Pokémon™
Omega Ruby
Pokémon™
Alpha Sapphire
THE OFFICIAL NATIONAL
POKÉDEX™

Mega Sceptile

1 Height: 6'03"

2 Note: Missing chunks on the "wings" of the arms and head have a visible facet

3 Lower in position than the other four leaves

4 No pads on feet

5 No fangs

6 Eyes when closed

7 Pattern is flat

8 Always aimed in the foe's direction

9 Head-on illustration

10 Center is round

11 Spheres used for firing tail are red (next set is orange)

12 Leaves on tails:
- Four leaves in a row, each ending in two lobes
- Gets narrower as it gets toward the end

13 Illustration of Mega Sceptile using its unique move

14 Three leaves on top

15 Two leaves on bottom

16 Wings on arms:
- Upper wing is longer
- The angle between the upper and lower wings where they attach is 90 degrees

17 Tail goes flying due to air pressure

18 Default is to always have its back turned

19 Flat

20 △(Stands up)

21 Flat

22 Spheres on the back:
- Five on each side (right and left)
- All are the same size
- Lined up along back

Summary Mega Sceptile's basic fighting stance always positions it with its back toward its opponent. Its tail is also kept aimed at the opponent. It has two sets of spheres along its back, five on the right and five on the left. They are all the same size. With the right move, it can use air pressure to shoot the leafy end of its tail at a target.

Mega Blaziken

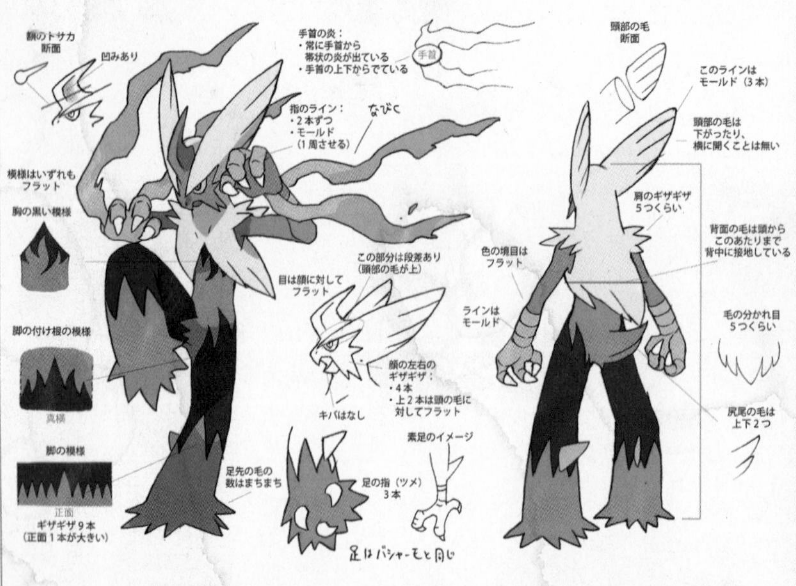

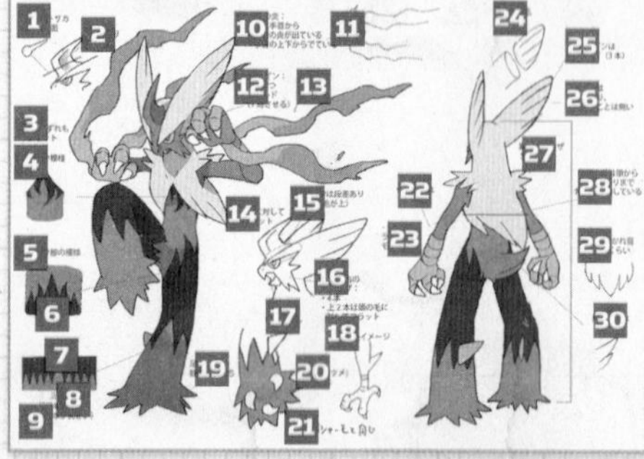

1 Cross section of cockscomb on forehead

2 A depression here

3 All patterns are flat

4 Black pattern on chest

5 Pattern where legs attach to torso

6 Straight from the side

7 Pattern on legs

8 View from straight on

9 Nine spiky points (the one on the front is tallest)

10 Flames on wrists:
- Streamers of flame always extending from wrists
- Extend from above and below wrists

11 Wrist

12 Lines on fingers:
- Two on each
- Molded (go all the way around fingers)

13 Fluttering

14 Eyes are flat against face

15 This part sticks up from the head (hair on the head is higher)

16 Jagged tufts on sides of face:
- Four per side
- The upper two lie flat against the hair sticking up from head

17 No fangs

18 Illustration of bare feet

19 Fur tufts on feet are diverse in number

20 Toes (three claws per foot)

21 Feet are same as Blaziken's

22 No height difference where colors meet

23 Lines are molded

24 Cross section of hair on head

25 These lines are molded (three lines)

26 Hair on head isn't lowered or spread to the sides

27 About five tufts of hair on each shoulder

28 Hair on the back is attached to the back down to about this point

29 Hair is split into about five tufts

30 Two tufts (upper and lower) on tail

Summary Mega Blaziken is easy to spot by the long streamers of flame flowing from its wrists. The flames stream from above and below its wrists and flutter freely. Its feet are hidden by down that covers them, but each foot features three claws just like Blaziken's.

Mega Swampert

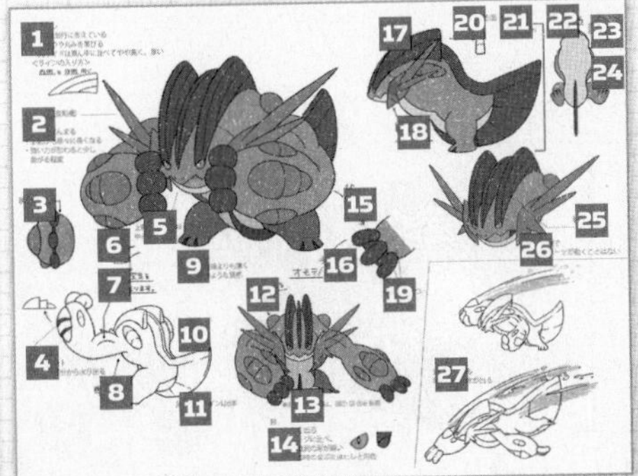

1. Fins on head:
   - Three fins sprout from its head in parallel
   - Edges are slightly rounded
   - Two on the sides are somewhat taller and thicker than the one in the middle
   - Lines are drawn the same on the inside as they are on the outside
2. Three spikes (sensors):
   - Conical
   - In cross section, perfectly round
   - Grow longer as you move from front to back
   - Could be bent slightly if you put a lot of strength into it
3. Arm (from straight on)
4. Gray parts:
   - Flat
   - Water comes out from here
5. Center protrusion on upper jaw is larger than others
6. Air tube
7. Sends air from back to arms
8. Arm joint
9. Toe fins:
   - Slightly thinner than toes
   - Webbing-like material
10. Illustration 3
11. Tail fin has six lines on it
12. Air enters here
13. Note: For pattern on stomach, see Illustrations 1, 2, and 3
14. Eyes:
    - Protrude outward with slight roundness
    - Compared to Swampert, the inner and outer corners of the eyes are sharper looking
    - When eyes are closed, its eyelids are the same color as its fins
15. Hand when open
16. Hand parts are the same on front and back
17. Illustration 2
18. Attachment point
19. Two joints
20. Fin from behind
21. Height: 6'03"
22. View from below
23. Illustration 1
24. Can be splayed
25. Cross section
26. Cheek parts do not move when the mouth opens or closes
27. Also expels water from thrusters when swimming

Summary

The muscle-bound Mega Swampert stands most often on two legs, but it sometimes walks on all fours. When unleashing attacks, it shoots water from its arms to make its attacks jet-powered. It also propels itself using the same method when swimming.

Mega Gallade

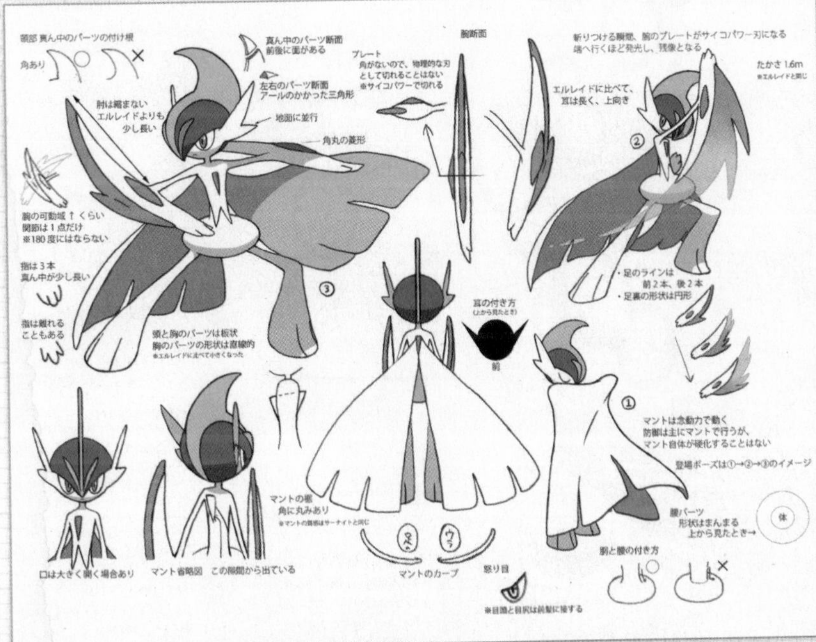

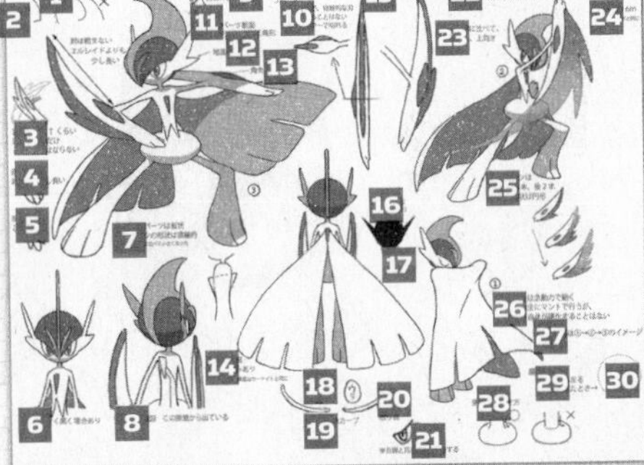

1. How part on head attaches
2. Has an angle
3. Range of motion for arms is like above
   Only connects at one point
   Note: Can't move a whole 180 degrees
4. Three fingers
   Middle is slightly longer
5. Fingers can be splayed
6. Mouth can open widely
7. Parts on head and chest are shaped like plates
   Chest part is shaped like a straight line
   Note: Smaller than on Gallade
8. Cape is omitted, but flows out from this part
9. Cross section of middle part
   Has a face on front and back
10. Plates have no edge, so cannot be used to cut foes as a physical blade
    Note: Able to cut with psychic power
11. Cross section of right and left parts
    Curved pyramid in shape
12. Parallel to ground
13. Round-cornered diamond
14. Angles on cape's hem are rounded
    Note: Cape's texture is same as Gardevoir's
15. Arm cross section
16. How ears attach to head (when seen from above)
17. Front
18. Bottom of feet
19. Curve of cape
20. Angry eyes
21. Note: Inner corner and outer corner of the eyes touch the "bangs"
22. The instant it slashes out, the arm plates become blades of psychic power. It emits more light as it reaches the farthest edge, and leaves an afterimage behind it.
23. Ears are longer and point upward more than on Gallade
24. Height: 5'03"
    Note: Same as Gallade
25. Lines on legs:
    - Two on front and two on back
    - Feet are round on the back
26. Cape moves with telekinetic power
    Uses cape primarily for defense, but cape itself doesn't harden
27. When appearing, strikes poses 1, 2, then 3!
28. How torso attaches to hips
29. Hip parts:
    - Round in shape
    - View from above
30. Body

Summary

Mega Gallade's large cape is controlled by its telekinesis and used mostly for defense. The instant that it slashes out at an opponent, its arm plates become blades of psychic power.

Mega Metagross

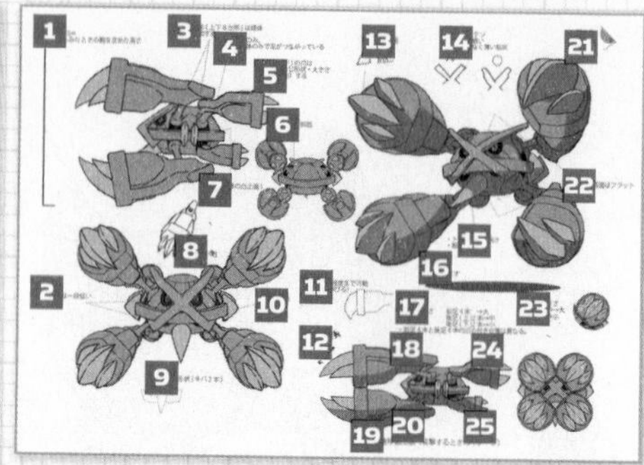

1. Height: 8'02"
Height when looked at from the front, including arms
2. Black parts are lower in elevation
3. Arm connection joints (eight in total, above and below) are spherical
Has a limited range of motion
4. The lower back arms alone are attached only with ball joints
5. Back legs (upper and lower) claws:
   - All three are the same shape and size
   - Can be spread apart (can be moved)
6. These faces are slanted
7. This face (where it sticks out from body) has a slight slope
8. Underside of arms
9. Mouth opens
Lower jaw shape (two fangs)
10. Hexagonal in cross section
11. Claws can move about this much (base parts extend)
12. Claws can move
13. Cross section of claws on front limbs
14. Cross on face:
    - Narrower at the ends
    - Thin plates without much heft
15. - Horn points downward diagonally
    - Round in cross section
16. Note: Floating in midair
17. Arm sizes:
    - Front four → large
    - Back (upper) two → medium
    - Back (lower) two → small
    - Positions of claws are different on the front four arms than on the back four arms
18. Large
19. High-speed form (like when used for charging foes)
20. Large
21. Closed eyes
22. Upper and lower faces are flat
23. Size of claws:
Middle claw → larger
Right and left claws → smaller
24. Medium
25. Small

Summary Mega Metagross floats in midair with four arms that thrust imposingly forward. It also has four arms which extend out from its back. When charging a foe, it flattens its arms to make itself aerodynamic enough for high-speed movement.

Primal Groudon

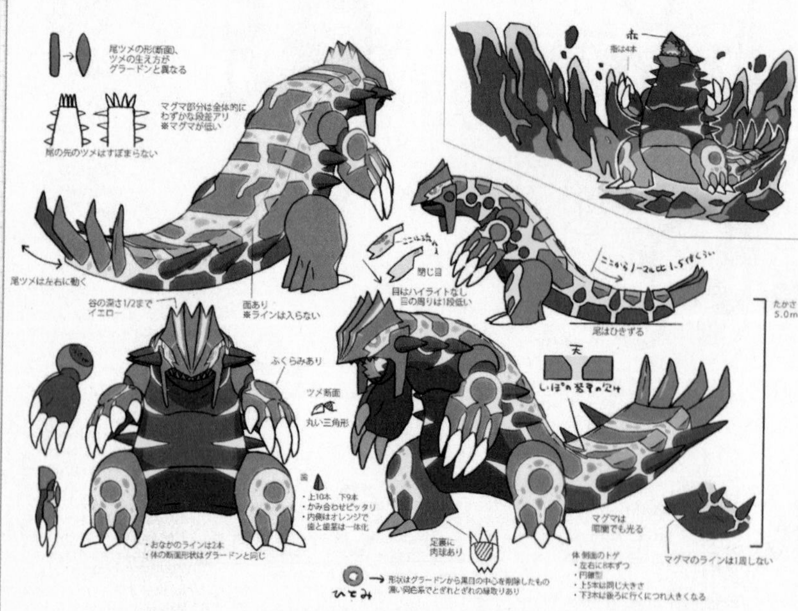

1. - Cross section of shape of claws on tail
   - Claws grow in a different way than Groudon's
2. There's a slight difference in height for the magma parts overall
Note: Magma parts are set deeper
3. Claws at tip of tail don't come in together
4. Claws on tail move left and right
5. Lower half of "valleys" are yellow
6. Attachment point
7. - Two lines seen on stomach
   - Its body shape in cross section is the same as Groudon's
8. A face here (but no lines will be drawn)
9. Rounded on top
10. Cross section of claw
11. A rounded pyramid
12. Tooth
13. - Ten on top, nine on bottom
    - Fit together without gaps
    - Orange on the inside, and teeth are one with gums
14. Iris
15. Flowing here
16. Eye closed
17. No highlight in eyes
Area around eye is set deeper
18. - Shape is the same as Groudon's eye, but with the black pupil omitted
    - Outlines are not solid but broken in places, and are a deeper shade of the same color
19. Pad on bottom of feet
20. Red
21. Four fingers
22. This part is about 1.5× bigger than on normal Groudon
23. Tail drags on ground
24. Surface
25. Gaps in plates on tail
26. Magma glows even in the dark
27. Spikes extending from sides of body:
    - Eight per side (right and left)
    - Round spikes
    - Upper five are the same size
    - Lower three get bigger the farther back they go
28. Height: 16'05"
29. Lines of magma do not continue in a full circle around the body

Summary Magma flows slightly under the surface of Primal Groudon's body, appearing below the outer layer. The claws on the end of its tail can be spread and moved right and left. It has 10 teeth in its upper jaw and nine in its lower jaw, so that its bite fits together perfectly.

Primal Kyogre

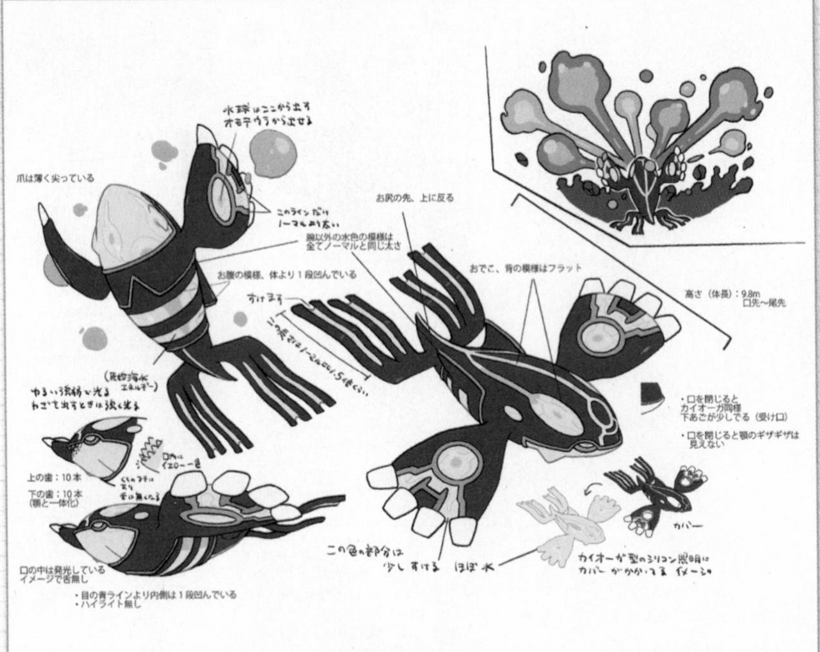

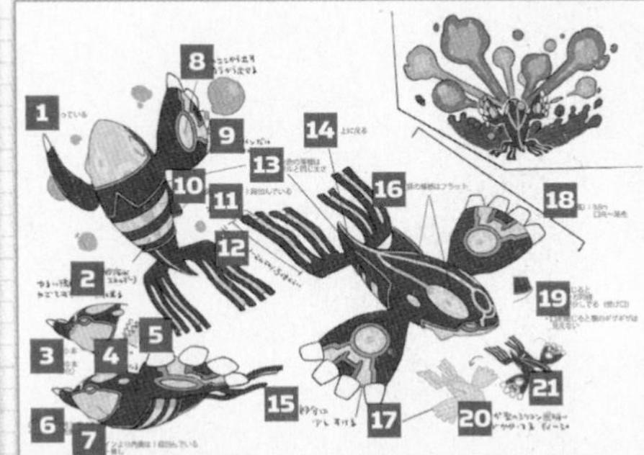

1. Claws are thin and taper to a point
2. Primal seawater energy:
   - Glows with a gentle power
   - Light grows when using a move
3. Upper teeth: 10
   Lower teeth: 10 (fused with jaw)
4. Mouth has an edge, but not a tongue
5. Interior of mouth is yellow
6. Interior of mouth appears to emit light
   No tongue
7. - Parts inside the blue line around eye are set a bit lower
   - No highlights in eye
8. Spheres of water come out here, from both front and back
9. These lines alone are thicker than normal
10. Patterns on the stomach are slightly less raised than the ones on the body
11. Transparent
12. These are 50% longer than on normal Kyogre
13. Light blue patterns on the body (other than those on the arms) are the same size as the ones on normal Kyogre
14. End of tail curves upward
15. The color of these parts is somewhat transparent
16. Patterns on forehead and back are flat
17. Practically water
18. Height: 32′02″ (length from tip of mouth to end of tail)
19. - When it closes its mouth, its lower jaw sticks out slightly just as it does on Kyogre (underbite)
    - When it closes its mouth, the jagged protrusions on its jaw can't be seen
20. Idea is that Kyogre is a molded silicone light encased in a cover
21. Cover

Summary

The inner part of Primal Kyogre's body glows with a gentle power. The light grows when it unleashes an attack. It also emits light from its open mouth. When its mouth is closed, its lower jaw juts out slightly just like Kyogre's.

Diancie

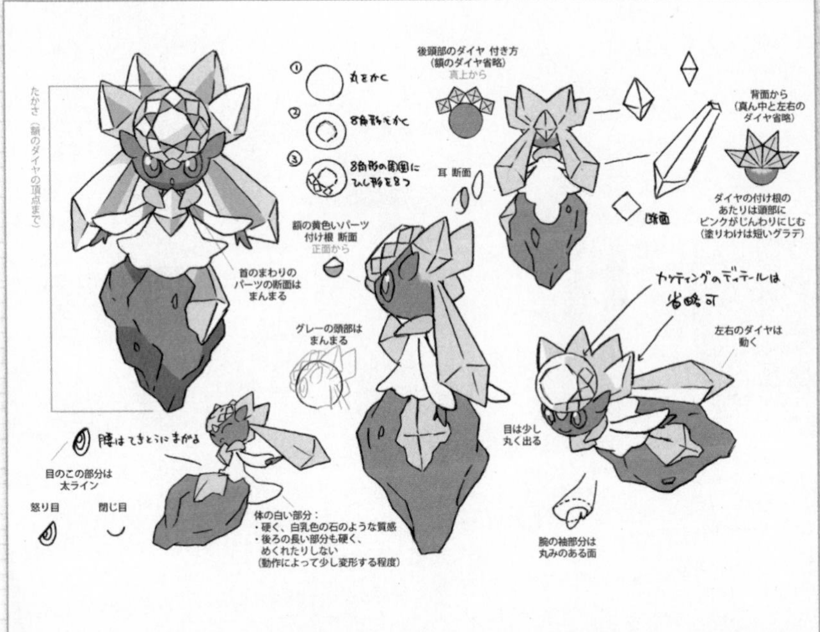

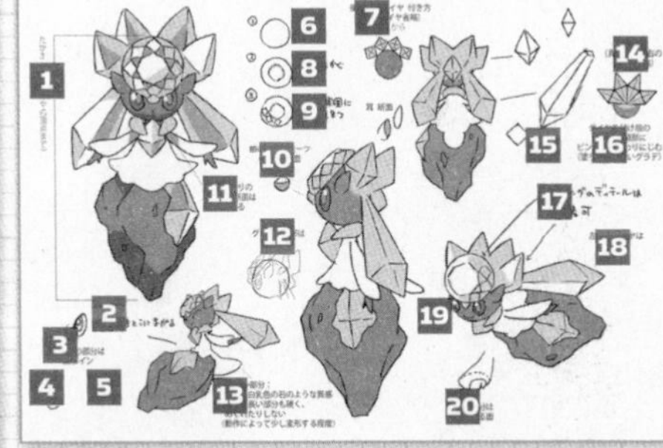

1. Height (all the way to the top of the diamonds)
2. Waist bends as needed
3. Thick line on this part of eye
4. Angry eyes
5. Closed eyes
6. Draw a circle
7. How rear diamonds attach to back of head
   (Diamond on top of head is omitted)
   (From above)
8. Draw an octagon
9. Draw eight diamonds around the points of the octagon
10. Cross section of where the yellow part on the forehead attaches (From front)
11. Part around the neck is round in cross section
12. Gray part of head is completely round
13. White part of body:
    - Made of a milky, stone-like substance
    - Longer part at back is also hard and does not flutter (though it can slightly change shape due to movements)
14. From back
    (Center diamond and diamonds on the right and left are omitted)
15. Cross section
16. Pink color bleeds out gradually from the point where the diamonds attach to the head
    (Brief gradation used to show color differentiation)
17. Details of the facet's cuts can be omitted
18. Diamonds on the right and left move
19. Eyes are round and bulge out slightly
20. Sleeve part of arm has a round face

Summary

Diancie's head is bedecked with diamonds, but is actually perfectly round beneath them. The white portions on its torso are rigid, composed of a milky substance that's as hard as stone. They do not move or flutter when Diancie flies through the air.

Mega Diancie

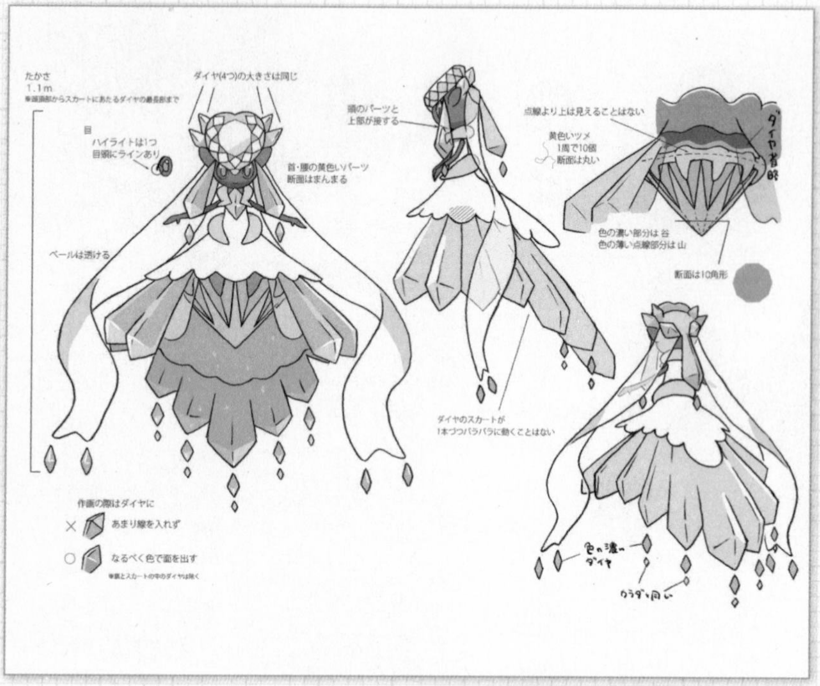

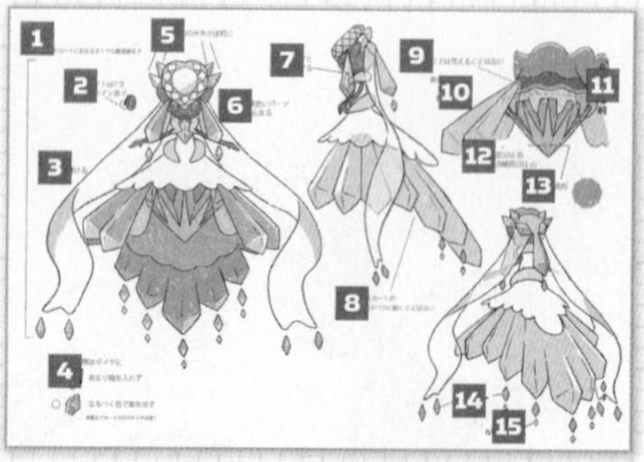

1 Height: 3'07"
Note: From top of head to longest part of diamonds making up the skirt

2 Eyes:
- One highlight in eyes
- Line at corner of eyes

3 Veil is transparent

4 When illustrating the diamonds:
X Don't draw a lot of lines in
O Use color as much as possible to show the facets
Note: Excludes diamonds making up head and in the skirt

5 All these diamonds (four) are same size

6 Yellow parts on neck and hips are round in cross section

7 Top of this part touches the head part

8 Diamond skirt's individual parts do not move independently

9 Area above the dotted line cannot be seen

10 Yellow "clasps":
- Ten in total around the perimeter
- Round in cross section

11 Diamonds are not shown

12 Deeper-colored parts are "valleys" (cut into facets)
Lighter parts with dotted lines jut outward

13 Ten facets

14 Diamonds with a deeper color

15 Same color as body

Summary
Mega Diancie sparkles in a beautiful diamond skirt. The four diamonds that extend from its head are all the same size. The veil that flows over its whole body is transparent.

Pikachu Rock Star

1 Tail not included

2 Matching outfits

Summary
Pikachu Rock Star has the same aggressive red color in its jacket, belt, shoes, and the accessories over its eyes, which expresses the fighting spirit that burns within it. There is a heart-shaped mark at the end of its tail in its usual illustrations. This mark is shared by Cosplay Pikachu in all of its different costumes.

Pikachu Belle

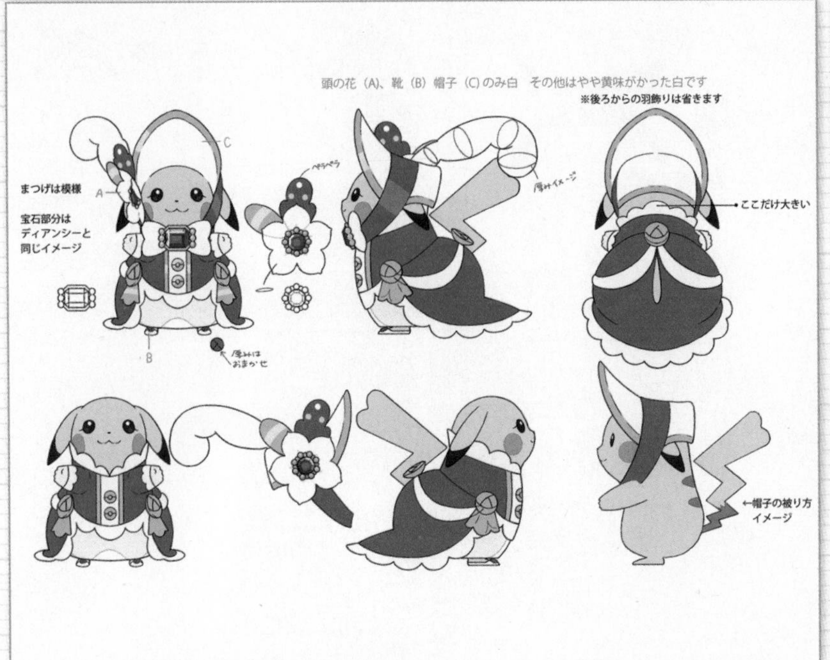

1. Eyelashes are just a pattern
2. Jeweled parts have the same image as Diancie
3. Only the flower on the face (A), the shoes (B), and the hat (C) are white. The rest are a slightly yellowed off-white.
4. Thin and fluttery
5. Will leave the thickness up to your interpretation
6. Note: Feather accessory is not shown in back view
7. Representation of how thick it is
8. This frill is longer
9. Illustration of how the hat fits on

Summary Pikachu Belle's design includes many details—the flower it wears on its head, its shoes, and its bonnet. Its eyes are adorned with a pattern resembling eyelashes, and its bonnet-covered ears are laid flat, changing its image drastically from that of a standard Pikachu. It also has a heart-shaped marking on the tip of its tail.

Pikachu Pop Star

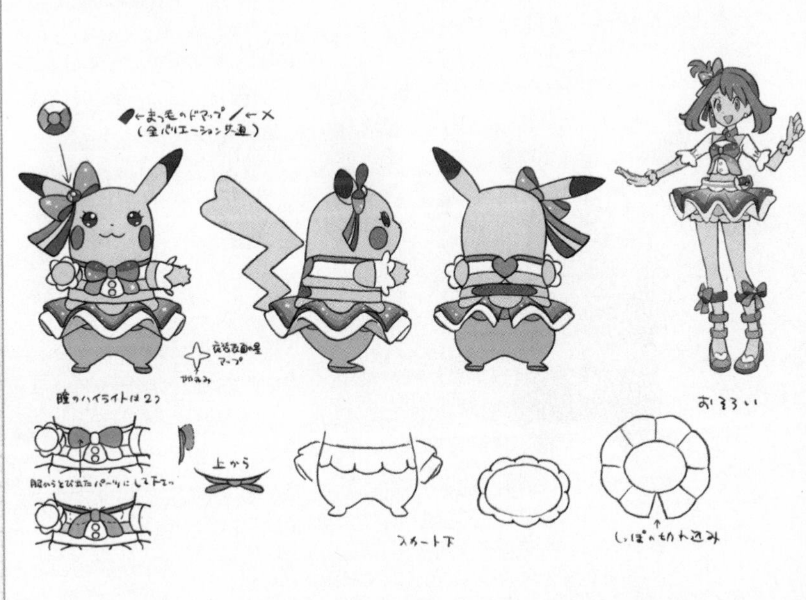

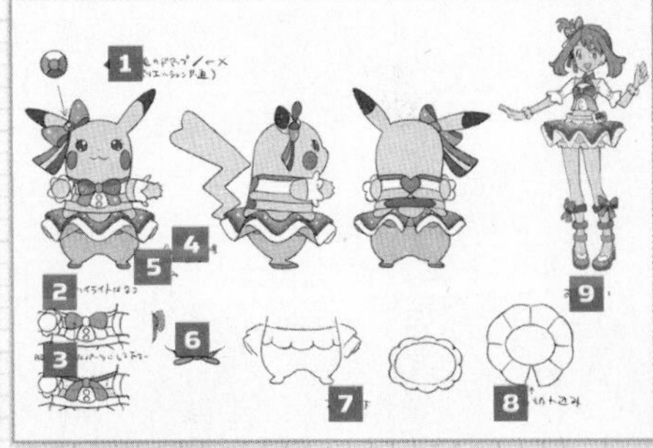

1. Super zoomed-in view of eyelashes (Not just /) (Same for all variations)
2. Two highlights in each eye
3. Make these parts stick out from the clothes
4. Zoomed-in view of stars on surface of clothes
5. Slightly rounded
6. From above
7. Below skirt
8. Cut out for tail
9. Matching outfits

Summary Pikachu Pop Star was designed to have a very cute costume with particular attention given to the coloration. The stars that bedeck its costume have round edges, which highlight its cuteness. Even the way that its ribbons are tied is planned in great detail. It also has a heart-shaped marking on the tip of its tail.

Pikachu, Ph.D.

1 Pocket Contents
2 • Toy Pokéblock Case
• Pencil
• Notebook
• Toy Pokédex
• Rare Candy
• Pecha Berry
3 Full reveal
4 Would love it if the force of moves made the glasses and wig slip a bit. Underneath it all, she's actually a beauty...
5 Drag, drag
6 My image
7 Want to have the white coat dragging behind her

Summary Pikachu, Ph.D., is the very image of a scholar in its thick and nerdy glasses and white lab coat. You'll find pencils, notepads, and more crammed in its pockets. Beneath the glasses, though, you'll see the stunning eyes of a true beauty.

Pikachu Libre

Summary Pikachu Libre's transformation is all about the mask and the costume. Its costume is fitted to its body, allowing for agile movement. In the front view, you can see the black tip of Cosplay Pikachu's distinctive tail sticking up.

For more GAME FREAK Concept Art, see *Pokémon Omega Ruby* & *Pokémon Alpha Sapphire*: The Official Hoenn Region Strategy Guide, available now.

THE OFFICIAL NATIONAL POKÉDEX™

Contents

National Pokédex Checklist

Alphabetical Index of Mega-Evolved Pokémon & Primal Pokémon

Catching Pokémon in the Hoenn region

The map on the following pages covers all of the wild Pokémon that you can catch in the Hoenn region. Each Pokémon is listed in just one location, either because it appears only there or is found more commonly in that location than it is in other places. This map also clumps Pokémon together in as few stops as possible, so you can make a quick circuit around the region and fill your Pokédex!

If you encounter a Pokémon that you haven't yet caught in a location other than the one listed here, don't let the opportunity go to waste! Try to catch new Pokémon whenever you have the chance. Remember, one way you can easily tell whether you have obtained a Pokémon is checking to see if there is a Poké Ball icon beside its name in battle.

No Poké Ball icon means you haven't caught this Pokémon

A Poké Ball icon means you have caught this Pokémon

Use the DexNav to confirm which Pokémon you've caught in each area

You can also quickly review whether you've caught all the easy-to-catch Pokémon in a given location using your DexNav. Open up the DexNav on your lower screen and check out the Pokémon that appear. If the Pokémon appears there in full color, then you've already caught it. For example, if you went to Route 101 to catch Wurmple, Zigzagoon, and Poochyena, and you saw a screen like the one above, you could easily confirm that you'd already caught all three! But you haven't yet caught Zorua or Lillipup, so start looking for any rustling patches of grass that might contain them!

The Pokémon not included on the following map are obtained by a variety of means other than catching them in the wild, such as leveling up and evolving the Pokémon you catch, leaving certain Pokémon at a Pokémon Day Care and discovering new Eggs that will hatch into other Pokémon, getting them from another character in the game, or receiving them as a trade from a different Pokémon game.

Note: Legendary and Mythical Pokémon are not included because they often have special requirements that need to be met before you can encounter them. Also not listed are the Pokémon obtained through particular events. Check out each Pokémon's specific Pokédex page to learn how to obtain them.

Pokémon obtained through events: Chikorita, Cyndaquil, Totodile, Lileep, Anorith, Castform, Beldum, Turtwig, Chimchar, Piplup, Spiritomb, Snivy, Tepig, and Oshawott.

Legendary and Mythical Pokémon: Raikou, Entei, Suicune, Lugia, Ho-Oh, Regirock, Regice, Registeel, Latias, Latios, Kyogre, Groudon, Rayquaza, Deoxys, Uxie, Mesprit, Azelf, Dialga, Palkia, Heatran, Regigigas, Giratina, Cresselia, Cobalion, Terrakion, Virizion, Tornadus, Thundurus, Reshiram, Zekrom, Landorus, and Kyurem.

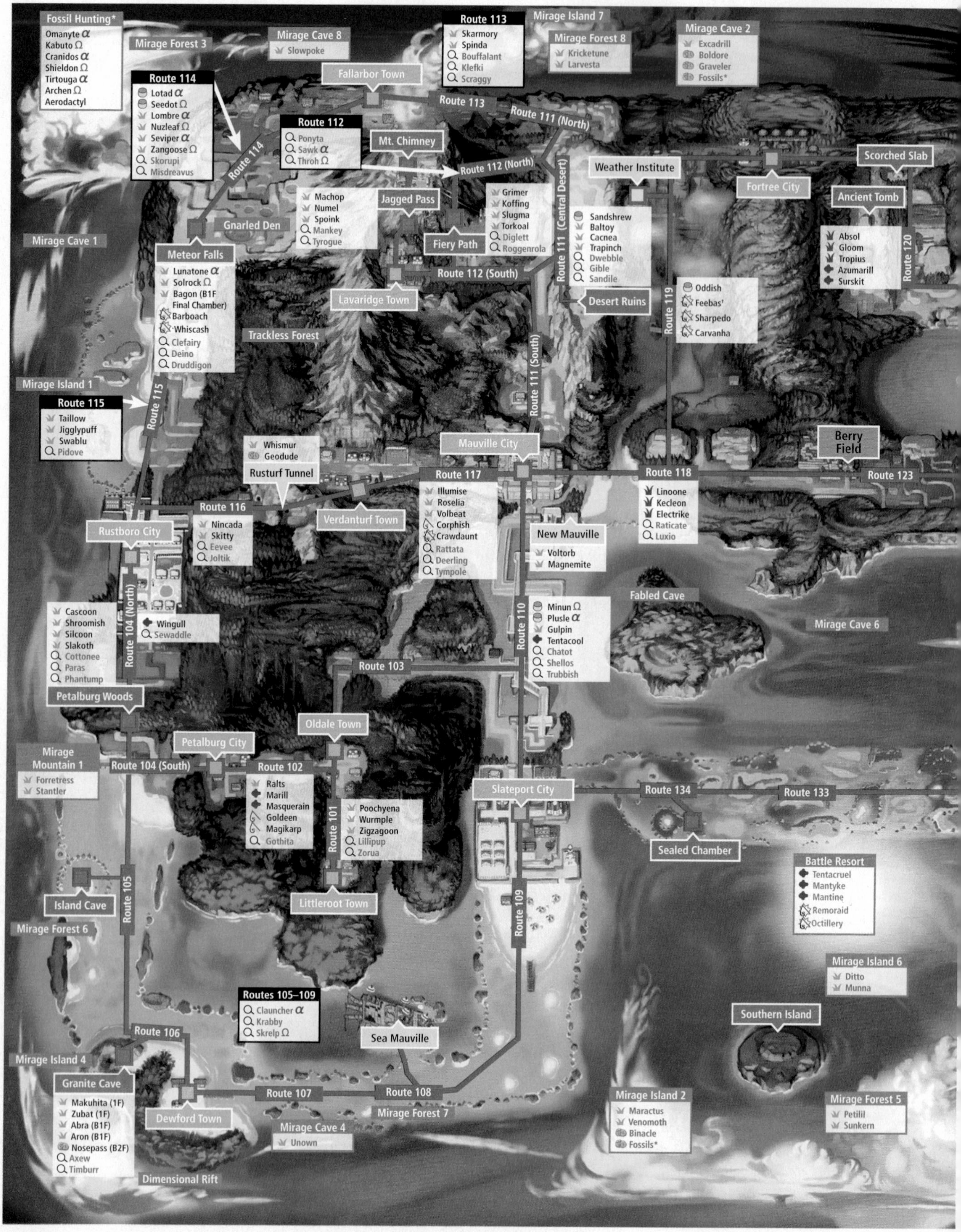

Pokémon Omega Ruby · Pokémon Alpha Sapphire

Fossil Hunting*
- Omanyte α
- Kabuto Ω
- Cranidos α
- Shieldon Ω
- Tirtouga α
- Archen Ω
- Aerodactyl

Mirage Forest 3

Mirage Cave 8
- Slowpoke

Route 114
- Lotad α
- Seedot Ω
- Lombre α
- Nuzleaf Ω
- Seviper α
- Zangoose Ω
- Skorupi
- Misdreavus

Route 114

Fallarbor Town

Route 113
- Skarmory
- Spinda
- Bouffalant
- Klefki
- Scraggy

Mirage Island 7

Mirage Forest 8
- Kricketune
- Larvesta

Mirage Cave 2
- Excadrill
- Boldore
- Graveler
- Fossils*

Route 113

Route 111 (North)

Route 112
- Ponyta
- Sawk α
- Throh Ω

Mt. Chimney

Route 112 (North)

Weather Institute

Scorched Slab

Fortree City

Ancient Tomb

Jagged Pass
- Machop
- Numel
- Spoink
- Mankey
- Tyrogue

Gnarled Den

Fiery Path
- Grimer
- Koffing
- Slugma
- Torkoal
- Diglett
- Roggenrola

Route 111 (Central Desert)

- Sandshrew
- Baltoy
- Cacnea
- Trapinch
- Dwebble
- Gible
- Sandile

Route 120
- Absol
- Gloom
- Tropius
- Azumarill
- Surskit

Mirage Cave 1

Meteor Falls
- Lunatone α
- Solrock Ω
- Bagon (B1F Final Chamber)
- Barboach
- Whiscash
- Clefairy
- Deino
- Druddigon

Route 112 (South)

Lavaridge Town

Desert Ruins

Route 119
- Oddish
- Feebas'
- Sharpedo
- Carvanha

Trackless Forest

Route 111 (South)

Mirage Island 1

Route 115
- Taillow
- Jigglypuff
- Swablu
- Pidove

Rusturf Tunnel
- Whismur
- Geodude

Mauville City

Berry Field

Route 117
- Illumise
- Roselia
- Volbeat
- Corphish
- Crawdaunt
- Rattata
- Deerling
- Tympole

Route 118
- Linoone
- Kecleon
- Electrike
- Raticate
- Luxio

Route 123

Route 116
- Nincada
- Skitty
- Eevee
- Joltik

Verdanturf Town

Rustboro City

New Mauville
- Voltorb
- Magnemite

Fabled Cave

Mirage Cave 6

Route 104 (North)
- Cascoon
- Shroomish
- Silcoon
- Slakoth
- Cottonee
- Paras
- Phantump
- Wingull
- Sewaddle

Route 110
- Minun Ω
- Plusle α
- Gulpin
- Tentacool
- Chatot
- Shellos
- Trubbish

Route 103

Petalburg Woods

Oldale Town

Mirage Mountain 1
- Forretress
- Stantler

Petalburg City

Route 104 (South)

Route 102
- Ralts
- Marill
- Masquerain
- Goldeen
- Magikarp
- Gothita

Route 101
- Poochyena
- Wurmple
- Zigzagoon
- Lillipup
- Zorua

Slateport City

Route 134

Route 133

Sealed Chamber

Battle Resort
- Tentacruel
- Mantyke
- Mantine
- Remoraid
- Octillery

Island Cave

Route 105

Littleroot Town

Route 109

Mirage Forest 6

Mirage Island 6
- Ditto
- Munna

Routes 105–109
- Clauncher α
- Krabby
- Skrelp Ω

Southern Island

Route 106

Sea Mauville

Mirage Island 4

Granite Cave
- Makuhita (1F)
- Zubat (1F)
- Abra (B1F)
- Aron (B1F)
- Nosepass (B2F)
- Axew
- Timburr

Dewford Town

Route 107

Route 108

Mirage Forest 7

Mirage Cave 4
- Unown

Mirage Island 2
- Maractus
- Venomoth
- Binacle
- Fossils*

Mirage Forest 5
- Petilil
- Sunkern

Dimensional Rift

Hoenn Region Pokémon Map

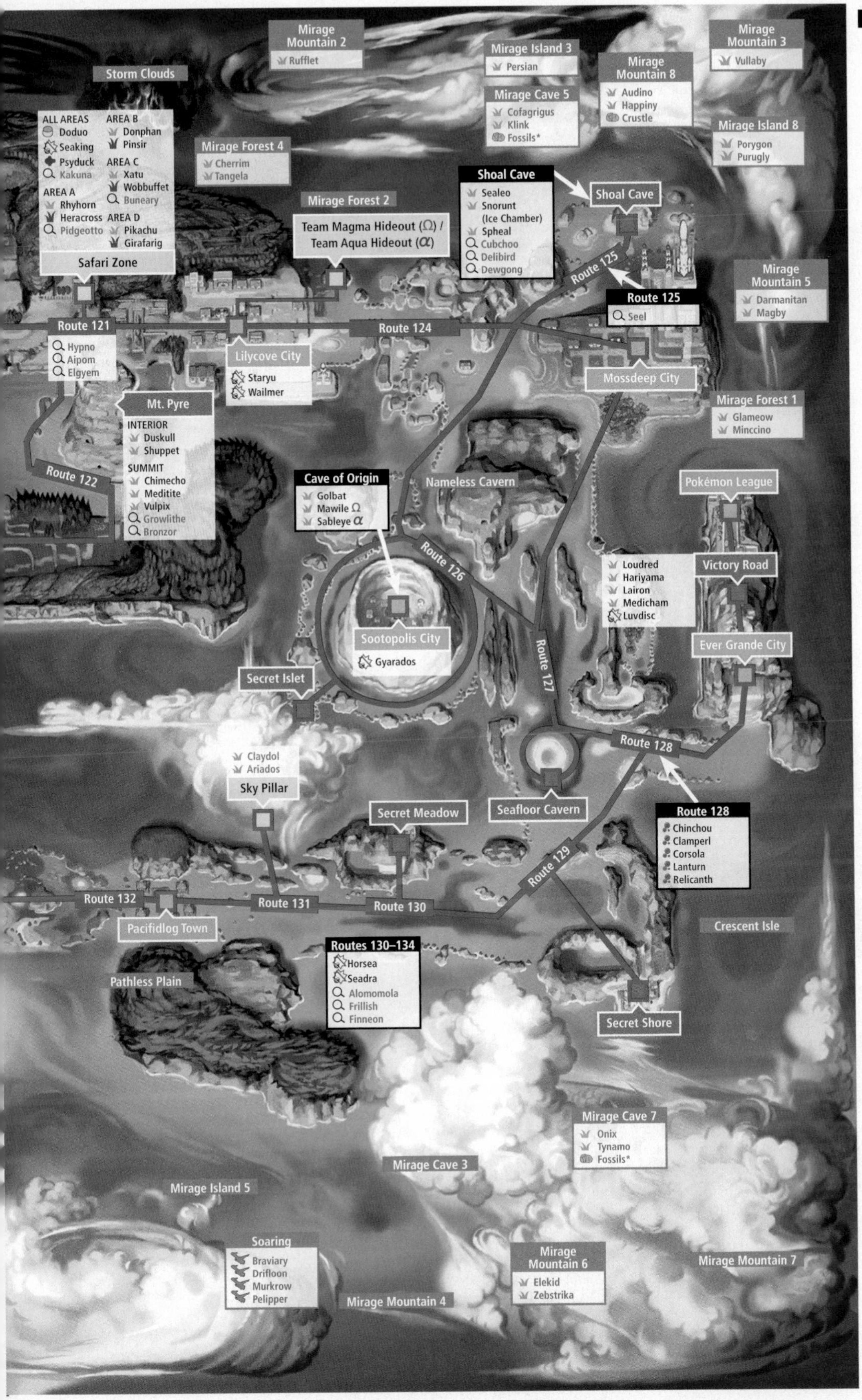

Mirage Mountain 2
Rufflet

Mirage Island 3
Persian

Mirage Mountain 8
Audino
Happiny
Crustle

Mirage Mountain 3
Vullaby

Storm Clouds

Mirage Cave 5
Cofagrigus
Klink
Fossils*

Mirage Island 8
Porygon
Purugly

ALL AREAS
Doduo
Seaking
Psyduck
Kakuna

AREA A
Rhyhorn
Heracross
Pidgeotto

AREA B
Donphan
Pinsir

AREA C
Xatu
Wobbuffet
Buneary

AREA D
Pikachu
Girafarig

Safari Zone

Mirage Forest 4
Cherrim
Tangela

Mirage Forest 2

Team Magma Hideout (Ω) / Team Aqua Hideout (α)

Shoal Cave
Sealeo
Snorunt (Ice Chamber)
Spheal
Cubchoo
Delibird
Dewgong

Shoal Cave

Mirage Mountain 5
Darmanitan
Magby

Route 125
Seel

Route 121
Hypno
Aipom
Elgyem

Route 124

Lilycove City
Staryu
Wailmer

Mossdeep City

Mirage Forest 1
Glameow
Minccino

Mt. Pyre
INTERIOR
Duskull
Shuppet
SUMMIT
Chimecho
Meditite
Vulpix
Growlithe
Bronzor

Route 122

Cave of Origin
Golbat
Mawile Ω
Sableye α

Nameless Cavern

Pokémon League

Route 126

Loudred
Hariyama
Lairon
Medicham
Luvdisc

Victory Road

Sootopolis City
Gyarados

Route 127

Ever Grande City

Secret Islet

Route 128

Claydol
Ariados
Sky Pillar

Secret Meadow

Seafloor Cavern

Route 128
Chinchou
Clamperl
Corsola
Lanturn
Relicanth

Route 129

Route 132
Route 131
Route 130

Pacifidlog Town

Crescent Isle

Routes 130–134
Horsea
Seadra
Alomomola
Frillish
Finneon

Pathless Plain

Secret Shore

Mirage Cave 7
Onix
Tynamo
Fossils*

Mirage Cave 3

Mirage Island 5

Soaring
Braviary
Drifloon
Murkrow
Pelipper

Mirage Mountain 6
Elekid
Zebstrika

Mirage Mountain 4

Mirage Mountain 7

Key

- Horde Encounters (Use Honey to trigger!)
- Normal encounters (tall grass / cave / desert)
- Encounters in very tall grass
- Encounters triggered by using Rock Smash
- Encounters on the water surface (using Surf)
- Caught with the Old Rod
- Caught with the Super Rod
- Caught underwater while using Dive
- Encounters while Soaring in the sky
- Encounters found hiding in the wild
- Ω Pokémon only available in *Pokémon Omega Ruby*
- α Pokémon only available in *Pokémon Alpha Sapphire*

Green Text / Purple Text
Pokémon names in green only appear after subduing Groudon/Kyogre, while purple names identify Pokémon only available after entering the Hall of Fame

*Fossil Hunting

Try to get Fossils by using Rock Smash in cracked rocks in Mirage Cave 2, Mirage Cave 5, Mirage Cave 7, and on Mirage Island 2.

†Catching Feebas

Use any rod in the shadow of the northern bridge while surfing during daytime hours.

How to Use the Pokédex

Pokémon

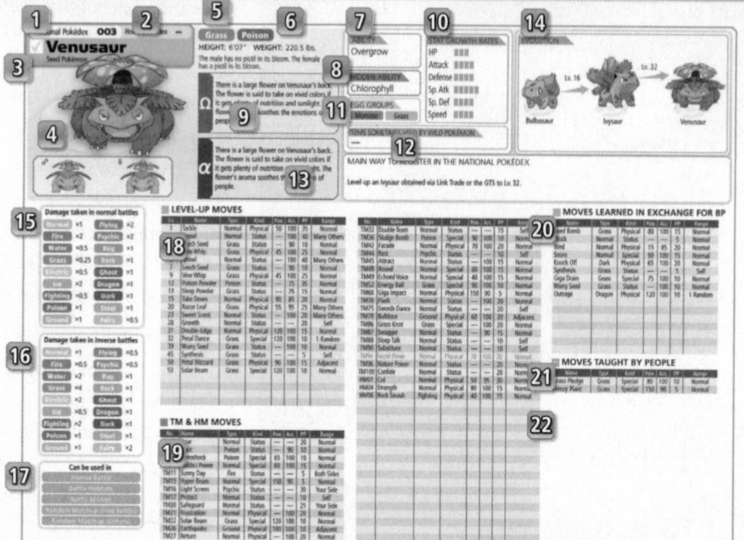

Mega Evolution / Primal Reversion

Pokémon

1 National Pokédex number

The National Pokédex number of the Pokémon.

2 Hoenn Pokédex number

The Hoenn Pokédex number of the Pokémon if it is included in the Hoenn Pokédex.

3 Pokémon category and species

A Pokémon's category, such as Young Fowl, may provide a pointer to its traits or attributes. Pokémon of different species, such as Treecko and Grovyle, may belong to the same category (in this case, Wood Gecko Pokémon).

4 Appearance

Here you can see how the Pokémon looks from the front. You can also see which genders, if any, the Pokémon has. If the male and female have different appearances, the differences will be explained in writing.

5 Type

The Pokémon's type. Some Pokémon have two types.

6 Height, weight, and gender

The height and weight of the Pokémon, as well as which genders, if any, the Pokémon has.

7 Abilities

The Pokémon's Ability. If two Abilities are listed, each Pokémon will have one of the two.

8 Hidden Ability

Some Pokémon have Hidden Abilities. Hidden Abilities are Abilities that hidden Pokémon or Pokémon in Horde Encounters may have. If a new Hidden Ability for a Pokémon included in the Kalos Pokédex has been discovered since *Pokémon X* and *Pokémon Y*, the Hidden Ability is shown in blue.

9 Pokédex entry

This is the summary of the Pokémon's characteristics given in the Hoenn Pokédex. The summary in *Pokémon Omega Ruby* usually differs from that in *Pokémon Alpha Sapphire*.

10 Stat growth rates

The growth rates of the Pokémon's stats are listed here. They are calculated by comparing the stat to the stats of other Pokémon in the National Pokédex. The first 5 are shown in green, and 6–10 are shown in red.

11 Egg Groups

The Egg Group the Pokémon belongs to. When two Egg Groups are listed, the Pokémon belongs to both.

12 Held item

Some wild Pokémon will have a held item. An item that the Pokémon may be holding is shown. If you use a Poké Ball to catch that Pokémon when it has a held item, you will also receive the item.

13 Main ways to register in the National Pokédex

Methods for adding Pokémon to the Hoenn Pokédex are shown. These are not the only ways to obtain the Pokémon. If you need to trade Pokémon by PSS (Player Search System), it will be indicated here.

14 Evolution

If the Pokémon evolves, this shows the course of Evolution for the Pokémon as well as any conditions governing its Evolution.

15 Damage taken in normal battles

Damage taken when the Pokémon is attacked by a move in a normal battle. It increases or decreases depending on the move type. If the effect of an Ability changes damage, ❶ is shown. If the data changes after Mega Evolution or Primal Reversion, it's shown in blue.

16 Damage taken in Inverse Battles

Damage taken when the Pokémon is attacked by a move in an Inverse Battle. If the effect of an Ability changes damage, ❶ is shown. If the data changes after Mega Evolution or Primal Reversion, it's shown in blue. You can try the battle once per day at the Inverse Battle Stop in Mauville City with the manager, Inver.

17 Can be used in

The battle formats and facilities that the Pokémon can join are listed here. There are five types: Inverse Battle, Battle Institute, Battle Maison, Random Matchup (Free), and Random Matchup (Other).

18 Level-up moves

A list of moves that the Pokémon can learn by leveling up. If a move has been newly added for a Pokémon included in the Kalos Pokédex since *Pokémon X* and *Pokémon Y*, the move is shown in pink, and if the level to learn a move has changed, the move name is shown in blue.

19 TM & HM moves

A list of moves the Pokémon can learn by using a TM or an HM. TMs and HMs do not go away once used, so they can be used to teach Pokémon moves as many times as you like. Moves that have been added since *Pokémon X* and *Pokémon Y* for Pokémon included in the Kalos Pokédex are shown in pink.

20 Moves that can be learned in exchange for BP

A list of moves that can be learned at the Battle Resort by using BP (Battle Points) that you earned by challenging the Battle Institute or Battle Maison.

21 Moves taught by people

A list of moves that people can teach Pokémon. There are ultimate moves, battle-combo moves, the strongest Dragon-type move, and moves necessary for Forme changes.

22 Egg Moves

These moves are occasionally learned by Pokémon upon hatching from a Pokémon Egg as long as the moves are known by either parent you left at the Pokémon Day Care. Newly added moves for Pokémon that appeared in *Pokémon X* and *Pokémon Y* are shown in pink. Some hidden Pokémon that you catch may also know Egg Moves.

Mega Evolution / Primal Reversion

23 Mega Evolution / Primal Reversion symbol

This symbol shows whether the Pokémon is capable of Mega Evolution or Primal Reversion.

24 Type

The Pokémon's type. If the data changes after Mega Evolution or Primal Reversion, it's shown in blue.

25 Height, weight, and gender

The height and weight of the Pokémon, as well as which genders, if any, the Pokémon has. If the data changes after Mega Evolution or Primal Reversion, it's shown in blue.

26 Mega Stone required

It shows the Mega Stone necessary for the Pokémon to Mega Evolve and how to obtain it, how to obtain the item necessary for Kyogre and Groudon to undergo Primal Reversion, and the move necessary for Rayquaza's special Mega Evolution.

27 Abilities

The Pokémon's Ability. If the Ability changes after Mega Evolution or Primal Reversion, it's shown in blue.

28 Stat growth rates

The growth rates of the Pokémon's stats are listed here. They are calculated by comparing the stat to the stats of other Pokémon in the National Pokédex. There are 10 stat growth rates. The first 5 are shown in green, and 6–10 are shown in red. If the stats change after Mega Evolution or Primal Reversion, they are shown in blue.

29 Mega-Evolved Pokémon moves

Please refer to the move list for the Pokémon before it Mega Evolved.

Move List Key

Lv.	The level at which the move can be learned
No.	The TM or HM's number
Type	The move's type
Kind	Whether the move is a physical, special, or status move

Physical Move:	Does more damage the higher the Attack stat is
Special Move:	Does more damage the higher the Sp. Atk stat is
Status Move:	Damages stats or inflicts status conditions on the target(s), or has various other effects

Pow.	The move's attack power
Acc.	The move's accuracy
PP	How many times the move can be used
Range	The number and range of targets the move can affect

Range Guide

- **Normal** The move affects the selected target. If the move is used by a Pokémon in the middle position during a Triple Battle, the move can target any of the other five Pokémon (including allies). If the move is used by a Pokémon in the left or right position during a Triple Battle, or during a Double Battle or Multi Battle, the move can target any of the three surrounding Pokémon (including its ally).
- **Self** This move affects only the user.
- **1 Ally** This move affects an adjacent ally during a Double Battle, Triple Battle, or Multi Battle. It has no effect in a Single Battle.
- **Self/Ally** This move affects the user or one of its allies. In a Single Battle, it affects only the user. In a Double Battle, Triple Battle, or Multi Battle it affects one of the allies (including the user).
- **Your Party** This move affects your entire party, including Pokémon that are in their Poké Balls.
- **1 Random** The move affects one of the opposing Pokémon at random.
- **Many Others** The move affects multiple Pokémon at the same time. If the move is used by a Pokémon in the middle position during a Triple Battle, the move will affect all three opposing Pokémon. If the move is used by a Pokémon in the left or right position during a Triple Battle, or during a Double Battle or Multi Battle, the move will affect two opposing Pokémon at the same time.
- **Adjacent** The move affects the surrounding Pokémon at the same time. If the move is used by a Pokémon in the middle position during a Triple Battle, the move will affect the other five Pokémon (including allies) simultaneously. If the move is used by a Pokémon in the left or right position during a Triple Battle, or during a Double Battle or Multi Battle, the move will affect the three surrounding Pokémon (including its ally) simultaneously.
- **Your Side** The move affects all Pokémon on your side of the field. Since the move affects the field, the move's effects continue even if the Pokémon are swapped out (except for moves that only work for one turn).
- **Other Side** The move affects all Pokémon on the opponent's side of the field. Since the move affects the field, the move's effects continue even if the Pokémon are swapped out (except for moves that only work for one turn).
- **Both Sides** The move affects all Pokémon on the field, regardless of which side they are on. Since the move affects the field, the move's effects continue even if the Pokémon are swapped out.
- **Varies** The move is influenced by factors such as the opposing Pokémon's move or the user's type, so the range is not fixed.

National Pokédex	001	Hoenn Pokédex	—

Bulbasaur

Seed Pokémon

Grass **Poison**

HEIGHT: 2'04" WEIGHT: 15.2 lbs.

Same form for ♂ / ♀

Ω Bulbasaur can be seen napping in bright sunlight. There is a seed on its back. By soaking up the sun's rays, the seed grows progressively larger.

α Bulbasaur can be seen napping in bright sunlight. There is a seed on its back. By soaking up the sun's rays, the seed grows progressively larger.

ABILITY
Overgrow

HIDDEN ABILITY
Chlorophyll

EGG GROUPS
Monster / Grass

STAT GROWTH RATES
HP
Attack
Defense
Sp. Atk
Sp. Def
Speed

ITEMS SOMETIMES HELD BY WILD POKÉMON
—

EVOLUTION
Bulbasaur → Lv. 16 → Ivysaur → Lv. 32 → Venusaur

MAIN WAY TO REGISTER IN THE NATIONAL POKÉDEX

Obtain in *Pokémon X* or *Pokémon Y*. Bring it to your game using Link Trade or the GTS.

Damage taken in normal battles

Type		Type	
Normal	×1	Flying	×2
Fire	×2	Psychic	×2
Water	×0.5	Bug	×1
Grass	×0.25	Rock	×1
Electric	×0.5	Ghost	×1
Ice	×2	Dragon	×1
Fighting	×0.5	Dark	×1
Poison	×1	Steel	×1
Ground	×1	Fairy	×0.5

Damage taken in Inverse battles

Type		Type	
Normal	×1	Flying	×0.5
Fire	×0.5	Psychic	×0.5
Water	×2	Bug	×1
Grass	×4	Rock	×1
Electric	×2	Ghost	×1
Ice	×0.5	Dragon	×1
Fighting	×2	Dark	×1
Poison	×1	Steel	×1
Ground	×1	Fairy	×2

Can be used in
- Inverse Battle
- Battle Institute
- Battle Maison
- Random Matchup (Free Battle)
- Random Matchup (Others)

LEVEL-UP MOVES

Lv.	Name	Type	Kind	Pow.	Acc.	PP	Range
1	Tackle	Normal	Physical	50	100	35	Normal
3	Growl	Normal	Status	—	100	40	Many Others
7	Leech Seed	Grass	Status	—	90	10	Normal
9	Vine Whip	Grass	Physical	45	100	25	Normal
13	Poison Powder	Poison	Status	—	75	35	Normal
13	Sleep Powder	Grass	Status	—	75	15	Normal
15	Take Down	Normal	Physical	90	85	20	Normal
19	Razor Leaf	Grass	Physical	55	95	25	Many Others
21	Sweet Scent	Normal	Status	—	100	20	Many Others
25	Growth	Normal	Status	—	—	20	Self
27	Double-Edge	Normal	Physical	120	100	15	Normal
31	Worry Seed	Grass	Status	—	100	10	Normal
33	Synthesis	Grass	Status	—	—	5	Self
37	Seed Bomb	Grass	Physical	80	100	15	Normal

TM & HM MOVES

No.	Name	Type	Kind	Pow.	Acc.	PP	Range
TM06	Toxic	Poison	Status	—	90	10	Normal
TM09	Venoshock	Poison	Special	65	100	10	Normal
TM10	Hidden Power	Normal	Special	60	100	15	Normal
TM11	Sunny Day	Fire	Status	—	—	5	Both Sides
TM16	Light Screen	Psychic	Status	—	—	30	Your Side
TM17	Protect	Normal	Status	—	—	10	Self
TM20	Safeguard	Normal	Status	—	—	25	Your Side
TM21	Frustration	Normal	Physical	—	100	20	Normal
TM22	Solar Beam	Grass	Special	120	100	10	Normal
TM27	Return	Normal	Physical	—	100	20	Normal
TM32	Double Team	Normal	Status	—	—	15	Self
TM36	Sludge Bomb	Poison	Special	90	100	10	Normal
TM42	Facade	Normal	Physical	70	100	20	Normal
TM44	Rest	Psychic	Status	—	—	10	Self
TM45	Attract	Normal	Status	—	100	15	Normal
TM48	Round	Normal	Special	60	100	15	Normal
TM49	Echoed Voice	Normal	Special	40	100	15	Normal
TM53	Energy Ball	Grass	Special	90	100	10	Normal
TM70	Flash	Normal	Status	—	100	20	Normal
TM75	Swords Dance	Normal	Status	—	—	20	Self
TM86	Grass Knot	Grass	Special	—	100	20	Normal
TM87	Swagger	Normal	Status	—	90	15	Normal
TM88	Sleep Talk	Normal	Status	—	—	10	Self
TM90	Substitute	Normal	Status	—	—	10	Self
TM94	Secret Power	Normal	Physical	70	100	20	Normal
TM96	Nature Power	Normal	Status	—	—	20	Normal
TM100	Confide	Normal	Status	—	—	20	Normal
HM01	Cut	Normal	Physical	50	95	30	Normal
HM04	Strength	Normal	Physical	80	100	15	Normal
HM06	Rock Smash	Fighting	Physical	40	100	15	Normal

MOVES LEARNED IN EXCHANGE FOR BP

Name	Type	Kind	Pow.	Acc.	PP	Range
Seed Bomb	Grass	Physical	80	100	15	Normal
Bind	Normal	Physical	15	85	20	Normal
Snore	Normal	Special	50	100	15	Normal
Knock Off	Dark	Physical	65	100	20	Normal
Synthesis	Grass	Status	—	—	5	Self
Giga Drain	Grass	Special	75	100	10	Normal
Worry Seed	Grass	Status	—	100	10	Normal

MOVES TAUGHT BY PEOPLE

Name	Type	Kind	Pow.	Acc.	PP	Range
Grass Pledge	Grass	Special	80	100	10	Normal

EGG MOVES

Name	Type	Kind	Pow.	Acc.	PP	Range
Skull Bash	Normal	Physical	130	100	10	Normal
Charm	Fairy	Status	—	100	20	Normal
Petal Dance	Grass	Special	120	100	10	1 Random
Magical Leaf	Grass	Special	60	—	20	Normal
Grass Whistle	Grass	Status	—	55	15	Normal
Curse	Ghost	Status	—	—	10	Varies
Ingrain	Grass	Status	—	—	20	Self
Nature Power	Normal	Status	—	—	20	Normal
Amnesia	Psychic	Status	—	—	20	Self
Leaf Storm	Grass	Special	130	90	5	Normal
Power Whip	Grass	Physical	120	85	10	Normal
Sludge	Poison	Special	65	100	20	Normal
Endure	Normal	Status	—	—	10	Self
Giga Drain	Grass	Special	75	100	10	Normal
Grassy Terrain	Grass	Status	—	—	10	Both Sides

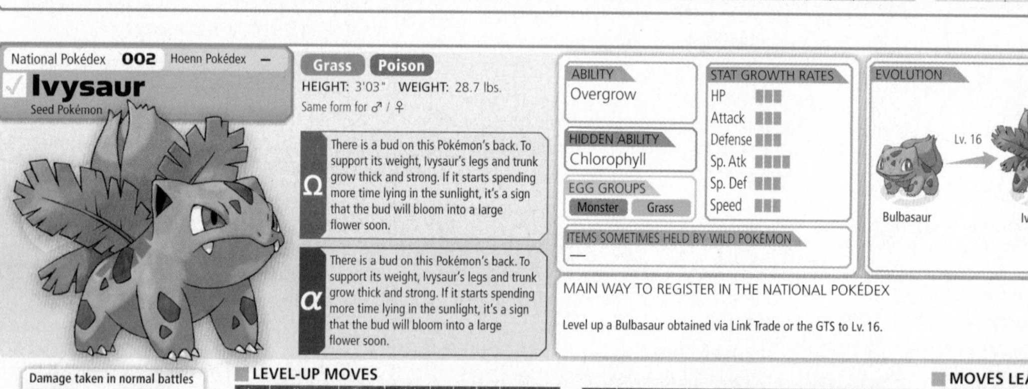

National Pokédex	002	Hoenn Pokédex	—

Ivysaur

Seed Pokémon

Grass **Poison**

HEIGHT: 3'03" WEIGHT: 28.7 lbs.

Same form for ♂ / ♀

Ω There is a bud on this Pokémon's back. To support its weight, Ivysaur's legs and trunk grow thick and strong. If it starts spending more time lying in the sunlight, it's a sign that the bud will bloom into a large flower soon.

α There is a bud on this Pokémon's back. To support its weight, Ivysaur's legs and trunk grow thick and strong. If it starts spending more time lying in the sunlight, it's a sign that the bud will bloom into a large flower soon.

ABILITY
Overgrow

HIDDEN ABILITY
Chlorophyll

EGG GROUPS
Monster / Grass

STAT GROWTH RATES
HP
Attack
Defense
Sp. Atk
Sp. Def
Speed

ITEMS SOMETIMES HELD BY WILD POKÉMON
—

EVOLUTION
Bulbasaur → Lv. 16 → Ivysaur → Lv. 32 → Venusaur

MAIN WAY TO REGISTER IN THE NATIONAL POKÉDEX

Level up a Bulbasaur obtained via Link Trade or the GTS to Lv. 16.

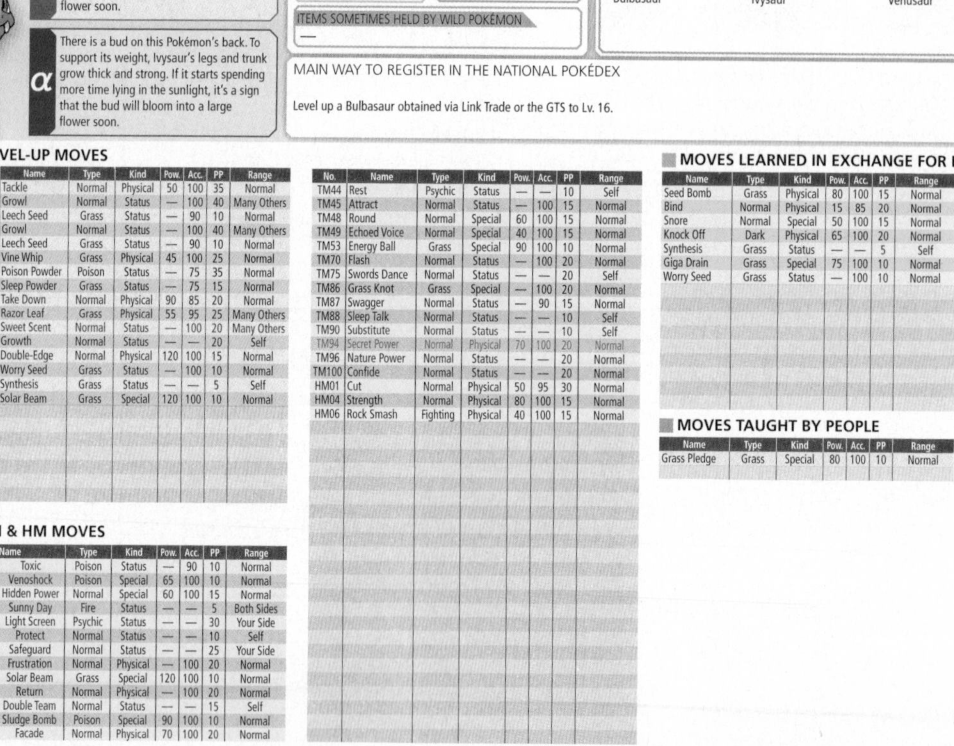

Damage taken in normal battles

Type		Type	
Normal	×1	Flying	×2
Fire	×2	Psychic	×2
Water	×0.5	Bug	×1
Grass	×0.25	Rock	×1
Electric	×0.5	Ghost	×1
Ice	×2	Dragon	×1
Fighting	×0.5	Dark	×1
Poison	×1	Steel	×1
Ground	×1	Fairy	×0.5

Damage taken in Inverse battles

Type		Type	
Normal	×1	Flying	×0.5
Fire	×0.5	Psychic	×0.5
Water	×2	Bug	×1
Grass	×4	Rock	×1
Electric	×2	Ghost	×1
Ice	×0.5	Dragon	×1
Fighting	×2	Dark	×1
Poison	×1	Steel	×1
Ground	×1	Fairy	×2

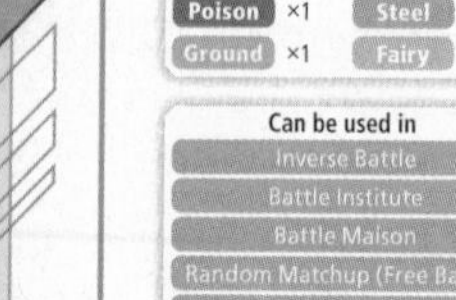

Can be used in
- Inverse Battle
- Battle Institute
- Battle Maison
- Random Matchup (Free Battle)
- Random Matchup (Others)

LEVEL-UP MOVES

Lv.	Name	Type	Kind	Pow.	Acc.	PP	Range
1	Tackle	Normal	Physical	50	100	35	Normal
1	Growl	Normal	Status	—	100	40	Many Others
1	Leech Seed	Grass	Status	—	90	10	Normal
3	Growl	Normal	Status	—	100	40	Many Others
7	Leech Seed	Grass	Status	—	90	10	Normal
9	Vine Whip	Grass	Physical	45	100	25	Normal
13	Poison Powder	Poison	Status	—	75	35	Normal
13	Sleep Powder	Grass	Status	—	75	15	Normal
15	Take Down	Normal	Physical	90	85	20	Normal
20	Razor Leaf	Grass	Physical	55	95	25	Many Others
23	Sweet Scent	Normal	Status	—	100	20	Many Others
28	Growth	Normal	Status	—	—	20	Self
31	Double-Edge	Normal	Physical	120	100	15	Normal
36	Worry Seed	Grass	Status	—	100	10	Normal
39	Synthesis	Grass	Status	—	—	5	Self
44	Solar Beam	Grass	Special	120	100	10	Normal

TM & HM MOVES

No.	Name	Type	Kind	Pow.	Acc.	PP	Range
TM06	Toxic	Poison	Status	—	90	10	Normal
TM09	Venoshock	Poison	Special	65	100	10	Normal
TM10	Hidden Power	Normal	Special	60	100	15	Normal
TM11	Sunny Day	Fire	Status	—	—	5	Both Sides
TM16	Light Screen	Psychic	Status	—	—	30	Your Side
TM17	Protect	Normal	Status	—	—	10	Self
TM20	Safeguard	Normal	Status	—	—	25	Your Side
TM21	Frustration	Normal	Physical	—	100	20	Normal
TM22	Solar Beam	Grass	Special	120	100	10	Normal
TM27	Return	Normal	Physical	—	100	20	Normal
TM32	Double Team	Normal	Status	—	—	15	Self
TM36	Sludge Bomb	Poison	Special	90	100	10	Normal
TM42	Facade	Normal	Physical	70	100	20	Normal
TM44	Rest	Psychic	Status	—	—	10	Self
TM45	Attract	Normal	Status	—	100	15	Normal
TM48	Round	Normal	Special	60	100	15	Normal
TM49	Echoed Voice	Normal	Special	40	100	15	Normal
TM53	Energy Ball	Grass	Special	90	100	10	Normal
TM70	Flash	Normal	Status	—	100	20	Normal
TM75	Swords Dance	Normal	Status	—	—	20	Self
TM86	Grass Knot	Grass	Special	—	100	20	Normal
TM87	Swagger	Normal	Status	—	90	15	Normal
TM88	Sleep Talk	Normal	Status	—	—	10	Self
TM90	Substitute	Normal	Status	—	—	10	Self
TM94	Secret Power	Normal	Physical	70	100	20	Normal
TM96	Nature Power	Normal	Status	—	—	20	Normal
TM100	Confide	Normal	Status	—	—	20	Normal
HM01	Cut	Normal	Physical	50	95	30	Normal
HM04	Strength	Normal	Physical	80	100	15	Normal
HM06	Rock Smash	Fighting	Physical	40	100	15	Normal

MOVES LEARNED IN EXCHANGE FOR BP

Name	Type	Kind	Pow.	Acc.	PP	Range
Seed Bomb	Grass	Physical	80	100	15	Normal
Bind	Normal	Physical	15	85	20	Normal
Snore	Normal	Special	50	100	15	Normal
Knock Off	Dark	Physical	65	100	20	Normal
Synthesis	Grass	Status	—	—	5	Self
Giga Drain	Grass	Special	75	100	10	Normal
Worry Seed	Grass	Status	—	100	10	Normal

MOVES TAUGHT BY PEOPLE

Name	Type	Kind	Pow.	Acc.	PP	Range
Grass Pledge	Grass	Special	80	100	10	Normal

National Pokédex **003** Hoenn Pokédex —

✓ Venusaur

Seed Pokémon

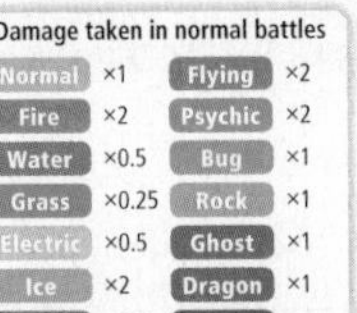

Grass | Poison

HEIGHT: 6'07" WEIGHT: 220.5 lbs.

The male has no pistil in its bloom. The female has a pistil in its bloom.

Ω There is a large flower on Venusaur's back. The flower is said to take on vivid colors if it gets plenty of nutrition and sunlight. The flower's aroma soothes the emotions of people.

α There is a large flower on Venusaur's back. The flower is said to take on vivid colors if it gets plenty of nutrition and sunlight. The flower's aroma soothes the emotions of people.

ABILITY
Overgrow

HIDDEN ABILITY
Chlorophyll

EGG GROUPS
Monster | Grass

STAT GROWTH RATES
HP ■■■
Attack ■■■■
Defense ■■■■
Sp. Atk ■■■■■
Sp. Def ■■■■
Speed ■■■■

ITEMS SOMETIMES HELD BY WILD POKÉMON
—

EVOLUTION

MAIN WAY TO REGISTER IN THE NATIONAL POKÉDEX

Level up an Ivysaur obtained via Link Trade or the GTS to Lv. 32.

Damage taken in normal battles

Type		Type	
Normal	×1	Flying	×2
Fire	×2	Psychic	×2
Water	×0.5	Bug	×1
Grass	×0.25	Rock	×1
Electric	×0.5	Ghost	×1
Ice	×2	Dragon	×1
Fighting	×0.5	Dark	×1
Poison	×1	Steel	×1
Ground	×1	Fairy	×0.5

Damage taken in Inverse battles

Type		Type	
Normal	×1	Flying	×0.5
Fire	×0.5	Psychic	×0.5
Water	×2	Bug	×1
Grass	×4	Rock	×1
Electric	×2	Ghost	×1
Ice	×0.5	Dragon	×1
Fighting	×2	Dark	×1
Poison	×1	Steel	×1
Ground	×1	Fairy	×2

Can be used in
- Inverse Battle
- Battle Institute
- Battle Maison
- Random Matchup (Free Battle)
- Random Matchup (Others)

LEVEL-UP MOVES

Lv.	Name	Type	Kind	Pow.	Acc.	PP	Range
1	Tackle	Normal	Physical	50	100	35	Normal
1	Growl	Normal	Status	—	100	40	Many Others
1	Leech Seed	Grass	Status	—	90	10	Normal
1	Vine Whip	Grass	Physical	45	100	25	Normal
3	Growl	Normal	Status	—	100	40	Many Others
7	Leech Seed	Grass	Status	—	90	10	Normal
9	Vine Whip	Grass	Physical	45	100	25	Normal
13	Poison Powder	Poison	Status	—	75	35	Normal
13	Sleep Powder	Grass	Status	—	75	15	Normal
15	Take Down	Normal	Physical	90	85	20	Normal
20	Razor Leaf	Grass	Physical	55	95	25	Many Others
23	Sweet Scent	Normal	Status	—	100	20	Many Others
28	Growth	Normal	Status	—	—	20	Self
31	Double-Edge	Normal	Physical	120	100	15	Normal
32	Petal Dance	Grass	Special	120	100	10	1 Random
39	Worry Seed	Grass	Status	—	100	10	Normal
45	Synthesis	Grass	Status	—	—	5	Self
50	Petal Blizzard	Grass	Physical	90	100	15	Adjacent
53	Solar Beam	Grass	Special	120	100	10	Normal

TM & HM MOVES

No.	Name	Type	Kind	Pow.	Acc.	PP	Range
TM05	Roar	Normal	Status	—	—	20	Normal
TM06	Toxic	Poison	Status	—	90	10	Normal
TM09	Venoshock	Poison	Special	65	100	10	Normal
TM10	Hidden Power	Normal	Special	60	100	15	Normal
TM11	Sunny Day	Fire	Status	—	—	5	Both Sides
TM15	Hyper Beam	Normal	Special	150	90	5	Normal
TM16	Light Screen	Psychic	Status	—	—	30	Your Side
TM17	Protect	Normal	Status	—	—	10	Self
TM20	Safeguard	Normal	Status	—	—	25	Your Side
TM21	Frustration	Normal	Physical	—	100	20	Normal
TM22	Solar Beam	Grass	Special	120	100	10	Normal
TM26	Earthquake	Ground	Physical	100	100	10	Adjacent
TM27	Return	Normal	Physical	—	100	20	Normal
TM32	Double Team	Normal	Status	—	—	15	Self
TM36	Sludge Bomb	Poison	Special	90	100	10	Normal
TM42	Facade	Normal	Physical	70	100	20	Normal
TM44	Rest	Psychic	Status	—	—	10	Self
TM45	Attract	Normal	Status	—	100	15	Normal
TM48	Round	Normal	Special	60	100	15	Normal
TM49	Echoed Voice	Normal	Special	40	100	15	Normal
TM53	Energy Ball	Grass	Special	90	100	10	Normal
TM68	Giga Impact	Normal	Physical	150	90	5	Normal
TM70	Flash	Normal	Status	—	100	20	Normal
TM75	Swords Dance	Normal	Status	—	—	20	Self
TM78	Bulldoze	Ground	Physical	60	100	20	Adjacent
TM86	Grass Knot	Grass	Special	—	100	20	Normal
TM87	Swagger	Normal	Status	—	90	15	Normal
TM88	Sleep Talk	Normal	Status	—	—	10	Self
TM90	Substitute	Normal	Status	—	—	10	Self
TM94	Secret Power	Normal	Physical	70	100	20	Normal
TM96	Nature Power	Normal	Status	—	—	20	Normal
TM100	Confide	Normal	Status	—	—	20	Normal
HM01	Cut	Normal	Physical	50	95	30	Normal
HM04	Strength	Normal	Physical	80	100	15	Normal
HM06	Rock Smash	Fighting	Physical	40	100	15	Normal

MOVES LEARNED IN EXCHANGE FOR BP

Name	Type	Kind	Pow.	Acc.	PP	Range
Seed Bomb	Grass	Physical	80	100	15	Normal
Block	Normal	Status	—	—	5	Normal
Bind	Normal	Physical	15	85	20	Normal
Snore	Normal	Special	50	100	15	Normal
Knock Off	Dark	Physical	65	100	20	Normal
Synthesis	Grass	Status	—	—	5	Self
Giga Drain	Grass	Special	75	100	10	Normal
Worry Seed	Grass	Status	—	100	10	Normal
Outrage	Dragon	Physical	120	100	10	1 Random

MOVES TAUGHT BY PEOPLE

Name	Type	Kind	Pow.	Acc.	PP	Range
Grass Pledge	Grass	Special	80	100	10	Normal
Frenzy Plant	Grass	Special	150	90	5	Normal

Mega Evolution

Mega Venusaur

Seed Pokémon

Grass | Poison

HEIGHT: 7'10" WEIGHT: 342.8 lbs.

Same form for ♂ / ♀

REQUIRED MEGA STONE
Venusaurite
Find on Route 119 (after battling Groudon or Kyogre).

ABILITY
Thick Fat

HIDDEN ABILITY
—

EGG GROUPS
—

STAT GROWTH RATES
HP ■■■
Attack ■■■■■
Defense ■■■■■
Sp. Atk ■■■■■■
Sp. Def ■■■■■
Speed ■■■■

Damage taken in normal battles

Type		Type	
Normal	×1	Flying	×2
! Fire	×2	Psychic	×2
Water	×0.5	Bug	×1
Grass	×0.25	Rock	×1
Electric	×0.5	Ghost	×1
! Ice	×2	Dragon	×1
Fighting	×0.5	Dark	×1
Poison	×1	Steel	×1
Ground	×1	Fairy	×0.5

Damage taken in Inverse battles

Type		Type	
Normal	×1	Flying	×0.5
! Fire	×0.5	Psychic	×0.5
Water	×2	Bug	×1
Grass	×4	Rock	×1
Electric	×2	Ghost	×1
! Ice	×0.5	Dragon	×1
Fighting	×2	Dark	×1
Poison	×1	Steel	×1
Ground	×1	Fairy	×2

Can be used in
- Inverse Battle
- Battle Institute
- Battle Maison
- Random Matchup (Free Battle)
- Random Matchup (Others)

National Pokédex **004** Hoenn Pokédex —

Charmander

Lizard Pokémon

Fire

HEIGHT: 2'00" WEIGHT: 18.7 lbs.

Same form for ♂ / ♀

Ω The flame that burns at the tip of its tail is an indication of its emotions. The flame wavers when Charmander is enjoying itself. If the Pokémon becomes enraged, the flame burns fiercely.

α The flame that burns at the tip of its tail is an indication of its emotions. The flame wavers when Charmander is enjoying itself. If the Pokémon becomes enraged, the flame burns fiercely.

ABILITY
Blaze

HIDDEN ABILITY
Solar Power

EGG GROUPS
Monster Dragon

STAT GROWTH RATES

HP	■■
Attack	■■■
Defense	■■
Sp. Atk	■■■
Sp. Def	■■
Speed	■■■■

ITEMS SOMETIMES HELD BY WILD POKÉMON
—

EVOLUTION

MAIN WAY TO REGISTER IN THE NATIONAL POKÉDEX

Obtain in *Pokémon X* or *Pokémon Y*. Bring it to your game using Link Trade or the GTS.

Damage taken in normal battles

Normal	×1	Flying	×1
Fire	×0.5	Psychic	×1
Water	×2	Bug	×0.5
Grass	×0.5	Rock	×2
Electric	×1	Ghost	×1
Ice	×0.5	Dragon	×1
Fighting	×1	Dark	×1
Poison	×1	Steel	×0.5
Ground	×2	Fairy	×0.5

Damage taken in Inverse battles

Normal	×1	Flying	×1
Fire	×2	Psychic	×1
Water	×0.5	Bug	×2
Grass	×2	Rock	×0.5
Electric	×1	Ghost	×1
Ice	×2	Dragon	×1
Fighting	×1	Dark	×1
Poison	×1	Steel	×2
Ground	×0.5	Fairy	×2

Can be used in

- Inverse Battle
- Battle Institute
- Battle Maison
- Random Matchup (Free Battle)
- Random Matchup (Others)

LEVEL-UP MOVES

Lv.	Name	Type	Kind	Pow.	Acc.	PP	Range
1	Scratch	Normal	Physical	40	100	35	Normal
1	Growl	Normal	Status	—	100	40	Many Others
7	Ember	Fire	Special	40	100	25	Normal
10	Smokescreen	Normal	Status	—	100	20	Normal
16	Dragon Rage	Dragon	Special	—	100	10	Normal
19	Scary Face	Normal	Status	—	100	10	Normal
25	Fire Fang	Fire	Physical	65	95	15	Normal
28	Flame Burst	Fire	Special	70	100	15	Normal
34	Slash	Normal	Physical	70	100	20	Normal
37	Flamethrower	Fire	Special	90	100	15	Normal
43	Fire Spin	Fire	Special	35	85	15	Normal
46	Inferno	Fire	Special	100	50	5	Normal

TM & HM MOVES

No.	Name	Type	Kind	Pow.	Acc.	PP	Range
TM01	Hone Claws	Dark	Status	—	—	15	Self
TM02	Dragon Claw	Dragon	Physical	80	100	15	Normal
TM06	Toxic	Poison	Status	—	90	10	Normal
TM10	Hidden Power	Normal	Special	60	100	15	Normal
TM11	Sunny Day	Fire	Status	—	—	5	Both Sides
TM17	Protect	Normal	Status	—	—	10	Self
TM21	Frustration	Normal	Physical	—	100	20	Normal
TM27	Return	Normal	Physical	—	100	20	Normal
TM28	Dig	Ground	Physical	80	100	10	Normal
TM31	Brick Break	Fighting	Physical	75	100	15	Normal
TM32	Double Team	Normal	Status	—	—	15	Self
TM35	Flamethrower	Fire	Special	90	100	15	Normal
TM38	Fire Blast	Fire	Special	110	85	5	Normal
TM39	Rock Tomb	Rock	Physical	60	95	15	Normal
TM40	Aerial Ace	Flying	Physical	60	—	20	Normal
TM42	Facade	Normal	Physical	70	100	20	Normal
TM43	Flame Charge	Fire	Physical	50	100	20	Normal
TM44	Rest	Psychic	Status	—	—	10	Self
TM45	Attract	Normal	Status	—	100	15	Normal
TM48	Round	Normal	Special	60	100	15	Normal
TM49	Echoed Voice	Normal	Special	40	100	15	Normal
TM50	Overheat	Fire	Special	130	90	5	Normal
TM56	Fling	Dark	Physical	—	100	10	Normal
TM59	Incinerate	Fire	Special	60	100	15	Many Others
TM61	Will-O-Wisp	Fire	Status	—	85	15	Normal
TM65	Shadow Claw	Ghost	Physical	70	100	15	Normal
TM75	Swords Dance	Normal	Status	—	—	20	Self
TM80	Rock Slide	Rock	Physical	75	90	10	Many Others
TM87	Swagger	Normal	Status	—	90	15	Normal
TM88	Sleep Talk	Normal	Status	—	—	10	Self
TM90	Substitute	Normal	Status	—	—	10	Self
TM94	Secret Power	Normal	Physical	70	100	20	Normal
TM98	Power-Up Punch	Fighting	Physical	40	100	20	Normal
TM100	Confide	Normal	Status	—	—	20	Normal
HM01	Cut	Normal	Physical	50	95	30	Normal
HM04	Strength	Normal	Physical	80	100	15	Normal
HM06	Rock Smash	Fighting	Physical	40	100	15	Normal

MOVES LEARNED IN EXCHANGE FOR BP

Name	Type	Kind	Pow.	Acc.	PP	Range
Thunder Punch	Electric	Physical	75	100	15	Normal
Fire Punch	Fire	Physical	75	100	15	Normal
Dragon Pulse	Dragon	Special	85	100	10	Normal
Iron Tail	Steel	Physical	100	75	15	Normal
Snore	Normal	Special	50	100	15	Normal
Heat Wave	Fire	Special	95	90	10	Many Others
Focus Punch	Fighting	Physical	150	100	20	Normal

MOVES TAUGHT BY PEOPLE

Name	Type	Kind	Pow.	Acc.	PP	Range
Fire Pledge	Fire	Special	80	100	10	Normal

EGG MOVES

Name	Type	Kind	Pow.	Acc.	PP	Range
Belly Drum	Normal	Status	—	—	10	Self
Ancient Power	Rock	Special	60	100	5	Normal
Bite	Dark	Physical	60	100	25	Normal
Outrage	Dragon	Physical	120	100	10	1 Random
Beat Up	Dark	Physical	—	100	10	Normal
Dragon Dance	Dragon	Status	—	—	20	Self
Crunch	Dark	Physical	80	100	15	Normal
Dragon Rush	Dragon	Physical	100	75	10	Normal
Metal Claw	Steel	Physical	50	95	35	Normal
Flare Blitz	Fire	Physical	120	100	15	Normal
Counter	Fighting	Physical	—	100	20	Varies
Dragon Pulse	Dragon	Special	85	100	10	Normal
Focus Punch	Fighting	Physical	150	100	20	Normal
Air Cutter	Flying	Special	60	95	25	Many Others

National Pokédex **005** Hoenn Pokédex —

Charmeleon

Flame Pokémon

Fire

HEIGHT: 3'07" WEIGHT: 41.9 lbs.

Same form for ♂ / ♀

Ω Charmeleon mercilessly destroys its foes using its sharp claws. If it encounters a strong foe, it turns aggressive. In this excited state, the flame at the tip of its tail flares with a bluish white color.

α Charmeleon mercilessly destroys its foes using its sharp claws. If it encounters a strong foe, it turns aggressive. In this excited state, the flame at the tip of its tail flares with a bluish white color.

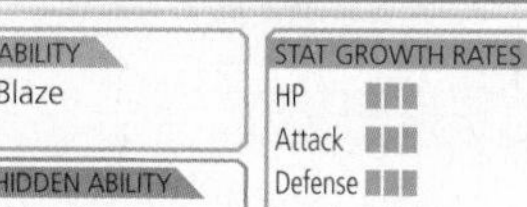

ABILITY
Blaze

HIDDEN ABILITY
Solar Power

EGG GROUPS
Monster Dragon

STAT GROWTH RATES

HP	■■■
Attack	■■■
Defense	■■■
Sp. Atk	■■■■
Sp. Def	■■■
Speed	■■■■

ITEMS SOMETIMES HELD BY WILD POKÉMON
—

EVOLUTION

Lv. 16 Lv. 36

Charmander Charmeleon Charizard

MAIN WAY TO REGISTER IN THE NATIONAL POKÉDEX

Level up a Charmander obtained via Link Trade or the GTS to Lv. 16.

Damage taken in normal battles

Normal	×1	Flying	×1
Fire	×0.5	Psychic	×1
Water	×2	Bug	×0.5
Grass	×0.5	Rock	×2
Electric	×1	Ghost	×1
Ice	×0.5	Dragon	×1
Fighting	×1	Dark	×1
Poison	×1	Steel	×0.5
Ground	×2	Fairy	×0.5

Damage taken in Inverse battles

Normal	×1	Flying	×1
Fire	×2	Psychic	×1
Water	×0.5	Bug	×2
Grass	×2	Rock	×0.5
Electric	×1	Ghost	×1
Ice	×2	Dragon	×1
Fighting	×1	Dark	×1
Poison	×1	Steel	×2
Ground	×0.5	Fairy	×2

Can be used in

- Inverse Battle
- Battle Institute
- Battle Maison
- Random Matchup (Free Battle)
- Random Matchup (Others)

LEVEL-UP MOVES

Lv.	Name	Type	Kind	Pow.	Acc.	PP	Range
1	Scratch	Normal	Physical	40	100	35	Normal
1	Growl	Normal	Status	—	100	40	Many Others
1	Ember	Fire	Special	40	100	25	Normal
7	Ember	Fire	Special	40	100	25	Normal
10	Smokescreen	Normal	Status	—	100	20	Normal
17	Dragon Rage	Dragon	Special	—	100	10	Normal
21	Scary Face	Normal	Status	—	100	10	Normal
28	Fire Fang	Fire	Physical	65	95	15	Normal
32	Flame Burst	Fire	Special	70	100	15	Normal
39	Slash	Normal	Physical	70	100	20	Normal
43	Flamethrower	Fire	Special	90	100	15	Normal
50	Fire Spin	Fire	Special	35	85	15	Normal
54	Inferno	Fire	Special	100	50	5	Normal

TM & HM MOVES

No.	Name	Type	Kind	Pow.	Acc.	PP	Range
TM01	Hone Claws	Dark	Status	—	—	15	Self
TM02	Dragon Claw	Dragon	Physical	80	100	15	Normal
TM06	Toxic	Poison	Status	—	90	10	Normal
TM10	Hidden Power	Normal	Special	60	100	15	Normal
TM11	Sunny Day	Fire	Status	—	—	5	Both Sides
TM17	Protect	Normal	Status	—	—	10	Self
TM21	Frustration	Normal	Physical	—	100	20	Normal
TM27	Return	Normal	Physical	—	100	20	Normal
TM28	Dig	Ground	Physical	80	100	10	Normal
TM31	Brick Break	Fighting	Physical	75	100	15	Normal
TM32	Double Team	Normal	Status	—	—	15	Self
TM35	Flamethrower	Fire	Special	90	100	15	Normal
TM38	Fire Blast	Fire	Special	110	85	5	Normal
TM39	Rock Tomb	Rock	Physical	60	95	15	Normal
TM40	Aerial Ace	Flying	Physical	60	—	20	Normal
TM42	Facade	Normal	Physical	70	100	20	Normal
TM43	Flame Charge	Fire	Physical	50	100	20	Normal
TM44	Rest	Psychic	Status	—	—	10	Self
TM45	Attract	Normal	Status	—	100	15	Normal
TM48	Round	Normal	Special	60	100	15	Normal
TM49	Echoed Voice	Normal	Special	40	100	15	Normal
TM50	Overheat	Fire	Special	130	90	5	Normal
TM56	Fling	Dark	Physical	—	100	10	Normal
TM59	Incinerate	Fire	Special	60	100	15	Many Others
TM61	Will-O-Wisp	Fire	Status	—	85	15	Normal
TM65	Shadow Claw	Ghost	Physical	70	100	15	Normal
TM75	Swords Dance	Normal	Status	—	—	20	Self
TM80	Rock Slide	Rock	Physical	75	90	10	Many Others
TM87	Swagger	Normal	Status	—	90	15	Normal
TM88	Sleep Talk	Normal	Status	—	—	10	Self
TM90	Substitute	Normal	Status	—	—	10	Self
TM94	Secret Power	Normal	Physical	70	100	20	Normal
TM98	Power-Up Punch	Fighting	Physical	40	100	20	Normal
TM100	Confide	Normal	Status	—	—	20	Normal
HM01	Cut	Normal	Physical	50	95	30	Normal
HM04	Strength	Normal	Physical	80	100	15	Normal
HM06	Rock Smash	Fighting	Physical	40	100	15	Normal

MOVES LEARNED IN EXCHANGE FOR BP

Name	Type	Kind	Pow.	Acc.	PP	Range
Thunder Punch	Electric	Physical	75	100	15	Normal
Fire Punch	Fire	Physical	75	100	15	Normal
Dragon Pulse	Dragon	Special	85	100	10	Normal
Iron Tail	Steel	Physical	100	75	15	Normal
Snore	Normal	Special	50	100	15	Normal
Heat Wave	Fire	Special	95	90	10	Many Others
Focus Punch	Fighting	Physical	150	100	20	Normal

MOVES TAUGHT BY PEOPLE

Name	Type	Kind	Pow.	Acc.	PP	Range
Fire Pledge	Fire	Special	80	100	10	Normal

National Pokédex **006** Hoenn Pokédex —

Charizard

Flame Pokémon

Fire | Flying

HEIGHT: 5'07" WEIGHT: 199.5 lbs.

Same form for ♂ / ♀

Ω Charizard flies around the sky in search of powerful opponents. It breathes fire of such great heat that it melts anything. However, it never turns its fiery breath on any opponent weaker than itself.

α Charizard flies around the sky in search of powerful opponents. It breathes fire of such great heat that it melts anything. However, it never turns its fiery breath on any opponent weaker than itself.

ABILITY
Blaze

HIDDEN ABILITY
Solar Power

EGG GROUPS
Monster | Dragon

STAT GROWTH RATES
HP
Attack
Defense
Sp. Atk
Sp. Def
Speed

ITEMS SOMETIMES HELD BY WILD POKÉMON
—

EVOLUTION

MAIN WAY TO REGISTER IN THE NATIONAL POKÉDEX

Level up a Charmeleon obtained via Link Trade or the GTS to Lv. 36.

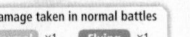

Damage taken in normal battles

Normal	×1	Flying	×1
Fire	×0.5	Psychic	×1
Water	×2	Bug	×0.25
Grass	×0.25	Rock	×4
Electric	×2	Ghost	×1
Ice	×1	Dragon	×1
Fighting	×0.5	Dark	×1
Poison	×1	Steel	×0.5
Ground	×0	Fairy	×0.5

Damage taken in Inverse battles

Normal	×1	Flying	×1
Fire	×2	Psychic	×1
Water	×0.5	Bug	×4
Grass	×4	Rock	×0.25
Electric	×0.5	Ghost	×1
Ice	×1	Dragon	×1
Fighting	×2	Dark	×1
Poison	×1	Steel	×2
Ground	×1	Fairy	×2

Can be used in
Inverse Battle
Battle Institute
Battle Maison
Random Matchup (Free Battle)
Random Matchup (Others)

LEVEL-UP MOVES

Lv.	Name	Type	Kind	Pow.	Acc.	PP	Range
1	Flare Blitz	Fire	Physical	120	100	15	Normal
1	Heat Wave	Fire	Special	95	90	10	Many Others
1	Dragon Claw	Dragon	Physical	80	100	15	Normal
1	Shadow Claw	Ghost	Physical	70	100	15	Normal
1	Air Slash	Flying	Special	75	95	15	Normal
1	Scratch	Normal	Physical	40	100	35	Normal
1	Growl	Normal	Status	—	100	40	Many Others
1	Ember	Fire	Special	40	100	25	Normal
1	Smokescreen	Normal	Status	—	100	20	Normal
7	Ember	Fire	Special	40	100	25	Normal
10	Smokescreen	Normal	Status	—	100	20	Normal
17	Dragon Rage	Dragon	Special	—	100	10	Normal
21	Scary Face	Normal	Status	—	100	10	Normal
28	Fire Fang	Fire	Physical	65	95	15	Normal
32	Flame Burst	Fire	Special	70	100	15	Normal
36	Wing Attack	Flying	Physical	60	100	35	Normal
41	Slash	Normal	Physical	70	100	20	Normal
47	Flamethrower	Fire	Special	90	100	15	Normal
56	Fire Spin	Fire	Special	35	85	15	Normal
62	Inferno	Fire	Special	100	50	5	Normal
71	Heat Wave	Fire	Special	95	90	10	Many Others
77	Flare Blitz	Fire	Physical	120	100	15	Normal

TM & HM MOVES

No.	Name	Type	Kind	Pow.	Acc.	PP	Range
TM01	Hone Claws	Dark	Status	—	—	15	Self
TM02	Dragon Claw	Dragon	Physical	80	100	15	Normal
TM05	Roar	Normal	Status	—	—	20	Normal
TM06	Toxic	Poison	Status	—	90	10	Normal
TM10	Hidden Power	Normal	Special	60	100	15	Normal
TM11	Sunny Day	Fire	Status	—	—	5	Both Sides
TM15	Hyper Beam	Normal	Special	150	90	5	Normal
TM17	Protect	Normal	Status	—	—	10	Self
TM19	Roost	Flying	Status	—	—	10	Self
TM21	Frustration	Normal	Physical	—	100	20	Normal
TM22	Solar Beam	Grass	Special	120	100	10	Normal
TM26	Earthquake	Ground	Physical	100	100	10	Adjacent
TM27	Return	Normal	Physical	—	100	20	Normal
TM28	Dig	Ground	Physical	80	100	10	Normal
TM31	Brick Break	Fighting	Physical	75	100	15	Normal
TM32	Double Team	Normal	Status	—	—	15	Self
TM35	Flamethrower	Fire	Special	90	100	15	Normal
TM38	Fire Blast	Fire	Special	110	85	5	Normal
TM39	Rock Tomb	Rock	Physical	60	95	15	Normal
TM40	Aerial Ace	Flying	Physical	60	—	20	Normal
TM42	Facade	Normal	Physical	70	100	20	Normal
TM43	Flame Charge	Fire	Physical	50	100	20	Normal
TM44	Rest	Psychic	Status	—	—	10	Self
TM45	Attract	Normal	Status	—	100	15	Normal
TM48	Round	Normal	Special	60	100	15	Normal
TM49	Echoed Voice	Normal	Special	40	100	15	Normal
TM50	Overheat	Fire	Special	130	90	5	Normal
TM51	Steel Wing	Steel	Physical	70	90	25	Normal
TM52	Focus Blast	Fighting	Special	120	70	5	Normal
TM56	Fling	Dark	Physical	—	100	10	Normal
TM58	Sky Drop	Flying	Physical	60	100	10	Normal
TM59	Incinerate	Fire	Special	60	100	15	Many Others
TM61	Will-O-Wisp	Fire	Status	—	85	15	Normal
TM65	Shadow Claw	Ghost	Physical	70	100	15	Normal
TM68	Giga Impact	Normal	Physical	150	90	5	Normal
TM75	Swords Dance	Normal	Status	—	—	20	Self
TM78	Bulldoze	Ground	Physical	60	100	20	Adjacent
TM80	Rock Slide	Rock	Physical	75	90	10	Many Others
TM82	Dragon Tail	Dragon	Physical	60	90	10	Normal
TM87	Swagger	Normal	Status	—	90	15	Normal
TM88	Sleep Talk	Normal	Status	—	—	10	Self
TM90	Substitute	Normal	Status	—	—	10	Self
TM94	Secret Power	Normal	Physical	70	100	20	Normal
TM98	Power-Up Punch	Fighting	Physical	40	100	20	Normal
TM100	Confide	Normal	Status	—	—	20	Normal
HM01	Cut	Normal	Physical	50	95	30	Normal
HM02	Fly	Flying	Physical	90	95	15	Normal
HM04	Strength	Normal	Physical	80	100	15	Normal
HM06	Rock Smash	Fighting	Physical	40	100	15	Normal

MOVES LEARNED IN EXCHANGE FOR BP

Name	Type	Kind	Pow.	Acc.	PP	Range
Thunder Punch	Electric	Physical	75	100	15	Normal
Fire Punch	Fire	Physical	75	100	15	Normal
Dragon Pulse	Dragon	Special	85	100	10	Normal
Iron Tail	Steel	Physical	100	75	15	Normal
Snore	Normal	Special	50	100	15	Normal
Heat Wave	Fire	Special	95	90	10	Many Others
Tailwind	Flying	Status	—	—	15	Your Side
Focus Punch	Fighting	Physical	150	100	20	Normal
Outrage	Dragon	Physical	120	100	10	1 Random

MOVES TAUGHT BY PEOPLE

Name	Type	Kind	Pow.	Acc.	PP	Range
Blast Burn	Fire	Special	150	90	5	Normal
Fire Pledge	Fire	Special	80	100	10	Normal

Mega Evolution

Mega Charizard X

Flame Pokémon

Fire | Dragon

HEIGHT: 5'07" WEIGHT: 243.6 lbs

Same form for ♂ / ♀

REQUIRED MEGA STONE
Charizardite X
Find on the Fiery Path (after battling Groudon or Kyogre).

ABILITY
Tough Claws

HIDDEN ABILITY
—

EGG GROUPS
—

STAT GROWTH RATES
HP
Attack
Defense
Sp. Atk
Sp. Def
Speed

Damage taken in normal battles

Normal	×1	Flying	×1
Fire	×0.25	Psychic	×1
Water	×1	Bug	×0.5
Grass	×0.25	Rock	×2
Electric	×0.5	Ghost	×1
Ice	×1	Dragon	×2
Fighting	×1	Dark	×1
Poison	×1	Steel	×0.5
Ground	×2	Fairy	×1

Damage taken in Inverse battles

Normal	×1	Flying	×1
Fire	×4	Psychic	×1
Water	×1	Bug	×2
Grass	×4	Rock	×0.5
Electric	×2	Ghost	×1
Ice	×1	Dragon	×0.5
Fighting	×1	Dark	×1
Poison	×1	Steel	×2
Ground	×0.5	Fairy	×1

Can be used in
Inverse Battle
Battle Institute
Battle Maison
Random Matchup (Free Battle)
Random Matchup (Others)

Mega Evolution

Mega Charizard Y

Flame Pokémon

Fire | Flying

HEIGHT: 5'07" WEIGHT: 221.6 lbs.

Same form for ♂ / ♀

REQUIRED MEGA STONE

Charizardite Y

Find on Scorched Slab B2F on Route 120 (after battling Groudon or Kyogre).

ABILITY

Drought

HIDDEN ABILITY

—

EGG GROUPS

—

STAT GROWTH RATES

HP	▮▮▮
Attack	▮▮▮▮▮
Defense	▮▮▮
Sp. Atk	▮▮▮▮▮▮▮▮
Sp. Def	▮▮▮▮▮
Speed	▮▮▮▮▮

Damage taken in normal battles

Type		Type	
Normal	×1	Flying	×1
Fire	×0.5	Psychic	×1
Water	×2	Bug	×0.25
Grass	×0.25	Rock	×4
Electric	×2	Ghost	×1
Ice	×1	Dragon	×1
Fighting	×0.5	Dark	×1
Poison	×1	Steel	×0.5
Ground	×0	Fairy	×0.5

Damage taken in Inverse battles

Type		Type	
Normal	×1	Flying	×1
Fire	×2	Psychic	×1
Water	×0.5	Bug	×4
Grass	×4	Rock	×0.25
Electric	×0.5	Ghost	×1
Ice	×1	Dragon	×1
Fighting	×2	Dark	×1
Poison	×1	Steel	×2
Ground	×1	Fairy	×2

Can be used in

Inverse Battle
Battle Institute
Battle Maison
Random Matchup (Free Battle)
Random Matchup (Others)

National Pokédex **007** Hoenn Pokédex **—**

Squirtle

Tiny Turtle Pokémon

Water

HEIGHT: 1'08" WEIGHT: 19.8 lbs.

Same form for ♂ / ♀

Ω Squirtle's shell is not merely used for protection. The shell's rounded shape and the grooves on its surface help minimize resistance in water, enabling this Pokémon to swim at high speeds.

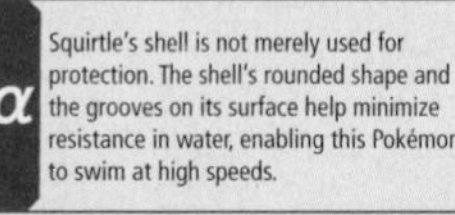

α Squirtle's shell is not merely used for protection. The shell's rounded shape and the grooves on its surface help minimize resistance in water, enabling this Pokémon to swim at high speeds.

ABILITY

Torrent

HIDDEN ABILITY

Rain Dish

EGG GROUPS

Monster | Water 1

STAT GROWTH RATES

HP	▮▮
Attack	▮▮▮
Defense	▮▮▮
Sp. Atk	▮▮
Sp. Def	▮▮▮
Speed	▮▮

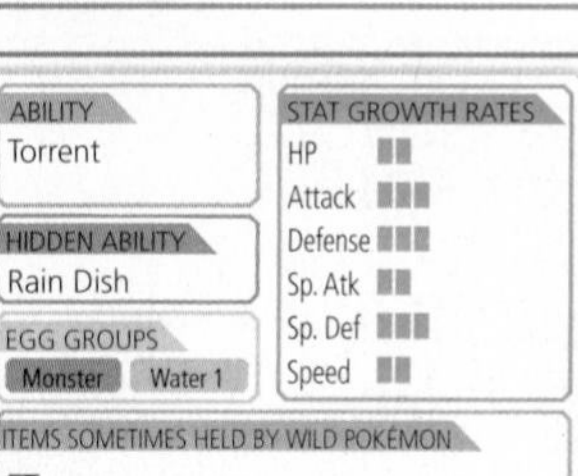

ITEMS SOMETIMES HELD BY WILD POKÉMON

—

EVOLUTION

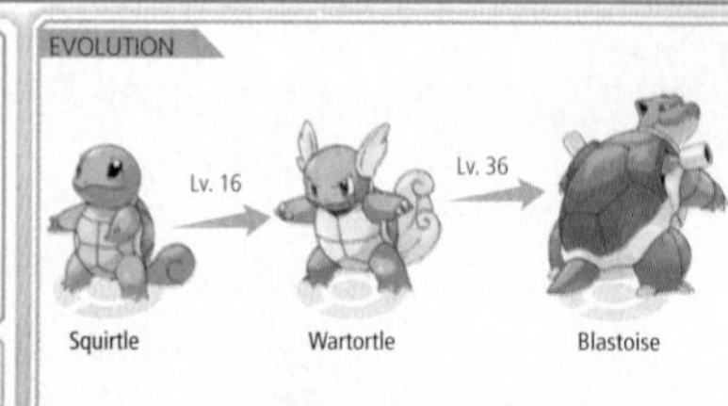

MAIN WAY TO REGISTER IN THE NATIONAL POKÉDEX

Obtain in *Pokémon X* or *Pokémon Y*. Bring it to your game using Link Trade or the GTS.

Damage taken in normal battles

Type		Type	
Normal	×1	Flying	×1
Fire	×0.5	Psychic	×1
Water	×0.5	Bug	×1
Grass	×2	Rock	×1
Electric	×2	Ghost	×1
Ice	×0.5	Dragon	×1
Fighting	×1	Dark	×1
Poison	×1	Steel	×0.5
Ground	×1	Fairy	×1

Damage taken in Inverse battles

Type		Type	
Normal	×1	Flying	×1
Fire	×2	Psychic	×1
Water	×2	Bug	×1
Grass	×0.5	Rock	×1
Electric	×0.5	Ghost	×1
Ice	×2	Dragon	×1
Fighting	×1	Dark	×1
Poison	×1	Steel	×2
Ground	×1	Fairy	×1

Can be used in

Inverse Battle
Battle Institute
Battle Maison
Random Matchup (Free Battle)
Random Matchup (Others)

LEVEL-UP MOVES

Lv.	Name	Type	Kind	Pow.	Acc.	PP	Range
1	Tackle	Normal	Physical	50	100	35	Normal
4	Tail Whip	Normal	Status	—	100	30	Many Others
7	Water Gun	Water	Special	40	100	25	Normal
10	Withdraw	Water	Status	—	—	40	Self
13	Bubble	Water	Special	40	100	30	Many Others
16	Bite	Dark	Physical	60	100	25	Normal
19	Rapid Spin	Normal	Physical	20	100	40	Normal
22	Protect	Normal	Status	—	—	10	Self
25	Water Pulse	Water	Special	60	100	20	Normal
28	Aqua Tail	Water	Physical	90	90	10	Normal
31	Skull Bash	Normal	Physical	130	100	10	Normal
34	Iron Defense	Steel	Status	—	—	15	Self
37	Rain Dance	Water	Status	—	—	5	Both Sides
40	Hydro Pump	Water	Special	110	80	5	Normal

TM & HM MOVES

No.	Name	Type	Kind	Pow.	Acc.	PP	Range
TM06	Toxic	Poison	Status	—	90	10	Normal
TM07	Hail	Ice	Status	—	—	10	Both Sides
TM10	Hidden Power	Normal	Special	60	100	15	Normal
TM13	Ice Beam	Ice	Special	90	100	10	Normal
TM14	Blizzard	Ice	Special	110	70	5	Many Others
TM17	Protect	Normal	Status	—	—	10	Self
TM18	Rain Dance	Water	Status	—	—	5	Both Sides
TM21	Frustration	Normal	Physical	—	100	20	Normal
TM27	Return	Normal	Physical	—	100	20	Normal
TM28	Dig	Ground	Physical	80	100	10	Normal
TM31	Brick Break	Fighting	Physical	75	100	15	Normal
TM32	Double Team	Normal	Status	—	—	15	Self
TM39	Rock Tomb	Rock	Physical	60	95	15	Normal
TM42	Facade	Normal	Physical	70	100	20	Normal
TM44	Rest	Psychic	Status	—	—	10	Self
TM45	Attract	Normal	Status	—	100	15	Normal
TM48	Round	Normal	Special	60	100	15	Normal
TM55	Scald	Water	Special	80	100	15	Normal
TM56	Fling	Dark	Physical	—	100	10	Normal
TM74	Gyro Ball	Steel	Physical	—	100	5	Normal
TM87	Swagger	Normal	Status	—	90	15	Normal
TM88	Sleep Talk	Normal	Status	—	—	10	Self
TM90	Substitute	Normal	Status	—	—	10	Self
TM94	Secret Power	Normal	Physical	70	100	20	Normal
TM98	Power-Up Punch	Fighting	Physical	40	100	20	Normal
TM100	Confide	Normal	Status	—	—	20	Normal
HM03	Surf	Water	Special	90	100	15	Adjacent
HM04	Strength	Normal	Physical	80	100	15	Normal
HM05	Waterfall	Water	Physical	80	100	15	Normal
HM06	Rock Smash	Fighting	Physical	40	100	15	Normal
HM07	Dive	Water	Physical	80	100	10	Normal

MOVES LEARNED IN EXCHANGE FOR BP

Name	Type	Kind	Pow.	Acc.	PP	Range
Ice Punch	Ice	Physical	75	100	15	Normal
Iron Defense	Steel	Status	—	—	15	Self
Icy Wind	Ice	Special	55	95	15	Many Others
Aqua Tail	Water	Physical	90	90	10	Normal
Zen Headbutt	Psychic	Physical	80	90	15	Normal
Dragon Pulse	Dragon	Special	85	100	10	Normal
Iron Tail	Steel	Physical	100	75	15	Normal
Snore	Normal	Special	50	100	15	Normal
Focus Punch	Fighting	Physical	150	100	20	Normal
Water Pulse	Water	Special	60	100	20	Normal

MOVES TAUGHT BY PEOPLE

Name	Type	Kind	Pow.	Acc.	PP	Range
Water Pledge	Water	Special	80	100	10	Normal

EGG MOVES

Name	Type	Kind	Pow.	Acc.	PP	Range
Mirror Coat	Psychic	Special		100	20	Varies
Haze	Ice	Status			30	Both Sides
Mist	Ice	Status			30	Your Side
Foresight	Normal	Status			40	Normal
Flail	Normal	Physical		100	15	Normal
Refresh	Normal	Status			20	Self
Mud Sport	Ground	Status			15	Both Sides
Yawn	Normal	Status			10	Normal
Muddy Water	Water	Special	90	85	10	Many Others
Fake Out	Normal	Physical	40	100	10	Normal
Aqua Ring	Water	Status			20	Self
Aqua Jet	Water	Physical	40	100	20	Normal
Water Spout	Water	Special	150	100	5	Many Others
Brine	Water	Special	65	100	10	Normal
Dragon Pulse	Dragon	Special	85	100	10	Normal
Aura Sphere	Fighting	Special	80		20	Normal

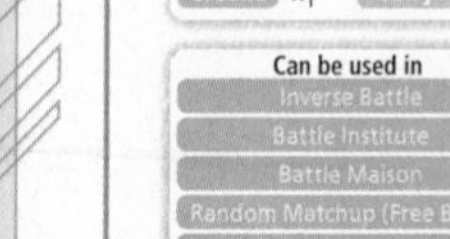

National Pokédex **008** Hoenn Pokédex —

Wartortle

Turtle Pokémon

Water

HEIGHT: 3'03" WEIGHT: 49.6 lbs.

Same form for ♂ / ♀

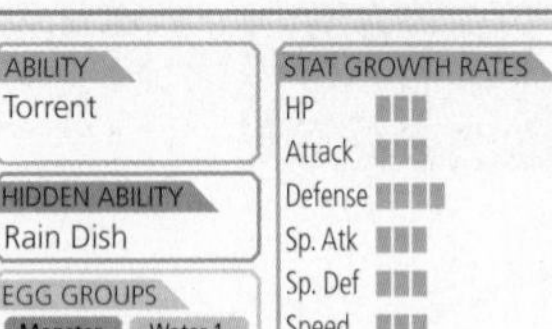

Ω Its tail is large and covered with a rich, thick fur. The tail becomes increasingly deeper in color as Wartortle ages. The scratches on its shell are evidence of this Pokémon's toughness as a battler.

α Its tail is large and covered with a rich, thick fur. The tail becomes increasingly deeper in color as Wartortle ages. The scratches on its shell are evidence of this Pokémon's toughness as a battler.

ABILITY
Torrent

HIDDEN ABILITY
Rain Dish

EGG GROUPS
Monster / Water 1

STAT GROWTH RATES
HP ■■■
Attack ■■■
Defense ■■■■
Sp. Atk ■■■
Sp. Def ■■■
Speed ■■■

ITEMS SOMETIMES HELD BY WILD POKÉMON
—

EVOLUTION
Squirtle → Lv. 16 → Wartortle → Lv. 36 → Blastoise

MAIN WAY TO REGISTER IN THE NATIONAL POKÉDEX

Level up a Squirtle obtained via Link Trade or the GTS to Lv. 16.

Damage taken in normal battles

Type		Type	
Normal	×1	Flying	×1
Fire	×0.5	Psychic	×1
Water	×0.5	Bug	×1
Grass	×2	Rock	×1
Electric	×2	Ghost	×1
Ice	×0.5	Dragon	×1
Fighting	×1	Dark	×1
Poison	×1	Steel	×0.5
Ground	×1	Fairy	×1

Damage taken in Inverse battles

Type		Type	
Normal	×1	Flying	×1
Fire	×2	Psychic	×1
Water	×2	Bug	×1
Grass	×0.5	Rock	×1
Electric	×0.5	Ghost	×1
Ice	×2	Dragon	×1
Fighting	×1	Dark	×1
Poison	×1	Steel	×2
Ground	×1	Fairy	×1

Can be used in
Inverse Battle
Battle Institute
Battle Maison
Random Matchup (Free Battle)
Random Matchup (Others)

LEVEL-UP MOVES

Lv.	Name	Type	Kind	Pow.	Acc.	PP	Range
1	Tackle	Normal	Physical	50	100	35	Normal
1	Tail Whip	Normal	Status	—	100	30	Many Others
1	Water Gun	Water	Special	40	100	25	Normal
4	Tail Whip	Normal	Status	—	100	30	Many Others
7	Water Gun	Water	Special	40	100	25	Normal
10	Withdraw	Water	Status	—	—	40	Self
13	Bubble	Water	Special	40	100	30	Many Others
16	Bite	Dark	Physical	60	100	25	Normal
20	Rapid Spin	Normal	Physical	20	100	40	Normal
24	Protect	Normal	Status	—	—	10	Self
28	Water Pulse	Water	Special	60	100	20	Normal
32	Aqua Tail	Water	Physical	90	90	10	Normal
36	Skull Bash	Normal	Physical	130	100	10	Normal
40	Iron Defense	Steel	Status	—	—	15	Self
44	Rain Dance	Water	Status	—	—	5	Both Sides
48	Hydro Pump	Water	Special	110	80	5	Normal

TM & HM MOVES

No.	Name	Type	Kind	Pow.	Acc.	PP	Range
TM06	Toxic	Poison	Status	—	90	10	Normal
TM07	Hail	Ice	Status	—	—	10	Both Sides
TM10	Hidden Power	Normal	Special	60	100	15	Normal
TM13	Ice Beam	Ice	Special	90	100	10	Normal
TM14	Blizzard	Ice	Special	110	70	5	Many Others
TM17	Protect	Normal	Status	—	—	10	Self
TM18	Rain Dance	Water	Status	—	—	5	Both Sides
TM21	Frustration	Normal	Physical	—	100	20	Normal
TM27	Return	Normal	Physical	—	100	20	Normal
TM28	Dig	Ground	Physical	80	100	10	Normal
TM31	Brick Break	Fighting	Physical	75	100	15	Normal
TM32	Double Team	Normal	Status	—	—	15	Self
TM39	Rock Tomb	Rock	Physical	60	95	15	Normal
TM42	Facade	Normal	Physical	70	100	20	Normal
TM44	Rest	Psychic	Status	—	—	10	Self
TM45	Attract	Normal	Status	—	100	15	Normal
TM48	Round	Normal	Special	60	100	15	Normal
TM55	Scald	Water	Special	80	100	15	Normal
TM56	Fling	Dark	Physical	—	100	10	Normal
TM74	Gyro Ball	Steel	Physical	—	100	5	Normal
TM87	Swagger	Normal	Status	—	90	15	Normal
TM88	Sleep Talk	Normal	Status	—	—	10	Self
TM90	Substitute	Normal	Status	—	—	10	Self
TM94	Secret Power	Normal	Physical	70	100	20	Normal
TM98	Power-Up Punch	Fighting	Physical	40	100	20	Normal
TM100	Confide	Normal	Status	—	—	20	Normal
HM03	Surf	Water	Special	90	100	15	Adjacent
HM04	Strength	Normal	Physical	80	100	15	Normal
HM05	Waterfall	Water	Physical	80	100	15	Normal
HM06	Rock Smash	Fighting	Physical	40	100	15	Normal
HM07	Dive	Water	Physical	80	100	10	Normal

MOVES LEARNED IN EXCHANGE FOR BP

Name	Type	Kind	Pow.	Acc.	PP	Range
Ice Punch	Ice	Physical	75	100	15	Normal
Iron Defense	Steel	Status	—	—	15	Self
Icy Wind	Ice	Special	55	95	15	Many Others
Aqua Tail	Water	Physical	90	90	10	Normal
Zen Headbutt	Psychic	Physical	80	90	15	Normal
Dragon Pulse	Dragon	Special	85	100	10	Normal
Iron Tail	Steel	Physical	100	75	15	Normal
Snore	Normal	Special	50	100	15	Normal
Focus Punch	Fighting	Physical	150	100	20	Normal
Water Pulse	Water	Special	60	100	20	Normal

MOVES TAUGHT BY PEOPLE

Name	Type	Kind	Pow.	Acc.	PP	Range
Water Pledge	Water	Special	80	100	10	Normal

National Pokédex **009** Hoenn Pokédex —

Blastoise

Shellfish Pokémon

Water

HEIGHT: 5'03" WEIGHT: 188.5 lbs.

Same form for ♂ / ♀

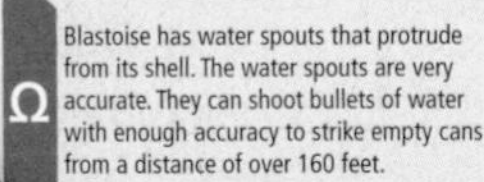

Ω Blastoise has water spouts that protrude from its shell. The water spouts are very accurate. They can shoot bullets of water with enough accuracy to strike empty cans from a distance of over 160 feet.

α Blastoise has water spouts that protrude from its shell. The water spouts are very accurate. They can shoot bullets of water with enough accuracy to strike empty cans from a distance of over 160 feet.

ABILITY
Torrent

HIDDEN ABILITY
Rain Dish

EGG GROUPS
Monster / Water 1

STAT GROWTH RATES
HP ■■■
Attack ■■■■
Defense ■■■■
Sp. Atk ■■■■
Sp. Def ■■■■
Speed ■■■■

ITEMS SOMETIMES HELD BY WILD POKÉMON
—

EVOLUTION
Squirtle → Lv. 16 → Wartortle → Lv. 36 → Blastoise

MAIN WAY TO REGISTER IN THE NATIONAL POKÉDEX

Level up a Wartortle obtained via Link Trade or the GTS to Lv. 36.

Damage taken in normal battles

Type		Type	
Normal	×1	Flying	×1
Fire	×0.5	Psychic	×1
Water	×0.5	Bug	×1
Grass	×2	Rock	×1
Electric	×2	Ghost	×1
Ice	×0.5	Dragon	×1
Fighting	×1	Dark	×1
Poison	×1	Steel	×0.5
Ground	×1	Fairy	×1

Damage taken in Inverse battles

Type		Type	
Normal	×1	Flying	×1
Fire	×2	Psychic	×1
Water	×2	Bug	×1
Grass	×0.5	Rock	×1
Electric	×0.5	Ghost	×1
Ice	×2	Dragon	×1
Fighting	×1	Dark	×1
Poison	×1	Steel	×2
Ground	×1	Fairy	×1

Can be used in
Inverse Battle
Battle Institute
Battle Maison
Random Matchup (Free Battle)
Random Matchup (Others)

LEVEL-UP MOVES

Lv.	Name	Type	Kind	Pow.	Acc.	PP	Range
1	Flash Cannon	Steel	Special	80	100	10	Normal
1	Tackle	Normal	Physical	50	100	35	Normal
1	Tail Whip	Normal	Status	—	100	30	Many Others
1	Water Gun	Water	Special	40	100	25	Normal
1	Withdraw	Water	Status	—	—	40	Self
4	Tail Whip	Normal	Status	—	100	30	Many Others
7	Water Gun	Water	Special	40	100	25	Normal
10	Withdraw	Water	Status	—	—	40	Self
13	Bubble	Water	Special	40	100	30	Many Others
16	Bite	Dark	Physical	60	100	25	Normal
20	Rapid Spin	Normal	Physical	20	100	40	Normal
24	Protect	Normal	Status	—	—	10	Self
28	Water Pulse	Water	Special	60	100	20	Normal
32	Aqua Tail	Water	Physical	90	90	10	Normal
39	Skull Bash	Normal	Physical	130	100	10	Normal
46	Iron Defense	Steel	Status	—	—	15	Self
53	Rain Dance	Water	Status	—	—	5	Both Sides
60	Hydro Pump	Water	Special	110	80	5	Normal

TM & HM MOVES

No.	Name	Type	Kind	Pow.	Acc.	PP	Range
TM05	Roar	Normal	Status	—	—	20	Normal
TM06	Toxic	Poison	Status	—	90	10	Normal
TM07	Hail	Ice	Status	—	—	10	Both Sides
TM10	Hidden Power	Normal	Special	60	100	15	Normal
TM13	Ice Beam	Ice	Special	90	100	10	Normal
TM14	Blizzard	Ice	Special	110	70	5	Many Others
TM15	Hyper Beam	Normal	Special	150	90	5	Normal
TM17	Protect	Normal	Status	—	—	10	Self
TM18	Rain Dance	Water	Status	—	—	5	Both Sides
TM21	Frustration	Normal	Physical	—	100	20	Normal
TM23	Smack Down	Rock	Physical	50	100	15	Normal
TM26	Earthquake	Ground	Physical	100	100	10	Adjacent
TM27	Return	Normal	Physical	—	100	20	Normal
TM28	Dig	Ground	Physical	80	100	10	Normal
TM31	Brick Break	Fighting	Physical	75	100	15	Normal
TM32	Double Team	Normal	Status	—	—	15	Self
TM39	Rock Tomb	Rock	Physical	60	95	15	Normal
TM42	Facade	Normal	Physical	70	100	20	Normal
TM44	Rest	Psychic	Status	—	—	10	Self
TM45	Attract	Normal	Status	—	100	15	Normal
TM48	Round	Normal	Special	60	100	15	Normal
TM52	Focus Blast	Fighting	Special	120	70	5	Normal
TM55	Scald	Water	Special	80	100	15	Normal
TM56	Fling	Dark	Physical	—	100	10	Normal
TM68	Giga Impact	Normal	Physical	150	90	5	Normal
TM74	Gyro Ball	Steel	Physical	—	100	5	Normal
TM78	Bulldoze	Ground	Physical	60	100	20	Adjacent
TM80	Rock Slide	Rock	Physical	75	90	10	Many Others
TM82	Dragon Tail	Dragon	Physical	60	90	10	Normal
TM87	Swagger	Normal	Status	—	90	15	Normal
TM88	Sleep Talk	Normal	Status	—	—	10	Self
TM90	Substitute	Normal	Status	—	—	10	Self
TM91	Flash Cannon	Steel	Special	80	100	10	Normal
TM94	Secret Power	Normal	Physical	70	100	20	Normal
TM97	Dark Pulse	Dark	Special	80	100	15	Normal
TM98	Power-Up Punch	Fighting	Physical	40	100	20	Normal
TM100	Confide	Normal	Status	—	—	20	Normal
HM03	Surf	Water	Special	90	100	15	Adjacent
HM04	Strength	Normal	Physical	80	100	15	Normal
HM05	Waterfall	Water	Physical	80	100	15	Normal
HM06	Rock Smash	Fighting	Physical	40	100	15	Normal
HM07	Dive	Water	Physical	80	100	10	Normal

MOVES LEARNED IN EXCHANGE FOR BP

Name	Type	Kind	Pow.	Acc.	PP	Range
Signal Beam	Bug	Special	75	100	15	Normal
Ice Punch	Ice	Physical	75	100	15	Normal
Iron Defense	Steel	Status	—	—	15	Self
Icy Wind	Ice	Special	55	95	15	Many Others
Aqua Tail	Water	Physical	90	90	10	Normal
Zen Headbutt	Psychic	Physical	80	90	15	Normal
Dragon Pulse	Dragon	Special	85	100	10	Normal
Iron Tail	Steel	Physical	100	75	15	Normal
Snore	Normal	Special	50	100	15	Normal
Focus Punch	Fighting	Physical	150	100	20	Normal
Water Pulse	Water	Special	60	100	20	Normal
Outrage	Dragon	Physical	120	100	10	1 Random

MOVES TAUGHT BY PEOPLE

Name	Type	Kind	Pow.	Acc.	PP	Range
Water Pledge	Water	Special	80	100	10	Normal
Hydro Cannon	Water	Special	150	90	5	Normal

Mega Evolution

Mega Blastoise

Shellfish Pokémon

Water

HEIGHT: 5'03" WEIGHT: 222.9 lbs.

Same form for ♂ / ♀

REQUIRED MEGA STONE

Blastoisinite

Find on the deck of the *S.S. Tidal* after completing the Delta Episode.

ABILITY

Mega Launcher

HIDDEN ABILITY

—

EGG GROUPS

—

STAT GROWTH RATES

HP	▮▮▮
Attack	▮▮▮▮▮
Defense	▮▮▮▮▮
Sp. Atk	▮▮▮▮▮▮▮
Sp. Def	▮▮▮▮▮
Speed	▮▮▮▮

Damage taken in normal battles

Normal	×1	Flying	×1
Fire	×0.5	Psychic	×1
Water	×0.5	Bug	×1
Grass	×2	Rock	×1
Electric	×2	Ghost	×1
Ice	×0.5	Dragon	×1
Fighting	×1	Dark	×1
Poison	×1	Steel	×0.5
Ground	×1	Fairy	×1

Damage taken in Inverse battles

Normal	×1	Flying	×1
Fire	×2	Psychic	×1
Water	×2	Bug	×1
Grass	×0.5	Rock	×1
Electric	×0.5	Ghost	×1
Ice	×2	Dragon	×1
Fighting	×1	Dark	×1
Poison	×1	Steel	×2
Ground	×1	Fairy	×1

Can be used in

- Inverse Battle
- Battle Institute
- Battle Maison
- Random Matchup (Free Battle)
- Random Matchup (Others)

National Pokédex **010** Hoenn Pokédex **—**

Caterpie

Worm Pokémon

Bug

HEIGHT: 1'00" WEIGHT: 6.4 lbs.

Same form for ♂ / ♀

Ω Caterpie has a voracious appetite. It can devour leaves bigger than its body right before your eyes. From its antenna, this Pokémon releases a terrifically strong odor.

α Caterpie has a voracious appetite. It can devour leaves bigger than its body right before your eyes. From its antenna, this Pokémon releases a terrifically strong odor.

ABILITY

Shield Dust

HIDDEN ABILITY

Run Away

EGG GROUPS

Bug

STAT GROWTH RATES

HP	▮▮
Attack	▮▮
Defense	▮▮
Sp. Atk	▮
Sp. Def	▮
Speed	▮▮▮

ITEMS SOMETIMES HELD BY WILD POKÉMON

—

EVOLUTION

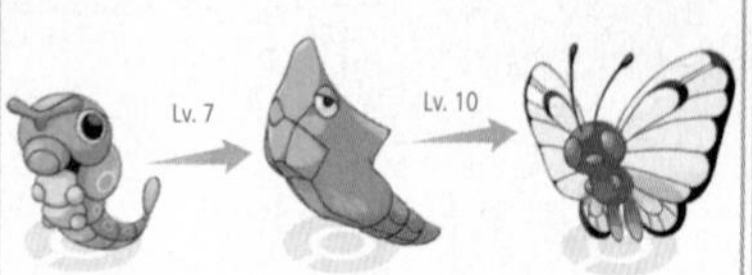

Caterpie → Lv. 7 → Metapod → Lv. 10 → Butterfree

MAIN WAY TO REGISTER IN THE NATIONAL POKÉDEX

Appears in *Pokémon X* and *Pokémon Y*. Bring it to your game using Link Trade or the GTS.

Damage taken in normal battles

Normal	×1	Flying	×2
Fire	×2	Psychic	×1
Water	×1	Bug	×1
Grass	×0.5	Rock	×2
Electric	×1	Ghost	×1
Ice	×1	Dragon	×1
Fighting	×0.5	Dark	×1
Poison	×1	Steel	×1
Ground	×0.5	Fairy	×1

Damage taken in Inverse battles

Normal	×1	Flying	×0.5
Fire	×0.5	Psychic	×1
Water	×1	Bug	×1
Grass	×2	Rock	×0.5
Electric	×1	Ghost	×1
Ice	×1	Dragon	×1
Fighting	×2	Dark	×1
Poison	×1	Steel	×1
Ground	×2	Fairy	×1

Can be used in

- Inverse Battle
- Battle Institute
- Battle Maison
- Random Matchup (Free Battle)
- Random Matchup (Others)

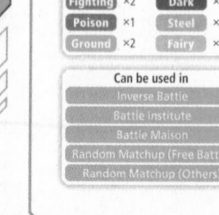

LEVEL-UP MOVES

Lv.	Name	Type	Kind	Pow.	Acc.	PP	Range
1	Tackle	Normal	Physical	50	100	35	Normal
1	String Shot	Bug	Status	—	95	40	Many Others
15	Bug Bite	Bug	Physical	60	100	20	Normal

TM & HM MOVES

No.	Name	Type	Kind	Pow.	Acc.	PP	Range

MOVES LEARNED IN EXCHANGE FOR BP

Name	Type	Kind	Pow.	Acc.	PP	Range
Bug Bite	Bug	Physical	60	100	20	Normal
Electroweb	Electric	Special	55	95	15	Many Others
Snore	Normal	Special	50	100	15	Normal

MOVES TAUGHT BY PEOPLE

Name	Type	Kind	Pow.	Acc.	PP	Range

National Pokédex **011** Hoenn Pokédex —

Metapod

Cocoon Pokémon

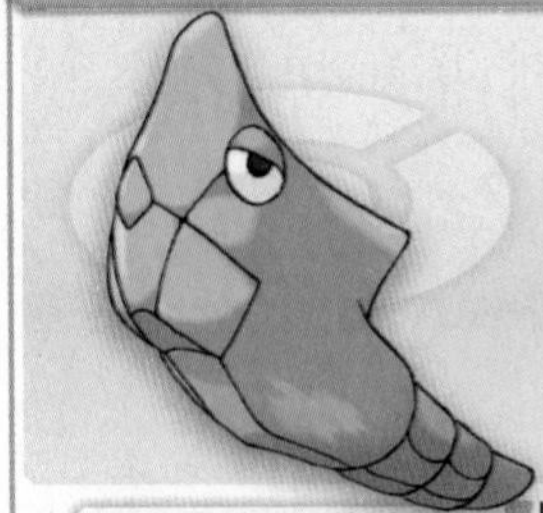

Bug

HEIGHT: 2'04" WEIGHT: 21.8 lbs.

Same form for ♂ / ♀

Ω The shell covering this Pokémon's body is as hard as an iron slab. Metapod does not move very much. It stays still because it is preparing its soft innards for evolution inside the hard shell.

α The shell covering this Pokémon's body is as hard as an iron slab. Metapod does not move very much. It stays still because it is preparing its soft innards for evolution inside the hard shell.

ABILITY
Shed Skin

HIDDEN ABILITY
—

EGG GROUPS
Bug

STAT GROWTH RATES
HP
Attack
Defense
Sp. Atk
Sp. Def
Speed

ITEMS SOMETIMES HELD BY WILD POKÉMON
—

EVOLUTION
Caterpie → Lv. 7 → Metapod → Lv. 10 → Butterfree

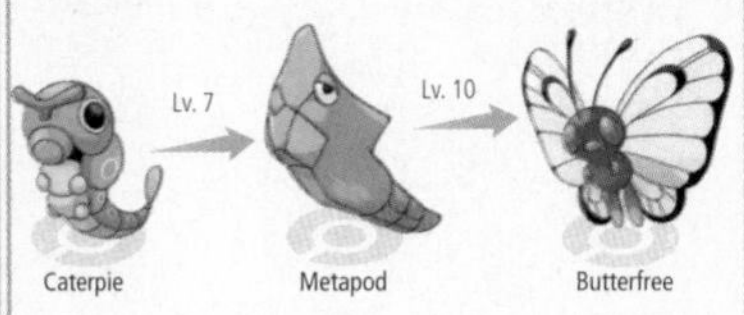

MAIN WAY TO REGISTER IN THE NATIONAL POKÉDEX

Level up a Caterpie obtained via Link Trade or the GTS to Lv. 7.

Damage taken in normal battles

Type		Type	
Normal	×1	Flying	×2
Fire	×2	Psychic	×1
Water	×1	Bug	×1
Grass	×0.5	Rock	×2
Electric	×1	Ghost	×1
Ice	×1	Dragon	×1
Fighting	×0.5	Dark	×1
Poison	×1	Steel	×1
Ground	×0.5	Fairy	×1

Damage taken in Inverse battles

Type		Type	
Normal	×1	Flying	×0.5
Fire	×0.5	Psychic	×1
Water	×1	Bug	×1
Grass	×2	Rock	×0.5
Electric	×1	Ghost	×1
Ice	×1	Dragon	×1
Fighting	×2	Dark	×1
Poison	×1	Steel	×1
Ground	×2	Fairy	×1

Can be used in
Inverse Battle
Battle Institute
Battle Maison
Random Matchup (Free Battle)
Random Matchup (Others)

LEVEL-UP MOVES

Lv.	Name	Type	Kind	Pow.	Acc.	PP	Range
1	Harden	Normal	Status	—	—	30	Self
7	Harden	Normal	Status	—	—	30	Self

TM & HM MOVES

No.	Name	Type	Kind	Pow.	Acc.	PP	Range

MOVES LEARNED IN EXCHANGE FOR BP

Name	Type	Kind	Pow.	Acc.	PP	Range
Bug Bite	Bug	Physical	60	100	20	Normal
Iron Defense	Steel	Status	—	—	15	Self
Electroweb	Electric	Special	55	95	15	Many Others

MOVES TAUGHT BY PEOPLE

Name	Type	Kind	Pow.	Acc.	PP	Range

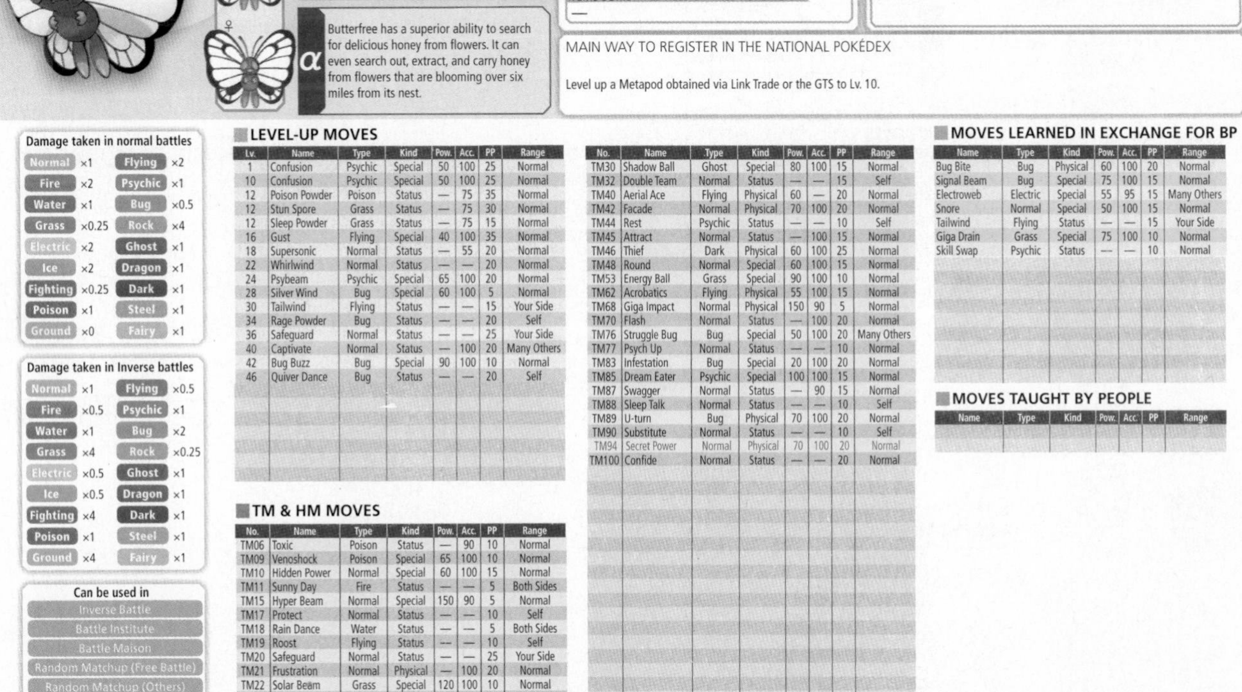

National Pokédex **012** Hoenn Pokédex —

Butterfree

Butterfly Pokémon

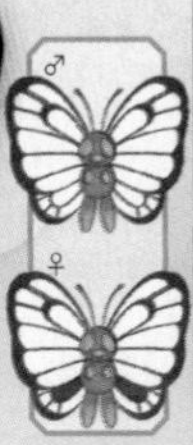

Bug **Flying**

HEIGHT: 3'07" WEIGHT: 70.5 lbs.

The base of the male's lower wings is white, while the female's is black.

♂ ♀

Ω Butterfree has a superior ability to search for delicious honey from flowers. It can even search out, extract, and carry honey from flowers that are blooming over six miles from its nest.

α Butterfree has a superior ability to search for delicious honey from flowers. It can even search out, extract, and carry honey from flowers that are blooming over six miles from its nest.

ABILITY
Compound Eyes

HIDDEN ABILITY
Tinted Lens

EGG GROUPS
Bug

STAT GROWTH RATES
HP
Attack
Defense
Sp. Atk
Sp. Def
Speed

ITEMS SOMETIMES HELD BY WILD POKÉMON
—

EVOLUTION
Caterpie → Lv. 7 → Metapod → Lv. 10 → Butterfree

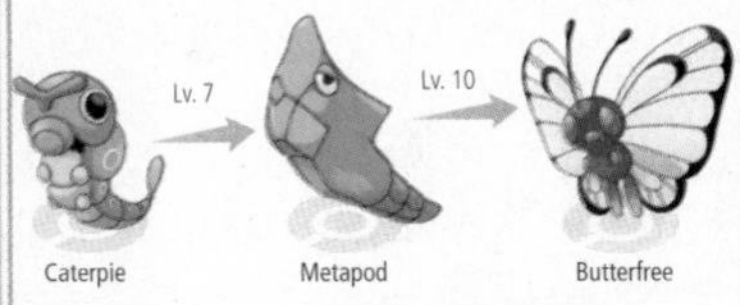

MAIN WAY TO REGISTER IN THE NATIONAL POKÉDEX

Level up a Metapod obtained via Link Trade or the GTS to Lv. 10.

Damage taken in normal battles

Type		Type	
Normal	×1	Flying	×2
Fire	×2	Psychic	×1
Water	×1	Bug	×0.5
Grass	×0.25	Rock	×4
Electric	×2	Ghost	×1
Ice	×2	Dragon	×1
Fighting	×0.25	Dark	×1
Poison	×1	Steel	×1
Ground	×0	Fairy	×1

Damage taken in Inverse battles

Type		Type	
Normal	×1	Flying	×0.5
Fire	×0.5	Psychic	×1
Water	×1	Bug	×2
Grass	×4	Rock	×0.25
Electric	×0.5	Ghost	×1
Ice	×0.5	Dragon	×1
Fighting	×4	Dark	×1
Poison	×1	Steel	×1
Ground	×4	Fairy	×1

Can be used in
Inverse Battle
Battle Institute
Battle Maison
Random Matchup (Free Battle)
Random Matchup (Others)

LEVEL-UP MOVES

Lv.	Name	Type	Kind	Pow.	Acc.	PP	Range
1	Confusion	Psychic	Special	50	100	25	Normal
10	Confusion	Psychic	Special	50	100	25	Normal
12	Poison Powder	Poison	Status	—	75	35	Normal
12	Stun Spore	Grass	Status	—	75	30	Normal
12	Sleep Powder	Grass	Status	—	75	15	Normal
16	Gust	Flying	Special	40	100	35	Normal
18	Supersonic	Normal	Status	—	55	20	Normal
22	Whirlwind	Normal	Status	—	—	20	Normal
24	Psybeam	Psychic	Special	65	100	20	Normal
28	Silver Wind	Bug	Special	60	100	5	Normal
30	Tailwind	Flying	Status	—	—	15	Your Side
34	Rage Powder	Bug	Status	—	—	20	Self
36	Safeguard	Normal	Status	—	—	25	Your Side
40	Captivate	Normal	Status	—	100	20	Many Others
42	Bug Buzz	Bug	Special	90	100	10	Normal
46	Quiver Dance	Bug	Status	—	—	20	Self

TM & HM MOVES

No.	Name	Type	Kind	Pow.	Acc.	PP	Range
TM06	Toxic	Poison	Status	—	90	10	Normal
TM09	Venoshock	Poison	Special	65	100	10	Normal
TM10	Hidden Power	Normal	Special	60	100	15	Normal
TM11	Sunny Day	Fire	Status	—	—	5	Both Sides
TM15	Hyper Beam	Normal	Special	150	90	5	Normal
TM17	Protect	Normal	Status	—	—	10	Self
TM18	Rain Dance	Water	Status	—	—	5	Both Sides
TM19	Roost	Flying	Status	—	—	10	Self
TM20	Safeguard	Normal	Status	—	—	25	Your Side
TM21	Frustration	Normal	Physical	—	100	20	Normal
TM22	Solar Beam	Grass	Special	120	100	10	Normal
TM27	Return	Normal	Physical	—	100	20	Normal
TM29	Psychic	Psychic	Special	90	100	10	Normal
TM30	Shadow Ball	Ghost	Special	80	100	15	Normal
TM32	Double Team	Normal	Status	—	—	15	Self
TM40	Aerial Ace	Flying	Physical	60	—	20	Normal
TM42	Facade	Normal	Physical	70	100	20	Normal
TM44	Rest	Psychic	Status	—	—	10	Self
TM45	Attract	Normal	Status	—	100	15	Normal
TM46	Thief	Dark	Physical	60	100	25	Normal
TM48	Round	Normal	Special	60	100	15	Normal
TM53	Energy Ball	Grass	Special	90	100	10	Normal
TM62	Acrobatics	Flying	Physical	55	100	15	Normal
TM68	Giga Impact	Normal	Physical	150	90	5	Normal
TM70	Flash	Normal	Status	—	100	20	Normal
TM76	Struggle Bug	Bug	Special	50	100	20	Many Others
TM77	Psych Up	Normal	Status	—	—	10	Normal
TM83	Infestation	Bug	Special	20	100	20	Normal
TM85	Dream Eater	Psychic	Special	100	100	15	Normal
TM87	Swagger	Normal	Status	—	90	15	Normal
TM88	Sleep Talk	Normal	Status	—	—	10	Self
TM89	U-turn	Bug	Physical	70	100	20	Normal
TM90	Substitute	Normal	Status	—	—	10	Self
TM94	Secret Power	Normal	Physical	70	100	20	Normal
TM100	Confide	Normal	Status	—	—	20	Normal

MOVES LEARNED IN EXCHANGE FOR BP

Name	Type	Kind	Pow.	Acc.	PP	Range
Bug Bite	Bug	Physical	60	100	20	Normal
Signal Beam	Bug	Special	75	100	15	Normal
Electroweb	Electric	Special	55	95	15	Many Others
Snore	Normal	Special	50	100	15	Normal
Tailwind	Flying	Status	—	—	15	Your Side
Giga Drain	Grass	Special	75	100	10	Normal
Skill Swap	Psychic	Status	—	—	10	Normal

MOVES TAUGHT BY PEOPLE

Name	Type	Kind	Pow.	Acc.	PP	Range

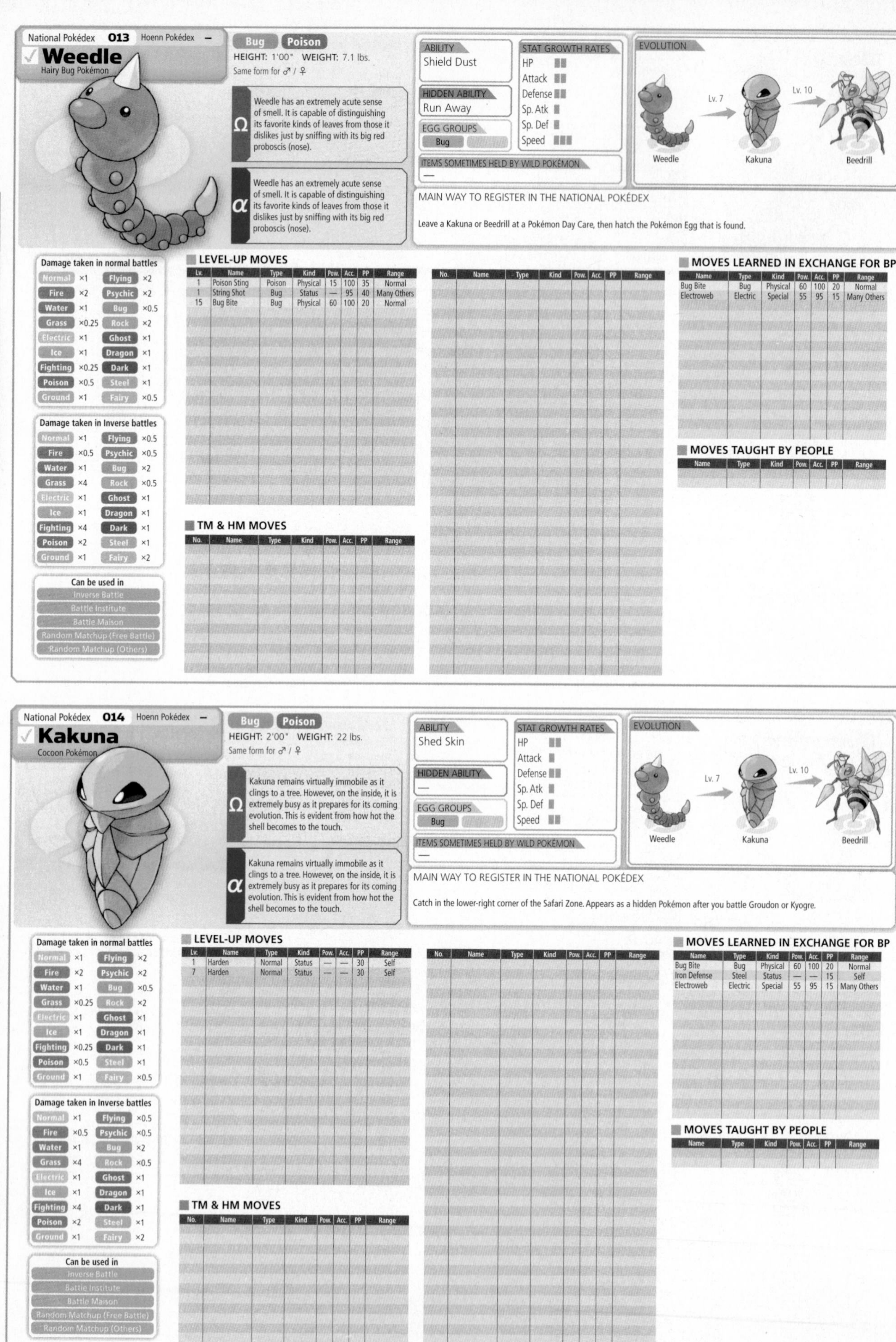

National Pokédex **013** Hoenn Pokédex —

Weedle

Hairy Bug Pokémon

Bug Poison

HEIGHT: 1'00" WEIGHT: 7.1 lbs.

Same form for ♂ / ♀

Ω Weedle has an extremely acute sense of smell. It is capable of distinguishing its favorite kinds of leaves from those it dislikes just by sniffing with its big red proboscis (nose).

α Weedle has an extremely acute sense of smell. It is capable of distinguishing its favorite kinds of leaves from those it dislikes just by sniffing with its big red proboscis (nose).

ABILITY: Shield Dust

HIDDEN ABILITY: Run Away

EGG GROUPS: Bug

STAT GROWTH RATES: HP, Attack, Defense, Sp. Atk, Sp. Def, Speed

ITEMS SOMETIMES HELD BY WILD POKÉMON: —

EVOLUTION

MAIN WAY TO REGISTER IN THE NATIONAL POKÉDEX

Leave a Kakuna or Beedrill at a Pokémon Day Care, then hatch the Pokémon Egg that is found.

Damage taken in normal battles

Type		Type	
Normal	×1	Flying	×2
Fire	×2	Psychic	×2
Water	×1	Bug	×0.5
Grass	×0.25	Rock	×2
Electric	×1	Ghost	×1
Ice	×1	Dragon	×1
Fighting	×0.25	Dark	×1
Poison	×0.5	Steel	×1
Ground	×1	Fairy	×0.5

Damage taken in Inverse battles

Type		Type	
Normal	×1	Flying	×0.5
Fire	×0.5	Psychic	×0.5
Water	×1	Bug	×2
Grass	×4	Rock	×0.5
Electric	×1	Ghost	×1
Ice	×1	Dragon	×1
Fighting	×4	Dark	×1
Poison	×2	Steel	×1
Ground	×1	Fairy	×2

Can be used in

- Inverse Battle
- Battle Institute
- Battle Maison
- Random Matchup (Free Battle)
- Random Matchup (Others)

LEVEL-UP MOVES

Lv.	Name	Type	Kind	Pow.	Acc.	PP	Range
1	Poison Sting	Poison	Physical	15	100	35	Normal
1	String Shot	Bug	Status	—	95	40	Many Others
15	Bug Bite	Bug	Physical	60	100	20	Normal

TM & HM MOVES

No.	Name	Type	Kind	Pow.	Acc.	PP	Range

No.	Name	Type	Kind	Pow.	Acc.	PP	Range

MOVES LEARNED IN EXCHANGE FOR BP

Name	Type	Kind	Pow.	Acc.	PP	Range
Bug Bite	Bug	Physical	60	100	20	Normal
Electroweb	Electric	Special	55	95	15	Many Others

MOVES TAUGHT BY PEOPLE

Name	Type	Kind	Pow.	Acc.	PP	Range

National Pokédex **014** Hoenn Pokédex —

Kakuna

Cocoon Pokémon

Bug Poison

HEIGHT: 2'00" WEIGHT: 22 lbs.

Same form for ♂ / ♀

Ω Kakuna remains virtually immobile as it clings to a tree. However, on the inside, it is extremely busy as it prepares for its coming evolution. This is evident from how hot the shell becomes to the touch.

α Kakuna remains virtually immobile as it clings to a tree. However, on the inside, it is extremely busy as it prepares for its coming evolution. This is evident from how hot the shell becomes to the touch.

ABILITY: Shed Skin

HIDDEN ABILITY: —

EGG GROUPS: Bug

STAT GROWTH RATES: HP, Attack, Defense, Sp. Atk, Sp. Def, Speed

ITEMS SOMETIMES HELD BY WILD POKÉMON: —

EVOLUTION

MAIN WAY TO REGISTER IN THE NATIONAL POKÉDEX

Catch in the lower-right corner of the Safari Zone. Appears as a hidden Pokémon after you battle Groudon or Kyogre.

Damage taken in normal battles

Type		Type	
Normal	×1	Flying	×2
Fire	×2	Psychic	×2
Water	×1	Bug	×0.5
Grass	×0.25	Rock	×2
Electric	×1	Ghost	×1
Ice	×1	Dragon	×1
Fighting	×0.25	Dark	×1
Poison	×0.5	Steel	×1
Ground	×1	Fairy	×0.5

Damage taken in Inverse battles

Type		Type	
Normal	×1	Flying	×0.5
Fire	×0.5	Psychic	×0.5
Water	×1	Bug	×2
Grass	×4	Rock	×0.5
Electric	×1	Ghost	×1
Ice	×1	Dragon	×1
Fighting	×4	Dark	×1
Poison	×2	Steel	×1
Ground	×1	Fairy	×2

Can be used in

- Inverse Battle
- Battle Institute
- Battle Maison
- Random Matchup (Free Battle)
- Random Matchup (Others)

LEVEL-UP MOVES

Lv.	Name	Type	Kind	Pow.	Acc.	PP	Range
1	Harden	Normal	Status	—	—	30	Self
7	Harden	Normal	Status	—	—	30	Self

TM & HM MOVES

No.	Name	Type	Kind	Pow.	Acc.	PP	Range

No.	Name	Type	Kind	Pow.	Acc.	PP	Range

MOVES LEARNED IN EXCHANGE FOR BP

Name	Type	Kind	Pow.	Acc.	PP	Range
Bug Bite	Bug	Physical	60	100	20	Normal
Iron Defense	Steel	Status	—	—	15	Self
Electroweb	Electric	Special	55	95	15	Many Others

MOVES TAUGHT BY PEOPLE

Name	Type	Kind	Pow.	Acc.	PP	Range

National Pokédex **015** Hoenn Pokédex —

✓ Beedrill

Poison Bee Pokémon

Bug | Poison

HEIGHT: 3'03" WEIGHT: 65 lbs.

Same form for ♂ / ♀

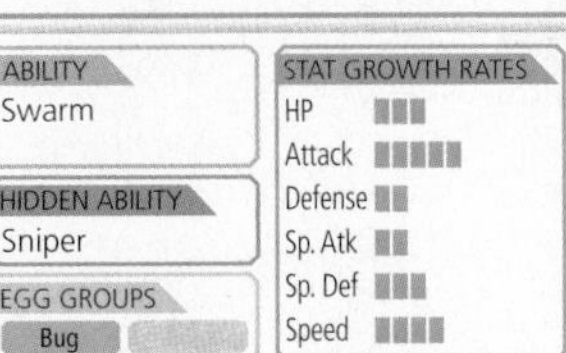

Ω Beedrill is extremely territorial. No one should ever approach its nest—this is for their own safety. If angered, they will attack in a furious swarm.

α Beedrill is extremely territorial. No one should ever approach its nest—this is for their own safety. If angered, they will attack in a furious swarm.

ABILITY
Swarm

HIDDEN ABILITY
Sniper

EGG GROUPS
Bug

ITEMS SOMETIMES HELD BY WILD POKÉMON
—

STAT GROWTH RATES
HP ■■■
Attack ■■■■■
Defense ■■
Sp. Atk ■■
Sp. Def ■■■
Speed ■■■■

EVOLUTION

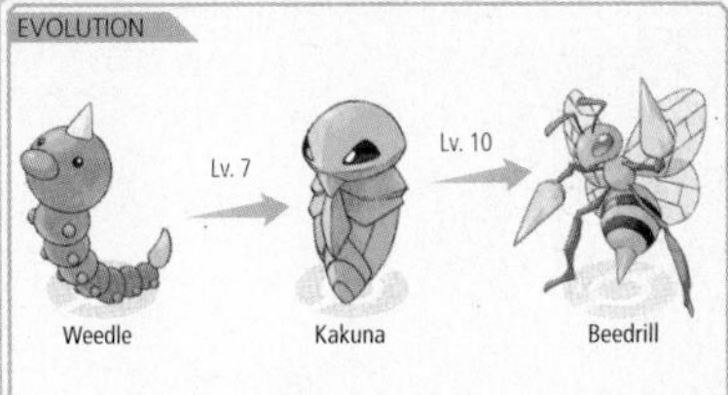

MAIN WAY TO REGISTER IN THE NATIONAL POKÉDEX

Level up Kakuna to Lv. 10.

Damage taken in normal battles

Type		Type	
Normal	×1	Flying	×2
Fire	×2	Psychic	×2
Water	×1	Bug	×0.5
Grass	×0.25	Rock	×2
Electric	×1	Ghost	×1
Ice	×1	Dragon	×1
Fighting	×0.25	Dark	×1
Poison	×0.5	Steel	×1
Ground	×1	Fairy	×0.5

Damage taken in Inverse battles

Type		Type	
Normal	×1	Flying	×0.5
Fire	×0.5	Psychic	×0.5
Water	×1	Bug	×2
Grass	×4	Rock	×0.5
Electric	×1	Ghost	×1
Ice	×1	Dragon	×1
Fighting	×4	Dark	×1
Poison	×2	Steel	×1
Ground	×1	Fairy	×2

Can be used in
Inverse Battle
Battle Institute
Battle Maison
Random Matchup (Free Battle)
Random Matchup (Others)

LEVEL-UP MOVES

Lv.	Name	Type	Kind	Pow.	Acc.	PP	Range
1	Fury Attack	Normal	Physical	15	85	20	Normal
10	Fury Attack	Normal	Physical	15	85	20	Normal
13	Focus Energy	Normal	Status	—	—	30	Self
16	Twineedle	Bug	Physical	25	100	20	Normal
19	Rage	Normal	Physical	20	100	20	Normal
22	Pursuit	Dark	Physical	40	100	20	Normal
25	Toxic Spikes	Poison	Status	—	—	20	Other Side
28	Pin Missile	Bug	Physical	25	95	20	Normal
31	Agility	Psychic	Status	—	—	30	Self
34	Assurance	Dark	Physical	60	100	10	Normal
37	Poison Jab	Poison	Physical	80	100	20	Normal
40	Endeavor	Normal	Physical	—	100	5	Normal
45	Fell Stinger	Bug	Physical	30	100	25	Normal

TM & HM MOVES

No.	Name	Type	Kind	Pow.	Acc.	PP	Range
TM06	Toxic	Poison	Status	—	90	10	Normal
TM09	Venoshock	Poison	Special	65	100	10	Normal
TM10	Hidden Power	Normal	Special	60	100	15	Normal
TM11	Sunny Day	Fire	Status	—	—	5	Both Sides
TM15	Hyper Beam	Normal	Special	150	90	5	Normal
TM17	Protect	Normal	Status	—	—	10	Self
TM19	Roost	Flying	Status	—	—	10	Self
TM21	Frustration	Normal	Physical	—	100	20	Normal
TM22	Solar Beam	Grass	Special	120	100	10	Normal
TM27	Return	Normal	Physical	—	100	20	Normal
TM31	Brick Break	Fighting	Physical	75	100	15	Normal
TM32	Double Team	Normal	Status	—	—	15	Self
TM36	Sludge Bomb	Poison	Special	90	100	10	Normal
TM40	Aerial Ace	Flying	Physical	60	—	20	Normal
TM42	Facade	Normal	Physical	70	100	20	Normal
TM44	Rest	Psychic	Status	—	—	10	Self
TM45	Attract	Normal	Status	—	100	15	Normal
TM46	Thief	Dark	Physical	60	100	25	Normal
TM48	Round	Normal	Special	60	100	15	Normal
TM54	False Swipe	Normal	Physical	40	100	40	Normal
TM62	Acrobatics	Flying	Physical	55	100	15	Normal
TM66	Payback	Dark	Physical	50	100	10	Normal
TM68	Giga Impact	Normal	Physical	150	90	5	Normal
TM70	Flash	Normal	Status	—	100	20	Normal
TM75	Swords Dance	Normal	Status	—	—	20	Self
TM76	Struggle Bug	Bug	Special	50	100	20	Many Others
TM81	X-Scissor	Bug	Physical	80	100	15	Normal
TM83	Infestation	Bug	Special	20	100	20	Normal
TM84	Poison Jab	Poison	Physical	80	100	20	Normal
TM87	Swagger	Normal	Status	—	90	15	Normal
TM88	Sleep Talk	Normal	Status	—	—	10	Self
TM89	U-turn	Bug	Physical	70	100	20	Normal
TM90	Substitute	Normal	Status	—	—	10	Self
TM94	Secret Power	Normal	Physical	70	100	20	Normal
TM100	Confide	Normal	Status	—	—	20	Normal
HM01	Cut	Normal	Physical	50	95	30	Normal
HM06	Rock Smash	Fighting	Physical	40	100	15	Normal

MOVES LEARNED IN EXCHANGE FOR BP

Name	Type	Kind	Pow.	Acc.	PP	Range
Bug Bite	Bug	Physical	60	100	20	Normal
Drill Run	Ground	Physical	80	95	10	Normal
Electroweb	Electric	Special	55	95	15	Many Others
Snore	Normal	Special	50	100	15	Normal
Knock Off	Dark	Physical	65	100	20	Normal
Tailwind	Flying	Status	—	—	15	Your Side
Giga Drain	Grass	Special	75	100	10	Normal
Endeavor	Normal	Physical	—	100	5	Normal

MOVES TAUGHT BY PEOPLE

Name	Type	Kind	Pow.	Acc.	PP	Range

Mega Evolution

Mega Beedrill

Poison Bee Pokémon

Bug | Poison

HEIGHT: 4'07" WEIGHT: 89.3 lbs.

Same form for ♂ / ♀

REQUIRED MEGA STONE
Beedrillite
Find in Sea Mauville (Storage).

ABILITY
Adaptability

HIDDEN ABILITY
—

EGG GROUPS
—

STAT GROWTH RATES
HP ■■■
Attack ■■■■■■■■
Defense ■■
Sp. Atk ■
Sp. Def ■■■
Speed ■■■■■■■■

Damage taken in normal battles

Type		Type	
Normal	×1	Flying	×2
Fire	×2	Psychic	×2
Water	×1	Bug	×0.5
Grass	×0.25	Rock	×2
Electric	×1	Ghost	×1
Ice	×1	Dragon	×1
Fighting	×0.25	Dark	×1
Poison	×0.5	Steel	×1
Ground	×1	Fairy	×0.5

Damage taken in Inverse battles

Type		Type	
Normal	×1	Flying	×0.5
Fire	×0.5	Psychic	×0.5
Water	×1	Bug	×2
Grass	×4	Rock	×0.5
Electric	×1	Ghost	×1
Ice	×1	Dragon	×1
Fighting	×4	Dark	×1
Poison	×2	Steel	×1
Ground	×1	Fairy	×2

Can be used in
Inverse Battle
Battle Institute
Battle Maison
Random Matchup (Free Battle)
Random Matchup (Others)

016

Pidgey

National Pokédex

National Pokédex **016** Hoenn Pokédex —

Pidgey

Tiny Bird Pokémon

Normal Flying

HEIGHT: 1'00" WEIGHT: 4 lbs.

Same form for ♂ / ♀

Ω Pidgey has an extremely sharp sense of direction. It is capable of unerringly returning home to its nest, however far it may be removed from its familiar surroundings.

α Pidgey has an extremely sharp sense of direction. It is capable of unerringly returning home to its nest, however far it may be removed from its familiar surroundings.

ABILITIES
Keen Eye
Tangled Feet

HIDDEN ABILITY
Big Pecks

EGG GROUPS
Flying

STAT GROWTH RATES
HP
Attack
Defense
Sp. Atk
Sp. Def
Speed

ITEMS SOMETIMES HELD BY WILD POKÉMON
—

EVOLUTION
Pidgey → Lv. 18 → Pidgeotto → Lv. 36 → Pidgeot

MAIN WAY TO REGISTER IN THE NATIONAL POKÉDEX

Leave a Pidgeotto or Pidgeot at a Pokémon Day Care, then hatch the Pokémon Egg that is found.

Damage taken in normal battles

Type		Type	
Normal	×1	Flying	×1
Fire	×1	Psychic	×1
Water	×1	Bug	×0.5
Grass	×0.5	Rock	×2
Electric	×2	Ghost	×0
Ice	×2	Dragon	×1
Fighting	×1	Dark	×1
Poison	×1	Steel	×1
Ground	×0	Fairy	×1

Damage taken in Inverse battles

Type		Type	
Normal	×1	Flying	×1
Fire	×1	Psychic	×1
Water	×1	Bug	×2
Grass	×2	Rock	×0.5
Electric	×0.5	Ghost	×2
Ice	×0.5	Dragon	×1
Fighting	×1	Dark	×1
Poison	×1	Steel	×1
Ground	×2	Fairy	×1

Can be used in
Inverse Battle
Battle Institute
Battle Maison
Random Matchup (Free Battle)
Random Matchup (Others)

LEVEL-UP MOVES

Lv.	Name	Type	Kind	Pow.	Acc.	PP	Range
1	Tackle	Normal	Physical	50	100	35	Normal
5	Sand Attack	Ground	Status	—	100	15	Normal
9	Gust	Flying	Special	40	100	35	Normal
13	Quick Attack	Normal	Physical	40	100	30	Normal
17	Whirlwind	Normal	Status	—	—	20	Normal
21	Twister	Dragon	Special	40	100	20	Many Others
25	Feather Dance	Flying	Status	—	100	15	Normal
29	Agility	Psychic	Status	—	—	30	Self
33	Wing Attack	Flying	Physical	60	100	35	Normal
37	Roost	Flying	Status	—	—	10	Self
41	Tailwind	Flying	Status	—	—	15	Your Side
45	Mirror Move	Flying	Status	—	—	20	Normal
49	Air Slash	Flying	Special	75	95	15	Normal
53	Hurricane	Flying	Special	110	70	10	Normal

TM & HM MOVES

No.	Name	Type	Kind	Pow.	Acc.	PP	Range
TM06	Toxic	Poison	Status	—	90	10	Normal
TM10	Hidden Power	Normal	Special	60	100	15	Normal
TM11	Sunny Day	Fire	Status	—	—	5	Both Sides
TM17	Protect	Normal	Status	—	—	10	Self
TM18	Rain Dance	Water	Status	—	—	5	Both Sides
TM19	Roost	Flying	Status	—	—	10	Self
TM21	Frustration	Normal	Physical	—	100	20	Normal
TM27	Return	Normal	Physical	—	100	20	Normal
TM32	Double Team	Normal	Status	—	—	15	Self
TM40	Aerial Ace	Flying	Physical	60	—	20	Normal
TM42	Facade	Normal	Physical	70	100	20	Normal
TM44	Rest	Psychic	Status	—	—	10	Self
TM45	Attract	Normal	Status	—	100	15	Normal
TM46	Thief	Dark	Physical	60	100	25	Normal
TM48	Round	Normal	Special	60	100	15	Normal
TM51	Steel Wing	Steel	Physical	70	90	25	Normal
TM87	Swagger	Normal	Status	—	90	15	Normal
TM88	Sleep Talk	Normal	Status	—	—	10	Self
TM89	U-turn	Bug	Physical	70	100	20	Normal
TM90	Substitute	Normal	Status	—	—	10	Self
TM94	Secret Power	Normal	Physical	70	100	20	Normal
TM100	Confide	Normal	Status	—	—	20	Normal
HM02	Fly	Flying	Physical	90	95	15	Normal

MOVES LEARNED IN EXCHANGE FOR BP

Name	Type	Kind	Pow.	Acc.	PP	Range
Uproar	Normal	Special	90	100	10	1 Random
Snore	Normal	Special	50	100	15	Normal
Heat Wave	Fire	Special	95	90	10	Many Others
Tailwind	Flying	Status	—	—	15	Your Side
Sky Attack	Flying	Physical	140	90	5	Normal

MOVES TAUGHT BY PEOPLE

Name	Type	Kind	Pow.	Acc.	PP	Range

EGG MOVES

Name	Type	Kind	Pow.	Acc.	PP	Range
Pursuit	Dark	Physical	40	100	20	Normal
Feint Attack	Dark	Physical	60	—	20	Normal
Foresight	Normal	Status	—	—	40	Normal
Steel Wing	Steel	Physical	70	90	25	Normal
Air Cutter	Flying	Special	60	95	25	Many Others
Air Slash	Flying	Special	75	95	15	Normal
Brave Bird	Flying	Physical	120	100	15	Normal
Uproar	Normal	Special	90	100	10	1 Random
Defog	Flying	Status	—	—	15	Normal

Pidgeotto

017

National Pokédex **017** Hoenn Pokédex —

Pidgeotto

Bird Pokémon

Normal Flying

HEIGHT: 3'07" WEIGHT: 66.1 lbs.

Same form for ♂ / ♀

Ω Pidgeotto claims a large area as its own territory. This Pokémon flies around, patrolling its living space. If its territory is violated, it shows no mercy in thoroughly punishing the foe with its sharp claws.

α Pidgeotto claims a large area as its own territory. This Pokémon flies around, patrolling its living space. If its territory is violated, it shows no mercy in thoroughly punishing the foe with its sharp claws.

ABILITIES
Keen Eye
Tangled Feet

HIDDEN ABILITY
Big Pecks

EGG GROUPS
Flying

STAT GROWTH RATES
HP
Attack
Defense
Sp. Atk
Sp. Def
Speed

ITEMS SOMETIMES HELD BY WILD POKÉMON
—

EVOLUTION
Pidgey → Lv. 18 → Pidgeotto → Lv. 36 → Pidgeot

MAIN WAY TO REGISTER IN THE NATIONAL POKÉDEX

Catch in the upper-right corner of the Safari Zone. Appears as a hidden Pokémon after you battle Groudon or Kyogre.

Damage taken in normal battles

Type		Type	
Normal	×1	Flying	×1
Fire	×1	Psychic	×1
Water	×1	Bug	×0.5
Grass	×0.5	Rock	×2
Electric	×2	Ghost	×0
Ice	×2	Dragon	×1
Fighting	×1	Dark	×1
Poison	×1	Steel	×1
Ground	×0	Fairy	×1

Damage taken in Inverse battles

Type		Type	
Normal	×1	Flying	×1
Fire	×1	Psychic	×1
Water	×1	Bug	×2
Grass	×2	Rock	×0.5
Electric	×0.5	Ghost	×2
Ice	×0.5	Dragon	×1
Fighting	×1	Dark	×1
Poison	×1	Steel	×1
Ground	×2	Fairy	×1

Can be used in
Inverse Battle
Battle Institute
Battle Maison
Random Matchup (Free Battle)
Random Matchup (Others)

LEVEL-UP MOVES

Lv.	Name	Type	Kind	Pow.	Acc.	PP	Range
1	Tackle	Normal	Physical	50	100	35	Normal
1	Sand Attack	Ground	Status	—	100	15	Normal
1	Gust	Flying	Special	40	100	35	Normal
5	Sand Attack	Ground	Status	—	100	15	Normal
9	Gust	Flying	Special	40	100	35	Normal
13	Quick Attack	Normal	Physical	40	100	30	Normal
17	Whirlwind	Normal	Status	—	—	20	Normal
22	Twister	Dragon	Special	40	100	20	Many Others
27	Feather Dance	Flying	Status	—	100	15	Normal
32	Agility	Psychic	Status	—	—	30	Self
37	Wing Attack	Flying	Physical	60	100	35	Normal
42	Roost	Flying	Status	—	—	10	Self
47	Tailwind	Flying	Status	—	—	15	Your Side
52	Mirror Move	Flying	Status	—	—	20	Normal
57	Air Slash	Flying	Special	75	95	15	Normal
62	Hurricane	Flying	Special	110	70	10	Normal

TM & HM MOVES

No.	Name	Type	Kind	Pow.	Acc.	PP	Range
TM06	Toxic	Poison	Status	—	90	10	Normal
TM10	Hidden Power	Normal	Special	60	100	15	Normal
TM11	Sunny Day	Fire	Status	—	—	5	Both Sides
TM17	Protect	Normal	Status	—	—	10	Self
TM18	Rain Dance	Water	Status	—	—	5	Both Sides
TM19	Roost	Flying	Status	—	—	10	Self
TM21	Frustration	Normal	Physical	—	100	20	Normal
TM27	Return	Normal	Physical	—	100	20	Normal
TM32	Double Team	Normal	Status	—	—	15	Self
TM40	Aerial Ace	Flying	Physical	60	—	20	Normal
TM42	Facade	Normal	Physical	70	100	20	Normal
TM44	Rest	Psychic	Status	—	—	10	Self
TM45	Attract	Normal	Status	—	100	15	Normal
TM46	Thief	Dark	Physical	60	100	25	Normal
TM48	Round	Normal	Special	60	100	15	Normal
TM51	Steel Wing	Steel	Physical	70	90	25	Normal
TM87	Swagger	Normal	Status	—	90	15	Normal
TM88	Sleep Talk	Normal	Status	—	—	10	Self
TM89	U-turn	Bug	Physical	70	100	20	Normal
TM90	Substitute	Normal	Status	—	—	10	Self
TM94	Secret Power	Normal	Physical	70	100	20	Normal
TM100	Confide	Normal	Status	—	—	20	Normal
HM02	Fly	Flying	Physical	90	95	15	Normal

MOVES LEARNED IN EXCHANGE FOR BP

Name	Type	Kind	Pow.	Acc.	PP	Range
Uproar	Normal	Special	90	100	10	1 Random
Snore	Normal	Special	50	100	15	Normal
Heat Wave	Fire	Special	95	90	10	Many Others
Tailwind	Flying	Status	—	—	15	Your Side
Sky Attack	Flying	Physical	140	90	5	Normal

MOVES TAUGHT BY PEOPLE

Name	Type	Kind	Pow.	Acc.	PP	Range

National Pokédex **018** Hoenn Pokédex —

Pidgeot

Bird Pokémon

Normal | Flying

HEIGHT: 4'11" WEIGHT: 87.1 lbs.

Same form for ♂ / ♀

Ω This Pokémon has a dazzling plumage of beautifully glossy feathers. Many Trainers are captivated by the striking beauty of the feathers on its head, compelling them to choose Pidgeot as their Pokémon.

α This Pokémon has a dazzling plumage of beautifully glossy feathers. Many Trainers are captivated by the striking beauty of the feathers on its head, compelling them to choose Pidgeot as their Pokémon.

ABILITIES
Keen Eye
Tangled Feet

HIDDEN ABILITY
Big Pecks

EGG GROUPS
Flying

STAT GROWTH RATES
HP ▮▮▮
Attack ▮▮▮▮
Defense ▮▮▮
Sp. Atk ▮▮▮
Sp. Def ▮▮▮
Speed ▮▮▮▮▮

ITEMS SOMETIMES HELD BY WILD POKÉMON
—

EVOLUTION

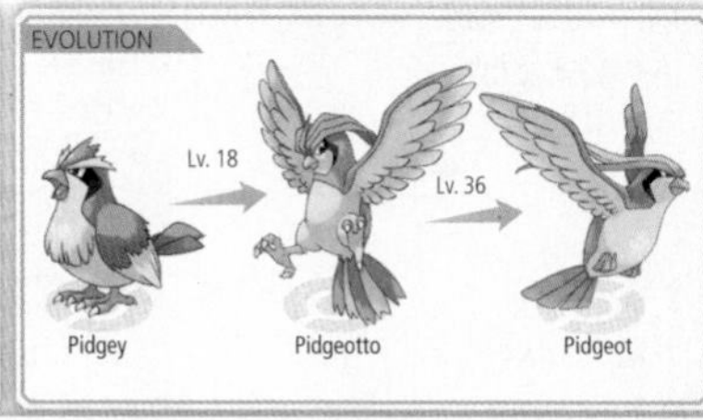

MAIN WAY TO REGISTER IN THE NATIONAL POKÉDEX

Level up Pidgeotto to Lv. 36.

Damage taken in normal battles

Type		Type	
Normal	×1	Flying	×1
Fire	×1	Psychic	×1
Water	×1	Bug	×0.5
Grass	×0.5	Rock	×2
Electric	×2	Ghost	×0
Ice	×2	Dragon	×1
Fighting	×1	Dark	×1
Poison	×1	Steel	×1
Ground	×0	Fairy	×1

Damage taken in Inverse battles

Type		Type	
Normal	×1	Flying	×1
Fire	×1	Psychic	×1
Water	×1	Bug	×2
Grass	×2	Rock	×0.5
Electric	×0.5	Ghost	×2
Ice	×0.5	Dragon	×1
Fighting	×1	Dark	×1
Poison	×1	Steel	×1
Ground	×2	Fairy	×1

Can be used in
Inverse Battle
Battle Institute
Battle Maison
Random Matchup (Free Battle)
Random Matchup (Others)

LEVEL-UP MOVES

Lv.	Name	Type	Kind	Pow.	Acc.	PP	Range
1	Hurricane	Flying	Special	110	70	10	Normal
1	Tackle	Normal	Physical	50	100	35	Normal
1	Sand Attack	Ground	Status	—	100	15	Normal
1	Gust	Flying	Special	40	100	35	Normal
1	Quick Attack	Normal	Physical	40	100	30	Normal
5	Sand Attack	Ground	Status	—	100	15	Normal
9	Gust	Flying	Special	40	100	35	Normal
13	Quick Attack	Normal	Physical	40	100	30	Normal
17	Whirlwind	Normal	Status	—	—	20	Normal
22	Twister	Dragon	Special	40	100	20	Many Others
27	Feather Dance	Flying	Status	—	100	15	Normal
32	Agility	Psychic	Status	—	—	30	Self
38	Wing Attack	Flying	Physical	60	100	35	Normal
44	Roost	Flying	Status	—	—	10	Self
50	Tailwind	Flying	Status	—	—	15	Your Side
56	Mirror Move	Flying	Status	—	—	20	Normal
62	Air Slash	Flying	Special	75	95	15	Normal
68	Hurricane	Flying	Special	110	70	10	Normal

TM & HM MOVES

No.	Name	Type	Kind	Pow.	Acc.	PP	Range
TM06	Toxic	Poison	Status	—	90	10	Normal
TM10	Hidden Power	Normal	Special	60	100	15	Normal
TM11	Sunny Day	Fire	Status	—	—	5	Both Sides
TM15	Hyper Beam	Normal	Special	150	90	5	Normal
TM17	Protect	Normal	Status	—	—	10	Self
TM18	Rain Dance	Water	Status	—	—	5	Both Sides
TM19	Roost	Flying	Status	—	—	10	Self
TM21	Frustration	Normal	Physical	—	100	20	Normal
TM27	Return	Normal	Physical	—	100	20	Normal
TM32	Double Team	Normal	Status	—	—	15	Self
TM40	Aerial Ace	Flying	Physical	60	—	20	Normal
TM42	Facade	Normal	Physical	70	100	20	Normal
TM44	Rest	Psychic	Status	—	—	10	Self
TM45	Attract	Normal	Status	—	100	15	Normal
TM46	Thief	Dark	Physical	60	100	25	Normal
TM48	Round	Normal	Special	60	100	15	Normal
TM51	Steel Wing	Steel	Physical	70	90	25	Normal
TM68	Giga Impact	Normal	Physical	150	90	5	Normal
TM87	Swagger	Normal	Status	—	90	15	Normal
TM88	Sleep Talk	Normal	Status	—	—	10	Self
TM89	U-turn	Bug	Physical	70	100	20	Normal
TM90	Substitute	Normal	Status	—	—	10	Self
TM94	Secret Power	Normal	Physical	70	100	20	Normal
TM100	Confide	Normal	Status	—	—	20	Normal
HM02	Fly	Flying	Physical	90	95	15	Normal

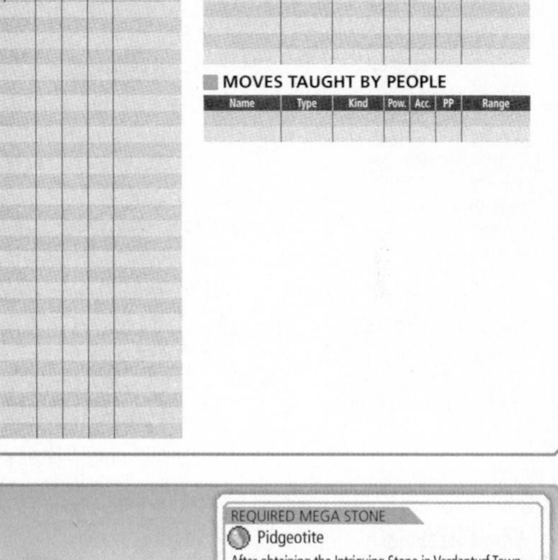

MOVES LEARNED IN EXCHANGE FOR BP

Name	Type	Kind	Pow.	Acc.	PP	Range
Uproar	Normal	Special	90	100	10	1 Random
Snore	Normal	Special	50	100	15	Normal
Heat Wave	Fire	Special	95	90	10	Many Others
Tailwind	Flying	Status	—	—	15	Your Side
Sky Attack	Flying	Physical	140	90	5	Normal

MOVES TAUGHT BY PEOPLE

Name	Type	Kind	Pow.	Acc.	PP	Range

Mega Evolution

Mega Pidgeot

Bird Pokémon

Normal | Flying

HEIGHT: 7'03" WEIGHT: 111.3 lbs.

Same form for ♂ / ♀

REQUIRED MEGA STONE
Pidgeotite
After obtaining the Intriguing Stone in Verdanturf Town, take it to the Devon Corporation in Rustboro City and talk to Mr. Stone on 3F, who will recognize it as a Pidgeotite.

ABILITY
No Guard

HIDDEN ABILITY
—

EGG GROUPS
—

STAT GROWTH RATES
HP ▮▮▮
Attack ▮▮▮▮
Defense ▮▮▮▮
Sp. Atk ▮▮▮▮▮▮▮
Sp. Def ▮▮▮
Speed ▮▮▮▮▮▮

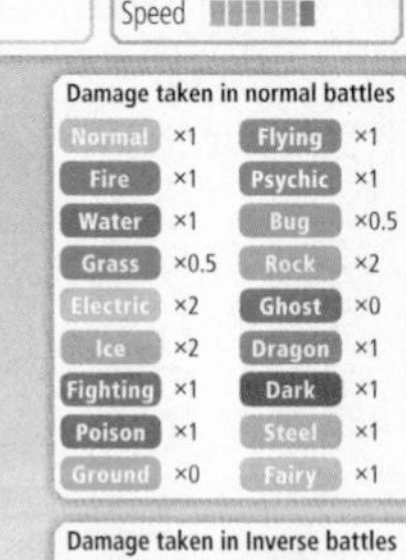

Damage taken in normal battles

Type		Type	
Normal	×1	Flying	×1
Fire	×1	Psychic	×1
Water	×1	Bug	×0.5
Grass	×0.5	Rock	×2
Electric	×2	Ghost	×0
Ice	×2	Dragon	×1
Fighting	×1	Dark	×1
Poison	×1	Steel	×1
Ground	×0	Fairy	×1

Damage taken in Inverse battles

Type		Type	
Normal	×1	Flying	×1
Fire	×1	Psychic	×1
Water	×1	Bug	×2
Grass	×2	Rock	×0.5
Electric	×0.5	Ghost	×2
Ice	×0.5	Dragon	×1
Fighting	×1	Dark	×1
Poison	×1	Steel	×1
Ground	×2	Fairy	×1

Can be used in
Inverse Battle
Battle Institute
Battle Maison
Random Matchup (Free Battle)
Random Matchup (Others)

National Pokédex **019** Hoenn Pokédex —

Rattata

Mouse Pokémon

Normal

HEIGHT: 1'00" WEIGHT: 7.7 lbs.

The male has longer whiskers than the female.

♂ ♀

Ω Rattata is cautious in the extreme. Even while it is asleep, it constantly listens by moving its ears around. It is not picky about where it lives—it will make its nest anywhere.

α Rattata is cautious in the extreme. Even while it is asleep, it constantly listens by moving its ears around. It is not picky about where it lives—it will make its nest anywhere.

ABILITIES
Run Away
Guts

HIDDEN ABILITY
Hustle

EGG GROUPS
Field

STAT GROWTH RATES
HP
Attack
Defense
Sp. Atk
Sp. Def
Speed

ITEMS SOMETIMES HELD BY WILD POKÉMON
—

EVOLUTION

Rattata → Lv. 20 → Raticate

MAIN WAY TO REGISTER IN THE NATIONAL POKÉDEX

Catch on Route 117. Appears as a hidden Pokémon after you battle Groudon or Kyogre.

Damage taken in normal battles

Type		Type	
Normal	×1	Flying	×1
Fire	×1	Psychic	×1
Water	×1	Bug	×1
Grass	×1	Rock	×1
Electric	×1	Ghost	×0
Ice	×1	Dragon	×1
Fighting	×2	Dark	×1
Poison	×1	Steel	×1
Ground	×1	Fairy	×1

Damage taken in Inverse battles

Type		Type	
Normal	×1	Flying	×1
Fire	×1	Psychic	×1
Water	×1	Bug	×1
Grass	×1	Rock	×1
Electric	×1	Ghost	×2
Ice	×1	Dragon	×1
Fighting	×0.5	Dark	×1
Poison	×1	Steel	×1
Ground	×1	Fairy	×1

Can be used in
Inverse Battle
Battle Institute
Battle Maison
Random Matchup (Free Battle)
Random Matchup (Others)

LEVEL-UP MOVES

Lv.	Name	Type	Kind	Pow.	Acc.	PP	Range
1	Tackle	Normal	Physical	50	100	35	Normal
1	Tail Whip	Normal	Status	—	100	30	Many Others
4	Quick Attack	Normal	Physical	40	100	30	Normal
7	Focus Energy	Normal	Status	—	—	30	Self
10	Bite	Dark	Physical	60	100	25	Normal
13	Pursuit	Dark	Physical	40	100	20	Normal
16	Hyper Fang	Normal	Physical	80	90	15	Normal
19	Sucker Punch	Dark	Physical	80	100	5	Normal
22	Crunch	Dark	Physical	80	100	15	Normal
25	Assurance	Dark	Physical	60	100	10	Normal
28	Super Fang	Normal	Physical	—	90	10	Normal
31	Double-Edge	Normal	Physical	120	100	15	Normal
34	Endeavor	Normal	Physical	—	100	5	Normal

TM & HM MOVES

No.	Name	Type	Kind	Pow.	Acc.	PP	Range
TM06	Toxic	Poison	Status	—	90	10	Normal
TM10	Hidden Power	Normal	Special	60	100	15	Normal
TM11	Sunny Day	Fire	Status	—	—	5	Both Sides
TM12	Taunt	Dark	Status	—	100	20	Normal
TM13	Ice Beam	Ice	Special	90	100	10	Normal
TM14	Blizzard	Ice	Special	110	70	5	Many Others
TM17	Protect	Normal	Status	—	—	10	Self
TM18	Rain Dance	Water	Status	—	—	5	Both Sides
TM21	Frustration	Normal	Physical	—	100	20	Normal
TM24	Thunderbolt	Electric	Special	90	100	15	Normal
TM25	Thunder	Electric	Special	110	70	10	Normal
TM27	Return	Normal	Physical	—	100	20	Normal
TM28	Dig	Ground	Physical	80	100	10	Normal
TM30	Shadow Ball	Ghost	Special	80	100	15	Normal
TM32	Double Team	Normal	Status	—	—	15	Self
TM42	Facade	Normal	Physical	70	100	20	Normal
TM44	Rest	Psychic	Status	—	—	10	Self
TM45	Attract	Normal	Status	—	100	15	Normal
TM46	Thief	Dark	Physical	60	100	25	Normal
TM48	Round	Normal	Special	60	100	15	Normal
TM57	Charge Beam	Electric	Special	50	90	10	Normal
TM67	Retaliate	Normal	Physical	70	100	5	Normal
TM73	Thunder Wave	Electric	Status	—	100	20	Normal
TM86	Grass Knot	Grass	Special	—	100	20	Normal
TM87	Swagger	Normal	Status	—	90	15	Normal
TM88	Sleep Talk	Normal	Status	—	—	10	Self
TM89	U-turn	Bug	Physical	70	100	20	Normal
TM90	Substitute	Normal	Status	—	—	10	Self
TM93	Wild Charge	Electric	Physical	90	100	15	Normal
TM94	Secret Power	Normal	Physical	70	100	20	Normal
TM100	Confide	Normal	Status	—	—	20	Normal
HM01	Cut	Normal	Physical	50	95	30	Normal
HM06	Rock Smash	Fighting	Physical	40	100	15	Normal

MOVES LEARNED IN EXCHANGE FOR BP

Name	Type	Kind	Pow.	Acc.	PP	Range
Covet	Normal	Physical	60	100	25	Normal
Super Fang	Normal	Physical	—	90	10	Normal
Uproar	Normal	Special	90	100	10	1 Random
Last Resort	Normal	Physical	140	100	5	Normal
Icy Wind	Ice	Special	55	95	15	Many Others
Zen Headbutt	Psychic	Physical	80	90	15	Normal
Iron Tail	Steel	Physical	100	75	15	Normal
Snore	Normal	Special	50	100	15	Normal
Shock Wave	Electric	Special	60	—	20	Normal
Endeavor	Normal	Physical	—	100	5	Normal

MOVES TAUGHT BY PEOPLE

Name	Type	Kind	Pow.	Acc.	PP	Range

EGG MOVES

Name	Type	Kind	Pow.	Acc.	PP	Range
Screech	Normal	Status	—	85	40	Normal
Flame Wheel	Fire	Physical	60	100	25	Normal
Fury Swipes	Normal	Physical	18	80	15	Normal
Bite	Dark	Physical	60	100	25	Normal
Counter	Fighting	Physical	—	100	20	Varies
Reversal	Fighting	Physical	—	100	15	Normal
Uproar	Normal	Special	90	100	10	1 Random
Last Resort	Normal	Physical	140	100	5	Normal
Me First	Normal	Status	—	—	20	Varies
Revenge	Fighting	Physical	60	100	10	Normal
Final Gambit	Fighting	Special	—	100	5	Normal

National Pokédex **020** Hoenn Pokédex —

Raticate

Mouse Pokémon

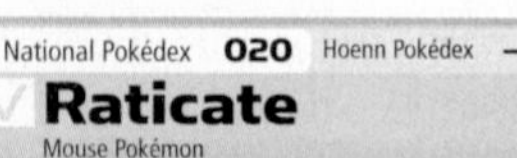

Normal

HEIGHT: 2'04" WEIGHT: 40.8 lbs.

The male has longer whiskers than the female.

♂ ♀

Ω Raticate's sturdy fangs grow steadily. To keep them ground down, it gnaws on rocks and logs. It may even chew on the walls of houses.

α Raticate's sturdy fangs grow steadily. To keep them ground down, it gnaws on rocks and logs. It may even chew on the walls of houses.

ABILITIES
Run Away
Guts

HIDDEN ABILITY
Hustle

EGG GROUPS
Field

STAT GROWTH RATES
HP
Attack
Defense
Sp. Atk
Sp. Def
Speed

ITEMS SOMETIMES HELD BY WILD POKÉMON
—

EVOLUTION

Rattata → Lv. 20 → Raticate

MAIN WAY TO REGISTER IN THE NATIONAL POKÉDEX

Catch on Route 118. Appears as a hidden Pokémon after you battle Groudon or Kyogre.

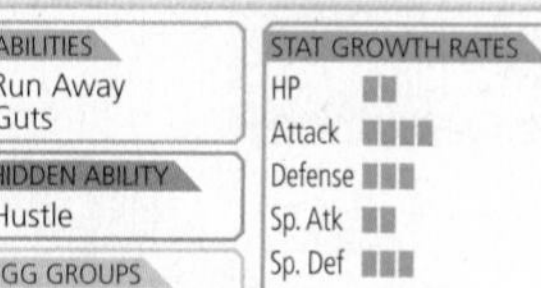

Damage taken in normal battles

Type		Type	
Normal	×1	Flying	×1
Fire	×1	Psychic	×1
Water	×1	Bug	×1
Grass	×1	Rock	×1
Electric	×1	Ghost	×0
Ice	×1	Dragon	×1
Fighting	×2	Dark	×1
Poison	×1	Steel	×1
Ground	×1	Fairy	×1

Damage taken in Inverse battles

Type		Type	
Normal	×1	Flying	×1
Fire	×1	Psychic	×1
Water	×1	Bug	×1
Grass	×1	Rock	×1
Electric	×1	Ghost	×2
Ice	×1	Dragon	×1
Fighting	×0.5	Dark	×1
Poison	×1	Steel	×1
Ground	×1	Fairy	×1

Can be used in
Inverse Battle
Battle Institute
Battle Maison
Random Matchup (Free Battle)
Random Matchup (Others)

LEVEL-UP MOVES

Lv.	Name	Type	Kind	Pow.	Acc.	PP	Range
1	Swords Dance	Normal	Status	—	—	20	Self
1	Tackle	Normal	Physical	50	100	35	Normal
1	Tail Whip	Normal	Status	—	100	30	Many Others
1	Quick Attack	Normal	Physical	40	100	30	Normal
1	Focus Energy	Normal	Status	—	—	30	Self
4	Quick Attack	Normal	Physical	40	100	30	Normal
7	Focus Energy	Normal	Status	—	—	30	Self
10	Bite	Dark	Physical	60	100	25	Normal
13	Pursuit	Dark	Physical	40	100	20	Normal
16	Hyper Fang	Normal	Physical	80	90	15	Normal
19	Sucker Punch	Dark	Physical	80	100	5	Normal
20	Scary Face	Normal	Status	—	100	10	Normal
24	Crunch	Dark	Physical	80	100	15	Normal
29	Assurance	Dark	Physical	60	100	10	Normal
34	Super Fang	Normal	Physical	—	90	10	Normal
39	Double-Edge	Normal	Physical	120	100	15	Normal
44	Endeavor	Normal	Physical	—	100	5	Normal

TM & HM MOVES

No.	Name	Type	Kind	Pow.	Acc.	PP	Range
TM05	Roar	Normal	Status	—	—	20	Normal
TM06	Toxic	Poison	Status	—	90	10	Normal
TM10	Hidden Power	Normal	Special	60	100	15	Normal
TM11	Sunny Day	Fire	Status	—	—	5	Both Sides
TM12	Taunt	Dark	Status	—	100	20	Normal
TM13	Ice Beam	Ice	Special	90	100	10	Normal
TM14	Blizzard	Ice	Special	110	70	5	Many Others
TM15	Hyper Beam	Normal	Special	150	90	5	Normal
TM17	Protect	Normal	Status	—	—	10	Self
TM18	Rain Dance	Water	Status	—	—	5	Both Sides
TM21	Frustration	Normal	Physical	—	100	20	Normal
TM24	Thunderbolt	Electric	Special	90	100	15	Normal
TM25	Thunder	Electric	Special	110	70	10	Normal
TM27	Return	Normal	Physical	—	100	20	Normal
TM28	Dig	Ground	Physical	80	100	10	Normal
TM30	Shadow Ball	Ghost	Special	80	100	15	Normal
TM32	Double Team	Normal	Status	—	—	15	Self
TM42	Facade	Normal	Physical	70	100	20	Normal
TM44	Rest	Psychic	Status	—	—	10	Self
TM45	Attract	Normal	Status	—	100	15	Normal
TM46	Thief	Dark	Physical	60	100	25	Normal
TM48	Round	Normal	Special	60	100	15	Normal
TM57	Charge Beam	Electric	Special	50	90	10	Normal
TM67	Retaliate	Normal	Physical	70	100	5	Normal
TM68	Giga Impact	Normal	Physical	150	90	5	Normal
TM73	Thunder Wave	Electric	Status	—	100	20	Normal
TM75	Swords Dance	Normal	Status	—	—	20	Self
TM86	Grass Knot	Grass	Special	—	100	20	Normal
TM87	Swagger	Normal	Status	—	90	15	Normal
TM88	Sleep Talk	Normal	Status	—	—	10	Self
TM89	U-turn	Bug	Physical	70	100	20	Normal
TM90	Substitute	Normal	Status	—	—	10	Self
TM93	Wild Charge	Electric	Physical	90	100	15	Normal
TM94	Secret Power	Normal	Physical	70	100	20	Normal
TM100	Confide	Normal	Status	—	—	20	Normal
HM01	Cut	Normal	Physical	50	95	30	Normal
HM04	Strength	Normal	Physical	80	100	15	Normal
HM06	Rock Smash	Fighting	Physical	40	100	15	Normal

MOVES LEARNED IN EXCHANGE FOR BP

Name	Type	Kind	Pow.	Acc.	PP	Range
Covet	Normal	Physical	60	100	25	Normal
Super Fang	Normal	Physical	—	90	10	Normal
Uproar	Normal	Special	90	100	10	1 Random
Last Resort	Normal	Physical	140	100	5	Normal
Icy Wind	Ice	Special	55	95	15	Many Others
Zen Headbutt	Psychic	Physical	80	90	15	Normal
Iron Tail	Steel	Physical	100	75	15	Normal
Snore	Normal	Special	50	100	15	Normal
Shock Wave	Electric	Special	60	—	20	Normal
Endeavor	Normal	Physical	—	100	5	Normal

MOVES TAUGHT BY PEOPLE

Name	Type	Kind	Pow.	Acc.	PP	Range

National Pokédex **021** Hoenn Pokédex —

Spearow

Tiny Bird Pokémon

Normal Flying

HEIGHT: 1'00" WEIGHT: 4.4 lbs.

Same form for ♂ / ♀

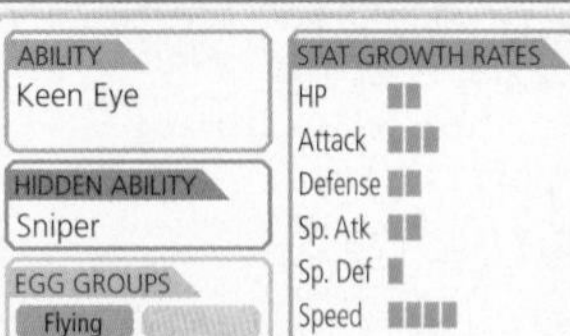

Ω Spearow has a very loud cry that can be heard over half a mile away. If its high, keening cry is heard echoing all around, it is a sign that they are warning each other of danger.

α Spearow has a very loud cry that can be heard over half a mile away. If its high, keening cry is heard echoing all around, it is a sign that they are warning each other of danger.

ABILITY
Keen Eye

HIDDEN ABILITY
Sniper

EGG GROUPS
Flying

STAT GROWTH RATES

HP	■■
Attack	■■
Defense	■■
Sp. Atk	■■
Sp. Def	■
Speed	■■■■

ITEMS SOMETIMES HELD BY WILD POKÉMON
—

EVOLUTION

MAIN WAY TO REGISTER IN THE NATIONAL POKÉDEX

Leave a Fearow obtained via Link Trade or the GTS at a Pokémon Day Care, then hatch the Pokémon Egg that is found.

Damage taken in normal battles

Normal	×1	Flying	×1
Fire	×1	Psychic	×1
Water	×1	Bug	×0.5
Grass	×0.5	Rock	×2
Electric	×2	Ghost	×0
Ice	×2	Dragon	×1
Fighting	×1	Dark	×1
Poison	×1	Steel	×1
Ground	×0	Fairy	×1

Damage taken in Inverse battles

Normal	×1	Flying	×1
Fire	×1	Psychic	×1
Water	×1	Bug	×2
Grass	×2	Rock	×0.5
Electric	×0.5	Ghost	×2
Ice	×0.5	Dragon	×1
Fighting	×1	Dark	×1
Poison	×1	Steel	×1
Ground	×2	Fairy	×1

Can be used in
- Inverse Battle
- Battle Institute
- Battle Maison
- Random Matchup (Free Battle)
- Random Matchup (Others)

LEVEL-UP MOVES

Lv.	Name	Type	Kind	Pow.	Acc.	PP	Range
1	Peck	Flying	Physical	35	100	35	Normal
1	Growl	Normal	Status	—	100	40	Many Others
5	Leer	Normal	Status	—	100	30	Many Others
9	Fury Attack	Normal	Physical	15	85	20	Normal
13	Pursuit	Dark	Physical	40	100	20	Normal
17	Aerial Ace	Flying	Physical	60	—	20	Normal
21	Mirror Move	Flying	Status	—	—	20	Normal
25	Agility	Psychic	Status	—	—	30	Self
29	Assurance	Dark	Physical	60	100	10	Normal
33	Roost	Flying	Status	—	—	10	Self
37	Drill Peck	Flying	Physical	80	100	20	Normal

TM & HM MOVES

No.	Name	Type	Kind	Pow.	Acc.	PP	Range
TM06	Toxic	Poison	Status	—	90	10	Normal
TM10	Hidden Power	Normal	Special	60	100	15	Normal
TM11	Sunny Day	Fire	Status	—	—	5	Both Sides
TM17	Protect	Normal	Status	—	—	10	Self
TM18	Rain Dance	Water	Status	—	—	5	Both Sides
TM19	Roost	Flying	Status	—	—	10	Self
TM21	Frustration	Normal	Physical	—	100	20	Normal
TM27	Return	Normal	Physical	—	100	20	Normal
TM32	Double Team	Normal	Status	—	—	15	Self
TM40	Aerial Ace	Flying	Physical	60	—	20	Normal
TM42	Facade	Normal	Physical	70	100	20	Normal
TM44	Rest	Psychic	Status	—	—	10	Self
TM45	Attract	Normal	Status	—	100	15	Normal
TM46	Thief	Dark	Physical	60	100	25	Normal
TM48	Round	Normal	Special	60	100	15	Normal
TM49	Echoed Voice	Normal	Special	40	100	15	Normal
TM51	Steel Wing	Steel	Physical	70	90	25	Normal
TM54	False Swipe	Normal	Physical	40	100	40	Normal
TM87	Swagger	Normal	Status	—	90	15	Normal
TM88	Sleep Talk	Normal	Status	—	—	10	Self
TM89	U-turn	Bug	Physical	70	100	20	Normal
TM90	Substitute	Normal	Status	—	—	10	Self
TM94	Secret Power	Normal	Physical	70	100	20	Normal
TM100	Confide	Normal	Status	—	—	20	Normal
HM02	Fly	Flying	Physical	90	95	15	Normal

MOVES LEARNED IN EXCHANGE FOR BP

Name	Type	Kind	Pow.	Acc.	PP	Range
Drill Run	Ground	Physical	80	95	10	Normal
Uproar	Normal	Special	90	100	10	1 Random
Snore	Normal	Special	50	100	15	Normal
Heat Wave	Fire	Special	95	90	10	Many Others
Tailwind	Flying	Status	—	—	15	Your Side
Sky Attack	Flying	Physical	140	90	5	Normal

MOVES TAUGHT BY PEOPLE

Name	Type	Kind	Pow.	Acc.	PP	Range

EGG MOVES

Name	Type	Kind	Pow.	Acc.	PP	Range
Feint Attack	Dark	Physical	60	—	20	Normal
Scary Face	Normal	Status	—	100	10	Normal
Quick Attack	Normal	Physical	40	100	30	Normal
Tri Attack	Normal	Special	80	100	10	Normal
Astonish	Ghost	Physical	30	100	15	Normal
Sky Attack	Flying	Physical	140	90	5	Normal
Whirlwind	Normal	Status	—	—	20	Normal
Uproar	Normal	Special	90	100	10	1 Random
Feather Dance	Flying	Status	—	100	15	Normal
Steel Wing	Steel	Physical	70	90	25	Normal
Razor Wind	Normal	Special	80	100	10	Many Others

National Pokédex **022** Hoenn Pokédex —

Fearow

Beak Pokémon

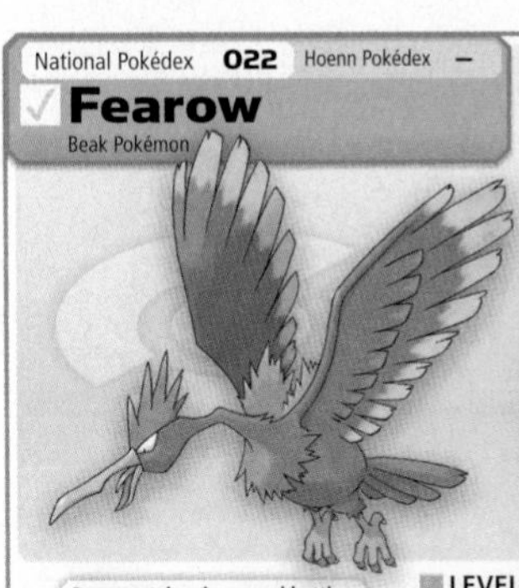

Normal Flying

HEIGHT: 3'11" WEIGHT: 83.8 lbs.

Same form for ♂ / ♀

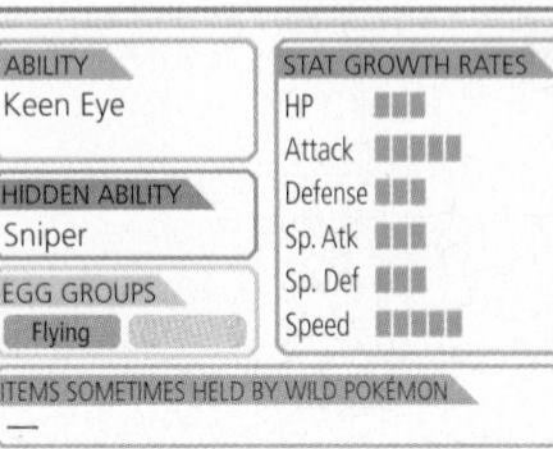

Ω Fearow is recognized by its long neck and elongated beak. They are conveniently shaped for catching prey in soil or water. It deftly moves its long and skinny beak to pluck prey.

α Fearow is recognized by its long neck and elongated beak. They are conveniently shaped for catching prey in soil or water. It deftly moves its long and skinny beak to pluck prey.

ABILITY
Keen Eye

HIDDEN ABILITY
Sniper

EGG GROUPS
Flying

STAT GROWTH RATES

HP	■■■
Attack	■■■■■
Defense	■■■
Sp. Atk	■■■
Sp. Def	■■■
Speed	■■■■■

ITEMS SOMETIMES HELD BY WILD POKÉMON
—

EVOLUTION

MAIN WAY TO REGISTER IN THE NATIONAL POKÉDEX

Appears in *Pokémon X* and *Pokémon Y*. Bring it to your game using Link Trade or the GTS.

Damage taken in normal battles

Normal	×1	Flying	×1
Fire	×1	Psychic	×1
Water	×1	Bug	×0.5
Grass	×0.5	Rock	×2
Electric	×2	Ghost	×0
Ice	×2	Dragon	×1
Fighting	×1	Dark	×1
Poison	×1	Steel	×1
Ground	×0	Fairy	×1

Damage taken in Inverse battles

Normal	×1	Flying	×1
Fire	×1	Psychic	×1
Water	×1	Bug	×2
Grass	×2	Rock	×0.5
Electric	×0.5	Ghost	×2
Ice	×0.5	Dragon	×1
Fighting	×1	Dark	×1
Poison	×1	Steel	×1
Ground	×2	Fairy	×1

Can be used in
- Inverse Battle
- Battle Institute
- Battle Maison
- Random Matchup (Free Battle)
- Random Matchup (Others)

LEVEL-UP MOVES

Lv.	Name	Type	Kind	Pow.	Acc.	PP	Range
1	Drill Run	Ground	Physical	80	95	10	Normal
1	Pluck	Flying	Physical	60	100	20	Normal
1	Peck	Flying	Physical	35	100	35	Normal
1	Growl	Normal	Status	—	100	40	Many Others
1	Leer	Normal	Status	—	100	30	Many Others
1	Fury Attack	Normal	Physical	15	85	20	Normal
5	Leer	Normal	Status	—	100	30	Many Others
9	Fury Attack	Normal	Physical	15	85	20	Normal
13	Pursuit	Dark	Physical	40	100	20	Normal
17	Aerial Ace	Flying	Physical	60	—	20	Normal
23	Mirror Move	Flying	Status	—	—	20	Normal
29	Agility	Psychic	Status	—	—	30	Self
35	Assurance	Dark	Physical	60	100	10	Normal
41	Roost	Flying	Status	—	—	10	Self
47	Drill Peck	Flying	Physical	80	100	20	Normal
53	Drill Run	Ground	Physical	80	95	10	Normal

TM & HM MOVES

No.	Name	Type	Kind	Pow.	Acc.	PP	Range
TM06	Toxic	Poison	Status	—	90	10	Normal
TM10	Hidden Power	Normal	Special	60	100	15	Normal
TM11	Sunny Day	Fire	Status	—	—	5	Both Sides
TM15	Hyper Beam	Normal	Special	150	90	5	Normal
TM17	Protect	Normal	Status	—	—	10	Self
TM18	Rain Dance	Water	Status	—	—	5	Both Sides
TM19	Roost	Flying	Status	—	—	10	Self
TM21	Frustration	Normal	Physical	—	100	20	Normal
TM27	Return	Normal	Physical	—	100	20	Normal
TM32	Double Team	Normal	Status	—	—	15	Self
TM40	Aerial Ace	Flying	Physical	60	—	20	Normal
TM42	Facade	Normal	Physical	70	100	20	Normal
TM44	Rest	Psychic	Status	—	—	10	Self
TM45	Attract	Normal	Status	—	100	15	Normal
TM46	Thief	Dark	Physical	60	100	25	Normal
TM48	Round	Normal	Special	60	100	15	Normal
TM49	Echoed Voice	Normal	Special	40	100	15	Normal
TM51	Steel Wing	Steel	Physical	70	90	25	Normal
TM54	False Swipe	Normal	Physical	40	100	40	Normal
TM68	Giga Impact	Normal	Physical	150	90	5	Normal
TM87	Swagger	Normal	Status	—	90	15	Normal
TM88	Sleep Talk	Normal	Status	—	—	10	Self
TM89	U-turn	Bug	Physical	70	100	20	Normal
TM90	Substitute	Normal	Status	—	—	10	Self
TM94	Secret Power	Normal	Physical	70	100	20	Normal
TM100	Confide	Normal	Status	—	—	20	Normal
HM02	Fly	Flying	Physical	90	95	15	Normal

MOVES LEARNED IN EXCHANGE FOR BP

Name	Type	Kind	Pow.	Acc.	PP	Range
Drill Run	Ground	Physical	80	95	10	Normal
Uproar	Normal	Special	90	100	10	1 Random
Snore	Normal	Special	50	100	15	Normal
Heat Wave	Fire	Special	95	90	10	Many Others
Tailwind	Flying	Status	—	—	15	Your Side
Sky Attack	Flying	Physical	140	90	5	Normal

MOVES TAUGHT BY PEOPLE

Name	Type	Kind	Pow.	Acc.	PP	Range

National Pokédex **023** Hoenn Pokédex —

Ekans

Snake Pokémon

Poison

HEIGHT: 6'07" WEIGHT: 15.2 lbs.

Same form for ♂ / ♀

Ω Ekans curls itself up in a spiral while it rests. Assuming this position allows it to quickly respond to a threat from any direction with a glare from its upraised head.

α Ekans curls itself up in a spiral while it rests. Assuming this position allows it to quickly respond to a threat from any direction with a glare from its upraised head.

ABILITIES
Intimidate
Shed Skin

HIDDEN ABILITY
Unnerve

EGG GROUPS
Field | Dragon

STAT GROWTH RATES
HP
Attack
Defense
Sp. Atk
Sp. Def
Speed

ITEMS SOMETIMES HELD BY WILD POKÉMON
—

EVOLUTION

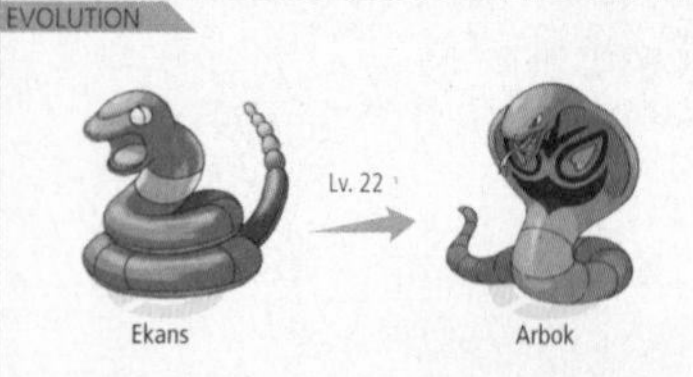

MAIN WAY TO REGISTER IN THE NATIONAL POKÉDEX

Appears in *Pokémon X* and *Pokémon Y*. Bring it to your game using Link Trade or the GTS.

Damage taken in normal battles

Type		Type	
Normal	×1	Flying	×1
Fire	×1	Psychic	×2
Water	×1	Bug	×0.5
Grass	×0.5	Rock	×1
Electric	×1	Ghost	×1
Ice	×1	Dragon	×1
Fighting	×0.5	Dark	×1
Poison	×0.5	Steel	×1
Ground	×2	Fairy	×0.5

Damage taken in Inverse battles

Type		Type	
Normal	×1	Flying	×1
Fire	×1	Psychic	×0.5
Water	×1	Bug	×2
Grass	×2	Rock	×1
Electric	×1	Ghost	×1
Ice	×1	Dragon	×1
Fighting	×2	Dark	×1
Poison	×2	Steel	×1
Ground	×0.5	Fairy	×2

Can be used in
Inverse Battle
Battle Institute
Battle Maison
Random Matchup (Free Battle)
Random Matchup (Others)

LEVEL-UP MOVES

Lv.	Name	Type	Kind	Pow.	Acc.	PP	Range
1	Wrap	Normal	Physical	15	90	20	Normal
1	Leer	Normal	Status	—	100	30	Many Others
4	Poison Sting	Poison	Physical	15	100	35	Normal
9	Bite	Dark	Physical	60	100	25	Normal
12	Glare	Normal	Status	—	100	30	Normal
17	Screech	Normal	Status	—	85	40	Normal
20	Acid	Poison	Special	40	100	30	Many Others
25	Stockpile	Normal	Status	—	—	20	Self
25	Swallow	Normal	Status	—	—	10	Self
25	Spit Up	Normal	Special	—	100	10	Normal
28	Acid Spray	Poison	Special	40	100	20	Normal
33	Mud Bomb	Ground	Special	65	85	10	Normal
36	Gastro Acid	Poison	Status	—	100	10	Normal
38	Belch	Poison	Special	120	90	10	Normal
41	Haze	Ice	Status	—	—	30	Both Sides
44	Coil	Poison	Status	—	—	20	Self
49	Gunk Shot	Poison	Physical	120	80	5	Normal

TM & HM MOVES

No.	Name	Type	Kind	Pow.	Acc.	PP	Range
TM06	Toxic	Poison	Status	—	90	10	Normal
TM09	Venoshock	Poison	Special	65	100	10	Normal
TM10	Hidden Power	Normal	Special	60	100	15	Normal
TM11	Sunny Day	Fire	Status	—	—	5	Both Sides
TM17	Protect	Normal	Status	—	—	10	Self
TM18	Rain Dance	Water	Status	—	—	5	Both Sides
TM21	Frustration	Normal	Physical	—	100	20	Normal
TM26	Earthquake	Ground	Physical	100	100	10	Adjacent
TM27	Return	Normal	Physical	—	100	20	Normal
TM28	Dig	Ground	Physical	80	100	10	Normal
TM32	Double Team	Normal	Status	—	—	15	Self
TM34	Sludge Wave	Poison	Special	95	100	10	Adjacent
TM36	Sludge Bomb	Poison	Special	90	100	10	Normal
TM39	Rock Tomb	Rock	Physical	60	95	15	Normal
TM41	Torment	Dark	Status	—	100	15	Normal
TM42	Facade	Normal	Physical	70	100	20	Normal
TM44	Rest	Psychic	Status	—	—	10	Self
TM45	Attract	Normal	Status	—	100	15	Normal
TM46	Thief	Dark	Physical	60	100	25	Normal
TM48	Round	Normal	Special	60	100	15	Normal
TM66	Payback	Dark	Physical	50	100	10	Normal
TM78	Bulldoze	Ground	Physical	60	100	20	Adjacent
TM80	Rock Slide	Rock	Physical	75	90	10	Many Others
TM83	Infestation	Bug	Special	20	100	20	Normal
TM84	Poison Jab	Poison	Physical	80	100	20	Normal
TM87	Swagger	Normal	Status	—	90	15	Normal
TM88	Sleep Talk	Normal	Status	—	—	10	Self
TM90	Substitute	Normal	Status	—	—	10	Self
TM94	Secret Power	Normal	Physical	70	100	20	Normal
TM97	Dark Pulse	Dark	Special	80	100	15	Normal
TM100	Confide	Normal	Status	—	—	20	Normal
HM04	Strength	Normal	Physical	80	100	15	Normal

MOVES LEARNED IN EXCHANGE FOR BP

Name	Type	Kind	Pow.	Acc.	PP	Range
Seed Bomb	Grass	Physical	80	100	15	Normal
Gunk Shot	Poison	Physical	120	80	5	Normal
Aqua Tail	Water	Physical	90	90	10	Normal
Iron Tail	Steel	Physical	100	75	15	Normal
Bind	Normal	Physical	15	85	20	Normal
Snore	Normal	Special	50	100	15	Normal
Giga Drain	Grass	Special	75	100	10	Normal
Gastro Acid	Poison	Status	—	100	10	Normal
Spite	Ghost	Status	—	100	10	Normal
Snatch	Dark	Status	—	—	10	Self

MOVES TAUGHT BY PEOPLE

Name	Type	Kind	Pow.	Acc.	PP	Range

EGG MOVES

Name	Type	Kind	Pow.	Acc.	PP	Range
Pursuit	Dark	Physical	40	100	20	Normal
Slam	Normal	Physical	80	75	20	Normal
Spite	Ghost	Status	—	100	10	Normal
Beat Up	Dark	Physical	—	100	10	Normal
Poison Fang	Poison	Physical	50	100	15	Normal
Scary Face	Normal	Status	—	100	10	Normal
Poison Tail	Poison	Physical	50	100	25	Normal
Disable	Normal	Status	—	100	20	Normal
Switcheroo	Dark	Status	—	100	10	Normal
Iron Tail	Steel	Physical	100	75	15	Normal
Sucker Punch	Dark	Physical	80	100	5	Normal
Snatch	Dark	Status	—	—	10	Self

National Pokédex **024** Hoenn Pokédex —

Arbok

Cobra Pokémon

Poison

HEIGHT: 11'06" WEIGHT: 143.3 lbs.

Same form for ♂ / ♀

Ω This Pokémon is terrifically strong in order to constrict things with its body. It can even flatten steel oil drums. Once Arbok wraps its body around its foe, escaping its crunching embrace is impossible.

α This Pokémon is terrifically strong in order to constrict things with its body. It can even flatten steel oil drums. Once Arbok wraps its body around its foe, escaping its crunching embrace is impossible.

ABILITIES
Intimidate
Shed Skin

HIDDEN ABILITY
Unnerve

EGG GROUPS
Field | Dragon

STAT GROWTH RATES
HP
Attack
Defense
Sp. Atk
Sp. Def
Speed

ITEMS SOMETIMES HELD BY WILD POKÉMON
—

EVOLUTION

Lv. 22
Ekans
Arbok

MAIN WAY TO REGISTER IN THE NATIONAL POKÉDEX

Appears in *Pokémon X* and *Pokémon Y*. Bring it to your game using Link Trade or the GTS.

Damage taken in normal battles

Type		Type	
Normal	×1	Flying	×1
Fire	×1	Psychic	×2
Water	×1	Bug	×0.5
Grass	×0.5	Rock	×1
Electric	×1	Ghost	×1
Ice	×1	Dragon	×1
Fighting	×0.5	Dark	×1
Poison	×0.5	Steel	×1
Ground	×2	Fairy	×0.5

Damage taken in Inverse battles

Type		Type	
Normal	×1	Flying	×1
Fire	×1	Psychic	×0.5
Water	×1	Bug	×2
Grass	×2	Rock	×1
Electric	×1	Ghost	×1
Ice	×1	Dragon	×1
Fighting	×2	Dark	×1
Poison	×2	Steel	×1
Ground	×0.5	Fairy	×2

Can be used in
Inverse Battle
Battle Institute
Battle Maison
Random Matchup (Free Battle)
Random Matchup (Others)

LEVEL-UP MOVES

Lv.	Name	Type	Kind	Pow.	Acc.	PP	Range
1	Ice Fang	Ice	Physical	65	95	15	Normal
1	Thunder Fang	Electric	Physical	65	95	15	Normal
1	Fire Fang	Fire	Physical	65	95	15	Normal
1	Wrap	Normal	Physical	15	90	20	Normal
1	Leer	Normal	Status	—	100	30	Many Others
1	Poison Sting	Poison	Physical	15	100	35	Normal
1	Bite	Dark	Physical	60	100	25	Normal
4	Poison Sting	Poison	Physical	15	100	35	Normal
9	Bite	Dark	Physical	60	100	25	Normal
12	Glare	Normal	Status	—	100	30	Normal
17	Screech	Normal	Status	—	85	40	Normal
20	Acid	Poison	Special	40	100	30	Many Others
22	Crunch	Dark	Physical	80	100	15	Normal
27	Stockpile	Normal	Status	—	—	20	Self
27	Swallow	Normal	Status	—	—	10	Self
27	Spit Up	Normal	Special	—	100	10	Normal
32	Acid Spray	Poison	Special	40	100	20	Normal
39	Mud Bomb	Ground	Special	65	85	10	Normal
44	Gastro Acid	Poison	Status	—	100	10	Normal
48	Belch	Poison	Special	120	90	10	Normal
51	Haze	Ice	Status	—	—	30	Both Sides
56	Coil	Poison	Status	—	—	20	Self
63	Gunk Shot	Poison	Physical	120	80	5	Normal

TM & HM MOVES

No.	Name	Type	Kind	Pow.	Acc.	PP	Range
TM06	Toxic	Poison	Status	—	90	10	Normal
TM09	Venoshock	Poison	Special	65	100	10	Normal
TM10	Hidden Power	Normal	Special	60	100	15	Normal
TM11	Sunny Day	Fire	Status	—	—	5	Both Sides
TM15	Hyper Beam	Normal	Special	150	90	5	Normal
TM17	Protect	Normal	Status	—	—	10	Self
TM18	Rain Dance	Water	Status	—	—	5	Both Sides
TM21	Frustration	Normal	Physical	—	100	20	Normal
TM26	Earthquake	Ground	Physical	100	100	10	Adjacent
TM27	Return	Normal	Physical	—	100	20	Normal
TM28	Dig	Ground	Physical	80	100	10	Normal
TM32	Double Team	Normal	Status	—	—	15	Self
TM34	Sludge Wave	Poison	Special	95	100	10	Adjacent
TM36	Sludge Bomb	Poison	Special	90	100	10	Normal
TM39	Rock Tomb	Rock	Physical	60	95	15	Normal
TM41	Torment	Dark	Status	—	100	15	Normal
TM42	Facade	Normal	Physical	70	100	20	Normal
TM44	Rest	Psychic	Status	—	—	10	Self
TM45	Attract	Normal	Status	—	100	15	Normal
TM46	Thief	Dark	Physical	60	100	25	Normal
TM48	Round	Normal	Special	60	100	15	Normal
TM66	Payback	Dark	Physical	50	100	10	Normal
TM68	Giga Impact	Normal	Physical	150	90	5	Normal
TM78	Bulldoze	Ground	Physical	60	100	20	Adjacent
TM80	Rock Slide	Rock	Physical	75	90	10	Many Others
TM82	Dragon Tail	Dragon	Physical	60	90	10	Normal
TM83	Infestation	Bug	Special	20	100	20	Normal
TM84	Poison Jab	Poison	Physical	80	100	20	Normal
TM87	Swagger	Normal	Status	—	90	15	Normal
TM88	Sleep Talk	Normal	Status	—	—	10	Self
TM90	Substitute	Normal	Status	—	—	10	Self
TM94	Secret Power	Normal	Physical	70	100	20	Normal
TM97	Dark Pulse	Dark	Special	80	100	15	Normal
TM100	Confide	Normal	Status	—	—	20	Normal
HM04	Strength	Normal	Physical	80	100	15	Normal

MOVES LEARNED IN EXCHANGE FOR BP

Name	Type	Kind	Pow.	Acc.	PP	Range
Seed Bomb	Grass	Physical	80	100	15	Normal
Gunk Shot	Poison	Physical	120	80	5	Normal
Aqua Tail	Water	Physical	90	90	10	Normal
Iron Tail	Steel	Physical	100	75	15	Normal
Bind	Normal	Physical	15	85	20	Normal
Snore	Normal	Special	50	100	15	Normal
Giga Drain	Grass	Special	75	100	10	Normal
Gastro Acid	Poison	Status	—	100	10	Normal
Spite	Ghost	Status	—	100	10	Normal
Snatch	Dark	Status	—	—	10	Self

MOVES TAUGHT BY PEOPLE

Name	Type	Kind	Pow.	Acc.	PP	Range

National Pokédex **025** Hoenn Pokédex **163**

✓ Pikachu

Mouse Pokémon

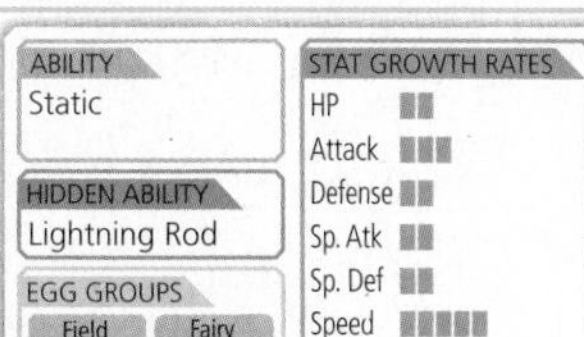

Electric

HEIGHT: 1'04" WEIGHT: 13.2 lbs.

The tip of the male's tail is straight. The female has a notch at the end of its tail.

♂ ♀

Ω Whenever Pikachu comes across something new, it blasts it with a jolt of electricity. If you come across a blackened berry, it's evidence that this Pokémon mistook the intensity of its charge.

α This Pokémon has electricity-storing pouches on its cheeks. These appear to become electrically charged during the night while Pikachu sleeps. It occasionally discharges electricity when it is dozy after waking up.

ABILITY
Static

HIDDEN ABILITY
Lightning Rod

EGG GROUPS
Field | Fairy

STAT GROWTH RATES
HP ■■
Attack ■■■
Defense ■■
Sp. Atk ■■
Sp. Def ■■
Speed ■■■■■

ITEMS SOMETIMES HELD BY WILD POKÉMON
Light Ball

EVOLUTION

Pichu → (Level up with high friendship) → Pikachu → (Thunder Stone) → Raichu

MAIN WAY TO REGISTER IN THE NATIONAL POKÉDEX

Catch in the tall grass in the lower-right corner of the Safari Zone.

Damage taken in normal battles

Type		Type	
Normal	×1	Flying	×0.5
Fire	×1	Psychic	×1
Water	×1	Bug	×1
Grass	×1	Rock	×1
Electric	×0.5	Ghost	×1
Ice	×1	Dragon	×1
Fighting	×1	Dark	×1
Poison	×1	Steel	×0.5
Ground	×2	Fairy	×1

Damage taken in Inverse battles

Type		Type	
Normal	×1	Flying	×2
Fire	×1	Psychic	×1
Water	×1	Bug	×1
Grass	×1	Rock	×1
Electric	×2	Ghost	×1
Ice	×1	Dragon	×1
Fighting	×1	Dark	×1
Poison	×1	Steel	×2
Ground	×0.5	Fairy	×1

Can be used in
Inverse Battle
Battle Institute
Battle Maison
Random Matchup (Free Battle)
Random Matchup (Others)

LEVEL-UP MOVES

Lv.	Name	Type	Kind	Pow.	Acc.	PP	Range
1	Tail Whip	Normal	Status	—	100	30	Many Others
1	Thunder Shock	Electric	Special	40	100	30	Normal
5	Growl	Normal	Status	—	100	40	Many Others
7	Play Nice	Normal	Status	—	—	20	Normal
10	Quick Attack	Normal	Physical	40	100	30	Normal
13	Electro Ball	Electric	Special	—	100	10	Normal
18	Thunder Wave	Electric	Status	—	100	20	Normal
21	Feint	Normal	Physical	30	100	10	Normal
23	Double Team	Normal	Status	—	—	15	Self
26	Spark	Electric	Physical	65	100	20	Normal
29	Nuzzle	Electric	Physical	20	100	20	Normal
34	Discharge	Electric	Special	80	100	15	Adjacent
37	Slam	Normal	Physical	80	75	20	Normal
42	Thunderbolt	Electric	Special	90	100	15	Normal
45	Agility	Psychic	Status	—	—	30	Self
50	Wild Charge	Electric	Physical	90	100	15	Normal
53	Light Screen	Psychic	Status	—	—	30	Your Side
58	Thunder	Electric	Special	110	70	10	Normal

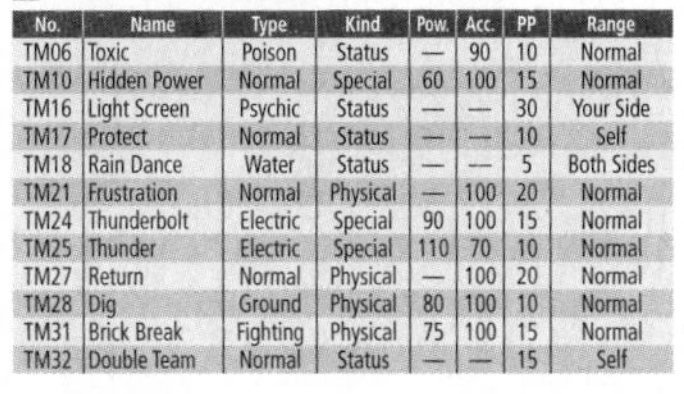

TM & HM MOVES

No.	Name	Type	Kind	Pow.	Acc.	PP	Range
TM06	Toxic	Poison	Status	—	90	10	Normal
TM10	Hidden Power	Normal	Special	60	100	15	Normal
TM16	Light Screen	Psychic	Status	—	—	30	Your Side
TM17	Protect	Normal	Status	—	—	10	Self
TM18	Rain Dance	Water	Status	—	—	5	Both Sides
TM21	Frustration	Normal	Physical	—	100	20	Normal
TM24	Thunderbolt	Electric	Special	90	100	15	Normal
TM25	Thunder	Electric	Special	110	70	10	Normal
TM27	Return	Normal	Physical	—	100	20	Normal
TM28	Dig	Ground	Physical	80	100	10	Normal
TM31	Brick Break	Fighting	Physical	75	100	15	Normal
TM32	Double Team	Normal	Status	—	—	15	Self
TM42	Facade	Normal	Physical	70	100	20	Normal
TM44	Rest	Psychic	Status	—	—	10	Self
TM45	Attract	Normal	Status	—	100	15	Normal
TM48	Round	Normal	Special	60	100	15	Normal
TM49	Echoed Voice	Normal	Special	40	100	15	Normal
TM56	Fling	Dark	Physical	—	100	10	Normal
TM57	Charge Beam	Electric	Special	50	90	10	Normal
TM70	Flash	Normal	Status	—	100	20	Normal
TM72	Volt Switch	Electric	Special	70	100	20	Normal
TM73	Thunder Wave	Electric	Status	—	100	20	Normal
TM86	Grass Knot	Grass	Special	—	100	20	Normal
TM87	Swagger	Normal	Status	—	90	15	Normal
TM88	Sleep Talk	Normal	Status	—	—	10	Self
TM90	Substitute	Normal	Status	—	—	10	Self
TM93	Wild Charge	Electric	Physical	90	100	15	Normal
TM94	Secret Power	Normal	Physical	70	100	20	Normal
TM100	Confide	Normal	Status	—	—	20	Normal
HM04	Strength	Normal	Physical	80	100	15	Normal
HM06	Rock Smash	Fighting	Physical	40	100	15	Normal

MOVES LEARNED IN EXCHANGE FOR BP

Name	Type	Kind	Pow.	Acc.	PP	Range
Covet	Normal	Physical	60	100	25	Normal
Signal Beam	Bug	Special	75	100	15	Normal
Thunder Punch	Electric	Physical	75	100	15	Normal
Magnet Rise	Electric	Status	—	—	10	Self
Electroweb	Electric	Special	55	95	15	Many Others
Iron Tail	Steel	Physical	100	75	15	Normal
Snore	Normal	Special	50	100	15	Normal
Knock Off	Dark	Physical	65	100	20	Normal
Focus Punch	Fighting	Physical	150	100	20	Normal
Shock Wave	Electric	Special	60	—	20	Normal
Helping Hand	Normal	Status	—	—	20	1 Ally

MOVES TAUGHT BY PEOPLE

Name	Type	Kind	Pow.	Acc.	PP	Range

National Pokédex **025** Hoenn Pokédex **163**

✓ Pikachu Pikachu Rock Star

Mouse Pokémon

Electric

HEIGHT: 1'04" WEIGHT: 13.2 lbs.

♀ only. Cosplay Pikachu has a black heart mark at the end of its tail.

Ω —

α —

ABILITY
—

HIDDEN ABILITY
Lightning Rod

EGG GROUPS
No Eggs Discovered

STAT GROWTH RATES
HP ■■
Attack ■■■
Defense ■■
Sp. Atk ■■
Sp. Def ■■
Speed ■■■■■

ITEMS SOMETIMES HELD BY WILD POKÉMON
—

EVOLUTION

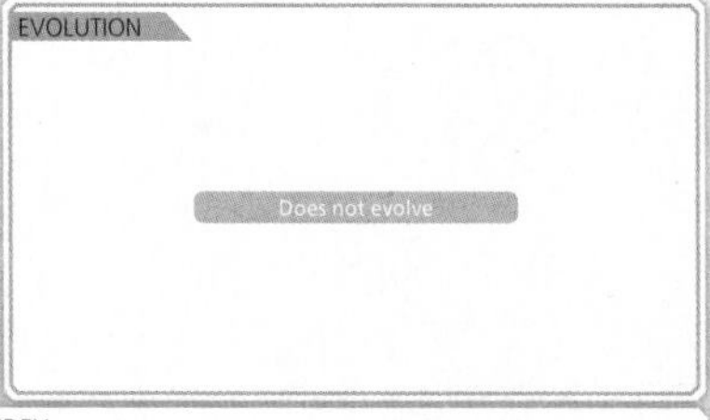

Does not evolve

MAIN WAY TO REGISTER IN THE NATIONAL POKÉDEX

Cosplay Pikachu can be obtained from a Breeder in any Contest Spectacular Hall after you take part in your first contest. Once you have Cosplay Pikachu in your party, talk to the Breeder again in the green room and have it change into a "cool" costume.

Damage taken in normal battles

Type		Type	
Normal	×1	Flying	×0.5
Fire	×1	Psychic	×1
Water	×1	Bug	×1
Grass	×1	Rock	×1
Electric	×0.5	Ghost	×1
Ice	×1	Dragon	×1
Fighting	×1	Dark	×1
Poison	×1	Steel	×0.5
Ground	×2	Fairy	×1

Damage taken in Inverse battles

Type		Type	
Normal	×1	Flying	×2
Fire	×1	Psychic	×1
Water	×1	Bug	×1
Grass	×1	Rock	×1
Electric	×2	Ghost	×1
Ice	×1	Dragon	×1
Fighting	×1	Dark	×1
Poison	×1	Steel	×2
Ground	×0.5	Fairy	×1

Can be used in
Inverse Battle
Battle Institute
Battle Maison
Random Matchup (Free Battle)
Random Matchup (Others)

LEVEL-UP MOVES

Lv.	Name	Type	Kind	Pow.	Acc.	PP	Range
1	Tail Whip	Normal	Status	—	100	30	Many Others
1	Thunder Shock	Electric	Special	40	100	30	Normal
5	Growl	Normal	Status	—	100	40	Many Others
7	Play Nice	Normal	Status	—	—	20	Normal
10	Quick Attack	Normal	Physical	40	100	30	Normal
13	Electro Ball	Electric	Special	—	100	10	Normal
18	Thunder Wave	Electric	Status	—	100	20	Normal
21	Feint	Normal	Physical	30	100	10	Normal
23	Double Team	Normal	Status	—	—	15	Self
26	Spark	Electric	Physical	65	100	20	Normal
29	Nuzzle	Electric	Physical	20	100	20	Normal
34	Discharge	Electric	Special	80	100	15	Adjacent
37	Slam	Normal	Physical	80	75	20	Normal
42	Thunderbolt	Electric	Special	90	100	15	Normal
45	Agility	Psychic	Status	—	—	30	Self
50	Wild Charge	Electric	Physical	90	100	15	Normal
53	Light Screen	Psychic	Status	—	—	30	Your Side
58	Thunder	Electric	Special	110	70	10	Normal
◆	Meteor Mash	Steel	Physical	90	90	10	Normal

TM & HM MOVES

No.	Name	Type	Kind	Pow.	Acc.	PP	Range
TM06	Toxic	Poison	Status	—	90	10	Normal
TM10	Hidden Power	Normal	Special	60	100	15	Normal
TM16	Light Screen	Psychic	Status	—	—	30	Your Side
TM17	Protect	Normal	Status	—	—	10	Self
TM18	Rain Dance	Water	Status	—	—	5	Both Sides
TM21	Frustration	Normal	Physical	—	100	20	Normal
TM24	Thunderbolt	Electric	Special	90	100	15	Normal
TM25	Thunder	Electric	Special	110	70	10	Normal
TM27	Return	Normal	Physical	—	100	20	Normal
TM28	Dig	Ground	Physical	80	100	10	Normal
TM31	Brick Break	Fighting	Physical	75	100	15	Normal
TM32	Double Team	Normal	Status	—	—	15	Self
TM42	Facade	Normal	Physical	70	100	20	Normal
TM44	Rest	Psychic	Status	—	—	10	Self
TM45	Attract	Normal	Status	—	100	15	Normal
TM48	Round	Normal	Special	60	100	15	Normal
TM49	Echoed Voice	Normal	Special	40	100	15	Normal
TM56	Fling	Dark	Physical	—	100	10	Normal
TM57	Charge Beam	Electric	Special	50	90	10	Normal
TM70	Flash	Normal	Status	—	100	20	Normal
TM72	Volt Switch	Electric	Special	70	100	20	Normal
TM73	Thunder Wave	Electric	Status	—	100	20	Normal
TM86	Grass Knot	Grass	Special	—	100	20	Normal
TM87	Swagger	Normal	Status	—	90	15	Normal
TM88	Sleep Talk	Normal	Status	—	—	10	Self
TM90	Substitute	Normal	Status	—	—	10	Self
TM93	Wild Charge	Electric	Physical	90	100	15	Normal
TM94	Secret Power	Normal	Physical	70	100	20	Normal
TM100	Confide	Normal	Status	—	—	20	Normal
HM04	Strength	Normal	Physical	80	100	15	Normal
HM06	Rock Smash	Fighting	Physical	40	100	15	Normal

MOVES LEARNED IN EXCHANGE FOR BP

Name	Type	Kind	Pow.	Acc.	PP	Range
Covet	Normal	Physical	60	100	25	Normal
Signal Beam	Bug	Special	75	100	15	Normal
Thunder Punch	Electric	Physical	75	100	15	Normal
Magnet Rise	Electric	Status	—	—	10	Self
Electroweb	Electric	Special	55	95	15	Many Others
Iron Tail	Steel	Physical	100	75	15	Normal
Snore	Normal	Special	50	100	15	Normal
Knock Off	Dark	Physical	65	100	20	Normal
Focus Punch	Fighting	Physical	150	100	20	Normal
Shock Wave	Electric	Special	60	—	20	Normal
Helping Hand	Normal	Status	—	—	20	1 Ally

MOVES TAUGHT BY PEOPLE

Name	Type	Kind	Pow.	Acc.	PP	Range

◆ When Cosplay Pikachu becomes Pikachu Rock Star, it learns the move Meteor Mash. It forgets this move if it removes or changes its costume.

National Pokédex **025** Hoenn Pokédex **163**

✓ Pikachu — Pikachu Belle

Mouse Pokémon

Electric

HEIGHT: 1'04" WEIGHT: 13.2 lbs.

♀ only. Cosplay Pikachu has a black heart mark at the end of its tail.

Ω —

α —

ABILITY
—

HIDDEN ABILITY
Lightning Rod

EGG GROUPS
No Eggs Discovered

STAT GROWTH RATES
HP ■■
Attack ■■■
Defense ■■
Sp. Atk ■■
Sp. Def ■■
Speed ■■■■■

ITEMS SOMETIMES HELD BY WILD POKÉMON
—

EVOLUTION
Does not evolve

MAIN WAY TO REGISTER IN THE NATIONAL POKÉDEX

Cosplay Pikachu can be obtained from a Breeder in any Contest Spectacular Hall after you take part in your first contest. Once you have Cosplay Pikachu in your party, talk to the Breeder again in the green room and have it change into a "beautiful" costume.

Damage taken in normal battles

Type		Type	
Normal	×1	Flying	×0.5
Fire	×1	Psychic	×1
Water	×1	Bug	×1
Grass	×1	Rock	×1
! Electric	×0.5	Ghost	×1
Ice	×1	Dragon	×1
Fighting	×1	Dark	×1
Poison	×1	Steel	×0.5
Ground	×2	Fairy	×1

Damage taken in Inverse battles

Type		Type	
Normal	×1	Flying	×2
Fire	×1	Psychic	×1
Water	×1	Bug	×1
Grass	×1	Rock	×1
! Electric	×2	Ghost	×1
Ice	×1	Dragon	×1
Fighting	×1	Dark	×1
Poison	×1	Steel	×2
Ground	×0.5	Fairy	×1

Can be used in
- Inverse Battle
- Battle Institute
- Battle Maison
- Random Matchup (Free Battle)
- Random Matchup (Others)

LEVEL-UP MOVES

Lv.	Name	Type	Kind	Pow.	Acc.	PP	Range
1	Tail Whip	Normal	Status	—	100	30	Many Others
1	Thunder Shock	Electric	Special	40	100	30	Normal
5	Growl	Normal	Status	—	100	40	Many Others
7	Play Nice	Normal	Status	—	—	20	Normal
10	Quick Attack	Normal	Physical	40	100	30	Normal
13	Electro Ball	Electric	Special	—	100	10	Normal
18	Thunder Wave	Electric	Status	—	100	20	Normal
21	Feint	Normal	Physical	30	100	10	Normal
23	Double Team	Normal	Status	—	—	15	Self
26	Spark	Electric	Physical	65	100	20	Normal
29	Nuzzle	Electric	Physical	20	100	20	Normal
34	Discharge	Electric	Special	80	100	15	Adjacent
37	Slam	Normal	Physical	80	75	20	Normal
42	Thunderbolt	Electric	Special	90	100	15	Normal
45	Agility	Psychic	Status	—	—	30	Self
50	Wild Charge	Electric	Physical	90	100	15	Normal
53	Light Screen	Psychic	Status	—	—	30	Your Side
58	Thunder	Electric	Special	110	70	10	Normal
◆	Icicle Crash	Ice	Physical	85	90	10	Normal

TM & HM MOVES

No.	Name	Type	Kind	Pow.	Acc.	PP	Range
TM06	Toxic	Poison	Status	—	90	10	Normal
TM10	Hidden Power	Normal	Special	60	100	15	Normal
TM16	Light Screen	Psychic	Status	—	—	30	Your Side
TM17	Protect	Normal	Status	—	—	10	Self
TM18	Rain Dance	Water	Status	—	—	5	Both Sides
TM21	Frustration	Normal	Physical	—	100	20	Normal
TM24	Thunderbolt	Electric	Special	90	100	15	Normal
TM25	Thunder	Electric	Special	110	70	10	Normal
TM27	Return	Normal	Physical	—	100	20	Normal
TM28	Dig	Ground	Physical	80	100	10	Normal
TM31	Brick Break	Fighting	Physical	75	100	15	Normal
TM32	Double Team	Normal	Status	—	—	15	Self
TM42	Facade	Normal	Physical	70	100	20	Normal
TM44	Rest	Psychic	Status	—	—	10	Self
TM45	Attract	Normal	Status	—	100	15	Normal
TM48	Round	Normal	Special	60	100	15	Normal
TM49	Echoed Voice	Normal	Special	40	100	15	Normal
TM56	Fling	Dark	Physical	—	100	10	Normal
TM57	Charge Beam	Electric	Special	50	90	10	Normal
TM70	Flash	Normal	Status	—	100	20	Normal
TM72	Volt Switch	Electric	Special	70	100	20	Normal
TM73	Thunder Wave	Electric	Status	—	100	20	Normal
TM86	Grass Knot	Grass	Special	—	100	20	Normal
TM87	Swagger	Normal	Status	—	90	15	Normal
TM88	Sleep Talk	Normal	Status	—	—	10	Self
TM90	Substitute	Normal	Status	—	—	10	Self
TM93	Wild Charge	Electric	Physical	90	100	15	Normal
TM94	Secret Power	Normal	Physical	70	100	20	Normal
TM100	Confide	Normal	Status	—	—	20	Normal
HM04	Strength	Normal	Physical	80	100	15	Normal
HM06	Rock Smash	Fighting	Physical	40	100	15	Normal

MOVES LEARNED IN EXCHANGE FOR BP

Name	Type	Kind	Pow.	Acc.	PP	Range
Covet	Normal	Physical	60	100	25	Normal
Signal Beam	Bug	Special	75	100	15	Normal
Thunder Punch	Electric	Physical	75	100	15	Normal
Magnet Rise	Electric	Status	—	—	10	Self
Electroweb	Electric	Special	55	95	15	Many Others
Iron Tail	Steel	Physical	100	75	15	Normal
Snore	Normal	Special	50	100	15	Normal
Knock Off	Dark	Physical	65	100	20	Normal
Focus Punch	Fighting	Physical	150	100	20	Normal
Shock Wave	Electric	Special	60	—	20	Normal
Helping Hand	Normal	Status	—	—	20	1 Ally

MOVES TAUGHT BY PEOPLE

Name	Type	Kind	Pow.	Acc.	PP	Range

◆ When Cosplay Pikachu becomes Pikachu Belle, it learns the move Icicle Crash. It forgets this move if it removes or changes its costume.

National Pokédex **025** Hoenn Pokédex **163**

✓ Pikachu — Pikachu Pop Star

Mouse Pokémon

Electric

HEIGHT: 1'04" WEIGHT: 13.2 lbs.

♀ only. Cosplay Pikachu has a black heart mark at the end of its tail.

Ω —

α —

ABILITY
—

HIDDEN ABILITY
Lightning Rod

EGG GROUPS
No Eggs Discovered

STAT GROWTH RATES
HP ■■
Attack ■■■
Defense ■■
Sp. Atk ■■
Sp. Def ■■
Speed ■■■■■

ITEMS SOMETIMES HELD BY WILD POKÉMON
—

EVOLUTION
Does not evolve

MAIN WAY TO REGISTER IN THE NATIONAL POKÉDEX

Cosplay Pikachu can be obtained from a Breeder in any Contest Spectacular Hall after you take part in your first contest. Once you have Cosplay Pikachu in your party, talk to the Breeder again in the green room and have it change into a "cute" costume.

Damage taken in normal battles

Type		Type	
Normal	×1	Flying	×0.5
Fire	×1	Psychic	×1
Water	×1	Bug	×1
Grass	×1	Rock	×1
! Electric	×0.5	Ghost	×1
Ice	×1	Dragon	×1
Fighting	×1	Dark	×1
Poison	×1	Steel	×0.5
Ground	×2	Fairy	×1

Damage taken in Inverse battles

Type		Type	
Normal	×1	Flying	×2
Fire	×1	Psychic	×1
Water	×1	Bug	×1
Grass	×1	Rock	×1
! Electric	×2	Ghost	×1
Ice	×1	Dragon	×1
Fighting	×1	Dark	×1
Poison	×1	Steel	×2
Ground	×0.5	Fairy	×1

Can be used in
- Inverse Battle
- Battle Institute
- Battle Maison
- Random Matchup (Free Battle)
- Random Matchup (Others)

LEVEL-UP MOVES

Lv.	Name	Type	Kind	Pow.	Acc.	PP	Range
1	Tail Whip	Normal	Status	—	100	30	Many Others
1	Thunder Shock	Electric	Special	40	100	30	Normal
5	Growl	Normal	Status	—	100	40	Many Others
7	Play Nice	Normal	Status	—	—	20	Normal
10	Quick Attack	Normal	Physical	40	100	30	Normal
13	Electro Ball	Electric	Special	—	100	10	Normal
18	Thunder Wave	Electric	Status	—	100	20	Normal
21	Feint	Normal	Physical	30	100	10	Normal
23	Double Team	Normal	Status	—	—	15	Self
26	Spark	Electric	Physical	65	100	20	Normal
29	Nuzzle	Electric	Physical	20	100	20	Normal
34	Discharge	Electric	Special	80	100	15	Adjacent
37	Slam	Normal	Physical	80	75	20	Normal
42	Thunderbolt	Electric	Special	90	100	15	Normal
45	Agility	Psychic	Status	—	—	30	Self
50	Wild Charge	Electric	Physical	90	100	15	Normal
53	Light Screen	Psychic	Status	—	—	30	Your Side
58	Thunder	Electric	Special	110	70	10	Normal
◆	Draining Kiss	Fairy	Special	50	100	10	Normal

TM & HM MOVES

No.	Name	Type	Kind	Pow.	Acc.	PP	Range
TM06	Toxic	Poison	Status	—	90	10	Normal
TM10	Hidden Power	Normal	Special	60	100	15	Normal
TM16	Light Screen	Psychic	Status	—	—	30	Your Side
TM17	Protect	Normal	Status	—	—	10	Self
TM18	Rain Dance	Water	Status	—	—	5	Both Sides
TM21	Frustration	Normal	Physical	—	100	20	Normal
TM24	Thunderbolt	Electric	Special	90	100	15	Normal
TM25	Thunder	Electric	Special	110	70	10	Normal
TM27	Return	Normal	Physical	—	100	20	Normal
TM28	Dig	Ground	Physical	80	100	10	Normal
TM31	Brick Break	Fighting	Physical	75	100	15	Normal
TM32	Double Team	Normal	Status	—	—	15	Self
TM42	Facade	Normal	Physical	70	100	20	Normal
TM44	Rest	Psychic	Status	—	—	10	Self
TM45	Attract	Normal	Status	—	100	15	Normal
TM48	Round	Normal	Special	60	100	15	Normal
TM49	Echoed Voice	Normal	Special	40	100	15	Normal
TM56	Fling	Dark	Physical	—	100	10	Normal
TM57	Charge Beam	Electric	Special	50	90	10	Normal
TM70	Flash	Normal	Status	—	100	20	Normal
TM72	Volt Switch	Electric	Special	70	100	20	Normal
TM73	Thunder Wave	Electric	Status	—	100	20	Normal
TM86	Grass Knot	Grass	Special	—	100	20	Normal
TM87	Swagger	Normal	Status	—	90	15	Normal
TM88	Sleep Talk	Normal	Status	—	—	10	Self
TM90	Substitute	Normal	Status	—	—	10	Self
TM93	Wild Charge	Electric	Physical	90	100	15	Normal
TM94	Secret Power	Normal	Physical	70	100	20	Normal
TM100	Confide	Normal	Status	—	—	20	Normal
HM04	Strength	Normal	Physical	80	100	15	Normal
HM06	Rock Smash	Fighting	Physical	40	100	15	Normal

MOVES LEARNED IN EXCHANGE FOR BP

Name	Type	Kind	Pow.	Acc.	PP	Range
Covet	Normal	Physical	60	100	25	Normal
Signal Beam	Bug	Special	75	100	15	Normal
Thunder Punch	Electric	Physical	75	100	15	Normal
Magnet Rise	Electric	Status	—	—	10	Self
Electroweb	Electric	Special	55	95	15	Many Others
Iron Tail	Steel	Physical	100	75	15	Normal
Snore	Normal	Special	50	100	15	Normal
Knock Off	Dark	Physical	65	100	20	Normal
Focus Punch	Fighting	Physical	150	100	20	Normal
Shock Wave	Electric	Special	60	—	20	Normal
Helping Hand	Normal	Status	—	—	20	1 Ally

MOVES TAUGHT BY PEOPLE

Name	Type	Kind	Pow.	Acc.	PP	Range

◆ When Cosplay Pikachu becomes Pikachu Pop Star, it learns the move Draining Kiss. It forgets this move if it removes or changes its costume.

National Pokédex **025** Hoenn Pokédex **163**

Pikachu Pikachu, Ph.D.

Mouse Pokémon

Electric

HEIGHT: 1'04" WEIGHT: 13.2 lbs.

♀ only. Cosplay Pikachu has a black heart mark at the end of its tail.

Ω —

α —

ABILITY
—

HIDDEN ABILITY
Lightning Rod

EGG GROUPS
No Eggs Discovered

STAT GROWTH RATES
HP ■■
Attack ■■■
Defense ■■
Sp. Atk ■■
Sp. Def ■■
Speed ■■■■■

ITEMS SOMETIMES HELD BY WILD POKÉMON
—

EVOLUTION
Does not evolve

MAIN WAY TO REGISTER IN THE NATIONAL POKÉDEX

Cosplay Pikachu can be obtained from a Breeder in any Contest Spectacular Hall after you take part in your first contest. Once you have Cosplay Pikachu in your party, talk to the Breeder again in the green room and have it change into a "clever" costume.

Damage taken in normal battles

Type		Type	
Normal	×1	Flying	×0.5
Fire	×1	Psychic	×1
Water	×1	Bug	×1
Grass	×1	Rock	×1
Electric	×0.5	Ghost	×1
Ice	×1	Dragon	×1
Fighting	×1	Dark	×1
Poison	×1	Steel	×0.5
Ground	×2	Fairy	×1

Damage taken in Inverse battles

Type		Type	
Normal	×1	Flying	×2
Fire	×1	Psychic	×1
Water	×1	Bug	×1
Grass	×1	Rock	×1
Electric	×2	Ghost	×1
Ice	×1	Dragon	×1
Fighting	×1	Dark	×1
Poison	×1	Steel	×2
Ground	×0.5	Fairy	×1

Can be used in
- Inverse Battle
- Battle Institute
- Battle Maison
- Random Matchup (Free Battle)
- Random Matchup (Others)

LEVEL-UP MOVES

Lv.	Name	Type	Kind	Pow.	Acc.	PP	Range
1	Tail Whip	Normal	Status	—	100	30	Many Others
1	Thunder Shock	Electric	Special	40	100	30	Normal
5	Growl	Normal	Status	—	100	40	Many Others
7	Play Nice	Normal	Status	—	—	20	Normal
10	Quick Attack	Normal	Physical	40	100	30	Normal
13	Electro Ball	Electric	Special	—	100	10	Normal
18	Thunder Wave	Electric	Status	—	100	20	Normal
21	Feint	Normal	Physical	30	100	10	Normal
23	Double Team	Normal	Status	—	—	15	Self
26	Spark	Electric	Physical	65	100	20	Normal
29	Nuzzle	Electric	Physical	20	100	20	Normal
34	Discharge	Electric	Special	80	100	15	Adjacent
37	Slam	Normal	Physical	80	75	20	Normal
42	Thunderbolt	Electric	Special	90	100	15	Normal
45	Agility	Psychic	Status	—	—	30	Self
50	Wild Charge	Electric	Physical	90	100	15	Normal
53	Light Screen	Psychic	Status	—	—	30	Your Side
58	Thunder	Electric	Special	110	70	10	Normal
◆	Electric Terrain	Electric	Status	-	-	10	Both Sides

TM & HM MOVES

No.	Name	Type	Kind	Pow.	Acc.	PP	Range
TM06	Toxic	Poison	Status	—	90	10	Normal
TM10	Hidden Power	Normal	Special	60	100	15	Normal
TM16	Light Screen	Psychic	Status	—	—	30	Your Side
TM17	Protect	Normal	Status	—	—	10	Self
TM18	Rain Dance	Water	Status	—	—	5	Both Sides
TM21	Frustration	Normal	Physical	—	100	20	Normal
TM24	Thunderbolt	Electric	Special	90	100	15	Normal
TM25	Thunder	Electric	Special	110	70	10	Normal
TM27	Return	Normal	Physical	—	100	20	Normal
TM28	Dig	Ground	Physical	80	100	10	Normal
TM31	Brick Break	Fighting	Physical	75	100	15	Normal
TM32	Double Team	Normal	Status	—	—	15	Self
TM42	Facade	Normal	Physical	70	100	20	Normal
TM44	Rest	Psychic	Status	—	—	10	Self
TM45	Attract	Normal	Status	—	100	15	Normal
TM48	Round	Normal	Special	60	100	15	Normal
TM49	Echoed Voice	Normal	Special	40	100	15	Normal
TM56	Fling	Dark	Physical	—	100	10	Normal
TM57	Charge Beam	Electric	Special	50	90	10	Normal
TM70	Flash	Normal	Status	—	100	20	Normal
TM72	Volt Switch	Electric	Special	70	100	20	Normal
TM73	Thunder Wave	Electric	Status	—	100	20	Normal
TM86	Grass Knot	Grass	Special	—	100	20	Normal
TM87	Swagger	Normal	Status	—	90	15	Normal
TM88	Sleep Talk	Normal	Status	—	—	10	Self
TM90	Substitute	Normal	Status	—	—	10	Self
TM93	Wild Charge	Electric	Physical	90	100	15	Normal
TM94	Secret Power	Normal	Physical	70	100	20	Normal
TM100	Confide	Normal	Status	—	—	20	Normal
HM04	Strength	Normal	Physical	80	100	15	Normal
HM06	Rock Smash	Fighting	Physical	40	100	15	Normal

MOVES LEARNED IN EXCHANGE FOR BP

Name	Type	Kind	Pow.	Acc.	PP	Range
Covet	Normal	Physical	60	100	25	Normal
Signal Beam	Bug	Special	75	100	15	Normal
Thunder Punch	Electric	Physical	75	100	15	Normal
Magnet Rise	Electric	Status	—	—	10	Self
Electroweb	Electric	Special	55	95	15	Many Others
Iron Tail	Steel	Physical	100	75	15	Normal
Snore	Normal	Special	50	100	15	Normal
Knock Off	Dark	Physical	65	100	20	Normal
Focus Punch	Fighting	Physical	150	100	20	Normal
Shock Wave	Electric	Special	60	—	20	Normal
Helping Hand	Normal	Status	—	—	20	1 Ally

MOVES TAUGHT BY PEOPLE

Name	Type	Kind	Pow.	Acc.	PP	Range

◆ When Cosplay Pikachu becomes Pikachu, Ph.D., it learns the move Electric Terrain. It forgets this move if it removes or changes its costume.

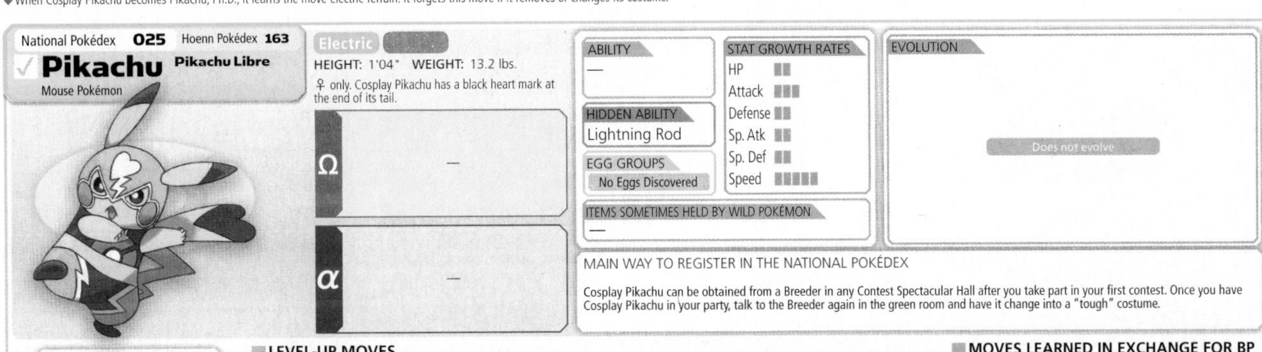

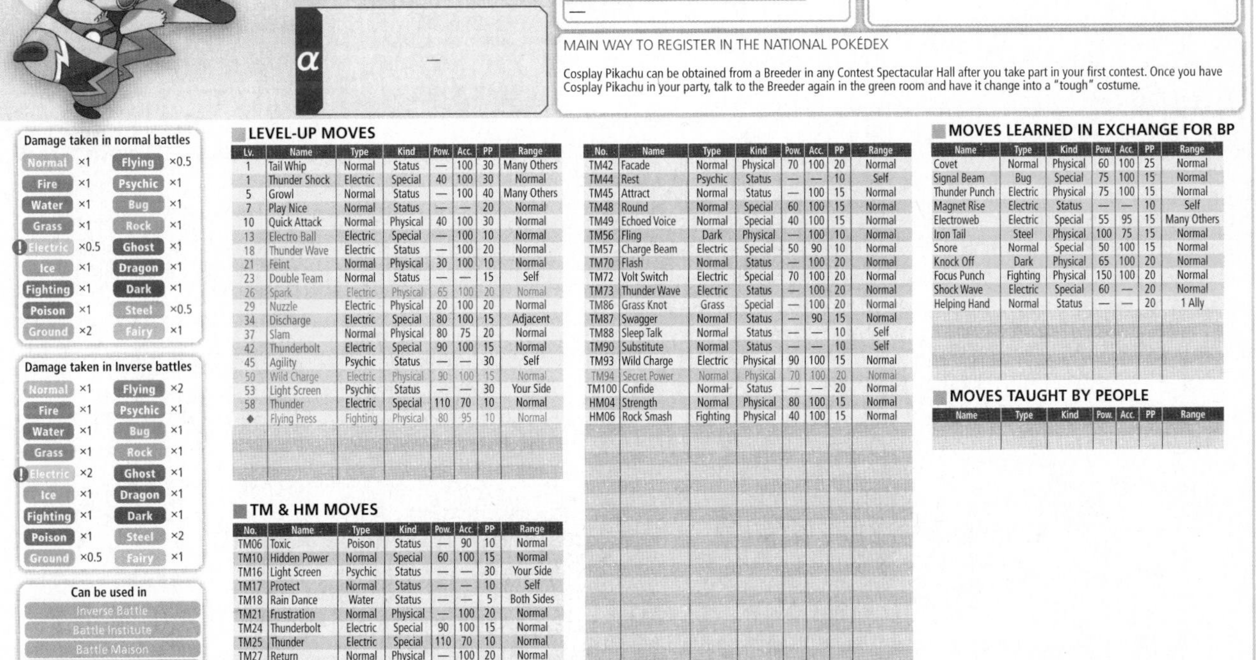

National Pokédex **025** Hoenn Pokédex **163**

Pikachu Pikachu Libre

Mouse Pokémon

Electric

HEIGHT: 1'04" WEIGHT: 13.2 lbs.

♀ only. Cosplay Pikachu has a black heart mark at the end of its tail.

Ω —

α —

ABILITY
—

HIDDEN ABILITY
Lightning Rod

EGG GROUPS
No Eggs Discovered

STAT GROWTH RATES
HP ■■
Attack ■■■
Defense ■■
Sp. Atk ■■
Sp. Def ■■
Speed ■■■■■

ITEMS SOMETIMES HELD BY WILD POKÉMON
—

EVOLUTION
Does not evolve

MAIN WAY TO REGISTER IN THE NATIONAL POKÉDEX

Cosplay Pikachu can be obtained from a Breeder in any Contest Spectacular Hall after you take part in your first contest. Once you have Cosplay Pikachu in your party, talk to the Breeder again in the green room and have it change into a "tough" costume.

Damage taken in normal battles

Type		Type	
Normal	×1	Flying	×0.5
Fire	×1	Psychic	×1
Water	×1	Bug	×1
Grass	×1	Rock	×1
Electric	×0.5	Ghost	×1
Ice	×1	Dragon	×1
Fighting	×1	Dark	×1
Poison	×1	Steel	×0.5
Ground	×2	Fairy	×1

Damage taken in Inverse battles

Type		Type	
Normal	×1	Flying	×2
Fire	×1	Psychic	×1
Water	×1	Bug	×1
Grass	×1	Rock	×1
Electric	×2	Ghost	×1
Ice	×1	Dragon	×1
Fighting	×1	Dark	×1
Poison	×1	Steel	×2
Ground	×0.5	Fairy	×1

Can be used in
- Inverse Battle
- Battle Institute
- Battle Maison
- Random Matchup (Free Battle)
- Random Matchup (Others)

LEVEL-UP MOVES

Lv.	Name	Type	Kind	Pow.	Acc.	PP	Range
1	Tail Whip	Normal	Status	—	100	30	Many Others
1	Thunder Shock	Electric	Special	40	100	30	Normal
5	Growl	Normal	Status	—	100	40	Many Others
7	Play Nice	Normal	Status	—	—	20	Normal
10	Quick Attack	Normal	Physical	40	100	30	Normal
13	Electro Ball	Electric	Special	—	100	10	Normal
18	Thunder Wave	Electric	Status	—	100	20	Normal
21	Feint	Normal	Physical	30	100	10	Normal
23	Double Team	Normal	Status	—	—	15	Self
26	Spark	Electric	Physical	65	100	20	Normal
29	Nuzzle	Electric	Physical	20	100	20	Normal
34	Discharge	Electric	Special	80	100	15	Adjacent
37	Slam	Normal	Physical	80	75	20	Normal
42	Thunderbolt	Electric	Special	90	100	15	Normal
45	Agility	Psychic	Status	—	—	30	Self
50	Wild Charge	Electric	Physical	90	100	15	Normal
53	Light Screen	Psychic	Status	—	—	30	Your Side
58	Thunder	Electric	Special	110	70	10	Normal
◆	Flying Press	Fighting	Physical	80	95	10	Normal

TM & HM MOVES

No.	Name	Type	Kind	Pow.	Acc.	PP	Range
TM06	Toxic	Poison	Status	—	90	10	Normal
TM10	Hidden Power	Normal	Special	60	100	15	Normal
TM16	Light Screen	Psychic	Status	—	—	30	Your Side
TM17	Protect	Normal	Status	—	—	10	Self
TM18	Rain Dance	Water	Status	—	—	5	Both Sides
TM21	Frustration	Normal	Physical	—	100	20	Normal
TM24	Thunderbolt	Electric	Special	90	100	15	Normal
TM25	Thunder	Electric	Special	110	70	10	Normal
TM27	Return	Normal	Physical	—	100	20	Normal
TM28	Dig	Ground	Physical	80	100	10	Normal
TM31	Brick Break	Fighting	Physical	75	100	15	Normal
TM32	Double Team	Normal	Status	—	—	15	Self
TM42	Facade	Normal	Physical	70	100	20	Normal
TM44	Rest	Psychic	Status	—	—	10	Self
TM45	Attract	Normal	Status	—	100	15	Normal
TM48	Round	Normal	Special	60	100	15	Normal
TM49	Echoed Voice	Normal	Special	40	100	15	Normal
TM56	Fling	Dark	Physical	—	100	10	Normal
TM57	Charge Beam	Electric	Special	50	90	10	Normal
TM70	Flash	Normal	Status	—	100	20	Normal
TM72	Volt Switch	Electric	Special	70	100	20	Normal
TM73	Thunder Wave	Electric	Status	—	100	20	Normal
TM86	Grass Knot	Grass	Special	—	100	20	Normal
TM87	Swagger	Normal	Status	—	90	15	Normal
TM88	Sleep Talk	Normal	Status	—	—	10	Self
TM90	Substitute	Normal	Status	—	—	10	Self
TM93	Wild Charge	Electric	Physical	90	100	15	Normal
TM94	Secret Power	Normal	Physical	70	100	20	Normal
TM100	Confide	Normal	Status	—	—	20	Normal
HM04	Strength	Normal	Physical	80	100	15	Normal
HM06	Rock Smash	Fighting	Physical	40	100	15	Normal

MOVES LEARNED IN EXCHANGE FOR BP

Name	Type	Kind	Pow.	Acc.	PP	Range
Covet	Normal	Physical	60	100	25	Normal
Signal Beam	Bug	Special	75	100	15	Normal
Thunder Punch	Electric	Physical	75	100	15	Normal
Magnet Rise	Electric	Status	—	—	10	Self
Electroweb	Electric	Special	55	95	15	Many Others
Iron Tail	Steel	Physical	100	75	15	Normal
Snore	Normal	Special	50	100	15	Normal
Knock Off	Dark	Physical	65	100	20	Normal
Focus Punch	Fighting	Physical	150	100	20	Normal
Shock Wave	Electric	Special	60	—	20	Normal
Helping Hand	Normal	Status	—	—	20	1 Ally

MOVES TAUGHT BY PEOPLE

Name	Type	Kind	Pow.	Acc.	PP	Range

◆ When Cosplay Pikachu becomes Pikachu Libre, it learns the move Flying Press. It forgets this move if it removes or changes its costume.

National Pokédex **026** Hoenn Pokédex **164**

Raichu

Mouse Pokémon

Electric

HEIGHT: 2'07" WEIGHT: 66.1 lbs.

The tip of the male's tail is longer than the female's.

Ω If the electrical sacs become excessively charged, Raichu plants its tail in the ground and discharges. Scorched patches of ground will be found near this Pokémon's nest.

α This Pokémon exudes a weak electrical charge from all over its body that makes it take on a slight glow in darkness. Raichu plants its tail in the ground to discharge electricity.

ABILITY
Static

HIDDEN ABILITY
Lightning Rod

EGG GROUPS
Field / Fairy

STAT GROWTH RATES
HP ▮▮▮
Attack ▮▮▮▮▮
Defense ▮▮▮
Sp. Atk ▮▮▮▮
Sp. Def ▮▮▮
Speed ▮▮▮▮▮▮

ITEMS SOMETIMES HELD BY WILD POKÉMON
—

EVOLUTION

MAIN WAY TO REGISTER IN THE NATIONAL POKÉDEX

Use a Thunder Stone on Pikachu.

Damage taken in normal battles

Type		Type	
Normal	×1	Flying	×0.5
Fire	×1	Psychic	×1
Water	×1	Bug	×1
Grass	×1	Rock	×1
Electric	×0.5	Ghost	×1
Ice	×1	Dragon	×1
Fighting	×1	Dark	×1
Poison	×1	Steel	×0.5
Ground	×2	Fairy	×1

Damage taken in Inverse battles

Type		Type	
Normal	×1	Flying	×2
Fire	×1	Psychic	×1
Water	×1	Bug	×1
Grass	×1	Rock	×1
Electric	×2	Ghost	×1
Ice	×1	Dragon	×1
Fighting	×1	Dark	×1
Poison	×1	Steel	×2
Ground	×0.5	Fairy	×1

Can be used in
Inverse Battle
Battle Institute
Battle Maison
Random Matchup (Free Battle)
Random Matchup (Others)

LEVEL-UP MOVES

Lv.	Name	Type	Kind	Pow.	Acc.	PP	Range
1	Thunder Shock	Electric	Special	40	100	30	Normal
1	Tail Whip	Normal	Status	—	100	30	Many Others
1	Quick Attack	Normal	Physical	40	100	30	Normal
1	Thunderbolt	Electric	Special	90	100	15	Normal

TM & HM MOVES

No.	Name	Type	Kind	Pow.	Acc.	PP	Range
TM06	Toxic	Poison	Status	—	90	10	Normal
TM10	Hidden Power	Normal	Special	60	100	15	Normal
TM15	Hyper Beam	Normal	Special	150	90	5	Normal
TM16	Light Screen	Psychic	Status	—	—	30	Your Side
TM17	Protect	Normal	Status	—	—	10	Self
TM18	Rain Dance	Water	Status	—	—	5	Both Sides
TM21	Frustration	Normal	Physical	—	100	20	Normal
TM24	Thunderbolt	Electric	Special	90	100	15	Normal
TM25	Thunder	Electric	Special	110	70	10	Normal
TM27	Return	Normal	Physical	—	100	20	Normal
TM28	Dig	Ground	Physical	80	100	10	Normal
TM31	Brick Break	Fighting	Physical	75	100	15	Normal
TM32	Double Team	Normal	Status	—	—	15	Self
TM42	Facade	Normal	Physical	70	100	20	Normal
TM44	Rest	Psychic	Status	—	—	10	Self
TM45	Attract	Normal	Status	—	100	15	Normal
TM46	Thief	Dark	Physical	60	100	25	Normal
TM48	Round	Normal	Special	60	100	15	Normal
TM49	Echoed Voice	Normal	Special	40	100	15	Normal
TM52	Focus Blast	Fighting	Special	120	70	5	Normal
TM56	Fling	Dark	Physical	—	100	10	Normal
TM57	Charge Beam	Electric	Special	50	90	10	Normal
TM68	Giga Impact	Normal	Physical	150	90	5	Normal
TM70	Flash	Normal	Status	—	100	20	Normal
TM72	Volt Switch	Electric	Special	70	100	20	Normal
TM73	Thunder Wave	Electric	Status	—	100	20	Normal
TM86	Grass Knot	Grass	Special	—	100	20	Normal
TM87	Swagger	Normal	Status	—	90	15	Normal
TM88	Sleep Talk	Normal	Status	—	—	10	Self
TM90	Substitute	Normal	Status	—	—	10	Self
TM93	Wild Charge	Electric	Physical	90	100	15	Normal
TM94	Secret Power	Normal	Physical	70	100	20	Normal
TM100	Confide	Normal	Status	—	—	20	Normal
HM04	Strength	Normal	Physical	80	100	15	Normal
HM06	Rock Smash	Fighting	Physical	40	100	15	Normal

MOVES LEARNED IN EXCHANGE FOR BP

Name	Type	Kind	Pow.	Acc.	PP	Range
Covet	Normal	Physical	60	100	25	Normal
Signal Beam	Bug	Special	75	100	15	Normal
Thunder Punch	Electric	Physical	75	100	15	Normal
Magnet Rise	Electric	Status	—	—	10	Self
Electroweb	Electric	Special	55	95	15	Many Others
Iron Tail	Steel	Physical	100	75	15	Normal
Snore	Normal	Special	50	100	15	Normal
Knock Off	Dark	Physical	65	100	20	Normal
Focus Punch	Fighting	Physical	150	100	20	Normal
Shock Wave	Electric	Special	60	—	20	Normal
Helping Hand	Normal	Status	—	—	20	1 Ally

MOVES TAUGHT BY PEOPLE

Name	Type	Kind	Pow.	Acc.	PP	Range

National Pokédex **027** Hoenn Pokédex **117**

Sandshrew

Mouse Pokémon

Ground

HEIGHT: 2'00" WEIGHT: 26.5 lbs.

Same form for ♂ / ♀

Ω Sandshrew's body is configured to absorb water without waste, enabling it to survive in an arid desert. This Pokémon curls up to protect itself from its enemies.

α Sandshrew has a very dry hide that is extremely tough. The Pokémon can roll into a ball that repels any attack. At night, it burrows into the desert sand to sleep.

ABILITY
Sand Veil

HIDDEN ABILITY
Sand Rush

EGG GROUPS
Field

STAT GROWTH RATES
HP ▮▮
Attack ▮▮▮▮
Defense ▮▮▮▮
Sp. Atk ▮
Sp. Def ▮
Speed ▮▮

ITEMS SOMETIMES HELD BY WILD POKÉMON
Grip Claw

EVOLUTION

Sandshrew → Lv. 22 → Sandslash

MAIN WAY TO REGISTER IN THE NATIONAL POKÉDEX

Catch on Route 113.

Damage taken in normal battles

Type		Type	
Normal	×1	Flying	×1
Fire	×1	Psychic	×1
Water	×2	Bug	×1
Grass	×2	Rock	×0.5
Electric	×0	Ghost	×1
Ice	×2	Dragon	×1
Fighting	×1	Dark	×1
Poison	×0.5	Steel	×1
Ground	×1	Fairy	×1

Damage taken in Inverse battles

Type		Type	
Normal	×1	Flying	×1
Fire	×1	Psychic	×1
Water	×0.5	Bug	×1
Grass	×0.5	Rock	×2
Electric	×2	Ghost	×1
Ice	×0.5	Dragon	×1
Fighting	×1	Dark	×1
Poison	×2	Steel	×1
Ground	×1	Fairy	×1

Can be used in
Inverse Battle
Battle Institute
Battle Maison
Random Matchup (Free Battle)
Random Matchup (Others)

LEVEL-UP MOVES

Lv.	Name	Type	Kind	Pow.	Acc.	PP	Range
1	Scratch	Normal	Physical	40	100	35	Normal
1	Defense Curl	Normal	Status	—	—	40	Self
3	Sand Attack	Ground	Status	—	100	15	Normal
5	Poison Sting	Poison	Physical	15	100	35	Normal
7	Rollout	Rock	Physical	30	90	20	Normal
9	Rapid Spin	Normal	Physical	20	100	40	Normal
11	Fury Cutter	Bug	Physical	40	95	20	Normal
14	Magnitude	Ground	Physical	—	100	30	Adjacent
17	Swift	Normal	Special	60	—	20	Many Others
20	Fury Swipes	Normal	Physical	18	80	15	Normal
23	Sand Tomb	Ground	Physical	35	85	15	Normal
26	Slash	Normal	Physical	70	100	20	Normal
30	Dig	Ground	Physical	80	100	10	Normal
34	Gyro Ball	Steel	Physical	—	100	5	Normal
38	Swords Dance	Normal	Status	—	—	20	Self
42	Sandstorm	Rock	Status	—	—	10	Both Sides
46	Earthquake	Ground	Physical	100	100	10	Adjacent

TM & HM MOVES

No.	Name	Type	Kind	Pow.	Acc.	PP	Range
TM01	Hone Claws	Dark	Status	—	—	15	Self
TM06	Toxic	Poison	Status	—	90	10	Normal
TM10	Hidden Power	Normal	Special	60	100	15	Normal
TM11	Sunny Day	Fire	Status	—	—	5	Both Sides
TM17	Protect	Normal	Status	—	—	10	Self
TM20	Safeguard	Normal	Status	—	—	25	Your Side
TM21	Frustration	Normal	Physical	—	100	20	Normal
TM26	Earthquake	Ground	Physical	100	100	10	Adjacent
TM27	Return	Normal	Physical	—	100	20	Normal
TM28	Dig	Ground	Physical	80	100	10	Normal
TM31	Brick Break	Fighting	Physical	75	100	15	Normal
TM32	Double Team	Normal	Status	—	—	15	Self
TM37	Sandstorm	Rock	Status	—	—	10	Both Sides
TM39	Rock Tomb	Rock	Physical	60	95	15	Normal
TM40	Aerial Ace	Flying	Physical	60	—	20	Normal
TM42	Facade	Normal	Physical	70	100	20	Normal
TM44	Rest	Psychic	Status	—	—	10	Self
TM45	Attract	Normal	Status	—	100	15	Normal
TM46	Thief	Dark	Physical	60	100	25	Normal
TM48	Round	Normal	Special	60	100	15	Normal
TM56	Fling	Dark	Physical	—	100	10	Normal
TM65	Shadow Claw	Ghost	Physical	70	100	15	Normal
TM74	Gyro Ball	Steel	Physical	—	100	5	Normal
TM75	Swords Dance	Normal	Status	—	—	20	Self
TM78	Bulldoze	Ground	Physical	60	100	20	Adjacent
TM80	Rock Slide	Rock	Physical	75	90	10	Many Others
TM81	X-Scissor	Bug	Physical	80	100	15	Normal
TM84	Poison Jab	Poison	Physical	80	100	20	Normal
TM87	Swagger	Normal	Status	—	90	15	Normal
TM88	Sleep Talk	Normal	Status	—	—	10	Self
TM90	Substitute	Normal	Status	—	—	10	Self
TM94	Secret Power	Normal	Physical	70	100	20	Normal
TM100	Confide	Normal	Status	—	—	20	Normal
HM01	Cut	Normal	Physical	50	95	30	Normal
HM04	Strength	Normal	Physical	80	100	15	Normal
HM06	Rock Smash	Fighting	Physical	40	100	15	Normal

MOVES LEARNED IN EXCHANGE FOR BP

Name	Type	Kind	Pow.	Acc.	PP	Range
Covet	Normal	Physical	60	100	25	Normal
Super Fang	Normal	Physical	—	90	10	Normal
Earth Power	Ground	Special	90	100	10	Normal
Iron Tail	Steel	Physical	100	75	15	Normal
Snore	Normal	Special	50	100	15	Normal
Knock Off	Dark	Physical	65	100	20	Normal
Focus Punch	Fighting	Physical	150	100	20	Normal
Stealth Rock	Rock	Status	—	—	20	Other Side

MOVES TAUGHT BY PEOPLE

Name	Type	Kind	Pow.	Acc.	PP	Range

EGG MOVES

Name	Type	Kind	Pow.	Acc.	PP	Range
Flail	Normal	Physical	—	100	15	Normal
Counter	Fighting	Physical	—	100	20	Varies
Rapid Spin	Normal	Physical	20	100	40	Normal
Metal Claw	Steel	Physical	50	95	35	Normal
Crush Claw	Normal	Physical	75	95	10	Normal
Night Slash	Dark	Physical	70	100	15	Normal
Mud Shot	Ground	Special	55	95	15	Normal
Endure	Normal	Status	—	—	10	Self
Chip Away	Normal	Physical	70	100	20	Normal
Rock Climb	Normal	Physical	90	85	20	Normal
Rototiller	Ground	Status	—	—	10	Adjacent

National Pokédex **028** Hoenn Pokédex **118**

Sandslash

Mouse Pokémon

Ground

HEIGHT: 3'03" WEIGHT: 65 lbs.

Same form for ♂ / ♀

Ω Sandslash's body is covered by tough spikes, which are hardened sections of its hide. Once a year, the old spikes fall out, to be replaced with new spikes that grow out from beneath the old ones.

α Sandslash can roll up its body as if it were a ball covered with large spikes. In battle, this Pokémon will try to make the foe flinch by jabbing it with its spines. It then leaps at the stunned foe to tear wildly with its sharp claws.

ABILITY
Sand Veil

HIDDEN ABILITY
Sand Rush

EGG GROUPS
Field

STAT GROWTH RATES

HP	■■■
Attack	■■■■■
Defense	■■■■■
Sp. Atk	■■
Sp. Def	■■
Speed	■■■■

ITEMS SOMETIMES HELD BY WILD POKÉMON
—

EVOLUTION

Sandshrew → Lv. 22 → Sandslash

MAIN WAY TO REGISTER IN THE NATIONAL POKÉDEX

Level up Sandshrew to Lv. 22.

Damage taken in normal battles

Type		Type	
Normal	×1	Flying	×1
Fire	×1	Psychic	×1
Water	×2	Bug	×1
Grass	×2	Rock	×0.5
Electric	×0	Ghost	×1
Ice	×2	Dragon	×1
Fighting	×1	Dark	×1
Poison	×0.5	Steel	×1
Ground	×1	Fairy	×1

Damage taken in Inverse battles

Type		Type	
Normal	×1	Flying	×1
Fire	×1	Psychic	×1
Water	×0.5	Bug	×1
Grass	×0.5	Rock	×2
Electric	×2	Ghost	×1
Ice	×0.5	Dragon	×1
Fighting	×1	Dark	×1
Poison	×2	Steel	×1
Ground	×1	Fairy	×1

Can be used in
Inverse Battle
Battle Institute
Battle Maison
Random Matchup (Free Battle)
Random Matchup (Others)

LEVEL-UP MOVES

Lv.	Name	Type	Kind	Pow.	Acc.	PP	Range
1	Scratch	Normal	Physical	40	100	35	Normal
1	Defense Curl	Normal	Status	—	—	40	Self
1	Sand Attack	Ground	Status	—	100	15	Normal
1	Poison Sting	Poison	Physical	15	100	35	Normal
3	Sand Attack	Ground	Status	—	100	15	Normal
5	Poison Sting	Poison	Physical	15	100	35	Normal
7	Rollout	Rock	Physical	30	90	20	Normal
9	Rapid Spin	Normal	Physical	20	100	40	Normal
11	Fury Cutter	Bug	Physical	40	95	20	Normal
14	Magnitude	Ground	Physical	—	100	30	Adjacent
17	Swift	Normal	Special	60	—	20	Many Others
20	Fury Swipes	Normal	Physical	18	80	15	Normal
22	Crush Claw	Normal	Physical	75	95	10	Normal
24	Sand Tomb	Ground	Physical	35	85	15	Normal
28	Slash	Normal	Physical	70	100	20	Normal
33	Dig	Ground	Physical	80	100	10	Normal
38	Gyro Ball	Steel	Physical	—	100	5	Normal
43	Swords Dance	Normal	Status	—	—	20	Self
48	Sandstorm	Rock	Status	—	—	10	Both Sides
53	Earthquake	Ground	Physical	100	100	10	Adjacent

TM & HM MOVES

No.	Name	Type	Kind	Pow.	Acc.	PP	Range
TM01	Hone Claws	Dark	Status	—	—	15	Self
TM06	Toxic	Poison	Status	—	90	10	Normal
TM10	Hidden Power	Normal	Special	60	100	15	Normal
TM11	Sunny Day	Fire	Status	—	—	5	Both Sides
TM15	Hyper Beam	Normal	Special	150	90	5	Normal
TM17	Protect	Normal	Status	—	—	10	Self
TM20	Safeguard	Normal	Status	—	—	25	Your Side
TM21	Frustration	Normal	Physical	—	100	20	Normal
TM26	Earthquake	Ground	Physical	100	100	10	Adjacent
TM27	Return	Normal	Physical	—	100	20	Normal
TM28	Dig	Ground	Physical	80	100	10	Normal
TM31	Brick Break	Fighting	Physical	75	100	15	Normal
TM32	Double Team	Normal	Status	—	—	15	Self
TM37	Sandstorm	Rock	Status	—	—	10	Both Sides
TM39	Rock Tomb	Rock	Physical	60	95	15	Normal
TM40	Aerial Ace	Flying	Physical	60	—	20	Normal
TM42	Facade	Normal	Physical	70	100	20	Normal
TM44	Rest	Psychic	Status	—	—	10	Self
TM45	Attract	Normal	Status	—	100	15	Normal
TM46	Thief	Dark	Physical	60	100	25	Normal
TM48	Round	Normal	Special	60	100	15	Normal
TM52	Focus Blast	Fighting	Special	120	70	5	Normal
TM56	Fling	Dark	Physical	—	100	10	Normal
TM65	Shadow Claw	Ghost	Physical	70	100	15	Normal
TM68	Giga Impact	Normal	Physical	150	90	5	Normal
TM71	Stone Edge	Rock	Physical	100	80	5	Normal
TM74	Gyro Ball	Steel	Physical	—	100	5	Normal
TM75	Swords Dance	Normal	Status	—	—	20	Self
TM78	Bulldoze	Ground	Physical	60	100	20	Adjacent
TM80	Rock Slide	Rock	Physical	75	90	10	Many Others
TM81	X-Scissor	Bug	Physical	80	100	15	Normal
TM84	Poison Jab	Poison	Physical	80	100	20	Normal
TM87	Swagger	Normal	Status	—	90	15	Normal
TM88	Sleep Talk	Normal	Status	—	—	10	Self
TM90	Substitute	Normal	Status	—	—	10	Self
TM94	Secret Power	Normal	Physical	70	100	20	Normal
TM100	Confide	Normal	Status	—	—	20	Normal
HM01	Cut	Normal	Physical	50	95	30	Normal
HM04	Strength	Normal	Physical	80	100	15	Normal
HM06	Rock Smash	Fighting	Physical	40	100	15	Normal

MOVES LEARNED IN EXCHANGE FOR BP

Name	Type	Kind	Pow.	Acc.	PP	Range
Covet	Normal	Physical	60	100	25	Normal
Super Fang	Normal	Physical	—	90	10	Normal
Earth Power	Ground	Special	90	100	10	Normal
Iron Tail	Steel	Physical	100	75	15	Normal
Snore	Normal	Special	50	100	15	Normal
Knock Off	Dark	Physical	65	100	20	Normal
Focus Punch	Fighting	Physical	150	100	20	Normal
Stealth Rock	Rock	Status	—	—	20	Other Side

MOVES TAUGHT BY PEOPLE

Name	Type	Kind	Pow.	Acc.	PP	Range

National Pokédex **029** Hoenn Pokédex **—**

Nidoran ♀

Poison Pin Pokémon

Poison

HEIGHT: 1'04" WEIGHT: 15.4 lbs.

♀ only

Ω Nidoran ♀ has barbs that secrete a powerful poison. They are thought to have developed as protection for this small-bodied Pokémon. When enraged, it releases a horrible toxin from its horn.

α Nidoran ♀ has barbs that secrete a powerful poison. They are thought to have developed as protection for this small-bodied Pokémon. When enraged, it releases a horrible toxin from its horn.

ABILITIES
Poison Point
Rivalry

HIDDEN ABILITY
Hustle

EGG GROUPS
Monster
Field

STAT GROWTH RATES

HP	■■
Attack	■■■
Defense	■■
Sp. Atk	■■
Sp. Def	■■
Speed	■■

ITEMS SOMETIMES HELD BY WILD POKÉMON
—

EVOLUTION

Nidoran ♀ → Lv. 16 → Nidorina → Moon Stone → Nidoqueen

MAIN WAY TO REGISTER IN THE NATIONAL POKÉDEX

Appears in *Pokémon X* and *Pokémon Y*. Bring it to your game using Link Trade or the GTS.

Damage taken in normal battles

Type		Type	
Normal	×1	Flying	×1
Fire	×1	Psychic	×2
Water	×1	Bug	×0.5
Grass	×0.5	Rock	×1
Electric	×1	Ghost	×1
Ice	×1	Dragon	×1
Fighting	×0.5	Dark	×1
Poison	×0.5	Steel	×1
Ground	×2	Fairy	×0.5

Damage taken in Inverse battles

Type		Type	
Normal	×1	Flying	×1
Fire	×1	Psychic	×0.5
Water	×1	Bug	×2
Grass	×2	Rock	×1
Electric	×1	Ghost	×1
Ice	×1	Dragon	×1
Fighting	×2	Dark	×1
Poison	×2	Steel	×1
Ground	×0.5	Fairy	×2

Can be used in
Inverse Battle
Battle Institute
Battle Maison
Random Matchup (Free Battle)
Random Matchup (Others)

LEVEL-UP MOVES

Lv.	Name	Type	Kind	Pow.	Acc.	PP	Range
1	Growl	Normal	Status	—	100	40	Many Others
1	Scratch	Normal	Physical	40	100	35	Normal
7	Tail Whip	Normal	Status	—	100	30	Many Others
9	Double Kick	Fighting	Physical	30	100	30	Normal
13	Poison Sting	Poison	Physical	15	100	35	Normal
19	Fury Swipes	Normal	Physical	18	80	15	Normal
21	Bite	Dark	Physical	60	100	25	Normal
25	Helping Hand	Normal	Status	—	—	20	1 Ally
31	Toxic Spikes	Poison	Status	—	—	20	Other Side
33	Flatter	Dark	Status	—	100	15	Normal
37	Crunch	Dark	Physical	80	100	15	Normal
43	Captivate	Normal	Status	—	100	20	Many Others
45	Poison Fang	Poison	Physical	50	100	15	Normal

TM & HM MOVES

No.	Name	Type	Kind	Pow.	Acc.	PP	Range
TM01	Hone Claws	Dark	Status	—	—	15	Self
TM06	Toxic	Poison	Status	—	90	10	Normal
TM09	Venoshock	Poison	Special	65	100	10	Normal
TM10	Hidden Power	Normal	Special	60	100	15	Normal
TM11	Sunny Day	Fire	Status	—	—	5	Both Sides
TM13	Ice Beam	Ice	Special	90	100	10	Normal
TM14	Blizzard	Ice	Special	110	70	5	Many Others
TM17	Protect	Normal	Status	—	—	10	Self
TM18	Rain Dance	Water	Status	—	—	5	Both Sides
TM21	Frustration	Normal	Physical	—	100	20	Normal
TM24	Thunderbolt	Electric	Special	90	100	15	Normal
TM25	Thunder	Electric	Special	110	70	10	Normal
TM27	Return	Normal	Physical	—	100	20	Normal
TM28	Dig	Ground	Physical	80	100	10	Normal
TM32	Double Team	Normal	Status	—	—	15	Self
TM36	Sludge Bomb	Poison	Special	90	100	10	Normal
TM40	Aerial Ace	Flying	Physical	60	—	20	Normal
TM42	Facade	Normal	Physical	70	100	20	Normal
TM44	Rest	Psychic	Status	—	—	10	Self
TM45	Attract	Normal	Status	—	100	15	Normal
TM46	Thief	Dark	Physical	60	100	25	Normal
TM48	Round	Normal	Special	60	100	15	Normal
TM49	Echoed Voice	Normal	Special	40	100	15	Normal
TM65	Shadow Claw	Ghost	Physical	70	100	15	Normal
TM84	Poison Jab	Poison	Physical	80	100	20	Normal
TM87	Swagger	Normal	Status	—	90	15	Normal
TM88	Sleep Talk	Normal	Status	—	—	10	Self
TM90	Substitute	Normal	Status	—	—	10	Self
TM94	Secret Power	Normal	Physical	70	100	20	Normal
TM100	Confide	Normal	Status	—	—	20	Normal
HM01	Cut	Normal	Physical	50	95	30	Normal
HM04	Strength	Normal	Physical	80	100	15	Normal
HM06	Rock Smash	Fighting	Physical	40	100	15	Normal

MOVES LEARNED IN EXCHANGE FOR BP

Name	Type	Kind	Pow.	Acc.	PP	Range
Super Fang	Normal	Physical	—	90	10	Normal
Iron Tail	Steel	Physical	100	75	15	Normal
Snore	Normal	Special	50	100	15	Normal
Shock Wave	Electric	Special	60	—	20	Normal
Water Pulse	Water	Special	60	100	20	Normal
Helping Hand	Normal	Status	—	—	20	1 Ally

MOVES TAUGHT BY PEOPLE

Name	Type	Kind	Pow.	Acc.	PP	Range

EGG MOVES

Name	Type	Kind	Pow.	Acc.	PP	Range
Supersonic	Normal	Status	—	55	20	Normal
Disable	Normal	Status	—	100	20	Normal
Take Down	Normal	Physical	90	85	20	Normal
Focus Energy	Normal	Status	—	—	30	Self
Charm	Fairy	Status	—	100	20	Normal
Counter	Fighting	Physical	—	100	20	Varies
Beat Up	Dark	Physical	—	100	10	Normal
Pursuit	Dark	Physical	40	100	20	Normal
Skull Bash	Normal	Physical	130	100	10	Normal
Iron Tail	Steel	Physical	100	75	15	Normal
Poison Tail	Poison	Physical	50	100	25	Normal
Endure	Normal	Status	—	—	10	Self
Chip Away	Normal	Physical	70	100	20	Normal
Venom Drench	Poison	Status	—	100	20	Many Others

National Pokédex **030** Hoenn Pokédex —

Nidorina

Poison Pin Pokémon

Poison

HEIGHT: 2'07" WEIGHT: 44.1 lbs.

♀ only

Ω When Nidorina are with their friends or family, they keep their barbs tucked away to prevent hurting each other. This Pokémon appears to become nervous if separated from the others.

α When Nidorina are with their friends or family, they keep their barbs tucked away to prevent hurting each other. This Pokémon appears to become nervous if separated from the others.

ABILITIES
Poison Point
Rivalry

HIDDEN ABILITY
Hustle

EGG GROUPS
No Eggs Discovered

STAT GROWTH RATES
HP
Attack
Defense
Sp. Atk
Sp. Def
Speed

ITEMS SOMETIMES HELD BY WILD POKÉMON
—

EVOLUTION
Nidoran♀ → Lv. 16 → Nidorina → Moon Stone → Nidoqueen

MAIN WAY TO REGISTER IN THE NATIONAL POKÉDEX

Appears in *Pokémon X* and *Pokémon Y*. Bring it to your game using Link Trade or the GTS.

Damage taken in normal battles

Type		Type	
Normal	×1	Flying	×1
Fire	×1	Psychic	×2
Water	×1	Bug	×0.5
Grass	×0.5	Rock	×1
Electric	×1	Ghost	×1
Ice	×1	Dragon	×1
Fighting	×0.5	Dark	×1
Poison	×0.5	Steel	×1
Ground	×2	Fairy	×0.5

Damage taken in Inverse battles

Type		Type	
Normal	×1	Flying	×1
Fire	×1	Psychic	×0.5
Water	×1	Bug	×2
Grass	×2	Rock	×1
Electric	×1	Ghost	×1
Ice	×1	Dragon	×1
Fighting	×2	Dark	×1
Poison	×2	Steel	×1
Ground	×0.5	Fairy	×2

Can be used in
Inverse Battle
Battle Institute
Battle Maison
Random Matchup (Free Battle)
Random Matchup (Others)

LEVEL-UP MOVES

Lv.	Name	Type	Kind	Pow.	Acc.	PP	Range
1	Growl	Normal	Status	—	100	40	Many Others
1	Scratch	Normal	Physical	40	100	35	Normal
7	Tail Whip	Normal	Status	—	100	30	Many Others
9	Double Kick	Fighting	Physical	30	100	30	Normal
13	Poison Sting	Poison	Physical	15	100	35	Normal
20	Fury Swipes	Normal	Physical	18	80	15	Normal
23	Bite	Dark	Physical	60	100	25	Normal
28	Helping Hand	Normal	Status	—	—	20	1 Ally
35	Toxic Spikes	Poison	Status	—	—	20	Other Side
38	Flatter	Dark	Status	—	100	15	Normal
43	Crunch	Dark	Physical	80	100	15	Normal
50	Captivate	Normal	Status	—	100	20	Many Others
58	Poison Fang	Poison	Physical	50	100	15	Normal

TM & HM MOVES

No.	Name	Type	Kind	Pow.	Acc.	PP	Range
TM01	Hone Claws	Dark	Status	—	—	15	Self
TM06	Toxic	Poison	Status	—	90	10	Normal
TM09	Venoshock	Poison	Special	65	100	10	Normal
TM10	Hidden Power	Normal	Special	60	100	15	Normal
TM11	Sunny Day	Fire	Status	—	—	5	Both Sides
TM13	Ice Beam	Ice	Special	90	100	10	Normal
TM14	Blizzard	Ice	Special	110	70	5	Many Others
TM17	Protect	Normal	Status	—	—	10	Self
TM18	Rain Dance	Water	Status	—	—	5	Both Sides
TM21	Frustration	Normal	Physical	—	100	20	Normal
TM24	Thunderbolt	Electric	Special	90	100	15	Normal
TM25	Thunder	Electric	Special	110	70	10	Normal
TM27	Return	Normal	Physical	—	100	20	Normal
TM28	Dig	Ground	Physical	80	100	10	Normal
TM32	Double Team	Normal	Status	—	—	15	Self
TM36	Sludge Bomb	Poison	Special	90	100	10	Normal
TM40	Aerial Ace	Flying	Physical	60	—	20	Normal
TM42	Facade	Normal	Physical	70	100	20	Normal
TM44	Rest	Psychic	Status	—	—	10	Self
TM45	Attract	Normal	Status	—	100	15	Normal
TM46	Thief	Dark	Physical	60	100	25	Normal
TM48	Round	Normal	Special	60	100	15	Normal
TM49	Echoed Voice	Normal	Special	40	100	15	Normal
TM65	Shadow Claw	Ghost	Physical	70	100	15	Normal
TM84	Poison Jab	Poison	Physical	80	100	20	Normal
TM87	Swagger	Normal	Status	—	90	15	Normal
TM88	Sleep Talk	Normal	Status	—	—	10	Self
TM90	Substitute	Normal	Status	—	—	10	Self
TM94	Secret Power	Normal	Physical	70	100	20	Normal
TM100	Confide	Normal	Status	—	—	20	Normal
HM01	Cut	Normal	Physical	50	95	30	Normal
HM04	Strength	Normal	Physical	80	100	15	Normal
HM06	Rock Smash	Fighting	Physical	40	100	15	Normal

MOVES LEARNED IN EXCHANGE FOR BP

Name	Type	Kind	Pow.	Acc.	PP	Range
Super Fang	Normal	Physical	—	90	10	Normal
Iron Tail	Steel	Physical	100	75	15	Normal
Snore	Normal	Special	50	100	15	Normal
Shock Wave	Electric	Special	60	—	20	Normal
Water Pulse	Water	Special	60	100	20	Normal
Helping Hand	Normal	Status	—	—	20	1 Ally

MOVES TAUGHT BY PEOPLE

Name	Type	Kind	Pow.	Acc.	PP	Range

National Pokédex **031** Hoenn Pokédex —

Nidoqueen

Drill Pokémon

Poison **Ground**

HEIGHT: 4'03" WEIGHT: 132.3 lbs.

♀ only

Ω Nidoqueen's body is encased in extremely hard scales. It is adept at sending foes flying with harsh tackles. This Pokémon is at its strongest when it is defending its young.

α Nidoqueen's body is encased in extremely hard scales. It is adept at sending foes flying with harsh tackles. This Pokémon is at its strongest when it is defending its young.

ABILITIES
Poison Point
Rivalry

HIDDEN ABILITY
Sheer Force

EGG GROUPS
No Eggs Discovered

STAT GROWTH RATES
HP
Attack
Defense
Sp. Atk
Sp. Def
Speed

ITEMS SOMETIMES HELD BY WILD POKÉMON
—

EVOLUTION
Nidoran♀ → Lv. 16 → Nidorina → Moon Stone → Nidoqueen

MAIN WAY TO REGISTER IN THE NATIONAL POKÉDEX

Use a Moon Stone on a Nidorina obtained via Link Trade or the GTS.

Damage taken in normal battles

Type		Type	
Normal	×1	Flying	×1
Fire	×1	Psychic	×2
Water	×2	Bug	×0.5
Grass	×1	Rock	×0.5
Electric	×0	Ghost	×1
Ice	×2	Dragon	×1
Fighting	×0.5	Dark	×1
Poison	×0.25	Steel	×1
Ground	×2	Fairy	×0.5

Damage taken in Inverse battles

Type		Type	
Normal	×1	Flying	×1
Fire	×1	Psychic	×0.5
Water	×0.5	Bug	×2
Grass	×1	Rock	×2
Electric	×2	Ghost	×1
Ice	×0.5	Dragon	×1
Fighting	×2	Dark	×1
Poison	×4	Steel	×1
Ground	×0.5	Fairy	×2

Can be used in
Inverse Battle
Battle Institute
Battle Maison
Random Matchup (Free Battle)
Random Matchup (Others)

LEVEL-UP MOVES

Lv.	Name	Type	Kind	Pow.	Acc.	PP	Range
1	Superpower	Fighting	Physical	120	100	5	Normal
1	Scratch	Normal	Physical	40	100	35	Normal
1	Tail Whip	Normal	Status	—	100	30	Many Others
1	Double Kick	Fighting	Physical	30	100	30	Normal
1	Poison Sting	Poison	Physical	15	100	35	Normal
23	Chip Away	Normal	Physical	70	100	20	Normal
35	Body Slam	Normal	Physical	85	100	15	Normal
43	Earth Power	Ground	Special	90	100	10	Normal
58	Superpower	Fighting	Physical	120	100	5	Normal

TM & HM MOVES

No.	Name	Type	Kind	Pow.	Acc.	PP	Range
TM01	Hone Claws	Dark	Status	—	—	15	Self
TM05	Roar	Normal	Status	—	—	20	Normal
TM06	Toxic	Poison	Status	—	90	10	Normal
TM09	Venoshock	Poison	Special	65	100	10	Normal
TM10	Hidden Power	Normal	Special	60	100	15	Normal
TM11	Sunny Day	Fire	Status	—	—	5	Both Sides
TM12	Taunt	Dark	Status	—	100	20	Normal
TM13	Ice Beam	Ice	Special	90	100	10	Normal
TM14	Blizzard	Ice	Special	110	70	5	Many Others
TM15	Hyper Beam	Normal	Special	150	90	5	Normal
TM17	Protect	Normal	Status	—	—	10	Self
TM18	Rain Dance	Water	Status	—	—	5	Both Sides
TM21	Frustration	Normal	Physical	—	100	20	Normal
TM23	Smack Down	Rock	Physical	50	100	15	Normal
TM24	Thunderbolt	Electric	Special	90	100	15	Normal
TM25	Thunder	Electric	Special	110	70	10	Normal
TM26	Earthquake	Ground	Physical	100	100	10	Adjacent
TM27	Return	Normal	Physical	—	100	20	Normal
TM28	Dig	Ground	Physical	80	100	10	Normal
TM30	Shadow Ball	Ghost	Special	80	100	15	Normal
TM31	Brick Break	Fighting	Physical	75	100	15	Normal
TM32	Double Team	Normal	Status	—	—	15	Self
TM34	Sludge Wave	Poison	Special	95	100	10	Adjacent
TM35	Flamethrower	Fire	Special	90	100	15	Normal
TM36	Sludge Bomb	Poison	Special	90	100	10	Normal
TM37	Sandstorm	Rock	Status	—	—	10	Both Sides
TM38	Fire Blast	Fire	Special	110	85	5	Normal
TM39	Rock Tomb	Rock	Physical	60	95	15	Normal
TM40	Aerial Ace	Flying	Physical	60	—	20	Normal
TM41	Torment	Dark	Status	—	100	15	Normal
TM42	Facade	Normal	Physical	70	100	20	Normal
TM44	Rest	Psychic	Status	—	—	10	Self
TM45	Attract	Normal	Status	—	100	15	Normal
TM46	Thief	Dark	Physical	60	100	25	Normal
TM48	Round	Normal	Special	60	100	15	Normal
TM49	Echoed Voice	Normal	Special	40	100	15	Normal
TM52	Focus Blast	Fighting	Special	120	70	5	Normal
TM56	Fling	Dark	Physical	—	100	10	Normal
TM59	Incinerate	Fire	Special	60	100	15	Many Others
TM60	Quash	Dark	Status	—	100	15	Normal
TM65	Shadow Claw	Ghost	Physical	70	100	15	Normal
TM68	Giga Impact	Normal	Physical	150	90	5	Normal
TM71	Stone Edge	Rock	Physical	100	80	5	Normal
TM78	Bulldoze	Ground	Physical	60	100	20	Adjacent
TM80	Rock Slide	Rock	Physical	75	90	10	Many Others
TM82	Dragon Tail	Dragon	Physical	60	90	10	Normal
TM84	Poison Jab	Poison	Physical	80	100	20	Normal
TM87	Swagger	Normal	Status	—	90	15	Normal
TM88	Sleep Talk	Normal	Status	—	—	10	Self
TM90	Substitute	Normal	Status	—	—	10	Self
TM94	Secret Power	Normal	Physical	70	100	20	Normal
TM98	Power-Up Punch	Fighting	Physical	40	100	20	Normal
TM100	Confide	Normal	Status	—	—	20	Normal
HM01	Cut	Normal	Physical	50	95	30	Normal
HM03	Surf	Water	Special	90	100	15	Adjacent
HM04	Strength	Normal	Physical	80	100	15	Normal
HM06	Rock Smash	Fighting	Physical	40	100	15	Normal

MOVES LEARNED IN EXCHANGE FOR BP

Name	Type	Kind	Pow.	Acc.	PP	Range
Super Fang	Normal	Physical	—	90	10	Normal
Drill Run	Ground	Physical	80	95	10	Normal
Uproar	Normal	Special	90	100	10	1 Random
Thunder Punch	Electric	Physical	75	100	15	Normal
Fire Punch	Fire	Physical	75	100	15	Normal
Ice Punch	Ice	Physical	75	100	15	Normal
Earth Power	Ground	Special	90	100	10	Normal
Superpower	Fighting	Physical	120	100	5	Normal
Icy Wind	Ice	Special	55	95	15	Many Others
Aqua Tail	Water	Physical	90	90	10	Normal
Dragon Pulse	Dragon	Special	85	100	10	Normal
Iron Tail	Steel	Physical	100	75	15	Normal
Snore	Normal	Special	50	100	15	Normal
Focus Punch	Fighting	Physical	150	100	20	Normal
Shock Wave	Electric	Special	60	—	20	Normal
Water Pulse	Water	Special	60	100	20	Normal
Helping Hand	Normal	Status	—	—	20	1 Ally
Outrage	Dragon	Physical	120	100	10	1 Random
Stealth Rock	Rock	Status	—	—	20	Other Side

MOVES TAUGHT BY PEOPLE

Name	Type	Kind	Pow.	Acc.	PP	Range

National Pokédex **032** Hoenn Pokédex —

Nidoran ♂

Poison Pin Pokémon

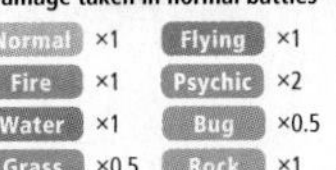

Poison

HEIGHT: 1'08" WEIGHT: 19.8 lbs.

♂ only

Ω Nidoran ♂ has developed muscles for moving its ears. Thanks to them, the ears can be freely moved in any direction. Even the slightest sound does not escape this Pokémon's notice.

α Nidoran ♂ has developed muscles for moving its ears. Thanks to them, the ears can be freely moved in any direction. Even the slightest sound does not escape this Pokémon's notice.

ABILITIES
Poison Point
Rivalry

HIDDEN ABILITY
Hustle

EGG GROUPS
Monster | Field

STAT GROWTH RATES
HP
Attack
Defense
Sp. Atk
Sp. Def
Speed

ITEMS SOMETIMES HELD BY WILD POKÉMON
—

EVOLUTION

MAIN WAY TO REGISTER IN THE NATIONAL POKÉDEX

Appears in *Pokémon X* and *Pokémon Y*. Bring it to your game using Link Trade or the GTS.

Damage taken in normal battles

Type		Type	
Normal	×1	Flying	×1
Fire	×1	Psychic	×2
Water	×1	Bug	×0.5
Grass	×0.5	Rock	×1
Electric	×1	Ghost	×1
Ice	×1	Dragon	×1
Fighting	×0.5	Dark	×1
Poison	×0.5	Steel	×1
Ground	×2	Fairy	×0.5

Damage taken in Inverse battles

Type		Type	
Normal	×1	Flying	×1
Fire	×1	Psychic	×0.5
Water	×1	Bug	×2
Grass	×2	Rock	×1
Electric	×1	Ghost	×1
Ice	×1	Dragon	×1
Fighting	×2	Dark	×1
Poison	×2	Steel	×1
Ground	×0.5	Fairy	×2

Can be used in
Inverse Battle
Battle Institute
Battle Maison
Random Matchup (Free Battle)
Random Matchup (Others)

LEVEL-UP MOVES

Lv.	Name	Type	Kind	Pow.	Acc.	PP	Range
1	Leer	Normal	Status	—	100	30	Many Others
1	Peck	Flying	Physical	35	100	35	Normal
7	Focus Energy	Normal	Status	—	—	30	Self
9	Double Kick	Fighting	Physical	30	100	30	Normal
13	Poison Sting	Poison	Physical	15	100	35	Normal
19	Fury Attack	Normal	Physical	15	85	20	Normal
21	Horn Attack	Normal	Physical	65	100	25	Normal
25	Helping Hand	Normal	Status	—	—	20	1 Ally
31	Toxic Spikes	Poison	Status	—	—	20	Other Side
33	Flatter	Dark	Status	—	100	15	Normal
37	Poison Jab	Poison	Physical	80	100	20	Normal
43	Captivate	Normal	Status	—	100	20	Many Others
45	Horn Drill	Normal	Physical	—	30	5	Normal

TM & HM MOVES

No.	Name	Type	Kind	Pow.	Acc.	PP	Range
TM01	Hone Claws	Dark	Status	—	—	15	Self
TM06	Toxic	Poison	Status	—	90	10	Normal
TM09	Venoshock	Poison	Special	65	100	10	Normal
TM10	Hidden Power	Normal	Special	60	100	15	Normal
TM11	Sunny Day	Fire	Status	—	—	5	Both Sides
TM13	Ice Beam	Ice	Special	90	100	10	Normal
TM14	Blizzard	Ice	Special	110	70	5	Many Others
TM17	Protect	Normal	Status	—	—	10	Self
TM18	Rain Dance	Water	Status	—	—	5	Both Sides
TM21	Frustration	Normal	Physical	—	100	20	Normal
TM24	Thunderbolt	Electric	Special	90	100	15	Normal
TM25	Thunder	Electric	Special	110	70	10	Normal
TM27	Return	Normal	Physical	—	100	20	Normal
TM28	Dig	Ground	Physical	80	100	10	Normal
TM32	Double Team	Normal	Status	—	—	15	Self
TM36	Sludge Bomb	Poison	Special	90	100	10	Normal
TM42	Facade	Normal	Physical	70	100	20	Normal
TM44	Rest	Psychic	Status	—	—	10	Self
TM45	Attract	Normal	Status	—	100	15	Normal
TM46	Thief	Dark	Physical	60	100	25	Normal
TM48	Round	Normal	Special	60	100	15	Normal
TM49	Echoed Voice	Normal	Special	40	100	15	Normal
TM65	Shadow Claw	Ghost	Physical	70	100	15	Normal
TM84	Poison Jab	Poison	Physical	80	100	20	Normal
TM87	Swagger	Normal	Status	—	90	15	Normal
TM88	Sleep Talk	Normal	Status	—	—	10	Self
TM90	Substitute	Normal	Status	—	—	10	Self
TM94	Secret Power	Normal	Physical	70	100	20	Normal
TM100	Confide	Normal	Status	—	—	20	Normal
HM01	Cut	Normal	Physical	50	95	30	Normal
HM04	Strength	Normal	Physical	80	100	15	Normal
HM06	Rock Smash	Fighting	Physical	40	100	15	Normal

MOVES LEARNED IN EXCHANGE FOR BP

Name	Type	Kind	Pow.	Acc.	PP	Range
Super Fang	Normal	Physical	—	90	10	Normal
Drill Run	Ground	Physical	80	95	10	Normal
Iron Tail	Steel	Physical	100	75	15	Normal
Snore	Normal	Special	50	100	15	Normal
Shock Wave	Electric	Special	60	—	20	Normal
Water Pulse	Water	Special	60	100	20	Normal
Helping Hand	Normal	Status	—	—	20	1 Ally

MOVES TAUGHT BY PEOPLE

Name	Type	Kind	Pow.	Acc.	PP	Range

EGG MOVES

Name	Type	Kind	Pow.	Acc.	PP	Range
Counter	Fighting	Physical	—	100	20	Varies
Disable	Normal	Status	—	100	20	Normal
Supersonic	Normal	Status	—	55	20	Normal
Take Down	Normal	Physical	90	85	20	Normal
Amnesia	Psychic	Status	—	—	20	Self
Confusion	Psychic	Special	50	100	25	Normal
Beat Up	Dark	Physical	—	100	10	Normal
Sucker Punch	Dark	Physical	80	100	5	Normal
Head Smash	Rock	Physical	150	80	5	Normal
Iron Tail	Steel	Physical	100	75	15	Normal
Poison Tail	Poison	Physical	50	100	25	Normal
Endure	Normal	Status	—	—	10	Self
Chip Away	Normal	Physical	70	100	20	Normal
Venom Drench	Poison	Status	—	100	20	Many Others

National Pokédex **033** Hoenn Pokédex —

Nidorino

Poison Pin Pokémon

Poison

HEIGHT: 2'11" WEIGHT: 43 lbs.

♂ only

Ω Nidorino has a horn that is harder than a diamond. If it senses a hostile presence, all the barbs on its back bristle up at once, and it challenges the foe with all its might.

α Nidorino has a horn that is harder than a diamond. If it senses a hostile presence, all the barbs on its back bristle up at once, and it challenges the foe with all its might.

ABILITIES
Poison Point
Rivalry

HIDDEN ABILITY
Hustle

EGG GROUPS
Monster | Field

STAT GROWTH RATES
HP
Attack
Defense
Sp. Atk
Sp. Def
Speed

ITEMS SOMETIMES HELD BY WILD POKÉMON
—

EVOLUTION
Lv. 16
Moon Stone
Nidoran♂
Nidorino
Nidoking

MAIN WAY TO REGISTER IN THE NATIONAL POKÉDEX

Appears in *Pokémon X* and *Pokémon Y*. Bring it to your game using Link Trade or the GTS.

Damage taken in normal battles

Type		Type	
Normal	×1	Flying	×1
Fire	×1	Psychic	×2
Water	×1	Bug	×0.5
Grass	×0.5	Rock	×1
Electric	×1	Ghost	×1
Ice	×1	Dragon	×1
Fighting	×0.5	Dark	×1
Poison	×0.5	Steel	×1
Ground	×2	Fairy	×0.5

Damage taken in Inverse battles

Type		Type	
Normal	×1	Flying	×1
Fire	×1	Psychic	×0.5
Water	×1	Bug	×2
Grass	×2	Rock	×1
Electric	×1	Ghost	×1
Ice	×1	Dragon	×1
Fighting	×2	Dark	×1
Poison	×2	Steel	×1
Ground	×0.5	Fairy	×2

Can be used in
Inverse Battle
Battle Institute
Battle Maison
Random Matchup (Free Battle)
Random Matchup (Others)

LEVEL-UP MOVES

Lv.	Name	Type	Kind	Pow.	Acc.	PP	Range
1	Leer	Normal	Status	—	100	30	Many Others
1	Peck	Flying	Physical	35	100	35	Normal
7	Focus Energy	Normal	Status	—	—	30	Self
9	Double Kick	Fighting	Physical	30	100	30	Normal
13	Poison Sting	Poison	Physical	15	100	35	Normal
20	Fury Attack	Normal	Physical	15	85	20	Normal
23	Horn Attack	Normal	Physical	65	100	25	Normal
28	Helping Hand	Normal	Status	—	—	20	1 Ally
35	Toxic Spikes	Poison	Status	—	—	20	Other Side
38	Flatter	Dark	Status	—	100	15	Normal
43	Poison Jab	Poison	Physical	80	100	20	Normal
50	Captivate	Normal	Status	—	100	20	Many Others
58	Horn Drill	Normal	Physical	—	30	5	Normal

TM & HM MOVES

No.	Name	Type	Kind	Pow.	Acc.	PP	Range
TM01	Hone Claws	Dark	Status	—	—	15	Self
TM06	Toxic	Poison	Status	—	90	10	Normal
TM09	Venoshock	Poison	Special	65	100	10	Normal
TM10	Hidden Power	Normal	Special	60	100	15	Normal
TM11	Sunny Day	Fire	Status	—	—	5	Both Sides
TM13	Ice Beam	Ice	Special	90	100	10	Normal
TM14	Blizzard	Ice	Special	110	70	5	Many Others
TM17	Protect	Normal	Status	—	—	10	Self
TM18	Rain Dance	Water	Status	—	—	5	Both Sides
TM21	Frustration	Normal	Physical	—	100	20	Normal
TM24	Thunderbolt	Electric	Special	90	100	15	Normal
TM25	Thunder	Electric	Special	110	70	10	Normal
TM27	Return	Normal	Physical	—	100	20	Normal
TM28	Dig	Ground	Physical	80	100	10	Normal
TM32	Double Team	Normal	Status	—	—	15	Self
TM36	Sludge Bomb	Poison	Special	90	100	10	Normal
TM42	Facade	Normal	Physical	70	100	20	Normal
TM44	Rest	Psychic	Status	—	—	10	Self
TM45	Attract	Normal	Status	—	100	15	Normal
TM46	Thief	Dark	Physical	60	100	25	Normal
TM48	Round	Normal	Special	60	100	15	Normal
TM49	Echoed Voice	Normal	Special	40	100	15	Normal
TM65	Shadow Claw	Ghost	Physical	70	100	15	Normal
TM84	Poison Jab	Poison	Physical	80	100	20	Normal
TM87	Swagger	Normal	Status	—	90	15	Normal
TM88	Sleep Talk	Normal	Status	—	—	10	Self
TM90	Substitute	Normal	Status	—	—	10	Self
TM94	Secret Power	Normal	Physical	70	100	20	Normal
TM100	Confide	Normal	Status	—	—	20	Normal
HM01	Cut	Normal	Physical	50	95	30	Normal
HM04	Strength	Normal	Physical	80	100	15	Normal
HM06	Rock Smash	Fighting	Physical	40	100	15	Normal

MOVES LEARNED IN EXCHANGE FOR BP

Name	Type	Kind	Pow.	Acc.	PP	Range
Super Fang	Normal	Physical	—	90	10	Normal
Drill Run	Ground	Physical	80	95	10	Normal
Iron Tail	Steel	Physical	100	75	15	Normal
Snore	Normal	Special	50	100	15	Normal
Shock Wave	Electric	Special	60	—	20	Normal
Water Pulse	Water	Special	60	100	20	Normal
Helping Hand	Normal	Status	—	—	20	1 Ally

MOVES TAUGHT BY PEOPLE

Name	Type	Kind	Pow.	Acc.	PP	Range

National Pokédex **034** Hoenn Pokédex –

Nidoking

Drill Pokémon

Poison | Ground

HEIGHT: 4'07" WEIGHT: 136.7 lbs.

♂ only

Ω Nidoking's thick tail packs enormously destructive power. With one swing, it can topple a metal transmission tower. Once this Pokémon goes on a rampage, there is no stopping it.

α Nidoking's thick tail packs enormously destructive power. With one swing, it can topple a metal transmission tower. Once this Pokémon goes on a rampage, there is no stopping it.

ABILITIES
Poison Point
Rivalry

HIDDEN ABILITY
Sheer Force

EGG GROUPS
Monster | Field

STAT GROWTH RATES
HP ■■■
Attack ■■■■■
Defense ■■■
Sp. Atk ■■■■
Sp. Def ■■■
Speed ■■■■■

ITEMS SOMETIMES HELD BY WILD POKÉMON
—

EVOLUTION

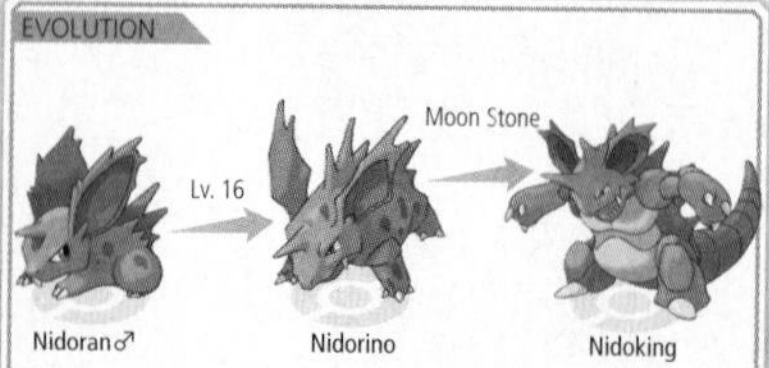

MAIN WAY TO REGISTER IN THE NATIONAL POKÉDEX

Use a Moon Stone on a Nidorino obtained via Link Trade or the GTS.

Damage taken in normal battles

Type		Type	
Normal	×1	Flying	×1
Fire	×1	Psychic	×2
Water	×2	Bug	×0.5
Grass	×1	Rock	×0.5
Electric	×0	Ghost	×1
Ice	×2	Dragon	×1
Fighting	×0.5	Dark	×1
Poison	×0.25	Steel	×1
Ground	×2	Fairy	×0.5

Damage taken in Inverse battles

Type		Type	
Normal	×1	Flying	×1
Fire	×1	Psychic	×0.5
Water	×0.5	Bug	×2
Grass	×1	Rock	×2
Electric	×2	Ghost	×1
Ice	×0.5	Dragon	×1
Fighting	×2	Dark	×1
Poison	×4	Steel	×1
Ground	×0.5	Fairy	×2

Can be used in
Inverse Battle
Battle Institute
Battle Maison
Random Matchup (Free Battle)
Random Matchup (Others)

LEVEL-UP MOVES

Lv.	Name	Type	Kind	Pow.	Acc.	PP	Range
1	Megahorn	Bug	Physical	120	85	10	Normal
1	Peck	Flying	Physical	35	100	35	Normal
1	Focus Energy	Normal	Status	—	—	30	Self
1	Double Kick	Fighting	Physical	30	100	30	Normal
1	Poison Sting	Poison	Physical	15	100	35	Normal
23	Chip Away	Normal	Physical	70	100	20	Normal
35	Thrash	Normal	Physical	120	100	10	1 Random
43	Earth Power	Ground	Special	90	100	10	Normal
58	Megahorn	Bug	Physical	120	85	10	Normal

TM & HM MOVES

No.	Name	Type	Kind	Pow.	Acc.	PP	Range
TM01	Hone Claws	Dark	Status	—	—	15	Self
TM05	Roar	Normal	Status	—	—	20	Normal
TM06	Toxic	Poison	Status	—	90	10	Normal
TM09	Venoshock	Poison	Special	65	100	10	Normal
TM10	Hidden Power	Normal	Special	60	100	15	Normal
TM11	Sunny Day	Fire	Status	—	—	5	Both Sides
TM12	Taunt	Dark	Status	—	100	20	Normal
TM13	Ice Beam	Ice	Special	90	100	10	Normal
TM14	Blizzard	Ice	Special	110	70	5	Many Others
TM15	Hyper Beam	Normal	Special	150	90	5	Normal
TM17	Protect	Normal	Status	—	—	10	Self
TM18	Rain Dance	Water	Status	—	—	5	Both Sides
TM21	Frustration	Normal	Physical	—	100	20	Normal
TM23	Smack Down	Rock	Physical	50	100	15	Normal
TM24	Thunderbolt	Electric	Special	90	100	15	Normal
TM25	Thunder	Electric	Special	110	70	10	Normal
TM26	Earthquake	Ground	Physical	100	100	10	Adjacent
TM27	Return	Normal	Physical	—	100	20	Normal
TM28	Dig	Ground	Physical	80	100	10	Normal
TM30	Shadow Ball	Ghost	Special	80	100	15	Normal
TM31	Brick Break	Fighting	Physical	75	100	15	Normal
TM32	Double Team	Normal	Status	—	—	15	Self
TM34	Sludge Wave	Poison	Special	95	100	10	Adjacent
TM35	Flamethrower	Fire	Special	90	100	15	Normal
TM36	Sludge Bomb	Poison	Special	90	100	10	Normal
TM37	Sandstorm	Rock	Status	—	—	10	Both Sides
TM38	Fire Blast	Fire	Special	110	85	5	Normal
TM39	Rock Tomb	Rock	Physical	60	95	15	Normal
TM41	Torment	Dark	Status	—	100	15	Normal
TM42	Facade	Normal	Physical	70	100	20	Normal
TM44	Rest	Psychic	Status	—	—	10	Self
TM45	Attract	Normal	Status	—	100	15	Normal
TM46	Thief	Dark	Physical	60	100	25	Normal
TM48	Round	Normal	Special	60	100	15	Normal
TM49	Echoed Voice	Normal	Special	40	100	15	Normal
TM52	Focus Blast	Fighting	Special	120	70	5	Normal
TM56	Fling	Dark	Physical	—	100	10	Normal
TM59	Incinerate	Fire	Special	60	100	15	Many Others
TM60	Quash	Dark	Status	—	100	15	Normal
TM65	Shadow Claw	Ghost	Physical	70	100	15	Normal
TM68	Giga Impact	Normal	Physical	150	90	5	Normal
TM71	Stone Edge	Rock	Physical	100	80	5	Normal
TM78	Bulldoze	Ground	Physical	60	100	20	Adjacent
TM80	Rock Slide	Rock	Physical	75	90	10	Many Others
TM82	Dragon Tail	Dragon	Physical	60	90	10	Normal
TM84	Poison Jab	Poison	Physical	80	100	20	Normal
TM87	Swagger	Normal	Status	—	90	15	Normal
TM88	Sleep Talk	Normal	Status	—	—	10	Self
TM90	Substitute	Normal	Status	—	—	10	Self
TM94	Secret Power	Normal	Physical	70	100	20	Normal
TM98	Power-Up Punch	Fighting	Physical	40	100	20	Normal
TM100	Confide	Normal	Status	—	—	20	Normal
HM01	Cut	Normal	Physical	50	95	30	Normal
HM03	Surf	Water	Special	90	100	15	Adjacent
HM04	Strength	Normal	Physical	80	100	15	Normal
HM06	Rock Smash	Fighting	Physical	40	100	15	Normal

MOVES LEARNED IN EXCHANGE FOR BP

Name	Type	Kind	Pow.	Acc.	PP	Range
Super Fang	Normal	Physical	—	90	10	Normal
Drill Run	Ground	Physical	80	95	10	Normal
Uproar	Normal	Special	90	100	10	1 Random
Thunder Punch	Electric	Physical	75	100	15	Normal
Fire Punch	Fire	Physical	75	100	15	Normal
Ice Punch	Ice	Physical	75	100	15	Normal
Earth Power	Ground	Special	90	100	10	Normal
Superpower	Fighting	Physical	120	100	5	Normal
Icy Wind	Ice	Special	55	95	15	Many Others
Aqua Tail	Water	Physical	90	90	10	Normal
Dragon Pulse	Dragon	Special	85	100	10	Normal
Iron Tail	Steel	Physical	100	75	15	Normal
Snore	Normal	Special	50	100	15	Normal
Focus Punch	Fighting	Physical	150	100	20	Normal
Shock Wave	Electric	Special	60	—	20	Normal
Water Pulse	Water	Special	60	100	20	Normal
Helping Hand	Normal	Status	—	—	20	1 Ally
Outrage	Dragon	Physical	120	100	10	1 Random
Stealth Rock	Rock	Status	—	—	20	Other Side

MOVES TAUGHT BY PEOPLE

Name	Type	Kind	Pow.	Acc.	PP	Range

National Pokédex **035** Hoenn Pokédex –

Clefairy

Fairy Pokémon

Fairy

HEIGHT: 2'00" WEIGHT: 16.5 lbs.

Same form for ♂ / ♀

Ω On every night of a full moon, groups of this Pokémon come out to play. When dawn arrives, the tired Clefairy return to their quiet mountain retreats and go to sleep nestled up against each other.

α On every night of a full moon, groups of this Pokémon come out to play. When dawn arrives, the tired Clefairy return to their quiet mountain retreats and go to sleep nestled up against each other.

ABILITIES
Cute Charm
Magic Guard

HIDDEN ABILITY
Friend Guard

EGG GROUPS
Fairy

STAT GROWTH RATES
HP ■■■
Attack ■■
Defense ■■
Sp. Atk ■■■
Sp. Def ■■■
Speed ■■

ITEMS SOMETIMES HELD BY WILD POKÉMON
Moon Stone

EVOLUTION

Cleffa → Level up with high friendship → Clefairy → Moon Stone → Clefable

MAIN WAY TO REGISTER IN THE NATIONAL POKÉDEX

Catch on Route 115. Appears as a hidden Pokémon after you battle Groudon or Kyogre.

Damage taken in normal battles

Type		Type	
Normal	×1	Flying	×1
Fire	×1	Psychic	×1
Water	×1	Bug	×0.5
Grass	×1	Rock	×1
Electric	×1	Ghost	×1
Ice	×1	Dragon	×0
Fighting	×0.5	Dark	×0.5
Poison	×2	Steel	×2
Ground	×1	Fairy	×1

Damage taken in Inverse battles

Type		Type	
Normal	×1	Flying	×1
Fire	×1	Psychic	×1
Water	×1	Bug	×2
Grass	×1	Rock	×1
Electric	×1	Ghost	×1
Ice	×1	Dragon	×2
Fighting	×2	Dark	×2
Poison	×0.5	Steel	×0.5
Ground	×1	Fairy	×1

Can be used in
Inverse Battle
Battle Institute
Battle Maison
Random Matchup (Free Battle)
Random Matchup (Others)

LEVEL-UP MOVES

Lv.	Name	Type	Kind	Pow.	Acc.	PP	Range
1	After You	Normal	Status	—	—	15	Normal
1	Healing Wish	Psychic	Status	—	—	10	Self
1	Disarming Voice	Fairy	Special	40	—	15	Many Others
1	Pound	Normal	Physical	40	100	35	Normal
1	Growl	Normal	Status	—	100	40	Many Others
1	Encore	Normal	Status	—	100	5	Normal
7	Sing	Normal	Status	—	55	15	Normal
10	Double Slap	Normal	Physical	15	85	10	Normal
13	Defense Curl	Normal	Status	—	—	40	Self
16	Follow Me	Normal	Status	—	—	20	Self
19	Bestow	Normal	Status	—	—	15	Normal
22	Wake-Up Slap	Fighting	Physical	70	100	10	Normal
25	Minimize	Normal	Status	—	—	10	Self
28	Stored Power	Psychic	Special	20	100	10	Normal
31	Metronome	Normal	Status	—	—	10	Self
34	Cosmic Power	Psychic	Status	—	—	20	Self
37	Lucky Chant	Normal	Status	—	—	30	Your Side
40	Body Slam	Normal	Physical	85	100	15	Normal
43	Moonlight	Fairy	Status	—	—	5	Self
46	Moonblast	Fairy	Special	95	100	15	Normal
49	Gravity	Psychic	Status	—	—	5	Both Sides
50	Meteor Mash	Steel	Physical	90	90	10	Normal
55	Healing Wish	Psychic	Status	—	—	10	Self
58	After You	Normal	Status	—	—	15	Normal

TM & HM MOVES

No.	Name	Type	Kind	Pow.	Acc.	PP	Range
TM03	Psyshock	Psychic	Special	80	100	10	Normal
TM04	Calm Mind	Psychic	Status	—	—	20	Self
TM06	Toxic	Poison	Status	—	90	10	Normal
TM10	Hidden Power	Normal	Special	60	100	15	Normal
TM11	Sunny Day	Fire	Status	—	—	5	Both Sides
TM13	Ice Beam	Ice	Special	90	100	10	Normal
TM14	Blizzard	Ice	Special	110	70	5	Many Others
TM16	Light Screen	Psychic	Status	—	—	30	Your Side
TM17	Protect	Normal	Status	—	—	10	Self
TM18	Rain Dance	Water	Status	—	—	5	Both Sides
TM20	Safeguard	Normal	Status	—	—	25	Your Side
TM21	Frustration	Normal	Physical	—	100	20	Normal
TM22	Solar Beam	Grass	Special	120	100	10	Normal
TM24	Thunderbolt	Electric	Special	90	100	15	Normal
TM25	Thunder	Electric	Special	110	70	10	Normal
TM27	Return	Normal	Physical	—	100	20	Normal
TM28	Dig	Ground	Physical	80	100	10	Normal
TM29	Psychic	Psychic	Special	90	100	10	Normal
TM30	Shadow Ball	Ghost	Special	80	100	15	Normal
TM31	Brick Break	Fighting	Physical	75	100	15	Normal
TM32	Double Team	Normal	Status	—	—	15	Self
TM33	Reflect	Psychic	Status	—	—	20	Your Side
TM35	Flamethrower	Fire	Special	90	100	15	Normal
TM38	Fire Blast	Fire	Special	110	85	5	Normal
TM42	Facade	Normal	Physical	70	100	20	Normal
TM44	Rest	Psychic	Status	—	—	10	Self
TM45	Attract	Normal	Status	—	100	15	Normal
TM48	Round	Normal	Special	60	100	15	Normal
TM49	Echoed Voice	Normal	Special	40	100	15	Normal
TM56	Fling	Dark	Physical	—	100	10	Normal
TM57	Charge Beam	Electric	Special	50	90	10	Normal
TM59	Incinerate	Fire	Special	60	100	15	Many Others
TM67	Retaliate	Normal	Physical	70	100	5	Normal
TM70	Flash	Normal	Status	—	100	20	Normal
TM73	Thunder Wave	Electric	Status	—	100	20	Normal
TM77	Psych Up	Normal	Status	—	—	10	Normal
TM85	Dream Eater	Psychic	Special	100	100	15	Normal
TM86	Grass Knot	Grass	Special	—	100	20	Normal
TM87	Swagger	Normal	Status	—	90	15	Normal
TM88	Sleep Talk	Normal	Status	—	—	10	Self
TM90	Substitute	Normal	Status	—	—	10	Self
TM94	Secret Power	Normal	Physical	70	100	20	Normal
TM98	Power-Up Punch	Fighting	Physical	40	100	20	Normal
TM99	Dazzling Gleam	Fairy	Special	80	100	10	Many Others
TM100	Confide	Normal	Status	—	—	20	Normal
HM04	Strength	Normal	Physical	80	100	15	Normal
HM06	Rock Smash	Fighting	Physical	40	100	15	Normal

MOVES LEARNED IN EXCHANGE FOR BP

Name	Type	Kind	Pow.	Acc.	PP	Range
Covet	Normal	Physical	60	100	25	Normal
Signal Beam	Bug	Special	75	100	15	Normal
Bounce	Flying	Physical	85	85	5	Normal
Thunder Punch	Electric	Physical	75	100	15	Normal
Fire Punch	Fire	Physical	75	100	15	Normal
Ice Punch	Ice	Physical	75	100	15	Normal
Magic Coat	Psychic	Status	—	—	15	Self
Gravity	Psychic	Status	—	—	5	Both Sides
Last Resort	Normal	Physical	140	100	5	Normal
Icy Wind	Ice	Special	55	95	15	Many Others
Zen Headbutt	Psychic	Physical	80	90	15	Normal
Hyper Voice	Normal	Special	90	100	10	Many Others
Iron Tail	Steel	Physical	100	75	15	Normal
Snore	Normal	Special	50	100	15	Normal
Knock Off	Dark	Physical	65	100	20	Normal
Role Play	Psychic	Status	—	—	10	Normal
Heal Bell	Normal	Status	—	—	5	Your Party
Drain Punch	Fighting	Physical	75	100	10	Normal
Focus Punch	Fighting	Physical	150	100	20	Normal
Shock Wave	Electric	Special	60	—	20	Normal
Water Pulse	Water	Special	60	100	20	Normal
After You	Normal	Status	—	—	15	Normal
Helping Hand	Normal	Status	—	—	20	1 Ally
Trick	Psychic	Status	—	100	10	Normal
Wonder Room	Psychic	Status	—	—	10	Both Sides
Endeavor	Normal	Physical	—	100	5	Normal
Recycle	Normal	Status	—	—	10	Self
Snatch	Dark	Status	—	—	10	Self
Stealth Rock	Rock	Status	—	—	20	Other Side

MOVES TAUGHT BY PEOPLE

Name	Type	Kind	Pow.	Acc.	PP	Range

National Pokédex **036** Hoenn Pokédex **—**

Clefable

Fairy Pokémon

Fairy

HEIGHT: 4'03" WEIGHT: 88.2 lbs.

Same form for ♂ / ♀

Ω Clefable moves by skipping lightly as if it were flying using its wings. Its bouncy step lets it even walk on water. It is known to take strolls on lakes on quiet, moonlit nights.

α Clefable moves by skipping lightly as if it were flying using its wings. Its bouncy step lets it even walk on water. It is known to take strolls on lakes on quiet, moonlit nights.

ABILITIES
Cute Charm
Magic Guard

HIDDEN ABILITY
Unaware

EGG GROUPS
Fairy

STAT GROWTH RATES
HP
Attack
Defense
Sp. Atk
Sp. Def
Speed

ITEMS SOMETIMES HELD BY WILD POKÉMON
—

EVOLUTION

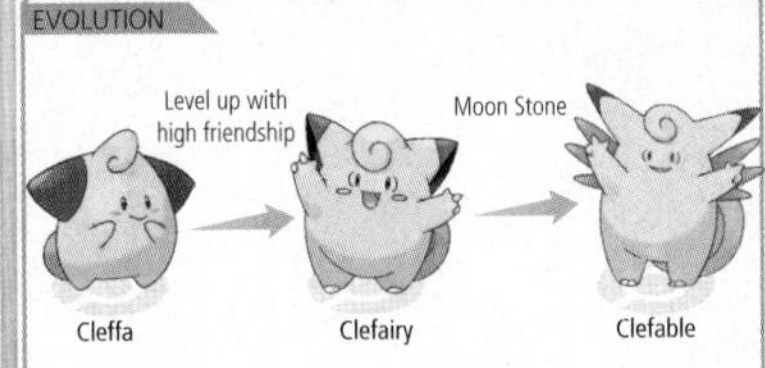

MAIN WAY TO REGISTER IN THE NATIONAL POKÉDEX

Use a Moon Stone on Clefairy.

Damage taken in normal battles

Type		Type	
Normal	×1	Flying	×1
Fire	×1	Psychic	×1
Water	×1	Bug	×0.5
Grass	×1	Rock	×1
Electric	×1	Ghost	×1
Ice	×1	Dragon	×0
Fighting	×0.5	Dark	×0.5
Poison	×2	Steel	×2
Ground	×1	Fairy	×1

Damage taken in Inverse battles

Type		Type	
Normal	×1	Flying	×1
Fire	×1	Psychic	×1
Water	×1	Bug	×2
Grass	×1	Rock	×1
Electric	×1	Ghost	×1
Ice	×1	Dragon	×2
Fighting	×2	Dark	×2
Poison	×0.5	Steel	×0.5
Ground	×1	Fairy	×1

Can be used in
Inverse Battle
Battle Institute
Battle Maison
Random Matchup (Free Battle)
Random Matchup (Others)

LEVEL-UP MOVES

Lv.	Name	Type	Kind	Pow.	Acc.	PP	Range
1	Disarming Voice	Fairy	Special	40	—	15	Many Others
1	Sing	Normal	Status	—	55	15	Normal
1	Double Slap	Normal	Physical	15	85	10	Normal
1	Minimize	Normal	Status	—	—	10	Self
1	Metronome	Normal	Status	—	—	10	Self

TM & HM MOVES

No.	Name	Type	Kind	Pow.	Acc.	PP	Range
TM03	Psyshock	Psychic	Special	80	100	10	Normal
TM04	Calm Mind	Psychic	Status	—	—	20	Self
TM06	Toxic	Poison	Status	—	90	10	Normal
TM10	Hidden Power	Normal	Special	60	100	15	Normal
TM11	Sunny Day	Fire	Status	—	—	5	Both Sides
TM13	Ice Beam	Ice	Special	90	100	10	Normal
TM14	Blizzard	Ice	Special	110	70	5	Many Others
TM15	Hyper Beam	Normal	Special	150	90	5	Normal
TM16	Light Screen	Psychic	Status	—	—	30	Your Side
TM17	Protect	Normal	Status	--	—	10	Self
TM18	Rain Dance	Water	Status	—	—	5	Both Sides
TM20	Safeguard	Normal	Status	—	—	25	Your Side
TM21	Frustration	Normal	Physical	—	100	20	Normal
TM22	Solar Beam	Grass	Special	120	100	10	Normal
TM24	Thunderbolt	Electric	Special	90	100	15	Normal
TM25	Thunder	Electric	Special	110	70	10	Normal
TM27	Return	Normal	Physical	—	100	20	Normal
TM28	Dig	Ground	Physical	80	100	10	Normal
TM29	Psychic	Psychic	Special	90	100	10	Normal
TM30	Shadow Ball	Ghost	Special	80	100	15	Normal
TM31	Brick Break	Fighting	Physical	75	100	15	Normal
TM32	Double Team	Normal	Status	—	—	15	Self
TM33	Reflect	Psychic	Status	—	—	20	Your Side
TM35	Flamethrower	Fire	Special	90	100	15	Normal
TM38	Fire Blast	Fire	Special	110	85	5	Normal
TM42	Facade	Normal	Physical	70	100	20	Normal
TM44	Rest	Psychic	Status	—	—	10	Self
TM45	Attract	Normal	Status	—	100	15	Normal
TM48	Round	Normal	Special	60	100	15	Normal
TM49	Echoed Voice	Normal	Special	40	100	15	Normal
TM52	Focus Blast	Fighting	Special	120	70	5	Normal
TM56	Fling	Dark	Physical	—	100	10	Normal
TM57	Charge Beam	Electric	Special	50	90	10	Normal
TM59	Incinerate	Fire	Special	60	100	15	Many Others
TM67	Retaliate	Normal	Physical	70	100	5	Normal
TM68	Giga Impact	Normal	Physical	150	90	5	Normal
TM70	Flash	Normal	Status	—	100	20	Normal
TM73	Thunder Wave	Electric	Status	—	100	20	Normal
TM77	Psych Up	Normal	Status	—	—	10	Normal
TM85	Dream Eater	Psychic	Special	100	100	15	Normal
TM86	Grass Knot	Grass	Special	—	100	20	Normal
TM87	Swagger	Normal	Status	—	90	15	Normal
TM88	Sleep Talk	Normal	Status	—	—	10	Self
TM90	Substitute	Normal	Status	—	—	10	Self
TM94	Secret Power	Normal	Physical	70	100	20	Normal
TM98	Power-Up Punch	Fighting	Physical	40	100	20	Normal
TM99	Dazzling Gleam	Fairy	Special	80	100	10	Many Others
TM100	Confide	Normal	Status	—	—	20	Normal
HM04	Strength	Normal	Physical	80	100	15	Normal
HM06	Rock Smash	Fighting	Physical	40	100	15	Normal

MOVES LEARNED IN EXCHANGE FOR BP

Name	Type	Kind	Pow.	Acc.	PP	Range
Covet	Normal	Physical	60	100	25	Normal
Signal Beam	Bug	Special	75	100	15	Normal
Bounce	Flying	Physical	85	85	5	Normal
Thunder Punch	Electric	Physical	75	100	15	Normal
Fire Punch	Fire	Physical	75	100	15	Normal
Ice Punch	Ice	Physical	75	100	15	Normal
Magic Coat	Psychic	Status	—	—	15	Self
Gravity	Psychic	Status	—	—	5	Both Sides
Last Resort	Normal	Physical	140	100	5	Normal
Icy Wind	Ice	Special	55	95	15	Many Others
Zen Headbutt	Psychic	Physical	80	90	15	Normal
Hyper Voice	Normal	Special	90	100	10	Many Others
Iron Tail	Steel	Physical	100	75	15	Normal
Snore	Normal	Special	50	100	15	Normal
Knock Off	Dark	Physical	65	100	20	Normal
Role Play	Psychic	Status	—	—	10	Normal
Heal Bell	Normal	Status	—	—	5	Your Party
Drain Punch	Fighting	Physical	75	100	10	Normal
Focus Punch	Fighting	Physical	150	100	20	Normal
Shock Wave	Electric	Special	60	—	20	Normal
Water Pulse	Water	Special	60	100	20	Normal
After You	Normal	Status	—	—	15	Normal
Helping Hand	Normal	Status	—	—	20	1 Ally
Trick	Psychic	Status	—	100	10	Normal
Wonder Room	Psychic	Status	—	—	10	Both Sides
Endeavor	Normal	Physical	—	100	5	Normal
Recycle	Normal	Status	—	—	10	Self
Snatch	Dark	Status	—	—	10	Self
Stealth Rock	Rock	Status	—	—	20	Other Side

MOVES TAUGHT BY PEOPLE

Name	Type	Kind	Pow.	Acc.	PP	Range

National Pokédex **037** Hoenn Pokédex **160**

Vulpix

Fox Pokémon

Fire

HEIGHT: 2'00" WEIGHT: 21.8 lbs.

Same form for ♂ / ♀

Ω At the time of its birth, Vulpix has one white tail. The tail separates into six if this Pokémon receives plenty of love from its Trainer. The six tails become magnificently curled.

α Inside Vulpix's body burns a flame that never goes out. During the daytime, when the temperatures rise, this Pokémon releases flames from its mouth to prevent its body from growing too hot.

ABILITY
Flash Fire

HIDDEN ABILITY
Drought

EGG GROUPS
Field

STAT GROWTH RATES
HP
Attack
Defense
Sp. Atk
Sp. Def
Speed

ITEMS SOMETIMES HELD BY WILD POKÉMON
Charcoal

EVOLUTION

Fire Stone

Vulpix → Ninetales

MAIN WAY TO REGISTER IN THE NATIONAL POKÉDEX

Catch on Mt. Pyre (Exterior).

Damage taken in normal battles

Type		Type	
Normal	×1	Flying	×1
Fire	×0.5	Psychic	×1
Water	×2	Bug	×0.5
Grass	×0.5	Rock	×2
Electric	×1	Ghost	×1
Ice	×0.5	Dragon	×1
Fighting	×1	Dark	×1
Poison	×1	Steel	×0.5
Ground	×2	Fairy	×0.5

Damage taken in Inverse battles

Type		Type	
Normal	×1	Flying	×1
Fire	×2	Psychic	×1
Water	×0.5	Bug	×2
Grass	×2	Rock	×0.5
Electric	×1	Ghost	×1
Ice	×2	Dragon	×1
Fighting	×1	Dark	×1
Poison	×1	Steel	×2
Ground	×0.5	Fairy	×2

Can be used in
Inverse Battle
Battle Institute
Battle Maison
Random Matchup (Free Battle)
Random Matchup (Others)

LEVEL-UP MOVES

Lv.	Name	Type	Kind	Pow.	Acc.	PP	Range
1	Ember	Fire	Special	40	100	25	Normal
4	Tail Whip	Normal	Status	—	100	30	Many Others
7	Roar	Normal	Status	—	—	20	Normal
9	Baby-Doll Eyes	Fairy	Status	—	100	30	Normal
10	Quick Attack	Normal	Physical	40	100	30	Normal
12	Confuse Ray	Ghost	Status	—	100	10	Normal
15	Fire Spin	Fire	Special	35	85	15	Normal
18	Payback	Dark	Physical	50	100	10	Normal
20	Will-O-Wisp	Fire	Status	—	85	15	Normal
23	Feint Attack	Dark	Physical	60	—	20	Normal
26	Hex	Ghost	Special	65	100	10	Normal
28	Flame Burst	Fire	Special	70	100	15	Normal
31	Extrasensory	Psychic	Special	80	100	20	Normal
34	Safeguard	Normal	Status	—	—	25	Your Side
36	Flamethrower	Fire	Special	90	100	15	Normal
39	Imprison	Psychic	Status	—	—	10	Self
42	Fire Blast	Fire	Special	110	85	5	Normal
44	Grudge	Ghost	Status	—	—	5	Self
47	Captivate	Normal	Status	—	100	20	Many Others
50	Inferno	Fire	Special	100	50	5	Normal

TM & HM MOVES

No.	Name	Type	Kind	Pow.	Acc.	PP	Range
TM05	Roar	Normal	Status	—	—	20	Normal
TM06	Toxic	Poison	Status	—	90	10	Normal
TM10	Hidden Power	Normal	Special	60	100	15	Normal
TM11	Sunny Day	Fire	Status	—	—	5	Both Sides
TM17	Protect	Normal	Status	—	—	10	Self
TM20	Safeguard	Normal	Status	—	—	25	Your Side
TM21	Frustration	Normal	Physical	—	100	20	Normal
TM27	Return	Normal	Physical	—	100	20	Normal
TM28	Dig	Ground	Physical	80	100	10	Normal
TM32	Double Team	Normal	Status	—	—	15	Self
TM35	Flamethrower	Fire	Special	90	100	15	Normal
TM38	Fire Blast	Fire	Special	110	85	5	Normal
TM42	Facade	Normal	Physical	70	100	20	Normal
TM43	Flame Charge	Fire	Physical	50	100	20	Normal
TM44	Rest	Psychic	Status	—	—	10	Self
TM45	Attract	Normal	Status	—	100	15	Normal
TM48	Round	Normal	Special	60	100	15	Normal
TM50	Overheat	Fire	Special	130	90	5	Normal
TM53	Energy Ball	Grass	Special	90	100	10	Normal
TM59	Incinerate	Fire	Special	60	100	15	Many Others
TM61	Will-O-Wisp	Fire	Status	—	85	15	Normal
TM66	Payback	Dark	Physical	50	100	10	Normal
TM77	Psych Up	Normal	Status	—	—	10	Normal
TM87	Swagger	Normal	Status	—	90	15	Normal
TM88	Sleep Talk	Normal	Status	—	—	10	Self
TM90	Substitute	Normal	Status	—	—	10	Self
TM94	Secret Power	Normal	Physical	70	100	20	Normal
TM97	Dark Pulse	Dark	Special	80	100	15	Normal
TM100	Confide	Normal	Status	—	—	20	Normal

MOVES LEARNED IN EXCHANGE FOR BP

Name	Type	Kind	Pow.	Acc.	PP	Range
Covet	Normal	Physical	60	100	25	Normal
Foul Play	Dark	Physical	95	100	15	Normal
Zen Headbutt	Psychic	Physical	80	90	15	Normal
Iron Tail	Steel	Physical	100	75	15	Normal
Snore	Normal	Special	50	100	15	Normal
Heat Wave	Fire	Special	95	90	10	Many Others
Role Play	Psychic	Status	—	—	10	Normal
Pain Split	Normal	Status	—	—	20	Normal
Spite	Ghost	Status	—	100	10	Normal

MOVES TAUGHT BY PEOPLE

Name	Type	Kind	Pow.	Acc.	PP	Range

EGG MOVES

Name	Type	Kind	Pow.	Acc.	PP	Range
Feint Attack	Dark	Physical	60	—	20	Normal
Hypnosis	Psychic	Status	—	60	20	Normal
Flail	Normal	Physical	—	100	15	Normal
Spite	Ghost	Status	—	100	10	Normal
Disable	Normal	Status	—	100	20	Normal
Howl	Normal	Status	—	—	40	Self
Heat Wave	Fire	Special	95	90	10	Many Others
Flare Blitz	Fire	Physical	120	100	15	Normal
Extrasensory	Psychic	Special	80	100	20	Normal
Power Swap	Psychic	Status	—	—	10	Normal
Secret Power	Normal	Physical	70	100	20	Normal
Hex	Ghost	Special	65	100	10	Normal
Tail Slap	Normal	Physical	25	85	10	Normal
Captivate	Normal	Status	—	100	20	Many Others

National Pokédex **038** Hoenn Pokédex **161**

Ninetales

Fox Pokémon

Fire

HEIGHT: 3'07" WEIGHT: 43.9 lbs.

Same form for ♂ / ♀

Ω Ninetales casts a sinister light from its bright red eyes to gain total control over its foe's mind. This Pokémon is said to live for a thousand years.

α Legend has it that Ninetales came into being when nine wizards possessing sacred powers merged into one. This Pokémon is highly intelligent—it can understand human speech.

ABILITY
Flash Fire

HIDDEN ABILITY
Drought

EGG GROUPS
Field

STAT GROWTH RATES
HP ■■■
Attack ■■■■
Defense ■■■
Sp. Atk ■■■■
Sp. Def ■■■■
Speed ■■■■■

ITEMS SOMETIMES HELD BY WILD POKÉMON
—

EVOLUTION

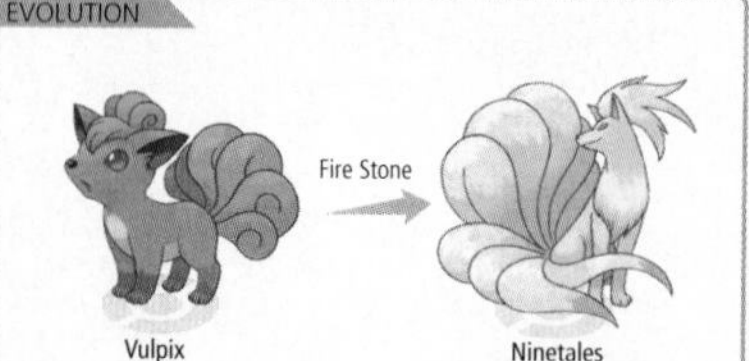

MAIN WAY TO REGISTER IN THE NATIONAL POKÉDEX

Use a Fire Stone on Vulpix.

Damage taken in normal battles

Type	×	Type	×
Normal	×1	Flying	×1
Fire	×0.5	Psychic	×1
Water	×2	Bug	×0.5
Grass	×0.5	Rock	×2
Electric	×1	Ghost	×1
Ice	×0.5	Dragon	×1
Fighting	×1	Dark	×1
Poison	×1	Steel	×0.5
Ground	×2	Fairy	×0.5

Damage taken in Inverse battles

Type	×	Type	×
Normal	×1	Flying	×1
Fire	×2	Psychic	×1
Water	×0.5	Bug	×2
Grass	×2	Rock	×0.5
Electric	×1	Ghost	×1
Ice	×2	Dragon	×1
Fighting	×1	Dark	×1
Poison	×1	Steel	×2
Ground	×0.5	Fairy	×2

Can be used in
Inverse Battle
Battle Institute
Battle Maison
Random Matchup (Free Battle)
Random Matchup (Others)

LEVEL-UP MOVES

Lv.	Name	Type	Kind	Pow.	Acc.	PP	Range
1	Imprison	Psychic	Status	—	—	10	Self
1	Nasty Plot	Dark	Status	—	—	20	Self
1	Flamethrower	Fire	Special	90	100	15	Normal
1	Quick Attack	Normal	Physical	40	100	30	Normal
1	Confuse Ray	Ghost	Status	—	100	10	Normal
1	Safeguard	Normal	Status	—	—	25	Your Side

TM & HM MOVES

No.	Name	Type	Kind	Pow.	Acc.	PP	Range
TM03	Psyshock	Psychic	Special	80	100	10	Normal
TM04	Calm Mind	Psychic	Status	—	—	20	Self
TM05	Roar	Normal	Status	—	—	20	Normal
TM06	Toxic	Poison	Status	—	90	10	Normal
TM10	Hidden Power	Normal	Special	60	100	15	Normal
TM11	Sunny Day	Fire	Status	—	—	5	Both Sides
TM15	Hyper Beam	Normal	Special	150	90	5	Normal
TM17	Protect	Normal	Status	—	—	10	Self
TM20	Safeguard	Normal	Status	—	—	25	Your Side
TM21	Frustration	Normal	Physical	—	100	20	Normal
TM22	Solar Beam	Grass	Special	120	100	10	Normal
TM27	Return	Normal	Physical	—	100	20	Normal
TM28	Dig	Ground	Physical	80	100	10	Normal
TM32	Double Team	Normal	Status	—	—	15	Self
TM35	Flamethrower	Fire	Special	90	100	15	Normal
TM38	Fire Blast	Fire	Special	110	85	5	Normal
TM42	Facade	Normal	Physical	70	100	20	Normal
TM43	Flame Charge	Fire	Physical	50	100	20	Normal
TM44	Rest	Psychic	Status	—	—	10	Self
TM45	Attract	Normal	Status	—	100	15	Normal
TM48	Round	Normal	Special	60	100	15	Normal
TM50	Overheat	Fire	Special	130	90	5	Normal
TM53	Energy Ball	Grass	Special	90	100	10	Normal
TM59	Incinerate	Fire	Special	60	100	15	Many Others
TM61	Will-O-Wisp	Fire	Status	—	85	15	Normal
TM66	Payback	Dark	Physical	50	100	10	Normal
TM68	Giga Impact	Normal	Physical	150	90	5	Normal
TM77	Psych Up	Normal	Status	—	—	10	Normal
TM85	Dream Eater	Psychic	Special	100	100	15	Normal
TM87	Swagger	Normal	Status	—	90	15	Normal
TM88	Sleep Talk	Normal	Status	—	—	10	Self
TM90	Substitute	Normal	Status	—	—	10	Self
TM94	Secret Power	Normal	Physical	70	100	20	Normal
TM97	Dark Pulse	Dark	Special	80	100	15	Normal
TM100	Confide	Normal	Status	—	—	20	Normal

MOVES LEARNED IN EXCHANGE FOR BP

Name	Type	Kind	Pow.	Acc.	PP	Range
Covet	Normal	Physical	60	100	25	Normal
Foul Play	Dark	Physical	95	100	15	Normal
Zen Headbutt	Psychic	Physical	80	90	15	Normal
Iron Tail	Steel	Physical	100	75	15	Normal
Snore	Normal	Special	50	100	15	Normal
Heat Wave	Fire	Special	95	90	10	Many Others
Role Play	Psychic	Status	—	—	10	Normal
Pain Split	Normal	Status	—	—	20	Normal
Spite	Ghost	Status	—	100	10	Normal

MOVES TAUGHT BY PEOPLE

Name	Type	Kind	Pow.	Acc.	PP	Range

National Pokédex **039** Hoenn Pokédex **143**

Jigglypuff

Balloon Pokémon

Normal Fairy

HEIGHT: 1'08" WEIGHT: 12.1 lbs.

Same form for ♂ / ♀

Ω Jigglypuff's vocal cords can freely adjust the wavelength of its voice. This Pokémon uses this ability to sing at precisely the right wavelength to make its foes most drowsy.

α When this Pokémon sings, it never pauses to breathe. If it is in a battle against an opponent that does not easily fall asleep, Jigglypuff cannot breathe, endangering its life.

ABILITIES
Cute Charm
Competitive

HIDDEN ABILITY
Friend Guard

EGG GROUPS
Fairy

STAT GROWTH RATES
HP ■■■■■
Attack ■■
Defense ■
Sp. Atk ■■
Sp. Def ■
Speed ■

ITEMS SOMETIMES HELD BY WILD POKÉMON
—

EVOLUTION

Igglybuff → (Level up with high friendship) → Jigglypuff → (Moon Stone) → Wigglytuff

MAIN WAY TO REGISTER IN THE NATIONAL POKÉDEX

Catch on Route 115.

Damage taken in normal battles

Type	×	Type	×
Normal	×1	Flying	×1
Fire	×1	Psychic	×1
Water	×1	Bug	×0.5
Grass	×1	Rock	×1
Electric	×1	Ghost	×0
Ice	×1	Dragon	×0
Fighting	×1	Dark	×0.5
Poison	×2	Steel	×2
Ground	×1	Fairy	×1

Damage taken in Inverse battles

Type	×	Type	×
Normal	×1	Flying	×1
Fire	×1	Psychic	×1
Water	×1	Bug	×2
Grass	×1	Rock	×1
Electric	×1	Ghost	×2
Ice	×1	Dragon	×2
Fighting	×1	Dark	×2
Poison	×0.5	Steel	×0.5
Ground	×1	Fairy	×1

Can be used in
Inverse Battle
Battle Institute
Battle Maison
Random Matchup (Free Battle)
Random Matchup (Others)

LEVEL-UP MOVES

Lv.	Name	Type	Kind	Pow.	Acc.	PP	Range
1	Sing	Normal	Status	—	55	15	Normal
3	Defense Curl	Normal	Status	—	—	40	Self
5	Pound	Normal	Physical	40	100	35	Normal
8	Play Nice	Normal	Status	—	—	20	Normal
11	Disarming Voice	Fairy	Special	40	—	15	Many Others
15	Disable	Normal	Status	—	100	20	Normal
18	Double Slap	Normal	Physical	15	85	10	Normal
21	Rollout	Rock	Physical	30	90	20	Normal
24	Round	Normal	Special	60	100	15	Normal
28	Wake-Up Slap	Fighting	Physical	70	100	10	Normal
32	Rest	Psychic	Status	—	—	10	Self
35	Body Slam	Normal	Physical	85	100	15	Normal
37	Mimic	Normal	Status	—	—	10	Normal
40	Gyro Ball	Steel	Physical	—	100	5	Normal
44	Hyper Voice	Normal	Special	90	100	10	Many Others
49	Double-Edge	Normal	Physical	120	100	15	Normal

TM & HM MOVES

No.	Name	Type	Kind	Pow.	Acc.	PP	Range
TM06	Toxic	Poison	Status	—	90	10	Normal
TM10	Hidden Power	Normal	Special	60	100	15	Normal
TM11	Sunny Day	Fire	Status	—	—	5	Both Sides
TM13	Ice Beam	Ice	Special	90	100	10	Normal
TM14	Blizzard	Ice	Special	110	70	5	Many Others
TM16	Light Screen	Psychic	Status	—	—	30	Your Side
TM17	Protect	Normal	Status	—	—	10	Self
TM18	Rain Dance	Water	Status	—	—	5	Both Sides
TM20	Safeguard	Normal	Status	—	—	25	Your Side
TM21	Frustration	Normal	Physical	—	100	20	Normal
TM22	Solar Beam	Grass	Special	120	100	10	Normal
TM24	Thunderbolt	Electric	Special	90	100	15	Normal
TM25	Thunder	Electric	Special	110	70	10	Normal
TM27	Return	Normal	Physical	—	100	20	Normal
TM28	Dig	Ground	Physical	80	100	10	Normal
TM29	Psychic	Psychic	Special	90	100	10	Normal
TM30	Shadow Ball	Ghost	Special	80	100	15	Normal
TM31	Brick Break	Fighting	Physical	75	100	15	Normal
TM32	Double Team	Normal	Status	—	—	15	Self
TM33	Reflect	Psychic	Status	—	—	20	Your Side
TM35	Flamethrower	Fire	Special	90	100	15	Normal
TM38	Fire Blast	Fire	Special	110	85	5	Normal
TM42	Facade	Normal	Physical	70	100	20	Normal
TM44	Rest	Psychic	Status	—	—	10	Self
TM45	Attract	Normal	Status	—	100	15	Normal
TM48	Round	Normal	Special	60	100	15	Normal
TM49	Echoed Voice	Normal	Special	40	100	15	Normal
TM56	Fling	Dark	Physical	—	100	10	Normal
TM57	Charge Beam	Electric	Special	50	90	10	Normal
TM59	Incinerate	Fire	Special	60	100	15	Many Others
TM67	Retaliate	Normal	Physical	70	100	5	Normal
TM70	Flash	Normal	Status	—	100	20	Normal
TM73	Thunder Wave	Electric	Status	—	100	20	Normal
TM74	Gyro Ball	Steel	Physical	—	100	5	Normal
TM77	Psych Up	Normal	Status	—	—	10	Normal
TM85	Dream Eater	Psychic	Special	100	100	15	Normal
TM86	Grass Knot	Grass	Special	—	100	20	Normal
TM87	Swagger	Normal	Status	—	90	15	Normal
TM88	Sleep Talk	Normal	Status	—	—	10	Self
TM90	Substitute	Normal	Status	—	—	10	Self
TM93	Wild Charge	Electric	Physical	90	100	15	Normal
TM94	Secret Power	Normal	Physical	70	100	20	Normal
TM98	Power-Up Punch	Fighting	Physical	40	100	20	Normal
TM99	Dazzling Gleam	Fairy	Special	80	100	10	Many Others
TM100	Confide	Normal	Status	—	—	20	Normal
HM04	Strength	Normal	Physical	80	100	15	Normal

MOVES LEARNED IN EXCHANGE FOR BP

Name	Type	Kind	Pow.	Acc.	PP	Range
Covet	Normal	Physical	60	100	25	Normal
Bounce	Flying	Physical	85	85	5	Normal
Thunder Punch	Electric	Physical	75	100	15	Normal
Fire Punch	Fire	Physical	75	100	15	Normal
Ice Punch	Ice	Physical	75	100	15	Normal
Magic Coat	Psychic	Status	—	—	15	Self
Gravity	Psychic	Status	—	—	5	Both Sides
Last Resort	Normal	Physical	140	100	5	Normal
Icy Wind	Ice	Special	55	95	15	Many Others
Hyper Voice	Normal	Special	90	100	10	Many Others
Snore	Normal	Special	50	100	15	Normal
Knock Off	Dark	Physical	65	100	20	Normal
Role Play	Psychic	Status	—	—	10	Normal
Heal Bell	Normal	Status	—	—	5	Your Party
Pain Split	Normal	Status	—	—	20	Normal
Drain Punch	Fighting	Physical	75	100	10	Normal
Focus Punch	Fighting	Physical	150	100	20	Normal
Shock Wave	Electric	Special	60	—	20	Normal
Water Pulse	Water	Special	60	100	20	Normal
Helping Hand	Normal	Status	—	—	20	1 Ally
Endeavor	Normal	Physical	—	100	5	Normal
Recycle	Normal	Status	—	—	10	Self
Snatch	Dark	Status	—	—	10	Self
Stealth Rock	Rock	Status	—	—	20	Other Side

MOVES TAUGHT BY PEOPLE

Name	Type	Kind	Pow.	Acc.	PP	Range

National Pokédex **040** Hoenn Pokédex **144**

Wigglytuff

Balloon Pokémon

Normal / Fairy

HEIGHT: 3'03" WEIGHT: 26.5 lbs.

Same form for ♂ / ♀

Ω Wigglytuff has large, saucerlike eyes. The surfaces of its eyes are alway covered with a thin layer of tears. If any dust gets in this Pokémon's eyes, it is quickly washed away.

α Wigglytuff's body is very flexible. By inhaling deeply, this Pokémon can inflate itself seemingly without end. Once inflated, Wigglytuff bounces along lightly like a balloon.

ABILITIES: Cute Charm, Competitive

HIDDEN ABILITY: Frisk

EGG GROUPS: Fairy

STAT GROWTH RATES: HP ■■■■■, Attack ■■■■, Defense ■■, Sp. Atk ■■■■, Sp. Def ■■, Speed ■■■

ITEMS SOMETIMES HELD BY WILD POKÉMON: —

EVOLUTION

MAIN WAY TO REGISTER IN THE NATIONAL POKÉDEX

Use a Moon Stone on Jigglypuff.

Damage taken in normal battles

Type		Type	
Normal	×1	Flying	×1
Fire	×1	Psychic	×1
Water	×1	Bug	×0.5
Grass	×1	Rock	×1
Electric	×1	Ghost	×0
Ice	×1	Dragon	×0
Fighting	×1	Dark	×0.5
Poison	×2	Steel	×2
Ground	×1	Fairy	×1

Damage taken in Inverse battles

Type		Type	
Normal	×1	Flying	×1
Fire	×1	Psychic	×1
Water	×1	Bug	×2
Grass	×1	Rock	×1
Electric	×1	Ghost	×2
Ice	×1	Dragon	×2
Fighting	×1	Dark	×2
Poison	×0.5	Steel	×0.5
Ground	×1	Fairy	×1

Can be used in
- Inverse Battle
- Battle Institute
- Battle Maison
- Random Matchup (Free Battle)
- Random Matchup (Others)

LEVEL-UP MOVES

Lv.	Name	Type	Kind	Pow.	Acc.	PP	Range
1	Double-Edge	Normal	Physical	120	100	15	Normal
1	Play Rough	Fairy	Physical	90	90	10	Normal
1	Sing	Normal	Status	—	55	15	Normal
1	Defense Curl	Normal	Status	—	—	40	Self
1	Disable	Normal	Status	—	100	20	Normal
1	Double Slap	Normal	Physical	15	85	10	Normal

TM & HM MOVES

No.	Name	Type	Kind	Pow.	Acc.	PP	Range
TM06	Toxic	Poison	Status	—	90	10	Normal
TM10	Hidden Power	Normal	Special	60	100	15	Normal
TM11	Sunny Day	Fire	Status	—	—	5	Both Sides
TM13	Ice Beam	Ice	Special	90	100	10	Normal
TM14	Blizzard	Ice	Special	110	70	5	Many Others
TM15	Hyper Beam	Normal	Special	150	90	5	Normal
TM16	Light Screen	Psychic	Status	—	—	30	Your Side
TM17	Protect	Normal	Status	—	—	10	Self
TM18	Rain Dance	Water	Status	—	—	5	Both Sides
TM20	Safeguard	Normal	Status	—	—	25	Your Side
TM21	Frustration	Normal	Physical	—	100	20	Normal
TM22	Solar Beam	Grass	Special	120	100	10	Normal
TM24	Thunderbolt	Electric	Special	90	100	15	Normal
TM25	Thunder	Electric	Special	110	70	10	Normal
TM27	Return	Normal	Physical	—	100	20	Normal
TM28	Dig	Ground	Physical	80	100	10	Normal
TM29	Psychic	Psychic	Special	90	100	10	Normal
TM30	Shadow Ball	Ghost	Special	80	100	15	Normal
TM31	Brick Break	Fighting	Physical	75	100	15	Normal
TM32	Double Team	Normal	Status	—	—	15	Self
TM33	Reflect	Psychic	Status	—	—	20	Your Side
TM35	Flamethrower	Fire	Special	90	100	15	Normal
TM38	Fire Blast	Fire	Special	110	85	5	Normal
TM42	Facade	Normal	Physical	70	100	20	Normal
TM44	Rest	Psychic	Status	—	—	10	Self
TM45	Attract	Normal	Status	—	100	15	Normal
TM48	Round	Normal	Special	60	100	15	Normal
TM49	Echoed Voice	Normal	Special	40	100	15	Normal
TM52	Focus Blast	Fighting	Special	120	70	5	Normal
TM56	Fling	Dark	Physical	—	100	10	Normal
TM57	Charge Beam	Electric	Special	50	90	10	Normal
TM59	Incinerate	Fire	Special	60	100	15	Many Others
TM67	Retaliate	Normal	Physical	70	100	5	Normal
TM68	Giga Impact	Normal	Physical	150	90	5	Normal
TM70	Flash	Normal	Status	—	100	20	Normal
TM73	Thunder Wave	Electric	Status	—	100	20	Normal
TM74	Gyro Ball	Steel	Physical	—	100	5	Normal
TM77	Psych Up	Normal	Status	—	—	10	Normal
TM85	Dream Eater	Psychic	Special	100	100	15	Normal
TM86	Grass Knot	Grass	Special	—	100	20	Normal
TM87	Swagger	Normal	Status	—	90	15	Normal
TM88	Sleep Talk	Normal	Status	—	—	10	Self
TM90	Substitute	Normal	Status	—	—	10	Self
TM93	Wild Charge	Electric	Physical	90	100	15	Normal
TM94	Secret Power	Normal	Physical	70	100	20	Normal
TM98	Power-Up Punch	Fighting	Physical	40	100	20	Normal
TM99	Dazzling Gleam	Fairy	Special	80	100	10	Many Others
TM100	Confide	Normal	Status	—	—	20	Normal
HM04	Strength	Normal	Physical	80	100	15	Normal

MOVES LEARNED IN EXCHANGE FOR BP

Name	Type	Kind	Pow.	Acc.	PP	Range
Covet	Normal	Physical	60	100	25	Normal
Bounce	Flying	Physical	85	85	5	Normal
Thunder Punch	Electric	Physical	75	100	15	Normal
Fire Punch	Fire	Physical	75	100	15	Normal
Ice Punch	Ice	Physical	75	100	15	Normal
Magic Coat	Psychic	Status	—	—	15	Self
Gravity	Psychic	Status	—	—	5	Both Sides
Last Resort	Normal	Physical	140	100	5	Normal
Icy Wind	Ice	Special	55	95	15	Many Others
Hyper Voice	Normal	Special	90	100	10	Many Others
Snore	Normal	Special	50	100	15	Normal
Knock Off	Dark	Physical	65	100	20	Normal
Role Play	Psychic	Status	—	—	10	Normal
Heal Bell	Normal	Status	—	—	5	Your Party
Pain Split	Normal	Status	—	—	20	Normal
Drain Punch	Fighting	Physical	75	100	10	Normal
Focus Punch	Fighting	Physical	150	100	20	Normal
Shock Wave	Electric	Special	60	—	20	Normal
Water Pulse	Water	Special	60	100	20	Normal
Helping Hand	Normal	Status	—	—	20	1 Ally
Magic Room	Psychic	Status	—	—	10	Both Sides
Endeavor	Normal	Physical	—	100	5	Normal
Recycle	Normal	Status	—	—	10	Self
Snatch	Dark	Status	—	—	10	Self
Stealth Rock	Rock	Status	—	—	20	Other Side

MOVES TAUGHT BY PEOPLE

Name	Type	Kind	Pow.	Acc.	PP	Range

National Pokédex **041** Hoenn Pokédex **065**

Zubat

Bat Pokémon

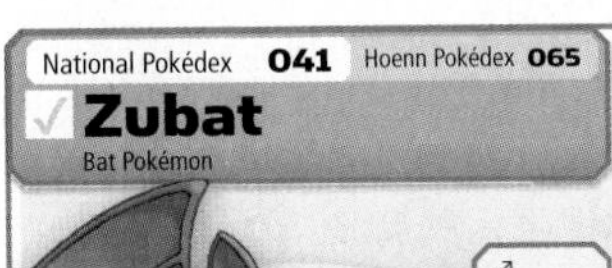

Poison / Flying

HEIGHT: 2'07" WEIGHT: 16.5 lbs.

The male has larger fangs. The female has smaller fangs.

♂ ♀

Ω Zubat remains quietly unmoving in a dark spot during the bright daylight hours. It does so because prolonged exposure to the sun causes its body to become slightly burned.

α Zubat avoids sunlight because exposure causes it to become unhealthy. During the daytime, it stays in caves or under the eaves of old houses, sleeping while hanging upside down.

ABILITY: Inner Focus

HIDDEN ABILITY: Infiltrator

EGG GROUPS: Flying

STAT GROWTH RATES: HP ■■, Attack ■■, Defense ■■, Sp. Atk ■, Sp. Def ■■, Speed ■■■

ITEMS SOMETIMES HELD BY WILD POKÉMON: —

EVOLUTION

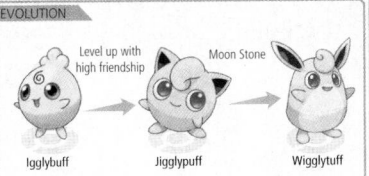

Zubat → Lv. 22 → Golbat → Level up with high friendship → Crobat

MAIN WAY TO REGISTER IN THE NATIONAL POKÉDEX

Catch in Granite Cave (1F).

Damage taken in normal battles

Type		Type	
Normal	×1	Flying	×1
Fire	×1	Psychic	×2
Water	×1	Bug	×0.25
Grass	×0.25	Rock	×2
Electric	×2	Ghost	×1
Ice	×2	Dragon	×1
Fighting	×0.25	Dark	×1
Poison	×0.5	Steel	×1
Ground	×0	Fairy	×0.5

Damage taken in Inverse battles

Type		Type	
Normal	×1	Flying	×1
Fire	×1	Psychic	×0.5
Water	×1	Bug	×4
Grass	×4	Rock	×0.5
Electric	×0.5	Ghost	×1
Ice	×0.5	Dragon	×1
Fighting	×4	Dark	×1
Poison	×2	Steel	×1
Ground	×1	Fairy	×2

Can be used in
- Inverse Battle
- Battle Institute
- Battle Maison
- Random Matchup (Free Battle)
- Random Matchup (Others)

LEVEL-UP MOVES

Lv.	Name	Type	Kind	Pow.	Acc.	PP	Range
1	Leech Life	Bug	Physical	20	100	15	Normal
5	Supersonic	Normal	Status	—	55	20	Normal
7	Astonish	Ghost	Physical	30	100	15	Normal
11	Bite	Dark	Physical	60	100	25	Normal
13	Wing Attack	Flying	Physical	60	100	35	Normal
17	Confuse Ray	Ghost	Status	—	100	10	Normal
19	Air Cutter	Flying	Special	60	95	25	Many Others
23	Swift	Normal	Special	60	—	20	Many Others
25	Poison Fang	Poison	Physical	50	100	15	Normal
29	Mean Look	Normal	Status	—	—	5	Normal
31	Acrobatics	Flying	Physical	55	100	15	Normal
35	Haze	Ice	Status	—	—	30	Both Sides
37	Venoshock	Poison	Special	65	100	10	Normal
41	Air Slash	Flying	Special	75	95	15	Normal
43	Quick Guard	Fighting	Status	—	—	15	Your Side

TM & HM MOVES

No.	Name	Type	Kind	Pow.	Acc.	PP	Range
TM06	Toxic	Poison	Status	—	90	10	Normal
TM09	Venoshock	Poison	Special	65	100	10	Normal
TM10	Hidden Power	Normal	Special	60	100	15	Normal
TM11	Sunny Day	Fire	Status	—	—	5	Both Sides
TM12	Taunt	Dark	Status	—	100	20	Normal
TM17	Protect	Normal	Status	—	—	10	Self
TM18	Rain Dance	Water	Status	—	—	5	Both Sides
TM19	Roost	Flying	Status	—	—	10	Self
TM21	Frustration	Normal	Physical	—	100	20	Normal
TM27	Return	Normal	Physical	—	100	20	Normal
TM30	Shadow Ball	Ghost	Special	80	100	15	Normal
TM32	Double Team	Normal	Status	—	—	15	Self
TM36	Sludge Bomb	Poison	Special	90	100	10	Normal
TM40	Aerial Ace	Flying	Physical	60	—	20	Normal
TM41	Torment	Dark	Status	—	100	15	Normal
TM42	Facade	Normal	Physical	70	100	20	Normal
TM44	Rest	Psychic	Status	—	—	10	Self
TM45	Attract	Normal	Status	—	100	15	Normal
TM46	Thief	Dark	Physical	60	100	25	Normal
TM48	Round	Normal	Special	60	100	15	Normal
TM51	Steel Wing	Steel	Physical	70	90	25	Normal
TM62	Acrobatics	Flying	Physical	55	100	15	Normal
TM66	Payback	Dark	Physical	50	100	10	Normal
TM87	Swagger	Normal	Status	—	90	15	Normal
TM88	Sleep Talk	Normal	Status	—	—	10	Self
TM89	U-turn	Bug	Physical	70	100	20	Normal
TM90	Substitute	Normal	Status	—	—	10	Self
TM94	Secret Power	Normal	Physical	70	100	20	Normal
TM100	Confide	Normal	Status	—	—	20	Normal
HM02	Fly	Flying	Physical	90	95	15	Normal

MOVES LEARNED IN EXCHANGE FOR BP

Name	Type	Kind	Pow.	Acc.	PP	Range
Super Fang	Normal	Physical	—	90	10	Normal
Uproar	Normal	Special	90	100	10	1 Random
Zen Headbutt	Psychic	Physical	80	90	15	Normal
Snore	Normal	Special	50	100	15	Normal
Heat Wave	Fire	Special	95	90	10	Many Others
Tailwind	Flying	Status	—	—	15	Your Side
Giga Drain	Grass	Special	75	100	10	Normal
Snatch	Dark	Status	—	—	10	Self

MOVES TAUGHT BY PEOPLE

Name	Type	Kind	Pow.	Acc.	PP	Range

EGG MOVES

Name	Type	Kind	Pow.	Acc.	PP	Range
Quick Attack	Normal	Physical	40	100	30	Normal
Pursuit	Dark	Physical	40	100	20	Normal
Feint Attack	Dark	Physical	60	—	20	Normal
Gust	Flying	Special	40	100	35	Normal
Whirlwind	Normal	Status	—	—	20	Normal
Curse	Ghost	Status	—	—	10	Varies
Nasty Plot	Dark	Status	—	—	20	Self
Hypnosis	Psychic	Status	—	60	20	Normal
Zen Headbutt	Psychic	Physical	80	90	15	Normal
Brave Bird	Flying	Physical	120	100	15	Normal
Giga Drain	Grass	Special	75	100	10	Normal
Steel Wing	Steel	Physical	70	90	25	Normal
Defog	Flying	Status	—	—	15	Normal
Venom Drench	Poison	Status	—	100	20	Many Others

National Pokédex **042** Hoenn Pokédex **066**

Golbat

Bat Pokémon

Poison | Flying

HEIGHT: 5'03" WEIGHT: 121.3 lbs.

The male has larger fangs. The female has smaller fangs.

Ω Golbat loves to drink the blood of living things. It is particularly active in the pitch black of night. This Pokémon flits around in the night skies, seeking fresh blood.

α Golbat bites down on prey with its four fangs and drinks the victim's blood. It becomes active on inky dark moonless nights, flying around to attack people and Pokémon.

ABILITY: Inner Focus

HIDDEN ABILITY: Infiltrator

EGG GROUPS: Flying

STAT GROWTH RATES: HP ■■■ / Attack ■■■■ / Defense ■■■ / Sp. Atk ■■■ / Sp. Def ■■■ / Speed ■■■■■

ITEMS SOMETIMES HELD BY WILD POKÉMON: —

EVOLUTION

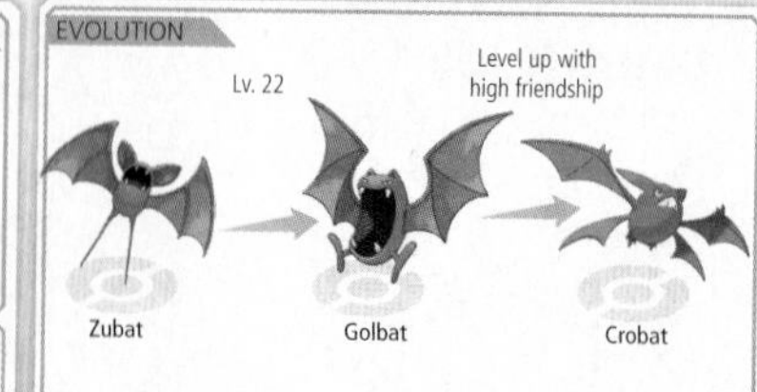

MAIN WAY TO REGISTER IN THE NATIONAL POKÉDEX

Catch in Shoal Cave (1F).

Damage taken in normal battles

Type		Type	
Normal	×1	Flying	×1
Fire	×1	Psychic	×2
Water	×1	Bug	×0.25
Grass	×0.25	Rock	×2
Electric	×2	Ghost	×1
Ice	×2	Dragon	×1
Fighting	×0.25	Dark	×1
Poison	×0.5	Steel	×1
Ground	×0	Fairy	×0.5

Damage taken in Inverse battles

Type		Type	
Normal	×1	Flying	×1
Fire	×1	Psychic	×0.5
Water	×1	Bug	×4
Grass	×4	Rock	×0.5
Electric	×0.5	Ghost	×1
Ice	×0.5	Dragon	×1
Fighting	×4	Dark	×1
Poison	×2	Steel	×1
Ground	×1	Fairy	×2

Can be used in
- Inverse Battle
- Battle Institute
- Battle Maison
- Random Matchup (Free Battle)
- Random Matchup (Others)

LEVEL-UP MOVES

Lv.	Name	Type	Kind	Pow.	Acc.	PP	Range
1	Screech	Normal	Status	—	85	40	Normal
1	Leech Life	Bug	Physical	20	100	15	Normal
1	Supersonic	Normal	Status	—	55	20	Normal
1	Astonish	Ghost	Physical	30	100	15	Normal
1	Bite	Dark	Physical	60	100	25	Normal
5	Supersonic	Normal	Status	—	55	20	Normal
7	Astonish	Ghost	Physical	30	100	15	Normal
11	Bite	Dark	Physical	60	100	25	Normal
13	Wing Attack	Flying	Physical	60	100	35	Normal
17	Confuse Ray	Ghost	Status	—	100	10	Normal
19	Air Cutter	Flying	Special	60	95	25	Many Others
24	Swift	Normal	Special	60	—	20	Many Others
27	Poison Fang	Poison	Physical	50	100	15	Normal
32	Mean Look	Normal	Status	—	—	5	Normal
35	Acrobatics	Flying	Physical	55	100	15	Normal
40	Haze	Ice	Status	—	—	30	Both Sides
43	Venoshock	Poison	Special	65	100	10	Normal
48	Air Slash	Flying	Special	75	95	15	Normal
51	Quick Guard	Fighting	Status	—	—	15	Your Side

TM & HM MOVES

No.	Name	Type	Kind	Pow.	Acc.	PP	Range
TM06	Toxic	Poison	Status	—	90	10	Normal
TM09	Venoshock	Poison	Special	65	100	10	Normal
TM10	Hidden Power	Normal	Special	60	100	15	Normal
TM11	Sunny Day	Fire	Status	—	—	5	Both Sides
TM12	Taunt	Dark	Status	—	100	20	Normal
TM15	Hyper Beam	Normal	Special	150	90	5	Normal
TM17	Protect	Normal	Status	—	—	10	Self
TM18	Rain Dance	Water	Status	—	—	5	Both Sides
TM19	Roost	Flying	Status	—	—	10	Self
TM21	Frustration	Normal	Physical	—	100	20	Normal
TM27	Return	Normal	Physical	—	100	20	Normal
TM30	Shadow Ball	Ghost	Special	80	100	15	Normal
TM32	Double Team	Normal	Status	—	—	15	Self
TM36	Sludge Bomb	Poison	Special	90	100	10	Normal
TM40	Aerial Ace	Flying	Physical	60	—	20	Normal
TM41	Torment	Dark	Status	—	100	15	Normal
TM42	Facade	Normal	Physical	70	100	20	Normal
TM44	Rest	Psychic	Status	—	—	10	Self
TM45	Attract	Normal	Status	—	100	15	Normal
TM46	Thief	Dark	Physical	60	100	25	Normal
TM48	Round	Normal	Special	60	100	15	Normal
TM51	Steel Wing	Steel	Physical	70	90	25	Normal
TM62	Acrobatics	Flying	Physical	55	100	15	Normal
TM66	Payback	Dark	Physical	50	100	10	Normal
TM68	Giga Impact	Normal	Physical	150	90	5	Normal
TM87	Swagger	Normal	Status	—	90	15	Normal
TM88	Sleep Talk	Normal	Status	—	—	10	Self
TM89	U-turn	Bug	Physical	70	100	20	Normal
TM90	Substitute	Normal	Status	—	—	10	Self
TM94	Secret Power	Normal	Physical	70	100	20	Normal
TM100	Confide	Normal	Status	—	—	20	Normal
HM02	Fly	Flying	Physical	90	95	15	Normal

MOVES LEARNED IN EXCHANGE FOR BP

Name	Type	Kind	Pow.	Acc.	PP	Range
Super Fang	Normal	Physical	—	90	10	Normal
Uproar	Normal	Special	90	100	10	1 Random
Zen Headbutt	Psychic	Physical	80	90	15	Normal
Snore	Normal	Special	50	100	15	Normal
Heat Wave	Fire	Special	95	90	10	Many Others
Tailwind	Flying	Status	—	—	15	Your Side
Giga Drain	Grass	Special	75	100	10	Normal
Snatch	Dark	Status	—	—	10	Self

MOVES TAUGHT BY PEOPLE

Name	Type	Kind	Pow.	Acc.	PP	Range

National Pokédex **043** Hoenn Pokédex **091**

Oddish

Weed Pokémon

Grass | Poison

HEIGHT: 1'08" WEIGHT: 11.9 lbs.

Same form for ♂ / ♀

Ω During the daytime, Oddish buries itself in soil to absorb nutrients from the ground using its entire body. The more fertile the soil, the glossier its leaves become.

α Oddish searches for fertile, nutrient-rich soil, then plants itself. During the daytime, while it is planted, this Pokémon's feet are thought to change shape and become similar to the roots of trees.

ABILITY: Chlorophyll

HIDDEN ABILITY: Run Away

EGG GROUPS: Grass

STAT GROWTH RATES: HP ■■ / Attack ■■■ / Defense ■■■ / Sp. Atk ■■■■ / Sp. Def ■■■ / Speed ■■

ITEMS SOMETIMES HELD BY WILD POKÉMON: Absorb Bulb

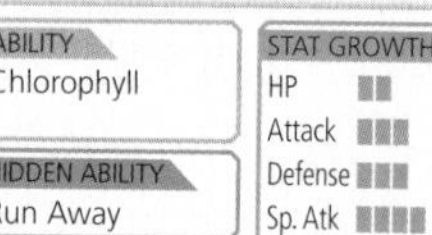

EVOLUTION

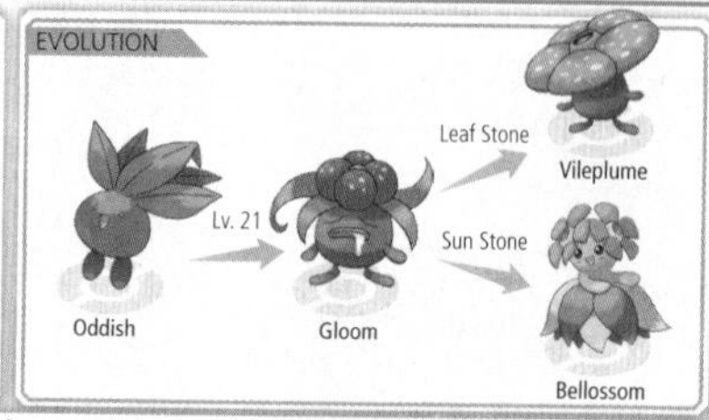

MAIN WAY TO REGISTER IN THE NATIONAL POKÉDEX

Catch on Route 110.

Damage taken in normal battles

Type		Type	
Normal	×1	Flying	×2
Fire	×2	Psychic	×2
Water	×0.5	Bug	×1
Grass	×0.25	Rock	×1
Electric	×0.5	Ghost	×1
Ice	×2	Dragon	×1
Fighting	×0.5	Dark	×1
Poison	×1	Steel	×1
Ground	×1	Fairy	×0.5

Damage taken in Inverse battles

Type		Type	
Normal	×1	Flying	×0.5
Fire	×0.5	Psychic	×0.5
Water	×2	Bug	×1
Grass	×4	Rock	×1
Electric	×2	Ghost	×1
Ice	×0.5	Dragon	×1
Fighting	×2	Dark	×1
Poison	×1	Steel	×1
Ground	×1	Fairy	×2

Can be used in
- Inverse Battle
- Battle Institute
- Battle Maison
- Random Matchup (Free Battle)
- Random Matchup (Others)

LEVEL-UP MOVES

Lv.	Name	Type	Kind	Pow.	Acc.	PP	Range
1	Absorb	Grass	Special	20	100	25	Normal
5	Sweet Scent	Normal	Status	—	100	20	Many Others
9	Acid	Poison	Special	40	100	30	Many Others
13	Poison Powder	Poison	Status	—	75	35	Normal
14	Stun Spore	Grass	Status	—	75	30	Normal
15	Sleep Powder	Grass	Status	—	75	15	Normal
19	Mega Drain	Grass	Special	40	100	15	Normal
23	Lucky Chant	Normal	Status	—	—	30	Your Side
27	Moonlight	Fairy	Status	—	—	5	Self
31	Giga Drain	Grass	Special	75	100	10	Normal
35	Toxic	Poison	Status	—	90	10	Normal
39	Natural Gift	Normal	Physical	—	100	15	Normal
43	Moonblast	Fairy	Special	95	100	15	Normal
47	Grassy Terrain	Grass	Status	—	—	10	Both Sides
51	Petal Dance	Grass	Special	120	100	10	1 Random

TM & HM MOVES

No.	Name	Type	Kind	Pow.	Acc.	PP	Range
TM06	Toxic	Poison	Status	—	90	10	Normal
TM09	Venoshock	Poison	Special	65	100	10	Normal
TM10	Hidden Power	Normal	Special	60	100	15	Normal
TM11	Sunny Day	Fire	Status	—	—	5	Both Sides
TM17	Protect	Normal	Status	—	—	10	Self
TM21	Frustration	Normal	Physical	—	100	20	Normal
TM22	Solar Beam	Grass	Special	120	100	10	Normal
TM27	Return	Normal	Physical	—	100	20	Normal
TM32	Double Team	Normal	Status	—	—	15	Self
TM36	Sludge Bomb	Poison	Special	90	100	10	Normal
TM42	Facade	Normal	Physical	70	100	20	Normal
TM44	Rest	Psychic	Status	—	—	10	Self
TM45	Attract	Normal	Status	—	100	15	Normal
TM48	Round	Normal	Special	60	100	15	Normal
TM53	Energy Ball	Grass	Special	90	100	10	Normal
TM70	Flash	Normal	Status	—	100	20	Normal
TM75	Swords Dance	Normal	Status	—	—	20	Self
TM83	Infestation	Bug	Special	20	100	20	Normal
TM86	Grass Knot	Grass	Special	—	100	20	Normal
TM87	Swagger	Normal	Status	—	90	15	Normal
TM88	Sleep Talk	Normal	Status	—	—	10	Self
TM90	Substitute	Normal	Status	—	—	10	Self
TM94	Secret Power	Normal	Physical	70	100	20	Normal
TM96	Nature Power	Normal	Status	—	—	20	Normal
TM99	Dazzling Gleam	Fairy	Special	80	100	10	Many Others
TM100	Confide	Normal	Status	—	—	20	Normal
HM01	Cut	Normal	Physical	50	95	30	Normal

MOVES LEARNED IN EXCHANGE FOR BP

Name	Type	Kind	Pow.	Acc.	PP	Range
Seed Bomb	Grass	Physical	80	100	15	Normal
Snore	Normal	Special	50	100	15	Normal
Synthesis	Grass	Status	—	—	5	Self
Giga Drain	Grass	Special	75	100	10	Normal
Gastro Acid	Poison	Status	—	100	10	Normal
Worry Seed	Grass	Status	—	100	10	Normal
After You	Normal	Status	—	—	15	Normal

MOVES TAUGHT BY PEOPLE

Name	Type	Kind	Pow.	Acc.	PP	Range

EGG MOVES

Name	Type	Kind	Pow.	Acc.	PP	Range
Razor Leaf	Grass	Physical	55	95	25	Many Others
Flail	Normal	Physical	—	100	15	Normal
Synthesis	Grass	Status	—	—	5	Self
Charm	Fairy	Status	—	100	20	Normal
Ingrain	Grass	Status	—	—	20	Self
Tickle	Normal	Status	—	100	20	Normal
Teeter Dance	Normal	Status	—	100	20	Adjacent
Secret Power	Normal	Physical	70	100	20	Normal
Nature Power	Normal	Status	—	—	20	Normal
After You	Normal	Status	—	—	15	Normal

National Pokédex **044** Hoenn Pokédex **092**

Gloom

Weed Pokémon

Grass Poison

HEIGHT: 2'07" WEIGHT: 19 lbs.

The male has a smaller-figured pattern.
The female has a larger-figured pattern.

♂ ♀

Ω Gloom releases a foul fragrance from the pistil of its flower. When faced with danger, the stench worsens. If this Pokémon is feeling calm and secure, it does not release its usual stinky aroma.

α From its mouth Gloom drips honey that smells absolutely horrible. Apparently, it loves the horrid stench. It sniffs the noxious fumes and then drools even more of its honey.

ABILITY
Chlorophyll

HIDDEN ABILITY
Stench

EGG GROUPS
Grass

STAT GROWTH RATES
HP ▮▮▮
Attack ▮▮▮
Defense ▮▮▮
Sp. Atk ▮▮▮▮
Sp. Def ▮▮▮
Speed ▮▮

ITEMS SOMETIMES HELD BY WILD POKÉMON
Absorb Bulb

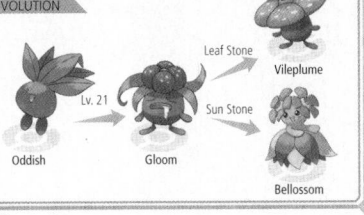

EVOLUTION
Oddish → Lv. 21 → Gloom → Leaf Stone → Vileplume
Gloom → Sun Stone → Bellossom

MAIN WAY TO REGISTER IN THE NATIONAL POKÉDEX

Catch in the very tall grass on Route 119.

Damage taken in normal battles

Normal	×1	Flying	×2
Fire	×2	Psychic	×2
Water	×0.5	Bug	×1
Grass	×0.25	Rock	×1
Electric	×0.5	Ghost	×1
Ice	×2	Dragon	×1
Fighting	×0.5	Dark	×1
Poison	×1	Steel	×1
Ground	×1	Fairy	×0.5

Damage taken in Inverse battles

Normal	×1	Flying	×0.5
Fire	×0.5	Psychic	×0.5
Water	×2	Bug	×1
Grass	×4	Rock	×1
Electric	×2	Ghost	×1
Ice	×0.5	Dragon	×1
Fighting	×2	Dark	×1
Poison	×1	Steel	×1
Ground	×1	Fairy	×2

Can be used in
Inverse Battle
Battle Institute
Battle Maison
Random Matchup (Free Battle)
Random Matchup (Others)

LEVEL-UP MOVES

Lv.	Name	Type	Kind	Pow.	Acc.	PP	Range
1	Absorb	Grass	Special	20	100	25	Normal
1	Sweet Scent	Normal	Status	—	100	20	Many Others
1	Acid	Poison	Special	40	100	30	Many Others
5	Sweet Scent	Normal	Status	—	100	20	Many Others
9	Acid	Poison	Special	40	100	30	Many Others
13	Poison Powder	Poison	Status	—	75	35	Normal
14	Stun Spore	Grass	Status	—	75	30	Normal
15	Sleep Powder	Grass	Status	—	75	15	Normal
19	Mega Drain	Grass	Special	40	100	15	Normal
24	Lucky Chant	Normal	Status	—	—	30	Your Side
29	Moonlight	Fairy	Status	—	—	5	Self
34	Giga Drain	Grass	Special	75	100	10	Normal
39	Toxic	Poison	Status	—	90	10	Normal
44	Natural Gift	Normal	Physical	—	100	15	Normal
49	Petal Blizzard	Grass	Physical	90	100	15	Adjacent
54	Grassy Terrain	Grass	Status	—	—	10	Both Sides
59	Petal Dance	Grass	Special	120	100	10	1 Random

TM & HM MOVES

No.	Name	Type	Kind	Pow.	Acc.	PP	Range
TM06	Toxic	Poison	Status	—	90	10	Normal
TM09	Venoshock	Poison	Special	65	100	10	Normal
TM10	Hidden Power	Normal	Special	60	100	15	Normal
TM11	Sunny Day	Fire	Status	—	—	5	Both Sides
TM17	Protect	Normal	Status	—	—	10	Self
TM21	Frustration	Normal	Physical	—	100	20	Normal
TM22	Solar Beam	Grass	Special	120	100	10	Normal
TM27	Return	Normal	Physical	—	100	20	Normal
TM32	Double Team	Normal	Status	—	—	15	Self
TM36	Sludge Bomb	Poison	Special	90	100	10	Normal
TM42	Facade	Normal	Physical	70	100	20	Normal
TM44	Rest	Psychic	Status	—	—	10	Self
TM45	Attract	Normal	Status	—	100	15	Normal
TM48	Round	Normal	Special	60	100	15	Normal
TM53	Energy Ball	Grass	Special	90	100	10	Normal
TM56	Fling	Dark	Physical	—	100	10	Normal
TM70	Flash	Normal	Status	—	100	20	Normal
TM75	Swords Dance	Normal	Status	—	—	20	Self
TM83	Infestation	Bug	Special	20	100	20	Normal
TM86	Grass Knot	Grass	Special	—	100	20	Normal
TM87	Swagger	Normal	Status	—	90	15	Normal
TM88	Sleep Talk	Normal	Status	—	—	10	Self
TM90	Substitute	Normal	Status	—	—	10	Self
TM94	Secret Power	Normal	Physical	70	100	20	Normal
TM96	Nature Power	Normal	Status	—	—	20	Normal
TM99	Dazzling Gleam	Fairy	Special	80	100	10	Many Others
TM100	Confide	Normal	Status	—	—	20	Normal
HM01	Cut	Normal	Physical	50	95	30	Normal

MOVES LEARNED IN EXCHANGE FOR BP

Name	Type	Kind	Pow.	Acc.	PP	Range
Seed Bomb	Grass	Physical	80	100	15	Normal
Snore	Normal	Special	50	100	15	Normal
Synthesis	Grass	Status	—	—	5	Self
Giga Drain	Grass	Special	75	100	10	Normal
Drain Punch	Fighting	Physical	75	100	10	Normal
Gastro Acid	Poison	Status	—	100	10	Normal
Worry Seed	Grass	Status	—	100	10	Normal
After You	Normal	Status	—	—	15	Normal

MOVES TAUGHT BY PEOPLE

Name	Type	Kind	Pow.	Acc.	PP	Range

National Pokédex **045** Hoenn Pokédex **093**

Vileplume

Flower Pokémon

Grass Poison

HEIGHT: 3'11" WEIGHT: 41 lbs.

The male has a smaller-figured pattern.
The female has a larger-figured pattern.

♂ ♀

Ω Vileplume's toxic pollen triggers atrocious allergy attacks. That's why it is advisable never to approach any attractive flowers in a jungle, however pretty they may be.

α Vileplume has the world's largest petals. They are used to attract prey that are then doused with toxic spores. Once the prey are immobilized, this Pokémon catches and devours them.

ABILITY
Chlorophyll

HIDDEN ABILITY
Effect Spore

EGG GROUPS
Grass

STAT GROWTH RATES
HP ▮▮▮
Attack ▮▮▮▮
Defense ▮▮▮▮
Sp. Atk ▮▮▮▮▮
Sp. Def ▮▮▮▮
Speed ▮▮▮

ITEMS SOMETIMES HELD BY WILD POKÉMON
—

EVOLUTION
Oddish → Lv. 21 → Gloom → Leaf Stone → Vileplume

MAIN WAY TO REGISTER IN THE NATIONAL POKÉDEX

Use a Leaf Stone on Gloom.

Damage taken in normal battles

Normal	×1	Flying	×2
Fire	×2	Psychic	×2
Water	×0.5	Bug	×1
Grass	×0.25	Rock	×1
Electric	×0.5	Ghost	×1
Ice	×2	Dragon	×1
Fighting	×0.5	Dark	×1
Poison	×1	Steel	×1
Ground	×1	Fairy	×0.5

Damage taken in Inverse battles

Normal	×1	Flying	×0.5
Fire	×0.5	Psychic	×0.5
Water	×2	Bug	×1
Grass	×4	Rock	×1
Electric	×2	Ghost	×1
Ice	×0.5	Dragon	×1
Fighting	×2	Dark	×1
Poison	×1	Steel	×1
Ground	×1	Fairy	×2

Can be used in
Inverse Battle
Battle Institute
Battle Maison
Random Matchup (Free Battle)
Random Matchup (Others)

LEVEL-UP MOVES

Lv.	Name	Type	Kind	Pow.	Acc.	PP	Range
1	Mega Drain	Grass	Special	40	100	15	Normal
1	Aromatherapy	Grass	Status	—	—	5	Your Party
1	Poison Powder	Poison	Status	—	75	35	Normal
1	Stun Spore	Grass	Status	—	75	30	Normal
49	Petal Blizzard	Grass	Physical	90	100	15	Adjacent
59	Petal Dance	Grass	Special	120	100	10	1 Random
64	Solar Beam	Grass	Special	120	100	10	Normal

TM & HM MOVES

No.	Name	Type	Kind	Pow.	Acc.	PP	Range
TM06	Toxic	Poison	Status	—	90	10	Normal
TM09	Venoshock	Poison	Special	65	100	10	Normal
TM10	Hidden Power	Normal	Special	60	100	15	Normal
TM11	Sunny Day	Fire	Status	—	—	5	Both Sides
TM15	Hyper Beam	Normal	Special	150	90	5	Normal
TM17	Protect	Normal	Status	—	—	10	Self
TM20	Safeguard	Normal	Status	—	—	25	Your Side
TM21	Frustration	Normal	Physical	—	100	20	Normal
TM22	Solar Beam	Grass	Special	120	100	10	Normal
TM27	Return	Normal	Physical	—	100	20	Normal
TM32	Double Team	Normal	Status	—	—	15	Self
TM36	Sludge Bomb	Poison	Special	90	100	10	Normal
TM42	Facade	Normal	Physical	70	100	20	Normal
TM44	Rest	Psychic	Status	—	—	10	Self
TM45	Attract	Normal	Status	—	100	15	Normal
TM48	Round	Normal	Special	60	100	15	Normal
TM53	Energy Ball	Grass	Special	90	100	10	Normal
TM56	Fling	Dark	Physical	—	100	10	Normal
TM68	Giga Impact	Normal	Physical	150	90	5	Normal
TM70	Flash	Normal	Status	—	100	20	Normal
TM75	Swords Dance	Normal	Status	—	—	20	Self
TM83	Infestation	Bug	Special	20	100	20	Normal
TM86	Grass Knot	Grass	Special	—	100	20	Normal
TM87	Swagger	Normal	Status	—	90	15	Normal
TM88	Sleep Talk	Normal	Status	—	—	10	Self
TM90	Substitute	Normal	Status	—	—	10	Self
TM94	Secret Power	Normal	Physical	70	100	20	Normal
TM96	Nature Power	Normal	Status	—	—	20	Normal
TM99	Dazzling Gleam	Fairy	Special	80	100	10	Many Others
TM100	Confide	Normal	Status	—	—	20	Normal
HM01	Cut	Normal	Physical	50	95	30	Normal

MOVES LEARNED IN EXCHANGE FOR BP

Name	Type	Kind	Pow.	Acc.	PP	Range
Seed Bomb	Grass	Physical	80	100	15	Normal
Snore	Normal	Special	50	100	15	Normal
Synthesis	Grass	Status	—	—	5	Self
Giga Drain	Grass	Special	75	100	10	Normal
Drain Punch	Fighting	Physical	75	100	10	Normal
Gastro Acid	Poison	Status	—	100	10	Normal
Worry Seed	Grass	Status	—	100	10	Normal
After You	Normal	Status	—	—	15	Normal

MOVES TAUGHT BY PEOPLE

Name	Type	Kind	Pow.	Acc.	PP	Range

National Pokédex **046** Hoenn Pokédex —

Paras

Mushroom Pokémon

Bug Grass

HEIGHT: 1'00" WEIGHT: 11.9 lbs.

Same form for ♂ / ♀

Ω Paras has parasitic mushrooms growing on its back called tochukaso. They grow large by drawing nutrients from this Bug Pokémon host. They are highly valued as a medicine for extending life.

α Paras has parasitic mushrooms growing on its back called tochukaso. They grow large by drawing nutrients from this Bug Pokémon host. They are highly valued as a medicine for extending life.

ABILITIES
Effect Spore
Dry Skin

HIDDEN ABILITY
Damp

EGG GROUPS
Bug Grass

STAT GROWTH RATES

HP	■■
Attack	■■■■
Defense	■■■
Sp. Atk	■■
Sp. Def	■■
Speed	■■

ITEMS SOMETIMES HELD BY WILD POKÉMON
Tiny Mushroom / Big Mushroom

EVOLUTION
Paras → Lv. 24 → Parasect

MAIN WAY TO REGISTER IN THE NATIONAL POKÉDEX

Catch in Petalburg Woods. Appears as a hidden Pokémon after you battle Groudon or Kyogre.

Damage taken in normal battles

Type		Type	
Normal	×1	Flying	×4
Fire	×4	Psychic	×1
Water	×0.5	Bug	×2
Grass	×0.25	Rock	×2
Electric	×0.5	Ghost	×1
Ice	×2	Dragon	×1
Fighting	×0.5	Dark	×1
Poison	×2	Steel	×1
Ground	×0.25	Fairy	×1

Damage taken in Inverse battles

Type		Type	
Normal	×1	Flying	×0.25
Fire	×0.25	Psychic	×1
Water	×2	Bug	×0.5
Grass	×4	Rock	×0.5
Electric	×2	Ghost	×1
Ice	×0.5	Dragon	×1
Fighting	×2	Dark	×1
Poison	×0.5	Steel	×1
Ground	×4	Fairy	×1

Can be used in
Inverse Battle
Battle Institute
Battle Maison
Random Matchup (Free Battle)
Random Matchup (Others)

LEVEL-UP MOVES

Lv.	Name	Type	Kind	Pow.	Acc.	PP	Range
1	Scratch	Normal	Physical	40	100	35	Normal
6	Stun Spore	Grass	Status	—	75	30	Normal
6	Poison Powder	Poison	Status	—	75	35	Normal
11	Leech Life	Bug	Physical	20	100	15	Normal
17	Fury Cutter	Bug	Physical	40	95	20	Normal
22	Spore	Grass	Status	—	100	15	Normal
27	Slash	Normal	Physical	70	100	20	Normal
33	Growth	Normal	Status	—	—	20	Self
38	Giga Drain	Grass	Special	75	100	10	Normal
43	Aromatherapy	Grass	Status	—	—	5	Your Party
49	Rage Powder	Bug	Status	—	—	20	Self
54	X-Scissor	Bug	Physical	80	100	15	Normal

TM & HM MOVES

No.	Name	Type	Kind	Pow.	Acc.	PP	Range
TM01	Hone Claws	Dark	Status	—	—	15	Self
TM06	Toxic	Poison	Status	—	90	10	Normal
TM09	Venoshock	Poison	Special	65	100	10	Normal
TM10	Hidden Power	Normal	Special	60	100	15	Normal
TM11	Sunny Day	Fire	Status	—	—	5	Both Sides
TM16	Light Screen	Psychic	Status	—	—	30	Your Side
TM17	Protect	Normal	Status	—	—	10	Self
TM21	Frustration	Normal	Physical	—	100	20	Normal
TM22	Solar Beam	Grass	Special	120	100	10	Normal
TM27	Return	Normal	Physical	—	100	20	Normal
TM28	Dig	Ground	Physical	80	100	10	Normal
TM31	Brick Break	Fighting	Physical	75	100	15	Normal
TM32	Double Team	Normal	Status	—	—	15	Self
TM36	Sludge Bomb	Poison	Special	90	100	10	Normal
TM40	Aerial Ace	Flying	Physical	60	—	20	Normal
TM42	Facade	Normal	Physical	70	100	20	Normal
TM44	Rest	Psychic	Status	—	—	10	Self
TM45	Attract	Normal	Status	—	100	15	Normal
TM46	Thief	Dark	Physical	60	100	25	Normal
TM48	Round	Normal	Special	60	100	15	Normal
TM53	Energy Ball	Grass	Special	90	100	10	Normal
TM54	False Swipe	Normal	Physical	40	100	40	Normal
TM70	Flash	Normal	Status	—	100	20	Normal
TM75	Swords Dance	Normal	Status	—	—	20	Self
TM76	Struggle Bug	Bug	Special	50	100	20	Many Others
TM81	X-Scissor	Bug	Physical	80	100	15	Normal
TM86	Grass Knot	Grass	Special	—	100	20	Normal
TM87	Swagger	Normal	Status	—	90	15	Normal
TM88	Sleep Talk	Normal	Status	—	—	10	Self
TM90	Substitute	Normal	Status	—	—	10	Self
TM94	Secret Power	Normal	Physical	70	100	20	Normal
TM96	Nature Power	Normal	Status	—	—	20	Normal
TM100	Confide	Normal	Status	—	—	20	Normal
HM01	Cut	Normal	Physical	50	95	30	Normal
HM06	Rock Smash	Fighting	Physical	40	100	15	Normal

MOVES LEARNED IN EXCHANGE FOR BP

Name	Type	Kind	Pow.	Acc.	PP	Range
Bug Bite	Bug	Physical	60	100	20	Normal
Seed Bomb	Grass	Physical	80	100	15	Normal
Snore	Normal	Special	50	100	15	Normal
Knock Off	Dark	Physical	65	100	20	Normal
Synthesis	Grass	Status	—	—	5	Self
Giga Drain	Grass	Special	75	100	10	Normal
Worry Seed	Grass	Status	—	100	10	Normal
After You	Normal	Status	—	—	15	Normal

MOVES TAUGHT BY PEOPLE

Name	Type	Kind	Pow.	Acc.	PP	Range

EGG MOVES

Name	Type	Kind	Pow.	Acc.	PP	Range
Screech	Normal	Status	—	85	40	Normal
Counter	Fighting	Physical	—	100	20	Varies
Psybeam	Psychic	Special	65	100	20	Normal
Flail	Normal	Physical	—	100	15	Normal
Sweet Scent	Normal	Status	—	100	20	Many Others
Pursuit	Dark	Physical	40	100	20	Normal
Metal Claw	Steel	Physical	50	95	35	Normal
Bug Bite	Bug	Physical	60	100	20	Normal
Cross Poison	Poison	Physical	70	100	20	Normal
Agility	Psychic	Status	—	—	30	Self
Endure	Normal	Status	—	—	10	Self
Natural Gift	Normal	Physical	—	100	15	Normal
Leech Seed	Grass	Status	—	90	10	Normal
Wide Guard	Rock	Status	—	—	10	Your Side
Rototiller	Ground	Status	—	—	10	Adjacent
Fell Stinger	Bug	Physical	30	100	25	Normal

National Pokédex **047** Hoenn Pokédex —

Parasect

Mushroom Pokémon

Bug Grass

HEIGHT: 3'03" WEIGHT: 65 lbs.

Same form for ♂ / ♀

Ω Parasect is known to infest large trees en masse and drain nutrients from the lower trunk and roots. When an infested tree dies, they move onto another tree all at once.

α Parasect is known to infest large trees en masse and drain nutrients from the lower trunk and roots. When an infested tree dies, they move onto another tree all at once.

ABILITIES
Effect Spore
Dry Skin

HIDDEN ABILITY
Damp

EGG GROUPS
Bug Grass

STAT GROWTH RATES

HP	■■■
Attack	■■■■■
Defense	■■■■
Sp. Atk	■■■
Sp. Def	■■■
Speed	■■

ITEMS SOMETIMES HELD BY WILD POKÉMON
—

EVOLUTION
Paras → Lv. 24 → Parasect

MAIN WAY TO REGISTER IN THE NATIONAL POKÉDEX

Level up Paras to Lv. 24.

Damage taken in normal battles

Type		Type	
Normal	×1	Flying	×4
Fire	×4	Psychic	×1
Water	×0.5	Bug	×2
Grass	×0.25	Rock	×2
Electric	×0.5	Ghost	×1
Ice	×2	Dragon	×1
Fighting	×0.5	Dark	×1
Poison	×2	Steel	×1
Ground	×0.25	Fairy	×1

Damage taken in Inverse battles

Type		Type	
Normal	×1	Flying	×0.25
Fire	×0.25	Psychic	×1
Water	×2	Bug	×0.5
Grass	×4	Rock	×0.5
Electric	×2	Ghost	×1
Ice	×0.5	Dragon	×1
Fighting	×2	Dark	×1
Poison	×0.5	Steel	×1
Ground	×4	Fairy	×1

Can be used in
Inverse Battle
Battle Institute
Battle Maison
Random Matchup (Free Battle)
Random Matchup (Others)

LEVEL-UP MOVES

Lv.	Name	Type	Kind	Pow.	Acc.	PP	Range
1	Cross Poison	Poison	Physical	70	100	20	Normal
1	Scratch	Normal	Physical	40	100	35	Normal
1	Stun Spore	Grass	Status	—	75	30	Normal
1	Poison Powder	Poison	Status	—	75	35	Normal
1	Leech Life	Bug	Physical	20	100	15	Normal
6	Stun Spore	Grass	Status	—	75	30	Normal
6	Poison Powder	Poison	Status	—	75	35	Normal
11	Leech Life	Bug	Physical	20	100	15	Normal
17	Fury Cutter	Bug	Physical	40	95	20	Normal
22	Spore	Grass	Status	—	100	15	Normal
29	Slash	Normal	Physical	70	100	20	Normal
37	Growth	Normal	Status	—	—	20	Self
44	Giga Drain	Grass	Special	75	100	10	Normal
51	Aromatherapy	Grass	Status	—	—	5	Your Party
59	Rage Powder	Bug	Status	—	—	20	Self
66	X-Scissor	Bug	Physical	80	100	15	Normal

TM & HM MOVES

No.	Name	Type	Kind	Pow.	Acc.	PP	Range
TM01	Hone Claws	Dark	Status	—	—	15	Self
TM06	Toxic	Poison	Status	—	90	10	Normal
TM09	Venoshock	Poison	Special	65	100	10	Normal
TM10	Hidden Power	Normal	Special	60	100	15	Normal
TM11	Sunny Day	Fire	Status	—	—	5	Both Sides
TM15	Hyper Beam	Normal	Special	150	90	5	Normal
TM16	Light Screen	Psychic	Status	—	—	30	Your Side
TM17	Protect	Normal	Status	—	—	10	Self
TM21	Frustration	Normal	Physical	—	100	20	Normal
TM22	Solar Beam	Grass	Special	120	100	10	Normal
TM27	Return	Normal	Physical	—	100	20	Normal
TM28	Dig	Ground	Physical	80	100	10	Normal
TM31	Brick Break	Fighting	Physical	75	100	15	Normal
TM32	Double Team	Normal	Status	—	—	15	Self
TM36	Sludge Bomb	Poison	Special	90	100	10	Normal
TM40	Aerial Ace	Flying	Physical	60	—	20	Normal
TM42	Facade	Normal	Physical	70	100	20	Normal
TM44	Rest	Psychic	Status	—	—	10	Self
TM45	Attract	Normal	Status	—	100	15	Normal
TM46	Thief	Dark	Physical	60	100	25	Normal
TM48	Round	Normal	Special	60	100	15	Normal
TM53	Energy Ball	Grass	Special	90	100	10	Normal
TM54	False Swipe	Normal	Physical	40	100	40	Normal
TM68	Giga Impact	Normal	Physical	150	90	5	Normal
TM70	Flash	Normal	Status	—	100	20	Normal
TM75	Swords Dance	Normal	Status	—	—	20	Self
TM76	Struggle Bug	Bug	Special	50	100	20	Many Others
TM81	X-Scissor	Bug	Physical	80	100	15	Normal
TM86	Grass Knot	Grass	Special	—	100	20	Normal
TM87	Swagger	Normal	Status	—	90	15	Normal
TM88	Sleep Talk	Normal	Status	—	—	10	Self
TM90	Substitute	Normal	Status	—	—	10	Self
TM94	Secret Power	Normal	Physical	70	100	20	Normal
TM96	Nature Power	Normal	Status	—	—	20	Normal
TM100	Confide	Normal	Status	—	—	20	Normal
HM01	Cut	Normal	Physical	50	95	30	Normal
HM06	Rock Smash	Fighting	Physical	40	100	15	Normal

MOVES LEARNED IN EXCHANGE FOR BP

Name	Type	Kind	Pow.	Acc.	PP	Range
Bug Bite	Bug	Physical	60	100	20	Normal
Seed Bomb	Grass	Physical	80	100	15	Normal
Snore	Normal	Special	50	100	15	Normal
Knock Off	Dark	Physical	65	100	20	Normal
Synthesis	Grass	Status	—	—	5	Self
Giga Drain	Grass	Special	75	100	10	Normal
Worry Seed	Grass	Status	—	100	10	Normal
After You	Normal	Status	—	—	15	Normal

MOVES TAUGHT BY PEOPLE

Name	Type	Kind	Pow.	Acc.	PP	Range

National Pokédex **048** Hoenn Pokédex **—**

Venonat

Insect Pokémon

Bug | Poison

HEIGHT: 3'03" WEIGHT: 66.1 lbs.

Same form for ♂ / ♀

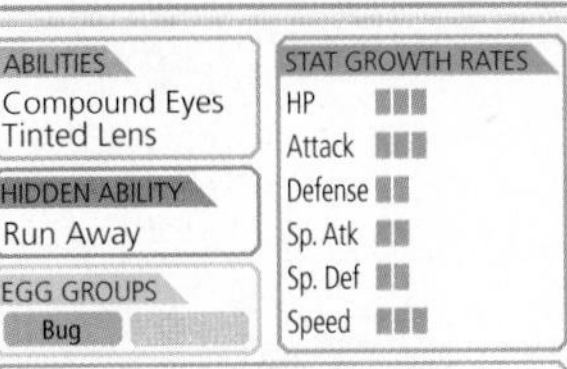

Ω Venonat is said to have evolved with a coat of thin, stiff hair that covers its entire body for protection. It possesses large eyes that never fail to spot even minuscule prey.

α Venonat is said to have evolved with a coat of thin, stiff hair that covers its entire body for protection. It possesses large eyes that never fail to spot even minuscule prey.

ABILITIES
Compound Eyes
Tinted Lens

HIDDEN ABILITY
Run Away

EGG GROUPS
Bug

STAT GROWTH RATES
HP ■■■
Attack ■■■
Defense ■■
Sp. Atk ■■
Sp. Def ■■
Speed ■■■

ITEMS SOMETIMES HELD BY WILD POKÉMON
—

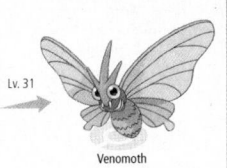

EVOLUTION
Venonat → Lv. 31 → Venomoth

MAIN WAY TO REGISTER IN THE NATIONAL POKÉDEX

Leave a Venomoth at a Pokémon Day Care, then hatch the Pokémon Egg that is found.

Damage taken in normal battles

Normal	×1	Flying	×2
Fire	×2	Psychic	×2
Water	×1	Bug	×0.5
Grass	×0.25	Rock	×2
Electric	×1	Ghost	×1
Ice	×1	Dragon	×1
Fighting	×0.25	Dark	×1
Poison	×0.5	Steel	×1
Ground	×1	Fairy	×0.5

Damage taken in Inverse battles

Normal	×1	Flying	×0.5
Fire	×0.5	Psychic	×0.5
Water	×1	Bug	×2
Grass	×4	Rock	×0.5
Electric	×1	Ghost	×1
Ice	×1	Dragon	×1
Fighting	×4	Dark	×1
Poison	×2	Steel	×1
Ground	×1	Fairy	×2

Can be used in
Inverse Battle
Battle Institute
Battle Maison
Random Matchup (Free Battle)
Random Matchup (Others)

LEVEL-UP MOVES

Lv.	Name	Type	Kind	Pow.	Acc.	PP	Range
1	Tackle	Normal	Physical	50	100	35	Normal
1	Disable	Normal	Status	—	100	20	Normal
1	Foresight	Normal	Status	—	—	40	Normal
5	Supersonic	Normal	Status	—	55	20	Normal
11	Confusion	Psychic	Special	50	100	25	Normal
13	Poison Powder	Poison	Status	—	75	35	Normal
17	Leech Life	Bug	Physical	20	100	15	Normal
23	Stun Spore	Grass	Status	—	75	30	Normal
25	Psybeam	Psychic	Special	65	100	20	Normal
29	Sleep Powder	Grass	Status	—	75	15	Normal
35	Signal Beam	Bug	Special	75	100	15	Normal
37	Zen Headbutt	Psychic	Physical	80	90	15	Normal
41	Poison Fang	Poison	Physical	50	100	15	Normal
47	Psychic	Psychic	Special	90	100	10	Normal

TM & HM MOVES

No.	Name	Type	Kind	Pow.	Acc.	PP	Range
TM06	Toxic	Poison	Status	—	90	10	Normal
TM09	Venoshock	Poison	Special	65	100	10	Normal
TM10	Hidden Power	Normal	Special	60	100	15	Normal
TM11	Sunny Day	Fire	Status	—	—	5	Both Sides
TM17	Protect	Normal	Status	—	—	10	Self
TM21	Frustration	Normal	Physical	—	100	20	Normal
TM22	Solar Beam	Grass	Special	120	100	10	Normal
TM27	Return	Normal	Physical	—	100	20	Normal
TM29	Psychic	Psychic	Special	90	100	10	Normal
TM32	Double Team	Normal	Status	—	—	15	Self
TM36	Sludge Bomb	Poison	Special	90	100	10	Normal
TM42	Facade	Normal	Physical	70	100	20	Normal
TM44	Rest	Psychic	Status	—	—	10	Self
TM45	Attract	Normal	Status	—	100	15	Normal
TM46	Thief	Dark	Physical	60	100	25	Normal
TM48	Round	Normal	Special	60	100	15	Normal
TM70	Flash	Normal	Status	—	100	20	Normal
TM76	Struggle Bug	Bug	Special	50	100	20	Many Others
TM83	Infestation	Bug	Special	20	100	20	Normal
TM87	Swagger	Normal	Status	—	90	15	Normal
TM88	Sleep Talk	Normal	Status	—	—	10	Self
TM90	Substitute	Normal	Status	—	—	10	Self
TM94	Secret Power	Normal	Physical	70	100	20	Normal
TM100	Confide	Normal	Status	—	—	20	Normal

MOVES LEARNED IN EXCHANGE FOR BP

Name	Type	Kind	Pow.	Acc.	PP	Range
Bug Bite	Bug	Physical	60	100	20	Normal
Signal Beam	Bug	Special	75	100	15	Normal
Zen Headbutt	Psychic	Physical	80	90	15	Normal
Snore	Normal	Special	50	100	15	Normal
Giga Drain	Grass	Special	75	100	10	Normal
Skill Swap	Psychic	Status	—	—	10	Normal

MOVES TAUGHT BY PEOPLE

Name	Type	Kind	Pow.	Acc.	PP	Range

EGG MOVES

Name	Type	Kind	Pow.	Acc.	PP	Range
Baton Pass	Normal	Status	—	—	40	Self
Screech	Normal	Status	—	85	40	Normal
Giga Drain	Grass	Special	75	100	10	Normal
Signal Beam	Bug	Special	75	100	15	Normal
Agility	Psychic	Status	—	—	30	Self
Morning Sun	Normal	Status	—	—	5	Self
Toxic Spikes	Poison	Status	—	—	20	Other Side
Bug Bite	Bug	Physical	60	100	20	Normal
Secret Power	Normal	Physical	70	100	20	Normal
Skill Swap	Psychic	Status	—	—	10	Normal
Rage Powder	Bug	Status	—	—	20	Self

National Pokédex **049** Hoenn Pokédex **—**

Venomoth

Poison Moth Pokémon

Bug | Poison

HEIGHT: 4'11" WEIGHT: 27.6 lbs.

Same form for ♂ / ♀

Ω Venomoth is nocturnal—it is a Pokémon that only becomes active at night. Its favorite prey are small insects that gather around streetlights, attracted by the light in the darkness.

α Venomoth is nocturnal—it is a Pokémon that only becomes active at night. Its favorite prey are small insects that gather around streetlights, attracted by the light in the darkness.

ABILITIES
Shield Dust
Tinted Lens

HIDDEN ABILITY
Wonder Skin

EGG GROUPS
Bug

STAT GROWTH RATES
HP ■■■
Attack ■■■
Defense ■■■
Sp. Atk ■■■■
Sp. Def ■■■
Speed ■■■■■

ITEMS SOMETIMES HELD BY WILD POKÉMON
Shed Shell

EVOLUTION
Venonat → Lv. 31 → Venomoth

MAIN WAY TO REGISTER IN THE NATIONAL POKÉDEX

Catch on Mirage Island 1.

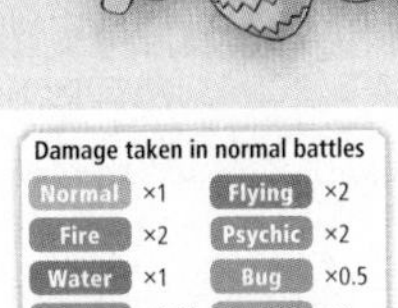

Damage taken in normal battles

Normal	×1	Flying	×2
Fire	×2	Psychic	×2
Water	×1	Bug	×0.5
Grass	×0.25	Rock	×2
Electric	×1	Ghost	×1
Ice	×1	Dragon	×1
Fighting	×0.25	Dark	×1
Poison	×0.5	Steel	×1
Ground	×1	Fairy	×0.5

Damage taken in Inverse battles

Normal	×1	Flying	×0.5
Fire	×0.5	Psychic	×0.5
Water	×1	Bug	×2
Grass	×4	Rock	×0.5
Electric	×1	Ghost	×1
Ice	×1	Dragon	×1
Fighting	×4	Dark	×1
Poison	×2	Steel	×1
Ground	×1	Fairy	×2

Can be used in
Inverse Battle
Battle Institute
Battle Maison
Random Matchup (Free Battle)
Random Matchup (Others)

LEVEL-UP MOVES

Lv.	Name	Type	Kind	Pow.	Acc.	PP	Range
1	Quiver Dance	Bug	Status	—	—	20	Self
1	Bug Buzz	Bug	Special	90	100	10	Normal
1	Silver Wind	Bug	Special	60	100	5	Normal
1	Tackle	Normal	Physical	50	100	35	Normal
1	Disable	Normal	Status	—	100	20	Normal
1	Foresight	Normal	Status	—	—	40	Normal
1	Supersonic	Normal	Status	—	55	20	Normal
5	Supersonic	Normal	Status	—	55	20	Normal
11	Confusion	Psychic	Special	50	100	25	Normal
13	Poison Powder	Poison	Status	—	75	35	Normal
17	Leech Life	Bug	Physical	20	100	15	Normal
23	Stun Spore	Grass	Status	—	75	30	Normal
25	Psybeam	Psychic	Special	65	100	20	Normal
29	Sleep Powder	Grass	Status	—	75	15	Normal
31	Gust	Flying	Special	40	100	35	Normal
37	Signal Beam	Bug	Special	75	100	15	Normal
41	Zen Headbutt	Psychic	Physical	80	90	15	Normal
47	Poison Fang	Poison	Physical	50	100	15	Normal
55	Psychic	Psychic	Special	90	100	10	Normal
59	Bug Buzz	Bug	Special	90	100	10	Normal
63	Quiver Dance	Bug	Status	—	—	20	Self

TM & HM MOVES

No.	Name	Type	Kind	Pow.	Acc.	PP	Range
TM06	Toxic	Poison	Status	—	90	10	Normal
TM09	Venoshock	Poison	Special	65	100	10	Normal
TM10	Hidden Power	Normal	Special	60	100	15	Normal
TM11	Sunny Day	Fire	Status	—	—	5	Both Sides
TM15	Hyper Beam	Normal	Special	150	90	5	Normal
TM17	Protect	Normal	Status	—	—	10	Self
TM19	Roost	Flying	Status	—	—	10	Self
TM21	Frustration	Normal	Physical	—	100	20	Normal
TM22	Solar Beam	Grass	Special	120	100	10	Normal
TM27	Return	Normal	Physical	—	100	20	Normal
TM29	Psychic	Psychic	Special	90	100	10	Normal
TM32	Double Team	Normal	Status	—	—	15	Self
TM36	Sludge Bomb	Poison	Special	90	100	10	Normal
TM40	Aerial Ace	Flying	Physical	60	—	20	Normal
TM42	Facade	Normal	Physical	70	100	20	Normal
TM44	Rest	Psychic	Status	—	—	10	Self
TM45	Attract	Normal	Status	—	100	15	Normal
TM46	Thief	Dark	Physical	60	100	25	Normal
TM48	Round	Normal	Special	60	100	15	Normal
TM53	Energy Ball	Grass	Special	90	100	10	Normal
TM62	Acrobatics	Flying	Physical	55	100	15	Normal
TM68	Giga Impact	Normal	Physical	150	90	5	Normal
TM70	Flash	Normal	Status	—	100	20	Normal
TM76	Struggle Bug	Bug	Special	50	100	20	Many Others
TM83	Infestation	Bug	Special	20	100	20	Normal
TM87	Swagger	Normal	Status	—	90	15	Normal
TM88	Sleep Talk	Normal	Status	—	—	10	Self
TM89	U-turn	Bug	Physical	70	100	20	Normal
TM90	Substitute	Normal	Status	—	—	10	Self
TM94	Secret Power	Normal	Physical	70	100	20	Normal
TM100	Confide	Normal	Status	—	—	20	Normal

MOVES LEARNED IN EXCHANGE FOR BP

Name	Type	Kind	Pow.	Acc.	PP	Range
Bug Bite	Bug	Physical	60	100	20	Normal
Signal Beam	Bug	Special	75	100	15	Normal
Zen Headbutt	Psychic	Physical	80	90	15	Normal
Snore	Normal	Special	50	100	15	Normal
Tailwind	Flying	Status	—	—	15	Your Side
Giga Drain	Grass	Special	75	100	10	Normal
Skill Swap	Psychic	Status	—	—	10	Normal

MOVES TAUGHT BY PEOPLE

Name	Type	Kind	Pow.	Acc.	PP	Range

National Pokédex **050** Hoenn Pokédex —

Diglett

Mole Pokémon

Ground

HEIGHT: 0'08" WEIGHT: 1.8 lbs.

Same form for ♂ / ♀

Ω Diglett are raised in most farms. The reason is simple—wherever this Pokémon burrows, the soil is left perfectly tilled for planting crops. This soil is made ideal for growing delicious vegetables.

α Diglett are raised in most farms. The reason is simple—wherever this Pokémon burrows, the soil is left perfectly tilled for planting crops. This soil is made ideal for growing delicious vegetables.

ABILITIES
Sand Veil
Arena Trap

HIDDEN ABILITY
Sand Force

EGG GROUPS
Field

STAT GROWTH RATES
HP ■
Attack ■■■
Defense ■
Sp. Atk ■■
Sp. Def ■■
Speed ■■■■■

ITEMS SOMETIMES HELD BY WILD POKÉMON
Soft Sand

EVOLUTION
Diglett → Lv. 26 → Dugtrio

MAIN WAY TO REGISTER IN THE NATIONAL POKÉDEX

Catch on the Fiery Path. Appears as a hidden Pokémon after you battle Groudon or Kyogre.

Damage taken in normal battles

Type		Type	
Normal	×1	Flying	×1
Fire	×1	Psychic	×1
Water	×2	Bug	×1
Grass	×2	Rock	×0.5
Electric	×0	Ghost	×1
Ice	×2	Dragon	×1
Fighting	×1	Dark	×1
Poison	×0.5	Steel	×1
Ground	×1	Fairy	×1

Damage taken in Inverse battles

Type		Type	
Normal	×1	Flying	×1
Fire	×1	Psychic	×1
Water	×0.5	Bug	×1
Grass	×0.5	Rock	×2
Electric	×2	Ghost	×1
Ice	×0.5	Dragon	×1
Fighting	×1	Dark	×1
Poison	×2	Steel	×1
Ground	×1	Fairy	×1

Can be used in
Inverse Battle
Battle Institute
Battle Maison
Random Matchup (Free Battle)
Random Matchup (Others)

LEVEL-UP MOVES

Lv.	Name	Type	Kind	Pow.	Acc.	PP	Range
1	Scratch	Normal	Physical	40	100	35	Normal
1	Sand Attack	Ground	Status	—	100	15	Normal
4	Growl	Normal	Status	—	100	40	Many Others
7	Astonish	Ghost	Physical	30	100	15	Normal
12	Mud-Slap	Ground	Special	20	100	10	Normal
15	Magnitude	Ground	Physical	—	100	30	Adjacent
18	Bulldoze	Ground	Physical	60	100	20	Adjacent
23	Sucker Punch	Dark	Physical	80	100	5	Normal
26	Mud Bomb	Ground	Special	65	85	10	Normal
29	Earth Power	Ground	Special	90	100	10	Normal
34	Dig	Ground	Physical	80	100	10	Normal
37	Slash	Normal	Physical	70	100	20	Normal
40	Earthquake	Ground	Physical	100	100	10	Adjacent
45	Fissure	Ground	Physical	—	30	5	Normal

TM & HM MOVES

No.	Name	Type	Kind	Pow.	Acc.	PP	Range
TM01	Hone Claws	Dark	Status	—	—	15	Self
TM06	Toxic	Poison	Status	—	90	10	Normal
TM10	Hidden Power	Normal	Special	60	100	15	Normal
TM11	Sunny Day	Fire	Status	—	—	5	Both Sides
TM17	Protect	Normal	Status	—	—	10	Self
TM21	Frustration	Normal	Physical	—	100	20	Normal
TM26	Earthquake	Ground	Physical	100	100	10	Adjacent
TM27	Return	Normal	Physical	—	100	20	Normal
TM28	Dig	Ground	Physical	80	100	10	Normal
TM32	Double Team	Normal	Status	—	—	15	Self
TM36	Sludge Bomb	Poison	Special	90	100	10	Normal
TM37	Sandstorm	Rock	Status	—	—	10	Both Sides
TM39	Rock Tomb	Rock	Physical	60	95	15	Normal
TM40	Aerial Ace	Flying	Physical	60	—	20	Normal
TM42	Facade	Normal	Physical	70	100	20	Normal
TM44	Rest	Psychic	Status	—	—	10	Self
TM45	Attract	Normal	Status	—	100	15	Normal
TM46	Thief	Dark	Physical	60	100	25	Normal
TM48	Round	Normal	Special	60	100	15	Normal
TM49	Echoed Voice	Normal	Special	40	100	15	Normal
TM65	Shadow Claw	Ghost	Physical	70	100	15	Normal
TM78	Bulldoze	Ground	Physical	60	100	20	Adjacent
TM80	Rock Slide	Rock	Physical	75	90	10	Many Others
TM87	Swagger	Normal	Status	—	90	15	Normal
TM88	Sleep Talk	Normal	Status	—	—	10	Self
TM90	Substitute	Normal	Status	—	—	10	Self
TM94	Secret Power	Normal	Physical	70	100	20	Normal
TM100	Confide	Normal	Status	—	—	20	Normal
HM01	Cut	Normal	Physical	50	95	30	Normal
HM06	Rock Smash	Fighting	Physical	40	100	15	Normal

MOVES LEARNED IN EXCHANGE FOR BP

Name	Type	Kind	Pow.	Acc.	PP	Range
Earth Power	Ground	Special	90	100	10	Normal
Snore	Normal	Special	50	100	15	Normal
Stealth Rock	Rock	Status	—	—	20	Other Side

MOVES TAUGHT BY PEOPLE

Name	Type	Kind	Pow.	Acc.	PP	Range

EGG MOVES

Name	Type	Kind	Pow.	Acc.	PP	Range
Feint Attack	Dark	Physical	60	—	20	Normal
Screech	Normal	Status	—	85	40	Normal
Ancient Power	Rock	Special	60	100	5	Normal
Pursuit	Dark	Physical	40	100	20	Normal
Beat Up	Dark	Physical	—	100	10	Normal
Uproar	Normal	Special	90	100	10	1 Random
Mud Bomb	Ground	Special	65	85	10	Normal
Astonish	Ghost	Physical	30	100	15	Normal
Reversal	Fighting	Physical	—	100	15	Normal
Headbutt	Normal	Physical	70	100	15	Normal
Endure	Normal	Status	—	—	10	Self
Final Gambit	Fighting	Special	—	100	5	Normal
Memento	Dark	Status	—	100	10	Normal

National Pokédex **051** Hoenn Pokédex —

Dugtrio

Mole Pokémon

Ground

HEIGHT: 2'04" WEIGHT: 73.4 lbs.

Same form for ♂ / ♀

Ω Dugtrio are actually triplets that emerged from one body. As a result, each triplet thinks exactly like the other two triplets. They work cooperatively to burrow endlessly.

α Dugtrio are actually triplets that emerged from one body. As a result, each triplet thinks exactly like the other two triplets. They work cooperatively to burrow endlessly.

ABILITIES
Sand Veil
Arena Trap

HIDDEN ABILITY
Sand Force

EGG GROUPS
Field

STAT GROWTH RATES
HP ■■
Attack ■■■■
Defense ■■
Sp. Atk ■■
Sp. Def ■■■
Speed ■■■■■■

ITEMS SOMETIMES HELD BY WILD POKÉMON
—

EVOLUTION
Diglett → Lv. 26 → Dugtrio

MAIN WAY TO REGISTER IN THE NATIONAL POKÉDEX

Level up Diglett to Lv. 26.

Damage taken in normal battles

Type		Type	
Normal	×1	Flying	×1
Fire	×1	Psychic	×1
Water	×2	Bug	×1
Grass	×2	Rock	×0.5
Electric	×0	Ghost	×1
Ice	×2	Dragon	×1
Fighting	×1	Dark	×1
Poison	×0.5	Steel	×1
Ground	×1	Fairy	×1

Damage taken in Inverse battles

Type		Type	
Normal	×1	Flying	×1
Fire	×1	Psychic	×1
Water	×0.5	Bug	×1
Grass	×0.5	Rock	×2
Electric	×2	Ghost	×1
Ice	×0.5	Dragon	×1
Fighting	×1	Dark	×1
Poison	×2	Steel	×1
Ground	×1	Fairy	×1

Can be used in
Inverse Battle
Battle Institute
Battle Maison
Random Matchup (Free Battle)
Random Matchup (Others)

LEVEL-UP MOVES

Lv.	Name	Type	Kind	Pow.	Acc.	PP	Range
1	Rototiller	Ground	Status	—	—	10	Adjacent
1	Night Slash	Dark	Physical	70	100	15	Normal
1	Tri Attack	Normal	Special	80	100	10	Normal
1	Scratch	Normal	Physical	40	100	35	Normal
1	Sand Attack	Ground	Status	—	100	15	Normal
1	Growl	Normal	Status	—	100	40	Many Others
4	Growl	Normal	Status	—	100	40	Many Others
7	Astonish	Ghost	Physical	30	100	15	Normal
12	Mud-Slap	Ground	Special	20	100	10	Normal
15	Magnitude	Ground	Physical	—	100	30	Adjacent
18	Bulldoze	Ground	Physical	60	100	20	Adjacent
23	Sucker Punch	Dark	Physical	80	100	5	Normal
26	Sand Tomb	Ground	Physical	35	85	15	Normal
28	Mud Bomb	Ground	Special	65	85	10	Normal
33	Earth Power	Ground	Special	90	100	10	Normal
40	Dig	Ground	Physical	80	100	10	Normal
45	Slash	Normal	Physical	70	100	20	Normal
50	Earthquake	Ground	Physical	100	100	10	Adjacent
57	Fissure	Ground	Physical	—	30	5	Normal

TM & HM MOVES

No.	Name	Type	Kind	Pow.	Acc.	PP	Range
TM01	Hone Claws	Dark	Status	—	—	15	Self
TM06	Toxic	Poison	Status	—	90	10	Normal
TM10	Hidden Power	Normal	Special	60	100	15	Normal
TM11	Sunny Day	Fire	Status	—	—	5	Both Sides
TM15	Hyper Beam	Normal	Special	150	90	5	Normal
TM17	Protect	Normal	Status	—	—	10	Self
TM21	Frustration	Normal	Physical	—	100	20	Normal
TM26	Earthquake	Ground	Physical	100	100	10	Adjacent
TM27	Return	Normal	Physical	—	100	20	Normal
TM28	Dig	Ground	Physical	80	100	10	Normal
TM32	Double Team	Normal	Status	—	—	15	Self
TM34	Sludge Wave	Poison	Special	95	100	10	Adjacent
TM36	Sludge Bomb	Poison	Special	90	100	10	Normal
TM37	Sandstorm	Rock	Status	—	—	10	Both Sides
TM39	Rock Tomb	Rock	Physical	60	95	15	Normal
TM40	Aerial Ace	Flying	Physical	60	—	20	Normal
TM42	Facade	Normal	Physical	70	100	20	Normal
TM44	Rest	Psychic	Status	—	—	10	Self
TM45	Attract	Normal	Status	—	100	15	Normal
TM46	Thief	Dark	Physical	60	100	25	Normal
TM48	Round	Normal	Special	60	100	15	Normal
TM49	Echoed Voice	Normal	Special	40	100	15	Normal
TM65	Shadow Claw	Ghost	Physical	70	100	15	Normal
TM68	Giga Impact	Normal	Physical	150	90	5	Normal
TM71	Stone Edge	Rock	Physical	100	80	5	Normal
TM78	Bulldoze	Ground	Physical	60	100	20	Adjacent
TM80	Rock Slide	Rock	Physical	75	90	10	Many Others
TM87	Swagger	Normal	Status	—	90	15	Normal
TM88	Sleep Talk	Normal	Status	—	—	10	Self
TM90	Substitute	Normal	Status	—	—	10	Self
TM94	Secret Power	Normal	Physical	70	100	20	Normal
TM100	Confide	Normal	Status	—	—	20	Normal
HM01	Cut	Normal	Physical	50	95	30	Normal
HM06	Rock Smash	Fighting	Physical	40	100	15	Normal

MOVES LEARNED IN EXCHANGE FOR BP

Name	Type	Kind	Pow.	Acc.	PP	Range
Earth Power	Ground	Special	90	100	10	Normal
Snore	Normal	Special	50	100	15	Normal
Stealth Rock	Rock	Status	—	—	20	Other Side

MOVES TAUGHT BY PEOPLE

Name	Type	Kind	Pow.	Acc.	PP	Range

National Pokédex **052** Hoenn Pokédex —

Meowth

Scratch Cat Pokémon

Normal

HEIGHT: 1'04" WEIGHT: 9.3 lbs.

Same form for ♂ / ♀

Ω Meowth withdraws its sharp claws into its paws to slinkily sneak about without making any incriminating footsteps. For some reason, this Pokémon loves shiny coins that glitter with light.

α Meowth withdraws its sharp claws into its paws to slinkily sneak about without making any incriminating footsteps. For some reason, this Pokémon loves shiny coins that glitter with light.

ABILITIES
Pickup
Technician

HIDDEN ABILITY
Unnerve

EGG GROUPS
Field

STAT GROWTH RATES
HP
Attack
Defense
Sp. Atk
Sp. Def
Speed

ITEMS SOMETIMES HELD BY WILD POKÉMON
—

EVOLUTION
Meowth → Lv. 28 → Persian

MAIN WAY TO REGISTER IN THE NATIONAL POKÉDEX

Leave a Persian at a Pokémon Day Care, then hatch the Pokémon Egg that is found.

Damage taken in normal battles

Type	×	Type	×
Normal	×1	Flying	×1
Fire	×1	Psychic	×1
Water	×1	Bug	×1
Grass	×1	Rock	×1
Electric	×1	Ghost	×0
Ice	×1	Dragon	×1
Fighting	×2	Dark	×1
Poison	×1	Steel	×1
Ground	×1	Fairy	×1

Damage taken in Inverse battles

Type	×	Type	×
Normal	×1	Flying	×1
Fire	×1	Psychic	×1
Water	×1	Bug	×1
Grass	×1	Rock	×1
Electric	×1	Ghost	×2
Ice	×1	Dragon	×1
Fighting	×0.5	Dark	×1
Poison	×1	Steel	×1
Ground	×1	Fairy	×1

Can be used in
Inverse Battle
Battle Institute
Battle Maison
Random Matchup (Free Battle)
Random Matchup (Others)

LEVEL-UP MOVES

Lv.	Name	Type	Kind	Pow.	Acc.	PP	Range
1	Scratch	Normal	Physical	40	100	35	Normal
1	Growl	Normal	Status	—	100	40	Many Others
6	Bite	Dark	Physical	60	100	25	Normal
9	Fake Out	Normal	Physical	40	100	10	Normal
14	Fury Swipes	Normal	Physical	18	80	15	Normal
17	Screech	Normal	Status	—	85	40	Normal
22	Feint Attack	Dark	Physical	60	—	20	Normal
25	Taunt	Dark	Status	—	100	20	Normal
30	Pay Day	Normal	Physical	40	100	20	Normal
33	Slash	Normal	Physical	70	100	20	Normal
38	Nasty Plot	Dark	Status	—	—	20	Self
41	Assurance	Dark	Physical	60	100	10	Normal
46	Captivate	Normal	Status	—	100	20	Many Others
49	Night Slash	Dark	Physical	70	100	15	Normal
50	Feint	Normal	Physical	30	100	10	Normal

TM & HM MOVES

No.	Name	Type	Kind	Pow.	Acc.	PP	Range
TM01	Hone Claws	Dark	Status	—	—	15	Self
TM06	Toxic	Poison	Status	—	90	10	Normal
TM10	Hidden Power	Normal	Special	60	100	15	Normal
TM11	Sunny Day	Fire	Status	—	—	5	Both Sides
TM12	Taunt	Dark	Status	—	100	20	Normal
TM17	Protect	Normal	Status	—	—	10	Self
TM18	Rain Dance	Water	Status	—	—	5	Both Sides
TM21	Frustration	Normal	Physical	—	100	20	Normal
TM24	Thunderbolt	Electric	Special	90	100	15	Normal
TM25	Thunder	Electric	Special	110	70	10	Normal
TM27	Return	Normal	Physical	—	100	20	Normal
TM28	Dig	Ground	Physical	80	100	10	Normal
TM30	Shadow Ball	Ghost	Special	80	100	15	Normal
TM32	Double Team	Normal	Status	—	—	15	Self
TM40	Aerial Ace	Flying	Physical	60	—	20	Normal
TM41	Torment	Dark	Status	—	100	15	Normal
TM42	Facade	Normal	Physical	70	100	20	Normal
TM44	Rest	Psychic	Status	—	—	10	Self
TM45	Attract	Normal	Status	—	100	15	Normal
TM46	Thief	Dark	Physical	60	100	25	Normal
TM48	Round	Normal	Special	60	100	15	Normal
TM49	Echoed Voice	Normal	Special	40	100	15	Normal
TM65	Shadow Claw	Ghost	Physical	70	100	15	Normal
TM66	Payback	Dark	Physical	50	100	10	Normal
TM67	Retaliate	Normal	Physical	70	100	5	Normal
TM70	Flash	Normal	Status	—	100	20	Normal
TM77	Psych Up	Normal	Status	—	—	10	Normal
TM85	Dream Eater	Psychic	Special	100	100	15	Normal
TM87	Swagger	Normal	Status	—	90	15	Normal
TM88	Sleep Talk	Normal	Status	—	—	10	Self
TM89	U-turn	Bug	Physical	70	100	20	Normal
TM90	Substitute	Normal	Status	—	—	10	Self
TM94	Secret Power	Normal	Physical	70	100	20	Normal
TM97	Dark Pulse	Dark	Special	80	100	15	Normal
TM100	Confide	Normal	Status	—	—	20	Normal
HM01	Cut	Normal	Physical	50	95	30	Normal

MOVES LEARNED IN EXCHANGE FOR BP

Name	Type	Kind	Pow.	Acc.	PP	Range
Covet	Normal	Physical	60	100	25	Normal
Seed Bomb	Grass	Physical	80	100	15	Normal
Gunk Shot	Poison	Physical	120	80	5	Normal
Uproar	Normal	Special	90	100	10	1 Random
Foul Play	Dark	Physical	95	100	15	Normal
Last Resort	Normal	Physical	140	100	5	Normal
Icy Wind	Ice	Special	55	95	15	Many Others
Hyper Voice	Normal	Special	90	100	10	Many Others
Iron Tail	Steel	Physical	100	75	15	Normal
Snore	Normal	Special	50	100	15	Normal
Knock Off	Dark	Physical	65	100	20	Normal
Shock Wave	Electric	Special	60	—	20	Normal
Water Pulse	Water	Special	60	100	20	Normal
Spite	Ghost	Status	—	100	10	Normal
Snatch	Dark	Status	—	—	10	Self

MOVES TAUGHT BY PEOPLE

Name	Type	Kind	Pow.	Acc.	PP	Range

EGG MOVES

Name	Type	Kind	Pow.	Acc.	PP	Range
Spite	Ghost	Status	—	100	10	Normal
Charm	Fairy	Status	—	100	20	Normal
Hypnosis	Psychic	Status	—	60	20	Normal
Amnesia	Psychic	Status	—	—	20	Self
Assist	Normal	Status	—	—	20	Self
Odor Sleuth	Normal	Status	—	—	40	Normal
Flail	Normal	Physical	—	100	15	Normal
Last Resort	Normal	Physical	140	100	5	Normal
Punishment	Dark	Physical	—	100	5	Normal
Tail Whip	Normal	Status	—	100	30	Many Others
Snatch	Dark	Status	—	—	10	Self
Iron Tail	Steel	Physical	100	75[1]	15	Normal
Foul Play	Dark	Physical	95	100	15	Normal

National Pokédex **053** Hoenn Pokédex —

Persian

Classy Cat Pokémon

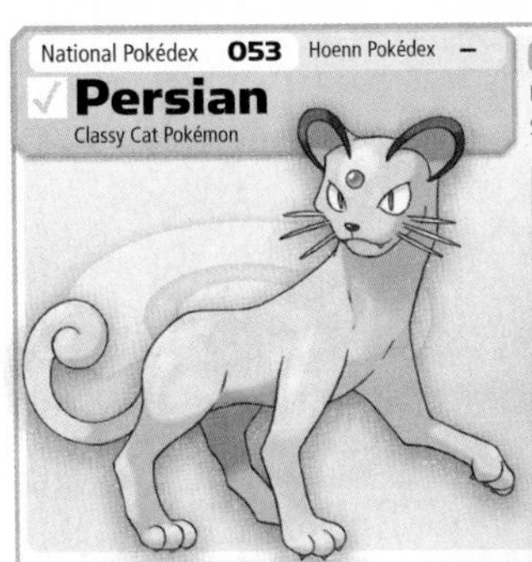

Normal

HEIGHT: 3'03" WEIGHT: 70.5 lbs.

Same form for ♂ / ♀

Ω Persian has six bold whiskers that give it a look of toughness. The whiskers sense air movements to determine what is in the Pokémon's surrounding vicinity. It becomes docile if grabbed by the whiskers.

α Persian has six bold whiskers that give it a look of toughness. The whiskers sense air movements to determine what is in the Pokémon's surrounding vicinity. It becomes docile if grabbed by the whiskers.

ABILITIES
Limber
Technician

HIDDEN ABILITY
Unnerve

EGG GROUPS
Field

STAT GROWTH RATES
HP
Attack
Defense
Sp. Atk
Sp. Def
Speed

ITEMS SOMETIMES HELD BY WILD POKÉMON
Quick Claw

EVOLUTION
Meowth → Lv. 28 → Persian

MAIN WAY TO REGISTER IN THE NATIONAL POKÉDEX

Catch on Mirage Island 3.

Damage taken in normal battles

Type	×	Type	×
Normal	×1	Flying	×1
Fire	×1	Psychic	×1
Water	×1	Bug	×1
Grass	×1	Rock	×1
Electric	×1	Ghost	×0
Ice	×1	Dragon	×1
Fighting	×2	Dark	×1
Poison	×1	Steel	×1
Ground	×1	Fairy	×1

Damage taken in Inverse battles

Type	×	Type	×
Normal	×1	Flying	×1
Fire	×1	Psychic	×1
Water	×1	Bug	×1
Grass	×1	Rock	×1
Electric	×1	Ghost	×2
Ice	×1	Dragon	×1
Fighting	×0.5	Dark	×1
Poison	×1	Steel	×1
Ground	×1	Fairy	×1

Can be used in
Inverse Battle
Battle Institute
Battle Maison
Random Matchup (Free Battle)
Random Matchup (Others)

LEVEL-UP MOVES

Lv.	Name	Type	Kind	Pow.	Acc.	PP	Range
1	Play Rough	Fairy	Physical	90	90	10	Normal
1	Switcheroo	Dark	Status	—	100	10	Normal
1	Scratch	Normal	Physical	40	100	35	Normal
1	Growl	Normal	Status	—	100	40	Many Others
1	Bite	Dark	Physical	60	100	25	Normal
1	Fake Out	Normal	Physical	40	100	10	Normal
6	Bite	Dark	Physical	60	100	25	Normal
9	Fake Out	Normal	Physical	40	100	10	Normal
14	Fury Swipes	Normal	Physical	18	80	15	Normal
17	Screech	Normal	Status	—	85	40	Normal
22	Feint Attack	Dark	Physical	60	—	20	Normal
25	Taunt	Dark	Status	—	100	20	Normal
28	Swift	Normal	Special	60	—	20	Many Others
32	Power Gem	Rock	Special	80	100	20	Normal
37	Slash	Normal	Physical	70	100	20	Normal
44	Nasty Plot	Dark	Status	—	—	20	Self
49	Assurance	Dark	Physical	60	100	10	Normal
56	Captivate	Normal	Status	—	100	20	Many Others
61	Night Slash	Dark	Physical	70	100	15	Normal
65	Feint	Normal	Physical	30	100	10	Normal

TM & HM MOVES

No.	Name	Type	Kind	Pow.	Acc.	PP	Range
TM01	Hone Claws	Dark	Status	—	—	15	Self
TM05	Roar	Normal	Status	—	—	20	Normal
TM06	Toxic	Poison	Status	—	90	10	Normal
TM10	Hidden Power	Normal	Special	60	100	15	Normal
TM11	Sunny Day	Fire	Status	—	—	5	Both Sides
TM12	Taunt	Dark	Status	—	100	20	Normal
TM15	Hyper Beam	Normal	Special	150	90	5	Normal
TM17	Protect	Normal	Status	—	—	10	Self
TM18	Rain Dance	Water	Status	—	—	5	Both Sides
TM21	Frustration	Normal	Physical	—	100	20	Normal
TM24	Thunderbolt	Electric	Special	90	100	15	Normal
TM25	Thunder	Electric	Special	110	70	10	Normal
TM27	Return	Normal	Physical	—	100	20	Normal
TM28	Dig	Ground	Physical	80	100	10	Normal
TM30	Shadow Ball	Ghost	Special	80	100	15	Normal
TM32	Double Team	Normal	Status	—	—	15	Self
TM40	Aerial Ace	Flying	Physical	60	—	20	Normal
TM41	Torment	Dark	Status	—	100	15	Normal
TM42	Facade	Normal	Physical	70	100	20	Normal
TM44	Rest	Psychic	Status	—	—	10	Self
TM45	Attract	Normal	Status	—	100	15	Normal
TM46	Thief	Dark	Physical	60	100	25	Normal
TM48	Round	Normal	Special	60	100	15	Normal
TM49	Echoed Voice	Normal	Special	40	100	15	Normal
TM63	Embargo	Dark	Status	—	100	15	Normal
TM65	Shadow Claw	Ghost	Physical	70	100	15	Normal
TM66	Payback	Dark	Physical	50	100	10	Normal
TM67	Retaliate	Normal	Physical	70	100	5	Normal
TM68	Giga Impact	Normal	Physical	150	90	5	Normal
TM70	Flash	Normal	Status	—	100	20	Normal
TM77	Psych Up	Normal	Status	—	—	10	Normal
TM85	Dream Eater	Psychic	Special	100	100	15	Normal
TM87	Swagger	Normal	Status	—	90	15	Normal
TM88	Sleep Talk	Normal	Status	—	—	10	Self
TM89	U-turn	Bug	Physical	70	100	20	Normal
TM90	Substitute	Normal	Status	—	—	10	Self
TM94	Secret Power	Normal	Physical	70	100	20	Normal
TM97	Dark Pulse	Dark	Special	80	100	15	Normal
TM100	Confide	Normal	Status	—	—	20	Normal
HM01	Cut	Normal	Physical	50	95	30	Normal

MOVES LEARNED IN EXCHANGE FOR BP

Name	Type	Kind	Pow.	Acc.	PP	Range
Covet	Normal	Physical	60	100	25	Normal
Seed Bomb	Grass	Physical	80	100	15	Normal
Gunk Shot	Poison	Physical	120	80	5	Normal
Uproar	Normal	Special	90	100	10	1 Random
Foul Play	Dark	Physical	95	100	15	Normal
Last Resort	Normal	Physical	140	100	5	Normal
Icy Wind	Ice	Special	55	95	15	Many Others
Hyper Voice	Normal	Special	90	100	10	Many Others
Iron Tail	Steel	Physical	100	75	15	Normal
Snore	Normal	Special	50	100	15	Normal
Knock Off	Dark	Physical	65	100	20	Normal
Shock Wave	Electric	Special	60	—	20	Normal
Water Pulse	Water	Special	60	100	20	Normal
Spite	Ghost	Status	—	100	10	Normal
Snatch	Dark	Status	—	—	10	Self

MOVES TAUGHT BY PEOPLE

Name	Type	Kind	Pow.	Acc.	PP	Range

National Pokédex **054** Hoenn Pokédex **165**

Psyduck

Duck Pokémon

Water

HEIGHT: 2'07" WEIGHT: 43.2 lbs.

Same form for ♂ / ♀

Ω Psyduck uses a mysterious power. When it does so, this Pokémon generates brain waves that are supposedly only seen in sleepers. This discovery spurred controversy among scholars.

α If it uses its mysterious power, Psyduck can't remember having done so. It apparently can't form a memory of such an event because it goes into an altered state that is much like deep sleep.

ABILITIES
Damp
Cloud Nine

HIDDEN ABILITY
Swift Swim

EGG GROUPS
Water 1 | Field

STAT GROWTH RATES
HP ■■
Attack ■■■
Defense ■■
Sp. Atk ■■■
Sp. Def ■■
Speed ■■■

ITEMS SOMETIMES HELD BY WILD POKÉMON
—

EVOLUTION
Psyduck → Lv. 33 → Golduck

MAIN WAY TO REGISTER IN THE NATIONAL POKÉDEX

Catch in the tall grass in the lower-right corner of the Safari Zone.

Damage taken in normal battles

Type		Type	
Normal	×1	Flying	×1
Fire	×0.5	Psychic	×1
Water	×0.5	Bug	×1
Grass	×2	Rock	×1
Electric	×2	Ghost	×1
Ice	×0.5	Dragon	×1
Fighting	×1	Dark	×1
Poison	×1	Steel	×0.5
Ground	×1	Fairy	×1

Damage taken in Inverse battles

Type		Type	
Normal	×1	Flying	×1
Fire	×2	Psychic	×1
Water	×2	Bug	×1
Grass	×0.5	Rock	×1
Electric	×0.5	Ghost	×1
Ice	×2	Dragon	×1
Fighting	×1	Dark	×1
Poison	×1	Steel	×2
Ground	×1	Fairy	×1

Can be used in
Inverse Battle
Battle Institute
Battle Maison
Random Matchup (Free Battle)
Random Matchup (Others)

LEVEL-UP MOVES

Lv.	Name	Type	Kind	Pow.	Acc.	PP	Range
1	Water Sport	Water	Status	—	—	15	Both Sides
1	Scratch	Normal	Physical	40	100	35	Normal
4	Tail Whip	Normal	Status	—	100	30	Many Others
8	Water Gun	Water	Special	40	100	25	Normal
11	Confusion	Psychic	Special	50	100	25	Normal
15	Fury Swipes	Normal	Physical	18	80	15	Normal
18	Water Pulse	Water	Special	60	100	20	Normal
22	Disable	Normal	Status	—	100	20	Normal
25	Screech	Normal	Status	—	85	40	Normal
29	Aqua Tail	Water	Physical	90	90	10	Normal
32	Zen Headbutt	Psychic	Physical	80	90	15	Normal
36	Soak	Water	Status	—	100	20	Normal
39	Psych Up	Normal	Status	—	—	10	Normal
43	Amnesia	Psychic	Status	—	—	20	Self
46	Hydro Pump	Water	Special	110	80	5	Normal
50	Wonder Room	Psychic	Status	—	—	10	Both Sides

TM & HM MOVES

No.	Name	Type	Kind	Pow.	Acc.	PP	Range
TM01	Hone Claws	Dark	Status	—	—	15	Self
TM03	Psyshock	Psychic	Special	80	100	10	Normal
TM04	Calm Mind	Psychic	Status	—	—	20	Self
TM06	Toxic	Poison	Status	—	90	10	Normal
TM07	Hail	Ice	Status	—	—	10	Both Sides
TM10	Hidden Power	Normal	Special	60	100	15	Normal
TM13	Ice Beam	Ice	Special	90	100	10	Normal
TM14	Blizzard	Ice	Special	110	70	5	Many Others
TM16	Light Screen	Psychic	Status	—	—	30	Your Side
TM17	Protect	Normal	Status	—	—	10	Self
TM18	Rain Dance	Water	Status	—	—	5	Both Sides
TM21	Frustration	Normal	Physical	—	100	20	Normal
TM27	Return	Normal	Physical	—	100	20	Normal
TM28	Dig	Ground	Physical	80	100	10	Normal
TM29	Psychic	Psychic	Special	90	100	10	Normal
TM31	Brick Break	Fighting	Physical	75	100	15	Normal
TM32	Double Team	Normal	Status	—	—	15	Self
TM40	Aerial Ace	Flying	Physical	60	—	20	Normal
TM42	Facade	Normal	Physical	70	100	20	Normal
TM44	Rest	Psychic	Status	—	—	10	Self
TM45	Attract	Normal	Status	—	100	15	Normal
TM48	Round	Normal	Special	60	100	15	Normal
TM55	Scald	Water	Special	80	100	15	Normal
TM56	Fling	Dark	Physical	—	100	10	Normal
TM65	Shadow Claw	Ghost	Physical	70	100	15	Normal
TM70	Flash	Normal	Status	—	100	20	Normal
TM77	Psych Up	Normal	Status	—	—	10	Normal
TM87	Swagger	Normal	Status	—	90	15	Normal
TM88	Sleep Talk	Normal	Status	—	—	10	Self
TM90	Substitute	Normal	Status	—	—	10	Self
TM94	Secret Power	Normal	Physical	70	100	20	Normal
TM98	Power-Up Punch	Fighting	Physical	40	100	20	Normal
TM100	Confide	Normal	Status	—	—	20	Normal
HM03	Surf	Water	Special	90	100	15	Adjacent
HM04	Strength	Normal	Physical	80	100	15	Normal
HM05	Waterfall	Water	Physical	80	100	15	Normal
HM06	Rock Smash	Fighting	Physical	40	100	15	Normal
HM07	Dive	Water	Physical	80	100	10	Normal

MOVES LEARNED IN EXCHANGE FOR BP

Name	Type	Kind	Pow.	Acc.	PP	Range
Signal Beam	Bug	Special	75	100	15	Normal
Ice Punch	Ice	Physical	75	100	15	Normal
Icy Wind	Ice	Special	55	95	15	Many Others
Aqua Tail	Water	Physical	90	90	10	Normal
Zen Headbutt	Psychic	Physical	80	90	15	Normal
Iron Tail	Steel	Physical	100	75	15	Normal
Snore	Normal	Special	50	100	15	Normal
Role Play	Psychic	Status	—	—	10	Normal
Focus Punch	Fighting	Physical	150	100	20	Normal
Water Pulse	Water	Special	60	100	20	Normal
Worry Seed	Grass	Status	—	100	10	Normal
Wonder Room	Psychic	Status	—	—	10	Both Sides

MOVES TAUGHT BY PEOPLE

Name	Type	Kind	Pow.	Acc.	PP	Range

EGG MOVES

Name	Type	Kind	Pow.	Acc.	PP	Range
Hypnosis	Psychic	Status	—	60	20	Normal
Psybeam	Psychic	Special	65	100	20	Normal
Foresight	Normal	Status	—	—	40	Normal
Future Sight	Psychic	Special	120	100	10	Normal
Cross Chop	Fighting	Physical	100	80	5	Normal
Refresh	Normal	Status	—	—	20	Self
Confuse Ray	Ghost	Status	—	100	10	Normal
Yawn	Normal	Status	—	—	10	Normal
Mud Bomb	Ground	Special	65	85	10	Normal
Encore	Normal	Status	—	100	5	Normal
Secret Power	Normal	Physical	70	100	20	Normal
Sleep Talk	Normal	Status	—	—	10	Self
Synchronoise	Psychic	Special	120	100	10	Adjacent
Simple Beam	Normal	Status	—	100	15	Normal
Clear Smog	Poison	Special	50	—	15	Normal

National Pokédex **055** Hoenn Pokédex **166**

Golduck

Duck Pokémon

Water

HEIGHT: 5'07" WEIGHT: 168.9 lbs.

Same form for ♂ / ♀

Ω The webbed flippers on its forelegs and hind legs and the streamlined body of Golduck give it frightening speed. This Pokémon is definitely much faster than even the most athletic swimmer.

α Golduck is the fastest swimmer among all Pokémon. It swims effortlessly, even in a rough, stormy sea. It sometimes rescues people from wrecked ships floundering in high seas.

ABILITIES
Damp
Cloud Nine

HIDDEN ABILITY
Swift Swim

EGG GROUPS
Water 1 | Field

STAT GROWTH RATES
HP ■■■
Attack ■■■■
Defense ■■■
Sp. Atk ■■■■■
Sp. Def ■■■
Speed ■■■■■

ITEMS SOMETIMES HELD BY WILD POKÉMON
—

EVOLUTION

Psyduck → Golduck

MAIN WAY TO REGISTER IN THE NATIONAL POKÉDEX

Level up Psyduck to Lv. 33.

Damage taken in normal battles

Type		Type	
Normal	×1	Flying	×1
Fire	×0.5	Psychic	×1
Water	×0.5	Bug	×1
Grass	×2	Rock	×1
Electric	×2	Ghost	×1
Ice	×0.5	Dragon	×1
Fighting	×1	Dark	×1
Poison	×1	Steel	×0.5
Ground	×1	Fairy	×1

Damage taken in Inverse battles

Type		Type	
Normal	×1	Flying	×1
Fire	×2	Psychic	×1
Water	×2	Bug	×1
Grass	×0.5	Rock	×1
Electric	×0.5	Ghost	×1
Ice	×2	Dragon	×1
Fighting	×1	Dark	×1
Poison	×1	Steel	×2
Ground	×1	Fairy	×1

Can be used in
Inverse Battle
Battle Institute
Battle Maison
Random Matchup (Free Battle)
Random Matchup (Others)

LEVEL-UP MOVES

Lv.	Name	Type	Kind	Pow.	Acc.	PP	Range
1	Aqua Jet	Water	Physical	40	100	20	Normal
1	Water Sport	Water	Status	—	—	15	Both Sides
1	Scratch	Normal	Physical	40	100	35	Normal
1	Tail Whip	Normal	Status	—	100	30	Many Others
1	Water Gun	Water	Special	40	100	25	Normal
4	Tail Whip	Normal	Status	—	100	30	Many Others
8	Water Gun	Water	Special	40	100	25	Normal
11	Confusion	Psychic	Special	50	100	25	Normal
15	Fury Swipes	Normal	Physical	18	80	15	Normal
18	Water Pulse	Water	Special	60	100	20	Normal
22	Disable	Normal	Status	—	100	20	Normal
25	Zen Headbutt	Psychic	Physical	80	90	15	Normal
29	Screech	Normal	Status	—	85	40	Normal
32	Aqua Tail	Water	Physical	90	90	10	Normal
38	Soak	Water	Status	—	100	20	Normal
43	Psych Up	Normal	Status	—	—	10	Normal
49	Amnesia	Psychic	Status	—	—	20	Self
54	Hydro Pump	Water	Special	110	80	5	Normal
60	Wonder Room	Psychic	Status	—	—	10	Both Sides

TM & HM MOVES

No.	Name	Type	Kind	Pow.	Acc.	PP	Range
TM01	Hone Claws	Dark	Status	—	—	15	Self
TM03	Psyshock	Psychic	Special	80	100	10	Normal
TM04	Calm Mind	Psychic	Status	—	—	20	Self
TM06	Toxic	Poison	Status	—	90	10	Normal
TM07	Hail	Ice	Status	—	—	10	Both Sides
TM10	Hidden Power	Normal	Special	60	100	15	Normal
TM13	Ice Beam	Ice	Special	90	100	10	Normal
TM14	Blizzard	Ice	Special	110	70	5	Many Others
TM15	Hyper Beam	Normal	Special	150	90	5	Normal
TM16	Light Screen	Psychic	Status	—	—	30	Your Side
TM17	Protect	Normal	Status	—	—	10	Self
TM18	Rain Dance	Water	Status	—	—	5	Both Sides
TM21	Frustration	Normal	Physical	—	100	20	Normal
TM27	Return	Normal	Physical	—	100	20	Normal
TM28	Dig	Ground	Physical	80	100	10	Normal
TM29	Psychic	Psychic	Special	90	100	10	Normal
TM31	Brick Break	Fighting	Physical	75	100	15	Normal
TM32	Double Team	Normal	Status	—	—	15	Self
TM40	Aerial Ace	Flying	Physical	60	—	20	Normal
TM42	Facade	Normal	Physical	70	100	20	Normal
TM44	Rest	Psychic	Status	—	—	10	Self
TM45	Attract	Normal	Status	—	100	15	Normal
TM47	Low Sweep	Fighting	Physical	65	100	20	Normal
TM48	Round	Normal	Special	60	100	15	Normal
TM52	Focus Blast	Fighting	Special	120	70	5	Normal
TM55	Scald	Water	Special	80	100	15	Normal
TM56	Fling	Dark	Physical	—	100	10	Normal
TM65	Shadow Claw	Ghost	Physical	70	100	15	Normal
TM68	Giga Impact	Normal	Physical	150	90	5	Normal
TM70	Flash	Normal	Status	—	100	20	Normal
TM77	Psych Up	Normal	Status	—	—	10	Normal
TM87	Swagger	Normal	Status	—	90	15	Normal
TM88	Sleep Talk	Normal	Status	—	—	10	Self
TM90	Substitute	Normal	Status	—	—	10	Self
TM94	Secret Power	Normal	Physical	70	100	20	Normal
TM98	Power-Up Punch	Fighting	Physical	40	100	20	Normal
TM100	Confide	Normal	Status	—	—	20	Normal
HM03	Surf	Water	Special	90	100	15	Adjacent
HM04	Strength	Normal	Physical	80	100	15	Normal
HM05	Waterfall	Water	Physical	80	100	15	Normal
HM06	Rock Smash	Fighting	Physical	40	100	15	Normal
HM07	Dive	Water	Physical	80	100	10	Normal

MOVES LEARNED IN EXCHANGE FOR BP

Name	Type	Kind	Pow.	Acc.	PP	Range
Signal Beam	Bug	Special	75	100	15	Normal
Low Kick	Fighting	Physical	—	100	20	Normal
Ice Punch	Ice	Physical	75	100	15	Normal
Icy Wind	Ice	Special	55	95	15	Many Others
Aqua Tail	Water	Physical	90	90	10	Normal
Zen Headbutt	Psychic	Physical	80	90	15	Normal
Iron Tail	Steel	Physical	100	75	15	Normal
Snore	Normal	Special	50	100	15	Normal
Role Play	Psychic	Status	—	—	10	Normal
Focus Punch	Fighting	Physical	150	100	20	Normal
Water Pulse	Water	Special	60	100	20	Normal
Worry Seed	Grass	Status	—	100	10	Normal
Wonder Room	Psychic	Status	—	—	10	Both Sides

MOVES TAUGHT BY PEOPLE

Name	Type	Kind	Pow.	Acc.	PP	Range

National Pokédex **056** Hoenn Pokédex —

Mankey

Pig Monkey Pokémon

Fighting

HEIGHT: 1'08" WEIGHT: 61.7 lbs.

Same form for ♂ / ♀

Ω When Mankey starts shaking and its nasal breathing turns rough, it's a sure sign that it is becoming angry. However, because it goes into a towering rage almost instantly, it is impossible for anyone to flee its wrath.

α When Mankey starts shaking and its nasal breathing turns rough, it's a sure sign that it is becoming angry. However, because it goes into a towering rage almost instantly, it is impossible for anyone to flee its wrath.

ABILITIES
Vital Spirit
Anger Point

HIDDEN ABILITY
Defiant

EGG GROUPS
Field

STAT GROWTH RATES
HP ■■
Attack ■■■■
Defense ■■
Sp. Atk ■■
Sp. Def ■■
Speed ■■■■

ITEMS SOMETIMES HELD BY WILD POKÉMON
—

EVOLUTION

Mankey Primeape

MAIN WAY TO REGISTER IN THE NATIONAL POKÉDEX

Catch on Jagged Pass. Appears as a hidden Pokémon after you battle Groudon or Kyogre.

Damage taken in normal battles

Type		Type	
Normal	×1	Flying	×2
Fire	×1	Psychic	×2
Water	×1	Bug	×0.5
Grass	×1	Rock	×0.5
Electric	×1	Ghost	×1
Ice	×1	Dragon	×1
Fighting	×1	Dark	×0.5
Poison	×1	Steel	×1
Ground	×1	Fairy	×2

Damage taken in Inverse battles

Type		Type	
Normal	×1	Flying	×0.5
Fire	×1	Psychic	×0.5
Water	×1	Bug	×2
Grass	×1	Rock	×2
Electric	×1	Ghost	×1
Ice	×1	Dragon	×1
Fighting	×1	Dark	×2
Poison	×1	Steel	×1
Ground	×1	Fairy	×0.5

Can be used in
Inverse Battle
Battle Institute
Battle Maison
Random Matchup (Free Battle)
Random Matchup (Others)

LEVEL-UP MOVES

Lv.	Name	Type	Kind	Pow.	Acc.	PP	Range
1	Covet	Normal	Physical	60	100	25	Normal
1	Scratch	Normal	Physical	40	100	35	Normal
1	Low Kick	Fighting	Physical	—	100	20	Normal
1	Leer	Normal	Status	—	100	30	Many Others
1	Focus Energy	Normal	Status	—	—	30	Self
9	Fury Swipes	Normal	Physical	18	80	15	Normal
13	Karate Chop	Fighting	Physical	50	100	25	Normal
17	Seismic Toss	Fighting	Physical	—	100	20	Normal
21	Screech	Normal	Status	—	85	40	Normal
25	Assurance	Dark	Physical	60	100	10	Normal
33	Swagger	Normal	Status	—	90	15	Normal
37	Cross Chop	Fighting	Physical	100	80	5	Normal
41	Thrash	Normal	Physical	120	100	10	1 Random
45	Punishment	Dark	Physical	—	100	5	Normal
49	Close Combat	Fighting	Physical	120	100	5	Normal
53	Final Gambit	Fighting	Special	—	100	5	Normal

TM & HM MOVES

No.	Name	Type	Kind	Pow.	Acc.	PP	Range
TM01	Hone Claws	Dark	Status	—	—	15	Self
TM06	Toxic	Poison	Status	—	90	10	Normal
TM08	Bulk Up	Fighting	Status	—	—	20	Self
TM10	Hidden Power	Normal	Special	60	100	15	Normal
TM11	Sunny Day	Fire	Status	—	—	5	Both Sides
TM12	Taunt	Dark	Status	—	100	20	Normal
TM17	Protect	Normal	Status	—	—	10	Self
TM18	Rain Dance	Water	Status	—	—	5	Both Sides
TM21	Frustration	Normal	Physical	—	100	20	Normal
TM23	Smack Down	Rock	Physical	50	100	15	Normal
TM24	Thunderbolt	Electric	Special	90	100	15	Normal
TM25	Thunder	Electric	Special	110	70	10	Normal
TM26	Earthquake	Ground	Physical	100	100	10	Adjacent
TM27	Return	Normal	Physical	—	100	20	Normal
TM28	Dig	Ground	Physical	80	100	10	Normal
TM31	Brick Break	Fighting	Physical	75	100	15	Normal
TM32	Double Team	Normal	Status	—	—	15	Self
TM39	Rock Tomb	Rock	Physical	60	95	15	Normal
TM40	Aerial Ace	Flying	Physical	60	—	20	Normal
TM42	Facade	Normal	Physical	70	100	20	Normal
TM44	Rest	Psychic	Status	—	—	10	Self
TM45	Attract	Normal	Status	—	100	15	Normal
TM46	Thief	Dark	Physical	60	100	25	Normal
TM47	Low Sweep	Fighting	Physical	65	100	20	Normal
TM48	Round	Normal	Special	60	100	15	Normal
TM50	Overheat	Fire	Special	130	90	5	Normal
TM52	Focus Blast	Fighting	Special	120	70	5	Normal
TM56	Fling	Dark	Physical	—	100	10	Normal
TM62	Acrobatics	Flying	Physical	55	100	15	Normal
TM66	Payback	Dark	Physical	50	100	10	Normal
TM67	Retaliate	Normal	Physical	70	100	5	Normal
TM78	Bulldoze	Ground	Physical	60	100	20	Adjacent
TM80	Rock Slide	Rock	Physical	75	90	10	Many Others
TM84	Poison Jab	Poison	Physical	80	100	20	Normal
TM87	Swagger	Normal	Status	—	90	15	Normal
TM88	Sleep Talk	Normal	Status	—	—	10	Self
TM89	U-turn	Bug	Physical	70	100	20	Normal
TM90	Substitute	Normal	Status	—	—	10	Self
TM94	Secret Power	Normal	Physical	70	100	20	Normal
TM98	Power-Up Punch	Fighting	Physical	40	100	20	Normal
TM100	Confide	Normal	Status	—	—	20	Normal
HM04	Strength	Normal	Physical	80	100	15	Normal
HM06	Rock Smash	Fighting	Physical	40	100	15	Normal

MOVES LEARNED IN EXCHANGE FOR BP

Name	Type	Kind	Pow.	Acc.	PP	Range
Covet	Normal	Physical	60	100	25	Normal
Dual Chop	Dragon	Physical	40	90	15	Normal
Seed Bomb	Grass	Physical	80	100	15	Normal
Low Kick	Fighting	Physical	—	100	20	Normal
Gunk Shot	Poison	Physical	120	80	5	Normal
Uproar	Normal	Special	90	100	10	1 Random
Thunder Punch	Electric	Physical	75	100	15	Normal
Fire Punch	Fire	Physical	75	100	15	Normal
Ice Punch	Ice	Physical	75	100	15	Normal
Iron Tail	Steel	Physical	100	75	15	Normal
Snore	Normal	Special	50	100	15	Normal
Role Play	Psychic	Status	—	—	10	Normal
Focus Punch	Fighting	Physical	150	100	20	Normal
Spite	Ghost	Status	—	100	10	Normal
Helping Hand	Normal	Status	—	—	20	1 Ally
Endeavor	Normal	Physical	—	100	5	Normal
Outrage	Dragon	Physical	120	100	10	1 Random

MOVES TAUGHT BY PEOPLE

Name	Type	Kind	Pow.	Acc.	PP	Range

EGG MOVES

Name	Type	Kind	Pow.	Acc.	PP	Range
Foresight	Normal	Status	—	—	40	Normal
Meditate	Psychic	Status	—	—	40	Self
Counter	Fighting	Physical	—	100	20	Varies
Reversal	Fighting	Physical	—	100	15	Normal
Beat Up	Dark	Physical	—	100	10	Normal
Revenge	Fighting	Physical	60	100	10	Normal
Smelling Salts	Normal	Physical	70	100	10	Normal
Close Combat	Fighting	Physical	120	100	5	Normal
Encore	Normal	Status	—	100	5	Normal
Focus Punch	Fighting	Physical	150	100	20	Normal
Sleep Talk	Normal	Status	—	—	10	Self
Night Slash	Dark	Physical	70	100	15	Normal

National Pokédex **057** Hoenn Pokédex —

Primeape

Pig Monkey Pokémon

Fighting

HEIGHT: 3'03" WEIGHT: 70.5 lbs.

Same form for ♂ / ♀

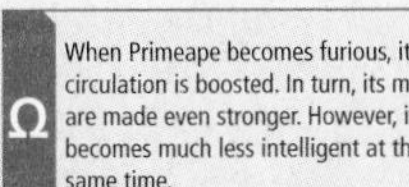

Ω When Primeape becomes furious, its blood circulation is boosted. In turn, its muscles are made even stronger. However, it also becomes much less intelligent at the same time.

α When Primeape becomes furious, its blood circulation is boosted. In turn, its muscles are made even stronger. However, it also becomes much less intelligent at the same time.

ABILITIES
Vital Spirit
Anger Point

HIDDEN ABILITY
Defiant

EGG GROUPS
Field

STAT GROWTH RATES
HP ■■■
Attack ■■■■■
Defense ■■■
Sp. Atk ■■■
Sp. Def ■■■
Speed ■■■■■

ITEMS SOMETIMES HELD BY WILD POKÉMON
—

EVOLUTION

Lv. 28

Mankey Primeape

MAIN WAY TO REGISTER IN THE NATIONAL POKÉDEX

Level up Mankey to Lv. 28.

Damage taken in normal battles

Type		Type	
Normal	×1	Flying	×2
Fire	×1	Psychic	×2
Water	×1	Bug	×0.5
Grass	×1	Rock	×0.5
Electric	×1	Ghost	×1
Ice	×1	Dragon	×1
Fighting	×1	Dark	×0.5
Poison	×1	Steel	×1
Ground	×1	Fairy	×2

Damage taken in Inverse battles

Type		Type	
Normal	×1	Flying	×0.5
Fire	×1	Psychic	×0.5
Water	×1	Bug	×2
Grass	×1	Rock	×2
Electric	×1	Ghost	×1
Ice	×1	Dragon	×1
Fighting	×1	Dark	×2
Poison	×1	Steel	×1
Ground	×1	Fairy	×0.5

Can be used in
Inverse Battle
Battle Institute
Battle Maison
Random Matchup (Free Battle)
Random Matchup (Others)

LEVEL-UP MOVES

Lv.	Name	Type	Kind	Pow.	Acc.	PP	Range
1	Final Gambit	Fighting	Special	—	100	5	Normal
1	Fling	Dark	Physical	—	100	10	Normal
1	Scratch	Normal	Physical	40	100	35	Normal
1	Low Kick	Fighting	Physical	—	100	20	Normal
1	Leer	Normal	Status	—	100	30	Many Others
1	Focus Energy	Normal	Status	—	—	30	Self
9	Fury Swipes	Normal	Physical	18	80	15	Normal
13	Karate Chop	Fighting	Physical	50	100	25	Normal
17	Seismic Toss	Fighting	Physical	—	100	20	Normal
21	Screech	Normal	Status	—	85	40	Normal
25	Assurance	Dark	Physical	60	100	10	Normal
28	Rage	Normal	Physical	20	100	20	Normal
35	Swagger	Normal	Status	—	90	15	Normal
41	Cross Chop	Fighting	Physical	100	80	5	Normal
47	Thrash	Normal	Physical	120	100	10	1 Random
53	Punishment	Dark	Physical	—	100	5	Normal
59	Close Combat	Fighting	Physical	120	100	5	Normal
63	Final Gambit	Fighting	Special	—	100	5	Normal

TM & HM MOVES

No.	Name	Type	Kind	Pow.	Acc.	PP	Range
TM01	Hone Claws	Dark	Status	—	—	15	Self
TM06	Toxic	Poison	Status	—	90	10	Normal
TM08	Bulk Up	Fighting	Status	—	—	20	Self
TM10	Hidden Power	Normal	Special	60	100	15	Normal
TM11	Sunny Day	Fire	Status	—	—	5	Both Sides
TM12	Taunt	Dark	Status	—	100	20	Normal
TM15	Hyper Beam	Normal	Special	150	90	5	Normal
TM17	Protect	Normal	Status	—	—	10	Self
TM18	Rain Dance	Water	Status	—	—	5	Both Sides
TM21	Frustration	Normal	Physical	—	100	20	Normal
TM23	Smack Down	Rock	Physical	50	100	15	Normal
TM24	Thunderbolt	Electric	Special	90	100	15	Normal
TM25	Thunder	Electric	Special	110	70	10	Normal
TM26	Earthquake	Ground	Physical	100	100	10	Adjacent
TM27	Return	Normal	Physical	—	100	20	Normal
TM28	Dig	Ground	Physical	80	100	10	Normal
TM31	Brick Break	Fighting	Physical	75	100	15	Normal
TM32	Double Team	Normal	Status	—	—	15	Self
TM39	Rock Tomb	Rock	Physical	60	95	15	Normal
TM40	Aerial Ace	Flying	Physical	60	—	20	Normal
TM42	Facade	Normal	Physical	70	100	20	Normal
TM44	Rest	Psychic	Status	—	—	10	Self
TM45	Attract	Normal	Status	—	100	15	Normal
TM46	Thief	Dark	Physical	60	100	25	Normal
TM47	Low Sweep	Fighting	Physical	65	100	20	Normal
TM48	Round	Normal	Special	60	100	15	Normal
TM50	Overheat	Fire	Special	130	90	5	Normal
TM52	Focus Blast	Fighting	Special	120	70	5	Normal
TM56	Fling	Dark	Physical	—	100	10	Normal
TM62	Acrobatics	Flying	Physical	55	100	15	Normal
TM66	Payback	Dark	Physical	50	100	10	Normal
TM67	Retaliate	Normal	Physical	70	100	5	Normal
TM68	Giga Impact	Normal	Physical	150	90	5	Normal
TM71	Stone Edge	Rock	Physical	100	80	5	Normal
TM78	Bulldoze	Ground	Physical	60	100	20	Adjacent
TM80	Rock Slide	Rock	Physical	75	90	10	Many Others
TM84	Poison Jab	Poison	Physical	80	100	20	Normal
TM87	Swagger	Normal	Status	—	90	15	Normal
TM88	Sleep Talk	Normal	Status	—	—	10	Self
TM89	U-turn	Bug	Physical	70	100	20	Normal
TM90	Substitute	Normal	Status	—	—	10	Self
TM94	Secret Power	Normal	Physical	70	100	20	Normal
TM98	Power-Up Punch	Fighting	Physical	40	100	20	Normal
TM100	Confide	Normal	Status	—	—	20	Normal
HM04	Strength	Normal	Physical	80	100	15	Normal
HM06	Rock Smash	Fighting	Physical	40	100	15	Normal

MOVES LEARNED IN EXCHANGE FOR BP

Name	Type	Kind	Pow.	Acc.	PP	Range
Covet	Normal	Physical	60	100	25	Normal
Dual Chop	Dragon	Physical	40	90	15	Normal
Seed Bomb	Grass	Physical	80	100	15	Normal
Low Kick	Fighting	Physical	—	100	20	Normal
Gunk Shot	Poison	Physical	120	80	5	Normal
Uproar	Normal	Special	90	100	10	1 Random
Thunder Punch	Electric	Physical	75	100	15	Normal
Fire Punch	Fire	Physical	75	100	15	Normal
Ice Punch	Ice	Physical	75	100	15	Normal
Iron Tail	Steel	Physical	100	75	15	Normal
Snore	Normal	Special	50	100	15	Normal
Role Play	Psychic	Status	—	—	10	Normal
Focus Punch	Fighting	Physical	150	100	20	Normal
Spite	Ghost	Status	—	100	10	Normal
Helping Hand	Normal	Status	—	—	20	1 Ally
Endeavor	Normal	Physical	—	100	5	Normal
Outrage	Dragon	Physical	120	100	10	1 Random

MOVES TAUGHT BY PEOPLE

Name	Type	Kind	Pow.	Acc.	PP	Range

National Pokédex **058** Hoenn Pokédex —

Growlithe

Puppy Pokémon

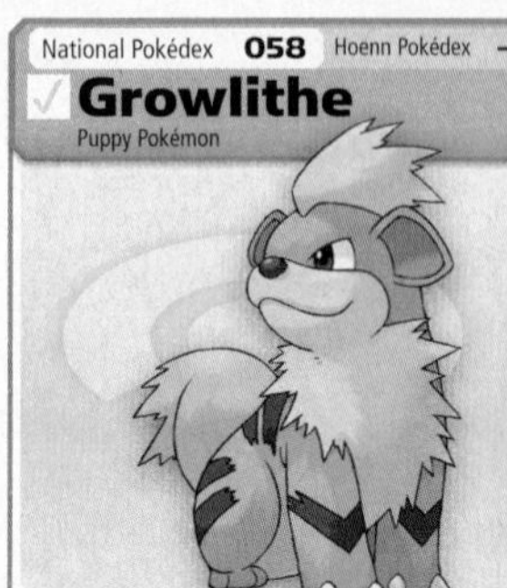

Fire

HEIGHT: 2'04" WEIGHT: 41.9 lbs.

Same form for ♂ / ♀

Ω Growlithe has a superb sense of smell. Once it smells anything, this Pokémon won't forget the scent, no matter what. It uses its advanced olfactory sense to determine the emotions of other living things.

α Growlithe has a superb sense of smell. Once it smells anything, this Pokémon won't forget the scent, no matter what. It uses its advanced olfactory sense to determine the emotions of other living things.

ABILITIES
Intimidate
Flash Fire

HIDDEN ABILITY
Justified

EGG GROUPS
Field

STAT GROWTH RATES
HP
Attack
Defense
Sp. Atk
Sp. Def
Speed

ITEMS SOMETIMES HELD BY WILD POKÉMON
—

EVOLUTION
Growlithe → Fire Stone → Arcanine

MAIN WAY TO REGISTER IN THE NATIONAL POKÉDEX

Catch on Mt. Pyre (Exterior). Appears as a hidden Pokémon after you battle Groudon or Kyogre.

Damage taken in normal battles

Type		Type	
Normal	×1	Flying	×1
Fire	×0.5	Psychic	×1
Water	×2	Bug	×0.5
Grass	×0.5	Rock	×2
Electric	×1	Ghost	×1
Ice	×0.5	Dragon	×1
Fighting	×1	Dark	×1
Poison	×1	Steel	×0.5
Ground	×2	Fairy	×0.5

Damage taken in Inverse battles

Type		Type	
Normal	×1	Flying	×1
Fire	×2	Psychic	×1
Water	×0.5	Bug	×2
Grass	×2	Rock	×0.5
Electric	×1	Ghost	×1
Ice	×2	Dragon	×1
Fighting	×1	Dark	×1
Poison	×1	Steel	×2
Ground	×0.5	Fairy	×2

Can be used in
Inverse Battle
Battle Institute
Battle Maison
Random Matchup (Free Battle)
Random Matchup (Others)

LEVEL-UP MOVES

Lv.	Name	Type	Kind	Pow.	Acc.	PP	Range
1	Bite	Dark	Physical	60	100	25	Normal
1	Roar	Normal	Status	—	—	20	Normal
6	Ember	Fire	Special	40	100	25	Normal
8	Leer	Normal	Status	—	100	30	Many Others
10	Odor Sleuth	Normal	Status	—	—	40	Normal
12	Helping Hand	Normal	Status	—	—	20	1 Ally
17	Flame Wheel	Fire	Physical	60	100	25	Normal
19	Reversal	Fighting	Physical	—	100	15	Normal
21	Fire Fang	Fire	Physical	65	95	15	Normal
23	Take Down	Normal	Physical	90	85	20	Normal
28	Flame Burst	Fire	Special	70	100	15	Normal
30	Agility	Psychic	Status	—	—	30	Self
32	Retaliate	Normal	Physical	70	100	5	Normal
34	Flamethrower	Fire	Special	90	100	15	Normal
39	Crunch	Dark	Physical	80	100	15	Normal
41	Heat Wave	Fire	Special	95	90	10	Many Others
43	Outrage	Dragon	Physical	120	100	10	1 Random
45	Flare Blitz	Fire	Physical	120	100	15	Normal

TM & HM MOVES

No.	Name	Type	Kind	Pow.	Acc.	PP	Range
TM05	Roar	Normal	Status	—	—	20	Normal
TM06	Toxic	Poison	Status	—	90	10	Normal
TM10	Hidden Power	Normal	Special	60	100	15	Normal
TM11	Sunny Day	Fire	Status	—	—	5	Both Sides
TM17	Protect	Normal	Status	—	—	10	Self
TM20	Safeguard	Normal	Status	—	—	25	Your Side
TM21	Frustration	Normal	Physical	—	100	20	Normal
TM27	Return	Normal	Physical	—	100	20	Normal
TM28	Dig	Ground	Physical	80	100	10	Normal
TM32	Double Team	Normal	Status	—	—	15	Self
TM35	Flamethrower	Fire	Special	90	100	15	Normal
TM38	Fire Blast	Fire	Special	110	85	5	Normal
TM40	Aerial Ace	Flying	Physical	60	—	20	Normal
TM42	Facade	Normal	Physical	70	100	20	Normal
TM43	Flame Charge	Fire	Physical	50	100	20	Normal
TM44	Rest	Psychic	Status	—	—	10	Self
TM45	Attract	Normal	Status	—	100	15	Normal
TM46	Thief	Dark	Physical	60	100	25	Normal
TM48	Round	Normal	Special	60	100	15	Normal
TM50	Overheat	Fire	Special	130	90	5	Normal
TM59	Incinerate	Fire	Special	60	100	15	Many Others
TM61	Will-O-Wisp	Fire	Status	—	85	15	Normal
TM67	Retaliate	Normal	Physical	70	100	5	Normal
TM87	Swagger	Normal	Status	—	90	15	Normal
TM88	Sleep Talk	Normal	Status	—	—	10	Self
TM90	Substitute	Normal	Status	—	—	10	Self
TM93	Wild Charge	Electric	Physical	90	100	15	Normal
TM94	Secret Power	Normal	Physical	70	100	20	Normal
TM95	Snarl	Dark	Special	55	95	15	Many Others
TM100	Confide	Normal	Status	—	—	20	Normal
HM04	Strength	Normal	Physical	80	100	15	Normal
HM06	Rock Smash	Fighting	Physical	40	100	15	Normal

MOVES LEARNED IN EXCHANGE FOR BP

Name	Type	Kind	Pow.	Acc.	PP	Range
Covet	Normal	Physical	60	100	25	Normal
Iron Tail	Steel	Physical	100	75	15	Normal
Snore	Normal	Special	50	100	15	Normal
Heat Wave	Fire	Special	95	90	10	Many Others
Helping Hand	Normal	Status	—	—	20	1 Ally
Outrage	Dragon	Physical	120	100	10	1 Random

MOVES TAUGHT BY PEOPLE

Name	Type	Kind	Pow.	Acc.	PP	Range

EGG MOVES

Name	Type	Kind	Pow.	Acc.	PP	Range
Body Slam	Normal	Physical	85	100	15	Normal
Crunch	Dark	Physical	80	100	15	Normal
Thrash	Normal	Physical	120	100	10	1 Random
Fire Spin	Fire	Special	35	85	15	Normal
Howl	Normal	Status	—	—	40	Self
Heat Wave	Fire	Special	95	90	10	Many Others
Double-Edge	Normal	Physical	120	100	15	Normal
Flare Blitz	Fire	Physical	120	100	15	Normal
Morning Sun	Normal	Status	—	—	5	Self
Covet	Normal	Physical	60	100	25	Normal
Iron Tail	Steel	Physical	100	75	15	Normal
Double Kick	Fighting	Physical	30	100	30	Normal
Close Combat	Fighting	Physical	120	100	5	Normal

National Pokédex **059** Hoenn Pokédex —

Arcanine

Legendary Pokémon

Fire

HEIGHT: 6'03" WEIGHT: 341.7 lbs.

Same form for ♂ / ♀

Ω Arcanine is known for its high speed. It is said to be capable of running over 6,200 miles in a single day and night. The fire that blazes wildly within this Pokémon's body is its source of power.

α Arcanine is known for its high speed. It is said to be capable of running over 6,200 miles in a single day and night. The fire that blazes wildly within this Pokémon's body is its source of power.

ABILITIES
Intimidate
Flash Fire

HIDDEN ABILITY
Justified

EGG GROUPS
Field

STAT GROWTH RATES
HP
Attack
Defense
Sp. Atk
Sp. Def
Speed

ITEMS SOMETIMES HELD BY WILD POKÉMON
—

EVOLUTION
Growlithe → Fire Stone → Arcanine

MAIN WAY TO REGISTER IN THE NATIONAL POKÉDEX

Use a Fire Stone on Growlithe.

Damage taken in normal battles

Type		Type	
Normal	×1	Flying	×1
Fire	×0.5	Psychic	×1
Water	×2	Bug	×0.5
Grass	×0.5	Rock	×2
Electric	×1	Ghost	×1
Ice	×0.5	Dragon	×1
Fighting	×1	Dark	×1
Poison	×1	Steel	×0.5
Ground	×2	Fairy	×0.5

Damage taken in Inverse battles

Type		Type	
Normal	×1	Flying	×1
Fire	×2	Psychic	×1
Water	×0.5	Bug	×2
Grass	×2	Rock	×0.5
Electric	×1	Ghost	×1
Ice	×2	Dragon	×1
Fighting	×1	Dark	×1
Poison	×1	Steel	×2
Ground	×0.5	Fairy	×2

Can be used in
Inverse Battle
Battle Institute
Battle Maison
Random Matchup (Free Battle)
Random Matchup (Others)

LEVEL-UP MOVES

Lv.	Name	Type	Kind	Pow.	Acc.	PP	Range
1	Thunder Fang	Electric	Physical	65	95	15	Normal
1	Bite	Dark	Physical	60	100	25	Normal
1	Roar	Normal	Status	—	—	20	Normal
1	Odor Sleuth	Normal	Status	—	—	40	Normal
1	Fire Fang	Fire	Physical	65	95	15	Normal
34	Extreme Speed	Normal	Physical	80	100	5	Normal

TM & HM MOVES

No.	Name	Type	Kind	Pow.	Acc.	PP	Range
TM05	Roar	Normal	Status	—	—	20	Normal
TM06	Toxic	Poison	Status	—	90	10	Normal
TM10	Hidden Power	Normal	Special	60	100	15	Normal
TM11	Sunny Day	Fire	Status	—	—	5	Both Sides
TM15	Hyper Beam	Normal	Special	150	90	5	Normal
TM17	Protect	Normal	Status	—	—	10	Self
TM20	Safeguard	Normal	Status	—	—	25	Your Side
TM21	Frustration	Normal	Physical	—	100	20	Normal
TM22	Solar Beam	Grass	Special	120	100	10	Normal
TM27	Return	Normal	Physical	—	100	20	Normal
TM28	Dig	Ground	Physical	80	100	10	Normal
TM32	Double Team	Normal	Status	—	—	15	Self
TM35	Flamethrower	Fire	Special	90	100	15	Normal
TM38	Fire Blast	Fire	Special	110	85	5	Normal
TM40	Aerial Ace	Flying	Physical	60	—	20	Normal
TM42	Facade	Normal	Physical	70	100	20	Normal
TM43	Flame Charge	Fire	Physical	50	100	20	Normal
TM44	Rest	Psychic	Status	—	—	10	Self
TM45	Attract	Normal	Status	—	100	15	Normal
TM46	Thief	Dark	Physical	60	100	25	Normal
TM48	Round	Normal	Special	60	100	15	Normal
TM50	Overheat	Fire	Special	130	90	5	Normal
TM59	Incinerate	Fire	Special	60	100	15	Many Others
TM61	Will-O-Wisp	Fire	Status	—	85	15	Normal
TM67	Retaliate	Normal	Physical	70	100	5	Normal
TM68	Giga Impact	Normal	Physical	150	90	5	Normal
TM78	Bulldoze	Ground	Physical	60	100	20	Adjacent
TM87	Swagger	Normal	Status	—	90	15	Normal
TM88	Sleep Talk	Normal	Status	—	—	10	Self
TM90	Substitute	Normal	Status	—	—	10	Self
TM93	Wild Charge	Electric	Physical	90	100	15	Normal
TM94	Secret Power	Normal	Physical	70	100	20	Normal
TM95	Snarl	Dark	Special	55	95	15	Many Others
TM100	Confide	Normal	Status	—	—	20	Normal
HM04	Strength	Normal	Physical	80	100	15	Normal
HM06	Rock Smash	Fighting	Physical	40	100	15	Normal

MOVES LEARNED IN EXCHANGE FOR BP

Name	Type	Kind	Pow.	Acc.	PP	Range
Covet	Normal	Physical	60	100	25	Normal
Iron Head	Steel	Physical	80	100	15	Normal
Dragon Pulse	Dragon	Special	85	100	10	Normal
Iron Tail	Steel	Physical	100	75	15	Normal
Snore	Normal	Special	50	100	15	Normal
Heat Wave	Fire	Special	95	90	10	Many Others
Helping Hand	Normal	Status	—	—	20	1 Ally
Outrage	Dragon	Physical	120	100	10	1 Random

MOVES TAUGHT BY PEOPLE

Name	Type	Kind	Pow.	Acc.	PP	Range

National Pokédex **060** Hoenn Pokédex —

Poliwag

Tadpole Pokémon

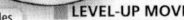

Water

HEIGHT: 2'00" WEIGHT: 27.3 lbs.

Same form for ♂ / ♀

Ω Poliwag has a very thin skin. It is possible to see the Pokémon's spiral innards right through the skin. Despite its thinness, however, the skin is also very flexible. Even sharp fangs bounce right off it.

α Poliwag has a very thin skin. It is possible to see the Pokémon's spiral innards right through the skin. Despite its thinness, however, the skin is also very flexible. Even sharp fangs bounce right off it.

ABILITIES
Water Absorb
Damp

HIDDEN ABILITY
Swift Swim

EGG GROUPS
Water 1

STAT GROWTH RATES
HP ■■
Attack ■■■
Defense ■■
Sp. Atk ■■
Sp. Def ■■
Speed ■■■■■

ITEMS SOMETIMES HELD BY WILD POKÉMON
—

EVOLUTION
Poliwag → Lv. 25 → Poliwhirl → Water Stone → Poliwrath
Poliwhirl → Link Trade with a King's Rock → Politoed

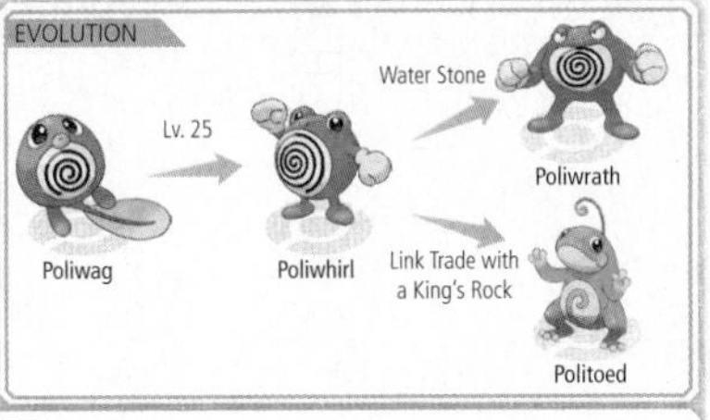

MAIN WAY TO REGISTER IN THE NATIONAL POKÉDEX

Appears in *Pokémon X* and *Pokémon Y*. Bring it to your game using Link Trade or the GTS.

Damage taken in normal battles

Type		Type	
Normal	×1	Flying	×1
Fire	×0.5	Psychic	×1
Water	×0.5	Bug	×1
Grass	×2	Rock	×1
Electric	×2	Ghost	×1
Ice	×0.5	Dragon	×1
Fighting	×1	Dark	×1
Poison	×1	Steel	×0.5
Ground	×1	Fairy	×1

Damage taken in Inverse battles

Type		Type	
Normal	×1	Flying	×1
Fire	×2	Psychic	×1
Water	×2	Bug	×1
Grass	×0.5	Rock	×1
Electric	×0.5	Ghost	×1
Ice	×2	Dragon	×1
Fighting	×1	Dark	×1
Poison	×1	Steel	×2
Ground	×1	Fairy	×1

Can be used in
Inverse Battle
Battle Institute
Battle Maison
Random Matchup (Free Battle)
Random Matchup (Others)

LEVEL-UP MOVES

Lv.	Name	Type	Kind	Pow.	Acc.	PP	Range
1	Water Sport	Water	Status	—	—	15	Both Sides
5	Water Gun	Water	Special	40	100	25	Normal
8	Hypnosis	Psychic	Status	—	60	20	Normal
11	Bubble	Water	Special	40	100	30	Many Others
15	Double Slap	Normal	Physical	15	85	10	Normal
18	Rain Dance	Water	Status	—	—	5	Both Sides
21	Body Slam	Normal	Physical	85	100	15	Normal
25	Bubble Beam	Water	Special	65	100	20	Normal
28	Mud Shot	Ground	Special	55	95	15	Normal
31	Belly Drum	Normal	Status	—	—	10	Self
35	Wake-Up Slap	Fighting	Physical	70	100	10	Normal
38	Hydro Pump	Water	Special	110	80	5	Normal
41	Mud Bomb	Ground	Special	65	85	10	Normal

TM & HM MOVES

No.	Name	Type	Kind	Pow.	Acc.	PP	Range
TM06	Toxic	Poison	Status	—	90	10	Normal
TM07	Hail	Ice	Status	—	—	10	Both Sides
TM10	Hidden Power	Normal	Special	60	100	15	Normal
TM13	Ice Beam	Ice	Special	90	100	10	Normal
TM14	Blizzard	Ice	Special	110	70	5	Many Others
TM17	Protect	Normal	Status	—	—	10	Self
TM18	Rain Dance	Water	Status	—	—	5	Both Sides
TM21	Frustration	Normal	Physical	—	100	20	Normal
TM27	Return	Normal	Physical	—	100	20	Normal
TM28	Dig	Ground	Physical	80	100	10	Normal
TM29	Psychic	Psychic	Special	90	100	10	Normal
TM32	Double Team	Normal	Status	—	—	15	Self
TM42	Facade	Normal	Physical	70	100	20	Normal
TM44	Rest	Psychic	Status	—	—	10	Self
TM45	Attract	Normal	Status	—	100	15	Normal
TM46	Thief	Dark	Physical	60	100	25	Normal
TM48	Round	Normal	Special	60	100	15	Normal
TM55	Scald	Water	Special	80	100	15	Normal
TM87	Swagger	Normal	Status	—	90	15	Normal
TM88	Sleep Talk	Normal	Status	—	—	10	Self
TM90	Substitute	Normal	Status	—	—	10	Self
TM94	Secret Power	Normal	Physical	70	100	20	Normal
TM100	Confide	Normal	Status	—	—	20	Normal
HM03	Surf	Water	Special	90	100	15	Adjacent
HM05	Waterfall	Water	Physical	80	100	15	Normal
HM07	Dive	Water	Physical	80	100	10	Normal

MOVES LEARNED IN EXCHANGE FOR BP

Name	Type	Kind	Pow.	Acc.	PP	Range
Icy Wind	Ice	Special	55	95	15	Many Others
Snore	Normal	Special	50	100	15	Normal
Water Pulse	Water	Special	60	100	20	Normal
Helping Hand	Normal	Status	—	—	20	1 Ally
Endeavor	Normal	Physical	—	100	5	Normal

MOVES TAUGHT BY PEOPLE

Name	Type	Kind	Pow.	Acc.	PP	Range

EGG MOVES

Name	Type	Kind	Pow.	Acc.	PP	Range
Mist	Ice	Status	—	—	30	Your Side
Splash	Normal	Status	—	—	40	Self
Bubble Beam	Water	Special	65	100	20	Normal
Haze	Ice	Status	—	—	30	Both Sides
Mind Reader	Normal	Status	—	—	5	Normal
Water Sport	Water	Status	—	—	15	Both Sides
Ice Ball	Ice	Physical	30	90	20	Normal
Mud Shot	Ground	Special	55	95	15	Normal
Refresh	Normal	Status	—	—	20	Self
Endeavor	Normal	Physical	—	100	5	Normal
Encore	Normal	Status	—	100	5	Normal
Endure	Normal	Status	—	—	10	Self
Water Pulse	Water	Special	60	100	20	Normal

National Pokédex **061** Hoenn Pokédex —

Poliwhirl

Tadpole Pokémon

Water

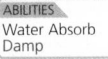

HEIGHT: 3'03" WEIGHT: 44.1 lbs.

Same form for ♂ / ♀

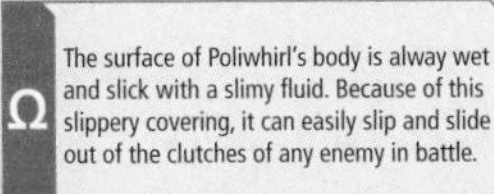

Ω The surface of Poliwhirl's body is alway wet and slick with a slimy fluid. Because of this slippery covering, it can easily slip and slide out of the clutches of any enemy in battle.

α The surface of Poliwhirl's body is alway wet and slick with a slimy fluid. Because of this slippery covering, it can easily slip and slide out of the clutches of any enemy in battle.

ABILITIES
Water Absorb
Damp

HIDDEN ABILITY
Swift Swim

EGG GROUPS
Water 1

STAT GROWTH RATES
HP ■■■
Attack ■■■
Defense ■■■
Sp. Atk ■■
Sp. Def ■■
Speed ■■■■■

ITEMS SOMETIMES HELD BY WILD POKÉMON
—

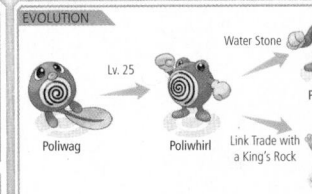

EVOLUTION
Poliwag → Lv. 25 → Poliwhirl → Water Stone → Poliwrath
Poliwhirl → Link Trade with a King's Rock → Politoed

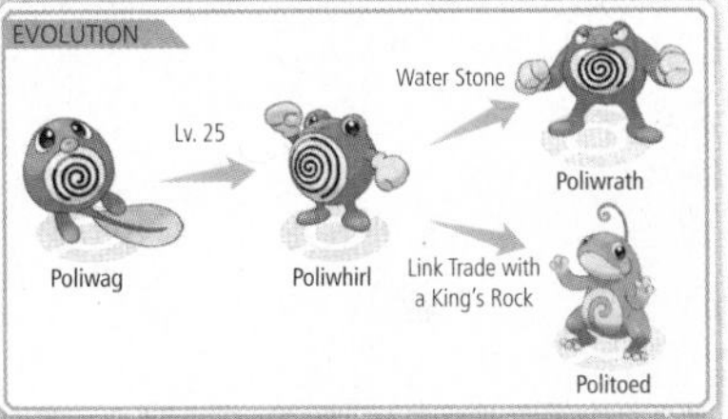

MAIN WAY TO REGISTER IN THE NATIONAL POKÉDEX

Appears in *Pokémon X* and *Pokémon Y*. Bring it to your game using Link Trade or the GTS.

Damage taken in normal battles

Type		Type	
Normal	×1	Flying	×1
Fire	×0.5	Psychic	×1
Water	×0.5	Bug	×1
Grass	×2	Rock	×1
Electric	×2	Ghost	×1
Ice	×0.5	Dragon	×1
Fighting	×1	Dark	×1
Poison	×1	Steel	×0.5
Ground	×1	Fairy	×1

Damage taken in Inverse battles

Type		Type	
Normal	×1	Flying	×1
Fire	×2	Psychic	×1
Water	×2	Bug	×1
Grass	×0.5	Rock	×1
Electric	×0.5	Ghost	×1
Ice	×2	Dragon	×1
Fighting	×1	Dark	×1
Poison	×1	Steel	×2
Ground	×1	Fairy	×1

Can be used in
Inverse Battle
Battle Institute
Battle Maison
Random Matchup (Free Battle)
Random Matchup (Others)

LEVEL-UP MOVES

Lv.	Name	Type	Kind	Pow.	Acc.	PP	Range
1	Water Sport	Water	Status	—	—	15	Both Sides
1	Water Gun	Water	Special	40	100	25	Normal
1	Hypnosis	Psychic	Status	—	60	20	Normal
5	Water Gun	Water	Special	40	100	25	Normal
8	Hypnosis	Psychic	Status	—	60	20	Normal
11	Bubble	Water	Special	40	100	30	Many Others
15	Double Slap	Normal	Physical	15	85	10	Normal
18	Rain Dance	Water	Status	—	—	5	Both Sides
21	Body Slam	Normal	Physical	85	100	15	Normal
27	Bubble Beam	Water	Special	65	100	20	Normal
32	Mud Shot	Ground	Special	55	95	15	Normal
37	Belly Drum	Normal	Status	—	—	10	Self
43	Wake-Up Slap	Fighting	Physical	70	100	10	Normal
48	Hydro Pump	Water	Special	110	80	5	Normal
53	Mud Bomb	Ground	Special	65	85	10	Normal

TM & HM MOVES

No.	Name	Type	Kind	Pow.	Acc.	PP	Range
TM06	Toxic	Poison	Status	—	90	10	Normal
TM07	Hail	Ice	Status	—	—	10	Both Sides
TM10	Hidden Power	Normal	Special	60	100	15	Normal
TM13	Ice Beam	Ice	Special	90	100	10	Normal
TM14	Blizzard	Ice	Special	110	70	5	Many Others
TM17	Protect	Normal	Status	—	—	10	Self
TM18	Rain Dance	Water	Status	—	—	5	Both Sides
TM21	Frustration	Normal	Physical	—	100	20	Normal
TM26	Earthquake	Ground	Physical	100	100	10	Adjacent
TM27	Return	Normal	Physical	—	100	20	Normal
TM28	Dig	Ground	Physical	80	100	10	Normal
TM29	Psychic	Psychic	Special	90	100	10	Normal
TM31	Brick Break	Fighting	Physical	75	100	15	Normal
TM32	Double Team	Normal	Status	—	—	15	Self
TM42	Facade	Normal	Physical	70	100	20	Normal
TM44	Rest	Psychic	Status	—	—	10	Self
TM45	Attract	Normal	Status	—	100	15	Normal
TM46	Thief	Dark	Physical	60	100	25	Normal
TM48	Round	Normal	Special	60	100	15	Normal
TM55	Scald	Water	Special	80	100	15	Normal
TM56	Fling	Dark	Physical	—	100	10	Normal
TM78	Bulldoze	Ground	Physical	60	100	20	Adjacent
TM87	Swagger	Normal	Status	—	90	15	Normal
TM88	Sleep Talk	Normal	Status	—	—	10	Self
TM90	Substitute	Normal	Status	—	—	10	Self
TM94	Secret Power	Normal	Physical	70	100	20	Normal
TM98	Power-Up Punch	Fighting	Physical	40	100	20	Normal
TM100	Confide	Normal	Status	—	—	20	Normal
HM03	Surf	Water	Special	90	100	15	Adjacent
HM04	Strength	Normal	Physical	80	100	15	Normal
HM05	Waterfall	Water	Physical	80	100	15	Normal
HM06	Rock Smash	Fighting	Physical	40	100	15	Normal
HM07	Dive	Water	Physical	80	100	10	Normal

MOVES LEARNED IN EXCHANGE FOR BP

Name	Type	Kind	Pow.	Acc.	PP	Range
Ice Punch	Ice	Physical	75	100	15	Normal
Icy Wind	Ice	Special	55	95	15	Many Others
Snore	Normal	Special	50	100	15	Normal
Focus Punch	Fighting	Physical	150	100	20	Normal
Water Pulse	Water	Special	60	100	20	Normal
Helping Hand	Normal	Status	—	—	20	1 Ally
Endeavor	Normal	Physical	—	100	5	Normal

MOVES TAUGHT BY PEOPLE

Name	Type	Kind	Pow.	Acc.	PP	Range

National Pokédex **062** Hoenn Pokédex —

Poliwrath

Tadpole Pokémon

Water | Fighting

HEIGHT: 4'03" WEIGHT: 119 lbs.

Same form for ♂ / ♀

Ω Poliwrath's highly developed, brawny muscles never grow fatigued, however much it exercises. It is so tirelessly strong, this Pokémon can swim back and forth across the ocean without effort.

α Poliwrath's highly developed, brawny muscles never grow fatigued, however much it exercises. It is so tirelessly strong, this Pokémon can swim back and forth across the ocean without effort.

ABILITIES
Water Absorb
Damp

HIDDEN ABILITY
Swift Swim

EGG GROUPS
Water 1

STAT GROWTH RATES
HP
Attack
Defense
Sp. Atk
Sp. Def
Speed

ITEMS SOMETIMES HELD BY WILD POKÉMON
—

EVOLUTION

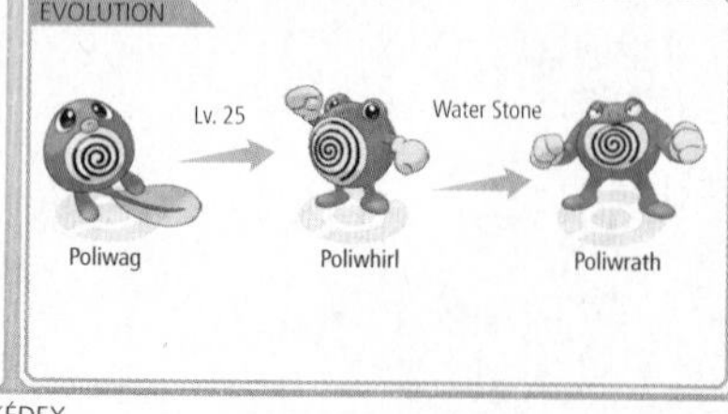

MAIN WAY TO REGISTER IN THE NATIONAL POKÉDEX

Appears in *Pokémon X* and *Pokémon Y*. Bring it to your game using Link Trade or the GTS.

Damage taken in normal battles

Type		Type	
Normal	×1	Flying	×2
Fire	×0.5	Psychic	×2
! Water	×0.5	Bug	×0.5
Grass	×2	Rock	×0.5
Electric	×2	Ghost	×1
Ice	×0.5	Dragon	×1
Fighting	×1	Dark	×0.5
Poison	×1	Steel	×0.5
Ground	×1	Fairy	×2

Damage taken in Inverse battles

Type		Type	
Normal	×1	Flying	×0.5
Fire	×2	Psychic	×0.5
! Water	×2	Bug	×2
Grass	×0.5	Rock	×2
Electric	×0.5	Ghost	×1
Ice	×2	Dragon	×1
Fighting	×1	Dark	×2
Poison	×1	Steel	×2
Ground	×1	Fairy	×0.5

Can be used in
Inverse Battle
Battle Institute
Battle Maison
Random Matchup (Free Battle)
Random Matchup (Others)

LEVEL-UP MOVES

Lv.	Name	Type	Kind	Pow.	Acc.	PP	Range
1	Circle Throw	Fighting	Physical	60	90	10	Normal
1	Bubble Beam	Water	Special	65	100	20	Normal
1	Hypnosis	Psychic	Status	—	60	20	Normal
1	Double Slap	Normal	Physical	15	85	10	Normal
1	Submission	Fighting	Physical	80	80	20	Normal
32	Dynamic Punch	Fighting	Physical	100	50	5	Normal
43	Mind Reader	Normal	Status	—	—	5	Normal
53	Circle Throw	Fighting	Physical	60	90	10	Normal

TM & HM MOVES

No.	Name	Type	Kind	Pow.	Acc.	PP	Range
TM06	Toxic	Poison	Status	—	90	10	Normal
TM07	Hail	Ice	Status	—	—	10	Both Sides
TM08	Bulk Up	Fighting	Status	—	—	20	Self
TM10	Hidden Power	Normal	Special	60	100	15	Normal
TM13	Ice Beam	Ice	Special	90	100	10	Normal
TM14	Blizzard	Ice	Special	110	70	5	Many Others
TM15	Hyper Beam	Normal	Special	150	90	5	Normal
TM17	Protect	Normal	Status	—	—	10	Self
TM18	Rain Dance	Water	Status	—	—	5	Both Sides
TM21	Frustration	Normal	Physical	—	100	20	Normal
TM26	Earthquake	Ground	Physical	100	100	10	Adjacent
TM27	Return	Normal	Physical	—	100	20	Normal
TM28	Dig	Ground	Physical	80	100	10	Normal
TM29	Psychic	Psychic	Special	90	100	10	Normal
TM31	Brick Break	Fighting	Physical	75	100	15	Normal
TM32	Double Team	Normal	Status	—	—	15	Self
TM39	Rock Tomb	Rock	Physical	60	95	15	Normal
TM42	Facade	Normal	Physical	70	100	20	Normal
TM44	Rest	Psychic	Status	—	—	10	Self
TM45	Attract	Normal	Status	—	100	15	Normal
TM46	Thief	Dark	Physical	60	100	25	Normal
TM47	Low Sweep	Fighting	Physical	65	100	20	Normal
TM48	Round	Normal	Special	60	100	15	Normal
TM52	Focus Blast	Fighting	Special	120	70	5	Normal
TM55	Scald	Water	Special	80	100	15	Normal
TM56	Fling	Dark	Physical	—	100	10	Normal
TM66	Payback	Dark	Physical	50	100	10	Normal
TM68	Giga Impact	Normal	Physical	150	90	5	Normal
TM78	Bulldoze	Ground	Physical	60	100	20	Adjacent
TM80	Rock Slide	Rock	Physical	75	90	10	Many Others
TM84	Poison Jab	Poison	Physical	80	100	20	Normal
TM87	Swagger	Normal	Status	—	90	15	Normal
TM88	Sleep Talk	Normal	Status	—	—	10	Self
TM90	Substitute	Normal	Status	—	—	10	Self
TM94	Secret Power	Normal	Physical	70	100	20	Normal
TM98	Power-Up Punch	Fighting	Physical	40	100	20	Normal
TM100	Confide	Normal	Status	—	—	20	Normal
HM03	Surf	Water	Special	90	100	15	Adjacent
HM04	Strength	Normal	Physical	80	100	15	Normal
HM05	Waterfall	Water	Physical	80	100	15	Normal
HM06	Rock Smash	Fighting	Physical	40	100	15	Normal
HM07	Dive	Water	Physical	80	100	10	Normal

MOVES LEARNED IN EXCHANGE FOR BP

Name	Type	Kind	Pow.	Acc.	PP	Range
Ice Punch	Ice	Physical	75	100	15	Normal
Icy Wind	Ice	Special	55	95	15	Many Others
Snore	Normal	Special	50	100	15	Normal
Focus Punch	Fighting	Physical	150	100	20	Normal
Water Pulse	Water	Special	60	100	20	Normal
Helping Hand	Normal	Status	—	—	20	1 Ally
Endeavor	Normal	Physical	—	100	5	Normal

MOVES TAUGHT BY PEOPLE

Name	Type	Kind	Pow.	Acc.	PP	Range

National Pokédex **063** Hoenn Pokédex **040**

Abra

Psi Pokémon

Psychic

HEIGHT: 2'11" WEIGHT: 43 lbs.

Same form for ♂ / ♀

Ω Abra sleeps for eighteen hours a day. However, it can sense the presence of foes even while it is sleeping. In such a situation, this Pokémon immediately teleports to safety.

α Abra needs to sleep for eighteen hours a day. If it doesn't, this Pokémon loses its ability to use telekinetic powers. If it is attacked, Abra escapes using Teleport while it is still sleeping.

ABILITIES
Synchronize
Inner Focus

HIDDEN ABILITY
Magic Guard

EGG GROUPS
Human-Like

STAT GROWTH RATES
HP
Attack
Defense
Sp. Atk
Sp. Def
Speed

ITEMS SOMETIMES HELD BY WILD POKÉMON
Twisted Spoon

EVOLUTION

Lv. 16 — Link Trade

Abra → Kadabra → Alakazam

MAIN WAY TO REGISTER IN THE NATIONAL POKÉDEX

Catch in Granite Cave (B1F).

Damage taken in normal battles

Type		Type	
Normal	×1	Flying	×1
Fire	×1	Psychic	×0.5
Water	×1	Bug	×2
Grass	×1	Rock	×1
Electric	×1	Ghost	×2
Ice	×1	Dragon	×1
Fighting	×0.5	Dark	×2
Poison	×1	Steel	×1
Ground	×1	Fairy	×1

Damage taken in Inverse battles

Type		Type	
Normal	×1	Flying	×1
Fire	×1	Psychic	×2
Water	×1	Bug	×0.5
Grass	×1	Rock	×1
Electric	×1	Ghost	×0.5
Ice	×1	Dragon	×1
Fighting	×2	Dark	×0.5
Poison	×1	Steel	×1
Ground	×1	Fairy	×1

Can be used in
Inverse Battle
Battle Institute
Battle Maison
Random Matchup (Free Battle)
Random Matchup (Others)

LEVEL-UP MOVES

Lv.	Name	Type	Kind	Pow.	Acc.	PP	Range
1	Teleport	Psychic	Status	—	—	20	Self

TM & HM MOVES

No.	Name	Type	Kind	Pow.	Acc.	PP	Range
TM03	Psyshock	Psychic	Special	80	100	10	Normal
TM04	Calm Mind	Psychic	Status	—	—	20	Self
TM06	Toxic	Poison	Status	—	90	10	Normal
TM10	Hidden Power	Normal	Special	60	100	15	Normal
TM11	Sunny Day	Fire	Status	—	—	5	Both Sides
TM12	Taunt	Dark	Status	—	100	20	Normal
TM16	Light Screen	Psychic	Status	—	—	30	Your Side
TM17	Protect	Normal	Status	—	—	10	Self
TM18	Rain Dance	Water	Status	—	—	5	Both Sides
TM20	Safeguard	Normal	Status	—	—	25	Your Side
TM21	Frustration	Normal	Physical	—	100	20	Normal
TM27	Return	Normal	Physical	—	100	20	Normal
TM29	Psychic	Psychic	Special	90	100	10	Normal
TM30	Shadow Ball	Ghost	Special	80	100	15	Normal
TM32	Double Team	Normal	Status	—	—	15	Self
TM33	Reflect	Psychic	Status	—	—	20	Your Side
TM41	Torment	Dark	Status	—	100	15	Normal
TM42	Facade	Normal	Physical	70	100	20	Normal
TM44	Rest	Psychic	Status	—	—	10	Self
TM45	Attract	Normal	Status	—	100	15	Normal
TM46	Thief	Dark	Physical	60	100	25	Normal
TM48	Round	Normal	Special	60	100	15	Normal
TM53	Energy Ball	Grass	Special	90	100	10	Normal
TM56	Fling	Dark	Physical	—	100	10	Normal
TM57	Charge Beam	Electric	Special	50	90	10	Normal
TM63	Embargo	Dark	Status	—	100	15	Normal
TM70	Flash	Normal	Status	—	100	20	Normal
TM73	Thunder Wave	Electric	Status	—	100	20	Normal
TM77	Psych Up	Normal	Status	—	—	10	Normal
TM85	Dream Eater	Psychic	Special	100	100	15	Normal
TM86	Grass Knot	Grass	Special	—	100	20	Normal
TM87	Swagger	Normal	Status	—	90	15	Normal
TM88	Sleep Talk	Normal	Status	—	—	10	Self
TM90	Substitute	Normal	Status	—	—	10	Self
TM92	Trick Room	Psychic	Status	—	—	5	Both Sides
TM94	Secret Power	Normal	Physical	70	100	20	Normal
TM99	Dazzling Gleam	Fairy	Special	80	100	10	Many Others
TM100	Confide	Normal	Status	—	—	20	Normal

MOVES LEARNED IN EXCHANGE FOR BP

Name	Type	Kind	Pow.	Acc.	PP	Range
Signal Beam	Bug	Special	75	100	15	Normal
Thunder Punch	Electric	Physical	75	100	15	Normal
Fire Punch	Fire	Physical	75	100	15	Normal
Ice Punch	Ice	Physical	75	100	15	Normal
Magic Coat	Psychic	Status	—	—	15	Self
Foul Play	Dark	Physical	95	100	15	Normal
Gravity	Psychic	Status	—	—	5	Both Sides
Zen Headbutt	Psychic	Physical	80	90	15	Normal
Iron Tail	Steel	Physical	100	75	15	Normal
Snore	Normal	Special	50	100	15	Normal
Knock Off	Dark	Physical	65	100	20	Normal
Role Play	Psychic	Status	—	—	10	Normal
Drain Punch	Fighting	Physical	75	100	10	Normal
Focus Punch	Fighting	Physical	150	100	20	Normal
Shock Wave	Electric	Special	60	—	20	Normal
Trick	Psychic	Status	—	100	10	Normal
Magic Room	Psychic	Status	—	—	10	Both Sides
Wonder Room	Psychic	Status	—	—	10	Both Sides
Recycle	Normal	Status	—	—	10	Self
Snatch	Dark	Status	—	—	10	Self
Skill Swap	Psychic	Status	—	—	10	Normal

MOVES TAUGHT BY PEOPLE

Name	Type	Kind	Pow.	Acc.	PP	Range

EGG MOVES

Name	Type	Kind	Pow.	Acc.	PP	Range
Encore	Normal	Status	—	100	5	Normal
Barrier	Psychic	Status	—	—	20	Self
Knock Off	Dark	Physical	65	100	20	Normal
Fire Punch	Fire	Physical	75	100	15	Normal
Thunder Punch	Electric	Physical	75	100	15	Normal
Ice Punch	Ice	Physical	75	100	15	Normal
Power Trick	Psychic	Status	—	—	10	Self
Guard Swap	Psychic	Status	—	—	10	Normal
Skill Swap	Psychic	Status	—	—	10	Normal
Guard Split	Psychic	Status	—	—	10	Normal
Psycho Shift	Psychic	Status	—	100	10	Normal
Ally Switch	Psychic	Status	—	—	15	Self

National Pokédex **064** Hoenn Pokédex **041**

Kadabra

Psi Pokémon

Psychic

HEIGHT: 4'03" WEIGHT: 124.6 lbs.

The male has longer whiskers than the female.

Ω Kadabra emits a peculiar alpha wave if it develops a headache. Only those people with a particularly strong psyche can hope to become a Trainer of this Pokémon.

α Kadabra holds a silver spoon in its hand. The spoon is used to amplify the alpha waves in its brain. Without the spoon, the Pokémon is said to be limited to half the usual amount of its telekinetic powers.

ABILITIES
Synchronize
Inner Focus

HIDDEN ABILITY
Magic Guard

EGG GROUPS
Human-Like

STAT GROWTH RATES
HP
Attack
Defense
Sp. Atk
Sp. Def
Speed

ITEMS SOMETIMES HELD BY WILD POKÉMON
—

EVOLUTION

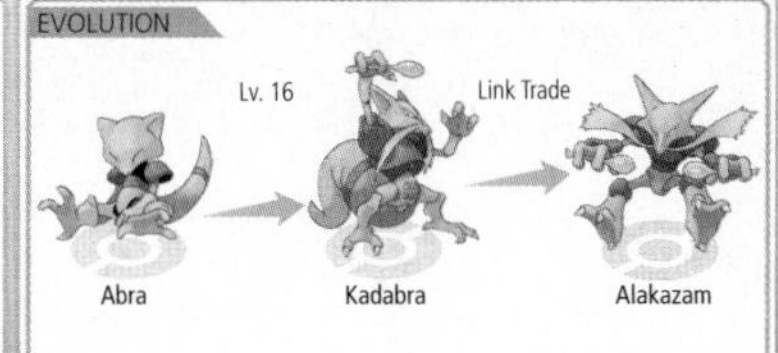

MAIN WAY TO REGISTER IN THE NATIONAL POKÉDEX

Level up Abra to Lv. 16.

Damage taken in normal battles

Type		Type	
Normal	×1	Flying	×1
Fire	×1	Psychic	×0.5
Water	×1	Bug	×2
Grass	×1	Rock	×1
Electric	×1	Ghost	×2
Ice	×1	Dragon	×1
Fighting	×0.5	Dark	×2
Poison	×1	Steel	×1
Ground	×1	Fairy	×1

Damage taken in Inverse battles

Type		Type	
Normal	×1	Flying	×1
Fire	×1	Psychic	×2
Water	×1	Bug	×0.5
Grass	×1	Rock	×1
Electric	×1	Ghost	×0.5
Ice	×1	Dragon	×1
Fighting	×2	Dark	×0.5
Poison	×1	Steel	×1
Ground	×1	Fairy	×1

Can be used in
Inverse Battle
Battle Institute
Battle Maison
Random Matchup (Free Battle)
Random Matchup (Others)

LEVEL-UP MOVES

Lv.	Name	Type	Kind	Pow.	Acc.	PP	Range
1	Teleport	Psychic	Status	—	—	20	Self
1	Kinesis	Psychic	Status	—	80	15	Normal
1	Confusion	Psychic	Special	50	100	25	Normal
16	Confusion	Psychic	Special	50	100	25	Normal
18	Disable	Normal	Status	—	100	20	Normal
21	Psybeam	Psychic	Special	65	100	20	Normal
23	Miracle Eye	Psychic	Status	—	—	40	Normal
26	Reflect	Psychic	Status	—	—	20	Your Side
28	Psycho Cut	Psychic	Physical	70	100	20	Normal
31	Recover	Normal	Status	—	—	10	Self
33	Telekinesis	Psychic	Status	—	—	15	Normal
36	Ally Switch	Psychic	Status	—	—	15	Self
38	Psychic	Psychic	Special	90	100	10	Normal
41	Role Play	Psychic	Status	—	—	10	Normal
43	Future Sight	Psychic	Special	120	100	10	Normal
46	Trick	Psychic	Status	—	100	10	Normal

TM & HM MOVES

No.	Name	Type	Kind	Pow.	Acc.	PP	Range
TM03	Psyshock	Psychic	Special	80	100	10	Normal
TM04	Calm Mind	Psychic	Status	—	—	20	Self
TM06	Toxic	Poison	Status	—	90	10	Normal
TM10	Hidden Power	Normal	Special	60	100	15	Normal
TM11	Sunny Day	Fire	Status	—	—	5	Both Sides
TM12	Taunt	Dark	Status	—	100	20	Normal
TM16	Light Screen	Psychic	Status	—	—	30	Your Side
TM17	Protect	Normal	Status	—	—	10	Self
TM18	Rain Dance	Water	Status	—	—	5	Both Sides
TM20	Safeguard	Normal	Status	—	—	25	Your Side
TM21	Frustration	Normal	Physical	—	100	20	Normal
TM27	Return	Normal	Physical	—	100	20	Normal
TM29	Psychic	Psychic	Special	90	100	10	Normal
TM30	Shadow Ball	Ghost	Special	80	100	15	Normal
TM32	Double Team	Normal	Status	—	—	15	Self
TM33	Reflect	Psychic	Status	—	—	20	Your Side
TM41	Torment	Dark	Status	—	100	15	Normal
TM42	Facade	Normal	Physical	70	100	20	Normal
TM44	Rest	Psychic	Status	—	—	10	Self
TM45	Attract	Normal	Status	—	100	15	Normal
TM46	Thief	Dark	Physical	60	100	25	Normal
TM48	Round	Normal	Special	60	100	15	Normal
TM53	Energy Ball	Grass	Special	90	100	10	Normal
TM56	Fling	Dark	Physical	—	100	10	Normal
TM57	Charge Beam	Electric	Special	50	90	10	Normal
TM63	Embargo	Dark	Status	—	100	15	Normal
TM70	Flash	Normal	Status	—	100	20	Normal
TM73	Thunder Wave	Electric	Status	—	100	20	Normal
TM77	Psych Up	Normal	Status	—	—	10	Normal
TM85	Dream Eater	Psychic	Special	100	100	15	Normal
TM86	Grass Knot	Grass	Special	—	100	20	Normal
TM87	Swagger	Normal	Status	—	90	15	Normal
TM88	Sleep Talk	Normal	Status	—	—	10	Self
TM90	Substitute	Normal	Status	—	—	10	Self
TM92	Trick Room	Psychic	Status	—	—	5	Both Sides
TM94	Secret Power	Normal	Physical	70	100	20	Normal
TM99	Dazzling Gleam	Fairy	Special	80	100	10	Many Others
TM100	Confide	Normal	Status	—	—	20	Normal

MOVES LEARNED IN EXCHANGE FOR BP

Name	Type	Kind	Pow.	Acc.	PP	Range
Signal Beam	Bug	Special	75	100	15	Normal
Thunder Punch	Electric	Physical	75	100	15	Normal
Fire Punch	Fire	Physical	75	100	15	Normal
Ice Punch	Ice	Physical	75	100	15	Normal
Magic Coat	Psychic	Status	—	—	15	Self
Foul Play	Dark	Physical	95	100	15	Normal
Gravity	Psychic	Status	—	—	5	Both Sides
Zen Headbutt	Psychic	Physical	80	90	15	Normal
Iron Tail	Steel	Physical	100	75	15	Normal
Snore	Normal	Special	50	100	15	Normal
Knock Off	Dark	Physical	65	100	20	Normal
Role Play	Psychic	Status	—	—	10	Normal
Drain Punch	Fighting	Physical	75	100	10	Normal
Focus Punch	Fighting	Physical	150	100	20	Normal
Shock Wave	Electric	Special	60	—	20	Normal
Trick	Psychic	Status	—	100	10	Normal
Magic Room	Psychic	Status	—	—	10	Both Sides
Wonder Room	Psychic	Status	—	—	10	Both Sides
Recycle	Normal	Status	—	—	10	Self
Snatch	Dark	Status	—	—	10	Self
Skill Swap	Psychic	Status	—	—	10	Normal

MOVES TAUGHT BY PEOPLE

Name	Type	Kind	Pow.	Acc.	PP	Range

National Pokédex **065** Hoenn Pokédex **042**

Alakazam

Psi Pokémon

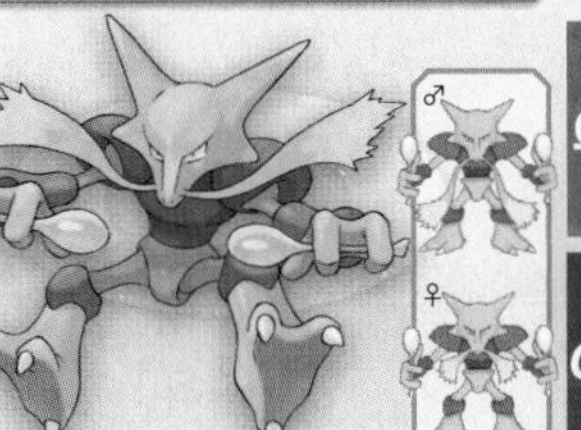

Psychic

HEIGHT: 4'11" WEIGHT: 105.8 lbs.

The male has longer whiskers than the female.

Ω Alakazam's brain continually grows, making its head far too heavy to support with its neck. This Pokémon holds its head up using its psychokinetic power instead.

α Alakazam's brain continually grows, infinitely multiplying brain cells. This amazing brain gives this Pokémon an astoundingly high IQ of 5,000. It has a thorough memory of everything that has occurred in the world.

ABILITIES
Synchronize
Inner Focus

HIDDEN ABILITY
Magic Guard

EGG GROUPS
Human-Like

STAT GROWTH RATES
HP
Attack
Defense
Sp. Atk
Sp. Def
Speed

ITEMS SOMETIMES HELD BY WILD POKÉMON
—

EVOLUTION

Lv. 16
Link Trade
Abra
Kadabra
Alakazam

MAIN WAY TO REGISTER IN THE NATIONAL POKÉDEX

Receive a Kadabra via Link Trade to have it evolve.

Damage taken in normal battles

Type		Type	
Normal	×1	Flying	×1
Fire	×1	Psychic	×0.5
Water	×1	Bug	×2
Grass	×1	Rock	×1
Electric	×1	Ghost	×2
Ice	×1	Dragon	×1
Fighting	×0.5	Dark	×2
Poison	×1	Steel	×1
Ground	×1	Fairy	×1

Damage taken in Inverse battles

Type		Type	
Normal	×1	Flying	×1
Fire	×1	Psychic	×2
Water	×1	Bug	×0.5
Grass	×1	Rock	×1
Electric	×1	Ghost	×0.5
Ice	×1	Dragon	×1
Fighting	×2	Dark	×0.5
Poison	×1	Steel	×1
Ground	×1	Fairy	×1

Can be used in
Inverse Battle
Battle Institute
Battle Maison
Random Matchup (Free Battle)
Random Matchup (Others)

LEVEL-UP MOVES

Lv.	Name	Type	Kind	Pow.	Acc.	PP	Range
1	Teleport	Psychic	Status	—	—	20	Self
1	Kinesis	Psychic	Status	—	80	15	Normal
1	Confusion	Psychic	Special	50	100	25	Normal
16	Confusion	Psychic	Special	50	100	25	Normal
18	Disable	Normal	Status	—	100	20	Normal
21	Psybeam	Psychic	Special	65	100	20	Normal
23	Miracle Eye	Psychic	Status	—	—	40	Normal
26	Reflect	Psychic	Status	—	—	20	Your Side
28	Psycho Cut	Psychic	Physical	70	100	20	Normal
31	Recover	Normal	Status	—	—	10	Self
33	Telekinesis	Psychic	Status	—	—	15	Normal
36	Ally Switch	Psychic	Status	—	—	15	Self
38	Psychic	Psychic	Special	90	100	10	Normal
41	Calm Mind	Psychic	Status	—	—	20	Self
43	Future Sight	Psychic	Special	120	100	10	Normal
46	Trick	Psychic	Status	—	100	10	Normal

TM & HM MOVES

No.	Name	Type	Kind	Pow.	Acc.	PP	Range
TM03	Psyshock	Psychic	Special	80	100	10	Normal
TM04	Calm Mind	Psychic	Status	—	—	20	Self
TM06	Toxic	Poison	Status	—	90	10	Normal
TM10	Hidden Power	Normal	Special	60	100	15	Normal
TM11	Sunny Day	Fire	Status	—	—	5	Both Sides
TM12	Taunt	Dark	Status	—	100	20	Normal
TM15	Hyper Beam	Normal	Special	150	90	5	Normal
TM16	Light Screen	Psychic	Status	—	—	30	Your Side
TM17	Protect	Normal	Status	—	—	10	Self
TM18	Rain Dance	Water	Status	—	—	5	Both Sides
TM20	Safeguard	Normal	Status	—	—	25	Your Side
TM21	Frustration	Normal	Physical	—	100	20	Normal
TM27	Return	Normal	Physical	—	100	20	Normal
TM29	Psychic	Psychic	Special	90	100	10	Normal
TM30	Shadow Ball	Ghost	Special	80	100	15	Normal
TM32	Double Team	Normal	Status	—	—	15	Self
TM33	Reflect	Psychic	Status	—	—	20	Your Side
TM41	Torment	Dark	Status	—	100	15	Normal
TM42	Facade	Normal	Physical	70	100	20	Normal
TM44	Rest	Psychic	Status	—	—	10	Self
TM45	Attract	Normal	Status	—	100	15	Normal
TM46	Thief	Dark	Physical	60	100	25	Normal
TM48	Round	Normal	Special	60	100	15	Normal
TM52	Focus Blast	Fighting	Special	120	70	5	Normal
TM53	Energy Ball	Grass	Special	90	100	10	Normal
TM56	Fling	Dark	Physical	—	100	10	Normal
TM57	Charge Beam	Electric	Special	50	90	10	Normal
TM63	Embargo	Dark	Status	—	100	15	Normal
TM68	Giga Impact	Normal	Physical	150	90	5	Normal
TM70	Flash	Normal	Status	—	100	20	Normal
TM73	Thunder Wave	Electric	Status	—	100	20	Normal
TM77	Psych Up	Normal	Status	—	—	10	Normal
TM85	Dream Eater	Psychic	Special	100	100	15	Normal
TM86	Grass Knot	Grass	Special	—	100	20	Normal
TM87	Swagger	Normal	Status	—	90	15	Normal
TM88	Sleep Talk	Normal	Status	—	—	10	Self
TM90	Substitute	Normal	Status	—	—	10	Self
TM92	Trick Room	Psychic	Status	—	—	5	Both Sides
TM94	Secret Power	Normal	Physical	70	100	20	Normal
TM99	Dazzling Gleam	Fairy	Special	80	100	10	Many Others
TM100	Confide	Normal	Status	—	—	20	Normal

MOVES LEARNED IN EXCHANGE FOR BP

Name	Type	Kind	Pow.	Acc.	PP	Range
Signal Beam	Bug	Special	75	100	15	Normal
Thunder Punch	Electric	Physical	75	100	15	Normal
Fire Punch	Fire	Physical	75	100	15	Normal
Ice Punch	Ice	Physical	75	100	15	Normal
Magic Coat	Psychic	Status	—	—	15	Self
Foul Play	Dark	Physical	95	100	15	Normal
Gravity	Psychic	Status	—	—	5	Both Sides
Zen Headbutt	Psychic	Physical	80	90	15	Normal
Iron Tail	Steel	Physical	100	75	15	Normal
Snore	Normal	Special	50	100	15	Normal
Knock Off	Dark	Physical	65	100	20	Normal
Role Play	Psychic	Status	—	—	10	Normal
Drain Punch	Fighting	Physical	75	100	10	Normal
Focus Punch	Fighting	Physical	150	100	20	Normal
Shock Wave	Electric	Special	60	—	20	Normal
Trick	Psychic	Status	—	100	10	Normal
Magic Room	Psychic	Status	—	—	10	Both Sides
Wonder Room	Psychic	Status	—	—	10	Both Sides
Recycle	Normal	Status	—	—	10	Self
Snatch	Dark	Status	—	—	10	Self
Skill Swap	Psychic	Status	—	—	10	Normal

MOVES TAUGHT BY PEOPLE

Name	Type	Kind	Pow.	Acc.	PP	Range

Mega Evolution

Mega Alakazam

Psi Pokémon

Psychic

HEIGHT: 3'11" WEIGHT: 105.8 lbs.

Same form for ♂ / ♀

REQUIRED MEGA STONE

Alakazite

Find it at the Slateport Market in Slateport City.

ABILITY
Trace

HIDDEN ABILITY
—

EGG GROUPS
—

STAT GROWTH RATES	
HP	■■
Attack	■■■
Defense	■■■
Sp. Atk	■■■■■■■■■■
Sp. Def	■■■■
Speed	■■■■■■■■

Damage taken in normal battles

Type		Type	
Normal	×1	Flying	×1
Fire	×1	Psychic	×0.5
Water	×1	Bug	×2
Grass	×1	Rock	×1
Electric	×1	Ghost	×2
Ice	×1	Dragon	×1
Fighting	×0.5	Dark	×2
Poison	×1	Steel	×1
Ground	×1	Fairy	×1

Damage taken in Inverse battles

Type		Type	
Normal	×1	Flying	×1
Fire	×1	Psychic	×2
Water	×1	Bug	×0.5
Grass	×1	Rock	×1
Electric	×1	Ghost	×0.5
Ice	×1	Dragon	×1
Fighting	×2	Dark	×0.5
Poison	×1	Steel	×1
Ground	×1	Fairy	×1

Can be used in

- Inverse Battle
- Battle Institute
- Battle Maison
- Random Matchup (Free Battle)
- Random Matchup (Others)

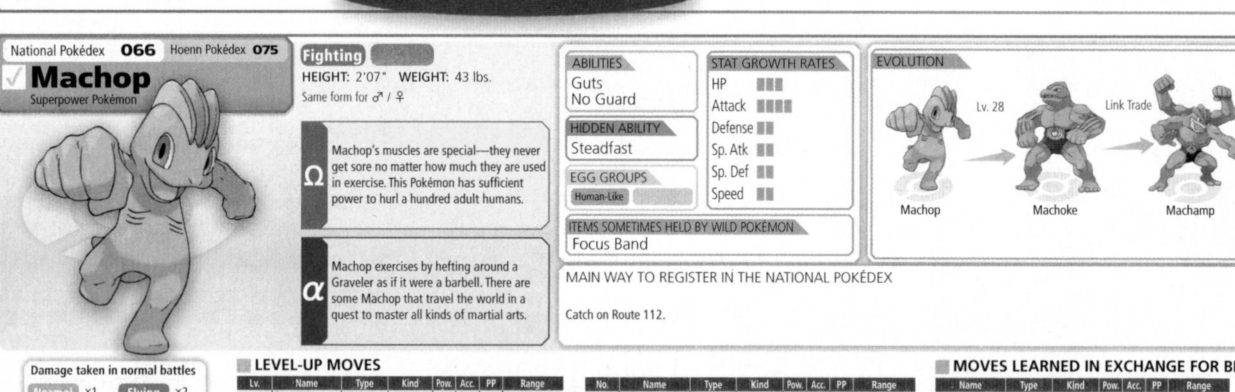

National Pokédex **066** Hoenn Pokédex **075**

Machop

Superpower Pokémon

Fighting

HEIGHT: 2'07" WEIGHT: 43 lbs.

Same form for ♂ / ♀

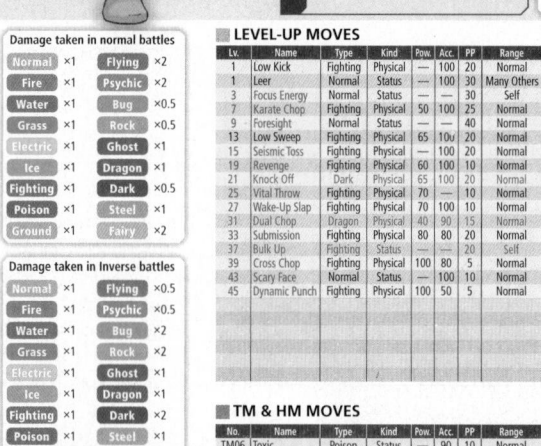

Ω Machop's muscles are special—they never get sore no matter how much they are used in exercise. This Pokémon has sufficient power to hurl a hundred adult humans.

α Machop exercises by hefting around a Graveler as if it were a barbell. There are some Machop that travel the world in a quest to master all kinds of martial arts.

ABILITIES
Guts
No Guard

HIDDEN ABILITY
Steadfast

EGG GROUPS
Human-Like

STAT GROWTH RATES	
HP	■■■
Attack	■■■■
Defense	■■
Sp. Atk	■■
Sp. Def	■■
Speed	■■

ITEMS SOMETIMES HELD BY WILD POKÉMON

Focus Band

EVOLUTION

Machop → Lv. 28 → Machoke → Link Trade → Machamp

MAIN WAY TO REGISTER IN THE NATIONAL POKÉDEX

Catch on Route 112.

Damage taken in normal battles

Type		Type	
Normal	×1	Flying	×2
Fire	×1	Psychic	×2
Water	×1	Bug	×0.5
Grass	×1	Rock	×0.5
Electric	×1	Ghost	×1
Ice	×1	Dragon	×1
Fighting	×1	Dark	×0.5
Poison	×1	Steel	×1
Ground	×1	Fairy	×2

Damage taken in Inverse battles

Type		Type	
Normal	×1	Flying	×0.5
Fire	×1	Psychic	×0.5
Water	×1	Bug	×2
Grass	×1	Rock	×2
Electric	×1	Ghost	×1
Ice	×1	Dragon	×1
Fighting	×1	Dark	×2
Poison	×1	Steel	×1
Ground	×1	Fairy	×0.5

Can be used in

- Inverse Battle
- Battle Institute
- Battle Maison
- Random Matchup (Free Battle)
- Random Matchup (Others)

LEVEL-UP MOVES

Lv.	Name	Type	Kind	Pow.	Acc.	PP	Range
1	Low Kick	Fighting	Physical	—	100	20	Normal
1	Leer	Normal	Status	—	100	30	Many Others
3	Focus Energy	Normal	Status	—	—	30	Self
7	Karate Chop	Fighting	Physical	50	100	25	Normal
9	Foresight	Normal	Status	—	—	40	Normal
13	Low Sweep	Fighting	Physical	65	100	20	Normal
15	Seismic Toss	Fighting	Physical	—	100	20	Normal
19	Revenge	Fighting	Physical	60	100	10	Normal
21	Knock Off	Dark	Physical	65	100	20	Normal
25	Vital Throw	Fighting	Physical	70	—	10	Normal
27	Wake-Up Slap	Fighting	Physical	70	100	10	Normal
31	Dual Chop	Dragon	Physical	40	90	15	Normal
33	Submission	Fighting	Physical	80	80	20	Normal
37	Bulk Up	Fighting	Status	—	—	20	Self
39	Cross Chop	Fighting	Physical	100	80	5	Normal
43	Scary Face	Normal	Status	—	100	10	Normal
45	Dynamic Punch	Fighting	Physical	100	50	5	Normal

TM & HM MOVES

No.	Name	Type	Kind	Pow.	Acc.	PP	Range
TM06	Toxic	Poison	Status	—	90	10	Normal
TM08	Bulk Up	Fighting	Status	—	—	20	Self
TM10	Hidden Power	Normal	Special	60	100	15	Normal
TM11	Sunny Day	Fire	Status	—	—	5	Both Sides
TM16	Light Screen	Psychic	Status	—	—	30	Your Side
TM17	Protect	Normal	Status	—	—	10	Self
TM18	Rain Dance	Water	Status	—	—	5	Both Sides
TM21	Frustration	Normal	Physical	—	100	20	Normal
TM23	Smack Down	Rock	Physical	50	100	15	Normal
TM26	Earthquake	Ground	Physical	100	100	10	Adjacent
TM27	Return	Normal	Physical	—	100	20	Normal
TM28	Dig	Ground	Physical	80	100	10	Normal
TM31	Brick Break	Fighting	Physical	75	100	15	Normal
TM32	Double Team	Normal	Status	—	—	15	Self
TM35	Flamethrower	Fire	Special	90	100	15	Normal
TM38	Fire Blast	Fire	Special	110	85	5	Normal
TM39	Rock Tomb	Rock	Physical	60	95	15	Normal
TM42	Facade	Normal	Physical	70	100	20	Normal
TM44	Rest	Psychic	Status	—	—	10	Self
TM45	Attract	Normal	Status	—	100	15	Normal
TM46	Thief	Dark	Physical	60	100	25	Normal
TM47	Low Sweep	Fighting	Physical	65	100	20	Normal
TM48	Round	Normal	Special	60	100	15	Normal
TM52	Focus Blast	Fighting	Special	120	70	5	Normal
TM56	Fling	Dark	Physical	—	100	10	Normal
TM59	Incinerate	Fire	Special	60	100	15	Many Others
TM66	Payback	Dark	Physical	50	100	10	Normal
TM67	Retaliate	Normal	Physical	70	100	5	Normal
TM78	Bulldoze	Ground	Physical	60	100	20	Adjacent
TM80	Rock Slide	Rock	Physical	75	90	10	Many Others
TM84	Poison Jab	Poison	Physical	80	100	20	Normal
TM87	Swagger	Normal	Status	—	90	15	Normal
TM88	Sleep Talk	Normal	Status	—	—	10	Self
TM90	Substitute	Normal	Status	—	—	10	Self
TM94	Secret Power	Normal	Physical	70	100	20	Normal
TM98	Power-Up Punch	Fighting	Physical	40	100	20	Normal
TM100	Confide	Normal	Status	—	—	20	Normal
HM04	Strength	Normal	Physical	80	100	15	Normal
HM06	Rock Smash	Fighting	Physical	40	100	15	Normal

MOVES LEARNED IN EXCHANGE FOR BP

Name	Type	Kind	Pow.	Acc.	PP	Range
Dual Chop	Dragon	Physical	40	90	15	Normal
Low Kick	Fighting	Physical	—	100	20	Normal
Thunder Punch	Electric	Physical	75	100	15	Normal
Fire Punch	Fire	Physical	75	100	15	Normal
Ice Punch	Ice	Physical	75	100	15	Normal
Superpower	Fighting	Physical	120	100	5	Normal
Snore	Normal	Special	50	100	15	Normal
Knock Off	Dark	Physical	65	100	20	Normal
Role Play	Psychic	Status	—	—	10	Normal
Focus Punch	Fighting	Physical	150	100	20	Normal
Helping Hand	Normal	Status	—	—	20	1 Ally

MOVES TAUGHT BY PEOPLE

Name	Type	Kind	Pow.	Acc.	PP	Range

EGG MOVES

Name	Type	Kind	Pow.	Acc.	PP	Range
Meditate	Psychic	Status	—	—	40	Self
Rolling Kick	Fighting	Physical	60	85	15	Normal
Encore	Normal	Status	—	100	5	Normal
Smelling Salts	Normal	Physical	70	100	10	Normal
Counter	Fighting	Physical	—	100	20	Varies
Close Combat	Fighting	Physical	120	100	5	Normal
Fire Punch	Fire	Physical	75	100	15	Normal
Thunder Punch	Electric	Physical	75	100	15	Normal
Ice Punch	Ice	Physical	75	100	15	Normal
Bullet Punch	Steel	Physical	40	100	30	Normal
Power Trick	Psychic	Status	—	—	10	Self
Heavy Slam	Steel	Physical	—	100	10	Normal
Knock Off	Dark	Physical	65	100	20	Normal
Tickle	Normal	Status	—	100	20	Normal
Quick Guard	Fighting	Status	—	—	15	Your Side

National Pokédex **067** Hoenn Pokédex **076**

Machoke

Superpower Pokémon

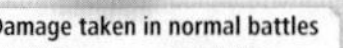

Fighting

HEIGHT: 4'11" WEIGHT: 155.4 lbs.

Same form for ♂ / ♀

Ω Machoke's thoroughly toned muscles possess the hardness of steel. This Pokémon has so much strength, it can easily hold aloft a sumo wrestler on just one finger.

α Machoke undertakes bodybuilding every day even as it helps people with tough, physically demanding labor. On its days off, this Pokémon heads to the fields and mountains to exercise and train.

ABILITIES
Guts
No Guard

HIDDEN ABILITY
Steadfast

EGG GROUPS
Human-Like

STAT GROWTH RATES
HP
Attack
Defense
Sp. Atk
Sp. Def
Speed

ITEMS SOMETIMES HELD BY WILD POKÉMON
—

EVOLUTION
Machop → Lv. 28 → Machoke → Link Trade → Machamp

MAIN WAY TO REGISTER IN THE NATIONAL POKÉDEX

Level up Machop to Lv. 28.

Damage taken in normal battles

Type		Type	
Normal	×1	Flying	×2
Fire	×1	Psychic	×2
Water	×1	Bug	×0.5
Grass	×1	Rock	×0.5
Electric	×1	Ghost	×1
Ice	×1	Dragon	×1
Fighting	×1	Dark	×0.5
Poison	×1	Steel	×1
Ground	×1	Fairy	×2

Damage taken in Inverse battles

Type		Type	
Normal	×1	Flying	×0.5
Fire	×1	Psychic	×0.5
Water	×1	Bug	×2
Grass	×1	Rock	×2
Electric	×1	Ghost	×1
Ice	×1	Dragon	×1
Fighting	×1	Dark	×2
Poison	×1	Steel	×1
Ground	×1	Fairy	×0.5

Can be used in
Inverse Battle
Battle Institute
Battle Maison
Random Matchup (Free Battle)
Random Matchup (Others)

LEVEL-UP MOVES

Lv.	Name	Type	Kind	Pow.	Acc.	PP	Range
1	Low Kick	Fighting	Physical	—	100	20	Normal
1	Leer	Normal	Status	—	100	30	Many Others
1	Focus Energy	Normal	Status	—	—	30	Self
1	Karate Chop	Fighting	Physical	50	100	25	Normal
3	Focus Energy	Normal	Status	—	—	30	Self
7	Karate Chop	Fighting	Physical	50	100	25	Normal
9	Foresight	Normal	Status	—	—	40	Normal
13	Low Sweep	Fighting	Physical	65	100	20	Normal
15	Seismic Toss	Fighting	Physical	—	100	20	Normal
19	Revenge	Fighting	Physical	60	100	10	Normal
21	Knock Off	Dark	Physical	65	100	20	Normal
25	Vital Throw	Fighting	Physical	70	—	10	Normal
27	Wake-Up Slap	Fighting	Physical	70	100	10	Normal
33	Dual Chop	Dragon	Physical	40	90	15	Normal
37	Submission	Fighting	Physical	80	80	20	Normal
43	Bulk Up	Fighting	Status	—	—	20	Self
47	Cross Chop	Fighting	Physical	100	80	5	Normal
53	Scary Face	Normal	Status	—	100	10	Normal
57	Dynamic Punch	Fighting	Physical	100	50	5	Normal

TM & HM MOVES

No.	Name	Type	Kind	Pow.	Acc.	PP	Range
TM06	Toxic	Poison	Status	—	90	10	Normal
TM08	Bulk Up	Fighting	Status	—	—	20	Self
TM10	Hidden Power	Normal	Special	60	100	15	Normal
TM11	Sunny Day	Fire	Status	—	—	5	Both Sides
TM16	Light Screen	Psychic	Status	—	—	30	Your Side
TM17	Protect	Normal	Status	—	—	10	Self
TM18	Rain Dance	Water	Status	—	—	5	Both Sides
TM21	Frustration	Normal	Physical	—	100	20	Normal
TM23	Smack Down	Rock	Physical	50	100	15	Normal
TM26	Earthquake	Ground	Physical	100	100	10	Adjacent
TM27	Return	Normal	Physical	—	100	20	Normal
TM28	Dig	Ground	Physical	80	100	10	Normal
TM31	Brick Break	Fighting	Physical	75	100	15	Normal
TM32	Double Team	Normal	Status	—	—	15	Self
TM35	Flamethrower	Fire	Special	90	100	15	Normal
TM38	Fire Blast	Fire	Special	110	85	5	Normal
TM39	Rock Tomb	Rock	Physical	60	95	15	Normal
TM42	Facade	Normal	Physical	70	100	20	Normal
TM44	Rest	Psychic	Status	—	—	10	Self
TM45	Attract	Normal	Status	—	100	15	Normal
TM46	Thief	Dark	Physical	60	100	25	Normal
TM47	Low Sweep	Fighting	Physical	65	100	20	Normal
TM48	Round	Normal	Special	60	100	15	Normal
TM52	Focus Blast	Fighting	Special	120	70	5	Normal
TM56	Fling	Dark	Physical	—	100	10	Normal
TM59	Incinerate	Fire	Special	60	100	15	Many Others
TM66	Payback	Dark	Physical	50	100	10	Normal
TM67	Retaliate	Normal	Physical	70	100	5	Normal
TM78	Bulldoze	Ground	Physical	60	100	20	Adjacent
TM80	Rock Slide	Rock	Physical	75	90	10	Many Others
TM84	Poison Jab	Poison	Physical	80	100	20	Normal
TM87	Swagger	Normal	Status	—	90	15	Normal
TM88	Sleep Talk	Normal	Status	—	—	10	Self
TM90	Substitute	Normal	Status	—	—	10	Self
TM94	Secret Power	Normal	Physical	70	100	20	Normal
TM98	Power-Up Punch	Fighting	Physical	40	100	20	Normal
TM100	Confide	Normal	Status	—	—	20	Normal
HM04	Strength	Normal	Physical	80	100	15	Normal
HM06	Rock Smash	Fighting	Physical	40	100	15	Normal

MOVES LEARNED IN EXCHANGE FOR BP

Name	Type	Kind	Pow.	Acc.	PP	Range
Dual Chop	Dragon	Physical	40	90	15	Normal
Low Kick	Fighting	Physical	—	100	20	Normal
Thunder Punch	Electric	Physical	75	100	15	Normal
Fire Punch	Fire	Physical	75	100	15	Normal
Ice Punch	Ice	Physical	75	100	15	Normal
Superpower	Fighting	Physical	120	100	5	Normal
Snore	Normal	Special	50	100	15	Normal
Knock Off	Dark	Physical	65	100	20	Normal
Role Play	Psychic	Status	—	—	10	Normal
Focus Punch	Fighting	Physical	150	100	20	Normal
Helping Hand	Normal	Status	—	—	20	1 Ally

MOVES TAUGHT BY PEOPLE

Name	Type	Kind	Pow.	Acc.	PP	Range

National Pokédex **068** Hoenn Pokédex **077**

Machamp

Superpower Pokémon

Fighting

HEIGHT: 5'03" WEIGHT: 286.6 lbs.

Same form for ♂ / ♀

Ω Machamp has the power to hurl anything aside. However, trying to do any work requiring care and dexterity causes its arms to get tangled. This Pokémon tends to leap into action before it thinks.

α Machamp is known as the Pokémon that has mastered every kind of martial arts. If it grabs hold of the foe with its four arms, the battle is all but over. The hapless foe is thrown far over the horizon.

ABILITIES
Guts
No Guard

HIDDEN ABILITY
Steadfast

EGG GROUPS
Human-Like

STAT GROWTH RATES
HP
Attack
Defense
Sp. Atk
Sp. Def
Speed

ITEMS SOMETIMES HELD BY WILD POKÉMON
—

EVOLUTION
Machop → Lv. 28 → Machoke → Link Trade → Machamp

MAIN WAY TO REGISTER IN THE NATIONAL POKÉDEX

Receive a Machoke via Link Trade to have it evolve.

Damage taken in normal battles

Type		Type	
Normal	×1	Flying	×2
Fire	×1	Psychic	×2
Water	×1	Bug	×0.5
Grass	×1	Rock	×0.5
Electric	×1	Ghost	×1
Ice	×1	Dragon	×1
Fighting	×1	Dark	×0.5
Poison	×1	Steel	×1
Ground	×1	Fairy	×2

Damage taken in Inverse battles

Type		Type	
Normal	×1	Flying	×0.5
Fire	×1	Psychic	×0.5
Water	×1	Bug	×2
Grass	×1	Rock	×2
Electric	×1	Ghost	×1
Ice	×1	Dragon	×1
Fighting	×1	Dark	×2
Poison	×1	Steel	×1
Ground	×1	Fairy	×0.5

Can be used in
Inverse Battle
Battle Institute
Battle Maison
Random Matchup (Free Battle)
Random Matchup (Others)

LEVEL-UP MOVES

Lv.	Name	Type	Kind	Pow.	Acc.	PP	Range
1	Wide Guard	Rock	Status	—	—	10	Your Side
1	Low Kick	Fighting	Physical	—	100	20	Normal
1	Leer	Normal	Status	—	100	30	Many Others
1	Focus Energy	Normal	Status	—	—	30	Self
1	Karate Chop	Fighting	Physical	50	100	25	Normal
3	Focus Energy	Normal	Status	—	—	30	Self
7	Karate Chop	Fighting	Physical	50	100	25	Normal
9	Foresight	Normal	Status	—	—	40	Normal
13	Low Sweep	Fighting	Physical	65	100	20	Normal
15	Seismic Toss	Fighting	Physical	—	100	20	Normal
19	Revenge	Fighting	Physical	60	100	10	Normal
21	Knock Off	Dark	Physical	65	100	20	Normal
25	Vital Throw	Fighting	Physical	70	—	10	Normal
27	Wake-Up Slap	Fighting	Physical	70	100	10	Normal
33	Dual Chop	Dragon	Physical	40	90	15	Normal
37	Submission	Fighting	Physical	80	80	20	Normal
43	Bulk Up	Fighting	Status	—	—	20	Self
47	Cross Chop	Fighting	Physical	100	80	5	Normal
53	Scary Face	Normal	Status	—	100	10	Normal
57	Dynamic Punch	Fighting	Physical	100	50	5	Normal

TM & HM MOVES

No.	Name	Type	Kind	Pow.	Acc.	PP	Range
TM06	Toxic	Poison	Status	—	90	10	Normal
TM08	Bulk Up	Fighting	Status	—	—	20	Self
TM10	Hidden Power	Normal	Special	60	100	15	Normal
TM11	Sunny Day	Fire	Status	—	—	5	Both Sides
TM15	Hyper Beam	Normal	Special	150	90	5	Normal
TM16	Light Screen	Psychic	Status	—	—	30	Your Side
TM17	Protect	Normal	Status	—	—	10	Self
TM18	Rain Dance	Water	Status	—	—	5	Both Sides
TM21	Frustration	Normal	Physical	—	100	20	Normal
TM23	Smack Down	Rock	Physical	50	100	15	Normal
TM26	Earthquake	Ground	Physical	100	100	10	Adjacent
TM27	Return	Normal	Physical	—	100	20	Normal
TM28	Dig	Ground	Physical	80	100	10	Normal
TM31	Brick Break	Fighting	Physical	75	100	15	Normal
TM32	Double Team	Normal	Status	—	—	15	Self
TM35	Flamethrower	Fire	Special	90	100	15	Normal
TM38	Fire Blast	Fire	Special	110	85	5	Normal
TM39	Rock Tomb	Rock	Physical	60	95	15	Normal
TM42	Facade	Normal	Physical	70	100	20	Normal
TM44	Rest	Psychic	Status	—	—	10	Self
TM45	Attract	Normal	Status	—	100	15	Normal
TM46	Thief	Dark	Physical	60	100	25	Normal
TM47	Low Sweep	Fighting	Physical	65	100	20	Normal
TM48	Round	Normal	Special	60	100	15	Normal
TM52	Focus Blast	Fighting	Special	120	70	5	Normal
TM56	Fling	Dark	Physical	—	100	10	Normal
TM59	Incinerate	Fire	Special	60	100	15	Many Others
TM66	Payback	Dark	Physical	50	100	10	Normal
TM67	Retaliate	Normal	Physical	70	100	5	Normal
TM68	Giga Impact	Normal	Physical	150	90	5	Normal
TM71	Stone Edge	Rock	Physical	100	80	5	Normal
TM78	Bulldoze	Ground	Physical	60	100	20	Adjacent
TM80	Rock Slide	Rock	Physical	75	90	10	Many Others
TM84	Poison Jab	Poison	Physical	80	100	20	Normal
TM87	Swagger	Normal	Status	—	90	15	Normal
TM88	Sleep Talk	Normal	Status	—	—	10	Self
TM90	Substitute	Normal	Status	—	—	10	Self
TM94	Secret Power	Normal	Physical	70	100	20	Normal
TM98	Power-Up Punch	Fighting	Physical	40	100	20	Normal
TM100	Confide	Normal	Status	—	—	20	Normal
HM04	Strength	Normal	Physical	80	100	15	Normal
HM06	Rock Smash	Fighting	Physical	40	100	15	Normal

MOVES LEARNED IN EXCHANGE FOR BP

Name	Type	Kind	Pow.	Acc.	PP	Range
Dual Chop	Dragon	Physical	40	90	15	Normal
Low Kick	Fighting	Physical	--	100	20	Normal
Thunder Punch	Electric	Physical	75	100	15	Normal
Fire Punch	Fire	Physical	75	100	15	Normal
Ice Punch	Ice	Physical	75	100	15	Normal
Superpower	Fighting	Physical	120	100	5	Normal
Snore	Normal	Special	50	100	15	Normal
Knock Off	Dark	Physical	65	100	20	Normal
Role Play	Psychic	Status	—	—	10	Normal
Focus Punch	Fighting	Physical	150	100	20	Normal
Helping Hand	Normal	Status	—	—	20	1 Ally

MOVES TAUGHT BY PEOPLE

Name	Type	Kind	Pow.	Acc.	PP	Range

National Pokédex **069** Hoenn Pokédex —

Bellsprout

Flower Pokémon

Grass **Poison**

HEIGHT: 2'04" WEIGHT: 8.8 lbs.

Same form for ♂ / ♀

Ω Bellsprout's thin and flexible body lets it bend and sway to avoid any attack, however strong it may be. From its mouth, this Pokémon spits a corrosive fluid that melts even iron.

α Bellsprout's thin and flexible body lets it bend and sway to avoid any attack, however strong it may be. From its mouth, this Pokémon spits a corrosive fluid that melts even iron.

ABILITY
Chlorophyll

HIDDEN ABILITY
Gluttony

EGG GROUPS
Grass

STAT GROWTH RATES
HP 3
Attack 4
Defense 2
Sp. Atk 3
Sp. Def 1
Speed 2

ITEMS SOMETIMES HELD BY WILD POKÉMON
—

EVOLUTION
Bellsprout → Lv. 21 → Weepinbell → Leaf Stone → Victreebel

MAIN WAY TO REGISTER IN THE NATIONAL POKÉDEX

Appears in *Pokémon X* and *Pokémon Y*. Bring it to your game using Link Trade or the GTS.

Damage taken in normal battles

Type		Type	
Normal	×1	Flying	×2
Fire	×2	Psychic	×2
Water	×0.5	Bug	×1
Grass	×0.25	Rock	×1
Electric	×0.5	Ghost	×1
Ice	×2	Dragon	×1
Fighting	×0.5	Dark	×1
Poison	×1	Steel	×1
Ground	×1	Fairy	×0.5

Damage taken in Inverse battles

Type		Type	
Normal	×1	Flying	×0.5
Fire	×0.5	Psychic	×0.5
Water	×2	Bug	×1
Grass	×4	Rock	×1
Electric	×2	Ghost	×1
Ice	×0.5	Dragon	×1
Fighting	×2	Dark	×1
Poison	×1	Steel	×1
Ground	×1	Fairy	×2

Can be used in
Inverse Battle
Battle Institute
Battle Maison
Random Matchup (Free Battle)
Random Matchup (Others)

LEVEL-UP MOVES

Lv.	Name	Type	Kind	Pow.	Acc.	PP	Range
1	Vine Whip	Grass	Physical	45	100	25	Normal
7	Growth	Normal	Status	—	—	20	Self
11	Wrap	Normal	Physical	15	90	20	Normal
13	Sleep Powder	Grass	Status	—	75	15	Normal
15	Poison Powder	Poison	Status	—	75	35	Normal
17	Stun Spore	Grass	Status	—	75	30	Normal
23	Acid	Poison	Special	40	100	30	Many Others
27	Knock Off	Dark	Physical	65	100	20	Normal
29	Sweet Scent	Normal	Status	—	100	20	Many Others
35	Gastro Acid	Poison	Status	—	100	10	Normal
39	Razor Leaf	Grass	Physical	55	95	25	Many Others
41	Slam	Normal	Physical	80	75	20	Normal
47	Wring Out	Normal	Special	—	100	5	Normal

TM & HM MOVES

No.	Name	Type	Kind	Pow.	Acc.	PP	Range
TM06	Toxic	Poison	Status	—	90	10	Normal
TM09	Venoshock	Poison	Special	65	100	10	Normal
TM10	Hidden Power	Normal	Special	60	100	15	Normal
TM11	Sunny Day	Fire	Status	—	—	5	Both Sides
TM17	Protect	Normal	Status	—	—	10	Self
TM21	Frustration	Normal	Physical	—	100	20	Normal
TM22	Solar Beam	Grass	Special	120	100	10	Normal
TM27	Return	Normal	Physical	—	100	20	Normal
TM32	Double Team	Normal	Status	—	—	15	Self
TM33	Reflect	Psychic	Status	—	—	20	Your Side
TM36	Sludge Bomb	Poison	Special	90	100	10	Normal
TM42	Facade	Normal	Physical	70	100	20	Normal
TM44	Rest	Psychic	Status	—	—	10	Self
TM45	Attract	Normal	Status	—	100	15	Normal
TM46	Thief	Dark	Physical	60	100	25	Normal
TM48	Round	Normal	Special	60	100	15	Normal
TM53	Energy Ball	Grass	Special	90	100	10	Normal
TM70	Flash	Normal	Status	—	100	20	Normal
TM75	Swords Dance	Normal	Status	—	—	20	Self
TM83	Infestation	Bug	Special	20	100	20	Normal
TM86	Grass Knot	Grass	Special	—	100	20	Normal
TM87	Swagger	Normal	Status	—	90	15	Normal
TM88	Sleep Talk	Normal	Status	—	—	10	Self
TM90	Substitute	Normal	Status	—	—	10	Self
TM94	Secret Power	Normal	Physical	70	100	20	Normal
TM96	Nature Power	Normal	Status	—	—	20	Normal
TM100	Confide	Normal	Status	—	—	20	Normal
HM01	Cut	Normal	Physical	50	95	30	Normal

MOVES LEARNED IN EXCHANGE FOR BP

Name	Type	Kind	Pow.	Acc.	PP	Range
Seed Bomb	Grass	Physical	80	100	15	Normal
Bind	Normal	Physical	15	85	20	Normal
Snore	Normal	Special	50	100	15	Normal
Knock Off	Dark	Physical	65	100	20	Normal
Synthesis	Grass	Status	—	—	5	Self
Giga Drain	Grass	Special	75	100	10	Normal
Gastro Acid	Poison	Status	—	100	10	Normal
Worry Seed	Grass	Status	—	100	10	Normal

MOVES TAUGHT BY PEOPLE

Name	Type	Kind	Pow.	Acc.	PP	Range

EGG MOVES

Name	Type	Kind	Pow.	Acc.	PP	Range
Encore	Normal	Status	—	100	5	Normal
Synthesis	Grass	Status	—	—	5	Self
Leech Life	Bug	Physical	20	100	15	Normal
Ingrain	Grass	Status	—	—	20	Self
Magical Leaf	Grass	Special	60	—	20	Normal
Worry Seed	Grass	Status	—	100	10	Normal
Tickle	Normal	Status	—	100	20	Normal
Weather Ball	Normal	Special	50	100	10	Normal
Bullet Seed	Grass	Physical	25	100	30	Normal
Natural Gift	Normal	Physical	—	100	15	Normal
Giga Drain	Grass	Special	75	100	10	Normal
Clear Smog	Poison	Special	50	—	15	Normal
Power Whip	Grass	Physical	120	85	10	Normal
Acid Spray	Poison	Special	40	100	20	Normal
Belch	Poison	Special	120	90	10	Normal

National Pokédex **070** Hoenn Pokédex —

Weepinbell

Flycatcher Pokémon

Grass **Poison**

HEIGHT: 3'03" WEIGHT: 14.1 lbs.

Same form for ♂ / ♀

Ω Weepinbell has a large hook on its rear end. At night, the Pokémon hooks on to a tree branch and goes to sleep. If it moves around in its sleep, it may wake up to find itself on the ground.

α Weepinbell has a large hook on its rear end. At night, the Pokémon hooks on to a tree branch and goes to sleep. If it moves around in its sleep, it may wake up to find itself on the ground.

ABILITY
Chlorophyll

HIDDEN ABILITY
Gluttony

EGG GROUPS
Grass

STAT GROWTH RATES
HP 3
Attack 5
Defense 2
Sp. Atk 4
Sp. Def 2
Speed 3

ITEMS SOMETIMES HELD BY WILD POKÉMON
—

EVOLUTION
Bellsprout → Lv. 21 → Weepinbell → Leaf Stone → Victreebel

MAIN WAY TO REGISTER IN THE NATIONAL POKÉDEX

Appears in *Pokémon X* and *Pokémon Y*. Bring it to your game using Link Trade or the GTS.

Damage taken in normal battles

Type		Type	
Normal	×1	Flying	×2
Fire	×2	Psychic	×2
Water	×0.5	Bug	×1
Grass	×0.25	Rock	×1
Electric	×0.5	Ghost	×1
Ice	×2	Dragon	×1
Fighting	×0.5	Dark	×1
Poison	×1	Steel	×1
Ground	×1	Fairy	×0.5

Damage taken in Inverse battles

Type		Type	
Normal	×1	Flying	×0.5
Fire	×0.5	Psychic	×0.5
Water	×2	Bug	×1
Grass	×4	Rock	×1
Electric	×2	Ghost	×1
Ice	×0.5	Dragon	×1
Fighting	×2	Dark	×1
Poison	×1	Steel	×1
Ground	×1	Fairy	×2

Can be used in
Inverse Battle
Battle Institute
Battle Maison
Random Matchup (Free Battle)
Random Matchup (Others)

LEVEL-UP MOVES

Lv.	Name	Type	Kind	Pow.	Acc.	PP	Range
1	Vine Whip	Grass	Physical	45	100	25	Normal
1	Growth	Normal	Status	—	—	20	Self
1	Wrap	Normal	Physical	15	90	20	Normal
7	Growth	Normal	Status	—	—	20	Self
11	Wrap	Normal	Physical	15	90	20	Normal
13	Sleep Powder	Grass	Status	—	75	15	Normal
15	Poison Powder	Poison	Status	—	75	35	Normal
17	Stun Spore	Grass	Status	—	75	30	Normal
23	Acid	Poison	Special	40	100	30	Many Others
27	Knock Off	Dark	Physical	65	100	20	Normal
29	Sweet Scent	Normal	Status	—	100	20	Many Others
35	Gastro Acid	Poison	Status	—	100	10	Normal
39	Razor Leaf	Grass	Physical	55	95	25	Many Others
41	Slam	Normal	Physical	80	75	20	Normal
47	Wring Out	Normal	Special	—	100	5	Normal

TM & HM MOVES

No.	Name	Type	Kind	Pow.	Acc.	PP	Range
TM06	Toxic	Poison	Status	—	90	10	Normal
TM09	Venoshock	Poison	Special	65	100	10	Normal
TM10	Hidden Power	Normal	Special	60	100	15	Normal
TM11	Sunny Day	Fire	Status	—	—	5	Both Sides
TM17	Protect	Normal	Status	—	—	10	Self
TM21	Frustration	Normal	Physical	—	100	20	Normal
TM22	Solar Beam	Grass	Special	120	100	10	Normal
TM27	Return	Normal	Physical	—	100	20	Normal
TM32	Double Team	Normal	Status	—	—	15	Self
TM33	Reflect	Psychic	Status	—	—	20	Your Side
TM36	Sludge Bomb	Poison	Special	90	100	10	Normal
TM42	Facade	Normal	Physical	70	100	20	Normal
TM44	Rest	Psychic	Status	—	—	10	Self
TM45	Attract	Normal	Status	—	100	15	Normal
TM46	Thief	Dark	Physical	60	100	25	Normal
TM48	Round	Normal	Special	60	100	15	Normal
TM53	Energy Ball	Grass	Special	90	100	10	Normal
TM70	Flash	Normal	Status	—	100	20	Normal
TM75	Swords Dance	Normal	Status	—	—	20	Self
TM83	Infestation	Bug	Special	20	100	20	Normal
TM86	Grass Knot	Grass	Special	—	100	20	Normal
TM87	Swagger	Normal	Status	—	90	15	Normal
TM88	Sleep Talk	Normal	Status	—	—	10	Self
TM90	Substitute	Normal	Status	—	—	10	Self
TM94	Secret Power	Normal	Physical	70	100	20	Normal
TM96	Nature Power	Normal	Status	—	—	20	Normal
TM100	Confide	Normal	Status	—	—	20	Normal
HM01	Cut	Normal	Physical	50	95	30	Normal

MOVES LEARNED IN EXCHANGE FOR BP

Name	Type	Kind	Pow.	Acc.	PP	Range
Seed Bomb	Grass	Physical	80	100	15	Normal
Bind	Normal	Physical	15	85	20	Normal
Snore	Normal	Special	50	100	15	Normal
Knock Off	Dark	Physical	65	100	20	Normal
Synthesis	Grass	Status	—	—	5	Self
Giga Drain	Grass	Special	75	100	10	Normal
Gastro Acid	Poison	Status	—	100	10	Normal
Worry Seed	Grass	Status	—	100	10	Normal

MOVES TAUGHT BY PEOPLE

Name	Type	Kind	Pow.	Acc.	PP	Range

National Pokédex **071** Hoenn Pokédex —

Victreebel

Flycatcher Pokémon

Grass Poison

HEIGHT: 5'07" WEIGHT: 34.2 lbs.

Same form for ♂ / ♀

Ω Victreebel has a long vine that extends from its head. This vine is waved and flicked about as if it were an animal to attract prey. When an unsuspecting prey draws near, this Pokémon swallows it whole.

α Victreebel has a long vine that extends from its head. This vine is waved and flicked about as if it were an animal to attract prey. When an unsuspecting prey draws near, this Pokémon swallows it whole.

ABILITY

Chlorophyll

HIDDEN ABILITY

Gluttony

EGG GROUPS

Grass

STAT GROWTH RATES

HP ■■■
Attack ■■■■■
Defense ■■■
Sp. Atk ■■■■■
Sp. Def ■■■
Speed ■■■■

ITEMS SOMETIMES HELD BY WILD POKÉMON

—

EVOLUTION

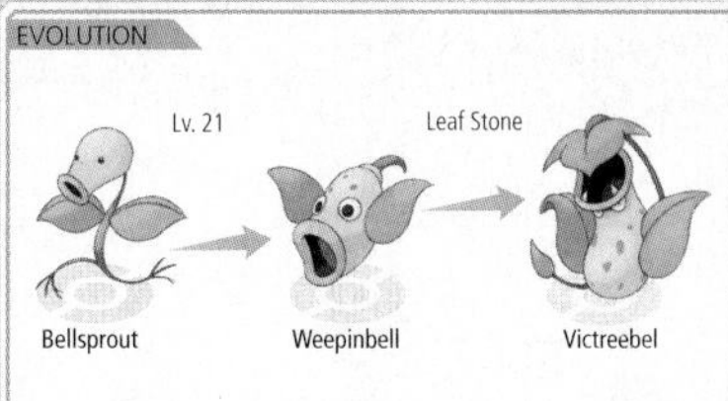

MAIN WAY TO REGISTER IN THE NATIONAL POKÉDEX

Use a Leaf Stone on a Weepinbell obtained via Link Trade or the GTS.

Damage taken in normal battles

Type		Type	
Normal	×1	Flying	×2
Fire	×2	Psychic	×2
Water	×0.5	Bug	×1
Grass	×0.25	Rock	×1
Electric	×0.5	Ghost	×1
Ice	×2	Dragon	×1
Fighting	×0.5	Dark	×1
Poison	×1	Steel	×1
Ground	×1	Fairy	×0.5

Damage taken in Inverse battles

Type		Type	
Normal	×1	Flying	×0.5
Fire	×0.5	Psychic	×0.5
Water	×2	Bug	×1
Grass	×4	Rock	×1
Electric	×2	Ghost	×1
Ice	×0.5	Dragon	×1
Fighting	×2	Dark	×1
Poison	×1	Steel	×1
Ground	×1	Fairy	×2

Can be used in

Inverse Battle
Battle Institute
Battle Maison
Random Matchup (Free Battle)
Random Matchup (Others)

LEVEL-UP MOVES

Lv.	Name	Type	Kind	Pow.	Acc.	PP	Range
1	Stockpile	Normal	Status	—	—	20	Self
1	Swallow	Normal	Status	—	—	10	Self
1	Spit Up	Normal	Special	—	100	10	Normal
1	Vine Whip	Grass	Physical	45	100	25	Normal
1	Sleep Powder	Grass	Status	—	75	15	Normal
1	Sweet Scent	Normal	Status	—	100	20	Many Others
1	Razor Leaf	Grass	Physical	55	95	25	Many Others
27	Leaf Tornado	Grass	Special	65	90	10	Normal
47	Leaf Storm	Grass	Special	130	90	5	Normal
47	Leaf Blade	Grass	Physical	90	100	15	Normal

TM & HM MOVES

No.	Name	Type	Kind	Pow.	Acc.	PP	Range
TM06	Toxic	Poison	Status	—	90	10	Normal
TM09	Venoshock	Poison	Special	65	100	10	Normal
TM10	Hidden Power	Normal	Special	60	100	15	Normal
TM11	Sunny Day	Fire	Status	—	—	5	Both Sides
TM15	Hyper Beam	Normal	Special	150	90	5	Normal
TM17	Protect	Normal	Status	—	—	10	Self
TM21	Frustration	Normal	Physical	—	100	20	Normal
TM22	Solar Beam	Grass	Special	120	100	10	Normal
TM27	Return	Normal	Physical	—	100	20	Normal
TM32	Double Team	Normal	Status	—	—	15	Self
TM33	Reflect	Psychic	Status	—	—	20	Your Side
TM36	Sludge Bomb	Poison	Special	90	100	10	Normal
TM42	Facade	Normal	Physical	70	100	20	Normal
TM44	Rest	Psychic	Status	—	—	10	Self
TM45	Attract	Normal	Status	—	100	15	Normal
TM46	Thief	Dark	Physical	60	100	25	Normal
TM48	Round	Normal	Special	60	100	15	Normal
TM53	Energy Ball	Grass	Special	90	100	10	Normal
TM68	Giga Impact	Normal	Physical	150	90	5	Normal
TM70	Flash	Normal	Status	—	100	20	Normal
TM75	Swords Dance	Normal	Status	—	—	20	Self
TM83	Infestation	Bug	Special	20	100	20	Normal
TM86	Grass Knot	Grass	Special	—	100	20	Normal
TM87	Swagger	Normal	Status	—	90	15	Normal
TM88	Sleep Talk	Normal	Status	—	—	10	Self
TM90	Substitute	Normal	Status	—	—	10	Self
TM94	Secret Power	Normal	Physical	70	100	20	Normal
TM96	Nature Power	Normal	Status	—	—	20	Normal
TM100	Confide	Normal	Status	—	—	20	Normal
HM01	Cut	Normal	Physical	50	95	30	Normal

MOVES LEARNED IN EXCHANGE FOR BP

Name	Type	Kind	Pow.	Acc.	PP	Range
Seed Bomb	Grass	Physical	80	100	15	Normal
Bind	Normal	Physical	15	85	20	Normal
Snore	Normal	Special	50	100	15	Normal
Knock Off	Dark	Physical	65	100	20	Normal
Synthesis	Grass	Status	--	—	5	Self
Giga Drain	Grass	Special	75	100	10	Normal
Gastro Acid	Poison	Status	—	100	10	Normal
Worry Seed	Grass	Status	—	100	10	Normal

MOVES TAUGHT BY PEOPLE

Name	Type	Kind	Pow.	Acc.	PP	Range

National Pokédex **072** Hoenn Pokédex **068**

Tentacool

Jellyfish Pokémon

Water Poison

HEIGHT: 2'11" WEIGHT: 100.3 lbs.

Same form for ♂ / ♀

Ω Tentacool's body is largely composed of water. If it is removed from the sea, it dries up like parchment. If this Pokémon happens to become dehydrated, put it back into the sea.

α Tentacool absorbs sunlight and refracts it using water inside its body to convert it into beam energy. This Pokémon shoots beams from the small round organ above its eyes.

ABILITIES

Clear Body
Liquid Ooze

HIDDEN ABILITY

Rain Dish

EGG GROUPS

Water 3

STAT GROWTH RATES

HP ■■
Attack ■■
Defense ■■
Sp. Atk ■■
Sp. Def ■■■■
Speed ■■■■

ITEMS SOMETIMES HELD BY WILD POKÉMON

Poison Barb

EVOLUTION

Lv. 30

Tentacool → Tentacruel

MAIN WAY TO REGISTER IN THE NATIONAL POKÉDEX

Catch on the water surface on Route 118.

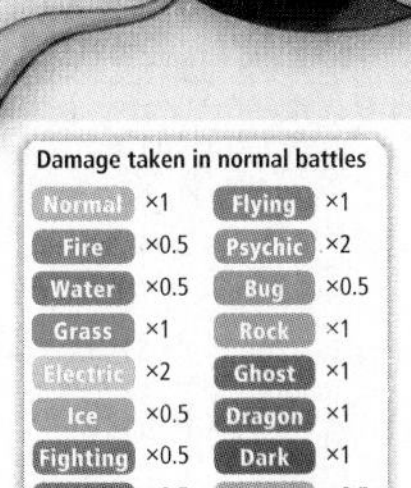

Damage taken in normal battles

Type		Type	
Normal	×1	Flying	×1
Fire	×0.5	Psychic	×2
Water	×0.5	Bug	×0.5
Grass	×1	Rock	×1
Electric	×2	Ghost	×1
Ice	×0.5	Dragon	×1
Fighting	×0.5	Dark	×1
Poison	×0.5	Steel	×0.5
Ground	×2	Fairy	×0.5

Damage taken in Inverse battles

Type		Type	
Normal	×1	Flying	×1
Fire	×2	Psychic	×0.5
Water	×2	Bug	×2
Grass	×1	Rock	×1
Electric	×0.5	Ghost	×1
Ice	×2	Dragon	×1
Fighting	×2	Dark	×1
Poison	×2	Steel	×2
Ground	×0.5	Fairy	×2

Can be used in

Inverse Battle
Battle Institute
Battle Maison
Random Matchup (Free Battle)
Random Matchup (Others)

LEVEL-UP MOVES

Lv.	Name	Type	Kind	Pow.	Acc.	PP	Range
1	Poison Sting	Poison	Physical	15	100	35	Normal
4	Supersonic	Normal	Status	—	55	20	Normal
7	Constrict	Normal	Physical	10	100	35	Normal
10	Acid	Poison	Special	40	100	30	Many Others
13	Toxic Spikes	Poison	Status	—	—	20	Other Side
16	Water Pulse	Water	Special	60	100	20	Normal
19	Wrap	Normal	Physical	15	90	20	Normal
22	Acid Spray	Poison	Special	40	100	20	Normal
25	Bubble Beam	Water	Special	65	100	20	Normal
28	Barrier	Psychic	Status	—	—	20	Self
31	Poison Jab	Poison	Physical	80	100	20	Normal
34	Brine	Water	Special	65	100	10	Normal
37	Screech	Normal	Status	—	85	40	Normal
40	Hex	Ghost	Special	65	100	10	Normal
43	Sludge Wave	Poison	Special	95	100	10	Adjacent
46	Hydro Pump	Water	Special	110	80	5	Normal
49	Wring Out	Normal	Special	—	100	5	Normal

TM & HM MOVES

No.	Name	Type	Kind	Pow.	Acc.	PP	Range
TM06	Toxic	Poison	Status	—	90	10	Normal
TM07	Hail	Ice	Status	—	—	10	Both Sides
TM09	Venoshock	Poison	Special	65	100	10	Normal
TM10	Hidden Power	Normal	Special	60	100	15	Normal
TM13	Ice Beam	Ice	Special	90	100	10	Normal
TM14	Blizzard	Ice	Special	110	70	5	Many Others
TM17	Protect	Normal	Status	—	—	10	Self
TM18	Rain Dance	Water	Status	—	—	5	Both Sides
TM20	Safeguard	Normal	Status	—	—	25	Your Side
TM21	Frustration	Normal	Physical	—	100	20	Normal
TM27	Return	Normal	Physical	—	100	20	Normal
TM32	Double Team	Normal	Status	—	—	15	Self
TM34	Sludge Wave	Poison	Special	95	100	10	Adjacent
TM36	Sludge Bomb	Poison	Special	90	100	10	Normal
TM42	Facade	Normal	Physical	70	100	20	Normal
TM44	Rest	Psychic	Status	—	—	10	Self
TM45	Attract	Normal	Status	—	100	15	Normal
TM46	Thief	Dark	Physical	60	100	25	Normal
TM48	Round	Normal	Special	60	100	15	Normal
TM55	Scald	Water	Special	80	100	15	Normal
TM66	Payback	Dark	Physical	50	100	10	Normal
TM75	Swords Dance	Normal	Status	—	—	20	Self
TM83	Infestation	Bug	Special	20	100	20	Normal
TM84	Poison Jab	Poison	Physical	80	100	20	Normal
TM87	Swagger	Normal	Status	—	90	15	Normal
TM88	Sleep Talk	Normal	Status	—	—	10	Self
TM90	Substitute	Normal	Status	—	—	10	Self
TM94	Secret Power	Normal	Physical	70	100	20	Normal
TM99	Dazzling Gleam	Fairy	Special	80	100	10	Many Others
TM100	Confide	Normal	Status	—	—	20	Normal
HM01	Cut	Normal	Physical	50	95	30	Normal
HM03	Surf	Water	Special	90	100	15	Adjacent
HM05	Waterfall	Water	Physical	80	100	15	Normal
HM07	Dive	Water	Physical	80	100	10	Normal

MOVES LEARNED IN EXCHANGE FOR BP

Name	Type	Kind	Pow.	Acc.	PP	Range
Magic Coat	Psychic	Status	—	—	15	Self
Icy Wind	Ice	Special	55	95	15	Many Others
Bind	Normal	Physical	15	85	20	Normal
Snore	Normal	Special	50	100	15	Normal
Knock Off	Dark	Physical	65	100	20	Normal
Giga Drain	Grass	Special	75	100	10	Normal
Water Pulse	Water	Special	60	100	20	Normal

MOVES TAUGHT BY PEOPLE

Name	Type	Kind	Pow.	Acc.	PP	Range

EGG MOVES

Name	Type	Kind	Pow.	Acc.	PP	Range
Aurora Beam	Ice	Special	65	100	20	Normal
Mirror Coat	Psychic	Special	—	100	20	Varies
Rapid Spin	Normal	Physical	20	100	40	Normal
Haze	Ice	Status	—	—	30	Both Sides
Confuse Ray	Ghost	Status	—	100	10	Normal
Knock Off	Dark	Physical	65	100	20	Normal
Acupressure	Normal	Status	—	—	30	Self/Ally
Muddy Water	Water	Special	90	85	10	Many Others
Bubble	Water	Special	40	100	30	Many Others
Aqua Ring	Water	Status	—	—	20	Self
Tickle	Normal	Status	—	100	20	Normal

National Pokédex **073** Hoenn Pokédex **069**

Tentacruel

Jellyfish Pokémon

Water Poison

HEIGHT: 5'03" WEIGHT: 121.3 lbs.

Same form for ♂ / ♀

Ω Tentacruel has large red orbs on its head. The orbs glow before lashing the vicinity with a harsh ultrasonic blast. This Pokémon's outburst creates rough waves around it.

α Tentacruel has tentacles that can be freely elongated and shortened at will. It ensnares prey with its tentacles and weakens the prey by dosing it with a harsh toxin. It can catch up to 80 prey at the same time.

ABILITIES
Clear Body
Liquid Ooze

HIDDEN ABILITY
Rain Dish

EGG GROUPS
Water 3

STAT GROWTH RATES
HP, Attack, Defense, Sp. Atk, Sp. Def, Speed

ITEMS SOMETIMES HELD BY WILD POKÉMON
Poison Barb

EVOLUTION
Tentacool → Lv. 30 → Tentacruel

MAIN WAY TO REGISTER IN THE NATIONAL POKÉDEX

Catch on the water surface in the Seafloor Cavern (Entrance).

Damage taken in normal battles

Type		Type	
Normal	×1	Flying	×1
Fire	×0.5	Psychic	×2
Water	×0.5	Bug	×0.5
Grass	×1	Rock	×1
Electric	×2	Ghost	×1
Ice	×0.5	Dragon	×1
Fighting	×0.5	Dark	×1
Poison	×0.5	Steel	×0.5
Ground	×2	Fairy	×0.5

Damage taken in Inverse battles

Type		Type	
Normal	×1	Flying	×1
Fire	×2	Psychic	×0.5
Water	×2	Bug	×2
Grass	×1	Rock	×1
Electric	×0.5	Ghost	×1
Ice	×2	Dragon	×1
Fighting	×2	Dark	×1
Poison	×2	Steel	×2
Ground	×0.5	Fairy	×2

Can be used in
Inverse Battle
Battle Institute
Battle Maison
Random Matchup (Free Battle)
Random Matchup (Others)

LEVEL-UP MOVES

Lv.	Name	Type	Kind	Pow.	Acc.	PP	Range
1	Reflect Type	Normal	Status	—	—	15	Normal
1	Wring Out	Normal	Special	—	100	5	Normal
1	Poison Sting	Poison	Physical	15	100	35	Normal
1	Supersonic	Normal	Status	—	55	20	Normal
1	Constrict	Normal	Physical	10	100	35	Normal
1	Acid	Poison	Special	40	100	30	Many Others
4	Supersonic	Normal	Status	—	55	20	Normal
7	Constrict	Normal	Physical	10	100	35	Normal
10	Acid	Poison	Special	40	100	30	Many Others
13	Toxic Spikes	Poison	Status	—	—	20	Other Side
16	Water Pulse	Water	Special	60	100	20	Normal
19	Wrap	Normal	Physical	15	90	20	Normal
22	Acid Spray	Poison	Special	40	100	20	Normal
25	Bubble Beam	Water	Special	65	100	20	Normal
28	Barrier	Psychic	Status	—	—	20	Self
32	Poison Jab	Poison	Physical	80	100	20	Normal
36	Brine	Water	Special	65	100	10	Normal
40	Screech	Normal	Status	—	85	40	Normal
44	Hex	Ghost	Special	65	100	10	Normal
48	Sludge Wave	Poison	Special	95	100	10	Adjacent
52	Hydro Pump	Water	Special	110	80	5	Normal
56	Wring Out	Normal	Special	—	100	5	Normal

TM & HM MOVES

No.	Name	Type	Kind	Pow.	Acc.	PP	Range
TM06	Toxic	Poison	Status	—	90	10	Normal
TM07	Hail	Ice	Status	—	—	10	Both Sides
TM09	Venoshock	Poison	Special	65	100	10	Normal
TM10	Hidden Power	Normal	Special	60	100	15	Normal
TM13	Ice Beam	Ice	Special	90	100	10	Normal
TM14	Blizzard	Ice	Special	110	70	5	Many Others
TM15	Hyper Beam	Normal	Special	150	90	5	Normal
TM17	Protect	Normal	Status	—	—	10	Self
TM18	Rain Dance	Water	Status	—	—	5	Both Sides
TM20	Safeguard	Normal	Status	—	—	25	Your Side
TM21	Frustration	Normal	Physical	—	100	20	Normal
TM27	Return	Normal	Physical	—	100	20	Normal
TM32	Double Team	Normal	Status	—	—	15	Self
TM34	Sludge Wave	Poison	Special	95	100	10	Adjacent
TM36	Sludge Bomb	Poison	Special	90	100	10	Normal
TM42	Facade	Normal	Physical	70	100	20	Normal
TM44	Rest	Psychic	Status	—	—	10	Self
TM45	Attract	Normal	Status	—	100	15	Normal
TM46	Thief	Dark	Physical	60	100	25	Normal
TM48	Round	Normal	Special	60	100	15	Normal
TM55	Scald	Water	Special	80	100	15	Normal
TM66	Payback	Dark	Physical	50	100	10	Normal
TM68	Giga Impact	Normal	Physical	150	90	5	Normal
TM75	Swords Dance	Normal	Status	—	—	20	Self
TM83	Infestation	Bug	Special	20	100	20	Normal
TM84	Poison Jab	Poison	Physical	80	100	20	Normal
TM87	Swagger	Normal	Status	—	90	15	Normal
TM88	Sleep Talk	Normal	Status	—	—	10	Self
TM90	Substitute	Normal	Status	—	—	10	Self
TM94	Secret Power	Normal	Physical	70	100	20	Normal
TM99	Dazzling Gleam	Fairy	Special	80	100	10	Many Others
TM100	Confide	Normal	Status	—	—	20	Normal
HM01	Cut	Normal	Physical	50	95	30	Normal
HM03	Surf	Water	Special	90	100	15	Adjacent
HM05	Waterfall	Water	Physical	80	100	15	Normal
HM07	Dive	Water	Physical	80	100	10	Normal

MOVES LEARNED IN EXCHANGE FOR BP

Name	Type	Kind	Pow.	Acc.	PP	Range
Magic Coat	Psychic	Status	—	—	15	Self
Icy Wind	Ice	Special	55	95	15	Many Others
Bind	Normal	Physical	15	85	20	Normal
Snore	Normal	Special	50	100	15	Normal
Knock Off	Dark	Physical	65	100	20	Normal
Giga Drain	Grass	Special	75	100	10	Normal
Water Pulse	Water	Special	60	100	20	Normal

MOVES TAUGHT BY PEOPLE

Name	Type	Kind	Pow.	Acc.	PP	Range

National Pokédex **074** Hoenn Pokédex **058**

Geodude

Rock Pokémon

Rock Ground

HEIGHT: 1'04" WEIGHT: 44.1 lbs.

Same form for ♂ / ♀

Ω The longer a Geodude lives, the more its edges are chipped and worn away, making it more rounded in appearance. However, this Pokémon's heart will remain hard, craggy, and rough alway.

α When Geodude sleeps deeply, it buries itself halfway into the ground. It will not awaken even if hikers step on it unwittingly. In the morning, this Pokémon rolls downhill in search of food.

ABILITIES
Rock Head
Sturdy

HIDDEN ABILITY
Sand Veil

EGG GROUPS
Mineral

STAT GROWTH RATES
HP, Attack, Defense, Sp. Atk, Sp. Def, Speed

ITEMS SOMETIMES HELD BY WILD POKÉMON
Everstone

EVOLUTION
Geodude → Lv. 25 → Graveler → Link Trade → Golem

MAIN WAY TO REGISTER IN THE NATIONAL POKÉDEX

Catch when it appears from a cracked rock in Rusturf Tunnel (using Rock Smash).

Damage taken in normal battles

Type		Type	
Normal	×0.5	Flying	×0.5
Fire	×0.5	Psychic	×1
Water	×4	Bug	×1
Grass	×4	Rock	×0.5
Electric	×0	Ghost	×1
Ice	×2	Dragon	×1
Fighting	×2	Dark	×1
Poison	×0.25	Steel	×2
Ground	×2	Fairy	×1

Damage taken in Inverse battles

Type		Type	
Normal	×2	Flying	×2
Fire	×2	Psychic	×1
Water	×0.25	Bug	×1
Grass	×0.25	Rock	×2
Electric	×2	Ghost	×1
Ice	×0.5	Dragon	×1
Fighting	×0.5	Dark	×1
Poison	×4	Steel	×0.5
Ground	×0.5	Fairy	×1

Can be used in
Inverse Battle
Battle Institute
Battle Maison
Random Matchup (Free Battle)
Random Matchup (Others)

LEVEL-UP MOVES

Lv.	Name	Type	Kind	Pow.	Acc.	PP	Range
1	Tackle	Normal	Physical	50	100	35	Normal
1	Defense Curl	Normal	Status	—	—	40	Self
4	Mud Sport	Ground	Status	—	—	15	Both Sides
6	Rock Polish	Rock	Status	—	—	20	Self
10	Rollout	Rock	Physical	30	90	20	Normal
12	Magnitude	Ground	Physical	—	100	30	Adjacent
16	Rock Throw	Rock	Physical	50	90	15	Normal
18	Smack Down	Rock	Physical	50	100	15	Normal
22	Bulldoze	Ground	Physical	60	100	20	Adjacent
24	Self-Destruct	Normal	Physical	200	100	5	Adjacent
28	Stealth Rock	Rock	Status	—	—	20	Other Side
30	Rock Blast	Rock	Physical	25	90	10	Normal
34	Earthquake	Ground	Physical	100	100	10	Adjacent
36	Explosion	Normal	Physical	250	100	5	Adjacent
40	Double-Edge	Normal	Physical	120	100	15	Normal
42	Stone Edge	Rock	Physical	100	80	5	Normal

TM & HM MOVES

No.	Name	Type	Kind	Pow.	Acc.	PP	Range
TM06	Toxic	Poison	Status	—	90	10	Normal
TM10	Hidden Power	Normal	Special	60	100	15	Normal
TM11	Sunny Day	Fire	Status	—	—	5	Both Sides
TM17	Protect	Normal	Status	—	—	10	Self
TM21	Frustration	Normal	Physical	—	100	20	Normal
TM23	Smack Down	Rock	Physical	50	100	15	Normal
TM26	Earthquake	Ground	Physical	100	100	10	Adjacent
TM27	Return	Normal	Physical	—	100	20	Normal
TM28	Dig	Ground	Physical	80	100	10	Normal
TM31	Brick Break	Fighting	Physical	75	100	15	Normal
TM32	Double Team	Normal	Status	—	—	15	Self
TM35	Flamethrower	Fire	Special	90	100	15	Normal
TM37	Sandstorm	Rock	Status	—	—	10	Both Sides
TM38	Fire Blast	Fire	Special	110	85	5	Normal
TM39	Rock Tomb	Rock	Physical	60	95	15	Normal
TM42	Facade	Normal	Physical	70	100	20	Normal
TM44	Rest	Psychic	Status	—	—	10	Self
TM45	Attract	Normal	Status	—	100	15	Normal
TM48	Round	Normal	Special	60	100	15	Normal
TM56	Fling	Dark	Physical	—	100	10	Normal
TM59	Incinerate	Fire	Special	60	100	15	Many Others
TM64	Explosion	Normal	Physical	250	100	5	Adjacent
TM69	Rock Polish	Rock	Status	—	—	20	Self
TM71	Stone Edge	Rock	Physical	100	80	5	Normal
TM74	Gyro Ball	Steel	Physical	—	100	5	Normal
TM78	Bulldoze	Ground	Physical	60	100	20	Adjacent
TM80	Rock Slide	Rock	Physical	75	90	10	Many Others
TM87	Swagger	Normal	Status	—	90	15	Normal
TM88	Sleep Talk	Normal	Status	—	—	10	Self
TM90	Substitute	Normal	Status	—	—	10	Self
TM94	Secret Power	Normal	Physical	70	100	20	Normal
TM96	Nature Power	Normal	Status	—	—	20	Normal
TM98	Power-Up Punch	Fighting	Physical	40	100	20	Normal
TM100	Confide	Normal	Status	—	—	20	Normal
HM04	Strength	Normal	Physical	80	100	15	Normal
HM06	Rock Smash	Fighting	Physical	40	100	15	Normal

MOVES LEARNED IN EXCHANGE FOR BP

Name	Type	Kind	Pow.	Acc.	PP	Range
Thunder Punch	Electric	Physical	75	100	15	Normal
Fire Punch	Fire	Physical	75	100	15	Normal
Block	Normal	Status	—	—	5	Normal
Earth Power	Ground	Special	90	100	10	Normal
Iron Defense	Steel	Status	—	—	15	Self
Superpower	Fighting	Physical	120	100	5	Normal
Snore	Normal	Special	50	100	15	Normal
Focus Punch	Fighting	Physical	150	100	20	Normal
Stealth Rock	Rock	Status	—	—	20	Other Side

MOVES TAUGHT BY PEOPLE

Name	Type	Kind	Pow.	Acc.	PP	Range

EGG MOVES

Name	Type	Kind	Pow.	Acc.	PP	Range
Mega Punch	Normal	Physical	80	85	20	Normal
Block	Normal	Status	—	—	5	Normal
Hammer Arm	Fighting	Physical	100	90	10	Normal
Flail	Normal	Physical	—	100	15	Normal
Curse	Ghost	Status	—	—	10	Varies
Focus Punch	Fighting	Physical	150	100	20	Normal
Rock Climb	Normal	Physical	90	85	20	Normal
Endure	Normal	Status	—	—	10	Self
Autotomize	Steel	Status	—	—	15	Self
Wide Guard	Rock	Status	—	—	10	Your Side

National Pokédex **075** Hoenn Pokédex **059**

Graveler

Rock Pokémon

Rock / Ground

HEIGHT: 3'03" WEIGHT: 231.5 lbs.

Same form for ♂ / ♀

Ω Graveler grows by feeding on rocks. Apparently, it prefers to eat rocks that are covered in moss. This Pokémon eats its way through a ton of rocks on a daily basis.

α Rocks are Graveler's favorite food. This Pokémon will climb a mountain from the base to the summit, crunchingly feasting on rocks all the while. Upon reaching the peak, it rolls back down to the bottom.

ABILITIES
Rock Head
Sturdy

HIDDEN ABILITY
Sand Veil

EGG GROUPS
Mineral

STAT GROWTH RATES
HP
Attack
Defense
Sp. Atk
Sp. Def
Speed

ITEMS SOMETIMES HELD BY WILD POKÉMON
Everstone

EVOLUTION
Geodude → Lv. 25 → Graveler → Link Trade → Golem

MAIN WAY TO REGISTER IN THE NATIONAL POKÉDEX

Catch when it appears from a cracked rock in Lilycove City (using Rock Smash).

Damage taken in normal battles

Type		Type	
Normal	×0.5	Flying	×0.5
Fire	×0.5	Psychic	×1
Water	×4	Bug	×1
Grass	×4	Rock	×0.5
Electric	×0	Ghost	×1
Ice	×2	Dragon	×1
Fighting	×2	Dark	×1
Poison	×0.25	Steel	×2
Ground	×2	Fairy	×1

Damage taken in Inverse battles

Type		Type	
Normal	×2	Flying	×2
Fire	×2	Psychic	×1
Water	×0.25	Bug	×1
Grass	×0.25	Rock	×2
Electric	×2	Ghost	×1
Ice	×0.5	Dragon	×1
Fighting	×0.5	Dark	×1
Poison	×4	Steel	×0.5
Ground	×0.5	Fairy	×1

Can be used in
Inverse Battle
Battle Institute
Battle Maison
Random Matchup (Free Battle)
Random Matchup (Others)

LEVEL-UP MOVES

Lv.	Name	Type	Kind	Pow.	Acc.	PP	Range
1	Tackle	Normal	Physical	50	100	35	Normal
1	Defense Curl	Normal	Status	—	—	40	Self
1	Mud Sport	Ground	Status	—	—	15	Both Sides
1	Rock Polish	Rock	Status	—	—	20	Self
4	Mud Sport	Ground	Status	—	—	15	Both Sides
6	Rock Polish	Rock	Status	—	—	20	Self
10	Rollout	Rock	Physical	30	90	20	Normal
12	Magnitude	Ground	Physical	—	100	30	Adjacent
16	Rock Throw	Rock	Physical	50	90	15	Normal
18	Smack Down	Rock	Physical	50	100	15	Normal
22	Bulldoze	Ground	Physical	60	100	20	Adjacent
24	Self-Destruct	Normal	Physical	200	100	5	Adjacent
30	Stealth Rock	Rock	Status	—	—	20	Other Side
34	Rock Blast	Rock	Physical	25	90	10	Normal
40	Earthquake	Ground	Physical	100	100	10	Adjacent
44	Explosion	Normal	Physical	250	100	5	Adjacent
50	Double-Edge	Normal	Physical	120	100	15	Normal
54	Stone Edge	Rock	Physical	100	80	5	Normal

TM & HM MOVES

No.	Name	Type	Kind	Pow.	Acc.	PP	Range
TM06	Toxic	Poison	Status	—	90	10	Normal
TM10	Hidden Power	Normal	Special	60	100	15	Normal
TM11	Sunny Day	Fire	Status	—	—	5	Both Sides
TM17	Protect	Normal	Status	—	—	10	Self
TM21	Frustration	Normal	Physical	—	100	20	Normal
TM23	Smack Down	Rock	Physical	50	100	15	Normal
TM26	Earthquake	Ground	Physical	100	100	10	Adjacent
TM27	Return	Normal	Physical	—	100	20	Normal
TM28	Dig	Ground	Physical	80	100	10	Normal
TM31	Brick Break	Fighting	Physical	75	100	15	Normal
TM32	Double Team	Normal	Status	—	—	15	Self
TM35	Flamethrower	Fire	Special	90	100	15	Normal
TM37	Sandstorm	Rock	Status	—	—	10	Both Sides
TM38	Fire Blast	Fire	Special	110	85	5	Normal
TM39	Rock Tomb	Rock	Physical	60	95	15	Normal
TM42	Facade	Normal	Physical	70	100	20	Normal
TM44	Rest	Psychic	Status	—	—	10	Self
TM45	Attract	Normal	Status	—	100	15	Normal
TM48	Round	Normal	Special	60	100	15	Normal
TM56	Fling	Dark	Physical	—	100	10	Normal
TM59	Incinerate	Fire	Special	60	100	15	Many Others
TM64	Explosion	Normal	Physical	250	100	5	Adjacent
TM69	Rock Polish	Rock	Status	—	—	20	Self
TM71	Stone Edge	Rock	Physical	100	80	5	Normal
TM74	Gyro Ball	Steel	Physical	—	100	5	Normal
TM78	Bulldoze	Ground	Physical	60	100	20	Adjacent
TM80	Rock Slide	Rock	Physical	75	90	10	Many Others
TM87	Swagger	Normal	Status	—	90	15	Normal
TM88	Sleep Talk	Normal	Status	—	—	10	Self
TM90	Substitute	Normal	Status	—	—	10	Self
TM94	Secret Power	Normal	Physical	70	100	20	Normal
TM96	Nature Power	Normal	Status	—	—	20	Normal
TM98	Power-Up Punch	Fighting	Physical	40	100	20	Normal
TM100	Confide	Normal	Status	—	—	20	Normal
HM04	Strength	Normal	Physical	80	100	15	Normal
HM06	Rock Smash	Fighting	Physical	40	100	15	Normal

MOVES LEARNED IN EXCHANGE FOR BP

Name	Type	Kind	Pow.	Acc.	PP	Range
Thunder Punch	Electric	Physical	75	100	15	Normal
Fire Punch	Fire	Physical	75	100	15	Normal
Block	Normal	Status	—	—	5	Normal
Earth Power	Ground	Special	90	100	10	Normal
Iron Defense	Steel	Status	—	—	15	Self
Superpower	Fighting	Physical	120	100	5	Normal
Snore	Normal	Special	50	100	15	Normal
Focus Punch	Fighting	Physical	150	100	20	Normal
Stealth Rock	Rock	Status	—	—	20	Other Side

MOVES TAUGHT BY PEOPLE

Name	Type	Kind	Pow.	Acc.	PP	Range

National Pokédex **076** Hoenn Pokédex **060**

Golem

Megaton Pokémon

Rock / Ground

HEIGHT: 4'07" WEIGHT: 661.4 lbs.

Same form for ♂ / ♀

Ω Golem live up on mountains. If there is a large earthquake, these Pokémon will come rolling down off the mountains en masse to the foothills below.

α Golem is known for rolling down from mountains. To prevent them from rolling into the homes of people downhill, grooves have been dug into the sides of mountains to serve as guideway for diverting this Pokémon's course.

ABILITIES
Rock Head
Sturdy

HIDDEN ABILITY
Sand Veil

EGG GROUPS
Mineral

STAT GROWTH RATES
HP
Attack
Defense
Sp. Atk
Sp. Def
Speed

ITEMS SOMETIMES HELD BY WILD POKÉMON
—

EVOLUTION
Geodude → Lv. 25 → Graveler → Link Trade → Golem

MAIN WAY TO REGISTER IN THE NATIONAL POKÉDEX

Receive a Graveler via Link Trade to have it evolve.

Damage taken in normal battles

Type		Type	
Normal	×0.5	Flying	×0.5
Fire	×0.5	Psychic	×1
Water	×4	Bug	×1
Grass	×4	Rock	×0.5
Electric	×0	Ghost	×1
Ice	×2	Dragon	×1
Fighting	×2	Dark	×1
Poison	×0.25	Steel	×2
Ground	×2	Fairy	×1

Damage taken in Inverse battles

Type		Type	
Normal	×2	Flying	×2
Fire	×2	Psychic	×1
Water	×0.25	Bug	×1
Grass	×0.25	Rock	×2
Electric	×2	Ghost	×1
Ice	×0.5	Dragon	×1
Fighting	×0.5	Dark	×1
Poison	×4	Steel	×0.5
Ground	×0.5	Fairy	×1

Can be used in
Inverse Battle
Battle Institute
Battle Maison
Random Matchup (Free Battle)
Random Matchup (Others)

LEVEL-UP MOVES

Lv.	Name	Type	Kind	Pow.	Acc.	PP	Range
1	Heavy Slam	Steel	Physical	—	100	10	Normal
1	Tackle	Normal	Physical	50	100	35	Normal
1	Defense Curl	Normal	Status	—	—	40	Self
1	Mud Sport	Ground	Status	—	—	15	Both Sides
1	Rock Polish	Rock	Status	—	—	20	Self
4	Mud Sport	Ground	Status	—	—	15	Both Sides
6	Rock Polish	Rock	Status	—	—	20	Self
10	Steamroller	Bug	Physical	65	100	20	Normal
12	Magnitude	Ground	Physical	—	100	30	Adjacent
16	Rock Throw	Rock	Physical	50	90	15	Normal
18	Smack Down	Rock	Physical	50	100	15	Normal
22	Bulldoze	Ground	Physical	60	100	20	Adjacent
24	Self-Destruct	Normal	Physical	200	100	5	Adjacent
30	Stealth Rock	Rock	Status	—	—	20	Other Side
34	Rock Blast	Rock	Physical	25	90	10	Normal
40	Earthquake	Ground	Physical	100	100	10	Adjacent
44	Explosion	Normal	Physical	250	100	5	Adjacent
50	Double-Edge	Normal	Physical	120	100	15	Normal
54	Stone Edge	Rock	Physical	100	80	5	Normal
60	Heavy Slam	Steel	Physical	—	100	10	Normal

TM & HM MOVES

No.	Name	Type	Kind	Pow.	Acc.	PP	Range
TM05	Roar	Normal	Status	—	—	20	Normal
TM06	Toxic	Poison	Status	—	90	10	Normal
TM10	Hidden Power	Normal	Special	60	100	15	Normal
TM11	Sunny Day	Fire	Status	—	—	5	Both Sides
TM15	Hyper Beam	Normal	Special	150	90	5	Normal
TM17	Protect	Normal	Status	—	—	10	Self
TM21	Frustration	Normal	Physical	—	100	20	Normal
TM23	Smack Down	Rock	Physical	50	100	15	Normal
TM26	Earthquake	Ground	Physical	100	100	10	Adjacent
TM27	Return	Normal	Physical	—	100	20	Normal
TM28	Dig	Ground	Physical	80	100	10	Normal
TM31	Brick Break	Fighting	Physical	75	100	15	Normal
TM32	Double Team	Normal	Status	—	—	15	Self
TM35	Flamethrower	Fire	Special	90	100	15	Normal
TM37	Sandstorm	Rock	Status	—	—	10	Both Sides
TM38	Fire Blast	Fire	Special	110	85	5	Normal
TM39	Rock Tomb	Rock	Physical	60	95	15	Normal
TM42	Facade	Normal	Physical	70	100	20	Normal
TM44	Rest	Psychic	Status	—	—	10	Self
TM45	Attract	Normal	Status	—	100	15	Normal
TM48	Round	Normal	Special	60	100	15	Normal
TM52	Focus Blast	Fighting	Special	120	70	5	Normal
TM56	Fling	Dark	Physical	—	100	10	Normal
TM59	Incinerate	Fire	Special	60	100	15	Many Others
TM64	Explosion	Normal	Physical	250	100	5	Adjacent
TM68	Giga Impact	Normal	Physical	150	90	5	Normal
TM69	Rock Polish	Rock	Status	—	—	20	Self
TM71	Stone Edge	Rock	Physical	100	80	5	Normal
TM74	Gyro Ball	Steel	Physical	—	100	5	Normal
TM78	Bulldoze	Ground	Physical	60	100	20	Adjacent
TM80	Rock Slide	Rock	Physical	75	90	10	Many Others
TM87	Swagger	Normal	Status	—	90	15	Normal
TM88	Sleep Talk	Normal	Status	—	—	10	Self
TM90	Substitute	Normal	Status	—	—	10	Self
TM94	Secret Power	Normal	Physical	70	100	20	Normal
TM96	Nature Power	Normal	Status	—	—	20	Normal
TM98	Power-Up Punch	Fighting	Physical	40	100	20	Normal
TM100	Confide	Normal	Status	—	—	20	Normal
HM04	Strength	Normal	Physical	80	100	15	Normal
HM06	Rock Smash	Fighting	Physical	40	100	15	Normal

MOVES LEARNED IN EXCHANGE FOR BP

Name	Type	Kind	Pow.	Acc.	PP	Range
Iron Head	Steel	Physical	80	100	15	Normal
Thunder Punch	Electric	Physical	75	100	15	Normal
Fire Punch	Fire	Physical	75	100	15	Normal
Block	Normal	Status	—	—	5	Normal
Earth Power	Ground	Special	90	100	10	Normal
Iron Defense	Steel	Status	—	—	15	Self
Superpower	Fighting	Physical	120	100	5	Normal
Snore	Normal	Special	50	100	15	Normal
Focus Punch	Fighting	Physical	150	100	20	Normal
Stealth Rock	Rock	Status	—	—	20	Other Side

MOVES TAUGHT BY PEOPLE

Name	Type	Kind	Pow.	Acc.	PP	Range

National Pokédex **077** Hoenn Pokédex —

Ponyta

Fire Horse Pokémon

Fire

HEIGHT: 3'03" WEIGHT: 66.1 lbs.

Same form for ♂ / ♀

Ω Ponyta is very weak at birth. It can barely stand up. This Pokémon becomes stronger by stumbling and falling to keep up with its parent.

α Ponyta is very weak at birth. It can barely stand up. This Pokémon becomes stronger by stumbling and falling to keep up with its parent.

ABILITIES
Run Away
Flash Fire

HIDDEN ABILITY
Flame Body

EGG GROUPS
Field

STAT GROWTH RATES
HP
Attack
Defense
Sp. Atk
Sp. Def
Speed

ITEMS SOMETIMES HELD BY WILD POKÉMON
—

EVOLUTION
Ponyta → Lv. 40 → Rapidash

MAIN WAY TO REGISTER IN THE NATIONAL POKÉDEX

Catch on Route 112. Appears as a hidden Pokémon after you battle Groudon or Kyogre.

Damage taken in normal battles

Type		Type	
Normal	×1	Flying	×1
Fire	×0.5	Psychic	×1
Water	×2	Bug	×0.5
Grass	×0.5	Rock	×2
Electric	×1	Ghost	×1
Ice	×0.5	Dragon	×1
Fighting	×1	Dark	×1
Poison	×1	Steel	×0.5
Ground	×2	Fairy	×0.5

Damage taken in Inverse battles

Type		Type	
Normal	×1	Flying	×1
Fire	×2	Psychic	×1
Water	×0.5	Bug	×2
Grass	×2	Rock	×0.5
Electric	×1	Ghost	×1
Ice	×2	Dragon	×1
Fighting	×1	Dark	×1
Poison	×1	Steel	×2
Ground	×0.5	Fairy	×2

Can be used in
Inverse Battle
Battle Institute
Battle Maison
Random Matchup (Free Battle)
Random Matchup (Others)

LEVEL-UP MOVES

Lv.	Name	Type	Kind	Pow.	Acc.	PP	Range
1	Growl	Normal	Status	—	100	40	Many Others
1	Tackle	Normal	Physical	50	100	35	Normal
4	Tail Whip	Normal	Status	—	100	30	Many Others
9	Ember	Fire	Special	40	100	25	Normal
13	Flame Wheel	Fire	Physical	60	100	25	Normal
17	Stomp	Normal	Physical	65	100	20	Normal
21	Flame Charge	Fire	Physical	50	100	20	Normal
25	Fire Spin	Fire	Special	35	85	15	Normal
29	Take Down	Normal	Physical	90	85	20	Normal
33	Inferno	Fire	Special	100	50	5	Normal
37	Agility	Psychic	Status	—	—	30	Self
41	Fire Blast	Fire	Special	110	85	5	Normal
45	Bounce	Flying	Physical	85	85	5	Normal
49	Flare Blitz	Fire	Physical	120	100	15	Normal

TM & HM MOVES

No.	Name	Type	Kind	Pow.	Acc.	PP	Range
TM06	Toxic	Poison	Status	—	90	10	Normal
TM10	Hidden Power	Normal	Special	60	100	15	Normal
TM11	Sunny Day	Fire	Status	—	—	5	Both Sides
TM17	Protect	Normal	Status	—	—	10	Self
TM21	Frustration	Normal	Physical	—	100	20	Normal
TM22	Solar Beam	Grass	Special	120	100	10	Normal
TM27	Return	Normal	Physical	—	100	20	Normal
TM32	Double Team	Normal	Status	—	—	15	Self
TM35	Flamethrower	Fire	Special	90	100	15	Normal
TM38	Fire Blast	Fire	Special	110	85	5	Normal
TM42	Facade	Normal	Physical	70	100	20	Normal
TM43	Flame Charge	Fire	Physical	50	100	20	Normal
TM44	Rest	Psychic	Status	—	—	10	Self
TM45	Attract	Normal	Status	—	100	15	Normal
TM48	Round	Normal	Special	60	100	15	Normal
TM49	Echoed Voice	Normal	Special	40	100	15	Normal
TM50	Overheat	Fire	Special	130	90	5	Normal
TM59	Incinerate	Fire	Special	60	100	15	Many Others
TM61	Will-O-Wisp	Fire	Status	—	85	15	Normal
TM87	Swagger	Normal	Status	—	90	15	Normal
TM88	Sleep Talk	Normal	Status	—	—	10	Self
TM90	Substitute	Normal	Status	—	—	10	Self
TM93	Wild Charge	Electric	Physical	90	100	15	Normal
TM94	Secret Power	Normal	Physical	70	100	20	Normal
TM100	Confide	Normal	Status	—	—	20	Normal
HM04	Strength	Normal	Physical	80	100	15	Normal

MOVES LEARNED IN EXCHANGE FOR BP

Name	Type	Kind	Pow.	Acc.	PP	Range
Bounce	Flying	Physical	85	85	5	Normal
Low Kick	Fighting	Physical	—	100	20	Normal
Iron Tail	Steel	Physical	100	75	15	Normal
Snore	Normal	Special	50	100	15	Normal
Heat Wave	Fire	Special	95	90	10	Many Others

MOVES TAUGHT BY PEOPLE

Name	Type	Kind	Pow.	Acc.	PP	Range

EGG MOVES

Name	Type	Kind	Pow.	Acc.	PP	Range
Flame Wheel	Fire	Physical	60	100	25	Normal
Thrash	Normal	Physical	120	100	10	1 Random
Double Kick	Fighting	Physical	30	100	30	Normal
Hypnosis	Psychic	Status	—	60	20	Normal
Charm	Fairy	Status	—	100	20	Normal
Double-Edge	Normal	Physical	120	100	15	Normal
Horn Drill	Normal	Physical	—	30	5	Normal
Morning Sun	Normal	Status	—	—	5	Self
Low Kick	Fighting	Physical	—	100	20	Normal
Captivate	Normal	Status	—	100	20	Many Others
Ally Switch	Psychic	Status	—	—	15	Self

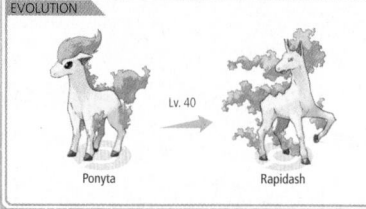

National Pokédex **078** Hoenn Pokédex —

Rapidash

Fire Horse Pokémon

Fire

HEIGHT: 5'07" WEIGHT: 209.4 lbs.

Same form for ♂ / ♀

Ω Rapidash usually can be seen casually cantering in the fields and plains. However, when this Pokémon turns serious, its fiery manes flare and blaze as it gallops its way up to 150 mph.

α Rapidash usually can be seen casually cantering in the fields and plains. However, when this Pokémon turns serious, its fiery manes flare and blaze as it gallops its way up to 150 mph.

ABILITIES
Run Away
Flash Fire

HIDDEN ABILITY
Flame Body

EGG GROUPS
Field

STAT GROWTH RATES
HP
Attack
Defense
Sp. Atk
Sp. Def
Speed

ITEMS SOMETIMES HELD BY WILD POKÉMON
—

EVOLUTION
Ponyta → Lv. 40 → Rapidash

MAIN WAY TO REGISTER IN THE NATIONAL POKÉDEX

Level up Ponyta to Lv. 40.

Damage taken in normal battles

Type		Type	
Normal	×1	Flying	×1
Fire	×0.5	Psychic	×1
Water	×2	Bug	×0.5
Grass	×0.5	Rock	×2
Electric	×1	Ghost	×1
Ice	×0.5	Dragon	×1
Fighting	×1	Dark	×1
Poison	×1	Steel	×0.5
Ground	×2	Fairy	×0.5

Damage taken in Inverse battles

Type		Type	
Normal	×1	Flying	×1
Fire	×2	Psychic	×1
Water	×0.5	Bug	×2
Grass	×2	Rock	×0.5
Electric	×1	Ghost	×1
Ice	×2	Dragon	×1
Fighting	×1	Dark	×1
Poison	×1	Steel	×2
Ground	×0.5	Fairy	×2

Can be used in
Inverse Battle
Battle Institute
Battle Maison
Random Matchup (Free Battle)
Random Matchup (Others)

LEVEL-UP MOVES

Lv.	Name	Type	Kind	Pow.	Acc.	PP	Range
1	Poison Jab	Poison	Physical	80	100	20	Normal
1	Megahorn	Bug	Physical	120	85	10	Normal
1	Growl	Normal	Status	—	100	40	Many Others
1	Quick Attack	Normal	Physical	40	100	30	Normal
1	Tail Whip	Normal	Status	—	100	30	Many Others
1	Ember	Fire	Special	40	100	25	Normal
4	Tail Whip	Normal	Status	—	100	30	Many Others
9	Ember	Fire	Special	40	100	25	Normal
13	Flame Wheel	Fire	Physical	60	100	25	Normal
17	Stomp	Normal	Physical	65	100	20	Normal
21	Flame Charge	Fire	Physical	50	100	20	Normal
25	Fire Spin	Fire	Special	35	85	15	Normal
29	Take Down	Normal	Physical	90	85	20	Normal
33	Inferno	Fire	Special	100	50	5	Normal
37	Agility	Psychic	Status	—	—	30	Self
40	Fury Attack	Normal	Physical	15	85	20	Normal
41	Fire Blast	Fire	Special	110	85	5	Normal
45	Bounce	Flying	Physical	85	85	5	Normal
49	Flare Blitz	Fire	Physical	120	100	15	Normal

TM & HM MOVES

No.	Name	Type	Kind	Pow.	Acc.	PP	Range
TM06	Toxic	Poison	Status	—	90	10	Normal
TM10	Hidden Power	Normal	Special	60	100	15	Normal
TM11	Sunny Day	Fire	Status	—	—	5	Both Sides
TM15	Hyper Beam	Normal	Special	150	90	5	Normal
TM17	Protect	Normal	Status	—	—	10	Self
TM21	Frustration	Normal	Physical	—	100	20	Normal
TM22	Solar Beam	Grass	Special	120	100	10	Normal
TM27	Return	Normal	Physical	—	100	20	Normal
TM32	Double Team	Normal	Status	—	—	15	Self
TM35	Flamethrower	Fire	Special	90	100	15	Normal
TM38	Fire Blast	Fire	Special	110	85	5	Normal
TM42	Facade	Normal	Physical	70	100	20	Normal
TM43	Flame Charge	Fire	Physical	50	100	20	Normal
TM44	Rest	Psychic	Status	—	—	10	Self
TM45	Attract	Normal	Status	—	100	15	Normal
TM48	Round	Normal	Special	60	100	15	Normal
TM49	Echoed Voice	Normal	Special	40	100	15	Normal
TM50	Overheat	Fire	Special	130	90	5	Normal
TM59	Incinerate	Fire	Special	60	100	15	Many Others
TM61	Will-O-Wisp	Fire	Status	—	85	15	Normal
TM68	Giga Impact	Normal	Physical	150	90	5	Normal
TM84	Poison Jab	Poison	Physical	80	100	20	Normal
TM87	Swagger	Normal	Status	—	90	15	Normal
TM88	Sleep Talk	Normal	Status	—	—	10	Self
TM90	Substitute	Normal	Status	—	—	10	Self
TM93	Wild Charge	Electric	Physical	90	100	15	Normal
TM94	Secret Power	Normal	Physical	70	100	20	Normal
TM100	Confide	Normal	Status	—	—	20	Normal
HM04	Strength	Normal	Physical	80	100	15	Normal

MOVES LEARNED IN EXCHANGE FOR BP

Name	Type	Kind	Pow.	Acc.	PP	Range
Drill Run	Ground	Physical	80	95	10	Normal
Bounce	Flying	Physical	85	85	5	Normal
Low Kick	Fighting	Physical	—	100	20	Normal
Iron Tail	Steel	Physical	100	75	15	Normal
Snore	Normal	Special	50	100	15	Normal
Heat Wave	Fire	Special	95	90	10	Many Others

MOVES TAUGHT BY PEOPLE

Name	Type	Kind	Pow.	Acc.	PP	Range

National Pokédex **079** Hoenn Pokédex —

Slowpoke

Dopey Pokémon

Water Psychic

HEIGHT: 3'11" WEIGHT: 79.4 lbs.

Same form for ♂ / ♀

Ω Slowpoke uses its tail to catch prey by dipping it in water at the side of a river. However, this Pokémon often forgets what it's doing and often spends entire days just loafing at water's edge.

α Slowpoke uses its tail to catch prey by dipping it in water at the side of a river. However, this Pokémon often forgets what it's doing and often spends entire days just loafing at water's edge.

ABILITIES
Oblivious
Own Tempo

HIDDEN ABILITY
Regenerator

EGG GROUPS
Monster Water 1

STAT GROWTH RATES
HP ■■■■
Attack ■■■
Defense ■■■
Sp. Atk ■■
Sp. Def ■■
Speed ■

ITEMS SOMETIMES HELD BY WILD POKÉMON
Lagging Tail

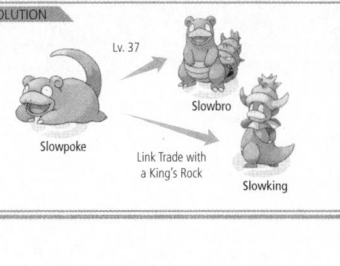

EVOLUTION
Slowpoke → Lv. 37 → Slowbro
Slowpoke → Link Trade with a King's Rock → Slowking

MAIN WAY TO REGISTER IN THE NATIONAL POKÉDEX

Catch in Mirage Cave 8.

Damage taken in normal battles

Type		Type	
Normal	×1	Flying	×1
Fire	×0.5	Psychic	×0.5
Water	×0.5	Bug	×2
Grass	×2	Rock	×1
Electric	×2	Ghost	×2
Ice	×0.5	Dragon	×1
Fighting	×0.5	Dark	×2
Poison	×1	Steel	×0.5
Ground	×1	Fairy	×1

Damage taken in Inverse battles

Type		Type	
Normal	×1	Flying	×1
Fire	×2	Psychic	×2
Water	×2	Bug	×0.5
Grass	×0.5	Rock	×1
Electric	×0.5	Ghost	×0.5
Ice	×2	Dragon	×1
Fighting	×2	Dark	×0.5
Poison	×1	Steel	×2
Ground	×1	Fairy	×1

Can be used in
Inverse Battle
Battle Institute
Battle Maison
Random Matchup (Free Battle)
Random Matchup (Others)

LEVEL-UP MOVES

Lv.	Name	Type	Kind	Pow.	Acc.	PP	Range
1	Curse	Ghost	Status	—	—	10	Varies
1	Yawn	Normal	Status	—	—	10	Normal
1	Tackle	Normal	Physical	50	100	35	Normal
5	Growl	Normal	Status	—	100	40	Many Others
9	Water Gun	Water	Special	40	100	25	Normal
14	Confusion	Psychic	Special	50	100	25	Normal
19	Disable	Normal	Status	—	100	20	Normal
23	Headbutt	Normal	Physical	70	100	15	Normal
28	Water Pulse	Water	Special	60	100	20	Normal
32	Zen Headbutt	Psychic	Physical	80	90	15	Normal
36	Slack Off	Normal	Status	—	—	10	Self
41	Amnesia	Psychic	Status	—	—	20	Self
45	Psychic	Psychic	Special	90	100	10	Normal
49	Rain Dance	Water	Status	—	—	5	Both Sides
54	Psych Up	Normal	Status	—	—	10	Normal
58	Heal Pulse	Psychic	Status	—	—	10	Normal

TM & HM MOVES

No.	Name	Type	Kind	Pow.	Acc.	PP	Range
TM03	Psyshock	Psychic	Special	80	100	10	Normal
TM04	Calm Mind	Psychic	Status	—	—	20	Self
TM06	Toxic	Poison	Status	—	90	10	Normal
TM07	Hail	Ice	Status	—	—	10	Both Sides
TM10	Hidden Power	Normal	Special	60	100	15	Normal
TM11	Sunny Day	Fire	Status	—	—	5	Both Sides
TM13	Ice Beam	Ice	Special	90	100	10	Normal
TM14	Blizzard	Ice	Special	110	70	5	Many Others
TM16	Light Screen	Psychic	Status	—	—	30	Your Side
TM17	Protect	Normal	Status	—	—	10	Self
TM18	Rain Dance	Water	Status	—	—	5	Both Sides
TM20	Safeguard	Normal	Status	—	—	25	Your Side
TM21	Frustration	Normal	Physical	—	100	20	Normal
TM26	Earthquake	Ground	Physical	100	100	10	Adjacent
TM27	Return	Normal	Physical	—	100	20	Normal
TM28	Dig	Ground	Physical	80	100	10	Normal
TM29	Psychic	Psychic	Special	90	100	10	Normal
TM30	Shadow Ball	Ghost	Special	80	100	15	Normal
TM32	Double Team	Normal	Status	—	—	15	Self
TM35	Flamethrower	Fire	Special	90	100	15	Normal
TM38	Fire Blast	Fire	Special	110	85	5	Normal
TM42	Facade	Normal	Physical	70	100	20	Normal
TM44	Rest	Psychic	Status	—	—	10	Self
TM45	Attract	Normal	Status	—	100	15	Normal
TM48	Round	Normal	Special	60	100	15	Normal
TM49	Echoed Voice	Normal	Special	40	100	15	Normal
TM55	Scald	Water	Special	80	100	15	Normal
TM59	Incinerate	Fire	Special	60	100	15	Many Others
TM70	Flash	Normal	Status	—	100	20	Normal
TM73	Thunder Wave	Electric	Status	—	100	20	Normal
TM77	Psych Up	Normal	Status	—	—	10	Normal
TM78	Bulldoze	Ground	Physical	60	100	20	Adjacent
TM85	Dream Eater	Psychic	Special	100	100	15	Normal
TM86	Grass Knot	Grass	Special	—	100	20	Normal
TM87	Swagger	Normal	Status	—	90	15	Normal
TM88	Sleep Talk	Normal	Status	—	—	10	Self
TM90	Substitute	Normal	Status	—	—	10	Self
TM92	Trick Room	Psychic	Status	—	—	5	Both Sides
TM94	Secret Power	Normal	Physical	70	100	20	Normal
TM100	Confide	Normal	Status	—	—	20	Normal
HM03	Surf	Water	Special	90	100	15	Adjacent
HM04	Strength	Normal	Physical	80	100	15	Normal
HM07	Dive	Water	Physical	80	100	10	Normal

MOVES LEARNED IN EXCHANGE FOR BP

Name	Type	Kind	Pow.	Acc.	PP	Range
Signal Beam	Bug	Special	75	100	15	Normal
Magic Coat	Psychic	Status	—	—	15	Self
Block	Normal	Status	—	—	5	Normal
Icy Wind	Ice	Special	55	95	15	Many Others
Aqua Tail	Water	Physical	90	90	10	Normal
Zen Headbutt	Psychic	Physical	80	90	15	Normal
Iron Tail	Steel	Physical	100	75	15	Normal
Snore	Normal	Special	50	100	15	Normal
Water Pulse	Water	Special	60	100	20	Normal
After You	Normal	Status	—	—	15	Normal
Trick	Psychic	Status	—	100	10	Normal
Wonder Room	Psychic	Status	—	—	10	Both Sides
Recycle	Normal	Status	—	—	10	Self
Skill Swap	Psychic	Status	—	—	10	Normal

MOVES TAUGHT BY PEOPLE

Name	Type	Kind	Pow.	Acc.	PP	Range

EGG MOVES

Name	Type	Kind	Pow.	Acc.	PP	Range
Belly Drum	Normal	Status	—	—	10	Self
Future Sight	Psychic	Special	120	100	10	Normal
Stomp	Normal	Physical	65	100	20	Normal
Mud Sport	Ground	Status	—	—	15	Both Sides
Sleep Talk	Normal	Status	—	—	10	Self
Snore	Normal	Special	50	100	15	Normal
Me First	Normal	Status	—	—	20	Varies
Block	Normal	Status	—	—	5	Normal
Zen Headbutt	Psychic	Physical	80	90	15	Normal
Wonder Room	Psychic	Status	—	—	10	Both Sides
Belch	Poison	Special	120	90	10	Normal

079 Slowpoke National Pokédex

National Pokédex **080** Hoenn Pokédex —

Slowbro

Hermit Crab Pokémon

Water Psychic

HEIGHT: 5'03" WEIGHT: 173.1 lbs.

Same form for ♂ / ♀

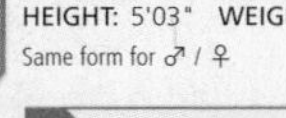

Ω Slowbro's tail has a Shellder firmly attached with a bite. As a result, the tail can't be used for fishing anymore. This causes Slowbro to grudgingly swim and catch prey instead.

α Slowbro's tail has a Shellder firmly attached with a bite. As a result, the tail can't be used for fishing anymore. This causes Slowbro to grudgingly swim and catch prey instead.

ABILITIES
Oblivious
Own Tempo

HIDDEN ABILITY
Regenerator

EGG GROUPS
Monster Water 1

STAT GROWTH RATES
HP ■■■■
Attack ■■■■
Defense ■■■■■
Sp. Atk ■■■■■
Sp. Def ■■■
Speed ■■

ITEMS SOMETIMES HELD BY WILD POKÉMON
—

EVOLUTION
Slowpoke → Lv. 37 → Slowbro

MAIN WAY TO REGISTER IN THE NATIONAL POKÉDEX

Level up Slowpoke to Lv. 37.

Damage taken in normal battles

Type		Type	
Normal	×1	Flying	×1
Fire	×0.5	Psychic	×0.5
Water	×0.5	Bug	×2
Grass	×2	Rock	×1
Electric	×2	Ghost	×2
Ice	×0.5	Dragon	×1
Fighting	×0.5	Dark	×2
Poison	×1	Steel	×0.5
Ground	×1	Fairy	×1

Damage taken in Inverse battles

Type		Type	
Normal	×1	Flying	×1
Fire	×2	Psychic	×2
Water	×2	Bug	×0.5
Grass	×0.5	Rock	×1
Electric	×0.5	Ghost	×0.5
Ice	×2	Dragon	×1
Fighting	×2	Dark	×0.5
Poison	×1	Steel	×2
Ground	×1	Fairy	×1

Can be used in
Inverse Battle
Battle Institute
Battle Maison
Random Matchup (Free Battle)
Random Matchup (Others)

LEVEL-UP MOVES

Lv.	Name	Type	Kind	Pow.	Acc.	PP	Range
1	Heal Pulse	Psychic	Status	—	—	10	Normal
1	Curse	Ghost	Status	—	—	10	Varies
1	Yawn	Normal	Status	—	—	10	Normal
1	Tackle	Normal	Physical	50	100	35	Normal
1	Growl	Normal	Status	—	100	40	Many Others
5	Growl	Normal	Status	—	100	40	Many Others
9	Water Gun	Water	Special	40	100	25	Normal
14	Confusion	Psychic	Special	50	100	25	Normal
19	Disable	Normal	Status	—	100	20	Normal
23	Headbutt	Normal	Physical	70	100	15	Normal
28	Water Pulse	Water	Special	60	100	20	Normal
32	Zen Headbutt	Psychic	Physical	80	90	15	Normal
36	Slack Off	Normal	Status	—	—	10	Self
37	Withdraw	Water	Status	—	—	40	Self
43	Amnesia	Psychic	Status	—	—	20	Self
49	Psychic	Psychic	Special	90	100	10	Normal
55	Rain Dance	Water	Status	—	—	5	Both Sides
62	Psych Up	Normal	Status	—	—	10	Normal
68	Heal Pulse	Psychic	Status	—	—	10	Normal

TM & HM MOVES

No.	Name	Type	Kind	Pow.	Acc.	PP	Range
TM03	Psyshock	Psychic	Special	80	100	10	Normal
TM04	Calm Mind	Psychic	Status	—	—	20	Self
TM06	Toxic	Poison	Status	—	90	10	Normal
TM07	Hail	Ice	Status	—	—	10	Both Sides
TM10	Hidden Power	Normal	Special	60	100	15	Normal
TM11	Sunny Day	Fire	Status	—	—	5	Both Sides
TM13	Ice Beam	Ice	Special	90	100	10	Normal
TM14	Blizzard	Ice	Special	110	70	5	Many Others
TM15	Hyper Beam	Normal	Special	150	90	5	Normal
TM16	Light Screen	Psychic	Status	—	—	30	Your Side
TM17	Protect	Normal	Status	—	—	10	Self
TM18	Rain Dance	Water	Status	—	—	5	Both Sides
TM20	Safeguard	Normal	Status	—	—	25	Your Side
TM21	Frustration	Normal	Physical	—	100	20	Normal
TM26	Earthquake	Ground	Physical	100	100	10	Adjacent
TM27	Return	Normal	Physical	—	100	20	Normal
TM28	Dig	Ground	Physical	80	100	10	Normal
TM29	Psychic	Psychic	Special	90	100	10	Normal
TM30	Shadow Ball	Ghost	Special	80	100	15	Normal
TM31	Brick Break	Fighting	Physical	75	100	15	Normal
TM32	Double Team	Normal	Status	—	—	15	Self
TM35	Flamethrower	Fire	Special	90	100	15	Normal
TM38	Fire Blast	Fire	Special	110	85	5	Normal
TM40	Aerial Ace	Flying	Physical	60	—	20	Normal
TM42	Facade	Normal	Physical	70	100	20	Normal
TM44	Rest	Psychic	Status	—	—	10	Self
TM45	Attract	Normal	Status	—	100	15	Normal
TM48	Round	Normal	Special	60	100	15	Normal
TM49	Echoed Voice	Normal	Special	40	100	15	Normal
TM52	Focus Blast	Fighting	Special	120	70	5	Normal
TM55	Scald	Water	Special	80	100	15	Normal
TM56	Fling	Dark	Physical	—	100	10	Normal
TM59	Incinerate	Fire	Special	60	100	15	Many Others
TM68	Giga Impact	Normal	Physical	150	90	5	Normal
TM70	Flash	Normal	Status	—	100	20	Normal
TM73	Thunder Wave	Electric	Status	—	100	20	Normal
TM77	Psych Up	Normal	Status	—	—	10	Normal
TM78	Bulldoze	Ground	Physical	60	100	20	Adjacent
TM85	Dream Eater	Psychic	Special	100	100	15	Normal
TM86	Grass Knot	Grass	Special	—	100	20	Normal
TM87	Swagger	Normal	Status	—	90	15	Normal
TM88	Sleep Talk	Normal	Status	—	—	10	Self
TM90	Substitute	Normal	Status	—	—	10	Self
TM92	Trick Room	Psychic	Status	—	—	5	Both Sides
TM94	Secret Power	Normal	Physical	70	100	20	Normal
TM100	Confide	Normal	Status	—	—	20	Normal
HM03	Surf	Water	Special	90	100	15	Adjacent
HM04	Strength	Normal	Physical	80	100	15	Normal
HM06	Rock Smash	Fighting	Physical	40	100	15	Normal
HM07	Dive	Water	Physical	80	100	10	Normal

MOVES LEARNED IN EXCHANGE FOR BP

Name	Type	Kind	Pow.	Acc.	PP	Range
Signal Beam	Bug	Special	75	100	15	Normal
Ice Punch	Ice	Physical	75	100	15	Normal
Magic Coat	Psychic	Status	—	—	15	Self
Block	Normal	Status	—	—	5	Normal
Foul Play	Dark	Physical	95	100	15	Normal
Iron Defense	Steel	Status	—	—	15	Self
Icy Wind	Ice	Special	55	95	15	Many Others
Aqua Tail	Water	Physical	90	90	10	Normal
Zen Headbutt	Psychic	Physical	80	90	15	Normal
Iron Tail	Steel	Physical	100	75	15	Normal
Snore	Normal	Special	50	100	15	Normal
Drain Punch	Fighting	Physical	75	100	10	Normal
Focus Punch	Fighting	Physical	150	100	20	Normal
Water Pulse	Water	Special	60	100	20	Normal
After You	Normal	Status	—	—	15	Normal
Trick	Psychic	Status	—	100	10	Normal
Wonder Room	Psychic	Status	—	—	10	Both Sides
Recycle	Normal	Status	—	—	10	Self
Skill Swap	Psychic	Status	—	—	10	Normal

MOVES TAUGHT BY PEOPLE

Name	Type	Kind	Pow.	Acc.	PP	Range

Slowbro 080

Mega Evolution

Mega Slowbro

Hermit Crab Pokémon

Water Psychic

HEIGHT: 6'07" WEIGHT: 264.6 lbs.
Same form for ♂ / ♀

REQUIRED MEGA STONE
Slowbronite
Receive from the old man in Shoal Cave (after you receive your first Shell Bell from him).

ABILITY
Shell Armor

HIDDEN ABILITY
—

EGG GROUPS
—

STAT GROWTH RATES

HP	■■■■
Attack	■■■■
Defense	■■■■■■■■
Sp. Atk	■■■■■■
Sp. Def	■■■
Speed	■■

Damage taken in normal battles

Normal	×1	Flying	×1
Fire	×0.5	Psychic	×0.5
Water	×0.5	Bug	×2
Grass	×2	Rock	×1
Electric	×2	Ghost	×2
Ice	×0.5	Dragon	×1
Fighting	×0.5	Dark	×2
Poison	×1	Steel	×0.5
Ground	×1	Fairy	×1

Damage taken in Inverse battles

Normal	×1	Flying	×1
Fire	×2	Psychic	×2
Water	×2	Bug	×0.5
Grass	×0.5	Rock	×1
Electric	×0.5	Ghost	×0.5
Ice	×2	Dragon	×1
Fighting	×2	Dark	×0.5
Poison	×1	Steel	×2
Ground	×1	Fairy	×1

Can be used in
Inverse Battle
Battle Institute
Battle Maison
Random Matchup (Free Battle)
Random Matchup (Others)

National Pokédex **081** Hoenn Pokédex **084**

Magnemite

Magnet Pokémon

Electric Steel

HEIGHT: 1'00" WEIGHT: 13.2 lbs.
Gender unknown

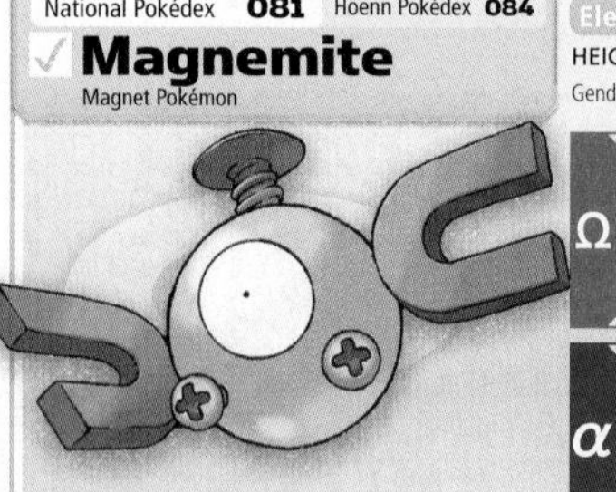

Ω Magnemite attaches itself to power lines to feed on electricity. If your house has a power outage, check your circuit breakers. You may find a large number of this Pokémon clinging to the breaker box.

α Magnemite floats in the air by emitting electromagnetic waves from the units at its sides. These waves block gravity. This Pokémon becomes incapable of flight if its internal electrical supply is depleted.

ABILITIES
Magnet Pull
Sturdy

HIDDEN ABILITY
Analytic

EGG GROUPS
Mineral

STAT GROWTH RATES

HP	■
Attack	■■
Defense	■■■
Sp. Atk	■■■■■
Sp. Def	■■
Speed	■■■

ITEMS SOMETIMES HELD BY WILD POKÉMON
Metal Coat

EVOLUTION
Magnemite → Lv. 30 → Magneton → Level up in New Mauville → Magnezone

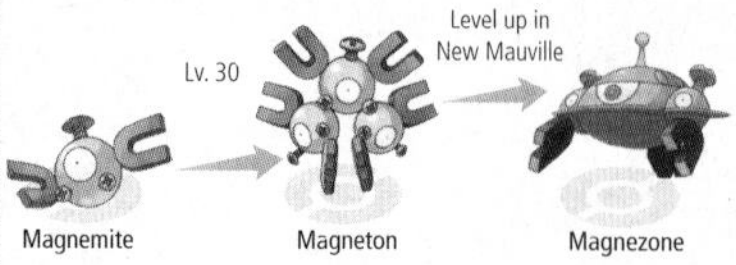

MAIN WAY TO REGISTER IN THE NATIONAL POKÉDEX
Catch in New Mauville.

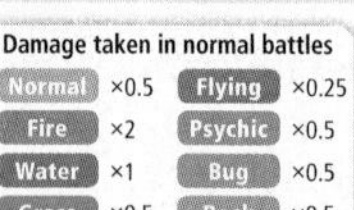

Damage taken in normal battles

Normal	×0.5	Flying	×0.25
Fire	×2	Psychic	×0.5
Water	×1	Bug	×0.5
Grass	×0.5	Rock	×0.5
Electric	×0.5	Ghost	×1
Ice	×0.5	Dragon	×0.5
Fighting	×2	Dark	×1
Poison	×0	Steel	×0.25
Ground	×4	Fairy	×0.5

Damage taken in Inverse battles

Normal	×2	Flying	×4
Fire	×0.5	Psychic	×2
Water	×1	Bug	×2
Grass	×2	Rock	×2
Electric	×2	Ghost	×1
Ice	×2	Dragon	×2
Fighting	×0.5	Dark	×1
Poison	×2	Steel	×4
Ground	×0.25	Fairy	×2

Can be used in
Inverse Battle
Battle Institute
Battle Maison
Random Matchup (Free Battle)
Random Matchup (Others)

LEVEL-UP MOVES

Lv.	Name	Type	Kind	Pow.	Acc.	PP	Range
1	Tackle	Normal	Physical	50	100	35	Normal
5	Supersonic	Normal	Status	—	55	20	Normal
7	Thunder Shock	Electric	Special	40	100	30	Normal
11	Sonic Boom	Normal	Special	—	90	20	Normal
13	Thunder Wave	Electric	Status	—	100	20	Normal
17	Magnet Bomb	Steel	Physical	60	—	20	Normal
19	Spark	Electric	Physical	65	100	20	Normal
23	Mirror Shot	Steel	Special	65	85	10	Normal
25	Metal Sound	Steel	Status	—	85	40	Normal
29	Electro Ball	Electric	Special	—	100	10	Normal
31	Flash Cannon	Steel	Special	80	100	10	Normal
35	Screech	Normal	Status	—	85	40	Normal
37	Discharge	Electric	Special	80	100	15	Adjacent
41	Lock-On	Normal	Status	—	—	5	Normal
43	Magnet Rise	Electric	Status	—	—	10	Self
47	Gyro Ball	Steel	Physical	—	100	5	Normal
49	Zap Cannon	Electric	Special	120	50	5	Normal

TM & HM MOVES

No.	Name	Type	Kind	Pow.	Acc.	PP	Range
TM06	Toxic	Poison	Status	—	90	10	Normal
TM10	Hidden Power	Normal	Special	60	100	15	Normal
TM11	Sunny Day	Fire	Status	—	—	5	Both Sides
TM16	Light Screen	Psychic	Status	—	—	30	Your Side
TM17	Protect	Normal	Status	—	—	10	Self
TM18	Rain Dance	Water	Status	—	—	5	Both Sides
TM21	Frustration	Normal	Physical	—	100	20	Normal
TM24	Thunderbolt	Electric	Special	90	100	15	Normal
TM25	Thunder	Electric	Special	110	70	10	Normal
TM27	Return	Normal	Physical	—	100	20	Normal
TM32	Double Team	Normal	Status	—	—	15	Self
TM33	Reflect	Psychic	Status	—	—	20	Your Side
TM42	Facade	Normal	Physical	70	100	20	Normal
TM44	Rest	Psychic	Status	—	—	10	Self
TM48	Round	Normal	Special	60	100	15	Normal
TM57	Charge Beam	Electric	Special	50	90	10	Normal
TM64	Explosion	Normal	Physical	250	100	5	Adjacent
TM70	Flash	Normal	Status	—	100	20	Normal
TM72	Volt Switch	Electric	Special	70	100	20	Normal
TM73	Thunder Wave	Electric	Status	—	100	20	Normal
TM74	Gyro Ball	Steel	Physical	—	100	5	Normal
TM77	Psych Up	Normal	Status	—	—	10	Normal
TM87	Swagger	Normal	Status	—	90	15	Normal
TM88	Sleep Talk	Normal	Status	—	—	10	Self
TM90	Substitute	Normal	Status	—	—	10	Self
TM91	Flash Cannon	Steel	Special	80	100	10	Normal
TM93	Wild Charge	Electric	Physical	90	100	15	Normal
TM94	Secret Power	Normal	Physical	70	100	20	Normal
TM100	Confide	Normal	Status	—	—	20	Normal

MOVES LEARNED IN EXCHANGE FOR BP

Name	Type	Kind	Pow.	Acc.	PP	Range
Signal Beam	Bug	Special	75	100	15	Normal
Magic Coat	Psychic	Status	—	—	15	Self
Gravity	Psychic	Status	—	—	5	Both Sides
Magnet Rise	Electric	Status	—	—	10	Self
Iron Defense	Steel	Status	—	—	15	Self
Electroweb	Electric	Special	55	95	15	Many Others
Snore	Normal	Special	50	100	15	Normal
Shock Wave	Electric	Special	60	—	20	Normal
Recycle	Normal	Status	—	—	10	Self

MOVES TAUGHT BY PEOPLE

Name	Type	Kind	Pow.	Acc.	PP	Range

National Pokédex **082** Hoenn Pokédex **085**

Magneton

Magnet Pokémon

Electric Steel

HEIGHT: 3'03" WEIGHT: 132.3 lbs.

Gender unknown

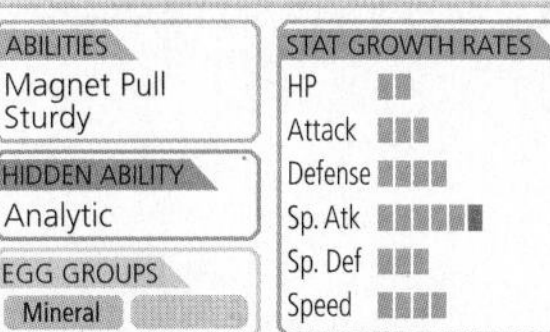

Ω Magneton emits a powerful magnetic force that is fatal to mechanical devices. As a result, large cities sound sirens to warn citizens of large-scale outbreaks of this Pokémon.

α Magneton emits a powerful magnetic force that is fatal to electronics and precision instruments. Because of this, it is said that some towns warn people to keep this Pokémon inside a Poké Ball.

ABILITIES
Magnet Pull
Sturdy

HIDDEN ABILITY
Analytic

EGG GROUPS
Mineral

STAT GROWTH RATES
HP ■■
Attack ■■■
Defense ■■■■
Sp. Atk ■■■■■■
Sp. Def ■■■
Speed ■■■■

ITEMS SOMETIMES HELD BY WILD POKÉMON
—

EVOLUTION

MAIN WAY TO REGISTER IN THE NATIONAL POKÉDEX

Level up Magnemite to Lv. 30.

Damage taken in normal battles

Type		Type	
Normal	×0.5	Flying	×0.25
Fire	×2	Psychic	×0.5
Water	×1	Bug	×0.5
Grass	×0.5	Rock	×0.5
Electric	×0.5	Ghost	×1
Ice	×0.5	Dragon	×0.5
Fighting	×2	Dark	×1
Poison	×0	Steel	×0.25
Ground	×4	Fairy	×0.5

Damage taken in Inverse battles

Type		Type	
Normal	×2	Flying	×4
Fire	×0.5	Psychic	×2
Water	×1	Bug	×2
Grass	×2	Rock	×2
Electric	×2	Ghost	×1
Ice	×2	Dragon	×2
Fighting	×0.5	Dark	×1
Poison	×2	Steel	×4
Ground	×0.25	Fairy	×2

Can be used in
Inverse Battle
Battle Institute
Battle Maison
Random Matchup (Free Battle)
Random Matchup (Others)

LEVEL-UP MOVES

Lv.	Name	Type	Kind	Pow.	Acc.	PP	Range
1	Zap Cannon	Electric	Special	120	50	5	Normal
1	Electric Terrain	Electric	Status	—	—	10	Both Sides
1	Tackle	Normal	Physical	50	100	35	Normal
1	Supersonic	Normal	Status	—	55	20	Normal
1	Thunder Shock	Electric	Special	40	100	30	Normal
1	Sonic Boom	Normal	Special	—	90	20	Normal
5	Supersonic	Normal	Status	—	55	20	Normal
7	Thunder Shock	Electric	Special	40	100	30	Normal
11	Sonic Boom	Normal	Special	—	90	20	Normal
13	Thunder Wave	Electric	Status	—	100	20	Normal
17	Magnet Bomb	Steel	Physical	60	—	20	Normal
19	Spark	Electric	Physical	65	100	20	Normal
23	Mirror Shot	Steel	Special	65	85	10	Normal
25	Metal Sound	Steel	Status	—	85	40	Normal
29	Electro Ball	Electric	Special	—	100	10	Normal
30	Tri Attack	Normal	Special	80	100	10	Normal
33	Flash Cannon	Steel	Special	80	100	10	Normal
39	Screech	Normal	Status	—	85	40	Normal
43	Discharge	Electric	Special	80	100	15	Adjacent
49	Lock-On	Normal	Status	—	—	5	Normal
53	Magnet Rise	Electric	Status	—	—	10	Self
59	Gyro Ball	Steel	Physical	—	100	5	Normal
63	Zap Cannon	Electric	Special	120	50	5	Normal

TM & HM MOVES

No.	Name	Type	Kind	Pow.	Acc.	PP	Range
TM06	Toxic	Poison	Status	—	90	10	Normal
TM10	Hidden Power	Normal	Special	60	100	15	Normal
TM11	Sunny Day	Fire	Status	—	—	5	Both Sides
TM15	Hyper Beam	Normal	Special	150	90	5	Normal
TM16	Light Screen	Psychic	Status	—	—	30	Your Side
TM17	Protect	Normal	Status	—	—	10	Self
TM18	Rain Dance	Water	Status	—	—	5	Both Sides
TM21	Frustration	Normal	Physical	—	100	20	Normal
TM24	Thunderbolt	Electric	Special	90	100	15	Normal
TM25	Thunder	Electric	Special	110	70	10	Normal
TM27	Return	Normal	Physical	—	100	20	Normal
TM32	Double Team	Normal	Status	—	—	15	Self
TM33	Reflect	Psychic	Status	—	—	20	Your Side
TM42	Facade	Normal	Physical	70	100	20	Normal
TM44	Rest	Psychic	Status	—	—	10	Self
TM48	Round	Normal	Special	60	100	15	Normal
TM57	Charge Beam	Electric	Special	50	90	10	Normal
TM64	Explosion	Normal	Physical	250	100	5	Adjacent
TM68	Giga Impact	Normal	Physical	150	90	5	Normal
TM70	Flash	Normal	Status	—	100	20	Normal
TM72	Volt Switch	Electric	Special	70	100	20	Normal
TM73	Thunder Wave	Electric	Status	—	100	20	Normal
TM74	Gyro Ball	Steel	Physical	—	100	5	Normal
TM77	Psych Up	Normal	Status	—	—	10	Normal
TM87	Swagger	Normal	Status	—	90	15	Normal
TM88	Sleep Talk	Normal	Status	—	—	10	Self
TM90	Substitute	Normal	Status	—	—	10	Self
TM91	Flash Cannon	Steel	Special	80	100	10	Normal
TM93	Wild Charge	Electric	Physical	90	100	15	Normal
TM94	Secret Power	Normal	Physical	70	100	20	Normal
TM100	Confide	Normal	Status	—	—	20	Normal

MOVES LEARNED IN EXCHANGE FOR BP

Name	Type	Kind	Pow.	Acc.	PP	Range
Signal Beam	Bug	Special	75	100	15	Normal
Magic Coat	Psychic	Status	—	—	15	Self
Gravity	Psychic	Status	—	—	5	Both Sides
Magnet Rise	Electric	Status	—	—	10	Self
Iron Defense	Steel	Status	—	—	15	Self
Electroweb	Electric	Special	55	95	15	Many Others
Snore	Normal	Special	50	100	15	Normal
Shock Wave	Electric	Special	60	—	20	Normal
Recycle	Normal	Status	—	—	10	Self

MOVES TAUGHT BY PEOPLE

Name	Type	Kind	Pow.	Acc.	PP	Range

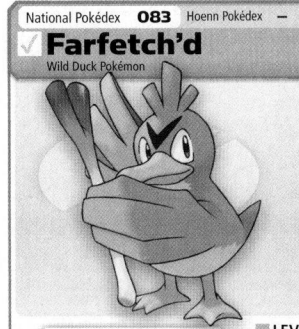

National Pokédex **083** Hoenn Pokédex **—**

Farfetch'd

Wild Duck Pokémon

Normal Flying

HEIGHT: 2'07" WEIGHT: 33.1 lbs.

Same form for ♂ / ♀

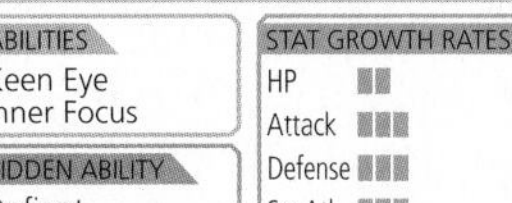

Ω Farfetch'd is alway seen with a stalk from a plant of some sort. Apparently, there are good stalks and bad stalks. This Pokémon has been known to fight with others over stalks.

α Farfetch'd is alway seen with a stalk from a plant of some sort. Apparently, there are good stalks and bad stalks. This Pokémon has been known to fight with others over stalks.

ABILITIES
Keen Eye
Inner Focus

HIDDEN ABILITY
Defiant

EGG GROUPS
Flying Field

STAT GROWTH RATES
HP ■■
Attack ■■■
Defense ■■■
Sp. Atk ■■■
Sp. Def ■■■
Speed ■■■

ITEMS SOMETIMES HELD BY WILD POKÉMON
—

EVOLUTION

Does not evolve

MAIN WAY TO REGISTER IN THE NATIONAL POKÉDEX

Appears in *Pokémon X* and *Pokémon Y*. Bring it to your game using Link Trade or the GTS.

Damage taken in normal battles

Type		Type	
Normal	×1	Flying	×1
Fire	×1	Psychic	×1
Water	×1	Bug	×0.5
Grass	×0.5	Rock	×2
Electric	×2	Ghost	×0
Ice	×2	Dragon	×1
Fighting	×1	Dark	×1
Poison	×1	Steel	×1
Ground	×0	Fairy	×1

Damage taken in Inverse battles

Type		Type	
Normal	×1	Flying	×1
Fire	×1	Psychic	×1
Water	×1	Bug	×2
Grass	×2	Rock	×0.5
Electric	×0.5	Ghost	×2
Ice	×0.5	Dragon	×1
Fighting	×1	Dark	×1
Poison	×1	Steel	×1
Ground	×2	Fairy	×1

Can be used in
Inverse Battle
Battle Institute
Battle Maison
Random Matchup (Free Battle)
Random Matchup (Others)

LEVEL-UP MOVES

Lv.	Name	Type	Kind	Pow.	Acc.	PP	Range
1	Brave Bird	Flying	Physical	120	100	15	Normal
1	Poison Jab	Poison	Physical	80	100	20	Normal
1	Peck	Flying	Physical	35	100	35	Normal
1	Sand Attack	Ground	Status	—	100	15	Normal
1	Leer	Normal	Status	—	100	30	Many Others
1	Fury Cutter	Bug	Physical	40	95	20	Normal
7	Fury Attack	Normal	Physical	15	85	20	Normal
9	Aerial Ace	Flying	Physical	60	—	20	Normal
13	Knock Off	Dark	Physical	65	100	20	Normal
19	Slash	Normal	Physical	70	100	20	Normal
21	Air Cutter	Flying	Special	60	95	25	Many Others
25	Swords Dance	Normal	Status	—	—	20	Self
31	Agility	Psychic	Status	—	—	30	Self
33	Night Slash	Dark	Physical	70	100	15	Normal
37	Acrobatics	Flying	Physical	55	100	15	Normal
43	Feint	Normal	Physical	30	100	10	Normal
45	False Swipe	Normal	Physical	40	100	40	Normal
49	Air Slash	Flying	Special	75	95	15	Normal
55	Brave Bird	Flying	Physical	120	100	15	Normal

TM & HM MOVES

No.	Name	Type	Kind	Pow.	Acc.	PP	Range
TM06	Toxic	Poison	Status	—	90	10	Normal
TM10	Hidden Power	Normal	Special	60	100	15	Normal
TM11	Sunny Day	Fire	Status	—	—	5	Both Sides
TM17	Protect	Normal	Status	—	—	10	Self
TM19	Roost	Flying	Status	—	—	10	Self
TM21	Frustration	Normal	Physical	—	100	20	Normal
TM27	Return	Normal	Physical	—	100	20	Normal
TM32	Double Team	Normal	Status	—	—	15	Self
TM40	Aerial Ace	Flying	Physical	60	—	20	Normal
TM42	Facade	Normal	Physical	70	100	20	Normal
TM44	Rest	Psychic	Status	—	—	10	Self
TM45	Attract	Normal	Status	—	100	15	Normal
TM46	Thief	Dark	Physical	60	100	25	Normal
TM48	Round	Normal	Special	60	100	15	Normal
TM51	Steel Wing	Steel	Physical	70	90	25	Normal
TM54	False Swipe	Normal	Physical	40	100	40	Normal
TM62	Acrobatics	Flying	Physical	55	100	15	Normal
TM67	Retaliate	Normal	Physical	70	100	5	Normal
TM75	Swords Dance	Normal	Status	—	—	20	Self
TM77	Psych Up	Normal	Status	—	—	10	Normal
TM84	Poison Jab	Poison	Physical	80	100	20	Normal
TM87	Swagger	Normal	Status	—	90	15	Normal
TM88	Sleep Talk	Normal	Status	—	—	10	Self
TM89	U-turn	Bug	Physical	70	100	20	Normal
TM90	Substitute	Normal	Status	—	—	10	Self
TM94	Secret Power	Normal	Physical	70	100	20	Normal
TM100	Confide	Normal	Status	—	—	20	Normal
HM01	Cut	Normal	Physical	50	95	30	Normal
HM02	Fly	Flying	Physical	90	95	15	Normal

MOVES LEARNED IN EXCHANGE FOR BP

Name	Type	Kind	Pow.	Acc.	PP	Range
Covet	Normal	Physical	60	100	25	Normal
Uproar	Normal	Special	90	100	10	1 Random
Last Resort	Normal	Physical	140	100	5	Normal
Iron Tail	Steel	Physical	100	75	15	Normal
Snore	Normal	Special	50	100	15	Normal
Knock Off	Dark	Physical	65	100	20	Normal
Heat Wave	Fire	Special	95	90	10	Many Others
Tailwind	Flying	Status	—	—	15	Your Side
Sky Attack	Flying	Physical	140	90	5	Normal
Helping Hand	Normal	Status	—	—	20	1 Ally

MOVES TAUGHT BY PEOPLE

Name	Type	Kind	Pow.	Acc.	PP	Range

EGG MOVES

Name	Type	Kind	Pow.	Acc.	PP	Range
Steel Wing	Steel	Physical	70	90	25	Normal
Foresight	Normal	Status	—	—	40	Normal
Mirror Move	Flying	Status	—	—	20	Normal
Gust	Flying	Special	40	100	35	Normal
Quick Attack	Normal	Physical	40	100	30	Normal
Flail	Normal	Physical	—	100	15	Normal
Feather Dance	Flying	Status	—	100	15	Normal
Curse	Ghost	Status	—	—	10	Varies
Covet	Normal	Physical	60	100	25	Normal
Mud-Slap	Ground	Special	20	100	10	Normal
Night Slash	Dark	Physical	70	100	15	Normal
Leaf Blade	Grass	Physical	90	100	15	Normal
Revenge	Fighting	Physical	60	100	10	Normal
Roost	Flying	Status	—	—	10	Self
Trump Card	Normal	Special	—	—	5	Normal
Simple Beam	Normal	Status	—	100	15	Normal

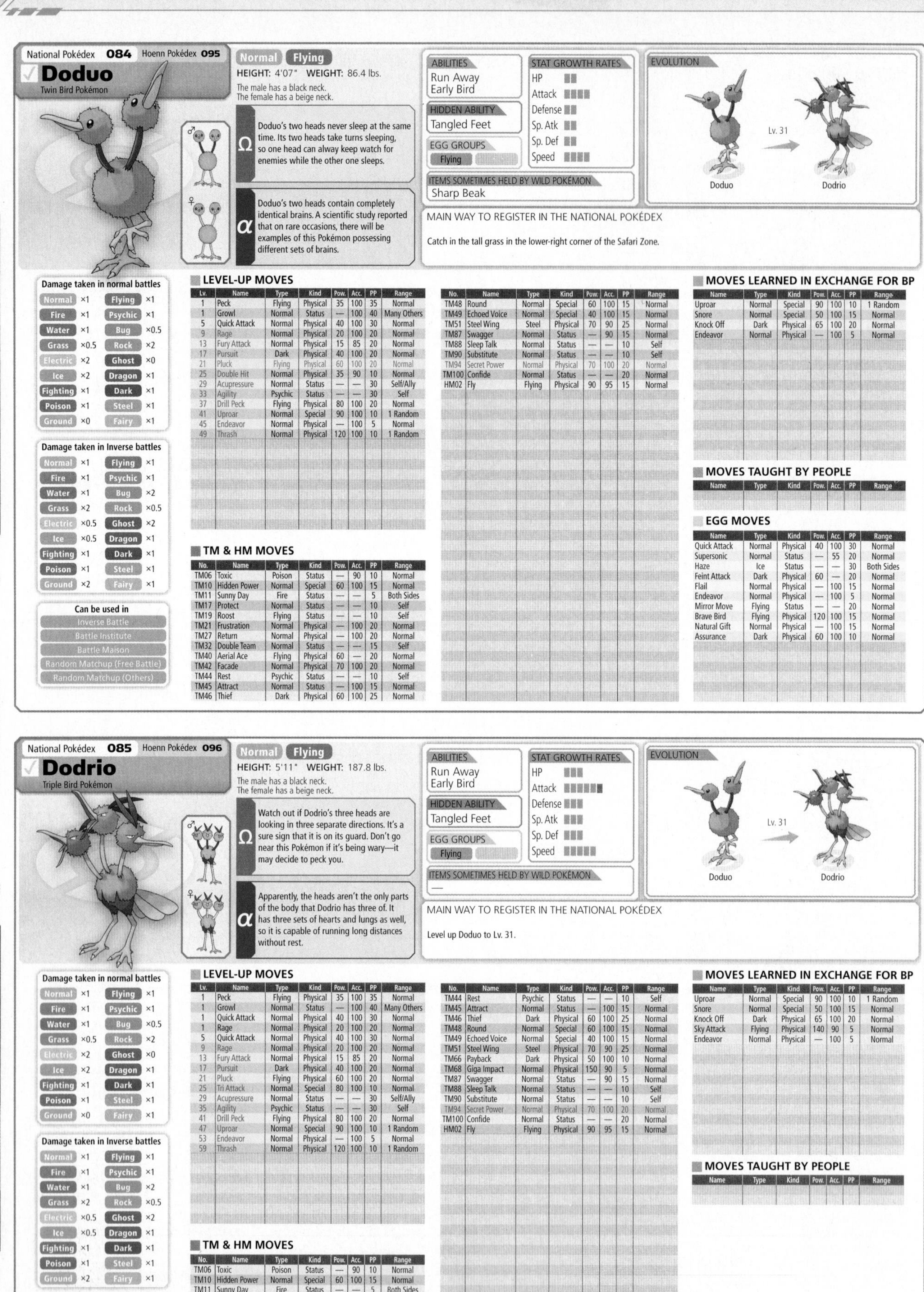

National Pokédex **084** Hoenn Pokédex **095**

Doduo

Twin Bird Pokémon

Normal Flying

HEIGHT: 4'07" WEIGHT: 86.4 lbs.

The male has a black neck.
The female has a beige neck.

Ω Doduo's two heads never sleep at the same time. Its two heads take turns sleeping, so one head can alway keep watch for enemies while the other one sleeps.

α Doduo's two heads contain completely identical brains. A scientific study reported that on rare occasions, there will be examples of this Pokémon possessing different sets of brains.

ABILITIES
Run Away
Early Bird

HIDDEN ABILITY
Tangled Feet

EGG GROUPS
Flying

STAT GROWTH RATES
HP
Attack
Defense
Sp. Atk
Sp. Def
Speed

ITEMS SOMETIMES HELD BY WILD POKÉMON
Sharp Beak

EVOLUTION
Doduo → Lv. 31 → Dodrio

MAIN WAY TO REGISTER IN THE NATIONAL POKÉDEX

Catch in the tall grass in the lower-right corner of the Safari Zone.

Damage taken in normal battles

Type		Type	
Normal	×1	Flying	×1
Fire	×1	Psychic	×1
Water	×1	Bug	×0.5
Grass	×0.5	Rock	×2
Electric	×2	Ghost	×0
Ice	×2	Dragon	×1
Fighting	×1	Dark	×1
Poison	×1	Steel	×1
Ground	×0	Fairy	×1

Damage taken in Inverse battles

Type		Type	
Normal	×1	Flying	×1
Fire	×1	Psychic	×1
Water	×1	Bug	×2
Grass	×2	Rock	×0.5
Electric	×0.5	Ghost	×2
Ice	×0.5	Dragon	×1
Fighting	×1	Dark	×1
Poison	×1	Steel	×1
Ground	×2	Fairy	×1

Can be used in
Inverse Battle
Battle Institute
Battle Maison
Random Matchup (Free Battle)
Random Matchup (Others)

LEVEL-UP MOVES

Lv.	Name	Type	Kind	Pow.	Acc.	PP	Range
1	Peck	Flying	Physical	35	100	35	Normal
1	Growl	Normal	Status	—	100	40	Many Others
5	Quick Attack	Normal	Physical	40	100	30	Normal
9	Rage	Normal	Physical	20	100	20	Normal
13	Fury Attack	Normal	Physical	15	85	20	Normal
17	Pursuit	Dark	Physical	40	100	20	Normal
21	Pluck	Flying	Physical	60	100	20	Normal
25	Double Hit	Normal	Physical	35	90	10	Normal
29	Acupressure	Normal	Status	—	—	30	Self/Ally
33	Agility	Psychic	Status	—	—	30	Self
37	Drill Peck	Flying	Physical	80	100	20	Normal
41	Uproar	Normal	Special	90	100	10	1 Random
45	Endeavor	Normal	Physical	—	100	5	Normal
49	Thrash	Normal	Physical	120	100	10	1 Random

TM & HM MOVES

No.	Name	Type	Kind	Pow.	Acc.	PP	Range
TM06	Toxic	Poison	Status	—	90	10	Normal
TM10	Hidden Power	Normal	Special	60	100	15	Normal
TM11	Sunny Day	Fire	Status	—	—	5	Both Sides
TM17	Protect	Normal	Status	—	—	10	Self
TM19	Roost	Flying	Status	—	—	10	Self
TM21	Frustration	Normal	Physical	—	100	20	Normal
TM27	Return	Normal	Physical	—	100	20	Normal
TM32	Double Team	Normal	Status	—	—	15	Self
TM40	Aerial Ace	Flying	Physical	60	—	20	Normal
TM42	Facade	Normal	Physical	70	100	20	Normal
TM44	Rest	Psychic	Status	—	—	10	Self
TM45	Attract	Normal	Status	—	100	15	Normal
TM46	Thief	Dark	Physical	60	100	25	Normal
TM48	Round	Normal	Special	60	100	15	Normal
TM49	Echoed Voice	Normal	Special	40	100	15	Normal
TM51	Steel Wing	Steel	Physical	70	90	25	Normal
TM87	Swagger	Normal	Status	—	90	15	Normal
TM88	Sleep Talk	Normal	Status	—	—	10	Self
TM90	Substitute	Normal	Status	—	—	10	Self
TM94	Secret Power	Normal	Physical	70	100	20	Normal
TM100	Confide	Normal	Status	—	—	20	Normal
HM02	Fly	Flying	Physical	90	95	15	Normal

MOVES LEARNED IN EXCHANGE FOR BP

Name	Type	Kind	Pow.	Acc.	PP	Range
Uproar	Normal	Special	90	100	10	1 Random
Snore	Normal	Special	50	100	15	Normal
Knock Off	Dark	Physical	65	100	20	Normal
Endeavor	Normal	Physical	—	100	5	Normal

MOVES TAUGHT BY PEOPLE

Name	Type	Kind	Pow.	Acc.	PP	Range

EGG MOVES

Name	Type	Kind	Pow.	Acc.	PP	Range
Quick Attack	Normal	Physical	40	100	30	Normal
Supersonic	Normal	Status	—	55	20	Normal
Haze	Ice	Status	—	—	30	Both Sides
Feint Attack	Dark	Physical	60	—	20	Normal
Flail	Normal	Physical	—	100	15	Normal
Endeavor	Normal	Physical	—	100	5	Normal
Mirror Move	Flying	Status	—	—	20	Normal
Brave Bird	Flying	Physical	120	100	15	Normal
Natural Gift	Normal	Physical	—	100	15	Normal
Assurance	Dark	Physical	60	100	10	Normal

National Pokédex **085** Hoenn Pokédex **096**

Dodrio

Triple Bird Pokémon

Normal Flying

HEIGHT: 5'11" WEIGHT: 187.8 lbs.

The male has a black neck.
The female has a beige neck.

Ω Watch out if Dodrio's three heads are looking in three separate directions. It's a sure sign that it is on its guard. Don't go near this Pokémon if it's being wary—it may decide to peck you.

α Apparently, the heads aren't the only parts of the body that Dodrio has three of. It has three sets of hearts and lungs as well, so it is capable of running long distances without rest.

ABILITIES
Run Away
Early Bird

HIDDEN ABILITY
Tangled Feet

EGG GROUPS
Flying

STAT GROWTH RATES
HP
Attack
Defense
Sp. Atk
Sp. Def
Speed

ITEMS SOMETIMES HELD BY WILD POKÉMON
—

EVOLUTION
Doduo → Lv. 31 → Dodrio

MAIN WAY TO REGISTER IN THE NATIONAL POKÉDEX

Level up Doduo to Lv. 31.

Damage taken in normal battles

Type		Type	
Normal	×1	Flying	×1
Fire	×1	Psychic	×1
Water	×1	Bug	×0.5
Grass	×0.5	Rock	×2
Electric	×2	Ghost	×0
Ice	×2	Dragon	×1
Fighting	×1	Dark	×1
Poison	×1	Steel	×1
Ground	×0	Fairy	×1

Damage taken in Inverse battles

Type		Type	
Normal	×1	Flying	×1
Fire	×1	Psychic	×1
Water	×1	Bug	×2
Grass	×2	Rock	×0.5
Electric	×0.5	Ghost	×2
Ice	×0.5	Dragon	×1
Fighting	×1	Dark	×1
Poison	×1	Steel	×1
Ground	×2	Fairy	×1

Can be used in
Inverse Battle
Battle Institute
Battle Maison
Random Matchup (Free Battle)
Random Matchup (Others)

LEVEL-UP MOVES

Lv.	Name	Type	Kind	Pow.	Acc.	PP	Range
1	Peck	Flying	Physical	35	100	35	Normal
1	Growl	Normal	Status	—	100	40	Many Others
1	Quick Attack	Normal	Physical	40	100	30	Normal
1	Rage	Normal	Physical	20	100	20	Normal
5	Quick Attack	Normal	Physical	40	100	30	Normal
9	Rage	Normal	Physical	20	100	20	Normal
13	Fury Attack	Normal	Physical	15	85	20	Normal
17	Pursuit	Dark	Physical	40	100	20	Normal
21	Pluck	Flying	Physical	60	100	20	Normal
25	Tri Attack	Normal	Special	80	100	10	Normal
29	Acupressure	Normal	Status	—	—	30	Self/Ally
35	Agility	Psychic	Status	—	—	30	Self
41	Drill Peck	Flying	Physical	80	100	20	Normal
47	Uproar	Normal	Special	90	100	10	1 Random
53	Endeavor	Normal	Physical	—	100	5	Normal
59	Thrash	Normal	Physical	120	100	10	1 Random

TM & HM MOVES

No.	Name	Type	Kind	Pow.	Acc.	PP	Range
TM06	Toxic	Poison	Status	—	90	10	Normal
TM10	Hidden Power	Normal	Special	60	100	15	Normal
TM11	Sunny Day	Fire	Status	—	—	5	Both Sides
TM12	Taunt	Dark	Status	—	100	20	Normal
TM15	Hyper Beam	Normal	Special	150	90	5	Normal
TM17	Protect	Normal	Status	—	—	10	Self
TM19	Roost	Flying	Status	—	—	10	Self
TM21	Frustration	Normal	Physical	—	100	20	Normal
TM27	Return	Normal	Physical	—	100	20	Normal
TM32	Double Team	Normal	Status	—	—	15	Self
TM40	Aerial Ace	Flying	Physical	60	—	20	Normal
TM41	Torment	Dark	Status	—	100	15	Normal
TM42	Facade	Normal	Physical	70	100	20	Normal
TM44	Rest	Psychic	Status	—	—	10	Self
TM45	Attract	Normal	Status	—	100	15	Normal
TM46	Thief	Dark	Physical	60	100	25	Normal
TM48	Round	Normal	Special	60	100	15	Normal
TM49	Echoed Voice	Normal	Special	40	100	15	Normal
TM51	Steel Wing	Steel	Physical	70	90	25	Normal
TM66	Payback	Dark	Physical	50	100	10	Normal
TM68	Giga Impact	Normal	Physical	150	90	5	Normal
TM87	Swagger	Normal	Status	—	90	15	Normal
TM88	Sleep Talk	Normal	Status	—	—	10	Self
TM90	Substitute	Normal	Status	—	—	10	Self
TM94	Secret Power	Normal	Physical	70	100	20	Normal
TM100	Confide	Normal	Status	—	—	20	Normal
HM02	Fly	Flying	Physical	90	95	15	Normal

MOVES LEARNED IN EXCHANGE FOR BP

Name	Type	Kind	Pow.	Acc.	PP	Range
Uproar	Normal	Special	90	100	10	1 Random
Snore	Normal	Special	50	100	15	Normal
Knock Off	Dark	Physical	65	100	20	Normal
Sky Attack	Flying	Physical	140	90	5	Normal
Endeavor	Normal	Physical	—	100	5	Normal

MOVES TAUGHT BY PEOPLE

Name	Type	Kind	Pow.	Acc.	PP	Range

National Pokédex **086** Hoenn Pokédex —

Seel

Sea Lion Pokémon

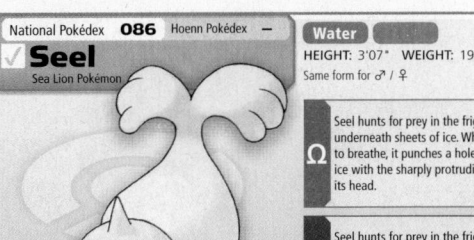

Water

HEIGHT: 3'07" WEIGHT: 198.4 lbs.

Same form for ♂ / ♀

Ω Seel hunts for prey in the frigid sea underneath sheets of ice. When it needs to breathe, it punches a hole through the ice with the sharply protruding section of its head.

α Seel hunts for prey in the frigid sea underneath sheets of ice. When it needs to breathe, it punches a hole through the ice with the sharply protruding section of its head.

ABILITIES
Thick Fat
Hydration

HIDDEN ABILITY
Ice Body

EGG GROUPS
Water 1 | Field

STAT GROWTH RATES
HP
Attack
Defense
Sp. Atk
Sp. Def
Speed

ITEMS SOMETIMES HELD BY WILD POKÉMON
—

EVOLUTION
Seel → Lv. 34 → Dewgong

MAIN WAY TO REGISTER IN THE NATIONAL POKÉDEX

Catch on the water surface on Route 125. Appears as a hidden Pokémon after you battle Groudon or Kyogre.

Damage taken in normal battles

Type		Type	
Normal	×1	Flying	×1
Fire	×0.5	Psychic	×1
Water	×0.5	Bug	×1
Grass	×2	Rock	×1
Electric	×2	Ghost	×1
Ice	×0.5	Dragon	×1
Fighting	×1	Dark	×1
Poison	×1	Steel	×0.5
Ground	×1	Fairy	×1

Damage taken in Inverse battles

Type		Type	
Normal	×1	Flying	×1
Fire	×2	Psychic	×1
Water	×2	Bug	×1
Grass	×0.5	Rock	×1
Electric	×0.5	Ghost	×1
Ice	×2	Dragon	×1
Fighting	×1	Dark	×1
Poison	×1	Steel	×2
Ground	×1	Fairy	×1

Can be used in
Inverse Battle
Battle Institute
Battle Maison
Random Matchup (Free Battle)
Random Matchup (Others)

LEVEL-UP MOVES

Lv.	Name	Type	Kind	Pow.	Acc.	PP	Range
1	Headbutt	Normal	Physical	70	100	15	Normal
3	Growl	Normal	Status	—	100	40	Many Others
7	Water Sport	Water	Status	—	—	15	Both Sides
11	Icy Wind	Ice	Special	55	95	15	Many Others
13	Encore	Normal	Status	—	100	5	Normal
17	Ice Shard	Ice	Physical	40	100	30	Normal
21	Rest	Psychic	Status	—	—	10	Self
23	Aqua Ring	Water	Status	—	—	20	Self
27	Aurora Beam	Ice	Special	65	100	20	Normal
31	Aqua Jet	Water	Physical	40	100	20	Normal
33	Brine	Water	Special	65	100	10	Normal
37	Take Down	Normal	Physical	90	85	20	Normal
41	Dive	Water	Physical	80	100	10	Normal
43	Aqua Tail	Water	Physical	90	90	10	Normal
47	Ice Beam	Ice	Special	90	100	10	Normal
51	Safeguard	Normal	Status	—	—	25	Your Side
53	Hail	Ice	Status	—	—	10	Both Sides

TM & HM MOVES

No.	Name	Type	Kind	Pow.	Acc.	PP	Range
TM06	Toxic	Poison	Status	—	90	10	Normal
TM07	Hail	Ice	Status	—	—	10	Both Sides
TM10	Hidden Power	Normal	Special	60	100	15	Normal
TM13	Ice Beam	Ice	Special	90	100	10	Normal
TM14	Blizzard	Ice	Special	110	70	5	Many Others
TM17	Protect	Normal	Status	—	—	10	Self
TM18	Rain Dance	Water	Status	—	—	5	Both Sides
TM20	Safeguard	Normal	Status	—	—	25	Your Side
TM21	Frustration	Normal	Physical	—	100	20	Normal
TM27	Return	Normal	Physical	—	100	20	Normal
TM32	Double Team	Normal	Status	—	—	15	Self
TM42	Facade	Normal	Physical	70	100	20	Normal
TM44	Rest	Psychic	Status	—	—	10	Self
TM45	Attract	Normal	Status	—	100	15	Normal
TM46	Thief	Dark	Physical	60	100	25	Normal
TM48	Round	Normal	Special	60	100	15	Normal
TM49	Echoed Voice	Normal	Special	40	100	15	Normal
TM56	Fling	Dark	Physical	—	100	10	Normal
TM87	Swagger	Normal	Status	—	90	15	Normal
TM88	Sleep Talk	Normal	Status	—	—	10	Self
TM90	Substitute	Normal	Status	—	—	10	Self
TM94	Secret Power	Normal	Physical	70	100	20	Normal
TM100	Confide	Normal	Status	—	—	20	Normal
HM03	Surf	Water	Special	90	100	15	Adjacent
HM05	Waterfall	Water	Physical	80	100	15	Normal
HM07	Dive	Water	Physical	80	100	10	Normal

MOVES LEARNED IN EXCHANGE FOR BP

Name	Type	Kind	Pow.	Acc.	PP	Range
Signal Beam	Bug	Special	75	100	15	Normal
Drill Run	Ground	Physical	80	95	10	Normal
Icy Wind	Ice	Special	55	95	15	Many Others
Aqua Tail	Water	Physical	90	90	10	Normal
Iron Tail	Steel	Physical	100	75	15	Normal
Snore	Normal	Special	50	100	15	Normal
Water Pulse	Water	Special	60	100	20	Normal

MOVES TAUGHT BY PEOPLE

Name	Type	Kind	Pow.	Acc.	PP	Range

EGG MOVES

Name	Type	Kind	Pow.	Acc.	PP	Range
Lick	Ghost	Physical	30	100	30	Normal
Perish Song	Normal	Status	—	—	5	Adjacent
Disable	Normal	Status	—	100	20	Normal
Horn Drill	Normal	Physical	—	30	5	Normal
Slam	Normal	Physical	80	75	20	Normal
Encore	Normal	Status	—	100	5	Normal
Fake Out	Normal	Physical	40	100	10	Normal
Icicle Spear	Ice	Physical	25	100	30	Normal
Signal Beam	Bug	Special	75	100	15	Normal
Stockpile	Normal	Status	—	—	20	Self
Swallow	Normal	Status	—	—	10	Self
Spit Up	Normal	Special	—	100	10	Normal
Water Pulse	Water	Special	60	100	20	Normal
Iron Tail	Steel	Physical	100	75	15	Normal
Sleep Talk	Normal	Status	—	—	10	Self
Belch	Poison	Special	120	90	10	Normal
Entrainment	Normal	Status	—	100	15	Normal

National Pokédex **087** Hoenn Pokédex —

Dewgong

Sea Lion Pokémon

Water | Ice

HEIGHT: 5'07" WEIGHT: 264.6 lbs.

Same form for ♂ / ♀

Ω Dewgong loves to snooze on bitterly cold ice. The sight of this Pokémon sleeping on a glacier was mistakenly thought to be a mermaid by a mariner long ago.

α Dewgong loves to snooze on bitterly cold ice. The sight of this Pokémon sleeping on a glacier was mistakenly thought to be a mermaid by a mariner long ago.

ABILITIES
Thick Fat
Hydration

HIDDEN ABILITY
Ice Body

EGG GROUPS
Water 1 | Field

STAT GROWTH RATES
HP
Attack
Defense
Sp. Atk
Sp. Def
Speed

ITEMS SOMETIMES HELD BY WILD POKÉMON
—

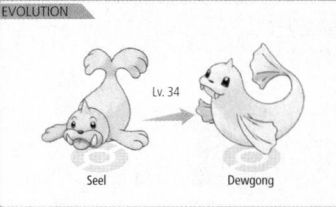

EVOLUTION
Seel → Lv. 34 → Dewgong

MAIN WAY TO REGISTER IN THE NATIONAL POKÉDEX

Catch in Shoal Cave. Appears as a hidden Pokémon after you battle Groudon or Kyogre.

Damage taken in normal battles

Type		Type	
Normal	×1	Flying	×1
Fire	×1	Psychic	×1
Water	×0.5	Bug	×1
Grass	×2	Rock	×2
Electric	×2	Ghost	×1
Ice	×0.25	Dragon	×1
Fighting	×2	Dark	×1
Poison	×1	Steel	×1
Ground	×1	Fairy	×1

Damage taken in Inverse battles

Type		Type	
Normal	×1	Flying	×1
Fire	×1	Psychic	×1
Water	×2	Bug	×1
Grass	×0.5	Rock	×0.5
Electric	×0.5	Ghost	×1
Ice	×4	Dragon	×1
Fighting	×0.5	Dark	×1
Poison	×1	Steel	×1
Ground	×1	Fairy	×1

Can be used in
Inverse Battle
Battle Institute
Battle Maison
Random Matchup (Free Battle)
Random Matchup (Others)

LEVEL-UP MOVES

Lv.	Name	Type	Kind	Pow.	Acc.	PP	Range
1	Headbutt	Normal	Physical	70	100	15	Normal
1	Growl	Normal	Status	—	100	40	Many Others
1	Signal Beam	Bug	Special	75	100	15	Normal
1	Icy Wind	Ice	Special	55	95	15	Many Others
3	Growl	Normal	Status	—	100	40	Many Others
7	Signal Beam	Bug	Special	75	100	15	Normal
11	Icy Wind	Ice	Special	55	95	15	Many Others
13	Encore	Normal	Status	—	100	5	Normal
17	Ice Shard	Ice	Physical	40	100	30	Normal
21	Rest	Psychic	Status	—	—	10	Self
23	Aqua Ring	Water	Status	—	—	20	Self
27	Aurora Beam	Ice	Special	65	100	20	Normal
31	Aqua Jet	Water	Physical	40	100	20	Normal
33	Brine	Water	Special	65	100	10	Normal
34	Sheer Cold	Ice	Special	—	30	5	Normal
39	Take Down	Normal	Physical	90	85	20	Normal
45	Dive	Water	Physical	80	100	10	Normal
49	Aqua Tail	Water	Physical	90	90	10	Normal
55	Ice Beam	Ice	Special	90	100	10	Normal
61	Safeguard	Normal	Status	—	—	25	Your Side
65	Hail	Ice	Status	—	—	10	Both Sides

TM & HM MOVES

No.	Name	Type	Kind	Pow.	Acc.	PP	Range
TM06	Toxic	Poison	Status	—	90	10	Normal
TM07	Hail	Ice	Status	—	—	10	Both Sides
TM10	Hidden Power	Normal	Special	60	100	15	Normal
TM13	Ice Beam	Ice	Special	90	100	10	Normal
TM14	Blizzard	Ice	Special	110	70	5	Many Others
TM15	Hyper Beam	Normal	Special	150	90	5	Normal
TM17	Protect	Normal	Status	—	—	10	Self
TM18	Rain Dance	Water	Status	—	—	5	Both Sides
TM20	Safeguard	Normal	Status	—	—	25	Your Side
TM21	Frustration	Normal	Physical	—	100	20	Normal
TM27	Return	Normal	Physical	—	100	20	Normal
TM32	Double Team	Normal	Status	—	—	15	Self
TM42	Facade	Normal	Physical	70	100	20	Normal
TM44	Rest	Psychic	Status	—	—	10	Self
TM45	Attract	Normal	Status	—	100	15	Normal
TM46	Thief	Dark	Physical	60	100	25	Normal
TM48	Round	Normal	Special	60	100	15	Normal
TM49	Echoed Voice	Normal	Special	40	100	15	Normal
TM56	Fling	Dark	Physical	—	100	10	Normal
TM68	Giga Impact	Normal	Physical	150	90	5	Normal
TM79	Frost Breath	Ice	Special	60	90	10	Normal
TM87	Swagger	Normal	Status	—	90	15	Normal
TM88	Sleep Talk	Normal	Status	—	—	10	Self
TM90	Substitute	Normal	Status	—	—	10	Self
TM94	Secret Power	Normal	Physical	70	100	20	Normal
TM100	Confide	Normal	Status	—	—	20	Normal
HM03	Surf	Water	Special	90	100	15	Adjacent
HM05	Waterfall	Water	Physical	80	100	15	Normal
HM07	Dive	Water	Physical	80	100	10	Normal

MOVES LEARNED IN EXCHANGE FOR BP

Name	Type	Kind	Pow.	Acc.	PP	Range
Signal Beam	Bug	Special	75	100	15	Normal
Drill Run	Ground	Physical	80	95	10	Normal
Icy Wind	Ice	Special	55	95	15	Many Others
Aqua Tail	Water	Physical	90	90	10	Normal
Iron Tail	Steel	Physical	100	75	15	Normal
Snore	Normal	Special	50	100	15	Normal
Water Pulse	Water	Special	60	100	20	Normal

MOVES TAUGHT BY PEOPLE

Name	Type	Kind	Pow.	Acc.	PP	Range

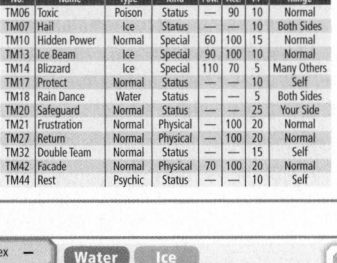

National Pokédex **088** Hoenn Pokédex **111**

Grimer

Sludge Pokémon

Poison

HEIGHT: 2'11" WEIGHT: 66.1 lbs.

Same form for ♂ / ♀

Ω Grimer's sludgy and rubbery body can be forced through any opening, however small it may be. This Pokémon enters sewer pipes to drink filthy wastewater.

α Grimer emerged from the sludge that settled on a polluted seabed. This Pokémon loves anything filthy. It constantly leaks a horribly germ-infested fluid from all over its body.

ABILITIES
Stench
Sticky Hold

HIDDEN ABILITY
Poison Touch

EGG GROUPS
Amorphous

STAT GROWTH RATES

HP	■■■
Attack	■■■■
Defense	■■
Sp. Atk	■■
Sp. Def	■■
Speed	■■

ITEMS SOMETIMES HELD BY WILD POKÉMON
Black Sludge

EVOLUTION

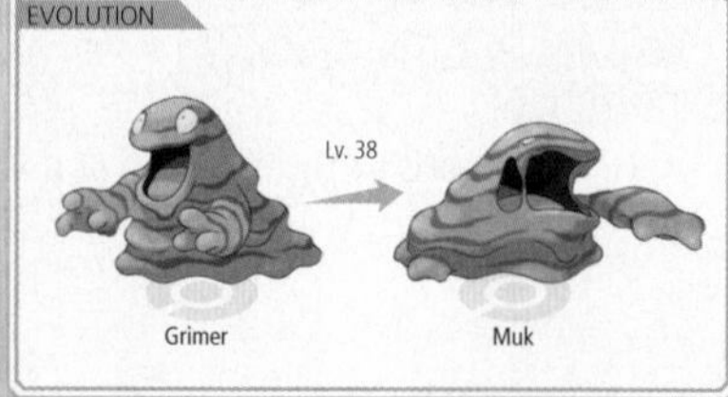

MAIN WAY TO REGISTER IN THE NATIONAL POKÉDEX

Catch on the Fiery Path.

Damage taken in normal battles

Type		Type	
Normal	×1	Flying	×1
Fire	×1	Psychic	×2
Water	×1	Bug	×0.5
Grass	×0.5	Rock	×1
Electric	×1	Ghost	×1
Ice	×1	Dragon	×1
Fighting	×0.5	Dark	×1
Poison	×0.5	Steel	×1
Ground	×2	Fairy	×0.5

Damage taken in Inverse battles

Type		Type	
Normal	×1	Flying	×1
Fire	×1	Psychic	×0.5
Water	×1	Bug	×2
Grass	×2	Rock	×1
Electric	×1	Ghost	×1
Ice	×1	Dragon	×1
Fighting	×2	Dark	×1
Poison	×2	Steel	×1
Ground	×0.5	Fairy	×2

Can be used in
Inverse Battle
Battle Institute
Random Matchup (Free Battle)
Random Matchup (Others)
Random Matchup (Others)

LEVEL-UP MOVES

Lv.	Name	Type	Kind	Pow.	Acc.	PP	Range
1	Pound	Normal	Physical	40	100	35	Normal
1	Poison Gas	Poison	Status	—	90	40	Many Others
4	Harden	Normal	Status	—	—	30	Self
7	Mud-Slap	Ground	Special	20	100	10	Normal
12	Disable	Normal	Status	—	100	20	Normal
15	Sludge	Poison	Special	65	100	20	Normal
18	Mud Bomb	Ground	Special	65	85	10	Normal
21	Minimize	Normal	Status	—	—	10	Self
26	Fling	Dark	Physical	—	100	10	Normal
29	Sludge Bomb	Poison	Special	90	100	10	Normal
32	Sludge Wave	Poison	Special	95	100	10	Adjacent
37	Screech	Normal	Status	—	85	40	Normal
40	Gunk Shot	Poison	Physical	120	80	5	Normal
43	Acid Armor	Poison	Status	—	—	20	Self
46	Belch	Poison	Special	120	90	10	Normal
48	Memento	Dark	Status	—	100	10	Normal

TM & HM MOVES

No.	Name	Type	Kind	Pow.	Acc.	PP	Range
TM06	Toxic	Poison	Status	—	90	10	Normal
TM09	Venoshock	Poison	Special	65	100	10	Normal
TM10	Hidden Power	Normal	Special	60	100	15	Normal
TM11	Sunny Day	Fire	Status	—	—	5	Both Sides
TM12	Taunt	Dark	Status	—	100	20	Normal
TM17	Protect	Normal	Status	—	—	10	Self
TM18	Rain Dance	Water	Status	—	—	5	Both Sides
TM21	Frustration	Normal	Physical	—	100	20	Normal
TM24	Thunderbolt	Electric	Special	90	100	15	Normal
TM25	Thunder	Electric	Special	110	70	10	Normal
TM27	Return	Normal	Physical	—	100	20	Normal
TM28	Dig	Ground	Physical	80	100	10	Normal
TM30	Shadow Ball	Ghost	Special	80	100	15	Normal
TM32	Double Team	Normal	Status	—	—	15	Self
TM34	Sludge Wave	Poison	Special	95	100	10	Adjacent
TM35	Flamethrower	Fire	Special	90	100	15	Normal
TM36	Sludge Bomb	Poison	Special	90	100	10	Normal
TM38	Fire Blast	Fire	Special	110	85	5	Normal
TM39	Rock Tomb	Rock	Physical	60	95	15	Normal
TM41	Torment	Dark	Status	—	100	15	Normal
TM42	Facade	Normal	Physical	70	100	20	Normal
TM44	Rest	Psychic	Status	—	—	10	Self
TM45	Attract	Normal	Status	—	100	15	Normal
TM46	Thief	Dark	Physical	60	100	25	Normal
TM48	Round	Normal	Special	60	100	15	Normal
TM56	Fling	Dark	Physical	—	100	10	Normal
TM59	Incinerate	Fire	Special	60	100	15	Many Others
TM64	Explosion	Normal	Physical	250	100	5	Adjacent
TM66	Payback	Dark	Physical	50	100	10	Normal
TM80	Rock Slide	Rock	Physical	75	90	10	Many Others
TM83	Infestation	Bug	Special	20	100	20	Normal
TM84	Poison Jab	Poison	Physical	80	100	20	Normal
TM87	Swagger	Normal	Status	—	90	15	Normal
TM88	Sleep Talk	Normal	Status	—	—	10	Self
TM90	Substitute	Normal	Status	—	—	10	Self
TM94	Secret Power	Normal	Physical	70	100	20	Normal
TM98	Power-Up Punch	Fighting	Physical	40	100	20	Normal
TM100	Confide	Normal	Status	—	—	20	Normal
HM04	Strength	Normal	Physical	80	100	15	Normal

MOVES LEARNED IN EXCHANGE FOR BP

Name	Type	Kind	Pow.	Acc.	PP	Range
Gunk Shot	Poison	Physical	120	80	5	Normal
Thunder Punch	Electric	Physical	75	100	15	Normal
Fire Punch	Fire	Physical	75	100	15	Normal
Ice Punch	Ice	Physical	75	100	15	Normal
Snore	Normal	Special	50	100	15	Normal
Pain Split	Normal	Status	—	—	20	Normal
Giga Drain	Grass	Special	75	100	10	Normal
Shock Wave	Electric	Special	60	—	20	Normal

MOVES TAUGHT BY PEOPLE

Name	Type	Kind	Pow.	Acc.	PP	Range

EGG MOVES

Name	Type	Kind	Pow.	Acc.	PP	Range
Haze	Ice	Status	—	—	30	Both Sides
Mean Look	Normal	Status	—	—	5	Normal
Lick	Ghost	Physical	30	100	30	Normal
Imprison	Psychic	Status	—	—	10	Self
Curse	Ghost	Status	—	—	10	Varies
Shadow Punch	Ghost	Physical	60	—	20	Normal
Shadow Sneak	Ghost	Physical	40	100	30	Normal
Stockpile	Normal	Status	—	—	20	Self
Swallow	Normal	Status	—	—	10	Self
Spit Up	Normal	Special	—	100	10	Normal
Scary Face	Normal	Status	—	100	10	Normal
Acid Spray	Poison	Special	40	100	20	Normal

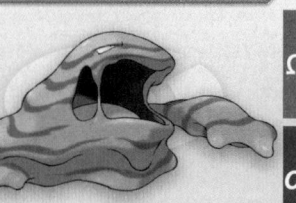

National Pokédex **089** Hoenn Pokédex **112**

Muk

Sludge Pokémon

Poison

HEIGHT: 3'11" WEIGHT: 66.1 lbs.

Same form for ♂ / ♀

Ω From Muk's body seeps a foul fluid that gives off a nose-bendingly horrible stench. Just one drop of this Pokémon's body fluid can turn a pool stagnant and rancid.

α This Pokémon's favorite food is anything that is repugnantly filthy. In dirty towns where people think nothing of throwing away litter on the streets, Muk are certain to gather.

ABILITIES
Stench
Sticky Hold

HIDDEN ABILITY
Poison Touch

EGG GROUPS
Amorphous

STAT GROWTH RATES

HP	■■■■
Attack	■■■■■
Defense	■■■
Sp. Atk	■■■
Sp. Def	■■■■
Speed	■■■

ITEMS SOMETIMES HELD BY WILD POKÉMON
—

EVOLUTION

Lv. 38
Grimer
Muk

MAIN WAY TO REGISTER IN THE NATIONAL POKÉDEX

Level up Grimer to Lv. 38.

Damage taken in normal battles

Type		Type	
Normal	×1	Flying	×1
Fire	×1	Psychic	×2
Water	×1	Bug	×0.5
Grass	×0.5	Rock	×1
Electric	×1	Ghost	×1
Ice	×1	Dragon	×1
Fighting	×0.5	Dark	×1
Poison	×0.5	Steel	×1
Ground	×2	Fairy	×0.5

Damage taken in Inverse battles

Type		Type	
Normal	×1	Flying	×1
Fire	×1	Psychic	×0.5
Water	×1	Bug	×2
Grass	×2	Rock	×1
Electric	×1	Ghost	×1
Ice	×1	Dragon	×1
Fighting	×2	Dark	×1
Poison	×2	Steel	×1
Ground	×0.5	Fairy	×2

Can be used in
Inverse Battle
Battle Institute
Random Matchup (Free Battle)
Random Matchup (Others)
Random Matchup (Others)

LEVEL-UP MOVES

Lv.	Name	Type	Kind	Pow.	Acc.	PP	Range
1	Pound	Normal	Physical	40	100	35	Normal
1	Poison Gas	Poison	Status	—	90	40	Many Others
1	Harden	Normal	Status	—	—	30	Self
1	Mud-Slap	Ground	Special	20	100	10	Normal
4	Harden	Normal	Status	—	—	30	Self
7	Mud-Slap	Ground	Special	20	100	10	Normal
12	Disable	Normal	Status	—	100	20	Normal
15	Sludge	Poison	Special	65	100	20	Normal
18	Mud Bomb	Ground	Special	65	85	10	Normal
21	Minimize	Normal	Status	—	—	10	Self
26	Fling	Dark	Physical	—	100	10	Normal
29	Sludge Bomb	Poison	Special	90	100	10	Normal
32	Sludge Wave	Poison	Special	95	100	10	Adjacent
37	Screech	Normal	Status	—	85	40	Normal
38	Venom Drench	Poison	Status	—	100	20	Many Others
40	Gunk Shot	Poison	Physical	120	80	5	Normal
46	Acid Armor	Poison	Status	—	—	20	Self
52	Belch	Poison	Special	120	90	10	Normal
57	Memento	Dark	Status	—	100	10	Normal

TM & HM MOVES

No.	Name	Type	Kind	Pow.	Acc.	PP	Range
TM06	Toxic	Poison	Status	—	90	10	Normal
TM09	Venoshock	Poison	Special	65	100	10	Normal
TM10	Hidden Power	Normal	Special	60	100	15	Normal
TM11	Sunny Day	Fire	Status	—	—	5	Both Sides
TM12	Taunt	Dark	Status	—	100	20	Normal
TM15	Hyper Beam	Normal	Special	150	90	5	Normal
TM17	Protect	Normal	Status	—	—	10	Self
TM18	Rain Dance	Water	Status	—	—	5	Both Sides
TM21	Frustration	Normal	Physical	—	100	20	Normal
TM24	Thunderbolt	Electric	Special	90	100	15	Normal
TM25	Thunder	Electric	Special	110	70	10	Normal
TM27	Return	Normal	Physical	—	100	20	Normal
TM28	Dig	Ground	Physical	80	100	10	Normal
TM30	Shadow Ball	Ghost	Special	80	100	15	Normal
TM31	Brick Break	Fighting	Physical	75	100	15	Normal
TM32	Double Team	Normal	Status	—	—	15	Self
TM34	Sludge Wave	Poison	Special	95	100	10	Adjacent
TM35	Flamethrower	Fire	Special	90	100	15	Normal
TM36	Sludge Bomb	Poison	Special	90	100	10	Normal
TM38	Fire Blast	Fire	Special	110	85	5	Normal
TM39	Rock Tomb	Rock	Physical	60	95	15	Normal
TM41	Torment	Dark	Status	—	100	15	Normal
TM42	Facade	Normal	Physical	70	100	20	Normal
TM44	Rest	Psychic	Status	—	—	10	Self
TM45	Attract	Normal	Status	—	100	15	Normal
TM46	Thief	Dark	Physical	60	100	25	Normal
TM48	Round	Normal	Special	60	100	15	Normal
TM52	Focus Blast	Fighting	Special	120	70	5	Normal
TM56	Fling	Dark	Physical	—	100	10	Normal
TM59	Incinerate	Fire	Special	60	100	15	Many Others
TM64	Explosion	Normal	Physical	250	100	5	Adjacent
TM66	Payback	Dark	Physical	50	100	10	Normal
TM68	Giga Impact	Normal	Physical	150	90	5	Normal
TM80	Rock Slide	Rock	Physical	75	90	10	Many Others
TM83	Infestation	Bug	Special	20	100	20	Normal
TM84	Poison Jab	Poison	Physical	80	100	20	Normal
TM87	Swagger	Normal	Status	—	90	15	Normal
TM88	Sleep Talk	Normal	Status	—	—	10	Self
TM90	Substitute	Normal	Status	—	—	10	Self
TM94	Secret Power	Normal	Physical	70	100	20	Normal
TM97	Dark Pulse	Dark	Special	80	100	15	Normal
TM98	Power-Up Punch	Fighting	Physical	40	100	20	Normal
TM100	Confide	Normal	Status	—	—	20	Normal
HM04	Strength	Normal	Physical	80	100	15	Normal
HM06	Rock Smash	Fighting	Physical	40	100	15	Normal

MOVES LEARNED IN EXCHANGE FOR BP

Name	Type	Kind	Pow.	Acc.	PP	Range
Gunk Shot	Poison	Physical	120	80	5	Normal
Thunder Punch	Electric	Physical	75	100	15	Normal
Fire Punch	Fire	Physical	75	100	15	Normal
Ice Punch	Ice	Physical	75	100	15	Normal
Block	Normal	Status	—	—	5	Normal
Snore	Normal	Special	50	100	15	Normal
Pain Split	Normal	Status	—	—	20	Normal
Giga Drain	Grass	Special	75	100	10	Normal
Focus Punch	Fighting	Physical	150	100	20	Normal
Shock Wave	Electric	Special	60	—	20	Normal

MOVES TAUGHT BY PEOPLE

Name	Type	Kind	Pow.	Acc.	PP	Range

National Pokédex **090** Hoenn Pokédex —

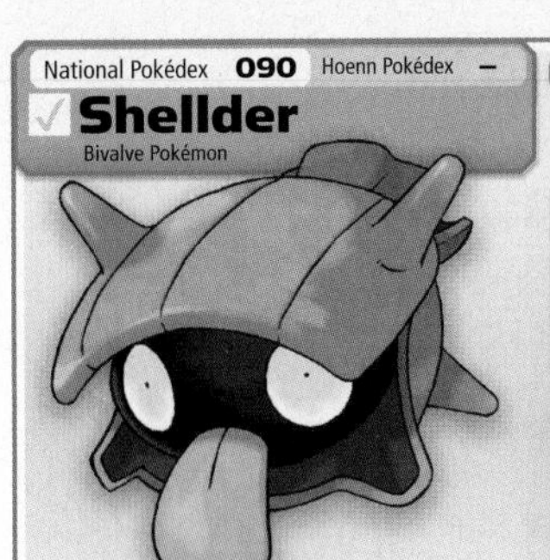

✓ Shellder

Bivalve Pokémon

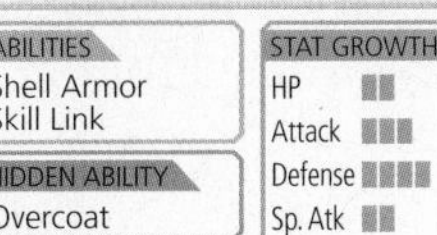

Water

HEIGHT: 1'00" WEIGHT: 8.8 lbs.

Same form for ♂ / ♀

Ω At night, this Pokémon uses its broad tongue to burrow a hole in the seafloor sand and then sleep in it. While it is sleeping, Shellder closes its shell, but leaves its tongue hanging out.

α At night, this Pokémon uses its broad tongue to burrow a hole in the seafloor sand and then sleep in it. While it is sleeping, Shellder closes its shell, but leaves its tongue hanging out.

ABILITIES
Shell Armor
Skill Link

HIDDEN ABILITY
Overcoat

EGG GROUPS
Water 3

STAT GROWTH RATES
HP
Attack
Defense
Sp. Atk
Sp. Def
Speed

ITEMS SOMETIMES HELD BY WILD POKÉMON
—

EVOLUTION

MAIN WAY TO REGISTER IN THE NATIONAL POKÉDEX

Appears in *Pokémon Y*. Bring it to your game using Link Trade or the GTS.

Damage taken in normal battles

Type		Type	
Normal	×1	Flying	×1
Fire	×0.5	Psychic	×1
Water	×0.5	Bug	×1
Grass	×2	Rock	×1
Electric	×2	Ghost	×1
Ice	×0.5	Dragon	×1
Fighting	×1	Dark	×1
Poison	×1	Steel	×0.5
Ground	×1	Fairy	×1

Damage taken in Inverse battles

Type		Type	
Normal	×1	Flying	×1
Fire	×2	Psychic	×1
Water	×2	Bug	×1
Grass	×0.5	Rock	×1
Electric	×0.5	Ghost	×1
Ice	×2	Dragon	×1
Fighting	×1	Dark	×1
Poison	×1	Steel	×2
Ground	×1	Fairy	×1

Can be used in
Inverse Battle
Battle Institute
Battle Maison
Random Matchup (Free Battle)
Random Matchup (Others)

LEVEL-UP MOVES

Lv.	Name	Type	Kind	Pow.	Acc.	PP	Range
1	Tackle	Normal	Physical	50	100	35	Normal
4	Withdraw	Water	Status	—	—	40	Self
8	Supersonic	Normal	Status	—	55	20	Normal
13	Icicle Spear	Ice	Physical	25	100	30	Normal
16	Protect	Normal	Status	—	—	10	Self
20	Leer	Normal	Status	—	100	30	Many Others
25	Clamp	Water	Physical	35	85	15	Normal
28	Ice Shard	Ice	Physical	40	100	30	Normal
32	Razor Shell	Water	Physical	75	95	10	Normal
37	Aurora Beam	Ice	Special	65	100	20	Normal
40	Whirlpool	Water	Special	35	85	15	Normal
44	Brine	Water	Special	65	100	10	Normal
49	Iron Defense	Steel	Status	—	—	15	Self
52	Ice Beam	Ice	Special	90	100	10	Normal
56	Shell Smash	Normal	Status	—	—	15	Self
61	Hydro Pump	Water	Special	110	80	5	Normal

TM & HM MOVES

No.	Name	Type	Kind	Pow.	Acc.	PP	Range
TM06	Toxic	Poison	Status	—	90	10	Normal
TM07	Hail	Ice	Status	—	—	10	Both Sides
TM10	Hidden Power	Normal	Special	60	100	15	Normal
TM13	Ice Beam	Ice	Special	90	100	10	Normal
TM14	Blizzard	Ice	Special	110	70	5	Many Others
TM17	Protect	Normal	Status	—	—	10	Self
TM18	Rain Dance	Water	Status	—	—	5	Both Sides
TM21	Frustration	Normal	Physical	—	100	20	Normal
TM27	Return	Normal	Physical	—	100	20	Normal
TM32	Double Team	Normal	Status	—	—	15	Self
TM42	Facade	Normal	Physical	70	100	20	Normal
TM44	Rest	Psychic	Status	—	—	10	Self
TM45	Attract	Normal	Status	—	100	15	Normal
TM48	Round	Normal	Special	60	100	15	Normal
TM64	Explosion	Normal	Physical	250	100	5	Adjacent
TM66	Payback	Dark	Physical	50	100	10	Normal
TM87	Swagger	Normal	Status	—	90	15	Normal
TM88	Sleep Talk	Normal	Status	—	—	10	Self
TM90	Substitute	Normal	Status	—	—	10	Self
TM94	Secret Power	Normal	Physical	70	100	20	Normal
TM100	Confide	Normal	Status	—	—	20	Normal
HM03	Surf	Water	Special	90	100	15	Adjacent
HM07	Dive	Water	Physical	80	100	10	Normal

MOVES LEARNED IN EXCHANGE FOR BP

Name	Type	Kind	Pow.	Acc.	PP	Range
Iron Defense	Steel	Status	—	—	15	Self
Icy Wind	Ice	Special	55	95	15	Many Others
Snore	Normal	Special	50	100	15	Normal
Water Pulse	Water	Special	60	100	20	Normal

MOVES TAUGHT BY PEOPLE

Name	Type	Kind	Pow.	Acc.	PP	Range

EGG MOVES

Name	Type	Kind	Pow.	Acc.	PP	Range
Bubble Beam	Water	Special	65	100	20	Normal
Take Down	Normal	Physical	90	85	20	Normal
Barrier	Psychic	Status	—	—	20	Self
Rapid Spin	Normal	Physical	20	100	40	Normal
Screech	Normal	Status	—	85	40	Normal
Icicle Spear	Ice	Physical	25	100	30	Normal
Mud Shot	Ground	Special	55	95	15	Normal
Rock Blast	Rock	Physical	25	90	10	Normal
Water Pulse	Water	Special	60	100	20	Normal
Aqua Ring	Water	Status	—	—	20	Self
Avalanche	Ice	Physical	60	100	10	Normal
Twineedle	Bug	Physical	25	100	20	Normal

National Pokédex **091** Hoenn Pokédex —

✓ Cloyster

Bivalve Pokémon

Water Ice

HEIGHT: 4'11" WEIGHT: 292.1 lbs.

Same form for ♂ / ♀

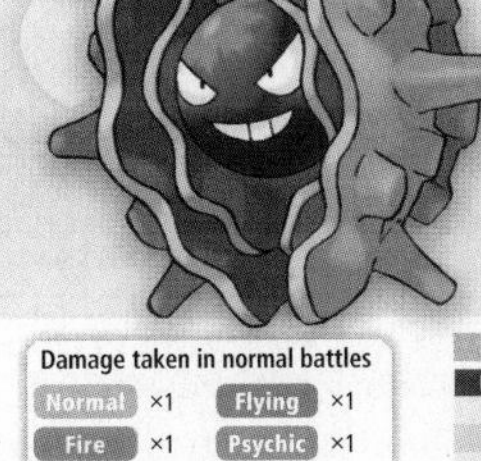

Ω Cloyster is capable of swimming in the sea. It does so by swallowing water, then jetting it out toward the rear. This Pokémon shoots spikes from its shell using the same system.

α Cloyster is capable of swimming in the sea. It does so by swallowing water, then jetting it out toward the rear. This Pokémon shoots spikes from its shell using the same system.

ABILITIES
Shell Armor
Skill Link

HIDDEN ABILITY
Overcoat

EGG GROUPS
Water 3

STAT GROWTH RATES
HP
Attack
Defense
Sp. Atk
Sp. Def
Speed

ITEMS SOMETIMES HELD BY WILD POKÉMON
—

EVOLUTION

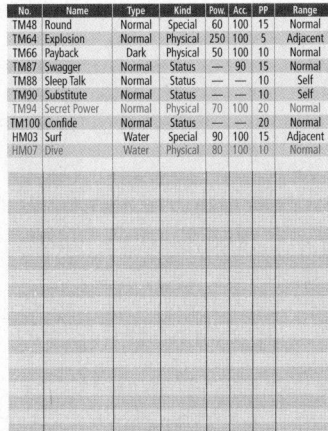

Water Stone
Shellder
Cloyster

MAIN WAY TO REGISTER IN THE NATIONAL POKÉDEX

Appears in *Pokémon Y*. Bring it to your game using Link Trade or the GTS.

Damage taken in normal battles

Type		Type	
Normal	×1	Flying	×1
Fire	×1	Psychic	×1
Water	×0.5	Bug	×1
Grass	×2	Rock	×2
Electric	×2	Ghost	×1
Ice	×0.25	Dragon	×1
Fighting	×2	Dark	×1
Poison	×1	Steel	×1
Ground	×1	Fairy	×1

Damage taken in Inverse battles

Type		Type	
Normal	×1	Flying	×1
Fire	×1	Psychic	×1
Water	×2	Bug	×1
Grass	×0.5	Rock	×0.5
Electric	×0.5	Ghost	×1
Ice	×4	Dragon	×1
Fighting	×0.5	Dark	×1
Poison	×1	Steel	×1
Ground	×1	Fairy	×1

Can be used in
Inverse Battle
Battle Institute
Battle Maison
Random Matchup (Free Battle)
Random Matchup (Others)

LEVEL-UP MOVES

Lv.	Name	Type	Kind	Pow.	Acc.	PP	Range
1	Hydro Pump	Water	Special	110	80	5	Normal
1	Shell Smash	Normal	Status	—	—	15	Self
1	Toxic Spikes	Poison	Status	—	—	20	Other Side
1	Withdraw	Water	Status	—	—	40	Self
1	Supersonic	Normal	Status	—	55	20	Normal
1	Protect	Normal	Status	—	—	10	Self
1	Aurora Beam	Ice	Special	65	100	20	Normal
13	Spike Cannon	Normal	Physical	20	100	15	Normal
28	Spikes	Ground	Status	—	—	20	Other Side
50	Icicle Crash	Ice	Physical	85	90	10	Normal

TM & HM MOVES

No.	Name	Type	Kind	Pow.	Acc.	PP	Range
TM06	Toxic	Poison	Status	—	90	10	Normal
TM07	Hail	Ice	Status	—	—	10	Both Sides
TM10	Hidden Power	Normal	Special	60	100	15	Normal
TM13	Ice Beam	Ice	Special	90	100	10	Normal
TM14	Blizzard	Ice	Special	110	70	5	Many Others
TM15	Hyper Beam	Normal	Special	150	90	5	Normal
TM17	Protect	Normal	Status	—	—	10	Self
TM18	Rain Dance	Water	Status	—	—	5	Both Sides
TM21	Frustration	Normal	Physical	—	100	20	Normal
TM27	Return	Normal	Physical	—	100	20	Normal
TM32	Double Team	Normal	Status	—	—	15	Self
TM41	Torment	Dark	Status	—	100	15	Normal
TM42	Facade	Normal	Physical	70	100	20	Normal
TM44	Rest	Psychic	Status	—	—	10	Self
TM45	Attract	Normal	Status	—	100	15	Normal
TM48	Round	Normal	Special	60	100	15	Normal
TM64	Explosion	Normal	Physical	250	100	5	Adjacent
TM66	Payback	Dark	Physical	50	100	10	Normal
TM68	Giga Impact	Normal	Physical	150	90	5	Normal
TM79	Frost Breath	Ice	Special	60	90	10	Normal
TM84	Poison Jab	Poison	Physical	80	100	20	Normal
TM87	Swagger	Normal	Status	—	90	15	Normal
TM88	Sleep Talk	Normal	Status	—	—	10	Self
TM90	Substitute	Normal	Status	—	—	10	Self
TM94	Secret Power	Normal	Physical	70	100	20	Normal
TM100	Confide	Normal	Status	—	—	20	Normal
HM03	Surf	Water	Special	90	100	15	Adjacent
HM07	Dive	Water	Physical	80	100	10	Normal

MOVES LEARNED IN EXCHANGE FOR BP

Name	Type	Kind	Pow.	Acc.	PP	Range
Signal Beam	Bug	Special	75	100	15	Normal
Iron Defense	Steel	Status	—	—	15	Self
Icy Wind	Ice	Special	55	95	15	Many Others
Snore	Normal	Special	50	100	15	Normal
Water Pulse	Water	Special	60	100	20	Normal

MOVES TAUGHT BY PEOPLE

Name	Type	Kind	Pow.	Acc.	PP	Range

National Pokédex **092** Hoenn Pokédex —

Gastly

Gas Pokémon

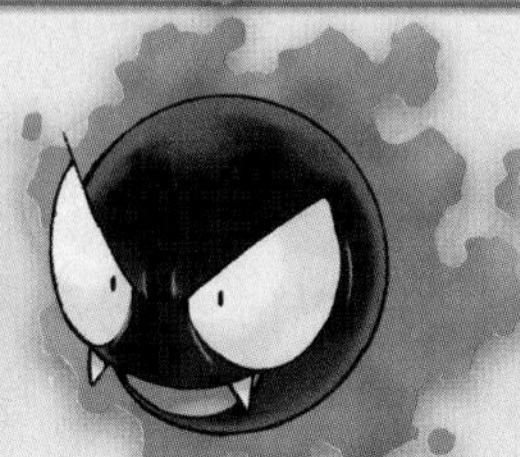

Ghost **Poison**

HEIGHT: 4'03" WEIGHT: 0.2 lbs.

Same form for ♂ / ♀

Ω Gastly is largely composed of gaseous matter. When exposed to a strong wind, the gaseous body quickly dwindles away. Groups of this Pokémon cluster under the eaves of houses to escape the ravages of wind.

α Gastly is largely composed of gaseous matter. When exposed to a strong wind, the gaseous body quickly dwindles away. Groups of this Pokémon cluster under the eaves of houses to escape the ravages of wind.

ABILITY

Levitate

HIDDEN ABILITY

—

EGG GROUPS

Amorphous

STAT GROWTH RATES

HP

Attack

Defense

Sp. Atk

Sp. Def

Speed

ITEMS SOMETIMES HELD BY WILD POKÉMON

—

EVOLUTION

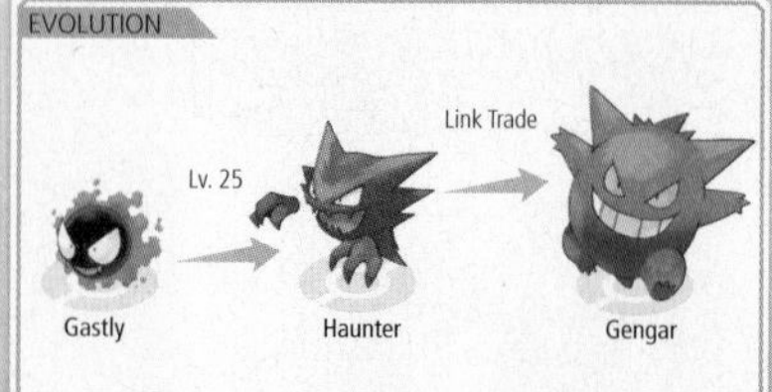

MAIN WAY TO REGISTER IN THE NATIONAL POKÉDEX

Leave a Haunter or Gengar obtained via Link Trade or the GTS at a Pokémon Day Care, then hatch the Pokémon Egg that is found.

Damage taken in normal battles

Normal	×0	Flying	×1
Fire	×1	Psychic	×2
Water	×1	Bug	×0.25
Grass	×0.5	Rock	×1
Electric	×1	Ghost	×2
Ice	×1	Dragon	×1
Fighting	×0	Dark	×2
Poison	×0.25	Steel	×1
! Ground	×2	Fairy	×0.5

Damage taken in Inverse battles

Normal	×2	Flying	×1
Fire	×1	Psychic	×0.5
Water	×1	Bug	×4
Grass	×2	Rock	×1
Electric	×1	Ghost	×0.5
Ice	×1	Dragon	×1
Fighting	×4	Dark	×0.5
Poison	×4	Steel	×1
! Ground	×0.5	Fairy	×2

Can be used in

Inverse Battle

Battle Institute

Battle Maison

Random Matchup (Free Battle)

Random Matchup (Others)

LEVEL-UP MOVES

Lv.	Name	Type	Kind	Pow.	Acc.	PP	Range
1	Hypnosis	Psychic	Status	—	60	20	Normal
1	Lick	Ghost	Physical	30	100	30	Normal
5	Spite	Ghost	Status	—	100	10	Normal
8	Mean Look	Normal	Status	—	—	5	Normal
12	Curse	Ghost	Status	—	—	10	Varies
15	Night Shade	Ghost	Special	—	100	15	Normal
19	Confuse Ray	Ghost	Status	—	100	10	Normal
22	Sucker Punch	Dark	Physical	80	100	5	Normal
26	Payback	Dark	Physical	50	100	10	Normal
29	Shadow Ball	Ghost	Special	80	100	15	Normal
33	Dream Eater	Psychic	Special	100	100	15	Normal
36	Dark Pulse	Dark	Special	80	100	15	Normal
40	Destiny Bond	Ghost	Status	—	—	5	Self
43	Hex	Ghost	Special	65	100	10	Normal
47	Nightmare	Ghost	Status	—	100	15	Normal

TM & HM MOVES

No.	Name	Type	Kind	Pow.	Acc.	PP	Range
TM06	Toxic	Poison	Status	—	90	10	Normal
TM09	Venoshock	Poison	Special	65	100	10	Normal
TM10	Hidden Power	Normal	Special	60	100	15	Normal
TM11	Sunny Day	Fire	Status	—	—	5	Both Sides
TM12	Taunt	Dark	Status	—	100	20	Normal
TM17	Protect	Normal	Status	—	—	10	Self
TM18	Rain Dance	Water	Status	—	—	5	Both Sides
TM21	Frustration	Normal	Physical	—	100	20	Normal
TM24	Thunderbolt	Electric	Special	90	100	15	Normal
TM27	Return	Normal	Physical	—	100	20	Normal
TM29	Psychic	Psychic	Special	90	100	10	Normal
TM30	Shadow Ball	Ghost	Special	80	100	15	Normal
TM32	Double Team	Normal	Status	—	—	15	Self
TM36	Sludge Bomb	Poison	Special	90	100	10	Normal
TM41	Torment	Dark	Status	—	100	15	Normal
TM42	Facade	Normal	Physical	70	100	20	Normal
TM44	Rest	Psychic	Status	—	—	10	Self
TM45	Attract	Normal	Status	—	100	15	Normal
TM46	Thief	Dark	Physical	60	100	25	Normal
TM48	Round	Normal	Special	60	100	15	Normal
TM53	Energy Ball	Grass	Special	90	100	10	Normal
TM61	Will-O-Wisp	Fire	Status	—	85	15	Normal
TM63	Embargo	Dark	Status	—	100	15	Normal
TM64	Explosion	Normal	Physical	250	100	5	Adjacent
TM66	Payback	Dark	Physical	50	100	10	Normal
TM77	Psych Up	Normal	Status	—	—	10	Normal
TM83	Infestation	Bug	Special	20	100	20	Normal
TM85	Dream Eater	Psychic	Special	100	100	15	Normal
TM87	Swagger	Normal	Status	—	90	15	Normal
TM88	Sleep Talk	Normal	Status	—	—	10	Self
TM90	Substitute	Normal	Status	—	—	10	Self
TM92	Trick Room	Psychic	Status	—	—	5	Both Sides
TM94	Secret Power	Normal	Physical	70	100	20	Normal
TM97	Dark Pulse	Dark	Special	80	100	15	Normal
TM99	Dazzling Gleam	Fairy	Special	80	100	10	Many Others
TM100	Confide	Normal	Status	—	—	20	Normal

MOVES LEARNED IN EXCHANGE FOR BP

Name	Type	Kind	Pow.	Acc.	PP	Range
Uproar	Normal	Special	90	100	10	1 Random
Thunder Punch	Electric	Physical	75	100	15	Normal
Fire Punch	Fire	Physical	75	100	15	Normal
Ice Punch	Ice	Physical	75	100	15	Normal
Foul Play	Dark	Physical	95	100	15	Normal
Icy Wind	Ice	Special	55	95	15	Many Others
Snore	Normal	Special	50	100	15	Normal
Knock Off	Dark	Physical	65	100	20	Normal
Pain Split	Normal	Status	—	—	20	Normal
Giga Drain	Grass	Special	75	100	10	Normal
Spite	Ghost	Status	—	100	10	Normal
Trick	Psychic	Status	—	100	10	Normal
Wonder Room	Psychic	Status	—	—	10	Both Sides
Snatch	Dark	Status	—	—	10	Self
Skill Swap	Psychic	Status	—	—	10	Normal

MOVES TAUGHT BY PEOPLE

Name	Type	Kind	Pow.	Acc.	PP	Range

EGG MOVES

Name	Type	Kind	Pow.	Acc.	PP	Range
Psywave	Psychic	Special	—	100	15	Normal
Perish Song	Normal	Status	—	—	5	Adjacent
Haze	Ice	Status	—	—	30	Both Sides
Astonish	Ghost	Physical	30	100	15	Normal
Grudge	Ghost	Status	—	—	5	Self
Fire Punch	Fire	Physical	75	100	15	Normal
Ice Punch	Ice	Physical	75	100	15	Normal
Thunder Punch	Electric	Physical	75	100	15	Normal
Disable	Normal	Status	—	100	20	Normal
Scary Face	Normal	Status	—	100	10	Normal
Clear Smog	Poison	Special	50	—	15	Normal
Smog	Poison	Special	30	70	20	Normal
Reflect Type	Normal	Status	—	—	15	Normal

National Pokédex **093** Hoenn Pokédex —

Haunter

Gas Pokémon

Ghost **Poison**

HEIGHT: 5'03" WEIGHT: 0.2 lbs.

Same form for ♂ / ♀

Ω Hunter is a dangerous Pokémon. If one beckons you while floating in darkness, you must never approach it. This Pokémon will try to lick you with its tongue and steal your life away.

α Haunter is a dangerous Pokémon. If one beckons you while floating in darkness, you must never approach it. This Pokémon will try to lick you with its tongue and steal your life away.

ABILITY

Levitate

HIDDEN ABILITY

—

EGG GROUPS

Amorphous

STAT GROWTH RATES

HP

Attack

Defense

Sp. Atk

Sp. Def

Speed

ITEMS SOMETIMES HELD BY WILD POKÉMON

—

EVOLUTION

Lv. 25

Link Trade

Gastly

Haunter

Gengar

MAIN WAY TO REGISTER IN THE NATIONAL POKÉDEX

Appears in *Pokémon X* and *Pokémon Y.* Bring it to your game using Link Trade or the GTS.

Damage taken in normal battles

Normal	×0	Flying	×1
Fire	×1	Psychic	×2
Water	×1	Bug	×0.25
Grass	×0.5	Rock	×1
Electric	×1	Ghost	×2
Ice	×1	Dragon	×1
Fighting	×0	Dark	×2
Poison	×0.25	Steel	×1
! Ground	×2	Fairy	×0.5

Damage taken in Inverse battles

Normal	×2	Flying	×1
Fire	×1	Psychic	×0.5
Water	×1	Bug	×4
Grass	×2	Rock	×1
Electric	×1	Ghost	×0.5
Ice	×1	Dragon	×1
Fighting	×4	Dark	×0.5
Poison	×4	Steel	×1
! Ground	×0.5	Fairy	×2

Can be used in

Inverse Battle

Battle Institute

Battle Maison

Random Matchup (Free Battle)

Random Matchup (Others)

LEVEL-UP MOVES

Lv.	Name	Type	Kind	Pow.	Acc.	PP	Range
1	Hypnosis	Psychic	Status	—	60	20	Normal
1	Lick	Ghost	Physical	30	100	30	Normal
1	Spite	Ghost	Status	—	100	10	Normal
5	Spite	Ghost	Status	—	100	10	Normal
8	Mean Look	Normal	Status	—	—	5	Normal
12	Curse	Ghost	Status	—	—	10	Varies
15	Night Shade	Ghost	Special	—	100	15	Normal
19	Confuse Ray	Ghost	Status	—	100	10	Normal
22	Sucker Punch	Dark	Physical	80	100	5	Normal
25	Shadow Punch	Ghost	Physical	60	—	20	Normal
28	Payback	Dark	Physical	50	100	10	Normal
33	Shadow Ball	Ghost	Special	80	100	15	Normal
39	Dream Eater	Psychic	Special	100	100	15	Normal
44	Dark Pulse	Dark	Special	80	100	15	Normal
50	Destiny Bond	Ghost	Status	—	—	5	Self
55	Hex	Ghost	Special	65	100	10	Normal
61	Nightmare	Ghost	Status	—	100	15	Normal

TM & HM MOVES

No.	Name	Type	Kind	Pow.	Acc.	PP	Range
TM06	Toxic	Poison	Status	—	90	10	Normal
TM09	Venoshock	Poison	Special	65	100	10	Normal
TM10	Hidden Power	Normal	Special	60	100	15	Normal
TM11	Sunny Day	Fire	Status	—	—	5	Both Sides
TM12	Taunt	Dark	Status	—	100	20	Normal
TM17	Protect	Normal	Status	—	—	10	Self
TM18	Rain Dance	Water	Status	—	—	5	Both Sides
TM21	Frustration	Normal	Physical	—	100	20	Normal
TM24	Thunderbolt	Electric	Special	90	100	15	Normal
TM27	Return	Normal	Physical	—	100	20	Normal
TM29	Psychic	Psychic	Special	90	100	10	Normal
TM30	Shadow Ball	Ghost	Special	80	100	15	Normal
TM32	Double Team	Normal	Status	—	—	15	Self
TM36	Sludge Bomb	Poison	Special	90	100	10	Normal
TM41	Torment	Dark	Status	—	100	15	Normal
TM42	Facade	Normal	Physical	70	100	20	Normal
TM44	Rest	Psychic	Status	—	—	10	Self
TM45	Attract	Normal	Status	—	100	15	Normal
TM46	Thief	Dark	Physical	60	100	25	Normal
TM48	Round	Normal	Special	60	100	15	Normal
TM53	Energy Ball	Grass	Special	90	100	10	Normal
TM56	Fling	Dark	Physical	—	100	10	Normal
TM61	Will-O-Wisp	Fire	Status	—	85	15	Normal
TM63	Embargo	Dark	Status	—	100	15	Normal
TM64	Explosion	Normal	Physical	250	100	5	Adjacent
TM65	Shadow Claw	Ghost	Physical	70	100	15	Normal
TM66	Payback	Dark	Physical	50	100	10	Normal
TM77	Psych Up	Normal	Status	—	—	10	Normal
TM83	Infestation	Bug	Special	20	100	20	Normal
TM84	Poison Jab	Poison	Physical	80	100	20	Normal
TM85	Dream Eater	Psychic	Special	100	100	15	Normal
TM87	Swagger	Normal	Status	—	90	15	Normal
TM88	Sleep Talk	Normal	Status	—	—	10	Self
TM90	Substitute	Normal	Status	—	—	10	Self
TM92	Trick Room	Psychic	Status	—	—	5	Both Sides
TM94	Secret Power	Normal	Physical	70	100	20	Normal
TM97	Dark Pulse	Dark	Special	80	100	15	Normal
TM99	Dazzling Gleam	Fairy	Special	80	100	10	Many Others
TM100	Confide	Normal	Status	—	—	20	Normal

MOVES LEARNED IN EXCHANGE FOR BP

Name	Type	Kind	Pow.	Acc.	PP	Range
Uproar	Normal	Special	90	100	10	1 Random
Thunder Punch	Electric	Physical	75	100	15	Normal
Fire Punch	Fire	Physical	75	100	15	Normal
Ice Punch	Ice	Physical	75	100	15	Normal
Foul Play	Dark	Physical	95	100	15	Normal
Icy Wind	Ice	Special	55	95	15	Many Others
Snore	Normal	Special	50	100	15	Normal
Knock Off	Dark	Physical	65	100	20	Normal
Pain Split	Normal	Status	—	—	20	Normal
Giga Drain	Grass	Special	75	100	10	Normal
Spite	Ghost	Status	—	100	10	Normal
Trick	Psychic	Status	—	100	10	Normal
Wonder Room	Psychic	Status	—	—	10	Both Sides
Snatch	Dark	Status	—	—	10	Self
Skill Swap	Psychic	Status	—	—	10	Normal

MOVES TAUGHT BY PEOPLE

Name	Type	Kind	Pow.	Acc.	PP	Range

National Pokédex **094** Hoenn Pokédex —

Gengar

Shadow Pokémon

Ghost | Poison

HEIGHT: 4'11" WEIGHT: 89.3 lbs.

Same form for ♂ / ♀

Ω Sometimes, on a dark night, your shadow thrown by a streetlight will suddenly and startlingly overtake you. It is actually a Gengar running past you, pretending to be your shadow.

α Sometimes, on a dark night, your shadow thrown by a streetlight will suddenly and startlingly overtake you. It is actually a Gengar running past you, pretending to be your shadow.

ABILITY
Levitate

HIDDEN ABILITY
—

EGG GROUPS
Amorphous

STAT GROWTH RATES
HP
Attack
Defense
Sp. Atk
Sp. Def
Speed

ITEMS SOMETIMES HELD BY WILD POKÉMON
—

EVOLUTION

MAIN WAY TO REGISTER IN THE NATIONAL POKÉDEX

Receive a Haunter via Link Trade or the GTS to have it evolve.

Damage taken in normal battles

Type		Type	
Normal	×0	Flying	×1
Fire	×1	Psychic	×2
Water	×1	Bug	×0.25
Grass	×0.5	Rock	×1
Electric	×1	Ghost	×2
Ice	×1	Dragon	×1
Fighting	×0	Dark	×2
Poison	×0.25	Steel	×1
! Ground	×2	Fairy	×0.5

Damage taken in Inverse battles

Type		Type	
Normal	×2	Flying	×1
Fire	×1	Psychic	×0.5
Water	×1	Bug	×4
Grass	×2	Rock	×1
Electric	×1	Ghost	×0.5
Ice	×1	Dragon	×1
Fighting	×4	Dark	×0.5
Poison	×4	Steel	×1
! Ground	×0.5	Fairy	×2

Can be used in
Inverse Battle
Battle Institute
Battle Maison
Random Matchup (Free Battle)
Random Matchup (Others)

LEVEL-UP MOVES

Lv.	Name	Type	Kind	Pow.	Acc.	PP	Range
1	Hypnosis	Psychic	Status	—	60	20	Normal
1	Lick	Ghost	Physical	30	100	30	Normal
1	Spite	Ghost	Status	—	100	10	Normal
5	Spite	Ghost	Status	—	100	10	Normal
8	Mean Look	Normal	Status	—	—	5	Normal
12	Curse	Ghost	Status	—	—	10	Varies
15	Night Shade	Ghost	Special	—	100	15	Normal
19	Confuse Ray	Ghost	Status	—	100	10	Normal
22	Sucker Punch	Dark	Physical	80	100	5	Normal
25	Shadow Punch	Ghost	Physical	60	—	20	Normal
28	Payback	Dark	Physical	50	100	10	Normal
33	Shadow Ball	Ghost	Special	80	100	15	Normal
39	Dream Eater	Psychic	Special	100	100	15	Normal
44	Dark Pulse	Dark	Special	80	100	15	Normal
50	Destiny Bond	Ghost	Status	—	—	5	Self
55	Hex	Ghost	Special	65	100	10	Normal
61	Nightmare	Ghost	Status	—	100	15	Normal

TM & HM MOVES

No.	Name	Type	Kind	Pow.	Acc.	PP	Range
TM06	Toxic	Poison	Status	—	90	10	Normal
TM09	Venoshock	Poison	Special	65	100	10	Normal
TM10	Hidden Power	Normal	Special	60	100	15	Normal
TM11	Sunny Day	Fire	Status	—	—	5	Both Sides
TM12	Taunt	Dark	Status	—	100	20	Normal
TM15	Hyper Beam	Normal	Special	150	90	5	Normal
TM17	Protect	Normal	Status	—	—	10	Self
TM18	Rain Dance	Water	Status	—	—	5	Both Sides
TM21	Frustration	Normal	Physical	—	100	20	Normal
TM24	Thunderbolt	Electric	Special	90	100	15	Normal
TM25	Thunder	Electric	Special	110	70	10	Normal
TM27	Return	Normal	Physical	—	100	20	Normal
TM29	Psychic	Psychic	Special	90	100	10	Normal
TM30	Shadow Ball	Ghost	Special	80	100	15	Normal
TM31	Brick Break	Fighting	Physical	75	100	15	Normal
TM32	Double Team	Normal	Status	—	—	15	Self
TM36	Sludge Bomb	Poison	Special	90	100	10	Normal
TM41	Torment	Dark	Status	—	100	15	Normal
TM42	Facade	Normal	Physical	70	100	20	Normal
TM44	Rest	Psychic	Status	—	—	10	Self
TM45	Attract	Normal	Status	—	100	15	Normal
TM46	Thief	Dark	Physical	60	100	25	Normal
TM48	Round	Normal	Special	60	100	15	Normal
TM52	Focus Blast	Fighting	Special	120	70	5	Normal
TM53	Energy Ball	Grass	Special	90	100	10	Normal
TM56	Fling	Dark	Physical	—	100	10	Normal
TM61	Will-O-Wisp	Fire	Status	—	85	15	Normal
TM63	Embargo	Dark	Status	—	100	15	Normal
TM64	Explosion	Normal	Physical	250	100	5	Adjacent
TM65	Shadow Claw	Ghost	Physical	70	100	15	Normal
TM66	Payback	Dark	Physical	50	100	10	Normal
TM68	Giga Impact	Normal	Physical	150	90	5	Normal
TM77	Psych Up	Normal	Status	—	—	10	Normal
TM83	Infestation	Bug	Special	20	100	20	Normal
TM84	Poison Jab	Poison	Physical	80	100	20	Normal
TM85	Dream Eater	Psychic	Special	100	100	15	Normal
TM87	Swagger	Normal	Status	—	90	15	Normal
TM88	Sleep Talk	Normal	Status	—	—	10	Self
TM90	Substitute	Normal	Status	—	—	10	Self
TM92	Trick Room	Psychic	Status	—	—	5	Both Sides
TM94	Secret Power	Normal	Physical	70	100	20	Normal
TM97	Dark Pulse	Dark	Special	80	100	15	Normal
TM98	Power-Up Punch	Fighting	Physical	40	100	20	Normal
TM99	Dazzling Gleam	Fairy	Special	80	100	10	Many Others
TM100	Confide	Normal	Status	—	—	20	Normal
HM04	Strength	Normal	Physical	80	100	15	Normal
HM06	Rock Smash	Fighting	Physical	40	100	15	Normal

MOVES LEARNED IN EXCHANGE FOR BP

Name	Type	Kind	Pow.	Acc.	PP	Range
Uproar	Normal	Special	90	100	10	1 Random
Thunder Punch	Electric	Physical	75	100	15	Normal
Fire Punch	Fire	Physical	75	100	15	Normal
Ice Punch	Ice	Physical	75	100	15	Normal
Foul Play	Dark	Physical	95	100	15	Normal
Icy Wind	Ice	Special	55	95	15	Many Others
Snore	Normal	Special	50	100	15	Normal
Knock Off	Dark	Physical	65	100	20	Normal
Role Play	Psychic	Status	—	—	10	Normal
Pain Split	Normal	Status	—	—	20	Normal
Giga Drain	Grass	Special	75	100	10	Normal
Drain Punch	Fighting	Physical	75	100	10	Normal
Focus Punch	Fighting	Physical	150	100	20	Normal
Spite	Ghost	Status	—	100	10	Normal
Trick	Psychic	Status	—	100	10	Normal
Wonder Room	Psychic	Status	—	—	10	Both Sides
Snatch	Dark	Status	—	—	10	Self
Skill Swap	Psychic	Status	—	—	10	Normal

MOVES TAUGHT BY PEOPLE

Name	Type	Kind	Pow.	Acc.	PP	Range

Mega Evolution

Mega Gengar

Shadow Pokémon

Ghost | Poison

HEIGHT: 4'07" WEIGHT: 89.3 lbs.

Same form for ♂ / ♀

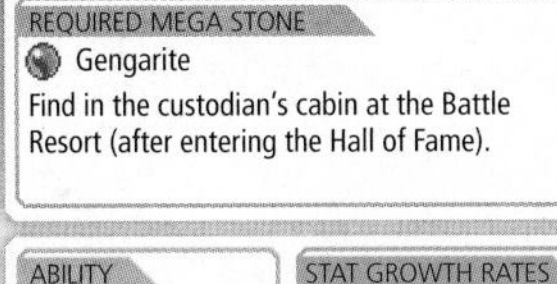

REQUIRED MEGA STONE
Gengarite
Find in the custodian's cabin at the Battle Resort (after entering the Hall of Fame).

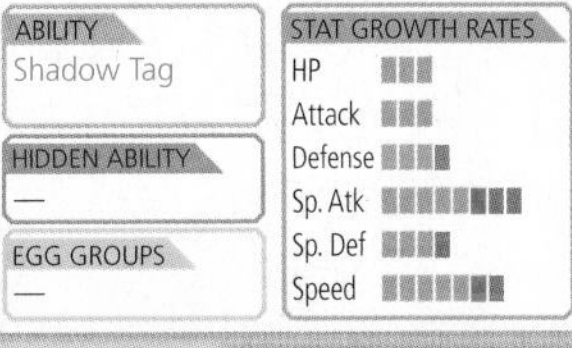

ABILITY
Shadow Tag

HIDDEN ABILITY
—

EGG GROUPS
—

STAT GROWTH RATES
HP
Attack
Defense
Sp. Atk
Sp. Def
Speed

Damage taken in normal battles

Type		Type	
Normal	×0	Flying	×1
Fire	×1	Psychic	×2
Water	×1	Bug	×0.25
Grass	×0.5	Rock	×1
Electric	×1	Ghost	×2
Ice	×1	Dragon	×1
Fighting	×0	Dark	×2
Poison	×0.25	Steel	×1
Ground	×2	Fairy	×0.5

Damage taken in Inverse battles

Type		Type	
Normal	×2	Flying	×1
Fire	×1	Psychic	×0.5
Water	×1	Bug	×4
Grass	×2	Rock	×1
Electric	×1	Ghost	×0.5
Ice	×1	Dragon	×1
Fighting	×4	Dark	×0.5
Poison	×4	Steel	×1
Ground	×0.5	Fairy	×2

Can be used in
Inverse Battle
Battle Institute
Battle Maison
Random Matchup (Free Battle)
Random Matchup (Others)

National Pokédex **095** Hoenn Pokédex —

Onix

Rock Snake Pokémon

Rock | Ground

HEIGHT: 28'10" WEIGHT: 463 lbs.

Same form for ♂ / ♀

Ω Onix has a magnet in its brain. It acts as a compass so that this Pokémon does not lose direction while it is tunneling. As it grows older, its body becomes increasingly rounder and smoother.

α Onix has a magnet in its brain. It acts as a compass so that this Pokémon does not lose direction while it is tunneling. As it grows older, its body becomes increasingly rounder and smoother.

ABILITIES
Rock Head
Sturdy

HIDDEN ABILITY
Weak Armor

EGG GROUPS
Mineral

STAT GROWTH RATES
HP
Attack
Defense
Sp. Atk
Sp. Def
Speed

ITEMS SOMETIMES HELD BY WILD POKÉMON
—

EVOLUTION

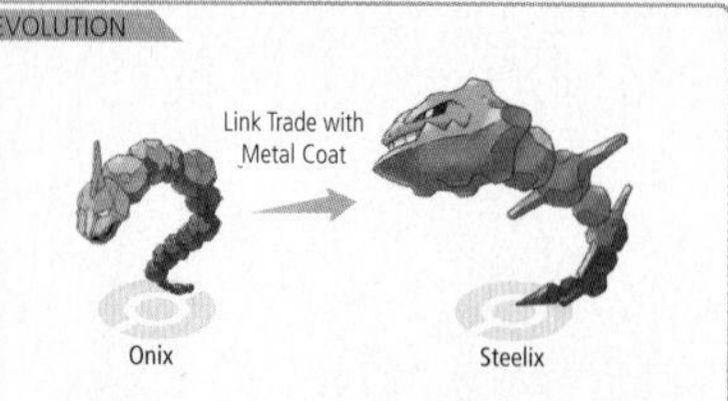

MAIN WAY TO REGISTER IN THE NATIONAL POKÉDEX

Catch in Granite Cave (1F). Appears as a hidden Pokémon after you battle Groudon or Kyogre.

Damage taken in normal battles

Type		Type	
Normal	×0.5	Flying	×0.5
Fire	×0.5	Psychic	×1
Water	×4	Bug	×1
Grass	×4	Rock	×0.5
Electric	×0	Ghost	×1
Ice	×2	Dragon	×1
Fighting	×2	Dark	×1
Poison	×0.25	Steel	×2
Ground	×2	Fairy	×1

Damage taken in Inverse battles

Type		Type	
Normal	×2	Flying	×2
Fire	×2	Psychic	×1
Water	×0.25	Bug	×1
Grass	×0.25	Rock	×2
Electric	×2	Ghost	×1
Ice	×0.5	Dragon	×1
Fighting	×0.5	Dark	×1
Poison	×4	Steel	×0.5
Ground	×0.5	Fairy	×1

Can be used in
Inverse Battle
Battle Institute
Battle Maison
Random Matchup (Free Battle)
Random Matchup (Others)

LEVEL-UP MOVES

Lv.	Name	Type	Kind	Pow.	Acc.	PP	Range
1	Mud Sport	Ground	Status	—	—	15	Both Sides
1	Tackle	Normal	Physical	50	100	35	Normal
1	Harden	Normal	Status	—	—	30	Self
1	Bind	Normal	Physical	15	85	20	Normal
4	Curse	Ghost	Status	—	—	10	Varies
7	Rock Throw	Rock	Physical	50	90	15	Normal
10	Rock Tomb	Rock	Physical	60	95	15	Normal
13	Rage	Normal	Physical	20	100	20	Normal
16	Stealth Rock	Rock	Status	—	—	20	Other Side
19	Rock Polish	Rock	Status	—	—	20	Self
20	Gyro Ball	Steel	Physical	—	100	5	Normal
22	Smack Down	Rock	Physical	50	100	15	Normal
25	Dragon Breath	Dragon	Special	60	100	20	Normal
28	Slam	Normal	Physical	80	75	20	Normal
31	Screech	Normal	Status	—	85	40	Normal
34	Rock Slide	Rock	Physical	75	90	10	Many Others
37	Sand Tomb	Ground	Physical	35	85	15	Normal
40	Iron Tail	Steel	Physical	100	75	15	Normal
43	Dig	Ground	Physical	80	100	10	Normal
46	Stone Edge	Rock	Physical	100	80	5	Normal
49	Double-Edge	Normal	Physical	120	100	15	Normal
52	Sandstorm	Rock	Status	—	—	10	Both Sides

TM & HM MOVES

No.	Name	Type	Kind	Pow.	Acc.	PP	Range
TM05	Roar	Normal	Status	—	—	20	Normal
TM06	Toxic	Poison	Status	—	90	10	Normal
TM10	Hidden Power	Normal	Special	60	100	15	Normal
TM11	Sunny Day	Fire	Status	—	—	5	Both Sides
TM12	Taunt	Dark	Status	—	100	20	Normal
TM17	Protect	Normal	Status	—	—	10	Self
TM21	Frustration	Normal	Physical	—	100	20	Normal
TM23	Smack Down	Rock	Physical	50	100	15	Normal
TM26	Earthquake	Ground	Physical	100	100	10	Adjacent
TM27	Return	Normal	Physical	—	100	20	Normal
TM28	Dig	Ground	Physical	80	100	10	Normal
TM32	Double Team	Normal	Status	—	—	15	Self
TM37	Sandstorm	Rock	Status	—	—	10	Both Sides
TM39	Rock Tomb	Rock	Physical	60	95	15	Normal
TM41	Torment	Dark	Status	—	100	15	Normal
TM42	Facade	Normal	Physical	70	100	20	Normal
TM44	Rest	Psychic	Status	—	—	10	Self
TM45	Attract	Normal	Status	—	100	15	Normal
TM48	Round	Normal	Special	60	100	15	Normal
TM64	Explosion	Normal	Physical	250	100	5	Adjacent
TM66	Payback	Dark	Physical	50	100	10	Normal
TM69	Rock Polish	Rock	Status	—	—	20	Self
TM71	Stone Edge	Rock	Physical	100	80	5	Normal
TM74	Gyro Ball	Steel	Physical	—	100	5	Normal
TM77	Psych Up	Normal	Status	—	—	10	Normal
TM78	Bulldoze	Ground	Physical	60	100	20	Adjacent
TM80	Rock Slide	Rock	Physical	75	90	10	Many Others
TM82	Dragon Tail	Dragon	Physical	60	90	10	Normal
TM87	Swagger	Normal	Status	—	90	15	Normal
TM88	Sleep Talk	Normal	Status	—	—	10	Self
TM90	Substitute	Normal	Status	—	—	10	Self
TM91	Flash Cannon	Steel	Special	80	100	10	Normal
TM94	Secret Power	Normal	Physical	70	100	20	Normal
TM96	Nature Power	Normal	Status	—	—	20	Normal
TM100	Confide	Normal	Status	—	—	20	Normal
HM04	Strength	Normal	Physical	80	100	15	Normal
HM06	Rock Smash	Fighting	Physical	40	100	15	Normal

MOVES LEARNED IN EXCHANGE FOR BP

Name	Type	Kind	Pow.	Acc.	PP	Range
Iron Head	Steel	Physical	80	100	15	Normal
Block	Normal	Status	—	—	5	Normal
Earth Power	Ground	Special	90	100	10	Normal
Dragon Pulse	Dragon	Special	85	100	10	Normal
Iron Tail	Steel	Physical	100	75	15	Normal
Bind	Normal	Physical	15	85	20	Normal
Snore	Normal	Special	50	100	15	Normal
Stealth Rock	Rock	Status	—	—	20	Other Side

MOVES TAUGHT BY PEOPLE

Name	Type	Kind	Pow.	Acc.	PP	Range

EGG MOVES

Name	Type	Kind	Pow.	Acc.	PP	Range
Flail	Normal	Physical	—	100	15	Normal
Block	Normal	Status	—	—	5	Normal
Defense Curl	Normal	Status	—	—	40	Self
Rollout	Rock	Physical	30	90	20	Normal
Rock Blast	Rock	Physical	25	90	10	Normal
Rock Climb	Normal	Physical	90	85	20	Normal
Heavy Slam	Steel	Physical	—	100	10	Normal
Stealth Rock	Rock	Status	—	—	20	Other Side
Rototiller	Ground	Status	—	—	10	Adjacent

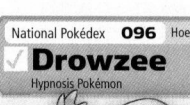

National Pokédex **096** Hoenn Pokédex —

Drowzee

Hypnosis Pokémon

Psychic

HEIGHT: 3'03" WEIGHT: 71.4 lbs.

Same form for ♂ / ♀

Ω If your nose becomes itchy while you are sleeping, it's a sure sign that one of these Pokémon is standing above your pillow and trying to eat your dream through your nostrils.

α If your nose becomes itchy while you are sleeping, it's a sure sign that one of these Pokémon is standing above your pillow and trying to eat your dream through your nostrils.

ABILITIES
Insomnia
Forewarn

HIDDEN ABILITY
Inner Focus

EGG GROUPS
Human-Like

STAT GROWTH RATES
HP
Attack
Defense
Sp. Atk
Sp. Def
Speed

ITEMS SOMETIMES HELD BY WILD POKÉMON
—

EVOLUTION

MAIN WAY TO REGISTER IN THE NATIONAL POKÉDEX

Leave a Hypno at a Pokémon Day Care, then hatch the Pokémon Egg that is found.

Damage taken in normal battles

Type		Type	
Normal	×1	Flying	×1
Fire	×1	Psychic	×0.5
Water	×1	Bug	×2
Grass	×1	Rock	×1
Electric	×1	Ghost	×2
Ice	×1	Dragon	×1
Fighting	×0.5	Dark	×2
Poison	×1	Steel	×1
Ground	×1	Fairy	×1

Damage taken in Inverse battles

Type		Type	
Normal	×1	Flying	×1
Fire	×1	Psychic	×2
Water	×1	Bug	×0.5
Grass	×1	Rock	×1
Electric	×1	Ghost	×0.5
Ice	×1	Dragon	×1
Fighting	×2	Dark	×0.5
Poison	×1	Steel	×1
Ground	×1	Fairy	×1

Can be used in
Inverse Battle
Battle Institute
Battle Maison
Random Matchup (Free Battle)
Random Matchup (Others)

LEVEL-UP MOVES

Lv.	Name	Type	Kind	Pow.	Acc.	PP	Range
1	Pound	Normal	Physical	40	100	35	Normal
1	Hypnosis	Psychic	Status	—	60	20	Normal
5	Disable	Normal	Status	—	100	20	Normal
9	Confusion	Psychic	Special	50	100	25	Normal
13	Headbutt	Normal	Physical	70	100	15	Normal
17	Poison Gas	Poison	Status	—	90	40	Many Others
21	Meditate	Psychic	Status	—	—	40	Self
25	Psybeam	Psychic	Special	65	100	20	Normal
29	Headbutt	Normal	Physical	70	100	15	Normal
33	Psych Up	Normal	Status	—	—	10	Normal
37	Synchronoise	Psychic	Special	120	100	10	Adjacent
41	Zen Headbutt	Psychic	Physical	80	90	15	Normal
45	Swagger	Normal	Status	—	90	15	Normal
49	Psychic	Psychic	Special	90	100	10	Normal
53	Nasty Plot	Dark	Status	—	—	20	Self
57	Psyshock	Psychic	Special	80	100	10	Normal
61	Future Sight	Psychic	Special	120	100	10	Normal

TM & HM MOVES

No.	Name	Type	Kind	Pow.	Acc.	PP	Range
TM03	Psyshock	Psychic	Special	80	100	10	Normal
TM04	Calm Mind	Psychic	Status	—	—	20	Self
TM06	Toxic	Poison	Status	—	90	10	Normal
TM10	Hidden Power	Normal	Special	60	100	15	Normal
TM11	Sunny Day	Fire	Status	—	—	5	Both Sides
TM12	Taunt	Dark	Status	—	100	20	Normal
TM16	Light Screen	Psychic	Status	—	—	30	Your Side
TM17	Protect	Normal	Status	—	—	10	Self
TM18	Rain Dance	Water	Status	—	—	5	Both Sides
TM20	Safeguard	Normal	Status	—	—	25	Your Side
TM21	Frustration	Normal	Physical	—	100	20	Normal
TM27	Return	Normal	Physical	—	100	20	Normal
TM29	Psychic	Psychic	Special	90	100	10	Normal
TM30	Shadow Ball	Ghost	Special	80	100	15	Normal
TM31	Brick Break	Fighting	Physical	75	100	15	Normal
TM32	Double Team	Normal	Status	—	—	15	Self
TM33	Reflect	Psychic	Status	—	—	20	Your Side
TM41	Torment	Dark	Status	—	100	15	Normal
TM42	Facade	Normal	Physical	70	100	20	Normal
TM44	Rest	Psychic	Status	—	—	10	Self
TM45	Attract	Normal	Status	—	100	15	Normal
TM46	Thief	Dark	Physical	60	100	25	Normal
TM47	Low Sweep	Fighting	Physical	65	100	20	Normal
TM48	Round	Normal	Special	60	100	15	Normal
TM56	Fling	Dark	Physical	—	100	10	Normal
TM70	Flash	Normal	Status	—	100	20	Normal
TM73	Thunder Wave	Electric	Status	—	100	20	Normal
TM77	Psych Up	Normal	Status	—	—	10	Normal
TM85	Dream Eater	Psychic	Special	100	100	15	Normal
TM86	Grass Knot	Grass	Special	—	100	20	Normal
TM87	Swagger	Normal	Status	—	90	15	Normal
TM88	Sleep Talk	Normal	Status	—	—	10	Self
TM90	Substitute	Normal	Status	—	—	10	Self
TM92	Trick Room	Psychic	Status	—	—	5	Both Sides
TM94	Secret Power	Normal	Physical	70	100	20	Normal
TM98	Power-Up Punch	Fighting	Physical	40	100	20	Normal
TM99	Dazzling Gleam	Fairy	Special	80	100	10	Many Others
TM100	Confide	Normal	Status	—	—	20	Normal

MOVES LEARNED IN EXCHANGE FOR BP

Name	Type	Kind	Pow.	Acc.	PP	Range
Signal Beam	Bug	Special	75	100	15	Normal
Low Kick	Fighting	Physical	—	100	20	Normal
Thunder Punch	Electric	Physical	75	100	15	Normal
Fire Punch	Fire	Physical	75	100	15	Normal
Ice Punch	Ice	Physical	75	100	15	Normal
Magic Coat	Psychic	Status	—	—	15	Self
Foul Play	Dark	Physical	95	100	15	Normal
Zen Headbutt	Psychic	Physical	80	90	15	Normal
Snore	Normal	Special	50	100	15	Normal
Role Play	Psychic	Status	—	—	10	Normal
Drain Punch	Fighting	Physical	75	100	10	Normal
Focus Punch	Fighting	Physical	150	100	20	Normal
Trick	Psychic	Status	—	100	10	Normal
Magic Room	Psychic	Status	—	—	10	Both Sides
Recycle	Normal	Status	—	—	10	Self
Snatch	Dark	Status	—	—	10	Self
Skill Swap	Psychic	Status	—	—	10	Normal

MOVES TAUGHT BY PEOPLE

Name	Type	Kind	Pow.	Acc.	PP	Range

EGG MOVES

Name	Type	Kind	Pow.	Acc.	PP	Range
Barrier	Psychic	Status	—	—	20	Self
Assist	Normal	Status	—	—	20	Self
Role Play	Psychic	Status	—	—	10	Normal
Fire Punch	Fire	Physical	75	100	15	Normal
Thunder Punch	Electric	Physical	75	100	15	Normal
Ice Punch	Ice	Physical	75	100	15	Normal
Nasty Plot	Dark	Status	—	—	20	Self
Flatter	Dark	Status	—	100	15	Normal
Psycho Cut	Psychic	Physical	70	100	20	Normal
Guard Swap	Psychic	Status	—	—	10	Normal
Secret Power	Normal	Physical	70	100	20	Normal
Skill Swap	Psychic	Status	—	—	10	Normal

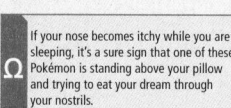

National Pokédex **097** Hoenn Pokédex —

Hypno

Hypnosis Pokémon

Psychic

HEIGHT: 5'03" WEIGHT: 166.7 lbs.

The fur around the male's neck is shorter.
The fur around the female's neck is longer.

♂ ♀

Ω Hypno holds a pendulum in its hand. The arcing movement and glitter of the pendulum lull the foe into a deep state of hypnosis. While this Pokémon searches for prey, it polishes the pendulum.

α Hypno holds a pendulum in its hand. The arcing movement and glitter of the pendulum lull the foe into a deep state of hypnosis. While this Pokémon searches for prey, it polishes the pendulum.

ABILITIES
Insomnia
Forewarn

HIDDEN ABILITY
Inner Focus

EGG GROUPS
Human-Like

STAT GROWTH RATES

HP	■■■
Attack	■■■■
Defense	■■■
Sp. Atk	■■■■
Sp. Def	■■■■■
Speed	■■■■

ITEMS SOMETIMES HELD BY WILD POKÉMON
—

EVOLUTION

Drowzee → Hypno

MAIN WAY TO REGISTER IN THE NATIONAL POKÉDEX

Catch on Route 121. Appears as a hidden Pokémon after you battle Groudon or Kyogre.

Damage taken in normal battles

Type		Type	
Normal	×1	Flying	×1
Fire	×1	Psychic	×0.5
Water	×1	Bug	×2
Grass	×1	Rock	×1
Electric	×1	Ghost	×2
Ice	×1	Dragon	×1
Fighting	×0.5	Dark	×2
Poison	×1	Steel	×1
Ground	×1	Fairy	×1

Damage taken in Inverse battles

Type		Type	
Normal	×1	Flying	×1
Fire	×1	Psychic	×2
Water	×1	Bug	×0.5
Grass	×1	Rock	×1
Electric	×1	Ghost	×0.5
Ice	×1	Dragon	×1
Fighting	×2	Dark	×0.5
Poison	×1	Steel	×1
Ground	×1	Fairy	×1

Can be used in
Inverse Battle
Battle Institute
Battle Maison
Random Matchup (Free Battle)
Random Matchup (Others)

LEVEL-UP MOVES

Lv.	Name	Type	Kind	Pow.	Acc.	PP	Range
1	Future Sight	Psychic	Special	120	100	10	Normal
1	Nasty Plot	Dark	Status	—	—	20	Self
1	Nightmare	Ghost	Status	—	100	15	Normal
1	Switcheroo	Dark	Status	—	100	10	Normal
1	Pound	Normal	Physical	40	100	35	Normal
1	Hypnosis	Psychic	Status	—	60	20	Normal
1	Disable	Normal	Status	—	100	20	Normal
1	Confusion	Psychic	Special	50	100	25	Normal
5	Disable	Normal	Status	—	100	20	Normal
9	Confusion	Psychic	Special	50	100	25	Normal
13	Headbutt	Normal	Physical	70	100	15	Normal
17	Poison Gas	Poison	Status	—	90	40	Many Others
21	Meditate	Psychic	Status	—	—	40	Self
25	Psybeam	Psychic	Special	65	100	20	Normal
29	Headbutt	Normal	Physical	70	100	15	Normal
33	Psych Up	Normal	Status	—	—	10	Normal
37	Synchronoise	Psychic	Special	120	100	10	Adjacent
41	Zen Headbutt	Psychic	Physical	80	90	15	Normal
45	Swagger	Normal	Status	—	90	15	Normal
49	Psychic	Psychic	Special	90	100	10	Normal
53	Nasty Plot	Dark	Status	—	—	20	Self
57	Psyshock	Psychic	Special	80	100	10	Normal
61	Future Sight	Psychic	Special	120	100	10	Normal

TM & HM MOVES

No.	Name	Type	Kind	Pow.	Acc.	PP	Range
TM03	Psyshock	Psychic	Special	80	100	10	Normal
TM04	Calm Mind	Psychic	Status	—	—	20	Self
TM06	Toxic	Poison	Status	—	90	10	Normal
TM10	Hidden Power	Normal	Special	60	100	15	Normal
TM11	Sunny Day	Fire	Status	—	—	5	Both Sides
TM12	Taunt	Dark	Status	—	100	20	Normal
TM15	Hyper Beam	Normal	Special	150	90	5	Normal
TM16	Light Screen	Psychic	Status	—	—	30	Your Side
TM17	Protect	Normal	Status	—	—	10	Self
TM18	Rain Dance	Water	Status	—	—	5	Both Sides
TM20	Safeguard	Normal	Status	—	—	25	Your Side
TM21	Frustration	Normal	Physical	—	100	20	Normal
TM27	Return	Normal	Physical	—	100	20	Normal
TM29	Psychic	Psychic	Special	90	100	10	Normal
TM30	Shadow Ball	Ghost	Special	80	100	15	Normal
TM31	Brick Break	Fighting	Physical	75	100	15	Normal
TM32	Double Team	Normal	Status	—	—	15	Self
TM33	Reflect	Psychic	Status	—	—	20	Your Side
TM41	Torment	Dark	Status	—	100	15	Normal
TM42	Facade	Normal	Physical	70	100	20	Normal
TM44	Rest	Psychic	Status	—	—	10	Self
TM45	Attract	Normal	Status	—	100	15	Normal
TM46	Thief	Dark	Physical	60	100	25	Normal
TM47	Low Sweep	Fighting	Physical	65	100	20	Normal
TM48	Round	Normal	Special	60	100	15	Normal
TM52	Focus Blast	Fighting	Special	120	70	5	Normal
TM56	Fling	Dark	Physical	—	100	10	Normal
TM68	Giga Impact	Normal	Physical	150	90	5	Normal
TM70	Flash	Normal	Status	—	100	20	Normal
TM73	Thunder Wave	Electric	Status	—	100	20	Normal
TM77	Psych Up	Normal	Status	—	—	10	Normal
TM85	Dream Eater	Psychic	Special	100	100	15	Normal
TM86	Grass Knot	Grass	Special	—	100	20	Normal
TM87	Swagger	Normal	Status	—	90	15	Normal
TM88	Sleep Talk	Normal	Status	—	—	10	Self
TM90	Substitute	Normal	Status	—	—	10	Self
TM92	Trick Room	Psychic	Status	—	—	5	Both Sides
TM94	Secret Power	Normal	Physical	70	100	20	Normal
TM98	Power-Up Punch	Fighting	Physical	40	100	20	Normal
TM99	Dazzling Gleam	Fairy	Special	80	100	10	Many Others
TM100	Confide	Normal	Status	—	—	20	Normal

MOVES LEARNED IN EXCHANGE FOR BP

Name	Type	Kind	Pow.	Acc.	PP	Range
Signal Beam	Bug	Special	75	100	15	Normal
Low Kick	Fighting	Physical	—	100	20	Normal
Thunder Punch	Electric	Physical	75	100	15	Normal
Fire Punch	Fire	Physical	75	100	15	Normal
Ice Punch	Ice	Physical	75	100	15	Normal
Magic Coat	Psychic	Status	—	—	15	Self
Foul Play	Dark	Physical	95	100	15	Normal
Zen Headbutt	Psychic	Physical	80	90	15	Normal
Snore	Normal	Special	50	100	15	Normal
Role Play	Psychic	Status	—	—	10	Normal
Drain Punch	Fighting	Physical	75	100	10	Normal
Focus Punch	Fighting	Physical	150	100	20	Normal
Trick	Psychic	Status	—	100	10	Normal
Magic Room	Psychic	Status	—	—	10	Both Sides
Recycle	Normal	Status	—	—	10	Self
Snatch	Dark	Status	—	—	10	Self
Skill Swap	Psychic	Status	—	—	10	Normal

MOVES TAUGHT BY PEOPLE

Name	Type	Kind	Pow.	Acc.	PP	Range

National Pokédex **098** Hoenn Pokédex —

Krabby

River Crab Pokémon

Water

HEIGHT: 1'04" WEIGHT: 14.3 lbs.

Same form for ♂ / ♀

Ω Krabby live on beaches, burrowed inside holes dug into the sand. On sandy beaches with little in the way of food, these Pokémon can be seen squabbling with each other over territory.

α Krabby live on beaches, burrowed inside holes dug into the sand. On sandy beaches with little in the way of food, these Pokémon can be seen squabbling with each other over territory.

ABILITIES
Hyper Cutter
Shell Armor

HIDDEN ABILITY
Sheer Force

EGG GROUPS
Water 3

STAT GROWTH RATES

HP	■■
Attack	■■■■■
Defense	■■■■
Sp. Atk	■
Sp. Def	■
Speed	■■■

ITEMS SOMETIMES HELD BY WILD POKÉMON
—

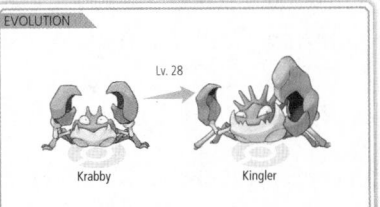

EVOLUTION

Lv. 28

Krabby → Kingler

MAIN WAY TO REGISTER IN THE NATIONAL POKÉDEX

Catch on the water surface on Route 105. Appears as a hidden Pokémon after you battle Groudon or Kyogre.

Damage taken in normal battles

Type		Type	
Normal	×1	Flying	×1
Fire	×0.5	Psychic	×1
Water	×0.5	Bug	×1
Grass	×2	Rock	×1
Electric	×2	Ghost	×1
Ice	×0.5	Dragon	×1
Fighting	×1	Dark	×1
Poison	×1	Steel	×0.5
Ground	×1	Fairy	×1

Damage taken in Inverse battles

Type		Type	
Normal	×1	Flying	×1
Fire	×2	Psychic	×1
Water	×2	Bug	×1
Grass	×0.5	Rock	×1
Electric	×0.5	Ghost	×1
Ice	×2	Dragon	×1
Fighting	×1	Dark	×1
Poison	×1	Steel	×2
Ground	×1	Fairy	×1

Can be used in
Inverse Battle
Battle Institute
Battle Maison
Random Matchup (Free Battle)
Random Matchup (Others)

LEVEL-UP MOVES

Lv.	Name	Type	Kind	Pow.	Acc.	PP	Range
1	Mud Sport	Ground	Status	—	—	15	Both Sides
1	Bubble	Water	Special	40	100	30	Many Others
5	Vice Grip	Normal	Physical	55	100	30	Normal
9	Leer	Normal	Status	—	100	30	Many Others
11	Harden	Normal	Status	—	—	30	Self
15	Bubble Beam	Water	Special	65	100	20	Normal
19	Mud Shot	Ground	Special	55	95	15	Normal
21	Metal Claw	Steel	Physical	50	95	35	Normal
25	Stomp	Normal	Physical	65	100	20	Normal
29	Protect	Normal	Status	—	—	10	Self
31	Guillotine	Normal	Physical	—	30	5	Normal
35	Slam	Normal	Physical	80	75	20	Normal
39	Brine	Water	Special	65	100	10	Normal
41	Crabhammer	Water	Physical	100	90	10	Normal
45	Flail	Normal	Physical	—	100	15	Normal

TM & HM MOVES

No.	Name	Type	Kind	Pow.	Acc.	PP	Range
TM01	Hone Claws	Dark	Status	—	—	15	Self
TM06	Toxic	Poison	Status	—	90	10	Normal
TM07	Hail	Ice	Status	—	—	10	Both Sides
TM10	Hidden Power	Normal	Special	60	100	15	Normal
TM13	Ice Beam	Ice	Special	90	100	10	Normal
TM14	Blizzard	Ice	Special	110	70	5	Many Others
TM17	Protect	Normal	Status	—	—	10	Self
TM18	Rain Dance	Water	Status	—	—	5	Both Sides
TM21	Frustration	Normal	Physical	—	100	20	Normal
TM27	Return	Normal	Physical	—	100	20	Normal
TM28	Dig	Ground	Physical	80	100	10	Normal
TM31	Brick Break	Fighting	Physical	75	100	15	Normal
TM32	Double Team	Normal	Status	—	—	15	Self
TM39	Rock Tomb	Rock	Physical	60	95	15	Normal
TM42	Facade	Normal	Physical	70	100	20	Normal
TM44	Rest	Psychic	Status	—	—	10	Self
TM45	Attract	Normal	Status	—	100	15	Normal
TM46	Thief	Dark	Physical	60	100	25	Normal
TM48	Round	Normal	Special	60	100	15	Normal
TM54	False Swipe	Normal	Physical	40	100	40	Normal
TM55	Scald	Water	Special	80	100	15	Normal
TM56	Fling	Dark	Physical	—	100	10	Normal
TM75	Swords Dance	Normal	Status	—	—	20	Self
TM80	Rock Slide	Rock	Physical	75	90	10	Many Others
TM81	X-Scissor	Bug	Physical	80	100	15	Normal
TM87	Swagger	Normal	Status	—	90	15	Normal
TM88	Sleep Talk	Normal	Status	—	—	10	Self
TM90	Substitute	Normal	Status	—	—	10	Self
TM94	Secret Power	Normal	Physical	70	100	20	Normal
TM100	Confide	Normal	Status	—	—	20	Normal
HM01	Cut	Normal	Physical	50	95	30	Normal
HM03	Surf	Water	Special	90	100	15	Adjacent
HM04	Strength	Normal	Physical	80	100	15	Normal
HM06	Rock Smash	Fighting	Physical	40	100	15	Normal
HM07	Dive	Water	Physical	80	100	10	Normal

MOVES LEARNED IN EXCHANGE FOR BP

Name	Type	Kind	Pow.	Acc.	PP	Range
Iron Defense	Steel	Status	—	—	15	Self
Superpower	Fighting	Physical	120	100	5	Normal
Icy Wind	Ice	Special	55	95	15	Many Others
Snore	Normal	Special	50	100	15	Normal
Knock Off	Dark	Physical	65	100	20	Normal
Water Pulse	Water	Special	60	100	20	Normal

MOVES TAUGHT BY PEOPLE

Name	Type	Kind	Pow.	Acc.	PP	Range

EGG MOVES

Name	Type	Kind	Pow.	Acc.	PP	Range
Haze	Ice	Status	—	—	30	Both Sides
Amnesia	Psychic	Status	—	—	20	Self
Flail	Normal	Physical	—	100	15	Normal
Slam	Normal	Physical	80	75	20	Normal
Knock Off	Dark	Physical	65	100	20	Normal
Tickle	Normal	Status	—	100	20	Normal
Ancient Power	Rock	Special	60	100	5	Normal
Agility	Psychic	Status	—	—	30	Self
Endure	Normal	Status	—	—	10	Self
Chip Away	Normal	Physical	70	100	20	Normal
Bide	Normal	Physical	—	—	10	Self
Ally Switch	Psychic	Status	—	—	15	Self

National Pokédex **099** Hoenn Pokédex –

Kingler

Pincer Pokémon

Water

HEIGHT: 4'03" WEIGHT: 132.3 lbs.

Same form for ♂ / ♀

Ω Kingler has an enormous, oversized claw. It waves this huge claw in the air to communicate with others. However, because the claw is so heavy, the Pokémon quickly tires.

α Kingler has an enormous, oversized claw. It waves this huge claw in the air to communicate with others. However, because the claw is so heavy, the Pokémon quickly tires.

ABILITIES
Hyper Cutter
Shell Armor

HIDDEN ABILITY
Sheer Force

EGG GROUPS
Water 3

STAT GROWTH RATES
HP, Attack, Defense, Sp. Atk, Sp. Def, Speed

ITEMS SOMETIMES HELD BY WILD POKÉMON
—

EVOLUTION

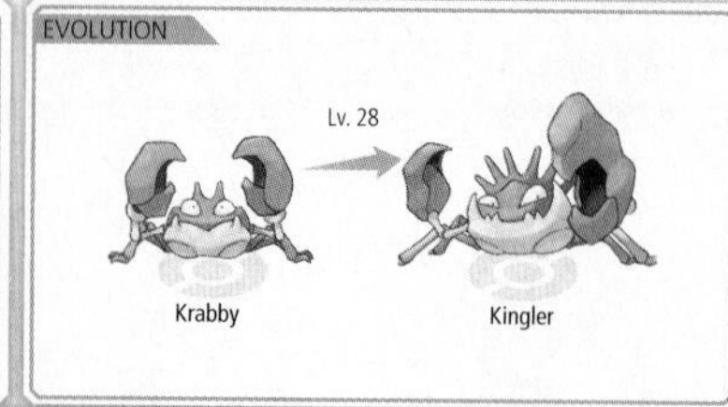

MAIN WAY TO REGISTER IN THE NATIONAL POKÉDEX

Level up Krabby to Lv. 28.

Damage taken in normal battles

Type	×	Type	×
Normal	×1	Flying	×1
Fire	×0.5	Psychic	×1
Water	×0.5	Bug	×1
Grass	×2	Rock	×1
Electric	×2	Ghost	×1
Ice	×0.5	Dragon	×1
Fighting	×1	Dark	×1
Poison	×1	Steel	×0.5
Ground	×1	Fairy	×1

Damage taken in Inverse battles

Type	×	Type	×
Normal	×1	Flying	×1
Fire	×2	Psychic	×1
Water	×2	Bug	×1
Grass	×0.5	Rock	×1
Electric	×0.5	Ghost	×1
Ice	×2	Dragon	×1
Fighting	×1	Dark	×1
Poison	×1	Steel	×2
Ground	×1	Fairy	×1

Can be used in
Inverse Battle
Battle Institute
Battle Maison
Random Matchup (Free Battle)
Random Matchup (Others)

LEVEL-UP MOVES

Lv.	Name	Type	Kind	Pow.	Acc.	PP	Range
1	Wide Guard	Rock	Status	—	—	10	Your Side
1	Mud Sport	Ground	Status	—	—	15	Both Sides
1	Bubble	Water	Special	40	100	30	Many Others
1	Vice Grip	Normal	Physical	55	100	30	Normal
1	Leer	Normal	Status	—	100	30	Many Others
5	Vice Grip	Normal	Physical	55	100	30	Normal
9	Leer	Normal	Status	—	100	30	Many Others
11	Harden	Normal	Status	—	—	30	Self
15	Bubble Beam	Water	Special	65	100	20	Normal
19	Mud Shot	Ground	Special	55	95	15	Normal
21	Metal Claw	Steel	Physical	50	95	35	Normal
25	Stomp	Normal	Physical	65	100	20	Normal
32	Protect	Normal	Status	—	—	10	Self
37	Guillotine	Normal	Physical	—	30	5	Normal
44	Slam	Normal	Physical	80	75	20	Normal
51	Brine	Water	Special	65	100	10	Normal
56	Crabhammer	Water	Physical	100	90	10	Normal
63	Flail	Normal	Physical	—	100	15	Normal

TM & HM MOVES

No.	Name	Type	Kind	Pow.	Acc.	PP	Range
TM01	Hone Claws	Dark	Status	—	—	15	Self
TM06	Toxic	Poison	Status	—	90	10	Normal
TM07	Hail	Ice	Status	—	—	10	Both Sides
TM10	Hidden Power	Normal	Special	60	100	15	Normal
TM13	Ice Beam	Ice	Special	90	100	10	Normal
TM14	Blizzard	Ice	Special	110	70	5	Many Others
TM15	Hyper Beam	Normal	Special	150	90	5	Normal
TM17	Protect	Normal	Status	—	—	10	Self
TM18	Rain Dance	Water	Status	—	—	5	Both Sides
TM21	Frustration	Normal	Physical	—	100	20	Normal
TM27	Return	Normal	Physical	—	100	20	Normal
TM28	Dig	Ground	Physical	80	100	10	Normal
TM31	Brick Break	Fighting	Physical	75	100	15	Normal
TM32	Double Team	Normal	Status	—	—	15	Self
TM39	Rock Tomb	Rock	Physical	60	95	15	Normal
TM42	Facade	Normal	Physical	70	100	20	Normal
TM44	Rest	Psychic	Status	—	—	10	Self
TM45	Attract	Normal	Status	—	100	15	Normal
TM46	Thief	Dark	Physical	60	100	25	Normal
TM48	Round	Normal	Special	60	100	15	Normal
TM54	False Swipe	Normal	Physical	40	100	40	Normal
TM55	Scald	Water	Special	80	100	15	Normal
TM56	Fling	Dark	Physical	—	100	10	Normal
TM60	Quash	Dark	Status	—	100	15	Normal
TM68	Giga Impact	Normal	Physical	150	90	5	Normal
TM75	Swords Dance	Normal	Status	—	—	20	Self
TM80	Rock Slide	Rock	Physical	75	90	10	Many Others
TM81	X-Scissor	Bug	Physical	80	100	15	Normal
TM87	Swagger	Normal	Status	—	90	15	Normal
TM88	Sleep Talk	Normal	Status	—	—	10	Self
TM90	Substitute	Normal	Status	—	—	10	Self
TM94	Secret Power	Normal	Physical	70	100	20	Normal
TM100	Confide	Normal	Status	—	—	20	Normal
HM01	Cut	Normal	Physical	50	95	30	Normal
HM03	Surf	Water	Special	90	100	15	Adjacent
HM04	Strength	Normal	Physical	80	100	15	Normal
HM06	Rock Smash	Fighting	Physical	40	100	15	Normal
HM07	Dive	Water	Physical	80	100	10	Normal

MOVES LEARNED IN EXCHANGE FOR BP

Name	Type	Kind	Pow.	Acc.	PP	Range
Iron Defense	Steel	Status	—	—	15	Self
Superpower	Fighting	Physical	120	100	5	Normal
Icy Wind	Ice	Special	55	95	15	Many Others
Snore	Normal	Special	50	100	15	Normal
Knock Off	Dark	Physical	65	100	20	Normal
Water Pulse	Water	Special	60	100	20	Normal

MOVES TAUGHT BY PEOPLE

Name	Type	Kind	Pow.	Acc.	PP	Range

National Pokédex **100** Hoenn Pokédex **087**

Voltorb

Ball Pokémon

Electric

HEIGHT: 1'08" WEIGHT: 22.9 lbs.

Gender unknown

Ω Voltorb was first sighted at a company that manufactures Poké Balls. The link between that sighting and the fact that this Pokémon looks very similar to a Poké Ball remains a mystery.

α Voltorb is extremely sensitive—it explodes at the slightest of shocks. It is rumored that it was first created when a Poké Ball was exposed to a powerful pulse of energy.

ABILITIES
Soundproof
Static

HIDDEN ABILITY
Aftermath

EGG GROUPS
Mineral

STAT GROWTH RATES
HP, Attack, Defense, Sp. Atk, Sp. Def, Speed

ITEMS SOMETIMES HELD BY WILD POKÉMON
—

EVOLUTION

Voltorb → Lv. 30 → Electrode

MAIN WAY TO REGISTER IN THE NATIONAL POKÉDEX

Catch in New Mauville.

Damage taken in normal battles

Type	×	Type	×
Normal	×1	Flying	×0.5
Fire	×1	Psychic	×1
Water	×1	Bug	×1
Grass	×1	Rock	×1
Electric	×0.5	Ghost	×1
Ice	×1	Dragon	×1
Fighting	×1	Dark	×1
Poison	×1	Steel	×0.5
Ground	×2	Fairy	×1

Damage taken in Inverse battles

Type	×	Type	×
Normal	×1	Flying	×2
Fire	×1	Psychic	×1
Water	×1	Bug	×1
Grass	×1	Rock	×1
Electric	×2	Ghost	×1
Ice	×1	Dragon	×1
Fighting	×1	Dark	×1
Poison	×1	Steel	×2
Ground	×0.5	Fairy	×1

Can be used in
Inverse Battle
Battle Institute
Battle Maison
Random Matchup (Free Battle)
Random Matchup (Others)

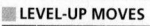

LEVEL-UP MOVES

Lv.	Name	Type	Kind	Pow.	Acc.	PP	Range
1	Charge	Electric	Status	—	—	20	Self
1	Tackle	Normal	Physical	50	100	35	Normal
4	Sonic Boom	Normal	Special	—	90	20	Normal
6	Eerie Impulse	Electric	Status	—	100	15	Normal
9	Spark	Electric	Physical	65	100	20	Normal
11	Rollout	Rock	Physical	30	90	20	Normal
13	Screech	Normal	Status	—	85	40	Normal
16	Charge Beam	Electric	Special	50	90	10	Normal
20	Swift	Normal	Special	60	—	20	Many Others
22	Electro Ball	Electric	Special	—	100	10	Normal
26	Self-Destruct	Normal	Physical	200	100	5	Adjacent
29	Light Screen	Psychic	Status	—	—	30	Your Side
34	Magnet Rise	Electric	Status	—	—	10	Self
37	Discharge	Electric	Special	80	100	15	Adjacent
41	Explosion	Normal	Physical	250	100	5	Adjacent
46	Gyro Ball	Steel	Physical	—	100	5	Normal
48	Mirror Coat	Psychic	Special	—	100	20	Varies

TM & HM MOVES

No.	Name	Type	Kind	Pow.	Acc.	PP	Range
TM06	Toxic	Poison	Status	—	90	10	Normal
TM10	Hidden Power	Normal	Special	60	100	15	Normal
TM12	Taunt	Dark	Status	—	100	20	Normal
TM16	Light Screen	Psychic	Status	—	—	30	Your Side
TM17	Protect	Normal	Status	—	—	10	Self
TM18	Rain Dance	Water	Status	—	—	5	Both Sides
TM21	Frustration	Normal	Physical	—	100	20	Normal
TM24	Thunderbolt	Electric	Special	90	100	15	Normal
TM25	Thunder	Electric	Special	110	70	10	Normal
TM27	Return	Normal	Physical	—	100	20	Normal
TM32	Double Team	Normal	Status	—	—	15	Self
TM41	Torment	Dark	Status	—	100	15	Normal
TM42	Facade	Normal	Physical	70	100	20	Normal
TM44	Rest	Psychic	Status	—	—	10	Self
TM46	Thief	Dark	Physical	60	100	25	Normal
TM48	Round	Normal	Special	60	100	15	Normal
TM57	Charge Beam	Electric	Special	50	90	10	Normal
TM64	Explosion	Normal	Physical	250	100	5	Adjacent
TM70	Flash	Normal	Status	—	100	20	Normal
TM72	Volt Switch	Electric	Special	70	100	20	Normal
TM73	Thunder Wave	Electric	Status	—	100	20	Normal
TM74	Gyro Ball	Steel	Physical	—	100	5	Normal
TM87	Swagger	Normal	Status	—	90	15	Normal
TM88	Sleep Talk	Normal	Status	—	—	10	Self
TM90	Substitute	Normal	Status	—	—	10	Self
TM93	Wild Charge	Electric	Physical	90	100	15	Normal
TM94	Secret Power	Normal	Physical	70	100	20	Normal
TM100	Confide	Normal	Status	—	—	20	Normal

MOVES LEARNED IN EXCHANGE FOR BP

Name	Type	Kind	Pow.	Acc.	PP	Range
Signal Beam	Bug	Special	75	100	15	Normal
Magic Coat	Psychic	Status	—	—	15	Self
Foul Play	Dark	Physical	95	100	15	Normal
Magnet Rise	Electric	Status	—	—	10	Self
Snore	Normal	Special	50	100	15	Normal
Shock Wave	Electric	Special	60	—	20	Normal

MOVES TAUGHT BY PEOPLE

Name	Type	Kind	Pow.	Acc.	PP	Range

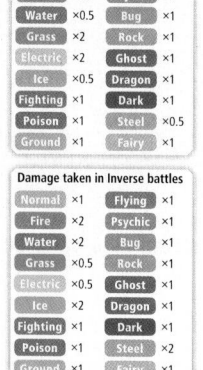

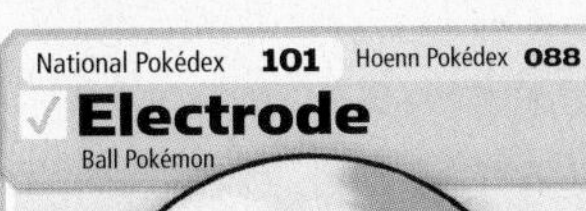

National Pokédex **101** Hoenn Pokédex **088**

Electrode

Ball Pokémon

Electric

HEIGHT: 3'11" WEIGHT: 146.8 lbs.
Gender unknown

Ω Electrode eats electricity in the atmosphere. On days when lightning strikes, you can see this Pokémon exploding all over the place from eating too much electricity.

α One of Electrode's characteristics is its attraction to electricity. It is a problematical Pokémon that congregates mostly at electrical power plants to feed on electricity that has just been generated.

ABILITIES
Soundproof
Static

HIDDEN ABILITY
Aftermath

EGG GROUPS
Mineral

ITEMS SOMETIMES HELD BY WILD POKÉMON
—

STAT GROWTH RATES
HP
Attack
Defense
Sp. Atk
Sp. Def
Speed

EVOLUTION

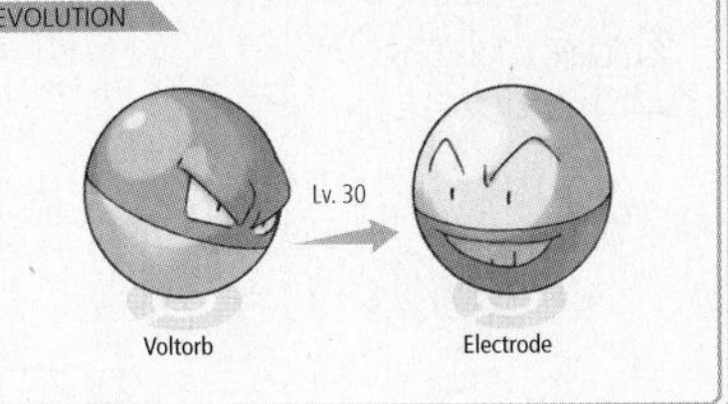

MAIN WAY TO REGISTER IN THE NATIONAL POKÉDEX

Level up Voltorb to Lv. 30.

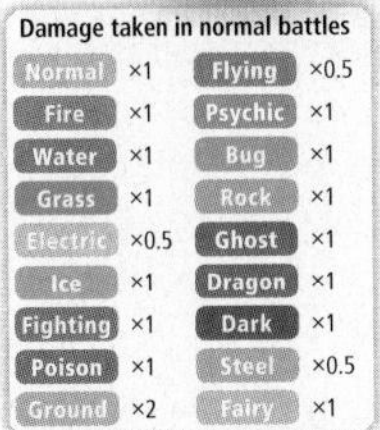

Damage taken in normal battles

Type		Type	
Normal	×1	Flying	×0.5
Fire	×1	Psychic	×1
Water	×1	Bug	×1
Grass	×1	Rock	×1
Electric	×0.5	Ghost	×1
Ice	×1	Dragon	×1
Fighting	×1	Dark	×1
Poison	×1	Steel	×0.5
Ground	×2	Fairy	×1

Damage taken in Inverse battles

Type		Type	
Normal	×1	Flying	×2
Fire	×1	Psychic	×1
Water	×1	Bug	×1
Grass	×1	Rock	×1
Electric	×2	Ghost	×1
Ice	×1	Dragon	×1
Fighting	×1	Dark	×1
Poison	×1	Steel	×2
Ground	×0.5	Fairy	×1

Can be used in
Inverse Battle
Battle Institute
Battle Maison
Random Matchup (Free Battle)
Random Matchup (Others)

LEVEL-UP MOVES

Lv.	Name	Type	Kind	Pow.	Acc.	PP	Range
1	Magnetic Flux	Electric	Status	—	—	20	Your Party
1	Charge	Electric	Status	—	—	20	Self
1	Tackle	Normal	Physical	50	100	35	Normal
1	Sonic Boom	Normal	Special	—	90	20	Normal
1	Spark	Electric	Physical	65	100	20	Normal
4	Sonic Boom	Normal	Special	—	90	20	Normal
6	Eerie Impulse	Electric	Status	—	100	15	Normal
9	Spark	Electric	Physical	65	100	20	Normal
11	Rollout	Rock	Physical	30	90	20	Normal
13	Screech	Normal	Status	—	85	40	Normal
16	Charge Beam	Electric	Special	50	90	10	Normal
20	Swift	Normal	Special	60	—	20	Many Others
22	Electro Ball	Electric	Special	—	100	10	Normal
26	Self-Destruct	Normal	Physical	200	100	5	Adjacent
29	Light Screen	Psychic	Status	—	—	30	Your Side
36	Magnet Rise	Electric	Status	—	—	10	Self
41	Discharge	Electric	Special	80	100	15	Adjacent
47	Explosion	Normal	Physical	250	100	5	Adjacent
54	Gyro Ball	Steel	Physical	—	100	5	Normal
58	Mirror Coat	Psychic	Special	—	100	20	Varies

TM & HM MOVES

No.	Name	Type	Kind	Pow.	Acc.	PP	Range
TM06	Toxic	Poison	Status	—	90	10	Normal
TM10	Hidden Power	Normal	Special	60	100	15	Normal
TM12	Taunt	Dark	Status	—	100	20	Normal
TM15	Hyper Beam	Normal	Special	150	90	5	Normal
TM16	Light Screen	Psychic	Status	—	—	30	Your Side
TM17	Protect	Normal	Status	—	—	10	Self
TM18	Rain Dance	Water	Status	—	—	5	Both Sides
TM21	Frustration	Normal	Physical	—	100	20	Normal
TM24	Thunderbolt	Electric	Special	90	100	15	Normal
TM25	Thunder	Electric	Special	110	70	10	Normal
TM27	Return	Normal	Physical	—	100	20	Normal
TM32	Double Team	Normal	Status	—	—	15	Self
TM41	Torment	Dark	Status	—	100	15	Normal
TM42	Facade	Normal	Physical	70	100	20	Normal
TM44	Rest	Psychic	Status	—	—	10	Self
TM46	Thief	Dark	Physical	60	100	25	Normal
TM48	Round	Normal	Special	60	100	15	Normal
TM57	Charge Beam	Electric	Special	50	90	10	Normal
TM64	Explosion	Normal	Physical	250	100	5	Adjacent
TM68	Giga Impact	Normal	Physical	150	90	5	Normal
TM70	Flash	Normal	Status	—	100	20	Normal
TM72	Volt Switch	Electric	Special	70	100	20	Normal
TM73	Thunder Wave	Electric	Status	—	100	20	Normal
TM74	Gyro Ball	Steel	Physical	—	100	5	Normal
TM87	Swagger	Normal	Status	—	90	15	Normal
TM88	Sleep Talk	Normal	Status	—	—	10	Self
TM90	Substitute	Normal	Status	—	—	10	Self
TM93	Wild Charge	Electric	Physical	90	100	15	Normal
TM94	Secret Power	Normal	Physical	70	100	20	Normal
TM100	Confide	Normal	Status	—	—	20	Normal

MOVES LEARNED IN EXCHANGE FOR BP

Name	Type	Kind	Pow.	Acc.	PP	Range
Signal Beam	Bug	Special	75	100	15	Normal
Magic Coat	Psychic	Status	—	—	15	Self
Foul Play	Dark	Physical	95	100	15	Normal
Magnet Rise	Electric	Status	—	—	10	Self
Snore	Normal	Special	50	100	15	Normal
Shock Wave	Electric	Special	60	—	20	Normal

MOVES TAUGHT BY PEOPLE

Name	Type	Kind	Pow.	Acc.	PP	Range

National Pokédex **102** Hoenn Pokédex **—**

Exeggcute

Egg Pokémon

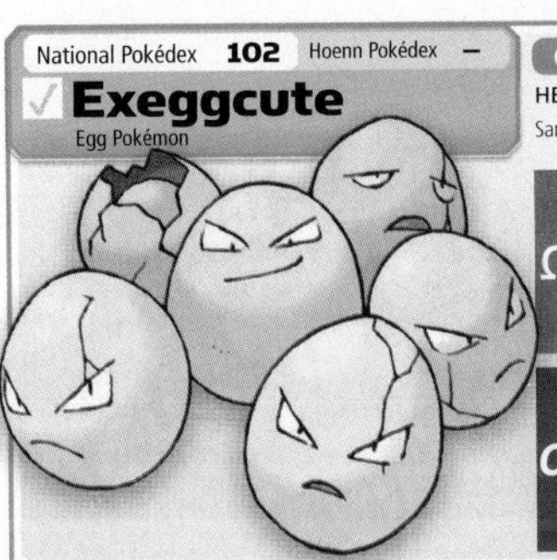

Grass Psychic

HEIGHT: 1'04" WEIGHT: 5.5 lbs.
Same form for ♂ / ♀

Ω This Pokémon consists of six eggs that form a closely knit cluster. The six eggs attract each other and spin around. When cracks increasingly appear on the eggs, Exeggcute is close to evolution.

α This Pokémon consists of six eggs that form a closely knit cluster. The six eggs attract each other and spin around. When cracks increasingly appear on the eggs, Exeggcute is close to evolution.

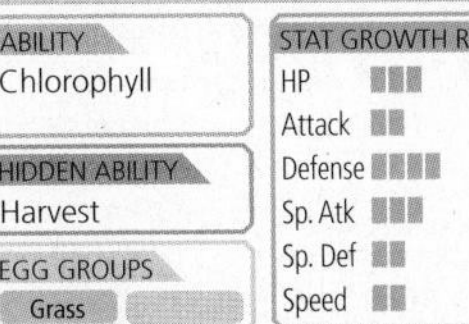

ABILITY
Chlorophyll

HIDDEN ABILITY
Harvest

EGG GROUPS
Grass

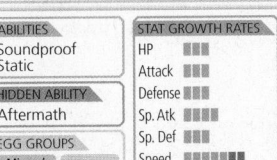

ITEMS SOMETIMES HELD BY WILD POKÉMON
—

STAT GROWTH RATES
HP
Attack
Defense
Sp. Atk
Sp. Def
Speed

EVOLUTION

MAIN WAY TO REGISTER IN THE NATIONAL POKÉDEX

Appears in *Pokémon X* and *Pokémon Y.* Bring it to your game using Link Trade or the GTS.

Damage taken in normal battles

Type		Type	
Normal	×1	Flying	×2
Fire	×2	Psychic	×0.5
Water	×0.5	Bug	×4
Grass	×0.5	Rock	×1
Electric	×0.5	Ghost	×2
Ice	×2	Dragon	×1
Fighting	×0.5	Dark	×2
Poison	×2	Steel	×1
Ground	×0.5	Fairy	×1

Damage taken in Inverse battles

Type		Type	
Normal	×1	Flying	×0.5
Fire	×0.5	Psychic	×2
Water	×2	Bug	×0.25
Grass	×2	Rock	×1
Electric	×2	Ghost	×0.5
Ice	×0.5	Dragon	×1
Fighting	×2	Dark	×0.5
Poison	×0.5	Steel	×1
Ground	×2	Fairy	×1

Can be used in
Inverse Battle
Battle Institute
Battle Maison
Random Matchup (Free Battle)
Random Matchup (Others)

LEVEL-UP MOVES

Lv.	Name	Type	Kind	Pow.	Acc.	PP	Range
1	Barrage	Normal	Physical	15	85	20	Normal
1	Uproar	Normal	Special	90	100	10	1 Random
1	Hypnosis	Psychic	Status	—	60	20	Normal
7	Reflect	Psychic	Status	—	—	20	Your Side
11	Leech Seed	Grass	Status	—	90	10	Normal
17	Bullet Seed	Grass	Physical	25	100	30	Normal
19	Stun Spore	Grass	Status	—	75	30	Normal
21	Poison Powder	Poison	Status	—	75	35	Normal
23	Sleep Powder	Grass	Status	—	75	15	Normal
27	Confusion	Psychic	Special	50	100	25	Normal
33	Worry Seed	Grass	Status	—	100	10	Normal
37	Natural Gift	Normal	Physical	—	100	15	Normal
43	Solar Beam	Grass	Special	120	100	10	Normal
47	Extrasensory	Psychic	Special	80	100	20	Normal
50	Bestow	Normal	Status	—	—	15	Normal

TM & HM MOVES

No.	Name	Type	Kind	Pow.	Acc.	PP	Range
TM06	Toxic	Poison	Status	—	90	10	Normal
TM10	Hidden Power	Normal	Special	60	100	15	Normal
TM11	Sunny Day	Fire	Status	—	—	5	Both Sides
TM16	Light Screen	Psychic	Status	—	—	30	Your Side
TM17	Protect	Normal	Status	—	—	10	Self
TM21	Frustration	Normal	Physical	—	100	20	Normal
TM22	Solar Beam	Grass	Special	120	100	10	Normal
TM27	Return	Normal	Physical	—	100	20	Normal
TM29	Psychic	Psychic	Special	90	100	10	Normal
TM32	Double Team	Normal	Status	—	—	15	Self
TM33	Reflect	Psychic	Status	—	—	20	Your Side
TM36	Sludge Bomb	Poison	Special	90	100	10	Normal
TM42	Facade	Normal	Physical	70	100	20	Normal
TM44	Rest	Psychic	Status	—	—	10	Self
TM45	Attract	Normal	Status	—	100	15	Normal
TM46	Thief	Dark	Physical	60	100	25	Normal
TM48	Round	Normal	Special	60	100	15	Normal
TM53	Energy Ball	Grass	Special	90	100	10	Normal
TM64	Explosion	Normal	Physical	250	100	5	Adjacent
TM70	Flash	Normal	Status	—	100	20	Normal
TM75	Swords Dance	Normal	Status	—	—	20	Self
TM77	Psych Up	Normal	Status	—	—	10	Normal
TM83	Infestation	Bug	Special	20	100	20	Normal
TM85	Dream Eater	Psychic	Special	100	100	15	Normal
TM86	Grass Knot	Grass	Special	—	100	20	Normal
TM87	Swagger	Normal	Status	—	90	15	Normal
TM88	Sleep Talk	Normal	Status	—	—	10	Self
TM90	Substitute	Normal	Status	—	—	10	Self
TM92	Trick Room	Psychic	Status	—	—	5	Both Sides
TM94	Secret Power	Normal	Physical	70	100	20	Normal
TM96	Nature Power	Normal	Status	—	—	20	Normal
TM100	Confide	Normal	Status	—	—	20	Normal
HM04	Strength	Normal	Physical	80	100	15	Normal

MOVES LEARNED IN EXCHANGE FOR BP

Name	Type	Kind	Pow.	Acc.	PP	Range
Seed Bomb	Grass	Physical	80	100	15	Normal
Uproar	Normal	Special	90	100	10	1 Random
Block	Normal	Status	—	—	5	Normal
Gravity	Psychic	Status	—	—	5	Both Sides
Snore	Normal	Special	50	100	15	Normal
Synthesis	Grass	Status	—	—	5	Self
Giga Drain	Grass	Special	75	100	10	Normal
Worry Seed	Grass	Status	—	100	10	Normal
Skill Swap	Psychic	Status	—	—	10	Normal

MOVES TAUGHT BY PEOPLE

Name	Type	Kind	Pow.	Acc.	PP	Range

EGG MOVES

Name	Type	Kind	Pow.	Acc.	PP	Range
Synthesis	Grass	Status	—	—	5	Self
Moonlight	Fairy	Status	—	—	5	Self
Ancient Power	Rock	Special	60	100	5	Normal
Ingrain	Grass	Status	—	—	20	Self
Curse	Ghost	Status	—	—	10	Varies
Nature Power	Normal	Status	—	—	20	Normal
Lucky Chant	Normal	Status	—	—	30	Your Side
Leaf Storm	Grass	Special	130	90	5	Normal
Power Swap	Psychic	Status	—	—	10	Normal
Giga Drain	Grass	Special	75	100	10	Normal
Skill Swap	Psychic	Status	—	—	10	Normal
Natural Gift	Normal	Physical	—	100	15	Normal
Block	Normal	Status	—	—	5	Normal
Grassy Terrain	Grass	Status	—	—	10	Both Sides

National Pokédex **103** Hoenn Pokédex —

Exeggutor

Coconut Pokémon

Grass Psychic

HEIGHT: 6'07" WEIGHT: 264.6 lbs.

Same form for ♂ / ♀

Ω Exeggutor originally came from the tropics. Its heads steadily grow larger from exposure to strong sunlight. It is said that when the heads fall off, they group together to form Exeggcute.

α Exeggutor originally came from the tropics. Its heads steadily grow larger from exposure to strong sunlight. It is said that when the heads fall off, they group together to form Exeggcute.

ABILITY
Chlorophyll

HIDDEN ABILITY
Harvest

EGG GROUPS
Grass

STAT GROWTH RATES
HP ■■■■
Attack ■■■■■
Defense ■■■■
Sp. Atk ■■■■■■
Sp. Def ■■■
Speed ■■■

ITEMS SOMETIMES HELD BY WILD POKÉMON
—

EVOLUTION
Exeggcute → Leaf Stone → Exeggutor

MAIN WAY TO REGISTER IN THE NATIONAL POKÉDEX

Use a Leaf Stone on an Exeggcute obtained via Link Trade or the GTS.

Damage taken in normal battles

Type		Type	
Normal	×1	Flying	×2
Fire	×2	Psychic	×0.5
Water	×0.5	Bug	×4
Grass	×0.5	Rock	×1
Electric	×0.5	Ghost	×2
Ice	×2	Dragon	×1
Fighting	×0.5	Dark	×2
Poison	×2	Steel	×1
Ground	×0.5	Fairy	×1

Damage taken in Inverse battles

Type		Type	
Normal	×1	Flying	×0.5
Fire	×0.5	Psychic	×2
Water	×2	Bug	×0.25
Grass	×2	Rock	×1
Electric	×2	Ghost	×0.5
Ice	×0.5	Dragon	×0.5
Fighting	×2	Dark	×0.5
Poison	×0.5	Steel	×1
Ground	×2	Fairy	×1

Can be used in
Inverse Battle
Battle Institute
Battle Maison
Random Matchup (Free Battle)
Random Matchup (Others)

LEVEL-UP MOVES

Lv.	Name	Type	Kind	Pow.	Acc.	PP	Range
1	Seed Bomb	Grass	Physical	80	100	15	Normal
1	Barrage	Normal	Physical	15	85	20	Normal
1	Hypnosis	Psychic	Status	—	60	20	Normal
1	Confusion	Psychic	Special	50	100	25	Normal
1	Stomp	Normal	Physical	65	100	20	Normal
17	Psyshock	Psychic	Special	80	100	10	Normal
27	Egg Bomb	Normal	Physical	100	75	10	Normal
37	Wood Hammer	Grass	Physical	120	100	15	Normal
47	Leaf Storm	Grass	Special	130	90	5	Normal

TM & HM MOVES

No.	Name	Type	Kind	Pow.	Acc.	PP	Range
TM03	Psyshock	Psychic	Special	80	100	10	Normal
TM06	Toxic	Poison	Status	—	90	10	Normal
TM10	Hidden Power	Normal	Special	60	100	15	Normal
TM11	Sunny Day	Fire	Status	—	—	5	Both Sides
TM15	Hyper Beam	Normal	Special	150	90	5	Normal
TM16	Light Screen	Psychic	Status	—	—	30	Your Side
TM17	Protect	Normal	Status	—	—	10	Self
TM21	Frustration	Normal	Physical	—	100	20	Normal
TM22	Solar Beam	Grass	Special	120	100	10	Normal
TM27	Return	Normal	Physical	—	100	20	Normal
TM29	Psychic	Psychic	Special	90	100	10	Normal
TM32	Double Team	Normal	Status	—	—	15	Self
TM33	Reflect	Psychic	Status	—	—	20	Your Side
TM36	Sludge Bomb	Poison	Special	90	100	10	Normal
TM42	Facade	Normal	Physical	70	100	20	Normal
TM44	Rest	Psychic	Status	—	—	10	Self
TM45	Attract	Normal	Status	—	100	15	Normal
TM46	Thief	Dark	Physical	60	100	25	Normal
TM48	Round	Normal	Special	60	100	15	Normal
TM53	Energy Ball	Grass	Special	90	100	10	Normal
TM64	Explosion	Normal	Physical	250	100	5	Adjacent
TM68	Giga Impact	Normal	Physical	150	90	5	Normal
TM70	Flash	Normal	Status	—	100	20	Normal
TM75	Swords Dance	Normal	Status	—	—	20	Self
TM77	Psych Up	Normal	Status	—	—	10	Normal
TM83	Infestation	Bug	Special	20	100	20	Normal
TM85	Dream Eater	Psychic	Special	100	100	15	Normal
TM86	Grass Knot	Grass	Special	—	100	20	Normal
TM87	Swagger	Normal	Status	—	90	15	Normal
TM88	Sleep Talk	Normal	Status	—	—	10	Self
TM90	Substitute	Normal	Status	—	—	10	Self
TM92	Trick Room	Psychic	Status	—	—	5	Both Sides
TM94	Secret Power	Normal	Physical	70	100	20	Normal
TM96	Nature Power	Normal	Status	—	—	20	Normal
TM100	Confide	Normal	Status	—	—	20	Normal
HM04	Strength	Normal	Physical	80	100	15	Normal

MOVES LEARNED IN EXCHANGE FOR BP

Name	Type	Kind	Pow.	Acc.	PP	Range
Seed Bomb	Grass	Physical	80	100	15	Normal
Low Kick	Fighting	Physical	—	100	20	Normal
Block	Normal	Status	—	—	5	Normal
Gravity	Psychic	Status	—	—	5	Both Sides
Zen Headbutt	Psychic	Physical	80	90	15	Normal
Snore	Normal	Special	50	100	15	Normal
Synthesis	Grass	Status	—	—	5	Self
Giga Drain	Grass	Special	75	100	10	Normal
Worry Seed	Grass	Status	—	100	10	Normal
Skill Swap	Psychic	Status	—	—	10	Normal

MOVES TAUGHT BY PEOPLE

Name	Type	Kind	Pow.	Acc.	PP	Range

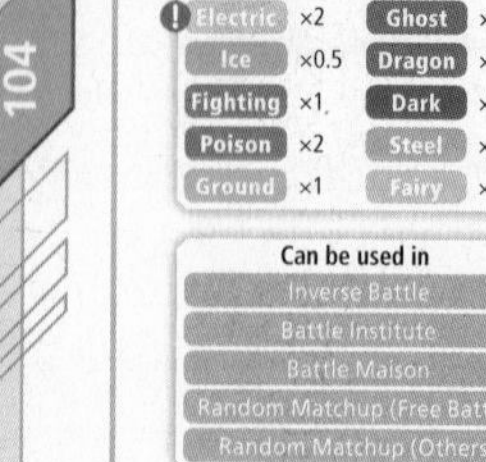

National Pokédex **104** Hoenn Pokédex —

Cubone

Lonely Pokémon

Ground

HEIGHT: 1'04" WEIGHT: 14.3 lbs.

Same form for ♂ / ♀

Ω Cubone pines for the mother it will never see again. Seeing a likeness of its mother in the full moon, it cries. The stains on the skull the Pokémon wears are made by the tears it sheds.

α Cubone pines for the mother it will never see again. Seeing a likeness of its mother in the full moon, it cries. The stains on the skull the Pokémon wears are made by the tears it sheds.

ABILITIES
Rock Head
Lightning Rod

HIDDEN ABILITY
Battle Armor

EGG GROUPS
Monster

STAT GROWTH RATES
HP ■■
Attack ■■■
Defense ■■■■
Sp. Atk ■■
Sp. Def ■■
Speed ■■

ITEMS SOMETIMES HELD BY WILD POKÉMON
—

EVOLUTION

MAIN WAY TO REGISTER IN THE NATIONAL POKÉDEX

Appears in *Pokémon X* and *Pokémon Y.* Bring it to your game using Link Trade or the GTS.

Damage taken in normal battles

Type		Type	
Normal	×1	Flying	×1
Fire	×1	Psychic	×1
Water	×2	Bug	×1
Grass	×2	Rock	×0.5
Electric	×0	Ghost	×1
Ice	×2	Dragon	×1
Fighting	×1	Dark	×1
Poison	×0.5	Steel	×1
Ground	×1	Fairy	×1

Damage taken in Inverse battles

Type		Type	
Normal	×1	Flying	×1
Fire	×1	Psychic	×1
Water	×0.5	Bug	×1
Grass	×0.5	Rock	×2
Electric	×2	Ghost	×1
Ice	×0.5	Dragon	×1
Fighting	×1	Dark	×1
Poison	×2	Steel	×1
Ground	×1	Fairy	×1

Can be used in
Inverse Battle
Battle Institute
Battle Maison
Random Matchup (Free Battle)
Random Matchup (Others)

LEVEL-UP MOVES

Lv.	Name	Type	Kind	Pow.	Acc.	PP	Range
1	Growl	Normal	Status	—	100	40	Many Others
3	Tail Whip	Normal	Status	—	100	30	Many Others
7	Bone Club	Ground	Physical	65	85	20	Normal
11	Headbutt	Normal	Physical	70	100	15	Normal
13	Leer	Normal	Status	—	100	30	Many Others
17	Focus Energy	Normal	Status	—	—	30	Self
21	Bonemerang	Ground	Physical	50	90	10	Normal
23	Rage	Normal	Physical	20	100	20	Normal
27	False Swipe	Normal	Physical	40	100	40	Normal
31	Thrash	Normal	Physical	120	100	10	1 Random
33	Fling	Dark	Physical	—	100	10	Normal
37	Bone Rush	Ground	Physical	25	90	10	Normal
41	Endeavor	Normal	Physical	—	100	5	Normal
43	Double-Edge	Normal	Physical	120	100	15	Normal
47	Retaliate	Normal	Physical	70	100	5	Normal

TM & HM MOVES

No.	Name	Type	Kind	Pow.	Acc.	PP	Range
TM06	Toxic	Poison	Status	—	90	10	Normal
TM10	Hidden Power	Normal	Special	60	100	15	Normal
TM11	Sunny Day	Fire	Status	—	—	5	Both Sides
TM13	Ice Beam	Ice	Special	90	100	10	Normal
TM14	Blizzard	Ice	Special	110	70	5	Many Others
TM17	Protect	Normal	Status	—	—	10	Self
TM21	Frustration	Normal	Physical	—	100	20	Normal
TM23	Smack Down	Rock	Physical	50	100	15	Normal
TM26	Earthquake	Ground	Physical	100	100	10	Adjacent
TM27	Return	Normal	Physical	—	100	20	Normal
TM28	Dig	Ground	Physical	80	100	10	Normal
TM31	Brick Break	Fighting	Physical	75	100	15	Normal
TM32	Double Team	Normal	Status	—	—	15	Self
TM35	Flamethrower	Fire	Special	90	100	15	Normal
TM37	Sandstorm	Rock	Status	—	—	10	Both Sides
TM38	Fire Blast	Fire	Special	110	85	5	Normal
TM39	Rock Tomb	Rock	Physical	60	95	15	Normal
TM40	Aerial Ace	Flying	Physical	60	—	20	Normal
TM42	Facade	Normal	Physical	70	100	20	Normal
TM44	Rest	Psychic	Status	—	—	10	Self
TM45	Attract	Normal	Status	—	100	15	Normal
TM46	Thief	Dark	Physical	60	100	25	Normal
TM48	Round	Normal	Special	60	100	15	Normal
TM49	Echoed Voice	Normal	Special	40	100	15	Normal
TM54	False Swipe	Normal	Physical	40	100	40	Normal
TM56	Fling	Dark	Physical	—	100	10	Normal
TM59	Incinerate	Fire	Special	60	100	15	Many Others
TM67	Retaliate	Normal	Physical	70	100	5	Normal
TM75	Swords Dance	Normal	Status	—	—	20	Self
TM78	Bulldoze	Ground	Physical	60	100	20	Adjacent
TM80	Rock Slide	Rock	Physical	75	90	10	Many Others
TM87	Swagger	Normal	Status	—	90	15	Normal
TM88	Sleep Talk	Normal	Status	—	—	10	Self
TM90	Substitute	Normal	Status	—	—	10	Self
TM94	Secret Power	Normal	Physical	70	100	20	Normal
TM98	Power-Up Punch	Fighting	Physical	40	100	20	Normal
TM100	Confide	Normal	Status	—	—	20	Normal
HM04	Strength	Normal	Physical	80	100	15	Normal
HM06	Rock Smash	Fighting	Physical	40	100	15	Normal

MOVES LEARNED IN EXCHANGE FOR BP

Name	Type	Kind	Pow.	Acc.	PP	Range
Iron Head	Steel	Physical	80	100	15	Normal
Low Kick	Fighting	Physical	—	100	20	Normal
Uproar	Normal	Special	90	100	10	1 Random
Thunder Punch	Electric	Physical	75	100	15	Normal
Fire Punch	Fire	Physical	75	100	15	Normal
Earth Power	Ground	Special	90	100	10	Normal
Iron Defense	Steel	Status	—	—	15	Self
Icy Wind	Ice	Special	55	95	15	Many Others
Iron Tail	Steel	Physical	100	75	15	Normal
Snore	Normal	Special	50	100	15	Normal
Knock Off	Dark	Physical	65	100	20	Normal
Focus Punch	Fighting	Physical	150	100	20	Normal
Endeavor	Normal	Physical	—	100	5	Normal
Stealth Rock	Rock	Status	—	—	20	Other Side

MOVES TAUGHT BY PEOPLE

Name	Type	Kind	Pow.	Acc.	PP	Range

EGG MOVES

Name	Type	Kind	Pow.	Acc.	PP	Range
Ancient Power	Rock	Special	60	100	5	Normal
Belly Drum	Normal	Status	—	—	10	Self
Screech	Normal	Status	—	85	40	Normal
Skull Bash	Normal	Physical	130	100	10	Normal
Perish Song	Normal	Status	—	—	5	Adjacent
Double Kick	Fighting	Physical	30	100	30	Normal
Iron Head	Steel	Physical	80	100	15	Normal
Detect	Fighting	Status	—	—	5	Self
Endure	Normal	Status	—	—	10	Self
Chip Away	Normal	Physical	70	100	20	Normal

National Pokédex **105** Hoenn Pokédex —

Marowak

Bone Keeper Pokémon

Ground

HEIGHT: 3'03" WEIGHT: 99.2 lbs.

Same form for ♂ / ♀

Ω Marowak is the evolved form of a Cubone that has overcome its sadness at the loss of its mother and grown tough. This Pokémon's tempered and hardened spirit is not easily broken.

α Marowak is the evolved form of a Cubone that has overcome its sadness at the loss of its mother and grown tough. This Pokémon's tempered and hardened spirit is not easily broken.

ABILITIES
Rock Head
Lightning Rod

HIDDEN ABILITY
Battle Armor

EGG GROUPS
Monster

STAT GROWTH RATES
HP ■■■
Attack ■■■■
Defense ■■■■■
Sp. Atk ■■
Sp. Def ■■■
Speed ■■■

ITEMS SOMETIMES HELD BY WILD POKÉMON
—

EVOLUTION

Cubone → Marowak

MAIN WAY TO REGISTER IN THE NATIONAL POKÉDEX

Level up a Cubone obtained via Link Trade or the GTS to Lv. 28.

Damage taken in normal battles

Type		Type	
Normal	×1	Flying	×1
Fire	×1	Psychic	×1
Water	×2	Bug	×1
Grass	×2	Rock	×0.5
Electric	×0	Ghost	×1
Ice	×2	Dragon	×1
Fighting	×1	Dark	×1
Poison	×0.5	Steel	×1
Ground	×1	Fairy	×1

Damage taken in Inverse battles

Type		Type	
Normal	×1	Flying	×1
Fire	×1	Psychic	×1
Water	×0.5	Bug	×1
Grass	×0.5	Rock	×2
! Electric	×2	Ghost	×1
Ice	×0.5	Dragon	×1
Fighting	×1	Dark	×1
Poison	×2	Steel	×1
Ground	×1	Fairy	×1

Can be used in
- Inverse Battle
- Battle Institute
- Battle Maison
- Random Matchup (Free Battle)
- Random Matchup (Others)

LEVEL-UP MOVES

Lv.	Name	Type	Kind	Pow.	Acc.	PP	Range
1	Growl	Normal	Status	—	100	40	Many Others
1	Tail Whip	Normal	Status	—	100	30	Many Others
1	Bone Club	Ground	Physical	65	85	20	Normal
1	Headbutt	Normal	Physical	70	100	15	Normal
3	Tail Whip	Normal	Status	—	100	30	Many Others
7	Bone Club	Ground	Physical	65	85	20	Normal
11	Headbutt	Normal	Physical	70	100	15	Normal
13	Leer	Normal	Status	—	100	30	Many Others
17	Focus Energy	Normal	Status	—	—	30	Self
21	Bonemerang	Ground	Physical	50	90	10	Normal
23	Rage	Normal	Physical	20	100	20	Normal
27	False Swipe	Normal	Physical	40	100	40	Normal
33	Thrash	Normal	Physical	120	100	10	1 Random
37	Fling	Dark	Physical	—	100	10	Normal
43	Bone Rush	Ground	Physical	25	90	10	Normal
49	Endeavor	Normal	Physical	—	100	5	Normal
53	Double-Edge	Normal	Physical	120	100	15	Normal
59	Retaliate	Normal	Physical	70	100	5	Normal

TM & HM MOVES

No.	Name	Type	Kind	Pow.	Acc.	PP	Range
TM06	Toxic	Poison	Status	—	90	10	Normal
TM10	Hidden Power	Normal	Special	60	100	15	Normal
TM11	Sunny Day	Fire	Status	—	—	5	Both Sides
TM13	Ice Beam	Ice	Special	90	100	10	Normal
TM14	Blizzard	Ice	Special	110	70	5	Many Others
TM15	Hyper Beam	Normal	Special	150	90	5	Normal
TM17	Protect	Normal	Status	—	—	10	Self
TM21	Frustration	Normal	Physical	—	100	20	Normal
TM23	Smack Down	Rock	Physical	50	100	15	Normal
TM26	Earthquake	Ground	Physical	100	100	10	Adjacent
TM27	Return	Normal	Physical	—	100	20	Normal
TM28	Dig	Ground	Physical	80	100	10	Normal
TM31	Brick Break	Fighting	Physical	75	100	15	Normal
TM32	Double Team	Normal	Status	—	—	15	Self
TM35	Flamethrower	Fire	Special	90	100	15	Normal
TM37	Sandstorm	Rock	Status	—	—	10	Both Sides
TM38	Fire Blast	Fire	Special	110	85	5	Normal
TM39	Rock Tomb	Rock	Physical	60	95	15	Normal
TM40	Aerial Ace	Flying	Physical	60	—	20	Normal
TM42	Facade	Normal	Physical	70	100	20	Normal
TM44	Rest	Psychic	Status	—	—	10	Self
TM45	Attract	Normal	Status	—	100	15	Normal
TM46	Thief	Dark	Physical	60	100	25	Normal
TM48	Round	Normal	Special	60	100	15	Normal
TM49	Echoed Voice	Normal	Special	40	100	15	Normal
TM52	Focus Blast	Fighting	Special	120	70	5	Normal
TM54	False Swipe	Normal	Physical	40	100	40	Normal
TM56	Fling	Dark	Physical	—	100	10	Normal
TM59	Incinerate	Fire	Special	60	100	15	Many Others
TM67	Retaliate	Normal	Physical	70	100	5	Normal
TM68	Giga Impact	Normal	Physical	150	90	5	Normal
TM71	Stone Edge	Rock	Physical	100	80	5	Normal
TM75	Swords Dance	Normal	Status	—	—	20	Self
TM78	Bulldoze	Ground	Physical	60	100	20	Adjacent
TM80	Rock Slide	Rock	Physical	75	90	10	Many Others
TM87	Swagger	Normal	Status	—	90	15	Normal
TM88	Sleep Talk	Normal	Status	—	—	10	Self
TM90	Substitute	Normal	Status	—	—	10	Self
TM94	Secret Power	Normal	Physical	70	100	20	Normal
TM98	Power-Up Punch	Fighting	Physical	40	100	20	Normal
TM100	Confide	Normal	Status	—	—	20	Normal
HM04	Strength	Normal	Physical	80	100	15	Normal
HM06	Rock Smash	Fighting	Physical	40	100	15	Normal

MOVES LEARNED IN EXCHANGE FOR BP

Name	Type	Kind	Pow.	Acc.	PP	Range
Iron Head	Steel	Physical	80	100	15	Normal
Low Kick	Fighting	Physical	—	100	20	Normal
Uproar	Normal	Special	90	100	10	1 Random
Thunder Punch	Electric	Physical	75	100	15	Normal
Fire Punch	Fire	Physical	75	100	15	Normal
Earth Power	Ground	Special	90	100	10	Normal
Iron Defense	Steel	Status	—	—	15	Self
Icy Wind	Ice	Special	55	95	15	Many Others
Iron Tail	Steel	Physical	100	75	15	Normal
Snore	Normal	Special	50	100	15	Normal
Knock Off	Dark	Physical	65	100	20	Normal
Focus Punch	Fighting	Physical	150	100	20	Normal
Endeavor	Normal	Physical	—	100	5	Normal
Outrage	Dragon	Physical	120	100	10	1 Random
Stealth Rock	Rock	Status	—	—	20	Other Side

MOVES TAUGHT BY PEOPLE

Name	Type	Kind	Pow.	Acc.	PP	Range

National Pokédex **106** Hoenn Pokédex —

Hitmonlee

Kicking Pokémon

Fighting

HEIGHT: 4'11" WEIGHT: 109.8 lbs.

♂ only

Ω Hitmonlee's legs freely contract and stretch. Using these springlike legs, it bowls over foes with devastating kicks. After battle, it rubs down its legs and loosens the muscles to overcome fatigue.

α Hitmonlee's legs freely contract and stretch. Using these springlike legs, it bowls over foes with devastating kicks. After battle, it rubs down its legs and loosens the muscles to overcome fatigue.

ABILITIES
Limber
Reckless

HIDDEN ABILITY
Unburden

EGG GROUPS
Human-Like

STAT GROWTH RATES
HP ■■
Attack ■■■■■■
Defense ■■
Sp. Atk ■■
Sp. Def ■■■■■
Speed ■■■■■

ITEMS SOMETIMES HELD BY WILD POKÉMON
—

EVOLUTION

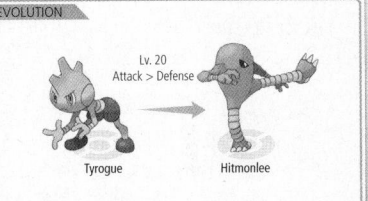

Tyrogue → (Lv. 20, Attack > Defense) → Hitmonlee

MAIN WAY TO REGISTER IN THE NATIONAL POKÉDEX

Level up Tyrogue to Lv. 20 with its Attack higher than its Defense.

Damage taken in normal battles

Type		Type	
Normal	×1	Flying	×2
Fire	×1	Psychic	×2
Water	×1	Bug	×0.5
Grass	×1	Rock	×0.5
Electric	×1	Ghost	×1
Ice	×1	Dragon	×1
Fighting	×1	Dark	×0.5
Poison	×1	Steel	×1
Ground	×1	Fairy	×2

Damage taken in Inverse battles

Type		Type	
Normal	×1	Flying	×0.5
Fire	×1	Psychic	×0.5
Water	×1	Bug	×2
Grass	×1	Rock	×2
Electric	×1	Ghost	×1
Ice	×1	Dragon	×1
Fighting	×1	Dark	×2
Poison	×1	Steel	×1
Ground	×1	Fairy	×0.5

Can be used in
- Inverse Battle
- Battle Institute
- Battle Maison
- Random Matchup (Free Battle)
- Random Matchup (Others)

LEVEL-UP MOVES

Lv.	Name	Type	Kind	Pow.	Acc.	PP	Range
1	Reversal	Fighting	Physical	—	100	15	Normal
1	Close Combat	Fighting	Physical	120	100	5	Normal
1	Mega Kick	Normal	Physical	120	75	5	Normal
1	Revenge	Fighting	Physical	60	100	10	Normal
1	Double Kick	Fighting	Physical	30	100	30	Normal
5	Meditate	Psychic	Status	—	—	40	Self
9	Rolling Kick	Fighting	Physical	60	85	15	Normal
13	Jump Kick	Fighting	Physical	100	95	10	Normal
17	Brick Break	Fighting	Physical	75	100	15	Normal
21	Focus Energy	Normal	Status	—	—	30	Self
25	Feint	Normal	Physical	30	100	10	Normal
29	High Jump Kick	Fighting	Physical	130	90	10	Normal
33	Mind Reader	Normal	Status	—	—	5	Normal
37	Foresight	Normal	Status	—	—	40	Normal
41	Wide Guard	Rock	Status	—	—	10	Your Side
45	Blaze Kick	Fire	Physical	85	90	10	Normal
49	Endure	Normal	Status	—	—	10	Self
53	Mega Kick	Normal	Physical	120	75	5	Normal
57	Close Combat	Fighting	Physical	120	100	5	Normal
61	Reversal	Fighting	Physical	—	100	15	Normal

TM & HM MOVES

No.	Name	Type	Kind	Pow.	Acc.	PP	Range
TM06	Toxic	Poison	Status	—	90	10	Normal
TM08	Bulk Up	Fighting	Status	—	—	20	Self
TM10	Hidden Power	Normal	Special	60	100	15	Normal
TM11	Sunny Day	Fire	Status	—	—	5	Both Sides
TM17	Protect	Normal	Status	—	—	10	Self
TM18	Rain Dance	Water	Status	—	—	5	Both Sides
TM21	Frustration	Normal	Physical	—	100	20	Normal
TM26	Earthquake	Ground	Physical	100	100	10	Adjacent
TM27	Return	Normal	Physical	—	100	20	Normal
TM31	Brick Break	Fighting	Physical	75	100	15	Normal
TM32	Double Team	Normal	Status	—	—	15	Self
TM39	Rock Tomb	Rock	Physical	60	95	15	Normal
TM42	Facade	Normal	Physical	70	100	20	Normal
TM44	Rest	Psychic	Status	—	—	10	Self
TM45	Attract	Normal	Status	—	100	15	Normal
TM46	Thief	Dark	Physical	60	100	25	Normal
TM47	Low Sweep	Fighting	Physical	65	100	20	Normal
TM48	Round	Normal	Special	60	100	15	Normal
TM52	Focus Blast	Fighting	Special	120	70	5	Normal
TM56	Fling	Dark	Physical	—	100	10	Normal
TM67	Retaliate	Normal	Physical	70	100	5	Normal
TM71	Stone Edge	Rock	Physical	100	80	5	Normal
TM78	Bulldoze	Ground	Physical	60	100	20	Adjacent
TM80	Rock Slide	Rock	Physical	75	90	10	Many Others
TM84	Poison Jab	Poison	Physical	80	100	20	Normal
TM87	Swagger	Normal	Status	—	90	15	Normal
TM88	Sleep Talk	Normal	Status	—	—	10	Self
TM90	Substitute	Normal	Status	—	—	10	Self
TM94	Secret Power	Normal	Physical	70	100	20	Normal
TM98	Power-Up Punch	Fighting	Physical	40	100	20	Normal
TM100	Confide	Normal	Status	—	—	20	Normal
HM04	Strength	Normal	Physical	80	100	15	Normal
HM06	Rock Smash	Fighting	Physical	40	100	15	Normal

MOVES LEARNED IN EXCHANGE FOR BP

Name	Type	Kind	Pow.	Acc.	PP	Range
Covet	Normal	Physical	60	100	25	Normal
Bounce	Flying	Physical	85	85	5	Normal
Low Kick	Fighting	Physical	—	100	20	Normal
Superpower	Fighting	Physical	120	100	5	Normal
Snore	Normal	Special	50	100	15	Normal
Knock Off	Dark	Physical	65	100	20	Normal
Role Play	Psychic	Status	—	—	10	Normal
Focus Punch	Fighting	Physical	150	100	20	Normal
Helping Hand	Normal	Status	—	—	20	1 Ally

MOVES TAUGHT BY PEOPLE

Name	Type	Kind	Pow.	Acc.	PP	Range

National Pokédex **107** Hoenn Pokédex —

Hitmonchan

Punching Pokémon

Fighting

HEIGHT: 4'07" WEIGHT: 110.7 lbs.

♂ only

Ω Hitmonchan is said to possess the spirit of a boxer who had been working toward a world championship. This Pokémon has an indomitable spirit and will never give up in the face of adversity.

α Hitmonchan is said to possess the spirit of a boxer who had been working toward a world championship. This Pokémon has an indomitable spirit and will never give up in the face of adversity.

ABILITIES
Keen Eye
Iron Fist

HIDDEN ABILITY
Inner Focus

EGG GROUPS
Human-Like

STAT GROWTH RATES
HP
Attack
Defense
Sp. Atk
Sp. Def
Speed

ITEMS SOMETIMES HELD BY WILD POKÉMON
—

EVOLUTION

Tyrogue → Lv. 20 Defense > Attack → Hitmonchan

MAIN WAY TO REGISTER IN THE NATIONAL POKÉDEX

Level up Tyrogue to Lv. 20 with its Defense higher than its Attack.

Damage taken in normal battles

Type		Type	
Normal	×1	Flying	×2
Fire	×1	Psychic	×2
Water	×1	Bug	×0.5
Grass	×1	Rock	×0.5
Electric	×1	Ghost	×1
Ice	×1	Dragon	×1
Fighting	×1	Dark	×0.5
Poison	×1	Steel	×1
Ground	×1	Fairy	×2

Damage taken in Inverse battles

Type		Type	
Normal	×1	Flying	×0.5
Fire	×1	Psychic	×0.5
Water	×1	Bug	×2
Grass	×1	Rock	×2
Electric	×1	Ghost	×1
Ice	×1	Dragon	×1
Fighting	×1	Dark	×2
Poison	×1	Steel	×1
Ground	×1	Fairy	×0.5

Can be used in
Inverse Battle
Battle Institute
Battle Maison
Random Matchup (Free Battle)
Random Matchup (Others)

LEVEL-UP MOVES

Lv.	Name	Type	Kind	Pow.	Acc.	PP	Range
1	Close Combat	Fighting	Physical	120	100	5	Normal
1	Counter	Fighting	Physical	—	100	20	Varies
1	Focus Punch	Fighting	Physical	150	100	20	Normal
1	Revenge	Fighting	Physical	60	100	10	Normal
1	Comet Punch	Normal	Physical	18	85	15	Normal
6	Agility	Psychic	Status	—	—	30	Self
11	Pursuit	Dark	Physical	40	100	20	Normal
16	Mach Punch	Fighting	Physical	40	100	30	Normal
16	Bullet Punch	Steel	Physical	40	100	30	Normal
21	Feint	Normal	Physical	30	100	10	Normal
26	Vacuum Wave	Fighting	Special	40	100	30	Normal
31	Quick Guard	Fighting	Status	—	—	15	Your Side
36	Thunder Punch	Electric	Physical	75	100	15	Normal
36	Ice Punch	Ice	Physical	75	100	15	Normal
36	Fire Punch	Fire	Physical	75	100	15	Normal
41	Sky Uppercut	Fighting	Physical	85	90	15	Normal
46	Mega Punch	Normal	Physical	80	85	20	Normal
50	Detect	Fighting	Status	—	—	5	Self
56	Focus Punch	Fighting	Physical	150	100	20	Normal
61	Counter	Fighting	Physical	—	100	20	Varies
66	Close Combat	Fighting	Physical	120	100	5	Normal

TM & HM MOVES

No.	Name	Type	Kind	Pow.	Acc.	PP	Range
TM06	Toxic	Poison	Status	—	90	10	Normal
TM08	Bulk Up	Fighting	Status	—	—	20	Self
TM10	Hidden Power	Normal	Special	60	100	15	Normal
TM11	Sunny Day	Fire	Status	—	—	5	Both Sides
TM17	Protect	Normal	Status	—	—	10	Self
TM18	Rain Dance	Water	Status	—	—	5	Both Sides
TM21	Frustration	Normal	Physical	—	100	20	Normal
TM26	Earthquake	Ground	Physical	100	100	10	Adjacent
TM27	Return	Normal	Physical	—	100	20	Normal
TM31	Brick Break	Fighting	Physical	75	100	15	Normal
TM32	Double Team	Normal	Status	—	—	15	Self
TM39	Rock Tomb	Rock	Physical	60	95	15	Normal
TM42	Facade	Normal	Physical	70	100	20	Normal
TM44	Rest	Psychic	Status	—	—	10	Self
TM45	Attract	Normal	Status	—	100	15	Normal
TM46	Thief	Dark	Physical	60	100	25	Normal
TM47	Low Sweep	Fighting	Physical	65	100	20	Normal
TM48	Round	Normal	Special	60	100	15	Normal
TM52	Focus Blast	Fighting	Special	120	70	5	Normal
TM56	Fling	Dark	Physical	—	100	10	Normal
TM67	Retaliate	Normal	Physical	70	100	5	Normal
TM71	Stone Edge	Rock	Physical	100	80	5	Normal
TM78	Bulldoze	Ground	Physical	60	100	20	Adjacent
TM80	Rock Slide	Rock	Physical	75	90	10	Many Others
TM87	Swagger	Normal	Status	—	90	15	Normal
TM88	Sleep Talk	Normal	Status	—	—	10	Self
TM90	Substitute	Normal	Status	—	—	10	Self
TM94	Secret Power	Normal	Physical	70	100	20	Normal
TM98	Power-Up Punch	Fighting	Physical	40	100	20	Normal
TM100	Confide	Normal	Status	—	—	20	Normal
HM04	Strength	Normal	Physical	80	100	15	Normal
HM06	Rock Smash	Fighting	Physical	40	100	15	Normal

MOVES LEARNED IN EXCHANGE FOR BP

Name	Type	Kind	Pow.	Acc.	PP	Range
Covet	Normal	Physical	60	100	25	Normal
Low Kick	Fighting	Physical	—	100	20	Normal
Thunder Punch	Electric	Physical	75	100	15	Normal
Fire Punch	Fire	Physical	75	100	15	Normal
Ice Punch	Ice	Physical	75	100	15	Normal
Snore	Normal	Special	50	100	15	Normal
Role Play	Psychic	Status	—	—	10	Normal
Drain Punch	Fighting	Physical	75	100	10	Normal
Focus Punch	Fighting	Physical	150	100	20	Normal
Helping Hand	Normal	Status	—	—	20	1 Ally

MOVES TAUGHT BY PEOPLE

Name	Type	Kind	Pow.	Acc.	PP	Range

National Pokédex **108** Hoenn Pokédex —

Lickitung

Licking Pokémon

Normal

HEIGHT: 3'11" WEIGHT: 144.4 lbs.

Same form for ♂ / ♀

Ω Whenever Lickitung comes across something new, it will unfailingly give it a lick. It does so because it memorizes things by texture and by taste. It is somewhat put off by sour things.

α Whenever Lickitung comes across something new, it will unfailingly give it a lick. It does so because it memorizes things by texture and by taste. It is somewhat put off by sour things.

ABILITIES
Own Tempo
Oblivious

HIDDEN ABILITY
Cloud Nine

EGG GROUPS
Monster

STAT GROWTH RATES
HP
Attack
Defense
Sp. Atk
Sp. Def
Speed

ITEMS SOMETIMES HELD BY WILD POKÉMON
—

EVOLUTION

MAIN WAY TO REGISTER IN THE NATIONAL POKÉDEX

Appears in *Pokémon X* and *Pokémon Y*. Bring it to your game using Link Trade or the GTS.

Damage taken in normal battles

Type		Type	
Normal	×1	Flying	×1
Fire	×1	Psychic	×1
Water	×1	Bug	×1
Grass	×1	Rock	×1
Electric	×1	Ghost	×0
Ice	×1	Dragon	×1
Fighting	×2	Dark	×1
Poison	×1	Steel	×1
Ground	×1	Fairy	×1

Damage taken in Inverse battles

Type		Type	
Normal	×1	Flying	×1
Fire	×1	Psychic	×1
Water	×1	Bug	×1
Grass	×1	Rock	×1
Electric	×1	Ghost	×2
Ice	×1	Dragon	×1
Fighting	×0.5	Dark	×1
Poison	×1	Steel	×1
Ground	×1	Fairy	×1

Can be used in
Inverse Battle
Battle Institute
Battle Maison
Random Matchup (Free Battle)
Random Matchup (Others)

LEVEL-UP MOVES

Lv.	Name	Type	Kind	Pow.	Acc.	PP	Range
1	Lick	Ghost	Physical	30	100	30	Normal
5	Supersonic	Normal	Status	—	55	20	Normal
9	Defense Curl	Normal	Status	—	—	40	Self
13	Knock Off	Dark	Physical	65	100	20	Normal
17	Wrap	Normal	Physical	15	90	20	Normal
21	Stomp	Normal	Physical	65	100	20	Normal
25	Disable	Normal	Status	—	100	20	Normal
29	Slam	Normal	Physical	80	75	20	Normal
33	Rollout	Rock	Physical	30	90	20	Normal
37	Chip Away	Normal	Physical	70	100	20	Normal
41	Me First	Normal	Status	—	—	20	Varies
45	Refresh	Normal	Status	—	—	20	Self
49	Screech	Normal	Status	—	85	40	Normal
53	Power Whip	Grass	Physical	120	85	10	Normal
57	Wring Out	Normal	Special	—	100	5	Normal

TM & HM MOVES

No.	Name	Type	Kind	Pow.	Acc.	PP	Range
TM06	Toxic	Poison	Status	—	90	10	Normal
TM10	Hidden Power	Normal	Special	60	100	15	Normal
TM11	Sunny Day	Fire	Status	—	—	5	Both Sides
TM13	Ice Beam	Ice	Special	90	100	10	Normal
TM14	Blizzard	Ice	Special	110	70	5	Many Others
TM15	Hyper Beam	Normal	Special	150	90	5	Normal
TM17	Protect	Normal	Status	—	—	10	Self
TM18	Rain Dance	Water	Status	—	—	5	Both Sides
TM21	Frustration	Normal	Physical	—	100	20	Normal
TM22	Solar Beam	Grass	Special	120	100	10	Normal
TM24	Thunderbolt	Electric	Special	90	100	15	Normal
TM25	Thunder	Electric	Special	110	70	10	Normal
TM26	Earthquake	Ground	Physical	100	100	10	Adjacent
TM27	Return	Normal	Physical	—	100	20	Normal
TM28	Dig	Ground	Physical	80	100	10	Normal
TM30	Shadow Ball	Ghost	Special	80	100	15	Normal
TM31	Brick Break	Fighting	Physical	75	100	15	Normal
TM32	Double Team	Normal	Status	—	—	15	Self
TM35	Flamethrower	Fire	Special	90	100	15	Normal
TM37	Sandstorm	Rock	Status	—	—	10	Both Sides
TM38	Fire Blast	Fire	Special	110	85	5	Normal
TM39	Rock Tomb	Rock	Physical	60	95	15	Normal
TM42	Facade	Normal	Physical	70	100	20	Normal
TM44	Rest	Psychic	Status	—	—	10	Self
TM45	Attract	Normal	Status	—	100	15	Normal
TM46	Thief	Dark	Physical	60	100	25	Normal
TM48	Round	Normal	Special	60	100	15	Normal
TM56	Fling	Dark	Physical	—	100	10	Normal
TM59	Incinerate	Fire	Special	60	100	15	Many Others
TM67	Retaliate	Normal	Physical	70	100	5	Normal
TM68	Giga Impact	Normal	Physical	150	90	5	Normal
TM75	Swords Dance	Normal	Status	—	—	20	Self
TM77	Psych Up	Normal	Status	—	—	10	Normal
TM78	Bulldoze	Ground	Physical	60	100	20	Adjacent
TM80	Rock Slide	Rock	Physical	75	90	10	Many Others
TM82	Dragon Tail	Dragon	Physical	60	90	10	Normal
TM85	Dream Eater	Psychic	Special	100	100	15	Normal
TM87	Swagger	Normal	Status	—	90	15	Normal
TM88	Sleep Talk	Normal	Status	—	—	10	Self
TM90	Substitute	Normal	Status	—	—	10	Self
TM94	Secret Power	Normal	Physical	70	100	20	Normal
TM98	Power-Up Punch	Fighting	Physical	40	100	20	Normal
TM100	Confide	Normal	Status	—	—	20	Normal
HM01	Cut	Normal	Physical	50	95	30	Normal
HM03	Surf	Water	Special	90	100	15	Adjacent
HM04	Strength	Normal	Physical	80	100	15	Normal
HM06	Rock Smash	Fighting	Physical	40	100	15	Normal

MOVES LEARNED IN EXCHANGE FOR BP

Name	Type	Kind	Pow.	Acc.	PP	Range
Thunder Punch	Electric	Physical	75	100	15	Normal
Fire Punch	Fire	Physical	75	100	15	Normal
Ice Punch	Ice	Physical	75	100	15	Normal
Icy Wind	Ice	Special	55	95	15	Many Others
Aqua Tail	Water	Physical	90	90	10	Normal
Zen Headbutt	Psychic	Physical	80	90	15	Normal
Iron Tail	Steel	Physical	100	75	15	Normal
Bind	Normal	Physical	15	85	20	Normal
Snore	Normal	Special	50	100	15	Normal
Knock Off	Dark	Physical	65	100	20	Normal
Focus Punch	Fighting	Physical	150	100	20	Normal
Shock Wave	Electric	Special	60	—	20	Normal
Water Pulse	Water	Special	60	100	20	Normal

MOVES TAUGHT BY PEOPLE

Name	Type	Kind	Pow.	Acc.	PP	Range

EGG MOVES

Name	Type	Kind	Pow.	Acc.	PP	Range
Belly Drum	Normal	Status	—	—	10	Self
Magnitude	Ground	Physical	—	100	30	Adjacent
Body Slam	Normal	Physical	85	100	15	Normal
Curse	Ghost	Status	—	—	10	Varies
Smelling Salts	Normal	Physical	70	100	10	Normal
Sleep Talk	Normal	Status	—	—	10	Self
Snore	Normal	Special	50	100	15	Normal
Amnesia	Psychic	Status	—	—	20	Self
Hammer Arm	Fighting	Physical	100	90	10	Normal
Muddy Water	Water	Special	90	85	10	Many Others
Zen Headbutt	Psychic	Physical	80	90	15	Normal
Belch	Poison	Special	120	90	10	Normal

National Pokédex **109** Hoenn Pokédex **113**

Koffing

Poison Gas Pokémon

Poison

HEIGHT: 2'00" WEIGHT: 2.2 lbs.
Same form for ♂ / ♀

Ω If Koffing becomes agitated, it raises the toxicity of its internal gases and jets them out from all over its body. This Pokémon may also overinflate its round body, then explode.

α Koffing embodies toxic substances. It mixes the toxins with raw garbage to set off a chemical reaction that results in a terribly powerful poison gas. The higher the temperature, the more gas is concocted by this Pokémon.

ABILITY
Levitate

HIDDEN ABILITY

EGG GROUPS
Amorphous

STAT GROWTH RATES
HP ■■
Attack ■■■
Defense ■■■■
Sp. Atk ■■■
Sp. Def ■■
Speed ■■

ITEMS SOMETIMES HELD BY WILD POKÉMON
Smoke Ball

EVOLUTION
Koffing → Lv. 35 → Weezing

MAIN WAY TO REGISTER IN THE NATIONAL POKÉDEX
Catch on the Fiery Path.

Damage taken in normal battles

Type		Type	
Normal	×1	Flying	×1
Fire	×1	Psychic	×2
Water	×1	Bug	×0.5
Grass	×0.5	Rock	×1
Electric	×1	Ghost	×1
Ice	×1	Dragon	×1
Fighting	×0.5	Dark	×1
Poison	×0.5	Steel	×1
! Ground	×2	Fairy	×0.5

Damage taken in Inverse battles

Type		Type	
Normal	×1	Flying	×1
Fire	×1	Psychic	×0.5
Water	×1	Bug	×2
Grass	×2	Rock	×1
Electric	×1	Ghost	×1
Ice	×1	Dragon	×1
Fighting	×2	Dark	×1
Poison	×2	Steel	×1
! Ground	×0.5	Fairy	×2

Can be used in
Inverse Battle
Battle Institute
Battle Maison
Random Matchup (Free Battle)
Random Matchup (Others)

LEVEL-UP MOVES

Lv.	Name	Type	Kind	Pow.	Acc.	PP	Range
1	Poison Gas	Poison	Status	—	90	40	Many Others
1	Tackle	Normal	Physical	50	100	35	Normal
4	Smog	Poison	Special	30	70	20	Normal
7	Smokescreen	Normal	Status	—	100	20	Normal
12	Assurance	Dark	Physical	60	100	10	Normal
15	Clear Smog	Poison	Special	50	—	15	Normal
18	Sludge	Poison	Special	65	100	20	Normal
23	Self-Destruct	Normal	Physical	200	100	5	Adjacent
26	Haze	Ice	Status	—	—	30	Both Sides
29	Gyro Ball	Steel	Physical	—	100	5	Normal
34	Sludge Bomb	Poison	Special	90	100	10	Normal
37	Explosion	Normal	Physical	250	100	5	Adjacent
40	Destiny Bond	Ghost	Status	—	—	5	Self
42	Belch	Poison	Special	120	90	10	Normal
45	Memento	Dark	Status	—	100	10	Normal

TM & HM MOVES

No.	Name	Type	Kind	Pow.	Acc.	PP	Range
TM06	Toxic	Poison	Status	—	90	10	Normal
TM09	Venoshock	Poison	Special	65	100	10	Normal
TM10	Hidden Power	Normal	Special	60	100	15	Normal
TM11	Sunny Day	Fire	Status	—	—	5	Both Sides
TM12	Taunt	Dark	Status	—	100	20	Normal
TM17	Protect	Normal	Status	—	—	10	Self
TM18	Rain Dance	Water	Status	—	—	5	Both Sides
TM21	Frustration	Normal	Physical	—	100	20	Normal
TM24	Thunderbolt	Electric	Special	90	100	15	Normal
TM25	Thunder	Electric	Special	110	70	10	Normal
TM27	Return	Normal	Physical	—	100	20	Normal
TM30	Shadow Ball	Ghost	Special	80	100	15	Normal
TM32	Double Team	Normal	Status	—	—	15	Self
TM35	Flamethrower	Fire	Special	90	100	15	Normal
TM36	Sludge Bomb	Poison	Special	90	100	10	Normal
TM38	Fire Blast	Fire	Special	110	85	5	Normal
TM41	Torment	Dark	Status	—	100	15	Normal
TM42	Facade	Normal	Physical	70	100	20	Normal
TM44	Rest	Psychic	Status	—	—	10	Self
TM45	Attract	Normal	Status	—	100	15	Normal
TM46	Thief	Dark	Physical	60	100	25	Normal
TM48	Round	Normal	Special	60	100	15	Normal
TM59	Incinerate	Fire	Special	60	100	15	Many Others
TM61	Will-O-Wisp	Fire	Status	—	85	15	Normal
TM64	Explosion	Normal	Physical	250	100	5	Adjacent
TM66	Payback	Dark	Physical	50	100	10	Normal
TM70	Flash	Normal	Status	—	100	20	Normal
TM74	Gyro Ball	Steel	Physical	—	100	5	Normal
TM83	Infestation	Bug	Special	20	100	20	Normal
TM87	Swagger	Normal	Status	—	90	15	Normal
TM88	Sleep Talk	Normal	Status	—	—	10	Self
TM90	Substitute	Normal	Status	—	—	10	Self
TM94	Secret Power	Normal	Physical	70	100	20	Normal
TM97	Dark Pulse	Dark	Special	80	100	15	Normal
TM100	Confide	Normal	Status	—	—	20	Normal

MOVES LEARNED IN EXCHANGE FOR BP

Name	Type	Kind	Pow.	Acc.	PP	Range
Uproar	Normal	Special	90	100	10	1 Random
Snore	Normal	Special	50	100	15	Normal
Pain Split	Normal	Status	—	—	20	Normal
Shock Wave	Electric	Special	60	—	20	Normal
Spite	Ghost	Status	—	100	10	Normal

MOVES TAUGHT BY PEOPLE

Name	Type	Kind	Pow.	Acc.	PP	Range

EGG MOVES

Name	Type	Kind	Pow.	Acc.	PP	Range
Screech	Normal	Status	—	85	40	Normal
Psywave	Psychic	Special	—	100	15	Normal
Psybeam	Psychic	Special	65	100	20	Normal
Destiny Bond	Ghost	Status	—	—	5	Self
Pain Split	Normal	Status	—	—	20	Normal
Grudge	Ghost	Status	—	—	5	Self
Spite	Ghost	Status	—	100	10	Normal
Curse	Ghost	Status	—	—	10	Varies
Stockpile	Normal	Status	—	—	20	Self
Swallow	Normal	Status	—	—	10	Self
Spit Up	Normal	Special	—	100	10	Normal
Toxic Spikes	Poison	Status	—	—	20	Other Side

National Pokédex **110** Hoenn Pokédex **114**

Weezing

Poison Gas Pokémon

Poison

HEIGHT: 3'11" WEIGHT: 20.9 lbs.
Same form for ♂ / ♀

Ω Weezing loves the gases given off by rotted kitchen garbage. This Pokémon will find a dirty, unkempt house and make it its home. At night, when the people in the house are asleep, it will go through the trash.

α Weezing alternately shrinks and inflates its twin bodies to mix together toxic gases inside. The more the gases are mixed, the more powerful the toxins become. The Pokémon also becomes more putrid.

ABILITY
Levitate

HIDDEN ABILITY

EGG GROUPS
Amorphous

STAT GROWTH RATES
HP ■■■
Attack ■■■■■
Defense ■■■■■
Sp. Atk ■■■■
Sp. Def ■■■
Speed ■■■

ITEMS SOMETIMES HELD BY WILD POKÉMON
—

EVOLUTION
Koffing → Lv. 35 → Weezing

MAIN WAY TO REGISTER IN THE NATIONAL POKÉDEX
Level up Koffing to Lv. 35.

Damage taken in normal battles

Type		Type	
Normal	×1	Flying	×1
Fire	×1	Psychic	×2
Water	×1	Bug	×0.5
Grass	×0.5	Rock	×1
Electric	×1	Ghost	×1
Ice	×1	Dragon	×1
Fighting	×0.5	Dark	×1
Poison	×0.5	Steel	×1
! Ground	×2	Fairy	×0.5

Damage taken in Inverse battles

Type		Type	
Normal	×1	Flying	×1
Fire	×1	Psychic	×0.5
Water	×1	Bug	×2
Grass	×2	Rock	×1
Electric	×1	Ghost	×1
Ice	×1	Dragon	×1
Fighting	×2	Dark	×1
Poison	×2	Steel	×1
! Ground	×0.5	Fairy	×2

Can be used in
Inverse Battle
Battle Institute
Battle Maison
Random Matchup (Free Battle)
Random Matchup (Others)

LEVEL-UP MOVES

Lv.	Name	Type	Kind	Pow.	Acc.	PP	Range
1	Poison Gas	Poison	Status	—	90	40	Many Others
1	Tackle	Normal	Physical	50	100	35	Normal
1	Smog	Poison	Special	30	70	20	Normal
1	Smokescreen	Normal	Status	—	100	20	Normal
4	Smog	Poison	Special	30	70	20	Normal
7	Smokescreen	Normal	Status	—	100	20	Normal
12	Assurance	Dark	Physical	60	100	10	Normal
15	Clear Smog	Poison	Special	50	—	15	Normal
18	Sludge	Poison	Special	65	100	20	Normal
23	Self-Destruct	Normal	Physical	200	100	5	Adjacent
26	Haze	Ice	Status	—	—	30	Both Sides
29	Double Hit	Normal	Physical	35	90	10	Normal
34	Sludge Bomb	Poison	Special	90	100	10	Normal
40	Explosion	Normal	Physical	250	100	5	Adjacent
46	Destiny Bond	Ghost	Status	—	—	5	Self
51	Belch	Poison	Special	120	90	10	Normal
57	Memento	Dark	Status	—	100	10	Normal

TM & HM MOVES

No.	Name	Type	Kind	Pow.	Acc.	PP	Range
TM06	Toxic	Poison	Status	—	90	10	Normal
TM09	Venoshock	Poison	Special	65	100	10	Normal
TM10	Hidden Power	Normal	Special	60	100	15	Normal
TM11	Sunny Day	Fire	Status	—	—	5	Both Sides
TM12	Taunt	Dark	Status	—	100	20	Normal
TM15	Hyper Beam	Normal	Special	150	90	5	Normal
TM17	Protect	Normal	Status	—	—	10	Self
TM18	Rain Dance	Water	Status	—	—	5	Both Sides
TM21	Frustration	Normal	Physical	—	100	20	Normal
TM24	Thunderbolt	Electric	Special	90	100	15	Normal
TM25	Thunder	Electric	Special	110	70	10	Normal
TM27	Return	Normal	Physical	—	100	20	Normal
TM30	Shadow Ball	Ghost	Special	80	100	15	Normal
TM32	Double Team	Normal	Status	—	—	15	Self
TM35	Flamethrower	Fire	Special	90	100	15	Normal
TM36	Sludge Bomb	Poison	Special	90	100	10	Normal
TM38	Fire Blast	Fire	Special	110	85	5	Normal
TM41	Torment	Dark	Status	—	100	15	Normal
TM42	Facade	Normal	Physical	70	100	20	Normal
TM44	Rest	Psychic	Status	—	—	10	Self
TM45	Attract	Normal	Status	—	100	15	Normal
TM46	Thief	Dark	Physical	60	100	25	Normal
TM48	Round	Normal	Special	60	100	15	Normal
TM59	Incinerate	Fire	Special	60	100	15	Many Others
TM61	Will-O-Wisp	Fire	Status	—	85	15	Normal
TM64	Explosion	Normal	Physical	250	100	5	Adjacent
TM66	Payback	Dark	Physical	50	100	10	Normal
TM68	Giga Impact	Normal	Physical	150	90	5	Normal
TM70	Flash	Normal	Status	—	100	20	Normal
TM74	Gyro Ball	Steel	Physical	—	100	5	Normal
TM83	Infestation	Bug	Special	20	100	20	Normal
TM87	Swagger	Normal	Status	—	90	15	Normal
TM88	Sleep Talk	Normal	Status	—	—	10	Self
TM90	Substitute	Normal	Status	—	—	10	Self
TM94	Secret Power	Normal	Physical	70	100	20	Normal
TM97	Dark Pulse	Dark	Special	80	100	15	Normal
TM100	Confide	Normal	Status	—	—	20	Normal

MOVES LEARNED IN EXCHANGE FOR BP

Name	Type	Kind	Pow.	Acc.	PP	Range
Uproar	Normal	Special	90	100	10	1 Random
Snore	Normal	Special	50	100	15	Normal
Pain Split	Normal	Status	—	—	20	Normal
Shock Wave	Electric	Special	60	—	20	Normal
Spite	Ghost	Status	—	100	10	Normal

MOVES TAUGHT BY PEOPLE

Name	Type	Kind	Pow.	Acc.	PP	Range

National Pokédex **111** Hoenn Pokédex **176**

Rhyhorn

Spikes Pokémon

Ground Rock

HEIGHT: 3'03" WEIGHT: 253.5 lbs.

The male has a longer horn on its face.
The female has a shorter horn on its face.

♂ Ω Rhyhorn runs in a straight line, smashing everything in its path. It is not bothered even if it rushes headlong into a block of steel. This Pokémon may feel some pain from the collision the next day, however.

♀ α Rhyhorn's brain is very small. It is so dense, while on a run it forgets why it started running in the first place. It apparently remembers sometimes if it demolishes something.

ABILITIES
Lightning Rod
Rock Head

HIDDEN ABILITY
Reckless

EGG GROUPS
Monster Field

STAT GROWTH RATES
HP
Attack
Defense
Sp. Atk
Sp. Def
Speed

ITEMS SOMETIMES HELD BY WILD POKÉMON
—

EVOLUTION
Rhyhorn → Lv. 42 → Rhydon → Link Trade with Protector → Rhyperior

MAIN WAY TO REGISTER IN THE NATIONAL POKÉDEX

Catch in the tall grass in the upper-left corner of the Safari Zone.

Damage taken in normal battles

Type		Type	
Normal	×0.5	Flying	×0.5
Fire	×0.5	Psychic	×1
Water	×4	Bug	×1
Grass	×4	Rock	×0.5
Electric	×0	Ghost	×1
Ice	×2	Dragon	×1
Fighting	×2	Dark	×1
Poison	×0.25	Steel	×2
Ground	×2	Fairy	×1

Damage taken in Inverse battles

Type		Type	
Normal	×2	Flying	×2
Fire	×2	Psychic	×1
Water	×0.25	Bug	×1
Grass	×0.25	Rock	×2
Electric	×2	Ghost	×1
Ice	×0.5	Dragon	×1
Fighting	×0.5	Dark	×1
Poison	×4	Steel	×0.5
Ground	×0.5	Fairy	×1

Can be used in
Inverse Battle
Battle Institute
Battle Maison
Random Matchup (Free Battle)
Random Matchup (Others)

LEVEL-UP MOVES

Lv.	Name	Type	Kind	Pow.	Acc.	PP	Range
1	Horn Attack	Normal	Physical	65	100	25	Normal
1	Tail Whip	Normal	Status	—	100	30	Many Others
5	Fury Attack	Normal	Physical	15	85	20	Normal
9	Scary Face	Normal	Status	—	100	10	Normal
13	Smack Down	Rock	Physical	50	100	15	Normal
17	Stomp	Normal	Physical	65	100	20	Normal
21	Bulldoze	Ground	Physical	60	100	20	Adjacent
25	Chip Away	Normal	Physical	70	100	20	Normal
29	Rock Blast	Rock	Physical	25	90	10	Normal
33	Drill Run	Ground	Physical	80	95	10	Normal
37	Take Down	Normal	Physical	90	85	20	Normal
41	Stone Edge	Rock	Physical	100	80	5	Normal
45	Earthquake	Ground	Physical	100	100	10	Adjacent
49	Megahorn	Bug	Physical	120	85	10	Normal
53	Horn Drill	Normal	Physical	—	30	5	Normal

TM & HM MOVES

No.	Name	Type	Kind	Pow.	Acc.	PP	Range
TM05	Roar	Normal	Status	—	—	20	Normal
TM06	Toxic	Poison	Status	—	90	10	Normal
TM10	Hidden Power	Normal	Special	60	100	15	Normal
TM11	Sunny Day	Fire	Status	—	—	5	Both Sides
TM13	Ice Beam	Ice	Special	90	100	10	Normal
TM14	Blizzard	Ice	Special	110	70	5	Many Others
TM17	Protect	Normal	Status	—	—	10	Self
TM18	Rain Dance	Water	Status	—	—	5	Both Sides
TM21	Frustration	Normal	Physical	—	100	20	Normal
TM23	Smack Down	Rock	Physical	50	100	15	Normal
TM24	Thunderbolt	Electric	Special	90	100	15	Normal
TM25	Thunder	Electric	Special	110	70	10	Normal
TM26	Earthquake	Ground	Physical	100	100	10	Adjacent
TM27	Return	Normal	Physical	—	100	20	Normal
TM28	Dig	Ground	Physical	80	100	10	Normal
TM32	Double Team	Normal	Status	—	—	15	Self
TM35	Flamethrower	Fire	Special	90	100	15	Normal
TM37	Sandstorm	Rock	Status	—	—	10	Both Sides
TM38	Fire Blast	Fire	Special	110	85	5	Normal
TM39	Rock Tomb	Rock	Physical	60	95	15	Normal
TM42	Facade	Normal	Physical	70	100	20	Normal
TM44	Rest	Psychic	Status	—	—	10	Self
TM45	Attract	Normal	Status	—	100	15	Normal
TM46	Thief	Dark	Physical	60	100	25	Normal
TM48	Round	Normal	Special	60	100	15	Normal
TM59	Incinerate	Fire	Special	60	100	15	Many Others
TM66	Payback	Dark	Physical	50	100	10	Normal
TM69	Rock Polish	Rock	Status	—	—	20	Self
TM71	Stone Edge	Rock	Physical	100	80	5	Normal
TM75	Swords Dance	Normal	Status	—	—	20	Self
TM78	Bulldoze	Ground	Physical	60	100	20	Adjacent
TM80	Rock Slide	Rock	Physical	75	90	10	Many Others
TM84	Poison Jab	Poison	Physical	80	100	20	Normal
TM87	Swagger	Normal	Status	—	90	15	Normal
TM88	Sleep Talk	Normal	Status	—	—	10	Self
TM90	Substitute	Normal	Status	—	—	10	Self
TM94	Secret Power	Normal	Physical	70	100	20	Normal
TM100	Confide	Normal	Status	—	—	20	Normal
HM04	Strength	Normal	Physical	80	100	15	Normal
HM06	Rock Smash	Fighting	Physical	40	100	15	Normal

MOVES LEARNED IN EXCHANGE FOR BP

Name	Type	Kind	Pow.	Acc.	PP	Range
Drill Run	Ground	Physical	80	95	10	Normal
Uproar	Normal	Special	90	100	10	1 Random
Earth Power	Ground	Special	90	100	10	Normal
Superpower	Fighting	Physical	120	100	5	Normal
Icy Wind	Ice	Special	55	95	15	Many Others
Aqua Tail	Water	Physical	90	90	10	Normal
Dragon Pulse	Dragon	Special	85	100	10	Normal
Iron Tail	Steel	Physical	100	75	15	Normal
Snore	Normal	Special	50	100	15	Normal
Shock Wave	Electric	Special	60	—	20	Normal
Spite	Ghost	Status	—	100	10	Normal
Endeavor	Normal	Physical	—	100	5	Normal
Stealth Rock	Rock	Status	—	—	20	Other Side

MOVES TAUGHT BY PEOPLE

Name	Type	Kind	Pow.	Acc.	PP	Range

EGG MOVES

Name	Type	Kind	Pow.	Acc.	PP	Range
Crunch	Dark	Physical	80	100	15	Normal
Reversal	Fighting	Physical	—	100	15	Normal
Counter	Fighting	Physical	—	100	20	Varies
Magnitude	Ground	Physical	—	100	30	Adjacent
Curse	Ghost	Status	—	—	10	Varies
Crush Claw	Normal	Physical	75	95	10	Normal
Dragon Rush	Dragon	Physical	100	75	10	Normal
Ice Fang	Ice	Physical	65	95	15	Normal
Fire Fang	Fire	Physical	65	95	15	Normal
Thunder Fang	Electric	Physical	65	95	15	Normal
Skull Bash	Normal	Physical	130	100	10	Normal
Iron Tail	Steel	Physical	100	75	15	Normal
Rock Climb	Normal	Physical	90	85	20	Normal
Rototiller	Ground	Status	—	—	10	Adjacent
Metal Burst	Steel	Physical	—	100	10	Varies
Guard Split	Psychic	Status	—	—	10	Normal

National Pokédex **112** Hoenn Pokédex **177**

Rhydon

Drill Pokémon

Ground Rock

HEIGHT: 6'03" WEIGHT: 264.6 lbs.

The male has a longer horn on its face.
The female has a shorter horn on its face.

♂ Ω Rhydon's horn can crush even uncut diamonds. One sweeping blow of its tail can topple a building. This Pokémon's hide is extremely tough. Even direct cannon hits don't leave a scratch.

♀ α Rhydon has a horn that serves as a drill. It is used for destroying rocks and boulders. This Pokémon occasionally rams into streams of magma, but the armor-like hide prevents it from feeling the heat.

ABILITIES
Lightning Rod
Rock Head

HIDDEN ABILITY
Reckless

EGG GROUPS
Monster Field

STAT GROWTH RATES
HP
Attack
Defense
Sp. Atk
Sp. Def
Speed

ITEMS SOMETIMES HELD BY WILD POKÉMON
—

EVOLUTION
Rhyhorn → Lv. 42 → Rhydon → Link Trade with Protector → Rhyperior

MAIN WAY TO REGISTER IN THE NATIONAL POKÉDEX

Level up Rhyhorn to Lv. 42.

Damage taken in normal battles

Type		Type	
Normal	×0.5	Flying	×0.5
Fire	×0.5	Psychic	×1
Water	×4	Bug	×1
Grass	×4	Rock	×0.5
Electric	×0	Ghost	×1
Ice	×2	Dragon	×1
Fighting	×2	Dark	×1
Poison	×0.25	Steel	×2
Ground	×2	Fairy	×1

Damage taken in Inverse battles

Type		Type	
Normal	×2	Flying	×2
Fire	×2	Psychic	×1
Water	×0.25	Bug	×1
Grass	×0.25	Rock	×2
Electric	×2	Ghost	×1
Ice	×0.5	Dragon	×1
Fighting	×0.5	Dark	×1
Poison	×4	Steel	×0.5
Ground	×0.5	Fairy	×1

Can be used in
Inverse Battle
Battle Institute
Battle Maison
Random Matchup (Free Battle)
Random Matchup (Others)

LEVEL-UP MOVES

Lv.	Name	Type	Kind	Pow.	Acc.	PP	Range
1	Horn Drill	Normal	Physical	—	30	5	Normal
1	Horn Attack	Normal	Physical	65	100	25	Normal
1	Tail Whip	Normal	Status	—	100	30	Many Others
1	Fury Attack	Normal	Physical	15	85	20	Normal
1	Scary Face	Normal	Status	—	100	10	Normal
5	Fury Attack	Normal	Physical	15	85	20	Normal
9	Scary Face	Normal	Status	—	100	10	Normal
13	Smack Down	Rock	Physical	50	100	15	Normal
17	Stomp	Normal	Physical	65	100	20	Normal
21	Bulldoze	Ground	Physical	60	100	20	Adjacent
25	Chip Away	Normal	Physical	70	100	20	Normal
29	Rock Blast	Rock	Physical	25	90	10	Normal
33	Drill Run	Ground	Physical	80	95	10	Normal
37	Take Down	Normal	Physical	90	85	20	Normal
41	Stone Edge	Rock	Physical	100	80	5	Normal
42	Hammer Arm	Fighting	Physical	100	90	10	Normal
48	Earthquake	Ground	Physical	100	100	10	Adjacent
55	Megahorn	Bug	Physical	120	85	10	Normal
62	Horn Drill	Normal	Physical	—	30	5	Normal

TM & HM MOVES

No.	Name	Type	Kind	Pow.	Acc.	PP	Range
TM05	Roar	Normal	Status	—	—	20	Normal
TM06	Toxic	Poison	Status	—	90	10	Normal
TM10	Hidden Power	Normal	Special	60	100	15	Normal
TM11	Sunny Day	Fire	Status	—	—	5	Both Sides
TM13	Ice Beam	Ice	Special	90	100	10	Normal
TM14	Blizzard	Ice	Special	110	70	5	Many Others
TM15	Hyper Beam	Normal	Special	150	90	5	Normal
TM17	Protect	Normal	Status	—	—	10	Self
TM18	Rain Dance	Water	Status	—	—	5	Both Sides
TM21	Frustration	Normal	Physical	—	100	20	Normal
TM23	Smack Down	Rock	Physical	50	100	15	Normal
TM24	Thunderbolt	Electric	Special	90	100	15	Normal
TM25	Thunder	Electric	Special	110	70	10	Normal
TM26	Earthquake	Ground	Physical	100	100	10	Adjacent
TM27	Return	Normal	Physical	—	100	20	Normal
TM28	Dig	Ground	Physical	80	100	10	Normal
TM31	Brick Break	Fighting	Physical	75	100	15	Normal
TM32	Double Team	Normal	Status	—	—	15	Self
TM35	Flamethrower	Fire	Special	90	100	15	Normal
TM37	Sandstorm	Rock	Status	—	—	10	Both Sides
TM38	Fire Blast	Fire	Special	110	85	5	Normal
TM39	Rock Tomb	Rock	Physical	60	95	15	Normal
TM42	Facade	Normal	Physical	70	100	20	Normal
TM44	Rest	Psychic	Status	—	—	10	Self
TM45	Attract	Normal	Status	—	100	15	Normal
TM46	Thief	Dark	Physical	60	100	25	Normal
TM48	Round	Normal	Special	60	100	15	Normal
TM52	Focus Blast	Fighting	Special	120	70	5	Normal
TM56	Fling	Dark	Physical	—	100	10	Normal
TM59	Incinerate	Fire	Special	60	100	15	Many Others
TM65	Shadow Claw	Ghost	Physical	70	100	15	Normal
TM66	Payback	Dark	Physical	50	100	10	Normal
TM68	Giga Impact	Normal	Physical	150	90	5	Normal
TM69	Rock Polish	Rock	Status	—	—	20	Self
TM71	Stone Edge	Rock	Physical	100	80	5	Normal
TM75	Swords Dance	Normal	Status	—	—	20	Self
TM78	Bulldoze	Ground	Physical	60	100	20	Adjacent
TM80	Rock Slide	Rock	Physical	75	90	10	Many Others
TM82	Dragon Tail	Dragon	Physical	60	90	10	Normal
TM84	Poison Jab	Poison	Physical	80	100	20	Normal
TM87	Swagger	Normal	Status	—	90	15	Normal
TM88	Sleep Talk	Normal	Status	—	—	10	Self
TM90	Substitute	Normal	Status	—	—	10	Self
TM94	Secret Power	Normal	Physical	70	100	20	Normal
TM98	Power-Up Punch	Fighting	Physical	40	100	20	Normal
TM100	Confide	Normal	Status	—	—	20	Normal
HM01	Cut	Normal	Physical	50	95	30	Normal
HM03	Surf	Water	Special	90	100	15	Adjacent
HM04	Strength	Normal	Physical	80	100	15	Normal
HM06	Rock Smash	Fighting	Physical	40	100	15	Normal

MOVES LEARNED IN EXCHANGE FOR BP

Name	Type	Kind	Pow.	Acc.	PP	Range
Drill Run	Ground	Physical	80	95	10	Normal
Uproar	Normal	Special	90	100	10	1 Random
Thunder Punch	Electric	Physical	75	100	15	Normal
Fire Punch	Fire	Physical	75	100	15	Normal
Ice Punch	Ice	Physical	75	100	15	Normal
Block	Normal	Status	—	—	5	Normal
Earth Power	Ground	Special	90	100	10	Normal
Superpower	Fighting	Physical	120	100	5	Normal
Icy Wind	Ice	Special	55	95	15	Many Others
Aqua Tail	Water	Physical	90	90	10	Normal
Dragon Pulse	Dragon	Special	85	100	10	Normal
Iron Tail	Steel	Physical	100	75	15	Normal
Snore	Normal	Special	50	100	15	Normal
Focus Punch	Fighting	Physical	150	100	20	Normal
Shock Wave	Electric	Special	60	—	20	Normal
Spite	Ghost	Status	—	100	10	Normal
Endeavor	Normal	Physical	—	100	5	Normal
Outrage	Dragon	Physical	120	100	10	1 Random
Stealth Rock	Rock	Status	—	—	20	Other Side

MOVES TAUGHT BY PEOPLE

Name	Type	Kind	Pow.	Acc.	PP	Range

National Pokédex **113** Hoenn Pokédex —

Chansey

Egg Pokémon

Normal

HEIGHT: 3'07" WEIGHT: 76.3 lbs.

♀ only

Ω Chansey lays nutritionally excellent eggs on an everyday basis. The eggs are so delicious, they are easily and eagerly devoured by even those people who have lost their appetite.

α Chansey lays nutritionally excellent eggs on an everyday basis. The eggs are so delicious, they are easily and eagerly devoured by even those people who have lost their appetite.

ABILITIES
Natural Cure
Serene Grace

HIDDEN ABILITY
Healer

EGG GROUPS
Fairy

STAT GROWTH RATES
HP
Attack
Defense
Sp. Atk
Sp. Def
Speed

ITEMS SOMETIMES HELD BY WILD POKÉMON
—

EVOLUTION

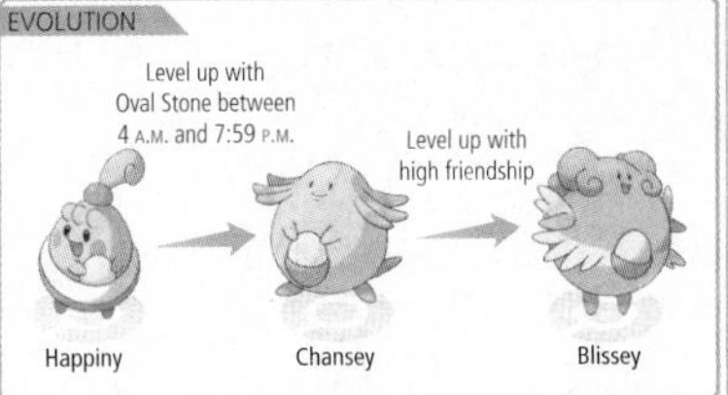

MAIN WAY TO REGISTER IN THE NATIONAL POKÉDEX

Have Happiny hold an Oval Stone, then level it up between 4:00 A.M. and 7:59 P.M.

Damage taken in normal battles

Type		Type	
Normal	×1	Flying	×1
Fire	×1	Psychic	×1
Water	×1	Bug	×1
Grass	×1	Rock	×1
Electric	×1	Ghost	×0
Ice	×1	Dragon	×1
Fighting	×2	Dark	×1
Poison	×1	Steel	×1
Ground	×1	Fairy	×1

Damage taken in Inverse battles

Type		Type	
Normal	×1	Flying	×1
Fire	×1	Psychic	×1
Water	×1	Bug	×1
Grass	×1	Rock	×1
Electric	×1	Ghost	×2
Ice	×1	Dragon	×1
Fighting	×0.5	Dark	×1
Poison	×1	Steel	×1
Ground	×1	Fairy	×1

Can be used in
Inverse Battle
Battle Institute
Battle Maison
Random Matchup (Free Battle)
Random Matchup (Others)

LEVEL-UP MOVES

Lv.	Name	Type	Kind	Pow.	Acc.	PP	Range
1	Double-Edge	Normal	Physical	120	100	15	Normal
1	Defense Curl	Normal	Status	—	—	40	Self
1	Pound	Normal	Physical	40	100	35	Normal
1	Growl	Normal	Status	—	100	40	Many Others
5	Tail Whip	Normal	Status	—	100	30	Many Others
9	Refresh	Normal	Status	—	—	20	Self
12	Double Slap	Normal	Physical	15	85	10	Normal
16	Soft-Boiled	Normal	Status	—	—	10	Self
20	Bestow	Normal	Status	—	—	15	Normal
23	Minimize	Normal	Status	—	—	10	Self
27	Take Down	Normal	Physical	90	85	20	Normal
31	Sing	Normal	Status	—	55	15	Normal
34	Fling	Dark	Physical	—	100	10	Normal
38	Heal Pulse	Psychic	Status	—	—	10	Normal
42	Egg Bomb	Normal	Physical	100	75	10	Normal
46	Light Screen	Psychic	Status	—	—	30	Your Side
50	Healing Wish	Psychic	Status	—	—	10	Self
54	Double-Edge	Normal	Physical	120	100	15	Normal

TM & HM MOVES

No.	Name	Type	Kind	Pow.	Acc.	PP	Range
TM04	Calm Mind	Psychic	Status	—	—	20	Self
TM06	Toxic	Poison	Status	—	90	10	Normal
TM07	Hail	Ice	Status	—	—	10	Both Sides
TM10	Hidden Power	Normal	Special	60	100	15	Normal
TM11	Sunny Day	Fire	Status	—	—	5	Both Sides
TM13	Ice Beam	Ice	Special	90	100	10	Normal
TM14	Blizzard	Ice	Special	110	70	5	Many Others
TM15	Hyper Beam	Normal	Special	150	90	5	Normal
TM16	Light Screen	Psychic	Status	—	—	30	Your Side
TM17	Protect	Normal	Status	—	—	10	Self
TM18	Rain Dance	Water	Status	—	—	5	Both Sides
TM20	Safeguard	Normal	Status	—	—	25	Your Side
TM21	Frustration	Normal	Physical	—	100	20	Normal
TM22	Solar Beam	Grass	Special	120	100	10	Normal
TM24	Thunderbolt	Electric	Special	90	100	15	Normal
TM25	Thunder	Electric	Special	110	70	10	Normal
TM26	Earthquake	Ground	Physical	100	100	10	Adjacent
TM27	Return	Normal	Physical	—	100	20	Normal
TM29	Psychic	Psychic	Special	90	100	10	Normal
TM30	Shadow Ball	Ghost	Special	80	100	15	Normal
TM31	Brick Break	Fighting	Physical	75	100	15	Normal
TM32	Double Team	Normal	Status	—	—	15	Self
TM35	Flamethrower	Fire	Special	90	100	15	Normal
TM37	Sandstorm	Rock	Status	—	—	10	Both Sides
TM38	Fire Blast	Fire	Special	110	85	5	Normal
TM39	Rock Tomb	Rock	Physical	60	95	15	Normal
TM42	Facade	Normal	Physical	70	100	20	Normal
TM44	Rest	Psychic	Status	—	—	10	Self
TM45	Attract	Normal	Status	—	100	15	Normal
TM48	Round	Normal	Special	60	100	15	Normal
TM49	Echoed Voice	Normal	Special	40	100	15	Normal
TM56	Fling	Dark	Physical	—	100	10	Normal
TM57	Charge Beam	Electric	Special	50	90	10	Normal
TM59	Incinerate	Fire	Special	60	100	15	Many Others
TM67	Retaliate	Normal	Physical	70	100	5	Normal
TM68	Giga Impact	Normal	Physical	150	90	5	Normal
TM70	Flash	Normal	Status	—	100	20	Normal
TM73	Thunder Wave	Electric	Status	—	100	20	Normal
TM77	Psych Up	Normal	Status	—	—	10	Normal
TM78	Bulldoze	Ground	Physical	60	100	20	Adjacent
TM80	Rock Slide	Rock	Physical	75	90	10	Many Others
TM85	Dream Eater	Psychic	Special	100	100	15	Normal
TM86	Grass Knot	Grass	Special	—	100	20	Normal
TM87	Swagger	Normal	Status	—	90	15	Normal
TM88	Sleep Talk	Normal	Status	—	—	10	Self
TM90	Substitute	Normal	Status	—	—	10	Self
TM93	Wild Charge	Electric	Physical	90	100	15	Normal
TM94	Secret Power	Normal	Physical	70	100	20	Normal
TM98	Power-Up Punch	Fighting	Physical	40	100	20	Normal
TM99	Dazzling Gleam	Fairy	Special	80	100	10	Many Others
TM100	Confide	Normal	Status	—	—	20	Normal
HM04	Strength	Normal	Physical	80	100	15	Normal
HM06	Rock Smash	Fighting	Physical	40	100	15	Normal

MOVES LEARNED IN EXCHANGE FOR BP

Name	Type	Kind	Pow.	Acc.	PP	Range
Covet	Normal	Physical	60	100	25	Normal
Thunder Punch	Electric	Physical	75	100	15	Normal
Fire Punch	Fire	Physical	75	100	15	Normal
Ice Punch	Ice	Physical	75	100	15	Normal
Gravity	Psychic	Status	—	—	5	Both Sides
Last Resort	Normal	Physical	140	100	5	Normal
Icy Wind	Ice	Special	55	95	15	Many Others
Zen Headbutt	Psychic	Physical	80	90	15	Normal
Hyper Voice	Normal	Special	90	100	10	Many Others
Iron Tail	Steel	Physical	100	75	15	Normal
Snore	Normal	Special	50	100	15	Normal
Heal Bell	Normal	Status	—	—	5	Your Party
Drain Punch	Fighting	Physical	75	100	10	Normal
Focus Punch	Fighting	Physical	150	100	20	Normal
Shock Wave	Electric	Special	60	—	20	Normal
Water Pulse	Water	Special	60	100	20	Normal
Helping Hand	Normal	Status	—	—	20	1 Ally
Endeavor	Normal	Physical	—	100	5	Normal
Recycle	Normal	Status	—	—	10	Self
Snatch	Dark	Status	—	—	10	Self
Stealth Rock	Rock	Status	—	—	20	Other Side
Skill Swap	Psychic	Status	—	—	10	Normal

MOVES TAUGHT BY PEOPLE

Name	Type	Kind	Pow.	Acc.	PP	Range

EGG MOVES

Name	Type	Kind	Pow.	Acc.	PP	Range
Present	Normal	Physical	—	90	15	Normal
Metronome	Normal	Status	—	—	10	Self
Heal Bell	Normal	Status	—	—	5	Your Party
Aromatherapy	Grass	Status	—	—	5	Your Party
Counter	Fighting	Physical	—	100	20	Varies
Helping Hand	Normal	Status	—	—	20	1 Ally
Gravity	Psychic	Status	—	—	5	Both Sides
Mud Bomb	Ground	Special	65	85	10	Normal
Natural Gift	Normal	Physical	—	100	15	Normal
Endure	Normal	Status	—	—	10	Self
Seismic Toss	Fighting	Physical	—	100	20	Normal

National Pokédex **114** Hoenn Pokédex —

Tangela

Vine Pokémon

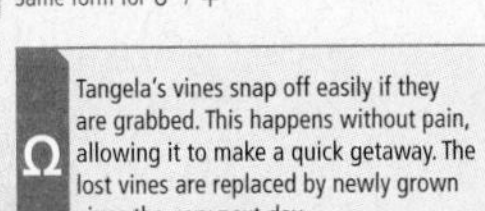

Grass

HEIGHT: 3'03" WEIGHT: 77.2 lbs.

Same form for ♂ / ♀

Ω Tangela's vines snap off easily if they are grabbed. This happens without pain, allowing it to make a quick getaway. The lost vines are replaced by newly grown vines the very next day.

α Tangela's vines snap off easily if they are grabbed. This happens without pain, allowing it to make a quick getaway. The lost vines are replaced by newly grown vines the very next day.

ABILITIES
Chlorophyll
Leaf Guard

HIDDEN ABILITY
Regenerator

EGG GROUPS
Grass

STAT GROWTH RATES
HP
Attack
Defense
Sp. Atk
Sp. Def
Speed

ITEMS SOMETIMES HELD BY WILD POKÉMON
—

EVOLUTION

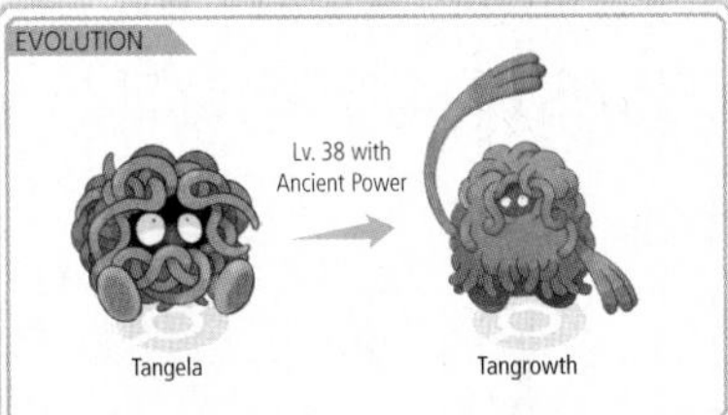

MAIN WAY TO REGISTER IN THE NATIONAL POKÉDEX

Catch in Mirage Forest 1.

Damage taken in normal battles

Type		Type	
Normal	×1	Flying	×2
Fire	×2	Psychic	×1
Water	×0.5	Bug	×2
Grass	×0.5	Rock	×1
Electric	×0.5	Ghost	×1
Ice	×2	Dragon	×1
Fighting	×1	Dark	×1
Poison	×2	Steel	×1
Ground	×0.5	Fairy	×1

Damage taken in Inverse battles

Type		Type	
Normal	×1	Flying	×0.5
Fire	×0.5	Psychic	×1
Water	×2	Bug	×0.5
Grass	×2	Rock	×1
Electric	×2	Ghost	×1
Ice	×0.5	Dragon	×1
Fighting	×1	Dark	×1
Poison	×0.5	Steel	×1
Ground	×2	Fairy	×1

Can be used in
Inverse Battle
Battle Institute
Battle Maison
Random Matchup (Free Battle)
Random Matchup (Others)

LEVEL-UP MOVES

Lv.	Name	Type	Kind	Pow.	Acc.	PP	Range
1	Ingrain	Grass	Status	—	—	20	Self
1	Constrict	Normal	Physical	10	100	35	Normal
4	Sleep Powder	Grass	Status	—	75	15	Normal
7	Vine Whip	Grass	Physical	45	100	25	Normal
10	Absorb	Grass	Special	20	100	25	Normal
14	Poison Powder	Poison	Status	—	75	35	Normal
17	Bind	Normal	Physical	15	85	20	Normal
20	Growth	Normal	Status	—	—	20	Self
23	Mega Drain	Grass	Special	40	100	15	Normal
27	Knock Off	Dark	Physical	65	100	20	Normal
30	Stun Spore	Grass	Status	—	75	30	Normal
33	Natural Gift	Normal	Physical	—	100	15	Normal
36	Giga Drain	Grass	Special	75	100	10	Normal
38	Ancient Power	Rock	Special	60	100	5	Normal
41	Slam	Normal	Physical	80	75	20	Normal
44	Tickle	Normal	Status	—	100	20	Normal
46	Wring Out	Normal	Special	—	100	5	Normal
48	Grassy Terrain	Grass	Status	—	—	10	Both Sides
50	Power Whip	Grass	Physical	120	85	10	Normal

TM & HM MOVES

No.	Name	Type	Kind	Pow.	Acc.	PP	Range
TM06	Toxic	Poison	Status	—	90	10	Normal
TM10	Hidden Power	Normal	Special	60	100	15	Normal
TM11	Sunny Day	Fire	Status	—	—	5	Both Sides
TM15	Hyper Beam	Normal	Special	150	90	5	Normal
TM17	Protect	Normal	Status	—	—	10	Self
TM21	Frustration	Normal	Physical	—	100	20	Normal
TM22	Solar Beam	Grass	Special	120	100	10	Normal
TM27	Return	Normal	Physical	—	100	20	Normal
TM32	Double Team	Normal	Status	—	—	15	Self
TM33	Reflect	Psychic	Status	—	—	20	Your Side
TM36	Sludge Bomb	Poison	Special	90	100	10	Normal
TM42	Facade	Normal	Physical	70	100	20	Normal
TM44	Rest	Psychic	Status	—	—	10	Self
TM45	Attract	Normal	Status	—	100	15	Normal
TM46	Thief	Dark	Physical	60	100	25	Normal
TM48	Round	Normal	Special	60	100	15	Normal
TM53	Energy Ball	Grass	Special	90	100	10	Normal
TM68	Giga Impact	Normal	Physical	150	90	5	Normal
TM70	Flash	Normal	Status	—	100	20	Normal
TM75	Swords Dance	Normal	Status	—	—	20	Self
TM77	Psych Up	Normal	Status	—	—	10	Normal
TM83	Infestation	Bug	Special	20	100	20	Normal
TM86	Grass Knot	Grass	Special	—	100	20	Normal
TM87	Swagger	Normal	Status	—	90	15	Normal
TM88	Sleep Talk	Normal	Status	—	—	10	Self
TM90	Substitute	Normal	Status	—	—	10	Self
TM94	Secret Power	Normal	Physical	70	100	20	Normal
TM96	Nature Power	Normal	Status	—	—	20	Normal
TM100	Confide	Normal	Status	—	—	20	Normal
HM01	Cut	Normal	Physical	50	95	30	Normal
HM06	Rock Smash	Fighting	Physical	40	100	15	Normal

MOVES LEARNED IN EXCHANGE FOR BP

Name	Type	Kind	Pow.	Acc.	PP	Range
Seed Bomb	Grass	Physical	80	100	15	Normal
Bind	Normal	Physical	15	85	20	Normal
Snore	Normal	Special	50	100	15	Normal
Knock Off	Dark	Physical	65	100	20	Normal
Synthesis	Grass	Status	—	—	5	Self
Pain Split	Normal	Status	—	—	20	Normal
Giga Drain	Grass	Special	75	100	10	Normal
Shock Wave	Electric	Special	60	—	20	Normal
Worry Seed	Grass	Status	—	100	10	Normal
Endeavor	Normal	Physical	—	100	5	Normal

MOVES TAUGHT BY PEOPLE

Name	Type	Kind	Pow.	Acc.	PP	Range

EGG MOVES

Name	Type	Kind	Pow.	Acc.	PP	Range
Flail	Normal	Physical	—	100	15	Normal
Confusion	Psychic	Special	50	100	25	Normal
Mega Drain	Grass	Special	40	100	15	Normal
Amnesia	Psychic	Status	—	—	20	Self
Leech Seed	Grass	Status	—	90	10	Normal
Nature Power	Normal	Status	—	—	20	Normal
Endeavor	Normal	Physical	—	100	5	Normal
Leaf Storm	Grass	Special	130	90	5	Normal
Power Swap	Psychic	Status	—	—	10	Normal
Giga Drain	Grass	Special	75	100	10	Normal
Rage Powder	Bug	Status	—	—	20	Self
Natural Gift	Normal	Physical	—	100	15	Normal

National Pokédex **115** Hoenn Pokédex —

Kangaskhan

Parent Pokémon

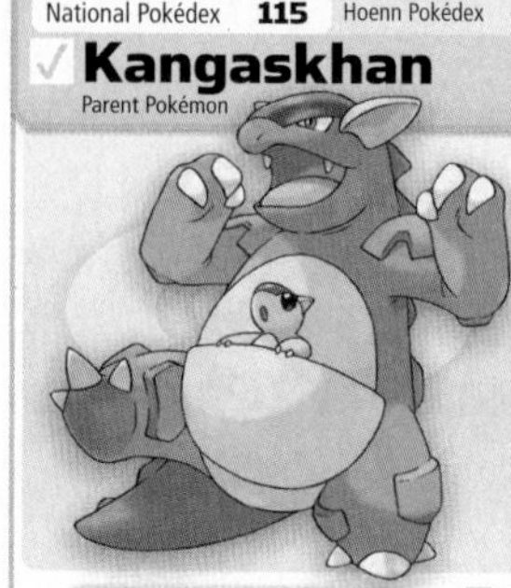

Normal

HEIGHT: 7'03" WEIGHT: 176.4 lbs.

♀ only

Ω If you come across a young Kangaskhan playing by itself, you must never disturb it or attempt to catch it. The baby Pokémon's parent is sure to be in the area, and it will become violently enraged at you.

α If you come across a young Kangaskhan playing by itself, you must never disturb it or attempt to catch it. The baby Pokémon's parent is sure to be in the area, and it will become violently enraged at you.

ABILITIES
Early Bird
Scrappy

HIDDEN ABILITY
Inner Focus

EGG GROUPS
Monster

STAT GROWTH RATES
HP
Attack
Defense
Sp. Atk
Sp. Def
Speed

ITEMS SOMETIMES HELD BY WILD POKÉMON
—

EVOLUTION
Does not evolve

MAIN WAY TO REGISTER IN THE NATIONAL POKÉDEX

Appears in *Pokémon X* and *Pokémon Y.* Bring it to your game using Link Trade or the GTS.

Damage taken in normal battles

Normal	×1	Flying	×1
Fire	×1	Psychic	×1
Water	×1	Bug	×1
Grass	×1	Rock	×1
Electric	×1	Ghost	×0
Ice	×1	Dragon	×1
Fighting	×2	Dark	×1
Poison	×1	Steel	×1
Ground	×1	Fairy	×1

Damage taken in Inverse battles

Normal	×1	Flying	×1
Fire	×1	Psychic	×1
Water	×1	Bug	×1
Grass	×1	Rock	×1
Electric	×1	Ghost	×2
Ice	×1	Dragon	×1
Fighting	×0.5	Dark	×1
Poison	×1	Steel	×1
Ground	×1	Fairy	×1

Can be used in
Inverse Battle
Battle Institute
Battle Maison
Random Matchup (Free Battle)
Random Matchup (Others)

LEVEL-UP MOVES

Lv.	Name	Type	Kind	Pow.	Acc.	PP	Range
1	Comet Punch	Normal	Physical	18	85	15	Normal
1	Leer	Normal	Status	—	100	30	Many Others
7	Fake Out	Normal	Physical	40	100	10	Normal
10	Tail Whip	Normal	Status	—	100	30	Many Others
13	Bite	Dark	Physical	60	100	25	Normal
19	Double Hit	Normal	Physical	35	90	10	Normal
22	Rage	Normal	Physical	20	100	20	Normal
25	Mega Punch	Normal	Physical	80	85	20	Normal
31	Chip Away	Normal	Physical	70	100	20	Normal
34	Dizzy Punch	Normal	Physical	70	100	10	Normal
37	Crunch	Dark	Physical	80	100	15	Normal
43	Endure	Normal	Status	—	—	10	Self
46	Outrage	Dragon	Physical	120	100	10	1 Random
49	Sucker Punch	Dark	Physical	80	100	5	Normal
50	Reversal	Fighting	Physical	—	100	15	Normal

TM & HM MOVES

No.	Name	Type	Kind	Pow.	Acc.	PP	Range
TM05	Roar	Normal	Status	—	—	20	Normal
TM06	Toxic	Poison	Status	—	90	10	Normal
TM07	Hail	Ice	Status	—	—	10	Both Sides
TM10	Hidden Power	Normal	Special	60	100	15	Normal
TM11	Sunny Day	Fire	Status	—	—	5	Both Sides
TM13	Ice Beam	Ice	Special	90	100	10	Normal
TM14	Blizzard	Ice	Special	110	70	5	Many Others
TM15	Hyper Beam	Normal	Special	150	90	5	Normal
TM17	Protect	Normal	Status	—	—	10	Self
TM18	Rain Dance	Water	Status	—	—	5	Both Sides
TM20	Safeguard	Normal	Status	—	—	25	Your Side
TM21	Frustration	Normal	Physical	—	100	20	Normal
TM22	Solar Beam	Grass	Special	120	100	10	Normal
TM24	Thunderbolt	Electric	Special	90	100	15	Normal
TM25	Thunder	Electric	Special	110	70	10	Normal
TM26	Earthquake	Ground	Physical	100	100	10	Adjacent
TM27	Return	Normal	Physical	—	100	20	Normal
TM28	Dig	Ground	Physical	80	100	10	Normal
TM30	Shadow Ball	Ghost	Special	80	100	15	Normal
TM31	Brick Break	Fighting	Physical	75	100	15	Normal
TM32	Double Team	Normal	Status	—	—	15	Self
TM35	Flamethrower	Fire	Special	90	100	15	Normal
TM37	Sandstorm	Rock	Status	—	—	10	Both Sides
TM38	Fire Blast	Fire	Special	110	85	5	Normal
TM39	Rock Tomb	Rock	Physical	60	95	15	Normal
TM40	Aerial Ace	Flying	Physical	60	—	20	Normal
TM42	Facade	Normal	Physical	70	100	20	Normal
TM44	Rest	Psychic	Status	—	—	10	Self
TM45	Attract	Normal	Status	—	100	15	Normal
TM46	Thief	Dark	Physical	60	100	25	Normal
TM48	Round	Normal	Special	60	100	15	Normal
TM52	Focus Blast	Fighting	Special	120	70	5	Normal
TM56	Fling	Dark	Physical	—	100	10	Normal
TM59	Incinerate	Fire	Special	60	100	15	Many Others
TM65	Shadow Claw	Ghost	Physical	70	100	15	Normal
TM67	Retaliate	Normal	Physical	70	100	5	Normal
TM68	Giga Impact	Normal	Physical	150	90	5	Normal
TM78	Bulldoze	Ground	Physical	60	100	20	Adjacent
TM80	Rock Slide	Rock	Physical	75	90	10	Many Others
TM87	Swagger	Normal	Status	—	90	15	Normal
TM88	Sleep Talk	Normal	Status	—	—	10	Self
TM90	Substitute	Normal	Status	—	—	10	Self
TM94	Secret Power	Normal	Physical	70	100	20	Normal
TM98	Power-Up Punch	Fighting	Physical	40	100	20	Normal
TM100	Confide	Normal	Status	—	—	20	Normal
HM01	Cut	Normal	Physical	50	95	30	Normal
HM03	Surf	Water	Special	90	100	15	Adjacent
HM04	Strength	Normal	Physical	80	100	15	Normal
HM06	Rock Smash	Fighting	Physical	40	100	15	Normal

MOVES LEARNED IN EXCHANGE FOR BP

Name	Type	Kind	Pow.	Acc.	PP	Range
Covet	Normal	Physical	60	100	25	Normal
Low Kick	Fighting	Physical	—	100	20	Normal
Uproar	Normal	Special	90	100	10	1 Random
Thunder Punch	Electric	Physical	75	100	15	Normal
Fire Punch	Fire	Physical	75	100	15	Normal
Ice Punch	Ice	Physical	75	100	15	Normal
Icy Wind	Ice	Special	55	95	15	Many Others
Aqua Tail	Water	Physical	90	90	10	Normal
Iron Tail	Steel	Physical	100	75	15	Normal
Snore	Normal	Special	50	100	15	Normal
Drain Punch	Fighting	Physical	75	100	10	Normal
Focus Punch	Fighting	Physical	150	100	20	Normal
Shock Wave	Electric	Special	60	—	20	Normal
Water Pulse	Water	Special	60	100	20	Normal
Spite	Ghost	Status	—	100	10	Normal
Helping Hand	Normal	Status	—	—	20	1 Ally
Endeavor	Normal	Physical	—	100	5	Normal
Outrage	Dragon	Physical	120	100	10	1 Random

MOVES TAUGHT BY PEOPLE

Name	Type	Kind	Pow.	Acc.	PP	Range

EGG MOVES

Name	Type	Kind	Pow.	Acc.	PP	Range
Stomp	Normal	Physical	65	100	20	Normal
Foresight	Normal	Status	—	—	40	Normal
Focus Energy	Normal	Status	—	—	30	Self
Disable	Normal	Status	—	100	20	Normal
Counter	Fighting	Physical	—	100	20	Varies
Crush Claw	Normal	Physical	75	95	10	Normal
Double-Edge	Normal	Physical	120	100	15	Normal
Endeavor	Normal	Physical	—	100	5	Normal
Hammer Arm	Fighting	Physical	100	90	10	Normal
Focus Punch	Fighting	Physical	150	100	20	Normal
Trump Card	Normal	Special	—	—	5	Normal
Uproar	Normal	Special	90	100	10	1 Random
Circle Throw	Fighting	Physical	60	90	10	Normal

Mega Evolution

Mega Kangaskhan

Parent Pokémon

Normal

HEIGHT: 7'03" WEIGHT: **220.5 lbs.**

♀ only

REQUIRED MEGA STONE
Kangaskhanite
Find in Pacifidlog Town (after battling Groudon or Kyogre).

ABILITY
Parental Bond

HIDDEN ABILITY
—

EGG GROUPS
—

STAT GROWTH RATES
HP
Attack
Defense
Sp. Atk
Sp. Def
Speed

Damage taken in normal battles

Normal	×1	Flying	×1
Fire	×1	Psychic	×1
Water	×1	Bug	×1
Grass	×1	Rock	×1
Electric	×1	Ghost	×0
Ice	×1	Dragon	×1
Fighting	×2	Dark	×1
Poison	×1	Steel	×1
Ground	×1	Fairy	×1

Damage taken in Inverse battles

Normal	×1	Flying	×1
Fire	×1	Psychic	×1
Water	×1	Bug	×1
Grass	×1	Rock	×1
Electric	×1	Ghost	×2
Ice	×1	Dragon	×1
Fighting	×0.5	Dark	×1
Poison	×1	Steel	×1
Ground	×1	Fairy	×1

Can be used in
Inverse Battle
Battle Institute
Battle Maison
Random Matchup (Free Battle)
Random Matchup (Others)

National Pokédex **116** Hoenn Pokédex **193**

Horsea

Dragon Pokémon

Water

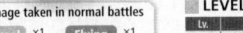

HEIGHT: 1'04" WEIGHT: 17.6 lbs.

Same form for ♂ / ♀

Ω Horsea eats small insects and moss off of rocks. If the ocean current turns fast, this Pokémon anchors itself by wrapping its tail around rocks or coral to prevent being washed away.

α If Horsea senses danger, it will reflexively spray a dense black ink from its mouth and try to escape. This Pokémon swims by cleverly flapping the fin on its back.

ABILITIES
Swift Swim
Sniper

HIDDEN ABILITY
Damp

EGG GROUPS
Water 1 | Dragon

STAT GROWTH RATES
HP ■■
Attack ■■
Defense ■■■
Sp. Atk ■■■
Sp. Def ■
Speed ■■■

ITEMS SOMETIMES HELD BY WILD POKÉMON
Dragon Scale

EVOLUTION
Horsea → Lv. 32 → Seadra → Link Trade with a Dragon Scale → Kingdra

MAIN WAY TO REGISTER IN THE NATIONAL POKÉDEX

Catch using a Super Rod on Route 130.

Damage taken in normal battles

Type		Type	
Normal	×1	Flying	×1
Fire	×0.5	Psychic	×1
Water	×0.5	Bug	×1
Grass	×2	Rock	×1
Electric	×2	Ghost	×1
Ice	×0.5	Dragon	×1
Fighting	×1	Dark	×1
Poison	×1	Steel	×0.5
Ground	×1	Fairy	×1

Damage taken in Inverse battles

Type		Type	
Normal	×1	Flying	×1
Fire	×2	Psychic	×1
Water	×2	Bug	×1
Grass	×0.5	Rock	×1
Electric	×0.5	Ghost	×1
Ice	×2	Dragon	×1
Fighting	×1	Dark	×1
Poison	×1	Steel	×2
Ground	×1	Fairy	×1

Can be used in
Inverse Battle
Battle Institute
Battle Maison
Random Matchup (Free Battle)
Random Matchup (Others)

LEVEL-UP MOVES

Lv.	Name	Type	Kind	Pow.	Acc.	PP	Range
1	Bubble	Water	Special	40	100	30	Many Others
5	Smokescreen	Normal	Status	—	100	20	Normal
9	Leer	Normal	Status	—	100	30	Many Others
13	Water Gun	Water	Special	40	100	25	Normal
17	Twister	Dragon	Special	40	100	20	Many Others
21	Bubble Beam	Water	Special	65	100	20	Normal
26	Focus Energy	Normal	Status	—	—	30	Self
31	Brine	Water	Special	65	100	10	Normal
36	Agility	Psychic	Status	—	—	30	Self
41	Dragon Pulse	Dragon	Special	85	100	10	Normal
46	Dragon Dance	Dragon	Status	—	—	20	Self
52	Hydro Pump	Water	Special	110	80	5	Normal

TM & HM MOVES

No.	Name	Type	Kind	Pow.	Acc.	PP	Range
TM06	Toxic	Poison	Status	—	90	10	Normal
TM07	Hail	Ice	Status	—	—	10	Both Sides
TM10	Hidden Power	Normal	Special	60	100	15	Normal
TM13	Ice Beam	Ice	Special	90	100	10	Normal
TM14	Blizzard	Ice	Special	110	70	5	Many Others
TM17	Protect	Normal	Status	—	—	10	Self
TM18	Rain Dance	Water	Status	—	—	5	Both Sides
TM21	Frustration	Normal	Physical	—	100	20	Normal
TM27	Return	Normal	Physical	—	100	20	Normal
TM32	Double Team	Normal	Status	—	—	15	Self
TM42	Facade	Normal	Physical	70	100	20	Normal
TM44	Rest	Psychic	Status	—	—	10	Self
TM45	Attract	Normal	Status	—	100	15	Normal
TM48	Round	Normal	Special	60	100	15	Normal
TM55	Scald	Water	Special	80	100	15	Normal
TM87	Swagger	Normal	Status	—	90	15	Normal
TM88	Sleep Talk	Normal	Status	—	—	10	Self
TM90	Substitute	Normal	Status	—	—	10	Self
TM91	Flash Cannon	Steel	Special	80	100	10	Normal
TM94	Secret Power	Normal	Physical	70	100	20	Normal
TM100	Confide	Normal	Status	—	—	20	Normal
HM03	Surf	Water	Special	90	100	15	Adjacent
HM05	Waterfall	Water	Physical	80	100	15	Normal
HM07	Dive	Water	Physical	80	100	10	Normal

MOVES LEARNED IN EXCHANGE FOR BP

Name	Type	Kind	Pow.	Acc.	PP	Range
Signal Beam	Bug	Special	75	100	15	Normal
Bounce	Flying	Physical	85	85	5	Normal
Icy Wind	Ice	Special	55	95	15	Many Others
Dragon Pulse	Dragon	Special	85	100	10	Normal
Snore	Normal	Special	50	100	15	Normal
Water Pulse	Water	Special	60	100	20	Normal
Outrage	Dragon	Physical	120	100	10	1 Random

MOVES TAUGHT BY PEOPLE

Name	Type	Kind	Pow.	Acc.	PP	Range

EGG MOVES

Name	Type	Kind	Pow.	Acc.	PP	Range
Flail	Normal	Physical	—	100	15	Normal
Aurora Beam	Ice	Special	65	100	20	Normal
Octazooka	Water	Special	65	85	10	Normal
Disable	Normal	Status	—	100	20	Normal
Splash	Normal	Status	—	—	40	Self
Dragon Rage	Dragon	Special	—	100	10	Normal
Dragon Breath	Dragon	Special	60	100	20	Normal
Signal Beam	Bug	Special	75	100	15	Normal
Razor Wind	Normal	Special	80	100	10	Many Others
Muddy Water	Water	Special	90	85	10	Many Others
Water Pulse	Water	Special	60	100	20	Normal
Clear Smog	Poison	Special	50	—	15	Normal
Outrage	Dragon	Physical	120	100	10	1 Random

National Pokédex **117** Hoenn Pokédex **194**

Seadra

Dragon Pokémon

Water

HEIGHT: 3'11" WEIGHT: 55.1 lbs.

Same form for ♂ / ♀

Ω Seadra sleeps after wriggling itself between the branches of coral. Those trying to harvest coral are occasionally stung by this Pokémon's poison barbs if they fail to notice it.

α Seadra generates whirlpools by spinning its body. The whirlpools are strong enough to swallow even fishing boats. This Pokémon weakens prey with these currents, then swallows it whole.

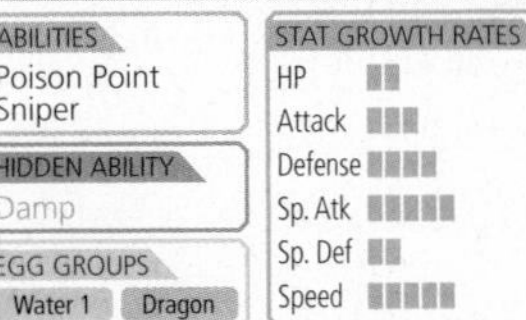

ABILITIES
Poison Point
Sniper

HIDDEN ABILITY
Damp

EGG GROUPS
Water 1 | Dragon

STAT GROWTH RATES
HP ■■
Attack ■■■
Defense ■■■■
Sp. Atk ■■■■■
Sp. Def ■■
Speed ■■■■■

ITEMS SOMETIMES HELD BY WILD POKÉMON
Dragon Scale

EVOLUTION
Horsea → Lv. 32 → Seadra → Link Trade with a Dragon Scale → Kingdra

MAIN WAY TO REGISTER IN THE NATIONAL POKÉDEX

Catch using a Super Rod on Route 130.

Damage taken in normal battles

Type		Type	
Normal	×1	Flying	×1
Fire	×0.5	Psychic	×1
Water	×0.5	Bug	×1
Grass	×2	Rock	×1
Electric	×2	Ghost	×1
Ice	×0.5	Dragon	×1
Fighting	×1	Dark	×1
Poison	×1	Steel	×0.5
Ground	×1	Fairy	×1

Damage taken in Inverse battles

Type		Type	
Normal	×1	Flying	×1
Fire	×2	Psychic	×1
Water	×2	Bug	×1
Grass	×0.5	Rock	×1
Electric	×0.5	Ghost	×1
Ice	×2	Dragon	×1
Fighting	×1	Dark	×1
Poison	×1	Steel	×2
Ground	×1	Fairy	×1

Can be used in
Inverse Battle
Battle Institute
Battle Maison
Random Matchup (Free Battle)
Random Matchup (Others)

LEVEL-UP MOVES

Lv.	Name	Type	Kind	Pow.	Acc.	PP	Range
1	Hydro Pump	Water	Special	110	80	5	Normal
1	Bubble	Water	Special	40	100	30	Many Others
1	Smokescreen	Normal	Status	—	100	20	Normal
1	Leer	Normal	Status	—	100	30	Many Others
1	Water Gun	Water	Special	40	100	25	Normal
5	Smokescreen	Normal	Status	—	100	20	Normal
9	Leer	Normal	Status	—	100	30	Many Others
13	Water Gun	Water	Special	40	100	25	Normal
17	Twister	Dragon	Special	40	100	20	Many Others
21	Bubble Beam	Water	Special	65	100	20	Normal
26	Focus Energy	Normal	Status	—	—	30	Self
31	Brine	Water	Special	65	100	10	Normal
38	Agility	Psychic	Status	—	—	30	Self
45	Dragon Pulse	Dragon	Special	85	100	10	Normal
52	Dragon Dance	Dragon	Status	—	—	20	Self
60	Hydro Pump	Water	Special	110	80	5	Normal

TM & HM MOVES

No.	Name	Type	Kind	Pow.	Acc.	PP	Range
TM06	Toxic	Poison	Status	—	90	10	Normal
TM07	Hail	Ice	Status	—	—	10	Both Sides
TM10	Hidden Power	Normal	Special	60	100	15	Normal
TM13	Ice Beam	Ice	Special	90	100	10	Normal
TM14	Blizzard	Ice	Special	110	70	5	Many Others
TM15	Hyper Beam	Normal	Special	150	90	5	Normal
TM17	Protect	Normal	Status	—	—	10	Self
TM18	Rain Dance	Water	Status	—	—	5	Both Sides
TM21	Frustration	Normal	Physical	—	100	20	Normal
TM27	Return	Normal	Physical	—	100	20	Normal
TM32	Double Team	Normal	Status	—	—	15	Self
TM42	Facade	Normal	Physical	70	100	20	Normal
TM44	Rest	Psychic	Status	—	—	10	Self
TM45	Attract	Normal	Status	—	100	15	Normal
TM48	Round	Normal	Special	60	100	15	Normal
TM55	Scald	Water	Special	80	100	15	Normal
TM68	Giga Impact	Normal	Physical	150	90	5	Normal
TM87	Swagger	Normal	Status	—	90	15	Normal
TM88	Sleep Talk	Normal	Status	—	—	10	Self
TM90	Substitute	Normal	Status	—	—	10	Self
TM91	Flash Cannon	Steel	Special	80	100	10	Normal
TM94	Secret Power	Normal	Physical	70	100	20	Normal
TM100	Confide	Normal	Status	—	—	20	Normal
HM03	Surf	Water	Special	90	100	15	Adjacent
HM05	Waterfall	Water	Physical	80	100	15	Normal
HM07	Dive	Water	Physical	80	100	10	Normal

MOVES LEARNED IN EXCHANGE FOR BP

Name	Type	Kind	Pow.	Acc.	PP	Range
Signal Beam	Bug	Special	75	100	15	Normal
Bounce	Flying	Physical	85	85	5	Normal
Icy Wind	Ice	Special	55	95	15	Many Others
Dragon Pulse	Dragon	Special	85	100	10	Normal
Snore	Normal	Special	50	100	15	Normal
Water Pulse	Water	Special	60	100	20	Normal
Outrage	Dragon	Physical	120	100	10	1 Random

MOVES TAUGHT BY PEOPLE

Name	Type	Kind	Pow.	Acc.	PP	Range

National Pokédex **118** Hoenn Pokédex **051**

Goldeen

Goldfish Pokémon

Water

HEIGHT: 2'00" WEIGHT: 33.1 lbs.

The male has a longer horn.
The female has a shorter horn.

Ω Goldeen is a very beautiful Pokémon with fins that billow elegantly in water. However, don't let your guard down around this Pokémon—it could ram you powerfully with its horn.

α Goldeen loves swimming wild and free in rivers and ponds. If one of these Pokémon is placed in an aquarium, it will shatter even the thickest glass with one ram of its horn and make its escape.

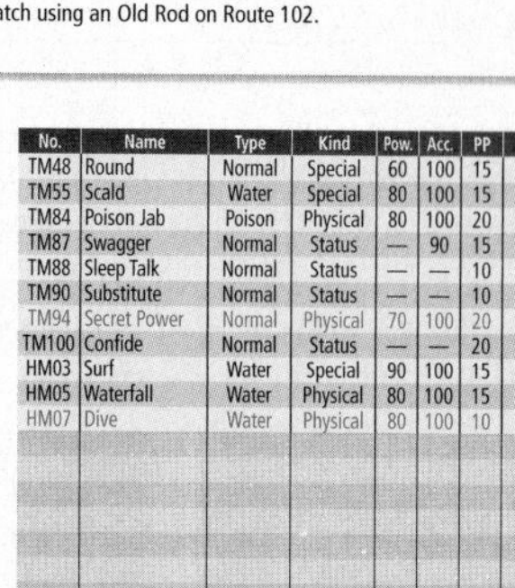

ABILITIES
Swift Swim
Water Veil

HIDDEN ABILITY
Lightning Rod

EGG GROUPS
Water 2

STAT GROWTH RATES
HP ■■
Attack ■■■■
Defense ■■■
Sp. Atk ■■
Sp. Def ■■
Speed ■■■

ITEMS SOMETIMES HELD BY WILD POKÉMON
Mystic Water

EVOLUTION
Goldeen → Lv. 33 → Seaking

MAIN WAY TO REGISTER IN THE NATIONAL POKÉDEX

Catch using an Old Rod on Route 102.

Damage taken in normal battles

Type		Type	
Normal	×1	Flying	×1
Fire	×0.5	Psychic	×1
Water	×0.5	Bug	×1
Grass	×2	Rock	×1
! Electric	×2	Ghost	×1
Ice	×0.5	Dragon	×1
Fighting	×1	Dark	×1
Poison	×1	Steel	×0.5
Ground	×1	Fairy	×1

Damage taken in Inverse battles

Type		Type	
Normal	×1	Flying	×1
Fire	×2	Psychic	×1
Water	×2	Bug	×1
Grass	×0.5	Rock	×1
! Electric	×0.5	Ghost	×1
Ice	×2	Dragon	×1
Fighting	×1	Dark	×1
Poison	×1	Steel	×2
Ground	×1	Fairy	×1

Can be used in
Inverse Battle
Battle Institute
Battle Maison
Random Matchup (Free Battle)
Random Matchup (Others)

LEVEL-UP MOVES

Lv.	Name	Type	Kind	Pow.	Acc.	PP	Range
1	Peck	Flying	Physical	35	100	35	Normal
1	Tail Whip	Normal	Status	—	100	30	Many Others
1	Water Sport	Water	Status	—	—	15	Both Sides
5	Supersonic	Normal	Status	—	55	20	Normal
8	Horn Attack	Normal	Physical	65	100	25	Normal
13	Flail	Normal	Physical	—	100	15	Normal
16	Water Pulse	Water	Special	60	100	20	Normal
21	Aqua Ring	Water	Status	—	—	20	Self
24	Fury Attack	Normal	Physical	15	85	20	Normal
29	Agility	Psychic	Status	—	—	30	Self
32	Waterfall	Water	Physical	80	100	15	Normal
37	Horn Drill	Normal	Physical	—	30	5	Normal
40	Soak	Water	Status	—	100	20	Normal
45	Megahorn	Bug	Physical	120	85	10	Normal

TM & HM MOVES

No.	Name	Type	Kind	Pow.	Acc.	PP	Range
TM06	Toxic	Poison	Status	—	90	10	Normal
TM07	Hail	Ice	Status	—	—	10	Both Sides
TM10	Hidden Power	Normal	Special	60	100	15	Normal
TM13	Ice Beam	Ice	Special	90	100	10	Normal
TM14	Blizzard	Ice	Special	110	70	5	Many Others
TM17	Protect	Normal	Status	—	—	10	Self
TM18	Rain Dance	Water	Status	—	—	5	Both Sides
TM21	Frustration	Normal	Physical	—	100	20	Normal
TM27	Return	Normal	Physical	—	100	20	Normal
TM32	Double Team	Normal	Status	—	—	15	Self
TM42	Facade	Normal	Physical	70	100	20	Normal
TM44	Rest	Psychic	Status	—	—	10	Self
TM45	Attract	Normal	Status	—	100	15	Normal
TM48	Round	Normal	Special	60	100	15	Normal
TM55	Scald	Water	Special	80	100	15	Normal
TM84	Poison Jab	Poison	Physical	80	100	20	Normal
TM87	Swagger	Normal	Status	—	90	15	Normal
TM88	Sleep Talk	Normal	Status	—	—	10	Self
TM90	Substitute	Normal	Status	—	—	10	Self
TM94	Secret Power	Normal	Physical	70	100	20	Normal
TM100	Confide	Normal	Status	—	—	20	Normal
HM03	Surf	Water	Special	90	100	15	Adjacent
HM05	Waterfall	Water	Physical	80	100	15	Normal
HM07	Dive	Water	Physical	80	100	10	Normal

MOVES LEARNED IN EXCHANGE FOR BP

Name	Type	Kind	Pow.	Acc.	PP	Range
Signal Beam	Bug	Special	75	100	15	Normal
Drill Run	Ground	Physical	80	95	10	Normal
Bounce	Flying	Physical	85	85	5	Normal
Icy Wind	Ice	Special	55	95	15	Many Others
Aqua Tail	Water	Physical	90	90	10	Normal
Snore	Normal	Special	50	100	15	Normal
Knock Off	Dark	Physical	65	100	20	Normal
Water Pulse	Water	Special	60	100	20	Normal

MOVES TAUGHT BY PEOPLE

Name	Type	Kind	Pow.	Acc.	PP	Range

EGG MOVES

Name	Type	Kind	Pow.	Acc.	PP	Range
Psybeam	Psychic	Special	65	100	20	Normal
Haze	Ice	Status	—	—	30	Both Sides
Hydro Pump	Water	Special	110	80	5	Normal
Sleep Talk	Normal	Status	—	—	10	Self
Mud Sport	Ground	Status	—	—	15	Both Sides
Mud-Slap	Ground	Special	20	100	10	Normal
Aqua Tail	Water	Physical	90	90	10	Normal
Body Slam	Normal	Physical	85	100	15	Normal
Mud Shot	Ground	Special	55	95	15	Normal
Skull Bash	Normal	Physical	130	100	10	Normal
Signal Beam	Bug	Special	75	100	15	Normal

National Pokédex **119** Hoenn Pokédex **052**

Seaking

Goldfish Pokémon

Water

HEIGHT: 4'03" WEIGHT: 86 lbs.

The male has a longer horn.
The female has a shorter horn.

Ω In the autumn, Seaking males can be seen performing courtship dances in riverbeds to woo females. During this season, this Pokémon's body coloration is at its most beautiful.

α Seaking is very protective of its eggs. The male and female will take turns patrolling around their nest and eggs. The guarding of eggs by these Pokémon goes on for over a month.

ABILITIES
Swift Swim
Water Veil

HIDDEN ABILITY
Lightning Rod

EGG GROUPS
Water 2

STAT GROWTH RATES
HP ■■■
Attack ■■■■■
Defense ■■■
Sp. Atk ■■■
Sp. Def ■■■
Speed ■■■■

ITEMS SOMETIMES HELD BY WILD POKÉMON
Mystic Water

EVOLUTION
Goldeen → Lv. 33 → Seaking

MAIN WAY TO REGISTER IN THE NATIONAL POKÉDEX

Catch using a Super Rod in the lower-left corner of the Safari Zone.

Damage taken in normal battles

Type		Type	
Normal	×1	Flying	×1
Fire	×0.5	Psychic	×1
Water	×0.5	Bug	×1
Grass	×2	Rock	×1
! Electric	×2	Ghost	×1
Ice	×0.5	Dragon	×1
Fighting	×1	Dark	×1
Poison	×1	Steel	×0.5
Ground	×1	Fairy	×1

Damage taken in Inverse battles

Type		Type	
Normal	×1	Flying	×1
Fire	×2	Psychic	×1
Water	×2	Bug	×1
Grass	×0.5	Rock	×1
! Electric	×0.5	Ghost	×1
Ice	×2	Dragon	×1
Fighting	×1	Dark	×1
Poison	×1	Steel	×2
Ground	×1	Fairy	×1

Can be used in
Inverse Battle
Battle Institute
Battle Maison
Random Matchup (Free Battle)
Random Matchup (Others)

LEVEL-UP MOVES

Lv.	Name	Type	Kind	Pow.	Acc.	PP	Range
1	Megahorn	Bug	Physical	120	85	10	Normal
1	Poison Jab	Poison	Physical	80	100	20	Normal
1	Peck	Flying	Physical	35	100	35	Normal
1	Tail Whip	Normal	Status	—	100	30	Many Others
1	Water Sport	Water	Status	—	—	15	Both Sides
1	Supersonic	Normal	Status	—	55	20	Normal
5	Supersonic	Normal	Status	—	55	20	Normal
8	Horn Attack	Normal	Physical	65	100	25	Normal
13	Flail	Normal	Physical	—	100	15	Normal
16	Water Pulse	Water	Special	60	100	20	Normal
21	Aqua Ring	Water	Status	—	—	20	Self
24	Fury Attack	Normal	Physical	15	85	20	Normal
29	Agility	Psychic	Status	—	—	30	Self
32	Waterfall	Water	Physical	80	100	15	Normal
40	Horn Drill	Normal	Physical	—	30	5	Normal
46	Soak	Water	Status	—	100	20	Normal
54	Megahorn	Bug	Physical	120	85	10	Normal

TM & HM MOVES

No.	Name	Type	Kind	Pow.	Acc.	PP	Range
TM06	Toxic	Poison	Status	—	90	10	Normal
TM07	Hail	Ice	Status	—	—	10	Both Sides
TM10	Hidden Power	Normal	Special	60	100	15	Normal
TM13	Ice Beam	Ice	Special	90	100	10	Normal
TM14	Blizzard	Ice	Special	110	70	5	Many Others
TM15	Hyper Beam	Normal	Special	150	90	5	Normal
TM17	Protect	Normal	Status	—	—	10	Self
TM18	Rain Dance	Water	Status	—	—	5	Both Sides
TM21	Frustration	Normal	Physical	—	100	20	Normal
TM27	Return	Normal	Physical	—	100	20	Normal
TM32	Double Team	Normal	Status	—	—	15	Self
TM42	Facade	Normal	Physical	70	100	20	Normal
TM44	Rest	Psychic	Status	—	—	10	Self
TM45	Attract	Normal	Status	—	100	15	Normal
TM48	Round	Normal	Special	60	100	15	Normal
TM55	Scald	Water	Special	80	100	15	Normal
TM68	Giga Impact	Normal	Physical	150	90	5	Normal
TM84	Poison Jab	Poison	Physical	80	100	20	Normal
TM87	Swagger	Normal	Status	—	90	15	Normal
TM88	Sleep Talk	Normal	Status	—	—	10	Self
TM90	Substitute	Normal	Status	—	—	10	Self
TM94	Secret Power	Normal	Physical	70	100	20	Normal
TM100	Confide	Normal	Status	—	—	20	Normal
HM03	Surf	Water	Special	90	100	15	Adjacent
HM05	Waterfall	Water	Physical	80	100	15	Normal
HM07	Dive	Water	Physical	80	100	10	Normal

MOVES LEARNED IN EXCHANGE FOR BP

Name	Type	Kind	Pow.	Acc.	PP	Range
Signal Beam	Bug	Special	75	100	15	Normal
Drill Run	Ground	Physical	80	95	10	Normal
Bounce	Flying	Physical	85	85	5	Normal
Icy Wind	Ice	Special	55	95	15	Many Others
Aqua Tail	Water	Physical	90	90	10	Normal
Snore	Normal	Special	50	100	15	Normal
Knock Off	Dark	Physical	65	100	20	Normal
Water Pulse	Water	Special	60	100	20	Normal

MOVES TAUGHT BY PEOPLE

Name	Type	Kind	Pow.	Acc.	PP	Range

National Pokédex **120** Hoenn Pokédex **148**

Staryu

Star Shape Pokémon

Water

HEIGHT: 2'07" WEIGHT: 76.1 lbs.

Gender unknown

Ω Staryu's center section has an organ called the core that shines bright red. If you go to a beach toward the end of summer, the glowing cores of these Pokémon look like the stars in the sky.

α Staryu apparently communicates with the stars in the night sky by flashing the red core at the center of its body. If parts of its body are torn, this Pokémon simply regenerates the missing pieces and limbs.

ABILITIES
Illuminate
Natural Cure

HIDDEN ABILITY
Analytic

EGG GROUPS
Water 3

STAT GROWTH RATES
HP
Attack
Defense
Sp. Atk
Sp. Def
Speed

ITEMS SOMETIMES HELD BY WILD POKÉMON
Star Piece / Stardust

EVOLUTION
Staryu → Water Stone → Starmie

MAIN WAY TO REGISTER IN THE NATIONAL POKÉDEX

Catch using a Super Rod in Lilycove City.

Damage taken in normal battles

Type		Type	
Normal	×1	Flying	×1
Fire	×0.5	Psychic	×1
Water	×0.5	Bug	×1
Grass	×2	Rock	×1
Electric	×2	Ghost	×1
Ice	×0.5	Dragon	×1
Fighting	×1	Dark	×1
Poison	×1	Steel	×0.5
Ground	×1	Fairy	×1

Damage taken in Inverse battles

Type		Type	
Normal	×1	Flying	×1
Fire	×2	Psychic	×1
Water	×2	Bug	×1
Grass	×0.5	Rock	×1
Electric	×0.5	Ghost	×1
Ice	×2	Dragon	×1
Fighting	×1	Dark	×1
Poison	×1	Steel	×2
Ground	×1	Fairy	×1

Can be used in
Inverse Battle
Battle Institute
Battle Maison
Random Matchup (Free Battle)
Random Matchup (Others)

LEVEL-UP MOVES

Lv.	Name	Type	Kind	Pow.	Acc.	PP	Range
1	Tackle	Normal	Physical	50	100	35	Normal
1	Harden	Normal	Status	—	—	30	Self
4	Water Gun	Water	Special	40	100	25	Normal
7	Rapid Spin	Normal	Physical	20	100	40	Normal
10	Recover	Normal	Status	—	—	10	Self
13	Psywave	Psychic	Special	—	100	15	Normal
16	Swift	Normal	Special	60	—	20	Many Others
18	Bubble Beam	Water	Special	65	100	20	Normal
22	Camouflage	Normal	Status	—	—	20	Self
24	Gyro Ball	Steel	Physical	—	100	5	Normal
28	Brine	Water	Special	65	100	10	Normal
31	Minimize	Normal	Status	—	—	10	Self
35	Reflect Type	Normal	Status	—	—	15	Normal
37	Power Gem	Rock	Special	80	100	20	Normal
40	Confuse Ray	Ghost	Status	—	100	10	Normal
42	Psychic	Psychic	Special	90	100	10	Normal
46	Light Screen	Psychic	Status	—	—	30	Your Side
49	Cosmic Power	Psychic	Status	—	—	20	Self
53	Hydro Pump	Water	Special	110	80	5	Normal

TM & HM MOVES

No.	Name	Type	Kind	Pow.	Acc.	PP	Range
TM06	Toxic	Poison	Status	—	90	10	Normal
TM07	Hail	Ice	Status	—	—	10	Both Sides
TM10	Hidden Power	Normal	Special	60	100	15	Normal
TM13	Ice Beam	Ice	Special	90	100	10	Normal
TM14	Blizzard	Ice	Special	110	70	5	Many Others
TM16	Light Screen	Psychic	Status	—	—	30	Your Side
TM17	Protect	Normal	Status	—	—	10	Self
TM18	Rain Dance	Water	Status	—	—	5	Both Sides
TM21	Frustration	Normal	Physical	—	100	20	Normal
TM24	Thunderbolt	Electric	Special	90	100	15	Normal
TM25	Thunder	Electric	Special	110	70	10	Normal
TM27	Return	Normal	Physical	—	100	20	Normal
TM29	Psychic	Psychic	Special	90	100	10	Normal
TM32	Double Team	Normal	Status	—	—	15	Self
TM33	Reflect	Psychic	Status	—	—	20	Your Side
TM42	Facade	Normal	Physical	70	100	20	Normal
TM44	Rest	Psychic	Status	—	—	10	Self
TM48	Round	Normal	Special	60	100	15	Normal
TM55	Scald	Water	Special	80	100	15	Normal
TM70	Flash	Normal	Status	—	100	20	Normal
TM73	Thunder Wave	Electric	Status	—	100	20	Normal
TM74	Gyro Ball	Steel	Physical	—	100	5	Normal
TM77	Psych Up	Normal	Status	—	—	10	Normal
TM87	Swagger	Normal	Status	—	90	15	Normal
TM88	Sleep Talk	Normal	Status	—	—	10	Self
TM90	Substitute	Normal	Status	—	—	10	Self
TM91	Flash Cannon	Steel	Special	80	100	10	Normal
TM94	Secret Power	Normal	Physical	70	100	20	Normal
TM99	Dazzling Gleam	Fairy	Special	80	100	10	Many Others
TM100	Confide	Normal	Status	—	—	20	Normal
HM03	Surf	Water	Special	90	100	15	Adjacent
HM05	Waterfall	Water	Physical	80	100	15	Normal
HM07	Dive	Water	Physical	80	100	10	Normal

MOVES LEARNED IN EXCHANGE FOR BP

Name	Type	Kind	Pow.	Acc.	PP	Range
Signal Beam	Bug	Special	75	100	15	Normal
Magic Coat	Psychic	Status	—	—	15	Self
Gravity	Psychic	Status	—	—	5	Both Sides
Icy Wind	Ice	Special	55	95	15	Many Others
Snore	Normal	Special	50	100	15	Normal
Pain Split	Normal	Status	—	—	20	Normal
Water Pulse	Water	Special	60	100	20	Normal
Recycle	Normal	Status	—	—	10	Self

MOVES TAUGHT BY PEOPLE

Name	Type	Kind	Pow.	Acc.	PP	Range

National Pokédex **121** Hoenn Pokédex **149**

Starmie

Mysterious Pokémon

Water Psychic

HEIGHT: 3'07" WEIGHT: 176.4 lbs.

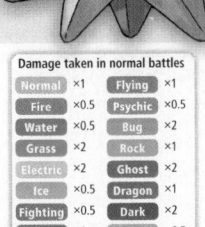

Gender unknown

Ω Starmie's center section—the core—glows brightly in seven colors. Because of its luminous nature, this Pokémon has been given the nickname "the gem of the sea."

α Starmie swims through water by spinning its star-shaped body as if it were a propeller on a ship. The core at the center of this Pokémon's body glows in seven colors.

ABILITIES
Illuminate
Natural Cure

HIDDEN ABILITY
Analytic

EGG GROUPS
Water 3

STAT GROWTH RATES
HP
Attack
Defense
Sp. Atk
Sp. Def
Speed

ITEMS SOMETIMES HELD BY WILD POKÉMON
—

EVOLUTION
Staryu → Water Stone → Starmie

MAIN WAY TO REGISTER IN THE NATIONAL POKÉDEX

Use a Water Stone on Staryu.

Damage taken in normal battles

Type		Type	
Normal	×1	Flying	×1
Fire	×0.5	Psychic	×0.5
Water	×0.5	Bug	×2
Grass	×2	Rock	×1
Electric	×2	Ghost	×2
Ice	×0.5	Dragon	×1
Fighting	×0.5	Dark	×2
Poison	×1	Steel	×0.5
Ground	×1	Fairy	×1

Damage taken in Inverse battles

Type		Type	
Normal	×1	Flying	×1
Fire	×2	Psychic	×2
Water	×2	Bug	×0.5
Grass	×0.5	Rock	×1
Electric	×0.5	Ghost	×0.5
Ice	×2	Dragon	×1
Fighting	×2	Dark	×0.5
Poison	×1	Steel	×2
Ground	×1	Fairy	×1

Can be used in
Inverse Battle
Battle Institute
Battle Maison
Random Matchup (Free Battle)
Random Matchup (Others)

LEVEL-UP MOVES

Lv.	Name	Type	Kind	Pow.	Acc.	PP	Range
1	Hydro Pump	Water	Special	110	80	5	Normal
1	Water Gun	Water	Special	40	100	25	Normal
1	Rapid Spin	Normal	Physical	20	100	40	Normal
1	Recover	Normal	Status	—	—	10	Self
1	Swift	Normal	Special	60	—	20	Many Others
40	Confuse Ray	Ghost	Status	—	100	10	Normal

TM & HM MOVES

No.	Name	Type	Kind	Pow.	Acc.	PP	Range
TM03	Psyshock	Psychic	Special	80	100	10	Normal
TM06	Toxic	Poison	Status	—	90	10	Normal
TM07	Hail	Ice	Status	—	—	10	Both Sides
TM10	Hidden Power	Normal	Special	60	100	15	Normal
TM13	Ice Beam	Ice	Special	90	100	10	Normal
TM14	Blizzard	Ice	Special	110	70	5	Many Others
TM15	Hyper Beam	Normal	Special	150	90	5	Normal
TM16	Light Screen	Psychic	Status	—	—	30	Your Side
TM17	Protect	Normal	Status	—	—	10	Self
TM18	Rain Dance	Water	Status	—	—	5	Both Sides
TM21	Frustration	Normal	Physical	—	100	20	Normal
TM24	Thunderbolt	Electric	Special	90	100	15	Normal
TM25	Thunder	Electric	Special	110	70	10	Normal
TM27	Return	Normal	Physical	—	100	20	Normal
TM29	Psychic	Psychic	Special	90	100	10	Normal
TM32	Double Team	Normal	Status	—	—	15	Self
TM33	Reflect	Psychic	Status	—	—	20	Your Side
TM42	Facade	Normal	Physical	70	100	20	Normal
TM44	Rest	Psychic	Status	—	—	10	Self
TM48	Round	Normal	Special	60	100	15	Normal
TM55	Scald	Water	Special	80	100	15	Normal
TM68	Giga Impact	Normal	Physical	150	90	5	Normal
TM70	Flash	Normal	Status	—	100	20	Normal
TM73	Thunder Wave	Electric	Status	—	100	20	Normal
TM74	Gyro Ball	Steel	Physical	—	100	5	Normal
TM77	Psych Up	Normal	Status	—	—	10	Normal
TM85	Dream Eater	Psychic	Special	100	100	15	Normal
TM86	Grass Knot	Grass	Special	—	100	20	Normal
TM87	Swagger	Normal	Status	—	90	15	Normal
TM88	Sleep Talk	Normal	Status	—	—	10	Self
TM90	Substitute	Normal	Status	—	—	10	Self
TM91	Flash Cannon	Steel	Special	80	100	10	Normal
TM92	Trick Room	Psychic	Status	—	—	5	Both Sides
TM94	Secret Power	Normal	Physical	70	100	20	Normal
TM99	Dazzling Gleam	Fairy	Special	80	100	10	Many Others
TM100	Confide	Normal	Status	—	—	20	Normal
HM03	Surf	Water	Special	90	100	15	Adjacent
HM05	Waterfall	Water	Physical	80	100	15	Normal
HM07	Dive	Water	Physical	80	100	10	Normal

MOVES LEARNED IN EXCHANGE FOR BP

Name	Type	Kind	Pow.	Acc.	PP	Range
Signal Beam	Bug	Special	75	100	15	Normal
Magic Coat	Psychic	Status	—	—	15	Self
Gravity	Psychic	Status	—	—	5	Both Sides
Icy Wind	Ice	Special	55	95	15	Many Others
Snore	Normal	Special	50	100	15	Normal
Pain Split	Normal	Status	—	—	20	Normal
Water Pulse	Water	Special	60	100	20	Normal
Trick	Psychic	Status	—	100	10	Normal
Wonder Room	Psychic	Status	—	—	10	Both Sides
Recycle	Normal	Status	—	—	10	Self
Skill Swap	Psychic	Status	—	—	10	Normal

MOVES TAUGHT BY PEOPLE

Name	Type	Kind	Pow.	Acc.	PP	Range

National Pokédex **122** Hoenn Pokédex —

Mr. Mime

Barrier Pokémon

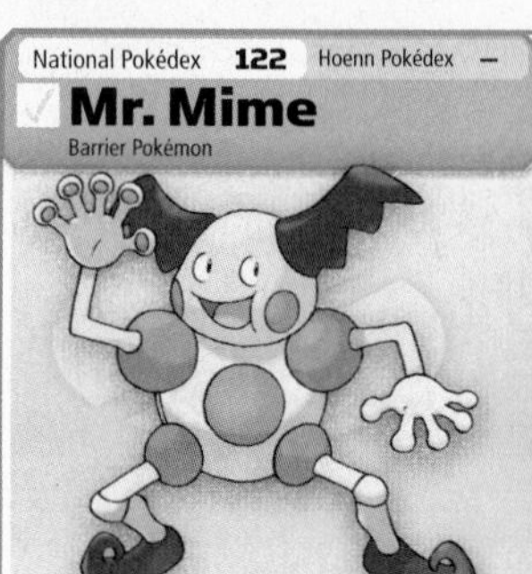

Psychic / Fairy

HEIGHT: 4'03" WEIGHT: 120.1 lbs.

Same form for ♂ / ♀

Ω Mr. Mime is a master of pantomime. Its gestures and motions convince watchers that something unseeable actually exists. Once the watchers are convinced, the unseeable thing exists as if it were real.

α Mr. Mime is a master of pantomime. Its gestures and motions convince watchers that something unseeable actually exists. Once the watchers are convinced, the unseeable thing exists as if it were real.

ABILITIES
Soundproof
Filter

HIDDEN ABILITY
Technician

EGG GROUPS
Human-Like

STAT GROWTH RATES
HP ▮▮
Attack ▮▮
Defense ▮▮▮
Sp. Atk ▮▮▮▮▮
Sp. Def ▮▮▮▮▮
Speed ▮▮▮▮▮

ITEMS SOMETIMES HELD BY WILD POKÉMON
—

EVOLUTION

MAIN WAY TO REGISTER IN THE NATIONAL POKÉDEX

Appears in *Pokémon X* and *Pokémon Y*. Bring it to your game using Link Trade or the GTS.

Damage taken in normal battles

Type		Type	
Normal	×1	Flying	×1
Fire	×1	Psychic	×0.5
Water	×1	Bug	×1
Grass	×1	Rock	×1
Electric	×1	Ghost	×2
Ice	×1	Dragon	×0
Fighting	×0.25	Dark	×1
Poison	×2	Steel	×2
Ground	×1	Fairy	×1

Damage taken in Inverse battles

Type		Type	
Normal	×1	Flying	×1
Fire	×1	Psychic	×2
Water	×1	Bug	×1
Grass	×1	Rock	×1
Electric	×1	Ghost	×0.5
Ice	×1	Dragon	×2
Fighting	×4	Dark	×1
Poison	×0.5	Steel	×0.5
Ground	×1	Fairy	×1

Can be used in
Inverse Battle
Battle Institute
Battle Maison
Random Matchup (Free Battle)
Random Matchup (Others)

LEVEL-UP MOVES

Lv.	Name	Type	Kind	Pow.	Acc.	PP	Range
1	Misty Terrain	Fairy	Status	—	—	10	Both Sides
1	Magical Leaf	Grass	Special	60	—	20	Normal
1	Quick Guard	Fighting	Status	—	—	15	Your Side
1	Wide Guard	Rock	Status	—	—	10	Your Side
1	Power Swap	Psychic	Status	—	—	10	Normal
1	Guard Swap	Psychic	Status	—	—	10	Normal
1	Barrier	Psychic	Status	—	—	20	Self
1	Confusion	Psychic	Special	50	100	25	Normal
4	Copycat	Normal	Status	—	—	20	Self
8	Meditate	Psychic	Status	—	—	40	Self
11	Double Slap	Normal	Physical	15	85	10	Normal
15	Mimic	Normal	Status	—	—	10	Normal
15	Psywave	Psychic	Special	—	100	15	Normal
18	Encore	Normal	Status	—	100	5	Normal
22	Light Screen	Psychic	Status	—	—	30	Your Side
22	Reflect	Psychic	Status	—	—	20	Your Side
25	Psybeam	Psychic	Special	65	100	20	Normal
29	Substitute	Normal	Status	—	—	10	Self
32	Recycle	Normal	Status	—	—	10	Self
36	Trick	Psychic	Status	—	100	10	Normal
39	Psychic	Psychic	Special	90	100	10	Normal
43	Role Play	Psychic	Status	—	—	10	Normal
46	Baton Pass	Normal	Status	—	--	40	Self
50	Safeguard	Normal	Status	—	—	25	Your Side

TM & HM MOVES

No.	Name	Type	Kind	Pow.	Acc.	PP	Range
TM03	Psyshock	Psychic	Special	80	100	10	Normal
TM04	Calm Mind	Psychic	Status	—	—	20	Self
TM06	Toxic	Poison	Status	—	90	10	Normal
TM10	Hidden Power	Normal	Special	60	100	15	Normal
TM11	Sunny Day	Fire	Status	—	—	5	Both Sides
TM12	Taunt	Dark	Status	—	100	20	Normal
TM15	Hyper Beam	Normal	Special	150	90	5	Normal
TM16	Light Screen	Psychic	Status	—	—	30	Your Side
TM17	Protect	Normal	Status	—	—	10	Self
TM18	Rain Dance	Water	Status	—	—	5	Both Sides
TM20	Safeguard	Normal	Status	—	—	25	Your Side
TM21	Frustration	Normal	Physical	—	100	20	Normal
TM22	Solar Beam	Grass	Special	120	100	10	Normal
TM24	Thunderbolt	Electric	Special	90	100	15	Normal
TM25	Thunder	Electric	Special	110	70	10	Normal
TM27	Return	Normal	Physical	—	100	20	Normal
TM29	Psychic	Psychic	Special	90	100	10	Normal
TM30	Shadow Ball	Ghost	Special	80	100	15	Normal
TM31	Brick Break	Fighting	Physical	75	100	15	Normal
TM32	Double Team	Normal	Status	—	—	15	Self
TM33	Reflect	Psychic	Status	--	—	20	Your Side
TM40	Aerial Ace	Flying	Physical	60	—	20	Normal
TM41	Torment	Dark	Status	—	100	15	Normal
TM42	Facade	Normal	Physical	70	100	20	Normal
TM44	Rest	Psychic	Status	—	—	10	Self
TM45	Attract	Normal	Status	—	100	15	Normal
TM46	Thief	Dark	Physical	60	100	25	Normal
TM48	Round	Normal	Special	60	100	15	Normal
TM52	Focus Blast	Fighting	Special	120	70	5	Normal
TM53	Energy Ball	Grass	Special	90	100	10	Normal
TM56	Fling	Dark	Physical	—	100	10	Normal
TM57	Charge Beam	Electric	Special	50	90	10	Normal
TM66	Payback	Dark	Physical	50	100	10	Normal
TM68	Giga Impact	Normal	Physical	150	90	5	Normal
TM70	Flash	Normal	Status	—	100	20	Normal
TM73	Thunder Wave	Electric	Status	—	100	20	Normal
TM77	Psych Up	Normal	Status	—	—	10	Normal
TM83	Infestation	Bug	Special	20	100	20	Normal
TM85	Dream Eater	Psychic	Special	100	100	15	Normal
TM86	Grass Knot	Grass	Special	—	100	20	Normal
TM87	Swagger	Normal	Status	—	90	15	Normal
TM88	Sleep Talk	Normal	Status	—	—	10	Self
TM90	Substitute	Normal	Status	—	—	10	Self
TM92	Trick Room	Psychic	Status	—	—	5	Both Sides
TM94	Secret Power	Normal	Physical	70	100	20	Normal
TM98	Power-Up Punch	Fighting	Physical	40	100	20	Normal
TM99	Dazzling Gleam	Fairy	Special	80	100	10	Many Others
TM100	Confide	Normal	Status	—	—	20	Normal

MOVES LEARNED IN EXCHANGE FOR BP

Name	Type	Kind	Pow.	Acc.	PP	Range
Covet	Normal	Physical	60	100	25	Normal
Signal Beam	Bug	Special	75	100	15	Normal
Thunder Punch	Electric	Physical	75	100	15	Normal
Fire Punch	Fire	Physical	75	100	15	Normal
Ice Punch	Ice	Physical	75	100	15	Normal
Magic Coat	Psychic	Status	—	—	15	Self
Foul Play	Dark	Physical	95	100	15	Normal
Iron Defense	Steel	Status	—	—	15	Self
Icy Wind	Ice	Special	55	95	15	Many Others
Zen Headbutt	Psychic	Physical	80	90	15	Normal
Snore	Normal	Special	50	100	15	Normal
Role Play	Psychic	Status	—	—	10	Normal
Drain Punch	Fighting	Physical	75	100	10	Normal
Focus Punch	Fighting	Physical	150	100	20	Normal
Shock Wave	Electric	Special	60	—	20	Normal
Helping Hand	Normal	Status	—	—	20	1 Ally
Trick	Psychic	Status	—	100	10	Normal
Magic Room	Psychic	Status	—	—	10	Both Sides
Wonder Room	Psychic	Status	—	—	10	Both Sides
Recycle	Normal	Status	—	—	10	Self
Snatch	Dark	Status	—	—	10	Self
Skill Swap	Psychic	Status	—	—	10	Normal

MOVES TAUGHT BY PEOPLE

Name	Type	Kind	Pow.	Acc.	PP	Range

EGG MOVES

Name	Type	Kind	Pow.	Acc.	PP	Range
Future Sight	Psychic	Special	120	100	10	Normal
Hypnosis	Psychic	Status	—	60	20	Normal
Mimic	Normal	Status	—	—	10	Normal
Fake Out	Normal	Physical	40	100	10	Normal
Trick	Psychic	Status	—	100	10	Normal
Confuse Ray	Ghost	Status	—	100	10	Normal
Wake-Up Slap	Fighting	Physical	70	100	10	Normal
Teeter Dance	Normal	Status	—	100	20	Adjacent
Nasty Plot	Dark	Status	—	—	20	Self
Power Split	Psychic	Status	—	—	10	Normal
Magic Room	Psychic	Status	—	—	10	Both Sides
Icy Wind	Ice	Special	55	95	15	Many Others

National Pokédex **123** Hoenn Pokédex —

Scyther

Mantis Pokémon

Bug / Flying

HEIGHT: 4'11" WEIGHT: 123.5 lbs.

The male has a shorter abdomen.
The female has a longer abdomen.

Ω Scyther is blindingly fast. Its blazing speed enhances the effectiveness of the twin scythes on its forearms. This Pokémon's scythes are so effective, they can slice through thick logs in one wicked stroke.

α Scyther is blindingly fast. Its blazing speed enhances the effectiveness of the twin scythes on its forearms. This Pokémon's scythes are so effective, they can slice through thick logs in one wicked stroke.

ABILITIES
Swarm
Technician

HIDDEN ABILITY
Steadfast

EGG GROUPS
Bug

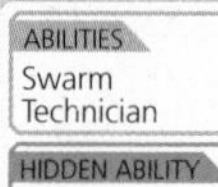

STAT GROWTH RATES
HP ▮▮▮
Attack ▮▮▮▮▮▮
Defense ▮▮▮▮
Sp. Atk ▮▮▮
Sp. Def ▮▮▮
Speed ▮▮▮▮▮▮

ITEMS SOMETIMES HELD BY WILD POKÉMON
—

EVOLUTION

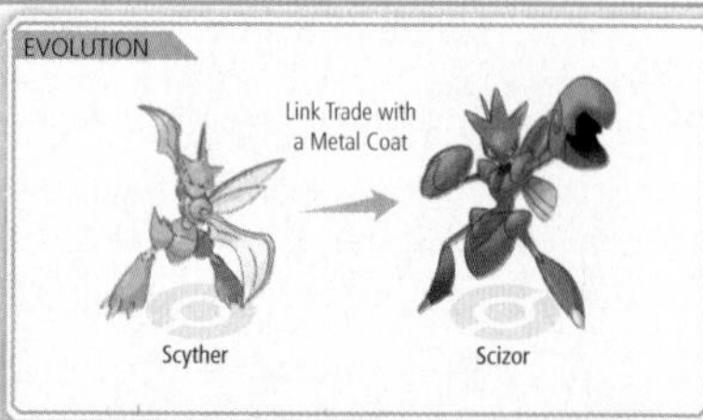

MAIN WAY TO REGISTER IN THE NATIONAL POKÉDEX

Appears in *Pokémon X* and *Pokémon Y*. Bring it to your game using Link Trade or the GTS.

Damage taken in normal battles

Type		Type	
Normal	×1	Flying	×2
Fire	×2	Psychic	×1
Water	×1	Bug	×0.5
Grass	×0.25	Rock	×4
Electric	×2	Ghost	×1
Ice	×2	Dragon	×1
Fighting	×0.25	Dark	×1
Poison	×1	Steel	×1
Ground	×0	Fairy	×1

Damage taken in Inverse battles

Type		Type	
Normal	×1	Flying	×0.5
Fire	×0.5	Psychic	×1
Water	×1	Bug	×2
Grass	×4	Rock	×0.25
Electric	×0.5	Ghost	×1
Ice	×0.5	Dragon	×1
Fighting	×4	Dark	×1
Poison	×1	Steel	×1
Ground	×4	Fairy	×1

Can be used in
Inverse Battle
Battle Institute
Battle Maison
Random Matchup (Free Battle)
Random Matchup (Others)

LEVEL-UP MOVES

Lv.	Name	Type	Kind	Pow.	Acc.	PP	Range
1	Vacuum Wave	Fighting	Special	40	100	30	Normal
1	Quick Attack	Normal	Physical	40	100	30	Normal
1	Leer	Normal	Status	—	100	30	Many Others
5	Focus Energy	Normal	Status	—	—	30	Self
9	Pursuit	Dark	Physical	40	100	20	Normal
13	False Swipe	Normal	Physical	40	100	40	Normal
17	Agility	Psychic	Status	—	—	30	Self
21	Wing Attack	Flying	Physical	60	100	35	Normal
25	Fury Cutter	Bug	Physical	40	95	20	Normal
29	Slash	Normal	Physical	70	100	20	Normal
33	Razor Wind	Normal	Special	80	100	10	Many Others
37	Double Team	Normal	Status	—	—	15	Self
41	X-Scissor	Bug	Physical	80	100	15	Normal
45	Night Slash	Dark	Physical	70	100	15	Normal
49	Double Hit	Normal	Physical	35	90	10	Normal
50	Air Slash	Flying	Special	75	95	15	Normal
57	Swords Dance	Normal	Status	—	—	20	Self
61	Feint	Normal	Physical	30	100	10	Normal

TM & HM MOVES

No.	Name	Type	Kind	Pow.	Acc.	PP	Range
TM06	Toxic	Poison	Status	—	90	10	Normal
TM10	Hidden Power	Normal	Special	60	100	15	Normal
TM11	Sunny Day	Fire	Status	—	—	5	Both Sides
TM15	Hyper Beam	Normal	Special	150	90	5	Normal
TM16	Light Screen	Psychic	Status	—	—	30	Your Side
TM17	Protect	Normal	Status	—	—	10	Self
TM18	Rain Dance	Water	Status	—	—	5	Both Sides
TM19	Roost	Flying	Status	—	—	10	Self
TM20	Safeguard	Normal	Status	—	—	25	Your Side
TM21	Frustration	Normal	Physical	—	100	20	Normal
TM27	Return	Normal	Physical	—	100	20	Normal
TM31	Brick Break	Fighting	Physical	75	100	15	Normal
TM32	Double Team	Normal	Status	—	—	15	Self
TM40	Aerial Ace	Flying	Physical	60	—	20	Normal
TM42	Facade	Normal	Physical	70	100	20	Normal
TM44	Rest	Psychic	Status	—	—	10	Self
TM45	Attract	Normal	Status	—	100	15	Normal
TM46	Thief	Dark	Physical	60	100	25	Normal
TM48	Round	Normal	Special	60	100	15	Normal
TM51	Steel Wing	Steel	Physical	70	90	25	Normal
TM54	False Swipe	Normal	Physical	40	100	40	Normal
TM68	Giga Impact	Normal	Physical	150	90	5	Normal
TM75	Swords Dance	Normal	Status	—	—	20	Self
TM76	Struggle Bug	Bug	Special	50	100	20	Many Others
TM81	X-Scissor	Bug	Physical	80	100	15	Normal
TM87	Swagger	Normal	Status	—	90	15	Normal
TM88	Sleep Talk	Normal	Status	—	—	10	Self
TM89	U-turn	Bug	Physical	70	100	20	Normal
TM90	Substitute	Normal	Status	—	—	10	Self
TM94	Secret Power	Normal	Physical	70	100	20	Normal
TM100	Confide	Normal	Status	—	—	20	Normal
HM01	Cut	Normal	Physical	50	95	30	Normal
HM06	Rock Smash	Fighting	Physical	40	100	15	Normal

MOVES LEARNED IN EXCHANGE FOR BP

Name	Type	Kind	Pow.	Acc.	PP	Range
Bug Bite	Bug	Physical	60	100	20	Normal
Snore	Normal	Special	50	100	15	Normal
Knock Off	Dark	Physical	65	100	20	Normal
Tailwind	Flying	Status	—	—	15	Your Side

MOVES TAUGHT BY PEOPLE

Name	Type	Kind	Pow.	Acc.	PP	Range

EGG MOVES

Name	Type	Kind	Pow.	Acc.	PP	Range
Counter	Fighting	Physical	—	100	20	Varies
Baton Pass	Normal	Status	—	—	40	Self
Razor Wind	Normal	Special	80	100	10	Many Others
Reversal	Fighting	Physical	—	100	15	Normal
Endure	Normal	Status	—	—	10	Self
Silver Wind	Bug	Special	60	100	5	Normal
Bug Buzz	Bug	Special	90	100	10	Normal
Night Slash	Dark	Physical	70	100	15	Normal
Defog	Flying	Status	—	—	15	Normal
Steel Wing	Steel	Physical	70	90	25	Normal
Quick Guard	Fighting	Status	—	—	15	Your Side

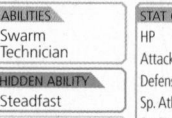

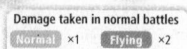

National Pokédex **124** Hoenn Pokédex —

Jynx

Human Shape Pokémon

Ice Psychic

HEIGHT: 4'07" WEIGHT: 89.5 lbs.

♀ only

Ω Jynx walks rhythmically, swaying and shaking its hips as if it were dancing. Its motions are so bouncingly alluring, people seeing it are compelled to shake their hips without giving any thought to what they are doing.

α Jynx walks rhythmically, swaying and shaking its hips as if it were dancing. Its motions are so bouncingly alluring, people seeing it are compelled to shake their hips without giving any thought to what they are doing.

ABILITIES
Oblivious
Forewarn

HIDDEN ABILITY
Dry Skin

EGG GROUPS
Human-Like

STAT GROWTH RATES
HP
Attack
Defense
Sp. Atk
Sp. Def
Speed

ITEMS SOMETIMES HELD BY WILD POKÉMON
—

EVOLUTION

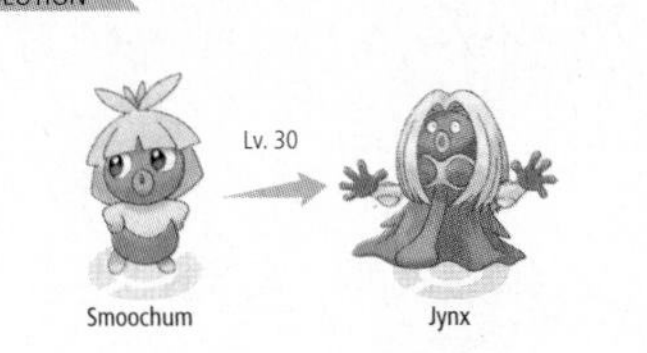

MAIN WAY TO REGISTER IN THE NATIONAL POKÉDEX

Appears in *Pokémon X* and *Pokémon Y*. Bring it to your game using Link Trade or the GTS.

Damage taken in normal battles

Type		Type	
Normal	×1	Flying	×1
Fire	×2	Psychic	×0.5
Water	×1	Bug	×2
Grass	×1	Rock	×2
Electric	×1	Ghost	×2
Ice	×0.5	Dragon	×1
Fighting	×1	Dark	×2
Poison	×1	Steel	×2
Ground	×1	Fairy	×1

Damage taken in Inverse battles

Type		Type	
Normal	×1	Flying	×1
Fire	×0.5	Psychic	×2
Water	×1	Bug	×0.5
Grass	×1	Rock	×0.5
Electric	×1	Ghost	×0.5
Ice	×2	Dragon	×1
Fighting	×1	Dark	×0.5
Poison	×1	Steel	×0.5
Ground	×1	Fairy	×1

Can be used in
Inverse Battle
Battle Institute
Battle Maison
Random Matchup (Free Battle)
Random Matchup (Others)

LEVEL-UP MOVES

Lv.	Name	Type	Kind	Pow.	Acc.	PP	Range
1	Draining Kiss	Fairy	Special	50	100	10	Normal
1	Perish Song	Normal	Status	—	—	5	Adjacent
1	Pound	Normal	Physical	40	100	35	Normal
1	Lick	Ghost	Physical	30	100	30	Normal
1	Lovely Kiss	Normal	Status	—	75	10	Normal
1	Powder Snow	Ice	Special	40	100	25	Many Others
5	Lick	Ghost	Physical	30	100	30	Normal
8	Lovely Kiss	Normal	Status	—	75	10	Normal
11	Powder Snow	Ice	Special	40	100	25	Many Others
15	Double Slap	Normal	Physical	15	85	10	Normal
18	Ice Punch	Ice	Physical	75	100	15	Normal
21	Heart Stamp	Psychic	Physical	60	100	25	Normal
25	Mean Look	Normal	Status	—	—	5	Normal
28	Fake Tears	Dark	Status	—	100	20	Normal
33	Wake-Up Slap	Fighting	Physical	70	100	10	Normal
39	Avalanche	Ice	Physical	60	100	10	Normal
44	Body Slam	Normal	Physical	85	100	15	Normal
49	Wring Out	Normal	Special	—	100	5	Normal
55	Perish Song	Normal	Status	—	—	5	Adjacent
60	Blizzard	Ice	Special	110	70	5	Many Others

TM & HM MOVES

No.	Name	Type	Kind	Pow.	Acc.	PP	Range
TM03	Psyshock	Psychic	Special	80	100	10	Normal
TM04	Calm Mind	Psychic	Status	—	—	20	Self
TM06	Toxic	Poison	Status	—	90	10	Normal
TM07	Hail	Ice	Status	—	—	10	Both Sides
TM10	Hidden Power	Normal	Special	60	100	15	Normal
TM12	Taunt	Dark	Status	—	100	20	Normal
TM13	Ice Beam	Ice	Special	90	100	10	Normal
TM14	Blizzard	Ice	Special	110	70	5	Many Others
TM15	Hyper Beam	Normal	Special	150	90	5	Normal
TM16	Light Screen	Psychic	Status	—	—	30	Your Side
TM17	Protect	Normal	Status	—	—	10	Self
TM18	Rain Dance	Water	Status	—	—	5	Both Sides
TM21	Frustration	Normal	Physical	—	100	20	Normal
TM27	Return	Normal	Physical	—	100	20	Normal
TM29	Psychic	Psychic	Special	90	100	10	Normal
TM30	Shadow Ball	Ghost	Special	80	100	15	Normal
TM31	Brick Break	Fighting	Physical	75	100	15	Normal
TM32	Double Team	Normal	Status	—	—	15	Self
TM33	Reflect	Psychic	Status	—	—	20	Your Side
TM41	Torment	Dark	Status	—	100	15	Normal
TM42	Facade	Normal	Physical	70	100	20	Normal
TM44	Rest	Psychic	Status	—	—	10	Self
TM45	Attract	Normal	Status	—	100	15	Normal
TM46	Thief	Dark	Physical	60	100	25	Normal
TM48	Round	Normal	Special	60	100	15	Normal
TM49	Echoed Voice	Normal	Special	40	100	15	Normal
TM52	Focus Blast	Fighting	Special	120	70	5	Normal
TM53	Energy Ball	Grass	Special	90	100	10	Normal
TM56	Fling	Dark	Physical	—	100	10	Normal
TM66	Payback	Dark	Physical	50	100	10	Normal
TM68	Giga Impact	Normal	Physical	150	90	5	Normal
TM70	Flash	Normal	Status	—	100	20	Normal
TM77	Psych Up	Normal	Status	—	—	10	Normal
TM79	Frost Breath	Ice	Special	60	90	10	Normal
TM85	Dream Eater	Psychic	Special	100	100	15	Normal
TM86	Grass Knot	Grass	Special	—	100	20	Normal
TM87	Swagger	Normal	Status	—	90	15	Normal
TM88	Sleep Talk	Normal	Status	—	—	10	Self
TM90	Substitute	Normal	Status	—	—	10	Self
TM92	Trick Room	Psychic	Status	—	—	5	Both Sides
TM94	Secret Power	Normal	Physical	70	100	20	Normal
TM98	Power-Up Punch	Fighting	Physical	40	100	20	Normal
TM100	Confide	Normal	Status	—	—	20	Normal

MOVES LEARNED IN EXCHANGE FOR BP

Name	Type	Kind	Pow.	Acc.	PP	Range
Covet	Normal	Physical	60	100	25	Normal
Signal Beam	Bug	Special	75	100	15	Normal
Ice Punch	Ice	Physical	75	100	15	Normal
Magic Coat	Psychic	Status	—	—	15	Self
Icy Wind	Ice	Special	55	95	15	Many Others
Zen Headbutt	Psychic	Physical	80	90	15	Normal
Hyper Voice	Normal	Special	90	100	10	Many Others
Snore	Normal	Special	50	100	15	Normal
Role Play	Psychic	Status	—	—	10	Normal
Heal Bell	Normal	Status	—	—	5	Your Party
Drain Punch	Fighting	Physical	75	100	10	Normal
Focus Punch	Fighting	Physical	150	100	20	Normal
Water Pulse	Water	Special	60	100	20	Normal
Helping Hand	Normal	Status	—	—	20	1 Ally
Trick	Psychic	Status	—	100	10	Normal
Magic Room	Psychic	Status	—	—	10	Both Sides
Recycle	Normal	Status	—	—	10	Self
Skill Swap	Psychic	Status	—	—	10	Normal

MOVES TAUGHT BY PEOPLE

Name	Type	Kind	Pow.	Acc.	PP	Range

National Pokédex **125** Hoenn Pokédex —

Electabuzz

Electric Pokémon

Electric

HEIGHT: 3'07" WEIGHT: 66.1 lbs.

Same form for ♂ / ♀

Ω When a storm arrives, gangs of this Pokémon compete with each other to scale heights that are likely to be stricken by lightning bolts. Some towns use Electabuzz in place of lightning rods.

α When a storm arrives, gangs of this Pokémon compete with each other to scale heights that are likely to be stricken by lightning bolts. Some towns use Electabuzz in place of lightning rods.

ABILITY
Static

HIDDEN ABILITY
Vital Spirit

EGG GROUPS
Human-Like

STAT GROWTH RATES
HP
Attack
Defense
Sp. Atk
Sp. Def
Speed

ITEMS SOMETIMES HELD BY WILD POKÉMON
—

EVOLUTION

Lv. 30
Link Trade with an Electrizer
Elekid
Electabuzz
Electivire

MAIN WAY TO REGISTER IN THE NATIONAL POKÉDEX

Level up Elekid to Lv. 30.

Damage taken in normal battles

Type		Type	
Normal	×1	Flying	×0.5
Fire	×1	Psychic	×1
Water	×1	Bug	×1
Grass	×1	Rock	×1
Electric	×0.5	Ghost	×1
Ice	×1	Dragon	×1
Fighting	×1	Dark	×1
Poison	×1	Steel	×0.5
Ground	×2	Fairy	×1

Damage taken in Inverse battles

Type		Type	
Normal	×1	Flying	×2
Fire	×1	Psychic	×1
Water	×1	Bug	×1
Grass	×1	Rock	×1
Electric	×2	Ghost	×1
Ice	×1	Dragon	×1
Fighting	×1	Dark	×1
Poison	×1	Steel	×2
Ground	×0.5	Fairy	×1

Can be used in
Inverse Battle
Battle Institute
Battle Maison
Random Matchup (Free Battle)
Random Matchup (Others)

LEVEL-UP MOVES

Lv.	Name	Type	Kind	Pow.	Acc.	PP	Range
1	Quick Attack	Normal	Physical	40	100	30	Normal
1	Leer	Normal	Status	—	100	30	Many Others
1	Thunder Shock	Electric	Special	40	100	30	Normal
5	Thunder Shock	Electric	Special	40	100	30	Normal
8	Low Kick	Fighting	Physical	—	100	20	Normal
12	Swift	Normal	Special	60	—	20	Many Others
15	Shock Wave	Electric	Special	60	—	20	Normal
19	Thunder Wave	Electric	Status	—	100	20	Normal
22	Electro Ball	Electric	Special	—	100	10	Normal
26	Light Screen	Psychic	Status	—	—	30	Your Side
29	Thunder Punch	Electric	Physical	75	100	15	Normal
36	Discharge	Electric	Special	80	100	15	Adjacent
42	Screech	Normal	Status	—	85	40	Normal
49	Thunderbolt	Electric	Special	90	100	15	Normal
55	Thunder	Electric	Special	110	70	10	Normal

TM & HM MOVES

No.	Name	Type	Kind	Pow.	Acc.	PP	Range
TM06	Toxic	Poison	Status	—	90	10	Normal
TM10	Hidden Power	Normal	Special	60	100	15	Normal
TM15	Hyper Beam	Normal	Special	150	90	5	Normal
TM16	Light Screen	Psychic	Status	—	—	30	Your Side
TM17	Protect	Normal	Status	—	—	10	Self
TM18	Rain Dance	Water	Status	—	—	5	Both Sides
TM21	Frustration	Normal	Physical	—	100	20	Normal
TM24	Thunderbolt	Electric	Special	90	100	15	Normal
TM25	Thunder	Electric	Special	110	70	10	Normal
TM27	Return	Normal	Physical	—	100	20	Normal
TM29	Psychic	Psychic	Special	90	100	10	Normal
TM31	Brick Break	Fighting	Physical	75	100	15	Normal
TM32	Double Team	Normal	Status	—	—	15	Self
TM42	Facade	Normal	Physical	70	100	20	Normal
TM44	Rest	Psychic	Status	—	—	10	Self
TM45	Attract	Normal	Status	—	100	15	Normal
TM46	Thief	Dark	Physical	60	100	25	Normal
TM47	Low Sweep	Fighting	Physical	65	100	20	Normal
TM48	Round	Normal	Special	60	100	15	Normal
TM52	Focus Blast	Fighting	Special	120	70	5	Normal
TM56	Fling	Dark	Physical	—	100	10	Normal
TM57	Charge Beam	Electric	Special	50	90	10	Normal
TM68	Giga Impact	Normal	Physical	150	90	5	Normal
TM70	Flash	Normal	Status	—	100	20	Normal
TM72	Volt Switch	Electric	Special	70	100	20	Normal
TM73	Thunder Wave	Electric	Status	—	100	20	Normal
TM87	Swagger	Normal	Status	—	90	15	Normal
TM88	Sleep Talk	Normal	Status	—	—	10	Self
TM90	Substitute	Normal	Status	—	—	10	Self
TM93	Wild Charge	Electric	Physical	90	100	15	Normal
TM94	Secret Power	Normal	Physical	70	100	20	Normal
TM98	Power-Up Punch	Fighting	Physical	40	100	20	Normal
TM100	Confide	Normal	Status	—	—	20	Normal
HM04	Strength	Normal	Physical	80	100	15	Normal
HM06	Rock Smash	Fighting	Physical	40	100	15	Normal

MOVES LEARNED IN EXCHANGE FOR BP

Name	Type	Kind	Pow.	Acc.	PP	Range
Covet	Normal	Physical	60	100	25	Normal
Dual Chop	Dragon	Physical	40	90	15	Normal
Signal Beam	Bug	Special	75	100	15	Normal
Low Kick	Fighting	Physical	—	100	20	Normal
Thunder Punch	Electric	Physical	75	100	15	Normal
Fire Punch	Fire	Physical	75	100	15	Normal
Ice Punch	Ice	Physical	75	100	15	Normal
Magnet Rise	Electric	Status	—	—	10	Self
Electroweb	Electric	Special	55	95	15	Many Others
Iron Tail	Steel	Physical	100	75	15	Normal
Snore	Normal	Special	50	100	15	Normal
Focus Punch	Fighting	Physical	150	100	20	Normal
Shock Wave	Electric	Special	60	—	20	Normal
Helping Hand	Normal	Status	—	—	20	1 Ally

MOVES TAUGHT BY PEOPLE

Name	Type	Kind	Pow.	Acc.	PP	Range

National Pokédex **126** Hoenn Pokédex —

Magmar

Spitfire Pokémon

Fire

HEIGHT: 4'03" WEIGHT: 98.1 lbs.

Same form for ♂ / ♀

Ω In battle, Magmar blows out intensely hot flames from all over its body to intimidate its opponent. This Pokémon's fiery bursts create heat waves that ignite grass and trees in its surroundings.

α In battle, Magmar blows out intensely hot flames from all over its body to intimidate its opponent. This Pokémon's fiery bursts create heat waves that ignite grass and trees in its surroundings.

ABILITY
Flame Body

HIDDEN ABILITY
Vital Spirit

EGG GROUPS
Human-Like

STAT GROWTH RATES
HP
Attack
Defense
Sp. Atk
Sp. Def
Speed

ITEMS SOMETIMES HELD BY WILD POKÉMON
—

EVOLUTION

Magby → Lv. 30 → Magmar → Link Trade with a Magmarizer → Magmortar

MAIN WAY TO REGISTER IN THE NATIONAL POKÉDEX

Level up Magby to Lv. 30.

Damage taken in normal battles

Type		Type	
Normal	×1	Flying	×1
Fire	×0.5	Psychic	×1
Water	×2	Bug	×0.5
Grass	×0.5	Rock	×2
Electric	×1	Ghost	×1
Ice	×0.5	Dragon	×1
Fighting	×1	Dark	×1
Poison	×1	Steel	×0.5
Ground	×2	Fairy	×0.5

Damage taken in Inverse battles

Type		Type	
Normal	×1	Flying	×1
Fire	×2	Psychic	×1
Water	×0.5	Bug	×2
Grass	×2	Rock	×0.5
Electric	×1	Ghost	×1
Ice	×2	Dragon	×1
Fighting	×1	Dark	×1
Poison	×1	Steel	×2
Ground	×0.5	Fairy	×2

Can be used in
- Inverse Battle
- Battle Institute
- Battle Maison
- Random Matchup (Free Battle)
- Random Matchup (Others)

LEVEL-UP MOVES

Lv.	Name	Type	Kind	Pow.	Acc.	PP	Range
1	Smog	Poison	Special	30	70	20	Normal
1	Leer	Normal	Status	—	100	30	Many Others
1	Ember	Fire	Special	40	100	25	Normal
5	Ember	Fire	Special	40	100	25	Normal
8	Smokescreen	Normal	Status	—	100	20	Normal
12	Feint Attack	Dark	Physical	60	—	20	Normal
15	Fire Spin	Fire	Special	35	85	15	Normal
19	Clear Smog	Poison	Special	50	—	15	Normal
22	Flame Burst	Fire	Special	70	100	15	Normal
26	Confuse Ray	Ghost	Status	—	100	10	Normal
29	Fire Punch	Fire	Physical	75	100	15	Normal
36	Lava Plume	Fire	Special	80	100	15	Adjacent
42	Sunny Day	Fire	Status	—	—	5	Both Sides
49	Flamethrower	Fire	Special	90	100	15	Normal
55	Fire Blast	Fire	Special	110	85	5	Normal

TM & HM MOVES

No.	Name	Type	Kind	Pow.	Acc.	PP	Range
TM06	Toxic	Poison	Status	—	90	10	Normal
TM10	Hidden Power	Normal	Special	60	100	15	Normal
TM11	Sunny Day	Fire	Status	—	—	5	Both Sides
TM15	Hyper Beam	Normal	Special	150	90	5	Normal
TM17	Protect	Normal	Status	—	—	10	Self
TM21	Frustration	Normal	Physical	—	100	20	Normal
TM27	Return	Normal	Physical	—	100	20	Normal
TM29	Psychic	Psychic	Special	90	100	10	Normal
TM31	Brick Break	Fighting	Physical	75	100	15	Normal
TM32	Double Team	Normal	Status	—	—	15	Self
TM35	Flamethrower	Fire	Special	90	100	15	Normal
TM38	Fire Blast	Fire	Special	110	85	5	Normal
TM42	Facade	Normal	Physical	70	100	20	Normal
TM43	Flame Charge	Fire	Physical	50	100	20	Normal
TM44	Rest	Psychic	Status	—	—	10	Self
TM45	Attract	Normal	Status	—	100	15	Normal
TM46	Thief	Dark	Physical	60	100	25	Normal
TM47	Low Sweep	Fighting	Physical	65	100	20	Normal
TM48	Round	Normal	Special	60	100	15	Normal
TM50	Overheat	Fire	Special	130	90	5	Normal
TM52	Focus Blast	Fighting	Special	120	70	5	Normal
TM56	Fling	Dark	Physical	—	100	10	Normal
TM59	Incinerate	Fire	Special	60	100	15	Many Others
TM61	Will-O-Wisp	Fire	Status	—	85	15	Normal
TM68	Giga Impact	Normal	Physical	150	90	5	Normal
TM87	Swagger	Normal	Status	—	90	15	Normal
TM88	Sleep Talk	Normal	Status	—	—	10	Self
TM90	Substitute	Normal	Status	—	—	10	Self
TM94	Secret Power	Normal	Physical	70	100	20	Normal
TM98	Power-Up Punch	Fighting	Physical	40	100	20	Normal
TM100	Confide	Normal	Status	—	—	20	Normal
HM04	Strength	Normal	Physical	80	100	15	Normal
HM06	Rock Smash	Fighting	Physical	40	100	15	Normal

MOVES LEARNED IN EXCHANGE FOR BP

Name	Type	Kind	Pow.	Acc.	PP	Range
Covet	Normal	Physical	60	100	25	Normal
Dual Chop	Dragon	Physical	40	90	15	Normal
Low Kick	Fighting	Physical	—	100	20	Normal
Thunder Punch	Electric	Physical	75	100	15	Normal
Fire Punch	Fire	Physical	75	100	15	Normal
Iron Tail	Steel	Physical	100	75	15	Normal
Snore	Normal	Special	50	100	15	Normal
Heat Wave	Fire	Special	95	90	10	Many Others
Focus Punch	Fighting	Physical	150	100	20	Normal
Helping Hand	Normal	Status	—	—	20	1 Ally

MOVES TAUGHT BY PEOPLE

Name	Type	Kind	Pow.	Acc.	PP	Range

National Pokédex **127** Hoenn Pokédex **174**

Pinsir

Stag Beetle Pokémon

Bug

HEIGHT: 4'11"" WEIGHT: 121.3 lbs.

Same form for ♂ / ♀

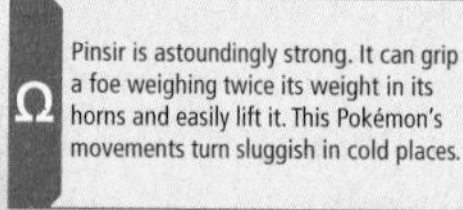

Ω Pinsir is astoundingly strong. It can grip a foe weighing twice its weight in its horns and easily lift it. This Pokémon's movements turn sluggish in cold places.

α Pinsir has a pair of massive horns. Protruding from the surface of these horns are thorns. These thorns are driven deeply into the foe's body when the pincer closes, making it tough for the foe to escape.

ABILITIES
Hyper Cutter
Mold Breaker

HIDDEN ABILITY
Moxie

EGG GROUPS
Bug

STAT GROWTH RATES
HP
Attack
Defense
Sp. Atk
Sp. Def
Speed

ITEMS SOMETIMES HELD BY WILD POKÉMON
—

EVOLUTION

Does not evolve

MAIN WAY TO REGISTER IN THE NATIONAL POKÉDEX

Catch in the very tall grass in the upper-right corner of the Safari Zone.

Damage taken in normal battles

Type		Type	
Normal	×1	Flying	×2
Fire	×2	Psychic	×1
Water	×1	Bug	×1
Grass	×0.5	Rock	×2
Electric	×1	Ghost	×1
Ice	×1	Dragon	×1
Fighting	×0.5	Dark	×1
Poison	×1	Steel	×1
Ground	×0.5	Fairy	×1

Damage taken in Inverse battles

Type		Type	
Normal	×1	Flying	×0.5
Fire	×0.5	Psychic	×1
Water	×1	Bug	×1
Grass	×2	Rock	×0.5
Electric	×1	Ghost	×1
Ice	×1	Dragon	×1
Fighting	×2	Dark	×1
Poison	×1	Steel	×1
Ground	×2	Fairy	×1

Can be used in
- Inverse Battle
- Battle Institute
- Battle Maison
- Random Matchup (Free Battle)
- Random Matchup (Others)

LEVEL-UP MOVES

Lv.	Name	Type	Kind	Pow.	Acc.	PP	Range
1	Vice Grip	Normal	Physical	55	100	30	Normal
1	Focus Energy	Normal	Status	—	—	30	Self
4	Bind	Normal	Physical	15	85	20	Normal
8	Seismic Toss	Fighting	Physical	—	100	20	Normal
11	Harden	Normal	Status	—	—	30	Self
15	Revenge	Fighting	Physical	60	100	10	Normal
18	Vital Throw	Fighting	Physical	70	—	10	Normal
22	Double Hit	Normal	Physical	35	90	10	Normal
26	Brick Break	Fighting	Physical	75	100	15	Normal
29	Submission	Fighting	Physical	80	80	20	Normal
33	X-Scissor	Bug	Physical	80	100	15	Normal
36	Storm Throw	Fighting	Physical	60	100	10	Normal
40	Swords Dance	Normal	Status	—	—	20	Self
43	Thrash	Normal	Physical	120	100	10	1 Random
47	Superpower	Fighting	Physical	120	100	5	Normal
50	Guillotine	Normal	Physical	—	30	5	Normal

TM & HM MOVES

No.	Name	Type	Kind	Pow.	Acc.	PP	Range
TM06	Toxic	Poison	Status	—	90	10	Normal
TM08	Bulk Up	Fighting	Status	—	—	20	Self
TM10	Hidden Power	Normal	Special	60	100	15	Normal
TM11	Sunny Day	Fire	Status	—	—	5	Both Sides
TM15	Hyper Beam	Normal	Special	150	90	5	Normal
TM17	Protect	Normal	Status	—	—	10	Self
TM18	Rain Dance	Water	Status	—	—	5	Both Sides
TM21	Frustration	Normal	Physical	—	100	20	Normal
TM23	Smack Down	Rock	Physical	50	100	15	Normal
TM26	Earthquake	Ground	Physical	100	100	10	Adjacent
TM27	Return	Normal	Physical	—	100	20	Normal
TM28	Dig	Ground	Physical	80	100	10	Normal
TM31	Brick Break	Fighting	Physical	75	100	15	Normal
TM32	Double Team	Normal	Status	—	—	15	Self
TM39	Rock Tomb	Rock	Physical	60	95	15	Normal
TM42	Facade	Normal	Physical	70	100	20	Normal
TM44	Rest	Psychic	Status	—	—	10	Self
TM45	Attract	Normal	Status	—	100	15	Normal
TM46	Thief	Dark	Physical	60	100	25	Normal
TM48	Round	Normal	Special	60	100	15	Normal
TM52	Focus Blast	Fighting	Special	120	70	5	Normal
TM54	False Swipe	Normal	Physical	40	100	40	Normal
TM56	Fling	Dark	Physical	—	100	10	Normal
TM68	Giga Impact	Normal	Physical	150	90	5	Normal
TM71	Stone Edge	Rock	Physical	100	80	5	Normal
TM75	Swords Dance	Normal	Status	—	—	20	Self
TM76	Struggle Bug	Bug	Special	50	100	20	Many Others
TM78	Bulldoze	Ground	Physical	60	100	20	Adjacent
TM80	Rock Slide	Rock	Physical	75	90	10	Many Others
TM81	X-Scissor	Bug	Physical	80	100	15	Normal
TM87	Swagger	Normal	Status	—	90	15	Normal
TM88	Sleep Talk	Normal	Status	—	—	10	Self
TM90	Substitute	Normal	Status	—	—	10	Self
TM94	Secret Power	Normal	Physical	70	100	20	Normal
TM100	Confide	Normal	Status	—	—	20	Normal
HM01	Cut	Normal	Physical	50	95	30	Normal
HM04	Strength	Normal	Physical	80	100	15	Normal
HM06	Rock Smash	Fighting	Physical	40	100	15	Normal

MOVES LEARNED IN EXCHANGE FOR BP

Name	Type	Kind	Pow.	Acc.	PP	Range
Bug Bite	Bug	Physical	60	100	20	Normal
Iron Defense	Steel	Status	—	—	15	Self
Superpower	Fighting	Physical	120	100	5	Normal
Bind	Normal	Physical	15	85	20	Normal
Snore	Normal	Special	50	100	15	Normal
Knock Off	Dark	Physical	65	100	20	Normal
Focus Punch	Fighting	Physical	150	100	20	Normal
Stealth Rock	Rock	Status	—	—	20	Other Side

MOVES TAUGHT BY PEOPLE

Name	Type	Kind	Pow.	Acc.	PP	Range

EGG MOVES

Name	Type	Kind	Pow.	Acc.	PP	Range
Fury Attack	Normal	Physical	15	85	20	Normal
Flail	Normal	Physical	—	100	15	Normal
Feint Attack	Dark	Physical	60	—	20	Normal
Quick Attack	Normal	Physical	40	100	30	Normal
Close Combat	Fighting	Physical	120	100	5	Normal
Feint	Normal	Physical	30	100	10	Normal
Me First	Normal	Status	—	—	20	Varies
Bug Bite	Bug	Physical	60	100	20	Normal
Superpower	Fighting	Physical	120	100	5	Normal

Mega Evolution

Mega Pinsir

Stag Beetle Pokémon

Bug / Flying

HEIGHT: 5'07" WEIGHT: 130.1 lbs.

Same form for ♂ / ♀

REQUIRED MEGA STONE

Pinsirite

Find on Route 124.

ABILITY

Aerilate

HIDDEN ABILITY

—

EGG GROUPS

—

STAT GROWTH RATES

HP

Attack

Defense

Sp. Atk

Sp. Def

Speed

Damage taken in normal battles

Type		Type	
Normal	×1	Flying	×2
Fire	×2	Psychic	×1
Water	×1	Bug	×0.5
Grass	×0.25	Rock	×4
Electric	×2	Ghost	×1
Ice	×2	Dragon	×1
Fighting	×0.25	Dark	×1
Poison	×1	Steel	×1
Ground	×0	Fairy	×1

Damage taken in Inverse battles

Type		Type	
Normal	×1	Flying	×0.5
Fire	×0.5	Psychic	×1
Water	×1	Bug	×2
Grass	×4	Rock	×0.25
Electric	×0.5	Ghost	×1
Ice	×0.5	Dragon	×1
Fighting	×4	Dark	×1
Poison	×1	Steel	×1
Ground	×4	Fairy	×1

Can be used in

Inverse Battle

Battle Institute

Battle Maison

Random Matchup (Free Battle)

Random Matchup (Others)

National Pokédex **128** Hoenn Pokédex —

Tauros

Wild Bull Pokémon

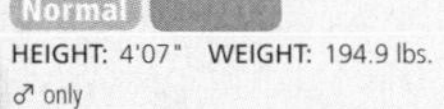

Normal

HEIGHT: 4'07" WEIGHT: 194.9 lbs.

♂ only

Ω This Pokémon is not satisfied unless it is rampaging at all times. If there is no opponent for Tauros to battle, it will charge at thick trees and knock them down to calm itself.

α This Pokémon is not satisfied unless it is rampaging at all times. If there is no opponent for Tauros to battle, it will charge at thick trees and knock them down to calm itself.

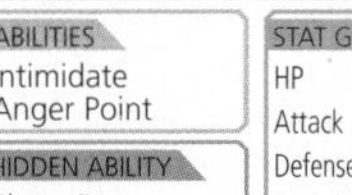

ABILITIES

Intimidate

Anger Point

HIDDEN ABILITY

Sheer Force

EGG GROUPS

Field

STAT GROWTH RATES

HP

Attack

Defense

Sp. Atk

Sp. Def

Speed

ITEMS SOMETIMES HELD BY WILD POKÉMON

—

EVOLUTION

Does not evolve

MAIN WAY TO REGISTER IN THE NATIONAL POKÉDEX

Appears in *Pokémon X* and *Pokémon Y.* Bring it to your game using Link Trade or the GTS.

Damage taken in normal battles

Type		Type	
Normal	×1	Flying	×1
Fire	×1	Psychic	×1
Water	×1	Bug	×1
Grass	×1	Rock	×1
Electric	×1	Ghost	×0
Ice	×1	Dragon	×1
Fighting	×2	Dark	×1
Poison	×1	Steel	×1
Ground	×1	Fairy	×1

Damage taken in Inverse battles

Type		Type	
Normal	×1	Flying	×1
Fire	×1	Psychic	×1
Water	×1	Bug	×1
Grass	×1	Rock	×1
Electric	×1	Ghost	×2
Ice	×1	Dragon	×1
Fighting	×0.5	Dark	×1
Poison	×1	Steel	×1
Ground	×1	Fairy	×1

Can be used in

Inverse Battle

Battle Institute

Battle Maison

Random Matchup (Free Battle)

Random Matchup (Others)

LEVEL-UP MOVES

Lv.	Name	Type	Kind	Pow.	Acc.	PP	Range
1	Tackle	Normal	Physical	50	100	35	Normal
3	Tail Whip	Normal	Status	—	100	30	Many Others
5	Rage	Normal	Physical	20	100	20	Normal
8	Horn Attack	Normal	Physical	65	100	25	Normal
11	Scary Face	Normal	Status	—	100	10	Normal
15	Pursuit	Dark	Physical	40	100	20	Normal
19	Rest	Psychic	Status	—	—	10	Self
24	Payback	Dark	Physical	50	100	10	Normal
29	Work Up	Normal	Status	—	—	30	Self
35	Zen Headbutt	Psychic	Physical	80	90	15	Normal
41	Take Down	Normal	Physical	90	85	20	Normal
48	Swagger	Normal	Status	—	90	15	Normal
50	Thrash	Normal	Physical	120	100	10	1 Random
63	Giga Impact	Normal	Physical	150	90	5	Normal

TM & HM MOVES

No.	Name	Type	Kind	Pow.	Acc.	PP	Range
TM06	Toxic	Poison	Status	—	90	10	Normal
TM10	Hidden Power	Normal	Special	60	100	15	Normal
TM11	Sunny Day	Fire	Status	—	—	5	Both Sides
TM13	Ice Beam	Ice	Special	90	100	10	Normal
TM14	Blizzard	Ice	Special	110	70	5	Many Others
TM15	Hyper Beam	Normal	Special	150	90	5	Normal
TM17	Protect	Normal	Status	—	—	10	Self
TM18	Rain Dance	Water	Status	—	—	5	Both Sides
TM21	Frustration	Normal	Physical	—	100	20	Normal
TM22	Solar Beam	Grass	Special	120	100	10	Normal
TM24	Thunderbolt	Electric	Special	90	100	15	Normal
TM25	Thunder	Electric	Special	110	70	10	Normal
TM26	Earthquake	Ground	Physical	100	100	10	Adjacent
TM27	Return	Normal	Physical	—	100	20	Normal
TM32	Double Team	Normal	Status	—	—	15	Self
TM35	Flamethrower	Fire	Special	90	100	15	Normal
TM37	Sandstorm	Rock	Status	—	—	10	Both Sides
TM38	Fire Blast	Fire	Special	110	85	5	Normal
TM39	Rock Tomb	Rock	Physical	60	95	15	Normal
TM42	Facade	Normal	Physical	70	100	20	Normal
TM44	Rest	Psychic	Status	—	—	10	Self
TM45	Attract	Normal	Status	—	100	15	Normal
TM48	Round	Normal	Special	60	100	15	Normal
TM59	Incinerate	Fire	Special	60	100	15	Many Others
TM66	Payback	Dark	Physical	50	100	10	Normal
TM67	Retaliate	Normal	Physical	70	100	5	Normal
TM68	Giga Impact	Normal	Physical	150	90	5	Normal
TM71	Stone Edge	Rock	Physical	100	80	5	Normal
TM78	Bulldoze	Ground	Physical	60	100	20	Adjacent
TM80	Rock Slide	Rock	Physical	75	90	10	Many Others
TM87	Swagger	Normal	Status	—	90	15	Normal
TM88	Sleep Talk	Normal	Status	—	—	10	Self
TM90	Substitute	Normal	Status	—	—	10	Self
TM93	Wild Charge	Electric	Physical	90	100	15	Normal
TM94	Secret Power	Normal	Physical	70	100	20	Normal
TM100	Confide	Normal	Status	—	—	20	Normal
HM03	Surf	Water	Special	90	100	15	Adjacent
HM04	Strength	Normal	Physical	80	100	15	Normal
HM06	Rock Smash	Fighting	Physical	40	100	15	Normal

MOVES LEARNED IN EXCHANGE FOR BP

Name	Type	Kind	Pow.	Acc.	PP	Range
Iron Head	Steel	Physical	80	100	15	Normal
Uproar	Normal	Special	90	100	10	1 Random
Icy Wind	Ice	Special	55	95	15	Many Others
Zen Headbutt	Psychic	Physical	80	90	15	Normal
Iron Tail	Steel	Physical	100	75	15	Normal
Snore	Normal	Special	50	100	15	Normal
Role Play	Psychic	Status	—	—	10	Normal
Shock Wave	Electric	Special	60	—	20	Normal
Water Pulse	Water	Special	60	100	20	Normal
Spite	Ghost	Status	—	100	10	Normal
Helping Hand	Normal	Status	—	—	20	1 Ally
Endeavor	Normal	Physical	—	100	5	Normal
Outrage	Dragon	Physical	120	100	10	1 Random

MOVES TAUGHT BY PEOPLE

Name	Type	Kind	Pow.	Acc.	PP	Range

National Pokédex **129** Hoenn Pokédex **053**

Magikarp

Fish Pokémon

Water

HEIGHT: 2'11" WEIGHT: 22 lbs.

The male has yellow whiskers.
The female has white whiskers.

Ω Magikarp is a pathetic excuse for a Pokémon that is only capable of flopping and splashing. This behavior prompted scientists to undertake research into it.

α Magikarp is virtually useless in battle as it can only splash around. As a result, it is considered to be weak. However, it is actually a very hardy Pokémon that can survive in any body of water no matter how polluted it is.

ABILITY: Swift Swim

HIDDEN ABILITY: Rattled

EGG GROUPS: Water 2, Dragon

STAT GROWTH RATES: HP, Attack, Defense, Sp. Atk, Sp. Def, Speed

ITEMS SOMETIMES HELD BY WILD POKÉMON: —

EVOLUTION: Magikarp → Lv. 20 → Gyarados

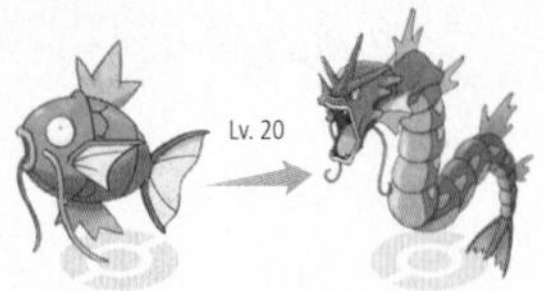

MAIN WAY TO REGISTER IN THE NATIONAL POKÉDEX

Catch using an Old Rod in Dewford Town.

Damage taken in normal battles

Type		Type	
Normal	×1	Flying	×1
Fire	×0.5	Psychic	×1
Water	×0.5	Bug	×1
Grass	×2	Rock	×1
Electric	×2	Ghost	×1
Ice	×0.5	Dragon	×1
Fighting	×1	Dark	×1
Poison	×1	Steel	×0.5
Ground	×1	Fairy	×1

Damage taken in Inverse battles

Type		Type	
Normal	×1	Flying	×1
Fire	×2	Psychic	×1
Water	×2	Bug	×1
Grass	×0.5	Rock	×1
Electric	×0.5	Ghost	×1
Ice	×2	Dragon	×1
Fighting	×1	Dark	×1
Poison	×1	Steel	×2
Ground	×1	Fairy	×1

Can be used in
Inverse Battle
Battle Institute
Battle Maison
Random Matchup (Free Battle)
Random Matchup (Others)

LEVEL-UP MOVES

Lv.	Name	Type	Kind	Pow.	Acc.	PP	Range
1	Splash	Normal	Status	—	—	40	Self
15	Tackle	Normal	Physical	50	100	35	Normal
30	Flail	Normal	Physical	—	100	15	Normal

TM & HM MOVES

No.	Name	Type	Kind	Pow.	Acc.	PP	Range

MOVES LEARNED IN EXCHANGE FOR BP

Name	Type	Kind	Pow.	Acc.	PP	Range
Bounce	Flying	Physical	85	85	5	Normal

MOVES TAUGHT BY PEOPLE

Name	Type	Kind	Pow.	Acc.	PP	Range

National Pokédex **130** Hoenn Pokédex **054**

Gyarados

Atrocious Pokémon

Water Flying

HEIGHT: 21'04" WEIGHT: 518.1 lbs.

The male has blue whiskers.
The female has white whiskers.

Ω When Magikarp evolves into Gyarados, its brain cells undergo a structural transformation. It is said that this transformation is to blame for this Pokémon's wildly violent nature.

α Once Gyarados goes on a rampage, its ferociously violent blood doesn't calm until it has burned everything down. There are records of this Pokémon's rampages lasting a whole month.

ABILITY: Intimidate

HIDDEN ABILITY: Moxie

EGG GROUPS: Water 2, Dragon

STAT GROWTH RATES: HP, Attack, Defense, Sp. Atk, Sp. Def, Speed

ITEMS SOMETIMES HELD BY WILD POKÉMON: —

EVOLUTION: Magikarp → Lv. 20 → Gyarados

MAIN WAY TO REGISTER IN THE NATIONAL POKÉDEX

Catch using a Super Rod in Sootopolis City.

Damage taken in normal battles

Type		Type	
Normal	×1	Flying	×1
Fire	×0.5	Psychic	×1
Water	×0.5	Bug	×0.5
Grass	×1	Rock	×2
Electric	×4	Ghost	×1
Ice	×1	Dragon	×1
Fighting	×0.5	Dark	×1
Poison	×1	Steel	×0.5
Ground	×0	Fairy	×1

Damage taken in Inverse battles

Type		Type	
Normal	×1	Flying	×1
Fire	×2	Psychic	×1
Water	×2	Bug	×2
Grass	×1	Rock	×0.5
Electric	×0.25	Ghost	×1
Ice	×1	Dragon	×1
Fighting	×2	Dark	×1
Poison	×1	Steel	×2
Ground	×2	Fairy	×1

Can be used in
Inverse Battle
Battle Institute
Battle Maison
Random Matchup (Free Battle)
Random Matchup (Others)

LEVEL-UP MOVES

Lv.	Name	Type	Kind	Pow.	Acc.	PP	Range
1	Thrash	Normal	Physical	120	100	10	1 Random
20	Bite	Dark	Physical	60	100	25	Normal
23	Dragon Rage	Dragon	Special	—	100	10	Normal
26	Leer	Normal	Status	—	100	30	Many Others
29	Twister	Dragon	Special	40	100	20	Many Others
32	Ice Fang	Ice	Physical	65	95	15	Normal
35	Aqua Tail	Water	Physical	90	90	10	Normal
38	Rain Dance	Water	Status	—	—	5	Both Sides
41	Crunch	Dark	Physical	80	100	15	Normal
44	Hydro Pump	Water	Special	110	80	5	Normal
47	Dragon Dance	Dragon	Status	—	—	20	Self
50	Hyper Beam	Normal	Special	150	90	5	Normal

TM & HM MOVES

No.	Name	Type	Kind	Pow.	Acc.	PP	Range
TM05	Roar	Normal	Status	—	—	20	Normal
TM06	Toxic	Poison	Status	—	90	10	Normal
TM07	Hail	Ice	Status	—	—	10	Both Sides
TM10	Hidden Power	Normal	Special	60	100	15	Normal
TM12	Taunt	Dark	Status	—	100	20	Normal
TM13	Ice Beam	Ice	Special	90	100	10	Normal
TM14	Blizzard	Ice	Special	110	70	5	Many Others
TM15	Hyper Beam	Normal	Special	150	90	5	Normal
TM17	Protect	Normal	Status	—	—	10	Self
TM18	Rain Dance	Water	Status	—	—	5	Both Sides
TM21	Frustration	Normal	Physical	—	100	20	Normal
TM24	Thunderbolt	Electric	Special	90	100	15	Normal
TM25	Thunder	Electric	Special	110	70	10	Normal
TM26	Earthquake	Ground	Physical	100	100	10	Adjacent
TM27	Return	Normal	Physical	—	100	20	Normal
TM32	Double Team	Normal	Status	—	—	15	Self
TM35	Flamethrower	Fire	Special	90	100	15	Normal
TM37	Sandstorm	Rock	Status	—	—	10	Both Sides
TM38	Fire Blast	Fire	Special	110	85	5	Normal
TM41	Torment	Dark	Status	—	100	15	Normal
TM42	Facade	Normal	Physical	70	100	20	Normal
TM44	Rest	Psychic	Status	—	—	10	Self
TM45	Attract	Normal	Status	—	100	15	Normal
TM48	Round	Normal	Special	60	100	15	Normal
TM55	Scald	Water	Special	80	100	15	Normal
TM59	Incinerate	Fire	Special	60	100	15	Many Others
TM66	Payback	Dark	Physical	50	100	10	Normal
TM68	Giga Impact	Normal	Physical	150	90	5	Normal
TM71	Stone Edge	Rock	Physical	100	80	5	Normal
TM73	Thunder Wave	Electric	Status	—	100	20	Normal
TM78	Bulldoze	Ground	Physical	60	100	20	Adjacent
TM82	Dragon Tail	Dragon	Physical	60	90	10	Normal
TM87	Swagger	Normal	Status	—	90	15	Normal
TM88	Sleep Talk	Normal	Status	—	—	10	Self
TM90	Substitute	Normal	Status	—	—	10	Self
TM94	Secret Power	Normal	Physical	70	100	20	Normal
TM97	Dark Pulse	Dark	Special	80	100	15	Normal
TM100	Confide	Normal	Status	—	—	20	Normal
HM03	Surf	Water	Special	90	100	15	Adjacent
HM04	Strength	Normal	Physical	80	100	15	Normal
HM05	Waterfall	Water	Physical	80	100	15	Normal
HM06	Rock Smash	Fighting	Physical	40	100	15	Normal
HM07	Dive	Water	Physical	80	100	10	Normal

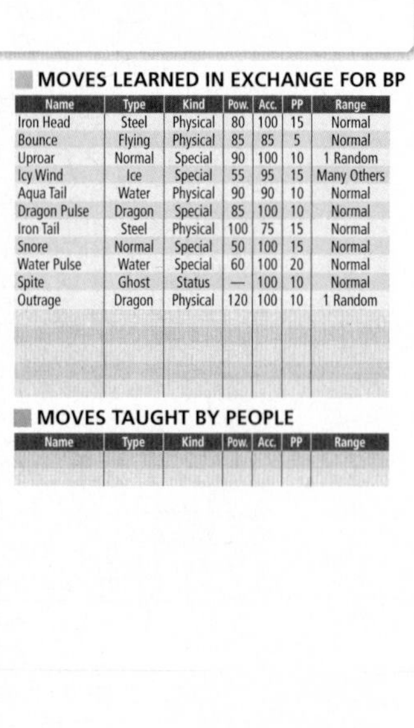

MOVES LEARNED IN EXCHANGE FOR BP

Name	Type	Kind	Pow.	Acc.	PP	Range
Iron Head	Steel	Physical	80	100	15	Normal
Bounce	Flying	Physical	85	85	5	Normal
Uproar	Normal	Special	90	100	10	1 Random
Icy Wind	Ice	Special	55	95	15	Many Others
Aqua Tail	Water	Physical	90	90	10	Normal
Dragon Pulse	Dragon	Special	85	100	10	Normal
Iron Tail	Steel	Physical	100	75	15	Normal
Snore	Normal	Special	50	100	15	Normal
Water Pulse	Water	Special	60	100	20	Normal
Spite	Ghost	Status	—	100	10	Normal
Outrage	Dragon	Physical	120	100	10	1 Random

MOVES TAUGHT BY PEOPLE

Name	Type	Kind	Pow.	Acc.	PP	Range

Mega Evolution

Mega Gyarados

Atrocious Pokémon

Water Dark

HEIGHT: 21'04" WEIGHT: 672.4 lbs.

Same form for ♂ / ♀

REQUIRED MEGA STONE

Gyaradosite

Talk to the Poochyena at 123 Go Fish on Route 123 and select "Yes" to obtain it.

ABILITY

Mold Breaker

HIDDEN ABILITY

—

EGG GROUPS

—

STAT GROWTH RATES

HP

Attack

Defense

Sp. Atk

Sp. Def

Speed

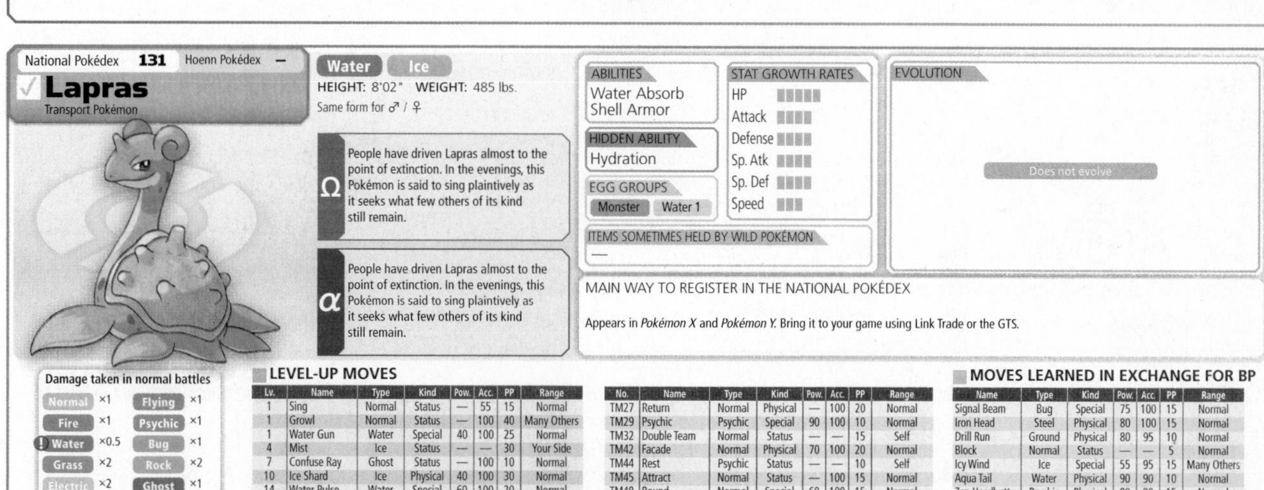

Damage taken in normal battles

Type		Type	
Normal	×1	Flying	×1
Fire	×0.5	Psychic	×0
Water	×0.5	Bug	×2
Grass	×2	Rock	×1
Electric	×2	Ghost	×0.5
Ice	×0.5	Dragon	×1
Fighting	×2	Dark	×0.5
Poison	×1	Steel	×0.5
Ground	×1	Fairy	×2

Damage taken in Inverse battles

Type		Type	
Normal	×1	Flying	×1
Fire	×2	Psychic	×2
Water	×2	Bug	×0.5
Grass	×0.5	Rock	×1
Electric	×0.5	Ghost	×2
Ice	×2	Dragon	×1
Fighting	×0.5	Dark	×2
Poison	×1	Steel	×2
Ground	×1	Fairy	×0.5

Can be used in

Inverse Battle

Battle Institute

Battle Maison

Random Matchup (Free Battle)

Random Matchup (Others)

National Pokédex 131 Hoenn Pokédex —

Lapras

Transport Pokémon

Water Ice

HEIGHT: 8'02" WEIGHT: 485 lbs.

Same form for ♂ / ♀

Ω People have driven Lapras almost to the point of extinction. In the evenings, this Pokémon is said to sing plaintively as it seeks what few others of its kind still remain.

α People have driven Lapras almost to the point of extinction. In the evenings, this Pokémon is said to sing plaintively as it seeks what few others of its kind still remain.

ABILITIES

Water Absorb

Shell Armor

HIDDEN ABILITY

Hydration

EGG GROUPS

Monster Water 1

STAT GROWTH RATES

HP

Attack

Defense

Sp. Atk

Sp. Def

Speed

ITEMS SOMETIMES HELD BY WILD POKÉMON

—

EVOLUTION

Does not evolve

MAIN WAY TO REGISTER IN THE NATIONAL POKÉDEX

Appears in *Pokémon X* and *Pokémon Y*. Bring it to your game using Link Trade or the GTS.

Damage taken in normal battles

Type		Type	
Normal	×1	Flying	×1
Fire	×1	Psychic	×1
! Water	×0.5	Bug	×1
Grass	×2	Rock	×2
Electric	×2	Ghost	×1
Ice	×0.25	Dragon	×1
Fighting	×2	Dark	×1
Poison	×1	Steel	×1
Ground	×1	Fairy	×1

Damage taken in Inverse battles

Type		Type	
Normal	×1	Flying	×1
Fire	×1	Psychic	×1
! Water	×2	Bug	×1
Grass	×0.5	Rock	×0.5
Electric	×0.5	Ghost	×1
Ice	×4	Dragon	×1
Fighting	×0.5	Dark	×1
Poison	×1	Steel	×1
Ground	×1	Fairy	×1

Can be used in

Inverse Battle

Battle Institute

Battle Maison

Random Matchup (Free Battle)

Random Matchup (Others)

LEVEL-UP MOVES

Lv.	Name	Type	Kind	Pow.	Acc.	PP	Range
1	Sing	Normal	Status	—	55	15	Normal
1	Growl	Normal	Status	—	100	40	Many Others
1	Water Gun	Water	Special	40	100	25	Normal
4	Mist	Ice	Status	—	—	30	Your Side
7	Confuse Ray	Ghost	Status	—	100	10	Normal
10	Ice Shard	Ice	Physical	40	100	30	Normal
14	Water Pulse	Water	Special	60	100	20	Normal
18	Body Slam	Normal	Physical	85	100	15	Normal
22	Rain Dance	Water	Status	—	—	5	Both Sides
27	Perish Song	Normal	Status	—	—	5	Adjacent
32	Ice Beam	Ice	Special	90	100	10	Normal
37	Brine	Water	Special	65	100	10	Normal
43	Safeguard	Normal	Status	—	—	25	Your Side
47	Hydro Pump	Water	Special	110	80	5	Normal
50	Sheer Cold	Ice	Special	—	30	5	Normal

TM & HM MOVES

No.	Name	Type	Kind	Pow.	Acc.	PP	Range
TM05	Roar	Normal	Status	—	—	20	Normal
TM06	Toxic	Poison	Status	—	90	10	Normal
TM07	Hail	Ice	Status	—	—	10	Both Sides
TM10	Hidden Power	Normal	Special	60	100	15	Normal
TM13	Ice Beam	Ice	Special	90	100	10	Normal
TM14	Blizzard	Ice	Special	110	70	5	Many Others
TM15	Hyper Beam	Normal	Special	150	90	5	Normal
TM17	Protect	Normal	Status	—	—	10	Self
TM18	Rain Dance	Water	Status	—	—	5	Both Sides
TM20	Safeguard	Normal	Status	—	—	25	Your Side
TM21	Frustration	Normal	Physical	—	100	20	Normal
TM24	Thunderbolt	Electric	Special	90	100	15	Normal
TM25	Thunder	Electric	Special	110	70	10	Normal
TM27	Return	Normal	Physical	—	100	20	Normal
TM29	Psychic	Psychic	Special	90	100	10	Normal
TM32	Double Team	Normal	Status	—	—	15	Self
TM42	Facade	Normal	Physical	70	100	20	Normal
TM44	Rest	Psychic	Status	—	—	10	Self
TM45	Attract	Normal	Status	—	100	15	Normal
TM48	Round	Normal	Special	60	100	15	Normal
TM49	Echoed Voice	Normal	Special	40	100	15	Normal
TM68	Giga Impact	Normal	Physical	150	90	5	Normal
TM78	Bulldoze	Ground	Physical	60	100	20	Adjacent
TM79	Frost Breath	Ice	Special	60	90	10	Normal
TM85	Dream Eater	Psychic	Special	100	100	15	Normal
TM87	Swagger	Normal	Status	—	90	15	Normal
TM88	Sleep Talk	Normal	Status	—	—	10	Self
TM90	Substitute	Normal	Status	—	—	10	Self
TM94	Secret Power	Normal	Physical	70	100	20	Normal
TM100	Confide	Normal	Status	—	—	20	Normal
HM03	Surf	Water	Special	90	100	15	Adjacent
HM04	Strength	Normal	Physical	80	100	15	Normal
HM05	Waterfall	Water	Physical	80	100	15	Normal
HM06	Rock Smash	Fighting	Physical	40	100	15	Normal
HM07	Dive	Water	Physical	80	100	10	Normal

MOVES LEARNED IN EXCHANGE FOR BP

Name	Type	Kind	Pow.	Acc.	PP	Range
Signal Beam	Bug	Special	75	100	15	Normal
Iron Head	Steel	Physical	80	100	15	Normal
Drill Run	Ground	Physical	80	95	10	Normal
Block	Normal	Status	—	—	5	Normal
Icy Wind	Ice	Special	55	95	15	Many Others
Aqua Tail	Water	Physical	90	90	10	Normal
Zen Headbutt	Psychic	Physical	80	90	15	Normal
Dragon Pulse	Dragon	Special	85	100	10	Normal
Hyper Voice	Normal	Special	90	100	10	Many Others
Iron Tail	Steel	Physical	100	75	15	Normal
Snore	Normal	Special	50	100	15	Normal
Heal Bell	Normal	Status	—	—	5	Your Party
Shock Wave	Electric	Special	60	—	20	Normal
Water Pulse	Water	Special	60	100	20	Normal
Outrage	Dragon	Physical	120	100	10	1 Random

MOVES TAUGHT BY PEOPLE

Name	Type	Kind	Pow.	Acc.	PP	Range

EGG MOVES

Name	Type	Kind	Pow.	Acc.	PP	Range
Foresight	Normal	Status	—	—	40	Normal
Tickle	Normal	Status	—	100	20	Normal
Refresh	Normal	Status	—	—	20	Self
Dragon Dance	Dragon	Status	—	—	20	Self
Curse	Ghost	Status	—	—	10	Varies
Sleep Talk	Normal	Status	—	—	10	Self
Horn Drill	Normal	Physical	—	30	5	Normal
Ancient Power	Rock	Special	60	100	5	Normal
Whirlpool	Water	Special	35	85	15	Normal
Fissure	Ground	Physical	—	30	5	Normal
Dragon Pulse	Dragon	Special	85	100	10	Normal
Avalanche	Ice	Physical	60	100	10	Normal
Future Sight	Psychic	Special	120	100	10	Normal
Freeze-Dry	Ice	Special	70	100	20	Normal

National Pokédex **132** Hoenn Pokédex —

Ditto

Transform Pokémon

Normal

HEIGHT: 1'00" WEIGHT: 8.8 lbs.

Gender unknown

Ω Ditto rearranges its cell structure to transform itself into other shapes. However, if it tries to transform itself into something by relying on its memory, this Pokémon manages to get details wrong.

α Ditto rearranges its cell structure to transform itself into other shapes. However, if it tries to transform itself into something by relying on its memory, this Pokémon manages to get details wrong.

ABILITY
Limber

HIDDEN ABILITY
Imposter

EGG GROUPS
Ditto

STAT GROWTH RATES
HP
Attack
Defense
Sp. Atk
Sp. Def
Speed

ITEMS SOMETIMES HELD BY WILD POKÉMON
Quick Powder / Metal Powder

EVOLUTION
Does not evolve

MAIN WAY TO REGISTER IN THE NATIONAL POKÉDEX

Catch on Mirage Island 6.

Damage taken in normal battles

Type		Type	
Normal	×1	Flying	×1
Fire	×1	Psychic	×1
Water	×1	Bug	×1
Grass	×1	Rock	×1
Electric	×1	Ghost	×0
Ice	×1	Dragon	×1
Fighting	×2	Dark	×1
Poison	×1	Steel	×1
Ground	×1	Fairy	×1

Damage taken in Inverse battles

Type		Type	
Normal	×1	Flying	×1
Fire	×1	Psychic	×1
Water	×1	Bug	×1
Grass	×1	Rock	×1
Electric	×1	Ghost	×2
Ice	×1	Dragon	×1
Fighting	×0.5	Dark	×1
Poison	×1	Steel	×1
Ground	×1	Fairy	×1

Can be used in
Inverse Battle
Battle Institute
Battle Maison
Random Matchup (Free Battle)
Random Matchup (Others)

LEVEL-UP MOVES

Lv.	Name	Type	Kind	Pow.	Acc.	PP	Range
1	Transform	Normal	Status	—	—	10	Normal

TM & HM MOVES

No.	Name	Type	Kind	Pow.	Acc.	PP	Range

MOVES LEARNED IN EXCHANGE FOR BP

Name	Type	Kind	Pow.	Acc.	PP	Range

MOVES TAUGHT BY PEOPLE

Name	Type	Kind	Pow.	Acc.	PP	Range

National Pokédex **133** Hoenn Pokédex —

Eevee

Evolution Pokémon

Normal

HEIGHT: 1'00" WEIGHT: 14.3 lbs.

Same form for ♂ / ♀

Ω Eevee has an unstable genetic makeup that suddenly mutates due to the environment in which it lives. Radiation from various stones causes this Pokémon to evolve.

α Eevee has an unstable genetic makeup that suddenly mutates due to the environment in which it lives. Radiation from various stones causes this Pokémon to evolve.

ABILITIES
Run Away
Adaptability

HIDDEN ABILITY
Anticipation

EGG GROUPS
Field

STAT GROWTH RATES
HP
Attack
Defense
Sp. Atk
Sp. Def
Speed

ITEMS SOMETIMES HELD BY WILD POKÉMON
—

EVOLUTION
Eevee
Vaporeon
Jolteon
Flareon
Espeon
Umbreon
Leafeon
Glaceon
Sylveon

MAIN WAY TO REGISTER IN THE NATIONAL POKÉDEX

Catch on Route 116. Appears as a hidden Pokémon after you battle Groudon or Kyogre.

Damage taken in normal battles

Type		Type	
Normal	×1	Flying	×1
Fire	×1	Psychic	×1
Water	×1	Bug	×1
Grass	×1	Rock	×1
Electric	×1	Ghost	×0
Ice	×1	Dragon	×1
Fighting	×2	Dark	×1
Poison	×1	Steel	×1
Ground	×1	Fairy	×1

Damage taken in Inverse battles

Type		Type	
Normal	×1	Flying	×1
Fire	×1	Psychic	×1
Water	×1	Bug	×1
Grass	×1	Rock	×1
Electric	×1	Ghost	×2
Ice	×1	Dragon	×1
Fighting	×0.5	Dark	×1
Poison	×1	Steel	×1
Ground	×1	Fairy	×1

Can be used in
Inverse Battle
Battle Institute
Battle Maison
Random Matchup (Free Battle)
Random Matchup (Others)

LEVEL-UP MOVES

Lv.	Name	Type	Kind	Pow.	Acc.	PP	Range
1	Helping Hand	Normal	Status	—	—	20	1 Ally
1	Growl	Normal	Status	—	100	40	Many Others
1	Tackle	Normal	Physical	50	100	35	Normal
1	Tail Whip	Normal	Status	—	100	30	Many Others
5	Sand Attack	Ground	Status	—	100	15	Normal
9	Baby-Doll Eyes	Fairy	Status	—	100	30	Normal
10	Swift	Normal	Special	60	—	20	Many Others
13	Quick Attack	Normal	Physical	40	100	30	Normal
17	Bite	Dark	Physical	60	100	25	Normal
20	Refresh	Normal	Status	—	—	20	Self
23	Covet	Normal	Physical	60	100	25	Normal
25	Take Down	Normal	Physical	90	85	20	Normal
29	Charm	Fairy	Status	—	100	20	Normal
33	Baton Pass	Normal	Status	—	—	40	Self
37	Double-Edge	Normal	Physical	120	100	15	Normal
41	Last Resort	Normal	Physical	140	100	5	Normal
45	Trump Card	Normal	Special	—	—	5	Normal

TM & HM MOVES

No.	Name	Type	Kind	Pow.	Acc.	PP	Range
TM06	Toxic	Poison	Status	—	90	10	Normal
TM10	Hidden Power	Normal	Special	60	100	15	Normal
TM11	Sunny Day	Fire	Status	—	—	5	Both Sides
TM17	Protect	Normal	Status	—	—	10	Self
TM18	Rain Dance	Water	Status	—	—	5	Both Sides
TM21	Frustration	Normal	Physical	—	100	20	Normal
TM27	Return	Normal	Physical	—	100	20	Normal
TM28	Dig	Ground	Physical	80	100	10	Normal
TM30	Shadow Ball	Ghost	Special	80	100	15	Normal
TM32	Double Team	Normal	Status	—	—	15	Self
TM42	Facade	Normal	Physical	70	100	20	Normal
TM44	Rest	Psychic	Status	—	—	10	Self
TM45	Attract	Normal	Status	—	100	15	Normal
TM48	Round	Normal	Special	60	100	15	Normal
TM49	Echoed Voice	Normal	Special	40	100	15	Normal
TM67	Retaliate	Normal	Physical	70	100	5	Normal
TM87	Swagger	Normal	Status	—	90	15	Normal
TM88	Sleep Talk	Normal	Status	—	—	10	Self
TM90	Substitute	Normal	Status	—	—	10	Self
TM94	Secret Power	Normal	Physical	70	100	20	Normal
TM100	Confide	Normal	Status	—	—	20	Normal

MOVES LEARNED IN EXCHANGE FOR BP

Name	Type	Kind	Pow.	Acc.	PP	Range
Covet	Normal	Physical	60	100	25	Normal
Last Resort	Normal	Physical	140	100	5	Normal
Hyper Voice	Normal	Special	90	100	10	Many Others
Iron Tail	Steel	Physical	100	75	15	Normal
Snore	Normal	Special	50	100	15	Normal
Heal Bell	Normal	Status	—	—	5	Your Party
Helping Hand	Normal	Status	—	—	20	1 Ally

MOVES TAUGHT BY PEOPLE

Name	Type	Kind	Pow.	Acc.	PP	Range

EGG MOVES

Name	Type	Kind	Pow.	Acc.	PP	Range
Charm	Fairy	Status	—	100	20	Normal
Flail	Normal	Physical	—	100	15	Normal
Endure	Normal	Status	—	—	10	Self
Curse	Ghost	Status	—	—	10	Varies
Tickle	Normal	Status	—	100	20	Normal
Wish	Normal	Status	—	—	10	Self
Yawn	Normal	Status	—	—	10	Normal
Fake Tears	Dark	Status	—	100	20	Normal
Covet	Normal	Physical	60	100	25	Normal
Detect	Fighting	Status	—	—	5	Self
Natural Gift	Normal	Physical	—	100	15	Normal
Stored Power	Psychic	Special	20	100	10	Normal
Synchronoise	Psychic	Special	120	100	10	Adjacent
Captivate	Normal	Status	—	100	20	Many Others

National Pokédex **134** Hoenn Pokédex —

Vaporeon

Bubble Jet Pokémon

Water

HEIGHT: 3'03" WEIGHT: 63.9 lbs.

Same form for ♂ / ♀

Ω Vaporeon underwent a spontaneous mutation and grew fins and gills that allow it to live underwater. This Pokémon has the ability to freely control water.

α Vaporeon underwent a spontaneous mutation and grew fins and gills that allow it to live underwater. This Pokémon has the ability to freely control water.

ABILITY: Water Absorb

HIDDEN ABILITY: Hydration

EGG GROUPS: Field

STAT GROWTH RATES: HP, Attack, Defense, Sp. Atk, Sp. Def, Speed

ITEMS SOMETIMES HELD BY WILD POKÉMON: —

EVOLUTION

Eevee → (Water Stone) → Vaporeon

MAIN WAY TO REGISTER IN THE NATIONAL POKÉDEX

Use a Water Stone on Eevee.

134 Vaporeon

Damage taken in normal battles

Normal	×1	Flying	×1
Fire	×0.5	Psychic	×1
Water	×0.5	Bug	×1
Grass	×2	Rock	×1
Electric	×2	Ghost	×1
Ice	×0.5	Dragon	×1
Fighting	×1	Dark	×1
Poison	×1	Steel	×0.5
Ground	×1	Fairy	×1

Damage taken in Inverse battles

Normal	×1	Flying	×1
Fire	×2	Psychic	×1
Water	×2	Bug	×1
Grass	×0.5	Rock	×1
Electric	×0.5	Ghost	×1
Ice	×2	Dragon	×1
Fighting	×1	Dark	×1
Poison	×1	Steel	×2
Ground	×1	Fairy	×1

Can be used in

Inverse Battle
Battle Institute
Battle Maison
Random Matchup (Free Battle)
Random Matchup (Others)

LEVEL-UP MOVES

Lv.	Name	Type	Kind	Pow.	Acc.	PP	Range
1	Helping Hand	Normal	Status	—	—	20	1 Ally
1	Tackle	Normal	Physical	50	100	35	Normal
1	Tail Whip	Normal	Status	—	100	30	Many Others
5	Sand Attack	Ground	Status	—	100	15	Normal
9	Water Gun	Water	Special	40	100	25	Normal
13	Quick Attack	Normal	Physical	40	100	30	Normal
17	Water Pulse	Water	Special	60	100	20	Normal
20	Aurora Beam	Ice	Special	65	100	20	Normal
25	Aqua Ring	Water	Status	—	—	20	Self
29	Acid Armor	Poison	Status	—	—	20	Self
33	Haze	Ice	Status	—	—	30	Both Sides
37	Muddy Water	Water	Special	90	85	10	Many Others
41	Last Resort	Normal	Physical	140	100	5	Normal
45	Hydro Pump	Water	Special	110	80	5	Normal

TM & HM MOVES

No.	Name	Type	Kind	Pow.	Acc.	PP	Range
TM05	Roar	Normal	Status	—	—	20	Normal
TM06	Toxic	Poison	Status	—	90	10	Normal
TM07	Hail	Ice	Status	—	—	10	Both Sides
TM10	Hidden Power	Normal	Special	60	100	15	Normal
TM11	Sunny Day	Fire	Status	—	—	5	Both Sides
TM13	Ice Beam	Ice	Special	90	100	10	Normal
TM14	Blizzard	Ice	Special	110	70	5	Many Others
TM15	Hyper Beam	Normal	Special	150	90	5	Normal
TM17	Protect	Normal	Status	—	—	10	Self
TM18	Rain Dance	Water	Status	—	—	5	Both Sides
TM21	Frustration	Normal	Physical	—	100	20	Normal
TM27	Return	Normal	Physical	—	100	20	Normal
TM28	Dig	Ground	Physical	80	100	10	Normal
TM30	Shadow Ball	Ghost	Special	80	100	15	Normal
TM32	Double Team	Normal	Status	—	—	15	Self
TM42	Facade	Normal	Physical	70	100	20	Normal
TM44	Rest	Psychic	Status	—	—	10	Self
TM45	Attract	Normal	Status	—	100	15	Normal
TM48	Round	Normal	Special	60	100	15	Normal
TM49	Echoed Voice	Normal	Special	40	100	15	Normal
TM55	Scald	Water	Special	80	100	15	Normal
TM67	Retaliate	Normal	Physical	70	100	5	Normal
TM68	Giga Impact	Normal	Physical	150	90	5	Normal
TM87	Swagger	Normal	Status	—	90	15	Normal
TM88	Sleep Talk	Normal	Status	—	—	10	Self
TM90	Substitute	Normal	Status	—	—	10	Self
TM94	Secret Power	Normal	Physical	70	100	20	Normal
TM100	Confide	Normal	Status	—	—	20	Normal
HM03	Surf	Water	Special	90	100	15	Adjacent
HM04	Strength	Normal	Physical	80	100	15	Normal
HM05	Waterfall	Water	Physical	80	100	15	Normal
HM06	Rock Smash	Fighting	Physical	40	100	15	Normal
HM07	Dive	Water	Physical	80	100	10	Normal

MOVES LEARNED IN EXCHANGE FOR BP

Name	Type	Kind	Pow.	Acc.	PP	Range
Covet	Normal	Physical	60	100	25	Normal
Signal Beam	Bug	Special	75	100	15	Normal
Last Resort	Normal	Physical	140	100	5	Normal
Icy Wind	Ice	Special	55	95	15	Many Others
Aqua Tail	Water	Physical	90	90	10	Normal
Hyper Voice	Normal	Special	90	100	10	Many Others
Iron Tail	Steel	Physical	100	75	15	Normal
Snore	Normal	Special	50	100	15	Normal
Heal Bell	Normal	Status	—	—	5	Your Party
Water Pulse	Water	Special	60	100	20	Normal
Helping Hand	Normal	Status	—	—	20	1 Ally

MOVES TAUGHT BY PEOPLE

Name	Type	Kind	Pow.	Acc.	PP	Range

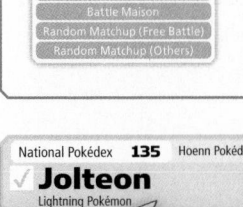

National Pokédex **135** Hoenn Pokédex —

Jolteon

Lightning Pokémon

Electric

HEIGHT: 2'07" WEIGHT: 54 lbs.

Same form for ♂ / ♀

Ω Jolteon's cells generate a low level of electricity. This power is amplified by the static electricity of its fur, enabling the Pokémon to drop thunderbolts. The bristling fur is made of electrically charged needles.

α Jolteon's cells generate a low level of electricity. This power is amplified by the static electricity of its fur, enabling the Pokémon to drop thunderbolts. The bristling fur is made of electrically charged needles.

ABILITY: Volt Absorb

HIDDEN ABILITY: Quick Feet

EGG GROUPS: Field

STAT GROWTH RATES: HP, Attack, Defense, Sp. Atk, Sp. Def, Speed

ITEMS SOMETIMES HELD BY WILD POKÉMON: —

EVOLUTION

Eevee → (Thunder Stone) → Jolteon

MAIN WAY TO REGISTER IN THE NATIONAL POKÉDEX

Use a Thunder Stone on Eevee.

National Pokédex

Jolteon 135

Damage taken in normal battles

Normal	×1	Flying	×0.5
Fire	×1	Psychic	×1
Water	×1	Bug	×1
Grass	×1	Rock	×1
Electric	×0.5	Ghost	×1
Ice	×1	Dragon	×1
Fighting	×1	Dark	×1
Poison	×1	Steel	×0.5
Ground	×2	Fairy	×1

Damage taken in Inverse battles

Normal	×1	Flying	×2
Fire	×1	Psychic	×1
Water	×1	Bug	×1
Grass	×1	Rock	×1
Electric	×2	Ghost	×1
Ice	×1	Dragon	×1
Fighting	×1	Dark	×1
Poison	×1	Steel	×2
Ground	×0.5	Fairy	×1

Can be used in

Inverse Battle
Battle Institute
Battle Maison
Random Matchup (Free Battle)
Random Matchup (Others)

LEVEL-UP MOVES

Lv.	Name	Type	Kind	Pow.	Acc.	PP	Range
1	Helping Hand	Normal	Status	—	—	20	1 Ally
1	Tackle	Normal	Physical	50	100	35	Normal
1	Tail Whip	Normal	Status	—	100	30	Many Others
5	Sand Attack	Ground	Status	—	100	15	Normal
9	Thunder Shock	Electric	Special	40	100	30	Normal
13	Quick Attack	Normal	Physical	40	100	30	Normal
17	Double Kick	Fighting	Physical	30	100	30	Normal
20	Thunder Fang	Electric	Physical	65	95	15	Normal
25	Pin Missile	Bug	Physical	25	95	20	Normal
29	Agility	Psychic	Status	—	—	30	Self
33	Thunder Wave	Electric	Status	—	100	20	Normal
37	Discharge	Electric	Special	80	100	15	Adjacent
41	Last Resort	Normal	Physical	140	100	5	Normal
45	Thunder	Electric	Special	110	70	10	Normal

TM & HM MOVES

No.	Name	Type	Kind	Pow.	Acc.	PP	Range
TM05	Roar	Normal	Status	—	—	20	Normal
TM06	Toxic	Poison	Status	—	90	10	Normal
TM10	Hidden Power	Normal	Special	60	100	15	Normal
TM11	Sunny Day	Fire	Status	—	—	5	Both Sides
TM15	Hyper Beam	Normal	Special	150	90	5	Normal
TM16	Light Screen	Psychic	Status	—	—	30	Your Side
TM17	Protect	Normal	Status	—	—	10	Self
TM18	Rain Dance	Water	Status	—	—	5	Both Sides
TM21	Frustration	Normal	Physical	—	100	20	Normal
TM24	Thunderbolt	Electric	Special	90	100	15	Normal
TM25	Thunder	Electric	Special	110	70	10	Normal
TM27	Return	Normal	Physical	—	100	20	Normal
TM28	Dig	Ground	Physical	80	100	10	Normal
TM30	Shadow Ball	Ghost	Special	80	100	15	Normal
TM32	Double Team	Normal	Status	—	—	15	Self
TM42	Facade	Normal	Physical	70	100	20	Normal
TM44	Rest	Psychic	Status	—	—	10	Self
TM45	Attract	Normal	Status	—	100	15	Normal
TM48	Round	Normal	Special	60	100	15	Normal
TM49	Echoed Voice	Normal	Special	40	100	15	Normal
TM57	Charge Beam	Electric	Special	50	90	10	Normal
TM67	Retaliate	Normal	Physical	70	100	5	Normal
TM68	Giga Impact	Normal	Physical	150	90	5	Normal
TM70	Flash	Normal	Status	—	100	20	Normal
TM72	Volt Switch	Electric	Special	70	100	20	Normal
TM73	Thunder Wave	Electric	Status	—	100	20	Normal
TM87	Swagger	Normal	Status	—	90	15	Normal
TM88	Sleep Talk	Normal	Status	—	—	10	Self
TM90	Substitute	Normal	Status	—	—	10	Self
TM93	Wild Charge	Electric	Physical	90	100	15	Normal
TM94	Secret Power	Normal	Physical	70	100	20	Normal
TM100	Confide	Normal	Status	—	—	20	Normal
HM04	Strength	Normal	Physical	80	100	15	Normal
HM06	Rock Smash	Fighting	Physical	40	100	15	Normal

MOVES LEARNED IN EXCHANGE FOR BP

Name	Type	Kind	Pow.	Acc.	PP	Range
Covet	Normal	Physical	60	100	25	Normal
Signal Beam	Bug	Special	75	100	15	Normal
Magnet Rise	Electric	Status	—	—	10	Self
Last Resort	Normal	Physical	140	100	5	Normal
Hyper Voice	Normal	Special	90	100	10	Many Others
Iron Tail	Steel	Physical	100	75	15	Normal
Snore	Normal	Special	50	100	15	Normal
Heal Bell	Normal	Status	—	—	5	Your Party
Shock Wave	Electric	Special	60	—	20	Normal
Helping Hand	Normal	Status	—	—	20	1 Ally

MOVES TAUGHT BY PEOPLE

Name	Type	Kind	Pow.	Acc.	PP	Range

National Pokédex **136** Hoenn Pokédex —

Flareon

Flame Pokémon

Fire

HEIGHT: 2'11" WEIGHT: 55.1 lbs.

Same form for ♂ / ♀

Ω Flareon's fluffy fur has a functional purpose—it releases heat into the air so that its body does not get excessively hot. This Pokémon's body temperature can rise to a maximum of 1,650 degrees Fahrenheit.

α Flareon's fluffy fur has a functional purpose—it releases heat into the air so that its body does not get excessively hot. This Pokémon's body temperature can rise to a maximum of 1,650 degrees Fahrenheit.

ABILITY
Flash Fire

HIDDEN ABILITY
Guts

EGG GROUPS
Field

STAT GROWTH RATES
HP
Attack
Defense
Sp. Atk
Sp. Def
Speed

ITEMS SOMETIMES HELD BY WILD POKÉMON
—

EVOLUTION
Eevee → Fire Stone → Flareon

MAIN WAY TO REGISTER IN THE NATIONAL POKÉDEX

Use a Fire Stone on Eevee.

Damage taken in normal battles

Type		Type	
Normal	×1	Flying	×1
Fire	×0.5	Psychic	×1
Water	×2	Bug	×0.5
Grass	×0.5	Rock	×2
Electric	×1	Ghost	×1
Ice	×0.5	Dragon	×1
Fighting	×1	Dark	×1
Poison	×1	Steel	×0.5
Ground	×2	Fairy	×0.5

Damage taken in Inverse battles

Type		Type	
Normal	×1	Flying	×1
Fire	×2	Psychic	×1
Water	×0.5	Bug	×2
Grass	×2	Rock	×0.5
Electric	×1	Ghost	×1
Ice	×2	Dragon	×1
Fighting	×1	Dark	×1
Poison	×1	Steel	×2
Ground	×0.5	Fairy	×2

Can be used in
Inverse Battle
Battle Institute
Battle Maison
Random Matchup (Free Battle)
Random Matchup (Others)

LEVEL-UP MOVES

Lv.	Name	Type	Kind	Pow.	Acc.	PP	Range
1	Helping Hand	Normal	Status	—	—	20	1 Ally
1	Tackle	Normal	Physical	50	100	35	Normal
1	Tail Whip	Normal	Status	—	100	30	Many Others
5	Sand Attack	Ground	Status	—	100	15	Normal
9	Ember	Fire	Special	40	100	25	Normal
13	Quick Attack	Normal	Physical	40	100	30	Normal
17	Bite	Dark	Physical	60	100	25	Normal
20	Fire Fang	Fire	Physical	65	95	15	Normal
25	Fire Spin	Fire	Special	35	85	15	Normal
29	Scary Face	Normal	Status	—	100	10	Normal
33	Smog	Poison	Special	30	70	20	Normal
37	Lava Plume	Fire	Special	80	100	15	Adjacent
41	Last Resort	Normal	Physical	140	100	5	Normal
45	Flare Blitz	Fire	Physical	120	100	15	Normal

TM & HM MOVES

No.	Name	Type	Kind	Pow.	Acc.	PP	Range
TM05	Roar	Normal	Status	—	—	20	Normal
TM06	Toxic	Poison	Status	—	90	10	Normal
TM10	Hidden Power	Normal	Special	60	100	15	Normal
TM11	Sunny Day	Fire	Status	—	—	5	Both Sides
TM15	Hyper Beam	Normal	Special	150	90	5	Normal
TM17	Protect	Normal	Status	—	—	10	Self
TM18	Rain Dance	Water	Status	—	—	5	Both Sides
TM21	Frustration	Normal	Physical	—	100	20	Normal
TM27	Return	Normal	Physical	—	100	20	Normal
TM28	Dig	Ground	Physical	80	100	10	Normal
TM30	Shadow Ball	Ghost	Special	80	100	15	Normal
TM32	Double Team	Normal	Status	—	—	15	Self
TM35	Flamethrower	Fire	Special	90	100	15	Normal
TM38	Fire Blast	Fire	Special	110	85	5	Normal
TM42	Facade	Normal	Physical	70	100	20	Normal
TM43	Flame Charge	Fire	Physical	50	100	20	Normal
TM44	Rest	Psychic	Status	—	—	10	Self
TM45	Attract	Normal	Status	—	100	15	Normal
TM48	Round	Normal	Special	60	100	15	Normal
TM49	Echoed Voice	Normal	Special	40	100	15	Normal
TM50	Overheat	Fire	Special	130	90	5	Normal
TM59	Incinerate	Fire	Special	60	100	15	Many Others
TM61	Will-O-Wisp	Fire	Status	—	85	15	Normal
TM67	Retaliate	Normal	Physical	70	100	5	Normal
TM68	Giga Impact	Normal	Physical	150	90	5	Normal
TM87	Swagger	Normal	Status	—	90	15	Normal
TM88	Sleep Talk	Normal	Status	—	—	10	Self
TM90	Substitute	Normal	Status	—	—	10	Self
TM94	Secret Power	Normal	Physical	70	100	20	Normal
TM100	Confide	Normal	Status	—	—	20	Normal
HM04	Strength	Normal	Physical	80	100	15	Normal
HM06	Rock Smash	Fighting	Physical	40	100	15	Normal

MOVES LEARNED IN EXCHANGE FOR BP

Name	Type	Kind	Pow.	Acc.	PP	Range
Covet	Normal	Physical	60	100	25	Normal
Last Resort	Normal	Physical	140	100	5	Normal
Superpower	Fighting	Physical	120	100	5	Normal
Hyper Voice	Normal	Special	90	100	10	Many Others
Iron Tail	Steel	Physical	100	75	15	Normal
Snore	Normal	Special	50	100	15	Normal
Heat Wave	Fire	Special	95	90	10	Many Others
Heal Bell	Normal	Status	—	—	5	Your Party
Helping Hand	Normal	Status	—	—	20	1 Ally

MOVES TAUGHT BY PEOPLE

Name	Type	Kind	Pow.	Acc.	PP	Range

National Pokédex **137** Hoenn Pokédex —

Porygon

Virtual Pokémon

Normal

HEIGHT: 2'07" WEIGHT: 80.5 lbs.

Gender unknown

Ω Porygon is capable of reverting itself entirely back to program data and entering cyberspace. This Pokémon is copy protected so it cannot be duplicated by copying.

α Porygon is capable of reverting itself entirely back to program data and entering cyberspace. This Pokémon is copy protected so it cannot be duplicated by copying.

ABILITIES
Trace
Download

HIDDEN ABILITY
Analytic

EGG GROUPS
Mineral

STAT GROWTH RATES
HP
Attack
Defense
Sp. Atk
Sp. Def
Speed

ITEMS SOMETIMES HELD BY WILD POKÉMON
—

EVOLUTION
Porygon → Link Trade with an Upgrade → Porygon2 → Link Trade with a Dubious Disk → Porygon-Z

MAIN WAY TO REGISTER IN THE NATIONAL POKÉDEX

Catch on Mirage Island 8.

Damage taken in normal battles

Type		Type	
Normal	×1	Flying	×1
Fire	×1	Psychic	×1
Water	×1	Bug	×1
Grass	×1	Rock	×1
Electric	×1	Ghost	×0
Ice	×1	Dragon	×1
Fighting	×2	Dark	×1
Poison	×1	Steel	×1
Ground	×1	Fairy	×1

Damage taken in Inverse battles

Type		Type	
Normal	×1	Flying	×1
Fire	×1	Psychic	×1
Water	×1	Bug	×1
Grass	×1	Rock	×1
Electric	×1	Ghost	×2
Ice	×1	Dragon	×1
Fighting	×0.5	Dark	×1
Poison	×1	Steel	×1
Ground	×1	Fairy	×1

Can be used in
Inverse Battle
Battle Institute
Battle Maison
Random Matchup (Free Battle)
Random Matchup (Others)

LEVEL-UP MOVES

Lv.	Name	Type	Kind	Pow.	Acc.	PP	Range
1	Conversion 2	Normal	Status	—	—	30	Normal
1	Tackle	Normal	Physical	50	100	35	Normal
1	Conversion	Normal	Status	—	—	30	Self
1	Sharpen	Normal	Status	—	—	30	Self
7	Psybeam	Psychic	Special	65	100	20	Normal
12	Agility	Psychic	Status	—	—	30	Self
18	Recover	Normal	Status	—	—	10	Self
23	Magnet Rise	Electric	Status	—	—	10	Self
29	Signal Beam	Bug	Special	75	100	15	Normal
34	Recycle	Normal	Status	—	—	10	Self
40	Discharge	Electric	Special	80	100	15	Adjacent
45	Lock-On	Normal	Status	—	—	5	Normal
50	Tri Attack	Normal	Special	80	100	10	Normal
56	Magic Coat	Psychic	Status	—	—	15	Self
62	Zap Cannon	Electric	Special	120	50	5	Normal

TM & HM MOVES

No.	Name	Type	Kind	Pow.	Acc.	PP	Range
TM03	Psyshock	Psychic	Special	80	100	10	Normal
TM06	Toxic	Poison	Status	—	90	10	Normal
TM10	Hidden Power	Normal	Special	60	100	15	Normal
TM11	Sunny Day	Fire	Status	—	—	5	Both Sides
TM13	Ice Beam	Ice	Special	90	100	10	Normal
TM14	Blizzard	Ice	Special	110	70	5	Many Others
TM15	Hyper Beam	Normal	Special	150	90	5	Normal
TM17	Protect	Normal	Status	—	—	10	Self
TM18	Rain Dance	Water	Status	—	—	5	Both Sides
TM21	Frustration	Normal	Physical	—	100	20	Normal
TM22	Solar Beam	Grass	Special	120	100	10	Normal
TM24	Thunderbolt	Electric	Special	90	100	15	Normal
TM25	Thunder	Electric	Special	110	70	10	Normal
TM27	Return	Normal	Physical	—	100	20	Normal
TM29	Psychic	Psychic	Special	90	100	10	Normal
TM30	Shadow Ball	Ghost	Special	80	100	15	Normal
TM32	Double Team	Normal	Status	—	—	15	Self
TM40	Aerial Ace	Flying	Physical	60	—	20	Normal
TM42	Facade	Normal	Physical	70	100	20	Normal
TM44	Rest	Psychic	Status	—	—	10	Self
TM46	Thief	Dark	Physical	60	100	25	Normal
TM48	Round	Normal	Special	60	100	15	Normal
TM57	Charge Beam	Electric	Special	50	90	10	Normal
TM68	Giga Impact	Normal	Physical	150	90	5	Normal
TM70	Flash	Normal	Status	—	100	20	Normal
TM73	Thunder Wave	Electric	Status	—	100	20	Normal
TM77	Psych Up	Normal	Status	—	—	10	Normal
TM85	Dream Eater	Psychic	Special	100	100	15	Normal
TM87	Swagger	Normal	Status	—	90	15	Normal
TM88	Sleep Talk	Normal	Status	—	—	10	Self
TM90	Substitute	Normal	Status	—	—	10	Self
TM92	Trick Room	Psychic	Status	—	—	5	Both Sides
TM94	Secret Power	Normal	Physical	70	100	20	Normal
TM100	Confide	Normal	Status	—	—	20	Normal

MOVES LEARNED IN EXCHANGE FOR BP

Name	Type	Kind	Pow.	Acc.	PP	Range
Signal Beam	Bug	Special	75	100	15	Normal
Magic Coat	Psychic	Status	—	—	15	Self
Foul Play	Dark	Physical	95	100	15	Normal
Gravity	Psychic	Status	—	—	5	Both Sides
Magnet Rise	Electric	Status	—	—	10	Self
Last Resort	Normal	Physical	140	100	5	Normal
Electroweb	Electric	Special	55	95	15	Many Others
Icy Wind	Ice	Special	55	95	15	Many Others
Zen Headbutt	Psychic	Physical	80	90	15	Normal
Iron Tail	Steel	Physical	100	75	15	Normal
Snore	Normal	Special	50	100	15	Normal
Pain Split	Normal	Status	—	—	20	Normal
Shock Wave	Electric	Special	60	—	20	Normal
Trick	Psychic	Status	—	100	10	Normal
Wonder Room	Psychic	Status	—	—	10	Both Sides
Recycle	Normal	Status	—	—	10	Self

MOVES TAUGHT BY PEOPLE

Name	Type	Kind	Pow.	Acc.	PP	Range

National Pokédex **138** Hoenn Pokédex —

Omanyte

Spiral Pokémon

Rock Water

HEIGHT: 1'04" WEIGHT: 16.5 lbs.

Same form for ♂ / ♀

Ω Omanyte is one of the ancient and long-since-extinct Pokémon that have been regenerated from fossils by people. If attacked by an enemy, it withdraws itself inside its hard shell.

α Omanyte is one of the ancient and long-since-extinct Pokémon that have been regenerated from fossils by people. If attacked by an enemy, it withdraws itself inside its hard shell.

ABILITIES
Swift Swim
Shell Armor

HIDDEN ABILITY
Weak Armor

EGG GROUPS
Water 1 Water 3

STAT GROWTH RATES
HP
Attack
Defense
Sp. Atk
Sp. Def
Speed

ITEMS SOMETIMES HELD BY WILD POKÉMON
—

EVOLUTION
Omanyte → Lv. 40 → Omastar

MAIN WAYS TO REGISTER IN THE NATIONAL POKÉDEX
Ω Bring it to your game using Link Trade or the GTS.
α Obtain a Helix Fossil from a cracked rock in a Mirage spot by using Rock Smash, then have it restored at the Devon Corporation (2F) in Rustboro City.

Damage taken in normal battles

Type		Type	
Normal	×0.5	Flying	×0.5
Fire	×0.25	Psychic	×1
Water	×1	Bug	×1
Grass	×4	Rock	×1
Electric	×2	Ghost	×1
Ice	×0.5	Dragon	×1
Fighting	×2	Dark	×1
Poison	×0.5	Steel	×1
Ground	×2	Fairy	×1

Damage taken in Inverse battles

Type		Type	
Normal	×2	Flying	×2
Fire	×4	Psychic	×1
Water	×1	Bug	×1
Grass	×0.25	Rock	×1
Electric	×0.5	Ghost	×1
Ice	×2	Dragon	×1
Fighting	×0.5	Dark	×1
Poison	×2	Steel	×1
Ground	×0.5	Fairy	×1

Can be used in
Inverse Battle
Battle Institute
Battle Maison
Random Matchup (Free Battle)
Random Matchup (Others)

LEVEL-UP MOVES

Lv.	Name	Type	Kind	Pow.	Acc.	PP	Range
1	Constrict	Normal	Physical	10	100	35	Normal
1	Withdraw	Water	Status	—	—	40	Self
7	Bite	Dark	Physical	60	100	25	Normal
10	Water Gun	Water	Special	40	100	25	Normal
16	Rollout	Rock	Physical	30	90	20	Normal
19	Leer	Normal	Status	—	100	30	Many Others
25	Mud Shot	Ground	Special	55	95	15	Normal
28	Brine	Water	Special	65	100	10	Normal
34	Protect	Normal	Status	—	—	10	Self
37	Ancient Power	Rock	Special	60	100	5	Normal
43	Tickle	Normal	Status	—	100	20	Normal
46	Rock Blast	Rock	Physical	25	90	10	Normal
50	Shell Smash	Normal	Status	—	—	15	Self
55	Hydro Pump	Water	Special	110	80	5	Normal

TM & HM MOVES

No.	Name	Type	Kind	Pow.	Acc.	PP	Range
TM06	Toxic	Poison	Status	—	90	10	Normal
TM07	Hail	Ice	Status	—	—	10	Both Sides
TM10	Hidden Power	Normal	Special	60	100	15	Normal
TM13	Ice Beam	Ice	Special	90	100	10	Normal
TM14	Blizzard	Ice	Special	110	70	5	Many Others
TM17	Protect	Normal	Status	—	—	10	Self
TM18	Rain Dance	Water	Status	—	—	5	Both Sides
TM21	Frustration	Normal	Physical	—	100	20	Normal
TM23	Smack Down	Rock	Physical	50	100	15	Normal
TM27	Return	Normal	Physical	—	100	20	Normal
TM32	Double Team	Normal	Status	—	—	15	Self
TM37	Sandstorm	Rock	Status	—	—	10	Both Sides
TM39	Rock Tomb	Rock	Physical	60	95	15	Normal
TM42	Facade	Normal	Physical	70	100	20	Normal
TM44	Rest	Psychic	Status	—	—	10	Self
TM45	Attract	Normal	Status	—	100	15	Normal
TM46	Thief	Dark	Physical	60	100	25	Normal
TM48	Round	Normal	Special	60	100	15	Normal
TM55	Scald	Water	Special	80	100	15	Normal
TM69	Rock Polish	Rock	Status	—	—	20	Self
TM74	Gyro Ball	Steel	Physical	—	100	5	Normal
TM80	Rock Slide	Rock	Physical	75	90	10	Many Others
TM87	Swagger	Normal	Status	—	90	15	Normal
TM88	Sleep Talk	Normal	Status	—	—	10	Self
TM90	Substitute	Normal	Status	—	—	10	Self
TM94	Secret Power	Normal	Physical	70	100	20	Normal
TM100	Confide	Normal	Status	—	—	20	Normal
HM03	Surf	Water	Special	90	100	15	Adjacent
HM05	Waterfall	Water	Physical	80	100	15	Normal
HM06	Rock Smash	Fighting	Physical	40	100	15	Normal
HM07	Dive	Water	Physical	80	100	10	Normal

MOVES LEARNED IN EXCHANGE FOR BP

Name	Type	Kind	Pow.	Acc.	PP	Range
Earth Power	Ground	Special	90	100	10	Normal
Iron Defense	Steel	Status	—	—	15	Self
Icy Wind	Ice	Special	55	95	15	Many Others
Bind	Normal	Physical	15	85	20	Normal
Snore	Normal	Special	50	100	15	Normal
Knock Off	Dark	Physical	65	100	20	Normal
Water Pulse	Water	Special	60	100	20	Normal
Stealth Rock	Rock	Status	—	—	20	Other Side

MOVES TAUGHT BY PEOPLE

Name	Type	Kind	Pow.	Acc.	PP	Range

EGG MOVES

Name	Type	Kind	Pow.	Acc.	PP	Range
Bubble Beam	Water	Special	65	100	20	Normal
Aurora Beam	Ice	Special	65	100	20	Normal
Slam	Normal	Physical	80	75	20	Normal
Supersonic	Normal	Status	—	55	20	Normal
Haze	Ice	Status	—	—	30	Both Sides
Spikes	Ground	Status	—	—	20	Other Side
Knock Off	Dark	Physical	65	100	20	Normal
Wring Out	Normal	Special	—	100	5	Normal
Toxic Spikes	Poison	Status	—	—	20	Other Side
Muddy Water	Water	Special	90	85	10	Many Others
Bide	Normal	Physical	—	—	10	Self
Water Pulse	Water	Special	60	100	20	Normal
Whirlpool	Water	Special	35	85	15	Normal
Reflect Type	Normal	Status	—	—	15	Normal

National Pokédex **139** Hoenn Pokédex —

Omastar

Spiral Pokémon

Rock Water

HEIGHT: 3'03" WEIGHT: 77.2 lbs.

Same form for ♂ / ♀

Ω Omastar uses its tentacles to capture its prey. It is believed to have become extinct because its shell grew too large and heavy, causing its movements to become too slow and ponderous.

α Omastar uses its tentacles to capture its prey. It is believed to have become extinct because its shell grew too large and heavy, causing its movements to become too slow and ponderous.

ABILITIES
Swift Swim
Shell Armor

HIDDEN ABILITY
Weak Armor

EGG GROUPS
Water 1 Water 3

STAT GROWTH RATES
HP
Attack
Defense
Sp. Atk
Sp. Def
Speed

ITEMS SOMETIMES HELD BY WILD POKÉMON
—

EVOLUTION
Omanyte → Lv. 40 → Omastar

MAIN WAYS TO REGISTER IN THE NATIONAL POKÉDEX
Ω Bring it to your game using Link Trade or the GTS.
α Level up Omanyte to Lv. 40.

Damage taken in normal battles

Type		Type	
Normal	×0.5	Flying	×0.5
Fire	×0.25	Psychic	×1
Water	×1	Bug	×1
Grass	×4	Rock	×1
Electric	×2	Ghost	×1
Ice	×0.5	Dragon	×1
Fighting	×2	Dark	×1
Poison	×0.5	Steel	×1
Ground	×2	Fairy	×1

Damage taken in Inverse battles

Type		Type	
Normal	×2	Flying	×2
Fire	×4	Psychic	×1
Water	×1	Bug	×1
Grass	×0.25	Rock	×1
Electric	×0.5	Ghost	×1
Ice	×2	Dragon	×1
Fighting	×0.5	Dark	×1
Poison	×2	Steel	×1
Ground	×0.5	Fairy	×1

Can be used in
Inverse Battle
Battle Institute
Battle Maison
Random Matchup (Free Battle)
Random Matchup (Others)

LEVEL-UP MOVES

Lv.	Name	Type	Kind	Pow.	Acc.	PP	Range
1	Hydro Pump	Water	Special	110	80	5	Normal
1	Constrict	Normal	Physical	10	100	35	Normal
1	Withdraw	Water	Status	—	—	40	Self
1	Bite	Dark	Physical	60	100	25	Normal
7	Bite	Dark	Physical	60	100	25	Normal
10	Water Gun	Water	Special	40	100	25	Normal
16	Rollout	Rock	Physical	30	90	20	Normal
19	Leer	Normal	Status	—	100	30	Many Others
25	Mud Shot	Ground	Special	55	95	15	Normal
28	Brine	Water	Special	65	100	10	Normal
34	Protect	Normal	Status	—	—	10	Self
37	Ancient Power	Rock	Special	60	100	5	Normal
40	Spike Cannon	Normal	Physical	20	100	15	Normal
48	Tickle	Normal	Status	—	100	20	Normal
56	Rock Blast	Rock	Physical	25	90	10	Normal
67	Shell Smash	Normal	Status	—	—	15	Self
75	Hydro Pump	Water	Special	110	80	5	Normal

TM & HM MOVES

No.	Name	Type	Kind	Pow.	Acc.	PP	Range
TM06	Toxic	Poison	Status	—	90	10	Normal
TM07	Hail	Ice	Status	—	—	10	Both Sides
TM10	Hidden Power	Normal	Special	60	100	15	Normal
TM13	Ice Beam	Ice	Special	90	100	10	Normal
TM14	Blizzard	Ice	Special	110	70	5	Many Others
TM15	Hyper Beam	Normal	Special	150	90	5	Normal
TM17	Protect	Normal	Status	—	—	10	Self
TM18	Rain Dance	Water	Status	—	—	5	Both Sides
TM21	Frustration	Normal	Physical	—	100	20	Normal
TM23	Smack Down	Rock	Physical	50	100	15	Normal
TM27	Return	Normal	Physical	—	100	20	Normal
TM32	Double Team	Normal	Status	—	—	15	Self
TM37	Sandstorm	Rock	Status	—	—	10	Both Sides
TM39	Rock Tomb	Rock	Physical	60	95	15	Normal
TM42	Facade	Normal	Physical	70	100	20	Normal
TM44	Rest	Psychic	Status	—	—	10	Self
TM45	Attract	Normal	Status	—	100	15	Normal
TM46	Thief	Dark	Physical	60	100	25	Normal
TM48	Round	Normal	Special	60	100	15	Normal
TM55	Scald	Water	Special	80	100	15	Normal
TM68	Giga Impact	Normal	Physical	150	90	5	Normal
TM69	Rock Polish	Rock	Status	—	—	20	Self
TM71	Stone Edge	Rock	Physical	100	80	5	Normal
TM74	Gyro Ball	Steel	Physical	—	100	5	Normal
TM80	Rock Slide	Rock	Physical	75	90	10	Many Others
TM87	Swagger	Normal	Status	—	90	15	Normal
TM88	Sleep Talk	Normal	Status	—	—	10	Self
TM90	Substitute	Normal	Status	—	—	10	Self
TM94	Secret Power	Normal	Physical	70	100	20	Normal
TM100	Confide	Normal	Status	—	—	20	Normal
HM03	Surf	Water	Special	90	100	15	Adjacent
HM05	Waterfall	Water	Physical	80	100	15	Normal
HM06	Rock Smash	Fighting	Physical	40	100	15	Normal
HM07	Dive	Water	Physical	80	100	10	Normal

MOVES LEARNED IN EXCHANGE FOR BP

Name	Type	Kind	Pow.	Acc.	PP	Range
Earth Power	Ground	Special	90	100	10	Normal
Iron Defense	Steel	Status	—	—	15	Self
Icy Wind	Ice	Special	55	95	15	Many Others
Bind	Normal	Physical	15	85	20	Normal
Snore	Normal	Special	50	100	15	Normal
Knock Off	Dark	Physical	65	100	20	Normal
Water Pulse	Water	Special	60	100	20	Normal
Stealth Rock	Rock	Status	—	—	20	Other Side

MOVES TAUGHT BY PEOPLE

Name	Type	Kind	Pow.	Acc.	PP	Range

National Pokédex **140** Hoenn Pokédex —

Kabuto

Shellfish Pokémon

Rock Water

HEIGHT: 1'08" WEIGHT: 25.4 lbs.

Same form for ♂ / ♀

Ω Kabuto is a Pokémon that has been regenerated from a fossil. However, in extremely rare cases, living examples have been discovered. The Pokémon has not changed at all for 300 million years.

α Kabuto is a Pokémon that has been regenerated from a fossil. However, in extremely rare cases, living examples have been discovered. The Pokémon has not changed at all for 300 million years.

ABILITIES
Swift Swim
Battle Armor

HIDDEN ABILITY
Weak Armor

EGG GROUPS
Water 1 Water 3

STAT GROWTH RATES
HP
Attack
Defense
Sp. Atk
Sp. Def
Speed

ITEMS SOMETIMES HELD BY WILD POKÉMON
—

EVOLUTION

MAIN WAYS TO REGISTER IN THE NATIONAL POKÉDEX

Ω Obtain a Dome Fossil from a cracked rock in a Mirage spot by using Rock Smash, then have it restored at the Devon Corporation (2F) in Rustboro City.

α Bring it to your game using Link Trade or the GTS.

Damage taken in normal battles

Type		Type	
Normal	×0.5	Flying	×0.5
Fire	×0.25	Psychic	×1
Water	×1	Bug	×1
Grass	×4	Rock	×1
Electric	×2	Ghost	×1
Ice	×0.5	Dragon	×1
Fighting	×2	Dark	×1
Poison	×0.5	Steel	×1
Ground	×2	Fairy	×1

Damage taken in Inverse battles

Type		Type	
Normal	×2	Flying	×2
Fire	×4	Psychic	×1
Water	×1	Bug	×1
Grass	×0.25	Rock	×1
Electric	×0.5	Ghost	×1
Ice	×2	Dragon	×1
Fighting	×0.5	Dark	×1
Poison	×2	Steel	×1
Ground	×0.5	Fairy	×1

Can be used in
Inverse Battle
Battle Institute
Battle Maison
Random Matchup (Free Battle)
Random Matchup (Others)

LEVEL-UP MOVES

Lv.	Name	Type	Kind	Pow.	Acc.	PP	Range
1	Scratch	Normal	Physical	40	100	35	Normal
1	Harden	Normal	Status	—	—	30	Self
6	Absorb	Grass	Special	20	100	25	Normal
11	Leer	Normal	Status	—	100	30	Many Others
16	Mud Shot	Ground	Special	55	95	15	Normal
21	Sand Attack	Ground	Status	—	100	15	Normal
26	Endure	Normal	Status	—	—	10	Self
31	Aqua Jet	Water	Physical	40	100	20	Normal
36	Mega Drain	Grass	Special	40	100	15	Normal
41	Metal Sound	Steel	Status	—	85	40	Normal
46	Ancient Power	Rock	Special	60	100	5	Normal
50	Wring Out	Normal	Special	—	100	5	Normal

TM & HM MOVES

No.	Name	Type	Kind	Pow.	Acc.	PP	Range
TM01	Hone Claws	Dark	Status	—	—	15	Self
TM06	Toxic	Poison	Status	—	90	10	Normal
TM07	Hail	Ice	Status	—	—	10	Both Sides
TM10	Hidden Power	Normal	Special	60	100	15	Normal
TM13	Ice Beam	Ice	Special	90	100	10	Normal
TM14	Blizzard	Ice	Special	110	70	5	Many Others
TM17	Protect	Normal	Status	—	—	10	Self
TM18	Rain Dance	Water	Status	—	—	5	Both Sides
TM21	Frustration	Normal	Physical	—	100	20	Normal
TM23	Smack Down	Rock	Physical	50	100	15	Normal
TM27	Return	Normal	Physical	—	100	20	Normal
TM28	Dig	Ground	Physical	80	100	10	Normal
TM32	Double Team	Normal	Status	—	—	15	Self
TM37	Sandstorm	Rock	Status	—	—	10	Both Sides
TM39	Rock Tomb	Rock	Physical	60	95	15	Normal
TM40	Aerial Ace	Flying	Physical	60	—	20	Normal
TM42	Facade	Normal	Physical	70	100	20	Normal
TM44	Rest	Psychic	Status	—	—	10	Self
TM45	Attract	Normal	Status	—	100	15	Normal
TM46	Thief	Dark	Physical	60	100	25	Normal
TM48	Round	Normal	Special	60	100	15	Normal
TM55	Scald	Water	Special	80	100	15	Normal
TM69	Rock Polish	Rock	Status	—	—	20	Self
TM80	Rock Slide	Rock	Physical	75	90	10	Many Others
TM87	Swagger	Normal	Status	—	90	15	Normal
TM88	Sleep Talk	Normal	Status	—	—	10	Self
TM90	Substitute	Normal	Status	—	—	10	Self
TM94	Secret Power	Normal	Physical	70	100	20	Normal
TM100	Confide	Normal	Status	—	—	20	Normal
HM03	Surf	Water	Special	90	100	15	Adjacent
HM05	Waterfall	Water	Physical	80	100	15	Normal
HM06	Rock Smash	Fighting	Physical	40	100	15	Normal

MOVES LEARNED IN EXCHANGE FOR BP

Name	Type	Kind	Pow.	Acc.	PP	Range
Earth Power	Ground	Special	90	100	10	Normal
Iron Defense	Steel	Status	—	—	15	Self
Icy Wind	Ice	Special	55	95	15	Many Others
Snore	Normal	Special	50	100	15	Normal
Knock Off	Dark	Physical	65	100	20	Normal
Giga Drain	Grass	Special	75	100	10	Normal
Water Pulse	Water	Special	60	100	20	Normal
Stealth Rock	Rock	Status	—	—	20	Other Side

MOVES TAUGHT BY PEOPLE

Name	Type	Kind	Pow.	Acc.	PP	Range

EGG MOVES

Name	Type	Kind	Pow.	Acc.	PP	Range
Bubble Beam	Water	Special	65	100	20	Normal
Aurora Beam	Ice	Special	65	100	20	Normal
Rapid Spin	Normal	Physical	20	100	40	Normal
Flail	Normal	Physical	—	100	15	Normal
Knock Off	Dark	Physical	65	100	20	Normal
Confuse Ray	Ghost	Status	—	100	10	Normal
Mud Shot	Ground	Special	55	95	15	Normal
Icy Wind	Ice	Special	55	95	15	Many Others
Screech	Normal	Status	—	85	40	Normal
Giga Drain	Grass	Special	75	100	10	Normal
Foresight	Normal	Status	—	—	40	Normal
Take Down	Normal	Physical	90	85	20	Normal

National Pokédex **141** Hoenn Pokédex —

Kabutops

Shellfish Pokémon

Rock Water

HEIGHT: 4'03" WEIGHT: 89.3 lbs.

Same form for ♂ / ♀

Ω Kabutops swam underwater to hunt for its prey in ancient times. The Pokémon was apparently evolving from being a water dweller to living on land as evident from the beginnings of change in its gills and legs.

α Kabutops swam underwater to hunt for its prey in ancient times. The Pokémon was apparently evolving from being a water dweller to living on land as evident from the beginnings of change in its gills and legs.

ABILITIES
Swift Swim
Battle Armor

HIDDEN ABILITY
Weak Armor

EGG GROUPS
Water 1 Water 3

STAT GROWTH RATES
HP
Attack
Defense
Sp. Atk
Sp. Def
Speed

ITEMS SOMETIMES HELD BY WILD POKÉMON
—

EVOLUTION

Lv. 40
Kabuto
Kabutops

MAIN WAYS TO REGISTER IN THE NATIONAL POKÉDEX

Ω Level up Kabuto to Lv. 40.

α Bring it to your game using Link Trade or the GTS.

Damage taken in normal battles

Type		Type	
Normal	×0.5	Flying	×0.5
Fire	×0.25	Psychic	×1
Water	×1	Bug	×1
Grass	×4	Rock	×1
Electric	×2	Ghost	×1
Ice	×0.5	Dragon	×1
Fighting	×2	Dark	×1
Poison	×0.5	Steel	×1
Ground	×2	Fairy	×1

Damage taken in Inverse battles

Type		Type	
Normal	×2	Flying	×2
Fire	×4	Psychic	×1
Water	×1	Bug	×1
Grass	×0.25	Rock	×1
Electric	×0.5	Ghost	×1
Ice	×2	Dragon	×1
Fighting	×0.5	Dark	×1
Poison	×2	Steel	×1
Ground	×0.5	Fairy	×1

Can be used in
Inverse Battle
Battle Institute
Battle Maison
Random Matchup (Free Battle)
Random Matchup (Others)

LEVEL-UP MOVES

Lv.	Name	Type	Kind	Pow.	Acc.	PP	Range
1	Night Slash	Dark	Physical	70	100	15	Normal
1	Feint	Normal	Physical	30	100	10	Normal
1	Scratch	Normal	Physical	40	100	35	Normal
1	Harden	Normal	Status	—	—	30	Self
1	Absorb	Grass	Special	20	100	25	Normal
1	Leer	Normal	Status	—	100	30	Many Others
6	Absorb	Grass	Special	20	100	25	Normal
11	Leer	Normal	Status	—	100	30	Many Others
16	Mud Shot	Ground	Special	55	95	15	Normal
21	Sand Attack	Ground	Status	—	100	15	Normal
26	Endure	Normal	Status	—	—	10	Self
31	Aqua Jet	Water	Physical	40	100	20	Normal
36	Mega Drain	Grass	Special	40	100	15	Normal
40	Slash	Normal	Physical	70	100	20	Normal
45	Metal Sound	Steel	Status	—	85	40	Normal
54	Ancient Power	Rock	Special	60	100	5	Normal
63	Wring Out	Normal	Special	—	100	5	Normal
72	Night Slash	Dark	Physical	70	100	15	Normal

TM & HM MOVES

No.	Name	Type	Kind	Pow.	Acc.	PP	Range
TM01	Hone Claws	Dark	Status	—	—	15	Self
TM06	Toxic	Poison	Status	—	90	10	Normal
TM07	Hail	Ice	Status	—	—	10	Both Sides
TM10	Hidden Power	Normal	Special	60	100	15	Normal
TM13	Ice Beam	Ice	Special	90	100	10	Normal
TM14	Blizzard	Ice	Special	110	70	5	Many Others
TM15	Hyper Beam	Normal	Special	150	90	5	Normal
TM17	Protect	Normal	Status	—	—	10	Self
TM18	Rain Dance	Water	Status	—	—	5	Both Sides
TM21	Frustration	Normal	Physical	—	100	20	Normal
TM23	Smack Down	Rock	Physical	50	100	15	Normal
TM27	Return	Normal	Physical	—	100	20	Normal
TM28	Dig	Ground	Physical	80	100	10	Normal
TM31	Brick Break	Fighting	Physical	75	100	15	Normal
TM32	Double Team	Normal	Status	—	—	15	Self
TM37	Sandstorm	Rock	Status	—	—	10	Both Sides
TM39	Rock Tomb	Rock	Physical	60	95	15	Normal
TM40	Aerial Ace	Flying	Physical	60	—	20	Normal
TM42	Facade	Normal	Physical	70	100	20	Normal
TM44	Rest	Psychic	Status	—	—	10	Self
TM45	Attract	Normal	Status	—	100	15	Normal
TM46	Thief	Dark	Physical	60	100	25	Normal
TM48	Round	Normal	Special	60	100	15	Normal
TM55	Scald	Water	Special	80	100	15	Normal
TM68	Giga Impact	Normal	Physical	150	90	5	Normal
TM69	Rock Polish	Rock	Status	—	—	20	Self
TM71	Stone Edge	Rock	Physical	100	80	5	Normal
TM75	Swords Dance	Normal	Status	—	—	20	Self
TM80	Rock Slide	Rock	Physical	75	90	10	Many Others
TM81	X-Scissor	Bug	Physical	80	100	15	Normal
TM87	Swagger	Normal	Status	—	90	15	Normal
TM88	Sleep Talk	Normal	Status	—	—	10	Self
TM90	Substitute	Normal	Status	—	—	10	Self
TM94	Secret Power	Normal	Physical	70	100	20	Normal
TM96	Nature Power	Normal	Status	—	—	20	Normal
TM100	Confide	Normal	Status	—	—	20	Normal
HM01	Cut	Normal	Physical	50	95	30	Normal
HM03	Surf	Water	Special	90	100	15	Adjacent
HM05	Waterfall	Water	Physical	80	100	15	Normal
HM06	Rock Smash	Fighting	Physical	40	100	15	Normal
HM07	Dive	Water	Physical	80	100	10	Normal

MOVES LEARNED IN EXCHANGE FOR BP

Name	Type	Kind	Pow.	Acc.	PP	Range
Low Kick	Fighting	Physical	—	100	20	Normal
Earth Power	Ground	Special	90	100	10	Normal
Iron Defense	Steel	Status	—	—	15	Self
Superpower	Fighting	Physical	120	100	5	Normal
Icy Wind	Ice	Special	55	95	15	Many Others
Aqua Tail	Water	Physical	90	90	10	Normal
Snore	Normal	Special	50	100	15	Normal
Knock Off	Dark	Physical	65	100	20	Normal
Giga Drain	Grass	Special	75	100	10	Normal
Water Pulse	Water	Special	60	100	20	Normal
Stealth Rock	Rock	Status	—	—	20	Other Side

MOVES TAUGHT BY PEOPLE

Name	Type	Kind	Pow.	Acc.	PP	Range

National Pokédex **142** Hoenn Pokédex —

Aerodactyl

Fossil Pokémon

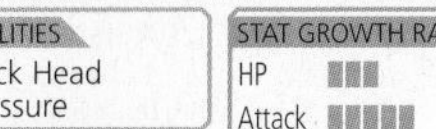

HEIGHT: 5'11" WEIGHT: 130.1 lbs.

Same form for ♂ / ♀

Ω Aerodactyl is a Pokémon from the age of dinosaurs. It was regenerated from genetic material extracted from amber. It is imagined to have been the king of the skies in ancient times.

α Aerodactyl is a Pokémon from the age of dinosaurs. It was regenerated from genetic material extracted from amber. It is imagined to have been the king of the skies in ancient times.

ABILITIES
Rock Head
Pressure

HIDDEN ABILITY
Unnerve

EGG GROUPS
Flying

STAT GROWTH RATES
HP
Attack
Defense
Sp. Atk
Sp. Def
Speed

ITEMS SOMETIMES HELD BY WILD POKÉMON
—

EVOLUTION

MAIN WAY TO REGISTER IN THE NATIONAL POKÉDEX

Obtain an Old Amber from a cracked rock in a Mirage spot by using Rock Smash, then have it restored at the Devon Corporation (2F) in Rustboro City.

Damage taken in normal battles

Type		Type	
Normal	×0.5	Flying	×0.5
Fire	×0.5	Psychic	×1
Water	×2	Bug	×0.5
Grass	×1	Rock	×2
Electric	×2	Ghost	×1
Ice	×2	Dragon	×1
Fighting	×1	Dark	×1
Poison	×0.5	Steel	×2
Ground	×0	Fairy	×1

Damage taken in Inverse battles

Type		Type	
Normal	×2	Flying	×2
Fire	×2	Psychic	×1
Water	×0.5	Bug	×2
Grass	×1	Rock	×0.5
Electric	×0.5	Ghost	×1
Ice	×0.5	Dragon	×1
Fighting	×1	Dark	×1
Poison	×2	Steel	×0.5
Ground	×1	Fairy	×1

Can be used in
Inverse Battle
Battle Institute
Battle Maison
Random Matchup (Free Battle)
Random Matchup (Others)

LEVEL-UP MOVES

Lv.	Name	Type	Kind	Pow.	Acc.	PP	Range
1	Iron Head	Steel	Physical	80	100	15	Normal
1	Ice Fang	Ice	Physical	65	95	15	Normal
1	Fire Fang	Fire	Physical	65	95	15	Normal
1	Thunder Fang	Electric	Physical	65	95	15	Normal
1	Wing Attack	Flying	Physical	60	100	35	Normal
1	Supersonic	Normal	Status	—	55	20	Normal
1	Bite	Dark	Physical	60	100	25	Normal
1	Scary Face	Normal	Status	—	100	10	Normal
9	Roar	Normal	Status	—	—	20	Normal
17	Agility	Psychic	Status	—	—	30	Self
25	Ancient Power	Rock	Special	60	100	5	Normal
33	Crunch	Dark	Physical	80	100	15	Normal
41	Take Down	Normal	Physical	90	85	20	Normal
49	Sky Drop	Flying	Physical	60	100	10	Normal
57	Iron Head	Steel	Physical	80	100	15	Normal
65	Hyper Beam	Normal	Special	150	90	5	Normal
73	Rock Slide	Rock	Physical	75	90	10	Many Others
81	Giga Impact	Normal	Physical	150	90	5	Normal

TM & HM MOVES

No.	Name	Type	Kind	Pow.	Acc.	PP	Range
TM01	Hone Claws	Dark	Status	—	—	15	Self
TM02	Dragon Claw	Dragon	Physical	80	100	15	Normal
TM05	Roar	Normal	Status	—	—	20	Normal
TM06	Toxic	Poison	Status	—	90	10	Normal
TM10	Hidden Power	Normal	Special	60	100	15	Normal
TM11	Sunny Day	Fire	Status	—	—	5	Both Sides
TM12	Taunt	Dark	Status	—	100	20	Normal
TM15	Hyper Beam	Normal	Special	150	90	5	Normal
TM17	Protect	Normal	Status	—	—	10	Self
TM18	Rain Dance	Water	Status	—	—	5	Both Sides
TM19	Roost	Flying	Status	—	—	10	Self
TM21	Frustration	Normal	Physical	—	100	20	Normal
TM23	Smack Down	Rock	Physical	50	100	15	Normal
TM26	Earthquake	Ground	Physical	100	100	10	Adjacent
TM27	Return	Normal	Physical	—	100	20	Normal
TM32	Double Team	Normal	Status	—	—	15	Self
TM35	Flamethrower	Fire	Special	90	100	15	Normal
TM37	Sandstorm	Rock	Status	—	—	10	Both Sides
TM38	Fire Blast	Fire	Special	110	85	5	Normal
TM39	Rock Tomb	Rock	Physical	60	95	15	Normal
TM40	Aerial Ace	Flying	Physical	60	—	20	Normal
TM41	Torment	Dark	Status	—	100	15	Normal
TM42	Facade	Normal	Physical	70	100	20	Normal
TM44	Rest	Psychic	Status	—	—	10	Self
TM45	Attract	Normal	Status	—	100	15	Normal
TM46	Thief	Dark	Physical	60	100	25	Normal
TM48	Round	Normal	Special	60	100	15	Normal
TM51	Steel Wing	Steel	Physical	70	90	25	Normal
TM58	Sky Drop	Flying	Physical	60	100	10	Normal
TM59	Incinerate	Fire	Special	60	100	15	Many Others
TM66	Payback	Dark	Physical	50	100	10	Normal
TM68	Giga Impact	Normal	Physical	150	90	5	Normal
TM69	Rock Polish	Rock	Status	—	—	20	Self
TM71	Stone Edge	Rock	Physical	100	80	5	Normal
TM78	Bulldoze	Ground	Physical	60	100	20	Adjacent
TM80	Rock Slide	Rock	Physical	75	90	10	Many Others
TM87	Swagger	Normal	Status	—	90	15	Normal
TM88	Sleep Talk	Normal	Status	—	—	10	Self
TM90	Substitute	Normal	Status	—	—	10	Self
TM94	Secret Power	Normal	Physical	70	100	20	Normal
TM100	Confide	Normal	Status	—	—	20	Normal
HM02	Fly	Flying	Physical	90	95	15	Normal
HM04	Strength	Normal	Physical	80	100	15	Normal
HM06	Rock Smash	Fighting	Physical	40	100	15	Normal

MOVES LEARNED IN EXCHANGE FOR BP

Name	Type	Kind	Pow.	Acc.	PP	Range
Iron Head	Steel	Physical	80	100	15	Normal
Earth Power	Ground	Special	90	100	10	Normal
Aqua Tail	Water	Physical	90	90	10	Normal
Dragon Pulse	Dragon	Special	85	100	10	Normal
Iron Tail	Steel	Physical	100	75	15	Normal
Snore	Normal	Special	50	100	15	Normal
Heat Wave	Fire	Special	95	90	10	Many Others
Tailwind	Flying	Status	—	—	15	Your Side
Sky Attack	Flying	Physical	140	90	5	Normal
Stealth Rock	Rock	Status	—	—	20	Other Side

MOVES TAUGHT BY PEOPLE

Name	Type	Kind	Pow.	Acc.	PP	Range

EGG MOVES

Name	Type	Kind	Pow.	Acc.	PP	Range
Whirlwind	Normal	Status	—	—	20	Normal
Pursuit	Dark	Physical	40	100	20	Normal
Foresight	Normal	Status	—	—	40	Normal
Steel Wing	Steel	Physical	70	90	25	Normal
Dragon Breath	Dragon	Special	60	100	20	Normal
Curse	Ghost	Status	—	—	10	Varies
Assurance	Dark	Physical	60	100	10	Normal
Roost	Flying	Status	—	—	10	Self
Tailwind	Flying	Status	—	—	15	Your Side
Wide Guard	Rock	Status	—	—	10	Your Side

Mega Evolution

Mega Aerodactyl

Fossil Pokémon

Rock Flying

HEIGHT: 6'11" WEIGHT: 174.2 lbs.

Same form for ♂ / ♀

REQUIRED MEGA STONE
Aerodactylite
Find in the Back chamber of Meteor Falls (after battling Groudon or Kyogre).

ABILITY
Tough Claws

HIDDEN ABILITY
—

EGG GROUPS
—

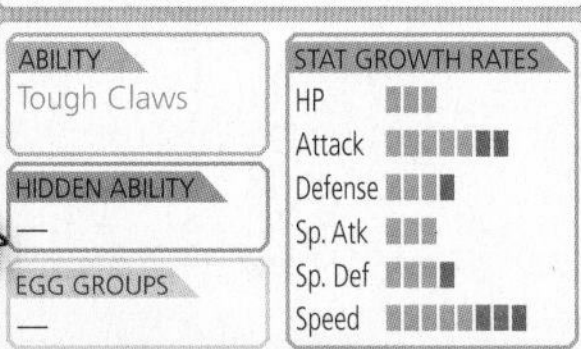

STAT GROWTH RATES
HP
Attack
Defense
Sp. Atk
Sp. Def
Speed

Damage taken in normal battles

Type		Type	
Normal	×0.5	Flying	×0.5
Fire	×0.5	Psychic	×1
Water	×2	Bug	×0.5
Grass	×1	Rock	×2
Electric	×2	Ghost	×1
Ice	×2	Dragon	×1
Fighting	×1	Dark	×1
Poison	×0.5	Steel	×2
Ground	×0	Fairy	×1

Damage taken in Inverse battles

Type		Type	
Normal	×2	Flying	×2
Fire	×2	Psychic	×1
Water	×0.5	Bug	×2
Grass	×1	Rock	×0.5
Electric	×0.5	Ghost	×1
Ice	×0.5	Dragon	×1
Fighting	×1	Dark	×1
Poison	×2	Steel	×0.5
Ground	×1	Fairy	×1

Can be used in
Inverse Battle
Battle Institute
Battle Maison
Random Matchup (Free Battle)
Random Matchup (Others)

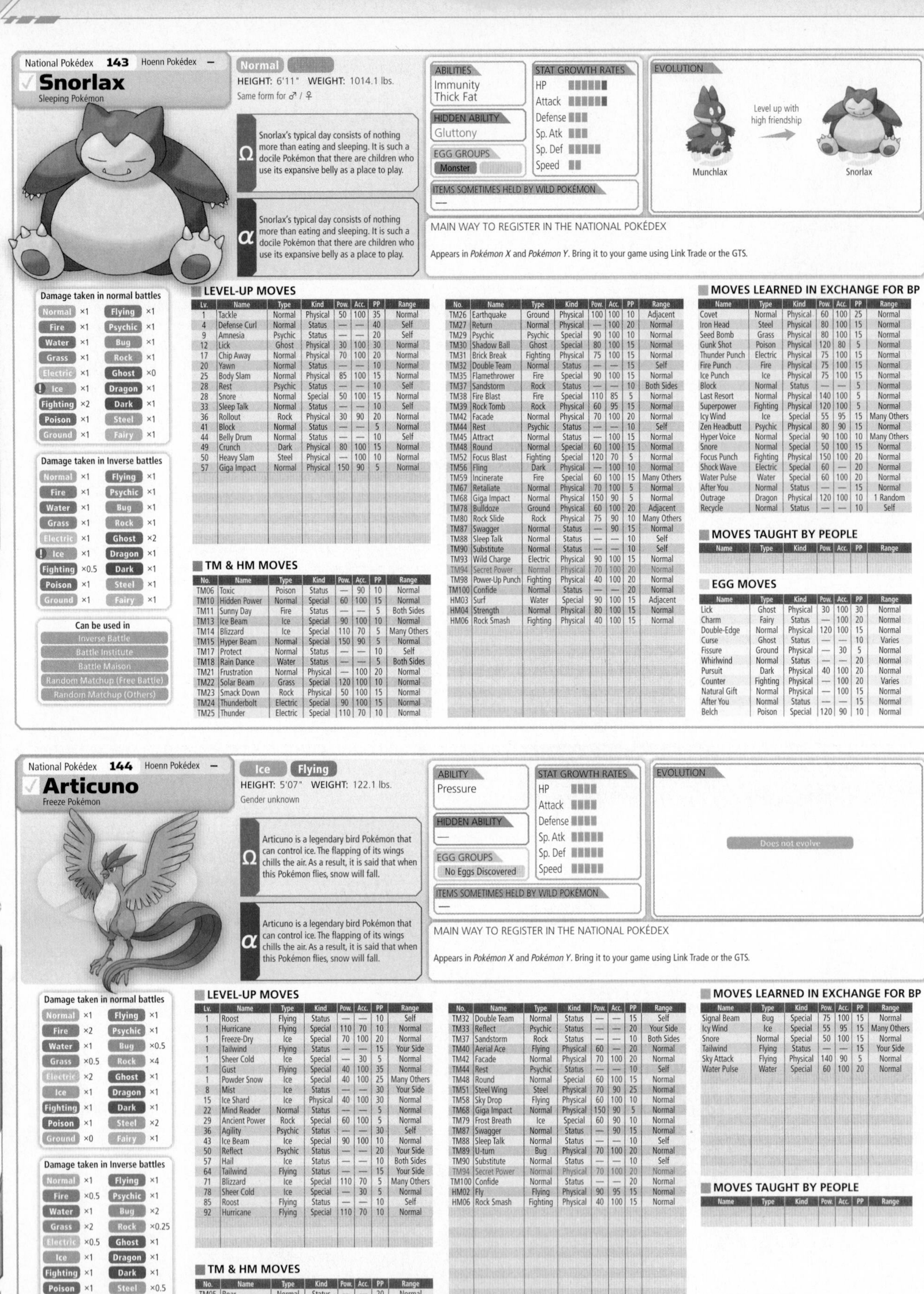

National Pokédex **143** Hoenn Pokédex —

Snorlax

Sleeping Pokémon

Normal

HEIGHT: 6'11" WEIGHT: 1014.1 lbs.

Same form for ♂ / ♀

Ω Snorlax's typical day consists of nothing more than eating and sleeping. It is such a docile Pokémon that there are children who use its expansive belly as a place to play.

α Snorlax's typical day consists of nothing more than eating and sleeping. It is such a docile Pokémon that there are children who use its expansive belly as a place to play.

ABILITIES
Immunity
Thick Fat

HIDDEN ABILITY
Gluttony

EGG GROUPS
Monster

STAT GROWTH RATES
HP ▮▮▮▮▮▮
Attack ▮▮▮▮▮▮
Defense ▮▮▮
Sp. Atk ▮▮▮
Sp. Def ▮▮▮▮▮
Speed ▮▮

ITEMS SOMETIMES HELD BY WILD POKÉMON
—

EVOLUTION
Munchlax → Level up with high friendship → Snorlax

MAIN WAY TO REGISTER IN THE NATIONAL POKÉDEX
Appears in *Pokémon X* and *Pokémon Y*. Bring it to your game using Link Trade or the GTS.

Damage taken in normal battles

Type		Type	
Normal	×1	Flying	×1
Fire	×1	Psychic	×1
Water	×1	Bug	×1
Grass	×1	Rock	×1
Electric	×1	Ghost	×0
Ice	×1	Dragon	×1
Fighting	×2	Dark	×1
Poison	×1	Steel	×1
Ground	×1	Fairy	×1

Damage taken in Inverse battles

Type		Type	
Normal	×1	Flying	×1
Fire	×1	Psychic	×1
Water	×1	Bug	×1
Grass	×1	Rock	×1
Electric	×1	Ghost	×2
Ice	×1	Dragon	×1
Fighting	×0.5	Dark	×1
Poison	×1	Steel	×1
Ground	×1	Fairy	×1

Can be used in
Inverse Battle
Battle Institute
Battle Maison
Random Matchup (Free Battle)
Random Matchup (Others)

LEVEL-UP MOVES

Lv.	Name	Type	Kind	Pow.	Acc.	PP	Range
1	Tackle	Normal	Physical	50	100	35	Normal
4	Defense Curl	Normal	Status	—	—	40	Self
9	Amnesia	Psychic	Status	—	—	20	Self
12	Lick	Ghost	Physical	30	100	30	Normal
17	Chip Away	Normal	Physical	70	100	20	Normal
20	Yawn	Normal	Status	—	—	10	Normal
25	Body Slam	Normal	Physical	85	100	15	Normal
28	Rest	Psychic	Status	—	—	10	Self
28	Snore	Normal	Special	50	100	15	Normal
33	Sleep Talk	Normal	Status	—	—	10	Self
36	Rollout	Rock	Physical	30	90	20	Normal
41	Block	Normal	Status	—	—	5	Normal
44	Belly Drum	Normal	Status	—	—	10	Self
49	Crunch	Dark	Physical	80	100	15	Normal
50	Heavy Slam	Steel	Physical	—	100	10	Normal
57	Giga Impact	Normal	Physical	150	90	5	Normal

TM & HM MOVES

No.	Name	Type	Kind	Pow.	Acc.	PP	Range
TM06	Toxic	Poison	Status	—	90	10	Normal
TM10	Hidden Power	Normal	Special	60	100	15	Normal
TM11	Sunny Day	Fire	Status	—	—	5	Both Sides
TM13	Ice Beam	Ice	Special	90	100	10	Normal
TM14	Blizzard	Ice	Special	110	70	5	Many Others
TM15	Hyper Beam	Normal	Special	150	90	5	Normal
TM17	Protect	Normal	Status	—	—	10	Self
TM18	Rain Dance	Water	Status	—	—	5	Both Sides
TM21	Frustration	Normal	Physical	—	100	20	Normal
TM22	Solar Beam	Grass	Special	120	100	10	Normal
TM23	Smack Down	Rock	Physical	50	100	15	Normal
TM24	Thunderbolt	Electric	Special	90	100	15	Normal
TM25	Thunder	Electric	Special	110	70	10	Normal
TM26	Earthquake	Ground	Physical	100	100	10	Adjacent
TM27	Return	Normal	Physical	—	100	20	Normal
TM29	Psychic	Psychic	Special	90	100	10	Normal
TM30	Shadow Ball	Ghost	Special	80	100	15	Normal
TM31	Brick Break	Fighting	Physical	75	100	15	Normal
TM32	Double Team	Normal	Status	—	—	15	Self
TM35	Flamethrower	Fire	Special	90	100	15	Normal
TM37	Sandstorm	Rock	Status	—	—	10	Both Sides
TM38	Fire Blast	Fire	Special	110	85	5	Normal
TM39	Rock Tomb	Rock	Physical	60	95	15	Normal
TM42	Facade	Normal	Physical	70	100	20	Normal
TM44	Rest	Psychic	Status	—	—	10	Self
TM45	Attract	Normal	Status	—	100	15	Normal
TM48	Round	Normal	Special	60	100	15	Normal
TM52	Focus Blast	Fighting	Special	120	70	5	Normal
TM56	Fling	Dark	Physical	—	100	10	Normal
TM59	Incinerate	Fire	Special	60	100	15	Many Others
TM67	Retaliate	Normal	Physical	70	100	5	Normal
TM68	Giga Impact	Normal	Physical	150	90	5	Normal
TM78	Bulldoze	Ground	Physical	60	100	20	Adjacent
TM80	Rock Slide	Rock	Physical	75	90	10	Many Others
TM87	Swagger	Normal	Status	—	90	15	Normal
TM88	Sleep Talk	Normal	Status	—	—	10	Self
TM90	Substitute	Normal	Status	—	—	10	Self
TM93	Wild Charge	Electric	Physical	90	100	15	Normal
TM94	Secret Power	Normal	Physical	70	100	20	Normal
TM98	Power-Up Punch	Fighting	Physical	40	100	20	Normal
TM100	Confide	Normal	Status	—	—	20	Normal
HM03	Surf	Water	Special	90	100	15	Adjacent
HM04	Strength	Normal	Physical	80	100	15	Normal
HM06	Rock Smash	Fighting	Physical	40	100	15	Normal

MOVES LEARNED IN EXCHANGE FOR BP

Name	Type	Kind	Pow.	Acc.	PP	Range
Covet	Normal	Physical	60	100	25	Normal
Iron Head	Steel	Physical	80	100	15	Normal
Seed Bomb	Grass	Physical	80	100	15	Normal
Gunk Shot	Poison	Physical	120	80	5	Normal
Thunder Punch	Electric	Physical	75	100	15	Normal
Fire Punch	Fire	Physical	75	100	15	Normal
Ice Punch	Ice	Physical	75	100	15	Normal
Block	Normal	Status	—	—	5	Normal
Last Resort	Normal	Physical	140	100	5	Normal
Superpower	Fighting	Physical	120	100	5	Normal
Icy Wind	Ice	Special	55	95	15	Many Others
Zen Headbutt	Psychic	Physical	80	90	15	Normal
Hyper Voice	Normal	Special	90	100	10	Many Others
Snore	Normal	Special	50	100	15	Normal
Focus Punch	Fighting	Physical	150	100	20	Normal
Shock Wave	Electric	Special	60	—	20	Normal
Water Pulse	Water	Special	60	100	20	Normal
After You	Normal	Status	—	—	15	Normal
Outrage	Dragon	Physical	120	100	10	1 Random
Recycle	Normal	Status	—	—	10	Self

MOVES TAUGHT BY PEOPLE

Name	Type	Kind	Pow.	Acc.	PP	Range

EGG MOVES

Name	Type	Kind	Pow.	Acc.	PP	Range
Lick	Ghost	Physical	30	100	30	Normal
Charm	Fairy	Status	—	100	20	Normal
Double-Edge	Normal	Physical	120	100	15	Normal
Curse	Ghost	Status	—	—	10	Varies
Fissure	Ground	Physical	—	30	5	Normal
Whirlwind	Normal	Status	—	—	20	Normal
Pursuit	Dark	Physical	40	100	20	Normal
Counter	Fighting	Physical	—	100	20	Varies
Natural Gift	Normal	Physical	—	100	15	Normal
After You	Normal	Status	—	—	15	Normal
Belch	Poison	Special	120	90	10	Normal

National Pokédex **144** Hoenn Pokédex —

Articuno

Freeze Pokémon

Ice Flying

HEIGHT: 5'07" WEIGHT: 122.1 lbs.

Gender unknown

Ω Articuno is a legendary bird Pokémon that can control ice. The flapping of its wings chills the air. As a result, it is said that when this Pokémon flies, snow will fall.

α Articuno is a legendary bird Pokémon that can control ice. The flapping of its wings chills the air. As a result, it is said that when this Pokémon flies, snow will fall.

ABILITY
Pressure

HIDDEN ABILITY
—

EGG GROUPS
No Eggs Discovered

STAT GROWTH RATES
HP ▮▮▮▮
Attack ▮▮▮▮
Defense ▮▮▮▮
Sp. Atk ▮▮▮▮▮
Sp. Def ▮▮▮▮▮
Speed ▮▮▮▮▮

ITEMS SOMETIMES HELD BY WILD POKÉMON
—

EVOLUTION
Does not evolve

MAIN WAY TO REGISTER IN THE NATIONAL POKÉDEX
Appears in *Pokémon X* and *Pokémon Y*. Bring it to your game using Link Trade or the GTS.

Damage taken in normal battles

Type		Type	
Normal	×1	Flying	×1
Fire	×2	Psychic	×1
Water	×1	Bug	×0.5
Grass	×0.5	Rock	×4
Electric	×2	Ghost	×1
Ice	×1	Dragon	×1
Fighting	×1	Dark	×1
Poison	×1	Steel	×2
Ground	×0	Fairy	×1

Damage taken in Inverse battles

Type		Type	
Normal	×1	Flying	×1
Fire	×0.5	Psychic	×1
Water	×1	Bug	×2
Grass	×2	Rock	×0.25
Electric	×0.5	Ghost	×1
Ice	×1	Dragon	×1
Fighting	×1	Dark	×1
Poison	×1	Steel	×0.5
Ground	×2	Fairy	×1

Can be used in
Inverse Battle
Battle Institute
Battle Maison
Random Matchup (Free Battle)
Random Matchup (Others)

LEVEL-UP MOVES

Lv.	Name	Type	Kind	Pow.	Acc.	PP	Range
1	Roost	Flying	Status	—	—	10	Self
1	Hurricane	Flying	Special	110	70	10	Normal
1	Freeze-Dry	Ice	Special	70	100	20	Normal
1	Tailwind	Flying	Status	—	—	15	Your Side
1	Sheer Cold	Ice	Special	—	30	5	Normal
1	Gust	Flying	Special	40	100	35	Normal
1	Powder Snow	Ice	Special	40	100	25	Many Others
8	Mist	Ice	Status	—	—	30	Your Side
15	Ice Shard	Ice	Physical	40	100	30	Normal
22	Mind Reader	Normal	Status	—	—	5	Normal
29	Ancient Power	Rock	Special	60	100	5	Normal
36	Agility	Psychic	Status	—	—	30	Self
43	Ice Beam	Ice	Special	90	100	10	Normal
50	Reflect	Psychic	Status	—	—	20	Your Side
57	Hail	Ice	Status	—	—	10	Both Sides
64	Tailwind	Flying	Status	—	—	15	Your Side
71	Blizzard	Ice	Special	110	70	5	Many Others
78	Sheer Cold	Ice	Special	—	30	5	Normal
85	Roost	Flying	Status	—	—	10	Self
92	Hurricane	Flying	Special	110	70	10	Normal

TM & HM MOVES

No.	Name	Type	Kind	Pow.	Acc.	PP	Range
TM05	Roar	Normal	Status	—	—	20	Normal
TM06	Toxic	Poison	Status	—	90	10	Normal
TM07	Hail	Ice	Status	—	—	10	Both Sides
TM10	Hidden Power	Normal	Special	60	100	15	Normal
TM11	Sunny Day	Fire	Status	—	—	5	Both Sides
TM13	Ice Beam	Ice	Special	90	100	10	Normal
TM14	Blizzard	Ice	Special	110	70	5	Many Others
TM15	Hyper Beam	Normal	Special	150	90	5	Normal
TM17	Protect	Normal	Status	—	—	10	Self
TM18	Rain Dance	Water	Status	—	—	5	Both Sides
TM19	Roost	Flying	Status	—	—	10	Self
TM21	Frustration	Normal	Physical	—	100	20	Normal
TM27	Return	Normal	Physical	—	100	20	Normal
TM32	Double Team	Normal	Status	—	—	15	Self
TM33	Reflect	Psychic	Status	—	—	20	Your Side
TM37	Sandstorm	Rock	Status	—	—	10	Both Sides
TM40	Aerial Ace	Flying	Physical	60	—	20	Normal
TM42	Facade	Normal	Physical	70	100	20	Normal
TM44	Rest	Psychic	Status	—	—	10	Self
TM48	Round	Normal	Special	60	100	15	Normal
TM51	Steel Wing	Steel	Physical	70	90	25	Normal
TM58	Sky Drop	Flying	Physical	60	100	10	Normal
TM68	Giga Impact	Normal	Physical	150	90	5	Normal
TM79	Frost Breath	Ice	Special	60	90	10	Normal
TM87	Swagger	Normal	Status	—	90	15	Normal
TM88	Sleep Talk	Normal	Status	—	—	10	Self
TM89	U-turn	Bug	Physical	70	100	20	Normal
TM90	Substitute	Normal	Status	—	—	10	Self
TM94	Secret Power	Normal	Physical	70	100	20	Normal
TM100	Confide	Normal	Status	—	—	20	Normal
HM02	Fly	Flying	Physical	90	95	15	Normal
HM06	Rock Smash	Fighting	Physical	40	100	15	Normal

MOVES LEARNED IN EXCHANGE FOR BP

Name	Type	Kind	Pow.	Acc.	PP	Range
Signal Beam	Bug	Special	75	100	15	Normal
Icy Wind	Ice	Special	55	95	15	Many Others
Snore	Normal	Special	50	100	15	Normal
Tailwind	Flying	Status	—	—	15	Your Side
Sky Attack	Flying	Physical	140	90	5	Normal
Water Pulse	Water	Special	60	100	20	Normal

MOVES TAUGHT BY PEOPLE

Name	Type	Kind	Pow.	Acc.	PP	Range

143 Snorlax National Pokédex Articuno 144

National Pokédex **145** Hoenn Pokédex —

Zapdos

Electric Pokémon

Electric Flying

HEIGHT: 5'03" WEIGHT: 116 lbs.

Gender unknown

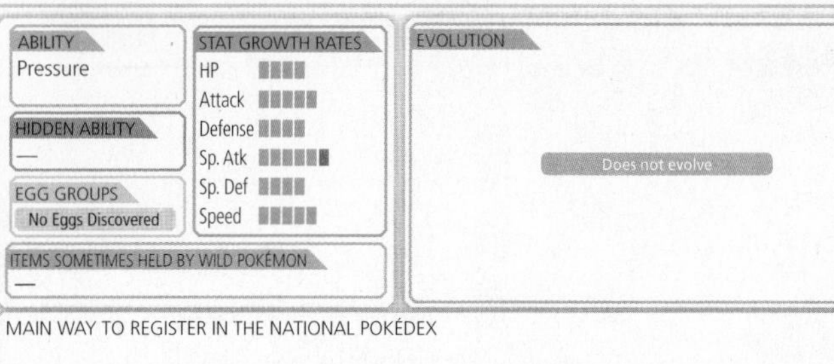

ABILITY: Pressure

HIDDEN ABILITY: —

EGG GROUPS: No Eggs Discovered

STAT GROWTH RATES: HP, Attack, Defense, Sp. Atk, Sp. Def, Speed

ITEMS SOMETIMES HELD BY WILD POKÉMON: —

EVOLUTION: Does not evolve

Ω Zapdos is a legendary bird Pokémon that has the ability to control electricity. It usually lives in thunderclouds. The Pokémon gains power if it is stricken by lightning bolts.

α Zapdos is a legendary bird Pokémon that has the ability to control electricity. It usually lives in thunderclouds. The Pokémon gains power if it is stricken by lightning bolts.

MAIN WAY TO REGISTER IN THE NATIONAL POKÉDEX

Appears in *Pokémon X* and *Pokémon Y*. Bring it to your game using Link Trade or the GTS.

Damage taken in normal battles

Type		Type	
Normal	×1	Flying	×0.5
Fire	×1	Psychic	×1
Water	×1	Bug	×0.5
Grass	×0.5	Rock	×2
Electric	×1	Ghost	×1
Ice	×2	Dragon	×1
Fighting	×0.5	Dark	×1
Poison	×1	Steel	×0.5
Ground	×0	Fairy	×1

Damage taken in Inverse battles

Type		Type	
Normal	×1	Flying	×2
Fire	×1	Psychic	×1
Water	×1	Bug	×2
Grass	×2	Rock	×0.5
Electric	×1	Ghost	×1
Ice	×0.5	Dragon	×1
Fighting	×2	Dark	×1
Poison	×1	Steel	×2
Ground	×1	Fairy	×1

Can be used in

Inverse Battle
Battle Institute
Battle Maison
Random Matchup (Free Battle)
Random Matchup (Others)

LEVEL-UP MOVES

Lv.	Name	Type	Kind	Pow.	Acc.	PP	Range
1	Roost	Flying	Status	—	—	10	Self
1	Zap Cannon	Electric	Special	120	50	5	Normal
1	Drill Peck	Flying	Physical	80	100	20	Normal
1	Peck	Flying	Physical	35	100	35	Normal
1	Thunder Shock	Electric	Special	40	100	30	Normal
8	Thunder Wave	Electric	Status	—	100	20	Normal
15	Detect	Fighting	Status	—	—	5	Self
22	Pluck	Flying	Physical	60	100	20	Normal
29	Ancient Power	Rock	Special	60	100	5	Normal
36	Charge	Electric	Status	—	—	20	Self
43	Agility	Psychic	Status	—	—	30	Self
50	Discharge	Electric	Special	80	100	15	Adjacent
57	Rain Dance	Water	Status	—	—	5	Both Sides
64	Light Screen	Psychic	Status	—	—	30	Your Side
71	Drill Peck	Flying	Physical	80	100	20	Normal
78	Thunder	Electric	Special	110	70	10	Normal
85	Roost	Flying	Status	—	—	10	Self
92	Zap Cannon	Electric	Special	120	50	5	Normal

TM & HM MOVES

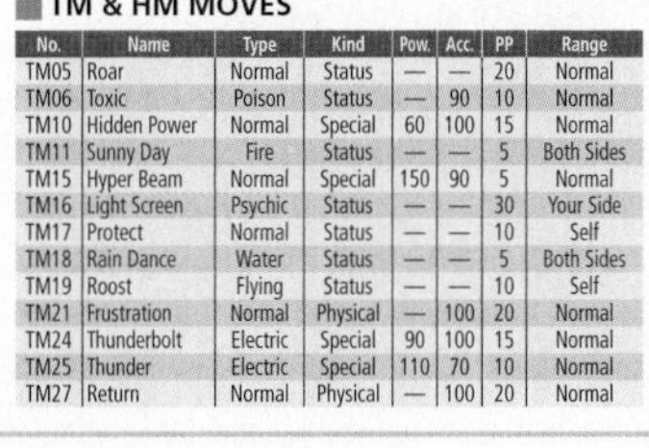

No.	Name	Type	Kind	Pow.	Acc.	PP	Range
TM05	Roar	Normal	Status	—	—	20	Normal
TM06	Toxic	Poison	Status	—	90	10	Normal
TM10	Hidden Power	Normal	Special	60	100	15	Normal
TM11	Sunny Day	Fire	Status	—	—	5	Both Sides
TM15	Hyper Beam	Normal	Special	150	90	5	Normal
TM16	Light Screen	Psychic	Status	—	—	30	Your Side
TM17	Protect	Normal	Status	—	—	10	Self
TM18	Rain Dance	Water	Status	—	—	5	Both Sides
TM19	Roost	Flying	Status	—	—	10	Self
TM21	Frustration	Normal	Physical	—	100	20	Normal
TM24	Thunderbolt	Electric	Special	90	100	15	Normal
TM25	Thunder	Electric	Special	110	70	10	Normal
TM27	Return	Normal	Physical	—	100	20	Normal
TM32	Double Team	Normal	Status	—	—	15	Self
TM37	Sandstorm	Rock	Status	—	—	10	Both Sides
TM40	Aerial Ace	Flying	Physical	60	—	20	Normal
TM42	Facade	Normal	Physical	70	100	20	Normal
TM44	Rest	Psychic	Status	—	—	10	Self
TM48	Round	Normal	Special	60	100	15	Normal
TM51	Steel Wing	Steel	Physical	70	90	25	Normal
TM57	Charge Beam	Electric	Special	50	90	10	Normal
TM58	Sky Drop	Flying	Physical	60	100	10	Normal
TM68	Giga Impact	Normal	Physical	150	90	5	Normal
TM70	Flash	Normal	Status	—	100	20	Normal
TM72	Volt Switch	Electric	Special	70	100	20	Normal
TM73	Thunder Wave	Electric	Status	—	100	20	Normal
TM87	Swagger	Normal	Status	—	90	15	Normal
TM88	Sleep Talk	Normal	Status	—	—	10	Self
TM89	U-turn	Bug	Physical	70	100	20	Normal
TM90	Substitute	Normal	Status	—	—	10	Self
TM93	Wild Charge	Electric	Physical	90	100	15	Normal
TM94	Secret Power	Normal	Physical	70	100	20	Normal
TM100	Confide	Normal	Status	—	—	20	Normal
HM02	Fly	Flying	Physical	90	95	15	Normal
HM06	Rock Smash	Fighting	Physical	40	100	15	Normal

MOVES LEARNED IN EXCHANGE FOR BP

Name	Type	Kind	Pow.	Acc.	PP	Range
Signal Beam	Bug	Special	75	100	15	Normal
Snore	Normal	Special	50	100	15	Normal
Heat Wave	Fire	Special	95	90	10	Many Others
Tailwind	Flying	Status	—	—	15	Your Side
Sky Attack	Flying	Physical	140	90	5	Normal
Shock Wave	Electric	Special	60	—	20	Normal

MOVES TAUGHT BY PEOPLE

Name	Type	Kind	Pow.	Acc.	PP	Range

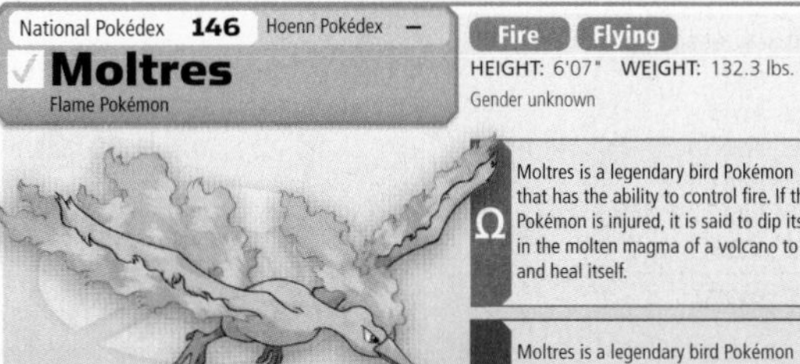

National Pokédex **146** Hoenn Pokédex —

Moltres

Flame Pokémon

Fire Flying

HEIGHT: 6'07" WEIGHT: 132.3 lbs.

Gender unknown

ABILITY: Pressure

HIDDEN ABILITY: —

EGG GROUPS: No Eggs Discovered

STAT GROWTH RATES: HP, Attack, Defense, Sp. Atk, Sp. Def, Speed

ITEMS SOMETIMES HELD BY WILD POKÉMON: —

EVOLUTION: Does not evolve

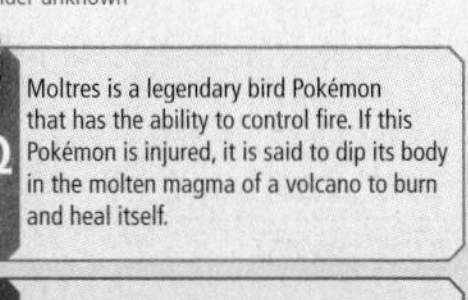

Ω Moltres is a legendary bird Pokémon that has the ability to control fire. If this Pokémon is injured, it is said to dip its body in the molten magma of a volcano to burn and heal itself.

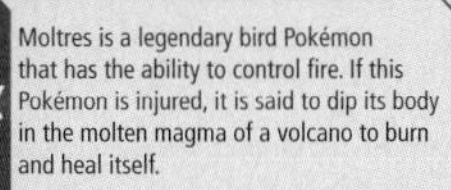

α Moltres is a legendary bird Pokémon that has the ability to control fire. If this Pokémon is injured, it is said to dip its body in the molten magma of a volcano to burn and heal itself.

MAIN WAY TO REGISTER IN THE NATIONAL POKÉDEX

Appears in *Pokémon X* and *Pokémon Y*. Bring it to your game using Link Trade or the GTS.

Damage taken in normal battles

Type		Type	
Normal	×1	Flying	×1
Fire	×0.5	Psychic	×1
Water	×2	Bug	×0.25
Grass	×0.25	Rock	×4
Electric	×2	Ghost	×1
Ice	×1	Dragon	×1
Fighting	×0.5	Dark	×1
Poison	×1	Steel	×0.5
Ground	×0	Fairy	×0.5

Damage taken in Inverse battles

Type		Type	
Normal	×1	Flying	×1
Fire	×2	Psychic	×1
Water	×0.5	Bug	×4
Grass	×4	Rock	×0.25
Electric	×0.5	Ghost	×1
Ice	×1	Dragon	×1
Fighting	×2	Dark	×1
Poison	×1	Steel	×2
Ground	×1	Fairy	×2

Can be used in

Inverse Battle
Battle Institute
Battle Maison
Random Matchup (Free Battle)
Random Matchup (Others)

LEVEL-UP MOVES

Lv.	Name	Type	Kind	Pow.	Acc.	PP	Range
1	Roost	Flying	Status	—	—	10	Self
1	Hurricane	Flying	Special	110	70	10	Normal
1	Sky Attack	Flying	Physical	140	90	5	Normal
1	Heat Wave	Fire	Special	95	90	10	Many Others
1	Wing Attack	Flying	Physical	60	100	35	Normal
1	Ember	Fire	Special	40	100	25	Normal
8	Fire Spin	Fire	Special	35	85	15	Normal
15	Agility	Psychic	Status	—	—	30	Self
22	Endure	Normal	Status	—	—	10	Self
29	Ancient Power	Rock	Special	60	100	5	Normal
36	Flamethrower	Fire	Special	90	100	15	Normal
43	Safeguard	Normal	Status	—	—	25	Your Side
50	Air Slash	Flying	Special	75	95	15	Normal
57	Sunny Day	Fire	Status	—	—	5	Both Sides
64	Heat Wave	Fire	Special	95	90	10	Many Others
71	Solar Beam	Grass	Special	120	100	10	Normal
78	Sky Attack	Flying	Physical	140	90	5	Normal
85	Roost	Flying	Status	—	—	10	Self
92	Hurricane	Flying	Special	110	70	10	Normal

TM & HM MOVES

No.	Name	Type	Kind	Pow.	Acc.	PP	Range
TM05	Roar	Normal	Status	—	—	20	Normal
TM06	Toxic	Poison	Status	—	90	10	Normal
TM10	Hidden Power	Normal	Special	60	100	15	Normal
TM11	Sunny Day	Fire	Status	—	—	5	Both Sides
TM15	Hyper Beam	Normal	Special	150	90	5	Normal
TM17	Protect	Normal	Status	—	—	10	Self
TM18	Rain Dance	Water	Status	—	—	5	Both Sides
TM19	Roost	Flying	Status	—	—	10	Self
TM20	Safeguard	Normal	Status	—	—	25	Your Side
TM21	Frustration	Normal	Physical	—	100	20	Normal
TM22	Solar Beam	Grass	Special	120	100	10	Normal
TM27	Return	Normal	Physical	—	100	20	Normal
TM32	Double Team	Normal	Status	—	—	15	Self
TM35	Flamethrower	Fire	Special	90	100	15	Normal
TM37	Sandstorm	Rock	Status	—	—	10	Both Sides
TM38	Fire Blast	Fire	Special	110	85	5	Normal
TM40	Aerial Ace	Flying	Physical	60	—	20	Normal
TM42	Facade	Normal	Physical	70	100	20	Normal
TM43	Flame Charge	Fire	Physical	50	100	20	Normal
TM44	Rest	Psychic	Status	—	—	10	Self
TM48	Round	Normal	Special	60	100	15	Normal
TM50	Overheat	Fire	Special	130	90	5	Normal
TM51	Steel Wing	Steel	Physical	70	90	25	Normal
TM58	Sky Drop	Flying	Physical	60	100	10	Normal
TM59	Incinerate	Fire	Special	60	100	15	Many Others
TM61	Will-O-Wisp	Fire	Status	—	85	15	Normal
TM68	Giga Impact	Normal	Physical	150	90	5	Normal
TM87	Swagger	Normal	Status	—	90	15	Normal
TM88	Sleep Talk	Normal	Status	—	—	10	Self
TM89	U-turn	Bug	Physical	70	100	20	Normal
TM90	Substitute	Normal	Status	—	—	10	Self
TM94	Secret Power	Normal	Physical	70	100	20	Normal
TM100	Confide	Normal	Status	—	—	20	Normal
HM02	Fly	Flying	Physical	90	95	15	Normal
HM06	Rock Smash	Fighting	Physical	40	100	15	Normal

MOVES LEARNED IN EXCHANGE FOR BP

Name	Type	Kind	Pow.	Acc.	PP	Range
Snore	Normal	Special	50	100	15	Normal
Heat Wave	Fire	Special	95	90	10	Many Others
Tailwind	Flying	Status	—	—	15	Your Side
Sky Attack	Flying	Physical	140	90	5	Normal

MOVES TAUGHT BY PEOPLE

Name	Type	Kind	Pow.	Acc.	PP	Range

National Pokédex **147** Hoenn Pokédex —

Dratini

Dragon Pokémon

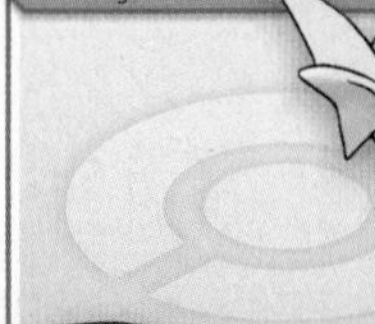

Dragon

HEIGHT: 5'11" WEIGHT: 7.3 lbs.

Same form for ♂ / ♀

Ω Dratini continually molts and sloughs off its old skin. It does so because the life energy within its body steadily builds to reach uncontrollable levels.

α Dratini continually molts and sloughs off its old skin. It does so because the life energy within its body steadily builds to reach uncontrollable levels.

ABILITY
Shed Skin

HIDDEN ABILITY
Marvel Scale

EGG GROUPS
Water 1 | Dragon

STAT GROWTH RATES
HP
Attack
Defense
Sp. Atk
Sp. Def
Speed

ITEMS SOMETIMES HELD BY WILD POKÉMON
—

EVOLUTION
Dratini → Lv. 30 → Dragonair → Lv. 55 → Dragonite

MAIN WAY TO REGISTER IN THE NATIONAL POKÉDEX

Appears in *Pokémon X* and *Pokémon Y*. Bring it to your game using Link Trade or the GTS.

Damage taken in normal battles

Normal	×1	Flying	×1
Fire	×0.5	Psychic	×1
Water	×0.5	Bug	×1
Grass	×0.5	Rock	×1
Electric	×0.5	Ghost	×1
Ice	×2	Dragon	×2
Fighting	×1	Dark	×1
Poison	×1	Steel	×1
Ground	×1	Fairy	×2

Damage taken in Inverse battles

Normal	×1	Flying	×1
Fire	×2	Psychic	×1
Water	×2	Bug	×1
Grass	×2	Rock	×1
Electric	×2	Ghost	×1
Ice	×0.5	Dragon	×0.5
Fighting	×1	Dark	×1
Poison	×1	Steel	×1
Ground	×1	Fairy	×0.5

Can be used in
Inverse Battle
Battle Institute
Battle Maison
Random Matchup (Free Battle)
Random Matchup (Others)

LEVEL-UP MOVES

Lv.	Name	Type	Kind	Pow.	Acc.	PP	Range
1	Wrap	Normal	Physical	15	90	20	Normal
1	Leer	Normal	Status	—	100	30	Many Others
5	Thunder Wave	Electric	Status	—	100	20	Normal
11	Twister	Dragon	Special	40	100	20	Many Others
15	Dragon Rage	Dragon	Special	—	100	10	Normal
21	Slam	Normal	Physical	80	75	20	Normal
25	Agility	Psychic	Status	—	—	30	Self
31	Dragon Tail	Dragon	Physical	60	90	10	Normal
35	Aqua Tail	Water	Physical	90	90	10	Normal
41	Dragon Rush	Dragon	Physical	100	75	10	Normal
45	Safeguard	Normal	Status	—	—	25	Your Side
51	Dragon Dance	Dragon	Status	—	—	20	Self
55	Outrage	Dragon	Physical	120	100	10	1 Random
61	Hyper Beam	Normal	Special	150	90	5	Normal

TM & HM MOVES

No.	Name	Type	Kind	Pow.	Acc.	PP	Range
TM06	Toxic	Poison	Status	—	90	10	Normal
TM07	Hail	Ice	Status	—	—	10	Both Sides
TM10	Hidden Power	Normal	Special	60	100	15	Normal
TM11	Sunny Day	Fire	Status	—	—	5	Both Sides
TM13	Ice Beam	Ice	Special	90	100	10	Normal
TM14	Blizzard	Ice	Special	110	70	5	Many Others
TM15	Hyper Beam	Normal	Special	150	90	5	Normal
TM16	Light Screen	Psychic	Status	—	—	30	Your Side
TM17	Protect	Normal	Status	—	—	10	Self
TM18	Rain Dance	Water	Status	—	—	5	Both Sides
TM20	Safeguard	Normal	Status	—	—	25	Your Side
TM21	Frustration	Normal	Physical	—	100	20	Normal
TM24	Thunderbolt	Electric	Special	90	100	15	Normal
TM25	Thunder	Electric	Special	110	70	10	Normal
TM27	Return	Normal	Physical	—	100	20	Normal
TM32	Double Team	Normal	Status	—	—	15	Self
TM35	Flamethrower	Fire	Special	90	100	15	Normal
TM38	Fire Blast	Fire	Special	110	85	5	Normal
TM42	Facade	Normal	Physical	70	100	20	Normal
TM44	Rest	Psychic	Status	—	—	10	Self
TM45	Attract	Normal	Status	—	100	15	Normal
TM48	Round	Normal	Special	60	100	15	Normal
TM59	Incinerate	Fire	Special	60	100	15	Many Others
TM73	Thunder Wave	Electric	Status	—	100	20	Normal
TM82	Dragon Tail	Dragon	Physical	60	90	10	Normal
TM87	Swagger	Normal	Status	—	90	15	Normal
TM88	Sleep Talk	Normal	Status	—	—	10	Self
TM90	Substitute	Normal	Status	—	—	10	Self
TM94	Secret Power	Normal	Physical	70	100	20	Normal
TM100	Confide	Normal	Status	—	—	20	Normal
HM03	Surf	Water	Special	90	100	15	Adjacent
HM05	Waterfall	Water	Physical	80	100	15	Normal

MOVES LEARNED IN EXCHANGE FOR BP

Name	Type	Kind	Pow.	Acc.	PP	Range
Icy Wind	Ice	Special	55	95	15	Many Others
Aqua Tail	Water	Physical	90	90	10	Normal
Dragon Pulse	Dragon	Special	85	100	10	Normal
Iron Tail	Steel	Physical	100	75	15	Normal
Bind	Normal	Physical	15	85	20	Normal
Snore	Normal	Special	50	100	15	Normal
Shock Wave	Electric	Special	60	—	20	Normal
Water Pulse	Water	Special	60	100	20	Normal
Outrage	Dragon	Physical	120	100	10	1 Random

MOVES TAUGHT BY PEOPLE

Name	Type	Kind	Pow.	Acc.	PP	Range
Draco Meteor	Dragon	Special	130	90	5	Normal

EGG MOVES

Name	Type	Kind	Pow.	Acc.	PP	Range
Mist	Ice	Status	—	—	30	Your Side
Haze	Ice	Status	—	—	30	Both Sides
Supersonic	Normal	Status	—	55	20	Normal
Dragon Breath	Dragon	Special	60	100	20	Normal
Dragon Dance	Dragon	Status	—	—	20	Self
Dragon Rush	Dragon	Physical	100	75	10	Normal
Extreme Speed	Normal	Physical	80	100	5	Normal
Water Pulse	Water	Special	60	100	20	Normal
Aqua Jet	Water	Physical	40	100	20	Normal
Dragon Pulse	Dragon	Special	85	100	10	Normal
Iron Tail	Steel	Physical	100	75	15	Normal

National Pokédex **148** Hoenn Pokédex —

Dragonair

Dragon Pokémon

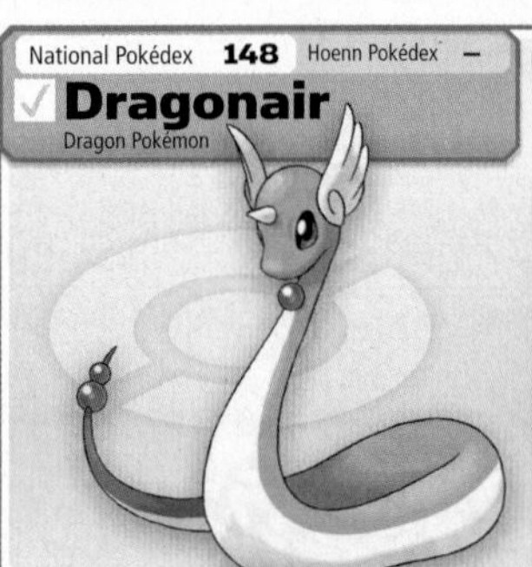

Dragon

HEIGHT: 13'01" WEIGHT: 36.4 lbs.

Same form for ♂ / ♀

Ω Dragonair stores an enormous amount of energy inside its body. It is said to alter weather conditions in its vicinity by discharging energy from the crystals on its neck and tail.

α Dragonair stores an enormous amount of energy inside its body. It is said to alter weather conditions in its vicinity by discharging energy from the crystals on its neck and tail.

ABILITY
Shed Skin

HIDDEN ABILITY
Marvel Scale

EGG GROUPS
Water 1 | Dragon

STAT GROWTH RATES
HP
Attack
Defense
Sp. Atk
Sp. Def
Speed

ITEMS SOMETIMES HELD BY WILD POKÉMON
—

EVOLUTION
Dratini → Lv. 30 → Dragonair → Lv. 55 → Dragonite

MAIN WAY TO REGISTER IN THE NATIONAL POKÉDEX

Appears in *Pokémon X* and *Pokémon Y*. Bring it to your game using Link Trade or the GTS.

Damage taken in normal battles

Normal	×1	Flying	×1
Fire	×0.5	Psychic	×1
Water	×0.5	Bug	×1
Grass	×0.5	Rock	×1
Electric	×0.5	Ghost	×1
Ice	×2	Dragon	×2
Fighting	×1	Dark	×1
Poison	×1	Steel	×1
Ground	×1	Fairy	×2

Damage taken in Inverse battles

Normal	×1	Flying	×1
Fire	×2	Psychic	×1
Water	×2	Bug	×1
Grass	×2	Rock	×1
Electric	×2	Ghost	×1
Ice	×0.5	Dragon	×0.5
Fighting	×1	Dark	×1
Poison	×1	Steel	×1
Ground	×1	Fairy	×0.5

Can be used in
Inverse Battle
Battle Institute
Battle Maison
Random Matchup (Free Battle)
Random Matchup (Others)

LEVEL-UP MOVES

Lv.	Name	Type	Kind	Pow.	Acc.	PP	Range
1	Wrap	Normal	Physical	15	90	20	Normal
1	Leer	Normal	Status	—	100	30	Many Others
1	Thunder Wave	Electric	Status	—	100	20	Normal
1	Twister	Dragon	Special	40	100	20	Many Others
5	Thunder Wave	Electric	Status	—	100	20	Normal
11	Twister	Dragon	Special	40	100	20	Many Others
15	Dragon Rage	Dragon	Special	—	100	10	Normal
21	Slam	Normal	Physical	80	75	20	Normal
25	Agility	Psychic	Status	—	—	30	Self
33	Dragon Tail	Dragon	Physical	60	90	10	Normal
39	Aqua Tail	Water	Physical	90	90	10	Normal
47	Dragon Rush	Dragon	Physical	100	75	10	Normal
53	Safeguard	Normal	Status	—	—	25	Your Side
61	Dragon Dance	Dragon	Status	—	—	20	Self
67	Outrage	Dragon	Physical	120	100	10	1 Random
75	Hyper Beam	Normal	Special	150	90	5	Normal

TM & HM MOVES

No.	Name	Type	Kind	Pow.	Acc.	PP	Range
TM06	Toxic	Poison	Status	—	90	10	Normal
TM07	Hail	Ice	Status	—	—	10	Both Sides
TM10	Hidden Power	Normal	Special	60	100	15	Normal
TM11	Sunny Day	Fire	Status	—	—	5	Both Sides
TM13	Ice Beam	Ice	Special	90	100	10	Normal
TM14	Blizzard	Ice	Special	110	70	5	Many Others
TM15	Hyper Beam	Normal	Special	150	90	5	Normal
TM16	Light Screen	Psychic	Status	—	—	30	Your Side
TM17	Protect	Normal	Status	—	—	10	Self
TM18	Rain Dance	Water	Status	—	—	5	Both Sides
TM20	Safeguard	Normal	Status	—	—	25	Your Side
TM21	Frustration	Normal	Physical	—	100	20	Normal
TM24	Thunderbolt	Electric	Special	90	100	15	Normal
TM25	Thunder	Electric	Special	110	70	10	Normal
TM27	Return	Normal	Physical	—	100	20	Normal
TM32	Double Team	Normal	Status	—	—	15	Self
TM35	Flamethrower	Fire	Special	90	100	15	Normal
TM38	Fire Blast	Fire	Special	110	85	5	Normal
TM42	Facade	Normal	Physical	70	100	20	Normal
TM44	Rest	Psychic	Status	—	—	10	Self
TM45	Attract	Normal	Status	—	100	15	Normal
TM48	Round	Normal	Special	60	100	15	Normal
TM59	Incinerate	Fire	Special	60	100	15	Many Others
TM73	Thunder Wave	Electric	Status	—	100	20	Normal
TM82	Dragon Tail	Dragon	Physical	60	90	10	Normal
TM87	Swagger	Normal	Status	—	90	15	Normal
TM88	Sleep Talk	Normal	Status	—	—	10	Self
TM90	Substitute	Normal	Status	—	—	10	Self
TM94	Secret Power	Normal	Physical	70	100	20	Normal
TM100	Confide	Normal	Status	—	—	20	Normal
HM03	Surf	Water	Special	90	100	15	Adjacent
HM05	Waterfall	Water	Physical	80	100	15	Normal

MOVES LEARNED IN EXCHANGE FOR BP

Name	Type	Kind	Pow.	Acc.	PP	Range
Icy Wind	Ice	Special	55	95	15	Many Others
Aqua Tail	Water	Physical	90	90	10	Normal
Dragon Pulse	Dragon	Special	85	100	10	Normal
Iron Tail	Steel	Physical	100	75	15	Normal
Bind	Normal	Physical	15	85	20	Normal
Snore	Normal	Special	50	100	15	Normal
Shock Wave	Electric	Special	60	—	20	Normal
Water Pulse	Water	Special	60	100	20	Normal
Outrage	Dragon	Physical	120	100	10	1 Random

MOVES TAUGHT BY PEOPLE

Name	Type	Kind	Pow.	Acc.	PP	Range
Draco Meteor	Dragon	Special	130	90	5	Normal

National Pokédex **149** Hoenn Pokédex —

Dragonite

Dragon Pokémon

Dragon | Flying

HEIGHT: 7'03" WEIGHT: 463 lbs.

Same form for ♂ / ♀

Ω Dragonite is capable of circling the globe in just 16 hours. It is a kindhearted Pokémon that leads lost and foundering ships in a storm to the safety of land.

α Dragonite is capable of circling the globe in just 16 hours. It is a kindhearted Pokémon that leads lost and foundering ships in a storm to the safety of land.

ABILITY
Inner Focus

HIDDEN ABILITY
Multiscale

EGG GROUPS
Water 1 | Dragon

STAT GROWTH RATES
HP ■■■■
Attack ■■■■■■■■
Defense ■■■■
Sp. Atk ■■■■■
Sp. Def ■■■■
Speed ■■■■

ITEMS SOMETIMES HELD BY WILD POKÉMON
—

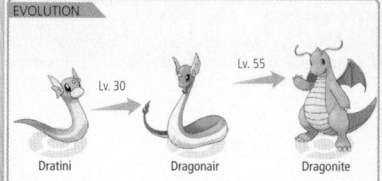

EVOLUTION
Dratini → Lv. 30 → Dragonair → Lv. 55 → Dragonite

MAIN WAY TO REGISTER IN THE NATIONAL POKÉDEX

Level up a Dragonair obtained via Link Trade or the GTS to Lv. 55.

149 Dragonite

Damage taken in normal battles

Type		Type	
Normal	×1	Flying	×1
Fire	×0.5	Psychic	×1
Water	×0.5	Bug	×0.5
Grass	×0.25	Rock	×2
Electric	×1	Ghost	×1
Ice	×4	Dragon	×2
Fighting	×0.5	Dark	×1
Poison	×1	Steel	×1
Ground	×0	Fairy	×2

Damage taken in Inverse battles

Type		Type	
Normal	×1	Flying	×1
Fire	×2	Psychic	×1
Water	×2	Bug	×2
Grass	×4	Rock	×0.5
Electric	×1	Ghost	×1
Ice	×0.25	Dragon	×0.5
Fighting	×2	Dark	×1
Poison	×1	Steel	×1
Ground	×2	Fairy	×0.5

Can be used in
- Inverse Battle
- Battle Institute
- Battle Maison
- Random Matchup (Free Battle)
- Random Matchup (Others)

LEVEL-UP MOVES

Lv.	Name	Type	Kind	Pow.	Acc.	PP	Range
1	Hurricane	Flying	Special	110	70	10	Normal
1	Fire Punch	Fire	Physical	75	100	15	Normal
1	Thunder Punch	Electric	Physical	75	100	15	Normal
1	Roost	Flying	Status	—	—	10	Self
1	Wrap	Normal	Physical	15	90	20	Normal
1	Leer	Normal	Status	—	100	30	Many Others
1	Thunder Wave	Electric	Status	—	100	20	Normal
1	Twister	Dragon	Special	40	100	20	Many Others
5	Thunder Wave	Electric	Status	—	100	20	Normal
11	Twister	Dragon	Special	40	100	20	Many Others
15	Dragon Rage	Dragon	Special	—	100	10	Normal
21	Slam	Normal	Physical	80	75	20	Normal
25	Agility	Psychic	Status	—	—	30	Self
33	Dragon Tail	Dragon	Physical	60	90	10	Normal
39	Aqua Tail	Water	Physical	90	90	10	Normal
47	Dragon Rush	Dragon	Physical	100	75	10	Normal
53	Safeguard	Normal	Status	—	—	25	Your Side
55	Wing Attack	Flying	Physical	60	100	35	Normal
61	Dragon Dance	Dragon	Status	—	—	20	Self
67	Outrage	Dragon	Physical	120	100	10	1 Random
75	Hyper Beam	Normal	Special	150	90	5	Normal
81	Hurricane	Flying	Special	110	70	10	Normal

TM & HM MOVES

No.	Name	Type	Kind	Pow.	Acc.	PP	Range
TM01	Hone Claws	Dark	Status	—	—	15	Self
TM02	Dragon Claw	Dragon	Physical	80	100	15	Normal
TM05	Roar	Normal	Status	—	—	20	Normal
TM06	Toxic	Poison	Status	—	90	10	Normal
TM07	Hail	Ice	Status	—	—	10	Both Sides
TM10	Hidden Power	Normal	Special	60	100	15	Normal
TM11	Sunny Day	Fire	Status	—	—	5	Both Sides
TM13	Ice Beam	Ice	Special	90	100	10	Normal
TM14	Blizzard	Ice	Special	110	70	5	Many Others
TM15	Hyper Beam	Normal	Special	150	90	5	Normal
TM16	Light Screen	Psychic	Status	—	—	30	Your Side
TM17	Protect	Normal	Status	—	—	10	Self
TM18	Rain Dance	Water	Status	—	—	5	Both Sides
TM19	Roost	Flying	Status	—	—	10	Self
TM20	Safeguard	Normal	Status	—	—	25	Your Side
TM21	Frustration	Normal	Physical	—	100	20	Normal
TM24	Thunderbolt	Electric	Special	90	100	15	Normal
TM25	Thunder	Electric	Special	110	70	10	Normal
TM26	Earthquake	Ground	Physical	100	100	10	Adjacent
TM27	Return	Normal	Physical	—	100	20	Normal
TM31	Brick Break	Fighting	Physical	75	100	15	Normal
TM32	Double Team	Normal	Status	—	—	15	Self
TM35	Flamethrower	Fire	Special	90	100	15	Normal
TM37	Sandstorm	Rock	Status	—	—	10	Both Sides
TM38	Fire Blast	Fire	Special	110	85	5	Normal
TM39	Rock Tomb	Rock	Physical	60	95	15	Normal
TM40	Aerial Ace	Flying	Physical	60	—	20	Normal
TM42	Facade	Normal	Physical	70	100	20	Normal
TM44	Rest	Psychic	Status	—	—	10	Self
TM45	Attract	Normal	Status	—	100	15	Normal
TM48	Round	Normal	Special	60	100	15	Normal
TM51	Steel Wing	Steel	Physical	70	90	25	Normal
TM52	Focus Blast	Fighting	Special	120	70	5	Normal
TM56	Fling	Dark	Physical	—	100	10	Normal
TM58	Sky Drop	Flying	Physical	60	100	10	Normal
TM59	Incinerate	Fire	Special	60	100	15	Many Others
TM68	Giga Impact	Normal	Physical	150	90	5	Normal
TM71	Stone Edge	Rock	Physical	100	80	5	Normal
TM73	Thunder Wave	Electric	Status	—	100	20	Normal
TM78	Bulldoze	Ground	Physical	60	100	20	Adjacent
TM80	Rock Slide	Rock	Physical	75	90	10	Many Others
TM82	Dragon Tail	Dragon	Physical	60	90	10	Normal
TM87	Swagger	Normal	Status	—	90	15	Normal
TM88	Sleep Talk	Normal	Status	—	—	10	Self
TM90	Substitute	Normal	Status	—	—	10	Self
TM94	Secret Power	Normal	Physical	70	100	20	Normal
TM98	Power-Up Punch	Fighting	Physical	40	100	20	Normal
TM100	Confide	Normal	Status	—	—	20	Normal
HM01	Cut	Normal	Physical	50	95	30	Normal
HM02	Fly	Flying	Physical	90	95	15	Normal
HM03	Surf	Water	Special	90	100	15	Adjacent
HM04	Strength	Normal	Physical	80	100	15	Normal
HM05	Waterfall	Water	Physical	80	100	15	Normal
HM06	Rock Smash	Fighting	Physical	40	100	15	Normal
HM07	Dive	Water	Physical	80	100	10	Normal

MOVES LEARNED IN EXCHANGE FOR BP

Name	Type	Kind	Pow.	Acc.	PP	Range
Iron Head	Steel	Physical	80	100	15	Normal
Thunder Punch	Electric	Physical	75	100	15	Normal
Fire Punch	Fire	Physical	75	100	15	Normal
Ice Punch	Ice	Physical	75	100	15	Normal
Superpower	Fighting	Physical	120	100	5	Normal
Icy Wind	Ice	Special	55	95	15	Many Others
Aqua Tail	Water	Physical	90	90	10	Normal
Dragon Pulse	Dragon	Special	85	100	10	Normal
Iron Tail	Steel	Physical	100	75	15	Normal
Bind	Normal	Physical	15	85	20	Normal
Snore	Normal	Special	50	100	15	Normal
Heat Wave	Fire	Special	95	90	10	Many Others
Tailwind	Flying	Status	—	—	15	Your Side
Focus Punch	Fighting	Physical	150	100	20	Normal
Shock Wave	Electric	Special	60	—	20	Normal
Water Pulse	Water	Special	60	100	20	Normal
Outrage	Dragon	Physical	120	100	10	1 Random

MOVES TAUGHT BY PEOPLE

Name	Type	Kind	Pow.	Acc.	PP	Range
Draco Meteor	Dragon	Special	130	90	5	Normal

National Pokédex **150** Hoenn Pokédex —

Mewtwo

Genetic Pokémon

Psychic

HEIGHT: 6'07" WEIGHT: 269 lbs.

Gender unknown

Ω Mewtwo is a Pokémon that was created by genetic manipulation. However, even though the scientific power of humans created this Pokémon's body, they failed to endow Mewtwo with a compassionate heart.

α Mewtwo is a Pokémon that was created by genetic manipulation. However, even though the scientific power of humans created this Pokémon's body, they failed to endow Mewtwo with a compassionate heart.

ABILITY
Pressure

HIDDEN ABILITY
Unnerve

EGG GROUPS
No Eggs Discovered

STAT GROWTH RATES
HP ■■■■
Attack ■■■■■■
Defense ■■■■
Sp. Atk ■■■■■■■■
Sp. Def ■■■■
Speed ■■■■■■■

ITEMS SOMETIMES HELD BY WILD POKÉMON
—

EVOLUTION
Does not evolve

MAIN WAY TO REGISTER IN THE NATIONAL POKÉDEX

Appears in *Pokémon X* and *Pokémon Y*. Bring it to your game using Link Trade or the GTS.

Damage taken in normal battles

Type		Type	
Normal	×1	Flying	×1
Fire	×1	Psychic	×0.5
Water	×1	Bug	×2
Grass	×1	Rock	×1
Electric	×1	Ghost	×2
Ice	×1	Dragon	×1
Fighting	×0.5	Dark	×2
Poison	×1	Steel	×1
Ground	×1	Fairy	×1

Damage taken in Inverse battles

Type		Type	
Normal	×1	Flying	×1
Fire	×1	Psychic	×2
Water	×1	Bug	×0.5
Grass	×1	Rock	×1
Electric	×1	Ghost	×0.5
Ice	×1	Dragon	×1
Fighting	×2	Dark	×0.5
Poison	×1	Steel	×1
Ground	×1	Fairy	×1

Can be used in
- Inverse Battle
- Battle Institute
- Battle Maison
- Random Matchup (Free Battle)
- Random Matchup (Others)

LEVEL-UP MOVES

Lv.	Name	Type	Kind	Pow.	Acc.	PP	Range
1	Confusion	Psychic	Special	50	100	25	Normal
1	Disable	Normal	Status	—	100	20	Normal
1	Safeguard	Normal	Status	—	—	25	Your Side
8	Swift	Normal	Special	60	—	20	Many Others
15	Future Sight	Psychic	Special	120	100	10	Normal
22	Psych Up	Normal	Status	—	—	10	Normal
29	Miracle Eye	Psychic	Status	—	—	40	Normal
36	Psycho Cut	Psychic	Physical	70	100	20	Normal
43	Power Swap	Psychic	Status	—	—	10	Normal
43	Guard Swap	Psychic	Status	—	—	10	Normal
50	Recover	Normal	Status	—	—	10	Self
57	Psychic	Psychic	Special	90	100	10	Normal
64	Barrier	Psychic	Status	—	—	20	Self
70	Aura Sphere	Fighting	Special	80	—	20	Normal
79	Amnesia	Psychic	Status	—	—	20	Self
86	Mist	Ice	Status	—	—	30	Your Side
93	Me First	Normal	Status	—	—	20	Varies
100	Psystrike	Psychic	Special	100	100	10	Normal

TM & HM MOVES

No.	Name	Type	Kind	Pow.	Acc.	PP	Range
TM03	Psyshock	Psychic	Special	80	100	10	Normal
TM04	Calm Mind	Psychic	Status	—	—	20	Self
TM06	Toxic	Poison	Status	—	90	10	Normal
TM07	Hail	Ice	Status	—	—	10	Both Sides
TM08	Bulk Up	Fighting	Status	—	—	20	Self
TM10	Hidden Power	Normal	Special	60	100	15	Normal
TM11	Sunny Day	Fire	Status	—	—	5	Both Sides
TM12	Taunt	Dark	Status	—	100	20	Normal
TM13	Ice Beam	Ice	Special	90	100	10	Normal
TM14	Blizzard	Ice	Special	110	70	5	Many Others
TM15	Hyper Beam	Normal	Special	150	90	5	Normal
TM16	Light Screen	Psychic	Status	—	—	30	Your Side
TM17	Protect	Normal	Status	—	—	10	Self
TM18	Rain Dance	Water	Status	—	—	5	Both Sides
TM20	Safeguard	Normal	Status	—	—	25	Your Side
TM21	Frustration	Normal	Physical	—	100	20	Normal
TM22	Solar Beam	Grass	Special	120	100	10	Normal
TM24	Thunderbolt	Electric	Special	90	100	15	Normal
TM25	Thunder	Electric	Special	110	70	10	Normal
TM26	Earthquake	Ground	Physical	100	100	10	Adjacent
TM27	Return	Normal	Physical	—	100	20	Normal
TM29	Psychic	Psychic	Special	90	100	10	Normal
TM30	Shadow Ball	Ghost	Special	80	100	15	Normal
TM31	Brick Break	Fighting	Physical	75	100	15	Normal
TM32	Double Team	Normal	Status	—	—	15	Self
TM33	Reflect	Psychic	Status	—	—	20	Your Side
TM35	Flamethrower	Fire	Special	90	100	15	Normal
TM37	Sandstorm	Rock	Status	—	—	10	Both Sides
TM38	Fire Blast	Fire	Special	110	85	5	Normal
TM39	Rock Tomb	Rock	Physical	60	95	15	Normal
TM40	Aerial Ace	Flying	Physical	60	—	20	Normal
TM41	Torment	Dark	Status	—	100	15	Normal
TM42	Facade	Normal	Physical	70	100	20	Normal
TM44	Rest	Psychic	Status	—	—	10	Self
TM47	Low Sweep	Fighting	Physical	65	100	20	Normal
TM48	Round	Normal	Special	60	100	15	Normal
TM52	Focus Blast	Fighting	Special	120	70	5	Normal
TM53	Energy Ball	Grass	Special	90	100	10	Normal
TM56	Fling	Dark	Physical	—	100	10	Normal
TM57	Charge Beam	Electric	Special	50	90	10	Normal
TM59	Incinerate	Fire	Special	60	100	15	Many Others
TM61	Will-O-Wisp	Fire	Status	—	85	15	Normal
TM63	Embargo	Dark	Status	—	100	15	Normal
TM68	Giga Impact	Normal	Physical	150	90	5	Normal
TM70	Flash	Normal	Status	—	100	20	Normal
TM71	Stone Edge	Rock	Physical	100	80	5	Normal
TM73	Thunder Wave	Electric	Status	—	100	20	Normal
TM77	Psych Up	Normal	Status	—	—	10	Normal
TM78	Bulldoze	Ground	Physical	60	100	20	Adjacent
TM80	Rock Slide	Rock	Physical	75	90	10	Many Others
TM84	Poison Jab	Poison	Physical	80	100	20	Normal
TM85	Dream Eater	Psychic	Special	100	100	15	Normal
TM86	Grass Knot	Grass	Special	—	100	20	Normal
TM87	Swagger	Normal	Status	—	90	15	Normal
TM88	Sleep Talk	Normal	Status	—	—	10	Self
TM90	Substitute	Normal	Status	—	—	10	Self
TM92	Trick Room	Psychic	Status	—	—	5	Both Sides
TM94	Secret Power	Normal	Physical	70	100	20	Normal
TM98	Power-Up Punch	Fighting	Physical	40	100	20	Normal
TM100	Confide	Normal	Status	—	—	20	Normal
HM04	Strength	Normal	Physical	80	100	15	Normal
HM06	Rock Smash	Fighting	Physical	40	100	15	Normal
HM07	Dive	Water	Physical	80	100	10	Normal

MOVES LEARNED IN EXCHANGE FOR BP

Name	Type	Kind	Pow.	Acc.	PP	Range
Signal Beam	Bug	Special	75	100	15	Normal
Low Kick	Fighting	Physical	—	100	20	Normal
Thunder Punch	Electric	Physical	75	100	15	Normal
Fire Punch	Fire	Physical	75	100	15	Normal
Ice Punch	Ice	Physical	75	100	15	Normal
Magic Coat	Psychic	Status	—	—	15	Self
Foul Play	Dark	Physical	95	100	15	Normal
Gravity	Psychic	Status	—	—	5	Both Sides
Icy Wind	Ice	Special	55	95	15	Many Others
Aqua Tail	Water	Physical	90	90	10	Normal
Zen Headbutt	Psychic	Physical	80	90	15	Normal
Iron Tail	Steel	Physical	100	75	15	Normal
Snore	Normal	Special	50	100	15	Normal
Role Play	Psychic	Status	—	—	10	Normal
Drain Punch	Fighting	Physical	75	100	10	Normal
Focus Punch	Fighting	Physical	150	100	20	Normal
Shock Wave	Electric	Special	60	—	20	Normal
Water Pulse	Water	Special	60	100	20	Normal
Trick	Psychic	Status	—	100	10	Normal
Magic Room	Psychic	Status	—	—	10	Both Sides
Wonder Room	Psychic	Status	—	—	10	Both Sides
Recycle	Normal	Status	—	—	10	Self
Snatch	Dark	Status	—	—	10	Self
Skill Swap	Psychic	Status	—	—	10	Normal

MOVES TAUGHT BY PEOPLE

Name	Type	Kind	Pow.	Acc.	PP	Range

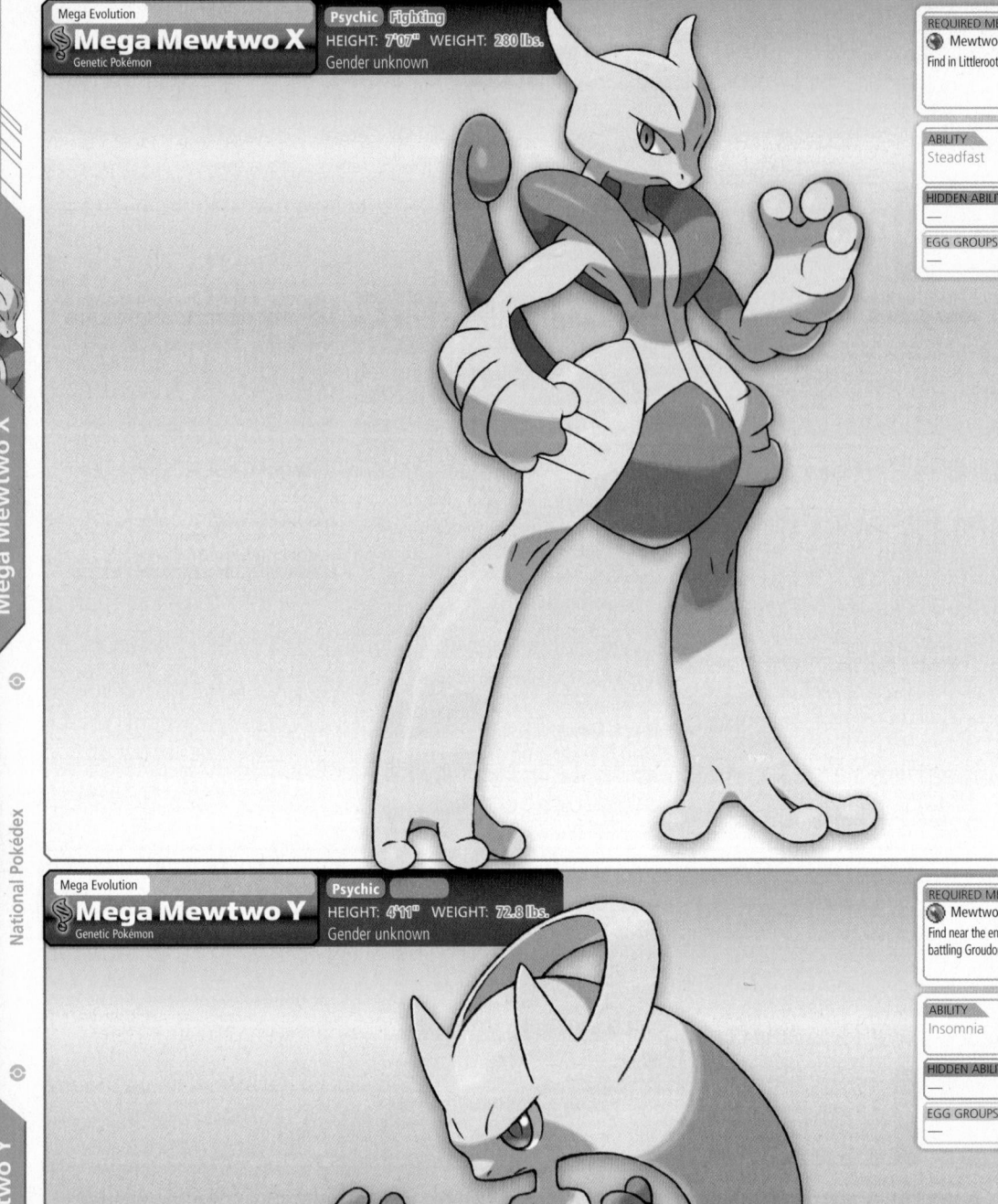

Mega Evolution

Mega Mewtwo X

Genetic Pokémon

Psychic Fighting

HEIGHT: 7'07" WEIGHT: 280 lbs.

Gender unknown

REQUIRED MEGA STONE

Mewtwonite X

Find in Littleroot Town (after battling Groudon or Kyogre).

ABILITY

Steadfast

HIDDEN ABILITY

—

EGG GROUPS

—

STAT GROWTH RATES

HP
Attack
Defense
Sp. Atk
Sp. Def
Speed

Damage taken in normal battles

Type		Type	
Normal	×1	Flying	×2
Fire	×1	Psychic	×1
Water	×1	Bug	×1
Grass	×1	Rock	×0.5
Electric	×1	Ghost	×2
Ice	×1	Dragon	×1
Fighting	×0.5	Dark	×1
Poison	×1	Steel	×1
Ground	×1	Fairy	×2

Damage taken in Inverse battles

Type		Type	
Normal	×1	Flying	×0.5
Fire	×1	Psychic	×1
Water	×1	Bug	×1
Grass	×1	Rock	×2
Electric	×1	Ghost	×0.5
Ice	×1	Dragon	×1
Fighting	×2	Dark	×1
Poison	×1	Steel	×1
Ground	×1	Fairy	×0.5

Can be used in

Inverse Battle
Battle Institute
Battle Maison
Random Matchup (Free Battle)
Random Matchup (Others)

Mega Evolution

Mega Mewtwo Y

Genetic Pokémon

Psychic

HEIGHT: 4'11" WEIGHT: 72.8 lbs.

Gender unknown

REQUIRED MEGA STONE

Mewtwonite Y

Find near the entrance of the Pokémon League (after battling Groudon or Kyogre).

ABILITY

Insomnia

HIDDEN ABILITY

—

EGG GROUPS

—

STAT GROWTH RATES

HP
Attack
Defense
Sp. Atk
Sp. Def
Speed

Damage taken in normal battles

Type		Type	
Normal	×1	Flying	×1
Fire	×1	Psychic	×0.5
Water	×1	Bug	×2
Grass	×1	Rock	×1
Electric	×1	Ghost	×2
Ice	×1	Dragon	×1
Fighting	×0.5	Dark	×2
Poison	×1	Steel	×1
Ground	×1	Fairy	×1

Damage taken in Inverse battles

Type		Type	
Normal	×1	Flying	×1
Fire	×1	Psychic	×2
Water	×1	Bug	×0.5
Grass	×1	Rock	×1
Electric	×1	Ghost	×0.5
Ice	×1	Dragon	×1
Fighting	×2	Dark	×0.5
Poison	×1	Steel	×1
Ground	×1	Fairy	×1

Can be used in

Inverse Battle
Battle Institute
Battle Maison
Random Matchup (Free Battle)
Random Matchup (Others)

National Pokédex **151** Hoenn Pokédex —

Mew

New Species Pokémon

Psychic

HEIGHT: 1'04" WEIGHT: 8.8 lbs.

Gender unknown

Ω Mew is said to possess the genetic composition of all Pokémon. It is capable of making itself invisible at will, so it entirely avoids notice even if it approaches people.

α Mew is said to possess the genetic composition of all Pokémon. It is capable of making itself invisible at will, so it entirely avoids notice even if it approaches people.

ABILITY
Synchronize

HIDDEN ABILITY
—

EGG GROUPS
No Eggs Discovered

STAT GROWTH RATES
HP ■■■■
Attack ■■■■■
Defense ■■■■
Sp. Atk ■■■■■
Sp. Def ■■■■
Speed ■■■■■

ITEMS SOMETIMES HELD BY WILD POKÉMON
—

EVOLUTION
Does not evolve

MAIN WAY TO REGISTER IN THE NATIONAL POKÉDEX

Previously obtainable through a special distribution. There may be more announcements to come regarding future opportunities to obtain it, so keep checking the official Pokémon website.

Damage taken in normal battles

Type		Type	
Normal	×1	Flying	×1
Fire	×1	Psychic	×0.5
Water	×1	Bug	×2
Grass	×1	Rock	×1
Electric	×1	Ghost	×2
Ice	×1	Dragon	×1
Fighting	×0.5	Dark	×2
Poison	×1	Steel	×1
Ground	×1	Fairy	×1

Damage taken in Inverse battles

Type		Type	
Normal	×1	Flying	×1
Fire	×1	Psychic	×2
Water	×1	Bug	×0.5
Grass	×1	Rock	×1
Electric	×1	Ghost	×0.5
Ice	×1	Dragon	×1
Fighting	×2	Dark	×0.5
Poison	×1	Steel	×1
Ground	×1	Fairy	×1

Can be used in
Inverse Battle
Battle Institute
Battle Maison
Random Matchup (Free Battle)
Random Matchup (Others)

LEVEL-UP MOVES

Lv.	Name	Type	Kind	Pow.	Acc.	PP	Range
1	Pound	Normal	Physical	40	100	35	Normal
1	Reflect Type	Normal	Status	—	—	15	Normal
1	Transform	Normal	Status	—	—	10	Normal
10	Mega Punch	Normal	Physical	80	85	20	Normal
20	Metronome	Normal	Status	—	—	10	Self
30	Psychic	Psychic	Special	90	100	10	Normal
40	Barrier	Psychic	Status	—	—	20	Self
50	Ancient Power	Rock	Special	60	100	5	Normal
60	Amnesia	Psychic	Status	—	—	20	Self
70	Me First	Normal	Status	—	—	20	Varies
80	Baton Pass	Normal	Status	—	—	40	Self
90	Nasty Plot	Dark	Status	—	—	20	Self
100	Aura Sphere	Fighting	Special	80	—	20	Normal

TM & HM MOVES

No.	Name	Type	Kind	Pow.	Acc.	PP	Range

Mew can learn all the moves taught with TMs and HMs.

MOVES LEARNED IN EXCHANGE FOR BP

Name	Type	Kind	Pow.	Acc.	PP	Range

Mew can learn all the moves taught for BPs.

MOVES TAUGHT BY PEOPLE

Name	Type	Kind	Pow.	Acc.	PP	Range

National Pokédex **152** Hoenn Pokédex —

Chikorita

Leaf Pokémon

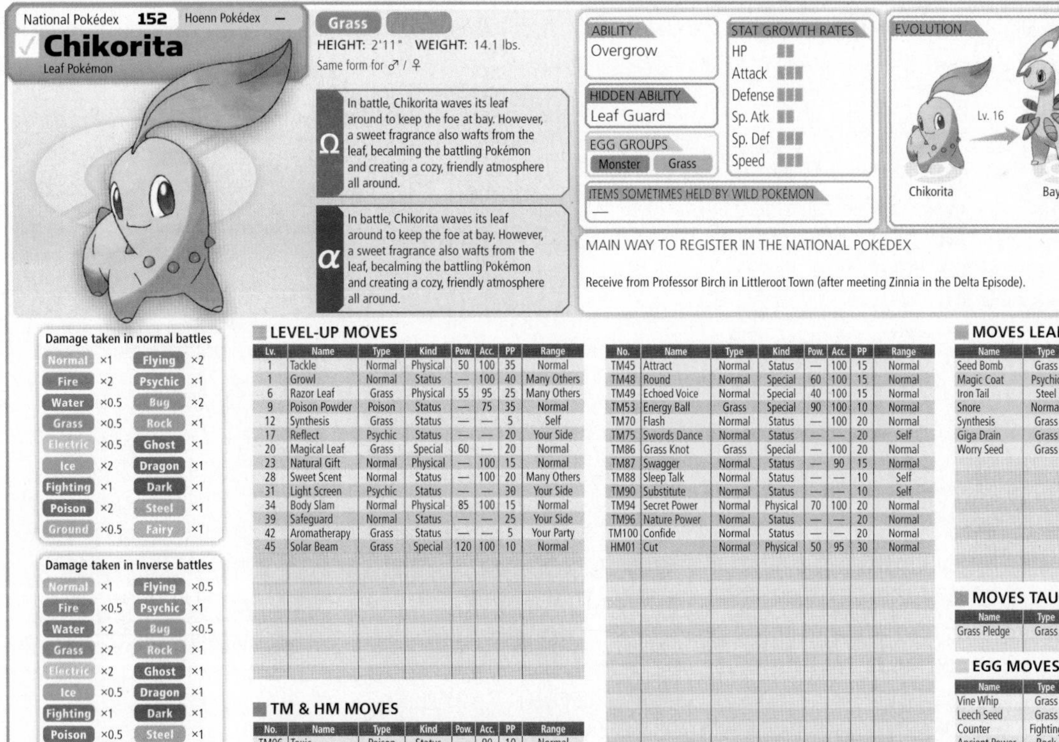

Grass

HEIGHT: 2'11" WEIGHT: 14.1 lbs.

Same form for ♂ / ♀

Ω In battle, Chikorita waves its leaf around to keep the foe at bay. However, a sweet fragrance also wafts from the leaf, becalming the battling Pokémon and creating a cozy, friendly atmosphere all around.

α In battle, Chikorita waves its leaf around to keep the foe at bay. However, a sweet fragrance also wafts from the leaf, becalming the battling Pokémon and creating a cozy, friendly atmosphere all around.

ABILITY
Overgrow

HIDDEN ABILITY
Leaf Guard

EGG GROUPS
Monster / Grass

STAT GROWTH RATES
HP ■■
Attack ■■■
Defense ■■■
Sp. Atk ■■
Sp. Def ■■■
Speed ■■■

ITEMS SOMETIMES HELD BY WILD POKÉMON
—

EVOLUTION
Chikorita → Lv. 16 → Bayleef → Lv. 32 → Meganium

MAIN WAY TO REGISTER IN THE NATIONAL POKÉDEX

Receive from Professor Birch in Littleroot Town (after meeting Zinnia in the Delta Episode).

Damage taken in normal battles

Type		Type	
Normal	×1	Flying	×2
Fire	×2	Psychic	×1
Water	×0.5	Bug	×2
Grass	×0.5	Rock	×1
Electric	×0.5	Ghost	×1
Ice	×2	Dragon	×1
Fighting	×1	Dark	×1
Poison	×2	Steel	×1
Ground	×0.5	Fairy	×1

Damage taken in Inverse battles

Type		Type	
Normal	×1	Flying	×0.5
Fire	×0.5	Psychic	×1
Water	×2	Bug	×0.5
Grass	×2	Rock	×1
Electric	×2	Ghost	×1
Ice	×0.5	Dragon	×1
Fighting	×1	Dark	×1
Poison	×0.5	Steel	×1
Ground	×2	Fairy	×1

Can be used in
Inverse Battle
Battle Institute
Battle Maison
Random Matchup (Free Battle)
Random Matchup (Others)

LEVEL-UP MOVES

Lv.	Name	Type	Kind	Pow.	Acc.	PP	Range
1	Tackle	Normal	Physical	50	100	35	Normal
1	Growl	Normal	Status	—	100	40	Many Others
6	Razor Leaf	Grass	Physical	55	95	25	Many Others
9	Poison Powder	Poison	Status	—	75	35	Normal
12	Synthesis	Grass	Status	—	—	5	Self
17	Reflect	Psychic	Status	—	—	20	Your Side
20	Magical Leaf	Grass	Special	60	—	20	Normal
23	Natural Gift	Normal	Physical	—	100	15	Normal
28	Sweet Scent	Normal	Status	—	100	20	Many Others
31	Light Screen	Psychic	Status	—	—	30	Your Side
34	Body Slam	Normal	Physical	85	100	15	Normal
39	Safeguard	Normal	Status	—	—	25	Your Side
42	Aromatherapy	Grass	Status	—	—	5	Your Party
45	Solar Beam	Grass	Special	120	100	10	Normal

TM & HM MOVES

No.	Name	Type	Kind	Pow.	Acc.	PP	Range
TM06	Toxic	Poison	Status	—	90	10	Normal
TM10	Hidden Power	Normal	Special	60	100	15	Normal
TM11	Sunny Day	Fire	Status	—	—	5	Both Sides
TM16	Light Screen	Psychic	Status	—	—	30	Your Side
TM17	Protect	Normal	Status	—	—	10	Self
TM20	Safeguard	Normal	Status	—	—	25	Your Side
TM21	Frustration	Normal	Physical	—	100	20	Normal
TM22	Solar Beam	Grass	Special	120	100	10	Normal
TM27	Return	Normal	Physical	—	100	20	Normal
TM32	Double Team	Normal	Status	—	—	15	Self
TM33	Reflect	Psychic	Status	—	—	20	Your Side
TM42	Facade	Normal	Physical	70	100	20	Normal
TM44	Rest	Psychic	Status	—	—	10	Self
TM45	Attract	Normal	Status	—	100	15	Normal
TM48	Round	Normal	Special	60	100	15	Normal
TM49	Echoed Voice	Normal	Special	40	100	15	Normal
TM53	Energy Ball	Grass	Special	90	100	10	Normal
TM70	Flash	Normal	Status	—	100	20	Normal
TM75	Swords Dance	Normal	Status	—	—	20	Self
TM86	Grass Knot	Grass	Special	—	100	20	Normal
TM87	Swagger	Normal	Status	—	90	15	Normal
TM88	Sleep Talk	Normal	Status	—	—	10	Self
TM90	Substitute	Normal	Status	—	—	10	Self
TM94	Secret Power	Normal	Physical	70	100	20	Normal
TM96	Nature Power	Normal	Status	—	—	20	Normal
TM100	Confide	Normal	Status	—	—	20	Normal
HM01	Cut	Normal	Physical	50	95	30	Normal

MOVES LEARNED IN EXCHANGE FOR BP

Name	Type	Kind	Pow.	Acc.	PP	Range
Seed Bomb	Grass	Physical	80	100	15	Normal
Magic Coat	Psychic	Status	—	—	15	Self
Iron Tail	Steel	Physical	100	75	15	Normal
Snore	Normal	Special	50	100	15	Normal
Synthesis	Grass	Status	—	—	5	Self
Giga Drain	Grass	Special	75	100	10	Normal
Worry Seed	Grass	Status	—	100	10	Normal

MOVES TAUGHT BY PEOPLE

Name	Type	Kind	Pow.	Acc.	PP	Range
Grass Pledge	Grass	Special	80	100	10	Normal

EGG MOVES

Name	Type	Kind	Pow.	Acc.	PP	Range
Vine Whip	Grass	Physical	45	100	25	Normal
Leech Seed	Grass	Status	—	90	10	Normal
Counter	Fighting	Physical	—	100	20	Varies
Ancient Power	Rock	Special	60	100	5	Normal
Flail	Normal	Physical	—	100	15	Normal
Nature Power	Normal	Status	—	—	20	Normal
Ingrain	Grass	Status	—	—	20	Self
Grass Whistle	Grass	Status	—	55	15	Normal
Leaf Storm	Grass	Special	130	90	5	Normal
Aromatherapy	Grass	Status	—	—	5	Your Party
Wring Out	Normal	Special	—	100	5	Normal
Body Slam	Normal	Physical	85	100	15	Normal
Refresh	Normal	Status	—	—	20	Self
Heal Pulse	Psychic	Status	—	—	10	Normal
Grassy Terrain	Grass	Status	—	—	10	Both Sides

National Pokédex **153** Hoenn Pokédex —

Bayleef

Leaf Pokémon

Grass

HEIGHT: 3'11" WEIGHT: 34.8 lbs.

Same form for ♂ / ♀

Ω Bayleef's neck is ringed by curled-up leaves. Inside each tubular leaf is a small shoot of a tree. The fragrance of this shoot makes people peppy.

α Bayleef's neck is ringed by curled-up leaves. Inside each tubular leaf is a small shoot of a tree. The fragrance of this shoot makes people peppy.

ABILITY
Overgrow

HIDDEN ABILITY
Leaf Guard

EGG GROUPS
Monster, Grass

STAT GROWTH RATES
HP
Attack
Defense
Sp. Atk
Sp. Def
Speed

ITEMS SOMETIMES HELD BY WILD POKÉMON
—

EVOLUTION
Chikorita → Lv. 16 → Bayleef → Lv. 32 → Meganium

MAIN WAY TO REGISTER IN THE NATIONAL POKÉDEX

Level up Chikorita to Lv. 16.

Damage taken in normal battles

Type		Type	
Normal	×1	Flying	×2
Fire	×2	Psychic	×1
Water	×0.5	Bug	×2
Grass	×0.5	Rock	×1
Electric	×0.5	Ghost	×1
Ice	×2	Dragon	×1
Fighting	×1	Dark	×1
Poison	×2	Steel	×1
Ground	×0.5	Fairy	×1

Damage taken in Inverse battles

Type		Type	
Normal	×1	Flying	×0.5
Fire	×0.5	Psychic	×1
Water	×2	Bug	×0.5
Grass	×2	Rock	×1
Electric	×2	Ghost	×1
Ice	×0.5	Dragon	×1
Fighting	×1	Dark	×1
Poison	×0.5	Steel	×1
Ground	×2	Fairy	×1

Can be used in
Inverse Battle
Battle Institute
Battle Maison
Random Matchup (Free Battle)
Random Matchup (Others)

LEVEL-UP MOVES

Lv.	Name	Type	Kind	Pow.	Acc.	PP	Range
1	Tackle	Normal	Physical	50	100	35	Normal
1	Growl	Normal	Status	—	100	40	Many Others
1	Razor Leaf	Grass	Physical	55	95	25	Many Others
1	Poison Powder	Poison	Status	—	75	35	Normal
6	Razor Leaf	Grass	Physical	55	95	25	Many Others
9	Poison Powder	Poison	Status	—	75	35	Normal
12	Synthesis	Grass	Status	—	—	5	Self
18	Reflect	Psychic	Status	—	—	20	Your Side
22	Magical Leaf	Grass	Special	60	—	20	Normal
26	Natural Gift	Normal	Physical	—	100	15	Normal
32	Sweet Scent	Normal	Status	—	100	20	Many Others
36	Light Screen	Psychic	Status	—	—	30	Your Side
40	Body Slam	Normal	Physical	85	100	15	Normal
46	Safeguard	Normal	Status	—	—	25	Your Side
50	Aromatherapy	Grass	Status	—	—	5	Your Party
54	Solar Beam	Grass	Special	120	100	10	Normal

TM & HM MOVES

No.	Name	Type	Kind	Pow.	Acc.	PP	Range
TM06	Toxic	Poison	Status	—	90	10	Normal
TM10	Hidden Power	Normal	Special	60	100	15	Normal
TM11	Sunny Day	Fire	Status	—	—	5	Both Sides
TM16	Light Screen	Psychic	Status	—	—	30	Your Side
TM17	Protect	Normal	Status	—	—	10	Self
TM20	Safeguard	Normal	Status	—	—	25	Your Side
TM21	Frustration	Normal	Physical	—	100	20	Normal
TM22	Solar Beam	Grass	Special	120	100	10	Normal
TM27	Return	Normal	Physical	—	100	20	Normal
TM32	Double Team	Normal	Status	—	—	15	Self
TM33	Reflect	Psychic	Status	—	—	20	Your Side
TM42	Facade	Normal	Physical	70	100	20	Normal
TM44	Rest	Psychic	Status	—	—	10	Self
TM45	Attract	Normal	Status	—	100	15	Normal
TM48	Round	Normal	Special	60	100	15	Normal
TM49	Echoed Voice	Normal	Special	40	100	15	Normal
TM53	Energy Ball	Grass	Special	90	100	10	Normal
TM70	Flash	Normal	Status	—	100	20	Normal
TM75	Swords Dance	Normal	Status	—	—	20	Self
TM86	Grass Knot	Grass	Special	—	100	20	Normal
TM87	Swagger	Normal	Status	—	90	15	Normal
TM88	Sleep Talk	Normal	Status	—	—	10	Self
TM90	Substitute	Normal	Status	—	—	10	Self
TM94	Secret Power	Normal	Physical	70	100	20	Normal
TM96	Nature Power	Normal	Status	—	—	20	Normal
TM100	Confide	Normal	Status	—	—	20	Normal
HM01	Cut	Normal	Physical	50	95	30	Normal
HM04	Strength	Normal	Physical	80	100	15	Normal
HM06	Rock Smash	Fighting	Physical	40	100	15	Normal

MOVES LEARNED IN EXCHANGE FOR BP

Name	Type	Kind	Pow.	Acc.	PP	Range
Seed Bomb	Grass	Physical	80	100	15	Normal
Magic Coat	Psychic	Status	—	—	15	Self
Iron Tail	Steel	Physical	100	75	15	Normal
Snore	Normal	Special	50	100	15	Normal
Synthesis	Grass	Status	—	—	5	Self
Giga Drain	Grass	Special	75	100	10	Normal
Worry Seed	Grass	Status	—	100	10	Normal

MOVES TAUGHT BY PEOPLE

Name	Type	Kind	Pow.	Acc.	PP	Range
Grass Pledge	Grass	Special	80	100	10	Normal

National Pokédex **154** Hoenn Pokédex —

Meganium

Herb Pokémon

Grass

HEIGHT: 5'11" WEIGHT: 221.6 lbs.

The male has longer feelers. The female has shorter feelers.

Ω The fragrance of Meganium's flower soothes and calms emotions. In battle, this Pokémon gives off more of its becalming scent to blunt the foe's fighting spirit.

α The fragrance of Meganium's flower soothes and calms emotions. In battle, this Pokémon gives off more of its becalming scent to blunt the foe's fighting spirit.

ABILITY
Overgrow

HIDDEN ABILITY
Leaf Guard

EGG GROUPS
Monster, Grass

STAT GROWTH RATES
HP
Attack
Defense
Sp. Atk
Sp. Def
Speed

ITEMS SOMETIMES HELD BY WILD POKÉMON
—

EVOLUTION
Chikorita → Lv. 16 → Bayleef → Lv. 32 → Meganium

MAIN WAY TO REGISTER IN THE NATIONAL POKÉDEX

Level up Bayleef to Lv. 32.

Damage taken in normal battles

Type		Type	
Normal	×1	Flying	×2
Fire	×2	Psychic	×1
Water	×0.5	Bug	×2
Grass	×0.5	Rock	×1
Electric	×0.5	Ghost	×1
Ice	×2	Dragon	×1
Fighting	×1	Dark	×1
Poison	×2	Steel	×1
Ground	×0.5	Fairy	×1

Damage taken in Inverse battles

Type		Type	
Normal	×1	Flying	×0.5
Fire	×0.5	Psychic	×1
Water	×2	Bug	×0.5
Grass	×2	Rock	×1
Electric	×2	Ghost	×1
Ice	×0.5	Dragon	×1
Fighting	×1	Dark	×1
Poison	×0.5	Steel	×1
Ground	×2	Fairy	×1

Can be used in
Inverse Battle
Battle Institute
Battle Maison
Random Matchup (Free Battle)
Random Matchup (Others)

LEVEL-UP MOVES

Lv.	Name	Type	Kind	Pow.	Acc.	PP	Range
1	Petal Blizzard	Grass	Physical	90	100	15	Adjacent
1	Tackle	Normal	Physical	50	100	35	Normal
1	Growl	Normal	Status	—	100	40	Many Others
1	Razor Leaf	Grass	Physical	55	95	25	Many Others
1	Poison Powder	Poison	Status	—	75	35	Normal
6	Razor Leaf	Grass	Physical	55	95	25	Many Others
9	Poison Powder	Poison	Status	—	75	35	Normal
12	Synthesis	Grass	Status	—	—	5	Self
18	Reflect	Psychic	Status	—	—	20	Your Side
22	Magical Leaf	Grass	Special	60	—	20	Normal
26	Natural Gift	Normal	Physical	—	100	15	Normal
32	Petal Dance	Grass	Special	120	100	10	1 Random
34	Sweet Scent	Normal	Status	—	100	20	Many Others
40	Light Screen	Psychic	Status	—	—	30	Your Side
46	Body Slam	Normal	Physical	85	100	15	Normal
54	Safeguard	Normal	Status	—	—	25	Your Side
60	Aromatherapy	Grass	Status	—	—	5	Your Party
66	Solar Beam	Grass	Special	120	100	10	Normal
70	Petal Blizzard	Grass	Physical	90	100	15	Adjacent

TM & HM MOVES

No.	Name	Type	Kind	Pow.	Acc.	PP	Range
TM06	Toxic	Poison	Status	—	90	10	Normal
TM10	Hidden Power	Normal	Special	60	100	15	Normal
TM11	Sunny Day	Fire	Status	—	—	5	Both Sides
TM15	Hyper Beam	Normal	Special	150	90	5	Normal
TM16	Light Screen	Psychic	Status	—	—	30	Your Side
TM17	Protect	Normal	Status	—	—	10	Self
TM20	Safeguard	Normal	Status	—	—	25	Your Side
TM21	Frustration	Normal	Physical	—	100	20	Normal
TM22	Solar Beam	Grass	Special	120	100	10	Normal
TM26	Earthquake	Ground	Physical	100	100	10	Adjacent
TM27	Return	Normal	Physical	—	100	20	Normal
TM32	Double Team	Normal	Status	—	—	15	Self
TM33	Reflect	Psychic	Status	—	—	20	Your Side
TM42	Facade	Normal	Physical	70	100	20	Normal
TM44	Rest	Psychic	Status	—	—	10	Self
TM45	Attract	Normal	Status	—	100	15	Normal
TM48	Round	Normal	Special	60	100	15	Normal
TM49	Echoed Voice	Normal	Special	40	100	15	Normal
TM53	Energy Ball	Grass	Special	90	100	10	Normal
TM68	Giga Impact	Normal	Physical	150	90	5	Normal
TM70	Flash	Normal	Status	—	100	20	Normal
TM75	Swords Dance	Normal	Status	—	—	20	Self
TM78	Bulldoze	Ground	Physical	60	100	20	Adjacent
TM82	Dragon Tail	Dragon	Physical	60	90	10	Normal
TM86	Grass Knot	Grass	Special	—	100	20	Normal
TM87	Swagger	Normal	Status	—	90	15	Normal
TM88	Sleep Talk	Normal	Status	—	—	10	Self
TM90	Substitute	Normal	Status	—	—	10	Self
TM94	Secret Power	Normal	Physical	70	100	20	Normal
TM96	Nature Power	Normal	Status	—	—	20	Normal
TM100	Confide	Normal	Status	—	—	20	Normal
HM01	Cut	Normal	Physical	50	95	30	Normal
HM04	Strength	Normal	Physical	80	100	15	Normal
HM06	Rock Smash	Fighting	Physical	40	100	15	Normal

MOVES LEARNED IN EXCHANGE FOR BP

Name	Type	Kind	Pow.	Acc.	PP	Range
Seed Bomb	Grass	Physical	80	100	15	Normal
Magic Coat	Psychic	Status	—	—	15	Self
Iron Tail	Steel	Physical	100	75	15	Normal
Snore	Normal	Special	50	100	15	Normal
Synthesis	Grass	Status	—	—	5	Self
Giga Drain	Grass	Special	75	100	10	Normal
Worry Seed	Grass	Status	—	100	10	Normal
Outrage	Dragon	Physical	120	100	10	1 Random

MOVES TAUGHT BY PEOPLE

Name	Type	Kind	Pow.	Acc.	PP	Range
Grass Pledge	Grass	Special	80	100	10	Normal
Frenzy Plant	Grass	Special	150	90	5	Normal

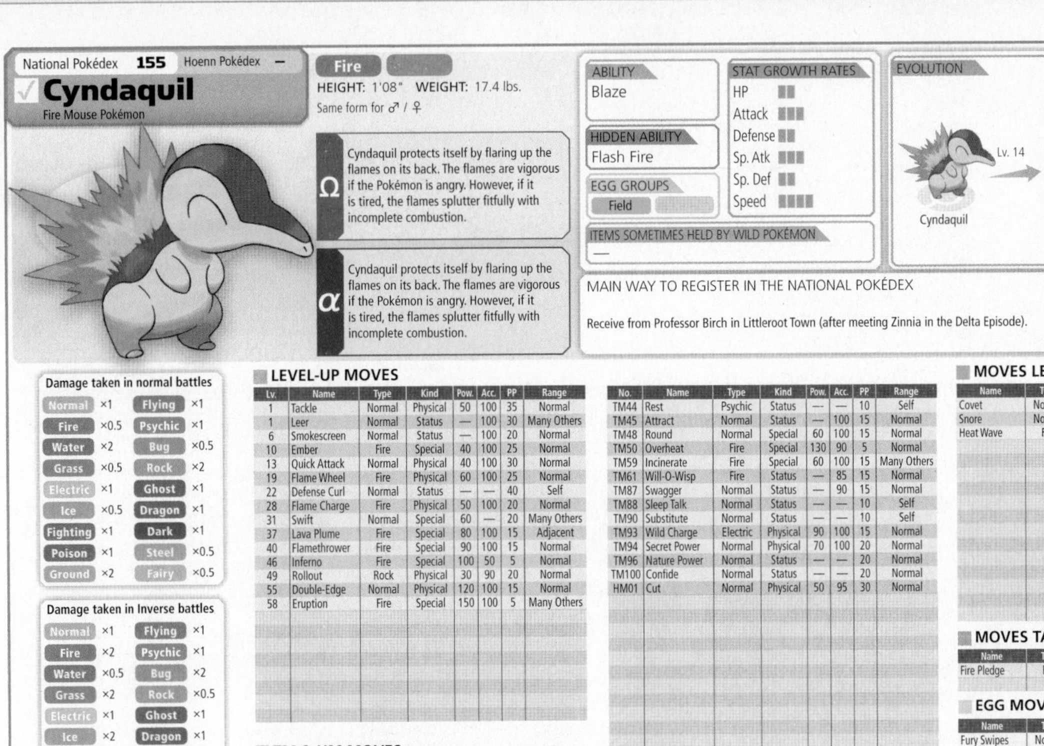

National Pokédex **155** Hoenn Pokédex —

Cyndaquil

Fire Mouse Pokémon

Fire

HEIGHT: 1'08" WEIGHT: 17.4 lbs.

Same form for ♂ / ♀

Ω Cyndaquil protects itself by flaring up the flames on its back. The flames are vigorous if the Pokémon is angry. However, if it is tired, the flames splutter fitfully with incomplete combustion.

α Cyndaquil protects itself by flaring up the flames on its back. The flames are vigorous if the Pokémon is angry. However, if it is tired, the flames splutter fitfully with incomplete combustion.

ABILITY: Blaze

HIDDEN ABILITY: Flash Fire

EGG GROUPS: Field

STAT GROWTH RATES: HP, Attack, Defense, Sp. Atk, Sp. Def, Speed

ITEMS SOMETIMES HELD BY WILD POKÉMON: —

EVOLUTION: Cyndaquil → Lv. 14 → Quilava → Lv. 36 → Typhlosion

MAIN WAY TO REGISTER IN THE NATIONAL POKÉDEX

Receive from Professor Birch in Littleroot Town (after meeting Zinnia in the Delta Episode).

Damage taken in normal battles

Type		Type	
Normal	×1	Flying	×1
Fire	×0.5	Psychic	×1
Water	×2	Bug	×0.5
Grass	×0.5	Rock	×2
Electric	×1	Ghost	×1
Ice	×0.5	Dragon	×1
Fighting	×1	Dark	×1
Poison	×1	Steel	×0.5
Ground	×2	Fairy	×0.5

Damage taken in Inverse battles

Type		Type	
Normal	×1	Flying	×1
Fire	×2	Psychic	×1
Water	×0.5	Bug	×2
Grass	×2	Rock	×0.5
Electric	×1	Ghost	×1
Ice	×2	Dragon	×1
Fighting	×1	Dark	×1
Poison	×1	Steel	×2
Ground	×0.5	Fairy	×2

Can be used in

Inverse Battle
Battle Institute
Battle Maison
Random Matchup (Free Battle)
Random Matchup (Others)

LEVEL-UP MOVES

Lv.	Name	Type	Kind	Pow.	Acc.	PP	Range
1	Tackle	Normal	Physical	50	100	35	Normal
1	Leer	Normal	Status	—	100	30	Many Others
6	Smokescreen	Normal	Status	—	100	20	Normal
10	Ember	Fire	Special	40	100	25	Normal
13	Quick Attack	Normal	Physical	40	100	30	Normal
19	Flame Wheel	Fire	Physical	60	100	25	Normal
22	Defense Curl	Normal	Status	—	—	40	Self
28	Flame Charge	Fire	Physical	50	100	20	Normal
31	Swift	Normal	Special	60	—	20	Many Others
37	Lava Plume	Fire	Special	80	100	15	Adjacent
40	Flamethrower	Fire	Special	90	100	15	Normal
46	Inferno	Fire	Special	100	50	5	Normal
49	Rollout	Rock	Physical	30	90	20	Normal
55	Double-Edge	Normal	Physical	120	100	15	Normal
58	Eruption	Fire	Special	150	100	5	Many Others

TM & HM MOVES

No.	Name	Type	Kind	Pow.	Acc.	PP	Range
TM06	Toxic	Poison	Status	—	90	10	Normal
TM10	Hidden Power	Normal	Special	60	100	15	Normal
TM11	Sunny Day	Fire	Status	—	—	5	Both Sides
TM17	Protect	Normal	Status	—	—	10	Self
TM21	Frustration	Normal	Physical	—	100	20	Normal
TM27	Return	Normal	Physical	—	100	20	Normal
TM28	Dig	Ground	Physical	80	100	10	Normal
TM32	Double Team	Normal	Status	—	—	15	Self
TM35	Flamethrower	Fire	Special	90	100	15	Normal
TM38	Fire Blast	Fire	Special	110	85	5	Normal
TM40	Aerial Ace	Flying	Physical	60	—	20	Normal
TM42	Facade	Normal	Physical	70	100	20	Normal
TM43	Flame Charge	Fire	Physical	50	100	20	Normal
TM44	Rest	Psychic	Status	—	—	10	Self
TM45	Attract	Normal	Status	—	100	15	Normal
TM48	Round	Normal	Special	60	100	15	Normal
TM50	Overheat	Fire	Special	130	90	5	Normal
TM59	Incinerate	Fire	Special	60	100	15	Many Others
TM61	Will-O-Wisp	Fire	Status	—	85	15	Normal
TM87	Swagger	Normal	Status	—	90	15	Normal
TM88	Sleep Talk	Normal	Status	—	—	10	Self
TM90	Substitute	Normal	Status	—	—	10	Self
TM93	Wild Charge	Electric	Physical	90	100	15	Normal
TM94	Secret Power	Normal	Physical	70	100	20	Normal
TM96	Nature Power	Normal	Status	—	—	20	Normal
TM100	Confide	Normal	Status	—	—	20	Normal
HM01	Cut	Normal	Physical	50	95	30	Normal

MOVES LEARNED IN EXCHANGE FOR BP

Name	Type	Kind	Pow.	Acc.	PP	Range
Covet	Normal	Physical	60	100	25	Normal
Snore	Normal	Special	50	100	15	Normal
Heat Wave	Fire	Special	95	90	10	Many Others

MOVES TAUGHT BY PEOPLE

Name	Type	Kind	Pow.	Acc.	PP	Range
Fire Pledge	Fire	Special	80	100	10	Normal

EGG MOVES

Name	Type	Kind	Pow.	Acc.	PP	Range
Fury Swipes	Normal	Physical	18	80	15	Normal
Quick Attack	Normal	Physical	40	100	30	Normal
Reversal	Fighting	Physical	—	100	15	Normal
Thrash	Normal	Physical	120	100	10	1 Random
Foresight	Normal	Status	—	—	40	Normal
Covet	Normal	Physical	60	100	25	Normal
Howl	Normal	Status	—	—	40	Self
Crush Claw	Normal	Physical	75	95	10	Normal
Double-Edge	Normal	Physical	120	100	15	Normal
Double Kick	Fighting	Physical	30	100	30	Normal
Flare Blitz	Fire	Physical	120	100	15	Normal
Extrasensory	Psychic	Special	80	100	20	Normal
Nature Power	Normal	Status	—	—	20	Normal
Flame Burst	Fire	Special	70	100	15	Normal

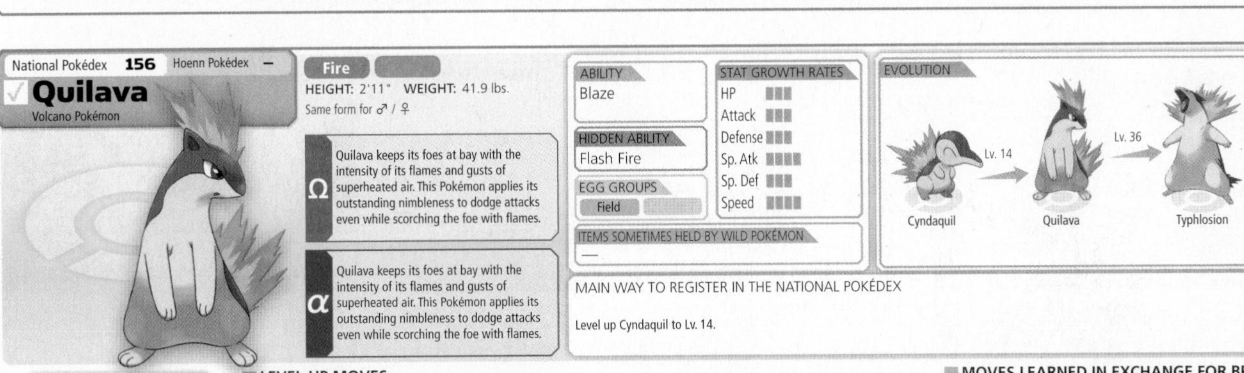

National Pokédex **156** Hoenn Pokédex —

Quilava

Volcano Pokémon

Fire

HEIGHT: 2'11" WEIGHT: 41.9 lbs.

Same form for ♂ / ♀

Ω Quilava keeps its foes at bay with the intensity of its flames and gusts of superheated air. This Pokémon applies its outstanding nimbleness to dodge attacks even while scorching the foe with flames.

α Quilava keeps its foes at bay with the intensity of its flames and gusts of superheated air. This Pokémon applies its outstanding nimbleness to dodge attacks even while scorching the foe with flames.

ABILITY: Blaze

HIDDEN ABILITY: Flash Fire

EGG GROUPS: Field

STAT GROWTH RATES: HP, Attack, Defense, Sp. Atk, Sp. Def, Speed

ITEMS SOMETIMES HELD BY WILD POKÉMON: —

EVOLUTION: Cyndaquil → Lv. 14 → Quilava → Lv. 36 → Typhlosion

MAIN WAY TO REGISTER IN THE NATIONAL POKÉDEX

Level up Cyndaquil to Lv. 14.

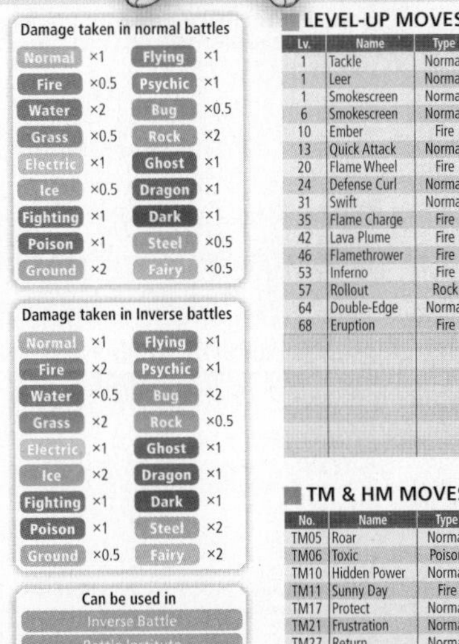

Damage taken in normal battles

Type		Type	
Normal	×1	Flying	×1
Fire	×0.5	Psychic	×1
Water	×2	Bug	×0.5
Grass	×0.5	Rock	×2
Electric	×1	Ghost	×1
Ice	×0.5	Dragon	×1
Fighting	×1	Dark	×1
Poison	×1	Steel	×0.5
Ground	×2	Fairy	×0.5

Damage taken in Inverse battles

Type		Type	
Normal	×1	Flying	×1
Fire	×2	Psychic	×1
Water	×0.5	Bug	×2
Grass	×2	Rock	×0.5
Electric	×1	Ghost	×1
Ice	×2	Dragon	×1
Fighting	×1	Dark	×1
Poison	×1	Steel	×2
Ground	×0.5	Fairy	×2

Can be used in

Inverse Battle
Battle Institute
Battle Maison
Random Matchup (Free Battle)
Random Matchup (Others)

LEVEL-UP MOVES

Lv.	Name	Type	Kind	Pow.	Acc.	PP	Range
1	Tackle	Normal	Physical	50	100	35	Normal
1	Leer	Normal	Status	—	100	30	Many Others
1	Smokescreen	Normal	Status	—	100	20	Normal
6	Smokescreen	Normal	Status	—	100	20	Normal
10	Ember	Fire	Special	40	100	25	Normal
13	Quick Attack	Normal	Physical	40	100	30	Normal
20	Flame Wheel	Fire	Physical	60	100	25	Normal
24	Defense Curl	Normal	Status	—	—	40	Self
31	Swift	Normal	Special	60	—	20	Many Others
35	Flame Charge	Fire	Physical	50	100	20	Normal
42	Lava Plume	Fire	Special	80	100	15	Adjacent
46	Flamethrower	Fire	Special	90	100	15	Normal
53	Inferno	Fire	Special	100	50	5	Normal
57	Rollout	Rock	Physical	30	90	20	Normal
64	Double-Edge	Normal	Physical	120	100	15	Normal
68	Eruption	Fire	Special	150	100	5	Many Others

TM & HM MOVES

No.	Name	Type	Kind	Pow.	Acc.	PP	Range
TM05	Roar	Normal	Status	—	—	20	Normal
TM06	Toxic	Poison	Status	—	90	10	Normal
TM10	Hidden Power	Normal	Special	60	100	15	Normal
TM11	Sunny Day	Fire	Status	—	—	5	Both Sides
TM17	Protect	Normal	Status	—	—	10	Self
TM21	Frustration	Normal	Physical	—	100	20	Normal
TM27	Return	Normal	Physical	—	100	20	Normal
TM28	Dig	Ground	Physical	80	100	10	Normal
TM31	Brick Break	Fighting	Physical	75	100	15	Normal
TM32	Double Team	Normal	Status	—	—	15	Self
TM35	Flamethrower	Fire	Special	90	100	15	Normal
TM38	Fire Blast	Fire	Special	110	85	5	Normal
TM40	Aerial Ace	Flying	Physical	60	—	20	Normal
TM42	Facade	Normal	Physical	70	100	20	Normal
TM43	Flame Charge	Fire	Physical	50	100	20	Normal
TM44	Rest	Psychic	Status	—	—	10	Self
TM45	Attract	Normal	Status	—	100	15	Normal
TM48	Round	Normal	Special	60	100	15	Normal
TM50	Overheat	Fire	Special	130	90	5	Normal
TM59	Incinerate	Fire	Special	60	100	15	Many Others
TM61	Will-O-Wisp	Fire	Status	—	85	15	Normal
TM87	Swagger	Normal	Status	—	90	15	Normal
TM88	Sleep Talk	Normal	Status	—	—	10	Self
TM90	Substitute	Normal	Status	—	—	10	Self
TM93	Wild Charge	Electric	Physical	90	100	15	Normal
TM94	Secret Power	Normal	Physical	70	100	20	Normal
TM96	Nature Power	Normal	Status	—	—	20	Normal
TM100	Confide	Normal	Status	—	—	20	Normal
HM01	Cut	Normal	Physical	50	95	30	Normal
HM04	Strength	Normal	Physical	80	100	15	Normal
HM06	Rock Smash	Fighting	Physical	40	100	15	Normal

MOVES LEARNED IN EXCHANGE FOR BP

Name	Type	Kind	Pow.	Acc.	PP	Range
Covet	Normal	Physical	60	100	25	Normal
Snore	Normal	Special	50	100	15	Normal
Heat Wave	Fire	Special	95	90	10	Many Others
Focus Punch	Fighting	Physical	150	100	20	Normal

MOVES TAUGHT BY PEOPLE

Name	Type	Kind	Pow.	Acc.	PP	Range
Fire Pledge	Fire	Special	80	100	10	Normal

National Pokédex **157** Hoenn Pokédex —

Typhlosion

Volcano Pokémon

Fire

HEIGHT: 5'07" WEIGHT: 175.3 lbs.

Same form for ♂ / ♀

Ω Typhlosion obscures itself behind a shimmering heat haze that it creates using its intensely hot flames. This Pokémon creates blazing explosive blasts that burn everything to cinders.

α Typhlosion obscures itself behind a shimmering heat haze that it creates using its intensely hot flames. This Pokémon creates blazing explosive blasts that burn everything to cinders.

ABILITY
Blaze

HIDDEN ABILITY
Flash Fire

EGG GROUPS
Field

STAT GROWTH RATES
HP
Attack
Defense
Sp. Atk
Sp. Def
Speed

ITEMS SOMETIMES HELD BY WILD POKÉMON
—

EVOLUTION
Cyndaquil → Lv. 14 → Quilava → Lv. 36 → Typhlosion

MAIN WAY TO REGISTER IN THE NATIONAL POKÉDEX

Level up Quilava to Lv. 36.

Damage taken in normal battles

Type		Type	
Normal	×1	Flying	×1
Fire	×0.5	Psychic	×1
Water	×2	Bug	×0.5
Grass	×0.5	Rock	×2
Electric	×1	Ghost	×1
Ice	×0.5	Dragon	×1
Fighting	×1	Dark	×1
Poison	×1	Steel	×0.5
Ground	×2	Fairy	×0.5

Damage taken in Inverse battles

Type		Type	
Normal	×1	Flying	×1
Fire	×2	Psychic	×1
Water	×0.5	Bug	×2
Grass	×2	Rock	×0.5
Electric	×1	Ghost	×1
Ice	×2	Dragon	×1
Fighting	×1	Dark	×1
Poison	×1	Steel	×2
Ground	×0.5	Fairy	×2

Can be used in

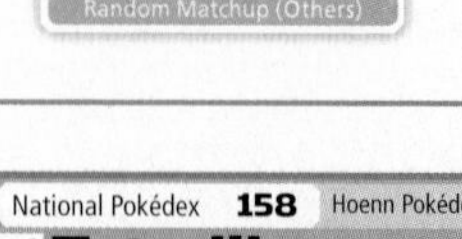

Inverse Battle
Battle Institute
Battle Maison
Random Matchup (Free Battle)
Random Matchup (Others)

LEVEL-UP MOVES

Lv.	Name	Type	Kind	Pow.	Acc.	PP	Range
1	Eruption	Fire	Special	150	100	5	Many Others
1	Double-Edge	Normal	Physical	120	100	15	Normal
1	Gyro Ball	Steel	Physical	—	100	5	Normal
1	Tackle	Normal	Physical	50	100	35	Normal
1	Leer	Normal	Status	—	100	30	Many Others
1	Smokescreen	Normal	Status	—	100	20	Normal
1	Ember	Fire	Special	40	100	25	Normal
6	Smokescreen	Normal	Status	—	100	20	Normal
10	Ember	Fire	Special	40	100	25	Normal
13	Quick Attack	Normal	Physical	40	100	30	Normal
20	Flame Wheel	Fire	Physical	60	100	25	Normal
24	Defense Curl	Normal	Status	—	—	40	Self
31	Swift	Normal	Special	60	—	20	Many Others
35	Flame Charge	Fire	Physical	50	100	20	Normal
43	Lava Plume	Fire	Special	80	100	15	Adjacent
48	Flamethrower	Fire	Special	90	100	15	Normal
56	Inferno	Fire	Special	100	50	5	Normal
61	Rollout	Rock	Physical	30	90	20	Normal
69	Double-Edge	Normal	Physical	120	100	15	Normal
74	Eruption	Fire	Special	150	100	5	Many Others

TM & HM MOVES

No.	Name	Type	Kind	Pow.	Acc.	PP	Range
TM05	Roar	Normal	Status	—	—	20	Normal
TM06	Toxic	Poison	Status	—	90	10	Normal
TM10	Hidden Power	Normal	Special	60	100	15	Normal
TM11	Sunny Day	Fire	Status	—	—	5	Both Sides
TM15	Hyper Beam	Normal	Special	150	90	5	Normal
TM17	Protect	Normal	Status	—	—	10	Self
TM21	Frustration	Normal	Physical	—	100	20	Normal
TM22	Solar Beam	Grass	Special	120	100	10	Normal
TM26	Earthquake	Ground	Physical	100	100	10	Adjacent
TM27	Return	Normal	Physical	—	100	20	Normal
TM28	Dig	Ground	Physical	80	100	10	Normal
TM31	Brick Break	Fighting	Physical	75	100	15	Normal
TM32	Double Team	Normal	Status	—	—	15	Self
TM35	Flamethrower	Fire	Special	90	100	15	Normal
TM38	Fire Blast	Fire	Special	110	85	5	Normal
TM39	Rock Tomb	Rock	Physical	60	95	15	Normal
TM40	Aerial Ace	Flying	Physical	60	—	20	Normal
TM42	Facade	Normal	Physical	70	100	20	Normal
TM43	Flame Charge	Fire	Physical	50	100	20	Normal
TM44	Rest	Psychic	Status	—	—	10	Self
TM45	Attract	Normal	Status	—	100	15	Normal
TM48	Round	Normal	Special	60	100	15	Normal
TM50	Overheat	Fire	Special	130	90	5	Normal
TM52	Focus Blast	Fighting	Special	120	70	5	Normal
TM56	Fling	Dark	Physical	—	100	10	Normal
TM59	Incinerate	Fire	Special	60	100	15	Many Others
TM61	Will-O-Wisp	Fire	Status	—	85	15	Normal
TM65	Shadow Claw	Ghost	Physical	70	100	15	Normal
TM68	Giga Impact	Normal	Physical	150	90	5	Normal
TM74	Gyro Ball	Steel	Physical	—	100	5	Normal
TM78	Bulldoze	Ground	Physical	60	100	20	Adjacent
TM80	Rock Slide	Rock	Physical	75	90	10	Many Others
TM87	Swagger	Normal	Status	—	90	15	Normal
TM88	Sleep Talk	Normal	Status	—	—	10	Self
TM90	Substitute	Normal	Status	—	—	10	Self
TM93	Wild Charge	Electric	Physical	90	100	15	Normal
TM94	Secret Power	Normal	Physical	70	100	20	Normal
TM96	Nature Power	Normal	Status	—	—	20	Normal
TM98	Power-Up Punch	Fighting	Physical	40	100	20	Normal
TM100	Confide	Normal	Status	—	—	20	Normal
HM01	Cut	Normal	Physical	50	95	30	Normal
HM04	Strength	Normal	Physical	80	100	15	Normal
HM06	Rock Smash	Fighting	Physical	40	100	15	Normal

MOVES LEARNED IN EXCHANGE FOR BP

Name	Type	Kind	Pow.	Acc.	PP	Range
Covet	Normal	Physical	60	100	25	Normal
Low Kick	Fighting	Physical	—	100	20	Normal
Thunder Punch	Electric	Physical	75	100	15	Normal
Fire Punch	Fire	Physical	75	100	15	Normal
Snore	Normal	Special	50	100	15	Normal
Heat Wave	Fire	Special	95	90	10	Many Others
Focus Punch	Fighting	Physical	150	100	20	Normal

MOVES TAUGHT BY PEOPLE

Name	Type	Kind	Pow.	Acc.	PP	Range
Fire Pledge	Fire	Special	80	100	10	Normal
Blast Burn	Fire	Special	150	90	5	Normal

National Pokédex **158** Hoenn Pokédex —

Totodile

Big Jaw Pokémon

Water

HEIGHT: 2'00" WEIGHT: 20.9 lbs.

Same form for ♂ / ♀

Ω Despite the smallness of its body, Totodile's jaws are very powerful. While the Pokémon may think it is just playfully nipping, its bite has enough power to cause serious injury.

α Despite the smallness of its body, Totodile's jaws are very powerful. While the Pokémon may think it is just playfully nipping, its bite has enough power to cause serious injury.

ABILITY
Torrent

HIDDEN ABILITY
Sheer Force

EGG GROUPS
Monster, Water 1

STAT GROWTH RATES
HP
Attack
Defense
Sp. Atk
Sp. Def
Speed

ITEMS SOMETIMES HELD BY WILD POKÉMON
—

EVOLUTION
Totodile → Lv. 18 → Croconaw → Lv. 30 → Feraligatr

MAIN WAY TO REGISTER IN THE NATIONAL POKÉDEX

Receive from Professor Birch in Littleroot Town (after meeting Zinnia in the Delta Episode).

Damage taken in normal battles

Type		Type	
Normal	×1	Flying	×1
Fire	×0.5	Psychic	×1
Water	×0.5	Bug	×1
Grass	×2	Rock	×1
Electric	×2	Ghost	×1
Ice	×0.5	Dragon	×1
Fighting	×1	Dark	×1
Poison	×1	Steel	×0.5
Ground	×1	Fairy	×1

Damage taken in Inverse battles

Type		Type	
Normal	×1	Flying	×1
Fire	×2	Psychic	×1
Water	×2	Bug	×1
Grass	×0.5	Rock	×1
Electric	×0.5	Ghost	×1
Ice	×2	Dragon	×1
Fighting	×1	Dark	×1
Poison	×1	Steel	×2
Ground	×1	Fairy	×1

Can be used in

Inverse Battle
Battle Institute
Battle Maison
Random Matchup (Free Battle)
Random Matchup (Others)

LEVEL-UP MOVES

Lv.	Name	Type	Kind	Pow.	Acc.	PP	Range
1	Scratch	Normal	Physical	40	100	35	Normal
1	Leer	Normal	Status	—	100	30	Many Others
6	Water Gun	Water	Special	40	100	25	Normal
8	Rage	Normal	Physical	20	100	20	Normal
13	Bite	Dark	Physical	60	100	25	Normal
15	Scary Face	Normal	Status	—	100	10	Normal
20	Ice Fang	Ice	Physical	65	95	15	Normal
22	Flail	Normal	Physical	—	100	15	Normal
27	Crunch	Dark	Physical	80	100	15	Normal
29	Chip Away	Normal	Physical	70	100	20	Normal
34	Slash	Normal	Physical	70	100	20	Normal
36	Screech	Normal	Status	—	85	40	Normal
41	Thrash	Normal	Physical	120	100	10	1 Random
43	Aqua Tail	Water	Physical	90	90	10	Normal
48	Superpower	Fighting	Physical	120	100	5	Normal
50	Hydro Pump	Water	Special	110	80	5	Normal

TM & HM MOVES

No.	Name	Type	Kind	Pow.	Acc.	PP	Range
TM01	Hone Claws	Dark	Status	—	—	15	Self
TM02	Dragon Claw	Dragon	Physical	80	100	15	Normal
TM06	Toxic	Poison	Status	—	90	10	Normal
TM07	Hail	Ice	Status	—	—	10	Both Sides
TM10	Hidden Power	Normal	Special	60	100	15	Normal
TM13	Ice Beam	Ice	Special	90	100	10	Normal
TM14	Blizzard	Ice	Special	110	70	5	Many Others
TM17	Protect	Normal	Status	—	—	10	Self
TM18	Rain Dance	Water	Status	—	—	5	Both Sides
TM21	Frustration	Normal	Physical	—	100	20	Normal
TM27	Return	Normal	Physical	—	100	20	Normal
TM28	Dig	Ground	Physical	80	100	10	Normal
TM31	Brick Break	Fighting	Physical	75	100	15	Normal
TM32	Double Team	Normal	Status	—	—	15	Self
TM39	Rock Tomb	Rock	Physical	60	95	15	Normal
TM40	Aerial Ace	Flying	Physical	60	—	20	Normal
TM42	Facade	Normal	Physical	70	100	20	Normal
TM44	Rest	Psychic	Status	—	—	10	Self
TM45	Attract	Normal	Status	—	100	15	Normal
TM48	Round	Normal	Special	60	100	15	Normal
TM55	Scald	Water	Special	80	100	15	Normal
TM56	Fling	Dark	Physical	—	100	10	Normal
TM65	Shadow Claw	Ghost	Physical	70	100	15	Normal
TM75	Swords Dance	Normal	Status	—	—	20	Self
TM80	Rock Slide	Rock	Physical	75	90	10	Many Others
TM87	Swagger	Normal	Status	—	90	15	Normal
TM88	Sleep Talk	Normal	Status	—	—	10	Self
TM90	Substitute	Normal	Status	—	—	10	Self
TM94	Secret Power	Normal	Physical	70	100	20	Normal
TM98	Power-Up Punch	Fighting	Physical	40	100	20	Normal
TM100	Confide	Normal	Status	—	—	20	Normal
HM01	Cut	Normal	Physical	50	95	30	Normal
HM03	Surf	Water	Special	90	100	15	Adjacent
HM05	Waterfall	Water	Physical	80	100	15	Normal
HM07	Dive	Water	Physical	80	100	10	Normal

MOVES LEARNED IN EXCHANGE FOR BP

Name	Type	Kind	Pow.	Acc.	PP	Range
Low Kick	Fighting	Physical	—	100	20	Normal
Uproar	Normal	Special	90	100	10	1 Random
Ice Punch	Ice	Physical	75	100	15	Normal
Block	Normal	Status	—	—	5	Normal
Superpower	Fighting	Physical	120	100	5	Normal
Icy Wind	Ice	Special	55	95	15	Many Others
Aqua Tail	Water	Physical	90	90	10	Normal
Iron Tail	Steel	Physical	100	75	15	Normal
Snore	Normal	Special	50	100	15	Normal
Focus Punch	Fighting	Physical	150	100	20	Normal
Water Pulse	Water	Special	60	100	20	Normal
Spite	Ghost	Status	—	100	10	Normal

MOVES TAUGHT BY PEOPLE

Name	Type	Kind	Pow.	Acc.	PP	Range
Water Pledge	Water	Special	80	100	10	Normal

EGG MOVES

Name	Type	Kind	Pow.	Acc.	PP	Range
Crunch	Dark	Physical	80	100	15	Normal
Thrash	Normal	Physical	120	100	10	1 Random
Hydro Pump	Water	Special	110	80	5	Normal
Ancient Power	Rock	Special	60	100	5	Normal
Mud Sport	Ground	Status	—	—	15	Both Sides
Water Sport	Water	Status	—	—	15	Both Sides
Ice Punch	Ice	Physical	75	100	15	Normal
Metal Claw	Steel	Physical	50	95	35	Normal
Dragon Dance	Dragon	Status	—	—	20	Self
Aqua Jet	Water	Physical	40	100	20	Normal
Fake Tears	Dark	Status	—	100	20	Normal
Block	Normal	Status	—	—	5	Normal
Water Pulse	Water	Special	60	100	20	Normal
Flatter	Dark	Status	—	100	15	Normal

National Pokédex **159** Hoenn Pokédex –

✓ Croconaw

Big Jaw Pokémon

Water

HEIGHT: 3'07" WEIGHT: 55.1 lbs.

Same form for ♂ / ♀

Ω Once Croconaw has clamped its jaws on its foe, it will absolutely not let go. Because the tips of its fangs are forked back like barbed fishhooks, they become impossible to remove when they have sunk in.

α Once Croconaw has clamped its jaws on its foe, it will absolutely not let go. Because the tips of its fangs are forked back like barbed fishhooks, they become impossible to remove when they have sunk in.

ABILITY
Torrent

HIDDEN ABILITY
Sheer Force

EGG GROUPS
Monster | Water 1

STAT GROWTH RATES
HP ■■■
Attack ■■■■
Defense ■■■■
Sp. Atk ■■■
Sp. Def ■■■
Speed ■■■

ITEMS SOMETIMES HELD BY WILD POKÉMON
—

EVOLUTION

MAIN WAY TO REGISTER IN THE NATIONAL POKÉDEX

Level up Totodile to Lv. 18.

Damage taken in normal battles

Type		Type	
Normal	×1	Flying	×1
Fire	×0.5	Psychic	×1
Water	×0.5	Bug	×1
Grass	×2	Rock	×1
Electric	×2	Ghost	×1
Ice	×0.5	Dragon	×1
Fighting	×1	Dark	×1
Poison	×1	Steel	×0.5
Ground	×1	Fairy	×1

Damage taken in Inverse battles

Type		Type	
Normal	×1	Flying	×1
Fire	×2	Psychic	×1
Water	×2	Bug	×1
Grass	×0.5	Rock	×1
Electric	×0.5	Ghost	×1
Ice	×2	Dragon	×1
Fighting	×1	Dark	×1
Poison	×1	Steel	×2
Ground	×1	Fairy	×1

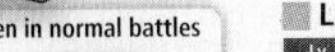

Can be used in
Inverse Battle
Battle Institute
Battle Maison
Random Matchup (Free Battle)
Random Matchup (Others)

LEVEL-UP MOVES

Lv.	Name	Type	Kind	Pow.	Acc.	PP	Range
1	Scratch	Normal	Physical	40	100	35	Normal
1	Leer	Normal	Status	—	100	30	Many Others
1	Water Gun	Water	Special	40	100	25	Normal
6	Water Gun	Water	Special	40	100	25	Normal
8	Rage	Normal	Physical	20	100	20	Normal
13	Bite	Dark	Physical	60	100	25	Normal
15	Scary Face	Normal	Status	—	100	10	Normal
21	Ice Fang	Ice	Physical	65	95	15	Normal
24	Flail	Normal	Physical	—	100	15	Normal
30	Crunch	Dark	Physical	80	100	15	Normal
33	Chip Away	Normal	Physical	70	100	20	Normal
39	Slash	Normal	Physical	70	100	20	Normal
42	Screech	Normal	Status	—	85	40	Normal
48	Thrash	Normal	Physical	120	100	10	1 Random
51	Aqua Tail	Water	Physical	90	90	10	Normal
57	Superpower	Fighting	Physical	120	100	5	Normal
60	Hydro Pump	Water	Special	110	80	5	Normal

TM & HM MOVES

No.	Name	Type	Kind	Pow.	Acc.	PP	Range
TM01	Hone Claws	Dark	Status	—	—	15	Self
TM02	Dragon Claw	Dragon	Physical	80	100	15	Normal
TM05	Roar	Normal	Status	—	—	20	Normal
TM06	Toxic	Poison	Status	—	90	10	Normal
TM07	Hail	Ice	Status	—	—	10	Both Sides
TM10	Hidden Power	Normal	Special	60	100	15	Normal
TM13	Ice Beam	Ice	Special	90	100	10	Normal
TM14	Blizzard	Ice	Special	110	70	5	Many Others
TM17	Protect	Normal	Status	—	—	10	Self
TM18	Rain Dance	Water	Status	—	—	5	Both Sides
TM21	Frustration	Normal	Physical	—	100	20	Normal
TM27	Return	Normal	Physical	—	100	20	Normal
TM28	Dig	Ground	Physical	80	100	10	Normal
TM31	Brick Break	Fighting	Physical	75	100	15	Normal
TM32	Double Team	Normal	Status	—	—	15	Self
TM39	Rock Tomb	Rock	Physical	60	95	15	Normal
TM40	Aerial Ace	Flying	Physical	60	—	20	Normal
TM42	Facade	Normal	Physical	70	100	20	Normal
TM44	Rest	Psychic	Status	—	—	10	Self
TM45	Attract	Normal	Status	—	100	15	Normal
TM48	Round	Normal	Special	60	100	15	Normal
TM55	Scald	Water	Special	80	100	15	Normal
TM56	Fling	Dark	Physical	—	100	10	Normal
TM65	Shadow Claw	Ghost	Physical	70	100	15	Normal
TM75	Swords Dance	Normal	Status	—	—	20	Self
TM80	Rock Slide	Rock	Physical	75	90	10	Many Others
TM87	Swagger	Normal	Status	—	90	15	Normal
TM88	Sleep Talk	Normal	Status	—	—	10	Self
TM90	Substitute	Normal	Status	—	—	10	Self
TM94	Secret Power	Normal	Physical	70	100	20	Normal
TM98	Power-Up Punch	Fighting	Physical	40	100	20	Normal
TM100	Confide	Normal	Status	—	—	20	Normal
HM01	Cut	Normal	Physical	50	95	30	Normal
HM03	Surf	Water	Special	90	100	15	Adjacent
HM04	Strength	Normal	Physical	80	100	15	Normal
HM05	Waterfall	Water	Physical	80	100	15	Normal
HM06	Rock Smash	Fighting	Physical	40	100	15	Normal
HM07	Dive	Water	Physical	80	100	10	Normal

MOVES LEARNED IN EXCHANGE FOR BP

Name	Type	Kind	Pow.	Acc.	PP	Range
Low Kick	Fighting	Physical	—	100	20	Normal
Uproar	Normal	Special	90	100	10	1 Random
Ice Punch	Ice	Physical	75	100	15	Normal
Block	Normal	Status	—	—	5	Normal
Superpower	Fighting	Physical	120	100	5	Normal
Icy Wind	Ice	Special	55	95	15	Many Others
Aqua Tail	Water	Physical	90	90	10	Normal
Iron Tail	Steel	Physical	100	75	15	Normal
Snore	Normal	Special	50	100	15	Normal
Focus Punch	Fighting	Physical	150	100	20	Normal
Water Pulse	Water	Special	60	100	20	Normal
Spite	Ghost	Status	—	100	10	Normal

MOVES TAUGHT BY PEOPLE

Name	Type	Kind	Pow.	Acc.	PP	Range
Water Pledge	Water	Special	80	100	10	Normal

National Pokédex **160** Hoenn Pokédex –

✓ Feraligatr

Big Jaw Pokémon

Water

HEIGHT: 7'07" WEIGHT: 195.8 lbs.

Same form for ♂ / ♀

Ω Feraligatr intimidates its foes by opening its huge mouth. In battle, it will kick the ground hard with its thick and powerful hind legs to charge at the foe at an incredible speed.

α Feraligatr intimidates its foes by opening its huge mouth. In battle, it will kick the ground hard with its thick and powerful hind legs to charge at the foe at an incredible speed.

ABILITY
Torrent

HIDDEN ABILITY
Sheer Force

EGG GROUPS
Monster | Water 1

STAT GROWTH RATES
HP ■■■
Attack ■■■■■
Defense ■■■■
Sp. Atk ■■■■
Sp. Def ■■■
Speed ■■■■

ITEMS SOMETIMES HELD BY WILD POKÉMON
—

EVOLUTION

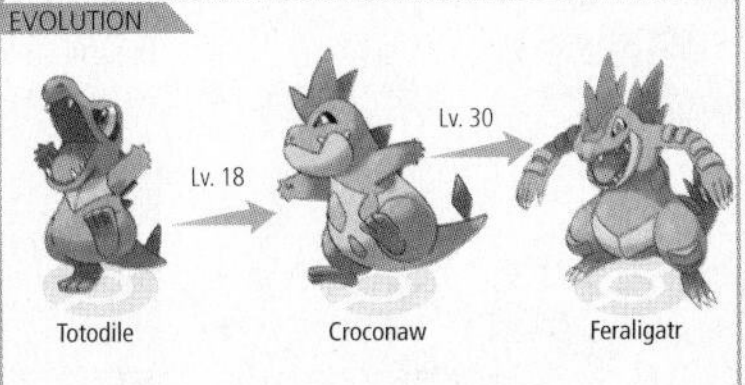

MAIN WAY TO REGISTER IN THE NATIONAL POKÉDEX

Level up Croconaw to Lv. 30.

Damage taken in normal battles

Type		Type	
Normal	×1	Flying	×1
Fire	×0.5	Psychic	×1
Water	×0.5	Bug	×1
Grass	×2	Rock	×1
Electric	×2	Ghost	×1
Ice	×0.5	Dragon	×1
Fighting	×1	Dark	×1
Poison	×1	Steel	×0.5
Ground	×1	Fairy	×1

Damage taken in Inverse battles

Type		Type	
Normal	×1	Flying	×1
Fire	×2	Psychic	×1
Water	×2	Bug	×1
Grass	×0.5	Rock	×1
Electric	×0.5	Ghost	×1
Ice	×2	Dragon	×1
Fighting	×1	Dark	×1
Poison	×1	Steel	×2
Ground	×1	Fairy	×1

Can be used in
Inverse Battle
Battle Institute
Battle Maison
Random Matchup (Free Battle)
Random Matchup (Others)

LEVEL-UP MOVES

Lv.	Name	Type	Kind	Pow.	Acc.	PP	Range
1	Scratch	Normal	Physical	40	100	35	Normal
1	Leer	Normal	Status	—	100	30	Many Others
1	Water Gun	Water	Special	40	100	25	Normal
1	Rage	Normal	Physical	20	100	20	Normal
6	Water Gun	Water	Special	40	100	25	Normal
8	Rage	Normal	Physical	20	100	20	Normal
13	Bite	Dark	Physical	60	100	25	Normal
15	Scary Face	Normal	Status	—	100	10	Normal
21	Ice Fang	Ice	Physical	65	95	15	Normal
24	Flail	Normal	Physical	—	100	15	Normal
30	Agility	Psychic	Status	—	—	30	Self
32	Crunch	Dark	Physical	80	100	15	Normal
37	Chip Away	Normal	Physical	70	100	20	Normal
45	Slash	Normal	Physical	70	100	20	Normal
50	Screech	Normal	Status	—	85	40	Normal
58	Thrash	Normal	Physical	120	100	10	1 Random
63	Aqua Tail	Water	Physical	90	90	10	Normal
71	Superpower	Fighting	Physical	120	100	5	Normal
76	Hydro Pump	Water	Special	110	80	5	Normal

TM & HM MOVES

No.	Name	Type	Kind	Pow.	Acc.	PP	Range
TM01	Hone Claws	Dark	Status	—	—	15	Self
TM02	Dragon Claw	Dragon	Physical	80	100	15	Normal
TM05	Roar	Normal	Status	—	—	20	Normal
TM06	Toxic	Poison	Status	—	90	10	Normal
TM07	Hail	Ice	Status	—	—	10	Both Sides
TM10	Hidden Power	Normal	Special	60	100	15	Normal
TM13	Ice Beam	Ice	Special	90	100	10	Normal
TM14	Blizzard	Ice	Special	110	70	5	Many Others
TM15	Hyper Beam	Normal	Special	150	90	5	Normal
TM17	Protect	Normal	Status	—	—	10	Self
TM18	Rain Dance	Water	Status	—	—	5	Both Sides
TM21	Frustration	Normal	Physical	—	100	20	Normal
TM26	Earthquake	Ground	Physical	100	100	10	Adjacent
TM27	Return	Normal	Physical	—	100	20	Normal
TM28	Dig	Ground	Physical	80	100	10	Normal
TM31	Brick Break	Fighting	Physical	75	100	15	Normal
TM32	Double Team	Normal	Status	—	—	15	Self
TM39	Rock Tomb	Rock	Physical	60	95	15	Normal
TM40	Aerial Ace	Flying	Physical	60	—	20	Normal
TM42	Facade	Normal	Physical	70	100	20	Normal
TM44	Rest	Psychic	Status	—	—	10	Self
TM45	Attract	Normal	Status	—	100	15	Normal
TM48	Round	Normal	Special	60	100	15	Normal
TM52	Focus Blast	Fighting	Special	120	70	5	Normal
TM55	Scald	Water	Special	80	100	15	Normal
TM56	Fling	Dark	Physical	—	100	10	Normal
TM65	Shadow Claw	Ghost	Physical	70	100	15	Normal
TM68	Giga Impact	Normal	Physical	150	90	5	Normal
TM75	Swords Dance	Normal	Status	—	—	20	Self
TM78	Bulldoze	Ground	Physical	60	100	20	Adjacent
TM80	Rock Slide	Rock	Physical	75	90	10	Many Others
TM82	Dragon Tail	Dragon	Physical	60	90	10	Normal
TM87	Swagger	Normal	Status	—	90	15	Normal
TM88	Sleep Talk	Normal	Status	—	—	10	Self
TM90	Substitute	Normal	Status	—	—	10	Self
TM94	Secret Power	Normal	Physical	70	100	20	Normal
TM98	Power-Up Punch	Fighting	Physical	40	100	20	Normal
TM100	Confide	Normal	Status	—	—	20	Normal
HM01	Cut	Normal	Physical	50	95	30	Normal
HM03	Surf	Water	Special	90	100	15	Adjacent
HM04	Strength	Normal	Physical	80	100	15	Normal
HM05	Waterfall	Water	Physical	80	100	15	Normal
HM06	Rock Smash	Fighting	Physical	40	100	15	Normal
HM07	Dive	Water	Physical	80	100	10	Normal

MOVES LEARNED IN EXCHANGE FOR BP

Name	Type	Kind	Pow.	Acc.	PP	Range
Low Kick	Fighting	Physical	—	100	20	Normal
Uproar	Normal	Special	90	100	10	1 Random
Ice Punch	Ice	Physical	75	100	15	Normal
Block	Normal	Status	—	—	5	Normal
Superpower	Fighting	Physical	120	100	5	Normal
Icy Wind	Ice	Special	55	95	15	Many Others
Aqua Tail	Water	Physical	90	90	10	Normal
Dragon Pulse	Dragon	Special	85	100	10	Normal
Iron Tail	Steel	Physical	100	75	15	Normal
Snore	Normal	Special	50	100	15	Normal
Focus Punch	Fighting	Physical	150	100	20	Normal
Water Pulse	Water	Special	60	100	20	Normal
Spite	Ghost	Status	—	100	10	Normal
Outrage	Dragon	Physical	120	100	10	1 Random

MOVES TAUGHT BY PEOPLE

Name	Type	Kind	Pow.	Acc.	PP	Range
Water Pledge	Water	Special	80	100	10	Normal
Hydro Cannon	Water	Special	150	90	5	Normal

National Pokédex **161** Hoenn Pokédex –

Sentret

Scout Pokémon

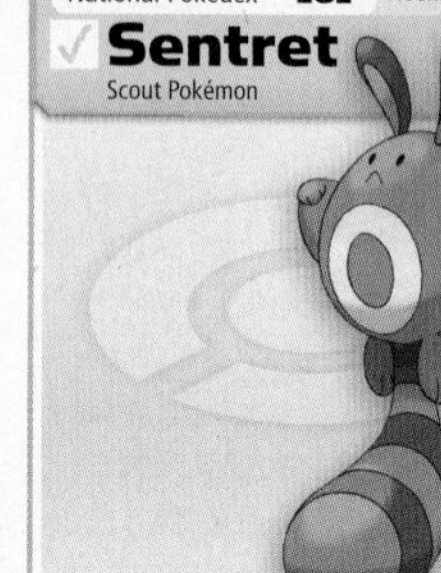

Normal

HEIGHT: 2'07" WEIGHT: 13.2 lbs.

Same form for ♂ / ♀

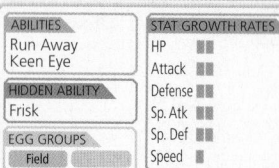

Ω When Sentret sleeps, it does so while another stands guard. The sentry wakes the others at the first sign of danger. When this Pokémon becomes separated from its pack, it becomes incapable of sleep due to fear.

α When Sentret sleeps, it does so while another stands guard. The sentry wakes the others at the first sign of danger. When this Pokémon becomes separated from its pack, it becomes incapable of sleep due to fear.

ABILITIES
Run Away
Keen Eye

HIDDEN ABILITY
Frisk

EGG GROUPS
Field

STAT GROWTH RATES
HP
Attack
Defense
Sp. Atk
Sp. Def
Speed

ITEMS SOMETIMES HELD BY WILD POKÉMON
—

EVOLUTION

Sentret → Furret

MAIN WAY TO REGISTER IN THE NATIONAL POKÉDEX

Appears in *Pokémon X* and *Pokémon Y*. Bring it to your game using Link Trade or the GTS.

Damage taken in normal battles

Type		Type	
Normal	×1	Flying	×1
Fire	×1	Psychic	×1
Water	×1	Bug	×1
Grass	×1	Rock	×1
Electric	×1	Ghost	×0
Ice	×1	Dragon	×1
Fighting	×2	Dark	×1
Poison	×1	Steel	×1
Ground	×1	Fairy	×1

Damage taken in Inverse battles

Type		Type	
Normal	×1	Flying	×1
Fire	×1	Psychic	×1
Water	×1	Bug	×1
Grass	×1	Rock	×1
Electric	×1	Ghost	×2
Ice	×1	Dragon	×1
Fighting	×0.5	Dark	×1
Poison	×1	Steel	×1
Ground	×1	Fairy	×1

Can be used in
Inverse Battle
Battle Institute
Battle Maison
Random Matchup (Free Battle)
Random Matchup (Others)

LEVEL-UP MOVES

Lv.	Name	Type	Kind	Pow.	Acc.	PP	Range
1	Scratch	Normal	Physical	40	100	35	Normal
1	Foresight	Normal	Status	—	—	40	Normal
4	Defense Curl	Normal	Status	—	—	40	Self
7	Quick Attack	Normal	Physical	40	100	30	Normal
13	Fury Swipes	Normal	Physical	18	80	15	Normal
16	Helping Hand	Normal	Status	—	—	20	1 Ally
19	Follow Me	Normal	Status	—	—	20	Self
25	Slam	Normal	Physical	80	75	20	Normal
28	Rest	Psychic	Status	—	—	10	Self
31	Sucker Punch	Dark	Physical	80	100	5	Normal
36	Amnesia	Psychic	Status	—	—	20	Self
39	Baton Pass	Normal	Status	—	—	40	Self
42	Me First	Normal	Status	—	—	20	Varies
47	Hyper Voice	Normal	Special	90	100	10	Many Others

TM & HM MOVES

No.	Name	Type	Kind	Pow.	Acc.	PP	Range
TM01	Hone Claws	Dark	Status	—	—	15	Self
TM06	Toxic	Poison	Status	—	90	10	Normal
TM10	Hidden Power	Normal	Special	60	100	15	Normal
TM11	Sunny Day	Fire	Status	—	—	5	Both Sides
TM13	Ice Beam	Ice	Special	90	100	10	Normal
TM17	Protect	Normal	Status	—	—	10	Self
TM18	Rain Dance	Water	Status	—	—	5	Both Sides
TM21	Frustration	Normal	Physical	—	100	20	Normal
TM22	Solar Beam	Grass	Special	120	100	10	Normal
TM24	Thunderbolt	Electric	Special	90	100	15	Normal
TM27	Return	Normal	Physical	—	100	20	Normal
TM28	Dig	Ground	Physical	80	100	10	Normal
TM30	Shadow Ball	Ghost	Special	80	100	15	Normal
TM31	Brick Break	Fighting	Physical	75	100	15	Normal
TM32	Double Team	Normal	Status	—	—	15	Self
TM35	Flamethrower	Fire	Special	90	100	15	Normal
TM42	Facade	Normal	Physical	70	100	20	Normal
TM44	Rest	Psychic	Status	—	—	10	Self
TM45	Attract	Normal	Status	—	100	15	Normal
TM46	Thief	Dark	Physical	60	100	25	Normal
TM48	Round	Normal	Special	60	100	15	Normal
TM49	Echoed Voice	Normal	Special	40	100	15	Normal
TM56	Fling	Dark	Physical	—	100	10	Normal
TM57	Charge Beam	Electric	Special	50	90	10	Normal
TM65	Shadow Claw	Ghost	Physical	70	100	15	Normal
TM67	Retaliate	Normal	Physical	70	100	5	Normal
TM86	Grass Knot	Grass	Special	—	100	20	Normal
TM87	Swagger	Normal	Status	—	90	15	Normal
TM88	Sleep Talk	Normal	Status	—	—	10	Self
TM89	U-turn	Bug	Physical	70	100	20	Normal
TM90	Substitute	Normal	Status	—	—	10	Self
TM94	Secret Power	Normal	Physical	70	100	20	Normal
TM98	Power-Up Punch	Fighting	Physical	40	100	20	Normal
TM100	Confide	Normal	Status	—	—	20	Normal
HM01	Cut	Normal	Physical	50	95	30	Normal
HM03	Surf	Water	Special	90	100	15	Adjacent

MOVES LEARNED IN EXCHANGE FOR BP

Name	Type	Kind	Pow.	Acc.	PP	Range
Covet	Normal	Physical	60	100	25	Normal
Super Fang	Normal	Physical	—	90	10	Normal
Uproar	Normal	Special	90	100	10	1 Random
Thunder Punch	Electric	Physical	75	100	15	Normal
Fire Punch	Fire	Physical	75	100	15	Normal
Ice Punch	Ice	Physical	75	100	15	Normal
Last Resort	Normal	Physical	140	100	5	Normal
Aqua Tail	Water	Physical	90	90	10	Normal
Hyper Voice	Normal	Special	90	100	10	Many Others
Iron Tail	Steel	Physical	100	75	15	Normal
Snore	Normal	Special	50	100	15	Normal
Knock Off	Dark	Physical	65	100	20	Normal
Focus Punch	Fighting	Physical	150	100	20	Normal
Shock Wave	Electric	Special	60	—	20	Normal
Water Pulse	Water	Special	60	100	20	Normal
Helping Hand	Normal	Status	—	—	20	1 Ally
Trick	Psychic	Status	—	100	10	Normal

MOVES TAUGHT BY PEOPLE

Name	Type	Kind	Pow.	Acc.	PP	Range

EGG MOVES

Name	Type	Kind	Pow.	Acc.	PP	Range
Double-Edge	Normal	Physical	120	100	15	Normal
Pursuit	Dark	Physical	40	100	20	Normal
Slash	Normal	Physical	70	100	20	Normal
Focus Energy	Normal	Status	—	—	30	Self
Reversal	Fighting	Physical	—	100	15	Normal
Trick	Psychic	Status	—	100	10	Normal
Assist	Normal	Status	—	—	20	Self
Last Resort	Normal	Physical	140	100	5	Normal
Charm	Fairy	Status	—	100	20	Normal
Covet	Normal	Physical	60	100	25	Normal
Natural Gift	Normal	Physical	—	100	15	Normal
Iron Tail	Steel	Physical	100	75	15	Normal
Captivate	Normal	Status	—	100	20	Many Others

National Pokédex **162** Hoenn Pokédex –

Furret

Long Body Pokémon

Normal

HEIGHT: 5'11" WEIGHT: 71.6 lbs.

Same form for ♂ / ♀

Ω Furret has a very slim build. When under attack, it can slickly squirm through narrow spaces and get away. In spite of its short limbs, this Pokémon is very nimble and fleet.

α Furret has a very slim build. When under attack, it can slickly squirm through narrow spaces and get away. In spite of its short limbs, this Pokémon is very nimble and fleet.

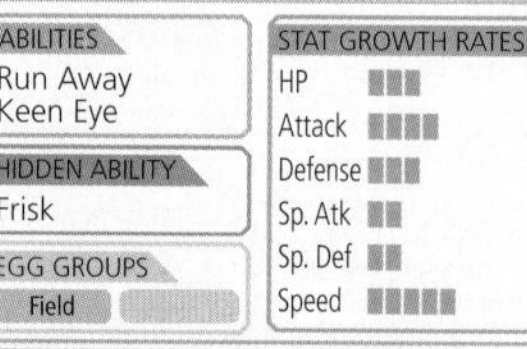

ABILITIES
Run Away
Keen Eye

HIDDEN ABILITY
Frisk

EGG GROUPS
Field

STAT GROWTH RATES
HP
Attack
Defense
Sp. Atk
Sp. Def
Speed

ITEMS SOMETIMES HELD BY WILD POKÉMON
—

EVOLUTION

Lv. 15

Sentret → Furret

MAIN WAY TO REGISTER IN THE NATIONAL POKÉDEX

Level up a Sentret obtained via Link Trade or the GTS to Lv. 15.

Damage taken in normal battles

Type		Type	
Normal	×1	Flying	×1
Fire	×1	Psychic	×1
Water	×1	Bug	×1
Grass	×1	Rock	×1
Electric	×1	Ghost	×0
Ice	×1	Dragon	×1
Fighting	×2	Dark	×1
Poison	×1	Steel	×1
Ground	×1	Fairy	×1

Damage taken in Inverse battles

Type		Type	
Normal	×1	Flying	×1
Fire	×1	Psychic	×1
Water	×1	Bug	×1
Grass	×1	Rock	×1
Electric	×1	Ghost	×2
Ice	×1	Dragon	×1
Fighting	×0.5	Dark	×1
Poison	×1	Steel	×1
Ground	×1	Fairy	×1

Can be used in
Inverse Battle
Battle Institute
Battle Maison
Random Matchup (Free Battle)
Random Matchup (Others)

LEVEL-UP MOVES

Lv.	Name	Type	Kind	Pow.	Acc.	PP	Range
1	Scratch	Normal	Physical	40	100	35	Normal
1	Foresight	Normal	Status	—	—	40	Normal
1	Defense Curl	Normal	Status	—	—	40	Self
1	Quick Attack	Normal	Physical	40	100	30	Normal
4	Defense Curl	Normal	Status	—	—	40	Self
7	Quick Attack	Normal	Physical	40	100	30	Normal
13	Fury Swipes	Normal	Physical	18	80	15	Normal
17	Helping Hand	Normal	Status	—	—	20	1 Ally
21	Follow Me	Normal	Status	—	—	20	Self
28	Slam	Normal	Physical	80	75	20	Normal
32	Rest	Psychic	Status	—	—	10	Self
36	Sucker Punch	Dark	Physical	80	100	5	Normal
42	Amnesia	Psychic	Status	—	—	20	Self
46	Baton Pass	Normal	Status	—	—	40	Self
50	Me First	Normal	Status	—	—	20	Varies
56	Hyper Voice	Normal	Special	90	100	10	Many Others

TM & HM MOVES

No.	Name	Type	Kind	Pow.	Acc.	PP	Range
TM01	Hone Claws	Dark	Status	—	—	15	Self
TM06	Toxic	Poison	Status	—	90	10	Normal
TM10	Hidden Power	Normal	Special	60	100	15	Normal
TM11	Sunny Day	Fire	Status	—	—	5	Both Sides
TM13	Ice Beam	Ice	Special	90	100	10	Normal
TM14	Blizzard	Ice	Special	110	70	5	Many Others
TM15	Hyper Beam	Normal	Special	150	90	5	Normal
TM17	Protect	Normal	Status	—	—	10	Self
TM18	Rain Dance	Water	Status	—	—	5	Both Sides
TM21	Frustration	Normal	Physical	—	100	20	Normal
TM22	Solar Beam	Grass	Special	120	100	10	Normal
TM24	Thunderbolt	Electric	Special	90	100	15	Normal
TM25	Thunder	Electric	Special	110	70	10	Normal
TM27	Return	Normal	Physical	—	100	20	Normal
TM28	Dig	Ground	Physical	80	100	10	Normal
TM30	Shadow Ball	Ghost	Special	80	100	15	Normal
TM31	Brick Break	Fighting	Physical	75	100	15	Normal
TM32	Double Team	Normal	Status	—	—	15	Self
TM35	Flamethrower	Fire	Special	90	100	15	Normal
TM42	Facade	Normal	Physical	70	100	20	Normal
TM44	Rest	Psychic	Status	—	—	10	Self
TM45	Attract	Normal	Status	—	100	15	Normal
TM46	Thief	Dark	Physical	60	100	25	Normal
TM48	Round	Normal	Special	60	100	15	Normal
TM49	Echoed Voice	Normal	Special	40	100	15	Normal
TM52	Focus Blast	Fighting	Special	120	70	5	Normal
TM56	Fling	Dark	Physical	—	100	10	Normal
TM57	Charge Beam	Electric	Special	50	90	10	Normal
TM65	Shadow Claw	Ghost	Physical	70	100	15	Normal
TM67	Retaliate	Normal	Physical	70	100	5	Normal
TM68	Giga Impact	Normal	Physical	150	90	5	Normal
TM86	Grass Knot	Grass	Special	—	100	20	Normal
TM87	Swagger	Normal	Status	—	90	15	Normal
TM88	Sleep Talk	Normal	Status	—	—	10	Self
TM89	U-turn	Bug	Physical	70	100	20	Normal
TM90	Substitute	Normal	Status	—	—	10	Self
TM94	Secret Power	Normal	Physical	70	100	20	Normal
TM98	Power-Up Punch	Fighting	Physical	40	100	20	Normal
TM100	Confide	Normal	Status	—	—	20	Normal
HM01	Cut	Normal	Physical	50	95	30	Normal
HM03	Surf	Water	Special	90	100	15	Adjacent
HM04	Strength	Normal	Physical	80	100	15	Normal
HM06	Rock Smash	Fighting	Physical	40	100	15	Normal

MOVES LEARNED IN EXCHANGE FOR BP

Name	Type	Kind	Pow.	Acc.	PP	Range
Covet	Normal	Physical	60	100	25	Normal
Super Fang	Normal	Physical	—	90	10	Normal
Uproar	Normal	Special	90	100	10	1 Random
Thunder Punch	Electric	Physical	75	100	15	Normal
Fire Punch	Fire	Physical	75	100	15	Normal
Ice Punch	Ice	Physical	75	100	15	Normal
Last Resort	Normal	Physical	140	100	5	Normal
Aqua Tail	Water	Physical	90	90	10	Normal
Hyper Voice	Normal	Special	90	100	10	Many Others
Iron Tail	Steel	Physical	100	75	15	Normal
Snore	Normal	Special	50	100	15	Normal
Knock Off	Dark	Physical	65	100	20	Normal
Focus Punch	Fighting	Physical	150	100	20	Normal
Shock Wave	Electric	Special	60	—	20	Normal
Water Pulse	Water	Special	60	100	20	Normal
Helping Hand	Normal	Status	—	—	20	1 Ally
Trick	Psychic	Status	—	100	10	Normal

MOVES TAUGHT BY PEOPLE

Name	Type	Kind	Pow.	Acc.	PP	Range

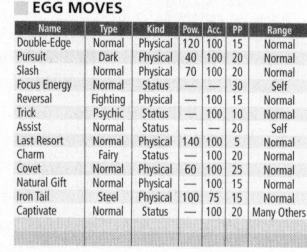

National Pokédex **163** Hoenn Pokédex —

✓ Hoothoot
Owl Pokémon

Normal | Flying

HEIGHT: 2'04" WEIGHT: 46.7 lbs.

Same form for ♂ / ♀

Ω Hoothoot has an internal organ that senses and tracks the earth's rotation. Using this special organ, this Pokémon begins hooting at precisely the same time every day.

α Hoothoot has an internal organ that senses and tracks the earth's rotation. Using this special organ, this Pokémon begins hooting at precisely the same time every day.

ABILITIES
Insomnia
Keen Eye

HIDDEN ABILITY
Tinted Lens

EGG GROUPS
Flying

STAT GROWTH RATES
HP ■■■
Attack ■■
Defense ■■
Sp. Atk ■■
Sp. Def ■■
Speed ■■■

ITEMS SOMETIMES HELD BY WILD POKÉMON
—

EVOLUTION

MAIN WAY TO REGISTER IN THE NATIONAL POKÉDEX

Leave a Noctowl obtained via Link Trade or the GTS at a Pokémon Day Care, then hatch the Pokémon Egg that is found.

Damage taken in normal battles

Type		Type	
Normal	×1	Flying	×1
Fire	×1	Psychic	×1
Water	×1	Bug	×0.5
Grass	×0.5	Rock	×2
Electric	×2	Ghost	×0
Ice	×2	Dragon	×1
Fighting	×1	Dark	×1
Poison	×1	Steel	×1
Ground	×0	Fairy	×1

Damage taken in Inverse battles

Type		Type	
Normal	×1	Flying	×1
Fire	×1	Psychic	×1
Water	×1	Bug	×2
Grass	×2	Rock	×0.5
Electric	×0.5	Ghost	×2
Ice	×0.5	Dragon	×1
Fighting	×1	Dark	×1
Poison	×1	Steel	×1
Ground	×2	Fairy	×1

Can be used in
Inverse Battle
Battle Institute
Battle Maison
Random Matchup (Free Battle)
Random Matchup (Others)

LEVEL-UP MOVES

Lv.	Name	Type	Kind	Pow.	Acc.	PP	Range
1	Tackle	Normal	Physical	50	100	35	Normal
1	Growl	Normal	Status	—	100	40	Many Others
1	Foresight	Normal	Status	—	—	40	Normal
5	Hypnosis	Psychic	Status	—	60	20	Normal
9	Peck	Flying	Physical	35	100	35	Normal
13	Uproar	Normal	Special	90	100	10	1 Random
17	Reflect	Psychic	Status	—	—	20	Your Side
21	Confusion	Psychic	Special	50	100	25	Normal
25	Echoed Voice	Normal	Special	40	100	15	Normal
29	Take Down	Normal	Physical	90	85	20	Normal
33	Air Slash	Flying	Special	75	95	15	Normal
37	Zen Headbutt	Psychic	Physical	80	90	15	Normal
41	Synchronoise	Psychic	Special	120	100	10	Adjacent
45	Extrasensory	Psychic	Special	80	100	20	Normal
49	Psycho Shift	Psychic	Status	—	100	10	Normal
53	Roost	Flying	Status	—	—	10	Self
57	Dream Eater	Psychic	Special	100	100	15	Normal

TM & HM MOVES

No.	Name	Type	Kind	Pow.	Acc.	PP	Range
TM06	Toxic	Poison	Status	—	90	10	Normal
TM10	Hidden Power	Normal	Special	60	100	15	Normal
TM11	Sunny Day	Fire	Status	—	—	5	Both Sides
TM17	Protect	Normal	Status	—	—	10	Self
TM18	Rain Dance	Water	Status	—	—	5	Both Sides
TM19	Roost	Flying	Status	—	—	10	Self
TM21	Frustration	Normal	Physical	—	100	20	Normal
TM27	Return	Normal	Physical	—	100	20	Normal
TM29	Psychic	Psychic	Special	90	100	10	Normal
TM30	Shadow Ball	Ghost	Special	80	100	15	Normal
TM32	Double Team	Normal	Status	—	—	15	Self
TM33	Reflect	Psychic	Status	—	—	20	Your Side
TM40	Aerial Ace	Flying	Physical	60	—	20	Normal
TM42	Facade	Normal	Physical	70	100	20	Normal
TM44	Rest	Psychic	Status	—	—	10	Self
TM45	Attract	Normal	Status	—	100	15	Normal
TM46	Thief	Dark	Physical	60	100	25	Normal
TM48	Round	Normal	Special	60	100	15	Normal
TM49	Echoed Voice	Normal	Special	40	100	15	Normal
TM51	Steel Wing	Steel	Physical	70	90	25	Normal
TM77	Psych Up	Normal	Status	—	—	10	Normal
TM85	Dream Eater	Psychic	Special	100	100	15	Normal
TM87	Swagger	Normal	Status	—	90	15	Normal
TM88	Sleep Talk	Normal	Status	—	—	10	Self
TM90	Substitute	Normal	Status	—	—	10	Self
TM94	Secret Power	Normal	Physical	70	100	20	Normal
TM100	Confide	Normal	Status	—	—	20	Normal
HM02	Fly	Flying	Physical	90	95	15	Normal

MOVES LEARNED IN EXCHANGE FOR BP

Name	Type	Kind	Pow.	Acc.	PP	Range
Uproar	Normal	Special	90	100	10	1 Random
Magic Coat	Psychic	Status	—	—	15	Self
Zen Headbutt	Psychic	Physical	80	90	15	Normal
Hyper Voice	Normal	Special	90	100	10	Many Others
Snore	Normal	Special	50	100	15	Normal
Heat Wave	Fire	Special	95	90	10	Many Others
Tailwind	Flying	Status	—	—	15	Your Side
Sky Attack	Flying	Physical	140	90	5	Normal
Recycle	Normal	Status	—	—	10	Self

MOVES TAUGHT BY PEOPLE

Name	Type	Kind	Pow.	Acc.	PP	Range

EGG MOVES

Name	Type	Kind	Pow.	Acc.	PP	Range
Mirror Move	Flying	Status	—	—	20	Normal
Supersonic	Normal	Status	—	55	20	Normal
Feint Attack	Dark	Physical	60	—	20	Normal
Wing Attack	Flying	Physical	60	100	35	Normal
Whirlwind	Normal	Status	—	—	20	Normal
Sky Attack	Flying	Physical	140	90	5	Normal
Feather Dance	Flying	Status	—	100	15	Normal
Agility	Psychic	Status	—	—	30	Self
Night Shade	Ghost	Special	—	100	15	Normal
Defog	Flying	Status	—	—	15	Normal

National Pokédex **164** Hoenn Pokédex —

✓ Noctowl
Owl Pokémon

Normal | Flying

HEIGHT: 5'03" WEIGHT: 89.9 lbs.

Same form for ♂ / ♀

Ω Noctowl never fails at catching prey in darkness. This Pokémon owes its success to its superior vision that allows it to see in minimal light, and to its soft, supple wings that make no sound in flight.

α Noctowl never fails at catching prey in darkness. This Pokémon owes its success to its superior vision that allows it to see in minimal light, and to its soft, supple wings that make no sound in flight.

ABILITIES
Insomnia
Keen Eye

HIDDEN ABILITY
Tinted Lens

EGG GROUPS
Flying

STAT GROWTH RATES
HP ■■■■
Attack ■■■
Defense ■■
Sp. Atk ■■■■
Sp. Def ■■■■
Speed ■■■■

ITEMS SOMETIMES HELD BY WILD POKÉMON
—

EVOLUTION

MAIN WAY TO REGISTER IN THE NATIONAL POKÉDEX

Appears in *Pokémon X* and *Pokémon Y*. Bring it to your game using Link Trade or the GTS.

Damage taken in normal battles

Type		Type	
Normal	×1	Flying	×1
Fire	×1	Psychic	×1
Water	×1	Bug	×0.5
Grass	×0.5	Rock	×2
Electric	×2	Ghost	×0
Ice	×2	Dragon	×1
Fighting	×1	Dark	×1
Poison	×1	Steel	×1
Ground	×0	Fairy	×1

Damage taken in Inverse battles

Type		Type	
Normal	×1	Flying	×1
Fire	×1	Psychic	×1
Water	×1	Bug	×2
Grass	×2	Rock	×0.5
Electric	×0.5	Ghost	×2
Ice	×0.5	Dragon	×1
Fighting	×1	Dark	×1
Poison	×1	Steel	×1
Ground	×2	Fairy	×1

Can be used in
Inverse Battle
Battle Institute
Battle Maison
Random Matchup (Free Battle)
Random Matchup (Others)

LEVEL-UP MOVES

Lv.	Name	Type	Kind	Pow.	Acc.	PP	Range
1	Dream Eater	Psychic	Special	100	100	15	Normal
1	Sky Attack	Flying	Physical	140	90	5	Normal
1	Tackle	Normal	Physical	50	100	35	Normal
1	Growl	Normal	Status	—	100	40	Many Others
1	Foresight	Normal	Status	—	—	40	Normal
1	Hypnosis	Psychic	Status	—	60	20	Normal
5	Hypnosis	Psychic	Status	—	60	20	Normal
9	Peck	Flying	Physical	35	100	35	Normal
13	Uproar	Normal	Special	90	100	10	1 Random
17	Reflect	Psychic	Status	—	—	20	Your Side
22	Confusion	Psychic	Special	50	100	25	Normal
27	Echoed Voice	Normal	Special	40	100	15	Normal
32	Take Down	Normal	Physical	90	85	20	Normal
37	Air Slash	Flying	Special	75	95	15	Normal
42	Zen Headbutt	Psychic	Physical	80	90	15	Normal
47	Synchronoise	Psychic	Special	120	100	10	Adjacent
52	Extrasensory	Psychic	Special	80	100	20	Normal
57	Psycho Shift	Psychic	Status	—	100	10	Normal
62	Roost	Flying	Status	—	—	10	Self
67	Dream Eater	Psychic	Special	100	100	15	Normal

TM & HM MOVES

No.	Name	Type	Kind	Pow.	Acc.	PP	Range
TM06	Toxic	Poison	Status	—	90	10	Normal
TM10	Hidden Power	Normal	Special	60	100	15	Normal
TM11	Sunny Day	Fire	Status	—	—	5	Both Sides
TM15	Hyper Beam	Normal	Special	150	90	5	Normal
TM17	Protect	Normal	Status	—	—	10	Self
TM18	Rain Dance	Water	Status	—	—	5	Both Sides
TM19	Roost	Flying	Status	—	—	10	Self
TM21	Frustration	Normal	Physical	—	100	20	Normal
TM27	Return	Normal	Physical	—	100	20	Normal
TM29	Psychic	Psychic	Special	90	100	10	Normal
TM30	Shadow Ball	Ghost	Special	80	100	15	Normal
TM32	Double Team	Normal	Status	—	—	15	Self
TM33	Reflect	Psychic	Status	—	—	20	Your Side
TM40	Aerial Ace	Flying	Physical	60	—	20	Normal
TM42	Facade	Normal	Physical	70	100	20	Normal
TM44	Rest	Psychic	Status	—	—	10	Self
TM45	Attract	Normal	Status	—	100	15	Normal
TM46	Thief	Dark	Physical	60	100	25	Normal
TM48	Round	Normal	Special	60	100	15	Normal
TM49	Echoed Voice	Normal	Special	40	100	15	Normal
TM51	Steel Wing	Steel	Physical	70	90	25	Normal
TM68	Giga Impact	Normal	Physical	150	90	5	Normal
TM77	Psych Up	Normal	Status	—	—	10	Normal
TM85	Dream Eater	Psychic	Special	100	100	15	Normal
TM87	Swagger	Normal	Status	—	90	15	Normal
TM88	Sleep Talk	Normal	Status	—	—	10	Self
TM90	Substitute	Normal	Status	—	—	10	Self
TM94	Secret Power	Normal	Physical	70	100	20	Normal
TM100	Confide	Normal	Status	—	—	20	Normal
HM02	Fly	Flying	Physical	90	95	15	Normal

MOVES LEARNED IN EXCHANGE FOR BP

Name	Type	Kind	Pow.	Acc.	PP	Range
Uproar	Normal	Special	90	100	10	1 Random
Magic Coat	Psychic	Status	—	—	15	Self
Zen Headbutt	Psychic	Physical	80	90	15	Normal
Hyper Voice	Normal	Special	90	100	10	Many Others
Snore	Normal	Special	50	100	15	Normal
Heat Wave	Fire	Special	95	90	10	Many Others
Tailwind	Flying	Status	—	—	15	Your Side
Sky Attack	Flying	Physical	140	90	5	Normal
Recycle	Normal	Status	—	—	10	Self

MOVES TAUGHT BY PEOPLE

Name	Type	Kind	Pow.	Acc.	PP	Range

National Pokédex **165** Hoenn Pokédex —

Ledyba

Five Star Pokémon

♂ ♀

Bug | Flying

HEIGHT: 3'03" WEIGHT: 23.8 lbs.

The male has longer antennae. The female has shorter antennae.

Ω Ledyba secretes an aromatic fluid from where its legs join its body. This fluid is used for communicating with others. This Pokémon conveys its feelings to others by altering the fluid's scent.

α Ledyba secretes an aromatic fluid from where its legs join its body. This fluid is used for communicating with others. This Pokémon conveys its feelings to others by altering the fluid's scent.

ABILITIES
Swarm
Early Bird

HIDDEN ABILITY
Rattled

EGG GROUPS
Bug

STAT GROWTH RATES
HP ■■
Attack ■
Defense ■■
Sp. Atk ■■
Sp. Def ■■■
Speed ■■■

ITEMS SOMETIMES HELD BY WILD POKÉMON
—

EVOLUTION

Ledyba → Lv. 18 → Ledian

MAIN WAY TO REGISTER IN THE NATIONAL POKÉDEX

Appears in *Pokémon X* and *Pokémon Y*. Bring it to your game using Link Trade or the GTS.

Damage taken in normal battles

Type		Type	
Normal	×1	Flying	×2
Fire	×2	Psychic	×1
Water	×1	Bug	×0.5
Grass	×0.25	Rock	×4
Electric	×2	Ghost	×1
Ice	×2	Dragon	×1
Fighting	×0.25	Dark	×1
Poison	×1	Steel	×1
Ground	×0	Fairy	×1

Damage taken in Inverse battles

Type		Type	
Normal	×1	Flying	×0.5
Fire	×0.5	Psychic	×1
Water	×1	Bug	×2
Grass	×4	Rock	×0.25
Electric	×0.5	Ghost	×1
Ice	×0.5	Dragon	×1
Fighting	×4	Dark	×1
Poison	×1	Steel	×1
Ground	×4	Fairy	×1

Can be used in
Inverse Battle
Battle Institute
Battle Maison
Random Matchup (Free Battle)
Random Matchup (Others)

LEVEL-UP MOVES

Lv.	Name	Type	Kind	Pow.	Acc.	PP	Range
1	Tackle	Normal	Physical	50	100	35	Normal
6	Supersonic	Normal	Status	—	55	20	Normal
9	Comet Punch	Normal	Physical	18	85	15	Normal
14	Light Screen	Psychic	Status	—	—	30	Your Side
14	Reflect	Psychic	Status	—	—	20	Your Side
14	Safeguard	Normal	Status	—	—	25	Your Side
17	Mach Punch	Fighting	Physical	40	100	30	Normal
22	Baton Pass	Normal	Status	—	—	40	Self
25	Silver Wind	Bug	Special	60	100	5	Normal
30	Agility	Psychic	Status	—	—	30	Self
33	Swift	Normal	Special	60	—	20	Many Others
38	Double-Edge	Normal	Physical	120	100	15	Normal
41	Bug Buzz	Bug	Special	90	100	10	Normal

TM & HM MOVES

No.	Name	Type	Kind	Pow.	Acc.	PP	Range
TM06	Toxic	Poison	Status	—	90	10	Normal
TM10	Hidden Power	Normal	Special	60	100	15	Normal
TM11	Sunny Day	Fire	Status	—	—	5	Both Sides
TM16	Light Screen	Psychic	Status	—	—	30	Your Side
TM17	Protect	Normal	Status	—	—	10	Self
TM19	Roost	Flying	Status	—	—	10	Self
TM20	Safeguard	Normal	Status	—	—	25	Your Side
TM21	Frustration	Normal	Physical	—	100	20	Normal
TM22	Solar Beam	Grass	Special	120	100	10	Normal
TM27	Return	Normal	Physical	—	100	20	Normal
TM28	Dig	Ground	Physical	80	100	10	Normal
TM31	Brick Break	Fighting	Physical	75	100	15	Normal
TM32	Double Team	Normal	Status	—	—	15	Self
TM33	Reflect	Psychic	Status	—	—	20	Your Side
TM40	Aerial Ace	Flying	Physical	60	—	20	Normal
TM42	Facade	Normal	Physical	70	100	20	Normal
TM44	Rest	Psychic	Status	—	—	10	Self
TM45	Attract	Normal	Status	—	100	15	Normal
TM46	Thief	Dark	Physical	60	100	25	Normal
TM48	Round	Normal	Special	60	100	15	Normal
TM56	Fling	Dark	Physical	—	100	10	Normal
TM62	Acrobatics	Flying	Physical	55	100	15	Normal
TM70	Flash	Normal	Status	—	100	20	Normal
TM75	Swords Dance	Normal	Status	—	—	20	Self
TM76	Struggle Bug	Bug	Special	50	100	20	Many Others
TM83	Infestation	Bug	Special	20	100	20	Normal
TM87	Swagger	Normal	Status	—	90	15	Normal
TM88	Sleep Talk	Normal	Status	—	—	10	Self
TM89	U-turn	Bug	Physical	70	100	20	Normal
TM90	Substitute	Normal	Status	—	—	10	Self
TM94	Secret Power	Normal	Physical	70	100	20	Normal
TM98	Power-Up Punch	Fighting	Physical	40	100	20	Normal
TM100	Confide	Normal	Status	—	—	20	Normal

MOVES LEARNED IN EXCHANGE FOR BP

Name	Type	Kind	Pow.	Acc.	PP	Range
Bug Bite	Bug	Physical	60	100	20	Normal
Uproar	Normal	Special	90	100	10	1 Random
Thunder Punch	Electric	Physical	75	100	15	Normal
Ice Punch	Ice	Physical	75	100	15	Normal
Snore	Normal	Special	50	100	15	Normal
Knock Off	Dark	Physical	65	100	20	Normal
Tailwind	Flying	Status	—	—	15	Your Side
Giga Drain	Grass	Special	75	100	10	Normal
Drain Punch	Fighting	Physical	75	100	10	Normal
Focus Punch	Fighting	Physical	150	100	20	Normal

MOVES TAUGHT BY PEOPLE

Name	Type	Kind	Pow.	Acc.	PP	Range

EGG MOVES

Name	Type	Kind	Pow.	Acc.	PP	Range
Psybeam	Psychic	Special	65	100	20	Normal
Bide	Normal	Physical	—	—	10	Self
Silver Wind	Bug	Special	60	100	5	Normal
Bug Buzz	Bug	Special	90	100	10	Normal
Screech	Normal	Status	—	85	40	Normal
Encore	Normal	Status	—	100	5	Normal
Knock Off	Dark	Physical	65	100	20	Normal
Bug Bite	Bug	Physical	60	100	20	Normal
Focus Punch	Fighting	Physical	150	100	20	Normal
Drain Punch	Fighting	Physical	75	100	10	Normal
Dizzy Punch	Normal	Physical	70	100	10	Normal
Tailwind	Flying	Status	—	—	15	Your Side

National Pokédex **166** Hoenn Pokédex —

Ledian

Five Star Pokémon

♂ ♀

Bug | Flying

HEIGHT: 4'07" WEIGHT: 78.5 lbs.

The male has longer antennae. The female has shorter antennae.

Ω It is said that in lands with clean air, where the stars fill the sky, there live Ledian in countless numbers. There is a good reason for this—the Pokémon uses the light of the stars as its energy.

α It is said that in lands with clean air, where the stars fill the sky, there live Ledian in countless numbers. There is a good reason for this—the Pokémon uses the light of the stars as its energy.

ABILITIES
Swarm
Early Bird

HIDDEN ABILITY
Iron Fist

EGG GROUPS
Bug

STAT GROWTH RATES
HP ■■
Attack ■■
Defense ■■
Sp. Atk ■■■
Sp. Def ■■■■■
Speed ■■■■■

ITEMS SOMETIMES HELD BY WILD POKÉMON
—

EVOLUTION

Ledyba → Lv. 18 → Ledian

MAIN WAY TO REGISTER IN THE NATIONAL POKÉDEX

Level up a Ledyba obtained via Link Trade or the GTS to Lv. 18.

Damage taken in normal battles

Type		Type	
Normal	×1	Flying	×2
Fire	×2	Psychic	×1
Water	×1	Bug	×0.5
Grass	×0.25	Rock	×4
Electric	×2	Ghost	×1
Ice	×2	Dragon	×1
Fighting	×0.25	Dark	×1
Poison	×1	Steel	×1
Ground	×0	Fairy	×1

Damage taken in Inverse battles

Type		Type	
Normal	×1	Flying	×0.5
Fire	×0.5	Psychic	×1
Water	×1	Bug	×2
Grass	×4	Rock	×0.25
Electric	×0.5	Ghost	×1
Ice	×0.5	Dragon	×1
Fighting	×4	Dark	×1
Poison	×1	Steel	×1
Ground	×4	Fairy	×1

Can be used in
Inverse Battle
Battle Institute
Battle Maison
Random Matchup (Free Battle)
Random Matchup (Others)

LEVEL-UP MOVES

Lv.	Name	Type	Kind	Pow.	Acc.	PP	Range
1	Tackle	Normal	Physical	50	100	35	Normal
1	Supersonic	Normal	Status	—	55	20	Normal
1	Comet Punch	Normal	Physical	18	85	15	Normal
6	Supersonic	Normal	Status	—	55	20	Normal
9	Comet Punch	Normal	Physical	18	85	15	Normal
14	Light Screen	Psychic	Status	—	—	30	Your Side
14	Reflect	Psychic	Status	—	—	20	Your Side
14	Safeguard	Normal	Status	—	—	25	Your Side
17	Mach Punch	Fighting	Physical	40	100	30	Normal
24	Baton Pass	Normal	Status	—	—	40	Self
29	Silver Wind	Bug	Special	60	100	5	Normal
36	Agility	Psychic	Status	—	—	30	Self
41	Swift	Normal	Special	60	—	20	Many Others
48	Double-Edge	Normal	Physical	120	100	15	Normal
53	Bug Buzz	Bug	Special	90	100	10	Normal

TM & HM MOVES

No.	Name	Type	Kind	Pow.	Acc.	PP	Range
TM06	Toxic	Poison	Status	—	90	10	Normal
TM10	Hidden Power	Normal	Special	60	100	15	Normal
TM11	Sunny Day	Fire	Status	—	—	5	Both Sides
TM15	Hyper Beam	Normal	Special	150	90	5	Normal
TM16	Light Screen	Psychic	Status	—	—	30	Your Side
TM17	Protect	Normal	Status	—	—	10	Self
TM19	Roost	Flying	Status	—	—	10	Self
TM20	Safeguard	Normal	Status	—	—	25	Your Side
TM21	Frustration	Normal	Physical	—	100	20	Normal
TM22	Solar Beam	Grass	Special	120	100	10	Normal
TM27	Return	Normal	Physical	—	100	20	Normal
TM28	Dig	Ground	Physical	80	100	10	Normal
TM31	Brick Break	Fighting	Physical	75	100	15	Normal
TM32	Double Team	Normal	Status	—	—	15	Self
TM33	Reflect	Psychic	Status	—	—	20	Your Side
TM40	Aerial Ace	Flying	Physical	60	—	20	Normal
TM42	Facade	Normal	Physical	70	100	20	Normal
TM44	Rest	Psychic	Status	—	—	10	Self
TM45	Attract	Normal	Status	—	100	15	Normal
TM46	Thief	Dark	Physical	60	100	25	Normal
TM48	Round	Normal	Special	60	100	15	Normal
TM52	Focus Blast	Fighting	Special	120	70	5	Normal
TM56	Fling	Dark	Physical	—	100	10	Normal
TM62	Acrobatics	Flying	Physical	55	100	15	Normal
TM68	Giga Impact	Normal	Physical	150	90	5	Normal
TM70	Flash	Normal	Status	—	100	20	Normal
TM75	Swords Dance	Normal	Status	—	—	20	Self
TM76	Struggle Bug	Bug	Special	50	100	20	Many Others
TM83	Infestation	Bug	Special	20	100	20	Normal
TM87	Swagger	Normal	Status	—	90	15	Normal
TM88	Sleep Talk	Normal	Status	—	—	10	Self
TM89	U-turn	Bug	Physical	70	100	20	Normal
TM90	Substitute	Normal	Status	—	—	10	Self
TM94	Secret Power	Normal	Physical	70	100	20	Normal
TM98	Power-Up Punch	Fighting	Physical	40	100	20	Normal
TM100	Confide	Normal	Status	—	—	20	Normal
HM04	Strength	Normal	Physical	80	100	15	Normal
HM06	Rock Smash	Fighting	Physical	40	100	15	Normal

MOVES LEARNED IN EXCHANGE FOR BP

Name	Type	Kind	Pow.	Acc.	PP	Range
Bug Bite	Bug	Physical	60	100	20	Normal
Uproar	Normal	Special	90	100	10	1 Random
Thunder Punch	Electric	Physical	75	100	15	Normal
Ice Punch	Ice	Physical	75	100	15	Normal
Snore	Normal	Special	50	100	15	Normal
Knock Off	Dark	Physical	65	100	20	Normal
Tailwind	Flying	Status	—	—	15	Your Side
Giga Drain	Grass	Special	75	100	10	Normal
Drain Punch	Fighting	Physical	75	100	10	Normal
Focus Punch	Fighting	Physical	150	100	20	Normal

MOVES TAUGHT BY PEOPLE

Name	Type	Kind	Pow.	Acc.	PP	Range

National Pokédex **167** Hoenn Pokédex —

Spinarak

String Spit Pokémon

Bug Poison

HEIGHT: 1'08" WEIGHT: 18.7 lbs.

Same form for ♂ / ♀

Ω The web spun by Spinarak can be considered its second nervous system. It is said that this Pokémon can determine what kind of prey is touching its web just by the tiny vibrations it feels through the web's strands.

α The web spun by Spinarak can be considered its second nervous system. It is said that this Pokémon can determine what kind of prey is touchingt its web just by the tiny vibrations it feels through the web's strands.

ABILITIES: Swarm, Insomnia

HIDDEN ABILITY: Sniper

EGG GROUPS: Bug

STAT GROWTH RATES: HP ■■ / Attack ■■■ / Defense ■■ / Sp. Atk ■■ / Sp. Def ■■ / Speed ■■

ITEMS SOMETIMES HELD BY WILD POKÉMON: —

EVOLUTION

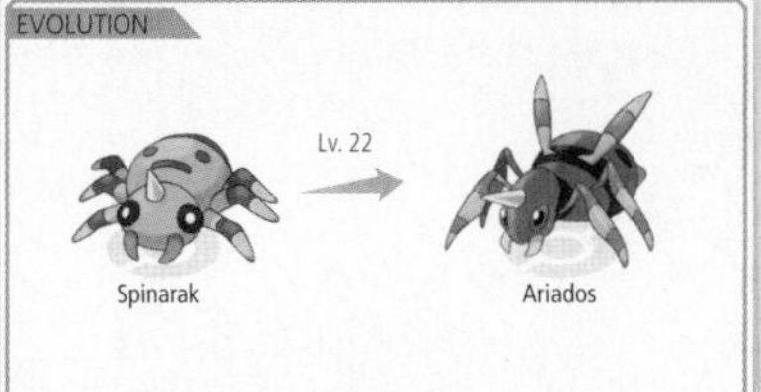

MAIN WAY TO REGISTER IN THE NATIONAL POKÉDEX

Leave an Ariados at a Pokémon Day Care, then hatch the Pokémon Egg that is found.

Damage taken in normal battles

Normal	×1	Flying	×2
Fire	×2	Psychic	×2
Water	×1	Bug	×0.5
Grass	×0.25	Rock	×2
Electric	×1	Ghost	×1
Ice	×1	Dragon	×1
Fighting	×0.25	Dark	×1
Poison	×0.5	Steel	×1
Ground	×1	Fairy	×0.5

Damage taken in Inverse battles

Normal	×1	Flying	×0.5
Fire	×0.5	Psychic	×0.5
Water	×1	Bug	×2
Grass	×4	Rock	×0.5
Electric	×1	Ghost	×1
Ice	×1	Dragon	×1
Fighting	×4	Dark	×1
Poison	×2	Steel	×1
Ground	×1	Fairy	×2

Can be used in

- Inverse Battle
- Battle Institute
- Battle Maison
- Random Matchup (Free Battle)
- Random Matchup (Others)

LEVEL-UP MOVES

Lv.	Name	Type	Kind	Pow.	Acc.	PP	Range
1	Poison Sting	Poison	Physical	15	100	35	Normal
1	String Shot	Bug	Status	—	95	40	Many Others
5	Scary Face	Normal	Status	—	100	10	Normal
8	Constrict	Normal	Physical	10	100	35	Normal
12	Leech Life	Bug	Physical	20	100	15	Normal
15	Night Shade	Ghost	Special	—	100	15	Normal
19	Shadow Sneak	Ghost	Physical	40	100	30	Normal
22	Fury Swipes	Normal	Physical	18	80	15	Normal
26	Sucker Punch	Dark	Physical	80	100	5	Normal
29	Spider Web	Bug	Status	—	—	10	Normal
33	Agility	Psychic	Status	—	—	30	Self
36	Pin Missile	Bug	Physical	25	95	20	Normal
40	Psychic	Psychic	Special	90	100	10	Normal
43	Poison Jab	Poison	Physical	80	100	20	Normal
47	Cross Poison	Poison	Physical	70	100	20	Normal
50	Sticky Web	Bug	Status	—	—	20	Other Side

TM & HM MOVES

No.	Name	Type	Kind	Pow.	Acc.	PP	Range
TM01	Hone Claws	Dark	Status	—	—	15	Self
TM06	Toxic	Poison	Status	—	90	10	Normal
TM09	Venoshock	Poison	Special	65	100	10	Normal
TM10	Hidden Power	Normal	Special	60	100	15	Normal
TM11	Sunny Day	Fire	Status	—	—	5	Both Sides
TM17	Protect	Normal	Status	—	—	10	Self
TM21	Frustration	Normal	Physical	—	100	20	Normal
TM22	Solar Beam	Grass	Special	120	100	10	Normal
TM27	Return	Normal	Physical	—	100	20	Normal
TM28	Dig	Ground	Physical	80	100	10	Normal
TM29	Psychic	Psychic	Special	90	100	10	Normal
TM32	Double Team	Normal	Status	—	—	15	Self
TM36	Sludge Bomb	Poison	Special	90	100	10	Normal
TM42	Facade	Normal	Physical	70	100	20	Normal
TM44	Rest	Psychic	Status	—	—	10	Self
TM45	Attract	Normal	Status	—	100	15	Normal
TM46	Thief	Dark	Physical	60	100	25	Normal
TM48	Round	Normal	Special	60	100	15	Normal
TM70	Flash	Normal	Status	—	100	20	Normal
TM76	Struggle Bug	Bug	Special	50	100	20	Many Others
TM81	X-Scissor	Bug	Physical	80	100	15	Normal
TM83	Infestation	Bug	Special	20	100	20	Normal
TM84	Poison Jab	Poison	Physical	80	100	20	Normal
TM87	Swagger	Normal	Status	—	90	15	Normal
TM88	Sleep Talk	Normal	Status	—	—	10	Self
TM90	Substitute	Normal	Status	—	—	10	Self
TM94	Secret Power	Normal	Physical	70	100	20	Normal
TM100	Confide	Normal	Status	—	—	20	Normal

MOVES LEARNED IN EXCHANGE FOR BP

Name	Type	Kind	Pow.	Acc.	PP	Range
Bug Bite	Bug	Physical	60	100	20	Normal
Signal Beam	Bug	Special	75	100	15	Normal
Bounce	Flying	Physical	85	85	5	Normal
Foul Play	Dark	Physical	95	100	15	Normal
Electroweb	Electric	Special	55	95	15	Many Others
Snore	Normal	Special	50	100	15	Normal
Giga Drain	Grass	Special	75	100	10	Normal

MOVES TAUGHT BY PEOPLE

Name	Type	Kind	Pow.	Acc.	PP	Range

EGG MOVES

Name	Type	Kind	Pow.	Acc.	PP	Range
Psybeam	Psychic	Special	65	100	20	Normal
Disable	Normal	Status	—	100	20	Normal
Sonic Boom	Normal	Special	—	90	20	Normal
Baton Pass	Normal	Status	—	—	40	Self
Pursuit	Dark	Physical	40	100	20	Normal
Signal Beam	Bug	Special	75	100	15	Normal
Toxic Spikes	Poison	Status	—	—	20	Other Side
Twineedle	Bug	Physical	25	100	20	Normal
Electroweb	Electric	Special	55	95	15	Many Others
Rage Powder	Bug	Status	—	—	20	Self
Night Slash	Dark	Physical	70	100	15	Normal
Megahorn	Bug	Physical	120	85	10	Normal

National Pokédex **168** Hoenn Pokédex —

Ariados

Long Leg Pokémon

HEIGHT: 3'07" WEIGHT: 73.9 lbs.

Same form for ♂ / ♀

Ω Ariados's feet are tipped with tiny hooked claws that enable it to scuttle on ceilings and vertical walls. This Pokémon constricts the foe with thin and strong silk webbing.

α Ariados's feet are tipped with tiny hooked claws that enable it to scuttle on ceilings and vertical walls. This Pokémon constricts the foe with thin and strong silk webbing.

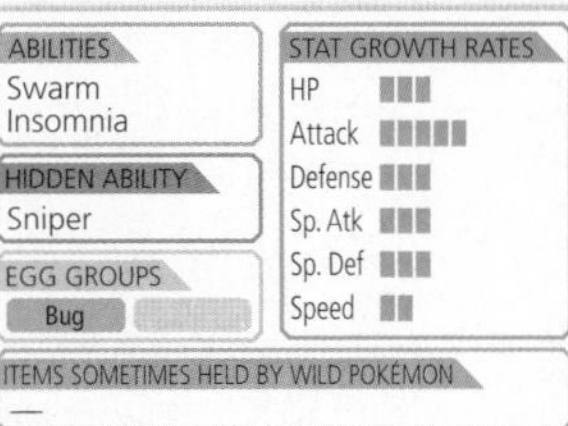

ABILITIES: Swarm, Insomnia

HIDDEN ABILITY: Sniper

EGG GROUPS: Bug

STAT GROWTH RATES: HP ■■■ / Attack ■■■■■ / Defense ■■■ / Sp. Atk ■■■ / Sp. Def ■■■ / Speed ■■

ITEMS SOMETIMES HELD BY WILD POKÉMON: —

EVOLUTION

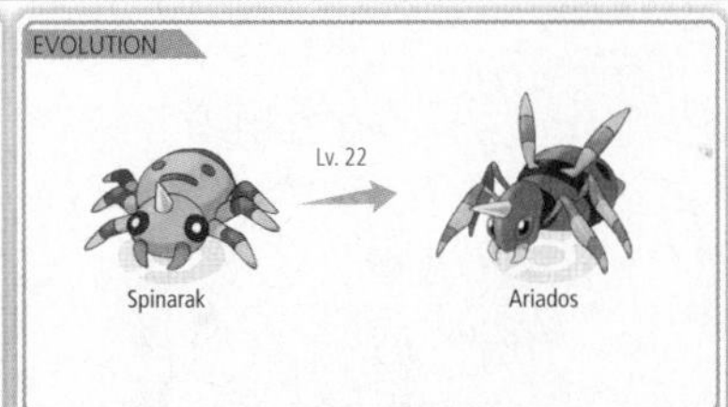

MAIN WAY TO REGISTER IN THE NATIONAL POKÉDEX

Catch at the Sky Pillar.

Damage taken in normal battles

Normal	×1	Flying	×2
Fire	×2	Psychic	×2
Water	×1	Bug	×0.5
Grass	×0.25	Rock	×2
Electric	×1	Ghost	×1
Ice	×1	Dragon	×1
Fighting	×0.25	Dark	×1
Poison	×0.5	Steel	×1
Ground	×1	Fairy	×0.5

Damage taken in Inverse battles

Normal	×1	Flying	×0.5
Fire	×0.5	Psychic	×0.5
Water	×1	Bug	×2
Grass	×4	Rock	×0.5
Electric	×1	Ghost	×1
Ice	×1	Dragon	×1
Fighting	×4	Dark	×1
Poison	×2	Steel	×1
Ground	×1	Fairy	×2

Can be used in

- Inverse Battle
- Battle Institute
- Battle Maison
- Random Matchup (Free Battle)
- Random Matchup (Others)

LEVEL-UP MOVES

Lv.	Name	Type	Kind	Pow.	Acc.	PP	Range
1	Venom Drench	Poison	Status	—	100	20	Many Others
1	Fell Stinger	Bug	Physical	30	100	25	Normal
1	Bug Bite	Bug	Physical	60	100	20	Normal
1	Poison Sting	Poison	Physical	15	100	35	Normal
1	String Shot	Bug	Status	—	95	40	Many Others
1	Scary Face	Normal	Status	—	100	10	Normal
1	Constrict	Normal	Physical	10	100	35	Normal
5	Scary Face	Normal	Status	—	100	10	Normal
8	Constrict	Normal	Physical	10	100	35	Normal
12	Leech Life	Bug	Physical	20	100	15	Normal
15	Night Shade	Ghost	Special	—	100	15	Normal
19	Shadow Sneak	Ghost	Physical	40	100	30	Normal
23	Fury Swipes	Normal	Physical	18	80	15	Normal
28	Sucker Punch	Dark	Physical	80	100	5	Normal
32	Spider Web	Bug	Status	—	—	10	Normal
37	Agility	Psychic	Status	—	—	30	Self
41	Pin Missile	Bug	Physical	25	95	20	Normal
46	Psychic	Psychic	Special	90	100	10	Normal
50	Poison Jab	Poison	Physical	80	100	20	Normal
55	Cross Poison	Poison	Physical	70	100	20	Normal
58	Sticky Web	Bug	Status	—	—	20	Other Side

TM & HM MOVES

No.	Name	Type	Kind	Pow.	Acc.	PP	Range
TM01	Hone Claws	Dark	Status	—	—	15	Self
TM06	Toxic	Poison	Status	—	90	10	Normal
TM09	Venoshock	Poison	Special	65	100	10	Normal
TM10	Hidden Power	Normal	Special	60	100	15	Normal
TM11	Sunny Day	Fire	Status	—	—	5	Both Sides
TM15	Hyper Beam	Normal	Special	150	90	5	Normal
TM17	Protect	Normal	Status	—	—	10	Self
TM21	Frustration	Normal	Physical	—	100	20	Normal
TM22	Solar Beam	Grass	Special	120	100	10	Normal
TM27	Return	Normal	Physical	—	100	20	Normal
TM28	Dig	Ground	Physical	80	100	10	Normal
TM29	Psychic	Psychic	Special	90	100	10	Normal
TM32	Double Team	Normal	Status	—	—	15	Self
TM36	Sludge Bomb	Poison	Special	90	100	10	Normal
TM42	Facade	Normal	Physical	70	100	20	Normal
TM44	Rest	Psychic	Status	—	—	10	Self
TM45	Attract	Normal	Status	—	100	15	Normal
TM46	Thief	Dark	Physical	60	100	25	Normal
TM48	Round	Normal	Special	60	100	15	Normal
TM68	Giga Impact	Normal	Physical	150	90	5	Normal
TM70	Flash	Normal	Status	—	100	20	Normal
TM76	Struggle Bug	Bug	Special	50	100	20	Many Others
TM81	X-Scissor	Bug	Physical	80	100	15	Normal
TM83	Infestation	Bug	Special	20	100	20	Normal
TM84	Poison Jab	Poison	Physical	80	100	20	Normal
TM87	Swagger	Normal	Status	—	90	15	Normal
TM88	Sleep Talk	Normal	Status	—	—	10	Self
TM90	Substitute	Normal	Status	—	—	10	Self
TM94	Secret Power	Normal	Physical	70	100	20	Normal
TM100	Confide	Normal	Status	—	—	20	Normal

MOVES LEARNED IN EXCHANGE FOR BP

Name	Type	Kind	Pow.	Acc.	PP	Range
Bug Bite	Bug	Physical	60	100	20	Normal
Signal Beam	Bug	Special	75	100	15	Normal
Bounce	Flying	Physical	85	85	5	Normal
Foul Play	Dark	Physical	95	100	15	Normal
Electroweb	Electric	Special	55	95	15	Many Others
Snore	Normal	Special	50	100	15	Normal
Giga Drain	Grass	Special	75	100	10	Normal

MOVES TAUGHT BY PEOPLE

Name	Type	Kind	Pow.	Acc.	PP	Range

National Pokédex **169** Hoenn Pokédex **067**

Crobat

Bat Pokémon

Poison Flying

HEIGHT: 5'11" WEIGHT: 165.3 lbs.

Same form for ♂ / ♀

Ω If this Pokémon is flying by fluttering only a pair of wings on either the forelegs or hind legs, it's proof that Crobat has been flying a long distance. It switches the wings it uses if it is tired.

α Crobat sneaks up on its intended prey using wings that barely make a sound. This Pokémon rests by hanging on a tree branch with its rear legs that serve as wings.

ABILITY
Inner Focus

HIDDEN ABILITY
Infiltrator

EGG GROUPS
Flying

STAT GROWTH RATES
HP
Attack
Defense
Sp. Atk
Sp. Def
Speed

EVOLUTION

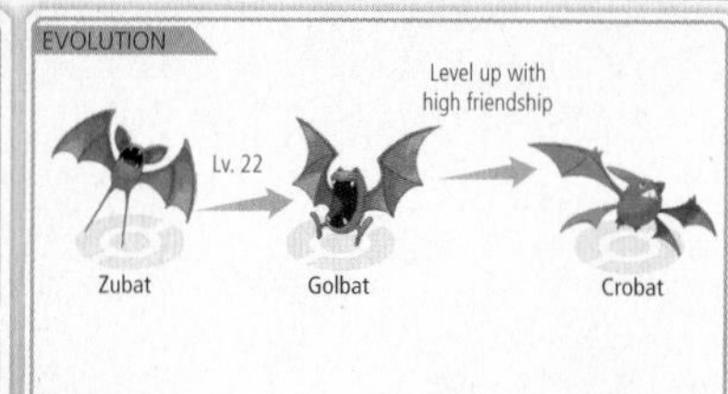

ITEMS SOMETIMES HELD BY WILD POKÉMON
—

MAIN WAY TO REGISTER IN THE NATIONAL POKÉDEX

Level up Golbat with high friendship.

Damage taken in normal battles

Type	Multiplier	Type	Multiplier
Normal	×1	Flying	×1
Fire	×1	Psychic	×2
Water	×1	Bug	×0.25
Grass	×0.25	Rock	×2
Electric	×2	Ghost	×1
Ice	×2	Dragon	×1
Fighting	×0.25	Dark	×1
Poison	×0.5	Steel	×1
Ground	×0	Fairy	×0.5

Damage taken in Inverse battles

Type	Multiplier	Type	Multiplier
Normal	×1	Flying	×1
Fire	×1	Psychic	×0.5
Water	×1	Bug	×4
Grass	×4	Rock	×0.5
Electric	×0.5	Ghost	×1
Ice	×0.5	Dragon	×1
Fighting	×4	Dark	×1
Poison	×2	Steel	×1
Ground	×1	Fairy	×2

Can be used in
- Inverse Battle
- Battle Institute
- Battle Maison
- Random Matchup (Free Battle)
- Random Matchup (Others)

LEVEL-UP MOVES

Lv.	Name	Type	Kind	Pow.	Acc.	PP	Range
1	Cross Poison	Poison	Physical	70	100	20	Normal
1	Screech	Normal	Status	—	85	40	Normal
1	Leech Life	Bug	Physical	20	100	15	Normal
1	Supersonic	Normal	Status	—	55	20	Normal
1	Astonish	Ghost	Physical	30	100	15	Normal
1	Bite	Dark	Physical	60	100	25	Normal
5	Supersonic	Normal	Status	—	55	20	Normal
7	Astonish	Ghost	Physical	30	100	15	Normal
11	Bite	Dark	Physical	60	100	25	Normal
13	Wing Attack	Flying	Physical	60	100	35	Normal
17	Confuse Ray	Ghost	Status	—	100	10	Normal
19	Air Cutter	Flying	Special	60	95	25	Many Others
24	Swift	Normal	Special	60	—	20	Many Others
27	Poison Fang	Poison	Physical	50	100	15	Normal
32	Mean Look	Normal	Status	—	—	5	Normal
35	Acrobatics	Flying	Physical	55	100	15	Normal
40	Haze	Ice	Status	—	—	30	Both Sides
43	Venoshock	Poison	Special	65	100	10	Normal
48	Air Slash	Flying	Special	75	95	15	Normal
51	Quick Guard	Fighting	Status	—	—	15	Your Side

TM & HM MOVES

No.	Name	Type	Kind	Pow.	Acc.	PP	Range
TM06	Toxic	Poison	Status	—	90	10	Normal
TM09	Venoshock	Poison	Special	65	100	10	Normal
TM10	Hidden Power	Normal	Special	60	100	15	Normal
TM11	Sunny Day	Fire	Status	—	—	5	Both Sides
TM12	Taunt	Dark	Status	—	100	20	Normal
TM15	Hyper Beam	Normal	Special	150	90	5	Normal
TM17	Protect	Normal	Status	—	—	10	Self
TM18	Rain Dance	Water	Status	—	—	5	Both Sides
TM19	Roost	Flying	Status	—	—	10	Self
TM21	Frustration	Normal	Physical	—	100	20	Normal
TM27	Return	Normal	Physical	—	100	20	Normal
TM30	Shadow Ball	Ghost	Special	80	100	15	Normal
TM32	Double Team	Normal	Status	—	—	15	Self
TM36	Sludge Bomb	Poison	Special	90	100	10	Normal
TM40	Aerial Ace	Flying	Physical	60	—	20	Normal
TM41	Torment	Dark	Status	—	100	15	Normal
TM42	Facade	Normal	Physical	70	100	20	Normal
TM44	Rest	Psychic	Status	—	—	10	Self
TM45	Attract	Normal	Status	—	100	15	Normal
TM46	Thief	Dark	Physical	60	100	25	Normal
TM48	Round	Normal	Special	60	100	15	Normal
TM51	Steel Wing	Steel	Physical	70	90	25	Normal
TM62	Acrobatics	Flying	Physical	55	100	15	Normal
TM66	Payback	Dark	Physical	50	100	10	Normal
TM68	Giga Impact	Normal	Physical	150	90	5	Normal
TM81	X-Scissor	Bug	Physical	80	100	15	Normal
TM87	Swagger	Normal	Status	—	90	15	Normal
TM88	Sleep Talk	Normal	Status	—	—	10	Self
TM89	U-turn	Bug	Physical	70	100	20	Normal
TM90	Substitute	Normal	Status	—	—	10	Self
TM94	Secret Power	Normal	Physical	70	100	20	Normal
TM97	Dark Pulse	Dark	Special	80	100	15	Normal
TM100	Confide	Normal	Status	—	—	20	Normal
HM02	Fly	Flying	Physical	90	95	15	Normal

MOVES LEARNED IN EXCHANGE FOR BP

Name	Type	Kind	Pow.	Acc.	PP	Range
Super Fang	Normal	Physical	—	90	10	Normal
Uproar	Normal	Special	90	100	10	1 Random
Zen Headbutt	Psychic	Physical	80	90	15	Normal
Snore	Normal	Special	50	100	15	Normal
Heat Wave	Fire	Special	95	90	10	Many Others
Tailwind	Flying	Status	—	—	15	Your Side
Sky Attack	Flying	Physical	140	90	5	Normal
Giga Drain	Grass	Special	75	100	10	Normal
Snatch	Dark	Status	—	—	10	Self

MOVES TAUGHT BY PEOPLE

Name	Type	Kind	Pow.	Acc.	PP	Range

National Pokédex **170** Hoenn Pokédex **190**

Chinchou

Angler Pokémon

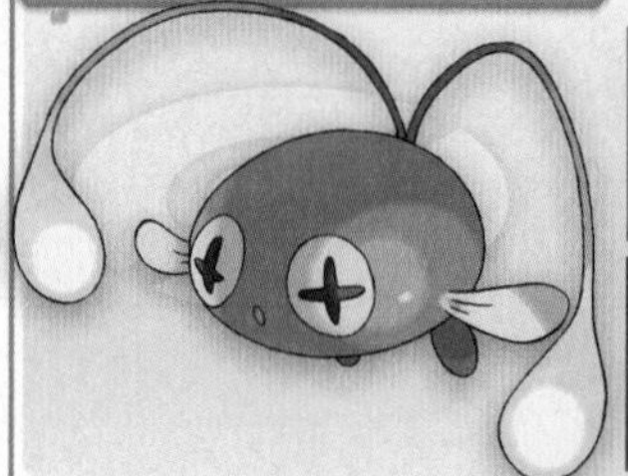

Water Electric

HEIGHT: 1'08" WEIGHT: 26.5 lbs.

Same form for ♂ / ♀

Ω Chinchou lets loose positive and negative electrical charges from its two antennas to make its prey faint. This Pokémon flashes its electric lights to exchange signals with others.

α Chinchou's two antennas are filled with cells that generate strong electricity. This Pokémon's cells create so much electrical power, it even makes itself tingle slightly.

ABILITIES
Volt Absorb
Illuminate

HIDDEN ABILITY
Water Absorb

EGG GROUPS
Water 2

STAT GROWTH RATES
HP
Attack
Defense
Sp. Atk
Sp. Def
Speed

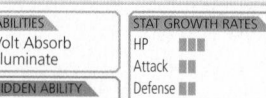

EVOLUTION
Chinchou → Lv. 27 → Lanturn

ITEMS SOMETIMES HELD BY WILD POKÉMON
Deep Sea Scale

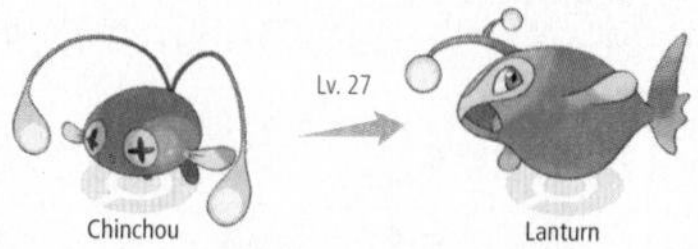

MAIN WAY TO REGISTER IN THE NATIONAL POKÉDEX

Catch at the bottom of the sea beneath Route 124.

Damage taken in normal battles

Type	Multiplier	Type	Multiplier
Normal	×1	Flying	×0.5
Fire	×0.5	Psychic	×1
! Water	×0.5	Bug	×1
Grass	×2	Rock	×1
! Electric	×1	Ghost	×1
Ice	×0.5	Dragon	×1
Fighting	×1	Dark	×1
Poison	×1	Steel	×0.25
Ground	×2	Fairy	×1

Damage taken in Inverse battles

Type	Multiplier	Type	Multiplier
Normal	×1	Flying	×2
Fire	×2	Psychic	×1
! Water	×2	Bug	×1
Grass	×0.5	Rock	×1
! Electric	×1	Ghost	×1
Ice	×2	Dragon	×1
Fighting	×1	Dark	×1
Poison	×1	Steel	×4
Ground	×0.5	Fairy	×1

Can be used in
- Inverse Battle
- Battle Institute
- Battle Maison
- Random Matchup (Free Battle)
- Random Matchup (Others)

LEVEL-UP MOVES

Lv.	Name	Type	Kind	Pow.	Acc.	PP	Range
1	Bubble	Water	Special	40	100	30	Many Others
1	Supersonic	Normal	Status	—	55	20	Normal
6	Thunder Wave	Electric	Status	—	100	20	Normal
9	Electro Ball	Electric	Special	—	100	10	Normal
12	Water Gun	Water	Special	40	100	25	Normal
17	Confuse Ray	Ghost	Status	—	100	10	Normal
20	Bubble Beam	Water	Special	65	100	20	Normal
23	Spark	Electric	Physical	65	100	20	Normal
28	Signal Beam	Bug	Special	75	100	15	Normal
31	Flail	Normal	Physical	—	100	15	Normal
34	Discharge	Electric	Special	80	100	15	Adjacent
39	Take Down	Normal	Physical	90	85	20	Normal
42	Aqua Ring	Water	Status	—	—	20	Self
45	Hydro Pump	Water	Special	110	80	5	Normal
47	Ion Deluge	Electric	Status	—	—	25	Both Sides
50	Charge	Electric	Status	—	—	20	Self

TM & HM MOVES

No.	Name	Type	Kind	Pow.	Acc.	PP	Range
TM06	Toxic	Poison	Status	—	90	10	Normal
TM07	Hail	Ice	Status	—	—	10	Both Sides
TM10	Hidden Power	Normal	Special	60	100	15	Normal
TM13	Ice Beam	Ice	Special	90	100	10	Normal
TM14	Blizzard	Ice	Special	110	70	5	Many Others
TM17	Protect	Normal	Status	—	—	10	Self
TM18	Rain Dance	Water	Status	—	—	5	Both Sides
TM21	Frustration	Normal	Physical	—	100	20	Normal
TM24	Thunderbolt	Electric	Special	90	100	15	Normal
TM25	Thunder	Electric	Special	110	70	10	Normal
TM27	Return	Normal	Physical	—	100	20	Normal
TM32	Double Team	Normal	Status	—	—	15	Self
TM42	Facade	Normal	Physical	70	100	20	Normal
TM44	Rest	Psychic	Status	—	—	10	Self
TM45	Attract	Normal	Status	—	100	15	Normal
TM48	Round	Normal	Special	60	100	15	Normal
TM55	Scald	Water	Special	80	100	15	Normal
TM57	Charge Beam	Electric	Special	50	90	10	Normal
TM70	Flash	Normal	Status	—	100	20	Normal
TM72	Volt Switch	Electric	Special	70	100	20	Normal
TM73	Thunder Wave	Electric	Status	—	100	20	Normal
TM87	Swagger	Normal	Status	—	90	15	Normal
TM88	Sleep Talk	Normal	Status	—	—	10	Self
TM90	Substitute	Normal	Status	—	—	10	Self
TM93	Wild Charge	Electric	Physical	90	100	15	Normal
TM94	Secret Power	Normal	Physical	70	100	20	Normal
TM99	Dazzling Gleam	Fairy	Special	80	100	10	Many Others
TM100	Confide	Normal	Status	—	—	20	Normal
HM03	Surf	Water	Special	90	100	15	Adjacent
HM05	Waterfall	Water	Physical	80	100	15	Normal
HM07	Dive	Water	Physical	80	100	10	Normal

MOVES LEARNED IN EXCHANGE FOR BP

Name	Type	Kind	Pow.	Acc.	PP	Range
Signal Beam	Bug	Special	75	100	15	Normal
Bounce	Flying	Physical	85	85	5	Normal
Icy Wind	Ice	Special	55	95	15	Many Others
Snore	Normal	Special	50	100	15	Normal
Heal Bell	Normal	Status	—	—	5	Your Party
Shock Wave	Electric	Special	60	—	20	Normal
Water Pulse	Water	Special	60	100	20	Normal

MOVES TAUGHT BY PEOPLE

Name	Type	Kind	Pow.	Acc.	PP	Range

EGG MOVES

Name	Type	Kind	Pow.	Acc.	PP	Range
Flail	Normal	Physical	—	100	15	Normal
Screech	Normal	Status	—	85	40	Normal
Amnesia	Psychic	Status	—	—	20	Self
Psybeam	Psychic	Special	65	100	20	Normal
Whirlpool	Water	Special	35	85	15	Normal
Agility	Psychic	Status	—	—	30	Self
Mist	Ice	Status	—	—	30	Your Side
Shock Wave	Electric	Special	60	—	20	Normal
Brine	Water	Special	65	100	10	Normal
Water Pulse	Water	Special	60	100	20	Normal
Soak	Water	Status	—	100	20	Normal

National Pokédex **171** Hoenn Pokédex **191**

Lanturn

Light Pokémon

Water / Electric

HEIGHT: 3'11" WEIGHT: 49.6 lbs.

Same form for ♂ / ♀

Ω Lanturn is nicknamed "the deep-sea star" for its illuminated antenna. This Pokémon produces light by causing a chemical reaction between bacteria and its bodily fluids inside the antenna.

α Lanturn is known to emit light. If you peer down into the dark sea from a ship at night, you can sometimes see this Pokémon's light rising from the depths where it swims. It gives the sea an appearance of a starlit night.

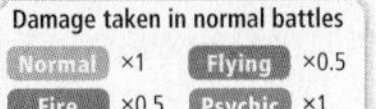

ABILITIES
Volt Absorb
Illuminate

HIDDEN ABILITY
Water Absorb

EGG GROUPS
Water 2

STAT GROWTH RATES
HP
Attack
Defense
Sp. Atk
Sp. Def
Speed

ITEMS SOMETIMES HELD BY WILD POKÉMON
Deep Sea Scale

EVOLUTION
Chinchou → Lv. 27 → Lanturn

MAIN WAY TO REGISTER IN THE NATIONAL POKÉDEX

Catch at the bottom of the sea beneath Route 124.

Damage taken in normal battles

Type		Type	
Normal	×1	Flying	×0.5
Fire	×0.5	Psychic	×1
Water	×0.5	Bug	×1
Grass	×2	Rock	×1
Electric	×1	Ghost	×1
Ice	×0.5	Dragon	×1
Fighting	×1	Dark	×1
Poison	×1	Steel	×0.25
Ground	×2	Fairy	×1

Damage taken in Inverse battles

Type		Type	
Normal	×1	Flying	×2
Fire	×2	Psychic	×1
Water	×2	Bug	×1
Grass	×0.5	Rock	×1
Electric	×1	Ghost	×1
Ice	×2	Dragon	×1
Fighting	×1	Dark	×1
Poison	×1	Steel	×4
Ground	×0.5	Fairy	×1

Can be used in
Inverse Battle
Battle Institute
Battle Maison
Random Matchup (Free Battle)
Random Matchup (Others)

LEVEL-UP MOVES

Lv.	Name	Type	Kind	Pow.	Acc.	PP	Range
1	Eerie Impulse	Electric	Status	—	100	15	Normal
1	Bubble	Water	Special	40	100	30	Many Others
1	Supersonic	Normal	Status	—	55	20	Normal
1	Thunder Wave	Electric	Status	—	100	20	Normal
1	Electro Ball	Electric	Special	—	100	10	Normal
6	Thunder Wave	Electric	Status	—	100	20	Normal
9	Electro Ball	Electric	Special	—	100	10	Normal
12	Water Gun	Water	Special	40	100	25	Normal
17	Confuse Ray	Ghost	Status	—	100	10	Normal
20	Bubble Beam	Water	Special	65	100	20	Normal
23	Spark	Electric	Physical	65	100	20	Normal
27	Stockpile	Normal	Status	—	—	20	Self
27	Swallow	Normal	Status	—	—	10	Self
27	Spit Up	Normal	Special	—	100	10	Normal
29	Signal Beam	Bug	Special	75	100	15	Normal
33	Flail	Normal	Physical	—	100	15	Normal
37	Discharge	Electric	Special	80	100	15	Adjacent
43	Take Down	Normal	Physical	90	85	20	Normal
47	Aqua Ring	Water	Status	—	—	20	Self
51	Hydro Pump	Water	Special	110	80	5	Normal
54	Ion Deluge	Electric	Status	—	—	25	Both Sides
58	Charge	Electric	Status	—	—	20	Self

TM & HM MOVES

No.	Name	Type	Kind	Pow.	Acc.	PP	Range
TM06	Toxic	Poison	Status	—	90	10	Normal
TM07	Hail	Ice	Status	—	—	10	Both Sides
TM10	Hidden Power	Normal	Special	60	100	15	Normal
TM13	Ice Beam	Ice	Special	90	100	10	Normal
TM14	Blizzard	Ice	Special	110	70	5	Many Others
TM15	Hyper Beam	Normal	Special	150	90	5	Normal
TM17	Protect	Normal	Status	—	—	10	Self
TM18	Rain Dance	Water	Status	—	—	5	Both Sides
TM21	Frustration	Normal	Physical	—	100	20	Normal
TM24	Thunderbolt	Electric	Special	90	100	15	Normal
TM25	Thunder	Electric	Special	110	70	10	Normal
TM27	Return	Normal	Physical	—	100	20	Normal
TM32	Double Team	Normal	Status	—	—	15	Self
TM42	Facade	Normal	Physical	70	100	20	Normal
TM44	Rest	Psychic	Status	—	—	10	Self
TM45	Attract	Normal	Status	—	100	15	Normal
TM48	Round	Normal	Special	60	100	15	Normal
TM55	Scald	Water	Special	80	100	15	Normal
TM57	Charge Beam	Electric	Special	50	90	10	Normal
TM68	Giga Impact	Normal	Physical	150	90	5	Normal
TM70	Flash	Normal	Status	—	100	20	Normal
TM72	Volt Switch	Electric	Special	70	100	20	Normal
TM73	Thunder Wave	Electric	Status	—	100	20	Normal
TM87	Swagger	Normal	Status	—	90	15	Normal
TM88	Sleep Talk	Normal	Status	—	—	10	Self
TM90	Substitute	Normal	Status	—	—	10	Self
TM93	Wild Charge	Electric	Physical	90	100	15	Normal
TM94	Secret Power	Normal	Physical	70	100	20	Normal
TM99	Dazzling Gleam	Fairy	Special	80	100	10	Many Others
TM100	Confide	Normal	Status	—	—	20	Normal
HM03	Surf	Water	Special	90	100	15	Adjacent
HM05	Waterfall	Water	Physical	80	100	15	Normal
HM07	Dive	Water	Physical	80	100	10	Normal

MOVES LEARNED IN EXCHANGE FOR BP

Name	Type	Kind	Pow.	Acc.	PP	Range
Signal Beam	Bug	Special	75	100	15	Normal
Bounce	Flying	Physical	85	85	5	Normal
Icy Wind	Ice	Special	55	95	15	Many Others
Aqua Tail	Water	Physical	90	90	10	Normal
Snore	Normal	Special	50	100	15	Normal
Heal Bell	Normal	Status	—	—	5	Your Party
Shock Wave	Electric	Special	60	—	20	Normal
Water Pulse	Water	Special	60	100	20	Normal

MOVES TAUGHT BY PEOPLE

Name	Type	Kind	Pow.	Acc.	PP	Range

National Pokédex **172** Hoenn Pokédex **162**

Pichu

Tiny Mouse Pokémon

Electric

HEIGHT: 1'00" WEIGHT: 4.4 lbs.

Same form for ♂ / ♀

Ω Pichu charges itself with electricity more easily on days with thunderclouds or when the air is very dry. You can hear the crackling of static electricity coming off this Pokémon.

α When Pichu plays with others, it may short out electricity with another Pichu, creating a shower of sparks. In that event, this Pokémon will begin crying, startled by the flash of sparks.

ABILITY
Static

HIDDEN ABILITY
Lightning Rod

EGG GROUPS
No Eggs Discovered

STAT GROWTH RATES
HP
Attack
Defense
Sp. Atk
Sp. Def
Speed

ITEMS SOMETIMES HELD BY WILD POKÉMON
—

EVOLUTION
Pichu → Level up with high friendship → Pikachu → Thunder Stone → Raichu

MAIN WAY TO REGISTER IN THE NATIONAL POKÉDEX

Leave a Pikachu or Raichu at a Pokémon Day Care, then hatch the Pokémon Egg that is found.

Damage taken in normal battles

Type		Type	
Normal	×1	Flying	×0.5
Fire	×1	Psychic	×1
Water	×1	Bug	×1
Grass	×1	Rock	×1
Electric	×0.5	Ghost	×1
Ice	×1	Dragon	×1
Fighting	×1	Dark	×1
Poison	×1	Steel	×0.5
Ground	×2	Fairy	×1

Damage taken in Inverse battles

Type		Type	
Normal	×1	Flying	×2
Fire	×1	Psychic	×1
Water	×1	Bug	×1
Grass	×1	Rock	×1
Electric	×2	Ghost	×1
Ice	×1	Dragon	×1
Fighting	×1	Dark	×1
Poison	×1	Steel	×2
Ground	×0.5	Fairy	×1

Can be used in
Inverse Battle
Battle Institute
Battle Maison
Random Matchup (Free Battle)
Random Matchup (Others)

LEVEL-UP MOVES

Lv.	Name	Type	Kind	Pow.	Acc.	PP	Range
1	Thunder Shock	Electric	Special	40	100	30	Normal
1	Charm	Fairy	Status	—	100	20	Normal
5	Tail Whip	Normal	Status	—	100	30	Many Others
10	Sweet Kiss	Fairy	Status	—	75	10	Normal
13	Nasty Plot	Dark	Status	—	—	20	Self
18	Thunder Wave	Electric	Status	—	100	20	Normal

TM & HM MOVES

No.	Name	Type	Kind	Pow.	Acc.	PP	Range
TM06	Toxic	Poison	Status	—	90	10	Normal
TM10	Hidden Power	Normal	Special	60	100	15	Normal
TM16	Light Screen	Psychic	Status	—	—	30	Your Side
TM17	Protect	Normal	Status	—	—	10	Self
TM18	Rain Dance	Water	Status	—	—	5	Both Sides
TM21	Frustration	Normal	Physical	—	100	20	Normal
TM24	Thunderbolt	Electric	Special	90	100	15	Normal
TM25	Thunder	Electric	Special	110	70	10	Normal
TM27	Return	Normal	Physical	—	100	20	Normal
TM32	Double Team	Normal	Status	—	—	15	Self
TM42	Facade	Normal	Physical	70	100	20	Normal
TM44	Rest	Psychic	Status	—	—	10	Self
TM45	Attract	Normal	Status	—	100	15	Normal
TM48	Round	Normal	Special	60	100	15	Normal
TM49	Echoed Voice	Normal	Special	40	100	15	Normal
TM56	Fling	Dark	Physical	—	100	10	Normal
TM57	Charge Beam	Electric	Special	50	90	10	Normal
TM70	Flash	Normal	Status	—	100	20	Normal
TM72	Volt Switch	Electric	Special	70	100	20	Normal
TM73	Thunder Wave	Electric	Status	—	100	20	Normal
TM86	Grass Knot	Grass	Special	—	100	20	Normal
TM87	Swagger	Normal	Status	—	90	15	Normal
TM88	Sleep Talk	Normal	Status	—	—	10	Self
TM90	Substitute	Normal	Status	—	—	10	Self
TM93	Wild Charge	Electric	Physical	90	100	15	Normal
TM94	Secret Power	Normal	Physical	70	100	20	Normal
TM100	Confide	Normal	Status	—	—	20	Normal

MOVES LEARNED IN EXCHANGE FOR BP

Name	Type	Kind	Pow.	Acc.	PP	Range
Covet	Normal	Physical	60	100	25	Normal
Signal Beam	Bug	Special	75	100	15	Normal
Uproar	Normal	Special	90	100	10	1 Random
Thunder Punch	Electric	Physical	75	100	15	Normal
Magnet Rise	Electric	Status	—	—	10	Self
Electroweb	Electric	Special	55	95	15	Many Others
Iron Tail	Steel	Physical	100	75	15	Normal
Snore	Normal	Special	50	100	15	Normal
Shock Wave	Electric	Special	60	—	20	Normal
Helping Hand	Normal	Status	—	—	20	1 Ally

MOVES TAUGHT BY PEOPLE

Name	Type	Kind	Pow.	Acc.	PP	Range

EGG MOVES

Name	Type	Kind	Pow.	Acc.	PP	Range
Reversal	Fighting	Physical	—	100	15	Normal
Bide	Normal	Physical	—	—	10	Self
Present	Normal	Physical	—	90	15	Normal
Encore	Normal	Status	—	100	5	Normal
Double Slap	Normal	Physical	15	85	10	Normal
Wish	Normal	Status	—	—	10	Self
Charge	Electric	Status	—	—	20	Self
Fake Out	Normal	Physical	40	100	10	Normal
Thunder Punch	Electric	Physical	75	100	15	Normal
Tickle	Normal	Status	—	100	20	Normal
Flail	Normal	Physical	—	100	15	Normal
Endure	Normal	Status	—	—	10	Self
Lucky Chant	Normal	Status	—	—	30	Your Side
Bestow	Normal	Status	—	—	15	Normal
Disarming Voice	Fairy	Special	40	—	15	Many Others
Volt Tackle ◆	Electric	Physical	120	100	15	Normal

◆ To obtain a Pichu that knows Volt Tackle from a Pokémon Egg, one of the Pokémon at the Pokémon Day Care needs to be a Pikachu or Raichu holding the Light Ball. Sometimes wild Pikachu are holding this item.

National Pokédex **173** Hoenn Pokédex —

Cleffa

Star Shape Pokémon

Fairy

HEIGHT: 1'00" WEIGHT: 6.6 lbs.

Same form for ♂ / ♀

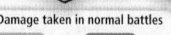

Ω On nights with many shooting stars, Cleffa can be seen dancing in a ring. They dance through the night and stop only at the break of day, when these Pokémon quench their thirst with the morning dew.

α On nights with many shooting stars, Cleffa can be seen dancing in a ring. They dance through the night and stop only at the break of day, when these Pokémon quench their thirst with the morning dew.

ABILITIES
Cute Charm
Magic Guard

HIDDEN ABILITY
Friend Guard

EGG GROUPS
No Eggs Discovered

STAT GROWTH RATES

Stat	Rate
HP	■■
Attack	■
Defense	■
Sp. Atk	■■
Sp. Def	■■
Speed	■

ITEMS SOMETIMES HELD BY WILD POKÉMON
—

EVOLUTION

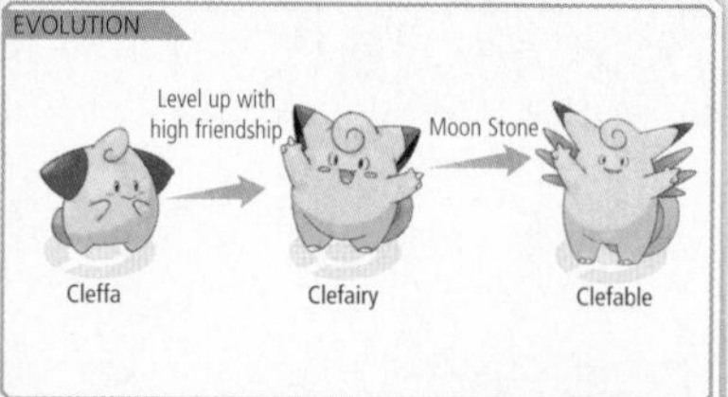

MAIN WAY TO REGISTER IN THE NATIONAL POKÉDEX

Leave a Clefairy or Clefable at a Pokémon Day Care, then hatch the Pokémon Egg that is found.

Damage taken in normal battles

Type		Type	
Normal	×1	Flying	×1
Fire	×1	Psychic	×1
Water	×1	Bug	×0.5
Grass	×1	Rock	×1
Electric	×1	Ghost	×1
Ice	×1	Dragon	×0
Fighting	×0.5	Dark	×0.5
Poison	×2	Steel	×2
Ground	×1	Fairy	×1

Damage taken in Inverse battles

Type		Type	
Normal	×1	Flying	×1
Fire	×1	Psychic	×1
Water	×1	Bug	×2
Grass	×1	Rock	×1
Electric	×1	Ghost	×1
Ice	×1	Dragon	×2
Fighting	×2	Dark	×2
Poison	×0.5	Steel	×0.5
Ground	×1	Fairy	×1

Can be used in
Inverse Battle
Battle Institute
Battle Maison
Random Matchup (Free Battle)
Random Matchup (Others)

LEVEL-UP MOVES

Lv.	Name	Type	Kind	Pow.	Acc.	PP	Range
1	Pound	Normal	Physical	40	100	35	Normal
1	Charm	Fairy	Status	—	100	20	Normal
4	Encore	Normal	Status	—	100	5	Normal
7	Sing	Normal	Status	—	55	15	Normal
10	Sweet Kiss	Fairy	Status	—	75	10	Normal
13	Copycat	Normal	Status	—	—	20	Self
16	Magical Leaf	Grass	Special	60	—	20	Normal

TM & HM MOVES

No.	Name	Type	Kind	Pow.	Acc.	PP	Range
TM03	Psyshock	Psychic	Special	80	100	10	Normal
TM06	Toxic	Poison	Status	—	90	10	Normal
TM10	Hidden Power	Normal	Special	60	100	15	Normal
TM11	Sunny Day	Fire	Status	—	—	5	Both Sides
TM16	Light Screen	Psychic	Status	—	—	30	Your Side
TM17	Protect	Normal	Status	—	—	10	Self
TM18	Rain Dance	Water	Status	—	—	5	Both Sides
TM20	Safeguard	Normal	Status	—	—	25	Your Side
TM21	Frustration	Normal	Physical	—	100	20	Normal
TM22	Solar Beam	Grass	Special	120	100	10	Normal
TM27	Return	Normal	Physical	—	100	20	Normal
TM28	Dig	Ground	Physical	80	100	10	Normal
TM29	Psychic	Psychic	Special	90	100	10	Normal
TM30	Shadow Ball	Ghost	Special	80	100	15	Normal
TM32	Double Team	Normal	Status	—	—	15	Self
TM33	Reflect	Psychic	Status	—	—	20	Your Side
TM35	Flamethrower	Fire	Special	90	100	15	Normal
TM38	Fire Blast	Fire	Special	110	85	5	Normal
TM42	Facade	Normal	Physical	70	100	20	Normal
TM44	Rest	Psychic	Status	—	—	10	Self
TM45	Attract	Normal	Status	—	100	15	Normal
TM48	Round	Normal	Special	60	100	15	Normal
TM49	Echoed Voice	Normal	Special	40	100	15	Normal
TM56	Fling	Dark	Physical	—	100	10	Normal
TM59	Incinerate	Fire	Special	60	100	15	Many Others
TM70	Flash	Normal	Status	—	100	20	Normal
TM73	Thunder Wave	Electric	Status	—	100	20	Normal
TM77	Psych Up	Normal	Status	—	—	10	Normal
TM85	Dream Eater	Psychic	Special	100	100	15	Normal
TM86	Grass Knot	Grass	Special	—	100	20	Normal
TM87	Swagger	Normal	Status	—	90	15	Normal
TM88	Sleep Talk	Normal	Status	—	—	10	Self
TM90	Substitute	Normal	Status	—	—	10	Self
TM94	Secret Power	Normal	Physical	70	100	20	Normal
TM100	Confide	Normal	Status	—	—	20	Normal

MOVES LEARNED IN EXCHANGE FOR BP

Name	Type	Kind	Pow.	Acc.	PP	Range
Covet	Normal	Physical	60	100	25	Normal
Signal Beam	Bug	Special	75	100	15	Normal
Uproar	Normal	Special	90	100	10	1 Random
Magic Coat	Psychic	Status	—	—	15	Self
Gravity	Psychic	Status	—	—	5	Both Sides
Last Resort	Normal	Physical	140	100	5	Normal
Icy Wind	Ice	Special	55	95	15	Many Others
Zen Headbutt	Psychic	Physical	80	90	15	Normal
Hyper Voice	Normal	Special	90	100	10	Many Others
Iron Tail	Steel	Physical	100	75	15	Normal
Snore	Normal	Special	50	100	15	Normal
Role Play	Psychic	Status	—	—	10	Normal
Shock Wave	Electric	Special	60	—	20	Normal
Water Pulse	Water	Special	60	100	20	Normal
After You	Normal	Status	—	—	15	Normal
Helping Hand	Normal	Status	—	—	20	1 Ally
Trick	Psychic	Status	—	100	10	Normal
Wonder Room	Psychic	Status	—	—	10	Both Sides
Endeavor	Normal	Physical	—	100	5	Normal
Recycle	Normal	Status	—	—	10	Self

MOVES TAUGHT BY PEOPLE

Name	Type	Kind	Pow.	Acc.	PP	Range

EGG MOVES

Name	Type	Kind	Pow.	Acc.	PP	Range
Present	Normal	Physical	—	90	15	Normal
Metronome	Normal	Status	—	—	10	Self
Amnesia	Psychic	Status	—	—	20	Self
Belly Drum	Normal	Status	—	—	10	Self
Splash	Normal	Status	—	—	40	Self
Mimic	Normal	Status	—	—	10	Normal
Wish	Normal	Status	—	—	10	Self
Fake Tears	Dark	Status	—	100	20	Normal
Covet	Normal	Physical	60	100	25	Normal
Aromatherapy	Grass	Status	—	—	5	Your Party
Stored Power	Psychic	Special	20	100	10	Normal
Tickle	Normal	Status	—	100	20	Normal
Misty Terrain	Fairy	Status	—	—	10	Both Sides
Heal Pulse	Psychic	Status	—	—	10	Normal

National Pokédex **174** Hoenn Pokédex **142**

Igglybuff

Balloon Pokémon

Normal Fairy

HEIGHT: 1'00" WEIGHT: 2.2 lbs.

Same form for ♂ / ♀

Ω Igglybuff's vocal cords are not sufficiently developed. It would hurt its throat if it were to sing too much. This Pokémon gargles with freshwater from a clean stream.

α Igglybuff has a soft and plushy body that feels very much like a marshmallow. From this body wafts a gently sweet fragrance that soothes and calms the emotions of its foes.

ABILITIES
Cute Charm
Competitive

HIDDEN ABILITY
Friend Guard

EGG GROUPS
No Eggs Discovered

STAT GROWTH RATES

Stat	Rate
HP	■■■■
Attack	■■
Defense	■
Sp. Atk	■■
Sp. Def	■
Speed	■

ITEMS SOMETIMES HELD BY WILD POKÉMON
—

EVOLUTION

Level up with high friendship → Moon Stone

Igglybuff → Jigglypuff → Wigglytuff

MAIN WAY TO REGISTER IN THE NATIONAL POKÉDEX

Leave a Jigglypuff or Wigglytuff at a Pokémon Day Care, then hatch the Pokémon Egg that is found.

Damage taken in normal battles

Type		Type	
Normal	×1	Flying	×1
Fire	×1	Psychic	×1
Water	×1	Bug	×0.5
Grass	×1	Rock	×1
Electric	×1	Ghost	×0
Ice	×1	Dragon	×0
Fighting	×1	Dark	×0.5
Poison	×2	Steel	×2
Ground	×1	Fairy	×1

Damage taken in Inverse battles

Type		Type	
Normal	×1	Flying	×1
Fire	×1	Psychic	×1
Water	×1	Bug	×2
Grass	×1	Rock	×1
Electric	×1	Ghost	×2
Ice	×1	Dragon	×2
Fighting	×1	Dark	×2
Poison	×0.5	Steel	×0.5
Ground	×1	Fairy	×1

Can be used in
Inverse Battle
Battle Institute
Battle Maison
Random Matchup (Free Battle)
Random Matchup (Others)

LEVEL-UP MOVES

Lv.	Name	Type	Kind	Pow.	Acc.	PP	Range
1	Sing	Normal	Status	—	55	15	Normal
1	Charm	Fairy	Status	—	100	20	Normal
3	Defense Curl	Normal	Status	—	—	40	Self
5	Pound	Normal	Physical	40	100	35	Normal
9	Sweet Kiss	Fairy	Status	—	75	10	Normal
11	Copycat	Normal	Status	—	—	20	Self

TM & HM MOVES

No.	Name	Type	Kind	Pow.	Acc.	PP	Range
TM06	Toxic	Poison	Status	—	90	10	Normal
TM10	Hidden Power	Normal	Special	60	100	15	Normal
TM11	Sunny Day	Fire	Status	—	—	5	Both Sides
TM16	Light Screen	Psychic	Status	—	—	30	Your Side
TM17	Protect	Normal	Status	—	—	10	Self
TM18	Rain Dance	Water	Status	—	—	5	Both Sides
TM20	Safeguard	Normal	Status	—	—	25	Your Side
TM21	Frustration	Normal	Physical	—	100	20	Normal
TM22	Solar Beam	Grass	Special	120	100	10	Normal
TM27	Return	Normal	Physical	—	100	20	Normal
TM28	Dig	Ground	Physical	80	100	10	Normal
TM29	Psychic	Psychic	Special	90	100	10	Normal
TM30	Shadow Ball	Ghost	Special	80	100	15	Normal
TM32	Double Team	Normal	Status	—	—	15	Self
TM33	Reflect	Psychic	Status	—	—	20	Your Side
TM35	Flamethrower	Fire	Special	90	100	15	Normal
TM38	Fire Blast	Fire	Special	110	85	5	Normal
TM42	Facade	Normal	Physical	70	100	20	Normal
TM44	Rest	Psychic	Status	—	—	10	Self
TM45	Attract	Normal	Status	—	100	15	Normal
TM48	Round	Normal	Special	60	100	15	Normal
TM49	Echoed Voice	Normal	Special	40	100	15	Normal
TM56	Fling	Dark	Physical	—	100	10	Normal
TM59	Incinerate	Fire	Special	60	100	15	Many Others
TM70	Flash	Normal	Status	—	100	20	Normal
TM73	Thunder Wave	Electric	Status	—	100	20	Normal
TM77	Psych Up	Normal	Status	—	—	10	Normal
TM85	Dream Eater	Psychic	Special	100	100	15	Normal
TM86	Grass Knot	Grass	Special	—	100	20	Normal
TM87	Swagger	Normal	Status	—	90	15	Normal
TM88	Sleep Talk	Normal	Status	—	—	10	Self
TM90	Substitute	Normal	Status	—	—	10	Self
TM93	Wild Charge	Electric	Physical	90	100	15	Normal
TM94	Secret Power	Normal	Physical	70	100	20	Normal
TM100	Confide	Normal	Status	—	—	20	Normal

MOVES LEARNED IN EXCHANGE FOR BP

Name	Type	Kind	Pow.	Acc.	PP	Range
Covet	Normal	Physical	60	100	25	Normal
Bounce	Flying	Physical	85	85	5	Normal
Uproar	Normal	Special	90	100	10	1 Random
Magic Coat	Psychic	Status	—	—	15	Self
Gravity	Psychic	Status	—	—	5	Both Sides
Last Resort	Normal	Physical	140	100	5	Normal
Icy Wind	Ice	Special	55	95	15	Many Others
Hyper Voice	Normal	Special	90	100	10	Many Others
Snore	Normal	Special	50	100	15	Normal
Role Play	Psychic	Status	—	—	10	Normal
Heal Bell	Normal	Status	—	—	5	Your Party
Pain Split	Normal	Status	—	—	20	Normal
Shock Wave	Electric	Special	60	—	20	Normal
Water Pulse	Water	Special	60	100	20	Normal
Helping Hand	Normal	Status	—	—	20	1 Ally
Endeavor	Normal	Physical	—	100	5	Normal
Recycle	Normal	Status	—	—	10	Self

MOVES TAUGHT BY PEOPLE

Name	Type	Kind	Pow.	Acc.	PP	Range

EGG MOVES

Name	Type	Kind	Pow.	Acc.	PP	Range
Perish Song	Normal	Status	—	—	5	Adjacent
Present	Normal	Physical	—	90	15	Normal
Feint Attack	Dark	Physical	60	—	20	Normal
Wish	Normal	Status	—	—	10	Self
Fake Tears	Dark	Status	—	100	20	Normal
Last Resort	Normal	Physical	140	100	5	Normal
Covet	Normal	Physical	60	100	25	Normal
Gravity	Psychic	Status	—	—	5	Both Sides
Sleep Talk	Normal	Status	—	—	10	Self
Captivate	Normal	Status	—	100	20	Many Others
Punishment	Dark	Physical	—	100	5	Normal
Misty Terrain	Fairy	Status	—	—	10	Both Sides
Heal Pulse	Psychic	Status	—	—	10	Normal

National Pokédex **175** Hoenn Pokédex —

Togepi

Spike Ball Pokémon

Fairy

HEIGHT: 1'00" WEIGHT: 3.3 lbs.

Same form for ♂ / ♀

Ω As its energy, Togepi uses the positive emotions of compassion and pleasure exuded by people and Pokémon. This Pokémon stores up feelings of happiness inside its shell, then shares them with others.

α As its energy, Togepi uses the positive emotions of compassion and pleasure exuded by people and Pokémon. This Pokémon stores up feelings of happiness inside its shell, then shares them with others.

ABILITIES

Hustle
Serene Grace

HIDDEN ABILITY

Super Luck

EGG GROUPS

No Eggs Discovered

STAT GROWTH RATES

HP
Attack
Defense
Sp. Atk
Sp. Def
Speed

ITEMS SOMETIMES HELD BY WILD POKÉMON

—

EVOLUTION

Togepi → Level up with high friendship → Togetic → Shiny Stone → Togekiss

MAIN WAY TO REGISTER IN THE NATIONAL POKÉDEX

Receive a second Pokémon Egg from an old woman in Lavaridge Town (after battling Groudon or Kyogre) and hatch it.

Damage taken in normal battles

Type		Type	
Normal	×1	Flying	×1
Fire	×1	Psychic	×1
Water	×1	Bug	×0.5
Grass	×1	Rock	×1
Electric	×1	Ghost	×1
Ice	×1	Dragon	×0
Fighting	×0.5	Dark	×0.5
Poison	×2	Steel	×2
Ground	×1	Fairy	×1

Damage taken in Inverse battles

Type		Type	
Normal	×1	Flying	×1
Fire	×1	Psychic	×1
Water	×1	Bug	×2
Grass	×1	Rock	×1
Electric	×1	Ghost	×1
Ice	×1	Dragon	×2
Fighting	×2	Dark	×2
Poison	×0.5	Steel	×0.5
Ground	×1	Fairy	×1

Can be used in

Inverse Battle
Battle Institute
Battle Maison
Random Matchup (Free Battle)
Random Matchup (Others)

LEVEL-UP MOVES

Lv.	Name	Type	Kind	Pow.	Acc.	PP	Range
1	Growl	Normal	Status	—	100	40	Many Others
1	Charm	Fairy	Status	—	100	20	Normal
5	Metronome	Normal	Status	—	—	10	Self
9	Sweet Kiss	Fairy	Status	—	75	10	Normal
13	Yawn	Normal	Status	—	—	10	Normal
17	Encore	Normal	Status	—	100	5	Normal
21	Follow Me	Normal	Status	—	—	20	Self
25	Bestow	Normal	Status	—	—	15	Normal
29	Wish	Normal	Status	—	—	10	Self
33	Ancient Power	Rock	Special	60	100	5	Normal
37	Safeguard	Normal	Status	—	—	25	Your Side
41	Baton Pass	Normal	Status	—	—	40	Self
45	Double-Edge	Normal	Physical	120	100	15	Normal
49	Last Resort	Normal	Physical	140	100	5	Normal
53	After You	Normal	Status	—	—	15	Normal

TM & HM MOVES

No.	Name	Type	Kind	Pow.	Acc.	PP	Range
TM03	Psyshock	Psychic	Special	80	100	10	Normal
TM06	Toxic	Poison	Status	—	90	10	Normal
TM10	Hidden Power	Normal	Special	60	100	15	Normal
TM11	Sunny Day	Fire	Status	—	—	5	Both Sides
TM16	Light Screen	Psychic	Status	—	—	30	Your Side
TM17	Protect	Normal	Status	—	—	10	Self
TM18	Rain Dance	Water	Status	—	—	5	Both Sides
TM20	Safeguard	Normal	Status	—	—	25	Your Side
TM21	Frustration	Normal	Physical	—	100	20	Normal
TM22	Solar Beam	Grass	Special	120	100	10	Normal
TM27	Return	Normal	Physical	—	100	20	Normal
TM29	Psychic	Psychic	Special	90	100	10	Normal
TM30	Shadow Ball	Ghost	Special	80	100	15	Normal
TM32	Double Team	Normal	Status	—	—	15	Self
TM33	Reflect	Psychic	Status	—	—	20	Your Side
TM35	Flamethrower	Fire	Special	90	100	15	Normal
TM38	Fire Blast	Fire	Special	110	85	5	Normal
TM42	Facade	Normal	Physical	70	100	20	Normal
TM44	Rest	Psychic	Status	—	—	10	Self
TM45	Attract	Normal	Status	—	100	15	Normal
TM48	Round	Normal	Special	60	100	15	Normal
TM49	Echoed Voice	Normal	Special	40	100	15	Normal
TM56	Fling	Dark	Physical	—	100	10	Normal
TM59	Incinerate	Fire	Special	60	100	15	Many Others
TM70	Flash	Normal	Status	—	100	20	Normal
TM73	Thunder Wave	Electric	Status	—	100	20	Normal
TM77	Psych Up	Normal	Status	—	—	10	Normal
TM85	Dream Eater	Psychic	Special	100	100	15	Normal
TM86	Grass Knot	Grass	Special	—	100	20	Normal
TM87	Swagger	Normal	Status	—	90	15	Normal
TM88	Sleep Talk	Normal	Status	—	—	10	Self
TM90	Substitute	Normal	Status	—	—	10	Self
TM94	Secret Power	Normal	Physical	70	100	20	Normal
TM99	Dazzling Gleam	Fairy	Special	80	100	10	Many Others
TM100	Confide	Normal	Status	—	—	20	Normal
HM06	Rock Smash	Fighting	Physical	40	100	15	Normal

MOVES LEARNED IN EXCHANGE FOR BP

Name	Type	Kind	Pow.	Acc.	PP	Range
Covet	Normal	Physical	60	100	25	Normal
Signal Beam	Bug	Special	75	100	15	Normal
Uproar	Normal	Special	90	100	10	1 Random
Magic Coat	Psychic	Status	—	—	15	Self
Last Resort	Normal	Physical	140	100	5	Normal
Zen Headbutt	Psychic	Physical	80	90	15	Normal
Hyper Voice	Normal	Special	90	100	10	Many Others
Snore	Normal	Special	50	100	15	Normal
Heal Bell	Normal	Status	—	—	5	Your Party
Shock Wave	Electric	Special	60	—	20	Normal
Water Pulse	Water	Special	60	100	20	Normal
After You	Normal	Status	—	—	15	Normal
Trick	Psychic	Status	—	100	10	Normal
Endeavor	Normal	Physical	—	100	5	Normal

MOVES TAUGHT BY PEOPLE

Name	Type	Kind	Pow.	Acc.	PP	Range

EGG MOVES

Name	Type	Kind	Pow.	Acc.	PP	Range
Present	Normal	Physical	—	90	15	Normal
Mirror Move	Flying	Status	—	—	20	Normal
Peck	Flying	Physical	35	100	35	Normal
Foresight	Normal	Status	—	—	40	Normal
Future Sight	Psychic	Special	120	100	10	Normal
Nasty Plot	Dark	Status	—	—	20	Self
Psycho Shift	Psychic	Status	—	100	10	Normal
Lucky Chant	Normal	Status	—	—	30	Your Side
Extrasensory	Psychic	Special	80	100	20	Normal
Secret Power	Normal	Physical	70	100	20	Normal
Stored Power	Psychic	Special	20	100	10	Normal
Morning Sun	Normal	Status	—	—	5	Self

National Pokédex **176** Hoenn Pokédex —

Togetic

Happiness Pokémon

Fairy Flying

HEIGHT: 2'00" WEIGHT: 7.1 lbs.

Same form for ♂ / ♀

Ω Togetic is said to be a Pokémon that brings good fortune. When the Pokémon spots someone who is pure of heart, it is said to appear and share its happiness with that person.

α Togetic is said to be a Pokémon that brings good fortune. When the Pokémon spots someone who is pure of heart, it is said to appear and share its happiness with that person.

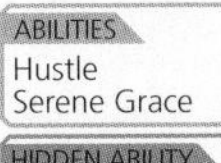

ABILITIES

Hustle
Serene Grace

HIDDEN ABILITY

Super Luck

EGG GROUPS

Flying Fairy

STAT GROWTH RATES

HP
Attack
Defense
Sp. Atk
Sp. Def
Speed

ITEMS SOMETIMES HELD BY WILD POKÉMON

—

EVOLUTION

Togepi → Level up with high friendship → Togetic → Shiny Stone → Togekiss

MAIN WAY TO REGISTER IN THE NATIONAL POKÉDEX

Level up Togepi with high friendship.

Damage taken in normal battles

Type		Type	
Normal	×1	Flying	×1
Fire	×1	Psychic	×1
Water	×1	Bug	×0.25
Grass	×0.5	Rock	×2
Electric	×2	Ghost	×1
Ice	×2	Dragon	×0
Fighting	×0.25	Dark	×0.5
Poison	×2	Steel	×2
Ground	×0	Fairy	×1

Damage taken in Inverse battles

Type		Type	
Normal	×1	Flying	×1
Fire	×1	Psychic	×1
Water	×1	Bug	×4
Grass	×2	Rock	×0.5
Electric	×0.5	Ghost	×1
Ice	×0.5	Dragon	×2
Fighting	×4	Dark	×2
Poison	×0.5	Steel	×0.5
Ground	×2	Fairy	×1

Can be used in

Inverse Battle
Battle Institute
Battle Maison
Random Matchup (Free Battle)
Random Matchup (Others)

LEVEL-UP MOVES

Lv.	Name	Type	Kind	Pow.	Acc.	PP	Range
1	Magical Leaf	Grass	Special	60	—	20	Normal
1	Growl	Normal	Status	—	100	40	Many Others
1	Charm	Fairy	Status	—	100	20	Normal
1	Metronome	Normal	Status	—	—	10	Self
1	Sweet Kiss	Fairy	Status	—	75	10	Normal
5	Metronome	Normal	Status	—	—	10	Self
9	Sweet Kiss	Fairy	Status	—	75	10	Normal
13	Yawn	Normal	Status	—	—	10	Normal
14	Fairy Wind	Fairy	Special	40	100	30	Normal
17	Encore	Normal	Status	—	100	5	Normal
21	Follow Me	Normal	Status	—	—	20	Self
25	Bestow	Normal	Status	—	—	15	Normal
29	Wish	Normal	Status	—	—	10	Self
33	Ancient Power	Rock	Special	60	100	5	Normal
37	Safeguard	Normal	Status	—	—	25	Your Side
41	Baton Pass	Normal	Status	—	—	40	Self
45	Double-Edge	Normal	Physical	120	100	15	Normal
49	Last Resort	Normal	Physical	140	100	5	Normal
53	After You	Normal	Status	—	—	15	Normal

TM & HM MOVES

No.	Name	Type	Kind	Pow.	Acc.	PP	Range
TM03	Psyshock	Psychic	Special	80	100	10	Normal
TM06	Toxic	Poison	Status	—	90	10	Normal
TM10	Hidden Power	Normal	Special	60	100	15	Normal
TM11	Sunny Day	Fire	Status	—	—	5	Both Sides
TM15	Hyper Beam	Normal	Special	150	90	5	Normal
TM16	Light Screen	Psychic	Status	—	—	30	Your Side
TM17	Protect	Normal	Status	—	—	10	Self
TM18	Rain Dance	Water	Status	—	—	5	Both Sides
TM19	Roost	Flying	Status	—	—	10	Self
TM20	Safeguard	Normal	Status	—	—	25	Your Side
TM21	Frustration	Normal	Physical	—	100	20	Normal
TM22	Solar Beam	Grass	Special	120	100	10	Normal
TM27	Return	Normal	Physical	—	100	20	Normal
TM29	Psychic	Psychic	Special	90	100	10	Normal
TM30	Shadow Ball	Ghost	Special	80	100	15	Normal
TM31	Brick Break	Fighting	Physical	75	100	15	Normal
TM32	Double Team	Normal	Status	—	—	15	Self
TM33	Reflect	Psychic	Status	—	—	20	Your Side
TM35	Flamethrower	Fire	Special	90	100	15	Normal
TM38	Fire Blast	Fire	Special	110	85	5	Normal
TM40	Aerial Ace	Flying	Physical	60	—	20	Normal
TM42	Facade	Normal	Physical	70	100	20	Normal
TM44	Rest	Psychic	Status	—	—	10	Self
TM45	Attract	Normal	Status	—	100	15	Normal
TM48	Round	Normal	Special	60	100	15	Normal
TM49	Echoed Voice	Normal	Special	40	100	15	Normal
TM51	Steel Wing	Steel	Physical	70	90	25	Normal
TM56	Fling	Dark	Physical	—	100	10	Normal
TM59	Incinerate	Fire	Special	60	100	15	Many Others
TM67	Retaliate	Normal	Physical	70	100	5	Normal
TM68	Giga Impact	Normal	Physical	150	90	5	Normal
TM70	Flash	Normal	Status	—	100	20	Normal
TM73	Thunder Wave	Electric	Status	—	100	20	Normal
TM77	Psych Up	Normal	Status	—	—	10	Normal
TM85	Dream Eater	Psychic	Special	100	100	15	Normal
TM86	Grass Knot	Grass	Special	—	100	20	Normal
TM87	Swagger	Normal	Status	—	90	15	Normal
TM88	Sleep Talk	Normal	Status	—	—	10	Self
TM90	Substitute	Normal	Status	—	—	10	Self
TM94	Secret Power	Normal	Physical	70	100	20	Normal
TM99	Dazzling Gleam	Fairy	Special	80	100	10	Many Others
TM100	Confide	Normal	Status	—	—	20	Normal
HM02	Fly	Flying	Physical	90	95	15	Normal
HM06	Rock Smash	Fighting	Physical	40	100	15	Normal

MOVES LEARNED IN EXCHANGE FOR BP

Name	Type	Kind	Pow.	Acc.	PP	Range
Covet	Normal	Physical	60	100	25	Normal
Signal Beam	Bug	Special	75	100	15	Normal
Magic Coat	Psychic	Status	—	—	15	Self
Last Resort	Normal	Physical	140	100	5	Normal
Zen Headbutt	Psychic	Physical	80	90	15	Normal
Hyper Voice	Normal	Special	90	100	10	Many Others
Snore	Normal	Special	50	100	15	Normal
Heat Wave	Fire	Special	95	90	10	Many Others
Heal Bell	Normal	Status	—	—	5	Your Party
Tailwind	Flying	Status	—	—	15	Your Side
Drain Punch	Fighting	Physical	75	100	10	Normal
Focus Punch	Fighting	Physical	150	100	20	Normal
Shock Wave	Electric	Special	60	—	20	Normal
Water Pulse	Water	Special	60	100	20	Normal
After You	Normal	Status	—	—	15	Normal
Trick	Psychic	Status	—	100	10	Normal
Endeavor	Normal	Physical	—	100	5	Normal

MOVES TAUGHT BY PEOPLE

Name	Type	Kind	Pow.	Acc.	PP	Range

National Pokédex **177** Hoenn Pokédex **169**

Natu

Tiny Bird Pokémon

Psychic Flying

HEIGHT: 0'08" WEIGHT: 4.4 lbs.

Same form for ♂ / ♀

Ω Natu cannot fly because its wings are not yet fully grown. If your eyes meet with this Pokémon's eyes, it will stare back intently at you. But if you move even slightly, it will hop away to safety.

α Natu has a highly developed jumping ability. The Pokémon flaps and leaps onto tree branches that are taller than grown-up people to pick at the tree's new shoots.

ABILITIES
Synchronize
Early Bird

HIDDEN ABILITY
Magic Bounce

EGG GROUPS
Flying

STAT GROWTH RATES
HP ■■
Attack ■■■
Defense ■■
Sp. Atk ■■■
Sp. Def ■■
Speed ■■■■

ITEMS SOMETIMES HELD BY WILD POKÉMON
—

EVOLUTION
Natu → Lv. 25 → Xatu

MAIN WAY TO REGISTER IN THE NATIONAL POKÉDEX

Leave a Xatu at a Pokémon Day Care, then hatch the Pokémon Egg that is found.

Damage taken in normal battles

Type		Type	
Normal	×1	Flying	×1
Fire	×1	Psychic	×0.5
Water	×1	Bug	×1
Grass	×0.5	Rock	×2
Electric	×2	Ghost	×2
Ice	×2	Dragon	×1
Fighting	×0.25	Dark	×2
Poison	×1	Steel	×1
Ground	×0	Fairy	×1

Damage taken in Inverse battles

Type		Type	
Normal	×1	Flying	×1
Fire	×1	Psychic	×2
Water	×1	Bug	×1
Grass	×2	Rock	×0.5
Electric	×0.5	Ghost	×0.5
Ice	×0.5	Dragon	×1
Fighting	×4	Dark	×0.5
Poison	×1	Steel	×1
Ground	×2	Fairy	×1

Can be used in
- Inverse Battle
- Battle Institute
- Battle Maison
- Random Matchup (Free Battle)
- Random Matchup (Others)

LEVEL-UP MOVES

Lv.	Name	Type	Kind	Pow.	Acc.	PP	Range
1	Peck	Flying	Physical	35	100	35	Normal
1	Leer	Normal	Status	—	100	30	Many Others
6	Night Shade	Ghost	Special	—	100	15	Normal
9	Teleport	Psychic	Status	—	—	20	Self
12	Lucky Chant	Normal	Status	—	—	30	Your Side
17	Stored Power	Psychic	Special	20	100	10	Normal
20	Ominous Wind	Ghost	Special	60	100	5	Normal
23	Confuse Ray	Ghost	Status	—	100	10	Normal
28	Wish	Normal	Status	—	—	10	Self
33	Psychic	Psychic	Special	90	100	10	Normal
36	Miracle Eye	Psychic	Status	—	—	40	Normal
39	Psycho Shift	Psychic	Status	—	100	10	Normal
44	Future Sight	Psychic	Special	120	100	10	Normal
47	Power Swap	Psychic	Status	—	—	10	Normal
47	Guard Swap	Psychic	Status	—	—	10	Normal
50	Me First	Normal	Status	—	—	20	Varies

TM & HM MOVES

No.	Name	Type	Kind	Pow.	Acc.	PP	Range
TM03	Psyshock	Psychic	Special	80	100	10	Normal
TM04	Calm Mind	Psychic	Status	—	—	20	Self
TM06	Toxic	Poison	Status	—	90	10	Normal
TM10	Hidden Power	Normal	Special	60	100	15	Normal
TM11	Sunny Day	Fire	Status	—	—	5	Both Sides
TM16	Light Screen	Psychic	Status	—	—	30	Your Side
TM17	Protect	Normal	Status	—	—	10	Self
TM18	Rain Dance	Water	Status	—	—	5	Both Sides
TM19	Roost	Flying	Status	—	—	10	Self
TM21	Frustration	Normal	Physical	—	100	20	Normal
TM22	Solar Beam	Grass	Special	120	100	10	Normal
TM27	Return	Normal	Physical	—	100	20	Normal
TM29	Psychic	Psychic	Special	90	100	10	Normal
TM30	Shadow Ball	Ghost	Special	80	100	15	Normal
TM32	Double Team	Normal	Status	—	—	15	Self
TM33	Reflect	Psychic	Status	—	—	20	Your Side
TM40	Aerial Ace	Flying	Physical	60	—	20	Normal
TM42	Facade	Normal	Physical	70	100	20	Normal
TM44	Rest	Psychic	Status	—	—	10	Self
TM45	Attract	Normal	Status	—	100	15	Normal
TM46	Thief	Dark	Physical	60	100	25	Normal
TM48	Round	Normal	Special	60	100	15	Normal
TM51	Steel Wing	Steel	Physical	70	90	25	Normal
TM70	Flash	Normal	Status	—	100	20	Normal
TM73	Thunder Wave	Electric	Status	—	100	20	Normal
TM77	Psych Up	Normal	Status	—	—	10	Normal
TM85	Dream Eater	Psychic	Special	100	100	15	Normal
TM86	Grass Knot	Grass	Special	—	100	20	Normal
TM87	Swagger	Normal	Status	—	90	15	Normal
TM88	Sleep Talk	Normal	Status	—	—	10	Self
TM89	U-turn	Bug	Physical	70	100	20	Normal
TM90	Substitute	Normal	Status	—	—	10	Self
TM92	Trick Room	Psychic	Status	—	—	5	Both Sides
TM94	Secret Power	Normal	Physical	70	100	20	Normal
TM99	Dazzling Gleam	Fairy	Special	80	100	10	Many Others
TM100	Confide	Normal	Status	—	—	20	Normal

MOVES LEARNED IN EXCHANGE FOR BP

Name	Type	Kind	Pow.	Acc.	PP	Range
Signal Beam	Bug	Special	75	100	15	Normal
Magic Coat	Psychic	Status	—	—	15	Self
Zen Headbutt	Psychic	Physical	80	90	15	Normal
Snore	Normal	Special	50	100	15	Normal
Heat Wave	Fire	Special	95	90	10	Many Others
Tailwind	Flying	Status	—	—	15	Your Side
Sky Attack	Flying	Physical	140	90	5	Normal
Pain Split	Normal	Status	—	—	20	Normal
Giga Drain	Grass	Special	75	100	10	Normal
Trick	Psychic	Status	—	100	10	Normal
Magic Room	Psychic	Status	—	—	10	Both Sides
Skill Swap	Psychic	Status	—	—	10	Normal

MOVES TAUGHT BY PEOPLE

Name	Type	Kind	Pow.	Acc.	PP	Range

EGG MOVES

Name	Type	Kind	Pow.	Acc.	PP	Range
Haze	Ice	Status	—	—	30	Both Sides
Drill Peck	Flying	Physical	80	100	20	Normal
Quick Attack	Normal	Physical	40	100	30	Normal
Feint Attack	Dark	Physical	60	—	20	Normal
Steel Wing	Steel	Physical	70	90	25	Normal
Feather Dance	Flying	Status	—	100	15	Normal
Refresh	Normal	Status	—	—	20	Self
Zen Headbutt	Psychic	Physical	80	90	15	Normal
Sucker Punch	Dark	Physical	80	100	5	Normal
Synchronoise	Psychic	Special	120	100	10	Adjacent
Roost	Flying	Status	—	—	10	Self
Skill Swap	Psychic	Status	—	—	10	Normal
Simple Beam	Normal	Status	—	100	15	Normal
Ally Switch	Psychic	Status	—	—	15	Self

National Pokédex **178** Hoenn Pokédex **170**

Xatu

Mystic Pokémon

Psychic Flying

HEIGHT: 4'11" WEIGHT: 33.1 lbs.

The male has three lines on its body. The female has two lines on its body.

♂ ♀

Ω Xatu stands rooted and still in one spot all day long. People believe that this Pokémon does so out of fear of the terrible things it has foreseen in the future.

α Xatu is known to stand motionless while staring at the sun all day long. Some people revere it as a mystical Pokémon out of their belief that Xatu is in possession of the power to see into the future.

ABILITIES
Synchronize
Early Bird

HIDDEN ABILITY
Magic Bounce

EGG GROUPS
Flying

STAT GROWTH RATES
HP ■■■
Attack ■■■■
Defense ■■■
Sp. Atk ■■■■■
Sp. Def ■■■
Speed ■■■■■

ITEMS SOMETIMES HELD BY WILD POKÉMON
—

EVOLUTION
Natu → Lv. 25 → Xatu

MAIN WAY TO REGISTER IN THE NATIONAL POKÉDEX

Catch in the tall grass in the lower-left corner of the Safari Zone.

Damage taken in normal battles

Type		Type	
Normal	×1	Flying	×1
Fire	×1	Psychic	×0.5
Water	×1	Bug	×1
Grass	×0.5	Rock	×2
Electric	×2	Ghost	×2
Ice	×2	Dragon	×1
Fighting	×0.25	Dark	×2
Poison	×1	Steel	×1
Ground	×0	Fairy	×1

Damage taken in Inverse battles

Type		Type	
Normal	×1	Flying	×1
Fire	×1	Psychic	×2
Water	×1	Bug	×1
Grass	×2	Rock	×0.5
Electric	×0.5	Ghost	×0.5
Ice	×0.5	Dragon	×1
Fighting	×4	Dark	×0.5
Poison	×1	Steel	×1
Ground	×2	Fairy	×1

Can be used in
- Inverse Battle
- Battle Institute
- Battle Maison
- Random Matchup (Free Battle)
- Random Matchup (Others)

LEVEL-UP MOVES

Lv.	Name	Type	Kind	Pow.	Acc.	PP	Range
1	Tailwind	Flying	Status	—	—	15	Your Side
1	Peck	Flying	Physical	35	100	35	Normal
1	Leer	Normal	Status	—	100	30	Many Others
1	Night Shade	Ghost	Special	—	100	15	Normal
1	Teleport	Psychic	Status	—	—	20	Self
6	Night Shade	Ghost	Special	—	100	15	Normal
9	Teleport	Psychic	Status	—	—	20	Self
12	Lucky Chant	Normal	Status	—	—	30	Your Side
17	Stored Power	Psychic	Special	20	100	10	Normal
20	Ominous Wind	Ghost	Special	60	100	5	Normal
23	Confuse Ray	Ghost	Status	—	100	10	Normal
25	Air Slash	Flying	Special	75	95	15	Normal
29	Wish	Normal	Status	—	—	10	Self
35	Psychic	Psychic	Special	90	100	10	Normal
39	Miracle Eye	Psychic	Status	—	—	40	Normal
43	Psycho Shift	Psychic	Status	—	100	10	Normal
49	Future Sight	Psychic	Special	120	100	10	Normal
53	Power Swap	Psychic	Status	—	—	10	Normal
53	Guard Swap	Psychic	Status	—	—	10	Normal
57	Me First	Normal	Status	—	—	20	Varies

TM & HM MOVES

No.	Name	Type	Kind	Pow.	Acc.	PP	Range
TM03	Psyshock	Psychic	Special	80	100	10	Normal
TM04	Calm Mind	Psychic	Status	—	—	20	Self
TM06	Toxic	Poison	Status	—	90	10	Normal
TM10	Hidden Power	Normal	Special	60	100	15	Normal
TM11	Sunny Day	Fire	Status	—	—	5	Both Sides
TM15	Hyper Beam	Normal	Special	150	90	5	Normal
TM16	Light Screen	Psychic	Status	—	—	30	Your Side
TM17	Protect	Normal	Status	—	—	10	Self
TM18	Rain Dance	Water	Status	—	—	5	Both Sides
TM19	Roost	Flying	Status	—	—	10	Self
TM21	Frustration	Normal	Physical	—	100	20	Normal
TM22	Solar Beam	Grass	Special	120	100	10	Normal
TM27	Return	Normal	Physical	—	100	20	Normal
TM29	Psychic	Psychic	Special	90	100	10	Normal
TM30	Shadow Ball	Ghost	Special	80	100	15	Normal
TM32	Double Team	Normal	Status	—	—	15	Self
TM33	Reflect	Psychic	Status	—	—	20	Your Side
TM40	Aerial Ace	Flying	Physical	60	—	20	Normal
TM42	Facade	Normal	Physical	70	100	20	Normal
TM44	Rest	Psychic	Status	—	—	10	Self
TM45	Attract	Normal	Status	—	100	15	Normal
TM46	Thief	Dark	Physical	60	100	25	Normal
TM48	Round	Normal	Special	60	100	15	Normal
TM51	Steel Wing	Steel	Physical	70	90	25	Normal
TM68	Giga Impact	Normal	Physical	150	90	5	Normal
TM70	Flash	Normal	Status	—	100	20	Normal
TM73	Thunder Wave	Electric	Status	—	100	20	Normal
TM77	Psych Up	Normal	Status	—	—	10	Normal
TM85	Dream Eater	Psychic	Special	100	100	15	Normal
TM86	Grass Knot	Grass	Special	—	100	20	Normal
TM87	Swagger	Normal	Status	—	90	15	Normal
TM88	Sleep Talk	Normal	Status	—	—	10	Self
TM89	U-turn	Bug	Physical	70	100	20	Normal
TM90	Substitute	Normal	Status	—	—	10	Self
TM92	Trick Room	Psychic	Status	—	—	5	Both Sides
TM94	Secret Power	Normal	Physical	70	100	20	Normal
TM99	Dazzling Gleam	Fairy	Special	80	100	10	Many Others
TM100	Confide	Normal	Status	—	—	20	Normal
HM02	Fly	Flying	Physical	90	95	15	Normal

MOVES LEARNED IN EXCHANGE FOR BP

Name	Type	Kind	Pow.	Acc.	PP	Range
Signal Beam	Bug	Special	75	100	15	Normal
Magic Coat	Psychic	Status	—	—	15	Self
Foul Play	Dark	Physical	95	100	15	Normal
Zen Headbutt	Psychic	Physical	80	90	15	Normal
Snore	Normal	Special	50	100	15	Normal
Heat Wave	Fire	Special	95	90	10	Many Others
Tailwind	Flying	Status	—	—	15	Your Side
Sky Attack	Flying	Physical	140	90	5	Normal
Pain Split	Normal	Status	—	—	20	Normal
Giga Drain	Grass	Special	75	100	10	Normal
Trick	Psychic	Status	—	100	10	Normal
Magic Room	Psychic	Status	—	—	10	Both Sides
Skill Swap	Psychic	Status	—	—	10	Normal

MOVES TAUGHT BY PEOPLE

Name	Type	Kind	Pow.	Acc.	PP	Range

National Pokédex **179** Hoenn Pokédex —

Mareep

Wool Pokémon

Electric

HEIGHT: 2'00" WEIGHT: 17.2 lbs.

Same form for ♂ / ♀

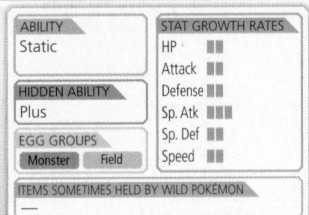

Ω Mareep's fluffy coat of wool rubs together and builds a static charge. The more static electricity is charged, the more brightly the lightbulb at the tip of its tail glows.

α Mareep's fluffy coat of wool rubs together and builds a static charge. The more static electricity is charged, the more brightly the lightbulb at the tip of its tail glows.

ABILITY
Static

HIDDEN ABILITY
Plus

EGG GROUPS
Monster / Field

STAT GROWTH RATES
HP ■■
Attack ■■
Defense ■■
Sp. Atk ■■■
Sp. Def ■■
Speed ■■

ITEMS SOMETIMES HELD BY WILD POKÉMON
—

EVOLUTION

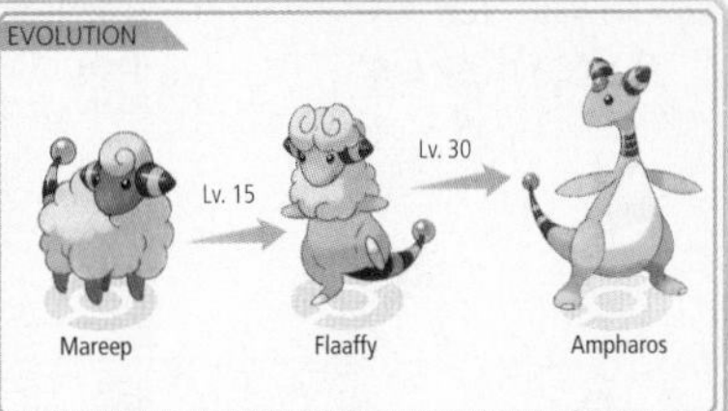

MAIN WAY TO REGISTER IN THE NATIONAL POKÉDEX

Appears in *Pokémon X* and *Pokémon Y*. Bring it to your game using Link Trade or the GTS.

Damage taken in normal battles

Type		Type	
Normal	×1	Flying	×0.5
Fire	×1	Psychic	×1
Water	×1	Bug	×1
Grass	×1	Rock	×1
Electric	×0.5	Ghost	×1
Ice	×1	Dragon	×1
Fighting	×1	Dark	×1
Poison	×1	Steel	×0.5
Ground	×2	Fairy	×1

Damage taken in Inverse battles

Type		Type	
Normal	×1	Flying	×2
Fire	×1	Psychic	×1
Water	×1	Bug	×1
Grass	×1	Rock	×1
Electric	×2	Ghost	×1
Ice	×1	Dragon	×1
Fighting	×1	Dark	×1
Poison	×1	Steel	×2
Ground	×0.5	Fairy	×1

Can be used in
- Inverse Battle
- Battle Institute
- Battle Maison
- Random Matchup (Free Battle)
- Random Matchup (Others)

LEVEL-UP MOVES

Lv.	Name	Type	Kind	Pow.	Acc.	PP	Range
1	Tackle	Normal	Physical	50	100	35	Normal
1	Growl	Normal	Status	—	100	40	Many Others
4	Thunder Wave	Electric	Status	—	100	20	Normal
8	Thunder Shock	Electric	Special	40	100	30	Normal
11	Cotton Spore	Grass	Status	—	100	40	Many Others
15	Charge	Electric	Status	—	—	20	Self
18	Take Down	Normal	Physical	90	85	20	Normal
22	Electro Ball	Electric	Special	—	100	10	Normal
25	Confuse Ray	Ghost	Status	—	100	10	Normal
29	Power Gem	Rock	Special	80	100	20	Normal
32	Discharge	Electric	Special	80	100	15	Adjacent
36	Cotton Guard	Grass	Status	—	—	10	Self
39	Signal Beam	Bug	Special	75	100	15	Normal
43	Light Screen	Psychic	Status	—	—	30	Your Side
46	Thunder	Electric	Special	110	70	10	Normal

TM & HM MOVES

No.	Name	Type	Kind	Pow.	Acc.	PP	Range
TM06	Toxic	Poison	Status	—	90	10	Normal
TM10	Hidden Power	Normal	Special	60	100	15	Normal
TM16	Light Screen	Psychic	Status	—	—	30	Your Side
TM17	Protect	Normal	Status	—	—	10	Self
TM18	Rain Dance	Water	Status	—	—	5	Both Sides
TM20	Safeguard	Normal	Status	—	—	25	Your Side
TM21	Frustration	Normal	Physical	—	100	20	Normal
TM24	Thunderbolt	Electric	Special	90	100	15	Normal
TM25	Thunder	Electric	Special	110	70	10	Normal
TM27	Return	Normal	Physical	—	100	20	Normal
TM32	Double Team	Normal	Status	—	—	15	Self
TM42	Facade	Normal	Physical	70	100	20	Normal
TM44	Rest	Psychic	Status	—	—	10	Self
TM45	Attract	Normal	Status	—	100	15	Normal
TM48	Round	Normal	Special	60	100	15	Normal
TM49	Echoed Voice	Normal	Special	40	100	15	Normal
TM57	Charge Beam	Electric	Special	50	90	10	Normal
TM70	Flash	Normal	Status	—	100	20	Normal
TM73	Thunder Wave	Electric	Status	—	100	20	Normal
TM87	Swagger	Normal	Status	—	90	15	Normal
TM88	Sleep Talk	Normal	Status	—	—	10	Self
TM90	Substitute	Normal	Status	—	—	10	Self
TM93	Wild Charge	Electric	Physical	90	100	15	Normal
TM94	Secret Power	Normal	Physical	70	100	20	Normal
TM100	Confide	Normal	Status	—	—	20	Normal

MOVES LEARNED IN EXCHANGE FOR BP

Name	Type	Kind	Pow.	Acc.	PP	Range
Signal Beam	Bug	Special	75	100	15	Normal
Magnet Rise	Electric	Status	—	—	10	Self
Electroweb	Electric	Special	55	95	15	Many Others
Iron Tail	Steel	Physical	100	75	15	Normal
Snore	Normal	Special	50	100	15	Normal
Heal Bell	Normal	Status	—	—	5	Your Party
Shock Wave	Electric	Special	60	—	20	Normal
After You	Normal	Status	—	—	15	Normal

MOVES TAUGHT BY PEOPLE

Name	Type	Kind	Pow.	Acc.	PP	Range

EGG MOVES

Name	Type	Kind	Pow.	Acc.	PP	Range
Take Down	Normal	Physical	90	85	20	Normal
Body Slam	Normal	Physical	85	100	15	Normal
Screech	Normal	Status	—	85	40	Normal
Odor Sleuth	Normal	Status	—	—	40	Normal
Charge	Electric	Status	—	—	20	Self
Flatter	Dark	Status	—	100	15	Normal
Sand Attack	Ground	Status	—	100	15	Normal
Iron Tail	Steel	Physical	100	75	15	Normal
After You	Normal	Status	—	—	15	Normal
Agility	Psychic	Status	—	—	30	Self
Eerie Impulse	Electric	Status	—	100	15	Normal
Electric Terrain	Electric	Status	—	—	10	Both Sides

National Pokédex **180** Hoenn Pokédex —

Flaaffy

Wool Pokémon

Electric

HEIGHT: 2'07" WEIGHT: 29.3 lbs.

Same form for ♂ / ♀

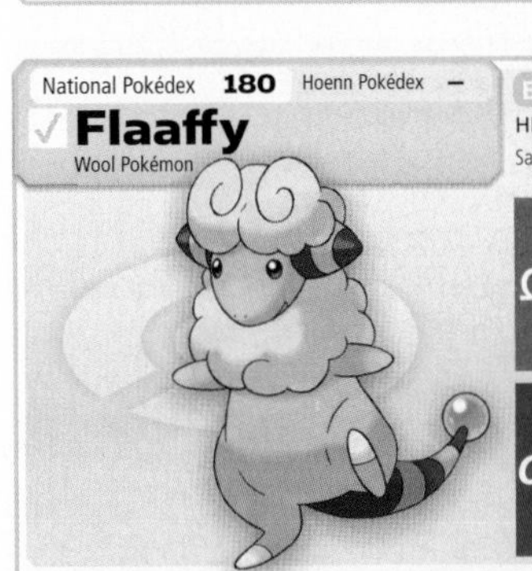

Ω Flaaffy's wool quality changes so that it can generate a high amount of static electricity with a small amount of wool. The bare and slick parts of its hide are shielded against electricity.

α Flaaffy's wool quality changes so that it can generate a high amount of static electricity with a small amount of wool. The bare and slick parts of its hide are shielded against electricity.

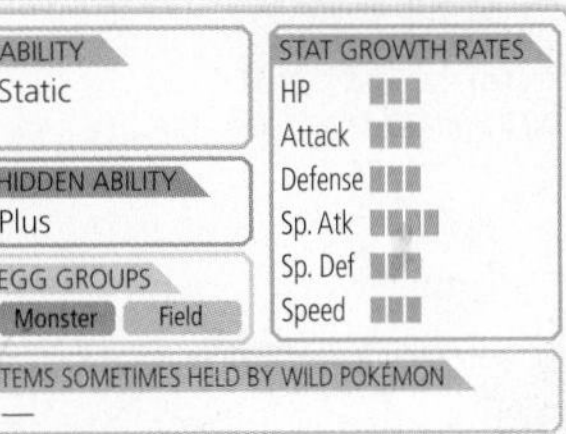

ABILITY
Static

HIDDEN ABILITY
Plus

EGG GROUPS
Monster / Field

STAT GROWTH RATES
HP ■■■
Attack ■■■
Defense ■■■
Sp. Atk ■■■■
Sp. Def ■■■
Speed ■■■

ITEMS SOMETIMES HELD BY WILD POKÉMON
—

EVOLUTION

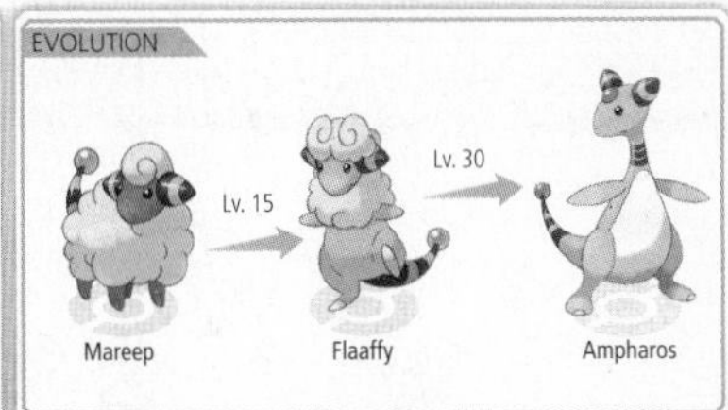

MAIN WAY TO REGISTER IN THE NATIONAL POKÉDEX

Level up a Mareep obtained via Link Trade or the GTS to Lv. 15.

Damage taken in normal battles

Type		Type	
Normal	×1	Flying	×0.5
Fire	×1	Psychic	×1
Water	×1	Bug	×1
Grass	×1	Rock	×1
Electric	×0.5	Ghost	×1
Ice	×1	Dragon	×1
Fighting	×1	Dark	×1
Poison	×1	Steel	×0.5
Ground	×2	Fairy	×1

Damage taken in Inverse battles

Type		Type	
Normal	×1	Flying	×2
Fire	×1	Psychic	×1
Water	×1	Bug	×1
Grass	×1	Rock	×1
Electric	×2	Ghost	×1
Ice	×1	Dragon	×1
Fighting	×1	Dark	×1
Poison	×1	Steel	×2
Ground	×0.5	Fairy	×1

Can be used in
- Inverse Battle
- Battle Institute
- Battle Maison
- Random Matchup (Free Battle)
- Random Matchup (Others)

LEVEL-UP MOVES

Lv.	Name	Type	Kind	Pow.	Acc.	PP	Range
1	Tackle	Normal	Physical	50	100	35	Normal
1	Growl	Normal	Status	—	100	40	Many Others
1	Thunder Wave	Electric	Status	—	100	20	Normal
1	Thunder Shock	Electric	Special	40	100	30	Normal
4	Thunder Wave	Electric	Status	—	100	20	Normal
8	Thunder Shock	Electric	Special	40	100	30	Normal
11	Cotton Spore	Grass	Status	—	100	40	Many Others
16	Charge	Electric	Status	—	—	20	Self
20	Take Down	Normal	Physical	90	85	20	Normal
25	Electro Ball	Electric	Special	—	100	10	Normal
29	Confuse Ray	Ghost	Status	—	100	10	Normal
34	Power Gem	Rock	Special	80	100	20	Normal
38	Discharge	Electric	Special	80	100	15	Adjacent
43	Cotton Guard	Grass	Status	—	—	10	Self
47	Signal Beam	Bug	Special	75	100	15	Normal
52	Light Screen	Psychic	Status	—	—	30	Your Side
56	Thunder	Electric	Special	110	70	10	Normal

TM & HM MOVES

No.	Name	Type	Kind	Pow.	Acc.	PP	Range
TM06	Toxic	Poison	Status	—	90	10	Normal
TM10	Hidden Power	Normal	Special	60	100	15	Normal
TM16	Light Screen	Psychic	Status	—	—	30	Your Side
TM17	Protect	Normal	Status	—	—	10	Self
TM18	Rain Dance	Water	Status	—	—	5	Both Sides
TM20	Safeguard	Normal	Status	—	—	25	Your Side
TM21	Frustration	Normal	Physical	—	100	20	Normal
TM24	Thunderbolt	Electric	Special	90	100	15	Normal
TM25	Thunder	Electric	Special	110	70	10	Normal
TM27	Return	Normal	Physical	—	100	20	Normal
TM31	Brick Break	Fighting	Physical	75	100	15	Normal
TM32	Double Team	Normal	Status	—	—	15	Self
TM42	Facade	Normal	Physical	70	100	20	Normal
TM44	Rest	Psychic	Status	—	—	10	Self
TM45	Attract	Normal	Status	—	100	15	Normal
TM48	Round	Normal	Special	60	100	15	Normal
TM49	Echoed Voice	Normal	Special	40	100	15	Normal
TM56	Fling	Dark	Physical	—	100	10	Normal
TM57	Charge Beam	Electric	Special	50	90	10	Normal
TM70	Flash	Normal	Status	—	100	20	Normal
TM72	Volt Switch	Electric	Special	70	100	20	Normal
TM73	Thunder Wave	Electric	Status	—	100	20	Normal
TM87	Swagger	Normal	Status	—	90	15	Normal
TM88	Sleep Talk	Normal	Status	—	—	10	Self
TM90	Substitute	Normal	Status	—	—	10	Self
TM93	Wild Charge	Electric	Physical	90	100	15	Normal
TM94	Secret Power	Normal	Physical	70	100	20	Normal
TM98	Power-Up Punch	Fighting	Physical	40	100	20	Normal
TM100	Confide	Normal	Status	—	—	20	Normal
HM04	Strength	Normal	Physical	80	100	15	Normal
HM06	Rock Smash	Fighting	Physical	40	100	15	Normal

MOVES LEARNED IN EXCHANGE FOR BP

Name	Type	Kind	Pow.	Acc.	PP	Range
Signal Beam	Bug	Special	75	100	15	Normal
Thunder Punch	Electric	Physical	75	100	15	Normal
Fire Punch	Fire	Physical	75	100	15	Normal
Magnet Rise	Electric	Status	—	—	10	Self
Electroweb	Electric	Special	55	95	15	Many Others
Iron Tail	Steel	Physical	100	75	15	Normal
Snore	Normal	Special	50	100	15	Normal
Heal Bell	Normal	Status	—	—	5	Your Party
Focus Punch	Fighting	Physical	150	100	20	Normal
Shock Wave	Electric	Special	60	—	20	Normal
After You	Normal	Status	—	—	15	Normal

MOVES TAUGHT BY PEOPLE

Name	Type	Kind	Pow.	Acc.	PP	Range

National Pokédex **181** Hoenn Pokédex —

Ampharos

Light Pokémon

Electric

HEIGHT: 4'07" WEIGHT: 135.6 lbs.

Same form for ♂ / ♀

Ω Ampharos gives off so much light that it can be seen even from space. People in the old days used the light of this Pokémon to send signals back and forth with others far away.

α Ampharos gives off so much light that it can be seen even from space. People in the old days used the light of this Pokémon to send signals back and forth with others far away.

ABILITY
Static

HIDDEN ABILITY
Plus

EGG GROUPS
Monster | Field

STAT GROWTH RATES
HP
Attack
Defense
Sp. Atk
Sp. Def
Speed

ITEMS SOMETIMES HELD BY WILD POKÉMON
—

EVOLUTION
Mareep → Lv. 15 → Flaaffy → Lv. 30 → Ampharos

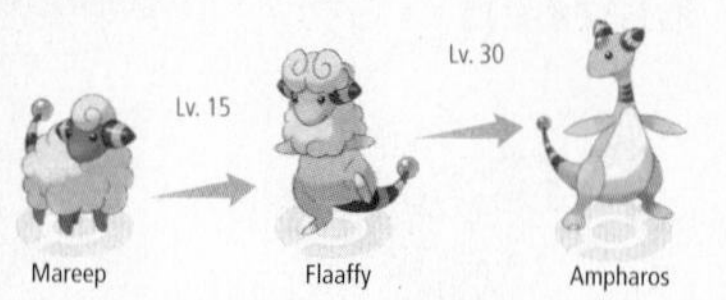

MAIN WAY TO REGISTER IN THE NATIONAL POKÉDEX

Level up a Flaaffy obtained via Link Trade or the GTS to Lv. 30.

Damage taken in normal battles

Type		Type	
Normal	×1	Flying	×0.5
Fire	×1	Psychic	×1
Water	×1	Bug	×1
Grass	×1	Rock	×1
Electric	×0.5	Ghost	×1
Ice	×1	Dragon	×1
Fighting	×1	Dark	×1
Poison	×1	Steel	×0.5
Ground	×2	Fairy	×1

Damage taken in Inverse battles

Type		Type	
Normal	×1	Flying	×2
Fire	×1	Psychic	×1
Water	×1	Bug	×1
Grass	×1	Rock	×1
Electric	×2	Ghost	×1
Ice	×1	Dragon	×1
Fighting	×1	Dark	×1
Poison	×1	Steel	×2
Ground	×0.5	Fairy	×1

Can be used in
Inverse Battle
Battle Institute
Battle Maison
Random Matchup (Free Battle)
Random Matchup (Others)

LEVEL-UP MOVES

Lv.	Name	Type	Kind	Pow.	Acc.	PP	Range
1	Zap Cannon	Electric	Special	120	50	5	Normal
1	Magnetic Flux	Electric	Status	—	—	20	Your Party
1	Ion Deluge	Electric	Status	—	—	25	Both Sides
1	Dragon Pulse	Dragon	Special	85	100	10	Normal
1	Fire Punch	Fire	Physical	75	100	15	Normal
1	Tackle	Normal	Physical	50	100	35	Normal
1	Growl	Normal	Status	—	100	40	Many Others
1	Thunder Wave	Electric	Status	—	100	20	Normal
1	Thunder Shock	Electric	Special	40	100	30	Normal
4	Thunder Wave	Electric	Status	—	100	20	Normal
8	Thunder Shock	Electric	Special	40	100	30	Normal
11	Cotton Spore	Grass	Status	—	100	40	Many Others
16	Charge	Electric	Status	—	—	20	Self
20	Take Down	Normal	Physical	90	85	20	Normal
25	Electro Ball	Electric	Special	—	100	10	Normal
29	Confuse Ray	Ghost	Status	—	100	10	Normal
30	Thunder Punch	Electric	Physical	75	100	15	Normal
35	Power Gem	Rock	Special	80	100	20	Normal
40	Discharge	Electric	Special	80	100	15	Adjacent
46	Cotton Guard	Grass	Status	—	—	10	Self
51	Signal Beam	Bug	Special	75	100	15	Normal
57	Light Screen	Psychic	Status	—	—	30	Your Side
62	Thunder	Electric	Special	110	70	10	Normal
65	Dragon Pulse	Dragon	Special	85	100	10	Normal

TM & HM MOVES

No.	Name	Type	Kind	Pow.	Acc.	PP	Range
TM06	Toxic	Poison	Status	—	90	10	Normal
TM10	Hidden Power	Normal	Special	60	100	15	Normal
TM15	Hyper Beam	Normal	Special	150	90	5	Normal
TM16	Light Screen	Psychic	Status	—	—	30	Your Side
TM17	Protect	Normal	Status	—	—	10	Self
TM18	Rain Dance	Water	Status	—	—	5	Both Sides
TM20	Safeguard	Normal	Status	—	—	25	Your Side
TM21	Frustration	Normal	Physical	—	100	20	Normal
TM24	Thunderbolt	Electric	Special	90	100	15	Normal
TM25	Thunder	Electric	Special	110	70	10	Normal
TM27	Return	Normal	Physical	—	100	20	Normal
TM31	Brick Break	Fighting	Physical	75	100	15	Normal
TM32	Double Team	Normal	Status	—	—	15	Self
TM42	Facade	Normal	Physical	70	100	20	Normal
TM44	Rest	Psychic	Status	—	—	10	Self
TM45	Attract	Normal	Status	—	100	15	Normal
TM48	Round	Normal	Special	60	100	15	Normal
TM49	Echoed Voice	Normal	Special	40	100	15	Normal
TM52	Focus Blast	Fighting	Special	120	70	5	Normal
TM56	Fling	Dark	Physical	—	100	10	Normal
TM57	Charge Beam	Electric	Special	50	90	10	Normal
TM68	Giga Impact	Normal	Physical	150	90	5	Normal
TM70	Flash	Normal	Status	—	100	20	Normal
TM72	Volt Switch	Electric	Special	70	100	20	Normal
TM73	Thunder Wave	Electric	Status	—	100	20	Normal
TM78	Bulldoze	Ground	Physical	60	100	20	Adjacent
TM87	Swagger	Normal	Status	—	90	15	Normal
TM88	Sleep Talk	Normal	Status	—	—	10	Self
TM90	Substitute	Normal	Status	—	—	10	Self
TM93	Wild Charge	Electric	Physical	90	100	15	Normal
TM94	Secret Power	Normal	Physical	70	100	20	Normal
TM98	Power-Up Punch	Fighting	Physical	40	100	20	Normal
TM100	Confide	Normal	Status	—	—	20	Normal
HM04	Strength	Normal	Physical	80	100	15	Normal
HM06	Rock Smash	Fighting	Physical	40	100	15	Normal

MOVES LEARNED IN EXCHANGE FOR BP

Name	Type	Kind	Pow.	Acc.	PP	Range
Signal Beam	Bug	Special	75	100	15	Normal
Thunder Punch	Electric	Physical	75	100	15	Normal
Fire Punch	Fire	Physical	75	100	15	Normal
Magnet Rise	Electric	Status	—	—	10	Self
Electroweb	Electric	Special	55	95	15	Many Others
Dragon Pulse	Dragon	Special	85	100	10	Normal
Iron Tail	Steel	Physical	100	75	15	Normal
Snore	Normal	Special	50	100	15	Normal
Heal Bell	Normal	Status	—	—	5	Your Party
Focus Punch	Fighting	Physical	150	100	20	Normal
Shock Wave	Electric	Special	60	—	20	Normal
After You	Normal	Status	—	—	15	Normal
Outrage	Dragon	Physical	120	100	10	1 Random

MOVES TAUGHT BY PEOPLE

Name	Type	Kind	Pow.	Acc.	PP	Range

Mega Evolution

Mega Ampharos

Light Pokémon

Electric Dragon

HEIGHT: 4'07" WEIGHT: 135.6 lbs.

Same form for ♂ / ♀

REQUIRED MEGA STONE
Ampharosite
Find in New Mauville (after battling Groudon or Kyogre).

ABILITY
Mold Breaker

HIDDEN ABILITY
—

EGG GROUPS
—

STAT GROWTH RATES
HP
Attack
Defense
Sp. Atk
Sp. Def
Speed

Damage taken in normal battles

Type		Type	
Normal	×1	Flying	×0.5
Fire	×0.5	Psychic	×1
Water	×0.5	Bug	×1
Grass	×0.5	Rock	×1
Electric	×0.25	Ghost	×1
Ice	×2	Dragon	×2
Fighting	×1	Dark	×1
Poison	×1	Steel	×0.5
Ground	×2	Fairy	×2

Damage taken in Inverse battles

Type		Type	
Normal	×1	Flying	×2
Fire	×2	Psychic	×1
Water	×2	Bug	×1
Grass	×2	Rock	×1
Electric	×4	Ghost	×1
Ice	×0.5	Dragon	×0.5
Fighting	×1	Dark	×1
Poison	×1	Steel	×2
Ground	×0.5	Fairy	×0.5

Can be used in
Inverse Battle
Battle Institute
Battle Maison
Random Matchup (Free Battle)
Random Matchup (Others)

National Pokédex **182** Hoenn Pokédex **094**

Bellossom

Flower Pokémon

Grass

HEIGHT: 1'04" WEIGHT: 12.8 lbs.

Same form for ♂ / ♀

Ω When Bellossom gets exposed to plenty of sunlight, the leaves ringing its body begin to spin around. This Pokémon's dancing is renowned in the southern lands.

α A Bellossom grows flowers more beautifully if it has evolved from a smelly Gloom—the more stinky the better. At night, this Pokémon closes its petals and goes to sleep.

ABILITY
Chlorophyll

HIDDEN ABILITY
Healer

EGG GROUPS
Grass

STAT GROWTH RATES

HP	▮▮▮
Attack	▮▮▮▮
Defense	▮▮▮▮
Sp. Atk	▮▮▮▮
Sp. Def	▮▮▮▮
Speed	▮▮▮

ITEMS SOMETIMES HELD BY WILD POKÉMON
—

EVOLUTION

Oddish → Lv. 21 → Gloom → Sun Stone → Bellossom

MAIN WAY TO REGISTER IN THE NATIONAL POKÉDEX

Use a Sun Stone on Gloom.

Damage taken in normal battles

Type		Type	
Normal	×1	Flying	×2
Fire	×2	Psychic	×1
Water	×0.5	Bug	×2
Grass	×0.5	Rock	×1
Electric	×0.5	Ghost	×1
Ice	×2	Dragon	×1
Fighting	×1	Dark	×1
Poison	×2	Steel	×1
Ground	×0.5	Fairy	×1

Damage taken in Inverse battles

Type		Type	
Normal	×1	Flying	×0.5
Fire	×0.5	Psychic	×1
Water	×2	Bug	×0.5
Grass	×2	Rock	×1
Electric	×2	Ghost	×1
Ice	×0.5	Dragon	×1
Fighting	×1	Dark	×1
Poison	×0.5	Steel	×1
Ground	×2	Fairy	×1

Can be used in
- Inverse Battle
- Battle Institute
- Battle Maison
- Random Matchup (Free Battle)
- Random Matchup (Others)

LEVEL-UP MOVES

Lv.	Name	Type	Kind	Pow.	Acc.	PP	Range
1	Leaf Storm	Grass	Special	130	90	5	Normal
1	Leaf Blade	Grass	Physical	90	100	15	Normal
1	Mega Drain	Grass	Special	40	100	15	Normal
1	Sweet Scent	Normal	Status	—	100	20	Many Others
1	Stun Spore	Grass	Status	—	75	30	Normal
1	Sunny Day	Fire	Status	—	—	5	Both Sides
24	Magical Leaf	Grass	Special	60	—	20	Normal
49	Petal Blizzard	Grass	Physical	90	100	15	Adjacent
64	Leaf Storm	Grass	Special	130	90	5	Normal

TM & HM MOVES

No.	Name	Type	Kind	Pow.	Acc.	PP	Range
TM06	Toxic	Poison	Status	—	90	10	Normal
TM09	Venoshock	Poison	Special	65	100	10	Normal
TM10	Hidden Power	Normal	Special	60	100	15	Normal
TM11	Sunny Day	Fire	Status	—	—	5	Both Sides
TM15	Hyper Beam	Normal	Special	150	90	5	Normal
TM17	Protect	Normal	Status	—	—	10	Self
TM20	Safeguard	Normal	Status	—	—	25	Your Side
TM21	Frustration	Normal	Physical	—	100	20	Normal
TM22	Solar Beam	Grass	Special	120	100	10	Normal
TM27	Return	Normal	Physical	—	100	20	Normal
TM32	Double Team	Normal	Status	—	—	15	Self
TM36	Sludge Bomb	Poison	Special	90	100	10	Normal
TM42	Facade	Normal	Physical	70	100	20	Normal
TM44	Rest	Psychic	Status	—	—	10	Self
TM45	Attract	Normal	Status	—	100	15	Normal
TM48	Round	Normal	Special	60	100	15	Normal
TM53	Energy Ball	Grass	Special	90	100	10	Normal
TM56	Fling	Dark	Physical	—	100	10	Normal
TM68	Giga Impact	Normal	Physical	150	90	5	Normal
TM70	Flash	Normal	Status	—	100	20	Normal
TM75	Swords Dance	Normal	Status	—	—	20	Self
TM83	Infestation	Bug	Special	20	100	20	Normal
TM86	Grass Knot	Grass	Special	—	100	20	Normal
TM87	Swagger	Normal	Status	—	90	15	Normal
TM88	Sleep Talk	Normal	Status	—	—	10	Self
TM90	Substitute	Normal	Status	—	—	10	Self
TM94	Secret Power	Normal	Physical	70	100	20	Normal
TM96	Nature Power	Normal	Status	—	—	20	Normal
TM99	Dazzling Gleam	Fairy	Special	80	100	10	Many Others
TM100	Confide	Normal	Status	—	—	20	Normal
HM01	Cut	Normal	Physical	50	95	30	Normal

MOVES LEARNED IN EXCHANGE FOR BP

Name	Type	Kind	Pow.	Acc.	PP	Range
Seed Bomb	Grass	Physical	80	100	15	Normal
Uproar	Normal	Special	90	100	10	1 Random
Snore	Normal	Special	50	100	15	Normal
Synthesis	Grass	Status	—	—	5	Self
Giga Drain	Grass	Special	75	100	10	Normal
Drain Punch	Fighting	Physical	75	100	10	Normal
Gastro Acid	Poison	Status	—	100	10	Normal
Worry Seed	Grass	Status	—	100	10	Normal
After You	Normal	Status	—	—	15	Normal

MOVES TAUGHT BY PEOPLE

Name	Type	Kind	Pow.	Acc.	PP	Range

National Pokédex **183** Hoenn Pokédex **056**

Marill

Aqua Mouse Pokémon

Water Fairy

HEIGHT: 1'04" WEIGHT: 18.7 lbs.

Same form for ♂ / ♀

Ω Marill's oil-filled tail acts much like a life preserver. If you see just its tail bobbing on the water's surface, it's a sure indication that this Pokémon is diving beneath the water to feed on aquatic plants.

α When fishing for food at the edge of a fast-running stream, Marill wraps its tail around the trunk of a tree. This Pokémon's tail is flexible and configured to stretch.

ABILITIES
Thick Fat
Huge Power

HIDDEN ABILITY
Sap Sipper

EGG GROUPS
Water 1 Fairy

STAT GROWTH RATES

HP	▮▮▮
Attack	▮
Defense	▮▮
Sp. Atk	▮
Sp. Def	▮▮
Speed	▮▮

ITEMS SOMETIMES HELD BY WILD POKÉMON
—

EVOLUTION

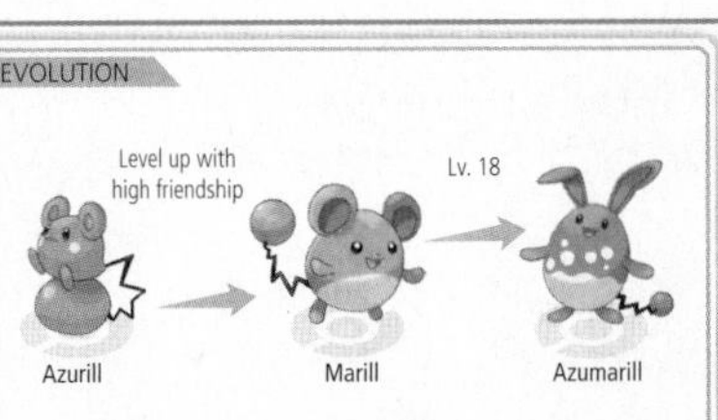

MAIN WAY TO REGISTER IN THE NATIONAL POKÉDEX

Catch on the water surface on Route 102.

Damage taken in normal battles

Type		Type	
Normal	×1	Flying	×1
Fire	×0.5	Psychic	×1
Water	×0.5	Bug	×0.5
Grass	×2	Rock	×1
Electric	×2	Ghost	×1
Ice	×0.5	Dragon	×0
Fighting	×0.5	Dark	×0.5
Poison	×2	Steel	×1
Ground	×1	Fairy	×1

Damage taken in Inverse battles

Type		Type	
Normal	×1	Flying	×1
Fire	×2	Psychic	×1
Water	×2	Bug	×2
Grass	×0.5	Rock	×1
Electric	×0.5	Ghost	×1
Ice	×2	Dragon	×2
Fighting	×2	Dark	×2
Poison	×0.5	Steel	×1
Ground	×1	Fairy	×1

Can be used in
- Inverse Battle
- Battle Institute
- Battle Maison
- Random Matchup (Free Battle)
- Random Matchup (Others)

LEVEL-UP MOVES

Lv.	Name	Type	Kind	Pow.	Acc.	PP	Range
1	Tackle	Normal	Physical	50	100	35	Normal
1	Water Gun	Water	Special	40	100	25	Normal
2	Tail Whip	Normal	Status	—	100	30	Many Others
5	Water Sport	Water	Status	—	—	15	Both Sides
7	Bubble	Water	Special	40	100	30	Many Others
10	Defense Curl	Normal	Status	—	—	40	Self
10	Rollout	Rock	Physical	30	90	20	Normal
13	Bubble Beam	Water	Special	65	100	20	Normal
16	Helping Hand	Normal	Status	—	—	20	1 Ally
20	Aqua Tail	Water	Physical	90	90	10	Normal
23	Play Rough	Fairy	Physical	90	90	10	Normal
28	Aqua Ring	Water	Status	—	—	20	Self
31	Rain Dance	Water	Status	—	—	5	Both Sides
37	Double-Edge	Normal	Physical	120	100	15	Normal
40	Superpower	Fighting	Physical	120	100	5	Normal
47	Hydro Pump	Water	Special	110	80	5	Normal

TM & HM MOVES

No.	Name	Type	Kind	Pow.	Acc.	PP	Range
TM06	Toxic	Poison	Status	—	90	10	Normal
TM07	Hail	Ice	Status	—	—	10	Both Sides
TM10	Hidden Power	Normal	Special	60	100	15	Normal
TM13	Ice Beam	Ice	Special	90	100	10	Normal
TM14	Blizzard	Ice	Special	110	70	5	Many Others
TM16	Light Screen	Psychic	Status	—	—	30	Your Side
TM17	Protect	Normal	Status	—	—	10	Self
TM18	Rain Dance	Water	Status	—	—	5	Both Sides
TM21	Frustration	Normal	Physical	—	100	20	Normal
TM27	Return	Normal	Physical	—	100	20	Normal
TM28	Dig	Ground	Physical	80	100	10	Normal
TM31	Brick Break	Fighting	Physical	75	100	15	Normal
TM32	Double Team	Normal	Status	—	—	15	Self
TM42	Facade	Normal	Physical	70	100	20	Normal
TM44	Rest	Psychic	Status	—	—	10	Self
TM45	Attract	Normal	Status	—	100	15	Normal
TM48	Round	Normal	Special	60	100	15	Normal
TM55	Scald	Water	Special	80	100	15	Normal
TM56	Fling	Dark	Physical	—	100	10	Normal
TM86	Grass Knot	Grass	Special	—	100	20	Normal
TM87	Swagger	Normal	Status	—	90	15	Normal
TM88	Sleep Talk	Normal	Status	—	—	10	Self
TM90	Substitute	Normal	Status	—	—	10	Self
TM94	Secret Power	Normal	Physical	70	100	20	Normal
TM98	Power-Up Punch	Fighting	Physical	40	100	20	Normal
TM100	Confide	Normal	Status	—	—	20	Normal
HM03	Surf	Water	Special	90	100	15	Adjacent
HM04	Strength	Normal	Physical	80	100	15	Normal
HM05	Waterfall	Water	Physical	80	100	15	Normal
HM06	Rock Smash	Fighting	Physical	40	100	15	Normal
HM07	Dive	Water	Physical	80	100	10	Normal

MOVES LEARNED IN EXCHANGE FOR BP

Name	Type	Kind	Pow.	Acc.	PP	Range
Covet	Normal	Physical	60	100	25	Normal
Bounce	Flying	Physical	85	85	5	Normal
Ice Punch	Ice	Physical	75	100	15	Normal
Superpower	Fighting	Physical	120	100	5	Normal
Icy Wind	Ice	Special	55	95	15	Many Others
Aqua Tail	Water	Physical	90	90	10	Normal
Hyper Voice	Normal	Special	90	100	10	Many Others
Iron Tail	Steel	Physical	100	75	15	Normal
Snore	Normal	Special	50	100	15	Normal
Knock Off	Dark	Physical	65	100	20	Normal
Focus Punch	Fighting	Physical	150	100	20	Normal
Water Pulse	Water	Special	60	100	20	Normal
Helping Hand	Normal	Status	—	—	20	1 Ally

MOVES TAUGHT BY PEOPLE

Name	Type	Kind	Pow.	Acc.	PP	Range

EGG MOVES

Name	Type	Kind	Pow.	Acc.	PP	Range
Present	Normal	Physical	—	90	15	Normal
Amnesia	Psychic	Status	—	—	20	Self
Future Sight	Psychic	Special	120	100	10	Normal
Belly Drum	Normal	Status	—	—	10	Self
Perish Song	Normal	Status	—	—	5	Adjacent
Supersonic	Normal	Status	—	55	20	Normal
Aqua Jet	Water	Physical	40	100	20	Normal
Superpower	Fighting	Physical	120	100	5	Normal
Refresh	Normal	Status	—	—	20	Self
Body Slam	Normal	Physical	85	100	15	Normal
Water Sport	Water	Status	—	—	15	Both Sides
Muddy Water	Water	Special	90	85	10	Many Others
Camouflage	Normal	Status	—	—	20	Self

National Pokédex **184** Hoenn Pokédex **057**

Azumarill

Aqua Rabbit Pokémon

Water | Fairy

HEIGHT: 2'07" WEIGHT: 62.8 lbs.

Same form for ♂ / ♀

Ω Azumarill's long ears are indispensable sensors. By focusing its hearing, this Pokémon can identify what kinds of prey are around, even in rough and fast-running rivers.

α Azumarill can make balloons out of air. It makes these air balloons if it spots a drowning Pokémon. The air balloons enable the Pokémon in trouble to breathe.

ABILITIES
Thick Fat
Huge Power

HIDDEN ABILITY
Sap Sipper

EGG GROUPS
Water 1 | Fairy

STAT GROWTH RATES
HP
Attack
Defense
Sp. Atk
Sp. Def
Speed

ITEMS SOMETIMES HELD BY WILD POKÉMON
—

EVOLUTION

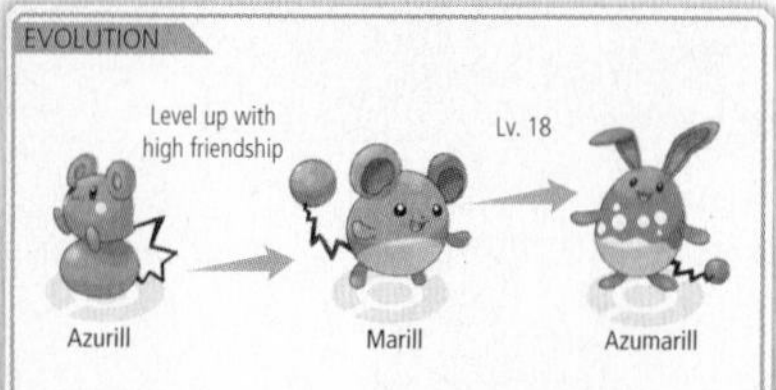

MAIN WAY TO REGISTER IN THE NATIONAL POKÉDEX

Catch on the water surface on Route 120.

Damage taken in normal battles

Type		Type	
Normal	×1	Flying	×1
Fire	×0.5	Psychic	×1
Water	×0.5	Bug	×0.5
Grass	×2	Rock	×1
Electric	×2	Ghost	×1
Ice	×0.5	Dragon	×0
Fighting	×0.5	Dark	×0.5
Poison	×2	Steel	×1
Ground	×1	Fairy	×1

Damage taken in Inverse battles

Type		Type	
Normal	×1	Flying	×1
Fire	×2	Psychic	×1
Water	×2	Bug	×2
Grass	×0.5	Rock	×1
Electric	×0.5	Ghost	×1
Ice	×2	Dragon	×2
Fighting	×2	Dark	×2
Poison	×0.5	Steel	×1
Ground	×1	Fairy	×1

Can be used in
- Inverse Battle
- Battle Institute
- Battle Maison
- Random Matchup (Free Battle)
- Random Matchup (Others)

LEVEL-UP MOVES

Lv.	Name	Type	Kind	Pow.	Acc.	PP	Range
1	Tackle	Normal	Physical	50	100	35	Normal
1	Water Gun	Water	Special	40	100	25	Normal
1	Tail Whip	Normal	Status	—	100	30	Many Others
1	Water Sport	Water	Status	—	—	15	Both Sides
2	Tail Whip	Normal	Status	—	100	30	Many Others
5	Water Sport	Water	Status	—	—	15	Both Sides
7	Bubble	Water	Special	40	100	30	Many Others
10	Defense Curl	Normal	Status	—	—	40	Self
10	Rollout	Rock	Physical	30	90	20	Normal
13	Bubble Beam	Water	Special	65	100	20	Normal
16	Helping Hand	Normal	Status	—	—	20	1 Ally
21	Aqua Tail	Water	Physical	90	90	10	Normal
25	Play Rough	Fairy	Physical	90	90	10	Normal
31	Aqua Ring	Water	Status	—	—	20	Self
35	Rain Dance	Water	Status	—	—	5	Both Sides
42	Double-Edge	Normal	Physical	120	100	15	Normal
46	Superpower	Fighting	Physical	120	100	5	Normal
55	Hydro Pump	Water	Special	110	80	5	Normal

TM & HM MOVES

No.	Name	Type	Kind	Pow.	Acc.	PP	Range
TM06	Toxic	Poison	Status	—	90	10	Normal
TM07	Hail	Ice	Status	—	—	10	Both Sides
TM10	Hidden Power	Normal	Special	60	100	15	Normal
TM13	Ice Beam	Ice	Special	90	100	10	Normal
TM14	Blizzard	Ice	Special	110	70	5	Many Others
TM15	Hyper Beam	Normal	Special	150	90	5	Normal
TM16	Light Screen	Psychic	Status	—	—	30	Your Side
TM17	Protect	Normal	Status	—	—	10	Self
TM18	Rain Dance	Water	Status	—	—	5	Both Sides
TM21	Frustration	Normal	Physical	—	100	20	Normal
TM27	Return	Normal	Physical	—	100	20	Normal
TM28	Dig	Ground	Physical	80	100	10	Normal
TM31	Brick Break	Fighting	Physical	75	100	15	Normal
TM32	Double Team	Normal	Status	—	—	15	Self
TM42	Facade	Normal	Physical	70	100	20	Normal
TM44	Rest	Psychic	Status	—	—	10	Self
TM45	Attract	Normal	Status	—	100	15	Normal
TM48	Round	Normal	Special	60	100	15	Normal
TM52	Focus Blast	Fighting	Special	120	70	5	Normal
TM55	Scald	Water	Special	80	100	15	Normal
TM56	Fling	Dark	Physical	—	100	10	Normal
TM68	Giga Impact	Normal	Physical	150	90	5	Normal
TM78	Bulldoze	Ground	Physical	60	100	20	Adjacent
TM86	Grass Knot	Grass	Special	—	100	20	Normal
TM87	Swagger	Normal	Status	—	90	15	Normal
TM88	Sleep Talk	Normal	Status	—	—	10	Self
TM90	Substitute	Normal	Status	—	—	10	Self
TM94	Secret Power	Normal	Physical	70	100	20	Normal
TM98	Power-Up Punch	Fighting	Physical	40	100	20	Normal
TM100	Confide	Normal	Status	—	—	20	Normal
HM03	Surf	Water	Special	90	100	15	Adjacent
HM04	Strength	Normal	Physical	80	100	15	Normal
HM05	Waterfall	Water	Physical	80	100	15	Normal
HM06	Rock Smash	Fighting	Physical	40	100	15	Normal
HM07	Dive	Water	Physical	80	100	10	Normal

MOVES LEARNED IN EXCHANGE FOR BP

Name	Type	Kind	Pow.	Acc.	PP	Range
Covet	Normal	Physical	60	100	25	Normal
Bounce	Flying	Physical	85	85	5	Normal
Ice Punch	Ice	Physical	75	100	15	Normal
Superpower	Fighting	Physical	120	100	5	Normal
Icy Wind	Ice	Special	55	95	15	Many Others
Aqua Tail	Water	Physical	90	90	10	Normal
Hyper Voice	Normal	Special	90	100	10	Many Others
Iron Tail	Steel	Physical	100	75	15	Normal
Snore	Normal	Special	50	100	15	Normal
Knock Off	Dark	Physical	65	100	20	Normal
Focus Punch	Fighting	Physical	150	100	20	Normal
Water Pulse	Water	Special	60	100	20	Normal
Helping Hand	Normal	Status	—	—	20	1 Ally

MOVES TAUGHT BY PEOPLE

Name	Type	Kind	Pow.	Acc.	PP	Range

National Pokédex **185** Hoenn Pokédex **—**

Sudowoodo

Imitation Pokémon

Rock

HEIGHT: 3'11" WEIGHT: 83.8 lbs.

The male has larger horns.
The female has smaller horns.

♂ ♀

Ω Sudowoodo camouflages itself as a tree to avoid being attacked by enemies. However, because its hands remain green throughout the year, the Pokémon is easily identified as a fake during the winter.

α Sudowoodo camouflages itself as a tree to avoid being attacked by enemies. However, because its hands remain green throughout the year, the Pokémon is easily identified as a fake during the winter.

ABILITIES
Sturdy
Rock Head

HIDDEN ABILITY
Rattled

EGG GROUPS
Mineral

STAT GROWTH RATES
HP
Attack
Defense
Sp. Atk
Sp. Def
Speed

ITEMS SOMETIMES HELD BY WILD POKÉMON
—

EVOLUTION

Bonsly → Lv. 15 with Mimic → Sudowoodo

MAIN WAY TO REGISTER IN THE NATIONAL POKÉDEX

Appears in *Pokémon X* and *Pokémon Y*. Bring it to your game using Link Trade or the GTS.

Damage taken in normal battles

Type		Type	
Normal	×0.5	Flying	×0.5
Fire	×0.5	Psychic	×1
Water	×2	Bug	×1
Grass	×2	Rock	×1
Electric	×1	Ghost	×1
Ice	×1	Dragon	×1
Fighting	×2	Dark	×1
Poison	×0.5	Steel	×2
Ground	×2	Fairy	×1

Damage taken in Inverse battles

Type		Type	
Normal	×2	Flying	×2
Fire	×2	Psychic	×1
Water	×0.5	Bug	×1
Grass	×0.5	Rock	×1
Electric	×1	Ghost	×1
Ice	×1	Dragon	×1
Fighting	×0.5	Dark	×1
Poison	×2	Steel	×0.5
Ground	×0.5	Fairy	×1

Can be used in
- Inverse Battle
- Battle Institute
- Battle Maison
- Random Matchup (Free Battle)
- Random Matchup (Others)

LEVEL-UP MOVES

Lv.	Name	Type	Kind	Pow.	Acc.	PP	Range
1	Wood Hammer	Grass	Physical	120	100	15	Normal
1	Copycat	Normal	Status	—	—	20	Self
1	Flail	Normal	Physical	—	100	15	Normal
1	Low Kick	Fighting	Physical	—	100	20	Normal
1	Rock Throw	Rock	Physical	50	90	15	Normal
5	Flail	Normal	Physical	—	100	15	Normal
8	Low Kick	Fighting	Physical	—	100	20	Normal
12	Rock Throw	Rock	Physical	50	90	15	Normal
15	Mimic	Normal	Status	—	—	10	Normal
15	Slam	Normal	Physical	80	75	20	Normal
19	Feint Attack	Dark	Physical	60	—	20	Normal
22	Rock Tomb	Rock	Physical	60	95	15	Normal
26	Block	Normal	Status	—	—	5	Normal
29	Rock Slide	Rock	Physical	75	90	10	Many Others
33	Counter	Fighting	Physical	—	100	20	Varies
36	Sucker Punch	Dark	Physical	80	100	5	Normal
40	Double-Edge	Normal	Physical	120	100	15	Normal
43	Stone Edge	Rock	Physical	100	80	5	Normal
47	Hammer Arm	Fighting	Physical	100	90	10	Normal

TM & HM MOVES

No.	Name	Type	Kind	Pow.	Acc.	PP	Range
TM04	Calm Mind	Psychic	Status	—	—	20	Self
TM06	Toxic	Poison	Status	—	90	10	Normal
TM10	Hidden Power	Normal	Special	60	100	15	Normal
TM11	Sunny Day	Fire	Status	—	—	5	Both Sides
TM12	Taunt	Dark	Status	—	100	20	Normal
TM17	Protect	Normal	Status	—	—	10	Self
TM21	Frustration	Normal	Physical	—	100	20	Normal
TM23	Smack Down	Rock	Physical	50	100	15	Normal
TM26	Earthquake	Ground	Physical	100	100	10	Adjacent
TM27	Return	Normal	Physical	—	100	20	Normal
TM28	Dig	Ground	Physical	80	100	10	Normal
TM31	Brick Break	Fighting	Physical	75	100	15	Normal
TM32	Double Team	Normal	Status	—	—	15	Self
TM37	Sandstorm	Rock	Status	—	—	10	Both Sides
TM39	Rock Tomb	Rock	Physical	60	95	15	Normal
TM41	Torment	Dark	Status	—	100	15	Normal
TM42	Facade	Normal	Physical	70	100	20	Normal
TM44	Rest	Psychic	Status	—	—	10	Self
TM45	Attract	Normal	Status	—	100	15	Normal
TM46	Thief	Dark	Physical	60	100	25	Normal
TM48	Round	Normal	Special	60	100	15	Normal
TM56	Fling	Dark	Physical	—	100	10	Normal
TM64	Explosion	Normal	Physical	250	100	5	Adjacent
TM69	Rock Polish	Rock	Status	—	—	20	Self
TM71	Stone Edge	Rock	Physical	100	80	5	Normal
TM77	Psych Up	Normal	Status	—	—	10	Normal
TM78	Bulldoze	Ground	Physical	60	100	20	Adjacent
TM80	Rock Slide	Rock	Physical	75	90	10	Many Others
TM87	Swagger	Normal	Status	—	90	15	Normal
TM88	Sleep Talk	Normal	Status	—	—	10	Self
TM90	Substitute	Normal	Status	—	—	10	Self
TM94	Secret Power	Normal	Physical	70	100	20	Normal
TM96	Nature Power	Normal	Status	—	—	20	Normal
TM98	Power-Up Punch	Fighting	Physical	40	100	20	Normal
TM100	Confide	Normal	Status	—	—	20	Normal
HM04	Strength	Normal	Physical	80	100	15	Normal
HM06	Rock Smash	Fighting	Physical	40	100	15	Normal

MOVES LEARNED IN EXCHANGE FOR BP

Name	Type	Kind	Pow.	Acc.	PP	Range
Covet	Normal	Physical	60	100	25	Normal
Low Kick	Fighting	Physical	—	100	20	Normal
Thunder Punch	Electric	Physical	75	100	15	Normal
Fire Punch	Fire	Physical	75	100	15	Normal
Ice Punch	Ice	Physical	75	100	15	Normal
Block	Normal	Status	—	—	5	Normal
Earth Power	Ground	Special	90	100	10	Normal
Foul Play	Dark	Physical	95	100	15	Normal
Snore	Normal	Special	50	100	15	Normal
Role Play	Psychic	Status	—	—	10	Normal
Focus Punch	Fighting	Physical	150	100	20	Normal
After You	Normal	Status	—	—	15	Normal
Helping Hand	Normal	Status	—	—	20	1 Ally
Stealth Rock	Rock	Status	—	—	20	Other Side

MOVES TAUGHT BY PEOPLE

Name	Type	Kind	Pow.	Acc.	PP	Range

EGG MOVES

Name	Type	Kind	Pow.	Acc.	PP	Range
Self-Destruct	Normal	Physical	200	100	5	Adjacent
Headbutt	Normal	Physical	70	100	15	Normal
Harden	Normal	Status	—	—	30	Self
Defense Curl	Normal	Status	—	—	40	Self
Rollout	Rock	Physical	30	90	20	Normal
Sand Tomb	Ground	Physical	35	85	15	Normal
Stealth Rock	Rock	Status	—	—	20	Other Side
Curse	Ghost	Status	—	—	10	Varies
Endure	Normal	Status	—	—	10	Self

National Pokédex **186** Hoenn Pokédex —

Politoed

Frog Pokémon

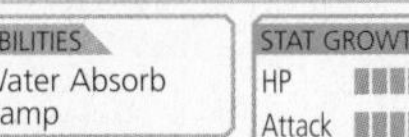

Water

HEIGHT: 3'07" WEIGHT: 74.7 lbs.

The male has larger vocal sacs on its cheeks.
The female has smaller vocal sacs on its cheeks.

Ω The curled hair on Politoed's head is proof of its status as a king. It is said that the longer and more curled the hair, the more respect this Pokémon earns from its peers.

α The curled hair on Politoed's head is proof of its status as a king. It is said that the longer and more curled the hair, the more respect this Pokémon earns from its peers.

ABILITIES
Water Absorb
Damp

HIDDEN ABILITY
Drizzle

EGG GROUPS
Water 1

STAT GROWTH RATES
HP
Attack
Defense
Sp. Atk
Sp. Def
Speed

ITEMS SOMETIMES HELD BY WILD POKÉMON
—

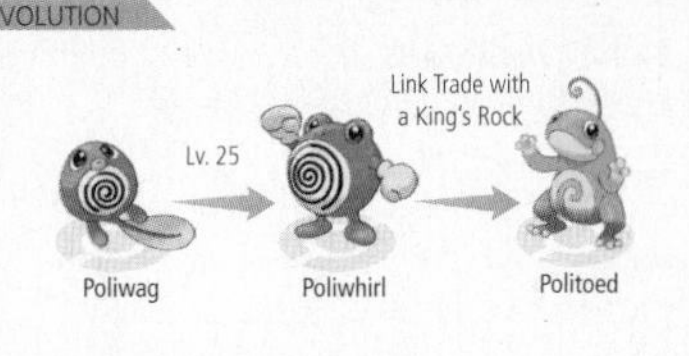

MAIN WAY TO REGISTER IN THE NATIONAL POKÉDEX

Appears in *Pokémon X* and *Pokémon Y*. Bring it to your game using Link Trade or the GTS.

Damage taken in normal battles

Type		Type	
Normal	×1	Flying	×1
Fire	×0.5	Psychic	×1
Water	×0.5	Bug	×1
Grass	×2	Rock	×1
Electric	×2	Ghost	×1
Ice	×0.5	Dragon	×1
Fighting	×1	Dark	×1
Poison	×1	Steel	×0.5
Ground	×1	Fairy	×1

Damage taken in Inverse battles

Type		Type	
Normal	×1	Flying	×1
Fire	×2	Psychic	×1
Water	×2	Bug	×1
Grass	×0.5	Rock	×1
Electric	×0.5	Ghost	×1
Ice	×2	Dragon	×1
Fighting	×1	Dark	×1
Poison	×1	Steel	×2
Ground	×1	Fairy	×1

Can be used in
Inverse Battle
Battle Institute
Battle Maison
Random Matchup (Free Battle)
Random Matchup (Others)

LEVEL-UP MOVES

Lv.	Name	Type	Kind	Pow.	Acc.	PP	Range
1	Bubble Beam	Water	Special	65	100	20	Normal
1	Hypnosis	Psychic	Status	—	60	20	Normal
1	Double Slap	Normal	Physical	15	85	10	Normal
1	Perish Song	Normal	Status	—	—	5	Adjacent
27	Swagger	Normal	Status	—	90	15	Normal
37	Bounce	Flying	Physical	85	85	5	Normal
48	Hyper Voice	Normal	Special	90	100	10	Many Others

TM & HM MOVES

No.	Name	Type	Kind	Pow.	Acc.	PP	Range
TM06	Toxic	Poison	Status	—	90	10	Normal
TM07	Hail	Ice	Status	—	—	10	Both Sides
TM10	Hidden Power	Normal	Special	60	100	15	Normal
TM13	Ice Beam	Ice	Special	90	100	10	Normal
TM14	Blizzard	Ice	Special	110	70	5	Many Others
TM15	Hyper Beam	Normal	Special	150	90	5	Normal
TM17	Protect	Normal	Status	—	—	10	Self
TM18	Rain Dance	Water	Status	—	—	5	Both Sides
TM21	Frustration	Normal	Physical	—	100	20	Normal
TM26	Earthquake	Ground	Physical	100	100	10	Adjacent
TM27	Return	Normal	Physical	—	100	20	Normal
TM28	Dig	Ground	Physical	80	100	10	Normal
TM29	Psychic	Psychic	Special	90	100	10	Normal
TM31	Brick Break	Fighting	Physical	75	100	15	Normal
TM32	Double Team	Normal	Status	—	—	15	Self
TM42	Facade	Normal	Physical	70	100	20	Normal
TM44	Rest	Psychic	Status	—	—	10	Self
TM45	Attract	Normal	Status	—	100	15	Normal
TM46	Thief	Dark	Physical	60	100	25	Normal
TM48	Round	Normal	Special	60	100	15	Normal
TM49	Echoed Voice	Normal	Special	40	100	15	Normal
TM52	Focus Blast	Fighting	Special	120	70	5	Normal
TM55	Scald	Water	Special	80	100	15	Normal
TM56	Fling	Dark	Physical	—	100	10	Normal
TM66	Payback	Dark	Physical	50	100	10	Normal
TM68	Giga Impact	Normal	Physical	150	90	5	Normal
TM78	Bulldoze	Ground	Physical	60	100	20	Adjacent
TM87	Swagger	Normal	Status	—	90	15	Normal
TM88	Sleep Talk	Normal	Status	—	—	10	Self
TM90	Substitute	Normal	Status	—	—	10	Self
TM94	Secret Power	Normal	Physical	70	100	20	Normal
TM98	Power-Up Punch	Fighting	Physical	40	100	20	Normal
TM100	Confide	Normal	Status	—	—	20	Normal
HM03	Surf	Water	Special	90	100	15	Adjacent
HM04	Strength	Normal	Physical	80	100	15	Normal
HM05	Waterfall	Water	Physical	80	100	15	Normal
HM06	Rock Smash	Fighting	Physical	40	100	15	Normal
HM07	Dive	Water	Physical	80	100	10	Normal

MOVES LEARNED IN EXCHANGE FOR BP

Name	Type	Kind	Pow.	Acc.	PP	Range
Bounce	Flying	Physical	85	85	5	Normal
Ice Punch	Ice	Physical	75	100	15	Normal
Icy Wind	Ice	Special	55	95	15	Many Others
Hyper Voice	Normal	Special	90	100	10	Many Others
Snore	Normal	Special	50	100	15	Normal
Focus Punch	Fighting	Physical	150	100	20	Normal
Water Pulse	Water	Special	60	100	20	Normal
Helping Hand	Normal	Status	—	—	20	1 Ally
Endeavor	Normal	Physical	—	100	5	Normal

MOVES TAUGHT BY PEOPLE

Name	Type	Kind	Pow.	Acc.	PP	Range

National Pokédex **187** Hoenn Pokédex —

Hoppip

Cottonweed Pokémon

Grass Flying

HEIGHT: 1'04" WEIGHT: 1.1 lbs.

Same form for ♂ / ♀

Ω This Pokémon drifts and floats with the wind. If it senses the approach of strong winds, Hoppip links its leaves with other Hoppip to prepare against being blown away.

α This Pokémon drifts and floats with the wind. If it senses the approach of strong winds, Hoppip links its leaves with other Hoppip to prepare against being blown away.

ABILITIES
Chlorophyll
Leaf Guard

HIDDEN ABILITY
Infiltrator

EGG GROUPS
Fairy
Grass

STAT GROWTH RATES
HP
Attack
Defense
Sp. Atk
Sp. Def
Speed

ITEMS SOMETIMES HELD BY WILD POKÉMON
—

EVOLUTION
Lv. 18
Lv. 27
Hoppip
Skiploom
Jumpluff

MAIN WAY TO REGISTER IN THE NATIONAL POKÉDEX

Appears in *Pokémon X* and *Pokémon Y*. Bring it to your game using Link Trade or the GTS.

Damage taken in normal battles

Type		Type	
Normal	×1	Flying	×2
Fire	×2	Psychic	×1
Water	×0.5	Bug	×1
Grass	×0.25	Rock	×2
Electric	×1	Ghost	×1
Ice	×4	Dragon	×1
Fighting	×0.5	Dark	×1
Poison	×2	Steel	×1
Ground	×0	Fairy	×1

Damage taken in Inverse battles

Type		Type	
Normal	×1	Flying	×0.5
Fire	×0.5	Psychic	×1
Water	×2	Bug	×1
Grass	×4	Rock	×0.5
Electric	×1	Ghost	×1
Ice	×0.25	Dragon	×1
Fighting	×2	Dark	×1
Poison	×0.5	Steel	×1
Ground	×4	Fairy	×1

Can be used in
Inverse Battle
Battle Institute
Battle Maison
Random Matchup (Free Battle)
Random Matchup (Others)

LEVEL-UP MOVES

Lv.	Name	Type	Kind	Pow.	Acc.	PP	Range
1	Splash	Normal	Status	—	—	40	Self
4	Synthesis	Grass	Status	—	—	5	Self
6	Tail Whip	Normal	Status	—	100	30	Many Others
8	Tackle	Normal	Physical	50	100	35	Normal
10	Fairy Wind	Fairy	Special	40	100	30	Normal
12	Poison Powder	Poison	Status	—	75	35	Normal
14	Stun Spore	Grass	Status	—	75	30	Normal
16	Sleep Powder	Grass	Status	—	75	15	Normal
19	Bullet Seed	Grass	Physical	25	100	30	Normal
22	Leech Seed	Grass	Status	—	90	10	Normal
25	Mega Drain	Grass	Special	40	100	15	Normal
28	Acrobatics	Flying	Physical	55	100	15	Normal
31	Rage Powder	Bug	Status	—	—	20	Self
34	Cotton Spore	Grass	Status	—	100	40	Many Others
37	U-turn	Bug	Physical	70	100	20	Normal
40	Worry Seed	Grass	Status	—	100	10	Normal
43	Giga Drain	Grass	Special	75	100	10	Normal
46	Bounce	Flying	Physical	85	85	5	Normal
49	Memento	Dark	Status	—	100	10	Normal

TM & HM MOVES

No.	Name	Type	Kind	Pow.	Acc.	PP	Range
TM06	Toxic	Poison	Status	—	90	10	Normal
TM10	Hidden Power	Normal	Special	60	100	15	Normal
TM11	Sunny Day	Fire	Status	—	—	5	Both Sides
TM17	Protect	Normal	Status	—	—	10	Self
TM21	Frustration	Normal	Physical	—	100	20	Normal
TM22	Solar Beam	Grass	Special	120	100	10	Normal
TM27	Return	Normal	Physical	—	100	20	Normal
TM32	Double Team	Normal	Status	—	—	15	Self
TM33	Reflect	Psychic	Status	—	—	20	Your Side
TM40	Aerial Ace	Flying	Physical	60	—	20	Normal
TM42	Facade	Normal	Physical	70	100	20	Normal
TM44	Rest	Psychic	Status	—	—	10	Self
TM45	Attract	Normal	Status	—	100	15	Normal
TM48	Round	Normal	Special	60	100	15	Normal
TM53	Energy Ball	Grass	Special	90	100	10	Normal
TM62	Acrobatics	Flying	Physical	55	100	15	Normal
TM70	Flash	Normal	Status	—	100	20	Normal
TM75	Swords Dance	Normal	Status	—	—	20	Self
TM77	Psych Up	Normal	Status	—	—	10	Normal
TM83	Infestation	Bug	Special	20	100	20	Normal
TM86	Grass Knot	Grass	Special	—	100	20	Normal
TM87	Swagger	Normal	Status	—	90	15	Normal
TM88	Sleep Talk	Normal	Status	—	—	10	Self
TM89	U-turn	Bug	Physical	70	100	20	Normal
TM90	Substitute	Normal	Status	—	—	10	Self
TM94	Secret Power	Normal	Physical	70	100	20	Normal
TM99	Dazzling Gleam	Fairy	Special	80	100	10	Many Others
TM100	Confide	Normal	Status	—	—	20	Normal

MOVES LEARNED IN EXCHANGE FOR BP

Name	Type	Kind	Pow.	Acc.	PP	Range
Seed Bomb	Grass	Physical	80	100	15	Normal
Bounce	Flying	Physical	85	85	5	Normal
Snore	Normal	Special	50	100	15	Normal
Synthesis	Grass	Status	—	—	5	Self
Giga Drain	Grass	Special	75	100	10	Normal
Worry Seed	Grass	Status	—	100	10	Normal
Helping Hand	Normal	Status	—	—	20	1 Ally

MOVES TAUGHT BY PEOPLE

Name	Type	Kind	Pow.	Acc.	PP	Range

EGG MOVES

Name	Type	Kind	Pow.	Acc.	PP	Range
Confusion	Psychic	Special	50	100	25	Normal
Encore	Normal	Status	—	100	5	Normal
Double-Edge	Normal	Physical	120	100	15	Normal
Amnesia	Psychic	Status	—	—	20	Self
Helping Hand	Normal	Status	—	—	20	1 Ally
Aromatherapy	Grass	Status	—	—	5	Your Party
Worry Seed	Grass	Status	—	100	10	Normal
Cotton Guard	Grass	Status	—	—	10	Self
Seed Bomb	Grass	Physical	80	100	15	Normal
Endure	Normal	Status	—	—	10	Self
Grassy Terrain	Grass	Status	—	—	10	Both Sides

National Pokédex **188** Hoenn Pokédex —

Skiploom

Cottonweed Pokémon

Grass Flying

HEIGHT: 2'00" WEIGHT: 2.2 lbs.

Same form for ♂ / ♀

Ω Skiploom's flower blossoms when the temperature rises above 64 degrees Fahrenheit. How much the flower opens depends on the temperature. For that reason, this Pokémon is sometimes used as a thermometer.

α Skiploom's flower blossoms when the temperature rises above 64 degrees Fahrenheit. How much the flower opens depends on the temperature. For that reason, this Pokémon is sometimes used as a thermometer.

ABILITIES
Chlorophyll
Leaf Guard

HIDDEN ABILITY
Infiltrator

EGG GROUPS
Fairy Grass

STAT GROWTH RATES
HP
Attack
Defense
Sp. Atk
Sp. Def
Speed

ITEMS SOMETIMES HELD BY WILD POKÉMON
—

EVOLUTION

Hoppip → Lv. 18 → Skiploom → Lv. 27 → Jumpluff

MAIN WAY TO REGISTER IN THE NATIONAL POKÉDEX

Level up a Hoppip obtained via Link Trade or the GTS to Lv. 18.

Damage taken in normal battles

Type		Type	
Normal	×1	Flying	×2
Fire	×2	Psychic	×1
Water	×0.5	Bug	×1
Grass	×0.25	Rock	×2
Electric	×1	Ghost	×1
Ice	×4	Dragon	×1
Fighting	×0.5	Dark	×1
Poison	×2	Steel	×1
Ground	×0	Fairy	×1

Damage taken in Inverse battles

Type		Type	
Normal	×1	Flying	×0.5
Fire	×0.5	Psychic	×1
Water	×2	Bug	×1
Grass	×4	Rock	×0.5
Electric	×1	Ghost	×1
Ice	×0.25	Dragon	×1
Fighting	×2	Dark	×1
Poison	×0.5	Steel	×1
Ground	×4	Fairy	×1

Can be used in
Inverse Battle
Battle Institute
Battle Maison
Random Matchup (Free Battle)
Random Matchup (Others)

LEVEL-UP MOVES

Lv.	Name	Type	Kind	Pow.	Acc.	PP	Range
1	Splash	Normal	Status	—	—	40	Self
1	Synthesis	Grass	Status	—	—	5	Self
1	Tail Whip	Normal	Status	—	100	30	Many Others
1	Tackle	Normal	Physical	50	100	35	Normal
4	Synthesis	Grass	Status	—	—	5	Self
6	Tail Whip	Normal	Status	—	100	30	Many Others
8	Tackle	Normal	Physical	50	100	35	Normal
10	Fairy Wind	Fairy	Special	40	100	30	Normal
12	Poison Powder	Poison	Status	—	75	35	Normal
14	Stun Spore	Grass	Status	—	75	30	Normal
16	Sleep Powder	Grass	Status	—	75	15	Normal
20	Bullet Seed	Grass	Physical	25	100	30	Normal
24	Leech Seed	Grass	Status	—	90	10	Normal
28	Mega Drain	Grass	Special	40	100	15	Normal
32	Acrobatics	Flying	Physical	55	100	15	Normal
36	Rage Powder	Bug	Status	—	—	20	Self
40	Cotton Spore	Grass	Status	—	100	40	Many Others
44	U-turn	Bug	Physical	70	100	20	Normal
48	Worry Seed	Grass	Status	—	100	10	Normal
52	Giga Drain	Grass	Special	75	100	10	Normal
56	Bounce	Flying	Physical	85	85	5	Normal
60	Memento	Dark	Status	—	100	10	Normal

TM & HM MOVES

No.	Name	Type	Kind	Pow.	Acc.	PP	Range
TM06	Toxic	Poison	Status	—	90	10	Normal
TM10	Hidden Power	Normal	Special	60	100	15	Normal
TM11	Sunny Day	Fire	Status	—	—	5	Both Sides
TM17	Protect	Normal	Status	—	—	10	Self
TM21	Frustration	Normal	Physical	—	100	20	Normal
TM22	Solar Beam	Grass	Special	120	100	10	Normal
TM27	Return	Normal	Physical	—	100	20	Normal
TM32	Double Team	Normal	Status	—	—	15	Self
TM33	Reflect	Psychic	Status	—	—	20	Your Side
TM40	Aerial Ace	Flying	Physical	60	—	20	Normal
TM42	Facade	Normal	Physical	70	100	20	Normal
TM44	Rest	Psychic	Status	—	—	10	Self
TM45	Attract	Normal	Status	—	100	15	Normal
TM48	Round	Normal	Special	60	100	15	Normal
TM53	Energy Ball	Grass	Special	90	100	10	Normal
TM62	Acrobatics	Flying	Physical	55	100	15	Normal
TM70	Flash	Normal	Status	—	100	20	Normal
TM75	Swords Dance	Normal	Status	—	—	20	Self
TM77	Psych Up	Normal	Status	—	—	10	Normal
TM83	Infestation	Bug	Special	20	100	20	Normal
TM86	Grass Knot	Grass	Special	—	100	20	Normal
TM87	Swagger	Normal	Status	—	90	15	Normal
TM88	Sleep Talk	Normal	Status	—	—	10	Self
TM89	U-turn	Bug	Physical	70	100	20	Normal
TM90	Substitute	Normal	Status	—	—	10	Self
TM94	Secret Power	Normal	Physical	70	100	20	Normal
TM99	Dazzling Gleam	Fairy	Special	80	100	10	Many Others
TM100	Confide	Normal	Status	—	—	20	Normal

MOVES LEARNED IN EXCHANGE FOR BP

Name	Type	Kind	Pow.	Acc.	PP	Range
Seed Bomb	Grass	Physical	80	100	15	Normal
Bounce	Flying	Physical	85	85	5	Normal
Snore	Normal	Special	50	100	15	Normal
Synthesis	Grass	Status	—	—	5	Self
Giga Drain	Grass	Special	75	100	10	Normal
Worry Seed	Grass	Status	—	100	10	Normal
Helping Hand	Normal	Status	—	—	20	1 Ally

MOVES TAUGHT BY PEOPLE

Name	Type	Kind	Pow.	Acc.	PP	Range

National Pokédex **189** Hoenn Pokédex —

Jumpluff

Cottonweed Pokémon

Grass Flying

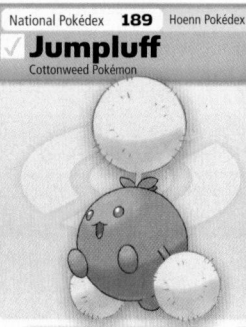

HEIGHT: 2'07" WEIGHT: 6.6 lbs.

Same form for ♂ / ♀

Ω Jumpluff rides warm southern winds to cross the sea and fly to foreign lands. The Pokémon descends to the ground when it encounters cold air while it is floating.

α Jumpluff rides warm southern winds to cross the sea and fly to foreign lands. The Pokémon descends to the ground when it encounters cold air while it is floating.

ABILITIES
Chlorophyll
Leaf Guard

HIDDEN ABILITY
Infiltrator

EGG GROUPS
Fairy Grass

STAT GROWTH RATES
HP
Attack
Defense
Sp. Atk
Sp. Def
Speed

ITEMS SOMETIMES HELD BY WILD POKÉMON
—

EVOLUTION

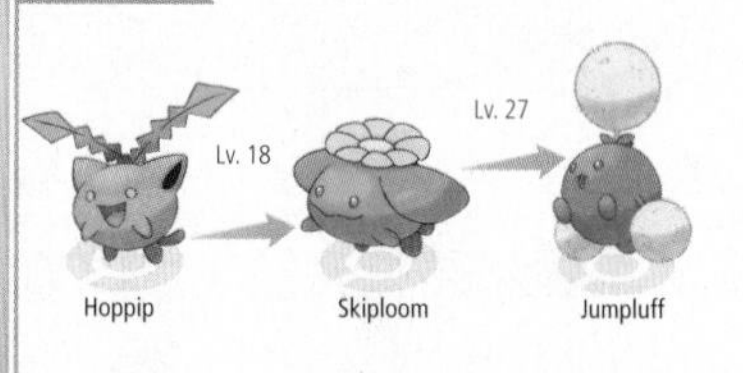

MAIN WAY TO REGISTER IN THE NATIONAL POKÉDEX

Level up a Skiploom obtained via Link Trade or the GTS to Lv. 27.

Damage taken in normal battles

Type		Type	
Normal	×1	Flying	×2
Fire	×2	Psychic	×1
Water	×0.5	Bug	×1
Grass	×0.25	Rock	×2
Electric	×1	Ghost	×1
Ice	×4	Dragon	×1
Fighting	×0.5	Dark	×1
Poison	×2	Steel	×1
Ground	×0	Fairy	×1

Damage taken in Inverse battles

Type		Type	
Normal	×1	Flying	×0.5
Fire	×0.5	Psychic	×1
Water	×2	Bug	×1
Grass	×4	Rock	×0.5
Electric	×1	Ghost	×1
Ice	×0.25	Dragon	×1
Fighting	×2	Dark	×1
Poison	×0.5	Steel	×1
Ground	×4	Fairy	×1

Can be used in
Inverse Battle
Battle Institute
Battle Maison
Random Matchup (Free Battle)
Random Matchup (Others)

LEVEL-UP MOVES

Lv.	Name	Type	Kind	Pow.	Acc.	PP	Range
1	Splash	Normal	Status	—	—	40	Self
1	Synthesis	Grass	Status	—	—	5	Self
1	Tail Whip	Normal	Status	—	100	30	Many Others
1	Tackle	Normal	Physical	50	100	35	Normal
4	Synthesis	Grass	Status	—	—	5	Self
6	Tail Whip	Normal	Status	—	100	30	Many Others
8	Tackle	Normal	Physical	50	100	35	Normal
10	Fairy Wind	Fairy	Special	40	100	30	Normal
12	Poison Powder	Poison	Status	—	75	35	Normal
14	Stun Spore	Grass	Status	—	75	30	Normal
16	Sleep Powder	Grass	Status	—	75	15	Normal
20	Bullet Seed	Grass	Physical	25	100	30	Normal
24	Leech Seed	Grass	Status	—	90	10	Normal
29	Mega Drain	Grass	Special	40	100	15	Normal
34	Acrobatics	Flying	Physical	55	100	15	Normal
39	Rage Powder	Bug	Status	—	—	20	Self
44	Cotton Spore	Grass	Status	—	100	40	Many Others
49	U-turn	Bug	Physical	70	100	20	Normal
54	Worry Seed	Grass	Status	—	100	10	Normal
59	Giga Drain	Grass	Special	75	100	10	Normal
64	Bounce	Flying	Physical	85	85	5	Normal
69	Memento	Dark	Status	—	100	10	Normal

TM & HM MOVES

No.	Name	Type	Kind	Pow.	Acc.	PP	Range
TM06	Toxic	Poison	Status	—	90	10	Normal
TM10	Hidden Power	Normal	Special	60	100	15	Normal
TM11	Sunny Day	Fire	Status	—	—	5	Both Sides
TM15	Hyper Beam	Normal	Special	150	90	5	Normal
TM17	Protect	Normal	Status	—	—	10	Self
TM21	Frustration	Normal	Physical	—	100	20	Normal
TM22	Solar Beam	Grass	Special	120	100	10	Normal
TM27	Return	Normal	Physical	—	100	20	Normal
TM32	Double Team	Normal	Status	—	—	15	Self
TM33	Reflect	Psychic	Status	—	—	20	Your Side
TM40	Aerial Ace	Flying	Physical	60	—	20	Normal
TM42	Facade	Normal	Physical	70	100	20	Normal
TM44	Rest	Psychic	Status	—	—	10	Self
TM45	Attract	Normal	Status	—	100	15	Normal
TM48	Round	Normal	Special	60	100	15	Normal
TM53	Energy Ball	Grass	Special	90	100	10	Normal
TM62	Acrobatics	Flying	Physical	55	100	15	Normal
TM68	Giga Impact	Normal	Physical	150	90	5	Normal
TM70	Flash	Normal	Status	—	100	20	Normal
TM75	Swords Dance	Normal	Status	—	—	20	Self
TM77	Psych Up	Normal	Status	—	—	10	Normal
TM83	Infestation	Bug	Special	20	100	20	Normal
TM86	Grass Knot	Grass	Special	—	100	20	Normal
TM87	Swagger	Normal	Status	—	90	15	Normal
TM88	Sleep Talk	Normal	Status	—	—	10	Self
TM89	U-turn	Bug	Physical	70	100	20	Normal
TM90	Substitute	Normal	Status	—	—	10	Self
TM94	Secret Power	Normal	Physical	70	100	20	Normal
TM99	Dazzling Gleam	Fairy	Special	80	100	10	Many Others
TM100	Confide	Normal	Status	—	—	20	Normal

MOVES LEARNED IN EXCHANGE FOR BP

Name	Type	Kind	Pow.	Acc.	PP	Range
Seed Bomb	Grass	Physical	80	100	15	Normal
Bounce	Flying	Physical	85	85	5	Normal
Snore	Normal	Special	50	100	15	Normal
Synthesis	Grass	Status	—	—	5	Self
Giga Drain	Grass	Special	75	100	10	Normal
Worry Seed	Grass	Status	—	100	10	Normal
Helping Hand	Normal	Status	—	—	20	1 Ally

MOVES TAUGHT BY PEOPLE

Name	Type	Kind	Pow.	Acc.	PP	Range

National Pokédex **190** Hoenn Pokédex —

Aipom

Long Tail Pokémon

Normal

HEIGHT: 2'07" WEIGHT: 25.4 lbs.

The male has shorter hair on its head.
The female has longer hair on its head.

Ω Aipom's tail ends in a hand-like appendage that can be cleverly manipulated. However, because the Pokémon uses its tail so much, its real hands have become rather clumsy.

α Aipom's tail ends in a hand-like appendage that can be cleverly manipulated. However, because the Pokémon uses its tail so much, its real hands have become rather clumsy.

ABILITIES
Run Away
Pickup

HIDDEN ABILITY
Skill Link

EGG GROUPS
Field

STAT GROWTH RATES
HP ■■
Attack ■■■■
Defense ■■■
Sp. Atk ■■
Sp. Def ■■
Speed ■■■■■

ITEMS SOMETIMES HELD BY WILD POKÉMON
—

EVOLUTION

MAIN WAY TO REGISTER IN THE NATIONAL POKÉDEX

Catch on Route 118. Appears as a hidden Pokémon after you battle Groudon or Kyogre.

Damage taken in normal battles

Type	×	Type	×
Normal	×1	Flying	×1
Fire	×1	Psychic	×1
Water	×1	Bug	×1
Grass	×1	Rock	×1
Electric	×1	Ghost	×0
Ice	×1	Dragon	×1
Fighting	×2	Dark	×1
Poison	×1	Steel	×1
Ground	×1	Fairy	×1

Damage taken in Inverse battles

Type	×	Type	×
Normal	×1	Flying	×1
Fire	×1	Psychic	×1
Water	×1	Bug	×1
Grass	×1	Rock	×1
Electric	×1	Ghost	×2
Ice	×1	Dragon	×1
Fighting	×0.5	Dark	×1
Poison	×1	Steel	×1
Ground	×1	Fairy	×1

Can be used in
Inverse Battle
Battle Institute
Battle Maison
Random Matchup (Free Battle)
Random Matchup (Others)

LEVEL-UP MOVES

Lv.	Name	Type	Kind	Pow.	Acc.	PP	Range
1	Scratch	Normal	Physical	40	100	35	Normal
1	Tail Whip	Normal	Status	—	100	30	Many Others
4	Sand Attack	Ground	Status	—	100	15	Normal
8	Astonish	Ghost	Physical	30	100	15	Normal
11	Baton Pass	Normal	Status	—	—	40	Self
15	Tickle	Normal	Status	—	100	20	Normal
18	Fury Swipes	Normal	Physical	18	80	15	Normal
22	Swift	Normal	Special	60	—	20	Many Others
25	Screech	Normal	Status	—	85	40	Normal
29	Agility	Psychic	Status	—	—	30	Self
32	Double Hit	Normal	Physical	35	90	10	Normal
36	Fling	Dark	Physical	—	100	10	Normal
39	Nasty Plot	Dark	Status	—	—	20	Self
43	Last Resort	Normal	Physical	140	100	5	Normal

TM & HM MOVES

No.	Name	Type	Kind	Pow.	Acc.	PP	Range
TM01	Hone Claws	Dark	Status	—	—	15	Self
TM06	Toxic	Poison	Status	—	90	10	Normal
TM10	Hidden Power	Normal	Special	60	100	15	Normal
TM11	Sunny Day	Fire	Status	—	—	5	Both Sides
TM12	Taunt	Dark	Status	—	100	20	Normal
TM17	Protect	Normal	Status	—	—	10	Self
TM18	Rain Dance	Water	Status	—	—	5	Both Sides
TM21	Frustration	Normal	Physical	—	100	20	Normal
TM22	Solar Beam	Grass	Special	120	100	10	Normal
TM24	Thunderbolt	Electric	Special	90	100	15	Normal
TM25	Thunder	Electric	Special	110	70	10	Normal
TM27	Return	Normal	Physical	—	100	20	Normal
TM28	Dig	Ground	Physical	80	100	10	Normal
TM30	Shadow Ball	Ghost	Special	80	100	15	Normal
TM31	Brick Break	Fighting	Physical	75	100	15	Normal
TM32	Double Team	Normal	Status	—	—	15	Self
TM40	Aerial Ace	Flying	Physical	60	—	20	Normal
TM42	Facade	Normal	Physical	70	100	20	Normal
TM44	Rest	Psychic	Status	—	—	10	Self
TM45	Attract	Normal	Status	—	100	15	Normal
TM46	Thief	Dark	Physical	60	100	25	Normal
TM47	Low Sweep	Fighting	Physical	65	100	20	Normal
TM48	Round	Normal	Special	60	100	15	Normal
TM56	Fling	Dark	Physical	—	100	10	Normal
TM62	Acrobatics	Flying	Physical	55	100	15	Normal
TM65	Shadow Claw	Ghost	Physical	70	100	15	Normal
TM66	Payback	Dark	Physical	50	100	10	Normal
TM67	Retaliate	Normal	Physical	70	100	5	Normal
TM73	Thunder Wave	Electric	Status	—	100	20	Normal
TM85	Dream Eater	Psychic	Special	100	100	15	Normal
TM86	Grass Knot	Grass	Special	—	100	20	Normal
TM87	Swagger	Normal	Status	—	90	15	Normal
TM88	Sleep Talk	Normal	Status	—	—	10	Self
TM89	U-turn	Bug	Physical	70	100	20	Normal
TM90	Substitute	Normal	Status	—	—	10	Self
TM94	Secret Power	Normal	Physical	70	100	20	Normal
TM98	Power-Up Punch	Fighting	Physical	40	100	20	Normal
TM100	Confide	Normal	Status	—	—	20	Normal
HM01	Cut	Normal	Physical	50	95	30	Normal
HM04	Strength	Normal	Physical	80	100	15	Normal
HM06	Rock Smash	Fighting	Physical	40	100	15	Normal

MOVES LEARNED IN EXCHANGE FOR BP

Name	Type	Kind	Pow.	Acc.	PP	Range
Covet	Normal	Physical	60	100	25	Normal
Seed Bomb	Grass	Physical	80	100	15	Normal
Bounce	Flying	Physical	85	85	5	Normal
Low Kick	Fighting	Physical	—	100	20	Normal
Gunk Shot	Poison	Physical	120	80	5	Normal
Uproar	Normal	Special	90	100	10	1 Random
Thunder Punch	Electric	Physical	75	100	15	Normal
Fire Punch	Fire	Physical	75	100	15	Normal
Ice Punch	Ice	Physical	75	100	15	Normal
Foul Play	Dark	Physical	95	100	15	Normal
Last Resort	Normal	Physical	140	100	5	Normal
Iron Tail	Steel	Physical	100	75	15	Normal
Snore	Normal	Special	50	100	15	Normal
Knock Off	Dark	Physical	65	100	20	Normal
Role Play	Psychic	Status	—	—	10	Normal
Focus Punch	Fighting	Physical	150	100	20	Normal
Shock Wave	Electric	Special	60	—	20	Normal
Water Pulse	Water	Special	60	100	20	Normal
Spite	Ghost	Status	—	100	10	Normal
Snatch	Dark	Status	—	—	10	Self

MOVES TAUGHT BY PEOPLE

Name	Type	Kind	Pow.	Acc.	PP	Range

EGG MOVES

Name	Type	Kind	Pow.	Acc.	PP	Range
Counter	Fighting	Physical	—	100	20	Varies
Screech	Normal	Status	—	85	40	Normal
Pursuit	Dark	Physical	40	100	20	Normal
Agility	Psychic	Status	—	—	30	Self
Spite	Ghost	Status	—	100	10	Normal
Slam	Normal	Physical	80	75	20	Normal
Double Slap	Normal	Physical	15	85	10	Normal
Beat Up	Dark	Physical	—	100	10	Normal
Fake Out	Normal	Physical	40	100	10	Normal
Covet	Normal	Physical	60	100	25	Normal
Bounce	Flying	Physical	85	85	5	Normal
Revenge	Fighting	Physical	60	100	10	Normal
Switcheroo	Dark	Status	—	100	10	Normal
Quick Guard	Fighting	Status	—	—	15	Your Side

National Pokédex **191** Hoenn Pokédex —

Sunkern

Seed Pokémon

Grass

HEIGHT: 1'00" WEIGHT: 4 lbs.

Same form for ♂ / ♀

Ω Sunkern tries to move as little as it possibly can. It does so because it tries to conserve all the nutrients it has stored in its body for its evolution. It will not eat a thing, subsisting only on morning dew.

α Sunkern tries to move as little as it possibly can. It does so because it tries to conserve all the nutrients it has stored in its body for its evolution. It will not eat a thing, subsisting only on morning dew.

ABILITIES
Chlorophyll
Solar Power

HIDDEN ABILITY
Early Bird

EGG GROUPS
Grass

STAT GROWTH RATES
HP ■■
Attack ■■
Defense ■■
Sp. Atk ■
Sp. Def ■
Speed ■■

ITEMS SOMETIMES HELD BY WILD POKÉMON
—

EVOLUTION

Sun Stone
Sunkern → Sunflora

MAIN WAY TO REGISTER IN THE NATIONAL POKÉDEX

Catch in Mirage Forest 5.

Damage taken in normal battles

Type	×	Type	×
Normal	×1	Flying	×2
Fire	×2	Psychic	×1
Water	×0.5	Bug	×2
Grass	×0.5	Rock	×1
Electric	×0.5	Ghost	×1
Ice	×2	Dragon	×1
Fighting	×1	Dark	×1
Poison	×2	Steel	×1
Ground	×0.5	Fairy	×1

Damage taken in Inverse battles

Type	×	Type	×
Normal	×1	Flying	×0.5
Fire	×0.5	Psychic	×1
Water	×2	Bug	×0.5
Grass	×2	Rock	×1
Electric	×2	Ghost	×1
Ice	×0.5	Dragon	×1
Fighting	×1	Dark	×1
Poison	×0.5	Steel	×1
Ground	×2	Fairy	×1

Can be used in
Inverse Battle
Battle Institute
Battle Maison
Random Matchup (Free Battle)
Random Matchup (Others)

LEVEL-UP MOVES

Lv.	Name	Type	Kind	Pow.	Acc.	PP	Range
1	Absorb	Grass	Special	20	100	25	Normal
1	Growth	Normal	Status	—	—	20	Self
4	Ingrain	Grass	Status	—	—	20	Self
7	Grass Whistle	Grass	Status	—	55	15	Normal
10	Mega Drain	Grass	Special	40	100	15	Normal
13	Leech Seed	Grass	Status	—	90	10	Normal
16	Razor Leaf	Grass	Physical	55	95	25	Many Others
19	Worry Seed	Grass	Status	—	100	10	Normal
22	Giga Drain	Grass	Special	75	100	10	Normal
25	Endeavor	Normal	Physical	—	100	5	Normal
28	Synthesis	Grass	Status	—	—	5	Self
31	Natural Gift	Normal	Physical	—	100	15	Normal
34	Solar Beam	Grass	Special	120	100	10	Normal
37	Double-Edge	Normal	Physical	120	100	15	Normal
40	Sunny Day	Fire	Status	—	—	5	Both Sides
43	Seed Bomb	Grass	Physical	80	100	15	Normal

TM & HM MOVES

No.	Name	Type	Kind	Pow.	Acc.	PP	Range
TM06	Toxic	Poison	Status	—	90	10	Normal
TM10	Hidden Power	Normal	Special	60	100	15	Normal
TM11	Sunny Day	Fire	Status	—	—	5	Both Sides
TM16	Light Screen	Psychic	Status	—	—	30	Your Side
TM17	Protect	Normal	Status	—	—	10	Self
TM20	Safeguard	Normal	Status	—	—	25	Your Side
TM21	Frustration	Normal	Physical	—	100	20	Normal
TM22	Solar Beam	Grass	Special	120	100	10	Normal
TM27	Return	Normal	Physical	—	100	20	Normal
TM32	Double Team	Normal	Status	—	—	15	Self
TM36	Sludge Bomb	Poison	Special	90	100	10	Normal
TM42	Facade	Normal	Physical	70	100	20	Normal
TM44	Rest	Psychic	Status	—	—	10	Self
TM45	Attract	Normal	Status	—	100	15	Normal
TM48	Round	Normal	Special	60	100	15	Normal
TM53	Energy Ball	Grass	Special	90	100	10	Normal
TM70	Flash	Normal	Status	—	100	20	Normal
TM75	Swords Dance	Normal	Status	—	—	20	Self
TM86	Grass Knot	Grass	Special	—	100	20	Normal
TM87	Swagger	Normal	Status	—	90	15	Normal
TM88	Sleep Talk	Normal	Status	—	—	10	Self
TM90	Substitute	Normal	Status	—	—	10	Self
TM94	Secret Power	Normal	Physical	70	100	20	Normal
TM96	Nature Power	Normal	Status	—	—	20	Normal
TM100	Confide	Normal	Status	—	—	20	Normal
HM01	Cut	Normal	Physical	50	95	30	Normal

MOVES LEARNED IN EXCHANGE FOR BP

Name	Type	Kind	Pow.	Acc.	PP	Range
Seed Bomb	Grass	Physical	80	100	15	Normal
Uproar	Normal	Special	90	100	10	1 Random
Earth Power	Ground	Special	90	100	10	Normal
Snore	Normal	Special	50	100	15	Normal
Synthesis	Grass	Status	—	—	5	Self
Giga Drain	Grass	Special	75	100	10	Normal
Worry Seed	Grass	Status	—	100	10	Normal
After You	Normal	Status	—	—	15	Normal
Helping Hand	Normal	Status	—	—	20	1 Ally
Endeavor	Normal	Physical	—	100	5	Normal

MOVES TAUGHT BY PEOPLE

Name	Type	Kind	Pow.	Acc.	PP	Range

EGG MOVES

Name	Type	Kind	Pow.	Acc.	PP	Range
Grass Whistle	Grass	Status	—	55	15	Normal
Encore	Normal	Status	—	100	5	Normal
Leech Seed	Grass	Status	—	90	10	Normal
Nature Power	Normal	Status	—	—	20	Normal
Curse	Ghost	Status	—	—	10	Varies
Helping Hand	Normal	Status	—	—	20	1 Ally
Ingrain	Grass	Status	—	—	20	Self
Sweet Scent	Normal	Status	—	100	20	Many Others
Endure	Normal	Status	—	—	10	Self
Bide	Normal	Physical	—	—	10	Self
Natural Gift	Normal	Physical	—	100	15	Normal
Morning Sun	Normal	Status	—	—	5	Self
Grassy Terrain	Grass	Status	—	—	10	Both Sides

National Pokédex **192** Hoenn Pokédex —

Sunflora

Sun Pokémon

Grass

HEIGHT: 2'07" WEIGHT: 18.7 lbs.

Same form for ♂ / ♀

Ω Sunflora converts solar energy into nutrition. It moves around actively in the daytime when it is warm. It stops moving as soon as the sun goes down for the night.

α Sunflora converts solar energy into nutrition. It moves around actively in the daytime when it is warm. It stops moving as soon as the sun goes down for the night.

ABILITIES
Chlorophyll
Solar Power

HIDDEN ABILITY
Early Bird

EGG GROUPS
Grass

STAT GROWTH RATES
HP ■■■
Attack ■■■■
Defense ■■■
Sp. Atk ■■■■■
Sp. Def ■■■■
Speed ■■

ITEMS SOMETIMES HELD BY WILD POKÉMON
—

EVOLUTION
Sunkern → Sun Stone → Sunflora

MAIN WAY TO REGISTER IN THE NATIONAL POKÉDEX

Use a Sun Stone on Sunkern.

Damage taken in normal battles

Type		Type	
Normal	×1	Flying	×2
Fire	×2	Psychic	×1
Water	×0.5	Bug	×2
Grass	×0.5	Rock	×1
Electric	×0.5	Ghost	×1
Ice	×2	Dragon	×1
Fighting	×1	Dark	×1
Poison	×2	Steel	×1
Ground	×0.5	Fairy	×1

Damage taken in Inverse battles

Type		Type	
Normal	×1	Flying	×0.5
Fire	×0.5	Psychic	×1
Water	×2	Bug	×0.5
Grass	×2	Rock	×1
Electric	×2	Ghost	×1
Ice	×0.5	Dragon	×1
Fighting	×1	Dark	×1
Poison	×0.5	Steel	×1
Ground	×2	Fairy	×1

Can be used in
Inverse Battle
Battle Institute
Battle Maison
Random Matchup (Free Battle)
Random Matchup (Others)

LEVEL-UP MOVES

Lv.	Name	Type	Kind	Pow.	Acc.	PP	Range
1	Flower Shield	Fairy	Status	—	—	10	Adjacent
1	Absorb	Grass	Special	20	100	25	Normal
1	Pound	Normal	Physical	40	100	35	Normal
1	Growth	Normal	Status	—	—	20	Self
4	Ingrain	Grass	Status	—	—	20	Self
7	Grass Whistle	Grass	Status	—	55	15	Normal
10	Mega Drain	Grass	Special	40	100	15	Normal
13	Leech Seed	Grass	Status	—	90	10	Normal
16	Razor Leaf	Grass	Physical	55	95	25	Many Others
19	Worry Seed	Grass	Status	—	100	10	Normal
22	Giga Drain	Grass	Special	75	100	10	Normal
25	Bullet Seed	Grass	Physical	25	100	30	Normal
28	Petal Dance	Grass	Special	120	100	10	1 Random
31	Natural Gift	Normal	Physical	—	100	15	Normal
34	Solar Beam	Grass	Special	120	100	10	Normal
37	Double-Edge	Normal	Physical	120	100	15	Normal
40	Sunny Day	Fire	Status	—	—	5	Both Sides
43	Leaf Storm	Grass	Special	130	90	5	Normal
50	Petal Blizzard	Grass	Physical	90	100	15	Adjacent

TM & HM MOVES

No.	Name	Type	Kind	Pow.	Acc.	PP	Range
TM06	Toxic	Poison	Status	—	90	10	Normal
TM10	Hidden Power	Normal	Special	60	100	15	Normal
TM11	Sunny Day	Fire	Status	—	—	5	Both Sides
TM15	Hyper Beam	Normal	Special	150	90	5	Normal
TM16	Light Screen	Psychic	Status	—	—	30	Your Side
TM17	Protect	Normal	Status	—	—	10	Self
TM20	Safeguard	Normal	Status	—	—	25	Your Side
TM21	Frustration	Normal	Physical	—	100	20	Normal
TM22	Solar Beam	Grass	Special	120	100	10	Normal
TM27	Return	Normal	Physical	—	100	20	Normal
TM32	Double Team	Normal	Status	—	—	15	Self
TM36	Sludge Bomb	Poison	Special	90	100	10	Normal
TM42	Facade	Normal	Physical	70	100	20	Normal
TM44	Rest	Psychic	Status	—	—	10	Self
TM45	Attract	Normal	Status	—	100	15	Normal
TM48	Round	Normal	Special	60	100	15	Normal
TM53	Energy Ball	Grass	Special	90	100	10	Normal
TM68	Giga Impact	Normal	Physical	150	90	5	Normal
TM70	Flash	Normal	Status	—	100	20	Normal
TM75	Swords Dance	Normal	Status	—	—	20	Self
TM86	Grass Knot	Grass	Special	—	100	20	Normal
TM87	Swagger	Normal	Status	—	90	15	Normal
TM88	Sleep Talk	Normal	Status	—	—	10	Self
TM90	Substitute	Normal	Status	—	—	10	Self
TM94	Secret Power	Normal	Physical	70	100	20	Normal
TM96	Nature Power	Normal	Status	—	—	20	Normal
TM100	Confide	Normal	Status	—	—	20	Normal
HM01	Cut	Normal	Physical	50	95	30	Normal

MOVES LEARNED IN EXCHANGE FOR BP

Name	Type	Kind	Pow.	Acc.	PP	Range
Seed Bomb	Grass	Physical	80	100	15	Normal
Uproar	Normal	Special	90	100	10	1 Random
Earth Power	Ground	Special	90	100	10	Normal
Snore	Normal	Special	50	100	15	Normal
Synthesis	Grass	Status	—	—	5	Self
Giga Drain	Grass	Special	75	100	10	Normal
Worry Seed	Grass	Status	—	100	10	Normal
After You	Normal	Status	—	—	15	Normal
Helping Hand	Normal	Status	—	—	20	1 Ally
Endeavor	Normal	Physical	—	100	5	Normal

MOVES TAUGHT BY PEOPLE

Name	Type	Kind	Pow.	Acc.	PP	Range

National Pokédex **193** Hoenn Pokédex —

Yanma

Clear Wing Pokémon

Bug Flying

HEIGHT: 3'11" WEIGHT: 83.8 lbs.

Same form for ♂ / ♀

Ω Yanma is capable of seeing 360 degrees without having to move its eyes. It is a great flier that is adept at making sudden stops and turning midair. This Pokémon uses its flying ability to quickly chase down targeted prey.

α Yanma is capable of seeing 360 degrees without having to move its eyes. It is a great flier that is adept at making sudden stops and turning midair. This Pokémon uses its flying ability to quickly chase down targeted prey.

ABILITIES
Speed Boost
Compound Eyes

HIDDEN ABILITY
Frisk

EGG GROUPS
Bug

STAT GROWTH RATES
HP ■■■
Attack ■■■
Defense ■■
Sp. Atk ■■■■
Sp. Def ■■
Speed ■■■■■

ITEMS SOMETIMES HELD BY WILD POKÉMON
—

EVOLUTION
Yanma → Lv. 33 with Ancient Power → Yanmega

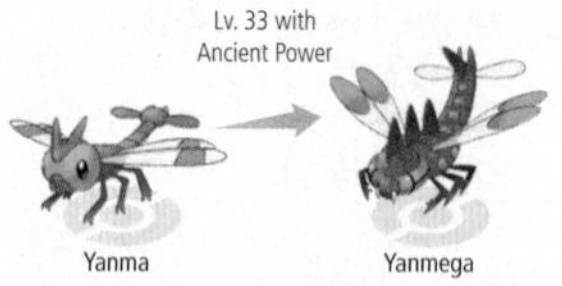

MAIN WAY TO REGISTER IN THE NATIONAL POKÉDEX

Appears in *Pokémon X* and *Pokémon Y*. Bring it to your game using Link Trade or the GTS.

Damage taken in normal battles

Type		Type	
Normal	×1	Flying	×2
Fire	×2	Psychic	×1
Water	×1	Bug	×0.5
Grass	×0.25	Rock	×4
Electric	×2	Ghost	×1
Ice	×2	Dragon	×1
Fighting	×0.25	Dark	×1
Poison	×1	Steel	×1
Ground	×0	Fairy	×1

Damage taken in Inverse battles

Type		Type	
Normal	×1	Flying	×0.5
Fire	×0.5	Psychic	×1
Water	×1	Bug	×2
Grass	×4	Rock	×0.25
Electric	×0.5	Ghost	×1
Ice	×0.5	Dragon	×1
Fighting	×4	Dark	×1
Poison	×1	Steel	×1
Ground	×4	Fairy	×1

Can be used in
Inverse Battle
Battle Institute
Battle Maison
Random Matchup (Free Battle)
Random Matchup (Others)

LEVEL-UP MOVES

Lv.	Name	Type	Kind	Pow.	Acc.	PP	Range
1	Tackle	Normal	Physical	50	100	35	Normal
1	Foresight	Normal	Status	—	—	40	Normal
6	Quick Attack	Normal	Physical	40	100	30	Normal
11	Double Team	Normal	Status	—	—	15	Self
14	Sonic Boom	Normal	Special	—	90	20	Normal
17	Detect	Fighting	Status	—	—	5	Self
22	Supersonic	Normal	Status	—	55	20	Normal
27	Uproar	Normal	Special	90	100	10	1 Random
30	Pursuit	Dark	Physical	40	100	20	Normal
33	Ancient Power	Rock	Special	60	100	5	Normal
38	Hypnosis	Psychic	Status	—	60	20	Normal
43	Wing Attack	Flying	Physical	60	100	35	Normal
46	Screech	Normal	Status	—	85	40	Normal
49	U-turn	Bug	Physical	70	100	20	Normal
54	Air Slash	Flying	Special	75	95	15	Normal
57	Bug Buzz	Bug	Special	90	100	10	Normal

TM & HM MOVES

No.	Name	Type	Kind	Pow.	Acc.	PP	Range
TM06	Toxic	Poison	Status	—	90	10	Normal
TM10	Hidden Power	Normal	Special	60	100	15	Normal
TM11	Sunny Day	Fire	Status	—	—	5	Both Sides
TM17	Protect	Normal	Status	—	—	10	Self
TM19	Roost	Flying	Status	—	—	10	Self
TM21	Frustration	Normal	Physical	—	100	20	Normal
TM22	Solar Beam	Grass	Special	120	100	10	Normal
TM27	Return	Normal	Physical	—	100	20	Normal
TM29	Psychic	Psychic	Special	90	100	10	Normal
TM30	Shadow Ball	Ghost	Special	80	100	15	Normal
TM32	Double Team	Normal	Status	—	—	15	Self
TM40	Aerial Ace	Flying	Physical	60	—	20	Normal
TM42	Facade	Normal	Physical	70	100	20	Normal
TM44	Rest	Psychic	Status	—	—	10	Self
TM45	Attract	Normal	Status	—	100	15	Normal
TM46	Thief	Dark	Physical	60	100	25	Normal
TM48	Round	Normal	Special	60	100	15	Normal
TM51	Steel Wing	Steel	Physical	70	90	25	Normal
TM70	Flash	Normal	Status	—	100	20	Normal
TM85	Dream Eater	Psychic	Special	100	100	15	Normal
TM87	Swagger	Normal	Status	—	90	15	Normal
TM88	Sleep Talk	Normal	Status	—	—	10	Self
TM89	U-turn	Bug	Physical	70	100	20	Normal
TM90	Substitute	Normal	Status	—	—	10	Self
TM94	Secret Power	Normal	Physical	70	100	20	Normal
TM100	Confide	Normal	Status	—	—	20	Normal

MOVES LEARNED IN EXCHANGE FOR BP

Name	Type	Kind	Pow.	Acc.	PP	Range
Bug Bite	Bug	Physical	60	100	20	Normal
Signal Beam	Bug	Special	75	100	15	Normal
Uproar	Normal	Special	90	100	10	1 Random
Snore	Normal	Special	50	100	15	Normal
Tailwind	Flying	Status	—	—	15	Your Side
Giga Drain	Grass	Special	75	100	10	Normal

MOVES TAUGHT BY PEOPLE

Name	Type	Kind	Pow.	Acc.	PP	Range

EGG MOVES

Name	Type	Kind	Pow.	Acc.	PP	Range
Whirlwind	Normal	Status	—	—	20	Normal
Reversal	Fighting	Physical	—	100	15	Normal
Leech Life	Bug	Physical	20	100	15	Normal
Signal Beam	Bug	Special	75	100	15	Normal
Silver Wind	Bug	Special	60	100	5	Normal
Feint	Normal	Physical	30	100	10	Normal
Feint Attack	Dark	Physical	60	—	20	Normal
Pursuit	Dark	Physical	40	100	20	Normal
Double-Edge	Normal	Physical	120	100	15	Normal
Secret Power	Normal	Physical	70	100	20	Normal

National Pokédex **194** Hoenn Pokédex —

Wooper

Water Fish Pokémon

Water | Ground

HEIGHT: 1'04" WEIGHT: 18.7 lbs.

The male has more abundant frills on its head.
The female has less abundant frills on its head.

Ω Wooper usually lives in water. However, it occasionally comes out onto land in search of food. On land, it coats its body with a gooey, toxic film.

α Wooper usually lives in water. However, it occasionally comes out onto land in search of food. On land, it coats its body with a gooey, toxic film.

ABILITIES
Damp
Water Absorb

HIDDEN ABILITY
Unaware

EGG GROUPS
Water 1 | Field

STAT GROWTH RATES
HP ■■
Attack ■■
Defense ■■
Sp. Atk ■
Sp. Def ■
Speed ■

ITEMS SOMETIMES HELD BY WILD POKÉMON
—

EVOLUTION

MAIN WAY TO REGISTER IN THE NATIONAL POKÉDEX

Leave a Quagsire obtained via Link Trade or the GTS at a Pokémon Day Care, then hatch the Pokémon Egg that is found.

Damage taken in normal battles

Type		Type	
Normal	×1	Flying	×1
Fire	×0.5	Psychic	×1
Water	×1	Bug	×1
Grass	×4	Rock	×0.5
Electric	×0	Ghost	×1
Ice	×1	Dragon	×1
Fighting	×1	Dark	×1
Poison	×0.5	Steel	×0.5
Ground	×1	Fairy	×1

Damage taken in Inverse battles

Type		Type	
Normal	×1	Flying	×1
Fire	×2	Psychic	×1
Water	×1	Bug	×1
Grass	×0.25	Rock	×2
Electric	×1	Ghost	×1
Ice	×1	Dragon	×1
Fighting	×1	Dark	×1
Poison	×2	Steel	×2
Ground	×1	Fairy	×1

Can be used in
Inverse Battle
Battle Institute
Battle Maison
Random Matchup (Free Battle)
Random Matchup (Others)

LEVEL-UP MOVES

Lv.	Name	Type	Kind	Pow.	Acc.	PP	Range
1	Water Gun	Water	Special	40	100	25	Normal
1	Tail Whip	Normal	Status	—	100	30	Many Others
5	Mud Sport	Ground	Status	—	—	15	Both Sides
9	Mud Shot	Ground	Special	55	95	15	Normal
15	Slam	Normal	Physical	80	75	20	Normal
19	Mud Bomb	Ground	Special	65	85	10	Normal
23	Amnesia	Psychic	Status	—	—	20	Self
29	Yawn	Normal	Status	—	—	10	Normal
33	Earthquake	Ground	Physical	100	100	10	Adjacent
37	Rain Dance	Water	Status	—	—	5	Both Sides
43	Mist	Ice	Status	—	—	30	Your Side
43	Haze	Ice	Status	—	—	30	Both Sides
47	Muddy Water	Water	Special	90	85	10	Many Others

TM & HM MOVES

No.	Name	Type	Kind	Pow.	Acc.	PP	Range
TM06	Toxic	Poison	Status	—	90	10	Normal
TM07	Hail	Ice	Status	—	—	10	Both Sides
TM10	Hidden Power	Normal	Special	60	100	15	Normal
TM13	Ice Beam	Ice	Special	90	100	10	Normal
TM14	Blizzard	Ice	Special	110	70	5	Many Others
TM17	Protect	Normal	Status	—	—	10	Self
TM18	Rain Dance	Water	Status	—	—	5	Both Sides
TM20	Safeguard	Normal	Status	—	—	25	Your Side
TM21	Frustration	Normal	Physical	—	100	20	Normal
TM26	Earthquake	Ground	Physical	100	100	10	Adjacent
TM27	Return	Normal	Physical	—	100	20	Normal
TM28	Dig	Ground	Physical	80	100	10	Normal
TM32	Double Team	Normal	Status	—	—	15	Self
TM34	Sludge Wave	Poison	Special	95	100	10	Adjacent
TM36	Sludge Bomb	Poison	Special	90	100	10	Normal
TM37	Sandstorm	Rock	Status	—	—	10	Both Sides
TM42	Facade	Normal	Physical	70	100	20	Normal
TM44	Rest	Psychic	Status	—	—	10	Self
TM45	Attract	Normal	Status	—	100	15	Normal
TM48	Round	Normal	Special	60	100	15	Normal
TM55	Scald	Water	Special	80	100	15	Normal
TM70	Flash	Normal	Status	—	100	20	Normal
TM78	Bulldoze	Ground	Physical	60	100	20	Adjacent
TM83	Infestation	Bug	Special	20	100	20	Normal
TM87	Swagger	Normal	Status	—	90	15	Normal
TM88	Sleep Talk	Normal	Status	—	—	10	Self
TM90	Substitute	Normal	Status	—	—	10	Self
TM94	Secret Power	Normal	Physical	70	100	20	Normal
TM100	Confide	Normal	Status	—	—	20	Normal
HM03	Surf	Water	Special	90	100	15	Adjacent
HM05	Waterfall	Water	Physical	80	100	15	Normal
HM06	Rock Smash	Fighting	Physical	40	100	15	Normal
HM07	Dive	Water	Physical	80	100	10	Normal

MOVES LEARNED IN EXCHANGE FOR BP

Name	Type	Kind	Pow.	Acc.	PP	Range
Ice Punch	Ice	Physical	75	100	15	Normal
Earth Power	Ground	Special	90	100	10	Normal
Icy Wind	Ice	Special	55	95	15	Many Others
Aqua Tail	Water	Physical	90	90	10	Normal
Iron Tail	Steel	Physical	100	75	15	Normal
Snore	Normal	Special	50	100	15	Normal
Water Pulse	Water	Special	60	100	20	Normal
After You	Normal	Status	—	—	15	Normal

MOVES TAUGHT BY PEOPLE

Name	Type	Kind	Pow.	Acc.	PP	Range

EGG MOVES

Name	Type	Kind	Pow.	Acc.	PP	Range
Body Slam	Normal	Physical	85	100	15	Normal
Ancient Power	Rock	Special	60	100	5	Normal
Curse	Ghost	Status	—	—	10	Varies
Mud Sport	Ground	Status	—	—	15	Both Sides
Stockpile	Normal	Status	—	—	20	Self
Swallow	Normal	Status	—	—	10	Self
Spit Up	Normal	Special	—	100	10	Normal
Counter	Fighting	Physical	—	100	20	Varies
Encore	Normal	Status	—	100	5	Normal
Double Kick	Fighting	Physical	30	100	30	Normal
Recover	Normal	Status	—	—	10	Self
After You	Normal	Status	—	—	15	Normal
Sleep Talk	Normal	Status	—	—	10	Self
Acid Spray	Poison	Special	40	100	20	Normal
Guard Swap	Psychic	Status	—	—	10	Normal
Eerie Impulse	Electric	Status	—	100	15	Normal

National Pokédex **195** Hoenn Pokédex —

Quagsire

Water Fish Pokémon

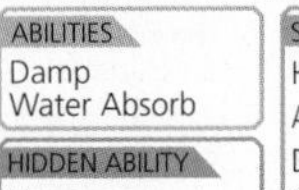

Water | Ground

HEIGHT: 4'07" WEIGHT: 165.3 lbs.

The male has larger fins on its back.
The female has smaller fins on its back.

Ω Quagsire hunts for food by leaving its mouth wide open in water and waiting for its prey to blunder in unaware. Because the Pokémon does not move, it does not get very hungry.

α Quagsire hunts for food by leaving its mouth wide open in water and waiting for its prey to blunder in unaware. Because the Pokémon does not move, it does not get very hungry.

ABILITIES
Damp
Water Absorb

HIDDEN ABILITY
Unaware

EGG GROUPS
Water 1 | Field

STAT GROWTH RATES
HP ■■■■
Attack ■■■■
Defense ■■■■
Sp. Atk ■■■
Sp. Def ■■■
Speed ■■

ITEMS SOMETIMES HELD BY WILD POKÉMON
—

EVOLUTION

MAIN WAY TO REGISTER IN THE NATIONAL POKÉDEX

Appears in *Pokémon X* and *Pokémon Y*. Bring it to your game using Link Trade or the GTS.

Damage taken in normal battles

Type		Type	
Normal	×1	Flying	×1
Fire	×0.5	Psychic	×1
Water	×1	Bug	×1
Grass	×4	Rock	×0.5
Electric	×0	Ghost	×1
Ice	×1	Dragon	×1
Fighting	×1	Dark	×1
Poison	×0.5	Steel	×0.5
Ground	×1	Fairy	×1

Damage taken in Inverse battles

Type		Type	
Normal	×1	Flying	×1
Fire	×2	Psychic	×1
Water	×1	Bug	×1
Grass	×0.25	Rock	×2
Electric	×1	Ghost	×1
Ice	×1	Dragon	×1
Fighting	×1	Dark	×1
Poison	×2	Steel	×2
Ground	×1	Fairy	×1

Can be used in
Inverse Battle
Battle Institute
Battle Maison
Random Matchup (Free Battle)
Random Matchup (Others)

LEVEL-UP MOVES

Lv.	Name	Type	Kind	Pow.	Acc.	PP	Range
1	Water Gun	Water	Special	40	100	25	Normal
1	Tail Whip	Normal	Status	—	100	30	Many Others
1	Mud Sport	Ground	Status	—	—	15	Both Sides
5	Mud Sport	Ground	Status	—	—	15	Both Sides
9	Mud Shot	Ground	Special	55	95	15	Normal
15	Slam	Normal	Physical	80	75	20	Normal
19	Mud Bomb	Ground	Special	65	85	10	Normal
24	Amnesia	Psychic	Status	—	—	20	Self
31	Yawn	Normal	Status	—	—	10	Normal
36	Earthquake	Ground	Physical	100	100	10	Adjacent
41	Rain Dance	Water	Status	—	—	5	Both Sides
48	Mist	Ice	Status	—	—	30	Your Side
48	Haze	Ice	Status	—	—	30	Both Sides
53	Muddy Water	Water	Special	90	85	10	Many Others

TM & HM MOVES

No.	Name	Type	Kind	Pow.	Acc.	PP	Range
TM06	Toxic	Poison	Status	—	90	10	Normal
TM07	Hail	Ice	Status	—	—	10	Both Sides
TM10	Hidden Power	Normal	Special	60	100	15	Normal
TM13	Ice Beam	Ice	Special	90	100	10	Normal
TM14	Blizzard	Ice	Special	110	70	5	Many Others
TM15	Hyper Beam	Normal	Special	150	90	5	Normal
TM17	Protect	Normal	Status	—	—	10	Self
TM18	Rain Dance	Water	Status	—	—	5	Both Sides
TM20	Safeguard	Normal	Status	—	—	25	Your Side
TM21	Frustration	Normal	Physical	—	100	20	Normal
TM26	Earthquake	Ground	Physical	100	100	10	Adjacent
TM27	Return	Normal	Physical	—	100	20	Normal
TM28	Dig	Ground	Physical	80	100	10	Normal
TM31	Brick Break	Fighting	Physical	75	100	15	Normal
TM32	Double Team	Normal	Status	—	—	15	Self
TM34	Sludge Wave	Poison	Special	95	100	10	Adjacent
TM36	Sludge Bomb	Poison	Special	90	100	10	Normal
TM37	Sandstorm	Rock	Status	—	—	10	Both Sides
TM39	Rock Tomb	Rock	Physical	60	95	15	Normal
TM42	Facade	Normal	Physical	70	100	20	Normal
TM44	Rest	Psychic	Status	—	—	10	Self
TM45	Attract	Normal	Status	—	100	15	Normal
TM46	Thief	Dark	Physical	60	100	25	Normal
TM48	Round	Normal	Special	60	100	15	Normal
TM52	Focus Blast	Fighting	Special	120	70	5	Normal
TM55	Scald	Water	Special	80	100	15	Normal
TM56	Fling	Dark	Physical	—	100	10	Normal
TM68	Giga Impact	Normal	Physical	150	90	5	Normal
TM70	Flash	Normal	Status	—	100	20	Normal
TM71	Stone Edge	Rock	Physical	100	80	5	Normal
TM78	Bulldoze	Ground	Physical	60	100	20	Adjacent
TM80	Rock Slide	Rock	Physical	75	90	10	Many Others
TM83	Infestation	Bug	Special	20	100	20	Normal
TM87	Swagger	Normal	Status	—	90	15	Normal
TM88	Sleep Talk	Normal	Status	—	—	10	Self
TM90	Substitute	Normal	Status	—	—	10	Self
TM94	Secret Power	Normal	Physical	70	100	20	Normal
TM98	Power-Up Punch	Fighting	Physical	40	100	20	Normal
TM100	Confide	Normal	Status	—	—	20	Normal
HM03	Surf	Water	Special	90	100	15	Adjacent
HM04	Strength	Normal	Physical	80	100	15	Normal
HM05	Waterfall	Water	Physical	80	100	15	Normal
HM06	Rock Smash	Fighting	Physical	40	100	15	Normal
HM07	Dive	Water	Physical	80	100	10	Normal

MOVES LEARNED IN EXCHANGE FOR BP

Name	Type	Kind	Pow.	Acc.	PP	Range
Ice Punch	Ice	Physical	75	100	15	Normal
Earth Power	Ground	Special	90	100	10	Normal
Icy Wind	Ice	Special	55	95	15	Many Others
Aqua Tail	Water	Physical	90	90	10	Normal
Iron Tail	Steel	Physical	100	75	15	Normal
Snore	Normal	Special	50	100	15	Normal
Focus Punch	Fighting	Physical	150	100	20	Normal
Water Pulse	Water	Special	60	100	20	Normal
After You	Normal	Status	—	—	15	Normal

MOVES TAUGHT BY PEOPLE

Name	Type	Kind	Pow.	Acc.	PP	Range

National Pokédex **196** Hoenn Pokédex —

Espeon

Sun Pokémon

Psychic

HEIGHT: 2'11" WEIGHT: 58.4 lbs.

Same form for ♂ / ♀

Ω Espeon is extremely loyal to any Trainer it considers to be worthy. It is said that this Pokémon developed its precognitive powers to protect its Trainer from harm.

α Espeon is extremely loyal to any Trainer it considers to be worthy. It is said that this Pokémon developed its precognitive powers to protect its Trainer from harm.

ABILITY
Synchronize

HIDDEN ABILITY
Magic Bounce

EGG GROUPS
Field

STAT GROWTH RATES
HP
Attack
Defense
Sp. Atk
Sp. Def
Speed

ITEMS SOMETIMES HELD BY WILD POKÉMON
—

EVOLUTION

MAIN WAY TO REGISTER IN THE NATIONAL POKÉDEX

Level up Eevee with high friendship between 4:00 A.M. and 7:59 P.M.

Damage taken in normal battles

Normal	×1	Flying	×1
Fire	×1	Psychic	×0.5
Water	×1	Bug	×2
Grass	×1	Rock	×1
Electric	×1	Ghost	×2
Ice	×1	Dragon	×1
Fighting	×0.5	Dark	×2
Poison	×1	Steel	×1
Ground	×1	Fairy	×1

Damage taken in Inverse battles

Normal	×1	Flying	×1
Fire	×1	Psychic	×2
Water	×1	Bug	×0.5
Grass	×1	Rock	×1
Electric	×1	Ghost	×0.5
Ice	×1	Dragon	×1
Fighting	×2	Dark	×0.5
Poison	×1	Steel	×1
Ground	×1	Fairy	×1

Can be used in
Inverse Battle
Battle Institute
Battle Maison
Random Matchup (Free Battle)
Random Matchup (Others)

LEVEL-UP MOVES

Lv.	Name	Type	Kind	Pow.	Acc.	PP	Range
1	Helping Hand	Normal	Status	—	—	20	1 Ally
1	Tackle	Normal	Physical	50	100	35	Normal
1	Tail Whip	Normal	Status	—	100	30	Many Others
5	Sand Attack	Ground	Status	—	100	15	Normal
9	Confusion	Psychic	Special	50	100	25	Normal
13	Quick Attack	Normal	Physical	40	100	30	Normal
17	Swift	Normal	Special	60	—	20	Many Others
20	Psybeam	Psychic	Special	65	100	20	Normal
25	Future Sight	Psychic	Special	120	100	10	Normal
29	Psych Up	Normal	Status	—	—	10	Normal
33	Morning Sun	Normal	Status	—	—	5	Self
37	Psychic	Psychic	Special	90	100	10	Normal
41	Last Resort	Normal	Physical	140	100	5	Normal
45	Power Swap	Psychic	Status	—	—	10	Normal

TM & HM MOVES

No.	Name	Type	Kind	Pow.	Acc.	PP	Range
TM03	Psyshock	Psychic	Special	80	100	10	Normal
TM04	Calm Mind	Psychic	Status	—	—	20	Self
TM06	Toxic	Poison	Status	—	90	10	Normal
TM10	Hidden Power	Normal	Special	60	100	15	Normal
TM11	Sunny Day	Fire	Status	—	—	5	Both Sides
TM15	Hyper Beam	Normal	Special	150	90	5	Normal
TM16	Light Screen	Psychic	Status	—	—	30	Your Side
TM17	Protect	Normal	Status	—	—	10	Self
TM18	Rain Dance	Water	Status	—	—	5	Both Sides
TM21	Frustration	Normal	Physical	—	100	20	Normal
TM27	Return	Normal	Physical	—	100	20	Normal
TM28	Dig	Ground	Physical	80	100	10	Normal
TM29	Psychic	Psychic	Special	90	100	10	Normal
TM30	Shadow Ball	Ghost	Special	80	100	15	Normal
TM32	Double Team	Normal	Status	—	—	15	Self
TM33	Reflect	Psychic	Status	—	—	20	Your Side
TM42	Facade	Normal	Physical	70	100	20	Normal
TM44	Rest	Psychic	Status	—	—	10	Self
TM45	Attract	Normal	Status	—	100	15	Normal
TM48	Round	Normal	Special	60	100	15	Normal
TM49	Echoed Voice	Normal	Special	40	100	15	Normal
TM67	Retaliate	Normal	Physical	70	100	5	Normal
TM68	Giga Impact	Normal	Physical	150	90	5	Normal
TM70	Flash	Normal	Status	—	100	20	Normal
TM77	Psych Up	Normal	Status	—	—	10	Normal
TM85	Dream Eater	Psychic	Special	100	100	15	Normal
TM86	Grass Knot	Grass	Special	—	100	20	Normal
TM87	Swagger	Normal	Status	—	90	15	Normal
TM88	Sleep Talk	Normal	Status	—	—	10	Self
TM90	Substitute	Normal	Status	—	—	10	Self
TM92	Trick Room	Psychic	Status	—	—	5	Both Sides
TM94	Secret Power	Normal	Physical	70	100	20	Normal
TM99	Dazzling Gleam	Fairy	Special	80	100	10	Many Others
TM100	Confide	Normal	Status	—	—	20	Normal
HM01	Cut	Normal	Physical	50	95	30	Normal

MOVES LEARNED IN EXCHANGE FOR BP

Name	Type	Kind	Pow.	Acc.	PP	Range
Covet	Normal	Physical	60	100	25	Normal
Signal Beam	Bug	Special	75	100	15	Normal
Magic Coat	Psychic	Status	—	—	15	Self
Last Resort	Normal	Physical	140	100	5	Normal
Zen Headbutt	Psychic	Physical	80	90	15	Normal
Hyper Voice	Normal	Special	90	100	10	Many Others
Iron Tail	Steel	Physical	100	75	15	Normal
Snore	Normal	Special	50	100	15	Normal
Heal Bell	Normal	Status	—	—	5	Your Party
Helping Hand	Normal	Status	—	—	20	1 Ally
Trick	Psychic	Status	—	100	10	Normal
Magic Room	Psychic	Status	—	—	10	Both Sides
Skill Swap	Psychic	Status	—	—	10	Normal

MOVES TAUGHT BY PEOPLE

Name	Type	Kind	Pow.	Acc.	PP	Range

National Pokédex **197** Hoenn Pokédex —

Umbreon

Moonlight Pokémon

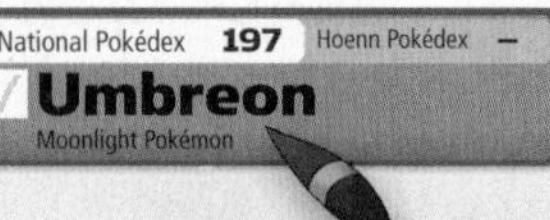

Dark

HEIGHT: 3'03" WEIGHT: 59.5 lbs.

Same form for ♂ / ♀

Ω Umbreon evolved as a result of exposure to the moon's waves. It hides silently in darkness and waits for its foes to make a move. The rings on its body glow when it leaps to attack.

α Umbreon evolved as a result of exposure to the moon's waves. It hides silently in darkness and waits for its foes to make a move. The rings on its body glow when it leaps to attack.

ABILITY
Synchronize

HIDDEN ABILITY
Inner Focus

EGG GROUPS
Field

STAT GROWTH RATES
HP
Attack
Defense
Sp. Atk
Sp. Def
Speed

ITEMS SOMETIMES HELD BY WILD POKÉMON
—

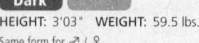

EVOLUTION

Level up between
8 P.M. and 3:59 A.M.
with high friendship

Eevee Umbreon

MAIN WAY TO REGISTER IN THE NATIONAL POKÉDEX

Level up Eevee with high friendship between 8:00 P.M. and 3:59 A.M.

Damage taken in normal battles

Normal	×1	Flying	×1
Fire	×1	Psychic	×0
Water	×1	Bug	×2
Grass	×1	Rock	×1
Electric	×1	Ghost	×0.5
Ice	×1	Dragon	×1
Fighting	×2	Dark	×0.5
Poison	×1	Steel	×1
Ground	×1	Fairy	×2

Damage taken in Inverse battles

Normal	×1	Flying	×1
Fire	×1	Psychic	×2
Water	×1	Bug	×0.5
Grass	×1	Rock	×1
Electric	×1	Ghost	×2
Ice	×1	Dragon	×1
Fighting	×0.5	Dark	×2
Poison	×1	Steel	×1
Ground	×1	Fairy	×0.5

Can be used in
Inverse Battle
Battle Institute
Battle Maison
Random Matchup (Free Battle)
Random Matchup (Others)

LEVEL-UP MOVES

Lv.	Name	Type	Kind	Pow.	Acc.	PP	Range
1	Helping Hand	Normal	Status	—	—	20	1 Ally
1	Tackle	Normal	Physical	50	100	35	Normal
1	Tail Whip	Normal	Status	—	100	30	Many Others
5	Sand Attack	Ground	Status	—	100	15	Normal
9	Pursuit	Dark	Physical	40	100	20	Normal
13	Quick Attack	Normal	Physical	40	100	30	Normal
17	Confuse Ray	Ghost	Status	—	100	10	Normal
20	Feint Attack	Dark	Physical	60	—	20	Normal
25	Assurance	Dark	Physical	60	100	10	Normal
29	Screech	Normal	Status	—	85	40	Normal
33	Moonlight	Fairy	Status	—	—	5	Self
37	Mean Look	Normal	Status	—	—	5	Normal
41	Last Resort	Normal	Physical	140	100	5	Normal
45	Guard Swap	Psychic	Status	—	—	10	Normal

TM & HM MOVES

No.	Name	Type	Kind	Pow.	Acc.	PP	Range
TM06	Toxic	Poison	Status	—	90	10	Normal
TM10	Hidden Power	Normal	Special	60	100	15	Normal
TM11	Sunny Day	Fire	Status	—	—	5	Both Sides
TM12	Taunt	Dark	Status	—	100	20	Normal
TM15	Hyper Beam	Normal	Special	150	90	5	Normal
TM17	Protect	Normal	Status	—	—	10	Self
TM18	Rain Dance	Water	Status	—	—	5	Both Sides
TM21	Frustration	Normal	Physical	—	100	20	Normal
TM27	Return	Normal	Physical	—	100	20	Normal
TM28	Dig	Ground	Physical	80	100	10	Normal
TM29	Psychic	Psychic	Special	90	100	10	Normal
TM30	Shadow Ball	Ghost	Special	80	100	15	Normal
TM32	Double Team	Normal	Status	—	—	15	Self
TM41	Torment	Dark	Status	—	100	15	Normal
TM42	Facade	Normal	Physical	70	100	20	Normal
TM44	Rest	Psychic	Status	—	—	10	Self
TM45	Attract	Normal	Status	—	100	15	Normal
TM48	Round	Normal	Special	60	100	15	Normal
TM49	Echoed Voice	Normal	Special	40	100	15	Normal
TM66	Payback	Dark	Physical	50	100	10	Normal
TM67	Retaliate	Normal	Physical	70	100	5	Normal
TM68	Giga Impact	Normal	Physical	150	90	5	Normal
TM70	Flash	Normal	Status	—	100	20	Normal
TM77	Psych Up	Normal	Status	—	—	10	Normal
TM85	Dream Eater	Psychic	Special	100	100	15	Normal
TM87	Swagger	Normal	Status	—	90	15	Normal
TM88	Sleep Talk	Normal	Status	—	—	10	Self
TM90	Substitute	Normal	Status	—	—	10	Self
TM94	Secret Power	Normal	Physical	70	100	20	Normal
TM95	Snarl	Dark	Special	55	95	15	Many Others
TM97	Dark Pulse	Dark	Special	80	100	15	Normal
TM100	Confide	Normal	Status	—	—	20	Normal
HM01	Cut	Normal	Physical	50	95	30	Normal

MOVES LEARNED IN EXCHANGE FOR BP

Name	Type	Kind	Pow.	Acc.	PP	Range
Covet	Normal	Physical	60	100	25	Normal
Foul Play	Dark	Physical	95	100	15	Normal
Last Resort	Normal	Physical	140	100	5	Normal
Hyper Voice	Normal	Special	90	100	10	Many Others
Iron Tail	Steel	Physical	100	75	15	Normal
Snore	Normal	Special	50	100	15	Normal
Heal Bell	Normal	Status	—	—	5	Your Party
Spite	Ghost	Status	—	100	10	Normal
Helping Hand	Normal	Status	—	—	20	1 Ally
Wonder Room	Psychic	Status	—	—	10	Both Sides
Snatch	Dark	Status	—	—	10	Self

MOVES TAUGHT BY PEOPLE

Name	Type	Kind	Pow.	Acc.	PP	Range

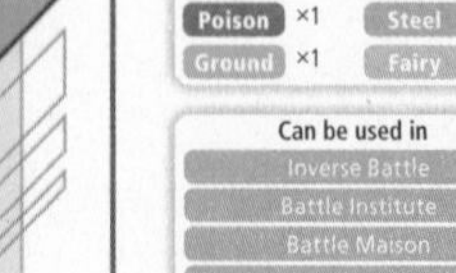

National Pokédex **198** Hoenn Pokédex —

Murkrow

Darkness Pokémon

Dark **Flying**

HEIGHT: 1'08" WEIGHT: 4.6 lbs.

The male has a larger crest.
The female has a smaller crest.

♂ ♀

Ω Murkrow was feared and loathed as the alleged bearer of ill fortune. This Pokémon shows strong interest in anything that sparkles or glitters. It will even try to steal rings from women.

α Murkrow was feared and loathed as the alleged bearer of ill fortune. This Pokémon shows strong interest in anything that sparkles or glitters. It will even try to steal rings from women.

ABILITIES
Insomnia
Super Luck

HIDDEN ABILITY
Prankster

EGG GROUPS
Flying

STAT GROWTH RATES

HP	■■■
Attack	■■■■
Defense	■■
Sp. Atk	■■■■
Sp. Def	■■
Speed	■■■■■

ITEMS SOMETIMES HELD BY WILD POKÉMON
—

EVOLUTION

MAIN WAY TO REGISTER IN THE NATIONAL POKÉDEX

While Soaring in the sky, approach the shadows of flying Pokémon, and catch it when it appears.

Damage taken in normal battles

Type		Type	
Normal	×1	Flying	×1
Fire	×1	Psychic	×0
Water	×1	Bug	×1
Grass	×0.5	Rock	×2
Electric	×2	Ghost	×0.5
Ice	×2	Dragon	×1
Fighting	×1	Dark	×0.5
Poison	×1	Steel	×1
Ground	×0	Fairy	×2

Damage taken in Inverse battles

Type		Type	
Normal	×1	Flying	×1
Fire	×1	Psychic	×2
Water	×1	Bug	×1
Grass	×2	Rock	×0.5
Electric	×0.5	Ghost	×2
Ice	×0.5	Dragon	×1
Fighting	×1	Dark	×2
Poison	×1	Steel	×1
Ground	×2	Fairy	×0.5

Can be used in
Inverse Battle
Battle Institute
Battle Maison
Random Matchup (Free Battle)
Random Matchup (Others)

LEVEL-UP MOVES

Lv.	Name	Type	Kind	Pow.	Acc.	PP	Range
1	Peck	Flying	Physical	35	100	35	Normal
1	Astonish	Ghost	Physical	30	100	15	Normal
5	Pursuit	Dark	Physical	40	100	20	Normal
11	Haze	Ice	Status	—	—	30	Both Sides
15	Wing Attack	Flying	Physical	60	100	35	Normal
21	Night Shade	Ghost	Special	—	100	15	Normal
25	Assurance	Dark	Physical	60	100	10	Normal
31	Taunt	Dark	Status	—	100	20	Normal
35	Feint Attack	Dark	Physical	60	—	20	Normal
41	Mean Look	Normal	Status	—	—	5	Normal
45	Foul Play	Dark	Physical	95	100	15	Normal
50	Tailwind	Flying	Status	—	—	15	Your Side
55	Sucker Punch	Dark	Physical	80	100	5	Normal
61	Torment	Dark	Status	—	100	15	Normal
65	Quash	Dark	Status	—	100	15	Normal

TM & HM MOVES

No.	Name	Type	Kind	Pow.	Acc.	PP	Range
TM04	Calm Mind	Psychic	Status	—	—	20	Self
TM06	Toxic	Poison	Status	—	90	10	Normal
TM10	Hidden Power	Normal	Special	60	100	15	Normal
TM11	Sunny Day	Fire	Status	—	—	5	Both Sides
TM12	Taunt	Dark	Status	—	100	20	Normal
TM17	Protect	Normal	Status	—	—	10	Self
TM18	Rain Dance	Water	Status	—	—	5	Both Sides
TM19	Roost	Flying	Status	—	—	10	Self
TM21	Frustration	Normal	Physical	—	100	20	Normal
TM27	Return	Normal	Physical	—	100	20	Normal
TM29	Psychic	Psychic	Special	90	100	10	Normal
TM30	Shadow Ball	Ghost	Special	80	100	15	Normal
TM32	Double Team	Normal	Status	—	—	15	Self
TM40	Aerial Ace	Flying	Physical	60	—	20	Normal
TM41	Torment	Dark	Status	—	100	15	Normal
TM42	Facade	Normal	Physical	70	100	20	Normal
TM44	Rest	Psychic	Status	—	—	10	Self
TM45	Attract	Normal	Status	—	100	15	Normal
TM46	Thief	Dark	Physical	60	100	25	Normal
TM48	Round	Normal	Special	60	100	15	Normal
TM51	Steel Wing	Steel	Physical	70	90	25	Normal
TM60	Quash	Dark	Status	—	100	15	Normal
TM63	Embargo	Dark	Status	—	100	15	Normal
TM66	Payback	Dark	Physical	50	100	10	Normal
TM67	Retaliate	Normal	Physical	70	100	5	Normal
TM73	Thunder Wave	Electric	Status	—	100	20	Normal
TM77	Psych Up	Normal	Status	—	—	10	Normal
TM85	Dream Eater	Psychic	Special	100	100	15	Normal
TM87	Swagger	Normal	Status	—	90	15	Normal
TM88	Sleep Talk	Normal	Status	—	—	10	Self
TM90	Substitute	Normal	Status	—	—	10	Self
TM94	Secret Power	Normal	Physical	70	100	20	Normal
TM95	Snarl	Dark	Special	55	95	15	Many Others
TM97	Dark Pulse	Dark	Special	80	100	15	Normal
TM100	Confide	Normal	Status	—	—	20	Normal
HM02	Fly	Flying	Physical	90	95	15	Normal

MOVES LEARNED IN EXCHANGE FOR BP

Name	Type	Kind	Pow.	Acc.	PP	Range
Uproar	Normal	Special	90	100	10	1 Random
Foul Play	Dark	Physical	95	100	15	Normal
Icy Wind	Ice	Special	55	95	15	Many Others
Snore	Normal	Special	50	100	15	Normal
Heat Wave	Fire	Special	95	90	10	Many Others
Tailwind	Flying	Status	—	—	15	Your Side
Sky Attack	Flying	Physical	140	90	5	Normal
Spite	Ghost	Status	—	100	10	Normal
Snatch	Dark	Status	—	—	10	Self

MOVES TAUGHT BY PEOPLE

Name	Type	Kind	Pow.	Acc.	PP	Range

EGG MOVES

Name	Type	Kind	Pow.	Acc.	PP	Range
Whirlwind	Normal	Status	—	—	20	Normal
Drill Peck	Flying	Physical	80	100	20	Normal
Mirror Move	Flying	Status	—	—	20	Normal
Wing Attack	Flying	Physical	60	100	35	Normal
Sky Attack	Flying	Physical	140	90	5	Normal
Confuse Ray	Ghost	Status	—	100	10	Normal
Feather Dance	Flying	Status	—	100	15	Normal
Perish Song	Normal	Status	—	—	5	Adjacent
Psycho Shift	Psychic	Status	—	100	10	Normal
Screech	Normal	Status	—	85	40	Normal
Feint Attack	Dark	Physical	60	—	20	Normal
Brave Bird	Flying	Physical	120	100	15	Normal
Roost	Flying	Status	—	—	10	Self
Assurance	Dark	Physical	60	100	10	Normal
Flatter	Dark	Status	—	100	15	Normal

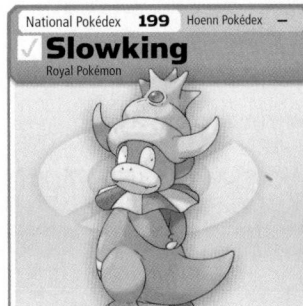

National Pokédex **199** Hoenn Pokédex —

Slowking

Royal Pokémon

Water **Psychic**

HEIGHT: 6'07" WEIGHT: 175.3 lbs.

Same form for ♂ / ♀

Ω Slowking undertakes research every day in an effort to solve the mysteries of the world. However, this Pokémon apparently forgets everything it has learned if the Shellder on its head comes off.

α Slowking undertakes research every day in an effort to solve the mysteries of the world. However, this Pokémon apparently forgets everything it has learned if the Shellder on its head comes off.

ABILITIES
Oblivious
Own Tempo

HIDDEN ABILITY
Regenerator

EGG GROUPS
Monster
Water 1

STAT GROWTH RATES

HP	■■■■
Attack	■■■■
Defense	■■■■
Sp. Atk	■■■■■
Sp. Def	■■■■■
Speed	■■

ITEMS SOMETIMES HELD BY WILD POKÉMON
—

EVOLUTION

Slowpoke → Link Trade with a King's Rock → Slowking

MAIN WAY TO REGISTER IN THE NATIONAL POKÉDEX

Receive a Slowpoke that is holding a King's Rock via Link Trade to have it evolve.

Damage taken in normal battles

Type		Type	
Normal	×1	Flying	×1
Fire	×0.5	Psychic	×0.5
Water	×0.5	Bug	×2
Grass	×2	Rock	×1
Electric	×2	Ghost	×2
Ice	×0.5	Dragon	×1
Fighting	×0.5	Dark	×2
Poison	×1	Steel	×0.5
Ground	×1	Fairy	×1

Damage taken in Inverse battles

Type		Type	
Normal	×1	Flying	×1
Fire	×2	Psychic	×2
Water	×2	Bug	×0.5
Grass	×0.5	Rock	×1
Electric	×0.5	Ghost	×0.5
Ice	×2	Dragon	×1
Fighting	×2	Dark	×0.5
Poison	×1	Steel	×2
Ground	×1	Fairy	×1

Can be used in
Inverse Battle
Battle Institute
Battle Maison
Random Matchup (Free Battle)
Random Matchup (Others)

LEVEL-UP MOVES

Lv.	Name	Type	Kind	Pow.	Acc.	PP	Range
1	Heal Pulse	Psychic	Status	—	—	10	Normal
1	Power Gem	Rock	Special	80	100	20	Normal
1	Hidden Power	Normal	Special	60	100	15	Normal
1	Curse	Ghost	Status	—	—	10	Varies
1	Yawn	Normal	Status	—	—	10	Normal
1	Tackle	Normal	Physical	50	100	35	Normal
5	Growl	Normal	Status	—	100	40	Many Others
9	Water Gun	Water	Special	40	100	25	Normal
14	Confusion	Psychic	Special	50	100	25	Normal
19	Disable	Normal	Status	—	100	20	Normal
23	Headbutt	Normal	Physical	70	100	15	Normal
28	Water Pulse	Water	Special	60	100	20	Normal
32	Zen Headbutt	Psychic	Physical	80	90	15	Normal
36	Nasty Plot	Dark	Status	—	—	20	Self
41	Swagger	Normal	Status	—	90	15	Normal
45	Psychic	Psychic	Special	90	100	10	Normal
49	Trump Card	Normal	Special	—	—	5	Normal
54	Psych Up	Normal	Status	—	—	10	Normal
58	Heal Pulse	Psychic	Status	—	—	10	Normal

TM & HM MOVES

No.	Name	Type	Kind	Pow.	Acc.	PP	Range
TM03	Psyshock	Psychic	Special	80	100	10	Normal
TM04	Calm Mind	Psychic	Status	—	—	20	Self
TM06	Toxic	Poison	Status	—	90	10	Normal
TM07	Hail	Ice	Status	—	—	10	Both Sides
TM10	Hidden Power	Normal	Special	60	100	15	Normal
TM11	Sunny Day	Fire	Status	—	—	5	Both Sides
TM13	Ice Beam	Ice	Special	90	100	10	Normal
TM14	Blizzard	Ice	Special	110	70	5	Many Others
TM15	Hyper Beam	Normal	Special	150	90	5	Normal
TM16	Light Screen	Psychic	Status	—	—	30	Your Side
TM17	Protect	Normal	Status	—	—	10	Self
TM18	Rain Dance	Water	Status	—	—	5	Both Sides
TM20	Safeguard	Normal	Status	—	—	25	Your Side
TM21	Frustration	Normal	Physical	—	100	20	Normal
TM26	Earthquake	Ground	Physical	100	100	10	Adjacent
TM27	Return	Normal	Physical	—	100	20	Normal
TM28	Dig	Ground	Physical	80	100	10	Normal
TM29	Psychic	Psychic	Special	90	100	10	Normal
TM30	Shadow Ball	Ghost	Special	80	100	15	Normal
TM31	Brick Break	Fighting	Physical	75	100	15	Normal
TM32	Double Team	Normal	Status	—	—	15	Self
TM35	Flamethrower	Fire	Special	90	100	15	Normal
TM38	Fire Blast	Fire	Special	110	85	5	Normal
TM42	Facade	Normal	Physical	70	100	20	Normal
TM44	Rest	Psychic	Status	—	—	10	Self
TM45	Attract	Normal	Status	—	100	15	Normal
TM48	Round	Normal	Special	60	100	15	Normal
TM49	Echoed Voice	Normal	Special	40	100	15	Normal
TM52	Focus Blast	Fighting	Special	120	70	5	Normal
TM55	Scald	Water	Special	80	100	15	Normal
TM56	Fling	Dark	Physical	—	100	10	Normal
TM59	Incinerate	Fire	Special	60	100	15	Many Others
TM60	Quash	Dark	Status	—	100	15	Normal
TM68	Giga Impact	Normal	Physical	150	90	5	Normal
TM70	Flash	Normal	Status	—	100	20	Normal
TM73	Thunder Wave	Electric	Status	—	100	20	Normal
TM77	Psych Up	Normal	Status	—	—	10	Normal
TM78	Bulldoze	Ground	Physical	60	100	20	Adjacent
TM82	Dragon Tail	Dragon	Physical	60	90	10	Normal
TM85	Dream Eater	Psychic	Special	100	100	15	Normal
TM86	Grass Knot	Grass	Special	—	100	20	Normal
TM87	Swagger	Normal	Status	—	90	15	Normal
TM88	Sleep Talk	Normal	Status	—	—	10	Self
TM90	Substitute	Normal	Status	—	—	10	Self
TM92	Trick Room	Psychic	Status	—	—	5	Both Sides
TM94	Secret Power	Normal	Physical	70	100	20	Normal
TM98	Power-Up Punch	Fighting	Physical	40	100	20	Normal
TM100	Confide	Normal	Status	—	—	20	Normal
HM03	Surf	Water	Special	90	100	15	Adjacent
HM04	Strength	Normal	Physical	80	100	15	Normal
HM06	Rock Smash	Fighting	Physical	40	100	15	Normal
HM07	Dive	Water	Physical	80	100	10	Normal

MOVES LEARNED IN EXCHANGE FOR BP

Name	Type	Kind	Pow.	Acc.	PP	Range
Signal Beam	Bug	Special	75	100	15	Normal
Ice Punch	Ice	Physical	75	100	15	Normal
Magic Coat	Psychic	Status	—	—	15	Self
Block	Normal	Status	—	—	5	Normal
Foul Play	Dark	Physical	95	100	15	Normal
Iron Defense	Steel	Status	—	—	15	Self
Icy Wind	Ice	Special	55	95	15	Many Others
Aqua Tail	Water	Physical	90	90	10	Normal
Zen Headbutt	Psychic	Physical	80	90	15	Normal
Iron Tail	Steel	Physical	100	75	15	Normal
Snore	Normal	Special	50	100	15	Normal
Drain Punch	Fighting	Physical	75	100	10	Normal
Focus Punch	Fighting	Physical	150	100	20	Normal
Water Pulse	Water	Special	60	100	20	Normal
After You	Normal	Status	—	—	15	Normal
Trick	Psychic	Status	—	100	10	Normal
Wonder Room	Psychic	Status	—	—	10	Both Sides
Recycle	Normal	Status	—	—	10	Self
Skill Swap	Psychic	Status	—	—	10	Normal

MOVES TAUGHT BY PEOPLE

Name	Type	Kind	Pow.	Acc.	PP	Range

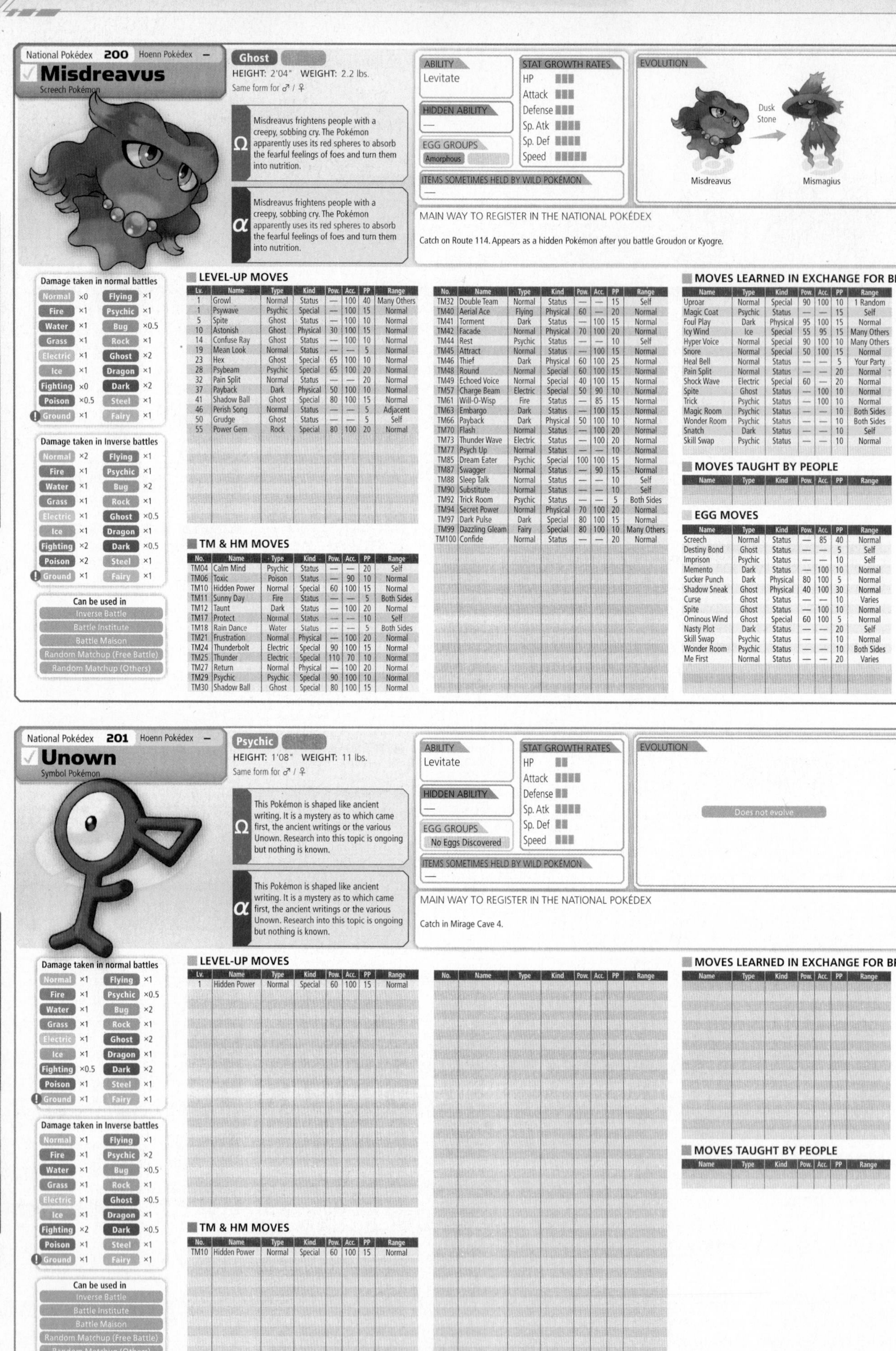

National Pokédex **200** Hoenn Pokédex —

Misdreavus

Screech Pokémon

Ghost

HEIGHT: 2'04" WEIGHT: 2.2 lbs.

Same form for ♂ / ♀

Ω Misdreavus frightens people with a creepy, sobbing cry. The Pokémon apparently uses its red spheres to absorb the fearful feelings of foes and turn them into nutrition.

α Misdreavus frightens people with a creepy, sobbing cry. The Pokémon apparently uses its red spheres to absorb the fearful feelings of foes and turn them into nutrition.

ABILITY
Levitate

HIDDEN ABILITY
—

EGG GROUPS
Amorphous

STAT GROWTH RATES
HP
Attack
Defense
Sp. Atk
Sp. Def
Speed

ITEMS SOMETIMES HELD BY WILD POKÉMON
—

EVOLUTION

Misdreavus → Dusk Stone → Mismagius

MAIN WAY TO REGISTER IN THE NATIONAL POKÉDEX

Catch on Route 114. Appears as a hidden Pokémon after you battle Groudon or Kyogre.

Damage taken in normal battles

Type		Type	
Normal	×0	Flying	×1
Fire	×1	Psychic	×1
Water	×1	Bug	×0.5
Grass	×1	Rock	×1
Electric	×1	Ghost	×2
Ice	×1	Dragon	×1
Fighting	×0	Dark	×2
Poison	×0.5	Steel	×1
Ground	×1	Fairy	×1

Damage taken in Inverse battles

Type		Type	
Normal	×2	Flying	×1
Fire	×1	Psychic	×1
Water	×1	Bug	×2
Grass	×1	Rock	×1
Electric	×1	Ghost	×0.5
Ice	×1	Dragon	×1
Fighting	×2	Dark	×0.5
Poison	×2	Steel	×1
Ground	×1	Fairy	×1

Can be used in
Inverse Battle
Battle Institute
Battle Maison
Random Matchup (Free Battle)
Random Matchup (Others)

LEVEL-UP MOVES

Lv.	Name	Type	Kind	Pow.	Acc.	PP	Range
1	Growl	Normal	Status	—	100	40	Many Others
1	Psywave	Psychic	Special	—	100	15	Normal
5	Spite	Ghost	Status	—	100	10	Normal
10	Astonish	Ghost	Physical	30	100	15	Normal
14	Confuse Ray	Ghost	Status	—	100	10	Normal
19	Mean Look	Normal	Status	—	—	5	Normal
23	Hex	Ghost	Special	65	100	10	Normal
28	Psybeam	Psychic	Special	65	100	20	Normal
32	Pain Split	Normal	Status	—	—	20	Normal
37	Payback	Dark	Physical	50	100	10	Normal
41	Shadow Ball	Ghost	Special	80	100	15	Normal
46	Perish Song	Normal	Status	—	—	5	Adjacent
50	Grudge	Ghost	Status	—	—	5	Self
55	Power Gem	Rock	Special	80	100	20	Normal

TM & HM MOVES

No.	Name	Type	Kind	Pow.	Acc.	PP	Range
TM04	Calm Mind	Psychic	Status	—	—	20	Self
TM06	Toxic	Poison	Status	—	90	10	Normal
TM10	Hidden Power	Normal	Special	60	100	15	Normal
TM11	Sunny Day	Fire	Status	—	—	5	Both Sides
TM12	Taunt	Dark	Status	—	100	20	Normal
TM17	Protect	Normal	Status	—	—	10	Self
TM18	Rain Dance	Water	Status	—	—	5	Both Sides
TM21	Frustration	Normal	Physical	—	100	20	Normal
TM24	Thunderbolt	Electric	Special	90	100	15	Normal
TM25	Thunder	Electric	Special	110	70	10	Normal
TM27	Return	Normal	Physical	—	100	20	Normal
TM29	Psychic	Psychic	Special	90	100	10	Normal
TM30	Shadow Ball	Ghost	Special	80	100	15	Normal
TM32	Double Team	Normal	Status	—	—	15	Self
TM40	Aerial Ace	Flying	Physical	60	—	20	Normal
TM41	Torment	Dark	Status	—	100	15	Normal
TM42	Facade	Normal	Physical	70	100	20	Normal
TM44	Rest	Psychic	Status	—	—	10	Self
TM45	Attract	Normal	Status	—	100	15	Normal
TM46	Thief	Dark	Physical	60	100	25	Normal
TM48	Round	Normal	Special	60	100	15	Normal
TM49	Echoed Voice	Normal	Special	40	100	15	Normal
TM57	Charge Beam	Electric	Special	50	90	10	Normal
TM61	Will-O-Wisp	Fire	Status	—	85	15	Normal
TM63	Embargo	Dark	Status	—	100	15	Normal
TM66	Payback	Dark	Physical	50	100	10	Normal
TM70	Flash	Normal	Status	—	100	20	Normal
TM73	Thunder Wave	Electric	Status	—	100	20	Normal
TM77	Psych Up	Normal	Status	—	—	10	Normal
TM85	Dream Eater	Psychic	Special	100	100	15	Normal
TM87	Swagger	Normal	Status	—	90	15	Normal
TM88	Sleep Talk	Normal	Status	—	—	10	Self
TM90	Substitute	Normal	Status	—	—	10	Self
TM92	Trick Room	Psychic	Status	—	—	5	Both Sides
TM94	Secret Power	Normal	Physical	70	100	20	Normal
TM97	Dark Pulse	Dark	Special	80	100	15	Normal
TM99	Dazzling Gleam	Fairy	Special	80	100	10	Many Others
TM100	Confide	Normal	Status	—	—	20	Normal

MOVES LEARNED IN EXCHANGE FOR BP

Name	Type	Kind	Pow.	Acc.	PP	Range
Uproar	Normal	Special	90	100	10	1 Random
Magic Coat	Psychic	Status	—	—	15	Self
Foul Play	Dark	Physical	95	100	15	Normal
Icy Wind	Ice	Special	55	95	15	Many Others
Hyper Voice	Normal	Special	90	100	10	Many Others
Snore	Normal	Special	50	100	15	Normal
Heal Bell	Normal	Status	—	—	5	Your Party
Pain Split	Normal	Status	—	—	20	Normal
Shock Wave	Electric	Special	60	—	20	Normal
Spite	Ghost	Status	—	100	10	Normal
Trick	Psychic	Status	—	100	10	Normal
Magic Room	Psychic	Status	—	—	10	Both Sides
Wonder Room	Psychic	Status	—	—	10	Both Sides
Snatch	Dark	Status	—	—	10	Self
Skill Swap	Psychic	Status	—	—	10	Normal

MOVES TAUGHT BY PEOPLE

Name	Type	Kind	Pow.	Acc.	PP	Range

EGG MOVES

Name	Type	Kind	Pow.	Acc.	PP	Range
Screech	Normal	Status	—	85	40	Normal
Destiny Bond	Ghost	Status	—	—	5	Self
Imprison	Psychic	Status	—	—	10	Self
Memento	Dark	Status	—	100	10	Normal
Sucker Punch	Dark	Physical	80	100	5	Normal
Shadow Sneak	Ghost	Physical	40	100	30	Normal
Curse	Ghost	Status	—	—	10	Varies
Spite	Ghost	Status	—	100	10	Normal
Ominous Wind	Ghost	Special	60	100	5	Normal
Nasty Plot	Dark	Status	—	—	20	Self
Skill Swap	Psychic	Status	—	—	10	Normal
Wonder Room	Psychic	Status	—	—	10	Both Sides
Me First	Normal	Status	—	—	20	Varies

National Pokédex **201** Hoenn Pokédex —

Unown

Symbol Pokémon

Psychic

HEIGHT: 1'08" WEIGHT: 11 lbs.

Same form for ♂ / ♀

Ω This Pokémon is shaped like ancient writing. It is a mystery as to which came first, the ancient writings or the various Unown. Research into this topic is ongoing but nothing is known.

α This Pokémon is shaped like ancient writing. It is a mystery as to which came first, the ancient writings or the various Unown. Research into this topic is ongoing but nothing is known.

ABILITY
Levitate

HIDDEN ABILITY
—

EGG GROUPS
No Eggs Discovered

STAT GROWTH RATES
HP
Attack
Defense
Sp. Atk
Sp. Def
Speed

ITEMS SOMETIMES HELD BY WILD POKÉMON
—

EVOLUTION

Does not evolve

MAIN WAY TO REGISTER IN THE NATIONAL POKÉDEX

Catch in Mirage Cave 4.

Damage taken in normal battles

Type		Type	
Normal	×1	Flying	×1
Fire	×1	Psychic	×0.5
Water	×1	Bug	×2
Grass	×1	Rock	×1
Electric	×1	Ghost	×2
Ice	×1	Dragon	×1
Fighting	×0.5	Dark	×2
Poison	×1	Steel	×1
Ground	×1	Fairy	×1

Damage taken in Inverse battles

Type		Type	
Normal	×1	Flying	×1
Fire	×1	Psychic	×2
Water	×1	Bug	×0.5
Grass	×1	Rock	×1
Electric	×1	Ghost	×0.5
Ice	×1	Dragon	×1
Fighting	×2	Dark	×0.5
Poison	×1	Steel	×1
Ground	×1	Fairy	×1

Can be used in
Inverse Battle
Battle Institute
Battle Maison
Random Matchup (Free Battle)
Random Matchup (Others)

LEVEL-UP MOVES

Lv.	Name	Type	Kind	Pow.	Acc.	PP	Range
1	Hidden Power	Normal	Special	60	100	15	Normal

TM & HM MOVES

No.	Name	Type	Kind	Pow.	Acc.	PP	Range
TM10	Hidden Power	Normal	Special	60	100	15	Normal

MOVES LEARNED IN EXCHANGE FOR BP

Name	Type	Kind	Pow.	Acc.	PP	Range

MOVES TAUGHT BY PEOPLE

Name	Type	Kind	Pow.	Acc.	PP	Range

National Pokédex **202** Hoenn Pokédex **168**

Wobbuffet

Patient Pokémon

Psychic

HEIGHT: 4'03" WEIGHT: 62.8 lbs.

The male has no marking on its mouth.
The female has a lipstick-like mark on its mouth.

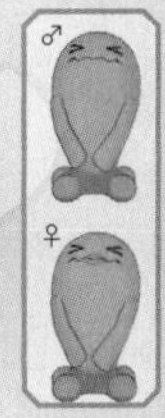

Ω If two or more Wobbuffet meet, they will turn competitive and try to outdo each other's endurance. However, they may try to see which one can endure the longest without food. Trainers need to beware of this habit.

α Wobbuffet does nothing but endure attacks—it won't attack on its own. However, it won't endure an attack on its tail. When that happens, the Pokémon will try to take the foe with it using Destiny Bond.

ABILITY
Shadow Tag

HIDDEN ABILITY
Telepathy

EGG GROUPS
Amorphous

STAT GROWTH RATES
HP
Attack
Defense
Sp. Atk
Sp. Def
Speed

ITEMS SOMETIMES HELD BY WILD POKÉMON
—

EVOLUTION
Wynaut → Lv. 15 → Wobbuffet

MAIN WAY TO REGISTER IN THE NATIONAL POKÉDEX

Catch in the very tall grass in the lower-left corner of the Safari Zone.

Damage taken in normal battles

Type		Type	
Normal	×1	Flying	×1
Fire	×1	Psychic	×0.5
Water	×1	Bug	×2
Grass	×1	Rock	×1
Electric	×1	Ghost	×2
Ice	×1	Dragon	×1
Fighting	×0.5	Dark	×2
Poison	×1	Steel	×1
Ground	×1	Fairy	×1

Damage taken in Inverse battles

Type		Type	
Normal	×1	Flying	×1
Fire	×1	Psychic	×2
Water	×1	Bug	×0.5
Grass	×1	Rock	×1
Electric	×1	Ghost	×0.5
Ice	×1	Dragon	×1
Fighting	×2	Dark	×0.5
Poison	×1	Steel	×1
Ground	×1	Fairy	×1

Can be used in
Inverse Battle
Battle Institute
Battle Maison
Random Matchup (Free Battle)
Random Matchup (Others)

LEVEL-UP MOVES

Lv.	Name	Type	Kind	Pow.	Acc.	PP	Range
1	Counter	Fighting	Physical	—	100	20	Varies
1	Mirror Coat	Psychic	Special	—	100	20	Varies
1	Safeguard	Normal	Status	—	—	25	Your Side
1	Destiny Bond	Ghost	Status	—	—	5	Self

TM & HM MOVES

No.	Name	Type	Kind	Pow.	Acc.	PP	Range
TM20	Safeguard	Normal	Status	—	—	25	Your Side

No.	Name	Type	Kind	Pow.	Acc.	PP	Range

MOVES LEARNED IN EXCHANGE FOR BP

Name	Type	Kind	Pow.	Acc.	PP	Range

MOVES TAUGHT BY PEOPLE

Name	Type	Kind	Pow.	Acc.	PP	Range

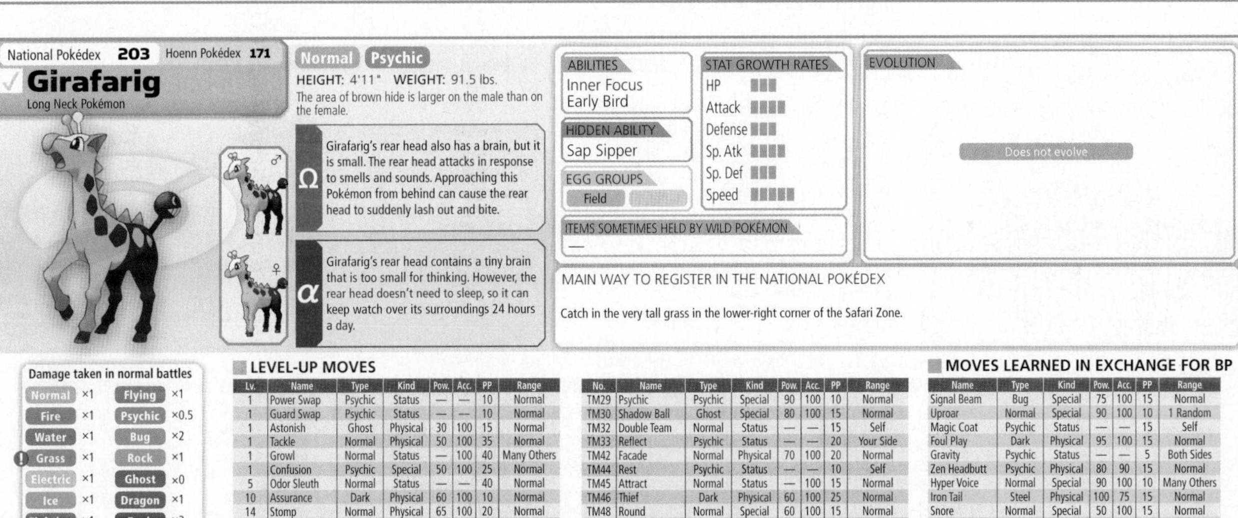

National Pokédex **203** Hoenn Pokédex **171**

Girafarig

Long Neck Pokémon

Normal **Psychic**

HEIGHT: 4'11" WEIGHT: 91.5 lbs.

The area of brown hide is larger on the male than on the female.

Ω Girafarig's rear head also has a brain, but it is small. The rear head attacks in response to smells and sounds. Approaching this Pokémon from behind can cause the rear head to suddenly lash out and bite.

α Girafarig's rear head contains a tiny brain that is too small for thinking. However, the rear head doesn't need to sleep, so it can keep watch over its surroundings 24 hours a day.

ABILITIES
Inner Focus
Early Bird

HIDDEN ABILITY
Sap Sipper

EGG GROUPS
Field

STAT GROWTH RATES
HP
Attack
Defense
Sp. Atk
Sp. Def
Speed

ITEMS SOMETIMES HELD BY WILD POKÉMON
—

EVOLUTION
Does not evolve

MAIN WAY TO REGISTER IN THE NATIONAL POKÉDEX

Catch in the very tall grass in the lower-right corner of the Safari Zone.

Damage taken in normal battles

Type		Type	
Normal	×1	Flying	×1
Fire	×1	Psychic	×0.5
Water	×1	Bug	×2
Grass	×1	Rock	×1
Electric	×1	Ghost	×0
Ice	×1	Dragon	×1
Fighting	×1	Dark	×2
Poison	×1	Steel	×1
Ground	×1	Fairy	×1

Damage taken in Inverse battles

Type		Type	
Normal	×1	Flying	×1
Fire	×1	Psychic	×2
Water	×1	Bug	×0.5
Grass	×1	Rock	×1
Electric	×1	Ghost	×1
Ice	×1	Dragon	×1
Fighting	×1	Dark	×0.5
Poison	×1	Steel	×1
Ground	×1	Fairy	×1

Can be used in
Inverse Battle
Battle Institute
Battle Maison
Random Matchup (Free Battle)
Random Matchup (Others)

LEVEL-UP MOVES

Lv.	Name	Type	Kind	Pow.	Acc.	PP	Range
1	Power Swap	Psychic	Status	—	—	10	Normal
1	Guard Swap	Psychic	Status	—	—	10	Normal
1	Astonish	Ghost	Physical	30	100	15	Normal
1	Tackle	Normal	Physical	50	100	35	Normal
1	Growl	Normal	Status	—	100	40	Many Others
1	Confusion	Psychic	Special	50	100	25	Normal
5	Odor Sleuth	Normal	Status	—	—	40	Normal
10	Assurance	Dark	Physical	60	100	10	Normal
14	Stomp	Normal	Physical	65	100	20	Normal
19	Psybeam	Psychic	Special	65	100	20	Normal
23	Agility	Psychic	Status	—	—	30	Self
28	Double Hit	Normal	Physical	35	90	10	Normal
32	Zen Headbutt	Psychic	Physical	80	90	15	Normal
37	Crunch	Dark	Physical	80	100	15	Normal
41	Baton Pass	Normal	Status	—	—	40	Self
46	Nasty Plot	Dark	Status	—	—	20	Self
50	Psychic	Psychic	Special	90	100	10	Normal

TM & HM MOVES

No.	Name	Type	Kind	Pow.	Acc.	PP	Range
TM03	Psyshock	Psychic	Special	80	100	10	Normal
TM04	Calm Mind	Psychic	Status	—	—	20	Self
TM06	Toxic	Poison	Status	—	90	10	Normal
TM10	Hidden Power	Normal	Special	60	100	15	Normal
TM11	Sunny Day	Fire	Status	—	—	5	Both Sides
TM16	Light Screen	Psychic	Status	—	—	30	Your Side
TM17	Protect	Normal	Status	—	—	10	Self
TM18	Rain Dance	Water	Status	—	—	5	Both Sides
TM21	Frustration	Normal	Physical	—	100	20	Normal
TM24	Thunderbolt	Electric	Special	90	100	15	Normal
TM25	Thunder	Electric	Special	110	70	10	Normal
TM26	Earthquake	Ground	Physical	100	100	10	Adjacent
TM27	Return	Normal	Physical	—	100	20	Normal

No.	Name	Type	Kind	Pow.	Acc.	PP	Range
TM29	Psychic	Psychic	Special	90	100	10	Normal
TM30	Shadow Ball	Ghost	Special	80	100	15	Normal
TM32	Double Team	Normal	Status	—	—	15	Self
TM33	Reflect	Psychic	Status	—	—	20	Your Side
TM42	Facade	Normal	Physical	70	100	20	Normal
TM44	Rest	Psychic	Status	—	—	10	Self
TM45	Attract	Normal	Status	—	100	15	Normal
TM46	Thief	Dark	Physical	60	100	25	Normal
TM48	Round	Normal	Special	60	100	15	Normal
TM49	Echoed Voice	Normal	Special	40	100	15	Normal
TM53	Energy Ball	Grass	Special	90	100	10	Normal
TM57	Charge Beam	Electric	Special	50	90	10	Normal
TM67	Retaliate	Normal	Physical	70	100	5	Normal
TM70	Flash	Normal	Status	—	100	20	Normal
TM73	Thunder Wave	Electric	Status	—	100	20	Normal
TM77	Psych Up	Normal	Status	—	—	10	Normal
TM78	Bulldoze	Ground	Physical	60	100	20	Adjacent
TM85	Dream Eater	Psychic	Special	100	100	15	Normal
TM86	Grass Knot	Grass	Special	—	100	20	Normal
TM87	Swagger	Normal	Status	—	90	15	Normal
TM88	Sleep Talk	Normal	Status	—	—	10	Self
TM90	Substitute	Normal	Status	—	—	10	Self
TM92	Trick Room	Psychic	Status	—	—	5	Both Sides
TM94	Secret Power	Normal	Physical	70	100	20	Normal
TM99	Dazzling Gleam	Fairy	Special	80	100	10	Many Others
TM100	Confide	Normal	Status	—	—	20	Normal
HM04	Strength	Normal	Physical	80	100	15	Normal
HM06	Rock Smash	Fighting	Physical	40	100	15	Normal

MOVES LEARNED IN EXCHANGE FOR BP

Name	Type	Kind	Pow.	Acc.	PP	Range
Signal Beam	Bug	Special	75	100	15	Normal
Uproar	Normal	Special	90	100	10	1 Random
Magic Coat	Psychic	Status	—	—	15	Self
Foul Play	Dark	Physical	95	100	15	Normal
Gravity	Psychic	Status	—	—	5	Both Sides
Zen Headbutt	Psychic	Physical	80	90	15	Normal
Hyper Voice	Normal	Special	90	100	10	Many Others
Iron Tail	Steel	Physical	100	75	15	Normal
Snore	Normal	Special	50	100	15	Normal
Shock Wave	Electric	Special	60	—	20	Normal
Trick	Psychic	Status	—	100	10	Normal
Recycle	Normal	Status	—	—	10	Self
Skill Swap	Psychic	Status	—	—	10	Normal

MOVES TAUGHT BY PEOPLE

Name	Type	Kind	Pow.	Acc.	PP	Range

EGG MOVES

Name	Type	Kind	Pow.	Acc.	PP	Range
Take Down	Normal	Physical	90	85	20	Normal
Amnesia	Psychic	Status	—	—	20	Self
Foresight	Normal	Status	—	—	40	Normal
Future Sight	Psychic	Special	120	100	10	Normal
Beat Up	Dark	Physical	—	100	10	Normal
Wish	Normal	Status	—	—	10	Self
Magic Coat	Psychic	Status	—	—	15	Self
Double Kick	Fighting	Physical	30	100	30	Normal
Mirror Coat	Psychic	Special	—	100	20	Varies
Razor Wind	Normal	Special	80	100	10	Many Others
Skill Swap	Psychic	Status	—	—	10	Normal
Secret Power	Normal	Physical	70	100	20	Normal
Mean Look	Normal	Status	—	—	5	Normal

National Pokédex **204** Hoenn Pokédex —

Pineco

Bagworm Pokémon

Bug

HEIGHT: 2'00" WEIGHT: 15.9 lbs.

Same form for ♂ / ♀

Ω Pineco hangs from a tree branch and patiently waits for prey to come along. If the Pokémon is disturbed while eating by someone shaking its tree, it drops down to the ground and explodes with no warning.

α Pineco hangs from a tree branch and patiently waits for prey to come along. If the Pokémon is disturbed while eating by someone shaking its tree, it drops down to the ground and explodes with no warning.

ABILITY

Sturdy

HIDDEN ABILITY

Overcoat

EGG GROUPS

Bug

STAT GROWTH RATES

HP ■■
Attack ■■■
Defense ■■■■
Sp. Atk ■■
Sp. Def ■■
Speed ■

ITEMS SOMETIMES HELD BY WILD POKÉMON

—

EVOLUTION

Pineco → Lv. 31 → Forretress

MAIN WAY TO REGISTER IN THE NATIONAL POKÉDEX

Leave a Forretress at a Pokémon Day Care, then hatch the Pokémon Egg that is found.

Damage taken in normal battles

Type		Type	
Normal	×1	Flying	×2
Fire	×2	Psychic	×1
Water	×1	Bug	×1
Grass	×0.5	Rock	×2
Electric	×1	Ghost	×1
Ice	×1	Dragon	×1
Fighting	×0.5	Dark	×1
Poison	×1	Steel	×1
Ground	×0.5	Fairy	×1

Damage taken in Inverse battles

Type		Type	
Normal	×1	Flying	×0.5
Fire	×0.5	Psychic	×1
Water	×1	Bug	×1
Grass	×2	Rock	×0.5
Electric	×1	Ghost	×1
Ice	×1	Dragon	×1
Fighting	×2	Dark	×1
Poison	×1	Steel	×1
Ground	×2	Fairy	×1

Can be used in

Inverse Battle
Battle Institute
Battle Maison
Random Matchup (Free Battle)
Random Matchup (Others)

LEVEL-UP MOVES

Lv.	Name	Type	Kind	Pow.	Acc.	PP	Range
1	Tackle	Normal	Physical	50	100	35	Normal
1	Protect	Normal	Status	—	—	10	Self
6	Self-Destruct	Normal	Physical	200	100	5	Adjacent
9	Bug Bite	Bug	Physical	60	100	20	Normal
12	Take Down	Normal	Physical	90	85	20	Normal
17	Rapid Spin	Normal	Physical	20	100	40	Normal
20	Bide	Normal	Physical	—	—	10	Self
23	Natural Gift	Normal	Physical	—	100	15	Normal
28	Spikes	Ground	Status	—	—	20	Other Side
31	Payback	Dark	Physical	50	100	10	Normal
34	Explosion	Normal	Physical	250	100	5	Adjacent
39	Iron Defense	Steel	Status	—	—	15	Self
42	Gyro Ball	Steel	Physical	—	100	5	Normal
45	Double-Edge	Normal	Physical	120	100	15	Normal

TM & HM MOVES

No.	Name	Type	Kind	Pow.	Acc.	PP	Range
TM06	Toxic	Poison	Status	—	90	10	Normal
TM09	Venoshock	Poison	Special	65	100	10	Normal
TM10	Hidden Power	Normal	Special	60	100	15	Normal
TM11	Sunny Day	Fire	Status	—	—	5	Both Sides
TM16	Light Screen	Psychic	Status	—	—	30	Your Side
TM17	Protect	Normal	Status	—	—	10	Self
TM21	Frustration	Normal	Physical	—	100	20	Normal
TM22	Solar Beam	Grass	Special	120	100	10	Normal
TM26	Earthquake	Ground	Physical	100	100	10	Adjacent
TM27	Return	Normal	Physical	—	100	20	Normal
TM28	Dig	Ground	Physical	80	100	10	Normal
TM32	Double Team	Normal	Status	—	—	15	Self
TM33	Reflect	Psychic	Status	—	—	20	Your Side
TM37	Sandstorm	Rock	Status	—	—	10	Both Sides
TM39	Rock Tomb	Rock	Physical	60	95	15	Normal
TM42	Facade	Normal	Physical	70	100	20	Normal
TM44	Rest	Psychic	Status	—	—	10	Self
TM45	Attract	Normal	Status	—	100	15	Normal
TM48	Round	Normal	Special	60	100	15	Normal
TM64	Explosion	Normal	Physical	250	100	5	Adjacent
TM66	Payback	Dark	Physical	50	100	10	Normal
TM74	Gyro Ball	Steel	Physical	—	100	5	Normal
TM76	Struggle Bug	Bug	Special	50	100	20	Many Others
TM78	Bulldoze	Ground	Physical	60	100	20	Adjacent
TM80	Rock Slide	Rock	Physical	75	90	10	Many Others
TM87	Swagger	Normal	Status	—	90	15	Normal
TM88	Sleep Talk	Normal	Status	—	—	10	Self
TM90	Substitute	Normal	Status	—	—	10	Self
TM94	Secret Power	Normal	Physical	70	100	20	Normal
TM100	Confide	Normal	Status	—	—	20	Normal
HM04	Strength	Normal	Physical	80	100	15	Normal
HM06	Rock Smash	Fighting	Physical	40	100	15	Normal

MOVES LEARNED IN EXCHANGE FOR BP

Name	Type	Kind	Pow.	Acc.	PP	Range
Bug Bite	Bug	Physical	60	100	20	Normal
Drill Run	Ground	Physical	80	95	10	Normal
Gravity	Psychic	Status	—	—	5	Both Sides
Iron Defense	Steel	Status	—	—	15	Self
Snore	Normal	Special	50	100	15	Normal
Pain Split	Normal	Status	—	—	20	Normal
Giga Drain	Grass	Special	75	100	10	Normal
Stealth Rock	Rock	Status	—	—	20	Other Side

MOVES TAUGHT BY PEOPLE

Name	Type	Kind	Pow.	Acc.	PP	Range

EGG MOVES

Name	Type	Kind	Pow.	Acc.	PP	Range
Pin Missile	Bug	Physical	25	95	20	Normal
Flail	Normal	Physical	—	100	15	Normal
Swift	Normal	Special	60	—	20	Many Others
Counter	Fighting	Physical	—	100	20	Varies
Sand Tomb	Ground	Physical	35	85	15	Normal
Revenge	Fighting	Physical	60	100	10	Normal
Double-Edge	Normal	Physical	120	100	15	Normal
Toxic Spikes	Poison	Status	—	—	20	Other Side
Power Trick	Psychic	Status	—	—	10	Self
Endure	Normal	Status	—	—	10	Self
Stealth Rock	Rock	Status	—	—	20	Other Side

National Pokédex **205** Hoenn Pokédex —

Forretress

Bagworm Pokémon

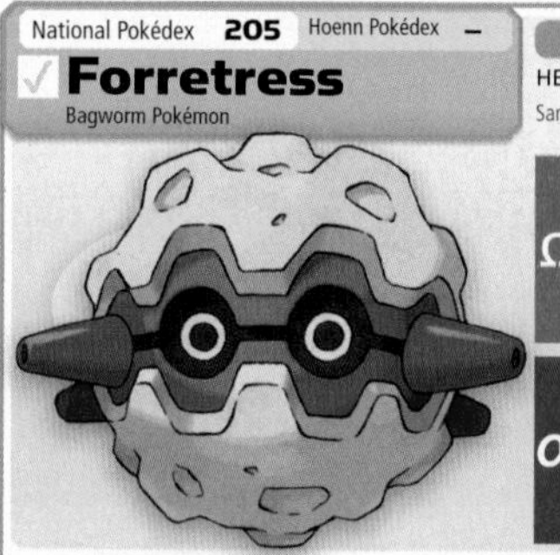

Bug Steel

HEIGHT: 3'11" WEIGHT: 277.3 lbs.

Same form for ♂ / ♀

Ω Forretress conceals itself inside its hardened steel shell. The shell is opened when the Pokémon is catching prey, but it does so at such a quick pace that the shell's inside cannot be seen.

α Forretress conceals itself inside its hardened steel shell. The shell is opened when the Pokémon is catching prey, but it does so at such a quick pace that the shell's inside cannot be seen.

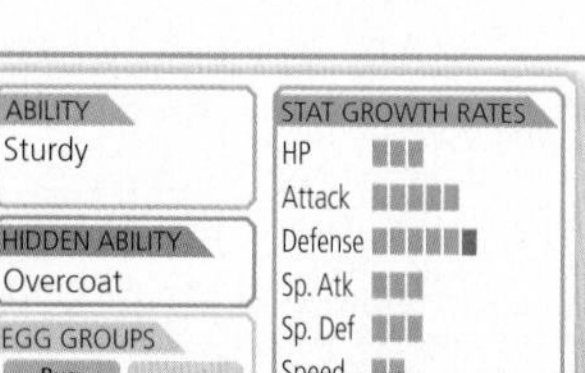

ABILITY

Sturdy

HIDDEN ABILITY

Overcoat

EGG GROUPS

Bug

STAT GROWTH RATES

HP ■■■
Attack ■■■■■
Defense ■■■■■■
Sp. Atk ■■■
Sp. Def ■■■
Speed ■■

ITEMS SOMETIMES HELD BY WILD POKÉMON

—

EVOLUTION

Pineco → Lv. 31 → Forretress

MAIN WAY TO REGISTER IN THE NATIONAL POKÉDEX

Catch in Mirage Forest 6.

Damage taken in normal battles

Type		Type	
Normal	×0.5	Flying	×1
Fire	×4	Psychic	×0.5
Water	×1	Bug	×0.5
Grass	×0.25	Rock	×1
Electric	×1	Ghost	×1
Ice	×0.5	Dragon	×0.5
Fighting	×1	Dark	×1
Poison	×0	Steel	×0.5
Ground	×1	Fairy	×0.5

Damage taken in Inverse battles

Type		Type	
Normal	×2	Flying	×1
Fire	×0.25	Psychic	×2
Water	×1	Bug	×2
Grass	×4	Rock	×1
Electric	×1	Ghost	×1
Ice	×2	Dragon	×2
Fighting	×1	Dark	×1
Poison	×2	Steel	×2
Ground	×1	Fairy	×2

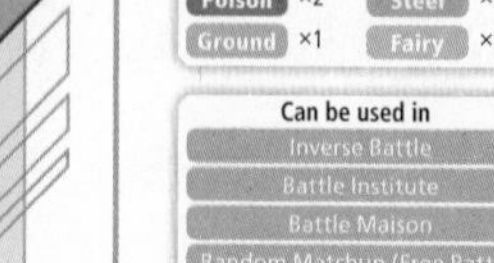

Can be used in

Inverse Battle
Battle Institute
Battle Maison
Random Matchup (Free Battle)
Random Matchup (Others)

LEVEL-UP MOVES

Lv.	Name	Type	Kind	Pow.	Acc.	PP	Range
1	Heavy Slam	Steel	Physical	—	100	10	Normal
1	Zap Cannon	Electric	Special	120	50	5	Normal
1	Magnet Rise	Electric	Status	—	—	10	Self
1	Toxic Spikes	Poison	Status	—	—	20	Other Side
1	Tackle	Normal	Physical	50	100	35	Normal
1	Protect	Normal	Status	—	—	10	Self
1	Self-Destruct	Normal	Physical	200	100	5	Adjacent
1	Bug Bite	Bug	Physical	60	100	20	Normal
12	Take Down	Normal	Physical	90	85	20	Normal
17	Rapid Spin	Normal	Physical	20	100	40	Normal
20	Bide	Normal	Physical	—	—	10	Self
23	Natural Gift	Normal	Physical	—	100	15	Normal
28	Spikes	Ground	Status	—	—	20	Other Side
31	Mirror Shot	Steel	Special	65	85	10	Normal
32	Autotomize	Steel	Status	—	—	15	Self
36	Payback	Dark	Physical	50	100	10	Normal
42	Explosion	Normal	Physical	250	100	5	Adjacent
46	Iron Defense	Steel	Status	—	—	15	Self
50	Gyro Ball	Steel	Physical	—	100	5	Normal
56	Double-Edge	Normal	Physical	120	100	15	Normal
60	Magnet Rise	Electric	Status	—	—	10	Self
64	Zap Cannon	Electric	Special	120	50	5	Normal
70	Heavy Slam	Steel	Physical	—	100	10	Normal

TM & HM MOVES

No.	Name	Type	Kind	Pow.	Acc.	PP	Range
TM06	Toxic	Poison	Status	—	90	10	Normal
TM09	Venoshock	Poison	Special	65	100	10	Normal
TM10	Hidden Power	Normal	Special	60	100	15	Normal
TM11	Sunny Day	Fire	Status	—	—	5	Both Sides
TM15	Hyper Beam	Normal	Special	150	90	5	Normal
TM16	Light Screen	Psychic	Status	—	—	30	Your Side
TM17	Protect	Normal	Status	—	—	10	Self
TM21	Frustration	Normal	Physical	—	100	20	Normal
TM22	Solar Beam	Grass	Special	120	100	10	Normal
TM26	Earthquake	Ground	Physical	100	100	10	Adjacent
TM27	Return	Normal	Physical	—	100	20	Normal
TM28	Dig	Ground	Physical	80	100	10	Normal
TM32	Double Team	Normal	Status	—	—	15	Self
TM33	Reflect	Psychic	Status	—	—	20	Your Side
TM37	Sandstorm	Rock	Status	—	—	10	Both Sides
TM39	Rock Tomb	Rock	Physical	60	95	15	Normal
TM42	Facade	Normal	Physical	70	100	20	Normal
TM44	Rest	Psychic	Status	—	—	10	Self
TM45	Attract	Normal	Status	—	100	15	Normal
TM48	Round	Normal	Special	60	100	15	Normal
TM64	Explosion	Normal	Physical	250	100	5	Adjacent
TM66	Payback	Dark	Physical	50	100	10	Normal
TM68	Giga Impact	Normal	Physical	150	90	5	Normal
TM69	Rock Polish	Rock	Status	—	—	20	Self
TM72	Volt Switch	Electric	Special	70	100	20	Normal
TM74	Gyro Ball	Steel	Physical	—	100	5	Normal
TM76	Struggle Bug	Bug	Special	50	100	20	Many Others
TM78	Bulldoze	Ground	Physical	60	100	20	Adjacent
TM80	Rock Slide	Rock	Physical	75	90	10	Many Others
TM87	Swagger	Normal	Status	—	90	15	Normal
TM88	Sleep Talk	Normal	Status	—	—	10	Self
TM90	Substitute	Normal	Status	—	—	10	Self
TM91	Flash Cannon	Steel	Special	80	100	10	Normal
TM94	Secret Power	Normal	Physical	70	100	20	Normal
TM100	Confide	Normal	Status	—	—	20	Normal
HM04	Strength	Normal	Physical	80	100	15	Normal
HM06	Rock Smash	Fighting	Physical	40	100	15	Normal

MOVES LEARNED IN EXCHANGE FOR BP

Name	Type	Kind	Pow.	Acc.	PP	Range
Bug Bite	Bug	Physical	60	100	20	Normal
Signal Beam	Bug	Special	75	100	15	Normal
Drill Run	Ground	Physical	80	95	10	Normal
Block	Normal	Status	—	—	5	Normal
Gravity	Psychic	Status	—	—	5	Both Sides
Magnet Rise	Electric	Status	—	—	10	Self
Iron Defense	Steel	Status	—	—	15	Self
Snore	Normal	Special	50	100	15	Normal
Pain Split	Normal	Status	—	—	20	Normal
Giga Drain	Grass	Special	75	100	10	Normal
Stealth Rock	Rock	Status	—	—	20	Other Side

MOVES TAUGHT BY PEOPLE

Name	Type	Kind	Pow.	Acc.	PP	Range

National Pokédex **206** Hoenn Pokédex —

Dunsparce

Land Snake Pokémon

Normal

HEIGHT: 4'11" WEIGHT: 30.9 lbs.

Same form for ♂ / ♀

Ω Dunsparce has a drill for its tail. It uses this tail to burrow into the ground backward. This Pokémon is known to make its nest in complex shapes deep under the ground.

α Dunsparce has a drill for its tail. It uses this tail to burrow into the ground backward. This Pokémon is known to make its nest in complex shapes deep under the ground.

ABILITIES
Serene Grace
Run Away

HIDDEN ABILITY
Rattled

EGG GROUPS
Field

STAT GROWTH RATES

HP	■■■■
Attack	■■■■
Defense	■■■
Sp. Atk	■■■
Sp. Def	■■■
Speed	■■■

ITEMS SOMETIMES HELD BY WILD POKÉMON
—

EVOLUTION

Does not evolve

MAIN WAY TO REGISTER IN THE NATIONAL POKÉDEX

Appears in *Pokémon X* and *Pokémon Y*. Bring it to your game using Link Trade or the GTS.

Damage taken in normal battles

Type		Type	
Normal	×1	Flying	×1
Fire	×1	Psychic	×1
Water	×1	Bug	×1
Grass	×1	Rock	×1
Electric	×1	Ghost	×0
Ice	×1	Dragon	×1
Fighting	×2	Dark	×1
Poison	×1	Steel	×1
Ground	×1	Fairy	×1

Damage taken in Inverse battles

Type		Type	
Normal	×1	Flying	×1
Fire	×1	Psychic	×1
Water	×1	Bug	×1
Grass	×1	Rock	×1
Electric	×1	Ghost	×2
Ice	×1	Dragon	×1
Fighting	×0.5	Dark	×1
Poison	×1	Steel	×1
Ground	×1	Fairy	×1

Can be used in
Inverse Battle
Battle Institute
Battle Maison
Random Matchup (Free Battle)
Random Matchup (Others)

LEVEL-UP MOVES

Lv.	Name	Type	Kind	Pow.	Acc.	PP	Range
1	Rage	Normal	Physical	20	100	20	Normal
1	Defense Curl	Normal	Status	—	—	40	Self
4	Rollout	Rock	Physical	30	90	20	Normal
7	Spite	Ghost	Status	—	100	10	Normal
10	Pursuit	Dark	Physical	40	100	20	Normal
13	Screech	Normal	Status	—	85	40	Normal
16	Yawn	Normal	Status	—	—	10	Normal
19	Ancient Power	Rock	Special	60	100	5	Normal
22	Take Down	Normal	Physical	90	85	20	Normal
25	Roost	Flying	Status	—	—	10	Self
28	Glare	Normal	Status	—	100	30	Normal
31	Dig	Ground	Physical	80	100	10	Normal
34	Double-Edge	Normal	Physical	120	100	15	Normal
37	Coil	Poison	Status	—	—	20	Self
40	Endure	Normal	Status	—	—	10	Self
43	Drill Run	Ground	Physical	80	95	10	Normal
46	Endeavor	Normal	Physical	—	100	5	Normal
49	Flail	Normal	Physical	—	100	15	Normal

TM & HM MOVES

No.	Name	Type	Kind	Pow.	Acc.	PP	Range
TM04	Calm Mind	Psychic	Status	—	—	20	Self
TM06	Toxic	Poison	Status	—	90	10	Normal
TM10	Hidden Power	Normal	Special	60	100	15	Normal
TM11	Sunny Day	Fire	Status	—	—	5	Both Sides
TM13	Ice Beam	Ice	Special	90	100	10	Normal
TM14	Blizzard	Ice	Special	110	70	5	Many Others
TM17	Protect	Normal	Status	—	—	10	Self
TM18	Rain Dance	Water	Status	—	—	5	Both Sides
TM19	Roost	Flying	Status	—	—	10	Self
TM21	Frustration	Normal	Physical	—	100	20	Normal
TM22	Solar Beam	Grass	Special	120	100	10	Normal
TM24	Thunderbolt	Electric	Special	90	100	15	Normal
TM25	Thunder	Electric	Special	110	70	10	Normal
TM26	Earthquake	Ground	Physical	100	100	10	Adjacent
TM27	Return	Normal	Physical	—	100	20	Normal
TM28	Dig	Ground	Physical	80	100	10	Normal
TM30	Shadow Ball	Ghost	Special	80	100	15	Normal
TM32	Double Team	Normal	Status	—	—	15	Self
TM35	Flamethrower	Fire	Special	90	100	15	Normal
TM38	Fire Blast	Fire	Special	110	85	5	Normal
TM39	Rock Tomb	Rock	Physical	60	95	15	Normal
TM42	Facade	Normal	Physical	70	100	20	Normal
TM44	Rest	Psychic	Status	—	—	10	Self
TM45	Attract	Normal	Status	—	100	15	Normal
TM46	Thief	Dark	Physical	60	100	25	Normal
TM48	Round	Normal	Special	60	100	15	Normal
TM57	Charge Beam	Electric	Special	50	90	10	Normal
TM59	Incinerate	Fire	Special	60	100	15	Many Others
TM67	Retaliate	Normal	Physical	70	100	5	Normal
TM73	Thunder Wave	Electric	Status	—	100	20	Normal
TM74	Gyro Ball	Steel	Physical	—	100	5	Normal
TM77	Psych Up	Normal	Status	—	—	10	Normal
TM78	Bulldoze	Ground	Physical	60	100	20	Adjacent
TM80	Rock Slide	Rock	Physical	75	90	10	Many Others
TM84	Poison Jab	Poison	Physical	80	100	20	Normal
TM85	Dream Eater	Psychic	Special	100	100	15	Normal
TM87	Swagger	Normal	Status	—	90	15	Normal
TM88	Sleep Talk	Normal	Status	—	—	10	Self
TM90	Substitute	Normal	Status	—	—	10	Self
TM93	Wild Charge	Electric	Physical	90	100	15	Normal
TM94	Secret Power	Normal	Physical	70	100	20	Normal
TM100	Confide	Normal	Status	—	—	20	Normal
HM04	Strength	Normal	Physical	80	100	15	Normal
HM06	Rock Smash	Fighting	Physical	40	100	15	Normal

MOVES LEARNED IN EXCHANGE FOR BP

Name	Type	Kind	Pow.	Acc.	PP	Range
Drill Run	Ground	Physical	80	95	10	Normal
Magic Coat	Psychic	Status	—	—	15	Self
Last Resort	Normal	Physical	140	100	5	Normal
Aqua Tail	Water	Physical	90	90	10	Normal
Zen Headbutt	Psychic	Physical	80	90	15	Normal
Iron Tail	Steel	Physical	100	75	15	Normal
Bind	Normal	Physical	15	85	20	Normal
Snore	Normal	Special	50	100	15	Normal
Pain Split	Normal	Status	—	—	20	Normal
Shock Wave	Electric	Special	60	—	20	Normal
Water Pulse	Water	Special	60	100	20	Normal
Spite	Ghost	Status	—	100	10	Normal
Endeavor	Normal	Physical	—	100	5	Normal
Stealth Rock	Rock	Status	—	—	20	Other Side

MOVES TAUGHT BY PEOPLE

Name	Type	Kind	Pow.	Acc.	PP	Range

EGG MOVES

Name	Type	Kind	Pow.	Acc.	PP	Range
Bide	Normal	Physical	—	—	10	Self
Ancient Power	Rock	Special	60	100	5	Normal
Bite	Dark	Physical	60	100	25	Normal
Headbutt	Normal	Physical	70	100	15	Normal
Astonish	Ghost	Physical	30	100	15	Normal
Curse	Ghost	Status	—	—	10	Varies
Trump Card	Normal	Special	—	—	5	Normal
Magic Coat	Psychic	Status	—	—	15	Self
Snore	Normal	Special	50	100	15	Normal
Agility	Psychic	Status	—	—	30	Self
Secret Power	Normal	Physical	70	100	20	Normal
Sleep Talk	Normal	Status	—	—	10	Self
Hex	Ghost	Special	65	100	10	Normal

National Pokédex **207** Hoenn Pokédex —

Gligar

Fly Scorpion Pokémon

Ground Flying

HEIGHT: 3'07" WEIGHT: 142.9 lbs.

The male has a larger stinger on its tail.
The female has a smaller stinger on its tail.

Ω Gligar glides through the air without a sound as if it were sliding. This Pokémon hangs on to the face of its foe using its clawed hind legs and the large pincers on its forelegs, then injects the prey with its poison barb.

α Gligar glides through the air without a sound as if it were sliding. This Pokémon hangs on to the face of its foe using its clawed hind legs and the large pincers on its forelegs, then injects the prey with its poison barb.

ABILITIES
Hyper Cutter
Sand Veil

HIDDEN ABILITY
Immunity

EGG GROUPS
Bug

STAT GROWTH RATES

HP	■■■
Attack	■■■■
Defense	■■■■■
Sp. Atk	■■
Sp. Def	■■■
Speed	■■■■■

ITEMS SOMETIMES HELD BY WILD POKÉMON
—

EVOLUTION

Gligar → Level up with a Razor Fang between 8 P.M. and 3:59 A.M. → Gliscor

MAIN WAY TO REGISTER IN THE NATIONAL POKÉDEX

Appears in *Pokémon X* and *Pokémon Y*. Bring it to your game using Link Trade or the GTS.

Damage taken in normal battles

Type		Type	
Normal	×1	Flying	×1
Fire	×1	Psychic	×1
Water	×2	Bug	×0.5
Grass	×1	Rock	×1
Electric	×0	Ghost	×1
Ice	×4	Dragon	×1
Fighting	×0.5	Dark	×1
Poison	×0.5	Steel	×1
Ground	×0	Fairy	×1

Damage taken in Inverse battles

Type		Type	
Normal	×1	Flying	×1
Fire	×1	Psychic	×1
Water	×0.5	Bug	×2
Grass	×1	Rock	×1
Electric	×1	Ghost	×1
Ice	×0.25	Dragon	×1
Fighting	×2	Dark	×1
Poison	×2	Steel	×1
Ground	×2	Fairy	×1

Can be used in
Inverse Battle
Battle Institute
Battle Maison
Random Matchup (Free Battle)
Random Matchup (Others)

LEVEL-UP MOVES

Lv.	Name	Type	Kind	Pow.	Acc.	PP	Range
1	Poison Sting	Poison	Physical	15	100	35	Normal
4	Sand Attack	Ground	Status	—	100	15	Normal
7	Harden	Normal	Status	—	—	30	Self
10	Knock Off	Dark	Physical	65	100	20	Normal
13	Quick Attack	Normal	Physical	40	100	30	Normal
16	Fury Cutter	Bug	Physical	40	95	20	Normal
19	Feint Attack	Dark	Physical	60	—	20	Normal
22	Acrobatics	Flying	Physical	55	100	15	Normal
27	Slash	Normal	Physical	70	100	20	Normal
30	U-turn	Bug	Physical	70	100	20	Normal
35	Screech	Normal	Status	—	85	40	Normal
40	X-Scissor	Bug	Physical	80	100	15	Normal
45	Sky Uppercut	Fighting	Physical	85	90	15	Normal
50	Swords Dance	Normal	Status	—	—	20	Self
55	Guillotine	Normal	Physical	—	30	5	Normal

TM & HM MOVES

No.	Name	Type	Kind	Pow.	Acc.	PP	Range
TM01	Hone Claws	Dark	Status	—	—	15	Self
TM06	Toxic	Poison	Status	—	90	10	Normal
TM09	Venoshock	Poison	Special	65	100	10	Normal
TM10	Hidden Power	Normal	Special	60	100	15	Normal
TM11	Sunny Day	Fire	Status	—	—	5	Both Sides
TM12	Taunt	Dark	Status	—	100	20	Normal
TM17	Protect	Normal	Status	—	—	10	Self
TM18	Rain Dance	Water	Status	—	—	5	Both Sides
TM19	Roost	Flying	Status	—	—	10	Self
TM21	Frustration	Normal	Physical	—	100	20	Normal
TM26	Earthquake	Ground	Physical	100	100	10	Adjacent
TM27	Return	Normal	Physical	—	100	20	Normal
TM28	Dig	Ground	Physical	80	100	10	Normal
TM31	Brick Break	Fighting	Physical	75	100	15	Normal
TM32	Double Team	Normal	Status	—	—	15	Self
TM36	Sludge Bomb	Poison	Special	90	100	10	Normal
TM37	Sandstorm	Rock	Status	—	—	10	Both Sides
TM39	Rock Tomb	Rock	Physical	60	95	15	Normal
TM40	Aerial Ace	Flying	Physical	60	—	20	Normal
TM41	Torment	Dark	Status	—	100	15	Normal
TM42	Facade	Normal	Physical	70	100	20	Normal
TM44	Rest	Psychic	Status	—	—	10	Self
TM45	Attract	Normal	Status	—	100	15	Normal
TM46	Thief	Dark	Physical	60	100	25	Normal
TM48	Round	Normal	Special	60	100	15	Normal
TM51	Steel Wing	Steel	Physical	70	90	25	Normal
TM54	False Swipe	Normal	Physical	40	100	40	Normal
TM56	Fling	Dark	Physical	—	100	10	Normal
TM62	Acrobatics	Flying	Physical	55	100	15	Normal
TM66	Payback	Dark	Physical	50	100	10	Normal
TM69	Rock Polish	Rock	Status	—	—	20	Self
TM71	Stone Edge	Rock	Physical	100	80	5	Normal
TM75	Swords Dance	Normal	Status	—	—	20	Self
TM76	Struggle Bug	Bug	Special	50	100	20	Many Others
TM78	Bulldoze	Ground	Physical	60	100	20	Adjacent
TM80	Rock Slide	Rock	Physical	75	90	10	Many Others
TM81	X-Scissor	Bug	Physical	80	100	15	Normal
TM84	Poison Jab	Poison	Physical	80	100	20	Normal
TM87	Swagger	Normal	Status	—	90	15	Normal
TM88	Sleep Talk	Normal	Status	—	—	10	Self
TM89	U-turn	Bug	Physical	70	100	20	Normal
TM90	Substitute	Normal	Status	—	—	10	Self
TM94	Secret Power	Normal	Physical	70	100	20	Normal
TM97	Dark Pulse	Dark	Special	80	100	15	Normal
TM100	Confide	Normal	Status	—	—	20	Normal
HM01	Cut	Normal	Physical	50	95	30	Normal
HM04	Strength	Normal	Physical	80	100	15	Normal
HM06	Rock Smash	Fighting	Physical	40	100	15	Normal

MOVES LEARNED IN EXCHANGE FOR BP

Name	Type	Kind	Pow.	Acc.	PP	Range
Bug Bite	Bug	Physical	60	100	20	Normal
Earth Power	Ground	Special	90	100	10	Normal
Aqua Tail	Water	Physical	90	90	10	Normal
Iron Tail	Steel	Physical	100	75	15	Normal
Snore	Normal	Special	50	100	15	Normal
Knock Off	Dark	Physical	65	100	20	Normal
Tailwind	Flying	Status	—	—	15	Your Side
Stealth Rock	Rock	Status	—	—	20	Other Side

MOVES TAUGHT BY PEOPLE

Name	Type	Kind	Pow.	Acc.	PP	Range

EGG MOVES

Name	Type	Kind	Pow.	Acc.	PP	Range
Metal Claw	Steel	Physical	50	95	35	Normal
Wing Attack	Flying	Physical	60	100	35	Normal
Razor Wind	Normal	Special	80	100	10	Many Others
Counter	Fighting	Physical	—	100	20	Varies
Sand Tomb	Ground	Physical	35	85	15	Normal
Agility	Psychic	Status	—	—	30	Self
Baton Pass	Normal	Status	—	—	40	Self
Double-Edge	Normal	Physical	120	100	15	Normal
Feint	Normal	Physical	30	100	10	Normal
Night Slash	Dark	Physical	70	100	15	Normal
Cross Poison	Poison	Physical	70	100	20	Normal
Power Trick	Psychic	Status	—	—	10	Self
Rock Climb	Normal	Physical	90	85	20	Normal
Poison Tail	Poison	Physical	50	100	25	Normal

National Pokédex **208** Hoenn Pokédex —

Steelix

Iron Snake Pokémon

Steel / Ground

HEIGHT: 30'02" WEIGHT: 881.8 lbs.

The male has two "fangs" on each side of its jaw. The female has one "fang" on each side of its jaw.

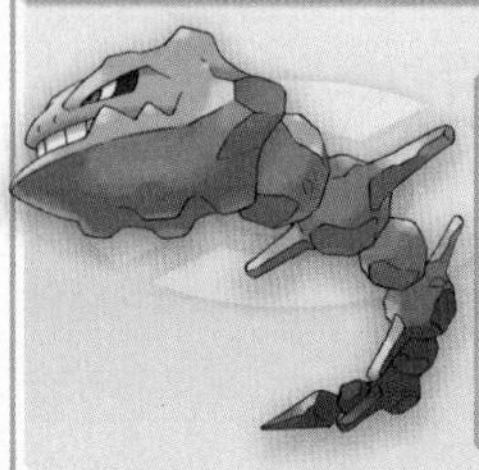

Steelix lives even further underground than Onix. This Pokémon is known to dig toward the earth's core. There are records of this Pokémon reaching a depth of over six-tenths of a mile underground.

Steelix lives even further underground than Onix. This Pokémon is known to dig toward the earth's core. There are records of this Pokémon reaching a depth of over six-tenths of a mile underground.

ABILITIES
Rock Head
Sturdy

HIDDEN ABILITY
Sheer Force

EGG GROUPS
Mineral

STAT GROWTH RATES
HP
Attack
Defense
Sp. Atk
Sp. Def
Speed

ITEMS SOMETIMES HELD BY WILD POKÉMON
—

EVOLUTION

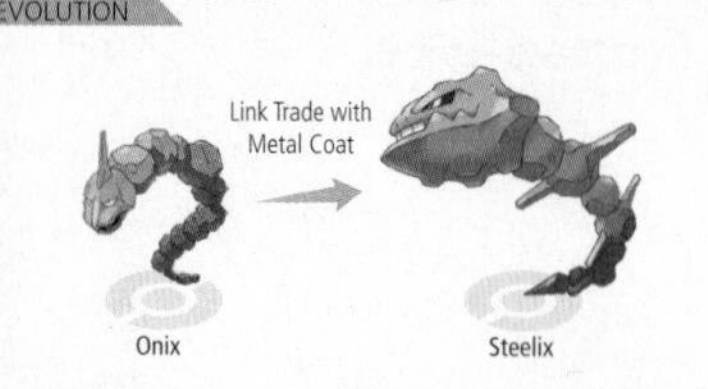

MAIN WAY TO REGISTER IN THE NATIONAL POKÉDEX

Receive an Onix that is holding a Metal Coat via Link Trade to have it evolve.

Damage taken in normal battles

Type		Type	
Normal	×0.5	Flying	×0.5
Fire	×2	Psychic	×0.5
Water	×2	Bug	×0.5
Grass	×1	Rock	×0.25
Electric	×0	Ghost	×1
Ice	×1	Dragon	×0.5
Fighting	×2	Dark	×1
Poison	×0	Steel	×0.5
Ground	×2	Fairy	×0.5

Damage taken in Inverse battles

Type		Type	
Normal	×2	Flying	×2
Fire	×0.5	Psychic	×2
Water	×0.5	Bug	×2
Grass	×1	Rock	×4
Electric	×2	Ghost	×1
Ice	×1	Dragon	×2
Fighting	×0.5	Dark	×1
Poison	×4	Steel	×2
Ground	×0.5	Fairy	×2

Can be used in
Inverse Battle
Battle Institute
Battle Maison
Random Matchup (Free Battle)
Random Matchup (Others)

LEVEL-UP MOVES

Lv.	Name	Type	Kind	Pow.	Acc.	PP	Range
1	Thunder Fang	Electric	Physical	65	95	15	Normal
1	Ice Fang	Ice	Physical	65	95	15	Normal
1	Fire Fang	Fire	Physical	65	95	15	Normal
1	Mud Sport	Ground	Status	—	—	15	Both Sides
1	Tackle	Normal	Physical	50	100	35	Normal
1	Harden	Normal	Status	—	—	30	Self
1	Bind	Normal	Physical	15	85	20	Normal
4	Curse	Ghost	Status	—	—	10	Varies
7	Rock Throw	Rock	Physical	50	90	15	Normal
10	Rock Tomb	Rock	Physical	60	95	15	Normal
13	Rage	Normal	Physical	20	100	20	Normal
16	Stealth Rock	Rock	Status	—	—	20	Other Side
19	Autotomize	Steel	Status	—	—	15	Self
20	Gyro Ball	Steel	Physical	—	100	5	Normal
22	Smack Down	Rock	Physical	50	100	15	Normal
25	Dragon Breath	Dragon	Special	60	100	20	Normal
28	Slam	Normal	Physical	80	75	20	Normal
31	Screech	Normal	Status	—	85	40	Normal
34	Rock Slide	Rock	Physical	75	90	10	Many Others
37	Crunch	Dark	Physical	80	100	15	Normal
40	Iron Tail	Steel	Physical	100	75	15	Normal
43	Dig	Ground	Physical	80	100	10	Normal
46	Stone Edge	Rock	Physical	100	80	5	Normal
49	Double-Edge	Normal	Physical	120	100	15	Normal
52	Sandstorm	Rock	Status	—	—	10	Both Sides

TM & HM MOVES

No.	Name	Type	Kind	Pow.	Acc.	PP	Range
TM05	Roar	Normal	Status	—	—	20	Normal
TM06	Toxic	Poison	Status	—	90	10	Normal
TM10	Hidden Power	Normal	Special	60	100	15	Normal
TM11	Sunny Day	Fire	Status	—	—	5	Both Sides
TM12	Taunt	Dark	Status	—	100	20	Normal
TM15	Hyper Beam	Normal	Special	150	90	5	Normal
TM17	Protect	Normal	Status	—	—	10	Self
TM21	Frustration	Normal	Physical	—	100	20	Normal
TM23	Smack Down	Rock	Physical	50	100	15	Normal
TM26	Earthquake	Ground	Physical	100	100	10	Adjacent
TM27	Return	Normal	Physical	—	100	20	Normal
TM28	Dig	Ground	Physical	80	100	10	Normal
TM32	Double Team	Normal	Status	—	—	15	Self
TM37	Sandstorm	Rock	Status	—	—	10	Both Sides
TM39	Rock Tomb	Rock	Physical	60	95	15	Normal
TM41	Torment	Dark	Status	—	100	15	Normal
TM42	Facade	Normal	Physical	70	100	20	Normal
TM44	Rest	Psychic	Status	—	—	10	Self
TM45	Attract	Normal	Status	—	100	15	Normal
TM48	Round	Normal	Special	60	100	15	Normal
TM64	Explosion	Normal	Physical	250	100	5	Adjacent
TM66	Payback	Dark	Physical	50	100	10	Normal
TM68	Giga Impact	Normal	Physical	150	90	5	Normal
TM69	Rock Polish	Rock	Status	—	—	20	Self
TM71	Stone Edge	Rock	Physical	100	80	5	Normal
TM74	Gyro Ball	Steel	Physical	—	100	5	Normal
TM77	Psych Up	Normal	Status	—	—	10	Normal
TM78	Bulldoze	Ground	Physical	60	100	20	Adjacent
TM80	Rock Slide	Rock	Physical	75	90	10	Many Others
TM82	Dragon Tail	Dragon	Physical	60	90	10	Normal
TM87	Swagger	Normal	Status	—	90	15	Normal
TM88	Sleep Talk	Normal	Status	—	—	10	Self
TM90	Substitute	Normal	Status	—	—	10	Self
TM91	Flash Cannon	Steel	Special	80	100	10	Normal
TM94	Secret Power	Normal	Physical	70	100	20	Normal
TM96	Nature Power	Normal	Status	—	—	20	Normal
TM97	Dark Pulse	Dark	Special	80	100	15	Normal
TM100	Confide	Normal	Status	—	—	20	Normal
HM01	Cut	Normal	Physical	50	95	30	Normal
HM04	Strength	Normal	Physical	80	100	15	Normal
HM06	Rock Smash	Fighting	Physical	40	100	15	Normal

MOVES LEARNED IN EXCHANGE FOR BP

Name	Type	Kind	Pow.	Acc.	PP	Range
Iron Head	Steel	Physical	80	100	15	Normal
Block	Normal	Status	—	—	5	Normal
Earth Power	Ground	Special	90	100	10	Normal
Magnet Rise	Electric	Status	—	—	10	Self
Aqua Tail	Water	Physical	90	90	10	Normal
Dragon Pulse	Dragon	Special	85	100	10	Normal
Iron Tail	Steel	Physical	100	75	15	Normal
Bind	Normal	Physical	15	85	20	Normal
Snore	Normal	Special	50	100	15	Normal
Stealth Rock	Rock	Status	—	—	20	Other Side

MOVES TAUGHT BY PEOPLE

Name	Type	Kind	Pow.	Acc.	PP	Range

Mega Evolution

Mega Steelix

Iron Snake Pokémon

Steel / Ground

HEIGHT: 34'05" WEIGHT: 1631.4 lbs.

Same form for ♂ / ♀

REQUIRED MEGA STONE
Steelixite
Find in Granite Cave (B2F).

ABILITY
Sand Force

HIDDEN ABILITY
—

EGG GROUPS
—

STAT GROWTH RATES
HP
Attack
Defense
Sp. Atk
Sp. Def
Speed

Damage taken in normal battles

Type		Type	
Normal	×0.5	Flying	×0.5
Fire	×2	Psychic	×0.5
Water	×2	Bug	×0.5
Grass	×1	Rock	×0.25
Electric	×0	Ghost	×1
Ice	×1	Dragon	×0.5
Fighting	×2	Dark	×1
Poison	×0	Steel	×0.5
Ground	×2	Fairy	×0.5

Damage taken in Inverse battles

Type		Type	
Normal	×2	Flying	×2
Fire	×0.5	Psychic	×2
Water	×0.5	Bug	×2
Grass	×1	Rock	×4
Electric	×2	Ghost	×1
Ice	×1	Dragon	×2
Fighting	×0.5	Dark	×1
Poison	×4	Steel	×2
Ground	×0.5	Fairy	×2

Can be used in
Inverse Battle
Battle Institute
Battle Maison
Random Matchup (Free Battle)
Random Matchup (Others)

National Pokédex **209** Hoenn Pokédex —

Snubbull

Fairy Pokémon

Fairy

HEIGHT: 2'00" WEIGHT: 17.2 lbs.

Same form for ♂ / ♀

Ω By baring its fangs and making a scary face, Snubbull sends smaller Pokémon scurrying away in terror. However, this Pokémon seems a little sad at making its foes flee.

α By baring its fangs and making a scary face, Snubbull sends smaller Pokémon scurrying away in terror. However, this Pokémon seems a little sad at making its foes flee.

ABILITIES
Intimidate
Run Away

HIDDEN ABILITY
Rattled

EGG GROUPS
Field | Fairy

STAT GROWTH RATES
HP
Attack
Defense
Sp. Atk
Sp. Def
Speed

ITEMS SOMETIMES HELD BY WILD POKÉMON
—

EVOLUTION
Snubbull → Lv. 23 → Granbull

MAIN WAY TO REGISTER IN THE NATIONAL POKÉDEX

Appears in *Pokémon X* and *Pokémon Y*. Bring it to your game using Link Trade or the GTS.

Damage taken in normal battles

Normal	×1	Flying	×1
Fire	×1	Psychic	×1
Water	×1	Bug	×0.5
Grass	×1	Rock	×1
Electric	×1	Ghost	×1
Ice	×1	Dragon	×0
Fighting	×0.5	Dark	×0.5
Poison	×2	Steel	×2
Ground	×1	Fairy	×1

Damage taken in Inverse battles

Normal	×1	Flying	×1
Fire	×1	Psychic	×1
Water	×1	Bug	×2
Grass	×1	Rock	×1
Electric	×1	Ghost	×1
Ice	×1	Dragon	×2
Fighting	×2	Dark	×2
Poison	×0.5	Steel	×0.5
Ground	×1	Fairy	×1

Can be used in
Inverse Battle
Battle Institute
Battle Maison
Random Matchup (Free Battle)
Random Matchup (Others)

LEVEL-UP MOVES

Lv.	Name	Type	Kind	Pow.	Acc.	PP	Range
1	Ice Fang	Ice	Physical	65	95	15	Normal
1	Fire Fang	Fire	Physical	65	95	15	Normal
1	Thunder Fang	Electric	Physical	65	95	15	Normal
1	Tackle	Normal	Physical	50	100	35	Normal
1	Scary Face	Normal	Status	—	100	10	Normal
1	Tail Whip	Normal	Status	—	100	30	Many Others
1	Charm	Fairy	Status	—	100	20	Normal
7	Bite	Dark	Physical	60	100	25	Normal
13	Lick	Ghost	Physical	30	100	30	Normal
19	Headbutt	Normal	Physical	70	100	15	Normal
25	Roar	Normal	Status	—	—	20	Normal
31	Rage	Normal	Physical	20	100	20	Normal
37	Play Rough	Fairy	Physical	90	90	10	Normal
43	Payback	Dark	Physical	50	100	10	Normal
49	Crunch	Dark	Physical	80	100	15	Normal

TM & HM MOVES

No.	Name	Type	Kind	Pow.	Acc.	PP	Range
TM05	Roar	Normal	Status	—	—	20	Normal
TM06	Toxic	Poison	Status	—	90	10	Normal
TM08	Bulk Up	Fighting	Status	—	—	20	Self
TM10	Hidden Power	Normal	Special	60	100	15	Normal
TM11	Sunny Day	Fire	Status	—	—	5	Both Sides
TM12	Taunt	Dark	Status	—	100	20	Normal
TM17	Protect	Normal	Status	—	—	10	Self
TM18	Rain Dance	Water	Status	—	—	5	Both Sides
TM21	Frustration	Normal	Physical	—	100	20	Normal
TM22	Solar Beam	Grass	Special	120	100	10	Normal
TM24	Thunderbolt	Electric	Special	90	100	15	Normal
TM25	Thunder	Electric	Special	110	70	10	Normal
TM26	Earthquake	Ground	Physical	100	100	10	Adjacent
TM27	Return	Normal	Physical	—	100	20	Normal
TM28	Dig	Ground	Physical	80	100	10	Normal
TM30	Shadow Ball	Ghost	Special	80	100	15	Normal
TM31	Brick Break	Fighting	Physical	75	100	15	Normal
TM32	Double Team	Normal	Status	—	—	15	Self
TM33	Reflect	Psychic	Status	—	—	20	Your Side
TM35	Flamethrower	Fire	Special	90	100	15	Normal
TM36	Sludge Bomb	Poison	Special	90	100	10	Normal
TM38	Fire Blast	Fire	Special	110	85	5	Normal
TM41	Torment	Dark	Status	—	100	15	Normal
TM42	Facade	Normal	Physical	70	100	20	Normal
TM44	Rest	Psychic	Status	—	—	10	Self
TM45	Attract	Normal	Status	—	100	15	Normal
TM46	Thief	Dark	Physical	60	100	25	Normal
TM48	Round	Normal	Special	60	100	15	Normal
TM50	Overheat	Fire	Special	130	90	5	Normal
TM56	Fling	Dark	Physical	—	100	10	Normal
TM59	Incinerate	Fire	Special	60	100	15	Many Others
TM66	Payback	Dark	Physical	50	100	10	Normal
TM67	Retaliate	Normal	Physical	70	100	5	Normal
TM73	Thunder Wave	Electric	Status	—	100	20	Normal
TM78	Bulldoze	Ground	Physical	60	100	20	Adjacent
TM87	Swagger	Normal	Status	—	90	15	Normal
TM88	Sleep Talk	Normal	Status	—	—	10	Self
TM90	Substitute	Normal	Status	—	—	10	Self
TM93	Wild Charge	Electric	Physical	90	100	15	Normal
TM94	Secret Power	Normal	Physical	70	100	20	Normal
TM95	Snarl	Dark	Special	55	95	15	Many Others
TM98	Power-Up Punch	Fighting	Physical	40	100	20	Normal
TM99	Dazzling Gleam	Fairy	Special	80	100	10	Many Others
TM100	Confide	Normal	Status	—	—	20	Normal
HM04	Strength	Normal	Physical	80	100	15	Normal
HM06	Rock Smash	Fighting	Physical	40	100	15	Normal

MOVES LEARNED IN EXCHANGE FOR BP

Name	Type	Kind	Pow.	Acc.	PP	Range
Covet	Normal	Physical	60	100	25	Normal
Super Fang	Normal	Physical	—	90	10	Normal
Low Kick	Fighting	Physical	—	100	20	Normal
Thunder Punch	Electric	Physical	75	100	15	Normal
Fire Punch	Fire	Physical	75	100	15	Normal
Ice Punch	Ice	Physical	75	100	15	Normal
Last Resort	Normal	Physical	140	100	5	Normal
Superpower	Fighting	Physical	120	100	5	Normal
Hyper Voice	Normal	Special	90	100	10	Many Others
Snore	Normal	Special	50	100	15	Normal
Heal Bell	Normal	Status	—	—	5	Your Party
Focus Punch	Fighting	Physical	150	100	20	Normal
Shock Wave	Electric	Special	60	—	20	Normal
Water Pulse	Water	Special	60	100	20	Normal

MOVES TAUGHT BY PEOPLE

Name	Type	Kind	Pow.	Acc.	PP	Range

EGG MOVES

Name	Type	Kind	Pow.	Acc.	PP	Range
Metronome	Normal	Status	—	—	10	Self
Feint Attack	Dark	Physical	60	—	20	Normal
Present	Normal	Physical	—	90	15	Normal
Crunch	Dark	Physical	80	100	15	Normal
Heal Bell	Normal	Status	—	—	5	Your Party
Snore	Normal	Special	50	100	15	Normal
Smelling Salts	Normal	Physical	70	100	10	Normal
Close Combat	Fighting	Physical	120	100	5	Normal
Ice Fang	Ice	Physical	65	95	15	Normal
Fire Fang	Fire	Physical	65	95	15	Normal
Thunder Fang	Electric	Physical	65	95	15	Normal
Focus Punch	Fighting	Physical	150	100	20	Normal
Double-Edge	Normal	Physical	120	100	15	Normal
Mimic	Normal	Status	—	—	10	Normal
Fake Tears	Dark	Status	—	100	20	Normal

National Pokédex **210** Hoenn Pokédex —

Granbull

Fairy Pokémon

Fairy

HEIGHT: 4'07" WEIGHT: 107.4 lbs.

Same form for ♂ / ♀

Ω Granbull has a particularly well-developed lower jaw. The enormous fangs are heavy, causing the Pokémon to tip its head back for balance. Unless it is startled, it will not try to bite indiscriminately.

α Granbull has a particularly well-developed lower jaw. The enormous fangs are heavy, causing the Pokémon to tip its head back for balance. Unless it is startled, it will not try to bite indiscriminately.

ABILITIES
Intimidate
Quick Feet

HIDDEN ABILITY
Rattled

EGG GROUPS
Field | Fairy

STAT GROWTH RATES
HP
Attack
Defense
Sp. Atk
Sp. Def
Speed

ITEMS SOMETIMES HELD BY WILD POKÉMON
—

EVOLUTION
Snubbull → Lv. 23 → Granbull

MAIN WAY TO REGISTER IN THE NATIONAL POKÉDEX

Level up a Snubbull obtained via Link Trade or the GTS to Lv. 23.

Damage taken in normal battles

Normal	×1	Flying	×1
Fire	×1	Psychic	×1
Water	×1	Bug	×0.5
Grass	×1	Rock	×1
Electric	×1	Ghost	×1
Ice	×1	Dragon	×0
Fighting	×0.5	Dark	×0.5
Poison	×2	Steel	×2
Ground	×1	Fairy	×1

Damage taken in Inverse battles

Normal	×1	Flying	×1
Fire	×1	Psychic	×1
Water	×1	Bug	×2
Grass	×1	Rock	×1
Electric	×1	Ghost	×1
Ice	×1	Dragon	×2
Fighting	×2	Dark	×2
Poison	×0.5	Steel	×0.5
Ground	×1	Fairy	×1

Can be used in
Inverse Battle
Battle Institute
Battle Maison
Random Matchup (Free Battle)
Random Matchup (Others)

LEVEL-UP MOVES

Lv.	Name	Type	Kind	Pow.	Acc.	PP	Range
1	Outrage	Dragon	Physical	120	100	10	1 Random
1	Ice Fang	Ice	Physical	65	95	15	Normal
1	Fire Fang	Fire	Physical	65	95	15	Normal
1	Thunder Fang	Electric	Physical	65	95	15	Normal
1	Tackle	Normal	Physical	50	100	35	Normal
1	Scary Face	Normal	Status	—	100	10	Normal
1	Tail Whip	Normal	Status	—	100	30	Many Others
1	Charm	Fairy	Status	—	100	20	Normal
7	Bite	Dark	Physical	60	100	25	Normal
13	Lick	Ghost	Physical	30	100	30	Normal
19	Headbutt	Normal	Physical	70	100	15	Normal
27	Roar	Normal	Status	—	—	20	Normal
35	Rage	Normal	Physical	20	100	20	Normal
43	Play Rough	Fairy	Physical	90	90	10	Normal
51	Payback	Dark	Physical	50	100	10	Normal
59	Crunch	Dark	Physical	80	100	15	Normal
67	Outrage	Dragon	Physical	120	100	10	1 Random

TM & HM MOVES

No.	Name	Type	Kind	Pow.	Acc.	PP	Range
TM05	Roar	Normal	Status	—	—	20	Normal
TM06	Toxic	Poison	Status	—	90	10	Normal
TM08	Bulk Up	Fighting	Status	—	—	20	Self
TM10	Hidden Power	Normal	Special	60	100	15	Normal
TM11	Sunny Day	Fire	Status	—	—	5	Both Sides
TM12	Taunt	Dark	Status	—	100	20	Normal
TM15	Hyper Beam	Normal	Special	150	90	5	Normal
TM17	Protect	Normal	Status	—	—	10	Self
TM18	Rain Dance	Water	Status	—	—	5	Both Sides
TM21	Frustration	Normal	Physical	—	100	20	Normal
TM22	Solar Beam	Grass	Special	120	100	10	Normal
TM24	Thunderbolt	Electric	Special	90	100	15	Normal
TM25	Thunder	Electric	Special	110	70	10	Normal
TM26	Earthquake	Ground	Physical	100	100	10	Adjacent
TM27	Return	Normal	Physical	—	100	20	Normal
TM28	Dig	Ground	Physical	80	100	10	Normal
TM30	Shadow Ball	Ghost	Special	80	100	15	Normal
TM31	Brick Break	Fighting	Physical	75	100	15	Normal
TM32	Double Team	Normal	Status	—	—	15	Self
TM33	Reflect	Psychic	Status	—	—	20	Your Side
TM35	Flamethrower	Fire	Special	90	100	15	Normal
TM36	Sludge Bomb	Poison	Special	90	100	10	Normal
TM38	Fire Blast	Fire	Special	110	85	5	Normal
TM39	Rock Tomb	Rock	Physical	60	95	15	Normal
TM41	Torment	Dark	Status	—	100	15	Normal
TM42	Facade	Normal	Physical	70	100	20	Normal
TM44	Rest	Psychic	Status	—	—	10	Self
TM45	Attract	Normal	Status	—	100	15	Normal
TM46	Thief	Dark	Physical	60	100	25	Normal
TM48	Round	Normal	Special	60	100	15	Normal
TM50	Overheat	Fire	Special	130	90	5	Normal
TM52	Focus Blast	Fighting	Special	120	70	5	Normal
TM56	Fling	Dark	Physical	—	100	10	Normal
TM59	Incinerate	Fire	Special	60	100	15	Many Others
TM66	Payback	Dark	Physical	50	100	10	Normal
TM67	Retaliate	Normal	Physical	70	100	5	Normal
TM68	Giga Impact	Normal	Physical	150	90	5	Normal
TM71	Stone Edge	Rock	Physical	100	80	5	Normal
TM73	Thunder Wave	Electric	Status	—	100	20	Normal
TM78	Bulldoze	Ground	Physical	60	100	20	Adjacent
TM80	Rock Slide	Rock	Physical	75	90	10	Many Others
TM87	Swagger	Normal	Status	—	90	15	Normal
TM88	Sleep Talk	Normal	Status	—	—	10	Self
TM90	Substitute	Normal	Status	—	—	10	Self
TM93	Wild Charge	Electric	Physical	90	100	15	Normal
TM94	Secret Power	Normal	Physical	70	100	20	Normal
TM95	Snarl	Dark	Special	55	95	15	Many Others
TM98	Power-Up Punch	Fighting	Physical	40	100	20	Normal
TM99	Dazzling Gleam	Fairy	Special	80	100	10	Many Others
TM100	Confide	Normal	Status	—	—	20	Normal
HM04	Strength	Normal	Physical	80	100	15	Normal
HM06	Rock Smash	Fighting	Physical	40	100	15	Normal

MOVES LEARNED IN EXCHANGE FOR BP

Name	Type	Kind	Pow.	Acc.	PP	Range
Covet	Normal	Physical	60	100	25	Normal
Super Fang	Normal	Physical	—	90	10	Normal
Low Kick	Fighting	Physical	—	100	20	Normal
Thunder Punch	Electric	Physical	75	100	15	Normal
Fire Punch	Fire	Physical	75	100	15	Normal
Ice Punch	Ice	Physical	75	100	15	Normal
Last Resort	Normal	Physical	140	100	5	Normal
Superpower	Fighting	Physical	120	100	5	Normal
Hyper Voice	Normal	Special	90	100	10	Many Others
Iron Tail	Steel	Physical	100	75	15	Normal
Snore	Normal	Special	50	100	15	Normal
Heal Bell	Normal	Status	—	—	5	Your Party
Focus Punch	Fighting	Physical	150	100	20	Normal
Shock Wave	Electric	Special	60	—	20	Normal
Water Pulse	Water	Special	60	100	20	Normal
Outrage	Dragon	Physical	120	100	10	1 Random

MOVES TAUGHT BY PEOPLE

Name	Type	Kind	Pow.	Acc.	PP	Range

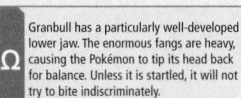

National Pokédex **211** Hoenn Pokédex —

Qwilfish

Balloon Pokémon

Water | Poison

HEIGHT: 1'08" WEIGHT: 8.6 lbs.

Same form for ♂ / ♀

Ω Qwilfish sucks in water, inflating itself. This Pokémon uses the pressure of the water it swallowed to shoot toxic quills all at once from all over its body. It finds swimming somewhat challenging.

α Qwilfish sucks in water, inflating itself. This Pokémon uses the pressure of the water it swallowed to shoot toxic quills all at once from all over its body. It finds swimming somewhat challenging.

ABILITIES
Poison Point
Swift Swim

HIDDEN ABILITY
Intimidate

EGG GROUPS
Water 2

STAT GROWTH RATES
HP ▮▮▮
Attack ▮▮▮▮▮
Defense ▮▮▮
Sp. Atk ▮▮▮
Sp. Def ▮▮
Speed ▮▮▮▮▮

ITEMS SOMETIMES HELD BY WILD POKÉMON
—

EVOLUTION
Does not evolve

MAIN WAY TO REGISTER IN THE NATIONAL POKÉDEX

Appears in *Pokémon X* and *Pokémon Y*. Bring it to your game using Link Trade or the GTS.

Damage taken in normal battles

Type		Type	
Normal	×1	Flying	×1
Fire	×0.5	Psychic	×2
Water	×0.5	Bug	×0.5
Grass	×1	Rock	×1
Electric	×2	Ghost	×1
Ice	×0.5	Dragon	×1
Fighting	×0.5	Dark	×1
Poison	×0.5	Steel	×0.5
Ground	×2	Fairy	×0.5

Damage taken in Inverse battles

Type		Type	
Normal	×1	Flying	×1
Fire	×2	Psychic	×0.5
Water	×2	Bug	×2
Grass	×1	Rock	×1
Electric	×0.5	Ghost	×1
Ice	×2	Dragon	×1
Fighting	×2	Dark	×1
Poison	×2	Steel	×2
Ground	×0.5	Fairy	×2

Can be used in
Inverse Battle
Battle Institute
Battle Maison
Random Matchup (Free Battle)
Random Matchup (Others)

LEVEL-UP MOVES

Lv.	Name	Type	Kind	Pow.	Acc.	PP	Range
1	Fell Stinger	Bug	Physical	30	100	25	Normal
1	Hydro Pump	Water	Special	110	80	5	Normal
1	Destiny Bond	Ghost	Status	—	—	5	Self
1	Water Gun	Water	Special	40	100	25	Normal
1	Spikes	Ground	Status	—	—	20	Other Side
1	Tackle	Normal	Physical	50	100	35	Normal
1	Poison Sting	Poison	Physical	15	100	35	Normal
9	Harden	Normal	Status	—	—	30	Self
9	Minimize	Normal	Status	—	—	10	Self
13	Bubble	Water	Special	40	100	30	Many Others
17	Rollout	Rock	Physical	30	90	20	Normal
21	Toxic Spikes	Poison	Status	—	—	20	Other Side
25	Stockpile	Normal	Status	—	—	20	Self
25	Spit Up	Normal	Special	—	100	10	Normal
29	Revenge	Fighting	Physical	60	100	10	Normal
33	Brine	Water	Special	65	100	10	Normal
37	Pin Missile	Bug	Physical	25	95	20	Normal
41	Take Down	Normal	Physical	90	85	20	Normal
45	Aqua Tail	Water	Physical	90	90	10	Normal
49	Poison Jab	Poison	Physical	80	100	20	Normal
53	Destiny Bond	Ghost	Status	—	—	5	Self
57	Hydro Pump	Water	Special	110	80	5	Normal
60	Fell Stinger	Bug	Physical	30	100	25	Normal

TM & HM MOVES

No.	Name	Type	Kind	Pow.	Acc.	PP	Range
TM06	Toxic	Poison	Status	—	90	10	Normal
TM07	Hail	Ice	Status	—	—	10	Both Sides
TM09	Venoshock	Poison	Special	65	100	10	Normal
TM10	Hidden Power	Normal	Special	60	100	15	Normal
TM12	Taunt	Dark	Status	—	100	20	Normal
TM13	Ice Beam	Ice	Special	90	100	10	Normal
TM14	Blizzard	Ice	Special	110	70	5	Many Others
TM17	Protect	Normal	Status	—	—	10	Self
TM18	Rain Dance	Water	Status	—	—	5	Both Sides
TM21	Frustration	Normal	Physical	—	100	20	Normal
TM27	Return	Normal	Physical	—	100	20	Normal
TM30	Shadow Ball	Ghost	Special	80	100	15	Normal
TM32	Double Team	Normal	Status	—	—	15	Self
TM34	Sludge Wave	Poison	Special	95	100	10	Adjacent
TM36	Sludge Bomb	Poison	Special	90	100	10	Normal
TM42	Facade	Normal	Physical	70	100	20	Normal
TM44	Rest	Psychic	Status	—	—	10	Self
TM45	Attract	Normal	Status	—	100	15	Normal
TM48	Round	Normal	Special	60	100	15	Normal
TM55	Scald	Water	Special	80	100	15	Normal
TM64	Explosion	Normal	Physical	250	100	5	Adjacent
TM66	Payback	Dark	Physical	50	100	10	Normal
TM73	Thunder Wave	Electric	Status	—	100	20	Normal
TM74	Gyro Ball	Steel	Physical	—	100	5	Normal
TM84	Poison Jab	Poison	Physical	80	100	20	Normal
TM87	Swagger	Normal	Status	—	90	15	Normal
TM88	Sleep Talk	Normal	Status	—	—	10	Self
TM90	Substitute	Normal	Status	—	—	10	Self
TM94	Secret Power	Normal	Physical	70	100	20	Normal
TM100	Confide	Normal	Status	—	—	20	Normal
HM03	Surf	Water	Special	90	100	15	Adjacent
HM05	Waterfall	Water	Physical	80	100	15	Normal
HM07	Dive	Water	Physical	80	100	10	Normal

MOVES LEARNED IN EXCHANGE FOR BP

Name	Type	Kind	Pow.	Acc.	PP	Range
Signal Beam	Bug	Special	75	100	15	Normal
Bounce	Flying	Physical	85	85	5	Normal
Icy Wind	Ice	Special	55	95	15	Many Others
Aqua Tail	Water	Physical	90	90	10	Normal
Snore	Normal	Special	50	100	15	Normal
Pain Split	Normal	Status	—	—	20	Normal
Shock Wave	Electric	Special	60	—	20	Normal
Water Pulse	Water	Special	60	100	20	Normal

MOVES TAUGHT BY PEOPLE

Name	Type	Kind	Pow.	Acc.	PP	Range

EGG MOVES

Name	Type	Kind	Pow.	Acc.	PP	Range
Flail	Normal	Physical	—	100	15	Normal
Haze	Ice	Status	—	—	30	Both Sides
Bubble Beam	Water	Special	65	100	20	Normal
Supersonic	Normal	Status	—	55	20	Normal
Astonish	Ghost	Physical	30	100	15	Normal
Signal Beam	Bug	Special	75	100	15	Normal
Aqua Jet	Water	Physical	40	100	20	Normal
Water Pulse	Water	Special	60	100	20	Normal
Brine	Water	Special	65	100	10	Normal
Acid Spray	Poison	Special	40	100	20	Normal

National Pokédex **212** Hoenn Pokédex —

Scizor

Pincer Pokémon

Bug | Steel

HEIGHT: 5'11" WEIGHT: 260.1 lbs.

The male has a shorter abdomen.
The female has a longer abdomen.

♂ ♀

Ω Scizor has a body with the hardness of steel. It is not easily fazed by ordinary sorts of attacks. This Pokémon flaps its wings to regulate its body temperature.

α Scizor has a body with the hardness of steel. It is not easily fazed by ordinary sorts of attacks. This Pokémon flaps its wings to regulate its body temperature.

ABILITIES
Swarm
Technician

HIDDEN ABILITY
Light Metal

EGG GROUPS
Bug

STAT GROWTH RATES
HP ▮▮▮
Attack ▮▮▮▮▮▮▮
Defense ▮▮▮▮
Sp. Atk ▮▮▮
Sp. Def ▮▮▮
Speed ▮▮▮▮

ITEMS SOMETIMES HELD BY WILD POKÉMON
—

EVOLUTION
Scyther → (Link Trade with Metal Coat) → Scizor

MAIN WAY TO REGISTER IN THE NATIONAL POKÉDEX

Receive a Scyther that is holding a Metal Coat via Link Trade or the GTS to have it evolve.

Damage taken in normal battles

Type		Type	
Normal	×0.5	Flying	×1
Fire	×4	Psychic	×0.5
Water	×1	Bug	×0.5
Grass	×0.25	Rock	×1
Electric	×1	Ghost	×1
Ice	×0.5	Dragon	×0.5
Fighting	×1	Dark	×1
Poison	×0	Steel	×0.5
Ground	×1	Fairy	×0.5

Damage taken in Inverse battles

Type		Type	
Normal	×2	Flying	×1
Fire	×0.25	Psychic	×2
Water	×1	Bug	×2
Grass	×4	Rock	×1
Electric	×1	Ghost	×1
Ice	×2	Dragon	×2
Fighting	×1	Dark	×1
Poison	×2	Steel	×2
Ground	×1	Fairy	×2

Can be used in
Inverse Battle
Battle Institute
Battle Maison
Random Matchup (Free Battle)
Random Matchup (Others)

LEVEL-UP MOVES

Lv.	Name	Type	Kind	Pow.	Acc.	PP	Range
1	Feint	Normal	Physical	30	100	10	Normal
1	Bullet Punch	Steel	Physical	40	100	30	Normal
1	Quick Attack	Normal	Physical	40	100	30	Normal
1	Leer	Normal	Status	—	100	30	Many Others
5	Focus Energy	Normal	Status	—	—	30	Self
9	Pursuit	Dark	Physical	40	100	20	Normal
13	False Swipe	Normal	Physical	40	100	40	Normal
17	Agility	Psychic	Status	—	—	30	Self
21	Metal Claw	Steel	Physical	50	95	35	Normal
25	Fury Cutter	Bug	Physical	40	95	20	Normal
29	Slash	Normal	Physical	70	100	20	Normal
33	Razor Wind	Normal	Special	80	100	10	Many Others
37	Iron Defense	Steel	Status	—	—	15	Self
41	X-Scissor	Bug	Physical	80	100	15	Normal
45	Night Slash	Dark	Physical	70	100	15	Normal
49	Double Hit	Normal	Physical	35	90	10	Normal
50	Iron Head	Steel	Physical	80	100	15	Normal
57	Swords Dance	Normal	Status	—	—	20	Self
61	Feint	Normal	Physical	30	100	10	Normal

TM & HM MOVES

No.	Name	Type	Kind	Pow.	Acc.	PP	Range
TM06	Toxic	Poison	Status	—	90	10	Normal
TM09	Venoshock	Poison	Special	65	100	10	Normal
TM10	Hidden Power	Normal	Special	60	100	15	Normal
TM11	Sunny Day	Fire	Status	—	—	5	Both Sides
TM15	Hyper Beam	Normal	Special	150	90	5	Normal
TM16	Light Screen	Psychic	Status	—	—	30	Your Side
TM17	Protect	Normal	Status	—	—	10	Self
TM18	Rain Dance	Water	Status	—	—	5	Both Sides
TM19	Roost	Flying	Status	—	—	10	Self
TM20	Safeguard	Normal	Status	—	—	25	Your Side
TM21	Frustration	Normal	Physical	—	100	20	Normal
TM27	Return	Normal	Physical	—	100	20	Normal
TM31	Brick Break	Fighting	Physical	75	100	15	Normal
TM32	Double Team	Normal	Status	—	—	15	Self
TM37	Sandstorm	Rock	Status	—	—	10	Both Sides
TM40	Aerial Ace	Flying	Physical	60	—	20	Normal
TM42	Facade	Normal	Physical	70	100	20	Normal
TM44	Rest	Psychic	Status	—	—	10	Self
TM45	Attract	Normal	Status	—	100	15	Normal
TM46	Thief	Dark	Physical	60	100	25	Normal
TM48	Round	Normal	Special	60	100	15	Normal
TM51	Steel Wing	Steel	Physical	70	90	25	Normal
TM54	False Swipe	Normal	Physical	40	100	40	Normal
TM56	Fling	Dark	Physical	—	100	10	Normal
TM62	Acrobatics	Flying	Physical	55	100	15	Normal
TM68	Giga Impact	Normal	Physical	150	90	5	Normal
TM75	Swords Dance	Normal	Status	—	—	20	Self
TM76	Struggle Bug	Bug	Special	50	100	20	Many Others
TM81	X-Scissor	Bug	Physical	80	100	15	Normal
TM87	Swagger	Normal	Status	—	90	15	Normal
TM88	Sleep Talk	Normal	Status	—	—	10	Self
TM89	U-turn	Bug	Physical	70	100	20	Normal
TM90	Substitute	Normal	Status	—	—	10	Self
TM91	Flash Cannon	Steel	Special	80	100	10	Normal
TM94	Secret Power	Normal	Physical	70	100	20	Normal
TM100	Confide	Normal	Status	—	—	20	Normal
HM01	Cut	Normal	Physical	50	95	30	Normal
HM04	Strength	Normal	Physical	80	100	15	Normal
HM06	Rock Smash	Fighting	Physical	40	100	15	Normal

MOVES LEARNED IN EXCHANGE FOR BP

Name	Type	Kind	Pow.	Acc.	PP	Range
Bug Bite	Bug	Physical	60	100	20	Normal
Iron Head	Steel	Physical	80	100	15	Normal
Iron Defense	Steel	Status	—	—	15	Self
Superpower	Fighting	Physical	120	100	5	Normal
Snore	Normal	Special	50	100	15	Normal
Knock Off	Dark	Physical	65	100	20	Normal
Tailwind	Flying	Status	—	—	15	Your Side

MOVES TAUGHT BY PEOPLE

Name	Type	Kind	Pow.	Acc.	PP	Range

Mega Evolution

Mega Scizor

Pincer Pokémon

Bug | Steel

HEIGHT: 6'07" WEIGHT: 275.6 lbs.

Same form for ♂ / ♀

REQUIRED MEGA STONE

Scizorite

Find in Petalburg Woods (after battling Groudon or Kyogre).

ABILITY: Technician

HIDDEN ABILITY: —

EGG GROUPS: —

STAT GROWTH RATES: HP, Attack, Defense, Sp. Atk, Sp. Def, Speed

Damage taken in normal battles

Type		Type	
Normal	×0.5	Flying	×1
Fire	×4	Psychic	×0.5
Water	×1	Bug	×0.5
Grass	×0.25	Rock	×1
Electric	×1	Ghost	×1
Ice	×0.5	Dragon	×0.5
Fighting	×1	Dark	×1
Poison	×0	Steel	×0.5
Ground	×1	Fairy	×0.5

Damage taken in Inverse battles

Type		Type	
Normal	×2	Flying	×1
Fire	×0.25	Psychic	×2
Water	×1	Bug	×2
Grass	×4	Rock	×1
Electric	×1	Ghost	×1
Ice	×2	Dragon	×2
Fighting	×1	Dark	×1
Poison	×2	Steel	×2
Ground	×1	Fairy	×2

Can be used in

- Inverse Battle
- Battle Institute
- Battle Maison
- Random Matchup (Free Battle)
- Random Matchup (Others)

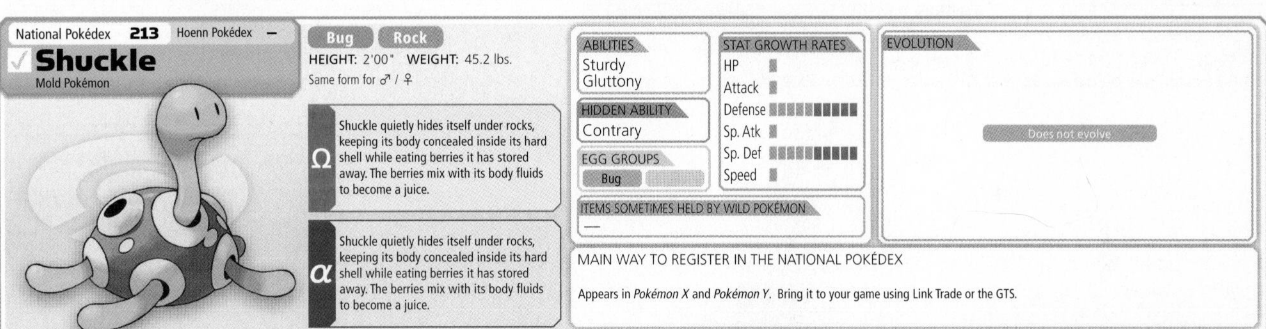

National Pokédex **213** Hoenn Pokédex —

Shuckle

Mold Pokémon

Bug | Rock

HEIGHT: 2'00" WEIGHT: 45.2 lbs.

Same form for ♂ / ♀

Ω Shuckle quietly hides itself under rocks, keeping its body concealed inside its hard shell while eating berries it has stored away. The berries mix with its body fluids to become a juice.

α Shuckle quietly hides itself under rocks, keeping its body concealed inside its hard shell while eating berries it has stored away. The berries mix with its body fluids to become a juice.

ABILITIES: Sturdy, Gluttony

HIDDEN ABILITY: Contrary

EGG GROUPS: Bug

STAT GROWTH RATES: HP, Attack, Defense, Sp. Atk, Sp. Def, Speed

ITEMS SOMETIMES HELD BY WILD POKÉMON: —

EVOLUTION

Does not evolve

MAIN WAY TO REGISTER IN THE NATIONAL POKÉDEX

Appears in *Pokémon X* and *Pokémon Y*. Bring it to your game using Link Trade or the GTS.

Damage taken in normal battles

Type		Type	
Normal	×0.5	Flying	×1
Fire	×1	Psychic	×1
Water	×2	Bug	×1
Grass	×1	Rock	×2
Electric	×1	Ghost	×1
Ice	×1	Dragon	×1
Fighting	×1	Dark	×1
Poison	×0.5	Steel	×2
Ground	×1	Fairy	×1

Damage taken in Inverse battles

Type		Type	
Normal	×2	Flying	×1
Fire	×1	Psychic	×1
Water	×0.5	Bug	×1
Grass	×1	Rock	×0.5
Electric	×1	Ghost	×1
Ice	×1	Dragon	×1
Fighting	×1	Dark	×1
Poison	×2	Steel	×0.5
Ground	×1	Fairy	×1

Can be used in

- Inverse Battle
- Battle Institute
- Battle Maison
- Random Matchup (Free Battle)
- Random Matchup (Others)

LEVEL-UP MOVES

Lv.	Name	Type	Kind	Pow.	Acc.	PP	Range
1	Sticky Web	Bug	Status	—	—	20	Other Side
1	Withdraw	Water	Status	—	—	40	Self
1	Constrict	Normal	Physical	10	100	35	Normal
1	Bide	Normal	Physical	—	—	10	Self
1	Rollout	Rock	Physical	30	90	20	Normal
5	Encore	Normal	Status	—	100	5	Normal
9	Wrap	Normal	Physical	15	90	20	Normal
12	Struggle Bug	Bug	Special	50	100	20	Many Others
16	Safeguard	Normal	Status	—	—	25	Your Side
20	Rest	Psychic	Status	—	—	10	Self
23	Rock Throw	Rock	Physical	50	90	15	Normal
27	Gastro Acid	Poison	Status	—	100	10	Normal
31	Power Trick	Psychic	Status	—	—	10	Self
34	Shell Smash	Normal	Status	—	—	15	Self
38	Rock Slide	Rock	Physical	75	90	10	Many Others
42	Bug Bite	Bug	Physical	60	100	20	Normal
45	Power Split	Psychic	Status	—	—	10	Normal
45	Guard Split	Psychic	Status	—	—	10	Normal
49	Stone Edge	Rock	Physical	100	80	5	Normal
53	Sticky Web	Bug	Status	—	—	20	Other Side

TM & HM MOVES

No.	Name	Type	Kind	Pow.	Acc.	PP	Range
TM06	Toxic	Poison	Status	—	90	10	Normal
TM09	Venoshock	Poison	Special	65	100	10	Normal
TM10	Hidden Power	Normal	Special	60	100	15	Normal
TM11	Sunny Day	Fire	Status	—	—	5	Both Sides
TM17	Protect	Normal	Status	—	—	10	Self
TM20	Safeguard	Normal	Status	—	—	25	Your Side
TM21	Frustration	Normal	Physical	—	100	20	Normal
TM23	Smack Down	Rock	Physical	50	100	15	Normal
TM26	Earthquake	Ground	Physical	100	100	10	Adjacent
TM27	Return	Normal	Physical	—	100	20	Normal
TM28	Dig	Ground	Physical	80	100	10	Normal
TM32	Double Team	Normal	Status	—	—	15	Self
TM34	Sludge Wave	Poison	Special	95	100	10	Adjacent
TM36	Sludge Bomb	Poison	Special	90	100	10	Normal
TM37	Sandstorm	Rock	Status	—	—	10	Both Sides
TM39	Rock Tomb	Rock	Physical	60	95	15	Normal
TM42	Facade	Normal	Physical	70	100	20	Normal
TM44	Rest	Psychic	Status	—	—	10	Self
TM45	Attract	Normal	Status	—	100	15	Normal
TM48	Round	Normal	Special	60	100	15	Normal
TM69	Rock Polish	Rock	Status	—	—	20	Self
TM70	Flash	Normal	Status	—	100	20	Normal
TM71	Stone Edge	Rock	Physical	100	80	5	Normal
TM74	Gyro Ball	Steel	Physical	—	100	5	Normal
TM76	Struggle Bug	Bug	Special	50	100	20	Many Others
TM78	Bulldoze	Ground	Physical	60	100	20	Adjacent
TM80	Rock Slide	Rock	Physical	75	90	10	Many Others
TM83	Infestation	Bug	Special	20	100	20	Normal
TM87	Swagger	Normal	Status	—	90	15	Normal
TM88	Sleep Talk	Normal	Status	—	—	10	Self
TM90	Substitute	Normal	Status	—	—	10	Self
TM94	Secret Power	Normal	Physical	70	100	20	Normal
TM100	Confide	Normal	Status	—	—	20	Normal
HM04	Strength	Normal	Physical	80	100	15	Normal
HM06	Rock Smash	Fighting	Physical	40	100	15	Normal

MOVES LEARNED IN EXCHANGE FOR BP

Name	Type	Kind	Pow.	Acc.	PP	Range
Bug Bite	Bug	Physical	60	100	20	Normal
Earth Power	Ground	Special	90	100	10	Normal
Bind	Normal	Physical	15	85	20	Normal
Snore	Normal	Special	50	100	15	Normal
Knock Off	Dark	Physical	65	100	20	Normal
Gastro Acid	Poison	Status	—	100	10	Normal
After You	Normal	Status	—	—	15	Normal
Helping Hand	Normal	Status	—	—	20	1 Ally
Stealth Rock	Rock	Status	—	—	20	Other Side

MOVES TAUGHT BY PEOPLE

Name	Type	Kind	Pow.	Acc.	PP	Range

EGG MOVES

Name	Type	Kind	Pow.	Acc.	PP	Range
Sweet Scent	Normal	Status	—	100	20	Many Others
Knock Off	Dark	Physical	65	100	20	Normal
Helping Hand	Normal	Status	—	—	20	1 Ally
Acupressure	Normal	Status	—	—	30	Self/Ally
Sand Tomb	Ground	Physical	35	85	15	Normal
Mud-Slap	Ground	Special	20	100	10	Normal
Acid	Poison	Special	40	100	30	Many Others
Rock Blast	Rock	Physical	25	90	10	Normal
Final Gambit	Fighting	Special	—	100	5	Normal

National Pokédex **214** Hoenn Pokédex **175**

Heracross

Single Horn Pokémon

Bug / Fighting

HEIGHT: 4'11" WEIGHT: 119 lbs.

The male has a larger horn with pointed tips.
The female has a smaller horn with rounded tips.

Ω Heracross charges in a straight line at its foe, slips beneath the foe's grasp, and then scoops up and hurls the opponent with its mighty horn. This Pokémon even has enough power to topple a massive tree.

α Heracross has sharp claws on its feet. These are planted firmly into the ground or the bark of a tree, giving the Pokémon a secure and solid footing to forcefully fling away foes with its proud horn.

ABILITIES
Swarm
Guts

HIDDEN ABILITY
Moxie

EGG GROUPS
Bug

STAT GROWTH RATES
HP
Attack
Defense
Sp. Atk
Sp. Def
Speed

ITEMS SOMETIMES HELD BY WILD POKÉMON
—

EVOLUTION
Does not evolve

MAIN WAY TO REGISTER IN THE NATIONAL POKÉDEX
Catch in the very tall grass in the upper-left corner of the Safari Zone.

Damage taken in normal battles

Type		Type	
Normal	×1	Flying	×4
Fire	×2	Psychic	×2
Water	×1	Bug	×0.5
Grass	×0.5	Rock	×1
Electric	×1	Ghost	×1
Ice	×1	Dragon	×1
Fighting	×0.5	Dark	×0.5
Poison	×1	Steel	×1
Ground	×0.5	Fairy	×2

Damage taken in Inverse battles

Type		Type	
Normal	×1	Flying	×0.25
Fire	×0.5	Psychic	×0.5
Water	×1	Bug	×2
Grass	×2	Rock	×1
Electric	×1	Ghost	×1
Ice	×1	Dragon	×1
Fighting	×2	Dark	×2
Poison	×1	Steel	×1
Ground	×2	Fairy	×0.5

Can be used in
Inverse Battle
Battle Institute
Battle Maison
Random Matchup (Free Battle)
Random Matchup (Others)

LEVEL-UP MOVES

Lv.	Name	Type	Kind	Pow.	Acc.	PP	Range
1	Arm Thrust	Fighting	Physical	15	100	20	Normal
1	Bullet Seed	Grass	Physical	25	100	30	Normal
1	Night Slash	Dark	Physical	70	100	15	Normal
1	Tackle	Normal	Physical	50	100	35	Normal
1	Leer	Normal	Status	—	100	30	Many Others
1	Horn Attack	Normal	Physical	65	100	25	Normal
1	Endure	Normal	Status	—	—	10	Self
7	Feint	Normal	Physical	30	100	10	Normal
10	Aerial Ace	Flying	Physical	60	—	20	Normal
16	Chip Away	Normal	Physical	70	100	20	Normal
19	Counter	Fighting	Physical	—	100	20	Varies
25	Fury Attack	Normal	Physical	15	85	20	Normal
28	Brick Break	Fighting	Physical	75	100	15	Normal
31	Pin Missile	Bug	Physical	25	95	20	Normal
34	Take Down	Normal	Physical	90	85	20	Normal
37	Megahorn	Bug	Physical	120	85	10	Normal
43	Close Combat	Fighting	Physical	120	100	5	Normal
46	Reversal	Fighting	Physical	—	100	15	Normal

TM & HM MOVES

No.	Name	Type	Kind	Pow.	Acc.	PP	Range
TM06	Toxic	Poison	Status	—	90	10	Normal
TM08	Bulk Up	Fighting	Status	—	—	20	Self
TM09	Venoshock	Poison	Special	65	100	10	Normal
TM10	Hidden Power	Normal	Special	60	100	15	Normal
TM11	Sunny Day	Fire	Status	—	—	5	Both Sides
TM15	Hyper Beam	Normal	Special	150	90	5	Normal
TM17	Protect	Normal	Status	—	—	10	Self
TM18	Rain Dance	Water	Status	—	—	5	Both Sides
TM21	Frustration	Normal	Physical	—	100	20	Normal
TM23	Smack Down	Rock	Physical	50	100	15	Normal
TM26	Earthquake	Ground	Physical	100	100	10	Adjacent
TM27	Return	Normal	Physical	—	100	20	Normal
TM28	Dig	Ground	Physical	80	100	10	Normal
TM31	Brick Break	Fighting	Physical	75	100	15	Normal
TM32	Double Team	Normal	Status	—	—	15	Self
TM39	Rock Tomb	Rock	Physical	60	95	15	Normal
TM40	Aerial Ace	Flying	Physical	60	—	20	Normal
TM42	Facade	Normal	Physical	70	100	20	Normal
TM44	Rest	Psychic	Status	—	—	10	Self
TM45	Attract	Normal	Status	—	100	15	Normal
TM46	Thief	Dark	Physical	60	100	25	Normal
TM48	Round	Normal	Special	60	100	15	Normal
TM52	Focus Blast	Fighting	Special	120	70	5	Normal
TM54	False Swipe	Normal	Physical	40	100	40	Normal
TM56	Fling	Dark	Physical	—	100	10	Normal
TM65	Shadow Claw	Ghost	Physical	70	100	15	Normal
TM67	Retaliate	Normal	Physical	70	100	5	Normal
TM68	Giga Impact	Normal	Physical	150	90	5	Normal
TM71	Stone Edge	Rock	Physical	100	80	5	Normal
TM75	Swords Dance	Normal	Status	—	—	20	Self
TM76	Struggle Bug	Bug	Special	50	100	20	Many Others
TM78	Bulldoze	Ground	Physical	60	100	20	Adjacent
TM80	Rock Slide	Rock	Physical	75	90	10	Many Others
TM87	Swagger	Normal	Status	—	90	15	Normal
TM88	Sleep Talk	Normal	Status	—	—	10	Self
TM90	Substitute	Normal	Status	—	—	10	Self
TM94	Secret Power	Normal	Physical	70	100	20	Normal
TM100	Confide	Normal	Status	—	—	20	Normal
HM01	Cut	Normal	Physical	50	95	30	Normal
HM04	Strength	Normal	Physical	80	100	15	Normal
HM06	Rock Smash	Fighting	Physical	40	100	15	Normal

MOVES LEARNED IN EXCHANGE FOR BP

Name	Type	Kind	Pow.	Acc.	PP	Range
Bug Bite	Bug	Physical	60	100	20	Normal
Low Kick	Fighting	Physical	—	100	20	Normal
Iron Defense	Steel	Status	—	—	15	Self
Snore	Normal	Special	50	100	15	Normal
Knock Off	Dark	Physical	65	100	20	Normal
Focus Punch	Fighting	Physical	150	100	20	Normal
Helping Hand	Normal	Status	—	—	20	1 Ally

MOVES TAUGHT BY PEOPLE

Name	Type	Kind	Pow.	Acc.	PP	Range

EGG MOVES

Name	Type	Kind	Pow.	Acc.	PP	Range
Harden	Normal	Status	—	—	30	Self
Bide	Normal	Physical	—	—	10	Self
Flail	Normal	Physical	—	100	15	Normal
Revenge	Fighting	Physical	60	100	10	Normal
Pursuit	Dark	Physical	40	100	20	Normal
Double-Edge	Normal	Physical	120	100	15	Normal
Seismic Toss	Fighting	Physical	—	100	20	Normal
Focus Punch	Fighting	Physical	150	100	20	Normal
Megahorn	Bug	Physical	120	85	10	Normal
Rock Blast	Rock	Physical	25	90	10	Normal

Mega Evolution

Mega Heracross

Single Horn Pokémon

Bug / Fighting

HEIGHT: 5'07" WEIGHT: 137.8 lbs.

Same form for ♂ / ♀

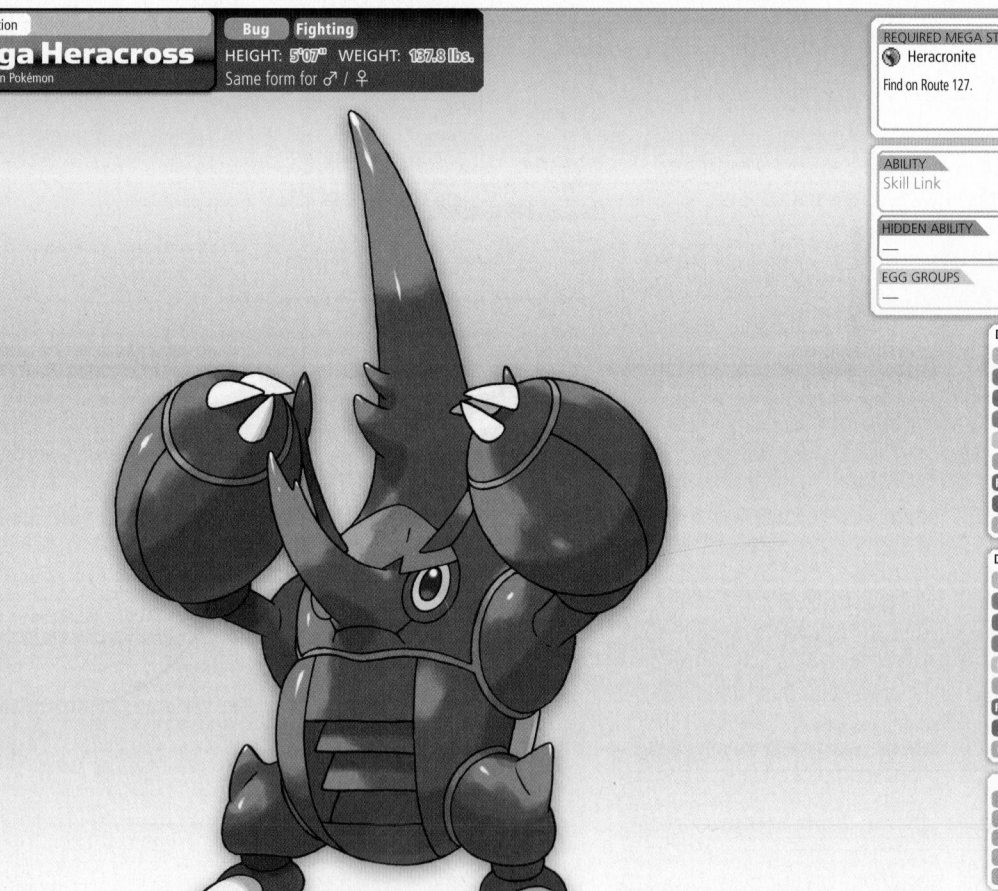

REQUIRED MEGA STONE
Heracronite
Find on Route 127.

ABILITY
Skill Link

HIDDEN ABILITY
—

EGG GROUPS
—

STAT GROWTH RATES
HP
Attack
Defense
Sp. Atk
Sp. Def
Speed

Damage taken in normal battles

Type		Type	
Normal	×1	Flying	×4
Fire	×2	Psychic	×2
Water	×1	Bug	×0.5
Grass	×0.5	Rock	×1
Electric	×1	Ghost	×1
Ice	×1	Dragon	×1
Fighting	×0.5	Dark	×0.5
Poison	×1	Steel	×1
Ground	×0.5	Fairy	×2

Damage taken in Inverse battles

Type		Type	
Normal	×1	Flying	×0.25
Fire	×0.5	Psychic	×0.5
Water	×1	Bug	×2
Grass	×2	Rock	×1
Electric	×1	Ghost	×1
Ice	×1	Dragon	×1
Fighting	×2	Dark	×2
Poison	×1	Steel	×1
Ground	×2	Fairy	×0.5

Can be used in
Inverse Battle
Battle Institute
Battle Maison
Random Matchup (Free Battle)
Random Matchup (Others)

National Pokédex **215** Hoenn Pokédex —

Sneasel

Sharp Claw Pokémon

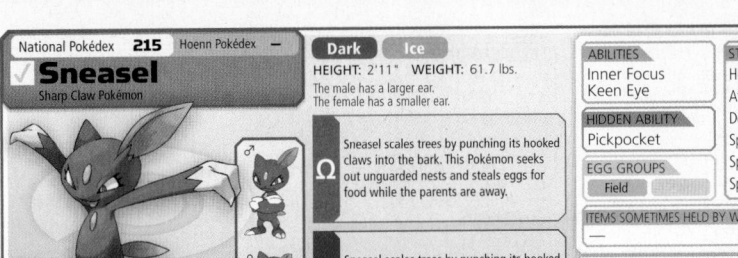

Dark / Ice

HEIGHT: 2'11" WEIGHT: 61.7 lbs.

The male has a larger ear.
The female has a smaller ear.

Ω Sneasel scales trees by punching its hooked claws into the bark. This Pokémon seeks out unguarded nests and steals eggs for food while the parents are away.

α Sneasel scales trees by punching its hooked claws into the bark. This Pokémon seeks out unguarded nests and steals eggs for food while the parents are away.

ABILITIES
Inner Focus
Keen Eye

HIDDEN ABILITY
Pickpocket

EGG GROUPS
Field

STAT GROWTH RATES
HP
Attack
Defense
Sp. Atk
Sp. Def
Speed

ITEMS SOMETIMES HELD BY WILD POKÉMON
—

EVOLUTION

MAIN WAY TO REGISTER IN THE NATIONAL POKÉDEX

Appears in *Pokémon X* and *Pokémon Y*. Bring it to your game using Link Trade or the GTS.

Damage taken in normal battles

Type		Type	
Normal	×1	Flying	×1
Fire	×2	Psychic	×0
Water	×1	Bug	×2
Grass	×1	Rock	×2
Electric	×1	Ghost	×0.5
Ice	×0.5	Dragon	×1
Fighting	×4	Dark	×0.5
Poison	×1	Steel	×2
Ground	×1	Fairy	×2

Damage taken in Inverse battles

Type		Type	
Normal	×1	Flying	×1
Fire	×0.5	Psychic	×2
Water	×1	Bug	×0.5
Grass	×1	Rock	×0.5
Electric	×1	Ghost	×2
Ice	×2	Dragon	×1
Fighting	×0.25	Dark	×2
Poison	×1	Steel	×0.5
Ground	×1	Fairy	×0.5

Can be used in
Inverse Battle
Battle Institute
Battle Maison
Random Matchup (Free Battle)
Random Matchup (Others)

LEVEL-UP MOVES

Lv.	Name	Type	Kind	Pow.	Acc.	PP	Range
1	Scratch	Normal	Physical	40	100	35	Normal
1	Leer	Normal	Status	—	100	30	Many Others
1	Taunt	Dark	Status	—	100	20	Normal
8	Quick Attack	Normal	Physical	40	100	30	Normal
10	Feint Attack	Dark	Physical	60	—	20	Normal
14	Icy Wind	Ice	Special	55	95	15	Many Others
16	Fury Swipes	Normal	Physical	18	80	15	Normal
20	Agility	Psychic	Status	—	—	30	Self
22	Metal Claw	Steel	Physical	50	95	35	Normal
25	Hone Claws	Dark	Status	—	—	15	Self
28	Beat Up	Dark	Physical	—	100	10	Normal
32	Screech	Normal	Status	—	85	40	Normal
35	Slash	Normal	Physical	70	100	20	Normal
40	Snatch	Dark	Status	—	—	10	Self
44	Punishment	Dark	Physical	—	100	5	Normal
47	Ice Shard	Ice	Physical	40	100	30	Normal

TM & HM MOVES

No.	Name	Type	Kind	Pow.	Acc.	PP	Range
TM01	Hone Claws	Dark	Status	—	—	15	Self
TM04	Calm Mind	Psychic	Status	—	—	20	Self
TM06	Toxic	Poison	Status	—	90	10	Normal
TM07	Hail	Ice	Status	—	—	10	Both Sides
TM10	Hidden Power	Normal	Special	60	100	15	Normal
TM11	Sunny Day	Fire	Status	—	—	5	Both Sides
TM12	Taunt	Dark	Status	—	100	20	Normal
TM13	Ice Beam	Ice	Special	90	100	10	Normal
TM14	Blizzard	Ice	Special	110	70	5	Many Others
TM17	Protect	Normal	Status	—	—	10	Self
TM18	Rain Dance	Water	Status	—	—	5	Both Sides
TM21	Frustration	Normal	Physical	—	100	20	Normal
TM27	Return	Normal	Physical	—	100	20	Normal
TM28	Dig	Ground	Physical	80	100	10	Normal
TM30	Shadow Ball	Ghost	Special	80	100	15	Normal
TM31	Brick Break	Fighting	Physical	75	100	15	Normal
TM32	Double Team	Normal	Status	—	—	15	Self
TM33	Reflect	Psychic	Status	—	—	20	Your Side
TM40	Aerial Ace	Flying	Physical	60	—	20	Normal
TM41	Torment	Dark	Status	—	100	15	Normal
TM42	Facade	Normal	Physical	70	100	20	Normal
TM44	Rest	Psychic	Status	—	—	10	Self
TM45	Attract	Normal	Status	—	100	15	Normal
TM46	Thief	Dark	Physical	60	100	25	Normal
TM47	Low Sweep	Fighting	Physical	65	100	20	Normal
TM48	Round	Normal	Special	60	100	15	Normal
TM54	False Swipe	Normal	Physical	40	100	40	Normal
TM56	Fling	Dark	Physical	—	100	10	Normal
TM63	Embargo	Dark	Status	—	100	15	Normal
TM65	Shadow Claw	Ghost	Physical	70	100	15	Normal
TM66	Payback	Dark	Physical	50	100	10	Normal
TM67	Retaliate	Normal	Physical	70	100	5	Normal
TM75	Swords Dance	Normal	Status	—	—	20	Self
TM77	Psych Up	Normal	Status	—	—	10	Self
TM81	X-Scissor	Bug	Physical	80	100	15	Normal
TM84	Poison Jab	Poison	Physical	80	100	20	Normal
TM85	Dream Eater	Psychic	Special	100	100	15	Normal
TM87	Swagger	Normal	Status	—	90	15	Normal
TM88	Sleep Talk	Normal	Status	—	—	10	Self
TM90	Substitute	Normal	Status	—	—	10	Self
TM94	Secret Power	Normal	Physical	70	100	20	Normal
TM95	Snarl	Dark	Special	55	95	15	Many Others
TM97	Dark Pulse	Dark	Special	80	100	15	Normal
TM98	Power-Up Punch	Fighting	Physical	40	100	20	Normal
TM100	Confide	Normal	Status	—	—	20	Normal
HM01	Cut	Normal	Physical	50	95	30	Normal
HM03	Surf	Water	Special	90	100	15	Adjacent
HM04	Strength	Normal	Physical	80	100	15	Normal
HM06	Rock Smash	Fighting	Physical	40	100	15	Normal

MOVES LEARNED IN EXCHANGE FOR BP

Name	Type	Kind	Pow.	Acc.	PP	Range
Low Kick	Fighting	Physical	—	100	20	Normal
Ice Punch	Ice	Physical	75	100	15	Normal
Foul Play	Dark	Physical	95	100	15	Normal
Icy Wind	Ice	Special	55	95	15	Many Others
Iron Tail	Steel	Physical	100	75	15	Normal
Snore	Normal	Special	50	100	15	Normal
Knock Off	Dark	Physical	65	100	20	Normal
Focus Punch	Fighting	Physical	150	100	20	Normal
Spite	Ghost	Status	—	100	10	Normal
Snatch	Dark	Status	—	—	10	Self

MOVES TAUGHT BY PEOPLE

Name	Type	Kind	Pow.	Acc.	PP	Range

EGG MOVES

Name	Type	Kind	Pow.	Acc.	PP	Range
Counter	Fighting	Physical	—	100	20	Varies
Spite	Ghost	Status	—	100	10	Normal
Foresight	Normal	Status	—	—	40	Normal
Bite	Dark	Physical	60	100	25	Normal
Crush Claw	Normal	Physical	75	95	10	Normal
Fake Out	Normal	Physical	40	100	10	Normal
Double Hit	Normal	Physical	35	90	10	Normal
Punishment	Dark	Physical	—	100	5	Normal
Pursuit	Dark	Physical	40	100	20	Normal
Ice Shard	Ice	Physical	40	100	30	Normal
Ice Punch	Ice	Physical	75	100	15	Normal
Assist	Normal	Status	—	—	20	Self
Avalanche	Ice	Physical	60	100	10	Normal
Feint	Normal	Physical	30	100	10	Normal
Icicle Crash	Ice	Physical	85	90	10	Normal

National Pokédex **216** Hoenn Pokédex —

Teddiursa

Little Bear Pokémon

Normal

HEIGHT: 2'00" WEIGHT: 19.4 lbs.

Same form for ♂ / ♀

Ω This Pokémon likes to lick its palms that are sweetened by being soaked in honey. Teddiursa concocts its own honey by blending fruits and pollen collected by Beedrill.

α This Pokémon likes to lick its palms that are sweetened by being soaked in honey. Teddiursa concocts its own honey by blending fruits and pollen collected by Beedrill.

ABILITIES
Pickup
Quick Feet

HIDDEN ABILITY
Honey Gather

EGG GROUPS
Field

STAT GROWTH RATES
HP
Attack
Defense
Sp. Atk
Sp. Def
Speed

ITEMS SOMETIMES HELD BY WILD POKÉMON
—

EVOLUTION

Teddiursa → Lv. 30 → Ursaring

MAIN WAY TO REGISTER IN THE NATIONAL POKÉDEX

Leave a Ursaring obtained via Link Trade or the GTS at a Pokémon Day Care, then hatch the Pokémon Egg that is found.

Damage taken in normal battles

Type		Type	
Normal	×1	Flying	×1
Fire	×1	Psychic	×1
Water	×1	Bug	×1
Grass	×1	Rock	×1
Electric	×1	Ghost	×0
Ice	×1	Dragon	×1
Fighting	×2	Dark	×1
Poison	×1	Steel	×1
Ground	×1	Fairy	×1

Damage taken in Inverse battles

Type		Type	
Normal	×1	Flying	×1
Fire	×1	Psychic	×1
Water	×1	Bug	×1
Grass	×1	Rock	×1
Electric	×1	Ghost	×2
Ice	×1	Dragon	×1
Fighting	×0.5	Dark	×1
Poison	×1	Steel	×1
Ground	×1	Fairy	×1

Can be used in
Inverse Battle
Battle Institute
Battle Maison
Random Matchup (Free Battle)
Random Matchup (Others)

LEVEL-UP MOVES

Lv.	Name	Type	Kind	Pow.	Acc.	PP	Range
1	Fling	Dark	Physical	—	100	10	Normal
1	Covet	Normal	Physical	60	100	25	Normal
1	Scratch	Normal	Physical	40	100	35	Normal
1	Baby-Doll Eyes	Fairy	Status	—	100	30	Normal
1	Lick	Ghost	Physical	30	100	30	Normal
1	Fake Tears	Dark	Status	—	100	20	Normal
8	Fury Swipes	Normal	Physical	18	80	15	Normal
15	Feint Attack	Dark	Physical	60	—	20	Normal
22	Sweet Scent	Normal	Status	—	100	20	Many Others
25	Play Nice	Normal	Status	—	—	20	Normal
29	Slash	Normal	Physical	70	100	20	Normal
36	Charm	Fairy	Status	—	100	20	Normal
43	Rest	Psychic	Status	—	—	10	Self
43	Snore	Normal	Special	50	100	15	Normal
50	Thrash	Normal	Physical	120	100	10	1 Random
57	Fling	Dark	Physical	—	100	10	Normal

TM & HM MOVES

No.	Name	Type	Kind	Pow.	Acc.	PP	Range
TM01	Hone Claws	Dark	Status	—	—	15	Self
TM05	Roar	Normal	Status	—	—	20	Normal
TM06	Toxic	Poison	Status	—	90	10	Normal
TM08	Bulk Up	Fighting	Status	—	—	20	Self
TM10	Hidden Power	Normal	Special	60	100	15	Normal
TM11	Sunny Day	Fire	Status	—	—	5	Both Sides
TM12	Taunt	Dark	Status	—	100	20	Normal
TM17	Protect	Normal	Status	—	—	10	Self
TM18	Rain Dance	Water	Status	—	—	5	Both Sides
TM21	Frustration	Normal	Physical	—	100	20	Normal
TM26	Earthquake	Ground	Physical	100	100	10	Adjacent
TM27	Return	Normal	Physical	—	100	20	Normal
TM28	Dig	Ground	Physical	80	100	10	Normal
TM31	Brick Break	Fighting	Physical	75	100	15	Normal
TM32	Double Team	Normal	Status	—	—	15	Self
TM39	Rock Tomb	Rock	Physical	60	95	15	Normal
TM40	Aerial Ace	Flying	Physical	60	—	20	Normal
TM41	Torment	Dark	Status	—	100	15	Normal
TM42	Facade	Normal	Physical	70	100	20	Normal
TM44	Rest	Psychic	Status	—	—	10	Self
TM45	Attract	Normal	Status	—	100	15	Normal
TM46	Thief	Dark	Physical	60	100	25	Normal
TM48	Round	Normal	Special	60	100	15	Normal
TM56	Fling	Dark	Physical	—	100	10	Normal
TM65	Shadow Claw	Ghost	Physical	70	100	15	Normal
TM66	Payback	Dark	Physical	50	100	10	Normal
TM67	Retaliate	Normal	Physical	70	100	5	Normal
TM75	Swords Dance	Normal	Status	—	—	20	Self
TM78	Bulldoze	Ground	Physical	60	100	20	Adjacent
TM80	Rock Slide	Rock	Physical	75	90	10	Many Others
TM87	Swagger	Normal	Status	—	90	15	Normal
TM88	Sleep Talk	Normal	Status	—	—	10	Self
TM90	Substitute	Normal	Status	—	—	10	Self
TM94	Secret Power	Normal	Physical	70	100	20	Normal
TM98	Power-Up Punch	Fighting	Physical	40	100	20	Normal
TM100	Confide	Normal	Status	—	—	20	Normal
HM01	Cut	Normal	Physical	50	95	30	Normal
HM04	Strength	Normal	Physical	80	100	15	Normal
HM06	Rock Smash	Fighting	Physical	40	100	15	Normal

MOVES LEARNED IN EXCHANGE FOR BP

Name	Type	Kind	Pow.	Acc.	PP	Range
Covet	Normal	Physical	60	100	25	Normal
Seed Bomb	Grass	Physical	80	100	15	Normal
Gunk Shot	Poison	Physical	120	80	5	Normal
Thunder Punch	Electric	Physical	75	100	15	Normal
Fire Punch	Fire	Physical	75	100	15	Normal
Ice Punch	Ice	Physical	75	100	15	Normal
Last Resort	Normal	Physical	140	100	5	Normal
Superpower	Fighting	Physical	120	100	5	Normal
Hyper Voice	Normal	Special	90	100	10	Many Others
Snore	Normal	Special	50	100	15	Normal
Focus Punch	Fighting	Physical	150	100	20	Normal

MOVES TAUGHT BY PEOPLE

Name	Type	Kind	Pow.	Acc.	PP	Range

EGG MOVES

Name	Type	Kind	Pow.	Acc.	PP	Range
Crunch	Dark	Physical	80	100	15	Normal
Take Down	Normal	Physical	90	85	20	Normal
Seismic Toss	Fighting	Physical	—	100	20	Normal
Counter	Fighting	Physical	—	100	20	Varies
Metal Claw	Steel	Physical	50	95	35	Normal
Fake Tears	Dark	Status	—	100	20	Normal
Yawn	Normal	Status	—	—	10	Normal
Sleep Talk	Normal	Status	—	—	10	Self
Cross Chop	Fighting	Physical	100	80	5	Normal
Double-Edge	Normal	Physical	120	100	15	Normal
Close Combat	Fighting	Physical	120	100	5	Normal
Night Slash	Dark	Physical	70	100	15	Normal
Belly Drum	Normal	Status	—	—	10	Self
Chip Away	Normal	Physical	70	100	20	Normal
Play Rough	Fairy	Physical	90	90	10	Normal

National Pokédex **217** Hoenn Pokédex —

Ursaring

Hibernator Pokémon

Normal

HEIGHT: 5'11" WEIGHT: 277.3 lbs.

The male has a shorter fringe on its shoulders. The female has a longer fringe on its shoulders.

♂ ♀

Ω In the forests inhabited by Ursaring, it is said that there are many streams and towering trees where they gather food. This Pokémon walks through its forest gathering food every day.

α In the forests inhabited by Ursaring, it is said that there are many streams and towering trees where they gather food. This Pokémon walks through its forest gathering food every day.

ABILITIES
Guts
Quick Feet

HIDDEN ABILITY
Unnerve

EGG GROUPS
Field

STAT GROWTH RATES
HP
Attack
Defense
Sp. Atk
Sp. Def
Speed

ITEMS SOMETIMES HELD BY WILD POKÉMON
—

EVOLUTION

Teddiursa

Lv. 30

Ursaring

MAIN WAY TO REGISTER IN THE NATIONAL POKÉDEX

Appears in *Pokémon X* and *Pokémon Y*. Bring it to your game using Link Trade or the GTS.

Damage taken in normal battles

Type		Type	
Normal	×1	Flying	×1
Fire	×1	Psychic	×1
Water	×1	Bug	×1
Grass	×1	Rock	×1
Electric	×1	Ghost	×0
Ice	×1	Dragon	×1
Fighting	×2	Dark	×1
Poison	×1	Steel	×1
Ground	×1	Fairy	×1

Damage taken in Inverse battles

Type		Type	
Normal	×1	Flying	×1
Fire	×1	Psychic	×1
Water	×1	Bug	×1
Grass	×1	Rock	×1
Electric	×1	Ghost	×2
Ice	×1	Dragon	×1
Fighting	×0.5	Dark	×1
Poison	×1	Steel	×1
Ground	×1	Fairy	×1

Can be used in
Inverse Battle
Battle Institute
Battle Maison
Random Matchup (Free Battle)
Random Matchup (Others)

LEVEL-UP MOVES

Lv.	Name	Type	Kind	Pow.	Acc.	PP	Range
1	Hammer Arm	Fighting	Physical	100	90	10	Normal
1	Covet	Normal	Physical	60	100	25	Normal
1	Scratch	Normal	Physical	40	100	35	Normal
1	Leer	Normal	Status	—	100	30	Many Others
1	Lick	Ghost	Physical	30	100	30	Normal
1	Fake Tears	Dark	Status	—	100	20	Normal
8	Fury Swipes	Normal	Physical	18	80	15	Normal
15	Feint Attack	Dark	Physical	60	—	20	Normal
22	Sweet Scent	Normal	Status	—	100	20	Many Others
25	Play Nice	Normal	Status	—	—	20	Normal
29	Slash	Normal	Physical	70	100	20	Normal
38	Scary Face	Normal	Status	—	100	10	Normal
47	Rest	Psychic	Status	—	—	10	Self
49	Snore	Normal	Special	50	100	15	Normal
58	Thrash	Normal	Physical	120	100	10	1 Random
67	Hammer Arm	Fighting	Physical	100	90	10	Normal

TM & HM MOVES

No.	Name	Type	Kind	Pow.	Acc.	PP	Range
TM01	Hone Claws	Dark	Status	—	—	15	Self
TM05	Roar	Normal	Status	—	—	20	Normal
TM06	Toxic	Poison	Status	—	90	10	Normal
TM08	Bulk Up	Fighting	Status	—	—	20	Self
TM10	Hidden Power	Normal	Special	60	100	15	Normal
TM11	Sunny Day	Fire	Status	—	—	5	Both Sides
TM12	Taunt	Dark	Status	—	100	20	Normal
TM15	Hyper Beam	Normal	Special	150	90	5	Normal
TM17	Protect	Normal	Status	—	—	10	Self
TM18	Rain Dance	Water	Status	—	—	5	Both Sides
TM21	Frustration	Normal	Physical	—	100	20	Normal
TM23	Smack Down	Rock	Physical	50	100	15	Normal
TM26	Earthquake	Ground	Physical	100	100	10	Adjacent
TM27	Return	Normal	Physical	—	100	20	Normal
TM28	Dig	Ground	Physical	80	100	10	Normal
TM31	Brick Break	Fighting	Physical	75	100	15	Normal
TM32	Double Team	Normal	Status	—	—	15	Self
TM39	Rock Tomb	Rock	Physical	60	95	15	Normal
TM40	Aerial Ace	Flying	Physical	60	—	20	Normal
TM41	Torment	Dark	Status	—	100	15	Normal
TM42	Facade	Normal	Physical	70	100	20	Normal
TM44	Rest	Psychic	Status	—	—	10	Self
TM45	Attract	Normal	Status	—	100	15	Normal
TM46	Thief	Dark	Physical	60	100	25	Normal
TM48	Round	Normal	Special	60	100	15	Normal
TM52	Focus Blast	Fighting	Special	120	70	5	Normal
TM56	Fling	Dark	Physical	—	100	10	Normal
TM65	Shadow Claw	Ghost	Physical	70	100	15	Normal
TM66	Payback	Dark	Physical	50	100	10	Normal
TM67	Retaliate	Normal	Physical	70	100	5	Normal
TM68	Giga Impact	Normal	Physical	150	90	5	Normal
TM71	Stone Edge	Rock	Physical	100	80	5	Normal
TM75	Swords Dance	Normal	Status	—	—	20	Self
TM78	Bulldoze	Ground	Physical	60	100	20	Adjacent
TM80	Rock Slide	Rock	Physical	75	90	10	Many Others
TM87	Swagger	Normal	Status	—	90	15	Normal
TM88	Sleep Talk	Normal	Status	—	—	10	Self
TM90	Substitute	Normal	Status	—	—	10	Self
TM94	Secret Power	Normal	Physical	70	100	20	Normal
TM98	Power-Up Punch	Fighting	Physical	40	100	20	Normal
TM100	Confide	Normal	Status	—	—	20	Normal
HM01	Cut	Normal	Physical	50	95	30	Normal
HM04	Strength	Normal	Physical	80	100	15	Normal
HM06	Rock Smash	Fighting	Physical	40	100	15	Normal

MOVES LEARNED IN EXCHANGE FOR BP

Name	Type	Kind	Pow.	Acc.	PP	Range
Covet	Normal	Physical	60	100	25	Normal
Seed Bomb	Grass	Physical	80	100	15	Normal
Low Kick	Fighting	Physical	—	100	20	Normal
Gunk Shot	Poison	Physical	120	80	5	Normal
Uproar	Normal	Special	90	100	10	1 Random
Thunder Punch	Electric	Physical	75	100	15	Normal
Fire Punch	Fire	Physical	75	100	15	Normal
Ice Punch	Ice	Physical	75	100	15	Normal
Last Resort	Normal	Physical	140	100	5	Normal
Superpower	Fighting	Physical	120	100	5	Normal
Hyper Voice	Normal	Special	90	100	10	Many Others
Snore	Normal	Special	50	100	15	Normal
Focus Punch	Fighting	Physical	150	100	20	Normal

MOVES TAUGHT BY PEOPLE

Name	Type	Kind	Pow.	Acc.	PP	Range

National Pokédex **218** Hoenn Pokédex **108**

Slugma

Lava Pokémon

Fire

HEIGHT: 2'04" WEIGHT: 77.2 lbs.

Same form for ♂ / ♀

Ω Molten magma courses throughout Slugma's circulatory system. If this Pokémon is chilled, the magma cools and hardens. Its body turns brittle and chunks fall off, reducing its size.

α Slugma does not have any blood in its body. Instead, intensely hot magma circulates throughout this Pokémon's body, carrying essential nutrients and oxygen to its organs.

ABILITIES
Magma Armor
Flame Body

HIDDEN ABILITY
Weak Armor

EGG GROUPS
Amorphous

STAT GROWTH RATES
HP
Attack
Defense
Sp. Atk
Sp. Def
Speed

ITEMS SOMETIMES HELD BY WILD POKÉMON
—

EVOLUTION

Slugma

Lv. 38

Magcargo

MAIN WAY TO REGISTER IN THE NATIONAL POKÉDEX

Catch on the Fiery Path.

Damage taken in normal battles

Type		Type	
Normal	×1	Flying	×1
Fire	×0.5	Psychic	×1
Water	×2	Bug	×0.5
Grass	×0.5	Rock	×2
Electric	×1	Ghost	×1
Ice	×0.5	Dragon	×1
Fighting	×1	Dark	×1
Poison	×1	Steel	×0.5
Ground	×2	Fairy	×0.5

Damage taken in Inverse battles

Type		Type	
Normal	×1	Flying	×1
Fire	×2	Psychic	×1
Water	×0.5	Bug	×2
Grass	×2	Rock	×0.5
Electric	×1	Ghost	×1
Ice	×2	Dragon	×1
Fighting	×1	Dark	×1
Poison	×1	Steel	×2
Ground	×0.5	Fairy	×2

Can be used in
Inverse Battle
Battle Institute
Battle Maison
Random Matchup (Free Battle)
Random Matchup (Others)

LEVEL-UP MOVES

Lv.	Name	Type	Kind	Pow.	Acc.	PP	Range
1	Yawn	Normal	Status	—	—	10	Normal
1	Smog	Poison	Special	30	70	20	Normal
6	Ember	Fire	Special	40	100	25	Normal
8	Rock Throw	Rock	Physical	50	90	15	Normal
13	Harden	Normal	Status	—	—	30	Self
15	Incinerate	Fire	Special	60	100	15	Many Others
20	Clear Smog	Poison	Special	50	—	15	Normal
22	Ancient Power	Rock	Special	60	100	5	Normal
27	Flame Burst	Fire	Special	70	100	15	Normal
29	Rock Slide	Rock	Physical	75	90	10	Many Others
34	Lava Plume	Fire	Special	80	100	15	Adjacent
36	Amnesia	Psychic	Status	—	—	20	Self
41	Body Slam	Normal	Physical	85	100	15	Normal
43	Recover	Normal	Status	—	—	10	Self
48	Flamethrower	Fire	Special	90	100	15	Normal
50	Earth Power	Ground	Special	90	100	10	Normal

TM & HM MOVES

No.	Name	Type	Kind	Pow.	Acc.	PP	Range
TM06	Toxic	Poison	Status	—	90	10	Normal
TM10	Hidden Power	Normal	Special	60	100	15	Normal
TM11	Sunny Day	Fire	Status	—	—	5	Both Sides
TM16	Light Screen	Psychic	Status	—	—	30	Your Side
TM17	Protect	Normal	Status	—	—	10	Self
TM21	Frustration	Normal	Physical	—	100	20	Normal
TM27	Return	Normal	Physical	—	100	20	Normal
TM32	Double Team	Normal	Status	—	—	15	Self
TM33	Reflect	Psychic	Status	—	—	20	Your Side
TM35	Flamethrower	Fire	Special	90	100	15	Normal
TM38	Fire Blast	Fire	Special	110	85	5	Normal
TM39	Rock Tomb	Rock	Physical	60	95	15	Normal
TM42	Facade	Normal	Physical	70	100	20	Normal
TM43	Flame Charge	Fire	Physical	50	100	20	Normal
TM44	Rest	Psychic	Status	—	—	10	Self
TM45	Attract	Normal	Status	—	100	15	Normal
TM48	Round	Normal	Special	60	100	15	Normal
TM50	Overheat	Fire	Special	130	90	5	Normal
TM59	Incinerate	Fire	Special	60	100	15	Many Others
TM61	Will-O-Wisp	Fire	Status	—	85	15	Normal
TM80	Rock Slide	Rock	Physical	75	90	10	Many Others
TM83	Infestation	Bug	Special	20	100	20	Normal
TM87	Swagger	Normal	Status	—	90	15	Normal
TM88	Sleep Talk	Normal	Status	—	—	10	Self
TM90	Substitute	Normal	Status	—	—	10	Self
TM94	Secret Power	Normal	Physical	70	100	20	Normal
TM96	Nature Power	Normal	Status	—	—	20	Normal
TM100	Confide	Normal	Status	—	—	20	Normal
HM06	Rock Smash	Fighting	Physical	40	100	15	Normal

MOVES LEARNED IN EXCHANGE FOR BP

Name	Type	Kind	Pow.	Acc.	PP	Range
Earth Power	Ground	Special	90	100	10	Normal
Iron Defense	Steel	Status	—	—	15	Self
Snore	Normal	Special	50	100	15	Normal
Heat Wave	Fire	Special	95	90	10	Many Others
Pain Split	Normal	Status	—	—	20	Normal
After You	Normal	Status	—	—	15	Normal

MOVES TAUGHT BY PEOPLE

Name	Type	Kind	Pow.	Acc.	PP	Range

EGG MOVES

Name	Type	Kind	Pow.	Acc.	PP	Range
Acid Armor	Poison	Status	—	—	20	Self
Heat Wave	Fire	Special	95	90	10	Many Others
Curse	Ghost	Status	—	—	10	Varies
Smokescreen	Normal	Status	—	100	20	Normal
Memento	Dark	Status	—	100	10	Normal
Stockpile	Normal	Status	—	—	20	Self
Spit Up	Normal	Special	—	100	10	Normal
Swallow	Normal	Status	—	—	10	Self
Rollout	Rock	Physical	30	90	20	Normal
Inferno	Fire	Special	100	50	5	Normal
Earth Power	Ground	Special	90	100	10	Normal
Guard Swap	Psychic	Status	—	—	10	Normal

National Pokédex **219** Hoenn Pokédex **109**

Magcargo

Lava Pokémon

Fire Rock

HEIGHT: 2'07" WEIGHT: 121.3 lbs.

Same form for ♂ / ♀

Ω Magcargo's shell is actually its skin that hardened as a result of cooling. Its shell is very brittle and fragile—just touching it causes it to crumble apart. This Pokémon returns to its original size by dipping itself in magma.

α Magcargo's body temperature is approximately 18,000 degrees Fahrenheit. Water is vaporized on contact. If this Pokémon is caught in the rain, the raindrops instantly turn into steam, cloaking the area in a thick fog.

ABILITIES
Magma Armor
Flame Body

HIDDEN ABILITY
Weak Armor

EGG GROUPS
Amorphous

STAT GROWTH RATES
HP
Attack
Defense
Sp. Atk
Sp. Def
Speed

ITEMS SOMETIMES HELD BY WILD POKÉMON
—

EVOLUTION

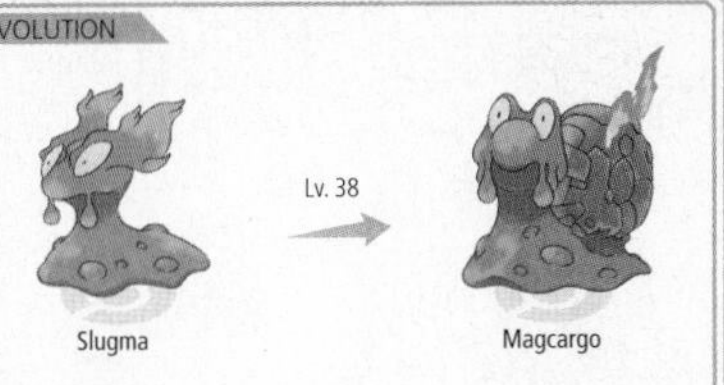

MAIN WAY TO REGISTER IN THE NATIONAL POKÉDEX

Level up Slugma to Lv. 38.

Damage taken in normal battles

Type	×	Type	×
Normal	×0.5	Flying	×0.5
Fire	×0.25	Psychic	×1
Water	×4	Bug	×0.5
Grass	×1	Rock	×2
Electric	×1	Ghost	×1
Ice	×0.5	Dragon	×1
Fighting	×2	Dark	×1
Poison	×0.5	Steel	×1
Ground	×4	Fairy	×0.5

Damage taken in Inverse battles

Type	×	Type	×
Normal	×2	Flying	×2
Fire	×4	Psychic	×1
Water	×0.25	Bug	×2
Grass	×1	Rock	×0.5
Electric	×1	Ghost	×1
Ice	×2	Dragon	×1
Fighting	×0.5	Dark	×1
Poison	×2	Steel	×1
Ground	×0.25	Fairy	×2

Can be used in
- Inverse Battle
- Battle Institute
- Battle Maison
- Random Matchup (Free Battle)
- Random Matchup (Others)

LEVEL-UP MOVES

Lv.	Name	Type	Kind	Pow.	Acc.	PP	Range
1	Earth Power	Ground	Special	90	100	10	Normal
1	Yawn	Normal	Status	—	—	10	Normal
1	Smog	Poison	Special	30	70	20	Normal
1	Ember	Fire	Special	40	100	25	Normal
1	Rock Throw	Rock	Physical	50	90	15	Normal
6	Ember	Fire	Special	40	100	25	Normal
8	Rock Throw	Rock	Physical	50	90	15	Normal
13	Harden	Normal	Status	—	—	30	Self
15	Incinerate	Fire	Special	60	100	15	Many Others
20	Clear Smog	Poison	Special	50	—	15	Normal
22	Ancient Power	Rock	Special	60	100	5	Normal
27	Flame Burst	Fire	Special	70	100	15	Normal
29	Rock Slide	Rock	Physical	75	90	10	Many Others
34	Lava Plume	Fire	Special	80	100	15	Adjacent
36	Amnesia	Psychic	Status	—	—	20	Self
38	Shell Smash	Normal	Status	—	—	15	Self
43	Body Slam	Normal	Physical	85	100	15	Normal
47	Recover	Normal	Status	—	—	10	Self
54	Flamethrower	Fire	Special	90	100	15	Normal
58	Earth Power	Ground	Special	90	100	10	Normal

TM & HM MOVES

No.	Name	Type	Kind	Pow.	Acc.	PP	Range
TM06	Toxic	Poison	Status	—	90	10	Normal
TM10	Hidden Power	Normal	Special	60	100	15	Normal
TM11	Sunny Day	Fire	Status	—	—	5	Both Sides
TM15	Hyper Beam	Normal	Special	150	90	5	Normal
TM16	Light Screen	Psychic	Status	—	—	30	Your Side
TM17	Protect	Normal	Status	—	—	10	Self
TM21	Frustration	Normal	Physical	—	100	20	Normal
TM22	Solar Beam	Grass	Special	120	100	10	Normal
TM23	Smack Down	Rock	Physical	50	100	15	Normal
TM26	Earthquake	Ground	Physical	100	100	10	Adjacent
TM27	Return	Normal	Physical	—	100	20	Normal
TM32	Double Team	Normal	Status	—	—	15	Self
TM33	Reflect	Psychic	Status	—	—	20	Your Side
TM35	Flamethrower	Fire	Special	90	100	15	Normal
TM37	Sandstorm	Rock	Status	—	—	10	Both Sides
TM38	Fire Blast	Fire	Special	110	85	5	Normal
TM39	Rock Tomb	Rock	Physical	60	95	15	Normal
TM42	Facade	Normal	Physical	70	100	20	Normal
TM43	Flame Charge	Fire	Physical	50	100	20	Normal
TM44	Rest	Psychic	Status	—	—	10	Self
TM45	Attract	Normal	Status	—	100	15	Normal
TM48	Round	Normal	Special	60	100	15	Normal
TM50	Overheat	Fire	Special	130	90	5	Normal
TM59	Incinerate	Fire	Special	60	100	15	Many Others
TM61	Will-O-Wisp	Fire	Status	—	85	15	Normal
TM64	Explosion	Normal	Physical	250	100	5	Adjacent
TM68	Giga Impact	Normal	Physical	150	90	5	Normal
TM69	Rock Polish	Rock	Status	—	—	20	Self
TM71	Stone Edge	Rock	Physical	100	80	5	Normal
TM74	Gyro Ball	Steel	Physical	—	100	5	Normal
TM78	Bulldoze	Ground	Physical	60	100	20	Adjacent
TM80	Rock Slide	Rock	Physical	75	90	10	Many Others
TM83	Infestation	Bug	Special	20	100	20	Normal
TM87	Swagger	Normal	Status	—	90	15	Normal
TM88	Sleep Talk	Normal	Status	—	—	10	Self
TM90	Substitute	Normal	Status	—	—	10	Self
TM94	Secret Power	Normal	Physical	70	100	20	Normal
TM96	Nature Power	Normal	Status	—	—	20	Normal
TM100	Confide	Normal	Status	—	—	20	Normal
HM04	Strength	Normal	Physical	80	100	15	Normal
HM06	Rock Smash	Fighting	Physical	40	100	15	Normal

MOVES LEARNED IN EXCHANGE FOR BP

Name	Type	Kind	Pow.	Acc.	PP	Range
Earth Power	Ground	Special	90	100	10	Normal
Iron Defense	Steel	Status	—	—	15	Self
Snore	Normal	Special	50	100	15	Normal
Heat Wave	Fire	Special	95	90	10	Many Others
Pain Split	Normal	Status	—	—	20	Normal
After You	Normal	Status	—	—	15	Normal
Stealth Rock	Rock	Status	—	—	20	Other Side

MOVES TAUGHT BY PEOPLE

Name	Type	Kind	Pow.	Acc.	PP	Range

National Pokédex **220** Hoenn Pokédex **—**

Swinub

Pig Pokémon

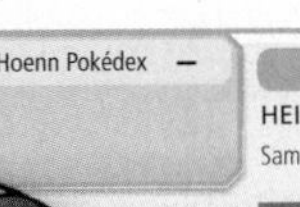

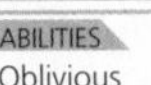

Ice Ground

HEIGHT: 1'04" WEIGHT: 14.3 lbs.

Same form for ♂ / ♀

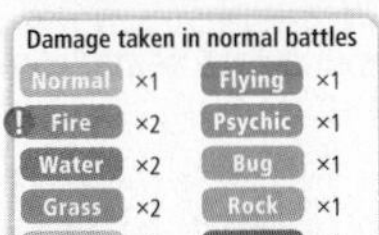

Ω Swinub roots for food by rubbing its snout against the ground. Its favorite food is a mushroom that grows under the cover of dead grass. This Pokémon occasionally roots out hot springs.

α Swinub roots for food by rubbing its snout against the ground. Its favorite food is a mushroom that grows under the cover of dead grass. This Pokémon occasionally roots out hot springs.

ABILITIES
Oblivious
Snow Cloak

HIDDEN ABILITY
Thick Fat

EGG GROUPS
Field

STAT GROWTH RATES
HP
Attack
Defense
Sp. Atk
Sp. Def
Speed

ITEMS SOMETIMES HELD BY WILD POKÉMON
—

EVOLUTION

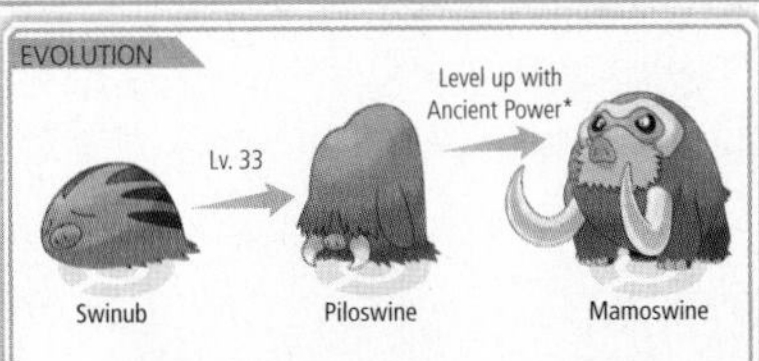

*If you wish to teach Piloswine the move Ancient Power, give the Move Maniac in Fallarbor Town a Heart Scale.

MAIN WAY TO REGISTER IN THE NATIONAL POKÉDEX

Leave a Piloswine obtained via Link Trade or the GTS at a Pokémon Day Care, then hatch the Pokémon Egg that is found.

Damage taken in normal battles

Type	×	Type	×
Normal	×1	Flying	×1
! Fire	×2	Psychic	×1
Water	×2	Bug	×1
Grass	×2	Rock	×1
Electric	×0	Ghost	×1
! Ice	×1	Dragon	×1
Fighting	×2	Dark	×1
Poison	×0.5	Steel	×2
Ground	×1	Fairy	×1

Damage taken in Inverse battles

Type	×	Type	×
Normal	×1	Flying	×1
! Fire	×0.5	Psychic	×1
Water	×0.5	Bug	×1
Grass	×0.5	Rock	×1
Electric	×2	Ghost	×1
! Ice	×1	Dragon	×1
Fighting	×0.5	Dark	×1
Poison	×2	Steel	×0.5
Ground	×1	Fairy	×1

Can be used in
- Inverse Battle
- Battle Institute
- Battle Maison
- Random Matchup (Free Battle)
- Random Matchup (Others)

LEVEL-UP MOVES

Lv.	Name	Type	Kind	Pow.	Acc.	PP	Range
1	Tackle	Normal	Physical	50	100	35	Normal
1	Odor Sleuth	Normal	Status	—	—	40	Normal
5	Mud Sport	Ground	Status	—	—	15	Both Sides
8	Powder Snow	Ice	Special	40	100	25	Many Others
11	Mud-Slap	Ground	Special	20	100	10	Normal
14	Endure	Normal	Status	—	—	10	Self
18	Mud Bomb	Ground	Special	65	85	10	Normal
21	Icy Wind	Ice	Special	55	95	15	Many Others
24	Ice Shard	Ice	Physical	40	100	30	Normal
28	Take Down	Normal	Physical	90	85	20	Normal
35	Mist	Ice	Status	—	—	30	Your Side
37	Earthquake	Ground	Physical	100	100	10	Adjacent
40	Flail	Normal	Physical	—	100	15	Normal
44	Blizzard	Ice	Special	110	70	5	Many Others
48	Amnesia	Psychic	Status	—	—	20	Self

TM & HM MOVES

No.	Name	Type	Kind	Pow.	Acc.	PP	Range
TM05	Roar	Normal	Status	—	—	20	Normal
TM06	Toxic	Poison	Status	—	90	10	Normal
TM07	Hail	Ice	Status	—	—	10	Both Sides
TM10	Hidden Power	Normal	Special	60	100	15	Normal
TM13	Ice Beam	Ice	Special	90	100	10	Normal
TM14	Blizzard	Ice	Special	110	70	5	Many Others
TM16	Light Screen	Psychic	Status	—	—	30	Your Side
TM17	Protect	Normal	Status	—	—	10	Self
TM18	Rain Dance	Water	Status	—	—	5	Both Sides
TM21	Frustration	Normal	Physical	—	100	20	Normal
TM26	Earthquake	Ground	Physical	100	100	10	Adjacent
TM27	Return	Normal	Physical	—	100	20	Normal
TM28	Dig	Ground	Physical	80	100	10	Normal
TM32	Double Team	Normal	Status	—	—	15	Self
TM33	Reflect	Psychic	Status	—	—	20	Your Side
TM37	Sandstorm	Rock	Status	—	—	10	Both Sides
TM39	Rock Tomb	Rock	Physical	60	95	15	Normal
TM42	Facade	Normal	Physical	70	100	20	Normal
TM44	Rest	Psychic	Status	—	—	10	Self
TM45	Attract	Normal	Status	—	100	15	Normal
TM48	Round	Normal	Special	60	100	15	Normal
TM78	Bulldoze	Ground	Physical	60	100	20	Adjacent
TM80	Rock Slide	Rock	Physical	75	90	10	Many Others
TM87	Swagger	Normal	Status	—	90	15	Normal
TM88	Sleep Talk	Normal	Status	—	—	10	Self
TM90	Substitute	Normal	Status	—	—	10	Self
TM94	Secret Power	Normal	Physical	70	100	20	Normal
TM100	Confide	Normal	Status	—	—	20	Normal
HM04	Strength	Normal	Physical	80	100	15	Normal
HM06	Rock Smash	Fighting	Physical	40	100	15	Normal

MOVES LEARNED IN EXCHANGE FOR BP

Name	Type	Kind	Pow.	Acc.	PP	Range
Earth Power	Ground	Special	90	100	10	Normal
Superpower	Fighting	Physical	120	100	5	Normal
Icy Wind	Ice	Special	55	95	15	Many Others
Snore	Normal	Special	50	100	15	Normal
Endeavor	Normal	Physical	—	100	5	Normal
Stealth Rock	Rock	Status	—	—	20	Other Side

MOVES TAUGHT BY PEOPLE

Name	Type	Kind	Pow.	Acc.	PP	Range

EGG MOVES

Name	Type	Kind	Pow.	Acc.	PP	Range
Take Down	Normal	Physical	90	85	20	Normal
Bite	Dark	Physical	60	100	25	Normal
Body Slam	Normal	Physical	85	100	15	Normal
Ancient Power	Rock	Special	60	100	5	Normal
Mud Shot	Ground	Special	55	95	15	Normal
Icicle Spear	Ice	Physical	25	100	30	Normal
Double-Edge	Normal	Physical	120	100	15	Normal
Fissure	Ground	Physical	—	30	5	Normal
Curse	Ghost	Status	—	—	10	Varies
Avalanche	Ice	Physical	60	100	10	Normal
Stealth Rock	Rock	Status	—	—	20	Other Side
Icicle Crash	Ice	Physical	85	90	10	Normal
Freeze-Dry	Ice	Special	70	100	20	Normal

National Pokédex **221** Hoenn Pokédex **—**

Piloswine

Swine Pokémon

Ice / Ground

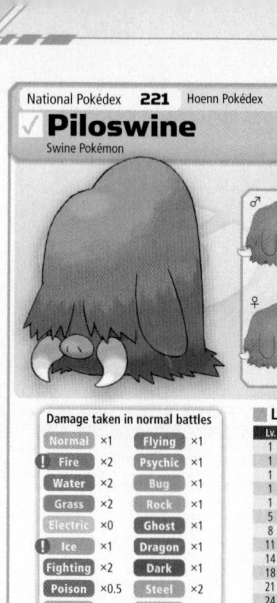

HEIGHT: 3'07" WEIGHT: 123 lbs.

The male has longer tusks. The female has shorter tusks.

♂ ♀

Ω: Piloswine is covered by a thick coat of long hair that enables it to endure the freezing cold. This Pokémon uses its tusks to dig up food that has been buried under ice.

α: Piloswine is covered by a thick coat of long hair that enables it to endure the freezing cold. This Pokémon uses its tusks to dig up food that has been buried under ice.

ABILITIES
Oblivious
Snow Cloak

HIDDEN ABILITY
Thick Fat

EGG GROUPS
Field

STAT GROWTH RATES
HP (4 bars)
Attack (5 bars)
Defense (4 bars)
Sp. Atk (3 bars)
Sp. Def (3 bars)
Speed (3 bars)

ITEMS SOMETIMES HELD BY WILD POKÉMON
—

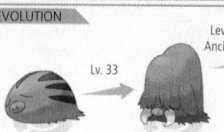

EVOLUTION
Swinub → Lv. 33 → Piloswine → Level up with Ancient Power* → Mamoswine

*If you wish to teach Piloswine the move Ancient Power, give the Move Maniac in Fallarbor Town a Heart Scale.

MAIN WAY TO REGISTER IN THE NATIONAL POKÉDEX

Appears in *Pokémon X* and *Pokémon Y*. Bring it to your game using Link Trade or the GTS.

Damage taken in normal battles

Type		Type	
Normal	×1	Flying	×1
Fire	×2	Psychic	×1
Water	×2	Bug	×1
Grass	×2	Rock	×1
Electric	×0	Ghost	×1
Ice	×1	Dragon	×1
Fighting	×2	Dark	×1
Poison	×0.5	Steel	×2
Ground	×1	Fairy	×1

Damage taken in Inverse battles

Type		Type	
Normal	×1	Flying	×1
Fire	×0.5	Psychic	×1
Water	×0.5	Bug	×1
Grass	×0.5	Rock	×1
Electric	×2	Ghost	×1
Ice	×1	Dragon	×1
Fighting	×0.5	Dark	×1
Poison	×2	Steel	×0.5
Ground	×1	Fairy	×1

Can be used in
Inverse Battle
Battle Institute
Battle Maison
Random Matchup (Free Battle)
Random Matchup (Others)

LEVEL-UP MOVES

Lv.	Name	Type	Kind	Pow.	Acc.	PP	Range
1	Ancient Power	Rock	Special	60	100	5	Normal
1	Peck	Flying	Physical	35	100	35	Normal
1	Odor Sleuth	Normal	Status	—	—	40	Normal
1	Mud Sport	Ground	Status	—	—	15	Both Sides
1	Powder Snow	Ice	Special	40	100	25	Many Others
5	Mud Sport	Ground	Status	—	—	15	Both Sides
8	Powder Snow	Ice	Special	40	100	25	Many Others
11	Mud-Slap	Ground	Special	20	100	10	Normal
14	Endure	Normal	Status	—	—	10	Self
18	Mud Bomb	Ground	Special	65	85	10	Normal
21	Icy Wind	Ice	Special	55	95	15	Many Others
24	Ice Fang	Ice	Physical	65	95	15	Normal
28	Take Down	Normal	Physical	90	85	20	Normal
33	Fury Attack	Normal	Physical	15	85	20	Normal
37	Mist	Ice	Status	—	—	30	Your Side
41	Thrash	Normal	Physical	120	100	10	1 Random
46	Earthquake	Ground	Physical	100	100	10	Adjacent
52	Blizzard	Ice	Special	110	70	5	Many Others
58	Amnesia	Psychic	Status	—	—	20	Self

TM & HM MOVES

No.	Name	Type	Kind	Pow.	Acc.	PP	Range
TM05	Roar	Normal	Status	—	—	20	Normal
TM06	Toxic	Poison	Status	—	90	10	Normal
TM07	Hail	Ice	Status	—	—	10	Both Sides
TM10	Hidden Power	Normal	Special	60	100	15	Normal
TM13	Ice Beam	Ice	Special	90	100	10	Normal
TM14	Blizzard	Ice	Special	110	70	5	Many Others
TM15	Hyper Beam	Normal	Special	150	90	5	Normal
TM16	Light Screen	Psychic	Status	—	—	30	Your Side
TM17	Protect	Normal	Status	—	—	10	Self
TM18	Rain Dance	Water	Status	—	—	5	Both Sides
TM21	Frustration	Normal	Physical	—	100	20	Normal
TM26	Earthquake	Ground	Physical	100	100	10	Adjacent
TM27	Return	Normal	Physical	—	100	20	Normal
TM28	Dig	Ground	Physical	80	100	10	Normal
TM32	Double Team	Normal	Status	—	—	15	Self
TM33	Reflect	Psychic	Status	—	—	20	Your Side
TM37	Sandstorm	Rock	Status	—	—	10	Both Sides
TM39	Rock Tomb	Rock	Physical	60	95	15	Normal
TM42	Facade	Normal	Physical	70	100	20	Normal
TM44	Rest	Psychic	Status	—	—	10	Self
TM45	Attract	Normal	Status	—	100	15	Normal
TM48	Round	Normal	Special	60	100	15	Normal
TM68	Giga Impact	Normal	Physical	150	90	5	Normal
TM71	Stone Edge	Rock	Physical	100	80	5	Normal
TM78	Bulldoze	Ground	Physical	60	100	20	Adjacent
TM80	Rock Slide	Rock	Physical	75	90	10	Many Others
TM87	Swagger	Normal	Status	—	90	15	Normal
TM88	Sleep Talk	Normal	Status	—	—	10	Self
TM90	Substitute	Normal	Status	—	—	10	Self
TM94	Secret Power	Normal	Physical	70	100	20	Normal
TM100	Confide	Normal	Status	—	—	20	Normal
HM04	Strength	Normal	Physical	80	100	15	Normal
HM06	Rock Smash	Fighting	Physical	40	100	15	Normal

MOVES LEARNED IN EXCHANGE FOR BP

Name	Type	Kind	Pow.	Acc.	PP	Range
Earth Power	Ground	Special	90	100	10	Normal
Superpower	Fighting	Physical	120	100	5	Normal
Icy Wind	Ice	Special	55	95	15	Many Others
Snore	Normal	Special	50	100	15	Normal
Endeavor	Normal	Physical	—	100	5	Normal
Stealth Rock	Rock	Status	—	—	20	Other Side

MOVES TAUGHT BY PEOPLE

Name	Type	Kind	Pow.	Acc.	PP	Range

National Pokédex **222** Hoenn Pokédex **189**

Corsola

Coral Pokémon

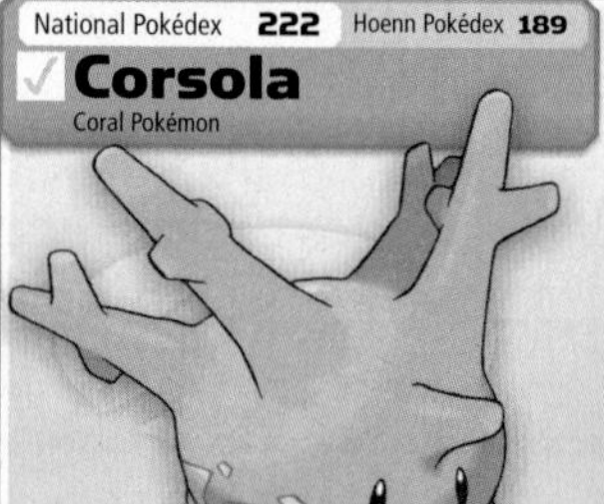

Water / Rock

HEIGHT: 2'00" WEIGHT: 11 lbs.

Same form for ♂ / ♀

Ω: Corsola's branches glitter very beautifully in seven colors when they catch sunlight. If any branch breaks off, this Pokémon grows it back in just one night.

α: Clusters of Corsola congregate in warm seas where they serve as ideal hiding places for smaller Pokémon. When the water temperature falls, this Pokémon migrates to the southern seas.

ABILITIES
Hustle
Natural Cure

HIDDEN ABILITY
Regenerator

EGG GROUPS
Water 1 / Water 3

STAT GROWTH RATES
HP (2 bars)
Attack (3 bars)
Defense (4 bars)
Sp. Atk (3 bars)
Sp. Def (4 bars)
Speed (2 bars)

ITEMS SOMETIMES HELD BY WILD POKÉMON
Luminous Moss

EVOLUTION
Does not evolve

MAIN WAY TO REGISTER IN THE NATIONAL POKÉDEX

Catch at the bottom of the sea beneath Route 128.

Damage taken in normal battles

Type		Type	
Normal	×0.5	Flying	×0.5
Fire	×0.25	Psychic	×1
Water	×1	Bug	×1
Grass	×4	Rock	×1
Electric	×2	Ghost	×1
Ice	×0.5	Dragon	×1
Fighting	×2	Dark	×1
Poison	×0.5	Steel	×1
Ground	×2	Fairy	×1

Damage taken in Inverse battles

Type		Type	
Normal	×2	Flying	×2
Fire	×4	Psychic	×1
Water	×1	Bug	×1
Grass	×0.25	Rock	×1
Electric	×0.5	Ghost	×1
Ice	×2	Dragon	×1
Fighting	×0.5	Dark	×1
Poison	×2	Steel	×1
Ground	×0.5	Fairy	×1

Can be used in
Inverse Battle
Battle Institute
Battle Maison
Random Matchup (Free Battle)
Random Matchup (Others)

LEVEL-UP MOVES

Lv.	Name	Type	Kind	Pow.	Acc.	PP	Range
1	Tackle	Normal	Physical	50	100	35	Normal
1	Harden	Normal	Status	—	—	30	Self
4	Bubble	Water	Special	40	100	30	Many Others
8	Recover	Normal	Status	—	—	10	Self
10	Bubble Beam	Water	Special	65	100	20	Normal
13	Refresh	Normal	Status	—	—	20	Self
17	Ancient Power	Rock	Special	60	100	5	Normal
20	Spike Cannon	Normal	Physical	20	100	15	Normal
23	Lucky Chant	Normal	Status	—	—	30	Your Side
27	Brine	Water	Special	65	100	10	Normal
29	Iron Defense	Steel	Status	—	—	15	Self
31	Rock Blast	Rock	Physical	25	90	10	Normal
35	Endure	Normal	Status	—	—	10	Self
38	Aqua Ring	Water	Status	—	—	20	Self
41	Power Gem	Rock	Special	80	100	20	Normal
45	Mirror Coat	Psychic	Special	—	100	20	Varies
47	Earth Power	Ground	Special	90	100	10	Normal
50	Flail	Normal	Physical	—	100	15	Normal

TM & HM MOVES

No.	Name	Type	Kind	Pow.	Acc.	PP	Range
TM04	Calm Mind	Psychic	Status	—	—	20	Self
TM06	Toxic	Poison	Status	—	90	10	Normal
TM07	Hail	Ice	Status	—	—	10	Both Sides
TM10	Hidden Power	Normal	Special	60	100	15	Normal
TM11	Sunny Day	Fire	Status	—	—	5	Both Sides
TM13	Ice Beam	Ice	Special	90	100	10	Normal
TM14	Blizzard	Ice	Special	110	70	5	Many Others
TM16	Light Screen	Psychic	Status	—	—	30	Your Side
TM17	Protect	Normal	Status	—	—	10	Self
TM18	Rain Dance	Water	Status	—	—	5	Both Sides
TM20	Safeguard	Normal	Status	—	—	25	Your Side
TM21	Frustration	Normal	Physical	—	100	20	Normal
TM26	Earthquake	Ground	Physical	100	100	10	Adjacent
TM27	Return	Normal	Physical	—	100	20	Normal
TM28	Dig	Ground	Physical	80	100	10	Normal
TM29	Psychic	Psychic	Special	90	100	10	Normal
TM30	Shadow Ball	Ghost	Special	80	100	15	Normal
TM32	Double Team	Normal	Status	—	—	15	Self
TM33	Reflect	Psychic	Status	—	—	20	Your Side
TM37	Sandstorm	Rock	Status	—	—	10	Both Sides
TM39	Rock Tomb	Rock	Physical	60	95	15	Normal
TM42	Facade	Normal	Physical	70	100	20	Normal
TM44	Rest	Psychic	Status	—	—	10	Self
TM45	Attract	Normal	Status	—	100	15	Normal
TM48	Round	Normal	Special	60	100	15	Normal
TM55	Scald	Water	Special	80	100	15	Normal
TM64	Explosion	Normal	Physical	250	100	5	Adjacent
TM69	Rock Polish	Rock	Status	—	—	20	Self
TM71	Stone Edge	Rock	Physical	100	80	5	Normal
TM78	Bulldoze	Ground	Physical	60	100	20	Adjacent
TM80	Rock Slide	Rock	Physical	75	90	10	Many Others
TM87	Swagger	Normal	Status	—	90	15	Normal
TM88	Sleep Talk	Normal	Status	—	—	10	Self
TM90	Substitute	Normal	Status	—	—	10	Self
TM94	Secret Power	Normal	Physical	70	100	20	Normal
TM96	Nature Power	Normal	Status	—	—	20	Normal
TM100	Confide	Normal	Status	—	—	20	Normal
HM03	Surf	Water	Special	90	100	15	Adjacent
HM04	Strength	Normal	Physical	80	100	15	Normal
HM06	Rock Smash	Fighting	Physical	40	100	15	Normal

MOVES LEARNED IN EXCHANGE FOR BP

Name	Type	Kind	Pow.	Acc.	PP	Range
Magic Coat	Psychic	Status	—	—	15	Self
Earth Power	Ground	Special	90	100	10	Normal
Iron Defense	Steel	Status	—	—	15	Self
Icy Wind	Ice	Special	55	95	15	Many Others
Snore	Normal	Special	50	100	15	Normal
Water Pulse	Water	Special	60	100	20	Normal
Endeavor	Normal	Physical	—	100	5	Normal
Stealth Rock	Rock	Status	—	—	20	Other Side

MOVES TAUGHT BY PEOPLE

Name	Type	Kind	Pow.	Acc.	PP	Range

EGG MOVES

Name	Type	Kind	Pow.	Acc.	PP	Range
Screech	Normal	Status	—	85	40	Normal
Mist	Ice	Status	—	—	30	Your Side
Amnesia	Psychic	Status	—	—	20	Self
Barrier	Psychic	Status	—	—	20	Self
Ingrain	Grass	Status	—	—	20	Self
Confuse Ray	Ghost	Status	—	100	10	Normal
Icicle Spear	Ice	Physical	25	100	30	Normal
Nature Power	Normal	Status	—	—	20	Normal
Aqua Ring	Water	Status	—	—	20	Self
Curse	Ghost	Status	—	—	10	Varies
Bide	Normal	Physical	—	—	10	Self
Water Pulse	Water	Special	60	100	20	Normal
Head Smash	Rock	Physical	150	80	5	Normal
Camouflage	Normal	Status	—	—	20	Self

National Pokédex **223** Hoenn Pokédex —

Remoraid

Jet Pokémon

Water

HEIGHT: 2'00" WEIGHT: 26.5 lbs.

Same form for ♂ / ♀

Ω Remoraid sucks in water, then expels it at high velocity using its abdominal muscles to shoot down flying prey. When evolution draws near, this Pokémon travels downstream from rivers.

α Remoraid sucks in water, then expels it at high velocity using its abdominal muscles to shoot down flying prey. When evolution draws near, this Pokémon travels downstream from rivers.

ABILITIES
Hustle
Sniper

HIDDEN ABILITY
Moody

EGG GROUPS
Water 1 | Water 2

STAT GROWTH RATES

HP	■■
Attack	■■■
Defense	■■
Sp. Atk	■■■
Sp. Def	■■
Speed	■■■■

ITEMS SOMETIMES HELD BY WILD POKÉMON
—

EVOLUTION

Remoraid → Lv. 25 → Octillery

MAIN WAY TO REGISTER IN THE NATIONAL POKÉDEX

Catch using a Super Rod in the Battle Resort.

Damage taken in normal battles

Type	×	Type	×
Normal	×1	Flying	×1
Fire	×0.5	Psychic	×1
Water	×0.5	Bug	×1
Grass	×2	Rock	×1
Electric	×2	Ghost	×1
Ice	×0.5	Dragon	×1
Fighting	×1	Dark	×1
Poison	×1	Steel	×0.5
Ground	×1	Fairy	×1

Damage taken in Inverse battles

Type	×	Type	×
Normal	×1	Flying	×1
Fire	×2	Psychic	×1
Water	×2	Bug	×1
Grass	×0.5	Rock	×1
Electric	×0.5	Ghost	×1
Ice	×2	Dragon	×1
Fighting	×1	Dark	×1
Poison	×1	Steel	×2
Ground	×1	Fairy	×1

Can be used in
Inverse Battle
Battle Institute
Battle Maison
Random Matchup (Free Battle)
Random Matchup (Others)

LEVEL-UP MOVES

Lv.	Name	Type	Kind	Pow.	Acc.	PP	Range
1	Water Gun	Water	Special	40	100	25	Normal
6	Lock-On	Normal	Status	—	—	5	Normal
10	Psybeam	Psychic	Special	65	100	20	Normal
14	Aurora Beam	Ice	Special	65	100	20	Normal
18	Bubble Beam	Water	Special	65	100	20	Normal
22	Focus Energy	Normal	Status	—	—	30	Self
26	Water Pulse	Water	Special	60	100	20	Normal
30	Signal Beam	Bug	Special	75	100	15	Normal
34	Ice Beam	Ice	Special	90	100	10	Normal
38	Bullet Seed	Grass	Physical	25	100	30	Normal
42	Hydro Pump	Water	Special	110	80	5	Normal
46	Hyper Beam	Normal	Special	150	90	5	Normal
50	Soak	Water	Status	—	100	20	Normal

TM & HM MOVES

No.	Name	Type	Kind	Pow.	Acc.	PP	Range
TM06	Toxic	Poison	Status	—	90	10	Normal
TM10	Hidden Power	Normal	Special	60	100	15	Normal
TM11	Sunny Day	Fire	Status	—	—	5	Both Sides
TM13	Ice Beam	Ice	Special	90	100	10	Normal
TM14	Blizzard	Ice	Special	110	70	5	Many Others
TM15	Hyper Beam	Normal	Special	150	90	5	Normal
TM17	Protect	Normal	Status	—	—	10	Self
TM18	Rain Dance	Water	Status	—	—	5	Both Sides
TM21	Frustration	Normal	Physical	—	100	20	Normal
TM23	Smack Down	Rock	Physical	50	100	15	Normal
TM27	Return	Normal	Physical	—	100	20	Normal
TM29	Psychic	Psychic	Special	90	100	10	Normal
TM32	Double Team	Normal	Status	—	—	15	Self
TM35	Flamethrower	Fire	Special	90	100	15	Normal
TM38	Fire Blast	Fire	Special	110	85	5	Normal
TM42	Facade	Normal	Physical	70	100	20	Normal
TM44	Rest	Psychic	Status	—	—	10	Self
TM45	Attract	Normal	Status	—	100	15	Normal
TM46	Thief	Dark	Physical	60	100	25	Normal
TM48	Round	Normal	Special	60	100	15	Normal
TM55	Scald	Water	Special	80	100	15	Normal
TM57	Charge Beam	Electric	Special	50	90	10	Normal
TM59	Incinerate	Fire	Special	60	100	15	Many Others
TM73	Thunder Wave	Electric	Status	—	100	20	Normal
TM87	Swagger	Normal	Status	—	90	15	Normal
TM88	Sleep Talk	Normal	Status	—	—	10	Self
TM90	Substitute	Normal	Status	—	—	10	Self
TM94	Secret Power	Normal	Physical	70	100	20	Normal
TM100	Confide	Normal	Status	—	—	20	Normal
HM03	Surf	Water	Special	90	100	15	Adjacent
HM05	Waterfall	Water	Physical	80	100	15	Normal
HM07	Dive	Water	Physical	80	100	10	Normal

MOVES LEARNED IN EXCHANGE FOR BP

Name	Type	Kind	Pow.	Acc.	PP	Range
Signal Beam	Bug	Special	75	100	15	Normal
Seed Bomb	Grass	Physical	80	100	15	Normal
Bounce	Flying	Physical	85	85	5	Normal
Gunk Shot	Poison	Physical	120	80	5	Normal
Icy Wind	Ice	Special	55	95	15	Many Others
Snore	Normal	Special	50	100	15	Normal
Water Pulse	Water	Special	60	100	20	Normal

MOVES TAUGHT BY PEOPLE

Name	Type	Kind	Pow.	Acc.	PP	Range

EGG MOVES

Name	Type	Kind	Pow.	Acc.	PP	Range
Aurora Beam	Ice	Special	65	100	20	Normal
Octazooka	Water	Special	65	85	10	Normal
Supersonic	Normal	Status	—	55	20	Normal
Haze	Ice	Status	—	—	30	Both Sides
Screech	Normal	Status	—	85	40	Normal
Rock Blast	Rock	Physical	25	90	10	Normal
Snore	Normal	Special	50	100	15	Normal
Flail	Normal	Physical	—	100	15	Normal
Water Spout	Water	Special	150	100	5	Many Others
Mud Shot	Ground	Special	55	95	15	Normal
Swift	Normal	Special	60	—	20	Many Others
Acid Spray	Poison	Special	40	100	20	Normal
Water Pulse	Water	Special	60	100	20	Normal
Entrainment	Normal	Status	—	100	15	Normal

National Pokédex **224** Hoenn Pokédex —

Octillery

Jet Pokémon

♂ ♀

Water

HEIGHT: 2'11" WEIGHT: 62.8 lbs.

The male has larger suckers. The female has smaller suckers.

Ω Octillery grabs onto its foe using its tentacles. This Pokémon tries to immobilize it before delivering the finishing blow. If the foe turns out to be too strong, Octillery spews ink to escape.

α Octillery grabs onto its foe using its tentacles. This Pokémon tries to immobilize it before delivering the finishing blow. If the foe turns out to be too strong, Octillery spews ink to escape.

ABILITIES
Suction Cups
Sniper

HIDDEN ABILITY
Moody

EGG GROUPS
Water 1 | Water 2

STAT GROWTH RATES

HP	■■■
Attack	■■■■■
Defense	■■■
Sp. Atk	■■■■■
Sp. Def	■■■
Speed	■■■

ITEMS SOMETIMES HELD BY WILD POKÉMON
—

EVOLUTION

Remoraid → Lv. 25 → Octillery

MAIN WAY TO REGISTER IN THE NATIONAL POKÉDEX

Catch using a Super Rod in the Battle Resort.

Damage taken in normal battles

Type	×	Type	×
Normal	×1	Flying	×1
Fire	×0.5	Psychic	×1
Water	×0.5	Bug	×1
Grass	×2	Rock	×1
Electric	×2	Ghost	×1
Ice	×0.5	Dragon	×1
Fighting	×1	Dark	×1
Poison	×1	Steel	×0.5
Ground	×1	Fairy	×1

Damage taken in Inverse battles

Type	×	Type	×
Normal	×1	Flying	×1
Fire	×2	Psychic	×1
Water	×2	Bug	×1
Grass	×0.5	Rock	×1
Electric	×0.5	Ghost	×1
Ice	×2	Dragon	×1
Fighting	×1	Dark	×1
Poison	×1	Steel	×2
Ground	×1	Fairy	×1

Can be used in
Inverse Battle
Battle Institute
Battle Maison
Random Matchup (Free Battle)
Random Matchup (Others)

LEVEL-UP MOVES

Lv.	Name	Type	Kind	Pow.	Acc.	PP	Range
1	Gunk Shot	Poison	Physical	120	80	5	Normal
1	Rock Blast	Rock	Physical	25	90	10	Normal
1	Water Gun	Water	Special	40	100	25	Normal
1	Constrict	Normal	Physical	10	100	35	Normal
1	Psybeam	Psychic	Special	65	100	20	Normal
1	Aurora Beam	Ice	Special	65	100	20	Normal
6	Constrict	Normal	Physical	10	100	35	Normal
10	Psybeam	Psychic	Special	65	100	20	Normal
14	Aurora Beam	Ice	Special	65	100	20	Normal
18	Bubble Beam	Water	Special	65	100	20	Normal
22	Focus Energy	Normal	Status	—	—	30	Self
25	Octazooka	Water	Special	65	85	10	Normal
28	Wring Out	Normal	Special	—	100	5	Normal
34	Signal Beam	Bug	Special	75	100	15	Normal
40	Ice Beam	Ice	Special	90	100	10	Normal
46	Bullet Seed	Grass	Physical	25	100	30	Normal
52	Hydro Pump	Water	Special	110	80	5	Normal
58	Hyper Beam	Normal	Special	150	90	5	Normal
64	Soak	Water	Status	—	100	20	Normal

TM & HM MOVES

No.	Name	Type	Kind	Pow.	Acc.	PP	Range
TM06	Toxic	Poison	Status	—	90	10	Normal
TM10	Hidden Power	Normal	Special	60	100	15	Normal
TM11	Sunny Day	Fire	Status	—	—	5	Both Sides
TM13	Ice Beam	Ice	Special	90	100	10	Normal
TM14	Blizzard	Ice	Special	110	70	5	Many Others
TM15	Hyper Beam	Normal	Special	150	90	5	Normal
TM17	Protect	Normal	Status	—	—	10	Self
TM18	Rain Dance	Water	Status	—	—	5	Both Sides
TM21	Frustration	Normal	Physical	—	100	20	Normal
TM23	Smack Down	Rock	Physical	50	100	15	Normal
TM27	Return	Normal	Physical	—	100	20	Normal
TM29	Psychic	Psychic	Special	90	100	10	Normal
TM32	Double Team	Normal	Status	—	—	15	Self
TM34	Sludge Wave	Poison	Special	95	100	10	Adjacent
TM35	Flamethrower	Fire	Special	90	100	15	Normal
TM36	Sludge Bomb	Poison	Special	90	100	10	Normal
TM38	Fire Blast	Fire	Special	110	85	5	Normal
TM42	Facade	Normal	Physical	70	100	20	Normal
TM44	Rest	Psychic	Status	—	—	10	Self
TM45	Attract	Normal	Status	—	100	15	Normal
TM46	Thief	Dark	Physical	60	100	25	Normal
TM48	Round	Normal	Special	60	100	15	Normal
TM53	Energy Ball	Grass	Special	90	100	10	Normal
TM55	Scald	Water	Special	80	100	15	Normal
TM57	Charge Beam	Electric	Special	50	90	10	Normal
TM59	Incinerate	Fire	Special	60	100	15	Many Others
TM66	Payback	Dark	Physical	50	100	10	Normal
TM68	Giga Impact	Normal	Physical	150	90	5	Normal
TM73	Thunder Wave	Electric	Status	—	100	20	Normal
TM87	Swagger	Normal	Status	—	90	15	Normal
TM88	Sleep Talk	Normal	Status	—	—	10	Self
TM90	Substitute	Normal	Status	—	—	10	Self
TM91	Flash Cannon	Steel	Special	80	100	10	Normal
TM94	Secret Power	Normal	Physical	70	100	20	Normal
TM100	Confide	Normal	Status	—	—	20	Normal
HM03	Surf	Water	Special	90	100	15	Adjacent
HM05	Waterfall	Water	Physical	80	100	15	Normal
HM07	Dive	Water	Physical	80	100	10	Normal

MOVES LEARNED IN EXCHANGE FOR BP

Name	Type	Kind	Pow.	Acc.	PP	Range
Signal Beam	Bug	Special	75	100	15	Normal
Seed Bomb	Grass	Physical	80	100	15	Normal
Bounce	Flying	Physical	85	85	5	Normal
Gunk Shot	Poison	Physical	120	80	5	Normal
Icy Wind	Ice	Special	55	95	15	Many Others
Bind	Normal	Physical	15	85	20	Normal
Snore	Normal	Special	50	100	15	Normal
Water Pulse	Water	Special	60	100	20	Normal

MOVES TAUGHT BY PEOPLE

Name	Type	Kind	Pow.	Acc.	PP	Range

225

Delibird

National Pokédex

National Pokédex **225** Hoenn Pokédex —

Delibird

Delivery Pokémon

Ice Flying

HEIGHT: 2'11" WEIGHT: 35.3 lbs.

Same form for ♂ / ♀

Ω Delibird carries its food bundled up in its tail. There once was a famous explorer who managed to reach the peak of the world's highest mountain, thanks to one of these Pokémon sharing its food.

α Delibird carries its food bundled up in its tail. There once was a famous explorer who managed to reach the peak of the world's highest mountain, thanks to one of these Pokémon sharing its food.

ABILITIES
Vital Spirit
Hustle

HIDDEN ABILITY
Insomnia

EGG GROUPS
Water 1 | Field

STAT GROWTH RATES

HP	■■
Attack	■■■
Defense	■■
Sp. Atk	■■■
Sp. Def	■■
Speed	■■■■

ITEMS SOMETIMES HELD BY WILD POKÉMON
—

EVOLUTION
Does not evolve

MAIN WAY TO REGISTER IN THE NATIONAL POKÉDEX

Catch in Shoal Cave. Appears as a hidden Pokémon after you battle Groudon or Kyogre.

Damage taken in normal battles

Type		Type	
Normal	×1	Flying	×1
Fire	×2	Psychic	×1
Water	×1	Bug	×0.5
Grass	×0.5	Rock	×4
Electric	×2	Ghost	×1
Ice	×1	Dragon	×1
Fighting	×1	Dark	×1
Poison	×1	Steel	×2
Ground	×0	Fairy	×1

Damage taken in Inverse battles

Type		Type	
Normal	×1	Flying	×1
Fire	×0.5	Psychic	×1
Water	×1	Bug	×2
Grass	×2	Rock	×0.25
Electric	×0.5	Ghost	×1
Ice	×1	Dragon	×1
Fighting	×1	Dark	×1
Poison	×1	Steel	×0.5
Ground	×2	Fairy	×1

Can be used in
Inverse Battle
Battle Institute
Battle Maison
Random Matchup (Free Battle)
Random Matchup (Others)

LEVEL-UP MOVES

Lv.	Name	Type	Kind	Pow.	Acc.	PP	Range
1	Present	Normal	Physical	—	90	15	Normal

TM & HM MOVES

No.	Name	Type	Kind	Pow.	Acc.	PP	Range
TM06	Toxic	Poison	Status	—	90	10	Normal
TM07	Hail	Ice	Status	—	—	10	Both Sides
TM10	Hidden Power	Normal	Special	60	100	15	Normal
TM13	Ice Beam	Ice	Special	90	100	10	Normal
TM14	Blizzard	Ice	Special	110	70	5	Many Others
TM17	Protect	Normal	Status	—	—	10	Self
TM18	Rain Dance	Water	Status	—	—	5	Both Sides
TM21	Frustration	Normal	Physical	—	100	20	Normal
TM27	Return	Normal	Physical	—	100	20	Normal
TM31	Brick Break	Fighting	Physical	75	100	15	Normal
TM32	Double Team	Normal	Status	—	—	15	Self
TM40	Aerial Ace	Flying	Physical	60	—	20	Normal
TM42	Facade	Normal	Physical	70	100	20	Normal
TM44	Rest	Psychic	Status	—	—	10	Self
TM45	Attract	Normal	Status	—	100	15	Normal
TM46	Thief	Dark	Physical	60	100	25	Normal
TM48	Round	Normal	Special	60	100	15	Normal
TM56	Fling	Dark	Physical	—	100	10	Normal
TM79	Frost Breath	Ice	Special	60	90	10	Normal
TM87	Swagger	Normal	Status	—	90	15	Normal
TM88	Sleep Talk	Normal	Status	—	—	10	Self
TM90	Substitute	Normal	Status	—	—	10	Self
TM94	Secret Power	Normal	Physical	70	100	20	Normal
TM98	Power-Up Punch	Fighting	Physical	40	100	20	Normal
TM100	Confide	Normal	Status	—	—	20	Normal
HM02	Fly	Flying	Physical	90	95	15	Normal

MOVES LEARNED IN EXCHANGE FOR BP

Name	Type	Kind	Pow.	Acc.	PP	Range
Signal Beam	Bug	Special	75	100	15	Normal
Seed Bomb	Grass	Physical	80	100	15	Normal
Bounce	Flying	Physical	85	85	5	Normal
Gunk Shot	Poison	Physical	120	80	5	Normal
Ice Punch	Ice	Physical	75	100	15	Normal
Icy Wind	Ice	Special	55	95	15	Many Others
Snore	Normal	Special	50	100	15	Normal
Sky Attack	Flying	Physical	140	90	5	Normal
Focus Punch	Fighting	Physical	150	100	20	Normal
Water Pulse	Water	Special	60	100	20	Normal
Recycle	Normal	Status	—	—	10	Self

MOVES TAUGHT BY PEOPLE

Name	Type	Kind	Pow.	Acc.	PP	Range

EGG MOVES

Name	Type	Kind	Pow.	Acc.	PP	Range
Aurora Beam	Ice	Special	65	100	20	Normal
Quick Attack	Normal	Physical	40	100	30	Normal
Future Sight	Psychic	Special	120	100	10	Normal
Splash	Normal	Status	—	—	40	Self
Rapid Spin	Normal	Physical	20	100	40	Normal
Ice Ball	Ice	Physical	30	90	20	Normal
Ice Shard	Ice	Physical	40	100	30	Normal
Ice Punch	Ice	Physical	75	100	15	Normal
Fake Out	Normal	Physical	40	100	10	Normal
Bestow	Normal	Status	—	—	15	Normal
Icy Wind	Ice	Special	55	95	15	Many Others
Freeze-Dry	Ice	Special	70	100	20	Normal
Destiny Bond	Ghost	Status	—	—	5	Self
Spikes	Ground	Status	—	—	20	Other Side

226

Mantine

National Pokédex **226** Hoenn Pokédex —

Mantine

Kite Pokémon

Water Flying

HEIGHT: 6'11" WEIGHT: 485 lbs.

Same form for ♂ / ♀

Ω On sunny days, schools of Mantine can be seen elegantly leaping over the sea's waves. This Pokémon is not bothered by the Remoraid that hitches rides.

α On sunny days, schools of Mantine can be seen elegantly leaping over the sea's waves. This Pokémon is not bothered by the Remoraid that hitches rides.

ABILITIES
Swift Swim
Water Absorb

HIDDEN ABILITY
Water Veil

EGG GROUPS
Water 1

STAT GROWTH RATES

HP	■■■
Attack	■■
Defense	■■■
Sp. Atk	■■■■
Sp. Def	■■■■■■
Speed	■■■■

ITEMS SOMETIMES HELD BY WILD POKÉMON
—

EVOLUTION

Mantyke → Level up with Remoraid in your party → Mantine

MAIN WAY TO REGISTER IN THE NATIONAL POKÉDEX

Catch on the water surface at the Battle Resort.

Damage taken in normal battles

Type		Type	
Normal	×1	Flying	×1
Fire	×0.5	Psychic	×1
Water	×0.5	Bug	×0.5
Grass	×1	Rock	×2
Electric	×4	Ghost	×1
Ice	×1	Dragon	×1
Fighting	×0.5	Dark	×1
Poison	×1	Steel	×0.5
Ground	×0	Fairy	×1

Damage taken in Inverse battles

Type		Type	
Normal	×1	Flying	×1
Fire	×2	Psychic	×1
Water	×2	Bug	×2
Grass	×1	Rock	×0.5
Electric	×0.25	Ghost	×1
Ice	×1	Dragon	×1
Fighting	×2	Dark	×1
Poison	×1	Steel	×2
Ground	×2	Fairy	×1

Can be used in
Inverse Battle
Battle Institute
Battle Maison
Random Matchup (Free Battle)
Random Matchup (Others)

LEVEL-UP MOVES

Lv.	Name	Type	Kind	Pow.	Acc.	PP	Range
1	Psybeam	Psychic	Special	65	100	20	Normal
1	Bullet Seed	Grass	Physical	25	100	30	Normal
1	Signal Beam	Bug	Special	75	100	15	Normal
1	Tackle	Normal	Physical	50	100	35	Normal
1	Bubble	Water	Special	40	100	30	Many Others
1	Supersonic	Normal	Status	—	55	20	Normal
1	Bubble Beam	Water	Special	65	100	20	Normal
3	Supersonic	Normal	Status	—	55	20	Normal
7	Bubble Beam	Water	Special	65	100	20	Normal
11	Confuse Ray	Ghost	Status	—	100	10	Normal
14	Wing Attack	Flying	Physical	60	100	35	Normal
16	Headbutt	Normal	Physical	70	100	15	Normal
19	Water Pulse	Water	Special	60	100	20	Normal
23	Wide Guard	Rock	Status	—	—	10	Your Side
27	Take Down	Normal	Physical	90	85	20	Normal
32	Agility	Psychic	Status	—	—	30	Self
36	Air Slash	Flying	Special	75	95	15	Normal
39	Aqua Ring	Water	Status	—	—	20	Self
46	Bounce	Flying	Physical	85	85	5	Normal
49	Hydro Pump	Water	Special	110	80	5	Normal

TM & HM MOVES

No.	Name	Type	Kind	Pow.	Acc.	PP	Range
TM06	Toxic	Poison	Status	—	90	10	Normal
TM07	Hail	Ice	Status	—	—	10	Both Sides
TM10	Hidden Power	Normal	Special	60	100	15	Normal
TM13	Ice Beam	Ice	Special	90	100	10	Normal
TM14	Blizzard	Ice	Special	110	70	5	Many Others
TM15	Hyper Beam	Normal	Special	150	90	5	Normal
TM17	Protect	Normal	Status	—	—	10	Self
TM18	Rain Dance	Water	Status	—	—	5	Both Sides
TM21	Frustration	Normal	Physical	—	100	20	Normal
TM26	Earthquake	Ground	Physical	100	100	10	Adjacent
TM27	Return	Normal	Physical	—	100	20	Normal
TM32	Double Team	Normal	Status	—	—	15	Self
TM39	Rock Tomb	Rock	Physical	60	95	15	Normal
TM40	Aerial Ace	Flying	Physical	60	—	20	Normal
TM42	Facade	Normal	Physical	70	100	20	Normal
TM44	Rest	Psychic	Status	—	—	10	Self
TM45	Attract	Normal	Status	—	100	15	Normal
TM48	Round	Normal	Special	60	100	15	Normal
TM55	Scald	Water	Special	80	100	15	Normal
TM62	Acrobatics	Flying	Physical	55	100	15	Normal
TM68	Giga Impact	Normal	Physical	150	90	5	Normal
TM78	Bulldoze	Ground	Physical	60	100	20	Adjacent
TM80	Rock Slide	Rock	Physical	75	90	10	Many Others
TM87	Swagger	Normal	Status	—	90	15	Normal
TM88	Sleep Talk	Normal	Status	—	—	10	Self
TM90	Substitute	Normal	Status	—	—	10	Self
TM94	Secret Power	Normal	Physical	70	100	20	Normal
TM100	Confide	Normal	Status	—	—	20	Normal
HM03	Surf	Water	Special	90	100	15	Adjacent
HM05	Waterfall	Water	Physical	80	100	15	Normal
HM07	Dive	Water	Physical	80	100	10	Normal

MOVES LEARNED IN EXCHANGE FOR BP

Name	Type	Kind	Pow.	Acc.	PP	Range
Signal Beam	Bug	Special	75	100	15	Normal
Iron Head	Steel	Physical	80	100	15	Normal
Seed Bomb	Grass	Physical	80	100	15	Normal
Bounce	Flying	Physical	85	85	5	Normal
Gunk Shot	Poison	Physical	120	80	5	Normal
Icy Wind	Ice	Special	55	95	15	Many Others
Aqua Tail	Water	Physical	90	90	10	Normal
Snore	Normal	Special	50	100	15	Normal
Tailwind	Flying	Status	—	—	15	Your Side
Water Pulse	Water	Special	60	100	20	Normal
Helping Hand	Normal	Status	—	—	20	1 Ally

MOVES TAUGHT BY PEOPLE

Name	Type	Kind	Pow.	Acc.	PP	Range

EGG MOVES

Name	Type	Kind	Pow.	Acc.	PP	Range
Twister	Dragon	Special	40	100	20	Many Others
Hydro Pump	Water	Special	110	80	5	Normal
Haze	Ice	Status	—	—	30	Both Sides
Slam	Normal	Physical	80	75	20	Normal
Mud Sport	Ground	Status	—	—	15	Both Sides
Mirror Coat	Psychic	Special	—	100	20	Varies
Water Sport	Water	Status	—	—	15	Both Sides
Splash	Normal	Status	—	—	40	Self
Wide Guard	Rock	Status	—	—	10	Your Side
Amnesia	Psychic	Status	—	—	20	Self

National Pokédex **227** Hoenn Pokédex **120**

Skarmory

Armor Bird Pokémon

Steel | Flying

HEIGHT: 5'07" WEIGHT: 111.3 lbs.

Same form for ♂ / ♀

Ω Skarmory is entirely encased in hard, protective armor. This Pokémon flies at close to 190 mph. It slashes foes with its wings that possess swordlike cutting edges.

α Skarmory's steel wings become tattered and bashed in from repeated battles. Once a year, the battered wings grow back completely, restoring the cutting edges to their pristine state.

ABILITIES
Keen Eye
Sturdy

HIDDEN ABILITY
Weak Armor

EGG GROUPS
Flying

STAT GROWTH RATES
HP ■■■
Attack ■■■■
Defense ■■■■■■
Sp. Atk ■■
Sp. Def ■■■
Speed ■■■■

ITEMS SOMETIMES HELD BY WILD POKÉMON
Metal Coat

EVOLUTION
Does not evolve

MAIN WAY TO REGISTER IN THE NATIONAL POKÉDEX

Catch on Route 113.

Damage taken in normal battles

Type		Type	
Normal	×0.5	Flying	×0.5
Fire	×2	Psychic	×0.5
Water	×1	Bug	×0.25
Grass	×0.25	Rock	×1
Electric	×2	Ghost	×1
Ice	×1	Dragon	×0.5
Fighting	×1	Dark	×1
Poison	×0	Steel	×0.5
Ground	×0	Fairy	×0.5

Damage taken in Inverse battles

Type		Type	
Normal	×2	Flying	×2
Fire	×0.5	Psychic	×2
Water	×1	Bug	×4
Grass	×4	Rock	×1
Electric	×0.5	Ghost	×1
Ice	×1	Dragon	×2
Fighting	×1	Dark	×1
Poison	×2	Steel	×2
Ground	×1	Fairy	×2

Can be used in
Inverse Battle
Battle Institute
Battle Maison
Random Matchup (Free Battle)
Random Matchup (Others)

LEVEL-UP MOVES

Lv.	Name	Type	Kind	Pow.	Acc.	PP	Range
1	Leer	Normal	Status	—	100	30	Many Others
1	Peck	Flying	Physical	35	100	35	Normal
6	Sand Attack	Ground	Status	—	100	15	Normal
9	Metal Claw	Steel	Physical	50	95	35	Normal
12	Air Cutter	Flying	Special	60	95	25	Many Others
17	Fury Attack	Normal	Physical	15	85	20	Normal
20	Feint	Normal	Physical	30	100	10	Normal
23	Swift	Normal	Special	60	—	20	Many Others
28	Spikes	Ground	Status	—	—	20	Other Side
31	Agility	Psychic	Status	—	—	30	Self
34	Steel Wing	Steel	Physical	70	90	25	Normal
39	Slash	Normal	Physical	70	100	20	Normal
42	Metal Sound	Steel	Status	—	85	40	Normal
45	Air Slash	Flying	Special	75	95	15	Normal
50	Autotomize	Steel	Status	—	—	15	Self
53	Night Slash	Dark	Physical	70	100	15	Normal

TM & HM MOVES

No.	Name	Type	Kind	Pow.	Acc.	PP	Range
TM05	Roar	Normal	Status	—	—	20	Normal
TM06	Toxic	Poison	Status	—	90	10	Normal
TM10	Hidden Power	Normal	Special	60	100	15	Normal
TM11	Sunny Day	Fire	Status	—	—	5	Both Sides
TM12	Taunt	Dark	Status	—	100	20	Normal
TM17	Protect	Normal	Status	—	—	10	Self
TM19	Roost	Flying	Status	—	—	10	Self
TM21	Frustration	Normal	Physical	—	100	20	Normal
TM27	Return	Normal	Physical	—	100	20	Normal
TM32	Double Team	Normal	Status	—	—	15	Self
TM37	Sandstorm	Rock	Status	—	—	10	Both Sides
TM39	Rock Tomb	Rock	Physical	60	95	15	Normal
TM40	Aerial Ace	Flying	Physical	60	—	20	Normal
TM41	Torment	Dark	Status	—	100	15	Normal
TM42	Facade	Normal	Physical	70	100	20	Normal
TM44	Rest	Psychic	Status	—	—	10	Self
TM45	Attract	Normal	Status	—	100	15	Normal
TM46	Thief	Dark	Physical	60	100	25	Normal
TM48	Round	Normal	Special	60	100	15	Normal
TM51	Steel Wing	Steel	Physical	70	90	25	Normal
TM58	Sky Drop	Flying	Physical	60	100	10	Normal
TM66	Payback	Dark	Physical	50	100	10	Normal
TM70	Flash	Normal	Status	—	100	20	Normal
TM75	Swords Dance	Normal	Status	—	—	20	Self
TM80	Rock Slide	Rock	Physical	75	90	10	Many Others
TM81	X-Scissor	Bug	Physical	80	100	15	Normal
TM87	Swagger	Normal	Status	—	90	15	Normal
TM88	Sleep Talk	Normal	Status	—	—	10	Self
TM90	Substitute	Normal	Status	—	—	10	Self
TM91	Flash Cannon	Steel	Special	80	100	10	Normal
TM94	Secret Power	Normal	Physical	70	100	20	Normal
TM97	Dark Pulse	Dark	Special	80	100	15	Normal
TM100	Confide	Normal	Status	—	—	20	Normal
HM01	Cut	Normal	Physical	50	95	30	Normal
HM02	Fly	Flying	Physical	90	95	15	Normal
HM06	Rock Smash	Fighting	Physical	40	100	15	Normal

MOVES LEARNED IN EXCHANGE FOR BP

Name	Type	Kind	Pow.	Acc.	PP	Range
Iron Head	Steel	Physical	80	100	15	Normal
Iron Defense	Steel	Status	—	—	15	Self
Icy Wind	Ice	Special	55	95	15	Many Others
Snore	Normal	Special	50	100	15	Normal
Tailwind	Flying	Status	—	—	15	Your Side
Sky Attack	Flying	Physical	140	90	5	Normal
Stealth Rock	Rock	Status	—	—	20	Other Side

MOVES TAUGHT BY PEOPLE

Name	Type	Kind	Pow.	Acc.	PP	Range

EGG MOVES

Name	Type	Kind	Pow.	Acc.	PP	Range
Drill Peck	Flying	Physical	80	100	20	Normal
Pursuit	Dark	Physical	40	100	20	Normal
Whirlwind	Normal	Status	—	—	20	Normal
Sky Attack	Flying	Physical	140	90	5	Normal
Curse	Ghost	Status	—	—	10	Varies
Brave Bird	Flying	Physical	120	100	15	Normal
Assurance	Dark	Physical	60	100	10	Normal
Guard Swap	Psychic	Status	—	—	10	Normal
Stealth Rock	Rock	Status	—	—	20	Other Side
Endure	Normal	Status	—	—	10	Self

National Pokédex **228** Hoenn Pokédex **—**

Houndour

Dark Pokémon

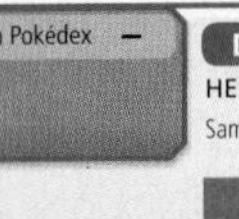

Dark | Fire

HEIGHT: 2'00" WEIGHT: 23.8 lbs.

Same form for ♂ / ♀

Ω Houndour hunt as a coordinated pack. They communicate with each other using a variety of cries to corner their prey. This Pokémon's remarkable teamwork is unparalleled.

α Houndour hunt as a coordinated pack. They communicate with each other using a variety of cries to corner their prey. This Pokémon's remarkable teamwork is unparalleled.

ABILITIES
Early Bird
Flash Fire

HIDDEN ABILITY
Unnerve

EGG GROUPS
Field

STAT GROWTH RATES
HP ■■
Attack ■■■
Defense ■■
Sp. Atk ■■■■
Sp. Def ■■
Speed ■■■■

ITEMS SOMETIMES HELD BY WILD POKÉMON
—

EVOLUTION
Houndour → Lv. 24 → Houndoom

MAIN WAY TO REGISTER IN THE NATIONAL POKÉDEX

Appears in *Pokémon X*. Bring it to your game using Link Trade or the GTS.

Damage taken in normal battles

Type		Type	
Normal	×1	Flying	×1
Fire	×0.5	Psychic	×0
Water	×2	Bug	×1
Grass	×0.5	Rock	×2
Electric	×1	Ghost	×0.5
Ice	×0.5	Dragon	×1
Fighting	×2	Dark	×0.5
Poison	×1	Steel	×0.5
Ground	×2	Fairy	×1

Damage taken in Inverse battles

Type		Type	
Normal	×1	Flying	×1
Fire	×2	Psychic	×2
Water	×0.5	Bug	×1
Grass	×2	Rock	×0.5
Electric	×1	Ghost	×2
Ice	×2	Dragon	×1
Fighting	×0.5	Dark	×2
Poison	×1	Steel	×2
Ground	×0.5	Fairy	×1

Can be used in
Inverse Battle
Battle Institute
Battle Maison
Random Matchup (Free Battle)
Random Matchup (Others)

LEVEL-UP MOVES

Lv.	Name	Type	Kind	Pow.	Acc.	PP	Range
1	Leer	Normal	Status	—	100	30	Many Others
1	Ember	Fire	Special	40	100	25	Normal
4	Howl	Normal	Status	—	—	40	Self
8	Smog	Poison	Special	30	70	20	Normal
13	Roar	Normal	Status	—	—	20	Normal
16	Bite	Dark	Physical	60	100	25	Normal
20	Odor Sleuth	Normal	Status	—	—	40	Normal
25	Beat Up	Dark	Physical	—	100	10	Normal
28	Fire Fang	Fire	Physical	65	95	15	Normal
32	Feint Attack	Dark	Physical	60	—	20	Normal
37	Embargo	Dark	Status	—	100	15	Normal
40	Foul Play	Dark	Physical	95	100	15	Normal
44	Flamethrower	Fire	Special	90	100	15	Normal
49	Crunch	Dark	Physical	80	100	15	Normal
52	Nasty Plot	Dark	Status	—	—	20	Self
56	Inferno	Fire	Special	100	50	5	Normal

TM & HM MOVES

No.	Name	Type	Kind	Pow.	Acc.	PP	Range
TM05	Roar	Normal	Status	—	—	20	Normal
TM06	Toxic	Poison	Status	—	90	10	Normal
TM10	Hidden Power	Normal	Special	60	100	15	Normal
TM11	Sunny Day	Fire	Status	—	—	5	Both Sides
TM12	Taunt	Dark	Status	—	100	20	Normal
TM17	Protect	Normal	Status	—	—	10	Self
TM21	Frustration	Normal	Physical	—	100	20	Normal
TM22	Solar Beam	Grass	Special	120	100	10	Normal
TM27	Return	Normal	Physical	—	100	20	Normal
TM30	Shadow Ball	Ghost	Special	80	100	15	Normal
TM32	Double Team	Normal	Status	—	—	15	Self
TM35	Flamethrower	Fire	Special	90	100	15	Normal
TM36	Sludge Bomb	Poison	Special	90	100	10	Normal
TM38	Fire Blast	Fire	Special	110	85	5	Normal
TM41	Torment	Dark	Status	—	100	15	Normal
TM42	Facade	Normal	Physical	70	100	20	Normal
TM43	Flame Charge	Fire	Physical	50	100	20	Normal
TM44	Rest	Psychic	Status	—	—	10	Self
TM45	Attract	Normal	Status	—	100	15	Normal
TM46	Thief	Dark	Physical	60	100	25	Normal
TM48	Round	Normal	Special	60	100	15	Normal
TM50	Overheat	Fire	Special	130	90	5	Normal
TM59	Incinerate	Fire	Special	60	100	15	Many Others
TM61	Will-O-Wisp	Fire	Status	—	85	15	Normal
TM63	Embargo	Dark	Status	—	100	15	Normal
TM66	Payback	Dark	Physical	50	100	10	Normal
TM67	Retaliate	Normal	Physical	70	100	5	Normal
TM85	Dream Eater	Psychic	Special	100	100	15	Normal
TM87	Swagger	Normal	Status	—	90	15	Normal
TM88	Sleep Talk	Normal	Status	—	—	10	Self
TM90	Substitute	Normal	Status	—	—	10	Self
TM94	Secret Power	Normal	Physical	70	100	20	Normal
TM95	Snarl	Dark	Special	55	95	15	Many Others
TM97	Dark Pulse	Dark	Special	80	100	15	Normal
TM100	Confide	Normal	Status	—	—	20	Normal
HM06	Rock Smash	Fighting	Physical	40	100	15	Normal

MOVES LEARNED IN EXCHANGE FOR BP

Name	Type	Kind	Pow.	Acc.	PP	Range
Super Fang	Normal	Physical	—	90	10	Normal
Uproar	Normal	Special	90	100	10	1 Random
Foul Play	Dark	Physical	95	100	15	Normal
Hyper Voice	Normal	Special	90	100	10	Many Others
Iron Tail	Steel	Physical	100	75	15	Normal
Snore	Normal	Special	50	100	15	Normal
Heat Wave	Fire	Special	95	90	10	Many Others
Role Play	Psychic	Status	—	—	10	Normal
Spite	Ghost	Status	—	100	10	Normal
Snatch	Dark	Status	—	—	10	Self

MOVES TAUGHT BY PEOPLE

Name	Type	Kind	Pow.	Acc.	PP	Range

EGG MOVES

Name	Type	Kind	Pow.	Acc.	PP	Range
Fire Spin	Fire	Special	35	85	15	Normal
Rage	Normal	Physical	20	100	20	Normal
Pursuit	Dark	Physical	40	100	20	Normal
Counter	Fighting	Physical	—	100	20	Varies
Spite	Ghost	Status	—	100	10	Normal
Reversal	Fighting	Physical	—	100	15	Normal
Beat Up	Dark	Physical	—	100	10	Normal
Fire Fang	Fire	Physical	65	95	15	Normal
Thunder Fang	Electric	Physical	65	95	15	Normal
Nasty Plot	Dark	Status	—	—	20	Self
Punishment	Dark	Physical	—	100	5	Normal
Feint	Normal	Physical	30	100	10	Normal
Sucker Punch	Dark	Physical	80	100	5	Normal
Destiny Bond	Ghost	Status	—	—	5	Self

National Pokédex **229** Hoenn Pokédex **—**

Houndoom

Dark Pokémon

Dark | Fire

HEIGHT: 4'07" WEIGHT: 77.2 lbs.

The male has larger horns. The female has smaller horns.

♂ ♀

Ω In a Houndoom pack, the one with its horns raked sharply toward the back serves a leadership role. These Pokémon choose their leader by fighting among themselves.

α In a Houndoom pack, the one with its horns raked sharply toward the back serves a leadership role. These Pokémon choose their leader by fighting among themselves.

ABILITIES
Early Bird
Flash Fire

HIDDEN ABILITY
Unnerve

EGG GROUPS
Field

STAT GROWTH RATES

HP	■■■
Attack	■■■■■
Defense	■■
Sp. Atk	■■■■■
Sp. Def	■■■
Speed	■■■■■

ITEMS SOMETIMES HELD BY WILD POKÉMON
—

EVOLUTION

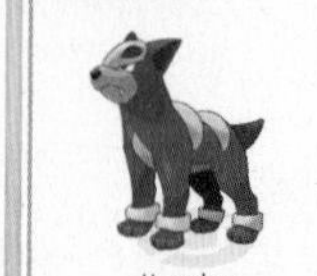
Houndour

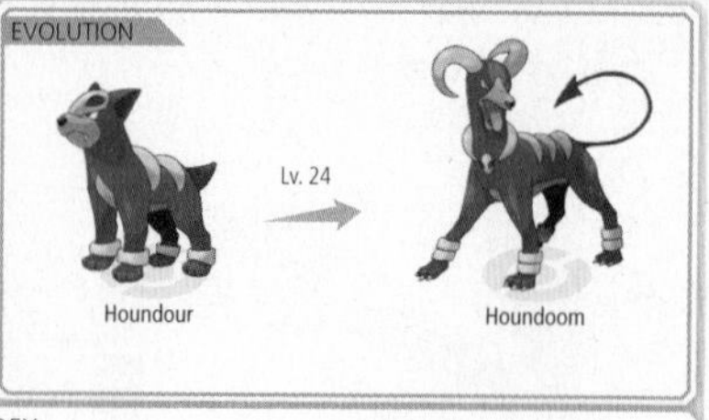

Lv. 24

Houndoom

MAIN WAY TO REGISTER IN THE NATIONAL POKÉDEX

Level up a Houndour obtained via Link Trade or the GTS to Lv. 24.

Damage taken in normal battles

Type		Type	
Normal	×1	Flying	×1
Fire	×0.5	Psychic	×0
Water	×2	Bug	×1
Grass	×0.5	Rock	×2
Electric	×1	Ghost	×0.5
Ice	×0.5	Dragon	×1
Fighting	×2	Dark	×0.5
Poison	×1	Steel	×0.5
Ground	×2	Fairy	×1

Damage taken in Inverse battles

Type		Type	
Normal	×1	Flying	×1
Fire	×2	Psychic	×2
Water	×0.5	Bug	×1
Grass	×2	Rock	×0.5
Electric	×1	Ghost	×2
Ice	×2	Dragon	×1
Fighting	×0.5	Dark	×2
Poison	×1	Steel	×2
Ground	×0.5	Fairy	×1

Can be used in
Inverse Battle
Battle Institute
Battle Maison
Random Matchup (Free Battle)
Random Matchup (Others)

LEVEL-UP MOVES

Lv.	Name	Type	Kind	Pow.	Acc.	PP	Range
1	Inferno	Fire	Special	100	50	5	Normal
1	Nasty Plot	Dark	Status	—	—	20	Self
1	Thunder Fang	Electric	Physical	65	95	15	Normal
1	Leer	Normal	Status	—	100	30	Many Others
1	Ember	Fire	Special	40	100	25	Normal
1	Howl	Normal	Status	—	—	40	Self
1	Smog	Poison	Special	30	70	20	Normal
4	Howl	Normal	Status	—	—	40	Self
8	Smog	Poison	Special	30	70	20	Normal
13	Roar	Normal	Status	—	—	20	Normal
16	Bite	Dark	Physical	60	100	25	Normal
20	Odor Sleuth	Normal	Status	—	—	40	Normal
26	Beat Up	Dark	Physical	—	100	10	Normal
30	Fire Fang	Fire	Physical	65	95	15	Normal
35	Feint Attack	Dark	Physical	60	—	20	Normal
41	Embargo	Dark	Status	—	100	15	Normal
45	Foul Play	Dark	Physical	95	100	15	Normal
50	Flamethrower	Fire	Special	90	100	15	Normal
56	Crunch	Dark	Physical	80	100	15	Normal
60	Nasty Plot	Dark	Status	—	—	20	Self
65	Inferno	Fire	Special	100	50	5	Normal

TM & HM MOVES

No.	Name	Type	Kind	Pow.	Acc.	PP	Range
TM05	Roar	Normal	Status	—	—	20	Normal
TM06	Toxic	Poison	Status	—	90	10	Normal
TM10	Hidden Power	Normal	Special	60	100	15	Normal
TM11	Sunny Day	Fire	Status	—	—	5	Both Sides
TM12	Taunt	Dark	Status	—	100	20	Normal
TM15	Hyper Beam	Normal	Special	150	90	5	Normal
TM17	Protect	Normal	Status	—	—	10	Self
TM21	Frustration	Normal	Physical	—	100	20	Normal
TM22	Solar Beam	Grass	Special	120	100	10	Normal
TM27	Return	Normal	Physical	—	100	20	Normal
TM30	Shadow Ball	Ghost	Special	80	100	15	Normal
TM32	Double Team	Normal	Status	—	—	15	Self
TM35	Flamethrower	Fire	Special	90	100	15	Normal
TM36	Sludge Bomb	Poison	Special	90	100	10	Normal
TM38	Fire Blast	Fire	Special	110	85	5	Normal
TM41	Torment	Dark	Status	—	100	15	Normal
TM42	Facade	Normal	Physical	70	100	20	Normal
TM43	Flame Charge	Fire	Physical	50	100	20	Normal
TM44	Rest	Psychic	Status	—	—	10	Self
TM45	Attract	Normal	Status	—	100	15	Normal
TM46	Thief	Dark	Physical	60	100	25	Normal
TM48	Round	Normal	Special	60	100	15	Normal
TM50	Overheat	Fire	Special	130	90	5	Normal
TM59	Incinerate	Fire	Special	60	100	15	Many Others
TM61	Will-O-Wisp	Fire	Status	—	85	15	Normal
TM63	Embargo	Dark	Status	—	100	15	Normal
TM66	Payback	Dark	Physical	50	100	10	Normal
TM67	Retaliate	Normal	Physical	70	100	5	Normal
TM68	Giga Impact	Normal	Physical	150	90	5	Normal
TM85	Dream Eater	Psychic	Special	100	100	15	Normal
TM87	Swagger	Normal	Status	—	90	15	Normal
TM88	Sleep Talk	Normal	Status	—	—	10	Self
TM90	Substitute	Normal	Status	—	—	10	Self
TM94	Secret Power	Normal	Physical	70	100	20	Normal
TM95	Snarl	Dark	Special	55	95	15	Many Others
TM97	Dark Pulse	Dark	Special	80	100	15	Normal
TM100	Confide	Normal	Status	—	—	20	Normal
HM04	Strength	Normal	Physical	80	100	15	Normal
HM06	Rock Smash	Fighting	Physical	40	100	15	Normal

MOVES LEARNED IN EXCHANGE FOR BP

Name	Type	Kind	Pow.	Acc.	PP	Range
Super Fang	Normal	Physical	—	90	10	Normal
Uproar	Normal	Special	90	100	10	1 Random
Foul Play	Dark	Physical	95	100	15	Normal
Hyper Voice	Normal	Special	90	100	10	Many Others
Iron Tail	Steel	Physical	100	75	15	Normal
Snore	Normal	Special	50	100	15	Normal
Heat Wave	Fire	Special	95	90	10	Many Others
Role Play	Psychic	Status	—	—	10	Normal
Spite	Ghost	Status	—	100	10	Normal
Snatch	Dark	Status	—	—	10	Self

MOVES TAUGHT BY PEOPLE

Name	Type	Kind	Pow.	Acc.	PP	Range

Mega Evolution

Mega Houndoom

Dark Pokémon

Dark | Fire

HEIGHT: 6'03" WEIGHT: 109.1 lbs.

Same form for ♂ / ♀

REQUIRED MEGA STONE
Houndoominite
Find in Lavaridge Town (after battling Groudon or Kyogre).

ABILITY
Solar Power

HIDDEN ABILITY
—

EGG GROUPS
—

STAT GROWTH RATES

HP	■■■
Attack	■■■■■
Defense	■■■■
Sp. Atk	■■■■■■■
Sp. Def	■■■■
Speed	■■■■■■

Damage taken in normal battles

Type		Type	
Normal	×1	Flying	×1
Fire	×0.5	Psychic	×0
Water	×2	Bug	×1
Grass	×0.5	Rock	×2
Electric	×1	Ghost	×0.5
Ice	×0.5	Dragon	×1
Fighting	×2	Dark	×0.5
Poison	×1	Steel	×0.5
Ground	×2	Fairy	×1

Damage taken in Inverse battles

Type		Type	
Normal	×1	Flying	×1
Fire	×2	Psychic	×2
Water	×0.5	Bug	×1
Grass	×2	Rock	×0.5
Electric	×1	Ghost	×2
Ice	×2	Dragon	×1
Fighting	×0.5	Dark	×2
Poison	×1	Steel	×2
Ground	×0.5	Fairy	×1

Can be used in
Inverse Battle
Battle Institute
Battle Maison
Random Matchup (Free Battle)
Random Matchup (Others)

National Pokédex **230** Hoenn Pokédex **195**

Kingdra

Dragon Pokémon

Water Dragon

HEIGHT: 5'11" WEIGHT: 335.1 lbs.

Same form for ♂ / ♀

Ω Kingdra lives at extreme ocean depths that are otherwise uninhabited. It has long been believed that the yawning of this Pokémon creates spiraling ocean currents.

α Kingdra sleeps on the seafloor where it is otherwise devoid of life. When a storm arrives, the Pokémon is said to awaken and wander about in search of prey.

ABILITIES
Swift Swim
Sniper

HIDDEN ABILITY
Damp

EGG GROUPS
Water 1 | Dragon

STAT GROWTH RATES
HP ■■■
Attack ■■■■■
Defense ■■■■
Sp. Atk ■■■■■
Sp. Def ■■■■
Speed ■■■■■

ITEMS SOMETIMES HELD BY WILD POKÉMON
—

EVOLUTION

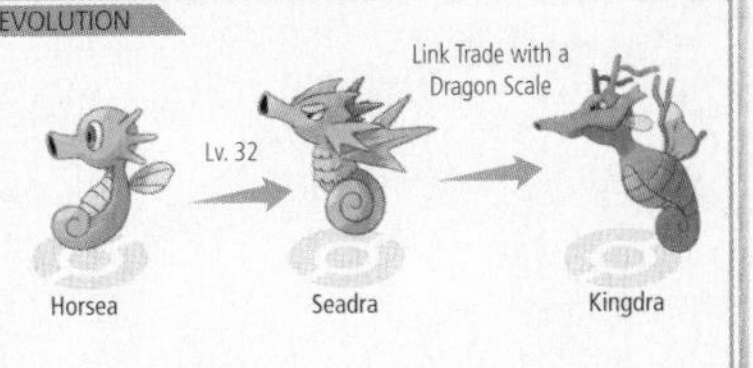

MAIN WAY TO REGISTER IN THE NATIONAL POKÉDEX

Receive a Seadra that is holding a Dragon Scale via Link Trade to have it evolve.

Damage taken in normal battles

Type		Type	
Normal	×1	Flying	×1
Fire	×0.25	Psychic	×1
Water	×0.25	Bug	×1
Grass	×1	Rock	×1
Electric	×1	Ghost	×1
Ice	×1	Dragon	×2
Fighting	×1	Dark	×1
Poison	×1	Steel	×0.5
Ground	×1	Fairy	×2

Damage taken in Inverse battles

Type		Type	
Normal	×1	Flying	×1
Fire	×4	Psychic	×1
Water	×4	Bug	×1
Grass	×1	Rock	×1
Electric	×1	Ghost	×1
Ice	×1	Dragon	×0.5
Fighting	×1	Dark	×1
Poison	×1	Steel	×2
Ground	×1	Fairy	×0.5

Can be used in
- Inverse Battle
- Battle Institute
- Battle Maison
- Random Matchup (Free Battle)
- Random Matchup (Others)

LEVEL-UP MOVES

Lv.	Name	Type	Kind	Pow.	Acc.	PP	Range
1	Hydro Pump	Water	Special	110	80	5	Normal
1	Yawn	Normal	Status	—	—	10	Normal
1	Bubble	Water	Special	40	100	30	Many Others
1	Smokescreen	Normal	Status	—	100	20	Normal
1	Leer	Normal	Status	—	100	30	Many Others
1	Water Gun	Water	Special	40	100	25	Normal
5	Smokescreen	Normal	Status	—	100	20	Normal
9	Leer	Normal	Status	—	100	30	Many Others
13	Water Gun	Water	Special	40	100	25	Normal
17	Twister	Dragon	Special	40	100	20	Many Others
21	Bubble Beam	Water	Special	65	100	20	Normal
26	Focus Energy	Normal	Status	—	—	30	Self
31	Brine	Water	Special	65	100	10	Normal
38	Agility	Psychic	Status	—	—	30	Self
45	Dragon Pulse	Dragon	Special	85	100	10	Normal
52	Dragon Dance	Dragon	Status	—	—	20	Self
60	Hydro Pump	Water	Special	110	80	5	Normal

TM & HM MOVES

No.	Name	Type	Kind	Pow.	Acc.	PP	Range
TM06	Toxic	Poison	Status	—	90	10	Normal
TM07	Hail	Ice	Status	—	—	10	Both Sides
TM10	Hidden Power	Normal	Special	60	100	15	Normal
TM13	Ice Beam	Ice	Special	90	100	10	Normal
TM14	Blizzard	Ice	Special	110	70	5	Many Others
TM15	Hyper Beam	Normal	Special	150	90	5	Normal
TM17	Protect	Normal	Status	—	—	10	Self
TM18	Rain Dance	Water	Status	—	—	5	Both Sides
TM21	Frustration	Normal	Physical	—	100	20	Normal
TM27	Return	Normal	Physical	—	100	20	Normal
TM32	Double Team	Normal	Status	—	—	15	Self
TM42	Facade	Normal	Physical	70	100	20	Normal
TM44	Rest	Psychic	Status	—	—	10	Self
TM45	Attract	Normal	Status	—	100	15	Normal
TM48	Round	Normal	Special	60	100	15	Normal
TM55	Scald	Water	Special	80	100	15	Normal
TM60	Quash	Dark	Status	—	100	15	Normal
TM68	Giga Impact	Normal	Physical	150	90	5	Normal
TM87	Swagger	Normal	Status	—	90	15	Normal
TM88	Sleep Talk	Normal	Status	—	—	10	Self
TM90	Substitute	Normal	Status	—	—	10	Self
TM91	Flash Cannon	Steel	Special	80	100	10	Normal
TM94	Secret Power	Normal	Physical	70	100	20	Normal
TM100	Confide	Normal	Status	—	—	20	Normal
HM03	Surf	Water	Special	90	100	15	Adjacent
HM05	Waterfall	Water	Physical	80	100	15	Normal
HM07	Dive	Water	Physical	80	100	10	Normal

MOVES LEARNED IN EXCHANGE FOR BP

Name	Type	Kind	Pow.	Acc.	PP	Range
Signal Beam	Bug	Special	75	100	15	Normal
Iron Head	Steel	Physical	80	100	15	Normal
Bounce	Flying	Physical	85	85	5	Normal
Icy Wind	Ice	Special	55	95	15	Many Others
Dragon Pulse	Dragon	Special	85	100	10	Normal
Snore	Normal	Special	50	100	15	Normal
Water Pulse	Water	Special	60	100	20	Normal
Outrage	Dragon	Physical	120	100	10	1 Random

MOVES TAUGHT BY PEOPLE

Name	Type	Kind	Pow.	Acc.	PP	Range
Draco Meteor	Dragon	Special	130	90	5	Normal

National Pokédex **231** Hoenn Pokédex **172**

Phanpy

Long Nose Pokémon

Ground

HEIGHT: 1'08" WEIGHT: 73.9 lbs.

Same form for ♂ / ♀

Ω For its nest, Phanpy digs a vertical pit in the ground at the edge of a river. It marks the area around its nest with its trunk to let the others know that the area has been claimed.

α Phanpy uses its long nose to shower itself. When others gather around, they thoroughly douse each other with water. These Pokémon can be seen drying their soaking-wet bodies at the edge of water.

ABILITY
Pickup

HIDDEN ABILITY
Sand Veil

EGG GROUPS
Field

STAT GROWTH RATES
HP ■■■■
Attack ■■■
Defense ■■■
Sp. Atk ■■
Sp. Def ■■
Speed ■■

ITEMS SOMETIMES HELD BY WILD POKÉMON
—

EVOLUTION

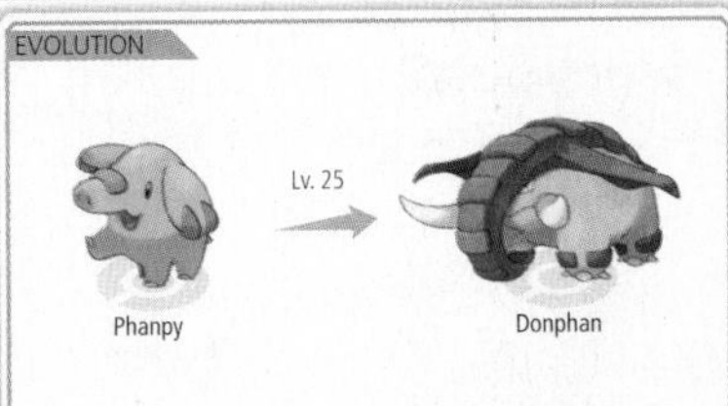

MAIN WAY TO REGISTER IN THE NATIONAL POKÉDEX

Leave a Donphan at a Pokémon Day Care, then hatch the Pokémon Egg that is found.

Damage taken in normal battles

Type		Type	
Normal	×1	Flying	×1
Fire	×1	Psychic	×1
Water	×2	Bug	×1
Grass	×2	Rock	×0.5
Electric	×0	Ghost	×1
Ice	×2	Dragon	×1
Fighting	×1	Dark	×1
Poison	×0.5	Steel	×1
Ground	×1	Fairy	×1

Damage taken in Inverse battles

Type		Type	
Normal	×1	Flying	×1
Fire	×1	Psychic	×1
Water	×0.5	Bug	×1
Grass	×0.5	Rock	×2
Electric	×2	Ghost	×1
Ice	×0.5	Dragon	×1
Fighting	×1	Dark	×1
Poison	×2	Steel	×1
Ground	×1	Fairy	×1

Can be used in
- Inverse Battle
- Battle Institute
- Battle Maison
- Random Matchup (Free Battle)
- Random Matchup (Others)

LEVEL-UP MOVES

Lv.	Name	Type	Kind	Pow.	Acc.	PP	Range
1	Odor Sleuth	Normal	Status	—	—	40	Normal
1	Tackle	Normal	Physical	50	100	35	Normal
1	Growl	Normal	Status	—	100	40	Many Others
1	Defense Curl	Normal	Status	—	—	40	Self
6	Flail	Normal	Physical	—	100	15	Normal
10	Rollout	Rock	Physical	30	90	20	Normal
15	Natural Gift	Normal	Physical	—	100	15	Normal
19	Endure	Normal	Status	—	—	10	Self
24	Slam	Normal	Physical	80	75	20	Normal
28	Take Down	Normal	Physical	90	85	20	Normal
33	Charm	Fairy	Status	—	100	20	Normal
37	Last Resort	Normal	Physical	140	100	5	Normal
42	Double-Edge	Normal	Physical	120	100	15	Normal

TM & HM MOVES

No.	Name	Type	Kind	Pow.	Acc.	PP	Range
TM05	Roar	Normal	Status	—	—	20	Normal
TM06	Toxic	Poison	Status	—	90	10	Normal
TM10	Hidden Power	Normal	Special	60	100	15	Normal
TM11	Sunny Day	Fire	Status	—	—	5	Both Sides
TM17	Protect	Normal	Status	—	—	10	Self
TM21	Frustration	Normal	Physical	—	100	20	Normal
TM26	Earthquake	Ground	Physical	100	100	10	Adjacent
TM27	Return	Normal	Physical	—	100	20	Normal
TM32	Double Team	Normal	Status	—	—	15	Self
TM37	Sandstorm	Rock	Status	—	—	10	Both Sides
TM39	Rock Tomb	Rock	Physical	60	95	15	Normal
TM42	Facade	Normal	Physical	70	100	20	Normal
TM44	Rest	Psychic	Status	—	—	10	Self
TM45	Attract	Normal	Status	—	100	15	Normal
TM48	Round	Normal	Special	60	100	15	Normal
TM49	Echoed Voice	Normal	Special	40	100	15	Normal
TM78	Bulldoze	Ground	Physical	60	100	20	Adjacent
TM80	Rock Slide	Rock	Physical	75	90	10	Many Others
TM87	Swagger	Normal	Status	—	90	15	Normal
TM88	Sleep Talk	Normal	Status	—	—	10	Self
TM90	Substitute	Normal	Status	—	—	10	Self
TM94	Secret Power	Normal	Physical	70	100	20	Normal
TM100	Confide	Normal	Status	—	—	20	Normal
HM04	Strength	Normal	Physical	80	100	15	Normal
HM06	Rock Smash	Fighting	Physical	40	100	15	Normal

MOVES LEARNED IN EXCHANGE FOR BP

Name	Type	Kind	Pow.	Acc.	PP	Range
Seed Bomb	Grass	Physical	80	100	15	Normal
Gunk Shot	Poison	Physical	120	80	5	Normal
Earth Power	Ground	Special	90	100	10	Normal
Last Resort	Normal	Physical	140	100	5	Normal
Superpower	Fighting	Physical	120	100	5	Normal
Hyper Voice	Normal	Special	90	100	10	Many Others
Iron Tail	Steel	Physical	100	75	15	Normal
Snore	Normal	Special	50	100	15	Normal
Knock Off	Dark	Physical	65	100	20	Normal
Endeavor	Normal	Physical	—	100	5	Normal
Stealth Rock	Rock	Status	—	—	20	Other Side

MOVES TAUGHT BY PEOPLE

Name	Type	Kind	Pow.	Acc.	PP	Range

EGG MOVES

Name	Type	Kind	Pow.	Acc.	PP	Range
Focus Energy	Normal	Status	—	—	30	Self
Body Slam	Normal	Physical	85	100	15	Normal
Ancient Power	Rock	Special	60	100	5	Normal
Snore	Normal	Special	50	100	15	Normal
Counter	Fighting	Physical	—	100	20	Varies
Fissure	Ground	Physical	—	30	5	Normal
Endeavor	Normal	Physical	—	100	5	Normal
Ice Shard	Ice	Physical	40	100	30	Normal
Head Smash	Rock	Physical	150	80	5	Normal
Mud-Slap	Ground	Special	20	100	10	Normal
Heavy Slam	Steel	Physical	—	100	10	Normal
Play Rough	Fairy	Physical	90	90	10	Normal

National Pokédex **232** Hoenn Pokédex **173**

Donphan

Armor Pokémon

♂ ♀

Ground

HEIGHT: 3'07" WEIGHT: 264.6 lbs.

The male has larger horns. The female has smaller horns.

Ω Donphan's favorite attack is curling its body into a ball, then charging at its foe while rolling at high speed. Once it starts rolling, this Pokémon can't stop very easily.

α If Donphan were to tackle with its hard body, even a house could be destroyed. Using its massive strength, the Pokémon helps clear rock and mud slides that block mountain trails.

ABILITY
Sturdy

HIDDEN ABILITY
Sand Veil

EGG GROUPS
Field

STAT GROWTH RATES
HP
Attack
Defense
Sp. Atk
Sp. Def
Speed

ITEMS SOMETIMES HELD BY WILD POKÉMON
—

EVOLUTION
Phanpy → Lv. 25 → Donphan

MAIN WAY TO REGISTER IN THE NATIONAL POKÉDEX

Catch in the tall grass in the upper-right corner of the Safari Zone.

Damage taken in normal battles

Normal	×1	Flying	×1
Fire	×1	Psychic	×1
Water	×2	Bug	×1
Grass	×2	Rock	×0.5
Electric	×0	Ghost	×1
Ice	×2	Dragon	×1
Fighting	×1	Dark	×1
Poison	×0.5	Steel	×1
Ground	×1	Fairy	×1

Damage taken in Inverse battles

Normal	×1	Flying	×1
Fire	×1	Psychic	×1
Water	×0.5	Bug	×1
Grass	×0.5	Rock	×2
Electric	×2	Ghost	×1
Ice	×0.5	Dragon	×1
Fighting	×1	Dark	×1
Poison	×2	Steel	×1
Ground	×1	Fairy	×1

Can be used in
Inverse Battle
Battle Institute
Battle Maison
Random Matchup (Free Battle)
Random Matchup (Others)

LEVEL-UP MOVES

Lv.	Name	Type	Kind	Pow.	Acc.	PP	Range
1	Fire Fang	Fire	Physical	65	95	15	Normal
1	Thunder Fang	Electric	Physical	65	95	15	Normal
1	Horn Attack	Normal	Physical	65	100	25	Normal
1	Bulldoze	Ground	Physical	60	100	20	Adjacent
1	Growl	Normal	Status	—	100	40	Many Others
1	Defense Curl	Normal	Status	—	—	40	Self
6	Rapid Spin	Normal	Physical	20	100	40	Normal
10	Rollout	Rock	Physical	30	90	20	Normal
15	Assurance	Dark	Physical	60	100	10	Normal
19	Knock Off	Dark	Physical	65	100	20	Normal
24	Slam	Normal	Physical	80	75	20	Normal
25	Fury Attack	Normal	Physical	15	85	20	Normal
30	Magnitude	Ground	Physical	—	100	30	Adjacent
37	Scary Face	Normal	Status	—	100	10	Normal
43	Earthquake	Ground	Physical	100	100	10	Adjacent
50	Giga Impact	Normal	Physical	150	90	5	Normal

TM & HM MOVES

No.	Name	Type	Kind	Pow.	Acc.	PP	Range
TM05	Roar	Normal	Status	—	—	20	Normal
TM06	Toxic	Poison	Status	—	90	10	Normal
TM10	Hidden Power	Normal	Special	60	100	15	Normal
TM11	Sunny Day	Fire	Status	—	—	5	Both Sides
TM15	Hyper Beam	Normal	Special	150	90	5	Normal
TM17	Protect	Normal	Status	—	—	10	Self
TM21	Frustration	Normal	Physical	—	100	20	Normal
TM26	Earthquake	Ground	Physical	100	100	10	Adjacent
TM27	Return	Normal	Physical	—	100	20	Normal
TM32	Double Team	Normal	Status	—	—	15	Self
TM37	Sandstorm	Rock	Status	—	—	10	Both Sides
TM39	Rock Tomb	Rock	Physical	60	95	15	Normal
TM42	Facade	Normal	Physical	70	100	20	Normal
TM44	Rest	Psychic	Status	—	—	10	Self
TM45	Attract	Normal	Status	—	100	15	Normal
TM48	Round	Normal	Special	60	100	15	Normal
TM49	Echoed Voice	Normal	Special	40	100	15	Normal
TM68	Giga Impact	Normal	Physical	150	90	5	Normal
TM69	Rock Polish	Rock	Status	—	—	20	Self
TM71	Stone Edge	Rock	Physical	100	80	5	Normal
TM74	Gyro Ball	Steel	Physical	—	100	5	Normal
TM78	Bulldoze	Ground	Physical	60	100	20	Adjacent
TM80	Rock Slide	Rock	Physical	75	90	10	Many Others
TM84	Poison Jab	Poison	Physical	80	100	20	Normal
TM87	Swagger	Normal	Status	—	90	15	Normal
TM88	Sleep Talk	Normal	Status	—	—	10	Self
TM90	Substitute	Normal	Status	—	—	10	Self
TM94	Secret Power	Normal	Physical	70	100	20	Normal
TM100	Confide	Normal	Status	—	—	20	Normal
HM04	Strength	Normal	Physical	80	100	15	Normal
HM06	Rock Smash	Fighting	Physical	40	100	15	Normal

MOVES LEARNED IN EXCHANGE FOR BP

Name	Type	Kind	Pow.	Acc.	PP	Range
Seed Bomb	Grass	Physical	80	100	15	Normal
Bounce	Flying	Physical	85	85	5	Normal
Gunk Shot	Poison	Physical	120	80	5	Normal
Block	Normal	Status	—	—	5	Normal
Earth Power	Ground	Special	90	100	10	Normal
Iron Defense	Steel	Status	—	—	15	Self
Last Resort	Normal	Physical	140	100	5	Normal
Superpower	Fighting	Physical	120	100	5	Normal
Hyper Voice	Normal	Special	90	100	10	Many Others
Iron Tail	Steel	Physical	100	75	15	Normal
Snore	Normal	Special	50	100	15	Normal
Knock Off	Dark	Physical	65	100	20	Normal
Endeavor	Normal	Physical	—	100	5	Normal
Stealth Rock	Rock	Status	—	—	20	Other Side

MOVES TAUGHT BY PEOPLE

Name	Type	Kind	Pow.	Acc.	PP	Range

National Pokédex **233** Hoenn Pokédex **—**

Porygon2

Virtual Pokémon

Normal

HEIGHT: 2'00" WEIGHT: 71.6 lbs.

Gender unknown

Ω Porygon2 was created by humans using the power of science. The man-made Pokémon has been endowed with artificial intelligence that enables it to learn new gestures and emotions on its own.

α Porygon2 was created by humans using the power of science. The man-made Pokémon has been endowed with artificial intelligence that enables it to learn new gestures and emotions on its own.

ABILITIES
Trace
Download

HIDDEN ABILITY
Analytic

EGG GROUPS
Mineral

STAT GROWTH RATES
HP
Attack
Defense
Sp. Atk
Sp. Def
Speed

ITEMS SOMETIMES HELD BY WILD POKÉMON
—

EVOLUTION
Porygon → Link Trade with an Up-Grade → Porygon2 → Link Trade with a Dubious Disk → Porygon-Z

MAIN WAY TO REGISTER IN THE NATIONAL POKÉDEX

Receive a Porygon that is holding an Up-Grade via Link Trade to have it evolve.

Damage taken in normal battles

Normal	×1	Flying	×1
Fire	×1	Psychic	×1
Water	×1	Bug	×1
Grass	×1	Rock	×1
Electric	×1	Ghost	×0
Ice	×1	Dragon	×1
Fighting	×2	Dark	×1
Poison	×1	Steel	×1
Ground	×1	Fairy	×1

Damage taken in Inverse battles

Normal	×1	Flying	×1
Fire	×1	Psychic	×1
Water	×1	Bug	×1
Grass	×1	Rock	×1
Electric	×1	Ghost	×2
Ice	×1	Dragon	×1
Fighting	×0.5	Dark	×1
Poison	×1	Steel	×1
Ground	×1	Fairy	×1

Can be used in
Inverse Battle
Battle Institute
Battle Maison
Random Matchup (Free Battle)
Random Matchup (Others)

LEVEL-UP MOVES

Lv.	Name	Type	Kind	Pow.	Acc.	PP	Range
1	Zap Cannon	Electric	Special	120	50	5	Normal
1	Magic Coat	Psychic	Status	—	—	15	Self
1	Conversion 2	Normal	Status	—	—	30	Normal
1	Tackle	Normal	Physical	50	100	35	Normal
1	Conversion	Normal	Status	—	—	30	Self
1	Defense Curl	Normal	Status	—	—	40	Self
7	Psybeam	Psychic	Special	65	100	20	Normal
12	Agility	Psychic	Status	—	—	30	Self
18	Recover	Normal	Status	—	—	10	Self
23	Magnet Rise	Electric	Status	—	—	10	Self
29	Signal Beam	Bug	Special	75	100	15	Normal
34	Recycle	Normal	Status	—	—	10	Self
40	Discharge	Electric	Special	80	100	15	Adjacent
45	Lock-On	Normal	Status	—	—	5	Normal
50	Tri Attack	Normal	Special	80	100	10	Normal
56	Magic Coat	Psychic	Status	—	—	15	Self
62	Zap Cannon	Electric	Special	120	50	5	Normal
67	Hyper Beam	Normal	Special	150	90	5	Normal

TM & HM MOVES

No.	Name	Type	Kind	Pow.	Acc.	PP	Range
TM03	Psyshock	Psychic	Special	80	100	10	Normal
TM06	Toxic	Poison	Status	—	90	10	Normal
TM10	Hidden Power	Normal	Special	60	100	15	Normal
TM11	Sunny Day	Fire	Status	—	—	5	Both Sides
TM13	Ice Beam	Ice	Special	90	100	10	Normal
TM14	Blizzard	Ice	Special	110	70	5	Many Others
TM15	Hyper Beam	Normal	Special	150	90	5	Normal
TM17	Protect	Normal	Status	—	—	10	Self
TM18	Rain Dance	Water	Status	—	—	5	Both Sides
TM21	Frustration	Normal	Physical	—	100	20	Normal
TM22	Solar Beam	Grass	Special	120	100	10	Normal
TM24	Thunderbolt	Electric	Special	90	100	15	Normal
TM25	Thunder	Electric	Special	110	70	10	Normal
TM27	Return	Normal	Physical	—	100	20	Normal
TM29	Psychic	Psychic	Special	90	100	10	Normal
TM30	Shadow Ball	Ghost	Special	80	100	15	Normal
TM32	Double Team	Normal	Status	—	—	15	Self
TM40	Aerial Ace	Flying	Physical	60	—	20	Normal
TM42	Facade	Normal	Physical	70	100	20	Normal
TM44	Rest	Psychic	Status	—	—	10	Self
TM46	Thief	Dark	Physical	60	100	25	Normal
TM48	Round	Normal	Special	60	100	15	Normal
TM57	Charge Beam	Electric	Special	50	90	10	Normal
TM68	Giga Impact	Normal	Physical	150	90	5	Normal
TM70	Flash	Normal	Status	—	100	20	Normal
TM73	Thunder Wave	Electric	Status	—	100	20	Normal
TM77	Psych Up	Normal	Status	—	—	10	Normal
TM85	Dream Eater	Psychic	Special	100	100	15	Normal
TM87	Swagger	Normal	Status	—	90	15	Normal
TM88	Sleep Talk	Normal	Status	—	—	10	Self
TM90	Substitute	Normal	Status	—	—	10	Self
TM92	Trick Room	Psychic	Status	—	—	5	Both Sides
TM94	Secret Power	Normal	Physical	70	100	20	Normal
TM100	Confide	Normal	Status	—	—	20	Normal

MOVES LEARNED IN EXCHANGE FOR BP

Name	Type	Kind	Pow.	Acc.	PP	Range
Signal Beam	Bug	Special	75	100	15	Normal
Magic Coat	Psychic	Status	—	—	15	Self
Foul Play	Dark	Physical	95	100	15	Normal
Gravity	Psychic	Status	—	—	5	Both Sides
Magnet Rise	Electric	Status	—	—	10	Self
Last Resort	Normal	Physical	140	100	5	Normal
Electroweb	Electric	Special	55	95	15	Many Others
Icy Wind	Ice	Special	55	95	15	Many Others
Zen Headbutt	Psychic	Physical	80	90	15	Normal
Iron Tail	Steel	Physical	100	75	15	Normal
Snore	Normal	Special	50	100	15	Normal
Pain Split	Normal	Status	—	—	20	Normal
Shock Wave	Electric	Special	60	—	20	Normal
Trick	Psychic	Status	—	100	10	Normal
Wonder Room	Psychic	Status	—	—	10	Both Sides
Recycle	Normal	Status	—	—	10	Self

MOVES TAUGHT BY PEOPLE

Name	Type	Kind	Pow.	Acc.	PP	Range

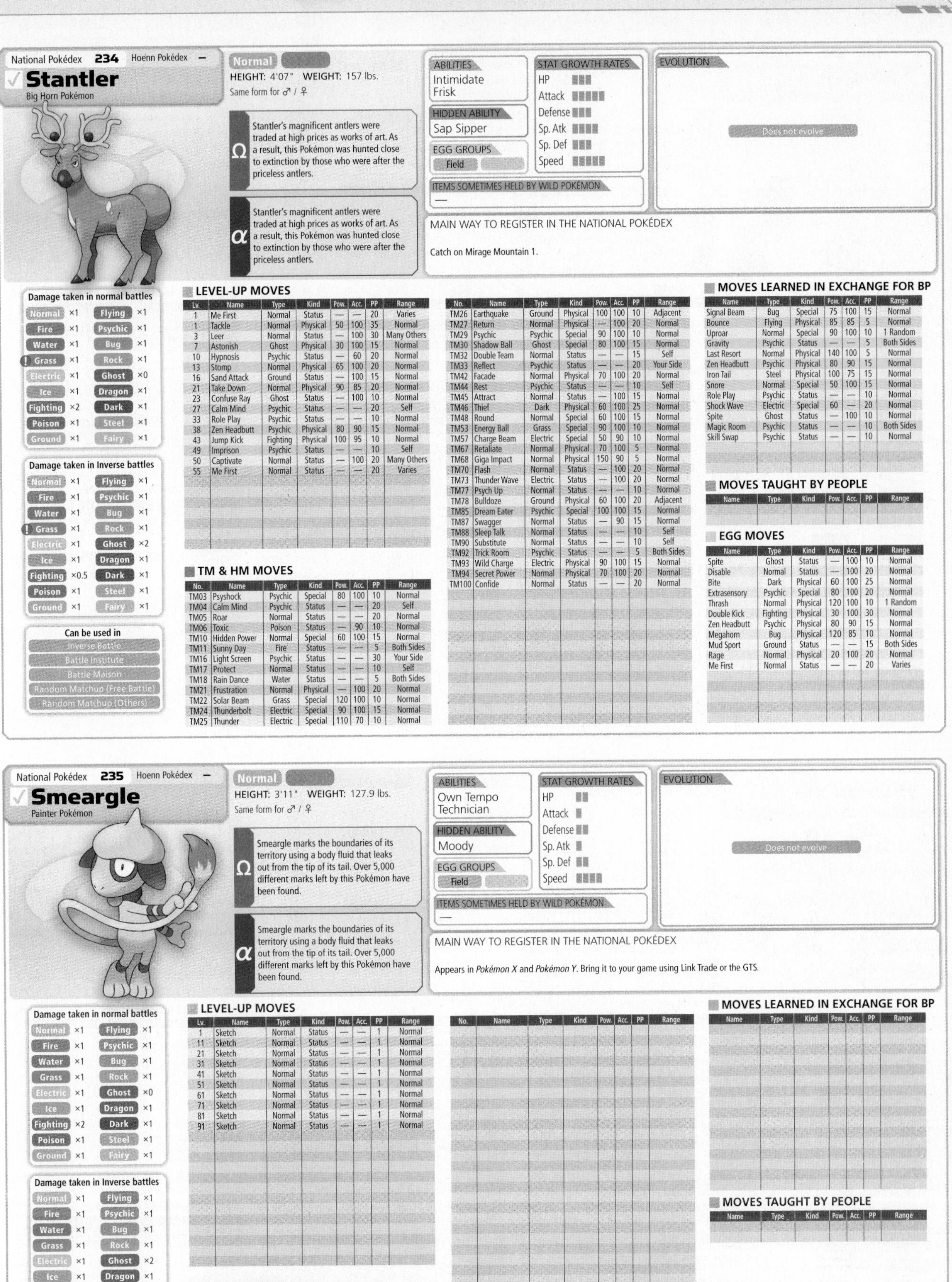

National Pokédex **234** Hoenn Pokédex —

Stantler

Big Horn Pokémon

Normal

HEIGHT: 4'07" WEIGHT: 157 lbs.

Same form for ♂ / ♀

Ω Stantler's magnificent antlers were traded at high prices as works of art. As a result, this Pokémon was hunted close to extinction by those who were after the priceless antlers.

α Stantler's magnificent antlers were traded at high prices as works of art. As a result, this Pokémon was hunted close to extinction by those who were after the priceless antlers.

ABILITIES
Intimidate
Frisk

HIDDEN ABILITY
Sap Sipper

EGG GROUPS
Field

STAT GROWTH RATES
HP
Attack
Defense
Sp. Atk
Sp. Def
Speed

ITEMS SOMETIMES HELD BY WILD POKÉMON
—

EVOLUTION
Does not evolve

MAIN WAY TO REGISTER IN THE NATIONAL POKÉDEX

Catch on Mirage Mountain 1.

Damage taken in normal battles

Type		Type	
Normal	×1	Flying	×1
Fire	×1	Psychic	×1
Water	×1	Bug	×1
Grass	×1	Rock	×1
Electric	×1	Ghost	×0
Ice	×1	Dragon	×1
Fighting	×2	Dark	×1
Poison	×1	Steel	×1
Ground	×1	Fairy	×1

Damage taken in Inverse battles

Type		Type	
Normal	×1	Flying	×1
Fire	×1	Psychic	×1
Water	×1	Bug	×1
Grass	×1	Rock	×1
Electric	×1	Ghost	×2
Ice	×1	Dragon	×1
Fighting	×0.5	Dark	×1
Poison	×1	Steel	×1
Ground	×1	Fairy	×1

Can be used in
Inverse Battle
Battle Institute
Battle Maison
Random Matchup (Free Battle)
Random Matchup (Others)

LEVEL-UP MOVES

Lv.	Name	Type	Kind	Pow.	Acc.	PP	Range
1	Me First	Normal	Status	—	—	20	Varies
1	Tackle	Normal	Physical	50	100	35	Normal
3	Leer	Normal	Status	—	100	30	Many Others
7	Astonish	Ghost	Physical	30	100	15	Normal
10	Hypnosis	Psychic	Status	—	60	20	Normal
13	Stomp	Normal	Physical	65	100	20	Normal
16	Sand Attack	Ground	Status	—	100	15	Normal
21	Take Down	Normal	Physical	90	85	20	Normal
23	Confuse Ray	Ghost	Status	—	100	10	Normal
27	Calm Mind	Psychic	Status	—	—	20	Self
33	Role Play	Psychic	Status	—	—	10	Normal
38	Zen Headbutt	Psychic	Physical	80	90	15	Normal
43	Jump Kick	Fighting	Physical	100	95	10	Normal
49	Imprison	Psychic	Status	—	—	10	Self
50	Captivate	Normal	Status	—	100	20	Many Others
55	Me First	Normal	Status	—	—	20	Varies

TM & HM MOVES

No.	Name	Type	Kind	Pow.	Acc.	PP	Range
TM03	Psyshock	Psychic	Special	80	100	10	Normal
TM04	Calm Mind	Psychic	Status	—	—	20	Self
TM05	Roar	Normal	Status	—	—	20	Normal
TM06	Toxic	Poison	Status	—	90	10	Normal
TM10	Hidden Power	Normal	Special	60	100	15	Normal
TM11	Sunny Day	Fire	Status	—	—	5	Both Sides
TM16	Light Screen	Psychic	Status	—	—	30	Your Side
TM17	Protect	Normal	Status	—	—	10	Self
TM18	Rain Dance	Water	Status	—	—	5	Both Sides
TM21	Frustration	Normal	Physical	—	100	20	Normal
TM22	Solar Beam	Grass	Special	120	100	10	Normal
TM24	Thunderbolt	Electric	Special	90	100	15	Normal
TM25	Thunder	Electric	Special	110	70	10	Normal
TM26	Earthquake	Ground	Physical	100	100	10	Adjacent
TM27	Return	Normal	Physical	—	100	20	Normal
TM29	Psychic	Psychic	Special	90	100	10	Normal
TM30	Shadow Ball	Ghost	Special	80	100	15	Normal
TM32	Double Team	Normal	Status	—	—	15	Self
TM33	Reflect	Psychic	Status	—	—	20	Your Side
TM42	Facade	Normal	Physical	70	100	20	Normal
TM44	Rest	Psychic	Status	—	—	10	Self
TM45	Attract	Normal	Status	—	100	15	Normal
TM46	Thief	Dark	Physical	60	100	25	Normal
TM48	Round	Normal	Special	60	100	15	Normal
TM53	Energy Ball	Grass	Special	90	100	10	Normal
TM57	Charge Beam	Electric	Special	50	90	10	Normal
TM67	Retaliate	Normal	Physical	70	100	5	Normal
TM68	Giga Impact	Normal	Physical	150	90	5	Normal
TM70	Flash	Normal	Status	—	100	20	Normal
TM73	Thunder Wave	Electric	Status	—	100	20	Normal
TM77	Psych Up	Normal	Status	—	—	10	Normal
TM78	Bulldoze	Ground	Physical	60	100	20	Adjacent
TM85	Dream Eater	Psychic	Special	100	100	15	Normal
TM87	Swagger	Normal	Status	—	90	15	Normal
TM88	Sleep Talk	Normal	Status	—	—	10	Self
TM90	Substitute	Normal	Status	—	—	10	Self
TM92	Trick Room	Psychic	Status	—	—	5	Both Sides
TM93	Wild Charge	Electric	Physical	90	100	15	Normal
TM94	Secret Power	Normal	Physical	70	100	20	Normal
TM100	Confide	Normal	Status	—	—	20	Normal

MOVES LEARNED IN EXCHANGE FOR BP

Name	Type	Kind	Pow.	Acc.	PP	Range
Signal Beam	Bug	Special	75	100	15	Normal
Bounce	Flying	Physical	85	85	5	Normal
Uproar	Normal	Special	90	100	10	1 Random
Gravity	Psychic	Status	—	—	5	Both Sides
Last Resort	Normal	Physical	140	100	5	Normal
Zen Headbutt	Psychic	Physical	80	90	15	Normal
Iron Tail	Steel	Physical	100	75	15	Normal
Snore	Normal	Special	50	100	15	Normal
Role Play	Psychic	Status	—	—	10	Normal
Shock Wave	Electric	Special	60	—	20	Normal
Spite	Ghost	Status	—	100	10	Normal
Magic Room	Psychic	Status	—	—	10	Both Sides
Skill Swap	Psychic	Status	—	—	10	Normal

MOVES TAUGHT BY PEOPLE

Name	Type	Kind	Pow.	Acc.	PP	Range

EGG MOVES

Name	Type	Kind	Pow.	Acc.	PP	Range
Spite	Ghost	Status	—	100	10	Normal
Disable	Normal	Status	—	100	20	Normal
Bite	Dark	Physical	60	100	25	Normal
Extrasensory	Psychic	Special	80	100	20	Normal
Thrash	Normal	Physical	120	100	10	1 Random
Double Kick	Fighting	Physical	30	100	30	Normal
Zen Headbutt	Psychic	Physical	80	90	15	Normal
Megahorn	Bug	Physical	120	85	10	Normal
Mud Sport	Ground	Status	—	—	15	Both Sides
Rage	Normal	Physical	20	100	20	Normal
Me First	Normal	Status	—	—	20	Varies

National Pokédex **235** Hoenn Pokédex —

Smeargle

Painter Pokémon

Normal

HEIGHT: 3'11" WEIGHT: 127.9 lbs.

Same form for ♂ / ♀

Ω Smeargle marks the boundaries of its territory using a body fluid that leaks out from the tip of its tail. Over 5,000 different marks left by this Pokémon have been found.

α Smeargle marks the boundaries of its territory using a body fluid that leaks out from the tip of its tail. Over 5,000 different marks left by this Pokémon have been found.

ABILITIES
Own Tempo
Technician

HIDDEN ABILITY
Moody

EGG GROUPS
Field

STAT GROWTH RATES
HP
Attack
Defense
Sp. Atk
Sp. Def
Speed

ITEMS SOMETIMES HELD BY WILD POKÉMON
—

EVOLUTION
Does not evolve

MAIN WAY TO REGISTER IN THE NATIONAL POKÉDEX

Appears in *Pokémon X* and *Pokémon Y*. Bring it to your game using Link Trade or the GTS.

Damage taken in normal battles

Type		Type	
Normal	×1	Flying	×1
Fire	×1	Psychic	×1
Water	×1	Bug	×1
Grass	×1	Rock	×1
Electric	×1	Ghost	×0
Ice	×1	Dragon	×1
Fighting	×2	Dark	×1
Poison	×1	Steel	×1
Ground	×1	Fairy	×1

Damage taken in Inverse battles

Type		Type	
Normal	×1	Flying	×1
Fire	×1	Psychic	×1
Water	×1	Bug	×1
Grass	×1	Rock	×1
Electric	×1	Ghost	×2
Ice	×1	Dragon	×1
Fighting	×0.5	Dark	×1
Poison	×1	Steel	×1
Ground	×1	Fairy	×1

Can be used in
Inverse Battle
Battle Institute
Battle Maison
Random Matchup (Free Battle)
Random Matchup (Others)

LEVEL-UP MOVES

Lv.	Name	Type	Kind	Pow.	Acc.	PP	Range
1	Sketch	Normal	Status	—	—	1	Normal
11	Sketch	Normal	Status	—	—	1	Normal
21	Sketch	Normal	Status	—	—	1	Normal
31	Sketch	Normal	Status	—	—	1	Normal
41	Sketch	Normal	Status	—	—	1	Normal
51	Sketch	Normal	Status	—	—	1	Normal
61	Sketch	Normal	Status	—	—	1	Normal
71	Sketch	Normal	Status	—	—	1	Normal
81	Sketch	Normal	Status	—	—	1	Normal
91	Sketch	Normal	Status	—	—	1	Normal

TM & HM MOVES

No.	Name	Type	Kind	Pow.	Acc.	PP	Range

MOVES LEARNED IN EXCHANGE FOR BP

Name	Type	Kind	Pow.	Acc.	PP	Range

MOVES TAUGHT BY PEOPLE

Name	Type	Kind	Pow.	Acc.	PP	Range

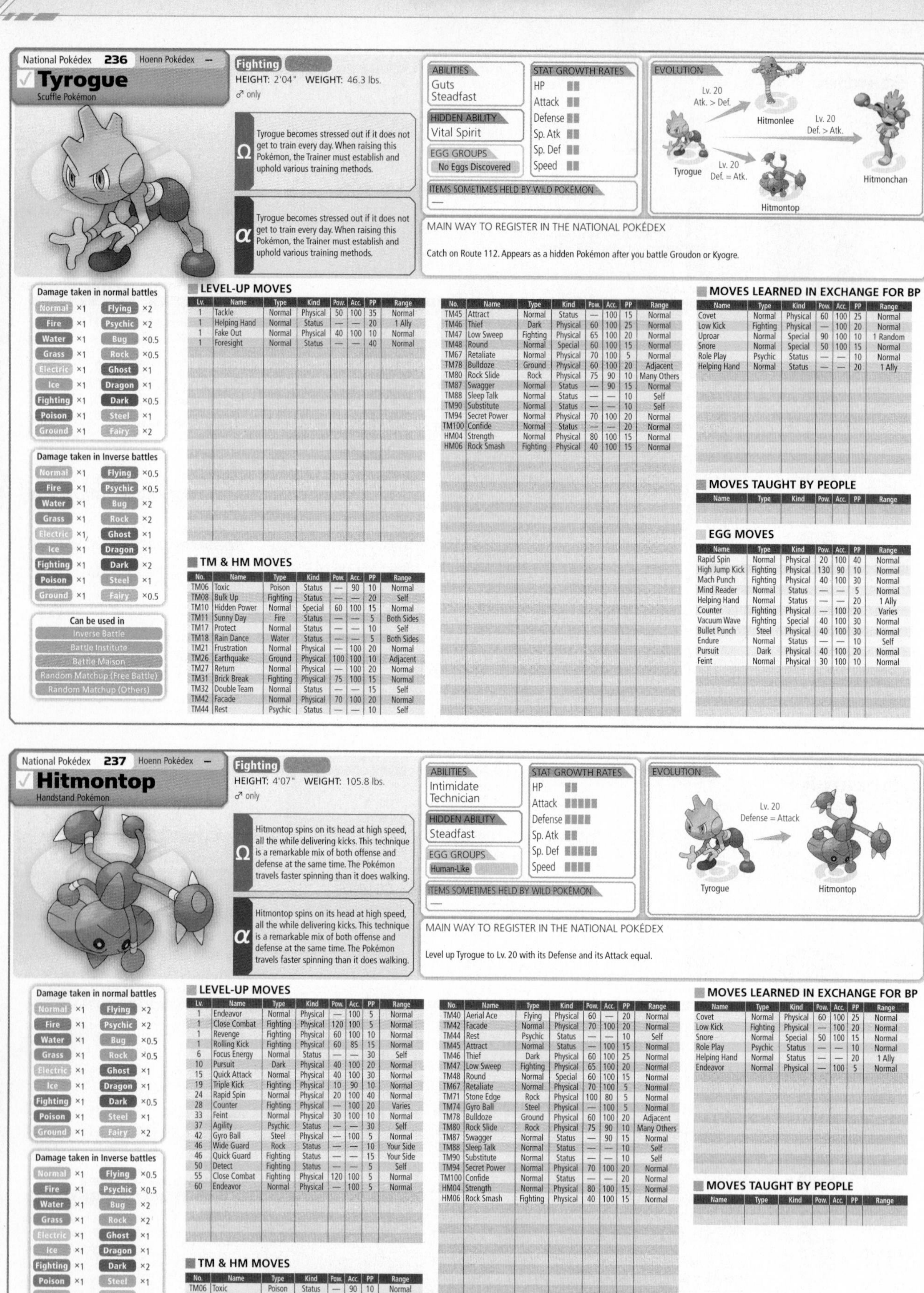

National Pokédex **236** Hoenn Pokédex —

Tyrogue

Scuffle Pokémon

Fighting

HEIGHT: 2'04" WEIGHT: 46.3 lbs.

♂ only

Ω Tyrogue becomes stressed out if it does not get to train every day. When raising this Pokémon, the Trainer must establish and uphold various training methods.

α Tyrogue becomes stressed out if it does not get to train every day. When raising this Pokémon, the Trainer must establish and uphold various training methods.

ABILITIES
Guts
Steadfast

HIDDEN ABILITY
Vital Spirit

EGG GROUPS
No Eggs Discovered

STAT GROWTH RATES
HP
Attack
Defense
Sp. Atk
Sp. Def
Speed

ITEMS SOMETIMES HELD BY WILD POKÉMON
—

EVOLUTION

MAIN WAY TO REGISTER IN THE NATIONAL POKÉDEX

Catch on Route 112. Appears as a hidden Pokémon after you battle Groudon or Kyogre.

Damage taken in normal battles

Type		Type	
Normal	×1	Flying	×2
Fire	×1	Psychic	×2
Water	×1	Bug	×0.5
Grass	×1	Rock	×0.5
Electric	×1	Ghost	×1
Ice	×1	Dragon	×1
Fighting	×1	Dark	×0.5
Poison	×1	Steel	×1
Ground	×1	Fairy	×2

Damage taken in Inverse battles

Type		Type	
Normal	×1	Flying	×0.5
Fire	×1	Psychic	×0.5
Water	×1	Bug	×2
Grass	×1	Rock	×2
Electric	×1	Ghost	×1
Ice	×1	Dragon	×1
Fighting	×1	Dark	×2
Poison	×1	Steel	×1
Ground	×1	Fairy	×0.5

Can be used in
Inverse Battle
Battle Institute
Battle Maison
Random Matchup (Free Battle)
Random Matchup (Others)

LEVEL-UP MOVES

Lv.	Name	Type	Kind	Pow.	Acc.	PP	Range
1	Tackle	Normal	Physical	50	100	35	Normal
1	Helping Hand	Normal	Status	—	—	20	1 Ally
1	Fake Out	Normal	Physical	40	100	10	Normal
1	Foresight	Normal	Status	—	—	40	Normal

TM & HM MOVES

No.	Name	Type	Kind	Pow.	Acc.	PP	Range
TM06	Toxic	Poison	Status	—	90	10	Normal
TM08	Bulk Up	Fighting	Status	—	—	20	Self
TM10	Hidden Power	Normal	Special	60	100	15	Normal
TM11	Sunny Day	Fire	Status	—	—	5	Both Sides
TM17	Protect	Normal	Status	—	—	10	Self
TM18	Rain Dance	Water	Status	—	—	5	Both Sides
TM21	Frustration	Normal	Physical	—	100	20	Normal
TM26	Earthquake	Ground	Physical	100	100	10	Adjacent
TM27	Return	Normal	Physical	—	100	20	Normal
TM31	Brick Break	Fighting	Physical	75	100	15	Normal
TM32	Double Team	Normal	Status	—	—	15	Self
TM42	Facade	Normal	Physical	70	100	20	Normal
TM44	Rest	Psychic	Status	—	—	10	Self
TM45	Attract	Normal	Status	—	100	15	Normal
TM46	Thief	Dark	Physical	60	100	25	Normal
TM47	Low Sweep	Fighting	Physical	65	100	20	Normal
TM48	Round	Normal	Special	60	100	15	Normal
TM67	Retaliate	Normal	Physical	70	100	5	Normal
TM78	Bulldoze	Ground	Physical	60	100	20	Adjacent
TM80	Rock Slide	Rock	Physical	75	90	10	Many Others
TM87	Swagger	Normal	Status	—	90	15	Normal
TM88	Sleep Talk	Normal	Status	—	—	10	Self
TM90	Substitute	Normal	Status	—	—	10	Self
TM94	Secret Power	Normal	Physical	70	100	20	Normal
TM100	Confide	Normal	Status	—	—	20	Normal
HM04	Strength	Normal	Physical	80	100	15	Normal
HM06	Rock Smash	Fighting	Physical	40	100	15	Normal

MOVES LEARNED IN EXCHANGE FOR BP

Name	Type	Kind	Pow.	Acc.	PP	Range
Covet	Normal	Physical	60	100	25	Normal
Low Kick	Fighting	Physical	—	100	20	Normal
Uproar	Normal	Special	90	100	10	1 Random
Snore	Normal	Special	50	100	15	Normal
Role Play	Psychic	Status	—	—	10	Normal
Helping Hand	Normal	Status	—	—	20	1 Ally

MOVES TAUGHT BY PEOPLE

Name	Type	Kind	Pow.	Acc.	PP	Range

EGG MOVES

Name	Type	Kind	Pow.	Acc.	PP	Range
Rapid Spin	Normal	Physical	20	100	40	Normal
High Jump Kick	Fighting	Physical	130	90	10	Normal
Mach Punch	Fighting	Physical	40	100	30	Normal
Mind Reader	Normal	Status	—	—	5	Normal
Helping Hand	Normal	Status	—	—	20	1 Ally
Counter	Fighting	Physical	—	100	20	Varies
Vacuum Wave	Fighting	Special	40	100	30	Normal
Bullet Punch	Steel	Physical	40	100	30	Normal
Endure	Normal	Status	—	—	10	Self
Pursuit	Dark	Physical	40	100	20	Normal
Feint	Normal	Physical	30	100	10	Normal

National Pokédex **237** Hoenn Pokédex —

Hitmontop

Handstand Pokémon

Fighting

HEIGHT: 4'07" WEIGHT: 105.8 lbs.

♂ only

Ω Hitmontop spins on its head at high speed, all the while delivering kicks. This technique is a remarkable mix of both offense and defense at the same time. The Pokémon travels faster spinning than it does walking.

α Hitmontop spins on its head at high speed, all the while delivering kicks. This technique is a remarkable mix of both offense and defense at the same time. The Pokémon travels faster spinning than it does walking.

ABILITIES
Intimidate
Technician

HIDDEN ABILITY
Steadfast

EGG GROUPS
Human-Like

STAT GROWTH RATES
HP
Attack
Defense
Sp. Atk
Sp. Def
Speed

ITEMS SOMETIMES HELD BY WILD POKÉMON
—

EVOLUTION

MAIN WAY TO REGISTER IN THE NATIONAL POKÉDEX

Level up Tyrogue to Lv. 20 with its Defense and its Attack equal.

Damage taken in normal battles

Type		Type	
Normal	×1	Flying	×2
Fire	×1	Psychic	×2
Water	×1	Bug	×0.5
Grass	×1	Rock	×0.5
Electric	×1	Ghost	×1
Ice	×1	Dragon	×1
Fighting	×1	Dark	×0.5
Poison	×1	Steel	×1
Ground	×1	Fairy	×2

Damage taken in Inverse battles

Type		Type	
Normal	×1	Flying	×0.5
Fire	×1	Psychic	×0.5
Water	×1	Bug	×2
Grass	×1	Rock	×2
Electric	×1	Ghost	×1
Ice	×1	Dragon	×1
Fighting	×1	Dark	×2
Poison	×1	Steel	×1
Ground	×1	Fairy	×0.5

Can be used in
Inverse Battle
Battle Institute
Battle Maison
Random Matchup (Free Battle)
Random Matchup (Others)

LEVEL-UP MOVES

Lv.	Name	Type	Kind	Pow.	Acc.	PP	Range
1	Endeavor	Normal	Physical	—	100	5	Normal
1	Close Combat	Fighting	Physical	120	100	5	Normal
1	Revenge	Fighting	Physical	60	100	10	Normal
1	Rolling Kick	Fighting	Physical	60	85	15	Normal
6	Focus Energy	Normal	Status	—	—	30	Self
10	Pursuit	Dark	Physical	40	100	20	Normal
15	Quick Attack	Normal	Physical	40	100	30	Normal
19	Triple Kick	Fighting	Physical	10	90	10	Normal
24	Rapid Spin	Normal	Physical	20	100	40	Normal
28	Counter	Fighting	Physical	—	100	20	Varies
33	Feint	Normal	Physical	30	100	10	Normal
37	Agility	Psychic	Status	—	—	30	Self
42	Gyro Ball	Steel	Physical	—	100	5	Normal
46	Wide Guard	Rock	Status	—	—	10	Your Side
46	Quick Guard	Fighting	Status	—	—	15	Your Side
50	Detect	Fighting	Status	—	—	5	Self
55	Close Combat	Fighting	Physical	120	100	5	Normal
60	Endeavor	Normal	Physical	—	100	5	Normal

TM & HM MOVES

No.	Name	Type	Kind	Pow.	Acc.	PP	Range
TM06	Toxic	Poison	Status	—	90	10	Normal
TM08	Bulk Up	Fighting	Status	—	—	20	Self
TM10	Hidden Power	Normal	Special	60	100	15	Normal
TM11	Sunny Day	Fire	Status	—	—	5	Both Sides
TM17	Protect	Normal	Status	—	—	10	Self
TM18	Rain Dance	Water	Status	—	—	5	Both Sides
TM21	Frustration	Normal	Physical	—	100	20	Normal
TM26	Earthquake	Ground	Physical	100	100	10	Adjacent
TM27	Return	Normal	Physical	—	100	20	Normal
TM28	Dig	Ground	Physical	80	100	10	Normal
TM31	Brick Break	Fighting	Physical	75	100	15	Normal
TM32	Double Team	Normal	Status	—	—	15	Self
TM37	Sandstorm	Rock	Status	—	—	10	Both Sides
TM40	Aerial Ace	Flying	Physical	60	—	20	Normal
TM42	Facade	Normal	Physical	70	100	20	Normal
TM44	Rest	Psychic	Status	—	—	10	Self
TM45	Attract	Normal	Status	—	100	15	Normal
TM46	Thief	Dark	Physical	60	100	25	Normal
TM47	Low Sweep	Fighting	Physical	65	100	20	Normal
TM48	Round	Normal	Special	60	100	15	Normal
TM67	Retaliate	Normal	Physical	70	100	5	Normal
TM71	Stone Edge	Rock	Physical	100	80	5	Normal
TM74	Gyro Ball	Steel	Physical	—	100	5	Normal
TM78	Bulldoze	Ground	Physical	60	100	20	Adjacent
TM80	Rock Slide	Rock	Physical	75	90	10	Many Others
TM87	Swagger	Normal	Status	—	90	15	Normal
TM88	Sleep Talk	Normal	Status	—	—	10	Self
TM90	Substitute	Normal	Status	—	—	10	Self
TM94	Secret Power	Normal	Physical	70	100	20	Normal
TM100	Confide	Normal	Status	—	—	20	Normal
HM04	Strength	Normal	Physical	80	100	15	Normal
HM06	Rock Smash	Fighting	Physical	40	100	15	Normal

MOVES LEARNED IN EXCHANGE FOR BP

Name	Type	Kind	Pow.	Acc.	PP	Range
Covet	Normal	Physical	60	100	25	Normal
Low Kick	Fighting	Physical	—	100	20	Normal
Snore	Normal	Special	50	100	15	Normal
Role Play	Psychic	Status	—	—	10	Normal
Helping Hand	Normal	Status	—	—	20	1 Ally
Endeavor	Normal	Physical	—	100	5	Normal

MOVES TAUGHT BY PEOPLE

Name	Type	Kind	Pow.	Acc.	PP	Range

National Pokédex **238** Hoenn Pokédex **—**

✓ Smoochum

Kiss Pokémon

Ice | Psychic

HEIGHT: 1'04" WEIGHT: 13.2 lbs.

♀ only

Ω Smoochum actively runs about, but also falls quite often. Whenever the chance arrives, it will look for its reflection to make sure its face hasn't become dirty.

α Smoochum actively runs about, but also falls quite often. Whenever the chance arrives, it will look for its reflection to make sure its face hasn't become dirty.

ABILITIES
Oblivious
Forewarn

HIDDEN ABILITY
Hydration

EGG GROUPS
No Eggs Discovered

STAT GROWTH RATES
HP ■■
Attack ■■
Defense ■
Sp. Atk ■■■■
Sp. Def ■■■
Speed ■■■■

ITEMS SOMETIMES HELD BY WILD POKÉMON
—

EVOLUTION

MAIN WAY TO REGISTER IN THE NATIONAL POKÉDEX

Appears in *Pokémon X* and *Pokémon Y*. Bring it to your game using Link Trade or the GTS.

Damage taken in normal battles

Type		Type	
Normal	×1	Flying	×1
Fire	×2	Psychic	×0.5
Water	×1	Bug	×2
Grass	×1	Rock	×2
Electric	×1	Ghost	×2
Ice	×0.5	Dragon	×1
Fighting	×1	Dark	×2
Poison	×1	Steel	×2
Ground	×1	Fairy	×1

Damage taken in Inverse battles

Type		Type	
Normal	×1	Flying	×1
Fire	×0.5	Psychic	×2
Water	×1	Bug	×0.5
Grass	×1	Rock	×0.5
Electric	×1	Ghost	×0.5
Ice	×2	Dragon	×1
Fighting	×1	Dark	×0.5
Poison	×1	Steel	×0.5
Ground	×1	Fairy	×1

Can be used in
Inverse Battle
Battle Institute
Battle Maison
Random Matchup (Free Battle)
Random Matchup (Others)

LEVEL-UP MOVES

Lv.	Name	Type	Kind	Pow.	Acc.	PP	Range
1	Pound	Normal	Physical	40	100	35	Normal
5	Lick	Ghost	Physical	30	100	30	Normal
8	Sweet Kiss	Fairy	Status	—	75	10	Normal
11	Powder Snow	Ice	Special	40	100	25	Many Others
15	Confusion	Psychic	Special	50	100	25	Normal
18	Sing	Normal	Status	—	55	15	Normal
21	Heart Stamp	Psychic	Physical	60	100	25	Normal
25	Mean Look	Normal	Status	—	—	5	Normal
28	Fake Tears	Dark	Status	—	100	20	Normal
31	Lucky Chant	Normal	Status	—	—	30	Your Side
35	Avalanche	Ice	Physical	60	100	10	Normal
38	Psychic	Psychic	Special	90	100	10	Normal
41	Copycat	Normal	Status	—	—	20	Self
45	Perish Song	Normal	Status	—	—	5	Adjacent
48	Blizzard	Ice	Special	110	70	5	Many Others

TM & HM MOVES

No.	Name	Type	Kind	Pow.	Acc.	PP	Range
TM03	Psyshock	Psychic	Special	80	100	10	Normal
TM04	Calm Mind	Psychic	Status	—	—	20	Self
TM06	Toxic	Poison	Status	—	90	10	Normal
TM07	Hail	Ice	Status	—	—	10	Both Sides
TM10	Hidden Power	Normal	Special	60	100	15	Normal
TM13	Ice Beam	Ice	Special	90	100	10	Normal
TM14	Blizzard	Ice	Special	110	70	5	Many Others
TM16	Light Screen	Psychic	Status	—	—	30	Your Side
TM17	Protect	Normal	Status	—	—	10	Self
TM18	Rain Dance	Water	Status	—	—	5	Both Sides
TM21	Frustration	Normal	Physical	—	100	20	Normal
TM27	Return	Normal	Physical	—	100	20	Normal
TM29	Psychic	Psychic	Special	90	100	10	Normal
TM30	Shadow Ball	Ghost	Special	80	100	15	Normal
TM32	Double Team	Normal	Status	—	—	15	Self
TM33	Reflect	Psychic	Status	—	—	20	Your Side
TM42	Facade	Normal	Physical	70	100	20	Normal
TM44	Rest	Psychic	Status	—	—	10	Self
TM45	Attract	Normal	Status	—	100	15	Normal
TM46	Thief	Dark	Physical	60	100	25	Normal
TM48	Round	Normal	Special	60	100	15	Normal
TM49	Echoed Voice	Normal	Special	40	100	15	Normal
TM56	Fling	Dark	Physical	—	100	10	Normal
TM66	Payback	Dark	Physical	50	100	10	Normal
TM70	Flash	Normal	Status	—	100	20	Normal
TM77	Psych Up	Normal	Status	—	—	10	Normal
TM79	Frost Breath	Ice	Special	60	90	10	Normal
TM85	Dream Eater	Psychic	Special	100	100	15	Normal
TM86	Grass Knot	Grass	Special	—	100	20	Normal
TM87	Swagger	Normal	Status	—	90	15	Normal
TM88	Sleep Talk	Normal	Status	—	—	10	Self
TM90	Substitute	Normal	Status	—	—	10	Self
TM92	Trick Room	Psychic	Status	—	—	5	Both Sides
TM94	Secret Power	Normal	Physical	70	100	20	Normal
TM100	Confide	Normal	Status	—	—	20	Normal

MOVES LEARNED IN EXCHANGE FOR BP

Name	Type	Kind	Pow.	Acc.	PP	Range
Covet	Normal	Physical	60	100	25	Normal
Signal Beam	Bug	Special	75	100	15	Normal
Uproar	Normal	Special	90	100	10	1 Random
Ice Punch	Ice	Physical	75	100	15	Normal
Magic Coat	Psychic	Status	—	—	15	Self
Icy Wind	Ice	Special	55	95	15	Many Others
Zen Headbutt	Psychic	Physical	80	90	15	Normal
Snore	Normal	Special	50	100	15	Normal
Role Play	Psychic	Status	—	—	10	Normal
Heal Bell	Normal	Status	—	—	5	Your Party
Water Pulse	Water	Special	60	100	20	Normal
Helping Hand	Normal	Status	—	—	20	1 Ally
Trick	Psychic	Status	—	100	10	Normal
Magic Room	Psychic	Status	—	—	10	Both Sides
Recycle	Normal	Status	—	—	10	Self
Skill Swap	Psychic	Status	—	—	10	Normal

MOVES TAUGHT BY PEOPLE

Name	Type	Kind	Pow.	Acc.	PP	Range

EGG MOVES

Name	Type	Kind	Pow.	Acc.	PP	Range
Meditate	Psychic	Status	—	—	40	Self
Fake Out	Normal	Physical	40	100	10	Normal
Wish	Normal	Status	—	—	10	Self
Ice Punch	Ice	Physical	75	100	15	Normal
Miracle Eye	Psychic	Status	—	—	40	Normal
Nasty Plot	Dark	Status	—	—	20	Self
Wake-Up Slap	Fighting	Physical	70	100	10	Normal
Captivate	Normal	Status	—	100	20	Many Others

National Pokédex **239** Hoenn Pokédex **—**

✓ Elekid

Electric Pokémon

Electric

HEIGHT: 2'00" WEIGHT: 51.8 lbs.

Same form for ♂ / ♀

Ω Elekid stores electricity in its body. If it touches metal and accidentally discharges all its built-up electricity, this Pokémon begins swinging its arms in circles to recharge itself.

α Elekid stores electricity in its body. If it touches metal and accidentally discharges all its built-up electricity, this Pokémon begins swinging its arms in circles to recharge itself.

ABILITY
Static

HIDDEN ABILITY
Vital Spirit

EGG GROUPS
No Eggs Discovered

STAT GROWTH RATES
HP ■■
Attack ■■■
Defense ■■
Sp. Atk ■■■
Sp. Def ■■
Speed ■■■■■

ITEMS SOMETIMES HELD BY WILD POKÉMON
Electirizer

EVOLUTION

Elekid → Lv. 30 → Electabuzz → Link Trade with an Electirizer → Electivire

MAIN WAY TO REGISTER IN THE NATIONAL POKÉDEX

Catch on Mirage Mountain 6.

Damage taken in normal battles

Type		Type	
Normal	×1	Flying	×0.5
Fire	×1	Psychic	×1
Water	×1	Bug	×1
Grass	×1	Rock	×1
Electric	×0.5	Ghost	×1
Ice	×1	Dragon	×1
Fighting	×1	Dark	×1
Poison	×1	Steel	×0.5
Ground	×2	Fairy	×1

Damage taken in Inverse battles

Type		Type	
Normal	×1	Flying	×2
Fire	×1	Psychic	×1
Water	×1	Bug	×1
Grass	×1	Rock	×1
Electric	×2	Ghost	×1
Ice	×1	Dragon	×1
Fighting	×1	Dark	×1
Poison	×1	Steel	×2
Ground	×0.5	Fairy	×1

Can be used in
Inverse Battle
Battle Institute
Battle Maison
Random Matchup (Free Battle)
Random Matchup (Others)

LEVEL-UP MOVES

Lv.	Name	Type	Kind	Pow.	Acc.	PP	Range
1	Quick Attack	Normal	Physical	40	100	30	Normal
1	Leer	Normal	Status	—	100	30	Many Others
5	Thunder Shock	Electric	Special	40	100	30	Normal
8	Low Kick	Fighting	Physical	—	100	20	Normal
12	Swift	Normal	Special	60	—	20	Many Others
15	Shock Wave	Electric	Special	60	—	20	Normal
19	Thunder Wave	Electric	Status	—	100	20	Normal
22	Electro Ball	Electric	Special	—	100	10	Normal
26	Light Screen	Psychic	Status	—	—	30	Your Side
29	Thunder Punch	Electric	Physical	75	100	15	Normal
33	Discharge	Electric	Special	80	100	15	Adjacent
36	Screech	Normal	Status	—	85	40	Normal
40	Thunderbolt	Electric	Special	90	100	15	Normal
43	Thunder	Electric	Special	110	70	10	Normal

TM & HM MOVES

No.	Name	Type	Kind	Pow.	Acc.	PP	Range
TM06	Toxic	Poison	Status	—	90	10	Normal
TM10	Hidden Power	Normal	Special	60	100	15	Normal
TM16	Light Screen	Psychic	Status	—	—	30	Your Side
TM17	Protect	Normal	Status	—	—	10	Self
TM18	Rain Dance	Water	Status	—	—	5	Both Sides
TM21	Frustration	Normal	Physical	—	100	20	Normal
TM24	Thunderbolt	Electric	Special	90	100	15	Normal
TM25	Thunder	Electric	Special	110	70	10	Normal
TM27	Return	Normal	Physical	—	100	20	Normal
TM29	Psychic	Psychic	Special	90	100	10	Normal
TM31	Brick Break	Fighting	Physical	75	100	15	Normal
TM32	Double Team	Normal	Status	—	—	15	Self
TM42	Facade	Normal	Physical	70	100	20	Normal
TM44	Rest	Psychic	Status	—	—	10	Self
TM45	Attract	Normal	Status	—	100	15	Normal
TM46	Thief	Dark	Physical	60	100	25	Normal
TM48	Round	Normal	Special	60	100	15	Normal
TM56	Fling	Dark	Physical	—	100	10	Normal
TM57	Charge Beam	Electric	Special	50	90	10	Normal
TM70	Flash	Normal	Status	—	100	20	Normal
TM72	Volt Switch	Electric	Special	70	100	20	Normal
TM73	Thunder Wave	Electric	Status	—	100	20	Normal
TM87	Swagger	Normal	Status	—	90	15	Normal
TM88	Sleep Talk	Normal	Status	—	—	10	Self
TM90	Substitute	Normal	Status	—	—	10	Self
TM93	Wild Charge	Electric	Physical	90	100	15	Normal
TM94	Secret Power	Normal	Physical	70	100	20	Normal
TM98	Power-Up Punch	Fighting	Physical	40	100	20	Normal
TM100	Confide	Normal	Status	—	—	20	Normal
HM06	Rock Smash	Fighting	Physical	40	100	15	Normal

MOVES LEARNED IN EXCHANGE FOR BP

Name	Type	Kind	Pow.	Acc.	PP	Range
Covet	Normal	Physical	60	100	25	Normal
Dual Chop	Dragon	Physical	40	90	15	Normal
Signal Beam	Bug	Special	75	100	15	Normal
Low Kick	Fighting	Physical	—	100	20	Normal
Uproar	Normal	Special	90	100	10	1 Random
Thunder Punch	Electric	Physical	75	100	15	Normal
Fire Punch	Fire	Physical	75	100	15	Normal
Ice Punch	Ice	Physical	75	100	15	Normal
Magnet Rise	Electric	Status	—	—	10	Self
Electroweb	Electric	Special	55	95	15	Many Others
Snore	Normal	Special	50	100	15	Normal
Focus Punch	Fighting	Physical	150	100	20	Normal
Shock Wave	Electric	Special	60	—	20	Normal
Helping Hand	Normal	Status	—	—	20	1 Ally

MOVES TAUGHT BY PEOPLE

Name	Type	Kind	Pow.	Acc.	PP	Range

EGG MOVES

Name	Type	Kind	Pow.	Acc.	PP	Range
Karate Chop	Fighting	Physical	50	100	25	Normal
Barrier	Psychic	Status	—	—	20	Self
Rolling Kick	Fighting	Physical	60	85	15	Normal
Meditate	Psychic	Status	—	—	40	Self
Cross Chop	Fighting	Physical	100	80	5	Normal
Fire Punch	Fire	Physical	75	100	15	Normal
Ice Punch	Ice	Physical	75	100	15	Normal
Dynamic Punch	Fighting	Physical	100	50	5	Normal
Feint	Normal	Physical	30	100	10	Normal
Hammer Arm	Fighting	Physical	100	90	10	Normal
Focus Punch	Fighting	Physical	150	100	20	Normal

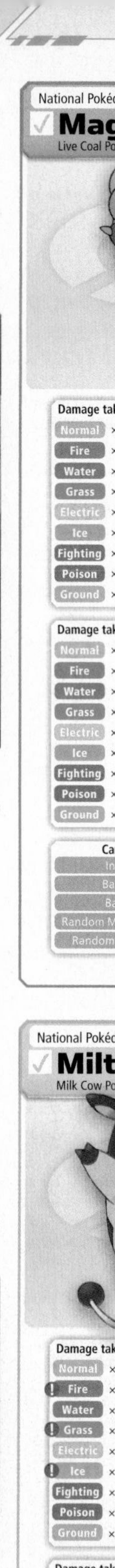

National Pokédex **240** Hoenn Pokédex —

Magby

Live Coal Pokémon

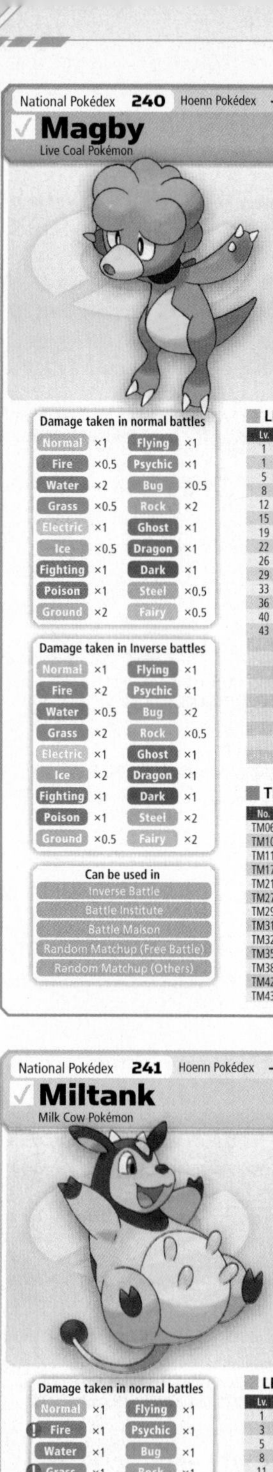

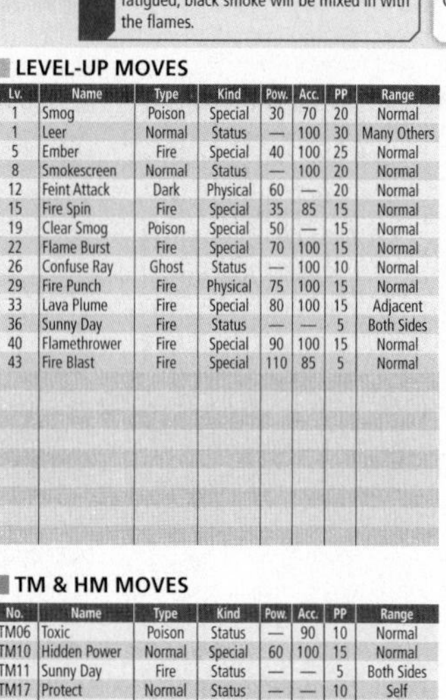

Fire

HEIGHT: 2'04" WEIGHT: 47.2 lbs.

Same form for ♂ / ♀

Ω Magby's state of health is determined by observing the fire it breathes. If the Pokémon is spouting yellow flames from its mouth, it is in good health. When it is fatigued, black smoke will be mixed in with the flames.

α Magby's state of health is determined by observing the fire it breathes. If the Pokémon is spouting yellow flames from its mouth, it is in good health. When it is fatigued, black smoke will be mixed in with the flames.

ABILITY: Flame Body

HIDDEN ABILITY: Vital Spirit

EGG GROUPS: No Eggs Discovered

STAT GROWTH RATES: HP, Attack, Defense, Sp. Atk, Sp. Def, Speed

ITEMS SOMETIMES HELD BY WILD POKÉMON: Magmarizer

EVOLUTION: Magby → Lv. 30 → Magmar → Link Trade with a Magmarizer → Magmortar

MAIN WAY TO REGISTER IN THE NATIONAL POKÉDEX

Catch on Mirage Mountain 5.

Damage taken in normal battles

Type		Type	
Normal	×1	Flying	×1
Fire	×0.5	Psychic	×1
Water	×2	Bug	×0.5
Grass	×0.5	Rock	×2
Electric	×1	Ghost	×1
Ice	×0.5	Dragon	×1
Fighting	×1	Dark	×1
Poison	×1	Steel	×0.5
Ground	×2	Fairy	×0.5

Damage taken in Inverse battles

Type		Type	
Normal	×1	Flying	×1
Fire	×2	Psychic	×1
Water	×0.5	Bug	×2
Grass	×2	Rock	×0.5
Electric	×1	Ghost	×1
Ice	×2	Dragon	×1
Fighting	×1	Dark	×1
Poison	×1	Steel	×2
Ground	×0.5	Fairy	×2

Can be used in

Inverse Battle
Battle Institute
Battle Maison
Random Matchup (Free Battle)
Random Matchup (Others)

LEVEL-UP MOVES

Lv.	Name	Type	Kind	Pow.	Acc.	PP	Range
1	Smog	Poison	Special	30	70	20	Normal
1	Leer	Normal	Status	—	100	30	Many Others
5	Ember	Fire	Special	40	100	25	Normal
8	Smokescreen	Normal	Status	—	100	20	Normal
12	Feint Attack	Dark	Physical	60	—	20	Normal
15	Fire Spin	Fire	Special	35	85	15	Normal
19	Clear Smog	Poison	Special	50	—	15	Normal
22	Flame Burst	Fire	Special	70	100	15	Normal
26	Confuse Ray	Ghost	Status	—	100	10	Normal
29	Fire Punch	Fire	Physical	75	100	15	Normal
33	Lava Plume	Fire	Special	80	100	15	Adjacent
36	Sunny Day	Fire	Status	—	—	5	Both Sides
40	Flamethrower	Fire	Special	90	100	15	Normal
43	Fire Blast	Fire	Special	110	85	5	Normal

TM & HM MOVES

No.	Name	Type	Kind	Pow.	Acc.	PP	Range
TM06	Toxic	Poison	Status	—	90	10	Normal
TM10	Hidden Power	Normal	Special	60	100	15	Normal
TM11	Sunny Day	Fire	Status	—	—	5	Both Sides
TM17	Protect	Normal	Status	—	—	10	Self
TM21	Frustration	Normal	Physical	—	100	20	Normal
TM27	Return	Normal	Physical	—	100	20	Normal
TM29	Psychic	Psychic	Special	90	100	10	Normal
TM31	Brick Break	Fighting	Physical	75	100	15	Normal
TM32	Double Team	Normal	Status	—	—	15	Self
TM35	Flamethrower	Fire	Special	90	100	15	Normal
TM38	Fire Blast	Fire	Special	110	85	5	Normal
TM42	Facade	Normal	Physical	70	100	20	Normal
TM43	Flame Charge	Fire	Physical	50	100	20	Normal
TM44	Rest	Psychic	Status	—	—	10	Self
TM45	Attract	Normal	Status	—	100	15	Normal
TM46	Thief	Dark	Physical	60	100	25	Normal
TM48	Round	Normal	Special	60	100	15	Normal
TM50	Overheat	Fire	Special	130	90	5	Normal
TM56	Fling	Dark	Physical	—	100	10	Normal
TM59	Incinerate	Fire	Special	60	100	15	Many Others
TM61	Will-O-Wisp	Fire	Status	—	85	15	Normal
TM87	Swagger	Normal	Status	—	90	15	Normal
TM88	Sleep Talk	Normal	Status	—	—	10	Self
TM90	Substitute	Normal	Status	—	—	10	Self
TM94	Secret Power	Normal	Physical	70	100	20	Normal
TM98	Power-Up Punch	Fighting	Physical	40	100	20	Normal
TM100	Confide	Normal	Status	—	—	20	Normal
HM06	Rock Smash	Fighting	Physical	40	100	15	Normal

MOVES LEARNED IN EXCHANGE FOR BP

Name	Type	Kind	Pow.	Acc.	PP	Range
Covet	Normal	Physical	60	100	25	Normal
Dual Chop	Dragon	Physical	40	90	15	Normal
Uproar	Normal	Special	90	100	10	1 Random
Thunder Punch	Electric	Physical	75	100	15	Normal
Fire Punch	Fire	Physical	75	100	15	Normal
Iron Tail	Steel	Physical	100	75	15	Normal
Snore	Normal	Special	50	100	15	Normal
Heat Wave	Fire	Special	95	90	10	Many Others
Focus Punch	Fighting	Physical	150	100	20	Normal
Helping Hand	Normal	Status	—	—	20	1 Ally

MOVES TAUGHT BY PEOPLE

Name	Type	Kind	Pow.	Acc.	PP	Range

EGG MOVES

Name	Type	Kind	Pow.	Acc.	PP	Range
Karate Chop	Fighting	Physical	50	100	25	Normal
Mega Punch	Normal	Physical	80	85	20	Normal
Barrier	Psychic	Status	—	—	20	Self
Screech	Normal	Status	—	85	40	Normal
Cross Chop	Fighting	Physical	100	80	5	Normal
Thunder Punch	Electric	Physical	75	100	15	Normal
Mach Punch	Fighting	Physical	40	100	30	Normal
Dynamic Punch	Fighting	Physical	100	50	5	Normal
Flare Blitz	Fire	Physical	120	100	15	Normal
Belly Drum	Normal	Status	—	—	10	Self
Iron Tail	Steel	Physical	100	75	15	Normal
Focus Energy	Normal	Status	—	—	30	Self
Power Swap	Psychic	Status	—	—	10	Normal
Belch	Poison	Special	120	90	10	Normal

National Pokédex **241** Hoenn Pokédex —

Miltank

Milk Cow Pokémon

Normal

HEIGHT: 3'11" WEIGHT: 166.4 lbs.

♀ only

Ω Miltank gives over five gallons of milk on a daily basis. Its sweet milk is enjoyed by children and grown-ups alike. People who can't drink milk turn it into yogurt and eat it instead.

α Miltank gives over five gallons of milk on a daily basis. Its sweet milk is enjoyed by children and grown-ups alike. People who can't drink milk turn it into yogurt and eat it instead.

ABILITIES: Thick Fat, Scrappy

HIDDEN ABILITY: Sap Sipper

EGG GROUPS: Field

STAT GROWTH RATES: HP, Attack, Defense, Sp. Atk, Sp. Def, Speed

ITEMS SOMETIMES HELD BY WILD POKÉMON: —

EVOLUTION: Does not evolve

MAIN WAY TO REGISTER IN THE NATIONAL POKÉDEX

Appears in *Pokémon X* and *Pokémon Y*. Bring it to your game using Link Trade or the GTS.

Damage taken in normal battles

Type		Type	
Normal	×1	Flying	×1
! Fire	×1	Psychic	×1
Water	×1	Bug	×1
! Grass	×1	Rock	×1
Electric	×1	Ghost	×0
! Ice	×1	Dragon	×1
Fighting	×2	Dark	×1
Poison	×1	Steel	×1
Ground	×1	Fairy	×1

Damage taken in Inverse battles

Type		Type	
Normal	×1	Flying	×1
! Fire	×1	Psychic	×1
Water	×1	Bug	×1
! Grass	×1	Rock	×1
Electric	×1	Ghost	×2
! Ice	×1	Dragon	×1
Fighting	×0.5	Dark	×1
Poison	×1	Steel	×1
Ground	×1	Fairy	×1

Can be used in

Inverse Battle
Battle Institute
Battle Maison
Random Matchup (Free Battle)
Random Matchup (Others)

LEVEL-UP MOVES

Lv.	Name	Type	Kind	Pow.	Acc.	PP	Range
1	Tackle	Normal	Physical	50	100	35	Normal
3	Growl	Normal	Status	—	100	40	Many Others
5	Defense Curl	Normal	Status	—	—	40	Self
8	Stomp	Normal	Physical	65	100	20	Normal
11	Milk Drink	Normal	Status	—	—	10	Self
15	Bide	Normal	Physical	—	—	10	Self
19	Rollout	Rock	Physical	30	90	20	Normal
24	Body Slam	Normal	Physical	85	100	15	Normal
29	Zen Headbutt	Psychic	Physical	80	90	15	Normal
35	Captivate	Normal	Status	—	100	20	Many Others
41	Gyro Ball	Steel	Physical	—	100	5	Normal
48	Heal Bell	Normal	Status	—	—	5	Your Party
50	Wake-Up Slap	Fighting	Physical	70	100	10	Normal

TM & HM MOVES

No.	Name	Type	Kind	Pow.	Acc.	PP	Range
TM06	Toxic	Poison	Status	—	90	10	Normal
TM10	Hidden Power	Normal	Special	60	100	15	Normal
TM11	Sunny Day	Fire	Status	—	—	5	Both Sides
TM13	Ice Beam	Ice	Special	90	100	10	Normal
TM14	Blizzard	Ice	Special	110	70	5	Many Others
TM15	Hyper Beam	Normal	Special	150	90	5	Normal
TM17	Protect	Normal	Status	—	—	10	Self
TM18	Rain Dance	Water	Status	—	—	5	Both Sides
TM21	Frustration	Normal	Physical	—	100	20	Normal
TM22	Solar Beam	Grass	Special	120	100	10	Normal
TM24	Thunderbolt	Electric	Special	90	100	15	Normal
TM25	Thunder	Electric	Special	110	70	10	Normal
TM26	Earthquake	Ground	Physical	100	100	10	Adjacent
TM27	Return	Normal	Physical	—	100	20	Normal
TM30	Shadow Ball	Ghost	Special	80	100	15	Normal
TM31	Brick Break	Fighting	Physical	75	100	15	Normal
TM32	Double Team	Normal	Status	—	—	15	Self
TM37	Sandstorm	Rock	Status	—	—	10	Both Sides
TM39	Rock Tomb	Rock	Physical	60	95	15	Normal
TM42	Facade	Normal	Physical	70	100	20	Normal
TM44	Rest	Psychic	Status	—	—	10	Self
TM45	Attract	Normal	Status	—	100	15	Normal
TM48	Round	Normal	Special	60	100	15	Normal
TM49	Echoed Voice	Normal	Special	40	100	15	Normal
TM52	Focus Blast	Fighting	Special	120	70	5	Normal
TM56	Fling	Dark	Physical	—	100	10	Normal
TM67	Retaliate	Normal	Physical	70	100	5	Normal
TM68	Giga Impact	Normal	Physical	150	90	5	Normal
TM73	Thunder Wave	Electric	Status	—	100	20	Normal
TM74	Gyro Ball	Steel	Physical	—	100	5	Normal
TM77	Psych Up	Normal	Status	—	—	10	Normal
TM78	Bulldoze	Ground	Physical	60	100	20	Adjacent
TM80	Rock Slide	Rock	Physical	75	90	10	Many Others
TM87	Swagger	Normal	Status	—	90	15	Normal
TM88	Sleep Talk	Normal	Status	—	—	10	Self
TM90	Substitute	Normal	Status	—	—	10	Self
TM94	Secret Power	Normal	Physical	70	100	20	Normal
TM98	Power-Up Punch	Fighting	Physical	40	100	20	Normal
TM100	Confide	Normal	Status	—	—	20	Normal
HM03	Surf	Water	Special	90	100	15	Adjacent
HM04	Strength	Normal	Physical	80	100	15	Normal
HM06	Rock Smash	Fighting	Physical	40	100	15	Normal

MOVES LEARNED IN EXCHANGE FOR BP

Name	Type	Kind	Pow.	Acc.	PP	Range
Iron Head	Steel	Physical	80	100	15	Normal
Thunder Punch	Electric	Physical	75	100	15	Normal
Fire Punch	Fire	Physical	75	100	15	Normal
Ice Punch	Ice	Physical	75	100	15	Normal
Block	Normal	Status	—	—	5	Normal
Icy Wind	Ice	Special	55	95	15	Many Others
Zen Headbutt	Psychic	Physical	80	90	15	Normal
Iron Tail	Steel	Physical	100	75	15	Normal
Snore	Normal	Special	50	100	15	Normal
Heal Bell	Normal	Status	—	—	5	Your Party
Focus Punch	Fighting	Physical	150	100	20	Normal
Shock Wave	Electric	Special	60	—	20	Normal
Water Pulse	Water	Special	60	100	20	Normal
After You	Normal	Status	—	—	15	Normal
Helping Hand	Normal	Status	—	—	20	1 Ally
Stealth Rock	Rock	Status	—	—	20	Other Side

MOVES TAUGHT BY PEOPLE

Name	Type	Kind	Pow.	Acc.	PP	Range

EGG MOVES

Name	Type	Kind	Pow.	Acc.	PP	Range
Present	Normal	Physical	—	90	15	Normal
Reversal	Fighting	Physical	—	100	15	Normal
Seismic Toss	Fighting	Physical	—	100	20	Normal
Endure	Normal	Status	—	—	10	Self
Curse	Ghost	Status	—	—	10	Varies
Helping Hand	Normal	Status	—	—	20	1 Ally
Sleep Talk	Normal	Status	—	—	10	Self
Dizzy Punch	Normal	Physical	70	100	10	Normal
Hammer Arm	Fighting	Physical	100	90	10	Normal
Double-Edge	Normal	Physical	120	100	15	Normal
Punishment	Dark	Physical	—	100	5	Normal
Natural Gift	Normal	Physical	—	100	15	Normal
Heart Stamp	Psychic	Physical	60	100	25	Normal
Belch	Poison	Special	120	90	10	Normal

National Pokédex **242** Hoenn Pokédex —

Blissey

Happiness Pokémon

Normal

HEIGHT: 4'11" WEIGHT: 103.2 lbs.

♀ only

Ω Blissey senses sadness with its fluffy coat of fur. If it does so, this Pokémon will rush over to a sad person, no matter how far away, to share a Lucky Egg that brings a smile to any face.

α Blissey senses sadness with its fluffy coat of fur. If it does so, this Pokémon will rush over to a sad person, no matter how far away, to share a Lucky Egg that brings a smile to any face.

ABILITIES
Natural Cure
Serene Grace

HIDDEN ABILITY
Healer

EGG GROUPS
Fairy

STAT GROWTH RATES
HP ▮▮▮▮▮▮▮▮▮▮
Attack ▮
Defense ▮
Sp. Atk ▮▮▮▮
Sp. Def ▮▮▮▮▮▮
Speed ▮▮▮

ITEMS SOMETIMES HELD BY WILD POKÉMON
—

EVOLUTION
Happiny → Level up with Oval Stone between 4 A.M. and 7:59 P.M. → Chansey → Level up with high friendship → Blissey

MAIN WAY TO REGISTER IN THE NATIONAL POKÉDEX

Level up Chansey with high friendship.

Damage taken in normal battles

Type		Type	
Normal	×1	Flying	×1
Fire	×1	Psychic	×1
Water	×1	Bug	×1
Grass	×1	Rock	×1
Electric	×1	Ghost	×0
Ice	×1	Dragon	×1
Fighting	×2	Dark	×1
Poison	×1	Steel	×1
Ground	×1	Fairy	×1

Damage taken in Inverse battles

Type		Type	
Normal	×1	Flying	×1
Fire	×1	Psychic	×1
Water	×1	Bug	×1
Grass	×1	Rock	×1
Electric	×1	Ghost	×2
Ice	×1	Dragon	×1
Fighting	×0.5	Dark	×1
Poison	×1	Steel	×1
Ground	×1	Fairy	×1

Can be used in
Inverse Battle
Battle Institute
Battle Maison
Random Matchup (Free Battle)
Random Matchup (Others)

LEVEL-UP MOVES

Lv.	Name	Type	Kind	Pow.	Acc.	PP	Range
1	Double-Edge	Normal	Physical	120	100	15	Normal
1	Defense Curl	Normal	Status	—	—	40	Self
1	Pound	Normal	Physical	40	100	35	Normal
1	Growl	Normal	Status	—	100	40	Many Others
5	Tail Whip	Normal	Status	—	100	30	Many Others
9	Refresh	Normal	Status	—	—	20	Self
12	Double Slap	Normal	Physical	15	85	10	Normal
16	Soft-Boiled	Normal	Status	—	—	10	Self
20	Bestow	Normal	Status	—	—	15	Normal
23	Minimize	Normal	Status	—	—	10	Self
27	Take Down	Normal	Physical	90	85	20	Normal
31	Sing	Normal	Status	—	55	15	Normal
34	Fling	Dark	Physical	—	100	10	Normal
38	Heal Pulse	Psychic	Status	—	—	10	Normal
42	Egg Bomb	Normal	Physical	100	75	10	Normal
46	Light Screen	Psychic	Status	—	—	30	Your Side
50	Healing Wish	Psychic	Status	—	—	10	Self
54	Double-Edge	Normal	Physical	120	100	15	Normal

TM & HM MOVES

No.	Name	Type	Kind	Pow.	Acc.	PP	Range
TM04	Calm Mind	Psychic	Status	—	—	20	Self
TM06	Toxic	Poison	Status	—	90	10	Normal
TM07	Hail	Ice	Status	—	—	10	Both Sides
TM10	Hidden Power	Normal	Special	60	100	15	Normal
TM11	Sunny Day	Fire	Status	—	—	5	Both Sides
TM13	Ice Beam	Ice	Special	90	100	10	Normal
TM14	Blizzard	Ice	Special	110	70	5	Many Others
TM15	Hyper Beam	Normal	Special	150	90	5	Normal
TM16	Light Screen	Psychic	Status	—	—	30	Your Side
TM17	Protect	Normal	Status	—	—	10	Self
TM18	Rain Dance	Water	Status	—	—	5	Both Sides
TM20	Safeguard	Normal	Status	—	—	25	Your Side
TM21	Frustration	Normal	Physical	—	100	20	Normal
TM22	Solar Beam	Grass	Special	120	100	10	Normal
TM24	Thunderbolt	Electric	Special	90	100	15	Normal
TM25	Thunder	Electric	Special	110	70	10	Normal
TM26	Earthquake	Ground	Physical	100	100	10	Adjacent
TM27	Return	Normal	Physical	—	100	20	Normal
TM29	Psychic	Psychic	Special	90	100	10	Normal
TM30	Shadow Ball	Ghost	Special	80	100	15	Normal
TM31	Brick Break	Fighting	Physical	75	100	15	Normal
TM32	Double Team	Normal	Status	—	—	15	Self
TM35	Flamethrower	Fire	Special	90	100	15	Normal
TM37	Sandstorm	Rock	Status	—	—	10	Both Sides
TM38	Fire Blast	Fire	Special	110	85	5	Normal
TM39	Rock Tomb	Rock	Physical	60	95	15	Normal
TM42	Facade	Normal	Physical	70	100	20	Normal
TM44	Rest	Psychic	Status	—	—	10	Self
TM45	Attract	Normal	Status	—	100	15	Normal
TM48	Round	Normal	Special	60	100	15	Normal
TM49	Echoed Voice	Normal	Special	40	100	15	Normal
TM52	Focus Blast	Fighting	Special	120	70	5	Normal
TM56	Fling	Dark	Physical	—	100	10	Normal
TM57	Charge Beam	Electric	Special	50	90	10	Normal
TM59	Incinerate	Fire	Special	60	100	15	Many Others
TM67	Retaliate	Normal	Physical	70	100	5	Normal
TM68	Giga Impact	Normal	Physical	150	90	5	Normal
TM70	Flash	Normal	Status	—	100	20	Normal
TM73	Thunder Wave	Electric	Status	—	100	20	Normal
TM77	Psych Up	Normal	Status	—	—	10	Normal
TM78	Bulldoze	Ground	Physical	60	100	20	Adjacent
TM80	Rock Slide	Rock	Physical	75	90	10	Many Others
TM85	Dream Eater	Psychic	Special	100	100	15	Normal
TM86	Grass Knot	Grass	Special	—	100	20	Normal
TM87	Swagger	Normal	Status	—	90	15	Normal
TM88	Sleep Talk	Normal	Status	—	—	10	Self
TM90	Substitute	Normal	Status	—	—	10	Self
TM93	Wild Charge	Electric	Physical	90	100	15	Normal
TM94	Secret Power	Normal	Physical	70	100	20	Normal
TM98	Power-Up Punch	Fighting	Physical	40	100	20	Normal
TM99	Dazzling Gleam	Fairy	Special	80	100	10	Many Others
TM100	Confide	Normal	Status	—	—	20	Normal
HM04	Strength	Normal	Physical	80	100	15	Normal
HM06	Rock Smash	Fighting	Physical	40	100	15	Normal

MOVES LEARNED IN EXCHANGE FOR BP

Name	Type	Kind	Pow.	Acc.	PP	Range
Covet	Normal	Physical	60	100	25	Normal
Thunder Punch	Electric	Physical	75	100	15	Normal
Fire Punch	Fire	Physical	75	100	15	Normal
Ice Punch	Ice	Physical	75	100	15	Normal
Block	Normal	Status	—	—	5	Normal
Gravity	Psychic	Status	—	—	5	Both Sides
Last Resort	Normal	Physical	140	100	5	Normal
Icy Wind	Ice	Special	55	95	15	Many Others
Zen Headbutt	Psychic	Physical	80	90	15	Normal
Hyper Voice	Normal	Special	90	100	10	Many Others
Iron Tail	Steel	Physical	100	75	15	Normal
Snore	Normal	Special	50	100	15	Normal
Heal Bell	Normal	Status	—	—	5	Your Party
Drain Punch	Fighting	Physical	75	100	10	Normal
Focus Punch	Fighting	Physical	150	100	20	Normal
Shock Wave	Electric	Special	60	—	20	Normal
Water Pulse	Water	Special	60	100	20	Normal
Helping Hand	Normal	Status	—	—	20	1 Ally
Endeavor	Normal	Physical	—	100	5	Normal
Recycle	Normal	Status	—	—	10	Self
Snatch	Dark	Status	—	—	10	Self
Stealth Rock	Rock	Status	—	—	20	Other Side
Skill Swap	Psychic	Status	—	—	10	Normal

MOVES TAUGHT BY PEOPLE

Name	Type	Kind	Pow.	Acc.	PP	Range

National Pokédex **243** Hoenn Pokédex —

Raikou

Thunder Pokémon

Electric

HEIGHT: 6'03" WEIGHT: 392.4 lbs.

Gender unknown

Ω Raikou embodies the speed of lightning. The roars of this Pokémon send shock waves shuddering through the air and shake the ground as if lightning bolts had come crashing down.

α Raikou embodies the speed of lightning. The roars of this Pokémon send shock waves shuddering through the air and shake the ground as if lightning bolts had come crashing down.

ABILITY
Pressure

HIDDEN ABILITY
—

EGG GROUPS
No Eggs Discovered

STAT GROWTH RATES
HP ▮▮▮▮
Attack ▮▮▮▮
Defense ▮▮▮
Sp. Atk ▮▮▮▮▮▮
Sp. Def ▮▮▮▮
Speed ▮▮▮▮▮▮

ITEMS SOMETIMES HELD BY WILD POKÉMON
—

EVOLUTION
Does not evolve

MAIN WAY TO REGISTER IN THE NATIONAL POKÉDEX

Catch in the Trackless Forest by Soaring in the sky during a certain time of day with either Ho-Oh or Lugia in your party.

Damage taken in normal battles

Type		Type	
Normal	×1	Flying	×0.5
Fire	×1	Psychic	×1
Water	×1	Bug	×1
Grass	×1	Rock	×1
Electric	×0.5	Ghost	×1
Ice	×1	Dragon	×1
Fighting	×1	Dark	×1
Poison	×1	Steel	×0.5
Ground	×2	Fairy	×1

Damage taken in Inverse battles

Type		Type	
Normal	×1	Flying	×2
Fire	×1	Psychic	×1
Water	×1	Bug	×1
Grass	×1	Rock	×1
Electric	×2	Ghost	×1
Ice	×1	Dragon	×1
Fighting	×1	Dark	×1
Poison	×1	Steel	×2
Ground	×0.5	Fairy	×1

Can be used in
Inverse Battle
Battle Institute
Battle Maison
Random Matchup (Free Battle)
Random Matchup (Others)

LEVEL-UP MOVES

Lv.	Name	Type	Kind	Pow.	Acc.	PP	Range
1	Extrasensory	Psychic	Special	80	100	20	Normal
1	Discharge	Electric	Special	80	100	15	Adjacent
1	Bite	Dark	Physical	60	100	25	Normal
1	Leer	Normal	Status	—	100	30	Many Others
8	Thunder Shock	Electric	Special	40	100	30	Normal
15	Roar	Normal	Status	—	—	20	Normal
22	Quick Attack	Normal	Physical	40	100	30	Normal
29	Spark	Electric	Physical	65	100	20	Normal
36	Reflect	Psychic	Status	—	—	20	Your Side
43	Crunch	Dark	Physical	80	100	15	Normal
50	Thunder Fang	Electric	Physical	65	95	15	Normal
57	Discharge	Electric	Special	80	100	15	Adjacent
64	Extrasensory	Psychic	Special	80	100	20	Normal
71	Rain Dance	Water	Status	—	—	5	Both Sides
78	Calm Mind	Psychic	Status	—	—	20	Self
85	Thunder	Electric	Special	110	70	10	Normal

TM & HM MOVES

No.	Name	Type	Kind	Pow.	Acc.	PP	Range
TM04	Calm Mind	Psychic	Status	—	—	20	Self
TM05	Roar	Normal	Status	—	—	20	Normal
TM06	Toxic	Poison	Status	—	90	10	Normal
TM10	Hidden Power	Normal	Special	60	100	15	Normal
TM11	Sunny Day	Fire	Status	—	—	5	Both Sides
TM15	Hyper Beam	Normal	Special	150	90	5	Normal
TM16	Light Screen	Psychic	Status	—	—	30	Your Side
TM17	Protect	Normal	Status	—	—	10	Self
TM18	Rain Dance	Water	Status	—	—	5	Both Sides
TM21	Frustration	Normal	Physical	—	100	20	Normal
TM24	Thunderbolt	Electric	Special	90	100	15	Normal
TM25	Thunder	Electric	Special	110	70	10	Normal
TM27	Return	Normal	Physical	—	100	20	Normal
TM28	Dig	Ground	Physical	80	100	10	Normal
TM30	Shadow Ball	Ghost	Special	80	100	15	Normal
TM32	Double Team	Normal	Status	—	—	15	Self
TM33	Reflect	Psychic	Status	—	—	20	Your Side
TM37	Sandstorm	Rock	Status	—	—	10	Both Sides
TM42	Facade	Normal	Physical	70	100	20	Normal
TM44	Rest	Psychic	Status	—	—	10	Self
TM48	Round	Normal	Special	60	100	15	Normal
TM57	Charge Beam	Electric	Special	50	90	10	Normal
TM60	Quash	Dark	Status	—	100	15	Normal
TM68	Giga Impact	Normal	Physical	150	90	5	Normal
TM70	Flash	Normal	Status	—	100	20	Normal
TM72	Volt Switch	Electric	Special	70	100	20	Normal
TM73	Thunder Wave	Electric	Status	—	100	20	Normal
TM77	Psych Up	Normal	Status	—	—	10	Normal
TM78	Bulldoze	Ground	Physical	60	100	20	Adjacent
TM87	Swagger	Normal	Status	—	90	15	Normal
TM88	Sleep Talk	Normal	Status	—	—	10	Self
TM90	Substitute	Normal	Status	—	—	10	Self
TM93	Wild Charge	Electric	Physical	90	100	15	Normal
TM94	Secret Power	Normal	Physical	70	100	20	Normal
TM95	Snarl	Dark	Special	55	95	15	Many Others
TM100	Confide	Normal	Status	—	—	20	Normal
HM01	Cut	Normal	Physical	50	95	30	Normal
HM04	Strength	Normal	Physical	80	100	15	Normal
HM06	Rock Smash	Fighting	Physical	40	100	15	Normal

MOVES LEARNED IN EXCHANGE FOR BP

Name	Type	Kind	Pow.	Acc.	PP	Range
Signal Beam	Bug	Special	75	100	15	Normal
Iron Head	Steel	Physical	80	100	15	Normal
Magnet Rise	Electric	Status	—	—	10	Self
Iron Tail	Steel	Physical	100	75	15	Normal
Snore	Normal	Special	50	100	15	Normal
Shock Wave	Electric	Special	60	—	20	Normal

MOVES TAUGHT BY PEOPLE

Name	Type	Kind	Pow.	Acc.	PP	Range

National Pokédex **244** Hoenn Pokédex **—**

✓ Entei

Volcano Pokémon

Fire

HEIGHT: 6'11" WEIGHT: 436.5 lbs.

Gender unknown

Ω Entei embodies the passion of magma. This Pokémon is thought to have been born in the eruption of a volcano. It sends up massive bursts of fire that utterly consume all that they touch.

α Entei embodies the passion of magma. This Pokémon is thought to have been born in the eruption of a volcano. It sends up massive bursts of fire that utterly consume all that they touch.

ABILITY
Pressure

HIDDEN ABILITY
—

EGG GROUPS
No Eggs Discovered

STAT GROWTH RATES
HP
Attack
Defense
Sp. Atk
Sp. Def
Speed

EVOLUTION
Does not evolve

ITEMS SOMETIMES HELD BY WILD POKÉMON
—

MAIN WAY TO REGISTER IN THE NATIONAL POKÉDEX

Catch in the Trackless Forest by Soaring in the sky during a certain time of day with either Ho-Oh or Lugia in your party.

Damage taken in normal battles

Type		Type	
Normal	×1	Flying	×1
Fire	×0.5	Psychic	×1
Water	×2	Bug	×0.5
Grass	×0.5	Rock	×2
Electric	×1	Ghost	×1
Ice	×0.5	Dragon	×1
Fighting	×1	Dark	×1
Poison	×1	Steel	×0.5
Ground	×2	Fairy	×0.5

Damage taken in Inverse battles

Type		Type	
Normal	×1	Flying	×1
Fire	×2	Psychic	×1
Water	×0.5	Bug	×2
Grass	×2	Rock	×0.5
Electric	×1	Ghost	×1
Ice	×2	Dragon	×1
Fighting	×1	Dark	×1
Poison	×1	Steel	×2
Ground	×0.5	Fairy	×2

Can be used in
Inverse Battle
Battle Institute
Battle Maison
Random Matchup (Free Battle)
Random Matchup (Others)

LEVEL-UP MOVES

Lv.	Name	Type	Kind	Pow.	Acc.	PP	Range
1	Sacred Fire	Fire	Physical	100	95	5	Normal
1	Eruption	Fire	Special	150	100	5	Many Others
1	Extrasensory	Psychic	Special	80	100	20	Normal
1	Lava Plume	Fire	Special	80	100	15	Adjacent
1	Bite	Dark	Physical	60	100	25	Normal
1	Leer	Normal	Status	—	100	30	Many Others
8	Ember	Fire	Special	40	100	25	Normal
15	Roar	Normal	Status	—	—	20	Normal
22	Fire Spin	Fire	Special	35	85	15	Normal
29	Stomp	Normal	Physical	65	100	20	Normal
36	Flamethrower	Fire	Special	90	100	15	Normal
43	Swagger	Normal	Status	—	90	15	Normal
50	Fire Fang	Fire	Physical	65	95	15	Normal
57	Lava Plume	Fire	Special	80	100	15	Adjacent
64	Extrasensory	Psychic	Special	80	100	20	Normal
71	Fire Blast	Fire	Special	110	85	5	Normal
78	Calm Mind	Psychic	Status	—	—	20	Self
85	Eruption	Fire	Special	150	100	5	Many Others

TM & HM MOVES

No.	Name	Type	Kind	Pow.	Acc.	PP	Range
TM04	Calm Mind	Psychic	Status	—	—	20	Self
TM05	Roar	Normal	Status	—	—	20	Normal
TM06	Toxic	Poison	Status	—	90	10	Normal
TM10	Hidden Power	Normal	Special	60	100	15	Normal
TM11	Sunny Day	Fire	Status	—	—	5	Both Sides
TM15	Hyper Beam	Normal	Special	150	90	5	Normal
TM17	Protect	Normal	Status	—	—	10	Self
TM18	Rain Dance	Water	Status	—	—	5	Both Sides
TM21	Frustration	Normal	Physical	—	100	20	Normal
TM22	Solar Beam	Grass	Special	120	100	10	Normal
TM27	Return	Normal	Physical	—	100	20	Normal
TM28	Dig	Ground	Physical	80	100	10	Normal
TM30	Shadow Ball	Ghost	Special	80	100	15	Normal
TM32	Double Team	Normal	Status	—	—	15	Self
TM33	Reflect	Psychic	Status	—	—	20	Your Side
TM35	Flamethrower	Fire	Special	90	100	15	Normal
TM37	Sandstorm	Rock	Status	—	—	10	Both Sides
TM38	Fire Blast	Fire	Special	110	85	5	Normal
TM42	Facade	Normal	Physical	70	100	20	Normal
TM43	Flame Charge	Fire	Physical	50	100	20	Normal
TM44	Rest	Psychic	Status	—	—	10	Self
TM48	Round	Normal	Special	60	100	15	Normal
TM50	Overheat	Fire	Special	130	90	5	Normal
TM59	Incinerate	Fire	Special	60	100	15	Many Others
TM60	Quash	Dark	Status	—	100	15	Normal
TM61	Will-O-Wisp	Fire	Status	—	85	15	Normal
TM68	Giga Impact	Normal	Physical	150	90	5	Normal
TM70	Flash	Normal	Status	—	100	20	Normal
TM71	Stone Edge	Rock	Physical	100	80	5	Normal
TM77	Psych Up	Normal	Status	—	—	10	Normal
TM78	Bulldoze	Ground	Physical	60	100	20	Adjacent
TM87	Swagger	Normal	Status	—	90	15	Normal
TM88	Sleep Talk	Normal	Status	—	—	10	Self
TM90	Substitute	Normal	Status	—	—	10	Self
TM94	Secret Power	Normal	Physical	70	100	20	Normal
TM95	Snarl	Dark	Special	55	95	15	Many Others
TM100	Confide	Normal	Status	—	—	20	Normal
HM01	Cut	Normal	Physical	50	95	30	Normal
HM04	Strength	Normal	Physical	80	100	15	Normal
HM06	Rock Smash	Fighting	Physical	40	100	15	Normal

MOVES LEARNED IN EXCHANGE FOR BP

Name	Type	Kind	Pow.	Acc.	PP	Range
Iron Head	Steel	Physical	80	100	15	Normal
Iron Tail	Steel	Physical	100	75	15	Normal
Snore	Normal	Special	50	100	15	Normal
Heat Wave	Fire	Special	95	90	10	Many Others

MOVES TAUGHT BY PEOPLE

Name	Type	Kind	Pow.	Acc.	PP	Range

National Pokédex **245** Hoenn Pokédex **—**

✓ Suicune

Aurora Pokémon

Water

HEIGHT: 6'07" WEIGHT: 412.3 lbs.

Gender unknown

Ω Suicune embodies the compassion of a pure spring of water. It runs across the land with gracefulness. This Pokémon has the power to purify dirty water.

α Suicune embodies the compassion of a pure spring of water. It runs across the land with gracefulness. This Pokémon has the power to purify dirty water.

ABILITY
Pressure

HIDDEN ABILITY
—

EGG GROUPS
No Eggs Discovered

STAT GROWTH RATES
HP
Attack
Defense
Sp. Atk
Sp. Def
Speed

EVOLUTION
Does not evolve

ITEMS SOMETIMES HELD BY WILD POKÉMON
—

MAIN WAY TO REGISTER IN THE NATIONAL POKÉDEX

Catch in the Trackless Forest by Soaring in the sky during a certain time of day with either Ho-Oh or Lugia in your party.

Damage taken in normal battles

Type		Type	
Normal	×1	Flying	×1
Fire	×0.5	Psychic	×1
Water	×0.5	Bug	×1
Grass	×2	Rock	×1
Electric	×2	Ghost	×1
Ice	×0.5	Dragon	×1
Fighting	×1	Dark	×1
Poison	×1	Steel	×0.5
Ground	×1	Fairy	×1

Damage taken in Inverse battles

Type		Type	
Normal	×1	Flying	×1
Fire	×2	Psychic	×1
Water	×2	Bug	×1
Grass	×0.5	Rock	×1
Electric	×0.5	Ghost	×1
Ice	×2	Dragon	×1
Fighting	×1	Dark	×1
Poison	×1	Steel	×2
Ground	×1	Fairy	×1

Can be used in
Inverse Battle
Battle Institute
Battle Maison
Random Matchup (Free Battle)
Random Matchup (Others)

LEVEL-UP MOVES

Lv.	Name	Type	Kind	Pow.	Acc.	PP	Range
1	Hydro Pump	Water	Special	110	80	5	Normal
1	Extrasensory	Psychic	Special	80	100	20	Normal
1	Tailwind	Flying	Status	—	—	15	Your Side
1	Bite	Dark	Physical	60	100	25	Normal
1	Leer	Normal	Status	—	100	30	Many Others
8	Bubble Beam	Water	Special	65	100	20	Normal
15	Rain Dance	Water	Status	—	—	5	Both Sides
22	Gust	Flying	Special	40	100	35	Normal
29	Aurora Beam	Ice	Special	65	100	20	Normal
36	Mist	Ice	Status	—	—	30	Your Side
43	Mirror Coat	Psychic	Special	—	100	20	Varies
50	Ice Fang	Ice	Physical	65	95	15	Normal
57	Tailwind	Flying	Status	—	—	15	Your Side
64	Extrasensory	Psychic	Special	80	100	20	Normal
71	Hydro Pump	Water	Special	110	80	5	Normal
78	Calm Mind	Psychic	Status	—	—	20	Self
85	Blizzard	Ice	Special	110	70	5	Many Others

TM & HM MOVES

No.	Name	Type	Kind	Pow.	Acc.	PP	Range
TM04	Calm Mind	Psychic	Status	—	—	20	Self
TM05	Roar	Normal	Status	—	—	20	Normal
TM06	Toxic	Poison	Status	—	90	10	Normal
TM07	Hail	Ice	Status	—	—	10	Both Sides
TM10	Hidden Power	Normal	Special	60	100	15	Normal
TM11	Sunny Day	Fire	Status	—	—	5	Both Sides
TM13	Ice Beam	Ice	Special	90	100	10	Normal
TM14	Blizzard	Ice	Special	110	70	5	Many Others
TM15	Hyper Beam	Normal	Special	150	90	5	Normal
TM17	Protect	Normal	Status	—	—	10	Self
TM18	Rain Dance	Water	Status	—	—	5	Both Sides
TM21	Frustration	Normal	Physical	—	100	20	Normal
TM27	Return	Normal	Physical	—	100	20	Normal
TM28	Dig	Ground	Physical	80	100	10	Normal
TM30	Shadow Ball	Ghost	Special	80	100	15	Normal
TM32	Double Team	Normal	Status	—	—	15	Self
TM33	Reflect	Psychic	Status	—	—	20	Your Side
TM37	Sandstorm	Rock	Status	—	—	10	Both Sides
TM42	Facade	Normal	Physical	70	100	20	Normal
TM44	Rest	Psychic	Status	—	—	10	Self
TM48	Round	Normal	Special	60	100	15	Normal
TM55	Scald	Water	Special	80	100	15	Normal
TM60	Quash	Dark	Status	—	100	15	Normal
TM68	Giga Impact	Normal	Physical	150	90	5	Normal
TM77	Psych Up	Normal	Status	—	—	10	Normal
TM78	Bulldoze	Ground	Physical	60	100	20	Adjacent
TM87	Swagger	Normal	Status	—	90	15	Normal
TM88	Sleep Talk	Normal	Status	—	—	10	Self
TM90	Substitute	Normal	Status	—	—	10	Self
TM94	Secret Power	Normal	Physical	70	100	20	Normal
TM95	Snarl	Dark	Special	55	95	15	Many Others
TM100	Confide	Normal	Status	—	—	20	Normal
HM01	Cut	Normal	Physical	50	95	30	Normal
HM03	Surf	Water	Special	90	100	15	Adjacent
HM05	Waterfall	Water	Physical	80	100	15	Normal
HM06	Rock Smash	Fighting	Physical	40	100	15	Normal
HM07	Dive	Water	Physical	80	100	10	Normal

MOVES LEARNED IN EXCHANGE FOR BP

Name	Type	Kind	Pow.	Acc.	PP	Range
Signal Beam	Bug	Special	75	100	15	Normal
Iron Head	Steel	Physical	80	100	15	Normal
Icy Wind	Ice	Special	55	95	15	Many Others
Iron Tail	Steel	Physical	100	75	15	Normal
Snore	Normal	Special	50	100	15	Normal
Tailwind	Flying	Status	—	—	15	Your Side
Water Pulse	Water	Special	60	100	20	Normal

MOVES TAUGHT BY PEOPLE

Name	Type	Kind	Pow.	Acc.	PP	Range

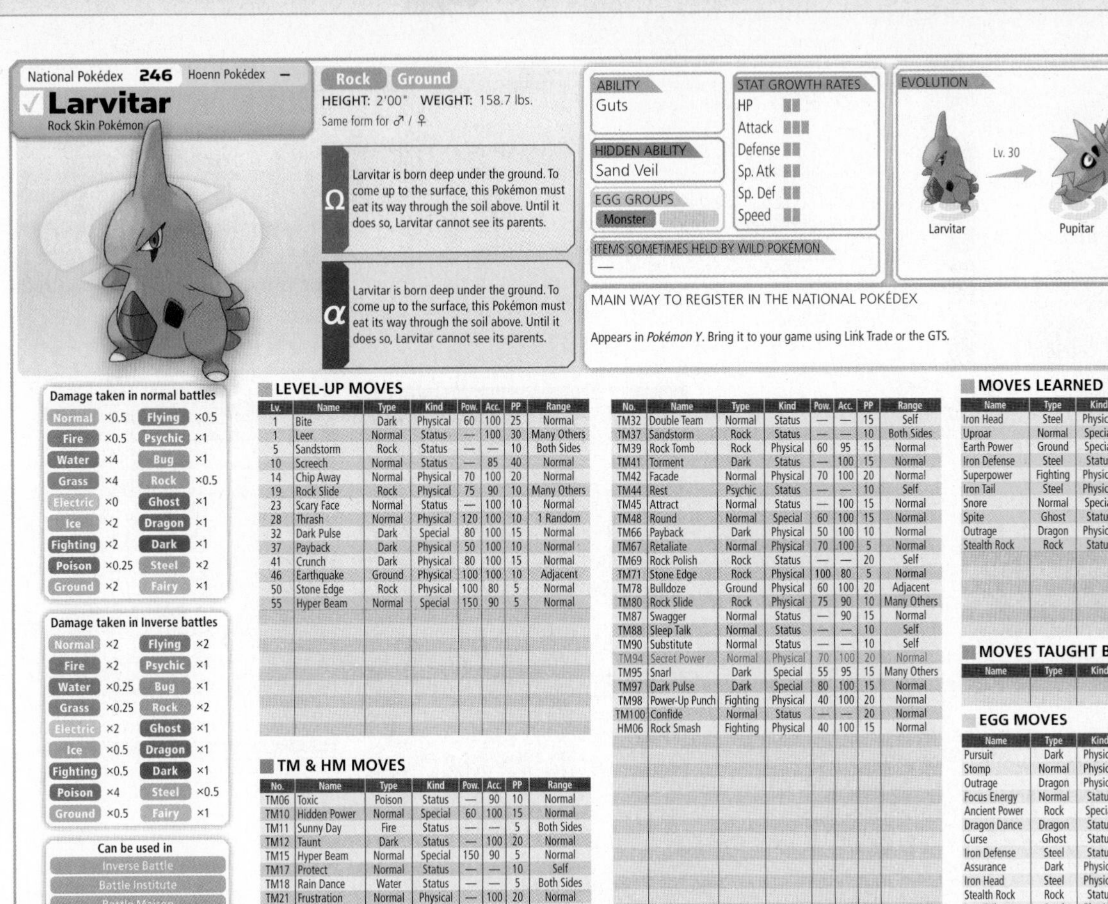

National Pokédex **246** Hoenn Pokédex —

Larvitar

Rock Skin Pokémon

Rock | Ground

HEIGHT: 2'00" WEIGHT: 158.7 lbs.

Same form for ♂ / ♀

Ω Larvitar is born deep under the ground. To come up to the surface, this Pokémon must eat its way through the soil above. Until it does so, Larvitar cannot see its parents.

α Larvitar is born deep under the ground. To come up to the surface, this Pokémon must eat its way through the soil above. Until it does so, Larvitar cannot see its parents.

ABILITY
Guts

HIDDEN ABILITY
Sand Veil

EGG GROUPS
Monster

STAT GROWTH RATES
HP
Attack
Defense
Sp. Atk
Sp. Def
Speed

ITEMS SOMETIMES HELD BY WILD POKÉMON
—

EVOLUTION
Larvitar → Lv. 30 → Pupitar → Lv. 55 → Tyranitar

MAIN WAY TO REGISTER IN THE NATIONAL POKÉDEX

Appears in *Pokémon Y*. Bring it to your game using Link Trade or the GTS.

Damage taken in normal battles

Type		Type	
Normal	×0.5	Flying	×0.5
Fire	×0.5	Psychic	×1
Water	×4	Bug	×1
Grass	×4	Rock	×0.5
Electric	×0	Ghost	×1
Ice	×2	Dragon	×1
Fighting	×2	Dark	×1
Poison	×0.25	Steel	×2
Ground	×2	Fairy	×1

Damage taken in Inverse battles

Type		Type	
Normal	×2	Flying	×2
Fire	×2	Psychic	×1
Water	×0.25	Bug	×1
Grass	×0.25	Rock	×2
Electric	×2	Ghost	×1
Ice	×0.5	Dragon	×1
Fighting	×0.5	Dark	×1
Poison	×4	Steel	×0.5
Ground	×0.5	Fairy	×1

Can be used in
- Inverse Battle
- Battle Institute
- Battle Maison
- Random Matchup (Free Battle)
- Random Matchup (Others)

LEVEL-UP MOVES

Lv.	Name	Type	Kind	Pow.	Acc.	PP	Range
1	Bite	Dark	Physical	60	100	25	Normal
1	Leer	Normal	Status	—	100	30	Many Others
5	Sandstorm	Rock	Status	—	—	10	Both Sides
10	Screech	Normal	Status	—	85	40	Normal
14	Chip Away	Normal	Physical	70	100	20	Normal
19	Rock Slide	Rock	Physical	75	90	10	Many Others
23	Scary Face	Normal	Status	—	100	10	Normal
28	Thrash	Normal	Physical	120	100	10	1 Random
32	Dark Pulse	Dark	Special	80	100	15	Normal
37	Payback	Dark	Physical	50	100	10	Normal
41	Crunch	Dark	Physical	80	100	15	Normal
46	Earthquake	Ground	Physical	100	100	10	Adjacent
50	Stone Edge	Rock	Physical	100	80	5	Normal
55	Hyper Beam	Normal	Special	150	90	5	Normal

TM & HM MOVES

No.	Name	Type	Kind	Pow.	Acc.	PP	Range
TM06	Toxic	Poison	Status	—	90	10	Normal
TM10	Hidden Power	Normal	Special	60	100	15	Normal
TM11	Sunny Day	Fire	Status	—	—	5	Both Sides
TM12	Taunt	Dark	Status	—	100	20	Normal
TM15	Hyper Beam	Normal	Special	150	90	5	Normal
TM17	Protect	Normal	Status	—	—	10	Self
TM18	Rain Dance	Water	Status	—	—	5	Both Sides
TM21	Frustration	Normal	Physical	—	100	20	Normal
TM23	Smack Down	Rock	Physical	50	100	15	Normal
TM26	Earthquake	Ground	Physical	100	100	10	Adjacent
TM27	Return	Normal	Physical	—	100	20	Normal
TM28	Dig	Ground	Physical	80	100	10	Normal
TM31	Brick Break	Fighting	Physical	75	100	15	Normal
TM32	Double Team	Normal	Status	—	—	15	Self
TM37	Sandstorm	Rock	Status	—	—	10	Both Sides
TM39	Rock Tomb	Rock	Physical	60	95	15	Normal
TM41	Torment	Dark	Status	—	100	15	Normal
TM42	Facade	Normal	Physical	70	100	20	Normal
TM44	Rest	Psychic	Status	—	—	10	Self
TM45	Attract	Normal	Status	—	100	15	Normal
TM48	Round	Normal	Special	60	100	15	Normal
TM66	Payback	Dark	Physical	50	100	10	Normal
TM67	Retaliate	Normal	Physical	70	100	5	Normal
TM69	Rock Polish	Rock	Status	—	—	20	Self
TM71	Stone Edge	Rock	Physical	100	80	5	Normal
TM78	Bulldoze	Ground	Physical	60	100	20	Adjacent
TM80	Rock Slide	Rock	Physical	75	90	10	Many Others
TM87	Swagger	Normal	Status	—	90	15	Normal
TM88	Sleep Talk	Normal	Status	—	—	10	Self
TM90	Substitute	Normal	Status	—	—	10	Self
TM94	Secret Power	Normal	Physical	70	100	20	Normal
TM95	Snarl	Dark	Special	55	95	15	Many Others
TM97	Dark Pulse	Dark	Special	80	100	15	Normal
TM98	Power-Up Punch	Fighting	Physical	40	100	20	Normal
TM100	Confide	Normal	Status	—	—	20	Normal
HM06	Rock Smash	Fighting	Physical	40	100	15	Normal

MOVES LEARNED IN EXCHANGE FOR BP

Name	Type	Kind	Pow.	Acc.	PP	Range
Iron Head	Steel	Physical	80	100	15	Normal
Uproar	Normal	Special	90	100	10	1 Random
Earth Power	Ground	Special	90	100	10	Normal
Iron Defense	Steel	Status	—	—	15	Self
Superpower	Fighting	Physical	120	100	5	Normal
Iron Tail	Steel	Physical	100	75	15	Normal
Snore	Normal	Special	50	100	15	Normal
Spite	Ghost	Status	—	100	10	Normal
Outrage	Dragon	Physical	120	100	10	1 Random
Stealth Rock	Rock	Status	—	—	20	Other Side

MOVES TAUGHT BY PEOPLE

Name	Type	Kind	Pow.	Acc.	PP	Range

EGG MOVES

Name	Type	Kind	Pow.	Acc.	PP	Range
Pursuit	Dark	Physical	40	100	20	Normal
Stomp	Normal	Physical	65	100	20	Normal
Outrage	Dragon	Physical	120	100	10	1 Random
Focus Energy	Normal	Status	—	—	30	Self
Ancient Power	Rock	Special	60	100	5	Normal
Dragon Dance	Dragon	Status	—	—	20	Self
Curse	Ghost	Status	—	—	10	Varies
Iron Defense	Steel	Status	—	—	15	Self
Assurance	Dark	Physical	60	100	10	Normal
Iron Head	Steel	Physical	80	100	15	Normal
Stealth Rock	Rock	Status	—	—	20	Other Side
Iron Tail	Steel	Physical	100	75	15	Normal

National Pokédex **247** Hoenn Pokédex —

Pupitar

Hard Shell Pokémon

Rock | Ground

HEIGHT: 3'11" WEIGHT: 335.1 lbs.

Same form for ♂ / ♀

Ω Pupitar creates a gas inside its body that it compresses and forcefully ejects to propel itself like a jet. The body is very durable—it avoids damage even if it hits solid steel.

α Pupitar creates a gas inside its body that it compresses and forcefully ejects to propel itself like a jet. The body is very durable—it avoids damage even if it hits solid steel.

ABILITY
Shed Skin

HIDDEN ABILITY
—

EGG GROUPS
Monster

STAT GROWTH RATES
HP
Attack
Defense
Sp. Atk
Sp. Def
Speed

ITEMS SOMETIMES HELD BY WILD POKÉMON
—

EVOLUTION
Larvitar → Lv. 30 → Pupitar → Lv. 55 → Tyranitar

MAIN WAY TO REGISTER IN THE NATIONAL POKÉDEX

Appears in *Pokémon Y*. Bring it to your game using Link Trade or the GTS.

Damage taken in normal battles

Type		Type	
Normal	×0.5	Flying	×0.5
Fire	×0.5	Psychic	×1
Water	×4	Bug	×1
Grass	×4	Rock	×0.5
Electric	×0	Ghost	×1
Ice	×2	Dragon	×1
Fighting	×2	Dark	×1
Poison	×0.25	Steel	×2
Ground	×2	Fairy	×1

Damage taken in Inverse battles

Type		Type	
Normal	×2	Flying	×2
Fire	×2	Psychic	×1
Water	×0.25	Bug	×1
Grass	×0.25	Rock	×2
Electric	×2	Ghost	×1
Ice	×0.5	Dragon	×1
Fighting	×0.5	Dark	×1
Poison	×4	Steel	×0.5
Ground	×0.5	Fairy	×1

Can be used in
- Inverse Battle
- Battle Institute
- Battle Maison
- Random Matchup (Free Battle)
- Random Matchup (Others)

LEVEL-UP MOVES

Lv.	Name	Type	Kind	Pow.	Acc.	PP	Range
1	Bite	Dark	Physical	60	100	25	Normal
1	Leer	Normal	Status	—	100	30	Many Others
1	Sandstorm	Rock	Status	—	—	10	Both Sides
1	Screech	Normal	Status	—	85	40	Normal
5	Sandstorm	Rock	Status	—	—	10	Both Sides
10	Screech	Normal	Status	—	85	40	Normal
14	Chip Away	Normal	Physical	70	100	20	Normal
19	Rock Slide	Rock	Physical	75	90	10	Many Others
23	Scary Face	Normal	Status	—	100	10	Normal
28	Thrash	Normal	Physical	120	100	10	1 Random
34	Dark Pulse	Dark	Special	80	100	15	Normal
41	Payback	Dark	Physical	50	100	10	Normal
47	Crunch	Dark	Physical	80	100	15	Normal
54	Earthquake	Ground	Physical	100	100	10	Adjacent
60	Stone Edge	Rock	Physical	100	80	5	Normal
67	Hyper Beam	Normal	Special	150	90	5	Normal

TM & HM MOVES

No.	Name	Type	Kind	Pow.	Acc.	PP	Range
TM06	Toxic	Poison	Status	—	90	10	Normal
TM10	Hidden Power	Normal	Special	60	100	15	Normal
TM11	Sunny Day	Fire	Status	—	—	5	Both Sides
TM12	Taunt	Dark	Status	—	100	20	Normal
TM15	Hyper Beam	Normal	Special	150	90	5	Normal
TM17	Protect	Normal	Status	—	—	10	Self
TM18	Rain Dance	Water	Status	—	—	5	Both Sides
TM21	Frustration	Normal	Physical	—	100	20	Normal
TM23	Smack Down	Rock	Physical	50	100	15	Normal
TM26	Earthquake	Ground	Physical	100	100	10	Adjacent
TM27	Return	Normal	Physical	—	100	20	Normal
TM28	Dig	Ground	Physical	80	100	10	Normal
TM31	Brick Break	Fighting	Physical	75	100	15	Normal
TM32	Double Team	Normal	Status	—	—	15	Self
TM37	Sandstorm	Rock	Status	—	—	10	Both Sides
TM39	Rock Tomb	Rock	Physical	60	95	15	Normal
TM41	Torment	Dark	Status	—	100	15	Normal
TM42	Facade	Normal	Physical	70	100	20	Normal
TM44	Rest	Psychic	Status	—	—	10	Self
TM45	Attract	Normal	Status	—	100	15	Normal
TM48	Round	Normal	Special	60	100	15	Normal
TM66	Payback	Dark	Physical	50	100	10	Normal
TM67	Retaliate	Normal	Physical	70	100	5	Normal
TM69	Rock Polish	Rock	Status	—	—	20	Self
TM71	Stone Edge	Rock	Physical	100	80	5	Normal
TM78	Bulldoze	Ground	Physical	60	100	20	Adjacent
TM80	Rock Slide	Rock	Physical	75	90	10	Many Others
TM87	Swagger	Normal	Status	—	90	15	Normal
TM88	Sleep Talk	Normal	Status	—	—	10	Self
TM90	Substitute	Normal	Status	—	—	10	Self
TM94	Secret Power	Normal	Physical	70	100	20	Normal
TM95	Snarl	Dark	Special	55	95	15	Many Others
TM97	Dark Pulse	Dark	Special	80	100	15	Normal
TM98	Power-Up Punch	Fighting	Physical	40	100	20	Normal
TM100	Confide	Normal	Status	—	—	20	Normal
HM06	Rock Smash	Fighting	Physical	40	100	15	Normal

MOVES LEARNED IN EXCHANGE FOR BP

Name	Type	Kind	Pow.	Acc.	PP	Range
Iron Head	Steel	Physical	80	100	15	Normal
Uproar	Normal	Special	90	100	10	1 Random
Earth Power	Ground	Special	90	100	10	Normal
Iron Defense	Steel	Status	—	—	15	Self
Superpower	Fighting	Physical	120	100	5	Normal
Iron Tail	Steel	Physical	100	75	15	Normal
Snore	Normal	Special	50	100	15	Normal
Spite	Ghost	Status	—	100	10	Normal
Outrage	Dragon	Physical	120	100	10	1 Random
Stealth Rock	Rock	Status	—	—	20	Other Side

MOVES TAUGHT BY PEOPLE

Name	Type	Kind	Pow.	Acc.	PP	Range

National Pokédex **248** Hoenn Pokédex —

Tyranitar

Armor Pokémon

Rock | Dark

HEIGHT: 6'07" WEIGHT: 445.3 lbs.

Same form for ♂ / ♀

Ω Tyranitar is so overwhelmingly powerful, it can bring down a whole mountain to make its nest. This Pokémon wanders about in mountains seeking new opponents to fight.

α Tyranitar is so overwhelmingly powerful, it can bring down a whole mountain to make its nest. This Pokémon wanders about in mountains seeking new opponents to fight.

ABILITY
Sand Stream

HIDDEN ABILITY
Unnerve

EGG GROUPS
Monster

STAT GROWTH RATES
HP ■■■■
Attack ■■■■■■■
Defense ■■■■■
Sp. Atk ■■■■■
Sp. Def ■■■■
Speed ■■■

ITEMS SOMETIMES HELD BY WILD POKÉMON
—

EVOLUTION
Larvitar → Lv. 30 → Pupitar → Lv. 55 → Tyranitar

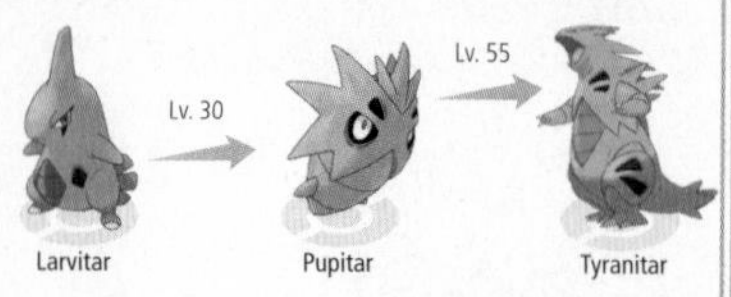

MAIN WAY TO REGISTER IN THE NATIONAL POKÉDEX

Level up a Pupitar obtained via Link Trade or the GTS to Lv. 55.

Damage taken in normal battles

Type		Type	
Normal	×0.5	Flying	×0.5
Fire	×0.5	Psychic	×0
Water	×2	Bug	×2
Grass	×2	Rock	×1
Electric	×1	Ghost	×0.5
Ice	×1	Dragon	×1
Fighting	×4	Dark	×0.5
Poison	×0.5	Steel	×2
Ground	×2	Fairy	×2

Damage taken in Inverse battles

Type		Type	
Normal	×2	Flying	×2
Fire	×2	Psychic	×2
Water	×0.5	Bug	×0.5
Grass	×0.5	Rock	×1
Electric	×1	Ghost	×2
Ice	×1	Dragon	×1
Fighting	×0.25	Dark	×2
Poison	×2	Steel	×0.5
Ground	×0.5	Fairy	×0.5

Can be used in
Inverse Battle
Battle Institute
Battle Maison
Random Matchup (Free Battle)
Random Matchup (Others)

LEVEL-UP MOVES

Lv.	Name	Type	Kind	Pow.	Acc.	PP	Range
1	Thunder Fang	Electric	Physical	65	95	15	Normal
1	Ice Fang	Ice	Physical	65	95	15	Normal
1	Fire Fang	Fire	Physical	65	95	15	Normal
1	Bite	Dark	Physical	60	100	25	Normal
1	Leer	Normal	Status	—	100	30	Many Others
1	Sandstorm	Rock	Status	—	—	10	Both Sides
1	Screech	Normal	Status	—	85	40	Normal
5	Sandstorm	Rock	Status	—	—	10	Both Sides
10	Screech	Normal	Status	—	85	40	Normal
14	Chip Away	Normal	Physical	70	100	20	Normal
19	Rock Slide	Rock	Physical	75	90	10	Many Others
23	Scary Face	Normal	Status	—	100	10	Normal
28	Thrash	Normal	Physical	120	100	10	1 Random
34	Dark Pulse	Dark	Special	80	100	15	Normal
41	Payback	Dark	Physical	50	100	10	Normal
47	Crunch	Dark	Physical	80	100	15	Normal
54	Earthquake	Ground	Physical	100	100	10	Adjacent
63	Stone Edge	Rock	Physical	100	80	5	Normal
73	Hyper Beam	Normal	Special	150	90	5	Normal
82	Giga Impact	Normal	Physical	150	90	5	Normal

TM & HM MOVES

No.	Name	Type	Kind	Pow.	Acc.	PP	Range
TM01	Hone Claws	Dark	Status	—	—	15	Self
TM02	Dragon Claw	Dragon	Physical	80	100	15	Normal
TM05	Roar	Normal	Status	—	—	20	Normal
TM06	Toxic	Poison	Status	—	90	10	Normal
TM10	Hidden Power	Normal	Special	60	100	15	Normal
TM11	Sunny Day	Fire	Status	—	—	5	Both Sides
TM12	Taunt	Dark	Status	—	100	20	Normal
TM13	Ice Beam	Ice	Special	90	100	10	Normal
TM14	Blizzard	Ice	Special	110	70	5	Many Others
TM15	Hyper Beam	Normal	Special	150	90	5	Normal
TM17	Protect	Normal	Status	—	—	10	Self
TM18	Rain Dance	Water	Status	—	—	5	Both Sides
TM21	Frustration	Normal	Physical	—	100	20	Normal
TM23	Smack Down	Rock	Physical	50	100	15	Normal
TM24	Thunderbolt	Electric	Special	90	100	15	Normal
TM25	Thunder	Electric	Special	110	70	10	Normal
TM26	Earthquake	Ground	Physical	100	100	10	Adjacent
TM27	Return	Normal	Physical	—	100	20	Normal
TM28	Dig	Ground	Physical	80	100	10	Normal
TM31	Brick Break	Fighting	Physical	75	100	15	Normal
TM32	Double Team	Normal	Status	—	—	15	Self
TM35	Flamethrower	Fire	Special	90	100	15	Normal
TM37	Sandstorm	Rock	Status	—	—	10	Both Sides
TM38	Fire Blast	Fire	Special	110	85	5	Normal
TM39	Rock Tomb	Rock	Physical	60	95	15	Normal
TM40	Aerial Ace	Flying	Physical	60	—	20	Normal
TM41	Torment	Dark	Status	—	100	15	Normal
TM42	Facade	Normal	Physical	70	100	20	Normal
TM44	Rest	Psychic	Status	—	—	10	Self
TM45	Attract	Normal	Status	—	100	15	Normal
TM48	Round	Normal	Special	60	100	15	Normal
TM52	Focus Blast	Fighting	Special	120	70	5	Normal
TM56	Fling	Dark	Physical	—	100	10	Normal
TM59	Incinerate	Fire	Special	60	100	15	Many Others
TM65	Shadow Claw	Ghost	Physical	70	100	15	Normal
TM66	Payback	Dark	Physical	50	100	10	Normal
TM67	Retaliate	Normal	Physical	70	100	5	Normal
TM68	Giga Impact	Normal	Physical	150	90	5	Normal
TM69	Rock Polish	Rock	Status	—	—	20	Self
TM71	Stone Edge	Rock	Physical	100	80	5	Normal
TM73	Thunder Wave	Electric	Status	—	100	20	Normal
TM78	Bulldoze	Ground	Physical	60	100	20	Adjacent
TM80	Rock Slide	Rock	Physical	75	90	10	Many Others
TM82	Dragon Tail	Dragon	Physical	60	90	10	Normal
TM87	Swagger	Normal	Status	—	90	15	Normal
TM88	Sleep Talk	Normal	Status	—	—	10	Self
TM90	Substitute	Normal	Status	—	—	10	Self
TM94	Secret Power	Normal	Physical	70	100	20	Normal
TM95	Snarl	Dark	Special	55	95	15	Many Others
TM97	Dark Pulse	Dark	Special	80	100	15	Normal
TM98	Power-Up Punch	Fighting	Physical	40	100	20	Normal
TM100	Confide	Normal	Status	—	—	20	Normal
HM01	Cut	Normal	Physical	50	95	30	Normal
HM03	Surf	Water	Special	90	100	15	Adjacent
HM04	Strength	Normal	Physical	80	100	15	Normal
HM06	Rock Smash	Fighting	Physical	40	100	15	Normal

MOVES LEARNED IN EXCHANGE FOR BP

Name	Type	Kind	Pow.	Acc.	PP	Range
Iron Head	Steel	Physical	80	100	15	Normal
Low Kick	Fighting	Physical	—	100	20	Normal
Uproar	Normal	Special	90	100	10	1 Random
Thunder Punch	Electric	Physical	75	100	15	Normal
Fire Punch	Fire	Physical	75	100	15	Normal
Ice Punch	Ice	Physical	75	100	15	Normal
Block	Normal	Status	—	—	5	Normal
Earth Power	Ground	Special	90	100	10	Normal
Foul Play	Dark	Physical	95	100	15	Normal
Iron Defense	Steel	Status	—	—	15	Self
Superpower	Fighting	Physical	120	100	5	Normal
Aqua Tail	Water	Physical	90	90	10	Normal
Dragon Pulse	Dragon	Special	85	100	10	Normal
Iron Tail	Steel	Physical	100	75	15	Normal
Snore	Normal	Special	50	100	15	Normal
Focus Punch	Fighting	Physical	150	100	20	Normal
Shock Wave	Electric	Special	60	—	20	Normal
Water Pulse	Water	Special	60	100	20	Normal
Spite	Ghost	Status	—	100	10	Normal
Outrage	Dragon	Physical	120	100	10	1 Random
Stealth Rock	Rock	Status	—	—	20	Other Side

MOVES TAUGHT BY PEOPLE

Name	Type	Kind	Pow.	Acc.	PP	Range

Mega Evolution

Mega Tyranitar

Armor Pokémon

Rock | Dark

HEIGHT: 8'02" WEIGHT: 562.2 lbs.

Same form for ♂ / ♀

REQUIRED MEGA STONE
Tyranitarite
Find on Jagged Pass (after battling Groudon or Kyogre).

ABILITY
Sand Stream

HIDDEN ABILITY
—

EGG GROUPS
—

STAT GROWTH RATES
HP ■■■■
Attack ■■■■■■■■
Defense ■■■■■■
Sp. Atk ■■■■■
Sp. Def ■■■■■
Speed ■■■■

Damage taken in normal battles

Type		Type	
Normal	×0.5	Flying	×0.5
Fire	×0.5	Psychic	×0
Water	×2	Bug	×2
Grass	×2	Rock	×1
Electric	×1	Ghost	×0.5
Ice	×1	Dragon	×1
Fighting	×4	Dark	×0.5
Poison	×0.5	Steel	×2
Ground	×2	Fairy	×2

Damage taken in Inverse battles

Type		Type	
Normal	×2	Flying	×2
Fire	×2	Psychic	×2
Water	×0.5	Bug	×0.5
Grass	×0.5	Rock	×1
Electric	×1	Ghost	×2
Ice	×1	Dragon	×1
Fighting	×0.25	Dark	×2
Poison	×2	Steel	×0.5
Ground	×0.5	Fairy	×0.5

Can be used in
Inverse Battle
Battle Institute
Battle Maison
Random Matchup (Free Battle)
Random Matchup (Others)

National Pokédex **249** Hoenn Pokédex —

Lugia

Diving Pokémon

Psychic Flying

HEIGHT: 17'01" WEIGHT: 476.2 lbs.

Gender unknown

Ω Lugia's wings pack devastating power—a light fluttering of its wings can blow apart regular houses. As a result, this Pokémon chooses to live out of sight deep under the sea.

α Lugia's wings pack devastating power—a light fluttering of its wings can blow apart regular houses. As a result, this Pokémon chooses to live out of sight deep under the sea.

ABILITY
Pressure

HIDDEN ABILITY
Multiscale

EGG GROUPS
No Eggs Discovered

STAT GROWTH RATES
HP
Attack
Defense
Sp. Atk
Sp. Def
Speed

ITEMS SOMETIMES HELD BY WILD POKÉMON
—

EVOLUTION
Does not evolve

MAIN WAYS TO REGISTER IN THE NATIONAL POKÉDEX

Ω Bring it to your game using Link Trade or the GTS.

α After obtaining the Tidal Bell from Stern in Slateport City, catch it in the flooded lower halls of Sea Mauville.

Damage taken in normal battles

Normal	×1	Flying	×1
Fire	×1	Psychic	×0.5
Water	×1	Bug	×1
Grass	×0.5	Rock	×2
Electric	×2	Ghost	×2
Ice	×2	Dragon	×1
Fighting	×0.25	Dark	×2
Poison	×1	Steel	×1
Ground	×0	Fairy	×1

Damage taken in Inverse battles

Normal	×1	Flying	×1
Fire	×1	Psychic	×2
Water	×1	Bug	×1
Grass	×2	Rock	×0.5
Electric	×0.5	Ghost	×0.5
Ice	×0.5	Dragon	×1
Fighting	×4	Dark	×0.5
Poison	×1	Steel	×1
Ground	×2	Fairy	×1

Can be used in
- Inverse Battle
- Battle Institute
- Battle Maison
- Random Matchup (Free Battle)
- Random Matchup (Others)

LEVEL-UP MOVES

Lv.	Name	Type	Kind	Pow.	Acc.	PP	Range
1	Whirlwind	Normal	Status	—	—	20	Normal
1	Weather Ball	Normal	Special	50	100	10	Normal
9	Gust	Flying	Special	40	100	35	Normal
15	Dragon Rush	Dragon	Physical	100	75	10	Normal
23	Extrasensory	Psychic	Special	80	100	20	Normal
29	Rain Dance	Water	Status	—	—	5	Both Sides
37	Hydro Pump	Water	Special	110	80	5	Normal
43	Aeroblast	Flying	Special	100	95	5	Normal
50	Punishment	Dark	Physical	—	100	5	Normal
57	Ancient Power	Rock	Special	60	100	5	Normal
65	Safeguard	Normal	Status	—	—	25	Your Side
71	Recover	Normal	Status	—	—	10	Self
79	Future Sight	Psychic	Special	120	100	10	Normal
85	Natural Gift	Normal	Physical	—	100	15	Normal
93	Calm Mind	Psychic	Status	—	—	20	Self
99	Sky Attack	Flying	Physical	140	90	5	Normal

TM & HM MOVES

No.	Name	Type	Kind	Pow.	Acc.	PP	Range
TM03	Psyshock	Psychic	Special	80	100	10	Normal
TM04	Calm Mind	Psychic	Status	—	—	20	Self
TM05	Roar	Normal	Status	—	—	20	Normal
TM06	Toxic	Poison	Status	—	90	10	Normal
TM07	Hail	Ice	Status	—	—	10	Both Sides
TM10	Hidden Power	Normal	Special	60	100	15	Normal
TM11	Sunny Day	Fire	Status	—	—	5	Both Sides
TM13	Ice Beam	Ice	Special	90	100	10	Normal
TM14	Blizzard	Ice	Special	110	70	5	Many Others
TM15	Hyper Beam	Normal	Special	150	90	5	Normal
TM16	Light Screen	Psychic	Status	—	—	30	Your Side
TM17	Protect	Normal	Status	—	—	10	Self
TM18	Rain Dance	Water	Status	—	—	5	Both Sides
TM19	Roost	Flying	Status	—	—	10	Self
TM20	Safeguard	Normal	Status	—	—	25	Your Side
TM21	Frustration	Normal	Physical	—	100	20	Normal
TM24	Thunderbolt	Electric	Special	90	100	15	Normal
TM25	Thunder	Electric	Special	110	70	10	Normal
TM26	Earthquake	Ground	Physical	100	100	10	Adjacent
TM27	Return	Normal	Physical	—	100	20	Normal
TM29	Psychic	Psychic	Special	90	100	10	Normal
TM30	Shadow Ball	Ghost	Special	80	100	15	Normal
TM32	Double Team	Normal	Status	—	—	15	Self
TM33	Reflect	Psychic	Status	—	—	20	Your Side
TM37	Sandstorm	Rock	Status	—	—	10	Both Sides
TM40	Aerial Ace	Flying	Physical	60	—	20	Normal
TM42	Facade	Normal	Physical	70	100	20	Normal
TM44	Rest	Psychic	Status	—	—	10	Self
TM48	Round	Normal	Special	60	100	15	Normal
TM49	Echoed Voice	Normal	Special	40	100	15	Normal
TM51	Steel Wing	Steel	Physical	70	90	25	Normal
TM57	Charge Beam	Electric	Special	50	90	10	Normal
TM58	Sky Drop	Flying	Physical	60	100	10	Normal
TM68	Giga Impact	Normal	Physical	150	90	5	Normal
TM70	Flash	Normal	Status	—	100	20	Normal
TM73	Thunder Wave	Electric	Status	—	100	20	Normal
TM77	Psych Up	Normal	Status	—	—	10	Normal
TM78	Bulldoze	Ground	Physical	60	100	20	Adjacent
TM82	Dragon Tail	Dragon	Physical	60	90	10	Normal
TM85	Dream Eater	Psychic	Special	100	100	15	Normal
TM87	Swagger	Normal	Status	—	90	15	Normal
TM88	Sleep Talk	Normal	Status	—	—	10	Self
TM90	Substitute	Normal	Status	—	—	10	Self
TM94	Secret Power	Normal	Physical	70	100	20	Normal
TM100	Confide	Normal	Status	—	—	20	Normal
HM02	Fly	Flying	Physical	90	95	15	Normal
HM03	Surf	Water	Special	90	100	15	Adjacent
HM04	Strength	Normal	Physical	80	100	15	Normal
HM05	Waterfall	Water	Physical	80	100	15	Normal
HM06	Rock Smash	Fighting	Physical	40	100	15	Normal
HM07	Dive	Water	Physical	80	100	10	Normal

MOVES LEARNED IN EXCHANGE FOR BP

Name	Type	Kind	Pow.	Acc.	PP	Range
Signal Beam	Bug	Special	75	100	15	Normal
Iron Head	Steel	Physical	80	100	15	Normal
Earth Power	Ground	Special	90	100	10	Normal
Icy Wind	Ice	Special	55	95	15	Many Others
Aqua Tail	Water	Physical	90	90	10	Normal
Zen Headbutt	Psychic	Physical	80	90	15	Normal
Dragon Pulse	Dragon	Special	85	100	10	Normal
Hyper Voice	Normal	Special	90	100	10	Many Others
Iron Tail	Steel	Physical	100	75	15	Normal
Snore	Normal	Special	50	100	15	Normal
Tailwind	Flying	Status	—	—	15	Your Side
Sky Attack	Flying	Physical	140	90	5	Normal
Giga Drain	Grass	Special	75	100	10	Normal
Shock Wave	Electric	Special	60	—	20	Normal
Water Pulse	Water	Special	60	100	20	Normal
Trick	Psychic	Status	—	100	10	Normal
Wonder Room	Psychic	Status	—	—	10	Both Sides
Skill Swap	Psychic	Status	—	—	10	Normal

MOVES TAUGHT BY PEOPLE

Name	Type	Kind	Pow.	Acc.	PP	Range

249 Lugia

National Pokédex

National Pokédex **250** Hoenn Pokédex —

Ho-Oh

Rainbow Pokémon

Fire Flying

HEIGHT: 12'06" WEIGHT: 438.7 lbs.

Gender unknown

Ω Ho-Oh's feathers glow in seven colors depending on the angle at which they are struck by light. These feathers are said to bring happiness to the bearers. This Pokémon is said to live at the foot of a rainbow.

α Ho-Oh's feathers glow in seven colors depending on the angle at which they are struck by light. These feathers are said to bring happiness to the bearers. This Pokémon is said to live at the foot of a rainbow.

ABILITY
Pressure

HIDDEN ABILITY
Regenerator

EGG GROUPS
No Eggs Discovered

STAT GROWTH RATES
HP
Attack
Defense
Sp. Atk
Sp. Def
Speed

ITEMS SOMETIMES HELD BY WILD POKÉMON
Sacred Ash

EVOLUTION

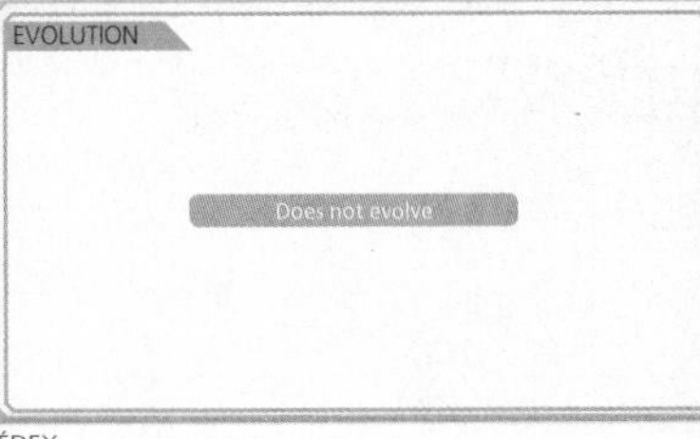

Does not evolve

MAIN WAYS TO REGISTER IN THE NATIONAL POKÉDEX

Ω After obtaining the Clear Bell from Stern in Slateport City, catch it near the entrance to Sea Mauville.

α Bring it to your game using Link Trade or the GTS.

Damage taken in normal battles

Normal	×1	Flying	×1
Fire	×0.5	Psychic	×1
Water	×2	Bug	×0.25
Grass	×0.25	Rock	×4
Electric	×2	Ghost	×1
Ice	×1	Dragon	×1
Fighting	×0.5	Dark	×1
Poison	×1	Steel	×0.5
Ground	×0	Fairy	×0.5

Damage taken in Inverse battles

Normal	×1	Flying	×1
Fire	×2	Psychic	×1
Water	×0.5	Bug	×4
Grass	×4	Rock	×0.25
Electric	×0.5	Ghost	×1
Ice	×1	Dragon	×1
Fighting	×2	Dark	×1
Poison	×1	Steel	×2
Ground	×1	Fairy	×2

Can be used in
- Inverse Battle
- Battle Institute
- Battle Maison
- Random Matchup (Free Battle)
- Random Matchup (Others)

LEVEL-UP MOVES

Lv.	Name	Type	Kind	Pow.	Acc.	PP	Range
1	Whirlwind	Normal	Status	—	—	20	Normal
1	Weather Ball	Normal	Special	50	100	10	Normal
9	Gust	Flying	Special	40	100	35	Normal
15	Brave Bird	Flying	Physical	120	100	15	Normal
23	Extrasensory	Psychic	Special	80	100	20	Normal
29	Sunny Day	Fire	Status	—	—	5	Both Sides
37	Fire Blast	Fire	Special	110	85	5	Normal
43	Sacred Fire	Fire	Physical	100	95	5	Normal
50	Punishment	Dark	Physical	—	100	5	Normal
57	Ancient Power	Rock	Special	60	100	5	Normal
65	Safeguard	Normal	Status	—	—	25	Your Side
71	Recover	Normal	Status	—	—	10	Self
79	Future Sight	Psychic	Special	120	100	10	Normal
85	Natural Gift	Normal	Physical	—	100	15	Normal
93	Calm Mind	Psychic	Status	—	—	20	Self
99	Sky Attack	Flying	Physical	140	90	5	Normal

TM & HM MOVES

No.	Name	Type	Kind	Pow.	Acc.	PP	Range
TM04	Calm Mind	Psychic	Status	—	—	20	Self
TM05	Roar	Normal	Status	—	—	20	Normal
TM06	Toxic	Poison	Status	—	90	10	Normal
TM10	Hidden Power	Normal	Special	60	100	15	Normal
TM11	Sunny Day	Fire	Status	—	—	5	Both Sides
TM15	Hyper Beam	Normal	Special	150	90	5	Normal
TM16	Light Screen	Psychic	Status	—	—	30	Your Side
TM17	Protect	Normal	Status	—	—	10	Self
TM18	Rain Dance	Water	Status	—	—	5	Both Sides
TM19	Roost	Flying	Status	—	—	10	Self
TM20	Safeguard	Normal	Status	—	—	25	Your Side
TM21	Frustration	Normal	Physical	—	100	20	Normal
TM22	Solar Beam	Grass	Special	120	100	10	Normal
TM24	Thunderbolt	Electric	Special	90	100	15	Normal
TM25	Thunder	Electric	Special	110	70	10	Normal
TM26	Earthquake	Ground	Physical	100	100	10	Adjacent
TM27	Return	Normal	Physical	—	100	20	Normal
TM29	Psychic	Psychic	Special	90	100	10	Normal
TM30	Shadow Ball	Ghost	Special	80	100	15	Normal
TM32	Double Team	Normal	Status	—	—	15	Self
TM33	Reflect	Psychic	Status	—	—	20	Your Side
TM35	Flamethrower	Fire	Special	90	100	15	Normal
TM37	Sandstorm	Rock	Status	—	—	10	Both Sides
TM38	Fire Blast	Fire	Special	110	85	5	Normal
TM40	Aerial Ace	Flying	Physical	60	—	20	Normal
TM42	Facade	Normal	Physical	70	100	20	Normal
TM43	Flame Charge	Fire	Physical	50	100	20	Normal
TM44	Rest	Psychic	Status	—	—	10	Self
TM48	Round	Normal	Special	60	100	15	Normal
TM49	Echoed Voice	Normal	Special	40	100	15	Normal
TM50	Overheat	Fire	Special	130	90	5	Normal
TM51	Steel Wing	Steel	Physical	70	90	25	Normal
TM57	Charge Beam	Electric	Special	50	90	10	Normal
TM58	Sky Drop	Flying	Physical	60	100	10	Normal
TM59	Incinerate	Fire	Special	60	100	15	Many Others
TM61	Will-O-Wisp	Fire	Status	—	85	15	Normal
TM68	Giga Impact	Normal	Physical	150	90	5	Normal
TM70	Flash	Normal	Status	—	100	20	Normal
TM73	Thunder Wave	Electric	Status	—	100	20	Normal
TM77	Psych Up	Normal	Status	—	—	10	Normal
TM78	Bulldoze	Ground	Physical	60	100	20	Adjacent
TM85	Dream Eater	Psychic	Special	100	100	15	Normal
TM87	Swagger	Normal	Status	—	90	15	Normal
TM88	Sleep Talk	Normal	Status	—	—	10	Self
TM90	Substitute	Normal	Status	—	—	10	Self
TM94	Secret Power	Normal	Physical	70	100	20	Normal
TM100	Confide	Normal	Status	—	—	20	Normal
HM02	Fly	Flying	Physical	90	95	15	Normal
HM04	Strength	Normal	Physical	80	100	15	Normal
HM06	Rock Smash	Fighting	Physical	40	100	15	Normal

MOVES LEARNED IN EXCHANGE FOR BP

Name	Type	Kind	Pow.	Acc.	PP	Range
Signal Beam	Bug	Special	75	100	15	Normal
Iron Head	Steel	Physical	80	100	15	Normal
Earth Power	Ground	Special	90	100	10	Normal
Zen Headbutt	Psychic	Physical	80	90	15	Normal
Hyper Voice	Normal	Special	90	100	10	Many Others
Snore	Normal	Special	50	100	15	Normal
Heat Wave	Fire	Special	95	90	10	Many Others
Tailwind	Flying	Status	—	—	15	Your Side
Sky Attack	Flying	Physical	140	90	5	Normal
Giga Drain	Grass	Special	75	100	10	Normal
Shock Wave	Electric	Special	60	—	20	Normal

MOVES TAUGHT BY PEOPLE

Name	Type	Kind	Pow.	Acc.	PP	Range

Ho-Oh 250

National Pokédex **251** Hoenn Pokédex **—**

Celebi

Time Travel Pokémon

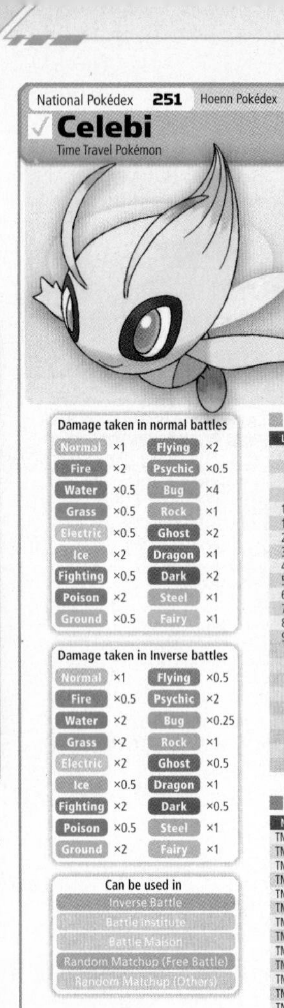

Psychic | Grass

HEIGHT: 2'00" WEIGHT: 11 lbs.

Gender unknown

Ω This Pokémon came from the future by crossing over time. It is thought that so long as Celebi appears, a bright and shining future awaits us.

α This Pokémon came from the future by crossing over time. It is thought that so long as Celebi appears, a bright and shining future awaits us.

ABILITY
Natural Cure

HIDDEN ABILITY
—

EGG GROUPS
No Eggs Discovered

STAT GROWTH RATES
HP
Attack
Defense
Sp. Atk
Sp. Def
Speed

ITEMS SOMETIMES HELD BY WILD POKÉMON
—

EVOLUTION
Does not evolve

MAIN WAY TO REGISTER IN THE NATIONAL POKÉDEX

Previously obtainable through a special distribution. There may be more announcements to come regarding future opportunities to obtain it, so keep checking the official Pokémon website.

Damage taken in normal battles

Type		Type	
Normal	×1	Flying	×2
Fire	×2	Psychic	×0.5
Water	×0.5	Bug	×4
Grass	×0.5	Rock	×1
Electric	×0.5	Ghost	×2
Ice	×2	Dragon	×1
Fighting	×0.5	Dark	×2
Poison	×2	Steel	×1
Ground	×0.5	Fairy	×1

Damage taken in Inverse battles

Type		Type	
Normal	×1	Flying	×0.5
Fire	×0.5	Psychic	×2
Water	×2	Bug	×0.25
Grass	×2	Rock	×1
Electric	×2	Ghost	×0.5
Ice	×0.5	Dragon	×1
Fighting	×2	Dark	×0.5
Poison	×0.5	Steel	×1
Ground	×2	Fairy	×1

Can be used in
Inverse Battle
Battle Institute
Battle Maison
Random Matchup (Free Battle)
Random Matchup (Others)

LEVEL-UP MOVES

Lv.	Name	Type	Kind	Pow.	Acc.	PP	Range
1	Leech Seed	Grass	Status	—	90	10	Normal
1	Confusion	Psychic	Special	50	100	25	Normal
1	Recover	Normal	Status	—	—	10	Self
1	Heal Bell	Normal	Status	—	—	5	Your Party
10	Safeguard	Normal	Status	—	—	25	Your Side
19	Magical Leaf	Grass	Special	60	—	20	Normal
28	Ancient Power	Rock	Special	60	100	5	Normal
37	Baton Pass	Normal	Status	—	—	40	Self
46	Natural Gift	Normal	Physical	—	100	15	Normal
55	Heal Block	Psychic	Status	—	100	15	Many Others
64	Future Sight	Psychic	Special	120	100	10	Normal
73	Healing Wish	Psychic	Status	—	—	10	Self
82	Leaf Storm	Grass	Special	130	90	5	Normal
91	Perish Song	Normal	Status	—	—	5	Adjacent

TM & HM MOVES

No.	Name	Type	Kind	Pow.	Acc.	PP	Range
TM04	Calm Mind	Psychic	Status	—	—	20	Self
TM06	Toxic	Poison	Status	—	90	10	Normal
TM10	Hidden Power	Normal	Special	60	100	15	Normal
TM11	Sunny Day	Fire	Status	—	—	5	Both Sides
TM15	Hyper Beam	Normal	Special	150	90	5	Normal
TM16	Light Screen	Psychic	Status	—	—	30	Your Side
TM17	Protect	Normal	Status	—	—	10	Self
TM18	Rain Dance	Water	Status	—	—	5	Both Sides
TM20	Safeguard	Normal	Status	—	—	25	Your Side
TM21	Frustration	Normal	Physical	—	100	20	Normal
TM22	Solar Beam	Grass	Special	120	100	10	Normal
TM27	Return	Normal	Physical	—	100	20	Normal
TM29	Psychic	Psychic	Special	90	100	10	Normal
TM30	Shadow Ball	Ghost	Special	80	100	15	Normal
TM32	Double Team	Normal	Status	—	—	15	Self
TM33	Reflect	Psychic	Status	—	—	20	Your Side
TM37	Sandstorm	Rock	Status	—	—	10	Both Sides
TM40	Aerial Ace	Flying	Physical	60	—	20	Normal
TM42	Facade	Normal	Physical	70	100	20	Normal
TM44	Rest	Psychic	Status	—	—	10	Self
TM48	Round	Normal	Special	60	100	15	Normal
TM49	Echoed Voice	Normal	Special	40	100	15	Normal
TM53	Energy Ball	Grass	Special	90	100	10	Normal
TM56	Fling	Dark	Physical	—	100	10	Normal
TM57	Charge Beam	Electric	Special	50	90	10	Normal
TM68	Giga Impact	Normal	Physical	150	90	5	Normal
TM70	Flash	Normal	Status	—	100	20	Normal
TM73	Thunder Wave	Electric	Status	—	100	20	Normal
TM75	Swords Dance	Normal	Status	—	—	20	Self
TM77	Psych Up	Normal	Status	—	—	10	Normal
TM85	Dream Eater	Psychic	Special	100	100	15	Normal
TM86	Grass Knot	Grass	Special	—	100	20	Normal
TM87	Swagger	Normal	Status	—	90	15	Normal
TM88	Sleep Talk	Normal	Status	—	—	10	Self
TM89	U-turn	Bug	Physical	70	100	20	Normal
TM90	Substitute	Normal	Status	—	—	10	Self
TM92	Trick Room	Psychic	Status	—	—	5	Both Sides
TM94	Secret Power	Normal	Physical	70	100	20	Normal
TM96	Nature Power	Normal	Status	—	—	20	Normal
TM99	Dazzling Gleam	Fairy	Special	80	100	10	Many Others
TM100	Confide	Normal	Status	—	—	20	Normal
HM01	Cut	Normal	Physical	50	95	30	Normal

MOVES LEARNED IN EXCHANGE FOR BP

Name	Type	Kind	Pow.	Acc.	PP	Range
Signal Beam	Bug	Special	75	100	15	Normal
Seed Bomb	Grass	Physical	80	100	15	Normal
Uproar	Normal	Special	90	100	10	1 Random
Magic Coat	Psychic	Status	—	—	15	Self
Earth Power	Ground	Special	90	100	10	Normal
Last Resort	Normal	Physical	140	100	5	Normal
Zen Headbutt	Psychic	Physical	80	90	15	Normal
Snore	Normal	Special	50	100	15	Normal
Synthesis	Grass	Status	—	—	5	Self
Heal Bell	Normal	Status	—	—	5	Your Party
Giga Drain	Grass	Special	75	100	10	Normal
Shock Wave	Electric	Special	60	—	20	Normal
Water Pulse	Water	Special	60	100	20	Normal
Worry Seed	Grass	Status	—	100	10	Normal
Helping Hand	Normal	Status	—	—	20	1 Ally
Trick	Psychic	Status	—	100	10	Normal
Magic Room	Psychic	Status	—	—	10	Both Sides
Wonder Room	Psychic	Status	—	—	10	Both Sides
Stealth Rock	Rock	Status	—	—	20	Other Side
Skill Swap	Psychic	Status	—	—	10	Normal

MOVES TAUGHT BY PEOPLE

Name	Type	Kind	Pow.	Acc.	PP	Range

National Pokédex **252** Hoenn Pokédex **001**

Treecko

Wood Gecko Pokémon

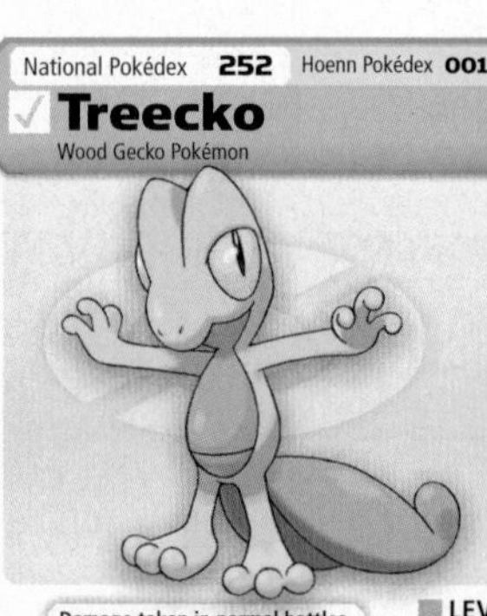

Grass

HEIGHT: 1'08" WEIGHT: 11 lbs.

Same form for ♂ / ♀

Ω Treecko has small hooks on the bottom of its feet that enable it to scale vertical walls. This Pokémon attacks by slamming foes with its thick tail.

α Treecko is cool, calm, and collected—it never panics under any situation. If a bigger foe were to glare at this Pokémon, it would glare right back without conceding an inch of ground.

ABILITY
Overgrow

HIDDEN ABILITY
Unburden

EGG GROUPS
Monster | Dragon

STAT GROWTH RATES
HP
Attack
Defense
Sp. Atk
Sp. Def
Speed

ITEMS SOMETIMES HELD BY WILD POKÉMON
—

EVOLUTION
Treecko → Lv. 16 → Grovyle → Lv. 36 → Sceptile

MAIN WAY TO REGISTER IN THE NATIONAL POKÉDEX

Receive from Professor Birch at his Pokémon Lab in Littleroot Town.

Damage taken in normal battles

Type		Type	
Normal	×1	Flying	×2
Fire	×2	Psychic	×1
Water	×0.5	Bug	×2
Grass	×0.5	Rock	×1
Electric	×0.5	Ghost	×1
Ice	×2	Dragon	×1
Fighting	×1	Dark	×1
Poison	×2	Steel	×1
Ground	×0.5	Fairy	×1

Damage taken in Inverse battles

Type		Type	
Normal	×1	Flying	×0.5
Fire	×0.5	Psychic	×1
Water	×2	Bug	×0.5
Grass	×2	Rock	×1
Electric	×2	Ghost	×1
Ice	×0.5	Dragon	×1
Fighting	×1	Dark	×1
Poison	×0.5	Steel	×1
Ground	×2	Fairy	×1

Can be used in
Inverse Battle
Battle Institute
Battle Maison
Random Matchup (Free Battle)
Random Matchup (Others)

LEVEL-UP MOVES

Lv.	Name	Type	Kind	Pow.	Acc.	PP	Range
1	Pound	Normal	Physical	40	100	35	Normal
1	Leer	Normal	Status	—	100	30	Many Others
5	Absorb	Grass	Special	20	100	25	Normal
9	Quick Attack	Normal	Physical	40	100	30	Normal
13	Mega Drain	Grass	Special	40	100	15	Normal
17	Pursuit	Dark	Physical	40	100	20	Normal
21	Giga Drain	Grass	Special	75	100	10	Normal
25	Agility	Psychic	Status	—	—	30	Self
29	Slam	Normal	Physical	80	75	20	Normal
33	Detect	Fighting	Status	—	—	5	Self
37	Energy Ball	Grass	Special	90	100	10	Normal
41	Quick Guard	Fighting	Status	—	—	15	Your Side
45	Endeavor	Normal	Physical	—	100	5	Normal
49	Screech	Normal	Status	—	85	40	Normal

TM & HM MOVES

No.	Name	Type	Kind	Pow.	Acc.	PP	Range
TM06	Toxic	Poison	Status	—	90	10	Normal
TM10	Hidden Power	Normal	Special	60	100	15	Normal
TM11	Sunny Day	Fire	Status	—	—	5	Both Sides
TM17	Protect	Normal	Status	—	—	10	Self
TM20	Safeguard	Normal	Status	—	—	25	Your Side
TM21	Frustration	Normal	Physical	—	100	20	Normal
TM22	Solar Beam	Grass	Special	120	100	10	Normal
TM27	Return	Normal	Physical	—	100	20	Normal
TM28	Dig	Ground	Physical	80	100	10	Normal
TM31	Brick Break	Fighting	Physical	75	100	15	Normal
TM32	Double Team	Normal	Status	—	—	15	Self
TM39	Rock Tomb	Rock	Physical	60	95	15	Normal
TM40	Aerial Ace	Flying	Physical	60	—	20	Normal
TM42	Facade	Normal	Physical	70	100	20	Normal
TM44	Rest	Psychic	Status	—	—	10	Self
TM45	Attract	Normal	Status	—	100	15	Normal
TM48	Round	Normal	Special	60	100	15	Normal
TM53	Energy Ball	Grass	Special	90	100	10	Normal
TM56	Fling	Dark	Physical	—	100	10	Normal
TM62	Acrobatics	Flying	Physical	55	100	15	Normal
TM70	Flash	Normal	Status	—	100	20	Normal
TM75	Swords Dance	Normal	Status	—	—	20	Self
TM80	Rock Slide	Rock	Physical	75	90	10	Many Others
TM86	Grass Knot	Grass	Special	—	100	20	Normal
TM87	Swagger	Normal	Status	—	90	15	Normal
TM88	Sleep Talk	Normal	Status	—	—	10	Self
TM90	Substitute	Normal	Status	—	—	10	Self
TM94	Secret Power	Normal	Physical	70	100	20	Normal
TM96	Nature Power	Normal	Status	—	—	20	Normal
TM98	Power-Up Punch	Fighting	Physical	40	100	20	Normal
TM100	Confide	Normal	Status	—	—	20	Normal
HM01	Cut	Normal	Physical	50	95	30	Normal
HM04	Strength	Normal	Physical	80	100	15	Normal
HM06	Rock Smash	Fighting	Physical	40	100	15	Normal

MOVES LEARNED IN EXCHANGE FOR BP

Name	Type	Kind	Pow.	Acc.	PP	Range
Seed Bomb	Grass	Physical	80	100	15	Normal
Low Kick	Fighting	Physical	—	100	20	Normal
Thunder Punch	Electric	Physical	75	100	15	Normal
Iron Tail	Steel	Physical	100	75	15	Normal
Snore	Normal	Special	50	100	15	Normal
Synthesis	Grass	Status	—	—	5	Self
Giga Drain	Grass	Special	75	100	10	Normal
Drain Punch	Fighting	Physical	75	100	10	Normal
Focus Punch	Fighting	Physical	150	100	20	Normal
Worry Seed	Grass	Status	—	100	10	Normal
Endeavor	Normal	Physical	—	100	5	Normal

MOVES TAUGHT BY PEOPLE

Name	Type	Kind	Pow.	Acc.	PP	Range
Grass Pledge	Grass	Special	80	100	10	Normal

EGG MOVES

Name	Type	Kind	Pow.	Acc.	PP	Range
Crunch	Dark	Physical	80	100	15	Normal
Mud Sport	Ground	Status	—	—	15	Both Sides
Endeavor	Normal	Physical	—	100	5	Normal
Leech Seed	Grass	Status	—	90	10	Normal
Dragon Breath	Dragon	Special	60	100	20	Normal
Crush Claw	Normal	Physical	75	95	10	Normal
Worry Seed	Grass	Status	—	100	10	Normal
Double Kick	Fighting	Physical	30	100	30	Normal
Grass Whistle	Grass	Status	—	55	15	Normal
Synthesis	Grass	Status	—	—	5	Self
Magical Leaf	Grass	Special	60	—	20	Normal
Leaf Storm	Grass	Special	130	90	5	Normal
Razor Wind	Normal	Special	80	100	10	Many Others
Bullet Seed	Grass	Physical	25	100	30	Normal
Natural Gift	Normal	Physical	—	100	15	Normal
Grassy Terrain	Grass	Status	—	—	10	Both Sides

National Pokédex **253** Hoenn Pokédex **002**

Grovyle

Wood Gecko Pokémon

Grass

HEIGHT: 2'11" WEIGHT: 47.6 lbs.

Same form for ♂ / ♀

Ω The leaves growing out of Grovyle's body are convenient for camouflaging it from enemies in the forest. This Pokémon is a master at climbing trees in jungles.

α This Pokémon adeptly flies from branch to branch in trees. In a forest, no Pokémon can ever hope to catch a fleeing Grovyle however fast they may be.

ABILITY: Overgrow

HIDDEN ABILITY: Unburden

EGG GROUPS: Monster, Dragon

STAT GROWTH RATES: HP ■■ / Attack ■■■ / Defense ■■ / Sp. Atk ■■■■ / Sp. Def ■■■ / Speed ■■■■■

ITEMS SOMETIMES HELD BY WILD POKÉMON: —

EVOLUTION

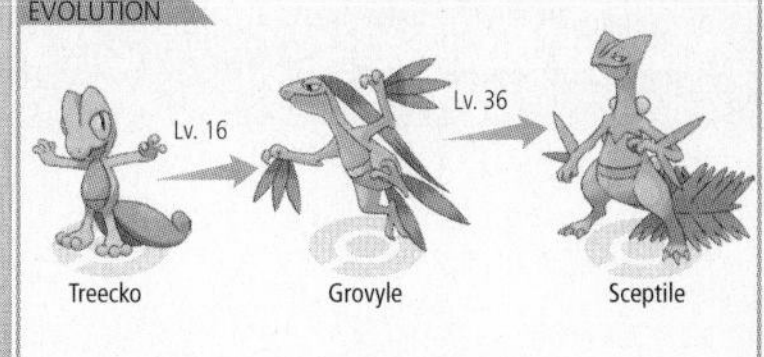

MAIN WAY TO REGISTER IN THE NATIONAL POKÉDEX

Level up Treecko to Lv. 16.

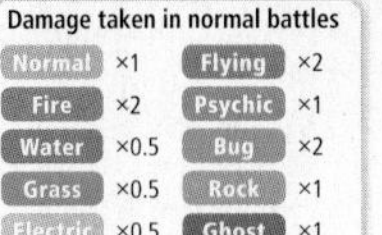

Damage taken in normal battles

Type		Type	
Normal	×1	Flying	×2
Fire	×2	Psychic	×1
Water	×0.5	Bug	×2
Grass	×0.5	Rock	×1
Electric	×0.5	Ghost	×1
Ice	×2	Dragon	×1
Fighting	×1	Dark	×1
Poison	×2	Steel	×1
Ground	×0.5	Fairy	×1

Damage taken in Inverse battles

Type		Type	
Normal	×1	Flying	×0.5
Fire	×0.5	Psychic	×1
Water	×2	Bug	×0.5
Grass	×2	Rock	×1
Electric	×2	Ghost	×1
Ice	×0.5	Dragon	×1
Fighting	×1	Dark	×1
Poison	×0.5	Steel	×1
Ground	×2	Fairy	×1

Can be used in

- Inverse Battle
- Battle Institute
- Battle Maison
- Random Matchup (Free Battle)
- Random Matchup (Others)

LEVEL-UP MOVES

Lv.	Name	Type	Kind	Pow.	Acc.	PP	Range
1	Pound	Normal	Physical	40	100	35	Normal
1	Leer	Normal	Status	—	100	30	Many Others
1	Absorb	Grass	Special	20	100	25	Normal
1	Quick Attack	Normal	Physical	40	100	30	Normal
5	Absorb	Grass	Special	20	100	25	Normal
9	Quick Attack	Normal	Physical	40	100	30	Normal
13	Mega Drain	Grass	Special	40	100	15	Normal
16	Fury Cutter	Bug	Physical	40	95	20	Normal
18	Pursuit	Dark	Physical	40	100	20	Normal
23	Leaf Blade	Grass	Physical	90	100	15	Normal
28	Agility	Psychic	Status	—	—	30	Self
33	Slam	Normal	Physical	80	75	20	Normal
38	Detect	Fighting	Status	—	—	5	Self
43	X-Scissor	Bug	Physical	80	100	15	Normal
48	False Swipe	Normal	Physical	40	100	40	Normal
53	Quick Guard	Fighting	Status	—	—	15	Your Side
58	Leaf Storm	Grass	Special	130	90	5	Normal
63	Screech	Normal	Status	—	85	40	Normal

TM & HM MOVES

No.	Name	Type	Kind	Pow.	Acc.	PP	Range
TM06	Toxic	Poison	Status	—	90	10	Normal
TM10	Hidden Power	Normal	Special	60	100	15	Normal
TM11	Sunny Day	Fire	Status	—	—	5	Both Sides
TM17	Protect	Normal	Status	—	—	10	Self
TM20	Safeguard	Normal	Status	—	—	25	Your Side
TM21	Frustration	Normal	Physical	—	100	20	Normal
TM22	Solar Beam	Grass	Special	120	100	10	Normal
TM27	Return	Normal	Physical	—	100	20	Normal
TM28	Dig	Ground	Physical	80	100	10	Normal
TM31	Brick Break	Fighting	Physical	75	100	15	Normal
TM32	Double Team	Normal	Status	—	—	15	Self
TM39	Rock Tomb	Rock	Physical	60	95	15	Normal
TM40	Aerial Ace	Flying	Physical	60	—	20	Normal
TM42	Facade	Normal	Physical	70	100	20	Normal
TM44	Rest	Psychic	Status	—	—	10	Self
TM45	Attract	Normal	Status	—	100	15	Normal
TM47	Low Sweep	Fighting	Physical	65	100	20	Normal
TM48	Round	Normal	Special	60	100	15	Normal
TM53	Energy Ball	Grass	Special	90	100	10	Normal
TM54	False Swipe	Normal	Physical	40	100	40	Normal
TM56	Fling	Dark	Physical	—	100	10	Normal
TM62	Acrobatics	Flying	Physical	55	100	15	Normal
TM70	Flash	Normal	Status	—	100	20	Normal
TM75	Swords Dance	Normal	Status	—	—	20	Self
TM80	Rock Slide	Rock	Physical	75	90	10	Many Others
TM81	X-Scissor	Bug	Physical	80	100	15	Normal
TM86	Grass Knot	Grass	Special	—	100	20	Normal
TM87	Swagger	Normal	Status	—	90	15	Normal
TM88	Sleep Talk	Normal	Status	—	—	10	Self
TM90	Substitute	Normal	Status	—	—	10	Self
TM94	Secret Power	Normal	Physical	70	100	20	Normal
TM96	Nature Power	Normal	Status	—	—	20	Normal
TM98	Power-Up Punch	Fighting	Physical	40	100	20	Normal
TM100	Confide	Normal	Status	—	—	20	Normal
HM01	Cut	Normal	Physical	50	95	30	Normal
HM04	Strength	Normal	Physical	80	100	15	Normal
HM06	Rock Smash	Fighting	Physical	40	100	15	Normal

MOVES LEARNED IN EXCHANGE FOR BP

Name	Type	Kind	Pow.	Acc.	PP	Range
Seed Bomb	Grass	Physical	80	100	15	Normal
Low Kick	Fighting	Physical	—	100	20	Normal
Thunder Punch	Electric	Physical	75	100	15	Normal
Iron Tail	Steel	Physical	100	75	15	Normal
Snore	Normal	Special	50	100	15	Normal
Synthesis	Grass	Status	—	—	5	Self
Giga Drain	Grass	Special	75	100	10	Normal
Drain Punch	Fighting	Physical	75	100	10	Normal
Focus Punch	Fighting	Physical	150	100	20	Normal
Worry Seed	Grass	Status	—	100	10	Normal
Endeavor	Normal	Physical	—	100	5	Normal

MOVES TAUGHT BY PEOPLE

Name	Type	Kind	Pow.	Acc.	PP	Range
Grass Pledge	Grass	Special	80	100	10	Normal

National Pokédex **254** Hoenn Pokédex **003**

Sceptile

Forest Pokémon

Grass

HEIGHT: 5'07" WEIGHT: 115.1 lbs.

Same form for ♂ / ♀

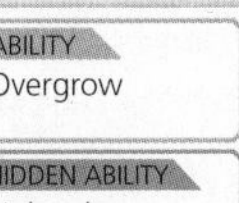

Ω The leaves growing on Sceptile's body are very sharp edged. This Pokémon is very agile—it leaps all over the branches of trees and jumps on its foe from above or behind.

α Sceptile has seeds growing on its back. They are said to be bursting with nutrients that revitalize trees. This Pokémon raises the trees in a forest with loving care.

ABILITY: Overgrow

HIDDEN ABILITY: Unburden

EGG GROUPS: Monster, Dragon

STAT GROWTH RATES: HP / Attack ■■■■ / Defense ■■■ / Sp. Atk ■■■■■ / Sp. Def ■■■■ / Speed ■■■■■■

ITEMS SOMETIMES HELD BY WILD POKÉMON: —

EVOLUTION

Lv. 16 Lv. 36

Treecko Grovyle Sceptile

MAIN WAY TO REGISTER IN THE NATIONAL POKÉDEX

Level up Grovyle to Lv. 36.

Damage taken in normal battles

Type		Type	
Normal	×1	Flying	×2
Fire	×2	Psychic	×1
Water	×0.5	Bug	×2
Grass	×0.5	Rock	×1
Electric	×0.5	Ghost	×1
Ice	×2	Dragon	×1
Fighting	×1	Dark	×1
Poison	×2	Steel	×1
Ground	×0.5	Fairy	×1

Damage taken in Inverse battles

Type		Type	
Normal	×1	Flying	×0.5
Fire	×0.5	Psychic	×1
Water	×2	Bug	×0.5
Grass	×2	Rock	×1
Electric	×2	Ghost	×1
Ice	×0.5	Dragon	×1
Fighting	×1	Dark	×1
Poison	×0.5	Steel	×1
Ground	×2	Fairy	×1

Can be used in

- Inverse Battle
- Battle Institute
- Battle Maison
- Random Matchup (Free Battle)
- Random Matchup (Others)

LEVEL-UP MOVES

Lv.	Name	Type	Kind	Pow.	Acc.	PP	Range
1	Leaf Storm	Grass	Special	130	90	5	Normal
1	Night Slash	Dark	Physical	70	100	15	Normal
1	Pound	Normal	Physical	40	100	35	Normal
1	Leer	Normal	Status	—	100	30	Many Others
1	Absorb	Grass	Special	20	100	25	Normal
1	Quick Attack	Normal	Physical	40	100	30	Normal
5	Absorb	Grass	Special	20	100	25	Normal
9	Quick Attack	Normal	Physical	40	100	30	Normal
13	Mega Drain	Grass	Special	40	100	15	Normal
16	Fury Cutter	Bug	Physical	40	95	20	Normal
18	Pursuit	Dark	Physical	40	100	20	Normal
23	Leaf Blade	Grass	Physical	90	100	15	Normal
28	Agility	Psychic	Status	—	—	30	Self
33	Slam	Normal	Physical	80	75	20	Normal
36	Dual Chop	Dragon	Physical	40	90	15	Normal
39	Detect	Fighting	Status	—	—	5	Self
45	X-Scissor	Bug	Physical	80	100	15	Normal
51	False Swipe	Normal	Physical	40	100	40	Normal
57	Quick Guard	Fighting	Status	—	—	15	Your Side
63	Leaf Storm	Grass	Special	130	90	5	Normal
69	Screech	Normal	Status	—	85	40	Normal

TM & HM MOVES

No.	Name	Type	Kind	Pow.	Acc.	PP	Range
TM01	Hone Claws	Dark	Status	—	—	15	Self
TM02	Dragon Claw	Dragon	Physical	80	100	15	Normal
TM05	Roar	Normal	Status	—	—	20	Normal
TM06	Toxic	Poison	Status	—	90	10	Normal
TM10	Hidden Power	Normal	Special	60	100	15	Normal
TM11	Sunny Day	Fire	Status	—	—	5	Both Sides
TM15	Hyper Beam	Normal	Special	150	90	5	Normal
TM17	Protect	Normal	Status	—	—	10	Self
TM20	Safeguard	Normal	Status	—	—	25	Your Side
TM21	Frustration	Normal	Physical	—	100	20	Normal
TM22	Solar Beam	Grass	Special	120	100	10	Normal
TM26	Earthquake	Ground	Physical	100	100	10	Adjacent
TM27	Return	Normal	Physical	—	100	20	Normal
TM28	Dig	Ground	Physical	80	100	10	Normal
TM31	Brick Break	Fighting	Physical	75	100	15	Normal
TM32	Double Team	Normal	Status	—	—	15	Self
TM39	Rock Tomb	Rock	Physical	60	95	15	Normal
TM40	Aerial Ace	Flying	Physical	60	—	20	Normal
TM42	Facade	Normal	Physical	70	100	20	Normal
TM44	Rest	Psychic	Status	—	—	10	Self
TM45	Attract	Normal	Status	—	100	15	Normal
TM47	Low Sweep	Fighting	Physical	65	100	20	Normal
TM48	Round	Normal	Special	60	100	15	Normal
TM52	Focus Blast	Fighting	Special	120	70	5	Normal
TM53	Energy Ball	Grass	Special	90	100	10	Normal
TM54	False Swipe	Normal	Physical	40	100	40	Normal
TM56	Fling	Dark	Physical	—	100	10	Normal
TM62	Acrobatics	Flying	Physical	55	100	15	Normal
TM68	Giga Impact	Normal	Physical	150	90	5	Normal
TM70	Flash	Normal	Status	—	100	20	Normal
TM75	Swords Dance	Normal	Status	—	—	20	Self
TM78	Bulldoze	Ground	Physical	60	100	20	Adjacent
TM80	Rock Slide	Rock	Physical	75	90	10	Many Others
TM81	X-Scissor	Bug	Physical	80	100	15	Normal
TM86	Grass Knot	Grass	Special	—	100	20	Normal
TM87	Swagger	Normal	Status	—	90	15	Normal
TM88	Sleep Talk	Normal	Status	—	—	10	Self
TM90	Substitute	Normal	Status	—	—	10	Self
TM94	Secret Power	Normal	Physical	70	100	20	Normal
TM96	Nature Power	Normal	Status	—	—	20	Normal
TM98	Power-Up Punch	Fighting	Physical	40	100	20	Normal
TM100	Confide	Normal	Status	—	—	20	Normal
HM01	Cut	Normal	Physical	50	95	30	Normal
HM04	Strength	Normal	Physical	80	100	15	Normal
HM06	Rock Smash	Fighting	Physical	40	100	15	Normal

MOVES LEARNED IN EXCHANGE FOR BP

Name	Type	Kind	Pow.	Acc.	PP	Range
Dual Chop	Dragon	Physical	40	90	15	Normal
Seed Bomb	Grass	Physical	80	100	15	Normal
Low Kick	Fighting	Physical	—	100	20	Normal
Thunder Punch	Electric	Physical	75	100	15	Normal
Dragon Pulse	Dragon	Special	85	100	10	Normal
Iron Tail	Steel	Physical	100	75	15	Normal
Snore	Normal	Special	50	100	15	Normal
Synthesis	Grass	Status	—	—	5	Self
Giga Drain	Grass	Special	75	100	10	Normal
Drain Punch	Fighting	Physical	75	100	10	Normal
Focus Punch	Fighting	Physical	150	100	20	Normal
Worry Seed	Grass	Status	—	100	10	Normal
Endeavor	Normal	Physical	—	100	5	Normal
Outrage	Dragon	Physical	120	100	10	1 Random

MOVES TAUGHT BY PEOPLE

Name	Type	Kind	Pow.	Acc.	PP	Range
Grass Pledge	Grass	Special	80	100	10	Normal
Frenzy Plant	Grass	Special	150	90	5	Normal

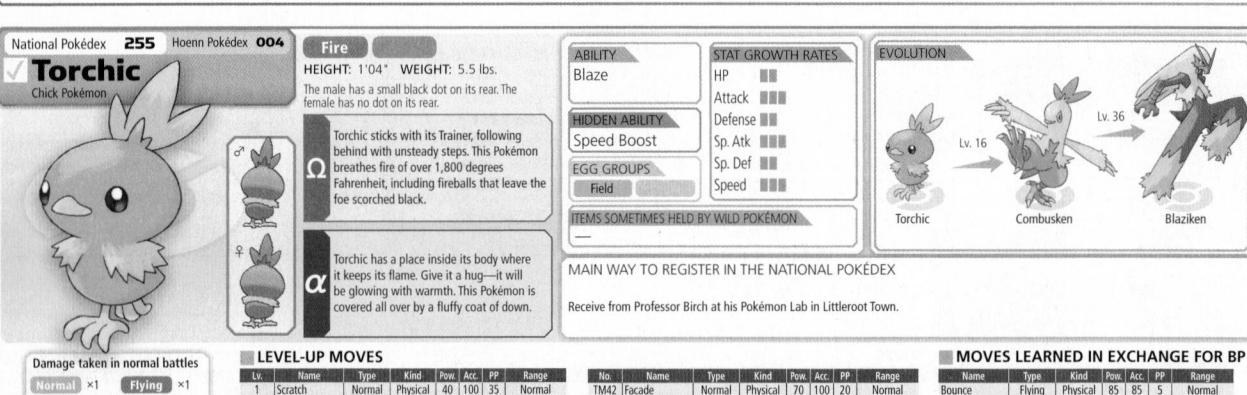

Mega Evolution

Mega Sceptile

Forest Pokémon

Grass | Dragon

HEIGHT: 6'03" WEIGHT: 121.7 lbs.

Same form for ♂ / ♀

REQUIRED MEGA STONE

Sceptilite

Receive from Steven on Route 120 (if you chose Treecko at the beginning of the game) / Purchase from the stone seller on Route 114 by selecting the piece titled "Withered Tree"

ABILITY

Lightning Rod

HIDDEN ABILITY

—

EGG GROUPS

—

STAT GROWTH RATES

HP

Attack

Defense

Sp. Atk

Sp. Def

Speed

Damage taken in normal battles

Type		Type	
Normal	×1	Flying	×2
Fire	×1	Psychic	×1
Water	×0.25	Bug	×2
Grass	×0.25	Rock	×1
! Electric	×0.25	Ghost	×1
Ice	×4	Dragon	×2
Fighting	×1	Dark	×1
Poison	×2	Steel	×1
Ground	×0.5	Fairy	×2

Damage taken in Inverse battles

Type		Type	
Normal	×1	Flying	×0.5
Fire	×1	Psychic	×1
Water	×4	Bug	×0.5
Grass	×4	Rock	×1
! Electric	×4	Ghost	×1
Ice	×0.25	Dragon	×0.5
Fighting	×1	Dark	×1
Poison	×0.5	Steel	×1
Ground	×2	Fairy	×0.5

Can be used in

Inverse Battle

Battle Institute

Battle Maison

Random Matchup (Free Battle)

Random Matchup (Others)

National Pokédex **255** Hoenn Pokédex **004**

Torchic

Chick Pokémon

Fire

HEIGHT: 1'04" WEIGHT: 5.5 lbs.

The male has a small black dot on its rear. The female has no dot on its rear.

♂ ♀

Ω Torchic sticks with its Trainer, following behind with unsteady steps. This Pokémon breathes fire of over 1,800 degrees Fahrenheit, including fireballs that leave the foe scorched black.

α Torchic has a place inside its body where it keeps its flame. Give it a hug—it will be glowing with warmth. This Pokémon is covered all over by a fluffy coat of down.

ABILITY

Blaze

HIDDEN ABILITY

Speed Boost

EGG GROUPS

Field

STAT GROWTH RATES

HP

Attack

Defense

Sp. Atk

Sp. Def

Speed

ITEMS SOMETIMES HELD BY WILD POKÉMON

—

EVOLUTION

MAIN WAY TO REGISTER IN THE NATIONAL POKÉDEX

Receive from Professor Birch at his Pokémon Lab in Littleroot Town.

Damage taken in normal battles

Type		Type	
Normal	×1	Flying	×1
Fire	×0.5	Psychic	×1
Water	×2	Bug	×0.5
Grass	×0.5	Rock	×2
Electric	×1	Ghost	×1
Ice	×0.5	Dragon	×1
Fighting	×1	Dark	×1
Poison	×1	Steel	×0.5
Ground	×2	Fairy	×0.5

Damage taken in Inverse battles

Type		Type	
Normal	×1	Flying	×1
Fire	×2	Psychic	×1
Water	×0.5	Bug	×2
Grass	×2	Rock	×0.5
Electric	×1	Ghost	×1
Ice	×2	Dragon	×1
Fighting	×1	Dark	×1
Poison	×1	Steel	×2
Ground	×0.5	Fairy	×2

Can be used in

Inverse Battle

Battle Institute

Battle Maison

Random Matchup (Free Battle)

Random Matchup (Others)

LEVEL-UP MOVES

Lv.	Name	Type	Kind	Pow.	Acc.	PP	Range
1	Scratch	Normal	Physical	40	100	35	Normal
1	Growl	Normal	Status	—	100	40	Many Others
5	Ember	Fire	Special	40	100	25	Normal
10	Sand Attack	Ground	Status	—	100	15	Normal
14	Peck	Flying	Physical	35	100	35	Normal
19	Fire Spin	Fire	Special	35	85	15	Normal
23	Quick Attack	Normal	Physical	40	100	30	Normal
28	Flame Burst	Fire	Special	70	100	15	Normal
32	Focus Energy	Normal	Status	—	—	30	Self
37	Slash	Normal	Physical	70	100	20	Normal
41	Mirror Move	Flying	Status	—	—	20	Normal
46	Flamethrower	Fire	Special	90	100	15	Normal

TM & HM MOVES

No.	Name	Type	Kind	Pow.	Acc.	PP	Range
TM01	Hone Claws	Dark	Status	—	—	15	Self
TM06	Toxic	Poison	Status	—	90	10	Normal
TM10	Hidden Power	Normal	Special	60	100	15	Normal
TM11	Sunny Day	Fire	Status	—	—	5	Both Sides
TM17	Protect	Normal	Status	—	—	10	Self
TM21	Frustration	Normal	Physical	—	100	20	Normal
TM27	Return	Normal	Physical	—	100	20	Normal
TM28	Dig	Ground	Physical	80	100	10	Normal
TM32	Double Team	Normal	Status	—	—	15	Self
TM35	Flamethrower	Fire	Special	90	100	15	Normal
TM38	Fire Blast	Fire	Special	110	85	5	Normal
TM39	Rock Tomb	Rock	Physical	60	95	15	Normal
TM40	Aerial Ace	Flying	Physical	60	—	20	Normal
TM42	Facade	Normal	Physical	70	100	20	Normal
TM43	Flame Charge	Fire	Physical	50	100	20	Normal
TM44	Rest	Psychic	Status	—	—	10	Self
TM45	Attract	Normal	Status	—	100	15	Normal
TM48	Round	Normal	Special	60	100	15	Normal
TM49	Echoed Voice	Normal	Special	40	100	15	Normal
TM50	Overheat	Fire	Special	130	90	5	Normal
TM59	Incinerate	Fire	Special	60	100	15	Many Others
TM61	Will-O-Wisp	Fire	Status	—	85	15	Normal
TM65	Shadow Claw	Ghost	Physical	70	100	15	Normal
TM75	Swords Dance	Normal	Status	—	—	20	Self
TM80	Rock Slide	Rock	Physical	75	90	10	Many Others
TM87	Swagger	Normal	Status	—	90	15	Normal
TM88	Sleep Talk	Normal	Status	—	—	10	Self
TM90	Substitute	Normal	Status	—	—	10	Self
TM94	Secret Power	Normal	Physical	70	100	20	Normal
TM100	Confide	Normal	Status	—	—	20	Normal
HM01	Cut	Normal	Physical	50	95	30	Normal
HM04	Strength	Normal	Physical	80	100	15	Normal
HM06	Rock Smash	Fighting	Physical	40	100	15	Normal

MOVES LEARNED IN EXCHANGE FOR BP

Name	Type	Kind	Pow.	Acc.	PP	Range
Bounce	Flying	Physical	85	85	5	Normal
Low Kick	Fighting	Physical	—	100	20	Normal
Last Resort	Normal	Physical	140	100	5	Normal
Snore	Normal	Special	50	100	15	Normal
Heat Wave	Fire	Special	95	90	10	Many Others
Helping Hand	Normal	Status	—	—	20	1 Ally

MOVES TAUGHT BY PEOPLE

Name	Type	Kind	Pow.	Acc.	PP	Range
Fire Pledge	Fire	Special	80	100	10	Normal

EGG MOVES

Name	Type	Kind	Pow.	Acc.	PP	Range
Counter	Fighting	Physical	—	100	20	Varies
Reversal	Fighting	Physical	—	100	15	Normal
Endure	Normal	Status	—	—	10	Self
Smelling Salts	Normal	Physical	70	100	10	Normal
Crush Claw	Normal	Physical	75	95	10	Normal
Baton Pass	Normal	Status	—	—	40	Self
Agility	Psychic	Status	—	—	30	Self
Night Slash	Dark	Physical	70	100	15	Normal
Last Resort	Normal	Physical	140	100	5	Normal
Feint	Normal	Physical	30	100	10	Normal
Feather Dance	Flying	Status	—	100	15	Normal
Curse	Ghost	Status	—	—	10	Varies
Flame Burst	Fire	Special	70	100	15	Normal
Low Kick	Fighting	Physical	—	100	20	Normal

National Pokédex **256** Hoenn Pokédex **005**

Combusken

Young Fowl Pokémon

Fire Fighting

HEIGHT: 2'11" WEIGHT: 43 lbs.

The male has a larger crest. The female has a smaller crest.

♂ ♀

Ω Combusken toughens up its legs and thighs by running through fields and mountains. This Pokémon's legs possess both speed and power, enabling it to dole out 10 kicks in one second.

α Combusken battles with the intensely hot flames it spews from its beak and with outstandingly destructive kicks. This Pokémon's cry is very loud and distracting.

ABILITY
Blaze

HIDDEN ABILITY
Speed Boost

EGG GROUPS
Field

STAT GROWTH RATES
HP
Attack
Defense
Sp. Atk
Sp. Def
Speed

ITEMS SOMETIMES HELD BY WILD POKÉMON
—

EVOLUTION

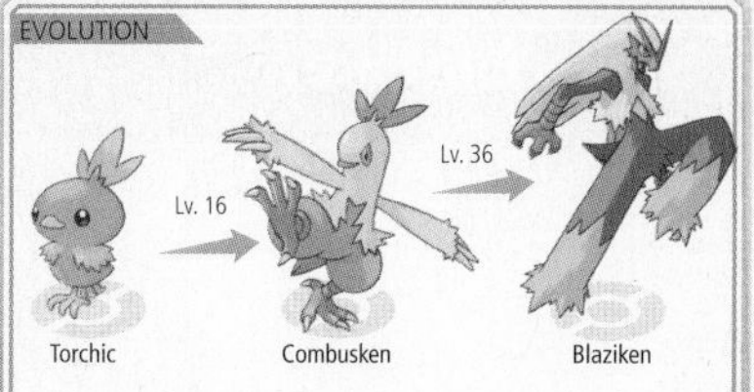

MAIN WAY TO REGISTER IN THE NATIONAL POKÉDEX

Level up Torchic to Lv. 16.

Damage taken in normal battles

Type		Type	
Normal	×1	Flying	×2
Fire	×0.5	Psychic	×2
Water	×2	Bug	×0.25
Grass	×0.5	Rock	×1
Electric	×1	Ghost	×1
Ice	×0.5	Dragon	×1
Fighting	×1	Dark	×0.5
Poison	×1	Steel	×0.5
Ground	×2	Fairy	×1

Damage taken in Inverse battles

Type		Type	
Normal	×1	Flying	×0.5
Fire	×2	Psychic	×0.5
Water	×0.5	Bug	×4
Grass	×2	Rock	×1
Electric	×1	Ghost	×1
Ice	×2	Dragon	×1
Fighting	×1	Dark	×2
Poison	×1	Steel	×2
Ground	×0.5	Fairy	×1

Can be used in
Inverse Battle
Battle Institute
Battle Maison
Random Matchup (Free Battle)
Random Matchup (Others)

LEVEL-UP MOVES

Lv.	Name	Type	Kind	Pow.	Acc.	PP	Range
1	Scratch	Normal	Physical	40	100	35	Normal
1	Growl	Normal	Status	—	100	40	Many Others
1	Ember	Fire	Special	40	100	25	Normal
1	Sand Attack	Ground	Status	—	100	15	Normal
5	Ember	Fire	Special	40	100	25	Normal
10	Sand Attack	Ground	Status	—	100	15	Normal
14	Peck	Flying	Physical	35	100	35	Normal
16	Double Kick	Fighting	Physical	30	100	30	Normal
20	Flame Charge	Fire	Physical	50	100	20	Normal
25	Quick Attack	Normal	Physical	40	100	30	Normal
31	Bulk Up	Fighting	Status	—	—	20	Self
36	Focus Energy	Normal	Status	—	—	30	Self
42	Slash	Normal	Physical	70	100	20	Normal
47	Mirror Move	Flying	Status	—	—	20	Normal
53	Sky Uppercut	Fighting	Physical	85	90	15	Normal
58	Flare Blitz	Fire	Physical	120	100	15	Normal

TM & HM MOVES

No.	Name	Type	Kind	Pow.	Acc.	PP	Range
TM01	Hone Claws	Dark	Status	—	—	15	Self
TM06	Toxic	Poison	Status	—	90	10	Normal
TM08	Bulk Up	Fighting	Status	—	—	20	Self
TM10	Hidden Power	Normal	Special	60	100	15	Normal
TM11	Sunny Day	Fire	Status	—	—	5	Both Sides
TM17	Protect	Normal	Status	—	—	10	Self
TM21	Frustration	Normal	Physical	—	100	20	Normal
TM27	Return	Normal	Physical	—	100	20	Normal
TM28	Dig	Ground	Physical	80	100	10	Normal
TM31	Brick Break	Fighting	Physical	75	100	15	Normal
TM32	Double Team	Normal	Status	—	—	15	Self
TM35	Flamethrower	Fire	Special	90	100	15	Normal
TM38	Fire Blast	Fire	Special	110	85	5	Normal
TM39	Rock Tomb	Rock	Physical	60	95	15	Normal
TM40	Aerial Ace	Flying	Physical	60	—	20	Normal
TM42	Facade	Normal	Physical	70	100	20	Normal
TM43	Flame Charge	Fire	Physical	50	100	20	Normal
TM44	Rest	Psychic	Status	—	—	10	Self
TM45	Attract	Normal	Status	—	100	15	Normal
TM47	Low Sweep	Fighting	Physical	65	100	20	Normal
TM48	Round	Normal	Special	60	100	15	Normal
TM49	Echoed Voice	Normal	Special	40	100	15	Normal
TM50	Overheat	Fire	Special	130	90	5	Normal
TM52	Focus Blast	Fighting	Special	120	70	5	Normal
TM56	Fling	Dark	Physical	—	100	10	Normal
TM59	Incinerate	Fire	Special	60	100	15	Many Others
TM61	Will-O-Wisp	Fire	Status	—	85	15	Normal
TM65	Shadow Claw	Ghost	Physical	70	100	15	Normal
TM75	Swords Dance	Normal	Status	—	—	20	Self
TM80	Rock Slide	Rock	Physical	75	90	10	Many Others
TM84	Poison Jab	Poison	Physical	80	100	20	Normal
TM87	Swagger	Normal	Status	—	90	15	Normal
TM88	Sleep Talk	Normal	Status	—	—	10	Self
TM90	Substitute	Normal	Status	—	—	10	Self
TM94	Secret Power	Normal	Physical	70	100	20	Normal
TM98	Power-Up Punch	Fighting	Physical	40	100	20	Normal
TM100	Confide	Normal	Status	—	—	20	Normal
HM01	Cut	Normal	Physical	50	95	30	Normal
HM04	Strength	Normal	Physical	80	100	15	Normal
HM06	Rock Smash	Fighting	Physical	40	100	15	Normal

MOVES LEARNED IN EXCHANGE FOR BP

Name	Type	Kind	Pow.	Acc.	PP	Range
Dual Chop	Dragon	Physical	40	90	15	Normal
Bounce	Flying	Physical	85	85	5	Normal
Low Kick	Fighting	Physical	—	100	20	Normal
Thunder Punch	Electric	Physical	75	100	15	Normal
Fire Punch	Fire	Physical	75	100	15	Normal
Last Resort	Normal	Physical	140	100	5	Normal
Snore	Normal	Special	50	100	15	Normal
Heat Wave	Fire	Special	95	90	10	Many Others
Focus Punch	Fighting	Physical	150	100	20	Normal
Helping Hand	Normal	Status	—	—	20	1 Ally

MOVES TAUGHT BY PEOPLE

Name	Type	Kind	Pow.	Acc.	PP	Range
Fire Pledge	Fire	Special	80	100	10	Normal

National Pokédex **257** Hoenn Pokédex **006**

Blaziken

Blaze Pokémon

Fire Fighting

HEIGHT: 6'03" WEIGHT: 114.6 lbs.

The hackles and feather crests are longer on the male than on the female.

♂ ♀

Ω In battle, Blaziken blows out intense flames from its wrists and attacks foes courageously. The stronger the foe, the more intensely this Pokémon's wrists burn.

α Blaziken has incredibly strong legs—it can easily clear a 30-story building in one leap. This Pokémon's blazing punches leave its foes scorched and blackened.

ABILITY
Blaze

HIDDEN ABILITY
Speed Boost

EGG GROUPS
Field

STAT GROWTH RATES
HP
Attack
Defense
Sp. Atk
Sp. Def
Speed

ITEMS SOMETIMES HELD BY WILD POKÉMON
—

EVOLUTION

Torchic
Lv. 16
Combusken
Lv. 36
Blaziken

MAIN WAY TO REGISTER IN THE NATIONAL POKÉDEX

Level up Combusken to Lv. 36.

Damage taken in normal battles

Type		Type	
Normal	×1	Flying	×2
Fire	×0.5	Psychic	×2
Water	×2	Bug	×0.25
Grass	×0.5	Rock	×1
Electric	×1	Ghost	×1
Ice	×0.5	Dragon	×1
Fighting	×1	Dark	×0.5
Poison	×1	Steel	×0.5
Ground	×2	Fairy	×1

Damage taken in Inverse battles

Type		Type	
Normal	×1	Flying	×0.5
Fire	×2	Psychic	×0.5
Water	×0.5	Bug	×4
Grass	×2	Rock	×1
Electric	×1	Ghost	×1
Ice	×2	Dragon	×1
Fighting	×1	Dark	×2
Poison	×1	Steel	×2
Ground	×0.5	Fairy	×1

Can be used in
Inverse Battle
Battle Institute
Battle Maison
Random Matchup (Free Battle)
Random Matchup (Others)

LEVEL-UP MOVES

Lv.	Name	Type	Kind	Pow.	Acc.	PP	Range
1	Flare Blitz	Fire	Physical	120	100	15	Normal
1	Fire Punch	Fire	Physical	75	100	15	Normal
1	High Jump Kick	Fighting	Physical	130	90	10	Normal
1	Scratch	Normal	Physical	40	100	35	Normal
1	Growl	Normal	Status	—	100	40	Many Others
1	Ember	Fire	Special	40	100	25	Normal
1	Sand Attack	Ground	Status	—	100	15	Normal
5	Ember	Fire	Special	40	100	25	Normal
10	Sand Attack	Ground	Status	—	100	15	Normal
14	Peck	Flying	Physical	35	100	35	Normal
16	Double Kick	Fighting	Physical	30	100	30	Normal
20	Flame Charge	Fire	Physical	50	100	20	Normal
25	Quick Attack	Normal	Physical	40	100	30	Normal
31	Bulk Up	Fighting	Status	—	—	20	Self
36	Blaze Kick	Fire	Physical	85	90	10	Normal
37	Focus Energy	Normal	Status	—	—	30	Self
44	Slash	Normal	Physical	70	100	20	Normal
50	Brave Bird	Flying	Physical	120	100	15	Normal
57	Sky Uppercut	Fighting	Physical	85	90	15	Normal
63	Flare Blitz	Fire	Physical	120	100	15	Normal

TM & HM MOVES

No.	Name	Type	Kind	Pow.	Acc.	PP	Range
TM01	Hone Claws	Dark	Status	—	—	15	Self
TM05	Roar	Normal	Status	—	—	20	Normal
TM06	Toxic	Poison	Status	—	90	10	Normal
TM08	Bulk Up	Fighting	Status	—	—	20	Self
TM10	Hidden Power	Normal	Special	60	100	15	Normal
TM11	Sunny Day	Fire	Status	—	—	5	Both Sides
TM15	Hyper Beam	Normal	Special	150	90	5	Normal
TM17	Protect	Normal	Status	—	—	10	Self
TM21	Frustration	Normal	Physical	—	100	20	Normal
TM22	Solar Beam	Grass	Special	120	100	10	Normal
TM26	Earthquake	Ground	Physical	100	100	10	Adjacent
TM27	Return	Normal	Physical	—	100	20	Normal
TM28	Dig	Ground	Physical	80	100	10	Normal
TM31	Brick Break	Fighting	Physical	75	100	15	Normal
TM32	Double Team	Normal	Status	—	—	15	Self
TM35	Flamethrower	Fire	Special	90	100	15	Normal
TM38	Fire Blast	Fire	Special	110	85	5	Normal
TM39	Rock Tomb	Rock	Physical	60	95	15	Normal
TM40	Aerial Ace	Flying	Physical	60	—	20	Normal
TM42	Facade	Normal	Physical	70	100	20	Normal
TM43	Flame Charge	Fire	Physical	50	100	20	Normal
TM44	Rest	Psychic	Status	—	—	10	Self
TM45	Attract	Normal	Status	—	100	15	Normal
TM47	Low Sweep	Fighting	Physical	65	100	20	Normal
TM48	Round	Normal	Special	60	100	15	Normal
TM49	Echoed Voice	Normal	Special	40	100	15	Normal
TM50	Overheat	Fire	Special	130	90	5	Normal
TM52	Focus Blast	Fighting	Special	120	70	5	Normal
TM56	Fling	Dark	Physical	—	100	10	Normal
TM59	Incinerate	Fire	Special	60	100	15	Many Others
TM61	Will-O-Wisp	Fire	Status	—	85	15	Normal
TM62	Acrobatics	Flying	Physical	55	100	15	Normal
TM65	Shadow Claw	Ghost	Physical	70	100	15	Normal
TM68	Giga Impact	Normal	Physical	150	90	5	Normal
TM71	Stone Edge	Rock	Physical	100	80	5	Normal
TM75	Swords Dance	Normal	Status	—	—	20	Self
TM78	Bulldoze	Ground	Physical	60	100	20	Adjacent
TM80	Rock Slide	Rock	Physical	75	90	10	Many Others
TM84	Poison Jab	Poison	Physical	80	100	20	Normal
TM87	Swagger	Normal	Status	—	90	15	Normal
TM88	Sleep Talk	Normal	Status	—	—	10	Self
TM90	Substitute	Normal	Status	—	—	10	Self
TM94	Secret Power	Normal	Physical	70	100	20	Normal
TM98	Power-Up Punch	Fighting	Physical	40	100	20	Normal
TM100	Confide	Normal	Status	—	—	20	Normal
HM01	Cut	Normal	Physical	50	95	30	Normal
HM04	Strength	Normal	Physical	80	100	15	Normal
HM06	Rock Smash	Fighting	Physical	40	100	15	Normal

MOVES LEARNED IN EXCHANGE FOR BP

Name	Type	Kind	Pow.	Acc.	PP	Range
Dual Chop	Dragon	Physical	40	90	15	Normal
Bounce	Flying	Physical	85	85	5	Normal
Low Kick	Fighting	Physical	—	100	20	Normal
Thunder Punch	Electric	Physical	75	100	15	Normal
Fire Punch	Fire	Physical	75	100	15	Normal
Last Resort	Normal	Physical	140	100	5	Normal
Superpower	Fighting	Physical	120	100	5	Normal
Snore	Normal	Special	50	100	15	Normal
Knock Off	Dark	Physical	65	100	20	Normal
Heat Wave	Fire	Special	95	90	10	Many Others
Role Play	Psychic	Status	—	—	10	Normal
Focus Punch	Fighting	Physical	150	100	20	Normal
Helping Hand	Normal	Status	—	—	20	1 Ally

MOVES TAUGHT BY PEOPLE

Name	Type	Kind	Pow.	Acc.	PP	Range
Fire Pledge	Fire	Special	80	100	10	Normal
Blast Burn	Fire	Special	150	90	5	Normal

Mega Evolution

Mega Blaziken

Blaze Pokémon

Fire | Fighting

HEIGHT: 6'03" WEIGHT: 114.6 lbs.

Same form for ♂ / ♀

REQUIRED MEGA STONE

Blazikenite

Receive from Steven on Route 120 (if you chose Torchic at the beginning of the game) / Purchase from the stone seller on Route 114 by selecting the piece titled "Fading Fire"

ABILITY

Speed Boost

HIDDEN ABILITY

—

EGG GROUPS

—

STAT GROWTH RATES

HP
Attack
Defense
Sp. Atk
Sp. Def
Speed

Damage taken in normal battles

Type		Type	
Normal	×1	Flying	×2
Fire	×0.5	Psychic	×2
Water	×2	Bug	×0.25
Grass	×0.5	Rock	×1
Electric	×1	Ghost	×1
Ice	×0.5	Dragon	×1
Fighting	×1	Dark	×0.5
Poison	×1	Steel	×0.5
Ground	×2	Fairy	×1

Damage taken in Inverse battles

Type		Type	
Normal	×1	Flying	×0.5
Fire	×2	Psychic	×0.5
Water	×0.5	Bug	×4
Grass	×2	Rock	×1
Electric	×1	Ghost	×1
Ice	×2	Dragon	×1
Fighting	×1	Dark	×2
Poison	×1	Steel	×2
Ground	×0.5	Fairy	×1

Can be used in

Inverse Battle
Battle Institute
Battle Maison
Random Matchup (Free Battle)
Random Matchup (Others)

National Pokédex **258** Hoenn Pokédex **007**

Mudkip

Mud Fish Pokémon

Water | -

HEIGHT: 1'04" WEIGHT: 16.8 lbs.

Same form for ♂ / ♀

Ω The fin on Mudkip's head acts as highly sensitive radar. Using this fin to sense movements of water and air, this Pokémon can determine what is taking place around it without using its eyes.

α In water, Mudkip breathes using the gills on its cheeks. If it is faced with a tight situation in battle, this Pokémon will unleash its amazing power—it can crush rocks bigger than itself.

ABILITY

Torrent

HIDDEN ABILITY

Damp

EGG GROUPS

Monster | Water 1

STAT GROWTH RATES

HP
Attack
Defense
Sp. Atk
Sp. Def
Speed

ITEMS SOMETIMES HELD BY WILD POKÉMON

—

EVOLUTION

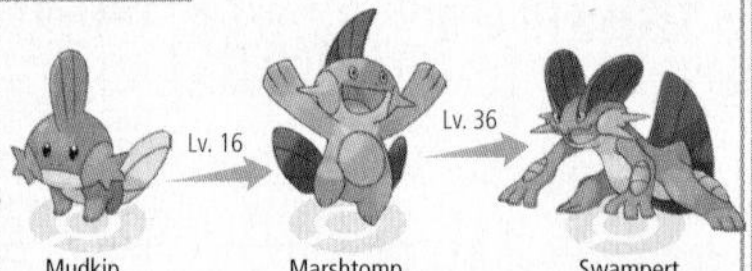

Mudkip → Lv. 16 → Marshtomp → Lv. 36 → Swampert

MAIN WAY TO REGISTER IN THE NATIONAL POKÉDEX

Receive from Professor Birch at his Pokémon Lab in Littleroot Town.

Damage taken in normal battles

Type		Type	
Normal	×1	Flying	×1
Fire	×0.5	Psychic	×1
Water	×0.5	Bug	×1
Grass	×2	Rock	×1
Electric	×2	Ghost	×1
Ice	×0.5	Dragon	×1
Fighting	×1	Dark	×1
Poison	×1	Steel	×0.5
Ground	×1	Fairy	×1

Damage taken in Inverse battles

Type		Type	
Normal	×1	Flying	×1
Fire	×2	Psychic	×1
Water	×2	Bug	×1
Grass	×0.5	Rock	×1
Electric	×0.5	Ghost	×1
Ice	×2	Dragon	×1
Fighting	×1	Dark	×1
Poison	×1	Steel	×2
Ground	×1	Fairy	×1

Can be used in

Inverse Battle
Battle Institute
Battle Maison
Random Matchup (Free Battle)
Random Matchup (Others)

LEVEL-UP MOVES

Lv.	Name	Type	Kind	Pow.	Acc.	PP	Range
1	Tackle	Normal	Physical	50	100	35	Normal
1	Growl	Normal	Status	—	100	40	Many Others
4	Water Gun	Water	Special	40	100	25	Normal
9	Mud-Slap	Ground	Special	20	100	10	Normal
12	Foresight	Normal	Status	—	—	40	Normal
17	Bide	Normal	Physical	—	—	10	Self
20	Mud Sport	Ground	Status	—	—	15	Both Sides
25	Rock Throw	Rock	Physical	50	90	15	Normal
28	Protect	Normal	Status	—	—	10	Self
33	Whirlpool	Water	Special	35	85	15	Normal
36	Take Down	Normal	Physical	90	85	20	Normal
41	Hydro Pump	Water	Special	110	80	5	Normal
44	Endeavor	Normal	Physical	—	100	5	Normal

TM & HM MOVES

No.	Name	Type	Kind	Pow.	Acc.	PP	Range
TM06	Toxic	Poison	Status	—	90	10	Normal
TM07	Hail	Ice	Status	—	—	10	Both Sides
TM10	Hidden Power	Normal	Special	60	100	15	Normal
TM13	Ice Beam	Ice	Special	90	100	10	Normal
TM14	Blizzard	Ice	Special	110	70	5	Many Others
TM17	Protect	Normal	Status	—	—	10	Self
TM18	Rain Dance	Water	Status	—	—	5	Both Sides
TM21	Frustration	Normal	Physical	—	100	20	Normal
TM27	Return	Normal	Physical	—	100	20	Normal
TM28	Dig	Ground	Physical	80	100	10	Normal
TM32	Double Team	Normal	Status	—	—	15	Self
TM34	Sludge Wave	Poison	Special	95	100	10	Adjacent
TM39	Rock Tomb	Rock	Physical	60	95	15	Normal
TM42	Facade	Normal	Physical	70	100	20	Normal
TM44	Rest	Psychic	Status	—	—	10	Self
TM45	Attract	Normal	Status	—	100	15	Normal
TM48	Round	Normal	Special	60	100	15	Normal
TM49	Echoed Voice	Normal	Special	40	100	15	Normal
TM55	Scald	Water	Special	80	100	15	Normal
TM80	Rock Slide	Rock	Physical	75	90	10	Many Others
TM87	Swagger	Normal	Status	—	90	15	Normal
TM88	Sleep Talk	Normal	Status	—	—	10	Self
TM90	Substitute	Normal	Status	—	—	10	Self
TM94	Secret Power	Normal	Physical	70	100	20	Normal
TM100	Confide	Normal	Status	—	—	20	Normal
HM03	Surf	Water	Special	90	100	15	Adjacent
HM04	Strength	Normal	Physical	80	100	15	Normal
HM05	Waterfall	Water	Physical	80	100	15	Normal
HM06	Rock Smash	Fighting	Physical	40	100	15	Normal
HM07	Dive	Water	Physical	80	100	10	Normal

MOVES LEARNED IN EXCHANGE FOR BP

Name	Type	Kind	Pow.	Acc.	PP	Range
Low Kick	Fighting	Physical	—	100	20	Normal
Uproar	Normal	Special	90	100	10	1 Random
Earth Power	Ground	Special	90	100	10	Normal
Superpower	Fighting	Physical	120	100	5	Normal
Icy Wind	Ice	Special	55	95	15	Many Others
Aqua Tail	Water	Physical	90	90	10	Normal
Iron Tail	Steel	Physical	100	75	15	Normal
Snore	Normal	Special	50	100	15	Normal
Water Pulse	Water	Special	60	100	20	Normal
Endeavor	Normal	Physical	—	100	5	Normal

MOVES TAUGHT BY PEOPLE

Name	Type	Kind	Pow.	Acc.	PP	Range
Water Pledge	Water	Special	80	100	10	Normal

EGG MOVES

Name	Type	Kind	Pow.	Acc.	PP	Range
Refresh	Normal	Status	—	—	20	Self
Uproar	Normal	Special	90	100	10	1 Random
Curse	Ghost	Status	—	—	10	Varies
Stomp	Normal	Physical	65	100	20	Normal
Ice Ball	Ice	Physical	30	90	20	Normal
Mirror Coat	Psychic	Special	—	100	20	Varies
Counter	Fighting	Physical	—	100	20	Varies
Ancient Power	Rock	Special	60	100	5	Normal
Whirlpool	Water	Special	35	85	15	Normal
Bite	Dark	Physical	60	100	25	Normal
Double-Edge	Normal	Physical	120	100	15	Normal
Mud Bomb	Ground	Special	65	85	10	Normal
Yawn	Normal	Status	—	—	10	Normal
Sludge	Poison	Special	65	100	20	Normal
Avalanche	Ice	Physical	60	100	10	Normal
Wide Guard	Rock	Status	—	—	10	Your Side
Barrier	Psychic	Status	—	—	20	Self

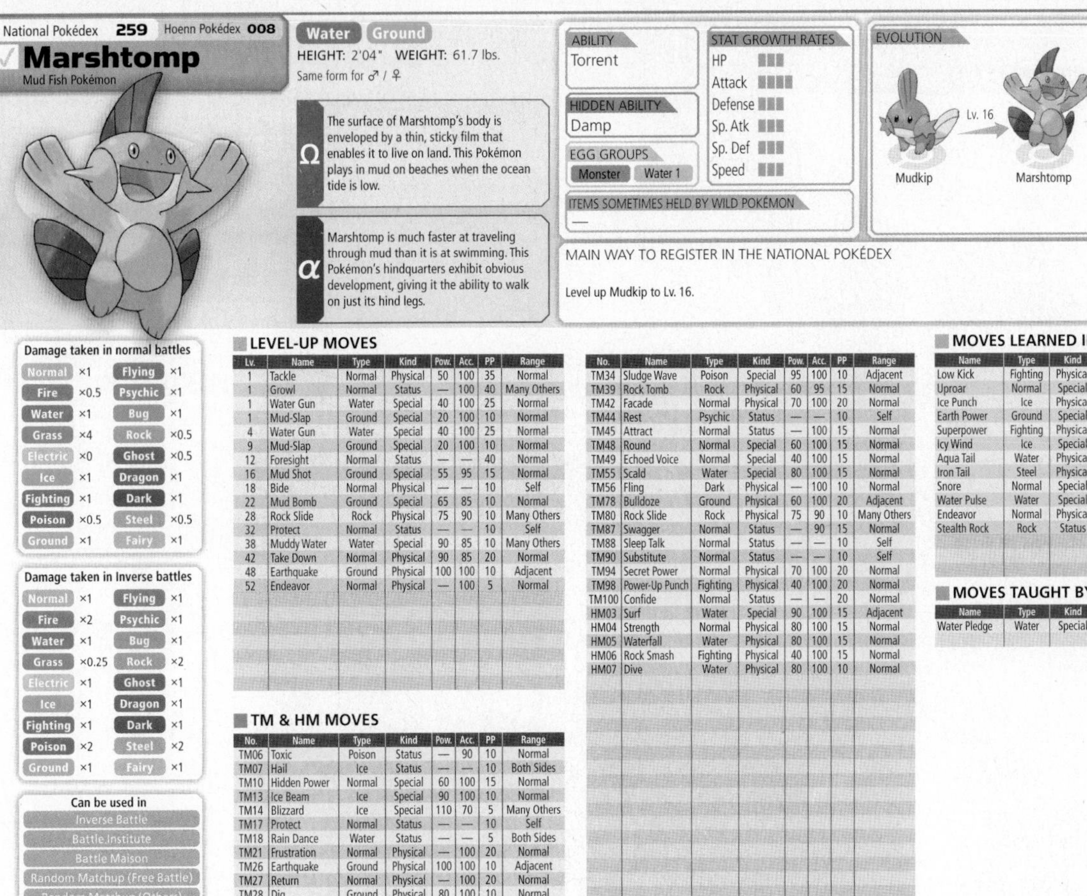

National Pokédex **259** Hoenn Pokédex **008**

Marshtomp

Mud Fish Pokémon

Water Ground

HEIGHT: 2'04" WEIGHT: 61.7 lbs.

Same form for ♂ / ♀

Ω The surface of Marshtomp's body is enveloped by a thin, sticky film that enables it to live on land. This Pokémon plays in mud on beaches when the ocean tide is low.

α Marshtomp is much faster at traveling through mud than it is at swimming. This Pokémon's hindquarters exhibit obvious development, giving it the ability to walk on just its hind legs.

ABILITY
Torrent

HIDDEN ABILITY
Damp

EGG GROUPS
Monster Water 1

STAT GROWTH RATES
HP
Attack
Defense
Sp. Atk
Sp. Def
Speed

ITEMS SOMETIMES HELD BY WILD POKÉMON
—

EVOLUTION

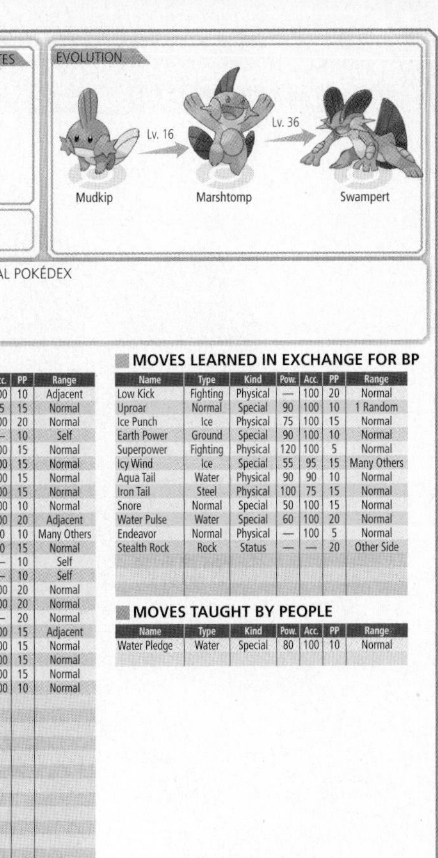

MAIN WAY TO REGISTER IN THE NATIONAL POKÉDEX

Level up Mudkip to Lv. 16.

Damage taken in normal battles

Normal	×1	Flying	×1
Fire	×0.5	Psychic	×1
Water	×1	Bug	×1
Grass	×4	Rock	×0.5
Electric	×0	Ghost	×0.5
Ice	×1	Dragon	×1
Fighting	×1	Dark	×1
Poison	×0.5	Steel	×0.5
Ground	×1	Fairy	×1

Damage taken in Inverse battles

Normal	×1	Flying	×1
Fire	×2	Psychic	×1
Water	×1	Bug	×1
Grass	×0.25	Rock	×2
Electric	×1	Ghost	×1
Ice	×1	Dragon	×1
Fighting	×1	Dark	×1
Poison	×2	Steel	×2
Ground	×1	Fairy	×1

Can be used in
Inverse Battle
Battle Institute
Battle Maison
Random Matchup (Free Battle)
Random Matchup (Others)

LEVEL-UP MOVES

Lv.	Name	Type	Kind	Pow.	Acc.	PP	Range
1	Tackle	Normal	Physical	50	100	35	Normal
1	Growl	Normal	Status	—	100	40	Many Others
1	Water Gun	Water	Special	40	100	25	Normal
1	Mud-Slap	Ground	Special	20	100	10	Normal
4	Water Gun	Water	Special	40	100	25	Normal
9	Mud-Slap	Ground	Special	20	100	10	Normal
12	Foresight	Normal	Status	—	—	40	Normal
16	Mud Shot	Ground	Special	55	95	15	Normal
18	Bide	Normal	Physical	—	—	10	Self
22	Mud Bomb	Ground	Special	65	85	10	Normal
28	Rock Slide	Rock	Physical	75	90	10	Many Others
32	Protect	Normal	Status	—	—	10	Self
38	Muddy Water	Water	Special	90	85	10	Many Others
42	Take Down	Normal	Physical	90	85	20	Normal
48	Earthquake	Ground	Physical	100	100	10	Adjacent
52	Endeavor	Normal	Physical	—	100	5	Normal

TM & HM MOVES

No.	Name	Type	Kind	Pow.	Acc.	PP	Range
TM06	Toxic	Poison	Status	—	90	10	Normal
TM07	Hail	Ice	Status	—	—	10	Both Sides
TM10	Hidden Power	Normal	Special	60	100	15	Normal
TM13	Ice Beam	Ice	Special	90	100	10	Normal
TM14	Blizzard	Ice	Special	110	70	5	Many Others
TM17	Protect	Normal	Status	—	—	10	Self
TM18	Rain Dance	Water	Status	—	—	5	Both Sides
TM21	Frustration	Normal	Physical	—	100	20	Normal
TM26	Earthquake	Ground	Physical	100	100	10	Adjacent
TM27	Return	Normal	Physical	—	100	20	Normal
TM28	Dig	Ground	Physical	80	100	10	Normal
TM31	Brick Break	Fighting	Physical	75	100	15	Normal
TM32	Double Team	Normal	Status	—	—	15	Self
TM34	Sludge Wave	Poison	Special	95	100	10	Adjacent
TM39	Rock Tomb	Rock	Physical	60	95	15	Normal
TM42	Facade	Normal	Physical	70	100	20	Normal
TM44	Rest	Psychic	Status	—	—	10	Self
TM45	Attract	Normal	Status	—	100	15	Normal
TM48	Round	Normal	Special	60	100	15	Normal
TM49	Echoed Voice	Normal	Special	40	100	15	Normal
TM55	Scald	Water	Special	80	100	15	Normal
TM56	Fling	Dark	Physical	—	100	10	Normal
TM78	Bulldoze	Ground	Physical	60	100	20	Adjacent
TM80	Rock Slide	Rock	Physical	75	90	10	Many Others
TM87	Swagger	Normal	Status	—	90	15	Normal
TM88	Sleep Talk	Normal	Status	—	—	10	Self
TM90	Substitute	Normal	Status	—	—	10	Self
TM94	Secret Power	Normal	Physical	70	100	20	Normal
TM98	Power-Up Punch	Fighting	Physical	40	100	20	Normal
TM100	Confide	Normal	Status	—	—	20	Normal
HM03	Surf	Water	Special	90	100	15	Adjacent
HM04	Strength	Normal	Physical	80	100	15	Normal
HM05	Waterfall	Water	Physical	80	100	15	Normal
HM06	Rock Smash	Fighting	Physical	40	100	15	Normal
HM07	Dive	Water	Physical	80	100	10	Normal

MOVES LEARNED IN EXCHANGE FOR BP

Name	Type	Kind	Pow.	Acc.	PP	Range
Low Kick	Fighting	Physical	—	100	20	Normal
Uproar	Normal	Special	90	100	10	1 Random
Ice Punch	Ice	Physical	75	100	15	Normal
Earth Power	Ground	Special	90	100	10	Normal
Superpower	Fighting	Physical	120	100	5	Normal
Icy Wind	Ice	Special	55	95	15	Many Others
Aqua Tail	Water	Physical	90	90	10	Normal
Iron Tail	Steel	Physical	100	75	15	Normal
Snore	Normal	Special	50	100	15	Normal
Water Pulse	Water	Special	60	100	20	Normal
Endeavor	Normal	Physical	—	100	5	Normal
Stealth Rock	Rock	Status	—	—	20	Other Side

MOVES TAUGHT BY PEOPLE

Name	Type	Kind	Pow.	Acc.	PP	Range
Water Pledge	Water	Special	80	100	10	Normal

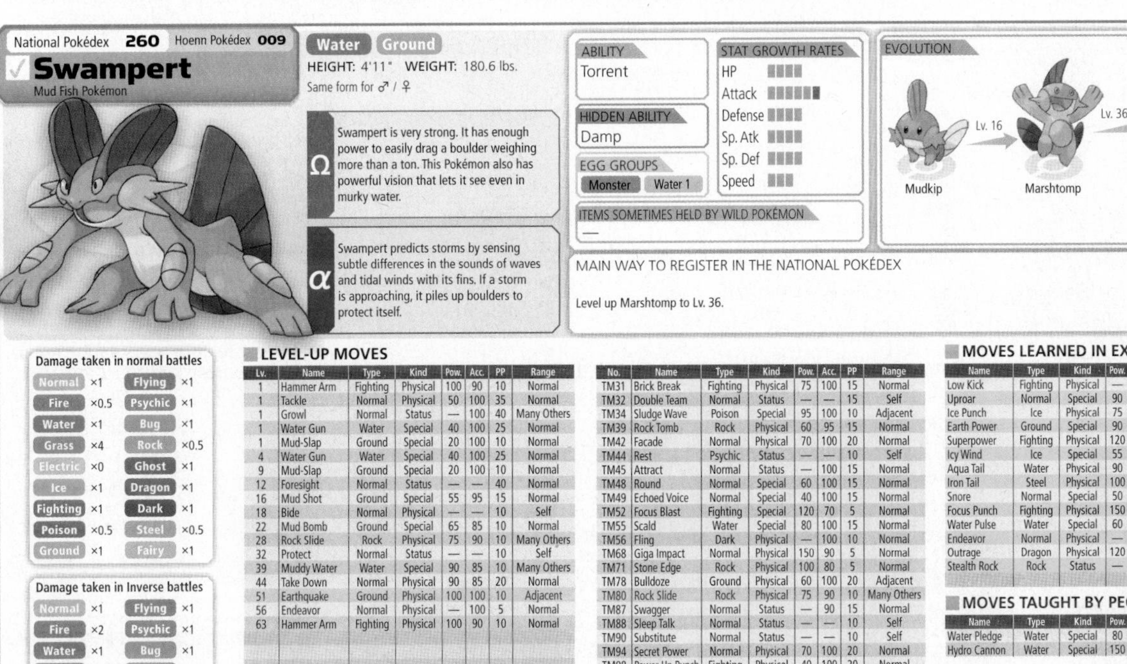

National Pokédex **260** Hoenn Pokédex **009**

Swampert

Mud Fish Pokémon

Water Ground

HEIGHT: 4'11" WEIGHT: 180.6 lbs.

Same form for ♂ / ♀

Ω Swampert is very strong. It has enough power to easily drag a boulder weighing more than a ton. This Pokémon also has powerful vision that lets it see even in murky water.

α Swampert predicts storms by sensing subtle differences in the sounds of waves and tidal winds with its fins. If a storm is approaching, it piles up boulders to protect itself.

ABILITY
Torrent

HIDDEN ABILITY
Damp

EGG GROUPS
Monster Water 1

STAT GROWTH RATES
HP
Attack
Defense
Sp. Atk
Sp. Def
Speed

ITEMS SOMETIMES HELD BY WILD POKÉMON
—

EVOLUTION

Mudkip → Lv. 16 → Marshtomp → Lv. 36 → Swampert

MAIN WAY TO REGISTER IN THE NATIONAL POKÉDEX

Level up Marshtomp to Lv. 36.

Damage taken in normal battles

Normal	×1	Flying	×1
Fire	×0.5	Psychic	×1
Water	×1	Bug	×1
Grass	×4	Rock	×0.5
Electric	×0	Ghost	×1
Ice	×1	Dragon	×1
Fighting	×1	Dark	×1
Poison	×0.5	Steel	×0.5
Ground	×1	Fairy	×1

Damage taken in Inverse battles

Normal	×1	Flying	×1
Fire	×2	Psychic	×1
Water	×1	Bug	×1
Grass	×0.25	Rock	×2
Electric	×1	Ghost	×1
Ice	×1	Dragon	×1
Fighting	×1	Dark	×1
Poison	×2	Steel	×2
Ground	×1	Fairy	×1

Can be used in
Inverse Battle
Battle Institute
Battle Maison
Random Matchup (Free Battle)
Random Matchup (Others)

LEVEL-UP MOVES

Lv.	Name	Type	Kind	Pow.	Acc.	PP	Range
1	Hammer Arm	Fighting	Physical	100	90	10	Normal
1	Tackle	Normal	Physical	50	100	35	Normal
1	Growl	Normal	Status	—	100	40	Many Others
1	Water Gun	Water	Special	40	100	25	Normal
1	Mud-Slap	Ground	Special	20	100	10	Normal
4	Water Gun	Water	Special	40	100	25	Normal
9	Mud-Slap	Ground	Special	20	100	10	Normal
12	Foresight	Normal	Status	—	—	40	Normal
16	Mud Shot	Ground	Special	55	95	15	Normal
18	Bide	Normal	Physical	—	—	10	Self
22	Mud Bomb	Ground	Special	65	85	10	Normal
28	Rock Slide	Rock	Physical	75	90	10	Many Others
32	Protect	Normal	Status	—	—	10	Self
39	Muddy Water	Water	Special	90	85	10	Many Others
44	Take Down	Normal	Physical	90	85	20	Normal
51	Earthquake	Ground	Physical	100	100	10	Adjacent
56	Endeavor	Normal	Physical	—	100	5	Normal
63	Hammer Arm	Fighting	Physical	100	90	10	Normal

TM & HM MOVES

No.	Name	Type	Kind	Pow.	Acc.	PP	Range
TM05	Roar	Normal	Status	—	—	20	Normal
TM06	Toxic	Poison	Status	—	90	10	Normal
TM07	Hail	Ice	Status	—	—	10	Both Sides
TM10	Hidden Power	Normal	Special	60	100	15	Normal
TM13	Ice Beam	Ice	Special	90	100	10	Normal
TM14	Blizzard	Ice	Special	110	70	5	Many Others
TM15	Hyper Beam	Normal	Special	150	90	5	Normal
TM17	Protect	Normal	Status	—	—	10	Self
TM18	Rain Dance	Water	Status	—	—	5	Both Sides
TM21	Frustration	Normal	Physical	—	100	20	Normal
TM26	Earthquake	Ground	Physical	100	100	10	Adjacent
TM27	Return	Normal	Physical	—	100	20	Normal
TM28	Dig	Ground	Physical	80	100	10	Normal
TM31	Brick Break	Fighting	Physical	75	100	15	Normal
TM32	Double Team	Normal	Status	—	—	15	Self
TM34	Sludge Wave	Poison	Special	95	100	10	Adjacent
TM39	Rock Tomb	Rock	Physical	60	95	15	Normal
TM42	Facade	Normal	Physical	70	100	20	Normal
TM44	Rest	Psychic	Status	—	—	10	Self
TM45	Attract	Normal	Status	—	100	15	Normal
TM48	Round	Normal	Special	60	100	15	Normal
TM49	Echoed Voice	Normal	Special	40	100	15	Normal
TM52	Focus Blast	Fighting	Special	120	70	5	Normal
TM55	Scald	Water	Special	80	100	15	Normal
TM56	Fling	Dark	Physical	—	100	10	Normal
TM68	Giga Impact	Normal	Physical	150	90	5	Normal
TM71	Stone Edge	Rock	Physical	100	80	5	Normal
TM78	Bulldoze	Ground	Physical	60	100	20	Adjacent
TM80	Rock Slide	Rock	Physical	75	90	10	Many Others
TM87	Swagger	Normal	Status	—	90	15	Normal
TM88	Sleep Talk	Normal	Status	—	—	10	Self
TM90	Substitute	Normal	Status	—	—	10	Self
TM94	Secret Power	Normal	Physical	70	100	20	Normal
TM98	Power-Up Punch	Fighting	Physical	40	100	20	Normal
TM100	Confide	Normal	Status	—	—	20	Normal
HM03	Surf	Water	Special	90	100	15	Adjacent
HM04	Strength	Normal	Physical	80	100	15	Normal
HM05	Waterfall	Water	Physical	80	100	15	Normal
HM06	Rock Smash	Fighting	Physical	40	100	15	Normal
HM07	Dive	Water	Physical	80	100	10	Normal

MOVES LEARNED IN EXCHANGE FOR BP

Name	Type	Kind	Pow.	Acc.	PP	Range
Low Kick	Fighting	Physical	—	100	20	Normal
Uproar	Normal	Special	90	100	10	1 Random
Ice Punch	Ice	Physical	75	100	15	Normal
Earth Power	Ground	Special	90	100	10	Normal
Superpower	Fighting	Physical	120	100	5	Normal
Icy Wind	Ice	Special	55	95	15	Many Others
Aqua Tail	Water	Physical	90	90	10	Normal
Iron Tail	Steel	Physical	100	75	15	Normal
Snore	Normal	Special	50	100	15	Normal
Focus Punch	Fighting	Physical	150	100	20	Normal
Water Pulse	Water	Special	60	100	20	Normal
Endeavor	Normal	Physical	—	100	5	Normal
Outrage	Dragon	Physical	120	100	10	1 Random
Stealth Rock	Rock	Status	—	—	20	Other Side

MOVES TAUGHT BY PEOPLE

Name	Type	Kind	Pow.	Acc.	PP	Range
Water Pledge	Water	Special	80	100	10	Normal
Hydro Cannon	Water	Special	150	90	5	Normal

Mega Evolution

Mega Swampert

Mud Fish Pokémon

Water Ground

HEIGHT: 6'03" WEIGHT: 224.9 lbs.

Same form for ♂ / ♀

REQUIRED MEGA STONE

Swampertite

Receive from Steven on Route 120 (if you chose Mudkip at the beginning of the game) / Purchase from the stone seller on Route 114 by selecting the piece titled "Ebb Tide"

ABILITY

Swift Swim

HIDDEN ABILITY

—

EGG GROUPS

—

STAT GROWTH RATES

HP

Attack

Defense

Sp. Atk

Sp. Def

Speed

Damage taken in normal battles

Type		Type	
Normal	×1	Flying	×1
Fire	×0.5	Psychic	×1
Water	×1	Bug	×1
Grass	×4	Rock	×0.5
Electric	×0	Ghost	×1
Ice	×1	Dragon	×1
Fighting	×1	Dark	×1
Poison	×0.5	Steel	×0.5
Ground	×1	Fairy	×1

Damage taken in Inverse battles

Type		Type	
Normal	×1	Flying	×1
Fire	×2	Psychic	×1
Water	×1	Bug	×1
Grass	×0.25	Rock	×2
Electric	×1	Ghost	×1
Ice	×1	Dragon	×1
Fighting	×1	Dark	×1
Poison	×2	Steel	×2
Ground	×1	Fairy	×1

Can be used in

Inverse Battle

Battle Institute

Battle Maison

Random Matchup (Free Battle)

Random Matchup (Others)

National Pokédex **261** Hoenn Pokédex **010**

Poochyena

Bite Pokémon

Dark

HEIGHT: 1'08" WEIGHT: 30 lbs.

Same form for ♂ / ♀

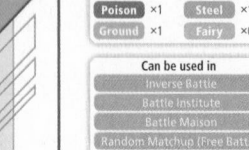

Ω At first sight, Poochyena takes a bite at anything that moves. This Pokémon chases after prey until the victim becomes exhausted. However, it may turn tail if the prey strikes back.

α Poochyena is an omnivore—it will eat anything. A distinguishing feature is how large its fangs are compared to its body. This Pokémon tries to intimidate its foes by making the hair on its tail bristle out.

ABILITIES

Run Away

Quick Feet

HIDDEN ABILITY

Rattled

EGG GROUPS

Field

STAT GROWTH RATES

HP

Attack

Defense

Sp. Atk

Sp. Def

Speed

EVOLUTION

Poochyena → Lv. 18 → Mightyena

ITEMS SOMETIMES HELD BY WILD POKÉMON

—

MAIN WAY TO REGISTER IN THE NATIONAL POKÉDEX

Catch on Route 101.

Damage taken in normal battles

Type		Type	
Normal	×1	Flying	×1
Fire	×1	Psychic	×0
Water	×1	Bug	×2
Grass	×1	Rock	×1
Electric	×1	Ghost	×0.5
Ice	×1	Dragon	×1
Fighting	×2	Dark	×0.5
Poison	×1	Steel	×1
Ground	×1	Fairy	×2

Damage taken in Inverse battles

Type		Type	
Normal	×1	Flying	×1
Fire	×1	Psychic	×2
Water	×1	Bug	×0.5
Grass	×1	Rock	×1
Electric	×1	Ghost	×2
Ice	×1	Dragon	×1
Fighting	×0.5	Dark	×2
Poison	×1	Steel	×1
Ground	×1	Fairy	×0.5

Can be used in

Inverse Battle

Battle Institute

Battle Maison

Random Matchup (Free Battle)

Random Matchup (Others)

LEVEL-UP MOVES

Lv.	Name	Type	Kind	Pow.	Acc.	PP	Range
1	Tackle	Normal	Physical	50	100	35	Normal
4	Howl	Normal	Status	—	—	40	Self
7	Sand Attack	Ground	Status	—	100	15	Normal
10	Bite	Dark	Physical	60	100	25	Normal
13	Odor Sleuth	Normal	Status	—	—	40	Normal
16	Roar	Normal	Status	—	—	20	Normal
19	Swagger	Normal	Status	—	90	15	Normal
22	Assurance	Dark	Physical	60	100	10	Normal
25	Scary Face	Normal	Status	—	100	10	Normal
28	Embargo	Dark	Status	—	100	15	Normal
31	Taunt	Dark	Status	—	100	20	Normal
34	Take Down	Normal	Physical	90	85	20	Normal
37	Crunch	Dark	Physical	80	100	15	Normal
40	Sucker Punch	Dark	Physical	80	100	5	Normal

TM & HM MOVES

No.	Name	Type	Kind	Pow.	Acc.	PP	Range
TM05	Roar	Normal	Status	—	—	20	Normal
TM06	Toxic	Poison	Status	—	90	10	Normal
TM10	Hidden Power	Normal	Special	60	100	15	Normal
TM11	Sunny Day	Fire	Status	—	—	5	Both Sides
TM12	Taunt	Dark	Status	—	100	20	Normal
TM17	Protect	Normal	Status	—	—	10	Self
TM18	Rain Dance	Water	Status	—	—	5	Both Sides
TM21	Frustration	Normal	Physical	—	100	20	Normal
TM27	Return	Normal	Physical	—	100	20	Normal
TM28	Dig	Ground	Physical	80	100	10	Normal
TM30	Shadow Ball	Ghost	Special	80	100	15	Normal
TM32	Double Team	Normal	Status	—	—	15	Self
TM41	Torment	Dark	Status	—	100	15	Normal
TM42	Facade	Normal	Physical	70	100	20	Normal
TM44	Rest	Psychic	Status	—	—	10	Self
TM45	Attract	Normal	Status	—	100	15	Normal
TM46	Thief	Dark	Physical	60	100	25	Normal
TM48	Round	Normal	Special	60	100	15	Normal
TM59	Incinerate	Fire	Special	60	100	15	Many Others
TM63	Embargo	Dark	Status	—	100	15	Normal
TM66	Payback	Dark	Physical	50	100	10	Normal
TM67	Retaliate	Normal	Physical	70	100	5	Normal
TM87	Swagger	Normal	Status	—	90	15	Normal
TM88	Sleep Talk	Normal	Status	—	—	10	Self
TM90	Substitute	Normal	Status	—	—	10	Self
TM94	Secret Power	Normal	Physical	70	100	20	Normal
TM95	Snarl	Dark	Special	55	95	15	Many Others
TM97	Dark Pulse	Dark	Special	80	100	15	Normal
TM100	Confide	Normal	Status	—	—	20	Normal
HM06	Rock Smash	Fighting	Physical	40	100	15	Normal

MOVES LEARNED IN EXCHANGE FOR BP

Name	Type	Kind	Pow.	Acc.	PP	Range
Covet	Normal	Physical	60	100	25	Normal
Super Fang	Normal	Physical	—	90	10	Normal
Uproar	Normal	Special	90	100	10	1 Random
Foul Play	Dark	Physical	95	100	15	Normal
Hyper Voice	Normal	Special	90	100	10	Many Others
Iron Tail	Steel	Physical	100	75	15	Normal
Snore	Normal	Special	50	100	15	Normal
Spite	Ghost	Status	—	100	10	Normal
Snatch	Dark	Status	—	—	10	Self

MOVES TAUGHT BY PEOPLE

Name	Type	Kind	Pow.	Acc.	PP	Range

EGG MOVES

Name	Type	Kind	Pow.	Acc.	PP	Range
Astonish	Ghost	Physical	30	100	15	Normal
Poison Fang	Poison	Physical	50	100	15	Normal
Covet	Normal	Physical	60	100	25	Normal
Leer	Normal	Status	—	100	30	Many Others
Yawn	Normal	Status	—	—	10	Normal
Sucker Punch	Dark	Physical	80	100	5	Normal
Ice Fang	Ice	Physical	65	95	15	Normal
Fire Fang	Fire	Physical	65	95	15	Normal
Thunder Fang	Electric	Physical	65	95	15	Normal
Me First	Normal	Status	—	—	20	Varies
Snatch	Dark	Status	—	—	10	Self
Sleep Talk	Normal	Status	—	—	10	Self
Play Rough	Fairy	Physical	90	90	10	Normal

National Pokédex **262** Hoenn Pokédex **011**

Mightyena

Bite Pokémon

Dark

HEIGHT: 3'03" WEIGHT: 81.6 lbs.

Same form for ♂ / ♀

Ω Mightyena gives obvious signals when it is preparing to attack. It starts to growl deeply and then flattens its body. This Pokémon will bite savagely with its sharply pointed fangs.

α Mightyena travel and act as a pack in the wild. The memory of its life in the wild compels the Pokémon to obey only those Trainers that it recognizes to possess superior skill.

ABILITIES
Intimidate
Quick Feet

HIDDEN ABILITY
Moxie

EGG GROUPS
Field

STAT GROWTH RATES
HP
Attack
Defense
Sp. Atk
Sp. Def
Speed

EVOLUTION

ITEMS SOMETIMES HELD BY WILD POKÉMON
—

MAIN WAY TO REGISTER IN THE NATIONAL POKÉDEX

Level up Poochyena to Lv. 18.

Damage taken in normal battles

Type		Type	
Normal	×1	Flying	×1
Fire	×1	Psychic	×0
Water	×1	Bug	×2
Grass	×1	Rock	×1
Electric	×1	Ghost	×0.5
Ice	×1	Dragon	×1
Fighting	×2	Dark	×0.5
Poison	×1	Steel	×1
Ground	×1	Fairy	×2

Damage taken in Inverse battles

Type		Type	
Normal	×1	Flying	×1
Fire	×1	Psychic	×2
Water	×1	Bug	×0.5
Grass	×1	Rock	×1
Electric	×1	Ghost	×2
Ice	×1	Dragon	×1
Fighting	×0.5	Dark	×2
Poison	×1	Steel	×1
Ground	×1	Fairy	×0.5

Can be used in
Inverse Battle
Battle Institute
Battle Maison
Random Matchup (Free Battle)
Random Matchup (Others)

LEVEL-UP MOVES

Lv.	Name	Type	Kind	Pow.	Acc.	PP	Range
1	Crunch	Dark	Physical	80	100	15	Normal
1	Thief	Dark	Physical	60	100	25	Normal
1	Tackle	Normal	Physical	50	100	35	Normal
1	Howl	Normal	Status	—	—	40	Self
1	Sand Attack	Ground	Status	—	100	15	Normal
1	Bite	Dark	Physical	60	100	25	Normal
4	Howl	Normal	Status	—	—	40	Self
7	Sand Attack	Ground	Status	—	100	15	Normal
10	Bite	Dark	Physical	60	100	25	Normal
13	Odor Sleuth	Normal	Status	—	—	40	Normal
16	Roar	Normal	Status	—	—	20	Normal
18	Snarl	Dark	Special	55	95	15	Many Others
20	Swagger	Normal	Status	—	90	15	Normal
24	Assurance	Dark	Physical	60	100	10	Normal
28	Scary Face	Normal	Status	—	100	10	Normal
32	Embargo	Dark	Status	—	100	15	Normal
36	Taunt	Dark	Status	—	100	20	Normal
40	Take Down	Normal	Physical	90	85	20	Normal
44	Crunch	Dark	Physical	80	100	15	Normal
48	Sucker Punch	Dark	Physical	80	100	5	Normal

TM & HM MOVES

No.	Name	Type	Kind	Pow.	Acc.	PP	Range
TM05	Roar	Normal	Status	—	—	20	Normal
TM06	Toxic	Poison	Status	—	90	10	Normal
TM10	Hidden Power	Normal	Special	60	100	15	Normal
TM11	Sunny Day	Fire	Status	—	—	5	Both Sides
TM12	Taunt	Dark	Status	—	100	20	Normal
TM15	Hyper Beam	Normal	Special	150	90	5	Normal
TM17	Protect	Normal	Status	—	—	10	Self
TM18	Rain Dance	Water	Status	—	—	5	Both Sides
TM21	Frustration	Normal	Physical	—	100	20	Normal
TM27	Return	Normal	Physical	—	100	20	Normal
TM28	Dig	Ground	Physical	80	100	10	Normal
TM30	Shadow Ball	Ghost	Special	80	100	15	Normal
TM32	Double Team	Normal	Status	—	—	15	Self
TM41	Torment	Dark	Status	—	100	15	Normal
TM42	Facade	Normal	Physical	70	100	20	Normal
TM44	Rest	Psychic	Status	—	—	10	Self
TM45	Attract	Normal	Status	—	100	15	Normal
TM46	Thief	Dark	Physical	60	100	25	Normal
TM48	Round	Normal	Special	60	100	15	Normal
TM59	Incinerate	Fire	Special	60	100	15	Many Others
TM63	Embargo	Dark	Status	—	100	15	Normal
TM66	Payback	Dark	Physical	50	100	10	Normal
TM67	Retaliate	Normal	Physical	70	100	5	Normal
TM68	Giga Impact	Normal	Physical	150	90	5	Normal
TM87	Swagger	Normal	Status	—	90	15	Normal
TM88	Sleep Talk	Normal	Status	—	—	10	Self
TM90	Substitute	Normal	Status	—	—	10	Self
TM94	Secret Power	Normal	Physical	70	100	20	Normal
TM95	Snarl	Dark	Special	55	95	15	Many Others
TM97	Dark Pulse	Dark	Special	80	100	15	Normal
TM100	Confide	Normal	Status	—	—	20	Normal
HM04	Strength	Normal	Physical	80	100	15	Normal
HM06	Rock Smash	Fighting	Physical	40	100	15	Normal

MOVES LEARNED IN EXCHANGE FOR BP

Name	Type	Kind	Pow.	Acc.	PP	Range
Covet	Normal	Physical	60	100	25	Normal
Super Fang	Normal	Physical	—	90	10	Normal
Uproar	Normal	Special	90	100	10	1 Random
Foul Play	Dark	Physical	95	100	15	Normal
Hyper Voice	Normal	Special	90	100	10	Many Others
Iron Tail	Steel	Physical	100	75	15	Normal
Snore	Normal	Special	50	100	15	Normal
Spite	Ghost	Status	—	100	10	Normal
Snatch	Dark	Status	—	—	10	Self

MOVES TAUGHT BY PEOPLE

Name	Type	Kind	Pow.	Acc.	PP	Range

National Pokédex **263** Hoenn Pokédex **012**

Zigzagoon

Tiny Raccoon Pokémon

Normal

HEIGHT: 1'04" WEIGHT: 38.6 lbs.

Same form for ♂ / ♀

Ω Zigzagoon restlessly wanders everywhere at all times. This Pokémon does so because it is very curious. It becomes interested in anything that it happens to see.

α The hair on Zigzagoon's back is bristly. It rubs the hard back hair against trees to leave its territorial markings. This Pokémon may play dead to fool foes in battle.

ABILITIES
Pickup
Gluttony

HIDDEN ABILITY
Quick Feet

EGG GROUPS
Field

STAT GROWTH RATES
HP
Attack
Defense
Sp. Atk
Sp. Def
Speed

EVOLUTION

Zigzagoon → Lv. 20 → Linoone

ITEMS SOMETIMES HELD BY WILD POKÉMON
Potion/Revive

MAIN WAY TO REGISTER IN THE NATIONAL POKÉDEX

Catch on Route 101.

Damage taken in normal battles

Type		Type	
Normal	×1	Flying	×1
Fire	×1	Psychic	×1
Water	×1	Bug	×1
Grass	×1	Rock	×1
Electric	×1	Ghost	×0
Ice	×1	Dragon	×1
Fighting	×2	Dark	×1
Poison	×1	Steel	×1
Ground	×1	Fairy	×1

Damage taken in Inverse battles

Type		Type	
Normal	×1	Flying	×1
Fire	×1	Psychic	×1
Water	×1	Bug	×1
Grass	×1	Rock	×1
Electric	×1	Ghost	×2
Ice	×1	Dragon	×1
Fighting	×0.5	Dark	×1
Poison	×1	Steel	×1
Ground	×1	Fairy	×1

Can be used in
Inverse Battle
Battle Institute
Battle Maison
Random Matchup (Free Battle)
Random Matchup (Others)

LEVEL-UP MOVES

Lv.	Name	Type	Kind	Pow.	Acc.	PP	Range
1	Tackle	Normal	Physical	50	100	35	Normal
1	Growl	Normal	Status	—	100	40	Many Others
5	Tail Whip	Normal	Status	—	100	30	Many Others
7	Sand Attack	Ground	Status	—	100	15	Normal
11	Headbutt	Normal	Physical	70	100	15	Normal
12	Baby-Doll Eyes	Fairy	Status	—	100	30	Normal
13	Odor Sleuth	Normal	Status	—	—	40	Normal
17	Mud Sport	Ground	Status	—	—	15	Both Sides
19	Pin Missile	Bug	Physical	25	95	20	Normal
23	Covet	Normal	Physical	60	100	25	Normal
25	Bestow	Normal	Status	—	—	15	Normal
29	Flail	Normal	Physical	—	100	15	Normal
31	Take Down	Normal	Physical	90	85	20	Normal
35	Rest	Psychic	Status	—	—	10	Self
37	Belly Drum	Normal	Status	—	—	10	Self
41	Fling	Dark	Physical	—	100	10	Normal

TM & HM MOVES

No.	Name	Type	Kind	Pow.	Acc.	PP	Range
TM01	Hone Claws	Dark	Status	—	—	15	Self
TM06	Toxic	Poison	Status	—	90	10	Normal
TM10	Hidden Power	Normal	Special	60	100	15	Normal
TM11	Sunny Day	Fire	Status	—	—	5	Both Sides
TM13	Ice Beam	Ice	Special	90	100	10	Normal
TM14	Blizzard	Ice	Special	110	70	5	Many Others
TM17	Protect	Normal	Status	—	—	10	Self
TM18	Rain Dance	Water	Status	—	—	5	Both Sides
TM21	Frustration	Normal	Physical	—	100	20	Normal
TM24	Thunderbolt	Electric	Special	90	100	15	Normal
TM25	Thunder	Electric	Special	110	70	10	Normal
TM27	Return	Normal	Physical	—	100	20	Normal
TM28	Dig	Ground	Physical	80	100	10	Normal
TM30	Shadow Ball	Ghost	Special	80	100	15	Normal
TM32	Double Team	Normal	Status	—	—	15	Self
TM42	Facade	Normal	Physical	70	100	20	Normal
TM44	Rest	Psychic	Status	—	—	10	Self
TM45	Attract	Normal	Status	—	100	15	Normal
TM46	Thief	Dark	Physical	60	100	25	Normal
TM48	Round	Normal	Special	60	100	15	Normal
TM49	Echoed Voice	Normal	Special	40	100	15	Normal
TM56	Fling	Dark	Physical	—	100	10	Normal
TM57	Charge Beam	Electric	Special	50	90	10	Normal
TM67	Retaliate	Normal	Physical	70	100	5	Normal
TM73	Thunder Wave	Electric	Status	—	100	20	Normal
TM86	Grass Knot	Grass	Special	—	100	20	Normal
TM87	Swagger	Normal	Status	—	90	15	Normal
TM88	Sleep Talk	Normal	Status	—	—	10	Self
TM90	Substitute	Normal	Status	—	—	10	Self
TM94	Secret Power	Normal	Physical	70	100	20	Normal
TM100	Confide	Normal	Status	—	—	20	Normal
HM01	Cut	Normal	Physical	50	95	30	Normal
HM03	Surf	Water	Special	90	100	15	Adjacent
HM06	Rock Smash	Fighting	Physical	40	100	15	Normal

MOVES LEARNED IN EXCHANGE FOR BP

Name	Type	Kind	Pow.	Acc.	PP	Range
Covet	Normal	Physical	60	100	25	Normal
Super Fang	Normal	Physical	—	90	10	Normal
Seed Bomb	Grass	Physical	80	100	15	Normal
Gunk Shot	Poison	Physical	120	80	5	Normal
Last Resort	Normal	Physical	140	100	5	Normal
Icy Wind	Ice	Special	55	95	15	Many Others
Hyper Voice	Normal	Special	90	100	10	Many Others
Iron Tail	Steel	Physical	100	75	15	Normal
Snore	Normal	Special	50	100	15	Normal
Shock Wave	Electric	Special	60	—	20	Normal
Water Pulse	Water	Special	60	100	20	Normal
Helping Hand	Normal	Status	—	—	20	1 Ally
Trick	Psychic	Status	—	100	10	Normal

MOVES TAUGHT BY PEOPLE

Name	Type	Kind	Pow.	Acc.	PP	Range

EGG MOVES

Name	Type	Kind	Pow.	Acc.	PP	Range
Charm	Fairy	Status	—	100	20	Normal
Pursuit	Dark	Physical	40	100	20	Normal
Tickle	Normal	Status	—	100	20	Normal
Trick	Psychic	Status	—	100	10	Normal
Helping Hand	Normal	Status	—	—	20	1 Ally
Mud-Slap	Ground	Special	20	100	10	Normal
Sleep Talk	Normal	Status	—	—	10	Self
Rock Climb	Normal	Physical	90	85	20	Normal
Simple Beam	Normal	Status	—	100	15	Normal

National Pokédex **264** Hoenn Pokédex **013**

Linoone

Rushing Pokémon

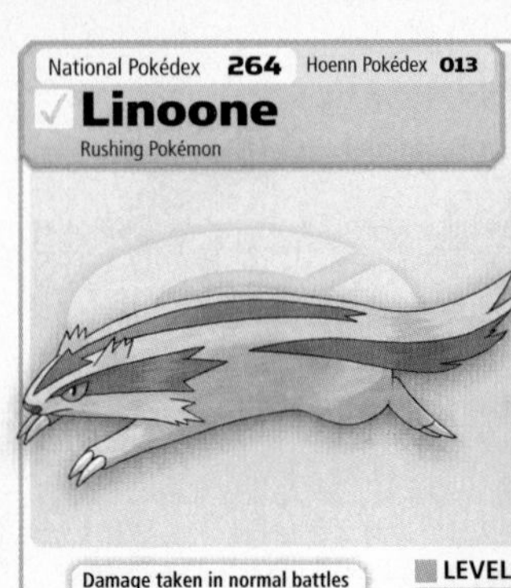

Normal

HEIGHT: 1'08" WEIGHT: 71.6 lbs.

Same form for ♂ / ♀

Ω Linoone always runs full speed and only in straight lines. If facing an obstacle, it makes a right-angle turn to evade it. This Pokémon is very challenged by gently curving roads.

α When hunting, Linoone will make a beeline straight for the prey at a full run. While this Pokémon is capable of topping 60 mph, it has to come to a screeching halt before it can turn.

ABILITIES
Pickup
Gluttony

HIDDEN ABILITY
Quick Feet

EGG GROUPS
Field

STAT GROWTH RATES
HP
Attack
Defense
Sp. Atk
Sp. Def
Speed

ITEMS SOMETIMES HELD BY WILD POKÉMON
Potion / Max Revive

EVOLUTION
Zigzagoon → Lv. 20 → Linoone

MAIN WAY TO REGISTER IN THE NATIONAL POKÉDEX

Catch in the very tall grass on Route 118.

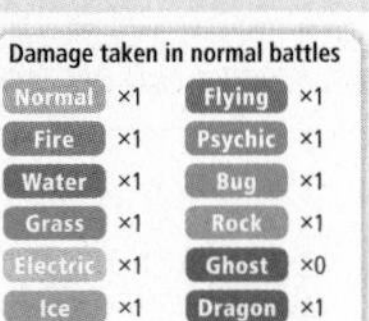

Damage taken in normal battles

Type		Type	
Normal	×1	Flying	×1
Fire	×1	Psychic	×1
Water	×1	Bug	×1
Grass	×1	Rock	×1
Electric	×1	Ghost	×0
Ice	×1	Dragon	×1
Fighting	×2	Dark	×1
Poison	×1	Steel	×1
Ground	×1	Fairy	×1

Damage taken in Inverse battles

Type		Type	
Normal	×1	Flying	×1
Fire	×1	Psychic	×1
Water	×1	Bug	×1
Grass	×1	Rock	×1
Electric	×1	Ghost	×2
Ice	×1	Dragon	×1
Fighting	×0.5	Dark	×1
Poison	×1	Steel	×1
Ground	×1	Fairy	×1

Can be used in
Inverse Battle
Battle Institute
Battle Maison
Random Matchup (Free Battle)
Random Matchup (Others)

LEVEL-UP MOVES

Lv.	Name	Type	Kind	Pow.	Acc.	PP	Range
1	Play Rough	Fairy	Physical	90	90	10	Normal
1	Rototiller	Ground	Status	—	—	10	Adjacent
1	Switcheroo	Dark	Status	—	100	10	Normal
1	Tackle	Normal	Physical	50	100	35	Normal
1	Growl	Normal	Status	—	100	40	Many Others
1	Tail Whip	Normal	Status	—	100	30	Many Others
1	Sand Attack	Ground	Status	—	100	15	Normal
5	Tail Whip	Normal	Status	—	100	30	Many Others
7	Sand Attack	Ground	Status	—	100	15	Normal
11	Headbutt	Normal	Physical	70	100	15	Normal
13	Odor Sleuth	Normal	Status	—	—	40	Normal
17	Mud Sport	Ground	Status	—	—	15	Both Sides
19	Fury Swipes	Normal	Physical	18	80	15	Normal
24	Covet	Normal	Physical	60	100	25	Normal
27	Bestow	Normal	Status	—	—	15	Normal
32	Slash	Normal	Physical	70	100	20	Normal
35	Double-Edge	Normal	Physical	120	100	15	Normal
40	Rest	Psychic	Status	—	—	10	Self
43	Belly Drum	Normal	Status	—	—	10	Self
48	Fling	Dark	Physical	—	100	10	Normal

TM & HM MOVES

No.	Name	Type	Kind	Pow.	Acc.	PP	Range
TM01	Hone Claws	Dark	Status	—	—	15	Self
TM05	Roar	Normal	Status	—	—	20	Normal
TM06	Toxic	Poison	Status	—	90	10	Normal
TM10	Hidden Power	Normal	Special	60	100	15	Normal
TM11	Sunny Day	Fire	Status	—	—	5	Both Sides
TM13	Ice Beam	Ice	Special	90	100	10	Normal
TM14	Blizzard	Ice	Special	110	70	5	Many Others
TM15	Hyper Beam	Normal	Special	150	90	5	Normal
TM17	Protect	Normal	Status	—	—	10	Self
TM18	Rain Dance	Water	Status	—	—	5	Both Sides
TM21	Frustration	Normal	Physical	—	100	20	Normal
TM24	Thunderbolt	Electric	Special	90	100	15	Normal
TM25	Thunder	Electric	Special	110	70	10	Normal
TM27	Return	Normal	Physical	—	100	20	Normal
TM28	Dig	Ground	Physical	80	100	10	Normal
TM30	Shadow Ball	Ghost	Special	80	100	15	Normal
TM32	Double Team	Normal	Status	—	—	15	Self
TM42	Facade	Normal	Physical	70	100	20	Normal
TM44	Rest	Psychic	Status	—	—	10	Self
TM45	Attract	Normal	Status	—	100	15	Normal
TM46	Thief	Dark	Physical	60	100	25	Normal
TM48	Round	Normal	Special	60	100	15	Normal
TM49	Echoed Voice	Normal	Special	40	100	15	Normal
TM56	Fling	Dark	Physical	—	100	10	Normal
TM57	Charge Beam	Electric	Special	50	90	10	Normal
TM65	Shadow Claw	Ghost	Physical	70	100	15	Normal
TM67	Retaliate	Normal	Physical	70	100	5	Normal
TM68	Giga Impact	Normal	Physical	150	90	5	Normal
TM73	Thunder Wave	Electric	Status	—	100	20	Normal
TM86	Grass Knot	Grass	Special	—	100	20	Normal
TM87	Swagger	Normal	Status	—	90	15	Normal
TM88	Sleep Talk	Normal	Status	—	—	10	Self
TM90	Substitute	Normal	Status	—	—	10	Self
TM94	Secret Power	Normal	Physical	70	100	20	Normal
TM100	Confide	Normal	Status	—	—	20	Normal
HM01	Cut	Normal	Physical	50	95	30	Normal
HM03	Surf	Water	Special	90	100	15	Adjacent
HM04	Strength	Normal	Physical	80	100	15	Normal
HM06	Rock Smash	Fighting	Physical	40	100	15	Normal

MOVES LEARNED IN EXCHANGE FOR BP

Name	Type	Kind	Pow.	Acc.	PP	Range
Covet	Normal	Physical	60	100	25	Normal
Super Fang	Normal	Physical	—	90	10	Normal
Seed Bomb	Grass	Physical	80	100	15	Normal
Gunk Shot	Poison	Physical	120	80	5	Normal
Last Resort	Normal	Physical	140	100	5	Normal
Icy Wind	Ice	Special	55	95	15	Many Others
Hyper Voice	Normal	Special	90	100	10	Many Others
Iron Tail	Steel	Physical	100	75	15	Normal
Snore	Normal	Special	50	100	15	Normal
Shock Wave	Electric	Special	60	—	20	Normal
Water Pulse	Water	Special	60	100	20	Normal
Helping Hand	Normal	Status	—	—	20	1 Ally
Trick	Psychic	Status	—	100	10	Normal

MOVES TAUGHT BY PEOPLE

Name	Type	Kind	Pow.	Acc.	PP	Range

National Pokédex **265** Hoenn Pokédex **014**

Wurmple

Worm Pokémon

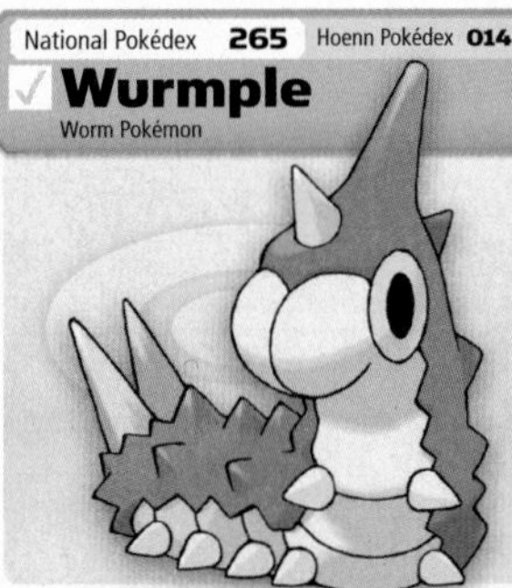

Bug

HEIGHT: 1'00" WEIGHT: 7.9 lbs.

Same form for ♂ / ♀

Ω Using the spikes on its rear end, Wurmple peels the bark off trees and feeds on the sap that oozes out. This Pokémon's feet are tipped with suction pads that allow it to cling to glass without slipping.

α Wurmple is targeted by Swellow as prey. This Pokémon will try to resist by pointing the spikes on its rear at the attacking predator. It will weaken the foe by leaking poison from the spikes.

ABILITY
Shield Dust

HIDDEN ABILITY
Run Away

EGG GROUPS
Bug

STAT GROWTH RATES
HP
Attack
Defense
Sp. Atk
Sp. Def
Speed

ITEMS SOMETIMES HELD BY WILD POKÉMON
Pecha Berry / Bright Powder

EVOLUTION
Wurmple → Lv. 7 → Silcoon → Lv. 10 → Beautifly
Wurmple → Lv. 7 → Cascoon → Lv. 10 → Dustox

MAIN WAY TO REGISTER IN THE NATIONAL POKÉDEX

Catch on Route 101.

Damage taken in normal battles

Type		Type	
Normal	×1	Flying	×2
Fire	×2	Psychic	×1
Water	×1	Bug	×1
Grass	×0.5	Rock	×2
Electric	×1	Ghost	×1
Ice	×1	Dragon	×1
Fighting	×0.5	Dark	×1
Poison	×1	Steel	×1
Ground	×0.5	Fairy	×1

Damage taken in Inverse battles

Type		Type	
Normal	×1	Flying	×0.5
Fire	×0.5	Psychic	×1
Water	×1	Bug	×1
Grass	×2	Rock	×0.5
Electric	×1	Ghost	×1
Ice	×1	Dragon	×1
Fighting	×2	Dark	×1
Poison	×1	Steel	×1
Ground	×2	Fairy	×1

Can be used in
Inverse Battle
Battle Institute
Battle Maison
Random Matchup (Free Battle)
Random Matchup (Others)

LEVEL-UP MOVES

Lv.	Name	Type	Kind	Pow.	Acc.	PP	Range
1	Tackle	Normal	Physical	50	100	35	Normal
1	String Shot	Bug	Status	—	95	40	Many Others
5	Poison Sting	Poison	Physical	15	100	35	Normal
15	Bug Bite	Bug	Physical	60	100	20	Normal

TM & HM MOVES

No.	Name	Type	Kind	Pow.	Acc.	PP	Range

MOVES LEARNED IN EXCHANGE FOR BP

Name	Type	Kind	Pow.	Acc.	PP	Range
Bug Bite	Bug	Physical	60	100	20	Normal
Electroweb	Electric	Special	55	95	15	Many Others
Snore	Normal	Special	50	100	15	Normal

MOVES TAUGHT BY PEOPLE

Name	Type	Kind	Pow.	Acc.	PP	Range

National Pokédex **266** Hoenn Pokédex **015**

Silcoon

Cocoon Pokémon

Bug

HEIGHT: 2'00" WEIGHT: 22 lbs.

Same form for ♂ / ♀

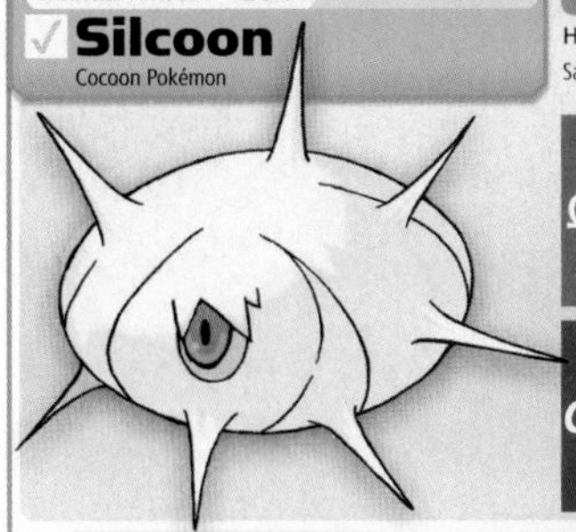

Ω Silcoon tethers itself to a tree branch using silk to keep from falling. There, this Pokémon hangs quietly while it awaits evolution. It peers out of the silk cocoon through a small hole.

α Silcoon was thought to endure hunger and not consume anything before its evolution. However, it is now thought that this Pokémon slakes its thirst by drinking rainwater that collects on its silk.

ABILITY
Shed Skin

HIDDEN ABILITY
—

EGG GROUPS
Bug

STAT GROWTH RATES

Stat	Rate
HP	■■
Attack	■■
Defense	■■■
Sp. Atk	■
Sp. Def	■
Speed	■

ITEMS SOMETIMES HELD BY WILD POKÉMON
—

EVOLUTION

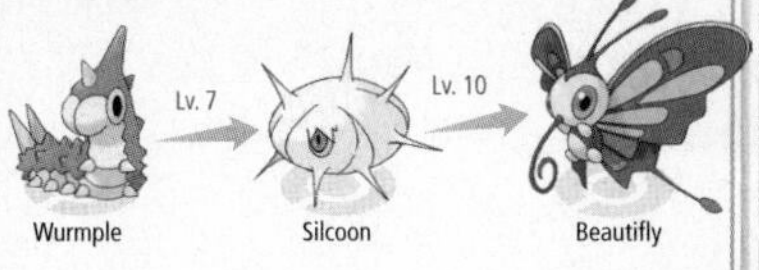

Wurmple → Lv. 7 → Silcoon → Lv. 10 → Beautifly

MAIN WAY TO REGISTER IN THE NATIONAL POKÉDEX

Catch in Petalburg Woods.

Damage taken in normal battles

Type	×	Type	×
Normal	×1	Flying	×2
Fire	×2	Psychic	×1
Water	×1	Bug	×1
Grass	×0.5	Rock	×2
Electric	×1	Ghost	×1
Ice	×1	Dragon	×1
Fighting	×0.5	Dark	×1
Poison	×1	Steel	×1
Ground	×0.5	Fairy	×1

Damage taken in Inverse battles

Type	×	Type	×
Normal	×1	Flying	×0.5
Fire	×0.5	Psychic	×1
Water	×1	Bug	×1
Grass	×2	Rock	×0.5
Electric	×1	Ghost	×1
Ice	×1	Dragon	×1
Fighting	×2	Dark	×1
Poison	×1	Steel	×1
Ground	×2	Fairy	×1

Can be used in

Inverse Battle
Battle Institute
Battle Maison
Random Matchup (Free Battle)
Random Matchup (Others)

LEVEL-UP MOVES

Lv.	Name	Type	Kind	Pow.	Acc.	PP	Range
1	Harden	Normal	Status	—	—	30	Self
7	Harden	Normal	Status	—	—	30	Self

TM & HM MOVES

No.	Name	Type	Kind	Pow.	Acc.	PP	Range

MOVES LEARNED IN EXCHANGE FOR BP

Name	Type	Kind	Pow.	Acc.	PP	Range
Bug Bite	Bug	Physical	60	100	20	Normal
Iron Defense	Steel	Status	—	—	15	Self
Electroweb	Electric	Special	55	95	15	Many Others

MOVES TAUGHT BY PEOPLE

Name	Type	Kind	Pow.	Acc.	PP	Range

National Pokédex **267** Hoenn Pokédex **016**

Beautifly

Butterfly Pokémon

Bug Flying

HEIGHT: 3'03" WEIGHT: 62.6 lbs.

The red patch on the male's wings is larger than the red patch on the female's wings.

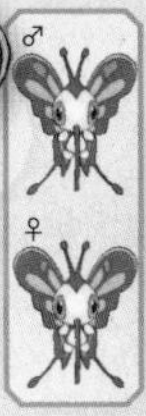

♂ ♀

Ω Beautifly's favorite food is the sweet pollen of flowers. If you want to see this Pokémon, just leave a potted flower by an open window. Beautifly is sure to come looking for pollen.

α Beautifly has a long mouth like a coiled needle, which is very convenient for collecting pollen from flowers. This Pokémon rides the spring winds as it flits around gathering pollen.

ABILITY
Swarm

HIDDEN ABILITY
Rivalry

EGG GROUPS
Bug

STAT GROWTH RATES

Stat	Rate
HP	■■■
Attack	■■■■
Defense	■■
Sp. Atk	■■■■■
Sp. Def	■■
Speed	■■■■

ITEMS SOMETIMES HELD BY WILD POKÉMON
—

EVOLUTION

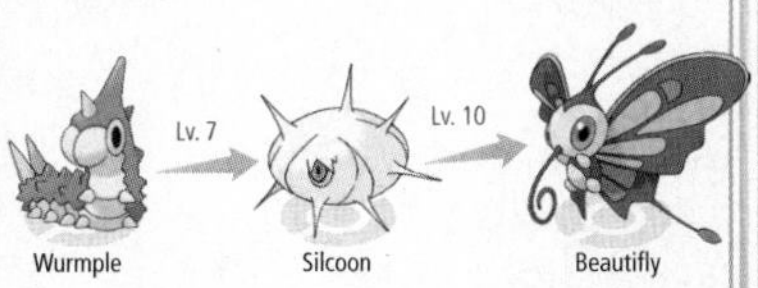

Wurmple → Lv. 7 → Silcoon → Lv. 10 → Beautifly

MAIN WAY TO REGISTER IN THE NATIONAL POKÉDEX

Level up Silcoon to Lv. 10.

Damage taken in normal battles

Type	×	Type	×
Normal	×1	Flying	×2
Fire	×2	Psychic	×1
Water	×1	Bug	×0.5
Grass	×0.25	Rock	×4
Electric	×2	Ghost	×1
Ice	×2	Dragon	×1
Fighting	×0.25	Dark	×1
Poison	×1	Steel	×1
Ground	×0	Fairy	×1

Damage taken in Inverse battles

Type	×	Type	×
Normal	×1	Flying	×0.5
Fire	×0.5	Psychic	×1
Water	×1	Bug	×2
Grass	×4	Rock	×0.25
Electric	×0.5	Ghost	×1
Ice	×0.5	Dragon	×1
Fighting	×4	Dark	×1
Poison	×1	Steel	×1
Ground	×4	Fairy	×1

Can be used in

Inverse Battle
Battle Institute
Battle Maison
Random Matchup (Free Battle)
Random Matchup (Others)

LEVEL-UP MOVES

Lv.	Name	Type	Kind	Pow.	Acc.	PP	Range
1	Gust	Flying	Special	40	100	35	Normal
10	Gust	Flying	Special	40	100	35	Normal
12	Absorb	Grass	Special	20	100	25	Normal
15	Stun Spore	Grass	Status	—	75	30	Normal
17	Morning Sun	Normal	Status	—	—	5	Self
20	Air Cutter	Flying	Special	60	95	25	Many Others
22	Mega Drain	Grass	Special	40	100	15	Normal
25	Silver Wind	Bug	Special	60	100	5	Normal
27	Attract	Normal	Status	—	100	15	Normal
30	Whirlwind	Normal	Status	—	—	20	Normal
32	Giga Drain	Grass	Special	75	100	10	Normal
35	Bug Buzz	Bug	Special	90	100	10	Normal
37	Rage	Normal	Physical	20	100	20	Normal
40	Quiver Dance	Bug	Status	—	—	20	Self

TM & HM MOVES

No.	Name	Type	Kind	Pow.	Acc.	PP	Range
TM06	Toxic	Poison	Status	—	90	10	Normal
TM09	Venoshock	Poison	Special	65	100	10	Normal
TM10	Hidden Power	Normal	Special	60	100	15	Normal
TM11	Sunny Day	Fire	Status	—	—	5	Both Sides
TM15	Hyper Beam	Normal	Special	150	90	5	Normal
TM17	Protect	Normal	Status	—	—	10	Self
TM19	Roost	Flying	Status	—	—	10	Self
TM20	Safeguard	Normal	Status	—	—	25	Your Side
TM21	Frustration	Normal	Physical	—	100	20	Normal
TM22	Solar Beam	Grass	Special	120	100	10	Normal
TM27	Return	Normal	Physical	—	100	20	Normal
TM29	Psychic	Psychic	Special	90	100	10	Normal
TM30	Shadow Ball	Ghost	Special	80	100	15	Normal
TM32	Double Team	Normal	Status	—	—	15	Self
TM40	Aerial Ace	Flying	Physical	60	—	20	Normal
TM42	Facade	Normal	Physical	70	100	20	Normal
TM44	Rest	Psychic	Status	—	—	10	Self
TM45	Attract	Normal	Status	—	100	15	Normal
TM46	Thief	Dark	Physical	60	100	25	Normal
TM48	Round	Normal	Special	60	100	15	Normal
TM53	Energy Ball	Grass	Special	90	100	10	Normal
TM62	Acrobatics	Flying	Physical	55	100	15	Normal
TM68	Giga Impact	Normal	Physical	150	90	5	Normal
TM70	Flash	Normal	Status	—	100	20	Normal
TM76	Struggle Bug	Bug	Special	50	100	20	Many Others
TM83	Infestation	Bug	Special	20	100	20	Normal
TM87	Swagger	Normal	Status	—	90	15	Normal
TM88	Sleep Talk	Normal	Status	—	—	10	Self
TM89	U-turn	Bug	Physical	70	100	20	Normal
TM90	Substitute	Normal	Status	—	—	10	Self
TM94	Secret Power	Normal	Physical	70	100	20	Normal
TM100	Confide	Normal	Status	—	—	20	Normal

MOVES LEARNED IN EXCHANGE FOR BP

Name	Type	Kind	Pow.	Acc.	PP	Range
Bug Bite	Bug	Physical	60	100	20	Normal
Signal Beam	Bug	Special	75	100	15	Normal
Electroweb	Electric	Special	55	95	15	Many Others
Snore	Normal	Special	50	100	15	Normal
Tailwind	Flying	Status	—	—	15	Your Side
Giga Drain	Grass	Special	75	100	10	Normal

MOVES TAUGHT BY PEOPLE

Name	Type	Kind	Pow.	Acc.	PP	Range

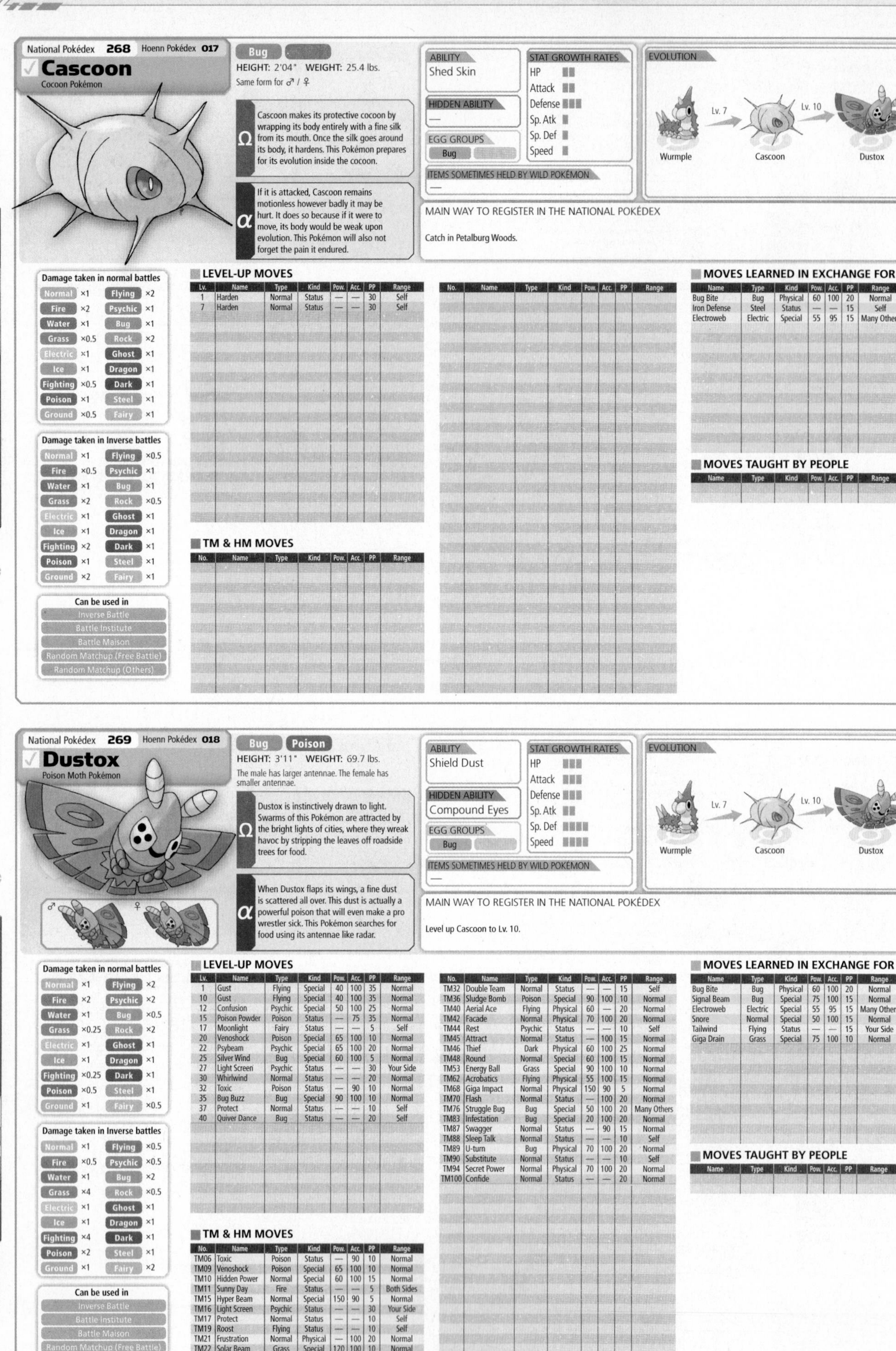

National Pokédex **268** Hoenn Pokédex **017**

Cascoon

Cocoon Pokémon

Bug

HEIGHT: 2'04" WEIGHT: 25.4 lbs.

Same form for ♂ / ♀

Ω Cascoon makes its protective cocoon by wrapping its body entirely with a fine silk from its mouth. Once the silk goes around its body, it hardens. This Pokémon prepares for its evolution inside the cocoon.

α If it is attacked, Cascoon remains motionless however badly it may be hurt. It does so because if it were to move, its body would be weak upon evolution. This Pokémon will also not forget the pain it endured.

ABILITY
Shed Skin

HIDDEN ABILITY
—

EGG GROUPS
Bug

STAT GROWTH RATES
HP
Attack
Defense
Sp. Atk
Sp. Def
Speed

ITEMS SOMETIMES HELD BY WILD POKÉMON
—

EVOLUTION
Wurmple → Lv. 7 → Cascoon → Lv. 10 → Dustox

MAIN WAY TO REGISTER IN THE NATIONAL POKÉDEX

Catch in Petalburg Woods.

Damage taken in normal battles

Type		Type	
Normal	×1	Flying	×2
Fire	×2	Psychic	×1
Water	×1	Bug	×1
Grass	×0.5	Rock	×2
Electric	×1	Ghost	×1
Ice	×1	Dragon	×1
Fighting	×0.5	Dark	×1
Poison	×1	Steel	×1
Ground	×0.5	Fairy	×1

Damage taken in Inverse battles

Type		Type	
Normal	×1	Flying	×0.5
Fire	×0.5	Psychic	×1
Water	×1	Bug	×1
Grass	×2	Rock	×0.5
Electric	×1	Ghost	×1
Ice	×1	Dragon	×1
Fighting	×2	Dark	×1
Poison	×1	Steel	×1
Ground	×2	Fairy	×1

Can be used in
Inverse Battle
Battle Institute
Battle Maison
Random Matchup (Free Battle)
Random Matchup (Others)

LEVEL-UP MOVES

Lv.	Name	Type	Kind	Pow.	Acc.	PP	Range
1	Harden	Normal	Status	—	—	30	Self
7	Harden	Normal	Status	—	—	30	Self

TM & HM MOVES

No.	Name	Type	Kind	Pow.	Acc.	PP	Range

MOVES LEARNED IN EXCHANGE FOR BP

Name	Type	Kind	Pow.	Acc.	PP	Range
Bug Bite	Bug	Physical	60	100	20	Normal
Iron Defense	Steel	Status	—	—	15	Self
Electroweb	Electric	Special	55	95	15	Many Others

MOVES TAUGHT BY PEOPLE

Name	Type	Kind	Pow.	Acc.	PP	Range

National Pokédex **269** Hoenn Pokédex **018**

Dustox

Poison Moth Pokémon

Bug Poison

HEIGHT: 3'11" WEIGHT: 69.7 lbs.

The male has larger antennae. The female has smaller antennae.

♂ ♀

Ω Dustox is instinctively drawn to light. Swarms of this Pokémon are attracted by the bright lights of cities, where they wreak havoc by stripping the leaves off roadside trees for food.

α When Dustox flaps its wings, a fine dust is scattered all over. This dust is actually a powerful poison that will even make a pro wrestler sick. This Pokémon searches for food using its antennae like radar.

ABILITY
Shield Dust

HIDDEN ABILITY
Compound Eyes

EGG GROUPS
Bug

STAT GROWTH RATES
HP
Attack
Defense
Sp. Atk
Sp. Def
Speed

ITEMS SOMETIMES HELD BY WILD POKÉMON
—

EVOLUTION
Wurmple → Lv. 7 → Cascoon → Lv. 10 → Dustox

MAIN WAY TO REGISTER IN THE NATIONAL POKÉDEX

Level up Cascoon to Lv. 10.

Damage taken in normal battles

Type		Type	
Normal	×1	Flying	×2
Fire	×2	Psychic	×2
Water	×1	Bug	×0.5
Grass	×0.25	Rock	×2
Electric	×1	Ghost	×1
Ice	×1	Dragon	×1
Fighting	×0.25	Dark	×1
Poison	×0.5	Steel	×1
Ground	×1	Fairy	×0.5

Damage taken in Inverse battles

Type		Type	
Normal	×1	Flying	×0.5
Fire	×0.5	Psychic	×0.5
Water	×1	Bug	×2
Grass	×4	Rock	×0.5
Electric	×1	Ghost	×1
Ice	×1	Dragon	×1
Fighting	×4	Dark	×1
Poison	×2	Steel	×1
Ground	×1	Fairy	×2

Can be used in
Inverse Battle
Battle Institute
Battle Maison
Random Matchup (Free Battle)
Random Matchup (Others)

LEVEL-UP MOVES

Lv.	Name	Type	Kind	Pow.	Acc.	PP	Range
1	Gust	Flying	Special	40	100	35	Normal
10	Gust	Flying	Special	40	100	35	Normal
12	Confusion	Psychic	Special	50	100	25	Normal
15	Poison Powder	Poison	Status	—	75	35	Normal
17	Moonlight	Fairy	Status	—	—	5	Self
20	Venoshock	Poison	Special	65	100	10	Normal
22	Psybeam	Psychic	Special	65	100	20	Normal
25	Silver Wind	Bug	Special	60	100	5	Normal
27	Light Screen	Psychic	Status	—	—	30	Your Side
30	Whirlwind	Normal	Status	—	—	20	Normal
32	Toxic	Poison	Status	—	90	10	Normal
35	Bug Buzz	Bug	Special	90	100	10	Normal
37	Protect	Normal	Status	—	—	10	Self
40	Quiver Dance	Bug	Status	—	—	20	Self

TM & HM MOVES

No.	Name	Type	Kind	Pow.	Acc.	PP	Range
TM06	Toxic	Poison	Status	—	90	10	Normal
TM09	Venoshock	Poison	Special	65	100	10	Normal
TM10	Hidden Power	Normal	Special	60	100	15	Normal
TM11	Sunny Day	Fire	Status	—	—	5	Both Sides
TM15	Hyper Beam	Normal	Special	150	90	5	Normal
TM16	Light Screen	Psychic	Status	—	—	30	Your Side
TM17	Protect	Normal	Status	—	—	10	Self
TM19	Roost	Flying	Status	—	—	10	Self
TM21	Frustration	Normal	Physical	—	100	20	Normal
TM22	Solar Beam	Grass	Special	120	100	10	Normal
TM27	Return	Normal	Physical	—	100	20	Normal
TM29	Psychic	Psychic	Special	90	100	10	Normal
TM30	Shadow Ball	Ghost	Special	80	100	15	Normal
TM32	Double Team	Normal	Status	—	—	15	Self
TM36	Sludge Bomb	Poison	Special	90	100	10	Normal
TM40	Aerial Ace	Flying	Physical	60	—	20	Normal
TM42	Facade	Normal	Physical	70	100	20	Normal
TM44	Rest	Psychic	Status	—	—	10	Self
TM45	Attract	Normal	Status	—	100	15	Normal
TM46	Thief	Dark	Physical	60	100	25	Normal
TM48	Round	Normal	Special	60	100	15	Normal
TM53	Energy Ball	Grass	Special	90	100	10	Normal
TM62	Acrobatics	Flying	Physical	55	100	15	Normal
TM68	Giga Impact	Normal	Physical	150	90	5	Normal
TM70	Flash	Normal	Status	—	100	20	Normal
TM76	Struggle Bug	Bug	Special	50	100	20	Many Others
TM83	Infestation	Bug	Special	20	100	20	Normal
TM87	Swagger	Normal	Status	—	90	15	Normal
TM88	Sleep Talk	Normal	Status	—	—	10	Self
TM89	U-turn	Bug	Physical	70	100	20	Normal
TM90	Substitute	Normal	Status	—	—	10	Self
TM94	Secret Power	Normal	Physical	70	100	20	Normal
TM100	Confide	Normal	Status	—	—	20	Normal

MOVES LEARNED IN EXCHANGE FOR BP

Name	Type	Kind	Pow.	Acc.	PP	Range
Bug Bite	Bug	Physical	60	100	20	Normal
Signal Beam	Bug	Special	75	100	15	Normal
Electroweb	Electric	Special	55	95	15	Many Others
Snore	Normal	Special	50	100	15	Normal
Tailwind	Flying	Status	—	—	15	Your Side
Giga Drain	Grass	Special	75	100	10	Normal

MOVES TAUGHT BY PEOPLE

Name	Type	Kind	Pow.	Acc.	PP	Range

National Pokédex **270** Hoenn Pokédex **019**

Lotad

Water Weed Pokémon

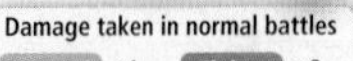

Water | Grass

HEIGHT: 1'08" WEIGHT: 5.7 lbs.

Same form for ♂ / ♀

Ω Lotad live in ponds and lakes, where they float on the surface. It grows weak if its broad leaf dies. On rare occasions, this Pokémon travels on land in search of clean water.

α Lotad is said to have dwelled on land before. However, this Pokémon is thought to have returned to water because the leaf on its head grew large and heavy. It now lives by floating atop the water.

ABILITIES
Swift Swim
Rain Dish

HIDDEN ABILITY
Own Tempo

EGG GROUPS
Water 1 | Grass

STAT GROWTH RATES
HP ■■
Attack ■■
Defense ■■
Sp. Atk ■■
Sp. Def ■■
Speed ■■

ITEMS SOMETIMES HELD BY WILD POKÉMON
Mental Herb

EVOLUTION
Lotad → Lv. 14 → Lombre → Water Stone → Ludicolo

MAIN WAYS TO REGISTER IN THE NATIONAL POKÉDEX
Ω Bring it to your game using Link Trade or the GTS.
α Catch on Route 102.

Damage taken in normal battles

Type		Type	
Normal	×1	Flying	×2
Fire	×1	Psychic	×1
Water	×0.25	Bug	×2
Grass	×1	Rock	×1
Electric	×1	Ghost	×1
Ice	×1	Dragon	×1
Fighting	×1	Dark	×1
Poison	×2	Steel	×0.5
Ground	×0.5	Fairy	×1

Damage taken in Inverse battles

Type		Type	
Normal	×1	Flying	×0.5
Fire	×1	Psychic	×1
Water	×4	Bug	×0.5
Grass	×1	Rock	×1
Electric	×1	Ghost	×1
Ice	×1	Dragon	×1
Fighting	×1	Dark	×1
Poison	×0.5	Steel	×2
Ground	×2	Fairy	×1

Can be used in
Inverse Battle
Battle Institute
Battle Maison
Random Matchup (Free Battle)
Random Matchup (Others)

LEVEL-UP MOVES

Lv.	Name	Type	Kind	Pow.	Acc.	PP	Range
1	Astonish	Ghost	Physical	30	100	15	Normal
3	Growl	Normal	Status	—	100	40	Many Others
6	Absorb	Grass	Special	20	100	25	Normal
9	Bubble	Water	Special	40	100	30	Many Others
12	Natural Gift	Normal	Physical	—	100	15	Normal
15	Mist	Ice	Status	—	—	30	Your Side
18	Mega Drain	Grass	Special	40	100	15	Normal
21	Bubble Beam	Water	Special	65	100	20	Normal
24	Nature Power	Normal	Status	—	—	20	Normal
27	Rain Dance	Water	Status	—	—	5	Both Sides
30	Giga Drain	Grass	Special	75	100	10	Normal
33	Zen Headbutt	Psychic	Physical	80	90	15	Normal
36	Energy Ball	Grass	Special	90	100	10	Normal

TM & HM MOVES

No.	Name	Type	Kind	Pow.	Acc.	PP	Range
TM06	Toxic	Poison	Status	—	90	10	Normal
TM07	Hail	Ice	Status	—	—	10	Both Sides
TM10	Hidden Power	Normal	Special	60	100	15	Normal
TM11	Sunny Day	Fire	Status	—	—	5	Both Sides
TM13	Ice Beam	Ice	Special	90	100	10	Normal
TM14	Blizzard	Ice	Special	110	70	5	Many Others
TM17	Protect	Normal	Status	—	—	10	Self
TM18	Rain Dance	Water	Status	—	—	5	Both Sides
TM21	Frustration	Normal	Physical	—	100	20	Normal
TM22	Solar Beam	Grass	Special	120	100	10	Normal
TM27	Return	Normal	Physical	—	100	20	Normal
TM32	Double Team	Normal	Status	—	—	15	Self
TM42	Facade	Normal	Physical	70	100	20	Normal
TM44	Rest	Psychic	Status	—	—	10	Self
TM45	Attract	Normal	Status	—	100	15	Normal
TM46	Thief	Dark	Physical	60	100	25	Normal
TM48	Round	Normal	Special	60	100	15	Normal
TM49	Echoed Voice	Normal	Special	40	100	15	Normal
TM53	Energy Ball	Grass	Special	90	100	10	Normal
TM55	Scald	Water	Special	80	100	15	Normal
TM70	Flash	Normal	Status	—	100	20	Normal
TM75	Swords Dance	Normal	Status	—	—	20	Self
TM86	Grass Knot	Grass	Special	—	100	20	Normal
TM87	Swagger	Normal	Status	—	90	15	Normal
TM88	Sleep Talk	Normal	Status	—	—	10	Self
TM90	Substitute	Normal	Status	—	—	10	Self
TM94	Secret Power	Normal	Physical	70	100	20	Normal
TM96	Nature Power	Normal	Status	—	—	20	Normal
TM100	Confide	Normal	Status	—	—	20	Normal
HM03	Surf	Water	Special	90	100	15	Adjacent

MOVES LEARNED IN EXCHANGE FOR BP

Name	Type	Kind	Pow.	Acc.	PP	Range
Seed Bomb	Grass	Physical	80	100	15	Normal
Uproar	Normal	Special	90	100	10	1 Random
Icy Wind	Ice	Special	55	95	15	Many Others
Zen Headbutt	Psychic	Physical	80	90	15	Normal
Snore	Normal	Special	50	100	15	Normal
Synthesis	Grass	Status	—	—	5	Self
Giga Drain	Grass	Special	75	100	10	Normal
Water Pulse	Water	Special	60	100	20	Normal

MOVES TAUGHT BY PEOPLE

Name	Type	Kind	Pow.	Acc.	PP	Range

EGG MOVES

Name	Type	Kind	Pow.	Acc.	PP	Range
Synthesis	Grass	Status	—	—	5	Self
Razor Leaf	Grass	Physical	55	95	25	Many Others
Sweet Scent	Normal	Status	—	100	20	Many Others
Leech Seed	Grass	Status	—	90	10	Normal
Flail	Normal	Physical	—	100	15	Normal
Water Gun	Water	Special	40	100	25	Normal
Tickle	Normal	Status	—	100	20	Normal
Counter	Fighting	Physical	—	100	20	Varies
Giga Drain	Grass	Special	75	100	10	Normal
Teeter Dance	Normal	Status	—	100	20	Adjacent

National Pokédex **271** Hoenn Pokédex **020**

Lombre

Jolly Pokémon

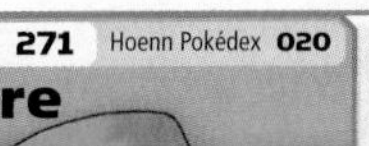

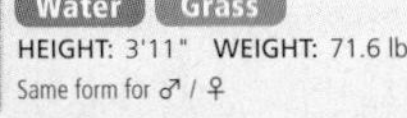

Water | Grass

HEIGHT: 3'11" WEIGHT: 71.6 lbs.

Same form for ♂ / ♀

Ω Lombre is nocturnal—it will get active after dusk. It is also a mischief maker. When this Pokémon spots anglers, it tugs on their fishing lines from beneath the surface and enjoys their consternation.

α Lombre's entire body is covered by a slippery, slimy film. It feels horribly unpleasant to be touched by this Pokémon's hands. Lombre is often mistaken for a human child.

ABILITIES
Swift Swim
Rain Dish

HIDDEN ABILITY
Own Tempo

EGG GROUPS
Water 1 | Grass

STAT GROWTH RATES
HP ■■■
Attack ■■■
Defense ■■
Sp. Atk ■■■
Sp. Def ■■■
Speed ■■■

ITEMS SOMETIMES HELD BY WILD POKÉMON
Mental Herb

EVOLUTION
Lotad → Lv. 14 → Lombre → Water Stone → Ludicolo

MAIN WAYS TO REGISTER IN THE NATIONAL POKÉDEX
Ω Bring it to your game using Link Trade or the GTS.
α Catch on Route 114.

Damage taken in normal battles

Type		Type	
Normal	×1	Flying	×2
Fire	×1	Psychic	×1
Water	×0.25	Bug	×2
Grass	×1	Rock	×1
Electric	×1	Ghost	×1
Ice	×1	Dragon	×1
Fighting	×1	Dark	×1
Poison	×2	Steel	×0.5
Ground	×0.5	Fairy	×1

Damage taken in Inverse battles

Type		Type	
Normal	×1	Flying	×0.5
Fire	×1	Psychic	×1
Water	×4	Bug	×0.5
Grass	×1	Rock	×1
Electric	×1	Ghost	×1
Ice	×1	Dragon	×1
Fighting	×1	Dark	×1
Poison	×0.5	Steel	×2
Ground	×2	Fairy	×1

Can be used in
Inverse Battle
Battle Institute
Battle Maison
Random Matchup (Free Battle)
Random Matchup (Others)

LEVEL-UP MOVES

Lv.	Name	Type	Kind	Pow.	Acc.	PP	Range
1	Astonish	Ghost	Physical	30	100	15	Normal
3	Growl	Normal	Status	—	100	40	Many Others
6	Absorb	Grass	Special	20	100	25	Normal
9	Bubble	Water	Special	40	100	30	Many Others
12	Fury Swipes	Normal	Physical	18	80	15	Normal
16	Fake Out	Normal	Physical	40	100	10	Normal
20	Water Sport	Water	Status	—	—	15	Both Sides
24	Bubble Beam	Water	Special	65	100	20	Normal
28	Nature Power	Normal	Status	—	—	20	Normal
32	Uproar	Normal	Special	90	100	10	1 Random
36	Knock Off	Dark	Physical	65	100	20	Normal
40	Zen Headbutt	Psychic	Physical	80	90	15	Normal
44	Hydro Pump	Water	Special	110	80	5	Normal

TM & HM MOVES

No.	Name	Type	Kind	Pow.	Acc.	PP	Range
TM01	Hone Claws	Dark	Status	—	—	15	Self
TM06	Toxic	Poison	Status	—	90	10	Normal
TM07	Hail	Ice	Status	—	—	10	Both Sides
TM10	Hidden Power	Normal	Special	60	100	15	Normal
TM11	Sunny Day	Fire	Status	—	—	5	Both Sides
TM13	Ice Beam	Ice	Special	90	100	10	Normal
TM14	Blizzard	Ice	Special	110	70	5	Many Others
TM17	Protect	Normal	Status	—	—	10	Self
TM18	Rain Dance	Water	Status	—	—	5	Both Sides
TM21	Frustration	Normal	Physical	—	100	20	Normal
TM22	Solar Beam	Grass	Special	120	100	10	Normal
TM27	Return	Normal	Physical	—	100	20	Normal
TM31	Brick Break	Fighting	Physical	75	100	15	Normal
TM32	Double Team	Normal	Status	—	—	15	Self
TM42	Facade	Normal	Physical	70	100	20	Normal
TM44	Rest	Psychic	Status	—	—	10	Self
TM45	Attract	Normal	Status	—	100	15	Normal
TM46	Thief	Dark	Physical	60	100	25	Normal
TM48	Round	Normal	Special	60	100	15	Normal
TM49	Echoed Voice	Normal	Special	40	100	15	Normal
TM53	Energy Ball	Grass	Special	90	100	10	Normal
TM55	Scald	Water	Special	80	100	15	Normal
TM56	Fling	Dark	Physical	—	100	10	Normal
TM70	Flash	Normal	Status	—	100	20	Normal
TM75	Swords Dance	Normal	Status	—	—	20	Self
TM86	Grass Knot	Grass	Special	—	100	20	Normal
TM87	Swagger	Normal	Status	—	90	15	Normal
TM88	Sleep Talk	Normal	Status	—	—	10	Self
TM90	Substitute	Normal	Status	—	—	10	Self
TM94	Secret Power	Normal	Physical	70	100	20	Normal
TM96	Nature Power	Normal	Status	—	—	20	Normal
TM98	Power-Up Punch	Fighting	Physical	40	100	20	Normal
TM100	Confide	Normal	Status	—	—	20	Normal
HM03	Surf	Water	Special	90	100	15	Adjacent
HM04	Strength	Normal	Physical	80	100	15	Normal
HM05	Waterfall	Water	Physical	80	100	15	Normal
HM06	Rock Smash	Fighting	Physical	40	100	15	Normal
HM07	Dive	Water	Physical	80	100	10	Normal

MOVES LEARNED IN EXCHANGE FOR BP

Name	Type	Kind	Pow.	Acc.	PP	Range
Seed Bomb	Grass	Physical	80	100	15	Normal
Uproar	Normal	Special	90	100	10	1 Random
Thunder Punch	Electric	Physical	75	100	15	Normal
Fire Punch	Fire	Physical	75	100	15	Normal
Ice Punch	Ice	Physical	75	100	15	Normal
Icy Wind	Ice	Special	55	95	15	Many Others
Zen Headbutt	Psychic	Physical	80	90	15	Normal
Hyper Voice	Normal	Special	90	100	10	Many Others
Snore	Normal	Special	50	100	15	Normal
Knock Off	Dark	Physical	65	100	20	Normal
Synthesis	Grass	Status	—	—	5	Self
Giga Drain	Grass	Special	75	100	10	Normal
Drain Punch	Fighting	Physical	75	100	10	Normal
Water Pulse	Water	Special	60	100	20	Normal

MOVES TAUGHT BY PEOPLE

Name	Type	Kind	Pow.	Acc.	PP	Range

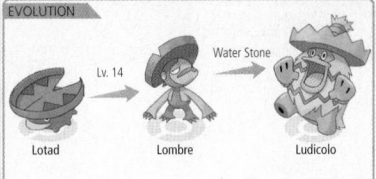

National Pokédex **272** Hoenn Pokédex **021**

Ludicolo

Carefree Pokémon

Water | Grass

HEIGHT: 4'11" WEIGHT: 121.3 lbs.

The zigzag patterns are larger on the male's body.
The zigzag patterns are smaller on the female's body.

Ω Ludicolo begins dancing as soon as it hears cheerful, festive music. This Pokémon is said to appear when it hears the singing of children on hiking outings.

α Upon hearing an upbeat and cheerful rhythm, the cells in Ludicolo's body become very energetic and active. Even in battle, this Pokémon will exhibit an amazing amount of power.

ABILITIES
Swift Swim
Rain Dish

HIDDEN ABILITY
Own Tempo

EGG GROUPS
Water 1 | Grass

STAT GROWTH RATES
HP
Attack
Defense
Sp. Atk
Sp. Def
Speed

ITEMS SOMETIMES HELD BY WILD POKÉMON
Mental Herb

EVOLUTION
Lotad → Lv. 14 → Lombre → Water Stone → Ludicolo

MAIN WAYS TO REGISTER IN THE NATIONAL POKÉDEX
Ω Bring it to your game using Link Trade or the GTS.
α Use a Water Stone on Lombre.

Damage taken in normal battles

Type		Type	
Normal	×1	Flying	×2
Fire	×1	Psychic	×1
Water	×0.25	Bug	×2
Grass	×1	Rock	×1
Electric	×1	Ghost	×1
Ice	×1	Dragon	×1
Fighting	×1	Dark	×1
Poison	×2	Steel	×0.5
Ground	×0.5	Fairy	×1

Damage taken in Inverse battles

Type		Type	
Normal	×1	Flying	×0.5
Fire	×1	Psychic	×1
Water	×4	Bug	×0.5
Grass	×1	Rock	×1
Electric	×1	Ghost	×1
Ice	×1	Dragon	×1
Fighting	×1	Dark	×1
Poison	×0.5	Steel	×2
Ground	×2	Fairy	×1

Can be used in
Inverse Battle
Battle Institute
Battle Maison
Random Matchup (Free Battle)
Random Matchup (Others)

LEVEL-UP MOVES

Lv.	Name	Type	Kind	Pow.	Acc.	PP	Range
1	Astonish	Ghost	Physical	30	100	15	Normal
1	Growl	Normal	Status	—	100	40	Many Others
1	Mega Drain	Grass	Special	40	100	15	Normal
1	Nature Power	Normal	Status	—	—	20	Normal

TM & HM MOVES

No.	Name	Type	Kind	Pow.	Acc.	PP	Range
TM01	Hone Claws	Dark	Status	—	—	15	Self
TM06	Toxic	Poison	Status	—	90	10	Normal
TM07	Hail	Ice	Status	—	—	10	Both Sides
TM10	Hidden Power	Normal	Special	60	100	15	Normal
TM11	Sunny Day	Fire	Status	—	—	5	Both Sides
TM13	Ice Beam	Ice	Special	90	100	10	Normal
TM14	Blizzard	Ice	Special	110	70	5	Many Others
TM15	Hyper Beam	Normal	Special	150	90	5	Normal
TM17	Protect	Normal	Status	—	—	10	Self
TM18	Rain Dance	Water	Status	—	—	5	Both Sides
TM21	Frustration	Normal	Physical	—	100	20	Normal
TM22	Solar Beam	Grass	Special	120	100	10	Normal
TM27	Return	Normal	Physical	—	100	20	Normal
TM31	Brick Break	Fighting	Physical	75	100	15	Normal
TM32	Double Team	Normal	Status	—	—	15	Self
TM42	Facade	Normal	Physical	70	100	20	Normal
TM44	Rest	Psychic	Status	—	—	10	Self
TM45	Attract	Normal	Status	—	100	15	Normal
TM46	Thief	Dark	Physical	60	100	25	Normal
TM48	Round	Normal	Special	60	100	15	Normal
TM49	Echoed Voice	Normal	Special	40	100	15	Normal
TM52	Focus Blast	Fighting	Special	120	70	5	Normal
TM53	Energy Ball	Grass	Special	90	100	10	Normal
TM55	Scald	Water	Special	80	100	15	Normal
TM56	Fling	Dark	Physical	—	100	10	Normal
TM68	Giga Impact	Normal	Physical	150	90	5	Normal
TM70	Flash	Normal	Status	—	100	20	Normal
TM75	Swords Dance	Normal	Status	—	—	20	Self
TM86	Grass Knot	Grass	Special	—	100	20	Normal
TM87	Swagger	Normal	Status	—	90	15	Normal
TM88	Sleep Talk	Normal	Status	—	—	10	Self
TM90	Substitute	Normal	Status	—	—	10	Self
TM94	Secret Power	Normal	Physical	70	100	20	Normal
TM96	Nature Power	Normal	Status	—	—	20	Normal
TM98	Power-Up Punch	Fighting	Physical	40	100	20	Normal
TM100	Confide	Normal	Status	—	—	20	Normal
HM03	Surf	Water	Special	90	100	15	Adjacent
HM04	Strength	Normal	Physical	80	100	15	Normal
HM05	Waterfall	Water	Physical	80	100	15	Normal
HM06	Rock Smash	Fighting	Physical	40	100	15	Normal
HM07	Dive	Water	Physical	80	100	10	Normal

MOVES LEARNED IN EXCHANGE FOR BP

Name	Type	Kind	Pow.	Acc.	PP	Range
Seed Bomb	Grass	Physical	80	100	15	Normal
Uproar	Normal	Special	90	100	10	1 Random
Thunder Punch	Electric	Physical	75	100	15	Normal
Fire Punch	Fire	Physical	75	100	15	Normal
Ice Punch	Ice	Physical	75	100	15	Normal
Icy Wind	Ice	Special	55	95	15	Many Others
Zen Headbutt	Psychic	Physical	80	90	15	Normal
Hyper Voice	Normal	Special	90	100	10	Many Others
Snore	Normal	Special	50	100	15	Normal
Knock Off	Dark	Physical	65	100	20	Normal
Synthesis	Grass	Status	—	—	5	Self
Giga Drain	Grass	Special	75	100	10	Normal
Drain Punch	Fighting	Physical	75	100	10	Normal
Focus Punch	Fighting	Physical	150	100	20	Normal
Water Pulse	Water	Special	60	100	20	Normal

MOVES TAUGHT BY PEOPLE

Name	Type	Kind	Pow.	Acc.	PP	Range

National Pokédex **273** Hoenn Pokédex **022**

Seedot

Acorn Pokémon

Grass

HEIGHT: 1'08" WEIGHT: 8.8 lbs.

Same form for ♂ / ♀

Ω Seedot attaches itself to a tree branch using the top of its head. It sucks moisture from the tree while hanging off the branch. The more water it drinks, the glossier this Pokémon's body becomes.

α Seedot looks exactly like an acorn when it is dangling from a tree branch. It startles other Pokémon by suddenly moving. This Pokémon polishes its body once a day using leaves.

ABILITIES
Chlorophyll
Early Bird

HIDDEN ABILITY
Pickpocket

EGG GROUPS
Field | Grass

STAT GROWTH RATES
HP
Attack
Defense
Sp. Atk
Sp. Def
Speed

ITEMS SOMETIMES HELD BY WILD POKÉMON
Power Herb

EVOLUTION
Seedot → Lv. 14 → Nuzleaf → Leaf Stone → Shiftry

MAIN WAYS TO REGISTER IN THE NATIONAL POKÉDEX
Ω Catch on Route 102.
α Bring it to your game using Link Trade or the GTS.

Damage taken in normal battles

Type		Type	
Normal	×1	Flying	×2
Fire	×2	Psychic	×1
Water	×0.5	Bug	×2
Grass	×0.5	Rock	×1
Electric	×0.5	Ghost	×1
Ice	×2	Dragon	×1
Fighting	×1	Dark	×1
Poison	×2	Steel	×1
Ground	×0.5	Fairy	×1

Damage taken in Inverse battles

Type		Type	
Normal	×1	Flying	×0.5
Fire	×0.5	Psychic	×1
Water	×2	Bug	×0.5
Grass	×2	Rock	×1
Electric	×2	Ghost	×1
Ice	×0.5	Dragon	×1
Fighting	×1	Dark	×1
Poison	×0.5	Steel	×1
Ground	×2	Fairy	×1

Can be used in
Inverse Battle
Battle Institute
Battle Maison
Random Matchup (Free Battle)
Random Matchup (Others)

LEVEL-UP MOVES

Lv.	Name	Type	Kind	Pow.	Acc.	PP	Range
1	Bide	Normal	Physical	—	—	10	Self
3	Harden	Normal	Status	—	—	30	Self
9	Growth	Normal	Status	—	—	20	Self
15	Nature Power	Normal	Status	—	—	20	Normal
21	Synthesis	Grass	Status	—	—	5	Self
27	Sunny Day	Fire	Status	—	—	5	Both Sides
33	Explosion	Normal	Physical	250	100	5	Adjacent

TM & HM MOVES

No.	Name	Type	Kind	Pow.	Acc.	PP	Range
TM06	Toxic	Poison	Status	—	90	10	Normal
TM10	Hidden Power	Normal	Special	60	100	15	Normal
TM11	Sunny Day	Fire	Status	—	—	5	Both Sides
TM17	Protect	Normal	Status	—	—	10	Self
TM21	Frustration	Normal	Physical	—	100	20	Normal
TM22	Solar Beam	Grass	Special	120	100	10	Normal
TM27	Return	Normal	Physical	—	100	20	Normal
TM28	Dig	Ground	Physical	80	100	10	Normal
TM30	Shadow Ball	Ghost	Special	80	100	15	Normal
TM32	Double Team	Normal	Status	—	—	15	Self
TM42	Facade	Normal	Physical	70	100	20	Normal
TM44	Rest	Psychic	Status	—	—	10	Self
TM45	Attract	Normal	Status	—	100	15	Normal
TM48	Round	Normal	Special	60	100	15	Normal
TM53	Energy Ball	Grass	Special	90	100	10	Normal
TM54	False Swipe	Normal	Physical	40	100	40	Normal
TM64	Explosion	Normal	Physical	250	100	5	Adjacent
TM67	Retaliate	Normal	Physical	70	100	5	Normal
TM70	Flash	Normal	Status	—	100	20	Normal
TM75	Swords Dance	Normal	Status	—	—	20	Self
TM86	Grass Knot	Grass	Special	—	100	20	Normal
TM87	Swagger	Normal	Status	—	90	15	Normal
TM88	Sleep Talk	Normal	Status	—	—	10	Self
TM90	Substitute	Normal	Status	—	—	10	Self
TM94	Secret Power	Normal	Physical	70	100	20	Normal
TM96	Nature Power	Normal	Status	—	—	20	Normal
TM100	Confide	Normal	Status	—	—	20	Normal
HM06	Rock Smash	Fighting	Physical	40	100	15	Normal

MOVES LEARNED IN EXCHANGE FOR BP

Name	Type	Kind	Pow.	Acc.	PP	Range
Seed Bomb	Grass	Physical	80	100	15	Normal
Foul Play	Dark	Physical	95	100	15	Normal
Snore	Normal	Special	50	100	15	Normal
Synthesis	Grass	Status	—	—	5	Self
Giga Drain	Grass	Special	75	100	10	Normal
Worry Seed	Grass	Status	—	100	10	Normal
Spite	Ghost	Status	—	100	10	Normal

MOVES TAUGHT BY PEOPLE

Name	Type	Kind	Pow.	Acc.	PP	Range

EGG MOVES

Name	Type	Kind	Pow.	Acc.	PP	Range
Leech Seed	Grass	Status	—	90	10	Normal
Amnesia	Psychic	Status	—	—	20	Self
Quick Attack	Normal	Physical	40	100	30	Normal
Razor Wind	Normal	Special	80	100	10	Many Others
Take Down	Normal	Physical	90	85	20	Normal
Worry Seed	Grass	Status	—	100	10	Normal
Nasty Plot	Dark	Status	—	—	20	Self
Power Swap	Psychic	Status	—	—	10	Normal
Defog	Flying	Status	—	—	15	Normal
Foul Play	Dark	Physical	95	100	15	Normal
Beat Up	Dark	Physical	—	100	10	Normal
Bullet Seed	Grass	Physical	25	100	30	Normal
Grassy Terrain	Grass	Status	—	—	10	Both Sides

National Pokédex **274** Hoenn Pokédex **023**

Nuzleaf

Wily Pokémon

Grass | Dark

HEIGHT: 3'03" WEIGHT: 61.7 lbs.

The male has a larger leaf on its head. The female has a smaller leaf on its head.

Ω Nuzleaf live in densely overgrown forests. They occasionally venture out of the forest to startle people. This Pokémon dislikes having its long nose pinched.

α This Pokémon pulls out the leaf on its head and makes a flute with it. The sound of Nuzleaf's flute strikes fear and uncertainty in the hearts of people lost in a forest.

ABILITIES
Chlorophyll
Early Bird

HIDDEN ABILITY
Pickpocket

EGG GROUPS
Field | Grass

STAT GROWTH RATES
HP
Attack
Defense
Sp. Atk
Sp. Def
Speed

ITEMS SOMETIMES HELD BY WILD POKÉMON
Power Herb

EVOLUTION

Seedot → Lv. 14 → Nuzleaf → Leaf Stone → Shiftry

MAIN WAYS TO REGISTER IN THE NATIONAL POKÉDEX

Ω Catch on Route 114.

α Bring it to your game using Link Trade or the GTS.

Damage taken in normal battles

Type	×	Type	×
Normal	×1	Flying	×2
Fire	×2	Psychic	×0
Water	×0.5	Bug	×4
Grass	×0.5	Rock	×1
Electric	×0.5	Ghost	×0.5
Ice	×2	Dragon	×1
Fighting	×2	Dark	×0.5
Poison	×2	Steel	×1
Ground	×0.5	Fairy	×2

Damage taken in Inverse battles

Type	×	Type	×
Normal	×1	Flying	×0.5
Fire	×0.5	Psychic	×2
Water	×2	Bug	×0.25
Grass	×2	Rock	×1
Electric	×2	Ghost	×2
Ice	×0.5	Dragon	×1
Fighting	×0.5	Dark	×2
Poison	×0.5	Steel	×1
Ground	×2	Fairy	×0.5

Can be used in
- Inverse Battle
- Battle Institute
- Battle Maison
- Random Matchup (Free Battle)
- Random Matchup (Others)

LEVEL-UP MOVES

Lv.	Name	Type	Kind	Pow.	Acc.	PP	Range
1	Pound	Normal	Physical	40	100	35	Normal
3	Harden	Normal	Status	—	—	30	Self
6	Growth	Normal	Status	—	—	20	Self
9	Nature Power	Normal	Status	—	—	20	Normal
12	Fake Out	Normal	Physical	40	100	10	Normal
14	Razor Leaf	Grass	Physical	55	95	25	Many Others
16	Torment	Dark	Status	—	100	15	Normal
20	Razor Wind	Normal	Special	80	100	10	Many Others
24	Feint Attack	Dark	Physical	60	—	20	Normal
28	Leaf Blade	Grass	Physical	90	100	15	Normal
32	Swagger	Normal	Status	—	90	15	Normal
36	Extrasensory	Psychic	Special	80	100	20	Normal

TM & HM MOVES

No.	Name	Type	Kind	Pow.	Acc.	PP	Range
TM06	Toxic	Poison	Status	—	90	10	Normal
TM10	Hidden Power	Normal	Special	60	100	15	Normal
TM11	Sunny Day	Fire	Status	—	—	5	Both Sides
TM15	Hyper Beam	Normal	Special	150	90	5	Normal
TM17	Protect	Normal	Status	—	—	10	Self
TM21	Frustration	Normal	Physical	—	100	20	Normal
TM22	Solar Beam	Grass	Special	120	100	10	Normal
TM27	Return	Normal	Physical	—	100	20	Normal
TM28	Dig	Ground	Physical	80	100	10	Normal
TM30	Shadow Ball	Ghost	Special	80	100	15	Normal
TM31	Brick Break	Fighting	Physical	75	100	15	Normal
TM32	Double Team	Normal	Status	—	—	15	Self
TM39	Rock Tomb	Rock	Physical	60	95	15	Normal
TM41	Torment	Dark	Status	—	100	15	Normal
TM42	Facade	Normal	Physical	70	100	20	Normal
TM44	Rest	Psychic	Status	—	—	10	Self
TM45	Attract	Normal	Status	—	100	15	Normal
TM46	Thief	Dark	Physical	60	100	25	Normal
TM47	Low Sweep	Fighting	Physical	65	100	20	Normal
TM48	Round	Normal	Special	60	100	15	Normal
TM53	Energy Ball	Grass	Special	90	100	10	Normal
TM54	False Swipe	Normal	Physical	40	100	40	Normal
TM56	Fling	Dark	Physical	—	100	10	Normal
TM63	Embargo	Dark	Status	—	100	15	Normal
TM64	Explosion	Normal	Physical	250	100	5	Adjacent
TM66	Payback	Dark	Physical	50	100	10	Normal
TM67	Retaliate	Normal	Physical	70	100	5	Normal
TM70	Flash	Normal	Status	—	100	20	Normal
TM75	Swords Dance	Normal	Status	—	—	20	Self
TM77	Psych Up	Normal	Status	—	—	10	Normal
TM80	Rock Slide	Rock	Physical	75	90	10	Many Others
TM86	Grass Knot	Grass	Special	—	100	20	Normal
TM87	Swagger	Normal	Status	—	90	15	Normal
TM88	Sleep Talk	Normal	Status	—	—	10	Self
TM90	Substitute	Normal	Status	—	—	10	Self
TM94	Secret Power	Normal	Physical	70	100	20	Normal
TM95	Snarl	Dark	Special	55	95	15	Many Others
TM96	Nature Power	Normal	Status	—	—	20	Normal
TM97	Dark Pulse	Dark	Special	80	100	15	Normal
TM98	Power-Up Punch	Fighting	Physical	40	100	20	Normal
TM100	Confide	Normal	Status	—	—	20	Normal
HM01	Cut	Normal	Physical	50	95	30	Normal
HM04	Strength	Normal	Physical	80	100	15	Normal
HM06	Rock Smash	Fighting	Physical	40	100	15	Normal

MOVES LEARNED IN EXCHANGE FOR BP

Name	Type	Kind	Pow.	Acc.	PP	Range
Seed Bomb	Grass	Physical	80	100	15	Normal
Low Kick	Fighting	Physical	—	100	20	Normal
Foul Play	Dark	Physical	95	100	15	Normal
Snore	Normal	Special	50	100	15	Normal
Synthesis	Grass	Status	—	—	5	Self
Giga Drain	Grass	Special	75	100	10	Normal
Worry Seed	Grass	Status	—	100	10	Normal
Spite	Ghost	Status	—	100	10	Normal

MOVES TAUGHT BY PEOPLE

Name	Type	Kind	Pow.	Acc.	PP	Range

National Pokédex **275** Hoenn Pokédex **024**

Shiftry

Wicked Pokémon

Grass | Dark

HEIGHT: 4'03" WEIGHT: 131.4 lbs.

The male has larger leaves on its hands. The female has smaller leaves on its hands.

Ω Shiftry is a mysterious Pokémon that is said to live atop towering trees dating back over a thousand years. It creates terrific windstorms with the fans it holds.

α Shiftry's large fans generate awesome gusts of wind at a speed close to 100 feet per second. The whipped-up wind blows anything away. This Pokémon chooses to live quietly deep in forests.

ABILITIES
Chlorophyll
Early Bird

HIDDEN ABILITY
Pickpocket

EGG GROUPS
Field | Grass

STAT GROWTH RATES
HP
Attack
Defense
Sp. Atk
Sp. Def
Speed

ITEMS SOMETIMES HELD BY WILD POKÉMON
—

EVOLUTION

Seedot → Lv. 14 → Nuzleaf → Leaf Stone → Shiftry

MAIN WAYS TO REGISTER IN THE NATIONAL POKÉDEX

Ω Use a Leaf Stone on Nuzleaf.

α Bring it to your game using Link Trade or the GTS.

Damage taken in normal battles

Type	×	Type	×
Normal	×1	Flying	×2
Fire	×2	Psychic	×0
Water	×0.5	Bug	×4
Grass	×0.5	Rock	×1
Electric	×0.5	Ghost	×0.5
Ice	×2	Dragon	×1
Fighting	×2	Dark	×0.5
Poison	×2	Steel	×1
Ground	×0.5	Fairy	×2

Damage taken in Inverse battles

Type	×	Type	×
Normal	×1	Flying	×0.5
Fire	×0.5	Psychic	×2
Water	×2	Bug	×0.25
Grass	×2	Rock	×1
Electric	×2	Ghost	×2
Ice	×0.5	Dragon	×1
Fighting	×0.5	Dark	×2
Poison	×0.5	Steel	×1
Ground	×2	Fairy	×0.5

Can be used in
- Inverse Battle
- Battle Institute
- Battle Maison
- Random Matchup (Free Battle)
- Random Matchup (Others)

LEVEL-UP MOVES

Lv.	Name	Type	Kind	Pow.	Acc.	PP	Range
1	Razor Leaf	Grass	Physical	55	95	25	Many Others
1	Feint Attack	Dark	Physical	60	—	20	Normal
1	Whirlwind	Normal	Status	—	—	20	Normal
1	Nasty Plot	Dark	Status	—	—	20	Self
20	Leaf Tornado	Grass	Special	65	90	10	Normal
32	Hurricane	Flying	Special	110	70	10	Normal
44	Leaf Storm	Grass	Special	130	90	5	Normal

TM & HM MOVES

No.	Name	Type	Kind	Pow.	Acc.	PP	Range
TM06	Toxic	Poison	Status	—	90	10	Normal
TM10	Hidden Power	Normal	Special	60	100	15	Normal
TM11	Sunny Day	Fire	Status	—	—	5	Both Sides
TM15	Hyper Beam	Normal	Special	150	90	5	Normal
TM17	Protect	Normal	Status	—	—	10	Self
TM21	Frustration	Normal	Physical	—	100	20	Normal
TM22	Solar Beam	Grass	Special	120	100	10	Normal
TM27	Return	Normal	Physical	—	100	20	Normal
TM28	Dig	Ground	Physical	80	100	10	Normal
TM30	Shadow Ball	Ghost	Special	80	100	15	Normal
TM31	Brick Break	Fighting	Physical	75	100	15	Normal
TM32	Double Team	Normal	Status	—	—	15	Self
TM39	Rock Tomb	Rock	Physical	60	95	15	Normal
TM40	Aerial Ace	Flying	Physical	60	—	20	Normal
TM41	Torment	Dark	Status	—	100	15	Normal
TM42	Facade	Normal	Physical	70	100	20	Normal
TM44	Rest	Psychic	Status	—	—	10	Self
TM45	Attract	Normal	Status	—	100	15	Normal
TM46	Thief	Dark	Physical	60	100	25	Normal
TM47	Low Sweep	Fighting	Physical	65	100	20	Normal
TM48	Round	Normal	Special	60	100	15	Normal
TM52	Focus Blast	Fighting	Special	120	70	5	Normal
TM53	Energy Ball	Grass	Special	90	100	10	Normal
TM54	False Swipe	Normal	Physical	40	100	40	Normal
TM56	Fling	Dark	Physical	—	100	10	Normal
TM63	Embargo	Dark	Status	—	100	15	Normal
TM64	Explosion	Normal	Physical	250	100	5	Adjacent
TM66	Payback	Dark	Physical	50	100	10	Normal
TM67	Retaliate	Normal	Physical	70	100	5	Normal
TM68	Giga Impact	Normal	Physical	150	90	5	Normal
TM70	Flash	Normal	Status	—	100	20	Normal
TM75	Swords Dance	Normal	Status	—	—	20	Self
TM77	Psych Up	Normal	Status	—	—	10	Normal
TM80	Rock Slide	Rock	Physical	75	90	10	Many Others
TM81	X-Scissor	Bug	Physical	80	100	15	Normal
TM86	Grass Knot	Grass	Special	—	100	20	Normal
TM87	Swagger	Normal	Status	—	90	15	Normal
TM88	Sleep Talk	Normal	Status	—	—	10	Self
TM90	Substitute	Normal	Status	—	—	10	Self
TM94	Secret Power	Normal	Physical	70	100	20	Normal
TM95	Snarl	Dark	Special	55	95	15	Many Others
TM96	Nature Power	Normal	Status	—	—	20	Normal
TM97	Dark Pulse	Dark	Special	80	100	15	Normal
TM98	Power-Up Punch	Fighting	Physical	40	100	20	Normal
TM100	Confide	Normal	Status	—	—	20	Normal
HM01	Cut	Normal	Physical	50	95	30	Normal
HM04	Strength	Normal	Physical	80	100	15	Normal
HM06	Rock Smash	Fighting	Physical	40	100	15	Normal

MOVES LEARNED IN EXCHANGE FOR BP

Name	Type	Kind	Pow.	Acc.	PP	Range
Seed Bomb	Grass	Physical	80	100	15	Normal
Bounce	Flying	Physical	85	85	5	Normal
Low Kick	Fighting	Physical	—	100	20	Normal
Foul Play	Dark	Physical	95	100	15	Normal
Icy Wind	Ice	Special	55	95	15	Many Others
Snore	Normal	Special	50	100	15	Normal
Knock Off	Dark	Physical	65	100	20	Normal
Synthesis	Grass	Status	—	—	5	Self
Tailwind	Flying	Status	—	—	15	Your Side
Giga Drain	Grass	Special	75	100	10	Normal
Worry Seed	Grass	Status	—	100	10	Normal
Spite	Ghost	Status	—	100	10	Normal

MOVES TAUGHT BY PEOPLE

Name	Type	Kind	Pow.	Acc.	PP	Range

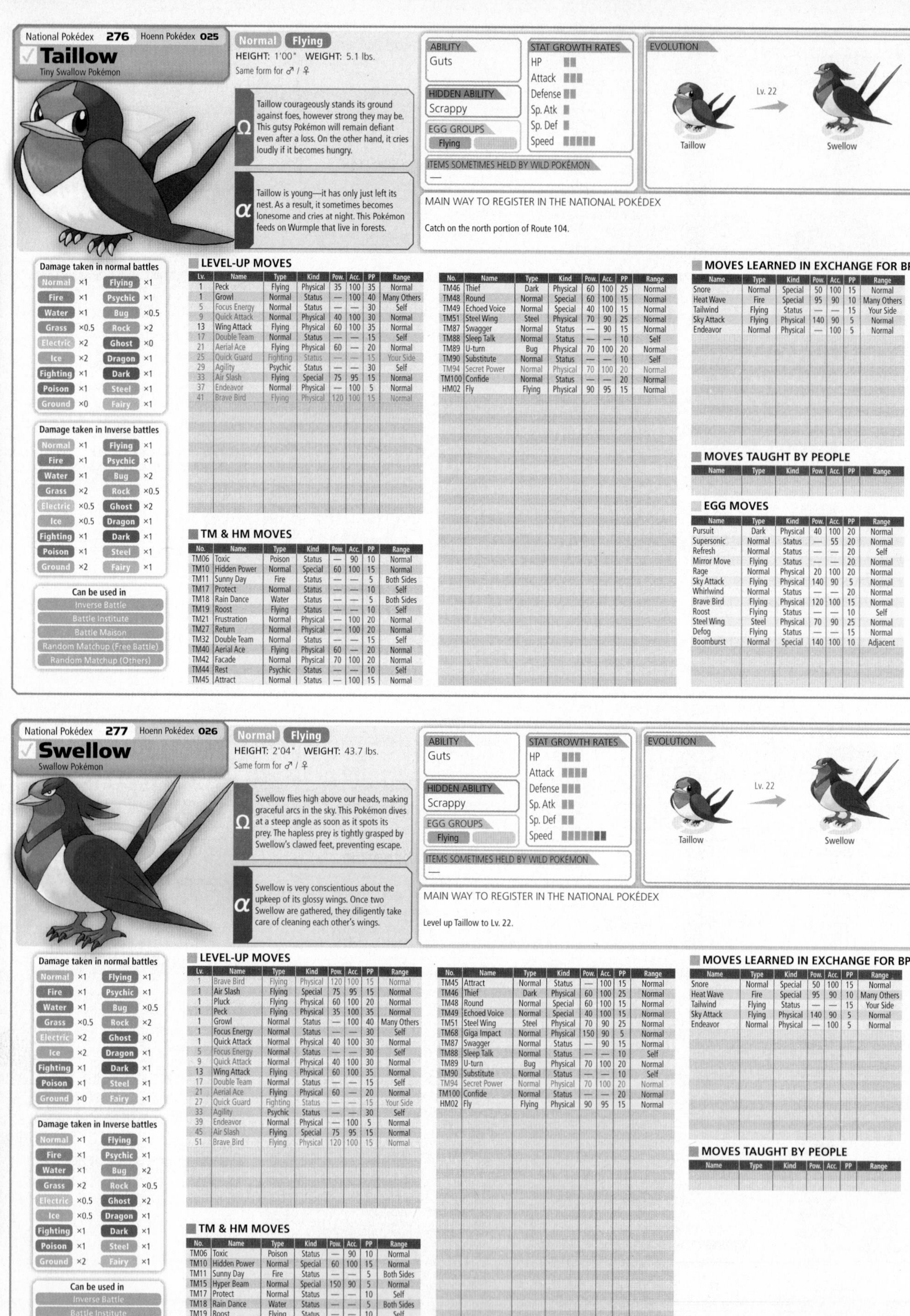

National Pokédex **276** Hoenn Pokédex **025**

Taillow

Tiny Swallow Pokémon

Normal | Flying

HEIGHT: 1'00" WEIGHT: 5.1 lbs.

Same form for ♂ / ♀

Ω Taillow courageously stands its ground against foes, however strong they may be. This gutsy Pokémon will remain defiant even after a loss. On the other hand, it cries loudly if it becomes hungry.

α Taillow is young—it has only just left its nest. As a result, it sometimes becomes lonesome and cries at night. This Pokémon feeds on Wurmple that live in forests.

ABILITY
Guts

HIDDEN ABILITY
Scrappy

EGG GROUPS
Flying

STAT GROWTH RATES
HP
Attack
Defense
Sp. Atk
Sp. Def
Speed

ITEMS SOMETIMES HELD BY WILD POKÉMON
—

EVOLUTION
Taillow → Lv. 22 → Swellow

MAIN WAY TO REGISTER IN THE NATIONAL POKÉDEX

Catch on the north portion of Route 104.

Damage taken in normal battles

Type		Type	
Normal	×1	Flying	×1
Fire	×1	Psychic	×1
Water	×1	Bug	×0.5
Grass	×0.5	Rock	×2
Electric	×2	Ghost	×0
Ice	×2	Dragon	×1
Fighting	×1	Dark	×1
Poison	×1	Steel	×1
Ground	×0	Fairy	×1

Damage taken in Inverse battles

Type		Type	
Normal	×1	Flying	×1
Fire	×1	Psychic	×1
Water	×1	Bug	×2
Grass	×2	Rock	×0.5
Electric	×0.5	Ghost	×2
Ice	×0.5	Dragon	×1
Fighting	×1	Dark	×1
Poison	×1	Steel	×1
Ground	×2	Fairy	×1

Can be used in
Inverse Battle
Battle Institute
Battle Maison
Random Matchup (Free Battle)
Random Matchup (Others)

LEVEL-UP MOVES

Lv.	Name	Type	Kind	Pow.	Acc.	PP	Range
1	Peck	Flying	Physical	35	100	35	Normal
1	Growl	Normal	Status	—	100	40	Many Others
5	Focus Energy	Normal	Status	—	—	30	Self
9	Quick Attack	Normal	Physical	40	100	30	Normal
13	Wing Attack	Flying	Physical	60	100	35	Normal
17	Double Team	Normal	Status	—	—	15	Self
21	Aerial Ace	Flying	Physical	60	—	20	Normal
25	Quick Guard	Fighting	Status	—	—	15	Your Side
29	Agility	Psychic	Status	—	—	30	Self
33	Air Slash	Flying	Special	75	95	15	Normal
37	Endeavor	Normal	Physical	—	100	5	Normal
41	Brave Bird	Flying	Physical	120	100	15	Normal

TM & HM MOVES

No.	Name	Type	Kind	Pow.	Acc.	PP	Range
TM06	Toxic	Poison	Status	—	90	10	Normal
TM10	Hidden Power	Normal	Special	60	100	15	Normal
TM11	Sunny Day	Fire	Status	—	—	5	Both Sides
TM17	Protect	Normal	Status	—	—	10	Self
TM18	Rain Dance	Water	Status	—	—	5	Both Sides
TM19	Roost	Flying	Status	—	—	10	Self
TM21	Frustration	Normal	Physical	—	100	20	Normal
TM27	Return	Normal	Physical	—	100	20	Normal
TM32	Double Team	Normal	Status	—	—	15	Self
TM40	Aerial Ace	Flying	Physical	60	—	20	Normal
TM42	Facade	Normal	Physical	70	100	20	Normal
TM44	Rest	Psychic	Status	—	—	10	Self
TM45	Attract	Normal	Status	—	100	15	Normal
TM46	Thief	Dark	Physical	60	100	25	Normal
TM48	Round	Normal	Special	60	100	15	Normal
TM49	Echoed Voice	Normal	Special	40	100	15	Normal
TM51	Steel Wing	Steel	Physical	70	90	25	Normal
TM87	Swagger	Normal	Status	—	90	15	Normal
TM88	Sleep Talk	Normal	Status	—	—	10	Self
TM89	U-turn	Bug	Physical	70	100	20	Normal
TM90	Substitute	Normal	Status	—	—	10	Self
TM94	Secret Power	Normal	Physical	70	100	20	Normal
TM100	Confide	Normal	Status	—	—	20	Normal
HM02	Fly	Flying	Physical	90	95	15	Normal

MOVES LEARNED IN EXCHANGE FOR BP

Name	Type	Kind	Pow.	Acc.	PP	Range
Snore	Normal	Special	50	100	15	Normal
Heat Wave	Fire	Special	95	90	10	Many Others
Tailwind	Flying	Status	—	—	15	Your Side
Sky Attack	Flying	Physical	140	90	5	Normal
Endeavor	Normal	Physical	—	100	5	Normal

MOVES TAUGHT BY PEOPLE

Name	Type	Kind	Pow.	Acc.	PP	Range

EGG MOVES

Name	Type	Kind	Pow.	Acc.	PP	Range
Pursuit	Dark	Physical	40	100	20	Normal
Supersonic	Normal	Status	—	55	20	Normal
Refresh	Normal	Status	—	—	20	Self
Mirror Move	Flying	Status	—	—	20	Normal
Rage	Normal	Physical	20	100	20	Normal
Sky Attack	Flying	Physical	140	90	5	Normal
Whirlwind	Normal	Status	—	—	20	Normal
Brave Bird	Flying	Physical	120	100	15	Normal
Roost	Flying	Status	—	—	10	Self
Steel Wing	Steel	Physical	70	90	25	Normal
Defog	Flying	Status	—	—	15	Normal
Boomburst	Normal	Special	140	100	10	Adjacent

National Pokédex **277** Hoenn Pokédex **026**

Swellow

Swallow Pokémon

Normal | Flying

HEIGHT: 2'04" WEIGHT: 43.7 lbs.

Same form for ♂ / ♀

Ω Swellow flies high above our heads, making graceful arcs in the sky. This Pokémon dives at a steep angle as soon as it spots its prey. The hapless prey is tightly grasped by Swellow's clawed feet, preventing escape.

α Swellow is very conscientious about the upkeep of its glossy wings. Once two Swellow are gathered, they diligently take care of cleaning each other's wings.

ABILITY
Guts

HIDDEN ABILITY
Scrappy

EGG GROUPS
Flying

STAT GROWTH RATES
HP
Attack
Defense
Sp. Atk
Sp. Def
Speed

ITEMS SOMETIMES HELD BY WILD POKÉMON
—

EVOLUTION
Taillow → Lv. 22 → Swellow

MAIN WAY TO REGISTER IN THE NATIONAL POKÉDEX

Level up Taillow to Lv. 22.

Damage taken in normal battles

Type		Type	
Normal	×1	Flying	×1
Fire	×1	Psychic	×1
Water	×1	Bug	×0.5
Grass	×0.5	Rock	×2
Electric	×2	Ghost	×0
Ice	×2	Dragon	×1
Fighting	×1	Dark	×1
Poison	×1	Steel	×1
Ground	×0	Fairy	×1

Damage taken in Inverse battles

Type		Type	
Normal	×1	Flying	×1
Fire	×1	Psychic	×1
Water	×1	Bug	×2
Grass	×2	Rock	×0.5
Electric	×0.5	Ghost	×2
Ice	×0.5	Dragon	×1
Fighting	×1	Dark	×1
Poison	×1	Steel	×1
Ground	×2	Fairy	×1

Can be used in
Inverse Battle
Battle Institute
Battle Maison
Random Matchup (Free Battle)
Random Matchup (Others)

LEVEL-UP MOVES

Lv.	Name	Type	Kind	Pow.	Acc.	PP	Range
1	Brave Bird	Flying	Physical	120	100	15	Normal
1	Air Slash	Flying	Special	75	95	15	Normal
1	Pluck	Flying	Physical	60	100	20	Normal
1	Peck	Flying	Physical	35	100	35	Normal
1	Growl	Normal	Status	—	100	40	Many Others
1	Focus Energy	Normal	Status	—	—	30	Self
1	Quick Attack	Normal	Physical	40	100	30	Normal
5	Focus Energy	Normal	Status	—	—	30	Self
9	Quick Attack	Normal	Physical	40	100	30	Normal
13	Wing Attack	Flying	Physical	60	100	35	Normal
17	Double Team	Normal	Status	—	—	15	Self
21	Aerial Ace	Flying	Physical	60	—	20	Normal
27	Quick Guard	Fighting	Status	—	—	15	Your Side
33	Agility	Psychic	Status	—	—	30	Self
39	Endeavor	Normal	Physical	—	100	5	Normal
45	Air Slash	Flying	Special	75	95	15	Normal
51	Brave Bird	Flying	Physical	120	100	15	Normal

TM & HM MOVES

No.	Name	Type	Kind	Pow.	Acc.	PP	Range
TM06	Toxic	Poison	Status	—	90	10	Normal
TM10	Hidden Power	Normal	Special	60	100	15	Normal
TM11	Sunny Day	Fire	Status	—	—	5	Both Sides
TM15	Hyper Beam	Normal	Special	150	90	5	Normal
TM17	Protect	Normal	Status	—	—	10	Self
TM18	Rain Dance	Water	Status	—	—	5	Both Sides
TM19	Roost	Flying	Status	—	—	10	Self
TM21	Frustration	Normal	Physical	—	100	20	Normal
TM27	Return	Normal	Physical	—	100	20	Normal
TM32	Double Team	Normal	Status	—	—	15	Self
TM40	Aerial Ace	Flying	Physical	60	—	20	Normal
TM42	Facade	Normal	Physical	70	100	20	Normal
TM44	Rest	Psychic	Status	—	—	10	Self
TM45	Attract	Normal	Status	—	100	15	Normal
TM46	Thief	Dark	Physical	60	100	25	Normal
TM48	Round	Normal	Special	60	100	15	Normal
TM49	Echoed Voice	Normal	Special	40	100	15	Normal
TM51	Steel Wing	Steel	Physical	70	90	25	Normal
TM68	Giga Impact	Normal	Physical	150	90	5	Normal
TM87	Swagger	Normal	Status	—	90	15	Normal
TM88	Sleep Talk	Normal	Status	—	—	10	Self
TM89	U-turn	Bug	Physical	70	100	20	Normal
TM90	Substitute	Normal	Status	—	—	10	Self
TM94	Secret Power	Normal	Physical	70	100	20	Normal
TM100	Confide	Normal	Status	—	—	20	Normal
HM02	Fly	Flying	Physical	90	95	15	Normal

MOVES LEARNED IN EXCHANGE FOR BP

Name	Type	Kind	Pow.	Acc.	PP	Range
Snore	Normal	Special	50	100	15	Normal
Heat Wave	Fire	Special	95	90	10	Many Others
Tailwind	Flying	Status	—	—	15	Your Side
Sky Attack	Flying	Physical	140	90	5	Normal
Endeavor	Normal	Physical	—	100	5	Normal

MOVES TAUGHT BY PEOPLE

Name	Type	Kind	Pow.	Acc.	PP	Range

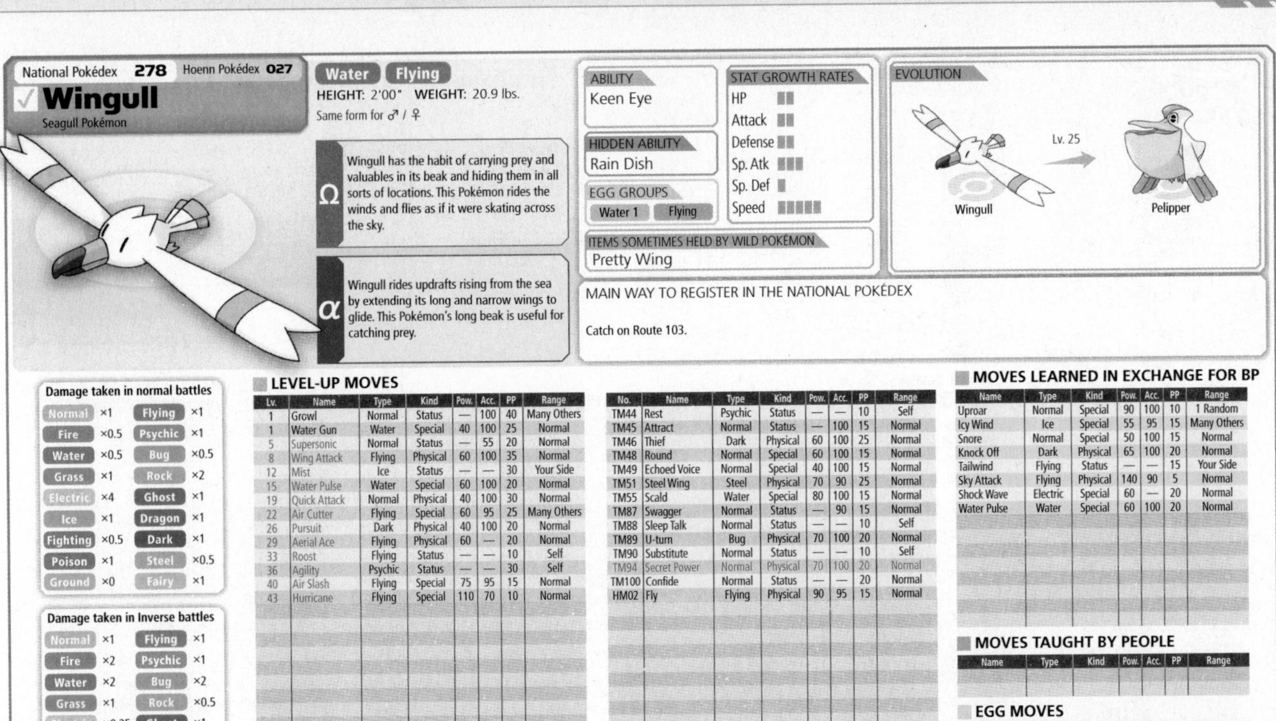

National Pokédex **278** Hoenn Pokédex **027**

Wingull

Seagull Pokémon

Water **Flying**

HEIGHT: 2'00" WEIGHT: 20.9 lbs.

Same form for ♂ / ♀

Ω Wingull has the habit of carrying prey and valuables in its beak and hiding them in all sorts of locations. This Pokémon rides the winds and flies as if it were skating across the sky.

α Wingull rides updrafts rising from the sea by extending its long and narrow wings to glide. This Pokémon's long beak is useful for catching prey.

ABILITY
Keen Eye

HIDDEN ABILITY
Rain Dish

EGG GROUPS
Water 1 | Flying

STAT GROWTH RATES
HP / Attack / Defense / Sp. Atk / Sp. Def / Speed

ITEMS SOMETIMES HELD BY WILD POKÉMON
Pretty Wing

EVOLUTION
Wingull → Lv. 25 → Pelipper

MAIN WAY TO REGISTER IN THE NATIONAL POKÉDEX

Catch on Route 103.

Damage taken in normal battles

Type	×	Type	×
Normal	×1	Flying	×1
Fire	×0.5	Psychic	×1
Water	×0.5	Bug	×0.5
Grass	×1	Rock	×2
Electric	×4	Ghost	×1
Ice	×1	Dragon	×1
Fighting	×0.5	Dark	×1
Poison	×1	Steel	×0.5
Ground	×0	Fairy	×1

Damage taken in Inverse battles

Type	×	Type	×
Normal	×1	Flying	×1
Fire	×2	Psychic	×1
Water	×2	Bug	×2
Grass	×1	Rock	×0.5
Electric	×0.25	Ghost	×1
Ice	×1	Dragon	×1
Fighting	×2	Dark	×1
Poison	×1	Steel	×2
Ground	×2	Fairy	×1

Can be used in
Inverse Battle
Battle Institute
Battle Maison
Random Matchup (Free Battle)
Random Matchup (Others)

LEVEL-UP MOVES

Lv.	Name	Type	Kind	Pow.	Acc.	PP	Range
1	Growl	Normal	Status	—	100	40	Many Others
1	Water Gun	Water	Special	40	100	25	Normal
5	Supersonic	Normal	Status	—	55	20	Normal
8	Wing Attack	Flying	Physical	60	100	35	Normal
12	Mist	Ice	Status	—	—	30	Your Side
15	Water Pulse	Water	Special	60	100	20	Normal
19	Quick Attack	Normal	Physical	40	100	30	Normal
22	Air Cutter	Flying	Special	60	95	25	Many Others
26	Pursuit	Dark	Physical	40	100	20	Normal
29	Aerial Ace	Flying	Physical	60	—	20	Normal
33	Roost	Flying	Status	—	—	10	Self
36	Agility	Psychic	Status	—	—	30	Self
40	Air Slash	Flying	Special	75	95	15	Normal
43	Hurricane	Flying	Special	110	70	10	Normal

TM & HM MOVES

No.	Name	Type	Kind	Pow.	Acc.	PP	Range
TM06	Toxic	Poison	Status	—	90	10	Normal
TM07	Hail	Ice	Status	—	—	10	Both Sides
TM10	Hidden Power	Normal	Special	60	100	15	Normal
TM13	Ice Beam	Ice	Special	90	100	10	Normal
TM14	Blizzard	Ice	Special	110	70	5	Many Others
TM17	Protect	Normal	Status	—	—	10	Self
TM18	Rain Dance	Water	Status	—	—	5	Both Sides
TM19	Roost	Flying	Status	—	—	10	Self
TM21	Frustration	Normal	Physical	—	100	20	Normal
TM27	Return	Normal	Physical	—	100	20	Normal
TM32	Double Team	Normal	Status	—	—	15	Self
TM40	Aerial Ace	Flying	Physical	60	—	20	Normal
TM42	Facade	Normal	Physical	70	100	20	Normal
TM44	Rest	Psychic	Status	—	—	10	Self
TM45	Attract	Normal	Status	—	100	15	Normal
TM46	Thief	Dark	Physical	60	100	25	Normal
TM48	Round	Normal	Special	60	100	15	Normal
TM49	Echoed Voice	Normal	Special	40	100	15	Normal
TM51	Steel Wing	Steel	Physical	70	90	25	Normal
TM55	Scald	Water	Special	80	100	15	Normal
TM87	Swagger	Normal	Status	—	90	15	Normal
TM88	Sleep Talk	Normal	Status	—	—	10	Self
TM89	U-turn	Bug	Physical	70	100	20	Normal
TM90	Substitute	Normal	Status	—	—	10	Self
TM94	Secret Power	Normal	Physical	70	100	20	Normal
TM100	Confide	Normal	Status	—	—	20	Normal
HM02	Fly	Flying	Physical	90	95	15	Normal

MOVES LEARNED IN EXCHANGE FOR BP

Name	Type	Kind	Pow.	Acc.	PP	Range
Uproar	Normal	Special	90	100	10	1 Random
Icy Wind	Ice	Special	55	95	15	Many Others
Snore	Normal	Special	50	100	15	Normal
Knock Off	Dark	Physical	65	100	20	Normal
Tailwind	Flying	Status	—	—	15	Your Side
Sky Attack	Flying	Physical	140	90	5	Normal
Shock Wave	Electric	Special	60	—	20	Normal
Water Pulse	Water	Special	60	100	20	Normal

MOVES TAUGHT BY PEOPLE

Name	Type	Kind	Pow.	Acc.	PP	Range

EGG MOVES

Name	Type	Kind	Pow.	Acc.	PP	Range
Mist	Ice	Status	—	—	30	Your Side
Twister	Dragon	Special	40	100	20	Many Others
Agility	Psychic	Status	—	—	30	Self
Gust	Flying	Special	40	100	35	Normal
Water Sport	Water	Status	—	—	15	Both Sides
Aqua Ring	Water	Status	—	—	20	Self
Knock Off	Dark	Physical	65	100	20	Normal
Brine	Water	Special	65	100	10	Normal
Roost	Flying	Status	—	—	10	Self
Soak	Water	Status	—	100	20	Normal
Wide Guard	Rock	Status	—	—	10	Your Side

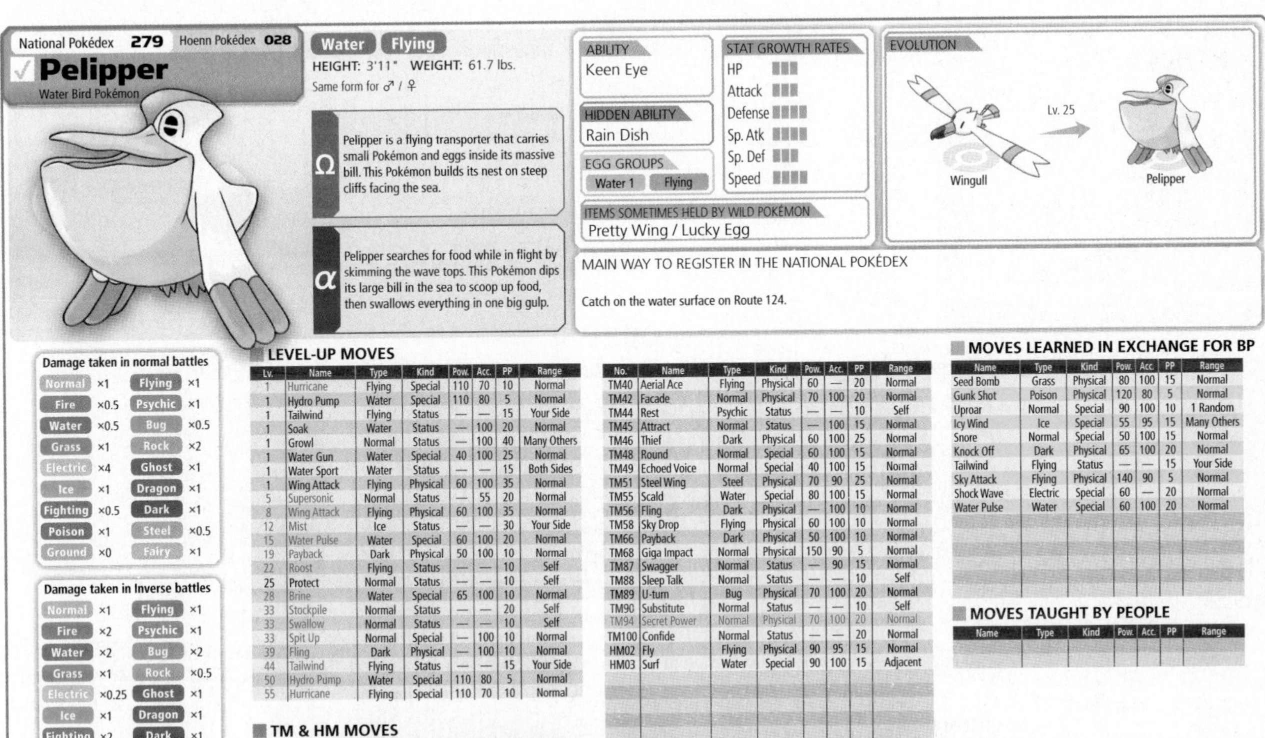

National Pokédex **279** Hoenn Pokédex **028**

Pelipper

Water Bird Pokémon

Water **Flying**

HEIGHT: 3'11" WEIGHT: 61.7 lbs.

Same form for ♂ / ♀

Ω Pelipper is a flying transporter that carries small Pokémon and eggs inside its massive bill. This Pokémon builds its nest on steep cliffs facing the sea.

α Pelipper searches for food while in flight by skimming the wave tops. This Pokémon dips its large bill in the sea to scoop up food, then swallows everything in one big gulp.

ABILITY
Keen Eye

HIDDEN ABILITY
Rain Dish

EGG GROUPS
Water 1 | Flying

STAT GROWTH RATES
HP / Attack / Defense / Sp. Atk / Sp. Def / Speed

ITEMS SOMETIMES HELD BY WILD POKÉMON
Pretty Wing / Lucky Egg

EVOLUTION
Wingull → Lv. 25 → Pelipper

MAIN WAY TO REGISTER IN THE NATIONAL POKÉDEX

Catch on the water surface on Route 124.

Damage taken in normal battles

Type	×	Type	×
Normal	×1	Flying	×1
Fire	×0.5	Psychic	×1
Water	×0.5	Bug	×0.5
Grass	×1	Rock	×2
Electric	×4	Ghost	×1
Ice	×1	Dragon	×1
Fighting	×0.5	Dark	×1
Poison	×1	Steel	×0.5
Ground	×0	Fairy	×1

Damage taken in Inverse battles

Type	×	Type	×
Normal	×1	Flying	×1
Fire	×2	Psychic	×1
Water	×2	Bug	×2
Grass	×1	Rock	×0.5
Electric	×0.25	Ghost	×1
Ice	×1	Dragon	×1
Fighting	×2	Dark	×1
Poison	×1	Steel	×2
Ground	×2	Fairy	×1

Can be used in
Inverse Battle
Battle Institute
Battle Maison
Random Matchup (Free Battle)
Random Matchup (Others)

LEVEL-UP MOVES

Lv.	Name	Type	Kind	Pow.	Acc.	PP	Range
1	Hurricane	Flying	Special	110	70	10	Normal
1	Hydro Pump	Water	Special	110	80	5	Normal
1	Tailwind	Flying	Status	—	—	15	Your Side
1	Soak	Water	Status	—	100	20	Normal
1	Growl	Normal	Status	—	100	40	Many Others
1	Water Gun	Water	Special	40	100	25	Normal
1	Water Sport	Water	Status	—	—	15	Both Sides
1	Wing Attack	Flying	Physical	60	100	35	Normal
5	Supersonic	Normal	Status	—	55	20	Normal
8	Wing Attack	Flying	Physical	60	100	35	Normal
12	Mist	Ice	Status	—	—	30	Your Side
15	Water Pulse	Water	Special	60	100	20	Normal
19	Payback	Dark	Physical	50	100	10	Normal
22	Roost	Flying	Status	—	—	10	Self
25	Protect	Normal	Status	—	—	10	Self
28	Brine	Water	Special	65	100	10	Normal
33	Stockpile	Normal	Status	—	—	20	Self
33	Swallow	Normal	Status	—	—	10	Self
33	Spit Up	Normal	Special	—	100	10	Normal
39	Fling	Dark	Physical	—	100	10	Normal
44	Tailwind	Flying	Status	—	—	15	Your Side
50	Hydro Pump	Water	Special	110	80	5	Normal
55	Hurricane	Flying	Special	110	70	10	Normal

TM & HM MOVES

No.	Name	Type	Kind	Pow.	Acc.	PP	Range
TM06	Toxic	Poison	Status	—	90	10	Normal
TM07	Hail	Ice	Status	—	—	10	Both Sides
TM10	Hidden Power	Normal	Special	60	100	15	Normal
TM13	Ice Beam	Ice	Special	90	100	10	Normal
TM14	Blizzard	Ice	Special	110	70	5	Many Others
TM15	Hyper Beam	Normal	Special	150	90	5	Normal
TM17	Protect	Normal	Status	—	—	10	Self
TM18	Rain Dance	Water	Status	—	—	5	Both Sides
TM19	Roost	Flying	Status	—	—	10	Self
TM21	Frustration	Normal	Physical	—	100	20	Normal
TM27	Return	Normal	Physical	—	100	20	Normal
TM32	Double Team	Normal	Status	—	—	15	Self
TM40	Aerial Ace	Flying	Physical	60	—	20	Normal
TM42	Facade	Normal	Physical	70	100	20	Normal
TM44	Rest	Psychic	Status	—	—	10	Self
TM45	Attract	Normal	Status	—	100	15	Normal
TM46	Thief	Dark	Physical	60	100	25	Normal
TM48	Round	Normal	Special	60	100	15	Normal
TM49	Echoed Voice	Normal	Special	40	100	15	Normal
TM51	Steel Wing	Steel	Physical	70	90	25	Normal
TM55	Scald	Water	Special	80	100	15	Normal
TM56	Fling	Dark	Physical	—	100	10	Normal
TM58	Sky Drop	Flying	Physical	60	100	10	Normal
TM66	Payback	Dark	Physical	50	100	10	Normal
TM68	Giga Impact	Normal	Physical	150	90	5	Normal
TM87	Swagger	Normal	Status	—	90	15	Normal
TM88	Sleep Talk	Normal	Status	—	—	10	Self
TM89	U-turn	Bug	Physical	70	100	20	Normal
TM90	Substitute	Normal	Status	—	—	10	Self
TM94	Secret Power	Normal	Physical	70	100	20	Normal
TM100	Confide	Normal	Status	—	—	20	Normal
HM02	Fly	Flying	Physical	90	95	15	Normal
HM03	Surf	Water	Special	90	100	15	Adjacent

MOVES LEARNED IN EXCHANGE FOR BP

Name	Type	Kind	Pow.	Acc.	PP	Range
Seed Bomb	Grass	Physical	80	100	15	Normal
Gunk Shot	Poison	Physical	120	80	5	Normal
Uproar	Normal	Special	90	100	10	1 Random
Icy Wind	Ice	Special	55	95	15	Many Others
Snore	Normal	Special	50	100	15	Normal
Knock Off	Dark	Physical	65	100	20	Normal
Tailwind	Flying	Status	—	—	15	Your Side
Sky Attack	Flying	Physical	140	90	5	Normal
Shock Wave	Electric	Special	60	—	20	Normal
Water Pulse	Water	Special	60	100	20	Normal

MOVES TAUGHT BY PEOPLE

Name	Type	Kind	Pow.	Acc.	PP	Range

National Pokédex **280** Hoenn Pokédex **029**

Ralts

Feeling Pokémon

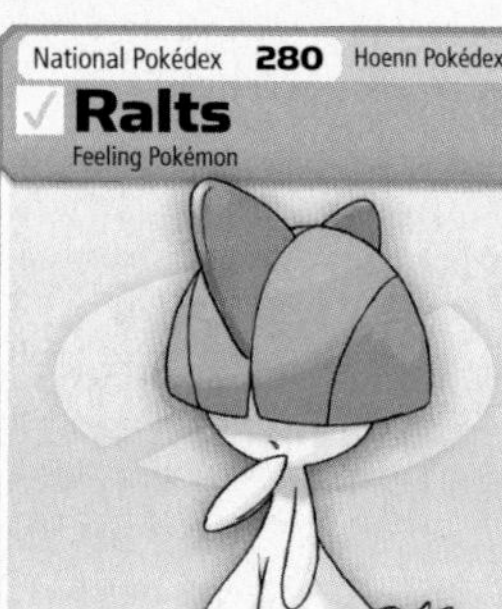

Psychic Fairy

HEIGHT: 1'04" WEIGHT: 14.6 lbs.

Same form for ♂ / ♀

Ω Ralts senses the emotions of people using the horns on its head. This Pokémon rarely appears before people. But when it does, it draws closer if it senses that the person has a positive disposition.

α Ralts has the ability to sense the emotions of people. If its Trainer is in a cheerful mood, this Pokémon grows cheerful and joyous in the same way.

ABILITIES
Synchronize
Trace

HIDDEN ABILITY
Telepathy

EGG GROUPS
Amorphous

STAT GROWTH RATES

Stat	Rate
HP	■
Attack	■
Defense	■
Sp. Atk	■■
Sp. Def	■■
Speed	■■

ITEMS SOMETIMES HELD BY WILD POKÉMON
—

EVOLUTION

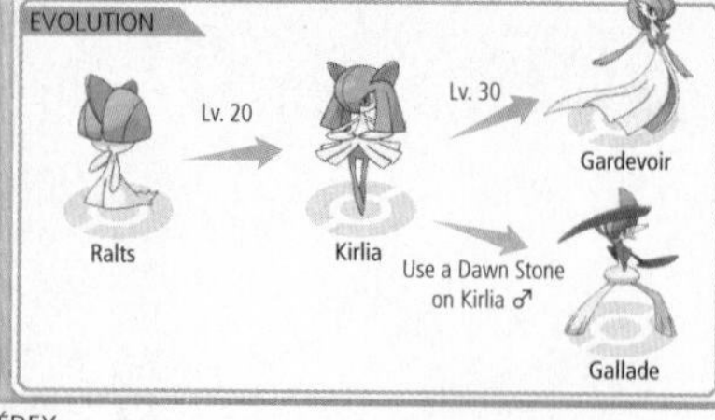

MAIN WAY TO REGISTER IN THE NATIONAL POKÉDEX

Catch on Route 102.

Damage taken in normal battles

Type	×	Type	×
Normal	×1	Flying	×1
Fire	×1	Psychic	×0.5
Water	×1	Bug	×1
Grass	×1	Rock	×1
Electric	×1	Ghost	×2
Ice	×1	Dragon	×0
Fighting	×0.25	Dark	×1
Poison	×2	Steel	×2
Ground	×1	Fairy	×1

Damage taken in Inverse battles

Type	×	Type	×
Normal	×1	Flying	×1
Fire	×1	Psychic	×2
Water	×1	Bug	×1
Grass	×1	Rock	×1
Electric	×1	Ghost	×0.5
Ice	×1	Dragon	×2
Fighting	×4	Dark	×1
Poison	×0.5	Steel	×0.5
Ground	×1	Fairy	×1

Can be used in
Inverse Battle
Battle Institute
Battle Maison
Random Matchup (Free Battle)
Random Matchup (Others)

LEVEL-UP MOVES

Lv.	Name	Type	Kind	Pow.	Acc.	PP	Range
1	Growl	Normal	Status	—	100	40	Many Others
4	Confusion	Psychic	Special	50	100	25	Normal
6	Double Team	Normal	Status	—	—	15	Self
9	Teleport	Psychic	Status	—	—	20	Self
11	Disarming Voice	Fairy	Special	40	—	15	Many Others
14	Lucky Chant	Normal	Status	—	—	30	Your Side
17	Magical Leaf	Grass	Special	60	—	20	Normal
19	Heal Pulse	Psychic	Status	—	—	10	Normal
22	Draining Kiss	Fairy	Special	50	100	10	Normal
24	Calm Mind	Psychic	Status	—	—	20	Self
27	Psychic	Psychic	Special	90	100	10	Normal
29	Imprison	Psychic	Status	—	—	10	Self
32	Future Sight	Psychic	Special	120	100	10	Normal
34	Charm	Fairy	Status	—	100	20	Normal
37	Hypnosis	Psychic	Status	—	60	20	Normal
39	Dream Eater	Psychic	Special	100	100	15	Normal
42	Stored Power	Psychic	Special	20	100	10	Normal

TM & HM MOVES

No.	Name	Type	Kind	Pow.	Acc.	PP	Range
TM03	Psyshock	Psychic	Special	80	100	10	Normal
TM04	Calm Mind	Psychic	Status	—	—	20	Self
TM06	Toxic	Poison	Status	—	90	10	Normal
TM10	Hidden Power	Normal	Special	60	100	15	Normal
TM11	Sunny Day	Fire	Status	—	—	5	Both Sides
TM12	Taunt	Dark	Status	—	100	20	Normal
TM16	Light Screen	Psychic	Status	—	—	30	Your Side
TM17	Protect	Normal	Status	—	—	10	Self
TM18	Rain Dance	Water	Status	—	—	5	Both Sides
TM20	Safeguard	Normal	Status	—	—	25	Your Side
TM21	Frustration	Normal	Physical	—	100	20	Normal
TM24	Thunderbolt	Electric	Special	90	100	15	Normal
TM27	Return	Normal	Physical	—	100	20	Normal
TM29	Psychic	Psychic	Special	90	100	10	Normal
TM30	Shadow Ball	Ghost	Special	80	100	15	Normal
TM32	Double Team	Normal	Status	—	—	15	Self
TM33	Reflect	Psychic	Status	—	—	20	Your Side
TM41	Torment	Dark	Status	—	100	15	Normal
TM42	Facade	Normal	Physical	70	100	20	Normal
TM44	Rest	Psychic	Status	—	—	10	Self
TM45	Attract	Normal	Status	—	100	15	Normal
TM46	Thief	Dark	Physical	60	100	25	Normal
TM48	Round	Normal	Special	60	100	15	Normal
TM49	Echoed Voice	Normal	Special	40	100	15	Normal
TM56	Fling	Dark	Physical	—	100	10	Normal
TM57	Charge Beam	Electric	Special	50	90	10	Normal
TM61	Will-O-Wisp	Fire	Status	—	85	15	Normal
TM70	Flash	Normal	Status	—	100	20	Normal
TM73	Thunder Wave	Electric	Status	—	100	20	Normal
TM77	Psych Up	Normal	Status	—	—	10	Normal
TM85	Dream Eater	Psychic	Special	100	100	15	Normal
TM86	Grass Knot	Grass	Special	—	100	20	Normal
TM87	Swagger	Normal	Status	—	90	15	Normal
TM88	Sleep Talk	Normal	Status	—	—	10	Self
TM90	Substitute	Normal	Status	—	—	10	Self
TM92	Trick Room	Psychic	Status	—	—	5	Both Sides
TM94	Secret Power	Normal	Physical	70	100	20	Normal
TM99	Dazzling Gleam	Fairy	Special	80	100	10	Many Others
TM100	Confide	Normal	Status	—	—	20	Normal

MOVES LEARNED IN EXCHANGE FOR BP

Name	Type	Kind	Pow.	Acc.	PP	Range
Signal Beam	Bug	Special	75	100	15	Normal
Thunder Punch	Electric	Physical	75	100	15	Normal
Fire Punch	Fire	Physical	75	100	15	Normal
Ice Punch	Ice	Physical	75	100	15	Normal
Magic Coat	Psychic	Status	—	—	15	Self
Icy Wind	Ice	Special	55	95	15	Many Others
Zen Headbutt	Psychic	Physical	80	90	15	Normal
Hyper Voice	Normal	Special	90	100	10	Many Others
Snore	Normal	Special	50	100	15	Normal
Pain Split	Normal	Status	—	—	20	Normal
Shock Wave	Electric	Special	60	—	20	Normal
Helping Hand	Normal	Status	—	—	20	1 Ally
Trick	Psychic	Status	—	100	10	Normal
Magic Room	Psychic	Status	—	—	10	Both Sides
Wonder Room	Psychic	Status	—	—	10	Both Sides
Recycle	Normal	Status	—	—	10	Self
Snatch	Dark	Status	—	—	10	Self
Skill Swap	Psychic	Status	—	—	10	Normal

MOVES TAUGHT BY PEOPLE

Name	Type	Kind	Pow.	Acc.	PP	Range

EGG MOVES

Name	Type	Kind	Pow.	Acc.	PP	Range
Disable	Normal	Status	—	100	20	Normal
Mean Look	Normal	Status	—	—	5	Normal
Memento	Dark	Status	—	100	10	Normal
Destiny Bond	Ghost	Status	—	—	5	Self
Grudge	Ghost	Status	—	—	5	Self
Shadow Sneak	Ghost	Physical	40	100	30	Normal
Confuse Ray	Ghost	Status	—	100	10	Normal
Encore	Normal	Status	—	100	5	Normal
Synchronoise	Psychic	Special	120	100	10	Adjacent
Skill Swap	Psychic	Status	—	—	10	Normal
Misty Terrain	Fairy	Status	—	—	10	Both Sides
Ally Switch	Psychic	Status	—	—	15	Self

National Pokédex **281** Hoenn Pokédex **030**

Kirlia

Emotion Pokémon

Psychic Fairy

HEIGHT: 2'07" WEIGHT: 44.5 lbs.

Same form for ♂ / ♀

Ω It is said that a Kirlia that is exposed to the positive emotions of its Trainer grows beautiful. This Pokémon controls psychokinetic powers with its highly developed brain.

α Kirlia uses the horns on its head to amplify its psychokinetic power. When the Pokémon uses its power, the air around it becomes distorted, creating mirages of nonexistent scenery.

ABILITIES
Synchronize
Trace

HIDDEN ABILITY
Telepathy

EGG GROUPS
Amorphous

STAT GROWTH RATES

Stat	Rate
HP	■■
Attack	■■
Defense	■■
Sp. Atk	■■■
Sp. Def	■■
Speed	■■■

ITEMS SOMETIMES HELD BY WILD POKÉMON
—

EVOLUTION

Lv. 20
Lv. 30
Gardevoir
Ralts
Kirlia
Use a Dawn Stone on Kirlia ♂
Gallade

MAIN WAY TO REGISTER IN THE NATIONAL POKÉDEX

Level up Ralts to Lv. 20.

Damage taken in normal battles

Type	×	Type	×
Normal	×1	Flying	×1
Fire	×1	Psychic	×0.5
Water	×1	Bug	×1
Grass	×1	Rock	×1
Electric	×1	Ghost	×2
Ice	×1	Dragon	×0
Fighting	×0.25	Dark	×1
Poison	×2	Steel	×2
Ground	×1	Fairy	×1

Damage taken in Inverse battles

Type	×	Type	×
Normal	×1	Flying	×1
Fire	×1	Psychic	×2
Water	×1	Bug	×1
Grass	×1	Rock	×1
Electric	×1	Ghost	×0.5
Ice	×1	Dragon	×2
Fighting	×4	Dark	×1
Poison	×0.5	Steel	×0.5
Ground	×1	Fairy	×1

Can be used in
Inverse Battle
Battle Institute
Battle Maison
Random Matchup (Free Battle)
Random Matchup (Others)

LEVEL-UP MOVES

Lv.	Name	Type	Kind	Pow.	Acc.	PP	Range
1	Growl	Normal	Status	—	100	40	Many Others
1	Confusion	Psychic	Special	50	100	25	Normal
1	Double Team	Normal	Status	—	—	15	Self
1	Teleport	Psychic	Status	—	—	20	Self
4	Confusion	Psychic	Special	50	100	25	Normal
6	Double Team	Normal	Status	—	—	15	Self
9	Teleport	Psychic	Status	—	—	20	Self
11	Disarming Voice	Fairy	Special	40	—	15	Many Others
14	Lucky Chant	Normal	Status	—	—	30	Your Side
17	Magical Leaf	Grass	Special	60	—	20	Normal
19	Heal Pulse	Psychic	Status	—	—	10	Normal
23	Draining Kiss	Fairy	Special	50	100	10	Normal
26	Calm Mind	Psychic	Status	—	—	20	Self
30	Psychic	Psychic	Special	90	100	10	Normal
33	Imprison	Psychic	Status	—	—	10	Self
37	Future Sight	Psychic	Special	120	100	10	Normal
40	Charm	Fairy	Status	—	100	20	Normal
44	Hypnosis	Psychic	Status	—	60	20	Normal
47	Dream Eater	Psychic	Special	100	100	15	Normal
51	Stored Power	Psychic	Special	20	100	10	Normal

TM & HM MOVES

No.	Name	Type	Kind	Pow.	Acc.	PP	Range
TM03	Psyshock	Psychic	Special	80	100	10	Normal
TM04	Calm Mind	Psychic	Status	—	—	20	Self
TM06	Toxic	Poison	Status	—	90	10	Normal
TM10	Hidden Power	Normal	Special	60	100	15	Normal
TM11	Sunny Day	Fire	Status	—	—	5	Both Sides
TM12	Taunt	Dark	Status	—	100	20	Normal
TM16	Light Screen	Psychic	Status	—	—	30	Your Side
TM17	Protect	Normal	Status	—	—	10	Self
TM18	Rain Dance	Water	Status	—	—	5	Both Sides
TM20	Safeguard	Normal	Status	—	—	25	Your Side
TM21	Frustration	Normal	Physical	—	100	20	Normal
TM24	Thunderbolt	Electric	Special	90	100	15	Normal
TM27	Return	Normal	Physical	—	100	20	Normal
TM29	Psychic	Psychic	Special	90	100	10	Normal
TM30	Shadow Ball	Ghost	Special	80	100	15	Normal
TM32	Double Team	Normal	Status	—	—	15	Self
TM33	Reflect	Psychic	Status	—	—	20	Your Side
TM41	Torment	Dark	Status	—	100	15	Normal
TM42	Facade	Normal	Physical	70	100	20	Normal
TM44	Rest	Psychic	Status	—	—	10	Self
TM45	Attract	Normal	Status	—	100	15	Normal
TM46	Thief	Dark	Physical	60	100	25	Normal
TM48	Round	Normal	Special	60	100	15	Normal
TM49	Echoed Voice	Normal	Special	40	100	15	Normal
TM56	Fling	Dark	Physical	—	100	10	Normal
TM57	Charge Beam	Electric	Special	50	90	10	Normal
TM61	Will-O-Wisp	Fire	Status	—	85	15	Normal
TM70	Flash	Normal	Status	—	100	20	Normal
TM73	Thunder Wave	Electric	Status	—	100	20	Normal
TM77	Psych Up	Normal	Status	—	—	10	Normal
TM85	Dream Eater	Psychic	Special	100	100	15	Normal
TM86	Grass Knot	Grass	Special	—	100	20	Normal
TM87	Swagger	Normal	Status	—	90	15	Normal
TM88	Sleep Talk	Normal	Status	—	—	10	Self
TM90	Substitute	Normal	Status	—	—	10	Self
TM92	Trick Room	Psychic	Status	—	—	5	Both Sides
TM94	Secret Power	Normal	Physical	70	100	20	Normal
TM99	Dazzling Gleam	Fairy	Special	80	100	10	Many Others
TM100	Confide	Normal	Status	—	—	20	Normal

MOVES LEARNED IN EXCHANGE FOR BP

Name	Type	Kind	Pow.	Acc.	PP	Range
Signal Beam	Bug	Special	75	100	15	Normal
Thunder Punch	Electric	Physical	75	100	15	Normal
Fire Punch	Fire	Physical	75	100	15	Normal
Ice Punch	Ice	Physical	75	100	15	Normal
Magic Coat	Psychic	Status	—	—	15	Self
Icy Wind	Ice	Special	55	95	15	Many Others
Zen Headbutt	Psychic	Physical	80	90	15	Normal
Hyper Voice	Normal	Special	90	100	10	Many Others
Snore	Normal	Special	50	100	15	Normal
Pain Split	Normal	Status	—	—	20	Normal
Shock Wave	Electric	Special	60	—	20	Normal
Helping Hand	Normal	Status	—	—	20	1 Ally
Trick	Psychic	Status	—	100	10	Normal
Magic Room	Psychic	Status	—	—	10	Both Sides
Wonder Room	Psychic	Status	—	—	10	Both Sides
Recycle	Normal	Status	—	—	10	Self
Snatch	Dark	Status	—	—	10	Self
Skill Swap	Psychic	Status	—	—	10	Normal

MOVES TAUGHT BY PEOPLE

Name	Type	Kind	Pow.	Acc.	PP	Range

National Pokédex **282** Hoenn Pokédex **031**

Gardevoir

Embrace Pokémon

Psychic | Fairy

HEIGHT: 5'03" WEIGHT: 106.7 lbs.

Same form for ♂ / ♀

Ω Gardevoir has the ability to read the future. If it senses impending danger to its Trainer, this Pokémon is said to unleash its psychokinetic energy at full power.

α Gardevoir has the psychokinetic power to distort the dimensions and create a small black hole. This Pokémon will try to protect its Trainer even at the risk of its own life.

ABILITES
Synchronize
Trace

HIDDEN ABILITY
Telepathy

EGG GROUPS
Amorphous

STAT GROWTH RATES
HP
Attack
Defense
Sp. Atk
Sp. Def
Speed

ITEMS SOMETIMES HELD BY WILD POKÉMON
—

EVOLUTION

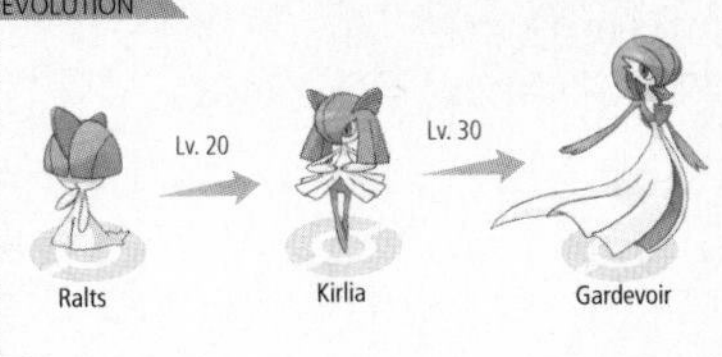

MAIN WAY TO REGISTER IN THE NATIONAL POKÉDEX

Level up Kirlia to Lv. 30.

Damage taken in normal battles

Normal	×1	Flying	×1
Fire	×1	Psychic	×0.5
Water	×1	Bug	×1
Grass	×1	Rock	×1
Electric	×1	Ghost	×2
Ice	×1	Dragon	×0
Fighting	×0.25	Dark	×1
Poison	×2	Steel	×2
Ground	×1	Fairy	×1

Damage taken in Inverse battles

Normal	×1	Flying	×1
Fire	×1	Psychic	×2
Water	×1	Bug	×1
Grass	×1	Rock	×1
Electric	×1	Ghost	×0.5
Ice	×1	Dragon	×2
Fighting	×4	Dark	×1
Poison	×0.5	Steel	×0.5
Ground	×1	Fairy	×1

Can be used in
Inverse Battle
Battle Institute
Battle Maison
Random Matchup (Free Battle)
Random Matchup (Others)

LEVEL-UP MOVES

Lv.	Name	Type	Kind	Pow.	Acc.	PP	Range
1	Moonblast	Fairy	Special	95	100	15	Normal
1	Stored Power	Psychic	Special	20	100	10	Normal
1	Misty Terrain	Fairy	Status	—	—	10	Both Sides
1	Healing Wish	Psychic	Status	—	—	10	Self
1	Growl	Normal	Status	—	100	40	Many Others
1	Confusion	Psychic	Special	50	100	25	Normal
1	Double Team	Normal	Status	—	—	15	Self
1	Teleport	Psychic	Status	—	—	20	Self
4	Confusion	Psychic	Special	50	100	25	Normal
6	Double Team	Normal	Status	—	—	15	Self
9	Teleport	Psychic	Status	—	—	20	Self
11	Disarming Voice	Fairy	Special	40	—	15	Many Others
14	Wish	Normal	Status	—	—	10	Self
17	Magical Leaf	Grass	Special	60	—	20	Normal
19	Heal Pulse	Psychic	Status	—	—	10	Normal
23	Draining Kiss	Fairy	Special	50	100	10	Normal
26	Calm Mind	Psychic	Status	—	—	20	Self
31	Psychic	Psychic	Special	90	100	10	Normal
35	Imprison	Psychic	Status	—	—	10	Self
40	Future Sight	Psychic	Special	120	100	10	Normal
44	Captivate	Normal	Status	—	100	20	Many Others
49	Hypnosis	Psychic	Status	—	60	20	Normal
53	Dream Eater	Psychic	Special	100	100	15	Normal
58	Stored Power	Psychic	Special	20	100	10	Normal
62	Moonblast	Fairy	Special	95	100	15	Normal

TM & HM MOVES

No.	Name	Type	Kind	Pow.	Acc.	PP	Range
TM03	Psyshock	Psychic	Special	80	100	10	Normal
TM04	Calm Mind	Psychic	Status	—	—	20	Self
TM06	Toxic	Poison	Status	—	90	10	Normal
TM10	Hidden Power	Normal	Special	60	100	15	Normal
TM11	Sunny Day	Fire	Status	—	—	5	Both Sides
TM12	Taunt	Dark	Status	—	100	20	Normal
TM15	Hyper Beam	Normal	Special	150	90	5	Normal
TM16	Light Screen	Psychic	Status	—	—	30	Your Side
TM17	Protect	Normal	Status	—	—	10	Self
TM18	Rain Dance	Water	Status	—	—	5	Both Sides
TM20	Safeguard	Normal	Status	—	—	25	Your Side
TM21	Frustration	Normal	Physical	—	100	20	Normal
TM24	Thunderbolt	Electric	Special	90	100	15	Normal
TM27	Return	Normal	Physical	—	100	20	Normal
TM29	Psychic	Psychic	Special	90	100	10	Normal
TM30	Shadow Ball	Ghost	Special	80	100	15	Normal
TM32	Double Team	Normal	Status	—	—	15	Self
TM33	Reflect	Psychic	Status	—	—	20	Your Side
TM41	Torment	Dark	Status	—	100	15	Normal
TM42	Facade	Normal	Physical	70	100	20	Normal
TM44	Rest	Psychic	Status	—	—	10	Self
TM45	Attract	Normal	Status	—	100	15	Normal
TM46	Thief	Dark	Physical	60	100	25	Normal
TM48	Round	Normal	Special	60	100	15	Normal
TM49	Echoed Voice	Normal	Special	40	100	15	Normal
TM52	Focus Blast	Fighting	Special	120	70	5	Normal
TM53	Energy Ball	Grass	Special	90	100	10	Normal
TM56	Fling	Dark	Physical	—	100	10	Normal
TM57	Charge Beam	Electric	Special	50	90	10	Normal
TM61	Will-O-Wisp	Fire	Status	—	85	15	Normal
TM68	Giga Impact	Normal	Physical	150	90	5	Normal
TM70	Flash	Normal	Status	—	100	20	Normal
TM73	Thunder Wave	Electric	Status	—	100	20	Normal
TM77	Psych Up	Normal	Status	—	—	10	Normal
TM85	Dream Eater	Psychic	Special	100	100	15	Normal
TM86	Grass Knot	Grass	Special	—	100	20	Normal
TM87	Swagger	Normal	Status	—	90	15	Normal
TM88	Sleep Talk	Normal	Status	—	—	10	Self
TM90	Substitute	Normal	Status	—	—	10	Self
TM92	Trick Room	Psychic	Status	—	—	5	Both Sides
TM94	Secret Power	Normal	Physical	70	100	20	Normal
TM99	Dazzling Gleam	Fairy	Special	80	100	10	Many Others
TM100	Confide	Normal	Status	—	—	20	Normal

MOVES LEARNED IN EXCHANGE FOR BP

Name	Type	Kind	Pow.	Acc.	PP	Range
Signal Beam	Bug	Special	75	100	15	Normal
Thunder Punch	Electric	Physical	75	100	15	Normal
Fire Punch	Fire	Physical	75	100	15	Normal
Ice Punch	Ice	Physical	75	100	15	Normal
Magic Coat	Psychic	Status	—	—	15	Self
Icy Wind	Ice	Special	55	95	15	Many Others
Zen Headbutt	Psychic	Physical	80	90	15	Normal
Hyper Voice	Normal	Special	90	100	10	Many Others
Snore	Normal	Special	50	100	15	Normal
Heal Bell	Normal	Status	—	—	5	Your Party
Pain Split	Normal	Status	—	—	20	Normal
Shock Wave	Electric	Special	60	—	20	Normal
Helping Hand	Normal	Status	—	—	20	1 Ally
Trick	Psychic	Status	—	100	10	Normal
Magic Room	Psychic	Status	—	—	10	Both Sides
Wonder Room	Psychic	Status	—	—	10	Both Sides
Recycle	Normal	Status	—	—	10	Self
Snatch	Dark	Status	—	—	10	Self
Skill Swap	Psychic	Status	—	—	10	Normal

MOVES TAUGHT BY PEOPLE

Name	Type	Kind	Pow.	Acc.	PP	Range

Mega Evolution

Mega Gardevoir

Embrace Pokémon

Psychic | Fairy

HEIGHT: 5'03" WEIGHT: 106.7 lbs.

Same form for ♂ / ♀

REQUIRED MEGA STONE
Gardevoirite
Receive from Wanda in her house in Verdanturf Town (after battling Groudon or Kyogre).

ABILITY
Pixilate

HIDDEN ABILITY
—

EGG GROUPS
—

STAT GROWTH RATES
HP
Attack
Defense
Sp. Atk
Sp. Def
Speed

Damage taken in normal battles

Normal	×1	Flying	×1
Fire	×1	Psychic	×0.5
Water	×1	Bug	×1
Grass	×1	Rock	×1
Electric	×1	Ghost	×2
Ice	×1	Dragon	×0
Fighting	×0.25	Dark	×1
Poison	×2	Steel	×2
Ground	×1	Fairy	×1

Damage taken in Inverse battles

Normal	×1	Flying	×1
Fire	×1	Psychic	×2
Water	×1	Bug	×1
Grass	×1	Rock	×1
Electric	×1	Ghost	×0.5
Ice	×1	Dragon	×2
Fighting	×4	Dark	×1
Poison	×0.5	Steel	×0.5
Ground	×1	Fairy	×1

Can be used in
Inverse Battle
Battle Institute
Battle Maison
Random Matchup (Free Battle)
Random Matchup (Others)

National Pokédex **283** Hoenn Pokédex **033**

✓ Surskit

Pond Skater Pokémon

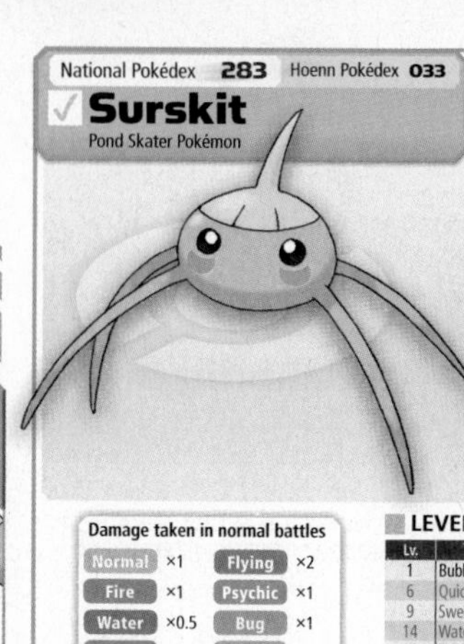

Bug | Water

HEIGHT: 1'08" WEIGHT: 3.7 lbs.

Same form for ♂ / ♀

Ω From the tips of its feet, Surskit secretes an oil that enables it to walk on water as if it were skating. This Pokémon feeds on microscopic organisms in ponds and lakes.

α If Surskit senses danger, it secretes a thick, sugary syrup from the tip of its head. There are some Pokémon that love eating this syrup.

ABILITY
Swift Swim

HIDDEN ABILITY
Rain Dish

EGG GROUPS
Water 1 | Bug

STAT GROWTH RATES
HP ■■
Attack ■■
Defense ■■
Sp. Atk ■■
Sp. Def ■■
Speed ■■■■

ITEMS SOMETIMES HELD BY WILD POKÉMON
Honey

EVOLUTION
Surskit → Lv. 22 → Masquerain

MAIN WAY TO REGISTER IN THE NATIONAL POKÉDEX
Catch on Route 102.

Damage taken in normal battles

Type		Type	
Normal	×1	Flying	×2
Fire	×1	Psychic	×1
Water	×0.5	Bug	×1
Grass	×1	Rock	×2
Electric	×2	Ghost	×1
Ice	×0.5	Dragon	×1
Fighting	×0.5	Dark	×1
Poison	×1	Steel	×0.5
Ground	×0.5	Fairy	×1

Damage taken in Inverse battles

Type		Type	
Normal	×1	Flying	×0.5
Fire	×1	Psychic	×1
Water	×2	Bug	×1
Grass	×1	Rock	×0.5
Electric	×0.5	Ghost	×1
Ice	×2	Dragon	×1
Fighting	×2	Dark	×1
Poison	×1	Steel	×2
Ground	×2	Fairy	×1

Can be used in
Inverse Battle
Battle Institute
Battle Maison
Random Matchup (Free Battle)
Random Matchup (Others)

LEVEL-UP MOVES

Lv.	Name	Type	Kind	Pow.	Acc.	PP	Range
1	Bubble	Water	Special	40	100	30	Many Others
6	Quick Attack	Normal	Physical	40	100	30	Normal
9	Sweet Scent	Normal	Status	—	100	20	Many Others
14	Water Sport	Water	Status	—	—	15	Both Sides
17	Bubble Beam	Water	Special	65	100	20	Normal
22	Agility	Psychic	Status	—	—	30	Self
25	Mist	Ice	Status	—	—	30	Your Side
25	Haze	Ice	Status	—	—	30	Both Sides
30	Aqua Jet	Water	Physical	40	100	20	Normal
35	Baton Pass	Normal	Status	—	—	40	Self
38	Sticky Web	Bug	Status	—	—	20	Other Side

TM & HM MOVES

No.	Name	Type	Kind	Pow.	Acc.	PP	Range
TM06	Toxic	Poison	Status	—	90	10	Normal
TM10	Hidden Power	Normal	Special	60	100	15	Normal
TM11	Sunny Day	Fire	Status	—	—	5	Both Sides
TM13	Ice Beam	Ice	Special	90	100	10	Normal
TM14	Blizzard	Ice	Special	110	70	5	Many Others
TM17	Protect	Normal	Status	—	—	10	Self
TM18	Rain Dance	Water	Status	—	—	5	Both Sides
TM21	Frustration	Normal	Physical	—	100	20	Normal
TM22	Solar Beam	Grass	Special	120	100	10	Normal
TM27	Return	Normal	Physical	—	100	20	Normal
TM30	Shadow Ball	Ghost	Special	80	100	15	Normal
TM32	Double Team	Normal	Status	—	—	15	Self
TM42	Facade	Normal	Physical	70	100	20	Normal
TM44	Rest	Psychic	Status	—	—	10	Self
TM45	Attract	Normal	Status	—	100	15	Normal
TM46	Thief	Dark	Physical	60	100	25	Normal
TM48	Round	Normal	Special	60	100	15	Normal
TM55	Scald	Water	Special	80	100	15	Normal
TM70	Flash	Normal	Status	—	100	20	Normal
TM76	Struggle Bug	Bug	Special	50	100	20	Many Others
TM77	Psych Up	Normal	Status	—	—	10	Normal
TM83	Infestation	Bug	Special	20	100	20	Normal
TM87	Swagger	Normal	Status	—	90	15	Normal
TM88	Sleep Talk	Normal	Status	—	—	10	Self
TM90	Substitute	Normal	Status	—	—	10	Self
TM94	Secret Power	Normal	Physical	70	100	20	Normal
TM100	Confide	Normal	Status	—	—	20	Normal

MOVES LEARNED IN EXCHANGE FOR BP

Name	Type	Kind	Pow.	Acc.	PP	Range
Bug Bite	Bug	Physical	60	100	20	Normal
Signal Beam	Bug	Special	75	100	15	Normal
Icy Wind	Ice	Special	55	95	15	Many Others
Snore	Normal	Special	50	100	15	Normal
Giga Drain	Grass	Special	75	100	10	Normal
Water Pulse	Water	Special	60	100	20	Normal

MOVES TAUGHT BY PEOPLE

Name	Type	Kind	Pow.	Acc.	PP	Range

EGG MOVES

Name	Type	Kind	Pow.	Acc.	PP	Range
Foresight	Normal	Status	—	—	40	Normal
Mud Shot	Ground	Special	55	95	15	Normal
Psybeam	Psychic	Special	65	100	20	Normal
Hydro Pump	Water	Special	110	80	5	Normal
Mind Reader	Normal	Status	—	—	5	Normal
Signal Beam	Bug	Special	75	100	15	Normal
Bug Bite	Bug	Physical	60	100	20	Normal
Aqua Jet	Water	Physical	40	100	20	Normal
Endure	Normal	Status	—	—	10	Self
Fell Stinger	Bug	Physical	30	100	25	Normal
Power Split	Psychic	Status	—	—	10	Normal

National Pokédex **284** Hoenn Pokédex **034**

✓ Masquerain

Eyeball Pokémon

Bug | Flying

HEIGHT: 2'07" WEIGHT: 7.9 lbs.

Same form for ♂ / ♀

Ω Masquerain intimidates enemies with the eyelike patterns on its antennas. This Pokémon flaps its four wings to freely fly in any direction—even sideways and backwards—as if it were a helicopter.

α Masquerain's antennas have eyelike patterns that usually give it an angry look. If the "eyes" are droopy and appear sad, it is said to be a sign that a heavy rainfall is on its way.

ABILITY
Intimidate

HIDDEN ABILITY
Unnerve

EGG GROUPS
Water 1 | Bug

STAT GROWTH RATES
HP ■■■
Attack ■■■
Defense ■■■
Sp. Atk ■■■■
Sp. Def ■■■
Speed ■■■

ITEMS SOMETIMES HELD BY WILD POKÉMON
Silver Powder

EVOLUTION
Surskit → Lv. 22 → Masquerain

MAIN WAY TO REGISTER IN THE NATIONAL POKÉDEX
Catch on the water surface on Route 120.

Damage taken in normal battles

Type		Type	
Normal	×1	Flying	×2
Fire	×2	Psychic	×1
Water	×1	Bug	×0.5
Grass	×0.25	Rock	×4
Electric	×2	Ghost	×1
Ice	×2	Dragon	×1
Fighting	×0.25	Dark	×1
Poison	×1	Steel	×1
Ground	×0	Fairy	×1

Damage taken in Inverse battles

Type		Type	
Normal	×1	Flying	×0.5
Fire	×0.5	Psychic	×1
Water	×1	Bug	×2
Grass	×4	Rock	×0.25
Electric	×0.5	Ghost	×1
Ice	×0.5	Dragon	×1
Fighting	×4	Dark	×1
Poison	×1	Steel	×1
Ground	×4	Fairy	×1

Can be used in
Inverse Battle
Battle Institute
Battle Maison
Random Matchup (Free Battle)
Random Matchup (Others)

LEVEL-UP MOVES

Lv.	Name	Type	Kind	Pow.	Acc.	PP	Range
1	Quiver Dance	Bug	Status	—	—	20	Self
1	Whirlwind	Normal	Status	—	—	20	Normal
1	Bug Buzz	Bug	Special	90	100	10	Normal
1	Ominous Wind	Ghost	Special	60	100	5	Normal
1	Bubble	Water	Special	40	100	30	Many Others
1	Quick Attack	Normal	Physical	40	100	30	Normal
1	Sweet Scent	Normal	Status	—	100	20	Many Others
1	Water Sport	Water	Status	—	—	15	Both Sides
6	Quick Attack	Normal	Physical	40	100	30	Normal
9	Sweet Scent	Normal	Status	—	100	20	Many Others
14	Water Sport	Water	Status	—	—	15	Both Sides
17	Gust	Flying	Special	40	100	35	Normal
22	Scary Face	Normal	Status	—	100	10	Normal
22	Air Cutter	Flying	Special	60	95	25	Many Others
26	Stun Spore	Grass	Status	—	75	30	Normal
32	Silver Wind	Bug	Special	60	100	5	Normal
38	Air Slash	Flying	Special	75	95	15	Normal
42	Bug Buzz	Bug	Special	90	100	10	Normal
48	Whirlwind	Normal	Status	—	—	20	Normal
52	Quiver Dance	Bug	Status	—	—	20	Self

TM & HM MOVES

No.	Name	Type	Kind	Pow.	Acc.	PP	Range
TM06	Toxic	Poison	Status	—	90	10	Normal
TM10	Hidden Power	Normal	Special	60	100	15	Normal
TM11	Sunny Day	Fire	Status	—	—	5	Both Sides
TM13	Ice Beam	Ice	Special	90	100	10	Normal
TM14	Blizzard	Ice	Special	110	70	5	Many Others
TM15	Hyper Beam	Normal	Special	150	90	5	Normal
TM17	Protect	Normal	Status	—	—	10	Self
TM18	Rain Dance	Water	Status	—	—	5	Both Sides
TM19	Roost	Flying	Status	—	—	10	Self
TM21	Frustration	Normal	Physical	—	100	20	Normal
TM22	Solar Beam	Grass	Special	120	100	10	Normal
TM27	Return	Normal	Physical	—	100	20	Normal
TM30	Shadow Ball	Ghost	Special	80	100	15	Normal
TM32	Double Team	Normal	Status	—	—	15	Self
TM40	Aerial Ace	Flying	Physical	60	—	20	Normal
TM42	Facade	Normal	Physical	70	100	20	Normal
TM44	Rest	Psychic	Status	—	—	10	Self
TM45	Attract	Normal	Status	—	100	15	Normal
TM46	Thief	Dark	Physical	60	100	25	Normal
TM48	Round	Normal	Special	60	100	15	Normal
TM53	Energy Ball	Grass	Special	90	100	10	Normal
TM55	Scald	Water	Special	80	100	15	Normal
TM68	Giga Impact	Normal	Physical	150	90	5	Normal
TM70	Flash	Normal	Status	—	100	20	Normal
TM76	Struggle Bug	Bug	Special	50	100	20	Many Others
TM77	Psych Up	Normal	Status	—	—	10	Normal
TM83	Infestation	Bug	Special	20	100	20	Normal
TM87	Swagger	Normal	Status	—	90	15	Normal
TM88	Sleep Talk	Normal	Status	—	—	10	Self
TM89	U-turn	Bug	Physical	70	100	20	Normal
TM90	Substitute	Normal	Status	—	—	10	Self
TM94	Secret Power	Normal	Physical	70	100	20	Normal
TM100	Confide	Normal	Status	—	—	20	Normal

MOVES LEARNED IN EXCHANGE FOR BP

Name	Type	Kind	Pow.	Acc.	PP	Range
Bug Bite	Bug	Physical	60	100	20	Normal
Signal Beam	Bug	Special	75	100	15	Normal
Icy Wind	Ice	Special	55	95	15	Many Others
Snore	Normal	Special	50	100	15	Normal
Tailwind	Flying	Status	—	—	15	Your Side
Giga Drain	Grass	Special	75	100	10	Normal
Water Pulse	Water	Special	60	100	20	Normal

MOVES TAUGHT BY PEOPLE

Name	Type	Kind	Pow.	Acc.	PP	Range

National Pokédex **285** Hoenn Pokédex **035**

Shroomish

Mushroom Pokémon

Grass

HEIGHT: 1'04" WEIGHT: 9.9 lbs.

Same form for ♂ / ♀

Ω Shroomish live in damp soil in the dark depths of forests. They are often found keeping still under fallen leaves. This Pokémon feeds on compost that is made up of fallen, rotted leaves.

α If Shroomish senses danger, it shakes its body and scatters spores from the top of its head. This Pokémon's spores are so toxic, they make trees and weeds wilt.

ABILITIES
Effect Spore
Poison Heal

HIDDEN ABILITY
Quick Feet

EGG GROUPS
Fairy | Grass

STAT GROWTH RATES
HP
Attack
Defense
Sp. Atk
Sp. Def
Speed

EVOLUTION
Shroomish → Lv. 23 → Breloom

ITEMS SOMETIMES HELD BY WILD POKÉMON
Tiny Mushroom / Big Mushroom

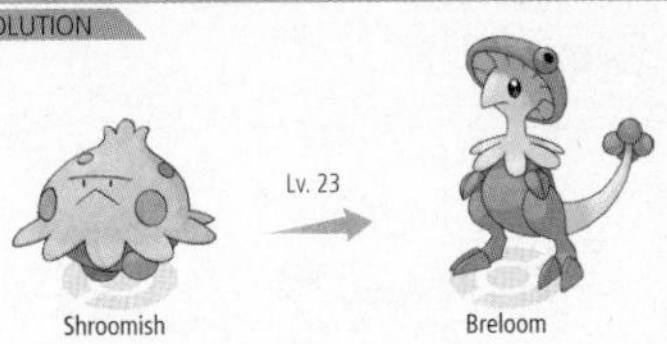

MAIN WAY TO REGISTER IN THE NATIONAL POKÉDEX
Catch in Petalburg Woods.

Damage taken in normal battles

Type		Type	
Normal	×1	Flying	×2
Fire	×2	Psychic	×1
Water	×0.5	Bug	×2
Grass	×0.5	Rock	×1
Electric	×0.5	Ghost	×1
Ice	×2	Dragon	×1
Fighting	×1	Dark	×1
Poison	×2	Steel	×1
Ground	×0.5	Fairy	×1

Damage taken in Inverse battles

Type		Type	
Normal	×1	Flying	×0.5
Fire	×0.5	Psychic	×1
Water	×2	Bug	×0.5
Grass	×2	Rock	×1
Electric	×2	Ghost	×1
Ice	×0.5	Dragon	×1
Fighting	×1	Dark	×1
Poison	×0.5	Steel	×1
Ground	×2	Fairy	×1

Can be used in
Inverse Battle
Battle Institute
Battle Maison
Random Matchup (Free Battle)
Random Matchup (Others)

LEVEL-UP MOVES

Lv.	Name	Type	Kind	Pow.	Acc.	PP	Range
1	Absorb	Grass	Special	20	100	25	Normal
1	Tackle	Normal	Physical	50	100	35	Normal
5	Stun Spore	Grass	Status	—	75	30	Normal
8	Leech Seed	Grass	Status	—	90	10	Normal
12	Mega Drain	Grass	Special	40	100	15	Normal
15	Headbutt	Normal	Physical	70	100	15	Normal
19	Poison Powder	Poison	Status	—	75	35	Normal
22	Worry Seed	Grass	Status	—	100	10	Normal
26	Giga Drain	Grass	Special	75	100	10	Normal
29	Growth	Normal	Status	—	—	20	Self
33	Toxic	Poison	Status	—	90	10	Normal
36	Seed Bomb	Grass	Physical	80	100	15	Normal
40	Spore	Grass	Status	—	100	15	Normal

TM & HM MOVES

No.	Name	Type	Kind	Pow.	Acc.	PP	Range
TM06	Toxic	Poison	Status	—	90	10	Normal
TM09	Venoshock	Poison	Special	65	100	10	Normal
TM10	Hidden Power	Normal	Special	60	100	15	Normal
TM11	Sunny Day	Fire	Status	—	—	5	Both Sides
TM17	Protect	Normal	Status	—	—	10	Self
TM20	Safeguard	Normal	Status	—	—	25	Your Side
TM21	Frustration	Normal	Physical	—	100	20	Normal
TM22	Solar Beam	Grass	Special	120	100	10	Normal
TM27	Return	Normal	Physical	—	100	20	Normal
TM32	Double Team	Normal	Status	—	—	15	Self
TM36	Sludge Bomb	Poison	Special	90	100	10	Normal
TM42	Facade	Normal	Physical	70	100	20	Normal
TM44	Rest	Psychic	Status	—	—	10	Self
TM45	Attract	Normal	Status	—	100	15	Normal
TM48	Round	Normal	Special	60	100	15	Normal
TM53	Energy Ball	Grass	Special	90	100	10	Normal
TM54	False Swipe	Normal	Physical	40	100	40	Normal
TM70	Flash	Normal	Status	—	100	20	Normal
TM75	Swords Dance	Normal	Status	—	—	20	Self
TM86	Grass Knot	Grass	Special	—	100	20	Normal
TM87	Swagger	Normal	Status	—	90	15	Normal
TM88	Sleep Talk	Normal	Status	—	—	10	Self
TM90	Substitute	Normal	Status	—	—	10	Self
TM94	Secret Power	Normal	Physical	70	100	20	Normal
TM100	Confide	Normal	Status	—	—	20	Normal

MOVES LEARNED IN EXCHANGE FOR BP

Name	Type	Kind	Pow.	Acc.	PP	Range
Seed Bomb	Grass	Physical	80	100	15	Normal
Snore	Normal	Special	50	100	15	Normal
Synthesis	Grass	Status	—	—	5	Self
Giga Drain	Grass	Special	75	100	10	Normal
Drain Punch	Fighting	Physical	75	100	10	Normal
Focus Punch	Fighting	Physical	150	100	20	Normal
Worry Seed	Grass	Status	—	100	10	Normal
Helping Hand	Normal	Status	—	—	20	1 Ally
Snatch	Dark	Status	—	—	10	Self

MOVES TAUGHT BY PEOPLE

Name	Type	Kind	Pow.	Acc.	PP	Range

EGG MOVES

Name	Type	Kind	Pow.	Acc.	PP	Range
Fake Tears	Dark	Status	—	100	20	Normal
Charm	Fairy	Status	—	100	20	Normal
Helping Hand	Normal	Status	—	—	20	1 Ally
Worry Seed	Grass	Status	—	100	10	Normal
Wake-Up Slap	Fighting	Physical	70	100	10	Normal
Seed Bomb	Grass	Physical	80	100	15	Normal
Bullet Seed	Grass	Physical	25	100	30	Normal
Focus Punch	Fighting	Physical	150	100	20	Normal
Natural Gift	Normal	Physical	—	100	15	Normal
Drain Punch	Fighting	Physical	75	100	10	Normal

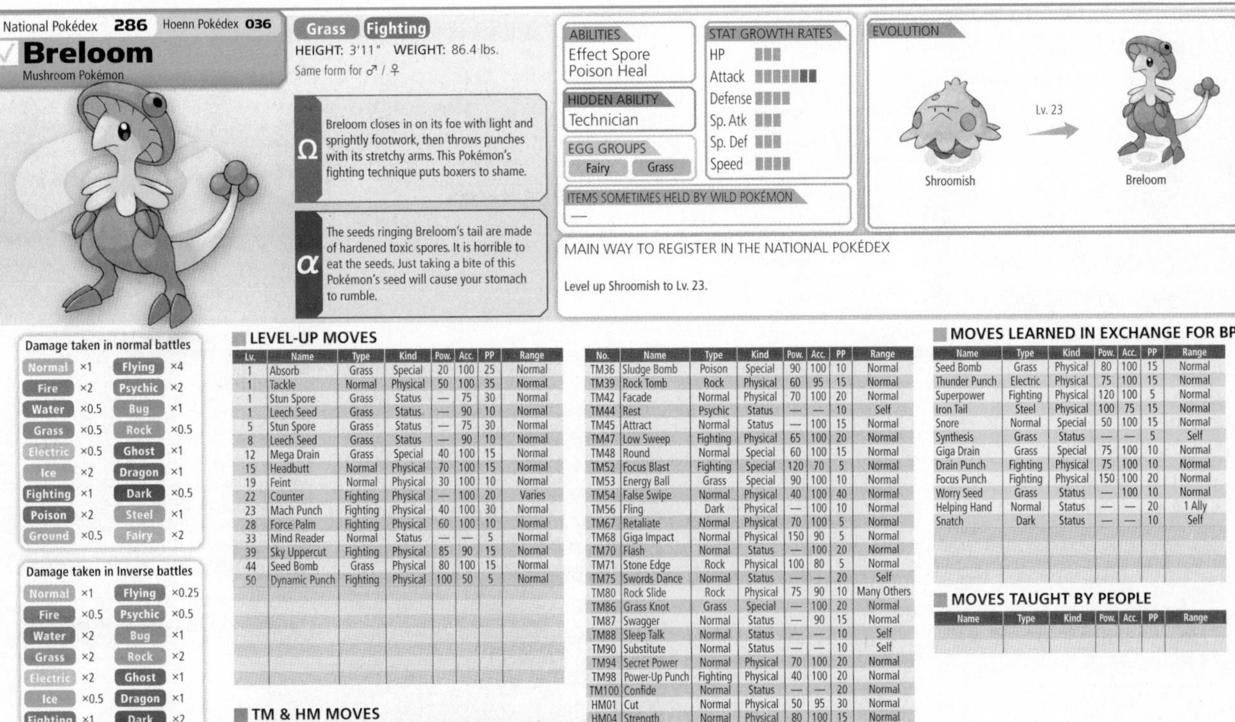

National Pokédex **286** Hoenn Pokédex **036**

Breloom

Mushroom Pokémon

Grass **Fighting**

HEIGHT: 3'11" WEIGHT: 86.4 lbs.

Same form for ♂ / ♀

Ω Breloom closes in on its foe with light and sprightly footwork, then throws punches with its stretchy arms. This Pokémon's fighting technique puts boxers to shame.

α The seeds ringing Breloom's tail are made of hardened toxic spores. It is horrible to eat the seeds. Just taking a bite of this Pokémon's seed will cause your stomach to rumble.

ABILITIES
Effect Spore
Poison Heal

HIDDEN ABILITY
Technician

EGG GROUPS
Fairy | Grass

STAT GROWTH RATES
HP
Attack
Defense
Sp. Atk
Sp. Def
Speed

EVOLUTION
Shroomish → Lv. 23 → Breloom

ITEMS SOMETIMES HELD BY WILD POKÉMON
—

MAIN WAY TO REGISTER IN THE NATIONAL POKÉDEX
Level up Shroomish to Lv. 23.

Damage taken in normal battles

Type		Type	
Normal	×1	Flying	×4
Fire	×2	Psychic	×2
Water	×0.5	Bug	×1
Grass	×0.5	Rock	×0.5
Electric	×0.5	Ghost	×1
Ice	×2	Dragon	×1
Fighting	×1	Dark	×0.5
Poison	×2	Steel	×1
Ground	×0.5	Fairy	×2

Damage taken in Inverse battles

Type		Type	
Normal	×1	Flying	×0.25
Fire	×0.5	Psychic	×0.5
Water	×2	Bug	×1
Grass	×2	Rock	×2
Electric	×2	Ghost	×1
Ice	×0.5	Dragon	×1
Fighting	×1	Dark	×2
Poison	×0.5	Steel	×1
Ground	×2	Fairy	×0.5

Can be used in
Inverse Battle
Battle Institute
Battle Maison
Random Matchup (Free Battle)
Random Matchup (Others)

LEVEL-UP MOVES

Lv.	Name	Type	Kind	Pow.	Acc.	PP	Range
1	Absorb	Grass	Special	20	100	25	Normal
1	Tackle	Normal	Physical	50	100	35	Normal
1	Stun Spore	Grass	Status	—	75	30	Normal
1	Leech Seed	Grass	Status	—	90	10	Normal
5	Stun Spore	Grass	Status	—	75	30	Normal
8	Leech Seed	Grass	Status	—	90	10	Normal
12	Mega Drain	Grass	Special	40	100	15	Normal
15	Headbutt	Normal	Physical	70	100	15	Normal
19	Feint	Normal	Physical	30	100	10	Normal
22	Counter	Fighting	Physical	—	100	20	Varies
23	Mach Punch	Fighting	Physical	40	100	30	Normal
28	Force Palm	Fighting	Physical	60	100	10	Normal
33	Mind Reader	Normal	Status	—	—	5	Normal
39	Sky Uppercut	Fighting	Physical	85	90	15	Normal
44	Seed Bomb	Grass	Physical	80	100	15	Normal
50	Dynamic Punch	Fighting	Physical	100	50	5	Normal

TM & HM MOVES

No.	Name	Type	Kind	Pow.	Acc.	PP	Range
TM06	Toxic	Poison	Status	—	90	10	Normal
TM08	Bulk Up	Fighting	Status	—	—	20	Self
TM09	Venoshock	Poison	Special	65	100	10	Normal
TM10	Hidden Power	Normal	Special	60	100	15	Normal
TM11	Sunny Day	Fire	Status	—	—	5	Both Sides
TM15	Hyper Beam	Normal	Special	150	90	5	Normal
TM17	Protect	Normal	Status	—	—	10	Self
TM20	Safeguard	Normal	Status	—	—	25	Your Side
TM21	Frustration	Normal	Physical	—	100	20	Normal
TM22	Solar Beam	Grass	Special	120	100	10	Normal
TM27	Return	Normal	Physical	—	100	20	Normal
TM31	Brick Break	Fighting	Physical	75	100	15	Normal
TM32	Double Team	Normal	Status	—	—	15	Self
TM36	Sludge Bomb	Poison	Special	90	100	10	Normal
TM39	Rock Tomb	Rock	Physical	60	95	15	Normal
TM42	Facade	Normal	Physical	70	100	20	Normal
TM44	Rest	Psychic	Status	—	—	10	Self
TM45	Attract	Normal	Status	—	100	15	Normal
TM47	Low Sweep	Fighting	Physical	65	100	20	Normal
TM48	Round	Normal	Special	60	100	15	Normal
TM52	Focus Blast	Fighting	Special	120	70	5	Normal
TM53	Energy Ball	Grass	Special	90	100	10	Normal
TM54	False Swipe	Normal	Physical	40	100	40	Normal
TM56	Fling	Dark	Physical	—	100	10	Normal
TM67	Retaliate	Normal	Physical	70	100	5	Normal
TM68	Giga Impact	Normal	Physical	150	90	5	Normal
TM70	Flash	Normal	Status	—	100	20	Normal
TM71	Stone Edge	Rock	Physical	100	80	5	Normal
TM75	Swords Dance	Normal	Status	—	—	20	Self
TM80	Rock Slide	Rock	Physical	75	90	10	Many Others
TM86	Grass Knot	Grass	Special	—	100	20	Normal
TM87	Swagger	Normal	Status	—	90	15	Normal
TM88	Sleep Talk	Normal	Status	—	—	10	Self
TM90	Substitute	Normal	Status	—	—	10	Self
TM94	Secret Power	Normal	Physical	70	100	20	Normal
TM98	Power-Up Punch	Fighting	Physical	40	100	20	Normal
TM100	Confide	Normal	Status	—	—	20	Normal
HM01	Cut	Normal	Physical	50	95	30	Normal
HM04	Strength	Normal	Physical	80	100	15	Normal
HM06	Rock Smash	Fighting	Physical	40	100	15	Normal

MOVES LEARNED IN EXCHANGE FOR BP

Name	Type	Kind	Pow.	Acc.	PP	Range
Seed Bomb	Grass	Physical	80	100	15	Normal
Thunder Punch	Electric	Physical	75	100	15	Normal
Superpower	Fighting	Physical	120	100	5	Normal
Iron Tail	Steel	Physical	100	75	15	Normal
Snore	Normal	Special	50	100	15	Normal
Synthesis	Grass	Status	—	—	5	Self
Giga Drain	Grass	Special	75	100	10	Normal
Drain Punch	Fighting	Physical	75	100	10	Normal
Focus Punch	Fighting	Physical	150	100	20	Normal
Worry Seed	Grass	Status	—	100	10	Normal
Helping Hand	Normal	Status	—	—	20	1 Ally
Snatch	Dark	Status	—	—	10	Self

MOVES TAUGHT BY PEOPLE

Name	Type	Kind	Pow.	Acc.	PP	Range

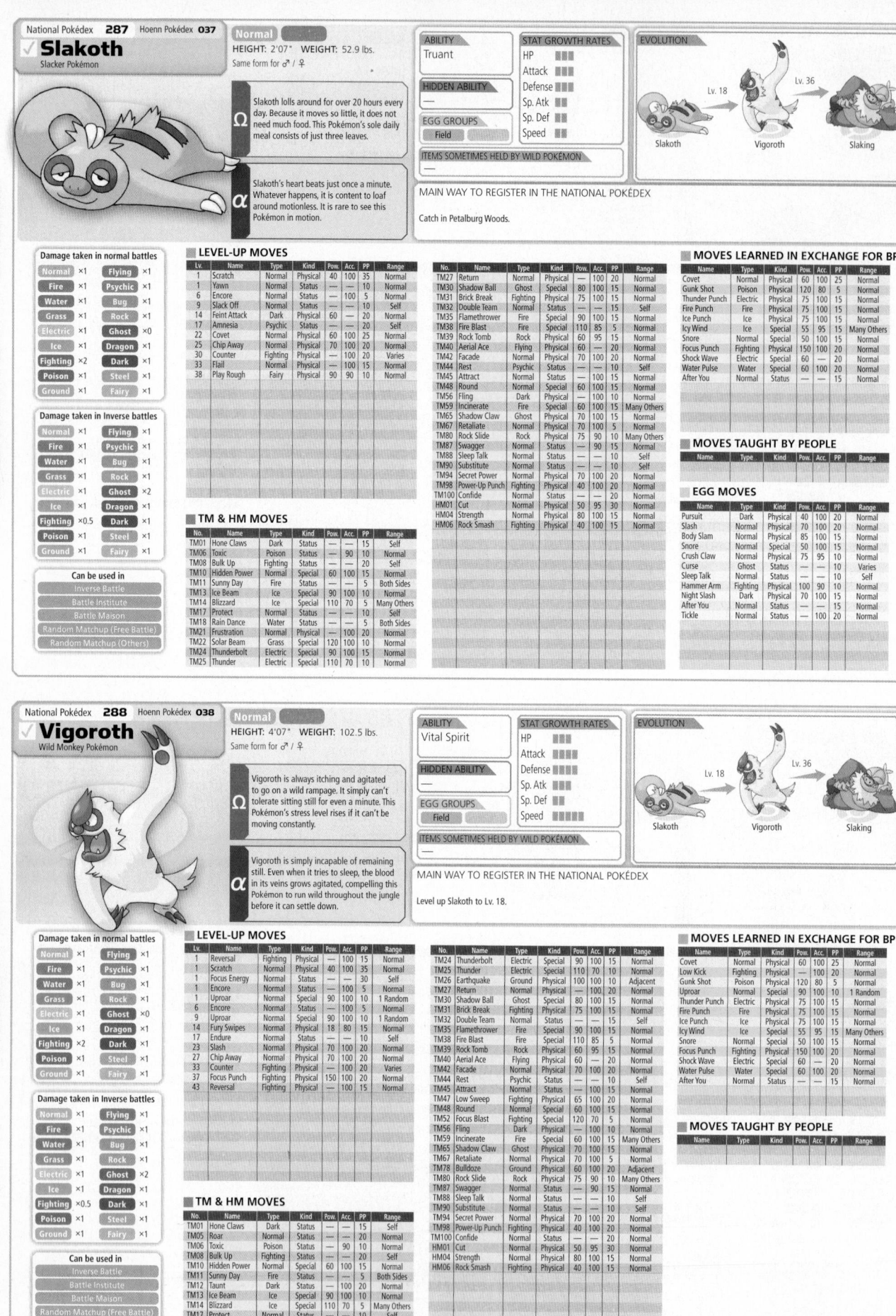

National Pokédex **287** Hoenn Pokédex **037**

Slakoth

Slacker Pokémon

Normal

HEIGHT: 2'07" WEIGHT: 52.9 lbs.

Same form for ♂ / ♀

Ω Slakoth lolls around for over 20 hours every day. Because it moves so little, it does not need much food. This Pokémon's sole daily meal consists of just three leaves.

α Slakoth's heart beats just once a minute. Whatever happens, it is content to loaf around motionless. It is rare to see this Pokémon in motion.

ABILITY
Truant

HIDDEN ABILITY
—

EGG GROUPS
Field

STAT GROWTH RATES
HP ■■■
Attack ■■■
Defense ■■■
Sp. Atk ■■
Sp. Def ■■
Speed ■■

ITEMS SOMETIMES HELD BY WILD POKÉMON
—

EVOLUTION
Slakoth → Lv. 18 → Vigoroth → Lv. 36 → Slaking

MAIN WAY TO REGISTER IN THE NATIONAL POKÉDEX

Catch in Petalburg Woods.

Damage taken in normal battles

Type		Type	
Normal	×1	Flying	×1
Fire	×1	Psychic	×1
Water	×1	Bug	×1
Grass	×1	Rock	×1
Electric	×1	Ghost	×0
Ice	×1	Dragon	×1
Fighting	×2	Dark	×1
Poison	×1	Steel	×1
Ground	×1	Fairy	×1

Damage taken in Inverse battles

Type		Type	
Normal	×1	Flying	×1
Fire	×1	Psychic	×1
Water	×1	Bug	×1
Grass	×1	Rock	×1
Electric	×1	Ghost	×2
Ice	×1	Dragon	×1
Fighting	×0.5	Dark	×1
Poison	×1	Steel	×1
Ground	×1	Fairy	×1

Can be used in
Inverse Battle
Battle Institute
Battle Maison
Random Matchup (Free Battle)
Random Matchup (Others)

LEVEL-UP MOVES

Lv.	Name	Type	Kind	Pow.	Acc.	PP	Range
1	Scratch	Normal	Physical	40	100	35	Normal
1	Yawn	Normal	Status	—	—	10	Normal
6	Encore	Normal	Status	—	100	5	Normal
9	Slack Off	Normal	Status	—	—	10	Self
14	Feint Attack	Dark	Physical	60	—	20	Normal
17	Amnesia	Psychic	Status	—	—	20	Self
22	Covet	Normal	Physical	60	100	25	Normal
25	Chip Away	Normal	Physical	70	100	20	Normal
30	Counter	Fighting	Physical	—	100	20	Varies
33	Flail	Normal	Physical	—	100	15	Normal
38	Play Rough	Fairy	Physical	90	90	10	Normal

TM & HM MOVES

No.	Name	Type	Kind	Pow.	Acc.	PP	Range
TM01	Hone Claws	Dark	Status	—	—	15	Self
TM06	Toxic	Poison	Status	—	90	10	Normal
TM08	Bulk Up	Fighting	Status	—	—	20	Self
TM10	Hidden Power	Normal	Special	60	100	15	Normal
TM11	Sunny Day	Fire	Status	—	—	5	Both Sides
TM13	Ice Beam	Ice	Special	90	100	10	Normal
TM14	Blizzard	Ice	Special	110	70	5	Many Others
TM17	Protect	Normal	Status	—	—	10	Self
TM18	Rain Dance	Water	Status	—	—	5	Both Sides
TM21	Frustration	Normal	Physical	—	100	20	Normal
TM22	Solar Beam	Grass	Special	120	100	10	Normal
TM24	Thunderbolt	Electric	Special	90	100	15	Normal
TM25	Thunder	Electric	Special	110	70	10	Normal
TM27	Return	Normal	Physical	—	100	20	Normal
TM30	Shadow Ball	Ghost	Special	80	100	15	Normal
TM31	Brick Break	Fighting	Physical	75	100	15	Normal
TM32	Double Team	Normal	Status	—	—	15	Self
TM35	Flamethrower	Fire	Special	90	100	15	Normal
TM38	Fire Blast	Fire	Special	110	85	5	Normal
TM39	Rock Tomb	Rock	Physical	60	95	15	Normal
TM40	Aerial Ace	Flying	Physical	60	—	20	Normal
TM42	Facade	Normal	Physical	70	100	20	Normal
TM44	Rest	Psychic	Status	—	—	10	Self
TM45	Attract	Normal	Status	—	100	15	Normal
TM48	Round	Normal	Special	60	100	15	Normal
TM56	Fling	Dark	Physical	—	100	10	Normal
TM59	Incinerate	Fire	Special	60	100	15	Many Others
TM65	Shadow Claw	Ghost	Physical	70	100	15	Normal
TM67	Retaliate	Normal	Physical	70	100	5	Normal
TM80	Rock Slide	Rock	Physical	75	90	10	Many Others
TM87	Swagger	Normal	Status	—	90	15	Normal
TM88	Sleep Talk	Normal	Status	—	—	10	Self
TM90	Substitute	Normal	Status	—	—	10	Self
TM94	Secret Power	Normal	Physical	70	100	20	Normal
TM98	Power-Up Punch	Fighting	Physical	40	100	20	Normal
TM100	Confide	Normal	Status	—	—	20	Normal
HM01	Cut	Normal	Physical	50	95	30	Normal
HM04	Strength	Normal	Physical	80	100	15	Normal
HM06	Rock Smash	Fighting	Physical	40	100	15	Normal

MOVES LEARNED IN EXCHANGE FOR BP

Name	Type	Kind	Pow.	Acc.	PP	Range
Covet	Normal	Physical	60	100	25	Normal
Gunk Shot	Poison	Physical	120	80	5	Normal
Thunder Punch	Electric	Physical	75	100	15	Normal
Fire Punch	Fire	Physical	75	100	15	Normal
Ice Punch	Ice	Physical	75	100	15	Normal
Icy Wind	Ice	Special	55	95	15	Many Others
Snore	Normal	Special	50	100	15	Normal
Focus Punch	Fighting	Physical	150	100	20	Normal
Shock Wave	Electric	Special	60	—	20	Normal
Water Pulse	Water	Special	60	100	20	Normal
After You	Normal	Status	—	—	15	Normal

MOVES TAUGHT BY PEOPLE

Name	Type	Kind	Pow.	Acc.	PP	Range

EGG MOVES

Name	Type	Kind	Pow.	Acc.	PP	Range
Pursuit	Dark	Physical	40	100	20	Normal
Slash	Normal	Physical	70	100	20	Normal
Body Slam	Normal	Physical	85	100	15	Normal
Snore	Normal	Special	50	100	15	Normal
Crush Claw	Normal	Physical	75	95	10	Normal
Curse	Ghost	Status	—	—	10	Varies
Sleep Talk	Normal	Status	—	—	10	Self
Hammer Arm	Fighting	Physical	100	90	10	Normal
Night Slash	Dark	Physical	70	100	15	Normal
After You	Normal	Status	—	—	15	Normal
Tickle	Normal	Status	—	100	20	Normal

National Pokédex **288** Hoenn Pokédex **038**

Vigoroth

Wild Monkey Pokémon

Normal

HEIGHT: 4'07" WEIGHT: 102.5 lbs.

Same form for ♂ / ♀

Ω Vigoroth is always itching and agitated to go on a wild rampage. It simply can't tolerate sitting still for even a minute. This Pokémon's stress level rises if it can't be moving constantly.

α Vigoroth is simply incapable of remaining still. Even when it tries to sleep, the blood in its veins grows agitated, compelling this Pokémon to run wild throughout the jungle before it can settle down.

ABILITY
Vital Spirit

HIDDEN ABILITY
—

EGG GROUPS
Field

STAT GROWTH RATES
HP ■■■
Attack ■■■■
Defense ■■■■
Sp. Atk ■■■
Sp. Def ■■
Speed ■■■■■

ITEMS SOMETIMES HELD BY WILD POKÉMON
—

EVOLUTION
Slakoth → Lv. 18 → Vigoroth → Lv. 36 → Slaking

MAIN WAY TO REGISTER IN THE NATIONAL POKÉDEX

Level up Slakoth to Lv. 18.

Damage taken in normal battles

Type		Type	
Normal	×1	Flying	×1
Fire	×1	Psychic	×1
Water	×1	Bug	×1
Grass	×1	Rock	×1
Electric	×1	Ghost	×0
Ice	×1	Dragon	×1
Fighting	×2	Dark	×1
Poison	×1	Steel	×1
Ground	×1	Fairy	×1

Damage taken in Inverse battles

Type		Type	
Normal	×1	Flying	×1
Fire	×1	Psychic	×1
Water	×1	Bug	×1
Grass	×1	Rock	×1
Electric	×1	Ghost	×2
Ice	×1	Dragon	×1
Fighting	×0.5	Dark	×1
Poison	×1	Steel	×1
Ground	×1	Fairy	×1

Can be used in
Inverse Battle
Battle Institute
Battle Maison
Random Matchup (Free Battle)
Random Matchup (Others)

LEVEL-UP MOVES

Lv.	Name	Type	Kind	Pow.	Acc.	PP	Range
1	Reversal	Fighting	Physical	—	100	15	Normal
1	Scratch	Normal	Physical	40	100	35	Normal
1	Focus Energy	Normal	Status	—	—	30	Self
1	Encore	Normal	Status	—	100	5	Normal
1	Uproar	Normal	Special	90	100	10	1 Random
6	Encore	Normal	Status	—	100	5	Normal
9	Uproar	Normal	Special	90	100	10	1 Random
14	Fury Swipes	Normal	Physical	18	80	15	Normal
17	Endure	Normal	Status	—	—	10	Self
23	Slash	Normal	Physical	70	100	20	Normal
27	Chip Away	Normal	Physical	70	100	20	Normal
33	Counter	Fighting	Physical	—	100	20	Varies
37	Focus Punch	Fighting	Physical	150	100	20	Normal
43	Reversal	Fighting	Physical	—	100	15	Normal

TM & HM MOVES

No.	Name	Type	Kind	Pow.	Acc.	PP	Range
TM01	Hone Claws	Dark	Status	—	—	15	Self
TM05	Roar	Normal	Status	—	—	20	Normal
TM06	Toxic	Poison	Status	—	90	10	Normal
TM08	Bulk Up	Fighting	Status	—	—	20	Self
TM10	Hidden Power	Normal	Special	60	100	15	Normal
TM11	Sunny Day	Fire	Status	—	—	5	Both Sides
TM12	Taunt	Dark	Status	—	100	20	Normal
TM13	Ice Beam	Ice	Special	90	100	10	Normal
TM14	Blizzard	Ice	Special	110	70	5	Many Others
TM17	Protect	Normal	Status	—	—	10	Self
TM18	Rain Dance	Water	Status	—	—	5	Both Sides
TM21	Frustration	Normal	Physical	—	100	20	Normal
TM22	Solar Beam	Grass	Special	120	100	10	Normal
TM24	Thunderbolt	Electric	Special	90	100	15	Normal
TM25	Thunder	Electric	Special	110	70	10	Normal
TM26	Earthquake	Ground	Physical	100	100	10	Adjacent
TM27	Return	Normal	Physical	—	100	20	Normal
TM30	Shadow Ball	Ghost	Special	80	100	15	Normal
TM31	Brick Break	Fighting	Physical	75	100	15	Normal
TM32	Double Team	Normal	Status	—	—	15	Self
TM35	Flamethrower	Fire	Special	90	100	15	Normal
TM38	Fire Blast	Fire	Special	110	85	5	Normal
TM39	Rock Tomb	Rock	Physical	60	95	15	Normal
TM40	Aerial Ace	Flying	Physical	60	—	20	Normal
TM42	Facade	Normal	Physical	70	100	20	Normal
TM44	Rest	Psychic	Status	—	—	10	Self
TM45	Attract	Normal	Status	—	100	15	Normal
TM47	Low Sweep	Fighting	Physical	65	100	20	Normal
TM48	Round	Normal	Special	60	100	15	Normal
TM52	Focus Blast	Fighting	Special	120	70	5	Normal
TM56	Fling	Dark	Physical	—	100	10	Normal
TM59	Incinerate	Fire	Special	60	100	15	Many Others
TM65	Shadow Claw	Ghost	Physical	70	100	15	Normal
TM67	Retaliate	Normal	Physical	70	100	5	Normal
TM78	Bulldoze	Ground	Physical	60	100	20	Adjacent
TM80	Rock Slide	Rock	Physical	75	90	10	Many Others
TM87	Swagger	Normal	Status	—	90	15	Normal
TM88	Sleep Talk	Normal	Status	—	—	10	Self
TM90	Substitute	Normal	Status	—	—	10	Self
TM94	Secret Power	Normal	Physical	70	100	20	Normal
TM98	Power-Up Punch	Fighting	Physical	40	100	20	Normal
TM100	Confide	Normal	Status	—	—	20	Normal
HM01	Cut	Normal	Physical	50	95	30	Normal
HM04	Strength	Normal	Physical	80	100	15	Normal
HM06	Rock Smash	Fighting	Physical	40	100	15	Normal

MOVES LEARNED IN EXCHANGE FOR BP

Name	Type	Kind	Pow.	Acc.	PP	Range
Covet	Normal	Physical	60	100	25	Normal
Low Kick	Fighting	Physical	—	100	20	Normal
Gunk Shot	Poison	Physical	120	80	5	Normal
Uproar	Normal	Special	90	100	10	1 Random
Thunder Punch	Electric	Physical	75	100	15	Normal
Fire Punch	Fire	Physical	75	100	15	Normal
Ice Punch	Ice	Physical	75	100	15	Normal
Icy Wind	Ice	Special	55	95	15	Many Others
Snore	Normal	Special	50	100	15	Normal
Focus Punch	Fighting	Physical	150	100	20	Normal
Shock Wave	Electric	Special	60	—	20	Normal
Water Pulse	Water	Special	60	100	20	Normal
After You	Normal	Status	—	—	15	Normal

MOVES TAUGHT BY PEOPLE

Name	Type	Kind	Pow.	Acc.	PP	Range

National Pokédex **289** Hoenn Pokédex **039**

Slaking

Lazy Pokémon

Normal

HEIGHT: 6'07" WEIGHT: 287.7 lbs.

Same form for ♂ / ♀

Ω Slaking spends all day lying down and lolling about. It eats grass growing within its reach. If it eats all the grass it can reach, this Pokémon reluctantly moves to another spot.

α Wherever Slaking live, rings of over a yard in diameter appear in grassy fields. They are made by the Pokémon as it eats all the grass within reach while lying prone on the ground.

ABILITY
Truant

HIDDEN ABILITY
—

EGG GROUPS
Field

STAT GROWTH RATES
HP
Attack
Defense
Sp. Atk
Sp. Def
Speed

ITEMS SOMETIMES HELD BY WILD POKÉMON
—

EVOLUTION

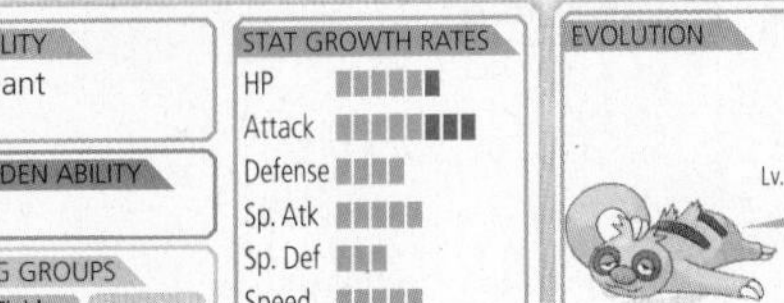

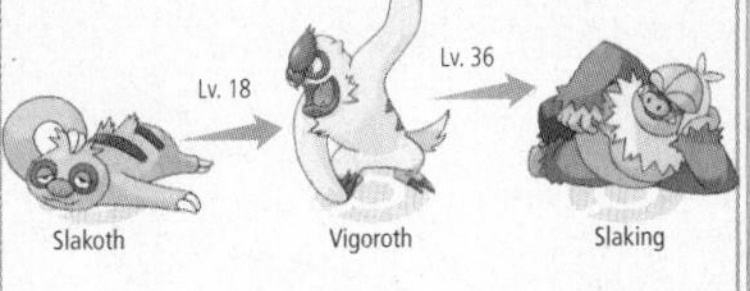

MAIN WAY TO REGISTER IN THE NATIONAL POKÉDEX

Level up Vigoroth to Lv. 36.

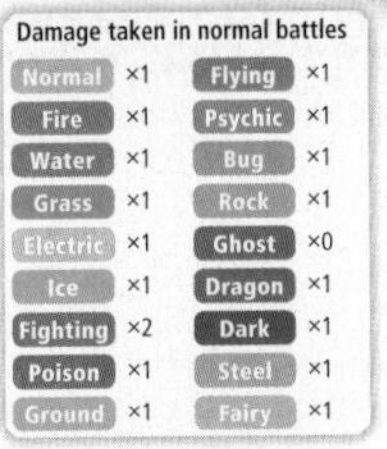

Damage taken in normal battles

Type		Type	
Normal	×1	Flying	×1
Fire	×1	Psychic	×1
Water	×1	Bug	×1
Grass	×1	Rock	×1
Electric	×1	Ghost	×0
Ice	×1	Dragon	×1
Fighting	×2	Dark	×1
Poison	×1	Steel	×1
Ground	×1	Fairy	×1

Damage taken in Inverse battles

Type		Type	
Normal	×1	Flying	×1
Fire	×1	Psychic	×1
Water	×1	Bug	×1
Grass	×1	Rock	×1
Electric	×1	Ghost	×2
Ice	×1	Dragon	×1
Fighting	×0.5	Dark	×1
Poison	×1	Steel	×1
Ground	×1	Fairy	×1

Can be used in
Inverse Battle
Battle Institute
Battle Maison
Random Matchup (Free Battle)
Random Matchup (Others)

LEVEL-UP MOVES

Lv.	Name	Type	Kind	Pow.	Acc.	PP	Range
1	Hammer Arm	Fighting	Physical	100	90	10	Normal
1	Punishment	Dark	Physical	—	100	5	Normal
1	Fling	Dark	Physical	—	100	10	Normal
1	Scratch	Normal	Physical	40	100	35	Normal
1	Yawn	Normal	Status	—	—	10	Normal
1	Encore	Normal	Status	—	100	5	Normal
1	Slack Off	Normal	Status	—	—	10	Self
6	Encore	Normal	Status	—	100	5	Normal
9	Slack Off	Normal	Status	—	—	10	Self
14	Feint Attack	Dark	Physical	60	—	20	Normal
17	Amnesia	Psychic	Status	—	—	20	Self
23	Covet	Normal	Physical	60	100	25	Normal
27	Chip Away	Normal	Physical	70	100	20	Normal
33	Counter	Fighting	Physical	—	100	20	Varies
36	Swagger	Normal	Status	—	90	15	Normal
39	Flail	Normal	Physical	—	100	15	Normal
47	Fling	Dark	Physical	—	100	10	Normal
53	Punishment	Dark	Physical	—	100	5	Normal
61	Hammer Arm	Fighting	Physical	100	90	10	Normal

TM & HM MOVES

No.	Name	Type	Kind	Pow.	Acc.	PP	Range
TM01	Hone Claws	Dark	Status	—	—	15	Self
TM05	Roar	Normal	Status	—	—	20	Normal
TM06	Toxic	Poison	Status	—	90	10	Normal
TM08	Bulk Up	Fighting	Status	—	—	20	Self
TM10	Hidden Power	Normal	Special	60	100	15	Normal
TM11	Sunny Day	Fire	Status	—	—	5	Both Sides
TM12	Taunt	Dark	Status	—	100	20	Normal
TM13	Ice Beam	Ice	Special	90	100	10	Normal
TM14	Blizzard	Ice	Special	110	70	5	Many Others
TM15	Hyper Beam	Normal	Special	150	90	5	Normal
TM17	Protect	Normal	Status	—	—	10	Self
TM18	Rain Dance	Water	Status	—	—	5	Both Sides
TM21	Frustration	Normal	Physical	—	100	20	Normal
TM22	Solar Beam	Grass	Special	120	100	10	Normal
TM23	Smack Down	Rock	Physical	50	100	15	Normal
TM24	Thunderbolt	Electric	Special	90	100	15	Normal
TM25	Thunder	Electric	Special	110	70	10	Normal
TM26	Earthquake	Ground	Physical	100	100	10	Adjacent
TM27	Return	Normal	Physical	—	100	20	Normal
TM30	Shadow Ball	Ghost	Special	80	100	15	Normal
TM31	Brick Break	Fighting	Physical	75	100	15	Normal
TM32	Double Team	Normal	Status	—	—	15	Self
TM35	Flamethrower	Fire	Special	90	100	15	Normal
TM38	Fire Blast	Fire	Special	110	85	5	Normal
TM39	Rock Tomb	Rock	Physical	60	95	15	Normal
TM40	Aerial Ace	Flying	Physical	60	—	20	Normal
TM42	Facade	Normal	Physical	70	100	20	Normal
TM44	Rest	Psychic	Status	—	—	10	Self
TM45	Attract	Normal	Status	—	100	15	Normal
TM47	Low Sweep	Fighting	Physical	65	100	20	Normal
TM48	Round	Normal	Special	60	100	15	Normal
TM52	Focus Blast	Fighting	Special	120	70	5	Normal
TM56	Fling	Dark	Physical	—	100	10	Normal
TM59	Incinerate	Fire	Special	60	100	15	Many Others
TM60	Quash	Dark	Status	—	100	15	Normal
TM65	Shadow Claw	Ghost	Physical	70	100	15	Normal
TM67	Retaliate	Normal	Physical	70	100	5	Normal
TM68	Giga Impact	Normal	Physical	150	90	5	Normal
TM78	Bulldoze	Ground	Physical	60	100	20	Adjacent
TM80	Rock Slide	Rock	Physical	75	90	10	Many Others
TM87	Swagger	Normal	Status	—	90	15	Normal
TM88	Sleep Talk	Normal	Status	—	—	10	Self
TM90	Substitute	Normal	Status	—	—	10	Self
TM94	Secret Power	Normal	Physical	70	100	20	Normal
TM98	Power-Up Punch	Fighting	Physical	40	100	20	Normal
TM100	Confide	Normal	Status	—	—	20	Normal
HM01	Cut	Normal	Physical	50	95	30	Normal
HM04	Strength	Normal	Physical	80	100	15	Normal
HM06	Rock Smash	Fighting	Physical	40	100	15	Normal

MOVES LEARNED IN EXCHANGE FOR BP

Name	Type	Kind	Pow.	Acc.	PP	Range
Covet	Normal	Physical	60	100	25	Normal
Low Kick	Fighting	Physical	—	100	20	Normal
Gunk Shot	Poison	Physical	120	80	5	Normal
Thunder Punch	Electric	Physical	75	100	15	Normal
Fire Punch	Fire	Physical	75	100	15	Normal
Ice Punch	Ice	Physical	75	100	15	Normal
Block	Normal	Status	—	—	5	Normal
Icy Wind	Ice	Special	55	95	15	Many Others
Snore	Normal	Special	50	100	15	Normal
Focus Punch	Fighting	Physical	150	100	20	Normal
Shock Wave	Electric	Special	60	—	20	Normal
Water Pulse	Water	Special	60	100	20	Normal
After You	Normal	Status	—	—	15	Normal

MOVES TAUGHT BY PEOPLE

Name	Type	Kind	Pow.	Acc.	PP	Range

National Pokédex **290** Hoenn Pokédex **043**

Nincada

Trainee Pokémon

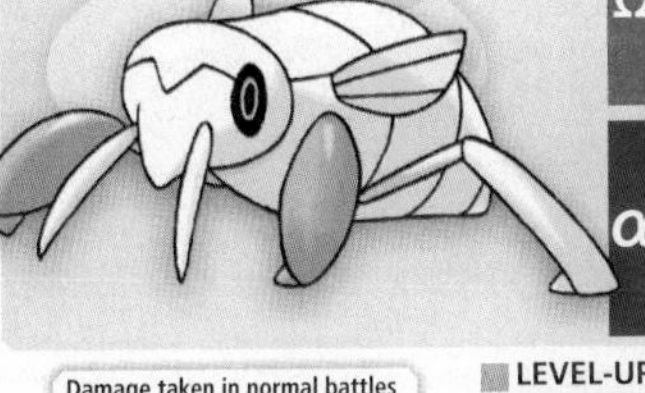

Bug Ground

HEIGHT: 1'08" WEIGHT: 12.1 lbs.

Same form for ♂ / ♀

Ω Nincada lives underground for many years in complete darkness. This Pokémon absorbs nutrients from the roots of trees. It stays motionless as it waits for evolution.

α Nincada lives underground. It uses its sharp claws to carve the roots of trees and absorb moisture and nutrients. This Pokémon can't withstand bright sunlight so avoids it.

ABILITY
Compound Eyes

HIDDEN ABILITY
Run Away

EGG GROUPS
Bug

STAT GROWTH RATES
HP
Attack
Defense
Sp. Atk
Sp. Def
Speed

ITEMS SOMETIMES HELD BY WILD POKÉMON
Run Away

EVOLUTION

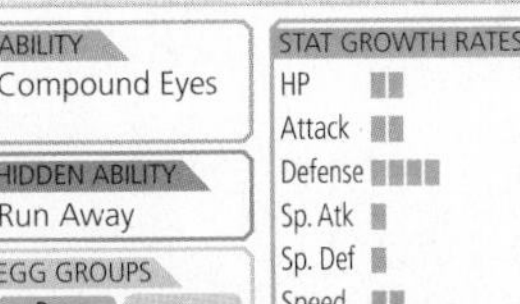

MAIN WAY TO REGISTER IN THE NATIONAL POKÉDEX

Catch on Route 116.

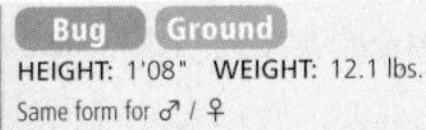

Damage taken in normal battles

Type		Type	
Normal	×1	Flying	×2
Fire	×2	Psychic	×1
Water	×2	Bug	×1
Grass	×1	Rock	×1
Electric	×0	Ghost	×1
Ice	×2	Dragon	×1
Fighting	×0.5	Dark	×1
Poison	×0.5	Steel	×1
Ground	×0.5	Fairy	×1

Damage taken in Inverse battles

Type		Type	
Normal	×1	Flying	×0.5
Fire	×0.5	Psychic	×1
Water	×0.5	Bug	×1
Grass	×1	Rock	×1
Electric	×2	Ghost	×1
Ice	×0.5	Dragon	×1
Fighting	×2	Dark	×1
Poison	×2	Steel	×1
Ground	×2	Fairy	×1

Can be used in
Inverse Battle
Battle Institute
Battle Maison
Random Matchup (Free Battle)
Random Matchup (Others)

LEVEL-UP MOVES

Lv.	Name	Type	Kind	Pow.	Acc.	PP	Range
1	Scratch	Normal	Physical	40	100	35	Normal
1	Harden	Normal	Status	—	—	30	Self
5	Leech Life	Bug	Physical	20	100	15	Normal
9	Sand Attack	Ground	Status	—	100	15	Normal
13	Fury Swipes	Normal	Physical	18	80	15	Normal
17	Mud-Slap	Ground	Special	20	100	10	Normal
21	Metal Claw	Steel	Physical	50	95	35	Normal
25	Mind Reader	Normal	Status	—	—	5	Normal
29	Bide	Normal	Physical	—	—	10	Self
33	False Swipe	Normal	Physical	40	100	40	Normal
37	Dig	Ground	Physical	80	100	10	Normal

TM & HM MOVES

No.	Name	Type	Kind	Pow.	Acc.	PP	Range
TM01	Hone Claws	Dark	Status	—	—	15	Self
TM06	Toxic	Poison	Status	—	90	10	Normal
TM10	Hidden Power	Normal	Special	60	100	15	Normal
TM11	Sunny Day	Fire	Status	—	—	5	Both Sides
TM17	Protect	Normal	Status	—	—	10	Self
TM21	Frustration	Normal	Physical	—	100	20	Normal
TM22	Solar Beam	Grass	Special	120	100	10	Normal
TM27	Return	Normal	Physical	—	100	20	Normal
TM28	Dig	Ground	Physical	80	100	10	Normal
TM30	Shadow Ball	Ghost	Special	80	100	15	Normal
TM32	Double Team	Normal	Status	—	—	15	Self
TM37	Sandstorm	Rock	Status	—	—	10	Both Sides
TM40	Aerial Ace	Flying	Physical	60	—	20	Normal
TM42	Facade	Normal	Physical	70	100	20	Normal
TM44	Rest	Psychic	Status	—	—	10	Self
TM48	Round	Normal	Special	60	100	15	Normal
TM54	False Swipe	Normal	Physical	40	100	40	Normal
TM70	Flash	Normal	Status	—	100	20	Normal
TM76	Struggle Bug	Bug	Special	50	100	20	Many Others
TM81	X-Scissor	Bug	Physical	80	100	15	Normal
TM87	Swagger	Normal	Status	—	90	15	Normal
TM88	Sleep Talk	Normal	Status	—	—	10	Self
TM90	Substitute	Normal	Status	—	—	10	Self
TM94	Secret Power	Normal	Physical	70	100	20	Normal
TM100	Confide	Normal	Status	—	—	20	Normal
HM01	Cut	Normal	Physical	50	95	30	Normal

MOVES LEARNED IN EXCHANGE FOR BP

Name	Type	Kind	Pow.	Acc.	PP	Range
Bug Bite	Bug	Physical	60	100	20	Normal
Snore	Normal	Special	50	100	15	Normal
Giga Drain	Grass	Special	75	100	10	Normal
Spite	Ghost	Status	—	100	10	Normal

MOVES TAUGHT BY PEOPLE

Name	Type	Kind	Pow.	Acc.	PP	Range

EGG MOVES

Name	Type	Kind	Pow.	Acc.	PP	Range
Endure	Normal	Status	—	—	10	Self
Feint Attack	Dark	Physical	60	—	20	Normal
Gust	Flying	Special	40	100	35	Normal
Silver Wind	Bug	Special	60	100	5	Normal
Bug Buzz	Bug	Special	90	100	10	Normal
Night Slash	Dark	Physical	70	100	15	Normal
Bug Bite	Bug	Physical	60	100	20	Normal
Final Gambit	Fighting	Special	—	100	5	Normal

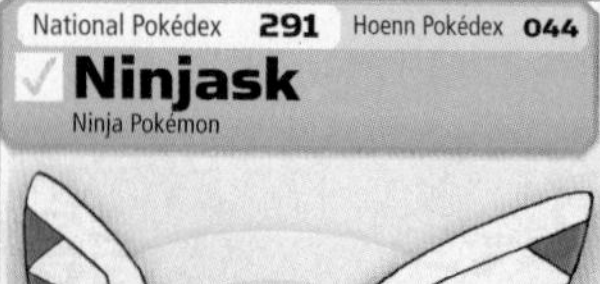

National Pokédex **291** Hoenn Pokédex **044**

Ninjask

Ninja Pokémon

Bug · Flying

HEIGHT: 2'07" WEIGHT: 26.5 lbs.

Same form for ♂ / ♀

Ω Ninjask moves around at such a high speed that it cannot be seen, even while its crying can be clearly heard. For that reason, this Pokémon was long believed to be invisible.

α If Ninjask is not trained properly, it will refuse to obey the Trainer and cry loudly continuously. Because of this quality, this Pokémon is said to be one that puts the Trainer's abilities to the test.

ABILITY
Speed Boost

HIDDEN ABILITY
Infiltrator

EGG GROUPS
Bug

STAT GROWTH RATES
HP · Attack · Defense · Sp. Atk · Sp. Def · Speed

ITEMS SOMETIMES HELD BY WILD POKÉMON
—

EVOLUTION

MAIN WAY TO REGISTER IN THE NATIONAL POKÉDEX

Level up Nincada to Lv. 20.

Damage taken in normal battles

Type		Type	
Normal	×1	Flying	×2
Fire	×2	Psychic	×1
Water	×1	Bug	×0.5
Grass	×0.25	Rock	×4
Electric	×2	Ghost	×1
Ice	×2	Dragon	×1
Fighting	×0.25	Dark	×1
Poison	×1	Steel	×1
Ground	×0	Fairy	×1

Damage taken in Inverse battles

Type		Type	
Normal	×1	Flying	×0.5
Fire	×0.5	Psychic	×1
Water	×1	Bug	×2
Grass	×4	Rock	×0.25
Electric	×0.5	Ghost	×1
Ice	×0.5	Dragon	×1
Fighting	×4	Dark	×1
Poison	×1	Steel	×1
Ground	×4	Fairy	×1

Can be used in
Inverse Battle
Battle Institute
Battle Maison
Random Matchup (Free Battle)
Random Matchup (Others)

LEVEL-UP MOVES

Lv.	Name	Type	Kind	Pow.	Acc.	PP	Range
1	Bug Bite	Bug	Physical	60	100	20	Normal
1	Scratch	Normal	Physical	40	100	35	Normal
1	Harden	Normal	Status	—	—	30	Self
1	Leech Life	Bug	Physical	20	100	15	Normal
1	Sand Attack	Ground	Status	—	100	15	Normal
5	Leech Life	Bug	Physical	20	100	15	Normal
9	Sand Attack	Ground	Status	—	100	15	Normal
13	Fury Swipes	Normal	Physical	18	80	15	Normal
17	Agility	Psychic	Status	—	—	30	Self
20	Double Team	Normal	Status	—	—	15	Self
20	Fury Cutter	Bug	Physical	40	95	20	Normal
20	Screech	Normal	Status	—	85	40	Normal
23	Slash	Normal	Physical	70	100	20	Normal
29	Mind Reader	Normal	Status	—	—	5	Normal
35	Baton Pass	Normal	Status	—	—	40	Self
41	Swords Dance	Normal	Status	—	—	20	Self
47	X-Scissor	Bug	Physical	80	100	15	Normal

TM & HM MOVES

No.	Name	Type	Kind	Pow.	Acc.	PP	Range
TM01	Hone Claws	Dark	Status	—	—	15	Self
TM06	Toxic	Poison	Status	—	90	10	Normal
TM10	Hidden Power	Normal	Special	60	100	15	Normal
TM11	Sunny Day	Fire	Status	—	—	5	Both Sides
TM15	Hyper Beam	Normal	Special	150	90	5	Normal
TM17	Protect	Normal	Status	—	—	10	Self
TM19	Roost	Flying	Status	—	—	10	Self
TM21	Frustration	Normal	Physical	—	100	20	Normal
TM22	Solar Beam	Grass	Special	120	100	10	Normal
TM27	Return	Normal	Physical	—	100	20	Normal
TM28	Dig	Ground	Physical	80	100	10	Normal
TM30	Shadow Ball	Ghost	Special	80	100	15	Normal
TM32	Double Team	Normal	Status	—	—	15	Self
TM37	Sandstorm	Rock	Status	—	—	10	Both Sides
TM40	Aerial Ace	Flying	Physical	60	—	20	Normal
TM42	Facade	Normal	Physical	70	100	20	Normal
TM44	Rest	Psychic	Status	—	—	10	Self
TM45	Attract	Normal	Status	—	100	15	Normal
TM46	Thief	Dark	Physical	60	100	25	Normal
TM48	Round	Normal	Special	60	100	15	Normal
TM54	False Swipe	Normal	Physical	40	100	40	Normal
TM68	Giga Impact	Normal	Physical	150	90	5	Normal
TM70	Flash	Normal	Status	—	100	20	Normal
TM75	Swords Dance	Normal	Status	—	—	20	Self
TM76	Struggle Bug	Bug	Special	50	100	20	Many Others
TM81	X-Scissor	Bug	Physical	80	100	15	Normal
TM87	Swagger	Normal	Status	—	90	15	Normal
TM88	Sleep Talk	Normal	Status	—	—	10	Self
TM89	U-turn	Bug	Physical	70	100	20	Normal
TM90	Substitute	Normal	Status	—	—	10	Self
TM94	Secret Power	Normal	Physical	70	100	20	Normal
TM100	Confide	Normal	Status	—	—	20	Normal
HM01	Cut	Normal	Physical	50	95	30	Normal

MOVES LEARNED IN EXCHANGE FOR BP

Name	Type	Kind	Pow.	Acc.	PP	Range
Bug Bite	Bug	Physical	60	100	20	Normal
Uproar	Normal	Special	90	100	10	1 Random
Snore	Normal	Special	50	100	15	Normal
Giga Drain	Grass	Special	75	100	10	Normal
Spite	Ghost	Status	—	100	10	Normal

MOVES TAUGHT BY PEOPLE

Name	Type	Kind	Pow.	Acc.	PP	Range

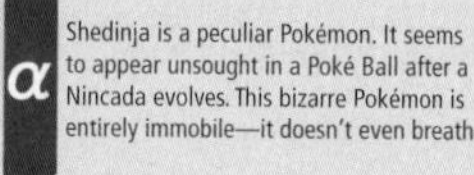

National Pokédex **292** Hoenn Pokédex **045**

Shedinja

Shed Pokémon

Bug · Ghost

HEIGHT: 2'07" WEIGHT: 2.6 lbs.

Gender unknown

Ω Shedinja's hard body doesn't move—not even a twitch. In fact, its body appears to be merely a hollow shell. It is believed that this Pokémon will steal the spirit of anyone peering into its hollow body from its back.

α Shedinja is a peculiar Pokémon. It seems to appear unsought in a Poké Ball after a Nincada evolves. This bizarre Pokémon is entirely immobile—it doesn't even breathe.

ABILITY
Wonder Guard

HIDDEN ABILITY
—

EGG GROUPS
Mineral

STAT GROWTH RATES
HP · Attack · Defense · Sp. Atk · Sp. Def · Speed

ITEMS SOMETIMES HELD BY WILD POKÉMON
—

EVOLUTION

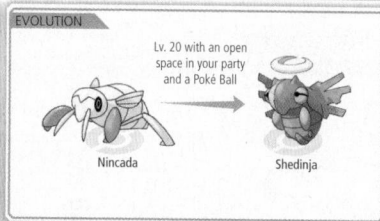

Lv. 20 with an open space in your party and a Poké Ball

Nincada → Shedinja

MAIN WAY TO REGISTER IN THE NATIONAL POKÉDEX

Level up Nincada to Lv. 20 while you have an empty space in your party and a spare Poké Ball in your Bag.

Damage taken in normal battles

Type		Type	
Normal	×0	Flying	×2
Fire	×2	! Psychic	×1
! Water	×1	! Bug	×0.5
! Grass	×0.5	Rock	×2
! Electric	×1	Ghost	×2
! Ice	×1	! Dragon	×1
Fighting	×0	Dark	×2
! Poison	×0.5	! Steel	×1
! Ground	×0.5	! Fairy	×1

Damage taken in Inverse battles

Type		Type	
Normal	×2	! Flying	×0.5
! Fire	×0.5	! Psychic	×1
! Water	×1	Bug	×2
Grass	×2	! Rock	×0.5
! Electric	×1	! Ghost	×0.5
! Ice	×1	! Dragon	×1
Fighting	×4	! Dark	×0.5
Poison	×2	! Steel	×1
Ground	×2	! Fairy	×1

Can be used in
Inverse Battle
Battle Institute
Battle Maison
Random Matchup (Free Battle)
Random Matchup (Others)

LEVEL-UP MOVES

Lv.	Name	Type	Kind	Pow.	Acc.	PP	Range
1	Scratch	Normal	Physical	40	100	35	Normal
1	Harden	Normal	Status	—	—	30	Self
5	Leech Life	Bug	Physical	20	100	15	Normal
9	Sand Attack	Ground	Status	—	100	15	Normal
13	Fury Swipes	Normal	Physical	18	80	15	Normal
17	Spite	Ghost	Status	—	100	10	Normal
21	Shadow Sneak	Ghost	Physical	40	100	30	Normal
25	Mind Reader	Normal	Status	—	—	5	Normal
29	Confuse Ray	Ghost	Status	—	100	10	Normal
33	Shadow Ball	Ghost	Special	80	100	15	Normal
37	Grudge	Ghost	Status	—	—	5	Self
41	Heal Block	Psychic	Status	—	100	15	Many Others
45	Phantom Force	Ghost	Physical	90	100	10	Normal

TM & HM MOVES

No.	Name	Type	Kind	Pow.	Acc.	PP	Range
TM01	Hone Claws	Dark	Status	—	—	15	Self
TM06	Toxic	Poison	Status	—	90	10	Normal
TM10	Hidden Power	Normal	Special	60	100	15	Normal
TM11	Sunny Day	Fire	Status	—	—	5	Both Sides
TM15	Hyper Beam	Normal	Special	150	90	5	Normal
TM17	Protect	Normal	Status	—	—	10	Self
TM21	Frustration	Normal	Physical	—	100	20	Normal
TM22	Solar Beam	Grass	Special	120	100	10	Normal
TM27	Return	Normal	Physical	—	100	20	Normal
TM28	Dig	Ground	Physical	80	100	10	Normal
TM30	Shadow Ball	Ghost	Special	80	100	15	Normal
TM32	Double Team	Normal	Status	—	—	15	Self
TM37	Sandstorm	Rock	Status	—	—	10	Both Sides
TM40	Aerial Ace	Flying	Physical	60	—	20	Normal
TM42	Facade	Normal	Physical	70	100	20	Normal
TM44	Rest	Psychic	Status	—	—	10	Self
TM46	Thief	Dark	Physical	60	100	25	Normal
TM48	Round	Normal	Special	60	100	15	Normal
TM54	False Swipe	Normal	Physical	40	100	40	Normal
TM61	Will-O-Wisp	Fire	Status	—	85	15	Normal
TM65	Shadow Claw	Ghost	Physical	70	100	15	Normal
TM68	Giga Impact	Normal	Physical	150	90	5	Normal
TM70	Flash	Normal	Status	—	100	20	Normal
TM76	Struggle Bug	Bug	Special	50	100	20	Many Others
TM81	X-Scissor	Bug	Physical	80	100	15	Normal
TM85	Dream Eater	Psychic	Special	100	100	15	Normal
TM87	Swagger	Normal	Status	—	90	15	Normal
TM88	Sleep Talk	Normal	Status	—	—	10	Self
TM90	Substitute	Normal	Status	—	—	10	Self
TM94	Secret Power	Normal	Physical	70	100	20	Normal
TM100	Confide	Normal	Status	—	—	20	Normal
HM01	Cut	Normal	Physical	50	95	30	Normal

MOVES LEARNED IN EXCHANGE FOR BP

Name	Type	Kind	Pow.	Acc.	PP	Range
Bug Bite	Bug	Physical	60	100	20	Normal
Snore	Normal	Special	50	100	15	Normal
Giga Drain	Grass	Special	75	100	10	Normal
Spite	Ghost	Status	—	100	10	Normal
Trick	Psychic	Status	—	100	10	Normal

MOVES TAUGHT BY PEOPLE

Name	Type	Kind	Pow.	Acc.	PP	Range

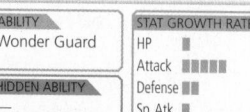

National Pokédex **293** Hoenn Pokédex **046**

✓ Whismur

Whisper Pokémon

Normal

HEIGHT: 2'00" WEIGHT: 35.9 lbs.

Same form for ♂ / ♀

Ω Normally, Whismur's voice is very quiet—it is barely audible even if one is paying close attention. However, if this Pokémon senses danger, it starts crying at an earsplitting volume.

α Whismur is very timid. If it starts to cry loudly, it becomes startled by its own crying and cries even harder. When it finally stops crying, the Pokémon goes to sleep, all tired out.

ABILITY: Soundproof

HIDDEN ABILITY: Rattled

EGG GROUPS: Monster, Field

STAT GROWTH RATES: HP ■■■ / Attack ■■■ / Defense ■ / Sp. Atk ■■■ / Sp. Def ■ / Speed ■■

ITEMS SOMETIMES HELD BY WILD POKÉMON: —

EVOLUTION: Whismur → Lv. 20 → Loudred → Lv. 40 → Exploud

MAIN WAY TO REGISTER IN THE NATIONAL POKÉDEX

Catch in Rusturf Tunnel.

Damage taken in normal battles

Type		Type	
Normal	×1	Flying	×1
Fire	×1	Psychic	×1
Water	×1	Bug	×1
Grass	×1	Rock	×1
Electric	×1	Ghost	×0
Ice	×1	Dragon	×1
Fighting	×2	Dark	×1
Poison	×1	Steel	×1
Ground	×1	Fairy	×1

Damage taken in Inverse battles

Type		Type	
Normal	×1	Flying	×1
Fire	×1	Psychic	×1
Water	×1	Bug	×1
Grass	×1	Rock	×1
Electric	×1	Ghost	×2
Ice	×1	Dragon	×1
Fighting	×0.5	Dark	×1
Poison	×1	Steel	×1
Ground	×1	Fairy	×1

Can be used in

Inverse Battle
Battle Institute
Battle Maison
Random Matchup (Free Battle)
Random Matchup (Others)

LEVEL-UP MOVES

Lv.	Name	Type	Kind	Pow.	Acc.	PP	Range
1	Pound	Normal	Physical	40	100	35	Normal
4	Echoed Voice	Normal	Special	40	100	15	Normal
8	Astonish	Ghost	Physical	30	100	15	Normal
11	Howl	Normal	Status	—	—	40	Self
15	Screech	Normal	Status	—	85	40	Normal
18	Supersonic	Normal	Status	—	55	20	Normal
22	Stomp	Normal	Physical	65	100	20	Normal
25	Uproar	Normal	Special	90	100	10	1 Random
29	Roar	Normal	Status	—	—	20	Normal
32	Rest	Psychic	Status	—	—	10	Self
36	Sleep Talk	Normal	Status	—	—	10	Self
39	Hyper Voice	Normal	Special	90	100	10	Many Others
43	Synchronoise	Psychic	Special	120	100	10	Adjacent

TM & HM MOVES

No.	Name	Type	Kind	Pow.	Acc.	PP	Range
TM05	Roar	Normal	Status	—	—	20	Normal
TM06	Toxic	Poison	Status	—	90	10	Normal
TM10	Hidden Power	Normal	Special	60	100	15	Normal
TM11	Sunny Day	Fire	Status	—	—	5	Both Sides
TM13	Ice Beam	Ice	Special	90	100	10	Normal
TM14	Blizzard	Ice	Special	110	70	5	Many Others
TM17	Protect	Normal	Status	—	—	10	Self
TM18	Rain Dance	Water	Status	—	—	5	Both Sides
TM21	Frustration	Normal	Physical	—	100	20	Normal
TM22	Solar Beam	Grass	Special	120	100	10	Normal
TM27	Return	Normal	Physical	—	100	20	Normal
TM30	Shadow Ball	Ghost	Special	80	100	15	Normal
TM32	Double Team	Normal	Status	—	—	15	Self
TM35	Flamethrower	Fire	Special	90	100	15	Normal
TM38	Fire Blast	Fire	Special	110	85	5	Normal
TM42	Facade	Normal	Physical	70	100	20	Normal
TM44	Rest	Psychic	Status	—	—	10	Self
TM45	Attract	Normal	Status	—	100	15	Normal
TM48	Round	Normal	Special	60	100	15	Normal
TM49	Echoed Voice	Normal	Special	40	100	15	Normal
TM56	Fling	Dark	Physical	—	100	10	Normal
TM59	Incinerate	Fire	Special	60	100	15	Many Others
TM67	Retaliate	Normal	Physical	70	100	5	Normal
TM87	Swagger	Normal	Status	—	90	15	Normal
TM88	Sleep Talk	Normal	Status	—	—	10	Self
TM90	Substitute	Normal	Status	—	—	10	Self
TM94	Secret Power	Normal	Physical	70	100	20	Normal
TM100	Confide	Normal	Status	—	—	20	Normal

MOVES LEARNED IN EXCHANGE FOR BP

Name	Type	Kind	Pow.	Acc.	PP	Range
Uproar	Normal	Special	90	100	10	1 Random
Thunder Punch	Electric	Physical	75	100	15	Normal
Fire Punch	Fire	Physical	75	100	15	Normal
Ice Punch	Ice	Physical	75	100	15	Normal
Icy Wind	Ice	Special	55	95	15	Many Others
Zen Headbutt	Psychic	Physical	80	90	15	Normal
Hyper Voice	Normal	Special	90	100	10	Many Others
Snore	Normal	Special	50	100	15	Normal
Shock Wave	Electric	Special	60	—	20	Normal
Water Pulse	Water	Special	60	100	20	Normal
Endeavor	Normal	Physical	—	100	5	Normal

MOVES TAUGHT BY PEOPLE

Name	Type	Kind	Pow.	Acc.	PP	Range

EGG MOVES

Name	Type	Kind	Pow.	Acc.	PP	Range
Take Down	Normal	Physical	90	85	20	Normal
Snore	Normal	Special	50	100	15	Normal
Extrasensory	Psychic	Special	80	100	20	Normal
Smelling Salts	Normal	Physical	70	100	10	Normal
Smokescreen	Normal	Status	—	100	20	Normal
Endeavor	Normal	Physical	—	100	5	Normal
Hammer Arm	Fighting	Physical	100	90	10	Normal
Fake Tears	Dark	Status	—	100	20	Normal
Circle Throw	Fighting	Physical	60	90	10	Normal
Disarming Voice	Fairy	Special	40	—	15	Many Others

National Pokédex **294** Hoenn Pokédex **047**

✓ Loudred

Big Voice Pokémon

Normal

HEIGHT: 3'03" WEIGHT: 89.3 lbs.

Same form for ♂ / ♀

Ω Loudred's bellowing can completely decimate a wood-frame house. It uses its voice to punish its foes. This Pokémon's round ears serve as loudspeakers.

α Loudred shouts while stamping its feet. After it finishes shouting, this Pokémon becomes incapable of hearing anything for a while. This is considered to be a weak point.

ABILITY: Soundproof

HIDDEN ABILITY: Scrappy

EGG GROUPS: Monster, Field

STAT GROWTH RATES: HP ■■■ / Attack ■■■■ / Defense ■■ / Sp. Atk ■■■ / Sp. Def ■■ / Speed ■■■

ITEMS SOMETIMES HELD BY WILD POKÉMON: —

EVOLUTION: Whismur → Lv. 20 → Loudred → Lv. 40 → Exploud

MAIN WAY TO REGISTER IN THE NATIONAL POKÉDEX

Catch on Victory Road (1F).

Damage taken in normal battles

Type		Type	
Normal	×1	Flying	×1
Fire	×1	Psychic	×1
Water	×1	Bug	×1
Grass	×1	Rock	×1
Electric	×1	Ghost	×0
Ice	×1	Dragon	×1
Fighting	×2	Dark	×1
Poison	×1	Steel	×1
Ground	×1	Fairy	×1

Damage taken in Inverse battles

Type		Type	
Normal	×1	Flying	×1
Fire	×1	Psychic	×1
Water	×1	Bug	×1
Grass	×1	Rock	×1
Electric	×1	Ghost	×2
Ice	×1	Dragon	×1
Fighting	×0.5	Dark	×1
Poison	×1	Steel	×1
Ground	×1	Fairy	×1

Can be used in

Inverse Battle
Battle Institute
Battle Maison
Random Matchup (Free Battle)
Random Matchup (Others)

LEVEL-UP MOVES

Lv.	Name	Type	Kind	Pow.	Acc.	PP	Range
1	Pound	Normal	Physical	40	100	35	Normal
1	Echoed Voice	Normal	Special	40	100	15	Normal
1	Astonish	Ghost	Physical	30	100	15	Normal
1	Howl	Normal	Status	—	—	40	Self
4	Echoed Voice	Normal	Special	40	100	15	Normal
9	Astonish	Ghost	Physical	30	100	15	Normal
11	Howl	Normal	Status	—	—	40	Self
15	Screech	Normal	Status	—	85	40	Normal
18	Supersonic	Normal	Status	—	55	20	Normal
20	Bite	Dark	Physical	60	100	25	Normal
23	Stomp	Normal	Physical	65	100	20	Normal
27	Uproar	Normal	Special	90	100	10	1 Random
32	Roar	Normal	Status	—	—	20	Normal
36	Rest	Psychic	Status	—	—	10	Self
41	Sleep Talk	Normal	Status	—	—	10	Self
45	Hyper Voice	Normal	Special	90	100	10	Many Others
50	Synchronoise	Psychic	Special	120	100	10	Adjacent

TM & HM MOVES

No.	Name	Type	Kind	Pow.	Acc.	PP	Range
TM05	Roar	Normal	Status	—	—	20	Normal
TM06	Toxic	Poison	Status	—	90	10	Normal
TM10	Hidden Power	Normal	Special	60	100	15	Normal
TM11	Sunny Day	Fire	Status	—	—	5	Both Sides
TM12	Taunt	Dark	Status	—	100	20	Normal
TM13	Ice Beam	Ice	Special	90	100	10	Normal
TM14	Blizzard	Ice	Special	110	70	5	Many Others
TM17	Protect	Normal	Status	—	—	10	Self
TM18	Rain Dance	Water	Status	—	—	5	Both Sides
TM21	Frustration	Normal	Physical	—	100	20	Normal
TM22	Solar Beam	Grass	Special	120	100	10	Normal
TM23	Smack Down	Rock	Physical	50	100	15	Normal
TM26	Earthquake	Ground	Physical	100	100	10	Adjacent
TM27	Return	Normal	Physical	—	100	20	Normal
TM30	Shadow Ball	Ghost	Special	80	100	15	Normal
TM31	Brick Break	Fighting	Physical	75	100	15	Normal
TM32	Double Team	Normal	Status	—	—	15	Self
TM35	Flamethrower	Fire	Special	90	100	15	Normal
TM38	Fire Blast	Fire	Special	110	85	5	Normal
TM39	Rock Tomb	Rock	Physical	60	95	15	Normal
TM41	Torment	Dark	Status	—	100	15	Normal
TM42	Facade	Normal	Physical	70	100	20	Normal
TM44	Rest	Psychic	Status	—	—	10	Self
TM45	Attract	Normal	Status	—	100	15	Normal
TM48	Round	Normal	Special	60	100	15	Normal
TM49	Echoed Voice	Normal	Special	40	100	15	Normal
TM50	Overheat	Fire	Special	130	90	5	Normal
TM56	Fling	Dark	Physical	—	100	10	Normal
TM59	Incinerate	Fire	Special	60	100	15	Many Others
TM67	Retaliate	Normal	Physical	70	100	5	Normal
TM78	Bulldoze	Ground	Physical	60	100	20	Adjacent
TM80	Rock Slide	Rock	Physical	75	90	10	Many Others
TM87	Swagger	Normal	Status	—	90	15	Normal
TM88	Sleep Talk	Normal	Status	—	—	10	Self
TM90	Substitute	Normal	Status	—	—	10	Self
TM94	Secret Power	Normal	Physical	70	100	20	Normal
TM98	Power-Up Punch	Fighting	Physical	40	100	20	Normal
TM100	Confide	Normal	Status	—	—	20	Normal
HM04	Strength	Normal	Physical	80	100	15	Normal
HM06	Rock Smash	Fighting	Physical	40	100	15	Normal

MOVES LEARNED IN EXCHANGE FOR BP

Name	Type	Kind	Pow.	Acc.	PP	Range
Low Kick	Fighting	Physical	—	100	20	Normal
Uproar	Normal	Special	90	100	10	1 Random
Thunder Punch	Electric	Physical	75	100	15	Normal
Fire Punch	Fire	Physical	75	100	15	Normal
Ice Punch	Ice	Physical	75	100	15	Normal
Icy Wind	Ice	Special	55	95	15	Many Others
Zen Headbutt	Psychic	Physical	80	90	15	Normal
Hyper Voice	Normal	Special	90	100	10	Many Others
Snore	Normal	Special	50	100	15	Normal
Shock Wave	Electric	Special	60	—	20	Normal
Water Pulse	Water	Special	60	100	20	Normal
Endeavor	Normal	Physical	—	100	5	Normal

MOVES TAUGHT BY PEOPLE

Name	Type	Kind	Pow.	Acc.	PP	Range

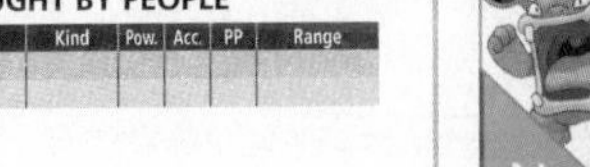

National Pokédex **295** Hoenn Pokédex **048**

Exploud

Loud Noise Pokémon

Normal

HEIGHT: 4'11" WEIGHT: 185.2 lbs.

Same form for ♂ / ♀

Ω Exploud triggers earthquakes with the tremors it creates by bellowing. If this Pokémon violently inhales from the ports on its body, it's a sign that it is preparing to let loose a huge bellow.

α Exploud communicates its feelings to the others by emitting whistle-like sounds from the tubes on its body. This Pokémon only raises its voice when it is in battle.

ABILITY
Soundproof

HIDDEN ABILITY
Scrappy

EGG GROUPS
Monster / Field

STAT GROWTH RATES
HP, Attack, Defense, Sp. Atk, Sp. Def, Speed

ITEMS SOMETIMES HELD BY WILD POKÉMON
—

EVOLUTION
Whismur → Lv. 20 → Loudred → Lv. 40 → Exploud

MAIN WAY TO REGISTER IN THE NATIONAL POKÉDEX

Level up Loudred to Lv. 40.

Damage taken in normal battles

Type	×	Type	×
Normal	×1	Flying	×1
Fire	×1	Psychic	×1
Water	×1	Bug	×1
Grass	×1	Rock	×1
Electric	×1	Ghost	×0
Ice	×1	Dragon	×1
Fighting	×2	Dark	×1
Poison	×1	Steel	×1
Ground	×1	Fairy	×1

Damage taken in Inverse battles

Type	×	Type	×
Normal	×1	Flying	×1
Fire	×1	Psychic	×1
Water	×1	Bug	×1
Grass	×1	Rock	×1
Electric	×1	Ghost	×2
Ice	×1	Dragon	×1
Fighting	×0.5	Dark	×1
Poison	×1	Steel	×1
Ground	×1	Fairy	×1

Can be used in
Inverse Battle
Battle Institute
Battle Maison
Random Matchup (Free Battle)
Random Matchup (Others)

LEVEL-UP MOVES

Lv.	Name	Type	Kind	Pow.	Acc.	PP	Range
1	Boomburst	Normal	Special	140	100	10	Adjacent
1	Ice Fang	Ice	Physical	65	95	15	Normal
1	Fire Fang	Fire	Physical	65	95	15	Normal
1	Thunder Fang	Electric	Physical	65	95	15	Normal
1	Pound	Normal	Physical	40	100	35	Normal
1	Echoed Voice	Normal	Special	40	100	15	Normal
1	Astonish	Ghost	Physical	30	100	15	Normal
1	Howl	Normal	Status	—	—	40	Self
4	Echoed Voice	Normal	Special	40	100	15	Normal
9	Astonish	Ghost	Physical	30	100	15	Normal
11	Howl	Normal	Status	—	—	40	Self
15	Screech	Normal	Status	—	85	40	Normal
18	Supersonic	Normal	Status	—	55	20	Normal
20	Bite	Dark	Physical	60	100	25	Normal
23	Stomp	Normal	Physical	65	100	20	Normal
27	Uproar	Normal	Special	90	100	10	1 Random
32	Roar	Normal	Status	—	—	20	Normal
36	Rest	Psychic	Status	—	—	10	Self
40	Crunch	Dark	Physical	80	100	15	Normal
42	Sleep Talk	Normal	Status	—	—	10	Self
47	Hyper Voice	Normal	Special	90	100	10	Many Others
53	Synchronoise	Psychic	Special	120	100	10	Adjacent
58	Boomburst	Normal	Special	140	100	10	Adjacent
64	Hyper Beam	Normal	Special	150	90	5	Normal

TM & HM MOVES

No.	Name	Type	Kind	Pow.	Acc.	PP	Range
TM05	Roar	Normal	Status	—	—	20	Normal
TM06	Toxic	Poison	Status	—	90	10	Normal
TM10	Hidden Power	Normal	Special	60	100	15	Normal
TM11	Sunny Day	Fire	Status	—	—	5	Both Sides
TM12	Taunt	Dark	Status	—	100	20	Normal
TM13	Ice Beam	Ice	Special	90	100	10	Normal
TM14	Blizzard	Ice	Special	110	70	5	Many Others
TM15	Hyper Beam	Normal	Special	150	90	5	Normal
TM17	Protect	Normal	Status	—	—	10	Self
TM18	Rain Dance	Water	Status	—	—	5	Both Sides
TM21	Frustration	Normal	Physical	—	100	20	Normal
TM22	Solar Beam	Grass	Special	120	100	10	Normal
TM23	Smack Down	Rock	Physical	50	100	15	Normal
TM26	Earthquake	Ground	Physical	100	100	10	Adjacent
TM27	Return	Normal	Physical	—	100	20	Normal
TM30	Shadow Ball	Ghost	Special	80	100	15	Normal
TM31	Brick Break	Fighting	Physical	75	100	15	Normal
TM32	Double Team	Normal	Status	—	—	15	Self
TM35	Flamethrower	Fire	Special	90	100	15	Normal
TM38	Fire Blast	Fire	Special	110	85	5	Normal
TM39	Rock Tomb	Rock	Physical	60	95	15	Normal
TM41	Torment	Dark	Status	—	100	15	Normal
TM42	Facade	Normal	Physical	70	100	20	Normal
TM44	Rest	Psychic	Status	—	—	10	Self
TM45	Attract	Normal	Status	—	100	15	Normal
TM48	Round	Normal	Special	60	100	15	Normal
TM49	Echoed Voice	Normal	Special	40	100	15	Normal
TM50	Overheat	Fire	Special	130	90	5	Normal
TM52	Focus Blast	Fighting	Special	120	70	5	Normal
TM56	Fling	Dark	Physical	—	100	10	Normal
TM59	Incinerate	Fire	Special	60	100	15	Many Others
TM67	Retaliate	Normal	Physical	70	100	5	Normal
TM68	Giga Impact	Normal	Physical	150	90	5	Normal
TM78	Bulldoze	Ground	Physical	60	100	20	Adjacent
TM80	Rock Slide	Rock	Physical	75	90	10	Many Others
TM87	Swagger	Normal	Status	—	90	15	Normal
TM88	Sleep Talk	Normal	Status	—	—	10	Self
TM90	Substitute	Normal	Status	—	—	10	Self
TM94	Secret Power	Normal	Physical	70	100	20	Normal
TM98	Power-Up Punch	Fighting	Physical	40	100	20	Normal
TM100	Confide	Normal	Status	—	—	20	Normal
HM03	Surf	Water	Special	90	100	15	Adjacent
HM04	Strength	Normal	Physical	80	100	15	Normal
HM06	Rock Smash	Fighting	Physical	40	100	15	Normal

MOVES LEARNED IN EXCHANGE FOR BP

Name	Type	Kind	Pow.	Acc.	PP	Range
Low Kick	Fighting	Physical	—	100	20	Normal
Uproar	Normal	Special	90	100	10	1 Random
Thunder Punch	Electric	Physical	75	100	15	Normal
Fire Punch	Fire	Physical	75	100	15	Normal
Ice Punch	Ice	Physical	75	100	15	Normal
Icy Wind	Ice	Special	55	95	15	Many Others
Zen Headbutt	Psychic	Physical	80	90	15	Normal
Hyper Voice	Normal	Special	90	100	10	Many Others
Snore	Normal	Special	50	100	15	Normal
Shock Wave	Electric	Special	60	—	20	Normal
Water Pulse	Water	Special	60	100	20	Normal
Endeavor	Normal	Physical	—	100	5	Normal
Outrage	Dragon	Physical	120	100	10	1 Random

MOVES TAUGHT BY PEOPLE

Name	Type	Kind	Pow.	Acc.	PP	Range

National Pokédex **296** Hoenn Pokédex **049**

Makuhita

Guts Pokémon

Fighting

HEIGHT: 3'03" WEIGHT: 190.5 lbs.

Same form for ♂ / ♀

Ω Makuhita is tenacious—it will keep getting up and attacking its foe however many times it is knocked down. Every time it gets back up, this Pokémon stores more energy in its body for evolving.

α Makuhita has a tireless spirit—it will never give up hope. It eats a lot of food, gets plenty of sleep, and it trains very rigorously. By living that way, this Pokémon packs its body with energy.

ABILITIES
Thick Fat
Guts

HIDDEN ABILITY
Sheer Force

EGG GROUPS
Human-Like

STAT GROWTH RATES
HP, Attack, Defense, Sp. Atk, Sp. Def, Speed

ITEMS SOMETIMES HELD BY WILD POKÉMON
Black Belt

EVOLUTION
Makuhita → Lv. 24 → Hariyama

MAIN WAY TO REGISTER IN THE NATIONAL POKÉDEX

Catch in Granite Cave (1F).

Damage taken in normal battles

Type	×	Type	×
Normal	×1	Flying	×2
Fire	×1	Psychic	×2
Water	×1	Bug	×0.5
Grass	×1	Rock	×0.5
Electric	×1	Ghost	×1
Ice	×1	Dragon	×1
Fighting	×1	Dark	×0.5
Poison	×1	Steel	×1
Ground	×1	Fairy	×2

Damage taken in Inverse battles

Type	×	Type	×
Normal	×1	Flying	×0.5
Fire	×1	Psychic	×0.5
Water	×1	Bug	×2
Grass	×1	Rock	×2
Electric	×1	Ghost	×1
Ice	×1	Dragon	×1
Fighting	×1	Dark	×2
Poison	×1	Steel	×1
Ground	×1	Fairy	×0.5

Can be used in
Inverse Battle
Battle Institute
Battle Maison
Random Matchup (Free Battle)
Random Matchup (Others)

LEVEL-UP MOVES

Lv.	Name	Type	Kind	Pow.	Acc.	PP	Range
1	Tackle	Normal	Physical	50	100	35	Normal
1	Focus Energy	Normal	Status	—	—	30	Self
4	Sand Attack	Ground	Status	—	100	15	Normal
7	Arm Thrust	Fighting	Physical	15	100	20	Normal
10	Fake Out	Normal	Physical	40	100	10	Normal
13	Force Palm	Fighting	Physical	60	100	10	Normal
16	Whirlwind	Normal	Status	—	—	20	Normal
19	Knock Off	Dark	Physical	65	100	20	Normal
22	Vital Throw	Fighting	Physical	70	—	10	Normal
25	Belly Drum	Normal	Status	—	—	10	Self
28	Smelling Salts	Normal	Physical	70	100	10	Normal
31	Seismic Toss	Fighting	Physical	—	100	20	Normal
34	Wake-Up Slap	Fighting	Physical	70	100	10	Normal
37	Endure	Normal	Status	—	—	10	Self
40	Close Combat	Fighting	Physical	120	100	5	Normal
43	Reversal	Fighting	Physical	—	100	15	Normal
46	Heavy Slam	Steel	Physical	—	100	10	Normal

TM & HM MOVES

No.	Name	Type	Kind	Pow.	Acc.	PP	Range
TM06	Toxic	Poison	Status	—	90	10	Normal
TM08	Bulk Up	Fighting	Status	—	—	20	Self
TM10	Hidden Power	Normal	Special	60	100	15	Normal
TM11	Sunny Day	Fire	Status	—	—	5	Both Sides
TM17	Protect	Normal	Status	—	—	10	Self
TM18	Rain Dance	Water	Status	—	—	5	Both Sides
TM21	Frustration	Normal	Physical	—	100	20	Normal
TM23	Smack Down	Rock	Physical	50	100	15	Normal
TM26	Earthquake	Ground	Physical	100	100	10	Adjacent
TM27	Return	Normal	Physical	—	100	20	Normal
TM28	Dig	Ground	Physical	80	100	10	Normal
TM31	Brick Break	Fighting	Physical	75	100	15	Normal
TM32	Double Team	Normal	Status	—	—	15	Self
TM39	Rock Tomb	Rock	Physical	60	95	15	Normal
TM42	Facade	Normal	Physical	70	100	20	Normal
TM44	Rest	Psychic	Status	—	—	10	Self
TM45	Attract	Normal	Status	—	100	15	Normal
TM47	Low Sweep	Fighting	Physical	65	100	20	Normal
TM48	Round	Normal	Special	60	100	15	Normal
TM52	Focus Blast	Fighting	Special	120	70	5	Normal
TM56	Fling	Dark	Physical	—	100	10	Normal
TM67	Retaliate	Normal	Physical	70	100	5	Normal
TM78	Bulldoze	Ground	Physical	60	100	20	Adjacent
TM80	Rock Slide	Rock	Physical	75	90	10	Many Others
TM84	Poison Jab	Poison	Physical	80	100	20	Normal
TM87	Swagger	Normal	Status	—	90	15	Normal
TM88	Sleep Talk	Normal	Status	—	—	10	Self
TM90	Substitute	Normal	Status	—	—	10	Self
TM94	Secret Power	Normal	Physical	70	100	20	Normal
TM98	Power-Up Punch	Fighting	Physical	40	100	20	Normal
TM100	Confide	Normal	Status	—	—	20	Normal
HM03	Surf	Water	Special	90	100	15	Adjacent
HM04	Strength	Normal	Physical	80	100	15	Normal
HM06	Rock Smash	Fighting	Physical	40	100	15	Normal

MOVES LEARNED IN EXCHANGE FOR BP

Name	Type	Kind	Pow.	Acc.	PP	Range
Low Kick	Fighting	Physical	—	100	20	Normal
Thunder Punch	Electric	Physical	75	100	15	Normal
Fire Punch	Fire	Physical	75	100	15	Normal
Ice Punch	Ice	Physical	75	100	15	Normal
Superpower	Fighting	Physical	120	100	5	Normal
Snore	Normal	Special	50	100	15	Normal
Knock Off	Dark	Physical	65	100	20	Normal
Role Play	Psychic	Status	—	—	10	Normal
Focus Punch	Fighting	Physical	150	100	20	Normal
Helping Hand	Normal	Status	—	—	20	1 Ally

MOVES TAUGHT BY PEOPLE

Name	Type	Kind	Pow.	Acc.	PP	Range

EGG MOVES

Name	Type	Kind	Pow.	Acc.	PP	Range
Feint Attack	Dark	Physical	60	—	20	Normal
Detect	Fighting	Status	—	—	5	Self
Foresight	Normal	Status	—	—	40	Normal
Helping Hand	Normal	Status	—	—	20	1 Ally
Cross Chop	Fighting	Physical	100	80	5	Normal
Revenge	Fighting	Physical	60	100	10	Normal
Dynamic Punch	Fighting	Physical	100	50	5	Normal
Counter	Fighting	Physical	—	100	20	Varies
Wake-Up Slap	Fighting	Physical	70	100	10	Normal
Bullet Punch	Steel	Physical	40	100	30	Normal
Feint	Normal	Physical	30	100	10	Normal
Wide Guard	Rock	Status	—	—	10	Your Side
Focus Punch	Fighting	Physical	150	100	20	Normal
Chip Away	Normal	Physical	70	100	20	Normal

National Pokédex **297** Hoenn Pokédex **050**

Hariyama

Arm Thrust Pokémon

Fighting

HEIGHT: 7'07" WEIGHT: 559.5 lbs.

Same form for ♂ / ♀

Ω Hariyama practices its straight-arm slaps in any number of locations. One hit of this Pokémon's powerful, openhanded, straight-arm punches could snap a telephone pole in two.

α Hariyama's thick body may appear fat, but it is actually a hunk of solid muscle. If this Pokémon bears down and tightens all its muscles, its body becomes as hard as a rock.

ABILITIES
Thick Fat
Guts

HIDDEN ABILITY
Sheer Force

EGG GROUPS
Human-Like

STAT GROWTH RATES
HP
Attack
Defense
Sp. Atk
Sp. Def
Speed

ITEMS SOMETIMES HELD BY WILD POKÉMON
King's Rock

EVOLUTION
Makuhita → Lv. 24 → Hariyama

MAIN WAY TO REGISTER IN THE NATIONAL POKÉDEX

Catch on Victory Road (1F).

Damage taken in normal battles

Type		Type	
Normal	×1	Flying	×2
Fire	×1	Psychic	×2
Water	×1	Bug	×0.5
Grass	×1	Rock	×0.5
Electric	×1	Ghost	×1
Ice	×1	Dragon	×1
Fighting	×1	Dark	×0.5
Poison	×1	Steel	×1
Ground	×1	Fairy	×2

Damage taken in Inverse battles

Type		Type	
Normal	×1	Flying	×0.5
Fire	×1	Psychic	×0.5
Water	×1	Bug	×2
Grass	×1	Rock	×2
Electric	×1	Ghost	×1
Ice	×1	Dragon	×1
Fighting	×1	Dark	×2
Poison	×1	Steel	×1
Ground	×1	Fairy	×0.5

Can be used in
Inverse Battle
Battle Institute
Battle Maison
Random Matchup (Free Battle)
Random Matchup (Others)

LEVEL-UP MOVES

Lv.	Name	Type	Kind	Pow.	Acc.	PP	Range
1	Brine	Water	Special	65	100	10	Normal
1	Tackle	Normal	Physical	50	100	35	Normal
1	Focus Energy	Normal	Status	—	—	30	Self
1	Sand Attack	Ground	Status	—	100	15	Normal
1	Arm Thrust	Fighting	Physical	15	100	20	Normal
4	Sand Attack	Ground	Status	—	100	15	Normal
7	Arm Thrust	Fighting	Physical	15	100	20	Normal
10	Fake Out	Normal	Physical	40	100	10	Normal
13	Force Palm	Fighting	Physical	60	100	10	Normal
16	Whirlwind	Normal	Status	—	—	20	Normal
19	Knock Off	Dark	Physical	65	100	20	Normal
22	Vital Throw	Fighting	Physical	70	—	10	Normal
26	Belly Drum	Normal	Status	—	—	10	Self
30	Smelling Salts	Normal	Physical	70	100	10	Normal
34	Seismic Toss	Fighting	Physical	—	100	20	Normal
38	Wake-Up Slap	Fighting	Physical	70	100	10	Normal
42	Endure	Normal	Status	—	—	10	Self
46	Close Combat	Fighting	Physical	120	100	5	Normal
50	Reversal	Fighting	Physical	—	100	15	Normal
54	Heavy Slam	Steel	Physical	—	100	10	Normal

TM & HM MOVES

No.	Name	Type	Kind	Pow.	Acc.	PP	Range
TM06	Toxic	Poison	Status	—	90	10	Normal
TM08	Bulk Up	Fighting	Status	—	—	20	Self
TM10	Hidden Power	Normal	Special	60	100	15	Normal
TM11	Sunny Day	Fire	Status	—	—	5	Both Sides
TM15	Hyper Beam	Normal	Special	150	90	5	Normal
TM17	Protect	Normal	Status	—	—	10	Self
TM18	Rain Dance	Water	Status	—	—	5	Both Sides
TM21	Frustration	Normal	Physical	—	100	20	Normal
TM23	Smack Down	Rock	Physical	50	100	15	Normal
TM26	Earthquake	Ground	Physical	100	100	10	Adjacent
TM27	Return	Normal	Physical	—	100	20	Normal
TM28	Dig	Ground	Physical	80	100	10	Normal
TM31	Brick Break	Fighting	Physical	75	100	15	Normal
TM32	Double Team	Normal	Status	—	—	15	Self
TM39	Rock Tomb	Rock	Physical	60	95	15	Normal
TM42	Facade	Normal	Physical	70	100	20	Normal
TM44	Rest	Psychic	Status	—	—	10	Self
TM45	Attract	Normal	Status	—	100	15	Normal
TM47	Low Sweep	Fighting	Physical	65	100	20	Normal
TM48	Round	Normal	Special	60	100	15	Normal
TM52	Focus Blast	Fighting	Special	120	70	5	Normal
TM56	Fling	Dark	Physical	—	100	10	Normal
TM66	Payback	Dark	Physical	50	100	10	Normal
TM67	Retaliate	Normal	Physical	70	100	5	Normal
TM68	Giga Impact	Normal	Physical	150	90	5	Normal
TM71	Stone Edge	Rock	Physical	100	80	5	Normal
TM78	Bulldoze	Ground	Physical	60	100	20	Adjacent
TM80	Rock Slide	Rock	Physical	75	90	10	Many Others
TM84	Poison Jab	Poison	Physical	80	100	20	Normal
TM87	Swagger	Normal	Status	—	90	15	Normal
TM88	Sleep Talk	Normal	Status	—	—	10	Self
TM90	Substitute	Normal	Status	—	—	10	Self
TM94	Secret Power	Normal	Physical	70	100	20	Normal
TM98	Power-Up Punch	Fighting	Physical	40	100	20	Normal
TM100	Confide	Normal	Status	—	—	20	Normal
HM03	Surf	Water	Special	90	100	15	Adjacent
HM04	Strength	Normal	Physical	80	100	15	Normal
HM06	Rock Smash	Fighting	Physical	40	100	15	Normal

MOVES LEARNED IN EXCHANGE FOR BP

Name	Type	Kind	Pow.	Acc.	PP	Range
Iron Head	Steel	Physical	80	100	15	Normal
Low Kick	Fighting	Physical	—	100	20	Normal
Thunder Punch	Electric	Physical	75	100	15	Normal
Fire Punch	Fire	Physical	75	100	15	Normal
Ice Punch	Ice	Physical	75	100	15	Normal
Superpower	Fighting	Physical	120	100	5	Normal
Snore	Normal	Special	50	100	15	Normal
Knock Off	Dark	Physical	65	100	20	Normal
Role Play	Psychic	Status	—	—	10	Normal
Focus Punch	Fighting	Physical	150	100	20	Normal
Helping Hand	Normal	Status	—	—	20	1 Ally

MOVES TAUGHT BY PEOPLE

Name	Type	Kind	Pow.	Acc.	PP	Range

National Pokédex **298** Hoenn Pokédex **055**

Azurill

Polka Dot Pokémon

Normal Fairy

HEIGHT: 0'08" WEIGHT: 4.4 lbs.

Same form for ♂ / ♀

Ω Azurill spins its tail as if it were a lasso, then hurls it far. The momentum of the throw sends its body flying, too. Using this unique action, one of these Pokémon managed to hurl itself a record 33 feet.

α Azurill's tail is large and bouncy. It is packed full of the nutrients this Pokémon needs to grow. Azurill can be seen bouncing and playing on its big, rubbery tail.

ABILITIES
Thick Fat
Huge Power

HIDDEN ABILITY
Sap Sipper

EGG GROUPS
No Eggs Discovered

STAT GROWTH RATES
HP
Attack
Defense
Sp. Atk
Sp. Def
Speed

ITEMS SOMETIMES HELD BY WILD POKÉMON
—

EVOLUTION
Azurill → Level up with high friendship → Marill → Lv. 18 → Azumarill

MAIN WAY TO REGISTER IN THE NATIONAL POKÉDEX

Leave a Marill or an Azumarill holding a Sea Incense at a Pokémon Day Care, then hatch the Pokémon Egg that is found.

Damage taken in normal battles

Type		Type	
Normal	×1	Flying	×1
Fire	×1	Psychic	×1
Water	×1	Bug	×0.5
Grass	×1	Rock	×1
Electric	×1	Ghost	×0
Ice	×1	Dragon	×0
Fighting	×1	Dark	×0.5
Poison	×2	Steel	×2
Ground	×1	Fairy	×1

Damage taken in Inverse battles

Type		Type	
Normal	×1	Flying	×1
Fire	×1	Psychic	×1
Water	×1	Bug	×2
Grass	×1	Rock	×1
Electric	×1	Ghost	×2
Ice	×1	Dragon	×2
Fighting	×1	Dark	×2
Poison	×0.5	Steel	×0.5
Ground	×1	Fairy	×1

Can be used in
Inverse Battle
Battle Institute
Battle Maison
Random Matchup (Free Battle)
Random Matchup (Others)

LEVEL-UP MOVES

Lv.	Name	Type	Kind	Pow.	Acc.	PP	Range
1	Splash	Normal	Status	—	—	40	Self
1	Water Gun	Water	Special	40	100	25	Normal
2	Tail Whip	Normal	Status	—	100	30	Many Others
5	Water Sport	Water	Status	—	—	15	Both Sides
7	Bubble	Water	Special	40	100	30	Many Others
10	Charm	Fairy	Status	—	100	20	Normal
13	Bubble Beam	Water	Special	65	100	20	Normal
16	Helping Hand	Normal	Status	—	—	20	1 Ally
20	Slam	Normal	Physical	80	75	20	Normal
23	Bounce	Flying	Physical	85	85	5	Normal

TM & HM MOVES

No.	Name	Type	Kind	Pow.	Acc.	PP	Range
TM06	Toxic	Poison	Status	—	90	10	Normal
TM07	Hail	Ice	Status	—	—	10	Both Sides
TM10	Hidden Power	Normal	Special	60	100	15	Normal
TM13	Ice Beam	Ice	Special	90	100	10	Normal
TM14	Blizzard	Ice	Special	110	70	5	Many Others
TM16	Light Screen	Psychic	Status	—	—	30	Your Side
TM17	Protect	Normal	Status	—	—	10	Self
TM18	Rain Dance	Water	Status	—	—	5	Both Sides
TM21	Frustration	Normal	Physical	—	100	20	Normal
TM27	Return	Normal	Physical	—	100	20	Normal
TM32	Double Team	Normal	Status	—	—	15	Self
TM42	Facade	Normal	Physical	70	100	20	Normal
TM44	Rest	Psychic	Status	—	—	10	Self
TM45	Attract	Normal	Status	—	100	15	Normal
TM48	Round	Normal	Special	60	100	15	Normal
TM55	Scald	Water	Special	80	100	15	Normal
TM87	Swagger	Normal	Status	—	90	15	Normal
TM88	Sleep Talk	Normal	Status	—	—	10	Self
TM90	Substitute	Normal	Status	—	—	10	Self
TM94	Secret Power	Normal	Physical	70	100	20	Normal
TM100	Confide	Normal	Status	—	—	20	Normal
HM03	Surf	Water	Special	90	100	15	Adjacent
HM05	Waterfall	Water	Physical	80	100	15	Normal

MOVES LEARNED IN EXCHANGE FOR BP

Name	Type	Kind	Pow.	Acc.	PP	Range
Covet	Normal	Physical	60	100	25	Normal
Bounce	Flying	Physical	85	85	5	Normal
Uproar	Normal	Special	90	100	10	1 Random
Icy Wind	Ice	Special	55	95	15	Many Others
Hyper Voice	Normal	Special	90	100	10	Many Others
Iron Tail	Steel	Physical	100	75	15	Normal
Snore	Normal	Special	50	100	15	Normal
Knock Off	Dark	Physical	65	100	20	Normal
Water Pulse	Water	Special	60	100	20	Normal
Helping Hand	Normal	Status	—	—	20	1 Ally

MOVES TAUGHT BY PEOPLE

Name	Type	Kind	Pow.	Acc.	PP	Range

EGG MOVES

Name	Type	Kind	Pow.	Acc.	PP	Range
Encore	Normal	Status	—	100	5	Normal
Sing	Normal	Status	—	55	15	Normal
Refresh	Normal	Status	—	—	20	Self
Slam	Normal	Physical	80	75	20	Normal
Tickle	Normal	Status	—	100	20	Normal
Fake Tears	Dark	Status	—	100	20	Normal
Body Slam	Normal	Physical	85	100	15	Normal
Water Sport	Water	Status	—	—	15	Both Sides
Soak	Water	Status	—	100	20	Normal
Muddy Water	Water	Special	90	85	10	Many Others
Copycat	Normal	Status	—	—	20	Self
Camouflage	Normal	Status	—	—	20	Self

National Pokédex **299** Hoenn Pokédex **061**

Nosepass

Compass Pokémon

Rock

HEIGHT: 3'03" WEIGHT: 213.8 lbs.

Same form for ♂ / ♀

Ω Nosepass's magnetic nose is always pointed to the north. If two of these Pokémon meet, they cannot turn their faces to each other when they are close because their magnetic noses repel one another.

α Nosepass had been said to be completely unmoving, with its magnetic nose pointed due north. However, close observation has revealed that the Pokémon actually moves by a little over 3/8 of an inch every year.

ABILITIES
Sturdy
Magnet Pull

HIDDEN ABILITY
Sand Force

EGG GROUPS
Mineral

STAT GROWTH RATES
HP ■■
Attack ■■
Defense ■■■■■■
Sp. Atk ■■
Sp. Def ■■■■
Speed ■■

ITEMS SOMETIMES HELD BY WILD POKÉMON
Hard Stone

EVOLUTION

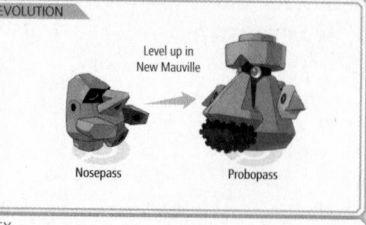

Nosepass → Level up in New Mauville → Probopass

MAIN WAY TO REGISTER IN THE NATIONAL POKÉDEX

Catch when it appears from a cracked rock in Granite Cave's B2F (using Rock Smash).

Damage taken in normal battles

Type		Type	
Normal	×0.5	Flying	×0.5
Fire	×0.5	Psychic	×1
Water	×2	Bug	×1
Grass	×2	Rock	×1
Electric	×1	Ghost	×1
Ice	×1	Dragon	×1
Fighting	×2	Dark	×1
Poison	×0.5	Steel	×2
Ground	×2	Fairy	×1

Damage taken in Inverse battles

Type		Type	
Normal	×2	Flying	×2
Fire	×2	Psychic	×1
Water	×0.5	Bug	×1
Grass	×0.5	Rock	×1
Electric	×1	Ghost	×1
Ice	×1	Dragon	×1
Fighting	×0.5	Dark	×1
Poison	×2	Steel	×0.5
Ground	×0.5	Fairy	×1

Can be used in
Inverse Battle
Battle Institute
Battle Maison
Random Matchup (Free Battle)
Random Matchup (Others)

LEVEL-UP MOVES

Lv.	Name	Type	Kind	Pow.	Acc.	PP	Range
1	Tackle	Normal	Physical	50	100	35	Normal
4	Harden	Normal	Status	—	—	30	Self
7	Block	Normal	Status	—	—	5	Normal
10	Rock Throw	Rock	Physical	50	90	15	Normal
13	Thunder Wave	Electric	Status	—	100	20	Normal
16	Rest	Psychic	Status	—	—	10	Self
19	Spark	Electric	Physical	65	100	20	Normal
22	Rock Slide	Rock	Physical	75	90	10	Many Others
25	Power Gem	Rock	Special	80	100	20	Normal
28	Rock Blast	Rock	Physical	25	90	10	Normal
31	Discharge	Electric	Special	80	100	15	Adjacent
34	Sandstorm	Rock	Status	—	—	10	Both Sides
37	Earth Power	Ground	Special	90	100	10	Normal
40	Stone Edge	Rock	Physical	100	80	5	Normal
43	Lock-On	Normal	Status	—	—	5	Normal
43	Zap Cannon	Electric	Special	120	50	5	Normal

TM & HM MOVES

No.	Name	Type	Kind	Pow.	Acc.	PP	Range
TM06	Toxic	Poison	Status	—	90	10	Normal
TM10	Hidden Power	Normal	Special	60	100	15	Normal
TM11	Sunny Day	Fire	Status	—	—	5	Both Sides
TM12	Taunt	Dark	Status	—	100	20	Normal
TM17	Protect	Normal	Status	—	—	10	Self
TM21	Frustration	Normal	Physical	—	100	20	Normal
TM23	Smack Down	Rock	Physical	50	100	15	Normal
TM24	Thunderbolt	Electric	Special	90	100	15	Normal
TM25	Thunder	Electric	Special	110	70	10	Normal
TM26	Earthquake	Ground	Physical	100	100	10	Adjacent
TM27	Return	Normal	Physical	—	100	20	Normal
TM32	Double Team	Normal	Status	—	—	15	Self
TM37	Sandstorm	Rock	Status	—	—	10	Both Sides
TM39	Rock Tomb	Rock	Physical	60	95	15	Normal
TM41	Torment	Dark	Status	—	100	15	Normal
TM42	Facade	Normal	Physical	70	100	20	Normal
TM44	Rest	Psychic	Status	—	—	10	Self
TM45	Attract	Normal	Status	—	100	15	Normal
TM48	Round	Normal	Special	60	100	15	Normal
TM64	Explosion	Normal	Physical	250	100	5	Adjacent
TM69	Rock Polish	Rock	Status	—	—	20	Self
TM71	Stone Edge	Rock	Physical	100	80	5	Normal
TM72	Volt Switch	Electric	Special	70	100	20	Normal
TM73	Thunder Wave	Electric	Status	—	100	20	Normal
TM78	Bulldoze	Ground	Physical	60	100	20	Adjacent
TM80	Rock Slide	Rock	Physical	75	90	10	Many Others
TM87	Swagger	Normal	Status	—	90	15	Normal
TM88	Sleep Talk	Normal	Status	—	—	10	Self
TM90	Substitute	Normal	Status	—	—	10	Self
TM94	Secret Power	Normal	Physical	70	100	20	Normal
TM99	Dazzling Gleam	Fairy	Special	80	100	10	Many Others
TM100	Confide	Normal	Status	—	—	20	Normal
HM04	Strength	Normal	Physical	80	100	15	Normal
HM06	Rock Smash	Fighting	Physical	40	100	15	Normal

MOVES LEARNED IN EXCHANGE FOR BP

Name	Type	Kind	Pow.	Acc.	PP	Range
Thunder Punch	Electric	Physical	75	100	15	Normal
Fire Punch	Fire	Physical	75	100	15	Normal
Ice Punch	Ice	Physical	75	100	15	Normal
Magic Coat	Psychic	Status	—	—	15	Self
Block	Normal	Status	—	—	5	Normal
Earth Power	Ground	Special	90	100	10	Normal
Gravity	Psychic	Status	—	—	5	Both Sides
Magnet Rise	Electric	Status	—	—	10	Self
Iron Defense	Steel	Status	—	—	15	Self
Snore	Normal	Special	50	100	15	Normal
Pain Split	Normal	Status	—	—	20	Normal
Shock Wave	Electric	Special	60	—	20	Normal
Stealth Rock	Rock	Status	—	—	20	Other Side

MOVES TAUGHT BY PEOPLE

Name	Type	Kind	Pow.	Acc.	PP	Range

EGG MOVES

Name	Type	Kind	Pow.	Acc.	PP	Range
Magnitude	Ground	Physical	—	100	30	Adjacent
Rollout	Rock	Physical	30	90	20	Normal
Double-Edge	Normal	Physical	120	100	15	Normal
Block	Normal	Status	—	—	5	Normal
Stealth Rock	Rock	Status	—	—	20	Other Side
Endure	Normal	Status	—	—	10	Self
Wide Guard	Rock	Status	—	—	10	Your Side

National Pokédex **300** Hoenn Pokédex **063**

Skitty

Kitten Pokémon

Normal

HEIGHT: 2'00" WEIGHT: 24.3 lbs.

Same form for ♂ / ♀

Ω Skitty has the habit of becoming fascinated by moving objects and chasing them around. This Pokémon is known to chase after its own tail and become dizzy.

α Skitty is known to chase around playfully after its own tail. In the wild, this Pokémon lives in holes in the trees of forests. It is very popular as a pet because of its adorable looks.

ABILITIES
Cute Charm
Normalize

HIDDEN ABILITY
Wonder Skin

EGG GROUPS
Field
Fairy

STAT GROWTH RATES
HP ■■
Attack ■■
Defense ■■
Sp. Atk ■■
Sp. Def ■■
Speed ■■■

ITEMS SOMETIMES HELD BY WILD POKÉMON
—

EVOLUTION

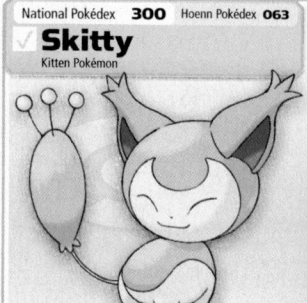

Skitty → Moon Stone → Delcatty

MAIN WAY TO REGISTER IN THE NATIONAL POKÉDEX

Catch on Route 116.

Damage taken in normal battles

Type		Type	
Normal	×1	Flying	×1
Fire	×1	Psychic	×1
Water	×1	Bug	×1
Grass	×1	Rock	×1
Electric	×1	Ghost	×0
Ice	×1	Dragon	×1
Fighting	×2	Dark	×1
Poison	×1	Steel	×1
Ground	×1	Fairy	×1

Damage taken in Inverse battles

Type		Type	
Normal	×1	Flying	×1
Fire	×1	Psychic	×1
Water	×1	Bug	×1
Grass	×1	Rock	×1
Electric	×1	Ghost	×2
Ice	×1	Dragon	×1
Fighting	×0.5	Dark	×1
Poison	×1	Steel	×1
Ground	×1	Fairy	×1

Can be used in
Inverse Battle
Battle Institute
Battle Maison
Random Matchup (Free Battle)
Random Matchup (Others)

LEVEL-UP MOVES

Lv.	Name	Type	Kind	Pow.	Acc.	PP	Range
1	Fake Out	Normal	Physical	40	100	10	Normal
1	Growl	Normal	Status	—	100	40	Many Others
1	Tail Whip	Normal	Status	—	100	30	Many Others
1	Tackle	Normal	Physical	50	100	35	Normal
4	Foresight	Normal	Status	—	—	40	Normal
7	Sing	Normal	Status	—	55	15	Normal
10	Attract	Normal	Status	—	100	15	Normal
13	Disarming Voice	Fairy	Special	40	—	15	Many Others
16	Double Slap	Normal	Physical	15	85	10	Normal
19	Copycat	Normal	Status	—	—	20	Self
22	Feint Attack	Dark	Physical	60	—	20	Normal
25	Charm	Fairy	Status	—	100	20	Normal
28	Wake-Up Slap	Fighting	Physical	70	100	10	Normal
31	Assist	Normal	Status	—	—	20	Self
34	Covet	Normal	Physical	60	100	25	Normal
37	Heal Bell	Normal	Status	—	—	5	Your Party
40	Double-Edge	Normal	Physical	120	100	15	Normal
43	Captivate	Normal	Status	—	100	20	Many Others
46	Play Rough	Fairy	Physical	90	90	10	Normal

TM & HM MOVES

No.	Name	Type	Kind	Pow.	Acc.	PP	Range
TM04	Calm Mind	Psychic	Status	—	—	20	Self
TM06	Toxic	Poison	Status	—	90	10	Normal
TM10	Hidden Power	Normal	Special	60	100	15	Normal
TM11	Sunny Day	Fire	Status	—	—	5	Both Sides
TM13	Ice Beam	Ice	Special	90	100	10	Normal
TM14	Blizzard	Ice	Special	110	70	5	Many Others
TM17	Protect	Normal	Status	—	—	10	Self
TM18	Rain Dance	Water	Status	—	—	5	Both Sides
TM20	Safeguard	Normal	Status	—	—	25	Your Side
TM21	Frustration	Normal	Physical	—	100	20	Normal
TM22	Solar Beam	Grass	Special	120	100	10	Normal
TM24	Thunderbolt	Electric	Special	90	100	15	Normal
TM25	Thunder	Electric	Special	110	70	10	Normal
TM27	Return	Normal	Physical	—	100	20	Normal
TM28	Dig	Ground	Physical	80	100	10	Normal
TM30	Shadow Ball	Ghost	Special	80	100	15	Normal
TM32	Double Team	Normal	Status	—	—	15	Self
TM42	Facade	Normal	Physical	70	100	20	Normal
TM44	Rest	Psychic	Status	—	—	10	Self
TM45	Attract	Normal	Status	—	100	15	Normal
TM48	Round	Normal	Special	60	100	15	Normal
TM49	Echoed Voice	Normal	Special	40	100	15	Normal
TM57	Charge Beam	Electric	Special	50	90	10	Normal
TM66	Payback	Dark	Physical	50	100	10	Normal
TM67	Retaliate	Normal	Physical	70	100	5	Normal
TM70	Flash	Normal	Status	—	100	20	Normal
TM73	Thunder Wave	Electric	Status	—	100	20	Normal
TM77	Psych Up	Normal	Status	—	—	10	Normal
TM85	Dream Eater	Psychic	Special	100	100	15	Normal
TM86	Grass Knot	Grass	Special	—	100	20	Normal
TM87	Swagger	Normal	Status	—	90	15	Normal
TM88	Sleep Talk	Normal	Status	—	—	10	Self
TM90	Substitute	Normal	Status	—	—	10	Self
TM93	Wild Charge	Electric	Physical	90	100	15	Normal
TM94	Secret Power	Normal	Physical	70	100	20	Normal
TM100	Confide	Normal	Status	—	—	20	Normal

MOVES LEARNED IN EXCHANGE FOR BP

Name	Type	Kind	Pow.	Acc.	PP	Range
Covet	Normal	Physical	60	100	25	Normal
Uproar	Normal	Special	90	100	10	1 Random
Last Resort	Normal	Physical	140	100	5	Normal
Icy Wind	Ice	Special	55	95	15	Many Others
Zen Headbutt	Psychic	Physical	80	90	15	Normal
Hyper Voice	Normal	Special	90	100	10	Many Others
Iron Tail	Steel	Physical	100	75	15	Normal
Snore	Normal	Special	50	100	15	Normal
Heal Bell	Normal	Status	—	—	5	Your Party
Shock Wave	Electric	Special	60	—	20	Normal
Water Pulse	Water	Special	60	100	20	Normal
Helping Hand	Normal	Status	—	—	20	1 Ally

MOVES TAUGHT BY PEOPLE

Name	Type	Kind	Pow.	Acc.	PP	Range

EGG MOVES

Name	Type	Kind	Pow.	Acc.	PP	Range
Helping Hand	Normal	Status	—	—	20	1 Ally
Uproar	Normal	Special	90	100	10	1 Random
Fake Tears	Dark	Status	—	100	20	Normal
Wish	Normal	Status	—	—	10	Self
Baton Pass	Normal	Status	—	—	40	Self
Tickle	Normal	Status	—	100	20	Normal
Last Resort	Normal	Physical	140	100	5	Normal
Fake Out	Normal	Physical	40	100	10	Normal
Zen Headbutt	Psychic	Physical	80	90	15	Normal
Sucker Punch	Dark	Physical	80	100	5	Normal
Mud Bomb	Ground	Special	65	85	10	Normal
Simple Beam	Normal	Status	—	100	15	Normal
Captivate	Normal	Status	—	100	20	Many Others
Cosmic Power	Psychic	Status	—	—	20	Self

National Pokédex **301** Hoenn Pokédex **064**

Delcatty

Prim Pokémon

Normal

HEIGHT: 3'07" WEIGHT: 71.9 lbs.

Same form for ♂ / ♀

Ω Delcatty prefers to live an unfettered existence in which it can do as it pleases at its own pace. Because this Pokémon eats and sleeps whenever it decides, its daily routines are completely random.

α Delcatty sleeps anywhere it wants without keeping a permanent nest. If other Pokémon approach it as it sleeps, this Pokémon will never fight—it will just move away somewhere else.

ABILITIES
Cute Charm
Normalize

HIDDEN ABILITY
Wonder Skin

EGG GROUPS
Field, Fairy

STAT GROWTH RATES
HP, Attack, Defense, Sp. Atk, Sp. Def, Speed

ITEMS SOMETIMES HELD BY WILD POKÉMON
—

EVOLUTION

MAIN WAY TO REGISTER IN THE NATIONAL POKÉDEX

Use a Moon Stone on Skitty.

Damage taken in normal battles

Type		Type	
Normal	×1	Flying	×1
Fire	×1	Psychic	×1
Water	×1	Bug	×1
Grass	×1	Rock	×1
Electric	×1	Ghost	×0
Ice	×1	Dragon	×1
Fighting	×2	Dark	×1
Poison	×1	Steel	×1
Ground	×1	Fairy	×1

Damage taken in Inverse battles

Type		Type	
Normal	×1	Flying	×1
Fire	×1	Psychic	×1
Water	×1	Bug	×1
Grass	×1	Rock	×1
Electric	×1	Ghost	×2
Ice	×1	Dragon	×1
Fighting	×0.5	Dark	×1
Poison	×1	Steel	×1
Ground	×1	Fairy	×1

Can be used in
Inverse Battle
Battle Institute
Battle Maison
Random Matchup (Free Battle)
Random Matchup (Others)

LEVEL-UP MOVES

Lv.	Name	Type	Kind	Pow.	Acc.	PP	Range
1	Fake Out	Normal	Physical	40	100	10	Normal
1	Sing	Normal	Status	—	55	15	Normal
1	Attract	Normal	Status	—	100	15	Normal
1	Double Slap	Normal	Physical	15	85	10	Normal

TM & HM MOVES

No.	Name	Type	Kind	Pow.	Acc.	PP	Range
TM04	Calm Mind	Psychic	Status	—	—	20	Self
TM06	Toxic	Poison	Status	—	90	10	Normal
TM10	Hidden Power	Normal	Special	60	100	15	Normal
TM11	Sunny Day	Fire	Status	—	—	5	Both Sides
TM13	Ice Beam	Ice	Special	90	100	10	Normal
TM14	Blizzard	Ice	Special	110	70	5	Many Others
TM15	Hyper Beam	Normal	Special	150	90	5	Normal
TM17	Protect	Normal	Status	—	—	10	Self
TM18	Rain Dance	Water	Status	—	—	5	Both Sides
TM20	Safeguard	Normal	Status	—	—	25	Your Side
TM21	Frustration	Normal	Physical	—	100	20	Normal
TM22	Solar Beam	Grass	Special	120	100	10	Normal
TM24	Thunderbolt	Electric	Special	90	100	15	Normal
TM25	Thunder	Electric	Special	110	70	10	Normal
TM27	Return	Normal	Physical	—	100	20	Normal
TM28	Dig	Ground	Physical	80	100	10	Normal
TM30	Shadow Ball	Ghost	Special	80	100	15	Normal
TM32	Double Team	Normal	Status	—	—	15	Self
TM42	Facade	Normal	Physical	70	100	20	Normal
TM44	Rest	Psychic	Status	—	—	10	Self
TM45	Attract	Normal	Status	—	100	15	Normal
TM48	Round	Normal	Special	60	100	15	Normal
TM49	Echoed Voice	Normal	Special	40	100	15	Normal
TM57	Charge Beam	Electric	Special	50	90	10	Normal
TM66	Payback	Dark	Physical	50	100	10	Normal
TM67	Retaliate	Normal	Physical	70	100	5	Normal
TM68	Giga Impact	Normal	Physical	150	90	5	Normal
TM70	Flash	Normal	Status	—	100	20	Normal
TM73	Thunder Wave	Electric	Status	—	100	20	Normal
TM77	Psych Up	Normal	Status	—	—	10	Normal
TM85	Dream Eater	Psychic	Special	100	100	15	Normal
TM86	Grass Knot	Grass	Special	—	100	20	Normal
TM87	Swagger	Normal	Status	—	90	15	Normal
TM88	Sleep Talk	Normal	Status	—	—	10	Self
TM90	Substitute	Normal	Status	—	—	10	Self
TM93	Wild Charge	Electric	Physical	90	100	15	Normal
TM94	Secret Power	Normal	Physical	70	100	20	Normal
TM100	Confide	Normal	Status	—	—	20	Normal
HM04	Strength	Normal	Physical	80	100	15	Normal
HM06	Rock Smash	Fighting	Physical	40	100	15	Normal

MOVES LEARNED IN EXCHANGE FOR BP

Name	Type	Kind	Pow.	Acc.	PP	Range
Covet	Normal	Physical	60	100	25	Normal
Uproar	Normal	Special	90	100	10	1 Random
Last Resort	Normal	Physical	140	100	5	Normal
Icy Wind	Ice	Special	55	95	15	Many Others
Zen Headbutt	Psychic	Physical	80	90	15	Normal
Hyper Voice	Normal	Special	90	100	10	Many Others
Iron Tail	Steel	Physical	100	75	15	Normal
Snore	Normal	Special	50	100	15	Normal
Heal Bell	Normal	Status	—	—	5	Your Party
Shock Wave	Electric	Special	60	—	20	Normal
Water Pulse	Water	Special	60	100	20	Normal
Helping Hand	Normal	Status	—	—	20	1 Ally

MOVES TAUGHT BY PEOPLE

Name	Type	Kind	Pow.	Acc.	PP	Range

National Pokédex **302** Hoenn Pokédex **070**

Sableye

Darkness Pokémon

Dark **Ghost**

HEIGHT: 1'08" WEIGHT: 24.3 lbs.

Same form for ♂ / ♀

Ω Sableye lead quiet lives deep inside caverns. They are feared, however, because these Pokémon are thought to steal the spirits of people when their eyes burn with a sinister glow in the darkness.

α Sableye digs the ground with sharpened claws to find rocks that it eats. Substances in the eaten rocks crystallize and rise up to the Pokémon's body surface.

ABILITIES
Keen Eye
Stall

HIDDEN ABILITY
Prankster

EGG GROUPS
Human-Like

STAT GROWTH RATES
HP, Attack, Defense, Sp. Atk, Sp. Def, Speed

ITEMS SOMETIMES HELD BY WILD POKÉMON
Wide Lens

EVOLUTION
Does not evolve

MAIN WAYS TO REGISTER IN THE NATIONAL POKÉDEX

Ω Bring it to your game using Link Trade or the GTS.

α Catch in Granite Cave (B2F).

Damage taken in normal battles

Type		Type	
Normal	×0	Flying	×1
Fire	×1	Psychic	×0
Water	×1	Bug	×1
Grass	×1	Rock	×1
Electric	×1	Ghost	×1
Ice	×1	Dragon	×1
Fighting	×0	Dark	×1
Poison	×0.5	Steel	×1
Ground	×1	Fairy	×2

Damage taken in Inverse battles

Type		Type	
Normal	×2	Flying	×1
Fire	×1	Psychic	×2
Water	×1	Bug	×1
Grass	×1	Rock	×1
Electric	×1	Ghost	×1
Ice	×1	Dragon	×1
Fighting	×1	Dark	×1
Poison	×2	Steel	×1
Ground	×1	Fairy	×0.5

Can be used in
Inverse Battle
Battle Institute
Battle Maison
Random Matchup (Free Battle)
Random Matchup (Others)

LEVEL-UP MOVES

Lv.	Name	Type	Kind	Pow.	Acc.	PP	Range
1	Leer	Normal	Status	—	100	30	Many Others
1	Scratch	Normal	Physical	40	100	35	Normal
4	Foresight	Normal	Status	—	—	40	Normal
6	Night Shade	Ghost	Special	—	100	15	Normal
9	Astonish	Ghost	Physical	30	100	15	Normal
11	Fury Swipes	Normal	Physical	18	80	15	Normal
14	Detect	Fighting	Status	—	—	5	Self
16	Shadow Sneak	Ghost	Physical	40	100	30	Normal
19	Feint Attack	Dark	Physical	60	—	20	Normal
21	Fake Out	Normal	Physical	40	100	10	Normal
24	Punishment	Dark	Physical	—	100	5	Normal
26	Knock Off	Dark	Physical	65	100	20	Normal
29	Shadow Claw	Ghost	Physical	70	100	15	Normal
31	Confuse Ray	Ghost	Status	—	100	10	Normal
34	Zen Headbutt	Psychic	Physical	80	90	15	Normal
36	Power Gem	Rock	Special	80	100	20	Normal
39	Shadow Ball	Ghost	Special	80	100	15	Normal
41	Foul Play	Dark	Physical	95	100	15	Normal
44	Quash	Dark	Status	—	100	15	Normal
46	Mean Look	Normal	Status	—	—	5	Normal

TM & HM MOVES

No.	Name	Type	Kind	Pow.	Acc.	PP	Range
TM01	Hone Claws	Dark	Status	—	—	15	Self
TM04	Calm Mind	Psychic	Status	—	—	20	Self
TM06	Toxic	Poison	Status	—	90	10	Normal
TM10	Hidden Power	Normal	Special	60	100	15	Normal
TM11	Sunny Day	Fire	Status	—	—	5	Both Sides
TM12	Taunt	Dark	Status	—	100	20	Normal
TM17	Protect	Normal	Status	—	—	10	Self
TM18	Rain Dance	Water	Status	—	—	5	Both Sides
TM21	Frustration	Normal	Physical	—	100	20	Normal
TM27	Return	Normal	Physical	—	100	20	Normal
TM28	Dig	Ground	Physical	80	100	10	Normal
TM29	Psychic	Psychic	Special	90	100	10	Normal
TM30	Shadow Ball	Ghost	Special	80	100	15	Normal
TM31	Brick Break	Fighting	Physical	75	100	15	Normal
TM32	Double Team	Normal	Status	—	—	15	Self
TM39	Rock Tomb	Rock	Physical	60	95	15	Normal
TM40	Aerial Ace	Flying	Physical	60	—	20	Normal
TM41	Torment	Dark	Status	—	100	15	Normal
TM42	Facade	Normal	Physical	70	100	20	Normal
TM44	Rest	Psychic	Status	—	—	10	Self
TM45	Attract	Normal	Status	—	100	15	Normal
TM46	Thief	Dark	Physical	60	100	25	Normal
TM47	Low Sweep	Fighting	Physical	65	100	20	Normal
TM48	Round	Normal	Special	60	100	15	Normal
TM56	Fling	Dark	Physical	—	100	10	Normal
TM59	Incinerate	Fire	Special	60	100	15	Many Others
TM60	Quash	Dark	Status	—	100	15	Normal
TM61	Will-O-Wisp	Fire	Status	—	85	15	Normal
TM63	Embargo	Dark	Status	—	100	15	Normal
TM65	Shadow Claw	Ghost	Physical	70	100	15	Normal
TM66	Payback	Dark	Physical	50	100	10	Normal
TM67	Retaliate	Normal	Physical	70	100	5	Normal
TM70	Flash	Normal	Status	—	100	20	Normal
TM77	Psych Up	Normal	Status	—	—	10	Normal
TM84	Poison Jab	Poison	Physical	80	100	20	Normal
TM85	Dream Eater	Psychic	Special	100	100	15	Normal
TM87	Swagger	Normal	Status	—	90	15	Normal
TM88	Sleep Talk	Normal	Status	—	—	10	Self
TM90	Substitute	Normal	Status	—	—	10	Self
TM94	Secret Power	Normal	Physical	70	100	20	Normal
TM95	Snarl	Dark	Special	55	95	15	Many Others
TM97	Dark Pulse	Dark	Special	80	100	15	Normal
TM98	Power-Up Punch	Fighting	Physical	40	100	20	Normal
TM99	Dazzling Gleam	Fairy	Special	80	100	10	Many Others
TM100	Confide	Normal	Status	—	—	20	Normal
HM01	Cut	Normal	Physical	50	95	30	Normal
HM06	Rock Smash	Fighting	Physical	40	100	15	Normal

MOVES LEARNED IN EXCHANGE FOR BP

Name	Type	Kind	Pow.	Acc.	PP	Range
Signal Beam	Bug	Special	75	100	15	Normal
Low Kick	Fighting	Physical	—	100	20	Normal
Thunder Punch	Electric	Physical	75	100	15	Normal
Fire Punch	Fire	Physical	75	100	15	Normal
Ice Punch	Ice	Physical	75	100	15	Normal
Magic Coat	Psychic	Status	—	—	15	Self
Foul Play	Dark	Physical	95	100	15	Normal
Gravity	Psychic	Status	—	—	5	Both Sides
Icy Wind	Ice	Special	55	95	15	Many Others
Zen Headbutt	Psychic	Physical	80	90	15	Normal
Snore	Normal	Special	50	100	15	Normal
Knock Off	Dark	Physical	65	100	20	Normal
Role Play	Psychic	Status	—	—	10	Normal
Pain Split	Normal	Status	—	—	20	Normal
Focus Punch	Fighting	Physical	150	100	20	Normal
Shock Wave	Electric	Special	60	—	20	Normal
Water Pulse	Water	Special	60	100	20	Normal
Spite	Ghost	Status	—	100	10	Normal
Trick	Psychic	Status	—	100	10	Normal
Wonder Room	Psychic	Status	—	—	10	Both Sides
Snatch	Dark	Status	—	—	10	Self

MOVES TAUGHT BY PEOPLE

Name	Type	Kind	Pow.	Acc.	PP	Range

EGG MOVES

Name	Type	Kind	Pow.	Acc.	PP	Range
Recover	Normal	Status	—	—	10	Self
Moonlight	Fairy	Status	—	—	5	Self
Nasty Plot	Dark	Status	—	—	20	Self
Flatter	Dark	Status	—	100	15	Normal
Feint	Normal	Physical	30	100	10	Normal
Sucker Punch	Dark	Physical	80	100	5	Normal
Trick	Psychic	Status	—	100	10	Normal
Captivate	Normal	Status	—	100	20	Many Others
Mean Look	Normal	Status	—	—	5	Normal
Metal Burst	Steel	Physical	—	100	10	Varies
Imprison	Psychic	Status	—	—	10	Self

Mega Evolution

Mega Sableye

Darkness Pokémon

Dark | Ghost

HEIGHT: 1'08" WEIGHT: 354.9 lbs.

Same form for ♂ / ♀

REQUIRED MEGA STONE

Sablenite

Find near the Cave of Origin in Sootopolis City.

ABILITY

Magic Bounce

HIDDEN ABILITY

—

EGG GROUPS

—

STAT GROWTH RATES

HP

Attack

Defense

Sp. Atk

Sp. Def

Speed

Damage taken in normal battles

Type		Type	
Normal	×0	Flying	×1
Fire	×1	Psychic	×0
Water	×1	Bug	×1
Grass	×1	Rock	×1
Electric	×1	Ghost	×1
Ice	×1	Dragon	×1
Fighting	×0	Dark	×1
Poison	×0.5	Steel	×1
Ground	×1	Fairy	×2

Damage taken in Inverse battles

Type		Type	
Normal	×2	Flying	×1
Fire	×1	Psychic	×2
Water	×1	Bug	×1
Grass	×1	Rock	×1
Electric	×1	Ghost	×1
Ice	×1	Dragon	×1
Fighting	×1	Dark	×1
Poison	×2	Steel	×1
Ground	×1	Fairy	×0.5

Can be used in

Inverse Battle

Battle Institute

Battle Maison

Random Matchup (Free Battle)

Random Matchup (Others)

National Pokédex **303** Hoenn Pokédex **071**

Mawile

Deceiver Pokémon

Steel | Fairy

HEIGHT: 2'00" WEIGHT: 25.4 lbs.

Same form for ♂ / ♀

Ω Mawile's huge jaws are actually steel horns that have been transformed. Its docile-looking face serves to lull its foe into letting down its guard. When the foe least expects it, Mawile chomps it with its gaping jaws.

α Don't be taken in by this Pokémon's cute face—it's very dangerous. Mawile fools the foe into letting down its guard, then chomps down with its massive jaws. The steel jaws are really horns that have been transformed.

ABILITIES

Hyper Cutter
Intimidate

HIDDEN ABILITY

Sheer Force

EGG GROUPS

Field | Fairy

STAT GROWTH RATES

HP

Attack

Defense

Sp. Atk

Sp. Def

Speed

ITEMS SOMETIMES HELD BY WILD POKÉMON

Iron Ball

EVOLUTION

Does not evolve

MAIN WAYS TO REGISTER IN THE NATIONAL POKÉDEX

Ω Catch in Granite Cave (B2F).

α Bring it to your game using Link Trade or the GTS.

Damage taken in normal battles

Type		Type	
Normal	×0.5	Flying	×0.5
Fire	×2	Psychic	×0.5
Water	×1	Bug	×0.25
Grass	×0.5	Rock	×0.5
Electric	×1	Ghost	×1
Ice	×0.5	Dragon	×0
Fighting	×1	Dark	×0.5
Poison	×0	Steel	×1
Ground	×2	Fairy	×0.5

Damage taken in Inverse battles

Type		Type	
Normal	×2	Flying	×2
Fire	×0.5	Psychic	×2
Water	×1	Bug	×4
Grass	×2	Rock	×2
Electric	×1	Ghost	×1
Ice	×2	Dragon	×4
Fighting	×1	Dark	×2
Poison	×1	Steel	×1
Ground	×0.5	Fairy	×2

Can be used in

Inverse Battle

Battle Institute

Battle Maison

Random Matchup (Free Battle)

Random Matchup (Others)

LEVEL-UP MOVES

Lv.	Name	Type	Kind	Pow.	Acc.	PP	Range
1	Play Rough	Fairy	Physical	90	90	10	Normal
1	Iron Head	Steel	Physical	80	100	15	Normal
1	Taunt	Dark	Status	—	100	20	Normal
1	Growl	Normal	Status	—	100	40	Many Others
1	Fairy Wind	Fairy	Special	40	100	30	Normal
1	Astonish	Ghost	Physical	30	100	15	Normal
5	Fake Tears	Dark	Status	—	100	20	Normal
9	Bite	Dark	Physical	60	100	25	Normal
13	Sweet Scent	Normal	Status	—	100	20	Many Others
17	Vice Grip	Normal	Physical	55	100	30	Normal
21	Feint Attack	Dark	Physical	60	—	20	Normal
25	Baton Pass	Normal	Status	—	—	40	Self
29	Crunch	Dark	Physical	80	100	15	Normal
33	Iron Defense	Steel	Status	—	—	15	Self
37	Sucker Punch	Dark	Physical	80	100	5	Normal
41	Stockpile	Normal	Status	—	—	20	Self
41	Swallow	Normal	Status	—	—	10	Self
41	Spit Up	Normal	Special	—	100	10	Normal
45	Iron Head	Steel	Physical	80	100	15	Normal
49	Play Rough	Fairy	Physical	90	90	10	Normal

TM & HM MOVES

No.	Name	Type	Kind	Pow.	Acc.	PP	Range
TM06	Toxic	Poison	Status	—	90	10	Normal
TM10	Hidden Power	Normal	Special	60	100	15	Normal
TM11	Sunny Day	Fire	Status	—	—	5	Both Sides
TM12	Taunt	Dark	Status	—	100	20	Normal
TM13	Ice Beam	Ice	Special	90	100	10	Normal
TM15	Hyper Beam	Normal	Special	150	90	5	Normal
TM17	Protect	Normal	Status	—	—	10	Self
TM18	Rain Dance	Water	Status	—	—	5	Both Sides
TM21	Frustration	Normal	Physical	—	100	20	Normal
TM22	Solar Beam	Grass	Special	120	100	10	Normal
TM27	Return	Normal	Physical	—	100	20	Normal
TM30	Shadow Ball	Ghost	Special	80	100	15	Normal
TM31	Brick Break	Fighting	Physical	75	100	15	Normal
TM32	Double Team	Normal	Status	—	—	15	Self
TM35	Flamethrower	Fire	Special	90	100	15	Normal
TM36	Sludge Bomb	Poison	Special	90	100	10	Normal
TM37	Sandstorm	Rock	Status	—	—	10	Both Sides
TM38	Fire Blast	Fire	Special	110	85	5	Normal
TM39	Rock Tomb	Rock	Physical	60	95	15	Normal
TM41	Torment	Dark	Status	—	100	15	Normal
TM42	Facade	Normal	Physical	70	100	20	Normal
TM44	Rest	Psychic	Status	—	—	10	Self
TM45	Attract	Normal	Status	—	100	15	Normal
TM48	Round	Normal	Special	60	100	15	Normal
TM52	Focus Blast	Fighting	Special	120	70	5	Normal
TM54	False Swipe	Normal	Physical	40	100	40	Normal
TM56	Fling	Dark	Physical	—	100	10	Normal
TM57	Charge Beam	Electric	Special	50	90	10	Normal
TM59	Incinerate	Fire	Special	60	100	15	Many Others
TM63	Embargo	Dark	Status	—	100	15	Normal
TM66	Payback	Dark	Physical	50	100	10	Normal
TM68	Giga Impact	Normal	Physical	150	90	5	Normal
TM71	Stone Edge	Rock	Physical	100	80	5	Normal
TM75	Swords Dance	Normal	Status	—	—	20	Self
TM77	Psych Up	Normal	Status	—	—	10	Normal
TM80	Rock Slide	Rock	Physical	75	90	10	Many Others
TM86	Grass Knot	Grass	Special	—	100	20	Normal
TM87	Swagger	Normal	Status	—	90	15	Normal
TM88	Sleep Talk	Normal	Status	—	—	10	Self
TM90	Substitute	Normal	Status	—	—	10	Self
TM91	Flash Cannon	Steel	Special	80	100	10	Normal
TM94	Secret Power	Normal	Physical	70	100	20	Normal
TM97	Dark Pulse	Dark	Special	80	100	15	Normal
TM98	Power-Up Punch	Fighting	Physical	40	100	20	Normal
TM100	Confide	Normal	Status	—	—	20	Normal
HM04	Strength	Normal	Physical	80	100	15	Normal
HM06	Rock Smash	Fighting	Physical	40	100	15	Normal

MOVES LEARNED IN EXCHANGE FOR BP

Name	Type	Kind	Pow.	Acc.	PP	Range
Super Fang	Normal	Physical	—	90	10	Normal
Iron Head	Steel	Physical	80	100	15	Normal
Thunder Punch	Electric	Physical	75	100	15	Normal
Ice Punch	Ice	Physical	75	100	15	Normal
Foul Play	Dark	Physical	95	100	15	Normal
Magnet Rise	Electric	Status	—	—	10	Self
Iron Defense	Steel	Status	—	—	15	Self
Last Resort	Normal	Physical	140	100	5	Normal
Icy Wind	Ice	Special	55	95	15	Many Others
Snore	Normal	Special	50	100	15	Normal
Knock Off	Dark	Physical	65	100	20	Normal
Pain Split	Normal	Status	—	—	20	Normal
Focus Punch	Fighting	Physical	150	100	20	Normal
Snatch	Dark	Status	—	—	10	Self
Stealth Rock	Rock	Status	—	—	20	Other Side

MOVES TAUGHT BY PEOPLE

Name	Type	Kind	Pow.	Acc.	PP	Range

EGG MOVES

Name	Type	Kind	Pow.	Acc.	PP	Range
Poison Fang	Poison	Physical	50	100	15	Normal
Ancient Power	Rock	Special	60	100	5	Normal
Tickle	Normal	Status	—	100	20	Normal
Sucker Punch	Dark	Physical	80	100	5	Normal
Ice Fang	Ice	Physical	65	95	15	Normal
Fire Fang	Fire	Physical	65	95	15	Normal
Thunder Fang	Electric	Physical	65	95	15	Normal
Punishment	Dark	Physical	—	100	5	Normal
Guard Swap	Psychic	Status	—	—	10	Normal
Captivate	Normal	Status	—	100	20	Many Others
Slam	Normal	Physical	80	75	20	Normal
Metal Burst	Steel	Physical	—	100	10	Varies
Misty Terrain	Fairy	Status	—	—	10	Both Sides
Seismic Toss	Fighting	Physical	—	100	20	Normal

Mega Evolution

Mega Mawile

Deceiver Pokémon

Steel | Fairy

HEIGHT: 3'03" WEIGHT: 51.8 lbs.

Same form for ♂ / ♀

REQUIRED MEGA STONE

Mawilite

Find on the east side of Verdanturf Town.

ABILITY

Huge Power

HIDDEN ABILITY

—

EGG GROUPS

—

STAT GROWTH RATES

HP, Attack, Defense, Sp. Atk, Sp. Def, Speed

Damage taken in normal battles

Type		Type	
Normal	×0.5	Flying	×0.5
Fire	×2	Psychic	×0.5
Water	×1	Bug	×0.25
Grass	×0.5	Rock	×0.5
Electric	×1	Ghost	×1
Ice	×0.5	Dragon	×0
Fighting	×1	Dark	×0.5
Poison	×0	Steel	×1
Ground	×2	Fairy	×0.5

Damage taken in Inverse battles

Type		Type	
Normal	×2	Flying	×2
Fire	×0.5	Psychic	×2
Water	×1	Bug	×4
Grass	×2	Rock	×2
Electric	×1	Ghost	×1
Ice	×2	Dragon	×4
Fighting	×1	Dark	×2
Poison	×1	Steel	×1
Ground	×0.5	Fairy	×2

Can be used in

Inverse Battle

Battle Institute

Battle Maison

Random Matchup (Free Battle)

Random Matchup (Others)

Mega Mawile

National Pokédex

National Pokédex 304 Hoenn Pokédex 072

Aron

Iron Armor Pokémon

Steel | Rock

HEIGHT: 1'04" WEIGHT: 132.3 lbs.

Same form for ♂ / ♀

Ω This Pokémon has a body of steel. To make its body, Aron feeds on iron ore that it digs from mountains. Occasionally, it causes major trouble by eating bridges and rails.

α Aron has a body of steel. With one all-out charge, this Pokémon can demolish even a heavy dump truck. The destroyed dump truck then becomes a handy meal for the Pokémon.

ABILITIES

Sturdy

Rock Head

HIDDEN ABILITY

Heavy Metal

EGG GROUPS

Monster

STAT GROWTH RATES

HP, Attack, Defense, Sp. Atk, Sp. Def, Speed

ITEMS SOMETIMES HELD BY WILD POKÉMON

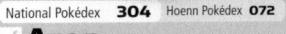

Hard Stone

EVOLUTION

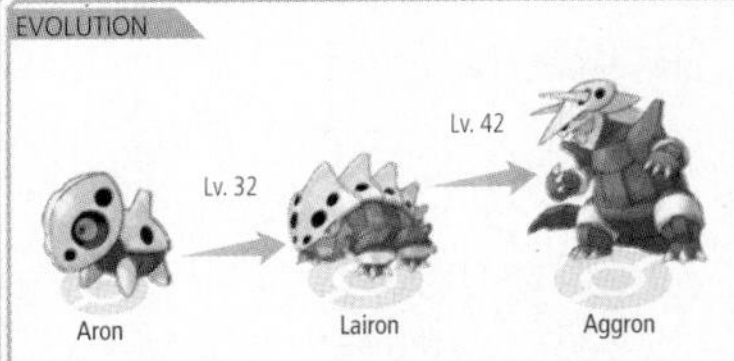

Aron → Lv. 32 → Lairon → Lv. 42 → Aggron

MAIN WAY TO REGISTER IN THE NATIONAL POKÉDEX

Catch in Granite Cave (B1F).

Damage taken in normal battles

Type		Type	
Normal	×0.25	Flying	×0.25
Fire	×1	Psychic	×0.5
Water	×2	Bug	×0.5
Grass	×1	Rock	×0.5
Electric	×1	Ghost	×1
Ice	×0.5	Dragon	×0.5
Fighting	×4	Dark	×1
Poison	×0	Steel	×1
Ground	×4	Fairy	×0.5

Damage taken in Inverse battles

Type		Type	
Normal	×4	Flying	×4
Fire	×1	Psychic	×2
Water	×0.5	Bug	×2
Grass	×1	Rock	×2
Electric	×1	Ghost	×1
Ice	×2	Dragon	×2
Fighting	×0.25	Dark	×1
Poison	×4	Steel	×1
Ground	×0.25	Fairy	×2

Can be used in

Inverse Battle

Battle Institute

Battle Maison

Random Matchup (Free Battle)

Random Matchup (Others)

LEVEL-UP MOVES

Lv.	Name	Type	Kind	Pow.	Acc.	PP	Range
1	Tackle	Normal	Physical	50	100	35	Normal
1	Harden	Normal	Status	—	—	30	Self
4	Mud-Slap	Ground	Special	20	100	10	Normal
7	Headbutt	Normal	Physical	70	100	15	Normal
10	Metal Claw	Steel	Physical	50	95	35	Normal
13	Rock Tomb	Rock	Physical	60	95	15	Normal
16	Protect	Normal	Status	—	—	10	Self
19	Roar	Normal	Status	—	—	20	Normal
22	Iron Head	Steel	Physical	80	100	15	Normal
25	Rock Slide	Rock	Physical	75	90	10	Many Others
28	Take Down	Normal	Physical	90	85	20	Normal
31	Metal Sound	Steel	Status	—	85	40	Normal
34	Iron Tail	Steel	Physical	100	75	15	Normal
37	Iron Defense	Steel	Status	—	—	15	Self
40	Double-Edge	Normal	Physical	120	100	15	Normal
43	Autotomize	Steel	Status	—	—	15	Self
46	Heavy Slam	Steel	Physical	—	100	10	Normal
49	Metal Burst	Steel	Physical	—	100	10	Varies

TM & HM MOVES

No.	Name	Type	Kind	Pow.	Acc.	PP	Range
TM01	Hone Claws	Dark	Status	—	—	15	Self
TM05	Roar	Normal	Status	—	—	20	Normal
TM06	Toxic	Poison	Status	—	90	10	Normal
TM10	Hidden Power	Normal	Special	60	100	15	Normal
TM11	Sunny Day	Fire	Status	—	—	5	Both Sides
TM17	Protect	Normal	Status	—	—	10	Self
TM18	Rain Dance	Water	Status	—	—	5	Both Sides
TM21	Frustration	Normal	Physical	—	100	20	Normal
TM26	Earthquake	Ground	Physical	100	100	10	Adjacent
TM27	Return	Normal	Physical	—	100	20	Normal
TM28	Dig	Ground	Physical	80	100	10	Normal
TM32	Double Team	Normal	Status	—	—	15	Self
TM37	Sandstorm	Rock	Status	—	—	10	Both Sides
TM39	Rock Tomb	Rock	Physical	60	95	15	Normal
TM40	Aerial Ace	Flying	Physical	60	—	20	Normal
TM42	Facade	Normal	Physical	70	100	20	Normal
TM44	Rest	Psychic	Status	—	—	10	Self
TM45	Attract	Normal	Status	—	100	15	Normal
TM48	Round	Normal	Special	60	100	15	Normal
TM65	Shadow Claw	Ghost	Physical	70	100	15	Normal
TM69	Rock Polish	Rock	Status	—	—	20	Self
TM78	Bulldoze	Ground	Physical	60	100	20	Adjacent
TM80	Rock Slide	Rock	Physical	75	90	10	Many Others
TM87	Swagger	Normal	Status	—	90	15	Normal
TM88	Sleep Talk	Normal	Status	—	—	10	Self
TM90	Substitute	Normal	Status	—	—	10	Self
TM94	Secret Power	Normal	Physical	70	100	20	Normal
TM100	Confide	Normal	Status	—	—	20	Normal
HM01	Cut	Normal	Physical	50	95	30	Normal
HM04	Strength	Normal	Physical	80	100	15	Normal
HM06	Rock Smash	Fighting	Physical	40	100	15	Normal

MOVES LEARNED IN EXCHANGE FOR BP

Name	Type	Kind	Pow.	Acc.	PP	Range
Iron Head	Steel	Physical	80	100	15	Normal
Uproar	Normal	Special	90	100	10	1 Random
Earth Power	Ground	Special	90	100	10	Normal
Magnet Rise	Electric	Status	—	—	10	Self
Iron Defense	Steel	Status	—	—	15	Self
Superpower	Fighting	Physical	120	100	5	Normal
Iron Tail	Steel	Physical	100	75	15	Normal
Snore	Normal	Special	50	100	15	Normal
Shock Wave	Electric	Special	60	—	20	Normal
Water Pulse	Water	Special	60	100	20	Normal
Spite	Ghost	Status	—	100	10	Normal
Endeavor	Normal	Physical	—	100	5	Normal
Stealth Rock	Rock	Status	—	—	20	Other Side

MOVES TAUGHT BY PEOPLE

Name	Type	Kind	Pow.	Acc.	PP	Range

EGG MOVES

Name	Type	Kind	Pow.	Acc.	PP	Range
Endeavor	Normal	Physical	—	100	5	Normal
Body Slam	Normal	Physical	85	100	15	Normal
Stomp	Normal	Physical	65	100	20	Normal
Smelling Salts	Normal	Physical	70	100	10	Normal
Curse	Ghost	Status	—	—	10	Varies
Screech	Normal	Status	—	85	40	Normal
Iron Head	Steel	Physical	80	100	15	Normal
Dragon Rush	Dragon	Physical	100	75	10	Normal
Head Smash	Rock	Physical	150	80	5	Normal
Superpower	Fighting	Physical	120	100	5	Normal
Stealth Rock	Rock	Status	—	—	20	Other Side
Reversal	Fighting	Physical	—	100	15	Normal

National Pokédex **305** Hoenn Pokédex **073**

✓ Lairon

Iron Armor Pokémon

Steel Rock

HEIGHT: 2'11" WEIGHT: 264.6 lbs.

Same form for ♂ / ♀

Ω Lairon tempers its steel body by drinking highly nutritious mineral springwater until it is bloated. This Pokémon makes its nest close to springs of delicious water.

α Lairon feeds on iron contained in rocks and water. It makes its nest on mountains where iron ore is buried. As a result, the Pokémon often clashes with humans mining the iron ore.

ABILITIES
Sturdy
Rock Head

HIDDEN ABILITY
Heavy Metal

EGG GROUPS
Monster

STAT GROWTH RATES
HP
Attack
Defense
Sp. Atk
Sp. Def
Speed

ITEMS SOMETIMES HELD BY WILD POKÉMON
Hard Stone

EVOLUTION
Aron → Lv. 32 → Lairon → Lv. 42 → Aggron

MAIN WAY TO REGISTER IN THE NATIONAL POKÉDEX

Catch on Victory Road (1F).

Damage taken in normal battles

Type		Type	
Normal	×0.25	Flying	×0.25
Fire	×1	Psychic	×0.5
Water	×2	Bug	×0.5
Grass	×1	Rock	×0.5
Electric	×1	Ghost	×1
Ice	×0.5	Dragon	×0.5
Fighting	×4	Dark	×1
Poison	×0	Steel	×1
Ground	×4	Fairy	×0.5

Damage taken in Inverse battles

Type		Type	
Normal	×4	Flying	×4
Fire	×1	Psychic	×2
Water	×0.5	Bug	×2
Grass	×1	Rock	×2
Electric	×1	Ghost	×1
Ice	×2	Dragon	×2
Fighting	×0.25	Dark	×1
Poison	×4	Steel	×1
Ground	×0.25	Fairy	×2

Can be used in
Inverse Battle
Battle Institute
Battle Maison
Random Matchup (Free Battle)
Random Matchup (Others)

LEVEL-UP MOVES

Lv.	Name	Type	Kind	Pow.	Acc.	PP	Range
1	Tackle	Normal	Physical	50	100	35	Normal
1	Harden	Normal	Status	—	—	30	Self
1	Mud-Slap	Ground	Special	20	100	10	Normal
1	Headbutt	Normal	Physical	70	100	15	Normal
4	Mud-Slap	Ground	Special	20	100	10	Normal
7	Headbutt	Normal	Physical	70	100	15	Normal
10	Metal Claw	Steel	Physical	50	95	35	Normal
13	Rock Tomb	Rock	Physical	60	95	15	Normal
16	Protect	Normal	Status	—	—	10	Self
19	Roar	Normal	Status	—	—	20	Normal
22	Iron Head	Steel	Physical	80	100	15	Normal
25	Rock Slide	Rock	Physical	75	90	10	Many Others
28	Take Down	Normal	Physical	90	85	20	Normal
31	Metal Sound	Steel	Status	—	85	40	Normal
35	Iron Tail	Steel	Physical	100	75	15	Normal
39	Iron Defense	Steel	Status	—	—	15	Self
43	Double-Edge	Normal	Physical	120	100	15	Normal
47	Autotomize	Steel	Status	—	—	15	Self
51	Heavy Slam	Steel	Physical	—	100	10	Normal
55	Metal Burst	Steel	Physical	—	100	10	Varies

TM & HM MOVES

No.	Name	Type	Kind	Pow.	Acc.	PP	Range
TM01	Hone Claws	Dark	Status	—	—	15	Self
TM05	Roar	Normal	Status	—	—	20	Normal
TM06	Toxic	Poison	Status	—	90	10	Normal
TM10	Hidden Power	Normal	Special	60	100	15	Normal
TM11	Sunny Day	Fire	Status	—	—	5	Both Sides
TM17	Protect	Normal	Status	—	—	10	Self
TM18	Rain Dance	Water	Status	—	—	5	Both Sides
TM21	Frustration	Normal	Physical	—	100	20	Normal
TM26	Earthquake	Ground	Physical	100	100	10	Adjacent
TM27	Return	Normal	Physical	—	100	20	Normal
TM28	Dig	Ground	Physical	80	100	10	Normal
TM32	Double Team	Normal	Status	—	—	15	Self
TM37	Sandstorm	Rock	Status	—	—	10	Both Sides
TM39	Rock Tomb	Rock	Physical	60	95	15	Normal
TM40	Aerial Ace	Flying	Physical	60	—	20	Normal
TM42	Facade	Normal	Physical	70	100	20	Normal
TM44	Rest	Psychic	Status	—	—	10	Self
TM45	Attract	Normal	Status	—	100	15	Normal
TM48	Round	Normal	Special	60	100	15	Normal
TM65	Shadow Claw	Ghost	Physical	70	100	15	Normal
TM69	Rock Polish	Rock	Status	—	—	20	Self
TM71	Stone Edge	Rock	Physical	100	80	5	Normal
TM78	Bulldoze	Ground	Physical	60	100	20	Adjacent
TM80	Rock Slide	Rock	Physical	75	90	10	Many Others
TM87	Swagger	Normal	Status	—	90	15	Normal
TM88	Sleep Talk	Normal	Status	—	—	10	Self
TM90	Substitute	Normal	Status	—	—	10	Self
TM94	Secret Power	Normal	Physical	70	100	20	Normal
TM100	Confide	Normal	Status	—	—	20	Normal
HM01	Cut	Normal	Physical	50	95	30	Normal
HM04	Strength	Normal	Physical	80	100	15	Normal
HM06	Rock Smash	Fighting	Physical	40	100	15	Normal

MOVES LEARNED IN EXCHANGE FOR BP

Name	Type	Kind	Pow.	Acc.	PP	Range
Iron Head	Steel	Physical	80	100	15	Normal
Uproar	Normal	Special	90	100	10	1 Random
Earth Power	Ground	Special	90	100	10	Normal
Magnet Rise	Electric	Status	—	—	10	Self
Iron Defense	Steel	Status	—	—	15	Self
Superpower	Fighting	Physical	120	100	5	Normal
Iron Tail	Steel	Physical	100	75	15	Normal
Snore	Normal	Special	50	100	15	Normal
Shock Wave	Electric	Special	60	—	20	Normal
Water Pulse	Water	Special	60	100	20	Normal
Spite	Ghost	Status	—	100	10	Normal
Endeavor	Normal	Physical	—	100	5	Normal
Stealth Rock	Rock	Status	—	—	20	Other Side

MOVES TAUGHT BY PEOPLE

Name	Type	Kind	Pow.	Acc.	PP	Range

National Pokédex **306** Hoenn Pokédex **074**

✓ Aggron

Iron Armor Pokémon

Steel Rock

HEIGHT: 6'11" WEIGHT: 793.7 lbs.

Same form for ♂ / ♀

Ω Aggron claims an entire mountain as its own territory. It mercilessly beats up anything that violates its environment. This Pokémon vigilantly patrols its territory at all times.

α Aggron is protective of its environment. If its mountain is ravaged by a landslide or a fire, this Pokémon will haul topsoil to the area, plant trees, and beautifully restore its own territory.

ABILITIES
Sturdy
Rock Head

HIDDEN ABILITY
Heavy Metal

EGG GROUPS
Monster

STAT GROWTH RATES
HP
Attack
Defense
Sp. Atk
Sp. Def
Speed

ITEMS SOMETIMES HELD BY WILD POKÉMON
—

EVOLUTION
Aron → Lv. 32 → Lairon → Lv. 42 → Aggron

MAIN WAY TO REGISTER IN THE NATIONAL POKÉDEX

Level up Lairon to Lv. 42.

Damage taken in normal battles

Type		Type	
Normal	×0.25	Flying	×0.25
Fire	×1	Psychic	×0.5
Water	×2	Bug	×0.5
Grass	×1	Rock	×0.5
Electric	×1	Ghost	×1
Ice	×0.5	Dragon	×0.5
Fighting	×4	Dark	×1
Poison	×0	Steel	×1
Ground	×4	Fairy	×0.5

Damage taken in Inverse battles

Type		Type	
Normal	×4	Flying	×4
Fire	×1	Psychic	×2
Water	×0.5	Bug	×2
Grass	×1	Rock	×2
Electric	×1	Ghost	×1
Ice	×2	Dragon	×2
Fighting	×0.25	Dark	×1
Poison	×4	Steel	×1
Ground	×0.25	Fairy	×2

Can be used in
Inverse Battle
Battle Institute
Battle Maison
Random Matchup (Free Battle)
Random Matchup (Others)

LEVEL-UP MOVES

Lv.	Name	Type	Kind	Pow.	Acc.	PP	Range
1	Tackle	Normal	Physical	50	100	35	Normal
1	Harden	Normal	Status	—	—	30	Self
1	Mud-Slap	Ground	Special	20	100	10	Normal
1	Headbutt	Normal	Physical	70	100	15	Normal
4	Mud-Slap	Ground	Special	20	100	10	Normal
7	Headbutt	Normal	Physical	70	100	15	Normal
10	Metal Claw	Steel	Physical	50	95	35	Normal
13	Rock Tomb	Rock	Physical	60	95	15	Normal
16	Protect	Normal	Status	—	—	10	Self
19	Roar	Normal	Status	—	—	20	Normal
22	Iron Head	Steel	Physical	80	100	15	Normal
25	Rock Slide	Rock	Physical	75	90	10	Many Others
28	Take Down	Normal	Physical	90	85	20	Normal
31	Metal Sound	Steel	Status	—	85	40	Normal
35	Iron Tail	Steel	Physical	100	75	15	Normal
39	Iron Defense	Steel	Status	—	—	15	Self
45	Double-Edge	Normal	Physical	120	100	15	Normal
51	Autotomize	Steel	Status	—	—	15	Self
57	Heavy Slam	Steel	Physical	—	100	10	Normal
63	Metal Burst	Steel	Physical	—	100	10	Varies

TM & HM MOVES

No.	Name	Type	Kind	Pow.	Acc.	PP	Range
TM01	Hone Claws	Dark	Status	—	—	15	Self
TM02	Dragon Claw	Dragon	Physical	80	100	15	Normal
TM05	Roar	Normal	Status	—	—	20	Normal
TM06	Toxic	Poison	Status	—	90	10	Normal
TM10	Hidden Power	Normal	Special	60	100	15	Normal
TM11	Sunny Day	Fire	Status	—	—	5	Both Sides
TM12	Taunt	Dark	Status	—	100	20	Normal
TM13	Ice Beam	Ice	Special	90	100	10	Normal
TM14	Blizzard	Ice	Special	110	70	5	Many Others
TM15	Hyper Beam	Normal	Special	150	90	5	Normal
TM17	Protect	Normal	Status	—	—	10	Self
TM18	Rain Dance	Water	Status	—	—	5	Both Sides
TM21	Frustration	Normal	Physical	—	100	20	Normal
TM22	Solar Beam	Grass	Special	120	100	10	Normal
TM23	Smack Down	Rock	Physical	50	100	15	Normal
TM24	Thunderbolt	Electric	Special	90	100	15	Normal
TM25	Thunder	Electric	Special	110	70	10	Normal
TM26	Earthquake	Ground	Physical	100	100	10	Adjacent
TM27	Return	Normal	Physical	—	100	20	Normal
TM28	Dig	Ground	Physical	80	100	10	Normal
TM31	Brick Break	Fighting	Physical	75	100	15	Normal
TM32	Double Team	Normal	Status	—	—	15	Self
TM35	Flamethrower	Fire	Special	90	100	15	Normal
TM37	Sandstorm	Rock	Status	—	—	10	Both Sides
TM38	Fire Blast	Fire	Special	110	85	5	Normal
TM39	Rock Tomb	Rock	Physical	60	95	15	Normal
TM40	Aerial Ace	Flying	Physical	60	—	20	Normal
TM42	Facade	Normal	Physical	70	100	20	Normal
TM44	Rest	Psychic	Status	—	—	10	Self
TM45	Attract	Normal	Status	—	100	15	Normal
TM48	Round	Normal	Special	60	100	15	Normal
TM52	Focus Blast	Fighting	Special	120	70	5	Normal
TM56	Fling	Dark	Physical	—	100	10	Normal
TM59	Incinerate	Fire	Special	60	100	15	Many Others
TM65	Shadow Claw	Ghost	Physical	70	100	15	Normal
TM66	Payback	Dark	Physical	50	100	10	Normal
TM68	Giga Impact	Normal	Physical	150	90	5	Normal
TM69	Rock Polish	Rock	Status	—	—	20	Self
TM71	Stone Edge	Rock	Physical	100	80	5	Normal
TM73	Thunder Wave	Electric	Status	—	100	20	Normal
TM78	Bulldoze	Ground	Physical	60	100	20	Adjacent
TM80	Rock Slide	Rock	Physical	75	90	10	Many Others
TM82	Dragon Tail	Dragon	Physical	60	90	10	Normal
TM87	Swagger	Normal	Status	—	90	15	Normal
TM88	Sleep Talk	Normal	Status	—	—	10	Self
TM90	Substitute	Normal	Status	—	—	10	Self
TM91	Flash Cannon	Steel	Special	80	100	10	Normal
TM94	Secret Power	Normal	Physical	70	100	20	Normal
TM97	Dark Pulse	Dark	Special	80	100	15	Normal
TM98	Power-Up Punch	Fighting	Physical	40	100	20	Normal
TM100	Confide	Normal	Status	—	—	20	Normal
HM01	Cut	Normal	Physical	50	95	30	Normal
HM03	Surf	Water	Special	90	100	15	Adjacent
HM04	Strength	Normal	Physical	80	100	15	Normal
HM06	Rock Smash	Fighting	Physical	40	100	15	Normal

MOVES LEARNED IN EXCHANGE FOR BP

Name	Type	Kind	Pow.	Acc.	PP	Range
Iron Head	Steel	Physical	80	100	15	Normal
Low Kick	Fighting	Physical	—	100	20	Normal
Uproar	Normal	Special	90	100	10	1 Random
Thunder Punch	Electric	Physical	75	100	15	Normal
Fire Punch	Fire	Physical	75	100	15	Normal
Ice Punch	Ice	Physical	75	100	15	Normal
Block	Normal	Status	—	—	5	Normal
Earth Power	Ground	Special	90	100	10	Normal
Magnet Rise	Electric	Status	—	—	10	Self
Iron Defense	Steel	Status	—	—	15	Self
Superpower	Fighting	Physical	120	100	5	Normal
Icy Wind	Ice	Special	55	95	15	Many Others
Aqua Tail	Water	Physical	90	90	10	Normal
Dragon Pulse	Dragon	Special	85	100	10	Normal
Iron Tail	Steel	Physical	100	75	15	Normal
Snore	Normal	Special	50	100	15	Normal
Focus Punch	Fighting	Physical	150	100	20	Normal
Shock Wave	Electric	Special	60	—	20	Normal
Water Pulse	Water	Special	60	100	20	Normal
Spite	Ghost	Status	—	100	10	Normal
Endeavor	Normal	Physical	—	100	5	Normal
Outrage	Dragon	Physical	120	100	10	1 Random
Stealth Rock	Rock	Status	—	—	20	Other Side

MOVES TAUGHT BY PEOPLE

Name	Type	Kind	Pow.	Acc.	PP	Range

Mega Evolution

Mega Aggron

Iron Armor Pokémon

Steel

HEIGHT: 7'03" WEIGHT: 870.8 lbs.

Same form for ♂ / ♀

REQUIRED MEGA STONE

Aggronite

Receive from the man in Rusturf Tunnel (after opening the tunnel with Rock Smash).

ABILITY

Filter

HIDDEN ABILITY

—

EGG GROUPS

—

STAT GROWTH RATES

HP

Attack

Defense

Sp. Atk

Sp. Def

Speed

Damage taken in normal battles

Type		Type	
Normal	×0.5	Flying	×0.5
Fire	×2	Psychic	×0.5
Water	×1	Bug	×0.5
Grass	×0.5	Rock	×0.5
Electric	×1	Ghost	×1
Ice	×0.5	Dragon	×0.5
Fighting	×2	Dark	×1
Poison	×0	Steel	×0.5
Ground	×2	Fairy	×0.5

Damage taken in Inverse battles

Type		Type	
Normal	×2	Flying	×2
Fire	×0.5	Psychic	×2
Water	×1	Bug	×2
Grass	×2	Rock	×2
Electric	×1	Ghost	×1
Ice	×2	Dragon	×2
Fighting	×0.5	Dark	×1
Poison	×2	Steel	×2
Ground	×0.5	Fairy	×2

Can be used in

Inverse Battle

Battle Institute

Battle Maison

Random Matchup (Free Battle)

Random Matchup (Others)

National Pokédex **307** Hoenn Pokédex **078**

Meditite

Meditate Pokémon

Fighting Psychic

HEIGHT: 2'00" WEIGHT: 24.7 lbs.

The bumps on the male's head are located higher. The bumps on the female's head are located lower.

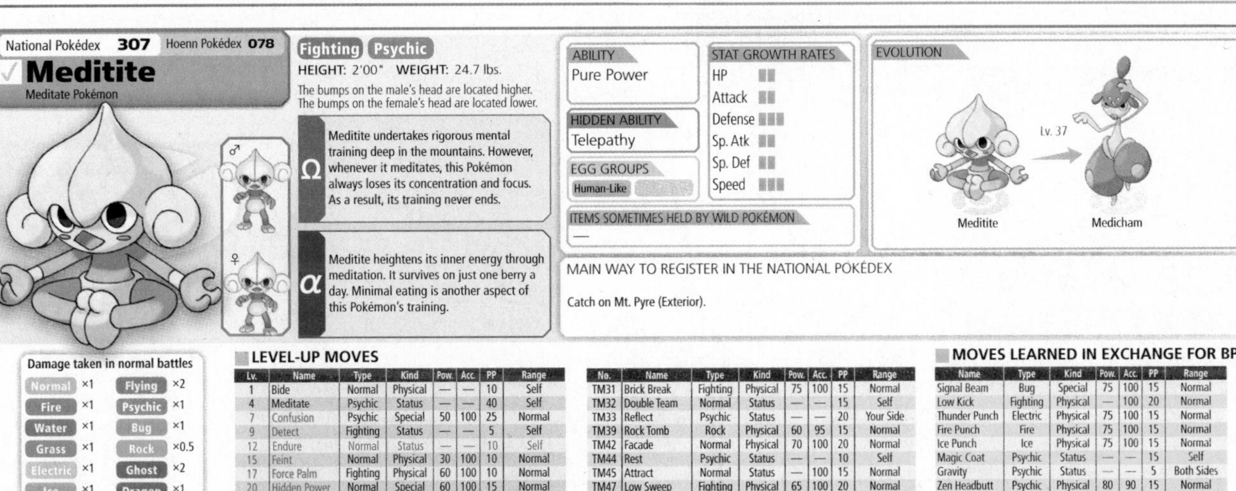

Ω Meditite undertakes rigorous mental training deep in the mountains. However, whenever it meditates, this Pokémon always loses its concentration and focus. As a result, its training never ends.

α Meditite heightens its inner energy through meditation. It survives on just one berry a day. Minimal eating is another aspect of this Pokémon's training.

ABILITY

Pure Power

HIDDEN ABILITY

Telepathy

EGG GROUPS

Human-Like

STAT GROWTH RATES

HP

Attack

Defense

Sp. Atk

Sp. Def

Speed

EVOLUTION

Meditite → Lv. 37 → Medicham

ITEMS SOMETIMES HELD BY WILD POKÉMON

—

MAIN WAY TO REGISTER IN THE NATIONAL POKÉDEX

Catch on Mt. Pyre (Exterior).

Damage taken in normal battles

Type		Type	
Normal	×1	Flying	×2
Fire	×1	Psychic	×1
Water	×1	Bug	×1
Grass	×1	Rock	×0.5
Electric	×1	Ghost	×2
Ice	×1	Dragon	×1
Fighting	×0.5	Dark	×1
Poison	×1	Steel	×1
Ground	×1	Fairy	×2

Damage taken in Inverse battles

Type		Type	
Normal	×1	Flying	×0.5
Fire	×1	Psychic	×1
Water	×1	Bug	×1
Grass	×1	Rock	×2
Electric	×1	Ghost	×0.5
Ice	×1	Dragon	×1
Fighting	×2	Dark	×1
Poison	×1	Steel	×1
Ground	×1	Fairy	×0.5

Can be used in

Inverse Battle

Battle Institute

Battle Maison

Random Matchup (Free Battle)

Random Matchup (Others)

LEVEL-UP MOVES

Lv.	Name	Type	Kind	Pow.	Acc.	PP	Range
1	Bide	Normal	Physical	—	—	10	Self
4	Meditate	Psychic	Status	—	—	40	Self
7	Confusion	Psychic	Special	50	100	25	Normal
9	Detect	Fighting	Status	—	—	5	Self
12	Endure	Normal	Status	—	—	10	Self
15	Feint	Normal	Physical	30	100	10	Normal
17	Force Palm	Fighting	Physical	60	100	10	Normal
20	Hidden Power	Normal	Special	60	100	15	Normal
23	Calm Mind	Psychic	Status	—	—	20	Self
25	Mind Reader	Normal	Status	—	—	5	Normal
28	High Jump Kick	Fighting	Physical	130	90	10	Normal
31	Psych Up	Normal	Status	—	—	10	Normal
33	Acupressure	Normal	Status	—	—	30	Self/Ally
36	Power Trick	Psychic	Status	—	—	10	Self
39	Reversal	Fighting	Physical	—	100	15	Normal
41	Recover	Normal	Status	—	—	10	Self
44	Counter	Fighting	Physical	—	100	20	Varies

TM & HM MOVES

No.	Name	Type	Kind	Pow.	Acc.	PP	Range
TM03	Psyshock	Psychic	Special	80	100	10	Normal
TM04	Calm Mind	Psychic	Status	—	—	20	Self
TM06	Toxic	Poison	Status	—	90	10	Normal
TM08	Bulk Up	Fighting	Status	—	—	20	Self
TM10	Hidden Power	Normal	Special	60	100	15	Normal
TM11	Sunny Day	Fire	Status	—	—	5	Both Sides
TM16	Light Screen	Psychic	Status	—	—	30	Your Side
TM17	Protect	Normal	Status	—	—	10	Self
TM18	Rain Dance	Water	Status	—	—	5	Both Sides
TM21	Frustration	Normal	Physical	—	100	20	Normal
TM27	Return	Normal	Physical	—	100	20	Normal
TM29	Psychic	Psychic	Special	90	100	10	Normal
TM30	Shadow Ball	Ghost	Special	80	100	15	Normal
TM31	Brick Break	Fighting	Physical	75	100	15	Normal
TM32	Double Team	Normal	Status	—	—	15	Self
TM33	Reflect	Psychic	Status	—	—	20	Your Side
TM39	Rock Tomb	Rock	Physical	60	95	15	Normal
TM42	Facade	Normal	Physical	70	100	20	Normal
TM44	Rest	Psychic	Status	—	—	10	Self
TM45	Attract	Normal	Status	—	100	15	Normal
TM47	Low Sweep	Fighting	Physical	65	100	20	Normal
TM48	Round	Normal	Special	60	100	15	Normal
TM52	Focus Blast	Fighting	Special	120	70	5	Normal
TM56	Fling	Dark	Physical	—	100	10	Normal
TM67	Retaliate	Normal	Physical	70	100	5	Normal
TM70	Flash	Normal	Status	—	100	20	Normal
TM77	Psych Up	Normal	Status	—	—	10	Normal
TM80	Rock Slide	Rock	Physical	75	90	10	Many Others
TM84	Poison Jab	Poison	Physical	80	100	20	Normal
TM85	Dream Eater	Psychic	Special	100	100	15	Normal
TM86	Grass Knot	Grass	Special	—	100	20	Normal
TM87	Swagger	Normal	Status	—	90	15	Normal
TM88	Sleep Talk	Normal	Status	—	—	10	Self
TM90	Substitute	Normal	Status	—	—	10	Self
TM94	Secret Power	Normal	Physical	70	100	20	Normal
TM98	Power-Up Punch	Fighting	Physical	40	100	20	Normal
TM100	Confide	Normal	Status	—	—	20	Normal
HM04	Strength	Normal	Physical	80	100	15	Normal
HM06	Rock Smash	Fighting	Physical	40	100	15	Normal

MOVES LEARNED IN EXCHANGE FOR BP

Name	Type	Kind	Pow.	Acc.	PP	Range
Signal Beam	Bug	Special	75	100	15	Normal
Low Kick	Fighting	Physical	—	100	20	Normal
Thunder Punch	Electric	Physical	75	100	15	Normal
Fire Punch	Fire	Physical	75	100	15	Normal
Ice Punch	Ice	Physical	75	100	15	Normal
Magic Coat	Psychic	Status	—	—	15	Self
Gravity	Psychic	Status	—	—	5	Both Sides
Zen Headbutt	Psychic	Physical	80	90	15	Normal
Snore	Normal	Special	50	100	15	Normal
Role Play	Psychic	Status	—	—	10	Normal
Pain Split	Normal	Status	—	—	20	Normal
Drain Punch	Fighting	Physical	75	100	10	Normal
Focus Punch	Fighting	Physical	150	100	20	Normal
Helping Hand	Normal	Status	—	—	20	1 Ally
Trick	Psychic	Status	—	100	10	Normal
Recycle	Normal	Status	—	—	10	Self

MOVES TAUGHT BY PEOPLE

Name	Type	Kind	Pow.	Acc.	PP	Range

EGG MOVES

Name	Type	Kind	Pow.	Acc.	PP	Range
Fire Punch	Fire	Physical	75	100	15	Normal
Thunder Punch	Electric	Physical	75	100	15	Normal
Ice Punch	Ice	Physical	75	100	15	Normal
Foresight	Normal	Status	—	—	40	Normal
Fake Out	Normal	Physical	40	100	10	Normal
Baton Pass	Normal	Status	—	—	40	Self
Dynamic Punch	Fighting	Physical	100	50	5	Normal
Power Swap	Psychic	Status	—	—	10	Normal
Guard Swap	Psychic	Status	—	—	10	Normal
Psycho Cut	Psychic	Physical	70	100	20	Normal
Bullet Punch	Steel	Physical	40	100	30	Normal
Drain Punch	Fighting	Physical	75	100	10	Normal
Secret Power	Normal	Physical	70	100	20	Normal
Quick Guard	Fighting	Status	—	—	15	Your Side

National Pokédex **308** Hoenn Pokédex **079**

Medicham

Meditate Pokémon

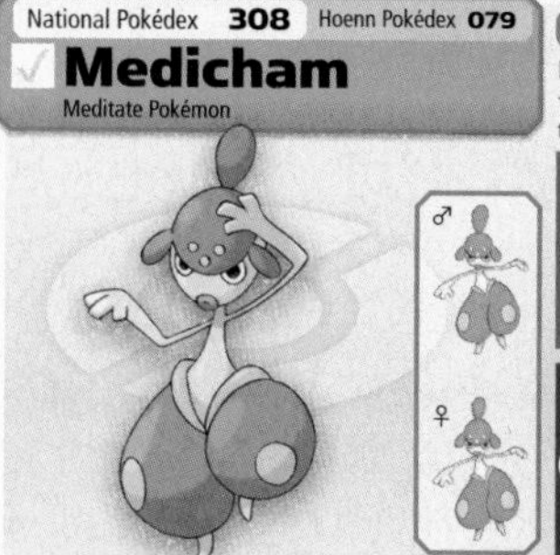

Fighting Psychic

HEIGHT: 4'03" WEIGHT: 69.4 lbs.

The male has a larger bulb on top of its head than the female.

♂ ♀

Ω It is said that through meditation, Medicham heightens energy inside its body and sharpens its sixth sense. This Pokémon hides its presence by merging itself with fields and mountains.

α Through the power of meditation, Medicham developed its sixth sense. It gained the ability to use psychokinetic powers. This Pokémon is known to meditate for a whole month without eating.

ABILITY
Pure Power

HIDDEN ABILITY
Telepathy

EGG GROUPS
Human-Like

STAT GROWTH RATES
HP
Attack
Defense
Sp. Atk
Sp. Def
Speed

ITEMS SOMETIMES HELD BY WILD POKÉMON
—

EVOLUTION
Meditite → Lv. 37 → Medicham

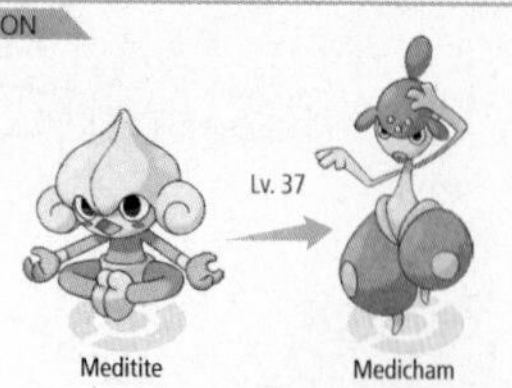

MAIN WAY TO REGISTER IN THE NATIONAL POKÉDEX
Catch on Victory Road (1F).

Damage taken in normal battles

Type		Type	
Normal	×1	Flying	×2
Fire	×1	Psychic	×1
Water	×1	Bug	×1
Grass	×1	Rock	×0.5
Electric	×1	Ghost	×2
Ice	×1	Dragon	×1
Fighting	×0.5	Dark	×1
Poison	×1	Steel	×1
Ground	×1	Fairy	×2

Damage taken in Inverse battles

Type		Type	
Normal	×1	Flying	×0.5
Fire	×1	Psychic	×1
Water	×1	Bug	×1
Grass	×1	Rock	×2
Electric	×1	Ghost	×0.5
Ice	×1	Dragon	×1
Fighting	×2	Dark	×1
Poison	×1	Steel	×1
Ground	×1	Fairy	×0.5

Can be used in
Inverse Battle
Battle Institute
Battle Maison
Random Matchup (Free Battle)
Random Matchup (Others)

LEVEL-UP MOVES

Lv.	Name	Type	Kind	Pow.	Acc.	PP	Range
1	Zen Headbutt	Psychic	Physical	80	90	15	Normal
1	Fire Punch	Fire	Physical	75	100	15	Normal
1	Thunder Punch	Electric	Physical	75	100	15	Normal
1	Ice Punch	Ice	Physical	75	100	15	Normal
1	Bide	Normal	Physical	—	—	10	Self
1	Meditate	Psychic	Status	—	—	40	Self
1	Confusion	Psychic	Special	50	100	25	Normal
1	Detect	Fighting	Status	—	—	5	Self
4	Meditate	Psychic	Status	—	—	40	Self
7	Confusion	Psychic	Special	50	100	25	Normal
9	Detect	Fighting	Status	—	—	5	Self
12	Endure	Normal	Status	—	—	10	Self
15	Feint	Normal	Physical	30	100	10	Normal
17	Force Palm	Fighting	Physical	60	100	10	Normal
20	Hidden Power	Normal	Special	60	100	15	Normal
23	Calm Mind	Psychic	Status	—	—	20	Self
25	Mind Reader	Normal	Status	—	—	5	Normal
28	High Jump Kick	Fighting	Physical	130	90	10	Normal
31	Psych Up	Normal	Status	—	—	10	Normal
33	Acupressure	Normal	Status	—	—	30	Self/Ally
36	Power Trick	Psychic	Status	—	—	10	Self
42	Reversal	Fighting	Physical	—	100	15	Normal
47	Recover	Normal	Status	—	—	10	Self
53	Counter	Fighting	Physical	—	100	20	Varies

TM & HM MOVES

No.	Name	Type	Kind	Pow.	Acc.	PP	Range
TM03	Psyshock	Psychic	Special	80	100	10	Normal
TM04	Calm Mind	Psychic	Status	—	—	20	Self
TM06	Toxic	Poison	Status	—	90	10	Normal
TM08	Bulk Up	Fighting	Status	—	—	20	Self
TM10	Hidden Power	Normal	Special	60	100	15	Normal
TM11	Sunny Day	Fire	Status	—	—	5	Both Sides
TM15	Hyper Beam	Normal	Special	150	90	5	Normal
TM16	Light Screen	Psychic	Status	—	—	30	Your Side
TM17	Protect	Normal	Status	—	—	10	Self
TM18	Rain Dance	Water	Status	—	—	5	Both Sides
TM21	Frustration	Normal	Physical	—	100	20	Normal
TM27	Return	Normal	Physical	—	100	20	Normal
TM29	Psychic	Psychic	Special	90	100	10	Normal
TM30	Shadow Ball	Ghost	Special	80	100	15	Normal
TM31	Brick Break	Fighting	Physical	75	100	15	Normal
TM32	Double Team	Normal	Status	—	—	15	Self
TM33	Reflect	Psychic	Status	—	—	20	Your Side
TM39	Rock Tomb	Rock	Physical	60	95	15	Normal
TM42	Facade	Normal	Physical	70	100	20	Normal
TM44	Rest	Psychic	Status	—	—	10	Self
TM45	Attract	Normal	Status	—	100	15	Normal
TM47	Low Sweep	Fighting	Physical	65	100	20	Normal
TM48	Round	Normal	Special	60	100	15	Normal
TM52	Focus Blast	Fighting	Special	120	70	5	Normal
TM53	Energy Ball	Grass	Special	90	100	10	Normal
TM56	Fling	Dark	Physical	—	100	10	Normal
TM67	Retaliate	Normal	Physical	70	100	5	Normal
TM68	Giga Impact	Normal	Physical	150	90	5	Normal
TM70	Flash	Normal	Status	—	100	20	Normal
TM77	Psych Up	Normal	Status	—	—	10	Normal
TM80	Rock Slide	Rock	Physical	75	90	10	Many Others
TM84	Poison Jab	Poison	Physical	80	100	20	Normal
TM85	Dream Eater	Psychic	Special	100	100	15	Normal
TM86	Grass Knot	Grass	Special	—	100	20	Normal
TM87	Swagger	Normal	Status	—	90	15	Normal
TM88	Sleep Talk	Normal	Status	—	—	10	Self
TM90	Substitute	Normal	Status	—	—	10	Self
TM94	Secret Power	Normal	Physical	70	100	20	Normal
TM98	Power-Up Punch	Fighting	Physical	40	100	20	Normal
TM100	Confide	Normal	Status	—	—	20	Normal
HM04	Strength	Normal	Physical	80	100	15	Normal
HM06	Rock Smash	Fighting	Physical	40	100	15	Normal

MOVES LEARNED IN EXCHANGE FOR BP

Name	Type	Kind	Pow.	Acc.	PP	Range
Signal Beam	Bug	Special	75	100	15	Normal
Low Kick	Fighting	Physical	—	100	20	Normal
Thunder Punch	Electric	Physical	75	100	15	Normal
Fire Punch	Fire	Physical	75	100	15	Normal
Ice Punch	Ice	Physical	75	100	15	Normal
Magic Coat	Psychic	Status	—	—	15	Self
Gravity	Psychic	Status	—	—	5	Both Sides
Zen Headbutt	Psychic	Physical	80	90	15	Normal
Snore	Normal	Special	50	100	15	Normal
Role Play	Psychic	Status	—	—	10	Normal
Pain Split	Normal	Status	—	—	20	Normal
Drain Punch	Fighting	Physical	75	100	10	Normal
Focus Punch	Fighting	Physical	150	100	20	Normal
Helping Hand	Normal	Status	—	—	20	1 Ally
Trick	Psychic	Status	—	100	10	Normal
Recycle	Normal	Status	—	—	10	Self

MOVES TAUGHT BY PEOPLE

Name	Type	Kind	Pow.	Acc.	PP	Range

Mega Evolution

Mega Medicham

Meditate Pokémon

Fighting Psychic

HEIGHT: 4'03" WEIGHT: 69.4 lbs.

Same form for ♂ / ♀

REQUIRED MEGA STONE
Medichamite
Find within Mt. Pyre (4F).

ABILITY
Pure Power

HIDDEN ABILITY
—

EGG GROUPS
—

STAT GROWTH RATES
HP
Attack
Defense
Sp. Atk
Sp. Def
Speed

Damage taken in normal battles

Type		Type	
Normal	×1	Flying	×2
Fire	×1	Psychic	×1
Water	×1	Bug	×1
Grass	×1	Rock	×0.5
Electric	×1	Ghost	×2
Ice	×1	Dragon	×1
Fighting	×0.5	Dark	×1
Poison	×1	Steel	×1
Ground	×1	Fairy	×2

Damage taken in Inverse battles

Type		Type	
Normal	×1	Flying	×0.5
Fire	×1	Psychic	×1
Water	×1	Bug	×1
Grass	×1	Rock	×2
Electric	×1	Ghost	×0.5
Ice	×1	Dragon	×1
Fighting	×2	Dark	×1
Poison	×1	Steel	×1
Ground	×1	Fairy	×0.5

Can be used in
Inverse Battle
Battle Institute
Battle Maison
Random Matchup (Free Battle)
Random Matchup (Others)

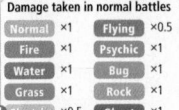

National Pokédex **309** Hoenn Pokédex **080**

Electrike

Lightning Pokémon

Electric

HEIGHT: 2'00" WEIGHT: 33.5 lbs.

Same form for ♂ / ♀

Ω Electrike stores electricity in its long body hair. This Pokémon stimulates its leg muscles with electric charges. These jolts of power give its legs explosive acceleration performance.

α Electrike runs faster than the human eye can follow. The friction from running is converted into electricity, which is then stored in this Pokémon's fur.

ABILITIES
Static
Lightning Rod

HIDDEN ABILITY
Minus

EGG GROUPS
Field

STAT GROWTH RATES
HP
Attack
Defense
Sp. Atk
Sp. Def
Speed

ITEMS SOMETIMES HELD BY WILD POKÉMON
—

EVOLUTION

MAIN WAY TO REGISTER IN THE NATIONAL POKÉDEX

Catch on Route 110.

Damage taken in normal battles

Normal	×1	Flying	×0.5
Fire	×1	Psychic	×1
Water	×1	Bug	×1
Grass	×1	Rock	×1
Electric	×0.5	Ghost	×1
Ice	×1	Dragon	×1
Fighting	×1	Dark	×1
Poison	×1	Steel	×0.5
Ground	×2	Fairy	×1

Damage taken in Inverse battles

Normal	×1	Flying	×2
Fire	×1	Psychic	×1
Water	×1	Bug	×1
Grass	×1	Rock	×1
Electric	×2	Ghost	×1
Ice	×1	Dragon	×1
Fighting	×1	Dark	×1
Poison	×1	Steel	×2
Ground	×0.5	Fairy	×1

Can be used in
- Inverse Battle
- Battle Institute
- Battle Maison
- Random Matchup (Free Battle)
- Random Matchup (Others)

LEVEL-UP MOVES

Lv.	Name	Type	Kind	Pow.	Acc.	PP	Range
1	Tackle	Normal	Physical	50	100	35	Normal
1	Thunder Wave	Electric	Status	—	100	20	Normal
4	Leer	Normal	Status	—	100	30	Many Others
7	Howl	Normal	Status	—	—	40	Self
10	Quick Attack	Normal	Physical	40	100	30	Normal
13	Spark	Electric	Physical	65	100	20	Normal
16	Odor Sleuth	Normal	Status	—	—	40	Normal
19	Thunder Fang	Electric	Physical	65	95	15	Normal
24	Bite	Dark	Physical	60	100	25	Normal
29	Discharge	Electric	Special	80	100	15	Adjacent
34	Roar	Normal	Status	—	—	20	Normal
39	Wild Charge	Electric	Physical	90	100	15	Normal
44	Charge	Electric	Status	—	—	20	Self
49	Thunder	Electric	Special	110	70	10	Normal

TM & HM MOVES

No.	Name	Type	Kind	Pow.	Acc.	PP	Range
TM05	Roar	Normal	Status	—	—	20	Normal
TM06	Toxic	Poison	Status	—	90	10	Normal
TM10	Hidden Power	Normal	Special	60	100	15	Normal
TM16	Light Screen	Psychic	Status	—	—	30	Your Side
TM17	Protect	Normal	Status	—	—	10	Self
TM18	Rain Dance	Water	Status	—	—	5	Both Sides
TM21	Frustration	Normal	Physical	—	100	20	Normal
TM24	Thunderbolt	Electric	Special	90	100	15	Normal
TM25	Thunder	Electric	Special	110	70	10	Normal
TM27	Return	Normal	Physical	—	100	20	Normal
TM32	Double Team	Normal	Status	—	—	15	Self
TM35	Flamethrower	Fire	Special	90	100	15	Normal
TM42	Facade	Normal	Physical	70	100	20	Normal
TM44	Rest	Psychic	Status	—	—	10	Self
TM45	Attract	Normal	Status	—	100	15	Normal
TM46	Thief	Dark	Physical	60	100	25	Normal
TM48	Round	Normal	Special	60	100	15	Normal
TM57	Charge Beam	Electric	Special	50	90	10	Normal
TM70	Flash	Normal	Status	—	100	20	Normal
TM72	Volt Switch	Electric	Special	70	100	20	Normal
TM73	Thunder Wave	Electric	Status	—	100	20	Normal
TM87	Swagger	Normal	Status	—	90	15	Normal
TM88	Sleep Talk	Normal	Status	—	—	10	Self
TM90	Substitute	Normal	Status	—	—	10	Self
TM93	Wild Charge	Electric	Physical	90	100	15	Normal
TM94	Secret Power	Normal	Physical	70	100	20	Normal
TM95	Snarl	Dark	Special	55	95	15	Many Others
TM100	Confide	Normal	Status	—	—	20	Normal
HM04	Strength	Normal	Physical	80	100	15	Normal

MOVES LEARNED IN EXCHANGE FOR BP

Name	Type	Kind	Pow.	Acc.	PP	Range
Signal Beam	Bug	Special	75	100	15	Normal
Uproar	Normal	Special	90	100	10	1 Random
Magnet Rise	Electric	Status	—	—	10	Self
Iron Tail	Steel	Physical	100	75	15	Normal
Snore	Normal	Special	50	100	15	Normal
Shock Wave	Electric	Special	60	—	20	Normal

MOVES TAUGHT BY PEOPLE

Name	Type	Kind	Pow.	Acc.	PP	Range

EGG MOVES

Name	Type	Kind	Pow.	Acc.	PP	Range
Crunch	Dark	Physical	80	100	15	Normal
Headbutt	Normal	Physical	70	100	15	Normal
Uproar	Normal	Special	90	100	10	1 Random
Curse	Ghost	Status	—	—	10	Varies
Swift	Normal	Special	60	—	20	Many Others
Discharge	Electric	Special	80	100	15	Adjacent
Ice Fang	Ice	Physical	65	95	15	Normal
Fire Fang	Fire	Physical	65	95	15	Normal
Thunder Fang	Electric	Physical	65	95	15	Normal
Switcheroo	Dark	Status	—	100	10	Normal
Electro Ball	Electric	Special	—	100	10	Normal
Shock Wave	Electric	Special	60	—	20	Normal
Flame Burst	Fire	Special	70	100	15	Normal
Eerie Impulse	Electric	Status	—	100	15	Normal

National Pokédex **310** Hoenn Pokédex **081**

Manectric

Discharge Pokémon

Electric

HEIGHT: 4'11" WEIGHT: 88.6 lbs.

Same form for ♂ / ♀

Ω Manectric is constantly discharging electricity from its mane. The sparks sometimes ignite forest fires. When it enters a battle, this Pokémon creates thunderclouds.

α Manectric discharges strong electricity from its mane. The mane is used for collecting electricity in the atmosphere. This Pokémon creates thunderclouds above its head.

ABILITIES
Static
Lightning Rod

HIDDEN ABILITY
Minus

EGG GROUPS
Field

STAT GROWTH RATES
HP
Attack
Defense
Sp. Atk
Sp. Def
Speed

ITEMS SOMETIMES HELD BY WILD POKÉMON
—

EVOLUTION

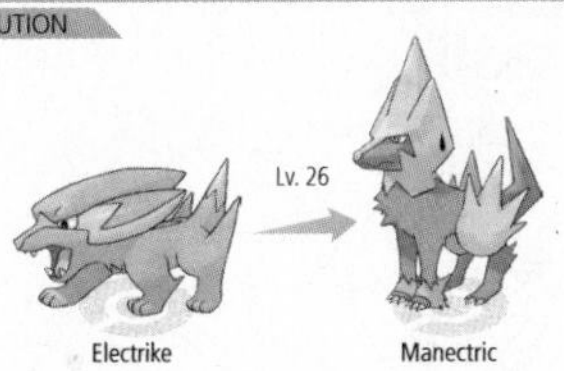

MAIN WAY TO REGISTER IN THE NATIONAL POKÉDEX

Level up Electrike to Lv. 26.

Damage taken in normal battles

Normal	×1	Flying	×0.5
Fire	×1	Psychic	×1
Water	×1	Bug	×1
Grass	×1	Rock	×1
Electric	×0.5	Ghost	×1
Ice	×1	Dragon	×1
Fighting	×1	Dark	×1
Poison	×1	Steel	×0.5
Ground	×2	Fairy	×1

Damage taken in Inverse battles

Normal	×1	Flying	×2
Fire	×1	Psychic	×1
Water	×1	Bug	×1
Grass	×1	Rock	×1
Electric	×2	Ghost	×1
Ice	×1	Dragon	×1
Fighting	×1	Dark	×1
Poison	×1	Steel	×2
Ground	×0.5	Fairy	×1

Can be used in
- Inverse Battle
- Battle Institute
- Battle Maison
- Random Matchup (Free Battle)
- Random Matchup (Others)

LEVEL-UP MOVES

Lv.	Name	Type	Kind	Pow.	Acc.	PP	Range
1	Electric Terrain	Electric	Status	—	—	10	Both Sides
1	Fire Fang	Fire	Physical	65	95	15	Normal
1	Tackle	Normal	Physical	50	100	35	Normal
1	Thunder Wave	Electric	Status	—	100	20	Normal
1	Leer	Normal	Status	—	100	30	Many Others
1	Howl	Normal	Status	—	—	40	Self
4	Leer	Normal	Status	—	100	30	Many Others
7	Howl	Normal	Status	—	—	40	Self
10	Quick Attack	Normal	Physical	40	100	30	Normal
13	Spark	Electric	Physical	65	100	20	Normal
16	Odor Sleuth	Normal	Status	—	—	40	Normal
19	Thunder Fang	Electric	Physical	65	95	15	Normal
24	Bite	Dark	Physical	60	100	25	Normal
30	Discharge	Electric	Special	80	100	15	Adjacent
36	Roar	Normal	Status	—	—	20	Normal
42	Wild Charge	Electric	Physical	90	100	15	Normal
48	Charge	Electric	Status	—	—	20	Self
54	Thunder	Electric	Special	110	70	10	Normal
60	Electric Terrain	Electric	Status	—	—	10	Both Sides

TM & HM MOVES

No.	Name	Type	Kind	Pow.	Acc.	PP	Range
TM05	Roar	Normal	Status	—	—	20	Normal
TM06	Toxic	Poison	Status	—	90	10	Normal
TM10	Hidden Power	Normal	Special	60	100	15	Normal
TM15	Hyper Beam	Normal	Special	150	90	5	Normal
TM16	Light Screen	Psychic	Status	—	—	30	Your Side
TM17	Protect	Normal	Status	—	—	10	Self
TM18	Rain Dance	Water	Status	—	—	5	Both Sides
TM21	Frustration	Normal	Physical	—	100	20	Normal
TM24	Thunderbolt	Electric	Special	90	100	15	Normal
TM25	Thunder	Electric	Special	110	70	10	Normal
TM27	Return	Normal	Physical	—	100	20	Normal
TM32	Double Team	Normal	Status	—	—	15	Self
TM35	Flamethrower	Fire	Special	90	100	15	Normal
TM42	Facade	Normal	Physical	70	100	20	Normal
TM44	Rest	Psychic	Status	—	—	10	Self
TM45	Attract	Normal	Status	—	100	15	Normal
TM46	Thief	Dark	Physical	60	100	25	Normal
TM48	Round	Normal	Special	60	100	15	Normal
TM50	Overheat	Fire	Special	130	90	5	Normal
TM57	Charge Beam	Electric	Special	50	90	10	Normal
TM68	Giga Impact	Normal	Physical	150	90	5	Normal
TM70	Flash	Normal	Status	—	100	20	Normal
TM72	Volt Switch	Electric	Special	70	100	20	Normal
TM73	Thunder Wave	Electric	Status	—	100	20	Normal
TM87	Swagger	Normal	Status	—	90	15	Normal
TM88	Sleep Talk	Normal	Status	—	—	10	Self
TM90	Substitute	Normal	Status	—	—	10	Self
TM93	Wild Charge	Electric	Physical	90	100	15	Normal
TM94	Secret Power	Normal	Physical	70	100	20	Normal
TM95	Snarl	Dark	Special	55	95	15	Many Others
TM100	Confide	Normal	Status	—	—	20	Normal
HM04	Strength	Normal	Physical	80	100	15	Normal

MOVES LEARNED IN EXCHANGE FOR BP

Name	Type	Kind	Pow.	Acc.	PP	Range
Signal Beam	Bug	Special	75	100	15	Normal
Uproar	Normal	Special	90	100	10	1 Random
Magnet Rise	Electric	Status	—	—	10	Self
Iron Tail	Steel	Physical	100	75	15	Normal
Snore	Normal	Special	50	100	15	Normal
Shock Wave	Electric	Special	60	—	20	Normal

MOVES TAUGHT BY PEOPLE

Name	Type	Kind	Pow.	Acc.	PP	Range

Mega Evolution

Mega Manectric

Discharge Pokémon

Electric

HEIGHT: 5'11" WEIGHT: 97 lbs.

Same form for ♂ / ♀

REQUIRED MEGA STONE

Manectite

Find near Cycling Road on Route 110 (after obtaining the Mach Bike or Acro Bike).

ABILITY

Intimidate

HIDDEN ABILITY

—

EGG GROUPS

—

STAT GROWTH RATES

HP, Attack, Defense, Sp. Atk, Sp. Def, Speed

Damage taken in normal battles

Type		Type	
Normal	×1	Flying	×0.5
Fire	×1	Psychic	×1
Water	×1	Bug	×1
Grass	×1	Rock	×1
Electric	×0.5	Ghost	×1
Ice	×1	Dragon	×1
Fighting	×1	Dark	×1
Poison	×1	Steel	×0.5
Ground	×2	Fairy	×1

Damage taken in Inverse battles

Type		Type	
Normal	×1	Flying	×2
Fire	×1	Psychic	×1
Water	×1	Bug	×1
Grass	×1	Rock	×1
Electric	×2	Ghost	×1
Ice	×1	Dragon	×1
Fighting	×1	Dark	×1
Poison	×1	Steel	×2
Ground	×0.5	Fairy	×1

Can be used in

Inverse Battle
Battle Institute
Battle Maison
Random Matchup (Free Battle)
Random Matchup (Others)

National Pokédex **311** Hoenn Pokédex **082**

Plusle

Cheering Pokémon

Electric

HEIGHT: 1'04" WEIGHT: 9.3 lbs.

Same form for ♂ / ♀

Ω Plusle alway acts as a cheerleader for its partners. Whenever a teammate puts out a good effort in battle, this Pokémon shorts out its body to create the crackling noises of sparks to show its joy.

α When Plusle is cheering on its partner, it flashes with electric sparks from all over its body. If its partner loses, this Pokémon cries loudly.

ABILITY

Plus

HIDDEN ABILITY

Lightning Rod

EGG GROUPS

Fairy

STAT GROWTH RATES

HP, Attack, Defense, Sp. Atk, Sp. Def, Speed

ITEMS SOMETIMES HELD BY WILD POKÉMON

Cell Battery

EVOLUTION

Does not evolve

MAIN WAYS TO REGISTER IN THE NATIONAL POKÉDEX

Ω Catch on Route 110 when it appears in a Horde Encounter.

α Catch on Route 110.

Damage taken in normal battles

Type		Type	
Normal	×1	Flying	×0.5
Fire	×1	Psychic	×1
Water	×1	Bug	×1
Grass	×1	Rock	×1
Electric	×0.5	Ghost	×1
Ice	×1	Dragon	×1
Fighting	×1	Dark	×1
Poison	×1	Steel	×0.5
Ground	×2	Fairy	×1

Damage taken in Inverse battles

Type		Type	
Normal	×1	Flying	×2
Fire	×1	Psychic	×1
Water	×1	Bug	×1
Grass	×1	Rock	×1
Electric	×2	Ghost	×1
Ice	×1	Dragon	×1
Fighting	×1	Dark	×1
Poison	×1	Steel	×2
Ground	×0.5	Fairy	×1

Can be used in

Inverse Battle
Battle Institute
Battle Maison
Random Matchup (Free Battle)
Random Matchup (Others)

LEVEL-UP MOVES

Lv.	Name	Type	Kind	Pow.	Acc.	PP	Range
1	Nuzzle	Electric	Physical	20	100	20	Normal
1	Play Nice	Normal	Status	—	—	20	Normal
1	Growl	Normal	Status	—	100	40	Many Others
1	Thunder Wave	Electric	Status	—	100	20	Normal
1	Quick Attack	Normal	Physical	40	100	30	Normal
4	Helping Hand	Normal	Status	—	—	20	1 Ally
7	Spark	Electric	Physical	65	100	20	Normal
10	Encore	Normal	Status	—	100	5	Normal
13	Bestow	Normal	Status	—	—	15	Normal
16	Swift	Normal	Special	60	—	20	Many Others
19	Electro Ball	Electric	Special	—	100	10	Normal
22	Copycat	Normal	Status	—	—	20	Self
25	Charm	Fairy	Status	—	100	20	Normal
28	Charge	Electric	Status	—	—	20	Self
31	Discharge	Electric	Special	80	100	15	Adjacent
34	Baton Pass	Normal	Status	—	—	40	Self
37	Agility	Psychic	Status	—	—	30	Self
40	Last Resort	Normal	Physical	140	100	5	Normal
43	Thunder	Electric	Special	110	70	10	Normal
46	Nasty Plot	Dark	Status	—	—	20	Self
49	Entrainment	Normal	Status	—	100	15	Normal

TM & HM MOVES

No.	Name	Type	Kind	Pow.	Acc.	PP	Range
TM06	Toxic	Poison	Status	—	90	10	Normal
TM10	Hidden Power	Normal	Special	60	100	15	Normal
TM16	Light Screen	Psychic	Status	—	—	30	Your Side
TM17	Protect	Normal	Status	—	—	10	Self
TM18	Rain Dance	Water	Status	—	—	5	Both Sides
TM21	Frustration	Normal	Physical	—	100	20	Normal
TM24	Thunderbolt	Electric	Special	90	100	15	Normal
TM25	Thunder	Electric	Special	110	70	10	Normal
TM27	Return	Normal	Physical	—	100	20	Normal
TM32	Double Team	Normal	Status	—	—	15	Self
TM42	Facade	Normal	Physical	70	100	20	Normal
TM44	Rest	Psychic	Status	—	—	10	Self
TM45	Attract	Normal	Status	—	100	15	Normal
TM48	Round	Normal	Special	60	100	15	Normal
TM49	Echoed Voice	Normal	Special	40	100	15	Normal
TM56	Fling	Dark	Physical	—	100	10	Normal
TM57	Charge Beam	Electric	Special	50	90	10	Normal
TM70	Flash	Normal	Status	—	100	20	Normal
TM72	Volt Switch	Electric	Special	70	100	20	Normal
TM73	Thunder Wave	Electric	Status	—	100	20	Normal
TM86	Grass Knot	Grass	Special	—	100	20	Normal
TM87	Swagger	Normal	Status	—	90	15	Normal
TM88	Sleep Talk	Normal	Status	—	—	10	Self
TM90	Substitute	Normal	Status	—	—	10	Self
TM93	Wild Charge	Electric	Physical	90	100	15	Normal
TM94	Secret Power	Normal	Physical	70	100	20	Normal
TM100	Confide	Normal	Status	—	—	20	Normal

MOVES LEARNED IN EXCHANGE FOR BP

Name	Type	Kind	Pow.	Acc.	PP	Range
Signal Beam	Bug	Special	75	100	15	Normal
Uproar	Normal	Special	90	100	10	1 Random
Thunder Punch	Electric	Physical	75	100	15	Normal
Magnet Rise	Electric	Status	—	—	10	Self
Last Resort	Normal	Physical	140	100	5	Normal
Electroweb	Electric	Special	55	95	15	Many Others
Iron Tail	Steel	Physical	100	75	15	Normal
Snore	Normal	Special	50	100	15	Normal
Shock Wave	Electric	Special	60	—	20	Normal
Helping Hand	Normal	Status	—	—	20	1 Ally

MOVES TAUGHT BY PEOPLE

Name	Type	Kind	Pow.	Acc.	PP	Range

EGG MOVES

Name	Type	Kind	Pow.	Acc.	PP	Range
Wish	Normal	Status	—	—	10	Self
Sing	Normal	Status	—	55	15	Normal
Sweet Kiss	Fairy	Status	—	75	10	Normal
Discharge	Electric	Special	80	100	15	Adjacent
Lucky Chant	Normal	Status	—	—	30	Your Side
Charm	Fairy	Status	—	100	20	Normal
Fake Tears	Dark	Status	—	100	20	Normal

National Pokédex **312** Hoenn Pokédex **083**

Minun

Cheering Pokémon

Electric

HEIGHT: 1'04" WEIGHT: 9.3 lbs.

Same form for ♂ / ♀

Ω Minun is more concerned about cheering on its partners than its own safety. It shorts out the electricity in its body to create brilliant showers of sparks to cheer on its teammates.

α Minun loves to cheer on its partner in battle. It gives off sparks from its body while it is doing so. If its partner is in trouble, this Pokémon gives off increasing amounts of sparks.

ABILITY
Minus

HIDDEN ABILITY
Volt Absorb

EGG GROUPS
Fairy

STAT GROWTH RATES
HP
Attack
Defense
Sp. Atk
Sp. Def
Speed

EVOLUTION
Does not evolve

ITEMS SOMETIMES HELD BY WILD POKÉMON
Cell Battery

MAIN WAYS TO REGISTER IN THE NATIONAL POKÉDEX
Ω Catch on Route 110.
α Catch on Route 110 when it appears in a Horde Encounter.

Damage taken in normal battles

Type		Type	
Normal	×1	Flying	×0.5
Fire	×1	Psychic	×1
Water	×1	Bug	×1
Grass	×1	Rock	×1
Electric	×0.5	Ghost	×1
Ice	×1	Dragon	×1
Fighting	×1	Dark	×1
Poison	×1	Steel	×0.5
Ground	×2	Fairy	×1

Damage taken in Inverse battles

Type		Type	
Normal	×1	Flying	×2
Fire	×1	Psychic	×1
Water	×1	Bug	×1
Grass	×1	Rock	×1
Electric	×2	Ghost	×1
Ice	×1	Dragon	×1
Fighting	×1	Dark	×1
Poison	×1	Steel	×2
Ground	×0.5	Fairy	×1

Can be used in
Inverse Battle
Battle Institute
Battle Maison
Random Matchup (Free Battle)
Random Matchup (Others)

LEVEL-UP MOVES

Lv.	Name	Type	Kind	Pow.	Acc.	PP	Range
1	Nuzzle	Electric	Physical	20	100	20	Normal
1	Play Nice	Normal	Status	—	—	20	Normal
1	Growl	Normal	Status	—	100	40	Many Others
1	Thunder Wave	Electric	Status	—	100	20	Normal
1	Quick Attack	Normal	Physical	40	100	30	Normal
4	Helping Hand	Normal	Status	—	—	20	1 Ally
7	Spark	Electric	Physical	65	100	20	Normal
10	Encore	Normal	Status	—	100	5	Normal
13	Switcheroo	Dark	Status	—	100	10	Normal
16	Swift	Normal	Special	60	—	20	Many Others
19	Electro Ball	Electric	Special	—	100	10	Normal
22	Copycat	Normal	Status	—	—	20	Self
25	Fake Tears	Dark	Status	—	100	20	Normal
28	Charge	Electric	Status	—	—	20	Self
31	Discharge	Electric	Special	80	100	15	Adjacent
34	Baton Pass	Normal	Status	—	—	40	Self
37	Agility	Psychic	Status	—	—	30	Self
40	Trump Card	Normal	Special	—	—	5	Normal
43	Thunder	Electric	Special	110	70	10	Normal
46	Nasty Plot	Dark	Status	—	—	20	Self
49	Entrainment	Normal	Status	—	100	15	Normal

TM & HM MOVES

No.	Name	Type	Kind	Pow.	Acc.	PP	Range
TM06	Toxic	Poison	Status	—	90	10	Normal
TM10	Hidden Power	Normal	Special	60	100	15	Normal
TM16	Light Screen	Psychic	Status	—	—	30	Your Side
TM17	Protect	Normal	Status	—	—	10	Self
TM18	Rain Dance	Water	Status	—	—	5	Both Sides
TM21	Frustration	Normal	Physical	—	100	20	Normal
TM24	Thunderbolt	Electric	Special	90	100	15	Normal
TM25	Thunder	Electric	Special	110	70	10	Normal
TM27	Return	Normal	Physical	—	100	20	Normal
TM32	Double Team	Normal	Status	—	—	15	Self
TM42	Facade	Normal	Physical	70	100	20	Normal
TM44	Rest	Psychic	Status	—	—	10	Self
TM45	Attract	Normal	Status	—	100	15	Normal
TM48	Round	Normal	Special	60	100	15	Normal
TM49	Echoed Voice	Normal	Special	40	100	15	Normal
TM56	Fling	Dark	Physical	—	100	10	Normal
TM57	Charge Beam	Electric	Special	50	90	10	Normal
TM70	Flash	Normal	Status	—	100	20	Normal
TM72	Volt Switch	Electric	Special	70	100	20	Normal
TM73	Thunder Wave	Electric	Status	—	100	20	Normal
TM86	Grass Knot	Grass	Special	—	100	20	Normal
TM87	Swagger	Normal	Status	—	90	15	Normal
TM88	Sleep Talk	Normal	Status	—	—	10	Self
TM90	Substitute	Normal	Status	—	—	10	Self
TM93	Wild Charge	Electric	Physical	90	100	15	Normal
TM94	Secret Power	Normal	Physical	70	100	20	Normal
TM100	Confide	Normal	Status	—	—	20	Normal

MOVES LEARNED IN EXCHANGE FOR BP

Name	Type	Kind	Pow.	Acc.	PP	Range
Signal Beam	Bug	Special	75	100	15	Normal
Uproar	Normal	Special	90	100	10	1 Random
Thunder Punch	Electric	Physical	75	100	15	Normal
Magnet Rise	Electric	Status	—	—	10	Self
Last Resort	Normal	Physical	140	100	5	Normal
Electroweb	Electric	Special	55	95	15	Many Others
Iron Tail	Steel	Physical	100	75	15	Normal
Snore	Normal	Special	50	100	15	Normal
Shock Wave	Electric	Special	60	—	20	Normal
Helping Hand	Normal	Status	—	—	20	1 Ally

MOVES TAUGHT BY PEOPLE

Name	Type	Kind	Pow.	Acc.	PP	Range

EGG MOVES

Name	Type	Kind	Pow.	Acc.	PP	Range
Wish	Normal	Status	—	—	10	Self
Sing	Normal	Status	—	55	15	Normal
Sweet Kiss	Fairy	Status	—	75	10	Normal
Discharge	Electric	Special	80	100	15	Adjacent
Lucky Chant	Normal	Status	—	—	30	Your Side
Charm	Fairy	Status	—	100	20	Normal
Fake Tears	Dark	Status	—	100	20	Normal

National Pokédex **313** Hoenn Pokédex **089**

Volbeat

Firefly Pokémon

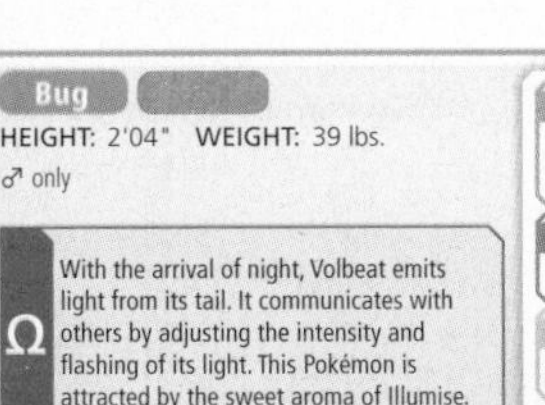

Bug

HEIGHT: 2'04" WEIGHT: 39 lbs.

♂ only

Ω With the arrival of night, Volbeat emits light from its tail. It communicates with others by adjusting the intensity and flashing of its light. This Pokémon is attracted by the sweet aroma of Illumise.

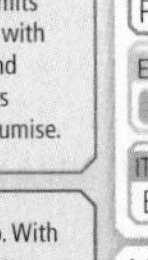

α Volbeat's tail glows like a lightbulb. With other Volbeat, it uses its tail to draw geometric shapes in the night sky. This Pokémon loves the sweet aroma given off by Illumise.

ABILITIES
Illuminate
Swarm

HIDDEN ABILITY
Prankster

EGG GROUPS
Bug
Human-Like

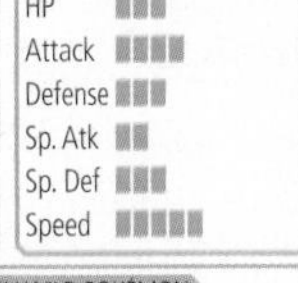

STAT GROWTH RATES
HP
Attack
Defense
Sp. Atk
Sp. Def
Speed

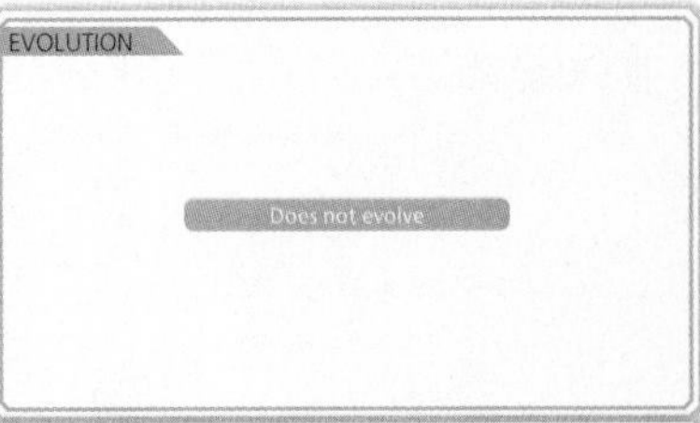

EVOLUTION
Does not evolve

ITEMS SOMETIMES HELD BY WILD POKÉMON
Bright Powder

MAIN WAY TO REGISTER IN THE NATIONAL POKÉDEX
Catch on Route 117.

Damage taken in normal battles

Type		Type	
Normal	×1	Flying	×2
Fire	×2	Psychic	×1
Water	×1	Bug	×1
Grass	×0.5	Rock	×2
Electric	×1	Ghost	×1
Ice	×1	Dragon	×1
Fighting	×0.5	Dark	×1
Poison	×1	Steel	×1
Ground	×0.5	Fairy	×1

Damage taken in Inverse battles

Type		Type	
Normal	×1	Flying	×0.5
Fire	×0.5	Psychic	×1
Water	×1	Bug	×1
Grass	×2	Rock	×0.5
Electric	×1	Ghost	×1
Ice	×1	Dragon	×1
Fighting	×2	Dark	×1
Poison	×1	Steel	×1
Ground	×2	Fairy	×1

Can be used in
Inverse Battle
Battle Institute
Battle Maison
Random Matchup (Free Battle)
Random Matchup (Others)

LEVEL-UP MOVES

Lv.	Name	Type	Kind	Pow.	Acc.	PP	Range
1	Flash	Normal	Status	—	100	20	Normal
1	Tackle	Normal	Physical	50	100	35	Normal
5	Double Team	Normal	Status	—	—	15	Self
8	Confuse Ray	Ghost	Status	—	100	10	Normal
12	Quick Attack	Normal	Physical	40	100	30	Normal
15	Struggle Bug	Bug	Special	50	100	20	Many Others
19	Moonlight	Fairy	Status	—	—	5	Self
22	Tail Glow	Bug	Status	—	—	20	Self
26	Signal Beam	Bug	Special	75	100	15	Normal
29	Protect	Normal	Status	—	—	10	Self
33	Zen Headbutt	Psychic	Physical	80	90	15	Normal
36	Helping Hand	Normal	Status	—	—	20	1 Ally
40	Bug Buzz	Bug	Special	90	100	10	Normal
43	Play Rough	Fairy	Physical	90	90	10	Normal
47	Double-Edge	Normal	Physical	120	100	15	Normal

TM & HM MOVES

No.	Name	Type	Kind	Pow.	Acc.	PP	Range
TM06	Toxic	Poison	Status	—	90	10	Normal
TM10	Hidden Power	Normal	Special	60	100	15	Normal
TM11	Sunny Day	Fire	Status	—	—	5	Both Sides
TM16	Light Screen	Psychic	Status	—	—	30	Your Side
TM17	Protect	Normal	Status	—	—	10	Self
TM18	Rain Dance	Water	Status	—	—	5	Both Sides
TM19	Roost	Flying	Status	—	—	10	Self
TM21	Frustration	Normal	Physical	—	100	20	Normal
TM22	Solar Beam	Grass	Special	120	100	10	Normal
TM24	Thunderbolt	Electric	Special	90	100	15	Normal
TM25	Thunder	Electric	Special	110	70	10	Normal
TM27	Return	Normal	Physical	—	100	20	Normal
TM30	Shadow Ball	Ghost	Special	80	100	15	Normal
TM31	Brick Break	Fighting	Physical	75	100	15	Normal
TM32	Double Team	Normal	Status	—	—	15	Self
TM40	Aerial Ace	Flying	Physical	60	—	20	Normal
TM42	Facade	Normal	Physical	70	100	20	Normal
TM44	Rest	Psychic	Status	—	—	10	Self
TM45	Attract	Normal	Status	—	100	15	Normal
TM46	Thief	Dark	Physical	60	100	25	Normal
TM48	Round	Normal	Special	60	100	15	Normal
TM56	Fling	Dark	Physical	—	100	10	Normal
TM57	Charge Beam	Electric	Special	50	90	10	Normal
TM62	Acrobatics	Flying	Physical	55	100	15	Normal
TM70	Flash	Normal	Status	—	100	20	Normal
TM73	Thunder Wave	Electric	Status	—	100	20	Normal
TM76	Struggle Bug	Bug	Special	50	100	20	Many Others
TM77	Psych Up	Normal	Status	—	—	10	Normal
TM87	Swagger	Normal	Status	—	90	15	Normal
TM88	Sleep Talk	Normal	Status	—	—	10	Self
TM89	U-turn	Bug	Physical	70	100	20	Normal
TM90	Substitute	Normal	Status	—	—	10	Self
TM94	Secret Power	Normal	Physical	70	100	20	Normal
TM98	Power-Up Punch	Fighting	Physical	40	100	20	Normal
TM99	Dazzling Gleam	Fairy	Special	80	100	10	Many Others
TM100	Confide	Normal	Status	—	—	20	Normal

MOVES LEARNED IN EXCHANGE FOR BP

Name	Type	Kind	Pow.	Acc.	PP	Range
Bug Bite	Bug	Physical	60	100	20	Normal
Signal Beam	Bug	Special	75	100	15	Normal
Thunder Punch	Electric	Physical	75	100	15	Normal
Ice Punch	Ice	Physical	75	100	15	Normal
Zen Headbutt	Psychic	Physical	80	90	15	Normal
Snore	Normal	Special	50	100	15	Normal
Tailwind	Flying	Status	—	—	15	Your Side
Giga Drain	Grass	Special	75	100	10	Normal
Focus Punch	Fighting	Physical	150	100	20	Normal
Shock Wave	Electric	Special	60	—	20	Normal
Water Pulse	Water	Special	60	100	20	Normal
Helping Hand	Normal	Status	—	—	20	1 Ally
Trick	Psychic	Status	—	100	10	Normal

MOVES TAUGHT BY PEOPLE

Name	Type	Kind	Pow.	Acc.	PP	Range

EGG MOVES

Name	Type	Kind	Pow.	Acc.	PP	Range
Baton Pass	Normal	Status	—	—	40	Self
Silver Wind	Bug	Special	60	100	5	Normal
Trick	Psychic	Status	—	100	10	Normal
Encore	Normal	Status	—	100	5	Normal
Bug Buzz	Bug	Special	90	100	10	Normal
Dizzy Punch	Normal	Physical	70	100	10	Normal
Seismic Toss	Fighting	Physical	—	100	20	Normal

National Pokédex **314** Hoenn Pokédex **090**

Illumise

Firefly Pokémon

Bug

HEIGHT: 2'00" WEIGHT: 39 lbs.

♀ only

Ω Illumise attracts a swarm of Volbeat using a sweet fragrance. Once the Volbeat have gathered, this Pokémon leads the lit-up swarm in drawing geometric designs on the canvas of the night sky.

α Illumise leads a flight of illuminated Volbeat to draw signs in the night sky. This Pokémon is said to earn greater respect from its peers by composing more complex designs in the sky.

ABILITIES
Oblivious
Tinted Lens

HIDDEN ABILITY
Prankster

EGG GROUPS
Bug, Human-Like

STAT GROWTH RATES

HP	■■■
Attack	■■■
Defense	■■■
Sp. Atk	■■■■
Sp. Def	■■■
Speed	■■■■■

ITEMS SOMETIMES HELD BY WILD POKÉMON
Bright Powder

EVOLUTION
Does not evolve

MAIN WAY TO REGISTER IN THE NATIONAL POKÉDEX
Catch on Route 117.

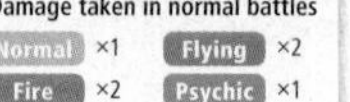

Damage taken in normal battles

Normal	×1	Flying	×2
Fire	×2	Psychic	×1
Water	×1	Bug	×1
Grass	×0.5	Rock	×2
Electric	×1	Ghost	×1
Ice	×1	Dragon	×1
Fighting	×0.5	Dark	×1
Poison	×1	Steel	×1
Ground	×0.5	Fairy	×1

Damage taken in Inverse battles

Normal	×1	Flying	×0.5
Fire	×0.5	Psychic	×1
Water	×1	Bug	×1
Grass	×2	Rock	×0.5
Electric	×1	Ghost	×1
Ice	×1	Dragon	×1
Fighting	×2	Dark	×1
Poison	×1	Steel	×1
Ground	×2	Fairy	×1

Can be used in
Inverse Battle
Battle Institute
Battle Maison
Random Matchup (Free Battle)
Random Matchup (Others)

LEVEL-UP MOVES

Lv.	Name	Type	Kind	Pow.	Acc.	PP	Range
1	Play Nice	Normal	Status	—	—	20	Normal
1	Tackle	Normal	Physical	50	100	35	Normal
5	Sweet Scent	Normal	Status	—	100	20	Many Others
9	Charm	Fairy	Status	—	100	20	Normal
12	Quick Attack	Normal	Physical	40	100	30	Normal
15	Struggle Bug	Bug	Special	50	100	20	Many Others
19	Moonlight	Fairy	Status	—	—	5	Self
22	Wish	Normal	Status	—	—	10	Self
26	Encore	Normal	Status	—	100	5	Normal
29	Flatter	Dark	Status	—	100	15	Normal
33	Zen Headbutt	Psychic	Physical	80	90	15	Normal
36	Helping Hand	Normal	Status	—	—	20	1 Ally
40	Bug Buzz	Bug	Special	90	100	10	Normal
43	Play Rough	Fairy	Physical	90	90	10	Normal
47	Covet	Normal	Physical	60	100	25	Normal

TM & HM MOVES

No.	Name	Type	Kind	Pow.	Acc.	PP	Range
TM06	Toxic	Poison	Status	—	90	10	Normal
TM10	Hidden Power	Normal	Special	60	100	15	Normal
TM11	Sunny Day	Fire	Status	—	—	5	Both Sides
TM16	Light Screen	Psychic	Status	—	—	30	Your Side
TM17	Protect	Normal	Status	—	—	10	Self
TM18	Rain Dance	Water	Status	—	—	5	Both Sides
TM19	Roost	Flying	Status	—	—	10	Self
TM21	Frustration	Normal	Physical	—	100	20	Normal
TM22	Solar Beam	Grass	Special	120	100	10	Normal
TM24	Thunderbolt	Electric	Special	90	100	15	Normal
TM25	Thunder	Electric	Special	110	70	10	Normal
TM27	Return	Normal	Physical	—	100	20	Normal
TM30	Shadow Ball	Ghost	Special	80	100	15	Normal
TM31	Brick Break	Fighting	Physical	75	100	15	Normal
TM32	Double Team	Normal	Status	—	—	15	Self
TM40	Aerial Ace	Flying	Physical	60	—	20	Normal
TM42	Facade	Normal	Physical	70	100	20	Normal
TM44	Rest	Psychic	Status	—	—	10	Self
TM45	Attract	Normal	Status	—	100	15	Normal
TM46	Thief	Dark	Physical	60	100	25	Normal
TM48	Round	Normal	Special	60	100	15	Normal
TM56	Fling	Dark	Physical	—	100	10	Normal
TM57	Charge Beam	Electric	Special	50	90	10	Normal
TM62	Acrobatics	Flying	Physical	55	100	15	Normal
TM70	Flash	Normal	Status	—	100	20	Normal
TM73	Thunder Wave	Electric	Status	—	100	20	Normal
TM76	Struggle Bug	Bug	Special	50	100	20	Many Others
TM77	Psych Up	Normal	Status	—	—	10	Normal
TM87	Swagger	Normal	Status	—	90	15	Normal
TM88	Sleep Talk	Normal	Status	—	—	10	Self
TM89	U-turn	Bug	Physical	70	100	20	Normal
TM90	Substitute	Normal	Status	—	—	10	Self
TM94	Secret Power	Normal	Physical	70	100	20	Normal
TM98	Power-Up Punch	Fighting	Physical	40	100	20	Normal
TM99	Dazzling Gleam	Fairy	Special	80	100	10	Many Others
TM100	Confide	Normal	Status	—	—	20	Normal

MOVES LEARNED IN EXCHANGE FOR BP

Name	Type	Kind	Pow.	Acc.	PP	Range
Bug Bite	Bug	Physical	60	100	20	Normal
Covet	Normal	Physical	60	100	25	Normal
Thunder Punch	Electric	Physical	75	100	15	Normal
Ice Punch	Ice	Physical	75	100	15	Normal
Zen Headbutt	Psychic	Physical	80	90	15	Normal
Snore	Normal	Special	50	100	15	Normal
Tailwind	Flying	Status	—	—	15	Your Side
Giga Drain	Grass	Special	75	100	10	Normal
Focus Punch	Fighting	Physical	150	100	20	Normal
Shock Wave	Electric	Special	60	—	20	Normal
Water Pulse	Water	Special	60	100	20	Normal
Helping Hand	Normal	Status	—	—	20	1 Ally

MOVES TAUGHT BY PEOPLE

Name	Type	Kind	Pow.	Acc.	PP	Range

EGG MOVES

Name	Type	Kind	Pow.	Acc.	PP	Range
Baton Pass	Normal	Status	—	—	40	Self
Silver Wind	Bug	Special	60	100	5	Normal
Growth	Normal	Status	—	—	20	Self
Encore	Normal	Status	—	100	5	Normal
Bug Buzz	Bug	Special	90	100	10	Normal
Captivate	Normal	Status	—	100	20	Many Others
Fake Tears	Dark	Status	—	100	20	Normal
Confuse Ray	Ghost	Status	—	100	10	Normal

National Pokédex **315** Hoenn Pokédex **098**

Roselia

Thorn Pokémon

Grass Poison

HEIGHT: 1'00" WEIGHT: 4.4 lbs.

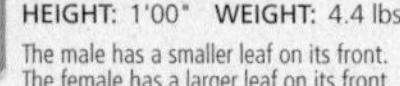

The male has a smaller leaf on its front.
The female has a larger leaf on its front.

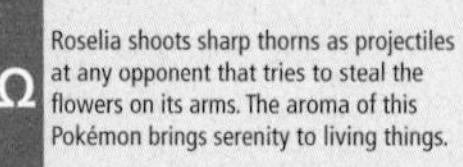

Ω Roselia shoots sharp thorns as projectiles at any opponent that tries to steal the flowers on its arms. The aroma of this Pokémon brings serenity to living things.

α On extremely rare occasions, a Roselia is said to appear with its flowers in unusual colors. The thorns on this Pokémon's head contain a vicious poison.

♂ ♀

ABILITIES
Natural Cure
Poison Point

HIDDEN ABILITY
Leaf Guard

EGG GROUPS
Fairy, Grass

STAT GROWTH RATES

HP	■■
Attack	■■■
Defense	■■
Sp. Atk	■■■■■
Sp. Def	■■■
Speed	■■■■

ITEMS SOMETIMES HELD BY WILD POKÉMON
Poison Barb

EVOLUTION
Budew → (Level up with high friendship between 4 A.M. and 7:59 P.M.) → Roselia → (Shiny Stone) → Roserade

MAIN WAY TO REGISTER IN THE NATIONAL POKÉDEX
Catch on Route 117.

Damage taken in normal battles

Normal	×1	Flying	×2
Fire	×2	Psychic	×2
Water	×0.5	Bug	×1
Grass	×0.25	Rock	×1
Electric	×0.5	Ghost	×1
Ice	×2	Dragon	×1
Fighting	×0.5	Dark	×1
Poison	×1	Steel	×1
Ground	×1	Fairy	×0.5

Damage taken in Inverse battles

Normal	×1	Flying	×0.5
Fire	×0.5	Psychic	×0.5
Water	×2	Bug	×1
Grass	×4	Rock	×1
Electric	×2	Ghost	×1
Ice	×0.5	Dragon	×1
Fighting	×2	Dark	×1
Poison	×1	Steel	×1
Ground	×1	Fairy	×2

Can be used in
Inverse Battle
Battle Institute
Battle Maison
Random Matchup (Free Battle)
Random Matchup (Others)

LEVEL-UP MOVES

Lv.	Name	Type	Kind	Pow.	Acc.	PP	Range
1	Absorb	Grass	Special	20	100	25	Normal
4	Growth	Normal	Status	—	—	20	Self
7	Poison Sting	Poison	Physical	15	100	35	Normal
10	Stun Spore	Grass	Status	—	75	30	Normal
13	Mega Drain	Grass	Special	40	100	15	Normal
16	Leech Seed	Grass	Status	—	90	10	Normal
19	Magical Leaf	Grass	Special	60	—	20	Normal
22	Grass Whistle	Grass	Status	—	55	15	Normal
25	Giga Drain	Grass	Special	75	100	10	Normal
28	Toxic Spikes	Poison	Status	—	—	20	Other Side
31	Sweet Scent	Normal	Status	—	100	20	Many Others
34	Ingrain	Grass	Status	—	—	20	Self
37	Petal Blizzard	Grass	Physical	90	100	15	Adjacent
40	Toxic	Poison	Status	—	90	10	Normal
43	Aromatherapy	Grass	Status	—	—	5	Your Party
46	Synthesis	Grass	Status	—	—	5	Self
50	Petal Dance	Grass	Special	120	100	10	1 Random

TM & HM MOVES

No.	Name	Type	Kind	Pow.	Acc.	PP	Range
TM06	Toxic	Poison	Status	—	90	10	Normal
TM09	Venoshock	Poison	Special	65	100	10	Normal
TM10	Hidden Power	Normal	Special	60	100	15	Normal
TM11	Sunny Day	Fire	Status	—	—	5	Both Sides
TM17	Protect	Normal	Status	—	—	10	Self
TM18	Rain Dance	Water	Status	—	—	5	Both Sides
TM21	Frustration	Normal	Physical	—	100	20	Normal
TM22	Solar Beam	Grass	Special	120	100	10	Normal
TM27	Return	Normal	Physical	—	100	20	Normal
TM30	Shadow Ball	Ghost	Special	80	100	15	Normal
TM32	Double Team	Normal	Status	—	—	15	Self
TM36	Sludge Bomb	Poison	Special	90	100	10	Normal
TM42	Facade	Normal	Physical	70	100	20	Normal
TM44	Rest	Psychic	Status	—	—	10	Self
TM45	Attract	Normal	Status	—	100	15	Normal
TM48	Round	Normal	Special	60	100	15	Normal
TM53	Energy Ball	Grass	Special	90	100	10	Normal
TM70	Flash	Normal	Status	—	100	20	Normal
TM75	Swords Dance	Normal	Status	—	—	20	Self
TM77	Psych Up	Normal	Status	—	—	10	Normal
TM84	Poison Jab	Poison	Physical	80	100	20	Normal
TM86	Grass Knot	Grass	Special	—	100	20	Normal
TM87	Swagger	Normal	Status	—	90	15	Normal
TM88	Sleep Talk	Normal	Status	—	—	10	Self
TM90	Substitute	Normal	Status	—	—	10	Self
TM94	Secret Power	Normal	Physical	70	100	20	Normal
TM96	Nature Power	Normal	Status	—	—	20	Normal
TM99	Dazzling Gleam	Fairy	Special	80	100	10	Many Others
TM100	Confide	Normal	Status	—	—	20	Normal
HM01	Cut	Normal	Physical	50	95	30	Normal

MOVES LEARNED IN EXCHANGE FOR BP

Name	Type	Kind	Pow.	Acc.	PP	Range
Covet	Normal	Physical	60	100	25	Normal
Seed Bomb	Grass	Physical	80	100	15	Normal
Snore	Normal	Special	50	100	15	Normal
Synthesis	Grass	Status	—	—	5	Self
Giga Drain	Grass	Special	75	100	10	Normal
Worry Seed	Grass	Status	—	100	10	Normal

MOVES TAUGHT BY PEOPLE

Name	Type	Kind	Pow.	Acc.	PP	Range

EGG MOVES

Name	Type	Kind	Pow.	Acc.	PP	Range
Spikes	Ground	Status	—	—	20	Other Side
Synthesis	Grass	Status	—	—	5	Self
Pin Missile	Bug	Physical	25	95	20	Normal
Cotton Spore	Grass	Status	—	100	40	Many Others
Sleep Powder	Grass	Status	—	75	15	Normal
Razor Leaf	Grass	Physical	55	95	25	Many Others
Mind Reader	Normal	Status	—	—	5	Normal
Leaf Storm	Grass	Special	130	90	5	Normal
Seed Bomb	Grass	Physical	80	100	15	Normal
Giga Drain	Grass	Special	75	100	10	Normal
Natural Gift	Normal	Physical	—	100	15	Normal
Grass Whistle	Grass	Status	—	55	15	Normal
Bullet Seed	Grass	Physical	25	100	30	Normal

National Pokédex **316** Hoenn Pokédex **100**

Gulpin

Stomach Pokémon

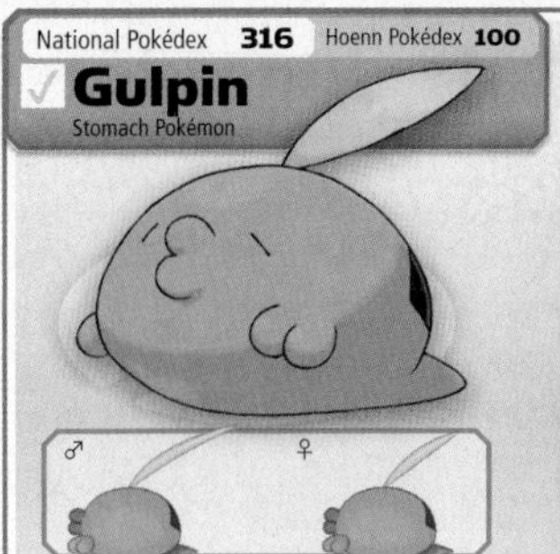

Poison

HEIGHT: 1'04" WEIGHT: 22.7 lbs.

The male has a longer antenna.
The female has a shorter antenna.

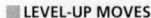

Ω Virtually all of Gulpin's body is its stomach. As a result, it can swallow something its own size. This Pokémon's stomach contains a special fluid that digests anything.

α Most of Gulpin's body is made up of its stomach—its heart and brain are very small in comparison. This Pokémon's stomach contains special enzymes that dissolve anything.

ABILITIES
Liquid Ooze
Sticky Hold

HIDDEN ABILITY
Gluttony

EGG GROUPS
Amorphous

STAT GROWTH RATES
HP ■■■
Attack ■■
Defense ■■
Sp. Atk ■■
Sp. Def ■■
Speed ■■

ITEMS SOMETIMES HELD BY WILD POKÉMON
Oran Berry / Sitrus Berry

EVOLUTION

MAIN WAY TO REGISTER IN THE NATIONAL POKÉDEX

Catch on Route 110.

Damage taken in normal battles

Type	×	Type	×
Normal	×1	Flying	×1
Fire	×1	Psychic	×2
Water	×1	Bug	×0.5
Grass	×0.5	Rock	×1
Electric	×1	Ghost	×1
Ice	×1	Dragon	×1
Fighting	×0.5	Dark	×1
Poison	×0.5	Steel	×1
Ground	×2	Fairy	×0.5

Damage taken in Inverse battles

Type	×	Type	×
Normal	×1	Flying	×1
Fire	×1	Psychic	×0.5
Water	×1	Bug	×2
Grass	×2	Rock	×1
Electric	×1	Ghost	×1
Ice	×1	Dragon	×1
Fighting	×2	Dark	×1
Poison	×2	Steel	×1
Ground	×0.5	Fairy	×2

Can be used in
- Inverse Battle
- Battle Institute
- Battle Maison
- Random Matchup (Free Battle)
- Random Matchup (Others)

LEVEL-UP MOVES

Lv.	Name	Type	Kind	Pow.	Acc.	PP	Range
1	Pound	Normal	Physical	40	100	35	Normal
5	Yawn	Normal	Status	—	—	10	Normal
8	Poison Gas	Poison	Status	—	90	40	Many Others
10	Sludge	Poison	Special	65	100	20	Normal
12	Amnesia	Psychic	Status	—	—	20	Self
17	Acid Spray	Poison	Special	40	100	20	Normal
20	Encore	Normal	Status	—	100	5	Normal
25	Toxic	Poison	Status	—	90	10	Normal
28	Stockpile	Normal	Status	—	—	20	Self
28	Spit Up	Normal	Special	—	100	10	Normal
28	Swallow	Normal	Status	—	—	10	Self
33	Sludge Bomb	Poison	Special	90	100	10	Normal
36	Gastro Acid	Poison	Status	—	100	10	Normal
41	Belch	Poison	Special	120	90	10	Normal
44	Wring Out	Normal	Special	—	100	5	Normal
49	Gunk Shot	Poison	Physical	120	80	5	Normal

TM & HM MOVES

No.	Name	Type	Kind	Pow.	Acc.	PP	Range
TM06	Toxic	Poison	Status	—	90	10	Normal
TM09	Venoshock	Poison	Special	65	100	10	Normal
TM10	Hidden Power	Normal	Special	60	100	15	Normal
TM11	Sunny Day	Fire	Status	—	—	5	Both Sides
TM13	Ice Beam	Ice	Special	90	100	10	Normal
TM17	Protect	Normal	Status	—	—	10	Self
TM18	Rain Dance	Water	Status	—	—	5	Both Sides
TM21	Frustration	Normal	Physical	—	100	20	Normal
TM22	Solar Beam	Grass	Special	120	100	10	Normal
TM27	Return	Normal	Physical	—	100	20	Normal
TM30	Shadow Ball	Ghost	Special	80	100	15	Normal
TM32	Double Team	Normal	Status	—	—	15	Self
TM34	Sludge Wave	Poison	Special	95	100	10	Adjacent
TM36	Sludge Bomb	Poison	Special	90	100	10	Normal
TM42	Facade	Normal	Physical	70	100	20	Normal
TM44	Rest	Psychic	Status	—	—	10	Self
TM45	Attract	Normal	Status	—	100	15	Normal
TM48	Round	Normal	Special	60	100	15	Normal
TM64	Explosion	Normal	Physical	250	100	5	Adjacent
TM83	Infestation	Bug	Special	20	100	20	Normal
TM85	Dream Eater	Psychic	Special	100	100	15	Normal
TM87	Swagger	Normal	Status	—	90	15	Normal
TM88	Sleep Talk	Normal	Status	—	—	10	Self
TM90	Substitute	Normal	Status	—	—	10	Self
TM94	Secret Power	Normal	Physical	70	100	20	Normal
TM98	Power-Up Punch	Fighting	Physical	40	100	20	Normal
TM100	Confide	Normal	Status	—	—	20	Normal
HM04	Strength	Normal	Physical	80	100	15	Normal
HM06	Rock Smash	Fighting	Physical	40	100	15	Normal

MOVES LEARNED IN EXCHANGE FOR BP

Name	Type	Kind	Pow.	Acc.	PP	Range
Seed Bomb	Grass	Physical	80	100	15	Normal
Gunk Shot	Poison	Physical	120	80	5	Normal
Thunder Punch	Electric	Physical	75	100	15	Normal
Fire Punch	Fire	Physical	75	100	15	Normal
Ice Punch	Ice	Physical	75	100	15	Normal
Snore	Normal	Special	50	100	15	Normal
Pain Split	Normal	Status	—	—	20	Normal
Giga Drain	Grass	Special	75	100	10	Normal
Shock Wave	Electric	Special	60	—	20	Normal
Water Pulse	Water	Special	60	100	20	Normal
Gastro Acid	Poison	Status	—	100	10	Normal
Snatch	Dark	Status	—	—	10	Self

MOVES TAUGHT BY PEOPLE

Name	Type	Kind	Pow.	Acc.	PP	Range

EGG MOVES

Name	Type	Kind	Pow.	Acc.	PP	Range
Acid Armor	Poison	Status	—	—	20	Self
Smog	Poison	Special	30	70	20	Normal
Pain Split	Normal	Status	—	—	20	Normal
Curse	Ghost	Status	—	—	10	Varies
Destiny Bond	Ghost	Status	—	—	5	Self
Mud-Slap	Ground	Special	20	100	10	Normal
Gunk Shot	Poison	Physical	120	80	5	Normal
Venom Drench	Poison	Status	—	100	20	Many Others

National Pokédex **317** Hoenn Pokédex **101**

Swalot

Poison Bag Pokémon

Poison

HEIGHT: 5'07" WEIGHT: 176.4 lbs.

The male has longer whiskers than the female.

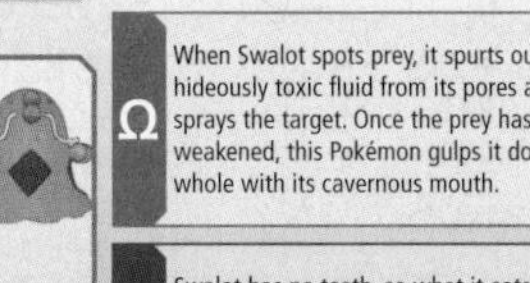

Ω When Swalot spots prey, it spurts out a hideously toxic fluid from its pores and sprays the target. Once the prey has weakened, this Pokémon gulps it down whole with its cavernous mouth.

α Swalot has no teeth, so what it eats, it swallows whole, no matter what. Its cavernous mouth yawns widely. An automobile tire could easily fit inside this Pokémon's mouth.

ABILITIES
Liquid Ooze
Sticky Hold

HIDDEN ABILITY
Gluttony

EGG GROUPS
Amorphous

STAT GROWTH RATES
HP ■■■■
Attack ■■■■
Defense ■■■■
Sp. Atk ■■■■
Sp. Def ■■■
Speed ■■■

ITEMS SOMETIMES HELD BY WILD POKÉMON
—

EVOLUTION

Lv. 26

Gulpin Swalot

MAIN WAY TO REGISTER IN THE NATIONAL POKÉDEX

Level up Gulpin to Lv. 26.

Damage taken in normal battles

Type	×	Type	×
Normal	×1	Flying	×1
Fire	×1	Psychic	×2
Water	×1	Bug	×0.5
Grass	×0.5	Rock	×1
Electric	×1	Ghost	×1
Ice	×1	Dragon	×1
Fighting	×0.5	Dark	×1
Poison	×0.5	Steel	×1
Ground	×2	Fairy	×0.5

Damage taken in Inverse battles

Type	×	Type	×
Normal	×1	Flying	×1
Fire	×1	Psychic	×0.5
Water	×1	Bug	×2
Grass	×2	Rock	×1
Electric	×1	Ghost	×1
Ice	×1	Dragon	×1
Fighting	×2	Dark	×1
Poison	×2	Steel	×1
Ground	×0.5	Fairy	×2

Can be used in
- Inverse Battle
- Battle Institute
- Battle Maison
- Random Matchup (Free Battle)
- Random Matchup (Others)

LEVEL-UP MOVES

Lv.	Name	Type	Kind	Pow.	Acc.	PP	Range
1	Gunk Shot	Poison	Physical	120	80	5	Normal
1	Wring Out	Normal	Special	—	100	5	Normal
1	Pound	Normal	Physical	40	100	35	Normal
1	Yawn	Normal	Status	—	—	10	Normal
1	Poison Gas	Poison	Status	—	90	40	Many Others
1	Sludge	Poison	Special	65	100	20	Normal
5	Yawn	Normal	Status	—	—	10	Normal
8	Poison Gas	Poison	Status	—	90	40	Many Others
10	Sludge	Poison	Special	65	100	20	Normal
12	Amnesia	Psychic	Status	—	—	20	Self
17	Acid Spray	Poison	Special	40	100	20	Normal
20	Encore	Normal	Status	—	100	5	Normal
25	Toxic	Poison	Status	—	90	10	Normal
26	Body Slam	Normal	Physical	85	100	15	Normal
30	Stockpile	Normal	Status	—	—	20	Self
30	Spit Up	Normal	Special	—	100	10	Normal
30	Swallow	Normal	Status	—	—	10	Self
37	Sludge Bomb	Poison	Special	90	100	10	Normal
42	Gastro Acid	Poison	Status	—	100	10	Normal
49	Belch	Poison	Special	120	90	10	Normal
54	Wring Out	Normal	Special	—	100	5	Normal
61	Gunk Shot	Poison	Physical	120	80	5	Normal

TM & HM MOVES

No.	Name	Type	Kind	Pow.	Acc.	PP	Range
TM06	Toxic	Poison	Status	—	90	10	Normal
TM09	Venoshock	Poison	Special	65	100	10	Normal
TM10	Hidden Power	Normal	Special	60	100	15	Normal
TM11	Sunny Day	Fire	Status	—	—	5	Both Sides
TM13	Ice Beam	Ice	Special	90	100	10	Normal
TM15	Hyper Beam	Normal	Special	150	90	5	Normal
TM17	Protect	Normal	Status	—	—	10	Self
TM18	Rain Dance	Water	Status	—	—	5	Both Sides
TM21	Frustration	Normal	Physical	—	100	20	Normal
TM22	Solar Beam	Grass	Special	120	100	10	Normal
TM26	Earthquake	Ground	Physical	100	100	10	Adjacent
TM27	Return	Normal	Physical	—	100	20	Normal
TM30	Shadow Ball	Ghost	Special	80	100	15	Normal
TM32	Double Team	Normal	Status	—	—	15	Self
TM34	Sludge Wave	Poison	Special	95	100	10	Adjacent
TM36	Sludge Bomb	Poison	Special	90	100	10	Normal
TM42	Facade	Normal	Physical	70	100	20	Normal
TM44	Rest	Psychic	Status	—	—	10	Self
TM45	Attract	Normal	Status	—	100	15	Normal
TM48	Round	Normal	Special	60	100	15	Normal
TM64	Explosion	Normal	Physical	250	100	5	Adjacent
TM68	Giga Impact	Normal	Physical	150	90	5	Normal
TM78	Bulldoze	Ground	Physical	60	100	20	Adjacent
TM83	Infestation	Bug	Special	20	100	20	Normal
TM85	Dream Eater	Psychic	Special	100	100	15	Normal
TM87	Swagger	Normal	Status	—	90	15	Normal
TM88	Sleep Talk	Normal	Status	—	—	10	Self
TM90	Substitute	Normal	Status	—	—	10	Self
TM94	Secret Power	Normal	Physical	70	100	20	Normal
TM98	Power-Up Punch	Fighting	Physical	40	100	20	Normal
TM100	Confide	Normal	Status	—	—	20	Normal
HM04	Strength	Normal	Physical	80	100	15	Normal
HM06	Rock Smash	Fighting	Physical	40	100	15	Normal

MOVES LEARNED IN EXCHANGE FOR BP

Name	Type	Kind	Pow.	Acc.	PP	Range
Seed Bomb	Grass	Physical	80	100	15	Normal
Gunk Shot	Poison	Physical	120	80	5	Normal
Thunder Punch	Electric	Physical	75	100	15	Normal
Fire Punch	Fire	Physical	75	100	15	Normal
Ice Punch	Ice	Physical	75	100	15	Normal
Block	Normal	Status	—	—	5	Normal
Snore	Normal	Special	50	100	15	Normal
Pain Split	Normal	Status	—	—	20	Normal
Giga Drain	Grass	Special	75	100	10	Normal
Shock Wave	Electric	Special	60	—	20	Normal
Water Pulse	Water	Special	60	100	20	Normal
Gastro Acid	Poison	Status	—	100	10	Normal
Snatch	Dark	Status	—	—	10	Self

MOVES TAUGHT BY PEOPLE

Name	Type	Kind	Pow.	Acc.	PP	Range

National Pokédex **318** Hoenn Pokédex **102**

Carvanha

Savage Pokémon

Water Dark

HEIGHT: 2'07" WEIGHT: 45.9 lbs.

Same form for ♂ / ♀

Ω Carvanha's strongly developed jaws and its sharply pointed fangs pack the destructive power to rip out boat hulls. Many boats have been attacked and sunk by this Pokémon.

α If anything invades Carvanha's territory, it will swarm and tear at the intruder with its pointed fangs. On its own, however, this Pokémon turns suddenly timid.

ABILITY: Rough Skin

HIDDEN ABILITY: Speed Boost

EGG GROUPS: Water 2

STAT GROWTH RATES: HP ■■ / Attack ■■■■■ / Defense ■ / Sp. Atk ■■■ / Sp. Def ■ / Speed ■■■■

ITEMS SOMETIMES HELD BY WILD POKÉMON: Deep Sea Tooth

EVOLUTION: Carvanha → Lv. 30 → Sharpedo

MAIN WAY TO REGISTER IN THE NATIONAL POKÉDEX

Catch using a Super Rod on Route 119.

Damage taken in normal battles

Type		Type	
Normal	×1	Flying	×1
Fire	×0.5	Psychic	×0
Water	×0.5	Bug	×2
Grass	×2	Rock	×1
Electric	×2	Ghost	×0.5
Ice	×0.5	Dragon	×1
Fighting	×2	Dark	×0.5
Poison	×1	Steel	×0.5
Ground	×1	Fairy	×2

Damage taken in Inverse battles

Type		Type	
Normal	×1	Flying	×1
Fire	×2	Psychic	×2
Water	×2	Bug	×0.5
Grass	×0.5	Rock	×1
Electric	×0.5	Ghost	×2
Ice	×2	Dragon	×1
Fighting	×0.5	Dark	×2
Poison	×1	Steel	×2
Ground	×1	Fairy	×0.5

Can be used in

Inverse Battle
Battle Institute
Battle Maison
Random Matchup (Free Battle)
Random Matchup (Others)

LEVEL-UP MOVES

Lv.	Name	Type	Kind	Pow.	Acc.	PP	Range
1	Leer	Normal	Status	—	100	30	Many Others
1	Bite	Dark	Physical	60	100	25	Normal
4	Rage	Normal	Physical	20	100	20	Normal
8	Focus Energy	Normal	Status	—	—	30	Self
11	Aqua Jet	Water	Physical	40	100	20	Normal
15	Assurance	Dark	Physical	60	100	10	Normal
18	Screech	Normal	Status	—	85	40	Normal
22	Swagger	Normal	Status	—	90	15	Normal
25	Ice Fang	Ice	Physical	65	95	15	Normal
29	Scary Face	Normal	Status	—	100	10	Normal
32	Poison Fang	Poison	Physical	50	100	15	Normal
36	Crunch	Dark	Physical	80	100	15	Normal
39	Agility	Psychic	Status	—	—	30	Self
43	Take Down	Normal	Physical	90	85	20	Normal

TM & HM MOVES

No.	Name	Type	Kind	Pow.	Acc.	PP	Range
TM06	Toxic	Poison	Status	—	90	10	Normal
TM07	Hail	Ice	Status	—	—	10	Both Sides
TM10	Hidden Power	Normal	Special	60	100	15	Normal
TM12	Taunt	Dark	Status	—	100	20	Normal
TM13	Ice Beam	Ice	Special	90	100	10	Normal
TM14	Blizzard	Ice	Special	110	70	5	Many Others
TM17	Protect	Normal	Status	—	—	10	Self
TM18	Rain Dance	Water	Status	—	—	5	Both Sides
TM21	Frustration	Normal	Physical	—	100	20	Normal
TM27	Return	Normal	Physical	—	100	20	Normal
TM32	Double Team	Normal	Status	—	—	15	Self
TM41	Torment	Dark	Status	—	100	15	Normal
TM42	Facade	Normal	Physical	70	100	20	Normal
TM44	Rest	Psychic	Status	—	—	10	Self
TM45	Attract	Normal	Status	—	100	15	Normal
TM46	Thief	Dark	Physical	60	100	25	Normal
TM48	Round	Normal	Special	60	100	15	Normal
TM55	Scald	Water	Special	80	100	15	Normal
TM66	Payback	Dark	Physical	50	100	10	Normal
TM67	Retaliate	Normal	Physical	70	100	5	Normal
TM87	Swagger	Normal	Status	—	90	15	Normal
TM88	Sleep Talk	Normal	Status	—	—	10	Self
TM90	Substitute	Normal	Status	—	—	10	Self
TM94	Secret Power	Normal	Physical	70	100	20	Normal
TM95	Snarl	Dark	Special	55	95	15	Many Others
TM97	Dark Pulse	Dark	Special	80	100	15	Normal
TM100	Confide	Normal	Status	—	—	20	Normal
HM03	Surf	Water	Special	90	100	15	Adjacent
HM05	Waterfall	Water	Physical	80	100	15	Normal
HM07	Dive	Water	Physical	80	100	10	Normal

MOVES LEARNED IN EXCHANGE FOR BP

Name	Type	Kind	Pow.	Acc.	PP	Range
Super Fang	Normal	Physical	—	90	10	Normal
Bounce	Flying	Physical	85	85	5	Normal
Uproar	Normal	Special	90	100	10	1 Random
Icy Wind	Ice	Special	55	95	15	Many Others
Zen Headbutt	Psychic	Physical	80	90	15	Normal
Snore	Normal	Special	50	100	15	Normal
Water Pulse	Water	Special	60	100	20	Normal
Spite	Ghost	Status	—	100	10	Normal

MOVES TAUGHT BY PEOPLE

Name	Type	Kind	Pow.	Acc.	PP	Range

EGG MOVES

Name	Type	Kind	Pow.	Acc.	PP	Range
Hydro Pump	Water	Special	110	80	5	Normal
Double-Edge	Normal	Physical	120	100	15	Normal
Thrash	Normal	Physical	120	100	10	1 Random
Ancient Power	Rock	Special	60	100	5	Normal
Swift	Normal	Special	60	—	20	Many Others
Brine	Water	Special	65	100	10	Normal
Destiny Bond	Ghost	Status	—	—	5	Self

National Pokédex **319** Hoenn Pokédex **103**

Sharpedo

Brutal Pokémon

Water Dark

HEIGHT: 5'11" WEIGHT: 195.8 lbs.

Same form for ♂ / ♀

Ω Nicknamed "the bully of the sea," Sharpedo is widely feared. Its cruel fangs grow back immediately if they snap off. Just one of these Pokémon can thoroughly tear apart a supertanker.

α Sharpedo can swim at speeds of up to 75 mph by jetting seawater out of its backside. This Pokémon's drawback is its inability to swim long distances.

ABILITY: Rough Skin

HIDDEN ABILITY: Speed Boost

EGG GROUPS: Water 2

STAT GROWTH RATES: HP ■■■ / Attack ■■■■■■ / Defense ■■ / Sp. Atk ■■■■■ / Sp. Def ■■ / Speed ■■■■■

ITEMS SOMETIMES HELD BY WILD POKÉMON: Deep Sea Tooth

EVOLUTION: Carvanha → Lv. 30 → Sharpedo

MAIN WAY TO REGISTER IN THE NATIONAL POKÉDEX

Catch using a Super Rod on Route 119.

Damage taken in normal battles

Type		Type	
Normal	×1	Flying	×1
Fire	×0.5	Psychic	×0
Water	×0.5	Bug	×2
Grass	×2	Rock	×1
Electric	×2	Ghost	×0.5
Ice	×0.5	Dragon	×1
Fighting	×2	Dark	×0.5
Poison	×1	Steel	×0.5
Ground	×1	Fairy	×2

Damage taken in Inverse battles

Type		Type	
Normal	×1	Flying	×1
Fire	×2	Psychic	×2
Water	×2	Bug	×0.5
Grass	×0.5	Rock	×1
Electric	×0.5	Ghost	×2
Ice	×2	Dragon	×1
Fighting	×0.5	Dark	×2
Poison	×1	Steel	×2
Ground	×1	Fairy	×0.5

Can be used in

Inverse Battle
Battle Institute
Battle Maison
Random Matchup (Free Battle)
Random Matchup (Others)

LEVEL-UP MOVES

Lv.	Name	Type	Kind	Pow.	Acc.	PP	Range
1	Night Slash	Dark	Physical	70	100	15	Normal
1	Feint	Normal	Physical	30	100	10	Normal
1	Leer	Normal	Status	—	100	30	Many Others
1	Bite	Dark	Physical	60	100	25	Normal
1	Rage	Normal	Physical	20	100	20	Normal
1	Focus Energy	Normal	Status	—	—	30	Self
4	Rage	Normal	Physical	20	100	20	Normal
8	Focus Energy	Normal	Status	—	—	30	Self
11	Aqua Jet	Water	Physical	40	100	20	Normal
15	Assurance	Dark	Physical	60	100	10	Normal
18	Screech	Normal	Status	—	85	40	Normal
22	Swagger	Normal	Status	—	90	15	Normal
25	Ice Fang	Ice	Physical	65	95	15	Normal
29	Scary Face	Normal	Status	—	100	10	Normal
30	Slash	Normal	Physical	70	100	20	Normal
34	Poison Fang	Poison	Physical	50	100	15	Normal
40	Crunch	Dark	Physical	80	100	15	Normal
45	Agility	Psychic	Status	—	—	30	Self
51	Skull Bash	Normal	Physical	130	100	10	Normal
56	Taunt	Dark	Status	—	100	20	Normal
62	Night Slash	Dark	Physical	70	100	15	Normal

TM & HM MOVES

No.	Name	Type	Kind	Pow.	Acc.	PP	Range
TM05	Roar	Normal	Status	—	—	20	Normal
TM06	Toxic	Poison	Status	—	90	10	Normal
TM07	Hail	Ice	Status	—	—	10	Both Sides
TM10	Hidden Power	Normal	Special	60	100	15	Normal
TM12	Taunt	Dark	Status	—	100	20	Normal
TM13	Ice Beam	Ice	Special	90	100	10	Normal
TM14	Blizzard	Ice	Special	110	70	5	Many Others
TM15	Hyper Beam	Normal	Special	150	90	5	Normal
TM17	Protect	Normal	Status	—	—	10	Self
TM18	Rain Dance	Water	Status	—	—	5	Both Sides
TM21	Frustration	Normal	Physical	—	100	20	Normal
TM26	Earthquake	Ground	Physical	100	100	10	Adjacent
TM27	Return	Normal	Physical	—	100	20	Normal
TM32	Double Team	Normal	Status	—	—	15	Self
TM39	Rock Tomb	Rock	Physical	60	95	15	Normal
TM41	Torment	Dark	Status	—	100	15	Normal
TM42	Facade	Normal	Physical	70	100	20	Normal
TM44	Rest	Psychic	Status	—	—	10	Self
TM45	Attract	Normal	Status	—	100	15	Normal
TM46	Thief	Dark	Physical	60	100	25	Normal
TM48	Round	Normal	Special	60	100	15	Normal
TM55	Scald	Water	Special	80	100	15	Normal
TM66	Payback	Dark	Physical	50	100	10	Normal
TM67	Retaliate	Normal	Physical	70	100	5	Normal
TM68	Giga Impact	Normal	Physical	150	90	5	Normal
TM78	Bulldoze	Ground	Physical	60	100	20	Adjacent
TM84	Poison Jab	Poison	Physical	80	100	20	Normal
TM87	Swagger	Normal	Status	—	90	15	Normal
TM88	Sleep Talk	Normal	Status	—	—	10	Self
TM90	Substitute	Normal	Status	—	—	10	Self
TM94	Secret Power	Normal	Physical	70	100	20	Normal
TM95	Snarl	Dark	Special	55	95	15	Many Others
TM97	Dark Pulse	Dark	Special	80	100	15	Normal
TM100	Confide	Normal	Status	—	—	20	Normal
HM03	Surf	Water	Special	90	100	15	Adjacent
HM04	Strength	Normal	Physical	80	100	15	Normal
HM05	Waterfall	Water	Physical	80	100	15	Normal
HM06	Rock Smash	Fighting	Physical	40	100	15	Normal
HM07	Dive	Water	Physical	80	100	10	Normal

MOVES LEARNED IN EXCHANGE FOR BP

Name	Type	Kind	Pow.	Acc.	PP	Range
Super Fang	Normal	Physical	—	90	10	Normal
Bounce	Flying	Physical	85	85	5	Normal
Uproar	Normal	Special	90	100	10	1 Random
Icy Wind	Ice	Special	55	95	15	Many Others
Zen Headbutt	Psychic	Physical	80	90	15	Normal
Snore	Normal	Special	50	100	15	Normal
Water Pulse	Water	Special	60	100	20	Normal
Spite	Ghost	Status	—	100	10	Normal

MOVES TAUGHT BY PEOPLE

Name	Type	Kind	Pow.	Acc.	PP	Range

Mega Evolution

Mega Sharpedo

Brutal Pokémon

Water | Dark

HEIGHT: 8'02" WEIGHT: 287.3 lbs.

Same form for ♂ / ♀

REQUIRED MEGA STONE

Sharpedonite

Receive from Team Aqua at the Battle Resort *(Pokémon Omega Ruby)* / Receive from Team Aqua during the Delta Episode *(Pokémon Alpha Sapphire)*

ABILITY

Strong Jaw

HIDDEN ABILITY

—

EGG GROUPS

—

STAT GROWTH RATES

HP	■■■
Attack	■■■■■■■
Defense	■■■
Sp. Atk	■■■■■
Sp. Def	■■■
Speed	■■■■■■

Damage taken in normal battles

Type		Type	
Normal	×1	Flying	×1
Fire	×0.5	Psychic	×0
Water	×0.5	Bug	×2
Grass	×2	Rock	×1
Electric	×2	Ghost	×0.5
Ice	×0.5	Dragon	×1
Fighting	×2	Dark	×0.5
Poison	×1	Steel	×0.5
Ground	×1	Fairy	×2

Damage taken in Inverse battles

Type		Type	
Normal	×1	Flying	×1
Fire	×2	Psychic	×2
Water	×2	Bug	×0.5
Grass	×0.5	Rock	×1
Electric	×0.5	Ghost	×2
Ice	×2	Dragon	×1
Fighting	×0.5	Dark	×2
Poison	×1	Steel	×2
Ground	×1	Fairy	×0.5

Can be used in

Inverse Battle

Battle Institute

Battle Maison

Random Matchup (Free Battle)

Random Matchup (Others)

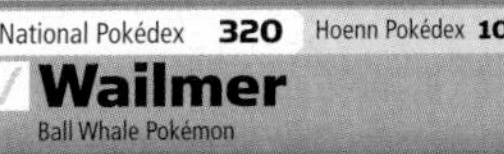

National Pokédex **320** Hoenn Pokédex **104**

✓ Wailmer

Ball Whale Pokémon

Water

HEIGHT: 6'07" WEIGHT: 286.6 lbs.

Same form for ♂ / ♀

Ω Wailmer's nostrils are located above its eyes. This playful Pokémon loves to startle people by forcefully snorting out seawater it stores inside its body out of its nostrils.

α Wailmer can store water inside its body to transform itself into a ball for bouncing around on the ground. By filling itself up with more water, this Pokémon can elevate the height of its bounces.

ABILITIES

Water Veil

Oblivious

HIDDEN ABILITY

Pressure

EGG GROUPS

Field | Water 2

STAT GROWTH RATES

HP	■■■■■
Attack	■■■■
Defense	■■
Sp. Atk	■■■
Sp. Def	■■
Speed	■■■

ITEMS SOMETIMES HELD BY WILD POKÉMON

—

EVOLUTION

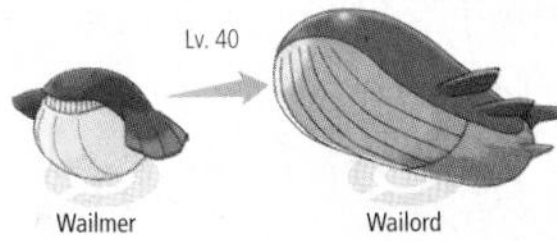

Wailmer → Lv. 40 → Wailord

MAIN WAY TO REGISTER IN THE NATIONAL POKÉDEX

Catch using a Super Rod in Mossdeep City.

Damage taken in normal battles

Type		Type	
Normal	×1	Flying	×1
Fire	×0.5	Psychic	×1
Water	×0.5	Bug	×1
Grass	×2	Rock	×1
Electric	×2	Ghost	×1
Ice	×0.5	Dragon	×1
Fighting	×1	Dark	×1
Poison	×1	Steel	×0.5
Ground	×1	Fairy	×1

Damage taken in Inverse battles

Type		Type	
Normal	×1	Flying	×1
Fire	×2	Psychic	×1
Water	×2	Bug	×1
Grass	×0.5	Rock	×1
Electric	×0.5	Ghost	×1
Ice	×2	Dragon	×1
Fighting	×1	Dark	×1
Poison	×1	Steel	×2
Ground	×1	Fairy	×1

Can be used in

Inverse Battle

Battle Institute

Battle Maison

Random Matchup (Free Battle)

Random Matchup (Others)

LEVEL-UP MOVES

Lv.	Name	Type	Kind	Pow.	Acc.	PP	Range
1	Splash	Normal	Status	—	—	40	Self
4	Growl	Normal	Status	—	100	40	Many Others
7	Water Gun	Water	Special	40	100	25	Normal
10	Rollout	Rock	Physical	30	90	20	Normal
13	Whirlpool	Water	Special	35	85	15	Normal
16	Astonish	Ghost	Physical	30	100	15	Normal
19	Water Pulse	Water	Special	60	100	20	Normal
22	Mist	Ice	Status	—	—	30	Your Side
25	Brine	Water	Special	65	100	10	Normal
29	Rest	Psychic	Status	—	—	10	Self
33	Dive	Water	Physical	80	100	10	Normal
37	Amnesia	Psychic	Status	—	—	20	Self
41	Water Spout	Water	Special	150	100	5	Many Others
45	Bounce	Flying	Physical	85	85	5	Normal
49	Hydro Pump	Water	Special	110	80	5	Normal
53	Heavy Slam	Steel	Physical	—	100	10	Normal

TM & HM MOVES

No.	Name	Type	Kind	Pow.	Acc.	PP	Range
TM05	Roar	Normal	Status	—	—	20	Normal
TM06	Toxic	Poison	Status	—	90	10	Normal
TM07	Hail	Ice	Status	—	—	10	Both Sides
TM10	Hidden Power	Normal	Special	60	100	15	Normal
TM13	Ice Beam	Ice	Special	90	100	10	Normal
TM14	Blizzard	Ice	Special	110	70	5	Many Others
TM17	Protect	Normal	Status	—	—	10	Self
TM18	Rain Dance	Water	Status	—	—	5	Both Sides
TM21	Frustration	Normal	Physical	—	100	20	Normal
TM26	Earthquake	Ground	Physical	100	100	10	Adjacent
TM27	Return	Normal	Physical	—	100	20	Normal
TM32	Double Team	Normal	Status	—	—	15	Self
TM39	Rock Tomb	Rock	Physical	60	95	15	Normal
TM42	Facade	Normal	Physical	70	100	20	Normal
TM44	Rest	Psychic	Status	—	—	10	Self
TM45	Attract	Normal	Status	—	100	15	Normal
TM48	Round	Normal	Special	60	100	15	Normal
TM49	Echoed Voice	Normal	Special	40	100	15	Normal
TM55	Scald	Water	Special	80	100	15	Normal
TM78	Bulldoze	Ground	Physical	60	100	20	Adjacent
TM87	Swagger	Normal	Status	—	90	15	Normal
TM88	Sleep Talk	Normal	Status	—	—	10	Self
TM90	Substitute	Normal	Status	—	—	10	Self
TM94	Secret Power	Normal	Physical	70	100	20	Normal
TM100	Confide	Normal	Status	—	—	20	Normal
HM03	Surf	Water	Special	90	100	15	Adjacent
HM04	Strength	Normal	Physical	80	100	15	Normal
HM05	Waterfall	Water	Physical	80	100	15	Normal
HM06	Rock Smash	Fighting	Physical	40	100	15	Normal
HM07	Dive	Water	Physical	80	100	10	Normal

MOVES LEARNED IN EXCHANGE FOR BP

Name	Type	Kind	Pow.	Acc.	PP	Range
Bounce	Flying	Physical	85	85	5	Normal
Icy Wind	Ice	Special	55	95	15	Many Others
Zen Headbutt	Psychic	Physical	80	90	15	Normal
Hyper Voice	Normal	Special	90	100	10	Many Others
Snore	Normal	Special	50	100	15	Normal
Water Pulse	Water	Special	60	100	20	Normal

MOVES TAUGHT BY PEOPLE

Name	Type	Kind	Pow.	Acc.	PP	Range

EGG MOVES

Name	Type	Kind	Pow.	Acc.	PP	Range
Double-Edge	Normal	Physical	120	100	15	Normal
Thrash	Normal	Physical	120	100	10	1 Random
Snore	Normal	Special	50	100	15	Normal
Sleep Talk	Normal	Status	—	—	10	Self
Curse	Ghost	Status	—	—	10	Varies
Fissure	Ground	Physical	—	30	5	Normal
Tickle	Normal	Status	—	100	20	Normal
Defense Curl	Normal	Status	—	—	40	Self
Body Slam	Normal	Physical	85	100	15	Normal
Aqua Ring	Water	Status	—	—	20	Self
Soak	Water	Status	—	100	20	Normal
Zen Headbutt	Psychic	Physical	80	90	15	Normal
Clear Smog	Poison	Special	50	—	15	Normal

National Pokédex **321** Hoenn Pokédex **105**

Wailord

Float Whale Pokémon

Water

HEIGHT: 47'07" WEIGHT: 877.4 lbs.

Same form for ♂ / ♀

Ω Wailord is the largest of all identified Pokémon up to now. This giant Pokémon swims languorously in the vast open sea, eating massive amounts of food at once with its enormous mouth.

α When chasing prey, Wailord herds them by leaping out of the water and making a humongous splash. It is breathtaking to see this Pokémon leaping out of the sea with others in its pod.

ABILITIES
Water Veil
Oblivious

HIDDEN ABILITY
Pressure

EGG GROUPS
Field Water 2

STAT GROWTH RATES
HP ▮▮▮▮▮▮
Attack ▮▮▮▮▮
Defense ▮▮
Sp. Atk ▮▮▮▮
Sp. Def ▮▮
Speed ▮▮▮

ITEMS SOMETIMES HELD BY WILD POKÉMON
—

EVOLUTION
Wailmer → Lv. 40 → Wailord

MAIN WAY TO REGISTER IN THE NATIONAL POKÉDEX

Level up Wailmer to Lv. 40.

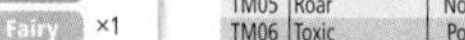

Damage taken in normal battles

Type		Type	
Normal	×1	Flying	×1
Fire	×0.5	Psychic	×1
Water	×0.5	Bug	×1
Grass	×2	Rock	×1
Electric	×2	Ghost	×1
Ice	×0.5	Dragon	×1
Fighting	×1	Dark	×1
Poison	×1	Steel	×0.5
Ground	×1	Fairy	×1

Damage taken in Inverse battles

Type		Type	
Normal	×1	Flying	×1
Fire	×2	Psychic	×1
Water	×2	Bug	×1
Grass	×0.5	Rock	×1
Electric	×0.5	Ghost	×1
Ice	×2	Dragon	×1
Fighting	×1	Dark	×1
Poison	×1	Steel	×2
Ground	×1	Fairy	×1

Can be used in
Inverse Battle
Battle Institute
Battle Maison
Random Matchup (Free Battle)
Random Matchup (Others)

LEVEL-UP MOVES

Lv.	Name	Type	Kind	Pow.	Acc.	PP	Range
1	Heavy Slam	Steel	Physical	—	100	10	Normal
1	Splash	Normal	Status	—	—	40	Self
1	Growl	Normal	Status	—	100	40	Many Others
1	Water Gun	Water	Special	40	100	25	Normal
1	Rollout	Rock	Physical	30	90	20	Normal
4	Growl	Normal	Status	—	100	40	Many Others
7	Water Gun	Water	Special	40	100	25	Normal
10	Rollout	Rock	Physical	30	90	20	Normal
13	Whirlpool	Water	Special	35	85	15	Normal
16	Astonish	Ghost	Physical	30	100	15	Normal
19	Water Pulse	Water	Special	60	100	20	Normal
22	Mist	Ice	Status	—	—	30	Your Side
25	Rest	Psychic	Status	—	—	10	Self
29	Brine	Water	Special	65	100	10	Normal
33	Water Spout	Water	Special	150	100	5	Many Others
37	Amnesia	Psychic	Status	—	—	20	Self
44	Dive	Water	Physical	80	100	10	Normal
51	Bounce	Flying	Physical	85	85	5	Normal
58	Hydro Pump	Water	Special	110	80	5	Normal
65	Heavy Slam	Steel	Physical	—	100	10	Normal

TM & HM MOVES

No.	Name	Type	Kind	Pow.	Acc.	PP	Range
TM05	Roar	Normal	Status	—	—	20	Normal
TM06	Toxic	Poison	Status	—	90	10	Normal
TM07	Hail	Ice	Status	—	—	10	Both Sides
TM10	Hidden Power	Normal	Special	60	100	15	Normal
TM13	Ice Beam	Ice	Special	90	100	10	Normal
TM14	Blizzard	Ice	Special	110	70	5	Many Others
TM15	Hyper Beam	Normal	Special	150	90	5	Normal
TM17	Protect	Normal	Status	—	—	10	Self
TM18	Rain Dance	Water	Status	—	—	5	Both Sides
TM21	Frustration	Normal	Physical	—	100	20	Normal
TM26	Earthquake	Ground	Physical	100	100	10	Adjacent
TM27	Return	Normal	Physical	—	100	20	Normal
TM32	Double Team	Normal	Status	—	—	15	Self
TM39	Rock Tomb	Rock	Physical	60	95	15	Normal
TM42	Facade	Normal	Physical	70	100	20	Normal
TM44	Rest	Psychic	Status	—	—	10	Self
TM45	Attract	Normal	Status	—	100	15	Normal
TM48	Round	Normal	Special	60	100	15	Normal
TM49	Echoed Voice	Normal	Special	40	100	15	Normal
TM55	Scald	Water	Special	80	100	15	Normal
TM68	Giga Impact	Normal	Physical	150	90	5	Normal
TM78	Bulldoze	Ground	Physical	60	100	20	Adjacent
TM87	Swagger	Normal	Status	—	90	15	Normal
TM88	Sleep Talk	Normal	Status	—	—	10	Self
TM90	Substitute	Normal	Status	—	—	10	Self
TM94	Secret Power	Normal	Physical	70	100	20	Normal
TM100	Confide	Normal	Status	—	—	20	Normal
HM03	Surf	Water	Special	90	100	15	Adjacent
HM04	Strength	Normal	Physical	80	100	15	Normal
HM05	Waterfall	Water	Physical	80	100	15	Normal
HM06	Rock Smash	Fighting	Physical	40	100	15	Normal
HM07	Dive	Water	Physical	80	100	10	Normal

MOVES LEARNED IN EXCHANGE FOR BP

Name	Type	Kind	Pow.	Acc.	PP	Range
Iron Head	Steel	Physical	80	100	15	Normal
Bounce	Flying	Physical	85	85	5	Normal
Block	Normal	Status	—	—	5	Normal
Icy Wind	Ice	Special	55	95	15	Many Others
Zen Headbutt	Psychic	Physical	80	90	15	Normal
Hyper Voice	Normal	Special	90	100	10	Many Others
Snore	Normal	Special	50	100	15	Normal
Water Pulse	Water	Special	60	100	20	Normal

MOVES TAUGHT BY PEOPLE

Name	Type	Kind	Pow.	Acc.	PP	Range

National Pokédex **322** Hoenn Pokédex **106**

Numel

Numb Pokémon

Fire Ground

HEIGHT: 2'04" WEIGHT: 52.9 lbs.

The male has a smaller hump.
The female has a larger hump.

Ω Numel is extremely dull witted—it doesn't notice being hit. However, it can't stand hunger for even a second. This Pokémon's body is a seething cauldron of boiling magma.

α Numel stores magma of almost 2,200 degrees Fahrenheit within its body. If it gets wet, the magma cools and hardens. In that event, the Pokémon's body grows heavy and its movements become sluggish.

ABILITIES
Oblivious
Simple

HIDDEN ABILITY
Own Tempo

EGG GROUPS
Field

STAT GROWTH RATES
HP ▮▮▮
Attack ▮▮▮
Defense ▮▮
Sp. Atk ▮▮▮
Sp. Def ▮▮
Speed ▮▮

ITEMS SOMETIMES HELD BY WILD POKÉMON
—

EVOLUTION
Numel → Lv. 33 → Camerupt

MAIN WAY TO REGISTER IN THE NATIONAL POKÉDEX

Catch on Route 112.

Damage taken in normal battles

Type		Type	
Normal	×1	Flying	×1
Fire	×0.5	Psychic	×1
Water	×4	Bug	×0.5
Grass	×1	Rock	×1
Electric	×0	Ghost	×1
Ice	×1	Dragon	×1
Fighting	×1	Dark	×1
Poison	×0.5	Steel	×0.5
Ground	×2	Fairy	×0.5

Damage taken in Inverse battles

Type		Type	
Normal	×1	Flying	×1
Fire	×2	Psychic	×1
Water	×0.25	Bug	×2
Grass	×1	Rock	×1
Electric	×2	Ghost	×1
Ice	×1	Dragon	×1
Fighting	×1	Dark	×1
Poison	×2	Steel	×2
Ground	×0.5	Fairy	×2

Can be used in
Inverse Battle
Battle Institute
Battle Maison
Random Matchup (Free Battle)
Random Matchup (Others)

LEVEL-UP MOVES

Lv.	Name	Type	Kind	Pow.	Acc.	PP	Range
1	Growl	Normal	Status	—	100	40	Many Others
1	Tackle	Normal	Physical	50	100	35	Normal
5	Ember	Fire	Special	40	100	25	Normal
8	Focus Energy	Normal	Status	—	—	30	Self
12	Magnitude	Ground	Physical	—	100	30	Adjacent
15	Flame Burst	Fire	Special	70	100	15	Normal
19	Amnesia	Psychic	Status	—	—	20	Self
22	Lava Plume	Fire	Special	80	100	15	Adjacent
26	Earth Power	Ground	Special	90	100	10	Normal
29	Curse	Ghost	Status	—	—	10	Varies
31	Take Down	Normal	Physical	90	85	20	Normal
36	Yawn	Normal	Status	—	—	10	Normal
40	Earthquake	Ground	Physical	100	100	10	Adjacent
43	Flamethrower	Fire	Special	90	100	15	Normal
47	Double-Edge	Normal	Physical	120	100	15	Normal

TM & HM MOVES

No.	Name	Type	Kind	Pow.	Acc.	PP	Range
TM06	Toxic	Poison	Status	—	90	10	Normal
TM10	Hidden Power	Normal	Special	60	100	15	Normal
TM11	Sunny Day	Fire	Status	—	—	5	Both Sides
TM17	Protect	Normal	Status	—	—	10	Self
TM21	Frustration	Normal	Physical	—	100	20	Normal
TM26	Earthquake	Ground	Physical	100	100	10	Adjacent
TM27	Return	Normal	Physical	—	100	20	Normal
TM28	Dig	Ground	Physical	80	100	10	Normal
TM32	Double Team	Normal	Status	—	—	15	Self
TM35	Flamethrower	Fire	Special	90	100	15	Normal
TM37	Sandstorm	Rock	Status	—	—	10	Both Sides
TM38	Fire Blast	Fire	Special	110	85	5	Normal
TM39	Rock Tomb	Rock	Physical	60	95	15	Normal
TM42	Facade	Normal	Physical	70	100	20	Normal
TM43	Flame Charge	Fire	Physical	50	100	20	Normal
TM44	Rest	Psychic	Status	—	—	10	Self
TM45	Attract	Normal	Status	—	100	15	Normal
TM48	Round	Normal	Special	60	100	15	Normal
TM49	Echoed Voice	Normal	Special	40	100	15	Normal
TM50	Overheat	Fire	Special	130	90	5	Normal
TM59	Incinerate	Fire	Special	60	100	15	Many Others
TM61	Will-O-Wisp	Fire	Status	—	85	15	Normal
TM78	Bulldoze	Ground	Physical	60	100	20	Adjacent
TM80	Rock Slide	Rock	Physical	75	90	10	Many Others
TM87	Swagger	Normal	Status	—	90	15	Normal
TM88	Sleep Talk	Normal	Status	—	—	10	Self
TM90	Substitute	Normal	Status	—	—	10	Self
TM94	Secret Power	Normal	Physical	70	100	20	Normal
TM96	Nature Power	Normal	Status	—	—	20	Normal
TM100	Confide	Normal	Status	—	—	20	Normal
HM04	Strength	Normal	Physical	80	100	15	Normal
HM06	Rock Smash	Fighting	Physical	40	100	15	Normal

MOVES LEARNED IN EXCHANGE FOR BP

Name	Type	Kind	Pow.	Acc.	PP	Range
Iron Head	Steel	Physical	80	100	15	Normal
Earth Power	Ground	Special	90	100	10	Normal
Snore	Normal	Special	50	100	15	Normal
Heat Wave	Fire	Special	95	90	10	Many Others
After You	Normal	Status	—	—	15	Normal
Stealth Rock	Rock	Status	—	—	20	Other Side

MOVES TAUGHT BY PEOPLE

Name	Type	Kind	Pow.	Acc.	PP	Range

EGG MOVES

Name	Type	Kind	Pow.	Acc.	PP	Range
Howl	Normal	Status	—	—	40	Self
Scary Face	Normal	Status	—	100	10	Normal
Body Slam	Normal	Physical	85	100	15	Normal
Rollout	Rock	Physical	30	90	20	Normal
Defense Curl	Normal	Status	—	—	40	Self
Stomp	Normal	Physical	65	100	20	Normal
Yawn	Normal	Status	—	—	10	Normal
Ancient Power	Rock	Special	60	100	5	Normal
Mud Bomb	Ground	Special	65	85	10	Normal
Heat Wave	Fire	Special	95	90	10	Many Others
Stockpile	Normal	Status	—	—	20	Self
Swallow	Normal	Status	—	—	10	Self
Spit Up	Normal	Special	—	100	10	Normal
Endure	Normal	Status	—	—	10	Self
Iron Head	Steel	Physical	80	100	15	Normal
Growth	Normal	Status	—	—	20	Self

National Pokédex **323** Hoenn Pokédex **107**

Camerupt

Eruption Pokémon

Fire | Ground

HEIGHT: 6'03" WEIGHT: 485 lbs.

The male has smaller humps.
The female has larger humps.

Ω Camerupt has a volcano inside its body. Magma of 18,000 degrees Fahrenheit courses through its body. Occasionally, the humps on this Pokémon's back erupt, spewing the superheated magma.

α The humps on Camerupt's back are formed by a transformation of its bones. They sometimes blast out molten magma. This Pokémon apparently erupts often when it is enraged.

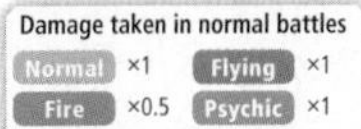

ABILITIES
Magma Armor
Solid Rock

HIDDEN ABILITY
Anger Point

EGG GROUPS
Field

STAT GROWTH RATES
HP
Attack
Defense
Sp. Atk
Sp. Def
Speed

ITEMS SOMETIMES HELD BY WILD POKÉMON
—

EVOLUTION

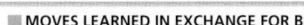

MAIN WAY TO REGISTER IN THE NATIONAL POKÉDEX

Level up Numel to Lv. 33.

Damage taken in normal battles

Type		Type	
Normal	×1	Flying	×1
Fire	×0.5	Psychic	×1
Water	×4	Bug	×0.5
Grass	×1	Rock	×1
Electric	×0	Ghost	×1
Ice	×1	Dragon	×1
Fighting	×1	Dark	×1
Poison	×0.5	Steel	×0.5
Ground	×2	Fairy	×0.5

Damage taken in Inverse battles

Type		Type	
Normal	×1	Flying	×1
Fire	×2	Psychic	×1
Water	×0.25	Bug	×2
Grass	×1	Rock	×1
Electric	×2	Ghost	×1
Ice	×1	Dragon	×1
Fighting	×1	Dark	×1
Poison	×2	Steel	×2
Ground	×0.5	Fairy	×2

Can be used in
Inverse Battle
Battle Institute
Battle Maison
Random Matchup (Free Battle)
Random Matchup (Others)

LEVEL-UP MOVES

Lv.	Name	Type	Kind	Pow.	Acc.	PP	Range
1	Fissure	Ground	Physical	—	30	5	Normal
1	Eruption	Fire	Special	150	100	5	Many Others
1	Growl	Normal	Status	—	100	40	Many Others
1	Tackle	Normal	Physical	50	100	35	Normal
1	Ember	Fire	Special	40	100	25	Normal
1	Focus Energy	Normal	Status	—	—	30	Self
5	Ember	Fire	Special	40	100	25	Normal
8	Focus Energy	Normal	Status	—	—	30	Self
12	Magnitude	Ground	Physical	—	100	30	Adjacent
15	Flame Burst	Fire	Special	70	100	15	Normal
19	Amnesia	Psychic	Status	—	—	20	Self
22	Lava Plume	Fire	Special	80	100	15	Adjacent
26	Earth Power	Ground	Special	90	100	10	Normal
29	Curse	Ghost	Status	—	—	10	Varies
31	Take Down	Normal	Physical	90	85	20	Normal
33	Rock Slide	Rock	Physical	75	90	10	Many Others
39	Yawn	Normal	Status	—	—	10	Normal
46	Earthquake	Ground	Physical	100	100	10	Adjacent
52	Eruption	Fire	Special	150	100	5	Many Others
59	Fissure	Ground	Physical	—	30	5	Normal

TM & HM MOVES

No.	Name	Type	Kind	Pow.	Acc.	PP	Range
TM05	Roar	Normal	Status	—	—	20	Normal
TM06	Toxic	Poison	Status	—	90	10	Normal
TM10	Hidden Power	Normal	Special	60	100	15	Normal
TM11	Sunny Day	Fire	Status	—	—	5	Both Sides
TM15	Hyper Beam	Normal	Special	150	90	5	Normal
TM17	Protect	Normal	Status	—	—	10	Self
TM21	Frustration	Normal	Physical	—	100	20	Normal
TM22	Solar Beam	Grass	Special	120	100	10	Normal
TM26	Earthquake	Ground	Physical	100	100	10	Adjacent
TM27	Return	Normal	Physical	—	100	20	Normal
TM28	Dig	Ground	Physical	80	100	10	Normal
TM32	Double Team	Normal	Status	—	—	15	Self
TM35	Flamethrower	Fire	Special	90	100	15	Normal
TM37	Sandstorm	Rock	Status	—	—	10	Both Sides
TM38	Fire Blast	Fire	Special	110	85	5	Normal
TM39	Rock Tomb	Rock	Physical	60	95	15	Normal
TM42	Facade	Normal	Physical	70	100	20	Normal
TM43	Flame Charge	Fire	Physical	50	100	20	Normal
TM44	Rest	Psychic	Status	—	—	10	Self
TM45	Attract	Normal	Status	—	100	15	Normal
TM48	Round	Normal	Special	60	100	15	Normal
TM49	Echoed Voice	Normal	Special	40	100	15	Normal
TM50	Overheat	Fire	Special	130	90	5	Normal
TM59	Incinerate	Fire	Special	60	100	15	Many Others
TM61	Will-O-Wisp	Fire	Status	—	85	15	Normal
TM64	Explosion	Normal	Physical	250	100	5	Adjacent
TM68	Giga Impact	Normal	Physical	150	90	5	Normal
TM69	Rock Polish	Rock	Status	—	—	20	Self
TM71	Stone Edge	Rock	Physical	100	80	5	Normal
TM78	Bulldoze	Ground	Physical	60	100	20	Adjacent
TM80	Rock Slide	Rock	Physical	75	90	10	Many Others
TM87	Swagger	Normal	Status	—	90	15	Normal
TM88	Sleep Talk	Normal	Status	—	—	10	Self
TM90	Substitute	Normal	Status	—	—	10	Self
TM91	Flash Cannon	Steel	Special	80	100	10	Normal
TM94	Secret Power	Normal	Physical	70	100	20	Normal
TM96	Nature Power	Normal	Status	—	—	20	Normal
TM100	Confide	Normal	Status	—	—	20	Normal
HM04	Strength	Normal	Physical	80	100	15	Normal
HM06	Rock Smash	Fighting	Physical	40	100	15	Normal

MOVES LEARNED IN EXCHANGE FOR BP

Name	Type	Kind	Pow.	Acc.	PP	Range
Iron Head	Steel	Physical	80	100	15	Normal
Earth Power	Ground	Special	90	100	10	Normal
Snore	Normal	Special	50	100	15	Normal
Heat Wave	Fire	Special	95	90	10	Many Others
After You	Normal	Status	—	—	15	Normal
Stealth Rock	Rock	Status	—	—	20	Other Side

MOVES TAUGHT BY PEOPLE

Name	Type	Kind	Pow.	Acc.	PP	Range

Mega Evolution

Mega Camerupt

Eruption Pokémon

Fire | Ground

HEIGHT: 8'02" WEIGHT: 706.6 lbs.

Same form for ♂ / ♀

REQUIRED MEGA STONE
Cameruptite
Receive from Team Magma during the Delta Episode *(Pokémon Omega Ruby)* / Receive from Team Magma at the Battle Resort *(Pokémon Alpha Sapphire)*

ABILITY
Sheer Force

HIDDEN ABILITY
—

EGG GROUPS
—

STAT GROWTH RATES
HP
Attack
Defense
Sp. Atk
Sp. Def
Speed

Damage taken in normal battles

Type		Type	
Normal	×1	Flying	×1
Fire	×0.5	Psychic	×1
Water	×4	Bug	×0.5
Grass	×1	Rock	×1
Electric	×0	Ghost	×1
Ice	×1	Dragon	×1
Fighting	×1	Dark	×1
Poison	×0.5	Steel	×0.5
Ground	×2	Fairy	×0.5

Damage taken in Inverse battles

Type		Type	
Normal	×1	Flying	×1
Fire	×2	Psychic	×1
Water	×0.25	Bug	×2
Grass	×1	Rock	×1
Electric	×2	Ghost	×1
Ice	×1	Dragon	×1
Fighting	×1	Dark	×1
Poison	×2	Steel	×2
Ground	×0.5	Fairy	×2

Can be used in
Inverse Battle
Battle Institute
Battle Maison
Random Matchup (Free Battle)
Random Matchup (Others)

National Pokédex **324** Hoenn Pokédex **110**

Torkoal

Coal Pokémon

Fire

HEIGHT: 1'08" WEIGHT: 177.2 lbs.

Same form for ♂ / ♀

Ω Torkoal digs through mountains in search of coal. If it finds some, it fills hollow spaces on its shell with the coal and burns it. If it is attacked, this Pokémon spouts thick black smoke to beat a retreat.

α Torkoal generates energy by burning coal. It grows weaker as the fire dies down. When it is preparing for battle, this Pokémon burns more coal.

ABILITY
White Smoke

HIDDEN ABILITY
Shell Armor

EGG GROUPS
Field

STAT GROWTH RATES
HP
Attack
Defense
Sp. Atk
Sp. Def
Speed

ITEMS SOMETIMES HELD BY WILD POKÉMON
Charcoal

EVOLUTION
Does not evolve

MAIN WAY TO REGISTER IN THE NATIONAL POKÉDEX

Catch on the Fiery Path.

Damage taken in normal battles

Type		Type	
Normal	×1	Flying	×1
Fire	×0.5	Psychic	×1
Water	×2	Bug	×0.5
Grass	×0.5	Rock	×2
Electric	×1	Ghost	×1
Ice	×0.5	Dragon	×1
Fighting	×1	Dark	×1
Poison	×1	Steel	×0.5
Ground	×2	Fairy	×0.5

Damage taken in Inverse battles

Type		Type	
Normal	×1	Flying	×1
Fire	×2	Psychic	×1
Water	×0.5	Bug	×2
Grass	×2	Rock	×0.5
Electric	×1	Ghost	×1
Ice	×2	Dragon	×1
Fighting	×1	Dark	×1
Poison	×1	Steel	×2
Ground	×0.5	Fairy	×2

Can be used in
Inverse Battle
Battle Institute
Battle Maison
Random Matchup (Free Battle)
Random Matchup (Others)

LEVEL-UP MOVES

Lv.	Name	Type	Kind	Pow.	Acc.	PP	Range
1	Ember	Fire	Special	40	100	25	Normal
4	Smog	Poison	Special	30	70	20	Normal
7	Withdraw	Water	Status	—	—	40	Self
10	Rapid Spin	Normal	Physical	20	100	40	Normal
13	Fire Spin	Fire	Special	35	85	15	Normal
15	Smokescreen	Normal	Status	—	100	20	Normal
18	Flame Wheel	Fire	Physical	60	100	25	Normal
22	Curse	Ghost	Status	—	—	10	Varies
25	Lava Plume	Fire	Special	80	100	15	Adjacent
27	Body Slam	Normal	Physical	85	100	15	Normal
30	Protect	Normal	Status	—	—	10	Self
34	Flamethrower	Fire	Special	90	100	15	Normal
38	Iron Defense	Steel	Status	—	—	15	Self
40	Amnesia	Psychic	Status	—	—	20	Self
42	Flail	Normal	Physical	—	100	15	Normal
45	Heat Wave	Fire	Special	95	90	10	Many Others
47	Shell Smash	Normal	Status	—	—	15	Self
50	Inferno	Fire	Special	100	50	5	Normal

TM & HM MOVES

No.	Name	Type	Kind	Pow.	Acc.	PP	Range
TM06	Toxic	Poison	Status	—	90	10	Normal
TM10	Hidden Power	Normal	Special	60	100	15	Normal
TM11	Sunny Day	Fire	Status	—	—	5	Both Sides
TM15	Hyper Beam	Normal	Special	150	90	5	Normal
TM17	Protect	Normal	Status	—	—	10	Self
TM21	Frustration	Normal	Physical	—	100	20	Normal
TM22	Solar Beam	Grass	Special	120	100	10	Normal
TM26	Earthquake	Ground	Physical	100	100	10	Adjacent
TM27	Return	Normal	Physical	—	100	20	Normal
TM32	Double Team	Normal	Status	—	—	15	Self
TM35	Flamethrower	Fire	Special	90	100	15	Normal
TM36	Sludge Bomb	Poison	Special	90	100	10	Normal
TM38	Fire Blast	Fire	Special	110	85	5	Normal
TM39	Rock Tomb	Rock	Physical	60	95	15	Normal
TM42	Facade	Normal	Physical	70	100	20	Normal
TM43	Flame Charge	Fire	Physical	50	100	20	Normal
TM44	Rest	Psychic	Status	—	—	10	Self
TM45	Attract	Normal	Status	—	100	15	Normal
TM48	Round	Normal	Special	60	100	15	Normal
TM50	Overheat	Fire	Special	130	90	5	Normal
TM59	Incinerate	Fire	Special	60	100	15	Many Others
TM61	Will-O-Wisp	Fire	Status	—	85	15	Normal
TM64	Explosion	Normal	Physical	250	100	5	Adjacent
TM68	Giga Impact	Normal	Physical	150	90	5	Normal
TM71	Stone Edge	Rock	Physical	100	80	5	Normal
TM74	Gyro Ball	Steel	Physical	—	100	5	Normal
TM78	Bulldoze	Ground	Physical	60	100	20	Adjacent
TM80	Rock Slide	Rock	Physical	75	90	10	Many Others
TM87	Swagger	Normal	Status	—	90	15	Normal
TM88	Sleep Talk	Normal	Status	—	—	10	Self
TM90	Substitute	Normal	Status	—	—	10	Self
TM94	Secret Power	Normal	Physical	70	100	20	Normal
TM96	Nature Power	Normal	Status	—	—	20	Normal
TM100	Confide	Normal	Status	—	—	20	Normal
HM04	Strength	Normal	Physical	80	100	15	Normal
HM06	Rock Smash	Fighting	Physical	40	100	15	Normal

MOVES LEARNED IN EXCHANGE FOR BP

Name	Type	Kind	Pow.	Acc.	PP	Range
Earth Power	Ground	Special	90	100	10	Normal
Iron Defense	Steel	Status	—	—	15	Self
Superpower	Fighting	Physical	120	100	5	Normal
Iron Tail	Steel	Physical	100	75	15	Normal
Snore	Normal	Special	50	100	15	Normal
Heat Wave	Fire	Special	95	90	10	Many Others
After You	Normal	Status	—	—	15	Normal
Stealth Rock	Rock	Status	—	—	20	Other Side

MOVES TAUGHT BY PEOPLE

Name	Type	Kind	Pow.	Acc.	PP	Range

EGG MOVES

Name	Type	Kind	Pow.	Acc.	PP	Range
Eruption	Fire	Special	150	100	5	Many Others
Endure	Normal	Status	—	—	10	Self
Sleep Talk	Normal	Status	—	—	10	Self
Yawn	Normal	Status	—	—	10	Normal
Fissure	Ground	Physical	—	30	5	Normal
Skull Bash	Normal	Physical	130	100	10	Normal
Flame Burst	Fire	Special	70	100	15	Normal
Clear Smog	Poison	Special	50	—	15	Normal
Superpower	Fighting	Physical	120	100	5	Normal

National Pokédex **325** Hoenn Pokédex **115**

Spoink

Bounce Pokémon

Psychic

HEIGHT: 2'04" WEIGHT: 67.5 lbs.

Same form for ♂ / ♀

Ω Spoink bounces around on its tail. The shock of its bouncing makes its heart pump. As a result, this Pokémon cannot afford to stop bouncing—if it stops, its heart will stop.

α Spoink keeps a pearl on top of its head. The pearl functions to amplify this Pokémon's psychokinetic powers. It is therefore on a constant search for a bigger pearl.

ABILITIES
Thick Fat
Own Tempo

HIDDEN ABILITY
Gluttony

EGG GROUPS
Field

STAT GROWTH RATES
HP
Attack
Defense
Sp. Atk
Sp. Def
Speed

ITEMS SOMETIMES HELD BY WILD POKÉMON
—

EVOLUTION
Spoink → Lv. 32 → Grumpig

MAIN WAY TO REGISTER IN THE NATIONAL POKÉDEX

Catch on Jagged Pass.

Damage taken in normal battles

Type		Type	
Normal	×1	Flying	×1
Fire	×1	Psychic	×0.5
Water	×1	Bug	×2
Grass	×1	Rock	×1
Electric	×1	Ghost	×2
Ice	×1	Dragon	×1
Fighting	×0.5	Dark	×2
Poison	×1	Steel	×1
Ground	×1	Fairy	×1

Damage taken in Inverse battles

Type		Type	
Normal	×1	Flying	×1
Fire	×1	Psychic	×2
Water	×1	Bug	×0.5
Grass	×1	Rock	×1
Electric	×1	Ghost	×0.5
Ice	×1	Dragon	×1
Fighting	×2	Dark	×0.5
Poison	×1	Steel	×1
Ground	×1	Fairy	×1

Can be used in
Inverse Battle
Battle Institute
Battle Maison
Random Matchup (Free Battle)
Random Matchup (Others)

LEVEL-UP MOVES

Lv.	Name	Type	Kind	Pow.	Acc.	PP	Range
1	Splash	Normal	Status	—	—	40	Self
7	Psywave	Psychic	Special	—	100	15	Normal
10	Odor Sleuth	Normal	Status	—	—	40	Normal
14	Psybeam	Psychic	Special	65	100	20	Normal
15	Psych Up	Normal	Status	—	—	10	Normal
18	Confuse Ray	Ghost	Status	—	100	10	Normal
21	Magic Coat	Psychic	Status	—	—	15	Self
26	Zen Headbutt	Psychic	Physical	80	90	15	Normal
29	Power Gem	Rock	Special	80	100	20	Normal
29	Rest	Psychic	Status	—	—	10	Self
33	Snore	Normal	Special	50	100	15	Normal
38	Psyshock	Psychic	Special	80	100	10	Normal
40	Payback	Dark	Physical	50	100	10	Normal
44	Psychic	Psychic	Special	90	100	10	Normal
50	Bounce	Flying	Physical	85	85	5	Normal

TM & HM MOVES

No.	Name	Type	Kind	Pow.	Acc.	PP	Range
TM03	Psyshock	Psychic	Special	80	100	10	Normal
TM04	Calm Mind	Psychic	Status	—	—	20	Self
TM06	Toxic	Poison	Status	—	90	10	Normal
TM10	Hidden Power	Normal	Special	60	100	15	Normal
TM11	Sunny Day	Fire	Status	—	—	5	Both Sides
TM12	Taunt	Dark	Status	—	100	20	Normal
TM16	Light Screen	Psychic	Status	—	—	30	Your Side
TM17	Protect	Normal	Status	—	—	10	Self
TM18	Rain Dance	Water	Status	—	—	5	Both Sides
TM21	Frustration	Normal	Physical	—	100	20	Normal
TM27	Return	Normal	Physical	—	100	20	Normal
TM29	Psychic	Psychic	Special	90	100	10	Normal
TM30	Shadow Ball	Ghost	Special	80	100	15	Normal
TM32	Double Team	Normal	Status	—	—	15	Self
TM33	Reflect	Psychic	Status	—	—	20	Your Side
TM41	Torment	Dark	Status	—	100	15	Normal
TM42	Facade	Normal	Physical	70	100	20	Normal
TM44	Rest	Psychic	Status	—	—	10	Self
TM45	Attract	Normal	Status	—	100	15	Normal
TM46	Thief	Dark	Physical	60	100	25	Normal
TM48	Round	Normal	Special	60	100	15	Normal
TM57	Charge Beam	Electric	Special	50	90	10	Normal
TM66	Payback	Dark	Physical	50	100	10	Normal
TM70	Flash	Normal	Status	—	100	20	Normal
TM73	Thunder Wave	Electric	Status	—	100	20	Normal
TM77	Psych Up	Normal	Status	—	—	10	Normal
TM85	Dream Eater	Psychic	Special	100	100	15	Normal
TM86	Grass Knot	Grass	Special	—	100	20	Normal
TM87	Swagger	Normal	Status	—	90	15	Normal
TM88	Sleep Talk	Normal	Status	—	—	10	Self
TM90	Substitute	Normal	Status	—	—	10	Self
TM92	Trick Room	Psychic	Status	—	—	5	Both Sides
TM94	Secret Power	Normal	Physical	70	100	20	Normal
TM100	Confide	Normal	Status	—	—	20	Normal

MOVES LEARNED IN EXCHANGE FOR BP

Name	Type	Kind	Pow.	Acc.	PP	Range
Covet	Normal	Physical	60	100	25	Normal
Signal Beam	Bug	Special	75	100	15	Normal
Bounce	Flying	Physical	85	85	5	Normal
Magic Coat	Psychic	Status	—	—	15	Self
Icy Wind	Ice	Special	55	95	15	Many Others
Zen Headbutt	Psychic	Physical	80	90	15	Normal
Iron Tail	Steel	Physical	100	75	15	Normal
Snore	Normal	Special	50	100	15	Normal
Role Play	Psychic	Status	—	—	10	Normal
Heal Bell	Normal	Status	—	—	5	Your Party
Shock Wave	Electric	Special	60	—	20	Normal
Trick	Psychic	Status	—	100	10	Normal
Recycle	Normal	Status	—	—	10	Self
Snatch	Dark	Status	—	—	10	Self
Skill Swap	Psychic	Status	—	—	10	Normal

MOVES TAUGHT BY PEOPLE

Name	Type	Kind	Pow.	Acc.	PP	Range

EGG MOVES

Name	Type	Kind	Pow.	Acc.	PP	Range
Future Sight	Psychic	Special	120	100	10	Normal
Extrasensory	Psychic	Special	80	100	20	Normal
Trick	Psychic	Status	—	100	10	Normal
Zen Headbutt	Psychic	Physical	80	90	15	Normal
Amnesia	Psychic	Status	—	—	20	Self
Mirror Coat	Psychic	Special	—	100	20	Varies
Skill Swap	Psychic	Status	—	—	10	Normal
Whirlwind	Normal	Status	—	—	20	Normal
Lucky Chant	Normal	Status	—	—	30	Your Side
Endure	Normal	Status	—	—	10	Self
Simple Beam	Normal	Status	—	100	15	Normal

National Pokédex **326** Hoenn Pokédex **116**

Grumpig

Manipulate Pokémon

Psychic

HEIGHT: 2'11" WEIGHT: 157.6 lbs.

Same form for ♂ / ♀

Ω Grumpig uses the black pearls on its body to amplify its psychic power waves for gaining total control over its foe. When this Pokémon uses its special power, its snorting breath grows labored.

α Grumpig uses the black pearls on its body to wield its fantastic powers. When it is doing so, it dances bizarrely. This Pokémon's black pearls are valuable as works of art.

ABILITIES
Thick Fat
Own Tempo

HIDDEN ABILITY
Gluttony

EGG GROUPS
Field

STAT GROWTH RATES
HP
Attack
Defense
Sp. Atk
Sp. Def
Speed

ITEMS SOMETIMES HELD BY WILD POKÉMON
—

EVOLUTION

MAIN WAY TO REGISTER IN THE NATIONAL POKÉDEX

Level up Spoink to Lv. 32.

Damage taken in normal battles

Normal	×1	Flying	×1
! Fire	×1	Psychic	×0.5
Water	×1	Bug	×2
Grass	×1	Rock	×1
Electric	×1	Ghost	×2
! Ice	×1	Dragon	×1
Fighting	×0.5	Dark	×2
Poison	×1	Steel	×1
Ground	×1	Fairy	×1

Damage taken in Inverse battles

Normal	×1	Flying	×1
! Fire	×1	Psychic	×2
Water	×1	Bug	×0.5
Grass	×1	Rock	×1
Electric	×1	Ghost	×0.5
! Ice	×1	Dragon	×1
Fighting	×2	Dark	×0.5
Poison	×1	Steel	×1
Ground	×1	Fairy	×1

Can be used in
Inverse Battle
Battle Institute
Battle Maison
Random Matchup (Free Battle)
Random Matchup (Others)

LEVEL-UP MOVES

Lv.	Name	Type	Kind	Pow.	Acc.	PP	Range
1	Splash	Normal	Status	—	—	40	Self
1	Psywave	Psychic	Special	—	100	15	Normal
1	Odor Sleuth	Normal	Status	—	—	40	Normal
1	Psybeam	Psychic	Special	65	100	20	Normal
7	Psywave	Psychic	Special	—	100	15	Normal
10	Odor Sleuth	Normal	Status	—	—	40	Normal
14	Psybeam	Psychic	Special	65	100	20	Normal
15	Psych Up	Normal	Status	—	—	10	Normal
18	Confuse Ray	Ghost	Status	—	100	10	Normal
21	Magic Coat	Psychic	Status	—	—	15	Self
26	Zen Headbutt	Psychic	Physical	80	90	15	Normal
29	Power Gem	Rock	Special	80	100	20	Normal
32	Teeter Dance	Normal	Status	—	100	20	Adjacent
35	Rest	Psychic	Status	—	—	10	Self
35	Snore	Normal	Special	50	100	15	Normal
42	Psyshock	Psychic	Special	80	100	10	Normal
46	Payback	Dark	Physical	50	100	10	Normal
52	Psychic	Psychic	Special	90	100	10	Normal
60	Bounce	Flying	Physical	85	85	5	Normal

TM & HM MOVES

No.	Name	Type	Kind	Pow.	Acc.	PP	Range
TM03	Psyshock	Psychic	Special	80	100	10	Normal
TM04	Calm Mind	Psychic	Status	—	—	20	Self
TM06	Toxic	Poison	Status	—	90	10	Normal
TM10	Hidden Power	Normal	Special	60	100	15	Normal
TM11	Sunny Day	Fire	Status	—	—	5	Both Sides
TM12	Taunt	Dark	Status	—	100	20	Normal
TM15	Hyper Beam	Normal	Special	150	90	5	Normal
TM16	Light Screen	Psychic	Status	—	—	30	Your Side
TM17	Protect	Normal	Status	—	—	10	Self
TM18	Rain Dance	Water	Status	—	—	5	Both Sides
TM21	Frustration	Normal	Physical	—	100	20	Normal
TM27	Return	Normal	Physical	—	100	20	Normal
TM29	Psychic	Psychic	Special	90	100	10	Normal
TM30	Shadow Ball	Ghost	Special	80	100	15	Normal
TM31	Brick Break	Fighting	Physical	75	100	15	Normal
TM32	Double Team	Normal	Status	—	—	15	Self
TM33	Reflect	Psychic	Status	—	—	20	Your Side
TM41	Torment	Dark	Status	—	100	15	Normal
TM42	Facade	Normal	Physical	70	100	20	Normal
TM44	Rest	Psychic	Status	—	—	10	Self
TM45	Attract	Normal	Status	—	100	15	Normal
TM46	Thief	Dark	Physical	60	100	25	Normal
TM48	Round	Normal	Special	60	100	15	Normal
TM52	Focus Blast	Fighting	Special	120	70	5	Normal
TM53	Energy Ball	Grass	Special	90	100	10	Normal
TM56	Fling	Dark	Physical	—	100	10	Normal
TM57	Charge Beam	Electric	Special	50	90	10	Normal
TM66	Payback	Dark	Physical	50	100	10	Normal
TM68	Giga Impact	Normal	Physical	150	90	5	Normal
TM70	Flash	Normal	Status	—	100	20	Normal
TM73	Thunder Wave	Electric	Status	—	100	20	Normal
TM77	Psych Up	Normal	Status	—	—	10	Normal
TM78	Bulldoze	Ground	Physical	60	100	20	Adjacent
TM85	Dream Eater	Psychic	Special	100	100	15	Normal
TM86	Grass Knot	Grass	Special	—	100	20	Normal
TM87	Swagger	Normal	Status	—	90	15	Normal
TM88	Sleep Talk	Normal	Status	—	—	10	Self
TM90	Substitute	Normal	Status	—	—	10	Self
TM92	Trick Room	Psychic	Status	—	—	5	Both Sides
TM94	Secret Power	Normal	Physical	70	100	20	Normal
TM98	Power-Up Punch	Fighting	Physical	40	100	20	Normal
TM100	Confide	Normal	Status	—	—	20	Normal

MOVES LEARNED IN EXCHANGE FOR BP

Name	Type	Kind	Pow.	Acc.	PP	Range
Covet	Normal	Physical	60	100	25	Normal
Signal Beam	Bug	Special	75	100	15	Normal
Bounce	Flying	Physical	85	85	5	Normal
Thunder Punch	Electric	Physical	75	100	15	Normal
Fire Punch	Fire	Physical	75	100	15	Normal
Ice Punch	Ice	Physical	75	100	15	Normal
Magic Coat	Psychic	Status	—	—	15	Self
Icy Wind	Ice	Special	55	95	15	Many Others
Zen Headbutt	Psychic	Physical	80	90	15	Normal
Iron Tail	Steel	Physical	100	75	15	Normal
Snore	Normal	Special	50	100	15	Normal
Role Play	Psychic	Status	—	—	10	Normal
Heal Bell	Normal	Status	—	—	5	Your Party
Drain Punch	Fighting	Physical	75	100	10	Normal
Focus Punch	Fighting	Physical	150	100	20	Normal
Shock Wave	Electric	Special	60	—	20	Normal
Trick	Psychic	Status	—	100	10	Normal
Recycle	Normal	Status	—	—	10	Self
Snatch	Dark	Status	—	—	10	Self
Skill Swap	Psychic	Status	—	—	10	Normal

MOVES TAUGHT BY PEOPLE

Name	Type	Kind	Pow.	Acc.	PP	Range

National Pokédex **327** Hoenn Pokédex **119**

Spinda

Spot Panda Pokémon

Normal

HEIGHT: 3'07" WEIGHT: 11 lbs.

Same form for ♂ / ♀

Ω All the Spinda that exist in the world are said to have utterly unique spot patterns. The shaky, tottering steps of this Pokémon give it the appearance of dancing.

α No two Spinda are said to have identical spot patterns on their hides. This Pokémon moves in a curious manner as if it is stumbling in dizziness. Its lurching movements can cause the opponent to become confused.

ABILITIES
Own Tempo
Tangled Feet

HIDDEN ABILITY
Contrary

EGG GROUPS
Field
Human-Like

STAT GROWTH RATES
HP
Attack
Defense
Sp. Atk
Sp. Def
Speed

ITEMS SOMETIMES HELD BY WILD POKÉMON
—

EVOLUTION

Does not evolve

MAIN WAY TO REGISTER IN THE NATIONAL POKÉDEX

Catch on Route 113.

Damage taken in normal battles

Normal	×1	Flying	×1
Fire	×1	Psychic	×1
Water	×1	Bug	×1
Grass	×1	Rock	×1
Electric	×1	Ghost	×0
Ice	×1	Dragon	×1
Fighting	×2	Dark	×1
Poison	×1	Steel	×1
Ground	×1	Fairy	×1

Damage taken in Inverse battles

Normal	×1	Flying	×1
Fire	×1	Psychic	×1
Water	×1	Bug	×1
Grass	×1	Rock	×1
Electric	×1	Ghost	×2
Ice	×1	Dragon	×1
Fighting	×0.5	Dark	×1
Poison	×1	Steel	×1
Ground	×1	Fairy	×1

Can be used in
Inverse Battle
Battle Institute
Battle Maison
Random Matchup (Free Battle)
Random Matchup (Others)

LEVEL-UP MOVES

Lv.	Name	Type	Kind	Pow.	Acc.	PP	Range
1	Tackle	Normal	Physical	50	100	35	Normal
5	Copycat	Normal	Status	—	—	20	Self
10	Feint Attack	Dark	Physical	60	—	20	Normal
14	Psybeam	Psychic	Special	65	100	20	Normal
19	Hypnosis	Psychic	Status	—	60	20	Normal
23	Dizzy Punch	Normal	Physical	70	100	10	Normal
28	Sucker Punch	Dark	Physical	80	100	5	Normal
32	Teeter Dance	Normal	Status	—	100	20	Adjacent
37	Uproar	Normal	Special	90	100	10	1 Random
41	Psych Up	Normal	Status	—	—	10	Normal
46	Double-Edge	Normal	Physical	120	100	15	Normal
50	Flail	Normal	Physical	—	100	15	Normal
55	Thrash	Normal	Physical	120	100	10	1 Random

TM & HM MOVES

No.	Name	Type	Kind	Pow.	Acc.	PP	Range
TM04	Calm Mind	Psychic	Status	—	—	20	Self
TM06	Toxic	Poison	Status	—	90	10	Normal
TM10	Hidden Power	Normal	Special	60	100	15	Normal
TM11	Sunny Day	Fire	Status	—	—	5	Both Sides
TM17	Protect	Normal	Status	—	—	10	Self
TM18	Rain Dance	Water	Status	—	—	5	Both Sides
TM20	Safeguard	Normal	Status	—	—	25	Your Side
TM21	Frustration	Normal	Physical	—	100	20	Normal
TM27	Return	Normal	Physical	—	100	20	Normal
TM28	Dig	Ground	Physical	80	100	10	Normal
TM29	Psychic	Psychic	Special	90	100	10	Normal
TM30	Shadow Ball	Ghost	Special	80	100	15	Normal
TM31	Brick Break	Fighting	Physical	75	100	15	Normal
TM32	Double Team	Normal	Status	—	—	15	Self
TM39	Rock Tomb	Rock	Physical	60	95	15	Normal
TM42	Facade	Normal	Physical	70	100	20	Normal
TM44	Rest	Psychic	Status	—	—	10	Self
TM45	Attract	Normal	Status	—	100	15	Normal
TM46	Thief	Dark	Physical	60	100	25	Normal
TM48	Round	Normal	Special	60	100	15	Normal
TM56	Fling	Dark	Physical	—	100	10	Normal
TM67	Retaliate	Normal	Physical	70	100	5	Normal
TM70	Flash	Normal	Status	—	100	20	Normal
TM77	Psych Up	Normal	Status	—	—	10	Normal
TM80	Rock Slide	Rock	Physical	75	90	10	Many Others
TM85	Dream Eater	Psychic	Special	100	100	15	Normal
TM87	Swagger	Normal	Status	—	90	15	Normal
TM88	Sleep Talk	Normal	Status	—	—	10	Self
TM90	Substitute	Normal	Status	—	—	10	Self
TM92	Trick Room	Psychic	Status	—	—	5	Both Sides
TM93	Wild Charge	Electric	Physical	90	100	15	Normal
TM94	Secret Power	Normal	Physical	70	100	20	Normal
TM98	Power-Up Punch	Fighting	Physical	40	100	20	Normal
TM100	Confide	Normal	Status	—	—	20	Normal
HM04	Strength	Normal	Physical	80	100	15	Normal
HM06	Rock Smash	Fighting	Physical	40	100	15	Normal

MOVES LEARNED IN EXCHANGE FOR BP

Name	Type	Kind	Pow.	Acc.	PP	Range
Covet	Normal	Physical	60	100	25	Normal
Low Kick	Fighting	Physical	—	100	20	Normal
Uproar	Normal	Special	90	100	10	1 Random
Thunder Punch	Electric	Physical	75	100	15	Normal
Fire Punch	Fire	Physical	75	100	15	Normal
Ice Punch	Ice	Physical	75	100	15	Normal
Last Resort	Normal	Physical	140	100	5	Normal
Icy Wind	Ice	Special	55	95	15	Many Others
Zen Headbutt	Psychic	Physical	80	90	15	Normal
Hyper Voice	Normal	Special	90	100	10	Many Others
Snore	Normal	Special	50	100	15	Normal
Role Play	Psychic	Status	—	—	10	Normal
Drain Punch	Fighting	Physical	75	100	10	Normal
Focus Punch	Fighting	Physical	150	100	20	Normal
Shock Wave	Electric	Special	60	—	20	Normal
Water Pulse	Water	Special	60	100	20	Normal
Helping Hand	Normal	Status	—	—	20	1 Ally
Trick	Psychic	Status	—	100	10	Normal
Recycle	Normal	Status	—	—	10	Self
Snatch	Dark	Status	—	—	10	Self
Skill Swap	Psychic	Status	—	—	10	Normal

MOVES TAUGHT BY PEOPLE

Name	Type	Kind	Pow.	Acc.	PP	Range

EGG MOVES

Name	Type	Kind	Pow.	Acc.	PP	Range
Encore	Normal	Status	—	100	5	Normal
Assist	Normal	Status	—	—	20	Self
Disable	Normal	Status	—	100	20	Normal
Baton Pass	Normal	Status	—	—	40	Self
Wish	Normal	Status	—	—	10	Self
Trick	Psychic	Status	—	100	10	Normal
Smelling Salts	Normal	Physical	70	100	10	Normal
Fake Out	Normal	Physical	40	100	10	Normal
Role Play	Psychic	Status	—	—	10	Normal
Psycho Cut	Psychic	Physical	70	100	20	Normal
Fake Tears	Dark	Status	—	100	20	Normal
Rapid Spin	Normal	Physical	20	100	40	Normal
Icy Wind	Ice	Special	55	95	15	Many Others
Water Pulse	Water	Special	60	100	20	Normal
Psycho Shift	Psychic	Status	—	100	10	Normal
Guard Split	Psychic	Status	—	—	10	Normal

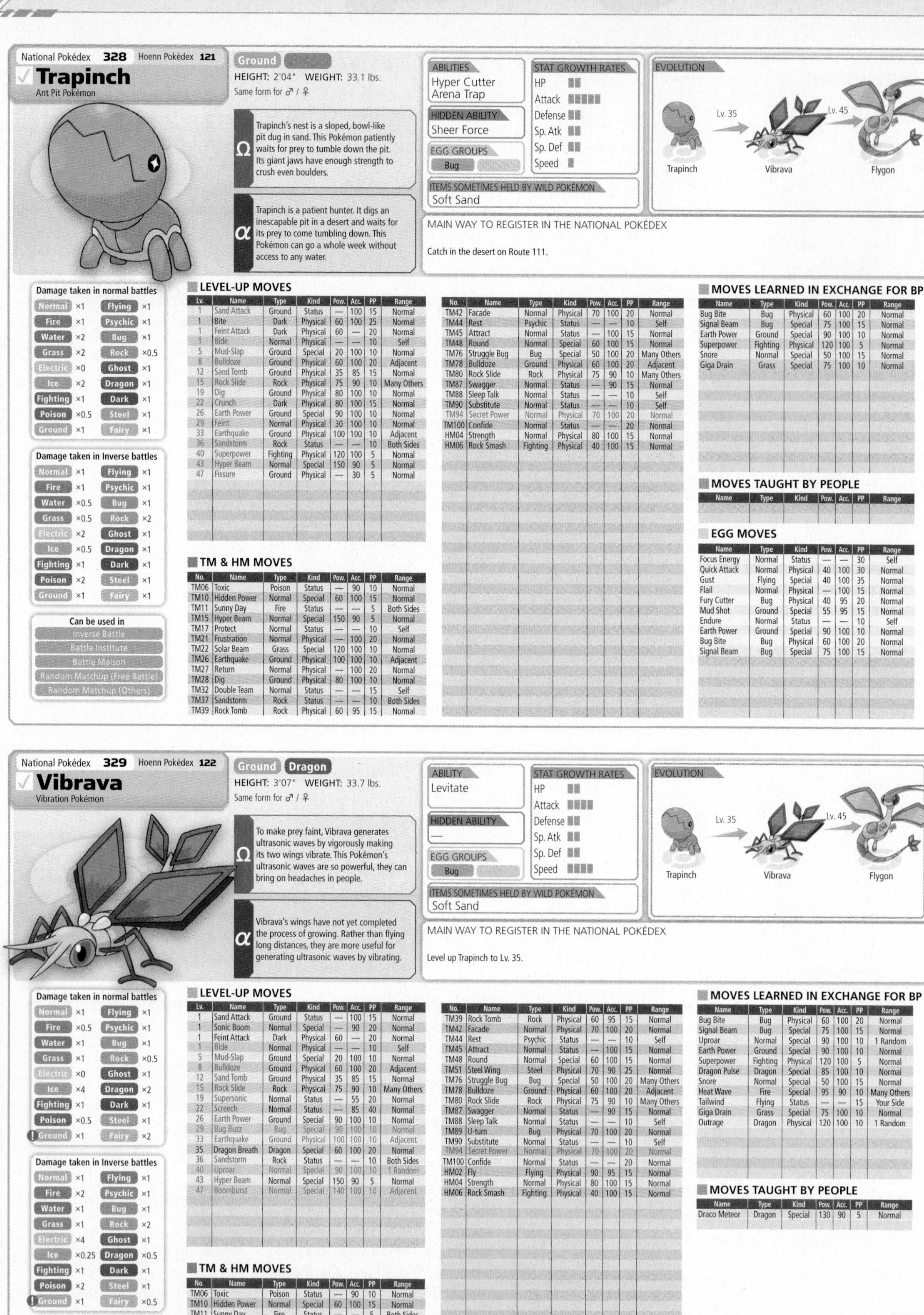

National Pokédex **328** Hoenn Pokédex **121**

Trapinch

Ant Pit Pokémon

Ground

HEIGHT: 2'04" WEIGHT: 33.1 lbs.

Same form for ♂ / ♀

Ω Trapinch's nest is a sloped, bowl-like pit dug in sand. This Pokémon patiently waits for prey to tumble down the pit. Its giant jaws have enough strength to crush even boulders.

α Trapinch is a patient hunter. It digs an inescapable pit in a desert and waits for its prey to come tumbling down. This Pokémon can go a whole week without access to any water.

ABILITIES
Hyper Cutter
Arena Trap

HIDDEN ABILITY
Sheer Force

EGG GROUPS
Bug

STAT GROWTH RATES
HP ■■
Attack ■■■■■
Defense ■■
Sp. Atk ■■
Sp. Def ■■
Speed ■

ITEMS SOMETIMES HELD BY WILD POKÉMON
Soft Sand

EVOLUTION
Trapinch → Lv. 35 → Vibrava → Lv. 45 → Flygon

MAIN WAY TO REGISTER IN THE NATIONAL POKÉDEX

Catch in the desert on Route 111.

Damage taken in normal battles

Type		Type	
Normal	×1	Flying	×1
Fire	×1	Psychic	×1
Water	×2	Bug	×1
Grass	×2	Rock	×0.5
Electric	×0	Ghost	×1
Ice	×2	Dragon	×1
Fighting	×1	Dark	×1
Poison	×0.5	Steel	×1
Ground	×1	Fairy	×1

Damage taken in Inverse battles

Type		Type	
Normal	×1	Flying	×1
Fire	×1	Psychic	×1
Water	×0.5	Bug	×1
Grass	×0.5	Rock	×2
Electric	×2	Ghost	×1
Ice	×0.5	Dragon	×1
Fighting	×1	Dark	×1
Poison	×2	Steel	×1
Ground	×1	Fairy	×1

Can be used in
Inverse Battle
Battle Institute
Battle Maison
Random Matchup (Free Battle)
Random Matchup (Others)

LEVEL-UP MOVES

Lv.	Name	Type	Kind	Pow.	Acc.	PP	Range
1	Sand Attack	Ground	Status	—	100	15	Normal
1	Bite	Dark	Physical	60	100	25	Normal
1	Feint Attack	Dark	Physical	60	—	20	Normal
1	Bide	Normal	Physical	—	—	10	Self
5	Mud-Slap	Ground	Special	20	100	10	Normal
8	Bulldoze	Ground	Physical	60	100	20	Adjacent
12	Sand Tomb	Ground	Physical	35	85	15	Normal
15	Rock Slide	Rock	Physical	75	90	10	Many Others
19	Dig	Ground	Physical	80	100	10	Normal
22	Crunch	Dark	Physical	80	100	15	Normal
26	Earth Power	Ground	Special	90	100	10	Normal
29	Feint	Normal	Physical	30	100	10	Normal
33	Earthquake	Ground	Physical	100	100	10	Adjacent
36	Sandstorm	Rock	Status	—	—	10	Both Sides
40	Superpower	Fighting	Physical	120	100	5	Normal
43	Hyper Beam	Normal	Special	150	90	5	Normal
47	Fissure	Ground	Physical	—	30	5	Normal

TM & HM MOVES

No.	Name	Type	Kind	Pow.	Acc.	PP	Range
TM06	Toxic	Poison	Status	—	90	10	Normal
TM10	Hidden Power	Normal	Special	60	100	15	Normal
TM11	Sunny Day	Fire	Status	—	—	5	Both Sides
TM15	Hyper Beam	Normal	Special	150	90	5	Normal
TM17	Protect	Normal	Status	—	—	10	Self
TM21	Frustration	Normal	Physical	—	100	20	Normal
TM22	Solar Beam	Grass	Special	120	100	10	Normal
TM26	Earthquake	Ground	Physical	100	100	10	Adjacent
TM27	Return	Normal	Physical	—	100	20	Normal
TM28	Dig	Ground	Physical	80	100	10	Normal
TM32	Double Team	Normal	Status	—	—	15	Self
TM37	Sandstorm	Rock	Status	—	—	10	Both Sides
TM39	Rock Tomb	Rock	Physical	60	95	15	Normal
TM42	Facade	Normal	Physical	70	100	20	Normal
TM44	Rest	Psychic	Status	—	—	10	Self
TM45	Attract	Normal	Status	—	100	15	Normal
TM48	Round	Normal	Special	60	100	15	Normal
TM76	Struggle Bug	Bug	Special	50	100	20	Many Others
TM78	Bulldoze	Ground	Physical	60	100	20	Adjacent
TM80	Rock Slide	Rock	Physical	75	90	10	Many Others
TM87	Swagger	Normal	Status	—	90	15	Normal
TM88	Sleep Talk	Normal	Status	—	—	10	Self
TM90	Substitute	Normal	Status	—	—	10	Self
TM94	Secret Power	Normal	Physical	70	100	20	Normal
TM100	Confide	Normal	Status	—	—	20	Normal
HM04	Strength	Normal	Physical	80	100	15	Normal
HM06	Rock Smash	Fighting	Physical	40	100	15	Normal

MOVES LEARNED IN EXCHANGE FOR BP

Name	Type	Kind	Pow.	Acc.	PP	Range
Bug Bite	Bug	Physical	60	100	20	Normal
Signal Beam	Bug	Special	75	100	15	Normal
Earth Power	Ground	Special	90	100	10	Normal
Superpower	Fighting	Physical	120	100	5	Normal
Snore	Normal	Special	50	100	15	Normal
Giga Drain	Grass	Special	75	100	10	Normal

MOVES TAUGHT BY PEOPLE

Name	Type	Kind	Pow.	Acc.	PP	Range

EGG MOVES

Name	Type	Kind	Pow.	Acc.	PP	Range
Focus Energy	Normal	Status	—	—	30	Self
Quick Attack	Normal	Physical	40	100	30	Normal
Gust	Flying	Special	40	100	35	Normal
Flail	Normal	Physical	—	100	15	Normal
Fury Cutter	Bug	Physical	40	95	20	Normal
Mud Shot	Ground	Special	55	95	15	Normal
Endure	Normal	Status	—	—	10	Self
Earth Power	Ground	Special	90	100	10	Normal
Bug Bite	Bug	Physical	60	100	20	Normal
Signal Beam	Bug	Special	75	100	15	Normal

National Pokédex **329** Hoenn Pokédex **122**

Vibrava

Vibration Pokémon

Ground Dragon

HEIGHT: 3'07" WEIGHT: 33.7 lbs.

Same form for ♂ / ♀

Ω To make prey faint, Vibrava generates ultrasonic waves by vigorously making its two wings vibrate. This Pokémon's ultrasonic waves are so powerful, they can bring on headaches in people.

α Vibrava's wings have not yet completed the process of growing. Rather than flying long distances, they are more useful for generating ultrasonic waves by vibrating.

ABILITY
Levitate

HIDDEN ABILITY
—

EGG GROUPS
Bug

STAT GROWTH RATES
HP ■■
Attack ■■■■
Defense ■■
Sp. Atk ■■
Sp. Def ■■
Speed ■■■■

ITEMS SOMETIMES HELD BY WILD POKÉMON
Soft Sand

EVOLUTION
Trapinch → Lv. 35 → Vibrava → Lv. 45 → Flygon

MAIN WAY TO REGISTER IN THE NATIONAL POKÉDEX

Level up Trapinch to Lv. 35.

Damage taken in normal battles

Type		Type	
Normal	×1	Flying	×1
Fire	×0.5	Psychic	×1
Water	×1	Bug	×1
Grass	×1	Rock	×0.5
Electric	×0	Ghost	×1
Ice	×4	Dragon	×2
Fighting	×1	Dark	×1
Poison	×0.5	Steel	×1
! Ground	×1	Fairy	×2

Damage taken in Inverse battles

Type		Type	
Normal	×1	Flying	×1
Fire	×2	Psychic	×1
Water	×1	Bug	×1
Grass	×1	Rock	×2
Electric	×4	Ghost	×1
Ice	×0.25	Dragon	×0.5
Fighting	×1	Dark	×1
Poison	×2	Steel	×1
! Ground	×1	Fairy	×0.5

Can be used in
Inverse Battle
Battle Institute
Battle Maison
Random Matchup (Free Battle)
Random Matchup (Others)

LEVEL-UP MOVES

Lv.	Name	Type	Kind	Pow.	Acc.	PP	Range
1	Sand Attack	Ground	Status	—	100	15	Normal
1	Sonic Boom	Normal	Special	—	90	20	Normal
1	Feint Attack	Dark	Physical	60	—	20	Normal
1	Bide	Normal	Physical	—	—	10	Self
5	Mud-Slap	Ground	Special	20	100	10	Normal
8	Bulldoze	Ground	Physical	60	100	20	Adjacent
12	Sand Tomb	Ground	Physical	35	85	15	Normal
15	Rock Slide	Rock	Physical	75	90	10	Many Others
19	Supersonic	Normal	Status	—	55	20	Normal
22	Screech	Normal	Status	—	85	40	Normal
26	Earth Power	Ground	Special	90	100	10	Normal
29	Bug Buzz	Bug	Special	90	100	10	Normal
33	Earthquake	Ground	Physical	100	100	10	Adjacent
35	Dragon Breath	Dragon	Special	60	100	20	Normal
36	Sandstorm	Rock	Status	—	—	10	Both Sides
40	Uproar	Normal	Special	90	100	10	1 Random
43	Hyper Beam	Normal	Special	150	90	5	Normal
47	Boomburst	Normal	Special	140	100	10	Adjacent

TM & HM MOVES

No.	Name	Type	Kind	Pow.	Acc.	PP	Range
TM06	Toxic	Poison	Status	—	90	10	Normal
TM10	Hidden Power	Normal	Special	60	100	15	Normal
TM11	Sunny Day	Fire	Status	—	—	5	Both Sides
TM15	Hyper Beam	Normal	Special	150	90	5	Normal
TM17	Protect	Normal	Status	—	—	10	Self
TM19	Roost	Flying	Status	—	—	10	Self
TM21	Frustration	Normal	Physical	—	100	20	Normal
TM22	Solar Beam	Grass	Special	120	100	10	Normal
TM26	Earthquake	Ground	Physical	100	100	10	Adjacent
TM27	Return	Normal	Physical	—	100	20	Normal
TM28	Dig	Ground	Physical	80	100	10	Normal
TM32	Double Team	Normal	Status	—	—	15	Self
TM37	Sandstorm	Rock	Status	—	—	10	Both Sides
TM39	Rock Tomb	Rock	Physical	60	95	15	Normal
TM42	Facade	Normal	Physical	70	100	20	Normal
TM44	Rest	Psychic	Status	—	—	10	Self
TM45	Attract	Normal	Status	—	100	15	Normal
TM48	Round	Normal	Special	60	100	15	Normal
TM51	Steel Wing	Steel	Physical	70	90	25	Normal
TM76	Struggle Bug	Bug	Special	50	100	20	Many Others
TM78	Bulldoze	Ground	Physical	60	100	20	Adjacent
TM80	Rock Slide	Rock	Physical	75	90	10	Many Others
TM87	Swagger	Normal	Status	—	90	15	Normal
TM88	Sleep Talk	Normal	Status	—	—	10	Self
TM89	U-turn	Bug	Physical	70	100	20	Normal
TM90	Substitute	Normal	Status	—	—	10	Self
TM94	Secret Power	Normal	Physical	70	100	20	Normal
TM100	Confide	Normal	Status	—	—	20	Normal
HM02	Fly	Flying	Physical	90	95	15	Normal
HM04	Strength	Normal	Physical	80	100	15	Normal
HM06	Rock Smash	Fighting	Physical	40	100	15	Normal

MOVES LEARNED IN EXCHANGE FOR BP

Name	Type	Kind	Pow.	Acc.	PP	Range
Bug Bite	Bug	Physical	60	100	20	Normal
Signal Beam	Bug	Special	75	100	15	Normal
Uproar	Normal	Special	90	100	10	1 Random
Earth Power	Ground	Special	90	100	10	Normal
Superpower	Fighting	Physical	120	100	5	Normal
Dragon Pulse	Dragon	Special	85	100	10	Normal
Snore	Normal	Special	50	100	15	Normal
Heat Wave	Fire	Special	95	90	10	Many Others
Tailwind	Flying	Status	—	—	15	Your Side
Giga Drain	Grass	Special	75	100	10	Normal
Outrage	Dragon	Physical	120	100	10	1 Random

MOVES TAUGHT BY PEOPLE

Name	Type	Kind	Pow.	Acc.	PP	Range
Draco Meteor	Dragon	Special	130	90	5	Normal

National Pokédex **330** Hoenn Pokédex **123**

Flygon

Mystic Pokémon

Ground | Dragon

HEIGHT: 6'07" WEIGHT: 108.8 lbs.

Same form for ♂ / ♀

Ω Flygon is nicknamed "the elemental spirit of the desert." Because its flapping wings whip up a cloud of sand, this Pokémon is always enveloped in a sandstorm while flying.

α Flygon whips up a sandstorm by flapping its wings. The wings create a series of notes that sound like singing. Because the "singing" is the only thing that can be heard in a sandstorm, this Pokémon is said to be the desert spirit.

ABILITY
Levitate

HIDDEN ABILITY
—

EGG GROUPS
Bug

STAT GROWTH RATES

HP	■■■
Attack	■■■■■
Defense	■■■■
Sp. Atk	■■■■
Sp. Def	■■■
Speed	■■■■■

ITEMS SOMETIMES HELD BY WILD POKÉMON
—

EVOLUTION

Trapinch → Lv. 35 → Vibrava → Lv. 45 → Flygon

MAIN WAY TO REGISTER IN THE NATIONAL POKÉDEX

Level up Vibrava to Lv. 45.

Damage taken in normal battles

Type		Type	
Normal	×1	Flying	×1
Fire	×0.5	Psychic	×1
Water	×1	Bug	×1
Grass	×1	Rock	×0.5
Electric	×0	Ghost	×1
Ice	×4	Dragon	×2
Fighting	×1	Dark	×1
Poison	×0.5	Steel	×1
Ground	×1	Fairy	×2

Damage taken in Inverse battles

Type		Type	
Normal	×1	Flying	×1
Fire	×2	Psychic	×1
Water	×1	Bug	×1
Grass	×1	Rock	×2
Electric	×4	Ghost	×1
Ice	×0.25	Dragon	×0.5
Fighting	×1	Dark	×1
Poison	×2	Steel	×1
Ground	×1	Fairy	×0.5

Can be used in
Inverse Battle
Battle Institute
Battle Maison
Random Matchup (Free Battle)
Random Matchup (Others)

LEVEL-UP MOVES

Lv.	Name	Type	Kind	Pow.	Acc.	PP	Range
1	Sand Attack	Ground	Status	—	100	15	Normal
1	Sonic Boom	Normal	Special	—	90	20	Normal
1	Feint Attack	Dark	Physical	60	—	20	Normal
1	Bide	Normal	Physical	—	—	10	Self
5	Mud-Slap	Ground	Special	20	100	10	Normal
8	Bulldoze	Ground	Physical	60	100	20	Adjacent
12	Sand Tomb	Ground	Physical	35	85	15	Normal
15	Rock Slide	Rock	Physical	75	90	10	Many Others
19	Supersonic	Normal	Status	—	55	20	Normal
22	Screech	Normal	Status	—	85	40	Normal
26	Earth Power	Ground	Special	90	100	10	Normal
29	Dragon Tail	Dragon	Physical	60	90	10	Normal
33	Earthquake	Ground	Physical	100	100	10	Adjacent
35	Dragon Breath	Dragon	Special	60	100	20	Normal
36	Sandstorm	Rock	Status	—	—	10	Both Sides
40	Uproar	Normal	Special	90	100	10	1 Random
43	Hyper Beam	Normal	Special	150	90	5	Normal
45	Dragon Claw	Dragon	Physical	80	100	15	Normal
47	Dragon Rush	Dragon	Physical	100	75	10	Normal

TM & HM MOVES

No.	Name	Type	Kind	Pow.	Acc.	PP	Range
TM01	Hone Claws	Dark	Status	—	—	15	Self
TM02	Dragon Claw	Dragon	Physical	80	100	15	Normal
TM06	Toxic	Poison	Status	—	90	10	Normal
TM10	Hidden Power	Normal	Special	60	100	15	Normal
TM11	Sunny Day	Fire	Status	—	—	5	Both Sides
TM15	Hyper Beam	Normal	Special	150	90	5	Normal
TM17	Protect	Normal	Status	—	—	10	Self
TM19	Roost	Flying	Status	—	—	10	Self
TM21	Frustration	Normal	Physical	—	100	20	Normal
TM22	Solar Beam	Grass	Special	120	100	10	Normal
TM26	Earthquake	Ground	Physical	100	100	10	Adjacent
TM27	Return	Normal	Physical	—	100	20	Normal
TM28	Dig	Ground	Physical	80	100	10	Normal
TM32	Double Team	Normal	Status	—	—	15	Self
TM35	Flamethrower	Fire	Special	90	100	15	Normal
TM37	Sandstorm	Rock	Status	—	—	10	Both Sides
TM38	Fire Blast	Fire	Special	110	85	5	Normal
TM39	Rock Tomb	Rock	Physical	60	95	15	Normal
TM40	Aerial Ace	Flying	Physical	60	—	20	Normal
TM42	Facade	Normal	Physical	70	100	20	Normal
TM44	Rest	Psychic	Status	—	—	10	Self
TM45	Attract	Normal	Status	—	100	15	Normal
TM48	Round	Normal	Special	60	100	15	Normal
TM51	Steel Wing	Steel	Physical	70	90	25	Normal
TM59	Incinerate	Fire	Special	60	100	15	Many Others
TM68	Giga Impact	Normal	Physical	150	90	5	Normal
TM71	Stone Edge	Rock	Physical	100	80	5	Normal
TM76	Struggle Bug	Bug	Special	50	100	20	Many Others
TM78	Bulldoze	Ground	Physical	60	100	20	Adjacent
TM80	Rock Slide	Rock	Physical	75	90	10	Many Others
TM82	Dragon Tail	Dragon	Physical	60	90	10	Normal
TM87	Swagger	Normal	Status	—	90	15	Normal
TM88	Sleep Talk	Normal	Status	—	—	10	Self
TM89	U-turn	Bug	Physical	70	100	20	Normal
TM90	Substitute	Normal	Status	—	—	10	Self
TM94	Secret Power	Normal	Physical	70	100	20	Normal
TM98	Power-Up Punch	Fighting	Physical	40	100	20	Normal
TM100	Confide	Normal	Status	—	—	20	Normal
HM02	Fly	Flying	Physical	90	95	15	Normal
HM04	Strength	Normal	Physical	80	100	15	Normal
HM06	Rock Smash	Fighting	Physical	40	100	15	Normal

MOVES LEARNED IN EXCHANGE FOR BP

Name	Type	Kind	Pow.	Acc.	PP	Range
Bug Bite	Bug	Physical	60	100	20	Normal
Signal Beam	Bug	Special	75	100	15	Normal
Uproar	Normal	Special	90	100	10	1 Random
Thunder Punch	Electric	Physical	75	100	15	Normal
Fire Punch	Fire	Physical	75	100	15	Normal
Earth Power	Ground	Special	90	100	10	Normal
Superpower	Fighting	Physical	120	100	5	Normal
Dragon Pulse	Dragon	Special	85	100	10	Normal
Iron Tail	Steel	Physical	100	75	15	Normal
Snore	Normal	Special	50	100	15	Normal
Heat Wave	Fire	Special	95	90	10	Many Others
Tailwind	Flying	Status	—	—	15	Your Side
Giga Drain	Grass	Special	75	100	10	Normal
Outrage	Dragon	Physical	120	100	10	1 Random

MOVES TAUGHT BY PEOPLE

Name	Type	Kind	Pow.	Acc.	PP	Range
Draco Meteor	Dragon	Special	130	90	5	Normal

National Pokédex **331** Hoenn Pokédex **124**

Cacnea

Cactus Pokémon

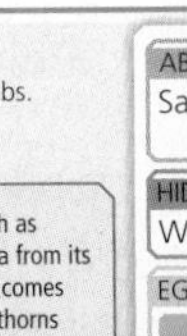

Grass

HEIGHT: 1'04" WEIGHT: 113.1 lbs.

Same form for ♂ / ♀

Ω Cacnea lives in arid locations such as deserts. It releases a strong aroma from its flower to attract prey. When prey comes near, this Pokémon shoots sharp thorns from its body to bring the victim down.

α The more arid and harsh the environment, the more pretty and fragrant a flower Cacnea grows. This Pokémon battles by wildly swinging its thorny arms.

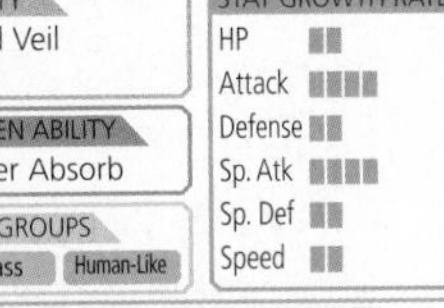

ABILITY
Sand Veil

HIDDEN ABILITY
Water Absorb

EGG GROUPS
Grass | Human-Like

STAT GROWTH RATES

HP	■■
Attack	■■■■
Defense	■■
Sp. Atk	■■■■
Sp. Def	■■
Speed	■■

ITEMS SOMETIMES HELD BY WILD POKÉMON
Sticky Barb

EVOLUTION

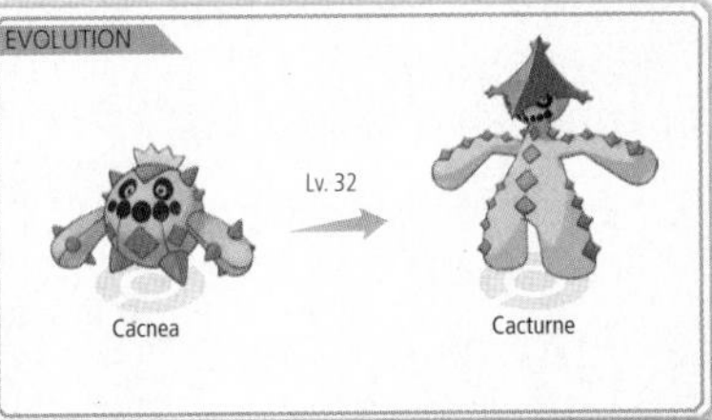

Cacnea → Lv. 32 → Cacturne

MAIN WAY TO REGISTER IN THE NATIONAL POKÉDEX

Catch in the desert on Route 111.

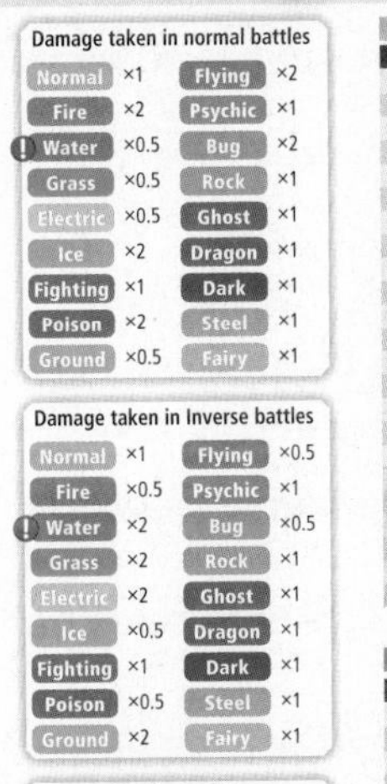

Damage taken in normal battles

Type		Type	
Normal	×1	Flying	×2
Fire	×2	Psychic	×1
Water	×0.5	Bug	×2
Grass	×0.5	Rock	×1
Electric	×0.5	Ghost	×1
Ice	×2	Dragon	×1
Fighting	×1	Dark	×1
Poison	×2	Steel	×1
Ground	×0.5	Fairy	×1

Damage taken in Inverse battles

Type		Type	
Normal	×1	Flying	×0.5
Fire	×0.5	Psychic	×1
Water	×2	Bug	×0.5
Grass	×2	Rock	×1
Electric	×2	Ghost	×1
Ice	×0.5	Dragon	×1
Fighting	×1	Dark	×1
Poison	×0.5	Steel	×1
Ground	×2	Fairy	×1

Can be used in
Inverse Battle
Battle Institute
Battle Maison
Random Matchup (Free Battle)
Random Matchup (Others)

LEVEL-UP MOVES

Lv.	Name	Type	Kind	Pow.	Acc.	PP	Range
1	Poison Sting	Poison	Physical	15	100	35	Normal
1	Leer	Normal	Status	—	100	30	Many Others
4	Absorb	Grass	Special	20	100	25	Normal
7	Growth	Normal	Status	—	—	20	Self
10	Leech Seed	Grass	Status	—	90	10	Normal
13	Sand Attack	Ground	Status	—	100	15	Normal
16	Needle Arm	Grass	Physical	60	100	15	Normal
19	Feint Attack	Dark	Physical	60	—	20	Normal
22	Ingrain	Grass	Status	—	—	20	Self
26	Payback	Dark	Physical	50	100	10	Normal
30	Spikes	Ground	Status	—	—	20	Other Side
34	Sucker Punch	Dark	Physical	80	100	5	Normal
38	Pin Missile	Bug	Physical	25	95	20	Normal
42	Energy Ball	Grass	Special	90	100	10	Normal
46	Cotton Spore	Grass	Status	—	100	40	Many Others
50	Sandstorm	Rock	Status	—	—	10	Both Sides
54	Destiny Bond	Ghost	Status	—	—	5	Self

TM & HM MOVES

No.	Name	Type	Kind	Pow.	Acc.	PP	Range
TM06	Toxic	Poison	Status	—	90	10	Normal
TM09	Venoshock	Poison	Special	65	100	10	Normal
TM10	Hidden Power	Normal	Special	60	100	15	Normal
TM11	Sunny Day	Fire	Status	—	—	5	Both Sides
TM17	Protect	Normal	Status	—	—	10	Self
TM21	Frustration	Normal	Physical	—	100	20	Normal
TM22	Solar Beam	Grass	Special	120	100	10	Normal
TM27	Return	Normal	Physical	—	100	20	Normal
TM31	Brick Break	Fighting	Physical	75	100	15	Normal
TM32	Double Team	Normal	Status	—	—	15	Self
TM37	Sandstorm	Rock	Status	—	—	10	Both Sides
TM42	Facade	Normal	Physical	70	100	20	Normal
TM44	Rest	Psychic	Status	—	—	10	Self
TM45	Attract	Normal	Status	—	100	15	Normal
TM48	Round	Normal	Special	60	100	15	Normal
TM53	Energy Ball	Grass	Special	90	100	10	Normal
TM56	Fling	Dark	Physical	—	100	10	Normal
TM66	Payback	Dark	Physical	50	100	10	Normal
TM70	Flash	Normal	Status	—	100	20	Normal
TM75	Swords Dance	Normal	Status	—	—	20	Self
TM84	Poison Jab	Poison	Physical	80	100	20	Normal
TM86	Grass Knot	Grass	Special	—	100	20	Normal
TM87	Swagger	Normal	Status	—	90	15	Normal
TM88	Sleep Talk	Normal	Status	—	—	10	Self
TM90	Substitute	Normal	Status	—	—	10	Self
TM94	Secret Power	Normal	Physical	70	100	20	Normal
TM96	Nature Power	Normal	Status	—	—	20	Normal
TM97	Dark Pulse	Dark	Special	80	100	15	Normal
TM98	Power-Up Punch	Fighting	Physical	40	100	20	Normal
TM100	Confide	Normal	Status	—	—	20	Normal
HM01	Cut	Normal	Physical	50	95	30	Normal

MOVES LEARNED IN EXCHANGE FOR BP

Name	Type	Kind	Pow.	Acc.	PP	Range
Seed Bomb	Grass	Physical	80	100	15	Normal
Low Kick	Fighting	Physical	—	100	20	Normal
Thunder Punch	Electric	Physical	75	100	15	Normal
Block	Normal	Status	—	—	5	Normal
Snore	Normal	Special	50	100	15	Normal
Synthesis	Grass	Status	—	—	5	Self
Role Play	Psychic	Status	—	—	10	Normal
Giga Drain	Grass	Special	75	100	10	Normal
Drain Punch	Fighting	Physical	75	100	10	Normal
Focus Punch	Fighting	Physical	150	100	20	Normal
Worry Seed	Grass	Status	—	100	10	Normal
Spite	Ghost	Status	—	100	10	Normal

MOVES TAUGHT BY PEOPLE

Name	Type	Kind	Pow.	Acc.	PP	Range

EGG MOVES

Name	Type	Kind	Pow.	Acc.	PP	Range
Grass Whistle	Grass	Status	—	55	15	Normal
Acid	Poison	Special	40	100	30	Many Others
Teeter Dance	Normal	Status	—	100	20	Adjacent
Dynamic Punch	Fighting	Physical	100	50	5	Normal
Counter	Fighting	Physical	—	100	20	Varies
Low Kick	Fighting	Physical	—	100	20	Normal
Smelling Salts	Normal	Physical	70	100	10	Normal
Magical Leaf	Grass	Special	60	—	20	Normal
Seed Bomb	Grass	Physical	80	100	15	Normal
Nasty Plot	Dark	Status	—	—	20	Self
Disable	Normal	Status	—	100	20	Normal
Block	Normal	Status	—	—	5	Normal
Worry Seed	Grass	Status	—	100	10	Normal
Switcheroo	Dark	Status	—	100	10	Normal
Fell Stinger	Bug	Physical	30	100	25	Normal
Belch	Poison	Special	120	90	10	Normal
Rototiller	Ground	Status	—	—	10	Adjacent

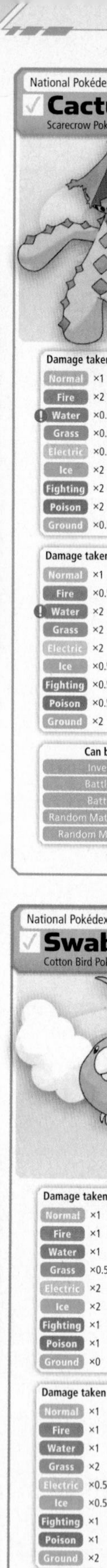

National Pokédex **332** Hoenn Pokédex **125**

Cacturne

Scarecrow Pokémon

Grass | Dark

HEIGHT: 4'03" WEIGHT: 170.6 lbs.

The male has four small diamonds on its front. The female has two small diamonds and one large diamond on its front.

♂ ♀

Ω During the daytime, Cacturne remains unmoving so that it does not lose any moisture to the harsh desert sun. This Pokémon becomes active at night when the temperature drops.

α If a traveler is going through a desert in the thick of night, Cacturne will follow in a ragtag group. The Pokémon are biding their time, waiting for the traveler to tire and become incapable of moving.

ABILITY
Sand Veil

HIDDEN ABILITY
Water Absorb

EGG GROUPS
Grass | Human-Like

STAT GROWTH RATES
HP
Attack
Defense
Sp. Atk
Sp. Def
Speed

ITEMS SOMETIMES HELD BY WILD POKÉMON
—

EVOLUTION
Cacnea → Lv. 32 → Cacturne

MAIN WAY TO REGISTER IN THE NATIONAL POKÉDEX

Level up Cacnea to Lv. 32.

Damage taken in normal battles

Normal	×1	Flying	×2
Fire	×2	Psychic	×0
! Water	×0.5	Bug	×4
Grass	×0.5	Rock	×1
Electric	×0.5	Ghost	×0.5
Ice	×2	Dragon	×1
Fighting	×2	Dark	×0.5
Poison	×2	Steel	×1
Ground	×0.5	Fairy	×2

Damage taken in Inverse battles

Normal	×1	Flying	×0.5
Fire	×0.5	Psychic	×2
! Water	×2	Bug	×0.25
Grass	×2	Rock	×1
Electric	×2	Ghost	×2
Ice	×0.5	Dragon	×1
Fighting	×0.5	Dark	×2
Poison	×0.5	Steel	×1
Ground	×2	Fairy	×0.5

Can be used in
- Inverse Battle
- Battle Institute
- Battle Maison
- Random Matchup (Free Battle)
- Random Matchup (Others)

LEVEL-UP MOVES

Lv.	Name	Type	Kind	Pow.	Acc.	PP	Range
1	Destiny Bond	Ghost	Status	—	—	5	Self
1	Revenge	Fighting	Physical	60	100	10	Normal
1	Poison Sting	Poison	Physical	15	100	35	Normal
1	Leer	Normal	Status	—	100	30	Many Others
1	Absorb	Grass	Special	20	100	25	Normal
1	Growth	Normal	Status	—	—	20	Self
4	Absorb	Grass	Special	20	100	25	Normal
7	Growth	Normal	Status	—	—	20	Self
10	Leech Seed	Grass	Status	—	90	10	Normal
13	Sand Attack	Ground	Status	—	100	15	Normal
16	Needle Arm	Grass	Physical	60	100	15	Normal
19	Feint Attack	Dark	Physical	60	—	20	Normal
22	Ingrain	Grass	Status	—	—	20	Self
26	Payback	Dark	Physical	50	100	10	Normal
30	Spikes	Ground	Status	—	—	20	Other Side
32	Spiky Shield	Grass	Status	—	—	10	Self
35	Sucker Punch	Dark	Physical	80	100	5	Normal
38	Pin Missile	Bug	Physical	25	95	20	Normal
44	Energy Ball	Grass	Special	90	100	10	Normal
49	Cotton Spore	Grass	Status	—	100	40	Many Others
54	Sandstorm	Rock	Status	—	—	10	Both Sides
59	Destiny Bond	Ghost	Status	—	—	5	Self

TM & HM MOVES

No.	Name	Type	Kind	Pow.	Acc.	PP	Range
TM06	Toxic	Poison	Status	—	90	10	Normal
TM09	Venoshock	Poison	Special	65	100	10	Normal
TM10	Hidden Power	Normal	Special	60	100	15	Normal
TM11	Sunny Day	Fire	Status	—	—	5	Both Sides
TM15	Hyper Beam	Normal	Special	150	90	5	Normal
TM17	Protect	Normal	Status	—	—	10	Self
TM21	Frustration	Normal	Physical	—	100	20	Normal
TM22	Solar Beam	Grass	Special	120	100	10	Normal
TM27	Return	Normal	Physical	—	100	20	Normal
TM31	Brick Break	Fighting	Physical	75	100	15	Normal
TM32	Double Team	Normal	Status	—	—	15	Self
TM37	Sandstorm	Rock	Status	—	—	10	Both Sides
TM42	Facade	Normal	Physical	70	100	20	Normal
TM44	Rest	Psychic	Status	—	—	10	Self
TM45	Attract	Normal	Status	—	100	15	Normal
TM48	Round	Normal	Special	60	100	15	Normal
TM52	Focus Blast	Fighting	Special	120	70	5	Normal
TM53	Energy Ball	Grass	Special	90	100	10	Normal
TM56	Fling	Dark	Physical	—	100	10	Normal
TM63	Embargo	Dark	Status	—	100	15	Normal
TM66	Payback	Dark	Physical	50	100	10	Normal
TM67	Retaliate	Normal	Physical	70	100	5	Normal
TM68	Giga Impact	Normal	Physical	150	90	5	Normal
TM70	Flash	Normal	Status	—	100	20	Normal
TM75	Swords Dance	Normal	Status	—	—	20	Self
TM84	Poison Jab	Poison	Physical	80	100	20	Normal
TM86	Grass Knot	Grass	Special	—	100	20	Normal
TM87	Swagger	Normal	Status	—	90	15	Normal
TM88	Sleep Talk	Normal	Status	—	—	10	Self
TM90	Substitute	Normal	Status	—	—	10	Self
TM94	Secret Power	Normal	Physical	70	100	20	Normal
TM96	Nature Power	Normal	Status	—	—	20	Normal
TM97	Dark Pulse	Dark	Special	80	100	15	Normal
TM98	Power-Up Punch	Fighting	Physical	40	100	20	Normal
TM100	Confide	Normal	Status	—	—	20	Normal
HM01	Cut	Normal	Physical	50	95	30	Normal
HM04	Strength	Normal	Physical	80	100	15	Normal

MOVES LEARNED IN EXCHANGE FOR BP

Name	Type	Kind	Pow.	Acc.	PP	Range
Seed Bomb	Grass	Physical	80	100	15	Normal
Low Kick	Fighting	Physical	—	100	20	Normal
Thunder Punch	Electric	Physical	75	100	15	Normal
Block	Normal	Status	—	—	5	Normal
Foul Play	Dark	Physical	95	100	15	Normal
Superpower	Fighting	Physical	120	100	5	Normal
Snore	Normal	Special	50	100	15	Normal
Synthesis	Grass	Status	—	—	5	Self
Role Play	Psychic	Status	—	—	10	Normal
Giga Drain	Grass	Special	75	100	10	Normal
Drain Punch	Fighting	Physical	75	100	10	Normal
Focus Punch	Fighting	Physical	150	100	20	Normal
Worry Seed	Grass	Status	—	100	10	Normal
Spite	Ghost	Status	—	100	10	Normal

MOVES TAUGHT BY PEOPLE

Name	Type	Kind	Pow.	Acc.	PP	Range

National Pokédex **333** Hoenn Pokédex **126**

Swablu

Cotton Bird Pokémon

Normal | Flying

HEIGHT: 1'04" WEIGHT: 2.6 lbs.

Same form for ♂ / ♀

Ω Swablu has light and fluffy wings that are like cottony clouds. This Pokémon is not frightened of people. It lands on the heads of people and sits there like a cotton-fluff hat.

α Swablu loves to make things clean. If it spots something dirty, it will wipe and polish it with its cottony wings. If its wings become dirty, this Pokémon finds a stream and showers itself.

ABILITY
Natural Cure

HIDDEN ABILITY
Cloud Nine

EGG GROUPS
Flying | Dragon

STAT GROWTH RATES
HP
Attack
Defense
Sp. Atk
Sp. Def
Speed

ITEMS SOMETIMES HELD BY WILD POKÉMON
—

EVOLUTION
Swablu → Lv. 35 → Altaria

MAIN WAY TO REGISTER IN THE NATIONAL POKÉDEX

Catch on Route 114.

Damage taken in normal battles

Normal	×1	Flying	×1
Fire	×1	Psychic	×1
Water	×1	Bug	×0.5
Grass	×0.5	Rock	×2
Electric	×2	Ghost	×0
Ice	×2	Dragon	×1
Fighting	×1	Dark	×1
Poison	×1	Steel	×1
Ground	×0	Fairy	×1

Damage taken in Inverse battles

Normal	×1	Flying	×1
Fire	×1	Psychic	×1
Water	×1	Bug	×2
Grass	×2	Rock	×0.5
Electric	×0.5	Ghost	×2
Ice	×0.5	Dragon	×1
Fighting	×1	Dark	×1
Poison	×1	Steel	×1
Ground	×2	Fairy	×1

Can be used in
- Inverse Battle
- Battle Institute
- Battle Maison
- Random Matchup (Free Battle)
- Random Matchup (Others)

LEVEL-UP MOVES

Lv.	Name	Type	Kind	Pow.	Acc.	PP	Range
1	Peck	Flying	Physical	35	100	35	Normal
1	Growl	Normal	Status	—	100	40	Many Others
3	Astonish	Ghost	Physical	30	100	15	Normal
5	Sing	Normal	Status	—	55	15	Normal
7	Fury Attack	Normal	Physical	15	85	20	Normal
9	Safeguard	Normal	Status	—	—	25	Your Side
11	Disarming Voice	Fairy	Special	40	—	15	Many Others
14	Mist	Ice	Status	—	—	30	Your Side
17	Round	Normal	Special	60	100	15	Normal
20	Natural Gift	Normal	Physical	—	100	15	Normal
23	Take Down	Normal	Physical	90	85	20	Normal
26	Refresh	Normal	Status	—	—	20	Self
30	Mirror Move	Flying	Status	—	—	20	Normal
34	Cotton Guard	Grass	Status	—	—	10	Self
38	Dragon Pulse	Dragon	Special	85	100	10	Normal
42	Perish Song	Normal	Status	—	—	5	Adjacent
46	Moonblast	Fairy	Special	95	100	15	Normal

TM & HM MOVES

No.	Name	Type	Kind	Pow.	Acc.	PP	Range
TM06	Toxic	Poison	Status	—	90	10	Normal
TM10	Hidden Power	Normal	Special	60	100	15	Normal
TM11	Sunny Day	Fire	Status	—	—	5	Both Sides
TM13	Ice Beam	Ice	Special	90	100	10	Normal
TM17	Protect	Normal	Status	—	—	10	Self
TM18	Rain Dance	Water	Status	—	—	5	Both Sides
TM19	Roost	Flying	Status	—	—	10	Self
TM20	Safeguard	Normal	Status	—	—	25	Your Side
TM21	Frustration	Normal	Physical	—	100	20	Normal
TM22	Solar Beam	Grass	Special	120	100	10	Normal
TM27	Return	Normal	Physical	—	100	20	Normal
TM32	Double Team	Normal	Status	—	—	15	Self
TM40	Aerial Ace	Flying	Physical	60	—	20	Normal
TM42	Facade	Normal	Physical	70	100	20	Normal
TM44	Rest	Psychic	Status	—	—	10	Self
TM45	Attract	Normal	Status	—	100	15	Normal
TM46	Thief	Dark	Physical	60	100	25	Normal
TM48	Round	Normal	Special	60	100	15	Normal
TM49	Echoed Voice	Normal	Special	40	100	15	Normal
TM51	Steel Wing	Steel	Physical	70	90	25	Normal
TM77	Psych Up	Normal	Status	—	—	10	Normal
TM85	Dream Eater	Psychic	Special	100	100	15	Normal
TM87	Swagger	Normal	Status	—	90	15	Normal
TM88	Sleep Talk	Normal	Status	—	—	10	Self
TM90	Substitute	Normal	Status	—	—	10	Self
TM94	Secret Power	Normal	Physical	70	100	20	Normal
TM99	Dazzling Gleam	Fairy	Special	80	100	10	Many Others
TM100	Confide	Normal	Status	—	—	20	Normal
HM02	Fly	Flying	Physical	90	95	15	Normal

MOVES LEARNED IN EXCHANGE FOR BP

Name	Type	Kind	Pow.	Acc.	PP	Range
Uproar	Normal	Special	90	100	10	1 Random
Dragon Pulse	Dragon	Special	85	100	10	Normal
Hyper Voice	Normal	Special	90	100	10	Many Others
Snore	Normal	Special	50	100	15	Normal
Heat Wave	Fire	Special	95	90	10	Many Others
Heal Bell	Normal	Status	—	—	5	Your Party
Tailwind	Flying	Status	—	—	15	Your Side
Sky Attack	Flying	Physical	140	90	5	Normal
Outrage	Dragon	Physical	120	100	10	1 Random

MOVES TAUGHT BY PEOPLE

Name	Type	Kind	Pow.	Acc.	PP	Range

EGG MOVES

Name	Type	Kind	Pow.	Acc.	PP	Range
Agility	Psychic	Status	—	—	30	Self
Haze	Ice	Status	—	—	30	Both Sides
Pursuit	Dark	Physical	40	100	20	Normal
Rage	Normal	Physical	20	100	20	Normal
Feather Dance	Flying	Status	—	100	15	Normal
Dragon Rush	Dragon	Physical	100	75	10	Normal
Power Swap	Psychic	Status	—	—	10	Normal
Roost	Flying	Status	—	—	10	Self
Hyper Voice	Normal	Special	90	100	10	Many Others
Steel Wing	Steel	Physical	70	90	25	Normal

National Pokédex **334** Hoenn Pokédex **127**

Altaria

Humming Pokémon

Dragon | Flying

HEIGHT: 3'07" WEIGHT: 45.4 lbs.

Same form for ♂ / ♀

Ω Altaria dances and wheels through the sky among billowing, cotton-like clouds. By singing melodies in its crystal-clear voice, this Pokémon makes its listeners experience dreamy wonderment.

α Altaria sings in a gorgeous soprano. Its wings are like cotton clouds. This Pokémon catches updrafts with its buoyant wings and soars way up into the wild blue yonder.

ABILITY
Natural Cure

HIDDEN ABILITY
Cloud Nine

EGG GROUPS
Flying | Dragon

STAT GROWTH RATES
HP
Attack
Defense
Sp. Atk
Sp. Def
Speed

ITEMS SOMETIMES HELD BY WILD POKÉMON
—

EVOLUTION

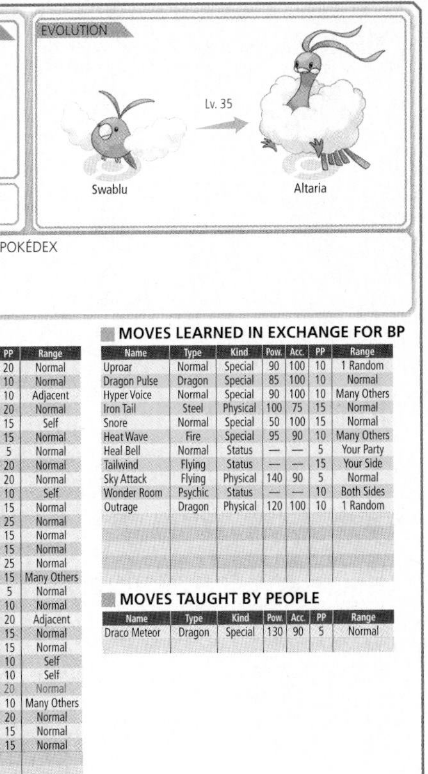

MAIN WAY TO REGISTER IN THE NATIONAL POKÉDEX

Level up Swablu to Lv. 35.

Damage taken in normal battles

Type		Type	
Normal	×1	Flying	×1
Fire	×0.5	Psychic	×1
Water	×0.5	Bug	×0.5
Grass	×0.25	Rock	×2
Electric	×1	Ghost	×1
Ice	×4	Dragon	×2
Fighting	×0.5	Dark	×1
Poison	×1	Steel	×1
Ground	×0	Fairy	×2

Damage taken in Inverse battles

Type		Type	
Normal	×1	Flying	×1
Fire	×2	Psychic	×1
Water	×2	Bug	×2
Grass	×4	Rock	×0.5
Electric	×1	Ghost	×1
Ice	×0.25	Dragon	×0.5
Fighting	×2	Dark	×1
Poison	×1	Steel	×1
Ground	×2	Fairy	×0.5

Can be used in
Inverse Battle
Battle Institute
Battle Maison
Random Matchup (Free Battle)
Random Matchup (Others)

LEVEL-UP MOVES

Lv.	Name	Type	Kind	Pow.	Acc.	PP	Range
1	Sky Attack	Flying	Physical	140	90	5	Normal
1	Pluck	Flying	Physical	60	100	20	Normal
1	Peck	Flying	Physical	35	100	35	Normal
1	Growl	Normal	Status	—	100	40	Many Others
1	Astonish	Ghost	Physical	30	100	15	Normal
1	Sing	Normal	Status	—	55	15	Normal
3	Astonish	Ghost	Physical	30	100	15	Normal
5	Sing	Normal	Status	—	55	15	Normal
7	Fury Attack	Normal	Physical	15	85	20	Normal
9	Safeguard	Normal	Status	—	—	25	Your Side
11	Disarming Voice	Fairy	Special	40	—	15	Many Others
14	Mist	Ice	Status	—	—	30	Your Side
17	Round	Normal	Special	60	100	15	Normal
20	Natural Gift	Normal	Physical	—	100	15	Normal
23	Take Down	Normal	Physical	90	85	20	Normal
26	Refresh	Normal	Status	—	—	20	Self
30	Dragon Dance	Dragon	Status	—	—	20	Self
34	Cotton Guard	Grass	Status	—	—	10	Self
35	Dragon Breath	Dragon	Special	60	100	20	Normal
40	Dragon Pulse	Dragon	Special	85	100	10	Normal
46	Perish Song	Normal	Status	—	—	5	Adjacent
52	Moonblast	Fairy	Special	95	100	15	Normal
59	Sky Attack	Flying	Physical	140	90	5	Normal

TM & HM MOVES

No.	Name	Type	Kind	Pow.	Acc.	PP	Range
TM01	Hone Claws	Dark	Status	—	—	15	Self
TM02	Dragon Claw	Dragon	Physical	80	100	15	Normal
TM05	Roar	Normal	Status	—	—	20	Normal
TM06	Toxic	Poison	Status	—	90	10	Normal
TM10	Hidden Power	Normal	Special	60	100	15	Normal
TM11	Sunny Day	Fire	Status	—	—	5	Both Sides
TM13	Ice Beam	Ice	Special	90	100	10	Normal
TM15	Hyper Beam	Normal	Special	150	90	5	Normal
TM17	Protect	Normal	Status	—	—	10	Self
TM18	Rain Dance	Water	Status	—	—	5	Both Sides
TM19	Roost	Flying	Status	—	—	10	Self
TM20	Safeguard	Normal	Status	—	—	25	Your Side
TM21	Frustration	Normal	Physical	—	100	20	Normal
TM22	Solar Beam	Grass	Special	120	100	10	Normal
TM26	Earthquake	Ground	Physical	100	100	10	Adjacent
TM27	Return	Normal	Physical	—	100	20	Normal
TM32	Double Team	Normal	Status	—	—	15	Self
TM35	Flamethrower	Fire	Special	90	100	15	Normal
TM38	Fire Blast	Fire	Special	110	85	5	Normal
TM40	Aerial Ace	Flying	Physical	60	—	20	Normal
TM42	Facade	Normal	Physical	70	100	20	Normal
TM44	Rest	Psychic	Status	—	—	10	Self
TM45	Attract	Normal	Status	—	100	15	Normal
TM46	Thief	Dark	Physical	60	100	25	Normal
TM48	Round	Normal	Special	60	100	15	Normal
TM49	Echoed Voice	Normal	Special	40	100	15	Normal
TM51	Steel Wing	Steel	Physical	70	90	25	Normal
TM59	Incinerate	Fire	Special	60	100	15	Many Others
TM68	Giga Impact	Normal	Physical	150	90	5	Normal
TM77	Psych Up	Normal	Status	—	—	10	Normal
TM78	Bulldoze	Ground	Physical	60	100	20	Adjacent
TM85	Dream Eater	Psychic	Special	100	100	15	Normal
TM87	Swagger	Normal	Status	—	90	15	Normal
TM88	Sleep Talk	Normal	Status	—	—	10	Self
TM90	Substitute	Normal	Status	—	—	10	Self
TM94	Secret Power	Normal	Physical	70	100	20	Normal
TM99	Dazzling Gleam	Fairy	Special	80	100	10	Many Others
TM100	Confide	Normal	Status	—	—	20	Normal
HM02	Fly	Flying	Physical	90	95	15	Normal
HM06	Rock Smash	Fighting	Physical	40	100	15	Normal

MOVES LEARNED IN EXCHANGE FOR BP

Name	Type	Kind	Pow.	Acc.	PP	Range
Uproar	Normal	Special	90	100	10	1 Random
Dragon Pulse	Dragon	Special	85	100	10	Normal
Hyper Voice	Normal	Special	90	100	10	Many Others
Iron Tail	Steel	Physical	100	75	15	Normal
Snore	Normal	Special	50	100	15	Normal
Heat Wave	Fire	Special	95	90	10	Many Others
Heal Bell	Normal	Status	—	—	5	Your Party
Tailwind	Flying	Status	—	—	15	Your Side
Sky Attack	Flying	Physical	140	90	5	Normal
Wonder Room	Psychic	Status	—	—	10	Both Sides
Outrage	Dragon	Physical	120	100	10	1 Random

MOVES TAUGHT BY PEOPLE

Name	Type	Kind	Pow.	Acc.	PP	Range
Draco Meteor	Dragon	Special	130	90	5	Normal

Mega Evolution

Mega Altaria

Humming Pokémon

Dragon | Fairy

HEIGHT: 4'11" WEIGHT: 45.4 lbs.

Same form for ♂ / ♀

REQUIRED MEGA STONE
Altarianite
Receive from a man in Lilycove City if you answer his question with "Altaria" and have an Altaria in your team

ABILITY
Pixilate

HIDDEN ABILITY
—

EGG GROUPS
—

STAT GROWTH RATES
HP
Attack
Defense
Sp. Atk
Sp. Def
Speed

Damage taken in normal battles

Type		Type	
Normal	×1	Flying	×1
Fire	×0.5	Psychic	×1
Water	×0.5	Bug	×0.5
Grass	×0.5	Rock	×1
Electric	×0.5	Ghost	×1
Ice	×2	Dragon	×0
Fighting	×0.5	Dark	×0.5
Poison	×2	Steel	×2
Ground	×1	Fairy	×2

Damage taken in Inverse battles

Type		Type	
Normal	×1	Flying	×1
Fire	×2	Psychic	×1
Water	×2	Bug	×2
Grass	×2	Rock	×1
Electric	×2	Ghost	×1
Ice	×0.5	Dragon	×1
Fighting	×2	Dark	×2
Poison	×0.5	Steel	×0.5
Ground	×1	Fairy	×0.5

Can be used in
Inverse Battle
Battle Institute
Battle Maison
Random Matchup (Free Battle)
Random Matchup (Others)

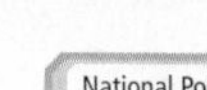

National Pokédex **335** Hoenn Pokédex **128**

Zangoose

Cat Ferret Pokémon

Normal

HEIGHT: 4'03" WEIGHT: 88.88 lbs.

Same form for ♂ / ♀

Ω Memories of battling its archrival Seviper are etched into every cell of Zangoose's body. This Pokémon adroitly dodges attacks with incredible agility.

α Zangoose usually stays on all fours, but when angered, it gets up on its hind legs and extends its claws. This Pokémon shares a bitter rivalry with Seviper that dates back over generations.

ABILITY
Immunity

HIDDEN ABILITY
Toxic Boost

EGG GROUPS
Field

STAT GROWTH RATES
HP ■■■
Attack ■■■■■■
Defense ■■■
Sp. Atk ■■■
Sp. Def ■■■
Speed ■■■■■

ITEMS SOMETIMES HELD BY WILD POKÉMON
Quick Claw

EVOLUTION
Does not evolve

MAIN WAYS TO REGISTER IN THE NATIONAL POKÉDEX
Ω Catch on Route 114.
α Bring it to your game using Link Trade or the GTS.

Damage taken in normal battles

Type		Type	
Normal	×1	Flying	×1
Fire	×1	Psychic	×1
Water	×1	Bug	×1
Grass	×1	Rock	×1
Electric	×1	Ghost	×0
Ice	×1	Dragon	×1
Fighting	×2	Dark	×1
Poison	×1	Steel	×1
Ground	×1	Fairy	×1

Damage taken in Inverse battles

Type		Type	
Normal	×1	Flying	×1
Fire	×1	Psychic	×1
Water	×1	Bug	×1
Grass	×1	Rock	×1
Electric	×1	Ghost	×2
Ice	×1	Dragon	×1
Fighting	×0.5	Dark	×1
Poison	×1	Steel	×1
Ground	×1	Fairy	×1

Can be used in
Inverse Battle
Battle Institute
Battle Maison
Random Matchup (Free Battle)
Random Matchup (Others)

LEVEL-UP MOVES

Lv.	Name	Type	Kind	Pow.	Acc.	PP	Range
1	Scratch	Normal	Physical	40	100	35	Normal
1	Leer	Normal	Status	—	100	30	Many Others
5	Quick Attack	Normal	Physical	40	100	30	Normal
8	Fury Cutter	Bug	Physical	40	95	20	Normal
12	Pursuit	Dark	Physical	40	100	20	Normal
15	Hone Claws	Dark	Status	—	—	15	Self
19	Slash	Normal	Physical	70	100	20	Normal
22	Revenge	Fighting	Physical	60	100	10	Normal
26	Crush Claw	Normal	Physical	75	95	10	Normal
29	False Swipe	Normal	Physical	40	100	40	Normal
33	Embargo	Dark	Status	—	100	15	Normal
36	Detect	Fighting	Status	—	—	5	Self
40	X-Scissor	Bug	Physical	80	100	15	Normal
43	Taunt	Dark	Status	—	100	20	Normal
47	Swords Dance	Normal	Status	—	—	20	Self
50	Close Combat	Fighting	Physical	120	100	5	Normal

TM & HM MOVES

No.	Name	Type	Kind	Pow.	Acc.	PP	Range
TM01	Hone Claws	Dark	Status	—	—	15	Self
TM05	Roar	Normal	Status	—	—	20	Normal
TM06	Toxic	Poison	Status	—	90	10	Normal
TM10	Hidden Power	Normal	Special	60	100	15	Normal
TM11	Sunny Day	Fire	Status	—	—	5	Both Sides
TM12	Taunt	Dark	Status	—	100	20	Normal
TM13	Ice Beam	Ice	Special	90	100	10	Normal
TM14	Blizzard	Ice	Special	110	70	5	Many Others
TM17	Protect	Normal	Status	—	—	10	Self
TM18	Rain Dance	Water	Status	—	—	5	Both Sides
TM21	Frustration	Normal	Physical	—	100	20	Normal
TM22	Solar Beam	Grass	Special	120	100	10	Normal
TM24	Thunderbolt	Electric	Special	90	100	15	Normal
TM25	Thunder	Electric	Special	110	70	10	Normal
TM27	Return	Normal	Physical	—	100	20	Normal
TM28	Dig	Ground	Physical	80	100	10	Normal
TM30	Shadow Ball	Ghost	Special	80	100	15	Normal
TM31	Brick Break	Fighting	Physical	75	100	15	Normal
TM32	Double Team	Normal	Status	—	—	15	Self
TM35	Flamethrower	Fire	Special	90	100	15	Normal
TM38	Fire Blast	Fire	Special	110	85	5	Normal
TM39	Rock Tomb	Rock	Physical	60	95	15	Normal
TM40	Aerial Ace	Flying	Physical	60	—	20	Normal
TM42	Facade	Normal	Physical	70	100	20	Normal
TM44	Rest	Psychic	Status	—	—	10	Self
TM45	Attract	Normal	Status	—	100	15	Normal
TM46	Thief	Dark	Physical	60	100	25	Normal
TM48	Round	Normal	Special	60	100	15	Normal
TM52	Focus Blast	Fighting	Special	120	70	5	Normal
TM54	False Swipe	Normal	Physical	40	100	40	Normal
TM56	Fling	Dark	Physical	—	100	10	Normal
TM59	Incinerate	Fire	Special	60	100	15	Many Others
TM63	Embargo	Dark	Status	—	100	15	Normal
TM65	Shadow Claw	Ghost	Physical	70	100	15	Normal
TM66	Payback	Dark	Physical	50	100	10	Normal
TM67	Retaliate	Normal	Physical	70	100	5	Normal
TM75	Swords Dance	Normal	Status	—	—	20	Self
TM80	Rock Slide	Rock	Physical	75	90	10	Many Others
TM81	X-Scissor	Bug	Physical	80	100	15	Normal
TM84	Poison Jab	Poison	Physical	80	100	20	Normal
TM87	Swagger	Normal	Status	—	90	15	Normal
TM88	Sleep Talk	Normal	Status	—	—	10	Self
TM90	Substitute	Normal	Status	—	—	10	Self
TM94	Secret Power	Normal	Physical	70	100	20	Normal
TM98	Power-Up Punch	Fighting	Physical	40	100	20	Normal
TM100	Confide	Normal	Status	—	—	20	Normal
HM04	Strength	Normal	Physical	80	100	15	Normal
HM06	Rock Smash	Fighting	Physical	40	100	15	Normal

MOVES LEARNED IN EXCHANGE FOR BP

Name	Type	Kind	Pow.	Acc.	PP	Range
Low Kick	Fighting	Physical	—	100	20	Normal
Thunder Punch	Electric	Physical	75	100	15	Normal
Fire Punch	Fire	Physical	75	100	15	Normal
Ice Punch	Ice	Physical	75	100	15	Normal
Last Resort	Normal	Physical	140	100	5	Normal
Icy Wind	Ice	Special	55	95	15	Many Others
Iron Tail	Steel	Physical	100	75	15	Normal
Snore	Normal	Special	50	100	15	Normal
Knock Off	Dark	Physical	65	100	20	Normal
Giga Drain	Grass	Special	75	100	10	Normal
Focus Punch	Fighting	Physical	150	100	20	Normal
Shock Wave	Electric	Special	60	—	20	Normal
Water Pulse	Water	Special	60	100	20	Normal
Endeavor	Normal	Physical	—	100	5	Normal

MOVES TAUGHT BY PEOPLE

Name	Type	Kind	Pow.	Acc.	PP	Range

EGG MOVES

Name	Type	Kind	Pow.	Acc.	PP	Range
Flail	Normal	Physical	—	100	15	Normal
Double Kick	Fighting	Physical	30	100	30	Normal
Razor Wind	Normal	Special	80	100	10	Many Others
Counter	Fighting	Physical	—	100	20	Varies
Curse	Ghost	Status	—	—	10	Varies
Fury Swipes	Normal	Physical	18	80	15	Normal
Night Slash	Dark	Physical	70	100	15	Normal
Metal Claw	Steel	Physical	50	95	35	Normal
Double Hit	Normal	Physical	35	90	10	Normal
Disable	Normal	Status	—	100	20	Normal
Iron Tail	Steel	Physical	100	75	15	Normal
Final Gambit	Fighting	Special	—	100	5	Normal
Feint	Normal	Physical	30	100	10	Normal
Quick Guard	Fighting	Status	—	—	15	Your Side

National Pokédex **336** Hoenn Pokédex **129**

Seviper

Fang Snake Pokémon

Poison

HEIGHT: 8'10" WEIGHT: 115.7 lbs.

Same form for ♂ / ♀

Ω Seviper shares a generations-long feud with Zangoose. The scars on its body are evidence of vicious battles. This Pokémon attacks using its sword-edged tail.

α Seviper's swordlike tail serves two purposes—it slashes foes and douses them with secreted poison. This Pokémon will not give up its long-running blood feud with Zangoose.

ABILITY
Shed Skin

HIDDEN ABILITY
Infiltrator

EGG GROUPS
Field Dragon

STAT GROWTH RATES
HP ■■■
Attack ■■■■■
Defense ■■■
Sp. Atk ■■■■■
Sp. Def ■■■
Speed ■■■■

ITEMS SOMETIMES HELD BY WILD POKÉMON
Shed Shell

EVOLUTION
Does not evolve

MAIN WAYS TO REGISTER IN THE NATIONAL POKÉDEX
Ω Bring it to your game using Link Trade or the GTS.
α Catch on Route 114.

Damage taken in normal battles

Type		Type	
Normal	×1	Flying	×1
Fire	×1	Psychic	×2
Water	×1	Bug	×0.5
Grass	×0.5	Rock	×1
Electric	×1	Ghost	×1
Ice	×1	Dragon	×1
Fighting	×0.5	Dark	×1
Poison	×0.5	Steel	×1
Ground	×2	Fairy	×0.5

Damage taken in Inverse battles

Type		Type	
Normal	×1	Flying	×1
Fire	×1	Psychic	×0.5
Water	×1	Bug	×2
Grass	×2	Rock	×1
Electric	×1	Ghost	×1
Ice	×1	Dragon	×1
Fighting	×2	Dark	×1
Poison	×2	Steel	×1
Ground	×0.5	Fairy	×2

Can be used in
Inverse Battle
Battle Institute
Battle Maison
Random Matchup (Free Battle)
Random Matchup (Others)

LEVEL-UP MOVES

Lv.	Name	Type	Kind	Pow.	Acc.	PP	Range
1	Wrap	Normal	Physical	15	90	20	Normal
1	Swagger	Normal	Status	—	90	15	Normal
4	Bite	Dark	Physical	60	100	25	Normal
7	Lick	Ghost	Physical	30	100	30	Normal
10	Poison Tail	Poison	Physical	50	100	25	Normal
13	Screech	Normal	Status	—	85	40	Normal
16	Venoshock	Poison	Special	65	100	10	Normal
19	Glare	Normal	Status	—	100	30	Normal
22	Poison Fang	Poison	Physical	50	100	15	Normal
25	Venom Drench	Poison	Status	—	100	20	Many Others
28	Night Slash	Dark	Physical	70	100	15	Normal
31	Gastro Acid	Poison	Status	—	100	10	Normal
34	Poison Jab	Poison	Physical	80	100	20	Normal
37	Haze	Ice	Status	—	—	30	Both Sides
40	Crunch	Dark	Physical	80	100	15	Normal
43	Belch	Poison	Special	120	90	10	Normal
46	Coil	Poison	Status	—	—	20	Self
49	Wring Out	Normal	Special	—	100	5	Normal

TM & HM MOVES

No.	Name	Type	Kind	Pow.	Acc.	PP	Range
TM06	Toxic	Poison	Status	—	90	10	Normal
TM09	Venoshock	Poison	Special	65	100	10	Normal
TM10	Hidden Power	Normal	Special	60	100	15	Normal
TM11	Sunny Day	Fire	Status	—	—	5	Both Sides
TM12	Taunt	Dark	Status	—	100	20	Normal
TM17	Protect	Normal	Status	—	—	10	Self
TM18	Rain Dance	Water	Status	—	—	5	Both Sides
TM21	Frustration	Normal	Physical	—	100	20	Normal
TM26	Earthquake	Ground	Physical	100	100	10	Adjacent
TM27	Return	Normal	Physical	—	100	20	Normal
TM28	Dig	Ground	Physical	80	100	10	Normal
TM32	Double Team	Normal	Status	—	—	15	Self
TM34	Sludge Wave	Poison	Special	95	100	10	Adjacent
TM35	Flamethrower	Fire	Special	90	100	15	Normal
TM36	Sludge Bomb	Poison	Special	90	100	10	Normal
TM42	Facade	Normal	Physical	70	100	20	Normal
TM44	Rest	Psychic	Status	—	—	10	Self
TM45	Attract	Normal	Status	—	100	15	Normal
TM46	Thief	Dark	Physical	60	100	25	Normal
TM48	Round	Normal	Special	60	100	15	Normal
TM66	Payback	Dark	Physical	50	100	10	Normal
TM67	Retaliate	Normal	Physical	70	100	5	Normal
TM78	Bulldoze	Ground	Physical	60	100	20	Adjacent
TM81	X-Scissor	Bug	Physical	80	100	15	Normal
TM82	Dragon Tail	Dragon	Physical	60	90	10	Normal
TM83	Infestation	Bug	Special	20	100	20	Normal
TM84	Poison Jab	Poison	Physical	80	100	20	Normal
TM87	Swagger	Normal	Status	—	90	15	Normal
TM88	Sleep Talk	Normal	Status	—	—	10	Self
TM90	Substitute	Normal	Status	—	—	10	Self
TM94	Secret Power	Normal	Physical	70	100	20	Normal
TM97	Dark Pulse	Dark	Special	80	100	15	Normal
TM100	Confide	Normal	Status	—	—	20	Normal
HM04	Strength	Normal	Physical	80	100	15	Normal
HM06	Rock Smash	Fighting	Physical	40	100	15	Normal

MOVES LEARNED IN EXCHANGE FOR BP

Name	Type	Kind	Pow.	Acc.	PP	Range
Aqua Tail	Water	Physical	90	90	10	Normal
Iron Tail	Steel	Physical	100	75	15	Normal
Bind	Normal	Physical	15	85	20	Normal
Snore	Normal	Special	50	100	15	Normal
Knock Off	Dark	Physical	65	100	20	Normal
Giga Drain	Grass	Special	75	100	10	Normal
Gastro Acid	Poison	Status	—	100	10	Normal
Snatch	Dark	Status	—	—	10	Self

MOVES TAUGHT BY PEOPLE

Name	Type	Kind	Pow.	Acc.	PP	Range

EGG MOVES

Name	Type	Kind	Pow.	Acc.	PP	Range
Stockpile	Normal	Status	—	—	20	Self
Swallow	Normal	Status	—	—	10	Self
Spit Up	Normal	Special	—	100	10	Normal
Body Slam	Normal	Physical	85	100	15	Normal
Scary Face	Normal	Status	—	100	10	Normal
Assurance	Dark	Physical	60	100	10	Normal
Night Slash	Dark	Physical	70	100	15	Normal
Switcheroo	Dark	Status	—	100	10	Normal
Iron Tail	Steel	Physical	100	75	15	Normal
Wring Out	Normal	Special	—	100	5	Normal
Punishment	Dark	Physical	—	100	5	Normal
Final Gambit	Fighting	Special	—	100	5	Normal

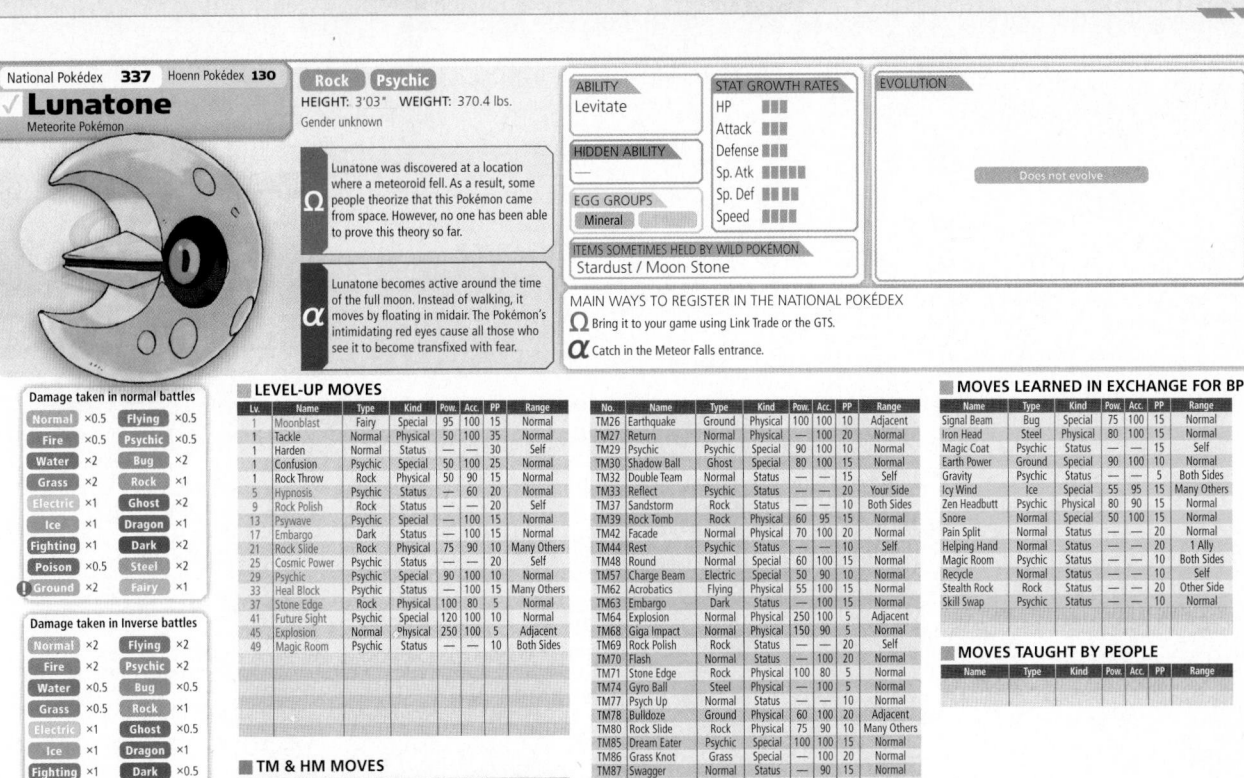

National Pokédex **337** Hoenn Pokédex **130**

✓ Lunatone

Meteorite Pokémon

Rock **Psychic**

HEIGHT: 3'03" WEIGHT: 370.4 lbs.

Gender unknown

Ω Lunatone was discovered at a location where a meteoroid fell. As a result, some people theorize that this Pokémon came from space. However, no one has been able to prove this theory so far.

α Lunatone becomes active around the time of the full moon. Instead of walking, it moves by floating in midair. The Pokémon's intimidating red eyes cause all those who see it to become transfixed with fear.

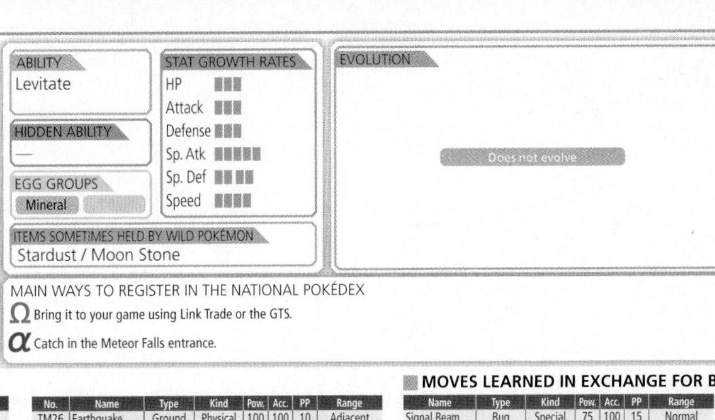

ABILITY: Levitate

HIDDEN ABILITY: —

EGG GROUPS: Mineral

STAT GROWTH RATES: HP, Attack, Defense, Sp. Atk, Sp. Def, Speed

ITEMS SOMETIMES HELD BY WILD POKÉMON: Stardust / Moon Stone

EVOLUTION: Does not evolve

MAIN WAYS TO REGISTER IN THE NATIONAL POKÉDEX

Ω Bring it to your game using Link Trade or the GTS.

α Catch in the Meteor Falls entrance.

Damage taken in normal battles

Type		Type	
Normal	×0.5	Flying	×0.5
Fire	×0.5	Psychic	×0.5
Water	×2	Bug	×2
Grass	×2	Rock	×1
Electric	×1	Ghost	×2
Ice	×1	Dragon	×1
Fighting	×1	Dark	×2
Poison	×0.5	Steel	×2
! Ground	×2	Fairy	×1

Damage taken in Inverse battles

Type		Type	
Normal	×2	Flying	×2
Fire	×2	Psychic	×2
Water	×0.5	Bug	×0.5
Grass	×0.5	Rock	×1
Electric	×1	Ghost	×0.5
Ice	×1	Dragon	×1
Fighting	×1	Dark	×0.5
Poison	×2	Steel	×0.5
! Ground	×0.5	Fairy	×1

Can be used in

- Inverse Battle
- Battle Institute
- Battle Maison
- Random Matchup (Free Battle)
- Random Matchup (Others)

LEVEL-UP MOVES

Lv.	Name	Type	Kind	Pow.	Acc.	PP	Range
1	Moonblast	Fairy	Special	95	100	15	Normal
1	Tackle	Normal	Physical	50	100	35	Normal
1	Harden	Normal	Status	—	—	30	Self
1	Confusion	Psychic	Special	50	100	25	Normal
1	Rock Throw	Rock	Physical	50	90	15	Normal
5	Hypnosis	Psychic	Status	—	60	20	Normal
9	Rock Polish	Rock	Status	—	—	20	Self
13	Psywave	Psychic	Special	—	100	15	Normal
17	Embargo	Dark	Status	—	100	15	Normal
21	Rock Slide	Rock	Physical	75	90	10	Many Others
25	Cosmic Power	Psychic	Status	—	—	20	Self
29	Psychic	Psychic	Special	90	100	10	Normal
33	Heal Block	Psychic	Status	—	100	15	Many Others
37	Stone Edge	Rock	Physical	100	80	5	Normal
41	Future Sight	Psychic	Special	120	100	10	Normal
45	Explosion	Normal	Physical	250	100	5	Adjacent
49	Magic Room	Psychic	Status	—	—	10	Both Sides

TM & HM MOVES

No.	Name	Type	Kind	Pow.	Acc.	PP	Range
TM03	Psyshock	Psychic	Special	80	100	10	Normal
TM04	Calm Mind	Psychic	Status	—	—	20	Self
TM06	Toxic	Poison	Status	—	90	10	Normal
TM10	Hidden Power	Normal	Special	60	100	15	Normal
TM13	Ice Beam	Ice	Special	90	100	10	Normal
TM14	Blizzard	Ice	Special	110	70	5	Many Others
TM15	Hyper Beam	Normal	Special	150	90	5	Normal
TM16	Light Screen	Psychic	Status	—	—	30	Your Side
TM17	Protect	Normal	Status	—	—	10	Self
TM18	Rain Dance	Water	Status	—	—	5	Both Sides
TM20	Safeguard	Normal	Status	—	—	25	Your Side
TM21	Frustration	Normal	Physical	—	100	20	Normal
TM23	Smack Down	Rock	Physical	50	100	15	Normal
TM26	Earthquake	Ground	Physical	100	100	10	Adjacent
TM27	Return	Normal	Physical	—	100	20	Normal
TM29	Psychic	Psychic	Special	90	100	10	Normal
TM30	Shadow Ball	Ghost	Special	80	100	15	Normal
TM32	Double Team	Normal	Status	—	—	15	Self
TM33	Reflect	Psychic	Status	—	—	20	Your Side
TM37	Sandstorm	Rock	Status	—	—	10	Both Sides
TM39	Rock Tomb	Rock	Physical	60	95	15	Normal
TM42	Facade	Normal	Physical	70	100	20	Normal
TM44	Rest	Psychic	Status	—	—	10	Self
TM48	Round	Normal	Special	60	100	15	Normal
TM57	Charge Beam	Electric	Special	50	90	10	Normal
TM62	Acrobatics	Flying	Physical	55	100	15	Normal
TM63	Embargo	Dark	Status	—	100	15	Normal
TM64	Explosion	Normal	Physical	250	100	5	Adjacent
TM68	Giga Impact	Normal	Physical	150	90	5	Normal
TM69	Rock Polish	Rock	Status	—	—	20	Self
TM70	Flash	Normal	Status	—	100	20	Normal
TM71	Stone Edge	Rock	Physical	100	80	5	Normal
TM74	Gyro Ball	Steel	Physical	—	100	5	Normal
TM77	Psych Up	Normal	Status	—	—	10	Normal
TM78	Bulldoze	Ground	Physical	60	100	20	Adjacent
TM80	Rock Slide	Rock	Physical	75	90	10	Many Others
TM85	Dream Eater	Psychic	Special	100	100	15	Normal
TM86	Grass Knot	Grass	Special	—	100	20	Normal
TM87	Swagger	Normal	Status	—	90	15	Normal
TM88	Sleep Talk	Normal	Status	—	—	10	Self
TM90	Substitute	Normal	Status	—	—	10	Self
TM92	Trick Room	Psychic	Status	—	—	5	Both Sides
TM94	Secret Power	Normal	Physical	70	100	20	Normal
TM100	Confide	Normal	Status	—	—	20	Normal

MOVES LEARNED IN EXCHANGE FOR BP

Name	Type	Kind	Pow.	Acc.	PP	Range
Signal Beam	Bug	Special	75	100	15	Normal
Iron Head	Steel	Physical	80	100	15	Normal
Magic Coat	Psychic	Status	—	—	15	Self
Earth Power	Ground	Special	90	100	10	Normal
Gravity	Psychic	Status	—	—	5	Both Sides
Icy Wind	Ice	Special	55	95	15	Many Others
Zen Headbutt	Psychic	Physical	80	90	15	Normal
Snore	Normal	Special	50	100	15	Normal
Pain Split	Normal	Status	—	—	20	Normal
Helping Hand	Normal	Status	—	—	20	1 Ally
Magic Room	Psychic	Status	—	—	10	Both Sides
Recycle	Normal	Status	—	—	10	Self
Stealth Rock	Rock	Status	—	—	20	Other Side
Skill Swap	Psychic	Status	—	—	10	Normal

MOVES TAUGHT BY PEOPLE

Name	Type	Kind	Pow.	Acc.	PP	Range

National Pokédex **338** Hoenn Pokédex **131**

✓ Solrock

Meteorite Pokémon

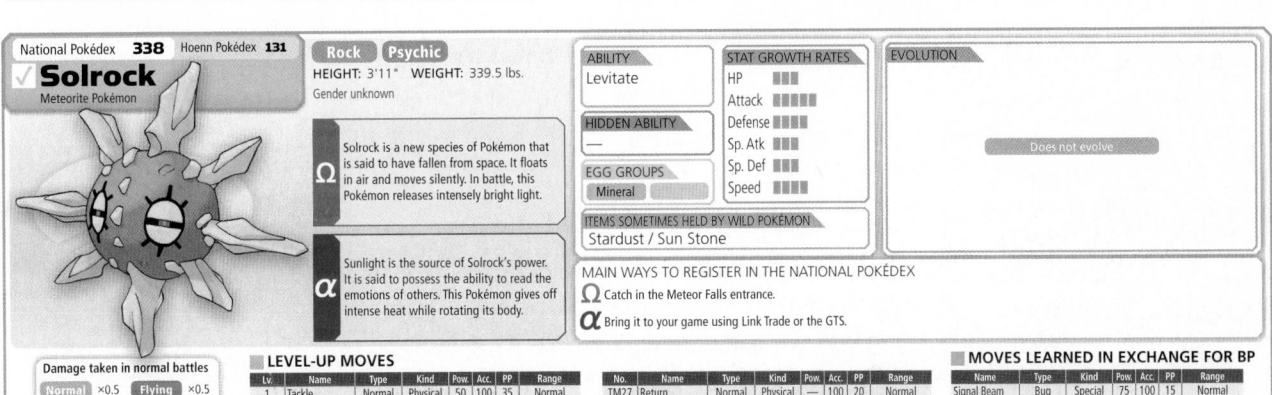

Rock **Psychic**

HEIGHT: 3'11" WEIGHT: 339.5 lbs.

Gender unknown

Ω Solrock is a new species of Pokémon that is said to have fallen from space. It floats in air and moves silently. In battle, this Pokémon releases intensely bright light.

α Sunlight is the source of Solrock's power. It is said to possess the ability to read the emotions of others. This Pokémon gives off intense heat while rotating its body.

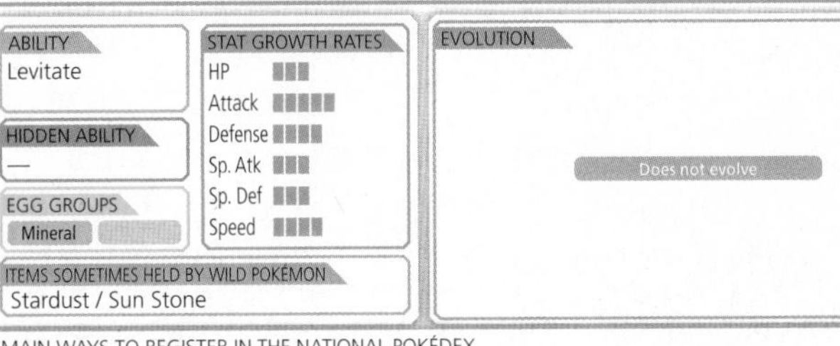

ABILITY: Levitate

HIDDEN ABILITY: —

EGG GROUPS: Mineral

STAT GROWTH RATES: HP, Attack, Defense, Sp. Atk, Sp. Def, Speed

ITEMS SOMETIMES HELD BY WILD POKÉMON: Stardust / Sun Stone

EVOLUTION: Does not evolve

MAIN WAYS TO REGISTER IN THE NATIONAL POKÉDEX

Ω Catch in the Meteor Falls entrance.

α Bring it to your game using Link Trade or the GTS.

Damage taken in normal battles

Type		Type	
Normal	×0.5	Flying	×0.5
Fire	×0.5	Psychic	×0.5
Water	×2	Bug	×2
Grass	×2	Rock	×1
Electric	×1	Ghost	×2
Ice	×1	Dragon	×1
Fighting	×1	Dark	×2
Poison	×0.5	Steel	×2
! Ground	×2	Fairy	×1

Damage taken in Inverse battles

Type		Type	
Normal	×2	Flying	×2
Fire	×2	Psychic	×2
Water	×0.5	Bug	×0.5
Grass	×0.5	Rock	×1
Electric	×1	Ghost	×0.5
Ice	×1	Dragon	×1
Fighting	×1	Dark	×0.5
Poison	×2	Steel	×0.5
! Ground	×0.5	Fairy	×1

Can be used in

- Inverse Battle
- Battle Institute
- Battle Maison
- Random Matchup (Free Battle)
- Random Matchup (Others)

LEVEL-UP MOVES

Lv.	Name	Type	Kind	Pow.	Acc.	PP	Range
1	Tackle	Normal	Physical	50	100	35	Normal
1	Harden	Normal	Status	—	—	30	Self
1	Confusion	Psychic	Special	50	100	25	Normal
1	Rock Throw	Rock	Physical	50	90	15	Normal
5	Fire Spin	Fire	Special	35	85	15	Normal
9	Rock Polish	Rock	Status	—	—	20	Self
13	Psywave	Psychic	Special	—	100	15	Normal
17	Embargo	Dark	Status	—	100	15	Normal
21	Rock Slide	Rock	Physical	75	90	10	Many Others
25	Cosmic Power	Psychic	Status	—	—	20	Self
29	Psychic	Psychic	Special	90	100	10	Normal
33	Heal Block	Psychic	Status	—	100	15	Many Others
37	Stone Edge	Rock	Physical	100	80	5	Normal
41	Solar Beam	Grass	Special	120	100	10	Normal
45	Explosion	Normal	Physical	250	100	5	Adjacent
49	Wonder Room	Psychic	Status	—	—	10	Both Sides

TM & HM MOVES

No.	Name	Type	Kind	Pow.	Acc.	PP	Range
TM03	Psyshock	Psychic	Special	80	100	10	Normal
TM04	Calm Mind	Psychic	Status	—	—	20	Self
TM06	Toxic	Poison	Status	—	90	10	Normal
TM10	Hidden Power	Normal	Special	60	100	15	Normal
TM11	Sunny Day	Fire	Status	—	—	5	Both Sides
TM15	Hyper Beam	Normal	Special	150	90	5	Normal
TM16	Light Screen	Psychic	Status	—	—	30	Your Side
TM17	Protect	Normal	Status	—	—	10	Self
TM20	Safeguard	Normal	Status	—	—	25	Your Side
TM21	Frustration	Normal	Physical	—	100	20	Normal
TM22	Solar Beam	Grass	Special	120	100	10	Normal
TM23	Smack Down	Rock	Physical	50	100	15	Normal
TM26	Earthquake	Ground	Physical	100	100	10	Adjacent
TM27	Return	Normal	Physical	—	100	20	Normal
TM29	Psychic	Psychic	Special	90	100	10	Normal
TM30	Shadow Ball	Ghost	Special	80	100	15	Normal
TM32	Double Team	Normal	Status	—	—	15	Self
TM33	Reflect	Psychic	Status	—	—	20	Your Side
TM35	Flamethrower	Fire	Special	90	100	15	Normal
TM37	Sandstorm	Rock	Status	—	—	10	Both Sides
TM38	Fire Blast	Fire	Special	110	85	5	Normal
TM39	Rock Tomb	Rock	Physical	60	95	15	Normal
TM42	Facade	Normal	Physical	70	100	20	Normal
TM44	Rest	Psychic	Status	—	—	10	Self
TM48	Round	Normal	Special	60	100	15	Normal
TM50	Overheat	Fire	Special	130	90	5	Normal
TM57	Charge Beam	Electric	Special	50	90	10	Normal
TM59	Incinerate	Fire	Special	60	100	15	Many Others
TM61	Will-O-Wisp	Fire	Status	—	85	15	Normal
TM62	Acrobatics	Flying	Physical	55	100	15	Normal
TM63	Embargo	Dark	Status	—	100	15	Normal
TM64	Explosion	Normal	Physical	250	100	5	Adjacent
TM68	Giga Impact	Normal	Physical	150	90	5	Normal
TM69	Rock Polish	Rock	Status	—	—	20	Self
TM70	Flash	Normal	Status	—	100	20	Normal
TM71	Stone Edge	Rock	Physical	100	80	5	Normal
TM74	Gyro Ball	Steel	Physical	—	100	5	Normal
TM77	Psych Up	Normal	Status	—	—	10	Normal
TM78	Bulldoze	Ground	Physical	60	100	20	Adjacent
TM80	Rock Slide	Rock	Physical	75	90	10	Many Others
TM85	Dream Eater	Psychic	Special	100	100	15	Normal
TM86	Grass Knot	Grass	Special	—	100	20	Normal
TM87	Swagger	Normal	Status	—	90	15	Normal
TM88	Sleep Talk	Normal	Status	—	—	10	Self
TM90	Substitute	Normal	Status	—	—	10	Self
TM92	Trick Room	Psychic	Status	—	—	5	Both Sides
TM94	Secret Power	Normal	Physical	70	100	20	Normal
TM100	Confide	Normal	Status	—	—	20	Normal

MOVES LEARNED IN EXCHANGE FOR BP

Name	Type	Kind	Pow.	Acc.	PP	Range
Signal Beam	Bug	Special	75	100	15	Normal
Iron Head	Steel	Physical	80	100	15	Normal
Magic Coat	Psychic	Status	—	—	15	Self
Earth Power	Ground	Special	90	100	10	Normal
Gravity	Psychic	Status	—	—	5	Both Sides
Iron Defense	Steel	Status	—	—	15	Self
Zen Headbutt	Psychic	Physical	80	90	15	Normal
Snore	Normal	Special	50	100	15	Normal
Heat Wave	Fire	Special	95	90	10	Many Others
Pain Split	Normal	Status	—	—	20	Normal
Helping Hand	Normal	Status	—	—	20	1 Ally
Wonder Room	Psychic	Status	—	—	10	Both Sides
Recycle	Normal	Status	—	—	10	Self
Stealth Rock	Rock	Status	—	—	20	Other Side
Skill Swap	Psychic	Status	—	—	10	Normal

MOVES TAUGHT BY PEOPLE

Name	Type	Kind	Pow.	Acc.	PP	Range

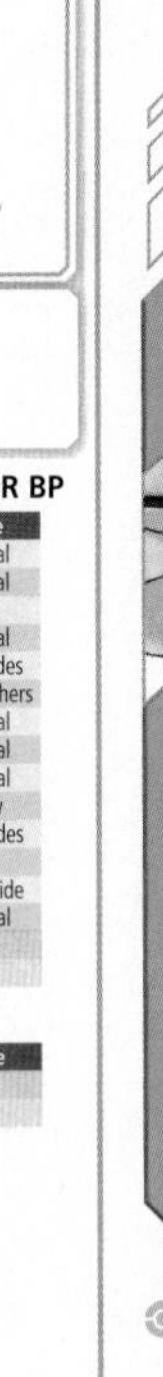

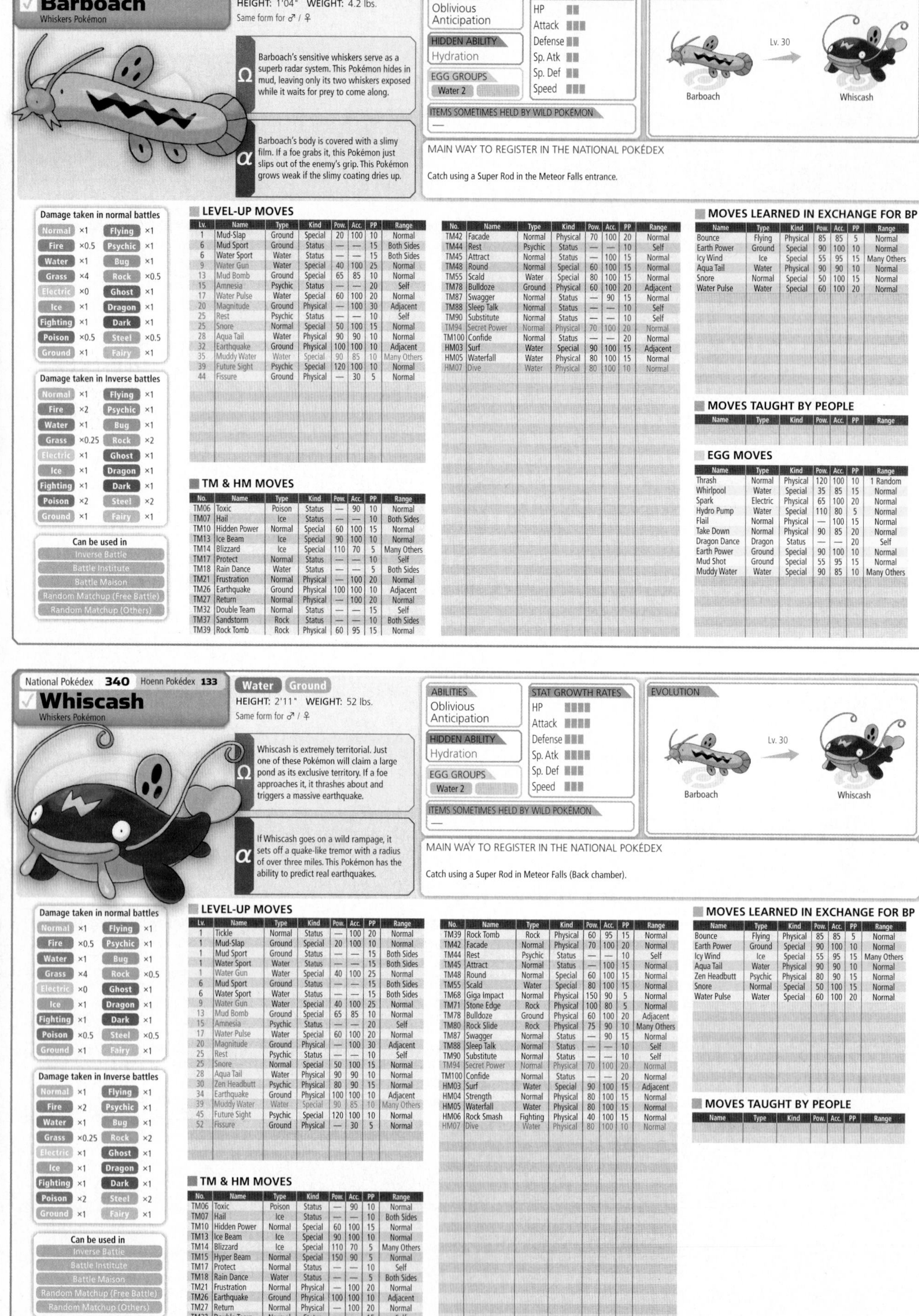

National Pokédex **339** Hoenn Pokédex **132**

Barboach

Whiskers Pokémon

Water **Ground**

HEIGHT: 1'04" WEIGHT: 4.2 lbs.

Same form for ♂ / ♀

Ω Barboach's sensitive whiskers serve as a superb radar system. This Pokémon hides in mud, leaving only its two whiskers exposed while it waits for prey to come along.

α Barboach's body is covered with a slimy film. If a foe grabs it, this Pokémon just slips out of the enemy's grip. This Pokémon grows weak if the slimy coating dries up.

ABILITIES
Oblivious
Anticipation

HIDDEN ABILITY
Hydration

EGG GROUPS
Water 2

STAT GROWTH RATES
HP
Attack
Defense
Sp. Atk
Sp. Def
Speed

ITEMS SOMETIMES HELD BY WILD POKÉMON
—

EVOLUTION
Barboach → Lv. 30 → Whiscash

MAIN WAY TO REGISTER IN THE NATIONAL POKÉDEX

Catch using a Super Rod in the Meteor Falls entrance.

Damage taken in normal battles

Type		Type	
Normal	×1	Flying	×1
Fire	×0.5	Psychic	×1
Water	×1	Bug	×1
Grass	×4	Rock	×0.5
Electric	×0	Ghost	×1
Ice	×1	Dragon	×1
Fighting	×1	Dark	×1
Poison	×0.5	Steel	×0.5
Ground	×1	Fairy	×1

Damage taken in Inverse battles

Type		Type	
Normal	×1	Flying	×1
Fire	×2	Psychic	×1
Water	×1	Bug	×1
Grass	×0.25	Rock	×2
Electric	×1	Ghost	×1
Ice	×1	Dragon	×1
Fighting	×1	Dark	×1
Poison	×2	Steel	×2
Ground	×1	Fairy	×1

Can be used in
Inverse Battle
Battle Institute
Battle Maison
Random Matchup (Free Battle)
Random Matchup (Others)

LEVEL-UP MOVES

Lv.	Name	Type	Kind	Pow.	Acc.	PP	Range
1	Mud-Slap	Ground	Special	20	100	10	Normal
6	Mud Sport	Ground	Status	—	—	15	Both Sides
6	Water Sport	Water	Status	—	—	15	Both Sides
9	Water Gun	Water	Special	40	100	25	Normal
13	Mud Bomb	Ground	Special	65	85	10	Normal
15	Amnesia	Psychic	Status	—	—	20	Self
17	Water Pulse	Water	Special	60	100	20	Normal
20	Magnitude	Ground	Physical	—	100	30	Adjacent
25	Rest	Psychic	Status	—	—	10	Self
25	Snore	Normal	Special	50	100	15	Normal
28	Aqua Tail	Water	Physical	90	90	10	Normal
32	Earthquake	Ground	Physical	100	100	10	Adjacent
35	Muddy Water	Water	Special	90	85	10	Many Others
39	Future Sight	Psychic	Special	120	100	10	Normal
44	Fissure	Ground	Physical	—	30	5	Normal

TM & HM MOVES

No.	Name	Type	Kind	Pow.	Acc.	PP	Range
TM06	Toxic	Poison	Status	—	90	10	Normal
TM07	Hail	Ice	Status	—	—	10	Both Sides
TM10	Hidden Power	Normal	Special	60	100	15	Normal
TM13	Ice Beam	Ice	Special	90	100	10	Normal
TM14	Blizzard	Ice	Special	110	70	5	Many Others
TM17	Protect	Normal	Status	—	—	10	Self
TM18	Rain Dance	Water	Status	—	—	5	Both Sides
TM21	Frustration	Normal	Physical	—	100	20	Normal
TM26	Earthquake	Ground	Physical	100	100	10	Adjacent
TM27	Return	Normal	Physical	—	100	20	Normal
TM32	Double Team	Normal	Status	—	—	15	Self
TM37	Sandstorm	Rock	Status	—	—	10	Both Sides
TM39	Rock Tomb	Rock	Physical	60	95	15	Normal
TM42	Facade	Normal	Physical	70	100	20	Normal
TM44	Rest	Psychic	Status	—	—	10	Self
TM45	Attract	Normal	Status	—	100	15	Normal
TM48	Round	Normal	Special	60	100	15	Normal
TM55	Scald	Water	Special	80	100	15	Normal
TM78	Bulldoze	Ground	Physical	60	100	20	Adjacent
TM87	Swagger	Normal	Status	—	90	15	Normal
TM88	Sleep Talk	Normal	Status	—	—	10	Self
TM90	Substitute	Normal	Status	—	—	10	Self
TM94	Secret Power	Normal	Physical	70	100	20	Normal
TM100	Confide	Normal	Status	—	—	20	Normal
HM03	Surf	Water	Special	90	100	15	Adjacent
HM05	Waterfall	Water	Physical	80	100	15	Normal
HM07	Dive	Water	Physical	80	100	10	Normal

MOVES LEARNED IN EXCHANGE FOR BP

Name	Type	Kind	Pow.	Acc.	PP	Range
Bounce	Flying	Physical	85	85	5	Normal
Earth Power	Ground	Special	90	100	10	Normal
Icy Wind	Ice	Special	55	95	15	Many Others
Aqua Tail	Water	Physical	90	90	10	Normal
Snore	Normal	Special	50	100	15	Normal
Water Pulse	Water	Special	60	100	20	Normal

MOVES TAUGHT BY PEOPLE

Name	Type	Kind	Pow.	Acc.	PP	Range

EGG MOVES

Name	Type	Kind	Pow.	Acc.	PP	Range
Thrash	Normal	Physical	120	100	10	1 Random
Whirlpool	Water	Special	35	85	15	Normal
Spark	Electric	Physical	65	100	20	Normal
Hydro Pump	Water	Special	110	80	5	Normal
Flail	Normal	Physical	—	100	15	Normal
Take Down	Normal	Physical	90	85	20	Normal
Dragon Dance	Dragon	Status	—	—	20	Self
Earth Power	Ground	Special	90	100	10	Normal
Mud Shot	Ground	Special	55	95	15	Normal
Muddy Water	Water	Special	90	85	10	Many Others

National Pokédex **340** Hoenn Pokédex **133**

Whiscash

Whiskers Pokémon

Water **Ground**

HEIGHT: 2'11" WEIGHT: 52 lbs.

Same form for ♂ / ♀

Ω Whiscash is extremely territorial. Just one of these Pokémon will claim a large pond as its exclusive territory. If a foe approaches it, it thrashes about and triggers a massive earthquake.

α If Whiscash goes on a wild rampage, it sets off a quake-like tremor with a radius of over three miles. This Pokémon has the ability to predict real earthquakes.

ABILITIES
Oblivious
Anticipation

HIDDEN ABILITY
Hydration

EGG GROUPS
Water 2

STAT GROWTH RATES
HP
Attack
Defense
Sp. Atk
Sp. Def
Speed

ITEMS SOMETIMES HELD BY WILD POKÉMON
—

EVOLUTION
Barboach → Lv. 30 → Whiscash

MAIN WAY TO REGISTER IN THE NATIONAL POKÉDEX

Catch using a Super Rod in Meteor Falls (Back chamber).

Damage taken in normal battles

Type		Type	
Normal	×1	Flying	×1
Fire	×0.5	Psychic	×1
Water	×1	Bug	×1
Grass	×4	Rock	×0.5
Electric	×0	Ghost	×1
Ice	×1	Dragon	×1
Fighting	×1	Dark	×1
Poison	×0.5	Steel	×0.5
Ground	×1	Fairy	×1

Damage taken in Inverse battles

Type		Type	
Normal	×1	Flying	×1
Fire	×2	Psychic	×1
Water	×1	Bug	×1
Grass	×0.25	Rock	×2
Electric	×1	Ghost	×1
Ice	×1	Dragon	×1
Fighting	×1	Dark	×1
Poison	×2	Steel	×2
Ground	×1	Fairy	×1

Can be used in
Inverse Battle
Battle Institute
Battle Maison
Random Matchup (Free Battle)
Random Matchup (Others)

LEVEL-UP MOVES

Lv.	Name	Type	Kind	Pow.	Acc.	PP	Range
1	Tickle	Normal	Status	—	100	20	Normal
1	Mud-Slap	Ground	Special	20	100	10	Normal
1	Mud Sport	Ground	Status	—	—	15	Both Sides
1	Water Sport	Water	Status	—	—	15	Both Sides
1	Water Gun	Water	Special	40	100	25	Normal
6	Mud Sport	Ground	Status	—	—	15	Both Sides
6	Water Sport	Water	Status	—	—	15	Both Sides
9	Water Gun	Water	Special	40	100	25	Normal
13	Mud Bomb	Ground	Special	65	85	10	Normal
15	Amnesia	Psychic	Status	—	—	20	Self
17	Water Pulse	Water	Special	60	100	20	Normal
20	Magnitude	Ground	Physical	—	100	30	Adjacent
25	Rest	Psychic	Status	—	—	10	Self
25	Snore	Normal	Special	50	100	15	Normal
28	Aqua Tail	Water	Physical	90	90	10	Normal
30	Zen Headbutt	Psychic	Physical	80	90	15	Normal
34	Earthquake	Ground	Physical	100	100	10	Adjacent
39	Muddy Water	Water	Special	90	85	10	Many Others
45	Future Sight	Psychic	Special	120	100	10	Normal
52	Fissure	Ground	Physical	—	30	5	Normal

TM & HM MOVES

No.	Name	Type	Kind	Pow.	Acc.	PP	Range
TM06	Toxic	Poison	Status	—	90	10	Normal
TM07	Hail	Ice	Status	—	—	10	Both Sides
TM10	Hidden Power	Normal	Special	60	100	15	Normal
TM13	Ice Beam	Ice	Special	90	100	10	Normal
TM14	Blizzard	Ice	Special	110	70	5	Many Others
TM15	Hyper Beam	Normal	Special	150	90	5	Normal
TM17	Protect	Normal	Status	—	—	10	Self
TM18	Rain Dance	Water	Status	—	—	5	Both Sides
TM21	Frustration	Normal	Physical	—	100	20	Normal
TM26	Earthquake	Ground	Physical	100	100	10	Adjacent
TM27	Return	Normal	Physical	—	100	20	Normal
TM32	Double Team	Normal	Status	—	—	15	Self
TM37	Sandstorm	Rock	Status	—	—	10	Both Sides
TM39	Rock Tomb	Rock	Physical	60	95	15	Normal
TM42	Facade	Normal	Physical	70	100	20	Normal
TM44	Rest	Psychic	Status	—	—	10	Self
TM45	Attract	Normal	Status	—	100	15	Normal
TM48	Round	Normal	Special	60	100	15	Normal
TM55	Scald	Water	Special	80	100	15	Normal
TM68	Giga Impact	Normal	Physical	150	90	5	Normal
TM71	Stone Edge	Rock	Physical	100	80	5	Normal
TM78	Bulldoze	Ground	Physical	60	100	20	Adjacent
TM80	Rock Slide	Rock	Physical	75	90	10	Many Others
TM87	Swagger	Normal	Status	—	90	15	Normal
TM88	Sleep Talk	Normal	Status	—	—	10	Self
TM90	Substitute	Normal	Status	—	—	10	Self
TM94	Secret Power	Normal	Physical	70	100	20	Normal
TM100	Confide	Normal	Status	—	—	20	Normal
HM03	Surf	Water	Special	90	100	15	Adjacent
HM04	Strength	Normal	Physical	80	100	15	Normal
HM05	Waterfall	Water	Physical	80	100	15	Normal
HM06	Rock Smash	Fighting	Physical	40	100	15	Normal
HM07	Dive	Water	Physical	80	100	10	Normal

MOVES LEARNED IN EXCHANGE FOR BP

Name	Type	Kind	Pow.	Acc.	PP	Range
Bounce	Flying	Physical	85	85	5	Normal
Earth Power	Ground	Special	90	100	10	Normal
Icy Wind	Ice	Special	55	95	15	Many Others
Aqua Tail	Water	Physical	90	90	10	Normal
Zen Headbutt	Psychic	Physical	80	90	15	Normal
Snore	Normal	Special	50	100	15	Normal
Water Pulse	Water	Special	60	100	20	Normal

MOVES TAUGHT BY PEOPLE

Name	Type	Kind	Pow.	Acc.	PP	Range

National Pokédex **341** Hoenn Pokédex **134**

Corphish

Ruffian Pokémon

Water

HEIGHT: 2'00" WEIGHT: 25.4 lbs.

Same form for ♂ / ♀

Ω Corphish were originally foreign Pokémon that were imported as pets. They eventually turned up in the wild. This Pokémon is very hardy and has greatly increased its population.

α Corphish catches prey with its sharp claws. It has no likes or dislikes when it comes to food—it will eat anything. This Pokémon has no trouble living in filthy water.

ABILITIES

Hyper Cutter
Shell Armor

HIDDEN ABILITY

Adaptability

EGG GROUPS

Water 1 | Water 3

STAT GROWTH RATES

HP
Attack
Defense
Sp. Atk
Sp. Def
Speed

ITEMS SOMETIMES HELD BY WILD POKÉMON

—

EVOLUTION

MAIN WAY TO REGISTER IN THE NATIONAL POKÉDEX

Catch using a Super Rod on Route 117.

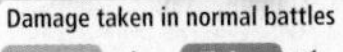

Damage taken in normal battles

Type		Type	
Normal	×1	Flying	×1
Fire	×0.5	Psychic	×1
Water	×0.5	Bug	×1
Grass	×2	Rock	×1
Electric	×2	Ghost	×1
Ice	×0.5	Dragon	×1
Fighting	×1	Dark	×1
Poison	×1	Steel	×0.5
Ground	×1	Fairy	×1

Damage taken in Inverse battles

Type		Type	
Normal	×1	Flying	×1
Fire	×2	Psychic	×1
Water	×2	Bug	×1
Grass	×0.5	Rock	×1
Electric	×0.5	Ghost	×1
Ice	×2	Dragon	×1
Fighting	×1	Dark	×1
Poison	×1	Steel	×2
Ground	×1	Fairy	×1

Can be used in

Inverse Battle
Battle Institute
Battle Maison
Random Matchup (Free Battle)
Random Matchup (Others)

LEVEL-UP MOVES

Lv.	Name	Type	Kind	Pow.	Acc.	PP	Range
1	Bubble	Water	Special	40	100	30	Many Others
5	Harden	Normal	Status	—	—	30	Self
7	Vice Grip	Normal	Physical	55	100	30	Normal
10	Leer	Normal	Status	—	100	30	Many Others
14	Bubble Beam	Water	Special	65	100	20	Normal
17	Protect	Normal	Status	—	—	10	Self
20	Double Hit	Normal	Physical	35	90	10	Normal
23	Knock Off	Dark	Physical	65	100	20	Normal
26	Night Slash	Dark	Physical	70	100	15	Normal
31	Razor Shell	Water	Physical	75	95	10	Normal
34	Taunt	Dark	Status	—	100	20	Normal
37	Swords Dance	Normal	Status	—	—	20	Self
39	Crunch	Dark	Physical	80	100	15	Normal
43	Crabhammer	Water	Physical	100	90	10	Normal
48	Guillotine	Normal	Physical	—	30	5	Normal

TM & HM MOVES

No.	Name	Type	Kind	Pow.	Acc.	PP	Range
TM01	Hone Claws	Dark	Status	—	—	15	Self
TM06	Toxic	Poison	Status	—	90	10	Normal
TM07	Hail	Ice	Status	—	—	10	Both Sides
TM10	Hidden Power	Normal	Special	60	100	15	Normal
TM12	Taunt	Dark	Status	—	100	20	Normal
TM13	Ice Beam	Ice	Special	90	100	10	Normal
TM14	Blizzard	Ice	Special	110	70	5	Many Others
TM17	Protect	Normal	Status	—	—	10	Self
TM18	Rain Dance	Water	Status	—	—	5	Both Sides
TM21	Frustration	Normal	Physical	—	100	20	Normal
TM27	Return	Normal	Physical	—	100	20	Normal
TM28	Dig	Ground	Physical	80	100	10	Normal
TM31	Brick Break	Fighting	Physical	75	100	15	Normal
TM32	Double Team	Normal	Status	—	—	15	Self
TM36	Sludge Bomb	Poison	Special	90	100	10	Normal
TM39	Rock Tomb	Rock	Physical	60	95	15	Normal
TM40	Aerial Ace	Flying	Physical	60	—	20	Normal
TM42	Facade	Normal	Physical	70	100	20	Normal
TM44	Rest	Psychic	Status	—	—	10	Self
TM45	Attract	Normal	Status	—	100	15	Normal
TM48	Round	Normal	Special	60	100	15	Normal
TM54	False Swipe	Normal	Physical	40	100	40	Normal
TM55	Scald	Water	Special	80	100	15	Normal
TM56	Fling	Dark	Physical	—	100	10	Normal
TM66	Payback	Dark	Physical	50	100	10	Normal
TM75	Swords Dance	Normal	Status	—	—	20	Self
TM80	Rock Slide	Rock	Physical	75	90	10	Many Others
TM81	X-Scissor	Bug	Physical	80	100	15	Normal
TM87	Swagger	Normal	Status	—	90	15	Normal
TM88	Sleep Talk	Normal	Status	—	—	10	Self
TM90	Substitute	Normal	Status	—	—	10	Self
TM94	Secret Power	Normal	Physical	70	100	20	Normal
TM100	Confide	Normal	Status	—	—	20	Normal
HM01	Cut	Normal	Physical	50	95	30	Normal
HM03	Surf	Water	Special	90	100	15	Adjacent
HM04	Strength	Normal	Physical	80	100	15	Normal
HM05	Waterfall	Water	Physical	80	100	15	Normal
HM06	Rock Smash	Fighting	Physical	40	100	15	Normal

MOVES LEARNED IN EXCHANGE FOR BP

Name	Type	Kind	Pow.	Acc.	PP	Range
Iron Defense	Steel	Status	—	—	15	Self
Superpower	Fighting	Physical	120	100	5	Normal
Icy Wind	Ice	Special	55	95	15	Many Others
Snore	Normal	Special	50	100	15	Normal
Knock Off	Dark	Physical	65	100	20	Normal
Water Pulse	Water	Special	60	100	20	Normal
Spite	Ghost	Status	—	100	10	Normal
Endeavor	Normal	Physical	—	100	5	Normal

MOVES TAUGHT BY PEOPLE

Name	Type	Kind	Pow.	Acc.	PP	Range

EGG MOVES

Name	Type	Kind	Pow.	Acc.	PP	Range
Mud Sport	Ground	Status	—	—	15	Both Sides
Endeavor	Normal	Physical	—	100	5	Normal
Body Slam	Normal	Physical	85	100	15	Normal
Ancient Power	Rock	Special	60	100	5	Normal
Knock Off	Dark	Physical	65	100	20	Normal
Superpower	Fighting	Physical	120	100	5	Normal
Metal Claw	Steel	Physical	50	95	35	Normal
Dragon Dance	Dragon	Status	—	—	20	Self
Trump Card	Normal	Special	—	—	5	Normal
Chip Away	Normal	Physical	70	100	20	Normal
Double-Edge	Normal	Physical	120	100	15	Normal
Aqua Jet	Water	Physical	40	100	20	Normal
Switcheroo	Dark	Status	—	100	10	Normal

National Pokédex **342** Hoenn Pokédex **135**

Crawdaunt

Rogue Pokémon

Water **Dark**

HEIGHT: 3'07" WEIGHT: 72.3 lbs.

Same form for ♂ / ♀

Ω Crawdaunt has an extremely violent nature that compels it to challenge other living things to battle. Other life-forms refuse to live in ponds inhabited by this Pokémon, making them desolate places.

α Crawdaunt molts (sheds) its shell regularly. Immediately after molting, its shell is soft and tender. Until the shell hardens, this Pokémon hides in its streambed burrow to avoid attack from its foes.

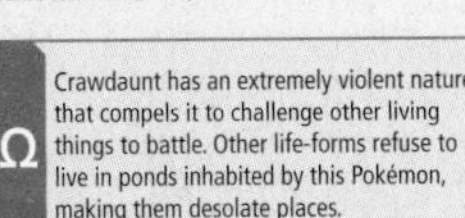

ABILITIES

Hyper Cutter
Shell Armor

HIDDEN ABILITY

Adaptability

EGG GROUPS

Water 1 | Water 3

STAT GROWTH RATES

HP
Attack
Defense
Sp. Atk
Sp. Def
Speed

ITEMS SOMETIMES HELD BY WILD POKÉMON

—

EVOLUTION

Corphish — Lv. 30 → Crawdaunt

MAIN WAY TO REGISTER IN THE NATIONAL POKÉDEX

Catch using a Super Rod on Route 117.

Damage taken in normal battles

Type		Type	
Normal	×1	Flying	×1
Fire	×0.5	Psychic	×0
Water	×0.5	Bug	×2
Grass	×2	Rock	×1
Electric	×2	Ghost	×0.5
Ice	×0.5	Dragon	×1
Fighting	×2	Dark	×0.5
Poison	×1	Steel	×0.5
Ground	×1	Fairy	×2

Damage taken in Inverse battles

Type		Type	
Normal	×1	Flying	×1
Fire	×2	Psychic	×2
Water	×2	Bug	×0.5
Grass	×0.5	Rock	×1
Electric	×0.5	Ghost	×2
Ice	×2	Dragon	×1
Fighting	×0.5	Dark	×2
Poison	×1	Steel	×2
Ground	×1	Fairy	×0.5

Can be used in

Inverse Battle
Battle Institute
Battle Maison
Random Matchup (Free Battle)
Random Matchup (Others)

LEVEL-UP MOVES

Lv.	Name	Type	Kind	Pow.	Acc.	PP	Range
1	Bubble	Water	Special	40	100	30	Many Others
1	Harden	Normal	Status	—	—	30	Self
1	Vice Grip	Normal	Physical	55	100	30	Normal
1	Leer	Normal	Status	—	100	30	Many Others
5	Harden	Normal	Status	—	—	30	Self
7	Vice Grip	Normal	Physical	55	100	30	Normal
10	Leer	Normal	Status	—	100	30	Many Others
14	Bubble Beam	Water	Special	65	100	20	Normal
17	Protect	Normal	Status	—	—	10	Self
20	Double Hit	Normal	Physical	35	90	10	Normal
23	Knock Off	Dark	Physical	65	100	20	Normal
26	Night Slash	Dark	Physical	70	100	15	Normal
30	Swift	Normal	Special	60	—	20	Many Others
32	Razor Shell	Water	Physical	75	95	10	Normal
36	Taunt	Dark	Status	—	100	20	Normal
40	Swords Dance	Normal	Status	—	—	20	Self
43	Crunch	Dark	Physical	80	100	15	Normal
48	Crabhammer	Water	Physical	100	90	10	Normal
54	Guillotine	Normal	Physical	—	30	5	Normal

TM & HM MOVES

No.	Name	Type	Kind	Pow.	Acc.	PP	Range
TM01	Hone Claws	Dark	Status	—	—	15	Self
TM06	Toxic	Poison	Status	—	90	10	Normal
TM07	Hail	Ice	Status	—	—	10	Both Sides
TM10	Hidden Power	Normal	Special	60	100	15	Normal
TM12	Taunt	Dark	Status	—	100	20	Normal
TM13	Ice Beam	Ice	Special	90	100	10	Normal
TM14	Blizzard	Ice	Special	110	70	5	Many Others
TM15	Hyper Beam	Normal	Special	150	90	5	Normal
TM17	Protect	Normal	Status	—	—	10	Self
TM18	Rain Dance	Water	Status	—	—	5	Both Sides
TM21	Frustration	Normal	Physical	—	100	20	Normal
TM27	Return	Normal	Physical	—	100	20	Normal
TM28	Dig	Ground	Physical	80	100	10	Normal
TM31	Brick Break	Fighting	Physical	75	100	15	Normal
TM32	Double Team	Normal	Status	—	—	15	Self
TM34	Sludge Wave	Poison	Special	95	100	10	Adjacent
TM36	Sludge Bomb	Poison	Special	90	100	10	Normal
TM39	Rock Tomb	Rock	Physical	60	95	15	Normal
TM40	Aerial Ace	Flying	Physical	60	—	20	Normal
TM42	Facade	Normal	Physical	70	100	20	Normal
TM44	Rest	Psychic	Status	—	—	10	Self
TM45	Attract	Normal	Status	—	100	15	Normal
TM48	Round	Normal	Special	60	100	15	Normal
TM54	False Swipe	Normal	Physical	40	100	40	Normal
TM55	Scald	Water	Special	80	100	15	Normal
TM56	Fling	Dark	Physical	—	100	10	Normal
TM66	Payback	Dark	Physical	50	100	10	Normal
TM67	Retaliate	Normal	Physical	70	100	5	Normal
TM68	Giga Impact	Normal	Physical	150	90	5	Normal
TM75	Swords Dance	Normal	Status	—	—	20	Self
TM80	Rock Slide	Rock	Physical	75	90	10	Many Others
TM81	X-Scissor	Bug	Physical	80	100	15	Normal
TM87	Swagger	Normal	Status	—	90	15	Normal
TM88	Sleep Talk	Normal	Status	—	—	10	Self
TM90	Substitute	Normal	Status	—	—	10	Self
TM94	Secret Power	Normal	Physical	70	100	20	Normal
TM95	Snarl	Dark	Special	55	95	15	Many Others
TM96	Nature Power	Normal	Status	—	—	20	Normal
TM97	Dark Pulse	Dark	Special	80	100	15	Normal
TM100	Confide	Normal	Status	—	—	20	Normal
HM01	Cut	Normal	Physical	50	95	30	Normal
HM03	Surf	Water	Special	90	100	15	Adjacent
HM04	Strength	Normal	Physical	80	100	15	Normal
HM05	Waterfall	Water	Physical	80	100	15	Normal
HM06	Rock Smash	Fighting	Physical	40	100	15	Normal
HM07	Dive	Water	Physical	80	100	10	Normal

MOVES LEARNED IN EXCHANGE FOR BP

Name	Type	Kind	Pow.	Acc.	PP	Range
Iron Defense	Steel	Status	—	—	15	Self
Superpower	Fighting	Physical	120	100	5	Normal
Icy Wind	Ice	Special	55	95	15	Many Others
Snore	Normal	Special	50	100	15	Normal
Knock Off	Dark	Physical	65	100	20	Normal
Water Pulse	Water	Special	60	100	20	Normal
Spite	Ghost	Status	—	100	10	Normal
Endeavor	Normal	Physical	—	100	5	Normal

MOVES TAUGHT BY PEOPLE

Name	Type	Kind	Pow.	Acc.	PP	Range

National Pokédex **343** Hoenn Pokédex **136**

Baltoy

Clay Doll Pokémon

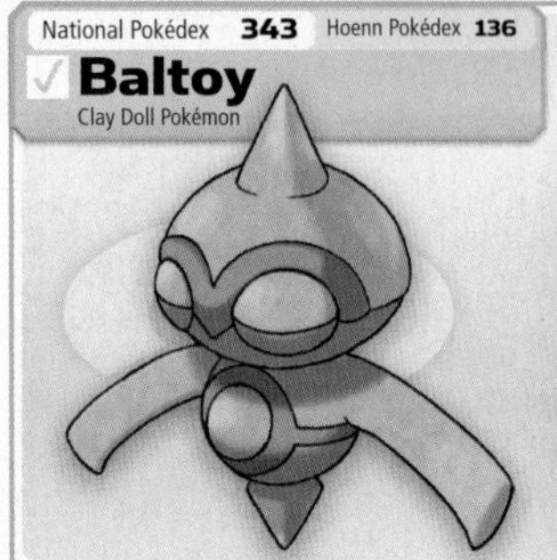

Ground Psychic

HEIGHT: 1'08" WEIGHT: 47.4 lbs.

Gender unknown

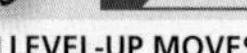

Ω Baltoy moves while spinning around on its one foot. Primitive wall paintings depicting this Pokémon living among people were discovered in some ancient ruins.

α As soon as it spots others of its kind, Baltoy congregates with them and then begins crying noisily in unison. This Pokémon sleeps while cleverly balancing itself on its one foot.

ABILITY
Levitate

HIDDEN ABILITY
—

EGG GROUPS
Mineral

STAT GROWTH RATES
HP ■■
Attack ■■
Defense ■■■
Sp. Atk ■■
Sp. Def ■■■
Speed ■■■

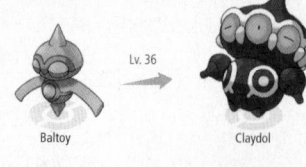

ITEMS SOMETIMES HELD BY WILD POKÉMON
Light Clay

EVOLUTION
Baltoy → Lv. 36 → Claydol

MAIN WAY TO REGISTER IN THE NATIONAL POKÉDEX
Catch in the desert on Route 111.

Damage taken in normal battles

Type		Type	
Normal	×1	Flying	×1
Fire	×1	Psychic	×0.5
Water	×2	Bug	×2
Grass	×2	Rock	×0.5
Electric	×0	Ghost	×2
Ice	×2	Dragon	×1
Fighting	×0.5	Dark	×2
Poison	×0.5	Steel	×1
! Ground	×1	Fairy	×1

Damage taken in Inverse battles

Type		Type	
Normal	×1	Flying	×1
Fire	×1	Psychic	×2
Water	×0.5	Bug	×0.5
Grass	×0.5	Rock	×2
Electric	×2	Ghost	×0.5
Ice	×0.5	Dragon	×1
Fighting	×2	Dark	×0.5
Poison	×2	Steel	×1
! Ground	×1	Fairy	×1

Can be used in
Inverse Battle
Battle Institute
Battle Maison
Random Matchup (Free Battle)
Random Matchup (Others)

LEVEL-UP MOVES

Lv.	Name	Type	Kind	Pow.	Acc.	PP	Range
1	Harden	Normal	Status	—	—	30	Self
1	Confusion	Psychic	Special	50	100	25	Normal
4	Rapid Spin	Normal	Physical	20	100	40	Normal
7	Mud-Slap	Ground	Special	20	100	10	Normal
10	Heal Block	Psychic	Status	—	100	15	Many Others
13	Rock Tomb	Rock	Physical	60	95	15	Normal
16	Psybeam	Psychic	Special	65	100	20	Normal
19	Ancient Power	Rock	Special	60	100	5	Normal
22	Cosmic Power	Psychic	Status	—	—	20	Self
25	Power Trick	Psychic	Status	—	—	10	Self
28	Self-Destruct	Normal	Physical	200	100	5	Adjacent
31	Extrasensory	Psychic	Special	80	100	20	Normal
34	Guard Split	Psychic	Status	—	—	10	Normal
34	Power Split	Psychic	Status	—	—	10	Normal
37	Earth Power	Ground	Special	90	100	10	Normal
40	Sandstorm	Rock	Status	—	—	10	Both Sides
43	Imprison	Psychic	Status	—	—	10	Self
46	Explosion	Normal	Physical	250	100	5	Adjacent

TM & HM MOVES

No.	Name	Type	Kind	Pow.	Acc.	PP	Range
TM03	Psyshock	Psychic	Special	80	100	10	Normal
TM04	Calm Mind	Psychic	Status	—	—	20	Self
TM06	Toxic	Poison	Status	—	90	10	Normal
TM10	Hidden Power	Normal	Special	60	100	15	Normal
TM11	Sunny Day	Fire	Status	—	—	5	Both Sides
TM13	Ice Beam	Ice	Special	90	100	10	Normal
TM16	Light Screen	Psychic	Status	—	—	30	Your Side
TM17	Protect	Normal	Status	—	—	10	Self
TM18	Rain Dance	Water	Status	—	—	5	Both Sides
TM20	Safeguard	Normal	Status	—	—	25	Your Side
TM21	Frustration	Normal	Physical	—	100	20	Normal
TM22	Solar Beam	Grass	Special	120	100	10	Normal
TM23	Smack Down	Rock	Physical	50	100	15	Normal
TM26	Earthquake	Ground	Physical	100	100	10	Adjacent
TM27	Return	Normal	Physical	—	100	20	Normal
TM28	Dig	Ground	Physical	80	100	10	Normal
TM29	Psychic	Psychic	Special	90	100	10	Normal
TM30	Shadow Ball	Ghost	Special	80	100	15	Normal
TM32	Double Team	Normal	Status	—	—	15	Self
TM33	Reflect	Psychic	Status	—	—	20	Your Side
TM37	Sandstorm	Rock	Status	—	—	10	Both Sides
TM39	Rock Tomb	Rock	Physical	60	95	15	Normal
TM42	Facade	Normal	Physical	70	100	20	Normal
TM44	Rest	Psychic	Status	—	—	10	Self
TM48	Round	Normal	Special	60	100	15	Normal
TM57	Charge Beam	Electric	Special	50	90	10	Normal
TM64	Explosion	Normal	Physical	250	100	5	Adjacent
TM69	Rock Polish	Rock	Status	—	—	20	Self
TM70	Flash	Normal	Status	—	100	20	Normal
TM74	Gyro Ball	Steel	Physical	—	100	5	Normal
TM77	Psych Up	Normal	Status	—	—	10	Normal
TM78	Bulldoze	Ground	Physical	60	100	20	Adjacent
TM80	Rock Slide	Rock	Physical	75	90	10	Many Others
TM85	Dream Eater	Psychic	Special	100	100	15	Normal
TM86	Grass Knot	Grass	Special	—	100	20	Normal
TM87	Swagger	Normal	Status	—	90	15	Normal
TM88	Sleep Talk	Normal	Status	—	—	10	Self
TM90	Substitute	Normal	Status	—	—	10	Self
TM92	Trick Room	Psychic	Status	—	—	5	Both Sides
TM94	Secret Power	Normal	Physical	70	100	20	Normal
TM99	Dazzling Gleam	Fairy	Special	80	100	10	Many Others
TM100	Confide	Normal	Status	—	—	20	Normal

MOVES LEARNED IN EXCHANGE FOR BP

Name	Type	Kind	Pow.	Acc.	PP	Range
Signal Beam	Bug	Special	75	100	15	Normal
Drill Run	Ground	Physical	80	95	10	Normal
Magic Coat	Psychic	Status	—	—	15	Self
Earth Power	Ground	Special	90	100	10	Normal
Gravity	Psychic	Status	—	—	5	Both Sides
Zen Headbutt	Psychic	Physical	80	90	15	Normal
Snore	Normal	Special	50	100	15	Normal
Trick	Psychic	Status	—	100	10	Normal
Wonder Room	Psychic	Status	—	—	10	Both Sides
Recycle	Normal	Status	—	—	10	Self
Stealth Rock	Rock	Status	—	—	20	Other Side
Skill Swap	Psychic	Status	—	—	10	Normal

MOVES TAUGHT BY PEOPLE

Name	Type	Kind	Pow.	Acc.	PP	Range

National Pokédex **344** Hoenn Pokédex **137**

Claydol

Clay Doll Pokémon

Ground Psychic

HEIGHT: 4'11" WEIGHT: 238.1 lbs.

Gender unknown

Ω Claydol are said to be dolls of mud made by primitive humans and brought to life by exposure to a mysterious ray. This Pokémon moves about while levitating.

α Claydol is an enigma that appeared from a clay statue made by an ancient civilization dating back 20,000 years. This Pokémon shoots beams from both its hands.

ABILITY
Levitate

HIDDEN ABILITY
—

EGG GROUPS
Mineral

STAT GROWTH RATES
HP ■■■
Attack ■■■■
Defense ■■■■■
Sp. Atk ■■■
Sp. Def ■■■■■
Speed ■■■■

ITEMS SOMETIMES HELD BY WILD POKÉMON
Light Clay

EVOLUTION
Baltoy → Lv. 36 → Claydol

MAIN WAY TO REGISTER IN THE NATIONAL POKÉDEX
Catch at the Sky Pillar.

Damage taken in normal battles

Type		Type	
Normal	×1	Flying	×1
Fire	×1	Psychic	×0.5
Water	×2	Bug	×2
Grass	×2	Rock	×0.5
Electric	×0	Ghost	×2
Ice	×2	Dragon	×1
Fighting	×0.5	Dark	×2
Poison	×0.5	Steel	×1
! Ground	×1	Fairy	×1

Damage taken in Inverse battles

Type		Type	
Normal	×1	Flying	×1
Fire	×1	Psychic	×2
Water	×0.5	Bug	×0.5
Grass	×0.5	Rock	×2
Electric	×2	Ghost	×0.5
Ice	×0.5	Dragon	×1
Fighting	×2	Dark	×0.5
Poison	×2	Steel	×1
! Ground	×1	Fairy	×1

Can be used in
Inverse Battle
Battle Institute
Battle Maison
Random Matchup (Free Battle)
Random Matchup (Others)

LEVEL-UP MOVES

Lv.	Name	Type	Kind	Pow.	Acc.	PP	Range
1	Teleport	Psychic	Status	—	—	20	Self
1	Harden	Normal	Status	—	—	30	Self
1	Confusion	Psychic	Special	50	100	25	Normal
1	Rapid Spin	Normal	Physical	20	100	40	Normal
4	Rapid Spin	Normal	Physical	20	100	40	Normal
7	Mud-Slap	Ground	Special	20	100	10	Normal
10	Heal Block	Psychic	Status	—	100	15	Many Others
13	Rock Tomb	Rock	Physical	60	95	15	Normal
16	Psybeam	Psychic	Special	65	100	20	Normal
19	Ancient Power	Rock	Special	60	100	5	Normal
22	Cosmic Power	Psychic	Status	—	—	20	Self
25	Power Trick	Psychic	Status	—	—	10	Self
28	Self-Destruct	Normal	Physical	200	100	5	Adjacent
31	Extrasensory	Psychic	Special	80	100	20	Normal
34	Guard Split	Psychic	Status	—	—	10	Normal
34	Power Split	Psychic	Status	—	—	10	Normal
36	Hyper Beam	Normal	Special	150	90	5	Normal
40	Earth Power	Ground	Special	90	100	10	Normal
46	Sandstorm	Rock	Status	—	—	10	Both Sides
52	Imprison	Psychic	Status	—	—	10	Self
58	Explosion	Normal	Physical	250	100	5	Adjacent

TM & HM MOVES

No.	Name	Type	Kind	Pow.	Acc.	PP	Range
TM03	Psyshock	Psychic	Special	80	100	10	Normal
TM04	Calm Mind	Psychic	Status	—	—	20	Self
TM06	Toxic	Poison	Status	—	90	10	Normal
TM10	Hidden Power	Normal	Special	60	100	15	Normal
TM11	Sunny Day	Fire	Status	—	—	5	Both Sides
TM13	Ice Beam	Ice	Special	90	100	10	Normal
TM15	Hyper Beam	Normal	Special	150	90	5	Normal
TM16	Light Screen	Psychic	Status	—	—	30	Your Side
TM17	Protect	Normal	Status	—	—	10	Self
TM18	Rain Dance	Water	Status	—	—	5	Both Sides
TM20	Safeguard	Normal	Status	—	—	25	Your Side
TM21	Frustration	Normal	Physical	—	100	20	Normal
TM22	Solar Beam	Grass	Special	120	100	10	Normal
TM23	Smack Down	Rock	Physical	50	100	15	Normal
TM26	Earthquake	Ground	Physical	100	100	10	Adjacent
TM27	Return	Normal	Physical	—	100	20	Normal
TM28	Dig	Ground	Physical	80	100	10	Normal
TM29	Psychic	Psychic	Special	90	100	10	Normal
TM30	Shadow Ball	Ghost	Special	80	100	15	Normal
TM32	Double Team	Normal	Status	—	—	15	Self
TM33	Reflect	Psychic	Status	—	—	20	Your Side
TM37	Sandstorm	Rock	Status	—	—	10	Both Sides
TM39	Rock Tomb	Rock	Physical	60	95	15	Normal
TM42	Facade	Normal	Physical	70	100	20	Normal
TM44	Rest	Psychic	Status	—	—	10	Self
TM48	Round	Normal	Special	60	100	15	Normal
TM57	Charge Beam	Electric	Special	50	90	10	Normal
TM64	Explosion	Normal	Physical	250	100	5	Adjacent
TM68	Giga Impact	Normal	Physical	150	90	5	Normal
TM69	Rock Polish	Rock	Status	—	—	20	Self
TM70	Flash	Normal	Status	—	100	20	Normal
TM71	Stone Edge	Rock	Physical	100	80	5	Normal
TM74	Gyro Ball	Steel	Physical	—	100	5	Normal
TM77	Psych Up	Normal	Status	—	—	10	Normal
TM78	Bulldoze	Ground	Physical	60	100	20	Adjacent
TM80	Rock Slide	Rock	Physical	75	90	10	Many Others
TM85	Dream Eater	Psychic	Special	100	100	15	Normal
TM86	Grass Knot	Grass	Special	—	100	20	Normal
TM87	Swagger	Normal	Status	—	90	15	Normal
TM88	Sleep Talk	Normal	Status	—	—	10	Self
TM90	Substitute	Normal	Status	—	—	10	Self
TM92	Trick Room	Psychic	Status	—	—	5	Both Sides
TM94	Secret Power	Normal	Physical	70	100	20	Normal
TM99	Dazzling Gleam	Fairy	Special	80	100	10	Many Others
TM100	Confide	Normal	Status	—	—	20	Normal
HM04	Strength	Normal	Physical	80	100	15	Normal
HM06	Rock Smash	Fighting	Physical	40	100	15	Normal

MOVES LEARNED IN EXCHANGE FOR BP

Name	Type	Kind	Pow.	Acc.	PP	Range
Signal Beam	Bug	Special	75	100	15	Normal
Drill Run	Ground	Physical	80	95	10	Normal
Magic Coat	Psychic	Status	—	—	15	Self
Earth Power	Ground	Special	90	100	10	Normal
Gravity	Psychic	Status	—	—	5	Both Sides
Zen Headbutt	Psychic	Physical	80	90	15	Normal
Snore	Normal	Special	50	100	15	Normal
Trick	Psychic	Status	—	100	10	Normal
Wonder Room	Psychic	Status	—	—	10	Both Sides
Recycle	Normal	Status	—	—	10	Self
Stealth Rock	Rock	Status	—	—	20	Other Side
Skill Swap	Psychic	Status	—	—	10	Normal

MOVES TAUGHT BY PEOPLE

Name	Type	Kind	Pow.	Acc.	PP	Range

National Pokédex **345** Hoenn Pokédex **138**

Lileep

Sea Lily Pokémon

Rock | Grass

HEIGHT: 3'03" WEIGHT: 52.5 lbs.

Same form for ♂ / ♀

Ω Lileep became extinct approximately a hundred million years ago. This ancient Pokémon attaches itself to a rock on the seafloor and catches approaching prey using tentacles shaped like flower petals.

α Lileep is an ancient Pokémon that was regenerated from a fossil. It remains permanently anchored to a rock. From its immobile perch, this Pokémon intently scans for prey with its two eyes.

ABILITY
Suction Cups

HIDDEN ABILITY
Storm Drain

EGG GROUPS
Water 3

STAT GROWTH RATES
HP ▮▮▮
Attack ▮▮
Defense ▮▮▮
Sp. Atk ▮▮▮
Sp. Def ▮▮▮▮
Speed ▮

ITEMS SOMETIMES HELD BY WILD POKÉMON
—

EVOLUTION

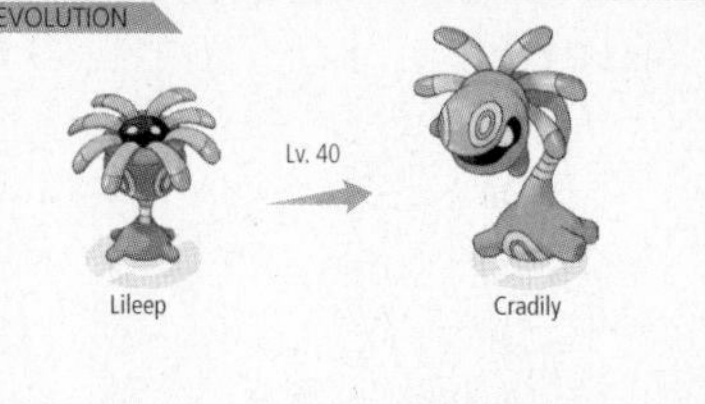

MAIN WAY TO REGISTER IN THE NATIONAL POKÉDEX

After obtaining the Root Fossil in the desert on Route 111, have it restored at the Devon Corporation (2F) in Rustboro City, or bring it to your game using Link Trade or the GTS.

Damage taken in normal battles

Type		Type	
Normal	×0.5	Flying	×1
Fire	×1	Psychic	×1
Water	×1	Bug	×2
Grass	×1	Rock	×1
Electric	×0.5	Ghost	×1
Ice	×2	Dragon	×1
Fighting	×2	Dark	×1
Poison	×1	Steel	×2
Ground	×1	Fairy	×1

Damage taken in Inverse battles

Type		Type	
Normal	×2	Flying	×1
Fire	×1	Psychic	×1
Water	×1	Bug	×0.5
Grass	×1	Rock	×1
Electric	×2	Ghost	×1
Ice	×0.5	Dragon	×1
Fighting	×0.5	Dark	×1
Poison	×1	Steel	×0.5
Ground	×1	Fairy	×1

Can be used in
Inverse Battle
Battle Institute
Battle Maison
Random Matchup (Free Battle)
Random Matchup (Others)

LEVEL-UP MOVES

Lv.	Name	Type	Kind	Pow.	Acc.	PP	Range
1	Astonish	Ghost	Physical	30	100	15	Normal
1	Constrict	Normal	Physical	10	100	35	Normal
5	Acid	Poison	Special	40	100	30	Many Others
9	Ingrain	Grass	Status	—	—	20	Self
13	Confuse Ray	Ghost	Status	—	100	10	Normal
17	Ancient Power	Rock	Special	60	100	5	Normal
21	Brine	Water	Special	65	100	10	Normal
26	Giga Drain	Grass	Special	75	100	10	Normal
31	Gastro Acid	Poison	Status	—	100	10	Normal
36	Amnesia	Psychic	Status	—	—	20	Self
41	Energy Ball	Grass	Special	90	100	10	Normal
46	Stockpile	Normal	Status	—	—	20	Self
46	Spit Up	Normal	Special	—	100	10	Normal
46	Swallow	Normal	Status	—	—	10	Self
52	Wring Out	Normal	Special	—	100	5	Normal

TM & HM MOVES

No.	Name	Type	Kind	Pow.	Acc.	PP	Range
TM06	Toxic	Poison	Status	—	90	10	Normal
TM10	Hidden Power	Normal	Special	60	100	15	Normal
TM11	Sunny Day	Fire	Status	—	—	5	Both Sides
TM17	Protect	Normal	Status	—	—	10	Self
TM21	Frustration	Normal	Physical	—	100	20	Normal
TM22	Solar Beam	Grass	Special	120	100	10	Normal
TM23	Smack Down	Rock	Physical	50	100	15	Normal
TM27	Return	Normal	Physical	—	100	20	Normal
TM32	Double Team	Normal	Status	—	—	15	Self
TM36	Sludge Bomb	Poison	Special	90	100	10	Normal
TM37	Sandstorm	Rock	Status	—	—	10	Both Sides
TM39	Rock Tomb	Rock	Physical	60	95	15	Normal
TM42	Facade	Normal	Physical	70	100	20	Normal
TM44	Rest	Psychic	Status	—	—	10	Self
TM45	Attract	Normal	Status	—	100	15	Normal
TM48	Round	Normal	Special	60	100	15	Normal
TM53	Energy Ball	Grass	Special	90	100	10	Normal
TM69	Rock Polish	Rock	Status	—	—	20	Self
TM70	Flash	Normal	Status	—	100	20	Normal
TM75	Swords Dance	Normal	Status	—	—	20	Self
TM80	Rock Slide	Rock	Physical	75	90	10	Many Others
TM83	Infestation	Bug	Special	20	100	20	Normal
TM86	Grass Knot	Grass	Special	—	100	20	Normal
TM87	Swagger	Normal	Status	—	90	15	Normal
TM88	Sleep Talk	Normal	Status	—	—	10	Self
TM90	Substitute	Normal	Status	—	—	10	Self
TM94	Secret Power	Normal	Physical	70	100	20	Normal
TM100	Confide	Normal	Status	—	—	20	Normal

MOVES LEARNED IN EXCHANGE FOR BP

Name	Type	Kind	Pow.	Acc.	PP	Range
Seed Bomb	Grass	Physical	80	100	15	Normal
Earth Power	Ground	Special	90	100	10	Normal
Bind	Normal	Physical	15	85	20	Normal
Snore	Normal	Special	50	100	15	Normal
Synthesis	Grass	Status	—	—	5	Self
Pain Split	Normal	Status	—	—	20	Normal
Giga Drain	Grass	Special	75	100	10	Normal
Gastro Acid	Poison	Status	—	100	10	Normal
Worry Seed	Grass	Status	—	100	10	Normal
Stealth Rock	Rock	Status	—	—	20	Other Side

MOVES TAUGHT BY PEOPLE

Name	Type	Kind	Pow.	Acc.	PP	Range

EGG MOVES

Name	Type	Kind	Pow.	Acc.	PP	Range
Barrier	Psychic	Status	—	—	20	Self
Recover	Normal	Status	—	—	10	Self
Mirror Coat	Psychic	Special	—	100	20	Varies
Wring Out	Normal	Special	—	100	5	Normal
Tickle	Normal	Status	—	100	20	Normal
Curse	Ghost	Status	—	—	10	Varies
Mega Drain	Grass	Special	40	100	15	Normal
Endure	Normal	Status	—	—	10	Self
Stealth Rock	Rock	Status	—	—	20	Other Side

National Pokédex **346** Hoenn Pokédex **139**

Cradily

Barnacle Pokémon

Rock | Grass

HEIGHT: 4'11" WEIGHT: 133.2 lbs.

Same form for ♂ / ♀

Ω Cradily roams around the ocean floor in search of food. This Pokémon freely extends its tree trunk-like neck and captures unwary prey using its eight tentacles.

α Cradily's body serves as an anchor, preventing it from being washed away in rough seas. This Pokémon secretes a strong digestive fluid from its tentacles.

ABILITY
Suction Cups

HIDDEN ABILITY
Storm Drain

EGG GROUPS
Water 3

STAT GROWTH RATES
HP ▮▮▮▮
Attack ▮▮▮▮
Defense ▮▮▮▮
Sp. Atk ▮▮▮▮
Sp. Def ▮▮▮▮
Speed ▮▮

ITEMS SOMETIMES HELD BY WILD POKÉMON
—

EVOLUTION

Lileep → Lv. 40 → Cradily

MAIN WAY TO REGISTER IN THE NATIONAL POKÉDEX

Level up Lileep to Lv. 40.

Damage taken in normal battles

Type		Type	
Normal	×0.5	Flying	×1
Fire	×1	Psychic	×1
Water	×1	Bug	×2
Grass	×1	Rock	×1
Electric	×0.5	Ghost	×1
Ice	×2	Dragon	×1
Fighting	×2	Dark	×1
Poison	×1	Steel	×2
Ground	×1	Fairy	×1

Damage taken in Inverse battles

Type		Type	
Normal	×2	Flying	×1
Fire	×1	Psychic	×1
Water	×1	Bug	×0.5
Grass	×1	Rock	×1
Electric	×2	Ghost	×1
Ice	×0.5	Dragon	×1
Fighting	×0.5	Dark	×1
Poison	×1	Steel	×0.5
Ground	×1	Fairy	×1

Can be used in
Inverse Battle
Battle Institute
Battle Maison
Random Matchup (Free Battle)
Random Matchup (Others)

LEVEL-UP MOVES

Lv.	Name	Type	Kind	Pow.	Acc.	PP	Range
1	Wring Out	Normal	Special	—	100	5	Normal
1	Astonish	Ghost	Physical	30	100	15	Normal
1	Constrict	Normal	Physical	10	100	35	Normal
1	Acid	Poison	Special	40	100	30	Many Others
1	Ingrain	Grass	Status	—	—	20	Self
5	Acid	Poison	Special	40	100	30	Many Others
9	Ingrain	Grass	Status	—	—	20	Self
13	Confuse Ray	Ghost	Status	—	100	10	Normal
17	Ancient Power	Rock	Special	60	100	5	Normal
21	Brine	Water	Special	65	100	10	Normal
26	Giga Drain	Grass	Special	75	100	10	Normal
31	Gastro Acid	Poison	Status	—	100	10	Normal
36	Amnesia	Psychic	Status	—	—	20	Self
44	Energy Ball	Grass	Special	90	100	10	Normal
52	Stockpile	Normal	Status	—	—	20	Self
52	Spit Up	Normal	Special	—	100	10	Normal
52	Swallow	Normal	Status	—	—	10	Self
61	Wring Out	Normal	Special	—	100	5	Normal

TM & HM MOVES

No.	Name	Type	Kind	Pow.	Acc.	PP	Range
TM06	Toxic	Poison	Status	—	90	10	Normal
TM10	Hidden Power	Normal	Special	60	100	15	Normal
TM11	Sunny Day	Fire	Status	—	—	5	Both Sides
TM15	Hyper Beam	Normal	Special	150	90	5	Normal
TM17	Protect	Normal	Status	—	—	10	Self
TM21	Frustration	Normal	Physical	—	100	20	Normal
TM22	Solar Beam	Grass	Special	120	100	10	Normal
TM23	Smack Down	Rock	Physical	50	100	15	Normal
TM26	Earthquake	Ground	Physical	100	100	10	Adjacent
TM27	Return	Normal	Physical	—	100	20	Normal
TM32	Double Team	Normal	Status	—	—	15	Self
TM34	Sludge Wave	Poison	Special	95	100	10	Adjacent
TM36	Sludge Bomb	Poison	Special	90	100	10	Normal
TM37	Sandstorm	Rock	Status	—	—	10	Both Sides
TM39	Rock Tomb	Rock	Physical	60	95	15	Normal
TM42	Facade	Normal	Physical	70	100	20	Normal
TM44	Rest	Psychic	Status	—	—	10	Self
TM45	Attract	Normal	Status	—	100	15	Normal
TM48	Round	Normal	Special	60	100	15	Normal
TM53	Energy Ball	Grass	Special	90	100	10	Normal
TM68	Giga Impact	Normal	Physical	150	90	5	Normal
TM69	Rock Polish	Rock	Status	—	—	20	Self
TM70	Flash	Normal	Status	—	100	20	Normal
TM71	Stone Edge	Rock	Physical	100	80	5	Normal
TM75	Swords Dance	Normal	Status	—	—	20	Self
TM78	Bulldoze	Ground	Physical	60	100	20	Adjacent
TM80	Rock Slide	Rock	Physical	75	90	10	Many Others
TM83	Infestation	Bug	Special	20	100	20	Normal
TM86	Grass Knot	Grass	Special	—	100	20	Normal
TM87	Swagger	Normal	Status	—	90	15	Normal
TM88	Sleep Talk	Normal	Status	—	—	10	Self
TM90	Substitute	Normal	Status	—	—	10	Self
TM94	Secret Power	Normal	Physical	70	100	20	Normal
TM100	Confide	Normal	Status	—	—	20	Normal
HM04	Strength	Normal	Physical	80	100	15	Normal
HM06	Rock Smash	Fighting	Physical	40	100	15	Normal

MOVES LEARNED IN EXCHANGE FOR BP

Name	Type	Kind	Pow.	Acc.	PP	Range
Seed Bomb	Grass	Physical	80	100	15	Normal
Block	Normal	Status	—	—	5	Normal
Earth Power	Ground	Special	90	100	10	Normal
Bind	Normal	Physical	15	85	20	Normal
Snore	Normal	Special	50	100	15	Normal
Synthesis	Grass	Status	—	—	5	Self
Pain Split	Normal	Status	—	—	20	Normal
Giga Drain	Grass	Special	75	100	10	Normal
Gastro Acid	Poison	Status	—	100	10	Normal
Worry Seed	Grass	Status	—	100	10	Normal
Stealth Rock	Rock	Status	—	—	20	Other Side

MOVES TAUGHT BY PEOPLE

Name	Type	Kind	Pow.	Acc.	PP	Range

National Pokédex **347** Hoenn Pokédex **140**

Anorith

Old Shrimp Pokémon

Rock | Bug

HEIGHT: 2'04" WEIGHT: 27.6 lbs.

Same form for ♂ / ♀

Ω Anorith was regenerated from a prehistoric fossil. This primitive Pokémon once lived in warm seas. It grips its prey firmly between its two large claws.

α Anorith is said to be a type of Pokémon predecessor, with eight wings at the sides of its body. This Pokémon swam in the primordial sea by undulating these eight wings.

ABILITY
Battle Armor

HIDDEN ABILITY
Swift Swim

EGG GROUPS
Water 3

STAT GROWTH RATES
HP
Attack
Defense
Sp. Atk
Sp. Def
Speed

ITEMS SOMETIMES HELD BY WILD POKÉMON
—

EVOLUTION

Anorith → Lv. 40 → Armaldo

MAIN WAY TO REGISTER IN THE NATIONAL POKÉDEX

After obtaining the Claw Fossil in the desert on Route 111, have it restored at the Devon Corporation (2F) in Rustboro City, or bring it to your game using Link Trade or the GTS.

Damage taken in normal battles

Type		Type	
Normal	×0.5	Flying	×1
Fire	×1	Psychic	×1
Water	×2	Bug	×1
Grass	×1	Rock	×2
Electric	×1	Ghost	×1
Ice	×1	Dragon	×1
Fighting	×1	Dark	×1
Poison	×0.5	Steel	×2
Ground	×1	Fairy	×1

Damage taken in Inverse battles

Type		Type	
Normal	×2	Flying	×1
Fire	×1	Psychic	×1
Water	×0.5	Bug	×1
Grass	×1	Rock	×0.5
Electric	×1	Ghost	×1
Ice	×1	Dragon	×1
Fighting	×1	Dark	×1
Poison	×2	Steel	×0.5
Ground	×1	Fairy	×1

Can be used in
Inverse Battle
Battle Institute
Battle Maison
Random Matchup (Free Battle)
Random Matchup (Others)

LEVEL-UP MOVES

Lv.	Name	Type	Kind	Pow.	Acc.	PP	Range
1	Scratch	Normal	Physical	40	100	35	Normal
1	Harden	Normal	Status	—	—	30	Self
4	Mud Sport	Ground	Status	—	—	15	Both Sides
7	Water Gun	Water	Special	40	100	25	Normal
10	Fury Cutter	Bug	Physical	40	95	20	Normal
13	Smack Down	Rock	Physical	50	100	15	Normal
17	Metal Claw	Steel	Physical	50	95	35	Normal
21	Ancient Power	Rock	Special	60	100	5	Normal
25	Bug Bite	Bug	Physical	60	100	20	Normal
29	Brine	Water	Special	65	100	10	Normal
34	Slash	Normal	Physical	70	100	20	Normal
39	Crush Claw	Normal	Physical	75	95	10	Normal
44	X-Scissor	Bug	Physical	80	100	15	Normal
49	Protect	Normal	Status	—	—	10	Self
55	Rock Blast	Rock	Physical	25	90	10	Normal

TM & HM MOVES

No.	Name	Type	Kind	Pow.	Acc.	PP	Range
TM01	Hone Claws	Dark	Status	—	—	15	Self
TM06	Toxic	Poison	Status	—	90	10	Normal
TM10	Hidden Power	Normal	Special	60	100	15	Normal
TM11	Sunny Day	Fire	Status	—	—	5	Both Sides
TM17	Protect	Normal	Status	—	—	10	Self
TM21	Frustration	Normal	Physical	—	100	20	Normal
TM23	Smack Down	Rock	Physical	50	100	15	Normal
TM27	Return	Normal	Physical	—	100	20	Normal
TM28	Dig	Ground	Physical	80	100	10	Normal
TM31	Brick Break	Fighting	Physical	75	100	15	Normal
TM32	Double Team	Normal	Status	—	—	15	Self
TM37	Sandstorm	Rock	Status	—	—	10	Both Sides
TM39	Rock Tomb	Rock	Physical	60	95	15	Normal
TM40	Aerial Ace	Flying	Physical	60	—	20	Normal
TM42	Facade	Normal	Physical	70	100	20	Normal
TM44	Rest	Psychic	Status	—	—	10	Self
TM45	Attract	Normal	Status	—	100	15	Normal
TM48	Round	Normal	Special	60	100	15	Normal
TM54	False Swipe	Normal	Physical	40	100	40	Normal
TM69	Rock Polish	Rock	Status	—	—	20	Self
TM75	Swords Dance	Normal	Status	—	—	20	Self
TM76	Struggle Bug	Bug	Special	50	100	20	Many Others
TM80	Rock Slide	Rock	Physical	75	90	10	Many Others
TM81	X-Scissor	Bug	Physical	80	100	15	Normal
TM87	Swagger	Normal	Status	—	90	15	Normal
TM88	Sleep Talk	Normal	Status	—	—	10	Self
TM90	Substitute	Normal	Status	—	—	10	Self
TM94	Secret Power	Normal	Physical	70	100	20	Normal
TM100	Confide	Normal	Status	—	—	20	Normal
HM01	Cut	Normal	Physical	50	95	30	Normal
HM06	Rock Smash	Fighting	Physical	40	100	15	Normal

MOVES LEARNED IN EXCHANGE FOR BP

Name	Type	Kind	Pow.	Acc.	PP	Range
Bug Bite	Bug	Physical	60	100	20	Normal
Earth Power	Ground	Special	90	100	10	Normal
Iron Defense	Steel	Status	—	—	15	Self
Snore	Normal	Special	50	100	15	Normal
Knock Off	Dark	Physical	65	100	20	Normal
Water Pulse	Water	Special	60	100	20	Normal
Stealth Rock	Rock	Status	—	—	20	Other Side

MOVES TAUGHT BY PEOPLE

Name	Type	Kind	Pow.	Acc.	PP	Range

EGG MOVES

Name	Type	Kind	Pow.	Acc.	PP	Range
Rapid Spin	Normal	Physical	20	100	40	Normal
Knock Off	Dark	Physical	65	100	20	Normal
Screech	Normal	Status	—	85	40	Normal
Sand Attack	Ground	Status	—	100	15	Normal
Cross Poison	Poison	Physical	70	100	20	Normal
Curse	Ghost	Status	—	—	10	Varies
Iron Defense	Steel	Status	—	—	15	Self
Water Pulse	Water	Special	60	100	20	Normal
Aqua Jet	Water	Physical	40	100	20	Normal

National Pokédex **348** Hoenn Pokédex **141**

Armaldo

Plate Pokémon

Rock | Bug

HEIGHT: 4'11" WEIGHT: 150.4 lbs.

Same form for ♂ / ♀

Ω Armaldo's tough armor makes all attacks bounce off. This Pokémon's two enormous claws can be freely extended or contracted. They have the power to punch right through a steel slab.

α Armaldo is a Pokémon species that became extinct in prehistoric times. This Pokémon is said to have walked on its hind legs, which would have been more convenient for life on land.

ABILITY
Battle Armor

HIDDEN ABILITY
Swift Swim

EGG GROUPS
Water 3

STAT GROWTH RATES
HP
Attack
Defense
Sp. Atk
Sp. Def
Speed

ITEMS SOMETIMES HELD BY WILD POKÉMON
—

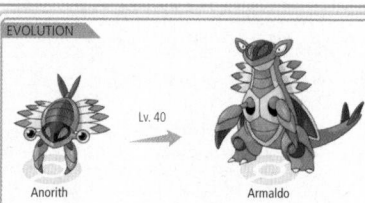

EVOLUTION

Anorith → Lv. 40 → Armaldo

MAIN WAY TO REGISTER IN THE NATIONAL POKÉDEX

Level up Anorith to Lv. 40.

Damage taken in normal battles

Type		Type	
Normal	×0.5	Flying	×1
Fire	×1	Psychic	×1
Water	×2	Bug	×1
Grass	×1	Rock	×2
Electric	×1	Ghost	×1
Ice	×1	Dragon	×1
Fighting	×1	Dark	×1
Poison	×0.5	Steel	×2
Ground	×1	Fairy	×1

Damage taken in Inverse battles

Type		Type	
Normal	×2	Flying	×1
Fire	×1	Psychic	×1
Water	×0.5	Bug	×1
Grass	×1	Rock	×0.5
Electric	×1	Ghost	×1
Ice	×1	Dragon	×1
Fighting	×1	Dark	×1
Poison	×2	Steel	×0.5
Ground	×1	Fairy	×1

Can be used in
Inverse Battle
Battle Institute
Battle Maison
Random Matchup (Free Battle)
Random Matchup (Others)

LEVEL-UP MOVES

Lv.	Name	Type	Kind	Pow.	Acc.	PP	Range
1	Scratch	Normal	Physical	40	100	35	Normal
1	Harden	Normal	Status	—	—	30	Self
1	Mud Sport	Ground	Status	—	—	15	Both Sides
1	Water Gun	Water	Special	40	100	25	Normal
4	Mud Sport	Ground	Status	—	—	15	Both Sides
7	Water Gun	Water	Special	40	100	25	Normal
10	Fury Cutter	Bug	Physical	40	95	20	Normal
13	Smack Down	Rock	Physical	50	100	15	Normal
17	Metal Claw	Steel	Physical	50	95	35	Normal
21	Ancient Power	Rock	Special	60	100	5	Normal
25	Slash	Normal	Physical	70	100	20	Normal
29	Brine	Water	Special	65	100	10	Normal
34	Slash	Normal	Physical	70	100	20	Normal
39	Crush Claw	Normal	Physical	75	95	10	Normal
46	X-Scissor	Bug	Physical	80	100	15	Normal
53	Protect	Normal	Status	—	—	10	Self
61	Rock Blast	Rock	Physical	25	90	10	Normal

TM & HM MOVES

No.	Name	Type	Kind	Pow.	Acc.	PP	Range
TM01	Hone Claws	Dark	Status	—	—	15	Self
TM06	Toxic	Poison	Status	—	90	10	Normal
TM10	Hidden Power	Normal	Special	60	100	15	Normal
TM11	Sunny Day	Fire	Status	—	—	5	Both Sides
TM15	Hyper Beam	Normal	Special	150	90	5	Normal
TM17	Protect	Normal	Status	—	—	10	Self
TM21	Frustration	Normal	Physical	—	100	20	Normal
TM23	Smack Down	Rock	Physical	50	100	15	Normal
TM26	Earthquake	Ground	Physical	100	100	10	Adjacent
TM27	Return	Normal	Physical	—	100	20	Normal
TM28	Dig	Ground	Physical	80	100	10	Normal
TM31	Brick Break	Fighting	Physical	75	100	15	Normal
TM32	Double Team	Normal	Status	—	—	15	Self
TM37	Sandstorm	Rock	Status	—	—	10	Both Sides
TM39	Rock Tomb	Rock	Physical	60	95	15	Normal
TM40	Aerial Ace	Flying	Physical	60	—	20	Normal
TM42	Facade	Normal	Physical	70	100	20	Normal
TM44	Rest	Psychic	Status	—	—	10	Self
TM45	Attract	Normal	Status	—	100	15	Normal
TM48	Round	Normal	Special	60	100	15	Normal
TM54	False Swipe	Normal	Physical	40	100	40	Normal
TM68	Giga Impact	Normal	Physical	150	90	5	Normal
TM69	Rock Polish	Rock	Status	—	—	20	Self
TM71	Stone Edge	Rock	Physical	100	80	5	Normal
TM75	Swords Dance	Normal	Status	—	—	20	Self
TM76	Struggle Bug	Bug	Special	50	100	20	Many Others
TM78	Bulldoze	Ground	Physical	60	100	20	Adjacent
TM80	Rock Slide	Rock	Physical	75	90	10	Many Others
TM81	X-Scissor	Bug	Physical	80	100	15	Normal
TM87	Swagger	Normal	Status	—	90	15	Normal
TM88	Sleep Talk	Normal	Status	—	—	10	Self
TM90	Substitute	Normal	Status	—	—	10	Self
TM91	Flash Cannon	Steel	Special	80	100	10	Normal
TM94	Secret Power	Normal	Physical	70	100	20	Normal
TM100	Confide	Normal	Status	—	—	20	Normal
HM01	Cut	Normal	Physical	50	95	30	Normal
HM04	Strength	Normal	Physical	80	100	15	Normal
HM06	Rock Smash	Fighting	Physical	40	100	15	Normal

MOVES LEARNED IN EXCHANGE FOR BP

Name	Type	Kind	Pow.	Acc.	PP	Range
Bug Bite	Bug	Physical	60	100	20	Normal
Low Kick	Fighting	Physical	—	100	20	Normal
Block	Normal	Status	—	—	5	Normal
Earth Power	Ground	Special	90	100	10	Normal
Iron Defense	Steel	Status	—	—	15	Self
Superpower	Fighting	Physical	120	100	5	Normal
Aqua Tail	Water	Physical	90	90	10	Normal
Iron Tail	Steel	Physical	100	75	15	Normal
Snore	Normal	Special	50	100	15	Normal
Knock Off	Dark	Physical	65	100	20	Normal
Water Pulse	Water	Special	60	100	20	Normal
Stealth Rock	Rock	Status	—	—	20	Other Side

MOVES TAUGHT BY PEOPLE

Name	Type	Kind	Pow.	Acc.	PP	Range

National Pokédex **349** Hoenn Pokédex **145**

Feebas

Fish Pokémon

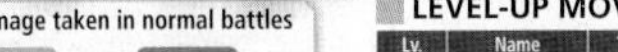

Water

HEIGHT: 2'00" WEIGHT: 16.3 lbs.

Same form for ♂ / ♀

Ω Feebas's fins are ragged and tattered from the start of its life. Because of its shoddy appearance, this Pokémon is largely ignored. It is capable of living in both the sea and in rivers.

α While Feebas's body is in tatters, it has a hardy and tenacious life force that enables it to live anywhere. However, this Pokémon is also slow and dimwitted, making it an easy catch.

ABILITIES
Swift Swim
Oblivious

HIDDEN ABILITY
Adaptability

EGG GROUPS
Water 1 | Dragon

STAT GROWTH RATES
HP
Attack
Defense
Sp. Atk
Sp. Def
Speed

ITEMS SOMETIMES HELD BY WILD POKÉMON
—

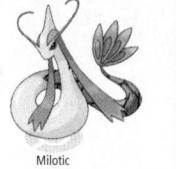

EVOLUTION

Feebas → Level up with high Beauty → Milotic

MAIN WAY TO REGISTER IN THE NATIONAL POKÉDEX

Catch using an Old Rod on Route 119.

Damage taken in normal battles

Type		Type	
Normal	×1	Flying	×1
Fire	×0.5	Psychic	×1
Water	×0.5	Bug	×1
Grass	×2	Rock	×1
Electric	×2	Ghost	×1
Ice	×0.5	Dragon	×1
Fighting	×1	Dark	×1
Poison	×1	Steel	×0.5
Ground	×1	Fairy	×1

Damage taken in Inverse battles

Type		Type	
Normal	×1	Flying	×1
Fire	×2	Psychic	×1
Water	×2	Bug	×1
Grass	×0.5	Rock	×1
Electric	×0.5	Ghost	×1
Ice	×2	Dragon	×1
Fighting	×1	Dark	×1
Poison	×1	Steel	×2
Ground	×1	Fairy	×1

Can be used in
Inverse Battle
Battle Institute
Battle Maison
Random Matchup (Free Battle)
Random Matchup (Others)

LEVEL-UP MOVES

Lv.	Name	Type	Kind	Pow.	Acc.	PP	Range
1	Splash	Normal	Status	—	—	40	Self
15	Tackle	Normal	Physical	50	100	35	Normal
30	Flail	Normal	Physical	—	100	15	Normal

TM & HM MOVES

No.	Name	Type	Kind	Pow.	Acc.	PP	Range
TM06	Toxic	Poison	Status	—	90	10	Normal
TM07	Hail	Ice	Status	—	—	10	Both Sides
TM10	Hidden Power	Normal	Special	60	100	15	Normal
TM13	Ice Beam	Ice	Special	90	100	10	Normal
TM14	Blizzard	Ice	Special	110	70	5	Many Others
TM16	Light Screen	Psychic	Status	—	—	30	Your Side
TM17	Protect	Normal	Status	—	—	10	Self
TM18	Rain Dance	Water	Status	—	—	5	Both Sides
TM21	Frustration	Normal	Physical	—	100	20	Normal
TM27	Return	Normal	Physical	—	100	20	Normal
TM32	Double Team	Normal	Status	—	—	15	Self
TM42	Facade	Normal	Physical	70	100	20	Normal
TM44	Rest	Psychic	Status	—	—	10	Self
TM45	Attract	Normal	Status	—	100	15	Normal
TM48	Round	Normal	Special	60	100	15	Normal
TM55	Scald	Water	Special	80	100	15	Normal
TM87	Swagger	Normal	Status	—	90	15	Normal
TM88	Sleep Talk	Normal	Status	—	—	10	Self
TM90	Substitute	Normal	Status	—	—	10	Self
TM94	Secret Power	Normal	Physical	70	100	20	Normal
TM100	Confide	Normal	Status	—	—	20	Normal
HM03	Surf	Water	Special	90	100	15	Adjacent
HM05	Waterfall	Water	Physical	80	100	15	Normal
HM07	Dive	Water	Physical	80	100	10	Normal

MOVES LEARNED IN EXCHANGE FOR BP

Name	Type	Kind	Pow.	Acc.	PP	Range
Icy Wind	Ice	Special	55	95	15	Many Others
Dragon Pulse	Dragon	Special	85	100	10	Normal
Iron Tail	Steel	Physical	100	75	15	Normal
Snore	Normal	Special	50	100	15	Normal
Water Pulse	Water	Special	60	100	20	Normal

MOVES TAUGHT BY PEOPLE

Name	Type	Kind	Pow.	Acc.	PP	Range

EGG MOVES

Name	Type	Kind	Pow.	Acc.	PP	Range
Mirror Coat	Psychic	Special	—	100	20	Varies
Dragon Breath	Dragon	Special	60	100	20	Normal
Mud Sport	Ground	Status	—	—	15	Both Sides
Hypnosis	Psychic	Status	—	60	20	Normal
Confuse Ray	Ghost	Status	—	100	10	Normal
Mist	Ice	Status	—	—	30	Your Side
Haze	Ice	Status	—	—	30	Both Sides
Tickle	Normal	Status	—	100	20	Normal
Brine	Water	Special	65	100	10	Normal
Iron Tail	Steel	Physical	100	75	15	Normal
Dragon Pulse	Dragon	Special	85	100	10	Normal
Captivate	Normal	Status	—	100	20	Many Others

National Pokédex **350** Hoenn Pokédex **146**

Milotic

Tender Pokémon

Water

HEIGHT: 20'04" WEIGHT: 357.1 lbs.

The male has shorter parts over its eyes. The female has longer parts over its eyes.

Ω Milotic is said to be the most beautiful of all the Pokémon. It has the power to becalm such emotions as anger and hostility to quell bitter feuding.

α Milotic live at the bottom of large lakes. When this Pokémon's body glows a vivid pink, it releases a pulsing wave of energy that brings soothing calm to troubled hearts.

ABILITIES
Marvel Scale
Competitive

HIDDEN ABILITY
Cute Charm

EGG GROUPS
Water 1 | Dragon

STAT GROWTH RATES
HP
Attack
Defense
Sp. Atk
Sp. Def
Speed

ITEMS SOMETIMES HELD BY WILD POKÉMON
—

EVOLUTION

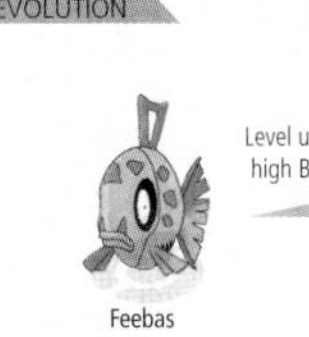

MAIN WAY TO REGISTER IN THE NATIONAL POKÉDEX

Level up Feebas with high beauty.

Damage taken in normal battles

Type		Type	
Normal	×1	Flying	×1
Fire	×0.5	Psychic	×1
Water	×0.5	Bug	×1
Grass	×2	Rock	×1
Electric	×2	Ghost	×1
Ice	×0.5	Dragon	×1
Fighting	×1	Dark	×1
Poison	×1	Steel	×0.5
Ground	×1	Fairy	×1

Damage taken in Inverse battles

Type		Type	
Normal	×1	Flying	×1
Fire	×2	Psychic	×1
Water	×2	Bug	×1
Grass	×0.5	Rock	×1
Electric	×0.5	Ghost	×1
Ice	×2	Dragon	×1
Fighting	×1	Dark	×1
Poison	×1	Steel	×2
Ground	×1	Fairy	×1

Can be used in
Inverse Battle
Battle Institute
Battle Maison
Random Matchup (Free Battle)
Random Matchup (Others)

LEVEL-UP MOVES

Lv.	Name	Type	Kind	Pow.	Acc.	PP	Range
1	Wrap	Normal	Physical	15	90	20	Normal
1	Water Gun	Water	Special	40	100	25	Normal
4	Water Sport	Water	Status	—	—	15	Both Sides
7	Refresh	Normal	Status	—	—	20	Self
11	Disarming Voice	Fairy	Special	40	—	15	Many Others
14	Twister	Dragon	Special	40	100	20	Many Others
17	Water Pulse	Water	Special	60	100	20	Normal
21	Aqua Ring	Water	Status	—	—	20	Self
24	Captivate	Normal	Status	—	100	20	Many Others
27	Dragon Tail	Dragon	Physical	60	90	10	Normal
31	Recover	Normal	Status	—	—	10	Self
34	Aqua Tail	Water	Physical	90	90	10	Normal
37	Attract	Normal	Status	—	100	15	Normal
41	Safeguard	Normal	Status	—	—	25	Your Side
44	Coil	Poison	Status	—	—	20	Self
47	Hydro Pump	Water	Special	110	80	5	Normal
51	Rain Dance	Water	Status	—	—	5	Both Sides

TM & HM MOVES

No.	Name	Type	Kind	Pow.	Acc.	PP	Range
TM06	Toxic	Poison	Status	—	90	10	Normal
TM07	Hail	Ice	Status	—	—	10	Both Sides
TM10	Hidden Power	Normal	Special	60	100	15	Normal
TM13	Ice Beam	Ice	Special	90	100	10	Normal
TM14	Blizzard	Ice	Special	110	70	5	Many Others
TM15	Hyper Beam	Normal	Special	150	90	5	Normal
TM16	Light Screen	Psychic	Status	—	—	30	Your Side
TM17	Protect	Normal	Status	—	—	10	Self
TM18	Rain Dance	Water	Status	—	—	5	Both Sides
TM20	Safeguard	Normal	Status	—	—	25	Your Side
TM21	Frustration	Normal	Physical	—	100	20	Normal
TM27	Return	Normal	Physical	—	100	20	Normal
TM32	Double Team	Normal	Status	—	—	15	Self
TM42	Facade	Normal	Physical	70	100	20	Normal
TM44	Rest	Psychic	Status	—	—	10	Self
TM45	Attract	Normal	Status	—	100	15	Normal
TM48	Round	Normal	Special	60	100	15	Normal
TM55	Scald	Water	Special	80	100	15	Normal
TM68	Giga Impact	Normal	Physical	150	90	5	Normal
TM77	Psych Up	Normal	Status	—	—	10	Normal
TM78	Bulldoze	Ground	Physical	60	100	20	Adjacent
TM82	Dragon Tail	Dragon	Physical	60	90	10	Normal
TM87	Swagger	Normal	Status	—	90	15	Normal
TM88	Sleep Talk	Normal	Status	—	—	10	Self
TM90	Substitute	Normal	Status	—	—	10	Self
TM94	Secret Power	Normal	Physical	70	100	20	Normal
TM100	Confide	Normal	Status	—	—	20	Normal
HM03	Surf	Water	Special	90	100	15	Adjacent
HM05	Waterfall	Water	Physical	80	100	15	Normal
HM07	Dive	Water	Physical	80	100	10	Normal

MOVES LEARNED IN EXCHANGE FOR BP

Name	Type	Kind	Pow.	Acc.	PP	Range
Iron Head	Steel	Physical	80	100	15	Normal
Magic Coat	Psychic	Status	—	—	15	Self
Icy Wind	Ice	Special	55	95	15	Many Others
Aqua Tail	Water	Physical	90	90	10	Normal
Dragon Pulse	Dragon	Special	85	100	10	Normal
Iron Tail	Steel	Physical	100	75	15	Normal
Bind	Normal	Physical	15	85	20	Normal
Snore	Normal	Special	50	100	15	Normal
Water Pulse	Water	Special	60	100	20	Normal

MOVES TAUGHT BY PEOPLE

Name	Type	Kind	Pow.	Acc.	PP	Range

National Pokédex **351** Hoenn Pokédex **147**

Castform

Weather Pokémon

Normal

HEIGHT: 1'00" WEIGHT: 1.8 lbs.

Same form for ♂ / ♀

Ω Castform's appearance changes with the weather. This Pokémon gained the ability to use the vast power of nature to protect its tiny body.

α Castform borrows the power of nature to transform itself into the guises of the sun, rain, and snow-clouds. This Pokémon's feelings change with the weather.

ABILITY

Forecast

HIDDEN ABILITY

—

EGG GROUPS

Fairy Amorphous

STAT GROWTH RATES

HP / Attack / Defense / Sp. Atk / Sp. Def / Speed

ITEMS SOMETIMES HELD BY WILD POKÉMON

—

EVOLUTION

Does not evolve

MAIN WAY TO REGISTER IN THE NATIONAL POKÉDEX

Receive from the head of the Weather Institute on Route 119.

Damage taken in normal battles

Type		Type	
Normal	×1	Flying	×1
Fire	×1	Psychic	×1
Water	×1	Bug	×1
Grass	×1	Rock	×1
Electric	×1	Ghost	×0
Ice	×1	Dragon	×1
Fighting	×2	Dark	×1
Poison	×1	Steel	×1
Ground	×1	Fairy	×1

Damage taken in Inverse battles

Type		Type	
Normal	×1	Flying	×1
Fire	×1	Psychic	×1
Water	×1	Bug	×1
Grass	×1	Rock	×1
Electric	×1	Ghost	×2
Ice	×1	Dragon	×1
Fighting	×0.5	Dark	×1
Poison	×1	Steel	×1
Ground	×1	Fairy	×1

Can be used in

- Inverse Battle
- Battle Institute
- Battle Maison
- Random Matchup (Free Battle)
- Random Matchup (Others)

LEVEL-UP MOVES

Lv.	Name	Type	Kind	Pow.	Acc.	PP	Range
1	Tackle	Normal	Physical	50	100	35	Normal
10	Water Gun	Water	Special	40	100	25	Normal
10	Ember	Fire	Special	40	100	25	Normal
10	Powder Snow	Ice	Special	40	100	25	Many Others
15	Headbutt	Normal	Physical	70	100	15	Normal
20	Rain Dance	Water	Status	—	—	5	Both Sides
20	Sunny Day	Fire	Status	—	—	5	Both Sides
20	Hail	Ice	Status	—	—	10	Both Sides
25	Weather Ball	Normal	Special	50	100	10	Normal
35	Hydro Pump	Water	Special	110	80	5	Normal
35	Fire Blast	Fire	Special	110	85	5	Normal
35	Blizzard	Ice	Special	110	70	5	Many Others
45	Hurricane	Flying	Special	110	70	10	Normal

TM & HM MOVES

No.	Name	Type	Kind	Pow.	Acc.	PP	Range
TM06	Toxic	Poison	Status	—	90	10	Normal
TM07	Hail	Ice	Status	—	—	10	Both Sides
TM10	Hidden Power	Normal	Special	60	100	15	Normal
TM11	Sunny Day	Fire	Status	—	—	5	Both Sides
TM13	Ice Beam	Ice	Special	90	100	10	Normal
TM14	Blizzard	Ice	Special	110	70	5	Many Others
TM17	Protect	Normal	Status	—	—	10	Self
TM18	Rain Dance	Water	Status	—	—	5	Both Sides
TM21	Frustration	Normal	Physical	—	100	20	Normal
TM22	Solar Beam	Grass	Special	120	100	10	Normal
TM24	Thunderbolt	Electric	Special	90	100	15	Normal
TM25	Thunder	Electric	Special	110	70	10	Normal
TM27	Return	Normal	Physical	—	100	20	Normal
TM30	Shadow Ball	Ghost	Special	80	100	15	Normal
TM32	Double Team	Normal	Status	—	—	15	Self
TM35	Flamethrower	Fire	Special	90	100	15	Normal
TM37	Sandstorm	Rock	Status	—	—	10	Both Sides
TM38	Fire Blast	Fire	Special	110	85	5	Normal
TM42	Facade	Normal	Physical	70	100	20	Normal
TM44	Rest	Psychic	Status	—	—	10	Self
TM45	Attract	Normal	Status	—	100	15	Normal
TM46	Thief	Dark	Physical	60	100	25	Normal
TM48	Round	Normal	Special	60	100	15	Normal
TM53	Energy Ball	Grass	Special	90	100	10	Normal
TM55	Scald	Water	Special	80	100	15	Normal
TM59	Incinerate	Fire	Special	60	100	15	Many Others
TM67	Retaliate	Normal	Physical	70	100	5	Normal
TM70	Flash	Normal	Status	—	100	20	Normal
TM73	Thunder Wave	Electric	Status	—	100	20	Normal
TM77	Psych Up	Normal	Status	—	—	10	Normal
TM87	Swagger	Normal	Status	—	90	15	Normal
TM88	Sleep Talk	Normal	Status	—	—	10	Self
TM90	Substitute	Normal	Status	—	—	10	Self
TM94	Secret Power	Normal	Physical	70	100	20	Normal
TM100	Confide	Normal	Status	—	—	20	Normal

MOVES LEARNED IN EXCHANGE FOR BP

Name	Type	Kind	Pow.	Acc.	PP	Range
Last Resort	Normal	Physical	140	100	5	Normal
Icy Wind	Ice	Special	55	95	15	Many Others
Snore	Normal	Special	50	100	15	Normal
Tailwind	Flying	Status	—	—	15	Your Side
Shock Wave	Electric	Special	60	—	20	Normal
Water Pulse	Water	Special	60	100	20	Normal

MOVES TAUGHT BY PEOPLE

Name	Type	Kind	Pow.	Acc.	PP	Range

EGG MOVES

Name	Type	Kind	Pow.	Acc.	PP	Range
Future Sight	Psychic	Special	120	100	10	Normal
Lucky Chant	Normal	Status	—	—	30	Your Side
Disable	Normal	Status	—	100	20	Normal
Amnesia	Psychic	Status	—	—	20	Self
Ominous Wind	Ghost	Special	60	100	5	Normal
Hex	Ghost	Special	65	100	10	Normal
Clear Smog	Poison	Special	50	—	15	Normal
Reflect Type	Normal	Status	—	—	15	Normal
Guard Swap	Psychic	Status	—	—	10	Normal
Cosmic Power	Psychic	Status	—	—	20	Self

National Pokédex **351** Hoenn Pokédex **147**

Castform Sunny Form

Weather Pokémon

Fire

HEIGHT: 1'00" WEIGHT: 1.8 lbs.

Same form for ♂ / ♀

Ω Castform's appearance changes with the weather. This Pokémon gained the ability to use the vast power of nature to protect its tiny body.

α Castform borrows the power of nature to transform itself into the guises of the sun, rain, and snow-clouds. This Pokémon's feelings change with the weather.

This Pokémon art is from in-game data.

ABILITY

Forecast

HIDDEN ABILITY

—

EGG GROUPS

Fairy Amorphous

STAT GROWTH RATES

HP / Attack / Defense / Sp. Atk / Sp. Def / Speed

ITEMS SOMETIMES HELD BY WILD POKÉMON

—

EVOLUTION

Does not evolve

MAIN WAY TO REGISTER IN THE NATIONAL POKÉDEX

Receive from the head of the Weather Institute on Route 119.

Damage taken in normal battles

Type		Type	
Normal	×1	Flying	×1
Fire	×0.5	Psychic	×1
Water	×2	Bug	×0.5
Grass	×0.5	Rock	×2
Electric	×1	Ghost	×1
Ice	×0.5	Dragon	×1
Fighting	×1	Dark	×1
Poison	×1	Steel	×0.5
Ground	×2	Fairy	×0.5

Damage taken in Inverse battles

Type		Type	
Normal	×1	Flying	×1
Fire	×2	Psychic	×1
Water	×0.5	Bug	×2
Grass	×2	Rock	×0.5
Electric	×1	Ghost	×1
Ice	×2	Dragon	×1
Fighting	×1	Dark	×1
Poison	×1	Steel	×2
Ground	×0.5	Fairy	×2

Can be used in

- Inverse Battle
- Battle Institute
- Battle Maison
- Random Matchup (Free Battle)
- Random Matchup (Others)

LEVEL-UP MOVES

Lv.	Name	Type	Kind	Pow.	Acc.	PP	Range
1	Tackle	Normal	Physical	50	100	35	Normal
10	Water Gun	Water	Special	40	100	25	Normal
10	Ember	Fire	Special	40	100	25	Normal
10	Powder Snow	Ice	Special	40	100	25	Many Others
15	Headbutt	Normal	Physical	70	100	15	Normal
20	Rain Dance	Water	Status	—	—	5	Both Sides
20	Sunny Day	Fire	Status	—	—	5	Both Sides
20	Hail	Ice	Status	—	—	10	Both Sides
25	Weather Ball	Normal	Special	50	100	10	Normal
35	Hydro Pump	Water	Special	110	80	5	Normal
35	Fire Blast	Fire	Special	110	85	5	Normal
35	Blizzard	Ice	Special	110	70	5	Many Others
45	Hurricane	Flying	Special	110	70	10	Normal

TM & HM MOVES

No.	Name	Type	Kind	Pow.	Acc.	PP	Range
TM06	Toxic	Poison	Status	—	90	10	Normal
TM07	Hail	Ice	Status	—	—	10	Both Sides
TM10	Hidden Power	Normal	Special	60	100	15	Normal
TM11	Sunny Day	Fire	Status	—	—	5	Both Sides
TM13	Ice Beam	Ice	Special	90	100	10	Normal
TM14	Blizzard	Ice	Special	110	70	5	Many Others
TM17	Protect	Normal	Status	—	—	10	Self
TM18	Rain Dance	Water	Status	—	—	5	Both Sides
TM21	Frustration	Normal	Physical	—	100	20	Normal
TM22	Solar Beam	Grass	Special	120	100	10	Normal
TM24	Thunderbolt	Electric	Special	90	100	15	Normal
TM25	Thunder	Electric	Special	110	70	10	Normal
TM27	Return	Normal	Physical	—	100	20	Normal
TM30	Shadow Ball	Ghost	Special	80	100	15	Normal
TM32	Double Team	Normal	Status	—	—	15	Self
TM35	Flamethrower	Fire	Special	90	100	15	Normal
TM37	Sandstorm	Rock	Status	—	—	10	Both Sides
TM38	Fire Blast	Fire	Special	110	85	5	Normal
TM42	Facade	Normal	Physical	70	100	20	Normal
TM44	Rest	Psychic	Status	—	—	10	Self
TM45	Attract	Normal	Status	—	100	15	Normal
TM46	Thief	Dark	Physical	60	100	25	Normal
TM48	Round	Normal	Special	60	100	15	Normal
TM53	Energy Ball	Grass	Special	90	100	10	Normal
TM55	Scald	Water	Special	80	100	15	Normal
TM59	Incinerate	Fire	Special	60	100	15	Many Others
TM67	Retaliate	Normal	Physical	70	100	5	Normal
TM70	Flash	Normal	Status	—	100	20	Normal
TM73	Thunder Wave	Electric	Status	—	100	20	Normal
TM77	Psych Up	Normal	Status	—	—	10	Normal
TM87	Swagger	Normal	Status	—	90	15	Normal
TM88	Sleep Talk	Normal	Status	—	—	10	Self
TM90	Substitute	Normal	Status	—	—	10	Self
TM94	Secret Power	Normal	Physical	70	100	20	Normal
TM100	Confide	Normal	Status	—	—	20	Normal

MOVES LEARNED IN EXCHANGE FOR BP

Name	Type	Kind	Pow.	Acc.	PP	Range
Last Resort	Normal	Physical	140	100	5	Normal
Icy Wind	Ice	Special	55	95	15	Many Others
Snore	Normal	Special	50	100	15	Normal
Tailwind	Flying	Status	—	—	15	Your Side
Shock Wave	Electric	Special	60	—	20	Normal
Water Pulse	Water	Special	60	100	20	Normal

MOVES TAUGHT BY PEOPLE

Name	Type	Kind	Pow.	Acc.	PP	Range

EGG MOVES

Name	Type	Kind	Pow.	Acc.	PP	Range
Future Sight	Psychic	Special	120	100	10	Normal
Lucky Chant	Normal	Status	—	—	30	Your Side
Disable	Normal	Status	—	100	20	Normal
Amnesia	Psychic	Status	—	—	20	Self
Ominous Wind	Ghost	Special	60	100	5	Normal
Hex	Ghost	Special	65	100	10	Normal
Clear Smog	Poison	Special	50	—	15	Normal
Reflect Type	Normal	Status	—	—	15	Normal
Guard Swap	Psychic	Status	—	—	10	Normal
Cosmic Power	Psychic	Status	—	—	20	Self

◆ Castform changes to its Sunny Form when the weather condition is sunny or extremely harsh sunlight.

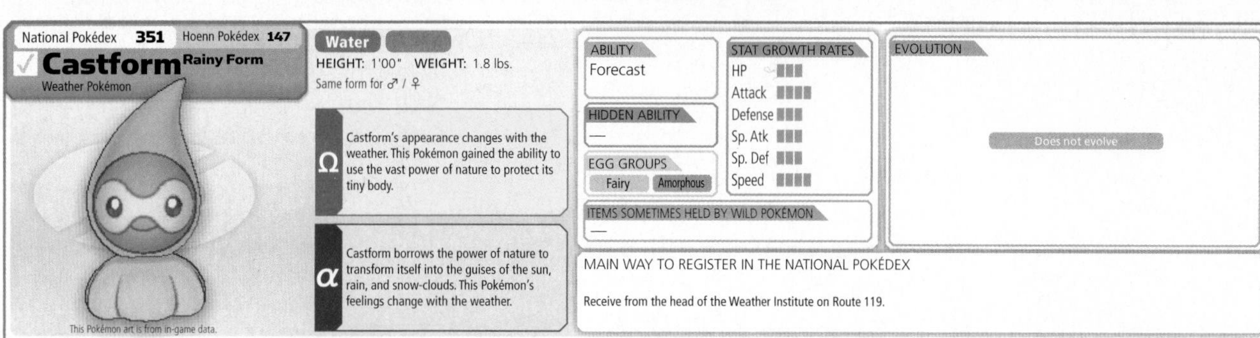

National Pokédex **351** Hoenn Pokédex **147**

Castform Rainy Form

Weather Pokémon

Water

HEIGHT: 1'00" WEIGHT: 1.8 lbs.

Same form for ♂ / ♀

Ω Castform's appearance changes with the weather. This Pokémon gained the ability to use the vast power of nature to protect its tiny body.

α Castform borrows the power of nature to transform itself into the guises of the sun, rain, and snow-clouds. This Pokémon's feelings change with the weather.

ABILITY
Forecast

HIDDEN ABILITY
—

EGG GROUPS
Fairy / Amorphous

STAT GROWTH RATES
HP ■■■
Attack ■■■■
Defense ■■■
Sp. Atk ■■■
Sp. Def ■■■
Speed ■■■■

ITEMS SOMETIMES HELD BY WILD POKÉMON
—

EVOLUTION
Does not evolve

MAIN WAY TO REGISTER IN THE NATIONAL POKÉDEX
Receive from the head of the Weather Institute on Route 119.

This Pokémon art is from in-game data.

Damage taken in normal battles

Type		Type	
Normal	×1	Flying	×1
Fire	×0.5	Psychic	×1
Water	×0.5	Bug	×1
Grass	×2	Rock	×1
Electric	×2	Ghost	×1
Ice	×0.5	Dragon	×1
Fighting	×1	Dark	×1
Poison	×1	Steel	×0.5
Ground	×1	Fairy	×1

Damage taken in Inverse battles

Type		Type	
Normal	×1	Flying	×1
Fire	×2	Psychic	×1
Water	×2	Bug	×1
Grass	×0.5	Rock	×1
Electric	×0.5	Ghost	×1
Ice	×2	Dragon	×1
Fighting	×1	Dark	×1
Poison	×1	Steel	×2
Ground	×1	Fairy	×1

Can be used in
Inverse Battle
Battle Institute
Battle Maison
Random Matchup (Free Battle)
Random Matchup (Others)

LEVEL-UP MOVES

Lv.	Name	Type	Kind	Pow.	Acc.	PP	Range
1	Tackle	Normal	Physical	50	100	35	Normal
10	Water Gun	Water	Special	40	100	25	Normal
10	Ember	Fire	Special	40	100	25	Normal
10	Powder Snow	Ice	Special	40	100	25	Many Others
15	Headbutt	Normal	Physical	70	100	15	Normal
20	Rain Dance	Water	Status	—	—	5	Both Sides
20	Sunny Day	Fire	Status	—	—	5	Both Sides
20	Hail	Ice	Status	—	—	10	Both Sides
25	Weather Ball	Normal	Special	50	100	10	Normal
35	Hydro Pump	Water	Special	110	80	5	Normal
35	Fire Blast	Fire	Special	110	85	5	Normal
35	Blizzard	Ice	Special	110	70	5	Many Others
45	Hurricane	Flying	Special	110	70	10	Normal

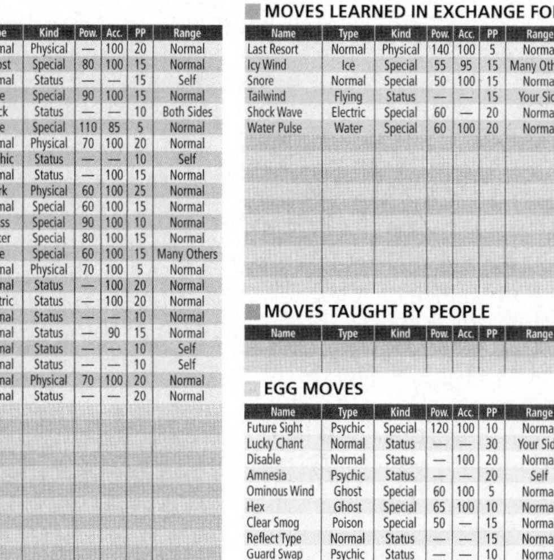

TM & HM MOVES

No.	Name	Type	Kind	Pow.	Acc.	PP	Range
TM06	Toxic	Poison	Status	—	90	10	Normal
TM07	Hail	Ice	Status	—	—	10	Both Sides
TM10	Hidden Power	Normal	Special	60	100	15	Normal
TM11	Sunny Day	Fire	Status	—	—	5	Both Sides
TM13	Ice Beam	Ice	Special	90	100	10	Normal
TM14	Blizzard	Ice	Special	110	70	5	Many Others
TM17	Protect	Normal	Status	—	—	10	Self
TM18	Rain Dance	Water	Status	—	—	5	Both Sides
TM21	Frustration	Normal	Physical	—	100	20	Normal
TM22	Solar Beam	Grass	Special	120	100	10	Normal
TM24	Thunderbolt	Electric	Special	90	100	15	Normal
TM25	Thunder	Electric	Special	110	70	10	Normal
TM27	Return	Normal	Physical	—	100	20	Normal
TM30	Shadow Ball	Ghost	Special	80	100	15	Normal
TM32	Double Team	Normal	Status	—	—	15	Self
TM35	Flamethrower	Fire	Special	90	100	15	Normal
TM37	Sandstorm	Rock	Status	—	—	10	Both Sides
TM38	Fire Blast	Fire	Special	110	85	5	Normal
TM42	Facade	Normal	Physical	70	100	20	Normal
TM44	Rest	Psychic	Status	—	—	10	Self
TM45	Attract	Normal	Status	—	100	15	Normal
TM46	Thief	Dark	Physical	60	100	25	Normal
TM48	Round	Normal	Special	60	100	15	Normal
TM53	Energy Ball	Grass	Special	90	100	10	Normal
TM55	Scald	Water	Special	80	100	15	Normal
TM59	Incinerate	Fire	Special	60	100	15	Many Others
TM67	Retaliate	Normal	Physical	70	100	5	Normal
TM70	Flash	Normal	Status	—	100	20	Normal
TM73	Thunder Wave	Electric	Status	—	100	20	Normal
TM77	Psych Up	Normal	Status	—	—	10	Normal
TM87	Swagger	Normal	Status	—	90	15	Normal
TM88	Sleep Talk	Normal	Status	—	—	10	Self
TM90	Substitute	Normal	Status	—	—	10	Self
TM94	Secret Power	Normal	Physical	70	100	20	Normal
TM100	Confide	Normal	Status	—	—	20	Normal

MOVES LEARNED IN EXCHANGE FOR BP

Name	Type	Kind	Pow.	Acc.	PP	Range
Last Resort	Normal	Physical	140	100	5	Normal
Icy Wind	Ice	Special	55	95	15	Many Others
Snore	Normal	Special	50	100	15	Normal
Tailwind	Flying	Status	—	—	15	Your Side
Shock Wave	Electric	Special	60	—	20	Normal
Water Pulse	Water	Special	60	100	20	Normal

MOVES TAUGHT BY PEOPLE

Name	Type	Kind	Pow.	Acc.	PP	Range

EGG MOVES

Name	Type	Kind	Pow.	Acc.	PP	Range
Future Sight	Psychic	Special	120	100	10	Normal
Lucky Chant	Normal	Status	—	—	30	Your Side
Disable	Normal	Status	—	100	20	Normal
Amnesia	Psychic	Status	—	—	20	Self
Ominous Wind	Ghost	Special	60	100	5	Normal
Hex	Ghost	Special	65	100	10	Normal
Clear Smog	Poison	Special	50	—	15	Normal
Reflect Type	Normal	Status	—	—	15	Normal
Guard Swap	Psychic	Status	—	—	10	Normal
Cosmic Power	Psychic	Status	—	—	20	Self

◆ Castform changes to its Rainy Form when the weather condition is rain.

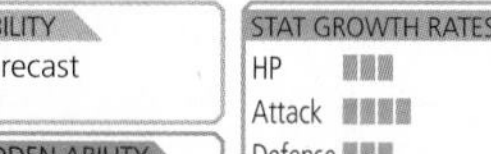

National Pokédex **351** Hoenn Pokédex **147**

Castform Snowy Form

Weather Pokémon

Ice

HEIGHT: 1'00" WEIGHT: 1.8 lbs.

Same form for ♂ / ♀

Ω Castform's appearance changes with the weather. This Pokémon gained the ability to use the vast power of nature to protect its tiny body.

α Castform borrows the power of nature to transform itself into the guises of the sun, rain, and snow-clouds. This Pokémon's feelings change with the weather.

ABILITY
Forecast

HIDDEN ABILITY
—

EGG GROUPS
Fairy / Amorphous

STAT GROWTH RATES
HP ■■■
Attack ■■■■
Defense ■■■
Sp. Atk ■■■
Sp. Def ■■■
Speed ■■■■

ITEMS SOMETIMES HELD BY WILD POKÉMON
—

EVOLUTION
Does not evolve

MAIN WAY TO REGISTER IN THE NATIONAL POKÉDEX
Receive from the head of the Weather Institute on Route 119.

This Pokémon art is from in-game data.

Damage taken in normal battles

Type		Type	
Normal	×1	Flying	×1
Fire	×2	Psychic	×1
Water	×1	Bug	×1
Grass	×1	Rock	×2
Electric	×1	Ghost	×1
Ice	×0.5	Dragon	×1
Fighting	×2	Dark	×1
Poison	×1	Steel	×2
Ground	×1	Fairy	×1

Damage taken in Inverse battles

Type		Type	
Normal	×1	Flying	×1
Fire	×0.5	Psychic	×1
Water	×1	Bug	×1
Grass	×1	Rock	×0.5
Electric	×1	Ghost	×1
Ice	×2	Dragon	×1
Fighting	×0.5	Dark	×1
Poison	×1	Steel	×0.5
Ground	×1	Fairy	×1

Can be used in
Inverse Battle
Battle Institute
Battle Maison
Random Matchup (Free Battle)
Random Matchup (Others)

LEVEL-UP MOVES

Lv.	Name	Type	Kind	Pow.	Acc.	PP	Range
1	Tackle	Normal	Physical	50	100	35	Normal
10	Water Gun	Water	Special	40	100	25	Normal
10	Ember	Fire	Special	40	100	25	Normal
10	Powder Snow	Ice	Special	40	100	25	Many Others
15	Headbutt	Normal	Physical	70	100	15	Normal
20	Rain Dance	Water	Status	—	—	5	Both Sides
20	Sunny Day	Fire	Status	—	—	5	Both Sides
20	Hail	Ice	Status	—	—	10	Both Sides
25	Weather Ball	Normal	Special	50	100	10	Normal
35	Hydro Pump	Water	Special	110	80	5	Normal
35	Fire Blast	Fire	Special	110	85	5	Normal
35	Blizzard	Ice	Special	110	70	5	Many Others
45	Hurricane	Flying	Special	110	70	10	Normal

TM & HM MOVES

No.	Name	Type	Kind	Pow.	Acc.	PP	Range
TM06	Toxic	Poison	Status	—	90	10	Normal
TM07	Hail	Ice	Status	—	—	10	Both Sides
TM10	Hidden Power	Normal	Special	60	100	15	Normal
TM11	Sunny Day	Fire	Status	—	—	5	Both Sides
TM13	Ice Beam	Ice	Special	90	100	10	Normal
TM14	Blizzard	Ice	Special	110	70	5	Many Others
TM17	Protect	Normal	Status	—	—	10	Self
TM18	Rain Dance	Water	Status	—	—	5	Both Sides
TM21	Frustration	Normal	Physical	—	100	20	Normal
TM22	Solar Beam	Grass	Special	120	100	10	Normal
TM24	Thunderbolt	Electric	Special	90	100	15	Normal
TM25	Thunder	Electric	Special	110	70	10	Normal
TM27	Return	Normal	Physical	—	100	20	Normal
TM30	Shadow Ball	Ghost	Special	80	100	15	Normal
TM32	Double Team	Normal	Status	—	—	15	Self
TM35	Flamethrower	Fire	Special	90	100	15	Normal
TM37	Sandstorm	Rock	Status	—	—	10	Both Sides
TM38	Fire Blast	Fire	Special	110	85	5	Normal
TM42	Facade	Normal	Physical	70	100	20	Normal
TM44	Rest	Psychic	Status	—	—	10	Self
TM45	Attract	Normal	Status	—	100	15	Normal
TM46	Thief	Dark	Physical	60	100	25	Normal
TM48	Round	Normal	Special	60	100	15	Normal
TM53	Energy Ball	Grass	Special	90	100	10	Normal
TM55	Scald	Water	Special	80	100	15	Normal
TM59	Incinerate	Fire	Special	60	100	15	Many Others
TM67	Retaliate	Normal	Physical	70	100	5	Normal
TM70	Flash	Normal	Status	—	100	20	Normal
TM73	Thunder Wave	Electric	Status	—	100	20	Normal
TM77	Psych Up	Normal	Status	—	—	10	Normal
TM87	Swagger	Normal	Status	—	90	15	Normal
TM88	Sleep Talk	Normal	Status	—	—	10	Self
TM90	Substitute	Normal	Status	—	—	10	Self
TM94	Secret Power	Normal	Physical	70	100	20	Normal
TM100	Confide	Normal	Status	—	—	20	Normal

MOVES LEARNED IN EXCHANGE FOR BP

Name	Type	Kind	Pow.	Acc.	PP	Range
Last Resort	Normal	Physical	140	100	5	Normal
Icy Wind	Ice	Special	55	95	15	Many Others
Snore	Normal	Special	50	100	15	Normal
Tailwind	Flying	Status	—	—	15	Your Side
Shock Wave	Electric	Special	60	—	20	Normal
Water Pulse	Water	Special	60	100	20	Normal

MOVES TAUGHT BY PEOPLE

Name	Type	Kind	Pow.	Acc.	PP	Range

EGG MOVES

Name	Type	Kind	Pow.	Acc.	PP	Range
Future Sight	Psychic	Special	120	100	10	Normal
Lucky Chant	Normal	Status	—	—	30	Your Side
Disable	Normal	Status	—	100	20	Normal
Amnesia	Psychic	Status	—	—	20	Self
Ominous Wind	Ghost	Special	60	100	5	Normal
Hex	Ghost	Special	65	100	10	Normal
Clear Smog	Poison	Special	50	—	15	Normal
Reflect Type	Normal	Status	—	—	15	Normal
Guard Swap	Psychic	Status	—	—	10	Normal
Cosmic Power	Psychic	Status	—	—	20	Self

◆ Castform changes to its Snowy Form when the weather condition is hail.

National Pokédex **352** Hoenn Pokédex **150**

Kecleon

Color Swap Pokémon

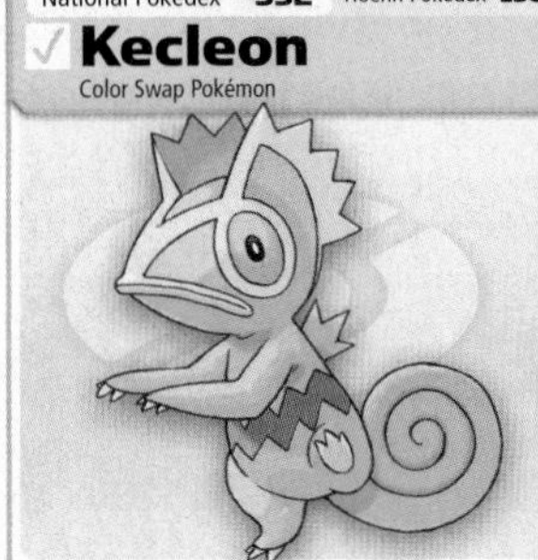

Normal

HEIGHT: 3'03" WEIGHT: 48.5 lbs.

Same form for ♂ / ♀

Ω Kecleon is capable of changing its body colors at will to blend in with its surroundings. There is one exception—this Pokémon can't change the zigzag pattern on its belly.

α Kecleon alters its body coloration to blend in with its surroundings, allowing it to sneak up on its prey unnoticed. Then it lashes out with its long, stretchy tongue to instantly ensnare the unsuspecting target.

ABILITY
Color Change

HIDDEN ABILITY
Protean

EGG GROUPS
Field

STAT GROWTH RATES
HP
Attack
Defense
Sp. Atk
Sp. Def
Speed

ITEMS SOMETIMES HELD BY WILD POKÉMON
—

EVOLUTION
Does not evolve

MAIN WAY TO REGISTER IN THE NATIONAL POKÉDEX

Catch in the tall grass on Route 118.

Damage taken in normal battles

Type		Type	
Normal	×1	Flying	×1
Fire	×1	Psychic	×1
Water	×1	Bug	×1
Grass	×1	Rock	×1
Electric	×1	Ghost	×0
Ice	×1	Dragon	×1
Fighting	×2	Dark	×1
Poison	×1	Steel	×1
Ground	×1	Fairy	×1

Damage taken in Inverse battles

Type		Type	
Normal	×1	Flying	×1
Fire	×1	Psychic	×1
Water	×1	Bug	×1
Grass	×1	Rock	×1
Electric	×1	Ghost	×2
Ice	×1	Dragon	×1
Fighting	×0.5	Dark	×1
Poison	×1	Steel	×1
Ground	×1	Fairy	×1

Can be used in
Inverse Battle
Battle Institute
Battle Maison
Random Matchup (Free Battle)
Random Matchup (Others)

LEVEL-UP MOVES

Lv.	Name	Type	Kind	Pow.	Acc.	PP	Range
1	Thief	Dark	Physical	60	100	25	Normal
1	Tail Whip	Normal	Status	—	100	30	Many Others
1	Astonish	Ghost	Physical	30	100	15	Normal
1	Lick	Ghost	Physical	30	100	30	Normal
1	Scratch	Normal	Physical	40	100	35	Normal
4	Bind	Normal	Physical	15	85	20	Normal
7	Shadow Sneak	Ghost	Physical	40	100	30	Normal
10	Feint	Normal	Physical	30	100	10	Normal
13	Fury Swipes	Normal	Physical	18	80	15	Normal
16	Feint Attack	Dark	Physical	60	—	20	Normal
18	Psybeam	Psychic	Special	65	100	20	Normal
21	Ancient Power	Rock	Special	60	100	5	Normal
25	Slash	Normal	Physical	70	100	20	Normal
30	Camouflage	Normal	Status	—	—	20	Self
33	Shadow Claw	Ghost	Physical	70	100	15	Normal
38	Screech	Normal	Status	—	85	40	Normal
42	Substitute	Normal	Status	—	—	10	Self
46	Sucker Punch	Dark	Physical	80	100	5	Normal
50	Synchronoise	Psychic	Special	120	100	10	Adjacent

TM & HM MOVES

No.	Name	Type	Kind	Pow.	Acc.	PP	Range
TM01	Hone Claws	Dark	Status	—	—	15	Self
TM06	Toxic	Poison	Status	—	90	10	Normal
TM10	Hidden Power	Normal	Special	60	100	15	Normal
TM11	Sunny Day	Fire	Status	—	—	5	Both Sides
TM13	Ice Beam	Ice	Special	90	100	10	Normal
TM14	Blizzard	Ice	Special	110	70	5	Many Others
TM17	Protect	Normal	Status	—	—	10	Self
TM18	Rain Dance	Water	Status	—	—	5	Both Sides
TM21	Frustration	Normal	Physical	—	100	20	Normal
TM22	Solar Beam	Grass	Special	120	100	10	Normal
TM24	Thunderbolt	Electric	Special	90	100	15	Normal
TM25	Thunder	Electric	Special	110	70	10	Normal
TM27	Return	Normal	Physical	—	100	20	Normal
TM28	Dig	Ground	Physical	80	100	10	Normal
TM30	Shadow Ball	Ghost	Special	80	100	15	Normal
TM31	Brick Break	Fighting	Physical	75	100	15	Normal
TM32	Double Team	Normal	Status	—	—	15	Self
TM35	Flamethrower	Fire	Special	90	100	15	Normal
TM38	Fire Blast	Fire	Special	110	85	5	Normal
TM39	Rock Tomb	Rock	Physical	60	95	15	Normal
TM40	Aerial Ace	Flying	Physical	60	—	20	Normal
TM42	Facade	Normal	Physical	70	100	20	Normal
TM44	Rest	Psychic	Status	—	—	10	Self
TM45	Attract	Normal	Status	—	100	15	Normal
TM46	Thief	Dark	Physical	60	100	25	Normal
TM48	Round	Normal	Special	60	100	15	Normal
TM56	Fling	Dark	Physical	—	100	10	Normal
TM57	Charge Beam	Electric	Special	50	90	10	Normal
TM59	Incinerate	Fire	Special	60	100	15	Many Others
TM65	Shadow Claw	Ghost	Physical	70	100	15	Normal
TM67	Retaliate	Normal	Physical	70	100	5	Normal
TM70	Flash	Normal	Status	—	100	20	Normal
TM73	Thunder Wave	Electric	Status	—	100	20	Normal
TM77	Psych Up	Normal	Status	—	—	10	Normal
TM80	Rock Slide	Rock	Physical	75	90	10	Many Others
TM86	Grass Knot	Grass	Special	—	100	20	Normal
TM87	Swagger	Normal	Status	—	90	15	Normal
TM88	Sleep Talk	Normal	Status	—	—	10	Self
TM90	Substitute	Normal	Status	—	—	10	Self
TM92	Trick Room	Psychic	Status	—	—	5	Both Sides
TM94	Secret Power	Normal	Physical	70	100	20	Normal
TM98	Power-Up Punch	Fighting	Physical	40	100	20	Normal
TM100	Confide	Normal	Status	—	—	20	Normal
HM01	Cut	Normal	Physical	50	95	30	Normal
HM04	Strength	Normal	Physical	80	100	15	Normal
HM06	Rock Smash	Fighting	Physical	40	100	15	Normal

MOVES LEARNED IN EXCHANGE FOR BP

Name	Type	Kind	Pow.	Acc.	PP	Range
Low Kick	Fighting	Physical	—	100	20	Normal
Thunder Punch	Electric	Physical	75	100	15	Normal
Fire Punch	Fire	Physical	75	100	15	Normal
Ice Punch	Ice	Physical	75	100	15	Normal
Magic Coat	Psychic	Status	—	—	15	Self
Foul Play	Dark	Physical	95	100	15	Normal
Last Resort	Normal	Physical	140	100	5	Normal
Icy Wind	Ice	Special	55	95	15	Many Others
Aqua Tail	Water	Physical	90	90	10	Normal
Iron Tail	Steel	Physical	100	75	15	Normal
Bind	Normal	Physical	15	85	20	Normal
Snore	Normal	Special	50	100	15	Normal
Knock Off	Dark	Physical	65	100	20	Normal
Role Play	Psychic	Status	—	—	10	Normal
Drain Punch	Fighting	Physical	75	100	10	Normal
Focus Punch	Fighting	Physical	150	100	20	Normal
Shock Wave	Electric	Special	60	—	20	Normal
Water Pulse	Water	Special	60	100	20	Normal
After You	Normal	Status	—	—	15	Normal
Trick	Psychic	Status	—	100	10	Normal
Wonder Room	Psychic	Status	—	—	10	Both Sides
Recycle	Normal	Status	—	—	10	Self
Snatch	Dark	Status	—	—	10	Self
Stealth Rock	Rock	Status	—	—	20	Other Side
Skill Swap	Psychic	Status	—	—	10	Normal

MOVES TAUGHT BY PEOPLE

Name	Type	Kind	Pow.	Acc.	PP	Range

EGG MOVES

Name	Type	Kind	Pow.	Acc.	PP	Range
Disable	Normal	Status	—	100	20	Normal
Magic Coat	Psychic	Status	—	—	15	Self
Trick	Psychic	Status	—	100	10	Normal
Fake Out	Normal	Physical	40	100	10	Normal
Nasty Plot	Dark	Status	—	—	20	Self
Dizzy Punch	Normal	Physical	70	100	10	Normal
Recover	Normal	Status	—	—	10	Self
Skill Swap	Psychic	Status	—	—	10	Normal
Snatch	Dark	Status	—	—	10	Self
Foul Play	Dark	Physical	95	100	15	Normal
Camouflage	Normal	Status	—	—	20	Self

National Pokédex **353** Hoenn Pokédex **151**

Shuppet

Puppet Pokémon

Ghost

HEIGHT: 2'00" WEIGHT: 5.1 lbs.

Same form for ♂ / ♀

Ω Shuppet is attracted by feelings of jealousy and vindictiveness. If someone develops strong feelings of vengeance, this Pokémon will appear in a swarm and line up beneath the eaves of that person's home.

α Shuppet grows by feeding on dark emotions, such as vengefulness and envy, in the hearts of people. It roams through cities in search of grudges that taint people.

ABILITIES
Insomnia
Frisk

HIDDEN ABILITY
Cursed Body

EGG GROUPS
Amorphous

STAT GROWTH RATES
HP
Attack
Defense
Sp. Atk
Sp. Def
Speed

ITEMS SOMETIMES HELD BY WILD POKÉMON
Spell Tag

EVOLUTION
Shuppet → Lv. 37 → Banette

MAIN WAY TO REGISTER IN THE NATIONAL POKÉDEX

Catch within Mt. Pyre (1F).

Damage taken in normal battles

Type		Type	
Normal	×0	Flying	×1
Fire	×1	Psychic	×1
Water	×1	Bug	×0.5
Grass	×1	Rock	×1
Electric	×1	Ghost	×2
Ice	×1	Dragon	×1
Fighting	×0	Dark	×2
Poison	×0.5	Steel	×1
Ground	×1	Fairy	×1

Damage taken in Inverse battles

Type		Type	
Normal	×2	Flying	×1
Fire	×1	Psychic	×1
Water	×1	Bug	×2
Grass	×1	Rock	×1
Electric	×1	Ghost	×0.5
Ice	×1	Dragon	×1
Fighting	×2	Dark	×0.5
Poison	×2	Steel	×1
Ground	×1	Fairy	×1

Can be used in
Inverse Battle
Battle Institute
Battle Maison
Random Matchup (Free Battle)
Random Matchup (Others)

LEVEL-UP MOVES

Lv.	Name	Type	Kind	Pow.	Acc.	PP	Range
1	Knock Off	Dark	Physical	65	100	20	Normal
4	Screech	Normal	Status	—	85	40	Normal
7	Night Shade	Ghost	Special	—	100	15	Normal
10	Spite	Ghost	Status	—	100	10	Normal
13	Shadow Sneak	Ghost	Physical	40	100	30	Normal
16	Will-O-Wisp	Fire	Status	—	85	15	Normal
19	Feint Attack	Dark	Physical	60	—	20	Normal
22	Hex	Ghost	Special	65	100	10	Normal
26	Curse	Ghost	Status	—	—	10	Varies
30	Shadow Ball	Ghost	Special	80	100	15	Normal
34	Embargo	Dark	Status	—	100	15	Normal
38	Sucker Punch	Dark	Physical	80	100	5	Normal
42	Snatch	Dark	Status	—	—	10	Self
46	Grudge	Ghost	Status	—	—	5	Self
50	Trick	Psychic	Status	—	100	10	Normal
54	Phantom Force	Ghost	Physical	90	100	10	Normal

TM & HM MOVES

No.	Name	Type	Kind	Pow.	Acc.	PP	Range
TM04	Calm Mind	Psychic	Status	—	—	20	Self
TM06	Toxic	Poison	Status	—	90	10	Normal
TM10	Hidden Power	Normal	Special	60	100	15	Normal
TM11	Sunny Day	Fire	Status	—	—	5	Both Sides
TM12	Taunt	Dark	Status	—	100	20	Normal
TM17	Protect	Normal	Status	—	—	10	Self
TM18	Rain Dance	Water	Status	—	—	5	Both Sides
TM21	Frustration	Normal	Physical	—	100	20	Normal
TM24	Thunderbolt	Electric	Special	90	100	15	Normal
TM25	Thunder	Electric	Special	110	70	10	Normal
TM27	Return	Normal	Physical	—	100	20	Normal
TM29	Psychic	Psychic	Special	90	100	10	Normal
TM30	Shadow Ball	Ghost	Special	80	100	15	Normal
TM32	Double Team	Normal	Status	—	—	15	Self
TM41	Torment	Dark	Status	—	100	15	Normal
TM42	Facade	Normal	Physical	70	100	20	Normal
TM44	Rest	Psychic	Status	—	—	10	Self
TM45	Attract	Normal	Status	—	100	15	Normal
TM46	Thief	Dark	Physical	60	100	25	Normal
TM48	Round	Normal	Special	60	100	15	Normal
TM57	Charge Beam	Electric	Special	50	90	10	Normal
TM61	Will-O-Wisp	Fire	Status	—	85	15	Normal
TM63	Embargo	Dark	Status	—	100	15	Normal
TM66	Payback	Dark	Physical	50	100	10	Normal
TM70	Flash	Normal	Status	—	100	20	Normal
TM73	Thunder Wave	Electric	Status	—	100	20	Normal
TM77	Psych Up	Normal	Status	—	—	10	Normal
TM85	Dream Eater	Psychic	Special	100	100	15	Normal
TM87	Swagger	Normal	Status	—	90	15	Normal
TM88	Sleep Talk	Normal	Status	—	—	10	Self
TM90	Substitute	Normal	Status	—	—	10	Self
TM92	Trick Room	Psychic	Status	—	—	5	Both Sides
TM94	Secret Power	Normal	Physical	70	100	20	Normal
TM97	Dark Pulse	Dark	Special	80	100	15	Normal
TM99	Dazzling Gleam	Fairy	Special	80	100	10	Many Others
TM100	Confide	Normal	Status	—	—	20	Normal

MOVES LEARNED IN EXCHANGE FOR BP

Name	Type	Kind	Pow.	Acc.	PP	Range
Magic Coat	Psychic	Status	—	—	15	Self
Foul Play	Dark	Physical	95	100	15	Normal
Icy Wind	Ice	Special	55	95	15	Many Others
Snore	Normal	Special	50	100	15	Normal
Knock Off	Dark	Physical	65	100	20	Normal
Role Play	Psychic	Status	—	—	10	Normal
Pain Split	Normal	Status	—	—	20	Normal
Shock Wave	Electric	Special	60	—	20	Normal
Spite	Ghost	Status	—	100	10	Normal
Trick	Psychic	Status	—	100	10	Normal
Magic Room	Psychic	Status	—	—	10	Both Sides
Snatch	Dark	Status	—	—	10	Self
Skill Swap	Psychic	Status	—	—	10	Normal

MOVES TAUGHT BY PEOPLE

Name	Type	Kind	Pow.	Acc.	PP	Range

EGG MOVES

Name	Type	Kind	Pow.	Acc.	PP	Range
Disable	Normal	Status	—	100	20	Normal
Destiny Bond	Ghost	Status	—	—	5	Self
Foresight	Normal	Status	—	—	40	Normal
Astonish	Ghost	Physical	30	100	15	Normal
Imprison	Psychic	Status	—	—	10	Self
Pursuit	Dark	Physical	40	100	20	Normal
Shadow Sneak	Ghost	Physical	40	100	30	Normal
Confuse Ray	Ghost	Status	—	100	10	Normal
Ominous Wind	Ghost	Special	60	100	5	Normal
Gunk Shot	Poison	Physical	120	80	5	Normal
Phantom Force	Ghost	Physical	90	100	10	Normal

National Pokédex **354** Hoenn Pokédex **152**

Banette

Marionette Pokémon

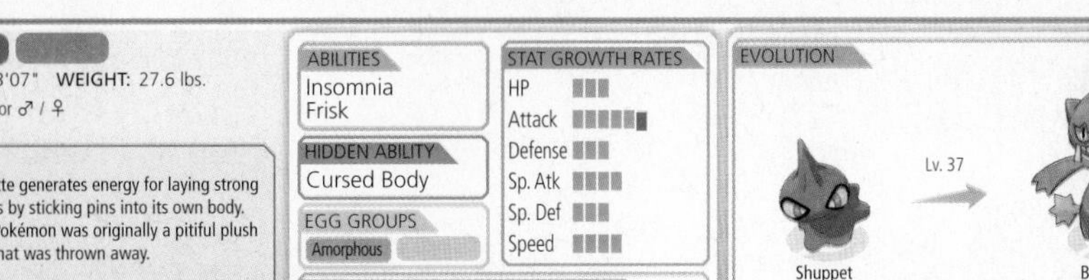

Ghost

HEIGHT: 3'07" WEIGHT: 27.6 lbs.

Same form for ♂ / ♀

Ω Banette generates energy for laying strong curses by sticking pins into its own body. This Pokémon was originally a pitiful plush doll that was thrown away.

α A cursed energy permeated the stuffing of a discarded and forgotten plush doll, giving it new life as Banette. The Pokémon's energy would escape if it were to ever open its mouth.

ABILITIES
Insomnia
Frisk

HIDDEN ABILITY
Cursed Body

EGG GROUPS
Amorphous

STAT GROWTH RATES
HP
Attack
Defense
Sp. Atk
Sp. Def
Speed

ITEMS SOMETIMES HELD BY WILD POKÉMON
—

EVOLUTION

Shuppet → Lv. 37 → Banette

MAIN WAY TO REGISTER IN THE NATIONAL POKÉDEX

Level up Shuppet to Lv. 37.

Damage taken in normal battles

Type	×	Type	×
Normal	×0	Flying	×1
Fire	×1	Psychic	×1
Water	×1	Bug	×0.5
Grass	×1	Rock	×1
Electric	×1	Ghost	×2
Ice	×1	Dragon	×1
Fighting	×0	Dark	×2
Poison	×0.5	Steel	×1
Ground	×1	Fairy	×1

Damage taken in Inverse battles

Type	×	Type	×
Normal	×2	Flying	×1
Fire	×1	Psychic	×1
Water	×1	Bug	×2
Grass	×1	Rock	×1
Electric	×1	Ghost	×0.5
Ice	×1	Dragon	×1
Fighting	×2	Dark	×0.5
Poison	×2	Steel	×1
Ground	×1	Fairy	×1

Can be used in
Inverse Battle
Battle Institute
Battle Maison
Random Matchup (Free Battle)
Random Matchup (Others)

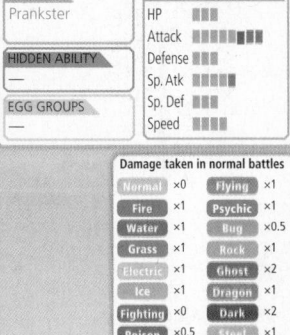

LEVEL-UP MOVES

Lv.	Name	Type	Kind	Pow.	Acc.	PP	Range
1	Phantom Force	Ghost	Physical	90	100	10	Normal
1	Knock Off	Dark	Physical	65	100	20	Normal
1	Screech	Normal	Status	—	85	40	Normal
1	Night Shade	Ghost	Special	—	100	15	Normal
1	Spite	Ghost	Status	—	100	10	Normal
4	Screech	Normal	Status	—	85	40	Normal
7	Night Shade	Ghost	Special	—	100	15	Normal
10	Spite	Ghost	Status	—	100	10	Normal
13	Shadow Sneak	Ghost	Physical	40	100	30	Normal
16	Will-O-Wisp	Fire	Status	—	85	15	Normal
19	Feint Attack	Dark	Physical	60	—	20	Normal
22	Hex	Ghost	Special	65	100	10	Normal
26	Curse	Ghost	Status	—	—	10	Varies
30	Shadow Ball	Ghost	Special	80	100	15	Normal
34	Embargo	Dark	Status	—	100	15	Normal
40	Sucker Punch	Dark	Physical	80	100	5	Normal
46	Snatch	Dark	Status	—	—	10	Self
52	Grudge	Ghost	Status	—	—	5	Self
58	Trick	Psychic	Status	—	100	10	Normal
64	Phantom Force	Ghost	Physical	90	100	10	Normal

TM & HM MOVES

No.	Name	Type	Kind	Pow.	Acc.	PP	Range
TM04	Calm Mind	Psychic	Status	—	—	20	Self
TM06	Toxic	Poison	Status	—	90	10	Normal
TM10	Hidden Power	Normal	Special	60	100	15	Normal
TM11	Sunny Day	Fire	Status	—	—	5	Both Sides
TM12	Taunt	Dark	Status	—	100	20	Normal
TM15	Hyper Beam	Normal	Special	150	90	5	Normal
TM17	Protect	Normal	Status	—	—	10	Self
TM18	Rain Dance	Water	Status	—	—	5	Both Sides
TM21	Frustration	Normal	Physical	—	100	20	Normal
TM24	Thunderbolt	Electric	Special	90	100	15	Normal
TM25	Thunder	Electric	Special	110	70	10	Normal
TM27	Return	Normal	Physical	—	100	20	Normal
TM29	Psychic	Psychic	Special	90	100	10	Normal
TM30	Shadow Ball	Ghost	Special	80	100	15	Normal
TM32	Double Team	Normal	Status	—	—	15	Self
TM41	Torment	Dark	Status	—	100	15	Normal
TM42	Facade	Normal	Physical	70	100	20	Normal
TM44	Rest	Psychic	Status	—	—	10	Self
TM45	Attract	Normal	Status	—	100	15	Normal
TM46	Thief	Dark	Physical	60	100	25	Normal
TM48	Round	Normal	Special	60	100	15	Normal
TM56	Fling	Dark	Physical	—	100	10	Normal
TM57	Charge Beam	Electric	Special	50	90	10	Normal
TM61	Will-O-Wisp	Fire	Status	—	85	15	Normal
TM63	Embargo	Dark	Status	—	100	15	Normal
TM65	Shadow Claw	Ghost	Physical	70	100	15	Normal
TM66	Payback	Dark	Physical	50	100	10	Normal
TM68	Giga Impact	Normal	Physical	150	90	5	Normal
TM70	Flash	Normal	Status	—	100	20	Normal
TM73	Thunder Wave	Electric	Status	—	100	20	Normal
TM77	Psych Up	Normal	Status	—	—	10	Normal
TM83	Infestation	Bug	Special	20	100	20	Normal
TM85	Dream Eater	Psychic	Special	100	100	15	Normal
TM87	Swagger	Normal	Status	—	90	15	Normal
TM88	Sleep Talk	Normal	Status	—	—	10	Self
TM90	Substitute	Normal	Status	—	—	10	Self
TM92	Trick Room	Psychic	Status	—	—	5	Both Sides
TM94	Secret Power	Normal	Physical	70	100	20	Normal
TM97	Dark Pulse	Dark	Special	80	100	15	Normal
TM99	Dazzling Gleam	Fairy	Special	80	100	10	Many Others
TM100	Confide	Normal	Status	—	—	20	Normal

MOVES LEARNED IN EXCHANGE FOR BP

Name	Type	Kind	Pow.	Acc.	PP	Range
Magic Coat	Psychic	Status	—	—	15	Self
Foul Play	Dark	Physical	95	100	15	Normal
Icy Wind	Ice	Special	55	95	15	Many Others
Snore	Normal	Special	50	100	15	Normal
Knock Off	Dark	Physical	65	100	20	Normal
Role Play	Psychic	Status	—	—	10	Normal
Pain Split	Normal	Status	—	—	20	Normal
Shock Wave	Electric	Special	60	—	20	Normal
Spite	Ghost	Status	—	100	10	Normal
Trick	Psychic	Status	—	100	10	Normal
Magic Room	Psychic	Status	—	—	10	Both Sides
Snatch	Dark	Status	—	—	10	Self
Skill Swap	Psychic	Status	—	—	10	Normal

MOVES TAUGHT BY PEOPLE

Name	Type	Kind	Pow.	Acc.	PP	Range

Mega Evolution

Mega Banette

Marionette Pokémon

Ghost

HEIGHT: 3'11" WEIGHT: 28.7 lbs.

Same form for ♂ / ♀

REQUIRED MEGA STONE
Banettite
Find on Mt. Pyre (Summit).

ABILITY
Prankster

HIDDEN ABILITY
—

EGG GROUPS
—

STAT GROWTH RATES
HP
Attack
Defense
Sp. Atk
Sp. Def
Speed

Damage taken in normal battles

Type	×	Type	×
Normal	×0	Flying	×1
Fire	×1	Psychic	×1
Water	×1	Bug	×0.5
Grass	×1	Rock	×1
Electric	×1	Ghost	×2
Ice	×1	Dragon	×1
Fighting	×0	Dark	×2
Poison	×0.5	Steel	×1
Ground	×1	Fairy	×1

Damage taken in Inverse battles

Type	×	Type	×
Normal	×2	Flying	×1
Fire	×1	Psychic	×1
Water	×1	Bug	×2
Grass	×1	Rock	×1
Electric	×1	Ghost	×0.5
Ice	×1	Dragon	×1
Fighting	×2	Dark	×0.5
Poison	×2	Steel	×1
Ground	×1	Fairy	×1

Can be used in
Inverse Battle
Battle Institute
Battle Maison
Random Matchup (Free Battle)
Random Matchup (Others)

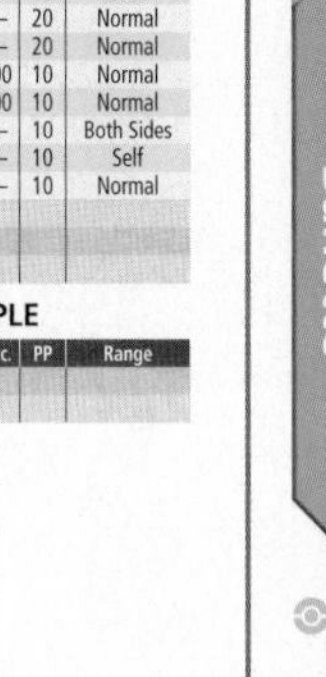

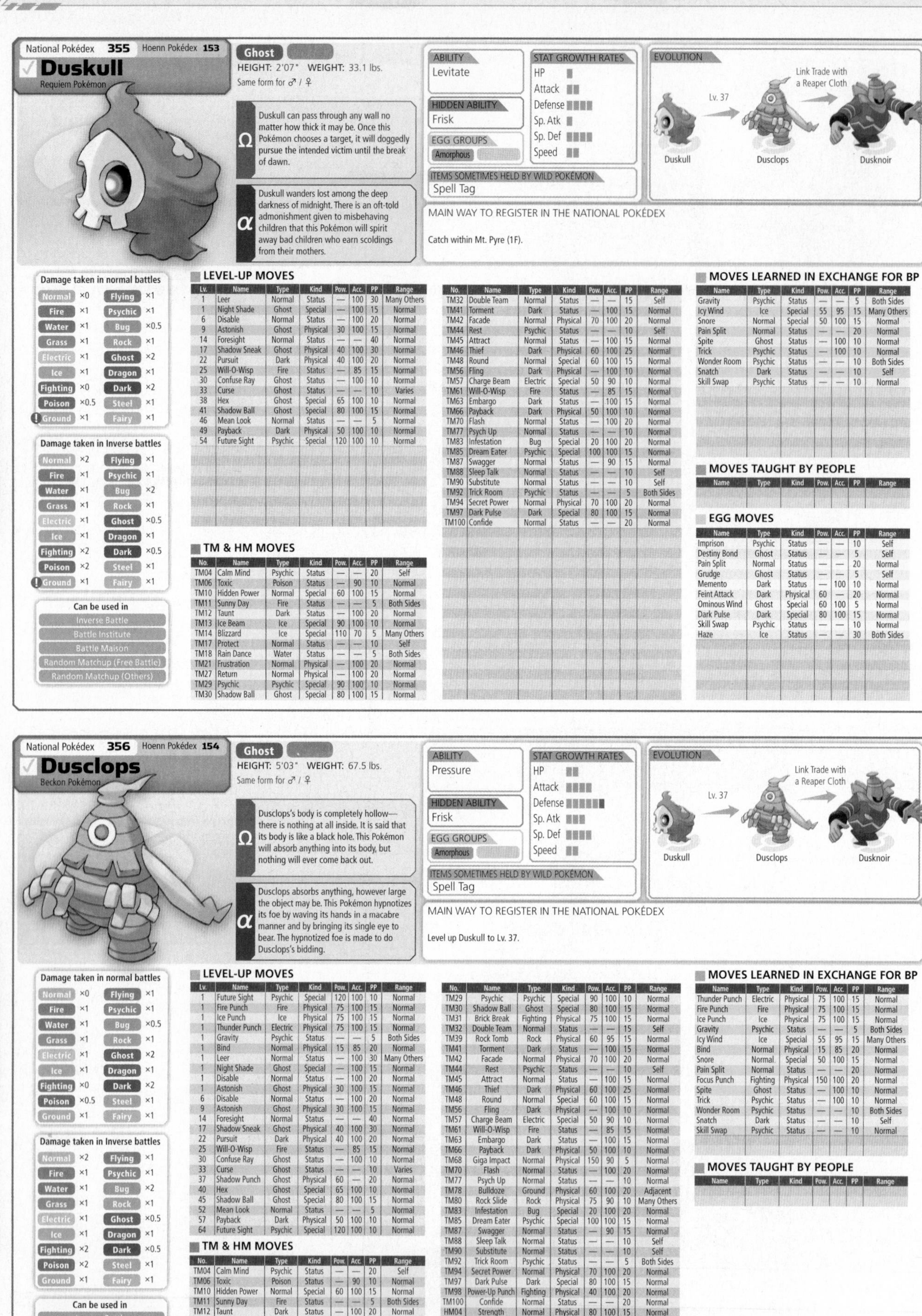

National Pokédex **355** Hoenn Pokédex **153**

Duskull

Requiem Pokémon

Ghost

HEIGHT: 2'07" WEIGHT: 33.1 lbs.

Same form for ♂ / ♀

Ω Duskull can pass through any wall no matter how thick it may be. Once this Pokémon chooses a target, it will doggedly pursue the intended victim until the break of dawn.

α Duskull wanders lost among the deep darkness of midnight. There is an oft-told admonishment given to misbehaving children that this Pokémon will spirit away bad children who earn scoldings from their mothers.

ABILITY
Levitate

HIDDEN ABILITY
Frisk

EGG GROUPS
Amorphous

STAT GROWTH RATES
HP, Attack, Defense, Sp. Atk, Sp. Def, Speed

ITEMS SOMETIMES HELD BY WILD POKÉMON
Spell Tag

EVOLUTION
Duskull → Lv. 37 → Dusclops → Link Trade with a Reaper Cloth → Dusknoir

MAIN WAY TO REGISTER IN THE NATIONAL POKÉDEX
Catch within Mt. Pyre (1F).

Damage taken in normal battles

Type		Type	
Normal	×0	Flying	×1
Fire	×1	Psychic	×1
Water	×1	Bug	×0.5
Grass	×1	Rock	×1
Electric	×1	Ghost	×2
Ice	×1	Dragon	×1
Fighting	×0	Dark	×2
Poison	×0.5	Steel	×1
! Ground	×1	Fairy	×1

Damage taken in Inverse battles

Type		Type	
Normal	×2	Flying	×1
Fire	×1	Psychic	×1
Water	×1	Bug	×2
Grass	×1	Rock	×1
Electric	×1	Ghost	×0.5
Ice	×1	Dragon	×1
Fighting	×2	Dark	×0.5
Poison	×2	Steel	×1
! Ground	×1	Fairy	×1

Can be used in
Inverse Battle
Battle Institute
Battle Maison
Random Matchup (Free Battle)
Random Matchup (Others)

LEVEL-UP MOVES

Lv.	Name	Type	Kind	Pow.	Acc.	PP	Range
1	Leer	Normal	Status	—	100	30	Many Others
1	Night Shade	Ghost	Special	—	100	15	Normal
6	Disable	Normal	Status	—	100	20	Normal
9	Astonish	Ghost	Physical	30	100	15	Normal
14	Foresight	Normal	Status	—	—	40	Normal
17	Shadow Sneak	Ghost	Physical	40	100	30	Normal
22	Pursuit	Dark	Physical	40	100	20	Normal
25	Will-O-Wisp	Fire	Status	—	85	15	Normal
30	Confuse Ray	Ghost	Status	—	100	10	Normal
33	Curse	Ghost	Status	—	—	10	Varies
38	Hex	Ghost	Special	65	100	10	Normal
41	Shadow Ball	Ghost	Special	80	100	15	Normal
46	Mean Look	Normal	Status	—	—	5	Normal
49	Payback	Dark	Physical	50	100	10	Normal
54	Future Sight	Psychic	Special	120	100	10	Normal

TM & HM MOVES

No.	Name	Type	Kind	Pow.	Acc.	PP	Range
TM04	Calm Mind	Psychic	Status	—	—	20	Self
TM06	Toxic	Poison	Status	—	90	10	Normal
TM10	Hidden Power	Normal	Special	60	100	15	Normal
TM11	Sunny Day	Fire	Status	—	—	5	Both Sides
TM12	Taunt	Dark	Status	—	100	20	Normal
TM13	Ice Beam	Ice	Special	90	100	10	Normal
TM14	Blizzard	Ice	Special	110	70	5	Many Others
TM17	Protect	Normal	Status	—	—	10	Self
TM18	Rain Dance	Water	Status	—	—	5	Both Sides
TM21	Frustration	Normal	Physical	—	100	20	Normal
TM27	Return	Normal	Physical	—	100	20	Normal
TM29	Psychic	Psychic	Special	90	100	10	Normal
TM30	Shadow Ball	Ghost	Special	80	100	15	Normal
TM32	Double Team	Normal	Status	—	—	15	Self
TM41	Torment	Dark	Status	—	100	15	Normal
TM42	Facade	Normal	Physical	70	100	20	Normal
TM44	Rest	Psychic	Status	—	—	10	Self
TM45	Attract	Normal	Status	—	100	15	Normal
TM46	Thief	Dark	Physical	60	100	25	Normal
TM48	Round	Normal	Special	60	100	15	Normal
TM56	Fling	Dark	Physical	—	100	10	Normal
TM57	Charge Beam	Electric	Special	50	90	10	Normal
TM61	Will-O-Wisp	Fire	Status	—	85	15	Normal
TM63	Embargo	Dark	Status	—	100	15	Normal
TM66	Payback	Dark	Physical	50	100	10	Normal
TM70	Flash	Normal	Status	—	100	20	Normal
TM77	Psych Up	Normal	Status	—	—	10	Normal
TM83	Infestation	Bug	Special	20	100	20	Normal
TM85	Dream Eater	Psychic	Special	100	100	15	Normal
TM87	Swagger	Normal	Status	—	90	15	Normal
TM88	Sleep Talk	Normal	Status	—	—	10	Self
TM90	Substitute	Normal	Status	—	—	10	Self
TM92	Trick Room	Psychic	Status	—	—	5	Both Sides
TM94	Secret Power	Normal	Physical	70	100	20	Normal
TM97	Dark Pulse	Dark	Special	80	100	15	Normal
TM100	Confide	Normal	Status	—	—	20	Normal

MOVES LEARNED IN EXCHANGE FOR BP

Name	Type	Kind	Pow.	Acc.	PP	Range
Gravity	Psychic	Status	—	—	5	Both Sides
Icy Wind	Ice	Special	55	95	15	Many Others
Snore	Normal	Special	50	100	15	Normal
Pain Split	Normal	Status	—	—	20	Normal
Spite	Ghost	Status	—	100	10	Normal
Trick	Psychic	Status	—	100	10	Normal
Wonder Room	Psychic	Status	—	—	10	Both Sides
Snatch	Dark	Status	—	—	10	Self
Skill Swap	Psychic	Status	—	—	10	Normal

MOVES TAUGHT BY PEOPLE

Name	Type	Kind	Pow.	Acc.	PP	Range

EGG MOVES

Name	Type	Kind	Pow.	Acc.	PP	Range
Imprison	Psychic	Status	—	—	10	Self
Destiny Bond	Ghost	Status	—	—	5	Self
Pain Split	Normal	Status	—	—	20	Normal
Grudge	Ghost	Status	—	—	5	Self
Memento	Dark	Status	—	100	10	Normal
Feint Attack	Dark	Physical	60	—	20	Normal
Ominous Wind	Ghost	Special	60	100	5	Normal
Dark Pulse	Dark	Special	80	100	15	Normal
Skill Swap	Psychic	Status	—	—	10	Normal
Haze	Ice	Status	—	—	30	Both Sides

National Pokédex **356** Hoenn Pokédex **154**

Dusclops

Beckon Pokémon

Ghost

HEIGHT: 5'03" WEIGHT: 67.5 lbs.

Same form for ♂ / ♀

Ω Dusclops's body is completely hollow—there is nothing at all inside. It is said that its body is like a black hole. This Pokémon will absorb anything into its body, but nothing will ever come back out.

α Dusclops absorbs anything, however large the object may be. This Pokémon hypnotizes its foe by waving its hands in a macabre manner and by bringing its single eye to bear. The hypnotized foe is made to do Dusclops's bidding.

ABILITY
Pressure

HIDDEN ABILITY
Frisk

EGG GROUPS
Amorphous

STAT GROWTH RATES
HP, Attack, Defense, Sp. Atk, Sp. Def, Speed

ITEMS SOMETIMES HELD BY WILD POKÉMON
Spell Tag

EVOLUTION
Duskull → Lv. 37 → Dusclops → Link Trade with a Reaper Cloth → Dusknoir

MAIN WAY TO REGISTER IN THE NATIONAL POKÉDEX
Level up Duskull to Lv. 37.

Damage taken in normal battles

Type		Type	
Normal	×0	Flying	×1
Fire	×1	Psychic	×1
Water	×1	Bug	×0.5
Grass	×1	Rock	×1
Electric	×1	Ghost	×2
Ice	×1	Dragon	×1
Fighting	×0	Dark	×2
Poison	×0.5	Steel	×1
Ground	×1	Fairy	×1

Damage taken in Inverse battles

Type		Type	
Normal	×2	Flying	×1
Fire	×1	Psychic	×1
Water	×1	Bug	×2
Grass	×1	Rock	×1
Electric	×1	Ghost	×0.5
Ice	×1	Dragon	×1
Fighting	×2	Dark	×0.5
Poison	×2	Steel	×1
Ground	×1	Fairy	×1

Can be used in
Inverse Battle
Battle Institute
Battle Maison
Random Matchup (Free Battle)
Random Matchup (Others)

LEVEL-UP MOVES

Lv.	Name	Type	Kind	Pow.	Acc.	PP	Range
1	Future Sight	Psychic	Special	120	100	10	Normal
1	Fire Punch	Fire	Physical	75	100	15	Normal
1	Ice Punch	Ice	Physical	75	100	15	Normal
1	Thunder Punch	Electric	Physical	75	100	15	Normal
1	Gravity	Psychic	Status	—	—	5	Both Sides
1	Bind	Normal	Physical	15	85	20	Normal
1	Leer	Normal	Status	—	100	30	Many Others
1	Night Shade	Ghost	Special	—	100	15	Normal
1	Disable	Normal	Status	—	100	20	Normal
1	Astonish	Ghost	Physical	30	100	15	Normal
6	Disable	Normal	Status	—	100	20	Normal
9	Astonish	Ghost	Physical	30	100	15	Normal
14	Foresight	Normal	Status	—	—	40	Normal
17	Shadow Sneak	Ghost	Physical	40	100	30	Normal
22	Pursuit	Dark	Physical	40	100	20	Normal
25	Will-O-Wisp	Fire	Status	—	85	15	Normal
30	Confuse Ray	Ghost	Status	—	100	10	Normal
33	Curse	Ghost	Status	—	—	10	Varies
37	Shadow Punch	Ghost	Physical	60	—	20	Normal
40	Hex	Ghost	Special	65	100	10	Normal
45	Shadow Ball	Ghost	Special	80	100	15	Normal
52	Mean Look	Normal	Status	—	—	5	Normal
57	Payback	Dark	Physical	50	100	10	Normal
64	Future Sight	Psychic	Special	120	100	10	Normal

TM & HM MOVES

No.	Name	Type	Kind	Pow.	Acc.	PP	Range
TM04	Calm Mind	Psychic	Status	—	—	20	Self
TM06	Toxic	Poison	Status	—	90	10	Normal
TM10	Hidden Power	Normal	Special	60	100	15	Normal
TM11	Sunny Day	Fire	Status	—	—	5	Both Sides
TM12	Taunt	Dark	Status	—	100	20	Normal
TM13	Ice Beam	Ice	Special	90	100	10	Normal
TM14	Blizzard	Ice	Special	110	70	5	Many Others
TM15	Hyper Beam	Normal	Special	150	90	5	Normal
TM17	Protect	Normal	Status	—	—	10	Self
TM18	Rain Dance	Water	Status	—	—	5	Both Sides
TM21	Frustration	Normal	Physical	—	100	20	Normal
TM26	Earthquake	Ground	Physical	100	100	10	Adjacent
TM27	Return	Normal	Physical	—	100	20	Normal
TM29	Psychic	Psychic	Special	90	100	10	Normal
TM30	Shadow Ball	Ghost	Special	80	100	15	Normal
TM31	Brick Break	Fighting	Physical	75	100	15	Normal
TM32	Double Team	Normal	Status	—	—	15	Self
TM39	Rock Tomb	Rock	Physical	60	95	15	Normal
TM41	Torment	Dark	Status	—	100	15	Normal
TM42	Facade	Normal	Physical	70	100	20	Normal
TM44	Rest	Psychic	Status	—	—	10	Self
TM45	Attract	Normal	Status	—	100	15	Normal
TM46	Thief	Dark	Physical	60	100	25	Normal
TM48	Round	Normal	Special	60	100	15	Normal
TM56	Fling	Dark	Physical	—	100	10	Normal
TM57	Charge Beam	Electric	Special	50	90	10	Normal
TM61	Will-O-Wisp	Fire	Status	—	85	15	Normal
TM63	Embargo	Dark	Status	—	100	15	Normal
TM66	Payback	Dark	Physical	50	100	10	Normal
TM68	Giga Impact	Normal	Physical	150	90	5	Normal
TM70	Flash	Normal	Status	—	100	20	Normal
TM77	Psych Up	Normal	Status	—	—	10	Normal
TM78	Bulldoze	Ground	Physical	60	100	20	Adjacent
TM80	Rock Slide	Rock	Physical	75	90	10	Many Others
TM83	Infestation	Bug	Special	20	100	20	Normal
TM85	Dream Eater	Psychic	Special	100	100	15	Normal
TM87	Swagger	Normal	Status	—	90	15	Normal
TM88	Sleep Talk	Normal	Status	—	—	10	Self
TM90	Substitute	Normal	Status	—	—	10	Self
TM92	Trick Room	Psychic	Status	—	—	5	Both Sides
TM94	Secret Power	Normal	Physical	70	100	20	Normal
TM97	Dark Pulse	Dark	Special	80	100	15	Normal
TM98	Power-Up Punch	Fighting	Physical	40	100	20	Normal
TM100	Confide	Normal	Status	—	—	20	Normal
HM04	Strength	Normal	Physical	80	100	15	Normal
HM06	Rock Smash	Fighting	Physical	40	100	15	Normal

MOVES LEARNED IN EXCHANGE FOR BP

Name	Type	Kind	Pow.	Acc.	PP	Range
Thunder Punch	Electric	Physical	75	100	15	Normal
Fire Punch	Fire	Physical	75	100	15	Normal
Ice Punch	Ice	Physical	75	100	15	Normal
Gravity	Psychic	Status	—	—	5	Both Sides
Icy Wind	Ice	Special	55	95	15	Many Others
Bind	Normal	Physical	15	85	20	Normal
Snore	Normal	Special	50	100	15	Normal
Pain Split	Normal	Status	—	—	20	Normal
Focus Punch	Fighting	Physical	150	100	20	Normal
Spite	Ghost	Status	—	100	10	Normal
Trick	Psychic	Status	—	100	10	Normal
Wonder Room	Psychic	Status	—	—	10	Both Sides
Snatch	Dark	Status	—	—	10	Self
Skill Swap	Psychic	Status	—	—	10	Normal

MOVES TAUGHT BY PEOPLE

Name	Type	Kind	Pow.	Acc.	PP	Range

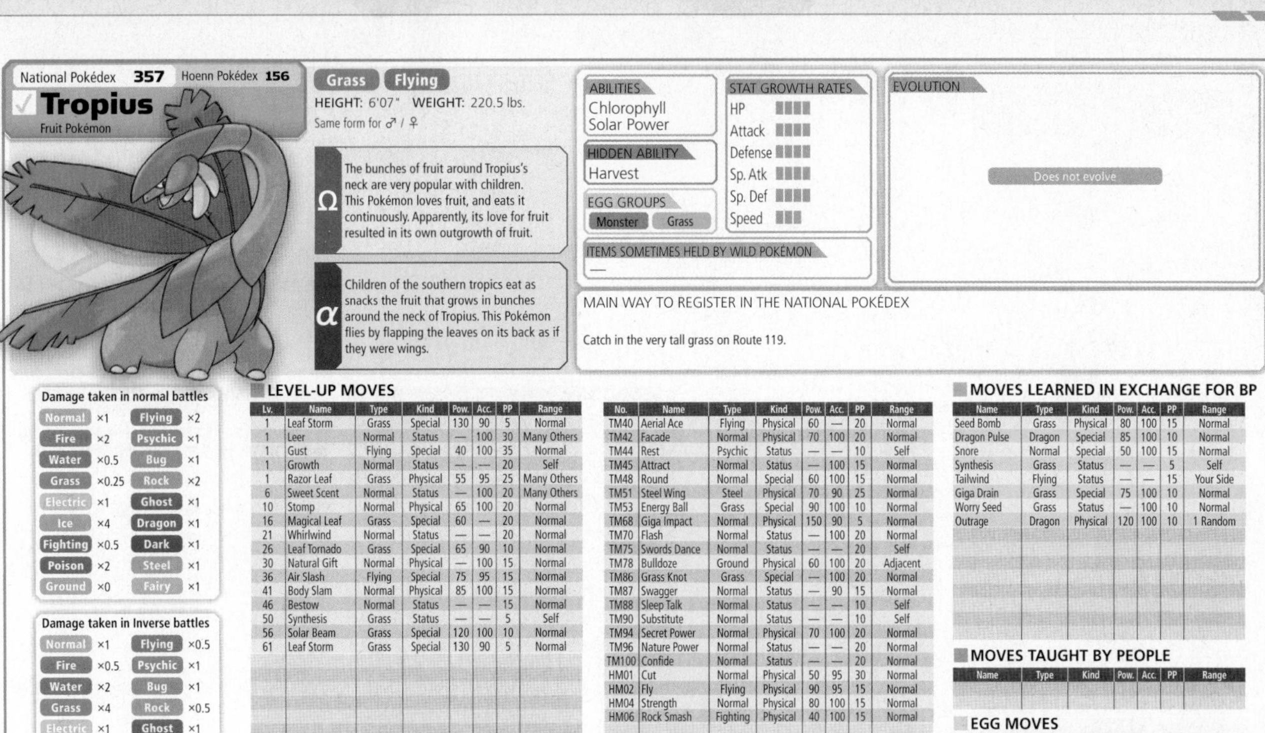

National Pokédex **357** Hoenn Pokédex **156**

Tropius

Fruit Pokémon

Grass | Flying

HEIGHT: 6'07" WEIGHT: 220.5 lbs.

Same form for ♂ / ♀

Ω The bunches of fruit around Tropius's neck are very popular with children. This Pokémon loves fruit, and eats it continuously. Apparently, its love for fruit resulted in its own outgrowth of fruit.

α Children of the southern tropics eat as snacks the fruit that grows in bunches around the neck of Tropius. This Pokémon flies by flapping the leaves on its back as if they were wings.

ABILITIES
Chlorophyll
Solar Power

HIDDEN ABILITY
Harvest

EGG GROUPS
Monster | Grass

STAT GROWTH RATES
HP ■■■■
Attack ■■■■
Defense ■■■■
Sp. Atk ■■■■
Sp. Def ■■■■
Speed ■■■

ITEMS SOMETIMES HELD BY WILD POKÉMON
—

EVOLUTION
Does not evolve

MAIN WAY TO REGISTER IN THE NATIONAL POKÉDEX

Catch in the very tall grass on Route 119.

Damage taken in normal battles

Type		Type	
Normal	×1	Flying	×2
Fire	×2	Psychic	×1
Water	×0.5	Bug	×1
Grass	×0.25	Rock	×2
Electric	×1	Ghost	×1
Ice	×4	Dragon	×1
Fighting	×0.5	Dark	×1
Poison	×2	Steel	×1
Ground	×0	Fairy	×1

Damage taken in Inverse battles

Type		Type	
Normal	×1	Flying	×0.5
Fire	×0.5	Psychic	×1
Water	×2	Bug	×1
Grass	×4	Rock	×0.5
Electric	×1	Ghost	×1
Ice	×0.25	Dragon	×1
Fighting	×2	Dark	×1
Poison	×0.5	Steel	×1
Ground	×4	Fairy	×1

Can be used in
Inverse Battle
Battle Institute
Battle Maison
Random Matchup (Free Battle)
Random Matchup (Others)

LEVEL-UP MOVES

Lv.	Name	Type	Kind	Pow.	Acc.	PP	Range
1	Leaf Storm	Grass	Special	130	90	5	Normal
1	Leer	Normal	Status	—	100	30	Many Others
1	Gust	Flying	Special	40	100	35	Normal
1	Growth	Normal	Status	—	—	20	Self
1	Razor Leaf	Grass	Physical	55	95	25	Many Others
6	Sweet Scent	Normal	Status	—	100	20	Many Others
10	Stomp	Normal	Physical	65	100	20	Normal
16	Magical Leaf	Grass	Special	60	—	20	Normal
21	Whirlwind	Normal	Status	—	—	20	Normal
26	Leaf Tornado	Grass	Special	65	90	10	Normal
30	Natural Gift	Normal	Physical	—	100	15	Normal
36	Air Slash	Flying	Special	75	95	15	Normal
41	Body Slam	Normal	Physical	85	100	15	Normal
46	Bestow	Normal	Status	—	—	15	Normal
50	Synthesis	Grass	Status	—	—	5	Self
56	Solar Beam	Grass	Special	120	100	10	Normal
61	Leaf Storm	Grass	Special	130	90	5	Normal

TM & HM MOVES

No.	Name	Type	Kind	Pow.	Acc.	PP	Range
TM05	Roar	Normal	Status	—	—	20	Normal
TM06	Toxic	Poison	Status	—	90	10	Normal
TM10	Hidden Power	Normal	Special	60	100	15	Normal
TM11	Sunny Day	Fire	Status	—	—	5	Both Sides
TM15	Hyper Beam	Normal	Special	150	90	5	Normal
TM17	Protect	Normal	Status	—	—	10	Self
TM19	Roost	Flying	Status	—	—	10	Self
TM20	Safeguard	Normal	Status	—	—	25	Your Side
TM21	Frustration	Normal	Physical	—	100	20	Normal
TM22	Solar Beam	Grass	Special	120	100	10	Normal
TM26	Earthquake	Ground	Physical	100	100	10	Adjacent
TM27	Return	Normal	Physical	—	100	20	Normal
TM32	Double Team	Normal	Status	—	—	15	Self
TM40	Aerial Ace	Flying	Physical	60	—	20	Normal
TM42	Facade	Normal	Physical	70	100	20	Normal
TM44	Rest	Psychic	Status	—	—	10	Self
TM45	Attract	Normal	Status	—	100	15	Normal
TM48	Round	Normal	Special	60	100	15	Normal
TM51	Steel Wing	Steel	Physical	70	90	25	Normal
TM53	Energy Ball	Grass	Special	90	100	10	Normal
TM68	Giga Impact	Normal	Physical	150	90	5	Normal
TM70	Flash	Normal	Status	—	100	20	Normal
TM75	Swords Dance	Normal	Status	—	—	20	Self
TM78	Bulldoze	Ground	Physical	60	100	20	Adjacent
TM86	Grass Knot	Grass	Special	—	100	20	Normal
TM87	Swagger	Normal	Status	—	90	15	Normal
TM88	Sleep Talk	Normal	Status	—	—	10	Self
TM90	Substitute	Normal	Status	—	—	10	Self
TM94	Secret Power	Normal	Physical	70	100	20	Normal
TM96	Nature Power	Normal	Status	—	—	20	Normal
TM100	Confide	Normal	Status	—	—	20	Normal
HM01	Cut	Normal	Physical	50	95	30	Normal
HM02	Fly	Flying	Physical	90	95	15	Normal
HM04	Strength	Normal	Physical	80	100	15	Normal
HM06	Rock Smash	Fighting	Physical	40	100	15	Normal

MOVES LEARNED IN EXCHANGE FOR BP

Name	Type	Kind	Pow.	Acc.	PP	Range
Seed Bomb	Grass	Physical	80	100	15	Normal
Dragon Pulse	Dragon	Special	85	100	10	Normal
Snore	Normal	Special	50	100	15	Normal
Synthesis	Grass	Status	—	—	5	Self
Tailwind	Flying	Status	—	—	15	Your Side
Giga Drain	Grass	Special	75	100	10	Normal
Worry Seed	Grass	Status	—	100	10	Normal
Outrage	Dragon	Physical	120	100	10	1 Random

MOVES TAUGHT BY PEOPLE

Name	Type	Kind	Pow.	Acc.	PP	Range

EGG MOVES

Name	Type	Kind	Pow.	Acc.	PP	Range
Headbutt	Normal	Physical	70	100	15	Normal
Slam	Normal	Physical	80	75	20	Normal
Razor Wind	Normal	Special	80	100	10	Many Others
Leech Seed	Grass	Status	—	90	10	Normal
Nature Power	Normal	Status	—	—	20	Normal
Leaf Storm	Grass	Special	130	90	5	Normal
Synthesis	Grass	Status	—	—	5	Self
Curse	Ghost	Status	—	—	10	Varies
Leaf Blade	Grass	Physical	90	100	15	Normal
Dragon Dance	Dragon	Status	—	—	20	Self
Bullet Seed	Grass	Physical	25	100	30	Normal
Natural Gift	Normal	Physical	—	100	15	Normal

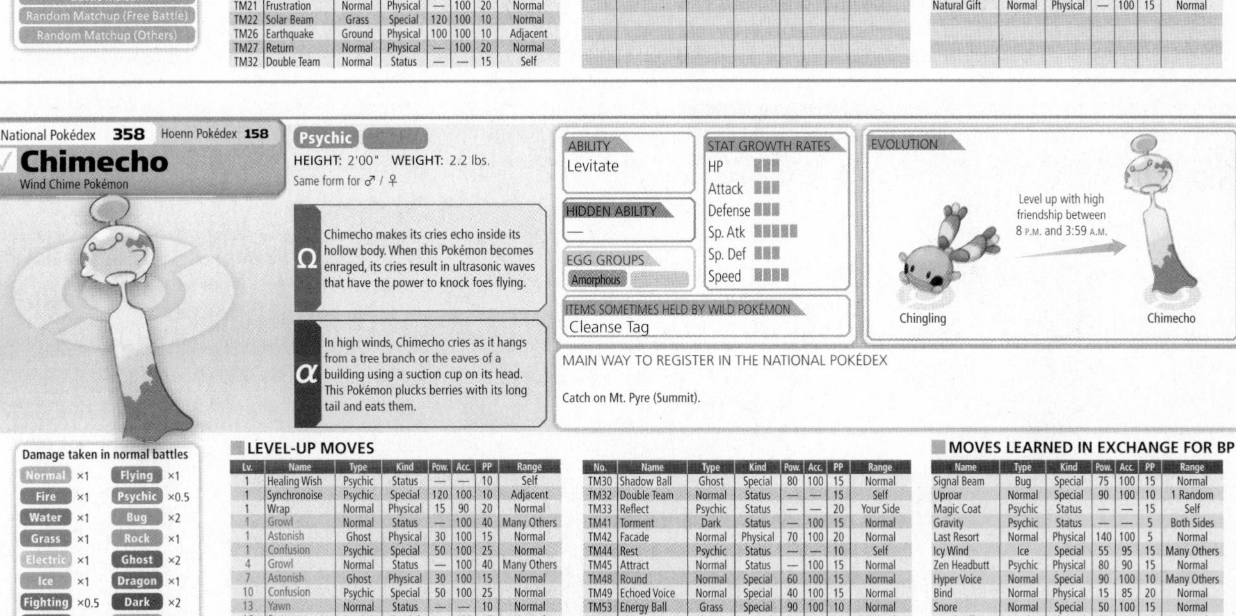

National Pokédex **358** Hoenn Pokédex **158**

Chimecho

Wind Chime Pokémon

Psychic

HEIGHT: 2'00" WEIGHT: 2.2 lbs.

Same form for ♂ / ♀

Ω Chimecho makes its cries echo inside its hollow body. When this Pokémon becomes enraged, its cries result in ultrasonic waves that have the power to knock foes flying.

α In high winds, Chimecho cries as it hangs from a tree branch or the eaves of a building using a suction cup on its head. This Pokémon plucks berries with its long tail and eats them.

ABILITY
Levitate

HIDDEN ABILITY
—

EGG GROUPS
Amorphous

STAT GROWTH RATES
HP ■■■
Attack ■■■
Defense ■■■
Sp. Atk ■■■■■
Sp. Def ■■■
Speed ■■■■

ITEMS SOMETIMES HELD BY WILD POKÉMON
Cleanse Tag

EVOLUTION

MAIN WAY TO REGISTER IN THE NATIONAL POKÉDEX

Catch on Mt. Pyre (Summit).

Damage taken in normal battles

Type		Type	
Normal	×1	Flying	×1
Fire	×1	Psychic	×0.5
Water	×1	Bug	×2
Grass	×1	Rock	×1
Electric	×1	Ghost	×2
Ice	×1	Dragon	×1
Fighting	×0.5	Dark	×2
Poison	×1	Steel	×1
! Ground	×1	Fairy	×1

Damage taken in Inverse battles

Type		Type	
Normal	×1	Flying	×1
Fire	×1	Psychic	×2
Water	×1	Bug	×0.5
Grass	×1	Rock	×1
Electric	×1	Ghost	×0.5
Ice	×1	Dragon	×1
Fighting	×2	Dark	×0.5
Poison	×1	Steel	×1
! Ground	×1	Fairy	×1

Can be used in
Inverse Battle
Battle Institute
Battle Maison
Random Matchup (Free Battle)
Random Matchup (Others)

LEVEL-UP MOVES

Lv.	Name	Type	Kind	Pow.	Acc.	PP	Range
1	Healing Wish	Psychic	Status	—	—	10	Self
1	Synchronoise	Psychic	Special	120	100	10	Adjacent
1	Wrap	Normal	Physical	15	90	20	Normal
1	Growl	Normal	Status	—	100	40	Many Others
1	Astonish	Ghost	Physical	30	100	15	Normal
1	Confusion	Psychic	Special	50	100	25	Normal
4	Growl	Normal	Status	—	100	40	Many Others
7	Astonish	Ghost	Physical	30	100	15	Normal
10	Confusion	Psychic	Special	50	100	25	Normal
13	Yawn	Normal	Status	—	—	10	Normal
16	Psywave	Psychic	Special	—	100	15	Normal
19	Take Down	Normal	Physical	90	85	20	Normal
22	Extrasensory	Psychic	Special	80	100	20	Normal
27	Heal Bell	Normal	Status	—	—	5	Your Party
32	Uproar	Normal	Special	90	100	10	1 Random
37	Safeguard	Normal	Status	—	—	25	Your Side
42	Double-Edge	Normal	Physical	120	100	15	Normal
47	Heal Pulse	Psychic	Status	—	—	10	Normal
52	Synchronoise	Psychic	Special	120	100	10	Adjacent
57	Healing Wish	Psychic	Status	—	—	10	Self

TM & HM MOVES

No.	Name	Type	Kind	Pow.	Acc.	PP	Range
TM03	Psyshock	Psychic	Special	80	100	10	Normal
TM04	Calm Mind	Psychic	Status	—	—	20	Self
TM06	Toxic	Poison	Status	—	90	10	Normal
TM10	Hidden Power	Normal	Special	60	100	15	Normal
TM11	Sunny Day	Fire	Status	—	—	5	Both Sides
TM12	Taunt	Dark	Status	—	100	20	Normal
TM16	Light Screen	Psychic	Status	—	—	30	Your Side
TM17	Protect	Normal	Status	—	—	10	Self
TM18	Rain Dance	Water	Status	—	—	5	Both Sides
TM20	Safeguard	Normal	Status	—	—	25	Your Side
TM21	Frustration	Normal	Physical	—	100	20	Normal
TM27	Return	Normal	Physical	—	100	20	Normal
TM29	Psychic	Psychic	Special	90	100	10	Normal
TM30	Shadow Ball	Ghost	Special	80	100	15	Normal
TM32	Double Team	Normal	Status	—	—	15	Self
TM33	Reflect	Psychic	Status	—	—	20	Your Side
TM41	Torment	Dark	Status	—	100	15	Normal
TM42	Facade	Normal	Physical	70	100	20	Normal
TM44	Rest	Psychic	Status	—	—	10	Self
TM45	Attract	Normal	Status	—	100	15	Normal
TM48	Round	Normal	Special	60	100	15	Normal
TM49	Echoed Voice	Normal	Special	40	100	15	Normal
TM53	Energy Ball	Grass	Special	90	100	10	Normal
TM57	Charge Beam	Electric	Special	50	90	10	Normal
TM70	Flash	Normal	Status	—	100	20	Normal
TM73	Thunder Wave	Electric	Status	—	100	20	Normal
TM77	Psych Up	Normal	Status	—	—	10	Normal
TM85	Dream Eater	Psychic	Special	100	100	15	Normal
TM86	Grass Knot	Grass	Special	—	100	20	Normal
TM87	Swagger	Normal	Status	—	90	15	Normal
TM88	Sleep Talk	Normal	Status	—	—	10	Self
TM90	Substitute	Normal	Status	—	—	10	Self
TM92	Trick Room	Psychic	Status	—	—	5	Both Sides
TM94	Secret Power	Normal	Physical	70	100	20	Normal
TM99	Dazzling Gleam	Fairy	Special	80	100	10	Many Others
TM100	Confide	Normal	Status	—	—	20	Normal

MOVES LEARNED IN EXCHANGE FOR BP

Name	Type	Kind	Pow.	Acc.	PP	Range
Signal Beam	Bug	Special	75	100	15	Normal
Uproar	Normal	Special	90	100	10	1 Random
Magic Coat	Psychic	Status	—	—	15	Self
Gravity	Psychic	Status	—	—	5	Both Sides
Last Resort	Normal	Physical	140	100	5	Normal
Icy Wind	Ice	Special	55	95	15	Many Others
Zen Headbutt	Psychic	Physical	80	90	15	Normal
Hyper Voice	Normal	Special	90	100	10	Many Others
Bind	Normal	Physical	15	85	20	Normal
Snore	Normal	Special	50	100	15	Normal
Knock Off	Dark	Physical	65	100	20	Normal
Heal Bell	Normal	Status	—	—	5	Your Party
Shock Wave	Electric	Special	60	—	20	Normal
Helping Hand	Normal	Status	—	—	20	1 Ally
Trick	Psychic	Status	—	100	10	Normal
Recycle	Normal	Status	—	—	10	Self
Snatch	Dark	Status	—	—	10	Self
Skill Swap	Psychic	Status	—	—	10	Normal

MOVES TAUGHT BY PEOPLE

Name	Type	Kind	Pow.	Acc.	PP	Range

EGG MOVES

Name	Type	Kind	Pow.	Acc.	PP	Range
Disable	Normal	Status	—	100	20	Normal
Curse	Ghost	Status	—	—	10	Varies
Hypnosis	Psychic	Status	—	60	20	Normal
Wish	Normal	Status	—	—	10	Self
Future Sight	Psychic	Special	120	100	10	Normal
Recover	Normal	Status	—	—	10	Self
Stored Power	Psychic	Special	20	100	10	Normal
Skill Swap	Psychic	Status	—	—	10	Normal
Cosmic Power	Psychic	Status	—	—	20	Self

National Pokédex **359** Hoenn Pokédex **159**

Absol

Disaster Pokémon

Dark

HEIGHT: 3'11" WEIGHT: 103.6 lbs.

Same form for ♂ / ♀

Ω Every time Absol appears before people, it is followed by a disaster such as an earthquake or a tidal wave. As a result, it came to be known as the disaster Pokémon.

α Absol has the ability to foretell the coming of natural disasters. It lives in a harsh, rugged mountain environment. This Pokémon very rarely ventures down from the mountains.

ABILITIES
Pressure
Super Luck

HIDDEN ABILITY
Justified

EGG GROUPS
Field

STAT GROWTH RATES
HP
Attack
Defense
Sp. Atk
Sp. Def
Speed

EVOLUTION
Does not evolve

ITEMS SOMETIMES HELD BY WILD POKÉMON
Life Orb

MAIN WAY TO REGISTER IN THE NATIONAL POKÉDEX

Catch in the very tall grass on Route 120.

Damage taken in normal battles

Type		Type	
Normal	×1	Flying	×1
Fire	×1	Psychic	×0
Water	×1	Bug	×2
Grass	×1	Rock	×1
Electric	×1	Ghost	×0.5
Ice	×1	Dragon	×1
Fighting	×2	Dark	×0.5
Poison	×1	Steel	×1
Ground	×1	Fairy	×2

Damage taken in Inverse battles

Type		Type	
Normal	×1	Flying	×1
Fire	×1	Psychic	×2
Water	×1	Bug	×0.5
Grass	×1	Rock	×1
Electric	×1	Ghost	×2
Ice	×1	Dragon	×1
Fighting	×0.5	Dark	×2
Poison	×1	Steel	×1
Ground	×1	Fairy	×0.5

Can be used in
Inverse Battle
Battle Institute
Battle Maison
Random Matchup (Free Battle)
Random Matchup (Others)

LEVEL-UP MOVES

Lv.	Name	Type	Kind	Pow.	Acc.	PP	Range
1	Perish Song	Normal	Status	—	—	5	Adjacent
1	Future Sight	Psychic	Special	120	100	10	Normal
1	Scratch	Normal	Physical	40	100	35	Normal
1	Feint	Normal	Physical	30	100	10	Normal
1	Leer	Normal	Status	—	100	30	Many Others
1	Quick Attack	Normal	Physical	40	100	30	Normal
4	Leer	Normal	Status	—	100	30	Many Others
7	Quick Attack	Normal	Physical	40	100	30	Normal
10	Pursuit	Dark	Physical	40	100	20	Normal
13	Taunt	Dark	Status	—	100	20	Normal
16	Bite	Dark	Physical	60	100	25	Normal
19	Double Team	Normal	Status	—	—	15	Self
22	Slash	Normal	Physical	70	100	20	Normal
25	Swords Dance	Normal	Status	—	—	20	Self
29	Night Slash	Dark	Physical	70	100	15	Normal
33	Detect	Fighting	Status	—	—	5	Self
37	Psycho Cut	Psychic	Physical	70	100	20	Normal
41	Me First	Normal	Status	—	—	20	Varies
45	Sucker Punch	Dark	Physical	80	100	5	Normal
49	Razor Wind	Normal	Special	80	100	10	Many Others
53	Future Sight	Psychic	Special	120	100	10	Normal
57	Perish Song	Normal	Status	—	—	5	Adjacent

TM & HM MOVES

No.	Name	Type	Kind	Pow.	Acc.	PP	Range
TM01	Hone Claws	Dark	Status	—	—	15	Self
TM04	Calm Mind	Psychic	Status	—	—	20	Self
TM06	Toxic	Poison	Status	—	90	10	Normal
TM07	Hail	Ice	Status	—	—	10	Both Sides
TM10	Hidden Power	Normal	Special	60	100	15	Normal
TM11	Sunny Day	Fire	Status	—	—	5	Both Sides
TM12	Taunt	Dark	Status	—	100	20	Normal
TM13	Ice Beam	Ice	Special	90	100	10	Normal
TM14	Blizzard	Ice	Special	110	70	5	Many Others
TM15	Hyper Beam	Normal	Special	150	90	5	Normal
TM17	Protect	Normal	Status	—	—	10	Self
TM18	Rain Dance	Water	Status	—	—	5	Both Sides
TM21	Frustration	Normal	Physical	—	100	20	Normal
TM24	Thunderbolt	Electric	Special	90	100	15	Normal
TM25	Thunder	Electric	Special	110	70	10	Normal
TM27	Return	Normal	Physical	—	100	20	Normal
TM30	Shadow Ball	Ghost	Special	80	100	15	Normal
TM32	Double Team	Normal	Status	—	—	15	Self
TM35	Flamethrower	Fire	Special	90	100	15	Normal
TM37	Sandstorm	Rock	Status	—	—	10	Both Sides
TM38	Fire Blast	Fire	Special	110	85	5	Normal
TM39	Rock Tomb	Rock	Physical	60	95	15	Normal
TM40	Aerial Ace	Flying	Physical	60	—	20	Normal
TM41	Torment	Dark	Status	—	100	15	Normal
TM42	Facade	Normal	Physical	70	100	20	Normal
TM44	Rest	Psychic	Status	—	—	10	Self
TM45	Attract	Normal	Status	—	100	15	Normal
TM46	Thief	Dark	Physical	60	100	25	Normal
TM48	Round	Normal	Special	60	100	15	Normal
TM49	Echoed Voice	Normal	Special	40	100	15	Normal
TM54	False Swipe	Normal	Physical	40	100	40	Normal
TM57	Charge Beam	Electric	Special	50	90	10	Normal
TM59	Incinerate	Fire	Special	60	100	15	Many Others
TM61	Will-O-Wisp	Fire	Status	—	85	15	Normal
TM65	Shadow Claw	Ghost	Physical	70	100	15	Normal
TM66	Payback	Dark	Physical	50	100	10	Normal
TM67	Retaliate	Normal	Physical	70	100	5	Normal
TM68	Giga Impact	Normal	Physical	150	90	5	Normal
TM70	Flash	Normal	Status	—	100	20	Normal
TM71	Stone Edge	Rock	Physical	100	80	5	Normal
TM73	Thunder Wave	Electric	Status	—	100	20	Normal
TM75	Swords Dance	Normal	Status	—	—	20	Self
TM77	Psych Up	Normal	Status	—	—	10	Normal
TM80	Rock Slide	Rock	Physical	75	90	10	Many Others
TM81	X-Scissor	Bug	Physical	80	100	15	Normal
TM85	Dream Eater	Psychic	Special	100	100	15	Normal
TM87	Swagger	Normal	Status	—	90	15	Normal
TM88	Sleep Talk	Normal	Status	—	—	10	Self
TM90	Substitute	Normal	Status	—	—	10	Self
TM94	Secret Power	Normal	Physical	70	100	20	Normal
TM95	Snarl	Dark	Special	55	95	15	Many Others
TM97	Dark Pulse	Dark	Special	80	100	15	Normal
TM100	Confide	Normal	Status	—	—	20	Normal
HM01	Cut	Normal	Physical	50	95	30	Normal
HM04	Strength	Normal	Physical	80	100	15	Normal
HM06	Rock Smash	Fighting	Physical	40	100	15	Normal

MOVES LEARNED IN EXCHANGE FOR BP

Name	Type	Kind	Pow.	Acc.	PP	Range
Bounce	Flying	Physical	85	85	5	Normal
Magic Coat	Psychic	Status	—	—	15	Self
Foul Play	Dark	Physical	95	100	15	Normal
Superpower	Fighting	Physical	120	100	5	Normal
Icy Wind	Ice	Special	55	95	15	Many Others
Zen Headbutt	Psychic	Physical	80	90	15	Normal
Iron Tail	Steel	Physical	100	75	15	Normal
Snore	Normal	Special	50	100	15	Normal
Knock Off	Dark	Physical	65	100	20	Normal
Role Play	Psychic	Status	—	—	10	Normal
Shock Wave	Electric	Special	60	—	20	Normal
Water Pulse	Water	Special	60	100	20	Normal
Spite	Ghost	Status	—	100	10	Normal
Snatch	Dark	Status	—	—	10	Self

MOVES TAUGHT BY PEOPLE

Name	Type	Kind	Pow.	Acc.	PP	Range

EGG MOVES

Name	Type	Kind	Pow.	Acc.	PP	Range
Baton Pass	Normal	Status	—	—	40	Self
Feint Attack	Dark	Physical	60	—	20	Normal
Double-Edge	Normal	Physical	120	100	15	Normal
Magic Coat	Psychic	Status	—	—	15	Self
Curse	Ghost	Status	—	—	10	Varies
Mean Look	Normal	Status	—	—	5	Normal
Zen Headbutt	Psychic	Physical	80	90	15	Normal
Punishment	Dark	Physical	—	100	5	Normal
Sucker Punch	Dark	Physical	80	100	5	Normal
Assurance	Dark	Physical	60	100	10	Normal
Me First	Normal	Status	—	—	20	Varies
Megahorn	Bug	Physical	120	85	10	Normal
Hex	Ghost	Special	65	100	10	Normal
Perish Song	Normal	Status	—	—	5	Adjacent
Play Rough	Fairy	Physical	90	90	10	Normal

Mega Evolution

Mega Absol

Disaster Pokémon

Dark

HEIGHT: 3'11" WEIGHT: 108 lbs.

Same form for ♂ / ♀

REQUIRED MEGA STONE
Absolite
Find in the Safari Zone.

ABILITY
Magic Bounce

HIDDEN ABILITY
—

EGG GROUPS
—

STAT GROWTH RATES
HP
Attack
Defense
Sp. Atk
Sp. Def
Speed

Damage taken in normal battles

Type		Type	
Normal	×1	Flying	×1
Fire	×1	Psychic	×0
Water	×1	Bug	×2
Grass	×1	Rock	×1
Electric	×1	Ghost	×0.5
Ice	×1	Dragon	×1
Fighting	×2	Dark	×0.5
Poison	×1	Steel	×1
Ground	×1	Fairy	×2

Damage taken in Inverse battles

Type		Type	
Normal	×1	Flying	×1
Fire	×1	Psychic	×2
Water	×1	Bug	×0.5
Grass	×1	Rock	×1
Electric	×1	Ghost	×2
Ice	×1	Dragon	×1
Fighting	×0.5	Dark	×2
Poison	×1	Steel	×1
Ground	×1	Fairy	×0.5

Can be used in
Inverse Battle
Battle Institute
Battle Maison
Random Matchup (Free Battle)
Random Matchup (Others)

National Pokédex 360	Hoenn Pokédex 167

Wynaut
Bright Pokémon

Psychic

HEIGHT: 2'00" WEIGHT: 30.9 lbs.
Same form for ♂ / ♀

Ω Wynaut can always be seen with a big, happy smile on its face. Look at its tail to determine if it is angry. When angered, this Pokémon will be slapping the ground with its tail.

α Wynaut gather on moonlit nights to play by squeezing up against each other. By being squeezed, this Pokémon gains endurance and is trained to dole out powerful counterattacks.

ABILITY
Shadow Tag

HIDDEN ABILITY
Telepathy

EGG GROUPS
No Eggs Discovered

STAT GROWTH RATES
HP ▮▮▮▮
Attack ▮
Defense ▮▮
Sp. Atk ▮
Sp. Def ▮▮
Speed ▮

ITEMS SOMETIMES HELD BY WILD POKÉMON
—

EVOLUTION
Wynaut → Lv. 15 → Wobbuffet

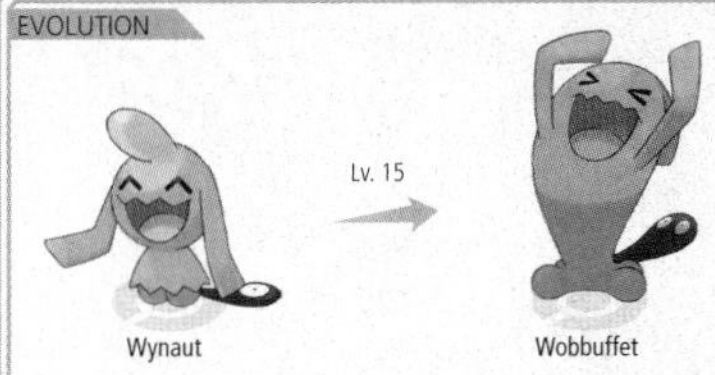

MAIN WAY TO REGISTER IN THE NATIONAL POKÉDEX

Receive a Pokémon Egg from an old woman in Lavaridge Town and hatch it.

Damage taken in normal battles

Type		Type	
Normal	×1	Flying	×1
Fire	×1	Psychic	×0.5
Water	×1	Bug	×2
Grass	×1	Rock	×1
Electric	×1	Ghost	×2
Ice	×1	Dragon	×1
Fighting	×0.5	Dark	×2
Poison	×1	Steel	×1
Ground	×1	Fairy	×1

Damage taken in Inverse battles

Type		Type	
Normal	×1	Flying	×1
Fire	×1	Psychic	×2
Water	×1	Bug	×0.5
Grass	×1	Rock	×1
Electric	×1	Ghost	×0.5
Ice	×1	Dragon	×1
Fighting	×2	Dark	×0.5
Poison	×1	Steel	×1
Ground	×1	Fairy	×1

Can be used in
Inverse Battle
Battle Institute
Battle Maison
Random Matchup (Free Battle)
Random Matchup (Others)

LEVEL-UP MOVES

Lv.	Name	Type	Kind	Pow.	Acc.	PP	Range
1	Splash	Normal	Status	—	—	40	Self
1	Charm	Fairy	Status	—	100	20	Normal
1	Encore	Normal	Status	—	100	5	Normal
15	Counter	Fighting	Physical	—	100	20	Varies
15	Mirror Coat	Psychic	Special	—	100	20	Varies
15	Safeguard	Normal	Status	—	—	25	Your Side
15	Destiny Bond	Ghost	Status	—	—	5	Self

TM & HM MOVES

No.	Name	Type	Kind	Pow.	Acc.	PP	Range
TM20	Safeguard	Normal	Status	—	—	25	Your Side

MOVES LEARNED IN EXCHANGE FOR BP

Name	Type	Kind	Pow.	Acc.	PP	Range

MOVES TAUGHT BY PEOPLE

Name	Type	Kind	Pow.	Acc.	PP	Range

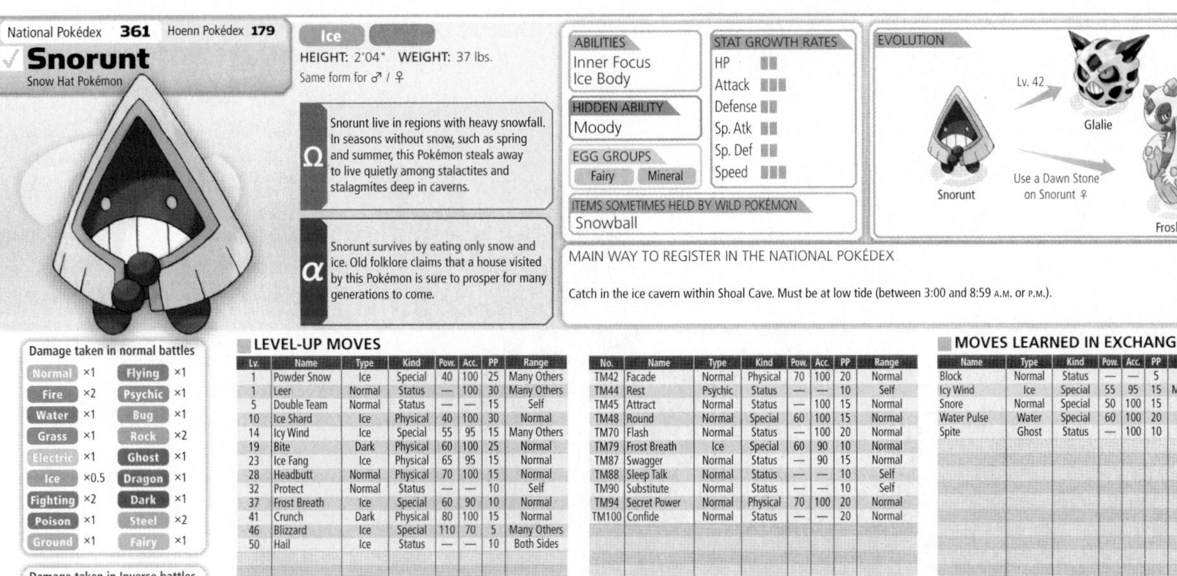

National Pokédex 361	Hoenn Pokédex 179

Snorunt
Snow Hat Pokémon

Ice

HEIGHT: 2'04" WEIGHT: 37 lbs.
Same form for ♂ / ♀

Ω Snorunt live in regions with heavy snowfall. In seasons without snow, such as spring and summer, this Pokémon steals away to live quietly among stalactites and stalagmites deep in caverns.

α Snorunt survives by eating only snow and ice. Old folklore claims that a house visited by this Pokémon is sure to prosper for many generations to come.

ABILITIES
Inner Focus
Ice Body

HIDDEN ABILITY
Moody

EGG GROUPS
Fairy / Mineral

STAT GROWTH RATES
HP ▮▮
Attack ▮▮▮
Defense ▮▮
Sp. Atk ▮▮
Sp. Def ▮▮
Speed ▮▮▮

ITEMS SOMETIMES HELD BY WILD POKÉMON
Snowball

EVOLUTION
Snorunt → Lv. 42 → Glalie
Snorunt → Use a Dawn Stone on Snorunt ♀ → Froslass

MAIN WAY TO REGISTER IN THE NATIONAL POKÉDEX

Catch in the ice cavern within Shoal Cave. Must be at low tide (between 3:00 and 8:59 A.M. or P.M.).

Damage taken in normal battles

Type		Type	
Normal	×1	Flying	×1
Fire	×2	Psychic	×1
Water	×1	Bug	×1
Grass	×1	Rock	×2
Electric	×1	Ghost	×1
Ice	×0.5	Dragon	×1
Fighting	×2	Dark	×1
Poison	×1	Steel	×2
Ground	×1	Fairy	×1

Damage taken in Inverse battles

Type		Type	
Normal	×1	Flying	×1
Fire	×0.5	Psychic	×1
Water	×1	Bug	×1
Grass	×1	Rock	×0.5
Electric	×1	Ghost	×1
Ice	×2	Dragon	×1
Fighting	×0.5	Dark	×1
Poison	×1	Steel	×0.5
Ground	×1	Fairy	×1

Can be used in
Inverse Battle
Battle Institute
Battle Maison
Random Matchup (Free Battle)
Random Matchup (Others)

LEVEL-UP MOVES

Lv.	Name	Type	Kind	Pow.	Acc.	PP	Range
1	Powder Snow	Ice	Special	40	100	25	Many Others
1	Leer	Normal	Status	—	100	30	Many Others
5	Double Team	Normal	Status	—	—	15	Self
10	Ice Shard	Ice	Physical	40	100	30	Normal
14	Icy Wind	Ice	Special	55	95	15	Many Others
19	Bite	Dark	Physical	60	100	25	Normal
23	Ice Fang	Ice	Physical	65	95	15	Normal
28	Headbutt	Normal	Physical	70	100	15	Normal
32	Protect	Normal	Status	—	—	10	Self
37	Frost Breath	Ice	Special	60	90	10	Normal
41	Crunch	Dark	Physical	80	100	15	Normal
46	Blizzard	Ice	Special	110	70	5	Many Others
50	Hail	Ice	Status	—	—	10	Both Sides

TM & HM MOVES

No.	Name	Type	Kind	Pow.	Acc.	PP	Range
TM06	Toxic	Poison	Status	—	90	10	Normal
TM07	Hail	Ice	Status	—	—	10	Both Sides
TM10	Hidden Power	Normal	Special	60	100	15	Normal
TM13	Ice Beam	Ice	Special	90	100	10	Normal
TM14	Blizzard	Ice	Special	110	70	5	Many Others
TM16	Light Screen	Psychic	Status	—	—	30	Your Side
TM17	Protect	Normal	Status	—	—	10	Self
TM18	Rain Dance	Water	Status	—	—	5	Both Sides
TM20	Safeguard	Normal	Status	—	—	25	Your Side
TM21	Frustration	Normal	Physical	—	100	20	Normal
TM27	Return	Normal	Physical	—	100	20	Normal
TM30	Shadow Ball	Ghost	Special	80	100	15	Normal
TM32	Double Team	Normal	Status	—	—	15	Self
TM42	Facade	Normal	Physical	70	100	20	Normal
TM44	Rest	Psychic	Status	—	—	10	Self
TM45	Attract	Normal	Status	—	100	15	Normal
TM48	Round	Normal	Special	60	100	15	Normal
TM70	Flash	Normal	Status	—	100	20	Normal
TM79	Frost Breath	Ice	Special	60	90	10	Normal
TM87	Swagger	Normal	Status	—	90	15	Normal
TM88	Sleep Talk	Normal	Status	—	—	10	Self
TM90	Substitute	Normal	Status	—	—	10	Self
TM94	Secret Power	Normal	Physical	70	100	20	Normal
TM100	Confide	Normal	Status	—	—	20	Normal

MOVES LEARNED IN EXCHANGE FOR BP

Name	Type	Kind	Pow.	Acc.	PP	Range
Block	Normal	Status	—	—	5	Normal
Icy Wind	Ice	Special	55	95	15	Many Others
Snore	Normal	Special	50	100	15	Normal
Water Pulse	Water	Special	60	100	20	Normal
Spite	Ghost	Status	—	100	10	Normal

MOVES TAUGHT BY PEOPLE

Name	Type	Kind	Pow.	Acc.	PP	Range

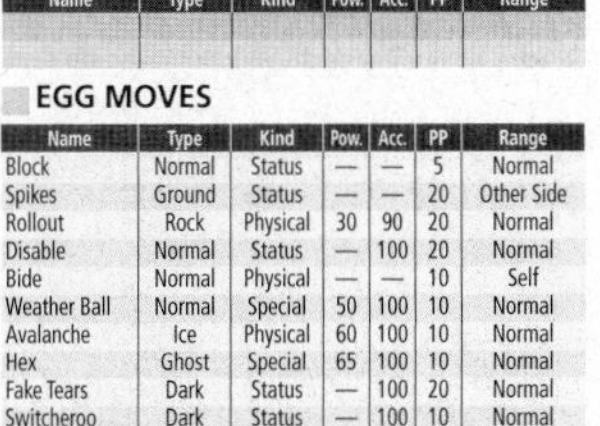

EGG MOVES

Name	Type	Kind	Pow.	Acc.	PP	Range
Block	Normal	Status	—	—	5	Normal
Spikes	Ground	Status	—	—	20	Other Side
Rollout	Rock	Physical	30	90	20	Normal
Disable	Normal	Status	—	100	20	Normal
Bide	Normal	Physical	—	—	10	Self
Weather Ball	Normal	Special	50	100	10	Normal
Avalanche	Ice	Physical	60	100	10	Normal
Hex	Ghost	Special	65	100	10	Normal
Fake Tears	Dark	Status	—	100	20	Normal
Switcheroo	Dark	Status	—	100	10	Normal

National Pokédex **362** Hoenn Pokédex **180**

✓ Glalie

Face Pokémon

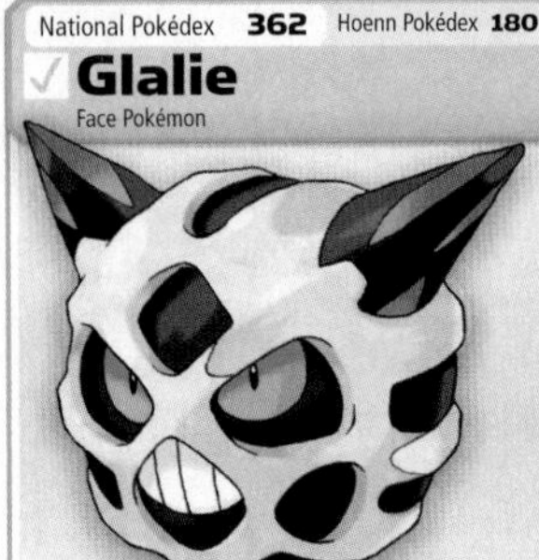

Ice

HEIGHT: 4'11" WEIGHT: 565.5 lbs.

Same form for ♂ / ♀

Ω Glalie has a body made of rock, which it hardens with an armor of ice. This Pokémon has the ability to freeze moisture in the atmosphere into any shape it desires.

α Glalie has the ability to freely control ice. For example, it can instantly freeze its prey solid. After immobilizing its prey in ice, this Pokémon enjoys eating it in leisurely fashion.

ABILITIES
Inner Focus
Ice Body

HIDDEN ABILITY
Moody

EGG GROUPS
Fairy | Mineral

STAT GROWTH RATES
HP
Attack
Defense
Sp. Atk
Sp. Def
Speed

ITEMS SOMETIMES HELD BY WILD POKÉMON
—

EVOLUTION

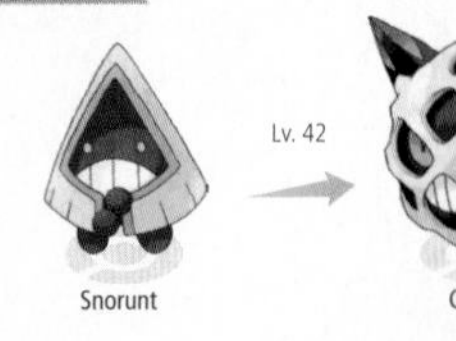

MAIN WAY TO REGISTER IN THE NATIONAL POKÉDEX

Level up Snorunt to Lv. 42.

Damage taken in normal battles

Normal	×1	Flying	×1
Fire	×2	Psychic	×1
Water	×1	Bug	×1
Grass	×1	Rock	×2
Electric	×1	Ghost	×1
Ice	×0.5	Dragon	×1
Fighting	×2	Dark	×1
Poison	×1	Steel	×2
Ground	×1	Fairy	×1

Damage taken in Inverse battles

Normal	×1	Flying	×1
Fire	×0.5	Psychic	×1
Water	×1	Bug	×1
Grass	×1	Rock	×0.5
Electric	×1	Ghost	×1
Ice	×2	Dragon	×1
Fighting	×0.5	Dark	×1
Poison	×1	Steel	×0.5
Ground	×1	Fairy	×1

Can be used in
Inverse Battle
Battle Institute
Battle Maison
Random Matchup (Free Battle)
Random Matchup (Others)

LEVEL-UP MOVES

Lv.	Name	Type	Kind	Pow.	Acc.	PP	Range
1	Sheer Cold	Ice	Special	—	30	5	Normal
1	Powder Snow	Ice	Special	40	100	25	Many Others
1	Leer	Normal	Status	—	100	30	Many Others
1	Double Team	Normal	Status	—	—	15	Self
1	Ice Shard	Ice	Physical	40	100	30	Normal
5	Double Team	Normal	Status	—	—	15	Self
10	Ice Shard	Ice	Physical	40	100	30	Normal
14	Icy Wind	Ice	Special	55	95	15	Many Others
19	Bite	Dark	Physical	60	100	25	Normal
23	Ice Fang	Ice	Physical	65	95	15	Normal
28	Headbutt	Normal	Physical	70	100	15	Normal
32	Protect	Normal	Status	—	—	10	Self
37	Frost Breath	Ice	Special	60	90	10	Normal
41	Crunch	Dark	Physical	80	100	15	Normal
42	Freeze-Dry	Ice	Special	70	100	20	Normal
48	Blizzard	Ice	Special	110	70	5	Many Others
54	Hail	Ice	Status	—	—	10	Both Sides
61	Sheer Cold	Ice	Special	—	30	5	Normal

TM & HM MOVES

No.	Name	Type	Kind	Pow.	Acc.	PP	Range
TM06	Toxic	Poison	Status	—	90	10	Normal
TM07	Hail	Ice	Status	—	—	10	Both Sides
TM10	Hidden Power	Normal	Special	60	100	15	Normal
TM12	Taunt	Dark	Status	—	100	20	Normal
TM13	Ice Beam	Ice	Special	90	100	10	Normal
TM14	Blizzard	Ice	Special	110	70	5	Many Others
TM15	Hyper Beam	Normal	Special	150	90	5	Normal
TM16	Light Screen	Psychic	Status	—	—	30	Your Side
TM17	Protect	Normal	Status	—	—	10	Self
TM18	Rain Dance	Water	Status	—	—	5	Both Sides
TM20	Safeguard	Normal	Status	—	—	25	Your Side
TM21	Frustration	Normal	Physical	—	100	20	Normal
TM26	Earthquake	Ground	Physical	100	100	10	Adjacent
TM27	Return	Normal	Physical	—	100	20	Normal
TM30	Shadow Ball	Ghost	Special	80	100	15	Normal
TM32	Double Team	Normal	Status	—	—	15	Self
TM41	Torment	Dark	Status	—	100	15	Normal
TM42	Facade	Normal	Physical	70	100	20	Normal
TM44	Rest	Psychic	Status	—	—	10	Self
TM45	Attract	Normal	Status	—	100	15	Normal
TM48	Round	Normal	Special	60	100	15	Normal
TM64	Explosion	Normal	Physical	250	100	5	Adjacent
TM66	Payback	Dark	Physical	50	100	10	Normal
TM68	Giga Impact	Normal	Physical	150	90	5	Normal
TM70	Flash	Normal	Status	—	100	20	Normal
TM74	Gyro Ball	Steel	Physical	—	100	5	Normal
TM78	Bulldoze	Ground	Physical	60	100	20	Adjacent
TM79	Frost Breath	Ice	Special	60	90	10	Normal
TM87	Swagger	Normal	Status	—	90	15	Normal
TM88	Sleep Talk	Normal	Status	—	—	10	Self
TM90	Substitute	Normal	Status	—	—	10	Self
TM94	Secret Power	Normal	Physical	70	100	20	Normal
TM97	Dark Pulse	Dark	Special	80	100	15	Normal
TM100	Confide	Normal	Status	—	—	20	Normal

MOVES LEARNED IN EXCHANGE FOR BP

Name	Type	Kind	Pow.	Acc.	PP	Range
Super Fang	Normal	Physical	—	90	10	Normal
Signal Beam	Bug	Special	75	100	15	Normal
Iron Head	Steel	Physical	80	100	15	Normal
Block	Normal	Status	—	—	5	Normal
Icy Wind	Ice	Special	55	95	15	Many Others
Snore	Normal	Special	50	100	15	Normal
Water Pulse	Water	Special	60	100	20	Normal
Spite	Ghost	Status	—	100	10	Normal

MOVES TAUGHT BY PEOPLE

Name	Type	Kind	Pow.	Acc.	PP	Range

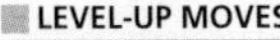

Mega Evolution

Mega Glalie

Face Pokémon

Ice

HEIGHT: 6'11" WEIGHT: 772.1 lbs.

Same form for ♂ / ♀

REQUIRED MEGA STONE
Glalitite
Find in the ice cavern within Shoal Cave. Must be at low tide (between 3:00 and 8:59 A.M. or P.M.).

ABILITY
Refrigerate

HIDDEN ABILITY
—

EGG GROUPS
—

STAT GROWTH RATES
HP
Attack
Defense
Sp. Atk
Sp. Def
Speed

Damage taken in normal battles

Normal	×1	Flying	×1
Fire	×2	Psychic	×1
Water	×1	Bug	×1
Grass	×1	Rock	×2
Electric	×1	Ghost	×1
Ice	×0.5	Dragon	×1
Fighting	×2	Dark	×1
Poison	×1	Steel	×2
Ground	×1	Fairy	×1

Damage taken in Inverse battles

Normal	×1	Flying	×1
Fire	×0.5	Psychic	×1
Water	×1	Bug	×1
Grass	×1	Rock	×0.5
Electric	×1	Ghost	×1
Ice	×2	Dragon	×1
Fighting	×0.5	Dark	×1
Poison	×1	Steel	×0.5
Ground	×1	Fairy	×1

Can be used in
Inverse Battle
Battle Institute
Battle Maison
Random Matchup (Free Battle)
Random Matchup (Others)

National Pokédex **363** Hoenn Pokédex **182**

✓ Spheal

Clap Pokémon

Ice | Water

HEIGHT: 2'07" WEIGHT: 87.1 lbs.

Same form for ♂ / ♀

Ω Spheal is much faster rolling than walking to get around. When groups of this Pokémon eat, they all clap at once to show their pleasure. Because of this, their mealtimes are noisy.

α Spheal always travels by rolling around on its ball-like body. When the season for ice floes arrives, this Pokémon can be seen rolling about on ice and crossing the sea.

ABILITIES
Thick Fat
Ice Body

HIDDEN ABILITY
Oblivious

EGG GROUPS
Water 1 | Field

STAT GROWTH RATES
HP
Attack
Defense
Sp. Atk
Sp. Def
Speed

ITEMS SOMETIMES HELD BY WILD POKÉMON
—

EVOLUTION

MAIN WAY TO REGISTER IN THE NATIONAL POKÉDEX

Catch in Shoal Cave (1F).

Damage taken in normal battles

Type		Type	
Normal	×1	Flying	×1
Fire	×1	Psychic	×1
Water	×0.5	Bug	×1
Grass	×2	Rock	×2
Electric	×2	Ghost	×1
Ice	×0.25	Dragon	×1
Fighting	×2	Dark	×1
Poison	×1	Steel	×1
Ground	×1	Fairy	×1

Damage taken in Inverse battles

Type		Type	
Normal	×1	Flying	×1
Fire	×1	Psychic	×1
Water	×2	Bug	×1
Grass	×0.5	Rock	×0.5
Electric	×0.5	Ghost	×1
Ice	×4	Dragon	×1
Fighting	×0.5	Dark	×1
Poison	×1	Steel	×1
Ground	×1	Fairy	×1

Can be used in
Inverse Battle
Battle Institute
Battle Maison
Random Matchup (Free Battle)
Random Matchup (Others)

LEVEL-UP MOVES

Lv.	Name	Type	Kind	Pow.	Acc.	PP	Range
1	Defense Curl	Normal	Status	—	—	40	Self
1	Powder Snow	Ice	Special	40	100	25	Many Others
1	Growl	Normal	Status	—	100	40	Many Others
1	Water Gun	Water	Special	40	100	25	Normal
5	Rollout	Rock	Physical	30	90	20	Normal
9	Encore	Normal	Status	—	100	5	Normal
13	Ice Ball	Ice	Physical	30	90	20	Normal
17	Brine	Water	Special	65	100	10	Normal
21	Aurora Beam	Ice	Special	65	100	20	Normal
26	Body Slam	Normal	Physical	85	100	15	Normal
31	Rest	Psychic	Status	—	—	10	Self
31	Snore	Normal	Special	50	100	15	Normal
36	Hail	Ice	Status	—	—	10	Both Sides
41	Blizzard	Ice	Special	110	70	5	Many Others
46	Sheer Cold	Ice	Special	—	30	5	Normal

TM & HM MOVES

No.	Name	Type	Kind	Pow.	Acc.	PP	Range
TM06	Toxic	Poison	Status	—	90	10	Normal
TM07	Hail	Ice	Status	—	—	10	Both Sides
TM10	Hidden Power	Normal	Special	60	100	15	Normal
TM13	Ice Beam	Ice	Special	90	100	10	Normal
TM14	Blizzard	Ice	Special	110	70	5	Many Others
TM17	Protect	Normal	Status	—	—	10	Self
TM18	Rain Dance	Water	Status	—	—	5	Both Sides
TM21	Frustration	Normal	Physical	—	100	20	Normal
TM26	Earthquake	Ground	Physical	100	100	10	Adjacent
TM27	Return	Normal	Physical	—	100	20	Normal
TM32	Double Team	Normal	Status	—	—	15	Self
TM39	Rock Tomb	Rock	Physical	60	95	15	Normal
TM42	Facade	Normal	Physical	70	100	20	Normal
TM44	Rest	Psychic	Status	—	—	10	Self
TM45	Attract	Normal	Status	—	100	15	Normal
TM48	Round	Normal	Special	60	100	15	Normal
TM49	Echoed Voice	Normal	Special	40	100	15	Normal
TM78	Bulldoze	Ground	Physical	60	100	20	Adjacent
TM79	Frost Breath	Ice	Special	60	90	10	Normal
TM80	Rock Slide	Rock	Physical	75	90	10	Many Others
TM87	Swagger	Normal	Status	—	90	15	Normal
TM88	Sleep Talk	Normal	Status	—	—	10	Self
TM90	Substitute	Normal	Status	—	—	10	Self
TM94	Secret Power	Normal	Physical	70	100	20	Normal
TM100	Confide	Normal	Status	—	—	20	Normal
HM03	Surf	Water	Special	90	100	15	Adjacent
HM04	Strength	Normal	Physical	80	100	15	Normal
HM05	Waterfall	Water	Physical	80	100	15	Normal
HM06	Rock Smash	Fighting	Physical	40	100	15	Normal
HM07	Dive	Water	Physical	80	100	10	Normal

MOVES LEARNED IN EXCHANGE FOR BP

Name	Type	Kind	Pow.	Acc.	PP	Range
Super Fang	Normal	Physical	—	90	10	Normal
Signal Beam	Bug	Special	75	100	15	Normal
Icy Wind	Ice	Special	55	95	15	Many Others
Aqua Tail	Water	Physical	90	90	10	Normal
Iron Tail	Steel	Physical	100	75	15	Normal
Snore	Normal	Special	50	100	15	Normal
Water Pulse	Water	Special	60	100	20	Normal

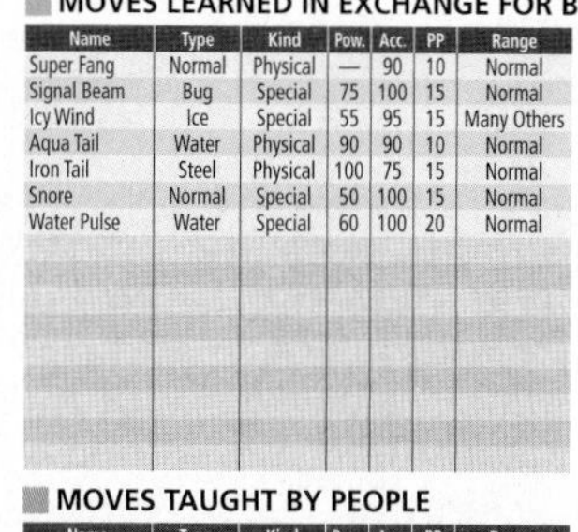

MOVES TAUGHT BY PEOPLE

Name	Type	Kind	Pow.	Acc.	PP	Range

EGG MOVES

Name	Type	Kind	Pow.	Acc.	PP	Range
Water Sport	Water	Status	—	—	15	Both Sides
Stockpile	Normal	Status	—	—	20	Self
Swallow	Normal	Status	—	—	10	Self
Spit Up	Normal	Special	—	100	10	Normal
Yawn	Normal	Status	—	—	10	Normal
Curse	Ghost	Status	—	—	10	Varies
Fissure	Ground	Physical	—	30	5	Normal
Signal Beam	Bug	Special	75	100	15	Normal
Aqua Ring	Water	Status	—	—	20	Self
Rollout	Rock	Physical	30	90	20	Normal
Sleep Talk	Normal	Status	—	—	10	Self
Water Pulse	Water	Special	60	100	20	Normal
Belly Drum	Normal	Status	—	—	10	Self

National Pokédex **364** Hoenn Pokédex **183**

✓ Sealeo

Ball Roll Pokémon

Ice | Water

HEIGHT: 3'07" WEIGHT: 193.1 lbs.

Same form for ♂ / ♀

Ω Sealeo has the habit of always juggling on the tip of its nose anything it sees for the first time. This Pokémon occasionally entertains itself by balancing and rolling a Spheal on its nose.

α Sealeo often balances and rolls things on the tip of its nose. While the Pokémon is rolling something, it checks the object's aroma and texture to determine whether it likes the object or not.

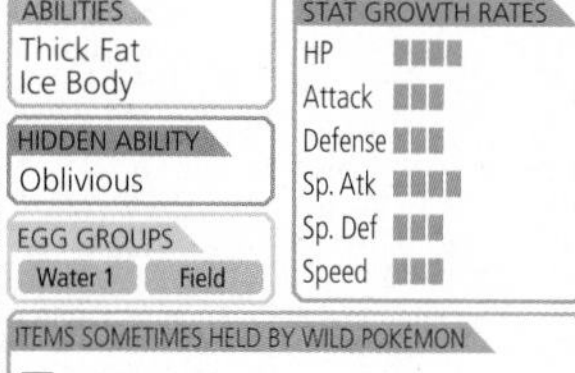

ABILITIES
Thick Fat
Ice Body

HIDDEN ABILITY
Oblivious

EGG GROUPS
Water 1 | Field

STAT GROWTH RATES
HP
Attack
Defense
Sp. Atk
Sp. Def
Speed

ITEMS SOMETIMES HELD BY WILD POKÉMON
—

EVOLUTION

MAIN WAY TO REGISTER IN THE NATIONAL POKÉDEX

Catch in Shoal Cave (1F).

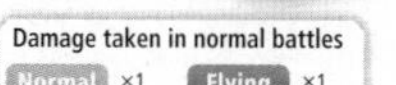

Damage taken in normal battles

Type		Type	
Normal	×1	Flying	×1
Fire	×1	Psychic	×1
Water	×0.5	Bug	×1
Grass	×2	Rock	×2
Electric	×2	Ghost	×1
Ice	×0.25	Dragon	×1
Fighting	×2	Dark	×1
Poison	×1	Steel	×1
Ground	×1	Fairy	×1

Damage taken in Inverse battles

Type		Type	
Normal	×1	Flying	×1
Fire	×1	Psychic	×1
Water	×2	Bug	×1
Grass	×0.5	Rock	×0.5
Electric	×0.5	Ghost	×1
Ice	×4	Dragon	×1
Fighting	×0.5	Dark	×1
Poison	×1	Steel	×1
Ground	×1	Fairy	×1

Can be used in
Inverse Battle
Battle Institute
Battle Maison
Random Matchup (Free Battle)
Random Matchup (Others)

LEVEL-UP MOVES

Lv.	Name	Type	Kind	Pow.	Acc.	PP	Range
1	Defense Curl	Normal	Status	—	—	40	Self
1	Powder Snow	Ice	Special	40	100	25	Many Others
1	Growl	Normal	Status	—	100	40	Many Others
1	Water Gun	Water	Special	40	100	25	Normal
5	Rollout	Rock	Physical	30	90	20	Normal
9	Encore	Normal	Status	—	100	5	Normal
13	Ice Ball	Ice	Physical	30	90	20	Normal
17	Brine	Water	Special	65	100	10	Normal
21	Aurora Beam	Ice	Special	65	100	20	Normal
26	Body Slam	Normal	Physical	85	100	15	Normal
31	Rest	Psychic	Status	—	—	10	Self
31	Snore	Normal	Special	50	100	15	Normal
32	Swagger	Normal	Status	—	90	15	Normal
38	Hail	Ice	Status	—	—	10	Both Sides
45	Blizzard	Ice	Special	110	70	5	Many Others
52	Sheer Cold	Ice	Special	—	30	5	Normal

TM & HM MOVES

No.	Name	Type	Kind	Pow.	Acc.	PP	Range
TM05	Roar	Normal	Status	—	—	20	Normal
TM06	Toxic	Poison	Status	—	90	10	Normal
TM07	Hail	Ice	Status	—	—	10	Both Sides
TM10	Hidden Power	Normal	Special	60	100	15	Normal
TM13	Ice Beam	Ice	Special	90	100	10	Normal
TM14	Blizzard	Ice	Special	110	70	5	Many Others
TM17	Protect	Normal	Status	—	—	10	Self
TM18	Rain Dance	Water	Status	—	—	5	Both Sides
TM21	Frustration	Normal	Physical	—	100	20	Normal
TM26	Earthquake	Ground	Physical	100	100	10	Adjacent
TM27	Return	Normal	Physical	—	100	20	Normal
TM32	Double Team	Normal	Status	—	—	15	Self
TM39	Rock Tomb	Rock	Physical	60	95	15	Normal
TM42	Facade	Normal	Physical	70	100	20	Normal
TM44	Rest	Psychic	Status	—	—	10	Self
TM45	Attract	Normal	Status	—	100	15	Normal
TM48	Round	Normal	Special	60	100	15	Normal
TM49	Echoed Voice	Normal	Special	40	100	15	Normal
TM78	Bulldoze	Ground	Physical	60	100	20	Adjacent
TM79	Frost Breath	Ice	Special	60	90	10	Normal
TM80	Rock Slide	Rock	Physical	75	90	10	Many Others
TM87	Swagger	Normal	Status	—	90	15	Normal
TM88	Sleep Talk	Normal	Status	—	—	10	Self
TM90	Substitute	Normal	Status	—	—	10	Self
TM94	Secret Power	Normal	Physical	70	100	20	Normal
TM100	Confide	Normal	Status	—	—	20	Normal
HM03	Surf	Water	Special	90	100	15	Adjacent
HM04	Strength	Normal	Physical	80	100	15	Normal
HM05	Waterfall	Water	Physical	80	100	15	Normal
HM06	Rock Smash	Fighting	Physical	40	100	15	Normal
HM07	Dive	Water	Physical	80	100	10	Normal

MOVES LEARNED IN EXCHANGE FOR BP

Name	Type	Kind	Pow.	Acc.	PP	Range
Super Fang	Normal	Physical	—	90	10	Normal
Signal Beam	Bug	Special	75	100	15	Normal
Icy Wind	Ice	Special	55	95	15	Many Others
Aqua Tail	Water	Physical	90	90	10	Normal
Iron Tail	Steel	Physical	100	75	15	Normal
Snore	Normal	Special	50	100	15	Normal
Water Pulse	Water	Special	60	100	20	Normal

MOVES TAUGHT BY PEOPLE

Name	Type	Kind	Pow.	Acc.	PP	Range

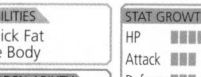

National Pokédex **365** Hoenn Pokédex **184**

✓ Walrein

Ice Break Pokémon

Ice | Water

HEIGHT: 4'07" WEIGHT: 332 lbs.

Same form for ♂ / ♀

Ω Walrein's two massively developed tusks can totally shatter blocks of ice weighing 10 tons with one blow. This Pokémon's thick coat of blubber insulates it from subzero temperatures.

α Walrein swims all over in frigid seawater while crushing icebergs with its grand, imposing tusks. Its thick layer of blubber makes enemy attacks bounce off harmlessly.

ABILITIES
Thick Fat
Ice Body

HIDDEN ABILITY
Oblivious

EGG GROUPS
Water 1 | Field

STAT GROWTH RATES
HP
Attack
Defense
Sp. Atk
Sp. Def
Speed

ITEMS SOMETIMES HELD BY WILD POKÉMON
—

EVOLUTION
Spheal → Lv. 32 → Sealeo → Lv. 44 → Walrein

MAIN WAY TO REGISTER IN THE NATIONAL POKÉDEX

Level up Sealeo to Lv. 44.

Damage taken in normal battles

Type	×	Type	×
Normal	×1	Flying	×1
! Fire	×1	Psychic	×1
Water	×0.5	Bug	×1
Grass	×2	Rock	×2
Electric	×2	Ghost	×1
! Ice	×0.25	Dragon	×1
Fighting	×2	Dark	×1
Poison	×1	Steel	×1
Ground	×1	Fairy	×1

Damage taken in Inverse battles

Type	×	Type	×
Normal	×1	Flying	×1
! Fire	×1	Psychic	×1
Water	×2	Bug	×1
Grass	×0.5	Rock	×0.5
Electric	×0.5	Ghost	×1
! Ice	×4	Dragon	×1
Fighting	×0.5	Dark	×1
Poison	×1	Steel	×1
Ground	×1	Fairy	×1

Can be used in
Inverse Battle
Battle Institute
Battle Maison
Random Matchup (Free Battle)
Random Matchup (Others)

LEVEL-UP MOVES

Lv.	Name	Type	Kind	Pow.	Acc.	PP	Range
1	Crunch	Dark	Physical	80	100	15	Normal
1	Defense Curl	Normal	Status	—	—	40	Self
1	Powder Snow	Ice	Special	40	100	25	Many Others
1	Growl	Normal	Status	—	100	40	Many Others
1	Water Gun	Water	Special	40	100	25	Normal
7	Rollout	Rock	Physical	30	90	20	Normal
7	Encore	Normal	Status	—	100	5	Normal
13	Ice Ball	Ice	Physical	30	90	20	Normal
19	Brine	Water	Special	65	100	10	Normal
19	Aurora Beam	Ice	Special	65	100	20	Normal
25	Body Slam	Normal	Physical	85	100	15	Normal
31	Rest	Psychic	Status	—	—	10	Self
31	Snore	Normal	Special	50	100	15	Normal
32	Swagger	Normal	Status	—	90	15	Normal
38	Hail	Ice	Status	—	—	10	Both Sides
44	Ice Fang	Ice	Physical	65	95	15	Normal
49	Blizzard	Ice	Special	110	70	5	Many Others
60	Sheer Cold	Ice	Special	—	30	5	Normal

TM & HM MOVES

No.	Name	Type	Kind	Pow.	Acc.	PP	Range
TM05	Roar	Normal	Status	—	—	20	Normal
TM06	Toxic	Poison	Status	—	90	10	Normal
TM07	Hail	Ice	Status	—	—	10	Both Sides
TM10	Hidden Power	Normal	Special	60	100	15	Normal
TM13	Ice Beam	Ice	Special	90	100	10	Normal
TM14	Blizzard	Ice	Special	110	70	5	Many Others
TM15	Hyper Beam	Normal	Special	150	90	5	Normal
TM17	Protect	Normal	Status	—	—	10	Self
TM18	Rain Dance	Water	Status	—	—	5	Both Sides
TM21	Frustration	Normal	Physical	—	100	20	Normal
TM26	Earthquake	Ground	Physical	100	100	10	Adjacent
TM27	Return	Normal	Physical	—	100	20	Normal
TM32	Double Team	Normal	Status	—	—	15	Self
TM39	Rock Tomb	Rock	Physical	60	95	15	Normal
TM42	Facade	Normal	Physical	70	100	20	Normal
TM44	Rest	Psychic	Status	—	—	10	Self
TM45	Attract	Normal	Status	—	100	15	Normal
TM48	Round	Normal	Special	60	100	15	Normal
TM49	Echoed Voice	Normal	Special	40	100	15	Normal
TM68	Giga Impact	Normal	Physical	150	90	5	Normal
TM78	Bulldoze	Ground	Physical	60	100	20	Adjacent
TM79	Frost Breath	Ice	Special	60	90	10	Normal
TM80	Rock Slide	Rock	Physical	75	90	10	Many Others
TM87	Swagger	Normal	Status	—	90	15	Normal
TM88	Sleep Talk	Normal	Status	—	—	10	Self
TM90	Substitute	Normal	Status	—	—	10	Self
TM94	Secret Power	Normal	Physical	70	100	20	Normal
TM100	Confide	Normal	Status	—	—	20	Normal
HM03	Surf	Water	Special	90	100	15	Adjacent
HM04	Strength	Normal	Physical	80	100	15	Normal
HM05	Waterfall	Water	Physical	80	100	15	Normal
HM06	Rock Smash	Fighting	Physical	40	100	15	Normal
HM07	Dive	Water	Physical	80	100	10	Normal

MOVES LEARNED IN EXCHANGE FOR BP

Name	Type	Kind	Pow.	Acc.	PP	Range
Super Fang	Normal	Physical	—	90	10	Normal
Signal Beam	Bug	Special	75	100	15	Normal
Iron Head	Steel	Physical	80	100	15	Normal
Block	Normal	Status	—	—	5	Normal
Icy Wind	Ice	Special	55	95	15	Many Others
Aqua Tail	Water	Physical	90	90	10	Normal
Iron Tail	Steel	Physical	100	75	15	Normal
Snore	Normal	Special	50	100	15	Normal
Water Pulse	Water	Special	60	100	20	Normal

MOVES TAUGHT BY PEOPLE

Name	Type	Kind	Pow.	Acc.	PP	Range

National Pokédex **366** Hoenn Pokédex **185**

✓ Clamperl

Bivalve Pokémon

Water

HEIGHT: 1'04" WEIGHT: 115.7 lbs.

Same form for ♂ / ♀

Ω Clamperl's sturdy shell is not only good for protection—it is also used for clamping and catching prey. A fully grown Clamperl's shell will be scored with nicks and scratches all over.

α Clamperl grows while being protected by its rock-hard shell. When its body becomes too large to fit inside the shell, it is sure evidence that this Pokémon is getting close to evolution.

ABILITY
Shell Armor

HIDDEN ABILITY
Rattled

EGG GROUPS
Water 1

STAT GROWTH RATES
HP
Attack
Defense
Sp. Atk
Sp. Def
Speed

ITEMS SOMETIMES HELD BY WILD POKÉMON
Pearl / Big Pearl

EVOLUTION
Clamperl → Link Trade with a Deep Sea Tooth → Huntail
Clamperl → Link Trade with a Deep Sea Scale → Gorebyss

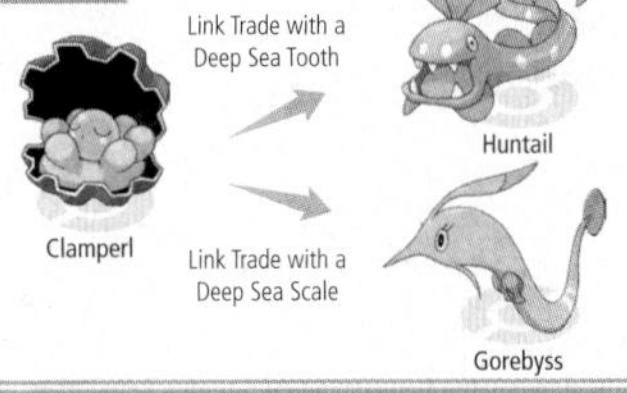

MAIN WAY TO REGISTER IN THE NATIONAL POKÉDEX

Catch at the bottom of the sea beneath Route 124.

Damage taken in normal battles

Type	×	Type	×
Normal	×1	Flying	×1
Fire	×0.5	Psychic	×1
Water	×0.5	Bug	×1
Grass	×2	Rock	×1
Electric	×2	Ghost	×1
Ice	×0.5	Dragon	×1
Fighting	×1	Dark	×1
Poison	×1	Steel	×0.5
Ground	×1	Fairy	×1

Damage taken in Inverse battles

Type	×	Type	×
Normal	×1	Flying	×1
Fire	×2	Psychic	×1
Water	×2	Bug	×1
Grass	×0.5	Rock	×1
Electric	×0.5	Ghost	×1
Ice	×2	Dragon	×1
Fighting	×1	Dark	×1
Poison	×1	Steel	×2
Ground	×1	Fairy	×1

Can be used in
Inverse Battle
Battle Institute
Battle Maison
Random Matchup (Free Battle)
Random Matchup (Others)

LEVEL-UP MOVES

Lv.	Name	Type	Kind	Pow.	Acc.	PP	Range
1	Clamp	Water	Physical	35	85	15	Normal
1	Water Gun	Water	Special	40	100	25	Normal
1	Whirlpool	Water	Special	35	85	15	Normal
1	Iron Defense	Steel	Status	—	—	15	Self
50	Shell Smash	Normal	Status	—	—	15	Self

TM & HM MOVES

No.	Name	Type	Kind	Pow.	Acc.	PP	Range
TM06	Toxic	Poison	Status	—	90	10	Normal
TM07	Hail	Ice	Status	—	—	10	Both Sides
TM10	Hidden Power	Normal	Special	60	100	15	Normal
TM13	Ice Beam	Ice	Special	90	100	10	Normal
TM14	Blizzard	Ice	Special	110	70	5	Many Others
TM17	Protect	Normal	Status	—	—	10	Self
TM18	Rain Dance	Water	Status	—	—	5	Both Sides
TM21	Frustration	Normal	Physical	—	100	20	Normal
TM27	Return	Normal	Physical	—	100	20	Normal
TM32	Double Team	Normal	Status	—	—	15	Self
TM42	Facade	Normal	Physical	70	100	20	Normal
TM44	Rest	Psychic	Status	—	—	10	Self
TM45	Attract	Normal	Status	—	100	15	Normal
TM48	Round	Normal	Special	60	100	15	Normal
TM55	Scald	Water	Special	80	100	15	Normal
TM87	Swagger	Normal	Status	—	90	15	Normal
TM88	Sleep Talk	Normal	Status	—	—	10	Self
TM90	Substitute	Normal	Status	—	—	10	Self
TM94	Secret Power	Normal	Physical	70	100	20	Normal
TM100	Confide	Normal	Status	—	—	20	Normal
HM03	Surf	Water	Special	90	100	15	Adjacent
HM05	Waterfall	Water	Physical	80	100	15	Normal
HM07	Dive	Water	Physical	80	100	10	Normal

MOVES LEARNED IN EXCHANGE FOR BP

Name	Type	Kind	Pow.	Acc.	PP	Range
Iron Defense	Steel	Status	—	—	15	Self
Icy Wind	Ice	Special	55	95	15	Many Others
Snore	Normal	Special	50	100	15	Normal
Water Pulse	Water	Special	60	100	20	Normal

MOVES TAUGHT BY PEOPLE

Name	Type	Kind	Pow.	Acc.	PP	Range

EGG MOVES

Name	Type	Kind	Pow.	Acc.	PP	Range
Refresh	Normal	Status	—	—	20	Self
Mud Sport	Ground	Status	—	—	15	Both Sides
Body Slam	Normal	Physical	85	100	15	Normal
Supersonic	Normal	Status	—	55	20	Normal
Barrier	Psychic	Status	—	—	20	Self
Confuse Ray	Ghost	Status	—	100	10	Normal
Aqua Ring	Water	Status	—	—	20	Self
Muddy Water	Water	Special	90	85	10	Many Others
Water Pulse	Water	Special	60	100	20	Normal
Brine	Water	Special	65	100	10	Normal
Endure	Normal	Status	—	—	10	Self

National Pokédex **367** Hoenn Pokédex **186**

Huntail

Deep Sea Pokémon

Water

HEIGHT: 5'07" WEIGHT: 59.5 lbs.

Same form for ♂ / ♀

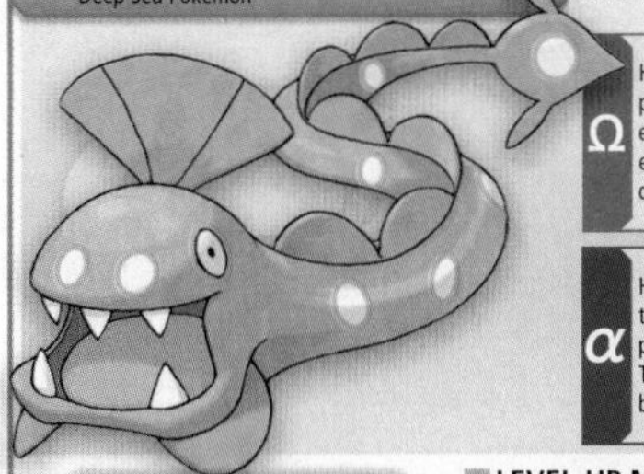

Ω Huntail's presence went unnoticed by people for a long time because it lives at extreme depths in the sea. This Pokémon's eyes can see clearly even in the murky dark depths of the ocean.

α Huntail's tail is shaped like a fish. It uses the tail to attract prey, then swallows the prey whole with its large, gaping mouth. This Pokémon swims by wiggling its slender body like a snake.

ABILITY: Swift Swim

HIDDEN ABILITY: Water Veil

EGG GROUPS: Water 1

STAT GROWTH RATES: HP ■■ / Attack ■■■■■ / Defense ■■■■■ / Sp. Atk ■■■■■ / Sp. Def ■■■ / Speed ■■■

ITEMS SOMETIMES HELD BY WILD POKÉMON: —

EVOLUTION: Clamperl → Link Trade with a Deep Sea Tooth → Huntail

MAIN WAY TO REGISTER IN THE NATIONAL POKÉDEX

Receive a Clamperl that is holding a Deep Sea Tooth via Link Trade to have it evolve.

Damage taken in normal battles

Type		Type	
Normal	×1	Flying	×1
Fire	×0.5	Psychic	×1
Water	×0.5	Bug	×1
Grass	×2	Rock	×1
Electric	×2	Ghost	×1
Ice	×0.5	Dragon	×1
Fighting	×1	Dark	×1
Poison	×1	Steel	×0.5
Ground	×1	Fairy	×1

Damage taken in Inverse battles

Type		Type	
Normal	×1	Flying	×1
Fire	×2	Psychic	×1
Water	×2	Bug	×1
Grass	×0.5	Rock	×1
Electric	×0.5	Ghost	×1
Ice	×2	Dragon	×1
Fighting	×1	Dark	×1
Poison	×1	Steel	×2
Ground	×1	Fairy	×1

Can be used in

Inverse Battle
Battle Institute
Battle Maison
Random Matchup (Free Battle)
Random Matchup (Others)

LEVEL-UP MOVES

Lv.	Name	Type	Kind	Pow.	Acc.	PP	Range
1	Whirlpool	Water	Special	35	85	15	Normal
1	Bite	Dark	Physical	60	100	25	Normal
5	Screech	Normal	Status	—	85	40	Normal
9	Scary Face	Normal	Status	—	100	10	Normal
11	Feint Attack	Dark	Physical	60	—	20	Normal
14	Water Pulse	Water	Special	60	100	20	Normal
16	Ice Fang	Ice	Physical	65	95	15	Normal
19	Brine	Water	Special	65	100	10	Normal
23	Sucker Punch	Dark	Physical	80	100	5	Normal
26	Dive	Water	Physical	80	100	10	Normal
29	Baton Pass	Normal	Status	—	—	40	Self
34	Crunch	Dark	Physical	80	100	15	Normal
39	Aqua Tail	Water	Physical	90	90	10	Normal
45	Coil	Poison	Status	—	—	20	Self
50	Hydro Pump	Water	Special	110	80	5	Normal

TM & HM MOVES

No.	Name	Type	Kind	Pow.	Acc.	PP	Range
TM06	Toxic	Poison	Status	—	90	10	Normal
TM07	Hail	Ice	Status	—	—	10	Both Sides
TM10	Hidden Power	Normal	Special	60	100	15	Normal
TM13	Ice Beam	Ice	Special	90	100	10	Normal
TM14	Blizzard	Ice	Special	110	70	5	Many Others
TM15	Hyper Beam	Normal	Special	150	90	5	Normal
TM17	Protect	Normal	Status	—	—	10	Self
TM18	Rain Dance	Water	Status	—	—	5	Both Sides
TM21	Frustration	Normal	Physical	—	100	20	Normal
TM27	Return	Normal	Physical	—	100	20	Normal
TM32	Double Team	Normal	Status	—	—	15	Self
TM39	Rock Tomb	Rock	Physical	60	95	15	Normal
TM42	Facade	Normal	Physical	70	100	20	Normal
TM44	Rest	Psychic	Status	—	—	10	Self
TM45	Attract	Normal	Status	—	100	15	Normal
TM48	Round	Normal	Special	60	100	15	Normal
TM55	Scald	Water	Special	80	100	15	Normal
TM68	Giga Impact	Normal	Physical	150	90	5	Normal
TM83	Infestation	Bug	Special	20	100	20	Normal
TM87	Swagger	Normal	Status	—	90	15	Normal
TM88	Sleep Talk	Normal	Status	—	—	10	Self
TM90	Substitute	Normal	Status	—	—	10	Self
TM94	Secret Power	Normal	Physical	70	100	20	Normal
TM100	Confide	Normal	Status	—	—	20	Normal
HM03	Surf	Water	Special	90	100	15	Adjacent
HM05	Waterfall	Water	Physical	80	100	15	Normal
HM07	Dive	Water	Physical	80	100	10	Normal

MOVES LEARNED IN EXCHANGE FOR BP

Name	Type	Kind	Pow.	Acc.	PP	Range
Super Fang	Normal	Physical	—	90	10	Normal
Bounce	Flying	Physical	85	85	5	Normal
Icy Wind	Ice	Special	55	95	15	Many Others
Aqua Tail	Water	Physical	90	90	10	Normal
Bind	Normal	Physical	15	85	20	Normal
Snore	Normal	Special	50	100	15	Normal
Water Pulse	Water	Special	60	100	20	Normal
Snatch	Dark	Status	—	—	10	Self

MOVES TAUGHT BY PEOPLE

Name	Type	Kind	Pow.	Acc.	PP	Range

National Pokédex **368** Hoenn Pokédex **187**

Gorebyss

South Sea Pokémon

Water

HEIGHT: 5'11" WEIGHT: 49.8 lbs.

Same form for ♂ / ♀

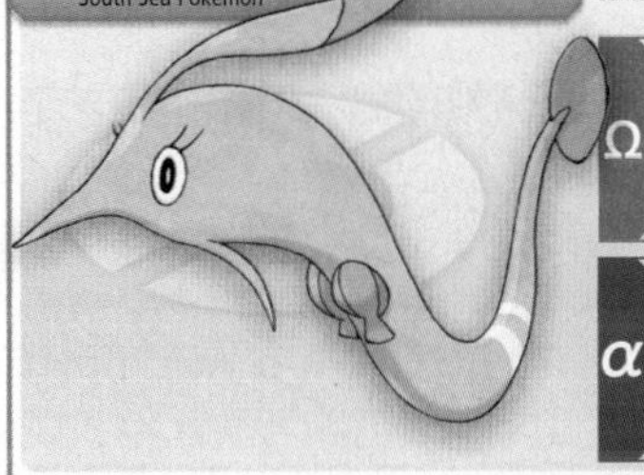

Ω Gorebyss lives in the southern seas at extreme depths. Its body is built to withstand the enormous pressure of water at incredible depths. Because of this, this Pokémon's body is unharmed by ordinary attacks.

α Although Gorebyss is the very picture of elegance and beauty while swimming, it is also cruel. When it spots prey, this Pokémon inserts its thin mouth into the prey's body and drains the prey of its body fluids.

ABILITY: Swift Swim

HIDDEN ABILITY: Hydration

EGG GROUPS: Water 1

STAT GROWTH RATES: HP ■■ / Attack ■■■■ / Defense ■■■■■ / Sp. Atk ■■■■■■ / Sp. Def ■■■ / Speed ■■■

ITEMS SOMETIMES HELD BY WILD POKÉMON: —

EVOLUTION: Clamperl → Link Trade with a Deep Sea Scale → Gorebyss

MAIN WAY TO REGISTER IN THE NATIONAL POKÉDEX

Receive a Clamperl that is holding a Deep Sea Scale via Link Trade to have it evolve.

Damage taken in normal battles

Type		Type	
Normal	×1	Flying	×1
Fire	×0.5	Psychic	×1
Water	×0.5	Bug	×1
Grass	×2	Rock	×1
Electric	×2	Ghost	×1
Ice	×0.5	Dragon	×1
Fighting	×1	Dark	×1
Poison	×1	Steel	×0.5
Ground	×1	Fairy	×1

Damage taken in Inverse battles

Type		Type	
Normal	×1	Flying	×1
Fire	×2	Psychic	×1
Water	×2	Bug	×1
Grass	×0.5	Rock	×1
Electric	×0.5	Ghost	×1
Ice	×2	Dragon	×1
Fighting	×1	Dark	×1
Poison	×1	Steel	×2
Ground	×1	Fairy	×1

Can be used in

Inverse Battle
Battle Institute
Battle Maison
Random Matchup (Free Battle)
Random Matchup (Others)

LEVEL-UP MOVES

Lv.	Name	Type	Kind	Pow.	Acc.	PP	Range
1	Whirlpool	Water	Special	35	85	15	Normal
1	Confusion	Psychic	Special	50	100	25	Normal
5	Water Sport	Water	Status	—	—	15	Both Sides
9	Agility	Psychic	Status	—	—	30	Self
11	Draining Kiss	Fairy	Special	50	100	10	Normal
14	Water Pulse	Water	Special	60	100	20	Normal
16	Amnesia	Psychic	Status	—	—	20	Self
19	Aqua Ring	Water	Status	—	—	20	Self
23	Captivate	Normal	Status	—	100	20	Many Others
26	Dive	Water	Physical	80	100	10	Normal
29	Baton Pass	Normal	Status	—	—	40	Self
34	Psychic	Psychic	Special	90	100	10	Normal
39	Aqua Tail	Water	Physical	90	90	10	Normal
45	Coil	Poison	Status	—	—	20	Self
50	Hydro Pump	Water	Special	110	80	5	Normal

TM & HM MOVES

No.	Name	Type	Kind	Pow.	Acc.	PP	Range
TM06	Toxic	Poison	Status	—	90	10	Normal
TM07	Hail	Ice	Status	—	—	10	Both Sides
TM10	Hidden Power	Normal	Special	60	100	15	Normal
TM13	Ice Beam	Ice	Special	90	100	10	Normal
TM14	Blizzard	Ice	Special	110	70	5	Many Others
TM15	Hyper Beam	Normal	Special	150	90	5	Normal
TM17	Protect	Normal	Status	—	—	10	Self
TM18	Rain Dance	Water	Status	—	—	5	Both Sides
TM20	Safeguard	Normal	Status	—	—	25	Your Side
TM21	Frustration	Normal	Physical	—	100	20	Normal
TM27	Return	Normal	Physical	—	100	20	Normal
TM29	Psychic	Psychic	Special	90	100	10	Normal
TM30	Shadow Ball	Ghost	Special	80	100	15	Normal
TM32	Double Team	Normal	Status	—	—	15	Self
TM42	Facade	Normal	Physical	70	100	20	Normal
TM44	Rest	Psychic	Status	—	—	10	Self
TM45	Attract	Normal	Status	—	100	15	Normal
TM48	Round	Normal	Special	60	100	15	Normal
TM55	Scald	Water	Special	80	100	15	Normal
TM68	Giga Impact	Normal	Physical	150	90	5	Normal
TM77	Psych Up	Normal	Status	—	—	10	Normal
TM83	Infestation	Bug	Special	20	100	20	Normal
TM87	Swagger	Normal	Status	—	90	15	Normal
TM88	Sleep Talk	Normal	Status	—	—	10	Self
TM90	Substitute	Normal	Status	—	—	10	Self
TM94	Secret Power	Normal	Physical	70	100	20	Normal
TM100	Confide	Normal	Status	—	—	20	Normal
HM03	Surf	Water	Special	90	100	15	Adjacent
HM05	Waterfall	Water	Physical	80	100	15	Normal
HM07	Dive	Water	Physical	80	100	10	Normal

MOVES LEARNED IN EXCHANGE FOR BP

Name	Type	Kind	Pow.	Acc.	PP	Range
Signal Beam	Bug	Special	75	100	15	Normal
Bounce	Flying	Physical	85	85	5	Normal
Icy Wind	Ice	Special	55	95	15	Many Others
Aqua Tail	Water	Physical	90	90	10	Normal
Bind	Normal	Physical	15	85	20	Normal
Snore	Normal	Special	50	100	15	Normal
Water Pulse	Water	Special	60	100	20	Normal

MOVES TAUGHT BY PEOPLE

Name	Type	Kind	Pow.	Acc.	PP	Range

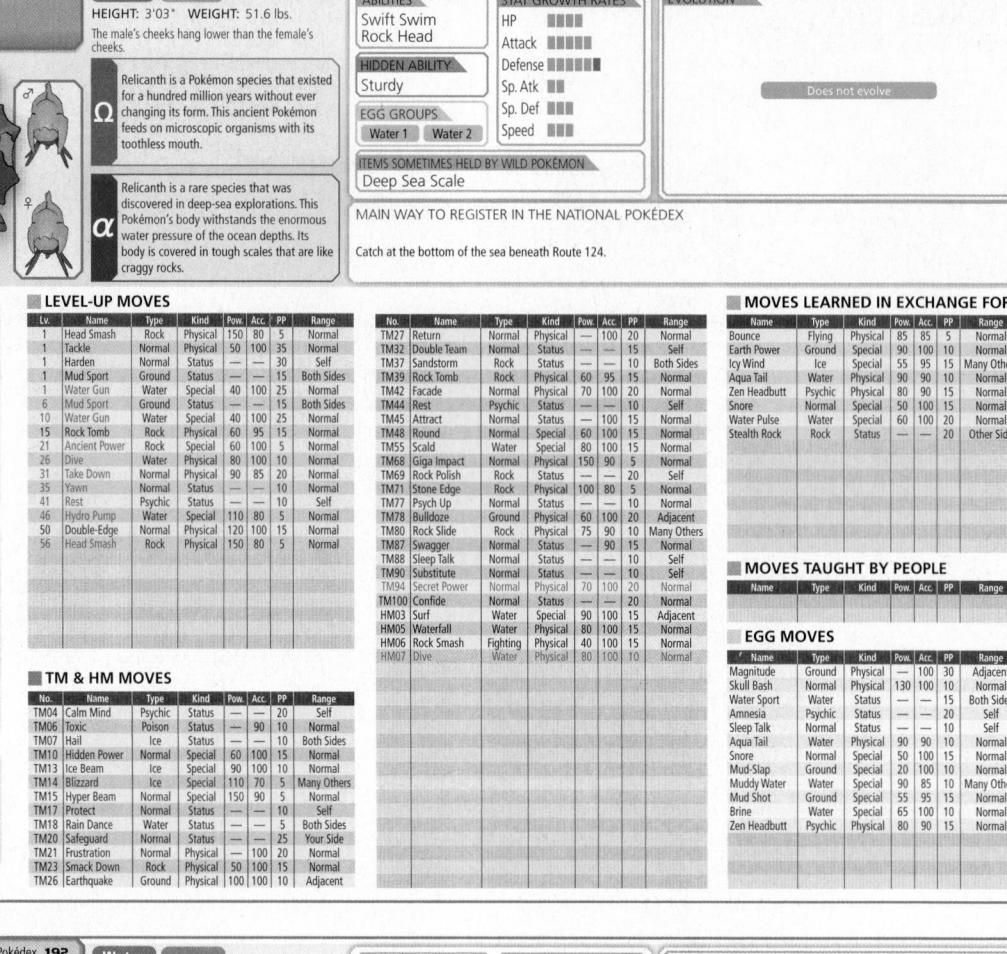

National Pokédex **369** Hoenn Pokédex **188**

Relicanth

Longevity Pokémon

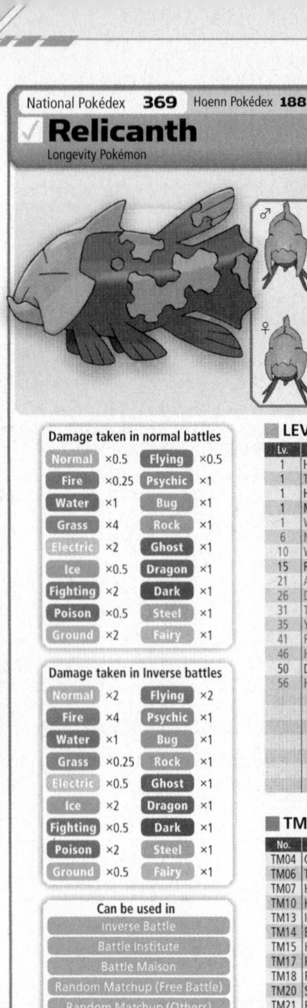

Water | Rock

HEIGHT: 3'03" WEIGHT: 51.6 lbs.

The male's cheeks hang lower than the female's cheeks.

Ω Relicanth is a Pokémon species that existed for a hundred million years without ever changing its form. This ancient Pokémon feeds on microscopic organisms with its toothless mouth.

α Relicanth is a rare species that was discovered in deep-sea explorations. This Pokémon's body withstands the enormous water pressure of the ocean depths. Its body is covered in tough scales that are like craggy rocks.

ABILITIES
Swift Swim
Rock Head

HIDDEN ABILITY
Sturdy

EGG GROUPS
Water 1 | Water 2

STAT GROWTH RATES
HP ■■■■
Attack ■■■■■
Defense ■■■■■■
Sp. Atk ■■
Sp. Def ■■■
Speed ■■■

ITEMS SOMETIMES HELD BY WILD POKÉMON
Deep Sea Scale

EVOLUTION
Does not evolve

MAIN WAY TO REGISTER IN THE NATIONAL POKÉDEX
Catch at the bottom of the sea beneath Route 124.

Damage taken in normal battles

Type		Type	
Normal	×0.5	Flying	×0.5
Fire	×0.25	Psychic	×1
Water	×1	Bug	×1
Grass	×4	Rock	×1
Electric	×2	Ghost	×1
Ice	×0.5	Dragon	×1
Fighting	×2	Dark	×1
Poison	×0.5	Steel	×1
Ground	×2	Fairy	×1

Damage taken in Inverse battles

Type		Type	
Normal	×2	Flying	×2
Fire	×4	Psychic	×1
Water	×1	Bug	×1
Grass	×0.25	Rock	×1
Electric	×0.5	Ghost	×1
Ice	×2	Dragon	×1
Fighting	×0.5	Dark	×1
Poison	×2	Steel	×1
Ground	×0.5	Fairy	×1

Can be used in
Inverse Battle
Battle Institute
Battle Maison
Random Matchup (Free Battle)
Random Matchup (Others)

LEVEL-UP MOVES

Lv.	Name	Type	Kind	Pow.	Acc.	PP	Range
1	Head Smash	Rock	Physical	150	80	5	Normal
1	Tackle	Normal	Physical	50	100	35	Normal
1	Harden	Normal	Status	—	—	30	Self
1	Mud Sport	Ground	Status	—	—	15	Both Sides
1	Water Gun	Water	Special	40	100	25	Normal
6	Mud Sport	Ground	Status	—	—	15	Both Sides
10	Water Gun	Water	Special	40	100	25	Normal
15	Rock Tomb	Rock	Physical	60	95	15	Normal
21	Ancient Power	Rock	Special	60	100	5	Normal
26	Dive	Water	Physical	80	100	10	Normal
31	Take Down	Normal	Physical	90	85	20	Normal
35	Yawn	Normal	Status	—	—	10	Normal
41	Rest	Psychic	Status	—	—	10	Self
46	Hydro Pump	Water	Special	110	80	5	Normal
50	Double-Edge	Normal	Physical	120	100	15	Normal
56	Head Smash	Rock	Physical	150	80	5	Normal

TM & HM MOVES

No.	Name	Type	Kind	Pow.	Acc.	PP	Range
TM04	Calm Mind	Psychic	Status	—	—	20	Self
TM06	Toxic	Poison	Status	—	90	10	Normal
TM07	Hail	Ice	Status	—	—	10	Both Sides
TM10	Hidden Power	Normal	Special	60	100	15	Normal
TM13	Ice Beam	Ice	Special	90	100	10	Normal
TM14	Blizzard	Ice	Special	110	70	5	Many Others
TM15	Hyper Beam	Normal	Special	150	90	5	Normal
TM17	Protect	Normal	Status	—	—	10	Self
TM18	Rain Dance	Water	Status	—	—	5	Both Sides
TM20	Safeguard	Normal	Status	—	—	25	Your Side
TM21	Frustration	Normal	Physical	—	100	20	Normal
TM23	Smack Down	Rock	Physical	50	100	15	Normal
TM26	Earthquake	Ground	Physical	100	100	10	Adjacent
TM27	Return	Normal	Physical	—	100	20	Normal
TM32	Double Team	Normal	Status	—	—	15	Self
TM37	Sandstorm	Rock	Status	—	—	10	Both Sides
TM39	Rock Tomb	Rock	Physical	60	95	15	Normal
TM42	Facade	Normal	Physical	70	100	20	Normal
TM44	Rest	Psychic	Status	—	—	10	Self
TM45	Attract	Normal	Status	—	100	15	Normal
TM48	Round	Normal	Special	60	100	15	Normal
TM55	Scald	Water	Special	80	100	15	Normal
TM68	Giga Impact	Normal	Physical	150	90	5	Normal
TM69	Rock Polish	Rock	Status	—	—	20	Self
TM71	Stone Edge	Rock	Physical	100	80	5	Normal
TM77	Psych Up	Normal	Status	—	—	10	Normal
TM78	Bulldoze	Ground	Physical	60	100	20	Adjacent
TM80	Rock Slide	Rock	Physical	75	90	10	Many Others
TM87	Swagger	Normal	Status	—	90	15	Normal
TM88	Sleep Talk	Normal	Status	—	—	10	Self
TM90	Substitute	Normal	Status	—	—	10	Self
TM94	Secret Power	Normal	Physical	70	100	20	Normal
TM100	Confide	Normal	Status	—	—	20	Normal
HM03	Surf	Water	Special	90	100	15	Adjacent
HM05	Waterfall	Water	Physical	80	100	15	Normal
HM06	Rock Smash	Fighting	Physical	40	100	15	Normal
HM07	Dive	Water	Physical	80	100	10	Normal

MOVES LEARNED IN EXCHANGE FOR BP

Name	Type	Kind	Pow.	Acc.	PP	Range
Bounce	Flying	Physical	85	85	5	Normal
Earth Power	Ground	Special	90	100	10	Normal
Icy Wind	Ice	Special	55	95	15	Many Others
Aqua Tail	Water	Physical	90	90	10	Normal
Zen Headbutt	Psychic	Physical	80	90	15	Normal
Snore	Normal	Special	50	100	15	Normal
Water Pulse	Water	Special	60	100	20	Normal
Stealth Rock	Rock	Status	—	—	20	Other Side

MOVES TAUGHT BY PEOPLE

Name	Type	Kind	Pow.	Acc.	PP	Range

EGG MOVES

Name	Type	Kind	Pow.	Acc.	PP	Range
Magnitude	Ground	Physical	—	100	30	Adjacent
Skull Bash	Normal	Physical	130	100	10	Normal
Water Sport	Water	Status	—	—	15	Both Sides
Amnesia	Psychic	Status	—	—	20	Self
Sleep Talk	Normal	Status	—	—	10	Self
Aqua Tail	Water	Physical	90	90	10	Normal
Snore	Normal	Special	50	100	15	Normal
Mud-Slap	Ground	Special	20	100	10	Normal
Muddy Water	Water	Special	90	85	10	Many Others
Mud Shot	Ground	Special	55	95	15	Normal
Brine	Water	Special	65	100	10	Normal
Zen Headbutt	Psychic	Physical	80	90	15	Normal

National Pokédex **370** Hoenn Pokédex **192**

Luvdisc

Rendezvous Pokémon

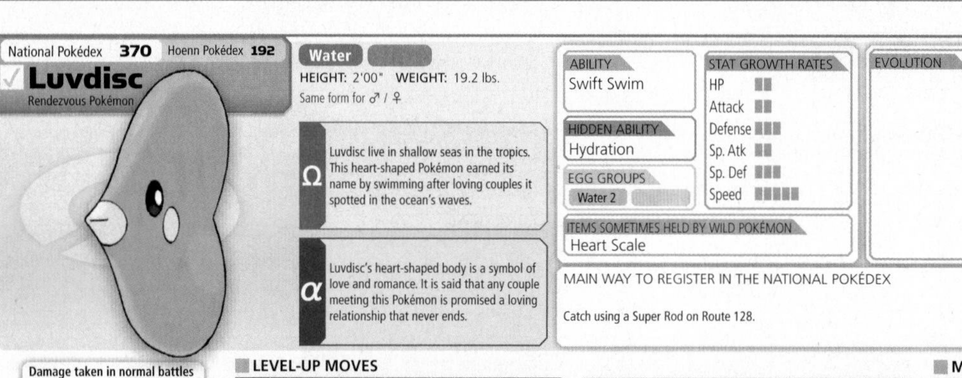

Water

HEIGHT: 2'00" WEIGHT: 19.2 lbs.

Same form for ♂ / ♀

Ω Luvdisc live in shallow seas in the tropics. This heart-shaped Pokémon earned its name by swimming after loving couples it spotted in the ocean's waves.

α Luvdisc's heart-shaped body is a symbol of love and romance. It is said that any couple meeting this Pokémon is promised a loving relationship that never ends.

ABILITY
Swift Swim

HIDDEN ABILITY
Hydration

EGG GROUPS
Water 2

STAT GROWTH RATES
HP ■■
Attack ■■
Defense ■■■
Sp. Atk ■■
Sp. Def ■■■
Speed ■■■■■

ITEMS SOMETIMES HELD BY WILD POKÉMON
Heart Scale

EVOLUTION
Does not evolve

MAIN WAY TO REGISTER IN THE NATIONAL POKÉDEX
Catch using a Super Rod on Route 128.

Damage taken in normal battles

Type		Type	
Normal	×1	Flying	×1
Fire	×0.5	Psychic	×1
Water	×0.5	Bug	×1
Grass	×2	Rock	×1
Electric	×2	Ghost	×1
Ice	×0.5	Dragon	×1
Fighting	×1	Dark	×1
Poison	×1	Steel	×0.5
Ground	×1	Fairy	×1

Damage taken in Inverse battles

Type		Type	
Normal	×1	Flying	×1
Fire	×2	Psychic	×1
Water	×2	Bug	×1
Grass	×0.5	Rock	×1
Electric	×0.5	Ghost	×1
Ice	×2	Dragon	×1
Fighting	×1	Dark	×1
Poison	×1	Steel	×2
Ground	×1	Fairy	×1

Can be used in
Inverse Battle
Battle Institute
Battle Maison
Random Matchup (Free Battle)
Random Matchup (Others)

LEVEL-UP MOVES

Lv.	Name	Type	Kind	Pow.	Acc.	PP	Range
1	Tackle	Normal	Physical	50	100	35	Normal
1	Charm	Fairy	Status	—	100	20	Normal
4	Water Gun	Water	Special	40	100	25	Normal
7	Agility	Psychic	Status	—	—	30	Self
9	Draining Kiss	Fairy	Special	50	100	10	Normal
14	Lucky Chant	Normal	Status	—	—	30	Your Side
17	Water Pulse	Water	Special	60	100	20	Normal
22	Attract	Normal	Status	—	100	15	Normal
27	Flail	Normal	Physical	—	100	15	Normal
31	Sweet Kiss	Fairy	Status	—	75	10	Normal
37	Take Down	Normal	Physical	90	85	20	Normal
40	Aqua Ring	Water	Status	—	—	20	Self
46	Captivate	Normal	Status	—	100	20	Many Others
50	Hydro Pump	Water	Special	110	80	5	Normal
55	Safeguard	Normal	Status	—	—	25	Your Side

TM & HM MOVES

No.	Name	Type	Kind	Pow.	Acc.	PP	Range
TM06	Toxic	Poison	Status	—	90	10	Normal
TM07	Hail	Ice	Status	—	—	10	Both Sides
TM10	Hidden Power	Normal	Special	60	100	15	Normal
TM13	Ice Beam	Ice	Special	90	100	10	Normal
TM14	Blizzard	Ice	Special	110	70	5	Many Others
TM17	Protect	Normal	Status	—	—	10	Self
TM18	Rain Dance	Water	Status	—	—	5	Both Sides
TM20	Safeguard	Normal	Status	—	—	25	Your Side
TM21	Frustration	Normal	Physical	—	100	20	Normal
TM27	Return	Normal	Physical	—	100	20	Normal
TM32	Double Team	Normal	Status	—	—	15	Self
TM42	Facade	Normal	Physical	70	100	20	Normal
TM44	Rest	Psychic	Status	—	—	10	Self
TM45	Attract	Normal	Status	—	100	15	Normal
TM48	Round	Normal	Special	60	100	15	Normal
TM55	Scald	Water	Special	80	100	15	Normal
TM77	Psych Up	Normal	Status	—	—	10	Normal
TM87	Swagger	Normal	Status	—	90	15	Normal
TM88	Sleep Talk	Normal	Status	—	—	10	Self
TM90	Substitute	Normal	Status	—	—	10	Self
TM94	Secret Power	Normal	Physical	70	100	20	Normal
TM100	Confide	Normal	Status	—	—	20	Normal
HM03	Surf	Water	Special	90	100	15	Adjacent
HM05	Waterfall	Water	Physical	80	100	15	Normal
HM07	Dive	Water	Physical	80	100	10	Normal

MOVES LEARNED IN EXCHANGE FOR BP

Name	Type	Kind	Pow.	Acc.	PP	Range
Bounce	Flying	Physical	85	85	5	Normal
Icy Wind	Ice	Special	55	95	15	Many Others
Snore	Normal	Special	50	100	15	Normal
Water Pulse	Water	Special	60	100	20	Normal

MOVES TAUGHT BY PEOPLE

Name	Type	Kind	Pow.	Acc.	PP	Range

EGG MOVES

Name	Type	Kind	Pow.	Acc.	PP	Range
Splash	Normal	Status	—	—	40	Self
Supersonic	Normal	Status	—	55	20	Normal
Water Sport	Water	Status	—	—	15	Both Sides
Mud Sport	Ground	Status	—	—	15	Both Sides
Captivate	Normal	Status	—	100	20	Many Others
Aqua Ring	Water	Status	—	—	20	Self
Aqua Jet	Water	Physical	40	100	20	Normal
Heal Pulse	Psychic	Status	—	—	10	Normal
Brine	Water	Special	65	100	10	Normal
Entrainment	Normal	Status	—	100	15	Normal

National Pokédex **371** Hoenn Pokédex **196**

Bagon

Rock Head Pokémon

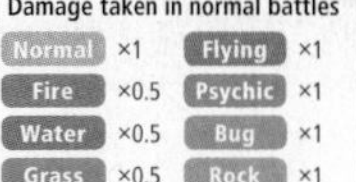

Dragon

HEIGHT: 2'00" WEIGHT: 92.8 lbs.

Same form for ♂ / ♀

Ω Bagon has a dream of one day soaring in the sky. In doomed efforts to fly, this Pokémon hurls itself off cliffs. As a result of its dives, its head has grown tough and as hard as tempered steel.

α Bagon harbors a never-ending dream of one day soaring high among the clouds. As if trying to dispel its frustration over its inability to fly, this Pokémon slams its hard head against huge rocks and shatters them into pebbles.

ABILITY: Rock Head

HIDDEN ABILITY: Sheer Force

EGG GROUPS: Dragon

STAT GROWTH RATES: HP ■■ / Attack ■■■■ / Defense ■■■ / Sp. Atk ■■ / Sp. Def ■ / Speed ■■■

ITEMS SOMETIMES HELD BY WILD POKÉMON: Dragon Fang

EVOLUTION: Bagon → Lv. 30 → Shelgon → Lv. 50 → Salamence

MAIN WAY TO REGISTER IN THE NATIONAL POKÉDEX

Catch at Meteor Falls (B1F Lower chamber).

Damage taken in normal battles

Type		Type	
Normal	×1	Flying	×1
Fire	×0.5	Psychic	×1
Water	×0.5	Bug	×1
Grass	×0.5	Rock	×1
Electric	×0.5	Ghost	×1
Ice	×2	Dragon	×2
Fighting	×1	Dark	×1
Poison	×1	Steel	×1
Ground	×1	Fairy	×2

Damage taken in Inverse battles

Type		Type	
Normal	×1	Flying	×1
Fire	×2	Psychic	×1
Water	×2	Bug	×1
Grass	×2	Rock	×1
Electric	×2	Ghost	×1
Ice	×0.5	Dragon	×0.5
Fighting	×1	Dark	×1
Poison	×1	Steel	×1
Ground	×1	Fairy	×0.5

Can be used in

- Inverse Battle
- Battle Institute
- Battle Maison
- Random Matchup (Free Battle)
- Random Matchup (Others)

LEVEL-UP MOVES

Lv.	Name	Type	Kind	Pow.	Acc.	PP	Range
1	Rage	Normal	Physical	20	100	20	Normal
4	Ember	Fire	Special	40	100	25	Normal
7	Leer	Normal	Status	—	100	30	Many Others
10	Bite	Dark	Physical	60	100	25	Normal
13	Dragon Breath	Dragon	Special	60	100	20	Normal
17	Headbutt	Normal	Physical	70	100	15	Normal
21	Focus Energy	Normal	Status	—	—	30	Self
25	Crunch	Dark	Physical	80	100	15	Normal
29	Dragon Claw	Dragon	Physical	80	100	15	Normal
34	Zen Headbutt	Psychic	Physical	80	90	15	Normal
39	Scary Face	Normal	Status	—	100	10	Normal
44	Flamethrower	Fire	Special	90	100	15	Normal
49	Double-Edge	Normal	Physical	120	100	15	Normal

TM & HM MOVES

No.	Name	Type	Kind	Pow.	Acc.	PP	Range
TM01	Hone Claws	Dark	Status	—	—	15	Self
TM02	Dragon Claw	Dragon	Physical	80	100	15	Normal
TM05	Roar	Normal	Status	—	—	20	Normal
TM06	Toxic	Poison	Status	—	90	10	Normal
TM10	Hidden Power	Normal	Special	60	100	15	Normal
TM11	Sunny Day	Fire	Status	—	—	5	Both Sides
TM17	Protect	Normal	Status	—	—	10	Self
TM18	Rain Dance	Water	Status	—	—	5	Both Sides
TM21	Frustration	Normal	Physical	—	100	20	Normal
TM27	Return	Normal	Physical	—	100	20	Normal
TM31	Brick Break	Fighting	Physical	75	100	15	Normal
TM32	Double Team	Normal	Status	—	—	15	Self
TM35	Flamethrower	Fire	Special	90	100	15	Normal
TM38	Fire Blast	Fire	Special	110	85	5	Normal
TM39	Rock Tomb	Rock	Physical	60	95	15	Normal
TM40	Aerial Ace	Flying	Physical	60	—	20	Normal
TM42	Facade	Normal	Physical	70	100	20	Normal
TM44	Rest	Psychic	Status	—	—	10	Self
TM45	Attract	Normal	Status	—	100	15	Normal
TM48	Round	Normal	Special	60	100	15	Normal
TM59	Incinerate	Fire	Special	60	100	15	Many Others
TM65	Shadow Claw	Ghost	Physical	70	100	15	Normal
TM80	Rock Slide	Rock	Physical	75	90	10	Many Others
TM87	Swagger	Normal	Status	—	90	15	Normal
TM88	Sleep Talk	Normal	Status	—	—	10	Self
TM90	Substitute	Normal	Status	—	—	10	Self
TM94	Secret Power	Normal	Physical	70	100	20	Normal
TM100	Confide	Normal	Status	—	—	20	Normal
HM01	Cut	Normal	Physical	50	95	30	Normal
HM04	Strength	Normal	Physical	80	100	15	Normal
HM06	Rock Smash	Fighting	Physical	40	100	15	Normal

MOVES LEARNED IN EXCHANGE FOR BP

Name	Type	Kind	Pow.	Acc.	PP	Range
Zen Headbutt	Psychic	Physical	80	90	15	Normal
Dragon Pulse	Dragon	Special	85	100	10	Normal
Hyper Voice	Normal	Special	90	100	10	Many Others
Snore	Normal	Special	50	100	15	Normal
Outrage	Dragon	Physical	120	100	10	1 Random

MOVES TAUGHT BY PEOPLE

Name	Type	Kind	Pow.	Acc.	PP	Range
Draco Meteor	Dragon	Special	130	90	5	Normal

EGG MOVES

Name	Type	Kind	Pow.	Acc.	PP	Range
Hydro Pump	Water	Special	110	80	5	Normal
Thrash	Normal	Physical	120	100	10	1 Random
Dragon Rage	Dragon	Special	—	100	10	Normal
Twister	Dragon	Special	40	100	20	Many Others
Dragon Dance	Dragon	Status	—	—	20	Self
Fire Fang	Fire	Physical	65	95	15	Normal
Dragon Rush	Dragon	Physical	100	75	10	Normal
Dragon Pulse	Dragon	Special	85	100	10	Normal
Endure	Normal	Status	—	—	10	Self
Defense Curl	Normal	Status	—	—	40	Self

National Pokédex **372** Hoenn Pokédex **197**

Shelgon

Endurance Pokémon

Dragon

HEIGHT: 3'07" WEIGHT: 243.6 lbs.

Same form for ♂ / ♀

Ω Inside Shelgon's armor-like shell, cells are in the midst of transformation to create an entirely new body. This Pokémon's shell is extremely heavy, making its movements sluggish.

α Covering Shelgon's body are outgrowths much like bones. The shell is very hard and bounces off enemy attacks. When awaiting evolution, this Pokémon hides away in a cavern.

ABILITY: Rock Head

HIDDEN ABILITY: Overcoat

EGG GROUPS: Dragon

STAT GROWTH RATES: HP ■■■ / Attack ■■■■■ / Defense ■■■■ / Sp. Atk ■■■ / Sp. Def ■■ / Speed ■■■

ITEMS SOMETIMES HELD BY WILD POKÉMON: —

EVOLUTION: Bagon → Lv. 30 → Shelgon → Lv. 50 → Salamence

MAIN WAY TO REGISTER IN THE NATIONAL POKÉDEX

Level up Bagon to Lv. 30.

Damage taken in normal battles

Type		Type	
Normal	×1	Flying	×1
Fire	×0.5	Psychic	×1
Water	×0.5	Bug	×1
Grass	×0.5	Rock	×1
Electric	×0.5	Ghost	×1
Ice	×2	Dragon	×2
Fighting	×1	Dark	×1
Poison	×1	Steel	×1
Ground	×1	Fairy	×2

Damage taken in Inverse battles

Type		Type	
Normal	×1	Flying	×1
Fire	×2	Psychic	×1
Water	×2	Bug	×1
Grass	×2	Rock	×1
Electric	×2	Ghost	×1
Ice	×0.5	Dragon	×0.5
Fighting	×1	Dark	×1
Poison	×1	Steel	×1
Ground	×1	Fairy	×0.5

Can be used in

- Inverse Battle
- Battle Institute
- Battle Maison
- Random Matchup (Free Battle)
- Random Matchup (Others)

LEVEL-UP MOVES

Lv.	Name	Type	Kind	Pow.	Acc.	PP	Range
1	Rage	Normal	Physical	20	100	20	Normal
1	Ember	Fire	Special	40	100	25	Normal
1	Leer	Normal	Status	—	100	30	Many Others
1	Bite	Dark	Physical	60	100	25	Normal
4	Ember	Fire	Special	40	100	25	Normal
7	Leer	Normal	Status	—	100	30	Many Others
10	Bite	Dark	Physical	60	100	25	Normal
13	Dragon Breath	Dragon	Special	60	100	20	Normal
17	Headbutt	Normal	Physical	70	100	15	Normal
21	Focus Energy	Normal	Status	—	—	30	Self
25	Crunch	Dark	Physical	80	100	15	Normal
29	Dragon Claw	Dragon	Physical	80	100	15	Normal
30	Protect	Normal	Status	—	—	10	Self
35	Zen Headbutt	Psychic	Physical	80	90	15	Normal
42	Scary Face	Normal	Status	—	100	10	Normal
49	Flamethrower	Fire	Special	90	100	15	Normal
56	Double-Edge	Normal	Physical	120	100	15	Normal

TM & HM MOVES

No.	Name	Type	Kind	Pow.	Acc.	PP	Range
TM01	Hone Claws	Dark	Status	—	—	15	Self
TM02	Dragon Claw	Dragon	Physical	80	100	15	Normal
TM05	Roar	Normal	Status	—	—	20	Normal
TM06	Toxic	Poison	Status	—	90	10	Normal
TM10	Hidden Power	Normal	Special	60	100	15	Normal
TM11	Sunny Day	Fire	Status	—	—	5	Both Sides
TM17	Protect	Normal	Status	—	—	10	Self
TM18	Rain Dance	Water	Status	—	—	5	Both Sides
TM21	Frustration	Normal	Physical	—	100	20	Normal
TM27	Return	Normal	Physical	—	100	20	Normal
TM31	Brick Break	Fighting	Physical	75	100	15	Normal
TM32	Double Team	Normal	Status	—	—	15	Self
TM35	Flamethrower	Fire	Special	90	100	15	Normal
TM38	Fire Blast	Fire	Special	110	85	5	Normal
TM39	Rock Tomb	Rock	Physical	60	95	15	Normal
TM40	Aerial Ace	Flying	Physical	60	—	20	Normal
TM42	Facade	Normal	Physical	70	100	20	Normal
TM44	Rest	Psychic	Status	—	—	10	Self
TM45	Attract	Normal	Status	—	100	15	Normal
TM48	Round	Normal	Special	60	100	15	Normal
TM59	Incinerate	Fire	Special	60	100	15	Many Others
TM65	Shadow Claw	Ghost	Physical	70	100	15	Normal
TM80	Rock Slide	Rock	Physical	75	90	10	Many Others
TM87	Swagger	Normal	Status	—	90	15	Normal
TM88	Sleep Talk	Normal	Status	—	—	10	Self
TM90	Substitute	Normal	Status	—	—	10	Self
TM94	Secret Power	Normal	Physical	70	100	20	Normal
TM100	Confide	Normal	Status	—	—	20	Normal
HM01	Cut	Normal	Physical	50	95	30	Normal
HM04	Strength	Normal	Physical	80	100	15	Normal
HM06	Rock Smash	Fighting	Physical	40	100	15	Normal

MOVES LEARNED IN EXCHANGE FOR BP

Name	Type	Kind	Pow.	Acc.	PP	Range
Iron Defense	Steel	Status	—	—	15	Self
Zen Headbutt	Psychic	Physical	80	90	15	Normal
Dragon Pulse	Dragon	Special	85	100	10	Normal
Hyper Voice	Normal	Special	90	100	10	Many Others
Snore	Normal	Special	50	100	15	Normal
Outrage	Dragon	Physical	120	100	10	1 Random

MOVES TAUGHT BY PEOPLE

Name	Type	Kind	Pow.	Acc.	PP	Range
Draco Meteor	Dragon	Special	130	90	5	Normal

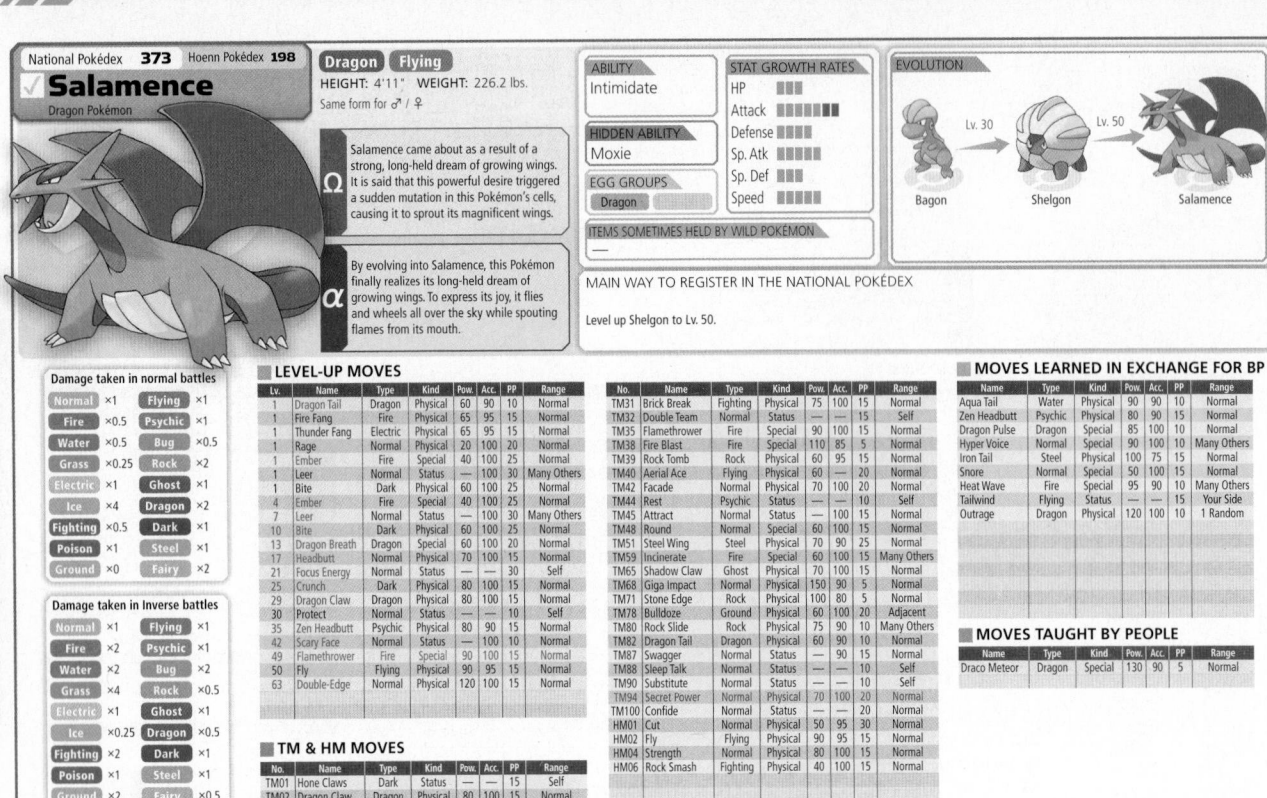

National Pokédex **373** Hoenn Pokédex **198**

✓ Salamence

Dragon Pokémon

Dragon **Flying**

HEIGHT: 4'11" WEIGHT: 226.2 lbs.

Same form for ♂ / ♀

Ω Salamence came about as a result of a strong, long-held dream of growing wings. It is said that this powerful desire triggered a sudden mutation in this Pokémon's cells, causing it to sprout its magnificent wings.

α By evolving into Salamence, this Pokémon finally realizes its long-held dream of growing wings. To express its joy, it flies and wheels all over the sky while spouting flames from its mouth.

ABILITY
Intimidate

HIDDEN ABILITY
Moxie

EGG GROUPS
Dragon

STAT GROWTH RATES
HP ▮▮▮
Attack ▮▮▮▮▮▮▮
Defense ▮▮▮▮
Sp. Atk ▮▮▮▮▮
Sp. Def ▮▮▮
Speed ▮▮▮▮▮

EVOLUTION
Bagon → Lv. 30 → Shelgon → Lv. 50 → Salamence

ITEMS SOMETIMES HELD BY WILD POKÉMON
—

MAIN WAY TO REGISTER IN THE NATIONAL POKÉDEX

Level up Shelgon to Lv. 50.

Damage taken in normal battles

Type		Type	
Normal	×1	Flying	×1
Fire	×0.5	Psychic	×1
Water	×0.5	Bug	×0.5
Grass	×0.25	Rock	×2
Electric	×1	Ghost	×1
Ice	×4	Dragon	×2
Fighting	×0.5	Dark	×1
Poison	×1	Steel	×1
Ground	×0	Fairy	×2

Damage taken in Inverse battles

Type		Type	
Normal	×1	Flying	×1
Fire	×2	Psychic	×1
Water	×2	Bug	×2
Grass	×4	Rock	×0.5
Electric	×1	Ghost	×1
Ice	×0.25	Dragon	×0.5
Fighting	×2	Dark	×1
Poison	×1	Steel	×1
Ground	×2	Fairy	×0.5

Can be used in
Inverse Battle
Battle Institute
Battle Maison
Random Matchup (Free Battle)
Random Matchup (Others)

LEVEL-UP MOVES

Lv.	Name	Type	Kind	Pow.	Acc.	PP	Range
1	Dragon Tail	Dragon	Physical	60	90	10	Normal
1	Fire Fang	Fire	Physical	65	95	15	Normal
1	Thunder Fang	Electric	Physical	65	95	15	Normal
1	Rage	Normal	Physical	20	100	20	Normal
1	Ember	Fire	Special	40	100	25	Normal
1	Leer	Normal	Status	—	100	30	Many Others
1	Bite	Dark	Physical	60	100	25	Normal
4	Ember	Fire	Special	40	100	25	Normal
7	Leer	Normal	Status	—	100	30	Many Others
10	Bite	Dark	Physical	60	100	25	Normal
13	Dragon Breath	Dragon	Special	60	100	20	Normal
17	Headbutt	Normal	Physical	70	100	15	Normal
21	Focus Energy	Normal	Status	—	—	30	Self
25	Crunch	Dark	Physical	80	100	15	Normal
29	Dragon Claw	Dragon	Physical	80	100	15	Normal
30	Protect	Normal	Status	—	—	10	Self
35	Zen Headbutt	Psychic	Physical	80	90	15	Normal
42	Scary Face	Normal	Status	—	100	10	Normal
49	Flamethrower	Fire	Special	90	100	15	Normal
50	Fly	Flying	Physical	90	95	15	Normal
63	Double-Edge	Normal	Physical	120	100	15	Normal

TM & HM MOVES

No.	Name	Type	Kind	Pow.	Acc.	PP	Range
TM01	Hone Claws	Dark	Status	—	—	15	Self
TM02	Dragon Claw	Dragon	Physical	80	100	15	Normal
TM05	Roar	Normal	Status	—	—	20	Normal
TM06	Toxic	Poison	Status	—	90	10	Normal
TM10	Hidden Power	Normal	Special	60	100	15	Normal
TM11	Sunny Day	Fire	Status	—	—	5	Both Sides
TM15	Hyper Beam	Normal	Special	150	90	5	Normal
TM17	Protect	Normal	Status	—	—	10	Self
TM18	Rain Dance	Water	Status	—	—	5	Both Sides
TM19	Roost	Flying	Status	—	—	10	Self
TM21	Frustration	Normal	Physical	—	100	20	Normal
TM26	Earthquake	Ground	Physical	100	100	10	Adjacent
TM27	Return	Normal	Physical	—	100	20	Normal
TM31	Brick Break	Fighting	Physical	75	100	15	Normal
TM32	Double Team	Normal	Status	—	—	15	Self
TM35	Flamethrower	Fire	Special	90	100	15	Normal
TM38	Fire Blast	Fire	Special	110	85	5	Normal
TM39	Rock Tomb	Rock	Physical	60	95	15	Normal
TM40	Aerial Ace	Flying	Physical	60	—	20	Normal
TM42	Facade	Normal	Physical	70	100	20	Normal
TM44	Rest	Psychic	Status	—	—	10	Self
TM45	Attract	Normal	Status	—	100	15	Normal
TM48	Round	Normal	Special	60	100	15	Normal
TM51	Steel Wing	Steel	Physical	70	90	25	Normal
TM59	Incinerate	Fire	Special	60	100	15	Many Others
TM65	Shadow Claw	Ghost	Physical	70	100	15	Normal
TM68	Giga Impact	Normal	Physical	150	90	5	Normal
TM71	Stone Edge	Rock	Physical	100	80	5	Normal
TM78	Bulldoze	Ground	Physical	60	100	20	Adjacent
TM80	Rock Slide	Rock	Physical	75	90	10	Many Others
TM82	Dragon Tail	Dragon	Physical	60	90	10	Normal
TM87	Swagger	Normal	Status	—	90	15	Normal
TM88	Sleep Talk	Normal	Status	—	—	10	Self
TM90	Substitute	Normal	Status	—	—	10	Self
TM94	Secret Power	Normal	Physical	70	100	20	Normal
TM100	Confide	Normal	Status	—	—	20	Normal
HM01	Cut	Normal	Physical	50	95	30	Normal
HM02	Fly	Flying	Physical	90	95	15	Normal
HM04	Strength	Normal	Physical	80	100	15	Normal
HM06	Rock Smash	Fighting	Physical	40	100	15	Normal

MOVES LEARNED IN EXCHANGE FOR BP

Name	Type	Kind	Pow.	Acc.	PP	Range
Aqua Tail	Water	Physical	90	90	10	Normal
Zen Headbutt	Psychic	Physical	80	90	15	Normal
Dragon Pulse	Dragon	Special	85	100	10	Normal
Hyper Voice	Normal	Special	90	100	10	Many Others
Iron Tail	Steel	Physical	100	75	15	Normal
Snore	Normal	Special	50	100	15	Normal
Heat Wave	Fire	Special	95	90	10	Many Others
Tailwind	Flying	Status	—	—	15	Your Side
Outrage	Dragon	Physical	120	100	10	1 Random

MOVES TAUGHT BY PEOPLE

Name	Type	Kind	Pow.	Acc.	PP	Range
Draco Meteor	Dragon	Special	130	90	5	Normal

Mega Evolution

Mega Salamence

Dragon Pokémon

Dragon **Flying**

HEIGHT: 5'11" WEIGHT: 248.2 lbs.

Same form for ♂ / ♀

REQUIRED MEGA STONE
Salamencite
Receive from old Draconid woman at Meteor Falls (after clearing the Delta Episode).

ABILITY
Aerilate

HIDDEN ABILITY
—

EGG GROUPS
—

STAT GROWTH RATES
HP ▮▮▮▮
Attack ▮▮▮▮▮▮▮
Defense ▮▮▮▮▮▮
Sp. Atk ▮▮▮▮▮▮
Sp. Def ▮▮▮▮
Speed ▮▮▮▮▮▮

Damage taken in normal battles

Type		Type	
Normal	×1	Flying	×1
Fire	×0.5	Psychic	×1
Water	×0.5	Bug	×0.5
Grass	×0.25	Rock	×2
Electric	×1	Ghost	×1
Ice	×4	Dragon	×2
Fighting	×0.5	Dark	×1
Poison	×1	Steel	×1
Ground	×0	Fairy	×2

Damage taken in Inverse battles

Type		Type	
Normal	×1	Flying	×1
Fire	×2	Psychic	×1
Water	×2	Bug	×2
Grass	×4	Rock	×0.5
Electric	×1	Ghost	×1
Ice	×0.25	Dragon	×0.5
Fighting	×2	Dark	×1
Poison	×1	Steel	×1
Ground	×2	Fairy	×0.5

Can be used in
Inverse Battle
Battle Institute
Battle Maison
Random Matchup (Free Battle)
Random Matchup (Others)

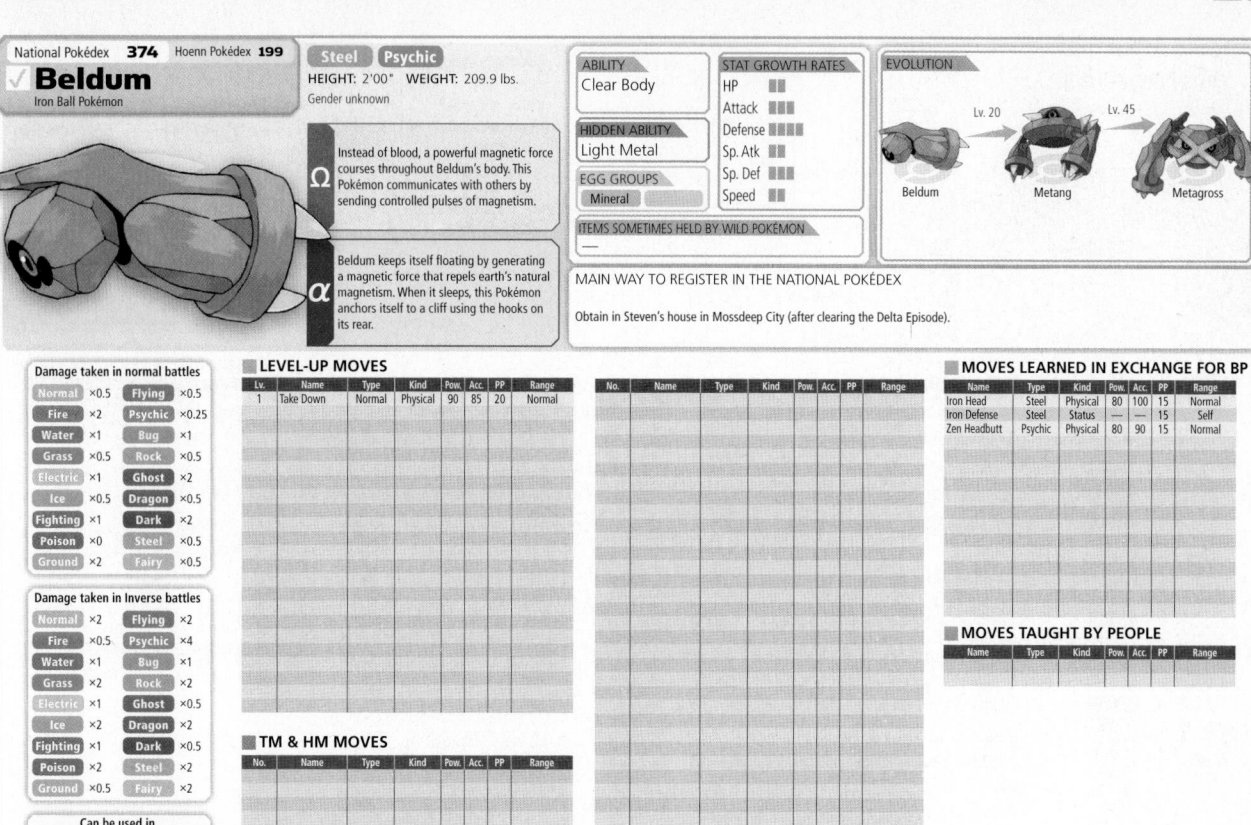

National Pokédex **374** Hoenn Pokédex **199**

Beldum

Iron Ball Pokémon

Steel | Psychic

HEIGHT: 2'00" WEIGHT: 209.9 lbs.

Gender unknown

Ω Instead of blood, a powerful magnetic force courses throughout Beldum's body. This Pokémon communicates with others by sending controlled pulses of magnetism.

α Beldum keeps itself floating by generating a magnetic force that repels earth's natural magnetism. When it sleeps, this Pokémon anchors itself to a cliff using the hooks on its rear.

ABILITY
Clear Body

HIDDEN ABILITY
Light Metal

EGG GROUPS
Mineral

STAT GROWTH RATES
HP
Attack
Defense
Sp. Atk
Sp. Def
Speed

ITEMS SOMETIMES HELD BY WILD POKÉMON
—

EVOLUTION
Beldum → Lv. 20 → Metang → Lv. 45 → Metagross

MAIN WAY TO REGISTER IN THE NATIONAL POKÉDEX

Obtain in Steven's house in Mossdeep City (after clearing the Delta Episode).

Damage taken in normal battles

Type		Type	
Normal	×0.5	Flying	×0.5
Fire	×2	Psychic	×0.25
Water	×1	Bug	×1
Grass	×0.5	Rock	×0.5
Electric	×1	Ghost	×2
Ice	×0.5	Dragon	×0.5
Fighting	×1	Dark	×2
Poison	×0	Steel	×0.5
Ground	×2	Fairy	×0.5

Damage taken in Inverse battles

Type		Type	
Normal	×2	Flying	×2
Fire	×0.5	Psychic	×4
Water	×1	Bug	×1
Grass	×2	Rock	×2
Electric	×1	Ghost	×0.5
Ice	×2	Dragon	×2
Fighting	×1	Dark	×0.5
Poison	×2	Steel	×2
Ground	×0.5	Fairy	×2

Can be used in
Inverse Battle
Battle Institute
Battle Maison
Random Matchup (Free Battle)
Random Matchup (Others)

LEVEL-UP MOVES

Lv.	Name	Type	Kind	Pow.	Acc.	PP	Range
1	Take Down	Normal	Physical	90	85	20	Normal

TM & HM MOVES

No.	Name	Type	Kind	Pow.	Acc.	PP	Range

MOVES LEARNED IN EXCHANGE FOR BP

Name	Type	Kind	Pow.	Acc.	PP	Range
Iron Head	Steel	Physical	80	100	15	Normal
Iron Defense	Steel	Status	—	—	15	Self
Zen Headbutt	Psychic	Physical	80	90	15	Normal

MOVES TAUGHT BY PEOPLE

Name	Type	Kind	Pow.	Acc.	PP	Range

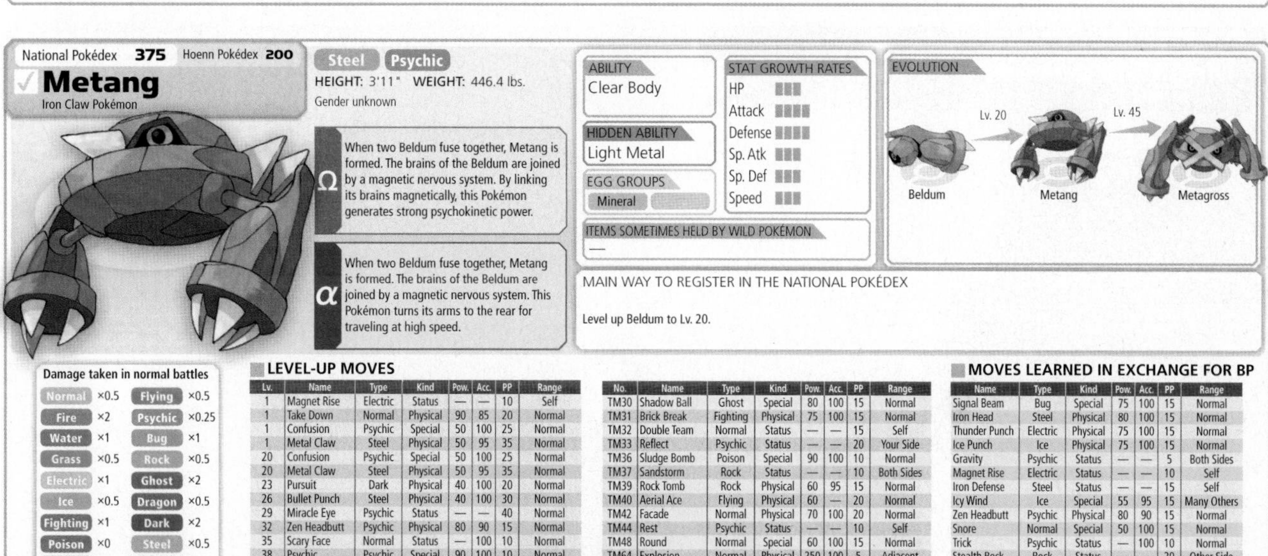

National Pokédex **375** Hoenn Pokédex **200**

Metang

Iron Claw Pokémon

Steel | Psychic

HEIGHT: 3'11" WEIGHT: 446.4 lbs.

Gender unknown

Ω When two Beldum fuse together, Metang is formed. The brains of the Beldum are joined by a magnetic nervous system. By linking its brains magnetically, this Pokémon generates strong psychokinetic power.

α When two Beldum fuse together, Metang is formed. The brains of the Beldum are joined by a magnetic nervous system. This Pokémon turns its arms to the rear for traveling at high speed.

ABILITY
Clear Body

HIDDEN ABILITY
Light Metal

EGG GROUPS
Mineral

STAT GROWTH RATES
HP
Attack
Defense
Sp. Atk
Sp. Def
Speed

ITEMS SOMETIMES HELD BY WILD POKÉMON
—

EVOLUTION
Beldum → Lv. 20 → Metang → Lv. 45 → Metagross

MAIN WAY TO REGISTER IN THE NATIONAL POKÉDEX

Level up Beldum to Lv. 20.

Damage taken in normal battles

Type		Type	
Normal	×0.5	Flying	×0.5
Fire	×2	Psychic	×0.25
Water	×1	Bug	×1
Grass	×0.5	Rock	×0.5
Electric	×1	Ghost	×2
Ice	×0.5	Dragon	×0.5
Fighting	×1	Dark	×2
Poison	×0	Steel	×0.5
Ground	×2	Fairy	×0.5

Damage taken in Inverse battles

Type		Type	
Normal	×2	Flying	×2
Fire	×0.5	Psychic	×4
Water	×1	Bug	×1
Grass	×2	Rock	×2
Electric	×1	Ghost	×0.5
Ice	×2	Dragon	×2
Fighting	×1	Dark	×0.5
Poison	×2	Steel	×2
Ground	×0.5	Fairy	×2

Can be used in
Inverse Battle
Battle Institute
Battle Maison
Random Matchup (Free Battle)
Random Matchup (Others)

LEVEL-UP MOVES

Lv.	Name	Type	Kind	Pow.	Acc.	PP	Range
1	Magnet Rise	Electric	Status	—	—	10	Self
1	Take Down	Normal	Physical	90	85	20	Normal
1	Confusion	Psychic	Special	50	100	25	Normal
1	Metal Claw	Steel	Physical	50	95	35	Normal
20	Confusion	Psychic	Special	50	100	25	Normal
20	Metal Claw	Steel	Physical	50	95	35	Normal
23	Pursuit	Dark	Physical	40	100	20	Normal
26	Bullet Punch	Steel	Physical	40	100	30	Normal
29	Miracle Eye	Psychic	Status	—	—	40	Normal
32	Zen Headbutt	Psychic	Physical	80	90	15	Normal
35	Scary Face	Normal	Status	—	100	10	Normal
38	Psychic	Psychic	Special	90	100	10	Normal
41	Agility	Psychic	Status	—	—	30	Self
44	Meteor Mash	Steel	Physical	90	90	10	Normal
47	Iron Defense	Steel	Status	—	—	15	Self
50	Hyper Beam	Normal	Special	150	90	5	Normal

TM & HM MOVES

No.	Name	Type	Kind	Pow.	Acc.	PP	Range
TM01	Hone Claws	Dark	Status	—	—	15	Self
TM03	Psyshock	Psychic	Special	80	100	10	Normal
TM06	Toxic	Poison	Status	—	90	10	Normal
TM10	Hidden Power	Normal	Special	60	100	15	Normal
TM11	Sunny Day	Fire	Status	—	—	5	Both Sides
TM15	Hyper Beam	Normal	Special	150	90	5	Normal
TM16	Light Screen	Psychic	Status	—	—	30	Your Side
TM17	Protect	Normal	Status	—	—	10	Self
TM18	Rain Dance	Water	Status	—	—	5	Both Sides
TM21	Frustration	Normal	Physical	—	100	20	Normal
TM26	Earthquake	Ground	Physical	100	100	10	Adjacent
TM27	Return	Normal	Physical	—	100	20	Normal
TM29	Psychic	Psychic	Special	90	100	10	Normal
TM30	Shadow Ball	Ghost	Special	80	100	15	Normal
TM31	Brick Break	Fighting	Physical	75	100	15	Normal
TM32	Double Team	Normal	Status	—	—	15	Self
TM33	Reflect	Psychic	Status	—	—	20	Your Side
TM36	Sludge Bomb	Poison	Special	90	100	10	Normal
TM37	Sandstorm	Rock	Status	—	—	10	Both Sides
TM39	Rock Tomb	Rock	Physical	60	95	15	Normal
TM40	Aerial Ace	Flying	Physical	60	—	20	Normal
TM42	Facade	Normal	Physical	70	100	20	Normal
TM44	Rest	Psychic	Status	—	—	10	Self
TM48	Round	Normal	Special	60	100	15	Normal
TM64	Explosion	Normal	Physical	250	100	5	Adjacent
TM69	Rock Polish	Rock	Status	—	—	20	Self
TM70	Flash	Normal	Status	—	100	20	Normal
TM74	Gyro Ball	Steel	Physical	—	100	5	Normal
TM77	Psych Up	Normal	Status	—	—	10	Normal
TM78	Bulldoze	Ground	Physical	60	100	20	Adjacent
TM80	Rock Slide	Rock	Physical	75	90	10	Many Others
TM86	Grass Knot	Grass	Special	—	100	20	Normal
TM87	Swagger	Normal	Status	—	90	15	Normal
TM88	Sleep Talk	Normal	Status	—	—	10	Self
TM90	Substitute	Normal	Status	—	—	10	Self
TM91	Flash Cannon	Steel	Special	80	100	10	Normal
TM94	Secret Power	Normal	Physical	70	100	20	Normal
TM98	Power-Up Punch	Fighting	Physical	40	100	20	Normal
TM100	Confide	Normal	Status	—	—	20	Normal
HM01	Cut	Normal	Physical	50	95	30	Normal
HM04	Strength	Normal	Physical	80	100	15	Normal
HM06	Rock Smash	Fighting	Physical	40	100	15	Normal

MOVES LEARNED IN EXCHANGE FOR BP

Name	Type	Kind	Pow.	Acc.	PP	Range
Signal Beam	Bug	Special	75	100	15	Normal
Iron Head	Steel	Physical	80	100	15	Normal
Thunder Punch	Electric	Physical	75	100	15	Normal
Ice Punch	Ice	Physical	75	100	15	Normal
Gravity	Psychic	Status	—	—	5	Both Sides
Magnet Rise	Electric	Status	—	—	10	Self
Iron Defense	Steel	Status	—	—	15	Self
Icy Wind	Ice	Special	55	95	15	Many Others
Zen Headbutt	Psychic	Physical	80	90	15	Normal
Snore	Normal	Special	50	100	15	Normal
Trick	Psychic	Status	—	100	10	Normal
Stealth Rock	Rock	Status	—	—	20	Other Side

MOVES TAUGHT BY PEOPLE

Name	Type	Kind	Pow.	Acc.	PP	Range

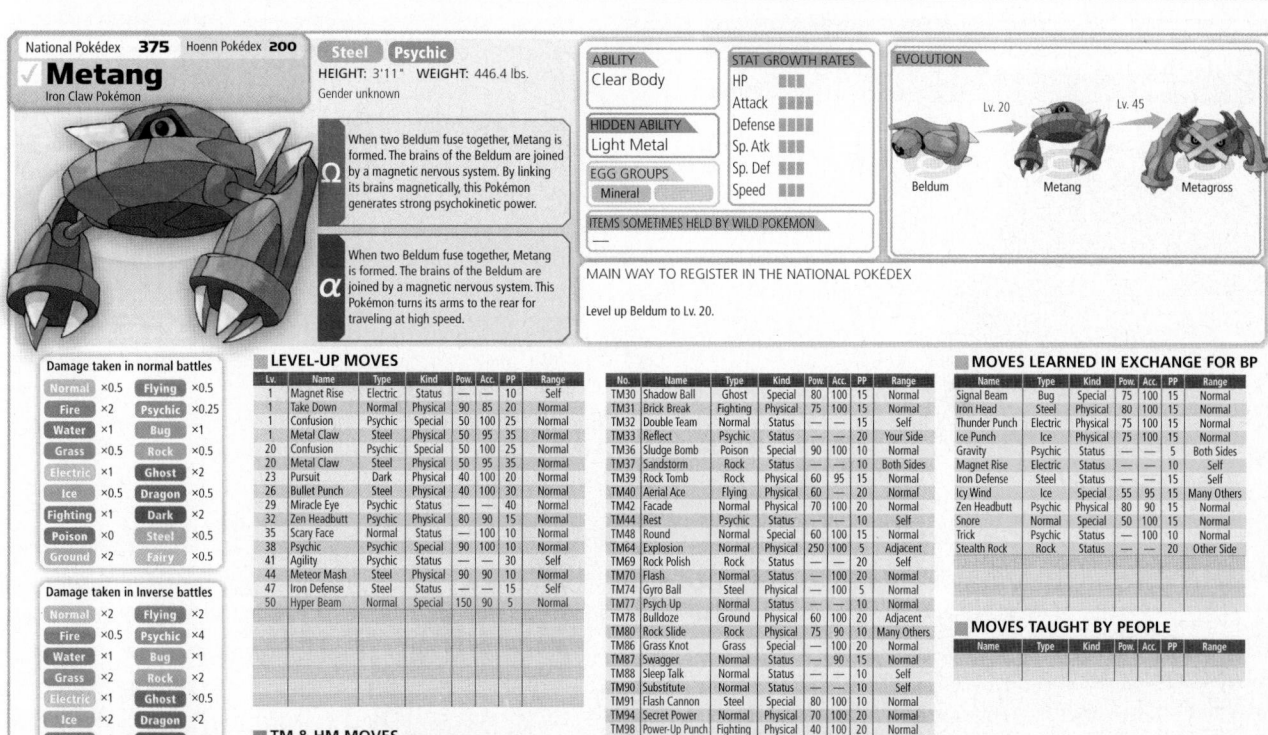

National Pokédex **376** Hoenn Pokédex **201**

✓ Metagross

Iron Leg Pokémon

Steel | Psychic

HEIGHT: 5'03" WEIGHT: 1212.5 lbs.

Gender unknown

Ω Metagross has four brains in total. Combined, the four brains can breeze through difficult calculations faster than a supercomputer. This Pokémon can float in the air by tucking in its four legs.

α Metagross is the result of two Metang achieving fusion. When hunting, this Pokémon pins the prey to the ground under its massive body. It then eats the helpless victim using the large mouth on its stomach.

ABILITY
Clear Body

HIDDEN ABILITY
Light Metal

EGG GROUPS
Mineral

STAT GROWTH RATES
HP ▮▮▮
Attack ▮▮▮▮▮▮▮
Defense ▮▮▮▮▮▮
Sp. Atk ▮▮▮▮▮
Sp. Def ▮▮▮▮
Speed ▮▮▮▮

ITEMS SOMETIMES HELD BY WILD POKÉMON
—

EVOLUTION
Beldum → Lv. 20 → Metang → Lv. 45 → Metagross

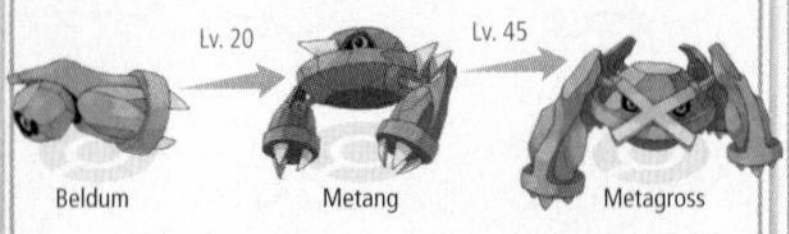

MAIN WAY TO REGISTER IN THE NATIONAL POKÉDEX

Level up Metang to Lv. 45.

Damage taken in normal battles

Type		Type	
Normal	×0.5	Flying	×0.5
Fire	×2	Psychic	×0.25
Water	×1	Bug	×1
Grass	×0.5	Rock	×0.5
Electric	×1	Ghost	×2
Ice	×0.5	Dragon	×0.5
Fighting	×1	Dark	×2
Poison	×0	Steel	×0.5
Ground	×2	Fairy	×0.5

Damage taken in Inverse battles

Type		Type	
Normal	×2	Flying	×2
Fire	×0.5	Psychic	×4
Water	×1	Bug	×1
Grass	×2	Rock	×2
Electric	×1	Ghost	×0.5
Ice	×2	Dragon	×2
Fighting	×1	Dark	×0.5
Poison	×2	Steel	×2
Ground	×0.5	Fairy	×2

Can be used in
Inverse Battle
Battle Institute
Battle Maison
Random Matchup (Free Battle)
Random Matchup (Others)

LEVEL-UP MOVES

Lv.	Name	Type	Kind	Pow.	Acc.	PP	Range
1	Magnet Rise	Electric	Status	—	—	10	Self
1	Take Down	Normal	Physical	90	85	20	Normal
1	Confusion	Psychic	Special	50	100	25	Normal
1	Metal Claw	Steel	Physical	50	95	35	Normal
20	Confusion	Psychic	Special	50	100	25	Normal
20	Metal Claw	Steel	Physical	50	95	35	Normal
23	Pursuit	Dark	Physical	40	100	20	Normal
26	Bullet Punch	Steel	Physical	40	100	30	Normal
29	Miracle Eye	Psychic	Status	—	—	40	Normal
32	Zen Headbutt	Psychic	Physical	80	90	15	Normal
35	Scary Face	Normal	Status	—	100	10	Normal
38	Psychic	Psychic	Special	90	100	10	Normal
41	Agility	Psychic	Status	—	—	30	Self
44	Meteor Mash	Steel	Physical	90	90	10	Normal
45	Hammer Arm	Fighting	Physical	100	90	10	Normal
52	Iron Defense	Steel	Status	—	—	15	Self
60	Hyper Beam	Normal	Special	150	90	5	Normal

TM & HM MOVES

No.	Name	Type	Kind	Pow.	Acc.	PP	Range
TM01	Hone Claws	Dark	Status	—	—	15	Self
TM03	Psyshock	Psychic	Special	80	100	10	Normal
TM06	Toxic	Poison	Status	—	90	10	Normal
TM10	Hidden Power	Normal	Special	60	100	15	Normal
TM11	Sunny Day	Fire	Status	—	—	5	Both Sides
TM15	Hyper Beam	Normal	Special	150	90	5	Normal
TM16	Light Screen	Psychic	Status	—	—	30	Your Side
TM17	Protect	Normal	Status	—	—	10	Self
TM18	Rain Dance	Water	Status	—	—	5	Both Sides
TM21	Frustration	Normal	Physical	—	100	20	Normal
TM26	Earthquake	Ground	Physical	100	100	10	Adjacent
TM27	Return	Normal	Physical	—	100	20	Normal
TM29	Psychic	Psychic	Special	90	100	10	Normal
TM30	Shadow Ball	Ghost	Special	80	100	15	Normal
TM31	Brick Break	Fighting	Physical	75	100	15	Normal
TM32	Double Team	Normal	Status	—	—	15	Self
TM33	Reflect	Psychic	Status	—	—	20	Your Side
TM36	Sludge Bomb	Poison	Special	90	100	10	Normal
TM37	Sandstorm	Rock	Status	—	—	10	Both Sides
TM39	Rock Tomb	Rock	Physical	60	95	15	Normal
TM40	Aerial Ace	Flying	Physical	60	—	20	Normal
TM42	Facade	Normal	Physical	70	100	20	Normal
TM44	Rest	Psychic	Status	—	—	10	Self
TM48	Round	Normal	Special	60	100	15	Normal
TM64	Explosion	Normal	Physical	250	100	5	Adjacent
TM68	Giga Impact	Normal	Physical	150	90	5	Normal
TM69	Rock Polish	Rock	Status	—	—	20	Self
TM70	Flash	Normal	Status	—	100	20	Normal
TM74	Gyro Ball	Steel	Physical	—	100	5	Normal
TM77	Psych Up	Normal	Status	—	—	10	Normal
TM78	Bulldoze	Ground	Physical	60	100	20	Adjacent
TM80	Rock Slide	Rock	Physical	75	90	10	Many Others
TM86	Grass Knot	Grass	Special	—	100	20	Normal
TM87	Swagger	Normal	Status	—	90	15	Normal
TM88	Sleep Talk	Normal	Status	—	—	10	Self
TM90	Substitute	Normal	Status	—	—	10	Self
TM91	Flash Cannon	Steel	Special	80	100	10	Normal
TM94	Secret Power	Normal	Physical	70	100	20	Normal
TM98	Power-Up Punch	Fighting	Physical	40	100	20	Normal
TM100	Confide	Normal	Status	—	—	20	Normal
HM01	Cut	Normal	Physical	50	95	30	Normal
HM04	Strength	Normal	Physical	80	100	15	Normal
HM06	Rock Smash	Fighting	Physical	40	100	15	Normal

MOVES LEARNED IN EXCHANGE FOR BP

Name	Type	Kind	Pow.	Acc.	PP	Range
Signal Beam	Bug	Special	75	100	15	Normal
Iron Head	Steel	Physical	80	100	15	Normal
Thunder Punch	Electric	Physical	75	100	15	Normal
Ice Punch	Ice	Physical	75	100	15	Normal
Block	Normal	Status	—	—	5	Normal
Gravity	Psychic	Status	—	—	5	Both Sides
Magnet Rise	Electric	Status	—	—	10	Self
Iron Defense	Steel	Status	—	—	15	Self
Icy Wind	Ice	Special	55	95	15	Many Others
Zen Headbutt	Psychic	Physical	80	90	15	Normal
Snore	Normal	Special	50	100	15	Normal
Trick	Psychic	Status	—	100	10	Normal
Stealth Rock	Rock	Status	—	—	20	Other Side

MOVES TAUGHT BY PEOPLE

Name	Type	Kind	Pow.	Acc.	PP	Range

Mega Evolution

Mega Metagross

Iron Leg Pokémon

Steel | Psychic

HEIGHT: 8'02" WEIGHT: 2078.7 lbs.

Gender unknown

REQUIRED MEGA STONE
Metagrossite
Receive from Champion Steven in the Pokémon League (if you defeat him again after clearing the Delta Episode).

ABILITY
Tough Claws

HIDDEN ABILITY
—

EGG GROUPS
—

STAT GROWTH RATES
HP ▮▮▮
Attack ▮▮▮▮▮▮▮
Defense ▮▮▮▮▮▮
Sp. Atk ▮▮▮▮▮
Sp. Def ▮▮▮▮▮
Speed ▮▮▮▮▮▮

Damage taken in normal battles

Type		Type	
Normal	×0.5	Flying	×0.5
Fire	×2	Psychic	×0.25
Water	×1	Bug	×1
Grass	×0.5	Rock	×0.5
Electric	×1	Ghost	×2
Ice	×0.5	Dragon	×0.5
Fighting	×1	Dark	×2
Poison	×0	Steel	×0.5
Ground	×2	Fairy	×0.5

Damage taken in Inverse battles

Type		Type	
Normal	×2	Flying	×2
Fire	×0.5	Psychic	×4
Water	×1	Bug	×1
Grass	×2	Rock	×2
Electric	×1	Ghost	×0.5
Ice	×2	Dragon	×2
Fighting	×1	Dark	×0.5
Poison	×2	Steel	×2
Ground	×0.5	Fairy	×2

Can be used in
Inverse Battle
Battle Institute
Battle Maison
Random Matchup (Free Battle)
Random Matchup (Others)

National Pokédex **377** Hoenn Pokédex **202**

Regirock

Rock Peak Pokémon

Rock

HEIGHT: 5'07" WEIGHT: 507.1 lbs.

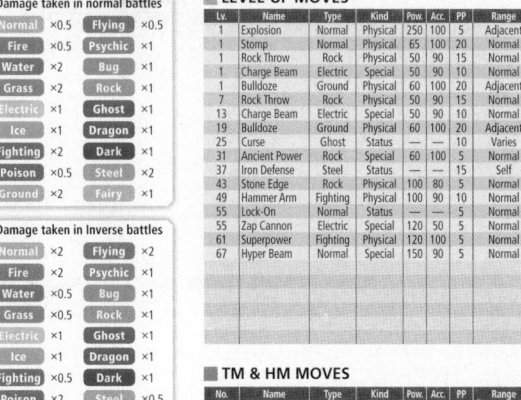

Gender unknown

Ω Regirock was sealed away by people long ago. If this Pokémon's body is damaged in battle, it is said to seek out suitable rocks on its own to repair itself.

α Regirock's body is composed entirely of rocks. Recently, a study made the startling discovery that the rocks were all unearthed from different locations.

ABILITY
Clear Body

HIDDEN ABILITY
—

EGG GROUPS
No Eggs Discovered

STAT GROWTH RATES
HP
Attack
Defense
Sp. Atk
Sp. Def
Speed

ITEMS SOMETIMES HELD BY WILD POKÉMON
—

EVOLUTION
Does not evolve

MAIN WAY TO REGISTER IN THE NATIONAL POKÉDEX

Catch in the Desert Ruins on Route 111 (after solving the secrets of the Sealed Chamber).

Damage taken in normal battles

Type		Type	
Normal	×0.5	Flying	×0.5
Fire	×0.5	Psychic	×1
Water	×2	Bug	×1
Grass	×2	Rock	×1
Electric	×1	Ghost	×1
Ice	×1	Dragon	×1
Fighting	×2	Dark	×1
Poison	×0.5	Steel	×2
Ground	×2	Fairy	×1

Damage taken in Inverse battles

Type		Type	
Normal	×2	Flying	×2
Fire	×2	Psychic	×1
Water	×0.5	Bug	×1
Grass	×0.5	Rock	×1
Electric	×1	Ghost	×1
Ice	×1	Dragon	×1
Fighting	×0.5	Dark	×1
Poison	×2	Steel	×0.5
Ground	×0.5	Fairy	×1

Can be used in
Inverse Battle
Battle Institute
Battle Maison
Random Matchup (Free Battle)
Random Matchup (Others)

LEVEL-UP MOVES

Lv.	Name	Type	Kind	Pow.	Acc.	PP	Range
1	Explosion	Normal	Physical	250	100	5	Adjacent
1	Stomp	Normal	Physical	65	100	20	Normal
1	Rock Throw	Rock	Physical	50	90	15	Normal
1	Charge Beam	Electric	Special	50	90	10	Normal
1	Bulldoze	Ground	Physical	60	100	20	Adjacent
7	Rock Throw	Rock	Physical	50	90	15	Normal
13	Charge Beam	Electric	Special	50	90	10	Normal
19	Bulldoze	Ground	Physical	60	100	20	Adjacent
25	Curse	Ghost	Status	—	—	10	Varies
31	Ancient Power	Rock	Special	60	100	5	Normal
37	Iron Defense	Steel	Status	—	—	15	Self
43	Stone Edge	Rock	Physical	100	80	5	Normal
49	Hammer Arm	Fighting	Physical	100	90	10	Normal
55	Lock-On	Normal	Status	—	—	5	Normal
55	Zap Cannon	Electric	Special	120	50	5	Normal
61	Superpower	Fighting	Physical	120	100	5	Normal
67	Hyper Beam	Normal	Special	150	90	5	Normal

TM & HM MOVES

No.	Name	Type	Kind	Pow.	Acc.	PP	Range
TM06	Toxic	Poison	Status	—	90	10	Normal
TM10	Hidden Power	Normal	Special	60	100	15	Normal
TM11	Sunny Day	Fire	Status	—	—	5	Both Sides
TM15	Hyper Beam	Normal	Special	150	90	5	Normal
TM17	Protect	Normal	Status	—	—	10	Self
TM20	Safeguard	Normal	Status	—	—	25	Your Side
TM21	Frustration	Normal	Physical	—	100	20	Normal
TM23	Smack Down	Rock	Physical	50	100	15	Normal
TM24	Thunderbolt	Electric	Special	90	100	15	Normal
TM25	Thunder	Electric	Special	110	70	10	Normal
TM26	Earthquake	Ground	Physical	100	100	10	Adjacent
TM27	Return	Normal	Physical	—	100	20	Normal
TM28	Dig	Ground	Physical	80	100	10	Normal
TM31	Brick Break	Fighting	Physical	75	100	15	Normal
TM32	Double Team	Normal	Status	—	—	15	Self
TM37	Sandstorm	Rock	Status	—	—	10	Both Sides
TM39	Rock Tomb	Rock	Physical	60	95	15	Normal
TM42	Facade	Normal	Physical	70	100	20	Normal
TM44	Rest	Psychic	Status	—	—	10	Self
TM48	Round	Normal	Special	60	100	15	Normal
TM52	Focus Blast	Fighting	Special	120	70	5	Normal
TM56	Fling	Dark	Physical	—	100	10	Normal
TM57	Charge Beam	Electric	Special	50	90	10	Normal
TM64	Explosion	Normal	Physical	250	100	5	Adjacent
TM68	Giga Impact	Normal	Physical	150	90	5	Normal
TM69	Rock Polish	Rock	Status	—	—	20	Self
TM71	Stone Edge	Rock	Physical	100	80	5	Normal
TM73	Thunder Wave	Electric	Status	—	100	20	Normal
TM77	Psych Up	Normal	Status	—	—	10	Normal
TM78	Bulldoze	Ground	Physical	60	100	20	Adjacent
TM80	Rock Slide	Rock	Physical	75	90	10	Many Others
TM87	Swagger	Normal	Status	—	90	15	Normal
TM88	Sleep Talk	Normal	Status	—	—	10	Self
TM90	Substitute	Normal	Status	—	—	10	Self
TM94	Secret Power	Normal	Physical	70	100	20	Normal
TM98	Power-Up Punch	Fighting	Physical	40	100	20	Normal
TM100	Confide	Normal	Status	—	—	20	Normal
HM04	Strength	Normal	Physical	80	100	15	Normal
HM06	Rock Smash	Fighting	Physical	40	100	15	Normal

MOVES LEARNED IN EXCHANGE FOR BP

Name	Type	Kind	Pow.	Acc.	PP	Range
Iron Head	Steel	Physical	80	100	15	Normal
Thunder Punch	Electric	Physical	75	100	15	Normal
Fire Punch	Fire	Physical	75	100	15	Normal
Ice Punch	Ice	Physical	75	100	15	Normal
Block	Normal	Status	—	—	5	Normal
Earth Power	Ground	Special	90	100	10	Normal
Gravity	Psychic	Status	—	—	5	Both Sides
Iron Defense	Steel	Status	—	—	15	Self
Superpower	Fighting	Physical	120	100	5	Normal
Snore	Normal	Special	50	100	15	Normal
Drain Punch	Fighting	Physical	75	100	10	Normal
Focus Punch	Fighting	Physical	150	100	20	Normal
Shock Wave	Electric	Special	60	—	20	Normal
Stealth Rock	Rock	Status	—	—	20	Other Side

MOVES TAUGHT BY PEOPLE

Name	Type	Kind	Pow.	Acc.	PP	Range

National Pokédex **378** Hoenn Pokédex **203**

Regice

Iceberg Pokémon

Ice

HEIGHT: 5'11" WEIGHT: 385.8 lbs.

Gender unknown

Ω Regice's body was made during an ice age. The deep-frozen body can't be melted, even by fire. This Pokémon controls frigid air of -328 degrees Fahrenheit.

α Regice cloaks itself with frigid air of -328 degrees Fahrenheit. Things will freeze solid just by going near this Pokémon. Its icy body is so cold, it will not melt even if it is immersed in magma.

ABILITY
Clear Body

HIDDEN ABILITY
—

EGG GROUPS
No Eggs Discovered

STAT GROWTH RATES
HP
Attack
Defense
Sp. Atk
Sp. Def
Speed

ITEMS SOMETIMES HELD BY WILD POKÉMON
—

EVOLUTION
Does not evolve

MAIN WAY TO REGISTER IN THE NATIONAL POKÉDEX

Catch in the Island Cave on Route 105 (after solving the secrets of the Sealed Chamber).

Damage taken in normal battles

Type		Type	
Normal	×1	Flying	×1
Fire	×2	Psychic	×1
Water	×1	Bug	×1
Grass	×1	Rock	×2
Electric	×1	Ghost	×1
Ice	×0.5	Dragon	×1
Fighting	×2	Dark	×1
Poison	×1	Steel	×2
Ground	×1	Fairy	×1

Damage taken in Inverse battles

Type		Type	
Normal	×1	Flying	×1
Fire	×0.5	Psychic	×1
Water	×1	Bug	×1
Grass	×1	Rock	×0.5
Electric	×1	Ghost	×1
Ice	×2	Dragon	×1
Fighting	×0.5	Dark	×1
Poison	×1	Steel	×0.5
Ground	×1	Fairy	×1

Can be used in
Inverse Battle
Battle Institute
Battle Maison
Random Matchup (Free Battle)
Random Matchup (Others)

LEVEL-UP MOVES

Lv.	Name	Type	Kind	Pow.	Acc.	PP	Range
1	Explosion	Normal	Physical	250	100	5	Adjacent
1	Stomp	Normal	Physical	65	100	20	Normal
1	Icy Wind	Ice	Special	55	95	15	Many Others
1	Charge Beam	Electric	Special	50	90	10	Normal
1	Bulldoze	Ground	Physical	60	100	20	Adjacent
7	Icy Wind	Ice	Special	55	95	15	Many Others
13	Charge Beam	Electric	Special	50	90	10	Normal
19	Bulldoze	Ground	Physical	60	100	20	Adjacent
25	Curse	Ghost	Status	—	—	10	Varies
31	Ancient Power	Rock	Special	60	100	5	Normal
37	Amnesia	Psychic	Status	—	—	20	Self
43	Ice Beam	Ice	Special	90	100	10	Normal
49	Hammer Arm	Fighting	Physical	100	90	10	Normal
55	Lock-On	Normal	Status	—	—	5	Normal
55	Zap Cannon	Electric	Special	120	50	5	Normal
61	Superpower	Fighting	Physical	120	100	5	Normal
67	Hyper Beam	Normal	Special	150	90	5	Normal

TM & HM MOVES

No.	Name	Type	Kind	Pow.	Acc.	PP	Range
TM06	Toxic	Poison	Status	—	90	10	Normal
TM07	Hail	Ice	Status	—	—	10	Both Sides
TM10	Hidden Power	Normal	Special	60	100	15	Normal
TM13	Ice Beam	Ice	Special	90	100	10	Normal
TM14	Blizzard	Ice	Special	110	70	5	Many Others
TM15	Hyper Beam	Normal	Special	150	90	5	Normal
TM17	Protect	Normal	Status	—	—	10	Self
TM18	Rain Dance	Water	Status	—	—	5	Both Sides
TM20	Safeguard	Normal	Status	—	—	25	Your Side
TM21	Frustration	Normal	Physical	—	100	20	Normal
TM24	Thunderbolt	Electric	Special	90	100	15	Normal
TM25	Thunder	Electric	Special	110	70	10	Normal
TM26	Earthquake	Ground	Physical	100	100	10	Adjacent
TM27	Return	Normal	Physical	—	100	20	Normal
TM31	Brick Break	Fighting	Physical	75	100	15	Normal
TM32	Double Team	Normal	Status	—	—	15	Self
TM39	Rock Tomb	Rock	Physical	60	95	15	Normal
TM42	Facade	Normal	Physical	70	100	20	Normal
TM44	Rest	Psychic	Status	—	—	10	Self
TM48	Round	Normal	Special	60	100	15	Normal
TM52	Focus Blast	Fighting	Special	120	70	5	Normal
TM56	Fling	Dark	Physical	—	100	10	Normal
TM57	Charge Beam	Electric	Special	50	90	10	Normal
TM64	Explosion	Normal	Physical	250	100	5	Adjacent
TM68	Giga Impact	Normal	Physical	150	90	5	Normal
TM69	Rock Polish	Rock	Status	—	—	20	Self
TM73	Thunder Wave	Electric	Status	—	100	20	Normal
TM77	Psych Up	Normal	Status	—	—	10	Normal
TM78	Bulldoze	Ground	Physical	60	100	20	Adjacent
TM79	Frost Breath	Ice	Special	60	90	10	Normal
TM80	Rock Slide	Rock	Physical	75	90	10	Many Others
TM87	Swagger	Normal	Status	—	90	15	Normal
TM88	Sleep Talk	Normal	Status	—	—	10	Self
TM90	Substitute	Normal	Status	—	—	10	Self
TM91	Flash Cannon	Steel	Special	80	100	10	Normal
TM94	Secret Power	Normal	Physical	70	100	20	Normal
TM98	Power-Up Punch	Fighting	Physical	40	100	20	Normal
TM100	Confide	Normal	Status	—	—	20	Normal
HM04	Strength	Normal	Physical	80	100	15	Normal
HM06	Rock Smash	Fighting	Physical	40	100	15	Normal

MOVES LEARNED IN EXCHANGE FOR BP

Name	Type	Kind	Pow.	Acc.	PP	Range
Signal Beam	Bug	Special	75	100	15	Normal
Iron Head	Steel	Physical	80	100	15	Normal
Thunder Punch	Electric	Physical	75	100	15	Normal
Ice Punch	Ice	Physical	75	100	15	Normal
Block	Normal	Status	—	—	5	Normal
Gravity	Psychic	Status	—	—	5	Both Sides
Superpower	Fighting	Physical	120	100	5	Normal
Icy Wind	Ice	Special	55	95	15	Many Others
Snore	Normal	Special	50	100	15	Normal
Focus Punch	Fighting	Physical	150	100	20	Normal
Shock Wave	Electric	Special	60	—	20	Normal

MOVES TAUGHT BY PEOPLE

Name	Type	Kind	Pow.	Acc.	PP	Range

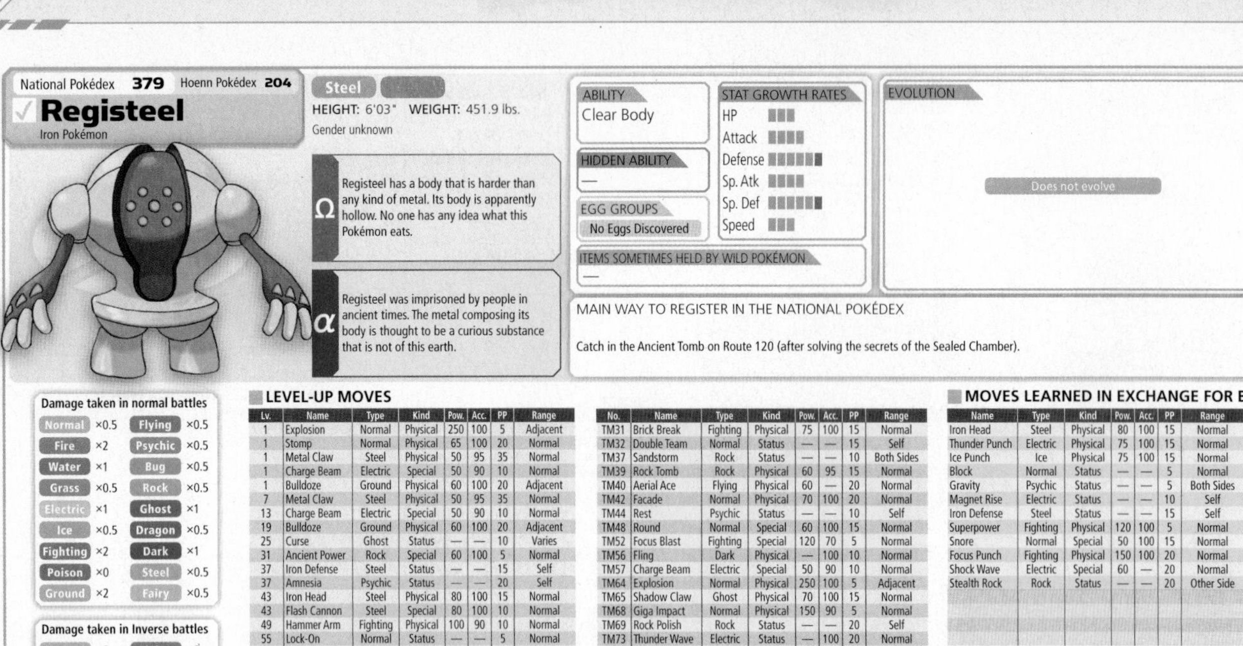

National Pokédex **379** Hoenn Pokédex **204**

Registeel

Iron Pokémon

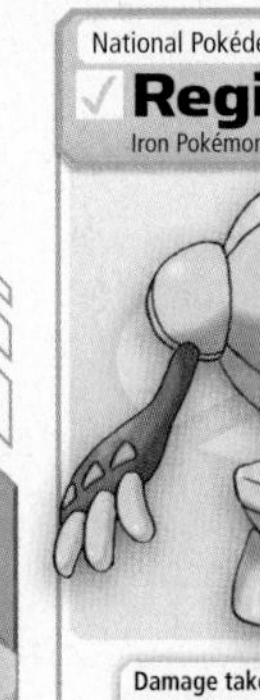

Steel

HEIGHT: 6'03" WEIGHT: 451.9 lbs.

Gender unknown

Ω Registeel has a body that is harder than any kind of metal. Its body is apparently hollow. No one has any idea what this Pokémon eats.

α Registeel was imprisoned by people in ancient times. The metal composing its body is thought to be a curious substance that is not of this earth.

ABILITY
Clear Body

HIDDEN ABILITY
—

EGG GROUPS
No Eggs Discovered

STAT GROWTH RATES
HP
Attack
Defense
Sp. Atk
Sp. Def
Speed

ITEMS SOMETIMES HELD BY WILD POKÉMON
—

EVOLUTION
Does not evolve

MAIN WAY TO REGISTER IN THE NATIONAL POKÉDEX

Catch in the Ancient Tomb on Route 120 (after solving the secrets of the Sealed Chamber).

Damage taken in normal battles

Type		Type	
Normal	×0.5	Flying	×0.5
Fire	×2	Psychic	×0.5
Water	×1	Bug	×0.5
Grass	×0.5	Rock	×0.5
Electric	×1	Ghost	×1
Ice	×0.5	Dragon	×0.5
Fighting	×2	Dark	×1
Poison	×0	Steel	×0.5
Ground	×2	Fairy	×0.5

Damage taken in Inverse battles

Type		Type	
Normal	×2	Flying	×2
Fire	×0.5	Psychic	×2
Water	×1	Bug	×2
Grass	×2	Rock	×2
Electric	×1	Ghost	×1
Ice	×2	Dragon	×2
Fighting	×0.5	Dark	×1
Poison	×2	Steel	×2
Ground	×0.5	Fairy	×2

Can be used in
- Inverse Battle
- Battle Institute
- Battle Maison
- Random Matchup (Free Battle)
- Random Matchup (Others)

LEVEL-UP MOVES

Lv.	Name	Type	Kind	Pow.	Acc.	PP	Range
1	Explosion	Normal	Physical	250	100	5	Adjacent
1	Stomp	Normal	Physical	65	100	20	Normal
1	Metal Claw	Steel	Physical	50	95	35	Normal
1	Charge Beam	Electric	Special	50	90	10	Normal
1	Bulldoze	Ground	Physical	60	100	20	Adjacent
7	Metal Claw	Steel	Physical	50	95	35	Normal
13	Charge Beam	Electric	Special	50	90	10	Normal
19	Bulldoze	Ground	Physical	60	100	20	Adjacent
25	Curse	Ghost	Status	—	—	10	Varies
31	Ancient Power	Rock	Special	60	100	5	Normal
37	Iron Defense	Steel	Status	—	—	15	Self
37	Amnesia	Psychic	Status	—	—	20	Self
43	Iron Head	Steel	Physical	80	100	15	Normal
43	Flash Cannon	Steel	Special	80	100	10	Normal
49	Hammer Arm	Fighting	Physical	100	90	10	Normal
55	Lock-On	Normal	Status	—	—	5	Normal
55	Zap Cannon	Electric	Special	120	50	5	Normal
61	Superpower	Fighting	Physical	120	100	5	Normal
67	Hyper Beam	Normal	Special	150	90	5	Normal

TM & HM MOVES

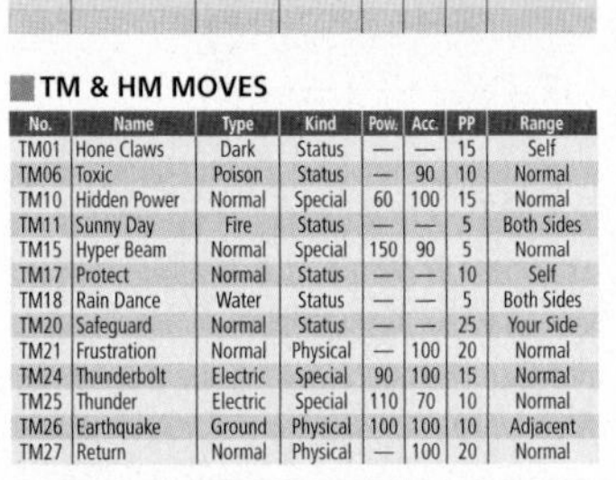

No.	Name	Type	Kind	Pow.	Acc.	PP	Range
TM01	Hone Claws	Dark	Status	—	—	15	Self
TM06	Toxic	Poison	Status	—	90	10	Normal
TM10	Hidden Power	Normal	Special	60	100	15	Normal
TM11	Sunny Day	Fire	Status	—	—	5	Both Sides
TM15	Hyper Beam	Normal	Special	150	90	5	Normal
TM17	Protect	Normal	Status	—	—	10	Self
TM18	Rain Dance	Water	Status	—	—	5	Both Sides
TM20	Safeguard	Normal	Status	—	—	25	Your Side
TM21	Frustration	Normal	Physical	—	100	20	Normal
TM24	Thunderbolt	Electric	Special	90	100	15	Normal
TM25	Thunder	Electric	Special	110	70	10	Normal
TM26	Earthquake	Ground	Physical	100	100	10	Adjacent
TM27	Return	Normal	Physical	—	100	20	Normal
TM31	Brick Break	Fighting	Physical	75	100	15	Normal
TM32	Double Team	Normal	Status	—	—	15	Self
TM37	Sandstorm	Rock	Status	—	—	10	Both Sides
TM39	Rock Tomb	Rock	Physical	60	95	15	Normal
TM40	Aerial Ace	Flying	Physical	60	—	20	Normal
TM42	Facade	Normal	Physical	70	100	20	Normal
TM44	Rest	Psychic	Status	—	—	10	Self
TM48	Round	Normal	Special	60	100	15	Normal
TM52	Focus Blast	Fighting	Special	120	70	5	Normal
TM56	Fling	Dark	Physical	—	100	10	Normal
TM57	Charge Beam	Electric	Special	50	90	10	Normal
TM64	Explosion	Normal	Physical	250	100	5	Adjacent
TM65	Shadow Claw	Ghost	Physical	70	100	15	Normal
TM68	Giga Impact	Normal	Physical	150	90	5	Normal
TM69	Rock Polish	Rock	Status	—	—	20	Self
TM73	Thunder Wave	Electric	Status	—	100	20	Normal
TM77	Psych Up	Normal	Status	—	—	10	Normal
TM78	Bulldoze	Ground	Physical	60	100	20	Adjacent
TM80	Rock Slide	Rock	Physical	75	90	10	Many Others
TM87	Swagger	Normal	Status	—	90	15	Normal
TM88	Sleep Talk	Normal	Status	—	—	10	Self
TM90	Substitute	Normal	Status	—	—	10	Self
TM91	Flash Cannon	Steel	Special	80	100	10	Normal
TM94	Secret Power	Normal	Physical	70	100	20	Normal
TM98	Power-Up Punch	Fighting	Physical	40	100	20	Normal
TM100	Confide	Normal	Status	—	—	20	Normal
HM04	Strength	Normal	Physical	80	100	15	Normal
HM06	Rock Smash	Fighting	Physical	40	100	15	Normal

MOVES LEARNED IN EXCHANGE FOR BP

Name	Type	Kind	Pow.	Acc.	PP	Range
Iron Head	Steel	Physical	80	100	15	Normal
Thunder Punch	Electric	Physical	75	100	15	Normal
Ice Punch	Ice	Physical	75	100	15	Normal
Block	Normal	Status	—	—	5	Normal
Gravity	Psychic	Status	—	—	5	Both Sides
Magnet Rise	Electric	Status	—	—	10	Self
Iron Defense	Steel	Status	—	—	15	Self
Superpower	Fighting	Physical	120	100	5	Normal
Snore	Normal	Special	50	100	15	Normal
Focus Punch	Fighting	Physical	150	100	20	Normal
Shock Wave	Electric	Special	60	—	20	Normal
Stealth Rock	Rock	Status	—	—	20	Other Side

MOVES TAUGHT BY PEOPLE

Name	Type	Kind	Pow.	Acc.	PP	Range

National Pokédex **380** Hoenn Pokédex **205**

Latias

Eon Pokémon

Dragon Psychic

HEIGHT: 4'07" WEIGHT: 88.2 lbs.

♀ only

Ω Latias is highly sensitive to the emotions of people. If it senses any hostility, this Pokémon ruffles the feathers all over its body and cries shrilly to intimidate the foe.

α Latias is highly intelligent and capable of understanding human speech. It is covered with a glass-like down. The Pokémon enfolds its body with its down and refracts light to alter its appearance.

ABILITY
Levitate

HIDDEN ABILITY
—

EGG GROUPS
No Eggs Discovered

STAT GROWTH RATES
HP
Attack
Defense
Sp. Atk
Sp. Def
Speed

ITEMS SOMETIMES HELD BY WILD POKÉMON
—

EVOLUTION
Does not evolve

MAIN WAYS TO REGISTER IN THE NATIONAL POKÉDEX

Ω Bring it to your game using Link Trade or the GTS.

α After the Delta Episode, catch it on Southern Island once you have obtained the Eon Ticket.

Damage taken in normal battles

Type		Type	
Normal	×1	Flying	×1
Fire	×0.5	Psychic	×0.5
Water	×0.5	Bug	×2
Grass	×0.5	Rock	×1
Electric	×0.5	Ghost	×2
Ice	×2	Dragon	×2
Fighting	×0.5	Dark	×2
Poison	×1	Steel	×1
! Ground	×1	Fairy	×2

Damage taken in Inverse battles

Type		Type	
Normal	×1	Flying	×1
Fire	×2	Psychic	×2
Water	×2	Bug	×0.5
Grass	×2	Rock	×1
Electric	×2	Ghost	×0.5
Ice	×0.5	Dragon	×0.5
Fighting	×2	Dark	×0.5
Poison	×1	Steel	×1
! Ground	×1	Fairy	×0.5

Can be used in
- Inverse Battle
- Battle Institute
- Battle Maison
- Random Matchup (Free Battle)
- Random Matchup (Others)

LEVEL-UP MOVES

Lv.	Name	Type	Kind	Pow.	Acc.	PP	Range
1	Healing Wish	Psychic	Status	—	—	10	Self
1	Helping Hand	Normal	Status	—	—	20	1 Ally
1	Wish	Normal	Status	—	—	10	Self
1	Psywave	Psychic	Special	—	100	15	Normal
1	Safeguard	Normal	Status	—	—	25	Your Side
4	Water Sport	Water	Status	—	—	15	Both Sides
7	Charm	Fairy	Status	—	100	20	Normal
10	Stored Power	Psychic	Special	20	100	10	Normal
13	Refresh	Normal	Status	—	—	20	Self
16	Heal Pulse	Psychic	Status	—	—	10	Normal
20	Dragon Breath	Dragon	Special	60	100	20	Normal
24	Mist Ball	Psychic	Special	70	100	5	Normal
28	Psycho Shift	Psychic	Status	—	100	10	Normal
32	Recover	Normal	Status	—	—	10	Self
36	Reflect Type	Normal	Status	—	—	15	Normal
41	Zen Headbutt	Psychic	Physical	80	90	15	Normal
46	Guard Split	Psychic	Status	—	—	10	Normal
51	Psychic	Psychic	Special	90	100	10	Normal
56	Dragon Pulse	Dragon	Special	85	100	10	Normal
61	Healing Wish	Psychic	Status	—	—	10	Self

TM & HM MOVES

No.	Name	Type	Kind	Pow.	Acc.	PP	Range
TM01	Hone Claws	Dark	Status	—	—	15	Self
TM02	Dragon Claw	Dragon	Physical	80	100	15	Normal
TM03	Psyshock	Psychic	Special	80	100	10	Normal
TM04	Calm Mind	Psychic	Status	—	—	20	Self
TM05	Roar	Normal	Status	—	—	20	Normal
TM06	Toxic	Poison	Status	—	90	10	Normal
TM10	Hidden Power	Normal	Special	60	100	15	Normal
TM11	Sunny Day	Fire	Status	—	—	5	Both Sides
TM13	Ice Beam	Ice	Special	90	100	10	Normal
TM15	Hyper Beam	Normal	Special	150	90	5	Normal
TM16	Light Screen	Psychic	Status	—	—	30	Your Side
TM17	Protect	Normal	Status	—	—	10	Self
TM18	Rain Dance	Water	Status	—	—	5	Both Sides
TM19	Roost	Flying	Status	—	—	10	Self
TM20	Safeguard	Normal	Status	—	—	25	Your Side
TM21	Frustration	Normal	Physical	—	100	20	Normal
TM22	Solar Beam	Grass	Special	120	100	10	Normal
TM24	Thunderbolt	Electric	Special	90	100	15	Normal
TM25	Thunder	Electric	Special	110	70	10	Normal
TM26	Earthquake	Ground	Physical	100	100	10	Adjacent
TM27	Return	Normal	Physical	—	100	20	Normal
TM29	Psychic	Psychic	Special	90	100	10	Normal
TM30	Shadow Ball	Ghost	Special	80	100	15	Normal
TM32	Double Team	Normal	Status	—	—	15	Self
TM33	Reflect	Psychic	Status	—	—	20	Your Side
TM37	Sandstorm	Rock	Status	—	—	10	Both Sides
TM40	Aerial Ace	Flying	Physical	60	—	20	Normal
TM42	Facade	Normal	Physical	70	100	20	Normal
TM44	Rest	Psychic	Status	—	—	10	Self
TM45	Attract	Normal	Status	—	100	15	Normal
TM48	Round	Normal	Special	60	100	15	Normal
TM51	Steel Wing	Steel	Physical	70	90	25	Normal
TM53	Energy Ball	Grass	Special	90	100	10	Normal
TM57	Charge Beam	Electric	Special	50	90	10	Normal
TM65	Shadow Claw	Ghost	Physical	70	100	15	Normal
TM67	Retaliate	Normal	Physical	70	100	5	Normal
TM68	Giga Impact	Normal	Physical	150	90	5	Normal
TM70	Flash	Normal	Status	—	100	20	Normal
TM73	Thunder Wave	Electric	Status	—	100	20	Normal
TM77	Psych Up	Normal	Status	—	—	10	Normal
TM78	Bulldoze	Ground	Physical	60	100	20	Adjacent
TM85	Dream Eater	Psychic	Special	100	100	15	Normal
TM86	Grass Knot	Grass	Special	—	100	20	Normal
TM87	Swagger	Normal	Status	—	90	15	Normal
TM88	Sleep Talk	Normal	Status	—	—	10	Self
TM90	Substitute	Normal	Status	—	—	10	Self
TM94	Secret Power	Normal	Physical	70	100	20	Normal
TM100	Confide	Normal	Status	—	—	20	Normal
HM01	Cut	Normal	Physical	50	95	30	Normal
HM02	Fly	Flying	Physical	90	95	15	Normal
HM03	Surf	Water	Special	90	100	15	Adjacent
HM05	Waterfall	Water	Physical	80	100	15	Normal
HM07	Dive	Water	Physical	80	100	10	Normal

MOVES LEARNED IN EXCHANGE FOR BP

Name	Type	Kind	Pow.	Acc.	PP	Range
Covet	Normal	Physical	60	100	25	Normal
Magic Coat	Psychic	Status	—	—	15	Self
Last Resort	Normal	Physical	140	100	5	Normal
Icy Wind	Ice	Special	55	95	15	Many Others
Zen Headbutt	Psychic	Physical	80	90	15	Normal
Dragon Pulse	Dragon	Special	85	100	10	Normal
Snore	Normal	Special	50	100	15	Normal
Role Play	Psychic	Status	—	—	10	Normal
Tailwind	Flying	Status	—	—	15	Your Side
Shock Wave	Electric	Special	60	—	20	Normal
Water Pulse	Water	Special	60	100	20	Normal
Helping Hand	Normal	Status	—	—	20	1 Ally
Trick	Psychic	Status	—	100	10	Normal
Magic Room	Psychic	Status	—	—	10	Both Sides
Outrage	Dragon	Physical	120	100	10	1 Random

MOVES TAUGHT BY PEOPLE

Name	Type	Kind	Pow.	Acc.	PP	Range
Draco Meteor	Dragon	Special	130	90	5	Normal

Mega Evolution

Mega Latias

Eon Pokémon

Dragon | Psychic

HEIGHT: 5'11" WEIGHT: 114.6 lbs.

♀ only

REQUIRED MEGA STONE

Latiasite

Receive from your mother in Littleroot Town after clearing the Delta Episode (*Pokémon Omega Ruby*) / Obtain on Southern Island (*Pokémon Alpha Sapphire*)

ABILITY

Levitate

HIDDEN ABILITY

—

EGG GROUPS

—

STAT GROWTH RATES

HP ▮▮▮
Attack ▮▮▮▮▮
Defense ▮▮▮▮▮
Sp. Atk ▮▮▮▮▮▮▮
Sp. Def ▮▮▮▮▮▮
Speed ▮▮▮▮▮▮

Damage taken in normal battles

Type		Type	
Normal	×1	Flying	×1
Fire	×0.5	Psychic	×0.5
Water	×0.5	Bug	×2
Grass	×0.5	Rock	×1
Electric	×0.5	Ghost	×2
Ice	×2	Dragon	×2
Fighting	×0.5	Dark	×2
Poison	×1	Steel	×1
! Ground	×1	Fairy	×2

Damage taken in Inverse battles

Type		Type	
Normal	×1	Flying	×1
Fire	×2	Psychic	×2
Water	×2	Bug	×0.5
Grass	×2	Rock	×1
Electric	×2	Ghost	×0.5
Ice	×0.5	Dragon	×0.5
Fighting	×2	Dark	×0.5
Poison	×1	Steel	×1
! Ground	×1	Fairy	×0.5

Can be used in

Inverse Battle
Battle Institute
Battle Maison
Random Matchup (Free Battle)
Random Matchup (Others)

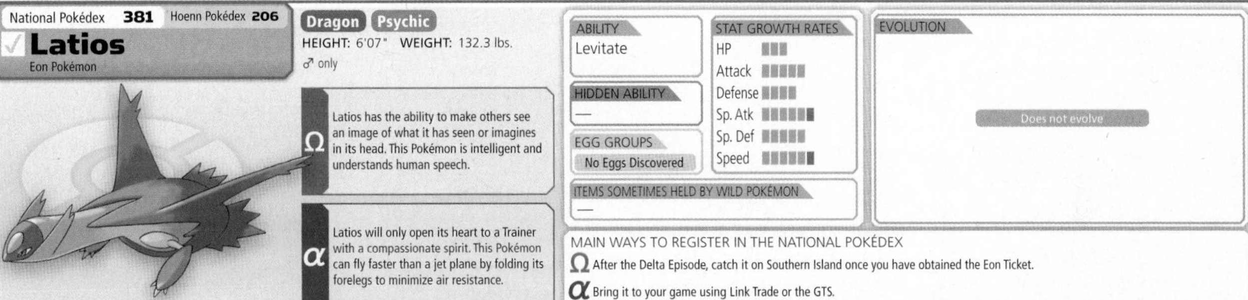

National Pokédex **381** Hoenn Pokédex **206**

Latios

Eon Pokémon

Dragon | Psychic

HEIGHT: 6'07" WEIGHT: 132.3 lbs.

♂ only

Ω Latios has the ability to make others see an image of what it has seen or imagines in its head. This Pokémon is intelligent and understands human speech.

α Latios will only open its heart to a Trainer with a compassionate spirit. This Pokémon can fly faster than a jet plane by folding its forelegs to minimize air resistance.

ABILITY

Levitate

HIDDEN ABILITY

—

EGG GROUPS

No Eggs Discovered

STAT GROWTH RATES

HP ▮▮▮
Attack ▮▮▮▮▮
Defense ▮▮▮▮
Sp. Atk ▮▮▮▮▮▮
Sp. Def ▮▮▮▮▮
Speed ▮▮▮▮▮▮

ITEMS SOMETIMES HELD BY WILD POKÉMON

—

EVOLUTION

Does not evolve

MAIN WAYS TO REGISTER IN THE NATIONAL POKÉDEX

Ω After the Delta Episode, catch it on Southern Island once you have obtained the Eon Ticket.

α Bring it to your game using Link Trade or the GTS.

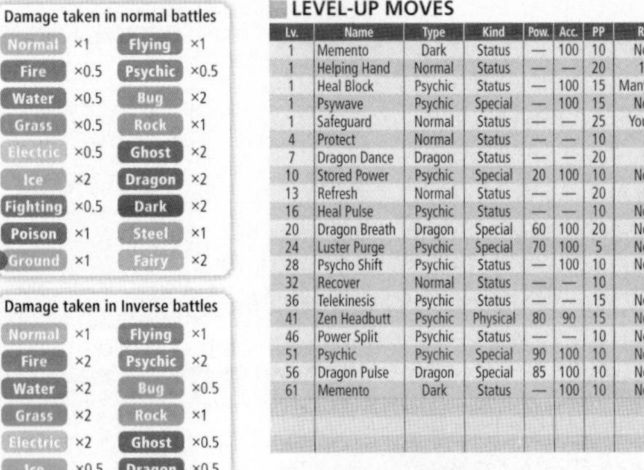

Damage taken in normal battles

Type		Type	
Normal	×1	Flying	×1
Fire	×0.5	Psychic	×0.5
Water	×0.5	Bug	×2
Grass	×0.5	Rock	×1
Electric	×0.5	Ghost	×2
Ice	×2	Dragon	×2
Fighting	×0.5	Dark	×2
Poison	×1	Steel	×1
! Ground	×1	Fairy	×2

Damage taken in Inverse battles

Type		Type	
Normal	×1	Flying	×1
Fire	×2	Psychic	×2
Water	×2	Bug	×0.5
Grass	×2	Rock	×1
Electric	×2	Ghost	×0.5
Ice	×0.5	Dragon	×0.5
Fighting	×2	Dark	×0.5
Poison	×1	Steel	×1
! Ground	×1	Fairy	×0.5

Can be used in

Inverse Battle
Battle Institute
Battle Maison
Random Matchup (Free Battle)
Random Matchup (Others)

LEVEL-UP MOVES

Lv.	Name	Type	Kind	Pow.	Acc.	PP	Range
1	Memento	Dark	Status	—	100	10	Normal
1	Helping Hand	Normal	Status	—	—	20	1 Ally
1	Heal Block	Psychic	Status	—	100	15	Many Others
1	Psywave	Psychic	Special	—	100	15	Normal
1	Safeguard	Normal	Status	—	—	25	Your Side
4	Protect	Normal	Status	—	—	10	Self
7	Dragon Dance	Dragon	Status	—	—	20	Self
10	Stored Power	Psychic	Special	20	100	10	Normal
13	Refresh	Normal	Status	—	—	20	Self
16	Heal Pulse	Psychic	Status	—	—	10	Normal
20	Dragon Breath	Dragon	Special	60	100	20	Normal
24	Luster Purge	Psychic	Special	70	100	5	Normal
28	Psycho Shift	Psychic	Status	—	100	10	Normal
32	Recover	Normal	Status	—	—	10	Self
36	Telekinesis	Psychic	Status	—	—	15	Normal
41	Zen Headbutt	Psychic	Physical	80	90	15	Normal
46	Power Split	Psychic	Status	—	—	10	Normal
51	Psychic	Psychic	Special	90	100	10	Normal
56	Dragon Pulse	Dragon	Special	85	100	10	Normal
61	Memento	Dark	Status	—	100	10	Normal

TM & HM MOVES

No.	Name	Type	Kind	Pow.	Acc.	PP	Range
TM01	Hone Claws	Dark	Status	—	—	15	Self
TM02	Dragon Claw	Dragon	Physical	80	100	15	Normal
TM03	Psyshock	Psychic	Special	80	100	10	Normal
TM04	Calm Mind	Psychic	Status	—	—	20	Self
TM05	Roar	Normal	Status	—	—	20	Normal
TM06	Toxic	Poison	Status	—	90	10	Normal
TM10	Hidden Power	Normal	Special	60	100	15	Normal
TM11	Sunny Day	Fire	Status	—	—	5	Both Sides
TM13	Ice Beam	Ice	Special	90	100	10	Normal
TM15	Hyper Beam	Normal	Special	150	90	5	Normal
TM16	Light Screen	Psychic	Status	—	—	30	Your Side
TM17	Protect	Normal	Status	—	—	10	Self
TM18	Rain Dance	Water	Status	—	—	5	Both Sides
TM19	Roost	Flying	Status	—	—	10	Self
TM20	Safeguard	Normal	Status	—	—	25	Your Side
TM21	Frustration	Normal	Physical	—	100	20	Normal
TM22	Solar Beam	Grass	Special	120	100	10	Normal
TM24	Thunderbolt	Electric	Special	90	100	15	Normal
TM25	Thunder	Electric	Special	110	70	10	Normal
TM26	Earthquake	Ground	Physical	100	100	10	Adjacent
TM27	Return	Normal	Physical	—	100	20	Normal
TM29	Psychic	Psychic	Special	90	100	10	Normal
TM30	Shadow Ball	Ghost	Special	80	100	15	Normal
TM32	Double Team	Normal	Status	—	—	15	Self
TM33	Reflect	Psychic	Status	—	—	20	Your Side
TM37	Sandstorm	Rock	Status	—	—	10	Both Sides
TM40	Aerial Ace	Flying	Physical	60	—	20	Normal
TM42	Facade	Normal	Physical	70	100	20	Normal
TM44	Rest	Psychic	Status	—	—	10	Self
TM45	Attract	Normal	Status	—	100	15	Normal
TM48	Round	Normal	Special	60	100	15	Normal
TM51	Steel Wing	Steel	Physical	70	90	25	Normal
TM53	Energy Ball	Grass	Special	90	100	10	Normal
TM57	Charge Beam	Electric	Special	50	90	10	Normal
TM65	Shadow Claw	Ghost	Physical	70	100	15	Normal
TM67	Retaliate	Normal	Physical	70	100	5	Normal
TM68	Giga Impact	Normal	Physical	150	90	5	Normal
TM70	Flash	Normal	Status	—	100	20	Normal
TM73	Thunder Wave	Electric	Status	—	100	20	Normal
TM77	Psych Up	Normal	Status	—	—	10	Normal
TM78	Bulldoze	Ground	Physical	60	100	20	Adjacent
TM85	Dream Eater	Psychic	Special	100	100	15	Normal
TM86	Grass Knot	Grass	Special	—	100	20	Normal
TM87	Swagger	Normal	Status	—	90	15	Normal
TM88	Sleep Talk	Normal	Status	—	—	10	Self
TM90	Substitute	Normal	Status	—	—	10	Self
TM94	Secret Power	Normal	Physical	70	100	20	Normal
TM100	Confide	Normal	Status	—	—	20	Normal
HM01	Cut	Normal	Physical	50	95	30	Normal
HM02	Fly	Flying	Physical	90	95	15	Normal
HM03	Surf	Water	Special	90	100	15	Adjacent
HM05	Waterfall	Water	Physical	80	100	15	Normal
HM07	Dive	Water	Physical	80	100	10	Normal

MOVES LEARNED IN EXCHANGE FOR BP

Name	Type	Kind	Pow.	Acc.	PP	Range
Magic Coat	Psychic	Status	—	—	15	Self
Last Resort	Normal	Physical	140	100	5	Normal
Icy Wind	Ice	Special	55	95	15	Many Others
Zen Headbutt	Psychic	Physical	80	90	15	Normal
Dragon Pulse	Dragon	Special	85	100	10	Normal
Snore	Normal	Special	50	100	15	Normal
Tailwind	Flying	Status	—	—	15	Your Side
Shock Wave	Electric	Special	60	—	20	Normal
Water Pulse	Water	Special	60	100	20	Normal
Helping Hand	Normal	Status	—	—	20	1 Ally
Trick	Psychic	Status	—	100	10	Normal
Wonder Room	Psychic	Status	—	—	10	Both Sides
Outrage	Dragon	Physical	120	100	10	1 Random

MOVES TAUGHT BY PEOPLE

Name	Type	Kind	Pow.	Acc.	PP	Range
Draco Meteor	Dragon	Special	130	90	5	Normal

Mega Evolution

Mega Latios

Eon Pokémon

Dragon | Psychic

HEIGHT: 7'07" WEIGHT: 154.3 lbs.

♂ only

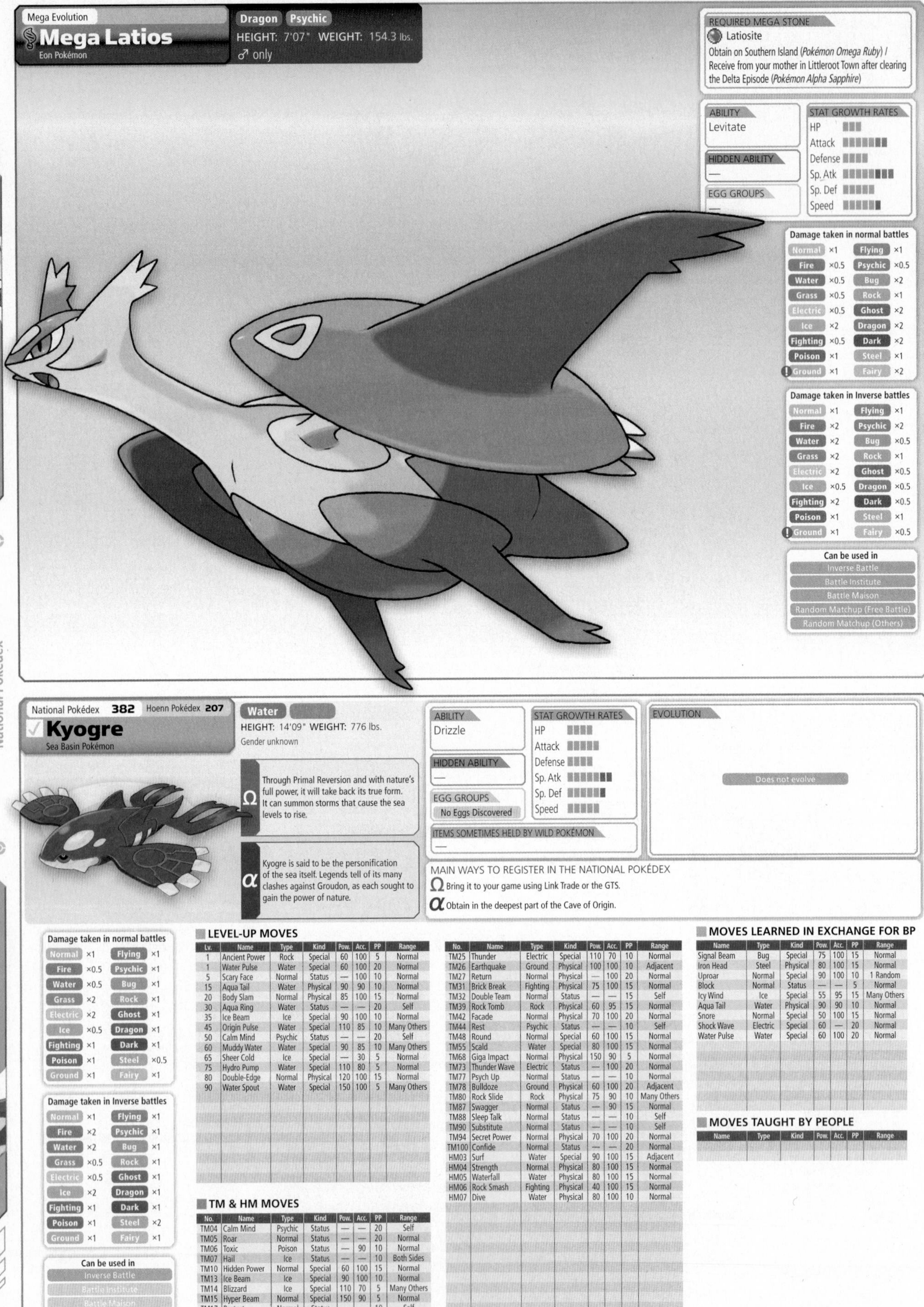

REQUIRED MEGA STONE

Latiosite

Obtain on Southern Island (*Pokémon Omega Ruby*) / Receive from your mother in Littleroot Town after clearing the Delta Episode (*Pokémon Alpha Sapphire*)

ABILITY

Levitate

HIDDEN ABILITY

—

EGG GROUPS

—

STAT GROWTH RATES

HP, Attack, Defense, Sp. Atk, Sp. Def, Speed

Damage taken in normal battles

Type		Type	
Normal	×1	Flying	×1
Fire	×0.5	Psychic	×0.5
Water	×0.5	Bug	×2
Grass	×0.5	Rock	×1
Electric	×0.5	Ghost	×2
Ice	×2	Dragon	×2
Fighting	×0.5	Dark	×2
Poison	×1	Steel	×1
! Ground	×1	Fairy	×2

Damage taken in Inverse battles

Type		Type	
Normal	×1	Flying	×1
Fire	×2	Psychic	×2
Water	×2	Bug	×0.5
Grass	×2	Rock	×1
Electric	×2	Ghost	×0.5
Ice	×0.5	Dragon	×0.5
Fighting	×2	Dark	×0.5
Poison	×1	Steel	×1
! Ground	×1	Fairy	×0.5

Can be used in

- Inverse Battle
- Battle Institute
- Battle Maison
- Random Matchup (Free Battle)
- Random Matchup (Others)

National Pokédex **382** Hoenn Pokédex **207**

Kyogre

Sea Basin Pokémon

Water

HEIGHT: 14'09" WEIGHT: 776 lbs.

Gender unknown

Ω Through Primal Reversion and with nature's full power, it will take back its true form. It can summon storms that cause the sea levels to rise.

α Kyogre is said to be the personification of the sea itself. Legends tell of its many clashes against Groudon, as each sought to gain the power of nature.

ABILITY

Drizzle

HIDDEN ABILITY

—

EGG GROUPS

No Eggs Discovered

STAT GROWTH RATES

HP, Attack, Defense, Sp. Atk, Sp. Def, Speed

ITEMS SOMETIMES HELD BY WILD POKÉMON

—

EVOLUTION

Does not evolve

MAIN WAYS TO REGISTER IN THE NATIONAL POKÉDEX

Ω Bring it to your game using Link Trade or the GTS.

α Obtain in the deepest part of the Cave of Origin.

Damage taken in normal battles

Type		Type	
Normal	×1	Flying	×1
Fire	×0.5	Psychic	×1
Water	×0.5	Bug	×1
Grass	×2	Rock	×1
Electric	×2	Ghost	×1
Ice	×0.5	Dragon	×1
Fighting	×1	Dark	×1
Poison	×1	Steel	×0.5
Ground	×1	Fairy	×1

Damage taken in Inverse battles

Type		Type	
Normal	×1	Flying	×1
Fire	×2	Psychic	×1
Water	×2	Bug	×1
Grass	×0.5	Rock	×1
Electric	×0.5	Ghost	×1
Ice	×2	Dragon	×1
Fighting	×1	Dark	×1
Poison	×1	Steel	×2
Ground	×1	Fairy	×1

Can be used in

- Inverse Battle
- Battle Institute
- Battle Maison
- Random Matchup (Free Battle)
- Random Matchup (Others)

LEVEL-UP MOVES

Lv.	Name	Type	Kind	Pow.	Acc.	PP	Range
1	Ancient Power	Rock	Special	60	100	5	Normal
1	Water Pulse	Water	Special	60	100	20	Normal
5	Scary Face	Normal	Status	—	100	10	Normal
15	Aqua Tail	Water	Physical	90	90	10	Normal
20	Body Slam	Normal	Physical	85	100	15	Normal
30	Aqua Ring	Water	Status	—	—	20	Self
35	Ice Beam	Ice	Special	90	100	10	Normal
45	Origin Pulse	Water	Special	110	85	10	Many Others
50	Calm Mind	Psychic	Status	—	—	20	Self
60	Muddy Water	Water	Special	90	85	10	Many Others
65	Sheer Cold	Ice	Special	—	30	5	Normal
75	Hydro Pump	Water	Special	110	80	5	Normal
80	Double-Edge	Normal	Physical	120	100	15	Normal
90	Water Spout	Water	Special	150	100	5	Many Others

TM & HM MOVES

No.	Name	Type	Kind	Pow.	Acc.	PP	Range
TM04	Calm Mind	Psychic	Status	—	—	20	Self
TM05	Roar	Normal	Status	—	—	20	Normal
TM06	Toxic	Poison	Status	—	90	10	Normal
TM07	Hail	Ice	Status	—	—	10	Both Sides
TM10	Hidden Power	Normal	Special	60	100	15	Normal
TM13	Ice Beam	Ice	Special	90	100	10	Normal
TM14	Blizzard	Ice	Special	110	70	5	Many Others
TM15	Hyper Beam	Normal	Special	150	90	5	Normal
TM17	Protect	Normal	Status	—	—	10	Self
TM18	Rain Dance	Water	Status	—	—	5	Both Sides
TM20	Safeguard	Normal	Status	—	—	25	Your Side
TM21	Frustration	Normal	Physical	—	100	20	Normal
TM24	Thunderbolt	Electric	Special	90	100	15	Normal
TM25	Thunder	Electric	Special	110	70	10	Normal
TM26	Earthquake	Ground	Physical	100	100	10	Adjacent
TM27	Return	Normal	Physical	—	100	20	Normal
TM31	Brick Break	Fighting	Physical	75	100	15	Normal
TM32	Double Team	Normal	Status	—	—	15	Self
TM39	Rock Tomb	Rock	Physical	60	95	15	Normal
TM42	Facade	Normal	Physical	70	100	20	Normal
TM44	Rest	Psychic	Status	—	—	10	Self
TM48	Round	Normal	Special	60	100	15	Normal
TM55	Scald	Water	Special	80	100	15	Normal
TM68	Giga Impact	Normal	Physical	150	90	5	Normal
TM73	Thunder Wave	Electric	Status	—	100	20	Normal
TM77	Psych Up	Normal	Status	—	—	10	Normal
TM78	Bulldoze	Ground	Physical	60	100	20	Adjacent
TM80	Rock Slide	Rock	Physical	75	90	10	Many Others
TM87	Swagger	Normal	Status	—	90	15	Normal
TM88	Sleep Talk	Normal	Status	—	—	10	Self
TM90	Substitute	Normal	Status	—	—	10	Self
TM94	Secret Power	Normal	Physical	70	100	20	Normal
TM100	Confide	Normal	Status	—	—	20	Normal
HM03	Surf	Water	Special	90	100	15	Adjacent
HM04	Strength	Normal	Physical	80	100	15	Normal
HM05	Waterfall	Water	Physical	80	100	15	Normal
HM06	Rock Smash	Fighting	Physical	40	100	15	Normal
HM07	Dive	Water	Physical	80	100	10	Normal

MOVES LEARNED IN EXCHANGE FOR BP

Name	Type	Kind	Pow.	Acc.	PP	Range
Signal Beam	Bug	Special	75	100	15	Normal
Iron Head	Steel	Physical	80	100	15	Normal
Uproar	Normal	Special	90	100	10	1 Random
Block	Normal	Status	—	—	5	Normal
Icy Wind	Ice	Special	55	95	15	Many Others
Aqua Tail	Water	Physical	90	90	10	Normal
Snore	Normal	Special	50	100	15	Normal
Shock Wave	Electric	Special	60	—	20	Normal
Water Pulse	Water	Special	60	100	20	Normal

MOVES TAUGHT BY PEOPLE

Name	Type	Kind	Pow.	Acc.	PP	Range

Primal Reversion

Primal Kyogre

Sea Basin Pokémon

Water

HEIGHT: 32'02" WEIGHT: 948 lbs.

Gender unknown

REQUIRED ORB

Blue Orb

Receive from the old lady at the peak of Mt. Pyre (*Pokémon Omega Ruby*) / Receive from Archie in Sootopolis City (*Pokémon Alpha Sapphire*)

ABILITY

Primordial Sea

HIDDEN ABILITY

—

EGG GROUPS

—

STAT GROWTH RATES

HP / Attack / Defense / Sp. Atk / Sp. Def / Speed

Damage taken in normal battles

Normal	×1	Flying	×1
Fire	×0.5	Psychic	×1
Water	×0.5	Bug	×1
Grass	×2	Rock	×1
Electric	×2	Ghost	×1
Ice	×0.5	Dragon	×1
Fighting	×1	Dark	×1
Poison	×1	Steel	×0.5
Ground	×1	Fairy	×1

Damage taken in Inverse battles

Normal	×1	Flying	×1
Fire	×2	Psychic	×1
Water	×2	Bug	×1
Grass	×0.5	Rock	×1
Electric	×0.5	Ghost	×1
Ice	×2	Dragon	×1
Fighting	×1	Dark	×1
Poison	×1	Steel	×2
Ground	×1	Fairy	×1

Can be used in

Inverse Battle
Battle Institute
Battle Maison
Random Matchup (Free Battle)
Random Matchup (Others)

National Pokédex **383** Hoenn Pokédex **208**

Groudon

Continent Pokémon

Ground

HEIGHT: 11'06" WEIGHT: 2094.4 lbs.

Gender unknown

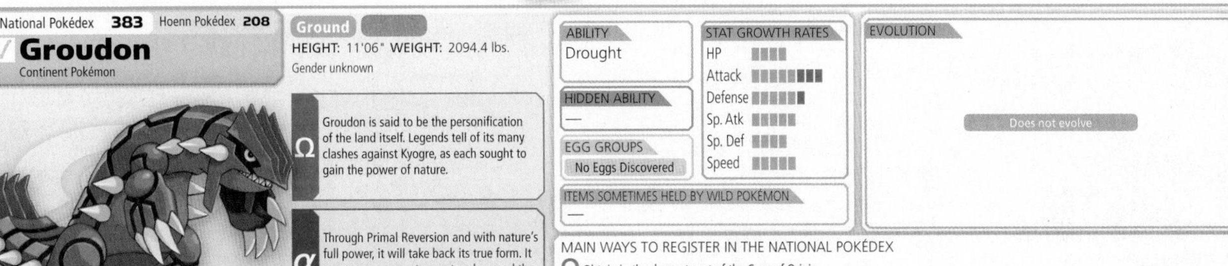

Ω Groudon is said to be the personification of the land itself. Legends tell of its many clashes against Kyogre, as each sought to gain the power of nature.

α Through Primal Reversion and with nature's full power, it will take back its true form. It can cause magma to erupt and expand the landmass of the world.

ABILITY

Drought

HIDDEN ABILITY

—

EGG GROUPS

No Eggs Discovered

STAT GROWTH RATES

HP / Attack / Defense / Sp. Atk / Sp. Def / Speed

ITEMS SOMETIMES HELD BY WILD POKÉMON

—

EVOLUTION

Does not evolve

MAIN WAYS TO REGISTER IN THE NATIONAL POKÉDEX

Ω Obtain in the deepest part of the Cave of Origin.

α Bring it to your game using Link Trade or the GTS.

Damage taken in normal battles

Normal	×1	Flying	×1
Fire	×1	Psychic	×1
Water	×2	Bug	×1
Grass	×2	Rock	×0.5
Electric	×0	Ghost	×1
Ice	×2	Dragon	×1
Fighting	×1	Dark	×1
Poison	×0.5	Steel	×1
Ground	×1	Fairy	×1

Damage taken in Inverse battles

Normal	×1	Flying	×1
Fire	×1	Psychic	×1
Water	×0.5	Bug	×1
Grass	×0.5	Rock	×2
Electric	×2	Ghost	×1
Ice	×0.5	Dragon	×1
Fighting	×1	Dark	×1
Poison	×2	Steel	×1
Ground	×1	Fairy	×1

Can be used in

Inverse Battle
Battle Institute
Battle Maison
Random Matchup (Free Battle)
Random Matchup (Others)

LEVEL-UP MOVES

Lv.	Name	Type	Kind	Pow.	Acc.	PP	Range
1	Ancient Power	Rock	Special	60	100	5	Normal
1	Mud Shot	Ground	Special	55	95	15	Normal
5	Scary Face	Normal	Status	—	100	10	Normal
15	Earth Power	Ground	Special	90	100	10	Normal
20	Lava Plume	Fire	Special	80	100	15	Adjacent
30	Rest	Psychic	Status	—	—	10	Self
35	Earthquake	Ground	Physical	100	100	10	Adjacent
45	Precipice Blades	Ground	Physical	120	85	10	Many Others
50	Bulk Up	Fighting	Status	—	—	20	Self
60	Solar Beam	Grass	Special	120	100	10	Normal
65	Fissure	Ground	Physical	—	30	5	Normal
75	Fire Blast	Fire	Special	110	85	5	Normal
80	Hammer Arm	Fighting	Physical	100	90	10	Normal
90	Eruption	Fire	Special	150	100	5	Many Others

TM & HM MOVES

No.	Name	Type	Kind	Pow.	Acc.	PP	Range
TM01	Hone Claws	Dark	Status	—	—	15	Self
TM02	Dragon Claw	Dragon	Physical	80	100	15	Normal
TM05	Roar	Normal	Status	—	—	20	Normal
TM06	Toxic	Poison	Status	—	90	10	Normal
TM08	Bulk Up	Fighting	Status	—	—	20	Self
TM10	Hidden Power	Normal	Special	60	100	15	Normal
TM11	Sunny Day	Fire	Status	—	—	5	Both Sides
TM15	Hyper Beam	Normal	Special	150	90	5	Normal
TM17	Protect	Normal	Status	—	—	10	Self
TM20	Safeguard	Normal	Status	—	—	25	Your Side
TM21	Frustration	Normal	Physical	—	100	20	Normal
TM22	Solar Beam	Grass	Special	120	100	10	Normal
TM23	Smack Down	Rock	Physical	50	100	15	Normal
TM24	Thunderbolt	Electric	Special	90	100	15	Normal
TM25	Thunder	Electric	Special	110	70	10	Normal
TM26	Earthquake	Ground	Physical	100	100	10	Adjacent
TM27	Return	Normal	Physical	—	100	20	Normal
TM28	Dig	Ground	Physical	80	100	10	Normal
TM31	Brick Break	Fighting	Physical	75	100	15	Normal
TM32	Double Team	Normal	Status	—	—	15	Self
TM35	Flamethrower	Fire	Special	90	100	15	Normal
TM37	Sandstorm	Rock	Status	—	—	10	Both Sides
TM38	Fire Blast	Fire	Special	110	85	5	Normal
TM39	Rock Tomb	Rock	Physical	60	95	15	Normal
TM40	Aerial Ace	Flying	Physical	60	—	20	Normal
TM42	Facade	Normal	Physical	70	100	20	Normal
TM44	Rest	Psychic	Status	—	—	10	Self
TM48	Round	Normal	Special	60	100	15	Normal
TM50	Overheat	Fire	Special	130	90	5	Normal
TM52	Focus Blast	Fighting	Special	120	70	5	Normal
TM56	Fling	Dark	Physical	—	100	10	Normal
TM59	Incinerate	Fire	Special	60	100	15	Many Others
TM65	Shadow Claw	Ghost	Physical	70	100	15	Normal
TM68	Giga Impact	Normal	Physical	150	90	5	Normal
TM69	Rock Polish	Rock	Status	—	—	20	Self
TM71	Stone Edge	Rock	Physical	100	80	5	Normal
TM73	Thunder Wave	Electric	Status	—	100	20	Normal
TM75	Swords Dance	Normal	Status	—	—	20	Self
TM77	Psych Up	Normal	Status	—	—	10	Normal
TM78	Bulldoze	Ground	Physical	60	100	20	Adjacent
TM80	Rock Slide	Rock	Physical	75	90	10	Many Others
TM82	Dragon Tail	Dragon	Physical	60	90	10	Normal
TM87	Swagger	Normal	Status	—	90	15	Normal
TM88	Sleep Talk	Normal	Status	—	—	10	Self
TM90	Substitute	Normal	Status	—	—	10	Self
TM94	Secret Power	Normal	Physical	70	100	20	Normal
TM98	Power-Up Punch	Fighting	Physical	40	100	20	Normal
TM100	Confide	Normal	Status	—	—	20	Normal
HM01	Cut	Normal	Physical	50	95	30	Normal
HM04	Strength	Normal	Physical	80	100	15	Normal
HM06	Rock Smash	Fighting	Physical	40	100	15	Normal

MOVES LEARNED IN EXCHANGE FOR BP

Name	Type	Kind	Pow.	Acc.	PP	Range
Iron Head	Steel	Physical	80	100	15	Normal
Uproar	Normal	Special	90	100	10	1 Random
Thunder Punch	Electric	Physical	75	100	15	Normal
Fire Punch	Fire	Physical	75	100	15	Normal
Block	Normal	Status	—	—	5	Normal
Earth Power	Ground	Special	90	100	10	Normal
Dragon Pulse	Dragon	Special	85	100	10	Normal
Iron Tail	Steel	Physical	100	75	15	Normal
Snore	Normal	Special	50	100	15	Normal
Shock Wave	Electric	Special	60	—	20	Normal
Stealth Rock	Rock	Status	—	—	20	Other Side

MOVES TAUGHT BY PEOPLE

Name	Type	Kind	Pow.	Acc.	PP	Range

Primal Reversion

Primal Groudon

Continent Pokémon

Ground / Fire

HEIGHT: 16'05" WEIGHT: 2204 lbs.

Gender unknown

REQUIRED ORB

Red Orb

Receive from Maxie in Sootopolis City (*Pokémon Omega Ruby*) / Receive from the old lady at the peak of Mt. Pyre (*Pokémon Alpha Sapphire*)

ABILITY

Desolate Land

HIDDEN ABILITY

—

EGG GROUPS

—

STAT GROWTH RATES

HP, Attack, Defense, Sp. Atk, Sp. Def, Speed

Damage taken in normal battles

Type		Type	
Normal	×1	Flying	×1
Fire	×0.5	Psychic	×1
! Water	×4	Bug	×0.5
Grass	×1	Rock	×1
Electric	×0	Ghost	×1
Ice	×1	Dragon	×1
Fighting	×1	Dark	×1
Poison	×0.5	Steel	×0.5
Ground	×2	Fairy	×0.5

Damage taken in Inverse battles

Type		Type	
Normal	×1	Flying	×1
Fire	×2	Psychic	×1
! Water	×0.25	Bug	×2
Grass	×1	Rock	×1
Electric	×2	Ghost	×1
Ice	×1	Dragon	×1
Fighting	×1	Dark	×1
Poison	×2	Steel	×2
Ground	×0.5	Fairy	×2

Can be used in

Inverse Battle
Battle Institute
Battle Maison
Random Matchup (Free Battle)
Random Matchup (Others)

National Pokédex **384** Hoenn Pokédex **209**

Rayquaza

Sky High Pokémon

Dragon / Flying

HEIGHT: 23'00" WEIGHT: 455.2 lbs.

Gender unknown

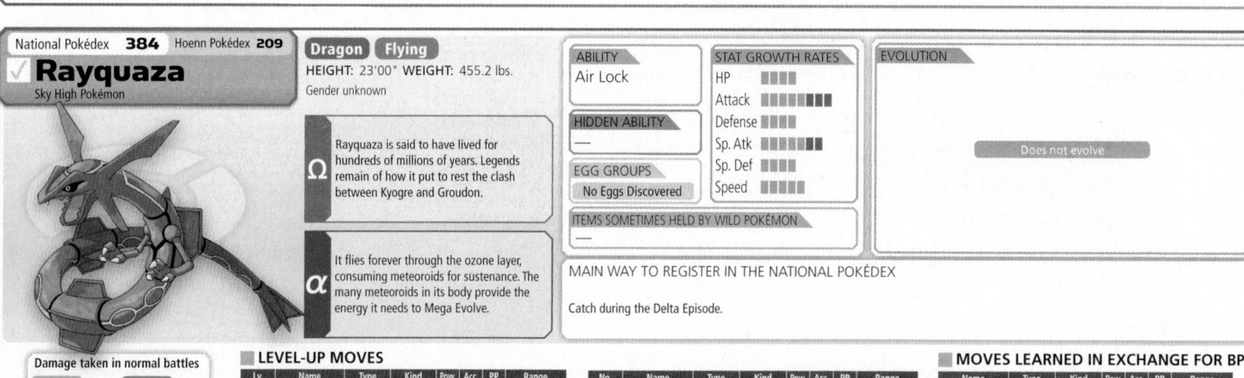

Ω Rayquaza is said to have lived for hundreds of millions of years. Legends remain of how it put to rest the clash between Kyogre and Groudon.

α It flies forever through the ozone layer, consuming meteoroids for sustenance. The many meteoroids in its body provide the energy it needs to Mega Evolve.

ABILITY

Air Lock

HIDDEN ABILITY

—

EGG GROUPS

No Eggs Discovered

STAT GROWTH RATES

HP, Attack, Defense, Sp. Atk, Sp. Def, Speed

ITEMS SOMETIMES HELD BY WILD POKÉMON

—

EVOLUTION

Does not evolve

MAIN WAY TO REGISTER IN THE NATIONAL POKÉDEX

Catch during the Delta Episode.

Damage taken in normal battles

Type		Type	
Normal	×1	Flying	×1
Fire	×0.5	Psychic	×1
Water	×0.5	Bug	×0.5
Grass	×0.25	Rock	×2
Electric	×1	Ghost	×1
Ice	×4	Dragon	×2
Fighting	×0.5	Dark	×1
Poison	×1	Steel	×1
Ground	×0	Fairy	×2

Damage taken in Inverse battles

Type		Type	
Normal	×1	Flying	×1
Fire	×2	Psychic	×1
Water	×2	Bug	×2
Grass	×4	Rock	×0.5
Electric	×1	Ghost	×1
Ice	×0.25	Dragon	×0.5
Fighting	×2	Dark	×1
Poison	×1	Steel	×1
Ground	×2	Fairy	×0.5

Can be used in

Inverse Battle
Battle Institute
Battle Maison
Random Matchup (Free Battle)
Random Matchup (Others)

LEVEL-UP MOVES

Lv.	Name	Type	Kind	Pow.	Acc.	PP	Range
1	Twister	Dragon	Special	40	100	20	Many Others
5	Scary Face	Normal	Status	—	100	10	Normal
15	Ancient Power	Rock	Special	60	100	5	Normal
20	Crunch	Dark	Physical	80	100	15	Normal
30	Air Slash	Flying	Special	75	95	15	Normal
35	Rest	Psychic	Status	—	—	10	Self
45	Extreme Speed	Normal	Physical	80	100	5	Normal
50	Dragon Pulse	Dragon	Special	85	100	10	Normal
60	Dragon Dance	Dragon	Status	—	—	20	Self
65	Fly	Flying	Physical	90	95	15	Normal
75	Hyper Voice	Normal	Special	90	100	10	Many Others
80	Outrage	Dragon	Physical	120	100	10	1 Random
90	Hyper Beam	Normal	Special	150	90	5	Normal

TM & HM MOVES

No.	Name	Type	Kind	Pow.	Acc.	PP	Range
TM01	Hone Claws	Dark	Status	—	—	15	Self
TM02	Dragon Claw	Dragon	Physical	80	100	15	Normal
TM05	Roar	Normal	Status	—	—	20	Normal
TM06	Toxic	Poison	Status	—	90	10	Normal
TM08	Bulk Up	Fighting	Status	—	—	20	Self
TM10	Hidden Power	Normal	Special	60	100	15	Normal
TM11	Sunny Day	Fire	Status	—	—	5	Both Sides
TM13	Ice Beam	Ice	Special	90	100	10	Normal
TM14	Blizzard	Ice	Special	110	70	5	Many Others
TM15	Hyper Beam	Normal	Special	150	90	5	Normal
TM17	Protect	Normal	Status	—	—	10	Self
TM18	Rain Dance	Water	Status	—	—	5	Both Sides
TM21	Frustration	Normal	Physical	—	100	20	Normal
TM22	Solar Beam	Grass	Special	120	100	10	Normal
TM24	Thunderbolt	Electric	Special	90	100	15	Normal
TM25	Thunder	Electric	Special	110	70	10	Normal
TM26	Earthquake	Ground	Physical	100	100	10	Adjacent
TM27	Return	Normal	Physical	—	100	20	Normal
TM31	Brick Break	Fighting	Physical	75	100	15	Normal
TM32	Double Team	Normal	Status	—	—	15	Self
TM35	Flamethrower	Fire	Special	90	100	15	Normal
TM37	Sandstorm	Rock	Status	—	—	10	Both Sides
TM38	Fire Blast	Fire	Special	110	85	5	Normal
TM39	Rock Tomb	Rock	Physical	60	95	15	Normal
TM40	Aerial Ace	Flying	Physical	60	—	20	Normal
TM42	Facade	Normal	Physical	70	100	20	Normal
TM44	Rest	Psychic	Status	—	—	10	Self
TM48	Round	Normal	Special	60	100	15	Normal
TM49	Echoed Voice	Normal	Special	40	100	15	Normal
TM50	Overheat	Fire	Special	130	90	5	Normal
TM52	Focus Blast	Fighting	Special	120	70	5	Normal
TM53	Energy Ball	Grass	Special	90	100	10	Normal
TM56	Fling	Dark	Physical	—	100	10	Normal
TM58	Sky Drop	Flying	Physical	60	100	10	Normal
TM59	Incinerate	Fire	Special	60	100	15	Many Others
TM65	Shadow Claw	Ghost	Physical	70	100	15	Normal
TM68	Giga Impact	Normal	Physical	150	90	5	Normal
TM71	Stone Edge	Rock	Physical	100	80	5	Normal
TM73	Thunder Wave	Electric	Status	—	100	20	Normal
TM74	Gyro Ball	Steel	Physical	—	100	5	Normal
TM75	Swords Dance	Normal	Status	—	—	20	Self
TM77	Psych Up	Normal	Status	—	—	10	Normal
TM78	Buildoze	Ground	Physical	60	100	20	Adjacent
TM80	Rock Slide	Rock	Physical	75	90	10	Many Others
TM82	Dragon Tail	Dragon	Physical	60	90	10	Normal
TM87	Swagger	Normal	Status	—	90	15	Normal
TM88	Sleep Talk	Normal	Status	—	—	10	Self
TM90	Substitute	Normal	Status	—	—	10	Self
TM94	Secret Power	Normal	Physical	70	100	20	Normal
TM100	Confide	Normal	Status	—	—	20	Normal
HM02	Fly	Flying	Physical	90	95	15	Normal
HM03	Surf	Water	Special	90	100	15	Adjacent
HM04	Strength	Normal	Physical	80	100	15	Normal
HM05	Waterfall	Water	Physical	80	100	15	Normal
HM06	Rock Smash	Fighting	Physical	40	100	15	Normal
HM07	Dive	Water	Physical	80	100	10	Normal

MOVES LEARNED IN EXCHANGE FOR BP

Name	Type	Kind	Pow.	Acc.	PP	Range
Iron Head	Steel	Physical	80	100	15	Normal
Uproar	Normal	Special	90	100	10	1 Random
Earth Power	Ground	Special	90	100	10	Normal
Icy Wind	Ice	Special	55	95	15	Many Others
Aqua Tail	Water	Physical	90	90	10	Normal
Dragon Pulse	Dragon	Special	85	100	10	Normal
Hyper Voice	Normal	Special	90	100	10	Many Others
Iron Tail	Steel	Physical	100	75	15	Normal
Bind	Normal	Physical	15	85	20	Normal
Snore	Normal	Special	50	100	15	Normal
Tailwind	Flying	Status	—	—	15	Your Side
Shock Wave	Electric	Special	60	—	20	Normal
Water Pulse	Water	Special	60	100	20	Normal
Outrage	Dragon	Physical	120	100	10	1 Random

MOVES TAUGHT BY PEOPLE

Name	Type	Kind	Pow.	Acc.	PP	Range
Draco Meteor	Dragon	Special	130	90	5	Normal
Dragon Ascent	Flying	Physical	120	100	5	Normal

Mega Evolution

Mega Rayquaza

Sky High Pokémon

Dragon | Flying

HEIGHT: 35'05" WEIGHT: 864.2 lbs.

Gender unknown

REQUIRED MOVE

Teach Rayquaza the Dragon Ascent move after catching it during the Delta Episode.

ABILITY

Delta Stream

HIDDEN ABILITY

—

EGG GROUPS

—

STAT GROWTH RATES

HP, Attack, Defense, Sp. Atk, Sp. Def, Speed

Damage taken in normal battles

Type		Type	
Normal	×1	Flying	×1
Fire	×0.5	Psychic	×1
Water	×0.5	Bug	×0.5
Grass	×0.25	! Rock	×2
! Electric	×1	Ghost	×1
! Ice	×4	Dragon	×2
Fighting	×0.5	Dark	×1
Poison	×1	Steel	×1
Ground	×0	Fairy	×2

Damage taken in Inverse battles

Type		Type	
Normal	×1	Flying	×1
Fire	×2	Psychic	×1
Water	×2	! Bug	×2
! Grass	×4	Rock	×0.5
Electric	×1	Ghost	×1
Ice	×0.25	Dragon	×0.5
! Fighting	×2	Dark	×1
Poison	×1	Steel	×1
! Ground	×2	Fairy	×0.5

Can be used in

Inverse Battle

Battle Institute

Battle Maison

Random Matchup (Free Battle)

Random Matchup (Others)

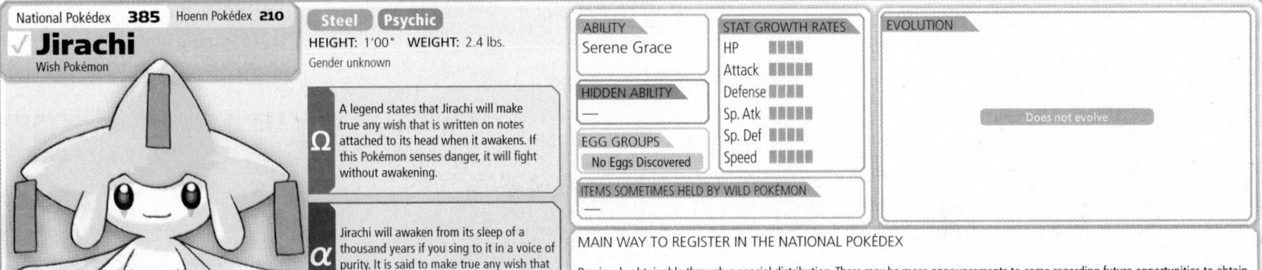

National Pokédex **385** Hoenn Pokédex **210**

✓ Jirachi

Wish Pokémon

Steel | Psychic

HEIGHT: 1'00" WEIGHT: 2.4 lbs.

Gender unknown

Ω A legend states that Jirachi will make true any wish that is written on notes attached to its head when it awakens. If this Pokémon senses danger, it will fight without awakening.

α Jirachi will awaken from its sleep of a thousand years if you sing to it in a voice of purity. It is said to make true any wish that people desire.

ABILITY

Serene Grace

HIDDEN ABILITY

—

EGG GROUPS

No Eggs Discovered

STAT GROWTH RATES

HP, Attack, Defense, Sp. Atk, Sp. Def, Speed

ITEMS SOMETIMES HELD BY WILD POKÉMON

—

EVOLUTION

Does not evolve

MAIN WAY TO REGISTER IN THE NATIONAL POKÉDEX

Previously obtainable through a special distribution. There may be more announcements to come regarding future opportunities to obtain it, so keep checking the official Pokémon website.

Damage taken in normal battles

Type		Type	
Normal	×0.5	Flying	×0.5
Fire	×2	Psychic	×0.25
Water	×1	Bug	×1
Grass	×0.5	Rock	×0.5
Electric	×1	Ghost	×2
Ice	×0.5	Dragon	×0.5
Fighting	×1	Dark	×2
Poison	×0	Steel	×0.5
Ground	×2	Fairy	×0.5

Damage taken in Inverse battles

Type		Type	
Normal	×2	Flying	×2
Fire	×0.5	Psychic	×4
Water	×1	Bug	×1
Grass	×2	Rock	×2
Electric	×1	Ghost	×0.5
Ice	×2	Dragon	×2
Fighting	×1	Dark	×0.5
Poison	×2	Steel	×2
Ground	×0.5	Fairy	×2

Can be used in

Inverse Battle

Battle Institute

Battle Maison

Random Matchup (Free Battle)

Random Matchup (Others)

LEVEL-UP MOVES

Lv.	Name	Type	Kind	Pow.	Acc.	PP	Range
1	Wish	Normal	Status	—	—	10	Self
1	Confusion	Psychic	Special	50	100	25	Normal
5	Rest	Psychic	Status	—	—	10	Self
10	Swift	Normal	Special	60	—	20	Many Others
15	Helping Hand	Normal	Status	—	—	20	1 Ally
20	Psychic	Psychic	Special	90	100	10	Normal
25	Refresh	Normal	Status	—	—	20	Self
30	Rest	Psychic	Status	—	—	10	Self
35	Zen Headbutt	Psychic	Physical	80	90	15	Normal
40	Double-Edge	Normal	Physical	120	100	15	Normal
45	Gravity	Psychic	Status	—	—	5	Both Sides
50	Healing Wish	Psychic	Status	—	—	10	Self
55	Future Sight	Psychic	Special	120	100	10	Normal
60	Cosmic Power	Psychic	Status	—	—	20	Self
65	Last Resort	Normal	Physical	140	100	5	Normal
70	Doom Desire	Steel	Special	140	100	5	Normal

TM & HM MOVES

No.	Name	Type	Kind	Pow.	Acc.	PP	Range
TM03	Psyshock	Psychic	Special	80	100	10	Normal
TM04	Calm Mind	Psychic	Status	—	—	20	Self
TM06	Toxic	Poison	Status	—	90	10	Normal
TM10	Hidden Power	Normal	Special	60	100	15	Normal
TM11	Sunny Day	Fire	Status	—	—	5	Both Sides
TM15	Hyper Beam	Normal	Special	150	90	5	Normal
TM16	Light Screen	Psychic	Status	—	—	30	Your Side
TM17	Protect	Normal	Status	—	—	10	Self
TM18	Rain Dance	Water	Status	—	—	5	Both Sides
TM20	Safeguard	Normal	Status	—	—	25	Your Side
TM21	Frustration	Normal	Physical	—	100	20	Normal
TM24	Thunderbolt	Electric	Special	90	100	15	Normal
TM25	Thunder	Electric	Special	110	70	10	Normal
TM27	Return	Normal	Physical	—	100	20	Normal
TM29	Psychic	Psychic	Special	90	100	10	Normal
TM30	Shadow Ball	Ghost	Special	80	100	15	Normal
TM32	Double Team	Normal	Status	—	—	15	Self
TM33	Reflect	Psychic	Status	—	—	20	Your Side
TM37	Sandstorm	Rock	Status	—	—	10	Both Sides
TM40	Aerial Ace	Flying	Physical	60	—	20	Normal
TM42	Facade	Normal	Physical	70	100	20	Normal
TM44	Rest	Psychic	Status	—	—	10	Self
TM48	Round	Normal	Special	60	100	15	Normal
TM53	Energy Ball	Grass	Special	90	100	10	Normal
TM56	Fling	Dark	Physical	—	100	10	Normal
TM57	Charge Beam	Electric	Special	50	90	10	Normal
TM68	Giga Impact	Normal	Physical	150	90	5	Normal
TM70	Flash	Normal	Status	—	100	20	Normal
TM73	Thunder Wave	Electric	Status	—	100	20	Normal
TM77	Psych Up	Normal	Status	—	—	10	Normal
TM85	Dream Eater	Psychic	Special	100	100	15	Normal
TM86	Grass Knot	Grass	Special	—	100	20	Normal
TM87	Swagger	Normal	Status	—	90	15	Normal
TM88	Sleep Talk	Normal	Status	—	—	10	Self
TM89	U-turn	Bug	Physical	70	100	20	Normal
TM90	Substitute	Normal	Status	—	—	10	Self
TM91	Flash Cannon	Steel	Special	80	100	10	Normal
TM92	Trick Room	Psychic	Status	—	—	5	Both Sides
TM94	Secret Power	Normal	Physical	70	100	20	Normal
TM98	Power-Up Punch	Fighting	Physical	40	100	20	Normal
TM99	Dazzling Gleam	Fairy	Special	80	100	10	Many Others
TM100	Confide	Normal	Status	—	—	20	Normal

MOVES LEARNED IN EXCHANGE FOR BP

Name	Type	Kind	Pow.	Acc.	PP	Range
Signal Beam	Bug	Special	75	100	15	Normal
Iron Head	Steel	Physical	80	100	15	Normal
Uproar	Normal	Special	90	100	10	1 Random
Thunder Punch	Electric	Physical	75	100	15	Normal
Fire Punch	Fire	Physical	75	100	15	Normal
Ice Punch	Ice	Physical	75	100	15	Normal
Magic Coat	Psychic	Status	—	—	15	Self
Gravity	Psychic	Status	—	—	5	Both Sides
Iron Defense	Steel	Status	—	—	15	Self
Last Resort	Normal	Physical	140	100	5	Normal
Icy Wind	Ice	Special	55	95	15	Many Others
Zen Headbutt	Psychic	Physical	80	90	15	Normal
Snore	Normal	Special	50	100	15	Normal
Drain Punch	Fighting	Physical	75	100	10	Normal
Shock Wave	Electric	Special	60	—	20	Normal
Water Pulse	Water	Special	60	100	20	Normal
Helping Hand	Normal	Status	—	—	20	1 Ally
Trick	Psychic	Status	—	100	10	Normal
Magic Room	Psychic	Status	—	—	10	Both Sides
Recycle	Normal	Status	—	—	10	Self
Stealth Rock	Rock	Status	—	—	20	Other Side
Skill Swap	Psychic	Status	—	—	10	Normal

MOVES TAUGHT BY PEOPLE

Name	Type	Kind	Pow.	Acc.	PP	Range

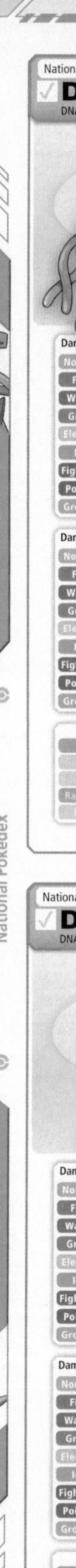

National Pokédex **386** Hoenn Pokédex **211**

✓ Deoxys — Normal Forme

DNA Pokémon

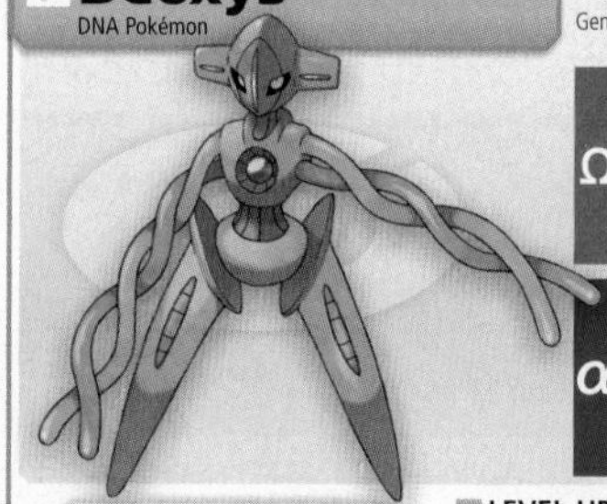

Psychic

HEIGHT: 5'07" WEIGHT: 134 lbs.

Gender unknown

Ω The DNA of a space virus underwent a sudden mutation upon exposure to a laser beam and resulted in Deoxys. The crystalline organ on this Pokémon's chest appears to be its brain.

α Deoxys emerged from a virus that came from space. It is highly intelligent and wields psychokinetic powers. This Pokémon shoots lasers from the crystalline organ on its chest.

ABILITY
Pressure

HIDDEN ABILITY
—

EGG GROUPS
No Eggs Discovered

STAT GROWTH RATES
HP
Attack
Defense
Sp. Atk
Sp. Def
Speed

ITEMS SOMETIMES HELD BY WILD POKÉMON
—

EVOLUTION
Does not evolve

MAIN WAY TO REGISTER IN THE NATIONAL POKÉDEX

Catch during the Delta Episode.

Damage taken in normal battles

Type		Type	
Normal	×1	Flying	×1
Fire	×1	Psychic	×0.5
Water	×1	Bug	×2
Grass	×1	Rock	×1
Electric	×1	Ghost	×2
Ice	×1	Dragon	×1
Fighting	×0.5	Dark	×2
Poison	×1	Steel	×1
Ground	×1	Fairy	×1

Damage taken in Inverse battles

Type		Type	
Normal	×1	Flying	×1
Fire	×1	Psychic	×2
Water	×1	Bug	×0.5
Grass	×1	Rock	×1
Electric	×1	Ghost	×0.5
Ice	×1	Dragon	×1
Fighting	×2	Dark	×0.5
Poison	×1	Steel	×1
Ground	×1	Fairy	×1

Can be used in

Inverse Battle
Battle Institute
Battle Maison
Random Matchup (Free Battle)
Random Matchup (Others)

LEVEL-UP MOVES

Lv.	Name	Type	Kind	Pow.	Acc.	PP	Range
1	Leer	Normal	Status	—	100	30	Many Others
1	Wrap	Normal	Physical	15	90	20	Normal
7	Night Shade	Ghost	Special	—	100	15	Normal
13	Teleport	Psychic	Status	—	—	20	Self
19	Knock Off	Dark	Physical	65	100	20	Normal
25	Pursuit	Dark	Physical	40	100	20	Normal
31	Psychic	Psychic	Special	90	100	10	Normal
37	Snatch	Dark	Status	—	—	10	Self
43	Psycho Shift	Psychic	Status	—	100	10	Normal
49	Zen Headbutt	Psychic	Physical	80	90	15	Normal
55	Cosmic Power	Psychic	Status	—	—	20	Self
61	Recover	Normal	Status	—	—	10	Self
67	Psycho Boost	Psychic	Special	140	90	5	Normal
73	Hyper Beam	Normal	Special	150	90	5	Normal

TM & HM MOVES

No.	Name	Type	Kind	Pow.	Acc.	PP	Range
TM03	Psyshock	Psychic	Special	80	100	10	Normal
TM04	Calm Mind	Psychic	Status	—	—	20	Self
TM06	Toxic	Poison	Status	—	90	10	Normal
TM10	Hidden Power	Normal	Special	60	100	15	Normal
TM11	Sunny Day	Fire	Status	—	—	5	Both Sides
TM12	Taunt	Dark	Status	—	100	20	Normal
TM13	Ice Beam	Ice	Special	90	100	10	Normal
TM15	Hyper Beam	Normal	Special	150	90	5	Normal
TM16	Light Screen	Psychic	Status	—	—	30	Your Side
TM17	Protect	Normal	Status	—	—	10	Self
TM18	Rain Dance	Water	Status	—	—	5	Both Sides
TM20	Safeguard	Normal	Status	—	—	25	Your Side
TM21	Frustration	Normal	Physical	—	100	20	Normal
TM22	Solar Beam	Grass	Special	120	100	10	Normal
TM24	Thunderbolt	Electric	Special	90	100	15	Normal
TM25	Thunder	Electric	Special	110	70	10	Normal
TM27	Return	Normal	Physical	—	100	20	Normal
TM29	Psychic	Psychic	Special	90	100	10	Normal
TM30	Shadow Ball	Ghost	Special	80	100	15	Normal
TM31	Brick Break	Fighting	Physical	75	100	15	Normal
TM32	Double Team	Normal	Status	—	—	15	Self
TM33	Reflect	Psychic	Status	—	—	20	Your Side
TM39	Rock Tomb	Rock	Physical	60	95	15	Normal
TM40	Aerial Ace	Flying	Physical	60	—	20	Normal
TM41	Torment	Dark	Status	—	100	15	Normal
TM42	Facade	Normal	Physical	70	100	20	Normal
TM44	Rest	Psychic	Status	—	—	10	Self
TM47	Low Sweep	Fighting	Physical	65	100	20	Normal
TM48	Round	Normal	Special	60	100	15	Normal
TM52	Focus Blast	Fighting	Special	120	70	5	Normal
TM53	Energy Ball	Grass	Special	90	100	10	Normal
TM56	Fling	Dark	Physical	—	100	10	Normal
TM57	Charge Beam	Electric	Special	50	90	10	Normal
TM68	Giga Impact	Normal	Physical	150	90	5	Normal
TM70	Flash	Normal	Status	—	100	20	Normal
TM73	Thunder Wave	Electric	Status	—	100	20	Normal
TM77	Psych Up	Normal	Status	—	—	10	Normal
TM80	Rock Slide	Rock	Physical	75	90	10	Many Others
TM84	Poison Jab	Poison	Physical	80	100	20	Normal
TM85	Dream Eater	Psychic	Special	100	100	15	Normal
TM86	Grass Knot	Grass	Special	—	100	20	Normal
TM87	Swagger	Normal	Status	—	90	15	Normal
TM88	Sleep Talk	Normal	Status	—	—	10	Self
TM90	Substitute	Normal	Status	—	—	10	Self
TM91	Flash Cannon	Steel	Special	80	100	10	Normal
TM92	Trick Room	Psychic	Status	—	—	5	Both Sides
TM94	Secret Power	Normal	Physical	70	100	20	Normal
TM97	Dark Pulse	Dark	Special	80	100	15	Normal
TM98	Power-Up Punch	Fighting	Physical	40	100	20	Normal
TM100	Confide	Normal	Status	—	—	20	Normal
HM01	Cut	Normal	Physical	50	95	30	Normal
HM04	Strength	Normal	Physical	80	100	15	Normal
HM06	Rock Smash	Fighting	Physical	40	100	15	Normal

MOVES LEARNED IN EXCHANGE FOR BP

Name	Type	Kind	Pow.	Acc.	PP	Range
Signal Beam	Bug	Special	75	100	15	Normal
Low Kick	Fighting	Physical	—	100	20	Normal
Thunder Punch	Electric	Physical	75	100	15	Normal
Fire Punch	Fire	Physical	75	100	15	Normal
Ice Punch	Ice	Physical	75	100	15	Normal
Magic Coat	Psychic	Status	—	—	15	Self
Gravity	Psychic	Status	—	—	5	Both Sides
Icy Wind	Ice	Special	55	95	15	Many Others
Zen Headbutt	Psychic	Physical	80	90	15	Normal
Bind	Normal	Physical	15	85	20	Normal
Snore	Normal	Special	50	100	15	Normal
Knock Off	Dark	Physical	65	100	20	Normal
Role Play	Psychic	Status	—	—	10	Normal
Drain Punch	Fighting	Physical	75	100	10	Normal
Focus Punch	Fighting	Physical	150	100	20	Normal
Shock Wave	Electric	Special	60	—	20	Normal
Water Pulse	Water	Special	60	100	20	Normal
Trick	Psychic	Status	—	100	10	Normal
Wonder Room	Psychic	Status	—	—	10	Both Sides
Recycle	Normal	Status	—	—	10	Self
Snatch	Dark	Status	—	—	10	Self
Stealth Rock	Rock	Status	—	—	20	Other Side
Skill Swap	Psychic	Status	—	—	10	Normal

MOVES TAUGHT BY PEOPLE

Name	Type	Kind	Pow.	Acc.	PP	Range

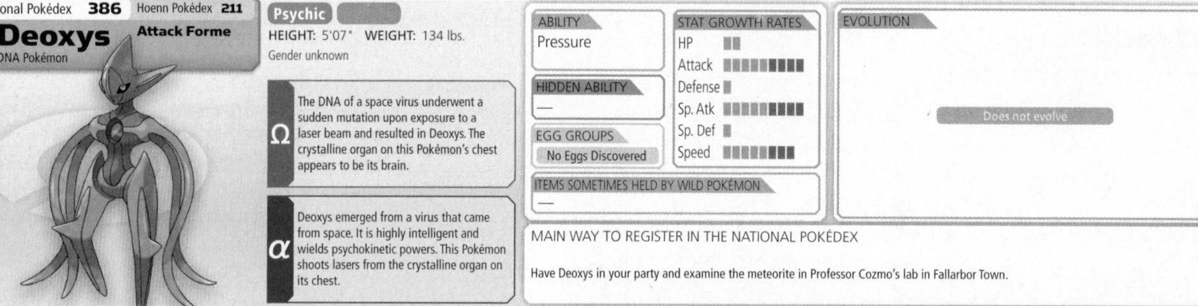

National Pokédex **386** Hoenn Pokédex **211**

✓ Deoxys — Attack Forme

DNA Pokémon

Psychic

HEIGHT: 5'07" WEIGHT: 134 lbs.

Gender unknown

Ω The DNA of a space virus underwent a sudden mutation upon exposure to a laser beam and resulted in Deoxys. The crystalline organ on this Pokémon's chest appears to be its brain.

α Deoxys emerged from a virus that came from space. It is highly intelligent and wields psychokinetic powers. This Pokémon shoots lasers from the crystalline organ on its chest.

ABILITY
Pressure

HIDDEN ABILITY
—

EGG GROUPS
No Eggs Discovered

STAT GROWTH RATES
HP
Attack
Defense
Sp. Atk
Sp. Def
Speed

ITEMS SOMETIMES HELD BY WILD POKÉMON
—

EVOLUTION
Does not evolve

MAIN WAY TO REGISTER IN THE NATIONAL POKÉDEX

Have Deoxys in your party and examine the meteorite in Professor Cozmo's lab in Fallarbor Town.

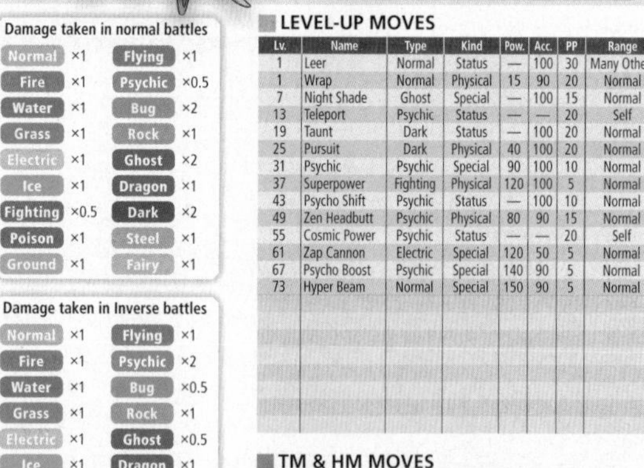

Damage taken in normal battles

Type		Type	
Normal	×1	Flying	×1
Fire	×1	Psychic	×0.5
Water	×1	Bug	×2
Grass	×1	Rock	×1
Electric	×1	Ghost	×2
Ice	×1	Dragon	×1
Fighting	×0.5	Dark	×2
Poison	×1	Steel	×1
Ground	×1	Fairy	×1

Damage taken in Inverse battles

Type		Type	
Normal	×1	Flying	×1
Fire	×1	Psychic	×2
Water	×1	Bug	×0.5
Grass	×1	Rock	×1
Electric	×1	Ghost	×0.5
Ice	×1	Dragon	×1
Fighting	×2	Dark	×0.5
Poison	×1	Steel	×1
Ground	×1	Fairy	×1

Can be used in

Inverse Battle
Battle Institute
Battle Maison
Random Matchup (Free Battle)
Random Matchup (Others)

LEVEL-UP MOVES

Lv.	Name	Type	Kind	Pow.	Acc.	PP	Range
1	Leer	Normal	Status	—	100	30	Many Others
1	Wrap	Normal	Physical	15	90	20	Normal
7	Night Shade	Ghost	Special	—	100	15	Normal
13	Teleport	Psychic	Status	—	—	20	Self
19	Taunt	Dark	Status	—	100	20	Normal
25	Pursuit	Dark	Physical	40	100	20	Normal
31	Psychic	Psychic	Special	90	100	10	Normal
37	Superpower	Fighting	Physical	120	100	5	Normal
43	Psycho Shift	Psychic	Status	—	100	10	Normal
49	Zen Headbutt	Psychic	Physical	80	90	15	Normal
55	Cosmic Power	Psychic	Status	—	—	20	Self
61	Zap Cannon	Electric	Special	120	50	5	Normal
67	Psycho Boost	Psychic	Special	140	90	5	Normal
73	Hyper Beam	Normal	Special	150	90	5	Normal

TM & HM MOVES

No.	Name	Type	Kind	Pow.	Acc.	PP	Range
TM03	Psyshock	Psychic	Special	80	100	10	Normal
TM04	Calm Mind	Psychic	Status	—	—	20	Self
TM06	Toxic	Poison	Status	—	90	10	Normal
TM10	Hidden Power	Normal	Special	60	100	15	Normal
TM11	Sunny Day	Fire	Status	—	—	5	Both Sides
TM12	Taunt	Dark	Status	—	100	20	Normal
TM13	Ice Beam	Ice	Special	90	100	10	Normal
TM15	Hyper Beam	Normal	Special	150	90	5	Normal
TM16	Light Screen	Psychic	Status	—	—	30	Your Side
TM17	Protect	Normal	Status	—	—	10	Self
TM18	Rain Dance	Water	Status	—	—	5	Both Sides
TM20	Safeguard	Normal	Status	—	—	25	Your Side
TM21	Frustration	Normal	Physical	—	100	20	Normal
TM22	Solar Beam	Grass	Special	120	100	10	Normal
TM24	Thunderbolt	Electric	Special	90	100	15	Normal
TM25	Thunder	Electric	Special	110	70	10	Normal
TM27	Return	Normal	Physical	—	100	20	Normal
TM29	Psychic	Psychic	Special	90	100	10	Normal
TM30	Shadow Ball	Ghost	Special	80	100	15	Normal
TM31	Brick Break	Fighting	Physical	75	100	15	Normal
TM32	Double Team	Normal	Status	—	—	15	Self
TM33	Reflect	Psychic	Status	—	—	20	Your Side
TM39	Rock Tomb	Rock	Physical	60	95	15	Normal
TM40	Aerial Ace	Flying	Physical	60	—	20	Normal
TM41	Torment	Dark	Status	—	100	15	Normal
TM42	Facade	Normal	Physical	70	100	20	Normal
TM44	Rest	Psychic	Status	—	—	10	Self
TM47	Low Sweep	Fighting	Physical	65	100	20	Normal
TM48	Round	Normal	Special	60	100	15	Normal
TM52	Focus Blast	Fighting	Special	120	70	5	Normal
TM53	Energy Ball	Grass	Special	90	100	10	Normal
TM56	Fling	Dark	Physical	—	100	10	Normal
TM57	Charge Beam	Electric	Special	50	90	10	Normal
TM68	Giga Impact	Normal	Physical	150	90	5	Normal
TM70	Flash	Normal	Status	—	100	20	Normal
TM73	Thunder Wave	Electric	Status	—	100	20	Normal
TM77	Psych Up	Normal	Status	—	—	10	Normal
TM80	Rock Slide	Rock	Physical	75	90	10	Many Others
TM84	Poison Jab	Poison	Physical	80	100	20	Normal
TM85	Dream Eater	Psychic	Special	100	100	15	Normal
TM86	Grass Knot	Grass	Special	—	100	20	Normal
TM87	Swagger	Normal	Status	—	90	15	Normal
TM88	Sleep Talk	Normal	Status	—	—	10	Self
TM90	Substitute	Normal	Status	—	—	10	Self
TM91	Flash Cannon	Steel	Special	80	100	10	Normal
TM92	Trick Room	Psychic	Status	—	—	5	Both Sides
TM94	Secret Power	Normal	Physical	70	100	20	Normal
TM97	Dark Pulse	Dark	Special	80	100	15	Normal
TM98	Power-Up Punch	Fighting	Physical	40	100	20	Normal
TM100	Confide	Normal	Status	—	—	20	Normal
HM01	Cut	Normal	Physical	50	95	30	Normal
HM04	Strength	Normal	Physical	80	100	15	Normal
HM06	Rock Smash	Fighting	Physical	40	100	15	Normal

MOVES LEARNED IN EXCHANGE FOR BP

Name	Type	Kind	Pow.	Acc.	PP	Range
Signal Beam	Bug	Special	75	100	15	Normal
Low Kick	Fighting	Physical	—	100	20	Normal
Magic Coat	Psychic	Status	—	—	15	Self
Gravity	Psychic	Status	—	—	5	Both Sides
Superpower	Fighting	Physical	120	100	5	Normal
Zen Headbutt	Psychic	Physical	80	90	15	Normal
Bind	Normal	Physical	15	85	20	Normal
Snore	Normal	Special	50	100	15	Normal
Role Play	Psychic	Status	—	—	10	Normal
Drain Punch	Fighting	Physical	75	100	10	Normal
Focus Punch	Fighting	Physical	150	100	20	Normal
Shock Wave	Electric	Special	60	—	20	Normal
Water Pulse	Water	Special	60	100	20	Normal
Trick	Psychic	Status	—	100	10	Normal
Wonder Room	Psychic	Status	—	—	10	Both Sides
Recycle	Normal	Status	—	—	10	Self
Snatch	Dark	Status	—	—	10	Self
Stealth Rock	Rock	Status	—	—	20	Other Side
Skill Swap	Psychic	Status	—	—	10	Normal

MOVES TAUGHT BY PEOPLE

Name	Type	Kind	Pow.	Acc.	PP	Range

National Pokédex **386** Hoenn Pokédex **211**

Deoxys Defense Forme

DNA Pokémon

Psychic

HEIGHT: 5'07" WEIGHT: 134 lbs.

Gender unknown

Ω The DNA of a space virus underwent a sudden mutation upon exposure to a laser beam and resulted in Deoxys. The crystalline organ on this Pokémon's chest appears to be its brain.

α Deoxys emerged from a virus that came from space. It is highly intelligent and wields psychokinetic powers. This Pokémon shoots lasers from the crystalline organ on its chest.

ABILITY
Pressure

HIDDEN ABILITY
—

EGG GROUPS
No Eggs Discovered

STAT GROWTH RATES

HP	■■
Attack	■■■■
Defense	■■■■■■■
Sp. Atk	■■■
Sp. Def	■■■■■■■
Speed	■■■■■

ITEMS SOMETIMES HELD BY WILD POKÉMON
—

EVOLUTION
Does not evolve

MAIN WAY TO REGISTER IN THE NATIONAL POKÉDEX

Have Deoxys in your party and examine the meteorite in Professor Cozmo's lab in Fallarbor Town.

Damage taken in normal battles

Type		Type	
Normal	×1	Flying	×1
Fire	×1	Psychic	×0.5
Water	×1	Bug	×2
Grass	×1	Rock	×1
Electric	×1	Ghost	×2
Ice	×1	Dragon	×1
Fighting	×0.5	Dark	×2
Poison	×1	Steel	×1
Ground	×1	Fairy	×1

Damage taken in Inverse battles

Type		Type	
Normal	×1	Flying	×1
Fire	×1	Psychic	×2
Water	×1	Bug	×0.5
Grass	×1	Rock	×1
Electric	×1	Ghost	×0.5
Ice	×1	Dragon	×1
Fighting	×2	Dark	×0.5
Poison	×1	Steel	×1
Ground	×1	Fairy	×1

Can be used in
Inverse Battle
Battle Institute
Battle Maison
Random Matchup (Free Battle)
Random Matchup (Others)

LEVEL-UP MOVES

Lv.	Name	Type	Kind	Pow.	Acc.	PP	Range
1	Leer	Normal	Status	—	100	30	Many Others
1	Wrap	Normal	Physical	15	90	20	Normal
7	Night Shade	Ghost	Special	—	100	15	Normal
13	Teleport	Psychic	Status	—	—	20	Self
19	Knock Off	Dark	Physical	65	100	20	Normal
25	Spikes	Ground	Status	—	—	20	Other Side
31	Psychic	Psychic	Special	90	100	10	Normal
37	Snatch	Dark	Status	—	—	10	Self
43	Psycho Shift	Psychic	Status	—	100	10	Normal
49	Zen Headbutt	Psychic	Physical	80	90	15	Normal
55	Iron Defense	Steel	Status	—	—	15	Self
55	Amnesia	Psychic	Status	—	—	20	Self
61	Recover	Normal	Status	—	—	10	Self
67	Psycho Boost	Psychic	Special	140	90	5	Normal
73	Counter	Fighting	Physical	—	100	20	Varies
73	Mirror Coat	Psychic	Special	—	100	20	Varies

TM & HM MOVES

No.	Name	Type	Kind	Pow.	Acc.	PP	Range
TM03	Psyshock	Psychic	Special	80	100	10	Normal
TM04	Calm Mind	Psychic	Status	—	—	20	Self
TM06	Toxic	Poison	Status	—	90	10	Normal
TM10	Hidden Power	Normal	Special	60	100	15	Normal
TM11	Sunny Day	Fire	Status	—	—	5	Both Sides
TM12	Taunt	Dark	Status	—	100	20	Normal
TM13	Ice Beam	Ice	Special	90	100	10	Normal
TM15	Hyper Beam	Normal	Special	150	90	5	Normal
TM16	Light Screen	Psychic	Status	—	—	30	Your Side
TM17	Protect	Normal	Status	—	—	10	Self
TM18	Rain Dance	Water	Status	—	—	5	Both Sides
TM20	Safeguard	Normal	Status	—	—	25	Your Side
TM21	Frustration	Normal	Physical	—	100	20	Normal
TM22	Solar Beam	Grass	Special	120	100	10	Normal
TM24	Thunderbolt	Electric	Special	90	100	15	Normal
TM25	Thunder	Electric	Special	110	70	10	Normal
TM27	Return	Normal	Physical	—	100	20	Normal
TM29	Psychic	Psychic	Special	90	100	10	Normal
TM30	Shadow Ball	Ghost	Special	80	100	15	Normal
TM31	Brick Break	Fighting	Physical	75	100	15	Normal
TM32	Double Team	Normal	Status	—	—	15	Self
TM33	Reflect	Psychic	Status	—	—	20	Your Side
TM39	Rock Tomb	Rock	Physical	60	95	15	Normal
TM40	Aerial Ace	Flying	Physical	60	—	20	Normal
TM41	Torment	Dark	Status	—	100	15	Normal
TM42	Facade	Normal	Physical	70	100	20	Normal
TM44	Rest	Psychic	Status	—	—	10	Self
TM47	Low Sweep	Fighting	Physical	65	100	20	Normal
TM48	Round	Normal	Special	60	100	15	Normal
TM52	Focus Blast	Fighting	Special	120	70	5	Normal
TM53	Energy Ball	Grass	Special	90	100	10	Normal
TM56	Fling	Dark	Physical	—	100	10	Normal
TM57	Charge Beam	Electric	Special	50	90	10	Normal
TM68	Giga Impact	Normal	Physical	150	90	5	Normal
TM70	Flash	Normal	Status	—	100	20	Normal
TM73	Thunder Wave	Electric	Status	—	100	20	Normal
TM77	Psych Up	Normal	Status	—	—	10	Normal
TM80	Rock Slide	Rock	Physical	75	90	10	Many Others
TM84	Poison Jab	Poison	Physical	80	100	20	Normal
TM85	Dream Eater	Psychic	Special	100	100	15	Normal
TM86	Grass Knot	Grass	Special	—	100	20	Normal
TM87	Swagger	Normal	Status	—	90	15	Normal
TM88	Sleep Talk	Normal	Status	—	—	10	Self
TM90	Substitute	Normal	Status	—	—	10	Self
TM91	Flash Cannon	Steel	Special	80	100	10	Normal
TM92	Trick Room	Psychic	Status	—	—	5	Both Sides
TM94	Secret Power	Normal	Physical	70	100	20	Normal
TM97	Dark Pulse	Dark	Special	80	100	15	Normal
TM98	Power-Up Punch	Fighting	Physical	40	100	20	Normal
TM100	Confide	Normal	Status	—	—	20	Normal
HM01	Cut	Normal	Physical	50	95	30	Normal
HM04	Strength	Normal	Physical	80	100	15	Normal
HM06	Rock Smash	Fighting	Physical	40	100	15	Normal

MOVES LEARNED IN EXCHANGE FOR BP

Name	Type	Kind	Pow.	Acc.	PP	Range
Signal Beam	Bug	Special	75	100	15	Normal
Low Kick	Fighting	Physical	—	100	20	Normal
Magic Coat	Psychic	Status	—	—	15	Self
Gravity	Psychic	Status	—	—	5	Both Sides
Iron Defense	Steel	Status	—	—	15	Self
Zen Headbutt	Psychic	Physical	80	90	15	Normal
Bind	Normal	Physical	15	85	20	Normal
Snore	Normal	Special	50	100	15	Normal
Knock Off	Dark	Physical	65	100	20	Normal
Role Play	Psychic	Status	—	—	10	Normal
Drain Punch	Fighting	Physical	75	100	10	Normal
Focus Punch	Fighting	Physical	150	100	20	Normal
Shock Wave	Electric	Special	60	—	20	Normal
Water Pulse	Water	Special	60	100	20	Normal
Trick	Psychic	Status	—	100	10	Normal
Wonder Room	Psychic	Status	—	—	10	Both Sides
Recycle	Normal	Status	—	—	10	Self
Snatch	Dark	Status	—	—	10	Self
Stealth Rock	Rock	Status	—	—	20	Other Side
Skill Swap	Psychic	Status	—	—	10	Normal

MOVES TAUGHT BY PEOPLE

Name	Type	Kind	Pow.	Acc.	PP	Range

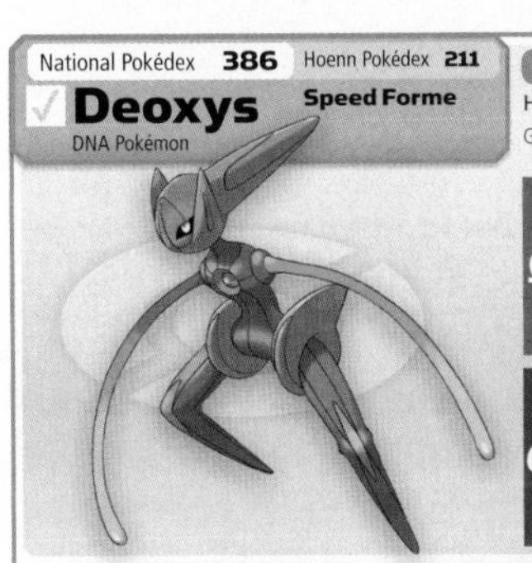

National Pokédex **386** Hoenn Pokédex **211**

Deoxys Speed Forme

DNA Pokémon

Psychic

HEIGHT: 5'07" WEIGHT: 134 lbs.

Gender unknown

Ω The DNA of a space virus underwent a sudden mutation upon exposure to a laser beam and resulted in Deoxys. The crystalline organ on this Pokémon's chest appears to be its brain.

α Deoxys emerged from a virus that came from space. It is highly intelligent and wields psychokinetic powers. This Pokémon shoots lasers from the crystalline organ on its chest.

ABILITY
Pressure

HIDDEN ABILITY
—

EGG GROUPS
No Eggs Discovered

STAT GROWTH RATES

HP	■■
Attack	■■■■■
Defense	■■■■
Sp. Atk	■■■■■
Sp. Def	■■■■
Speed	■■■■■■■■■■

ITEMS SOMETIMES HELD BY WILD POKÉMON
—

EVOLUTION
Does not evolve

MAIN WAY TO REGISTER IN THE NATIONAL POKÉDEX

Have Deoxys in your party and examine the meteorite in Professor Cozmo's lab in Fallarbor Town.

Damage taken in normal battles

Type		Type	
Normal	×1	Flying	×1
Fire	×1	Psychic	×0.5
Water	×1	Bug	×2
Grass	×1	Rock	×1
Electric	×1	Ghost	×2
Ice	×1	Dragon	×1
Fighting	×0.5	Dark	×2
Poison	×1	Steel	×1
Ground	×1	Fairy	×1

Damage taken in Inverse battles

Type		Type	
Normal	×1	Flying	×1
Fire	×1	Psychic	×2
Water	×1	Bug	×0.5
Grass	×1	Rock	×1
Electric	×1	Ghost	×0.5
Ice	×1	Dragon	×1
Fighting	×2	Dark	×0.5
Poison	×1	Steel	×1
Ground	×1	Fairy	×1

Can be used in
Inverse Battle
Battle Institute
Battle Maison
Random Matchup (Free Battle)
Random Matchup (Others)

LEVEL-UP MOVES

Lv.	Name	Type	Kind	Pow.	Acc.	PP	Range
1	Leer	Normal	Status	—	100	30	Many Others
1	Wrap	Normal	Physical	15	90	20	Normal
7	Night Shade	Ghost	Special	—	100	15	Normal
13	Double Team	Normal	Status	—	—	15	Self
19	Knock Off	Dark	Physical	65	100	20	Normal
25	Pursuit	Dark	Physical	40	100	20	Normal
31	Psychic	Psychic	Special	90	100	10	Normal
37	Swift	Normal	Special	60	—	20	Many Others
43	Psycho Shift	Psychic	Status	—	100	10	Normal
49	Zen Headbutt	Psychic	Physical	80	90	15	Normal
55	Agility	Psychic	Status	—	—	30	Self
61	Recover	Normal	Status	—	—	10	Self
67	Psycho Boost	Psychic	Special	140	90	5	Normal
73	Extreme Speed	Normal	Physical	80	100	5	Normal

TM & HM MOVES

No.	Name	Type	Kind	Pow.	Acc.	PP	Range
TM03	Psyshock	Psychic	Special	80	100	10	Normal
TM04	Calm Mind	Psychic	Status	—	—	20	Self
TM06	Toxic	Poison	Status	—	90	10	Normal
TM10	Hidden Power	Normal	Special	60	100	15	Normal
TM11	Sunny Day	Fire	Status	—	—	5	Both Sides
TM12	Taunt	Dark	Status	—	100	20	Normal
TM13	Ice Beam	Ice	Special	90	100	10	Normal
TM15	Hyper Beam	Normal	Special	150	90	5	Normal
TM16	Light Screen	Psychic	Status	—	—	30	Your Side
TM17	Protect	Normal	Status	—	—	10	Self
TM18	Rain Dance	Water	Status	—	—	5	Both Sides
TM20	Safeguard	Normal	Status	—	—	25	Your Side
TM21	Frustration	Normal	Physical	—	100	20	Normal
TM22	Solar Beam	Grass	Special	120	100	10	Normal
TM24	Thunderbolt	Electric	Special	90	100	15	Normal
TM25	Thunder	Electric	Special	110	70	10	Normal
TM27	Return	Normal	Physical	—	100	20	Normal
TM29	Psychic	Psychic	Special	90	100	10	Normal
TM30	Shadow Ball	Ghost	Special	80	100	15	Normal
TM31	Brick Break	Fighting	Physical	75	100	15	Normal
TM32	Double Team	Normal	Status	—	—	15	Self
TM33	Reflect	Psychic	Status	—	—	20	Your Side
TM39	Rock Tomb	Rock	Physical	60	95	15	Normal
TM40	Aerial Ace	Flying	Physical	60	—	20	Normal
TM41	Torment	Dark	Status	—	100	15	Normal
TM42	Facade	Normal	Physical	70	100	20	Normal
TM44	Rest	Psychic	Status	—	—	10	Self
TM47	Low Sweep	Fighting	Physical	65	100	20	Normal
TM48	Round	Normal	Special	60	100	15	Normal
TM52	Focus Blast	Fighting	Special	120	70	5	Normal
TM53	Energy Ball	Grass	Special	90	100	10	Normal
TM56	Fling	Dark	Physical	—	100	10	Normal
TM57	Charge Beam	Electric	Special	50	90	10	Normal
TM68	Giga Impact	Normal	Physical	150	90	5	Normal
TM70	Flash	Normal	Status	—	100	20	Normal
TM73	Thunder Wave	Electric	Status	—	100	20	Normal
TM77	Psych Up	Normal	Status	—	—	10	Normal
TM80	Rock Slide	Rock	Physical	75	90	10	Many Others
TM84	Poison Jab	Poison	Physical	80	100	20	Normal
TM85	Dream Eater	Psychic	Special	100	100	15	Normal
TM86	Grass Knot	Grass	Special	—	100	20	Normal
TM87	Swagger	Normal	Status	—	90	15	Normal
TM88	Sleep Talk	Normal	Status	—	—	10	Self
TM90	Substitute	Normal	Status	—	—	10	Self
TM91	Flash Cannon	Steel	Special	80	100	10	Normal
TM92	Trick Room	Psychic	Status	—	—	5	Both Sides
TM94	Secret Power	Normal	Physical	70	100	20	Normal
TM97	Dark Pulse	Dark	Special	80	100	15	Normal
TM98	Power-Up Punch	Fighting	Physical	40	100	20	Normal
TM100	Confide	Normal	Status	—	—	20	Normal
HM01	Cut	Normal	Physical	50	95	30	Normal
HM04	Strength	Normal	Physical	80	100	15	Normal
HM06	Rock Smash	Fighting	Physical	40	100	15	Normal

MOVES LEARNED IN EXCHANGE FOR BP

Name	Type	Kind	Pow.	Acc.	PP	Range
Signal Beam	Bug	Special	75	100	15	Normal
Low Kick	Fighting	Physical	—	100	20	Normal
Thunder Punch	Electric	Physical	75	100	15	Normal
Fire Punch	Fire	Physical	75	100	15	Normal
Ice Punch	Ice	Physical	75	100	15	Normal
Magic Coat	Psychic	Status	—	—	15	Self
Gravity	Psychic	Status	—	—	5	Both Sides
Zen Headbutt	Psychic	Physical	80	90	15	Normal
Bind	Normal	Physical	15	85	20	Normal
Snore	Normal	Special	50	100	15	Normal
Knock Off	Dark	Physical	65	100	20	Normal
Role Play	Psychic	Status	—	—	10	Normal
Drain Punch	Fighting	Physical	75	100	10	Normal
Focus Punch	Fighting	Physical	150	100	20	Normal
Shock Wave	Electric	Special	60	—	20	Normal
Water Pulse	Water	Special	60	100	20	Normal
Trick	Psychic	Status	—	100	10	Normal
Wonder Room	Psychic	Status	—	—	10	Both Sides
Recycle	Normal	Status	—	—	10	Self
Snatch	Dark	Status	—	—	10	Self
Stealth Rock	Rock	Status	—	—	20	Other Side
Skill Swap	Psychic	Status	—	—	10	Normal

MOVES TAUGHT BY PEOPLE

Name	Type	Kind	Pow.	Acc.	PP	Range

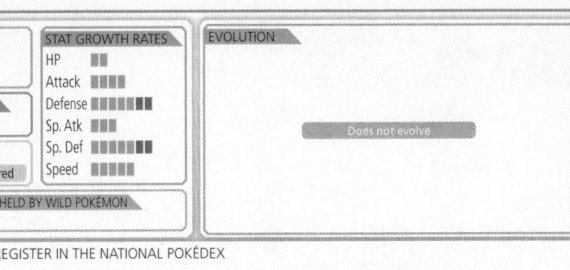

National Pokédex **387** Hoenn Pokédex —

✓ Turtwig

Tiny Leaf Pokémon

Grass

HEIGHT: 1'04" WEIGHT: 22.5 lbs.

Same form for ♂ / ♀

Ω Photosynthesis occurs across its body under the sun. The shell on its back is actually hardened soil.

α It undertakes photosynthesis with its body, making oxygen. The leaf on its head wilts if it is thirsty.

ABILITY
Overgrow

HIDDEN ABILITY
Shell Armor

EGG GROUPS
Monster | Grass

STAT GROWTH RATES
HP ■■
Attack ■■■■
Defense ■■■
Sp. Atk ■■
Sp. Def ■■
Speed ■■

ITEMS SOMETIMES HELD BY WILD POKÉMON
—

EVOLUTION

MAIN WAY TO REGISTER IN THE NATIONAL POKÉDEX

Receive from Professor Birch in Littleroot Town (after entering the Hall of Fame for the second time), or bring it to your game using Link Trade or the GTS.

Damage taken in normal battles

Type		Type	
Normal	×1	Flying	×2
Fire	×2	Psychic	×1
Water	×0.5	Bug	×2
Grass	×0.5	Rock	×1
Electric	×0.5	Ghost	×1
Ice	×2	Dragon	×1
Fighting	×1	Dark	×1
Poison	×2	Steel	×1
Ground	×0.5	Fairy	×1

Damage taken in Inverse battles

Type		Type	
Normal	×1	Flying	×0.5
Fire	×0.5	Psychic	×1
Water	×2	Bug	×0.5
Grass	×2	Rock	×1
Electric	×2	Ghost	×1
Ice	×0.5	Dragon	×1
Fighting	×1	Dark	×1
Poison	×0.5	Steel	×1
Ground	×2	Fairy	×1

Can be used in

- Inverse Battle
- Battle Institute
- Battle Maison
- Random Matchup (Free Battle)
- Random Matchup (Others)

LEVEL-UP MOVES

Lv.	Name	Type	Kind	Pow.	Acc.	PP	Range
1	Tackle	Normal	Physical	50	100	35	Normal
5	Withdraw	Water	Status	—	—	40	Self
9	Absorb	Grass	Special	20	100	25	Normal
13	Razor Leaf	Grass	Physical	55	95	25	Many Others
17	Curse	Ghost	Status	—	—	10	Varies
21	Bite	Dark	Physical	60	100	25	Normal
25	Mega Drain	Grass	Special	40	100	15	Normal
29	Leech Seed	Grass	Status	—	90	10	Normal
33	Synthesis	Grass	Status	—	—	5	Self
37	Crunch	Dark	Physical	80	100	15	Normal
41	Giga Drain	Grass	Special	75	100	10	Normal
45	Leaf Storm	Grass	Special	130	90	5	Normal

TM & HM MOVES

No.	Name	Type	Kind	Pow.	Acc.	PP	Range
TM06	Toxic	Poison	Status	—	90	10	Normal
TM10	Hidden Power	Normal	Special	60	100	15	Normal
TM11	Sunny Day	Fire	Status	—	—	5	Both Sides
TM16	Light Screen	Psychic	Status	—	—	30	Your Side
TM17	Protect	Normal	Status	—	—	10	Self
TM20	Safeguard	Normal	Status	—	—	25	Your Side
TM21	Frustration	Normal	Physical	—	100	20	Normal
TM22	Solar Beam	Grass	Special	120	100	10	Normal
TM27	Return	Normal	Physical	—	100	20	Normal
TM32	Double Team	Normal	Status	—	—	15	Self
TM33	Reflect	Psychic	Status	—	—	20	Your Side
TM42	Facade	Normal	Physical	70	100	20	Normal
TM44	Rest	Psychic	Status	—	—	10	Self
TM45	Attract	Normal	Status	—	100	15	Normal
TM48	Round	Normal	Special	60	100	15	Normal
TM53	Energy Ball	Grass	Special	90	100	10	Normal
TM70	Flash	Normal	Status	—	100	20	Normal
TM75	Swords Dance	Normal	Status	—	—	20	Self
TM86	Grass Knot	Grass	Special	—	100	20	Normal
TM87	Swagger	Normal	Status	—	90	15	Normal
TM88	Sleep Talk	Normal	Status	—	—	10	Self
TM90	Substitute	Normal	Status	—	—	10	Self
TM94	Secret Power	Normal	Physical	70	100	20	Normal
TM96	Nature Power	Normal	Status	—	—	20	Normal
TM100	Confide	Normal	Status	—	—	20	Normal
HM01	Cut	Normal	Physical	50	95	30	Normal
HM04	Strength	Normal	Physical	80	100	15	Normal
HM06	Rock Smash	Fighting	Physical	40	100	15	Normal

MOVES LEARNED IN EXCHANGE FOR BP

Name	Type	Kind	Pow.	Acc.	PP	Range
Seed Bomb	Grass	Physical	80	100	15	Normal
Earth Power	Ground	Special	90	100	10	Normal
Superpower	Fighting	Physical	120	100	5	Normal
Iron Tail	Steel	Physical	100	75	15	Normal
Snore	Normal	Special	50	100	15	Normal
Synthesis	Grass	Status	—	—	5	Self
Giga Drain	Grass	Special	75	100	10	Normal
Worry Seed	Grass	Status	—	100	10	Normal
Stealth Rock	Rock	Status	—	—	20	Other Side

MOVES TAUGHT BY PEOPLE

Name	Type	Kind	Pow.	Acc.	PP	Range
Grass Pledge	Grass	Special	80	100	10	Normal

EGG MOVES

Name	Type	Kind	Pow.	Acc.	PP	Range
Worry Seed	Grass	Status	—	100	10	Normal
Growth	Normal	Status	—	—	20	Self
Tickle	Normal	Status	—	100	20	Normal
Body Slam	Normal	Physical	85	100	15	Normal
Double-Edge	Normal	Physical	120	100	15	Normal
Sand Tomb	Ground	Physical	35	85	15	Normal
Seed Bomb	Grass	Physical	80	100	15	Normal
Thrash	Normal	Physical	120	100	10	1 Random
Amnesia	Psychic	Status	—	—	20	Self
Superpower	Fighting	Physical	120	100	5	Normal
Stockpile	Normal	Status	—	—	20	Self
Swallow	Normal	Status	—	—	10	Self
Spit Up	Normal	Special	—	100	10	Normal
Earth Power	Ground	Special	90	100	10	Normal
Wide Guard	Rock	Status	—	—	10	Your Side
Grassy Terrain	Grass	Status	—	—	10	Both Sides

National Pokédex **388** Hoenn Pokédex —

✓ Grotle

Grove Pokémon

Grass

HEIGHT: 3'07" WEIGHT: 213.8 lbs.

Same form for ♂ / ♀

Ω It lives along water in forests. In the daytime, it leaves the forest to sunbathe its treed shell.

α It knows where pure water wells up. It carries fellow Pokémon there on its back.

ABILITY
Overgrow

HIDDEN ABILITY
Shell Armor

EGG GROUPS
Monster | Grass

STAT GROWTH RATES
HP ■■■
Attack ■■■■■
Defense ■■■■
Sp. Atk ■■■
Sp. Def ■■■
Speed ■■

ITEMS SOMETIMES HELD BY WILD POKÉMON
—

EVOLUTION

Lv. 18 Lv. 32
Turtwig Grotle Torterra

MAIN WAY TO REGISTER IN THE NATIONAL POKÉDEX

Level up Turtwig to Lv. 18.

Damage taken in normal battles

Type		Type	
Normal	×1	Flying	×2
Fire	×2	Psychic	×1
Water	×0.5	Bug	×2
Grass	×0.5	Rock	×1
Electric	×0.5	Ghost	×1
Ice	×2	Dragon	×1
Fighting	×1	Dark	×1
Poison	×2	Steel	×1
Ground	×0.5	Fairy	×1

Damage taken in Inverse battles

Type		Type	
Normal	×1	Flying	×0.5
Fire	×0.5	Psychic	×1
Water	×2	Bug	×0.5
Grass	×2	Rock	×1
Electric	×2	Ghost	×1
Ice	×0.5	Dragon	×1
Fighting	×1	Dark	×1
Poison	×0.5	Steel	×1
Ground	×2	Fairy	×1

Can be used in

- Inverse Battle
- Battle Institute
- Battle Maison
- Random Matchup (Free Battle)
- Random Matchup (Others)

LEVEL-UP MOVES

Lv.	Name	Type	Kind	Pow.	Acc.	PP	Range
1	Tackle	Normal	Physical	50	100	35	Normal
1	Withdraw	Water	Status	—	—	40	Self
5	Withdraw	Water	Status	—	—	40	Self
9	Absorb	Grass	Special	20	100	25	Normal
13	Razor Leaf	Grass	Physical	55	95	25	Many Others
17	Curse	Ghost	Status	—	—	10	Varies
22	Bite	Dark	Physical	60	100	25	Normal
27	Mega Drain	Grass	Special	40	100	15	Normal
32	Leech Seed	Grass	Status	—	90	10	Normal
37	Synthesis	Grass	Status	—	—	5	Self
42	Crunch	Dark	Physical	80	100	15	Normal
47	Giga Drain	Grass	Special	75	100	10	Normal
52	Leaf Storm	Grass	Special	130	90	5	Normal

TM & HM MOVES

No.	Name	Type	Kind	Pow.	Acc.	PP	Range
TM06	Toxic	Poison	Status	—	90	10	Normal
TM10	Hidden Power	Normal	Special	60	100	15	Normal
TM11	Sunny Day	Fire	Status	—	—	5	Both Sides
TM16	Light Screen	Psychic	Status	—	—	30	Your Side
TM17	Protect	Normal	Status	—	—	10	Self
TM20	Safeguard	Normal	Status	—	—	25	Your Side
TM21	Frustration	Normal	Physical	—	100	20	Normal
TM22	Solar Beam	Grass	Special	120	100	10	Normal
TM27	Return	Normal	Physical	—	100	20	Normal
TM32	Double Team	Normal	Status	—	—	15	Self
TM33	Reflect	Psychic	Status	—	—	20	Your Side
TM42	Facade	Normal	Physical	70	100	20	Normal
TM44	Rest	Psychic	Status	—	—	10	Self
TM45	Attract	Normal	Status	—	100	15	Normal
TM48	Round	Normal	Special	60	100	15	Normal
TM53	Energy Ball	Grass	Special	90	100	10	Normal
TM70	Flash	Normal	Status	—	100	20	Normal
TM75	Swords Dance	Normal	Status	—	—	20	Self
TM86	Grass Knot	Grass	Special	—	100	20	Normal
TM87	Swagger	Normal	Status	—	90	15	Normal
TM88	Sleep Talk	Normal	Status	—	—	10	Self
TM90	Substitute	Normal	Status	—	—	10	Self
TM94	Secret Power	Normal	Physical	70	100	20	Normal
TM96	Nature Power	Normal	Status	—	—	20	Normal
TM100	Confide	Normal	Status	—	—	20	Normal
HM01	Cut	Normal	Physical	50	95	30	Normal
HM04	Strength	Normal	Physical	80	100	15	Normal
HM06	Rock Smash	Fighting	Physical	40	100	15	Normal

MOVES LEARNED IN EXCHANGE FOR BP

Name	Type	Kind	Pow.	Acc.	PP	Range
Seed Bomb	Grass	Physical	80	100	15	Normal
Earth Power	Ground	Special	90	100	10	Normal
Superpower	Fighting	Physical	120	100	5	Normal
Iron Tail	Steel	Physical	100	75	15	Normal
Snore	Normal	Special	50	100	15	Normal
Synthesis	Grass	Status	—	—	5	Self
Giga Drain	Grass	Special	75	100	10	Normal
Worry Seed	Grass	Status	—	100	10	Normal
Stealth Rock	Rock	Status	—	—	20	Other Side

MOVES TAUGHT BY PEOPLE

Name	Type	Kind	Pow.	Acc.	PP	Range
Grass Pledge	Grass	Special	80	100	10	Normal

National Pokédex **389** Hoenn Pokédex —

Torterra

Continent Pokémon

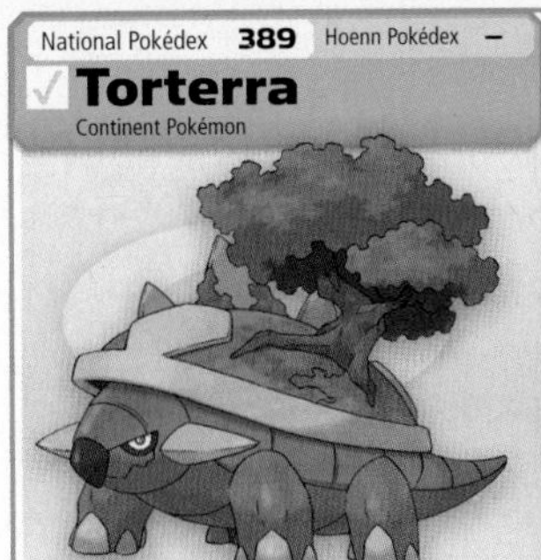

Grass | Ground

HEIGHT: 7'03" WEIGHT: 683.4 lbs.

Same form for ♂ / ♀

Ω Ancient people imagined that beneath the ground, a gigantic Torterra dwelled.

α Small Pokémon occasionally gather on its unmoving back to begin building their nests.

ABILITY
Overgrow

HIDDEN ABILITY
Shell Armor

EGG GROUPS
Monster | Grass

STAT GROWTH RATES
HP ■■■■
Attack ■■■■■■
Defense ■■■■■
Sp. Atk ■■■■
Sp. Def ■■■■
Speed ■■■

ITEMS SOMETIMES HELD BY WILD POKÉMON
—

EVOLUTION

MAIN WAY TO REGISTER IN THE NATIONAL POKÉDEX

Level up Grotle to Lv. 32.

Damage taken in normal battles

Type		Type	
Normal	×1	Flying	×2
Fire	×2	Psychic	×1
Water	×1	Bug	×2
Grass	×1	Rock	×0.5
Electric	×0	Ghost	×1
Ice	×4	Dragon	×1
Fighting	×1	Dark	×1
Poison	×1	Steel	×1
Ground	×0.5	Fairy	×1

Damage taken in Inverse battles

Type		Type	
Normal	×1	Flying	×0.5
Fire	×0.5	Psychic	×1
Water	×1	Bug	×0.5
Grass	×1	Rock	×2
Electric	×4	Ghost	×1
Ice	×0.25	Dragon	×1
Fighting	×1	Dark	×1
Poison	×1	Steel	×1
Ground	×2	Fairy	×1

Can be used in
Inverse Battle
Battle Institute
Battle Maison
Random Matchup (Free Battle)
Random Matchup (Others)

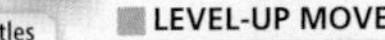

LEVEL-UP MOVES

Lv.	Name	Type	Kind	Pow.	Acc.	PP	Range
1	Wood Hammer	Grass	Physical	120	100	15	Normal
1	Tackle	Normal	Physical	50	100	35	Normal
1	Withdraw	Water	Status	—	—	40	Self
1	Absorb	Grass	Special	20	100	25	Normal
1	Razor Leaf	Grass	Physical	55	95	25	Many Others
5	Withdraw	Water	Status	—	—	40	Self
9	Absorb	Grass	Special	20	100	25	Normal
13	Razor Leaf	Grass	Physical	55	95	25	Many Others
17	Curse	Ghost	Status	—	—	10	Varies
22	Bite	Dark	Physical	60	100	25	Normal
27	Mega Drain	Grass	Special	40	100	15	Normal
32	Earthquake	Ground	Physical	100	100	10	Adjacent
33	Leech Seed	Grass	Status	—	90	10	Normal
39	Synthesis	Grass	Status	—	—	5	Self
45	Crunch	Dark	Physical	80	100	15	Normal
51	Giga Drain	Grass	Special	75	100	10	Normal
57	Leaf Storm	Grass	Special	130	90	5	Normal

TM & HM MOVES

No.	Name	Type	Kind	Pow.	Acc.	PP	Range
TM05	Roar	Normal	Status	—	—	20	Normal
TM06	Toxic	Poison	Status	—	90	10	Normal
TM10	Hidden Power	Normal	Special	60	100	15	Normal
TM11	Sunny Day	Fire	Status	—	—	5	Both Sides
TM15	Hyper Beam	Normal	Special	150	90	5	Normal
TM16	Light Screen	Psychic	Status	—	—	30	Your Side
TM17	Protect	Normal	Status	—	—	10	Self
TM20	Safeguard	Normal	Status	—	—	25	Your Side
TM21	Frustration	Normal	Physical	—	100	20	Normal
TM22	Solar Beam	Grass	Special	120	100	10	Normal
TM26	Earthquake	Ground	Physical	100	100	10	Adjacent
TM27	Return	Normal	Physical	—	100	20	Normal
TM32	Double Team	Normal	Status	—	—	15	Self
TM33	Reflect	Psychic	Status	—	—	20	Your Side
TM37	Sandstorm	Rock	Status	—	—	10	Both Sides
TM39	Rock Tomb	Rock	Physical	60	95	15	Normal
TM42	Facade	Normal	Physical	70	100	20	Normal
TM44	Rest	Psychic	Status	—	—	10	Self
TM45	Attract	Normal	Status	—	100	15	Normal
TM48	Round	Normal	Special	60	100	15	Normal
TM53	Energy Ball	Grass	Special	90	100	10	Normal
TM68	Giga Impact	Normal	Physical	150	90	5	Normal
TM69	Rock Polish	Rock	Status	—	—	20	Self
TM70	Flash	Normal	Status	—	100	20	Normal
TM71	Stone Edge	Rock	Physical	100	80	5	Normal
TM75	Swords Dance	Normal	Status	—	—	20	Self
TM78	Bulldoze	Ground	Physical	60	100	20	Adjacent
TM80	Rock Slide	Rock	Physical	75	90	10	Many Others
TM86	Grass Knot	Grass	Special	—	100	20	Normal
TM87	Swagger	Normal	Status	—	90	15	Normal
TM88	Sleep Talk	Normal	Status	—	—	10	Self
TM90	Substitute	Normal	Status	—	—	10	Self
TM94	Secret Power	Normal	Physical	70	100	20	Normal
TM96	Nature Power	Normal	Status	—	—	20	Normal
TM100	Confide	Normal	Status	—	—	20	Normal
HM01	Cut	Normal	Physical	50	95	30	Normal
HM04	Strength	Normal	Physical	80	100	15	Normal
HM06	Rock Smash	Fighting	Physical	40	100	15	Normal

MOVES LEARNED IN EXCHANGE FOR BP

Name	Type	Kind	Pow.	Acc.	PP	Range
Iron Head	Steel	Physical	80	100	15	Normal
Seed Bomb	Grass	Physical	80	100	15	Normal
Block	Normal	Status	—	—	5	Normal
Earth Power	Ground	Special	90	100	10	Normal
Superpower	Fighting	Physical	120	100	5	Normal
Iron Tail	Steel	Physical	100	75	15	Normal
Snore	Normal	Special	50	100	15	Normal
Synthesis	Grass	Status	—	—	5	Self
Giga Drain	Grass	Special	75	100	10	Normal
Worry Seed	Grass	Status	—	100	10	Normal
Outrage	Dragon	Physical	120	100	10	1 Random
Stealth Rock	Rock	Status	—	—	20	Other Side

MOVES TAUGHT BY PEOPLE

Name	Type	Kind	Pow.	Acc.	PP	Range
Grass Pledge	Grass	Special	80	100	10	Normal
Frenzy Plant	Grass	Special	150	90	5	Normal

National Pokédex **390** Hoenn Pokédex —

Chimchar

Chimp Pokémon

Fire

HEIGHT: 1'08" WEIGHT: 13.7 lbs.

Same form for ♂ / ♀

Ω Its fiery rear end is fueled by gas made in its belly. Even rain can't extinguish the fire.

α The gas made in its belly burns from its rear end. The fire burns weakly when it feels sick.

ABILITY
Blaze

HIDDEN ABILITY
Iron Fist

EGG GROUPS
Field | Human-Like

STAT GROWTH RATES
HP ■■
Attack ■■■
Defense ■■
Sp. Atk ■■■
Sp. Def ■■
Speed ■■■

ITEMS SOMETIMES HELD BY WILD POKÉMON
—

EVOLUTION

Lv. 14 — Lv. 36

Chimchar → Monferno → Infernape

MAIN WAY TO REGISTER IN THE NATIONAL POKÉDEX

Receive from Professor Birch in Littleroot Town (after entering the Hall of Fame for the second time), or bring it to your game using Link Trade or the GTS.

Damage taken in normal battles

Type		Type	
Normal	×1	Flying	×1
Fire	×0.5	Psychic	×1
Water	×2	Bug	×0.5
Grass	×0.5	Rock	×2
Electric	×1	Ghost	×1
Ice	×0.5	Dragon	×1
Fighting	×1	Dark	×1
Poison	×1	Steel	×0.5
Ground	×2	Fairy	×0.5

Damage taken in Inverse battles

Type		Type	
Normal	×1	Flying	×1
Fire	×2	Psychic	×1
Water	×0.5	Bug	×2
Grass	×2	Rock	×0.5
Electric	×1	Ghost	×1
Ice	×2	Dragon	×1
Fighting	×1	Dark	×1
Poison	×1	Steel	×2
Ground	×0.5	Fairy	×2

Can be used in
Inverse Battle
Battle Institute
Battle Maison
Random Matchup (Free Battle)
Random Matchup (Others)

LEVEL-UP MOVES

Lv.	Name	Type	Kind	Pow.	Acc.	PP	Range
1	Scratch	Normal	Physical	40	100	35	Normal
1	Leer	Normal	Status	—	100	30	Many Others
7	Ember	Fire	Special	40	100	25	Normal
9	Taunt	Dark	Status	—	100	20	Normal
15	Fury Swipes	Normal	Physical	18	80	15	Normal
17	Flame Wheel	Fire	Physical	60	100	25	Normal
23	Nasty Plot	Dark	Status	—	—	20	Self
25	Torment	Dark	Status	—	100	15	Normal
31	Facade	Normal	Physical	70	100	20	Normal
33	Fire Spin	Fire	Special	35	85	15	Normal
39	Acrobatics	Flying	Physical	55	100	15	Normal
41	Slack Off	Normal	Status	—	—	10	Self
47	Flamethrower	Fire	Special	90	100	15	Normal

TM & HM MOVES

No.	Name	Type	Kind	Pow.	Acc.	PP	Range
TM01	Hone Claws	Dark	Status	—	—	15	Self
TM06	Toxic	Poison	Status	—	90	10	Normal
TM08	Bulk Up	Fighting	Status	—	—	20	Self
TM10	Hidden Power	Normal	Special	60	100	15	Normal
TM11	Sunny Day	Fire	Status	—	—	5	Both Sides
TM12	Taunt	Dark	Status	—	100	20	Normal
TM17	Protect	Normal	Status	—	—	10	Self
TM21	Frustration	Normal	Physical	—	100	20	Normal
TM27	Return	Normal	Physical	—	100	20	Normal
TM28	Dig	Ground	Physical	80	100	10	Normal
TM31	Brick Break	Fighting	Physical	75	100	15	Normal
TM32	Double Team	Normal	Status	—	—	15	Self
TM35	Flamethrower	Fire	Special	90	100	15	Normal
TM38	Fire Blast	Fire	Special	110	85	5	Normal
TM40	Aerial Ace	Flying	Physical	60	—	20	Normal
TM41	Torment	Dark	Status	—	100	15	Normal
TM42	Facade	Normal	Physical	70	100	20	Normal
TM43	Flame Charge	Fire	Physical	50	100	20	Normal
TM44	Rest	Psychic	Status	—	—	10	Self
TM45	Attract	Normal	Status	—	100	15	Normal
TM47	Low Sweep	Fighting	Physical	65	100	20	Normal
TM48	Round	Normal	Special	60	100	15	Normal
TM50	Overheat	Fire	Special	130	90	5	Normal
TM56	Fling	Dark	Physical	—	100	10	Normal
TM59	Incinerate	Fire	Special	60	100	15	Many Others
TM61	Will-O-Wisp	Fire	Status	—	85	15	Normal
TM62	Acrobatics	Flying	Physical	55	100	15	Normal
TM65	Shadow Claw	Ghost	Physical	70	100	15	Normal
TM75	Swords Dance	Normal	Status	—	—	20	Self
TM86	Grass Knot	Grass	Special	—	100	20	Normal
TM87	Swagger	Normal	Status	—	90	15	Normal
TM88	Sleep Talk	Normal	Status	—	—	10	Self
TM89	U-turn	Bug	Physical	70	100	20	Normal
TM90	Substitute	Normal	Status	—	—	10	Self
TM94	Secret Power	Normal	Physical	70	100	20	Normal
TM98	Power-Up Punch	Fighting	Physical	40	100	20	Normal
TM100	Confide	Normal	Status	—	—	20	Normal
HM01	Cut	Normal	Physical	50	95	30	Normal
HM04	Strength	Normal	Physical	80	100	15	Normal
HM06	Rock Smash	Fighting	Physical	40	100	15	Normal

MOVES LEARNED IN EXCHANGE FOR BP

Name	Type	Kind	Pow.	Acc.	PP	Range
Covet	Normal	Physical	60	100	25	Normal
Low Kick	Fighting	Physical	—	100	20	Normal
Gunk Shot	Poison	Physical	120	80	5	Normal
Uproar	Normal	Special	90	100	10	1 Random
Thunder Punch	Electric	Physical	75	100	15	Normal
Fire Punch	Fire	Physical	75	100	15	Normal
Iron Tail	Steel	Physical	100	75	15	Normal
Snore	Normal	Special	50	100	15	Normal
Heat Wave	Fire	Special	95	90	10	Many Others
Role Play	Psychic	Status	—	—	10	Normal
Focus Punch	Fighting	Physical	150	100	20	Normal
Helping Hand	Normal	Status	—	—	20	1 Ally
Endeavor	Normal	Physical	—	100	5	Normal
Stealth Rock	Rock	Status	—	—	20	Other Side

MOVES TAUGHT BY PEOPLE

Name	Type	Kind	Pow.	Acc.	PP	Range
Fire Pledge	Fire	Special	80	100	10	Normal

EGG MOVES

Name	Type	Kind	Pow.	Acc.	PP	Range
Fire Punch	Fire	Physical	75	100	15	Normal
Thunder Punch	Electric	Physical	75	100	15	Normal
Double Kick	Fighting	Physical	30	100	30	Normal
Encore	Normal	Status	—	100	5	Normal
Heat Wave	Fire	Special	95	90	10	Many Others
Focus Energy	Normal	Status	—	—	30	Self
Helping Hand	Normal	Status	—	—	20	1 Ally
Fake Out	Normal	Physical	40	100	10	Normal
Blaze Kick	Fire	Physical	85	90	10	Normal
Counter	Fighting	Physical	—	100	20	Varies
Assist	Normal	Status	—	—	20	Self
Quick Guard	Fighting	Status	—	—	15	Your Side
Focus Punch	Fighting	Physical	150	100	20	Normal
Submission	Fighting	Physical	80	80	20	Normal

National Pokédex **391** Hoenn Pokédex —

Monferno

Playful Pokémon

Fire | Fighting

HEIGHT: 2'11" WEIGHT: 48.5 lbs.

Same form for ♂ / ♀

Ω It skillfully controls the intensity of the fire on its tail to keep its foes at an ideal distance.

α It uses ceilings and walls to launch aerial attacks. Its fiery tail is but one weapon.

ABILITY
Blaze

HIDDEN ABILITY
Iron Fist

EGG GROUPS
Field | Human-Like

STAT GROWTH RATES
HP ■■■
Attack ■■■■
Defense ■■
Sp. Atk ■■■■
Sp. Def ■■
Speed ■■■■

ITEMS SOMETIMES HELD BY WILD POKÉMON
—

EVOLUTION

MAIN WAY TO REGISTER IN THE NATIONAL POKÉDEX

Level up Chimchar to Lv. 14.

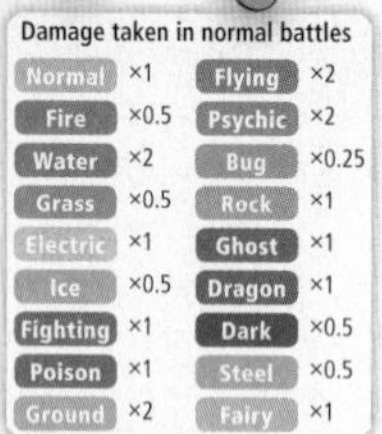

Damage taken in normal battles

Type		Type	
Normal	×1	Flying	×2
Fire	×0.5	Psychic	×2
Water	×2	Bug	×0.25
Grass	×0.5	Rock	×1
Electric	×1	Ghost	×1
Ice	×0.5	Dragon	×1
Fighting	×1	Dark	×0.5
Poison	×1	Steel	×0.5
Ground	×2	Fairy	×1

Damage taken in Inverse battles

Type		Type	
Normal	×1	Flying	×0.5
Fire	×2	Psychic	×0.5
Water	×0.5	Bug	×4
Grass	×2	Rock	×1
Electric	×1	Ghost	×1
Ice	×2	Dragon	×1
Fighting	×1	Dark	×2
Poison	×1	Steel	×2
Ground	×0.5	Fairy	×1

Can be used in
- Inverse Battle
- Battle Institute
- Battle Maison
- Random Matchup (Free Battle)
- Random Matchup (Others)

LEVEL-UP MOVES

Lv.	Name	Type	Kind	Pow.	Acc.	PP	Range
1	Scratch	Normal	Physical	40	100	35	Normal
1	Leer	Normal	Status	—	100	30	Many Others
1	Ember	Fire	Special	40	100	25	Normal
7	Ember	Fire	Special	40	100	25	Normal
9	Taunt	Dark	Status	—	100	20	Normal
14	Mach Punch	Fighting	Physical	40	100	30	Normal
16	Fury Swipes	Normal	Physical	18	80	15	Normal
19	Flame Wheel	Fire	Physical	60	100	25	Normal
26	Feint	Normal	Physical	30	100	10	Normal
29	Torment	Dark	Status	—	100	15	Normal
36	Close Combat	Fighting	Physical	120	100	5	Normal
39	Fire Spin	Fire	Special	35	85	15	Normal
46	Acrobatics	Flying	Physical	55	100	15	Normal
49	Slack Off	Normal	Status	—	—	10	Self
56	Flare Blitz	Fire	Physical	120	100	15	Normal

TM & HM MOVES

No.	Name	Type	Kind	Pow.	Acc.	PP	Range
TM01	Hone Claws	Dark	Status	—	—	15	Self
TM06	Toxic	Poison	Status	—	90	10	Normal
TM08	Bulk Up	Fighting	Status	—	—	20	Self
TM10	Hidden Power	Normal	Special	60	100	15	Normal
TM11	Sunny Day	Fire	Status	—	—	5	Both Sides
TM12	Taunt	Dark	Status	—	100	20	Normal
TM17	Protect	Normal	Status	—	—	10	Self
TM21	Frustration	Normal	Physical	—	100	20	Normal
TM27	Return	Normal	Physical	—	100	20	Normal
TM28	Dig	Ground	Physical	80	100	10	Normal
TM31	Brick Break	Fighting	Physical	75	100	15	Normal
TM32	Double Team	Normal	Status	—	—	15	Self
TM35	Flamethrower	Fire	Special	90	100	15	Normal
TM38	Fire Blast	Fire	Special	110	85	5	Normal
TM39	Rock Tomb	Rock	Physical	60	95	15	Normal
TM40	Aerial Ace	Flying	Physical	60	—	20	Normal
TM41	Torment	Dark	Status	—	100	15	Normal
TM42	Facade	Normal	Physical	70	100	20	Normal
TM43	Flame Charge	Fire	Physical	50	100	20	Normal
TM44	Rest	Psychic	Status	—	—	10	Self
TM45	Attract	Normal	Status	—	100	15	Normal
TM47	Low Sweep	Fighting	Physical	65	100	20	Normal
TM48	Round	Normal	Special	60	100	15	Normal
TM50	Overheat	Fire	Special	130	90	5	Normal
TM52	Focus Blast	Fighting	Special	120	70	5	Normal
TM56	Fling	Dark	Physical	—	100	10	Normal
TM59	Incinerate	Fire	Special	60	100	15	Many Others
TM61	Will-O-Wisp	Fire	Status	—	85	15	Normal
TM62	Acrobatics	Flying	Physical	55	100	15	Normal
TM65	Shadow Claw	Ghost	Physical	70	100	15	Normal
TM67	Retaliate	Normal	Physical	70	100	5	Normal
TM75	Swords Dance	Normal	Status	—	—	20	Self
TM80	Rock Slide	Rock	Physical	75	90	10	Many Others
TM84	Poison Jab	Poison	Physical	80	100	20	Normal
TM86	Grass Knot	Grass	Special	—	100	20	Normal
TM87	Swagger	Normal	Status	—	90	15	Normal
TM88	Sleep Talk	Normal	Status	—	—	10	Self
TM89	U-turn	Bug	Physical	70	100	20	Normal
TM90	Substitute	Normal	Status	—	—	10	Self
TM94	Secret Power	Normal	Physical	70	100	20	Normal
TM98	Power-Up Punch	Fighting	Physical	40	100	20	Normal
TM100	Confide	Normal	Status	—	—	20	Normal
HM01	Cut	Normal	Physical	50	95	30	Normal
HM04	Strength	Normal	Physical	80	100	15	Normal
HM06	Rock Smash	Fighting	Physical	40	100	15	Normal

MOVES LEARNED IN EXCHANGE FOR BP

Name	Type	Kind	Pow.	Acc.	PP	Range
Covet	Normal	Physical	60	100	25	Normal
Dual Chop	Dragon	Physical	40	90	15	Normal
Low Kick	Fighting	Physical	—	100	20	Normal
Gunk Shot	Poison	Physical	120	80	5	Normal
Thunder Punch	Electric	Physical	75	100	15	Normal
Fire Punch	Fire	Physical	75	100	15	Normal
Iron Tail	Steel	Physical	100	75	15	Normal
Snore	Normal	Special	50	100	15	Normal
Heat Wave	Fire	Special	95	90	10	Many Others
Role Play	Psychic	Status	—	—	10	Normal
Focus Punch	Fighting	Physical	150	100	20	Normal
Helping Hand	Normal	Status	—	—	20	1 Ally
Endeavor	Normal	Physical	—	100	5	Normal
Stealth Rock	Rock	Status	—	—	20	Other Side

MOVES TAUGHT BY PEOPLE

Name	Type	Kind	Pow.	Acc.	PP	Range
Fire Pledge	Fire	Special	80	100	10	Normal

National Pokédex **392** Hoenn Pokédex —

Infernape

Flame Pokémon

Fire | Fighting

HEIGHT: 3'11" WEIGHT: 121.3 lbs.

Same form for ♂ / ♀

Ω Its crown of fire is indicative of its fiery nature. It is beaten by none in terms of quickness.

α It tosses its enemies around with agility. It uses all its limbs to fight in its own unique style.

ABILITY
Blaze

HIDDEN ABILITY
Iron Fist

EGG GROUPS
Field | Human-Like

STAT GROWTH RATES
HP ■■■
Attack ■■■■■
Defense ■■■
Sp. Atk ■■■■■
Sp. Def ■■■
Speed ■■■■■■

ITEMS SOMETIMES HELD BY WILD POKÉMON
—

EVOLUTION

Chimchar → Lv. 14 → Monferno → Lv. 36 → Infernape

MAIN WAY TO REGISTER IN THE NATIONAL POKÉDEX

Level up Monferno to Lv. 36.

Damage taken in normal battles

Type		Type	
Normal	×1	Flying	×2
Fire	×0.5	Psychic	×2
Water	×2	Bug	×0.25
Grass	×0.5	Rock	×1
Electric	×1	Ghost	×1
Ice	×0.5	Dragon	×1
Fighting	×1	Dark	×0.5
Poison	×1	Steel	×0.5
Ground	×2	Fairy	×1

Damage taken in Inverse battles

Type		Type	
Normal	×1	Flying	×0.5
Fire	×2	Psychic	×0.5
Water	×0.5	Bug	×4
Grass	×2	Rock	×1
Electric	×1	Ghost	×1
Ice	×2	Dragon	×1
Fighting	×1	Dark	×2
Poison	×1	Steel	×2
Ground	×0.5	Fairy	×1

Can be used in
- Inverse Battle
- Battle Institute
- Battle Maison
- Random Matchup (Free Battle)
- Random Matchup (Others)

LEVEL-UP MOVES

Lv.	Name	Type	Kind	Pow.	Acc.	PP	Range
1	Flare Blitz	Fire	Physical	120	100	15	Normal
1	Scratch	Normal	Physical	40	100	35	Normal
1	Leer	Normal	Status	—	100	30	Many Others
1	Ember	Fire	Special	40	100	25	Normal
1	Taunt	Dark	Status	—	100	20	Normal
7	Ember	Fire	Special	40	100	25	Normal
9	Taunt	Dark	Status	—	100	20	Normal
14	Mach Punch	Fighting	Physical	40	100	30	Normal
16	Fury Swipes	Normal	Physical	18	80	15	Normal
19	Flame Wheel	Fire	Physical	60	100	25	Normal
26	Feint	Normal	Physical	30	100	10	Normal
29	Punishment	Dark	Physical	—	100	5	Normal
36	Close Combat	Fighting	Physical	120	100	5	Normal
42	Fire Spin	Fire	Special	35	85	15	Normal
52	Acrobatics	Flying	Physical	55	100	15	Normal
58	Calm Mind	Psychic	Status	—	—	20	Self
68	Flare Blitz	Fire	Physical	120	100	15	Normal

TM & HM MOVES

No.	Name	Type	Kind	Pow.	Acc.	PP	Range
TM01	Hone Claws	Dark	Status	—	—	15	Self
TM04	Calm Mind	Psychic	Status	—	—	20	Self
TM05	Roar	Normal	Status	—	—	20	Normal
TM06	Toxic	Poison	Status	—	90	10	Normal
TM08	Bulk Up	Fighting	Status	—	—	20	Self
TM10	Hidden Power	Normal	Special	60	100	15	Normal
TM11	Sunny Day	Fire	Status	—	—	5	Both Sides
TM12	Taunt	Dark	Status	—	100	20	Normal
TM15	Hyper Beam	Normal	Special	150	90	5	Normal
TM17	Protect	Normal	Status	—	—	10	Self
TM21	Frustration	Normal	Physical	—	100	20	Normal
TM22	Solar Beam	Grass	Special	120	100	10	Normal
TM26	Earthquake	Ground	Physical	100	100	10	Adjacent
TM27	Return	Normal	Physical	—	100	20	Normal
TM28	Dig	Ground	Physical	80	100	10	Normal
TM31	Brick Break	Fighting	Physical	75	100	15	Normal
TM32	Double Team	Normal	Status	—	—	15	Self
TM35	Flamethrower	Fire	Special	90	100	15	Normal
TM38	Fire Blast	Fire	Special	110	85	5	Normal
TM39	Rock Tomb	Rock	Physical	60	95	15	Normal
TM40	Aerial Ace	Flying	Physical	60	—	20	Normal
TM41	Torment	Dark	Status	—	100	15	Normal
TM42	Facade	Normal	Physical	70	100	20	Normal
TM43	Flame Charge	Fire	Physical	50	100	20	Normal
TM44	Rest	Psychic	Status	—	—	10	Self
TM45	Attract	Normal	Status	—	100	15	Normal
TM47	Low Sweep	Fighting	Physical	65	100	20	Normal
TM48	Round	Normal	Special	60	100	15	Normal
TM50	Overheat	Fire	Special	130	90	5	Normal
TM52	Focus Blast	Fighting	Special	120	70	5	Normal
TM56	Fling	Dark	Physical	—	100	10	Normal
TM59	Incinerate	Fire	Special	60	100	15	Many Others
TM61	Will-O-Wisp	Fire	Status	—	85	15	Normal
TM62	Acrobatics	Flying	Physical	55	100	15	Normal
TM65	Shadow Claw	Ghost	Physical	70	100	15	Normal
TM67	Retaliate	Normal	Physical	70	100	5	Normal
TM68	Giga Impact	Normal	Physical	150	90	5	Normal
TM71	Stone Edge	Rock	Physical	100	80	5	Normal
TM75	Swords Dance	Normal	Status	—	—	20	Self
TM78	Bulldoze	Ground	Physical	60	100	20	Adjacent
TM80	Rock Slide	Rock	Physical	75	90	10	Many Others
TM84	Poison Jab	Poison	Physical	80	100	20	Normal
TM86	Grass Knot	Grass	Special	—	100	20	Normal
TM87	Swagger	Normal	Status	—	90	15	Normal
TM88	Sleep Talk	Normal	Status	—	—	10	Self
TM89	U-turn	Bug	Physical	70	100	20	Normal
TM90	Substitute	Normal	Status	—	—	10	Self
TM94	Secret Power	Normal	Physical	70	100	20	Normal
TM98	Power-Up Punch	Fighting	Physical	40	100	20	Normal
TM100	Confide	Normal	Status	—	—	20	Normal
HM01	Cut	Normal	Physical	50	95	30	Normal
HM04	Strength	Normal	Physical	80	100	15	Normal
HM06	Rock Smash	Fighting	Physical	40	100	15	Normal

MOVES LEARNED IN EXCHANGE FOR BP

Name	Type	Kind	Pow.	Acc.	PP	Range
Covet	Normal	Physical	60	100	25	Normal
Dual Chop	Dragon	Physical	40	90	15	Normal
Low Kick	Fighting	Physical	—	100	20	Normal
Gunk Shot	Poison	Physical	120	80	5	Normal
Thunder Punch	Electric	Physical	75	100	15	Normal
Fire Punch	Fire	Physical	75	100	15	Normal
Iron Tail	Steel	Physical	100	75	15	Normal
Snore	Normal	Special	50	100	15	Normal
Heat Wave	Fire	Special	95	90	10	Many Others
Role Play	Psychic	Status	—	—	10	Normal
Focus Punch	Fighting	Physical	150	100	20	Normal
Helping Hand	Normal	Status	—	—	20	1 Ally
Endeavor	Normal	Physical	—	100	5	Normal
Stealth Rock	Rock	Status	—	—	20	Other Side

MOVES TAUGHT BY PEOPLE

Name	Type	Kind	Pow.	Acc.	PP	Range
Fire Pledge	Fire	Special	80	100	10	Normal
Blast Burn	Fire	Special	150	90	5	Normal

National Pokédex **393** Hoenn Pokédex —

Piplup

Penguin Pokémon

Water

HEIGHT: 1'04" WEIGHT: 11.5 lbs.

Same form for ♂ / ♀

Ω It doesn't like to be taken care of. It's difficult to bond with since it won't listen to its Trainer.

α Because it is very proud, it hates accepting food from people. Its thick down guards it from cold.

ABILITY
Torrent

HIDDEN ABILITY
Defiant

EGG GROUPS
Water 1 | Field

STAT GROWTH RATES

HP	■■
Attack	■■■
Defense	■■
Sp. Atk	■■■
Sp. Def	■■
Speed	■■

ITEMS SOMETIMES HELD BY WILD POKÉMON
—

EVOLUTION

MAIN WAY TO REGISTER IN THE NATIONAL POKÉDEX

Receive from Professor Birch in Littleroot Town (after entering the Hall of Fame for the second time), or bring it to your game using Link Trade or the GTS.

Damage taken in normal battles

Type	×	Type	×
Normal	×1	Flying	×1
Fire	×0.5	Psychic	×1
Water	×0.5	Bug	×1
Grass	×2	Rock	×1
Electric	×2	Ghost	×1
Ice	×0.5	Dragon	×1
Fighting	×1	Dark	×1
Poison	×1	Steel	×0.5
Ground	×1	Fairy	×1

Damage taken in Inverse battles

Type	×	Type	×
Normal	×1	Flying	×1
Fire	×2	Psychic	×1
Water	×2	Bug	×1
Grass	×0.5	Rock	×1
Electric	×0.5	Ghost	×1
Ice	×2	Dragon	×1
Fighting	×1	Dark	×1
Poison	×1	Steel	×2
Ground	×1	Fairy	×1

Can be used in

Inverse Battle
Battle Institute
Battle Maison
Random Matchup (Free Battle)
Random Matchup (Others)

LEVEL-UP MOVES

Lv.	Name	Type	Kind	Pow.	Acc.	PP	Range
1	Pound	Normal	Physical	40	100	35	Normal
4	Growl	Normal	Status	—	100	40	Many Others
8	Bubble	Water	Special	40	100	30	Many Others
11	Water Sport	Water	Status	—	—	15	Both Sides
15	Peck	Flying	Physical	35	100	35	Normal
18	Bubble Beam	Water	Special	65	100	20	Normal
22	Bide	Normal	Physical	—	—	10	Self
25	Fury Attack	Normal	Physical	15	85	20	Normal
29	Brine	Water	Special	65	100	10	Normal
32	Whirlpool	Water	Special	35	85	15	Normal
36	Mist	Ice	Status	—	—	30	Your Side
39	Drill Peck	Flying	Physical	80	100	20	Normal
43	Hydro Pump	Water	Special	110	80	5	Normal

TM & HM MOVES

No.	Name	Type	Kind	Pow.	Acc.	PP	Range
TM06	Toxic	Poison	Status	—	90	10	Normal
TM07	Hail	Ice	Status	—	—	10	Both Sides
TM10	Hidden Power	Normal	Special	60	100	15	Normal
TM13	Ice Beam	Ice	Special	90	100	10	Normal
TM14	Blizzard	Ice	Special	110	70	5	Many Others
TM17	Protect	Normal	Status	—	—	10	Self
TM18	Rain Dance	Water	Status	—	—	5	Both Sides
TM21	Frustration	Normal	Physical	—	100	20	Normal
TM27	Return	Normal	Physical	—	100	20	Normal
TM28	Dig	Ground	Physical	80	100	10	Normal
TM31	Brick Break	Fighting	Physical	75	100	15	Normal
TM32	Double Team	Normal	Status	—	—	15	Self
TM39	Rock Tomb	Rock	Physical	60	95	15	Normal
TM40	Aerial Ace	Flying	Physical	60	—	20	Normal
TM42	Facade	Normal	Physical	70	100	20	Normal
TM44	Rest	Psychic	Status	—	—	10	Self
TM45	Attract	Normal	Status	—	100	15	Normal
TM48	Round	Normal	Special	60	100	15	Normal
TM49	Echoed Voice	Normal	Special	40	100	15	Normal
TM55	Scald	Water	Special	80	100	15	Normal
TM56	Fling	Dark	Physical	—	100	10	Normal
TM60	Quash	Dark	Status	—	100	15	Normal
TM86	Grass Knot	Grass	Special	—	100	20	Normal
TM87	Swagger	Normal	Status	—	90	15	Normal
TM88	Sleep Talk	Normal	Status	—	—	10	Self
TM90	Substitute	Normal	Status	—	—	10	Self
TM94	Secret Power	Normal	Physical	70	100	20	Normal
TM100	Confide	Normal	Status	—	—	20	Normal
HM01	Cut	Normal	Physical	50	95	30	Normal
HM03	Surf	Water	Special	90	100	15	Adjacent
HM05	Waterfall	Water	Physical	80	100	15	Normal
HM07	Dive	Water	Physical	80	100	10	Normal

MOVES LEARNED IN EXCHANGE FOR BP

Name	Type	Kind	Pow.	Acc.	PP	Range
Covet	Normal	Physical	60	100	25	Normal
Signal Beam	Bug	Special	75	100	15	Normal
Icy Wind	Ice	Special	55	95	15	Many Others
Snore	Normal	Special	50	100	15	Normal
Water Pulse	Water	Special	60	100	20	Normal
Stealth Rock	Rock	Status	—	—	20	Other Side

MOVES TAUGHT BY PEOPLE

Name	Type	Kind	Pow.	Acc.	PP	Range
Water Pledge	Water	Special	80	100	10	Normal

EGG MOVES

Name	Type	Kind	Pow.	Acc.	PP	Range
Double Hit	Normal	Physical	35	90	10	Normal
Supersonic	Normal	Status	—	55	20	Normal
Yawn	Normal	Status	—	—	10	Normal
Mud Sport	Ground	Status	—	—	15	Both Sides
Mud-Slap	Ground	Special	20	100	10	Normal
Snore	Normal	Special	50	100	15	Normal
Flail	Normal	Physical	—	100	15	Normal
Agility	Psychic	Status	—	—	30	Self
Aqua Ring	Water	Status	—	—	20	Self
Hydro Pump	Water	Special	110	80	5	Normal
Feather Dance	Flying	Status	—	100	15	Normal
Bide	Normal	Physical	—	—	10	Self
Icy Wind	Ice	Special	55	95	15	Many Others

National Pokédex **394** Hoenn Pokédex —

Prinplup

Penguin Pokémon

Water

HEIGHT: 2'07" WEIGHT: 50.7 lbs.

Same form for ♂ / ♀

Ω It lives alone, away from others. Apparently, every one of them believes it is the most important.

α It lives a solitary life. Its wings deliver wicked blows that can snap even the thickest of trees.

ABILITY
Torrent

HIDDEN ABILITY
Defiant

EGG GROUPS
Water 1 | Field

STAT GROWTH RATES

HP	■■■
Attack	■■■
Defense	■■■
Sp. Atk	■■■■
Sp. Def	■■■
Speed	■■■

ITEMS SOMETIMES HELD BY WILD POKÉMON
—

EVOLUTION

Lv. 16 Lv. 36
Piplup Prinplup Empoleon

MAIN WAY TO REGISTER IN THE NATIONAL POKÉDEX

Level up Piplup to Lv. 16.

Damage taken in normal battles

Type	×	Type	×
Normal	×1	Flying	×1
Fire	×0.5	Psychic	×1
Water	×0.5	Bug	×1
Grass	×2	Rock	×1
Electric	×2	Ghost	×1
Ice	×0.5	Dragon	×1
Fighting	×1	Dark	×1
Poison	×1	Steel	×0.5
Ground	×1	Fairy	×1

Damage taken in Inverse battles

Type	×	Type	×
Normal	×1	Flying	×1
Fire	×2	Psychic	×1
Water	×2	Bug	×1
Grass	×0.5	Rock	×1
Electric	×0.5	Ghost	×1
Ice	×2	Dragon	×1
Fighting	×1	Dark	×1
Poison	×1	Steel	×2
Ground	×1	Fairy	×1

Can be used in

Inverse Battle
Battle Institute
Battle Maison
Random Matchup (Free Battle)
Random Matchup (Others)

LEVEL-UP MOVES

Lv.	Name	Type	Kind	Pow.	Acc.	PP	Range
1	Tackle	Normal	Physical	50	100	35	Normal
1	Growl	Normal	Status	—	100	40	Many Others
4	Growl	Normal	Status	—	100	40	Many Others
8	Bubble	Water	Special	40	100	30	Many Others
11	Water Sport	Water	Status	—	—	15	Both Sides
15	Peck	Flying	Physical	35	100	35	Normal
16	Metal Claw	Steel	Physical	50	95	35	Normal
19	Bubble Beam	Water	Special	65	100	20	Normal
24	Bide	Normal	Physical	—	—	10	Self
28	Fury Attack	Normal	Physical	15	85	20	Normal
33	Brine	Water	Special	65	100	10	Normal
37	Whirlpool	Water	Special	35	85	15	Normal
42	Mist	Ice	Status	—	—	30	Your Side
46	Drill Peck	Flying	Physical	80	100	20	Normal
50	Hydro Pump	Water	Special	110	80	5	Normal

TM & HM MOVES

No.	Name	Type	Kind	Pow.	Acc.	PP	Range
TM01	Hone Claws	Dark	Status	—	—	15	Self
TM06	Toxic	Poison	Status	—	90	10	Normal
TM07	Hail	Ice	Status	—	—	10	Both Sides
TM10	Hidden Power	Normal	Special	60	100	15	Normal
TM13	Ice Beam	Ice	Special	90	100	10	Normal
TM14	Blizzard	Ice	Special	110	70	5	Many Others
TM17	Protect	Normal	Status	—	—	10	Self
TM18	Rain Dance	Water	Status	—	—	5	Both Sides
TM21	Frustration	Normal	Physical	—	100	20	Normal
TM27	Return	Normal	Physical	—	100	20	Normal
TM28	Dig	Ground	Physical	80	100	10	Normal
TM31	Brick Break	Fighting	Physical	75	100	15	Normal
TM32	Double Team	Normal	Status	—	—	15	Self
TM39	Rock Tomb	Rock	Physical	60	95	15	Normal
TM40	Aerial Ace	Flying	Physical	60	—	20	Normal
TM42	Facade	Normal	Physical	70	100	20	Normal
TM44	Rest	Psychic	Status	—	—	10	Self
TM45	Attract	Normal	Status	—	100	15	Normal
TM48	Round	Normal	Special	60	100	15	Normal
TM49	Echoed Voice	Normal	Special	40	100	15	Normal
TM55	Scald	Water	Special	80	100	15	Normal
TM56	Fling	Dark	Physical	—	100	10	Normal
TM60	Quash	Dark	Status	—	100	15	Normal
TM65	Shadow Claw	Ghost	Physical	70	100	15	Normal
TM86	Grass Knot	Grass	Special	—	100	20	Normal
TM87	Swagger	Normal	Status	—	90	15	Normal
TM88	Sleep Talk	Normal	Status	—	—	10	Self
TM90	Substitute	Normal	Status	—	—	10	Self
TM94	Secret Power	Normal	Physical	70	100	20	Normal
TM100	Confide	Normal	Status	—	—	20	Normal
HM01	Cut	Normal	Physical	50	95	30	Normal
HM03	Surf	Water	Special	90	100	15	Adjacent
HM04	Strength	Normal	Physical	80	100	15	Normal
HM05	Waterfall	Water	Physical	80	100	15	Normal
HM06	Rock Smash	Fighting	Physical	40	100	15	Normal
HM07	Dive	Water	Physical	80	100	10	Normal

MOVES LEARNED IN EXCHANGE FOR BP

Name	Type	Kind	Pow.	Acc.	PP	Range
Covet	Normal	Physical	60	100	25	Normal
Signal Beam	Bug	Special	75	100	15	Normal
Icy Wind	Ice	Special	55	95	15	Many Others
Snore	Normal	Special	50	100	15	Normal
Water Pulse	Water	Special	60	100	20	Normal
Stealth Rock	Rock	Status	—	—	20	Other Side

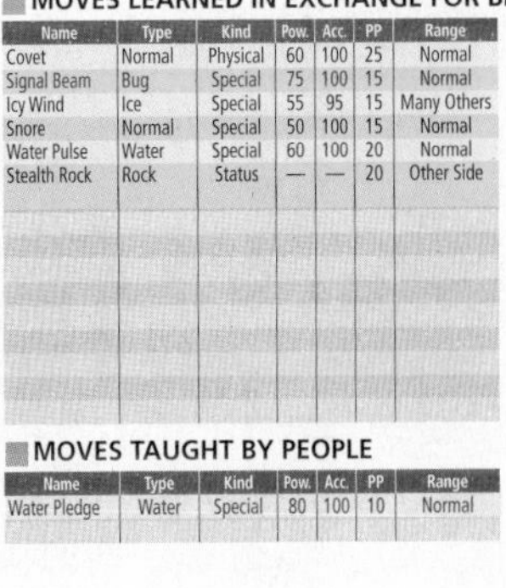

MOVES TAUGHT BY PEOPLE

Name	Type	Kind	Pow.	Acc.	PP	Range
Water Pledge	Water	Special	80	100	10	Normal

National Pokédex **395** Hoenn Pokédex —

Empoleon

Emperor Pokémon

Water / Steel

HEIGHT: 5'07" WEIGHT: 186.3 lbs.

Same form for ♂ / ♀

Ω It swims as fast as a jet boat. The edges of its wings are sharp and can slice apart drifting ice.

α The three horns that extend from its beak attest to its power. The leader has the biggest horns.

ABILITY
Torrent

HIDDEN ABILITY
Defiant

EGG GROUPS
Water 1 / Field

STAT GROWTH RATES

HP	■■■
Attack	■■■■
Defense	■■■■
Sp. Atk	■■■■■
Sp. Def	■■■■
Speed	■■■

ITEMS SOMETIMES HELD BY WILD POKÉMON
—

EVOLUTION

MAIN WAY TO REGISTER IN THE NATIONAL POKÉDEX

Level up Prinplup to Lv. 36.

Damage taken in normal battles

Type		Type	
Normal	×0.5	Flying	×0.5
Fire	×1	Psychic	×0.5
Water	×0.5	Bug	×0.5
Grass	×1	Rock	×0.5
Electric	×2	Ghost	×1
Ice	×0.25	Dragon	×0.5
Fighting	×2	Dark	×1
Poison	×0	Steel	×0.25
Ground	×2	Fairy	×0.5

Damage taken in Inverse battles

Type		Type	
Normal	×2	Flying	×2
Fire	×1	Psychic	×2
Water	×2	Bug	×2
Grass	×1	Rock	×2
Electric	×0.5	Ghost	×1
Ice	×4	Dragon	×2
Fighting	×0.5	Dark	×1
Poison	×2	Steel	×4
Ground	×0.5	Fairy	×2

Can be used in
- Inverse Battle
- Battle Institute
- Battle Maison
- Random Matchup (Free Battle)
- Random Matchup (Others)

LEVEL-UP MOVES

Lv.	Name	Type	Kind	Pow.	Acc.	PP	Range
1	Tackle	Normal	Physical	50	100	35	Normal
1	Growl	Normal	Status	—	100	40	Many Others
1	Bubble	Water	Special	40	100	30	Many Others
4	Growl	Normal	Status	—	100	40	Many Others
8	Bubble	Water	Special	40	100	30	Many Others
11	Swords Dance	Normal	Status	—	—	20	Self
15	Peck	Flying	Physical	35	100	35	Normal
16	Metal Claw	Steel	Physical	50	95	35	Normal
19	Bubble Beam	Water	Special	65	100	20	Normal
24	Swagger	Normal	Status	—	90	15	Normal
28	Fury Attack	Normal	Physical	15	85	20	Normal
33	Brine	Water	Special	65	100	10	Normal
36	Aqua Jet	Water	Physical	40	100	20	Normal
39	Whirlpool	Water	Special	35	85	15	Normal
46	Mist	Ice	Status	—	—	30	Your Side
52	Drill Peck	Flying	Physical	80	100	20	Normal
59	Hydro Pump	Water	Special	110	80	5	Normal

TM & HM MOVES

No.	Name	Type	Kind	Pow.	Acc.	PP	Range
TM01	Hone Claws	Dark	Status	—	—	15	Self
TM05	Roar	Normal	Status	—	—	20	Normal
TM06	Toxic	Poison	Status	—	90	10	Normal
TM07	Hail	Ice	Status	—	—	10	Both Sides
TM10	Hidden Power	Normal	Special	60	100	15	Normal
TM13	Ice Beam	Ice	Special	90	100	10	Normal
TM14	Blizzard	Ice	Special	110	70	5	Many Others
TM15	Hyper Beam	Normal	Special	150	90	5	Normal
TM17	Protect	Normal	Status	—	—	10	Self
TM18	Rain Dance	Water	Status	—	—	5	Both Sides
TM21	Frustration	Normal	Physical	—	100	20	Normal
TM26	Earthquake	Ground	Physical	100	100	10	Adjacent
TM27	Return	Normal	Physical	—	100	20	Normal
TM28	Dig	Ground	Physical	80	100	10	Normal
TM31	Brick Break	Fighting	Physical	75	100	15	Normal
TM32	Double Team	Normal	Status	—	—	15	Self
TM39	Rock Tomb	Rock	Physical	60	95	15	Normal
TM40	Aerial Ace	Flying	Physical	60	—	20	Normal
TM42	Facade	Normal	Physical	70	100	20	Normal
TM44	Rest	Psychic	Status	—	—	10	Self
TM45	Attract	Normal	Status	—	100	15	Normal
TM48	Round	Normal	Special	60	100	15	Normal
TM49	Echoed Voice	Normal	Special	40	100	15	Normal
TM51	Steel Wing	Steel	Physical	70	90	25	Normal
TM55	Scald	Water	Special	80	100	15	Normal
TM56	Fling	Dark	Physical	—	100	10	Normal
TM60	Quash	Dark	Status	—	100	15	Normal
TM65	Shadow Claw	Ghost	Physical	70	100	15	Normal
TM68	Giga Impact	Normal	Physical	150	90	5	Normal
TM75	Swords Dance	Normal	Status	—	—	20	Self
TM78	Bulldoze	Ground	Physical	60	100	20	Adjacent
TM80	Rock Slide	Rock	Physical	75	90	10	Many Others
TM86	Grass Knot	Grass	Special	—	100	20	Normal
TM87	Swagger	Normal	Status	—	90	15	Normal
TM88	Sleep Talk	Normal	Status	—	—	10	Self
TM90	Substitute	Normal	Status	—	—	10	Self
TM91	Flash Cannon	Steel	Special	80	100	10	Normal
TM94	Secret Power	Normal	Physical	70	100	20	Normal
TM100	Confide	Normal	Status	—	—	20	Normal
HM01	Cut	Normal	Physical	50	95	30	Normal
HM03	Surf	Water	Special	90	100	15	Adjacent
HM04	Strength	Normal	Physical	80	100	15	Normal
HM05	Waterfall	Water	Physical	80	100	15	Normal
HM06	Rock Smash	Fighting	Physical	40	100	15	Normal
HM07	Dive	Water	Physical	80	100	10	Normal

MOVES LEARNED IN EXCHANGE FOR BP

Name	Type	Kind	Pow.	Acc.	PP	Range
Covet	Normal	Physical	60	100	25	Normal
Signal Beam	Bug	Special	75	100	15	Normal
Iron Defense	Steel	Status	—	—	15	Self
Icy Wind	Ice	Special	55	95	15	Many Others
Snore	Normal	Special	50	100	15	Normal
Knock Off	Dark	Physical	65	100	20	Normal
Water Pulse	Water	Special	60	100	20	Normal
Stealth Rock	Rock	Status	—	—	20	Other Side

MOVES TAUGHT BY PEOPLE

Name	Type	Kind	Pow.	Acc.	PP	Range
Water Pledge	Water	Special	80	100	10	Normal
Hydro Cannon	Water	Special	150	90	5	Normal

National Pokédex **396** Hoenn Pokédex —

Starly

Starling Pokémon

Normal / Flying

HEIGHT: 1'00" WEIGHT: 4.4 lbs.

The pattern on the male's forehead is spread out more widely. The pattern on the female's forehead is narrower.

Ω They flock in great numbers. Though small, they flap their wings with great power.

α They flock around mountains and fields, chasing after bug Pokémon. Their singing is noisy and annoying.

ABILITY
Keen Eye

HIDDEN ABILITY
Reckless

EGG GROUPS
Flying

STAT GROWTH RATES

HP	■■
Attack	■■■
Defense	■■
Sp. Atk	■
Sp. Def	■
Speed	■■■

ITEMS SOMETIMES HELD BY WILD POKÉMON
—

EVOLUTION

Starly → Lv. 14 → Staravia → Lv. 34 → Staraptor

MAIN WAY TO REGISTER IN THE NATIONAL POKÉDEX

Appears in *Pokémon X* and *Pokémon Y*. Bring it to your game using Link Trade or the GTS.

Damage taken in normal battles

Type		Type	
Normal	×1	Flying	×1
Fire	×1	Psychic	×1
Water	×1	Bug	×0.5
Grass	×0.5	Rock	×2
Electric	×2	Ghost	×0
Ice	×2	Dragon	×1
Fighting	×1	Dark	×1
Poison	×1	Steel	×1
Ground	×0	Fairy	×1

Damage taken in Inverse battles

Type		Type	
Normal	×1	Flying	×1
Fire	×1	Psychic	×1
Water	×1	Bug	×2
Grass	×2	Rock	×0.5
Electric	×0.5	Ghost	×2
Ice	×0.5	Dragon	×1
Fighting	×1	Dark	×1
Poison	×1	Steel	×1
Ground	×2	Fairy	×1

Can be used in
- Inverse Battle
- Battle Institute
- Battle Maison
- Random Matchup (Free Battle)
- Random Matchup (Others)

LEVEL-UP MOVES

Lv.	Name	Type	Kind	Pow.	Acc.	PP	Range
1	Tackle	Normal	Physical	50	100	35	Normal
1	Growl	Normal	Status	—	100	40	Many Others
5	Quick Attack	Normal	Physical	40	100	30	Normal
9	Wing Attack	Flying	Physical	60	100	35	Normal
13	Double Team	Normal	Status	—	—	15	Self
17	Endeavor	Normal	Physical	—	100	5	Normal
21	Whirlwind	Normal	Status	—	—	20	Normal
25	Aerial Ace	Flying	Physical	60	—	20	Normal
29	Take Down	Normal	Physical	90	85	20	Normal
33	Agility	Psychic	Status	—	—	30	Self
37	Brave Bird	Flying	Physical	120	100	15	Normal
41	Final Gambit	Fighting	Special	—	100	5	Normal

TM & HM MOVES

No.	Name	Type	Kind	Pow.	Acc.	PP	Range
TM06	Toxic	Poison	Status	—	90	10	Normal
TM10	Hidden Power	Normal	Special	60	100	15	Normal
TM11	Sunny Day	Fire	Status	—	—	5	Both Sides
TM17	Protect	Normal	Status	—	—	10	Self
TM18	Rain Dance	Water	Status	—	—	5	Both Sides
TM19	Roost	Flying	Status	—	—	10	Self
TM21	Frustration	Normal	Physical	—	100	20	Normal
TM27	Return	Normal	Physical	—	100	20	Normal
TM32	Double Team	Normal	Status	—	—	15	Self
TM40	Aerial Ace	Flying	Physical	60	—	20	Normal
TM42	Facade	Normal	Physical	70	100	20	Normal
TM44	Rest	Psychic	Status	—	—	10	Self
TM45	Attract	Normal	Status	—	100	15	Normal
TM46	Thief	Dark	Physical	60	100	25	Normal
TM48	Round	Normal	Special	60	100	15	Normal
TM49	Echoed Voice	Normal	Special	40	100	15	Normal
TM51	Steel Wing	Steel	Physical	70	90	25	Normal
TM87	Swagger	Normal	Status	—	90	15	Normal
TM88	Sleep Talk	Normal	Status	—	—	10	Self
TM89	U-turn	Bug	Physical	70	100	20	Normal
TM90	Substitute	Normal	Status	—	—	10	Self
TM94	Secret Power	Normal	Physical	70	100	20	Normal
TM100	Confide	Normal	Status	—	—	20	Normal
HM02	Fly	Flying	Physical	90	95	15	Normal

MOVES LEARNED IN EXCHANGE FOR BP

Name	Type	Kind	Pow.	Acc.	PP	Range
Uproar	Normal	Special	90	100	10	1 Random
Snore	Normal	Special	50	100	15	Normal
Heat Wave	Fire	Special	95	90	10	Many Others
Tailwind	Flying	Status	—	—	15	Your Side
Endeavor	Normal	Physical	—	100	5	Normal

MOVES TAUGHT BY PEOPLE

Name	Type	Kind	Pow.	Acc.	PP	Range

EGG MOVES

Name	Type	Kind	Pow.	Acc.	PP	Range
Feather Dance	Flying	Status	—	100	15	Normal
Fury Attack	Normal	Physical	15	85	20	Normal
Pursuit	Dark	Physical	40	100	20	Normal
Astonish	Ghost	Physical	30	100	15	Normal
Sand Attack	Ground	Status	—	100	15	Normal
Foresight	Normal	Status	—	—	40	Normal
Double-Edge	Normal	Physical	120	100	15	Normal
Steel Wing	Steel	Physical	70	90	25	Normal
Uproar	Normal	Special	90	100	10	1 Random
Roost	Flying	Status	—	—	10	Self
Detect	Fighting	Status	—	—	5	Self
Revenge	Fighting	Physical	60	100	10	Normal
Mirror Move	Flying	Status	—	—	20	Normal

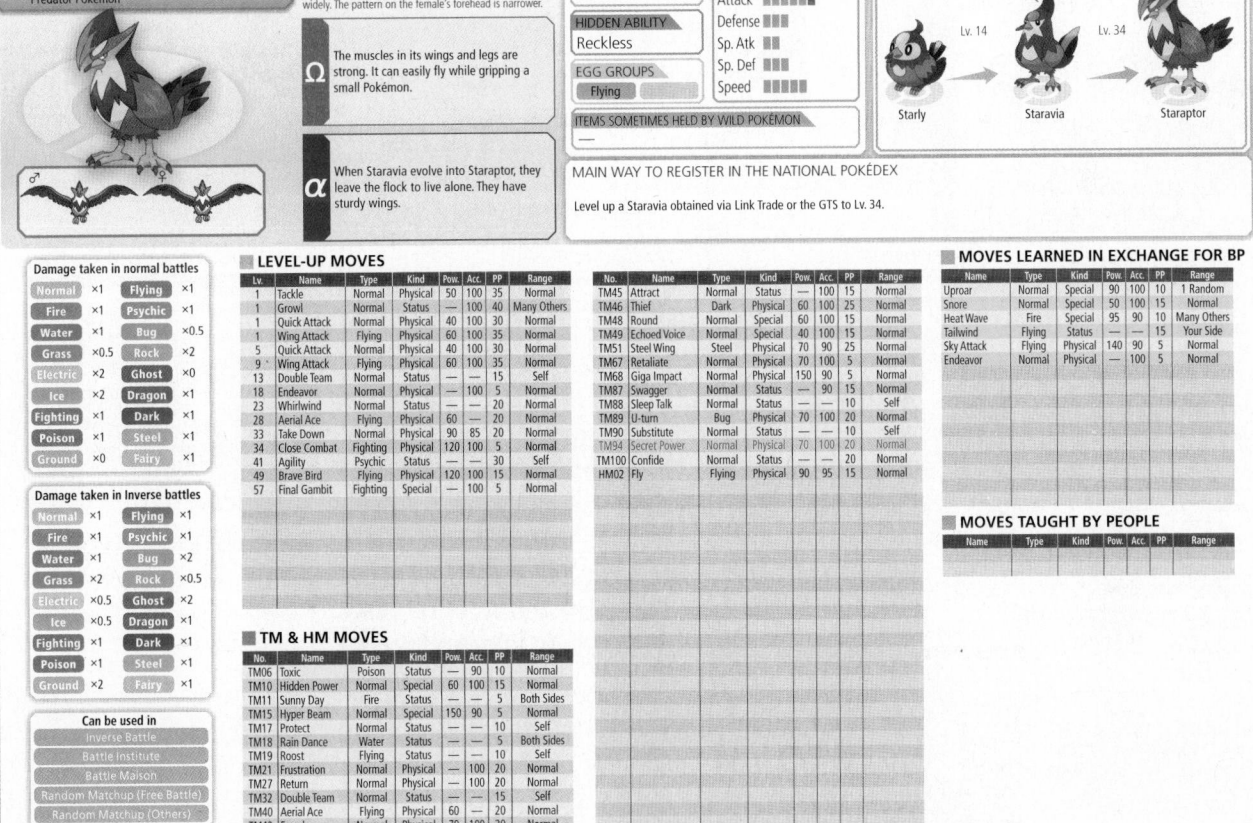

National Pokédex **397** Hoenn Pokédex —

Staravia

Starling Pokémon

Normal Flying

HEIGHT: 2'00" WEIGHT: 34.2 lbs.

The pattern on the male's forehead is spread out more widely. The pattern on the female's forehead is narrower.

Ω They maintain huge flocks, although fierce scuffles break out between various flocks.

α It lives in forests and fields. Squabbles over territory occur when flocks collide.

ABILITY: Intimidate

HIDDEN ABILITY: Reckless

EGG GROUPS: Flying

STAT GROWTH RATES

HP	■■
Attack	■■■■
Defense	■■
Sp. Atk	■■
Sp. Def	■■
Speed	■■■■

ITEMS SOMETIMES HELD BY WILD POKÉMON: —

EVOLUTION: Starly → Lv. 14 → Staravia → Lv. 34 → Staraptor

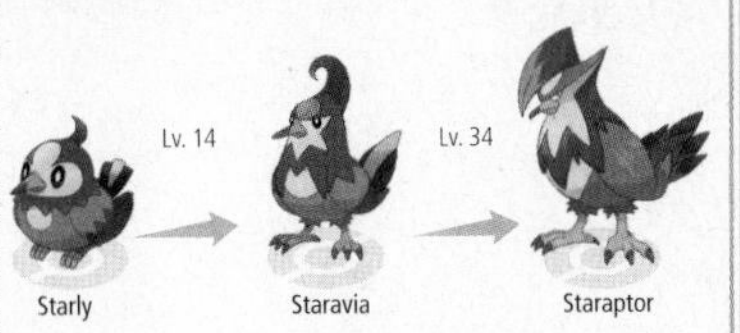

MAIN WAY TO REGISTER IN THE NATIONAL POKÉDEX

Appears in *Pokémon X* and *Pokémon Y*. Bring it to your game using Link Trade or the GTS.

Damage taken in normal battles

Type		Type	
Normal	×1	Flying	×1
Fire	×1	Psychic	×1
Water	×1	Bug	×0.5
Grass	×0.5	Rock	×2
Electric	×2	Ghost	×0
Ice	×2	Dragon	×1
Fighting	×1	Dark	×1
Poison	×1	Steel	×1
Ground	×0	Fairy	×1

Damage taken in Inverse battles

Type		Type	
Normal	×1	Flying	×1
Fire	×1	Psychic	×1
Water	×1	Bug	×2
Grass	×2	Rock	×0.5
Electric	×0.5	Ghost	×2
Ice	×0.5	Dragon	×1
Fighting	×1	Dark	×1
Poison	×1	Steel	×1
Ground	×2	Fairy	×1

Can be used in

- Inverse Battle
- Battle Institute
- Battle Maison
- Random Matchup (Free Battle)
- Random Matchup (Others)

LEVEL-UP MOVES

Lv.	Name	Type	Kind	Pow.	Acc.	PP	Range
1	Tackle	Normal	Physical	50	100	35	Normal
1	Growl	Normal	Status	—	100	40	Many Others
1	Quick Attack	Normal	Physical	40	100	30	Normal
5	Quick Attack	Normal	Physical	40	100	30	Normal
9	Wing Attack	Flying	Physical	60	100	35	Normal
13	Double Team	Normal	Status	—	—	15	Self
18	Endeavor	Normal	Physical	—	100	5	Normal
23	Whirlwind	Normal	Status	—	—	20	Normal
28	Aerial Ace	Flying	Physical	60	—	20	Normal
33	Take Down	Normal	Physical	90	85	20	Normal
38	Agility	Psychic	Status	—	—	30	Self
43	Brave Bird	Flying	Physical	120	100	15	Normal
48	Final Gambit	Fighting	Special	—	100	5	Normal

TM & HM MOVES

No.	Name	Type	Kind	Pow.	Acc.	PP	Range
TM06	Toxic	Poison	Status	—	90	10	Normal
TM10	Hidden Power	Normal	Special	60	100	15	Normal
TM11	Sunny Day	Fire	Status	—	—	5	Both Sides
TM17	Protect	Normal	Status	—	—	10	Self
TM18	Rain Dance	Water	Status	—	—	5	Both Sides
TM19	Roost	Flying	Status	—	—	10	Self
TM21	Frustration	Normal	Physical	—	100	20	Normal
TM27	Return	Normal	Physical	—	100	20	Normal
TM32	Double Team	Normal	Status	—	—	15	Self
TM40	Aerial Ace	Flying	Physical	60	—	20	Normal
TM42	Facade	Normal	Physical	70	100	20	Normal
TM44	Rest	Psychic	Status	—	—	10	Self
TM45	Attract	Normal	Status	—	100	15	Normal
TM46	Thief	Dark	Physical	60	100	25	Normal
TM48	Round	Normal	Special	60	100	15	Normal
TM49	Echoed Voice	Normal	Special	40	100	15	Normal
TM51	Steel Wing	Steel	Physical	70	90	25	Normal
TM67	Retaliate	Normal	Physical	70	100	5	Normal
TM87	Swagger	Normal	Status	—	90	15	Normal
TM88	Sleep Talk	Normal	Status	—	—	10	Self
TM89	U-turn	Bug	Physical	70	100	20	Normal
TM90	Substitute	Normal	Status	—	—	10	Self
TM94	Secret Power	Normal	Physical	70	100	20	Normal
TM100	Confide	Normal	Status	—	—	20	Normal
HM02	Fly	Flying	Physical	90	95	15	Normal

MOVES LEARNED IN EXCHANGE FOR BP

Name	Type	Kind	Pow.	Acc.	PP	Range
Uproar	Normal	Special	90	100	10	1 Random
Snore	Normal	Special	50	100	15	Normal
Heat Wave	Fire	Special	95	90	10	Many Others
Tailwind	Flying	Status	—	—	15	Your Side
Endeavor	Normal	Physical	—	100	5	Normal

MOVES TAUGHT BY PEOPLE

Name	Type	Kind	Pow.	Acc.	PP	Range

National Pokédex **398** Hoenn Pokédex —

Staraptor

Predator Pokémon

Normal Flying

HEIGHT: 3'11" WEIGHT: 54.9 lbs.

The pattern on the male's forehead is spread out more widely. The pattern on the female's forehead is narrower.

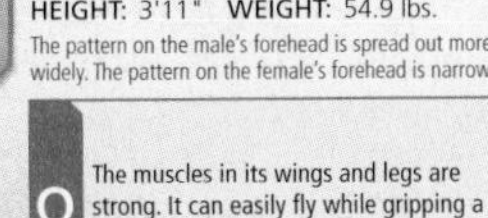

Ω The muscles in its wings and legs are strong. It can easily fly while gripping a small Pokémon.

α When Staravia evolve into Staraptor, they leave the flock to live alone. They have sturdy wings.

ABILITY: Intimidate

HIDDEN ABILITY: Reckless

EGG GROUPS: Flying

STAT GROWTH RATES

HP	■■■
Attack	■■■■■■
Defense	■■■
Sp. Atk	■■
Sp. Def	■■■
Speed	■■■■■

ITEMS SOMETIMES HELD BY WILD POKÉMON: —

EVOLUTION: Starly → Lv. 14 → Staravia → Lv. 34 → Staraptor

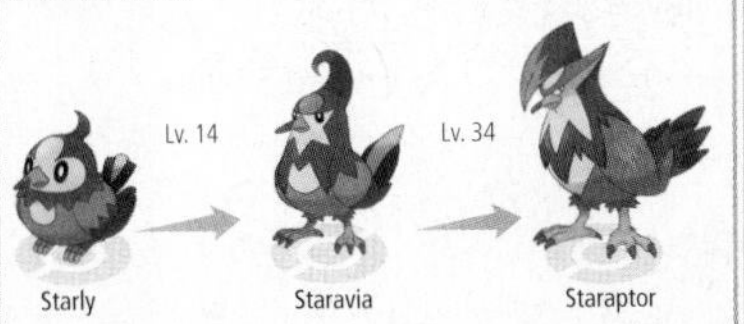

MAIN WAY TO REGISTER IN THE NATIONAL POKÉDEX

Level up a Staravia obtained via Link Trade or the GTS to Lv. 34.

Damage taken in normal battles

Type		Type	
Normal	×1	Flying	×1
Fire	×1	Psychic	×1
Water	×1	Bug	×0.5
Grass	×0.5	Rock	×2
Electric	×2	Ghost	×0
Ice	×2	Dragon	×1
Fighting	×1	Dark	×1
Poison	×1	Steel	×1
Ground	×0	Fairy	×1

Damage taken in Inverse battles

Type		Type	
Normal	×1	Flying	×1
Fire	×1	Psychic	×1
Water	×1	Bug	×2
Grass	×2	Rock	×0.5
Electric	×0.5	Ghost	×2
Ice	×0.5	Dragon	×1
Fighting	×1	Dark	×1
Poison	×1	Steel	×1
Ground	×2	Fairy	×1

Can be used in

- Inverse Battle
- Battle Institute
- Battle Maison
- Random Matchup (Free Battle)
- Random Matchup (Others)

LEVEL-UP MOVES

Lv.	Name	Type	Kind	Pow.	Acc.	PP	Range
1	Tackle	Normal	Physical	50	100	35	Normal
1	Growl	Normal	Status	—	100	40	Many Others
1	Quick Attack	Normal	Physical	40	100	30	Normal
1	Wing Attack	Flying	Physical	60	100	35	Normal
5	Quick Attack	Normal	Physical	40	100	30	Normal
9	Wing Attack	Flying	Physical	60	100	35	Normal
13	Double Team	Normal	Status	—	—	15	Self
18	Endeavor	Normal	Physical	—	100	5	Normal
23	Whirlwind	Normal	Status	—	—	20	Normal
28	Aerial Ace	Flying	Physical	60	—	20	Normal
33	Take Down	Normal	Physical	90	85	20	Normal
34	Close Combat	Fighting	Physical	120	100	5	Normal
41	Agility	Psychic	Status	—	—	30	Self
49	Brave Bird	Flying	Physical	120	100	15	Normal
57	Final Gambit	Fighting	Special	—	100	5	Normal

TM & HM MOVES

No.	Name	Type	Kind	Pow.	Acc.	PP	Range
TM06	Toxic	Poison	Status	—	90	10	Normal
TM10	Hidden Power	Normal	Special	60	100	15	Normal
TM11	Sunny Day	Fire	Status	—	—	5	Both Sides
TM15	Hyper Beam	Normal	Special	150	90	5	Normal
TM17	Protect	Normal	Status	—	—	10	Self
TM18	Rain Dance	Water	Status	—	—	5	Both Sides
TM19	Roost	Flying	Status	—	—	10	Self
TM21	Frustration	Normal	Physical	—	100	20	Normal
TM27	Return	Normal	Physical	—	100	20	Normal
TM32	Double Team	Normal	Status	—	—	15	Self
TM40	Aerial Ace	Flying	Physical	60	—	20	Normal
TM42	Facade	Normal	Physical	70	100	20	Normal
TM44	Rest	Psychic	Status	—	—	10	Self
TM45	Attract	Normal	Status	—	100	15	Normal
TM46	Thief	Dark	Physical	60	100	25	Normal
TM48	Round	Normal	Special	60	100	15	Normal
TM49	Echoed Voice	Normal	Special	40	100	15	Normal
TM51	Steel Wing	Steel	Physical	70	90	25	Normal
TM67	Retaliate	Normal	Physical	70	100	5	Normal
TM68	Giga Impact	Normal	Physical	150	90	5	Normal
TM87	Swagger	Normal	Status	—	90	15	Normal
TM88	Sleep Talk	Normal	Status	—	—	10	Self
TM89	U-turn	Bug	Physical	70	100	20	Normal
TM90	Substitute	Normal	Status	—	—	10	Self
TM94	Secret Power	Normal	Physical	70	100	20	Normal
TM100	Confide	Normal	Status	—	—	20	Normal
HM02	Fly	Flying	Physical	90	95	15	Normal

MOVES LEARNED IN EXCHANGE FOR BP

Name	Type	Kind	Pow.	Acc.	PP	Range
Uproar	Normal	Special	90	100	10	1 Random
Snore	Normal	Special	50	100	15	Normal
Heat Wave	Fire	Special	95	90	10	Many Others
Tailwind	Flying	Status	—	—	15	Your Side
Sky Attack	Flying	Physical	140	90	5	Normal
Endeavor	Normal	Physical	—	100	5	Normal

MOVES TAUGHT BY PEOPLE

Name	Type	Kind	Pow.	Acc.	PP	Range

National Pokédex **399** Hoenn Pokédex —

Bidoof

Plump Mouse Pokémon

Normal

HEIGHT: 1'08" WEIGHT: 44.1 lbs.

A male has more tufts on its tail than a female.

♂ ♀

Ω With nerves of steel, nothing can perturb it. It is more agile and active than it appears.

α It constantly gnaws on logs and rocks to whittle down its front teeth. It nests alongside water.

ABILITIES
Simple
Unaware

HIDDEN ABILITY
Moody

EGG GROUPS
Water 1 | Field

STAT GROWTH RATES
HP ■■■
Attack ■■
Defense ■■
Sp. Atk ■■
Sp. Def ■■
Speed ■■

ITEMS SOMETIMES HELD BY WILD POKÉMON
—

EVOLUTION
Bidoof → Lv. 15 → Bibarel

MAIN WAY TO REGISTER IN THE NATIONAL POKÉDEX

Appears in *Pokémon X* and *Pokémon Y*. Bring it to your game using Link Trade or the GTS.

Damage taken in normal battles

Type		Type	
Normal	×1	Flying	×1
Fire	×1	Psychic	×1
Water	×1	Bug	×1
Grass	×1	Rock	×1
Electric	×1	Ghost	×0
Ice	×1	Dragon	×1
Fighting	×2	Dark	×1
Poison	×1	Steel	×1
Ground	×1	Fairy	×1

Damage taken in Inverse battles

Type		Type	
Normal	×1	Flying	×1
Fire	×1	Psychic	×1
Water	×1	Bug	×1
Grass	×1	Rock	×1
Electric	×1	Ghost	×2
Ice	×1	Dragon	×1
Fighting	×0.5	Dark	×1
Poison	×1	Steel	×1
Ground	×1	Fairy	×1

Can be used in
Inverse Battle
Battle Institute
Battle Maison
Random Matchup (Free Battle)
Random Matchup (Others)

LEVEL-UP MOVES

Lv.	Name	Type	Kind	Pow.	Acc.	PP	Range
1	Tackle	Normal	Physical	50	100	35	Normal
5	Growl	Normal	Status	—	100	40	Many Others
9	Defense Curl	Normal	Status	—	—	40	Self
13	Rollout	Rock	Physical	30	90	20	Normal
17	Headbutt	Normal	Physical	70	100	15	Normal
21	Hyper Fang	Normal	Physical	80	90	15	Normal
25	Yawn	Normal	Status	—	—	10	Normal
29	Amnesia	Psychic	Status	—	—	20	Self
33	Take Down	Normal	Physical	90	85	20	Normal
37	Super Fang	Normal	Physical	—	90	10	Normal
41	Superpower	Fighting	Physical	120	100	5	Normal
45	Curse	Ghost	Status	—	—	10	Varies

TM & HM MOVES

No.	Name	Type	Kind	Pow.	Acc.	PP	Range
TM06	Toxic	Poison	Status	—	90	10	Normal
TM10	Hidden Power	Normal	Special	60	100	15	Normal
TM11	Sunny Day	Fire	Status	—	—	5	Both Sides
TM12	Taunt	Dark	Status	—	100	20	Normal
TM13	Ice Beam	Ice	Special	90	100	10	Normal
TM14	Blizzard	Ice	Special	110	70	5	Many Others
TM17	Protect	Normal	Status	—	—	10	Self
TM18	Rain Dance	Water	Status	—	—	5	Both Sides
TM21	Frustration	Normal	Physical	—	100	20	Normal
TM24	Thunderbolt	Electric	Special	90	100	15	Normal
TM25	Thunder	Electric	Special	110	70	10	Normal
TM27	Return	Normal	Physical	—	100	20	Normal
TM28	Dig	Ground	Physical	80	100	10	Normal
TM30	Shadow Ball	Ghost	Special	80	100	15	Normal
TM32	Double Team	Normal	Status	—	—	15	Self
TM42	Facade	Normal	Physical	70	100	20	Normal
TM44	Rest	Psychic	Status	—	—	10	Self
TM45	Attract	Normal	Status	—	100	15	Normal
TM46	Thief	Dark	Physical	60	100	25	Normal
TM48	Round	Normal	Special	60	100	15	Normal
TM49	Echoed Voice	Normal	Special	40	100	15	Normal
TM57	Charge Beam	Electric	Special	50	90	10	Normal
TM67	Retaliate	Normal	Physical	70	100	5	Normal
TM73	Thunder Wave	Electric	Status	—	100	20	Normal
TM86	Grass Knot	Grass	Special	—	100	20	Normal
TM87	Swagger	Normal	Status	—	90	15	Normal
TM88	Sleep Talk	Normal	Status	—	—	10	Self
TM90	Substitute	Normal	Status	—	—	10	Self
TM94	Secret Power	Normal	Physical	70	100	20	Normal
TM100	Confide	Normal	Status	—	—	20	Normal
HM01	Cut	Normal	Physical	50	95	30	Normal
HM06	Rock Smash	Fighting	Physical	40	100	15	Normal

MOVES LEARNED IN EXCHANGE FOR BP

Name	Type	Kind	Pow.	Acc.	PP	Range
Covet	Normal	Physical	60	100	25	Normal
Super Fang	Normal	Physical	—	90	10	Normal
Last Resort	Normal	Physical	140	100	5	Normal
Superpower	Fighting	Physical	120	100	5	Normal
Icy Wind	Ice	Special	55	95	15	Many Others
Aqua Tail	Water	Physical	90	90	10	Normal
Iron Tail	Steel	Physical	100	75	15	Normal
Snore	Normal	Special	50	100	15	Normal
Shock Wave	Electric	Special	60	—	20	Normal
Stealth Rock	Rock	Status	—	—	20	Other Side

MOVES TAUGHT BY PEOPLE

Name	Type	Kind	Pow.	Acc.	PP	Range

EGG MOVES

Name	Type	Kind	Pow.	Acc.	PP	Range
Quick Attack	Normal	Physical	40	100	30	Normal
Water Sport	Water	Status	—	—	15	Both Sides
Double-Edge	Normal	Physical	120	100	15	Normal
Fury Swipes	Normal	Physical	18	80	15	Normal
Defense Curl	Normal	Status	—	—	40	Self
Rollout	Rock	Physical	30	90	20	Normal
Odor Sleuth	Normal	Status	—	—	40	Normal
Aqua Tail	Water	Physical	90	90	10	Normal
Rock Climb	Normal	Physical	90	85	20	Normal
Sleep Talk	Normal	Status	—	—	10	Self
Endure	Normal	Status	—	—	10	Self
Skull Bash	Normal	Physical	130	100	10	Normal

National Pokédex **400** Hoenn Pokédex —

Bibarel

Beaver Pokémon

Normal | Water

HEIGHT: 3'03" WEIGHT: 69.4 lbs.

The patch of white fur on the male's face is larger.
The patch of white fur on the female's face is smaller.

♂ ♀

Ω It busily makes its nest with stacks of branches and roots it has cut up with its sharp incisors.

α It makes its nest by damming streams with bark and mud. It is known as an industrious worker.

ABILITIES
Simple
Unaware

HIDDEN ABILITY
Moody

EGG GROUPS
Water 1 | Field

STAT GROWTH RATES
HP ■■■
Attack ■■■■
Defense ■■■
Sp. Atk ■■■
Sp. Def ■■■
Speed ■■■■

ITEMS SOMETIMES HELD BY WILD POKÉMON
—

EVOLUTION
Bidoof → Lv. 15 → Bibarel

MAIN WAY TO REGISTER IN THE NATIONAL POKÉDEX

Appears in *Pokémon X* and *Pokémon Y*. Bring it to your game using Link Trade or the GTS.

Damage taken in normal battles

Type		Type	
Normal	×1	Flying	×1
Fire	×0.5	Psychic	×1
Water	×0.5	Bug	×1
Grass	×2	Rock	×1
Electric	×2	Ghost	×0
Ice	×0.5	Dragon	×1
Fighting	×2	Dark	×1
Poison	×1	Steel	×0.5
Ground	×1	Fairy	×1

Damage taken in Inverse battles

Type		Type	
Normal	×1	Flying	×1
Fire	×2	Psychic	×1
Water	×2	Bug	×1
Grass	×0.5	Rock	×1
Electric	×0.5	Ghost	×2
Ice	×2	Dragon	×1
Fighting	×0.5	Dark	×1
Poison	×1	Steel	×2
Ground	×1	Fairy	×1

Can be used in
Inverse Battle
Battle Institute
Battle Maison
Random Matchup (Free Battle)
Random Matchup (Others)

LEVEL-UP MOVES

Lv.	Name	Type	Kind	Pow.	Acc.	PP	Range
1	Rototiller	Ground	Status	—	—	10	Adjacent
1	Tackle	Normal	Physical	50	100	35	Normal
1	Growl	Normal	Status	—	100	40	Many Others
5	Growl	Normal	Status	—	100	40	Many Others
9	Defense Curl	Normal	Status	—	—	40	Self
13	Rollout	Rock	Physical	30	90	20	Normal
15	Water Gun	Water	Special	40	100	25	Normal
18	Headbutt	Normal	Physical	70	100	15	Normal
23	Hyper Fang	Normal	Physical	80	90	15	Normal
28	Yawn	Normal	Status	—	—	10	Normal
33	Amnesia	Psychic	Status	—	—	20	Self
38	Take Down	Normal	Physical	90	85	20	Normal
43	Super Fang	Normal	Physical	—	90	10	Normal
48	Superpower	Fighting	Physical	120	100	5	Normal
53	Curse	Ghost	Status	—	—	10	Varies

TM & HM MOVES

No.	Name	Type	Kind	Pow.	Acc.	PP	Range
TM06	Toxic	Poison	Status	—	90	10	Normal
TM10	Hidden Power	Normal	Special	60	100	15	Normal
TM11	Sunny Day	Fire	Status	—	—	5	Both Sides
TM12	Taunt	Dark	Status	—	100	20	Normal
TM13	Ice Beam	Ice	Special	90	100	10	Normal
TM14	Blizzard	Ice	Special	110	70	5	Many Others
TM15	Hyper Beam	Normal	Special	150	90	5	Normal
TM17	Protect	Normal	Status	—	—	10	Self
TM18	Rain Dance	Water	Status	—	—	5	Both Sides
TM21	Frustration	Normal	Physical	—	100	20	Normal
TM24	Thunderbolt	Electric	Special	90	100	15	Normal
TM25	Thunder	Electric	Special	110	70	10	Normal
TM27	Return	Normal	Physical	—	100	20	Normal
TM28	Dig	Ground	Physical	80	100	10	Normal
TM30	Shadow Ball	Ghost	Special	80	100	15	Normal
TM32	Double Team	Normal	Status	—	—	15	Self
TM42	Facade	Normal	Physical	70	100	20	Normal
TM44	Rest	Psychic	Status	—	—	10	Self
TM45	Attract	Normal	Status	—	100	15	Normal
TM46	Thief	Dark	Physical	60	100	25	Normal
TM48	Round	Normal	Special	60	100	15	Normal
TM49	Echoed Voice	Normal	Special	40	100	15	Normal
TM55	Scald	Water	Special	80	100	15	Normal
TM56	Fling	Dark	Physical	—	100	10	Normal
TM57	Charge Beam	Electric	Special	50	90	10	Normal
TM67	Retaliate	Normal	Physical	70	100	5	Normal
TM68	Giga Impact	Normal	Physical	150	90	5	Normal
TM73	Thunder Wave	Electric	Status	—	100	20	Normal
TM78	Bulldoze	Ground	Physical	60	100	20	Adjacent
TM86	Grass Knot	Grass	Special	—	100	20	Normal
TM87	Swagger	Normal	Status	—	90	15	Normal
TM88	Sleep Talk	Normal	Status	—	—	10	Self
TM90	Substitute	Normal	Status	—	—	10	Self
TM94	Secret Power	Normal	Physical	70	100	20	Normal
TM100	Confide	Normal	Status	—	—	20	Normal
HM01	Cut	Normal	Physical	50	95	30	Normal
HM03	Surf	Water	Special	90	100	15	Adjacent
HM04	Strength	Normal	Physical	80	100	15	Normal
HM05	Waterfall	Water	Physical	80	100	15	Normal
HM06	Rock Smash	Fighting	Physical	40	100	15	Normal
HM07	Dive	Water	Physical	80	100	10	Normal

MOVES LEARNED IN EXCHANGE FOR BP

Name	Type	Kind	Pow.	Acc.	PP	Range
Covet	Normal	Physical	60	100	25	Normal
Super Fang	Normal	Physical	—	90	10	Normal
Last Resort	Normal	Physical	140	100	5	Normal
Superpower	Fighting	Physical	120	100	5	Normal
Icy Wind	Ice	Special	55	95	15	Many Others
Aqua Tail	Water	Physical	90	90	10	Normal
Iron Tail	Steel	Physical	100	75	15	Normal
Snore	Normal	Special	50	100	15	Normal
Focus Punch	Fighting	Physical	150	100	20	Normal
Shock Wave	Electric	Special	60	—	20	Normal
Water Pulse	Water	Special	60	100	20	Normal
Stealth Rock	Rock	Status	—	—	20	Other Side

MOVES TAUGHT BY PEOPLE

Name	Type	Kind	Pow.	Acc.	PP	Range

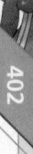

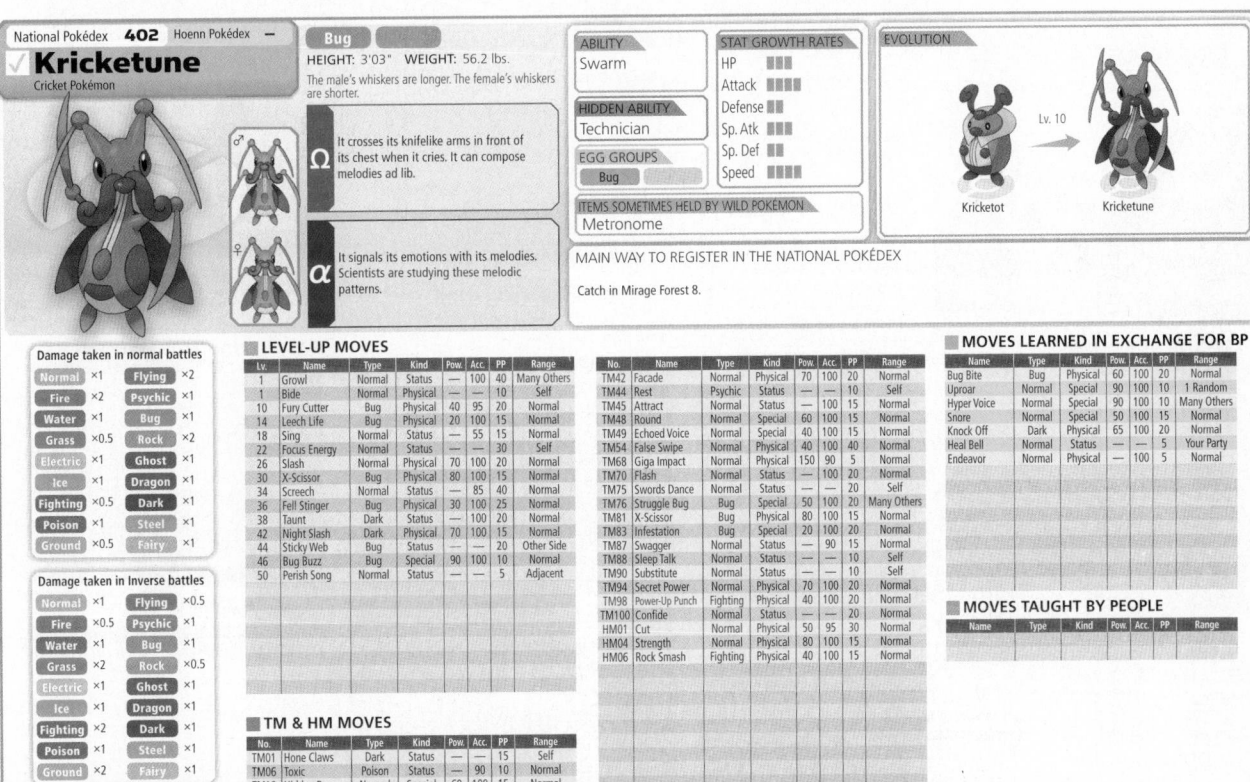

National Pokédex **401** Hoenn Pokédex —

Kricketot

Cricket Pokémon

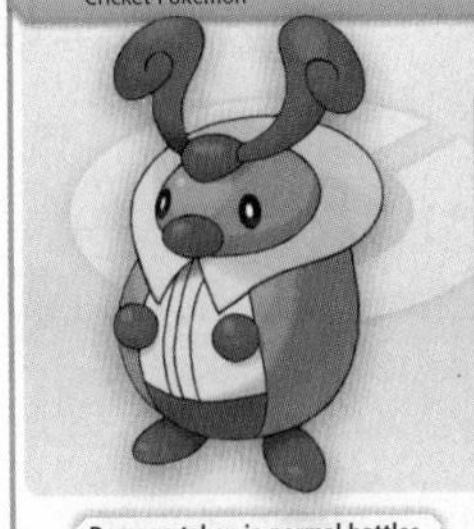

Bug

HEIGHT: 1'00" WEIGHT: 4.9 lbs.

The male's collar is thinner. The female's collar is thicker.

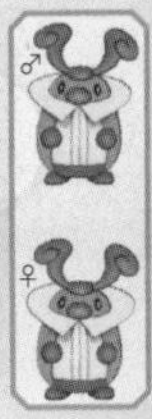

♂

Ω It chats with others using the sounds of its colliding antennae. These sounds are fall hallmarks.

♀

α When its antennae hit each other, it sounds like the music of a xylophone.

ABILITY

Shed Skin

HIDDEN ABILITY

Run Away

EGG GROUPS

Bug

STAT GROWTH RATES

HP

Attack

Defense

Sp. Atk

Sp. Def

Speed

ITEMS SOMETIMES HELD BY WILD POKÉMON

—

EVOLUTION

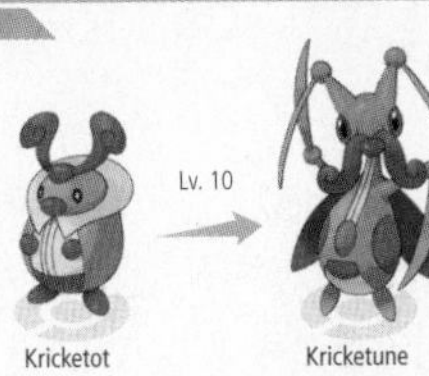

Kricketot → Lv. 10 → Kricketune

MAIN WAY TO REGISTER IN THE NATIONAL POKÉDEX

Leave a Kricketune at a Pokémon Day Care, then hatch the Pokémon Egg that is found.

Damage taken in normal battles

Normal	×1	Flying	×2
Fire	×2	Psychic	×1
Water	×1	Bug	×1
Grass	×0.5	Rock	×2
Electric	×1	Ghost	×1
Ice	×1	Dragon	×1
Fighting	×0.5	Dark	×1
Poison	×1	Steel	×1
Ground	×0.5	Fairy	×1

Damage taken in Inverse battles

Normal	×1	Flying	×0.5
Fire	×0.5	Psychic	×1
Water	×1	Bug	×1
Grass	×2	Rock	×0.5
Electric	×1	Ghost	×1
Ice	×1	Dragon	×1
Fighting	×2	Dark	×1
Poison	×1	Steel	×1
Ground	×2	Fairy	×1

Can be used in

- Inverse Battle
- Battle Institute
- Battle Maison
- Random Matchup (Free Battle)
- Random Matchup (Others)

LEVEL-UP MOVES

Lv.	Name	Type	Kind	Pow.	Acc.	PP	Range
1	Growl	Normal	Status	—	100	40	Many Others
1	Bide	Normal	Physical	—	—	10	Self
6	Struggle Bug	Bug	Special	50	100	20	Many Others
16	Bug Bite	Bug	Physical	60	100	20	Normal

TM & HM MOVES

No.	Name	Type	Kind	Pow.	Acc.	PP	Range
TM76	Struggle Bug	Bug	Special	50	100	20	Many Others

MOVES LEARNED IN EXCHANGE FOR BP

Name	Type	Kind	Pow.	Acc.	PP	Range
Bug Bite	Bug	Physical	60	100	20	Normal
Uproar	Normal	Special	90	100	10	1 Random
Snore	Normal	Special	50	100	15	Normal
Endeavor	Normal	Physical	—	100	5	Normal

MOVES TAUGHT BY PEOPLE

Name	Type	Kind	Pow.	Acc.	PP	Range

National Pokédex **402** Hoenn Pokédex —

Kricketune

Cricket Pokémon

Bug

HEIGHT: 3'03" WEIGHT: 56.2 lbs.

The male's whiskers are longer. The female's whiskers are shorter.

♂

Ω It crosses its knifelike arms in front of its chest when it cries. It can compose melodies ad lib.

♀

α It signals its emotions with its melodies. Scientists are studying these melodic patterns.

ABILITY

Swarm

HIDDEN ABILITY

Technician

EGG GROUPS

Bug

STAT GROWTH RATES

HP

Attack

Defense

Sp. Atk

Sp. Def

Speed

ITEMS SOMETIMES HELD BY WILD POKÉMON

Metronome

EVOLUTION

Kricketot → Lv. 10 → Kricketune

MAIN WAY TO REGISTER IN THE NATIONAL POKÉDEX

Catch in Mirage Forest 8.

Damage taken in normal battles

Normal	×1	Flying	×2
Fire	×2	Psychic	×1
Water	×1	Bug	×1
Grass	×0.5	Rock	×2
Electric	×1	Ghost	×1
Ice	×1	Dragon	×1
Fighting	×0.5	Dark	×1
Poison	×1	Steel	×1
Ground	×0.5	Fairy	×1

Damage taken in Inverse battles

Normal	×1	Flying	×0.5
Fire	×0.5	Psychic	×1
Water	×1	Bug	×1
Grass	×2	Rock	×0.5
Electric	×1	Ghost	×1
Ice	×1	Dragon	×1
Fighting	×2	Dark	×1
Poison	×1	Steel	×1
Ground	×2	Fairy	×1

Can be used in

- Inverse Battle
- Battle Institute
- Battle Maison
- Random Matchup (Free Battle)
- Random Matchup (Others)

LEVEL-UP MOVES

Lv.	Name	Type	Kind	Pow.	Acc.	PP	Range
1	Growl	Normal	Status	—	100	40	Many Others
1	Bide	Normal	Physical	—	—	10	Self
10	Fury Cutter	Bug	Physical	40	95	20	Normal
14	Leech Life	Bug	Physical	20	100	15	Normal
18	Sing	Normal	Status	—	55	15	Normal
22	Focus Energy	Normal	Status	—	—	30	Self
26	Slash	Normal	Physical	70	100	20	Normal
30	X-Scissor	Bug	Physical	80	100	15	Normal
34	Screech	Normal	Status	—	85	40	Normal
36	Fell Stinger	Bug	Physical	30	100	25	Normal
38	Taunt	Dark	Status	—	100	20	Normal
42	Night Slash	Dark	Physical	70	100	15	Normal
44	Sticky Web	Bug	Status	—	—	20	Other Side
46	Bug Buzz	Bug	Special	90	100	10	Normal
50	Perish Song	Normal	Status	—	—	5	Adjacent

TM & HM MOVES

No.	Name	Type	Kind	Pow.	Acc.	PP	Range
TM01	Hone Claws	Dark	Status	—	—	15	Self
TM06	Toxic	Poison	Status	—	90	10	Normal
TM10	Hidden Power	Normal	Special	60	100	15	Normal
TM11	Sunny Day	Fire	Status	—	—	5	Both Sides
TM12	Taunt	Dark	Status	—	100	20	Normal
TM15	Hyper Beam	Normal	Special	150	90	5	Normal
TM17	Protect	Normal	Status	—	—	10	Self
TM18	Rain Dance	Water	Status	—	—	5	Both Sides
TM21	Frustration	Normal	Physical	—	100	20	Normal
TM27	Return	Normal	Physical	—	100	20	Normal
TM31	Brick Break	Fighting	Physical	75	100	15	Normal
TM32	Double Team	Normal	Status	—	—	15	Self
TM40	Aerial Ace	Flying	Physical	60	—	20	Normal
TM42	Facade	Normal	Physical	70	100	20	Normal
TM44	Rest	Psychic	Status	—	—	10	Self
TM45	Attract	Normal	Status	—	100	15	Normal
TM48	Round	Normal	Special	60	100	15	Normal
TM49	Echoed Voice	Normal	Special	40	100	15	Normal
TM54	False Swipe	Normal	Physical	40	100	40	Normal
TM68	Giga Impact	Normal	Physical	150	90	5	Normal
TM70	Flash	Normal	Status	—	100	20	Normal
TM75	Swords Dance	Normal	Status	—	—	20	Self
TM76	Struggle Bug	Bug	Special	50	100	20	Many Others
TM81	X-Scissor	Bug	Physical	80	100	15	Normal
TM83	Infestation	Bug	Special	20	100	20	Normal
TM87	Swagger	Normal	Status	—	90	15	Normal
TM88	Sleep Talk	Normal	Status	—	—	10	Self
TM90	Substitute	Normal	Status	—	—	10	Self
TM94	Secret Power	Normal	Physical	70	100	20	Normal
TM98	Power-Up Punch	Fighting	Physical	40	100	20	Normal
TM100	Confide	Normal	Status	—	—	20	Normal
HM01	Cut	Normal	Physical	50	95	30	Normal
HM04	Strength	Normal	Physical	80	100	15	Normal
HM06	Rock Smash	Fighting	Physical	40	100	15	Normal

MOVES LEARNED IN EXCHANGE FOR BP

Name	Type	Kind	Pow.	Acc.	PP	Range
Bug Bite	Bug	Physical	60	100	20	Normal
Uproar	Normal	Special	90	100	10	1 Random
Hyper Voice	Normal	Special	90	100	10	Many Others
Snore	Normal	Special	50	100	15	Normal
Knock Off	Dark	Physical	65	100	20	Normal
Heal Bell	Normal	Status	—	—	5	Your Party
Endeavor	Normal	Physical	—	100	5	Normal

MOVES TAUGHT BY PEOPLE

Name	Type	Kind	Pow.	Acc.	PP	Range

National Pokédex **403** Hoenn Pokédex —

Shinx

Flash Pokémon

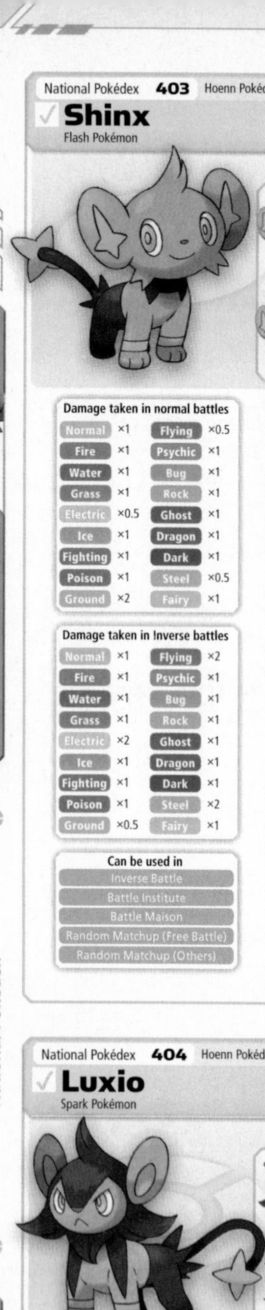

Electric

HEIGHT: 1'08" WEIGHT: 20.9 lbs.

The male has a longer tuft of fur on its head and the black fur on its rear legs extends all the way to its feet, while the female's does not.

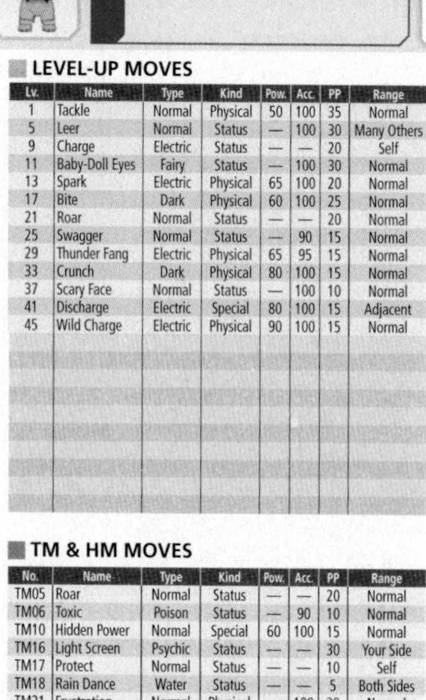

Ω The extension and contraction of its muscles generates electricity. It glows when in trouble.

α All of its fur dazzles if danger is sensed. It flees while the foe is momentarily blinded.

ABILITIES
Rivalry
Intimidate

HIDDEN ABILITY
Guts

EGG GROUPS
Field

STAT GROWTH RATES
HP ■■
Attack ■■■
Defense ■■
Sp. Atk ■■
Sp. Def ■
Speed ■■■

ITEMS SOMETIMES HELD BY WILD POKÉMON
—

EVOLUTION

MAIN WAY TO REGISTER IN THE NATIONAL POKÉDEX

Leave a Luxio or Luxray at a Pokémon Day Care, then hatch the Pokémon Egg that is found.

Damage taken in normal battles

Type		Type	
Normal	×1	Flying	×0.5
Fire	×1	Psychic	×1
Water	×1	Bug	×1
Grass	×1	Rock	×1
Electric	×0.5	Ghost	×1
Ice	×1	Dragon	×1
Fighting	×1	Dark	×1
Poison	×1	Steel	×0.5
Ground	×2	Fairy	×1

Damage taken in Inverse battles

Type		Type	
Normal	×1	Flying	×2
Fire	×1	Psychic	×1
Water	×1	Bug	×1
Grass	×1	Rock	×1
Electric	×2	Ghost	×1
Ice	×1	Dragon	×1
Fighting	×1	Dark	×1
Poison	×1	Steel	×2
Ground	×0.5	Fairy	×1

Can be used in
Inverse Battle
Battle Institute
Battle Maison
Random Matchup (Free Battle)
Random Matchup (Others)

LEVEL-UP MOVES

Lv.	Name	Type	Kind	Pow.	Acc.	PP	Range
1	Tackle	Normal	Physical	50	100	35	Normal
5	Leer	Normal	Status	—	100	30	Many Others
9	Charge	Electric	Status	—	—	20	Self
11	Baby-Doll Eyes	Fairy	Status	—	100	30	Normal
13	Spark	Electric	Physical	65	100	20	Normal
17	Bite	Dark	Physical	60	100	25	Normal
21	Roar	Normal	Status	—	—	20	Normal
25	Swagger	Normal	Status	—	90	15	Normal
29	Thunder Fang	Electric	Physical	65	95	15	Normal
33	Crunch	Dark	Physical	80	100	15	Normal
37	Scary Face	Normal	Status	—	100	10	Normal
41	Discharge	Electric	Special	80	100	15	Adjacent
45	Wild Charge	Electric	Physical	90	100	15	Normal

TM & HM MOVES

No.	Name	Type	Kind	Pow.	Acc.	PP	Range
TM05	Roar	Normal	Status	—	—	20	Normal
TM06	Toxic	Poison	Status	—	90	10	Normal
TM10	Hidden Power	Normal	Special	60	100	15	Normal
TM16	Light Screen	Psychic	Status	—	—	30	Your Side
TM17	Protect	Normal	Status	—	—	10	Self
TM18	Rain Dance	Water	Status	—	—	5	Both Sides
TM21	Frustration	Normal	Physical	—	100	20	Normal
TM24	Thunderbolt	Electric	Special	90	100	15	Normal
TM25	Thunder	Electric	Special	110	70	10	Normal
TM27	Return	Normal	Physical	—	100	20	Normal
TM32	Double Team	Normal	Status	—	—	15	Self
TM42	Facade	Normal	Physical	70	100	20	Normal
TM44	Rest	Psychic	Status	—	—	10	Self
TM45	Attract	Normal	Status	—	100	15	Normal
TM46	Thief	Dark	Physical	60	100	25	Normal
TM48	Round	Normal	Special	60	100	15	Normal
TM57	Charge Beam	Electric	Special	50	90	10	Normal
TM70	Flash	Normal	Status	—	100	20	Normal
TM72	Volt Switch	Electric	Special	70	100	20	Normal
TM73	Thunder Wave	Electric	Status	—	100	20	Normal
TM87	Swagger	Normal	Status	—	90	15	Normal
TM88	Sleep Talk	Normal	Status	—	—	10	Self
TM90	Substitute	Normal	Status	—	—	10	Self
TM93	Wild Charge	Electric	Physical	90	100	15	Normal
TM94	Secret Power	Normal	Physical	70	100	20	Normal
TM95	Snarl	Dark	Special	55	95	15	Many Others
TM100	Confide	Normal	Status	—	—	20	Normal
HM04	Strength	Normal	Physical	80	100	15	Normal

MOVES LEARNED IN EXCHANGE FOR BP

Name	Type	Kind	Pow.	Acc.	PP	Range
Signal Beam	Bug	Special	75	100	15	Normal
Magnet Rise	Electric	Status	—	—	10	Self
Iron Tail	Steel	Physical	100	75	15	Normal
Snore	Normal	Special	50	100	15	Normal
Shock Wave	Electric	Special	60	—	20	Normal
Helping Hand	Normal	Status	—	—	20	1 Ally

MOVES TAUGHT BY PEOPLE

Name	Type	Kind	Pow.	Acc.	PP	Range

EGG MOVES

Name	Type	Kind	Pow.	Acc.	PP	Range
Ice Fang	Ice	Physical	65	95	15	Normal
Fire Fang	Fire	Physical	65	95	15	Normal
Thunder Fang	Electric	Physical	65	95	15	Normal
Quick Attack	Normal	Physical	40	100	30	Normal
Howl	Normal	Status	—	—	40	Self
Take Down	Normal	Physical	90	85	20	Normal
Night Slash	Dark	Physical	70	100	15	Normal
Shock Wave	Electric	Special	60	—	20	Normal
Swift	Normal	Special	60	—	20	Many Others
Double Kick	Fighting	Physical	30	100	30	Normal
Signal Beam	Bug	Special	75	100	15	Normal
Helping Hand	Normal	Status	—	—	20	1 Ally
Eerie Impulse	Electric	Status	—	100	15	Normal
Fake Tears	Dark	Status	—	100	20	Normal

National Pokédex **404** Hoenn Pokédex —

Luxio

Spark Pokémon

Electric

HEIGHT: 2'11" WEIGHT: 67.2 lbs.

The male has a longer tuft of fur on its head and the black fur on its rear legs extends farther down than on the female's.

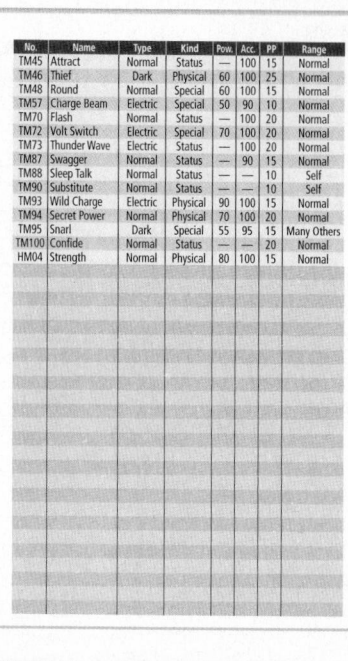

Ω Its claws loose electricity with enough amperage to cause fainting. They live in small groups.

α Strong electricity courses through the tips of its sharp claws. A light scratch causes fainting in foes.

ABILITIES
Rivalry
Intimidate

HIDDEN ABILITY
Guts

EGG GROUPS
Field

STAT GROWTH RATES
HP ■■■
Attack ■■■■
Defense ■■
Sp. Atk ■■■
Sp. Def ■■
Speed ■■■

ITEMS SOMETIMES HELD BY WILD POKÉMON
—

EVOLUTION

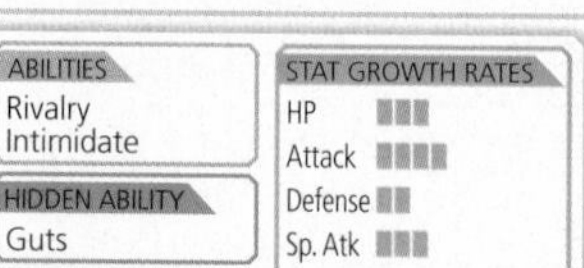

MAIN WAY TO REGISTER IN THE NATIONAL POKÉDEX

Catch on Route 118. Appears as a hidden Pokémon after you battle Groudon or Kyogre.

Damage taken in normal battles

Type		Type	
Normal	×1	Flying	×0.5
Fire	×1	Psychic	×1
Water	×1	Bug	×1
Grass	×1	Rock	×1
Electric	×0.5	Ghost	×1
Ice	×1	Dragon	×1
Fighting	×1	Dark	×1
Poison	×1	Steel	×0.5
Ground	×2	Fairy	×1

Damage taken in Inverse battles

Type		Type	
Normal	×1	Flying	×2
Fire	×1	Psychic	×1
Water	×1	Bug	×1
Grass	×1	Rock	×1
Electric	×2	Ghost	×1
Ice	×1	Dragon	×1
Fighting	×1	Dark	×1
Poison	×1	Steel	×2
Ground	×0.5	Fairy	×1

Can be used in
Inverse Battle
Battle Institute
Battle Maison
Random Matchup (Free Battle)
Random Matchup (Others)

LEVEL-UP MOVES

Lv.	Name	Type	Kind	Pow.	Acc.	PP	Range
1	Tackle	Normal	Physical	50	100	35	Normal
1	Leer	Normal	Status	—	100	30	Many Others
5	Leer	Normal	Status	—	100	30	Many Others
9	Charge	Electric	Status	—	—	20	Self
13	Spark	Electric	Physical	65	100	20	Normal
18	Bite	Dark	Physical	60	100	25	Normal
23	Roar	Normal	Status	—	—	20	Normal
28	Swagger	Normal	Status	—	90	15	Normal
33	Thunder Fang	Electric	Physical	65	95	15	Normal
38	Crunch	Dark	Physical	80	100	15	Normal
43	Scary Face	Normal	Status	—	100	10	Normal
48	Discharge	Electric	Special	80	100	15	Adjacent
53	Wild Charge	Electric	Physical	90	100	15	Normal

TM & HM MOVES

No.	Name	Type	Kind	Pow.	Acc.	PP	Range
TM05	Roar	Normal	Status	—	—	20	Normal
TM06	Toxic	Poison	Status	—	90	10	Normal
TM10	Hidden Power	Normal	Special	60	100	15	Normal
TM16	Light Screen	Psychic	Status	—	—	30	Your Side
TM17	Protect	Normal	Status	—	—	10	Self
TM18	Rain Dance	Water	Status	—	—	5	Both Sides
TM21	Frustration	Normal	Physical	—	100	20	Normal
TM24	Thunderbolt	Electric	Special	90	100	15	Normal
TM25	Thunder	Electric	Special	110	70	10	Normal
TM27	Return	Normal	Physical	—	100	20	Normal
TM32	Double Team	Normal	Status	—	—	15	Self
TM42	Facade	Normal	Physical	70	100	20	Normal
TM44	Rest	Psychic	Status	—	—	10	Self
TM45	Attract	Normal	Status	—	100	15	Normal
TM46	Thief	Dark	Physical	60	100	25	Normal
TM48	Round	Normal	Special	60	100	15	Normal
TM57	Charge Beam	Electric	Special	50	90	10	Normal
TM70	Flash	Normal	Status	—	100	20	Normal
TM72	Volt Switch	Electric	Special	70	100	20	Normal
TM73	Thunder Wave	Electric	Status	—	100	20	Normal
TM87	Swagger	Normal	Status	—	90	15	Normal
TM88	Sleep Talk	Normal	Status	—	—	10	Self
TM90	Substitute	Normal	Status	—	—	10	Self
TM93	Wild Charge	Electric	Physical	90	100	15	Normal
TM94	Secret Power	Normal	Physical	70	100	20	Normal
TM95	Snarl	Dark	Special	55	95	15	Many Others
TM100	Confide	Normal	Status	—	—	20	Normal
HM04	Strength	Normal	Physical	80	100	15	Normal

MOVES LEARNED IN EXCHANGE FOR BP

Name	Type	Kind	Pow.	Acc.	PP	Range
Signal Beam	Bug	Special	75	100	15	Normal
Magnet Rise	Electric	Status	—	—	10	Self
Iron Tail	Steel	Physical	100	75	15	Normal
Snore	Normal	Special	50	100	15	Normal
Shock Wave	Electric	Special	60	—	20	Normal
Helping Hand	Normal	Status	—	—	20	1 Ally

MOVES TAUGHT BY PEOPLE

Name	Type	Kind	Pow.	Acc.	PP	Range

National Pokédex **405** Hoenn Pokédex —

Luxray

Gleam Eyes Pokémon

Electric

HEIGHT: 4'07" WEIGHT: 92.6 lbs.

The male has a longer tuft of fur on its head than the female.

Ω When its eyes gleam gold, it can spot hiding prey—even those taking shelter behind a wall.

α Luxray's ability to see through objects comes in handy when it's scouting for danger.

ABILITIES
Rivalry
Intimidate

HIDDEN ABILITY
Guts

EGG GROUPS
Field

STAT GROWTH RATES
HP, Attack, Defense, Sp. Atk, Sp. Def, Speed

ITEMS SOMETIMES HELD BY WILD POKÉMON
—

EVOLUTION

MAIN WAY TO REGISTER IN THE NATIONAL POKÉDEX

Level up Luxio to Lv. 30.

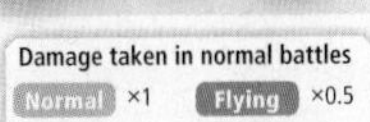

Damage taken in normal battles

Type		Type	
Normal	×1	Flying	×0.5
Fire	×1	Psychic	×1
Water	×1	Bug	×1
Grass	×1	Rock	×1
Electric	×0.5	Ghost	×1
Ice	×1	Dragon	×1
Fighting	×1	Dark	×1
Poison	×1	Steel	×0.5
Ground	×2	Fairy	×1

Damage taken in Inverse battles

Type		Type	
Normal	×1	Flying	×2
Fire	×1	Psychic	×1
Water	×1	Bug	×1
Grass	×1	Rock	×1
Electric	×2	Ghost	×1
Ice	×1	Dragon	×1
Fighting	×1	Dark	×1
Poison	×1	Steel	×2
Ground	×0.5	Fairy	×1

Can be used in
Inverse Battle
Battle Institute
Battle Maison
Random Matchup (Free Battle)
Random Matchup (Others)

LEVEL-UP MOVES

Lv.	Name	Type	Kind	Pow.	Acc.	PP	Range
1	Electric Terrain	Electric	Status	—	—	10	Both Sides
1	Tackle	Normal	Physical	50	100	35	Normal
1	Leer	Normal	Status	—	100	30	Many Others
1	Charge	Electric	Status	—	—	20	Self
5	Leer	Normal	Status	—	100	30	Many Others
9	Charge	Electric	Status	—	—	20	Self
13	Spark	Electric	Physical	65	100	20	Normal
18	Bite	Dark	Physical	60	100	25	Normal
23	Roar	Normal	Status	—	—	20	Normal
28	Swagger	Normal	Status	—	90	15	Normal
35	Thunder Fang	Electric	Physical	65	95	15	Normal
42	Crunch	Dark	Physical	80	100	15	Normal
49	Scary Face	Normal	Status	—	100	10	Normal
56	Discharge	Electric	Special	80	100	15	Adjacent
63	Wild Charge	Electric	Physical	90	100	15	Normal
67	Electric Terrain	Electric	Status	—	—	10	Both Sides

TM & HM MOVES

No.	Name	Type	Kind	Pow.	Acc.	PP	Range
TM05	Roar	Normal	Status	—	—	20	Normal
TM06	Toxic	Poison	Status	—	90	10	Normal
TM10	Hidden Power	Normal	Special	60	100	15	Normal
TM15	Hyper Beam	Normal	Special	150	90	5	Normal
TM16	Light Screen	Psychic	Status	—	—	30	Your Side
TM17	Protect	Normal	Status	—	—	10	Self
TM18	Rain Dance	Water	Status	—	—	5	Both Sides
TM21	Frustration	Normal	Physical	—	100	20	Normal
TM24	Thunderbolt	Electric	Special	90	100	15	Normal
TM25	Thunder	Electric	Special	110	70	10	Normal
TM27	Return	Normal	Physical	—	100	20	Normal
TM32	Double Team	Normal	Status	—	—	15	Self
TM42	Facade	Normal	Physical	70	100	20	Normal
TM44	Rest	Psychic	Status	—	—	10	Self
TM45	Attract	Normal	Status	—	100	15	Normal
TM46	Thief	Dark	Physical	60	100	25	Normal
TM48	Round	Normal	Special	60	100	15	Normal
TM57	Charge Beam	Electric	Special	50	90	10	Normal
TM68	Giga Impact	Normal	Physical	150	90	5	Normal
TM70	Flash	Normal	Status	—	100	20	Normal
TM72	Volt Switch	Electric	Special	70	100	20	Normal
TM73	Thunder Wave	Electric	Status	—	100	20	Normal
TM87	Swagger	Normal	Status	—	90	15	Normal
TM88	Sleep Talk	Normal	Status	—	—	10	Self
TM90	Substitute	Normal	Status	—	—	10	Self
TM93	Wild Charge	Electric	Physical	90	100	15	Normal
TM94	Secret Power	Normal	Physical	70	100	20	Normal
TM95	Snarl	Dark	Special	55	95	15	Many Others
TM100	Confide	Normal	Status	—	—	20	Normal
HM04	Strength	Normal	Physical	80	100	15	Normal

MOVES LEARNED IN EXCHANGE FOR BP

Name	Type	Kind	Pow.	Acc.	PP	Range
Signal Beam	Bug	Special	75	100	15	Normal
Magnet Rise	Electric	Status	—	—	10	Self
Superpower	Fighting	Physical	120	100	5	Normal
Iron Tail	Steel	Physical	100	75	15	Normal
Snore	Normal	Special	50	100	15	Normal
Shock Wave	Electric	Special	60	—	20	Normal
Helping Hand	Normal	Status	—	—	20	1 Ally

MOVES TAUGHT BY PEOPLE

Name	Type	Kind	Pow.	Acc.	PP	Range

National Pokédex **406** Hoenn Pokédex **097**

Budew

Bud Pokémon

Grass Poison

HEIGHT: 0'08" WEIGHT: 2.6 lbs.

Same form for ♂ / ♀

Ω When it feels the sun's warm touch, it opens its bud to release pollen. It lives alongside clear pools.

α Over the winter, it closes its bud and endures the cold. In spring, the bud opens and releases pollen.

ABILITIES
Natural Cure
Poison Point

HIDDEN ABILITY
Leaf Guard

EGG GROUPS
No Eggs Discovered

STAT GROWTH RATES
HP, Attack, Defense, Sp. Atk, Sp. Def, Speed

ITEMS SOMETIMES HELD BY WILD POKÉMON
—

EVOLUTION

Level up with high friendship between 4 A.M. and 7:59 P.M.

Shiny Stone

Budew → Roselia → Roserade

MAIN WAY TO REGISTER IN THE NATIONAL POKÉDEX

Leave a Roselia or Roserade holding a Rose Incense at a Pokémon Day Care, then hatch the Pokémon Egg that is found.

Damage taken in normal battles

Type		Type	
Normal	×1	Flying	×2
Fire	×2	Psychic	×2
Water	×0.5	Bug	×1
Grass	×0.25	Rock	×1
Electric	×0.5	Ghost	×1
Ice	×2	Dragon	×1
Fighting	×0.5	Dark	×1
Poison	×1	Steel	×1
Ground	×1	Fairy	×0.5

Damage taken in Inverse battles

Type		Type	
Normal	×1	Flying	×0.5
Fire	×0.5	Psychic	×0.5
Water	×2	Bug	×1
Grass	×4	Rock	×1
Electric	×2	Ghost	×1
Ice	×0.5	Dragon	×1
Fighting	×2	Dark	×1
Poison	×1	Steel	×1
Ground	×1	Fairy	×2

Can be used in
Inverse Battle
Battle Institute
Battle Maison
Random Matchup (Free Battle)
Random Matchup (Others)

LEVEL-UP MOVES

Lv.	Name	Type	Kind	Pow.	Acc.	PP	Range
1	Absorb	Grass	Special	20	100	25	Normal
4	Growth	Normal	Status	—	—	20	Self
7	Water Sport	Water	Status	—	—	15	Both Sides
10	Stun Spore	Grass	Status	—	75	30	Normal
13	Mega Drain	Grass	Special	40	100	15	Normal
16	Worry Seed	Grass	Status	—	100	10	Normal

TM & HM MOVES

No.	Name	Type	Kind	Pow.	Acc.	PP	Range
TM06	Toxic	Poison	Status	—	90	10	Normal
TM09	Venoshock	Poison	Special	65	100	10	Normal
TM10	Hidden Power	Normal	Special	60	100	15	Normal
TM11	Sunny Day	Fire	Status	—	—	5	Both Sides
TM17	Protect	Normal	Status	—	—	10	Self
TM18	Rain Dance	Water	Status	—	—	5	Both Sides
TM21	Frustration	Normal	Physical	—	100	20	Normal
TM22	Solar Beam	Grass	Special	120	100	10	Normal
TM27	Return	Normal	Physical	—	100	20	Normal
TM30	Shadow Ball	Ghost	Special	80	100	15	Normal
TM32	Double Team	Normal	Status	—	—	15	Self
TM36	Sludge Bomb	Poison	Special	90	100	10	Normal
TM42	Facade	Normal	Physical	70	100	20	Normal
TM44	Rest	Psychic	Status	—	—	10	Self
TM45	Attract	Normal	Status	—	100	15	Normal
TM48	Round	Normal	Special	60	100	15	Normal
TM53	Energy Ball	Grass	Special	90	100	10	Normal
TM70	Flash	Normal	Status	—	100	20	Normal
TM75	Swords Dance	Normal	Status	—	—	20	Self
TM77	Psych Up	Normal	Status	—	—	10	Normal
TM86	Grass Knot	Grass	Special	—	100	20	Normal
TM87	Swagger	Normal	Status	—	90	15	Normal
TM88	Sleep Talk	Normal	Status	—	—	10	Self
TM90	Substitute	Normal	Status	—	—	10	Self
TM94	Secret Power	Normal	Physical	70	100	20	Normal
TM96	Nature Power	Normal	Status	—	—	20	Normal
TM99	Dazzling Gleam	Fairy	Special	80	100	10	Many Others
TM100	Confide	Normal	Status	—	—	20	Normal
HM01	Cut	Normal	Physical	50	95	30	Normal

MOVES LEARNED IN EXCHANGE FOR BP

Name	Type	Kind	Pow.	Acc.	PP	Range
Covet	Normal	Physical	60	100	25	Normal
Seed Bomb	Grass	Physical	80	100	15	Normal
Uproar	Normal	Special	90	100	10	1 Random
Snore	Normal	Special	50	100	15	Normal
Synthesis	Grass	Status	—	—	5	Self
Giga Drain	Grass	Special	75	100	10	Normal
Worry Seed	Grass	Status	—	100	10	Normal

MOVES TAUGHT BY PEOPLE

Name	Type	Kind	Pow.	Acc.	PP	Range

EGG MOVES

Name	Type	Kind	Pow.	Acc.	PP	Range
Spikes	Ground	Status	—	—	20	Other Side
Synthesis	Grass	Status	—	—	5	Self
Pin Missile	Bug	Physical	25	95	20	Normal
Cotton Spore	Grass	Status	—	100	40	Many Others
Sleep Powder	Grass	Status	—	75	15	Normal
Razor Leaf	Grass	Physical	55	95	25	Many Others
Mind Reader	Normal	Status	—	—	5	Normal
Leaf Storm	Grass	Special	130	90	5	Normal
Extrasensory	Psychic	Special	80	100	20	Normal
Seed Bomb	Grass	Physical	80	100	15	Normal
Giga Drain	Grass	Special	75	100	10	Normal
Natural Gift	Normal	Physical	—	100	15	Normal
Grass Whistle	Grass	Status	—	55	15	Normal

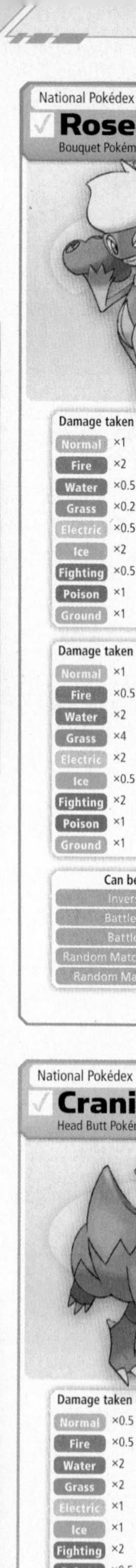

National Pokédex **407** Hoenn Pokédex **099**

Roserade

Bouquet Pokémon

Grass | Poison

HEIGHT: 2'11" WEIGHT: 32 lbs.

The male has a shorter cape-like attachment. The female has a longer cape-like attachment.

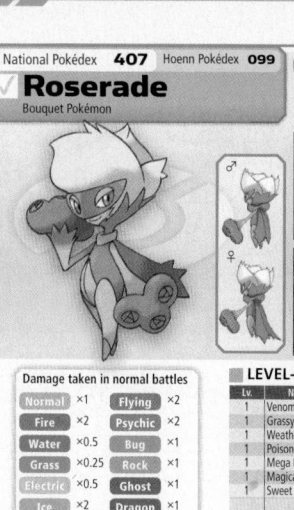

Ω Luring prey with a sweet scent, it uses poison whips on its arms to poison, bind, and finish off the prey.

α With the movements of a dancer, it strikes with whips that are densely lined with poison thorns.

ABILITIES
Natural Cure
Poison Point

HIDDEN ABILITY
Technician

EGG GROUPS
Fairy | Grass

STAT GROWTH RATES
HP ▮▮▮
Attack ▮▮▮▮
Defense ▮▮▮
Sp. Atk ▮▮▮▮▮▮
Sp. Def ▮▮▮▮
Speed ▮▮▮▮▮

ITEMS SOMETIMES HELD BY WILD POKÉMON
—

EVOLUTION
Budew → Level up with high friendship between 4 A.M. and 7:59 P.M. → Roselia → Shiny Stone → Roserade

MAIN WAY TO REGISTER IN THE NATIONAL POKÉDEX
Use a Shiny Stone on Roselia.

Damage taken in normal battles

Type		Type	
Normal	×1	Flying	×2
Fire	×2	Psychic	×2
Water	×0.5	Bug	×1
Grass	×0.25	Rock	×1
Electric	×0.5	Ghost	×1
Ice	×2	Dragon	×1
Fighting	×0.5	Dark	×1
Poison	×1	Steel	×1
Ground	×1	Fairy	×0.5

Damage taken in Inverse battles

Type		Type	
Normal	×1	Flying	×0.5
Fire	×0.5	Psychic	×0.5
Water	×2	Bug	×1
Grass	×4	Rock	×1
Electric	×2	Ghost	×1
Ice	×0.5	Dragon	×1
Fighting	×2	Dark	×1
Poison	×1	Steel	×1
Ground	×1	Fairy	×2

Can be used in
Inverse Battle
Battle Institute
Battle Maison
Random Matchup (Free Battle)
Random Matchup (Others)

LEVEL-UP MOVES

Lv.	Name	Type	Kind	Pow.	Acc.	PP	Range
1	Venom Drench	Poison	Status	—	100	20	Many Others
1	Grassy Terrain	Grass	Status	—	—	10	Both Sides
1	Weather Ball	Normal	Special	50	100	10	Normal
1	Poison Sting	Poison	Physical	15	100	35	Normal
1	Mega Drain	Grass	Special	40	100	15	Normal
1	Magical Leaf	Grass	Special	60	—	20	Normal
1	Sweet Scent	Normal	Status	—	100	20	Many Others

TM & HM MOVES

No.	Name	Type	Kind	Pow.	Acc.	PP	Range
TM06	Toxic	Poison	Status	—	90	10	Normal
TM09	Venoshock	Poison	Special	65	100	10	Normal
TM10	Hidden Power	Normal	Special	60	100	15	Normal
TM11	Sunny Day	Fire	Status	—	—	5	Both Sides
TM15	Hyper Beam	Normal	Special	150	90	5	Normal
TM17	Protect	Normal	Status	—	—	10	Self
TM18	Rain Dance	Water	Status	—	—	5	Both Sides
TM21	Frustration	Normal	Physical	—	100	20	Normal
TM22	Solar Beam	Grass	Special	120	100	10	Normal
TM27	Return	Normal	Physical	—	100	20	Normal
TM30	Shadow Ball	Ghost	Special	80	100	15	Normal
TM32	Double Team	Normal	Status	—	—	15	Self
TM36	Sludge Bomb	Poison	Special	90	100	10	Normal
TM42	Facade	Normal	Physical	70	100	20	Normal
TM44	Rest	Psychic	Status	—	—	10	Self
TM45	Attract	Normal	Status	—	100	15	Normal
TM48	Round	Normal	Special	60	100	15	Normal
TM53	Energy Ball	Grass	Special	90	100	10	Normal
TM68	Giga Impact	Normal	Physical	150	90	5	Normal
TM70	Flash	Normal	Status	—	100	20	Normal
TM75	Swords Dance	Normal	Status	—	—	20	Self
TM77	Psych Up	Normal	Status	—	—	10	Normal
TM84	Poison Jab	Poison	Physical	80	100	20	Normal
TM86	Grass Knot	Grass	Special	—	100	20	Normal
TM87	Swagger	Normal	Status	—	90	15	Normal
TM88	Sleep Talk	Normal	Status	—	—	10	Self
TM90	Substitute	Normal	Status	—	—	10	Self
TM94	Secret Power	Normal	Physical	70	100	20	Normal
TM96	Nature Power	Normal	Status	—	—	20	Normal
TM99	Dazzling Gleam	Fairy	Special	80	100	10	Many Others
TM100	Confide	Normal	Status	—	—	20	Normal
HM01	Cut	Normal	Physical	50	95	30	Normal

MOVES LEARNED IN EXCHANGE FOR BP

Name	Type	Kind	Pow.	Acc.	PP	Range
Covet	Normal	Physical	60	100	25	Normal
Seed Bomb	Grass	Physical	80	100	15	Normal
Snore	Normal	Special	50	100	15	Normal
Synthesis	Grass	Status	—	—	5	Self
Giga Drain	Grass	Special	75	100	10	Normal
Worry Seed	Grass	Status	—	100	10	Normal

MOVES TAUGHT BY PEOPLE

Name	Type	Kind	Pow.	Acc.	PP	Range

National Pokédex **408** Hoenn Pokédex **—**

Cranidos

Head Butt Pokémon

Rock

HEIGHT: 2'11" WEIGHT: 69.4 lbs.

Same form for ♂ / ♀

Ω It was resurrected from an iron ball-like fossil. It downs prey with its headbutts.

α A lifelong jungle dweller from 100 million years ago, it would snap obstructing trees with headbutts.

ABILITY
Mold Breaker

HIDDEN ABILITY
Sheer Force

EGG GROUPS
Monster

STAT GROWTH RATES
HP ▮▮▮
Attack ▮▮▮▮▮▮
Defense ▮▮
Sp. Atk ▮
Sp. Def ▮
Speed ▮▮▮

ITEMS SOMETIMES HELD BY WILD POKÉMON
—

EVOLUTION
Cranidos → Lv. 30 → Rampardos

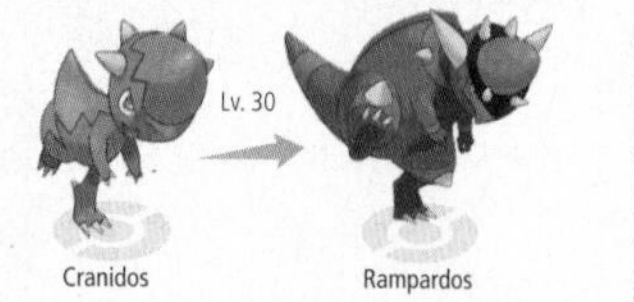

MAIN WAYS TO REGISTER IN THE NATIONAL POKÉDEX
Ω Bring it to your game using Link Trade or the GTS.
α After obtaining a Skull Fossil from a cracked rock in a Mirage spot by using Rock Smash, have it restored at the Devon Corporation (2F) in Rustboro City.

Damage taken in normal battles

Type		Type	
Normal	×0.5	Flying	×0.5
Fire	×0.5	Psychic	×1
Water	×2	Bug	×1
Grass	×2	Rock	×1
Electric	×1	Ghost	×1
Ice	×1	Dragon	×1
Fighting	×2	Dark	×1
Poison	×0.5	Steel	×2
Ground	×2	Fairy	×1

Damage taken in Inverse battles

Type		Type	
Normal	×2	Flying	×2
Fire	×2	Psychic	×1
Water	×0.5	Bug	×1
Grass	×0.5	Rock	×1
Electric	×1	Ghost	×1
Ice	×1	Dragon	×1
Fighting	×0.5	Dark	×1
Poison	×2	Steel	×0.5
Ground	×0.5	Fairy	×1

Can be used in
Inverse Battle
Battle Institute
Battle Maison
Random Matchup (Free Battle)
Random Matchup (Others)

LEVEL-UP MOVES

Lv.	Name	Type	Kind	Pow.	Acc.	PP	Range
1	Headbutt	Normal	Physical	70	100	15	Normal
1	Leer	Normal	Status	—	100	30	Many Others
6	Focus Energy	Normal	Status	—	—	30	Self
10	Pursuit	Dark	Physical	40	100	20	Normal
15	Take Down	Normal	Physical	90	85	20	Normal
19	Scary Face	Normal	Status	—	100	10	Normal
24	Assurance	Dark	Physical	60	100	10	Normal
28	Chip Away	Normal	Physical	70	100	20	Normal
33	Ancient Power	Rock	Special	60	100	5	Normal
37	Zen Headbutt	Psychic	Physical	80	90	15	Normal
42	Screech	Normal	Status	—	85	40	Normal
46	Head Smash	Rock	Physical	150	80	5	Normal

TM & HM MOVES

No.	Name	Type	Kind	Pow.	Acc.	PP	Range
TM05	Roar	Normal	Status	—	—	20	Normal
TM06	Toxic	Poison	Status	—	90	10	Normal
TM10	Hidden Power	Normal	Special	60	100	15	Normal
TM11	Sunny Day	Fire	Status	—	—	5	Both Sides
TM13	Ice Beam	Ice	Special	90	100	10	Normal
TM14	Blizzard	Ice	Special	110	70	5	Many Others
TM17	Protect	Normal	Status	—	—	10	Self
TM18	Rain Dance	Water	Status	—	—	5	Both Sides
TM21	Frustration	Normal	Physical	—	100	20	Normal
TM23	Smack Down	Rock	Physical	50	100	15	Normal
TM24	Thunderbolt	Electric	Special	90	100	15	Normal
TM25	Thunder	Electric	Special	110	70	10	Normal
TM26	Earthquake	Ground	Physical	100	100	10	Adjacent
TM27	Return	Normal	Physical	—	100	20	Normal
TM28	Dig	Ground	Physical	80	100	10	Normal
TM32	Double Team	Normal	Status	—	—	15	Self
TM35	Flamethrower	Fire	Special	90	100	15	Normal
TM37	Sandstorm	Rock	Status	—	—	10	Both Sides
TM38	Fire Blast	Fire	Special	110	85	5	Normal
TM39	Rock Tomb	Rock	Physical	60	95	15	Normal
TM42	Facade	Normal	Physical	70	100	20	Normal
TM44	Rest	Psychic	Status	—	—	10	Self
TM45	Attract	Normal	Status	—	100	15	Normal
TM46	Thief	Dark	Physical	60	100	25	Normal
TM48	Round	Normal	Special	60	100	15	Normal
TM56	Fling	Dark	Physical	—	100	10	Normal
TM59	Incinerate	Fire	Special	60	100	15	Many Others
TM66	Payback	Dark	Physical	50	100	10	Normal
TM69	Rock Polish	Rock	Status	—	—	20	Self
TM71	Stone Edge	Rock	Physical	100	80	5	Normal
TM75	Swords Dance	Normal	Status	—	—	20	Self
TM78	Bulldoze	Ground	Physical	60	100	20	Adjacent
TM80	Rock Slide	Rock	Physical	75	90	10	Many Others
TM87	Swagger	Normal	Status	—	90	15	Normal
TM88	Sleep Talk	Normal	Status	—	—	10	Self
TM90	Substitute	Normal	Status	—	—	10	Self
TM94	Secret Power	Normal	Physical	70	100	20	Normal
TM98	Power-Up Punch	Fighting	Physical	40	100	20	Normal
TM100	Confide	Normal	Status	—	—	20	Normal
HM04	Strength	Normal	Physical	80	100	15	Normal
HM06	Rock Smash	Fighting	Physical	40	100	15	Normal

MOVES LEARNED IN EXCHANGE FOR BP

Name	Type	Kind	Pow.	Acc.	PP	Range
Iron Head	Steel	Physical	80	100	15	Normal
Uproar	Normal	Special	90	100	10	1 Random
Thunder Punch	Electric	Physical	75	100	15	Normal
Fire Punch	Fire	Physical	75	100	15	Normal
Earth Power	Ground	Special	90	100	10	Normal
Superpower	Fighting	Physical	120	100	5	Normal
Zen Headbutt	Psychic	Physical	80	90	15	Normal
Dragon Pulse	Dragon	Special	85	100	10	Normal
Iron Tail	Steel	Physical	100	75	15	Normal
Snore	Normal	Special	50	100	15	Normal
Shock Wave	Electric	Special	60	—	20	Normal
Spite	Ghost	Status	—	100	10	Normal
Endeavor	Normal	Physical	—	100	5	Normal
Stealth Rock	Rock	Status	—	—	20	Other Side

MOVES TAUGHT BY PEOPLE

Name	Type	Kind	Pow.	Acc.	PP	Range

EGG MOVES

Name	Type	Kind	Pow.	Acc.	PP	Range
Crunch	Dark	Physical	80	100	15	Normal
Thrash	Normal	Physical	120	100	10	1 Random
Double-Edge	Normal	Physical	120	100	15	Normal
Leer	Normal	Status	—	100	30	Many Others
Slam	Normal	Physical	80	75	20	Normal
Stomp	Normal	Physical	65	100	20	Normal
Whirlwind	Normal	Status	—	—	20	Normal
Hammer Arm	Fighting	Physical	100	90	10	Normal
Curse	Ghost	Status	—	—	10	Varies
Iron Tail	Steel	Physical	100	75	15	Normal
Iron Head	Steel	Physical	80	100	15	Normal

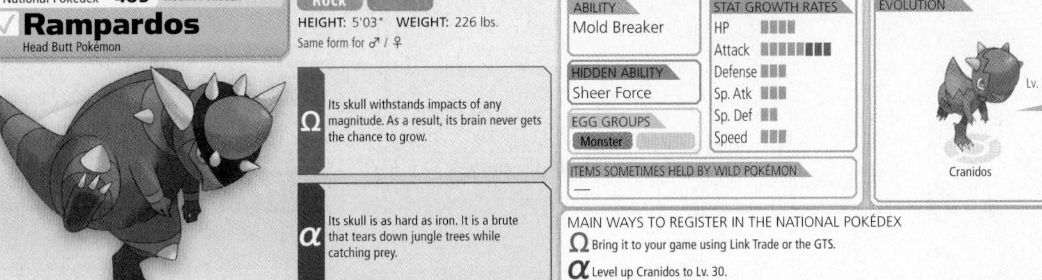

National Pokédex **409** Hoenn Pokédex —

Rampardos

Head Butt Pokémon

Rock

HEIGHT: 5'03" WEIGHT: 226 lbs.

Same form for ♂ / ♀

Ω Its skull withstands impacts of any magnitude. As a result, its brain never gets the chance to grow.

α Its skull is as hard as iron. It is a brute that tears down jungle trees while catching prey.

ABILITY: Mold Breaker

HIDDEN ABILITY: Sheer Force

EGG GROUPS: Monster

STAT GROWTH RATES: HP, Attack, Defense, Sp. Atk, Sp. Def, Speed

ITEMS SOMETIMES HELD BY WILD POKÉMON: —

EVOLUTION

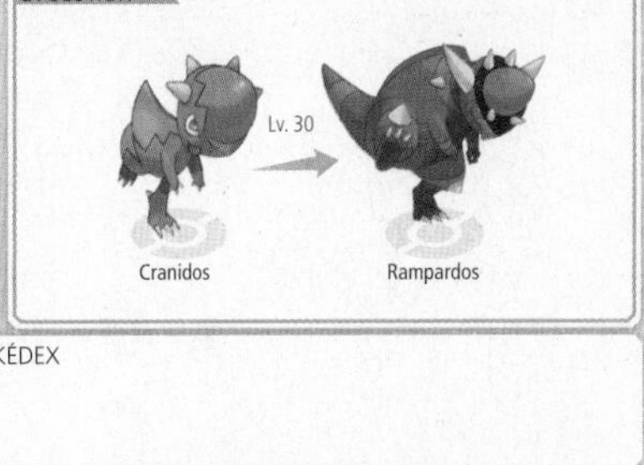

MAIN WAYS TO REGISTER IN THE NATIONAL POKÉDEX

Ω Bring it to your game using Link Trade or the GTS.

α Level up Cranidos to Lv. 30.

Damage taken in normal battles

Type	Multiplier	Type	Multiplier
Normal	×0.5	Flying	×0.5
Fire	×0.5	Psychic	×1
Water	×2	Bug	×1
Grass	×2	Rock	×1
Electric	×1	Ghost	×1
Ice	×1	Dragon	×1
Fighting	×2	Dark	×1
Poison	×0.5	Steel	×2
Ground	×2	Fairy	×1

Damage taken in Inverse battles

Type	Multiplier	Type	Multiplier
Normal	×2	Flying	×2
Fire	×2	Psychic	×1
Water	×0.5	Bug	×1
Grass	×0.5	Rock	×1
Electric	×1	Ghost	×1
Ice	×1	Dragon	×1
Fighting	×0.5	Dark	×1
Poison	×2	Steel	×0.5
Ground	×0.5	Fairy	×1

Can be used in

- Inverse Battle
- Battle Institute
- Battle Maison
- Random Matchup (Free Battle)
- Random Matchup (Others)

LEVEL-UP MOVES

Lv.	Name	Type	Kind	Pow.	Acc.	PP	Range
1	Headbutt	Normal	Physical	70	100	15	Normal
1	Leer	Normal	Status	—	100	30	Many Others
6	Focus Energy	Normal	Status	—	—	30	Self
10	Pursuit	Dark	Physical	40	100	20	Normal
15	Take Down	Normal	Physical	90	85	20	Normal
19	Scary Face	Normal	Status	—	100	10	Normal
24	Assurance	Dark	Physical	60	100	10	Normal
28	Chip Away	Normal	Physical	70	100	20	Normal
30	Endeavor	Normal	Physical	—	100	5	Normal
36	Ancient Power	Rock	Special	60	100	5	Normal
43	Zen Headbutt	Psychic	Physical	80	90	15	Normal
51	Screech	Normal	Status	—	85	40	Normal
58	Head Smash	Rock	Physical	150	80	5	Normal

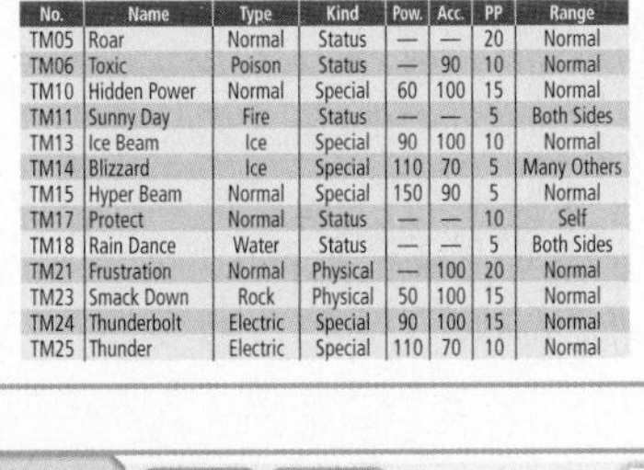

TM & HM MOVES

No.	Name	Type	Kind	Pow.	Acc.	PP	Range
TM05	Roar	Normal	Status	—	—	20	Normal
TM06	Toxic	Poison	Status	—	90	10	Normal
TM10	Hidden Power	Normal	Special	60	100	15	Normal
TM11	Sunny Day	Fire	Status	—	—	5	Both Sides
TM13	Ice Beam	Ice	Special	90	100	10	Normal
TM14	Blizzard	Ice	Special	110	70	5	Many Others
TM15	Hyper Beam	Normal	Special	150	90	5	Normal
TM17	Protect	Normal	Status	—	—	10	Self
TM18	Rain Dance	Water	Status	—	—	5	Both Sides
TM21	Frustration	Normal	Physical	—	100	20	Normal
TM23	Smack Down	Rock	Physical	50	100	15	Normal
TM24	Thunderbolt	Electric	Special	90	100	15	Normal
TM25	Thunder	Electric	Special	110	70	10	Normal
TM26	Earthquake	Ground	Physical	100	100	10	Adjacent
TM27	Return	Normal	Physical	—	100	20	Normal
TM28	Dig	Ground	Physical	80	100	10	Normal
TM31	Brick Break	Fighting	Physical	75	100	15	Normal
TM32	Double Team	Normal	Status	—	—	15	Self
TM35	Flamethrower	Fire	Special	90	100	15	Normal
TM37	Sandstorm	Rock	Status	—	—	10	Both Sides
TM38	Fire Blast	Fire	Special	110	85	5	Normal
TM39	Rock Tomb	Rock	Physical	60	95	15	Normal
TM42	Facade	Normal	Physical	70	100	20	Normal
TM44	Rest	Psychic	Status	—	—	10	Self
TM45	Attract	Normal	Status	—	100	15	Normal
TM46	Thief	Dark	Physical	60	100	25	Normal
TM48	Round	Normal	Special	60	100	15	Normal
TM52	Focus Blast	Fighting	Special	120	70	5	Normal
TM56	Fling	Dark	Physical	—	100	10	Normal
TM59	Incinerate	Fire	Special	60	100	15	Many Others
TM66	Payback	Dark	Physical	50	100	10	Normal
TM68	Giga Impact	Normal	Physical	150	90	5	Normal
TM69	Rock Polish	Rock	Status	—	—	20	Self
TM71	Stone Edge	Rock	Physical	100	80	5	Normal
TM75	Swords Dance	Normal	Status	—	—	20	Self
TM78	Bulldoze	Ground	Physical	60	100	20	Adjacent
TM80	Rock Slide	Rock	Physical	75	90	10	Many Others
TM82	Dragon Tail	Dragon	Physical	60	90	10	Normal
TM87	Swagger	Normal	Status	—	90	15	Normal
TM88	Sleep Talk	Normal	Status	—	—	10	Self
TM90	Substitute	Normal	Status	—	—	10	Self
TM94	Secret Power	Normal	Physical	70	100	20	Normal
TM98	Power-Up Punch	Fighting	Physical	40	100	20	Normal
TM100	Confide	Normal	Status	—	—	20	Normal
HM01	Cut	Normal	Physical	50	95	30	Normal
HM03	Surf	Water	Special	90	100	15	Adjacent
HM04	Strength	Normal	Physical	80	100	15	Normal
HM06	Rock Smash	Fighting	Physical	40	100	15	Normal

MOVES LEARNED IN EXCHANGE FOR BP

Name	Type	Kind	Pow.	Acc.	PP	Range
Iron Head	Steel	Physical	80	100	15	Normal
Uproar	Normal	Special	90	100	10	1 Random
Thunder Punch	Electric	Physical	75	100	15	Normal
Fire Punch	Fire	Physical	75	100	15	Normal
Earth Power	Ground	Special	90	100	10	Normal
Superpower	Fighting	Physical	120	100	5	Normal
Zen Headbutt	Psychic	Physical	80	90	15	Normal
Dragon Pulse	Dragon	Special	85	100	10	Normal
Iron Tail	Steel	Physical	100	75	15	Normal
Snore	Normal	Special	50	100	15	Normal
Pain Split	Normal	Status	—	—	20	Normal
Focus Punch	Fighting	Physical	150	100	20	Normal
Shock Wave	Electric	Special	60	—	20	Normal
Spite	Ghost	Status	—	100	10	Normal
Endeavor	Normal	Physical	—	100	5	Normal
Outrage	Dragon	Physical	120	100	10	1 Random
Stealth Rock	Rock	Status	—	—	20	Other Side

MOVES TAUGHT BY PEOPLE

Name	Type	Kind	Pow.	Acc.	PP	Range

National Pokédex **410** Hoenn Pokédex —

Shieldon

Shield Pokémon

Rock Steel

HEIGHT: 1'08" WEIGHT: 125.7 lbs.

Same form for ♂ / ♀

Ω It habitually polishes its face by rubbing it against tree trunks. It is weak to attacks from behind.

α It was generated from a fossil dug out of a layer of clay that was older than anyone knows. It has a sturdy face.

ABILITY: Sturdy

HIDDEN ABILITY: Soundproof

EGG GROUPS: Monster

STAT GROWTH RATES: HP, Attack, Defense, Sp. Atk, Sp. Def, Speed

ITEMS SOMETIMES HELD BY WILD POKÉMON: —

EVOLUTION

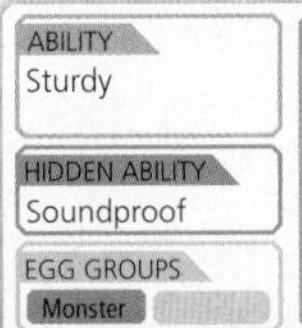

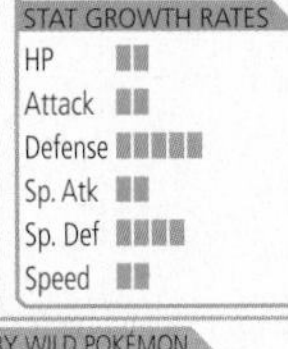

MAIN WAYS TO REGISTER IN THE NATIONAL POKÉDEX

Ω Obtain an Armor Fossil from a cracked rock in a Mirage spot by using Rock Smash, then have it restored at the Devon Corporation (2F) in Rustboro City.

α Bring it to your game using Link Trade or the GTS.

Damage taken in normal battles

Type	Multiplier	Type	Multiplier
Normal	×0.25	Flying	×0.25
Fire	×1	Psychic	×0.5
Water	×2	Bug	×0.5
Grass	×1	Rock	×0.5
Electric	×1	Ghost	×1
Ice	×0.5	Dragon	×0.5
Fighting	×4	Dark	×1
Poison	×0	Steel	×1
Ground	×4	Fairy	×0.5

Damage taken in Inverse battles

Type	Multiplier	Type	Multiplier
Normal	×4	Flying	×4
Fire	×1	Psychic	×2
Water	×0.5	Bug	×2
Grass	×1	Rock	×2
Electric	×1	Ghost	×1
Ice	×2	Dragon	×2
Fighting	×0.25	Dark	×1
Poison	×4	Steel	×1
Ground	×0.25	Fairy	×2

Can be used in

- Inverse Battle
- Battle Institute
- Battle Maison
- Random Matchup (Free Battle)
- Random Matchup (Others)

LEVEL-UP MOVES

Lv.	Name	Type	Kind	Pow.	Acc.	PP	Range
1	Tackle	Normal	Physical	50	100	35	Normal
1	Protect	Normal	Status	—	—	10	Self
6	Taunt	Dark	Status	—	100	20	Normal
10	Metal Sound	Steel	Status	—	85	40	Normal
15	Take Down	Normal	Physical	90	85	20	Normal
19	Iron Defense	Steel	Status	—	—	15	Self
24	Swagger	Normal	Status	—	90	15	Normal
28	Ancient Power	Rock	Special	60	100	5	Normal
33	Endure	Normal	Status	—	—	10	Self
37	Metal Burst	Steel	Physical	—	100	10	Varies
42	Iron Head	Steel	Physical	80	100	15	Normal
46	Heavy Slam	Steel	Physical	—	100	10	Normal

TM & HM MOVES

No.	Name	Type	Kind	Pow.	Acc.	PP	Range
TM05	Roar	Normal	Status	—	—	20	Normal
TM06	Toxic	Poison	Status	—	90	10	Normal
TM10	Hidden Power	Normal	Special	60	100	15	Normal
TM11	Sunny Day	Fire	Status	—	—	5	Both Sides
TM12	Taunt	Dark	Status	—	100	20	Normal
TM13	Ice Beam	Ice	Special	90	100	10	Normal
TM14	Blizzard	Ice	Special	110	70	5	Many Others
TM17	Protect	Normal	Status	—	—	10	Self
TM18	Rain Dance	Water	Status	—	—	5	Both Sides
TM21	Frustration	Normal	Physical	—	100	20	Normal
TM23	Smack Down	Rock	Physical	50	100	15	Normal
TM24	Thunderbolt	Electric	Special	90	100	15	Normal
TM25	Thunder	Electric	Special	110	70	10	Normal
TM26	Earthquake	Ground	Physical	100	100	10	Adjacent
TM27	Return	Normal	Physical	—	100	20	Normal
TM28	Dig	Ground	Physical	80	100	10	Normal
TM32	Double Team	Normal	Status	—	—	15	Self
TM35	Flamethrower	Fire	Special	90	100	15	Normal
TM37	Sandstorm	Rock	Status	—	—	10	Both Sides
TM38	Fire Blast	Fire	Special	110	85	5	Normal
TM39	Rock Tomb	Rock	Physical	60	95	15	Normal
TM41	Torment	Dark	Status	—	100	15	Normal
TM42	Facade	Normal	Physical	70	100	20	Normal
TM44	Rest	Psychic	Status	—	—	10	Self
TM45	Attract	Normal	Status	—	100	15	Normal
TM48	Round	Normal	Special	60	100	15	Normal
TM59	Incinerate	Fire	Special	60	100	15	Many Others
TM69	Rock Polish	Rock	Status	—	—	20	Self
TM71	Stone Edge	Rock	Physical	100	80	5	Normal
TM78	Bulldoze	Ground	Physical	60	100	20	Adjacent
TM80	Rock Slide	Rock	Physical	75	90	10	Many Others
TM87	Swagger	Normal	Status	—	90	15	Normal
TM88	Sleep Talk	Normal	Status	—	—	10	Self
TM90	Substitute	Normal	Status	—	—	10	Self
TM91	Flash Cannon	Steel	Special	80	100	10	Normal
TM94	Secret Power	Normal	Physical	70	100	20	Normal
TM100	Confide	Normal	Status	—	—	20	Normal
HM04	Strength	Normal	Physical	80	100	15	Normal
HM06	Rock Smash	Fighting	Physical	40	100	15	Normal

MOVES LEARNED IN EXCHANGE FOR BP

Name	Type	Kind	Pow.	Acc.	PP	Range
Iron Head	Steel	Physical	80	100	15	Normal
Earth Power	Ground	Special	90	100	10	Normal
Magnet Rise	Electric	Status	—	—	10	Self
Iron Defense	Steel	Status	—	—	15	Self
Iron Tail	Steel	Physical	100	75	15	Normal
Snore	Normal	Special	50	100	15	Normal
Shock Wave	Electric	Special	60	—	20	Normal
Stealth Rock	Rock	Status	—	—	20	Other Side

MOVES TAUGHT BY PEOPLE

Name	Type	Kind	Pow.	Acc.	PP	Range

EGG MOVES

Name	Type	Kind	Pow.	Acc.	PP	Range
Headbutt	Normal	Physical	70	100	15	Normal
Scary Face	Normal	Status	—	100	10	Normal
Focus Energy	Normal	Status	—	—	30	Self
Double-Edge	Normal	Physical	120	100	15	Normal
Rock Blast	Rock	Physical	25	90	10	Normal
Body Slam	Normal	Physical	85	100	15	Normal
Screech	Normal	Status	—	85	40	Normal
Curse	Ghost	Status	—	—	10	Varies
Fissure	Ground	Physical	—	30	5	Normal
Counter	Fighting	Physical	—	100	20	Varies
Stealth Rock	Rock	Status	—	—	20	Other Side
Wide Guard	Rock	Status	—	—	10	Your Side
Guard Split	Psychic	Status	—	—	10	Normal

National Pokédex **411** Hoenn Pokédex —

Bastiodon

Shield Pokémon

Rock Steel

HEIGHT: 4'03" WEIGHT: 329.6 lbs.

Same form for ♂ / ♀

Ω When they lined up side by side, no foe could break through. They shielded their young in that way.

α Any frontal attack is repulsed. It is a docile Pokémon that feeds on grass and berries.

ABILITY: Sturdy

HIDDEN ABILITY: Soundproof

EGG GROUPS: Monster

STAT GROWTH RATES: HP, Attack, Defense, Sp. Atk, Sp. Def, Speed

ITEMS SOMETIMES HELD BY WILD POKÉMON: —

EVOLUTION: Shieldon → Lv. 30 → Bastiodon

MAIN WAYS TO REGISTER IN THE NATIONAL POKÉDEX

Ω Level up Shieldon to Lv. 30.

α Bring it to your game using Link Trade or the GTS.

Damage taken in normal battles

Type	×	Type	×
Normal	×0.25	Flying	×0.25
Fire	×1	Psychic	×0.5
Water	×2	Bug	×0.5
Grass	×1	Rock	×0.5
Electric	×1	Ghost	×1
Ice	×0.5	Dragon	×0.5
Fighting	×4	Dark	×1
Poison	×0	Steel	×1
Ground	×4	Fairy	×0.5

Damage taken in Inverse battles

Type	×	Type	×
Normal	×4	Flying	×4
Fire	×1	Psychic	×2
Water	×0.5	Bug	×2
Grass	×1	Rock	×2
Electric	×1	Ghost	×1
Ice	×2	Dragon	×2
Fighting	×0.25	Dark	×1
Poison	×4	Steel	×1
Ground	×0.25	Fairy	×2

Can be used in

Inverse Battle
Battle Institute
Battle Maison
Random Matchup (Free Battle)
Random Matchup (Others)

LEVEL-UP MOVES

Lv.	Name	Type	Kind	Pow.	Acc.	PP	Range
1	Tackle	Normal	Physical	50	100	35	Normal
1	Protect	Normal	Status	—	—	10	Self
1	Taunt	Dark	Status	—	100	20	Normal
1	Metal Sound	Steel	Status	—	85	40	Normal
6	Taunt	Dark	Status	—	100	20	Normal
10	Metal Sound	Steel	Status	—	85	40	Normal
15	Take Down	Normal	Physical	90	85	20	Normal
19	Iron Defense	Steel	Status	—	—	15	Self
24	Swagger	Normal	Status	—	90	15	Normal
28	Ancient Power	Rock	Special	60	100	5	Normal
30	Block	Normal	Status	—	—	5	Normal
36	Endure	Normal	Status	—	—	10	Self
43	Metal Burst	Steel	Physical	—	100	10	Varies
51	Iron Head	Steel	Physical	80	100	15	Normal
58	Heavy Slam	Steel	Physical	—	100	10	Normal

TM & HM MOVES

No.	Name	Type	Kind	Pow.	Acc.	PP	Range
TM05	Roar	Normal	Status	—	—	20	Normal
TM06	Toxic	Poison	Status	—	90	10	Normal
TM10	Hidden Power	Normal	Special	60	100	15	Normal
TM11	Sunny Day	Fire	Status	—	—	5	Both Sides
TM12	Taunt	Dark	Status	—	100	20	Normal
TM13	Ice Beam	Ice	Special	90	100	10	Normal
TM14	Blizzard	Ice	Special	110	70	5	Many Others
TM15	Hyper Beam	Normal	Special	150	90	5	Normal
TM17	Protect	Normal	Status	—	—	10	Self
TM18	Rain Dance	Water	Status	—	—	5	Both Sides
TM21	Frustration	Normal	Physical	—	100	20	Normal
TM23	Smack Down	Rock	Physical	50	100	15	Normal
TM24	Thunderbolt	Electric	Special	90	100	15	Normal
TM25	Thunder	Electric	Special	110	70	10	Normal
TM26	Earthquake	Ground	Physical	100	100	10	Adjacent
TM27	Return	Normal	Physical	—	100	20	Normal
TM28	Dig	Ground	Physical	80	100	10	Normal
TM32	Double Team	Normal	Status	—	—	15	Self
TM35	Flamethrower	Fire	Special	90	100	15	Normal
TM37	Sandstorm	Rock	Status	—	—	10	Both Sides
TM38	Fire Blast	Fire	Special	110	85	5	Normal
TM39	Rock Tomb	Rock	Physical	60	95	15	Normal
TM41	Torment	Dark	Status	—	100	15	Normal
TM42	Facade	Normal	Physical	70	100	20	Normal
TM44	Rest	Psychic	Status	—	—	10	Self
TM45	Attract	Normal	Status	—	100	15	Normal
TM48	Round	Normal	Special	60	100	15	Normal
TM59	Incinerate	Fire	Special	60	100	15	Many Others
TM68	Giga Impact	Normal	Physical	150	90	5	Normal
TM69	Rock Polish	Rock	Status	—	—	20	Self
TM71	Stone Edge	Rock	Physical	100	80	5	Normal
TM78	Bulldoze	Ground	Physical	60	100	20	Adjacent
TM80	Rock Slide	Rock	Physical	75	90	10	Many Others
TM87	Swagger	Normal	Status	—	90	15	Normal
TM88	Sleep Talk	Normal	Status	—	—	10	Self
TM90	Substitute	Normal	Status	—	—	10	Self
TM91	Flash Cannon	Steel	Special	80	100	10	Normal
TM94	Secret Power	Normal	Physical	70	100	20	Normal
TM100	Confide	Normal	Status	—	—	20	Normal
HM04	Strength	Normal	Physical	80	100	15	Normal
HM06	Rock Smash	Fighting	Physical	40	100	15	Normal

MOVES LEARNED IN EXCHANGE FOR BP

Name	Type	Kind	Pow.	Acc.	PP	Range
Iron Head	Steel	Physical	80	100	15	Normal
Magic Coat	Psychic	Status	—	—	15	Self
Block	Normal	Status	—	—	5	Normal
Earth Power	Ground	Special	90	100	10	Normal
Magnet Rise	Electric	Status	—	—	10	Self
Iron Defense	Steel	Status	—	—	15	Self
Iron Tail	Steel	Physical	100	75	15	Normal
Snore	Normal	Special	50	100	15	Normal
Shock Wave	Electric	Special	60	—	20	Normal
Outrage	Dragon	Physical	120	100	10	1 Random
Stealth Rock	Rock	Status	—	—	20	Other Side

MOVES TAUGHT BY PEOPLE

Name	Type	Kind	Pow.	Acc.	PP	Range

National Pokédex **412** Hoenn Pokédex —

Burmy

Bagworm Pokémon

Bug

HEIGHT: 0'08" WEIGHT: 7.5 lbs.

Same form for ♂ / ♀

Ω To shelter itself from cold, wintry winds, it covers itself with a cloak made of twigs and leaves.

α If its cloak is broken in battle, it quickly remakes the cloak with materials nearby.

ABILITY: Shed Skin

HIDDEN ABILITY: Overcoat

EGG GROUPS: Bug

STAT GROWTH RATES: HP, Attack, Defense, Sp. Atk, Sp. Def, Speed

ITEMS SOMETIMES HELD BY WILD POKÉMON: —

EVOLUTION

Burmy ♀ Plant Cloak → Lv. 20 → Wormadam Plant Cloak

Burmy ♀ Sandy Cloak → Lv. 20 → Wormadam Sandy Cloak

Burmy ♀ Trash Cloak → Lv. 20 → Wormadam Trash Cloak

Burmy ♂ → Lv. 20 → Mothim

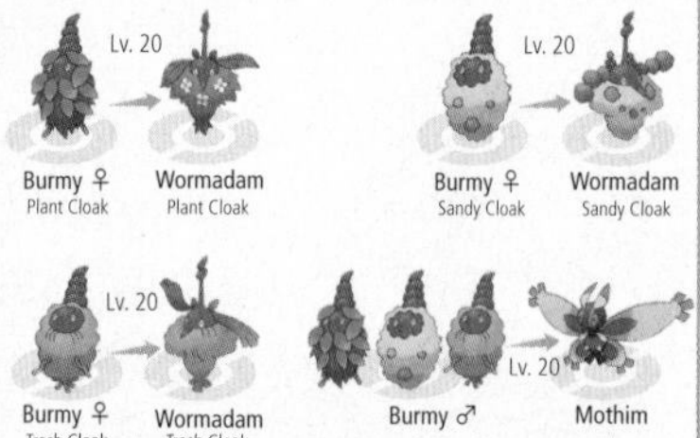

MAIN WAY TO REGISTER IN THE NATIONAL POKÉDEX

Appears in *Pokémon X* and *Pokémon Y*. Bring it to your game using Link Trade or the GTS.

Damage taken in normal battles

Type	×	Type	×
Normal	×1	Flying	×2
Fire	×2	Psychic	×1
Water	×1	Bug	×1
Grass	×0.5	Rock	×2
Electric	×1	Ghost	×1
Ice	×1	Dragon	×1
Fighting	×0.5	Dark	×1
Poison	×1	Steel	×1
Ground	×0.5	Fairy	×1

Damage taken in Inverse battles

Type	×	Type	×
Normal	×1	Flying	×0.5
Fire	×0.5	Psychic	×1
Water	×1	Bug	×1
Grass	×2	Rock	×0.5
Electric	×1	Ghost	×1
Ice	×1	Dragon	×1
Fighting	×2	Dark	×1
Poison	×1	Steel	×1
Ground	×2	Fairy	×1

Can be used in

Inverse Battle
Battle Institute
Battle Maison
Random Matchup (Free Battle)
Random Matchup (Others)

LEVEL-UP MOVES

Lv.	Name	Type	Kind	Pow.	Acc.	PP	Range
1	Protect	Normal	Status	—	—	10	Self
10	Tackle	Normal	Physical	50	100	35	Normal
15	Bug Bite	Bug	Physical	60	100	20	Normal
20	Hidden Power	Normal	Special	60	100	15	Normal

TM & HM MOVES

No.	Name	Type	Kind	Pow.	Acc.	PP	Range
TM10	Hidden Power	Normal	Special	60	100	15	Normal
TM17	Protect	Normal	Status	—	—	10	Self

MOVES LEARNED IN EXCHANGE FOR BP

Name	Type	Kind	Pow.	Acc.	PP	Range
Bug Bite	Bug	Physical	60	100	20	Normal
Electroweb	Electric	Special	55	95	15	Many Others
Snore	Normal	Special	50	100	15	Normal

MOVES TAUGHT BY PEOPLE

Name	Type	Kind	Pow.	Acc.	PP	Range

National Pokédex **413** Hoenn Pokédex —

Wormadam Plant Cloak

Bagworm Pokémon

Bug Grass

HEIGHT: 1'08" WEIGHT: 14.3 lbs.

♀ only

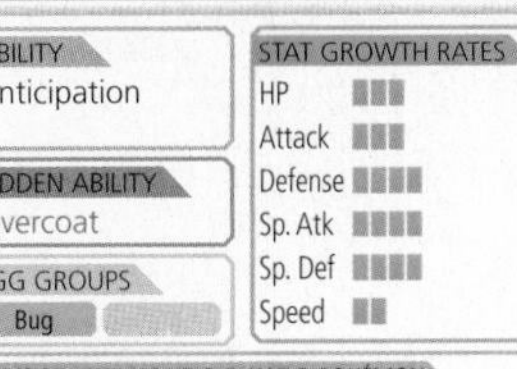

Ω Its appearance changes depending on where it evolved. The materials on hand become a part of its body.

α When Burmy evolved, its cloak became a part of this Pokémon's body. The cloak is never shed.

ABILITY
Anticipation

HIDDEN ABILITY
Overcoat

EGG GROUPS
Bug

STAT GROWTH RATES

HP	■■■
Attack	■■■
Defense	■■■■
Sp. Atk	■■■■
Sp. Def	■■■■
Speed	■■

ITEMS SOMETIMES HELD BY WILD POKÉMON
—

EVOLUTION

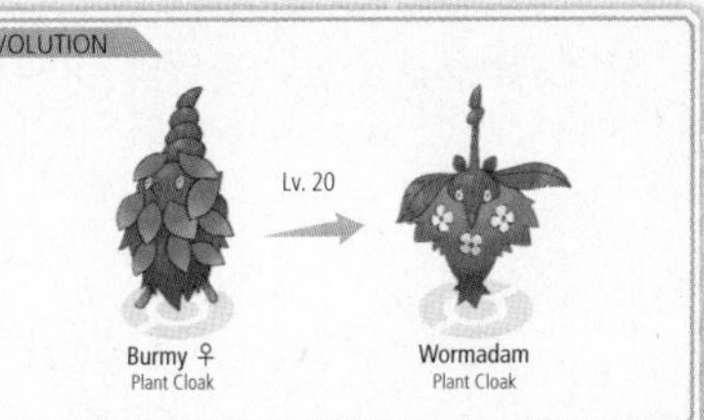

Burmy ♀ Plant Cloak → Lv. 20 → Wormadam Plant Cloak

MAIN WAY TO REGISTER IN THE NATIONAL POKÉDEX

Level up a female Burmy (Plant Cloak) obtained via Link Trade or the GTS to Lv. 20.

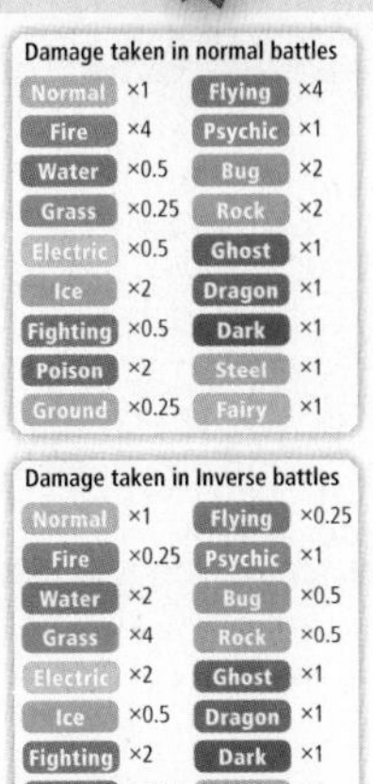

Damage taken in normal battles

Type		Type	
Normal	×1	Flying	×4
Fire	×4	Psychic	×1
Water	×0.5	Bug	×2
Grass	×0.25	Rock	×2
Electric	×0.5	Ghost	×1
Ice	×2	Dragon	×1
Fighting	×0.5	Dark	×1
Poison	×2	Steel	×1
Ground	×0.25	Fairy	×1

Damage taken in Inverse battles

Type		Type	
Normal	×1	Flying	×0.25
Fire	×0.25	Psychic	×1
Water	×2	Bug	×0.5
Grass	×4	Rock	×0.5
Electric	×2	Ghost	×1
Ice	×0.5	Dragon	×1
Fighting	×2	Dark	×1
Poison	×0.5	Steel	×1
Ground	×4	Fairy	×1

Can be used in

- Inverse Battle
- Battle Institute
- Battle Maison
- Random Matchup (Free Battle)
- Random Matchup (Others)

LEVEL-UP MOVES

Lv.	Name	Type	Kind	Pow.	Acc.	PP	Range
1	Tackle	Normal	Physical	50	100	35	Normal
10	Protect	Normal	Status	—	—	10	Self
15	Bug Bite	Bug	Physical	60	100	20	Normal
20	Hidden Power	Normal	Special	60	100	15	Normal
23	Confusion	Psychic	Special	50	100	25	Normal
26	Razor Leaf	Grass	Physical	55	95	25	Many Others
29	Growth	Normal	Status	—	—	20	Self
32	Psybeam	Psychic	Special	65	100	20	Normal
35	Captivate	Normal	Status	—	100	20	Many Others
38	Flail	Normal	Physical	—	100	15	Normal
41	Attract	Normal	Status	—	100	15	Normal
44	Psychic	Psychic	Special	90	100	10	Normal
47	Leaf Storm	Grass	Special	130	90	5	Normal

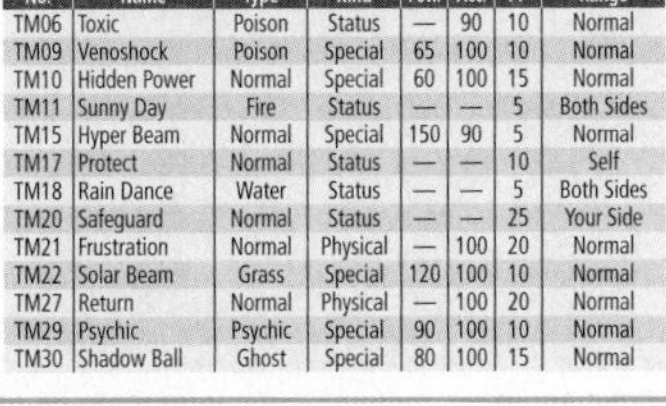

TM & HM MOVES

No.	Name	Type	Kind	Pow.	Acc.	PP	Range
TM06	Toxic	Poison	Status	—	90	10	Normal
TM09	Venoshock	Poison	Special	65	100	10	Normal
TM10	Hidden Power	Normal	Special	60	100	15	Normal
TM11	Sunny Day	Fire	Status	—	—	5	Both Sides
TM15	Hyper Beam	Normal	Special	150	90	5	Normal
TM17	Protect	Normal	Status	—	—	10	Self
TM18	Rain Dance	Water	Status	—	—	5	Both Sides
TM20	Safeguard	Normal	Status	—	—	25	Your Side
TM21	Frustration	Normal	Physical	—	100	20	Normal
TM22	Solar Beam	Grass	Special	120	100	10	Normal
TM27	Return	Normal	Physical	—	100	20	Normal
TM29	Psychic	Psychic	Special	90	100	10	Normal
TM30	Shadow Ball	Ghost	Special	80	100	15	Normal
TM32	Double Team	Normal	Status	—	—	15	Self
TM42	Facade	Normal	Physical	70	100	20	Normal
TM44	Rest	Psychic	Status	—	—	10	Self
TM45	Attract	Normal	Status	—	100	15	Normal
TM46	Thief	Dark	Physical	60	100	25	Normal
TM48	Round	Normal	Special	60	100	15	Normal
TM53	Energy Ball	Grass	Special	90	100	10	Normal
TM68	Giga Impact	Normal	Physical	150	90	5	Normal
TM70	Flash	Normal	Status	—	100	20	Normal
TM76	Struggle Bug	Bug	Special	50	100	20	Many Others
TM77	Psych Up	Normal	Status	—	—	10	Normal
TM83	Infestation	Bug	Special	20	100	20	Normal
TM85	Dream Eater	Psychic	Special	100	100	15	Normal
TM86	Grass Knot	Grass	Special	—	100	20	Normal
TM87	Swagger	Normal	Status	—	90	15	Normal
TM88	Sleep Talk	Normal	Status	—	—	10	Self
TM90	Substitute	Normal	Status	—	—	10	Self
TM94	Secret Power	Normal	Physical	70	100	20	Normal
TM100	Confide	Normal	Status	—	—	20	Normal

MOVES LEARNED IN EXCHANGE FOR BP

Name	Type	Kind	Pow.	Acc.	PP	Range
Bug Bite	Bug	Physical	60	100	20	Normal
Signal Beam	Bug	Special	75	100	15	Normal
Seed Bomb	Grass	Physical	80	100	15	Normal
Uproar	Normal	Special	90	100	10	1 Random
Electroweb	Electric	Special	55	95	15	Many Others
Snore	Normal	Special	50	100	15	Normal
Synthesis	Grass	Status	—	—	5	Self
Giga Drain	Grass	Special	75	100	10	Normal
Worry Seed	Grass	Status	—	100	10	Normal
Endeavor	Normal	Physical	—	100	5	Normal
Skill Swap	Psychic	Status	—	—	10	Normal

MOVES TAUGHT BY PEOPLE

Name	Type	Kind	Pow.	Acc.	PP	Range

National Pokédex **413** Hoenn Pokédex —

Wormadam Sandy Cloak

Bagworm Pokémon

Bug Ground

HEIGHT: 1'08" WEIGHT: 14.3 lbs.

♀ only

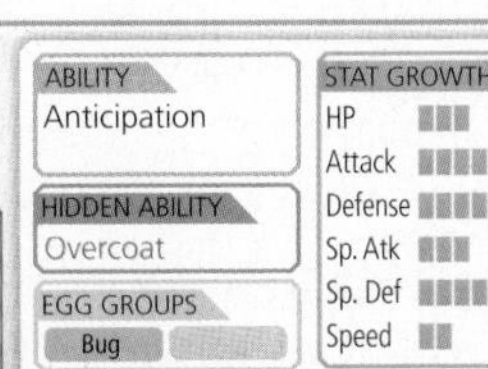

Ω Its appearance changes depending on where it evolved. The materials on hand become a part of its body.

α When Burmy evolved, its cloak became a part of this Pokémon's body. The cloak is never shed.

ABILITY
Anticipation

HIDDEN ABILITY
Overcoat

EGG GROUPS
Bug

STAT GROWTH RATES

HP	■■■
Attack	■■■■
Defense	■■■■■
Sp. Atk	■■■■
Sp. Def	■■■■
Speed	■■

ITEMS SOMETIMES HELD BY WILD POKÉMON
—

EVOLUTION

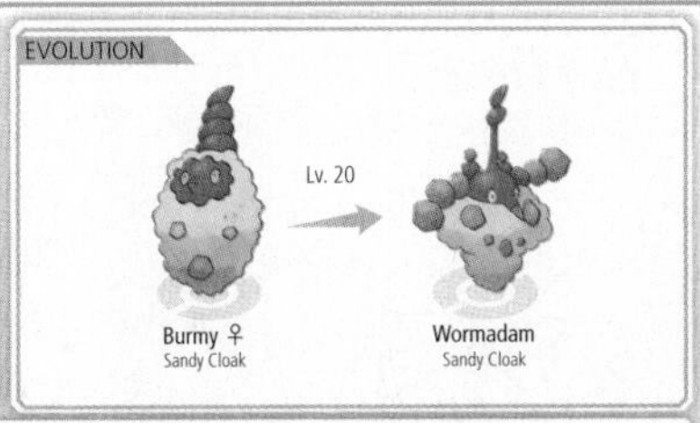

Burmy ♀ Sandy Cloak → Lv. 20 → Wormadam Sandy Cloak

MAIN WAY TO REGISTER IN THE NATIONAL POKÉDEX

Level up a female Burmy (Sandy Cloak) obtained via Link Trade or the GTS to Lv. 20.

Damage taken in normal battles

Type		Type	
Normal	×1	Flying	×2
Fire	×2	Psychic	×1
Water	×2	Bug	×1
Grass	×1	Rock	×1
Electric	×0	Ghost	×1
Ice	×2	Dragon	×1
Fighting	×0.5	Dark	×1
Poison	×0.5	Steel	×1
Ground	×0.5	Fairy	×1

Damage taken in Inverse battles

Type		Type	
Normal	×1	Flying	×0.5
Fire	×0.5	Psychic	×1
Water	×0.5	Bug	×1
Grass	×1	Rock	×1
Electric	×2	Ghost	×1
Ice	×0.5	Dragon	×1
Fighting	×2	Dark	×1
Poison	×2	Steel	×1
Ground	×2	Fairy	×1

Can be used in

- Inverse Battle
- Battle Institute
- Battle Maison
- Random Matchup (Free Battle)
- Random Matchup (Others)

LEVEL-UP MOVES

Lv.	Name	Type	Kind	Pow.	Acc.	PP	Range
1	Tackle	Normal	Physical	50	100	35	Normal
10	Protect	Normal	Status	—	—	10	Self
15	Bug Bite	Bug	Physical	60	100	20	Normal
20	Hidden Power	Normal	Special	60	100	15	Normal
23	Confusion	Psychic	Special	50	100	25	Normal
26	Rock Blast	Rock	Physical	25	90	10	Normal
29	Harden	Normal	Status	—	—	30	Self
32	Psybeam	Psychic	Special	65	100	20	Normal
35	Captivate	Normal	Status	—	100	20	Many Others
38	Flail	Normal	Physical	—	100	15	Normal
41	Attract	Normal	Status	—	100	15	Normal
44	Psychic	Psychic	Special	90	100	10	Normal
47	Fissure	Ground	Physical	—	30	5	Normal

TM & HM MOVES

No.	Name	Type	Kind	Pow.	Acc.	PP	Range
TM06	Toxic	Poison	Status	—	90	10	Normal
TM09	Venoshock	Poison	Special	65	100	10	Normal
TM10	Hidden Power	Normal	Special	60	100	15	Normal
TM11	Sunny Day	Fire	Status	—	—	5	Both Sides
TM15	Hyper Beam	Normal	Special	150	90	5	Normal
TM17	Protect	Normal	Status	—	—	10	Self
TM18	Rain Dance	Water	Status	—	—	5	Both Sides
TM20	Safeguard	Normal	Status	—	—	25	Your Side
TM21	Frustration	Normal	Physical	—	100	20	Normal
TM26	Earthquake	Ground	Physical	100	100	10	Adjacent
TM27	Return	Normal	Physical	—	100	20	Normal
TM28	Dig	Ground	Physical	80	100	10	Normal
TM29	Psychic	Psychic	Special	90	100	10	Normal
TM30	Shadow Ball	Ghost	Special	80	100	15	Normal
TM32	Double Team	Normal	Status	—	—	15	Self
TM37	Sandstorm	Rock	Status	—	—	10	Both Sides
TM39	Rock Tomb	Rock	Physical	60	95	15	Normal
TM42	Facade	Normal	Physical	70	100	20	Normal
TM44	Rest	Psychic	Status	—	—	10	Self
TM45	Attract	Normal	Status	—	100	15	Normal
TM46	Thief	Dark	Physical	60	100	25	Normal
TM48	Round	Normal	Special	60	100	15	Normal
TM68	Giga Impact	Normal	Physical	150	90	5	Normal
TM70	Flash	Normal	Status	—	100	20	Normal
TM76	Struggle Bug	Bug	Special	50	100	20	Many Others
TM77	Psych Up	Normal	Status	—	—	10	Normal
TM78	Bulldoze	Ground	Physical	60	100	20	Adjacent
TM83	Infestation	Bug	Special	20	100	20	Normal
TM85	Dream Eater	Psychic	Special	100	100	15	Normal
TM87	Swagger	Normal	Status	—	90	15	Normal
TM88	Sleep Talk	Normal	Status	—	—	10	Self
TM90	Substitute	Normal	Status	—	—	10	Self
TM94	Secret Power	Normal	Physical	70	100	20	Normal
TM100	Confide	Normal	Status	—	—	20	Normal

MOVES LEARNED IN EXCHANGE FOR BP

Name	Type	Kind	Pow.	Acc.	PP	Range
Bug Bite	Bug	Physical	60	100	20	Normal
Signal Beam	Bug	Special	75	100	15	Normal
Uproar	Normal	Special	90	100	10	1 Random
Earth Power	Ground	Special	90	100	10	Normal
Electroweb	Electric	Special	55	95	15	Many Others
Snore	Normal	Special	50	100	15	Normal
Endeavor	Normal	Physical	—	100	5	Normal
Stealth Rock	Rock	Status	—	—	20	Other Side
Skill Swap	Psychic	Status	—	—	10	Normal

MOVES TAUGHT BY PEOPLE

Name	Type	Kind	Pow.	Acc.	PP	Range

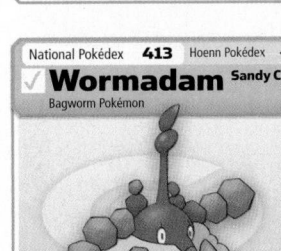

National Pokédex **413** Hoenn Pokédex —

Wormadam Trash Cloak

Bagworm Pokémon

Bug | Steel

HEIGHT: 1'08" WEIGHT: 14.3 lbs.

♀ only

Ω Its appearance changes depending on where it evolved. The materials on hand become a part of its body.

α When Burmy evolved, its cloak became a part of this Pokémon's body. The cloak is never shed.

ABILITY
Anticipation

HIDDEN ABILITY
Overcoat

EGG GROUPS
Bug

STAT GROWTH RATES

HP	■■■
Attack	■■■■
Defense	■■■■
Sp. Atk	■■■
Sp. Def	■■■■
Speed	■■

ITEMS SOMETIMES HELD BY WILD POKÉMON
—

EVOLUTION

Burmy ♀ Trash Cloak → Lv. 20 → Wormadam Trash Cloak

MAIN WAY TO REGISTER IN THE NATIONAL POKÉDEX

Level up a female Burmy (Trash Cloak) obtained via Link Trade or the GTS to Lv. 20.

Damage taken in normal battles

Normal	×0.5	Flying	×1
Fire	×4	Psychic	×0.5
Water	×1	Bug	×0.5
Grass	×0.25	Rock	×1
Electric	×1	Ghost	×1
Ice	×0.5	Dragon	×0.5
Fighting	×1	Dark	×1
Poison	×0	Steel	×0.5
Ground	×1	Fairy	×0.5

Damage taken in Inverse battles

Normal	×2	Flying	×1
Fire	×0.25	Psychic	×2
Water	×1	Bug	×2
Grass	×4	Rock	×1
Electric	×1	Ghost	×1
Ice	×2	Dragon	×2
Fighting	×1	Dark	×1
Poison	×2	Steel	×2
Ground	×1	Fairy	×2

Can be used in
- Inverse Battle
- Battle Institute
- Battle Maison
- Random Matchup (Free Battle)
- Random Matchup (Others)

LEVEL-UP MOVES

Lv.	Name	Type	Kind	Pow.	Acc.	PP	Range
1	Tackle	Normal	Physical	50	100	35	Normal
10	Protect	Normal	Status	—	—	10	Self
15	Bug Bite	Bug	Physical	60	100	20	Normal
20	Hidden Power	Normal	Special	60	100	15	Normal
23	Confusion	Psychic	Special	50	100	25	Normal
26	Mirror Shot	Steel	Special	65	85	10	Normal
29	Metal Sound	Steel	Status	—	85	40	Normal
32	Psybeam	Psychic	Special	65	100	20	Normal
35	Captivate	Normal	Status	—	100	20	Many Others
38	Flail	Normal	Physical	—	100	15	Normal
41	Attract	Normal	Status	—	100	15	Normal
44	Psychic	Psychic	Special	90	100	10	Normal
47	Iron Head	Steel	Physical	80	100	15	Normal

TM & HM MOVES

No.	Name	Type	Kind	Pow.	Acc.	PP	Range
TM06	Toxic	Poison	Status	—	90	10	Normal
TM09	Venoshock	Poison	Special	65	100	10	Normal
TM10	Hidden Power	Normal	Special	60	100	15	Normal
TM11	Sunny Day	Fire	Status	—	—	5	Both Sides
TM15	Hyper Beam	Normal	Special	150	90	5	Normal
TM17	Protect	Normal	Status	—	—	10	Self
TM18	Rain Dance	Water	Status	—	—	5	Both Sides
TM20	Safeguard	Normal	Status	—	—	25	Your Side
TM21	Frustration	Normal	Physical	—	100	20	Normal
TM27	Return	Normal	Physical	—	100	20	Normal
TM29	Psychic	Psychic	Special	90	100	10	Normal
TM30	Shadow Ball	Ghost	Special	80	100	15	Normal
TM32	Double Team	Normal	Status	—	—	15	Self
TM42	Facade	Normal	Physical	70	100	20	Normal
TM44	Rest	Psychic	Status	—	—	10	Self
TM45	Attract	Normal	Status	—	100	15	Normal
TM46	Thief	Dark	Physical	60	100	25	Normal
TM48	Round	Normal	Special	60	100	15	Normal
TM68	Giga Impact	Normal	Physical	150	90	5	Normal
TM70	Flash	Normal	Status	—	100	20	Normal
TM74	Gyro Ball	Steel	Physical	—	100	5	Normal
TM76	Struggle Bug	Bug	Special	50	100	20	Many Others
TM77	Psych Up	Normal	Status	—	—	10	Normal
TM83	Infestation	Bug	Special	20	100	20	Normal
TM85	Dream Eater	Psychic	Special	100	100	15	Normal
TM87	Swagger	Normal	Status	—	90	15	Normal
TM88	Sleep Talk	Normal	Status	—	—	10	Self
TM90	Substitute	Normal	Status	—	—	10	Self
TM91	Flash Cannon	Steel	Special	80	100	10	Normal
TM94	Secret Power	Normal	Physical	70	100	20	Normal
TM100	Confide	Normal	Status	—	—	20	Normal

MOVES LEARNED IN EXCHANGE FOR BP

Name	Type	Kind	Pow.	Acc.	PP	Range
Bug Bite	Bug	Physical	60	100	20	Normal
Signal Beam	Bug	Special	75	100	15	Normal
Iron Head	Steel	Physical	80	100	15	Normal
Gunk Shot	Poison	Physical	120	80	5	Normal
Uproar	Normal	Special	90	100	10	1 Random
Magnet Rise	Electric	Status	—	—	10	Self
Iron Defense	Steel	Status	—	—	15	Self
Electroweb	Electric	Special	55	95	15	Many Others
Snore	Normal	Special	50	100	15	Normal
Endeavor	Normal	Physical	—	100	5	Normal
Stealth Rock	Rock	Status	—	—	20	Other Side
Skill Swap	Psychic	Status	—	—	10	Normal

MOVES TAUGHT BY PEOPLE

Name	Type	Kind	Pow.	Acc.	PP	Range

National Pokédex **414** Hoenn Pokédex —

Mothim

Moth Pokémon

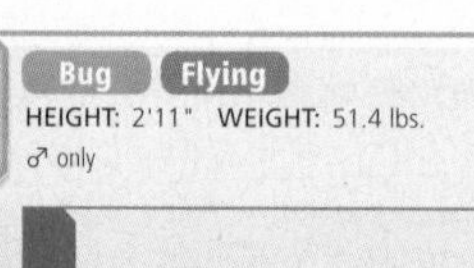

Bug | Flying

HEIGHT: 2'11" WEIGHT: 51.4 lbs.

♂ only

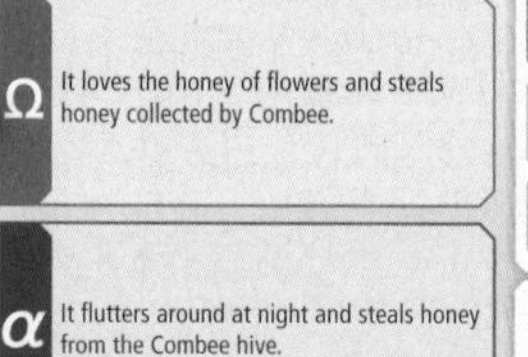

Ω It loves the honey of flowers and steals honey collected by Combee.

α It flutters around at night and steals honey from the Combee hive.

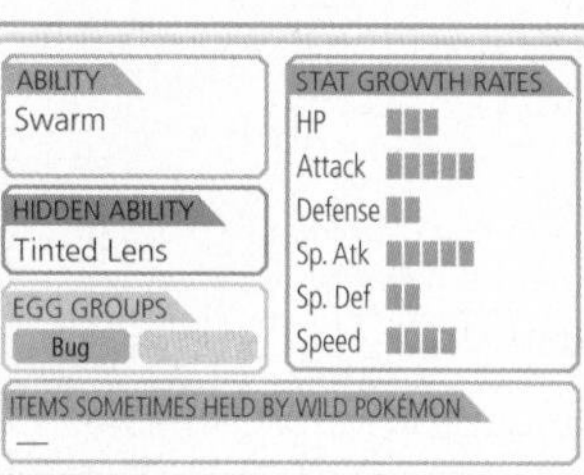

ABILITY
Swarm

HIDDEN ABILITY
Tinted Lens

EGG GROUPS
Bug

STAT GROWTH RATES

HP	■■■
Attack	■■■■■
Defense	■■
Sp. Atk	■■■■■
Sp. Def	■■
Speed	■■■■

ITEMS SOMETIMES HELD BY WILD POKÉMON
—

MAIN WAY TO REGISTER IN THE NATIONAL POKÉDEX

Level up a male Burmy obtained via Link Trade or the GTS to Lv. 20.

EVOLUTION

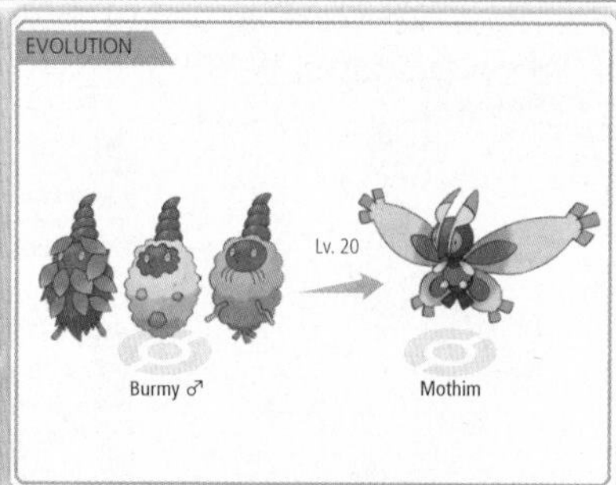

Damage taken in normal battles

Normal	×1	Flying	×2
Fire	×2	Psychic	×1
Water	×1	Bug	×0.5
Grass	×0.25	Rock	×4
Electric	×2	Ghost	×1
Ice	×2	Dragon	×1
Fighting	×0.25	Dark	×1
Poison	×1	Steel	×1
Ground	×0	Fairy	×1

Damage taken in Inverse battles

Normal	×1	Flying	×0.5
Fire	×0.5	Psychic	×1
Water	×1	Bug	×2
Grass	×4	Rock	×0.25
Electric	×0.5	Ghost	×1
Ice	×0.5	Dragon	×1
Fighting	×4	Dark	×1
Poison	×1	Steel	×1
Ground	×4	Fairy	×1

Can be used in
- Inverse Battle
- Battle Institute
- Battle Maison
- Random Matchup (Free Battle)
- Random Matchup (Others)

LEVEL-UP MOVES

Lv.	Name	Type	Kind	Pow.	Acc.	PP	Range
1	Tackle	Normal	Physical	50	100	35	Normal
10	Protect	Normal	Status	—	—	10	Self
15	Bug Bite	Bug	Physical	60	100	20	Normal
20	Hidden Power	Normal	Special	60	100	15	Normal
23	Confusion	Psychic	Special	50	100	25	Normal
26	Gust	Flying	Special	40	100	35	Normal
29	Poison Powder	Poison	Status	—	75	35	Normal
32	Psybeam	Psychic	Special	65	100	20	Normal
35	Camouflage	Normal	Status	—	—	20	Self
38	Silver Wind	Bug	Special	60	100	5	Normal
41	Air Slash	Flying	Special	75	95	15	Normal
44	Psychic	Psychic	Special	90	100	10	Normal
47	Bug Buzz	Bug	Special	90	100	10	Normal
50	Quiver Dance	Bug	Status	—	—	20	Self

TM & HM MOVES

No.	Name	Type	Kind	Pow.	Acc.	PP	Range
TM06	Toxic	Poison	Status	—	90	10	Normal
TM09	Venoshock	Poison	Special	65	100	10	Normal
TM10	Hidden Power	Normal	Special	60	100	15	Normal
TM11	Sunny Day	Fire	Status	—	—	5	Both Sides
TM15	Hyper Beam	Normal	Special	150	90	5	Normal
TM17	Protect	Normal	Status	—	—	10	Self
TM18	Rain Dance	Water	Status	—	—	5	Both Sides
TM19	Roost	Flying	Status	—	—	10	Self
TM20	Safeguard	Normal	Status	—	—	25	Your Side
TM21	Frustration	Normal	Physical	—	100	20	Normal
TM22	Solar Beam	Grass	Special	120	100	10	Normal
TM27	Return	Normal	Physical	—	100	20	Normal
TM29	Psychic	Psychic	Special	90	100	10	Normal
TM30	Shadow Ball	Ghost	Special	80	100	15	Normal
TM32	Double Team	Normal	Status	—	—	15	Self
TM40	Aerial Ace	Flying	Physical	60	—	20	Normal
TM42	Facade	Normal	Physical	70	100	20	Normal
TM44	Rest	Psychic	Status	—	—	10	Self
TM45	Attract	Normal	Status	—	100	15	Normal
TM46	Thief	Dark	Physical	60	100	25	Normal
TM48	Round	Normal	Special	60	100	15	Normal
TM53	Energy Ball	Grass	Special	90	100	10	Normal
TM62	Acrobatics	Flying	Physical	55	100	15	Normal
TM68	Giga Impact	Normal	Physical	150	90	5	Normal
TM70	Flash	Normal	Status	—	100	20	Normal
TM76	Struggle Bug	Bug	Special	50	100	20	Many Others
TM77	Psych Up	Normal	Status	—	—	10	Normal
TM83	Infestation	Bug	Special	20	100	20	Normal
TM85	Dream Eater	Psychic	Special	100	100	15	Normal
TM87	Swagger	Normal	Status	—	90	15	Normal
TM88	Sleep Talk	Normal	Status	—	—	10	Self
TM89	U-turn	Bug	Physical	70	100	20	Normal
TM90	Substitute	Normal	Status	—	—	10	Self
TM94	Secret Power	Normal	Physical	70	100	20	Normal
TM100	Confide	Normal	Status	—	—	20	Normal

MOVES LEARNED IN EXCHANGE FOR BP

Name	Type	Kind	Pow.	Acc.	PP	Range
Bug Bite	Bug	Physical	60	100	20	Normal
Signal Beam	Bug	Special	75	100	15	Normal
Electroweb	Electric	Special	55	95	15	Many Others
Snore	Normal	Special	50	100	15	Normal
Tailwind	Flying	Status	—	—	15	Your Side
Giga Drain	Grass	Special	75	100	10	Normal
Skill Swap	Psychic	Status	—	—	10	Normal

MOVES TAUGHT BY PEOPLE

Name	Type	Kind	Pow.	Acc.	PP	Range

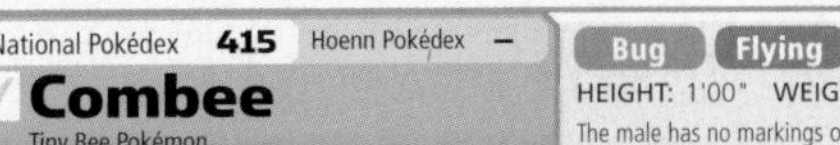

National Pokédex **415** Hoenn Pokédex —

Combee

Tiny Bee Pokémon

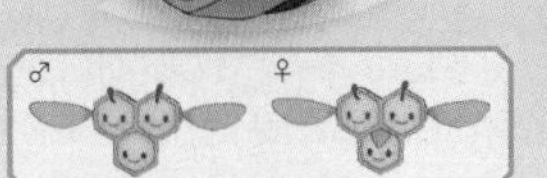

Bug **Flying**

HEIGHT: 1'00" WEIGHT: 12.1 lbs.

The male has no markings on its forehead. The female has a red mark on its forehead.

Ω The trio is together from birth. It constantly gathers honey from flowers to please Vespiquen.

α It collects and delivers honey to its colony. At night, they cluster to form a beehive and sleep.

ABILITY
Honey Gather

HIDDEN ABILITY
Hustle

EGG GROUPS
Bug

STAT GROWTH RATES
HP
Attack
Defense
Sp. Atk
Sp. Def
Speed

ITEMS SOMETIMES HELD BY WILD POKÉMON
—

EVOLUTION

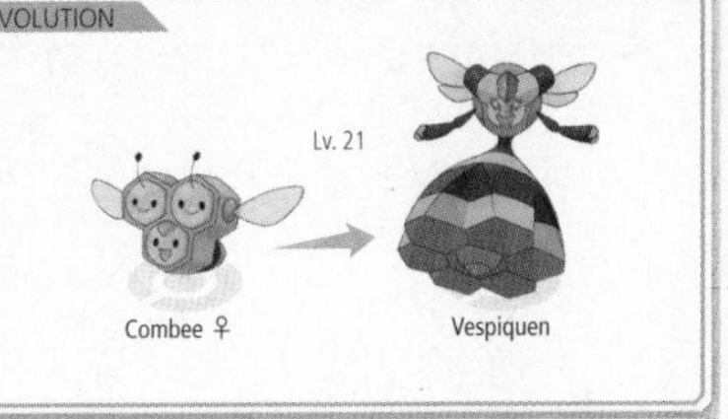

MAIN WAY TO REGISTER IN THE NATIONAL POKÉDEX

Appears in *Pokémon X* and *Pokémon Y*. Bring it to your game using Link Trade or the GTS.

Damage taken in normal battles

Type		Type	
Normal	×1	Flying	×2
Fire	×2	Psychic	×1
Water	×1	Bug	×0.5
Grass	×0.25	Rock	×4
Electric	×2	Ghost	×1
Ice	×2	Dragon	×1
Fighting	×0.25	Dark	×1
Poison	×1	Steel	×1
Ground	×0	Fairy	×1

Damage taken in Inverse battles

Type		Type	
Normal	×1	Flying	×0.5
Fire	×0.5	Psychic	×1
Water	×1	Bug	×2
Grass	×4	Rock	×0.25
Electric	×0.5	Ghost	×1
Ice	×0.5	Dragon	×1
Fighting	×4	Dark	×1
Poison	×1	Steel	×1
Ground	×4	Fairy	×1

Can be used in
Inverse Battle
Battle Institute
Battle Maison
Random Matchup (Free Battle)
Random Matchup (Others)

LEVEL-UP MOVES

Lv.	Name	Type	Kind	Pow.	Acc.	PP	Range
1	Sweet Scent	Normal	Status	—	100	20	Many Others
1	Gust	Flying	Special	40	100	35	Normal
13	Bug Bite	Bug	Physical	60	100	20	Normal
29	Bug Buzz	Bug	Special	90	100	10	Normal

TM & HM MOVES

No.	Name	Type	Kind	Pow.	Acc.	PP	Range

MOVES LEARNED IN EXCHANGE FOR BP

Name	Type	Kind	Pow.	Acc.	PP	Range
Bug Bite	Bug	Physical	60	100	20	Normal
Snore	Normal	Special	50	100	15	Normal
Tailwind	Flying	Status	—	—	15	Your Side
Endeavor	Normal	Physical	—	100	5	Normal

MOVES TAUGHT BY PEOPLE

Name	Type	Kind	Pow.	Acc.	PP	Range

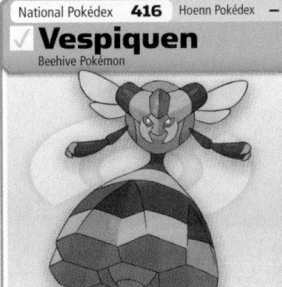

National Pokédex **416** Hoenn Pokédex —

Vespiquen

Beehive Pokémon

Bug **Flying**

HEIGHT: 3'11" WEIGHT: 84.9 lbs.

♀ only

Ω It houses its colony in cells in its body and releases various pheromones to make those grubs do its bidding.

α Its abdomen is a honeycomb for grubs. It raises its grubs on honey collected by Combee.

ABILITY
Pressure

HIDDEN ABILITY
Unnerve

EGG GROUPS
Bug

STAT GROWTH RATES
HP
Attack
Defense
Sp. Atk
Sp. Def
Speed

ITEMS SOMETIMES HELD BY WILD POKÉMON
—

EVOLUTION

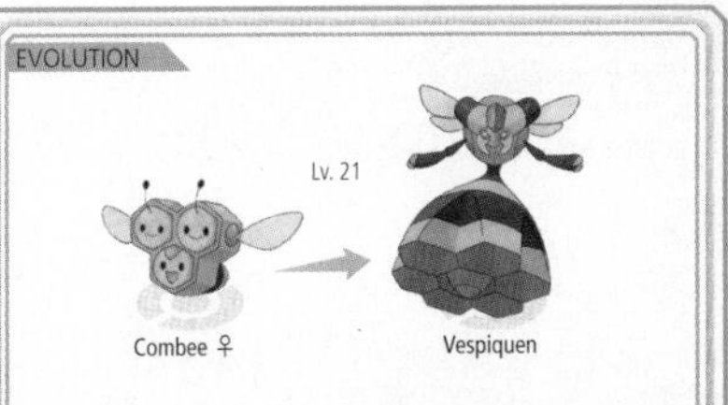

MAIN WAY TO REGISTER IN THE NATIONAL POKÉDEX

Level up a female Combee obtained via Link Trade or the GTS to Lv. 21.

Damage taken in normal battles

Type		Type	
Normal	×1	Flying	×2
Fire	×2	Psychic	×1
Water	×1	Bug	×0.5
Grass	×0.25	Rock	×4
Electric	×2	Ghost	×1
Ice	×2	Dragon	×1
Fighting	×0.25	Dark	×1
Poison	×1	Steel	×1
Ground	×0	Fairy	×1

Damage taken in Inverse battles

Type		Type	
Normal	×1	Flying	×0.5
Fire	×0.5	Psychic	×1
Water	×1	Bug	×2
Grass	×4	Rock	×0.25
Electric	×0.5	Ghost	×1
Ice	×0.5	Dragon	×1
Fighting	×4	Dark	×1
Poison	×1	Steel	×1
Ground	×4	Fairy	×1

Can be used in
Inverse Battle
Battle Institute
Battle Maison
Random Matchup (Free Battle)
Random Matchup (Others)

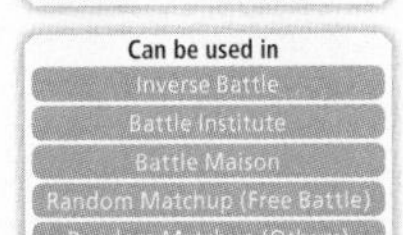

LEVEL-UP MOVES

Lv.	Name	Type	Kind	Pow.	Acc.	PP	Range
1	Fell Stinger	Bug	Physical	30	100	25	Normal
1	Destiny Bond	Ghost	Status	—	—	5	Self
1	Sweet Scent	Normal	Status	—	100	20	Many Others
1	Gust	Flying	Special	40	100	35	Normal
1	Poison Sting	Poison	Physical	15	100	35	Normal
1	Confuse Ray	Ghost	Status	—	100	10	Normal
5	Fury Cutter	Bug	Physical	40	95	20	Normal
9	Pursuit	Dark	Physical	40	100	20	Normal
13	Fury Swipes	Normal	Physical	18	80	15	Normal
17	Defend Order	Bug	Status	—	—	10	Self
21	Slash	Normal	Physical	70	100	20	Normal
25	Power Gem	Rock	Special	80	100	20	Normal
29	Heal Order	Bug	Status	—	—	10	Self
33	Toxic	Poison	Status	—	90	10	Normal
37	Air Slash	Flying	Special	75	95	15	Normal
41	Captivate	Normal	Status	—	100	20	Many Others
45	Attack Order	Bug	Physical	90	100	15	Normal
49	Swagger	Normal	Status	—	90	15	Normal
53	Destiny Bond	Ghost	Status	—	—	5	Self
57	Fell Stinger	Bug	Physical	30	100	25	Normal

TM & HM MOVES

No.	Name	Type	Kind	Pow.	Acc.	PP	Range
TM01	Hone Claws	Dark	Status	—	—	15	Self
TM06	Toxic	Poison	Status	—	90	10	Normal
TM09	Venoshock	Poison	Special	65	100	10	Normal
TM10	Hidden Power	Normal	Special	60	100	15	Normal
TM11	Sunny Day	Fire	Status	—	—	5	Both Sides
TM15	Hyper Beam	Normal	Special	150	90	5	Normal
TM17	Protect	Normal	Status	—	—	10	Self
TM18	Rain Dance	Water	Status	—	—	5	Both Sides
TM19	Roost	Flying	Status	—	—	10	Self
TM21	Frustration	Normal	Physical	—	100	20	Normal
TM27	Return	Normal	Physical	—	100	20	Normal
TM32	Double Team	Normal	Status	—	—	15	Self
TM36	Sludge Bomb	Poison	Special	90	100	10	Normal
TM40	Aerial Ace	Flying	Physical	60	—	20	Normal
TM42	Facade	Normal	Physical	70	100	20	Normal
TM44	Rest	Psychic	Status	—	—	10	Self
TM45	Attract	Normal	Status	—	100	15	Normal
TM46	Thief	Dark	Physical	60	100	25	Normal
TM48	Round	Normal	Special	60	100	15	Normal
TM56	Fling	Dark	Physical	—	100	10	Normal
TM60	Quash	Dark	Status	—	100	15	Normal
TM62	Acrobatics	Flying	Physical	55	100	15	Normal
TM68	Giga Impact	Normal	Physical	150	90	5	Normal
TM70	Flash	Normal	Status	—	100	20	Normal
TM76	Struggle Bug	Bug	Special	50	100	20	Many Others
TM81	X-Scissor	Bug	Physical	80	100	15	Normal
TM83	Infestation	Bug	Special	20	100	20	Normal
TM87	Swagger	Normal	Status	—	90	15	Normal
TM88	Sleep Talk	Normal	Status	—	—	10	Self
TM89	U-turn	Bug	Physical	70	100	20	Normal
TM90	Substitute	Normal	Status	—	—	10	Self
TM94	Secret Power	Normal	Physical	70	100	20	Normal
TM100	Confide	Normal	Status	—	—	20	Normal
HM01	Cut	Normal	Physical	50	95	30	Normal

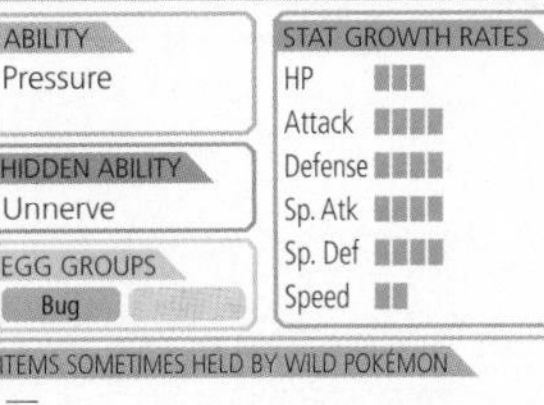

MOVES LEARNED IN EXCHANGE FOR BP

Name	Type	Kind	Pow.	Acc.	PP	Range
Bug Bite	Bug	Physical	60	100	20	Normal
Signal Beam	Bug	Special	75	100	15	Normal
Snore	Normal	Special	50	100	15	Normal
Tailwind	Flying	Status	—	—	15	Your Side
Endeavor	Normal	Physical	—	100	5	Normal

MOVES TAUGHT BY PEOPLE

Name	Type	Kind	Pow.	Acc.	PP	Range

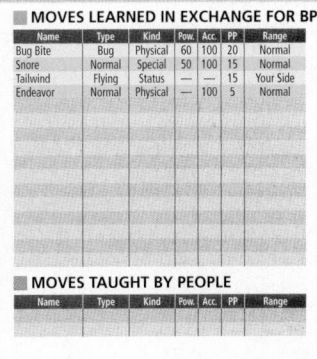

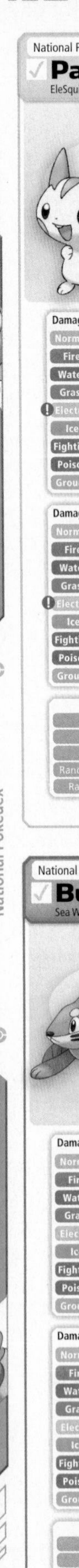

National Pokédex **417** Hoenn Pokédex —

Pachirisu

EleSquirrel Pokémon

Electric

HEIGHT: 1'04" WEIGHT: 8.6 lbs.

The pattern on the male's forehead extends farther down than the pattern on the female's.

Ω It makes fur balls that crackle with static electricity. It stores them with berries in tree holes.

α A pair may be seen rubbing their cheek pouches together in an effort to share stored electricity.

ABILITIES
Run Away
Pickup

HIDDEN ABILITY
Volt Absorb

EGG GROUPS
Field
Fairy

STAT GROWTH RATES
HP
Attack
Defense
Sp. Atk
Sp. Def
Speed

ITEMS SOMETIMES HELD BY WILD POKÉMON
—

EVOLUTION
Does not evolve

MAIN WAY TO REGISTER IN THE NATIONAL POKÉDEX

Appears in *Pokémon X* and *Pokémon Y*. Bring it to your game using Link Trade or the GTS.

Damage taken in normal battles

Type		Type	
Normal	×1	Flying	×0.5
Fire	×1	Psychic	×1
Water	×1	Bug	×1
Grass	×1	Rock	×1
Electric	×0.5	Ghost	×1
Ice	×1	Dragon	×1
Fighting	×1	Dark	×1
Poison	×1	Steel	×0.5
Ground	×2	Fairy	×1

Damage taken in Inverse battles

Type		Type	
Normal	×1	Flying	×2
Fire	×1	Psychic	×1
Water	×1	Bug	×1
Grass	×1	Rock	×1
Electric	×2	Ghost	×1
Ice	×1	Dragon	×1
Fighting	×1	Dark	×1
Poison	×1	Steel	×2
Ground	×0.5	Fairy	×1

Can be used in
Inverse Battle
Battle Institute
Battle Maison
Random Matchup (Free Battle)
Random Matchup (Others)

LEVEL-UP MOVES

Lv.	Name	Type	Kind	Pow.	Acc.	PP	Range
1	Growl	Normal	Status	—	100	40	Many Others
1	Bide	Normal	Physical	—	—	10	Self
5	Quick Attack	Normal	Physical	40	100	30	Normal
9	Charm	Fairy	Status	—	100	20	Normal
13	Spark	Electric	Physical	65	100	20	Normal
17	Endure	Normal	Status	—	—	10	Self
19	Nuzzle	Electric	Physical	20	100	20	Normal
21	Swift	Normal	Special	60	—	20	Many Others
25	Electro Ball	Electric	Special	—	100	10	Normal
29	Sweet Kiss	Fairy	Status	—	75	10	Normal
33	Thunder Wave	Electric	Status	—	100	20	Normal
37	Super Fang	Normal	Physical	—	90	10	Normal
41	Discharge	Electric	Special	80	100	15	Adjacent
45	Last Resort	Normal	Physical	140	100	5	Normal
49	Hyper Fang	Normal	Physical	80	90	15	Normal

TM & HM MOVES

No.	Name	Type	Kind	Pow.	Acc.	PP	Range
TM06	Toxic	Poison	Status	—	90	10	Normal
TM10	Hidden Power	Normal	Special	60	100	15	Normal
TM16	Light Screen	Psychic	Status	—	—	30	Your Side
TM17	Protect	Normal	Status	—	—	10	Self
TM18	Rain Dance	Water	Status	—	—	5	Both Sides
TM21	Frustration	Normal	Physical	—	100	20	Normal
TM24	Thunderbolt	Electric	Special	90	100	15	Normal
TM25	Thunder	Electric	Special	110	70	10	Normal
TM27	Return	Normal	Physical	—	100	20	Normal
TM28	Dig	Ground	Physical	80	100	10	Normal
TM32	Double Team	Normal	Status	—	—	15	Self
TM42	Facade	Normal	Physical	70	100	20	Normal
TM44	Rest	Psychic	Status	—	—	10	Self
TM45	Attract	Normal	Status	—	100	15	Normal
TM48	Round	Normal	Special	60	100	15	Normal
TM49	Echoed Voice	Normal	Special	40	100	15	Normal
TM56	Fling	Dark	Physical	—	100	10	Normal
TM57	Charge Beam	Electric	Special	50	90	10	Normal
TM70	Flash	Normal	Status	—	100	20	Normal
TM72	Volt Switch	Electric	Special	70	100	20	Normal
TM73	Thunder Wave	Electric	Status	—	100	20	Normal
TM86	Grass Knot	Grass	Special	—	100	20	Normal
TM87	Swagger	Normal	Status	—	90	15	Normal
TM88	Sleep Talk	Normal	Status	—	—	10	Self
TM89	U-turn	Bug	Physical	70	100	20	Normal
TM90	Substitute	Normal	Status	—	—	10	Self
TM94	Secret Power	Normal	Physical	70	100	20	Normal
TM100	Confide	Normal	Status	—	—	20	Normal
HM01	Cut	Normal	Physical	50	95	30	Normal

MOVES LEARNED IN EXCHANGE FOR BP

Name	Type	Kind	Pow.	Acc.	PP	Range
Covet	Normal	Physical	60	100	25	Normal
Super Fang	Normal	Physical	—	90	10	Normal
Seed Bomb	Grass	Physical	80	100	15	Normal
Gunk Shot	Poison	Physical	120	80	5	Normal
Uproar	Normal	Special	90	100	10	1 Random
Thunder Punch	Electric	Physical	75	100	15	Normal
Magnet Rise	Electric	Status	—	—	10	Self
Last Resort	Normal	Physical	140	100	5	Normal
Electroweb	Electric	Special	55	95	15	Many Others
Iron Tail	Steel	Physical	100	75	15	Normal
Snore	Normal	Special	50	100	15	Normal
Shock Wave	Electric	Special	60	—	20	Normal
Helping Hand	Normal	Status	—	—	20	1 Ally

MOVES TAUGHT BY PEOPLE

Name	Type	Kind	Pow.	Acc.	PP	Range

EGG MOVES

Name	Type	Kind	Pow.	Acc.	PP	Range
Covet	Normal	Physical	60	100	25	Normal
Bite	Dark	Physical	60	100	25	Normal
Fake Tears	Dark	Status	—	100	20	Normal
Defense Curl	Normal	Status	—	—	40	Self
Rollout	Rock	Physical	30	90	20	Normal
Flatter	Dark	Status	—	100	15	Normal
Flail	Normal	Physical	—	100	15	Normal
Iron Tail	Steel	Physical	100	75	15	Normal
Tail Whip	Normal	Status	—	100	30	Many Others
Follow Me	Normal	Status	—	—	20	Self
Charge	Electric	Status	—	—	20	Self
Bestow	Normal	Status	—	—	15	Normal
Ion Deluge	Electric	Status	—	—	25	Both Sides

National Pokédex **418** Hoenn Pokédex —

Buizel

Sea Weasel Pokémon

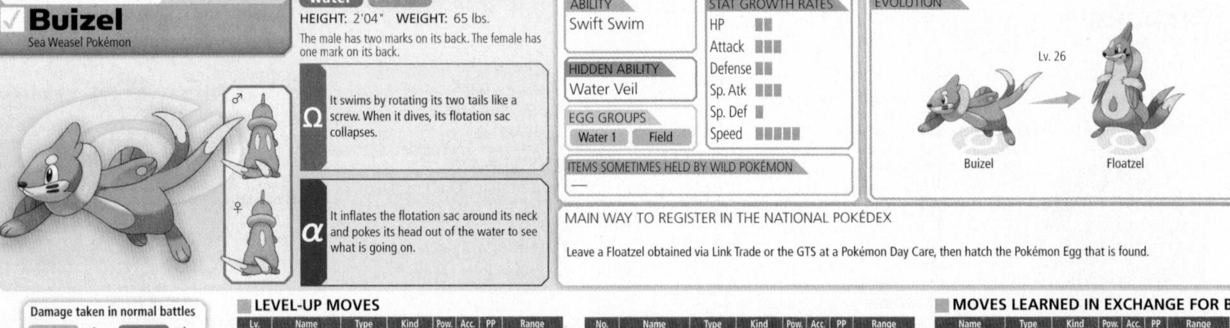

Water

HEIGHT: 2'04" WEIGHT: 65 lbs.

The male has two marks on its back. The female has one mark on its back.

Ω It swims by rotating its two tails like a screw. When it dives, its flotation sac collapses.

α It inflates the flotation sac around its neck and pokes its head out of the water to see what is going on.

ABILITY
Swift Swim

HIDDEN ABILITY
Water Veil

EGG GROUPS
Water 1
Field

STAT GROWTH RATES
HP
Attack
Defense
Sp. Atk
Sp. Def
Speed

ITEMS SOMETIMES HELD BY WILD POKÉMON
—

EVOLUTION

MAIN WAY TO REGISTER IN THE NATIONAL POKÉDEX

Leave a Floatzel obtained via Link Trade or the GTS at a Pokémon Day Care, then hatch the Pokémon Egg that is found.

Damage taken in normal battles

Type		Type	
Normal	×1	Flying	×1
Fire	×0.5	Psychic	×1
Water	×0.5	Bug	×1
Grass	×2	Rock	×1
Electric	×2	Ghost	×1
Ice	×0.5	Dragon	×1
Fighting	×1	Dark	×1
Poison	×1	Steel	×0.5
Ground	×1	Fairy	×1

Damage taken in Inverse battles

Type		Type	
Normal	×1	Flying	×1
Fire	×2	Psychic	×1
Water	×2	Bug	×1
Grass	×0.5	Rock	×1
Electric	×0.5	Ghost	×1
Ice	×2	Dragon	×1
Fighting	×1	Dark	×1
Poison	×1	Steel	×2
Ground	×1	Fairy	×1

Can be used in
Inverse Battle
Battle Institute
Battle Maison
Random Matchup (Free Battle)
Random Matchup (Others)

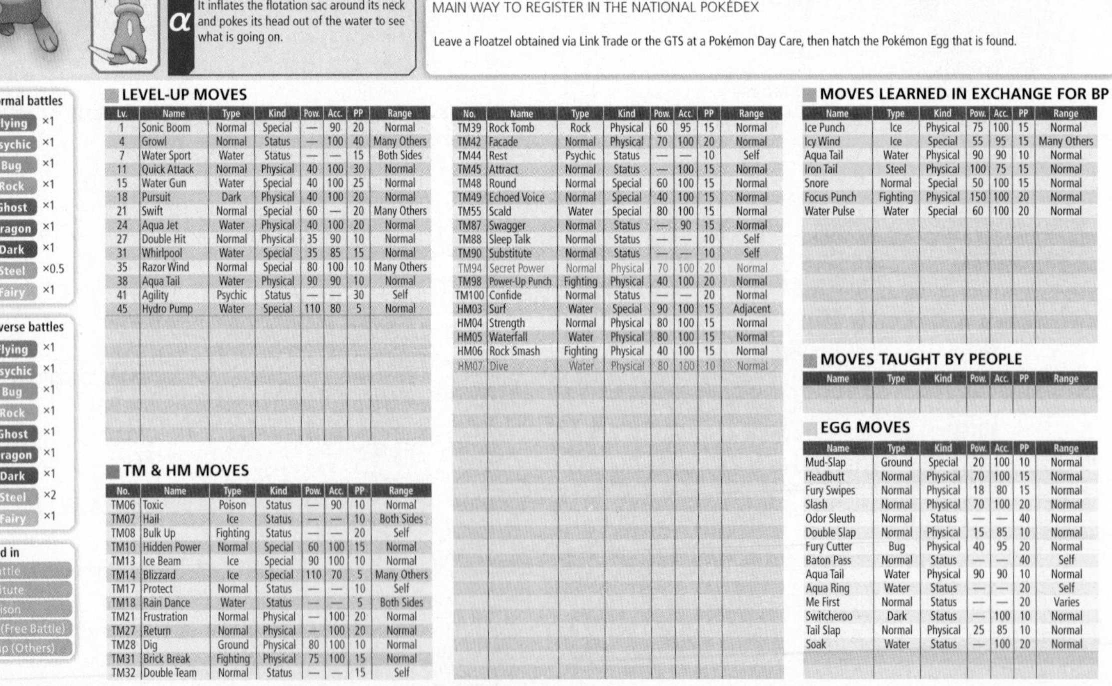

LEVEL-UP MOVES

Lv.	Name	Type	Kind	Pow.	Acc.	PP	Range
1	Sonic Boom	Normal	Special	—	90	20	Normal
4	Growl	Normal	Status	—	100	40	Many Others
7	Water Sport	Water	Status	—	—	15	Both Sides
11	Quick Attack	Normal	Physical	40	100	30	Normal
15	Water Gun	Water	Special	40	100	25	Normal
18	Pursuit	Dark	Physical	40	100	20	Normal
21	Swift	Normal	Special	60	—	20	Many Others
24	Aqua Jet	Water	Physical	40	100	20	Normal
27	Double Hit	Normal	Physical	35	90	10	Normal
31	Whirlpool	Water	Special	35	85	15	Normal
35	Razor Wind	Normal	Special	80	100	10	Many Others
38	Aqua Tail	Water	Physical	90	90	10	Normal
41	Agility	Psychic	Status	—	—	30	Self
45	Hydro Pump	Water	Special	110	80	5	Normal

TM & HM MOVES

No.	Name	Type	Kind	Pow.	Acc.	PP	Range
TM06	Toxic	Poison	Status	—	90	10	Normal
TM07	Hail	Ice	Status	—	—	10	Both Sides
TM08	Bulk Up	Fighting	Status	—	—	20	Self
TM10	Hidden Power	Normal	Special	60	100	15	Normal
TM13	Ice Beam	Ice	Special	90	100	10	Normal
TM14	Blizzard	Ice	Special	110	70	5	Many Others
TM17	Protect	Normal	Status	—	—	10	Self
TM18	Rain Dance	Water	Status	—	—	5	Both Sides
TM21	Frustration	Normal	Physical	—	100	20	Normal
TM27	Return	Normal	Physical	—	100	20	Normal
TM28	Dig	Ground	Physical	80	100	10	Normal
TM31	Brick Break	Fighting	Physical	75	100	15	Normal
TM32	Double Team	Normal	Status	—	—	15	Self
TM39	Rock Tomb	Rock	Physical	60	95	15	Normal
TM42	Facade	Normal	Physical	70	100	20	Normal
TM44	Rest	Psychic	Status	—	—	10	Self
TM45	Attract	Normal	Status	—	100	15	Normal
TM48	Round	Normal	Special	60	100	15	Normal
TM49	Echoed Voice	Normal	Special	40	100	15	Normal
TM55	Scald	Water	Special	80	100	15	Normal
TM87	Swagger	Normal	Status	—	90	15	Normal
TM88	Sleep Talk	Normal	Status	—	—	10	Self
TM90	Substitute	Normal	Status	—	—	10	Self
TM94	Secret Power	Normal	Physical	70	100	20	Normal
TM98	Power-Up Punch	Fighting	Physical	40	100	20	Normal
TM100	Confide	Normal	Status	—	—	20	Normal
HM03	Surf	Water	Special	90	100	15	Adjacent
HM04	Strength	Normal	Physical	80	100	15	Normal
HM05	Waterfall	Water	Physical	80	100	15	Normal
HM06	Rock Smash	Fighting	Physical	40	100	15	Normal
HM07	Dive	Water	Physical	80	100	10	Normal

MOVES LEARNED IN EXCHANGE FOR BP

Name	Type	Kind	Pow.	Acc.	PP	Range
Ice Punch	Ice	Physical	75	100	15	Normal
Icy Wind	Ice	Special	55	95	15	Many Others
Aqua Tail	Water	Physical	90	90	10	Normal
Iron Tail	Steel	Physical	100	75	15	Normal
Snore	Normal	Special	50	100	15	Normal
Focus Punch	Fighting	Physical	150	100	20	Normal
Water Pulse	Water	Special	60	100	20	Normal

MOVES TAUGHT BY PEOPLE

Name	Type	Kind	Pow.	Acc.	PP	Range

EGG MOVES

Name	Type	Kind	Pow.	Acc.	PP	Range
Mud-Slap	Ground	Special	20	100	10	Normal
Headbutt	Normal	Physical	70	100	15	Normal
Fury Swipes	Normal	Physical	18	80	15	Normal
Slash	Normal	Physical	70	100	20	Normal
Odor Sleuth	Normal	Status	—	—	40	Normal
Double Slap	Normal	Physical	15	85	10	Normal
Fury Cutter	Bug	Physical	40	95	20	Normal
Baton Pass	Normal	Status	—	—	40	Self
Aqua Tail	Water	Physical	90	90	10	Normal
Aqua Ring	Water	Status	—	—	20	Self
Me First	Normal	Status	—	—	20	Varies
Switcheroo	Dark	Status	—	100	10	Normal
Tail Slap	Normal	Physical	25	85	10	Normal
Soak	Water	Status	—	100	20	Normal

National Pokédex **419** Hoenn Pokédex —

Floatzel

Sea Weasel Pokémon

Water

HEIGHT: 3'07" WEIGHT: 73.9 lbs.

The male has two marks on its back. The female has one mark on its back.

Ω It floats using its well-developed flotation sac. It assists in the rescues of drowning people.

α Its flotation sac developed as a result of pursuing aquatic prey. It can double as a rubber raft.

ABILITY
Swift Swim

HIDDEN ABILITY
Water Veil

EGG GROUPS
Water 1 | Field

STAT GROWTH RATES
HP, Attack, Defense, Sp. Atk, Sp. Def, Speed

ITEMS SOMETIMES HELD BY WILD POKÉMON
—

EVOLUTION

MAIN WAY TO REGISTER IN THE NATIONAL POKÉDEX

Appears in *Pokémon X* and *Pokémon Y*. Bring it to your game using Link Trade or the GTS.

Damage taken in normal battles

Type		Type	
Normal	×1	Flying	×1
Fire	×0.5	Psychic	×1
Water	×0.5	Bug	×1
Grass	×2	Rock	×1
Electric	×2	Ghost	×1
Ice	×0.5	Dragon	×1
Fighting	×1	Dark	×1
Poison	×1	Steel	×0.5
Ground	×1	Fairy	×1

Damage taken in Inverse battles

Type		Type	
Normal	×1	Flying	×1
Fire	×2	Psychic	×1
Water	×2	Bug	×1
Grass	×0.5	Rock	×1
Electric	×0.5	Ghost	×1
Ice	×2	Dragon	×1
Fighting	×1	Dark	×1
Poison	×1	Steel	×2
Ground	×1	Fairy	×1

Can be used in
- Inverse Battle
- Battle Institute
- Battle Maison
- Random Matchup (Free Battle)
- Random Matchup (Others)

LEVEL-UP MOVES

Lv.	Name	Type	Kind	Pow.	Acc.	PP	Range
1	Ice Fang	Ice	Physical	65	95	15	Normal
1	Crunch	Dark	Physical	80	100	15	Normal
1	Sonic Boom	Normal	Special	—	90	20	Normal
1	Growl	Normal	Status	—	100	40	Many Others
1	Water Sport	Water	Status	—	—	15	Both Sides
1	Quick Attack	Normal	Physical	40	100	30	Normal
4	Growl	Normal	Status	—	100	40	Many Others
7	Water Sport	Water	Status	—	—	15	Both Sides
11	Quick Attack	Normal	Physical	40	100	30	Normal
15	Water Gun	Water	Special	40	100	25	Normal
18	Pursuit	Dark	Physical	40	100	20	Normal
21	Swift	Normal	Special	60	—	20	Many Others
24	Aqua Jet	Water	Physical	40	100	20	Normal
29	Double Hit	Normal	Physical	35	90	10	Normal
35	Whirlpool	Water	Special	35	85	15	Normal
41	Razor Wind	Normal	Special	80	100	10	Many Others
46	Aqua Tail	Water	Physical	90	90	10	Normal
51	Agility	Psychic	Status	—	—	30	Self
57	Hydro Pump	Water	Special	110	80	5	Normal

TM & HM MOVES

No.	Name	Type	Kind	Pow.	Acc.	PP	Range
TM05	Roar	Normal	Status	—	—	20	Normal
TM06	Toxic	Poison	Status	—	90	10	Normal
TM07	Hail	Ice	Status	—	—	10	Both Sides
TM08	Bulk Up	Fighting	Status	—	—	20	Self
TM10	Hidden Power	Normal	Special	60	100	15	Normal
TM12	Taunt	Dark	Status	—	100	20	Normal
TM13	Ice Beam	Ice	Special	90	100	10	Normal
TM14	Blizzard	Ice	Special	110	70	5	Many Others
TM15	Hyper Beam	Normal	Special	150	90	5	Normal
TM17	Protect	Normal	Status	—	—	10	Self
TM18	Rain Dance	Water	Status	—	—	5	Both Sides
TM21	Frustration	Normal	Physical	—	100	20	Normal
TM27	Return	Normal	Physical	—	100	20	Normal
TM28	Dig	Ground	Physical	80	100	10	Normal
TM31	Brick Break	Fighting	Physical	75	100	15	Normal
TM32	Double Team	Normal	Status	—	—	15	Self
TM39	Rock Tomb	Rock	Physical	60	95	15	Normal
TM41	Torment	Dark	Status	—	100	15	Normal
TM42	Facade	Normal	Physical	70	100	20	Normal
TM44	Rest	Psychic	Status	—	—	10	Self
TM45	Attract	Normal	Status	—	100	15	Normal
TM48	Round	Normal	Special	60	100	15	Normal
TM49	Echoed Voice	Normal	Special	40	100	15	Normal
TM52	Focus Blast	Fighting	Special	120	70	5	Normal
TM55	Scald	Water	Special	80	100	15	Normal
TM66	Payback	Dark	Physical	50	100	10	Normal
TM68	Giga Impact	Normal	Physical	150	90	5	Normal
TM87	Swagger	Normal	Status	—	90	15	Normal
TM88	Sleep Talk	Normal	Status	—	—	10	Self
TM90	Substitute	Normal	Status	—	—	10	Self
TM94	Secret Power	Normal	Physical	70	100	20	Normal
TM98	Power-Up Punch	Fighting	Physical	40	100	20	Normal
TM100	Confide	Normal	Status	—	—	20	Normal
HM03	Surf	Water	Special	90	100	15	Adjacent
HM04	Strength	Normal	Physical	80	100	15	Normal
HM05	Waterfall	Water	Physical	80	100	15	Normal
HM06	Rock Smash	Fighting	Physical	40	100	15	Normal
HM07	Dive	Water	Physical	80	100	10	Normal

MOVES LEARNED IN EXCHANGE FOR BP

Name	Type	Kind	Pow.	Acc.	PP	Range
Low Kick	Fighting	Physical	—	100	20	Normal
Ice Punch	Ice	Physical	75	100	15	Normal
Icy Wind	Ice	Special	55	95	15	Many Others
Aqua Tail	Water	Physical	90	90	10	Normal
Iron Tail	Steel	Physical	100	75	15	Normal
Snore	Normal	Special	50	100	15	Normal
Focus Punch	Fighting	Physical	150	100	20	Normal
Water Pulse	Water	Special	60	100	20	Normal

MOVES TAUGHT BY PEOPLE

Name	Type	Kind	Pow.	Acc.	PP	Range

419 Floatzel National Pokédex

National Pokédex **420** Hoenn Pokédex —

Cherubi

Cherry Pokémon

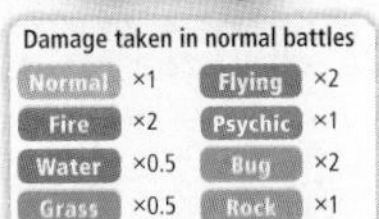

Grass

HEIGHT: 1'04" WEIGHT: 7.3 lbs.

Same form for ♂ / ♀

Ω Sunlight colors it red. When the small ball is drained of nutrients, it shrivels to herald evolution.

α It evolves by sucking the energy out of the small ball where it had been storing nutrients.

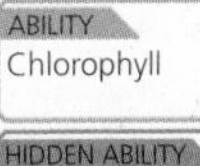

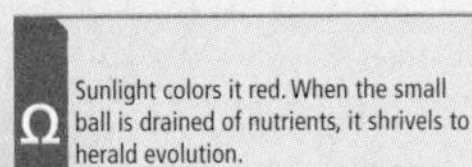

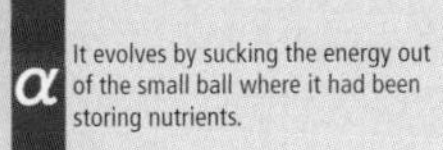

ABILITY
Chlorophyll

HIDDEN ABILITY
—

EGG GROUPS
Fairy | Grass

STAT GROWTH RATES
HP, Attack, Defense, Sp. Atk, Sp. Def, Speed

ITEMS SOMETIMES HELD BY WILD POKÉMON
—

EVOLUTION

MAIN WAY TO REGISTER IN THE NATIONAL POKÉDEX

Leave a Cherrim at a Pokémon Day Care, then hatch the Pokémon Egg that is found.

Damage taken in normal battles

Type		Type	
Normal	×1	Flying	×2
Fire	×2	Psychic	×1
Water	×0.5	Bug	×2
Grass	×0.5	Rock	×1
Electric	×0.5	Ghost	×1
Ice	×2	Dragon	×1
Fighting	×1	Dark	×1
Poison	×2	Steel	×1
Ground	×0.5	Fairy	×1

Damage taken in Inverse battles

Type		Type	
Normal	×1	Flying	×0.5
Fire	×0.5	Psychic	×1
Water	×2	Bug	×0.5
Grass	×2	Rock	×1
Electric	×2	Ghost	×1
Ice	×0.5	Dragon	×1
Fighting	×1	Dark	×1
Poison	×0.5	Steel	×1
Ground	×2	Fairy	×1

Can be used in
- Inverse Battle
- Battle Institute
- Battle Maison
- Random Matchup (Free Battle)
- Random Matchup (Others)

LEVEL-UP MOVES

Lv.	Name	Type	Kind	Pow.	Acc.	PP	Range
1	Morning Sun	Normal	Status	—	—	5	Self
1	Tackle	Normal	Physical	50	100	35	Normal
7	Growth	Normal	Status	—	—	20	Self
10	Leech Seed	Grass	Status	—	90	10	Normal
13	Helping Hand	Normal	Status	—	—	20	1 Ally
19	Magical Leaf	Grass	Special	60	—	20	Normal
22	Sunny Day	Fire	Status	—	—	5	Both Sides
28	Worry Seed	Grass	Status	—	100	10	Normal
31	Take Down	Normal	Physical	90	85	20	Normal
37	Solar Beam	Grass	Special	120	100	10	Normal
40	Lucky Chant	Normal	Status	—	—	30	Your Side
47	Petal Blizzard	Grass	Physical	90	100	15	Adjacent

TM & HM MOVES

No.	Name	Type	Kind	Pow.	Acc.	PP	Range
TM06	Toxic	Poison	Status	—	90	10	Normal
TM10	Hidden Power	Normal	Special	60	100	15	Normal
TM11	Sunny Day	Fire	Status	—	—	5	Both Sides
TM17	Protect	Normal	Status	—	—	10	Self
TM20	Safeguard	Normal	Status	—	—	25	Your Side
TM21	Frustration	Normal	Physical	—	100	20	Normal
TM22	Solar Beam	Grass	Special	120	100	10	Normal
TM27	Return	Normal	Physical	—	100	20	Normal
TM32	Double Team	Normal	Status	—	—	15	Self
TM42	Facade	Normal	Physical	70	100	20	Normal
TM44	Rest	Psychic	Status	—	—	10	Self
TM45	Attract	Normal	Status	—	100	15	Normal
TM48	Round	Normal	Special	60	100	15	Normal
TM53	Energy Ball	Grass	Special	90	100	10	Normal
TM70	Flash	Normal	Status	—	100	20	Normal
TM75	Swords Dance	Normal	Status	—	—	20	Self
TM86	Grass Knot	Grass	Special	—	100	20	Normal
TM87	Swagger	Normal	Status	—	90	15	Normal
TM88	Sleep Talk	Normal	Status	—	—	10	Self
TM90	Substitute	Normal	Status	—	—	10	Self
TM94	Secret Power	Normal	Physical	70	100	20	Normal
TM96	Nature Power	Normal	Status	—	—	20	Normal
TM99	Dazzling Gleam	Fairy	Special	80	100	10	Many Others
TM100	Confide	Normal	Status	—	—	20	Normal

MOVES LEARNED IN EXCHANGE FOR BP

Name	Type	Kind	Pow.	Acc.	PP	Range
Seed Bomb	Grass	Physical	80	100	15	Normal
Snore	Normal	Special	50	100	15	Normal
Synthesis	Grass	Status	—	—	5	Self
Giga Drain	Grass	Special	75	100	10	Normal
Worry Seed	Grass	Status	—	100	10	Normal
Helping Hand	Normal	Status	—	—	20	1 Ally

MOVES TAUGHT BY PEOPLE

Name	Type	Kind	Pow.	Acc.	PP	Range

EGG MOVES

Name	Type	Kind	Pow.	Acc.	PP	Range
Razor Leaf	Grass	Physical	55	95	25	Many Others
Sweet Scent	Normal	Status	—	100	20	Many Others
Tickle	Normal	Status	—	100	20	Normal
Nature Power	Normal	Status	—	—	20	Normal
Grass Whistle	Grass	Status	—	55	15	Normal
Aromatherapy	Grass	Status	—	—	5	Your Party
Weather Ball	Normal	Special	50	100	10	Normal
Heal Pulse	Psychic	Status	—	—	10	Normal
Healing Wish	Psychic	Status	—	—	10	Self
Seed Bomb	Grass	Physical	80	100	15	Normal
Natural Gift	Normal	Physical	—	100	15	Normal
Defense Curl	Normal	Status	—	—	40	Self
Rollout	Rock	Physical	30	90	20	Normal
Flower Shield	Fairy	Status	—	—	10	Adjacent

Cherubi 420

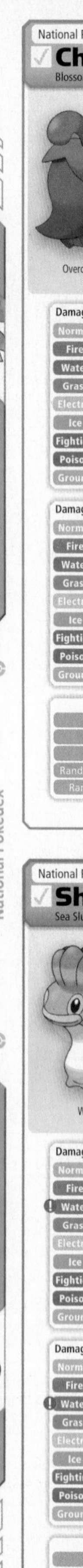
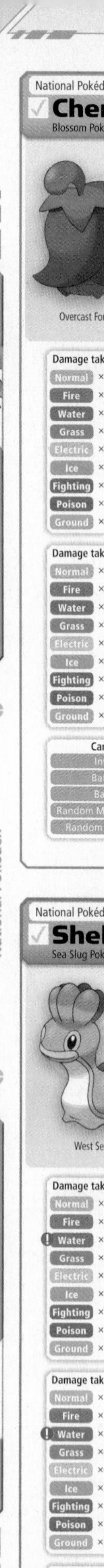

National Pokédex **421** Hoenn Pokédex —

Cherrim

Blossom Pokémon

Grass

HEIGHT: 1'08" WEIGHT: 20.5 lbs.

Same form for ♂ / ♀

Overcast Form | Sunshine Form

Ω During times of strong sunlight, its bud blooms, its petals open fully, and it becomes very active.

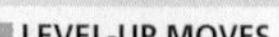

α If it senses strong sunlight, it opens its folded petals to absorb the sun's rays with its whole body.

ABILITY
Flower Gift

HIDDEN ABILITY
—

EGG GROUPS
Fairy | Grass

STAT GROWTH RATES
HP ■■■
Attack ■■■
Defense ■■■
Sp. Atk ■■■■
Sp. Def ■■■
Speed ■■■■■

ITEMS SOMETIMES HELD BY WILD POKÉMON
Miracle Seed

EVOLUTION
Cherubi → Lv. 25 → Cherrim

MAIN WAY TO REGISTER IN THE NATIONAL POKÉDEX
Catch in Mirage Forest 4.

Damage taken in normal battles

Type	×	Type	×
Normal	×1	Flying	×2
Fire	×2	Psychic	×1
Water	×0.5	Bug	×2
Grass	×0.5	Rock	×1
Electric	×0.5	Ghost	×1
Ice	×2	Dragon	×1
Fighting	×1	Dark	×1
Poison	×2	Steel	×1
Ground	×0.5	Fairy	×1

Damage taken in Inverse battles

Type	×	Type	×
Normal	×1	Flying	×0.5
Fire	×0.5	Psychic	×1
Water	×2	Bug	×0.5
Grass	×2	Rock	×1
Electric	×2	Ghost	×1
Ice	×0.5	Dragon	×1
Fighting	×1	Dark	×1
Poison	×0.5	Steel	×1
Ground	×2	Fairy	×1

Can be used in
Inverse Battle
Battle Institute
Battle Maison
Random Matchup (Free Battle)
Random Matchup (Others)

LEVEL-UP MOVES

Lv.	Name	Type	Kind	Pow.	Acc.	PP	Range
1	Morning Sun	Normal	Status	—	—	5	Self
1	Tackle	Normal	Physical	50	100	35	Normal
1	Growth	Normal	Status	—	—	20	Self
7	Growth	Normal	Status	—	—	20	Self
10	Leech Seed	Grass	Status	—	90	10	Normal
13	Helping Hand	Normal	Status	—	—	20	1 Ally
19	Magical Leaf	Grass	Special	60	—	20	Normal
22	Sunny Day	Fire	Status	—	—	5	Both Sides
25	Petal Dance	Grass	Special	120	100	10	1 Random
30	Worry Seed	Grass	Status	—	100	10	Normal
35	Take Down	Normal	Physical	90	85	20	Normal
43	Solar Beam	Grass	Special	120	100	10	Normal
48	Lucky Chant	Normal	Status	—	—	30	Your Side
50	Petal Blizzard	Grass	Physical	90	100	15	Adjacent

TM & HM MOVES

No.	Name	Type	Kind	Pow.	Acc.	PP	Range
TM06	Toxic	Poison	Status	—	90	10	Normal
TM10	Hidden Power	Normal	Special	60	100	15	Normal
TM11	Sunny Day	Fire	Status	—	—	5	Both Sides
TM15	Hyper Beam	Normal	Special	150	90	5	Normal
TM17	Protect	Normal	Status	—	—	10	Self
TM20	Safeguard	Normal	Status	—	—	25	Your Side
TM21	Frustration	Normal	Physical	—	100	20	Normal
TM22	Solar Beam	Grass	Special	120	100	10	Normal
TM27	Return	Normal	Physical	—	100	20	Normal
TM32	Double Team	Normal	Status	—	—	15	Self
TM42	Facade	Normal	Physical	70	100	20	Normal
TM44	Rest	Psychic	Status	—	—	10	Self
TM45	Attract	Normal	Status	—	100	15	Normal
TM48	Round	Normal	Special	60	100	15	Normal
TM53	Energy Ball	Grass	Special	90	100	10	Normal
TM68	Giga Impact	Normal	Physical	150	90	5	Normal
TM70	Flash	Normal	Status	—	100	20	Normal
TM75	Swords Dance	Normal	Status	—	—	20	Self
TM86	Grass Knot	Grass	Special	—	100	20	Normal
TM87	Swagger	Normal	Status	—	90	15	Normal
TM88	Sleep Talk	Normal	Status	—	—	10	Self
TM90	Substitute	Normal	Status	—	—	10	Self
TM94	Secret Power	Normal	Physical	70	100	20	Normal
TM96	Nature Power	Normal	Status	—	—	20	Normal
TM99	Dazzling Gleam	Fairy	Special	80	100	10	Many Others
TM100	Confide	Normal	Status	—	—	20	Normal

MOVES LEARNED IN EXCHANGE FOR BP

Name	Type	Kind	Pow.	Acc.	PP	Range
Seed Bomb	Grass	Physical	80	100	15	Normal
Snore	Normal	Special	50	100	15	Normal
Synthesis	Grass	Status	—	—	5	Self
Giga Drain	Grass	Special	75	100	10	Normal
Worry Seed	Grass	Status	—	100	10	Normal
Helping Hand	Normal	Status	—	—	20	1 Ally

MOVES TAUGHT BY PEOPLE

Name	Type	Kind	Pow.	Acc.	PP	Range

National Pokédex **422** Hoenn Pokédex —

Shellos

Sea Slug Pokémon

Water

HEIGHT: 1'00" WEIGHT: 13.9 lbs.

Same form for ♂ / ♀

West Sea | East Sea

Ω Beware of pushing strongly on its squishy body, as it makes a mysterious purple fluid ooze out.

α Its shape and coloration vary, depending on its habitat.

ABILITIES
Sticky Hold
Storm Drain

HIDDEN ABILITY
Sand Force

EGG GROUPS
Water 1 | Amorphous

STAT GROWTH RATES
HP ■■■
Attack ■■■
Defense ■■
Sp. Atk ■■■
Sp. Def ■■■
Speed ■■

ITEMS SOMETIMES HELD BY WILD POKÉMON
—

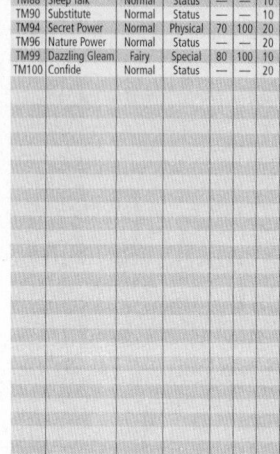

EVOLUTION
Shellos (West Sea) → Lv. 30 → Gastrodon (West Sea)
Shellos (East Sea) → Lv. 30 → Gastrodon (East Sea)

MAIN WAYS TO REGISTER SHELLOS (WEST SEA)
Ω Catch on Route 103. Appears as a hidden Pokémon after you battle Groudon or Kyogre.
α Bring it to your game using Link Trade or the GTS.

MAIN WAYS TO REGISTER SHELLOS (EAST SEA)
Ω Bring it to your game using Link Trade or the GTS.
α Catch on Route 103. Appears as a hidden Pokémon after you battle Groudon or Kyogre.

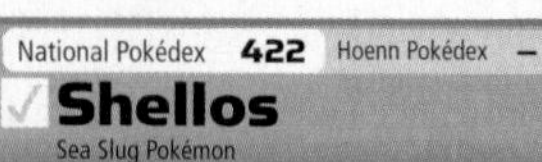

Damage taken in normal battles

Type	×	Type	×
Normal	×1	Flying	×1
Fire	×0.5	Psychic	×1
Water	×0.5	Bug	×1
Grass	×2	Rock	×1
Electric	×2	Ghost	×1
Ice	×0.5	Dragon	×1
Fighting	×1	Dark	×1
Poison	×1	Steel	×0.5
Ground	×1	Fairy	×1

Damage taken in Inverse battles

Type	×	Type	×
Normal	×1	Flying	×1
Fire	×2	Psychic	×1
Water	×2	Bug	×1
Grass	×0.5	Rock	×1
Electric	×0.5	Ghost	×1
Ice	×2	Dragon	×1
Fighting	×1	Dark	×1
Poison	×1	Steel	×2
Ground	×1	Fairy	×1

Can be used in
Inverse Battle
Battle Institute
Battle Maison
Random Matchup (Free Battle)
Random Matchup (Others)

LEVEL-UP MOVES

Lv.	Name	Type	Kind	Pow.	Acc.	PP	Range
1	Mud-Slap	Ground	Special	20	100	10	Normal
2	Mud Sport	Ground	Status	—	—	15	Both Sides
4	Harden	Normal	Status	—	—	30	Self
7	Water Pulse	Water	Special	60	100	20	Normal
11	Mud Bomb	Ground	Special	65	85	10	Normal
16	Hidden Power	Normal	Special	60	100	15	Normal
22	Rain Dance	Water	Status	—	—	5	Both Sides
29	Body Slam	Normal	Physical	85	100	15	Normal
37	Muddy Water	Water	Special	90	85	10	Many Others
46	Recover	Normal	Status	—	—	10	Self

TM & HM MOVES

No.	Name	Type	Kind	Pow.	Acc.	PP	Range
TM06	Toxic	Poison	Status	—	90	10	Normal
TM07	Hail	Ice	Status	—	—	10	Both Sides
TM10	Hidden Power	Normal	Special	60	100	15	Normal
TM13	Ice Beam	Ice	Special	90	100	10	Normal
TM14	Blizzard	Ice	Special	110	70	5	Many Others
TM17	Protect	Normal	Status	—	—	10	Self
TM18	Rain Dance	Water	Status	—	—	5	Both Sides
TM21	Frustration	Normal	Physical	—	100	20	Normal
TM27	Return	Normal	Physical	—	100	20	Normal
TM32	Double Team	Normal	Status	—	—	15	Self
TM42	Facade	Normal	Physical	70	100	20	Normal
TM44	Rest	Psychic	Status	—	—	10	Self
TM45	Attract	Normal	Status	—	100	15	Normal
TM48	Round	Normal	Special	60	100	15	Normal
TM55	Scald	Water	Special	80	100	15	Normal
TM83	Infestation	Bug	Special	20	100	20	Normal
TM87	Swagger	Normal	Status	—	90	15	Normal
TM88	Sleep Talk	Normal	Status	—	—	10	Self
TM90	Substitute	Normal	Status	—	—	10	Self
TM94	Secret Power	Normal	Physical	70	100	20	Normal
TM100	Confide	Normal	Status	—	—	20	Normal
HM03	Surf	Water	Special	90	100	15	Adjacent
HM07	Dive	Water	Physical	80	100	10	Normal

MOVES LEARNED IN EXCHANGE FOR BP

Name	Type	Kind	Pow.	Acc.	PP	Range
Earth Power	Ground	Special	90	100	10	Normal
Icy Wind	Ice	Special	55	95	15	Many Others
Snore	Normal	Special	50	100	15	Normal
Pain Split	Normal	Status	—	—	20	Normal
Water Pulse	Water	Special	60	100	20	Normal

MOVES TAUGHT BY PEOPLE

Name	Type	Kind	Pow.	Acc.	PP	Range

EGG MOVES

Name	Type	Kind	Pow.	Acc.	PP	Range
Counter	Fighting	Physical	—	100	20	Varies
Mirror Coat	Psychic	Special	—	100	20	Varies
Stockpile	Normal	Status	—	—	20	Self
Swallow	Normal	Status	—	—	10	Self
Spit Up	Normal	Special	—	100	10	Normal
Yawn	Normal	Status	—	—	10	Normal
Memento	Dark	Status	—	100	10	Normal
Curse	Ghost	Status	—	—	10	Varies
Amnesia	Psychic	Status	—	—	20	Self
Fissure	Ground	Physical	—	30	5	Normal
Trump Card	Normal	Special	—	—	5	Normal
Sludge	Poison	Special	65	100	20	Normal
Clear Smog	Poison	Special	50	—	15	Normal
Brine	Water	Special	65	100	10	Normal
Mist	Ice	Status	—	—	30	Your Side
Acid Armor	Poison	Status	—	—	20	Self

National Pokédex **423** Hoenn Pokédex —

Gastrodon

Sea Slug Pokémon

HEIGHT: 2'11" WEIGHT: 65.9 lbs.

Same form for ♂ / ♀

West Sea / East Sea

Ω When its natural enemy attacks, it oozes purple fluid and escapes.

α It apparently had a huge shell for protection in ancient times. It lives in shallow tidal pools.

ABILITIES
Sticky Hold
Storm Drain

HIDDEN ABILITY
Sand Force

EGG GROUPS
Water 1, Amorphous

STAT GROWTH RATES
HP ■■■■
Attack ■■■■
Defense ■■■
Sp. Atk ■■■■■
Sp. Def ■■■
Speed ■■

ITEMS SOMETIMES HELD BY WILD POKÉMON
—

EVOLUTION
Shellos (West Sea) → Lv. 30 → Gastrodon (West Sea)
Shellos (East Sea) → Lv. 30 → Gastrodon (East Sea)

MAIN WAYS TO REGISTER GASTRODON (WEST SEA)
Ω Level up Shellos (West Sea) to Lv. 30.
α Bring it to your game using Link Trade or the GTS.

MAIN WAYS TO GASTRODON SHELLOS (EAST SEA)
Ω Bring it to your game using Link Trade or the GTS.
α Level up Shellos (East Sea) to Lv. 30.

Damage taken in normal battles

Type		Type	
Normal	×1	Flying	×1
Fire	×0.5	Psychic	×1
! Water	×1	Bug	×1
Grass	×4	Rock	×0.5
Electric	×0	Ghost	×1
Ice	×1	Dragon	×1
Fighting	×1	Dark	×1
Poison	×0.5	Steel	×0.5
Ground	×1	Fairy	×1

Damage taken in Inverse battles

Type		Type	
Normal	×1	Flying	×1
Fire	×2	Psychic	×1
! Water	×1	Bug	×1
Grass	×0.25	Rock	×2
Electric	×1	Ghost	×1
Ice	×1	Dragon	×1
Fighting	×1	Dark	×1
Poison	×2	Steel	×2
Ground	×1	Fairy	×1

Can be used in
Inverse Battle
Battle Institute
Battle Maison
Random Matchup (Free Battle)
Random Matchup (Others)

LEVEL-UP MOVES

Lv.	Name	Type	Kind	Pow.	Acc.	PP	Range
1	Mud-Slap	Ground	Special	20	100	10	Normal
1	Mud Sport	Ground	Status	—	—	15	Both Sides
1	Harden	Normal	Status	—	—	30	Self
1	Water Pulse	Water	Special	60	100	20	Normal
2	Mud Sport	Ground	Status	—	—	15	Both Sides
4	Harden	Normal	Status	—	—	30	Self
7	Water Pulse	Water	Special	60	100	20	Normal
11	Mud Bomb	Ground	Special	65	85	10	Normal
16	Hidden Power	Normal	Special	60	100	15	Normal
22	Rain Dance	Water	Status	—	—	5	Both Sides
29	Body Slam	Normal	Physical	85	100	15	Normal
41	Muddy Water	Water	Special	90	85	10	Many Others
54	Recover	Normal	Status	—	—	10	Self

TM & HM MOVES

No.	Name	Type	Kind	Pow.	Acc.	PP	Range
TM06	Toxic	Poison	Status	—	90	10	Normal
TM07	Hail	Ice	Status	—	—	10	Both Sides
TM10	Hidden Power	Normal	Special	60	100	15	Normal
TM13	Ice Beam	Ice	Special	90	100	10	Normal
TM14	Blizzard	Ice	Special	110	70	5	Many Others
TM15	Hyper Beam	Normal	Special	150	90	5	Normal
TM17	Protect	Normal	Status	—	—	10	Self
TM18	Rain Dance	Water	Status	—	—	5	Both Sides
TM21	Frustration	Normal	Physical	—	100	20	Normal
TM26	Earthquake	Ground	Physical	100	100	10	Adjacent
TM27	Return	Normal	Physical	—	100	20	Normal
TM28	Dig	Ground	Physical	80	100	10	Normal
TM32	Double Team	Normal	Status	—	—	15	Self
TM34	Sludge Wave	Poison	Special	95	100	10	Adjacent
TM36	Sludge Bomb	Poison	Special	90	100	10	Normal
TM37	Sandstorm	Rock	Status	—	—	10	Both Sides
TM39	Rock Tomb	Rock	Physical	60	95	15	Normal
TM42	Facade	Normal	Physical	70	100	20	Normal
TM44	Rest	Psychic	Status	—	—	10	Self
TM45	Attract	Normal	Status	—	100	15	Normal
TM48	Round	Normal	Special	60	100	15	Normal
TM55	Scald	Water	Special	80	100	15	Normal
TM68	Giga Impact	Normal	Physical	150	90	5	Normal
TM70	Flash	Normal	Status	—	100	20	Normal
TM71	Stone Edge	Rock	Physical	100	80	5	Normal
TM78	Bulldoze	Ground	Physical	60	100	20	Adjacent
TM80	Rock Slide	Rock	Physical	75	90	10	Many Others
TM83	Infestation	Bug	Special	20	100	20	Normal
TM87	Swagger	Normal	Status	—	90	15	Normal
TM88	Sleep Talk	Normal	Status	—	—	10	Self
TM90	Substitute	Normal	Status	—	—	10	Self
TM94	Secret Power	Normal	Physical	70	100	20	Normal
TM100	Confide	Normal	Status	—	—	20	Normal
HM03	Surf	Water	Special	90	100	15	Adjacent
HM04	Strength	Normal	Physical	80	100	15	Normal
HM05	Waterfall	Water	Physical	80	100	15	Normal
HM06	Rock Smash	Fighting	Physical	40	100	15	Normal
HM07	Dive	Water	Physical	80	100	10	Normal

MOVES LEARNED IN EXCHANGE FOR BP

Name	Type	Kind	Pow.	Acc.	PP	Range
Block	Normal	Status	—	—	5	Normal
Earth Power	Ground	Special	90	100	10	Normal
Icy Wind	Ice	Special	55	95	15	Many Others
Snore	Normal	Special	50	100	15	Normal
Pain Split	Normal	Status	—	—	20	Normal
Water Pulse	Water	Special	60	100	20	Normal

MOVES TAUGHT BY PEOPLE

Name	Type	Kind	Pow.	Acc.	PP	Range

National Pokédex **424** Hoenn Pokédex —

Ambipom

Long Tail Pokémon

Normal

HEIGHT: 3'11" WEIGHT: 44.8 lbs.

The male has shorter tufts of fur on its head than the female.

♂ ♀

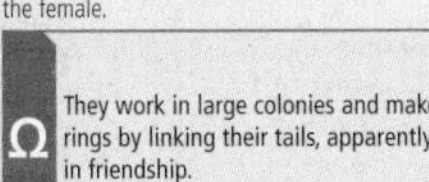

Ω They work in large colonies and make rings by linking their tails, apparently in friendship.

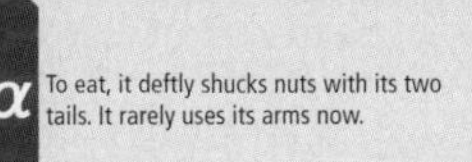

α To eat, it deftly shucks nuts with its two tails. It rarely uses its arms now.

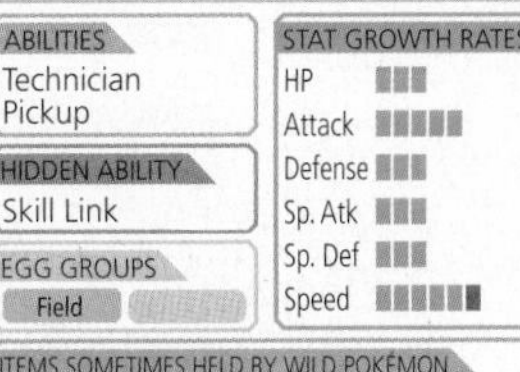

ABILITIES
Technician
Pickup

HIDDEN ABILITY
Skill Link

EGG GROUPS
Field

STAT GROWTH RATES
HP ■■■
Attack ■■■■■
Defense ■■■
Sp. Atk ■■■
Sp. Def ■■■
Speed ■■■■■■

ITEMS SOMETIMES HELD BY WILD POKÉMON
—

EVOLUTION

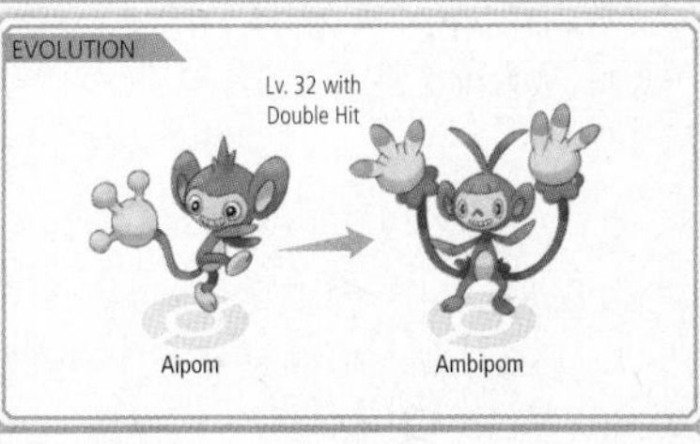

MAIN WAY TO REGISTER IN THE NATIONAL POKÉDEX

Level up Aipom to Lv. 32, then teach it the move Double Hit. Alternatively, teach it the move Double Hit first, then have it level up.

Damage taken in normal battles

Type		Type	
Normal	×1	Flying	×1
Fire	×1	Psychic	×1
Water	×1	Bug	×1
Grass	×1	Rock	×1
Electric	×1	Ghost	×0
Ice	×1	Dragon	×1
Fighting	×2	Dark	×1
Poison	×1	Steel	×1
Ground	×1	Fairy	×1

Damage taken in Inverse battles

Type		Type	
Normal	×1	Flying	×1
Fire	×1	Psychic	×1
Water	×1	Bug	×1
Grass	×1	Rock	×1
Electric	×1	Ghost	×2
Ice	×1	Dragon	×1
Fighting	×0.5	Dark	×1
Poison	×1	Steel	×1
Ground	×1	Fairy	×1

Can be used in
Inverse Battle
Battle Institute
Battle Maison
Random Matchup (Free Battle)
Random Matchup (Others)

LEVEL-UP MOVES

Lv.	Name	Type	Kind	Pow.	Acc.	PP	Range
1	Scratch	Normal	Physical	40	100	35	Normal
1	Tail Whip	Normal	Status	—	100	30	Many Others
1	Sand Attack	Ground	Status	—	100	15	Normal
1	Astonish	Ghost	Physical	30	100	15	Normal
4	Sand Attack	Ground	Status	—	100	15	Normal
8	Astonish	Ghost	Physical	30	100	15	Normal
11	Baton Pass	Normal	Status	—	—	40	Self
15	Tickle	Normal	Status	—	100	20	Normal
18	Fury Swipes	Normal	Physical	18	80	15	Normal
22	Swift	Normal	Special	60	—	20	Many Others
25	Screech	Normal	Status	—	85	40	Normal
29	Agility	Psychic	Status	—	—	30	Self
32	Double Hit	Normal	Physical	35	90	10	Normal
36	Fling	Dark	Physical	—	100	10	Normal
39	Nasty Plot	Dark	Status	—	—	20	Self
43	Last Resort	Normal	Physical	140	100	5	Normal

TM & HM MOVES

No.	Name	Type	Kind	Pow.	Acc.	PP	Range
TM01	Hone Claws	Dark	Status	—	—	15	Self
TM06	Toxic	Poison	Status	—	90	10	Normal
TM10	Hidden Power	Normal	Special	60	100	15	Normal
TM11	Sunny Day	Fire	Status	—	—	5	Both Sides
TM12	Taunt	Dark	Status	—	100	20	Normal
TM15	Hyper Beam	Normal	Special	150	90	5	Normal
TM17	Protect	Normal	Status	—	—	10	Self
TM18	Rain Dance	Water	Status	—	—	5	Both Sides
TM21	Frustration	Normal	Physical	—	100	20	Normal
TM22	Solar Beam	Grass	Special	120	100	10	Normal
TM24	Thunderbolt	Electric	Special	90	100	15	Normal
TM25	Thunder	Electric	Special	110	70	10	Normal
TM27	Return	Normal	Physical	—	100	20	Normal
TM28	Dig	Ground	Physical	80	100	10	Normal
TM30	Shadow Ball	Ghost	Special	80	100	15	Normal
TM31	Brick Break	Fighting	Physical	75	100	15	Normal
TM32	Double Team	Normal	Status	—	—	15	Self
TM40	Aerial Ace	Flying	Physical	60	—	20	Normal
TM42	Facade	Normal	Physical	70	100	20	Normal
TM44	Rest	Psychic	Status	—	—	10	Self
TM45	Attract	Normal	Status	—	100	15	Normal
TM46	Thief	Dark	Physical	60	100	25	Normal
TM47	Low Sweep	Fighting	Physical	65	100	20	Normal
TM48	Round	Normal	Special	60	100	15	Normal
TM56	Fling	Dark	Physical	—	100	10	Normal
TM62	Acrobatics	Flying	Physical	55	100	15	Normal
TM65	Shadow Claw	Ghost	Physical	70	100	15	Normal
TM66	Payback	Dark	Physical	50	100	10	Normal
TM67	Retaliate	Normal	Physical	70	100	5	Normal
TM68	Giga Impact	Normal	Physical	150	90	5	Normal
TM73	Thunder Wave	Electric	Status	—	100	20	Normal
TM85	Dream Eater	Psychic	Special	100	100	15	Normal
TM86	Grass Knot	Grass	Special	—	100	20	Normal
TM87	Swagger	Normal	Status	—	90	15	Normal
TM88	Sleep Talk	Normal	Status	—	—	10	Self
TM89	U-turn	Bug	Physical	70	100	20	Normal
TM90	Substitute	Normal	Status	—	—	10	Self
TM94	Secret Power	Normal	Physical	70	100	20	Normal
TM98	Power-Up Punch	Fighting	Physical	40	100	20	Normal
TM100	Confide	Normal	Status	—	—	20	Normal
HM01	Cut	Normal	Physical	50	95	30	Normal
HM04	Strength	Normal	Physical	80	100	15	Normal
HM06	Rock Smash	Fighting	Physical	40	100	15	Normal

MOVES LEARNED IN EXCHANGE FOR BP

Name	Type	Kind	Pow.	Acc.	PP	Range
Covet	Normal	Physical	60	100	25	Normal
Seed Bomb	Grass	Physical	80	100	15	Normal
Bounce	Flying	Physical	85	85	5	Normal
Low Kick	Fighting	Physical	—	100	20	Normal
Gunk Shot	Poison	Physical	120	80	5	Normal
Uproar	Normal	Special	90	100	10	1 Random
Thunder Punch	Electric	Physical	75	100	15	Normal
Fire Punch	Fire	Physical	75	100	15	Normal
Ice Punch	Ice	Physical	75	100	15	Normal
Foul Play	Dark	Physical	95	100	15	Normal
Last Resort	Normal	Physical	140	100	5	Normal
Iron Tail	Steel	Physical	100	75	15	Normal
Snore	Normal	Special	50	100	15	Normal
Knock Off	Dark	Physical	65	100	20	Normal
Role Play	Psychic	Status	—	—	10	Normal
Focus Punch	Fighting	Physical	150	100	20	Normal
Shock Wave	Electric	Special	60	—	20	Normal
Water Pulse	Water	Special	60	100	20	Normal
Spite	Ghost	Status	—	100	10	Normal
Snatch	Dark	Status	—	—	10	Self

MOVES TAUGHT BY PEOPLE

Name	Type	Kind	Pow.	Acc.	PP	Range

National Pokédex **425** Hoenn Pokédex —

Drifloon

Balloon Pokémon

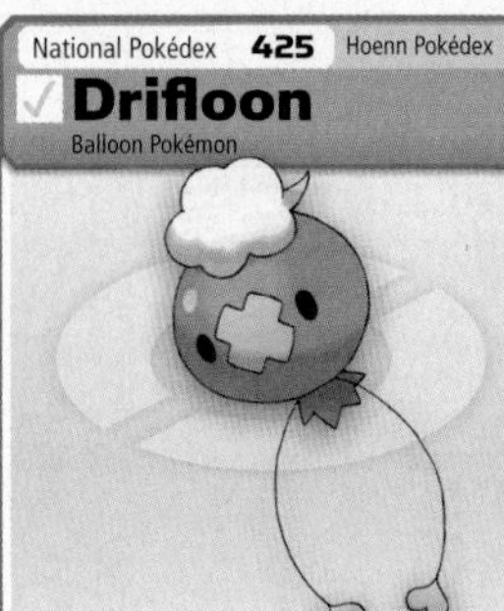

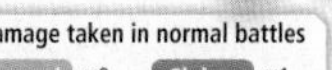

Ghost Flying

HEIGHT: 1'04" WEIGHT: 2.6 lbs.

Same form for ♂ / ♀

Ω A Pokémon formed by the spirits of people and Pokémon. It loves damp, humid seasons.

α These Pokémon are called the "Signpost for Wandering Spirits." Children holding them sometimes vanish.

ABILITIES
Aftermath
Unburden

HIDDEN ABILITY
Flare Boost

EGG GROUPS
Amorphous

STAT GROWTH RATES
HP
Attack
Defense
Sp. Atk
Sp. Def
Speed

ITEMS SOMETIMES HELD BY WILD POKÉMON
—

EVOLUTION
Drifloon → Lv. 28 → Drifblim

MAIN WAY TO REGISTER IN THE NATIONAL POKÉDEX

While Soaring in the sky, approach the shadows of flying Pokémon, and catch it when it appears.

Damage taken in normal battles

Type		Type	
Normal	×0	Flying	×1
Fire	×1	Psychic	×1
Water	×1	Bug	×0.25
Grass	×0.5	Rock	×2
Electric	×2	Ghost	×2
Ice	×2	Dragon	×1
Fighting	×0	Dark	×2
Poison	×0.5	Steel	×1
Ground	×0	Fairy	×1

Damage taken in Inverse battles

Type		Type	
Normal	×2	Flying	×1
Fire	×1	Psychic	×1
Water	×1	Bug	×4
Grass	×2	Rock	×0.5
Electric	×0.5	Ghost	×0.5
Ice	×0.5	Dragon	×1
Fighting	×4	Dark	×0.5
Poison	×2	Steel	×1
Ground	×2	Fairy	×1

Can be used in
Inverse Battle
Battle Institute
Battle Maison
Random Matchup (Free Battle)
Random Matchup (Others)

LEVEL-UP MOVES

Lv.	Name	Type	Kind	Pow.	Acc.	PP	Range
1	Constrict	Normal	Physical	10	100	35	Normal
1	Minimize	Normal	Status	—	—	10	Self
4	Astonish	Ghost	Physical	30	100	15	Normal
8	Gust	Flying	Special	40	100	35	Normal
13	Focus Energy	Normal	Status	—	—	30	Self
16	Payback	Dark	Physical	50	100	10	Normal
20	Ominous Wind	Ghost	Special	60	100	5	Normal
25	Stockpile	Normal	Status	—	—	20	Self
27	Hex	Ghost	Special	65	100	10	Normal
32	Swallow	Normal	Status	—	—	10	Self
32	Spit Up	Normal	Special	—	100	10	Normal
36	Shadow Ball	Ghost	Special	80	100	15	Normal
40	Amnesia	Psychic	Status	—	—	20	Self
44	Baton Pass	Normal	Status	—	—	40	Self
50	Explosion	Normal	Physical	250	100	5	Adjacent

TM & HM MOVES

No.	Name	Type	Kind	Pow.	Acc.	PP	Range
TM04	Calm Mind	Psychic	Status	—	—	20	Self
TM06	Toxic	Poison	Status	—	90	10	Normal
TM10	Hidden Power	Normal	Special	60	100	15	Normal
TM11	Sunny Day	Fire	Status	—	—	5	Both Sides
TM17	Protect	Normal	Status	—	—	10	Self
TM18	Rain Dance	Water	Status	—	—	5	Both Sides
TM21	Frustration	Normal	Physical	—	100	20	Normal
TM24	Thunderbolt	Electric	Special	90	100	15	Normal
TM25	Thunder	Electric	Special	110	70	10	Normal
TM27	Return	Normal	Physical	—	100	20	Normal
TM29	Psychic	Psychic	Special	90	100	10	Normal
TM30	Shadow Ball	Ghost	Special	80	100	15	Normal
TM32	Double Team	Normal	Status	—	—	15	Self
TM42	Facade	Normal	Physical	70	100	20	Normal
TM44	Rest	Psychic	Status	—	—	10	Self
TM45	Attract	Normal	Status	—	100	15	Normal
TM46	Thief	Dark	Physical	60	100	25	Normal
TM48	Round	Normal	Special	60	100	15	Normal
TM57	Charge Beam	Electric	Special	50	90	10	Normal
TM61	Will-O-Wisp	Fire	Status	—	85	15	Normal
TM62	Acrobatics	Flying	Physical	55	100	15	Normal
TM63	Embargo	Dark	Status	—	100	15	Normal
TM64	Explosion	Normal	Physical	250	100	5	Adjacent
TM66	Payback	Dark	Physical	50	100	10	Normal
TM70	Flash	Normal	Status	—	100	20	Normal
TM73	Thunder Wave	Electric	Status	—	100	20	Normal
TM74	Gyro Ball	Steel	Physical	—	100	5	Normal
TM77	Psych Up	Normal	Status	—	—	10	Normal
TM85	Dream Eater	Psychic	Special	100	100	15	Normal
TM87	Swagger	Normal	Status	—	90	15	Normal
TM88	Sleep Talk	Normal	Status	—	—	10	Self
TM90	Substitute	Normal	Status	—	—	10	Self
TM94	Secret Power	Normal	Physical	70	100	20	Normal
TM100	Confide	Normal	Status	—	—	20	Normal
HM01	Cut	Normal	Physical	50	95	30	Normal

MOVES LEARNED IN EXCHANGE FOR BP

Name	Type	Kind	Pow.	Acc.	PP	Range
Magic Coat	Psychic	Status	—	—	15	Self
Icy Wind	Ice	Special	55	95	15	Many Others
Bind	Normal	Physical	15	85	20	Normal
Snore	Normal	Special	50	100	15	Normal
Knock Off	Dark	Physical	65	100	20	Normal
Tailwind	Flying	Status	—	—	15	Your Side
Pain Split	Normal	Status	—	—	20	Normal
Shock Wave	Electric	Special	60	—	20	Normal
Spite	Ghost	Status	—	100	10	Normal
Trick	Psychic	Status	—	100	10	Normal
Recycle	Normal	Status	—	—	10	Self
Skill Swap	Psychic	Status	—	—	10	Normal

MOVES TAUGHT BY PEOPLE

Name	Type	Kind	Pow.	Acc.	PP	Range

EGG MOVES

Name	Type	Kind	Pow.	Acc.	PP	Range
Memento	Dark	Status	—	100	10	Normal
Body Slam	Normal	Physical	85	100	15	Normal
Destiny Bond	Ghost	Status	—	—	5	Self
Disable	Normal	Status	—	100	20	Normal
Haze	Ice	Status	—	—	30	Both Sides
Hypnosis	Psychic	Status	—	60	20	Normal
Weather Ball	Normal	Special	50	100	10	Normal
Clear Smog	Poison	Special	50	—	15	Normal
Defog	Flying	Status	—	—	15	Normal
Tailwind	Flying	Status	—	—	15	Your Side

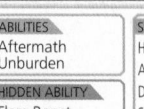

National Pokédex **426** Hoenn Pokédex —

Drifblim

Blimp Pokémon

Ghost Flying

HEIGHT: 3'11" WEIGHT: 33.1 lbs.

Same form for ♂ / ♀

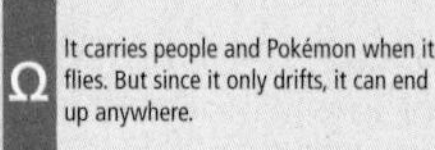

Ω It carries people and Pokémon when it flies. But since it only drifts, it can end up anywhere.

α It's drowsy in daytime, but flies off in the evening in big groups. No one knows where they go.

ABILITIES
Aftermath
Unburden

HIDDEN ABILITY
Flare Boost

EGG GROUPS
Amorphous

STAT GROWTH RATES
HP
Attack
Defense
Sp. Atk
Sp. Def
Speed

ITEMS SOMETIMES HELD BY WILD POKÉMON
—

EVOLUTION
Drifloon → Lv. 28 → Drifblim

MAIN WAY TO REGISTER IN THE NATIONAL POKÉDEX

Level up Drifloon to Lv. 28.

Damage taken in normal battles

Type		Type	
Normal	×0	Flying	×1
Fire	×1	Psychic	×1
Water	×1	Bug	×0.25
Grass	×0.5	Rock	×2
Electric	×2	Ghost	×2
Ice	×2	Dragon	×1
Fighting	×0	Dark	×2
Poison	×0.5	Steel	×1
Ground	×0	Fairy	×1

Damage taken in Inverse battles

Type		Type	
Normal	×2	Flying	×1
Fire	×1	Psychic	×1
Water	×1	Bug	×4
Grass	×2	Rock	×0.5
Electric	×0.5	Ghost	×0.5
Ice	×0.5	Dragon	×1
Fighting	×4	Dark	×0.5
Poison	×2	Steel	×1
Ground	×2	Fairy	×1

Can be used in
Inverse Battle
Battle Institute
Battle Maison
Random Matchup (Free Battle)
Random Matchup (Others)

LEVEL-UP MOVES

Lv.	Name	Type	Kind	Pow.	Acc.	PP	Range
1	Phantom Force	Ghost	Physical	90	100	10	Normal
1	Constrict	Normal	Physical	10	100	35	Normal
1	Minimize	Normal	Status	—	—	10	Self
1	Astonish	Ghost	Physical	30	100	15	Normal
1	Gust	Flying	Special	40	100	35	Normal
4	Astonish	Ghost	Physical	30	100	15	Normal
8	Gust	Flying	Special	40	100	35	Normal
13	Focus Energy	Normal	Status	—	—	30	Self
16	Payback	Dark	Physical	50	100	10	Normal
20	Ominous Wind	Ghost	Special	60	100	5	Normal
25	Stockpile	Normal	Status	—	—	20	Self
27	Hex	Ghost	Special	65	100	10	Normal
34	Swallow	Normal	Status	—	—	10	Self
34	Spit Up	Normal	Special	—	100	10	Normal
40	Shadow Ball	Ghost	Special	80	100	15	Normal
46	Amnesia	Psychic	Status	—	—	20	Self
52	Baton Pass	Normal	Status	—	—	40	Self
60	Explosion	Normal	Physical	250	100	5	Adjacent
65	Phantom Force	Ghost	Physical	90	100	10	Normal

TM & HM MOVES

No.	Name	Type	Kind	Pow.	Acc.	PP	Range
TM04	Calm Mind	Psychic	Status	—	—	20	Self
TM06	Toxic	Poison	Status	—	90	10	Normal
TM10	Hidden Power	Normal	Special	60	100	15	Normal
TM11	Sunny Day	Fire	Status	—	—	5	Both Sides
TM15	Hyper Beam	Normal	Special	150	90	5	Normal
TM17	Protect	Normal	Status	—	—	10	Self
TM18	Rain Dance	Water	Status	—	—	5	Both Sides
TM21	Frustration	Normal	Physical	—	100	20	Normal
TM24	Thunderbolt	Electric	Special	90	100	15	Normal
TM25	Thunder	Electric	Special	110	70	10	Normal
TM27	Return	Normal	Physical	—	100	20	Normal
TM29	Psychic	Psychic	Special	90	100	10	Normal
TM30	Shadow Ball	Ghost	Special	80	100	15	Normal
TM32	Double Team	Normal	Status	—	—	15	Self
TM42	Facade	Normal	Physical	70	100	20	Normal
TM44	Rest	Psychic	Status	—	—	10	Self
TM45	Attract	Normal	Status	—	100	15	Normal
TM46	Thief	Dark	Physical	60	100	25	Normal
TM48	Round	Normal	Special	60	100	15	Normal
TM57	Charge Beam	Electric	Special	50	90	10	Normal
TM61	Will-O-Wisp	Fire	Status	—	85	15	Normal
TM62	Acrobatics	Flying	Physical	55	100	15	Normal
TM63	Embargo	Dark	Status	—	100	15	Normal
TM64	Explosion	Normal	Physical	250	100	5	Adjacent
TM66	Payback	Dark	Physical	50	100	10	Normal
TM68	Giga Impact	Normal	Physical	150	90	5	Normal
TM70	Flash	Normal	Status	—	100	20	Normal
TM73	Thunder Wave	Electric	Status	—	100	20	Normal
TM74	Gyro Ball	Steel	Physical	—	100	5	Normal
TM77	Psych Up	Normal	Status	—	—	10	Normal
TM85	Dream Eater	Psychic	Special	100	100	15	Normal
TM87	Swagger	Normal	Status	—	90	15	Normal
TM88	Sleep Talk	Normal	Status	—	—	10	Self
TM90	Substitute	Normal	Status	—	—	10	Self
TM94	Secret Power	Normal	Physical	70	100	20	Normal
TM100	Confide	Normal	Status	—	—	20	Normal
HM01	Cut	Normal	Physical	50	95	30	Normal
HM02	Fly	Flying	Physical	90	95	15	Normal

MOVES LEARNED IN EXCHANGE FOR BP

Name	Type	Kind	Pow.	Acc.	PP	Range
Magic Coat	Psychic	Status	—	—	15	Self
Icy Wind	Ice	Special	55	95	15	Many Others
Bind	Normal	Physical	15	85	20	Normal
Snore	Normal	Special	50	100	15	Normal
Knock Off	Dark	Physical	65	100	20	Normal
Tailwind	Flying	Status	—	—	15	Your Side
Pain Split	Normal	Status	—	—	20	Normal
Shock Wave	Electric	Special	60	—	20	Normal
Spite	Ghost	Status	—	100	10	Normal
Trick	Psychic	Status	—	100	10	Normal
Recycle	Normal	Status	—	—	10	Self
Skill Swap	Psychic	Status	—	—	10	Normal

MOVES TAUGHT BY PEOPLE

Name	Type	Kind	Pow.	Acc.	PP	Range

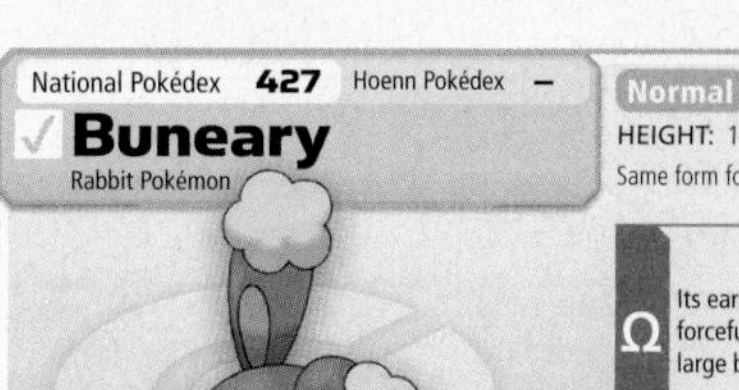

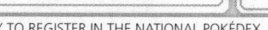

National Pokédex **427** Hoenn Pokédex —

Buneary

Rabbit Pokémon

Normal

HEIGHT: 1'04" WEIGHT: 12.1 lbs.

Same form for ♂ / ♀

Ω Its ears are always rolled up. They can be forcefully extended to shatter even a large boulder.

α When it senses danger, it perks up its ears. On cold nights, it sleeps with its head tucked into its fur.

ABILITIES
Run Away
Klutz

HIDDEN ABILITY
Limber

EGG GROUPS
Field | Human-Like

STAT GROWTH RATES
HP
Attack
Defense
Sp. Atk
Sp. Def
Speed

ITEMS SOMETIMES HELD BY WILD POKÉMON
—

EVOLUTION
Buneary → Level up with high friendship → Lopunny

MAIN WAY TO REGISTER IN THE NATIONAL POKÉDEX

Catch in the lower-right corner of the Safari Zone. Appears as a hidden Pokémon after you battle Groudon or Kyogre.

Damage taken in normal battles

Type		Type	
Normal	×1	Flying	×1
Fire	×1	Psychic	×1
Water	×1	Bug	×1
Grass	×1	Rock	×1
Electric	×1	Ghost	×0
Ice	×1	Dragon	×1
Fighting	×2	Dark	×1
Poison	×1	Steel	×1
Ground	×1	Fairy	×1

Damage taken in Inverse battles

Type		Type	
Normal	×1	Flying	×1
Fire	×1	Psychic	×1
Water	×1	Bug	×1
Grass	×1	Rock	×1
Electric	×1	Ghost	×2
Ice	×1	Dragon	×1
Fighting	×0.5	Dark	×1
Poison	×1	Steel	×1
Ground	×1	Fairy	×1

Can be used in
Inverse Battle
Battle Institute
Battle Maison
Random Matchup (Free Battle)
Random Matchup (Others)

LEVEL-UP MOVES

Lv.	Name	Type	Kind	Pow.	Acc.	PP	Range
1	Defense Curl	Normal	Status	—	—	40	Self
1	Splash	Normal	Status	—	—	40	Self
1	Pound	Normal	Physical	40	100	35	Normal
1	Foresight	Normal	Status	—	—	40	Normal
6	Endure	Normal	Status	—	—	10	Self
10	Baby-Doll Eyes	Fairy	Status	—	100	30	Normal
13	Frustration	Normal	Physical	—	100	20	Normal
16	Quick Attack	Normal	Physical	40	100	30	Normal
23	Jump Kick	Fighting	Physical	100	95	10	Normal
26	Baton Pass	Normal	Status	—	—	40	Self
33	Agility	Psychic	Status	—	—	30	Self
36	Dizzy Punch	Normal	Physical	70	100	10	Normal
43	After You	Normal	Status	—	—	15	Normal
46	Charm	Fairy	Status	—	100	20	Normal
50	Entrainment	Normal	Status	—	100	15	Normal
56	Bounce	Flying	Physical	85	85	5	Normal
63	Healing Wish	Psychic	Status	—	—	10	Self

TM & HM MOVES

No.	Name	Type	Kind	Pow.	Acc.	PP	Range
TM06	Toxic	Poison	Status	—	90	10	Normal
TM10	Hidden Power	Normal	Special	60	100	15	Normal
TM11	Sunny Day	Fire	Status	—	—	5	Both Sides
TM13	Ice Beam	Ice	Special	90	100	10	Normal
TM17	Protect	Normal	Status	—	—	10	Self
TM18	Rain Dance	Water	Status	—	—	5	Both Sides
TM21	Frustration	Normal	Physical	—	100	20	Normal
TM22	Solar Beam	Grass	Special	120	100	10	Normal
TM24	Thunderbolt	Electric	Special	90	100	15	Normal
TM27	Return	Normal	Physical	—	100	20	Normal
TM28	Dig	Ground	Physical	80	100	10	Normal
TM30	Shadow Ball	Ghost	Special	80	100	15	Normal
TM32	Double Team	Normal	Status	—	—	15	Self
TM42	Facade	Normal	Physical	70	100	20	Normal
TM44	Rest	Psychic	Status	—	—	10	Self
TM45	Attract	Normal	Status	—	100	15	Normal
TM48	Round	Normal	Special	60	100	15	Normal
TM56	Fling	Dark	Physical	—	100	10	Normal
TM57	Charge Beam	Electric	Special	50	90	10	Normal
TM67	Retaliate	Normal	Physical	70	100	5	Normal
TM73	Thunder Wave	Electric	Status	—	100	20	Normal
TM86	Grass Knot	Grass	Special	—	100	20	Normal
TM87	Swagger	Normal	Status	—	90	15	Normal
TM88	Sleep Talk	Normal	Status	—	—	10	Self
TM90	Substitute	Normal	Status	—	—	10	Self
TM94	Secret Power	Normal	Physical	70	100	20	Normal
TM98	Power-Up Punch	Fighting	Physical	40	100	20	Normal
TM100	Confide	Normal	Status	—	—	20	Normal
HM01	Cut	Normal	Physical	50	95	30	Normal
HM06	Rock Smash	Fighting	Physical	40	100	15	Normal

MOVES LEARNED IN EXCHANGE FOR BP

Name	Type	Kind	Pow.	Acc.	PP	Range
Covet	Normal	Physical	60	100	25	Normal
Bounce	Flying	Physical	85	85	5	Normal
Low Kick	Fighting	Physical	—	100	20	Normal
Uproar	Normal	Special	90	100	10	1 Random
Thunder Punch	Electric	Physical	75	100	15	Normal
Fire Punch	Fire	Physical	75	100	15	Normal
Ice Punch	Ice	Physical	75	100	15	Normal
Magic Coat	Psychic	Status	—	—	15	Self
Last Resort	Normal	Physical	140	100	5	Normal
Hyper Voice	Normal	Special	90	100	10	Many Others
Iron Tail	Steel	Physical	100	75	15	Normal
Snore	Normal	Special	50	100	15	Normal
Heal Bell	Normal	Status	—	—	5	Your Party
Drain Punch	Fighting	Physical	75	100	10	Normal
Focus Punch	Fighting	Physical	150	100	20	Normal
Shock Wave	Electric	Special	60	—	20	Normal
Water Pulse	Water	Special	60	100	20	Normal
After You	Normal	Status	—	—	15	Normal
Helping Hand	Normal	Status	—	—	20	1 Ally
Endeavor	Normal	Physical	—	100	5	Normal

MOVES TAUGHT BY PEOPLE

Name	Type	Kind	Pow.	Acc.	PP	Range

EGG MOVES

Name	Type	Kind	Pow.	Acc.	PP	Range
Fake Tears	Dark	Status	—	100	20	Normal
Fake Out	Normal	Physical	40	100	10	Normal
Encore	Normal	Status	—	100	5	Normal
Sweet Kiss	Fairy	Status	—	75	10	Normal
Double Hit	Normal	Physical	35	90	10	Normal
Low Kick	Fighting	Physical	—	100	20	Normal
Sky Uppercut	Fighting	Physical	85	90	15	Normal
Switcheroo	Dark	Status	—	100	10	Normal
Thunder Punch	Electric	Physical	75	100	15	Normal
Ice Punch	Ice	Physical	75	100	15	Normal
Fire Punch	Fire	Physical	75	100	15	Normal
Flail	Normal	Physical	—	100	15	Normal
Focus Punch	Fighting	Physical	150	100	20	Normal
Circle Throw	Fighting	Physical	60	90	10	Normal
Copycat	Normal	Status	—	—	20	Self
Teeter Dance	Normal	Status	—	100	20	Adjacent
Cosmic Power	Psychic	Status	—	—	20	Self
Mud Sport	Ground	Status	—	—	15	Both Sides

National Pokédex **428** Hoenn Pokédex —

Lopunny

Rabbit Pokémon

Normal

HEIGHT: 3'11" WEIGHT: 73.4 lbs.

Same form for ♂ / ♀

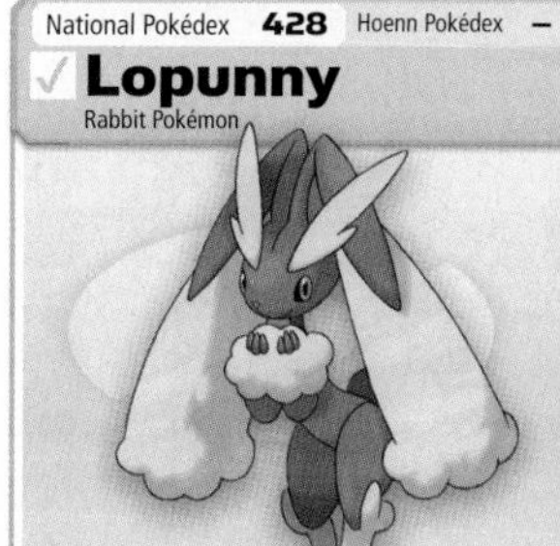

Ω Extremely cautious, it quickly bounds off when it senses danger.

α The ears appear to be delicate. If they are touched roughly, it kicks with its graceful legs.

ABILITIES
Cute Charm
Klutz

HIDDEN ABILITY
Limber

EGG GROUPS
Field | Human-Like

STAT GROWTH RATES
HP
Attack
Defense
Sp. Atk
Sp. Def
Speed

ITEMS SOMETIMES HELD BY WILD POKÉMON
—

EVOLUTION
Buneary → Level up with high friendship → Lopunny

MAIN WAY TO REGISTER IN THE NATIONAL POKÉDEX

Level up Buneary with high friendship.

Damage taken in normal battles

Type		Type	
Normal	×1	Flying	×1
Fire	×1	Psychic	×1
Water	×1	Bug	×1
Grass	×1	Rock	×1
Electric	×1	Ghost	×0
Ice	×1	Dragon	×1
Fighting	×2	Dark	×1
Poison	×1	Steel	×1
Ground	×1	Fairy	×1

Damage taken in Inverse battles

Type		Type	
Normal	×1	Flying	×1
Fire	×1	Psychic	×1
Water	×1	Bug	×1
Grass	×1	Rock	×1
Electric	×1	Ghost	×2
Ice	×1	Dragon	×1
Fighting	×0.5	Dark	×1
Poison	×1	Steel	×1
Ground	×1	Fairy	×1

Can be used in
Inverse Battle
Battle Institute
Battle Maison
Random Matchup (Free Battle)
Random Matchup (Others)

LEVEL-UP MOVES

Lv.	Name	Type	Kind	Pow.	Acc.	PP	Range
1	Healing Wish	Psychic	Status	—	—	10	Self
1	Bounce	Flying	Physical	85	85	5	Normal
1	Rototiller	Ground	Status	—	—	10	Adjacent
1	Mirror Coat	Psychic	Special	—	100	20	Varies
1	Magic Coat	Psychic	Status	—	—	15	Self
1	Defense Curl	Normal	Status	—	—	40	Self
1	Splash	Normal	Status	—	—	40	Self
1	Pound	Normal	Physical	40	100	35	Normal
1	Foresight	Normal	Status	—	—	40	Normal
6	Endure	Normal	Status	—	—	10	Self
13	Return	Normal	Physical	—	100	20	Normal
16	Quick Attack	Normal	Physical	40	100	30	Normal
23	Jump Kick	Fighting	Physical	100	95	10	Normal
26	Baton Pass	Normal	Status	—	—	40	Self
33	Agility	Psychic	Status	—	—	30	Self
36	Dizzy Punch	Normal	Physical	70	100	10	Normal
43	After You	Normal	Status	—	—	15	Normal
46	Charm	Fairy	Status	—	100	20	Normal
53	Entrainment	Normal	Status	—	100	15	Normal
56	Bounce	Flying	Physical	85	85	5	Normal
63	Healing Wish	Psychic	Status	—	—	10	Self
66	High Jump Kick	Fighting	Physical	130	90	10	Normal

TM & HM MOVES

No.	Name	Type	Kind	Pow.	Acc.	PP	Range
TM06	Toxic	Poison	Status	—	90	10	Normal
TM10	Hidden Power	Normal	Special	60	100	15	Normal
TM11	Sunny Day	Fire	Status	—	—	5	Both Sides
TM13	Ice Beam	Ice	Special	90	100	10	Normal
TM14	Blizzard	Ice	Special	110	70	5	Many Others
TM15	Hyper Beam	Normal	Special	150	90	5	Normal
TM17	Protect	Normal	Status	—	—	10	Self
TM18	Rain Dance	Water	Status	—	—	5	Both Sides
TM21	Frustration	Normal	Physical	—	100	20	Normal
TM22	Solar Beam	Grass	Special	120	100	10	Normal
TM24	Thunderbolt	Electric	Special	90	100	15	Normal
TM25	Thunder	Electric	Special	110	70	10	Normal
TM27	Return	Normal	Physical	—	100	20	Normal
TM28	Dig	Ground	Physical	80	100	10	Normal
TM30	Shadow Ball	Ghost	Special	80	100	15	Normal
TM32	Double Team	Normal	Status	—	—	15	Self
TM42	Facade	Normal	Physical	70	100	20	Normal
TM44	Rest	Psychic	Status	—	—	10	Self
TM45	Attract	Normal	Status	—	100	15	Normal
TM47	Low Sweep	Fighting	Physical	65	100	20	Normal
TM48	Round	Normal	Special	60	100	15	Normal
TM52	Focus Blast	Fighting	Special	120	70	5	Normal
TM56	Fling	Dark	Physical	—	100	10	Normal
TM57	Charge Beam	Electric	Special	50	90	10	Normal
TM67	Retaliate	Normal	Physical	70	100	5	Normal
TM68	Giga Impact	Normal	Physical	150	90	5	Normal
TM73	Thunder Wave	Electric	Status	—	100	20	Normal
TM86	Grass Knot	Grass	Special	—	100	20	Normal
TM87	Swagger	Normal	Status	—	90	15	Normal
TM88	Sleep Talk	Normal	Status	—	—	10	Self
TM90	Substitute	Normal	Status	—	—	10	Self
TM94	Secret Power	Normal	Physical	70	100	20	Normal
TM98	Power-Up Punch	Fighting	Physical	40	100	20	Normal
TM100	Confide	Normal	Status	—	—	20	Normal
HM01	Cut	Normal	Physical	50	95	30	Normal
HM04	Strength	Normal	Physical	80	100	15	Normal
HM06	Rock Smash	Fighting	Physical	40	100	15	Normal

MOVES LEARNED IN EXCHANGE FOR BP

Name	Type	Kind	Pow.	Acc.	PP	Range
Covet	Normal	Physical	60	100	25	Normal
Bounce	Flying	Physical	85	85	5	Normal
Low Kick	Fighting	Physical	—	100	20	Normal
Uproar	Normal	Special	90	100	10	1 Random
Thunder Punch	Electric	Physical	75	100	15	Normal
Fire Punch	Fire	Physical	75	100	15	Normal
Ice Punch	Ice	Physical	75	100	15	Normal
Magic Coat	Psychic	Status	—	—	15	Self
Last Resort	Normal	Physical	140	100	5	Normal
Hyper Voice	Normal	Special	90	100	10	Many Others
Iron Tail	Steel	Physical	100	75	15	Normal
Snore	Normal	Special	50	100	15	Normal
Heal Bell	Normal	Status	—	—	5	Your Party
Drain Punch	Fighting	Physical	75	100	10	Normal
Focus Punch	Fighting	Physical	150	100	20	Normal
Shock Wave	Electric	Special	60	—	20	Normal
Water Pulse	Water	Special	60	100	20	Normal
After You	Normal	Status	—	—	15	Normal
Helping Hand	Normal	Status	—	—	20	1 Ally
Endeavor	Normal	Physical	—	100	5	Normal

MOVES TAUGHT BY PEOPLE

Name	Type	Kind	Pow.	Acc.	PP	Range

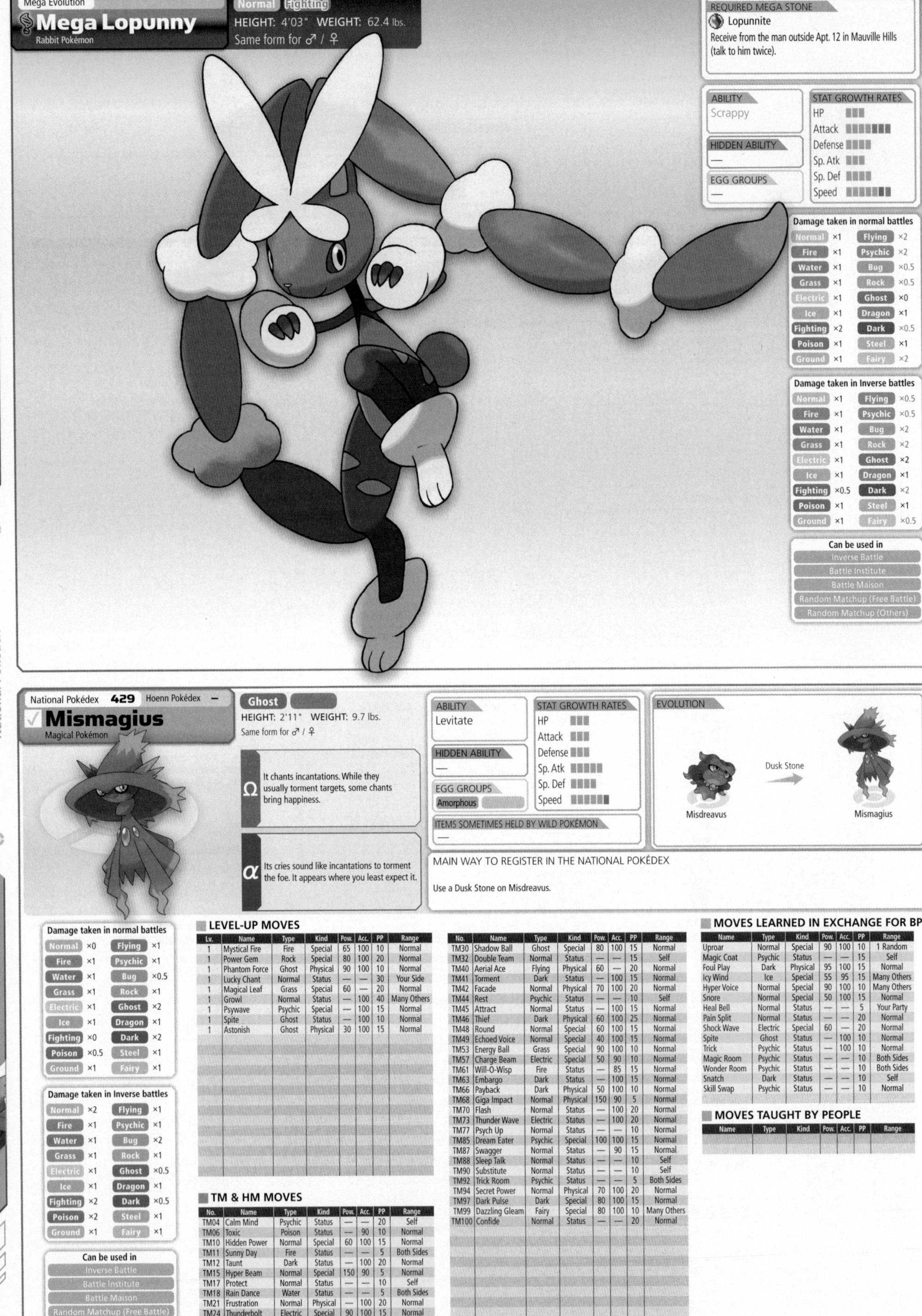

Mega Evolution

Mega Lopunny

Rabbit Pokémon

Normal Fighting

HEIGHT: 4'03" WEIGHT: 62.4 lbs.

Same form for ♂ / ♀

REQUIRED MEGA STONE

Lopunnite

Receive from the man outside Apt. 12 in Mauville Hills (talk to him twice).

ABILITY

Scrappy

HIDDEN ABILITY

—

EGG GROUPS

—

STAT GROWTH RATES

HP, Attack, Defense, Sp. Atk, Sp. Def, Speed

Damage taken in normal battles

Type		Type	
Normal	×1	Flying	×2
Fire	×1	Psychic	×2
Water	×1	Bug	×0.5
Grass	×1	Rock	×0.5
Electric	×1	Ghost	×0
Ice	×1	Dragon	×1
Fighting	×2	Dark	×0.5
Poison	×1	Steel	×1
Ground	×1	Fairy	×2

Damage taken in Inverse battles

Type		Type	
Normal	×1	Flying	×0.5
Fire	×1	Psychic	×0.5
Water	×1	Bug	×2
Grass	×1	Rock	×2
Electric	×1	Ghost	×2
Ice	×1	Dragon	×1
Fighting	×0.5	Dark	×2
Poison	×1	Steel	×1
Ground	×1	Fairy	×0.5

Can be used in

Inverse Battle
Battle Institute
Battle Maison
Random Matchup (Free Battle)
Random Matchup (Others)

National Pokédex **429** Hoenn Pokédex —

Mismagius

Magical Pokémon

Ghost

HEIGHT: 2'11" WEIGHT: 9.7 lbs.

Same form for ♂ / ♀

Ω It chants incantations. While they usually torment targets, some chants bring happiness.

α Its cries sound like incantations to torment the foe. It appears where you least expect it.

ABILITY

Levitate

HIDDEN ABILITY

—

EGG GROUPS

Amorphous

STAT GROWTH RATES

HP, Attack, Defense, Sp. Atk, Sp. Def, Speed

ITEMS SOMETIMES HELD BY WILD POKÉMON

—

EVOLUTION

Misdreavus → Dusk Stone → Mismagius

MAIN WAY TO REGISTER IN THE NATIONAL POKÉDEX

Use a Dusk Stone on Misdreavus.

Damage taken in normal battles

Type		Type	
Normal	×0	Flying	×1
Fire	×1	Psychic	×1
Water	×1	Bug	×0.5
Grass	×1	Rock	×1
Electric	×1	Ghost	×2
Ice	×1	Dragon	×1
Fighting	×0	Dark	×2
Poison	×0.5	Steel	×1
Ground	×1	Fairy	×1

Damage taken in Inverse battles

Type		Type	
Normal	×2	Flying	×1
Fire	×1	Psychic	×1
Water	×1	Bug	×2
Grass	×1	Rock	×1
Electric	×1	Ghost	×0.5
Ice	×1	Dragon	×1
Fighting	×2	Dark	×0.5
Poison	×2	Steel	×1
Ground	×1	Fairy	×1

Can be used in

Inverse Battle
Battle Institute
Battle Maison
Random Matchup (Free Battle)
Random Matchup (Others)

LEVEL-UP MOVES

Lv.	Name	Type	Kind	Pow.	Acc.	PP	Range
1	Mystical Fire	Fire	Special	65	100	10	Normal
1	Power Gem	Rock	Special	80	100	20	Normal
1	Phantom Force	Ghost	Physical	90	100	10	Normal
1	Lucky Chant	Normal	Status	—	—	30	Your Side
1	Magical Leaf	Grass	Special	60	—	20	Normal
1	Growl	Normal	Status	—	100	40	Many Others
1	Psywave	Psychic	Special	—	100	15	Normal
1	Spite	Ghost	Status	—	100	10	Normal
1	Astonish	Ghost	Physical	30	100	15	Normal

TM & HM MOVES

No.	Name	Type	Kind	Pow.	Acc.	PP	Range
TM04	Calm Mind	Psychic	Status	—	—	20	Self
TM06	Toxic	Poison	Status	—	90	10	Normal
TM10	Hidden Power	Normal	Special	60	100	15	Normal
TM11	Sunny Day	Fire	Status	—	—	5	Both Sides
TM12	Taunt	Dark	Status	—	100	20	Normal
TM15	Hyper Beam	Normal	Special	150	90	5	Normal
TM17	Protect	Normal	Status	—	—	10	Self
TM18	Rain Dance	Water	Status	—	—	5	Both Sides
TM21	Frustration	Normal	Physical	—	100	20	Normal
TM24	Thunderbolt	Electric	Special	90	100	15	Normal
TM25	Thunder	Electric	Special	110	70	10	Normal
TM27	Return	Normal	Physical	—	100	20	Normal
TM29	Psychic	Psychic	Special	90	100	10	Normal
TM30	Shadow Ball	Ghost	Special	80	100	15	Normal
TM32	Double Team	Normal	Status	—	—	15	Self
TM40	Aerial Ace	Flying	Physical	60	—	20	Normal
TM41	Torment	Dark	Status	—	100	15	Normal
TM42	Facade	Normal	Physical	70	100	20	Normal
TM44	Rest	Psychic	Status	—	—	10	Self
TM45	Attract	Normal	Status	—	100	15	Normal
TM46	Thief	Dark	Physical	60	100	25	Normal
TM48	Round	Normal	Special	60	100	15	Normal
TM49	Echoed Voice	Normal	Special	40	100	15	Normal
TM53	Energy Ball	Grass	Special	90	100	10	Normal
TM57	Charge Beam	Electric	Special	50	90	10	Normal
TM61	Will-O-Wisp	Fire	Status	—	85	15	Normal
TM63	Embargo	Dark	Status	—	100	15	Normal
TM66	Payback	Dark	Physical	50	100	10	Normal
TM68	Giga Impact	Normal	Physical	150	90	5	Normal
TM70	Flash	Normal	Status	—	100	20	Normal
TM73	Thunder Wave	Electric	Status	—	100	20	Normal
TM77	Psych Up	Normal	Status	—	—	10	Normal
TM85	Dream Eater	Psychic	Special	100	100	15	Normal
TM87	Swagger	Normal	Status	—	90	15	Normal
TM88	Sleep Talk	Normal	Status	—	—	10	Self
TM90	Substitute	Normal	Status	—	—	10	Self
TM92	Trick Room	Psychic	Status	—	—	5	Both Sides
TM94	Secret Power	Normal	Physical	70	100	20	Normal
TM97	Dark Pulse	Dark	Special	80	100	15	Normal
TM99	Dazzling Gleam	Fairy	Special	80	100	10	Many Others
TM100	Confide	Normal	Status	—	—	20	Normal

MOVES LEARNED IN EXCHANGE FOR BP

Name	Type	Kind	Pow.	Acc.	PP	Range
Uproar	Normal	Special	90	100	10	1 Random
Magic Coat	Psychic	Status	—	—	15	Self
Foul Play	Dark	Physical	95	100	15	Normal
Icy Wind	Ice	Special	55	95	15	Many Others
Hyper Voice	Normal	Special	90	100	10	Many Others
Snore	Normal	Special	50	100	15	Normal
Heal Bell	Normal	Status	—	—	5	Your Party
Pain Split	Normal	Status	—	—	20	Normal
Shock Wave	Electric	Special	60	—	20	Normal
Spite	Ghost	Status	—	100	10	Normal
Trick	Psychic	Status	—	100	10	Normal
Magic Room	Psychic	Status	—	—	10	Both Sides
Wonder Room	Psychic	Status	—	—	10	Both Sides
Snatch	Dark	Status	—	—	10	Self
Skill Swap	Psychic	Status	—	—	10	Normal

MOVES TAUGHT BY PEOPLE

Name	Type	Kind	Pow.	Acc.	PP	Range

National Pokédex **430** Hoenn Pokédex —

Honchkrow

Big Boss Pokémon

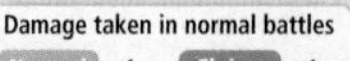

Dark | Flying

HEIGHT: 2'11" WEIGHT: 60.2 lbs.

Same form for ♂ / ♀

Ω If one utters a deep cry, many Murkrow gather quickly. For this, it is called "Summoner of Night."

α Becoming active at night, it is known to swarm with numerous Murkrow in tow.

ABILITIES
Insomnia
Super Luck

HIDDEN ABILITY
Moxie

EGG GROUPS
Flying

STAT GROWTH RATES
HP ■■■■
Attack ■■■■■■
Defense ■■
Sp. Atk ■■■■■
Sp. Def ■■
Speed ■■■■

ITEMS SOMETIMES HELD BY WILD POKÉMON
—

EVOLUTION
Murkrow → (Dusk Stone) → Honchkrow

MAIN WAY TO REGISTER IN THE NATIONAL POKÉDEX
Use a Dusk Stone on Murkrow.

Damage taken in normal battles

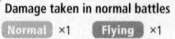

Type		Type	
Normal	×1	Flying	×1
Fire	×1	Psychic	×0
Water	×1	Bug	×1
Grass	×0.5	Rock	×2
Electric	×2	Ghost	×0.5
Ice	×2	Dragon	×1
Fighting	×1	Dark	×0.5
Poison	×1	Steel	×1
Ground	×0	Fairy	×2

Damage taken in Inverse battles

Type		Type	
Normal	×1	Flying	×1
Fire	×1	Psychic	×2
Water	×1	Bug	×1
Grass	×2	Rock	×0.5
Electric	×0.5	Ghost	×2
Ice	×0.5	Dragon	×1
Fighting	×1	Dark	×2
Poison	×1	Steel	×1
Ground	×2	Fairy	×0.5

Can be used in
Inverse Battle
Battle Institute
Battle Maison
Random Matchup (Free Battle)
Random Matchup (Others)

LEVEL-UP MOVES

Lv.	Name	Type	Kind	Pow.	Acc.	PP	Range
1	Night Slash	Dark	Physical	70	100	15	Normal
1	Sucker Punch	Dark	Physical	80	100	5	Normal
1	Astonish	Ghost	Physical	30	100	15	Normal
1	Pursuit	Dark	Physical	40	100	20	Normal
1	Haze	Ice	Status	—	—	30	Both Sides
1	Wing Attack	Flying	Physical	60	100	35	Normal
25	Swagger	Normal	Status	—	90	15	Normal
35	Nasty Plot	Dark	Status	—	—	20	Self
45	Foul Play	Dark	Physical	95	100	15	Normal
55	Night Slash	Dark	Physical	70	100	15	Normal
65	Quash	Dark	Status	—	100	15	Normal
75	Dark Pulse	Dark	Special	80	100	15	Normal

TM & HM MOVES

No.	Name	Type	Kind	Pow.	Acc.	PP	Range
TM04	Calm Mind	Psychic	Status	—	—	20	Self
TM06	Toxic	Poison	Status	—	90	10	Normal
TM10	Hidden Power	Normal	Special	60	100	15	Normal
TM11	Sunny Day	Fire	Status	—	—	5	Both Sides
TM12	Taunt	Dark	Status	—	100	20	Normal
TM15	Hyper Beam	Normal	Special	150	90	5	Normal
TM17	Protect	Normal	Status	—	—	10	Self
TM18	Rain Dance	Water	Status	—	—	5	Both Sides
TM19	Roost	Flying	Status	—	—	10	Self
TM21	Frustration	Normal	Physical	—	100	20	Normal
TM27	Return	Normal	Physical	—	100	20	Normal
TM29	Psychic	Psychic	Special	90	100	10	Normal
TM30	Shadow Ball	Ghost	Special	80	100	15	Normal
TM32	Double Team	Normal	Status	—	—	15	Self
TM40	Aerial Ace	Flying	Physical	60	—	20	Normal
TM41	Torment	Dark	Status	—	100	15	Normal
TM42	Facade	Normal	Physical	70	100	20	Normal
TM44	Rest	Psychic	Status	—	—	10	Self
TM45	Attract	Normal	Status	—	100	15	Normal
TM46	Thief	Dark	Physical	60	100	25	Normal
TM48	Round	Normal	Special	60	100	15	Normal
TM51	Steel Wing	Steel	Physical	70	90	25	Normal
TM59	Incinerate	Fire	Special	60	100	15	Many Others
TM60	Quash	Dark	Status	—	100	15	Normal
TM63	Embargo	Dark	Status	—	100	15	Normal
TM66	Payback	Dark	Physical	50	100	10	Normal
TM67	Retaliate	Normal	Physical	70	100	5	Normal
TM68	Giga Impact	Normal	Physical	150	90	5	Normal
TM73	Thunder Wave	Electric	Status	—	100	20	Normal
TM77	Psych Up	Normal	Status	—	—	10	Normal
TM85	Dream Eater	Psychic	Special	100	100	15	Normal
TM87	Swagger	Normal	Status	—	90	15	Normal
TM88	Sleep Talk	Normal	Status	—	—	10	Self
TM90	Substitute	Normal	Status	—	—	10	Self
TM94	Secret Power	Normal	Physical	70	100	20	Normal
TM95	Snarl	Dark	Special	55	95	15	Many Others
TM97	Dark Pulse	Dark	Special	80	100	15	Normal
TM100	Confide	Normal	Status	—	—	20	Normal
HM02	Fly	Flying	Physical	90	95	15	Normal

MOVES LEARNED IN EXCHANGE FOR BP

Name	Type	Kind	Pow.	Acc.	PP	Range
Uproar	Normal	Special	90	100	10	1 Random
Foul Play	Dark	Physical	95	100	15	Normal
Superpower	Fighting	Physical	120	100	5	Normal
Icy Wind	Ice	Special	55	95	15	Many Others
Snore	Normal	Special	50	100	15	Normal
Heat Wave	Fire	Special	95	90	10	Many Others
Tailwind	Flying	Status	—	—	15	Your Side
Sky Attack	Flying	Physical	140	90	5	Normal
Spite	Ghost	Status	—	100	10	Normal
Snatch	Dark	Status	—	—	10	Self

MOVES TAUGHT BY PEOPLE

Name	Type	Kind	Pow.	Acc.	PP	Range

National Pokédex **431** Hoenn Pokédex —

Glameow

Catty Pokémon

Normal

HEIGHT: 1'08" WEIGHT: 8.6 lbs.

Same form for ♂ / ♀

Ω It claws if displeased and purrs when affectionate. Its fickleness is very popular among some.

α When it's happy, Glameow demonstrates beautiful movements of its tail, like a dancing ribbon.

ABILITIES
Limber
Own Tempo

HIDDEN ABILITY
Keen Eye

EGG GROUPS
Field

STAT GROWTH RATES
HP ■■
Attack ■■■
Defense ■■
Sp. Atk ■■
Sp. Def ■■
Speed ■■■■■

ITEMS SOMETIMES HELD BY WILD POKÉMON
—

EVOLUTION
Glameow → (Lv. 38) → Purugly

MAIN WAY TO REGISTER IN THE NATIONAL POKÉDEX
Catch in Mirage Forest 1.

Damage taken in normal battles

Type		Type	
Normal	×1	Flying	×1
Fire	×1	Psychic	×1
Water	×1	Bug	×1
Grass	×1	Rock	×1
Electric	×1	Ghost	×0
Ice	×1	Dragon	×1
Fighting	×2	Dark	×1
Poison	×1	Steel	×1
Ground	×1	Fairy	×1

Damage taken in Inverse battles

Type		Type	
Normal	×1	Flying	×1
Fire	×1	Psychic	×1
Water	×1	Bug	×1
Grass	×1	Rock	×1
Electric	×1	Ghost	×2
Ice	×1	Dragon	×1
Fighting	×0.5	Dark	×1
Poison	×1	Steel	×1
Ground	×1	Fairy	×1

Can be used in
Inverse Battle
Battle Institute
Battle Maison
Random Matchup (Free Battle)
Random Matchup (Others)

LEVEL-UP MOVES

Lv.	Name	Type	Kind	Pow.	Acc.	PP	Range
1	Fake Out	Normal	Physical	40	100	10	Normal
5	Scratch	Normal	Physical	40	100	35	Normal
8	Growl	Normal	Status	—	100	40	Many Others
13	Hypnosis	Psychic	Status	—	60	20	Normal
17	Feint Attack	Dark	Physical	60	—	20	Normal
20	Fury Swipes	Normal	Physical	18	80	15	Normal
25	Charm	Fairy	Status	—	100	20	Normal
29	Assist	Normal	Status	—	—	20	Self
32	Captivate	Normal	Status	—	100	20	Many Others
37	Slash	Normal	Physical	70	100	20	Normal
41	Sucker Punch	Dark	Physical	80	100	5	Normal
44	Attract	Normal	Status	—	100	15	Normal
48	Hone Claws	Dark	Status	—	—	15	Self
50	Play Rough	Fairy	Physical	90	90	10	Normal

TM & HM MOVES

No.	Name	Type	Kind	Pow.	Acc.	PP	Range
TM01	Hone Claws	Dark	Status	—	—	15	Self
TM06	Toxic	Poison	Status	—	90	10	Normal
TM10	Hidden Power	Normal	Special	60	100	15	Normal
TM11	Sunny Day	Fire	Status	—	—	5	Both Sides
TM12	Taunt	Dark	Status	—	100	20	Normal
TM17	Protect	Normal	Status	—	—	10	Self
TM18	Rain Dance	Water	Status	—	—	5	Both Sides
TM21	Frustration	Normal	Physical	—	100	20	Normal
TM24	Thunderbolt	Electric	Special	90	100	15	Normal
TM25	Thunder	Electric	Special	110	70	10	Normal
TM27	Return	Normal	Physical	—	100	20	Normal
TM28	Dig	Ground	Physical	80	100	10	Normal
TM30	Shadow Ball	Ghost	Special	80	100	15	Normal
TM32	Double Team	Normal	Status	—	—	15	Self
TM40	Aerial Ace	Flying	Physical	60	—	20	Normal
TM41	Torment	Dark	Status	—	100	15	Normal
TM42	Facade	Normal	Physical	70	100	20	Normal
TM44	Rest	Psychic	Status	—	—	10	Self
TM45	Attract	Normal	Status	—	100	15	Normal
TM46	Thief	Dark	Physical	60	100	25	Normal
TM48	Round	Normal	Special	60	100	15	Normal
TM49	Echoed Voice	Normal	Special	40	100	15	Normal
TM65	Shadow Claw	Ghost	Physical	70	100	15	Normal
TM66	Payback	Dark	Physical	50	100	10	Normal
TM67	Retaliate	Normal	Physical	70	100	5	Normal
TM70	Flash	Normal	Status	—	100	20	Normal
TM77	Psych Up	Normal	Status	—	—	10	Normal
TM85	Dream Eater	Psychic	Special	100	100	15	Normal
TM87	Swagger	Normal	Status	—	90	15	Normal
TM88	Sleep Talk	Normal	Status	—	—	10	Self
TM89	U-turn	Bug	Physical	70	100	20	Normal
TM90	Substitute	Normal	Status	—	—	10	Self
TM94	Secret Power	Normal	Physical	70	100	20	Normal
TM100	Confide	Normal	Status	—	—	20	Normal
HM01	Cut	Normal	Physical	50	95	30	Normal

MOVES LEARNED IN EXCHANGE FOR BP

Name	Type	Kind	Pow.	Acc.	PP	Range
Covet	Normal	Physical	60	100	25	Normal
Super Fang	Normal	Physical	—	90	10	Normal
Foul Play	Dark	Physical	95	100	15	Normal
Last Resort	Normal	Physical	140	100	5	Normal
Hyper Voice	Normal	Special	90	100	10	Many Others
Iron Tail	Steel	Physical	100	75	15	Normal
Snore	Normal	Special	50	100	15	Normal
Knock Off	Dark	Physical	65	100	20	Normal
Shock Wave	Electric	Special	60	—	20	Normal
Water Pulse	Water	Special	60	100	20	Normal
Snatch	Dark	Status	—	—	10	Self

MOVES TAUGHT BY PEOPLE

Name	Type	Kind	Pow.	Acc.	PP	Range

EGG MOVES

Name	Type	Kind	Pow.	Acc.	PP	Range
Bite	Dark	Physical	60	100	25	Normal
Tail Whip	Normal	Status	—	100	30	Many Others
Quick Attack	Normal	Physical	40	100	30	Normal
Sand Attack	Ground	Status	—	100	15	Normal
Fake Tears	Dark	Status	—	100	20	Normal
Assurance	Dark	Physical	60	100	10	Normal
Flail	Normal	Physical	—	100	15	Normal
Snatch	Dark	Status	—	—	10	Self
Wake-Up Slap	Fighting	Physical	70	100	10	Normal
Last Resort	Normal	Physical	140	100	5	Normal

National Pokédex **432** Hoenn Pokédex —

Purugly

Tiger Cat Pokémon

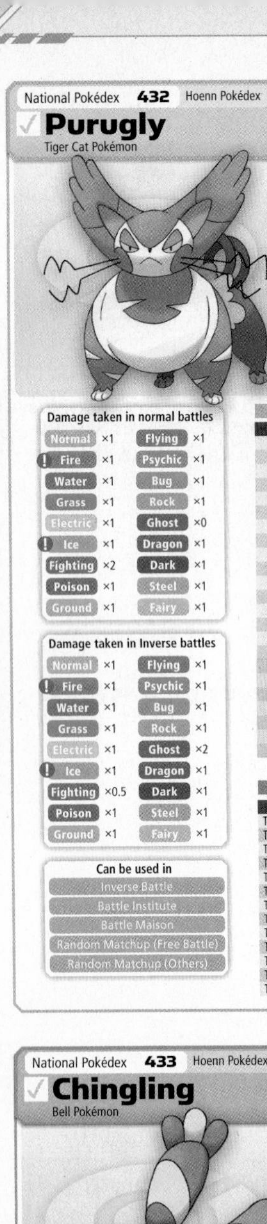

Normal

HEIGHT: 3'03" WEIGHT: 96.6 lbs.

Same form for ♂ / ♀

Ω It would claim another Pokémon's nest as its own if it finds a nest sufficiently comfortable.

α To make itself appear intimidatingly beefy, it tightly cinches its waist with its twin tails.

ABILITIES
Thick Fat
Own Tempo

HIDDEN ABILITY
Defiant

EGG GROUPS
Field

STAT GROWTH RATES
HP
Attack
Defense
Sp. Atk
Sp. Def
Speed

ITEMS SOMETIMES HELD BY WILD POKÉMON
—

EVOLUTION 
Glameow → Lv. 38 → Purugly

MAIN WAY TO REGISTER IN THE NATIONAL POKÉDEX

Catch on Mirage Island 8.

Damage taken in normal battles

Type		Type	
Normal	×1	Flying	×1
Fire	×1	Psychic	×1
Water	×1	Bug	×1
Grass	×1	Rock	×1
Electric	×1	Ghost	×0
Ice	×1	Dragon	×1
Fighting	×2	Dark	×1
Poison	×1	Steel	×1
Ground	×1	Fairy	×1

Damage taken in Inverse battles

Type		Type	
Normal	×1	Flying	×1
Fire	×1	Psychic	×1
Water	×1	Bug	×1
Grass	×1	Rock	×1
Electric	×1	Ghost	×2
Ice	×1	Dragon	×1
Fighting	×0.5	Dark	×1
Poison	×1	Steel	×1
Ground	×1	Fairy	×1

Can be used in
Inverse Battle
Battle Institute
Battle Maison
Random Matchup (Free Battle)
Random Matchup (Others)

LEVEL-UP MOVES

Lv.	Name	Type	Kind	Pow.	Acc.	PP	Range
1	Fake Out	Normal	Physical	40	100	10	Normal
1	Scratch	Normal	Physical	40	100	35	Normal
1	Growl	Normal	Status	—	100	40	Many Others
5	Scratch	Normal	Physical	40	100	35	Normal
8	Growl	Normal	Status	—	100	40	Many Others
13	Hypnosis	Psychic	Status	—	60	20	Normal
17	Feint Attack	Dark	Physical	60	—	20	Normal
20	Fury Swipes	Normal	Physical	18	80	15	Normal
25	Charm	Fairy	Status	—	100	20	Normal
29	Assist	Normal	Status	—	—	20	Self
32	Captivate	Normal	Status	—	100	20	Many Others
37	Slash	Normal	Physical	70	100	20	Normal
38	Swagger	Normal	Status	—	90	15	Normal
45	Body Slam	Normal	Physical	85	100	15	Normal
52	Attract	Normal	Status	—	100	15	Normal
60	Hone Claws	Dark	Status	—	—	15	Self

TM & HM MOVES

No.	Name	Type	Kind	Pow.	Acc.	PP	Range
TM01	Hone Claws	Dark	Status	—	—	15	Self
TM05	Roar	Normal	Status	—	—	20	Normal
TM06	Toxic	Poison	Status	—	90	10	Normal
TM10	Hidden Power	Normal	Special	60	100	15	Normal
TM11	Sunny Day	Fire	Status	—	—	5	Both Sides
TM12	Taunt	Dark	Status	—	100	20	Normal
TM15	Hyper Beam	Normal	Special	150	90	5	Normal
TM17	Protect	Normal	Status	—	—	10	Self
TM18	Rain Dance	Water	Status	—	—	5	Both Sides
TM21	Frustration	Normal	Physical	—	100	20	Normal
TM24	Thunderbolt	Electric	Special	90	100	15	Normal
TM25	Thunder	Electric	Special	110	70	10	Normal
TM27	Return	Normal	Physical	—	100	20	Normal
TM28	Dig	Ground	Physical	80	100	10	Normal
TM30	Shadow Ball	Ghost	Special	80	100	15	Normal
TM32	Double Team	Normal	Status	—	—	15	Self
TM40	Aerial Ace	Flying	Physical	60	—	20	Normal
TM41	Torment	Dark	Status	—	100	15	Normal
TM42	Facade	Normal	Physical	70	100	20	Normal
TM44	Rest	Psychic	Status	—	—	10	Self
TM45	Attract	Normal	Status	—	100	15	Normal
TM46	Thief	Dark	Physical	60	100	25	Normal
TM48	Round	Normal	Special	60	100	15	Normal
TM49	Echoed Voice	Normal	Special	40	100	15	Normal
TM65	Shadow Claw	Ghost	Physical	70	100	15	Normal
TM66	Payback	Dark	Physical	50	100	10	Normal
TM67	Retaliate	Normal	Physical	70	100	5	Normal
TM68	Giga Impact	Normal	Physical	150	90	5	Normal
TM70	Flash	Normal	Status	—	100	20	Normal
TM77	Psych Up	Normal	Status	—	—	10	Normal
TM78	Bulldoze	Ground	Physical	60	100	20	Adjacent
TM85	Dream Eater	Psychic	Special	100	100	15	Normal
TM87	Swagger	Normal	Status	—	90	15	Normal
TM88	Sleep Talk	Normal	Status	—	—	10	Self
TM89	U-turn	Bug	Physical	70	100	20	Normal
TM90	Substitute	Normal	Status	—	—	10	Self
TM94	Secret Power	Normal	Physical	70	100	20	Normal
TM100	Confide	Normal	Status	—	—	20	Normal
HM01	Cut	Normal	Physical	50	95	30	Normal

MOVES LEARNED IN EXCHANGE FOR BP

Name	Type	Kind	Pow.	Acc.	PP	Range
Covet	Normal	Physical	60	100	25	Normal
Super Fang	Normal	Physical	—	90	10	Normal
Foul Play	Dark	Physical	95	100	15	Normal
Last Resort	Normal	Physical	140	100	5	Normal
Hyper Voice	Normal	Special	90	100	10	Many Others
Iron Tail	Steel	Physical	100	75	15	Normal
Snore	Normal	Special	50	100	15	Normal
Knock Off	Dark	Physical	65	100	20	Normal
Shock Wave	Electric	Special	60	—	20	Normal
Water Pulse	Water	Special	60	100	20	Normal
Snatch	Dark	Status	—	—	10	Self

MOVES TAUGHT BY PEOPLE

Name	Type	Kind	Pow.	Acc.	PP	Range

National Pokédex **433** Hoenn Pokédex **157**

Chingling

Bell Pokémon

Psychic

HEIGHT: 0'08" WEIGHT: 1.3 lbs.

Same form for ♂ / ♀

Ω Each time it hops, it makes a ringing sound. It deafens foes by emitting high-frequency cries.

α There is an orb inside its mouth. When it hops, the orb bounces all over and makes a ringing sound.

ABILITY
Levitate

HIDDEN ABILITY
—

EGG GROUPS
No Eggs Discovered

STAT GROWTH RATES
HP
Attack
Defense
Sp. Atk
Sp. Def
Speed

ITEMS SOMETIMES HELD BY WILD POKÉMON
—

EVOLUTION 
Chingling → Level up with high friendship between 8 P.M. and 3:59 A.M. → Chimecho

MAIN WAY TO REGISTER IN THE NATIONAL POKÉDEX

Leave a Chimecho holding a Pure Incense at a Pokémon Day Care, then hatch the Pokémon Egg that is found.

Damage taken in normal battles

Type		Type	
Normal	×1	Flying	×1
Fire	×1	Psychic	×0.5
Water	×1	Bug	×2
Grass	×1	Rock	×1
Electric	×1	Ghost	×2
Ice	×1	Dragon	×1
Fighting	×0.5	Dark	×2
Poison	×1	Steel	×1
Ground	×1	Fairy	×1

Damage taken in Inverse battles

Type		Type	
Normal	×1	Flying	×1
Fire	×1	Psychic	×2
Water	×1	Bug	×0.5
Grass	×1	Rock	×1
Electric	×1	Ghost	×0.5
Ice	×1	Dragon	×1
Fighting	×2	Dark	×0.5
Poison	×1	Steel	×1
Ground	×1	Fairy	×1

Can be used in
Inverse Battle
Battle Institute
Battle Maison
Random Matchup (Free Battle)
Random Matchup (Others)

LEVEL-UP MOVES

Lv.	Name	Type	Kind	Pow.	Acc.	PP	Range
1	Wrap	Normal	Physical	15	90	20	Normal
4	Growl	Normal	Status	—	100	40	Many Others
7	Astonish	Ghost	Physical	30	100	15	Normal
10	Confusion	Psychic	Special	50	100	25	Normal
13	Yawn	Normal	Status	—	—	10	Normal
16	Last Resort	Normal	Physical	140	100	5	Normal
19	Entrainment	Normal	Status	—	100	15	Normal
32	Uproar	Normal	Special	90	100	10	1 Random

TM & HM MOVES

No.	Name	Type	Kind	Pow.	Acc.	PP	Range
TM03	Psyshock	Psychic	Special	80	100	10	Normal
TM04	Calm Mind	Psychic	Status	—	—	20	Self
TM06	Toxic	Poison	Status	—	90	10	Normal
TM10	Hidden Power	Normal	Special	60	100	15	Normal
TM11	Sunny Day	Fire	Status	—	—	5	Both Sides
TM12	Taunt	Dark	Status	—	100	20	Normal
TM16	Light Screen	Psychic	Status	—	—	30	Your Side
TM17	Protect	Normal	Status	—	—	10	Self
TM18	Rain Dance	Water	Status	—	—	5	Both Sides
TM20	Safeguard	Normal	Status	—	—	25	Your Side
TM21	Frustration	Normal	Physical	—	100	20	Normal
TM27	Return	Normal	Physical	—	100	20	Normal
TM29	Psychic	Psychic	Special	90	100	10	Normal
TM30	Shadow Ball	Ghost	Special	80	100	15	Normal
TM32	Double Team	Normal	Status	—	—	15	Self
TM33	Reflect	Psychic	Status	—	—	20	Your Side
TM41	Torment	Dark	Status	—	100	15	Normal
TM42	Facade	Normal	Physical	70	100	20	Normal
TM44	Rest	Psychic	Status	—	—	10	Self
TM45	Attract	Normal	Status	—	100	15	Normal
TM48	Round	Normal	Special	60	100	15	Normal
TM49	Echoed Voice	Normal	Special	40	100	15	Normal
TM57	Charge Beam	Electric	Special	50	90	10	Normal
TM70	Flash	Normal	Status	—	100	20	Normal
TM73	Thunder Wave	Electric	Status	—	100	20	Normal
TM77	Psych Up	Normal	Status	—	—	10	Normal
TM85	Dream Eater	Psychic	Special	100	100	15	Normal
TM86	Grass Knot	Grass	Special	—	100	20	Normal
TM87	Swagger	Normal	Status	—	90	15	Normal
TM88	Sleep Talk	Normal	Status	—	—	10	Self
TM90	Substitute	Normal	Status	—	—	10	Self
TM92	Trick Room	Psychic	Status	—	—	5	Both Sides
TM94	Secret Power	Normal	Physical	70	100	20	Normal
TM99	Dazzling Gleam	Fairy	Special	80	100	10	Many Others
TM100	Confide	Normal	Status	—	—	20	Normal

MOVES LEARNED IN EXCHANGE FOR BP

Name	Type	Kind	Pow.	Acc.	PP	Range
Signal Beam	Bug	Special	75	100	15	Normal
Uproar	Normal	Special	90	100	10	1 Random
Magic Coat	Psychic	Status	—	—	15	Self
Gravity	Psychic	Status	—	—	5	Both Sides
Last Resort	Normal	Physical	140	100	5	Normal
Icy Wind	Ice	Special	55	95	15	Many Others
Zen Headbutt	Psychic	Physical	80	90	15	Normal
Hyper Voice	Normal	Special	90	100	10	Many Others
Bind	Normal	Physical	15	85	20	Normal
Snore	Normal	Special	50	100	15	Normal
Knock Off	Dark	Physical	65	100	20	Normal
Heal Bell	Normal	Status	—	—	5	Your Party
Shock Wave	Electric	Special	60	—	20	Normal
Helping Hand	Normal	Status	—	—	20	1 Ally
Trick	Psychic	Status	—	100	10	Normal
Recycle	Normal	Status	—	—	10	Self
Snatch	Dark	Status	—	—	10	Self
Skill Swap	Psychic	Status	—	—	10	Normal

MOVES TAUGHT BY PEOPLE

Name	Type	Kind	Pow.	Acc.	PP	Range

EGG MOVES

Name	Type	Kind	Pow.	Acc.	PP	Range
Disable	Normal	Status	—	100	20	Normal
Curse	Ghost	Status	—	—	10	Varies
Hypnosis	Psychic	Status	—	60	20	Normal
Wish	Normal	Status	—	—	10	Self
Future Sight	Psychic	Special	120	100	10	Normal
Recover	Normal	Status	—	—	10	Self
Stored Power	Psychic	Special	20	100	10	Normal
Skill Swap	Psychic	Status	—	—	10	Normal
Cosmic Power	Psychic	Status	—	—	20	Self

National Pokédex **434** Hoenn Pokédex —

Stunky

Skunk Pokémon

Poison | Dark

HEIGHT: 1'04" WEIGHT: 42.3 lbs.

Same form for ♂ / ♀

Ω It sprays a foul fluid from its rear. Its stench spreads over a mile radius, driving Pokémon away.

α It protects itself by spraying a noxious fluid from its rear. The stench lingers for 24 hours.

ABILITIES
Stench
Aftermath

HIDDEN ABILITY
Keen Eye

EGG GROUPS
Field

STAT GROWTH RATES
HP ■■■
Attack ■■■
Defense ■■
Sp. Atk ■■
Sp. Def ■■
Speed ■■■■

ITEMS SOMETIMES HELD BY WILD POKÉMON
—

EVOLUTION

MAIN WAY TO REGISTER IN THE NATIONAL POKÉDEX

Appears in *Pokémon X* and *Pokémon Y*. Bring it to your game using Link Trade or the GTS.

Damage taken in normal battles

Type		Type	
Normal	×1	Flying	×1
Fire	×1	Psychic	×0
Water	×1	Bug	×1
Grass	×0.5	Rock	×1
Electric	×1	Ghost	×0.5
Ice	×1	Dragon	×1
Fighting	×1	Dark	×0.5
Poison	×0.5	Steel	×1
Ground	×2	Fairy	×1

Damage taken in Inverse battles

Type		Type	
Normal	×1	Flying	×1
Fire	×1	Psychic	×1
Water	×1	Bug	×1
Grass	×2	Rock	×1
Electric	×1	Ghost	×2
Ice	×1	Dragon	×1
Fighting	×1	Dark	×2
Poison	×2	Steel	×1
Ground	×0.5	Fairy	×1

Can be used in
Inverse Battle
Battle Institute
Battle Maison
Random Matchup (Free Battle)
Random Matchup (Others)

LEVEL-UP MOVES

Lv.	Name	Type	Kind	Pow.	Acc.	PP	Range
1	Scratch	Normal	Physical	40	100	35	Normal
1	Focus Energy	Normal	Status	—	—	30	Self
4	Poison Gas	Poison	Status	—	90	40	Many Others
7	Screech	Normal	Status	—	85	40	Normal
10	Fury Swipes	Normal	Physical	18	80	15	Normal
14	Smokescreen	Normal	Status	—	100	20	Normal
18	Feint	Normal	Physical	30	100	10	Normal
22	Slash	Normal	Physical	70	100	20	Normal
27	Toxic	Poison	Status	—	90	10	Normal
32	Acid Spray	Poison	Special	40	100	20	Normal
37	Night Slash	Dark	Physical	70	100	15	Normal
43	Memento	Dark	Status	—	100	10	Normal
46	Belch	Poison	Special	120	90	10	Normal
49	Explosion	Normal	Physical	250	100	5	Adjacent

TM & HM MOVES

No.	Name	Type	Kind	Pow.	Acc.	PP	Range
TM01	Hone Claws	Dark	Status	—	—	15	Self
TM05	Roar	Normal	Status	—	—	20	Normal
TM06	Toxic	Poison	Status	—	90	10	Normal
TM09	Venoshock	Poison	Special	65	100	10	Normal
TM10	Hidden Power	Normal	Special	60	100	15	Normal
TM11	Sunny Day	Fire	Status	—	—	5	Both Sides
TM12	Taunt	Dark	Status	—	100	20	Normal
TM17	Protect	Normal	Status	—	—	10	Self
TM18	Rain Dance	Water	Status	—	—	5	Both Sides
TM21	Frustration	Normal	Physical	—	100	20	Normal
TM27	Return	Normal	Physical	—	100	20	Normal
TM28	Dig	Ground	Physical	80	100	10	Normal
TM30	Shadow Ball	Ghost	Special	80	100	15	Normal
TM32	Double Team	Normal	Status	—	—	15	Self
TM35	Flamethrower	Fire	Special	90	100	15	Normal
TM36	Sludge Bomb	Poison	Special	90	100	10	Normal
TM38	Fire Blast	Fire	Special	110	85	5	Normal
TM41	Torment	Dark	Status	—	100	15	Normal
TM42	Facade	Normal	Physical	70	100	20	Normal
TM44	Rest	Psychic	Status	—	—	10	Self
TM45	Attract	Normal	Status	—	100	15	Normal
TM46	Thief	Dark	Physical	60	100	25	Normal
TM48	Round	Normal	Special	60	100	15	Normal
TM59	Incinerate	Fire	Special	60	100	15	Many Others
TM64	Explosion	Normal	Physical	250	100	5	Adjacent
TM65	Shadow Claw	Ghost	Physical	70	100	15	Normal
TM66	Payback	Dark	Physical	50	100	10	Normal
TM87	Swagger	Normal	Status	—	90	15	Normal
TM88	Sleep Talk	Normal	Status	—	—	10	Self
TM90	Substitute	Normal	Status	—	—	10	Self
TM94	Secret Power	Normal	Physical	70	100	20	Normal
TM95	Snarl	Dark	Special	55	95	15	Many Others
TM97	Dark Pulse	Dark	Special	80	100	15	Normal
TM100	Confide	Normal	Status	—	—	20	Normal
HM01	Cut	Normal	Physical	50	95	30	Normal
HM06	Rock Smash	Fighting	Physical	40	100	15	Normal

MOVES LEARNED IN EXCHANGE FOR BP

Name	Type	Kind	Pow.	Acc.	PP	Range
Foul Play	Dark	Physical	95	100	15	Normal
Iron Tail	Steel	Physical	100	75	15	Normal
Snore	Normal	Special	50	100	15	Normal
Snatch	Dark	Status	—	—	10	Self

MOVES TAUGHT BY PEOPLE

Name	Type	Kind	Pow.	Acc.	PP	Range

EGG MOVES

Name	Type	Kind	Pow.	Acc.	PP	Range
Pursuit	Dark	Physical	40	100	20	Normal
Leer	Normal	Status	—	100	30	Many Others
Smog	Poison	Special	30	70	20	Normal
Double-Edge	Normal	Physical	120	100	15	Normal
Crunch	Dark	Physical	80	100	15	Normal
Scary Face	Normal	Status	—	100	10	Normal
Astonish	Ghost	Physical	30	100	15	Normal
Punishment	Dark	Physical	—	100	5	Normal
Haze	Ice	Status	—	—	30	Both Sides
Iron Tail	Steel	Physical	100	75	15	Normal
Foul Play	Dark	Physical	95	100	15	Normal
Flame Burst	Fire	Special	70	100	15	Normal
Play Rough	Fairy	Physical	90	90	10	Normal

National Pokédex **435** Hoenn Pokédex —

Skuntank

Skunk Pokémon

Poison | Dark

HEIGHT: 3'03" WEIGHT: 83.8 lbs.

Same form for ♂ / ♀

Ω It sprays a vile-smelling fluid from the tip of its tail to attack. Its range is over 160 feet.

α It sprays a stinky fluid from its tail. The fluid smells worse the longer it is allowed to fester.

ABILITIES
Stench
Aftermath

HIDDEN ABILITY
Keen Eye

EGG GROUPS
Field

STAT GROWTH RATES
HP ■■■■
Attack ■■■■■
Defense ■■■
Sp. Atk ■■■
Sp. Def ■■■
Speed ■■■■■

ITEMS SOMETIMES HELD BY WILD POKÉMON
—

EVOLUTION

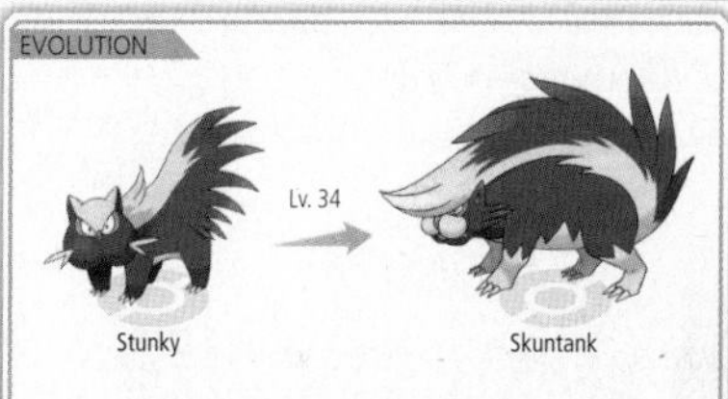

MAIN WAY TO REGISTER IN THE NATIONAL POKÉDEX

Level up a Stunky obtained via Link Trade or the GTS to Lv. 34.

Damage taken in normal battles

Type		Type	
Normal	×1	Flying	×1
Fire	×1	Psychic	×0
Water	×1	Bug	×1
Grass	×0.5	Rock	×1
Electric	×1	Ghost	×0.5
Ice	×1	Dragon	×1
Fighting	×1	Dark	×0.5
Poison	×0.5	Steel	×1
Ground	×2	Fairy	×1

Damage taken in Inverse battles

Type		Type	
Normal	×1	Flying	×1
Fire	×1	Psychic	×1
Water	×1	Bug	×1
Grass	×2	Rock	×1
Electric	×1	Ghost	×2
Ice	×1	Dragon	×1
Fighting	×1	Dark	×2
Poison	×2	Steel	×1
Ground	×0.5	Fairy	×1

Can be used in
Inverse Battle
Battle Institute
Battle Maison
Random Matchup (Free Battle)
Random Matchup (Others)

LEVEL-UP MOVES

Lv.	Name	Type	Kind	Pow.	Acc.	PP	Range
1	Scratch	Normal	Physical	40	100	35	Normal
1	Focus Energy	Normal	Status	—	—	30	Self
1	Poison Gas	Poison	Status	—	90	40	Many Others
4	Poison Gas	Poison	Status	—	90	40	Many Others
7	Screech	Normal	Status	—	85	40	Normal
10	Fury Swipes	Normal	Physical	18	80	15	Normal
14	Smokescreen	Normal	Status	—	100	20	Normal
18	Feint	Normal	Physical	30	100	10	Normal
22	Slash	Normal	Physical	70	100	20	Normal
27	Toxic	Poison	Status	—	90	10	Normal
32	Acid Spray	Poison	Special	40	100	20	Normal
34	Flamethrower	Fire	Special	90	100	15	Normal
41	Night Slash	Dark	Physical	70	100	15	Normal
51	Memento	Dark	Status	—	100	10	Normal
56	Belch	Poison	Special	120	90	10	Normal
61	Explosion	Normal	Physical	250	100	5	Adjacent

TM & HM MOVES

No.	Name	Type	Kind	Pow.	Acc.	PP	Range
TM01	Hone Claws	Dark	Status	—	—	15	Self
TM05	Roar	Normal	Status	—	—	20	Normal
TM06	Toxic	Poison	Status	—	90	10	Normal
TM09	Venoshock	Poison	Special	65	100	10	Normal
TM10	Hidden Power	Normal	Special	60	100	15	Normal
TM11	Sunny Day	Fire	Status	—	—	5	Both Sides
TM12	Taunt	Dark	Status	—	100	20	Normal
TM15	Hyper Beam	Normal	Special	150	90	5	Normal
TM17	Protect	Normal	Status	—	—	10	Self
TM18	Rain Dance	Water	Status	—	—	5	Both Sides
TM21	Frustration	Normal	Physical	—	100	20	Normal
TM27	Return	Normal	Physical	—	100	20	Normal
TM28	Dig	Ground	Physical	80	100	10	Normal
TM30	Shadow Ball	Ghost	Special	80	100	15	Normal
TM32	Double Team	Normal	Status	—	—	15	Self
TM35	Flamethrower	Fire	Special	90	100	15	Normal
TM36	Sludge Bomb	Poison	Special	90	100	10	Normal
TM38	Fire Blast	Fire	Special	110	85	5	Normal
TM41	Torment	Dark	Status	—	100	15	Normal
TM42	Facade	Normal	Physical	70	100	20	Normal
TM44	Rest	Psychic	Status	—	—	10	Self
TM45	Attract	Normal	Status	—	100	15	Normal
TM46	Thief	Dark	Physical	60	100	25	Normal
TM48	Round	Normal	Special	60	100	15	Normal
TM59	Incinerate	Fire	Special	60	100	15	Many Others
TM64	Explosion	Normal	Physical	250	100	5	Adjacent
TM65	Shadow Claw	Ghost	Physical	70	100	15	Normal
TM66	Payback	Dark	Physical	50	100	10	Normal
TM68	Giga Impact	Normal	Physical	150	90	5	Normal
TM84	Poison Jab	Poison	Physical	80	100	20	Normal
TM87	Swagger	Normal	Status	—	90	15	Normal
TM88	Sleep Talk	Normal	Status	—	—	10	Self
TM90	Substitute	Normal	Status	—	—	10	Self
TM94	Secret Power	Normal	Physical	70	100	20	Normal
TM95	Snarl	Dark	Special	55	95	15	Many Others
TM97	Dark Pulse	Dark	Special	80	100	15	Normal
TM100	Confide	Normal	Status	—	—	20	Normal
HM01	Cut	Normal	Physical	50	95	30	Normal
HM04	Strength	Normal	Physical	80	100	15	Normal
HM06	Rock Smash	Fighting	Physical	40	100	15	Normal

MOVES LEARNED IN EXCHANGE FOR BP

Name	Type	Kind	Pow.	Acc.	PP	Range
Foul Play	Dark	Physical	95	100	15	Normal
Iron Tail	Steel	Physical	100	75	15	Normal
Snore	Normal	Special	50	100	15	Normal
Snatch	Dark	Status	—	—	10	Self

MOVES TAUGHT BY PEOPLE

Name	Type	Kind	Pow.	Acc.	PP	Range

National Pokédex **436** Hoenn Pokédex —

Bronzor

Bronze Pokémon

Steel | Psychic

HEIGHT: 1'08" WEIGHT: 133.4 lbs.

Gender unknown

Ω Ancient people believed that the pattern on Bronzor's back contained a mysterious power.

α Implements shaped like it were discovered in ancient tombs. It is unknown if they are related.

ABILITIES
Levitate
Heatproof

HIDDEN ABILITY
Heavy Metal

EGG GROUPS
Mineral

STAT GROWTH RATES
HP
Attack
Defense
Sp. Atk
Sp. Def
Speed

ITEMS SOMETIMES HELD BY WILD POKÉMON
Metal Coat

EVOLUTION

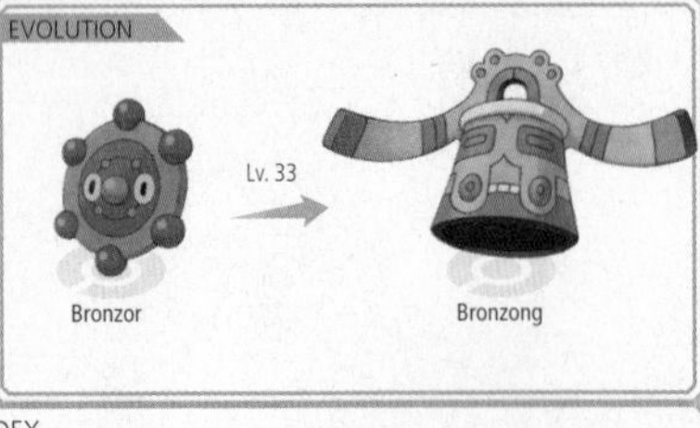

MAIN WAY TO REGISTER IN THE NATIONAL POKÉDEX

Catch on Mt. Pyre (Exterior). Appears as a hidden Pokémon after you battle Groudon or Kyogre.

Damage taken in normal battles

Type		Type	
Normal	×0.5	Flying	×0.5
Fire	×2	Psychic	×0.25
Water	×1	Bug	×1
Grass	×0.5	Rock	×0.5
Electric	×1	Ghost	×2
Ice	×0.5	Dragon	×0.5
Fighting	×1	Dark	×2
Poison	×0	Steel	×0.5
Ground	×2	Fairy	×0.5

Damage taken in Inverse battles

Type		Type	
Normal	×2	Flying	×2
Fire	×0.5	Psychic	×4
Water	×1	Bug	×1
Grass	×2	Rock	×2
Electric	×1	Ghost	×0.5
Ice	×2	Dragon	×2
Fighting	×1	Dark	×0.5
Poison	×2	Steel	×2
Ground	×0.5	Fairy	×2

Can be used in
Inverse Battle
Battle Institute
Battle Maison
Random Matchup (Free Battle)
Random Matchup (Others)

LEVEL-UP MOVES

Lv.	Name	Type	Kind	Pow.	Acc.	PP	Range
1	Tackle	Normal	Physical	50	100	35	Normal
1	Confusion	Psychic	Special	50	100	25	Normal
5	Hypnosis	Psychic	Status	—	60	20	Normal
9	Imprison	Psychic	Status	—	—	10	Self
11	Confuse Ray	Ghost	Status	—	100	10	Normal
15	Psywave	Psychic	Special	—	100	15	Normal
19	Iron Defense	Steel	Status	—	—	15	Self
21	Feint Attack	Dark	Physical	60	—	20	Normal
25	Safeguard	Normal	Status	—	—	25	Your Side
29	Future Sight	Psychic	Special	120	100	10	Normal
31	Metal Sound	Steel	Status	—	85	40	Normal
35	Gyro Ball	Steel	Physical	—	100	5	Normal
39	Extrasensory	Psychic	Special	80	100	20	Normal
41	Payback	Dark	Physical	50	100	10	Normal
45	Heal Block	Psychic	Status	—	100	15	Many Others
49	Heavy Slam	Steel	Physical	—	100	10	Normal

TM & HM MOVES

No.	Name	Type	Kind	Pow.	Acc.	PP	Range
TM03	Psyshock	Psychic	Special	80	100	10	Normal
TM04	Calm Mind	Psychic	Status	—	—	20	Self
TM06	Toxic	Poison	Status	—	90	10	Normal
TM10	Hidden Power	Normal	Special	60	100	15	Normal
TM11	Sunny Day	Fire	Status	—	—	5	Both Sides
TM16	Light Screen	Psychic	Status	—	—	30	Your Side
TM17	Protect	Normal	Status	—	—	10	Self
TM18	Rain Dance	Water	Status	—	—	5	Both Sides
TM20	Safeguard	Normal	Status	—	—	25	Your Side
TM21	Frustration	Normal	Physical	—	100	20	Normal
TM22	Solar Beam	Grass	Special	120	100	10	Normal
TM26	Earthquake	Ground	Physical	100	100	10	Adjacent
TM27	Return	Normal	Physical	—	100	20	Normal
TM29	Psychic	Psychic	Special	90	100	10	Normal
TM30	Shadow Ball	Ghost	Special	80	100	15	Normal
TM32	Double Team	Normal	Status	—	—	15	Self
TM33	Reflect	Psychic	Status	—	—	20	Your Side
TM37	Sandstorm	Rock	Status	—	—	10	Both Sides
TM39	Rock Tomb	Rock	Physical	60	95	15	Normal
TM42	Facade	Normal	Physical	70	100	20	Normal
TM44	Rest	Psychic	Status	—	—	10	Self
TM48	Round	Normal	Special	60	100	15	Normal
TM57	Charge Beam	Electric	Special	50	90	10	Normal
TM66	Payback	Dark	Physical	50	100	10	Normal
TM69	Rock Polish	Rock	Status	—	—	20	Self
TM70	Flash	Normal	Status	—	100	20	Normal
TM74	Gyro Ball	Steel	Physical	—	100	5	Normal
TM77	Psych Up	Normal	Status	—	—	10	Normal
TM78	Bulldoze	Ground	Physical	60	100	20	Adjacent
TM80	Rock Slide	Rock	Physical	75	90	10	Many Others
TM85	Dream Eater	Psychic	Special	100	100	15	Normal
TM86	Grass Knot	Grass	Special	—	100	20	Normal
TM87	Swagger	Normal	Status	—	90	15	Normal
TM88	Sleep Talk	Normal	Status	—	—	10	Self
TM90	Substitute	Normal	Status	—	—	10	Self
TM91	Flash Cannon	Steel	Special	80	100	10	Normal
TM92	Trick Room	Psychic	Status	—	—	5	Both Sides
TM94	Secret Power	Normal	Physical	70	100	20	Normal
TM100	Confide	Normal	Status	—	—	20	Normal

MOVES LEARNED IN EXCHANGE FOR BP

Name	Type	Kind	Pow.	Acc.	PP	Range
Signal Beam	Bug	Special	75	100	15	Normal
Gravity	Psychic	Status	—	—	5	Both Sides
Iron Defense	Steel	Status	—	—	15	Self
Snore	Normal	Special	50	100	15	Normal
Trick	Psychic	Status	—	100	10	Normal
Wonder Room	Psychic	Status	—	—	10	Both Sides
Recycle	Normal	Status	—	—	10	Self
Stealth Rock	Rock	Status	—	—	20	Other Side
Skill Swap	Psychic	Status	—	—	10	Normal

MOVES TAUGHT BY PEOPLE

Name	Type	Kind	Pow.	Acc.	PP	Range

National Pokédex **437** Hoenn Pokédex —

Bronzong

Bronze Bell Pokémon

Steel | Psychic

HEIGHT: 4'03" WEIGHT: 412.3 lbs.

Gender unknown

Ω In ages past, this Pokémon was revered as a bringer of rain. It was found buried in the ground.

α Ancient people believed that petitioning Bronzong for rain was the way to make crops grow.

ABILITIES
Levitate
Heatproof

HIDDEN ABILITY
Heavy Metal

EGG GROUPS
Mineral

STAT GROWTH RATES
HP
Attack
Defense
Sp. Atk
Sp. Def
Speed

ITEMS SOMETIMES HELD BY WILD POKÉMON
—

EVOLUTION

Lv. 33
Bronzor
Bronzong

MAIN WAY TO REGISTER IN THE NATIONAL POKÉDEX

Level up Bronzor to Lv. 33.

Damage taken in normal battles

Type		Type	
Normal	×0.5	Flying	×0.5
Fire	×2	Psychic	×0.25
Water	×1	Bug	×1
Grass	×0.5	Rock	×0.5
Electric	×1	Ghost	×2
Ice	×0.5	Dragon	×0.5
Fighting	×1	Dark	×2
Poison	×0	Steel	×0.5
Ground	×2	Fairy	×0.5

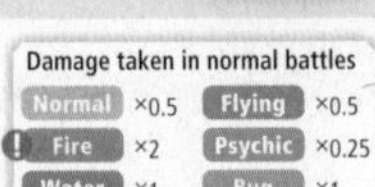

Damage taken in Inverse battles

Type		Type	
Normal	×2	Flying	×2
Fire	×0.5	Psychic	×4
Water	×1	Bug	×1
Grass	×2	Rock	×2
Electric	×1	Ghost	×0.5
Ice	×2	Dragon	×2
Fighting	×1	Dark	×0.5
Poison	×2	Steel	×2
Ground	×0.5	Fairy	×2

Can be used in
Inverse Battle
Battle Institute
Battle Maison
Random Matchup (Free Battle)
Random Matchup (Others)

LEVEL-UP MOVES

Lv.	Name	Type	Kind	Pow.	Acc.	PP	Range
1	Sunny Day	Fire	Status	—	—	5	Both Sides
1	Rain Dance	Water	Status	—	—	5	Both Sides
1	Tackle	Normal	Physical	50	100	35	Normal
1	Confusion	Psychic	Special	50	100	25	Normal
1	Hypnosis	Psychic	Status	—	60	20	Normal
1	Imprison	Psychic	Status	—	—	10	Self
5	Hypnosis	Psychic	Status	—	60	20	Normal
9	Imprison	Psychic	Status	—	—	10	Self
11	Confuse Ray	Ghost	Status	—	100	10	Normal
15	Psywave	Psychic	Special	—	100	15	Normal
19	Iron Defense	Steel	Status	—	—	15	Self
21	Feint Attack	Dark	Physical	60	—	20	Normal
25	Safeguard	Normal	Status	—	—	25	Your Side
29	Future Sight	Psychic	Special	120	100	10	Normal
31	Metal Sound	Steel	Status	—	85	40	Normal
33	Block	Normal	Status	—	—	5	Normal
36	Gyro Ball	Steel	Physical	—	100	5	Normal
42	Extrasensory	Psychic	Special	80	100	20	Normal
46	Payback	Dark	Physical	50	100	10	Normal
52	Heal Block	Psychic	Status	—	100	15	Many Others
58	Heavy Slam	Steel	Physical	—	100	10	Normal

TM & HM MOVES

No.	Name	Type	Kind	Pow.	Acc.	PP	Range
TM03	Psyshock	Psychic	Special	80	100	10	Normal
TM04	Calm Mind	Psychic	Status	—	—	20	Self
TM06	Toxic	Poison	Status	—	90	10	Normal
TM10	Hidden Power	Normal	Special	60	100	15	Normal
TM11	Sunny Day	Fire	Status	—	—	5	Both Sides
TM15	Hyper Beam	Normal	Special	150	90	5	Normal
TM16	Light Screen	Psychic	Status	—	—	30	Your Side
TM17	Protect	Normal	Status	—	—	10	Self
TM18	Rain Dance	Water	Status	—	—	5	Both Sides
TM20	Safeguard	Normal	Status	—	—	25	Your Side
TM21	Frustration	Normal	Physical	—	100	20	Normal
TM22	Solar Beam	Grass	Special	120	100	10	Normal
TM26	Earthquake	Ground	Physical	100	100	10	Adjacent
TM27	Return	Normal	Physical	—	100	20	Normal
TM29	Psychic	Psychic	Special	90	100	10	Normal
TM30	Shadow Ball	Ghost	Special	80	100	15	Normal
TM32	Double Team	Normal	Status	—	—	15	Self
TM33	Reflect	Psychic	Status	—	—	20	Your Side
TM37	Sandstorm	Rock	Status	—	—	10	Both Sides
TM39	Rock Tomb	Rock	Physical	60	95	15	Normal
TM42	Facade	Normal	Physical	70	100	20	Normal
TM44	Rest	Psychic	Status	—	—	10	Self
TM48	Round	Normal	Special	60	100	15	Normal
TM57	Charge Beam	Electric	Special	50	90	10	Normal
TM64	Explosion	Normal	Physical	250	100	5	Adjacent
TM66	Payback	Dark	Physical	50	100	10	Normal
TM68	Giga Impact	Normal	Physical	150	90	5	Normal
TM69	Rock Polish	Rock	Status	—	—	20	Self
TM70	Flash	Normal	Status	—	100	20	Normal
TM74	Gyro Ball	Steel	Physical	—	100	5	Normal
TM77	Psych Up	Normal	Status	—	—	10	Normal
TM78	Bulldoze	Ground	Physical	60	100	20	Adjacent
TM80	Rock Slide	Rock	Physical	75	90	10	Many Others
TM85	Dream Eater	Psychic	Special	100	100	15	Normal
TM86	Grass Knot	Grass	Special	—	100	20	Normal
TM87	Swagger	Normal	Status	—	90	15	Normal
TM88	Sleep Talk	Normal	Status	—	—	10	Self
TM90	Substitute	Normal	Status	—	—	10	Self
TM91	Flash Cannon	Steel	Special	80	100	10	Normal
TM92	Trick Room	Psychic	Status	—	—	5	Both Sides
TM94	Secret Power	Normal	Physical	70	100	20	Normal
TM100	Confide	Normal	Status	—	—	20	Normal
HM04	Strength	Normal	Physical	80	100	15	Normal
HM06	Rock Smash	Fighting	Physical	40	100	15	Normal

MOVES LEARNED IN EXCHANGE FOR BP

Name	Type	Kind	Pow.	Acc.	PP	Range
Signal Beam	Bug	Special	75	100	15	Normal
Iron Head	Steel	Physical	80	100	15	Normal
Block	Normal	Status	—	—	5	Normal
Gravity	Psychic	Status	—	—	5	Both Sides
Iron Defense	Steel	Status	—	—	15	Self
Zen Headbutt	Psychic	Physical	80	90	15	Normal
Snore	Normal	Special	50	100	15	Normal
Trick	Psychic	Status	—	100	10	Normal
Wonder Room	Psychic	Status	—	—	10	Both Sides
Recycle	Normal	Status	—	—	10	Self
Stealth Rock	Rock	Status	—	—	20	Other Side
Skill Swap	Psychic	Status	—	—	10	Normal

MOVES TAUGHT BY PEOPLE

Name	Type	Kind	Pow.	Acc.	PP	Range

National Pokédex **438** Hoenn Pokédex —

Bonsly

Bonsai Pokémon

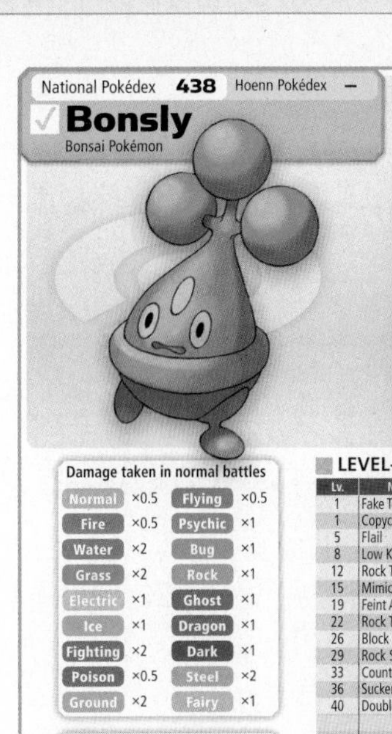

Rock

HEIGHT: 1'08" WEIGHT: 33.1 lbs.

Same form for ♂ / ♀

Ω It prefers arid environments. It leaks water from its eyes to adjust its body's fluid levels.

α It prefers an arid atmosphere. It leaks water that looks like tears when adjusting its moisture level.

ABILITIES
Sturdy
Rock Head

HIDDEN ABILITY
Rattled

EGG GROUPS
No Eggs Discovered

STAT GROWTH RATES
HP
Attack
Defense
Sp. Atk
Sp. Def
Speed

ITEMS SOMETIMES HELD BY WILD POKÉMON
—

EVOLUTION

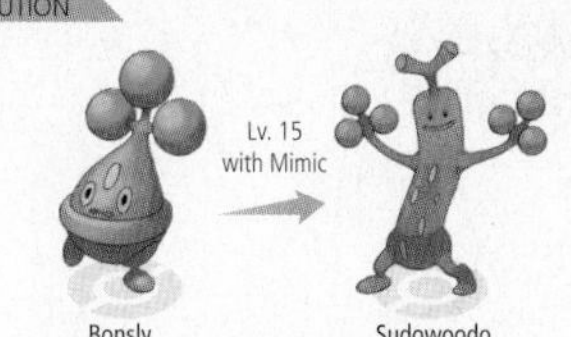

MAIN WAY TO REGISTER IN THE NATIONAL POKÉDEX

Leave a Sudowoodo obtained via Link Trade or the GTS at a Pokémon Day Care while holding a Rock Incense, then hatch the Pokémon Egg that is found.

Damage taken in normal battles

Normal	×0.5	Flying	×0.5
Fire	×0.5	Psychic	×1
Water	×2	Bug	×1
Grass	×2	Rock	×1
Electric	×1	Ghost	×1
Ice	×1	Dragon	×1
Fighting	×2	Dark	×1
Poison	×0.5	Steel	×2
Ground	×2	Fairy	×1

Damage taken in Inverse battles

Normal	×2	Flying	×2
Fire	×2	Psychic	×1
Water	×0.5	Bug	×1
Grass	×0.5	Rock	×1
Electric	×1	Ghost	×1
Ice	×1	Dragon	×1
Fighting	×0.5	Dark	×1
Poison	×2	Steel	×0.5
Ground	×0.5	Fairy	×1

Can be used in
Inverse Battle
Battle Institute
Battle Maison
Random Matchup (Free Battle)
Random Matchup (Others)

LEVEL-UP MOVES

Lv.	Name	Type	Kind	Pow.	Acc.	PP	Range
1	Fake Tears	Dark	Status	—	100	20	Normal
1	Copycat	Normal	Status	—	—	20	Self
5	Flail	Normal	Physical	—	100	15	Normal
8	Low Kick	Fighting	Physical	—	100	20	Normal
12	Rock Throw	Rock	Physical	50	90	15	Normal
15	Mimic	Normal	Status	—	—	10	Normal
19	Feint Attack	Dark	Physical	60	—	20	Normal
22	Rock Tomb	Rock	Physical	60	95	15	Normal
26	Block	Normal	Status	—	—	5	Normal
29	Rock Slide	Rock	Physical	75	90	10	Many Others
33	Counter	Fighting	Physical	—	100	20	Varies
36	Sucker Punch	Dark	Physical	80	100	5	Normal
40	Double-Edge	Normal	Physical	120	100	15	Normal

TM & HM MOVES

No.	Name	Type	Kind	Pow.	Acc.	PP	Range
TM04	Calm Mind	Psychic	Status	—	—	20	Self
TM06	Toxic	Poison	Status	—	90	10	Normal
TM10	Hidden Power	Normal	Special	60	100	15	Normal
TM11	Sunny Day	Fire	Status	—	—	5	Both Sides
TM17	Protect	Normal	Status	—	—	10	Self
TM21	Frustration	Normal	Physical	—	100	20	Normal
TM23	Smack Down	Rock	Physical	50	100	15	Normal
TM27	Return	Normal	Physical	—	100	20	Normal
TM28	Dig	Ground	Physical	80	100	10	Normal
TM31	Brick Break	Fighting	Physical	75	100	15	Normal
TM32	Double Team	Normal	Status	—	—	15	Self
TM37	Sandstorm	Rock	Status	—	—	10	Both Sides
TM39	Rock Tomb	Rock	Physical	60	95	15	Normal
TM42	Facade	Normal	Physical	70	100	20	Normal
TM44	Rest	Psychic	Status	—	—	10	Self
TM45	Attract	Normal	Status	—	100	15	Normal
TM46	Thief	Dark	Physical	60	100	25	Normal
TM48	Round	Normal	Special	60	100	15	Normal
TM64	Explosion	Normal	Physical	250	100	5	Adjacent
TM69	Rock Polish	Rock	Status	—	—	20	Self
TM77	Psych Up	Normal	Status	—	—	10	Normal
TM80	Rock Slide	Rock	Physical	75	90	10	Many Others
TM87	Swagger	Normal	Status	—	90	15	Normal
TM88	Sleep Talk	Normal	Status	—	—	10	Self
TM90	Substitute	Normal	Status	—	—	10	Self
TM94	Secret Power	Normal	Physical	70	100	20	Normal
TM96	Nature Power	Normal	Status	—	—	20	Normal
TM100	Confide	Normal	Status	—	—	20	Normal

MOVES LEARNED IN EXCHANGE FOR BP

Name	Type	Kind	Pow.	Acc.	PP	Range
Covet	Normal	Physical	60	100	25	Normal
Low Kick	Fighting	Physical	—	100	20	Normal
Uproar	Normal	Special	90	100	10	1 Random
Block	Normal	Status	—	—	5	Normal
Earth Power	Ground	Special	90	100	10	Normal
Foul Play	Dark	Physical	95	100	15	Normal
Snore	Normal	Special	50	100	15	Normal
Role Play	Psychic	Status	—	—	10	Normal
After You	Normal	Status	—	—	15	Normal
Helping Hand	Normal	Status	—	—	20	1 Ally
Stealth Rock	Rock	Status	—	—	20	Other Side

MOVES TAUGHT BY PEOPLE

Name	Type	Kind	Pow.	Acc.	PP	Range

EGG MOVES

Name	Type	Kind	Pow.	Acc.	PP	Range
Self-Destruct	Normal	Physical	200	100	5	Adjacent
Headbutt	Normal	Physical	70	100	15	Normal
Harden	Normal	Status	—	—	30	Self
Defense Curl	Normal	Status	—	—	40	Self
Rollout	Rock	Physical	30	90	20	Normal
Sand Tomb	Ground	Physical	35	85	15	Normal
Stealth Rock	Rock	Status	—	—	20	Other Side
Curse	Ghost	Status	—	—	10	Varies
Endure	Normal	Status	—	—	10	Self

National Pokédex **439** Hoenn Pokédex —

Mime Jr.

Mime Pokémon

Psychic Fairy

HEIGHT: 2'00" WEIGHT: 28.7 lbs.

Same form for ♂ / ♀

Ω In an attempt to confuse its enemy, it mimics the enemy's movements. Then it wastes no time in making itself scarce!

α It habitually mimics foes. Once mimicked, the foe cannot take its eyes off this Pokémon.

ABILITIES
Soundproof
Filter

HIDDEN ABILITY
Technician

EGG GROUPS
No Eggs Discovered

STAT GROWTH RATES
HP
Attack
Defense
Sp. Atk
Sp. Def
Speed

ITEMS SOMETIMES HELD BY WILD POKÉMON
—

EVOLUTION

MAIN WAY TO REGISTER IN THE NATIONAL POKÉDEX

Appears in *Pokémon X* and *Pokémon Y*. Bring it to your game using Link Trade or the GTS.

Damage taken in normal battles

Normal	×1	Flying	×1
Fire	×1	Psychic	×0.5
Water	×1	Bug	×1
Grass	×1	Rock	×1
Electric	×1	! Ghost	×2
Ice	×1	Dragon	×0
Fighting	×0.25	Dark	×1
! Poison	×2	! Steel	×2
Ground	×1	Fairy	×1

Damage taken in Inverse battles

Normal	×1	Flying	×1
Fire	×1	! Psychic	×2
Water	×1	Bug	×1
Grass	×1	Rock	×1
Electric	×1	Ghost	×0.5
Ice	×1	! Dragon	×2
! Fighting	×4	Dark	×1
Poison	×0.5	Steel	×0.5
Ground	×1	Fairy	×1

Can be used in
Inverse Battle
Battle Institute
Battle Maison
Random Matchup (Free Battle)
Random Matchup (Others)

LEVEL-UP MOVES

Lv.	Name	Type	Kind	Pow.	Acc.	PP	Range
1	Tickle	Normal	Status	—	100	20	Normal
1	Barrier	Psychic	Status	—	—	20	Self
1	Confusion	Psychic	Special	50	100	25	Normal
4	Copycat	Normal	Status	—	—	20	Self
8	Meditate	Psychic	Status	—	—	40	Self
11	Double Slap	Normal	Physical	15	85	10	Normal
15	Mimic	Normal	Status	—	—	10	Normal
18	Encore	Normal	Status	—	100	5	Normal
22	Light Screen	Psychic	Status	—	—	30	Your Side
22	Reflect	Psychic	Status	—	—	20	Your Side
25	Psybeam	Psychic	Special	65	100	20	Normal
29	Substitute	Normal	Status	—	—	10	Self
32	Recycle	Normal	Status	—	—	10	Self
36	Trick	Psychic	Status	—	100	10	Normal
39	Psychic	Psychic	Special	90	100	10	Normal
43	Role Play	Psychic	Status	—	—	10	Normal
46	Baton Pass	Normal	Status	—	—	40	Self
50	Safeguard	Normal	Status	—	—	25	Your Side

TM & HM MOVES

No.	Name	Type	Kind	Pow.	Acc.	PP	Range
TM03	Psyshock	Psychic	Special	80	100	10	Normal
TM04	Calm Mind	Psychic	Status	—	—	20	Self
TM06	Toxic	Poison	Status	—	90	10	Normal
TM10	Hidden Power	Normal	Special	60	100	15	Normal
TM11	Sunny Day	Fire	Status	—	—	5	Both Sides
TM12	Taunt	Dark	Status	—	100	20	Normal
TM16	Light Screen	Psychic	Status	—	—	30	Your Side
TM17	Protect	Normal	Status	—	—	10	Self
TM18	Rain Dance	Water	Status	—	—	5	Both Sides
TM20	Safeguard	Normal	Status	—	—	25	Your Side
TM21	Frustration	Normal	Physical	—	100	20	Normal
TM22	Solar Beam	Grass	Special	120	100	10	Normal
TM24	Thunderbolt	Electric	Special	90	100	15	Normal
TM25	Thunder	Electric	Special	110	70	10	Normal
TM27	Return	Normal	Physical	—	100	20	Normal
TM29	Psychic	Psychic	Special	90	100	10	Normal
TM30	Shadow Ball	Ghost	Special	80	100	15	Normal
TM31	Brick Break	Fighting	Physical	75	100	15	Normal
TM32	Double Team	Normal	Status	—	—	15	Self
TM33	Reflect	Psychic	Status	—	—	20	Your Side
TM41	Torment	Dark	Status	—	100	15	Normal
TM42	Facade	Normal	Physical	70	100	20	Normal
TM44	Rest	Psychic	Status	—	—	10	Self
TM45	Attract	Normal	Status	—	100	15	Normal
TM46	Thief	Dark	Physical	60	100	25	Normal
TM48	Round	Normal	Special	60	100	15	Normal
TM56	Fling	Dark	Physical	—	100	10	Normal
TM57	Charge Beam	Electric	Special	50	90	10	Normal
TM70	Flash	Normal	Status	—	100	20	Normal
TM73	Thunder Wave	Electric	Status	—	100	20	Normal
TM77	Psych Up	Normal	Status	—	—	10	Normal
TM83	Infestation	Bug	Special	20	100	20	Normal
TM85	Dream Eater	Psychic	Special	100	100	15	Normal
TM86	Grass Knot	Grass	Special	—	100	20	Normal
TM87	Swagger	Normal	Status	—	90	15	Normal
TM88	Sleep Talk	Normal	Status	—	—	10	Self
TM90	Substitute	Normal	Status	—	—	10	Self
TM92	Trick Room	Psychic	Status	—	—	5	Both Sides
TM94	Secret Power	Normal	Physical	70	100	20	Normal
TM100	Confide	Normal	Status	—	—	20	Normal

MOVES LEARNED IN EXCHANGE FOR BP

Name	Type	Kind	Pow.	Acc.	PP	Range
Covet	Normal	Physical	60	100	25	Normal
Signal Beam	Bug	Special	75	100	15	Normal
Uproar	Normal	Special	90	100	10	1 Random
Magic Coat	Psychic	Status	—	—	15	Self
Icy Wind	Ice	Special	55	95	15	Many Others
Snore	Normal	Special	50	100	15	Normal
Role Play	Psychic	Status	—	—	10	Normal
Drain Punch	Fighting	Physical	75	100	10	Normal
Focus Punch	Fighting	Physical	150	100	20	Normal
Shock Wave	Electric	Special	60	—	20	Normal
Helping Hand	Normal	Status	—	—	20	1 Ally
Trick	Psychic	Status	—	100	10	Normal
Magic Room	Psychic	Status	—	—	10	Both Sides
Wonder Room	Psychic	Status	—	—	10	Both Sides
Recycle	Normal	Status	—	—	10	Self
Snatch	Dark	Status	—	—	10	Self
Skill Swap	Psychic	Status	—	—	10	Normal

MOVES TAUGHT BY PEOPLE

Name	Type	Kind	Pow.	Acc.	PP	Range

EGG MOVES

Name	Type	Kind	Pow.	Acc.	PP	Range
Future Sight	Psychic	Special	120	100	10	Normal
Hypnosis	Psychic	Status	—	60	20	Normal
Mimic	Normal	Status	—	—	10	Normal
Fake Out	Normal	Physical	40	100	10	Normal
Trick	Psychic	Status	—	100	10	Normal
Confuse Ray	Ghost	Status	—	100	10	Normal
Wake-Up Slap	Fighting	Physical	70	100	10	Normal
Teeter Dance	Normal	Status	—	100	20	Adjacent
Healing Wish	Psychic	Status	—	—	10	Self
Charm	Fairy	Status	—	100	20	Normal
Nasty Plot	Dark	Status	—	—	20	Self
Power Split	Psychic	Status	—	—	10	Normal
Magic Room	Psychic	Status	—	—	10	Both Sides
Icy Wind	Ice	Special	55	95	15	Many Others

National Pokédex **440** Hoenn Pokédex —

Happiny

Playhouse Pokémon

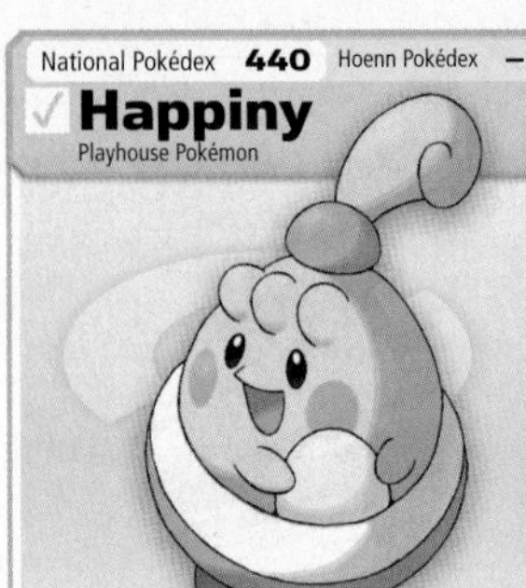

Normal

HEIGHT: 2'00" WEIGHT: 53.8 lbs.

♀ only

Ω It carries a round, egg-shaped rock in its belly pouch and gives the rock to its friends.

α It carefully carries a round, white rock that it thinks is an egg. It's bothered by how curly its hair looks.

ABILITIES
Natural Cure
Serene Grace

HIDDEN ABILITY
Friend Guard

EGG GROUPS
No Eggs Discovered

STAT GROWTH RATES

Stat	Rate
HP	■■■■
Attack	■
Defense	■
Sp. Atk	■
Sp. Def	■■■
Speed	■■

ITEMS SOMETIMES HELD BY WILD POKÉMON
Oval Stone / Lucky Egg

EVOLUTION

MAIN WAY TO REGISTER IN THE NATIONAL POKÉDEX

Catch in Mirage Forest 6.

Damage taken in normal battles

Normal	×1	Flying	×1
Fire	×1	Psychic	×1
Water	×1	Bug	×1
Grass	×1	Rock	×1
Electric	×1	Ghost	×0
Ice	×1	Dragon	×1
Fighting	×2	Dark	×1
Poison	×1	Steel	×1
Ground	×1	Fairy	×1

Damage taken in Inverse battles

Normal	×1	Flying	×1
Fire	×1	Psychic	×1
Water	×1	Bug	×1
Grass	×1	Rock	×1
Electric	×1	Ghost	×2
Ice	×1	Dragon	×1
Fighting	×0.5	Dark	×1
Poison	×1	Steel	×1
Ground	×1	Fairy	×1

Can be used in
Inverse Battle
Battle Institute
Battle Maison
Random Matchup (Free Battle)
Random Matchup (Others)

LEVEL-UP MOVES

Lv.	Name	Type	Kind	Pow.	Acc.	PP	Range
1	Pound	Normal	Physical	40	100	35	Normal
1	Charm	Fairy	Status	—	100	20	Normal
5	Copycat	Normal	Status	—	—	20	Self
9	Refresh	Normal	Status	—	—	20	Self
12	Sweet Kiss	Fairy	Status	—	75	10	Normal

TM & HM MOVES

No.	Name	Type	Kind	Pow.	Acc.	PP	Range
TM06	Toxic	Poison	Status	—	90	10	Normal
TM07	Hail	Ice	Status	—	—	10	Both Sides
TM10	Hidden Power	Normal	Special	60	100	15	Normal
TM11	Sunny Day	Fire	Status	—	—	5	Both Sides
TM16	Light Screen	Psychic	Status	—	—	30	Your Side
TM17	Protect	Normal	Status	—	—	10	Self
TM18	Rain Dance	Water	Status	—	—	5	Both Sides
TM20	Safeguard	Normal	Status	—	—	25	Your Side
TM21	Frustration	Normal	Physical	—	100	20	Normal
TM22	Solar Beam	Grass	Special	120	100	10	Normal
TM27	Return	Normal	Physical	—	100	20	Normal
TM29	Psychic	Psychic	Special	90	100	10	Normal
TM30	Shadow Ball	Ghost	Special	80	100	15	Normal
TM32	Double Team	Normal	Status	—	—	15	Self
TM35	Flamethrower	Fire	Special	90	100	15	Normal
TM38	Fire Blast	Fire	Special	110	85	5	Normal
TM42	Facade	Normal	Physical	70	100	20	Normal
TM44	Rest	Psychic	Status	—	—	10	Self
TM45	Attract	Normal	Status	—	100	15	Normal
TM48	Round	Normal	Special	60	100	15	Normal
TM49	Echoed Voice	Normal	Special	40	100	15	Normal
TM56	Fling	Dark	Physical	—	100	10	Normal
TM59	Incinerate	Fire	Special	60	100	15	Many Others
TM70	Flash	Normal	Status	—	100	20	Normal
TM73	Thunder Wave	Electric	Status	—	100	20	Normal
TM77	Psych Up	Normal	Status	—	—	10	Normal
TM85	Dream Eater	Psychic	Special	100	100	15	Normal
TM86	Grass Knot	Grass	Special	—	100	20	Normal
TM87	Swagger	Normal	Status	—	90	15	Normal
TM88	Sleep Talk	Normal	Status	—	—	10	Self
TM90	Substitute	Normal	Status	—	—	10	Self
TM94	Secret Power	Normal	Physical	70	100	20	Normal
TM100	Confide	Normal	Status	—	—	20	Normal

MOVES LEARNED IN EXCHANGE FOR BP

Name	Type	Kind	Pow.	Acc.	PP	Range
Covet	Normal	Physical	60	100	25	Normal
Uproar	Normal	Special	90	100	10	1 Random
Gravity	Psychic	Status	—	—	5	Both Sides
Last Resort	Normal	Physical	140	100	5	Normal
Icy Wind	Ice	Special	55	95	15	Many Others
Zen Headbutt	Psychic	Physical	80	90	15	Normal
Hyper Voice	Normal	Special	90	100	10	Many Others
Snore	Normal	Special	50	100	15	Normal
Heal Bell	Normal	Status	—	—	5	Your Party
Drain Punch	Fighting	Physical	75	100	10	Normal
Shock Wave	Electric	Special	60	—	20	Normal
Water Pulse	Water	Special	60	100	20	Normal
Helping Hand	Normal	Status	—	—	20	1 Ally
Endeavor	Normal	Physical	—	100	5	Normal
Recycle	Normal	Status	—	—	10	Self

MOVES TAUGHT BY PEOPLE

Name	Type	Kind	Pow.	Acc.	PP	Range

EGG MOVES

Name	Type	Kind	Pow.	Acc.	PP	Range
Present	Normal	Physical	—	90	15	Normal
Metronome	Normal	Status	—	—	10	Self
Heal Bell	Normal	Status	—	—	5	Your Party
Aromatherapy	Grass	Status	—	—	5	Your Party
Counter	Fighting	Physical	—	100	20	Varies
Helping Hand	Normal	Status	—	—	20	1 Ally
Gravity	Psychic	Status	—	—	5	Both Sides
Last Resort	Normal	Physical	140	100	5	Normal
Mud Bomb	Ground	Special	65	85	10	Normal
Natural Gift	Normal	Physical	—	100	15	Normal
Endure	Normal	Status	—	—	10	Self

National Pokédex **441** Hoenn Pokédex —

Chatot

Music Note Pokémon

Normal Flying

HEIGHT: 1'08" WEIGHT: 4.2 lbs.

Same form for ♂ / ♀

Ω It mimics the cries of other Pokémon to trick them into thinking it's one of them. This way they won't attack it.

α It can learn and speak human words. If they gather, they all learn the same saying.

ABILITIES
Keen Eye
Tangled Feet

HIDDEN ABILITY
Big Pecks

EGG GROUPS
Flying

STAT GROWTH RATES

Stat	Rate
HP	■■■
Attack	■■■
Defense	■■
Sp. Atk	■■■■■
Sp. Def	■■
Speed	■■■■■

ITEMS SOMETIMES HELD BY WILD POKÉMON
Metronome

EVOLUTION

Does not evolve

MAIN WAY TO REGISTER IN THE NATIONAL POKÉDEX

Catch on Route 103. Appears as a hidden Pokémon after you battle Groudon or Kyogre.

Damage taken in normal battles

Normal	×1	Flying	×1
Fire	×1	Psychic	×1
Water	×1	Bug	×0.5
Grass	×0.5	Rock	×2
Electric	×2	Ghost	×0
Ice	×2	Dragon	×1
Fighting	×1	Dark	×1
Poison	×1	Steel	×1
Ground	×0	Fairy	×1

Damage taken in Inverse battles

Normal	×1	Flying	×1
Fire	×1	Psychic	×1
Water	×1	Bug	×2
Grass	×2	Rock	×0.5
Electric	×0.5	Ghost	×2
Ice	×0.5	Dragon	×1
Fighting	×1	Dark	×1
Poison	×1	Steel	×1
Ground	×2	Fairy	×1

Can be used in
Inverse Battle
Battle Institute
Battle Maison
Random Matchup (Free Battle)
Random Matchup (Others)

LEVEL-UP MOVES

Lv.	Name	Type	Kind	Pow.	Acc.	PP	Range
1	Hyper Voice	Normal	Special	90	100	10	Many Others
1	Chatter	Flying	Special	65	100	20	Normal
1	Confide	Normal	Status	—	—	20	Normal
1	Taunt	Dark	Status	—	100	20	Normal
1	Peck	Flying	Physical	35	100	35	Normal
5	Growl	Normal	Status	—	100	40	Many Others
9	Mirror Move	Flying	Status	—	—	20	Normal
13	Sing	Normal	Status	—	55	15	Normal
17	Fury Attack	Normal	Physical	15	85	20	Normal
21	Chatter	Flying	Special	65	100	20	Normal
25	Taunt	Dark	Status	—	100	20	Normal
29	Round	Normal	Special	60	100	15	Normal
33	Mimic	Normal	Status	—	—	10	Normal
37	Echoed Voice	Normal	Special	40	100	15	Normal
41	Roost	Flying	Status	—	—	10	Self
45	Uproar	Normal	Special	90	100	10	1 Random
49	Synchronoise	Psychic	Special	120	100	10	Adjacent
50	Feather Dance	Flying	Status	—	100	15	Normal
57	Hyper Voice	Normal	Special	90	100	10	Many Others

TM & HM MOVES

No.	Name	Type	Kind	Pow.	Acc.	PP	Range
TM06	Toxic	Poison	Status	—	90	10	Normal
TM10	Hidden Power	Normal	Special	60	100	15	Normal
TM11	Sunny Day	Fire	Status	—	—	5	Both Sides
TM12	Taunt	Dark	Status	—	100	20	Normal
TM17	Protect	Normal	Status	—	—	10	Self
TM18	Rain Dance	Water	Status	—	—	5	Both Sides
TM19	Roost	Flying	Status	—	—	10	Self
TM21	Frustration	Normal	Physical	—	100	20	Normal
TM27	Return	Normal	Physical	—	100	20	Normal
TM32	Double Team	Normal	Status	—	—	15	Self
TM40	Aerial Ace	Flying	Physical	60	—	20	Normal
TM41	Torment	Dark	Status	—	100	15	Normal
TM42	Facade	Normal	Physical	70	100	20	Normal
TM44	Rest	Psychic	Status	—	—	10	Self
TM45	Attract	Normal	Status	—	100	15	Normal
TM46	Thief	Dark	Physical	60	100	25	Normal
TM48	Round	Normal	Special	60	100	15	Normal
TM49	Echoed Voice	Normal	Special	40	100	15	Normal
TM51	Steel Wing	Steel	Physical	70	90	25	Normal
TM87	Swagger	Normal	Status	—	90	15	Normal
TM88	Sleep Talk	Normal	Status	—	—	10	Self
TM89	U-turn	Bug	Physical	70	100	20	Normal
TM90	Substitute	Normal	Status	—	—	10	Self
TM94	Secret Power	Normal	Physical	70	100	20	Normal
TM100	Confide	Normal	Status	—	—	20	Normal
HM02	Fly	Flying	Physical	90	95	15	Normal

MOVES LEARNED IN EXCHANGE FOR BP

Name	Type	Kind	Pow.	Acc.	PP	Range
Uproar	Normal	Special	90	100	10	1 Random
Hyper Voice	Normal	Special	90	100	10	Many Others
Snore	Normal	Special	50	100	15	Normal
Heat Wave	Fire	Special	95	90	10	Many Others
Role Play	Psychic	Status	—	—	10	Normal
Tailwind	Flying	Status	—	—	15	Your Side
Sky Attack	Flying	Physical	140	90	5	Normal

MOVES TAUGHT BY PEOPLE

Name	Type	Kind	Pow.	Acc.	PP	Range

EGG MOVES

Name	Type	Kind	Pow.	Acc.	PP	Range
Encore	Normal	Status	—	100	5	Normal
Night Shade	Ghost	Special	—	100	15	Normal
Agility	Psychic	Status	—	—	30	Self
Nasty Plot	Dark	Status	—	—	20	Self
Supersonic	Normal	Status	—	55	20	Normal
Steel Wing	Steel	Physical	70	90	25	Normal
Sleep Talk	Normal	Status	—	—	10	Self
Defog	Flying	Status	—	—	15	Normal
Air Cutter	Flying	Special	60	95	25	Many Others
Boomburst	Normal	Special	140	100	10	Adjacent

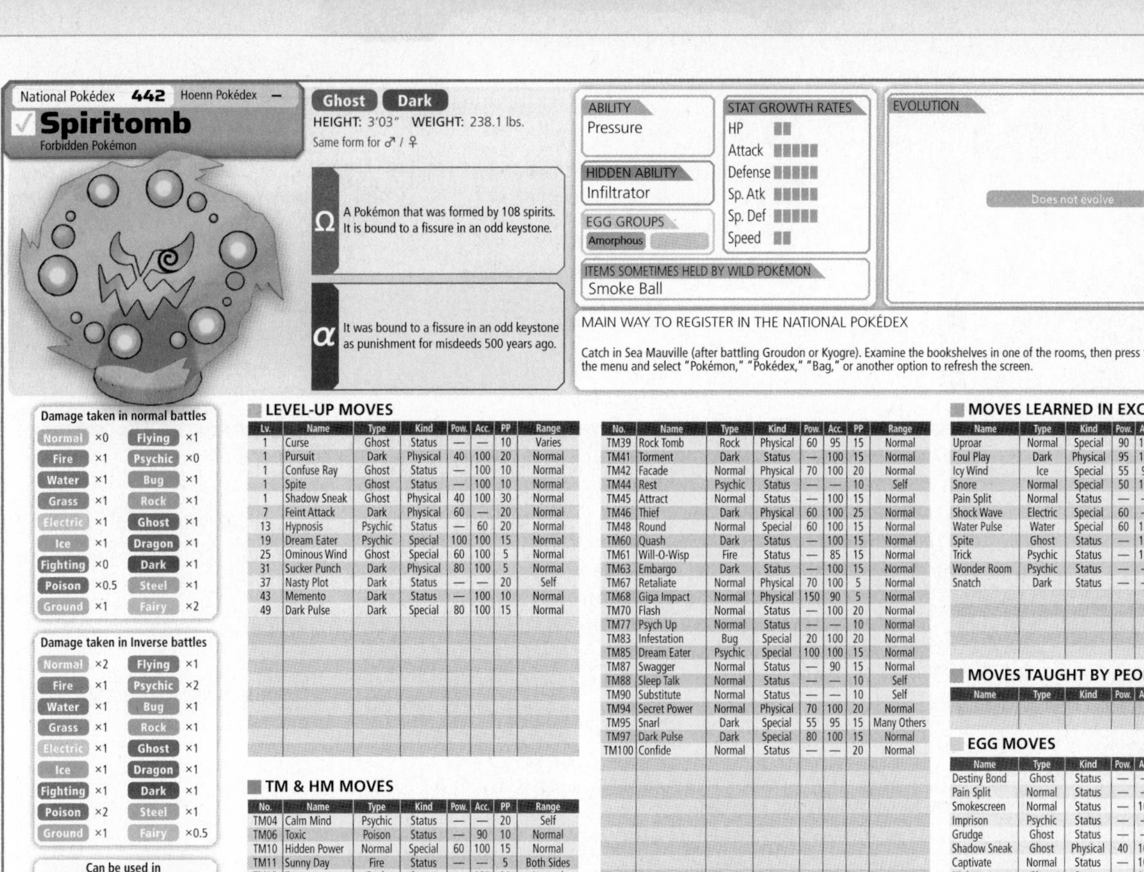

National Pokédex **442** Hoenn Pokédex —

Spiritomb

Forbidden Pokémon

Ghost **Dark**

HEIGHT: 3'03" WEIGHT: 238.1 lbs.

Same form for ♂ / ♀

Ω A Pokémon that was formed by 108 spirits. It is bound to a fissure in an odd keystone.

α It was bound to a fissure in an odd keystone as punishment for misdeeds 500 years ago.

ABILITY: Pressure

HIDDEN ABILITY: Infiltrator

EGG GROUPS: Amorphous

STAT GROWTH RATES: HP, Attack, Defense, Sp. Atk, Sp. Def, Speed

ITEMS SOMETIMES HELD BY WILD POKÉMON: Smoke Ball

EVOLUTION: Does not evolve

MAIN WAY TO REGISTER IN THE NATIONAL POKÉDEX

Catch in Sea Mauville (after battling Groudon or Kyogre). Examine the bookshelves in one of the rooms, then press the X Button to open the menu and select "Pokémon," "Pokédex," "Bag," or another option to refresh the screen.

Damage taken in normal battles

Type		Type	
Normal	×0	Flying	×1
Fire	×1	Psychic	×0
Water	×1	Bug	×1
Grass	×1	Rock	×1
Electric	×1	Ghost	×1
Ice	×1	Dragon	×1
Fighting	×0	Dark	×1
Poison	×0.5	Steel	×1
Ground	×1	Fairy	×2

Damage taken in Inverse battles

Type		Type	
Normal	×2	Flying	×1
Fire	×1	Psychic	×2
Water	×1	Bug	×1
Grass	×1	Rock	×1
Electric	×1	Ghost	×1
Ice	×1	Dragon	×1
Fighting	×1	Dark	×1
Poison	×2	Steel	×1
Ground	×1	Fairy	×0.5

Can be used in

Inverse Battle
Battle Institute
Battle Maison
Random Matchup (Free Battle)
Random Matchup (Others)

LEVEL-UP MOVES

Lv.	Name	Type	Kind	Pow.	Acc.	PP	Range
1	Curse	Ghost	Status	—	—	10	Varies
1	Pursuit	Dark	Physical	40	100	20	Normal
1	Confuse Ray	Ghost	Status	—	100	10	Normal
1	Spite	Ghost	Status	—	100	10	Normal
1	Shadow Sneak	Ghost	Physical	40	100	30	Normal
7	Feint Attack	Dark	Physical	60	—	20	Normal
13	Hypnosis	Psychic	Status	—	60	20	Normal
19	Dream Eater	Psychic	Special	100	100	15	Normal
25	Ominous Wind	Ghost	Special	60	100	5	Normal
31	Sucker Punch	Dark	Physical	80	100	5	Normal
37	Nasty Plot	Dark	Status	—	—	20	Self
43	Memento	Dark	Status	—	100	10	Normal
49	Dark Pulse	Dark	Special	80	100	15	Normal

TM & HM MOVES

No.	Name	Type	Kind	Pow.	Acc.	PP	Range
TM04	Calm Mind	Psychic	Status	—	—	20	Self
TM06	Toxic	Poison	Status	—	90	10	Normal
TM10	Hidden Power	Normal	Special	60	100	15	Normal
TM11	Sunny Day	Fire	Status	—	—	5	Both Sides
TM12	Taunt	Dark	Status	—	100	20	Normal
TM15	Hyper Beam	Normal	Special	150	90	5	Normal
TM17	Protect	Normal	Status	—	—	10	Self
TM18	Rain Dance	Water	Status	—	—	5	Both Sides
TM21	Frustration	Normal	Physical	—	100	20	Normal
TM27	Return	Normal	Physical	—	100	20	Normal
TM29	Psychic	Psychic	Special	90	100	10	Normal
TM30	Shadow Ball	Ghost	Special	80	100	15	Normal
TM32	Double Team	Normal	Status	—	—	15	Self
TM39	Rock Tomb	Rock	Physical	60	95	15	Normal
TM41	Torment	Dark	Status	—	100	15	Normal
TM42	Facade	Normal	Physical	70	100	20	Normal
TM44	Rest	Psychic	Status	—	—	10	Self
TM45	Attract	Normal	Status	—	100	15	Normal
TM46	Thief	Dark	Physical	60	100	25	Normal
TM48	Round	Normal	Special	60	100	15	Normal
TM60	Quash	Dark	Status	—	100	15	Normal
TM61	Will-O-Wisp	Fire	Status	—	85	15	Normal
TM63	Embargo	Dark	Status	—	100	15	Normal
TM67	Retaliate	Normal	Physical	70	100	5	Normal
TM68	Giga Impact	Normal	Physical	150	90	5	Normal
TM70	Flash	Normal	Status	—	100	20	Normal
TM77	Psych Up	Normal	Status	—	—	10	Normal
TM83	Infestation	Bug	Special	20	100	20	Normal
TM85	Dream Eater	Psychic	Special	100	100	15	Normal
TM87	Swagger	Normal	Status	—	90	15	Normal
TM88	Sleep Talk	Normal	Status	—	—	10	Self
TM90	Substitute	Normal	Status	—	—	10	Self
TM94	Secret Power	Normal	Physical	70	100	20	Normal
TM95	Snarl	Dark	Special	55	95	15	Many Others
TM97	Dark Pulse	Dark	Special	80	100	15	Normal
TM100	Confide	Normal	Status	—	—	20	Normal

MOVES LEARNED IN EXCHANGE FOR BP

Name	Type	Kind	Pow.	Acc.	PP	Range
Uproar	Normal	Special	90	100	10	1 Random
Foul Play	Dark	Physical	95	100	15	Normal
Icy Wind	Ice	Special	55	95	15	Many Others
Snore	Normal	Special	50	100	15	Normal
Pain Split	Normal	Status	—	—	20	Normal
Shock Wave	Electric	Special	60	—	20	Normal
Water Pulse	Water	Special	60	100	20	Normal
Spite	Ghost	Status	—	100	10	Normal
Trick	Psychic	Status	—	100	10	Normal
Wonder Room	Psychic	Status	—	—	10	Both Sides
Snatch	Dark	Status	—	—	10	Self

MOVES TAUGHT BY PEOPLE

Name	Type	Kind	Pow.	Acc.	PP	Range

EGG MOVES

Name	Type	Kind	Pow.	Acc.	PP	Range
Destiny Bond	Ghost	Status	—	—	5	Self
Pain Split	Normal	Status	—	—	20	Normal
Smokescreen	Normal	Status	—	100	20	Normal
Imprison	Psychic	Status	—	—	10	Self
Grudge	Ghost	Status	—	—	5	Self
Shadow Sneak	Ghost	Physical	40	100	30	Normal
Captivate	Normal	Status	—	100	20	Many Others
Nightmare	Ghost	Status	—	100	15	Normal
Foul Play	Dark	Physical	95	100	15	Normal

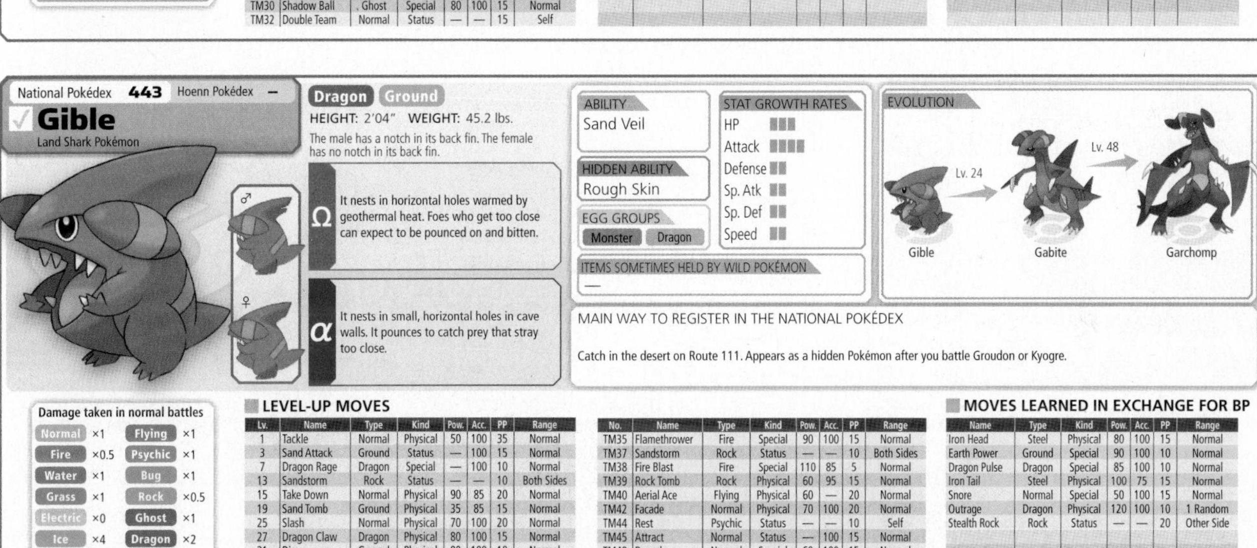

National Pokédex **443** Hoenn Pokédex —

Gible

Land Shark Pokémon

Dragon **Ground**

HEIGHT: 2'04" WEIGHT: 45.2 lbs.

The male has a notch in its back fin. The female has no notch in its back fin.

♂ ♀

Ω It nests in horizontal holes warmed by geothermal heat. Foes who get too close can expect to be pounced on and bitten.

α It nests in small, horizontal holes in cave walls. It pounces to catch prey that stray too close.

ABILITY: Sand Veil

HIDDEN ABILITY: Rough Skin

EGG GROUPS: Monster, Dragon

STAT GROWTH RATES: HP, Attack, Defense, Sp. Atk, Sp. Def, Speed

ITEMS SOMETIMES HELD BY WILD POKÉMON: —

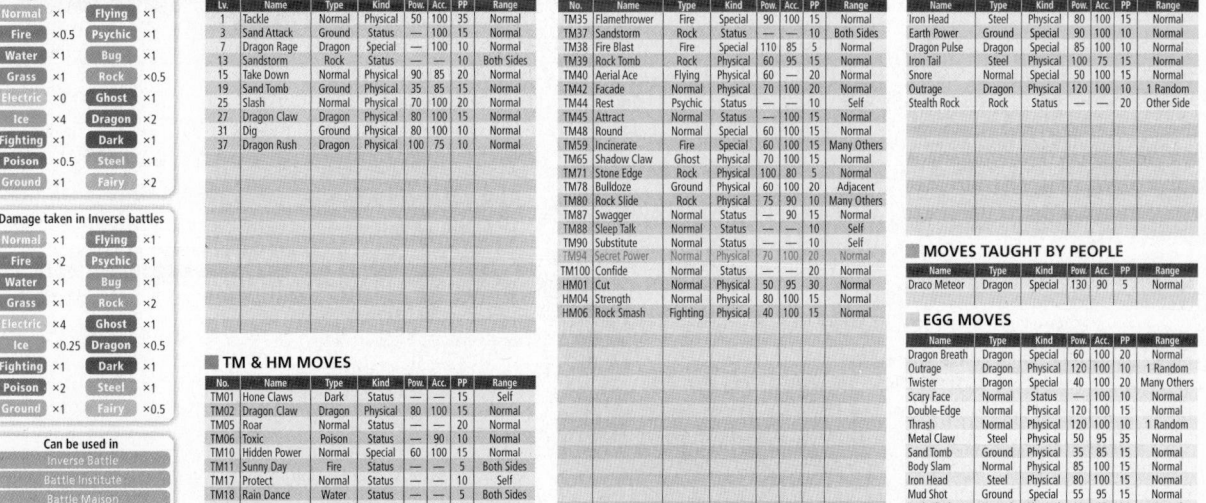

EVOLUTION: Gible → Lv. 24 → Gabite → Lv. 48 → Garchomp

MAIN WAY TO REGISTER IN THE NATIONAL POKÉDEX

Catch in the desert on Route 111. Appears as a hidden Pokémon after you battle Groudon or Kyogre.

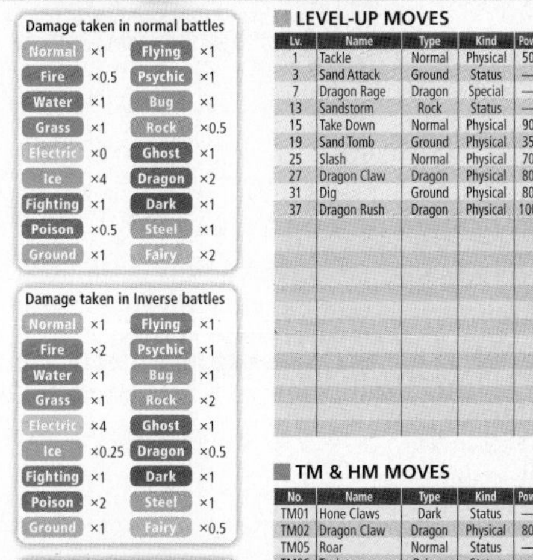

Damage taken in normal battles

Type		Type	
Normal	×1	Flying	×1
Fire	×0.5	Psychic	×1
Water	×1	Bug	×1
Grass	×1	Rock	×0.5
Electric	×0	Ghost	×1
Ice	×4	Dragon	×2
Fighting	×1	Dark	×1
Poison	×0.5	Steel	×1
Ground	×1	Fairy	×2

Damage taken in Inverse battles

Type		Type	
Normal	×1	Flying	×1
Fire	×2	Psychic	×1
Water	×1	Bug	×1
Grass	×1	Rock	×2
Electric	×4	Ghost	×1
Ice	×0.25	Dragon	×0.5
Fighting	×1	Dark	×1
Poison	×2	Steel	×1
Ground	×1	Fairy	×0.5

Can be used in

Inverse Battle
Battle Institute
Battle Maison
Random Matchup (Free Battle)
Random Matchup (Others)

LEVEL-UP MOVES

Lv.	Name	Type	Kind	Pow.	Acc.	PP	Range
1	Tackle	Normal	Physical	50	100	35	Normal
3	Sand Attack	Ground	Status	—	100	15	Normal
7	Dragon Rage	Dragon	Special	—	100	10	Normal
13	Sandstorm	Rock	Status	—	—	10	Both Sides
15	Take Down	Normal	Physical	90	85	20	Normal
19	Sand Tomb	Ground	Physical	35	85	15	Normal
25	Slash	Normal	Physical	70	100	20	Normal
27	Dragon Claw	Dragon	Physical	80	100	15	Normal
31	Dig	Ground	Physical	80	100	10	Normal
37	Dragon Rush	Dragon	Physical	100	75	10	Normal

TM & HM MOVES

No.	Name	Type	Kind	Pow.	Acc.	PP	Range
TM01	Hone Claws	Dark	Status	—	—	15	Self
TM02	Dragon Claw	Dragon	Physical	80	100	15	Normal
TM05	Roar	Normal	Status	—	—	20	Normal
TM06	Toxic	Poison	Status	—	90	10	Normal
TM10	Hidden Power	Normal	Special	60	100	15	Normal
TM11	Sunny Day	Fire	Status	—	—	5	Both Sides
TM17	Protect	Normal	Status	—	—	10	Self
TM18	Rain Dance	Water	Status	—	—	5	Both Sides
TM21	Frustration	Normal	Physical	—	100	20	Normal
TM26	Earthquake	Ground	Physical	100	100	10	Adjacent
TM27	Return	Normal	Physical	—	100	20	Normal
TM28	Dig	Ground	Physical	80	100	10	Normal
TM32	Double Team	Normal	Status	—	—	15	Self
TM35	Flamethrower	Fire	Special	90	100	15	Normal
TM37	Sandstorm	Rock	Status	—	—	10	Both Sides
TM38	Fire Blast	Fire	Special	110	85	5	Normal
TM39	Rock Tomb	Rock	Physical	60	95	15	Normal
TM40	Aerial Ace	Flying	Physical	60	—	20	Normal
TM42	Facade	Normal	Physical	70	100	20	Normal
TM44	Rest	Psychic	Status	—	—	10	Self
TM45	Attract	Normal	Status	—	100	15	Normal
TM48	Round	Normal	Special	60	100	15	Normal
TM59	Incinerate	Fire	Special	60	100	15	Many Others
TM65	Shadow Claw	Ghost	Physical	70	100	15	Normal
TM71	Stone Edge	Rock	Physical	100	80	5	Normal
TM78	Bulldoze	Ground	Physical	60	100	20	Adjacent
TM80	Rock Slide	Rock	Physical	75	90	10	Many Others
TM87	Swagger	Normal	Status	—	90	15	Normal
TM88	Sleep Talk	Normal	Status	—	—	10	Self
TM90	Substitute	Normal	Status	—	—	10	Self
TM94	Secret Power	Normal	Physical	70	100	20	Normal
TM100	Confide	Normal	Status	—	—	20	Normal
HM01	Cut	Normal	Physical	50	95	30	Normal
HM04	Strength	Normal	Physical	80	100	15	Normal
HM06	Rock Smash	Fighting	Physical	40	100	15	Normal

MOVES LEARNED IN EXCHANGE FOR BP

Name	Type	Kind	Pow.	Acc.	PP	Range
Iron Head	Steel	Physical	80	100	15	Normal
Earth Power	Ground	Special	90	100	10	Normal
Dragon Pulse	Dragon	Special	85	100	10	Normal
Iron Tail	Steel	Physical	100	75	15	Normal
Snore	Normal	Special	50	100	15	Normal
Outrage	Dragon	Physical	120	100	10	1 Random
Stealth Rock	Rock	Status	—	—	20	Other Side

MOVES TAUGHT BY PEOPLE

Name	Type	Kind	Pow.	Acc.	PP	Range
Draco Meteor	Dragon	Special	130	90	5	Normal

EGG MOVES

Name	Type	Kind	Pow.	Acc.	PP	Range
Dragon Breath	Dragon	Special	60	100	20	Normal
Outrage	Dragon	Physical	120	100	10	1 Random
Twister	Dragon	Special	40	100	20	Many Others
Scary Face	Normal	Status	—	100	10	Normal
Double-Edge	Normal	Physical	120	100	15	Normal
Thrash	Normal	Physical	120	100	10	1 Random
Metal Claw	Steel	Physical	50	95	35	Normal
Sand Tomb	Ground	Physical	35	85	15	Normal
Body Slam	Normal	Physical	85	100	15	Normal
Iron Head	Steel	Physical	80	100	15	Normal
Mud Shot	Ground	Special	55	95	15	Normal
Rock Climb	Normal	Physical	90	85	20	Normal
Iron Tail	Steel	Physical	100	75	15	Normal

National Pokédex **444** Hoenn Pokédex —

Gabite

Cave Pokémon

Dragon Ground

HEIGHT: 4'07" WEIGHT: 123.5 lbs.

The male has a notch in its back fin. The female has no notch in its back fin.

Ω It loves sparkly things. It seeks treasures in caves and hoards the loot in its nest.

α As it digs to expand its nest, it habitually digs up gems that it then hoards in its nest.

ABILITY
Sand Veil

HIDDEN ABILITY
Rough Skin

EGG GROUPS
Monster Dragon

STAT GROWTH RATES
HP
Attack
Defense
Sp. Atk
Sp. Def
Speed

ITEMS SOMETIMES HELD BY WILD POKÉMON
—

EVOLUTION
Gible → Lv. 24 → Gabite → Lv. 48 → Garchomp

MAIN WAY TO REGISTER IN THE NATIONAL POKÉDEX

Level up Gible to Lv. 24.

Damage taken in normal battles

Type		Type	
Normal	×1	Flying	×1
Fire	×0.5	Psychic	×1
Water	×1	Bug	×1
Grass	×1	Rock	×0.5
Electric	×0	Ghost	×1
Ice	×4	Dragon	×2
Fighting	×1	Dark	×1
Poison	×0.5	Steel	×1
Ground	×1	Fairy	×2

Damage taken in Inverse battles

Type		Type	
Normal	×1	Flying	×1
Fire	×2	Psychic	×1
Water	×1	Bug	×1
Grass	×1	Rock	×2
Electric	×4	Ghost	×1
Ice	×0.25	Dragon	×0.5
Fighting	×1	Dark	×1
Poison	×2	Steel	×1
Ground	×1	Fairy	×0.5

Can be used in
- Inverse Battle
- Battle Institute
- Battle Maison
- Random Matchup (Free Battle)
- Random Matchup (Others)

LEVEL-UP MOVES

Lv.	Name	Type	Kind	Pow.	Acc.	PP	Range
1	Tackle	Normal	Physical	50	100	35	Normal
1	Sand Attack	Ground	Status	—	100	15	Normal
3	Sand Attack	Ground	Status	—	100	15	Normal
7	Dragon Rage	Dragon	Special	—	100	10	Normal
13	Sandstorm	Rock	Status	—	—	10	Both Sides
15	Take Down	Normal	Physical	90	85	20	Normal
19	Sand Tomb	Ground	Physical	35	85	15	Normal
24	Dual Chop	Dragon	Physical	40	90	15	Normal
28	Slash	Normal	Physical	70	100	20	Normal
33	Dragon Claw	Dragon	Physical	80	100	15	Normal
40	Dig	Ground	Physical	80	100	10	Normal
49	Dragon Rush	Dragon	Physical	100	75	10	Normal

TM & HM MOVES

No.	Name	Type	Kind	Pow.	Acc.	PP	Range
TM01	Hone Claws	Dark	Status	—	—	15	Self
TM02	Dragon Claw	Dragon	Physical	80	100	15	Normal
TM05	Roar	Normal	Status	—	—	20	Normal
TM06	Toxic	Poison	Status	—	90	10	Normal
TM10	Hidden Power	Normal	Special	60	100	15	Normal
TM11	Sunny Day	Fire	Status	—	—	5	Both Sides
TM17	Protect	Normal	Status	—	—	10	Self
TM18	Rain Dance	Water	Status	—	—	5	Both Sides
TM21	Frustration	Normal	Physical	—	100	20	Normal
TM26	Earthquake	Ground	Physical	100	100	10	Adjacent
TM27	Return	Normal	Physical	—	100	20	Normal
TM28	Dig	Ground	Physical	80	100	10	Normal
TM32	Double Team	Normal	Status	—	—	15	Self
TM35	Flamethrower	Fire	Special	90	100	15	Normal
TM37	Sandstorm	Rock	Status	—	—	10	Both Sides
TM38	Fire Blast	Fire	Special	110	85	5	Normal
TM39	Rock Tomb	Rock	Physical	60	95	15	Normal
TM40	Aerial Ace	Flying	Physical	60	—	20	Normal
TM42	Facade	Normal	Physical	70	100	20	Normal
TM44	Rest	Psychic	Status	—	—	10	Self
TM45	Attract	Normal	Status	—	100	15	Normal
TM48	Round	Normal	Special	60	100	15	Normal
TM59	Incinerate	Fire	Special	60	100	15	Many Others
TM65	Shadow Claw	Ghost	Physical	70	100	15	Normal
TM71	Stone Edge	Rock	Physical	100	80	5	Normal
TM78	Bulldoze	Ground	Physical	60	100	20	Adjacent
TM80	Rock Slide	Rock	Physical	75	90	10	Many Others
TM87	Swagger	Normal	Status	—	90	15	Normal
TM88	Sleep Talk	Normal	Status	—	—	10	Self
TM90	Substitute	Normal	Status	—	—	10	Self
TM94	Secret Power	Normal	Physical	70	100	20	Normal
TM100	Confide	Normal	Status	—	—	20	Normal
HM01	Cut	Normal	Physical	50	95	30	Normal
HM04	Strength	Normal	Physical	80	100	15	Normal
HM06	Rock Smash	Fighting	Physical	40	100	15	Normal

MOVES LEARNED IN EXCHANGE FOR BP

Name	Type	Kind	Pow.	Acc.	PP	Range
Dual Chop	Dragon	Physical	40	90	15	Normal
Iron Head	Steel	Physical	80	100	15	Normal
Earth Power	Ground	Special	90	100	10	Normal
Dragon Pulse	Dragon	Special	85	100	10	Normal
Iron Tail	Steel	Physical	100	75	15	Normal
Snore	Normal	Special	50	100	15	Normal
Outrage	Dragon	Physical	120	100	10	1 Random
Stealth Rock	Rock	Status	—	—	20	Other Side

MOVES TAUGHT BY PEOPLE

Name	Type	Kind	Pow.	Acc.	PP	Range
Draco Meteor	Dragon	Special	130	90	5	Normal

National Pokédex **445** Hoenn Pokédex —

Garchomp

Mach Pokémon

Dragon Ground

HEIGHT: 6'03" WEIGHT: 209.4 lbs.

The male has a notch in its back fin. The female has no notch in its back fin.

Ω When it folds up its body and extends its wings, it looks like a jet plane. It flies at sonic speed.

α It flies at speeds equal to a jet fighter plane. It never allows its prey to escape.

ABILITY
Sand Veil

HIDDEN ABILITY
Rough Skin

EGG GROUPS
Monster Dragon

STAT GROWTH RATES
HP
Attack
Defense
Sp. Atk
Sp. Def
Speed

ITEMS SOMETIMES HELD BY WILD POKÉMON
—

EVOLUTION
Gible → Lv. 24 → Gabite → Lv. 48 → Garchomp

MAIN WAY TO REGISTER IN THE NATIONAL POKÉDEX

Level up Gabite to Lv. 48.

Damage taken in normal battles

Type		Type	
Normal	×1	Flying	×1
Fire	×0.5	Psychic	×1
Water	×1	Bug	×1
Grass	×1	Rock	×0.5
Electric	×0	Ghost	×1
Ice	×4	Dragon	×2
Fighting	×1	Dark	×1
Poison	×0.5	Steel	×1
Ground	×1	Fairy	×2

Damage taken in Inverse battles

Type		Type	
Normal	×1	Flying	×1
Fire	×2	Psychic	×1
Water	×1	Bug	×1
Grass	×1	Rock	×2
Electric	×4	Ghost	×1
Ice	×0.25	Dragon	×0.5
Fighting	×1	Dark	×1
Poison	×2	Steel	×1
Ground	×1	Fairy	×0.5

Can be used in
- Inverse Battle
- Battle Institute
- Battle Maison
- Random Matchup (Free Battle)
- Random Matchup (Others)

LEVEL-UP MOVES

Lv.	Name	Type	Kind	Pow.	Acc.	PP	Range
1	Fire Fang	Fire	Physical	65	95	15	Normal
1	Tackle	Normal	Physical	50	100	35	Normal
1	Sand Attack	Ground	Status	—	100	15	Normal
1	Dragon Rage	Dragon	Special	—	100	10	Normal
1	Sandstorm	Rock	Status	—	—	10	Both Sides
3	Sand Attack	Ground	Status	—	100	15	Normal
7	Dragon Rage	Dragon	Special	—	100	10	Normal
13	Sandstorm	Rock	Status	—	—	10	Both Sides
15	Take Down	Normal	Physical	90	85	20	Normal
19	Sand Tomb	Ground	Physical	35	85	15	Normal
24	Dual Chop	Dragon	Physical	40	90	15	Normal
28	Slash	Normal	Physical	70	100	20	Normal
33	Dragon Claw	Dragon	Physical	80	100	15	Normal
40	Dig	Ground	Physical	80	100	10	Normal
48	Crunch	Dark	Physical	80	100	15	Normal
55	Dragon Rush	Dragon	Physical	100	75	10	Normal

TM & HM MOVES

No.	Name	Type	Kind	Pow.	Acc.	PP	Range
TM01	Hone Claws	Dark	Status	—	—	15	Self
TM02	Dragon Claw	Dragon	Physical	80	100	15	Normal
TM05	Roar	Normal	Status	—	—	20	Normal
TM06	Toxic	Poison	Status	—	90	10	Normal
TM10	Hidden Power	Normal	Special	60	100	15	Normal
TM11	Sunny Day	Fire	Status	—	—	5	Both Sides
TM15	Hyper Beam	Normal	Special	150	90	5	Normal
TM17	Protect	Normal	Status	—	—	10	Self
TM18	Rain Dance	Water	Status	—	—	5	Both Sides
TM21	Frustration	Normal	Physical	—	100	20	Normal
TM26	Earthquake	Ground	Physical	100	100	10	Adjacent
TM27	Return	Normal	Physical	—	100	20	Normal
TM28	Dig	Ground	Physical	80	100	10	Normal
TM31	Brick Break	Fighting	Physical	75	100	15	Normal
TM32	Double Team	Normal	Status	—	—	15	Self
TM35	Flamethrower	Fire	Special	90	100	15	Normal
TM37	Sandstorm	Rock	Status	—	—	10	Both Sides
TM38	Fire Blast	Fire	Special	110	85	5	Normal
TM39	Rock Tomb	Rock	Physical	60	95	15	Normal
TM40	Aerial Ace	Flying	Physical	60	—	20	Normal
TM42	Facade	Normal	Physical	70	100	20	Normal
TM44	Rest	Psychic	Status	—	—	10	Self
TM45	Attract	Normal	Status	—	100	15	Normal
TM48	Round	Normal	Special	60	100	15	Normal
TM54	False Swipe	Normal	Physical	40	100	40	Normal
TM56	Fling	Dark	Physical	—	100	10	Normal
TM59	Incinerate	Fire	Special	60	100	15	Many Others
TM65	Shadow Claw	Ghost	Physical	70	100	15	Normal
TM68	Giga Impact	Normal	Physical	150	90	5	Normal
TM71	Stone Edge	Rock	Physical	100	80	5	Normal
TM75	Swords Dance	Normal	Status	—	—	20	Self
TM78	Bulldoze	Ground	Physical	60	100	20	Adjacent
TM80	Rock Slide	Rock	Physical	75	90	10	Many Others
TM82	Dragon Tail	Dragon	Physical	60	90	10	Normal
TM84	Poison Jab	Poison	Physical	80	100	20	Normal
TM87	Swagger	Normal	Status	—	90	15	Normal
TM88	Sleep Talk	Normal	Status	—	—	10	Self
TM90	Substitute	Normal	Status	—	—	10	Self
TM94	Secret Power	Normal	Physical	70	100	20	Normal
TM100	Confide	Normal	Status	—	—	20	Normal
HM01	Cut	Normal	Physical	50	95	30	Normal
HM03	Surf	Water	Special	90	100	15	Adjacent
HM04	Strength	Normal	Physical	80	100	15	Normal
HM06	Rock Smash	Fighting	Physical	40	100	15	Normal

MOVES LEARNED IN EXCHANGE FOR BP

Name	Type	Kind	Pow.	Acc.	PP	Range
Dual Chop	Dragon	Physical	40	90	15	Normal
Iron Head	Steel	Physical	80	100	15	Normal
Earth Power	Ground	Special	90	100	10	Normal
Aqua Tail	Water	Physical	90	90	10	Normal
Dragon Pulse	Dragon	Special	85	100	10	Normal
Iron Tail	Steel	Physical	100	75	15	Normal
Snore	Normal	Special	50	100	15	Normal
Outrage	Dragon	Physical	120	100	10	1 Random
Stealth Rock	Rock	Status	—	—	20	Other Side

MOVES TAUGHT BY PEOPLE

Name	Type	Kind	Pow.	Acc.	PP	Range
Draco Meteor	Dragon	Special	130	90	5	Normal

Mega Evolution

Mega Garchomp

Mach Pokémon

Dragon | Ground

HEIGHT: 6'03" WEIGHT: 209.4 lbs.

Same form for ♂ / ♀

REQUIRED MEGA STONE

Garchompite

Receive from Aarune in Fortree City's Secret Base Guild as a reward for your secret team reaching Platinum Rank.

ABILITY

Sand Force

HIDDEN ABILITY

—

EGG GROUPS

—

STAT GROWTH RATES

HP, Attack, Defense, Sp. Atk, Sp. Def, Speed

Damage taken in normal battles

Type		Type	
Normal	×1	Flying	×1
Fire	×0.5	Psychic	×1
Water	×1	Bug	×1
Grass	×1	Rock	×0.5
Electric	×0	Ghost	×1
Ice	×4	Dragon	×2
Fighting	×1	Dark	×1
Poison	×0.5	Steel	×1
Ground	×1	Fairy	×2

Damage taken in Inverse battles

Type		Type	
Normal	×1	Flying	×1
Fire	×2	Psychic	×1
Water	×1	Bug	×1
Grass	×1	Rock	×2
Electric	×4	Ghost	×1
Ice	×0.25	Dragon	×0.5
Fighting	×1	Dark	×1
Poison	×2	Steel	×1
Ground	×1	Fairy	×0.5

Can be used in

- Inverse Battle
- Battle Institute
- Battle Maison
- Random Matchup (Free Battle)
- Random Matchup (Others)

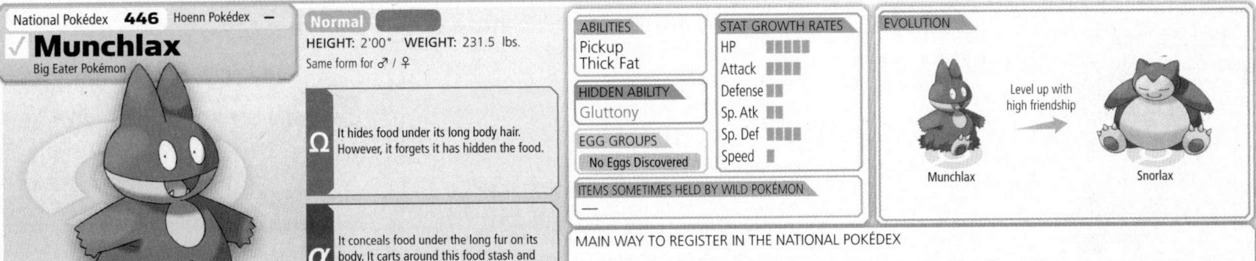

National Pokédex **446** Hoenn Pokédex —

Munchlax

Big Eater Pokémon

Normal

HEIGHT: 2'00" WEIGHT: 231.5 lbs.

Same form for ♂ / ♀

Ω It hides food under its long body hair. However, it forgets it has hidden the food.

α It conceals food under the long fur on its body. It carts around this food stash and swallows it without chewing.

ABILITIES

Pickup
Thick Fat

HIDDEN ABILITY

Gluttony

EGG GROUPS

No Eggs Discovered

STAT GROWTH RATES

HP, Attack, Defense, Sp. Atk, Sp. Def, Speed

ITEMS SOMETIMES HELD BY WILD POKÉMON

—

EVOLUTION

Munchlax → Level up with high friendship → Snorlax

MAIN WAY TO REGISTER IN THE NATIONAL POKÉDEX

Leave a Snorlax obtained via Link Trade or the GTS at a Pokémon Day Care while holding a Full Incense, then hatch the Pokémon Egg that is found.

Damage taken in normal battles

Type		Type	
Normal	×1	Flying	×1
Fire	×1	Psychic	×1
Water	×1	Bug	×1
Grass	×1	Rock	×1
Electric	×1	Ghost	×0
Ice	×1	Dragon	×1
Fighting	×2	Dark	×1
Poison	×1	Steel	×1
Ground	×1	Fairy	×1

Damage taken in Inverse battles

Type		Type	
Normal	×1	Flying	×1
Fire	×1	Psychic	×1
Water	×1	Bug	×1
Grass	×1	Rock	×1
Electric	×1	Ghost	×2
Ice	×1	Dragon	×1
Fighting	×0.5	Dark	×1
Poison	×1	Steel	×1
Ground	×1	Fairy	×1

Can be used in

- Inverse Battle
- Battle Institute
- Battle Maison
- Random Matchup (Free Battle)
- Random Matchup (Others)

LEVEL-UP MOVES

Lv.	Name	Type	Kind	Pow.	Acc.	PP	Range
1	Last Resort	Normal	Physical	140	100	5	Normal
1	Recycle	Normal	Status	—	—	10	Self
1	Lick	Ghost	Physical	30	100	30	Normal
1	Metronome	Normal	Status	—	—	10	Self
1	Odor Sleuth	Normal	Status	—	—	40	Normal
1	Tackle	Normal	Physical	50	100	35	Normal
4	Defense Curl	Normal	Status	—	—	40	Self
9	Amnesia	Psychic	Status	—	—	20	Self
12	Lick	Ghost	Physical	30	100	30	Normal
17	Chip Away	Normal	Physical	70	100	20	Normal
20	Screech	Normal	Status	—	85	40	Normal
25	Body Slam	Normal	Physical	85	100	15	Normal
28	Stockpile	Normal	Status	—	—	20	Self
33	Swallow	Normal	Status	—	—	10	Self
36	Rollout	Rock	Physical	30	90	20	Normal
41	Fling	Dark	Physical	—	100	10	Normal
44	Belly Drum	Normal	Status	—	—	10	Self
49	Natural Gift	Normal	Physical	—	100	15	Normal
50	Snatch	Dark	Status	—	—	10	Self
57	Last Resort	Normal	Physical	140	100	5	Normal

TM & HM MOVES

No.	Name	Type	Kind	Pow.	Acc.	PP	Range
TM06	Toxic	Poison	Status	—	90	10	Normal
TM10	Hidden Power	Normal	Special	60	100	15	Normal
TM11	Sunny Day	Fire	Status	—	—	5	Both Sides
TM13	Ice Beam	Ice	Special	90	100	10	Normal
TM14	Blizzard	Ice	Special	110	70	5	Many Others
TM17	Protect	Normal	Status	—	—	10	Self
TM18	Rain Dance	Water	Status	—	—	5	Both Sides
TM21	Frustration	Normal	Physical	—	100	20	Normal
TM22	Solar Beam	Grass	Special	120	100	10	Normal
TM24	Thunderbolt	Electric	Special	90	100	15	Normal
TM25	Thunder	Electric	Special	110	70	10	Normal
TM26	Earthquake	Ground	Physical	100	100	10	Adjacent
TM27	Return	Normal	Physical	—	100	20	Normal
TM29	Psychic	Psychic	Special	90	100	10	Normal
TM30	Shadow Ball	Ghost	Special	80	100	15	Normal
TM31	Brick Break	Fighting	Physical	75	100	15	Normal
TM32	Double Team	Normal	Status	—	—	15	Self
TM35	Flamethrower	Fire	Special	90	100	15	Normal
TM37	Sandstorm	Rock	Status	—	—	10	Both Sides
TM38	Fire Blast	Fire	Special	110	85	5	Normal
TM39	Rock Tomb	Rock	Physical	60	95	15	Normal
TM42	Facade	Normal	Physical	70	100	20	Normal
TM44	Rest	Psychic	Status	—	—	10	Self
TM45	Attract	Normal	Status	—	100	15	Normal
TM48	Round	Normal	Special	60	100	15	Normal
TM56	Fling	Dark	Physical	—	100	10	Normal
TM59	Incinerate	Fire	Special	60	100	15	Many Others
TM67	Retaliate	Normal	Physical	70	100	5	Normal
TM78	Bulldoze	Ground	Physical	60	100	20	Adjacent
TM80	Rock Slide	Rock	Physical	75	90	10	Many Others
TM87	Swagger	Normal	Status	—	90	15	Normal
TM88	Sleep Talk	Normal	Status	—	—	10	Self
TM90	Substitute	Normal	Status	—	—	10	Self
TM94	Secret Power	Normal	Physical	70	100	20	Normal
TM98	Power-Up Punch	Fighting	Physical	40	100	20	Normal
TM100	Confide	Normal	Status	—	—	20	Normal
HM03	Surf	Water	Special	90	100	15	Adjacent
HM04	Strength	Normal	Physical	80	100	15	Normal
HM06	Rock Smash	Fighting	Physical	40	100	15	Normal

MOVES LEARNED IN EXCHANGE FOR BP

Name	Type	Kind	Pow.	Acc.	PP	Range
Covet	Normal	Physical	60	100	25	Normal
Seed Bomb	Grass	Physical	80	100	15	Normal
Gunk Shot	Poison	Physical	120	80	5	Normal
Uproar	Normal	Special	90	100	10	1 Random
Thunder Punch	Electric	Physical	75	100	15	Normal
Fire Punch	Fire	Physical	75	100	15	Normal
Ice Punch	Ice	Physical	75	100	15	Normal
Last Resort	Normal	Physical	140	100	5	Normal
Superpower	Fighting	Physical	120	100	5	Normal
Icy Wind	Ice	Special	55	95	15	Many Others
Zen Headbutt	Psychic	Physical	80	90	15	Normal
Hyper Voice	Normal	Special	90	100	10	Many Others
Snore	Normal	Special	50	100	15	Normal
Focus Punch	Fighting	Physical	150	100	20	Normal
Shock Wave	Electric	Special	60	—	20	Normal
Water Pulse	Water	Special	60	100	20	Normal
After You	Normal	Status	—	—	15	Normal
Recycle	Normal	Status	—	—	10	Self
Snatch	Dark	Status	—	—	10	Self

MOVES TAUGHT BY PEOPLE

Name	Type	Kind	Pow.	Acc.	PP	Range

EGG MOVES

Name	Type	Kind	Pow.	Acc.	PP	Range
Lick	Ghost	Physical	30	100	30	Normal
Charm	Fairy	Status	—	100	20	Normal
Double-Edge	Normal	Physical	120	100	15	Normal
Curse	Ghost	Status	—	—	10	Varies
Whirlwind	Normal	Status	—	—	20	Normal
Pursuit	Dark	Physical	40	100	20	Normal
Zen Headbutt	Psychic	Physical	80	90	15	Normal
Counter	Fighting	Physical	—	100	20	Varies
Natural Gift	Normal	Physical	—	100	15	Normal
After You	Normal	Status	—	—	15	Normal
Self-Destruct	Normal	Physical	200	100	5	Adjacent
Belch	Poison	Special	120	90	10	Normal

National Pokédex **447** Hoenn Pokédex —

Riolu

Emanation Pokémon

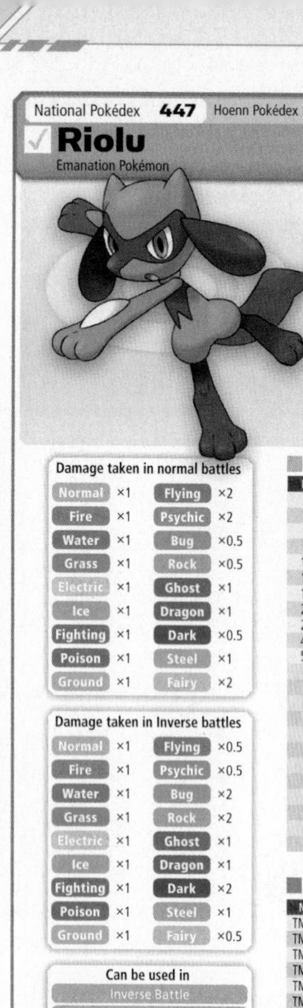

Fighting

HEIGHT: 2'04" WEIGHT: 44.5 lbs.

Same form for ♂ / ♀

Ω It uses the shapes of auras, which change according to emotion, to communicate with others.

α The aura that emanates from its body intensifies to alert others if it is afraid or sad.

ABILITIES
Steadfast
Inner Focus

HIDDEN ABILITY
Prankster

EGG GROUPS
No Eggs Discovered

STAT GROWTH RATES
HP ■■
Attack ■■■■
Defense ■■
Sp. Atk ■■
Sp. Def ■■
Speed ■■■

ITEMS SOMETIMES HELD BY WILD POKÉMON
—

EVOLUTION

Riolu → Level up with high friendship between 4 A.M. and 7:59 P.M. → Lucario

MAIN WAY TO REGISTER IN THE NATIONAL POKÉDEX

Appears in *Pokémon X* and *Pokémon Y*. Bring it to your game using Link Trade or the GTS.

Damage taken in normal battles

Type		Type	
Normal	×1	Flying	×2
Fire	×1	Psychic	×2
Water	×1	Bug	×0.5
Grass	×1	Rock	×0.5
Electric	×1	Ghost	×1
Ice	×1	Dragon	×1
Fighting	×1	Dark	×0.5
Poison	×1	Steel	×1
Ground	×1	Fairy	×2

Damage taken in Inverse battles

Type		Type	
Normal	×1	Flying	×0.5
Fire	×1	Psychic	×0.5
Water	×1	Bug	×2
Grass	×1	Rock	×2
Electric	×1	Ghost	×1
Ice	×1	Dragon	×1
Fighting	×1	Dark	×2
Poison	×1	Steel	×1
Ground	×1	Fairy	×0.5

Can be used in
Inverse Battle
Battle Institute
Battle Maison
Random Matchup (Free Battle)
Random Matchup (Others)

LEVEL-UP MOVES

Lv.	Name	Type	Kind	Pow.	Acc.	PP	Range
1	Foresight	Normal	Status	—	—	40	Normal
1	Quick Attack	Normal	Physical	40	100	30	Normal
1	Endure	Normal	Status	—	—	10	Self
6	Counter	Fighting	Physical	—	100	20	Varies
11	Feint	Normal	Physical	30	100	10	Normal
15	Force Palm	Fighting	Physical	60	100	10	Normal
19	Copycat	Normal	Status	—	—	20	Self
24	Screech	Normal	Status	—	85	40	Normal
29	Reversal	Fighting	Physical	—	100	15	Normal
47	Nasty Plot	Dark	Status	—	—	20	Self
50	Final Gambit	Fighting	Special	—	100	5	Normal

TM & HM MOVES

No.	Name	Type	Kind	Pow.	Acc.	PP	Range
TM05	Roar	Normal	Status	—	—	20	Normal
TM06	Toxic	Poison	Status	—	90	10	Normal
TM08	Bulk Up	Fighting	Status	—	—	20	Self
TM10	Hidden Power	Normal	Special	60	100	15	Normal
TM11	Sunny Day	Fire	Status	—	—	5	Both Sides
TM17	Protect	Normal	Status	—	—	10	Self
TM18	Rain Dance	Water	Status	—	—	5	Both Sides
TM21	Frustration	Normal	Physical	—	100	20	Normal
TM26	Earthquake	Ground	Physical	100	100	10	Adjacent
TM27	Return	Normal	Physical	—	100	20	Normal
TM28	Dig	Ground	Physical	80	100	10	Normal
TM31	Brick Break	Fighting	Physical	75	100	15	Normal
TM32	Double Team	Normal	Status	—	—	15	Self
TM39	Rock Tomb	Rock	Physical	60	95	15	Normal
TM42	Facade	Normal	Physical	70	100	20	Normal
TM44	Rest	Psychic	Status	—	—	10	Self
TM45	Attract	Normal	Status	—	100	15	Normal
TM47	Low Sweep	Fighting	Physical	65	100	20	Normal
TM48	Round	Normal	Special	60	100	15	Normal
TM52	Focus Blast	Fighting	Special	120	70	5	Normal
TM56	Fling	Dark	Physical	—	100	10	Normal
TM65	Shadow Claw	Ghost	Physical	70	100	15	Normal
TM66	Payback	Dark	Physical	50	100	10	Normal
TM67	Retaliate	Normal	Physical	70	100	5	Normal
TM75	Swords Dance	Normal	Status	—	—	20	Self
TM78	Bulldoze	Ground	Physical	60	100	20	Adjacent
TM80	Rock Slide	Rock	Physical	75	90	10	Many Others
TM84	Poison Jab	Poison	Physical	80	100	20	Normal
TM87	Swagger	Normal	Status	—	90	15	Normal
TM88	Sleep Talk	Normal	Status	—	—	10	Self
TM90	Substitute	Normal	Status	—	—	10	Self
TM94	Secret Power	Normal	Physical	70	100	20	Normal
TM98	Power-Up Punch	Fighting	Physical	40	100	20	Normal
TM100	Confide	Normal	Status	—	—	20	Normal
HM04	Strength	Normal	Physical	80	100	15	Normal
HM06	Rock Smash	Fighting	Physical	40	100	15	Normal

MOVES LEARNED IN EXCHANGE FOR BP

Name	Type	Kind	Pow.	Acc.	PP	Range
Dual Chop	Dragon	Physical	40	90	15	Normal
Low Kick	Fighting	Physical	—	100	20	Normal
Thunder Punch	Electric	Physical	75	100	15	Normal
Ice Punch	Ice	Physical	75	100	15	Normal
Magnet Rise	Electric	Status	—	—	10	Self
Iron Defense	Steel	Status	—	—	15	Self
Zen Headbutt	Psychic	Physical	80	90	15	Normal
Iron Tail	Steel	Physical	100	75	15	Normal
Snore	Normal	Special	50	100	15	Normal
Role Play	Psychic	Status	—	—	10	Normal
Drain Punch	Fighting	Physical	75	100	10	Normal
Focus Punch	Fighting	Physical	150	100	20	Normal
Helping Hand	Normal	Status	—	—	20	1 Ally

MOVES TAUGHT BY PEOPLE

Name	Type	Kind	Pow.	Acc.	PP	Range

EGG MOVES

Name	Type	Kind	Pow.	Acc.	PP	Range
Cross Chop	Fighting	Physical	100	80	5	Normal
Detect	Fighting	Status	—	—	5	Self
Bite	Dark	Physical	60	100	25	Normal
Mind Reader	Normal	Status	—	—	5	Normal
Sky Uppercut	Fighting	Physical	85	90	15	Normal
High Jump Kick	Fighting	Physical	130	90	10	Normal
Agility	Psychic	Status	—	—	30	Self
Vacuum Wave	Fighting	Special	40	100	30	Normal
Crunch	Dark	Physical	80	100	15	Normal
Low Kick	Fighting	Physical	—	100	20	Normal
Iron Defense	Steel	Status	—	—	15	Self
Blaze Kick	Fire	Physical	85	90	10	Normal
Bullet Punch	Steel	Physical	40	100	30	Normal
Follow Me	Normal	Status	—	—	20	Self
Circle Throw	Fighting	Physical	60	90	10	Normal

National Pokédex **448** Hoenn Pokédex —

Lucario

Aura Pokémon

Fighting Steel

HEIGHT: 3'11" WEIGHT: 119 lbs.

Same form for ♂ / ♀

Ω By catching the aura emanating from others, it can read their thoughts and movements.

α By reading the auras of all things, it can tell how others are feeling from over half a mile away.

ABILITIES
Steadfast
Inner Focus

HIDDEN ABILITY
Justified

EGG GROUPS
Field Human-Like

STAT GROWTH RATES
HP ■■■
Attack ■■■■■■
Defense ■■■
Sp. Atk ■■■■■■
Sp. Def ■■■
Speed ■■■■■

ITEMS SOMETIMES HELD BY WILD POKÉMON
—

EVOLUTION

Riolu → Level up with high friendship between 4 A.M. and 7:59 P.M. → Lucario

MAIN WAY TO REGISTER IN THE NATIONAL POKÉDEX

Obtain in *Pokémon X* or *Pokémon Y*. Bring it to your game using Link Trade or the GTS.

Damage taken in normal battles

Type		Type	
Normal	×0.5	Flying	×1
Fire	×2	Psychic	×1
Water	×1	Bug	×0.25
Grass	×0.5	Rock	×0.25
Electric	×1	Ghost	×1
Ice	×0.5	Dragon	×0.5
Fighting	×2	Dark	×0.5
Poison	×0	Steel	×0.5
Ground	×2	Fairy	×1

Damage taken in Inverse battles

Type		Type	
Normal	×2	Flying	×1
Fire	×0.5	Psychic	×1
Water	×1	Bug	×4
Grass	×2	Rock	×4
Electric	×1	Ghost	×1
Ice	×2	Dragon	×2
Fighting	×0.5	Dark	×2
Poison	×2	Steel	×2
Ground	×0.5	Fairy	×1

Can be used in
Inverse Battle
Battle Institute
Battle Maison
Random Matchup (Free Battle)
Random Matchup (Others)

LEVEL-UP MOVES

Lv.	Name	Type	Kind	Pow.	Acc.	PP	Range
1	Extreme Speed	Normal	Physical	80	100	5	Normal
1	Dragon Pulse	Dragon	Special	85	100	10	Normal
1	Close Combat	Fighting	Physical	120	100	5	Normal
1	Aura Sphere	Fighting	Special	80	—	20	Normal
1	Foresight	Normal	Status	—	—	40	Normal
1	Quick Attack	Normal	Physical	40	100	30	Normal
1	Detect	Fighting	Status	—	—	5	Self
1	Metal Claw	Steel	Physical	50	95	35	Normal
6	Counter	Fighting	Physical	—	100	20	Varies
11	Feint	Normal	Physical	30	100	10	Normal
15	Power-Up Punch	Fighting	Physical	40	100	20	Normal
19	Swords Dance	Normal	Status	—	—	20	Self
24	Metal Sound	Steel	Status	—	85	40	Normal
29	Bone Rush	Ground	Physical	25	90	10	Normal
33	Quick Guard	Fighting	Status	—	—	15	Your Side
37	Me First	Normal	Status	—	—	20	Varies
42	Aura Sphere	Fighting	Special	80	—	20	Normal
47	Calm Mind	Psychic	Status	—	—	20	Self
51	Heal Pulse	Psychic	Status	—	—	10	Normal
55	Close Combat	Fighting	Physical	120	100	5	Normal
60	Dragon Pulse	Dragon	Special	85	100	10	Normal
65	Extreme Speed	Normal	Physical	80	100	5	Normal

TM & HM MOVES

No.	Name	Type	Kind	Pow.	Acc.	PP	Range
TM01	Hone Claws	Dark	Status	—	—	15	Self
TM04	Calm Mind	Psychic	Status	—	—	20	Self
TM05	Roar	Normal	Status	—	—	20	Normal
TM06	Toxic	Poison	Status	—	90	10	Normal
TM08	Bulk Up	Fighting	Status	—	—	20	Self
TM10	Hidden Power	Normal	Special	60	100	15	Normal
TM11	Sunny Day	Fire	Status	—	—	5	Both Sides
TM15	Hyper Beam	Normal	Special	150	90	5	Normal
TM17	Protect	Normal	Status	—	—	10	Self
TM18	Rain Dance	Water	Status	—	—	5	Both Sides
TM21	Frustration	Normal	Physical	—	100	20	Normal
TM26	Earthquake	Ground	Physical	100	100	10	Adjacent
TM27	Return	Normal	Physical	—	100	20	Normal
TM28	Dig	Ground	Physical	80	100	10	Normal
TM29	Psychic	Psychic	Special	90	100	10	Normal
TM30	Shadow Ball	Ghost	Special	80	100	15	Normal
TM31	Brick Break	Fighting	Physical	75	100	15	Normal
TM32	Double Team	Normal	Status	—	—	15	Self
TM39	Rock Tomb	Rock	Physical	60	95	15	Normal
TM42	Facade	Normal	Physical	70	100	20	Normal
TM44	Rest	Psychic	Status	—	—	10	Self
TM45	Attract	Normal	Status	—	100	15	Normal
TM47	Low Sweep	Fighting	Physical	65	100	20	Normal
TM48	Round	Normal	Special	60	100	15	Normal
TM52	Focus Blast	Fighting	Special	120	70	5	Normal
TM56	Fling	Dark	Physical	—	100	10	Normal
TM65	Shadow Claw	Ghost	Physical	70	100	15	Normal
TM66	Payback	Dark	Physical	50	100	10	Normal
TM67	Retaliate	Normal	Physical	70	100	5	Normal
TM68	Giga Impact	Normal	Physical	150	90	5	Normal
TM71	Stone Edge	Rock	Physical	100	80	5	Normal
TM75	Swords Dance	Normal	Status	—	—	20	Self
TM78	Bulldoze	Ground	Physical	60	100	20	Adjacent
TM80	Rock Slide	Rock	Physical	75	90	10	Many Others
TM84	Poison Jab	Poison	Physical	80	100	20	Normal
TM87	Swagger	Normal	Status	—	90	15	Normal
TM88	Sleep Talk	Normal	Status	—	—	10	Self
TM90	Substitute	Normal	Status	—	—	10	Self
TM91	Flash Cannon	Steel	Special	80	100	10	Normal
TM94	Secret Power	Normal	Physical	70	100	20	Normal
TM97	Dark Pulse	Dark	Special	80	100	15	Normal
TM98	Power-Up Punch	Fighting	Physical	40	100	20	Normal
TM100	Confide	Normal	Status	—	—	20	Normal
HM04	Strength	Normal	Physical	80	100	15	Normal
HM06	Rock Smash	Fighting	Physical	40	100	15	Normal

MOVES LEARNED IN EXCHANGE FOR BP

Name	Type	Kind	Pow.	Acc.	PP	Range
Dual Chop	Dragon	Physical	40	90	15	Normal
Low Kick	Fighting	Physical	—	100	20	Normal
Thunder Punch	Electric	Physical	75	100	15	Normal
Ice Punch	Ice	Physical	75	100	15	Normal
Magnet Rise	Electric	Status	—	—	10	Self
Iron Defense	Steel	Status	—	—	15	Self
Zen Headbutt	Psychic	Physical	80	90	15	Normal
Dragon Pulse	Dragon	Special	85	100	10	Normal
Iron Tail	Steel	Physical	100	75	15	Normal
Snore	Normal	Special	50	100	15	Normal
Role Play	Psychic	Status	—	—	10	Normal
Drain Punch	Fighting	Physical	75	100	10	Normal
Focus Punch	Fighting	Physical	150	100	20	Normal
Water Pulse	Water	Special	60	100	20	Normal
Helping Hand	Normal	Status	—	—	20	1 Ally

MOVES TAUGHT BY PEOPLE

Name	Type	Kind	Pow.	Acc.	PP	Range

Mega Evolution

Mega Lucario

Aura Pokémon

Fighting | Steel

HEIGHT: 4'03" WEIGHT: 126.8 lbs.

Same form for ♂ / ♀

REQUIRED MEGA STONE

Lucarionite

Receive from Chaz in the Pokémon Contest Spectacular Hall (after winning in the Master Rank for all five contest conditions and defeating Lisia in a Master Rank contest).

ABILITY

Adaptability

HIDDEN ABILITY

—

EGG GROUPS

—

STAT GROWTH RATES

HP
Attack
Defense
Sp. Atk
Sp. Def
Speed

Damage taken in normal battles

Type		Type	
Normal	×0.5	Flying	×1
Fire	×2	Psychic	×1
Water	×1	Bug	×0.25
Grass	×0.5	Rock	×0.25
Electric	×1	Ghost	×1
Ice	×0.5	Dragon	×0.5
Fighting	×2	Dark	×0.5
Poison	×0	Steel	×0.5
Ground	×2	Fairy	×1

Damage taken in Inverse battles

Type		Type	
Normal	×2	Flying	×1
Fire	×0.5	Psychic	×1
Water	×1	Bug	×4
Grass	×2	Rock	×4
Electric	×1	Ghost	×1
Ice	×2	Dragon	×2
Fighting	×0.5	Dark	×2
Poison	×2	Steel	×2
Ground	×0.5	Fairy	×1

Can be used in

Inverse Battle
Battle Institute
Battle Maison
Random Matchup (Free Battle)
Random Matchup (Others)

Mega Lucario

National Pokédex

National Pokédex **449** Hoenn Pokédex —

Hippopotas

Hippo Pokémon

Ground

HEIGHT: 2'07" WEIGHT: 109.1 lbs.

The male's body is mainly beige. The female's body is mainly brown.

♂ ♀

Ω It lives in arid places. Instead of perspiration, it expels grainy sand from its body.

α It enshrouds itself with sand to protect itself from germs. It does not enjoy getting wet.

ABILITY

Sand Stream

HIDDEN ABILITY

Sand Force

EGG GROUPS

Field

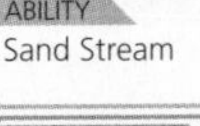

STAT GROWTH RATES

HP
Attack
Defense
Sp. Atk
Sp. Def
Speed

ITEMS SOMETIMES HELD BY WILD POKÉMON

—

EVOLUTION

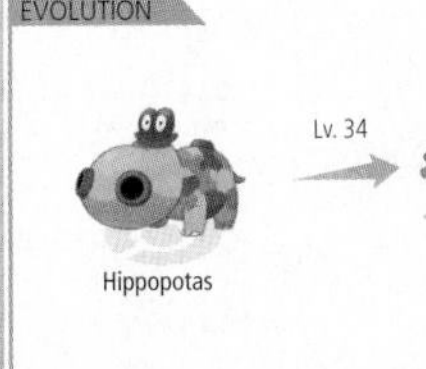

MAIN WAY TO REGISTER IN THE NATIONAL POKÉDEX

Appears in *Pokémon X* and *Pokémon Y*. Bring it to your game using Link Trade or the GTS.

Damage taken in normal battles

Type		Type	
Normal	×1	Flying	×1
Fire	×1	Psychic	×1
Water	×2	Bug	×1
Grass	×2	Rock	×0.5
Electric	×0	Ghost	×1
Ice	×2	Dragon	×1
Fighting	×1	Dark	×1
Poison	×0.5	Steel	×1
Ground	×1	Fairy	×1

Damage taken in Inverse battles

Type		Type	
Normal	×1	Flying	×1
Fire	×1	Psychic	×1
Water	×0.5	Bug	×1
Grass	×0.5	Rock	×2
Electric	×2	Ghost	×1
Ice	×0.5	Dragon	×1
Fighting	×1	Dark	×1
Poison	×2	Steel	×1
Ground	×1	Fairy	×1

Can be used in

Inverse Battle
Battle Institute
Battle Maison
Random Matchup (Free Battle)
Random Matchup (Others)

LEVEL-UP MOVES

Lv.	Name	Type	Kind	Pow.	Acc.	PP	Range
1	Tackle	Normal	Physical	50	100	35	Normal
1	Sand Attack	Ground	Status	—	100	15	Normal
7	Bite	Dark	Physical	60	100	25	Normal
13	Yawn	Normal	Status	—	—	10	Normal
19	Take Down	Normal	Physical	90	85	20	Normal
19	Dig	Ground	Physical	80	100	10	Normal
25	Sand Tomb	Ground	Physical	35	85	15	Normal
31	Crunch	Dark	Physical	80	100	15	Normal
37	Earthquake	Ground	Physical	100	100	10	Adjacent
44	Double-Edge	Normal	Physical	120	100	15	Normal
50	Fissure	Ground	Physical	—	30	5	Normal

TM & HM MOVES

No.	Name	Type	Kind	Pow.	Acc.	PP	Range
TM05	Roar	Normal	Status	—	—	20	Normal
TM06	Toxic	Poison	Status	—	90	10	Normal
TM10	Hidden Power	Normal	Special	60	100	15	Normal
TM11	Sunny Day	Fire	Status	—	—	5	Both Sides
TM17	Protect	Normal	Status	—	—	10	Self
TM21	Frustration	Normal	Physical	—	100	20	Normal
TM26	Earthquake	Ground	Physical	100	100	10	Adjacent
TM27	Return	Normal	Physical	—	100	20	Normal
TM28	Dig	Ground	Physical	80	100	10	Normal
TM32	Double Team	Normal	Status	—	—	15	Self
TM37	Sandstorm	Rock	Status	—	—	10	Both Sides
TM39	Rock Tomb	Rock	Physical	60	95	15	Normal
TM42	Facade	Normal	Physical	70	100	20	Normal
TM44	Rest	Psychic	Status	—	—	10	Self
TM45	Attract	Normal	Status	—	100	15	Normal
TM48	Round	Normal	Special	60	100	15	Normal
TM78	Bulldoze	Ground	Physical	60	100	20	Adjacent
TM80	Rock Slide	Rock	Physical	75	90	10	Many Others
TM87	Swagger	Normal	Status	—	90	15	Normal
TM88	Sleep Talk	Normal	Status	—	—	10	Self
TM90	Substitute	Normal	Status	—	—	10	Self
TM94	Secret Power	Normal	Physical	70	100	20	Normal
TM100	Confide	Normal	Status	—	—	20	Normal
HM04	Strength	Normal	Physical	80	100	15	Normal
HM06	Rock Smash	Fighting	Physical	40	100	15	Normal

MOVES LEARNED IN EXCHANGE FOR BP

Name	Type	Kind	Pow.	Acc.	PP	Range
Earth Power	Ground	Special	90	100	10	Normal
Superpower	Fighting	Physical	120	100	5	Normal
Iron Tail	Steel	Physical	100	75	15	Normal
Snore	Normal	Special	50	100	15	Normal
Water Pulse	Water	Special	60	100	20	Normal
Stealth Rock	Rock	Status	—	—	20	Other Side

MOVES TAUGHT BY PEOPLE

Name	Type	Kind	Pow.	Acc.	PP	Range

EGG MOVES

Name	Type	Kind	Pow.	Acc.	PP	Range
Stockpile	Normal	Status	—	—	20	Self
Swallow	Normal	Status	—	—	10	Self
Spit Up	Normal	Special	—	100	10	Normal
Curse	Ghost	Status	—	—	10	Varies
Slack Off	Normal	Status	—	—	10	Self
Body Slam	Normal	Physical	85	100	15	Normal
Sand Tomb	Ground	Physical	35	85	15	Normal
Revenge	Fighting	Physical	60	100	10	Normal
Sleep Talk	Normal	Status	—	—	10	Self
Whirlwind	Normal	Status	—	—	20	Normal

Hippopotas 449

National Pokédex **450** Hoenn Pokédex —

Hippowdon

Heavyweight Pokémon

Ground

HEIGHT: 6'07" WEIGHT: 661.4 lbs.

The male has a brownish body. The female has a blackish body.

♂ ♀

Ω It brandishes its gaping mouth in a display of fearsome strength. It raises vast quantities of sand while attacking.

α It blasts internally stored sand from ports on its body to create a towering twister for attack.

ABILITY
Sand Stream

HIDDEN ABILITY
Sand Force

EGG GROUPS
Field

STAT GROWTH RATES
HP, Attack, Defense, Sp. Atk, Sp. Def, Speed

ITEMS SOMETIMES HELD BY WILD POKÉMON
—

EVOLUTION
Hippopotas → Lv. 34 → Hippowdon

MAIN WAY TO REGISTER IN THE NATIONAL POKÉDEX

Level up a Hippopotas obtained via Link Trade or the GTS to Lv. 34.

Damage taken in normal battles

Type		Type	
Normal	×1	Flying	×1
Fire	×1	Psychic	×1
Water	×2	Bug	×1
Grass	×2	Rock	×0.5
Electric	×0	Ghost	×1
Ice	×2	Dragon	×1
Fighting	×1	Dark	×1
Poison	×0.5	Steel	×1
Ground	×1	Fairy	×1

Damage taken in Inverse battles

Type		Type	
Normal	×1	Flying	×1
Fire	×1	Psychic	×1
Water	×0.5	Bug	×1
Grass	×0.5	Rock	×2
Electric	×2	Ghost	×1
Ice	×0.5	Dragon	×1
Fighting	×1	Dark	×1
Poison	×2	Steel	×1
Ground	×1	Fairy	×1

Can be used in
Inverse Battle
Battle Institute
Battle Maison
Random Matchup (Free Battle)
Random Matchup (Others)

LEVEL-UP MOVES

Lv.	Name	Type	Kind	Pow.	Acc.	PP	Range
1	Ice Fang	Ice	Physical	65	95	15	Normal
1	Fire Fang	Fire	Physical	65	95	15	Normal
1	Thunder Fang	Electric	Physical	65	95	15	Normal
1	Tackle	Normal	Physical	50	100	35	Normal
1	Sand Attack	Ground	Status	—	100	15	Normal
1	Bite	Dark	Physical	60	100	25	Normal
1	Yawn	Normal	Status	—	—	10	Normal
7	Bite	Dark	Physical	60	100	25	Normal
13	Yawn	Normal	Status	—	—	10	Normal
19	Take Down	Normal	Physical	90	85	20	Normal
19	Dig	Ground	Physical	80	100	10	Normal
25	Sand Tomb	Ground	Physical	35	85	15	Normal
31	Crunch	Dark	Physical	80	100	15	Normal
40	Earthquake	Ground	Physical	100	100	10	Adjacent
50	Double-Edge	Normal	Physical	120	100	15	Normal
60	Fissure	Ground	Physical	—	30	5	Normal

TM & HM MOVES

No.	Name	Type	Kind	Pow.	Acc.	PP	Range
TM05	Roar	Normal	Status	—	—	20	Normal
TM06	Toxic	Poison	Status	—	90	10	Normal
TM10	Hidden Power	Normal	Special	60	100	15	Normal
TM11	Sunny Day	Fire	Status	—	—	5	Both Sides
TM15	Hyper Beam	Normal	Special	150	90	5	Normal
TM17	Protect	Normal	Status	—	—	10	Self
TM21	Frustration	Normal	Physical	—	100	20	Normal
TM26	Earthquake	Ground	Physical	100	100	10	Adjacent
TM27	Return	Normal	Physical	—	100	20	Normal
TM28	Dig	Ground	Physical	80	100	10	Normal
TM32	Double Team	Normal	Status	—	—	15	Self
TM37	Sandstorm	Rock	Status	—	—	10	Both Sides
TM39	Rock Tomb	Rock	Physical	60	95	15	Normal
TM42	Facade	Normal	Physical	70	100	20	Normal
TM44	Rest	Psychic	Status	—	—	10	Self
TM45	Attract	Normal	Status	—	100	15	Normal
TM48	Round	Normal	Special	60	100	15	Normal
TM68	Giga Impact	Normal	Physical	150	90	5	Normal
TM71	Stone Edge	Rock	Physical	100	80	5	Normal
TM78	Bulldoze	Ground	Physical	60	100	20	Adjacent
TM80	Rock Slide	Rock	Physical	75	90	10	Many Others
TM87	Swagger	Normal	Status	—	90	15	Normal
TM88	Sleep Talk	Normal	Status	—	—	10	Self
TM90	Substitute	Normal	Status	—	—	10	Self
TM94	Secret Power	Normal	Physical	70	100	20	Normal
TM100	Confide	Normal	Status	—	—	20	Normal
HM04	Strength	Normal	Physical	80	100	15	Normal
HM06	Rock Smash	Fighting	Physical	40	100	15	Normal

MOVES LEARNED IN EXCHANGE FOR BP

Name	Type	Kind	Pow.	Acc.	PP	Range
Iron Head	Steel	Physical	80	100	15	Normal
Earth Power	Ground	Special	90	100	10	Normal
Superpower	Fighting	Physical	120	100	5	Normal
Iron Tail	Steel	Physical	100	75	15	Normal
Snore	Normal	Special	50	100	15	Normal
Water Pulse	Water	Special	60	100	20	Normal
Stealth Rock	Rock	Status	—	—	20	Other Side

MOVES TAUGHT BY PEOPLE

Name	Type	Kind	Pow.	Acc.	PP	Range

National Pokédex **451** Hoenn Pokédex —

Skorupi

Scorpion Pokémon

Poison Bug

HEIGHT: 2'07" WEIGHT: 26.5 lbs.

Same form for ♂ / ♀

Ω It grips prey with its tail claws and injects poison. It tenaciously hangs on until the poison takes.

α It burrows under the sand to lie in wait for prey. Its tail claws can inject its prey with a savage poison.

ABILITIES
Battle Armor
Sniper

HIDDEN ABILITY
Keen Eye

EGG GROUPS
Bug, Water 3

STAT GROWTH RATES
HP, Attack, Defense, Sp. Atk, Sp. Def, Speed

ITEMS SOMETIMES HELD BY WILD POKÉMON
Poison Barb

EVOLUTION
Skorupi → Lv. 40 → Drapion

MAIN WAY TO REGISTER IN THE NATIONAL POKÉDEX

Catch on Route 114. Appears as a hidden Pokémon after you battle Groudon or Kyogre.

Damage taken in normal battles

Type		Type	
Normal	×1	Flying	×2
Fire	×2	Psychic	×2
Water	×1	Bug	×0.5
Grass	×0.25	Rock	×2
Electric	×1	Ghost	×1
Ice	×1	Dragon	×1
Fighting	×0.25	Dark	×1
Poison	×0.5	Steel	×1
Ground	×1	Fairy	×0.5

Damage taken in Inverse battles

Type		Type	
Normal	×1	Flying	×0.5
Fire	×0.5	Psychic	×0.5
Water	×1	Bug	×2
Grass	×4	Rock	×0.5
Electric	×1	Ghost	×1
Ice	×1	Dragon	×1
Fighting	×4	Dark	×1
Poison	×2	Steel	×1
Ground	×1	Fairy	×2

Can be used in
Inverse Battle
Battle Institute
Battle Maison
Random Matchup (Free Battle)
Random Matchup (Others)

LEVEL-UP MOVES

Lv.	Name	Type	Kind	Pow.	Acc.	PP	Range
1	Bite	Dark	Physical	60	100	25	Normal
1	Poison Sting	Poison	Physical	15	100	35	Normal
1	Leer	Normal	Status	—	100	30	Many Others
5	Knock Off	Dark	Physical	65	100	20	Normal
9	Pin Missile	Bug	Physical	25	95	20	Normal
13	Acupressure	Normal	Status	—	—	30	Self/Ally
16	Pursuit	Dark	Physical	40	100	20	Normal
20	Bug Bite	Bug	Physical	60	100	20	Normal
23	Poison Fang	Poison	Physical	50	100	15	Normal
27	Venoshock	Poison	Special	65	100	10	Normal
30	Hone Claws	Dark	Status	—	—	15	Self
34	Toxic Spikes	Poison	Status	—	—	20	Other Side
38	Night Slash	Dark	Physical	70	100	15	Normal
41	Scary Face	Normal	Status	—	100	10	Normal
45	Crunch	Dark	Physical	80	100	15	Normal
47	Fell Stinger	Bug	Physical	30	100	25	Normal
49	Cross Poison	Poison	Physical	70	100	20	Normal

TM & HM MOVES

No.	Name	Type	Kind	Pow.	Acc.	PP	Range
TM01	Hone Claws	Dark	Status	—	—	15	Self
TM06	Toxic	Poison	Status	—	90	10	Normal
TM09	Venoshock	Poison	Special	65	100	10	Normal
TM10	Hidden Power	Normal	Special	60	100	15	Normal
TM11	Sunny Day	Fire	Status	—	—	5	Both Sides
TM12	Taunt	Dark	Status	—	100	20	Normal
TM17	Protect	Normal	Status	—	—	10	Self
TM18	Rain Dance	Water	Status	—	—	5	Both Sides
TM21	Frustration	Normal	Physical	—	100	20	Normal
TM27	Return	Normal	Physical	—	100	20	Normal
TM28	Dig	Ground	Physical	80	100	10	Normal
TM30	Shadow Ball	Ghost	Special	80	100	15	Normal
TM31	Brick Break	Fighting	Physical	75	100	15	Normal
TM32	Double Team	Normal	Status	—	—	15	Self
TM36	Sludge Bomb	Poison	Special	90	100	10	Normal
TM39	Rock Tomb	Rock	Physical	60	95	15	Normal
TM40	Aerial Ace	Flying	Physical	60	—	20	Normal
TM41	Torment	Dark	Status	—	100	15	Normal
TM42	Facade	Normal	Physical	70	100	20	Normal
TM44	Rest	Psychic	Status	—	—	10	Self
TM45	Attract	Normal	Status	—	100	15	Normal
TM46	Thief	Dark	Physical	60	100	25	Normal
TM48	Round	Normal	Special	60	100	15	Normal
TM54	False Swipe	Normal	Physical	40	100	40	Normal
TM56	Fling	Dark	Physical	—	100	10	Normal
TM66	Payback	Dark	Physical	50	100	10	Normal
TM70	Flash	Normal	Status	—	100	20	Normal
TM75	Swords Dance	Normal	Status	—	—	20	Self
TM76	Struggle Bug	Bug	Special	50	100	20	Many Others
TM81	X-Scissor	Bug	Physical	80	100	15	Normal
TM83	Infestation	Bug	Special	20	100	20	Normal
TM84	Poison Jab	Poison	Physical	80	100	20	Normal
TM87	Swagger	Normal	Status	—	90	15	Normal
TM88	Sleep Talk	Normal	Status	—	—	10	Self
TM90	Substitute	Normal	Status	—	—	10	Self
TM94	Secret Power	Normal	Physical	70	100	20	Normal
TM97	Dark Pulse	Dark	Special	80	100	15	Normal
TM100	Confide	Normal	Status	—	—	20	Normal
HM01	Cut	Normal	Physical	50	95	30	Normal
HM04	Strength	Normal	Physical	80	100	15	Normal
HM06	Rock Smash	Fighting	Physical	40	100	15	Normal

MOVES LEARNED IN EXCHANGE FOR BP

Name	Type	Kind	Pow.	Acc.	PP	Range
Bug Bite	Bug	Physical	60	100	20	Normal
Aqua Tail	Water	Physical	90	90	10	Normal
Iron Tail	Steel	Physical	100	75	15	Normal
Snore	Normal	Special	50	100	15	Normal
Knock Off	Dark	Physical	65	100	20	Normal

MOVES TAUGHT BY PEOPLE

Name	Type	Kind	Pow.	Acc.	PP	Range

EGG MOVES

Name	Type	Kind	Pow.	Acc.	PP	Range
Feint Attack	Dark	Physical	60	—	20	Normal
Screech	Normal	Status	—	85	40	Normal
Sand Attack	Ground	Status	—	100	15	Normal
Slash	Normal	Physical	70	100	20	Normal
Confuse Ray	Ghost	Status	—	100	10	Normal
Whirlwind	Normal	Status	—	—	20	Normal
Agility	Psychic	Status	—	—	30	Self
Pursuit	Dark	Physical	40	100	20	Normal
Night Slash	Dark	Physical	70	100	15	Normal
Iron Tail	Steel	Physical	100	75	15	Normal
Twineedle	Bug	Physical	25	100	20	Normal
Poison Tail	Poison	Physical	50	100	25	Normal

National Pokédex **452** Hoenn Pokédex —

Drapion

Ogre Scorpion Pokémon

Poison **Dark**

HEIGHT: 4'03" WEIGHT: 135.6 lbs.

Same form for ♂ / ♀

Ω It takes pride in its strength. Even though it can tear foes apart, it finishes them off with powerful poison.

α It has the power in its clawed arms to make scrap of a car. The tips of its claws release poison.

ABILITIES
Battle Armor
Sniper

HIDDEN ABILITY
Keen Eye

EGG GROUPS
Bug | Water 3

STAT GROWTH RATES
HP ■■■
Attack ■■■■■
Defense ■■■■■
Sp. Atk ■■■
Sp. Def ■■■
Speed ■■■■■

ITEMS SOMETIMES HELD BY WILD POKÉMON
—

EVOLUTION

MAIN WAY TO REGISTER IN THE NATIONAL POKÉDEX

Level up Skorupi to Lv. 40.

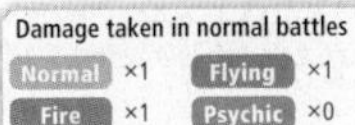

Damage taken in normal battles

Type	×	Type	×
Normal	×1	Flying	×1
Fire	×1	Psychic	×0
Water	×1	Bug	×1
Grass	×0.5	Rock	×1
Electric	×1	Ghost	×0.5
Ice	×1	Dragon	×1
Fighting	×1	Dark	×0.5
Poison	×0.5	Steel	×1
Ground	×2	Fairy	×1

Damage taken in Inverse battles

Type	×	Type	×
Normal	×1	Flying	×1
Fire	×1	Psychic	×1
Water	×1	Bug	×1
Grass	×2	Rock	×1
Electric	×1	Ghost	×2
Ice	×1	Dragon	×1
Fighting	×1	Dark	×2
Poison	×2	Steel	×1
Ground	×0.5	Fairy	×1

Can be used in
Inverse Battle
Battle Institute
Battle Maison
Random Matchup (Free Battle)
Random Matchup (Others)

LEVEL-UP MOVES

Lv.	Name	Type	Kind	Pow.	Acc.	PP	Range
1	Thunder Fang	Electric	Physical	65	95	15	Normal
1	Ice Fang	Ice	Physical	65	95	15	Normal
1	Fire Fang	Fire	Physical	65	95	15	Normal
1	Bite	Dark	Physical	60	100	25	Normal
1	Poison Sting	Poison	Physical	15	100	35	Normal
1	Leer	Normal	Status	—	100	30	Many Others
1	Knock Off	Dark	Physical	65	100	20	Normal
5	Knock Off	Dark	Physical	65	100	20	Normal
9	Pin Missile	Bug	Physical	25	95	20	Normal
13	Acupressure	Normal	Status	—	—	30	Self/Ally
16	Pursuit	Dark	Physical	40	100	20	Normal
20	Bug Bite	Bug	Physical	60	100	20	Normal
23	Poison Fang	Poison	Physical	50	100	15	Normal
27	Venoshock	Poison	Special	65	100	10	Normal
30	Hone Claws	Dark	Status	—	—	15	Self
34	Toxic Spikes	Poison	Status	—	—	20	Other Side
38	Night Slash	Dark	Physical	70	100	15	Normal
43	Scary Face	Normal	Status	—	100	10	Normal
49	Crunch	Dark	Physical	80	100	15	Normal
53	Fell Stinger	Bug	Physical	30	100	25	Normal
57	Cross Poison	Poison	Physical	70	100	20	Normal

TM & HM MOVES

No.	Name	Type	Kind	Pow.	Acc.	PP	Range
TM01	Hone Claws	Dark	Status	—	—	15	Self
TM05	Roar	Normal	Status	—	—	20	Normal
TM06	Toxic	Poison	Status	—	90	10	Normal
TM09	Venoshock	Poison	Special	65	100	10	Normal
TM10	Hidden Power	Normal	Special	60	100	15	Normal
TM11	Sunny Day	Fire	Status	—	—	5	Both Sides
TM12	Taunt	Dark	Status	—	100	20	Normal
TM15	Hyper Beam	Normal	Special	150	90	5	Normal
TM17	Protect	Normal	Status	—	—	10	Self
TM18	Rain Dance	Water	Status	—	—	5	Both Sides
TM21	Frustration	Normal	Physical	—	100	20	Normal
TM26	Earthquake	Ground	Physical	100	100	10	Adjacent
TM27	Return	Normal	Physical	—	100	20	Normal
TM28	Dig	Ground	Physical	80	100	10	Normal
TM30	Shadow Ball	Ghost	Special	80	100	15	Normal
TM31	Brick Break	Fighting	Physical	75	100	15	Normal
TM32	Double Team	Normal	Status	—	—	15	Self
TM36	Sludge Bomb	Poison	Special	90	100	10	Normal
TM39	Rock Tomb	Rock	Physical	60	95	15	Normal
TM40	Aerial Ace	Flying	Physical	60	—	20	Normal
TM41	Torment	Dark	Status	—	100	15	Normal
TM42	Facade	Normal	Physical	70	100	20	Normal
TM44	Rest	Psychic	Status	—	—	10	Self
TM45	Attract	Normal	Status	—	100	15	Normal
TM46	Thief	Dark	Physical	60	100	25	Normal
TM48	Round	Normal	Special	60	100	15	Normal
TM54	False Swipe	Normal	Physical	40	100	40	Normal
TM56	Fling	Dark	Physical	—	100	10	Normal
TM66	Payback	Dark	Physical	50	100	10	Normal
TM67	Retaliate	Normal	Physical	70	100	5	Normal
TM68	Giga Impact	Normal	Physical	150	90	5	Normal
TM70	Flash	Normal	Status	—	100	20	Normal
TM75	Swords Dance	Normal	Status	—	—	20	Self
TM76	Struggle Bug	Bug	Special	50	100	20	Many Others
TM78	Bulldoze	Ground	Physical	60	100	20	Adjacent
TM80	Rock Slide	Rock	Physical	75	90	10	Many Others
TM81	X-Scissor	Bug	Physical	80	100	15	Normal
TM83	Infestation	Bug	Special	20	100	20	Normal
TM84	Poison Jab	Poison	Physical	80	100	20	Normal
TM87	Swagger	Normal	Status	—	90	15	Normal
TM88	Sleep Talk	Normal	Status	—	—	10	Self
TM90	Substitute	Normal	Status	—	—	10	Self
TM94	Secret Power	Normal	Physical	70	100	20	Normal
TM95	Snarl	Dark	Special	55	95	15	Many Others
TM97	Dark Pulse	Dark	Special	80	100	15	Normal
TM100	Confide	Normal	Status	—	—	20	Normal
HM01	Cut	Normal	Physical	50	95	30	Normal
HM04	Strength	Normal	Physical	80	100	15	Normal
HM06	Rock Smash	Fighting	Physical	40	100	15	Normal

MOVES LEARNED IN EXCHANGE FOR BP

Name	Type	Kind	Pow.	Acc.	PP	Range
Bug Bite	Bug	Physical	60	100	20	Normal
Aqua Tail	Water	Physical	90	90	10	Normal
Iron Tail	Steel	Physical	100	75	15	Normal
Snore	Normal	Special	50	100	15	Normal
Knock Off	Dark	Physical	65	100	20	Normal

MOVES TAUGHT BY PEOPLE

Name	Type	Kind	Pow.	Acc.	PP	Range

National Pokédex **453** Hoenn Pokédex —

Croagunk

Toxic Mouth Pokémon

Poison **Fighting**

HEIGHT: 2'04" WEIGHT: 50.7 lbs.

The male's stripes on its abdomen are located lower than the female's stripes.

♂ ♀

Ω Its cheeks hold poison sacs. It tries to catch foes off guard to jab them with toxic fingers.

α Inflating its poison sacs, it fills the area with an odd sound and hits flinching opponents with a poison jab.

ABILITIES
Anticipation
Dry Skin

HIDDEN ABILITY
Poison Touch

EGG GROUPS
Human-Like

STAT GROWTH RATES
HP ■■
Attack ■■■
Defense ■■
Sp. Atk ■■■
Sp. Def ■■
Speed ■■■

ITEMS SOMETIMES HELD BY WILD POKÉMON
—

EVOLUTION

Croagunk → Lv. 37 → Toxicroak

MAIN WAY TO REGISTER IN THE NATIONAL POKÉDEX

Appears in *Pokémon X* and *Pokémon Y*. Bring it to your game using Link Trade or the GTS.

Damage taken in normal battles

Type	×	Type	×
Normal	×1	Flying	×2
! Fire	×1	Psychic	×4
! Water	×1	Bug	×0.25
Grass	×0.5	Rock	×0.5
Electric	×1	Ghost	×1
Ice	×1	Dragon	×1
Fighting	×0.5	Dark	×0.5
Poison	×0.5	Steel	×1
Ground	×2	Fairy	×1

Damage taken in Inverse battles

Type	×	Type	×
Normal	×1	Flying	×0.5
! Fire	×1	Psychic	×0.25
! Water	×1	Bug	×4
Grass	×2	Rock	×2
Electric	×1	Ghost	×1
Ice	×1	Dragon	×1
Fighting	×2	Dark	×2
Poison	×2	Steel	×1
Ground	×0.5	Fairy	×1

Can be used in
Inverse Battle
Battle Institute
Battle Maison
Random Matchup (Free Battle)
Random Matchup (Others)

LEVEL-UP MOVES

Lv.	Name	Type	Kind	Pow.	Acc.	PP	Range
1	Astonish	Ghost	Physical	30	100	15	Normal
3	Mud-Slap	Ground	Special	20	100	10	Normal
8	Poison Sting	Poison	Physical	15	100	35	Normal
10	Taunt	Dark	Status	—	100	20	Normal
15	Pursuit	Dark	Physical	40	100	20	Normal
17	Feint Attack	Dark	Physical	60	—	20	Normal
22	Revenge	Fighting	Physical	60	100	10	Normal
24	Swagger	Normal	Status	—	90	15	Normal
29	Mud Bomb	Ground	Special	65	85	10	Normal
31	Sucker Punch	Dark	Physical	80	100	5	Normal
36	Venoshock	Poison	Special	65	100	10	Normal
38	Nasty Plot	Dark	Status	—	—	20	Self
43	Poison Jab	Poison	Physical	80	100	20	Normal
45	Sludge Bomb	Poison	Special	90	100	10	Normal
47	Belch	Poison	Special	120	90	10	Normal
50	Flatter	Dark	Status	—	100	15	Normal

TM & HM MOVES

No.	Name	Type	Kind	Pow.	Acc.	PP	Range
TM06	Toxic	Poison	Status	—	90	10	Normal
TM08	Bulk Up	Fighting	Status	—	—	20	Self
TM09	Venoshock	Poison	Special	65	100	10	Normal
TM10	Hidden Power	Normal	Special	60	100	15	Normal
TM11	Sunny Day	Fire	Status	—	—	5	Both Sides
TM12	Taunt	Dark	Status	—	100	20	Normal
TM17	Protect	Normal	Status	—	—	10	Self
TM18	Rain Dance	Water	Status	—	—	5	Both Sides
TM21	Frustration	Normal	Physical	—	100	20	Normal
TM26	Earthquake	Ground	Physical	100	100	10	Adjacent
TM27	Return	Normal	Physical	—	100	20	Normal
TM28	Dig	Ground	Physical	80	100	10	Normal
TM30	Shadow Ball	Ghost	Special	80	100	15	Normal
TM31	Brick Break	Fighting	Physical	75	100	15	Normal
TM32	Double Team	Normal	Status	—	—	15	Self
TM34	Sludge Wave	Poison	Special	95	100	10	Adjacent
TM36	Sludge Bomb	Poison	Special	90	100	10	Normal
TM39	Rock Tomb	Rock	Physical	60	95	15	Normal
TM41	Torment	Dark	Status	—	100	15	Normal
TM42	Facade	Normal	Physical	70	100	20	Normal
TM44	Rest	Psychic	Status	—	—	10	Self
TM45	Attract	Normal	Status	—	100	15	Normal
TM46	Thief	Dark	Physical	60	100	25	Normal
TM47	Low Sweep	Fighting	Physical	65	100	20	Normal
TM48	Round	Normal	Special	60	100	15	Normal
TM52	Focus Blast	Fighting	Special	120	70	5	Normal
TM56	Fling	Dark	Physical	—	100	10	Normal
TM63	Embargo	Dark	Status	—	100	15	Normal
TM66	Payback	Dark	Physical	50	100	10	Normal
TM67	Retaliate	Normal	Physical	70	100	5	Normal
TM78	Bulldoze	Ground	Physical	60	100	20	Adjacent
TM80	Rock Slide	Rock	Physical	75	90	10	Many Others
TM81	X-Scissor	Bug	Physical	80	100	15	Normal
TM84	Poison Jab	Poison	Physical	80	100	20	Normal
TM87	Swagger	Normal	Status	—	90	15	Normal
TM88	Sleep Talk	Normal	Status	—	—	10	Self
TM90	Substitute	Normal	Status	—	—	10	Self
TM94	Secret Power	Normal	Physical	70	100	20	Normal
TM97	Dark Pulse	Dark	Special	80	100	15	Normal
TM98	Power-Up Punch	Fighting	Physical	40	100	20	Normal
TM100	Confide	Normal	Status	—	—	20	Normal
HM04	Strength	Normal	Physical	80	100	15	Normal
HM06	Rock Smash	Fighting	Physical	40	100	15	Normal

MOVES LEARNED IN EXCHANGE FOR BP

Name	Type	Kind	Pow.	Acc.	PP	Range
Super Fang	Normal	Physical	—	90	10	Normal
Dual Chop	Dragon	Physical	40	90	15	Normal
Bounce	Flying	Physical	85	85	5	Normal
Low Kick	Fighting	Physical	—	100	20	Normal
Gunk Shot	Poison	Physical	120	80	5	Normal
Thunder Punch	Electric	Physical	75	100	15	Normal
Ice Punch	Ice	Physical	75	100	15	Normal
Foul Play	Dark	Physical	95	100	15	Normal
Icy Wind	Ice	Special	55	95	15	Many Others
Snore	Normal	Special	50	100	15	Normal
Knock Off	Dark	Physical	65	100	20	Normal
Role Play	Psychic	Status	—	—	10	Normal
Drain Punch	Fighting	Physical	75	100	10	Normal
Focus Punch	Fighting	Physical	150	100	20	Normal
Spite	Ghost	Status	—	100	10	Normal
Helping Hand	Normal	Status	—	—	20	1 Ally
Snatch	Dark	Status	—	—	10	Self

MOVES TAUGHT BY PEOPLE

Name	Type	Kind	Pow.	Acc.	PP	Range

EGG MOVES

Name	Type	Kind	Pow.	Acc.	PP	Range
Me First	Normal	Status	—	—	20	Varies
Feint	Normal	Physical	30	100	10	Normal
Dynamic Punch	Fighting	Physical	100	50	5	Normal
Headbutt	Normal	Physical	70	100	15	Normal
Vacuum Wave	Fighting	Special	40	100	30	Normal
Meditate	Psychic	Status	—	—	40	Self
Fake Out	Normal	Physical	40	100	10	Normal
Wake-Up Slap	Fighting	Physical	70	100	10	Normal
Smelling Salts	Normal	Physical	70	100	10	Normal
Cross Chop	Fighting	Physical	100	80	5	Normal
Bullet Punch	Steel	Physical	40	100	30	Normal
Counter	Fighting	Physical	—	100	20	Varies
Drain Punch	Fighting	Physical	75	100	10	Normal
Acupressure	Normal	Status	—	—	30	Self/Ally
Quick Guard	Fighting	Status	—	—	15	Your Side

National Pokédex **454** Hoenn Pokédex —

Toxicroak

Toxic Mouth Pokémon

Poison Fighting

HEIGHT: 4'03" WEIGHT: 97.9 lbs.

The male has a bigger throat sac. The female has a smaller throat sac.

♂ ♀

Ω It has a poison sac at its throat. When it croaks, the stored poison is churned for greater potency.

α Its knuckle claws secrete a toxin so vile that even a scratch could prove fatal.

ABILITIES
Anticipation
Dry Skin

HIDDEN ABILITY
Poison Touch

EGG GROUPS
Human-Like

STAT GROWTH RATES
HP
Attack
Defense
Sp. Atk
Sp. Def
Speed

ITEMS SOMETIMES HELD BY WILD POKÉMON
—

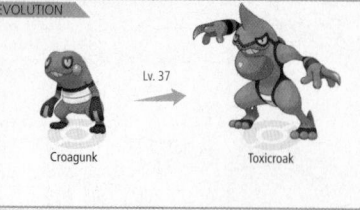

EVOLUTION
Croagunk → Lv. 37 → Toxicroak

MAIN WAY TO REGISTER IN THE NATIONAL POKÉDEX

Level up a Croagunk obtained via Link Trade or the GTS to Lv. 37.

Damage taken in normal battles

Normal	×1	Flying	×2
! Fire	×1	Psychic	×4
! Water	×1	Bug	×0.25
Grass	×0.5	Rock	×0.5
Electric	×1	Ghost	×1
Ice	×1	Dragon	×1
Fighting	×0.5	Dark	×0.5
Poison	×0.5	Steel	×1
Ground	×2	Fairy	×1

Damage taken in Inverse battles

Normal	×1	Flying	×0.5
! Fire	×1	Psychic	×0.25
! Water	×1	Bug	×4
Grass	×2	Rock	×2
Electric	×1	Ghost	×1
Ice	×1	Dragon	×1
Fighting	×2	Dark	×2
Poison	×2	Steel	×1
Ground	×0.5	Fairy	×1

Can be used in
Inverse Battle
Battle Institute
Battle Maison
Random Matchup (Free Battle)
Random Matchup (Others)

LEVEL-UP MOVES

Lv.	Name	Type	Kind	Pow.	Acc.	PP	Range
1	Astonish	Ghost	Physical	30	100	15	Normal
1	Mud-Slap	Ground	Special	20	100	10	Normal
1	Poison Sting	Poison	Physical	15	100	35	Normal
3	Mud-Slap	Ground	Special	20	100	10	Normal
8	Poison Sting	Poison	Physical	15	100	35	Normal
10	Taunt	Dark	Status	—	100	20	Normal
15	Pursuit	Dark	Physical	40	100	20	Normal
17	Feint Attack	Dark	Physical	60	—	20	Normal
22	Revenge	Fighting	Physical	60	100	10	Normal
24	Swagger	Normal	Status	—	90	15	Normal
29	Mud Bomb	Ground	Special	65	85	10	Normal
31	Sucker Punch	Dark	Physical	80	100	5	Normal
36	Venoshock	Poison	Special	65	100	10	Normal
41	Nasty Plot	Dark	Status	—	—	20	Self
49	Poison Jab	Poison	Physical	80	100	20	Normal
54	Sludge Bomb	Poison	Special	90	100	10	Normal
58	Belch	Poison	Special	120	90	10	Normal
62	Flatter	Dark	Status	—	100	15	Normal

TM & HM MOVES

No.	Name	Type	Kind	Pow.	Acc.	PP	Range
TM06	Toxic	Poison	Status	—	90	10	Normal
TM08	Bulk Up	Fighting	Status	—	—	20	Self
TM09	Venoshock	Poison	Special	65	100	10	Normal
TM10	Hidden Power	Normal	Special	60	100	15	Normal
TM11	Sunny Day	Fire	Status	—	—	5	Both Sides
TM12	Taunt	Dark	Status	—	100	20	Normal
TM15	Hyper Beam	Normal	Special	150	90	5	Normal
TM17	Protect	Normal	Status	—	—	10	Self
TM18	Rain Dance	Water	Status	—	—	5	Both Sides
TM21	Frustration	Normal	Physical	—	100	20	Normal
TM26	Earthquake	Ground	Physical	100	100	10	Adjacent
TM27	Return	Normal	Physical	—	100	20	Normal
TM28	Dig	Ground	Physical	80	100	10	Normal
TM30	Shadow Ball	Ghost	Special	80	100	15	Normal
TM31	Brick Break	Fighting	Physical	75	100	15	Normal
TM32	Double Team	Normal	Status	—	—	15	Self
TM34	Sludge Wave	Poison	Special	95	100	10	Adjacent
TM36	Sludge Bomb	Poison	Special	90	100	10	Normal
TM39	Rock Tomb	Rock	Physical	60	95	15	Normal
TM41	Torment	Dark	Status	—	100	15	Normal
TM42	Facade	Normal	Physical	70	100	20	Normal
TM44	Rest	Psychic	Status	—	—	10	Self
TM45	Attract	Normal	Status	—	100	15	Normal
TM46	Thief	Dark	Physical	60	100	25	Normal
TM47	Low Sweep	Fighting	Physical	65	100	20	Normal
TM48	Round	Normal	Special	60	100	15	Normal
TM52	Focus Blast	Fighting	Special	120	70	5	Normal
TM56	Fling	Dark	Physical	—	100	10	Normal
TM63	Embargo	Dark	Status	—	100	15	Normal
TM66	Payback	Dark	Physical	50	100	10	Normal
TM67	Retaliate	Normal	Physical	70	100	5	Normal
TM68	Giga Impact	Normal	Physical	150	90	5	Normal
TM71	Stone Edge	Rock	Physical	100	80	5	Normal
TM75	Swords Dance	Normal	Status	—	—	20	Self
TM78	Bulldoze	Ground	Physical	60	100	20	Adjacent
TM80	Rock Slide	Rock	Physical	75	90	10	Many Others
TM81	X-Scissor	Bug	Physical	80	100	15	Normal
TM84	Poison Jab	Poison	Physical	80	100	20	Normal
TM87	Swagger	Normal	Status	—	90	15	Normal
TM88	Sleep Talk	Normal	Status	—	—	10	Self
TM90	Substitute	Normal	Status	—	—	10	Self
TM94	Secret Power	Normal	Physical	70	100	20	Normal
TM97	Dark Pulse	Dark	Special	80	100	15	Normal
TM98	Power-Up Punch	Fighting	Physical	40	100	20	Normal
TM100	Confide	Normal	Status	—	—	20	Normal
HM01	Cut	Normal	Physical	50	95	30	Normal
HM04	Strength	Normal	Physical	80	100	15	Normal
HM06	Rock Smash	Fighting	Physical	40	100	15	Normal

MOVES LEARNED IN EXCHANGE FOR BP

Name	Type	Kind	Pow.	Acc.	PP	Range
Super Fang	Normal	Physical	—	90	10	Normal
Dual Chop	Dragon	Physical	40	90	15	Normal
Bounce	Flying	Physical	85	85	5	Normal
Low Kick	Fighting	Physical	—	100	20	Normal
Gunk Shot	Poison	Physical	120	80	5	Normal
Thunder Punch	Electric	Physical	75	100	15	Normal
Ice Punch	Ice	Physical	75	100	15	Normal
Foul Play	Dark	Physical	95	100	15	Normal
Icy Wind	Ice	Special	55	95	15	Many Others
Snore	Normal	Special	50	100	15	Normal
Knock Off	Dark	Physical	65	100	20	Normal
Role Play	Psychic	Status	—	—	10	Normal
Drain Punch	Fighting	Physical	75	100	10	Normal
Focus Punch	Fighting	Physical	150	100	20	Normal
Spite	Ghost	Status	—	100	10	Normal
Helping Hand	Normal	Status	—	—	20	1 Ally
Snatch	Dark	Status	—	—	10	Self

MOVES TAUGHT BY PEOPLE

Name	Type	Kind	Pow.	Acc.	PP	Range

National Pokédex **455** Hoenn Pokédex —

Carnivine

Bug Catcher Pokémon

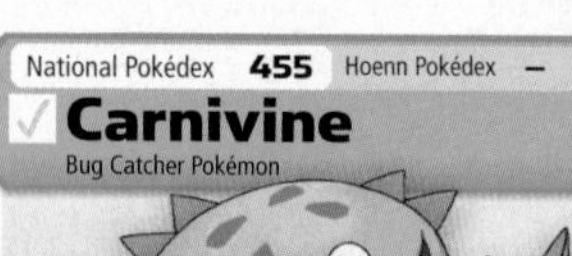

Grass

HEIGHT: 4'07" WEIGHT: 59.5 lbs.

Same form for ♂ / ♀

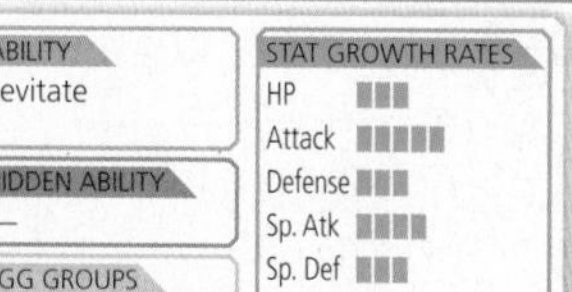

Ω It attracts prey with its sweet-smelling saliva, then chomps down. It takes a whole day to eat prey.

α It binds itself to trees in marshes. It attracts prey with its sweet-smelling drool and gulps them down.

ABILITY
Levitate

HIDDEN ABILITY
—

EGG GROUPS
Grass

STAT GROWTH RATES
HP
Attack
Defense
Sp. Atk
Sp. Def
Speed

ITEMS SOMETIMES HELD BY WILD POKÉMON
—

EVOLUTION
Does not evolve

MAIN WAY TO REGISTER IN THE NATIONAL POKÉDEX

Appears in *Pokémon X* and *Pokémon Y*. Bring it to your game using Link Trade or the GTS.

Damage taken in normal battles

Normal	×1	Flying	×2
Fire	×2	Psychic	×1
Water	×0.5	Bug	×2
Grass	×0.5	Rock	×1
Electric	×0.5	Ghost	×1
Ice	×2	Dragon	×1
Fighting	×1	Dark	×1
Poison	×2	Steel	×1
! Ground	×0.5	Fairy	×1

Damage taken in Inverse battles

Normal	×1	Flying	×0.5
Fire	×0.5	Psychic	×1
Water	×2	Bug	×0.5
Grass	×2	Rock	×1
Electric	×2	Ghost	×1
Ice	×0.5	Dragon	×1
Fighting	×1	Dark	×1
Poison	×0.5	Steel	×1
! Ground	×2	Fairy	×1

Can be used in
Inverse Battle
Battle Institute
Battle Maison
Random Matchup (Free Battle)
Random Matchup (Others)

LEVEL-UP MOVES

Lv.	Name	Type	Kind	Pow.	Acc.	PP	Range
1	Bind	Normal	Physical	15	85	20	Normal
1	Growth	Normal	Status	—	—	20	Self
7	Bite	Dark	Physical	60	100	25	Normal
11	Vine Whip	Grass	Physical	45	100	25	Normal
17	Sweet Scent	Normal	Status	—	100	20	Many Others
21	Ingrain	Grass	Status	—	—	20	Self
27	Feint Attack	Dark	Physical	60	—	20	Normal
31	Leaf Tornado	Grass	Special	65	90	10	Normal
37	Stockpile	Normal	Status	—	—	20	Self
37	Spit Up	Normal	Special	—	100	10	Normal
37	Swallow	Normal	Status	—	—	10	Self
41	Crunch	Dark	Physical	80	100	15	Normal
47	Wring Out	Normal	Special	—	100	5	Normal
50	Power Whip	Grass	Physical	120	85	10	Normal

TM & HM MOVES

No.	Name	Type	Kind	Pow.	Acc.	PP	Range
TM06	Toxic	Poison	Status	—	90	10	Normal
TM10	Hidden Power	Normal	Special	60	100	15	Normal
TM11	Sunny Day	Fire	Status	—	—	5	Both Sides
TM15	Hyper Beam	Normal	Special	150	90	5	Normal
TM17	Protect	Normal	Status	—	—	10	Self
TM21	Frustration	Normal	Physical	—	100	20	Normal
TM22	Solar Beam	Grass	Special	120	100	10	Normal
TM27	Return	Normal	Physical	—	100	20	Normal
TM32	Double Team	Normal	Status	—	—	15	Self
TM36	Sludge Bomb	Poison	Special	90	100	10	Normal
TM42	Facade	Normal	Physical	70	100	20	Normal
TM44	Rest	Psychic	Status	—	—	10	Self
TM45	Attract	Normal	Status	—	100	15	Normal
TM46	Thief	Dark	Physical	60	100	25	Normal
TM48	Round	Normal	Special	60	100	15	Normal
TM53	Energy Ball	Grass	Special	90	100	10	Normal
TM56	Fling	Dark	Physical	—	100	10	Normal
TM66	Payback	Dark	Physical	50	100	10	Normal
TM68	Giga Impact	Normal	Physical	150	90	5	Normal
TM70	Flash	Normal	Status	—	100	20	Normal
TM75	Swords Dance	Normal	Status	—	—	20	Self
TM83	Infestation	Bug	Special	20	100	20	Normal
TM86	Grass Knot	Grass	Special	—	100	20	Normal
TM87	Swagger	Normal	Status	—	90	15	Normal
TM88	Sleep Talk	Normal	Status	—	—	10	Self
TM90	Substitute	Normal	Status	—	—	10	Self
TM94	Secret Power	Normal	Physical	70	100	20	Normal
TM96	Nature Power	Normal	Status	—	—	20	Normal
TM100	Confide	Normal	Status	—	—	20	Normal
HM01	Cut	Normal	Physical	50	95	30	Normal

MOVES LEARNED IN EXCHANGE FOR BP

Name	Type	Kind	Pow.	Acc.	PP	Range
Bug Bite	Bug	Physical	60	100	20	Normal
Seed Bomb	Grass	Physical	80	100	15	Normal
Bind	Normal	Physical	15	85	20	Normal
Snore	Normal	Special	50	100	15	Normal
Knock Off	Dark	Physical	65	100	20	Normal
Synthesis	Grass	Status	—	—	5	Self
Giga Drain	Grass	Special	75	100	10	Normal
Gastro Acid	Poison	Status	—	100	10	Normal
Worry Seed	Grass	Status	—	100	10	Normal

MOVES TAUGHT BY PEOPLE

Name	Type	Kind	Pow.	Acc.	PP	Range

EGG MOVES

Name	Type	Kind	Pow.	Acc.	PP	Range
Sleep Powder	Grass	Status	—	75	15	Normal
Stun Spore	Grass	Status	—	75	30	Normal
Razor Leaf	Grass	Physical	55	95	25	Many Others
Slam	Normal	Physical	80	75	20	Normal
Synthesis	Grass	Status	—	—	5	Self
Magical Leaf	Grass	Special	60	—	20	Normal
Leech Seed	Grass	Status	—	90	10	Normal
Worry Seed	Grass	Status	—	100	10	Normal
Giga Drain	Grass	Special	75	100	10	Normal
Rage Powder	Bug	Status	—	—	20	Self
Grass Whistle	Grass	Status	—	55	15	Normal

National Pokédex **456** Hoenn Pokédex **—**

Finneon

Wing Fish Pokémon

Water

HEIGHT: 1'04" WEIGHT: 15.4 lbs.

The lower part of the male's tail fin is smaller.
The lower part of the female's tail fin is larger.

Ω The line running down its side can store sunlight. It shines vividly at night.

α After long exposure to sunlight, the patterns on its tail fins shine vividly when darkness arrives.

ABILITIES
Swift Swim
Storm Drain

HIDDEN ABILITY
Water Veil

EGG GROUPS
Water 2

STAT GROWTH RATES

HP	■■
Attack	■■■
Defense	■■■
Sp. Atk	■■
Sp. Def	■■■
Speed	■■■■

ITEMS SOMETIMES HELD BY WILD POKÉMON
—

EVOLUTION

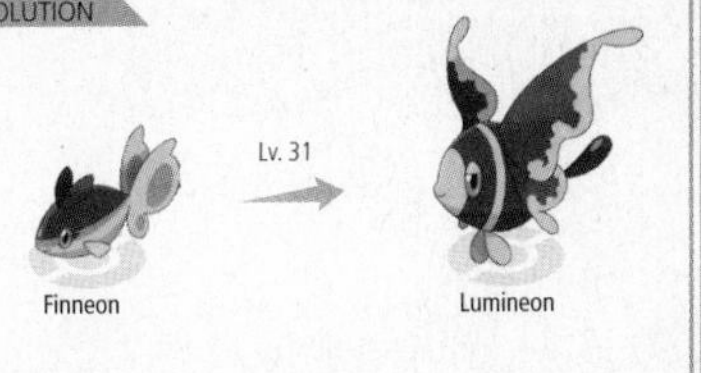

MAIN WAY TO REGISTER IN THE NATIONAL POKÉDEX

Catch on the water surface on Route 122. Appears as a hidden Pokémon after you battle Groudon or Kyogre.

Damage taken in normal battles

Type		Type	
Normal	×1	Flying	×1
Fire	×0.5	Psychic	×1
Water	×0.5	Bug	×1
Grass	×2	Rock	×1
Electric	×2	Ghost	×1
Ice	×0.5	Dragon	×1
Fighting	×1	Dark	×1
Poison	×1	Steel	×0.5
Ground	×1	Fairy	×1

Damage taken in Inverse battles

Type		Type	
Normal	×1	Flying	×1
Fire	×2	Psychic	×1
Water	×2	Bug	×1
Grass	×0.5	Rock	×1
Electric	×0.5	Ghost	×1
Ice	×2	Dragon	×1
Fighting	×1	Dark	×1
Poison	×1	Steel	×2
Ground	×1	Fairy	×1

Can be used in
- Inverse Battle
- Battle Institute
- Battle Maison
- Random Matchup (Free Battle)
- Random Matchup (Others)

LEVEL-UP MOVES

Lv.	Name	Type	Kind	Pow.	Acc.	PP	Range
1	Pound	Normal	Physical	40	100	35	Normal
6	Water Gun	Water	Special	40	100	25	Normal
10	Attract	Normal	Status	—	100	15	Normal
13	Rain Dance	Water	Status	—	—	5	Both Sides
17	Gust	Flying	Special	40	100	35	Normal
22	Water Pulse	Water	Special	60	100	20	Normal
26	Captivate	Normal	Status	—	100	20	Many Others
29	Safeguard	Normal	Status	—	—	25	Your Side
33	Aqua Ring	Water	Status	—	—	20	Self
38	Whirlpool	Water	Special	35	85	15	Normal
42	U-turn	Bug	Physical	70	100	20	Normal
45	Bounce	Flying	Physical	85	85	5	Normal
49	Silver Wind	Bug	Special	60	100	5	Normal
54	Soak	Water	Status	—	100	20	Normal

TM & HM MOVES

No.	Name	Type	Kind	Pow.	Acc.	PP	Range
TM06	Toxic	Poison	Status	—	90	10	Normal
TM07	Hail	Ice	Status	—	—	10	Both Sides
TM10	Hidden Power	Normal	Special	60	100	15	Normal
TM13	Ice Beam	Ice	Special	90	100	10	Normal
TM14	Blizzard	Ice	Special	110	70	5	Many Others
TM17	Protect	Normal	Status	—	—	10	Self
TM18	Rain Dance	Water	Status	—	—	5	Both Sides
TM20	Safeguard	Normal	Status	—	—	25	Your Side
TM21	Frustration	Normal	Physical	—	100	20	Normal
TM27	Return	Normal	Physical	—	100	20	Normal
TM32	Double Team	Normal	Status	—	—	15	Self
TM42	Facade	Normal	Physical	70	100	20	Normal
TM44	Rest	Psychic	Status	—	—	10	Self
TM45	Attract	Normal	Status	—	100	15	Normal
TM48	Round	Normal	Special	60	100	15	Normal
TM55	Scald	Water	Special	80	100	15	Normal
TM66	Payback	Dark	Physical	50	100	10	Normal
TM70	Flash	Normal	Status	—	100	20	Normal
TM77	Psych Up	Normal	Status	—	—	10	Normal
TM87	Swagger	Normal	Status	—	90	15	Normal
TM88	Sleep Talk	Normal	Status	—	—	10	Self
TM89	U-turn	Bug	Physical	70	100	20	Normal
TM90	Substitute	Normal	Status	—	—	10	Self
TM94	Secret Power	Normal	Physical	70	100	20	Normal
TM96	Nature Power	Normal	Status	—	—	20	Normal
TM100	Confide	Normal	Status	—	—	20	Normal
HM03	Surf	Water	Special	90	100	15	Adjacent
HM05	Waterfall	Water	Physical	80	100	15	Normal
HM07	Dive	Water	Physical	80	100	10	Normal

MOVES LEARNED IN EXCHANGE FOR BP

Name	Type	Kind	Pow.	Acc.	PP	Range
Signal Beam	Bug	Special	75	100	15	Normal
Bounce	Flying	Physical	85	85	5	Normal
Icy Wind	Ice	Special	55	95	15	Many Others
Aqua Tail	Water	Physical	90	90	10	Normal
Snore	Normal	Special	50	100	15	Normal
Tailwind	Flying	Status	—	—	15	Your Side
Water Pulse	Water	Special	60	100	20	Normal

MOVES TAUGHT BY PEOPLE

Name	Type	Kind	Pow.	Acc.	PP	Range

EGG MOVES

Name	Type	Kind	Pow.	Acc.	PP	Range
Sweet Kiss	Fairy	Status	—	75	10	Normal
Charm	Fairy	Status	—	100	20	Normal
Flail	Normal	Physical	—	100	15	Normal
Aqua Tail	Water	Physical	90	90	10	Normal
Splash	Normal	Status	—	—	40	Self
Psybeam	Psychic	Special	65	100	20	Normal
Tickle	Normal	Status	—	100	20	Normal
Agility	Psychic	Status	—	—	30	Self
Brine	Water	Special	65	100	10	Normal
Aurora Beam	Ice	Special	65	100	20	Normal
Signal Beam	Bug	Special	75	100	15	Normal

National Pokédex **457** Hoenn Pokédex **—**

Lumineon

Neon Pokémon

Water

HEIGHT: 13'11" WEIGHT: 52.9 lbs.

The male's pectoral fins are shorter on the bottom than the female's.

Ω It lives on the deep-sea floor. It attracts prey by flashing the patterns on its four tail fins.

α To avoid detection by predators, it crawls along the seafloor using the two fins on its chest.

ABILITIES
Swift Swim
Storm Drain

HIDDEN ABILITY
Water Veil

EGG GROUPS
Water 2

STAT GROWTH RATES

HP	■■■
Attack	■■■■
Defense	■■■■
Sp. Atk	■■■
Sp. Def	■■■■
Speed	■■■■■

ITEMS SOMETIMES HELD BY WILD POKÉMON
—

EVOLUTION

Lv. 31
Finneon → Lumineon

MAIN WAY TO REGISTER IN THE NATIONAL POKÉDEX

Level up Finneon to Lv. 31.

Damage taken in normal battles

Type		Type	
Normal	×1	Flying	×1
Fire	×0.5	Psychic	×1
Water	×0.5	Bug	×1
Grass	×2	Rock	×1
Electric	×2	Ghost	×1
Ice	×0.5	Dragon	×1
Fighting	×1	Dark	×1
Poison	×1	Steel	×0.5
Ground	×1	Fairy	×1

Damage taken in Inverse battles

Type		Type	
Normal	×1	Flying	×1
Fire	×2	Psychic	×1
Water	×2	Bug	×1
Grass	×0.5	Rock	×1
Electric	×0.5	Ghost	×1
Ice	×2	Dragon	×1
Fighting	×1	Dark	×1
Poison	×1	Steel	×2
Ground	×1	Fairy	×1

Can be used in
- Inverse Battle
- Battle Institute
- Battle Maison
- Random Matchup (Free Battle)
- Random Matchup (Others)

LEVEL-UP MOVES

Lv.	Name	Type	Kind	Pow.	Acc.	PP	Range
1	Soak	Water	Status	—	100	20	Normal
1	Gust	Flying	Special	40	100	35	Normal
1	Pound	Normal	Physical	40	100	35	Normal
1	Water Gun	Water	Special	40	100	25	Normal
1	Attract	Normal	Status	—	100	15	Normal
6	Water Gun	Water	Special	40	100	25	Normal
10	Attract	Normal	Status	—	100	15	Normal
13	Rain Dance	Water	Status	—	—	5	Both Sides
17	Gust	Flying	Special	40	100	35	Normal
22	Water Pulse	Water	Special	60	100	20	Normal
26	Captivate	Normal	Status	—	100	20	Many Others
29	Safeguard	Normal	Status	—	—	25	Your Side
35	Aqua Ring	Water	Status	—	—	20	Self
42	Whirlpool	Water	Special	35	85	15	Normal
48	U-turn	Bug	Physical	70	100	20	Normal
53	Bounce	Flying	Physical	85	85	5	Normal
59	Silver Wind	Bug	Special	60	100	5	Normal
66	Soak	Water	Status	—	100	20	Normal

TM & HM MOVES

No.	Name	Type	Kind	Pow.	Acc.	PP	Range
TM06	Toxic	Poison	Status	—	90	10	Normal
TM07	Hail	Ice	Status	—	—	10	Both Sides
TM10	Hidden Power	Normal	Special	60	100	15	Normal
TM13	Ice Beam	Ice	Special	90	100	10	Normal
TM14	Blizzard	Ice	Special	110	70	5	Many Others
TM15	Hyper Beam	Normal	Special	150	90	5	Normal
TM17	Protect	Normal	Status	—	—	10	Self
TM18	Rain Dance	Water	Status	—	—	5	Both Sides
TM20	Safeguard	Normal	Status	—	—	25	Your Side
TM21	Frustration	Normal	Physical	—	100	20	Normal
TM27	Return	Normal	Physical	—	100	20	Normal
TM32	Double Team	Normal	Status	—	—	15	Self
TM42	Facade	Normal	Physical	70	100	20	Normal
TM44	Rest	Psychic	Status	—	—	10	Self
TM45	Attract	Normal	Status	—	100	15	Normal
TM48	Round	Normal	Special	60	100	15	Normal
TM55	Scald	Water	Special	80	100	15	Normal
TM66	Payback	Dark	Physical	50	100	10	Normal
TM68	Giga Impact	Normal	Physical	150	90	5	Normal
TM70	Flash	Normal	Status	—	100	20	Normal
TM77	Psych Up	Normal	Status	—	—	10	Normal
TM87	Swagger	Normal	Status	—	90	15	Normal
TM88	Sleep Talk	Normal	Status	—	—	10	Self
TM89	U-turn	Bug	Physical	70	100	20	Normal
TM90	Substitute	Normal	Status	—	—	10	Self
TM94	Secret Power	Normal	Physical	70	100	20	Normal
TM100	Confide	Normal	Status	—	—	20	Normal
HM03	Surf	Water	Special	90	100	15	Adjacent
HM05	Waterfall	Water	Physical	80	100	15	Normal
HM07	Dive	Water	Physical	80	100	10	Normal

MOVES LEARNED IN EXCHANGE FOR BP

Name	Type	Kind	Pow.	Acc.	PP	Range
Signal Beam	Bug	Special	75	100	15	Normal
Bounce	Flying	Physical	85	85	5	Normal
Icy Wind	Ice	Special	55	95	15	Many Others
Aqua Tail	Water	Physical	90	90	10	Normal
Snore	Normal	Special	50	100	15	Normal
Tailwind	Flying	Status	—	—	15	Your Side
Water Pulse	Water	Special	60	100	20	Normal

MOVES TAUGHT BY PEOPLE

Name	Type	Kind	Pow.	Acc.	PP	Range

National Pokédex **458** Hoenn Pokédex —

Mantyke

Kite Pokémon

Water | Flying

HEIGHT: 3'03" WEIGHT: 143.3 lbs.

Same form for ♂ / ♀

Ω The pattern on its back varies by region. It often swims in a school of Remoraid.

α When it swims close to the surface of the ocean, people aboard ships are able to observe the pattern on its back.

ABILITIES
Swift Swim
Water Absorb

HIDDEN ABILITY
Water Veil

EGG GROUPS
No Eggs Discovered

STAT GROWTH RATES
HP
Attack
Defense
Sp. Atk
Sp. Def
Speed

ITEMS SOMETIMES HELD BY WILD POKÉMON
—

EVOLUTION
Mantyke → Level up with Remoraid in your party → Mantine

MAIN WAY TO REGISTER IN THE NATIONAL POKÉDEX

Catch on the water surface at the Battle Resort.

Damage taken in normal battles

Normal	×1	Flying	×1
Fire	×0.5	Psychic	×1
! Water	×0.5	Bug	×0.5
Grass	×1	Rock	×2
Electric	×4	Ghost	×1
Ice	×1	Dragon	×1
Fighting	×0.5	Dark	×1
Poison	×1	Steel	×0.5
Ground	×0	Fairy	×1

Damage taken in Inverse battles

Normal	×1	Flying	×1
Fire	×2	Psychic	×1
! Water	×2	Bug	×2
Grass	×1	Rock	×0.5
Electric	×0.25	Ghost	×1
Ice	×1	Dragon	×1
Fighting	×2	Dark	×1
Poison	×1	Steel	×2
Ground	×2	Fairy	×1

Can be used in
- Inverse Battle
- Battle Institute
- Battle Maison
- Random Matchup (Free Battle)
- Random Matchup (Others)

LEVEL-UP MOVES

Lv.	Name	Type	Kind	Pow.	Acc.	PP	Range
1	Tackle	Normal	Physical	50	100	35	Normal
1	Bubble	Water	Special	40	100	30	Many Others
3	Supersonic	Normal	Status	—	55	20	Normal
7	Bubble Beam	Water	Special	65	100	20	Normal
11	Confuse Ray	Ghost	Status	—	100	10	Normal
14	Wing Attack	Flying	Physical	60	100	35	Normal
16	Headbutt	Normal	Physical	70	100	15	Normal
19	Water Pulse	Water	Special	60	100	20	Normal
23	Wide Guard	Rock	Status	—	—	10	Your Side
27	Take Down	Normal	Physical	90	85	20	Normal
32	Agility	Psychic	Status	—	—	30	Self
36	Air Slash	Flying	Special	75	95	15	Normal
39	Aqua Ring	Water	Status	—	—	20	Self
46	Bounce	Flying	Physical	85	85	5	Normal
49	Hydro Pump	Water	Special	110	80	5	Normal

TM & HM MOVES

No.	Name	Type	Kind	Pow.	Acc.	PP	Range
TM06	Toxic	Poison	Status	—	90	10	Normal
TM07	Hail	Ice	Status	—	—	10	Both Sides
TM10	Hidden Power	Normal	Special	60	100	15	Normal
TM13	Ice Beam	Ice	Special	90	100	10	Normal
TM14	Blizzard	Ice	Special	110	70	5	Many Others
TM17	Protect	Normal	Status	—	—	10	Self
TM18	Rain Dance	Water	Status	—	—	5	Both Sides
TM21	Frustration	Normal	Physical	—	100	20	Normal
TM26	Earthquake	Ground	Physical	100	100	10	Adjacent
TM27	Return	Normal	Physical	—	100	20	Normal
TM32	Double Team	Normal	Status	—	—	15	Self
TM40	Aerial Ace	Flying	Physical	60	—	20	Normal
TM42	Facade	Normal	Physical	70	100	20	Normal
TM44	Rest	Psychic	Status	—	—	10	Self
TM45	Attract	Normal	Status	—	100	15	Normal
TM48	Round	Normal	Special	60	100	15	Normal
TM55	Scald	Water	Special	80	100	15	Normal
TM62	Acrobatics	Flying	Physical	55	100	15	Normal
TM78	Bulldoze	Ground	Physical	60	100	20	Adjacent
TM80	Rock Slide	Rock	Physical	75	90	10	Many Others
TM87	Swagger	Normal	Status	—	90	15	Normal
TM88	Sleep Talk	Normal	Status	—	—	10	Self
TM90	Substitute	Normal	Status	—	—	10	Self
TM94	Secret Power	Normal	Physical	70	100	20	Normal
TM100	Confide	Normal	Status	—	—	20	Normal
HM03	Surf	Water	Special	90	100	15	Adjacent
HM05	Waterfall	Water	Physical	80	100	15	Normal
HM07	Dive	Water	Physical	80	100	10	Normal

MOVES LEARNED IN EXCHANGE FOR BP

Name	Type	Kind	Pow.	Acc.	PP	Range
Signal Beam	Bug	Special	75	100	15	Normal
Bounce	Flying	Physical	85	85	5	Normal
Icy Wind	Ice	Special	55	95	15	Many Others
Snore	Normal	Special	50	100	15	Normal
Water Pulse	Water	Special	60	100	20	Normal
Helping Hand	Normal	Status	—	—	20	1 Ally

MOVES TAUGHT BY PEOPLE

Name	Type	Kind	Pow.	Acc.	PP	Range

EGG MOVES

Name	Type	Kind	Pow.	Acc.	PP	Range
Twister	Dragon	Special	40	100	20	Many Others
Hydro Pump	Water	Special	110	80	5	Normal
Haze	Ice	Status	—	—	30	Both Sides
Slam	Normal	Physical	80	75	20	Normal
Mud Sport	Ground	Status	—	—	15	Both Sides
Mirror Coat	Psychic	Special	—	100	20	Varies
Water Sport	Water	Status	—	—	15	Both Sides
Splash	Normal	Status	—	—	40	Self
Signal Beam	Bug	Special	75	100	15	Normal
Wide Guard	Rock	Status	—	—	10	Your Side
Amnesia	Psychic	Status	—	—	20	Self
Tailwind	Flying	Status	—	—	15	Your Side

National Pokédex **459** Hoenn Pokédex —

Snover

Frost Tree Pokémon

Grass | Ice

HEIGHT: 3'03" WEIGHT: 111.3 lbs.

The male has less white on its body. The female has more white on its body.

♂ ♀

Ω During cold seasons, it migrates to the mountain's lower reaches. It returns to the snow-covered summit in the spring.

α In the spring, it grows berries with the texture of frozen treats around its belly.

ABILITY
Snow Warning

HIDDEN ABILITY
Soundproof

EGG GROUPS
Monster | Grass

STAT GROWTH RATES
HP
Attack
Defense
Sp. Atk
Sp. Def
Speed

ITEMS SOMETIMES HELD BY WILD POKÉMON
—

EVOLUTION
Snover → Lv. 40 → Abomasnow

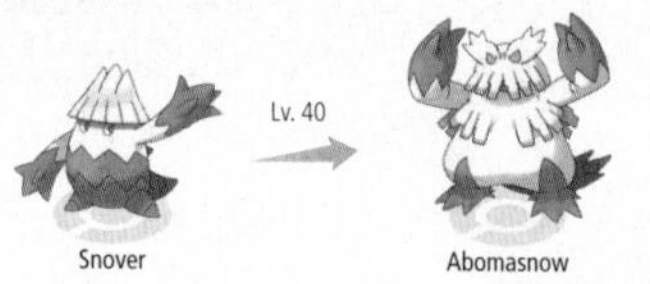

MAIN WAY TO REGISTER IN THE NATIONAL POKÉDEX

Appears in *Pokémon X* and *Pokémon Y*. Bring it to your game using Link Trade or the GTS.

Damage taken in normal battles

Normal	×1	Flying	×2
Fire	×4	Psychic	×1
Water	×0.5	Bug	×2
Grass	×0.5	Rock	×2
Electric	×0.5	Ghost	×1
Ice	×1	Dragon	×1
Fighting	×2	Dark	×1
Poison	×2	Steel	×2
Ground	×0.5	Fairy	×1

Damage taken in Inverse battles

Normal	×1	Flying	×0.5
Fire	×0.25	Psychic	×1
Water	×2	Bug	×0.5
Grass	×2	Rock	×0.5
Electric	×2	Ghost	×1
Ice	×1	Dragon	×1
Fighting	×0.5	Dark	×1
Poison	×0.5	Steel	×0.5
Ground	×2	Fairy	×1

Can be used in
- Inverse Battle
- Battle Institute
- Battle Maison
- Random Matchup (Free Battle)
- Random Matchup (Others)

LEVEL-UP MOVES

Lv.	Name	Type	Kind	Pow.	Acc.	PP	Range
1	Powder Snow	Ice	Special	40	100	25	Many Others
1	Leer	Normal	Status	—	100	30	Many Others
5	Razor Leaf	Grass	Physical	55	95	25	Many Others
9	Icy Wind	Ice	Special	55	95	15	Many Others
13	Grass Whistle	Grass	Status	—	55	15	Normal
17	Swagger	Normal	Status	—	90	15	Normal
21	Mist	Ice	Status	—	—	30	Your Side
26	Ice Shard	Ice	Physical	40	100	30	Normal
31	Ingrain	Grass	Status	—	—	20	Self
36	Wood Hammer	Grass	Physical	120	100	15	Normal
41	Blizzard	Ice	Special	110	70	5	Many Others
46	Sheer Cold	Ice	Special	—	30	5	Normal

TM & HM MOVES

No.	Name	Type	Kind	Pow.	Acc.	PP	Range
TM06	Toxic	Poison	Status	—	90	10	Normal
TM07	Hail	Ice	Status	—	—	10	Both Sides
TM10	Hidden Power	Normal	Special	60	100	15	Normal
TM13	Ice Beam	Ice	Special	90	100	10	Normal
TM14	Blizzard	Ice	Special	110	70	5	Many Others
TM16	Light Screen	Psychic	Status	—	—	30	Your Side
TM17	Protect	Normal	Status	—	—	10	Self
TM18	Rain Dance	Water	Status	—	—	5	Both Sides
TM20	Safeguard	Normal	Status	—	—	25	Your Side
TM21	Frustration	Normal	Physical	—	100	20	Normal
TM22	Solar Beam	Grass	Special	120	100	10	Normal
TM27	Return	Normal	Physical	—	100	20	Normal
TM30	Shadow Ball	Ghost	Special	80	100	15	Normal
TM32	Double Team	Normal	Status	—	—	15	Self
TM42	Facade	Normal	Physical	70	100	20	Normal
TM44	Rest	Psychic	Status	—	—	10	Self
TM45	Attract	Normal	Status	—	100	15	Normal
TM48	Round	Normal	Special	60	100	15	Normal
TM53	Energy Ball	Grass	Special	90	100	10	Normal
TM70	Flash	Normal	Status	—	100	20	Normal
TM75	Swords Dance	Normal	Status	—	—	20	Self
TM79	Frost Breath	Ice	Special	60	90	10	Normal
TM86	Grass Knot	Grass	Special	—	100	20	Normal
TM87	Swagger	Normal	Status	—	90	15	Normal
TM88	Sleep Talk	Normal	Status	—	—	10	Self
TM90	Substitute	Normal	Status	—	—	10	Self
TM94	Secret Power	Normal	Physical	70	100	20	Normal
TM100	Confide	Normal	Status	—	—	20	Normal

MOVES LEARNED IN EXCHANGE FOR BP

Name	Type	Kind	Pow.	Acc.	PP	Range
Seed Bomb	Grass	Physical	80	100	15	Normal
Ice Punch	Ice	Physical	75	100	15	Normal
Icy Wind	Ice	Special	55	95	15	Many Others
Iron Tail	Steel	Physical	100	75	15	Normal
Snore	Normal	Special	50	100	15	Normal
Synthesis	Grass	Status	—	—	5	Self
Role Play	Psychic	Status	—	—	10	Normal
Giga Drain	Grass	Special	75	100	10	Normal
Water Pulse	Water	Special	60	100	20	Normal
Worry Seed	Grass	Status	—	100	10	Normal

MOVES TAUGHT BY PEOPLE

Name	Type	Kind	Pow.	Acc.	PP	Range

EGG MOVES

Name	Type	Kind	Pow.	Acc.	PP	Range
Leech Seed	Grass	Status	—	90	10	Normal
Magical Leaf	Grass	Special	60	—	20	Normal
Seed Bomb	Grass	Physical	80	100	15	Normal
Growth	Normal	Status	—	—	20	Self
Double-Edge	Normal	Physical	120	100	15	Normal
Mist	Ice	Status	—	—	30	Your Side
Stomp	Normal	Physical	65	100	20	Normal
Skull Bash	Normal	Physical	130	100	10	Normal
Avalanche	Ice	Physical	60	100	10	Normal
Natural Gift	Normal	Physical	—	100	15	Normal
Bullet Seed	Grass	Physical	25	100	30	Normal

National Pokédex **460** Hoenn Pokédex —

Abomasnow

Frost Tree Pokémon

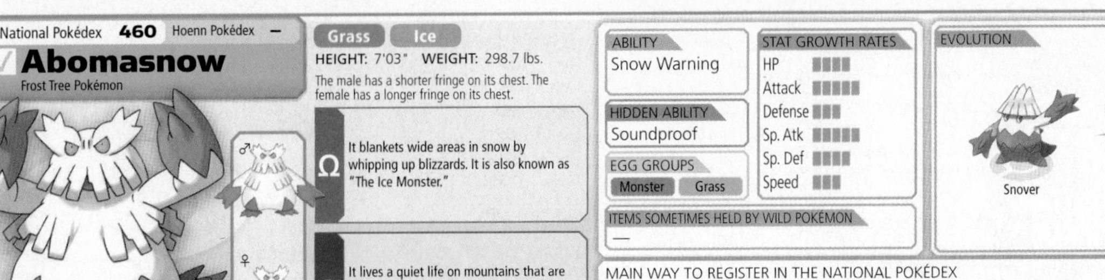

Grass | Ice

HEIGHT: 7'03" WEIGHT: 298.7 lbs.

The male has a shorter fringe on its chest. The female has a longer fringe on its chest.

Ω It blankets wide areas in snow by whipping up blizzards. It is also known as "The Ice Monster."

α It lives a quiet life on mountains that are perpetually covered in snow. It hides itself by whipping up blizzards.

ABILITY
Snow Warning

HIDDEN ABILITY
Soundproof

EGG GROUPS
Monster | Grass

STAT GROWTH RATES
HP ■■■■
Attack ■■■■■
Defense ■■■
Sp. Atk ■■■■■
Sp. Def ■■■■
Speed ■■■

ITEMS SOMETIMES HELD BY WILD POKÉMON
—

EVOLUTION
Snover → Lv. 40 → Abomasnow

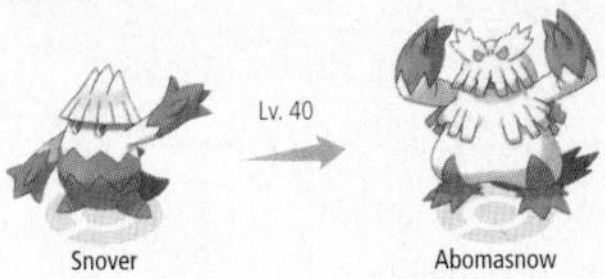

MAIN WAY TO REGISTER IN THE NATIONAL POKÉDEX

Appears in *Pokémon X* and *Pokémon Y*. Bring it to your game using Link Trade or the GTS.

Damage taken in normal battles

Type		Type	
Normal	×1	Flying	×2
Fire	×4	Psychic	×1
Water	×0.5	Bug	×2
Grass	×0.5	Rock	×2
Electric	×0.5	Ghost	×1
Ice	×1	Dragon	×1
Fighting	×2	Dark	×1
Poison	×2	Steel	×2
Ground	×0.5	Fairy	×1

Damage taken in Inverse battles

Type		Type	
Normal	×1	Flying	×0.5
Fire	×0.25	Psychic	×1
Water	×2	Bug	×0.5
Grass	×2	Rock	×0.5
Electric	×2	Ghost	×1
Ice	×1	Dragon	×1
Fighting	×0.5	Dark	×1
Poison	×0.5	Steel	×0.5
Ground	×2	Fairy	×1

Can be used in
Inverse Battle
Battle Institute
Battle Maison
Random Matchup (Free Battle)
Random Matchup (Others)

LEVEL-UP MOVES

Lv.	Name	Type	Kind	Pow.	Acc.	PP	Range
1	Ice Punch	Ice	Physical	75	100	15	Normal
1	Powder Snow	Ice	Special	40	100	25	Many Others
1	Leer	Normal	Status	—	100	30	Many Others
1	Razor Leaf	Grass	Physical	55	95	25	Many Others
1	Icy Wind	Ice	Special	55	95	15	Many Others
5	Razor Leaf	Grass	Physical	55	95	25	Many Others
9	Icy Wind	Ice	Special	55	95	15	Many Others
13	Grass Whistle	Grass	Status	—	55	15	Normal
17	Swagger	Normal	Status	—	90	15	Normal
21	Mist	Ice	Status	—	—	30	Your Side
26	Ice Shard	Ice	Physical	40	100	30	Normal
31	Ingrain	Grass	Status	—	—	20	Self
36	Wood Hammer	Grass	Physical	120	100	15	Normal
47	Blizzard	Ice	Special	110	70	5	Many Others
58	Sheer Cold	Ice	Special	—	30	5	Normal

TM & HM MOVES

No.	Name	Type	Kind	Pow.	Acc.	PP	Range
TM06	Toxic	Poison	Status	—	90	10	Normal
TM07	Hail	Ice	Status	—	—	10	Both Sides
TM10	Hidden Power	Normal	Special	60	100	15	Normal
TM13	Ice Beam	Ice	Special	90	100	10	Normal
TM14	Blizzard	Ice	Special	110	70	5	Many Others
TM15	Hyper Beam	Normal	Special	150	90	5	Normal
TM16	Light Screen	Psychic	Status	—	—	30	Your Side
TM17	Protect	Normal	Status	—	—	10	Self
TM18	Rain Dance	Water	Status	—	—	5	Both Sides
TM20	Safeguard	Normal	Status	—	—	25	Your Side
TM21	Frustration	Normal	Physical	—	100	20	Normal
TM22	Solar Beam	Grass	Special	120	100	10	Normal
TM26	Earthquake	Ground	Physical	100	100	10	Adjacent
TM27	Return	Normal	Physical	—	100	20	Normal
TM30	Shadow Ball	Ghost	Special	80	100	15	Normal
TM31	Brick Break	Fighting	Physical	75	100	15	Normal
TM32	Double Team	Normal	Status	—	—	15	Self
TM39	Rock Tomb	Rock	Physical	60	95	15	Normal
TM42	Facade	Normal	Physical	70	100	20	Normal
TM44	Rest	Psychic	Status	—	—	10	Self
TM45	Attract	Normal	Status	—	100	15	Normal
TM48	Round	Normal	Special	60	100	15	Normal
TM52	Focus Blast	Fighting	Special	120	70	5	Normal
TM53	Energy Ball	Grass	Special	90	100	10	Normal
TM56	Fling	Dark	Physical	—	100	10	Normal
TM68	Giga Impact	Normal	Physical	150	90	5	Normal
TM70	Flash	Normal	Status	—	100	20	Normal
TM75	Swords Dance	Normal	Status	—	—	20	Self
TM78	Bulldoze	Ground	Physical	60	100	20	Adjacent
TM79	Frost Breath	Ice	Special	60	90	10	Normal
TM80	Rock Slide	Rock	Physical	75	90	10	Many Others
TM86	Grass Knot	Grass	Special	—	100	20	Normal
TM87	Swagger	Normal	Status	—	90	15	Normal
TM88	Sleep Talk	Normal	Status	—	—	10	Self
TM90	Substitute	Normal	Status	—	—	10	Self
TM94	Secret Power	Normal	Physical	70	100	20	Normal
TM100	Confide	Normal	Status	—	—	20	Normal
HM04	Strength	Normal	Physical	80	100	15	Normal
HM06	Rock Smash	Fighting	Physical	40	100	15	Normal

MOVES LEARNED IN EXCHANGE FOR BP

Name	Type	Kind	Pow.	Acc.	PP	Range
Seed Bomb	Grass	Physical	80	100	15	Normal
Ice Punch	Ice	Physical	75	100	15	Normal
Block	Normal	Status	—	—	5	Normal
Icy Wind	Ice	Special	55	95	15	Many Others
Iron Tail	Steel	Physical	100	75	15	Normal
Snore	Normal	Special	50	100	15	Normal
Synthesis	Grass	Status	—	—	5	Self
Role Play	Psychic	Status	—	—	10	Normal
Giga Drain	Grass	Special	75	100	10	Normal
Focus Punch	Fighting	Physical	150	100	20	Normal
Water Pulse	Water	Special	60	100	20	Normal
Worry Seed	Grass	Status	—	100	10	Normal
Outrage	Dragon	Physical	120	100	10	1 Random

MOVES TAUGHT BY PEOPLE

Name	Type	Kind	Pow.	Acc.	PP	Range

Mega Evolution

Mega Abomasnow

Frost Tree Pokémon

Grass | Ice

HEIGHT: 8'10" WEIGHT: 407.9 lbs.

Same form for ♂ / ♀

REQUIRED MEGA STONE
Abomasite
Find it in the Berry fields on Route 123 (after battling Groudon or Kyogre).

ABILITY
Snow Warning

HIDDEN ABILITY
—

EGG GROUPS
—

STAT GROWTH RATES
HP ■■■■
Attack ■■■■■■■
Defense ■■■■■
Sp. Atk ■■■■■■
Sp. Def ■■■■
Speed ■■

Damage taken in normal battles

Type		Type	
Normal	×1	Flying	×2
Fire	×4	Psychic	×1
Water	×0.5	Bug	×2
Grass	×0.5	Rock	×2
Electric	×0.5	Ghost	×1
Ice	×1	Dragon	×1
Fighting	×2	Dark	×1
Poison	×2	Steel	×2
Ground	×0.5	Fairy	×1

Damage taken in Inverse battles

Type		Type	
Normal	×1	Flying	×0.5
Fire	×0.25	Psychic	×1
Water	×2	Bug	×0.5
Grass	×2	Rock	×0.5
Electric	×2	Ghost	×1
Ice	×1	Dragon	×1
Fighting	×0.5	Dark	×1
Poison	×0.5	Steel	×0.5
Ground	×2	Fairy	×1

Can be used in
Inverse Battle
Battle Institute
Battle Maison
Random Matchup (Free Battle)
Random Matchup (Others)

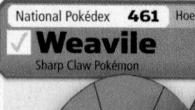

National Pokédex **461** Hoenn Pokédex —

Weavile

Sharp Claw Pokémon

Dark | Ice

HEIGHT: 3'07" WEIGHT: 75 lbs.

The male has larger ears. The female has smaller ears.

Ω It lives in snowy regions. It carves patterns in trees with its claws as a signal to others.

α They live in cold regions, forming groups of four or five that hunt prey with impressive coordination.

ABILITY
Pressure

HIDDEN ABILITY
Pickpocket

EGG GROUPS
Field

STAT GROWTH RATES

HP	■■■
Attack	■■■■■■
Defense	■■■
Sp. Atk	■■
Sp. Def	■■■■
Speed	■■■■■■■

ITEMS SOMETIMES HELD BY WILD POKÉMON
—

EVOLUTION

MAIN WAY TO REGISTER IN THE NATIONAL POKÉDEX

Have a Sneasel obtained via Link Trade or the GTS hold a Razor Claw, then level it up between 8:00 P.M. and 3:59 A.M.

Damage taken in normal battles

Type		Type	
Normal	×1	Flying	×1
Fire	×2	Psychic	×0
Water	×1	Bug	×2
Grass	×1	Rock	×2
Electric	×1	Ghost	×0.5
Ice	×0.5	Dragon	×1
Fighting	×4	Dark	×0.5
Poison	×1	Steel	×2
Ground	×1	Fairy	×2

Damage taken in Inverse battles

Type		Type	
Normal	×1	Flying	×1
Fire	×0.5	Psychic	×2
Water	×1	Bug	×0.5
Grass	×1	Rock	×0.5
Electric	×1	Ghost	×2
Ice	×2	Dragon	×1
Fighting	×0.25	Dark	×2
Poison	×1	Steel	×0.5
Ground	×1	Fairy	×0.5

Can be used in
Inverse Battle
Battle Institute
Battle Maison
Random Matchup (Free Battle)
Random Matchup (Others)

LEVEL-UP MOVES

Lv.	Name	Type	Kind	Pow.	Acc.	PP	Range
1	Embargo	Dark	Status	—	100	15	Normal
1	Revenge	Fighting	Physical	60	100	10	Normal
1	Assurance	Dark	Physical	60	100	10	Normal
1	Scratch	Normal	Physical	40	100	35	Normal
1	Leer	Normal	Status	—	100	30	Many Others
1	Taunt	Dark	Status	—	100	20	Normal
1	Quick Attack	Normal	Physical	40	100	30	Normal
8	Quick Attack	Normal	Physical	40	100	30	Normal
10	Feint Attack	Dark	Physical	60	—	20	Normal
14	Icy Wind	Ice	Special	55	95	15	Many Others
16	Fury Swipes	Normal	Physical	18	80	15	Normal
20	Nasty Plot	Dark	Status	—	—	20	Self
22	Metal Claw	Steel	Physical	50	95	35	Normal
25	Hone Claws	Dark	Status	—	—	15	Self
28	Fling	Dark	Physical	—	100	10	Normal
32	Screech	Normal	Status	—	85	40	Normal
35	Night Slash	Dark	Physical	70	100	15	Normal
40	Snatch	Dark	Status	—	—	10	Self
44	Punishment	Dark	Physical	—	100	5	Normal
47	Dark Pulse	Dark	Special	80	100	15	Normal

TM & HM MOVES

No.	Name	Type	Kind	Pow.	Acc.	PP	Range
TM01	Hone Claws	Dark	Status	—	—	15	Self
TM04	Calm Mind	Psychic	Status	—	—	20	Self
TM06	Toxic	Poison	Status	—	90	10	Normal
TM07	Hail	Ice	Status	—	—	10	Both Sides
TM10	Hidden Power	Normal	Special	60	100	15	Normal
TM11	Sunny Day	Fire	Status	—	—	5	Both Sides
TM12	Taunt	Dark	Status	—	100	20	Normal
TM13	Ice Beam	Ice	Special	90	100	10	Normal
TM14	Blizzard	Ice	Special	110	70	5	Many Others
TM15	Hyper Beam	Normal	Special	150	90	5	Normal
TM17	Protect	Normal	Status	—	—	10	Self
TM18	Rain Dance	Water	Status	—	—	5	Both Sides
TM21	Frustration	Normal	Physical	—	100	20	Normal
TM27	Return	Normal	Physical	—	100	20	Normal
TM28	Dig	Ground	Physical	80	100	10	Normal
TM30	Shadow Ball	Ghost	Special	80	100	15	Normal
TM31	Brick Break	Fighting	Physical	75	100	15	Normal
TM32	Double Team	Normal	Status	—	—	15	Self
TM33	Reflect	Psychic	Status	—	—	20	Your Side
TM40	Aerial Ace	Flying	Physical	60	—	20	Normal
TM41	Torment	Dark	Status	—	100	15	Normal
TM42	Facade	Normal	Physical	70	100	20	Normal
TM44	Rest	Psychic	Status	—	—	10	Self
TM45	Attract	Normal	Status	—	100	15	Normal
TM46	Thief	Dark	Physical	60	100	25	Normal
TM47	Low Sweep	Fighting	Physical	65	100	20	Normal
TM48	Round	Normal	Special	60	100	15	Normal
TM52	Focus Blast	Fighting	Special	120	70	5	Normal
TM54	False Swipe	Normal	Physical	40	100	40	Normal
TM56	Fling	Dark	Physical	—	100	10	Normal
TM63	Embargo	Dark	Status	—	100	15	Normal
TM65	Shadow Claw	Ghost	Physical	70	100	15	Normal
TM66	Payback	Dark	Physical	50	100	10	Normal
TM67	Retaliate	Normal	Physical	70	100	5	Normal
TM68	Giga Impact	Normal	Physical	150	90	5	Normal
TM75	Swords Dance	Normal	Status	—	—	20	Self
TM77	Psych Up	Normal	Status	—	—	10	Normal
TM81	X-Scissor	Bug	Physical	80	100	15	Normal
TM84	Poison Jab	Poison	Physical	80	100	20	Normal
TM85	Dream Eater	Psychic	Special	100	100	15	Normal
TM87	Swagger	Normal	Status	—	90	15	Normal
TM88	Sleep Talk	Normal	Status	—	—	10	Self
TM90	Substitute	Normal	Status	—	—	10	Self
TM94	Secret Power	Normal	Physical	70	100	20	Normal
TM95	Snarl	Dark	Special	55	95	15	Many Others
TM97	Dark Pulse	Dark	Special	80	100	15	Normal
TM98	Power-Up Punch	Fighting	Physical	40	100	20	Normal
TM100	Confide	Normal	Status	—	—	20	Normal
HM01	Cut	Normal	Physical	50	95	30	Normal
HM03	Surf	Water	Special	90	100	15	Adjacent
HM04	Strength	Normal	Physical	80	100	15	Normal
HM06	Rock Smash	Fighting	Physical	40	100	15	Normal

MOVES LEARNED IN EXCHANGE FOR BP

Name	Type	Kind	Pow.	Acc.	PP	Range
Low Kick	Fighting	Physical	—	100	20	Normal
Ice Punch	Ice	Physical	75	100	15	Normal
Foul Play	Dark	Physical	95	100	15	Normal
Icy Wind	Ice	Special	55	95	15	Many Others
Iron Tail	Steel	Physical	100	75	15	Normal
Snore	Normal	Special	50	100	15	Normal
Knock Off	Dark	Physical	65	100	20	Normal
Focus Punch	Fighting	Physical	150	100	20	Normal
Spite	Ghost	Status	—	100	10	Normal
Snatch	Dark	Status	—	—	10	Self

MOVES TAUGHT BY PEOPLE

Name	Type	Kind	Pow.	Acc.	PP	Range

National Pokédex **462** Hoenn Pokédex **086**

Magnezone

Magnet Area Pokémon

Electric | Steel

HEIGHT: 3'11" WEIGHT: 396.8 lbs.

Gender unknown

Ω Sometimes the magnetism emitted by Magnezone is too strong, making them attract each other so they cannot move.

α It evolved from exposure to a special magnetic field. Three units generate magnetism.

ABILITIES
Magnet Pull
Sturdy

HIDDEN ABILITY
Analytic

EGG GROUPS
Mineral

STAT GROWTH RATES

HP	■■■
Attack	■■■■
Defense	■■■■■
Sp. Atk	■■■■■■
Sp. Def	■■■■
Speed	■■■

ITEMS SOMETIMES HELD BY WILD POKÉMON
—

EVOLUTION

Magnepite → Lv. 30 → Magneton → Level up in New Mauville → Magnezone

MAIN WAY TO REGISTER IN THE NATIONAL POKÉDEX

Level up Magneton in New Mauville.

Damage taken in normal battles

Type		Type	
Normal	×0.5	Flying	×0.25
Fire	×2	Psychic	×0.5
Water	×1	Bug	×0.5
Grass	×0.5	Rock	×0.5
Electric	×0.5	Ghost	×1
Ice	×0.5	Dragon	×0.5
Fighting	×2	Dark	×1
Poison	×0	Steel	×0.25
Ground	×4	Fairy	×0.5

Damage taken in Inverse battles

Type		Type	
Normal	×2	Flying	×4
Fire	×0.5	Psychic	×2
Water	×1	Bug	×2
Grass	×2	Rock	×2
Electric	×2	Ghost	×1
Ice	×2	Dragon	×2
Fighting	×0.5	Dark	×1
Poison	×2	Steel	×4
Ground	×0.25	Fairy	×2

Can be used in
Inverse Battle
Battle Institute
Battle Maison
Random Matchup (Free Battle)
Random Matchup (Others)

LEVEL-UP MOVES

Lv.	Name	Type	Kind	Pow.	Acc.	PP	Range
1	Zap Cannon	Electric	Special	120	50	5	Normal
1	Magnetic Flux	Electric	Status	—	—	20	Your Party
1	Mirror Coat	Psychic	Special	—	100	20	Varies
1	Barrier	Psychic	Status	—	—	20	Self
1	Electric Terrain	Electric	Status	—	—	10	Both Sides
1	Tackle	Normal	Physical	50	100	35	Normal
1	Supersonic	Normal	Status	—	55	20	Normal
1	Thunder Shock	Electric	Special	40	100	30	Normal
1	Sonic Boom	Normal	Special	—	90	20	Normal
5	Supersonic	Normal	Status	—	55	20	Normal
7	Thunder Shock	Electric	Special	40	100	30	Normal
11	Sonic Boom	Normal	Special	—	90	20	Normal
13	Thunder Wave	Electric	Status	—	100	20	Normal
17	Magnet Bomb	Steel	Physical	60	—	20	Normal
19	Spark	Electric	Physical	65	100	20	Normal
23	Mirror Shot	Steel	Special	65	85	10	Normal
25	Metal Sound	Steel	Status	—	85	40	Normal
29	Electro Ball	Electric	Special	—	100	10	Normal
33	Flash Cannon	Steel	Special	80	100	10	Normal
39	Screech	Normal	Status	—	85	40	Normal
43	Discharge	Electric	Special	80	100	15	Adjacent
49	Lock-On	Normal	Status	—	—	5	Normal
53	Magnet Rise	Electric	Status	—	—	10	Self
59	Gyro Ball	Steel	Physical	—	100	5	Normal
63	Zap Cannon	Electric	Special	120	50	5	Normal

TM & HM MOVES

No.	Name	Type	Kind	Pow.	Acc.	PP	Range
TM06	Toxic	Poison	Status	—	90	10	Normal
TM10	Hidden Power	Normal	Special	60	100	15	Normal
TM11	Sunny Day	Fire	Status	—	—	5	Both Sides
TM15	Hyper Beam	Normal	Special	150	90	5	Normal
TM16	Light Screen	Psychic	Status	—	—	30	Your Side
TM17	Protect	Normal	Status	—	—	10	Self
TM18	Rain Dance	Water	Status	—	—	5	Both Sides
TM21	Frustration	Normal	Physical	—	100	20	Normal
TM24	Thunderbolt	Electric	Special	90	100	15	Normal
TM25	Thunder	Electric	Special	110	70	10	Normal
TM27	Return	Normal	Physical	—	100	20	Normal
TM32	Double Team	Normal	Status	—	—	15	Self
TM33	Reflect	Psychic	Status	—	—	20	Your Side
TM42	Facade	Normal	Physical	70	100	20	Normal
TM44	Rest	Psychic	Status	—	—	10	Self
TM48	Round	Normal	Special	60	100	15	Normal
TM57	Charge Beam	Electric	Special	50	90	10	Normal
TM64	Explosion	Normal	Physical	250	100	5	Adjacent
TM68	Giga Impact	Normal	Physical	150	90	5	Normal
TM70	Flash	Normal	Status	—	100	20	Normal
TM72	Volt Switch	Electric	Special	70	100	20	Normal
TM73	Thunder Wave	Electric	Status	—	100	20	Normal
TM74	Gyro Ball	Steel	Physical	—	100	5	Normal
TM77	Psych Up	Normal	Status	—	—	10	Normal
TM87	Swagger	Normal	Status	—	90	15	Normal
TM88	Sleep Talk	Normal	Status	—	—	10	Self
TM90	Substitute	Normal	Status	—	—	10	Self
TM91	Flash Cannon	Steel	Special	80	100	10	Normal
TM93	Wild Charge	Electric	Physical	90	100	15	Normal
TM94	Secret Power	Normal	Physical	70	100	20	Normal
TM100	Confide	Normal	Status	—	—	20	Normal

MOVES LEARNED IN EXCHANGE FOR BP

Name	Type	Kind	Pow.	Acc.	PP	Range
Signal Beam	Bug	Special	75	100	15	Normal
Iron Head	Steel	Physical	80	100	15	Normal
Magic Coat	Psychic	Status	—	—	15	Self
Gravity	Psychic	Status	—	—	5	Both Sides
Magnet Rise	Electric	Status	—	—	10	Self
Iron Defense	Steel	Status	—	—	15	Self
Electroweb	Electric	Special	55	95	15	Many Others
Snore	Normal	Special	50	100	15	Normal
Shock Wave	Electric	Special	60	—	20	Normal
Recycle	Normal	Status	—	—	10	Self

MOVES TAUGHT BY PEOPLE

Name	Type	Kind	Pow.	Acc.	PP	Range

National Pokédex **463** Hoenn Pokédex **—**

Lickilicky

Licking Pokémon

Normal

HEIGHT: 5'07" WEIGHT: 308.6 lbs.

Same form for ♂ / ♀

Ω It wraps things with its extensible tongue. Getting too close to it will leave you soaked with drool.

α Their saliva contains lots of components that can dissolve anything. The numbness caused by their lick does not dissipate.

ABILITIES
Own Tempo
Oblivious

HIDDEN ABILITY
Cloud Nine

EGG GROUPS
Monster

STAT GROWTH RATES
HP
Attack
Defense
Sp. Atk
Sp. Def
Speed

ITEMS SOMETIMES HELD BY WILD POKÉMON
—

EVOLUTION

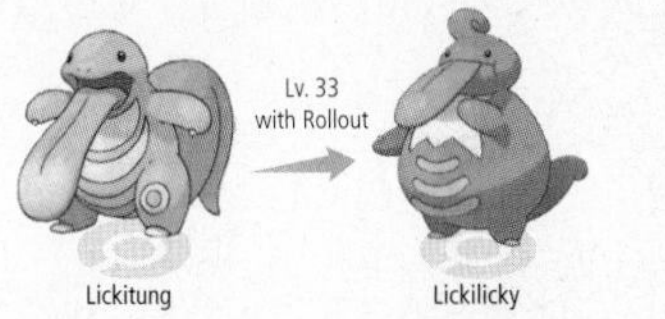

MAIN WAY TO REGISTER IN THE NATIONAL POKÉDEX

Level up a Lickitung obtained via Link Trade or the GTS to Lv. 33, then teach it the move Rollout. Alternatively, teach it the move Rollout first, then have it level up.

Damage taken in normal battles

Normal	×1	Flying	×1
Fire	×1	Psychic	×1
Water	×1	Bug	×1
Grass	×1	Rock	×1
Electric	×1	Ghost	×0
Ice	×1	Dragon	×1
Fighting	×2	Dark	×1
Poison	×1	Steel	×1
Ground	×1	Fairy	×1

Damage taken in Inverse battles

Normal	×1	Flying	×1
Fire	×1	Psychic	×1
Water	×1	Bug	×1
Grass	×1	Rock	×1
Electric	×1	Ghost	×2
Ice	×1	Dragon	×1
Fighting	×0.5	Dark	×1
Poison	×1	Steel	×1
Ground	×1	Fairy	×1

Can be used in

- Inverse Battle
- Battle Institute
- Battle Maison
- Random Matchup (Free Battle)
- Random Matchup (Others)

LEVEL-UP MOVES

Lv.	Name	Type	Kind	Pow.	Acc.	PP	Range
1	Wring Out	Normal	Special	—	100	5	Normal
1	Power Whip	Grass	Physical	120	85	10	Normal
1	Lick	Ghost	Physical	30	100	30	Normal
5	Supersonic	Normal	Status	—	55	20	Normal
9	Defense Curl	Normal	Status	—	—	40	Self
13	Knock Off	Dark	Physical	65	100	20	Normal
17	Wrap	Normal	Physical	15	90	20	Normal
21	Stomp	Normal	Physical	65	100	20	Normal
25	Disable	Normal	Status	—	100	20	Normal
29	Slam	Normal	Physical	80	75	20	Normal
33	Rollout	Rock	Physical	30	90	20	Normal
37	Chip Away	Normal	Physical	70	100	20	Normal
41	Me First	Normal	Status	—	—	20	Varies
45	Refresh	Normal	Status	—	—	20	Self
49	Screech	Normal	Status	—	85	40	Normal
53	Power Whip	Grass	Physical	120	85	10	Normal
57	Wring Out	Normal	Special	—	100	5	Normal
61	Gyro Ball	Steel	Physical	—	100	5	Normal

TM & HM MOVES

No.	Name	Type	Kind	Pow.	Acc.	PP	Range
TM06	Toxic	Poison	Status	—	90	10	Normal
TM10	Hidden Power	Normal	Special	60	100	15	Normal
TM11	Sunny Day	Fire	Status	—	—	5	Both Sides
TM13	Ice Beam	Ice	Special	90	100	10	Normal
TM14	Blizzard	Ice	Special	110	70	5	Many Others
TM15	Hyper Beam	Normal	Special	150	90	5	Normal
TM17	Protect	Normal	Status	—	—	10	Self
TM18	Rain Dance	Water	Status	—	—	5	Both Sides
TM21	Frustration	Normal	Physical	—	100	20	Normal
TM22	Solar Beam	Grass	Special	120	100	10	Normal
TM24	Thunderbolt	Electric	Special	90	100	15	Normal
TM25	Thunder	Electric	Special	110	70	10	Normal
TM26	Earthquake	Ground	Physical	100	100	10	Adjacent
TM27	Return	Normal	Physical	—	100	20	Normal
TM28	Dig	Ground	Physical	80	100	10	Normal
TM30	Shadow Ball	Ghost	Special	80	100	15	Normal
TM31	Brick Break	Fighting	Physical	75	100	15	Normal
TM32	Double Team	Normal	Status	—	—	15	Self
TM35	Flamethrower	Fire	Special	90	100	15	Normal
TM37	Sandstorm	Rock	Status	—	—	10	Both Sides
TM38	Fire Blast	Fire	Special	110	85	5	Normal
TM39	Rock Tomb	Rock	Physical	60	95	15	Normal
TM42	Facade	Normal	Physical	70	100	20	Normal
TM44	Rest	Psychic	Status	—	—	10	Self
TM45	Attract	Normal	Status	—	100	15	Normal
TM46	Thief	Dark	Physical	60	100	25	Normal
TM48	Round	Normal	Special	60	100	15	Normal
TM52	Focus Blast	Fighting	Special	120	70	5	Normal
TM56	Fling	Dark	Physical	—	100	10	Normal
TM59	Incinerate	Fire	Special	60	100	15	Many Others
TM64	Explosion	Normal	Physical	250	100	5	Adjacent
TM67	Retaliate	Normal	Physical	70	100	5	Normal
TM68	Giga Impact	Normal	Physical	150	90	5	Normal
TM74	Gyro Ball	Steel	Physical	—	100	5	Normal
TM75	Swords Dance	Normal	Status	—	—	20	Self
TM77	Psych Up	Normal	Status	—	—	10	Normal
TM78	Bulldoze	Ground	Physical	60	100	20	Adjacent
TM80	Rock Slide	Rock	Physical	75	90	10	Many Others
TM82	Dragon Tail	Dragon	Physical	60	90	10	Normal
TM85	Dream Eater	Psychic	Special	100	100	15	Normal
TM87	Swagger	Normal	Status	—	90	15	Normal
TM88	Sleep Talk	Normal	Status	—	—	10	Self
TM90	Substitute	Normal	Status	—	—	10	Self
TM94	Secret Power	Normal	Physical	70	100	20	Normal
TM98	Power-Up Punch	Fighting	Physical	40	100	20	Normal
TM100	Confide	Normal	Status	—	—	20	Normal
HM01	Cut	Normal	Physical	50	95	30	Normal
HM03	Surf	Water	Special	90	100	15	Adjacent
HM04	Strength	Normal	Physical	80	100	15	Normal
HM06	Rock Smash	Fighting	Physical	40	100	15	Normal

MOVES LEARNED IN EXCHANGE FOR BP

Name	Type	Kind	Pow.	Acc.	PP	Range
Thunder Punch	Electric	Physical	75	100	15	Normal
Fire Punch	Fire	Physical	75	100	15	Normal
Ice Punch	Ice	Physical	75	100	15	Normal
Block	Normal	Status	—	—	5	Normal
Icy Wind	Ice	Special	55	95	15	Many Others
Aqua Tail	Water	Physical	90	90	10	Normal
Zen Headbutt	Psychic	Physical	80	90	15	Normal
Iron Tail	Steel	Physical	100	75	15	Normal
Bind	Normal	Physical	15	85	20	Normal
Snore	Normal	Special	50	100	15	Normal
Knock Off	Dark	Physical	65	100	20	Normal
Focus Punch	Fighting	Physical	150	100	20	Normal
Shock Wave	Electric	Special	60	—	20	Normal
Water Pulse	Water	Special	60	100	20	Normal

MOVES TAUGHT BY PEOPLE

Name	Type	Kind	Pow.	Acc.	PP	Range

National Pokédex **464** Hoenn Pokédex **178**

Rhyperior

Drill Pokémon

Ground Rock

HEIGHT: 7'10" WEIGHT: 623.5 lbs.

The male has a longer horn on top of its head. The female has a shorter horn on top of its head.

Ω From holes in its palms, it fires out Geodude. Its carapace can withstand volcanic eruptions.

α It puts rocks in holes in its palms and uses its muscles to shoot them. Geodude are shot at rare times.

ABILITIES
Lightning Rod
Solid Rock

HIDDEN ABILITY
Reckless

EGG GROUPS
Monster Field

STAT GROWTH RATES
HP
Attack
Defense
Sp. Atk
Sp. Def
Speed

ITEMS SOMETIMES HELD BY WILD POKÉMON
—

EVOLUTION

MAIN WAY TO REGISTER IN THE NATIONAL POKÉDEX

Receive a Rhydon that is holding a Protector via Link Trade to have it evolve.

Damage taken in normal battles

Normal	×0.5	Flying	×0.5
Fire	×0.5	Psychic	×1
Water	×4	Bug	×1
Grass	×4	Rock	×0.5
Electric	×0	Ghost	×1
Ice	×2	Dragon	×1
Fighting	×2	Dark	×1
Poison	×0.25	Steel	×2
Ground	×2	Fairy	×1

Damage taken in Inverse battles

Normal	×2	Flying	×2
Fire	×2	Psychic	×1
Water	×0.25	Bug	×1
Grass	×0.25	Rock	×2
Electric	×2	Ghost	×1
Ice	×0.5	Dragon	×1
Fighting	×0.5	Dark	×1
Poison	×4	Steel	×0.5
Ground	×0.5	Fairy	×1

Can be used in

- Inverse Battle
- Battle Institute
- Battle Maison
- Random Matchup (Free Battle)
- Random Matchup (Others)

LEVEL-UP MOVES

Lv.	Name	Type	Kind	Pow.	Acc.	PP	Range
1	Rock Wrecker	Rock	Physical	150	90	5	Normal
1	Horn Drill	Normal	Physical	—	30	5	Normal
1	Poison Jab	Poison	Physical	80	100	20	Normal
1	Horn Attack	Normal	Physical	65	100	25	Normal
1	Tail Whip	Normal	Status	—	100	30	Many Others
1	Fury Attack	Normal	Physical	15	85	20	Normal
1	Scary Face	Normal	Status	—	100	10	Normal
5	Fury Attack	Normal	Physical	15	85	20	Normal
9	Scary Face	Normal	Status	—	100	10	Normal
13	Smack Down	Rock	Physical	50	100	15	Normal
17	Stomp	Normal	Physical	65	100	20	Normal
21	Bulldoze	Ground	Physical	60	100	20	Adjacent
25	Chip Away	Normal	Physical	70	100	20	Normal
29	Rock Blast	Rock	Physical	25	90	10	Normal
33	Drill Run	Ground	Physical	80	95	10	Normal
37	Take Down	Normal	Physical	90	85	20	Normal
41	Stone Edge	Rock	Physical	100	80	5	Normal
42	Hammer Arm	Fighting	Physical	100	90	10	Normal
48	Earthquake	Ground	Physical	100	100	10	Adjacent
55	Megahorn	Bug	Physical	120	85	10	Normal
62	Horn Drill	Normal	Physical	—	30	5	Normal
69	Rock Wrecker	Rock	Physical	150	90	5	Normal

TM & HM MOVES

No.	Name	Type	Kind	Pow.	Acc.	PP	Range
TM05	Roar	Normal	Status	—	—	20	Normal
TM06	Toxic	Poison	Status	—	90	10	Normal
TM10	Hidden Power	Normal	Special	60	100	15	Normal
TM11	Sunny Day	Fire	Status	—	—	5	Both Sides
TM13	Ice Beam	Ice	Special	90	100	10	Normal
TM14	Blizzard	Ice	Special	110	70	5	Many Others
TM15	Hyper Beam	Normal	Special	150	90	5	Normal
TM17	Protect	Normal	Status	—	—	10	Self
TM18	Rain Dance	Water	Status	—	—	5	Both Sides
TM21	Frustration	Normal	Physical	—	100	20	Normal
TM23	Smack Down	Rock	Physical	50	100	15	Normal
TM24	Thunderbolt	Electric	Special	90	100	15	Normal
TM25	Thunder	Electric	Special	110	70	10	Normal
TM26	Earthquake	Ground	Physical	100	100	10	Adjacent
TM27	Return	Normal	Physical	—	100	20	Normal
TM28	Dig	Ground	Physical	80	100	10	Normal
TM31	Brick Break	Fighting	Physical	75	100	15	Normal
TM32	Double Team	Normal	Status	—	—	15	Self
TM35	Flamethrower	Fire	Special	90	100	15	Normal
TM37	Sandstorm	Rock	Status	—	—	10	Both Sides
TM38	Fire Blast	Fire	Special	110	85	5	Normal
TM39	Rock Tomb	Rock	Physical	60	95	15	Normal
TM42	Facade	Normal	Physical	70	100	20	Normal
TM44	Rest	Psychic	Status	—	—	10	Self
TM45	Attract	Normal	Status	—	100	15	Normal
TM46	Thief	Dark	Physical	60	100	25	Normal
TM48	Round	Normal	Special	60	100	15	Normal
TM52	Focus Blast	Fighting	Special	120	70	5	Normal
TM56	Fling	Dark	Physical	—	100	10	Normal
TM59	Incinerate	Fire	Special	60	100	15	Many Others
TM65	Shadow Claw	Ghost	Physical	70	100	15	Normal
TM66	Payback	Dark	Physical	50	100	10	Normal
TM68	Giga Impact	Normal	Physical	150	90	5	Normal
TM69	Rock Polish	Rock	Status	—	—	20	Self
TM71	Stone Edge	Rock	Physical	100	80	5	Normal
TM75	Swords Dance	Normal	Status	—	—	20	Self
TM78	Bulldoze	Ground	Physical	60	100	20	Adjacent
TM80	Rock Slide	Rock	Physical	75	90	10	Many Others
TM82	Dragon Tail	Dragon	Physical	60	90	10	Normal
TM84	Poison Jab	Poison	Physical	80	100	20	Normal
TM87	Swagger	Normal	Status	—	90	15	Normal
TM88	Sleep Talk	Normal	Status	—	—	10	Self
TM90	Substitute	Normal	Status	—	—	10	Self
TM91	Flash Cannon	Steel	Special	80	100	10	Normal
TM94	Secret Power	Normal	Physical	70	100	20	Normal
TM98	Power-Up Punch	Fighting	Physical	40	100	20	Normal
TM100	Confide	Normal	Status	—	—	20	Normal
HM01	Cut	Normal	Physical	50	95	30	Normal
HM03	Surf	Water	Special	90	100	15	Adjacent
HM04	Strength	Normal	Physical	80	100	15	Normal
HM06	Rock Smash	Fighting	Physical	40	100	15	Normal

MOVES LEARNED IN EXCHANGE FOR BP

Name	Type	Kind	Pow.	Acc.	PP	Range
Iron Head	Steel	Physical	80	100	15	Normal
Drill Run	Ground	Physical	80	95	10	Normal
Uproar	Normal	Special	90	100	10	1 Random
Thunder Punch	Electric	Physical	75	100	15	Normal
Fire Punch	Fire	Physical	75	100	15	Normal
Ice Punch	Ice	Physical	75	100	15	Normal
Block	Normal	Status	—	—	5	Normal
Earth Power	Ground	Special	90	100	10	Normal
Superpower	Fighting	Physical	120	100	5	Normal
Icy Wind	Ice	Special	55	95	15	Many Others
Aqua Tail	Water	Physical	90	90	10	Normal
Dragon Pulse	Dragon	Special	85	100	10	Normal
Iron Tail	Steel	Physical	100	75	15	Normal
Snore	Normal	Special	50	100	15	Normal
Focus Punch	Fighting	Physical	150	100	20	Normal
Shock Wave	Electric	Special	60	—	20	Normal
Spite	Ghost	Status	—	100	10	Normal
Endeavor	Normal	Physical	—	100	5	Normal
Outrage	Dragon	Physical	120	100	10	1 Random
Stealth Rock	Rock	Status	—	—	20	Other Side

MOVES TAUGHT BY PEOPLE

Name	Type	Kind	Pow.	Acc.	PP	Range

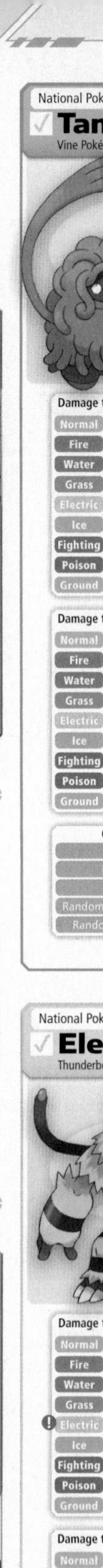

National Pokédex **465** Hoenn Pokédex —

Tangrowth

Vine Pokémon

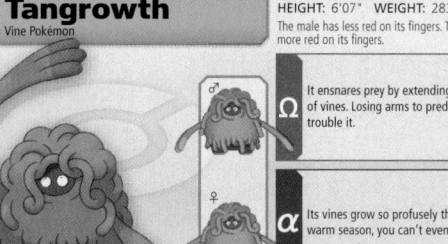

Grass

HEIGHT: 6'07" WEIGHT: 283.5 lbs.

The male has less red on its fingers. The female has more red on its fingers.

Ω It ensnares prey by extending arms made of vines. Losing arms to predators does not trouble it.

α Its vines grow so profusely that, in the warm season, you can't even see its eyes.

ABILITIES
Chlorophyll
Leaf Guard

HIDDEN ABILITY
Regenerator

EGG GROUPS
Grass

STAT GROWTH RATES
HP ■■■■
Attack ■■■■■
Defense ■■■■■
Sp. Atk ■■■■■
Sp. Def ■■
Speed ■■■

ITEMS SOMETIMES HELD BY WILD POKÉMON
—

EVOLUTION

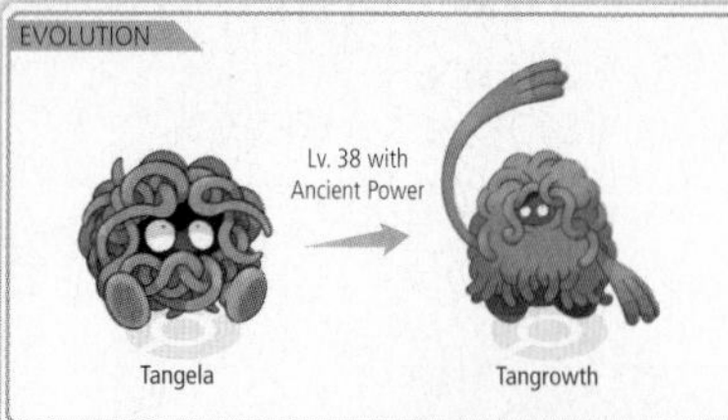

MAIN WAY TO REGISTER IN THE NATIONAL POKÉDEX

Level up Tangela to Lv. 38, then teach it the move Ancient Power. Alternatively, teach it the move Ancient Power first, then have it level up.

Damage taken in normal battles

Type		Type	
Normal	×1	Flying	×2
Fire	×2	Psychic	×1
Water	×0.5	Bug	×2
Grass	×0.5	Rock	×1
Electric	×0.5	Ghost	×1
Ice	×2	Dragon	×1
Fighting	×1	Dark	×1
Poison	×2	Steel	×1
Ground	×0.5	Fairy	×1

Damage taken in Inverse battles

Type		Type	
Normal	×1	Flying	×0.5
Fire	×0.5	Psychic	×1
Water	×2	Bug	×0.5
Grass	×2	Rock	×1
Electric	×2	Ghost	×1
Ice	×0.5	Dragon	×1
Fighting	×1	Dark	×1
Poison	×0.5	Steel	×1
Ground	×2	Fairy	×1

Can be used in
Inverse Battle
Battle Institute
Battle Maison
Random Matchup (Free Battle)
Random Matchup (Others)

LEVEL-UP MOVES

Lv.	Name	Type	Kind	Pow.	Acc.	PP	Range
1	Block	Normal	Status	—	—	5	Normal
1	Ingrain	Grass	Status	—	—	20	Self
1	Constrict	Normal	Physical	10	100	35	Normal
4	Sleep Powder	Grass	Status	—	75	15	Normal
7	Vine Whip	Grass	Physical	45	100	25	Normal
10	Absorb	Grass	Special	20	100	25	Normal
14	Poison Powder	Poison	Status	—	75	35	Normal
17	Bind	Normal	Physical	15	85	20	Normal
20	Growth	Normal	Status	—	—	20	Self
23	Mega Drain	Grass	Special	40	100	15	Normal
27	Knock Off	Dark	Physical	65	100	20	Normal
30	Stun Spore	Grass	Status	—	75	30	Normal
33	Natural Gift	Normal	Physical	—	100	15	Normal
36	Giga Drain	Grass	Special	75	100	10	Normal
40	Ancient Power	Rock	Special	60	100	5	Normal
43	Slam	Normal	Physical	80	75	20	Normal
46	Tickle	Normal	Status	—	100	20	Normal
49	Wring Out	Normal	Special	—	100	5	Normal
50	Grassy Terrain	Grass	Status	—	—	10	Both Sides
53	Power Whip	Grass	Physical	120	85	10	Normal
56	Block	Normal	Status	—	—	5	Normal

TM & HM MOVES

No.	Name	Type	Kind	Pow.	Acc.	PP	Range
TM06	Toxic	Poison	Status	—	90	10	Normal
TM10	Hidden Power	Normal	Special	60	100	15	Normal
TM11	Sunny Day	Fire	Status	—	—	5	Both Sides
TM15	Hyper Beam	Normal	Special	150	90	5	Normal
TM17	Protect	Normal	Status	—	—	10	Self
TM21	Frustration	Normal	Physical	—	100	20	Normal
TM22	Solar Beam	Grass	Special	120	100	10	Normal
TM26	Earthquake	Ground	Physical	100	100	10	Adjacent
TM27	Return	Normal	Physical	—	100	20	Normal
TM31	Brick Break	Fighting	Physical	75	100	15	Normal
TM32	Double Team	Normal	Status	—	—	15	Self
TM33	Reflect	Psychic	Status	—	—	20	Your Side
TM36	Sludge Bomb	Poison	Special	90	100	10	Normal
TM39	Rock Tomb	Rock	Physical	60	95	15	Normal
TM40	Aerial Ace	Flying	Physical	60	—	20	Normal
TM42	Facade	Normal	Physical	70	100	20	Normal
TM44	Rest	Psychic	Status	—	—	10	Self
TM45	Attract	Normal	Status	—	100	15	Normal
TM46	Thief	Dark	Physical	60	100	25	Normal
TM48	Round	Normal	Special	60	100	15	Normal
TM52	Focus Blast	Fighting	Special	120	70	5	Normal
TM53	Energy Ball	Grass	Special	90	100	10	Normal
TM56	Fling	Dark	Physical	—	100	10	Normal
TM66	Payback	Dark	Physical	50	100	10	Normal
TM68	Giga Impact	Normal	Physical	150	90	5	Normal
TM70	Flash	Normal	Status	—	100	20	Normal
TM75	Swords Dance	Normal	Status	—	—	20	Self
TM77	Psych Up	Normal	Status	—	—	10	Normal
TM78	Bulldoze	Ground	Physical	60	100	20	Adjacent
TM80	Rock Slide	Rock	Physical	75	90	10	Many Others
TM83	Infestation	Bug	Special	20	100	20	Normal
TM84	Poison Jab	Poison	Physical	80	100	20	Normal
TM86	Grass Knot	Grass	Special	—	100	20	Normal
TM87	Swagger	Normal	Status	—	90	15	Normal
TM88	Sleep Talk	Normal	Status	—	—	10	Self
TM90	Substitute	Normal	Status	—	—	10	Self
TM94	Secret Power	Normal	Physical	70	100	20	Normal
TM96	Nature Power	Normal	Status	—	—	20	Normal
TM100	Confide	Normal	Status	—	—	20	Normal
HM01	Cut	Normal	Physical	50	95	30	Normal
HM04	Strength	Normal	Physical	80	100	15	Normal
HM06	Rock Smash	Fighting	Physical	40	100	15	Normal

MOVES LEARNED IN EXCHANGE FOR BP

Name	Type	Kind	Pow.	Acc.	PP	Range
Seed Bomb	Grass	Physical	80	100	15	Normal
Block	Normal	Status	—	—	5	Normal
Bind	Normal	Physical	15	85	20	Normal
Snore	Normal	Special	50	100	15	Normal
Knock Off	Dark	Physical	65	100	20	Normal
Synthesis	Grass	Status	—	—	5	Self
Pain Split	Normal	Status	—	—	20	Normal
Giga Drain	Grass	Special	75	100	10	Normal
Shock Wave	Electric	Special	60	—	20	Normal
Worry Seed	Grass	Status	—	100	10	Normal
Endeavor	Normal	Physical	—	100	5	Normal

MOVES TAUGHT BY PEOPLE

Name	Type	Kind	Pow.	Acc.	PP	Range

National Pokédex **466** Hoenn Pokédex —

Electivire

Thunderbolt Pokémon

Electric

HEIGHT: 5'11" WEIGHT: 305.6 lbs.

Same form for ♂ / ♀

Ω As its electric charge amplifies, blue sparks begin to crackle between its horns.

α It pushes the tips of its two tails against the foe, then lets loose with over 20,000 volts of power.

ABILITY
Motor Drive

HIDDEN ABILITY
Vital Spirit

EGG GROUPS
Human-Like

STAT GROWTH RATES
HP ■■■
Attack ■■■■■■
Defense ■■■
Sp. Atk ■■■■■
Sp. Def ■■■■
Speed ■■■■■

ITEMS SOMETIMES HELD BY WILD POKÉMON
—

EVOLUTION

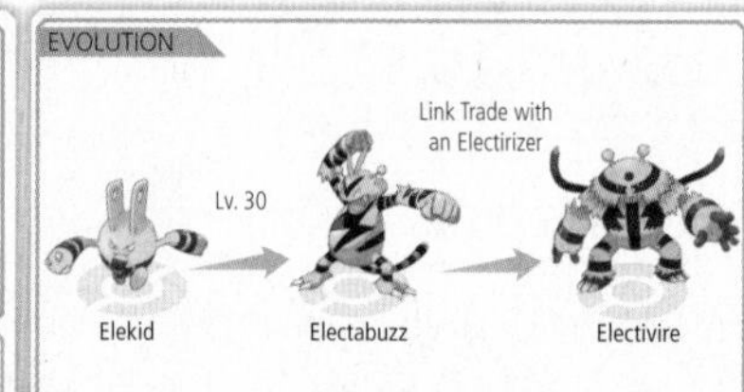

MAIN WAY TO REGISTER IN THE NATIONAL POKÉDEX

Receive an Electabuzz that is holding an Electirizer via Link Trade to have it evolve.

Damage taken in normal battles

Type		Type	
Normal	×1	Flying	×0.5
Fire	×1	Psychic	×1
Water	×1	Bug	×1
Grass	×1	Rock	×1
Electric	×0.5	Ghost	×1
Ice	×1	Dragon	×1
Fighting	×1	Dark	×1
Poison	×1	Steel	×0.5
Ground	×2	Fairy	×1

Damage taken in Inverse battles

Type		Type	
Normal	×1	Flying	×2
Fire	×1	Psychic	×1
Water	×1	Bug	×1
Grass	×1	Rock	×1
Electric	×2	Ghost	×1
Ice	×1	Dragon	×1
Fighting	×1	Dark	×1
Poison	×1	Steel	×2
Ground	×0.5	Fairy	×1

Can be used in
Inverse Battle
Battle Institute
Battle Maison
Random Matchup (Free Battle)
Random Matchup (Others)

LEVEL-UP MOVES

Lv.	Name	Type	Kind	Pow.	Acc.	PP	Range
1	Electric Terrain	Electric	Status	—	—	10	Both Sides
1	Ion Deluge	Electric	Status	—	—	25	Both Sides
1	Fire Punch	Fire	Physical	75	100	15	Normal
1	Quick Attack	Normal	Physical	40	100	30	Normal
1	Leer	Normal	Status	—	100	30	Many Others
1	Thunder Shock	Electric	Special	40	100	30	Normal
1	Low Kick	Fighting	Physical	—	100	20	Normal
5	Thunder Shock	Electric	Special	40	100	30	Normal
8	Low Kick	Fighting	Physical	—	100	20	Normal
12	Swift	Normal	Special	60	—	20	Many Others
15	Shock Wave	Electric	Special	60	—	20	Normal
19	Thunder Wave	Electric	Status	—	100	20	Normal
22	Electro Ball	Electric	Special	—	100	10	Normal
26	Light Screen	Psychic	Status	—	—	30	Your Side
29	Thunder Punch	Electric	Physical	75	100	15	Normal
36	Discharge	Electric	Special	80	100	15	Adjacent
42	Screech	Normal	Status	—	85	40	Normal
49	Thunderbolt	Electric	Special	90	100	15	Normal
55	Thunder	Electric	Special	110	70	10	Normal
62	Giga Impact	Normal	Physical	150	90	5	Normal
65	Electric Terrain	Electric	Status	—	—	10	Both Sides

TM & HM MOVES

No.	Name	Type	Kind	Pow.	Acc.	PP	Range
TM06	Toxic	Poison	Status	—	90	10	Normal
TM10	Hidden Power	Normal	Special	60	100	15	Normal
TM12	Taunt	Dark	Status	—	100	20	Normal
TM15	Hyper Beam	Normal	Special	150	90	5	Normal
TM16	Light Screen	Psychic	Status	—	—	30	Your Side
TM17	Protect	Normal	Status	—	—	10	Self
TM18	Rain Dance	Water	Status	—	—	5	Both Sides
TM21	Frustration	Normal	Physical	—	100	20	Normal
TM24	Thunderbolt	Electric	Special	90	100	15	Normal
TM25	Thunder	Electric	Special	110	70	10	Normal
TM26	Earthquake	Ground	Physical	100	100	10	Adjacent
TM27	Return	Normal	Physical	—	100	20	Normal
TM28	Dig	Ground	Physical	80	100	10	Normal
TM29	Psychic	Psychic	Special	90	100	10	Normal
TM31	Brick Break	Fighting	Physical	75	100	15	Normal
TM32	Double Team	Normal	Status	—	—	15	Self
TM35	Flamethrower	Fire	Special	90	100	15	Normal
TM39	Rock Tomb	Rock	Physical	60	95	15	Normal
TM41	Torment	Dark	Status	—	100	15	Normal
TM42	Facade	Normal	Physical	70	100	20	Normal
TM44	Rest	Psychic	Status	—	—	10	Self
TM45	Attract	Normal	Status	—	100	15	Normal
TM46	Thief	Dark	Physical	60	100	25	Normal
TM47	Low Sweep	Fighting	Physical	65	100	20	Normal
TM48	Round	Normal	Special	60	100	15	Normal
TM52	Focus Blast	Fighting	Special	120	70	5	Normal
TM56	Fling	Dark	Physical	—	100	10	Normal
TM57	Charge Beam	Electric	Special	50	90	10	Normal
TM68	Giga Impact	Normal	Physical	150	90	5	Normal
TM70	Flash	Normal	Status	—	100	20	Normal
TM72	Volt Switch	Electric	Special	70	100	20	Normal
TM73	Thunder Wave	Electric	Status	—	100	20	Normal
TM78	Bulldoze	Ground	Physical	60	100	20	Adjacent
TM80	Rock Slide	Rock	Physical	75	90	10	Many Others
TM87	Swagger	Normal	Status	—	90	15	Normal
TM88	Sleep Talk	Normal	Status	—	—	10	Self
TM90	Substitute	Normal	Status	—	—	10	Self
TM93	Wild Charge	Electric	Physical	90	100	15	Normal
TM94	Secret Power	Normal	Physical	70	100	20	Normal
TM98	Power-Up Punch	Fighting	Physical	40	100	20	Normal
TM100	Confide	Normal	Status	—	—	20	Normal
HM04	Strength	Normal	Physical	80	100	15	Normal
HM06	Rock Smash	Fighting	Physical	40	100	15	Normal

MOVES LEARNED IN EXCHANGE FOR BP

Name	Type	Kind	Pow.	Acc.	PP	Range
Covet	Normal	Physical	60	100	25	Normal
Dual Chop	Dragon	Physical	40	90	15	Normal
Signal Beam	Bug	Special	75	100	15	Normal
Low Kick	Fighting	Physical	—	100	20	Normal
Thunder Punch	Electric	Physical	75	100	15	Normal
Fire Punch	Fire	Physical	75	100	15	Normal
Ice Punch	Ice	Physical	75	100	15	Normal
Magnet Rise	Electric	Status	—	—	10	Self
Electroweb	Electric	Special	55	95	15	Many Others
Iron Tail	Steel	Physical	100	75	15	Normal
Snore	Normal	Special	50	100	15	Normal
Focus Punch	Fighting	Physical	150	100	20	Normal
Shock Wave	Electric	Special	60	—	20	Normal
Helping Hand	Normal	Status	—	—	20	1 Ally

MOVES TAUGHT BY PEOPLE

Name	Type	Kind	Pow.	Acc.	PP	Range

National Pokédex **467** Hoenn Pokédex —

Magmortar

Blast Pokémon

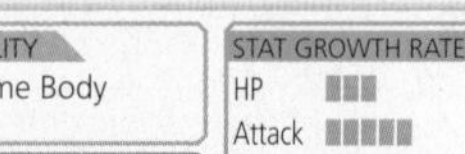

Fire

HEIGHT: 5'03" WEIGHT: 149.9 lbs.

Same form for ♂ / ♀

Ω It blasts fireballs of over 3,600 degrees Fahrenheit from the ends of its arms. It lives in volcanic craters.

α It blasts fireballs of over 3,600 degrees Fahrenheit out of its arms. Its breath also sears and sizzles.

ABILITY
Flame Body

HIDDEN ABILITY
Vital Spirit

EGG GROUPS
Human-Like

STAT GROWTH RATES
HP
Attack
Defense
Sp. Atk
Sp. Def
Speed

ITEMS SOMETIMES HELD BY WILD POKÉMON
—

EVOLUTION

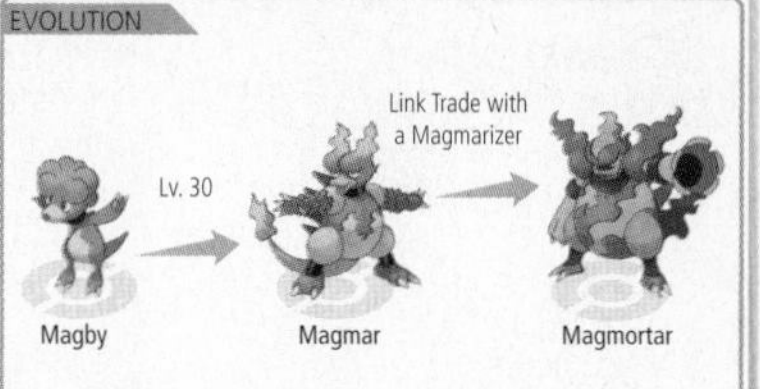

MAIN WAY TO REGISTER IN THE NATIONAL POKÉDEX

Receive a Magmar that is holding a Magmarizer via Link Trade to have it evolve.

Damage taken in normal battles

Type		Type	
Normal	×1	Flying	×1
Fire	×0.5	Psychic	×1
Water	×2	Bug	×0.5
Grass	×0.5	Rock	×2
Electric	×1	Ghost	×1
Ice	×0.5	Dragon	×1
Fighting	×1	Dark	×1
Poison	×1	Steel	×0.5
Ground	×2	Fairy	×0.5

Damage taken in Inverse battles

Type		Type	
Normal	×1	Flying	×1
Fire	×2	Psychic	×1
Water	×0.5	Bug	×2
Grass	×2	Rock	×0.5
Electric	×1	Ghost	×1
Ice	×2	Dragon	×1
Fighting	×1	Dark	×1
Poison	×1	Steel	×2
Ground	×0.5	Fairy	×2

Can be used in
- Inverse Battle
- Battle Institute
- Battle Maison
- Random Matchup (Free Battle)
- Random Matchup (Others)

LEVEL-UP MOVES

Lv.	Name	Type	Kind	Pow.	Acc.	PP	Range
1	Thunder Punch	Electric	Physical	75	100	15	Normal
1	Smog	Poison	Special	30	70	20	Normal
1	Leer	Normal	Status	—	100	30	Many Others
1	Ember	Fire	Special	40	100	25	Normal
1	Smokescreen	Normal	Status	—	100	20	Normal
5	Ember	Fire	Special	40	100	25	Normal
8	Smokescreen	Normal	Status	—	100	20	Normal
12	Feint Attack	Dark	Physical	60	—	20	Normal
15	Fire Spin	Fire	Special	35	85	15	Normal
19	Clear Smog	Poison	Special	50	—	15	Normal
22	Flame Burst	Fire	Special	70	100	15	Normal
26	Confuse Ray	Ghost	Status	—	100	10	Normal
29	Fire Punch	Fire	Physical	75	100	15	Normal
36	Lava Plume	Fire	Special	80	100	15	Adjacent
42	Sunny Day	Fire	Status	—	—	5	Both Sides
49	Flamethrower	Fire	Special	90	100	15	Normal
55	Fire Blast	Fire	Special	110	85	5	Normal
62	Hyper Beam	Normal	Special	150	90	5	Normal

TM & HM MOVES

No.	Name	Type	Kind	Pow.	Acc.	PP	Range
TM06	Toxic	Poison	Status	—	90	10	Normal
TM10	Hidden Power	Normal	Special	60	100	15	Normal
TM11	Sunny Day	Fire	Status	—	—	5	Both Sides
TM12	Taunt	Dark	Status	—	100	20	Normal
TM15	Hyper Beam	Normal	Special	150	90	5	Normal
TM17	Protect	Normal	Status	—	—	10	Self
TM21	Frustration	Normal	Physical	—	100	20	Normal
TM22	Solar Beam	Grass	Special	120	100	10	Normal
TM24	Thunderbolt	Electric	Special	90	100	15	Normal
TM26	Earthquake	Ground	Physical	100	100	10	Adjacent
TM27	Return	Normal	Physical	—	100	20	Normal
TM29	Psychic	Psychic	Special	90	100	10	Normal
TM31	Brick Break	Fighting	Physical	75	100	15	Normal
TM32	Double Team	Normal	Status	—	—	15	Self
TM35	Flamethrower	Fire	Special	90	100	15	Normal
TM38	Fire Blast	Fire	Special	110	85	5	Normal
TM39	Rock Tomb	Rock	Physical	60	95	15	Normal
TM41	Torment	Dark	Status	—	100	15	Normal
TM42	Facade	Normal	Physical	70	100	20	Normal
TM43	Flame Charge	Fire	Physical	50	100	20	Normal
TM44	Rest	Psychic	Status	—	—	10	Self
TM45	Attract	Normal	Status	—	100	15	Normal
TM46	Thief	Dark	Physical	60	100	25	Normal
TM47	Low Sweep	Fighting	Physical	65	100	20	Normal
TM48	Round	Normal	Special	60	100	15	Normal
TM50	Overheat	Fire	Special	130	90	5	Normal
TM52	Focus Blast	Fighting	Special	120	70	5	Normal
TM56	Fling	Dark	Physical	—	100	10	Normal
TM59	Incinerate	Fire	Special	60	100	15	Many Others
TM61	Will-O-Wisp	Fire	Status	—	85	15	Normal
TM68	Giga Impact	Normal	Physical	150	90	5	Normal
TM78	Bulldoze	Ground	Physical	60	100	20	Adjacent
TM80	Rock Slide	Rock	Physical	75	90	10	Many Others
TM87	Swagger	Normal	Status	—	90	15	Normal
TM88	Sleep Talk	Normal	Status	—	—	10	Self
TM90	Substitute	Normal	Status	—	—	10	Self
TM94	Secret Power	Normal	Physical	70	100	20	Normal
TM98	Power-Up Punch	Fighting	Physical	40	100	20	Normal
TM100	Confide	Normal	Status	—	—	20	Normal
HM04	Strength	Normal	Physical	80	100	15	Normal
HM06	Rock Smash	Fighting	Physical	40	100	15	Normal

MOVES LEARNED IN EXCHANGE FOR BP

Name	Type	Kind	Pow.	Acc.	PP	Range
Covet	Normal	Physical	60	100	25	Normal
Dual Chop	Dragon	Physical	40	90	15	Normal
Low Kick	Fighting	Physical	—	100	20	Normal
Thunder Punch	Electric	Physical	75	100	15	Normal
Fire Punch	Fire	Physical	75	100	15	Normal
Iron Tail	Steel	Physical	100	75	15	Normal
Snore	Normal	Special	50	100	15	Normal
Heat Wave	Fire	Special	95	90	10	Many Others
Focus Punch	Fighting	Physical	150	100	20	Normal
Helping Hand	Normal	Status	—	—	20	1 Ally

MOVES TAUGHT BY PEOPLE

Name	Type	Kind	Pow.	Acc.	PP	Range

National Pokédex **468** Hoenn Pokédex —

Togekiss

Jubilee Pokémon

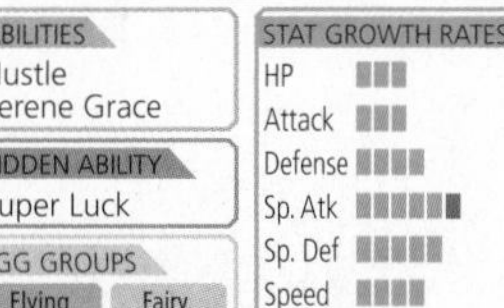

Fairy Flying

HEIGHT: 4'11" WEIGHT: 83.8 lbs.

Same form for ♂ / ♀

Ω As everyone knows, it visits peaceful regions, bringing them gifts of kindness and sweet blessings.

α It shares many blessings with people who respect one another's rights and avoid needless strife.

ABILITIES
Hustle
Serene Grace

HIDDEN ABILITY
Super Luck

EGG GROUPS
Flying Fairy

STAT GROWTH RATES
HP
Attack
Defense
Sp. Atk
Sp. Def
Speed

ITEMS SOMETIMES HELD BY WILD POKÉMON
—

EVOLUTION

Level up with high friendship → Shiny Stone

Togepi → Togetic → Togekiss

MAIN WAY TO REGISTER IN THE NATIONAL POKÉDEX

Use a Shiny Stone on Togetic.

Damage taken in normal battles

Type		Type	
Normal	×1	Flying	×1
Fire	×1	Psychic	×1
Water	×1	Bug	×0.25
Grass	×0.5	Rock	×2
Electric	×2	Ghost	×1
Ice	×2	Dragon	×0
Fighting	×0.25	Dark	×0.5
Poison	×2	Steel	×2
Ground	×0	Fairy	×1

Damage taken in Inverse battles

Type		Type	
Normal	×1	Flying	×1
Fire	×1	Psychic	×1
Water	×1	Bug	×4
Grass	×2	Rock	×0.5
Electric	×0.5	Ghost	×1
Ice	×0.5	Dragon	×2
Fighting	×4	Dark	×2
Poison	×0.5	Steel	×0.5
Ground	×2	Fairy	×1

Can be used in
- Inverse Battle
- Battle Institute
- Battle Maison
- Random Matchup (Free Battle)
- Random Matchup (Others)

LEVEL-UP MOVES

Lv.	Name	Type	Kind	Pow.	Acc.	PP	Range
1	After You	Normal	Status	—	—	15	Normal
1	Sky Attack	Flying	Physical	140	90	5	Normal
1	Extreme Speed	Normal	Physical	80	100	5	Normal
1	Aura Sphere	Fighting	Special	80	—	20	Normal
1	Air Slash	Flying	Special	75	95	15	Normal

TM & HM MOVES

No.	Name	Type	Kind	Pow.	Acc.	PP	Range
TM03	Psyshock	Psychic	Special	80	100	10	Normal
TM06	Toxic	Poison	Status	—	90	10	Normal
TM10	Hidden Power	Normal	Special	60	100	15	Normal
TM11	Sunny Day	Fire	Status	—	—	5	Both Sides
TM15	Hyper Beam	Normal	Special	150	90	5	Normal
TM16	Light Screen	Psychic	Status	—	—	30	Your Side
TM17	Protect	Normal	Status	—	—	10	Self
TM18	Rain Dance	Water	Status	—	—	5	Both Sides
TM19	Roost	Flying	Status	—	—	10	Self
TM20	Safeguard	Normal	Status	—	—	25	Your Side
TM21	Frustration	Normal	Physical	—	100	20	Normal
TM22	Solar Beam	Grass	Special	120	100	10	Normal
TM27	Return	Normal	Physical	—	100	20	Normal
TM29	Psychic	Psychic	Special	90	100	10	Normal
TM30	Shadow Ball	Ghost	Special	80	100	15	Normal
TM31	Brick Break	Fighting	Physical	75	100	15	Normal
TM32	Double Team	Normal	Status	—	—	15	Self
TM33	Reflect	Psychic	Status	—	—	20	Your Side
TM35	Flamethrower	Fire	Special	90	100	15	Normal
TM38	Fire Blast	Fire	Special	110	85	5	Normal
TM40	Aerial Ace	Flying	Physical	60	—	20	Normal
TM42	Facade	Normal	Physical	70	100	20	Normal
TM44	Rest	Psychic	Status	—	—	10	Self
TM45	Attract	Normal	Status	—	100	15	Normal
TM48	Round	Normal	Special	60	100	15	Normal
TM49	Echoed Voice	Normal	Special	40	100	15	Normal
TM51	Steel Wing	Steel	Physical	70	90	25	Normal
TM56	Fling	Dark	Physical	—	100	10	Normal
TM59	Incinerate	Fire	Special	60	100	15	Many Others
TM67	Retaliate	Normal	Physical	70	100	5	Normal
TM68	Giga Impact	Normal	Physical	150	90	5	Normal
TM70	Flash	Normal	Status	—	100	20	Normal
TM73	Thunder Wave	Electric	Status	—	100	20	Normal
TM77	Psych Up	Normal	Status	—	—	10	Normal
TM85	Dream Eater	Psychic	Special	100	100	15	Normal
TM86	Grass Knot	Grass	Special	—	100	20	Normal
TM87	Swagger	Normal	Status	—	90	15	Normal
TM88	Sleep Talk	Normal	Status	—	—	10	Self
TM90	Substitute	Normal	Status	—	—	10	Self
TM94	Secret Power	Normal	Physical	70	100	20	Normal
TM99	Dazzling Gleam	Fairy	Special	80	100	10	Many Others
TM100	Confide	Normal	Status	—	—	20	Normal
HM02	Fly	Flying	Physical	90	95	15	Normal
HM06	Rock Smash	Fighting	Physical	40	100	15	Normal

MOVES LEARNED IN EXCHANGE FOR BP

Name	Type	Kind	Pow.	Acc.	PP	Range
Covet	Normal	Physical	60	100	25	Normal
Signal Beam	Bug	Special	75	100	15	Normal
Magic Coat	Psychic	Status	—	—	15	Self
Last Resort	Normal	Physical	140	100	5	Normal
Zen Headbutt	Psychic	Physical	80	90	15	Normal
Hyper Voice	Normal	Special	90	100	10	Many Others
Snore	Normal	Special	50	100	15	Normal
Heat Wave	Fire	Special	95	90	10	Many Others
Heal Bell	Normal	Status	—	—	5	Your Party
Tailwind	Flying	Status	—	—	15	Your Side
Sky Attack	Flying	Physical	140	90	5	Normal
Drain Punch	Fighting	Physical	75	100	10	Normal
Focus Punch	Fighting	Physical	150	100	20	Normal
Shock Wave	Electric	Special	60	—	20	Normal
Water Pulse	Water	Special	60	100	20	Normal
After You	Normal	Status	—	—	15	Normal
Trick	Psychic	Status	—	100	10	Normal
Endeavor	Normal	Physical	—	100	5	Normal

MOVES TAUGHT BY PEOPLE

Name	Type	Kind	Pow.	Acc.	PP	Range

National Pokédex **469** Hoenn Pokédex —

Yanmega

Ogre Darner Pokémon

Bug | Flying

HEIGHT: 6'03" WEIGHT: 113.5 lbs.

Same form for ♂ / ♀

Ω It prefers to battle by biting apart foes' heads instantly while flying by at high speed.

α This six-legged Pokémon is easily capable of transporting an adult in flight. The wings on its tail help it stay balanced.

ABILITIES
Speed Boost
Tinted Lens

HIDDEN ABILITY
Frisk

EGG GROUPS
Bug

STAT GROWTH RATES
HP, Attack, Defense, Sp. Atk, Sp. Def, Speed

ITEMS SOMETIMES HELD BY WILD POKÉMON
—

EVOLUTION
Yanma → (Lv. 33 with Ancient Power) → Yanmega

MAIN WAY TO REGISTER IN THE NATIONAL POKÉDEX

Level up a Yanma obtained via Link Trade or the GTS to Lv. 33, then teach it the move Ancient Power. Alternatively, teach it the move Ancient Power first, then have it level up.

Damage taken in normal battles

Type	×	Type	×
Normal	×1	Flying	×2
Fire	×2	Psychic	×1
Water	×1	Bug	×0.5
Grass	×0.25	Rock	×4
Electric	×2	Ghost	×1
Ice	×2	Dragon	×1
Fighting	×0.25	Dark	×1
Poison	×1	Steel	×1
Ground	×0	Fairy	×1

Damage taken in Inverse battles

Type	×	Type	×
Normal	×1	Flying	×0.5
Fire	×0.5	Psychic	×1
Water	×1	Bug	×2
Grass	×4	Rock	×0.25
Electric	×0.5	Ghost	×1
Ice	×0.5	Dragon	×1
Fighting	×4	Dark	×1
Poison	×1	Steel	×1
Ground	×4	Fairy	×1

Can be used in
Inverse Battle
Battle Institute
Battle Maison
Random Matchup (Free Battle)
Random Matchup (Others)

LEVEL-UP MOVES

Lv.	Name	Type	Kind	Pow.	Acc.	PP	Range
1	Bug Buzz	Bug	Special	90	100	10	Normal
1	Air Slash	Flying	Special	75	95	15	Normal
1	Night Slash	Dark	Physical	70	100	15	Normal
1	Bug Bite	Bug	Physical	60	100	20	Normal
1	Tackle	Normal	Physical	50	100	35	Normal
1	Foresight	Normal	Status	—	—	40	Normal
1	Quick Attack	Normal	Physical	40	100	30	Normal
1	Double Team	Normal	Status	—	—	15	Self
6	Quick Attack	Normal	Physical	40	100	30	Normal
11	Double Team	Normal	Status	—	—	15	Self
14	Sonic Boom	Normal	Special	—	90	20	Normal
17	Detect	Fighting	Status	—	—	5	Self
22	Supersonic	Normal	Status	—	55	20	Normal
27	Uproar	Normal	Special	90	100	10	1 Random
30	Pursuit	Dark	Physical	40	100	20	Normal
33	Ancient Power	Rock	Special	60	100	5	Normal
38	Feint	Normal	Physical	30	100	10	Normal
43	Slash	Normal	Physical	70	100	20	Normal
46	Screech	Normal	Status	—	85	40	Normal
49	U-turn	Bug	Physical	70	100	20	Normal
54	Air Slash	Flying	Special	75	95	15	Normal
57	Bug Buzz	Bug	Special	90	100	10	Normal

TM & HM MOVES

No.	Name	Type	Kind	Pow.	Acc.	PP	Range
TM06	Toxic	Poison	Status	—	90	10	Normal
TM10	Hidden Power	Normal	Special	60	100	15	Normal
TM11	Sunny Day	Fire	Status	—	—	5	Both Sides
TM15	Hyper Beam	Normal	Special	150	90	5	Normal
TM17	Protect	Normal	Status	—	—	10	Self
TM19	Roost	Flying	Status	—	—	10	Self
TM21	Frustration	Normal	Physical	—	100	20	Normal
TM22	Solar Beam	Grass	Special	120	100	10	Normal
TM27	Return	Normal	Physical	—	100	20	Normal
TM29	Psychic	Psychic	Special	90	100	10	Normal
TM30	Shadow Ball	Ghost	Special	80	100	15	Normal
TM32	Double Team	Normal	Status	—	—	15	Self
TM40	Aerial Ace	Flying	Physical	60	—	20	Normal
TM42	Facade	Normal	Physical	70	100	20	Normal
TM44	Rest	Psychic	Status	—	—	10	Self
TM45	Attract	Normal	Status	—	100	15	Normal
TM46	Thief	Dark	Physical	60	100	25	Normal
TM48	Round	Normal	Special	60	100	15	Normal
TM51	Steel Wing	Steel	Physical	70	90	25	Normal
TM68	Giga Impact	Normal	Physical	150	90	5	Normal
TM70	Flash	Normal	Status	—	100	20	Normal
TM76	Struggle Bug	Bug	Special	50	100	20	Many Others
TM77	Psych Up	Normal	Status	—	—	10	Normal
TM85	Dream Eater	Psychic	Special	100	100	15	Normal
TM87	Swagger	Normal	Status	—	90	15	Normal
TM88	Sleep Talk	Normal	Status	—	—	10	Self
TM89	U-turn	Bug	Physical	70	100	20	Normal
TM90	Substitute	Normal	Status	—	—	10	Self
TM94	Secret Power	Normal	Physical	70	100	20	Normal
TM100	Confide	Normal	Status	—	—	20	Normal

MOVES LEARNED IN EXCHANGE FOR BP

Name	Type	Kind	Pow.	Acc.	PP	Range
Bug Bite	Bug	Physical	60	100	20	Normal
Signal Beam	Bug	Special	75	100	15	Normal
Uproar	Normal	Special	90	100	10	1 Random
Snore	Normal	Special	50	100	15	Normal
Tailwind	Flying	Status	—	—	15	Your Side
Giga Drain	Grass	Special	75	100	10	Normal

MOVES TAUGHT BY PEOPLE

Name	Type	Kind	Pow.	Acc.	PP	Range

National Pokédex **470** Hoenn Pokédex —

Leafeon

Verdant Pokémon

Grass

HEIGHT: 3'03" WEIGHT: 56.2 lbs.

Same form for ♂ / ♀

Ω When you see Leafeon asleep in a patch of sunshine, you'll know it is using photosynthesis to produce clean air.

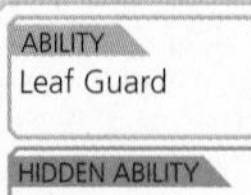

α Just like a plant, it uses photosynthesis. As a result, it is always enveloped in clear air.

ABILITY
Leaf Guard

HIDDEN ABILITY
Chlorophyll

EGG GROUPS
Field

STAT GROWTH RATES
HP, Attack, Defense, Sp. Atk, Sp. Def, Speed

ITEMS SOMETIMES HELD BY WILD POKÉMON
—

EVOLUTION
Eevee → (Level up in Petalburg Woods) → Leafeon

MAIN WAY TO REGISTER IN THE NATIONAL POKÉDEX

Level up Eevee in Petalburg Woods.

Damage taken in normal battles

Type	×	Type	×
Normal	×1	Flying	×2
Fire	×2	Psychic	×1
Water	×0.5	Bug	×2
Grass	×0.5	Rock	×1
Electric	×0.5	Ghost	×1
Ice	×2	Dragon	×1
Fighting	×1	Dark	×1
Poison	×2	Steel	×1
Ground	×0.5	Fairy	×1

Damage taken in Inverse battles

Type	×	Type	×
Normal	×1	Flying	×0.5
Fire	×0.5	Psychic	×1
Water	×2	Bug	×0.5
Grass	×2	Rock	×1
Electric	×2	Ghost	×1
Ice	×0.5	Dragon	×1
Fighting	×1	Dark	×1
Poison	×0.5	Steel	×1
Ground	×2	Fairy	×1

Can be used in
Inverse Battle
Battle Institute
Battle Maison
Random Matchup (Free Battle)
Random Matchup (Others)

LEVEL-UP MOVES

Lv.	Name	Type	Kind	Pow.	Acc.	PP	Range
1	Tail Whip	Normal	Status	—	100	30	Many Others
1	Tackle	Normal	Physical	50	100	35	Normal
1	Helping Hand	Normal	Status	—	—	20	1 Ally
5	Sand Attack	Ground	Status	—	100	15	Normal
9	Razor Leaf	Grass	Physical	55	95	25	Many Others
13	Quick Attack	Normal	Physical	40	100	30	Normal
17	Grass Whistle	Grass	Status	—	55	15	Normal
20	Magical Leaf	Grass	Special	60	—	20	Normal
25	Giga Drain	Grass	Special	75	100	10	Normal
29	Swords Dance	Normal	Status	—	—	20	Self
33	Synthesis	Grass	Status	—	—	5	Self
37	Sunny Day	Fire	Status	—	—	5	Both Sides
41	Last Resort	Normal	Physical	140	100	5	Normal
45	Leaf Blade	Grass	Physical	90	100	15	Normal

TM & HM MOVES

No.	Name	Type	Kind	Pow.	Acc.	PP	Range
TM05	Roar	Normal	Status	—	—	20	Normal
TM06	Toxic	Poison	Status	—	90	10	Normal
TM10	Hidden Power	Normal	Special	60	100	15	Normal
TM11	Sunny Day	Fire	Status	—	—	5	Both Sides
TM15	Hyper Beam	Normal	Special	150	90	5	Normal
TM17	Protect	Normal	Status	—	—	10	Self
TM18	Rain Dance	Water	Status	—	—	5	Both Sides
TM21	Frustration	Normal	Physical	—	100	20	Normal
TM22	Solar Beam	Grass	Special	120	100	10	Normal
TM27	Return	Normal	Physical	—	100	20	Normal
TM28	Dig	Ground	Physical	80	100	10	Normal
TM30	Shadow Ball	Ghost	Special	80	100	15	Normal
TM32	Double Team	Normal	Status	—	—	15	Self
TM40	Aerial Ace	Flying	Physical	60	—	20	Normal
TM42	Facade	Normal	Physical	70	100	20	Normal
TM44	Rest	Psychic	Status	—	—	10	Self
TM45	Attract	Normal	Status	—	100	15	Normal
TM48	Round	Normal	Special	60	100	15	Normal
TM49	Echoed Voice	Normal	Special	40	100	15	Normal
TM53	Energy Ball	Grass	Special	90	100	10	Normal
TM67	Retaliate	Normal	Physical	70	100	5	Normal
TM68	Giga Impact	Normal	Physical	150	90	5	Normal
TM70	Flash	Normal	Status	—	100	20	Normal
TM75	Swords Dance	Normal	Status	—	—	20	Self
TM81	X-Scissor	Bug	Physical	80	100	15	Normal
TM86	Grass Knot	Grass	Special	—	100	20	Normal
TM87	Swagger	Normal	Status	—	90	15	Normal
TM88	Sleep Talk	Normal	Status	—	—	10	Self
TM90	Substitute	Normal	Status	—	—	10	Self
TM94	Secret Power	Normal	Physical	70	100	20	Normal
TM96	Nature Power	Normal	Status	—	—	20	Normal
TM100	Confide	Normal	Status	—	—	20	Normal
HM04	Strength	Normal	Physical	80	100	15	Normal
HM06	Rock Smash	Fighting	Physical	40	100	15	Normal

MOVES LEARNED IN EXCHANGE FOR BP

Name	Type	Kind	Pow.	Acc.	PP	Range
Covet	Normal	Physical	60	100	25	Normal
Seed Bomb	Grass	Physical	80	100	15	Normal
Last Resort	Normal	Physical	140	100	5	Normal
Hyper Voice	Normal	Special	90	100	10	Many Others
Iron Tail	Steel	Physical	100	75	15	Normal
Snore	Normal	Special	50	100	15	Normal
Knock Off	Dark	Physical	65	100	20	Normal
Synthesis	Grass	Status	—	—	5	Self
Heal Bell	Normal	Status	—	—	5	Your Party
Giga Drain	Grass	Special	75	100	10	Normal
Worry Seed	Grass	Status	—	100	10	Normal
Helping Hand	Normal	Status	—	—	20	1 Ally

MOVES TAUGHT BY PEOPLE

Name	Type	Kind	Pow.	Acc.	PP	Range

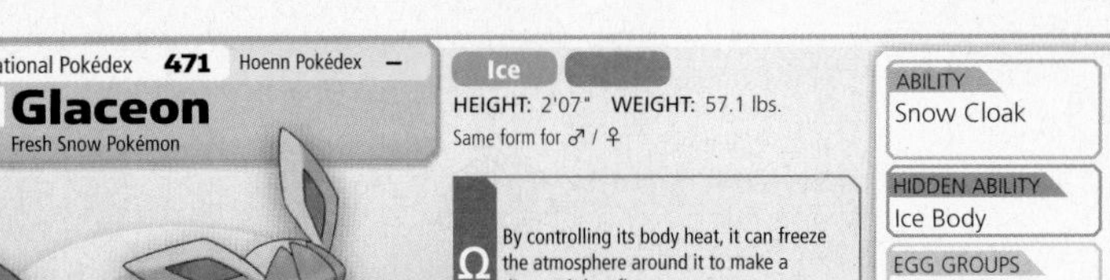

National Pokédex **471** Hoenn Pokédex —

Glaceon

Fresh Snow Pokémon

Ice

HEIGHT: 2'07" WEIGHT: 57.1 lbs.

Same form for ♂ / ♀

Ω By controlling its body heat, it can freeze the atmosphere around it to make a diamond-dust flurry.

α It lowers its body heat to freeze its fur. The hairs then become like needles it can fire.

ABILITY
Snow Cloak

HIDDEN ABILITY
Ice Body

EGG GROUPS
Field

STAT GROWTH RATES
HP
Attack
Defense
Sp. Atk
Sp. Def
Speed

ITEMS SOMETIMES HELD BY WILD POKÉMON
—

EVOLUTION

Level up Eevee in the ice cavern within Shoal Cave

Eevee → Glaceon

MAIN WAY TO REGISTER IN THE NATIONAL POKÉDEX

Level up Eevee in the ice cavern within Shoal Cave. Must be at low tide (between 3:00 and 8:59 A.M. or P.M.).

Damage taken in normal battles

Normal	×1	Flying	×1
Fire	×2	Psychic	×1
Water	×1	Bug	×1
Grass	×1	Rock	×2
Electric	×1	Ghost	×1
Ice	×0.5	Dragon	×1
Fighting	×2	Dark	×1
Poison	×1	Steel	×2
Ground	×1	Fairy	×1

Damage taken in Inverse battles

Normal	×1	Flying	×1
Fire	×0.5	Psychic	×1
Water	×1	Bug	×1
Grass	×1	Rock	×0.5
Electric	×1	Ghost	×1
Ice	×2	Dragon	×1
Fighting	×0.5	Dark	×1
Poison	×1	Steel	×0.5
Ground	×1	Fairy	×1

Can be used in
Inverse Battle
Battle Institute
Battle Maison
Random Matchup (Free Battle)
Random Matchup (Others)

LEVEL-UP MOVES

Lv.	Name	Type	Kind	Pow.	Acc.	PP	Range
1	Helping Hand	Normal	Status	—	—	20	1 Ally
1	Tackle	Normal	Physical	50	100	35	Normal
1	Tail Whip	Normal	Status	—	100	30	Many Others
5	Sand Attack	Ground	Status	—	100	15	Normal
9	Icy Wind	Ice	Special	55	95	15	Many Others
13	Quick Attack	Normal	Physical	40	100	30	Normal
17	Bite	Dark	Physical	60	100	25	Normal
20	Ice Fang	Ice	Physical	65	95	15	Normal
25	Ice Shard	Ice	Physical	40	100	30	Normal
29	Barrier	Psychic	Status	—	—	20	Self
33	Mirror Coat	Psychic	Special	—	100	20	Varies
37	Hail	Ice	Status	—	—	10	Both Sides
41	Last Resort	Normal	Physical	140	100	5	Normal
45	Blizzard	Ice	Special	110	70	5	Many Others

TM & HM MOVES

No.	Name	Type	Kind	Pow.	Acc.	PP	Range
TM05	Roar	Normal	Status	—	—	20	Normal
TM06	Toxic	Poison	Status	—	90	10	Normal
TM07	Hail	Ice	Status	—	—	10	Both Sides
TM10	Hidden Power	Normal	Special	60	100	15	Normal
TM11	Sunny Day	Fire	Status	—	—	5	Both Sides
TM13	Ice Beam	Ice	Special	90	100	10	Normal
TM14	Blizzard	Ice	Special	110	70	5	Many Others
TM15	Hyper Beam	Normal	Special	150	90	5	Normal
TM17	Protect	Normal	Status	—	—	10	Self
TM18	Rain Dance	Water	Status	—	—	5	Both Sides
TM21	Frustration	Normal	Physical	—	100	20	Normal
TM27	Return	Normal	Physical	—	100	20	Normal
TM28	Dig	Ground	Physical	80	100	10	Normal
TM30	Shadow Ball	Ghost	Special	80	100	15	Normal
TM32	Double Team	Normal	Status	—	—	15	Self
TM42	Facade	Normal	Physical	70	100	20	Normal
TM44	Rest	Psychic	Status	—	—	10	Self
TM45	Attract	Normal	Status	—	100	15	Normal
TM48	Round	Normal	Special	60	100	15	Normal
TM49	Echoed Voice	Normal	Special	40	100	15	Normal
TM67	Retaliate	Normal	Physical	70	100	5	Normal
TM68	Giga Impact	Normal	Physical	150	90	5	Normal
TM79	Frost Breath	Ice	Special	60	90	10	Normal
TM87	Swagger	Normal	Status	—	90	15	Normal
TM88	Sleep Talk	Normal	Status	—	—	10	Self
TM90	Substitute	Normal	Status	—	—	10	Self
TM94	Secret Power	Normal	Physical	70	100	20	Normal
TM100	Confide	Normal	Status	—	—	20	Normal
HM04	Strength	Normal	Physical	80	100	15	Normal
HM06	Rock Smash	Fighting	Physical	40	100	15	Normal

MOVES LEARNED IN EXCHANGE FOR BP

Name	Type	Kind	Pow.	Acc.	PP	Range
Covet	Normal	Physical	60	100	25	Normal
Signal Beam	Bug	Special	75	100	15	Normal
Last Resort	Normal	Physical	140	100	5	Normal
Icy Wind	Ice	Special	55	95	15	Many Others
Aqua Tail	Water	Physical	90	90	10	Normal
Hyper Voice	Normal	Special	90	100	10	Many Others
Iron Tail	Steel	Physical	100	75	15	Normal
Snore	Normal	Special	50	100	15	Normal
Heal Bell	Normal	Status	—	—	5	Your Party
Water Pulse	Water	Special	60	100	20	Normal
Helping Hand	Normal	Status	—	—	20	1 Ally

MOVES TAUGHT BY PEOPLE

Name	Type	Kind	Pow.	Acc.	PP	Range

National Pokédex **472** Hoenn Pokédex —

Gliscor

Fang Scorpion Pokémon

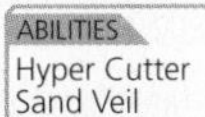

Ground Flying

HEIGHT: 6'07" WEIGHT: 93.7 lbs.

Same form for ♂ / ♀

Ω It observes prey while hanging inverted from branches. When the chance presents itself, it swoops!

α Its flight is soundless. It uses its lengthy tail to carry off its prey... Then its elongated fangs do the rest.

ABILITIES
Hyper Cutter
Sand Veil

HIDDEN ABILITY
Poison Heal

EGG GROUPS
Bug

STAT GROWTH RATES
HP
Attack
Defense
Sp. Atk
Sp. Def
Speed

ITEMS SOMETIMES HELD BY WILD POKÉMON
—

EVOLUTION

Level up with a Razor Fang between 8 P.M. and 3:59 A.M.

Gligar → Gliscor

MAIN WAY TO REGISTER IN THE NATIONAL POKÉDEX

Have a Gligar obtained via Link Trade or the GTS hold a Razor Fang, then level it up between 8:00 P.M. and 3:59 A.M.

Damage taken in normal battles

Normal	×1	Flying	×1
Fire	×1	Psychic	×1
Water	×2	Bug	×0.5
Grass	×1	Rock	×1
Electric	×0	Ghost	×1
Ice	×4	Dragon	×1
Fighting	×0.5	Dark	×1
Poison	×0.5	Steel	×1
Ground	×0	Fairy	×1

Damage taken in Inverse battles

Normal	×1	Flying	×1
Fire	×1	Psychic	×1
Water	×0.5	Bug	×2
Grass	×1	Rock	×1
Electric	×1	Ghost	×1
Ice	×0.25	Dragon	×1
Fighting	×2	Dark	×1
Poison	×2	Steel	×1
Ground	×2	Fairy	×1

Can be used in
Inverse Battle
Battle Institute
Battle Maison
Random Matchup (Free Battle)
Random Matchup (Others)

LEVEL-UP MOVES

Lv.	Name	Type	Kind	Pow.	Acc.	PP	Range
1	Guillotine	Normal	Physical	—	30	5	Normal
1	Thunder Fang	Electric	Physical	65	95	15	Normal
1	Ice Fang	Ice	Physical	65	95	15	Normal
1	Fire Fang	Fire	Physical	65	95	15	Normal
1	Poison Jab	Poison	Physical	80	100	20	Normal
1	Sand Attack	Ground	Status	—	100	15	Normal
1	Harden	Normal	Status	—	—	30	Self
1	Knock Off	Dark	Physical	65	100	20	Normal
4	Sand Attack	Ground	Status	—	100	15	Normal
7	Harden	Normal	Status	—	—	30	Self
10	Knock Off	Dark	Physical	65	100	20	Normal
13	Quick Attack	Normal	Physical	40	100	30	Normal
16	Fury Cutter	Bug	Physical	40	95	20	Normal
19	Feint Attack	Dark	Physical	60	—	20	Normal
22	Acrobatics	Flying	Physical	55	100	15	Normal
27	Night Slash	Dark	Physical	70	100	15	Normal
30	U-turn	Bug	Physical	70	100	20	Normal
35	Screech	Normal	Status	—	85	40	Normal
40	X-Scissor	Bug	Physical	80	100	15	Normal
45	Sky Uppercut	Fighting	Physical	85	90	15	Normal
50	Swords Dance	Normal	Status	—	—	20	Self
55	Guillotine	Normal	Physical	—	30	5	Normal

TM & HM MOVES

No.	Name	Type	Kind	Pow.	Acc.	PP	Range
TM01	Hone Claws	Dark	Status	—	—	15	Self
TM06	Toxic	Poison	Status	—	90	10	Normal
TM09	Venoshock	Poison	Special	65	100	10	Normal
TM10	Hidden Power	Normal	Special	60	100	15	Normal
TM11	Sunny Day	Fire	Status	—	—	5	Both Sides
TM12	Taunt	Dark	Status	—	100	20	Normal
TM15	Hyper Beam	Normal	Special	150	90	5	Normal
TM17	Protect	Normal	Status	—	—	10	Self
TM18	Rain Dance	Water	Status	—	—	5	Both Sides
TM19	Roost	Flying	Status	—	—	10	Self
TM21	Frustration	Normal	Physical	—	100	20	Normal
TM26	Earthquake	Ground	Physical	100	100	10	Adjacent
TM27	Return	Normal	Physical	—	100	20	Normal
TM28	Dig	Ground	Physical	80	100	10	Normal
TM31	Brick Break	Fighting	Physical	75	100	15	Normal
TM32	Double Team	Normal	Status	—	—	15	Self
TM36	Sludge Bomb	Poison	Special	90	100	10	Normal
TM37	Sandstorm	Rock	Status	—	—	10	Both Sides
TM39	Rock Tomb	Rock	Physical	60	95	15	Normal
TM40	Aerial Ace	Flying	Physical	60	—	20	Normal
TM41	Torment	Dark	Status	—	100	15	Normal
TM42	Facade	Normal	Physical	70	100	20	Normal
TM44	Rest	Psychic	Status	—	—	10	Self
TM45	Attract	Normal	Status	—	100	15	Normal
TM46	Thief	Dark	Physical	60	100	25	Normal
TM48	Round	Normal	Special	60	100	15	Normal
TM51	Steel Wing	Steel	Physical	70	90	25	Normal
TM54	False Swipe	Normal	Physical	40	100	40	Normal
TM56	Fling	Dark	Physical	—	100	10	Normal
TM62	Acrobatics	Flying	Physical	55	100	15	Normal
TM66	Payback	Dark	Physical	50	100	10	Normal
TM68	Giga Impact	Normal	Physical	150	90	5	Normal
TM69	Rock Polish	Rock	Status	—	—	20	Self
TM71	Stone Edge	Rock	Physical	100	80	5	Normal
TM75	Swords Dance	Normal	Status	—	—	20	Self
TM76	Struggle Bug	Bug	Special	50	100	20	Many Others
TM78	Bulldoze	Ground	Physical	60	100	20	Adjacent
TM80	Rock Slide	Rock	Physical	75	90	10	Many Others
TM81	X-Scissor	Bug	Physical	80	100	15	Normal
TM84	Poison Jab	Poison	Physical	80	100	20	Normal
TM87	Swagger	Normal	Status	—	90	15	Normal
TM88	Sleep Talk	Normal	Status	—	—	10	Self
TM89	U-turn	Bug	Physical	70	100	20	Normal
TM90	Substitute	Normal	Status	—	—	10	Self
TM94	Secret Power	Normal	Physical	70	100	20	Normal
TM97	Dark Pulse	Dark	Special	80	100	15	Normal
TM100	Confide	Normal	Status	—	—	20	Normal
HM01	Cut	Normal	Physical	50	95	30	Normal
HM04	Strength	Normal	Physical	80	100	15	Normal
HM06	Rock Smash	Fighting	Physical	40	100	15	Normal

MOVES LEARNED IN EXCHANGE FOR BP

Name	Type	Kind	Pow.	Acc.	PP	Range
Bug Bite	Bug	Physical	60	100	20	Normal
Earth Power	Ground	Special	90	100	10	Normal
Aqua Tail	Water	Physical	90	90	10	Normal
Iron Tail	Steel	Physical	100	75	15	Normal
Snore	Normal	Special	50	100	15	Normal
Knock Off	Dark	Physical	65	100	20	Normal
Tailwind	Flying	Status	—	—	15	Your Side
Sky Attack	Flying	Physical	140	90	5	Normal
Stealth Rock	Rock	Status	—	—	20	Other Side

MOVES TAUGHT BY PEOPLE

Name	Type	Kind	Pow.	Acc.	PP	Range

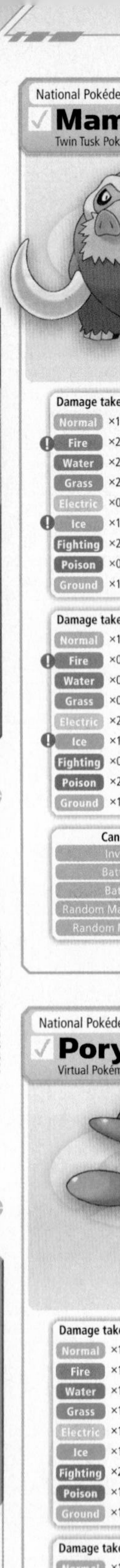

National Pokédex **473** Hoenn Pokédex —

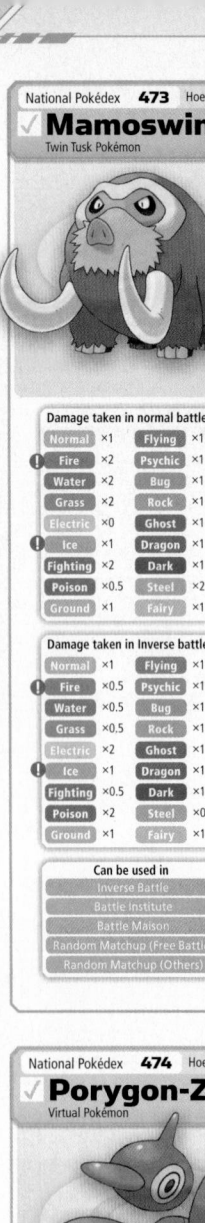

Mamoswine

Twin Tusk Pokémon

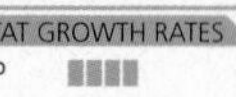

Ice | Ground

HEIGHT: 8'02" WEIGHT: 641.5 lbs.

The male has longer tusks. The female has shorter tusks.

Ω A frozen Mamoswine was dug from ice dating back 10,000 years. This Pokémon has been around a long, long, long time.

α Its impressive tusks are made of ice. The population thinned when it turned warm after the ice age.

ABILITIES
Oblivious
Snow Cloak

HIDDEN ABILITY
Thick Fat

EGG GROUPS
Field

STAT GROWTH RATES
HP
Attack
Defense
Sp. Atk
Sp. Def
Speed

ITEMS SOMETIMES HELD BY WILD POKÉMON
—

EVOLUTION

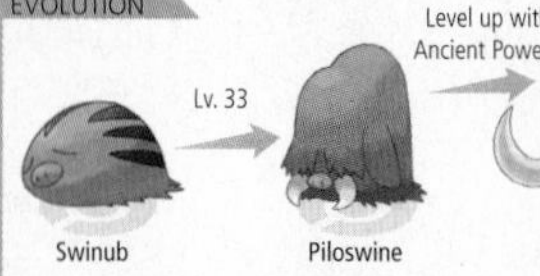

*If you wish to teach Piloswine the move Ancient Power, give the Move Maniac in Fallarbor Town a Heart Scale.

MAIN WAY TO REGISTER IN THE NATIONAL POKÉDEX

Teach Piloswine obtained via Link Trade or the GTS the move Ancient Power, and then have it level up.

Damage taken in normal battles

Type		Type	
Normal	×1	Flying	×1
Fire	×2	Psychic	×1
Water	×2	Bug	×1
Grass	×2	Rock	×1
Electric	×0	Ghost	×1
Ice	×1	Dragon	×1
Fighting	×2	Dark	×1
Poison	×0.5	Steel	×2
Ground	×1	Fairy	×1

Damage taken in Inverse battles

Type		Type	
Normal	×1	Flying	×1
Fire	×0.5	Psychic	×1
Water	×0.5	Bug	×1
Grass	×0.5	Rock	×1
Electric	×2	Ghost	×1
Ice	×1	Dragon	×1
Fighting	×0.5	Dark	×1
Poison	×2	Steel	×0.5
Ground	×1	Fairy	×1

Can be used in
- Inverse Battle
- Battle Institute
- Battle Maison
- Random Matchup (Free Battle)
- Random Matchup (Others)

LEVEL-UP MOVES

Lv.	Name	Type	Kind	Pow.	Acc.	PP	Range
1	Scary Face	Normal	Status	—	100	10	Normal
1	Ancient Power	Rock	Special	60	100	5	Normal
1	Peck	Flying	Physical	35	100	35	Normal
1	Odor Sleuth	Normal	Status	—	—	40	Normal
1	Mud Sport	Ground	Status	—	—	15	Both Sides
1	Powder Snow	Ice	Special	40	100	25	Many Others
5	Mud Sport	Ground	Status	—	—	15	Both Sides
8	Powder Snow	Ice	Special	40	100	25	Many Others
11	Mud-Slap	Ground	Special	20	100	10	Normal
14	Endure	Normal	Status	—	—	10	Self
18	Mud Bomb	Ground	Special	65	85	10	Normal
21	Hail	Ice	Status	—	—	10	Both Sides
24	Ice Fang	Ice	Physical	65	95	15	Normal
28	Take Down	Normal	Physical	90	85	20	Normal
33	Double Hit	Normal	Physical	35	90	10	Normal
37	Mist	Ice	Status	—	—	30	Your Side
41	Thrash	Normal	Physical	120	100	10	1 Random
46	Earthquake	Ground	Physical	100	100	10	Adjacent
52	Blizzard	Ice	Special	110	70	5	Many Others
58	Scary Face	Normal	Status	—	100	10	Normal

TM & HM MOVES

No.	Name	Type	Kind	Pow.	Acc.	PP	Range
TM05	Roar	Normal	Status	—	—	20	Normal
TM06	Toxic	Poison	Status	—	90	10	Normal
TM07	Hail	Ice	Status	—	—	10	Both Sides
TM10	Hidden Power	Normal	Special	60	100	15	Normal
TM13	Ice Beam	Ice	Special	90	100	10	Normal
TM14	Blizzard	Ice	Special	110	70	5	Many Others
TM15	Hyper Beam	Normal	Special	150	90	5	Normal
TM16	Light Screen	Psychic	Status	—	—	30	Your Side
TM17	Protect	Normal	Status	—	—	10	Self
TM18	Rain Dance	Water	Status	—	—	5	Both Sides
TM21	Frustration	Normal	Physical	—	100	20	Normal
TM26	Earthquake	Ground	Physical	100	100	10	Adjacent
TM27	Return	Normal	Physical	—	100	20	Normal
TM28	Dig	Ground	Physical	80	100	10	Normal
TM32	Double Team	Normal	Status	—	—	15	Self
TM33	Reflect	Psychic	Status	—	—	20	Your Side
TM37	Sandstorm	Rock	Status	—	—	10	Both Sides
TM39	Rock Tomb	Rock	Physical	60	95	15	Normal
TM42	Facade	Normal	Physical	70	100	20	Normal
TM44	Rest	Psychic	Status	—	—	10	Self
TM45	Attract	Normal	Status	—	100	15	Normal
TM48	Round	Normal	Special	60	100	15	Normal
TM68	Giga Impact	Normal	Physical	150	90	5	Normal
TM71	Stone Edge	Rock	Physical	100	80	5	Normal
TM78	Bulldoze	Ground	Physical	60	100	20	Adjacent
TM80	Rock Slide	Rock	Physical	75	90	10	Many Others
TM87	Swagger	Normal	Status	—	90	15	Normal
TM88	Sleep Talk	Normal	Status	—	—	10	Self
TM90	Substitute	Normal	Status	—	—	10	Self
TM94	Secret Power	Normal	Physical	70	100	20	Normal
TM100	Confide	Normal	Status	—	—	20	Normal
HM04	Strength	Normal	Physical	80	100	15	Normal
HM06	Rock Smash	Fighting	Physical	40	100	15	Normal

MOVES LEARNED IN EXCHANGE FOR BP

Name	Type	Kind	Pow.	Acc.	PP	Range
Iron Head	Steel	Physical	80	100	15	Normal
Block	Normal	Status	—	—	5	Normal
Earth Power	Ground	Special	90	100	10	Normal
Superpower	Fighting	Physical	120	100	5	Normal
Icy Wind	Ice	Special	55	95	15	Many Others
Snore	Normal	Special	50	100	15	Normal
Knock Off	Dark	Physical	65	100	20	Normal
Endeavor	Normal	Physical	—	100	5	Normal
Stealth Rock	Rock	Status	—	—	20	Other Side

MOVES TAUGHT BY PEOPLE

Name	Type	Kind	Pow.	Acc.	PP	Range

National Pokédex **474** Hoenn Pokédex —

Porygon-Z

Virtual Pokémon

Normal

HEIGHT: 2'11" WEIGHT: 75 lbs.

Gender unknown

Ω Additional software was installed to make it a better Pokémon. It began acting oddly, however.

α Its programming was modified to enable it to travel through alien dimensions. Seems there might have been an error...

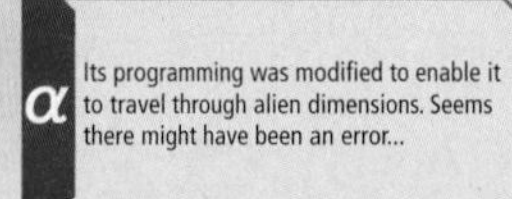

ABILITIES
Adaptability
Download

HIDDEN ABILITY
Analytic

EGG GROUPS
Mineral

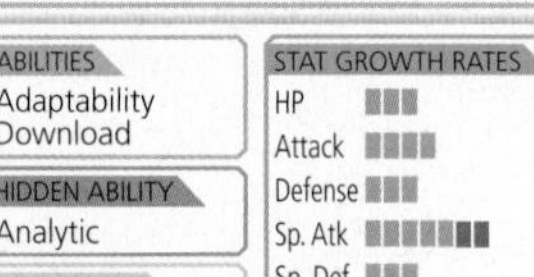

STAT GROWTH RATES
HP
Attack
Defense
Sp. Atk
Sp. Def
Speed

ITEMS SOMETIMES HELD BY WILD POKÉMON
—

EVOLUTION

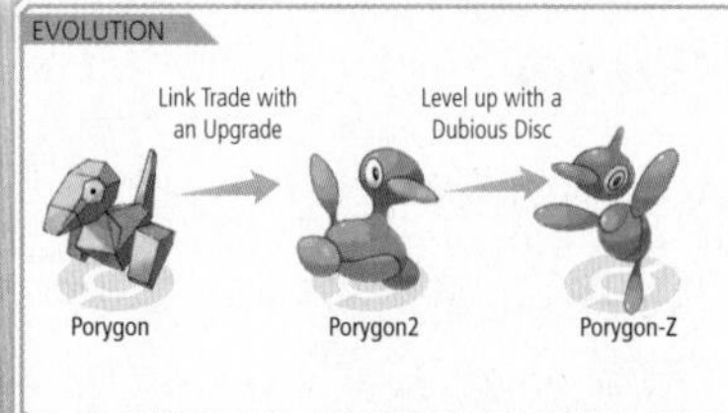

MAIN WAY TO REGISTER IN THE NATIONAL POKÉDEX

Receive a Porygon2 that is holding a Dubious Disc via Link Trade to have it evolve.

Damage taken in normal battles

Type		Type	
Normal	×1	Flying	×1
Fire	×1	Psychic	×1
Water	×1	Bug	×1
Grass	×1	Rock	×1
Electric	×1	Ghost	×0
Ice	×1	Dragon	×1
Fighting	×2	Dark	×1
Poison	×1	Steel	×1
Ground	×1	Fairy	×1

Damage taken in Inverse battles

Type		Type	
Normal	×1	Flying	×1
Fire	×1	Psychic	×1
Water	×1	Bug	×1
Grass	×1	Rock	×1
Electric	×1	Ghost	×2
Ice	×1	Dragon	×1
Fighting	×0.5	Dark	×1
Poison	×1	Steel	×1
Ground	×1	Fairy	×1

Can be used in
- Inverse Battle
- Battle Institute
- Battle Maison
- Random Matchup (Free Battle)
- Random Matchup (Others)

LEVEL-UP MOVES

Lv.	Name	Type	Kind	Pow.	Acc.	PP	Range
1	Trick Room	Psychic	Status	—	—	5	Both Sides
1	Zap Cannon	Electric	Special	120	50	5	Normal
1	Magic Coat	Psychic	Status	—	—	15	Self
1	Conversion 2	Normal	Status	—	—	30	Normal
1	Tackle	Normal	Physical	50	100	35	Normal
1	Conversion	Normal	Status	—	—	30	Self
1	Nasty Plot	Dark	Status	—	—	20	Self
7	Psybeam	Psychic	Special	65	100	20	Normal
12	Agility	Psychic	Status	—	—	30	Self
18	Recover	Normal	Status	—	—	10	Self
23	Magnet Rise	Electric	Status	—	—	10	Self
29	Signal Beam	Bug	Special	75	100	15	Normal
34	Embargo	Dark	Status	—	100	15	Normal
40	Discharge	Electric	Special	80	100	15	Adjacent
45	Lock-On	Normal	Status	—	—	5	Normal
50	Tri Attack	Normal	Special	80	100	10	Normal
56	Magic Coat	Psychic	Status	—	—	15	Self
62	Zap Cannon	Electric	Special	120	50	5	Normal
67	Hyper Beam	Normal	Special	150	90	5	Normal

TM & HM MOVES

No.	Name	Type	Kind	Pow.	Acc.	PP	Range
TM03	Psyshock	Psychic	Special	80	100	10	Normal
TM06	Toxic	Poison	Status	—	90	10	Normal
TM10	Hidden Power	Normal	Special	60	100	15	Normal
TM11	Sunny Day	Fire	Status	—	—	5	Both Sides
TM13	Ice Beam	Ice	Special	90	100	10	Normal
TM14	Blizzard	Ice	Special	110	70	5	Many Others
TM15	Hyper Beam	Normal	Special	150	90	5	Normal
TM17	Protect	Normal	Status	—	—	10	Self
TM18	Rain Dance	Water	Status	—	—	5	Both Sides
TM21	Frustration	Normal	Physical	—	100	20	Normal
TM22	Solar Beam	Grass	Special	120	100	10	Normal
TM24	Thunderbolt	Electric	Special	90	100	15	Normal
TM25	Thunder	Electric	Special	110	70	10	Normal
TM27	Return	Normal	Physical	—	100	20	Normal
TM29	Psychic	Psychic	Special	90	100	10	Normal
TM30	Shadow Ball	Ghost	Special	80	100	15	Normal
TM32	Double Team	Normal	Status	—	—	15	Self
TM40	Aerial Ace	Flying	Physical	60	—	20	Normal
TM42	Facade	Normal	Physical	70	100	20	Normal
TM44	Rest	Psychic	Status	—	—	10	Self
TM46	Thief	Dark	Physical	60	100	25	Normal
TM48	Round	Normal	Special	60	100	15	Normal
TM57	Charge Beam	Electric	Special	50	90	10	Normal
TM63	Embargo	Dark	Status	—	100	15	Normal
TM68	Giga Impact	Normal	Physical	150	90	5	Normal
TM70	Flash	Normal	Status	—	100	20	Normal
TM73	Thunder Wave	Electric	Status	—	100	20	Normal
TM77	Psych Up	Normal	Status	—	—	10	Normal
TM85	Dream Eater	Psychic	Special	100	100	15	Normal
TM87	Swagger	Normal	Status	—	90	15	Normal
TM88	Sleep Talk	Normal	Status	—	—	10	Self
TM90	Substitute	Normal	Status	—	—	10	Self
TM92	Trick Room	Psychic	Status	—	—	5	Both Sides
TM94	Secret Power	Normal	Physical	70	100	20	Normal
TM97	Dark Pulse	Dark	Special	80	100	15	Normal
TM100	Confide	Normal	Status	—	—	20	Normal

MOVES LEARNED IN EXCHANGE FOR BP

Name	Type	Kind	Pow.	Acc.	PP	Range
Signal Beam	Bug	Special	75	100	15	Normal
Uproar	Normal	Special	90	100	10	1 Random
Magic Coat	Psychic	Status	—	—	15	Self
Foul Play	Dark	Physical	95	100	15	Normal
Gravity	Psychic	Status	—	—	5	Both Sides
Magnet Rise	Electric	Status	—	—	10	Self
Last Resort	Normal	Physical	140	100	5	Normal
Electroweb	Electric	Special	55	95	15	Many Others
Icy Wind	Ice	Special	55	95	15	Many Others
Zen Headbutt	Psychic	Physical	80	90	15	Normal
Iron Tail	Steel	Physical	100	75	15	Normal
Snore	Normal	Special	50	100	15	Normal
Pain Split	Normal	Status	—	—	20	Normal
Shock Wave	Electric	Special	60	—	20	Normal
Trick	Psychic	Status	—	100	10	Normal
Recycle	Normal	Status	—	—	10	Self

MOVES TAUGHT BY PEOPLE

Name	Type	Kind	Pow.	Acc.	PP	Range

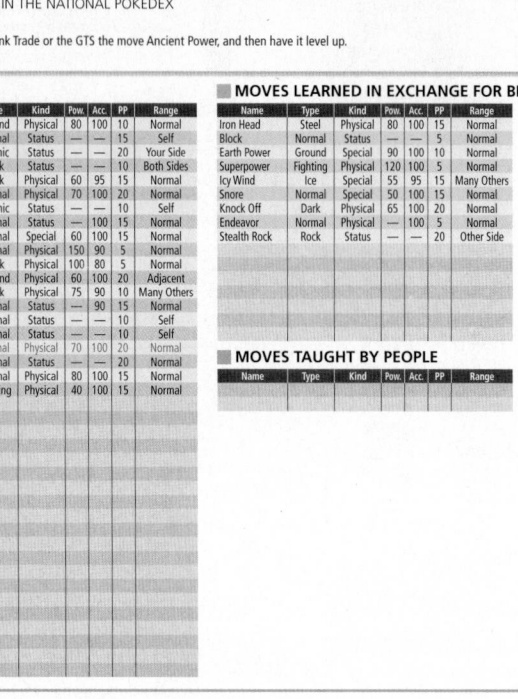

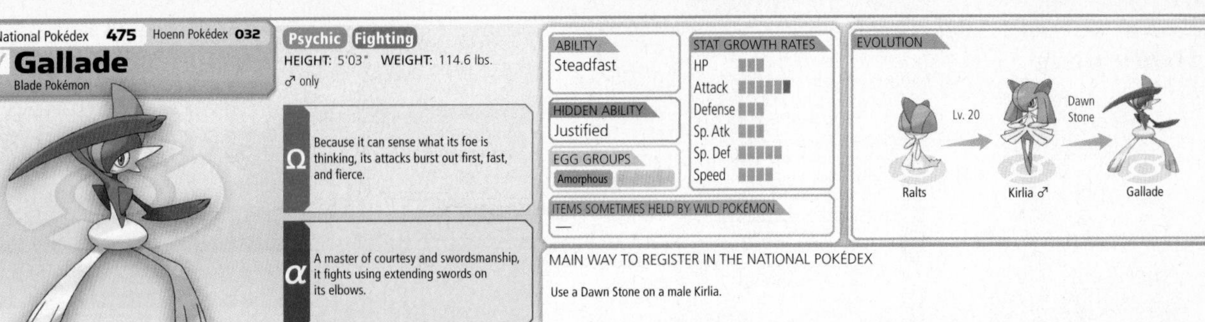

National Pokédex **475** Hoenn Pokédex **032**

✓ Gallade

Blade Pokémon

Psychic Fighting

HEIGHT: 5'03" WEIGHT: 114.6 lbs.

♂ only

Ω Because it can sense what its foe is thinking, its attacks burst out first, fast, and fierce.

α A master of courtesy and swordsmanship, it fights using extending swords on its elbows.

ABILITY
Steadfast

HIDDEN ABILITY
Justified

EGG GROUPS
Amorphous

STAT GROWTH RATES
HP
Attack
Defense
Sp. Atk
Sp. Def
Speed

EVOLUTION

ITEMS SOMETIMES HELD BY WILD POKÉMON
—

MAIN WAY TO REGISTER IN THE NATIONAL POKÉDEX

Use a Dawn Stone on a male Kirlia.

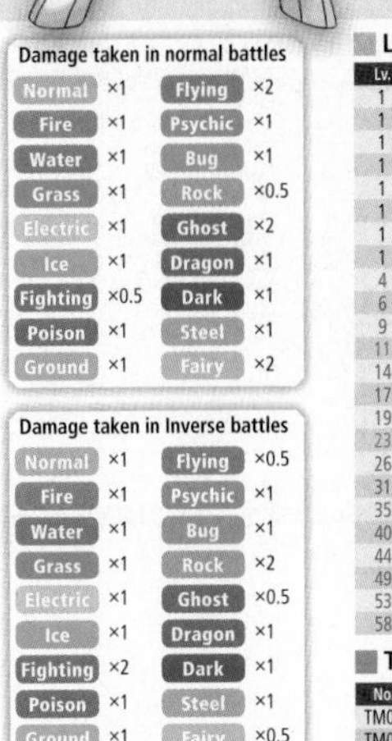

Damage taken in normal battles

Type		Type	
Normal	×1	Flying	×2
Fire	×1	Psychic	×1
Water	×1	Bug	×1
Grass	×1	Rock	×0.5
Electric	×1	Ghost	×2
Ice	×1	Dragon	×1
Fighting	×0.5	Dark	×1
Poison	×1	Steel	×1
Ground	×1	Fairy	×2

Damage taken in Inverse battles

Type		Type	
Normal	×1	Flying	×0.5
Fire	×1	Psychic	×1
Water	×1	Bug	×1
Grass	×1	Rock	×2
Electric	×1	Ghost	×0.5
Ice	×1	Dragon	×1
Fighting	×2	Dark	×1
Poison	×1	Steel	×1
Ground	×1	Fairy	×0.5

Can be used in
- Inverse Battle
- Battle Institute
- Battle Maison
- Random Matchup (Free Battle)
- Random Matchup (Others)

LEVEL-UP MOVES

Lv.	Name	Type	Kind	Pow.	Acc.	PP	Range
1	Stored Power	Psychic	Special	20	100	10	Normal
1	Close Combat	Fighting	Physical	120	100	5	Normal
1	Leaf Blade	Grass	Physical	90	100	15	Normal
1	Night Slash	Dark	Physical	70	100	15	Normal
1	Leer	Normal	Status	—	100	30	Many Others
1	Confusion	Psychic	Special	50	100	25	Normal
1	Double Team	Normal	Status	—	—	15	Self
1	Teleport	Psychic	Status	—	—	20	Self
4	Confusion	Psychic	Special	50	100	25	Normal
6	Double Team	Normal	Status	—	—	15	Self
9	Teleport	Psychic	Status	—	—	20	Self
11	Quick Guard	Fighting	Status	—	—	15	Your Side
14	Fury Cutter	Bug	Physical	40	95	20	Normal
17	Slash	Normal	Physical	70	100	20	Normal
19	Heal Pulse	Psychic	Status	—	—	10	Normal
23	Wide Guard	Rock	Status	—	—	10	Your Side
26	Swords Dance	Normal	Status	—	—	20	Self
31	Psycho Cut	Psychic	Physical	70	100	20	Normal
35	Helping Hand	Normal	Status	—	—	20	1 Ally
40	Feint	Normal	Physical	30	100	10	Normal
44	False Swipe	Normal	Physical	40	100	40	Normal
49	Protect	Normal	Status	—	—	10	Self
53	Close Combat	Fighting	Physical	120	100	5	Normal
58	Stored Power	Psychic	Special	20	100	10	Normal

TM & HM MOVES

No.	Name	Type	Kind	Pow.	Acc.	PP	Range
TM03	Psyshock	Psychic	Special	80	100	10	Normal
TM04	Calm Mind	Psychic	Status	—	—	20	Self
TM06	Toxic	Poison	Status	—	90	10	Normal
TM08	Bulk Up	Fighting	Status	—	—	20	Self
TM10	Hidden Power	Normal	Special	60	100	15	Normal
TM11	Sunny Day	Fire	Status	—	—	5	Both Sides
TM12	Taunt	Dark	Status	—	100	20	Normal
TM15	Hyper Beam	Normal	Special	150	90	5	Normal
TM16	Light Screen	Psychic	Status	—	—	30	Your Side
TM17	Protect	Normal	Status	—	—	10	Self
TM18	Rain Dance	Water	Status	—	—	5	Both Sides
TM20	Safeguard	Normal	Status	—	—	25	Your Side
TM21	Frustration	Normal	Physical	—	100	20	Normal
TM24	Thunderbolt	Electric	Special	90	100	15	Normal
TM26	Earthquake	Ground	Physical	100	100	10	Adjacent
TM27	Return	Normal	Physical	—	100	20	Normal
TM29	Psychic	Psychic	Special	90	100	10	Normal
TM30	Shadow Ball	Ghost	Special	80	100	15	Normal
TM31	Brick Break	Fighting	Physical	75	100	15	Normal
TM32	Double Team	Normal	Status	—	—	15	Self
TM33	Reflect	Psychic	Status	—	—	20	Your Side
TM39	Rock Tomb	Rock	Physical	60	95	15	Normal
TM40	Aerial Ace	Flying	Physical	60	—	20	Normal
TM41	Torment	Dark	Status	—	100	15	Normal
TM42	Facade	Normal	Physical	70	100	20	Normal
TM44	Rest	Psychic	Status	—	—	10	Self
TM45	Attract	Normal	Status	—	100	15	Normal
TM46	Thief	Dark	Physical	60	100	25	Normal
TM47	Low Sweep	Fighting	Physical	65	100	20	Normal
TM48	Round	Normal	Special	60	100	15	Normal
TM49	Echoed Voice	Normal	Special	40	100	15	Normal
TM52	Focus Blast	Fighting	Special	120	70	5	Normal
TM54	False Swipe	Normal	Physical	40	100	40	Normal
TM56	Fling	Dark	Physical	—	100	10	Normal
TM57	Charge Beam	Electric	Special	50	90	10	Normal
TM61	Will-O-Wisp	Fire	Status	—	85	15	Normal
TM67	Retaliate	Normal	Physical	70	100	5	Normal
TM68	Giga Impact	Normal	Physical	150	90	5	Normal
TM70	Flash	Normal	Status	—	100	20	Normal
TM71	Stone Edge	Rock	Physical	100	80	5	Normal
TM73	Thunder Wave	Electric	Status	—	100	20	Normal
TM75	Swords Dance	Normal	Status	—	—	20	Self
TM77	Psych Up	Normal	Status	—	—	10	Normal
TM78	Bulldoze	Ground	Physical	60	100	20	Adjacent
TM80	Rock Slide	Rock	Physical	75	90	10	Many Others
TM81	X-Scissor	Bug	Physical	80	100	15	Normal
TM84	Poison Jab	Poison	Physical	80	100	20	Normal
TM85	Dream Eater	Psychic	Special	100	100	15	Normal
TM86	Grass Knot	Grass	Special	—	100	20	Normal
TM87	Swagger	Normal	Status	—	90	15	Normal
TM88	Sleep Talk	Normal	Status	—	—	10	Self
TM90	Substitute	Normal	Status	—	—	10	Self
TM92	Trick Room	Psychic	Status	—	—	5	Both Sides
TM94	Secret Power	Normal	Physical	70	100	20	Normal
TM98	Power-Up Punch	Fighting	Physical	40	100	20	Normal
TM99	Dazzling Gleam	Fairy	Special	80	100	10	Many Others
TM100	Confide	Normal	Status	—	—	20	Normal
HM01	Cut	Normal	Physical	50	95	30	Normal
HM04	Strength	Normal	Physical	80	100	15	Normal
HM06	Rock Smash	Fighting	Physical	40	100	15	Normal

MOVES LEARNED IN EXCHANGE FOR BP

Name	Type	Kind	Pow.	Acc.	PP	Range
Dual Chop	Dragon	Physical	40	90	15	Normal
Signal Beam	Bug	Special	75	100	15	Normal
Low Kick	Fighting	Physical	—	100	20	Normal
Thunder Punch	Electric	Physical	75	100	15	Normal
Fire Punch	Fire	Physical	75	100	15	Normal
Ice Punch	Ice	Physical	75	100	15	Normal
Magic Coat	Psychic	Status	—	—	15	Self
Zen Headbutt	Psychic	Physical	80	90	15	Normal
Hyper Voice	Normal	Special	90	100	10	Many Others
Snore	Normal	Special	50	100	15	Normal
Knock Off	Dark	Physical	65	100	20	Normal
Pain Split	Normal	Status	—	—	20	Normal
Drain Punch	Fighting	Physical	75	100	10	Normal
Focus Punch	Fighting	Physical	150	100	20	Normal
Shock Wave	Electric	Special	60	—	20	Normal
Helping Hand	Normal	Status	—	—	20	1 Ally
Trick	Psychic	Status	—	100	10	Normal
Magic Room	Psychic	Status	—	—	10	Both Sides
Wonder Room	Psychic	Status	—	—	10	Both Sides
Recycle	Normal	Status	—	—	10	Self
Snatch	Dark	Status	—	—	10	Self
Skill Swap	Psychic	Status	—	—	10	Normal

MOVES TAUGHT BY PEOPLE

Name	Type	Kind	Pow.	Acc.	PP	Range

Mega Evolution

Mega Gallade

Blade Pokémon

Psychic Fighting

HEIGHT: 5'03" WEIGHT: 124.3 lbs.

♂ only

REQUIRED MEGA STONE
Galladite
Receive from Professor Cozmo in Fallarbor Town (after clearing the Delta Episode).

ABILITY
Inner Focus

HIDDEN ABILITY
—

EGG GROUPS
—

STAT GROWTH RATES
HP
Attack
Defense
Sp. Atk
Sp. Def
Speed

Damage taken in normal battles

Type		Type	
Normal	×1	Flying	×2
Fire	×1	Psychic	×1
Water	×1	Bug	×1
Grass	×1	Rock	×0.5
Electric	×1	Ghost	×2
Ice	×1	Dragon	×1
Fighting	×0.5	Dark	×1
Poison	×1	Steel	×1
Ground	×1	Fairy	×2

Damage taken in Inverse battles

Type		Type	
Normal	×1	Flying	×0.5
Fire	×1	Psychic	×1
Water	×1	Bug	×1
Grass	×1	Rock	×2
Electric	×1	Ghost	×0.5
Ice	×1	Dragon	×1
Fighting	×2	Dark	×1
Poison	×1	Steel	×1
Ground	×1	Fairy	×0.5

Can be used in
- Inverse Battle
- Battle Institute
- Battle Maison
- Random Matchup (Free Battle)
- Random Matchup (Others)

National Pokédex **476** Hoenn Pokédex **062**

Probopass

Compass Pokémon

Rock | Steel

HEIGHT: 4'07" WEIGHT: 749.6 lbs.

Same form for ♂ / ♀

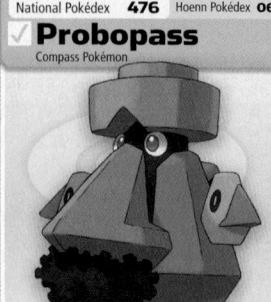

Ω It exudes strong magnetism from all over. It controls three small units called Mini-Noses.

α It freely controls three small units called Mini-Noses using magnetic force.

ABILITIES
Sturdy
Magnet Pull

HIDDEN ABILITY
Sand Force

EGG GROUPS
Mineral

STAT GROWTH RATES
HP ■■■
Attack ■■■
Defense ■■■■■■
Sp. Atk ■■■■
Sp. Def ■■■■■■
Speed ■■

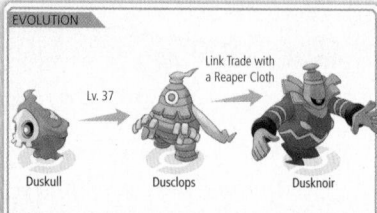

ITEMS SOMETIMES HELD BY WILD POKÉMON
—

EVOLUTION

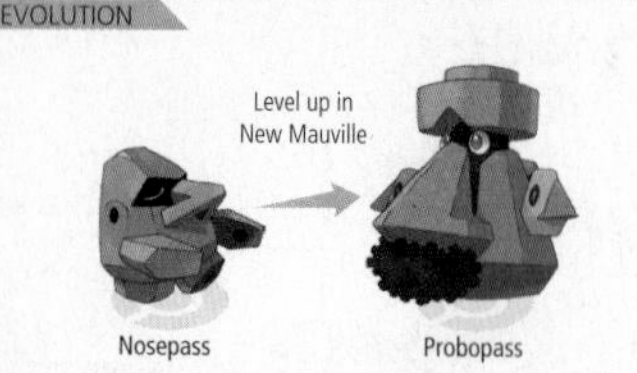

MAIN WAY TO REGISTER IN THE NATIONAL POKÉDEX

Level up Nosepass in New Mauville.

Damage taken in normal battles

Normal	×0.25	Flying	×0.25
Fire	×1	Psychic	×0.5
Water	×2	Bug	×0.5
Grass	×1	Rock	×0.5
Electric	×1	Ghost	×1
Ice	×0.5	Dragon	×0.5
Fighting	×4	Dark	×1
Poison	×0	Steel	×1
Ground	×4	Fairy	×0.5

Damage taken in Inverse battles

Normal	×4	Flying	×4
Fire	×1	Psychic	×2
Water	×0.5	Bug	×2
Grass	×1	Rock	×2
Electric	×1	Ghost	×1
Ice	×2	Dragon	×2
Fighting	×0.25	Dark	×1
Poison	×4	Steel	×1
Ground	×0.25	Fairy	×2

Can be used in
Inverse Battle
Battle Institute
Battle Maison
Random Matchup (Free Battle)
Random Matchup (Others)

LEVEL-UP MOVES

Lv.	Name	Type	Kind	Pow.	Acc.	PP	Range
1	Magnet Rise	Electric	Status	—	—	10	Self
1	Gravity	Psychic	Status	—	—	5	Both Sides
1	Wide Guard	Rock	Status	—	—	10	Your Side
1	Tackle	Normal	Physical	50	100	35	Normal
1	Iron Defense	Steel	Status	—	—	15	Self
1	Block	Normal	Status	—	—	5	Normal
1	Magnet Bomb	Steel	Physical	60	—	20	Normal
4	Iron Defense	Steel	Status	—	—	15	Self
7	Block	Normal	Status	—	—	5	Normal
10	Magnet Bomb	Steel	Physical	60	—	20	Normal
13	Thunder Wave	Electric	Status	—	100	20	Normal
16	Rest	Psychic	Status	—	—	10	Self
19	Spark	Electric	Physical	65	100	20	Normal
22	Rock Slide	Rock	Physical	75	90	10	Many Others
25	Power Gem	Rock	Special	80	100	20	Normal
28	Rock Blast	Rock	Physical	25	90	10	Normal
31	Discharge	Electric	Special	80	100	15	Adjacent
34	Sandstorm	Rock	Status	—	—	10	Both Sides
37	Earth Power	Ground	Special	90	100	10	Normal
40	Stone Edge	Rock	Physical	100	80	5	Normal
43	Lock-On	Normal	Status	—	—	5	Normal
43	Zap Cannon	Electric	Special	120	50	5	Normal

TM & HM MOVES

No.	Name	Type	Kind	Pow.	Acc.	PP	Range
TM06	Toxic	Poison	Status	—	90	10	Normal
TM10	Hidden Power	Normal	Special	60	100	15	Normal
TM11	Sunny Day	Fire	Status	—	—	5	Both Sides
TM12	Taunt	Dark	Status	—	100	20	Normal
TM15	Hyper Beam	Normal	Special	150	90	5	Normal
TM17	Protect	Normal	Status	—	—	10	Self
TM21	Frustration	Normal	Physical	—	100	20	Normal
TM23	Smack Down	Rock	Physical	50	100	15	Normal
TM24	Thunderbolt	Electric	Special	90	100	15	Normal
TM25	Thunder	Electric	Special	110	70	10	Normal
TM26	Earthquake	Ground	Physical	100	100	10	Adjacent
TM27	Return	Normal	Physical	—	100	20	Normal
TM32	Double Team	Normal	Status	—	—	15	Self
TM37	Sandstorm	Rock	Status	—	—	10	Both Sides
TM39	Rock Tomb	Rock	Physical	60	95	15	Normal
TM41	Torment	Dark	Status	—	100	15	Normal
TM42	Facade	Normal	Physical	70	100	20	Normal
TM44	Rest	Psychic	Status	—	—	10	Self
TM45	Attract	Normal	Status	—	100	15	Normal
TM48	Round	Normal	Special	60	100	15	Normal
TM64	Explosion	Normal	Physical	250	100	5	Adjacent
TM68	Giga Impact	Normal	Physical	150	90	5	Normal
TM69	Rock Polish	Rock	Status	—	—	20	Self
TM71	Stone Edge	Rock	Physical	100	80	5	Normal
TM72	Volt Switch	Electric	Special	70	100	20	Normal
TM73	Thunder Wave	Electric	Status	—	100	20	Normal
TM78	Bulldoze	Ground	Physical	60	100	20	Adjacent
TM80	Rock Slide	Rock	Physical	75	90	10	Many Others
TM87	Swagger	Normal	Status	—	90	15	Normal
TM88	Sleep Talk	Normal	Status	—	—	10	Self
TM90	Substitute	Normal	Status	—	—	10	Self
TM91	Flash Cannon	Steel	Special	80	100	10	Normal
TM94	Secret Power	Normal	Physical	70	100	20	Normal
TM99	Dazzling Gleam	Fairy	Special	80	100	10	Many Others
TM100	Confide	Normal	Status	—	—	20	Normal
HM04	Strength	Normal	Physical	80	100	15	Normal
HM06	Rock Smash	Fighting	Physical	40	100	15	Normal

MOVES LEARNED IN EXCHANGE FOR BP

Name	Type	Kind	Pow.	Acc.	PP	Range
Iron Head	Steel	Physical	80	100	15	Normal
Thunder Punch	Electric	Physical	75	100	15	Normal
Fire Punch	Fire	Physical	75	100	15	Normal
Ice Punch	Ice	Physical	75	100	15	Normal
Magic Coat	Psychic	Status	—	—	15	Self
Block	Normal	Status	—	—	5	Normal
Earth Power	Ground	Special	90	100	10	Normal
Gravity	Psychic	Status	—	—	5	Both Sides
Magnet Rise	Electric	Status	—	—	10	Self
Iron Defense	Steel	Status	—	—	15	Self
Snore	Normal	Special	50	100	15	Normal
Pain Split	Normal	Status	—	—	20	Normal
Shock Wave	Electric	Special	60	—	20	Normal
Stealth Rock	Rock	Status	—	—	20	Other Side

MOVES TAUGHT BY PEOPLE

Name	Type	Kind	Pow.	Acc.	PP	Range

National Pokédex **477** Hoenn Pokédex **155**

Dusknoir

Gripper Pokémon

Ghost

HEIGHT: 7'03" WEIGHT: 235 lbs.

Same form for ♂ / ♀

Ω It is said to take lost spirits into its pliant body and guide them home.

α The antenna on its head captures radio waves from the world of spirits that command it to take people there.

ABILITY
Pressure

HIDDEN ABILITY
Frisk

EGG GROUPS
Amorphous

STAT GROWTH RATES
HP ■■
Attack ■■■■■
Defense ■■■■■■
Sp. Atk ■■■
Sp. Def ■■■■■■
Speed ■■■

ITEMS SOMETIMES HELD BY WILD POKÉMON
—

EVOLUTION

Duskull → Lv. 37 → Dusclops → Link Trade with a Reaper Cloth → Dusknoir

MAIN WAY TO REGISTER IN THE NATIONAL POKÉDEX

Receive a Dusclops that is holding a Reaper Cloth via Link Trade to have it evolve.

Damage taken in normal battles

Normal	×0	Flying	×1
Fire	×1	Psychic	×1
Water	×1	Bug	×0.5
Grass	×1	Rock	×1
Electric	×1	Ghost	×2
Ice	×1	Dragon	×1
Fighting	×0	Dark	×2
Poison	×0.5	Steel	×1
Ground	×1	Fairy	×1

Damage taken in Inverse battles

Normal	×2	Flying	×1
Fire	×1	Psychic	×1
Water	×1	Bug	×2
Grass	×1	Rock	×1
Electric	×1	Ghost	×0.5
Ice	×1	Dragon	×1
Fighting	×2	Dark	×0.5
Poison	×2	Steel	×1
Ground	×1	Fairy	×1

Can be used in
Inverse Battle
Battle Institute
Battle Maison
Random Matchup (Free Battle)
Random Matchup (Others)

LEVEL-UP MOVES

Lv.	Name	Type	Kind	Pow.	Acc.	PP	Range
1	Future Sight	Psychic	Special	120	100	10	Normal
1	Fire Punch	Fire	Physical	75	100	15	Normal
1	Ice Punch	Ice	Physical	75	100	15	Normal
1	Thunder Punch	Electric	Physical	75	100	15	Normal
1	Gravity	Psychic	Status	—	—	5	Both Sides
1	Bind	Normal	Physical	15	85	20	Normal
1	Leer	Normal	Status	—	100	30	Many Others
1	Night Shade	Ghost	Special	—	100	15	Normal
1	Disable	Normal	Status	—	100	20	Normal
1	Astonish	Ghost	Physical	30	100	15	Normal
6	Disable	Normal	Status	—	100	20	Normal
9	Astonish	Ghost	Physical	30	100	15	Normal
14	Foresight	Normal	Status	—	—	40	Normal
17	Shadow Sneak	Ghost	Physical	40	100	30	Normal
22	Pursuit	Dark	Physical	40	100	20	Normal
25	Will-O-Wisp	Fire	Status	—	85	15	Normal
30	Confuse Ray	Ghost	Status	—	100	10	Normal
33	Curse	Ghost	Status	—	—	10	Varies
37	Shadow Punch	Ghost	Physical	60	—	20	Normal
40	Hex	Ghost	Special	65	100	10	Normal
45	Shadow Ball	Ghost	Special	80	100	15	Normal
52	Mean Look	Normal	Status	—	—	5	Normal
57	Payback	Dark	Physical	50	100	10	Normal
64	Future Sight	Psychic	Special	120	100	10	Normal

TM & HM MOVES

No.	Name	Type	Kind	Pow.	Acc.	PP	Range
TM04	Calm Mind	Psychic	Status	—	—	20	Self
TM06	Toxic	Poison	Status	—	90	10	Normal
TM10	Hidden Power	Normal	Special	60	100	15	Normal
TM11	Sunny Day	Fire	Status	—	—	5	Both Sides
TM12	Taunt	Dark	Status	—	100	20	Normal
TM13	Ice Beam	Ice	Special	90	100	10	Normal
TM14	Blizzard	Ice	Special	110	70	5	Many Others
TM15	Hyper Beam	Normal	Special	150	90	5	Normal
TM17	Protect	Normal	Status	—	—	10	Self
TM18	Rain Dance	Water	Status	—	—	5	Both Sides
TM21	Frustration	Normal	Physical	—	100	20	Normal
TM26	Earthquake	Ground	Physical	100	100	10	Adjacent
TM27	Return	Normal	Physical	—	100	20	Normal
TM29	Psychic	Psychic	Special	90	100	10	Normal
TM30	Shadow Ball	Ghost	Special	80	100	15	Normal
TM31	Brick Break	Fighting	Physical	75	100	15	Normal
TM32	Double Team	Normal	Status	—	—	15	Self
TM39	Rock Tomb	Rock	Physical	60	95	15	Normal
TM41	Torment	Dark	Status	—	100	15	Normal
TM42	Facade	Normal	Physical	70	100	20	Normal
TM44	Rest	Psychic	Status	—	—	10	Self
TM45	Attract	Normal	Status	—	100	15	Normal
TM46	Thief	Dark	Physical	60	100	25	Normal
TM48	Round	Normal	Special	60	100	15	Normal
TM52	Focus Blast	Fighting	Special	120	70	5	Normal
TM56	Fling	Dark	Physical	—	100	10	Normal
TM57	Charge Beam	Electric	Special	50	90	10	Normal
TM61	Will-O-Wisp	Fire	Status	—	85	15	Normal
TM63	Embargo	Dark	Status	—	100	15	Normal
TM66	Payback	Dark	Physical	50	100	10	Normal
TM68	Giga Impact	Normal	Physical	150	90	5	Normal
TM70	Flash	Normal	Status	—	100	20	Normal
TM77	Psych Up	Normal	Status	—	—	10	Normal
TM78	Bulldoze	Ground	Physical	60	100	20	Adjacent
TM80	Rock Slide	Rock	Physical	75	90	10	Many Others
TM83	Infestation	Bug	Special	20	100	20	Normal
TM85	Dream Eater	Psychic	Special	100	100	15	Normal
TM87	Swagger	Normal	Status	—	90	15	Normal
TM88	Sleep Talk	Normal	Status	—	—	10	Self
TM90	Substitute	Normal	Status	—	—	10	Self
TM92	Trick Room	Psychic	Status	—	—	5	Both Sides
TM94	Secret Power	Normal	Physical	70	100	20	Normal
TM97	Dark Pulse	Dark	Special	80	100	15	Normal
TM98	Power-Up Punch	Fighting	Physical	40	100	20	Normal
TM100	Confide	Normal	Status	—	—	20	Normal
HM04	Strength	Normal	Physical	80	100	15	Normal
HM06	Rock Smash	Fighting	Physical	40	100	15	Normal

MOVES LEARNED IN EXCHANGE FOR BP

Name	Type	Kind	Pow.	Acc.	PP	Range
Thunder Punch	Electric	Physical	75	100	15	Normal
Fire Punch	Fire	Physical	75	100	15	Normal
Ice Punch	Ice	Physical	75	100	15	Normal
Gravity	Psychic	Status	—	—	5	Both Sides
Icy Wind	Ice	Special	55	95	15	Many Others
Bind	Normal	Physical	15	85	20	Normal
Snore	Normal	Special	50	100	15	Normal
Pain Split	Normal	Status	—	—	20	Normal
Focus Punch	Fighting	Physical	150	100	20	Normal
Spite	Ghost	Status	—	100	10	Normal
Trick	Psychic	Status	—	100	10	Normal
Wonder Room	Psychic	Status	—	—	10	Both Sides
Snatch	Dark	Status	—	—	10	Self
Skill Swap	Psychic	Status	—	—	10	Normal

MOVES TAUGHT BY PEOPLE

Name	Type	Kind	Pow.	Acc.	PP	Range

National Pokédex **478** Hoenn Pokédex **181**

✓ Froslass

Snow Land Pokémon

Ice | Ghost

HEIGHT: 4'03" WEIGHT: 58.6 lbs.

♀ only

Ω It freezes foes with an icy breath nearly -60 degrees Fahrenheit. What seems to be its body is actually hollow.

α Legends in snowy regions say that a woman who was lost on an icy mountain was reborn as Froslass.

ABILITY
Snow Cloak

HIDDEN ABILITY
Cursed Body

EGG GROUPS
Fairy | Mineral

STAT GROWTH RATES

HP	■■■
Attack	■■■■
Defense	■■■
Sp. Atk	■■■■
Sp. Def	■■■
Speed	■■■■■■

ITEMS SOMETIMES HELD BY WILD POKÉMON
—

EVOLUTION

Snorunt ♀ → (Dawn Stone) → Froslass

MAIN WAY TO REGISTER IN THE NATIONAL POKÉDEX

Use a Dawn Stone on a female Snorunt.

Damage taken in normal battles

Type		Type	
Normal	×0	Flying	×1
Fire	×2	Psychic	×1
Water	×1	Bug	×0.5
Grass	×1	Rock	×2
Electric	×1	Ghost	×2
Ice	×0.5	Dragon	×1
Fighting	×0	Dark	×2
Poison	×0.5	Steel	×2
Ground	×1	Fairy	×1

Damage taken in Inverse battles

Type		Type	
Normal	×2	Flying	×1
Fire	×0.5	Psychic	×1
Water	×1	Bug	×2
Grass	×1	Rock	×0.5
Electric	×1	Ghost	×0.5
Ice	×2	Dragon	×1
Fighting	×1	Dark	×0.5
Poison	×2	Steel	×0.5
Ground	×1	Fairy	×1

Can be used in
Inverse Battle
Battle Institute
Battle Maison
Random Matchup (Free Battle)
Random Matchup (Others)

LEVEL-UP MOVES

Lv.	Name	Type	Kind	Pow.	Acc.	PP	Range
1	Destiny Bond	Ghost	Status	—	—	5	Self
1	Powder Snow	Ice	Special	40	100	25	Many Others
1	Leer	Normal	Status	—	100	30	Many Others
1	Double Team	Normal	Status	—	—	15	Self
1	Ice Shard	Ice	Physical	40	100	30	Normal
5	Double Team	Normal	Status	—	—	15	Self
10	Ice Shard	Ice	Physical	40	100	30	Normal
14	Icy Wind	Ice	Special	55	95	15	Many Others
19	Astonish	Ghost	Physical	30	100	15	Normal
23	Draining Kiss	Fairy	Special	50	100	10	Normal
28	Ominous Wind	Ghost	Special	60	100	5	Normal
32	Confuse Ray	Ghost	Status	—	100	10	Normal
37	Wake-Up Slap	Fighting	Physical	70	100	10	Normal
41	Captivate	Normal	Status	—	100	20	Many Others
42	Shadow Ball	Ghost	Special	80	100	15	Normal
48	Blizzard	Ice	Special	110	70	5	Many Others
54	Hail	Ice	Status	—	—	10	Both Sides
61	Destiny Bond	Ghost	Status	—	—	5	Self

TM & HM MOVES

No.	Name	Type	Kind	Pow.	Acc.	PP	Range
TM06	Toxic	Poison	Status	—	90	10	Normal
TM07	Hail	Ice	Status	—	—	10	Both Sides
TM10	Hidden Power	Normal	Special	60	100	15	Normal
TM12	Taunt	Dark	Status	—	100	20	Normal
TM13	Ice Beam	Ice	Special	90	100	10	Normal
TM14	Blizzard	Ice	Special	110	70	5	Many Others
TM15	Hyper Beam	Normal	Special	150	90	5	Normal
TM16	Light Screen	Psychic	Status	—	—	30	Your Side
TM17	Protect	Normal	Status	—	—	10	Self
TM18	Rain Dance	Water	Status	—	—	5	Both Sides
TM20	Safeguard	Normal	Status	—	—	25	Your Side
TM21	Frustration	Normal	Physical	—	100	20	Normal
TM24	Thunderbolt	Electric	Special	90	100	15	Normal
TM25	Thunder	Electric	Special	110	70	10	Normal
TM27	Return	Normal	Physical	—	100	20	Normal
TM29	Psychic	Psychic	Special	90	100	10	Normal
TM30	Shadow Ball	Ghost	Special	80	100	15	Normal
TM32	Double Team	Normal	Status	—	—	15	Self
TM41	Torment	Dark	Status	—	100	15	Normal
TM42	Facade	Normal	Physical	70	100	20	Normal
TM44	Rest	Psychic	Status	—	—	10	Self
TM45	Attract	Normal	Status	—	100	15	Normal
TM48	Round	Normal	Special	60	100	15	Normal
TM56	Fling	Dark	Physical	—	100	10	Normal
TM63	Embargo	Dark	Status	—	100	15	Normal
TM66	Payback	Dark	Physical	50	100	10	Normal
TM68	Giga Impact	Normal	Physical	150	90	5	Normal
TM70	Flash	Normal	Status	—	100	20	Normal
TM73	Thunder Wave	Electric	Status	—	100	20	Normal
TM77	Psych Up	Normal	Status	—	—	10	Normal
TM79	Frost Breath	Ice	Special	60	90	10	Normal
TM85	Dream Eater	Psychic	Special	100	100	15	Normal
TM87	Swagger	Normal	Status	—	90	15	Normal
TM88	Sleep Talk	Normal	Status	—	—	10	Self
TM90	Substitute	Normal	Status	—	—	10	Self
TM94	Secret Power	Normal	Physical	70	100	20	Normal
TM100	Confide	Normal	Status	—	—	20	Normal

MOVES LEARNED IN EXCHANGE FOR BP

Name	Type	Kind	Pow.	Acc.	PP	Range
Signal Beam	Bug	Special	75	100	15	Normal
Ice Punch	Ice	Physical	75	100	15	Normal
Block	Normal	Status	—	—	5	Normal
Icy Wind	Ice	Special	55	95	15	Many Others
Snore	Normal	Special	50	100	15	Normal
Pain Split	Normal	Status	—	—	20	Normal
Shock Wave	Electric	Special	60	—	20	Normal
Water Pulse	Water	Special	60	100	20	Normal
Spite	Ghost	Status	—	100	10	Normal
Trick	Psychic	Status	—	100	10	Normal
Snatch	Dark	Status	—	—	10	Self

MOVES TAUGHT BY PEOPLE

Name	Type	Kind	Pow.	Acc.	PP	Range

National Pokédex **479** Hoenn Pokédex **—**

✓ Rotom

Plasma Pokémon

Electric | Ghost

HEIGHT: 1'00" WEIGHT: 0.7 lbs.

Gender unknown

Ω Research continues on this Pokémon, which could be the power source of a unique motor.

α Its body is composed of plasma. It is known to infiltrate electronic devices and wreak havoc.

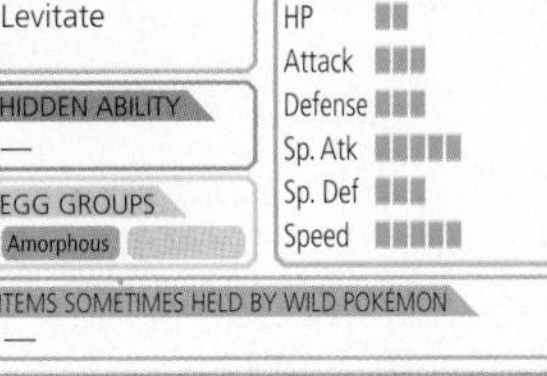

ABILITY
Levitate

HIDDEN ABILITY
—

EGG GROUPS
Amorphous

STAT GROWTH RATES

HP	■■
Attack	■■■
Defense	■■■
Sp. Atk	■■■■■
Sp. Def	■■■
Speed	■■■■■

ITEMS SOMETIMES HELD BY WILD POKÉMON
—

EVOLUTION

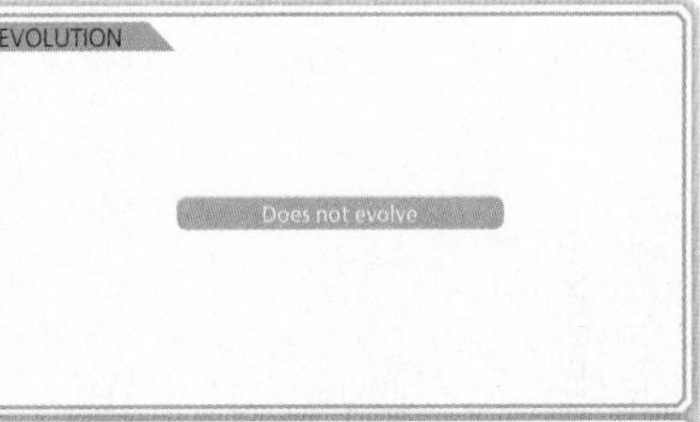

Does not evolve

MAIN WAY TO REGISTER IN THE NATIONAL POKÉDEX

Appears in *Pokémon X* and *Pokémon Y*. Bring it to your game using Link Trade or the GTS.

Damage taken in normal battles

Type		Type	
Normal	×0	Flying	×0.5
Fire	×1	Psychic	×1
Water	×1	Bug	×0.5
Grass	×1	Rock	×1
Electric	×0.5	Ghost	×2
Ice	×1	Dragon	×1
Fighting	×0	Dark	×2
Poison	×0.5	Steel	×0.5
! Ground	×2	Fairy	×1

Damage taken in Inverse battles

Type		Type	
Normal	×2	Flying	×2
Fire	×1	Psychic	×1
Water	×1	Bug	×2
Grass	×1	Rock	×1
Electric	×2	Ghost	×0.5
Ice	×1	Dragon	×1
Fighting	×2	Dark	×0.5
Poison	×2	Steel	×2
! Ground	×0.5	Fairy	×1

Can be used in
Inverse Battle
Battle Institute
Battle Maison
Random Matchup (Free Battle)
Random Matchup (Others)

LEVEL-UP MOVES

Lv.	Name	Type	Kind	Pow.	Acc.	PP	Range
1	Discharge	Electric	Special	80	100	15	Adjacent
1	Charge	Electric	Status	—	—	20	Self
1	Trick	Psychic	Status	—	100	10	Normal
1	Astonish	Ghost	Physical	30	100	15	Normal
1	Thunder Wave	Electric	Status	—	100	20	Normal
1	Thunder Shock	Electric	Special	40	100	30	Normal
1	Confuse Ray	Ghost	Status	—	100	10	Normal
8	Uproar	Normal	Special	90	100	10	1 Random
15	Double Team	Normal	Status	—	—	15	Self
22	Shock Wave	Electric	Special	60	—	20	Normal
29	Ominous Wind	Ghost	Special	60	100	5	Normal
36	Substitute	Normal	Status	—	—	10	Self
43	Electro Ball	Electric	Special	—	100	10	Normal
50	Hex	Ghost	Special	65	100	10	Normal
57	Charge	Electric	Status	—	—	20	Self
64	Discharge	Electric	Special	80	100	15	Adjacent

TM & HM MOVES

No.	Name	Type	Kind	Pow.	Acc.	PP	Range
TM06	Toxic	Poison	Status	—	90	10	Normal
TM10	Hidden Power	Normal	Special	60	100	15	Normal
TM11	Sunny Day	Fire	Status	—	—	5	Both Sides
TM16	Light Screen	Psychic	Status	—	—	30	Your Side
TM17	Protect	Normal	Status	—	—	10	Self
TM18	Rain Dance	Water	Status	—	—	5	Both Sides
TM21	Frustration	Normal	Physical	—	100	20	Normal
TM24	Thunderbolt	Electric	Special	90	100	15	Normal
TM25	Thunder	Electric	Special	110	70	10	Normal
TM27	Return	Normal	Physical	—	100	20	Normal
TM30	Shadow Ball	Ghost	Special	80	100	15	Normal
TM32	Double Team	Normal	Status	—	—	15	Self
TM33	Reflect	Psychic	Status	—	—	20	Your Side
TM42	Facade	Normal	Physical	70	100	20	Normal
TM44	Rest	Psychic	Status	—	—	10	Self
TM46	Thief	Dark	Physical	60	100	25	Normal
TM48	Round	Normal	Special	60	100	15	Normal
TM57	Charge Beam	Electric	Special	50	90	10	Normal
TM61	Will-O-Wisp	Fire	Status	—	85	15	Normal
TM70	Flash	Normal	Status	—	100	20	Normal
TM72	Volt Switch	Electric	Special	70	100	20	Normal
TM73	Thunder Wave	Electric	Status	—	100	20	Normal
TM77	Psych Up	Normal	Status	—	—	10	Normal
TM85	Dream Eater	Psychic	Special	100	100	15	Normal
TM87	Swagger	Normal	Status	—	90	15	Normal
TM88	Sleep Talk	Normal	Status	—	—	10	Self
TM90	Substitute	Normal	Status	—	—	10	Self
TM94	Secret Power	Normal	Physical	70	100	20	Normal
TM97	Dark Pulse	Dark	Special	80	100	15	Normal
TM100	Confide	Normal	Status	—	—	20	Normal

MOVES LEARNED IN EXCHANGE FOR BP

Name	Type	Kind	Pow.	Acc.	PP	Range
Signal Beam	Bug	Special	75	100	15	Normal
Uproar	Normal	Special	90	100	10	1 Random
Foul Play	Dark	Physical	95	100	15	Normal
Electroweb	Electric	Special	55	95	15	Many Others
Snore	Normal	Special	50	100	15	Normal
Pain Split	Normal	Status	—	—	20	Normal
Shock Wave	Electric	Special	60	—	20	Normal
Spite	Ghost	Status	—	100	10	Normal
Trick	Psychic	Status	—	100	10	Normal
Snatch	Dark	Status	—	—	10	Self

MOVES TAUGHT BY PEOPLE

Name	Type	Kind	Pow.	Acc.	PP	Range

National Pokédex **479** Hoenn Pokédex —

Rotom Heat Rotom

Plasma Pokémon

Electric Fire

HEIGHT: 1'00" WEIGHT: 0.7 lbs.

Gender unknown

Ω Research continues on this Pokémon, which could be the power source of a unique motor.

α Its body is composed of plasma. It is known to infiltrate electronic devices and wreak havoc.

ABILITY: Levitate

HIDDEN ABILITY: —

EGG GROUPS: Amorphous

STAT GROWTH RATES: HP ■■ / Attack ■■■ / Defense ■■■■■ / Sp. Atk ■■■■■ / Sp. Def ■■■■ / Speed ■■■■■

ITEMS SOMETIMES HELD BY WILD POKÉMON: —

EVOLUTION: Does not evolve

MAIN WAY TO REGISTER IN THE NATIONAL POKÉDEX

Have a Rotom received via Link Trade or the GTS in your party, then check out the cardboard boxes in Littleroot Town's Pokémon Lab and select "Microwave oven."

Damage taken in normal battles

Type		Type	
Normal	×1	Flying	×0.5
Fire	×0.5	Psychic	×1
Water	×2	Bug	×0.5
Grass	×0.5	Rock	×2
Electric	×0.5	Ghost	×1
Ice	×0.5	Dragon	×1
Fighting	×1	Dark	×1
Poison	×1	Steel	×0.25
! Ground	×4	Fairy	×0.5

Damage taken in Inverse battles

Type		Type	
Normal	×1	Flying	×2
Fire	×2	Psychic	×1
Water	×0.5	Bug	×2
Grass	×2	Rock	×0.5
Electric	×2	Ghost	×1
Ice	×2	Dragon	×1
Fighting	×1	Dark	×1
Poison	×1	Steel	×4
! Ground	×0.25	Fairy	×2

Can be used in

- Inverse Battle
- Battle Institute
- Battle Maison
- Random Matchup (Free Battle)
- Random Matchup (Others)

LEVEL-UP MOVES

Lv.	Name	Type	Kind	Pow.	Acc.	PP	Range
1	Discharge	Electric	Special	80	100	15	Adjacent
1	Charge	Electric	Status	—	—	20	Self
1	Trick	Psychic	Status	—	100	10	Normal
1	Astonish	Ghost	Physical	30	100	15	Normal
1	Thunder Wave	Electric	Status	—	100	20	Normal
1	Thunder Shock	Electric	Special	40	100	30	Normal
1	Confuse Ray	Ghost	Status	—	100	10	Normal
8	Uproar	Normal	Special	90	100	10	1 Random
15	Double Team	Normal	Status	—	—	15	Self
22	Shock Wave	Electric	Special	60	—	20	Normal
29	Ominous Wind	Ghost	Special	60	100	5	Normal
36	Substitute	Normal	Status	—	—	10	Self
43	Electro Ball	Electric	Special	—	100	10	Normal
50	Hex	Ghost	Special	65	100	10	Normal
57	Charge	Electric	Status	—	—	20	Self
64	Discharge	Electric	Special	80	100	15	Adjacent
◆	Overheat	Fire	Special	130	90	5	Normal

TM & HM MOVES

No.	Name	Type	Kind	Pow.	Acc.	PP	Range
TM06	Toxic	Poison	Status	—	90	10	Normal
TM10	Hidden Power	Normal	Special	60	100	15	Normal
TM11	Sunny Day	Fire	Status	—	—	5	Both Sides
TM16	Light Screen	Psychic	Status	—	—	30	Your Side
TM17	Protect	Normal	Status	—	—	10	Self
TM18	Rain Dance	Water	Status	—	—	5	Both Sides
TM21	Frustration	Normal	Physical	—	100	20	Normal
TM24	Thunderbolt	Electric	Special	90	100	15	Normal
TM25	Thunder	Electric	Special	110	70	10	Normal
TM27	Return	Normal	Physical	—	100	20	Normal
TM30	Shadow Ball	Ghost	Special	80	100	15	Normal
TM32	Double Team	Normal	Status	—	—	15	Self
TM33	Reflect	Psychic	Status	—	—	20	Your Side
TM42	Facade	Normal	Physical	70	100	20	Normal
TM44	Rest	Psychic	Status	—	—	10	Self
TM46	Thief	Dark	Physical	60	100	25	Normal
TM48	Round	Normal	Special	60	100	15	Normal
TM57	Charge Beam	Electric	Special	50	90	10	Normal
TM61	Will-O-Wisp	Fire	Status	—	85	15	Normal
TM70	Flash	Normal	Status	—	100	20	Normal
TM72	Volt Switch	Electric	Special	70	100	20	Normal
TM73	Thunder Wave	Electric	Status	—	100	20	Normal
TM77	Psych Up	Normal	Status	—	—	10	Normal
TM85	Dream Eater	Psychic	Special	100	100	15	Normal
TM87	Swagger	Normal	Status	—	90	15	Normal
TM88	Sleep Talk	Normal	Status	—	—	10	Self
TM90	Substitute	Normal	Status	—	—	10	Self
TM94	Secret Power	Normal	Physical	70	100	20	Normal
TM97	Dark Pulse	Dark	Special	80	100	15	Normal
TM100	Confide	Normal	Status	—	—	20	Normal

MOVES LEARNED IN EXCHANGE FOR BP

Name	Type	Kind	Pow.	Acc.	PP	Range
Signal Beam	Bug	Special	75	100	15	Normal
Uproar	Normal	Special	90	100	10	1 Random
Foul Play	Dark	Physical	95	100	15	Normal
Electroweb	Electric	Special	55	95	15	Many Others
Snore	Normal	Special	50	100	15	Normal
Pain Split	Normal	Status	—	—	20	Normal
Shock Wave	Electric	Special	60	—	20	Normal
Spite	Ghost	Status	—	100	10	Normal
Trick	Psychic	Status	—	100	10	Normal
Snatch	Dark	Status	—	—	10	Self

MOVES TAUGHT BY PEOPLE

Name	Type	Kind	Pow.	Acc.	PP	Range

◆ When Rotom becomes Heat Rotom, it learns the move Overheat. When it changes back to Rotom, it forgets the move.

National Pokédex **479** Hoenn Pokédex —

Rotom Wash Rotom

Plasma Pokémon

Electric Water

HEIGHT: 1'00" WEIGHT: 0.7 lbs.

Gender unknown

Ω Research continues on this Pokémon, which could be the power source of a unique motor.

α Its body is composed of plasma. It is known to infiltrate electronic devices and wreak havoc.

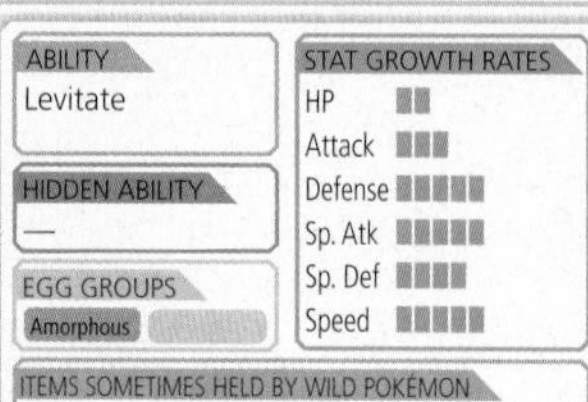

ABILITY: Levitate

HIDDEN ABILITY: —

EGG GROUPS: Amorphous

STAT GROWTH RATES: HP ■■ / Attack ■■■ / Defense ■■■■■ / Sp. Atk ■■■■■ / Sp. Def ■■■■ / Speed ■■■■■

ITEMS SOMETIMES HELD BY WILD POKÉMON: —

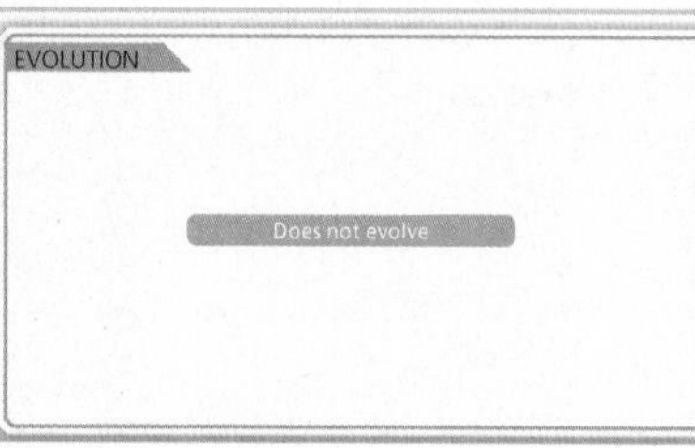

EVOLUTION: Does not evolve

MAIN WAY TO REGISTER IN THE NATIONAL POKÉDEX

Have a Rotom received via Link Trade or the GTS in your party, then check out the cardboard boxes in Littleroot Town's Pokémon Lab and select "Washing machine."

Damage taken in normal battles

Type		Type	
Normal	×1	Flying	×0.5
Fire	×0.5	Psychic	×1
Water	×0.5	Bug	×1
Grass	×2	Rock	×1
Electric	×1	Ghost	×1
Ice	×0.5	Dragon	×1
Fighting	×1	Dark	×1
Poison	×1	Steel	×0.25
! Ground	×2	Fairy	×1

Damage taken in Inverse battles

Type		Type	
Normal	×1	Flying	×2
Fire	×2	Psychic	×1
Water	×2	Bug	×1
Grass	×0.5	Rock	×1
Electric	×1	Ghost	×1
Ice	×2	Dragon	×1
Fighting	×1	Dark	×1
Poison	×1	Steel	×4
! Ground	×0.5	Fairy	×1

Can be used in

- Inverse Battle
- Battle Institute
- Battle Maison
- Random Matchup (Free Battle)
- Random Matchup (Others)

LEVEL-UP MOVES

Lv.	Name	Type	Kind	Pow.	Acc.	PP	Range
1	Discharge	Electric	Special	80	100	15	Adjacent
1	Charge	Electric	Status	—	—	20	Self
1	Trick	Psychic	Status	—	100	10	Normal
1	Astonish	Ghost	Physical	30	100	15	Normal
1	Thunder Wave	Electric	Status	—	100	20	Normal
1	Thunder Shock	Electric	Special	40	100	30	Normal
1	Confuse Ray	Ghost	Status	—	100	10	Normal
8	Uproar	Normal	Special	90	100	10	1 Random
15	Double Team	Normal	Status	—	—	15	Self
22	Shock Wave	Electric	Special	60	—	20	Normal
29	Ominous Wind	Ghost	Special	60	100	5	Normal
36	Substitute	Normal	Status	—	—	10	Self
43	Electro Ball	Electric	Special	—	100	10	Normal
50	Hex	Ghost	Special	65	100	10	Normal
57	Charge	Electric	Status	—	—	20	Self
64	Discharge	Electric	Special	80	100	15	Adjacent
◆	Hydro Pump	Water	Special	110	80	5	Normal

TM & HM MOVES

No.	Name	Type	Kind	Pow.	Acc.	PP	Range
TM06	Toxic	Poison	Status	—	90	10	Normal
TM10	Hidden Power	Normal	Special	60	100	15	Normal
TM11	Sunny Day	Fire	Status	—	—	5	Both Sides
TM16	Light Screen	Psychic	Status	—	—	30	Your Side
TM17	Protect	Normal	Status	—	—	10	Self
TM18	Rain Dance	Water	Status	—	—	5	Both Sides
TM21	Frustration	Normal	Physical	—	100	20	Normal
TM24	Thunderbolt	Electric	Special	90	100	15	Normal
TM25	Thunder	Electric	Special	110	70	10	Normal
TM27	Return	Normal	Physical	—	100	20	Normal
TM30	Shadow Ball	Ghost	Special	80	100	15	Normal
TM32	Double Team	Normal	Status	—	—	15	Self
TM33	Reflect	Psychic	Status	—	—	20	Your Side
TM42	Facade	Normal	Physical	70	100	20	Normal
TM44	Rest	Psychic	Status	—	—	10	Self
TM46	Thief	Dark	Physical	60	100	25	Normal
TM48	Round	Normal	Special	60	100	15	Normal
TM57	Charge Beam	Electric	Special	50	90	10	Normal
TM61	Will-O-Wisp	Fire	Status	—	85	15	Normal
TM70	Flash	Normal	Status	—	100	20	Normal
TM72	Volt Switch	Electric	Special	70	100	20	Normal
TM73	Thunder Wave	Electric	Status	—	100	20	Normal
TM77	Psych Up	Normal	Status	—	—	10	Normal
TM85	Dream Eater	Psychic	Special	100	100	15	Normal
TM87	Swagger	Normal	Status	—	90	15	Normal
TM88	Sleep Talk	Normal	Status	—	—	10	Self
TM90	Substitute	Normal	Status	—	—	10	Self
TM94	Secret Power	Normal	Physical	70	100	20	Normal
TM97	Dark Pulse	Dark	Special	80	100	15	Normal
TM100	Confide	Normal	Status	—	—	20	Normal

MOVES LEARNED IN EXCHANGE FOR BP

Name	Type	Kind	Pow.	Acc.	PP	Range
Signal Beam	Bug	Special	75	100	15	Normal
Uproar	Normal	Special	90	100	10	1 Random
Foul Play	Dark	Physical	95	100	15	Normal
Electroweb	Electric	Special	55	95	15	Many Others
Snore	Normal	Special	50	100	15	Normal
Pain Split	Normal	Status	—	—	20	Normal
Shock Wave	Electric	Special	60	—	20	Normal
Spite	Ghost	Status	—	100	10	Normal
Trick	Psychic	Status	—	100	10	Normal
Snatch	Dark	Status	—	—	10	Self

MOVES TAUGHT BY PEOPLE

Name	Type	Kind	Pow.	Acc.	PP	Range

◆ When Rotom becomes Wash Rotom, it learns the move Hydro Pump. When it changes back to Rotom, it forgets the move.

National Pokédex **479** Hoenn Pokédex —

✓ Rotom Frost Rotom

Plasma Pokémon

Electric Ice

HEIGHT: 1'00" WEIGHT: 0.7 lbs.

Gender unknown

Ω Research continues on this Pokémon, which could be the power source of a unique motor.

α Its body is composed of plasma. It is known to infiltrate electronic devices and wreak havoc.

ABILITY
Levitate

HIDDEN ABILITY
—

EGG GROUPS
Amorphous

STAT GROWTH RATES

HP	■■
Attack	■■■
Defense	■■■■■
Sp. Atk	■■■■■
Sp. Def	■■■■
Speed	■■■■■

ITEMS SOMETIMES HELD BY WILD POKÉMON
—

EVOLUTION
Does not evolve

MAIN WAY TO REGISTER IN THE NATIONAL POKÉDEX

Have a Rotom received via Link Trade or the GTS in your party, then check out the cardboard boxes in Littleroot Town's Pokémon Lab and select "Refrigerator."

Damage taken in normal battles

Normal	×1	Flying	×0.5
Fire	×2	Psychic	×1
Water	×1	Bug	×1
Grass	×1	Rock	×2
Electric	×0.5	Ghost	×1
Ice	×0.5	Dragon	×1
Fighting	×2	Dark	×1
Poison	×1	Steel	×1
! Ground	×2	Fairy	×1

Damage taken in Inverse battles

Normal	×1	Flying	×2
Fire	×0.5	Psychic	×1
Water	×1	Bug	×1
Grass	×1	Rock	×0.5
Electric	×2	Ghost	×1
Ice	×2	Dragon	×1
Fighting	×0.5	Dark	×1
Poison	×1	Steel	×1
! Ground	×0.5	Fairy	×1

Can be used in
Inverse Battle
Battle Institute
Battle Maison
Random Matchup (Free Battle)
Random Matchup (Others)

LEVEL-UP MOVES

Lv.	Name	Type	Kind	Pow.	Acc.	PP	Range
1	Discharge	Electric	Special	80	100	15	Adjacent
1	Charge	Electric	Status	—	—	20	Self
1	Trick	Psychic	Status	—	100	10	Normal
1	Astonish	Ghost	Physical	30	100	15	Normal
1	Thunder Wave	Electric	Status	—	100	20	Normal
1	Thunder Shock	Electric	Special	40	100	30	Normal
1	Confuse Ray	Ghost	Status	—	100	10	Normal
8	Uproar	Normal	Special	90	100	10	1 Random
15	Double Team	Normal	Status	—	—	15	Self
22	Shock Wave	Electric	Special	60	—	20	Normal
29	Ominous Wind	Ghost	Special	60	100	5	Normal
36	Substitute	Normal	Status	—	—	10	Self
43	Electro Ball	Electric	Special	—	100	10	Normal
50	Hex	Ghost	Special	65	100	10	Normal
57	Charge	Electric	Status	—	—	20	Self
64	Discharge	Electric	Special	80	100	15	Adjacent
◆	Blizzard	Ice	Special	110	70	5	Many Others

TM & HM MOVES

No.	Name	Type	Kind	Pow.	Acc.	PP	Range
TM06	Toxic	Poison	Status	—	90	10	Normal
TM10	Hidden Power	Normal	Special	60	100	15	Normal
TM11	Sunny Day	Fire	Status	—	—	5	Both Sides
TM16	Light Screen	Psychic	Status	—	—	30	Your Side
TM17	Protect	Normal	Status	—	—	10	Self
TM18	Rain Dance	Water	Status	—	—	5	Both Sides
TM21	Frustration	Normal	Physical	—	100	20	Normal
TM24	Thunderbolt	Electric	Special	90	100	15	Normal
TM25	Thunder	Electric	Special	110	70	10	Normal
TM27	Return	Normal	Physical	—	100	20	Normal
TM30	Shadow Ball	Ghost	Special	80	100	15	Normal
TM32	Double Team	Normal	Status	—	—	15	Self
TM33	Reflect	Psychic	Status	—	—	20	Your Side
TM42	Facade	Normal	Physical	70	100	20	Normal
TM44	Rest	Psychic	Status	—	—	10	Self
TM46	Thief	Dark	Physical	60	100	25	Normal
TM48	Round	Normal	Special	60	100	15	Normal
TM57	Charge Beam	Electric	Special	50	90	10	Normal
TM61	Will-O-Wisp	Fire	Status	—	85	15	Normal
TM70	Flash	Normal	Status	—	100	20	Normal
TM72	Volt Switch	Electric	Special	70	100	20	Normal
TM73	Thunder Wave	Electric	Status	—	100	20	Normal
TM77	Psych Up	Normal	Status	—	—	10	Normal
TM85	Dream Eater	Psychic	Special	100	100	15	Normal
TM87	Swagger	Normal	Status	—	90	15	Normal
TM88	Sleep Talk	Normal	Status	—	—	10	Self
TM90	Substitute	Normal	Status	—	—	10	Self
TM94	Secret Power	Normal	Physical	70	100	20	Normal
TM97	Dark Pulse	Dark	Special	80	100	15	Normal
TM100	Confide	Normal	Status	—	—	20	Normal

MOVES LEARNED IN EXCHANGE FOR BP

Name	Type	Kind	Pow.	Acc.	PP	Range
Signal Beam	Bug	Special	75	100	15	Normal
Uproar	Normal	Special	90	100	10	1 Random
Foul Play	Dark	Physical	95	100	15	Normal
Electroweb	Electric	Special	55	95	15	Many Others
Snore	Normal	Special	50	100	15	Normal
Pain Split	Normal	Status	—	—	20	Normal
Shock Wave	Electric	Special	60	—	20	Normal
Spite	Ghost	Status	—	100	10	Normal
Trick	Psychic	Status	—	100	10	Normal
Snatch	Dark	Status	—	—	10	Self

MOVES TAUGHT BY PEOPLE

Name	Type	Kind	Pow.	Acc.	PP	Range

◆ When Rotom becomes Frost Rotom, it learns the move Blizzard. When it changes back to Rotom, it forgets the move.

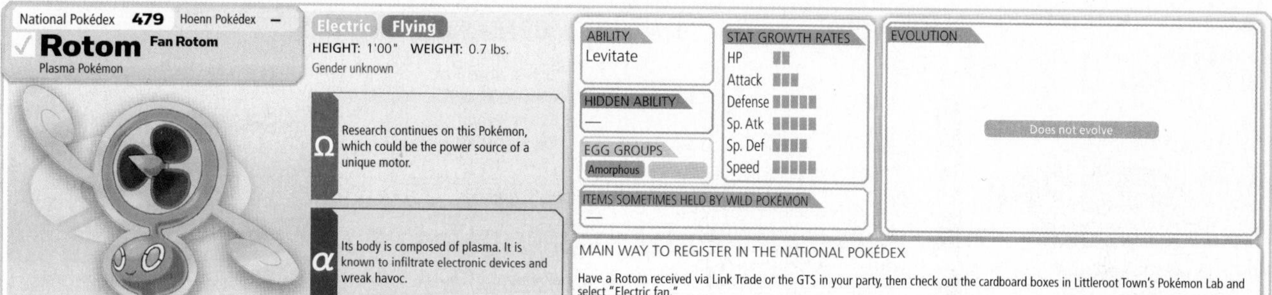

National Pokédex **479** Hoenn Pokédex —

✓ Rotom Fan Rotom

Plasma Pokémon

Electric Flying

HEIGHT: 1'00" WEIGHT: 0.7 lbs.

Gender unknown

Ω Research continues on this Pokémon, which could be the power source of a unique motor.

α Its body is composed of plasma. It is known to infiltrate electronic devices and wreak havoc.

ABILITY
Levitate

HIDDEN ABILITY
—

EGG GROUPS
Amorphous

STAT GROWTH RATES

HP	■■
Attack	■■■
Defense	■■■■■
Sp. Atk	■■■■■
Sp. Def	■■■■
Speed	■■■■■

ITEMS SOMETIMES HELD BY WILD POKÉMON
—

EVOLUTION
Does not evolve

MAIN WAY TO REGISTER IN THE NATIONAL POKÉDEX

Have a Rotom received via Link Trade or the GTS in your party, then check out the cardboard boxes in Littleroot Town's Pokémon Lab and select "Electric fan."

Damage taken in normal battles

Normal	×1	Flying	×0.5
Fire	×1	Psychic	×1
Water	×1	Bug	×0.5
Grass	×0.5	Rock	×2
Electric	×1	Ghost	×1
Ice	×2	Dragon	×1
Fighting	×0.5	Dark	×1
Poison	×1	Steel	×0.5
Ground	×0	Fairy	×1

Damage taken in Inverse battles

Normal	×1	Flying	×2
Fire	×1	Psychic	×1
Water	×1	Bug	×2
Grass	×2	Rock	×0.5
Electric	×1	Ghost	×1
Ice	×0.5	Dragon	×1
Fighting	×2	Dark	×1
Poison	×1	Steel	×2
! Ground	×1	Fairy	×1

Can be used in
Inverse Battle
Battle Institute
Battle Maison
Random Matchup (Free Battle)
Random Matchup (Others)

LEVEL-UP MOVES

Lv.	Name	Type	Kind	Pow.	Acc.	PP	Range
1	Discharge	Electric	Special	80	100	15	Adjacent
1	Charge	Electric	Status	—	—	20	Self
1	Trick	Psychic	Status	—	100	10	Normal
1	Astonish	Ghost	Physical	30	100	15	Normal
1	Thunder Wave	Electric	Status	—	100	20	Normal
1	Thunder Shock	Electric	Special	40	100	30	Normal
1	Confuse Ray	Ghost	Status	—	100	10	Normal
8	Uproar	Normal	Special	90	100	10	1 Random
15	Double Team	Normal	Status	—	—	15	Self
22	Shock Wave	Electric	Special	60	—	20	Normal
29	Ominous Wind	Ghost	Special	60	100	5	Normal
36	Substitute	Normal	Status	—	—	10	Self
43	Electro Ball	Electric	Special	—	100	10	Normal
50	Hex	Ghost	Special	65	100	10	Normal
57	Charge	Electric	Status	—	—	20	Self
64	Discharge	Electric	Special	80	100	15	Adjacent
◆	Air Slash	Flying	Special	75	95	15	Normal

TM & HM MOVES

No.	Name	Type	Kind	Pow.	Acc.	PP	Range
TM06	Toxic	Poison	Status	—	90	10	Normal
TM10	Hidden Power	Normal	Special	60	100	15	Normal
TM11	Sunny Day	Fire	Status	—	—	5	Both Sides
TM16	Light Screen	Psychic	Status	—	—	30	Your Side
TM17	Protect	Normal	Status	—	—	10	Self
TM18	Rain Dance	Water	Status	—	—	5	Both Sides
TM21	Frustration	Normal	Physical	—	100	20	Normal
TM24	Thunderbolt	Electric	Special	90	100	15	Normal
TM25	Thunder	Electric	Special	110	70	10	Normal
TM27	Return	Normal	Physical	—	100	20	Normal
TM30	Shadow Ball	Ghost	Special	80	100	15	Normal
TM32	Double Team	Normal	Status	—	—	15	Self
TM33	Reflect	Psychic	Status	—	—	20	Your Side
TM42	Facade	Normal	Physical	70	100	20	Normal
TM44	Rest	Psychic	Status	—	—	10	Self
TM46	Thief	Dark	Physical	60	100	25	Normal
TM48	Round	Normal	Special	60	100	15	Normal
TM57	Charge Beam	Electric	Special	50	90	10	Normal
TM61	Will-O-Wisp	Fire	Status	—	85	15	Normal
TM70	Flash	Normal	Status	—	100	20	Normal
TM72	Volt Switch	Electric	Special	70	100	20	Normal
TM73	Thunder Wave	Electric	Status	—	100	20	Normal
TM77	Psych Up	Normal	Status	—	—	10	Normal
TM85	Dream Eater	Psychic	Special	100	100	15	Normal
TM87	Swagger	Normal	Status	—	90	15	Normal
TM88	Sleep Talk	Normal	Status	—	—	10	Self
TM90	Substitute	Normal	Status	—	—	10	Self
TM94	Secret Power	Normal	Physical	70	100	20	Normal
TM97	Dark Pulse	Dark	Special	80	100	15	Normal
TM100	Confide	Normal	Status	—	—	20	Normal

MOVES LEARNED IN EXCHANGE FOR BP

Name	Type	Kind	Pow.	Acc.	PP	Range
Signal Beam	Bug	Special	75	100	15	Normal
Uproar	Normal	Special	90	100	10	1 Random
Foul Play	Dark	Physical	95	100	15	Normal
Electroweb	Electric	Special	55	95	15	Many Others
Snore	Normal	Special	50	100	15	Normal
Pain Split	Normal	Status	—	—	20	Normal
Shock Wave	Electric	Special	60	—	20	Normal
Spite	Ghost	Status	—	100	10	Normal
Trick	Psychic	Status	—	100	10	Normal
Snatch	Dark	Status	—	—	10	Self

MOVES TAUGHT BY PEOPLE

Name	Type	Kind	Pow.	Acc.	PP	Range

◆ When Rotom becomes Fan Rotom, it learns the move Air Slash. When it changes back to Rotom, it forgets the move.

National Pokédex **479** Hoenn Pokédex —

Rotom
Mow Rotom

Plasma Pokémon

Electric Grass

HEIGHT: 1'00" WEIGHT: 0.7 lbs.

Gender unknown

Ω Research continues on this Pokémon, which could be the power source of a unique motor.

α Its body is composed of plasma. It is known to infiltrate electronic devices and wreak havoc.

ABILITY
Levitate

HIDDEN ABILITY
—

EGG GROUPS
Amorphous

STAT GROWTH RATES
HP
Attack
Defense
Sp. Atk
Sp. Def
Speed

ITEMS SOMETIMES HELD BY WILD POKÉMON
—

EVOLUTION
Does not evolve

MAIN WAY TO REGISTER IN THE NATIONAL POKÉDEX

Have a Rotom received via Link Trade or the GTS in your party, then check out the cardboard boxes in Littleroot Town's Pokémon Lab and select "Lawnmower."

Damage taken in normal battles

Type		Type	
Normal	×1	Flying	×1
Fire	×2	Psychic	×1
Water	×0.5	Bug	×2
Grass	×0.5	Rock	×1
Electric	×0.25	Ghost	×1
Ice	×2	Dragon	×1
Fighting	×1	Dark	×1
Poison	×2	Steel	×0.5
! Ground	×1	Fairy	×1

Damage taken in Inverse battles

Type		Type	
Normal	×1	Flying	×1
Fire	×0.5	Psychic	×1
Water	×2	Bug	×0.5
Grass	×2	Rock	×1
Electric	×4	Ghost	×1
Ice	×0.5	Dragon	×1
Fighting	×1	Dark	×1
Poison	×0.5	Steel	×2
! Ground	×1	Fairy	×1

Can be used in
Inverse Battle
Battle Institute
Battle Maison
Random Matchup (Free Battle)
Random Matchup (Others)

LEVEL-UP MOVES

Lv.	Name	Type	Kind	Pow.	Acc.	PP	Range
1	Discharge	Electric	Special	80	100	15	Adjacent
1	Charge	Electric	Status	—	—	20	Self
1	Trick	Psychic	Status	—	100	10	Normal
1	Astonish	Ghost	Physical	30	100	15	Normal
1	Thunder Wave	Electric	Status	—	100	20	Normal
1	Thunder Shock	Electric	Special	40	100	30	Normal
1	Confuse Ray	Ghost	Status	—	100	10	Normal
8	Uproar	Normal	Special	90	100	10	1 Random
15	Double Team	Normal	Status	—	—	15	Self
22	Shock Wave	Electric	Special	60	—	20	Normal
29	Ominous Wind	Ghost	Special	60	100	5	Normal
36	Substitute	Normal	Status	—	—	10	Self
43	Electro Ball	Electric	Special	—	100	10	Normal
50	Hex	Ghost	Special	65	100	10	Normal
57	Charge	Electric	Status	—	—	20	Self
64	Discharge	Electric	Special	80	100	15	Adjacent
◆	Leaf Storm	Grass	Special	130	90	5	Normal

TM & HM MOVES

No.	Name	Type	Kind	Pow.	Acc.	PP	Range
TM06	Toxic	Poison	Status	—	90	10	Normal
TM10	Hidden Power	Normal	Special	60	100	15	Normal
TM11	Sunny Day	Fire	Status	—	—	5	Both Sides
TM16	Light Screen	Psychic	Status	—	—	30	Your Side
TM17	Protect	Normal	Status	—	—	10	Self
TM18	Rain Dance	Water	Status	—	—	5	Both Sides
TM21	Frustration	Normal	Physical	—	100	20	Normal
TM24	Thunderbolt	Electric	Special	90	100	15	Normal
TM25	Thunder	Electric	Special	110	70	10	Normal
TM27	Return	Normal	Physical	—	100	20	Normal
TM30	Shadow Ball	Ghost	Special	80	100	15	Normal
TM32	Double Team	Normal	Status	—	—	15	Self
TM33	Reflect	Psychic	Status	—	—	20	Your Side
TM42	Facade	Normal	Physical	70	100	20	Normal
TM44	Rest	Psychic	Status	—	—	10	Self
TM46	Thief	Dark	Physical	60	100	25	Normal
TM48	Round	Normal	Special	60	100	15	Normal
TM57	Charge Beam	Electric	Special	50	90	10	Normal
TM61	Will-O-Wisp	Fire	Status	—	85	15	Normal
TM70	Flash	Normal	Status	—	100	20	Normal
TM72	Volt Switch	Electric	Special	70	100	20	Normal
TM73	Thunder Wave	Electric	Status	—	100	20	Normal
TM77	Psych Up	Normal	Status	—	—	10	Normal
TM85	Dream Eater	Psychic	Special	100	100	15	Normal
TM87	Swagger	Normal	Status	—	90	15	Normal
TM88	Sleep Talk	Normal	Status	—	—	10	Self
TM90	Substitute	Normal	Status	—	—	10	Self
TM94	Secret Power	Normal	Physical	70	100	20	Normal
TM97	Dark Pulse	Dark	Special	80	100	15	Normal
TM100	Confide	Normal	Status	—	—	20	Normal

MOVES LEARNED IN EXCHANGE FOR BP

Name	Type	Kind	Pow.	Acc.	PP	Range
Signal Beam	Bug	Special	75	100	15	Normal
Uproar	Normal	Special	90	100	10	1 Random
Foul Play	Dark	Physical	95	100	15	Normal
Electroweb	Electric	Special	55	95	15	Many Others
Snore	Normal	Special	50	100	15	Normal
Pain Split	Normal	Status	—	—	20	Normal
Shock Wave	Electric	Special	60	—	20	Normal
Spite	Ghost	Status	—	100	10	Normal
Trick	Psychic	Status	—	100	10	Normal
Snatch	Dark	Status	—	—	10	Self

MOVES TAUGHT BY PEOPLE

Name	Type	Kind	Pow.	Acc.	PP	Range

◆ When Rotom becomes Mow Rotom, it learns the move Leaf Storm. When it changes back to Rotom, it forgets the move.

National Pokédex **480** Hoenn Pokédex —

Uxie

Knowledge Pokémon

Psychic

HEIGHT: 1'00" WEIGHT: 0.7 lbs.

Gender unknown

Ω Known as "The Being of Knowledge." It is said that it can wipe out the memory of those who see its eyes.

α It is said that its emergence gave humans the intelligence to improve their quality of life.

ABILITY
Levitate

HIDDEN ABILITY
—

EGG GROUPS
No Eggs Discovered

STAT GROWTH RATES
HP
Attack
Defense
Sp. Atk
Sp. Def
Speed

ITEMS SOMETIMES HELD BY WILD POKÉMON
—

EVOLUTION
Does not evolve

MAIN WAY TO REGISTER IN THE NATIONAL POKÉDEX

Catch in the Nameless Cavern Mirage spot by Soaring in the sky with at least three Pokémon in your party with maximum friendship.

Damage taken in normal battles

Type		Type	
Normal	×1	Flying	×1
Fire	×1	Psychic	×0.5
Water	×1	Bug	×2
Grass	×1	Rock	×1
Electric	×1	Ghost	×2
Ice	×1	Dragon	×1
Fighting	×0.5	Dark	×2
Poison	×1	Steel	×1
! Ground	×1	Fairy	×1

Damage taken in Inverse battles

Type		Type	
Normal	×1	Flying	×1
Fire	×1	Psychic	×2
Water	×1	Bug	×0.5
Grass	×1	Rock	×1
Electric	×1	Ghost	×0.5
Ice	×1	Dragon	×1
Fighting	×2	Dark	×0.5
Poison	×1	Steel	×1
! Ground	×1	Fairy	×1

Can be used in
Inverse Battle
Battle Institute
Battle Maison
Random Matchup (Free Battle)
Random Matchup (Others)

LEVEL-UP MOVES

Lv.	Name	Type	Kind	Pow.	Acc.	PP	Range
1	Memento	Dark	Status	—	100	10	Normal
1	Natural Gift	Normal	Physical	—	100	15	Normal
1	Flail	Normal	Physical	—	100	15	Normal
1	Rest	Psychic	Status	—	—	10	Self
1	Confusion	Psychic	Special	50	100	25	Normal
6	Imprison	Psychic	Status	—	—	10	Self
16	Endure	Normal	Status	—	—	10	Self
21	Swift	Normal	Special	60	—	20	Many Others
31	Yawn	Normal	Status	—	—	10	Normal
36	Future Sight	Psychic	Special	120	100	10	Normal
46	Amnesia	Psychic	Status	—	—	20	Self
50	Extrasensory	Psychic	Special	80	100	20	Normal
61	Flail	Normal	Physical	—	100	15	Normal
66	Natural Gift	Normal	Physical	—	100	15	Normal
76	Memento	Dark	Status	—	100	10	Normal

TM & HM MOVES

No.	Name	Type	Kind	Pow.	Acc.	PP	Range
TM03	Psyshock	Psychic	Special	80	100	10	Normal
TM04	Calm Mind	Psychic	Status	—	—	20	Self
TM06	Toxic	Poison	Status	—	90	10	Normal
TM10	Hidden Power	Normal	Special	60	100	15	Normal
TM11	Sunny Day	Fire	Status	—	—	5	Both Sides
TM15	Hyper Beam	Normal	Special	150	90	5	Normal
TM16	Light Screen	Psychic	Status	—	—	30	Your Side
TM17	Protect	Normal	Status	—	—	10	Self
TM18	Rain Dance	Water	Status	—	—	5	Both Sides
TM20	Safeguard	Normal	Status	—	—	25	Your Side
TM21	Frustration	Normal	Physical	—	100	20	Normal
TM22	Solar Beam	Grass	Special	120	100	10	Normal
TM24	Thunderbolt	Electric	Special	90	100	15	Normal
TM25	Thunder	Electric	Special	110	70	10	Normal
TM27	Return	Normal	Physical	—	100	20	Normal
TM29	Psychic	Psychic	Special	90	100	10	Normal
TM30	Shadow Ball	Ghost	Special	80	100	15	Normal
TM32	Double Team	Normal	Status	—	—	15	Self
TM33	Reflect	Psychic	Status	—	—	20	Your Side
TM37	Sandstorm	Rock	Status	—	—	10	Both Sides
TM42	Facade	Normal	Physical	70	100	20	Normal
TM44	Rest	Psychic	Status	—	—	10	Self
TM48	Round	Normal	Special	60	100	15	Normal
TM53	Energy Ball	Grass	Special	90	100	10	Normal
TM56	Fling	Dark	Physical	—	100	10	Normal
TM57	Charge Beam	Electric	Special	50	90	10	Normal
TM62	Acrobatics	Flying	Physical	55	100	15	Normal
TM68	Giga Impact	Normal	Physical	150	90	5	Normal
TM70	Flash	Normal	Status	—	100	20	Normal
TM73	Thunder Wave	Electric	Status	—	100	20	Normal
TM77	Psych Up	Normal	Status	—	—	10	Normal
TM85	Dream Eater	Psychic	Special	100	100	15	Normal
TM86	Grass Knot	Grass	Special	—	100	20	Normal
TM87	Swagger	Normal	Status	—	90	15	Normal
TM88	Sleep Talk	Normal	Status	—	—	10	Self
TM89	U-turn	Bug	Physical	70	100	20	Normal
TM90	Substitute	Normal	Status	—	—	10	Self
TM92	Trick Room	Psychic	Status	—	—	5	Both Sides
TM94	Secret Power	Normal	Physical	70	100	20	Normal
TM98	Power-Up Punch	Fighting	Physical	40	100	20	Normal
TM99	Dazzling Gleam	Fairy	Special	80	100	10	Many Others
TM100	Confide	Normal	Status	—	—	20	Normal

MOVES LEARNED IN EXCHANGE FOR BP

Name	Type	Kind	Pow.	Acc.	PP	Range
Signal Beam	Bug	Special	75	100	15	Normal
Thunder Punch	Electric	Physical	75	100	15	Normal
Fire Punch	Fire	Physical	75	100	15	Normal
Ice Punch	Ice	Physical	75	100	15	Normal
Magic Coat	Psychic	Status	—	—	15	Self
Foul Play	Dark	Physical	95	100	15	Normal
Zen Headbutt	Psychic	Physical	80	90	15	Normal
Iron Tail	Steel	Physical	100	75	15	Normal
Snore	Normal	Special	50	100	15	Normal
Knock Off	Dark	Physical	65	100	20	Normal
Role Play	Psychic	Status	—	—	10	Normal
Heal Bell	Normal	Status	—	—	5	Your Party
Giga Drain	Grass	Special	75	100	10	Normal
Shock Wave	Electric	Special	60	—	20	Normal
Water Pulse	Water	Special	60	100	20	Normal
Helping Hand	Normal	Status	—	—	20	1 Ally
Trick	Psychic	Status	—	100	10	Normal
Magic Room	Psychic	Status	—	—	10	Both Sides
Wonder Room	Psychic	Status	—	—	10	Both Sides
Recycle	Normal	Status	—	—	10	Self
Stealth Rock	Rock	Status	—	—	20	Other Side
Skill Swap	Psychic	Status	—	—	10	Normal

MOVES TAUGHT BY PEOPLE

Name	Type	Kind	Pow.	Acc.	PP	Range

National Pokédex **481** Hoenn Pokédex —

Mesprit

Emotion Pokémon

Psychic

HEIGHT: 1'00" WEIGHT: 0.7 lbs.

Gender unknown

Ω Known as "The Being of Emotion." It taught humans the nobility of sorrow, pain, and joy.

α It sleeps at the bottom of a lake. Its spirit is said to leave its body to fly on the lake's surface.

ABILITY: Levitate

HIDDEN ABILITY: —

EGG GROUPS: No Eggs Discovered

STAT GROWTH RATES: HP, Attack, Defense, Sp. Atk, Sp. Def, Speed

ITEMS SOMETIMES HELD BY WILD POKÉMON: —

EVOLUTION: Does not evolve

MAIN WAY TO REGISTER IN THE NATIONAL POKÉDEX

Catch in the Nameless Cavern Mirage spot by Soaring in the sky with at least three Pokémon in your party with maximum friendship.

Damage taken in normal battles

Normal	×1	Flying	×1
Fire	×1	Psychic	×0.5
Water	×1	Bug	×2
Grass	×1	Rock	×1
Electric	×1	Ghost	×2
Ice	×1	Dragon	×1
Fighting	×0.5	Dark	×2
Poison	×1	Steel	×1
Ground	×1	Fairy	×1

Damage taken in Inverse battles

Normal	×1	Flying	×1
Fire	×1	Psychic	×2
Water	×1	Bug	×0.5
Grass	×1	Rock	×1
Electric	×1	Ghost	×0.5
Ice	×1	Dragon	×1
Fighting	×2	Dark	×0.5
Poison	×1	Steel	×1
Ground	×1	Fairy	×1

Can be used in

Inverse Battle
Battle Institute
Battle Maison
Random Matchup (Free Battle)
Random Matchup (Others)

LEVEL-UP MOVES

Lv.	Name	Type	Kind	Pow.	Acc.	PP	Range
1	Healing Wish	Psychic	Status	—	—	10	Self
1	Natural Gift	Normal	Physical	—	100	15	Normal
1	Copycat	Normal	Status	—	—	20	Self
1	Rest	Psychic	Status	—	—	10	Self
1	Confusion	Psychic	Special	50	100	25	Normal
6	Imprison	Psychic	Status	—	—	10	Self
16	Protect	Normal	Status	—	—	10	Self
21	Swift	Normal	Special	60	—	20	Many Others
31	Lucky Chant	Normal	Status	—	—	30	Your Side
36	Future Sight	Psychic	Special	120	100	10	Normal
46	Charm	Fairy	Status	—	100	20	Normal
50	Extrasensory	Psychic	Special	80	100	20	Normal
61	Copycat	Normal	Status	—	—	20	Self
66	Natural Gift	Normal	Physical	—	100	15	Normal
76	Healing Wish	Psychic	Status	—	—	10	Self

TM & HM MOVES

No.	Name	Type	Kind	Pow.	Acc.	PP	Range
TM03	Psyshock	Psychic	Special	80	100	10	Normal
TM04	Calm Mind	Psychic	Status	—	—	20	Self
TM06	Toxic	Poison	Status	—	90	10	Normal
TM10	Hidden Power	Normal	Special	60	100	15	Normal
TM11	Sunny Day	Fire	Status	—	—	5	Both Sides
TM13	Ice Beam	Ice	Special	90	100	10	Normal
TM14	Blizzard	Ice	Special	110	70	5	Many Others
TM15	Hyper Beam	Normal	Special	150	90	5	Normal
TM16	Light Screen	Psychic	Status	—	—	30	Your Side
TM17	Protect	Normal	Status	—	—	10	Self
TM18	Rain Dance	Water	Status	—	—	5	Both Sides
TM20	Safeguard	Normal	Status	—	—	25	Your Side
TM21	Frustration	Normal	Physical	—	100	20	Normal
TM24	Thunderbolt	Electric	Special	90	100	15	Normal
TM25	Thunder	Electric	Special	110	70	10	Normal
TM27	Return	Normal	Physical	—	100	20	Normal
TM29	Psychic	Psychic	Special	90	100	10	Normal
TM30	Shadow Ball	Ghost	Special	80	100	15	Normal
TM32	Double Team	Normal	Status	—	—	15	Self
TM33	Reflect	Psychic	Status	—	—	20	Your Side
TM37	Sandstorm	Rock	Status	—	—	10	Both Sides
TM42	Facade	Normal	Physical	70	100	20	Normal
TM44	Rest	Psychic	Status	—	—	10	Self
TM48	Round	Normal	Special	60	100	15	Normal
TM53	Energy Ball	Grass	Special	90	100	10	Normal
TM56	Fling	Dark	Physical	—	100	10	Normal
TM57	Charge Beam	Electric	Special	50	90	10	Normal
TM62	Acrobatics	Flying	Physical	55	100	15	Normal
TM68	Giga Impact	Normal	Physical	150	90	5	Normal
TM70	Flash	Normal	Status	—	100	20	Normal
TM73	Thunder Wave	Electric	Status	—	100	20	Normal
TM77	Psych Up	Normal	Status	—	—	10	Normal
TM85	Dream Eater	Psychic	Special	100	100	15	Normal
TM86	Grass Knot	Grass	Special	—	100	20	Normal
TM87	Swagger	Normal	Status	—	90	15	Normal
TM88	Sleep Talk	Normal	Status	—	—	10	Self
TM89	U-turn	Bug	Physical	70	100	20	Normal
TM90	Substitute	Normal	Status	—	—	10	Self
TM92	Trick Room	Psychic	Status	—	—	5	Both Sides
TM94	Secret Power	Normal	Physical	70	100	20	Normal
TM98	Power-Up Punch	Fighting	Physical	40	100	20	Normal
TM99	Dazzling Gleam	Fairy	Special	80	100	10	Many Others
TM100	Confide	Normal	Status	—	—	20	Normal

MOVES LEARNED IN EXCHANGE FOR BP

Name	Type	Kind	Pow.	Acc.	PP	Range
Signal Beam	Bug	Special	75	100	15	Normal
Thunder Punch	Electric	Physical	75	100	15	Normal
Fire Punch	Fire	Physical	75	100	15	Normal
Ice Punch	Ice	Physical	75	100	15	Normal
Magic Coat	Psychic	Status	—	—	15	Self
Zen Headbutt	Psychic	Physical	80	90	15	Normal
Iron Tail	Steel	Physical	100	75	15	Normal
Snore	Normal	Special	50	100	15	Normal
Knock Off	Dark	Physical	65	100	20	Normal
Role Play	Psychic	Status	—	—	10	Normal
Shock Wave	Electric	Special	60	—	20	Normal
Water Pulse	Water	Special	60	100	20	Normal
Helping Hand	Normal	Status	—	—	20	1 Ally
Trick	Psychic	Status	—	100	10	Normal
Magic Room	Psychic	Status	—	—	10	Both Sides
Wonder Room	Psychic	Status	—	—	10	Both Sides
Recycle	Normal	Status	—	—	10	Self
Stealth Rock	Rock	Status	—	—	20	Other Side
Skill Swap	Psychic	Status	—	—	10	Normal

MOVES TAUGHT BY PEOPLE

Name	Type	Kind	Pow.	Acc.	PP	Range

National Pokédex **482** Hoenn Pokédex —

Azelf

Willpower Pokémon

Psychic

HEIGHT: 1'00" WEIGHT: 0.7 lbs.

Gender unknown

Ω Known as "The Being of Willpower." It sleeps at the bottom of a lake to keep the world in balance.

α It is thought that Uxie, Mesprit, and Azelf all came from the same egg.

ABILITY: Levitate

HIDDEN ABILITY: —

EGG GROUPS: No Eggs Discovered

STAT GROWTH RATES: HP, Attack, Defense, Sp. Atk, Sp. Def, Speed

ITEMS SOMETIMES HELD BY WILD POKÉMON: —

EVOLUTION: Does not evolve

MAIN WAY TO REGISTER IN THE NATIONAL POKÉDEX

Catch in the Nameless Cavern Mirage spot by Soaring in the sky with at least three Pokémon in your party with maximum friendship.

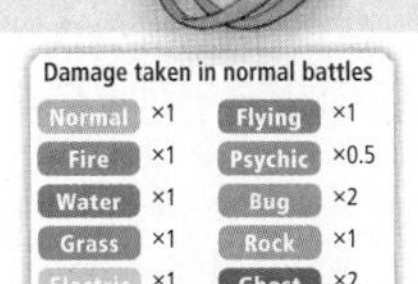

Damage taken in normal battles

Normal	×1	Flying	×1
Fire	×1	Psychic	×0.5
Water	×1	Bug	×2
Grass	×1	Rock	×1
Electric	×1	Ghost	×2
Ice	×1	Dragon	×1
Fighting	×0.5	Dark	×2
Poison	×1	Steel	×1
Ground	×1	Fairy	×1

Damage taken in Inverse battles

Normal	×1	Flying	×1
Fire	×1	Psychic	×2
Water	×1	Bug	×0.5
Grass	×1	Rock	×1
Electric	×1	Ghost	×0.5
Ice	×1	Dragon	×1
Fighting	×2	Dark	×0.5
Poison	×1	Steel	×1
Ground	×1	Fairy	×1

Can be used in

Inverse Battle
Battle Institute
Battle Maison
Random Matchup (Free Battle)
Random Matchup (Others)

LEVEL-UP MOVES

Lv.	Name	Type	Kind	Pow.	Acc.	PP	Range
1	Natural Gift	Normal	Physical	—	100	15	Normal
1	Last Resort	Normal	Physical	140	100	5	Normal
1	Rest	Psychic	Status	—	—	10	Self
1	Confusion	Psychic	Special	50	100	25	Normal
6	Imprison	Psychic	Status	—	—	10	Self
16	Detect	Fighting	Status	—	—	5	Self
21	Swift	Normal	Special	60	—	20	Many Others
31	Uproar	Normal	Special	90	100	10	1 Random
36	Future Sight	Psychic	Special	120	100	10	Normal
46	Nasty Plot	Dark	Status	—	—	20	Self
50	Extrasensory	Psychic	Special	80	100	20	Normal
61	Last Resort	Normal	Physical	140	100	5	Normal
66	Natural Gift	Normal	Physical	—	100	15	Normal
76	Explosion	Normal	Physical	250	100	5	Adjacent

TM & HM MOVES

No.	Name	Type	Kind	Pow.	Acc.	PP	Range
TM03	Psyshock	Psychic	Special	80	100	10	Normal
TM04	Calm Mind	Psychic	Status	—	—	20	Self
TM06	Toxic	Poison	Status	—	90	10	Normal
TM10	Hidden Power	Normal	Special	60	100	15	Normal
TM11	Sunny Day	Fire	Status	—	—	5	Both Sides
TM12	Taunt	Dark	Status	—	100	20	Normal
TM15	Hyper Beam	Normal	Special	150	90	5	Normal
TM16	Light Screen	Psychic	Status	—	—	30	Your Side
TM17	Protect	Normal	Status	—	—	10	Self
TM18	Rain Dance	Water	Status	—	—	5	Both Sides
TM20	Safeguard	Normal	Status	—	—	25	Your Side
TM21	Frustration	Normal	Physical	—	100	20	Normal
TM24	Thunderbolt	Electric	Special	90	100	15	Normal
TM25	Thunder	Electric	Special	110	70	10	Normal
TM27	Return	Normal	Physical	—	100	20	Normal
TM29	Psychic	Psychic	Special	90	100	10	Normal
TM30	Shadow Ball	Ghost	Special	80	100	15	Normal
TM32	Double Team	Normal	Status	—	—	15	Self
TM33	Reflect	Psychic	Status	—	—	20	Your Side
TM35	Flamethrower	Fire	Special	90	100	15	Normal
TM37	Sandstorm	Rock	Status	—	—	10	Both Sides
TM38	Fire Blast	Fire	Special	110	85	5	Normal
TM41	Torment	Dark	Status	—	100	15	Normal
TM42	Facade	Normal	Physical	70	100	20	Normal
TM44	Rest	Psychic	Status	—	—	10	Self
TM48	Round	Normal	Special	60	100	15	Normal
TM53	Energy Ball	Grass	Special	90	100	10	Normal
TM56	Fling	Dark	Physical	—	100	10	Normal
TM57	Charge Beam	Electric	Special	50	90	10	Normal
TM59	Incinerate	Fire	Special	60	100	15	Many Others
TM62	Acrobatics	Flying	Physical	55	100	15	Normal
TM64	Explosion	Normal	Physical	250	100	5	Adjacent
TM66	Payback	Dark	Physical	50	100	10	Normal
TM68	Giga Impact	Normal	Physical	150	90	5	Normal
TM70	Flash	Normal	Status	—	100	20	Normal
TM73	Thunder Wave	Electric	Status	—	100	20	Normal
TM77	Psych Up	Normal	Status	—	—	10	Normal
TM85	Dream Eater	Psychic	Special	100	100	15	Normal
TM86	Grass Knot	Grass	Special	—	100	20	Normal
TM87	Swagger	Normal	Status	—	90	15	Normal
TM88	Sleep Talk	Normal	Status	—	—	10	Self
TM89	U-turn	Bug	Physical	70	100	20	Normal
TM90	Substitute	Normal	Status	—	—	10	Self
TM92	Trick Room	Psychic	Status	—	—	5	Both Sides
TM94	Secret Power	Normal	Physical	70	100	20	Normal
TM98	Power-Up Punch	Fighting	Physical	40	100	20	Normal
TM99	Dazzling Gleam	Fairy	Special	80	100	10	Many Others
TM100	Confide	Normal	Status	—	—	20	Normal

MOVES LEARNED IN EXCHANGE FOR BP

Name	Type	Kind	Pow.	Acc.	PP	Range
Signal Beam	Bug	Special	75	100	15	Normal
Uproar	Normal	Special	90	100	10	1 Random
Thunder Punch	Electric	Physical	75	100	15	Normal
Fire Punch	Fire	Physical	75	100	15	Normal
Ice Punch	Ice	Physical	75	100	15	Normal
Magic Coat	Psychic	Status	—	—	15	Self
Last Resort	Normal	Physical	140	100	5	Normal
Zen Headbutt	Psychic	Physical	80	90	15	Normal
Iron Tail	Steel	Physical	100	75	15	Normal
Snore	Normal	Special	50	100	15	Normal
Knock Off	Dark	Physical	65	100	20	Normal
Role Play	Psychic	Status	—	—	10	Normal
Shock Wave	Electric	Special	60	—	20	Normal
Water Pulse	Water	Special	60	100	20	Normal
Helping Hand	Normal	Status	—	—	20	1 Ally
Trick	Psychic	Status	—	100	10	Normal
Magic Room	Psychic	Status	—	—	10	Both Sides
Wonder Room	Psychic	Status	—	—	10	Both Sides
Recycle	Normal	Status	—	—	10	Self
Stealth Rock	Rock	Status	—	—	20	Other Side
Skill Swap	Psychic	Status	—	—	10	Normal

MOVES TAUGHT BY PEOPLE

Name	Type	Kind	Pow.	Acc.	PP	Range

National Pokédex **483** Hoenn Pokédex —

✓ Dialga

Temporal Pokémon

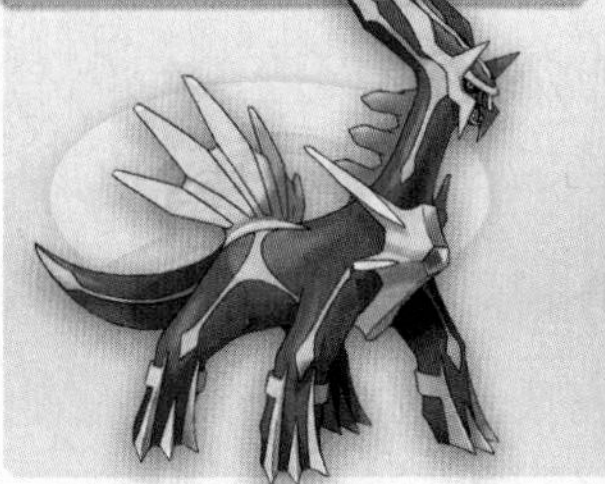

Steel **Dragon**

HEIGHT: 17'09" **WEIGHT:** 1505.8 lbs.

Gender unknown

Ω A Pokémon spoken of in legend. It is said that time began moving when Dialga was born.

α It has the power to control time. It appears in Sinnoh-region myths as an ancient deity.

ABILITY
Pressure

HIDDEN ABILITY
Telepathy

EGG GROUPS
No Eggs Discovered

STAT GROWTH RATES
HP ▮▮▮▮
Attack ▮▮▮▮▮▮
Defense ▮▮▮▮▮
Sp. Atk ▮▮▮▮▮▮▮
Sp. Def ▮▮▮▮
Speed ▮▮▮▮▮

ITEMS SOMETIMES HELD BY WILD POKÉMON
—

EVOLUTION
Does not evolve

MAIN WAYS TO REGISTER IN THE NATIONAL POKÉDEX

Ω Bring it to your game using Link Trade or the GTS.

α Catch in the Dimensional Rift Mirage spot that appears in the sky when Soaring with a certain Psychic trio of Legendary Pokemon in your party.

Damage taken in normal battles

Type		Type	
Normal	×0.5	Flying	×0.5
Fire	×1	Psychic	×0.5
Water	×0.5	Bug	×0.5
Grass	×0.25	Rock	×0.5
Electric	×0.5	Ghost	×1
Ice	×1	Dragon	×1
Fighting	×2	Dark	×1
Poison	×0	Steel	×0.5
Ground	×2	Fairy	×1

Damage taken in Inverse battles

Type		Type	
Normal	×2	Flying	×2
Fire	×1	Psychic	×2
Water	×2	Bug	×2
Grass	×4	Rock	×2
Electric	×2	Ghost	×1
Ice	×1	Dragon	×1
Fighting	×0.5	Dark	×1
Poison	×2	Steel	×2
Ground	×0.5	Fairy	×1

Can be used in
Inverse Battle
Battle Institute
Battle Maison
Random Matchup (Free Battle)
Random Matchup (Others)

LEVEL-UP MOVES

Lv.	Name	Type	Kind	Pow.	Acc.	PP	Range
1	Dragon Breath	Dragon	Special	60	100	20	Normal
1	Scary Face	Normal	Status	—	100	10	Normal
6	Metal Claw	Steel	Physical	50	95	35	Normal
10	Ancient Power	Rock	Special	60	100	5	Normal
15	Slash	Normal	Physical	70	100	20	Normal
19	Power Gem	Rock	Special	80	100	20	Normal
24	Metal Burst	Steel	Physical	—	100	10	Varies
28	Dragon Claw	Dragon	Physical	80	100	15	Normal
33	Earth Power	Ground	Special	90	100	10	Normal
37	Aura Sphere	Fighting	Special	80	—	20	Normal
42	Iron Tail	Steel	Physical	100	75	15	Normal
46	Roar of Time	Dragon	Special	150	90	5	Normal
50	Flash Cannon	Steel	Special	80	100	10	Normal

TM & HM MOVES

No.	Name	Type	Kind	Pow.	Acc.	PP	Range
TM01	Hone Claws	Dark	Status	—	—	15	Self
TM02	Dragon Claw	Dragon	Physical	80	100	15	Normal
TM05	Roar	Normal	Status	—	—	20	Normal
TM06	Toxic	Poison	Status	—	90	10	Normal
TM08	Bulk Up	Fighting	Status	—	—	20	Self
TM10	Hidden Power	Normal	Special	60	100	15	Normal
TM11	Sunny Day	Fire	Status	—	—	5	Both Sides
TM13	Ice Beam	Ice	Special	90	100	10	Normal
TM14	Blizzard	Ice	Special	110	70	5	Many Others
TM15	Hyper Beam	Normal	Special	150	90	5	Normal
TM17	Protect	Normal	Status	—	—	10	Self
TM18	Rain Dance	Water	Status	—	—	5	Both Sides
TM20	Safeguard	Normal	Status	—	—	25	Your Side
TM21	Frustration	Normal	Physical	—	100	20	Normal
TM24	Thunderbolt	Electric	Special	90	100	15	Normal
TM25	Thunder	Electric	Special	110	70	10	Normal
TM26	Earthquake	Ground	Physical	100	100	10	Adjacent
TM27	Return	Normal	Physical	—	100	20	Normal
TM31	Brick Break	Fighting	Physical	75	100	15	Normal
TM32	Double Team	Normal	Status	—	—	15	Self
TM35	Flamethrower	Fire	Special	90	100	15	Normal
TM37	Sandstorm	Rock	Status	—	—	10	Both Sides
TM38	Fire Blast	Fire	Special	110	85	5	Normal
TM39	Rock Tomb	Rock	Physical	60	95	15	Normal
TM40	Aerial Ace	Flying	Physical	60	—	20	Normal
TM42	Facade	Normal	Physical	70	100	20	Normal
TM44	Rest	Psychic	Status	—	—	10	Self
TM48	Round	Normal	Special	60	100	15	Normal
TM49	Echoed Voice	Normal	Special	40	100	15	Normal
TM50	Overheat	Fire	Special	130	90	5	Normal
TM59	Incinerate	Fire	Special	60	100	15	Many Others
TM65	Shadow Claw	Ghost	Physical	70	100	15	Normal
TM68	Giga Impact	Normal	Physical	150	90	5	Normal
TM70	Flash	Normal	Status	—	100	20	Normal
TM71	Stone Edge	Rock	Physical	100	80	5	Normal
TM73	Thunder Wave	Electric	Status	—	100	20	Normal
TM77	Psych Up	Normal	Status	—	—	10	Normal
TM78	Bulldoze	Ground	Physical	60	100	20	Adjacent
TM80	Rock Slide	Rock	Physical	75	90	10	Many Others
TM82	Dragon Tail	Dragon	Physical	60	90	10	Normal
TM87	Swagger	Normal	Status	—	90	15	Normal
TM88	Sleep Talk	Normal	Status	—	—	10	Self
TM90	Substitute	Normal	Status	—	—	10	Self
TM91	Flash Cannon	Steel	Special	80	100	10	Normal
TM92	Trick Room	Psychic	Status	—	—	5	Both Sides
TM94	Secret Power	Normal	Physical	70	100	20	Normal
TM100	Confide	Normal	Status	—	—	20	Normal
HM01	Cut	Normal	Physical	50	95	30	Normal
HM04	Strength	Normal	Physical	80	100	15	Normal
HM06	Rock Smash	Fighting	Physical	40	100	15	Normal

MOVES LEARNED IN EXCHANGE FOR BP

Name	Type	Kind	Pow.	Acc.	PP	Range
Iron Head	Steel	Physical	80	100	15	Normal
Earth Power	Ground	Special	90	100	10	Normal
Gravity	Psychic	Status	—	—	5	Both Sides
Magnet Rise	Electric	Status	—	—	10	Self
Iron Defense	Steel	Status	—	—	15	Self
Dragon Pulse	Dragon	Special	85	100	10	Normal
Hyper Voice	Normal	Special	90	100	10	Many Others
Iron Tail	Steel	Physical	100	75	15	Normal
Snore	Normal	Special	50	100	15	Normal
Shock Wave	Electric	Special	60	—	20	Normal
Outrage	Dragon	Physical	120	100	10	1 Random
Stealth Rock	Rock	Status	—	—	20	Other Side

MOVES TAUGHT BY PEOPLE

Name	Type	Kind	Pow.	Acc.	PP	Range
Draco Meteor	Dragon	Special	130	90	5	Normal

National Pokédex **484** Hoenn Pokédex —

✓ Palkia

Spatial Pokémon

Water **Dragon**

HEIGHT: 13'09" **WEIGHT:** 740.8 lbs.

Gender unknown

Ω It is said to live in a gap in the spatial dimension parallel to ours. It appears in mythology.

α It has the ability to distort space. It is described as a deity in Sinnoh-region mythology.

ABILITY
Pressure

HIDDEN ABILITY
Telepathy

EGG GROUPS
No Eggs Discovered

STAT GROWTH RATES
HP ▮▮▮▮
Attack ▮▮▮▮▮▮
Defense ▮▮▮▮
Sp. Atk ▮▮▮▮▮▮▮
Sp. Def ▮▮▮▮▮
Speed ▮▮▮▮▮

ITEMS SOMETIMES HELD BY WILD POKÉMON
—

EVOLUTION
Does not evolve

MAIN WAYS TO REGISTER IN THE NATIONAL POKÉDEX

Ω Catch in the Dimensional Rift Mirage spot that appears in the sky when Soaring with a certain Psychic trio of Legendary Pokémon in your party.

α Bring it to your game using Link Trade or the GTS.

Damage taken in normal battles

Type		Type	
Normal	×1	Flying	×1
Fire	×0.25	Psychic	×1
Water	×0.25	Bug	×1
Grass	×1	Rock	×1
Electric	×1	Ghost	×1
Ice	×1	Dragon	×2
Fighting	×1	Dark	×1
Poison	×1	Steel	×0.5
Ground	×1	Fairy	×2

Damage taken in Inverse battles

Type		Type	
Normal	×1	Flying	×1
Fire	×4	Psychic	×1
Water	×4	Bug	×1
Grass	×1	Rock	×1
Electric	×1	Ghost	×1
Ice	×1	Dragon	×0.5
Fighting	×1	Dark	×1
Poison	×1	Steel	×2
Ground	×1	Fairy	×0.5

Can be used in
Inverse Battle
Battle Institute
Battle Maison
Random Matchup (Free Battle)
Random Matchup (Others)

LEVEL-UP MOVES

Lv.	Name	Type	Kind	Pow.	Acc.	PP	Range
1	Dragon Breath	Dragon	Special	60	100	20	Normal
1	Scary Face	Normal	Status	—	100	10	Normal
6	Water Pulse	Water	Special	60	100	20	Normal
10	Ancient Power	Rock	Special	60	100	5	Normal
15	Slash	Normal	Physical	70	100	20	Normal
19	Power Gem	Rock	Special	80	100	20	Normal
24	Aqua Tail	Water	Physical	90	90	10	Normal
28	Dragon Claw	Dragon	Physical	80	100	15	Normal
33	Earth Power	Ground	Special	90	100	10	Normal
37	Aura Sphere	Fighting	Special	80	—	20	Normal
42	Aqua Tail	Water	Physical	90	90	10	Normal
46	Spacial Rend	Dragon	Special	100	95	5	Normal
50	Hydro Pump	Water	Special	110	80	5	Normal

TM & HM MOVES

No.	Name	Type	Kind	Pow.	Acc.	PP	Range
TM01	Hone Claws	Dark	Status	—	—	15	Self
TM02	Dragon Claw	Dragon	Physical	80	100	15	Normal
TM05	Roar	Normal	Status	—	—	20	Normal
TM06	Toxic	Poison	Status	—	90	10	Normal
TM07	Hail	Ice	Status	—	—	10	Both Sides
TM08	Bulk Up	Fighting	Status	—	—	20	Self
TM10	Hidden Power	Normal	Special	60	100	15	Normal
TM11	Sunny Day	Fire	Status	—	—	5	Both Sides
TM13	Ice Beam	Ice	Special	90	100	10	Normal
TM14	Blizzard	Ice	Special	110	70	5	Many Others
TM15	Hyper Beam	Normal	Special	150	90	5	Normal
TM17	Protect	Normal	Status	—	—	10	Self
TM18	Rain Dance	Water	Status	—	—	5	Both Sides
TM20	Safeguard	Normal	Status	—	—	25	Your Side
TM21	Frustration	Normal	Physical	—	100	20	Normal
TM24	Thunderbolt	Electric	Special	90	100	15	Normal
TM25	Thunder	Electric	Special	110	70	10	Normal
TM26	Earthquake	Ground	Physical	100	100	10	Adjacent
TM27	Return	Normal	Physical	—	100	20	Normal
TM31	Brick Break	Fighting	Physical	75	100	15	Normal
TM32	Double Team	Normal	Status	—	—	15	Self
TM35	Flamethrower	Fire	Special	90	100	15	Normal
TM37	Sandstorm	Rock	Status	—	—	10	Both Sides
TM38	Fire Blast	Fire	Special	110	85	5	Normal
TM39	Rock Tomb	Rock	Physical	60	95	15	Normal
TM40	Aerial Ace	Flying	Physical	60	—	20	Normal
TM42	Facade	Normal	Physical	70	100	20	Normal
TM44	Rest	Psychic	Status	—	—	10	Self
TM48	Round	Normal	Special	60	100	15	Normal
TM49	Echoed Voice	Normal	Special	40	100	15	Normal
TM52	Focus Blast	Fighting	Special	120	70	5	Normal
TM56	Fling	Dark	Physical	—	100	10	Normal
TM59	Incinerate	Fire	Special	60	100	15	Many Others
TM65	Shadow Claw	Ghost	Physical	70	100	15	Normal
TM68	Giga Impact	Normal	Physical	150	90	5	Normal
TM71	Stone Edge	Rock	Physical	100	80	5	Normal
TM73	Thunder Wave	Electric	Status	—	100	20	Normal
TM77	Psych Up	Normal	Status	—	—	10	Normal
TM78	Bulldoze	Ground	Physical	60	100	20	Adjacent
TM80	Rock Slide	Rock	Physical	75	90	10	Many Others
TM82	Dragon Tail	Dragon	Physical	60	90	10	Normal
TM87	Swagger	Normal	Status	—	90	15	Normal
TM88	Sleep Talk	Normal	Status	—	—	10	Self
TM90	Substitute	Normal	Status	—	—	10	Self
TM92	Trick Room	Psychic	Status	—	—	5	Both Sides
TM94	Secret Power	Normal	Physical	70	100	20	Normal
TM100	Confide	Normal	Status	—	—	20	Normal
HM01	Cut	Normal	Physical	50	95	30	Normal
HM03	Surf	Water	Special	90	100	15	Adjacent
HM04	Strength	Normal	Physical	80	100	15	Normal
HM06	Rock Smash	Fighting	Physical	40	100	15	Normal
HM07	Dive	Water	Physical	80	100	10	Normal

MOVES LEARNED IN EXCHANGE FOR BP

Name	Type	Kind	Pow.	Acc.	PP	Range
Earth Power	Ground	Special	90	100	10	Normal
Gravity	Psychic	Status	—	—	5	Both Sides
Aqua Tail	Water	Physical	90	90	10	Normal
Dragon Pulse	Dragon	Special	85	100	10	Normal
Hyper Voice	Normal	Special	90	100	10	Many Others
Snore	Normal	Special	50	100	15	Normal
Focus Punch	Fighting	Physical	150	100	20	Normal
Shock Wave	Electric	Special	60	—	20	Normal
Water Pulse	Water	Special	60	100	20	Normal
Outrage	Dragon	Physical	120	100	10	1 Random

MOVES TAUGHT BY PEOPLE

Name	Type	Kind	Pow.	Acc.	PP	Range
Draco Meteor	Dragon	Special	130	90	5	Normal

National Pokédex **485** Hoenn Pokédex —

Heatran

Lava Dome Pokémon

Fire | Steel

HEIGHT: 5'07" WEIGHT: 948 lbs.

Same form for ♂ / ♀

Ω It dwells in volcanic caves. It digs in with its cross-shaped feet to crawl on ceilings and walls.

α Boiling blood, like magma, circulates through its body. It makes its dwelling place in volcanic caves.

ABILITY
Flash Fire

HIDDEN ABILITY
—

EGG GROUPS
No Eggs Discovered

STAT GROWTH RATES
HP
Attack
Defense
Sp. Atk
Sp. Def
Speed

ITEMS SOMETIMES HELD BY WILD POKÉMON
—

EVOLUTION
Does not evolve

MAIN WAY TO REGISTER IN THE NATIONAL POKÉDEX

Catch on Scorched Slab B3F (after battling Groudon or Kyogre).

Damage taken in normal battles

Type		Type	
Normal	×0.5	Flying	×0.5
Fire	×1	Psychic	×0.5
Water	×2	Bug	×0.25
Grass	×0.25	Rock	×1
Electric	×1	Ghost	×1
Ice	×0.25	Dragon	×0.5
Fighting	×2	Dark	×1
Poison	×0	Steel	×0.25
Ground	×4	Fairy	×0.25

Damage taken in Inverse battles

Type		Type	
Normal	×2	Flying	×2
Fire	×1	Psychic	×2
Water	×0.5	Bug	×4
Grass	×4	Rock	×1
Electric	×1	Ghost	×1
Ice	×4	Dragon	×2
Fighting	×0.5	Dark	×1
Poison	×2	Steel	×4
Ground	×0.25	Fairy	×4

Can be used in
Inverse Battle
Battle Institute
Battle Maison
Random Matchup (Free Battle)
Random Matchup (Others)

LEVEL-UP MOVES

Lv.	Name	Type	Kind	Pow.	Acc.	PP	Range
1	Magma Storm	Fire	Special	100	75	5	Normal
1	Heat Wave	Fire	Special	95	90	10	Many Others
1	Earth Power	Ground	Special	90	100	10	Normal
1	Iron Head	Steel	Physical	80	100	15	Normal
1	Fire Spin	Fire	Special	35	85	15	Normal
1	Ancient Power	Rock	Special	60	100	5	Normal
9	Leer	Normal	Status	—	100	30	Many Others
17	Fire Fang	Fire	Physical	65	95	15	Normal
25	Metal Sound	Steel	Status	—	85	40	Normal
33	Crunch	Dark	Physical	80	100	15	Normal
41	Scary Face	Normal	Status	—	100	10	Normal
49	Lava Plume	Fire	Special	80	100	15	Adjacent
57	Fire Spin	Fire	Special	35	85	15	Normal
65	Iron Head	Steel	Physical	80	100	15	Normal
73	Earth Power	Ground	Special	90	100	10	Normal
81	Heat Wave	Fire	Special	95	90	10	Many Others
88	Stone Edge	Rock	Physical	100	80	5	Normal
96	Magma Storm	Fire	Special	100	75	5	Normal

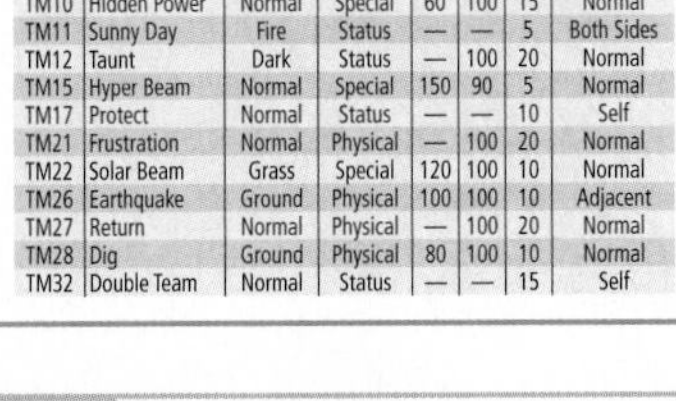

TM & HM MOVES

No.	Name	Type	Kind	Pow.	Acc.	PP	Range
TM05	Roar	Normal	Status	—	—	20	Normal
TM06	Toxic	Poison	Status	—	90	10	Normal
TM10	Hidden Power	Normal	Special	60	100	15	Normal
TM11	Sunny Day	Fire	Status	—	—	5	Both Sides
TM12	Taunt	Dark	Status	—	100	20	Normal
TM15	Hyper Beam	Normal	Special	150	90	5	Normal
TM17	Protect	Normal	Status	—	—	10	Self
TM21	Frustration	Normal	Physical	—	100	20	Normal
TM22	Solar Beam	Grass	Special	120	100	10	Normal
TM26	Earthquake	Ground	Physical	100	100	10	Adjacent
TM27	Return	Normal	Physical	—	100	20	Normal
TM28	Dig	Ground	Physical	80	100	10	Normal
TM32	Double Team	Normal	Status	—	—	15	Self
TM35	Flamethrower	Fire	Special	90	100	15	Normal
TM38	Fire Blast	Fire	Special	110	85	5	Normal
TM39	Rock Tomb	Rock	Physical	60	95	15	Normal
TM41	Torment	Dark	Status	—	100	15	Normal
TM42	Facade	Normal	Physical	70	100	20	Normal
TM43	Flame Charge	Fire	Physical	50	100	20	Normal
TM44	Rest	Psychic	Status	—	—	10	Self
TM45	Attract	Normal	Status	—	100	15	Normal
TM48	Round	Normal	Special	60	100	15	Normal
TM50	Overheat	Fire	Special	130	90	5	Normal
TM59	Incinerate	Fire	Special	60	100	15	Many Others
TM61	Will-O-Wisp	Fire	Status	—	85	15	Normal
TM64	Explosion	Normal	Physical	250	100	5	Adjacent
TM66	Payback	Dark	Physical	50	100	10	Normal
TM68	Giga Impact	Normal	Physical	150	90	5	Normal
TM71	Stone Edge	Rock	Physical	100	80	5	Normal
TM78	Bulldoze	Ground	Physical	60	100	20	Adjacent
TM80	Rock Slide	Rock	Physical	75	90	10	Many Others
TM87	Swagger	Normal	Status	—	90	15	Normal
TM88	Sleep Talk	Normal	Status	—	—	10	Self
TM90	Substitute	Normal	Status	—	—	10	Self
TM91	Flash Cannon	Steel	Special	80	100	10	Normal
TM94	Secret Power	Normal	Physical	70	100	20	Normal
TM96	Nature Power	Normal	Status	—	—	20	Normal
TM97	Dark Pulse	Dark	Special	80	100	15	Normal
TM100	Confide	Normal	Status	—	—	20	Normal
HM04	Strength	Normal	Physical	80	100	15	Normal
HM06	Rock Smash	Fighting	Physical	40	100	15	Normal

MOVES LEARNED IN EXCHANGE FOR BP

Name	Type	Kind	Pow.	Acc.	PP	Range
Bug Bite	Bug	Physical	60	100	20	Normal
Iron Head	Steel	Physical	80	100	15	Normal
Uproar	Normal	Special	90	100	10	1 Random
Earth Power	Ground	Special	90	100	10	Normal
Iron Defense	Steel	Status	—	—	15	Self
Dragon Pulse	Dragon	Special	85	100	10	Normal
Snore	Normal	Special	50	100	15	Normal
Heat Wave	Fire	Special	95	90	10	Many Others
Stealth Rock	Rock	Status	—	—	20	Other Side

MOVES TAUGHT BY PEOPLE

Name	Type	Kind	Pow.	Acc.	PP	Range

National Pokédex **486** Hoenn Pokédex —

Regigigas

Colossal Pokémon

Normal

HEIGHT: 12'02" WEIGHT: 925.9 lbs.

Gender unknown

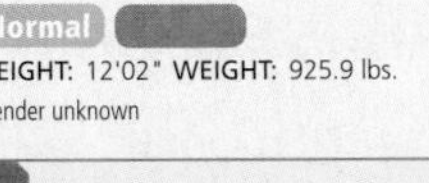

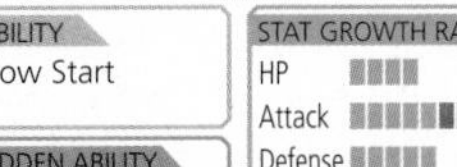

ABILITY
Slow Start

HIDDEN ABILITY
—

EGG GROUPS
No Eggs Discovered

STAT GROWTH RATES
HP
Attack
Defense
Sp. Atk
Sp. Def
Speed

ITEMS SOMETIMES HELD BY WILD POKÉMON
—

EVOLUTION
Does not evolve

Ω It is said to have made Pokémon that look like itself from a special ice mountain, rocks, and magma.

α There is an enduring legend that states this Pokémon towed continents with ropes.

MAIN WAY TO REGISTER IN THE NATIONAL POKÉDEX

Appears in the Island Cave Mirage spot after fulfilling five specific conditions: 1) Have Regirock, Regice, and Registeel present in your team; 2) Defeat Groudon/Kyogre; 3) Give Regice a Never-Melt Ice, a Casteliacone, an Icy Rock, an Icicle Plate, or a Snowball to hold; 4) Give a nickname to Regice; 5) Wait for one day after having caught Regirock, Regice, and Registeel.

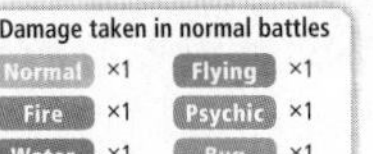

Damage taken in normal battles

Type		Type	
Normal	×1	Flying	×1
Fire	×1	Psychic	×1
Water	×1	Bug	×1
Grass	×1	Rock	×1
Electric	×1	Ghost	×0
Ice	×1	Dragon	×1
Fighting	×2	Dark	×1
Poison	×1	Steel	×1
Ground	×1	Fairy	×1

Damage taken in Inverse battles

Type		Type	
Normal	×1	Flying	×1
Fire	×1	Psychic	×1
Water	×1	Bug	×1
Grass	×1	Rock	×1
Electric	×1	Ghost	×2
Ice	×1	Dragon	×1
Fighting	×0.5	Dark	×1
Poison	×1	Steel	×1
Ground	×1	Fairy	×1

Can be used in
Inverse Battle
Battle Institute
Battle Maison
Random Matchup (Free Battle)
Random Matchup (Others)

LEVEL-UP MOVES

Lv.	Name	Type	Kind	Pow.	Acc.	PP	Range
1	Heavy Slam	Steel	Physical	—	100	10	Normal
1	Crush Grip	Normal	Physical	—	100	5	Normal
1	Fire Punch	Fire	Physical	75	100	15	Normal
1	Ice Punch	Ice	Physical	75	100	15	Normal
1	Thunder Punch	Electric	Physical	75	100	15	Normal
1	Dizzy Punch	Normal	Physical	70	100	10	Normal
1	Knock Off	Dark	Physical	65	100	20	Normal
1	Confuse Ray	Ghost	Status	—	100	10	Normal
1	Foresight	Normal	Status	—	—	40	Normal
25	Revenge	Fighting	Physical	60	100	10	Normal
40	Wide Guard	Rock	Status	—	—	10	Your Side
50	Zen Headbutt	Psychic	Physical	80	90	15	Normal
65	Payback	Dark	Physical	50	100	10	Normal
75	Crush Grip	Normal	Physical	—	100	5	Normal
90	Heavy Slam	Steel	Physical	—	100	10	Normal
100	Giga Impact	Normal	Physical	150	90	5	Normal

TM & HM MOVES

No.	Name	Type	Kind	Pow.	Acc.	PP	Range
TM06	Toxic	Poison	Status	—	90	10	Normal
TM10	Hidden Power	Normal	Special	60	100	15	Normal
TM11	Sunny Day	Fire	Status	—	—	5	Both Sides
TM15	Hyper Beam	Normal	Special	150	90	5	Normal
TM18	Rain Dance	Water	Status	—	—	5	Both Sides
TM20	Safeguard	Normal	Status	—	—	25	Your Side
TM21	Frustration	Normal	Physical	—	100	20	Normal
TM23	Smack Down	Rock	Physical	50	100	15	Normal
TM24	Thunderbolt	Electric	Special	90	100	15	Normal
TM25	Thunder	Electric	Special	110	70	10	Normal
TM26	Earthquake	Ground	Physical	100	100	10	Adjacent
TM27	Return	Normal	Physical	—	100	20	Normal
TM31	Brick Break	Fighting	Physical	75	100	15	Normal
TM32	Double Team	Normal	Status	—	—	15	Self
TM39	Rock Tomb	Rock	Physical	60	95	15	Normal
TM40	Aerial Ace	Flying	Physical	60	—	20	Normal
TM42	Facade	Normal	Physical	70	100	20	Normal
TM48	Round	Normal	Special	60	100	15	Normal
TM52	Focus Blast	Fighting	Special	120	70	5	Normal
TM56	Fling	Dark	Physical	—	100	10	Normal
TM66	Payback	Dark	Physical	50	100	10	Normal
TM67	Retaliate	Normal	Physical	70	100	5	Normal
TM68	Giga Impact	Normal	Physical	150	90	5	Normal
TM69	Rock Polish	Rock	Status	—	—	20	Self
TM71	Stone Edge	Rock	Physical	100	80	5	Normal
TM73	Thunder Wave	Electric	Status	—	100	20	Normal
TM77	Psych Up	Normal	Status	—	—	10	Normal
TM78	Bulldoze	Ground	Physical	60	100	20	Adjacent
TM80	Rock Slide	Rock	Physical	75	90	10	Many Others
TM87	Swagger	Normal	Status	—	90	15	Normal
TM88	Sleep Talk	Normal	Status	—	—	10	Self
TM90	Substitute	Normal	Status	—	—	10	Self
TM94	Secret Power	Normal	Physical	70	100	20	Normal
TM96	Nature Power	Normal	Status	—	—	20	Normal
TM98	Power-Up Punch	Fighting	Physical	40	100	20	Normal
TM100	Confide	Normal	Status	—	—	20	Normal
HM04	Strength	Normal	Physical	80	100	15	Normal
HM06	Rock Smash	Fighting	Physical	40	100	15	Normal

MOVES LEARNED IN EXCHANGE FOR BP

Name	Type	Kind	Pow.	Acc.	PP	Range
Iron Head	Steel	Physical	80	100	15	Normal
Thunder Punch	Electric	Physical	75	100	15	Normal
Fire Punch	Fire	Physical	75	100	15	Normal
Ice Punch	Ice	Physical	75	100	15	Normal
Block	Normal	Status	—	—	5	Normal
Earth Power	Ground	Special	90	100	10	Normal
Gravity	Psychic	Status	—	—	5	Both Sides
Superpower	Fighting	Physical	120	100	5	Normal
Icy Wind	Ice	Special	55	95	15	Many Others
Zen Headbutt	Psychic	Physical	80	90	15	Normal
Snore	Normal	Special	50	100	15	Normal
Knock Off	Dark	Physical	65	100	20	Normal
Drain Punch	Fighting	Physical	75	100	10	Normal
Focus Punch	Fighting	Physical	150	100	20	Normal
Shock Wave	Electric	Special	60	—	20	Normal

MOVES TAUGHT BY PEOPLE

Name	Type	Kind	Pow.	Acc.	PP	Range

National Pokédex **487** Hoenn Pokédex —

Giratina Altered Forme

Renegade Pokémon

Ghost **Dragon**

HEIGHT: 14'09" WEIGHT: 1653.5 lbs.

Gender unknown

Ω This Pokémon is said to live in a world on the reverse side of ours, where common knowledge is distorted and strange.

α It was banished for its violence. It silently gazed upon the old world from the Distortion World.

ABILITY
Pressure

HIDDEN ABILITY
Telepathy

EGG GROUPS
No Eggs Discovered

STAT GROWTH RATES
HP
Attack
Defense
Sp. Atk
Sp. Def
Speed

ITEMS SOMETIMES HELD BY WILD POKÉMON
—

EVOLUTION
Does not evolve

MAIN WAY TO REGISTER IN THE NATIONAL POKÉDEX

Catch in the Dimensional Rift Mirage spot that appears in the sky when Soaring with a pair of Legendary Pokémon that are said to control time and space in your party.

Damage taken in normal battles

Type		Type	
Normal	×0	Flying	×1
Fire	×0.5	Psychic	×1
Water	×0.5	Bug	×0.5
Grass	×0.5	Rock	×1
Electric	×0.5	Ghost	×2
Ice	×2	Dragon	×2
Fighting	×0	Dark	×2
Poison	×0.5	Steel	×1
Ground	×1	Fairy	×2

Damage taken in Inverse battles

Type		Type	
Normal	×2	Flying	×1
Fire	×2	Psychic	×1
Water	×2	Bug	×2
Grass	×2	Rock	×1
Electric	×2	Ghost	×0.5
Ice	×0.5	Dragon	×0.5
Fighting	×2	Dark	×0.5
Poison	×2	Steel	×1
Ground	×1	Fairy	×0.5

Can be used in
Inverse Battle
Battle Institute
Battle Maison
Random Matchup (Free Battle)
Random Matchup (Others)

LEVEL-UP MOVES

Lv.	Name	Type	Kind	Pow.	Acc.	PP	Range
1	Dragon Breath	Dragon	Special	60	100	20	Normal
1	Scary Face	Normal	Status	—	100	10	Normal
6	Ominous Wind	Ghost	Special	60	100	5	Normal
10	Ancient Power	Rock	Special	60	100	5	Normal
15	Slash	Normal	Physical	70	100	20	Normal
19	Shadow Sneak	Ghost	Physical	40	100	30	Normal
24	Destiny Bond	Ghost	Status	—	—	5	Self
28	Dragon Claw	Dragon	Physical	80	100	15	Normal
33	Earth Power	Ground	Special	90	100	10	Normal
37	Aura Sphere	Fighting	Special	80	—	20	Normal
42	Shadow Claw	Ghost	Physical	70	100	15	Normal
46	Shadow Force	Ghost	Physical	120	100	5	Normal
50	Hex	Ghost	Special	65	100	10	Normal

TM & HM MOVES

No.	Name	Type	Kind	Pow.	Acc.	PP	Range
TM01	Hone Claws	Dark	Status	—	—	15	Self
TM02	Dragon Claw	Dragon	Physical	80	100	15	Normal
TM04	Calm Mind	Psychic	Status	—	—	20	Self
TM05	Roar	Normal	Status	—	—	20	Normal
TM06	Toxic	Poison	Status	—	90	10	Normal
TM10	Hidden Power	Normal	Special	60	100	15	Normal
TM11	Sunny Day	Fire	Status	—	—	5	Both Sides
TM15	Hyper Beam	Normal	Special	150	90	5	Normal
TM17	Protect	Normal	Status	—	—	10	Self
TM18	Rain Dance	Water	Status	—	—	5	Both Sides
TM20	Safeguard	Normal	Status	—	—	25	Your Side
TM21	Frustration	Normal	Physical	—	100	20	Normal
TM24	Thunderbolt	Electric	Special	90	100	15	Normal
TM25	Thunder	Electric	Special	110	70	10	Normal
TM26	Earthquake	Ground	Physical	100	100	10	Adjacent
TM27	Return	Normal	Physical	—	100	20	Normal
TM29	Psychic	Psychic	Special	90	100	10	Normal
TM30	Shadow Ball	Ghost	Special	80	100	15	Normal
TM32	Double Team	Normal	Status	—	—	15	Self
TM40	Aerial Ace	Flying	Physical	60	—	20	Normal
TM42	Facade	Normal	Physical	70	100	20	Normal
TM44	Rest	Psychic	Status	—	—	10	Self
TM48	Round	Normal	Special	60	100	15	Normal
TM49	Echoed Voice	Normal	Special	40	100	15	Normal
TM51	Steel Wing	Steel	Physical	70	90	25	Normal
TM53	Energy Ball	Grass	Special	90	100	10	Normal
TM57	Charge Beam	Electric	Special	50	90	10	Normal
TM61	Will-O-Wisp	Fire	Status	—	85	15	Normal
TM65	Shadow Claw	Ghost	Physical	70	100	15	Normal
TM66	Payback	Dark	Physical	50	100	10	Normal
TM68	Giga Impact	Normal	Physical	150	90	5	Normal
TM71	Stone Edge	Rock	Physical	100	80	5	Normal
TM73	Thunder Wave	Electric	Status	—	100	20	Normal
TM77	Psych Up	Normal	Status	—	—	10	Normal
TM78	Bulldoze	Ground	Physical	60	100	20	Adjacent
TM82	Dragon Tail	Dragon	Physical	60	90	10	Normal
TM85	Dream Eater	Psychic	Special	100	100	15	Normal
TM87	Swagger	Normal	Status	—	90	15	Normal
TM88	Sleep Talk	Normal	Status	—	—	10	Self
TM90	Substitute	Normal	Status	—	—	10	Self
TM94	Secret Power	Normal	Physical	70	100	20	Normal
TM97	Dark Pulse	Dark	Special	80	100	15	Normal
TM100	Confide	Normal	Status	—	—	20	Normal
HM01	Cut	Normal	Physical	50	95	30	Normal
HM02	Fly	Flying	Physical	90	95	15	Normal
HM04	Strength	Normal	Physical	80	100	15	Normal
HM06	Rock Smash	Fighting	Physical	40	100	15	Normal

MOVES LEARNED IN EXCHANGE FOR BP

Name	Type	Kind	Pow.	Acc.	PP	Range
Iron Head	Steel	Physical	80	100	15	Normal
Earth Power	Ground	Special	90	100	10	Normal
Gravity	Psychic	Status	—	—	5	Both Sides
Icy Wind	Ice	Special	55	95	15	Many Others
Aqua Tail	Water	Physical	90	90	10	Normal
Dragon Pulse	Dragon	Special	85	100	10	Normal
Hyper Voice	Normal	Special	90	100	10	Many Others
Iron Tail	Steel	Physical	100	75	15	Normal
Snore	Normal	Special	50	100	15	Normal
Pain Split	Normal	Status	—	—	20	Normal
Shock Wave	Electric	Special	60	—	20	Normal
Spite	Ghost	Status	—	100	10	Normal
Outrage	Dragon	Physical	120	100	10	1 Random

MOVES TAUGHT BY PEOPLE

Name	Type	Kind	Pow.	Acc.	PP	Range
Draco Meteor	Dragon	Special	130	90	5	Normal

National Pokédex **487** Hoenn Pokédex —

Giratina Origin Forme

Renegade Pokémon

Ghost **Dragon**

HEIGHT: 22'08" WEIGHT: 1433 lbs.

Gender unknown

Ω This Pokémon is said to live in a world on the reverse side of ours, where common knowledge is distorted and strange.

α It was banished for its violence. It silently gazed upon the old world from the Distortion World.

ABILITY
Levitate

HIDDEN ABILITY
—

EGG GROUPS
No Eggs Discovered

STAT GROWTH RATES
HP
Attack
Defense
Sp. Atk
Sp. Def
Speed

ITEMS SOMETIMES HELD BY WILD POKÉMON
—

EVOLUTION
Does not evolve

MAIN WAY TO REGISTER IN THE NATIONAL POKÉDEX

Have Giratina (Altered Forme) hold a Griseous Orb.

Damage taken in normal battles

Type		Type	
Normal	×0	Flying	×1
Fire	×0.5	Psychic	×1
Water	×0.5	Bug	×0.5
Grass	×0.5	Rock	×1
Electric	×0.5	Ghost	×2
Ice	×2	Dragon	×2
Fighting	×0	Dark	×2
Poison	×0.5	Steel	×1
! Ground	×1	Fairy	×2

Damage taken in Inverse battles

Type		Type	
Normal	×2	Flying	×1
Fire	×2	Psychic	×1
Water	×2	Bug	×2
Grass	×2	Rock	×1
Electric	×2	Ghost	×0.5
Ice	×0.5	Dragon	×0.5
Fighting	×2	Dark	×0.5
Poison	×2	Steel	×1
! Ground	×1	Fairy	×0.5

Can be used in
Inverse Battle
Battle Institute
Battle Maison
Random Matchup (Free Battle)
Random Matchup (Others)

LEVEL-UP MOVES

Lv.	Name	Type	Kind	Pow.	Acc.	PP	Range
1	Dragon Breath	Dragon	Special	60	100	20	Normal
1	Scary Face	Normal	Status	—	100	10	Normal
6	Ominous Wind	Ghost	Special	60	100	5	Normal
10	Ancient Power	Rock	Special	60	100	5	Normal
15	Slash	Normal	Physical	70	100	20	Normal
19	Shadow Sneak	Ghost	Physical	40	100	30	Normal
24	Destiny Bond	Ghost	Status	—	—	5	Self
28	Dragon Claw	Dragon	Physical	80	100	15	Normal
33	Earth Power	Ground	Special	90	100	10	Normal
37	Aura Sphere	Fighting	Special	80	—	20	Normal
42	Shadow Claw	Ghost	Physical	70	100	15	Normal
46	Shadow Force	Ghost	Physical	120	100	5	Normal
50	Hex	Ghost	Special	65	100	10	Normal

TM & HM MOVES

No.	Name	Type	Kind	Pow.	Acc.	PP	Range
TM01	Hone Claws	Dark	Status	—	—	15	Self
TM02	Dragon Claw	Dragon	Physical	80	100	15	Normal
TM04	Calm Mind	Psychic	Status	—	—	20	Self
TM05	Roar	Normal	Status	—	—	20	Normal
TM06	Toxic	Poison	Status	—	90	10	Normal
TM10	Hidden Power	Normal	Special	60	100	15	Normal
TM11	Sunny Day	Fire	Status	—	—	5	Both Sides
TM15	Hyper Beam	Normal	Special	150	90	5	Normal
TM17	Protect	Normal	Status	—	—	10	Self
TM18	Rain Dance	Water	Status	—	—	5	Both Sides
TM20	Safeguard	Normal	Status	—	—	25	Your Side
TM21	Frustration	Normal	Physical	—	100	20	Normal
TM24	Thunderbolt	Electric	Special	90	100	15	Normal
TM25	Thunder	Electric	Special	110	70	10	Normal
TM26	Earthquake	Ground	Physical	100	100	10	Adjacent
TM27	Return	Normal	Physical	—	100	20	Normal
TM29	Psychic	Psychic	Special	90	100	10	Normal
TM30	Shadow Ball	Ghost	Special	80	100	15	Normal
TM32	Double Team	Normal	Status	—	—	15	Self
TM40	Aerial Ace	Flying	Physical	60	—	20	Normal
TM42	Facade	Normal	Physical	70	100	20	Normal
TM44	Rest	Psychic	Status	—	—	10	Self
TM48	Round	Normal	Special	60	100	15	Normal
TM49	Echoed Voice	Normal	Special	40	100	15	Normal
TM51	Steel Wing	Steel	Physical	70	90	25	Normal
TM53	Energy Ball	Grass	Special	90	100	10	Normal
TM57	Charge Beam	Electric	Special	50	90	10	Normal
TM61	Will-O-Wisp	Fire	Status	—	85	15	Normal
TM65	Shadow Claw	Ghost	Physical	70	100	15	Normal
TM66	Payback	Dark	Physical	50	100	10	Normal
TM68	Giga Impact	Normal	Physical	150	90	5	Normal
TM71	Stone Edge	Rock	Physical	100	80	5	Normal
TM73	Thunder Wave	Electric	Status	—	100	20	Normal
TM77	Psych Up	Normal	Status	—	—	10	Normal
TM78	Bulldoze	Ground	Physical	60	100	20	Adjacent
TM82	Dragon Tail	Dragon	Physical	60	90	10	Normal
TM85	Dream Eater	Psychic	Special	100	100	15	Normal
TM87	Swagger	Normal	Status	—	90	15	Normal
TM88	Sleep Talk	Normal	Status	—	—	10	Self
TM90	Substitute	Normal	Status	—	—	10	Self
TM94	Secret Power	Normal	Physical	70	100	20	Normal
TM97	Dark Pulse	Dark	Special	80	100	15	Normal
TM100	Confide	Normal	Status	—	—	20	Normal
HM01	Cut	Normal	Physical	50	95	30	Normal
HM02	Fly	Flying	Physical	90	95	15	Normal
HM04	Strength	Normal	Physical	80	100	15	Normal
HM06	Rock Smash	Fighting	Physical	40	100	15	Normal

MOVES LEARNED IN EXCHANGE FOR BP

Name	Type	Kind	Pow.	Acc.	PP	Range
Iron Head	Steel	Physical	80	100	15	Normal
Magic Coat	Psychic	Status	—	—	15	Self
Earth Power	Ground	Special	90	100	10	Normal
Gravity	Psychic	Status	—	—	5	Both Sides
Icy Wind	Ice	Special	55	95	15	Many Others
Aqua Tail	Water	Physical	90	90	10	Normal
Dragon Pulse	Dragon	Special	85	100	10	Normal
Hyper Voice	Normal	Special	90	100	10	Many Others
Iron Tail	Steel	Physical	100	75	15	Normal
Snore	Normal	Special	50	100	15	Normal
Tailwind	Flying	Status	—	—	15	Your Side
Shock Wave	Electric	Special	60	—	20	Normal
Spite	Ghost	Status	—	100	10	Normal
Outrage	Dragon	Physical	120	100	10	1 Random

MOVES TAUGHT BY PEOPLE

Name	Type	Kind	Pow.	Acc.	PP	Range
Draco Meteor	Dragon	Special	130	90	5	Normal

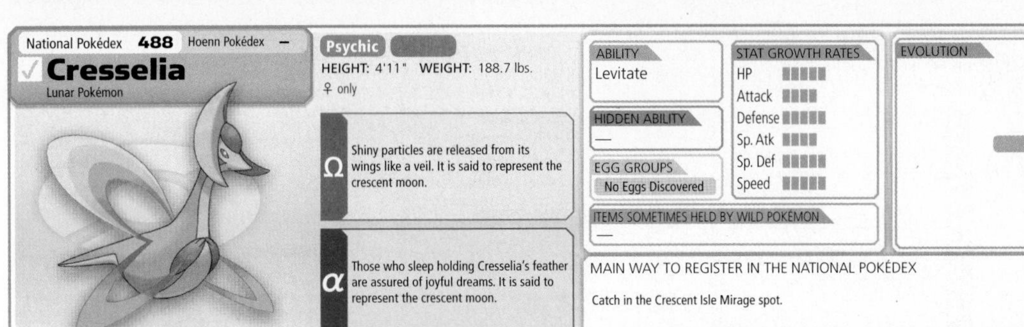

National Pokédex **488** Hoenn Pokédex —

Cresselia

Lunar Pokémon

Psychic

HEIGHT: 4'11" WEIGHT: 188.7 lbs.

♀ only

Ω Shiny particles are released from its wings like a veil. It is said to represent the crescent moon.

α Those who sleep holding Cresselia's feather are assured of joyful dreams. It is said to represent the crescent moon.

ABILITY
Levitate

HIDDEN ABILITY
—

EGG GROUPS
No Eggs Discovered

STAT GROWTH RATES
HP, Attack, Defense, Sp. Atk, Sp. Def, Speed

ITEMS SOMETIMES HELD BY WILD POKÉMON
—

EVOLUTION

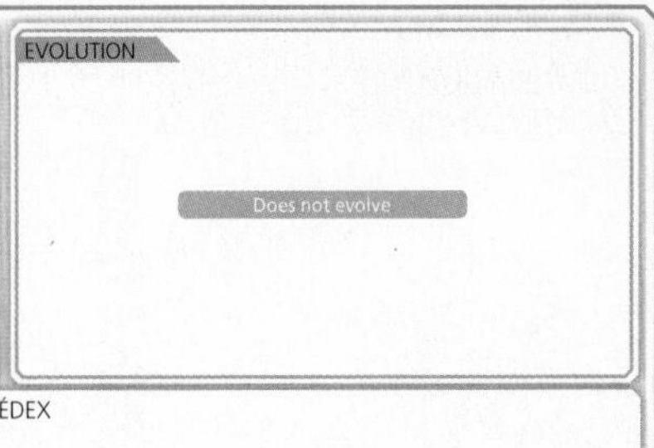

Does not evolve

MAIN WAY TO REGISTER IN THE NATIONAL POKÉDEX

Catch in the Crescent Isle Mirage spot.

Damage taken in normal battles

Type		Type	
Normal	×1	Flying	×1
Fire	×1	Psychic	×0.5
Water	×1	Bug	×2
Grass	×1	Rock	×1
Electric	×1	Ghost	×2
Ice	×1	Dragon	×1
Fighting	×0.5	Dark	×2
Poison	×1	Steel	×1
Ground	×1	Fairy	×1

Damage taken in Inverse battles

Type		Type	
Normal	×1	Flying	×1
Fire	×1	Psychic	×2
Water	×1	Bug	×0.5
Grass	×1	Rock	×1
Electric	×1	Ghost	×0.5
Ice	×1	Dragon	×1
Fighting	×2	Dark	×0.5
Poison	×1	Steel	×1
Ground	×1	Fairy	×1

Can be used in

- Inverse Battle
- Battle Institute
- Battle Maison
- Random Matchup (Free Battle)
- Random Matchup (Others)

LEVEL-UP MOVES

Lv.	Name	Type	Kind	Pow.	Acc.	PP	Range
1	Lunar Dance	Psychic	Status	—	—	10	Self
1	Psycho Shift	Psychic	Status	—	100	10	Normal
1	Psycho Cut	Psychic	Physical	70	100	20	Normal
1	Moonlight	Fairy	Status	—	—	5	Self
1	Confusion	Psychic	Special	50	100	25	Normal
1	Double Team	Normal	Status	—	—	15	Self
11	Safeguard	Normal	Status	—	—	25	Your Side
20	Mist	Ice	Status	—	—	30	Your Side
29	Aurora Beam	Ice	Special	65	100	20	Normal
38	Future Sight	Psychic	Special	120	100	10	Normal
47	Slash	Normal	Physical	70	100	20	Normal
57	Moonlight	Fairy	Status	—	—	5	Self
66	Psycho Cut	Psychic	Physical	70	100	20	Normal
75	Psycho Shift	Psychic	Status	—	100	10	Normal
84	Lunar Dance	Psychic	Status	—	—	10	Self
93	Psychic	Psychic	Special	90	100	10	Normal
99	Moonblast	Fairy	Special	95	100	15	Normal

TM & HM MOVES

No.	Name	Type	Kind	Pow.	Acc.	PP	Range
TM03	Psyshock	Psychic	Special	80	100	10	Normal
TM04	Calm Mind	Psychic	Status	—	—	20	Self
TM06	Toxic	Poison	Status	—	90	10	Normal
TM10	Hidden Power	Normal	Special	60	100	15	Normal
TM11	Sunny Day	Fire	Status	—	—	5	Both Sides
TM13	Ice Beam	Ice	Special	90	100	10	Normal
TM15	Hyper Beam	Normal	Special	150	90	5	Normal
TM16	Light Screen	Psychic	Status	—	—	30	Your Side
TM17	Protect	Normal	Status	—	—	10	Self
TM18	Rain Dance	Water	Status	—	—	5	Both Sides
TM20	Safeguard	Normal	Status	—	—	25	Your Side
TM21	Frustration	Normal	Physical	—	100	20	Normal
TM22	Solar Beam	Grass	Special	120	100	10	Normal
TM27	Return	Normal	Physical	—	100	20	Normal
TM29	Psychic	Psychic	Special	90	100	10	Normal
TM30	Shadow Ball	Ghost	Special	80	100	15	Normal
TM32	Double Team	Normal	Status	—	—	15	Self
TM33	Reflect	Psychic	Status	—	—	20	Your Side
TM42	Facade	Normal	Physical	70	100	20	Normal
TM44	Rest	Psychic	Status	—	—	10	Self
TM45	Attract	Normal	Status	—	100	15	Normal
TM48	Round	Normal	Special	60	100	15	Normal
TM53	Energy Ball	Grass	Special	90	100	10	Normal
TM57	Charge Beam	Electric	Special	50	90	10	Normal
TM68	Giga Impact	Normal	Physical	150	90	5	Normal
TM70	Flash	Normal	Status	—	100	20	Normal
TM73	Thunder Wave	Electric	Status	—	100	20	Normal
TM77	Psych Up	Normal	Status	—	—	10	Normal
TM85	Dream Eater	Psychic	Special	100	100	15	Normal
TM86	Grass Knot	Grass	Special	—	100	20	Normal
TM87	Swagger	Normal	Status	—	90	15	Normal
TM88	Sleep Talk	Normal	Status	—	—	10	Self
TM90	Substitute	Normal	Status	—	—	10	Self
TM92	Trick Room	Psychic	Status	—	—	5	Both Sides
TM94	Secret Power	Normal	Physical	70	100	20	Normal
TM100	Confide	Normal	Status	—	—	20	Normal

MOVES LEARNED IN EXCHANGE FOR BP

Name	Type	Kind	Pow.	Acc.	PP	Range
Signal Beam	Bug	Special	75	100	15	Normal
Magic Coat	Psychic	Status	—	—	15	Self
Gravity	Psychic	Status	—	—	5	Both Sides
Icy Wind	Ice	Special	55	95	15	Many Others
Zen Headbutt	Psychic	Physical	80	90	15	Normal
Snore	Normal	Special	50	100	15	Normal
Helping Hand	Normal	Status	—	—	20	1 Ally
Trick	Psychic	Status	—	100	10	Normal
Magic Room	Psychic	Status	—	—	10	Both Sides
Recycle	Normal	Status	—	—	10	Self
Skill Swap	Psychic	Status	—	—	10	Normal

MOVES TAUGHT BY PEOPLE

Name	Type	Kind	Pow.	Acc.	PP	Range

National Pokédex **489** Hoenn Pokédex —

Phione

Sea Drifter Pokémon

Water

HEIGHT: 1'04" WEIGHT: 6.8 lbs.

Gender unknown

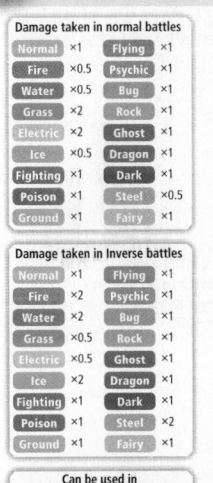

Ω When the water warms, they inflate the flotation sac on their heads and drift languidly on the sea in packs.

α It drifts in warm seas. It always returns to where it was born, no matter how far it may have drifted.

ABILITY
Hydration

HIDDEN ABILITY
—

EGG GROUPS
Water 1 / Fairy

STAT GROWTH RATES
HP, Attack, Defense, Sp. Atk, Sp. Def, Speed

ITEMS SOMETIMES HELD BY WILD POKÉMON
—

EVOLUTION

Does not evolve

MAIN WAY TO REGISTER IN THE NATIONAL POKÉDEX

Leave a Manaphy and Ditto at a Pokémon Day Care, then hatch the Pokémon Egg that is found.

Damage taken in normal battles

Type		Type	
Normal	×1	Flying	×1
Fire	×0.5	Psychic	×1
Water	×0.5	Bug	×1
Grass	×2	Rock	×1
Electric	×2	Ghost	×1
Ice	×0.5	Dragon	×1
Fighting	×1	Dark	×1
Poison	×1	Steel	×0.5
Ground	×1	Fairy	×1

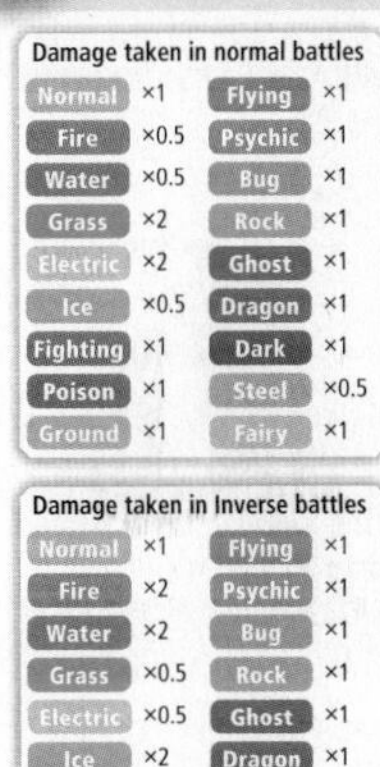

Damage taken in Inverse battles

Type		Type	
Normal	×1	Flying	×1
Fire	×2	Psychic	×1
Water	×2	Bug	×1
Grass	×0.5	Rock	×1
Electric	×0.5	Ghost	×1
Ice	×2	Dragon	×1
Fighting	×1	Dark	×1
Poison	×1	Steel	×2
Ground	×1	Fairy	×1

Can be used in

- Inverse Battle
- Battle Institute
- Battle Maison
- Random Matchup (Free Battle)
- Random Matchup (Others)

LEVEL-UP MOVES

Lv.	Name	Type	Kind	Pow.	Acc.	PP	Range
1	Bubble	Water	Special	40	100	30	Many Others
1	Water Sport	Water	Status	—	—	15	Both Sides
9	Charm	Fairy	Status	—	100	20	Normal
16	Supersonic	Normal	Status	—	55	20	Normal
24	Bubble Beam	Water	Special	65	100	20	Normal
31	Acid Armor	Poison	Status	—	—	20	Self
39	Whirlpool	Water	Special	35	85	15	Normal
46	Water Pulse	Water	Special	60	100	20	Normal
54	Aqua Ring	Water	Status	—	—	20	Self
61	Dive	Water	Physical	80	100	10	Normal
69	Rain Dance	Water	Status	—	—	5	Both Sides

TM & HM MOVES

No.	Name	Type	Kind	Pow.	Acc.	PP	Range
TM06	Toxic	Poison	Status	—	90	10	Normal
TM07	Hail	Ice	Status	—	—	10	Both Sides
TM10	Hidden Power	Normal	Special	60	100	15	Normal
TM13	Ice Beam	Ice	Special	90	100	10	Normal
TM14	Blizzard	Ice	Special	110	70	5	Many Others
TM17	Protect	Normal	Status	—	—	10	Self
TM18	Rain Dance	Water	Status	—	—	5	Both Sides
TM20	Safeguard	Normal	Status	—	—	25	Your Side
TM21	Frustration	Normal	Physical	—	100	20	Normal
TM27	Return	Normal	Physical	—	100	20	Normal
TM32	Double Team	Normal	Status	—	—	15	Self
TM42	Facade	Normal	Physical	70	100	20	Normal
TM44	Rest	Psychic	Status	—	—	10	Self
TM48	Round	Normal	Special	60	100	15	Normal
TM55	Scald	Water	Special	80	100	15	Normal
TM56	Fling	Dark	Physical	—	100	10	Normal
TM77	Psych Up	Normal	Status	—	—	10	Normal
TM86	Grass Knot	Grass	Special	—	100	20	Normal
TM87	Swagger	Normal	Status	—	90	15	Normal
TM88	Sleep Talk	Normal	Status	—	—	10	Self
TM89	U-turn	Bug	Physical	70	100	20	Normal
TM90	Substitute	Normal	Status	—	—	10	Self
TM94	Secret Power	Normal	Physical	70	100	20	Normal
TM99	Dazzling Gleam	Fairy	Special	80	100	10	Many Others
TM100	Confide	Normal	Status	—	—	20	Normal
HM03	Surf	Water	Special	90	100	15	Adjacent
HM05	Waterfall	Water	Physical	80	100	15	Normal
HM07	Dive	Water	Physical	80	100	10	Normal

MOVES LEARNED IN EXCHANGE FOR BP

Name	Type	Kind	Pow.	Acc.	PP	Range
Covet	Normal	Physical	60	100	25	Normal
Signal Beam	Bug	Special	75	100	15	Normal
Bounce	Flying	Physical	85	85	5	Normal
Uproar	Normal	Special	90	100	10	1 Random
Last Resort	Normal	Physical	140	100	5	Normal
Icy Wind	Ice	Special	55	95	15	Many Others
Snore	Normal	Special	50	100	15	Normal
Knock Off	Dark	Physical	65	100	20	Normal
Heal Bell	Normal	Status	—	—	5	Your Party
Water Pulse	Water	Special	60	100	20	Normal
Helping Hand	Normal	Status	—	—	20	1 Ally

MOVES TAUGHT BY PEOPLE

Name	Type	Kind	Pow.	Acc.	PP	Range

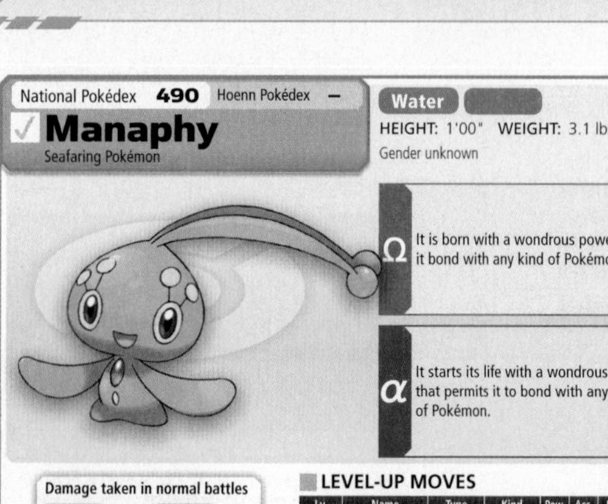

National Pokédex **490** Hoenn Pokédex —

Manaphy

Seafaring Pokémon

Water

HEIGHT: 1'00" WEIGHT: 3.1 lbs.

Gender unknown

Ω It is born with a wondrous power that lets it bond with any kind of Pokémon.

α It starts its life with a wondrous power that permits it to bond with any kind of Pokémon.

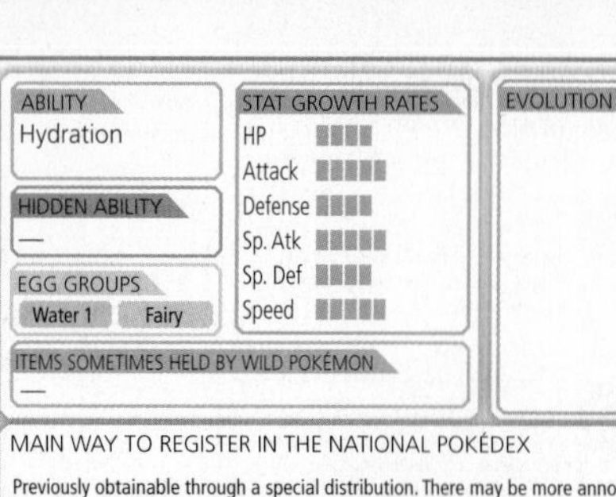

ABILITY
Hydration

HIDDEN ABILITY
—

EGG GROUPS
Water 1 | Fairy

STAT GROWTH RATES
HP
Attack
Defense
Sp. Atk
Sp. Def
Speed

ITEMS SOMETIMES HELD BY WILD POKÉMON
—

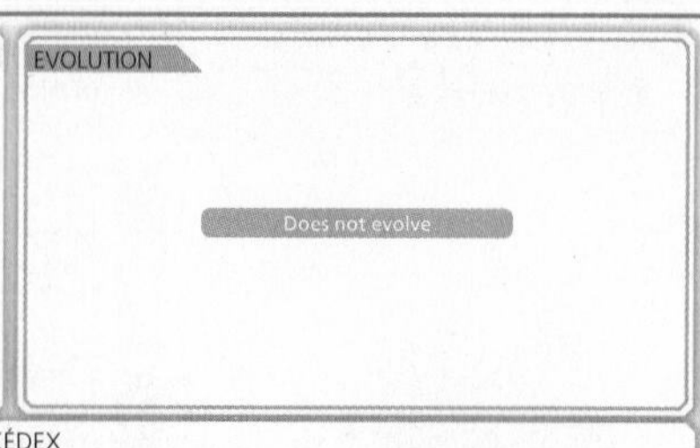

EVOLUTION
Does not evolve

MAIN WAY TO REGISTER IN THE NATIONAL POKÉDEX

Previously obtainable through a special distribution. There may be more announcements to come regarding future opportunities to obtain it, so keep checking the official Pokémon website.

Damage taken in normal battles

Type		Type	
Normal	×1	Flying	×1
Fire	×0.5	Psychic	×1
Water	×0.5	Bug	×1
Grass	×2	Rock	×1
Electric	×2	Ghost	×1
Ice	×0.5	Dragon	×1
Fighting	×1	Dark	×1
Poison	×1	Steel	×0.5
Ground	×1	Fairy	×1

Damage taken in Inverse battles

Type		Type	
Normal	×1	Flying	×1
Fire	×2	Psychic	×1
Water	×2	Bug	×1
Grass	×0.5	Rock	×1
Electric	×0.5	Ghost	×1
Ice	×2	Dragon	×1
Fighting	×1	Dark	×1
Poison	×1	Steel	×2
Ground	×1	Fairy	×1

Can be used in

Inverse Battle
Battle Institute
Battle Maison
Random Matchup (Free Battle)
Random Matchup (Others)

LEVEL-UP MOVES

Lv.	Name	Type	Kind	Pow.	Acc.	PP	Range
1	Tail Glow	Bug	Status	—	—	20	Self
1	Bubble	Water	Special	40	100	30	Many Others
1	Water Sport	Water	Status	—	—	15	Both Sides
9	Charm	Fairy	Status	—	100	20	Normal
16	Supersonic	Normal	Status	—	55	20	Normal
24	Bubble Beam	Water	Special	65	100	20	Normal
31	Acid Armor	Poison	Status	—	—	20	Self
39	Whirlpool	Water	Special	35	85	15	Normal
46	Water Pulse	Water	Special	60	100	20	Normal
54	Aqua Ring	Water	Status	—	—	20	Self
61	Dive	Water	Physical	80	100	10	Normal
69	Rain Dance	Water	Status	—	—	5	Both Sides
76	Heart Swap	Psychic	Status	—	—	10	Normal

TM & HM MOVES

No.	Name	Type	Kind	Pow.	Acc.	PP	Range
TM04	Calm Mind	Psychic	Status	—	—	20	Self
TM06	Toxic	Poison	Status	—	90	10	Normal
TM07	Hail	Ice	Status	—	—	10	Both Sides
TM10	Hidden Power	Normal	Special	60	100	15	Normal
TM13	Ice Beam	Ice	Special	90	100	10	Normal
TM14	Blizzard	Ice	Special	110	70	5	Many Others
TM15	Hyper Beam	Normal	Special	150	90	5	Normal
TM16	Light Screen	Psychic	Status	—	—	30	Your Side
TM17	Protect	Normal	Status	—	—	10	Self
TM18	Rain Dance	Water	Status	—	—	5	Both Sides
TM20	Safeguard	Normal	Status	—	—	25	Your Side
TM21	Frustration	Normal	Physical	—	100	20	Normal
TM27	Return	Normal	Physical	—	100	20	Normal
TM29	Psychic	Psychic	Special	90	100	10	Normal
TM30	Shadow Ball	Ghost	Special	80	100	15	Normal
TM32	Double Team	Normal	Status	—	—	15	Self
TM33	Reflect	Psychic	Status	—	—	20	Your Side
TM42	Facade	Normal	Physical	70	100	20	Normal
TM44	Rest	Psychic	Status	—	—	10	Self
TM48	Round	Normal	Special	60	100	15	Normal
TM53	Energy Ball	Grass	Special	90	100	10	Normal
TM55	Scald	Water	Special	80	100	15	Normal
TM56	Fling	Dark	Physical	—	100	10	Normal
TM68	Giga Impact	Normal	Physical	150	90	5	Normal
TM70	Flash	Normal	Status	—	100	20	Normal
TM77	Psych Up	Normal	Status	—	—	10	Normal
TM86	Grass Knot	Grass	Special	—	100	20	Normal
TM87	Swagger	Normal	Status	—	90	15	Normal
TM88	Sleep Talk	Normal	Status	—	—	10	Self
TM89	U-turn	Bug	Physical	70	100	20	Normal
TM90	Substitute	Normal	Status	—	—	10	Self
TM94	Secret Power	Normal	Physical	70	100	20	Normal
TM99	Dazzling Gleam	Fairy	Special	80	100	10	Many Others
TM100	Confide	Normal	Status	—	—	20	Normal
HM03	Surf	Water	Special	90	100	15	Adjacent
HM05	Waterfall	Water	Physical	80	100	15	Normal
HM07	Dive	Water	Physical	80	100	10	Normal

MOVES LEARNED IN EXCHANGE FOR BP

Name	Type	Kind	Pow.	Acc.	PP	Range
Covet	Normal	Physical	60	100	25	Normal
Signal Beam	Bug	Special	75	100	15	Normal
Bounce	Flying	Physical	85	85	5	Normal
Uproar	Normal	Special	90	100	10	1 Random
Last Resort	Normal	Physical	140	100	5	Normal
Icy Wind	Ice	Special	55	95	15	Many Others
Snore	Normal	Special	50	100	15	Normal
Knock Off	Dark	Physical	65	100	20	Normal
Heal Bell	Normal	Status	—	—	5	Your Party
Water Pulse	Water	Special	60	100	20	Normal
Helping Hand	Normal	Status	—	—	20	1 Ally
Skill Swap	Psychic	Status	—	—	10	Normal

MOVES TAUGHT BY PEOPLE

Name	Type	Kind	Pow.	Acc.	PP	Range

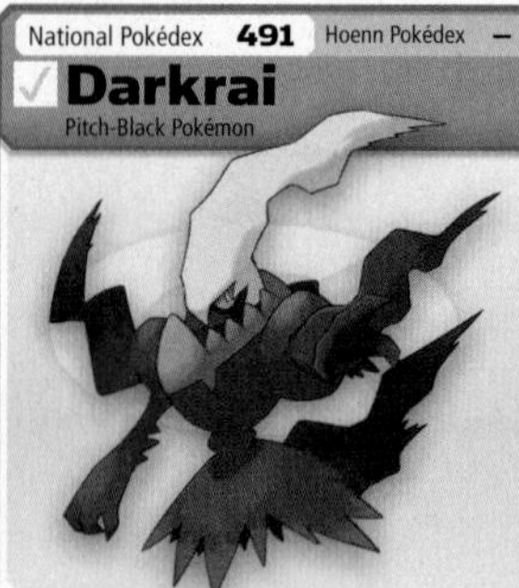

National Pokédex **491** Hoenn Pokédex —

Darkrai

Pitch-Black Pokémon

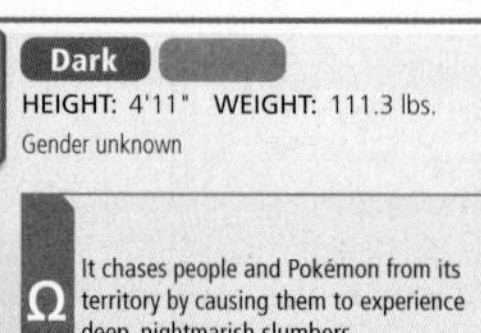

Dark

HEIGHT: 4'11" WEIGHT: 111.3 lbs.

Gender unknown

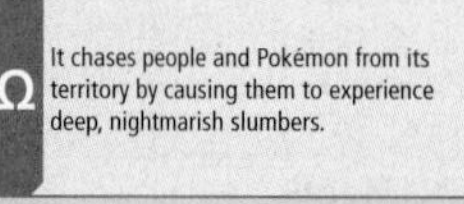

Ω It chases people and Pokémon from its territory by causing them to experience deep, nightmarish slumbers.

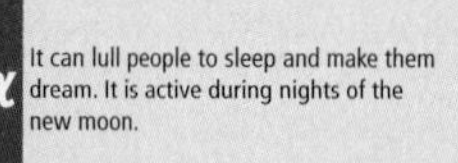

α It can lull people to sleep and make them dream. It is active during nights of the new moon.

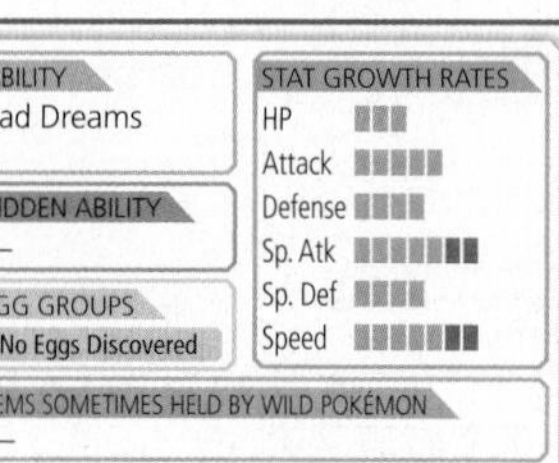

ABILITY
Bad Dreams

HIDDEN ABILITY
—

EGG GROUPS
No Eggs Discovered

STAT GROWTH RATES
HP
Attack
Defense
Sp. Atk
Sp. Def
Speed

ITEMS SOMETIMES HELD BY WILD POKÉMON
—

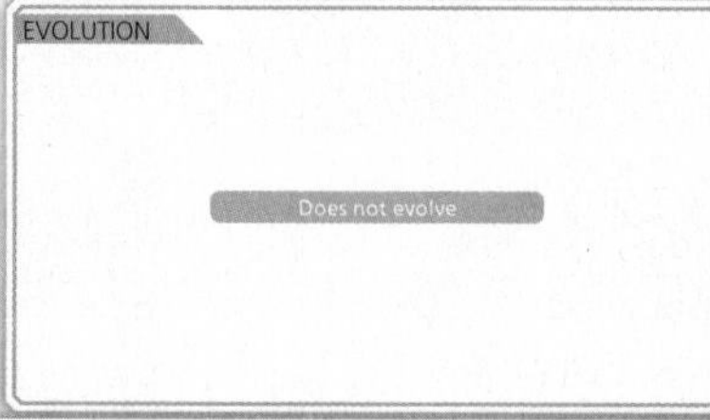

EVOLUTION
Does not evolve

MAIN WAY TO REGISTER IN THE NATIONAL POKÉDEX

Previously obtainable through a special distribution. There may be more announcements to come regarding future opportunities to obtain it, so keep checking the official Pokémon website.

Damage taken in normal battles

Type		Type	
Normal	×1	Flying	×1
Fire	×1	Psychic	×0
Water	×1	Bug	×2
Grass	×1	Rock	×1
Electric	×1	Ghost	×0.5
Ice	×1	Dragon	×1
Fighting	×2	Dark	×0.5
Poison	×1	Steel	×1
Ground	×1	Fairy	×2

Damage taken in Inverse battles

Type		Type	
Normal	×1	Flying	×1
Fire	×1	Psychic	×2
Water	×1	Bug	×0.5
Grass	×1	Rock	×1
Electric	×1	Ghost	×2
Ice	×1	Dragon	×1
Fighting	×0.5	Dark	×2
Poison	×1	Steel	×1
Ground	×1	Fairy	×0.5

Can be used in

Inverse Battle
Battle Institute
Battle Maison
Random Matchup (Free Battle)
Random Matchup (Others)

LEVEL-UP MOVES

Lv.	Name	Type	Kind	Pow.	Acc.	PP	Range
1	Ominous Wind	Ghost	Special	60	100	5	Normal
1	Disable	Normal	Status	—	100	20	Normal
11	Quick Attack	Normal	Physical	40	100	30	Normal
20	Hypnosis	Psychic	Status	—	60	20	Normal
29	Feint Attack	Dark	Physical	60	—	20	Normal
38	Nightmare	Ghost	Status	—	100	15	Normal
47	Double Team	Normal	Status	—	—	15	Self
57	Haze	Ice	Status	—	—	30	Both Sides
66	Dark Void	Dark	Status	—	80	10	Many Others
75	Nasty Plot	Dark	Status	—	—	20	Self
84	Dream Eater	Psychic	Special	100	100	15	Normal
93	Dark Pulse	Dark	Special	80	100	15	Normal

TM & HM MOVES

No.	Name	Type	Kind	Pow.	Acc.	PP	Range
TM04	Calm Mind	Psychic	Status	—	—	20	Self
TM06	Toxic	Poison	Status	—	90	10	Normal
TM10	Hidden Power	Normal	Special	60	100	15	Normal
TM11	Sunny Day	Fire	Status	—	—	5	Both Sides
TM12	Taunt	Dark	Status	—	100	20	Normal
TM13	Ice Beam	Ice	Special	90	100	10	Normal
TM14	Blizzard	Ice	Special	110	70	5	Many Others
TM15	Hyper Beam	Normal	Special	150	90	5	Normal
TM17	Protect	Normal	Status	—	—	10	Self
TM18	Rain Dance	Water	Status	—	—	5	Both Sides
TM21	Frustration	Normal	Physical	—	100	20	Normal
TM24	Thunderbolt	Electric	Special	90	100	15	Normal
TM25	Thunder	Electric	Special	110	70	10	Normal
TM27	Return	Normal	Physical	—	100	20	Normal
TM29	Psychic	Psychic	Special	90	100	10	Normal
TM30	Shadow Ball	Ghost	Special	80	100	15	Normal
TM31	Brick Break	Fighting	Physical	75	100	15	Normal
TM32	Double Team	Normal	Status	—	—	15	Self
TM36	Sludge Bomb	Poison	Special	90	100	10	Normal
TM39	Rock Tomb	Rock	Physical	60	95	15	Normal
TM40	Aerial Ace	Flying	Physical	60	—	20	Normal
TM41	Torment	Dark	Status	—	100	15	Normal
TM42	Facade	Normal	Physical	70	100	20	Normal
TM44	Rest	Psychic	Status	—	—	10	Self
TM46	Thief	Dark	Physical	60	100	25	Normal
TM48	Round	Normal	Special	60	100	15	Normal
TM52	Focus Blast	Fighting	Special	120	70	5	Normal
TM56	Fling	Dark	Physical	—	100	10	Normal
TM57	Charge Beam	Electric	Special	50	90	10	Normal
TM59	Incinerate	Fire	Special	60	100	15	Many Others
TM61	Will-O-Wisp	Fire	Status	—	85	15	Normal
TM63	Embargo	Dark	Status	—	100	15	Normal
TM65	Shadow Claw	Ghost	Physical	70	100	15	Normal
TM66	Payback	Dark	Physical	50	100	10	Normal
TM67	Retaliate	Normal	Physical	70	100	5	Normal
TM68	Giga Impact	Normal	Physical	150	90	5	Normal
TM70	Flash	Normal	Status	—	100	20	Normal
TM73	Thunder Wave	Electric	Status	—	100	20	Normal
TM75	Swords Dance	Normal	Status	—	—	20	Self
TM77	Psych Up	Normal	Status	—	—	10	Normal
TM80	Rock Slide	Rock	Physical	75	90	10	Many Others
TM81	X-Scissor	Bug	Physical	80	100	15	Normal
TM84	Poison Jab	Poison	Physical	80	100	20	Normal
TM85	Dream Eater	Psychic	Special	100	100	15	Normal
TM87	Swagger	Normal	Status	—	90	15	Normal
TM88	Sleep Talk	Normal	Status	—	—	10	Self
TM90	Substitute	Normal	Status	—	—	10	Self
TM94	Secret Power	Normal	Physical	70	100	20	Normal
TM95	Snarl	Dark	Special	55	95	15	Many Others
TM97	Dark Pulse	Dark	Special	80	100	15	Normal
TM98	Power-Up Punch	Fighting	Physical	40	100	20	Normal
TM100	Confide	Normal	Status	—	—	20	Normal
HM01	Cut	Normal	Physical	50	95	30	Normal
HM04	Strength	Normal	Physical	80	100	15	Normal
HM06	Rock Smash	Fighting	Physical	40	100	15	Normal

MOVES LEARNED IN EXCHANGE FOR BP

Name	Type	Kind	Pow.	Acc.	PP	Range
Foul Play	Dark	Physical	95	100	15	Normal
Last Resort	Normal	Physical	140	100	5	Normal
Icy Wind	Ice	Special	55	95	15	Many Others
Snore	Normal	Special	50	100	15	Normal
Knock Off	Dark	Physical	65	100	20	Normal
Drain Punch	Fighting	Physical	75	100	10	Normal
Focus Punch	Fighting	Physical	150	100	20	Normal
Shock Wave	Electric	Special	60	—	20	Normal
Spite	Ghost	Status	—	100	10	Normal
Trick	Psychic	Status	—	100	10	Normal
Wonder Room	Psychic	Status	—	—	10	Both Sides
Snatch	Dark	Status	—	—	10	Self

MOVES TAUGHT BY PEOPLE

Name	Type	Kind	Pow.	Acc.	PP	Range

National Pokédex 492 Hoenn Pokédex —

Shaymin Land Forme

Gratitude Pokémon

Grass

HEIGHT: 0'08" WEIGHT: 4.6 lbs.

Gender unknown

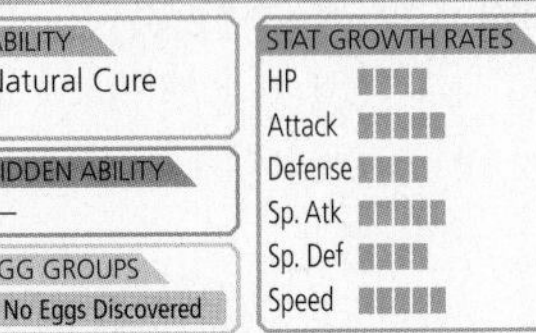

Ω It can dissolve toxins in the air to instantly transform ruined land into a lush field of flowers.

α The blooming of Gracidea flowers confers the power of flight upon it. Feelings of gratitude are the message it delivers.

ABILITY: Natural Cure

HIDDEN ABILITY: —

EGG GROUPS: No Eggs Discovered

STAT GROWTH RATES: HP, Attack, Defense, Sp. Atk, Sp. Def, Speed

ITEMS SOMETIMES HELD BY WILD POKÉMON: —

EVOLUTION: Does not evolve

MAIN WAY TO REGISTER IN THE NATIONAL POKÉDEX

Previously obtainable through a special distribution. There may be more announcements to come regarding future opportunities to obtain it, so keep checking the official Pokémon website.

Damage taken in normal battles

Type		Type	
Normal	×1	Flying	×2
Fire	×2	Psychic	×1
Water	×0.5	Bug	×2
Grass	×0.5	Rock	×1
Electric	×0.5	Ghost	×1
Ice	×2	Dragon	×1
Fighting	×1	Dark	×1
Poison	×2	Steel	×1
Ground	×0.5	Fairy	×1

Damage taken in Inverse battles

Type		Type	
Normal	×1	Flying	×0.5
Fire	×0.5	Psychic	×1
Water	×2	Bug	×0.5
Grass	×2	Rock	×1
Electric	×2	Ghost	×1
Ice	×0.5	Dragon	×1
Fighting	×1	Dark	×1
Poison	×0.5	Steel	×1
Ground	×2	Fairy	×1

Can be used in

Inverse Battle
Battle Institute
Battle Maison
Random Matchup (Free Battle)
Random Matchup (Others)

LEVEL-UP MOVES

Lv.	Name	Type	Kind	Pow.	Acc.	PP	Range
1	Growth	Normal	Status	—	—	20	Self
10	Magical Leaf	Grass	Special	60	—	20	Normal
19	Leech Seed	Grass	Status	—	90	10	Normal
28	Synthesis	Grass	Status	—	—	5	Self
37	Sweet Scent	Normal	Status	—	100	20	Many Others
46	Natural Gift	Normal	Physical	—	100	15	Normal
55	Worry Seed	Grass	Status	—	100	10	Normal
64	Aromatherapy	Grass	Status	—	—	5	Your Party
73	Energy Ball	Grass	Special	90	100	10	Normal
82	Sweet Kiss	Fairy	Status	—	75	10	Normal
91	Healing Wish	Psychic	Status	—	—	10	Self
100	Seed Flare	Grass	Special	120	85	5	Normal

TM & HM MOVES

No.	Name	Type	Kind	Pow.	Acc.	PP	Range
TM06	Toxic	Poison	Status	—	90	10	Normal
TM10	Hidden Power	Normal	Special	60	100	15	Normal
TM11	Sunny Day	Fire	Status	—	—	5	Both Sides
TM15	Hyper Beam	Normal	Special	150	90	5	Normal
TM17	Protect	Normal	Status	—	—	10	Self
TM20	Safeguard	Normal	Status	—	—	25	Your Side
TM21	Frustration	Normal	Physical	—	100	20	Normal
TM22	Solar Beam	Grass	Special	120	100	10	Normal
TM27	Return	Normal	Physical	—	100	20	Normal
TM29	Psychic	Psychic	Special	90	100	10	Normal
TM32	Double Team	Normal	Status	—	—	15	Self
TM42	Facade	Normal	Physical	70	100	20	Normal
TM44	Rest	Psychic	Status	—	—	10	Self
TM48	Round	Normal	Special	60	100	15	Normal
TM53	Energy Ball	Grass	Special	90	100	10	Normal
TM68	Giga Impact	Normal	Physical	150	90	5	Normal
TM70	Flash	Normal	Status	—	100	20	Normal
TM75	Swords Dance	Normal	Status	—	—	20	Self
TM77	Psych Up	Normal	Status	—	—	10	Normal
TM86	Grass Knot	Grass	Special	—	100	20	Normal
TM87	Swagger	Normal	Status	—	90	15	Normal
TM88	Sleep Talk	Normal	Status	—	—	10	Self
TM90	Substitute	Normal	Status	—	—	10	Self
TM94	Secret Power	Normal	Physical	70	100	20	Normal
TM96	Nature Power	Normal	Status	—	—	20	Normal
TM99	Dazzling Gleam	Fairy	Special	80	100	10	Many Others
TM100	Confide	Normal	Status	—	—	20	Normal

MOVES LEARNED IN EXCHANGE FOR BP

Name	Type	Kind	Pow.	Acc.	PP	Range
Covet	Normal	Physical	60	100	25	Normal
Seed Bomb	Grass	Physical	80	100	15	Normal
Earth Power	Ground	Special	90	100	10	Normal
Last Resort	Normal	Physical	140	100	5	Normal
Zen Headbutt	Psychic	Physical	80	90	15	Normal
Snore	Normal	Special	50	100	15	Normal
Synthesis	Grass	Status	—	—	5	Self
Giga Drain	Grass	Special	75	100	10	Normal
Worry Seed	Grass	Status	—	100	10	Normal
Endeavor	Normal	Physical	—	100	5	Normal

MOVES TAUGHT BY PEOPLE

Name	Type	Kind	Pow.	Acc.	PP	Range

◆ Several conditions will make Shaymin (Sky Forme) change back to its Land Forme: depositing it in your PC, leaving it at a Pokémon Day Care, using Link Trade or the GTS, changing from day to night or late night, or afflicting it with the Frozen status condition.

National Pokédex 492 Hoenn Pokédex —

Shaymin Sky Forme

Gratitude Pokémon

Grass Flying

HEIGHT: 1'04" WEIGHT: 11.5 lbs.

Gender unknown

Ω It can dissolve toxins in the air to instantly transform ruined land into a lush field of flowers.

α The blooming of Gracidea flowers confers the power of flight upon it. Feelings of gratitude are the message it delivers.

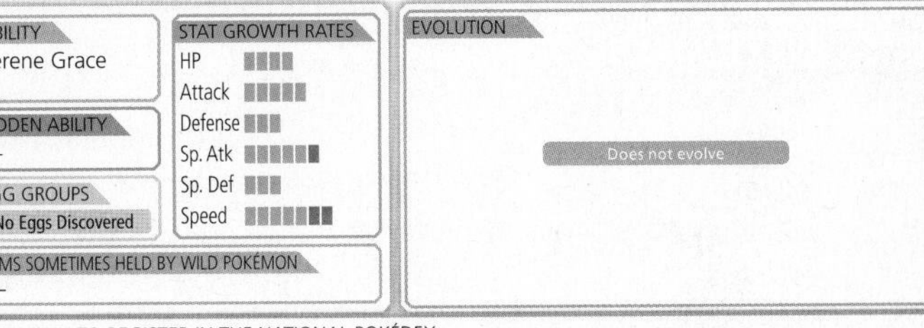

ABILITY: Serene Grace

HIDDEN ABILITY: —

EGG GROUPS: No Eggs Discovered

STAT GROWTH RATES: HP, Attack, Defense, Sp. Atk, Sp. Def, Speed

ITEMS SOMETIMES HELD BY WILD POKÉMON: —

EVOLUTION: Does not evolve

MAIN WAY TO REGISTER IN THE NATIONAL POKÉDEX

Use the Gracidea flower on Shaymin (Land Forme). The Gracidea flower can only be used between 4:00 A.M. and 7:59 P.M.

Damage taken in normal battles

Type		Type	
Normal	×1	Flying	×2
Fire	×2	Psychic	×1
Water	×0.5	Bug	×1
Grass	×0.25	Rock	×2
Electric	×1	Ghost	×1
Ice	×4	Dragon	×1
Fighting	×0.5	Dark	×1
Poison	×2	Steel	×1
Ground	×0	Fairy	×1

Damage taken in Inverse battles

Type		Type	
Normal	×1	Flying	×0.5
Fire	×0.5	Psychic	×1
Water	×2	Bug	×1
Grass	×4	Rock	×0.5
Electric	×1	Ghost	×1
Ice	×0.25	Dragon	×1
Fighting	×2	Dark	×1
Poison	×0.5	Steel	×1
Ground	×4	Fairy	×1

Can be used in

Inverse Battle
Battle Institute
Battle Maison
Random Matchup (Free Battle)
Random Matchup (Others)

LEVEL-UP MOVES

Lv.	Name	Type	Kind	Pow.	Acc.	PP	Range
1	Growth	Normal	Status	—	—	20	Self
10	Magical Leaf	Grass	Special	60	—	20	Normal
19	Leech Seed	Grass	Status	—	90	10	Normal
28	Quick Attack	Normal	Physical	40	100	30	Normal
37	Sweet Scent	Normal	Status	—	100	20	Many Others
46	Natural Gift	Normal	Physical	—	100	15	Normal
55	Worry Seed	Grass	Status	—	100	10	Normal
64	Air Slash	Flying	Special	75	95	15	Normal
73	Energy Ball	Grass	Special	90	100	10	Normal
82	Sweet Kiss	Fairy	Status	—	75	10	Normal
91	Leaf Storm	Grass	Special	130	90	5	Normal
100	Seed Flare	Grass	Special	120	85	5	Normal

TM & HM MOVES

No.	Name	Type	Kind	Pow.	Acc.	PP	Range
TM06	Toxic	Poison	Status	—	90	10	Normal
TM10	Hidden Power	Normal	Special	60	100	15	Normal
TM11	Sunny Day	Fire	Status	—	—	5	Both Sides
TM15	Hyper Beam	Normal	Special	150	90	5	Normal
TM17	Protect	Normal	Status	—	—	10	Self
TM20	Safeguard	Normal	Status	—	—	25	Your Side
TM21	Frustration	Normal	Physical	—	100	20	Normal
TM22	Solar Beam	Grass	Special	120	100	10	Normal
TM27	Return	Normal	Physical	—	100	20	Normal
TM29	Psychic	Psychic	Special	90	100	10	Normal
TM32	Double Team	Normal	Status	—	—	15	Self
TM42	Facade	Normal	Physical	70	100	20	Normal
TM44	Rest	Psychic	Status	—	—	10	Self
TM48	Round	Normal	Special	60	100	15	Normal
TM53	Energy Ball	Grass	Special	90	100	10	Normal
TM68	Giga Impact	Normal	Physical	150	90	5	Normal
TM70	Flash	Normal	Status	—	100	20	Normal
TM75	Swords Dance	Normal	Status	—	—	20	Self
TM77	Psych Up	Normal	Status	—	—	10	Normal
TM86	Grass Knot	Grass	Special	—	100	20	Normal
TM87	Swagger	Normal	Status	—	90	15	Normal
TM88	Sleep Talk	Normal	Status	—	—	10	Self
TM90	Substitute	Normal	Status	—	—	10	Self
TM94	Secret Power	Normal	Physical	70	100	20	Normal
TM96	Nature Power	Normal	Status	—	—	20	Normal
TM99	Dazzling Gleam	Fairy	Special	80	100	10	Many Others
TM100	Confide	Normal	Status	—	—	20	Normal

MOVES LEARNED IN EXCHANGE FOR BP

Name	Type	Kind	Pow.	Acc.	PP	Range
Covet	Normal	Physical	60	100	25	Normal
Seed Bomb	Grass	Physical	80	100	15	Normal
Last Resort	Normal	Physical	140	100	5	Normal
Zen Headbutt	Psychic	Physical	80	90	15	Normal
Snore	Normal	Special	50	100	15	Normal
Synthesis	Grass	Status	—	—	5	Self
Tailwind	Flying	Status	—	—	15	Your Side
Giga Drain	Grass	Special	75	100	10	Normal
Worry Seed	Grass	Status	—	100	10	Normal

MOVES TAUGHT BY PEOPLE

Name	Type	Kind	Pow.	Acc.	PP	Range

National Pokédex **493** Hoenn Pokédex —

Arceus

Alpha Pokémon

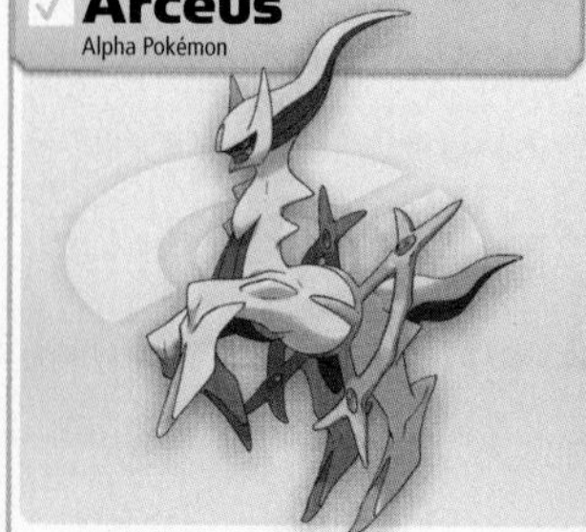

Normal

HEIGHT: 10'06" WEIGHT: 705.5 lbs.

Gender unknown

Ω According to the legends of Sinnoh, this Pokémon emerged from an egg and shaped all there is in this world.

α It is told in mythology that this Pokémon was born before the universe even existed.

ABILITY
Multitype

HIDDEN ABILITY
—

EGG GROUPS
No Eggs Discovered

STAT GROWTH RATES
HP
Attack
Defense
Sp. Atk
Sp. Def
Speed

ITEMS SOMETIMES HELD BY WILD POKÉMON
—

EVOLUTION
Does not evolve

MAIN WAY TO REGISTER IN THE NATIONAL POKÉDEX

Previously obtainable through a special distribution. There may be more announcements to come regarding future opportunities to obtain it, so keep checking the official Pokémon website.

Damage taken in normal battles

Normal	×1	Flying	×1
Fire	×1	Psychic	×1
Water	×1	Bug	×1
Grass	×1	Rock	×1
Electric	×1	Ghost	×0
Ice	×1	Dragon	×1
Fighting	×2	Dark	×1
Poison	×1	Steel	×1
Ground	×1	Fairy	×1

Damage taken in Inverse battles

Normal	×1	Flying	×1
Fire	×1	Psychic	×1
Water	×1	Bug	×1
Grass	×1	Rock	×1
Electric	×1	Ghost	×2
Ice	×1	Dragon	×1
Fighting	×0.5	Dark	×1
Poison	×1	Steel	×1
Ground	×1	Fairy	×1

Can be used in
Inverse Battle
Battle Institute
Battle Maison
Random Matchup (Free Battle)
Random Matchup (Others)

LEVEL-UP MOVES

Lv.	Name	Type	Kind	Pow.	Acc.	PP	Range
1	Seismic Toss	Fighting	Physical	—	100	20	Normal
1	Cosmic Power	Psychic	Status	—	—	20	Self
1	Natural Gift	Normal	Physical	—	100	15	Normal
1	Punishment	Dark	Physical	—	100	5	Normal
10	Gravity	Psychic	Status	—	—	5	Both Sides
20	Earth Power	Ground	Special	90	100	10	Normal
30	Hyper Voice	Normal	Special	90	100	10	Many Others
40	Extreme Speed	Normal	Physical	80	100	5	Normal
50	Refresh	Normal	Status	—	—	20	Self
60	Future Sight	Psychic	Special	120	100	10	Normal
70	Recover	Normal	Status	—	—	10	Self
80	Hyper Beam	Normal	Special	150	90	5	Normal
90	Perish Song	Normal	Status	—	—	5	Adjacent
100	Judgment	Normal	Special	100	100	10	Normal

TM & HM MOVES

No.	Name	Type	Kind	Pow.	Acc.	PP	Range
TM01	Hone Claws	Dark	Status	—	—	15	Self
TM02	Dragon Claw	Dragon	Physical	80	100	15	Normal
TM03	Psyshock	Psychic	Special	80	100	10	Normal
TM04	Calm Mind	Psychic	Status	—	—	20	Self
TM05	Roar	Normal	Status	—	—	20	Normal
TM06	Toxic	Poison	Status	—	90	10	Normal
TM07	Hail	Ice	Status	—	—	10	Both Sides
TM10	Hidden Power	Normal	Special	60	100	15	Normal
TM11	Sunny Day	Fire	Status	—	—	5	Both Sides
TM13	Ice Beam	Ice	Special	90	100	10	Normal
TM14	Blizzard	Ice	Special	110	70	5	Many Others
TM15	Hyper Beam	Normal	Special	150	90	5	Normal
TM16	Light Screen	Psychic	Status	—	—	30	Your Side
TM17	Protect	Normal	Status	—	—	10	Self
TM18	Rain Dance	Water	Status	—	—	5	Both Sides
TM20	Safeguard	Normal	Status	—	—	25	Your Side
TM21	Frustration	Normal	Physical	—	100	20	Normal
TM22	Solar Beam	Grass	Special	120	100	10	Normal
TM24	Thunderbolt	Electric	Special	90	100	15	Normal
TM25	Thunder	Electric	Special	110	70	10	Normal
TM26	Earthquake	Ground	Physical	100	100	10	Adjacent
TM27	Return	Normal	Physical	—	100	20	Normal
TM29	Psychic	Psychic	Special	90	100	10	Normal
TM30	Shadow Ball	Ghost	Special	80	100	15	Normal
TM31	Brick Break	Fighting	Physical	75	100	15	Normal
TM32	Double Team	Normal	Status	—	—	15	Self
TM33	Reflect	Psychic	Status	—	—	20	Your Side
TM35	Flamethrower	Fire	Special	90	100	15	Normal
TM36	Sludge Bomb	Poison	Special	90	100	10	Normal
TM37	Sandstorm	Rock	Status	—	—	10	Both Sides
TM38	Fire Blast	Fire	Special	110	85	5	Normal
TM39	Rock Tomb	Rock	Physical	60	95	15	Normal
TM40	Aerial Ace	Flying	Physical	60	—	20	Normal
TM42	Facade	Normal	Physical	70	100	20	Normal
TM44	Rest	Psychic	Status	—	—	10	Self
TM48	Round	Normal	Special	60	100	15	Normal
TM49	Echoed Voice	Normal	Special	40	100	15	Normal
TM50	Overheat	Fire	Special	130	90	5	Normal
TM52	Focus Blast	Fighting	Special	120	70	5	Normal
TM53	Energy Ball	Grass	Special	90	100	10	Normal
TM57	Charge Beam	Electric	Special	50	90	10	Normal
TM59	Incinerate	Fire	Special	60	100	15	Many Others
TM60	Quash	Dark	Status	—	100	15	Normal
TM61	Will-O-Wisp	Fire	Status	—	85	15	Normal
TM65	Shadow Claw	Ghost	Physical	70	100	15	Normal
TM66	Payback	Dark	Physical	50	100	10	Normal
TM67	Retaliate	Normal	Physical	70	100	5	Normal
TM68	Giga Impact	Normal	Physical	150	90	5	Normal
TM70	Flash	Normal	Status	—	100	20	Normal
TM71	Stone Edge	Rock	Physical	100	80	5	Normal
TM73	Thunder Wave	Electric	Status	—	100	20	Normal
TM75	Swords Dance	Normal	Status	—	—	20	Self
TM77	Psych Up	Normal	Status	—	—	10	Normal
TM78	Bulldoze	Ground	Physical	60	100	20	Adjacent
TM80	Rock Slide	Rock	Physical	75	90	10	Many Others
TM81	X-Scissor	Bug	Physical	80	100	15	Normal
TM84	Poison Jab	Poison	Physical	80	100	20	Normal
TM85	Dream Eater	Psychic	Special	100	100	15	Normal
TM86	Grass Knot	Grass	Special	—	100	20	Normal
TM87	Swagger	Normal	Status	—	90	15	Normal
TM88	Sleep Talk	Normal	Status	—	—	10	Self
TM90	Substitute	Normal	Status	—	—	10	Self
TM91	Flash Cannon	Steel	Special	80	100	10	Normal
TM92	Trick Room	Psychic	Status	—	—	5	Both Sides
TM94	Secret Power	Normal	Physical	70	100	20	Normal
TM95	Snarl	Dark	Special	55	95	15	Many Others
TM97	Dark Pulse	Dark	Special	80	100	15	Normal
TM100	Confide	Normal	Status	—	—	20	Normal
HM01	Cut	Normal	Physical	50	95	30	Normal
HM02	Fly	Flying	Physical	90	95	15	Normal
HM03	Surf	Water	Special	90	100	15	Adjacent
HM04	Strength	Normal	Physical	80	100	15	Normal
HM05	Waterfall	Water	Physical	80	100	15	Normal
HM06	Rock Smash	Fighting	Physical	40	100	15	Normal
HM07	Dive	Water	Physical	80	100	10	Normal

MOVES LEARNED IN EXCHANGE FOR BP

Name	Type	Kind	Pow.	Acc.	PP	Range
Signal Beam	Bug	Special	75	100	15	Normal
Iron Head	Steel	Physical	80	100	15	Normal
Magic Coat	Psychic	Status	—	—	15	Self
Earth Power	Ground	Special	90	100	10	Normal
Gravity	Psychic	Status	—	—	5	Both Sides
Iron Defense	Steel	Status	—	—	15	Self
Last Resort	Normal	Physical	140	100	5	Normal
Icy Wind	Ice	Special	55	95	15	Many Others
Aqua Tail	Water	Physical	90	90	10	Normal
Zen Headbutt	Psychic	Physical	80	90	15	Normal
Dragon Pulse	Dragon	Special	85	100	10	Normal
Hyper Voice	Normal	Special	90	100	10	Many Others
Iron Tail	Steel	Physical	100	75	15	Normal
Snore	Normal	Special	50	100	15	Normal
Heat Wave	Fire	Special	95	90	10	Many Others
Tailwind	Flying	Status	—	—	15	Your Side
Giga Drain	Grass	Special	75	100	10	Normal
Shock Wave	Electric	Special	60	—	20	Normal
Water Pulse	Water	Special	60	100	20	Normal
Trick	Psychic	Status	—	100	10	Normal
Outrage	Dragon	Physical	120	100	10	1 Random
Recycle	Normal	Status	—	—	10	Self
Stealth Rock	Rock	Status	—	—	20	Other Side

MOVES TAUGHT BY PEOPLE

Name	Type	Kind	Pow.	Acc.	PP	Range
◆Draco Meteor	Dragon	Special	130	90	5	Normal

◆ Holding one of 17 plates will shift Arceus's type. Arceus can learn the move Draco Meteor when it has a Draco Plate and is very friendly toward you.

National Pokédex **494** Hoenn Pokédex —

Victini

Victory Pokémon

Psychic Fire

HEIGHT: 1'04" WEIGHT: 8.8 lbs.

Gender unknown

Ω This Pokémon brings victory. It is said that Trainers with Victini always win, regardless of the type of encounter.

α When it shares the infinite energy it creates, that being's entire body will be overflowing with power.

ABILITY
Victory Star

HIDDEN ABILITY
—

EGG GROUPS
No Eggs Discovered

STAT GROWTH RATES
HP
Attack
Defense
Sp. Atk
Sp. Def
Speed

ITEMS SOMETIMES HELD BY WILD POKÉMON
—

EVOLUTION
Does not evolve

MAIN WAY TO REGISTER IN THE NATIONAL POKÉDEX

Previously obtainable through a special distribution. There may be more announcements to come regarding future opportunities to obtain it, so keep checking the official Pokémon website.

Damage taken in normal battles

Normal	×1	Flying	×1
Fire	×0.5	Psychic	×0.5
Water	×2	Bug	×1
Grass	×0.5	Rock	×2
Electric	×1	Ghost	×2
Ice	×0.5	Dragon	×1
Fighting	×0.5	Dark	×2
Poison	×1	Steel	×0.5
Ground	×2	Fairy	×0.5

Damage taken in Inverse battles

Normal	×1	Flying	×1
Fire	×2	Psychic	×2
Water	×0.5	Bug	×1
Grass	×2	Rock	×0.5
Electric	×1	Ghost	×0.5
Ice	×2	Dragon	×1
Fighting	×2	Dark	×0.5
Poison	×1	Steel	×2
Ground	×0.5	Fairy	×2

Can be used in
Inverse Battle
Battle Institute
Battle Maison
Random Matchup (Free Battle)
Random Matchup (Others)

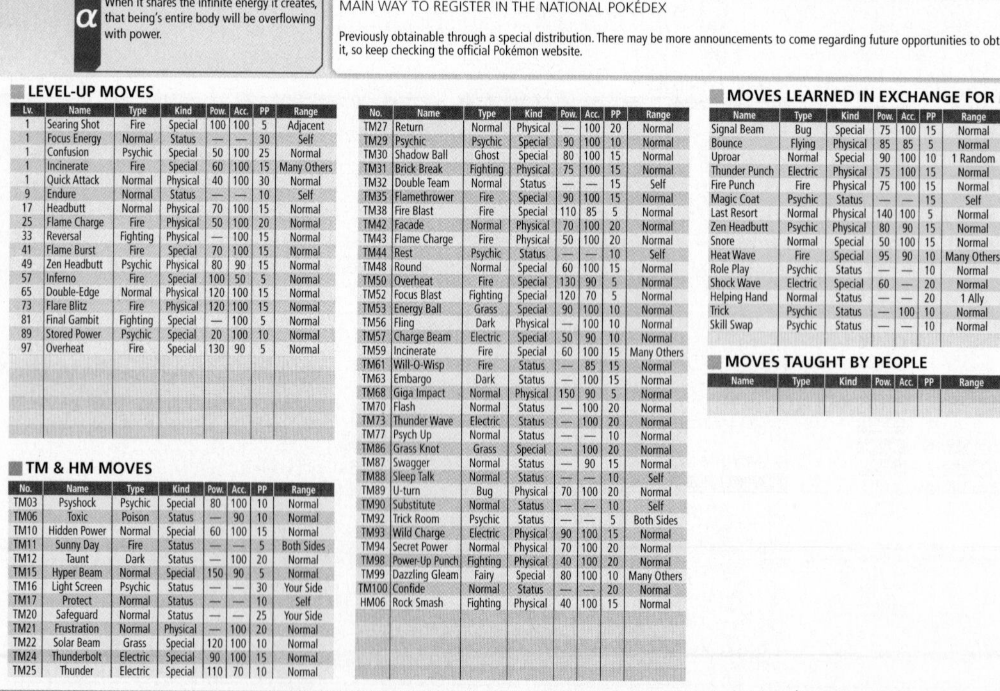

LEVEL-UP MOVES

Lv.	Name	Type	Kind	Pow.	Acc.	PP	Range
1	Searing Shot	Fire	Special	100	100	5	Adjacent
1	Focus Energy	Normal	Status	—	—	30	Self
1	Confusion	Psychic	Special	50	100	25	Normal
1	Incinerate	Fire	Special	60	100	15	Many Others
1	Quick Attack	Normal	Physical	40	100	30	Normal
9	Endure	Normal	Status	—	—	10	Self
17	Headbutt	Normal	Physical	70	100	15	Normal
25	Flame Charge	Fire	Physical	50	100	20	Normal
33	Reversal	Fighting	Physical	—	100	15	Normal
41	Flame Burst	Fire	Special	70	100	15	Normal
49	Zen Headbutt	Psychic	Physical	80	90	15	Normal
57	Inferno	Fire	Special	100	50	5	Normal
65	Double-Edge	Normal	Physical	120	100	15	Normal
73	Flare Blitz	Fire	Physical	120	100	15	Normal
81	Final Gambit	Fighting	Special	—	100	5	Normal
89	Stored Power	Psychic	Special	20	100	10	Normal
97	Overheat	Fire	Special	130	90	5	Normal

TM & HM MOVES

No.	Name	Type	Kind	Pow.	Acc.	PP	Range
TM03	Psyshock	Psychic	Special	80	100	10	Normal
TM06	Toxic	Poison	Status	—	90	10	Normal
TM10	Hidden Power	Normal	Special	60	100	15	Normal
TM11	Sunny Day	Fire	Status	—	—	5	Both Sides
TM12	Taunt	Dark	Status	—	100	20	Normal
TM15	Hyper Beam	Normal	Special	150	90	5	Normal
TM16	Light Screen	Psychic	Status	—	—	30	Your Side
TM17	Protect	Normal	Status	—	—	10	Self
TM20	Safeguard	Normal	Status	—	—	25	Your Side
TM21	Frustration	Normal	Physical	—	100	20	Normal
TM22	Solar Beam	Grass	Special	120	100	10	Normal
TM24	Thunderbolt	Electric	Special	90	100	15	Normal
TM25	Thunder	Electric	Special	110	70	10	Normal
TM27	Return	Normal	Physical	—	100	20	Normal
TM29	Psychic	Psychic	Special	90	100	10	Normal
TM30	Shadow Ball	Ghost	Special	80	100	15	Normal
TM31	Brick Break	Fighting	Physical	75	100	15	Normal
TM32	Double Team	Normal	Status	—	—	15	Self
TM35	Flamethrower	Fire	Special	90	100	15	Normal
TM38	Fire Blast	Fire	Special	110	85	5	Normal
TM42	Facade	Normal	Physical	70	100	20	Normal
TM43	Flame Charge	Fire	Physical	50	100	20	Normal
TM44	Rest	Psychic	Status	—	—	10	Self
TM48	Round	Normal	Special	60	100	15	Normal
TM50	Overheat	Fire	Special	130	90	5	Normal
TM52	Focus Blast	Fighting	Special	120	70	5	Normal
TM53	Energy Ball	Grass	Special	90	100	10	Normal
TM56	Fling	Dark	Physical	—	100	10	Normal
TM57	Charge Beam	Electric	Special	50	90	10	Normal
TM59	Incinerate	Fire	Special	60	100	15	Many Others
TM61	Will-O-Wisp	Fire	Status	—	85	15	Normal
TM63	Embargo	Dark	Status	—	100	15	Normal
TM68	Giga Impact	Normal	Physical	150	90	5	Normal
TM70	Flash	Normal	Status	—	100	20	Normal
TM73	Thunder Wave	Electric	Status	—	100	20	Normal
TM77	Psych Up	Normal	Status	—	—	10	Normal
TM86	Grass Knot	Grass	Special	—	100	20	Normal
TM87	Swagger	Normal	Status	—	90	15	Normal
TM88	Sleep Talk	Normal	Status	—	—	10	Self
TM89	U-turn	Bug	Physical	70	100	20	Normal
TM90	Substitute	Normal	Status	—	—	10	Self
TM92	Trick Room	Psychic	Status	—	—	5	Both Sides
TM93	Wild Charge	Electric	Physical	90	100	15	Normal
TM94	Secret Power	Normal	Physical	70	100	20	Normal
TM98	Power-Up Punch	Fighting	Physical	40	100	20	Normal
TM99	Dazzling Gleam	Fairy	Special	80	100	10	Many Others
TM100	Confide	Normal	Status	—	—	20	Normal
HM06	Rock Smash	Fighting	Physical	40	100	15	Normal

MOVES LEARNED IN EXCHANGE FOR BP

Name	Type	Kind	Pow.	Acc.	PP	Range
Signal Beam	Bug	Special	75	100	15	Normal
Bounce	Flying	Physical	85	85	5	Normal
Uproar	Normal	Special	90	100	10	1 Random
Thunder Punch	Electric	Physical	75	100	15	Normal
Fire Punch	Fire	Physical	75	100	15	Normal
Magic Coat	Psychic	Status	—	—	15	Self
Last Resort	Normal	Physical	140	100	5	Normal
Zen Headbutt	Psychic	Physical	80	90	15	Normal
Snore	Normal	Special	50	100	15	Normal
Heat Wave	Fire	Special	95	90	10	Many Others
Role Play	Psychic	Status	—	—	10	Normal
Shock Wave	Electric	Special	60	—	20	Normal
Helping Hand	Normal	Status	—	—	20	1 Ally
Trick	Psychic	Status	—	100	10	Normal
Skill Swap	Psychic	Status	—	—	10	Normal

MOVES TAUGHT BY PEOPLE

Name	Type	Kind	Pow.	Acc.	PP	Range

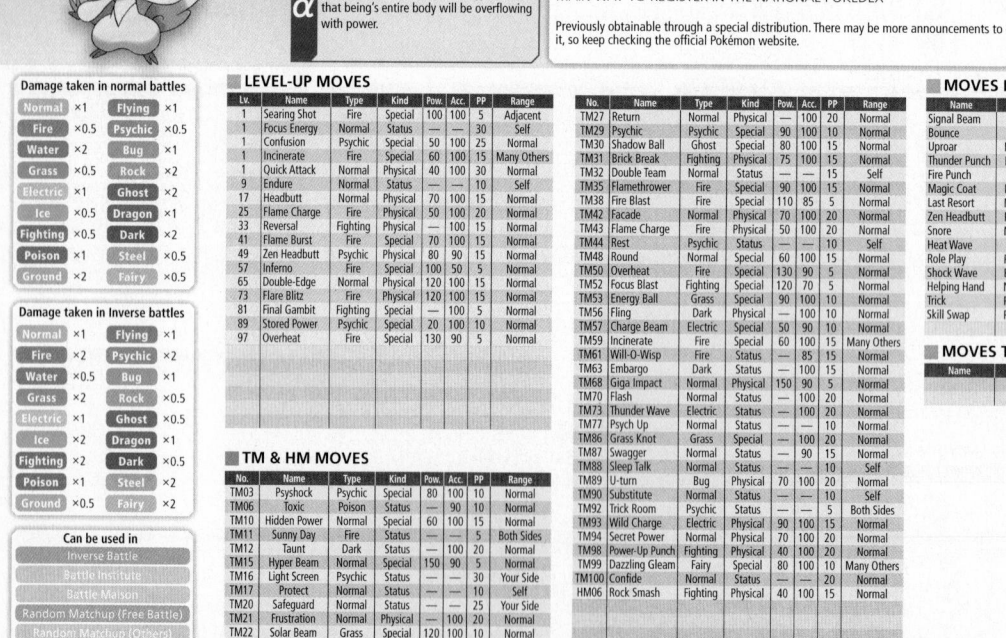

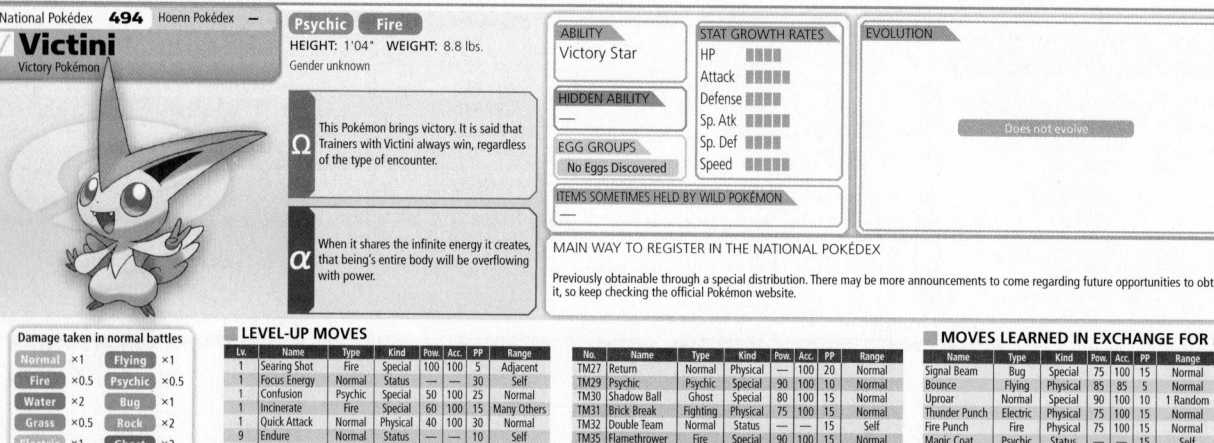

National Pokédex **495** Hoenn Pokédex —

Snivy

Grass Snake Pokémon

Grass

HEIGHT: 2'00" WEIGHT: 17.9 lbs.

Same form for ♂ / ♀

Ω Being exposed to sunlight makes its movements swifter. It uses vines more adeptly than its hands.

α They photosynthesize by bathing their tails in sunlight. When they are not feeling well, their tails droop.

ABILITY: Overgrow

HIDDEN ABILITY: Contrary

EGG GROUPS: Field, Grass

STAT GROWTH RATES: HP, Attack, Defense, Sp. Atk, Sp. Def, Speed

ITEMS SOMETIMES HELD BY WILD POKÉMON: —

EVOLUTION

MAIN WAY TO REGISTER IN THE NATIONAL POKÉDEX

Receive from Professor Birch in Littleroot Town (after clearing the Delta Episode), or bring it to your game using Link Trade or the GTS.

Damage taken in normal battles

Type		Type	
Normal	×1	Flying	×2
Fire	×2	Psychic	×1
Water	×0.5	Bug	×2
Grass	×0.5	Rock	×1
Electric	×0.5	Ghost	×1
Ice	×2	Dragon	×1
Fighting	×1	Dark	×1
Poison	×2	Steel	×1
Ground	×0.5	Fairy	×1

Damage taken in Inverse battles

Type		Type	
Normal	×1	Flying	×0.5
Fire	×0.5	Psychic	×1
Water	×2	Bug	×0.5
Grass	×2	Rock	×1
Electric	×2	Ghost	×1
Ice	×0.5	Dragon	×1
Fighting	×1	Dark	×1
Poison	×0.5	Steel	×1
Ground	×2	Fairy	×1

Can be used in

- Inverse Battle
- Battle Institute
- Battle Maison
- Random Matchup (Free Battle)
- Random Matchup (Others)

LEVEL-UP MOVES

Lv.	Name	Type	Kind	Pow.	Acc.	PP	Range
1	Tackle	Normal	Physical	50	100	35	Normal
4	Leer	Normal	Status	—	100	30	Many Others
7	Vine Whip	Grass	Physical	45	100	25	Normal
10	Wrap	Normal	Physical	15	90	20	Normal
13	Growth	Normal	Status	—	—	20	Self
16	Leaf Tornado	Grass	Special	65	90	10	Normal
19	Leech Seed	Grass	Status	—	90	10	Normal
22	Mega Drain	Grass	Special	40	100	15	Normal
25	Slam	Normal	Physical	80	75	20	Normal
28	Leaf Blade	Grass	Physical	90	100	15	Normal
31	Coil	Poison	Status	—	—	20	Self
34	Giga Drain	Grass	Special	75	100	10	Normal
37	Wring Out	Normal	Special	—	100	5	Normal
40	Gastro Acid	Poison	Status	—	100	10	Normal
43	Leaf Storm	Grass	Special	130	90	5	Normal

TM & HM MOVES

No.	Name	Type	Kind	Pow.	Acc.	PP	Range
TM04	Calm Mind	Psychic	Status	—	—	20	Self
TM06	Toxic	Poison	Status	—	90	10	Normal
TM10	Hidden Power	Normal	Special	60	100	15	Normal
TM11	Sunny Day	Fire	Status	—	—	5	Both Sides
TM12	Taunt	Dark	Status	—	100	20	Normal
TM16	Light Screen	Psychic	Status	—	—	30	Your Side
TM17	Protect	Normal	Status	—	—	10	Self
TM20	Safeguard	Normal	Status	—	—	25	Your Side
TM21	Frustration	Normal	Physical	—	100	20	Normal
TM22	Solar Beam	Grass	Special	120	100	10	Normal
TM27	Return	Normal	Physical	—	100	20	Normal
TM32	Double Team	Normal	Status	—	—	15	Self
TM33	Reflect	Psychic	Status	—	—	20	Your Side
TM40	Aerial Ace	Flying	Physical	60	—	20	Normal
TM41	Torment	Dark	Status	—	100	15	Normal
TM42	Facade	Normal	Physical	70	100	20	Normal
TM44	Rest	Psychic	Status	—	—	10	Self
TM45	Attract	Normal	Status	—	100	15	Normal
TM48	Round	Normal	Special	60	100	15	Normal
TM53	Energy Ball	Grass	Special	90	100	10	Normal
TM70	Flash	Normal	Status	—	100	20	Normal
TM75	Swords Dance	Normal	Status	—	—	20	Self
TM86	Grass Knot	Grass	Special	—	100	20	Normal
TM87	Swagger	Normal	Status	—	90	15	Normal
TM88	Sleep Talk	Normal	Status	—	—	10	Self
TM90	Substitute	Normal	Status	—	—	10	Self
TM94	Secret Power	Normal	Physical	70	100	20	Normal
TM96	Nature Power	Normal	Status	—	—	20	Normal
TM100	Confide	Normal	Status	—	—	20	Normal
HM01	Cut	Normal	Physical	50	95	30	Normal

MOVES LEARNED IN EXCHANGE FOR BP

Name	Type	Kind	Pow.	Acc.	PP	Range
Seed Bomb	Grass	Physical	80	100	15	Normal
Aqua Tail	Water	Physical	90	90	10	Normal
Iron Tail	Steel	Physical	100	75	15	Normal
Bind	Normal	Physical	15	85	20	Normal
Snore	Normal	Special	50	100	15	Normal
Knock Off	Dark	Physical	65	100	20	Normal
Synthesis	Grass	Status	—	—	5	Self
Giga Drain	Grass	Special	75	100	10	Normal
Gastro Acid	Poison	Status	—	100	10	Normal
Worry Seed	Grass	Status	—	100	10	Normal
Snatch	Dark	Status	—	—	10	Self

MOVES TAUGHT BY PEOPLE

Name	Type	Kind	Pow.	Acc.	PP	Range
Grass Pledge	Grass	Special	80	100	10	Normal

EGG MOVES

Name	Type	Kind	Pow.	Acc.	PP	Range
Captivate	Normal	Status	—	100	20	Many Others
Natural Gift	Normal	Physical	—	100	15	Normal
Glare	Normal	Status	—	100	30	Normal
Iron Tail	Steel	Physical	100	75	15	Normal
Magical Leaf	Grass	Special	60	—	20	Normal
Sweet Scent	Normal	Status	—	100	20	Many Others
Mirror Coat	Psychic	Special	—	100	20	Varies
Pursuit	Dark	Physical	40	100	20	Normal
Mean Look	Normal	Status	—	—	5	Normal
Twister	Dragon	Special	40	100	20	Many Others
Grassy Terrain	Grass	Status	—	—	10	Both Sides

National Pokédex **496** Hoenn Pokédex —

Servine

Grass Snake Pokémon

Grass

HEIGHT: 2'07" WEIGHT: 35.3 lbs.

Same form for ♂ / ♀

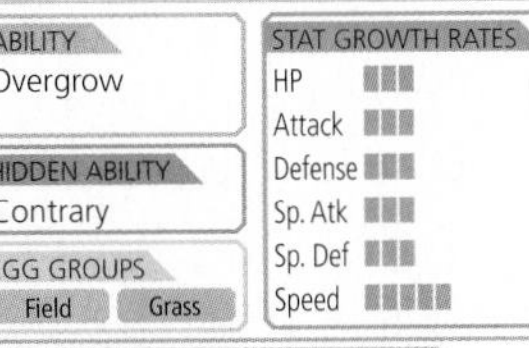

Ω It moves along the ground as if sliding. Its swift movements befuddle its foes, and it then attacks with a vine whip.

α When it gets dirty, its leaves can't be used in photosynthesis, so it always keeps itself clean.

ABILITY: Overgrow

HIDDEN ABILITY: Contrary

EGG GROUPS: Field, Grass

STAT GROWTH RATES: HP, Attack, Defense, Sp. Atk, Sp. Def, Speed

ITEMS SOMETIMES HELD BY WILD POKÉMON: —

EVOLUTION

Lv. 17 Lv. 36

Snivy Servine Serperior

MAIN WAY TO REGISTER IN THE NATIONAL POKÉDEX

Level up Snivy to Lv. 17.

Damage taken in normal battles

Type		Type	
Normal	×1	Flying	×2
Fire	×2	Psychic	×1
Water	×0.5	Bug	×2
Grass	×0.5	Rock	×1
Electric	×0.5	Ghost	×1
Ice	×2	Dragon	×1
Fighting	×1	Dark	×1
Poison	×2	Steel	×1
Ground	×0.5	Fairy	×1

Damage taken in Inverse battles

Type		Type	
Normal	×1	Flying	×0.5
Fire	×0.5	Psychic	×1
Water	×2	Bug	×0.5
Grass	×2	Rock	×1
Electric	×2	Ghost	×1
Ice	×0.5	Dragon	×1
Fighting	×1	Dark	×1
Poison	×0.5	Steel	×1
Ground	×2	Fairy	×1

Can be used in

- Inverse Battle
- Battle Institute
- Battle Maison
- Random Matchup (Free Battle)
- Random Matchup (Others)

LEVEL-UP MOVES

Lv.	Name	Type	Kind	Pow.	Acc.	PP	Range
1	Tackle	Normal	Physical	50	100	35	Normal
1	Leer	Normal	Status	—	100	30	Many Others
1	Vine Whip	Grass	Physical	45	100	25	Normal
1	Wrap	Normal	Physical	15	90	20	Normal
4	Leer	Normal	Status	—	100	30	Many Others
7	Vine Whip	Grass	Physical	45	100	25	Normal
10	Wrap	Normal	Physical	15	90	20	Normal
13	Growth	Normal	Status	—	—	20	Self
16	Leaf Tornado	Grass	Special	65	90	10	Normal
20	Leech Seed	Grass	Status	—	90	10	Normal
24	Mega Drain	Grass	Special	40	100	15	Normal
28	Slam	Normal	Physical	80	75	20	Normal
32	Leaf Blade	Grass	Physical	90	100	15	Normal
36	Coil	Poison	Status	—	—	20	Self
40	Giga Drain	Grass	Special	75	100	10	Normal
44	Wring Out	Normal	Special	—	100	5	Normal
48	Gastro Acid	Poison	Status	—	100	10	Normal
52	Leaf Storm	Grass	Special	130	90	5	Normal

TM & HM MOVES

No.	Name	Type	Kind	Pow.	Acc.	PP	Range
TM04	Calm Mind	Psychic	Status	—	—	20	Self
TM06	Toxic	Poison	Status	—	90	10	Normal
TM10	Hidden Power	Normal	Special	60	100	15	Normal
TM11	Sunny Day	Fire	Status	—	—	5	Both Sides
TM12	Taunt	Dark	Status	—	100	20	Normal
TM16	Light Screen	Psychic	Status	—	—	30	Your Side
TM17	Protect	Normal	Status	—	—	10	Self
TM20	Safeguard	Normal	Status	—	—	25	Your Side
TM21	Frustration	Normal	Physical	—	100	20	Normal
TM22	Solar Beam	Grass	Special	120	100	10	Normal
TM27	Return	Normal	Physical	—	100	20	Normal
TM32	Double Team	Normal	Status	—	—	15	Self
TM33	Reflect	Psychic	Status	—	—	20	Your Side
TM40	Aerial Ace	Flying	Physical	60	—	20	Normal
TM41	Torment	Dark	Status	—	100	15	Normal
TM42	Facade	Normal	Physical	70	100	20	Normal
TM44	Rest	Psychic	Status	—	—	10	Self
TM45	Attract	Normal	Status	—	100	15	Normal
TM48	Round	Normal	Special	60	100	15	Normal
TM53	Energy Ball	Grass	Special	90	100	10	Normal
TM70	Flash	Normal	Status	—	100	20	Normal
TM75	Swords Dance	Normal	Status	—	—	20	Self
TM86	Grass Knot	Grass	Special	—	100	20	Normal
TM87	Swagger	Normal	Status	—	90	15	Normal
TM88	Sleep Talk	Normal	Status	—	—	10	Self
TM90	Substitute	Normal	Status	—	—	10	Self
TM94	Secret Power	Normal	Physical	70	100	20	Normal
TM96	Nature Power	Normal	Status	—	—	20	Normal
TM100	Confide	Normal	Status	—	—	20	Normal
HM01	Cut	Normal	Physical	50	95	30	Normal

MOVES LEARNED IN EXCHANGE FOR BP

Name	Type	Kind	Pow.	Acc.	PP	Range
Seed Bomb	Grass	Physical	80	100	15	Normal
Aqua Tail	Water	Physical	90	90	10	Normal
Iron Tail	Steel	Physical	100	75	15	Normal
Bind	Normal	Physical	15	85	20	Normal
Snore	Normal	Special	50	100	15	Normal
Knock Off	Dark	Physical	65	100	20	Normal
Synthesis	Grass	Status	—	—	5	Self
Giga Drain	Grass	Special	75	100	10	Normal
Gastro Acid	Poison	Status	—	100	10	Normal
Worry Seed	Grass	Status	—	100	10	Normal
Snatch	Dark	Status	—	—	10	Self

MOVES TAUGHT BY PEOPLE

Name	Type	Kind	Pow.	Acc.	PP	Range
Grass Pledge	Grass	Special	80	100	10	Normal

National Pokédex **497** Hoenn Pokédex —

✓ Serperior

Regal Pokémon

Grass

HEIGHT: 10'10" WEIGHT: 138.9 lbs.

Same form for ♂ / ♀

Ω It only gives its all against strong opponents who are not fazed by the glare from Serperior's noble eyes.

α It can stop its opponents' movements with just a glare. It takes in solar energy and boosts it internally.

ABILITY
Overgrow

HIDDEN ABILITY
Contrary

EGG GROUPS
Field / Grass

STAT GROWTH RATES
HP / Attack / Defense / Sp. Atk / Sp. Def / Speed

ITEMS SOMETIMES HELD BY WILD POKÉMON
—

EVOLUTION

MAIN WAY TO REGISTER IN THE NATIONAL POKÉDEX

Level up Servine to Lv. 36.

Damage taken in normal battles

Type		Type	
Normal	×1	Flying	×2
Fire	×2	Psychic	×1
Water	×0.5	Bug	×2
Grass	×0.5	Rock	×1
Electric	×0.5	Ghost	×1
Ice	×2	Dragon	×1
Fighting	×1	Dark	×1
Poison	×2	Steel	×1
Ground	×0.5	Fairy	×1

Damage taken in Inverse battles

Type		Type	
Normal	×1	Flying	×0.5
Fire	×0.5	Psychic	×1
Water	×2	Bug	×0.5
Grass	×2	Rock	×1
Electric	×2	Ghost	×1
Ice	×0.5	Dragon	×1
Fighting	×1	Dark	×1
Poison	×0.5	Steel	×1
Ground	×2	Fairy	×1

Can be used in
- Inverse Battle
- Battle Institute
- Battle Maison
- Random Matchup (Free Battle)
- Random Matchup (Others)

LEVEL-UP MOVES

Lv.	Name	Type	Kind	Pow.	Acc.	PP	Range
1	Tackle	Normal	Physical	50	100	35	Normal
1	Leer	Normal	Status	—	100	30	Many Others
1	Vine Whip	Grass	Physical	45	100	25	Normal
1	Wrap	Normal	Physical	15	90	20	Normal
4	Leer	Normal	Status	—	100	30	Many Others
7	Vine Whip	Grass	Physical	45	100	25	Normal
10	Wrap	Normal	Physical	15	90	20	Normal
13	Growth	Normal	Status	—	—	20	Self
16	Leaf Tornado	Grass	Special	65	90	10	Normal
20	Leech Seed	Grass	Status	—	90	10	Normal
24	Mega Drain	Grass	Special	40	100	15	Normal
28	Slam	Normal	Physical	80	75	20	Normal
32	Leaf Blade	Grass	Physical	90	100	15	Normal
38	Coil	Poison	Status	—	—	20	Self
44	Giga Drain	Grass	Special	75	100	10	Normal
50	Wring Out	Normal	Special	—	100	5	Normal
56	Gastro Acid	Poison	Status	—	100	10	Normal
62	Leaf Storm	Grass	Special	130	90	5	Normal

TM & HM MOVES

No.	Name	Type	Kind	Pow.	Acc.	PP	Range
TM04	Calm Mind	Psychic	Status	—	—	20	Self
TM06	Toxic	Poison	Status	—	90	10	Normal
TM10	Hidden Power	Normal	Special	60	100	15	Normal
TM11	Sunny Day	Fire	Status	—	—	5	Both Sides
TM12	Taunt	Dark	Status	—	100	20	Normal
TM15	Hyper Beam	Normal	Special	150	90	5	Normal
TM16	Light Screen	Psychic	Status	—	—	30	Your Side
TM17	Protect	Normal	Status	—	—	10	Self
TM20	Safeguard	Normal	Status	—	—	25	Your Side
TM21	Frustration	Normal	Physical	—	100	20	Normal
TM22	Solar Beam	Grass	Special	120	100	10	Normal
TM27	Return	Normal	Physical	—	100	20	Normal
TM32	Double Team	Normal	Status	—	—	15	Self
TM33	Reflect	Psychic	Status	—	—	20	Your Side
TM40	Aerial Ace	Flying	Physical	60	—	20	Normal
TM41	Torment	Dark	Status	—	100	15	Normal
TM42	Facade	Normal	Physical	70	100	20	Normal
TM44	Rest	Psychic	Status	—	—	10	Self
TM45	Attract	Normal	Status	—	100	15	Normal
TM48	Round	Normal	Special	60	100	15	Normal
TM53	Energy Ball	Grass	Special	90	100	10	Normal
TM68	Giga Impact	Normal	Physical	150	90	5	Normal
TM70	Flash	Normal	Status	—	100	20	Normal
TM75	Swords Dance	Normal	Status	—	—	20	Self
TM82	Dragon Tail	Dragon	Physical	60	90	10	Normal
TM86	Grass Knot	Grass	Special	—	100	20	Normal
TM87	Swagger	Normal	Status	—	90	15	Normal
TM88	Sleep Talk	Normal	Status	—	—	10	Self
TM90	Substitute	Normal	Status	—	—	10	Self
TM94	Secret Power	Normal	Physical	70	100	20	Normal
TM96	Nature Power	Normal	Status	—	—	20	Normal
TM100	Confide	Normal	Status	—	—	20	Normal
HM01	Cut	Normal	Physical	50	95	30	Normal
HM04	Strength	Normal	Physical	80	100	15	Normal
HM06	Rock Smash	Fighting	Physical	40	100	15	Normal

MOVES LEARNED IN EXCHANGE FOR BP

Name	Type	Kind	Pow.	Acc.	PP	Range
Seed Bomb	Grass	Physical	80	100	15	Normal
Aqua Tail	Water	Physical	90	90	10	Normal
Dragon Pulse	Dragon	Special	85	100	10	Normal
Iron Tail	Steel	Physical	100	75	15	Normal
Bind	Normal	Physical	15	85	20	Normal
Snore	Normal	Special	50	100	15	Normal
Knock Off	Dark	Physical	65	100	20	Normal
Synthesis	Grass	Status	—	—	5	Self
Giga Drain	Grass	Special	75	100	10	Normal
Gastro Acid	Poison	Status	—	100	10	Normal
Worry Seed	Grass	Status	—	100	10	Normal
Outrage	Dragon	Physical	120	100	10	1 Random
Snatch	Dark	Status	—	—	10	Self

MOVES TAUGHT BY PEOPLE

Name	Type	Kind	Pow.	Acc.	PP	Range
Grass Pledge	Grass	Special	80	100	10	Normal
Frenzy Plant	Grass	Special	150	90	5	Normal

National Pokédex **498** Hoenn Pokédex —

✓ Tepig

Fire Pig Pokémon

Fire

HEIGHT: 1'08" WEIGHT: 21.8 lbs.

Same form for ♂ / ♀

Ω It can deftly dodge its foe's attacks while shooting fireballs from its nose. It roasts berries before it eats them.

α It loves to eat roasted berries, but sometimes it gets too excited and burns them to a crisp.

ABILITY
Blaze

HIDDEN ABILITY
Reckless

EGG GROUPS
Field

STAT GROWTH RATES
HP / Attack / Defense / Sp. Atk / Sp. Def / Speed

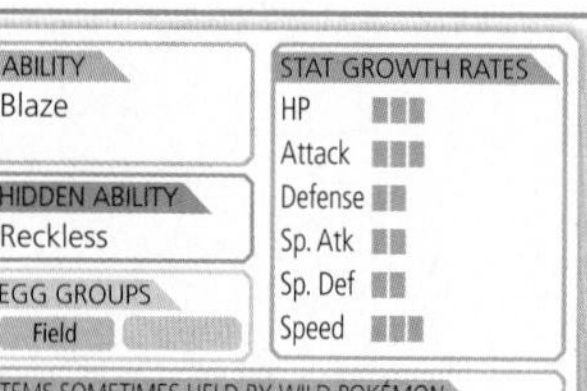

ITEMS SOMETIMES HELD BY WILD POKÉMON
—

EVOLUTION

Lv. 17 Lv. 36

Tepig → Pignite → Emboar

MAIN WAY TO REGISTER IN THE NATIONAL POKÉDEX

Receive from Professor Birch in Littleroot Town (after clearing the Delta Episode), or bring it to your game using Link Trade or the GTS.

Damage taken in normal battles

Type		Type	
Normal	×1	Flying	×1
Fire	×0.5	Psychic	×1
Water	×2	Bug	×0.5
Grass	×0.5	Rock	×2
Electric	×1	Ghost	×1
Ice	×0.5	Dragon	×1
Fighting	×1	Dark	×1
Poison	×1	Steel	×0.5
Ground	×2	Fairy	×0.5

Damage taken in Inverse battles

Type		Type	
Normal	×1	Flying	×1
Fire	×2	Psychic	×1
Water	×0.5	Bug	×2
Grass	×2	Rock	×0.5
Electric	×1	Ghost	×1
Ice	×2	Dragon	×1
Fighting	×1	Dark	×1
Poison	×1	Steel	×2
Ground	×0.5	Fairy	×2

Can be used in
- Inverse Battle
- Battle Institute
- Battle Maison
- Random Matchup (Free Battle)
- Random Matchup (Others)

LEVEL-UP MOVES

Lv.	Name	Type	Kind	Pow.	Acc.	PP	Range
1	Tackle	Normal	Physical	50	100	35	Normal
3	Tail Whip	Normal	Status	—	100	30	Many Others
7	Ember	Fire	Special	40	100	25	Normal
9	Odor Sleuth	Normal	Status	—	—	40	Normal
13	Defense Curl	Normal	Status	—	—	40	Self
15	Flame Charge	Fire	Physical	50	100	20	Normal
19	Smog	Poison	Special	30	70	20	Normal
21	Rollout	Rock	Physical	30	90	20	Normal
25	Take Down	Normal	Physical	90	85	20	Normal
27	Heat Crash	Fire	Physical	—	100	10	Normal
31	Assurance	Dark	Physical	60	100	10	Normal
33	Flamethrower	Fire	Special	90	100	15	Normal
37	Head Smash	Rock	Physical	150	80	5	Normal
39	Roar	Normal	Status	—	—	20	Normal
43	Flare Blitz	Fire	Physical	120	100	15	Normal

TM & HM MOVES

No.	Name	Type	Kind	Pow.	Acc.	PP	Range
TM05	Roar	Normal	Status	—	—	20	Normal
TM06	Toxic	Poison	Status	—	90	10	Normal
TM10	Hidden Power	Normal	Special	60	100	15	Normal
TM11	Sunny Day	Fire	Status	—	—	5	Both Sides
TM12	Taunt	Dark	Status	—	100	20	Normal
TM17	Protect	Normal	Status	—	—	10	Self
TM21	Frustration	Normal	Physical	—	100	20	Normal
TM22	Solar Beam	Grass	Special	120	100	10	Normal
TM27	Return	Normal	Physical	—	100	20	Normal
TM32	Double Team	Normal	Status	—	—	15	Self
TM35	Flamethrower	Fire	Special	90	100	15	Normal
TM38	Fire Blast	Fire	Special	110	85	5	Normal
TM39	Rock Tomb	Rock	Physical	60	95	15	Normal
TM42	Facade	Normal	Physical	70	100	20	Normal
TM43	Flame Charge	Fire	Physical	50	100	20	Normal
TM44	Rest	Psychic	Status	—	—	10	Self
TM45	Attract	Normal	Status	—	100	15	Normal
TM48	Round	Normal	Special	60	100	15	Normal
TM49	Echoed Voice	Normal	Special	40	100	15	Normal
TM50	Overheat	Fire	Special	130	90	5	Normal
TM59	Incinerate	Fire	Special	60	100	15	Many Others
TM61	Will-O-Wisp	Fire	Status	—	85	15	Normal
TM74	Gyro Ball	Steel	Physical	—	100	5	Normal
TM86	Grass Knot	Grass	Special	—	100	20	Normal
TM87	Swagger	Normal	Status	—	90	15	Normal
TM88	Sleep Talk	Normal	Status	—	—	10	Self
TM90	Substitute	Normal	Status	—	—	10	Self
TM93	Wild Charge	Electric	Physical	90	100	15	Normal
TM94	Secret Power	Normal	Physical	70	100	20	Normal
TM100	Confide	Normal	Status	—	—	20	Normal
HM04	Strength	Normal	Physical	80	100	15	Normal
HM06	Rock Smash	Fighting	Physical	40	100	15	Normal

MOVES LEARNED IN EXCHANGE FOR BP

Name	Type	Kind	Pow.	Acc.	PP	Range
Covet	Normal	Physical	60	100	25	Normal
Superpower	Fighting	Physical	120	100	5	Normal
Zen Headbutt	Psychic	Physical	80	90	15	Normal
Iron Tail	Steel	Physical	100	75	15	Normal
Snore	Normal	Special	50	100	15	Normal
Heat Wave	Fire	Special	95	90	10	Many Others
Helping Hand	Normal	Status	—	—	20	1 Ally
Endeavor	Normal	Physical	—	100	5	Normal

MOVES TAUGHT BY PEOPLE

Name	Type	Kind	Pow.	Acc.	PP	Range
Fire Pledge	Fire	Special	80	100	10	Normal

EGG MOVES

Name	Type	Kind	Pow.	Acc.	PP	Range
Covet	Normal	Physical	60	100	25	Normal
Body Slam	Normal	Physical	85	100	15	Normal
Thrash	Normal	Physical	120	100	10	1 Random
Magnitude	Ground	Physical	—	100	30	Adjacent
Superpower	Fighting	Physical	120	100	5	Normal
Curse	Ghost	Status	—	—	10	Varies
Endeavor	Normal	Physical	—	100	5	Normal
Yawn	Normal	Status	—	—	10	Normal
Sleep Talk	Normal	Status	—	—	10	Self
Heavy Slam	Steel	Physical	—	100	10	Normal
Sucker Punch	Dark	Physical	80	100	5	Normal

National Pokédex **499** Hoenn Pokédex —

Pignite

Fire Pig Pokémon

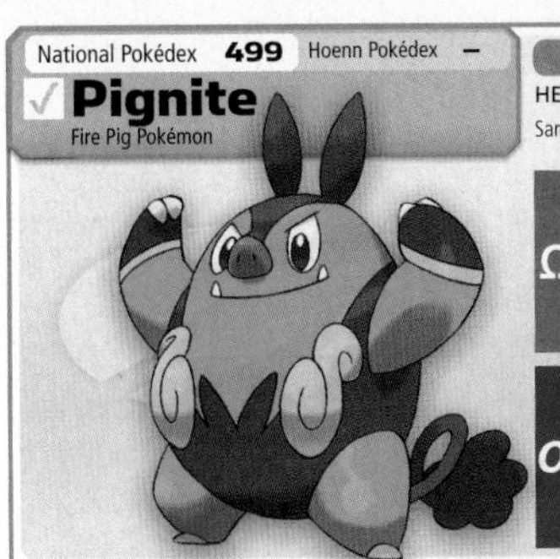

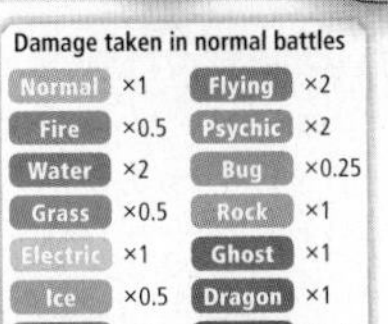

Fire Fighting

HEIGHT: 3'03" WEIGHT: 122.4 lbs.

Same form for ♂ / ♀

Ω The more it eats, the more fuel it has to make the fire in its stomach stronger. This fills it with even more power.

α When its internal fire flares up, its movements grow sharper and faster. When in trouble, it emits smoke.

ABILITY
Blaze

HIDDEN ABILITY
Reckless

EGG GROUPS
Field

STAT GROWTH RATES
HP
Attack
Defense
Sp. Atk
Sp. Def
Speed

ITEMS SOMETIMES HELD BY WILD POKÉMON
—

EVOLUTION

MAIN WAY TO REGISTER IN THE NATIONAL POKÉDEX

Level up Tepig to Lv. 17.

Damage taken in normal battles

Type		Type	
Normal	×1	Flying	×2
Fire	×0.5	Psychic	×2
Water	×2	Bug	×0.25
Grass	×0.5	Rock	×1
Electric	×1	Ghost	×1
Ice	×0.5	Dragon	×1
Fighting	×1	Dark	×0.5
Poison	×1	Steel	×0.5
Ground	×2	Fairy	×1

Damage taken in Inverse battles

Type		Type	
Normal	×1	Flying	×0.5
Fire	×2	Psychic	×0.5
Water	×0.5	Bug	×4
Grass	×2	Rock	×1
Electric	×1	Ghost	×1
Ice	×2	Dragon	×1
Fighting	×1	Dark	×2
Poison	×1	Steel	×2
Ground	×0.5	Fairy	×1

Can be used in
Inverse Battle
Battle Institute
Battle Maison
Random Matchup (Free Battle)
Random Matchup (Others)

LEVEL-UP MOVES

Lv.	Name	Type	Kind	Pow.	Acc.	PP	Range
1	Tackle	Normal	Physical	50	100	35	Normal
1	Tail Whip	Normal	Status	—	100	30	Many Others
1	Ember	Fire	Special	40	100	25	Normal
1	Odor Sleuth	Normal	Status	—	—	40	Normal
3	Tail Whip	Normal	Status	—	100	30	Many Others
7	Ember	Fire	Special	40	100	25	Normal
9	Odor Sleuth	Normal	Status	—	—	40	Normal
13	Defense Curl	Normal	Status	—	—	40	Self
15	Flame Charge	Fire	Physical	50	100	20	Normal
17	Arm Thrust	Fighting	Physical	15	100	20	Normal
20	Smog	Poison	Special	30	70	20	Normal
23	Rollout	Rock	Physical	30	90	20	Normal
28	Take Down	Normal	Physical	90	85	20	Normal
31	Heat Crash	Fire	Physical	—	100	10	Normal
36	Assurance	Dark	Physical	60	100	10	Normal
39	Flamethrower	Fire	Special	90	100	15	Normal
44	Head Smash	Rock	Physical	150	80	5	Normal
47	Roar	Normal	Status	—	—	20	Normal
52	Flare Blitz	Fire	Physical	120	100	15	Normal

TM & HM MOVES

No.	Name	Type	Kind	Pow.	Acc.	PP	Range
TM05	Roar	Normal	Status	—	—	20	Normal
TM06	Toxic	Poison	Status	—	90	10	Normal
TM10	Hidden Power	Normal	Special	60	100	15	Normal
TM11	Sunny Day	Fire	Status	—	—	5	Both Sides
TM12	Taunt	Dark	Status	—	100	20	Normal
TM17	Protect	Normal	Status	—	—	10	Self
TM21	Frustration	Normal	Physical	—	100	20	Normal
TM22	Solar Beam	Grass	Special	120	100	10	Normal
TM27	Return	Normal	Physical	—	100	20	Normal
TM31	Brick Break	Fighting	Physical	75	100	15	Normal
TM32	Double Team	Normal	Status	—	—	15	Self
TM35	Flamethrower	Fire	Special	90	100	15	Normal
TM38	Fire Blast	Fire	Special	110	85	5	Normal
TM39	Rock Tomb	Rock	Physical	60	95	15	Normal
TM42	Facade	Normal	Physical	70	100	20	Normal
TM43	Flame Charge	Fire	Physical	50	100	20	Normal
TM44	Rest	Psychic	Status	—	—	10	Self
TM45	Attract	Normal	Status	—	100	15	Normal
TM47	Low Sweep	Fighting	Physical	65	100	20	Normal
TM48	Round	Normal	Special	60	100	15	Normal
TM49	Echoed Voice	Normal	Special	40	100	15	Normal
TM50	Overheat	Fire	Special	130	90	5	Normal
TM52	Focus Blast	Fighting	Special	120	70	5	Normal
TM56	Fling	Dark	Physical	—	100	10	Normal
TM59	Incinerate	Fire	Special	60	100	15	Many Others
TM61	Will-O-Wisp	Fire	Status	—	85	15	Normal
TM71	Stone Edge	Rock	Physical	100	80	5	Normal
TM74	Gyro Ball	Steel	Physical	—	100	5	Normal
TM78	Bulldoze	Ground	Physical	60	100	20	Adjacent
TM80	Rock Slide	Rock	Physical	75	90	10	Many Others
TM84	Poison Jab	Poison	Physical	80	100	20	Normal
TM86	Grass Knot	Grass	Special	—	100	20	Normal
TM87	Swagger	Normal	Status	—	90	15	Normal
TM88	Sleep Talk	Normal	Status	—	—	10	Self
TM90	Substitute	Normal	Status	—	—	10	Self
TM93	Wild Charge	Electric	Physical	90	100	15	Normal
TM94	Secret Power	Normal	Physical	70	100	20	Normal
TM98	Power-Up Punch	Fighting	Physical	40	100	20	Normal
TM100	Confide	Normal	Status	—	—	20	Normal
HM04	Strength	Normal	Physical	80	100	15	Normal
HM06	Rock Smash	Fighting	Physical	40	100	15	Normal

MOVES LEARNED IN EXCHANGE FOR BP

Name	Type	Kind	Pow.	Acc.	PP	Range
Covet	Normal	Physical	60	100	25	Normal
Low Kick	Fighting	Physical	—	100	20	Normal
Thunder Punch	Electric	Physical	75	100	15	Normal
Fire Punch	Fire	Physical	75	100	15	Normal
Superpower	Fighting	Physical	120	100	5	Normal
Zen Headbutt	Psychic	Physical	80	90	15	Normal
Iron Tail	Steel	Physical	100	75	15	Normal
Snore	Normal	Special	50	100	15	Normal
Heat Wave	Fire	Special	95	90	10	Many Others
Focus Punch	Fighting	Physical	150	100	20	Normal
Helping Hand	Normal	Status	—	—	20	1 Ally
Endeavor	Normal	Physical	—	100	5	Normal

MOVES TAUGHT BY PEOPLE

Name	Type	Kind	Pow.	Acc.	PP	Range
Fire Pledge	Fire	Special	80	100	10	Normal

National Pokédex **500** Hoenn Pokédex —

Emboar

Mega Fire Pig Pokémon

Fire Fighting

HEIGHT: 5'03" WEIGHT: 330.7 lbs.

Same form for ♂ / ♀

Ω It can throw a fire punch by setting its fists on fire with its fiery chin. It cares deeply about its friends.

α It has mastered fast and powerful fighting moves. It grows a beard of fire.

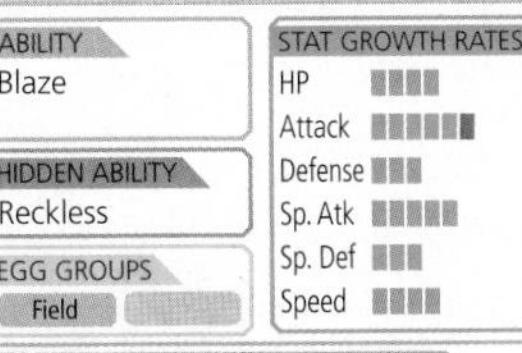

ABILITY
Blaze

HIDDEN ABILITY
Reckless

EGG GROUPS
Field

STAT GROWTH RATES
HP
Attack
Defense
Sp. Atk
Sp. Def
Speed

ITEMS SOMETIMES HELD BY WILD POKÉMON
—

EVOLUTION

Lv. 17
Lv. 36
Tepig
Pignite
Emboar

MAIN WAY TO REGISTER IN THE NATIONAL POKÉDEX

Level up Pignite to Lv. 36.

Damage taken in normal battles

Type		Type	
Normal	×1	Flying	×2
Fire	×0.5	Psychic	×2
Water	×2	Bug	×0.25
Grass	×0.5	Rock	×1
Electric	×1	Ghost	×1
Ice	×0.5	Dragon	×1
Fighting	×1	Dark	×0.5
Poison	×1	Steel	×0.5
Ground	×2	Fairy	×1

Damage taken in Inverse battles

Type		Type	
Normal	×1	Flying	×0.5
Fire	×2	Psychic	×0.5
Water	×0.5	Bug	×4
Grass	×2	Rock	×1
Electric	×1	Ghost	×1
Ice	×2	Dragon	×1
Fighting	×1	Dark	×2
Poison	×1	Steel	×2
Ground	×0.5	Fairy	×1

Can be used in
Inverse Battle
Battle Institute
Battle Maison
Random Matchup (Free Battle)
Random Matchup (Others)

LEVEL-UP MOVES

Lv.	Name	Type	Kind	Pow.	Acc.	PP	Range
1	Hammer Arm	Fighting	Physical	100	90	10	Normal
1	Tackle	Normal	Physical	50	100	35	Normal
1	Tail Whip	Normal	Status	—	100	30	Many Others
1	Ember	Fire	Special	40	100	25	Normal
1	Odor Sleuth	Normal	Status	—	—	40	Normal
3	Tail Whip	Normal	Status	—	100	30	Many Others
7	Ember	Fire	Special	40	100	25	Normal
9	Odor Sleuth	Normal	Status	—	—	40	Normal
13	Defense Curl	Normal	Status	—	—	40	Self
15	Flame Charge	Fire	Physical	50	100	20	Normal
17	Arm Thrust	Fighting	Physical	15	100	20	Normal
20	Smog	Poison	Special	30	70	20	Normal
23	Rollout	Rock	Physical	30	90	20	Normal
28	Take Down	Normal	Physical	90	85	20	Normal
31	Heat Crash	Fire	Physical	—	100	10	Normal
38	Assurance	Dark	Physical	60	100	10	Normal
43	Flamethrower	Fire	Special	90	100	15	Normal
50	Head Smash	Rock	Physical	150	80	5	Normal
55	Roar	Normal	Status	—	—	20	Normal
62	Flare Blitz	Fire	Physical	120	100	15	Normal

TM & HM MOVES

No.	Name	Type	Kind	Pow.	Acc.	PP	Range
TM05	Roar	Normal	Status	—	—	20	Normal
TM06	Toxic	Poison	Status	—	90	10	Normal
TM08	Bulk Up	Fighting	Status	—	—	20	Self
TM10	Hidden Power	Normal	Special	60	100	15	Normal
TM11	Sunny Day	Fire	Status	—	—	5	Both Sides
TM12	Taunt	Dark	Status	—	100	20	Normal
TM15	Hyper Beam	Normal	Special	150	90	5	Normal
TM17	Protect	Normal	Status	—	—	10	Self
TM21	Frustration	Normal	Physical	—	100	20	Normal
TM22	Solar Beam	Grass	Special	120	100	10	Normal
TM23	Smack Down	Rock	Physical	50	100	15	Normal
TM26	Earthquake	Ground	Physical	100	100	10	Adjacent
TM27	Return	Normal	Physical	—	100	20	Normal
TM31	Brick Break	Fighting	Physical	75	100	15	Normal
TM32	Double Team	Normal	Status	—	—	15	Self
TM35	Flamethrower	Fire	Special	90	100	15	Normal
TM38	Fire Blast	Fire	Special	110	85	5	Normal
TM39	Rock Tomb	Rock	Physical	60	95	15	Normal
TM42	Facade	Normal	Physical	70	100	20	Normal
TM43	Flame Charge	Fire	Physical	50	100	20	Normal
TM44	Rest	Psychic	Status	—	—	10	Self
TM45	Attract	Normal	Status	—	100	15	Normal
TM47	Low Sweep	Fighting	Physical	65	100	20	Normal
TM48	Round	Normal	Special	60	100	15	Normal
TM49	Echoed Voice	Normal	Special	40	100	15	Normal
TM50	Overheat	Fire	Special	130	90	5	Normal
TM52	Focus Blast	Fighting	Special	120	70	5	Normal
TM55	Scald	Water	Special	80	100	15	Normal
TM56	Fling	Dark	Physical	—	100	10	Normal
TM59	Incinerate	Fire	Special	60	100	15	Many Others
TM61	Will-O-Wisp	Fire	Status	—	85	15	Normal
TM68	Giga Impact	Normal	Physical	150	90	5	Normal
TM71	Stone Edge	Rock	Physical	100	80	5	Normal
TM74	Gyro Ball	Steel	Physical	—	100	5	Normal
TM78	Bulldoze	Ground	Physical	60	100	20	Adjacent
TM80	Rock Slide	Rock	Physical	75	90	10	Many Others
TM84	Poison Jab	Poison	Physical	80	100	20	Normal
TM86	Grass Knot	Grass	Special	—	100	20	Normal
TM87	Swagger	Normal	Status	—	90	15	Normal
TM88	Sleep Talk	Normal	Status	—	—	10	Self
TM90	Substitute	Normal	Status	—	—	10	Self
TM93	Wild Charge	Electric	Physical	90	100	15	Normal
TM94	Secret Power	Normal	Physical	70	100	20	Normal
TM98	Power-Up Punch	Fighting	Physical	40	100	20	Normal
TM100	Confide	Normal	Status	—	—	20	Normal
HM04	Strength	Normal	Physical	80	100	15	Normal
HM06	Rock Smash	Fighting	Physical	40	100	15	Normal

MOVES LEARNED IN EXCHANGE FOR BP

Name	Type	Kind	Pow.	Acc.	PP	Range
Covet	Normal	Physical	60	100	25	Normal
Iron Head	Steel	Physical	80	100	15	Normal
Low Kick	Fighting	Physical	—	100	20	Normal
Thunder Punch	Electric	Physical	75	100	15	Normal
Fire Punch	Fire	Physical	75	100	15	Normal
Block	Normal	Status	—	—	5	Normal
Superpower	Fighting	Physical	120	100	5	Normal
Zen Headbutt	Psychic	Physical	80	90	15	Normal
Iron Tail	Steel	Physical	100	75	15	Normal
Snore	Normal	Special	50	100	15	Normal
Heat Wave	Fire	Special	95	90	10	Many Others
Focus Punch	Fighting	Physical	150	100	20	Normal
Helping Hand	Normal	Status	—	—	20	1 Ally
Endeavor	Normal	Physical	—	100	5	Normal

MOVES TAUGHT BY PEOPLE

Name	Type	Kind	Pow.	Acc.	PP	Range
Fire Pledge	Fire	Special	80	100	10	Normal
Blast Burn	Fire	Special	150	90	5	Normal

National Pokédex **501** Hoenn Pokédex **—**

Oshawott

Sea Otter Pokémon

Water

HEIGHT: 1'08" WEIGHT: 13 lbs.

Same form for ♂ / ♀

Ω The scalchop on its stomach isn't just used for battle—it can be used to break open hard berries as well.

α It fights using the scalchop on its stomach. In response to an attack, it retaliates immediately by slashing.

ABILITY
Torrent

HIDDEN ABILITY
Shell Armor

EGG GROUPS
Field

STAT GROWTH RATES

HP	■■
Attack	■■■
Defense	■■
Sp. Atk	■■■
Sp. Def	■■
Speed	■■■

ITEMS SOMETIMES HELD BY WILD POKÉMON
—

EVOLUTION

Oshawott → Lv. 17 → Dewott → Lv. 36 → Samurott

MAIN WAY TO REGISTER IN THE NATIONAL POKÉDEX

Receive from Professor Birch in Littleroot Town (after clearing the Delta Episode), or bring it to your game using Link Trade or the GTS.

Damage taken in normal battles

Normal	×1	Flying	×1
Fire	×0.5	Psychic	×1
Water	×0.5	Bug	×1
Grass	×2	Rock	×1
Electric	×2	Ghost	×1
Ice	×0.5	Dragon	×1
Fighting	×1	Dark	×1
Poison	×1	Steel	×0.5
Ground	×1	Fairy	×1

Damage taken in Inverse battles

Normal	×1	Flying	×1
Fire	×2	Psychic	×1
Water	×2	Bug	×1
Grass	×0.5	Rock	×1
Electric	×0.5	Ghost	×1
Ice	×2	Dragon	×1
Fighting	×1	Dark	×1
Poison	×1	Steel	×2
Ground	×1	Fairy	×1

Can be used in
- Inverse Battle
- Battle Institute
- Battle Maison
- Random Matchup (Free Battle)
- Random Matchup (Others)

LEVEL-UP MOVES

Lv.	Name	Type	Kind	Pow.	Acc.	PP	Range
1	Tackle	Normal	Physical	50	100	35	Normal
5	Tail Whip	Normal	Status	—	100	30	Many Others
7	Water Gun	Water	Special	40	100	25	Normal
11	Water Sport	Water	Status	—	—	15	Both Sides
13	Focus Energy	Normal	Status	—	—	30	Self
17	Razor Shell	Water	Physical	75	95	10	Normal
19	Fury Cutter	Bug	Physical	40	95	20	Normal
23	Water Pulse	Water	Special	60	100	20	Normal
25	Revenge	Fighting	Physical	60	100	10	Normal
29	Aqua Jet	Water	Physical	40	100	20	Normal
31	Encore	Normal	Status	—	100	5	Normal
35	Aqua Tail	Water	Physical	90	90	10	Normal
37	Retaliate	Normal	Physical	70	100	5	Normal
41	Swords Dance	Normal	Status	—	—	20	Self
43	Hydro Pump	Water	Special	110	80	5	Normal

TM & HM MOVES

No.	Name	Type	Kind	Pow.	Acc.	PP	Range
TM06	Toxic	Poison	Status	—	90	10	Normal
TM07	Hail	Ice	Status	—	—	10	Both Sides
TM10	Hidden Power	Normal	Special	60	100	15	Normal
TM12	Taunt	Dark	Status	—	100	20	Normal
TM13	Ice Beam	Ice	Special	90	100	10	Normal
TM14	Blizzard	Ice	Special	110	70	5	Many Others
TM17	Protect	Normal	Status	—	—	10	Self
TM18	Rain Dance	Water	Status	—	—	5	Both Sides
TM21	Frustration	Normal	Physical	—	100	20	Normal
TM27	Return	Normal	Physical	—	100	20	Normal
TM28	Dig	Ground	Physical	80	100	10	Normal
TM32	Double Team	Normal	Status	—	—	15	Self
TM40	Aerial Ace	Flying	Physical	60	—	20	Normal
TM42	Facade	Normal	Physical	70	100	20	Normal
TM44	Rest	Psychic	Status	—	—	10	Self
TM45	Attract	Normal	Status	—	100	15	Normal
TM48	Round	Normal	Special	60	100	15	Normal
TM54	False Swipe	Normal	Physical	40	100	40	Normal
TM55	Scald	Water	Special	80	100	15	Normal
TM56	Fling	Dark	Physical	—	100	10	Normal
TM67	Retaliate	Normal	Physical	70	100	5	Normal
TM75	Swords Dance	Normal	Status	—	—	20	Self
TM81	X-Scissor	Bug	Physical	80	100	15	Normal
TM86	Grass Knot	Grass	Special	—	100	20	Normal
TM87	Swagger	Normal	Status	—	90	15	Normal
TM88	Sleep Talk	Normal	Status	—	—	10	Self
TM90	Substitute	Normal	Status	—	—	10	Self
TM94	Secret Power	Normal	Physical	70	100	20	Normal
TM100	Confide	Normal	Status	—	—	20	Normal
HM01	Cut	Normal	Physical	50	95	30	Normal
HM03	Surf	Water	Special	90	100	15	Adjacent
HM05	Waterfall	Water	Physical	80	100	15	Normal
HM06	Rock Smash	Fighting	Physical	40	100	15	Normal
HM07	Dive	Water	Physical	80	100	10	Normal

MOVES LEARNED IN EXCHANGE FOR BP

Name	Type	Kind	Pow.	Acc.	PP	Range
Covet	Normal	Physical	60	100	25	Normal
Icy Wind	Ice	Special	55	95	15	Many Others
Aqua Tail	Water	Physical	90	90	10	Normal
Iron Tail	Steel	Physical	100	75	15	Normal
Snore	Normal	Special	50	100	15	Normal
Water Pulse	Water	Special	60	100	20	Normal
Helping Hand	Normal	Status	—	—	20	1 Ally

MOVES TAUGHT BY PEOPLE

Name	Type	Kind	Pow.	Acc.	PP	Range
Water Pledge	Water	Special	80	100	10	Normal

EGG MOVES

Name	Type	Kind	Pow.	Acc.	PP	Range
Copycat	Normal	Status	—	—	20	Self
Detect	Fighting	Status	—	—	5	Self
Air Slash	Flying	Special	75	95	15	Normal
Assurance	Dark	Physical	60	100	10	Normal
Brine	Water	Special	65	100	10	Normal
Night Slash	Dark	Physical	70	100	15	Normal
Trump Card	Normal	Special	—	—	5	Normal
Screech	Normal	Status	—	85	40	Normal

National Pokédex **502** Hoenn Pokédex **—**

Dewott

Discipline Pokémon

Water

HEIGHT: 2'07" WEIGHT: 54 lbs.

Same form for ♂ / ♀

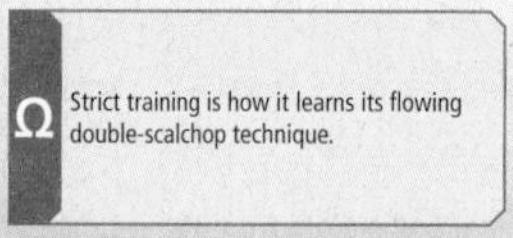

Ω Strict training is how it learns its flowing double-scalchop technique.

α As a result of strict training, each Dewott learns different forms for using the scalchops.

ABILITY
Torrent

HIDDEN ABILITY
Shell Armor

EGG GROUPS
Field

STAT GROWTH RATES

HP	■■■
Attack	■■■■
Defense	■■■
Sp. Atk	■■■■
Sp. Def	■■■
Speed	■■■

ITEMS SOMETIMES HELD BY WILD POKÉMON
—

EVOLUTION

Oshawott → Lv. 17 → Dewott → Lv. 36 → Samurott

MAIN WAY TO REGISTER IN THE NATIONAL POKÉDEX

Level up Oshawott to Lv. 17.

Damage taken in normal battles

Normal	×1	Flying	×1
Fire	×0.5	Psychic	×1
Water	×0.5	Bug	×1
Grass	×2	Rock	×1
Electric	×2	Ghost	×1
Ice	×0.5	Dragon	×1
Fighting	×1	Dark	×1
Poison	×1	Steel	×0.5
Ground	×1	Fairy	×1

Damage taken in Inverse battles

Normal	×1	Flying	×1
Fire	×2	Psychic	×1
Water	×2	Bug	×1
Grass	×0.5	Rock	×1
Electric	×0.5	Ghost	×1
Ice	×2	Dragon	×1
Fighting	×1	Dark	×1
Poison	×1	Steel	×2
Ground	×1	Fairy	×1

Can be used in
- Inverse Battle
- Battle Institute
- Battle Maison
- Random Matchup (Free Battle)
- Random Matchup (Others)

LEVEL-UP MOVES

Lv.	Name	Type	Kind	Pow.	Acc.	PP	Range
1	Tackle	Normal	Physical	50	100	35	Normal
1	Tail Whip	Normal	Status	—	100	30	Many Others
1	Water Gun	Water	Special	40	100	25	Normal
1	Water Sport	Water	Status	—	—	15	Both Sides
5	Tail Whip	Normal	Status	—	100	30	Many Others
7	Water Gun	Water	Special	40	100	25	Normal
11	Water Sport	Water	Status	—	—	15	Both Sides
13	Focus Energy	Normal	Status	—	—	30	Self
17	Razor Shell	Water	Physical	75	95	10	Normal
20	Fury Cutter	Bug	Physical	40	95	20	Normal
25	Water Pulse	Water	Special	60	100	20	Normal
28	Revenge	Fighting	Physical	60	100	10	Normal
33	Aqua Jet	Water	Physical	40	100	20	Normal
36	Encore	Normal	Status	—	100	5	Normal
41	Aqua Tail	Water	Physical	90	90	10	Normal
44	Retaliate	Normal	Physical	70	100	5	Normal
49	Swords Dance	Normal	Status	—	—	20	Self
52	Hydro Pump	Water	Special	110	80	5	Normal

TM & HM MOVES

No.	Name	Type	Kind	Pow.	Acc.	PP	Range
TM06	Toxic	Poison	Status	—	90	10	Normal
TM07	Hail	Ice	Status	—	—	10	Both Sides
TM10	Hidden Power	Normal	Special	60	100	15	Normal
TM12	Taunt	Dark	Status	—	100	20	Normal
TM13	Ice Beam	Ice	Special	90	100	10	Normal
TM14	Blizzard	Ice	Special	110	70	5	Many Others
TM17	Protect	Normal	Status	—	—	10	Self
TM18	Rain Dance	Water	Status	—	—	5	Both Sides
TM21	Frustration	Normal	Physical	—	100	20	Normal
TM27	Return	Normal	Physical	—	100	20	Normal
TM28	Dig	Ground	Physical	80	100	10	Normal
TM32	Double Team	Normal	Status	—	—	15	Self
TM40	Aerial Ace	Flying	Physical	60	—	20	Normal
TM42	Facade	Normal	Physical	70	100	20	Normal
TM44	Rest	Psychic	Status	—	—	10	Self
TM45	Attract	Normal	Status	—	100	15	Normal
TM48	Round	Normal	Special	60	100	15	Normal
TM54	False Swipe	Normal	Physical	40	100	40	Normal
TM55	Scald	Water	Special	80	100	15	Normal
TM56	Fling	Dark	Physical	—	100	10	Normal
TM67	Retaliate	Normal	Physical	70	100	5	Normal
TM75	Swords Dance	Normal	Status	—	—	20	Self
TM81	X-Scissor	Bug	Physical	80	100	15	Normal
TM86	Grass Knot	Grass	Special	—	100	20	Normal
TM87	Swagger	Normal	Status	—	90	15	Normal
TM88	Sleep Talk	Normal	Status	—	—	10	Self
TM90	Substitute	Normal	Status	—	—	10	Self
TM94	Secret Power	Normal	Physical	70	100	20	Normal
TM100	Confide	Normal	Status	—	—	20	Normal
HM01	Cut	Normal	Physical	50	95	30	Normal
HM03	Surf	Water	Special	90	100	15	Adjacent
HM05	Waterfall	Water	Physical	80	100	15	Normal
HM06	Rock Smash	Fighting	Physical	40	100	15	Normal
HM07	Dive	Water	Physical	80	100	10	Normal

MOVES LEARNED IN EXCHANGE FOR BP

Name	Type	Kind	Pow.	Acc.	PP	Range
Covet	Normal	Physical	60	100	25	Normal
Icy Wind	Ice	Special	55	95	15	Many Others
Aqua Tail	Water	Physical	90	90	10	Normal
Iron Tail	Steel	Physical	100	75	15	Normal
Snore	Normal	Special	50	100	15	Normal
Water Pulse	Water	Special	60	100	20	Normal
Helping Hand	Normal	Status	—	—	20	1 Ally

MOVES TAUGHT BY PEOPLE

Name	Type	Kind	Pow.	Acc.	PP	Range
Water Pledge	Water	Special	80	100	10	Normal

National Pokédex **503** Hoenn Pokédex —

Samurott

Formidable Pokémon

Water

HEIGHT: 4'11" WEIGHT: 208.6 lbs.

Same form for ♂ / ♀

Ω In the time it takes a foe to blink, it can draw and sheathe the seamitars attached to its front legs.

α One swing of the sword incorporated in its armor can fell an opponent. A simple glare from one of them quiets everybody.

ABILITY
Torrent

HIDDEN ABILITY
Shell Armor

EGG GROUPS
Field

STAT GROWTH RATES
HP ▮▮▮▮
Attack ▮▮▮▮▮
Defense ▮▮▮▮
Sp. Atk ▮▮▮▮▮
Sp. Def ▮▮▮
Speed ▮▮▮▮

ITEMS SOMETIMES HELD BY WILD POKÉMON
—

EVOLUTION
Oshawott → Lv. 17 → Dewott → Lv. 36 → Samurott

MAIN WAY TO REGISTER IN THE NATIONAL POKÉDEX

Level up Dewott to Lv. 36.

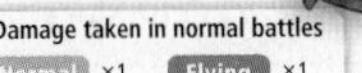

Damage taken in normal battles

Type		Type	
Normal	×1	Flying	×1
Fire	×0.5	Psychic	×1
Water	×0.5	Bug	×1
Grass	×2	Rock	×1
Electric	×2	Ghost	×1
Ice	×0.5	Dragon	×1
Fighting	×1	Dark	×1
Poison	×1	Steel	×0.5
Ground	×1	Fairy	×1

Damage taken in Inverse battles

Type		Type	
Normal	×1	Flying	×1
Fire	×2	Psychic	×1
Water	×2	Bug	×1
Grass	×0.5	Rock	×1
Electric	×0.5	Ghost	×1
Ice	×2	Dragon	×1
Fighting	×1	Dark	×1
Poison	×1	Steel	×2
Ground	×1	Fairy	×1

Can be used in
Inverse Battle
Battle Institute
Battle Maison
Random Matchup (Free Battle)
Random Matchup (Others)

LEVEL-UP MOVES

Lv.	Name	Type	Kind	Pow.	Acc.	PP	Range
1	Megahorn	Bug	Physical	120	85	10	Normal
1	Tackle	Normal	Physical	50	100	35	Normal
1	Tail Whip	Normal	Status	—	100	30	Many Others
1	Water Gun	Water	Special	40	100	25	Normal
1	Water Sport	Water	Status	—	—	15	Both Sides
5	Tail Whip	Normal	Status	—	100	30	Many Others
7	Water Gun	Water	Special	40	100	25	Normal
11	Water Sport	Water	Status	—	—	15	Both Sides
13	Focus Energy	Normal	Status	—	—	30	Self
17	Razor Shell	Water	Physical	75	95	10	Normal
20	Fury Cutter	Bug	Physical	40	95	20	Normal
25	Water Pulse	Water	Special	60	100	20	Normal
28	Revenge	Fighting	Physical	60	100	10	Normal
33	Aqua Jet	Water	Physical	40	100	20	Normal
36	Slash	Normal	Physical	70	100	20	Normal
38	Encore	Normal	Status	—	100	5	Normal
45	Aqua Tail	Water	Physical	90	90	10	Normal
50	Retaliate	Normal	Physical	70	100	5	Normal
57	Swords Dance	Normal	Status	—	—	20	Self
62	Hydro Pump	Water	Special	110	80	5	Normal

TM & HM MOVES

No.	Name	Type	Kind	Pow.	Acc.	PP	Range
TM06	Toxic	Poison	Status	—	90	10	Normal
TM07	Hail	Ice	Status	—	—	10	Both Sides
TM10	Hidden Power	Normal	Special	60	100	15	Normal
TM12	Taunt	Dark	Status	—	100	20	Normal
TM13	Ice Beam	Ice	Special	90	100	10	Normal
TM14	Blizzard	Ice	Special	110	70	5	Many Others
TM15	Hyper Beam	Normal	Special	150	90	5	Normal
TM17	Protect	Normal	Status	—	—	10	Self
TM18	Rain Dance	Water	Status	—	—	5	Both Sides
TM21	Frustration	Normal	Physical	—	100	20	Normal
TM27	Return	Normal	Physical	—	100	20	Normal
TM28	Dig	Ground	Physical	80	100	10	Normal
TM32	Double Team	Normal	Status	—	—	15	Self
TM40	Aerial Ace	Flying	Physical	60	—	20	Normal
TM42	Facade	Normal	Physical	70	100	20	Normal
TM44	Rest	Psychic	Status	—	—	10	Self
TM45	Attract	Normal	Status	—	100	15	Normal
TM48	Round	Normal	Special	60	100	15	Normal
TM54	False Swipe	Normal	Physical	40	100	40	Normal
TM55	Scald	Water	Special	80	100	15	Normal
TM56	Fling	Dark	Physical	—	100	10	Normal
TM67	Retaliate	Normal	Physical	70	100	5	Normal
TM68	Giga Impact	Normal	Physical	150	90	5	Normal
TM75	Swords Dance	Normal	Status	—	—	20	Self
TM81	X-Scissor	Bug	Physical	80	100	15	Normal
TM82	Dragon Tail	Dragon	Physical	60	90	10	Normal
TM86	Grass Knot	Grass	Special	—	100	20	Normal
TM87	Swagger	Normal	Status	—	90	15	Normal
TM88	Sleep Talk	Normal	Status	—	—	10	Self
TM90	Substitute	Normal	Status	—	—	10	Self
TM94	Secret Power	Normal	Physical	70	100	20	Normal
TM100	Confide	Normal	Status	—	—	20	Normal
HM01	Cut	Normal	Physical	50	95	30	Normal
HM03	Surf	Water	Special	90	100	15	Adjacent
HM04	Strength	Normal	Physical	80	100	15	Normal
HM05	Waterfall	Water	Physical	80	100	15	Normal
HM06	Rock Smash	Fighting	Physical	40	100	15	Normal
HM07	Dive	Water	Physical	80	100	10	Normal

MOVES LEARNED IN EXCHANGE FOR BP

Name	Type	Kind	Pow.	Acc.	PP	Range
Covet	Normal	Physical	60	100	25	Normal
Block	Normal	Status	—	—	5	Normal
Superpower	Fighting	Physical	120	100	5	Normal
Icy Wind	Ice	Special	55	95	15	Many Others
Aqua Tail	Water	Physical	90	90	10	Normal
Iron Tail	Steel	Physical	100	75	15	Normal
Snore	Normal	Special	50	100	15	Normal
Knock Off	Dark	Physical	65	100	20	Normal
Water Pulse	Water	Special	60	100	20	Normal
Helping Hand	Normal	Status	—	—	20	1 Ally

MOVES TAUGHT BY PEOPLE

Name	Type	Kind	Pow.	Acc.	PP	Range
Water Pledge	Water	Special	80	100	10	Normal
Hydro Cannon	Water	Special	150	90	5	Normal

National Pokédex **504** Hoenn Pokédex —

Patrat

Scout Pokémon

Normal

HEIGHT: 1'08" WEIGHT: 25.6 lbs.

Same form for ♂ / ♀

Ω Using food stored in cheek pouches, they can keep watch for days. They use their tails to communicate with others.

α Extremely cautious, one of them will always be on the lookout, but it won't notice a foe coming from behind.

ABILITIES
Run Away
Keen Eye

HIDDEN ABILITY
Analytic

EGG GROUPS
Field

STAT GROWTH RATES
HP ▮▮
Attack ▮▮▮
Defense ▮▮
Sp. Atk ▮▮
Sp. Def ▮▮
Speed ▮▮

ITEMS SOMETIMES HELD BY WILD POKÉMON
—

EVOLUTION
Patrat → Lv. 20 → Watchog

MAIN WAY TO REGISTER IN THE NATIONAL POKÉDEX

Leave a Watchog obtained via Link Trade or the GTS at a Pokémon Day Care, then hatch the Pokémon Egg that is found.

Damage taken in normal battles

Type		Type	
Normal	×1	Flying	×1
Fire	×1	Psychic	×1
Water	×1	Bug	×1
Grass	×1	Rock	×1
Electric	×1	Ghost	×0
Ice	×1	Dragon	×1
Fighting	×2	Dark	×1
Poison	×1	Steel	×1
Ground	×1	Fairy	×1

Damage taken in Inverse battles

Type		Type	
Normal	×1	Flying	×1
Fire	×1	Psychic	×1
Water	×1	Bug	×1
Grass	×1	Rock	×1
Electric	×1	Ghost	×2
Ice	×1	Dragon	×1
Fighting	×0.5	Dark	×1
Poison	×1	Steel	×1
Ground	×1	Fairy	×1

Can be used in
Inverse Battle
Battle Institute
Battle Maison
Random Matchup (Free Battle)
Random Matchup (Others)

LEVEL-UP MOVES

Lv.	Name	Type	Kind	Pow.	Acc.	PP	Range
1	Tackle	Normal	Physical	50	100	35	Normal
3	Leer	Normal	Status	—	100	30	Many Others
6	Bite	Dark	Physical	60	100	25	Normal
8	Bide	Normal	Physical	—	—	10	Self
11	Detect	Fighting	Status	—	—	5	Self
13	Sand Attack	Ground	Status	—	100	15	Normal
16	Crunch	Dark	Physical	80	100	15	Normal
18	Hypnosis	Psychic	Status	—	60	20	Normal
21	Super Fang	Normal	Physical	—	90	10	Normal
23	After You	Normal	Status	—	—	15	Normal
26	Work Up	Normal	Status	—	—	30	Self
28	Hyper Fang	Normal	Physical	80	90	15	Normal
31	Mean Look	Normal	Status	—	—	5	Normal
33	Baton Pass	Normal	Status	—	—	40	Self
36	Slam	Normal	Physical	80	75	20	Normal

TM & HM MOVES

No.	Name	Type	Kind	Pow.	Acc.	PP	Range
TM06	Toxic	Poison	Status	—	90	10	Normal
TM10	Hidden Power	Normal	Special	60	100	15	Normal
TM11	Sunny Day	Fire	Status	—	—	5	Both Sides
TM17	Protect	Normal	Status	—	—	10	Self
TM18	Rain Dance	Water	Status	—	—	5	Both Sides
TM21	Frustration	Normal	Physical	—	100	20	Normal
TM24	Thunderbolt	Electric	Special	90	100	15	Normal
TM27	Return	Normal	Physical	—	100	20	Normal
TM28	Dig	Ground	Physical	80	100	10	Normal
TM30	Shadow Ball	Ghost	Special	80	100	15	Normal
TM32	Double Team	Normal	Status	—	—	15	Self
TM42	Facade	Normal	Physical	70	100	20	Normal
TM44	Rest	Psychic	Status	—	—	10	Self
TM45	Attract	Normal	Status	—	100	15	Normal
TM48	Round	Normal	Special	60	100	15	Normal
TM56	Fling	Dark	Physical	—	100	10	Normal
TM67	Retaliate	Normal	Physical	70	100	5	Normal
TM75	Swords Dance	Normal	Status	—	—	20	Self
TM86	Grass Knot	Grass	Special	—	100	20	Normal
TM87	Swagger	Normal	Status	—	90	15	Normal
TM88	Sleep Talk	Normal	Status	—	—	10	Self
TM90	Substitute	Normal	Status	—	—	10	Self
TM94	Secret Power	Normal	Physical	70	100	20	Normal
TM100	Confide	Normal	Status	—	—	20	Normal
HM01	Cut	Normal	Physical	50	95	30	Normal

MOVES LEARNED IN EXCHANGE FOR BP

Name	Type	Kind	Pow.	Acc.	PP	Range
Covet	Normal	Physical	60	100	25	Normal
Super Fang	Normal	Physical	—	90	10	Normal
Seed Bomb	Grass	Physical	80	100	15	Normal
Low Kick	Fighting	Physical	—	100	20	Normal
Gunk Shot	Poison	Physical	120	80	5	Normal
Last Resort	Normal	Physical	140	100	5	Normal
Aqua Tail	Water	Physical	90	90	10	Normal
Zen Headbutt	Psychic	Physical	80	90	15	Normal
Iron Tail	Steel	Physical	100	75	15	Normal
Snore	Normal	Special	50	100	15	Normal
Shock Wave	Electric	Special	60	—	20	Normal
After You	Normal	Status	—	—	15	Normal
Helping Hand	Normal	Status	—	—	20	1 Ally
Endeavor	Normal	Physical	—	100	5	Normal

MOVES TAUGHT BY PEOPLE

Name	Type	Kind	Pow.	Acc.	PP	Range

EGG MOVES

Name	Type	Kind	Pow.	Acc.	PP	Range
Foresight	Normal	Status	—	—	40	Normal
Iron Tail	Steel	Physical	100	75	15	Normal
Screech	Normal	Status	—	85	40	Normal
Assurance	Dark	Physical	60	100	10	Normal
Pursuit	Dark	Physical	40	100	20	Normal
Revenge	Fighting	Physical	60	100	10	Normal
Flail	Normal	Physical	—	100	15	Normal

National Pokédex **505** Hoenn Pokédex —

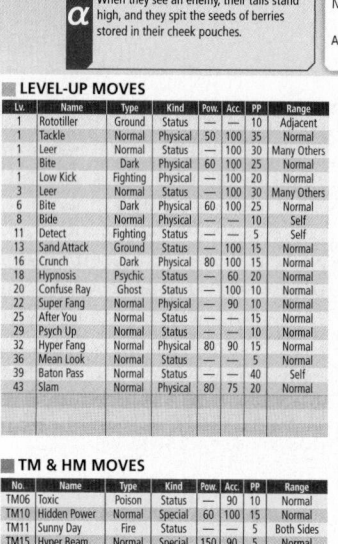

Watchog

Lookout Pokémon

Normal

HEIGHT: 3'07" WEIGHT: 59.5 lbs.

Same form for ♂ / ♀

Ω Using luminescent matter, it makes its eyes and body glow and stuns attacking opponents.

α When they see an enemy, their tails stand high, and they spit the seeds of berries stored in their cheek pouches.

ABILITIES
Illuminate
Keen Eye

HIDDEN ABILITY
Analytic

EGG GROUPS
Field

STAT GROWTH RATES
HP ■■■
Attack ■■■■
Defense ■■■
Sp. Atk ■■■
Sp. Def ■■■
Speed ■■■■

ITEMS SOMETIMES HELD BY WILD POKÉMON
—

EVOLUTION

MAIN WAY TO REGISTER IN THE NATIONAL POKÉDEX

Appears in *Pokémon X* and *Pokémon Y*. Bring it to your game using Link Trade or the GTS.

Damage taken in normal battles

Type	×	Type	×
Normal	×1	Flying	×1
Fire	×1	Psychic	×1
Water	×1	Bug	×1
Grass	×1	Rock	×1
Electric	×1	Ghost	×0
Ice	×1	Dragon	×1
Fighting	×2	Dark	×1
Poison	×1	Steel	×1
Ground	×1	Fairy	×1

Damage taken in Inverse battles

Type	×	Type	×
Normal	×1	Flying	×1
Fire	×1	Psychic	×1
Water	×1	Bug	×1
Grass	×1	Rock	×1
Electric	×1	Ghost	×2
Ice	×1	Dragon	×1
Fighting	×0.5	Dark	×1
Poison	×1	Steel	×1
Ground	×1	Fairy	×1

Can be used in
Inverse Battle
Battle Institute
Battle Maison
Random Matchup (Free Battle)
Random Matchup (Others)

LEVEL-UP MOVES

Lv.	Name	Type	Kind	Pow.	Acc.	PP	Range
1	Rototiller	Ground	Status	—	—	10	Adjacent
1	Tackle	Normal	Physical	50	100	35	Normal
1	Leer	Normal	Status	—	100	30	Many Others
1	Bite	Dark	Physical	60	100	25	Normal
1	Low Kick	Fighting	Physical	—	100	20	Normal
3	Leer	Normal	Status	—	100	30	Many Others
6	Bite	Dark	Physical	60	100	25	Normal
8	Bide	Normal	Physical	—	—	10	Self
11	Detect	Fighting	Status	—	—	5	Self
13	Sand Attack	Ground	Status	—	100	15	Normal
16	Crunch	Dark	Physical	80	100	15	Normal
18	Hypnosis	Psychic	Status	—	60	20	Normal
20	Confuse Ray	Ghost	Status	—	100	10	Normal
22	Super Fang	Normal	Physical	—	90	10	Normal
25	After You	Normal	Status	—	—	15	Normal
29	Psych Up	Normal	Status	—	—	10	Normal
32	Hyper Fang	Normal	Physical	80	90	15	Normal
36	Mean Look	Normal	Status	—	—	5	Normal
39	Baton Pass	Normal	Status	—	—	40	Self
43	Slam	Normal	Physical	80	75	20	Normal

TM & HM MOVES

No.	Name	Type	Kind	Pow.	Acc.	PP	Range
TM06	Toxic	Poison	Status	—	90	10	Normal
TM10	Hidden Power	Normal	Special	60	100	15	Normal
TM11	Sunny Day	Fire	Status	—	—	5	Both Sides
TM15	Hyper Beam	Normal	Special	150	90	5	Normal
TM16	Light Screen	Psychic	Status	—	—	30	Your Side
TM17	Protect	Normal	Status	—	—	10	Self
TM18	Rain Dance	Water	Status	—	—	5	Both Sides
TM21	Frustration	Normal	Physical	—	100	20	Normal
TM24	Thunderbolt	Electric	Special	90	100	15	Normal
TM25	Thunder	Electric	Special	110	70	10	Normal
TM27	Return	Normal	Physical	—	100	20	Normal
TM28	Dig	Ground	Physical	80	100	10	Normal
TM30	Shadow Ball	Ghost	Special	80	100	15	Normal
TM32	Double Team	Normal	Status	—	—	15	Self
TM35	Flamethrower	Fire	Special	90	100	15	Normal
TM42	Facade	Normal	Physical	70	100	20	Normal
TM44	Rest	Psychic	Status	—	—	10	Self
TM45	Attract	Normal	Status	—	100	15	Normal
TM48	Round	Normal	Special	60	100	15	Normal
TM52	Focus Blast	Fighting	Special	120	70	5	Normal
TM56	Fling	Dark	Physical	—	100	10	Normal
TM67	Retaliate	Normal	Physical	70	100	5	Normal
TM68	Giga Impact	Normal	Physical	150	90	5	Normal
TM70	Flash	Normal	Status	—	100	20	Normal
TM73	Thunder Wave	Electric	Status	—	100	20	Normal
TM75	Swords Dance	Normal	Status	—	—	20	Self
TM77	Psych Up	Normal	Status	—	—	10	Normal
TM85	Dream Eater	Psychic	Special	100	100	15	Normal
TM86	Grass Knot	Grass	Special	—	100	20	Normal
TM87	Swagger	Normal	Status	—	90	15	Normal
TM88	Sleep Talk	Normal	Status	—	—	10	Self
TM90	Substitute	Normal	Status	—	—	10	Self
TM94	Secret Power	Normal	Physical	70	100	20	Normal
TM98	Power-Up Punch	Fighting	Physical	40	100	20	Normal
TM100	Confide	Normal	Status	—	—	20	Normal
HM01	Cut	Normal	Physical	50	95	30	Normal
HM04	Strength	Normal	Physical	80	100	15	Normal
HM06	Rock Smash	Fighting	Physical	40	100	15	Normal

MOVES LEARNED IN EXCHANGE FOR BP

Name	Type	Kind	Pow.	Acc.	PP	Range
Covet	Normal	Physical	60	100	25	Normal
Super Fang	Normal	Physical	—	90	10	Normal
Signal Beam	Bug	Special	75	100	15	Normal
Seed Bomb	Grass	Physical	80	100	15	Normal
Low Kick	Fighting	Physical	—	100	20	Normal
Gunk Shot	Poison	Physical	120	80	5	Normal
Thunder Punch	Electric	Physical	75	100	15	Normal
Fire Punch	Fire	Physical	75	100	15	Normal
Ice Punch	Ice	Physical	75	100	15	Normal
Last Resort	Normal	Physical	140	100	5	Normal
Aqua Tail	Water	Physical	90	90	10	Normal
Zen Headbutt	Psychic	Physical	80	90	15	Normal
Iron Tail	Steel	Physical	100	75	15	Normal
Snore	Normal	Special	50	100	15	Normal
Knock Off	Dark	Physical	65	100	20	Normal
Focus Punch	Fighting	Physical	150	100	20	Normal
Shock Wave	Electric	Special	60	—	20	Normal
After You	Normal	Status	—	—	15	Normal
Helping Hand	Normal	Status	—	—	20	1 Ally
Endeavor	Normal	Physical	—	100	5	Normal

MOVES TAUGHT BY PEOPLE

Name	Type	Kind	Pow.	Acc.	PP	Range

National Pokédex **506** Hoenn Pokédex —

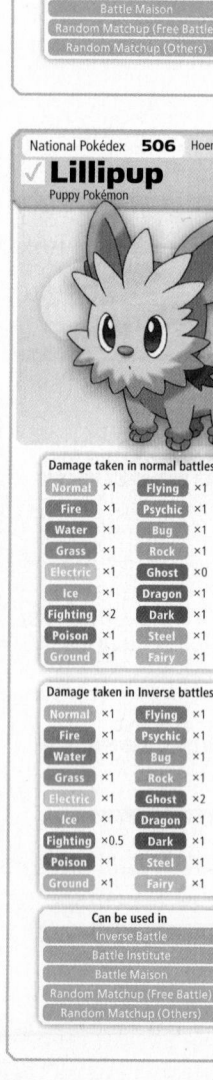

Lillipup

Puppy Pokémon

Normal

HEIGHT: 1'04" WEIGHT: 9 lbs.

Same form for ♂ / ♀

Ω The long hair around its face provides an amazing radar that lets it sense subtle changes in its surroundings.

α Though it is a very brave Pokémon, it's also smart enough to check its foe's strength and avoid battle.

ABILITIES
Vital Spirit
Pickup

HIDDEN ABILITY
Run Away

EGG GROUPS
Field

STAT GROWTH RATES
HP ■■
Attack ■■■
Defense ■■
Sp. Atk ■■
Sp. Def ■■
Speed ■■■

ITEMS SOMETIMES HELD BY WILD POKÉMON
—

EVOLUTION

MAIN WAY TO REGISTER IN THE NATIONAL POKÉDEX

Catch on Route 101. Appears as a hidden Pokémon after you battle Groudon or Kyogre.

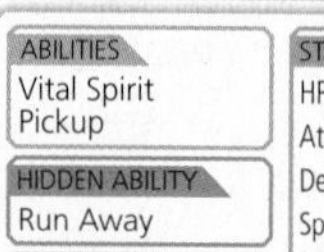

Damage taken in normal battles

Type	×	Type	×
Normal	×1	Flying	×1
Fire	×1	Psychic	×1
Water	×1	Bug	×1
Grass	×1	Rock	×1
Electric	×1	Ghost	×0
Ice	×1	Dragon	×1
Fighting	×2	Dark	×1
Poison	×1	Steel	×1
Ground	×1	Fairy	×1

Damage taken in Inverse battles

Type	×	Type	×
Normal	×1	Flying	×1
Fire	×1	Psychic	×1
Water	×1	Bug	×1
Grass	×1	Rock	×1
Electric	×1	Ghost	×2
Ice	×1	Dragon	×1
Fighting	×0.5	Dark	×1
Poison	×1	Steel	×1
Ground	×1	Fairy	×1

Can be used in
Inverse Battle
Battle Institute
Battle Maison
Random Matchup (Free Battle)
Random Matchup (Others)

LEVEL-UP MOVES

Lv.	Name	Type	Kind	Pow.	Acc.	PP	Range
1	Leer	Normal	Status	—	100	30	Many Others
1	Tackle	Normal	Physical	50	100	35	Normal
5	Odor Sleuth	Normal	Status	—	—	40	Normal
8	Bite	Dark	Physical	60	100	25	Normal
10	Baby-Doll Eyes	Fairy	Status	—	100	30	Normal
12	Helping Hand	Normal	Status	—	—	20	1 Ally
15	Take Down	Normal	Physical	90	85	20	Normal
19	Work Up	Normal	Status	—	—	30	Self
22	Crunch	Dark	Physical	80	100	15	Normal
26	Roar	Normal	Status	—	—	20	Normal
29	Retaliate	Normal	Physical	70	100	5	Normal
33	Reversal	Fighting	Physical	—	100	15	Normal
36	Last Resort	Normal	Physical	140	100	5	Normal
40	Giga Impact	Normal	Physical	150	90	5	Normal
45	Play Rough	Fairy	Physical	90	90	10	Normal

TM & HM MOVES

No.	Name	Type	Kind	Pow.	Acc.	PP	Range
TM05	Roar	Normal	Status	—	—	20	Normal
TM06	Toxic	Poison	Status	—	90	10	Normal
TM10	Hidden Power	Normal	Special	60	100	15	Normal
TM11	Sunny Day	Fire	Status	—	—	5	Both Sides
TM17	Protect	Normal	Status	—	—	10	Self
TM18	Rain Dance	Water	Status	—	—	5	Both Sides
TM21	Frustration	Normal	Physical	—	100	20	Normal
TM24	Thunderbolt	Electric	Special	90	100	15	Normal
TM27	Return	Normal	Physical	—	100	20	Normal
TM28	Dig	Ground	Physical	80	100	10	Normal
TM30	Shadow Ball	Ghost	Special	80	100	15	Normal
TM32	Double Team	Normal	Status	—	—	15	Self
TM39	Rock Tomb	Rock	Physical	60	95	15	Normal
TM40	Aerial Ace	Flying	Physical	60	—	20	Normal
TM42	Facade	Normal	Physical	70	100	20	Normal
TM44	Rest	Psychic	Status	—	—	10	Self
TM45	Attract	Normal	Status	—	100	15	Normal
TM48	Round	Normal	Special	60	100	15	Normal
TM67	Retaliate	Normal	Physical	70	100	5	Normal
TM68	Giga Impact	Normal	Physical	150	90	5	Normal
TM73	Thunder Wave	Electric	Status	—	100	20	Normal
TM87	Swagger	Normal	Status	—	90	15	Normal
TM88	Sleep Talk	Normal	Status	—	—	10	Self
TM90	Substitute	Normal	Status	—	—	10	Self
TM93	Wild Charge	Electric	Physical	90	100	15	Normal
TM94	Secret Power	Normal	Physical	70	100	20	Normal
TM95	Snarl	Dark	Special	55	95	15	Many Others
TM100	Confide	Normal	Status	—	—	20	Normal
HM06	Rock Smash	Fighting	Physical	40	100	15	Normal

MOVES LEARNED IN EXCHANGE FOR BP

Name	Type	Kind	Pow.	Acc.	PP	Range
Covet	Normal	Physical	60	100	25	Normal
Uproar	Normal	Special	90	100	10	1 Random
Last Resort	Normal	Physical	140	100	5	Normal
Hyper Voice	Normal	Special	90	100	10	Many Others
Snore	Normal	Special	50	100	15	Normal
Shock Wave	Electric	Special	60	—	20	Normal
After You	Normal	Status	—	—	15	Normal
Helping Hand	Normal	Status	—	—	20	1 Ally

MOVES TAUGHT BY PEOPLE

Name	Type	Kind	Pow.	Acc.	PP	Range

EGG MOVES

Name	Type	Kind	Pow.	Acc.	PP	Range
Howl	Normal	Status	—	—	40	Self
Sand Attack	Ground	Status	—	100	15	Normal
Mud-Slap	Ground	Special	20	100	10	Normal
Lick	Ghost	Physical	30	100	30	Normal
Charm	Fairy	Status	—	100	20	Normal
Endure	Normal	Status	—	—	10	Self
Yawn	Normal	Status	—	—	10	Normal
Pursuit	Dark	Physical	40	100	20	Normal
Fire Fang	Fire	Physical	65	95	15	Normal
Thunder Fang	Electric	Physical	65	95	15	Normal
Ice Fang	Ice	Physical	65	95	15	Normal
After You	Normal	Status	—	—	15	Normal

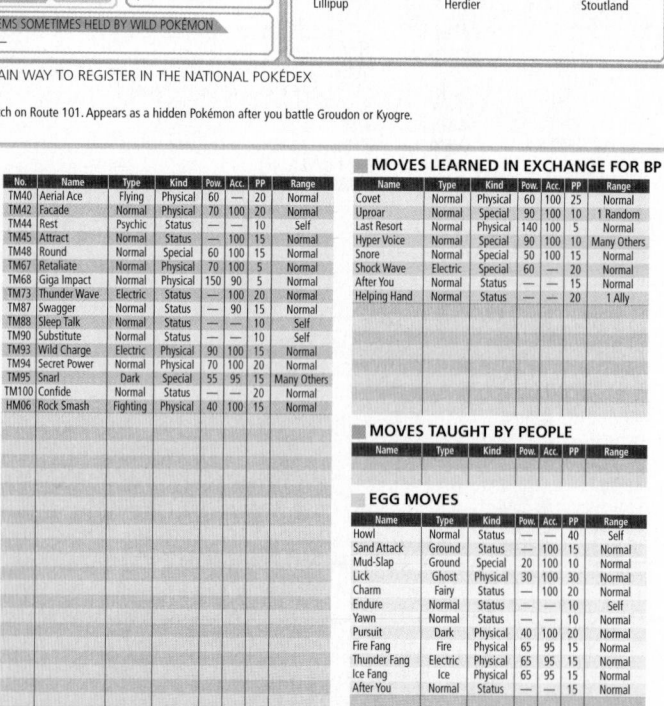

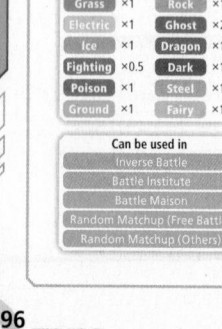

National Pokédex **507** Hoenn Pokédex —

✓ Herdier

Loyal Dog Pokémon

Normal

HEIGHT: 2'11" WEIGHT: 32.4 lbs.

Same form for ♂ / ♀

Ω This very loyal Pokémon helps Trainers, and it also takes care of other Pokémon.

α It has black, cape-like fur that is very hard and decreases the amount of damage it receives.

ABILITIES
Intimidate
Sand Rush

HIDDEN ABILITY
Scrappy

EGG GROUPS
Field

STAT GROWTH RATES

HP	■■■
Attack	■■■■
Defense	■■■
Sp. Atk	■■
Sp. Def	■■■
Speed	■■■

ITEMS SOMETIMES HELD BY WILD POKÉMON
—

EVOLUTION
Lillipup → Lv. 16 → Herdier → Lv. 32 → Stoutland

MAIN WAY TO REGISTER IN THE NATIONAL POKÉDEX

Level up Lillipup to Lv. 16.

Damage taken in normal battles

Type		Type	
Normal	×1	Flying	×1
Fire	×1	Psychic	×1
Water	×1	Bug	×1
Grass	×1	Rock	×1
Electric	×1	Ghost	×0
Ice	×1	Dragon	×1
Fighting	×2	Dark	×1
Poison	×1	Steel	×1
Ground	×1	Fairy	×1

Damage taken in Inverse battles

Type		Type	
Normal	×1	Flying	×1
Fire	×1	Psychic	×1
Water	×1	Bug	×1
Grass	×1	Rock	×1
Electric	×1	Ghost	×2
Ice	×1	Dragon	×1
Fighting	×0.5	Dark	×1
Poison	×1	Steel	×1
Ground	×1	Fairy	×1

Can be used in
Inverse Battle
Battle Institute
Battle Maison
Random Matchup (Free Battle)
Random Matchup (Others)

LEVEL-UP MOVES

Lv.	Name	Type	Kind	Pow.	Acc.	PP	Range
1	Leer	Normal	Status	—	100	30	Many Others
1	Tackle	Normal	Physical	50	100	35	Normal
1	Odor Sleuth	Normal	Status	—	—	40	Normal
1	Bite	Dark	Physical	60	100	25	Normal
5	Odor Sleuth	Normal	Status	—	—	40	Normal
8	Bite	Dark	Physical	60	100	25	Normal
12	Helping Hand	Normal	Status	—	—	20	1 Ally
15	Take Down	Normal	Physical	90	85	20	Normal
20	Work Up	Normal	Status	—	—	30	Self
24	Crunch	Dark	Physical	80	100	15	Normal
29	Roar	Normal	Status	—	—	20	Normal
33	Retaliate	Normal	Physical	70	100	5	Normal
38	Reversal	Fighting	Physical	—	100	15	Normal
42	Last Resort	Normal	Physical	140	100	5	Normal
47	Giga Impact	Normal	Physical	150	90	5	Normal
52	Play Rough	Fairy	Physical	90	90	10	Normal

TM & HM MOVES

No.	Name	Type	Kind	Pow.	Acc.	PP	Range
TM05	Roar	Normal	Status	—	—	20	Normal
TM06	Toxic	Poison	Status	—	90	10	Normal
TM10	Hidden Power	Normal	Special	60	100	15	Normal
TM11	Sunny Day	Fire	Status	—	—	5	Both Sides
TM17	Protect	Normal	Status	—	—	10	Self
TM18	Rain Dance	Water	Status	—	—	5	Both Sides
TM21	Frustration	Normal	Physical	—	100	20	Normal
TM24	Thunderbolt	Electric	Special	90	100	15	Normal
TM27	Return	Normal	Physical	—	100	20	Normal
TM28	Dig	Ground	Physical	80	100	10	Normal
TM30	Shadow Ball	Ghost	Special	80	100	15	Normal
TM32	Double Team	Normal	Status	—	—	15	Self
TM39	Rock Tomb	Rock	Physical	60	95	15	Normal
TM40	Aerial Ace	Flying	Physical	60	—	20	Normal
TM42	Facade	Normal	Physical	70	100	20	Normal
TM44	Rest	Psychic	Status	—	—	10	Self
TM45	Attract	Normal	Status	—	100	15	Normal
TM48	Round	Normal	Special	60	100	15	Normal
TM66	Payback	Dark	Physical	50	100	10	Normal
TM67	Retaliate	Normal	Physical	70	100	5	Normal
TM68	Giga Impact	Normal	Physical	150	90	5	Normal
TM73	Thunder Wave	Electric	Status	—	100	20	Normal
TM87	Swagger	Normal	Status	—	90	15	Normal
TM88	Sleep Talk	Normal	Status	—	—	10	Self
TM90	Substitute	Normal	Status	—	—	10	Self
TM93	Wild Charge	Electric	Physical	90	100	15	Normal
TM94	Secret Power	Normal	Physical	70	100	20	Normal
TM95	Snarl	Dark	Special	55	95	15	Many Others
TM100	Confide	Normal	Status	—	—	20	Normal
HM03	Surf	Water	Special	90	100	15	Adjacent
HM04	Strength	Normal	Physical	80	100	15	Normal
HM06	Rock Smash	Fighting	Physical	40	100	15	Normal

MOVES LEARNED IN EXCHANGE FOR BP

Name	Type	Kind	Pow.	Acc.	PP	Range
Covet	Normal	Physical	60	100	25	Normal
Uproar	Normal	Special	90	100	10	1 Random
Last Resort	Normal	Physical	140	100	5	Normal
Hyper Voice	Normal	Special	90	100	10	Many Others
Snore	Normal	Special	50	100	15	Normal
Shock Wave	Electric	Special	60	—	20	Normal
After You	Normal	Status	—	—	15	Normal
Helping Hand	Normal	Status	—	—	20	1 Ally

MOVES TAUGHT BY PEOPLE

Name	Type	Kind	Pow.	Acc.	PP	Range

National Pokédex **508** Hoenn Pokédex —

✓ Stoutland

Big-Hearted Pokémon

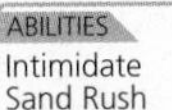

Normal

HEIGHT: 3'11" WEIGHT: 134.5 lbs.

Same form for ♂ / ♀

Ω It rescues people stranded by blizzards in the mountains. Its shaggy fur shields it from the cold.

α Being wrapped in its long fur is so comfortable that a person would be fine even overnight on a wintry mountain.

ABILITIES
Intimidate
Sand Rush

HIDDEN ABILITY
Scrappy

EGG GROUPS
Field

STAT GROWTH RATES

HP	■■■
Attack	■■■■■
Defense	■■■■
Sp. Atk	■■
Sp. Def	■■■■
Speed	■■■■

ITEMS SOMETIMES HELD BY WILD POKÉMON
—

EVOLUTION

Lillipup → Lv. 16 → Herdier → Lv. 32 → Stoutland

MAIN WAY TO REGISTER IN THE NATIONAL POKÉDEX

Level up Herdier to Lv. 32.

Damage taken in normal battles

Type		Type	
Normal	×1	Flying	×1
Fire	×1	Psychic	×1
Water	×1	Bug	×1
Grass	×1	Rock	×1
Electric	×1	Ghost	×0
Ice	×1	Dragon	×1
Fighting	×2	Dark	×1
Poison	×1	Steel	×1
Ground	×1	Fairy	×1

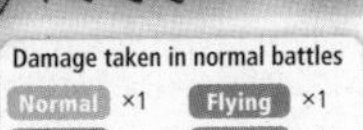

Damage taken in Inverse battles

Type		Type	
Normal	×1	Flying	×1
Fire	×1	Psychic	×1
Water	×1	Bug	×1
Grass	×1	Rock	×1
Electric	×1	Ghost	×2
Ice	×1	Dragon	×1
Fighting	×0.5	Dark	×1
Poison	×1	Steel	×1
Ground	×1	Fairy	×1

Can be used in
Inverse Battle
Battle Institute
Battle Maison
Random Matchup (Free Battle)
Random Matchup (Others)

LEVEL-UP MOVES

Lv.	Name	Type	Kind	Pow.	Acc.	PP	Range
1	Ice Fang	Ice	Physical	65	95	15	Normal
1	Fire Fang	Fire	Physical	65	95	15	Normal
1	Thunder Fang	Electric	Physical	65	95	15	Normal
1	Leer	Normal	Status	—	100	30	Many Others
1	Tackle	Normal	Physical	50	100	35	Normal
1	Odor Sleuth	Normal	Status	—	—	40	Normal
1	Bite	Dark	Physical	60	100	25	Normal
5	Odor Sleuth	Normal	Status	—	—	40	Normal
8	Bite	Dark	Physical	60	100	25	Normal
12	Helping Hand	Normal	Status	—	—	20	1 Ally
15	Take Down	Normal	Physical	90	85	20	Normal
20	Work Up	Normal	Status	—	—	30	Self
24	Crunch	Dark	Physical	80	100	15	Normal
29	Roar	Normal	Status	—	—	20	Normal
36	Retaliate	Normal	Physical	70	100	5	Normal
42	Reversal	Fighting	Physical	—	100	15	Normal
51	Last Resort	Normal	Physical	140	100	5	Normal
59	Giga Impact	Normal	Physical	150	90	5	Normal
63	Play Rough	Fairy	Physical	90	90	10	Normal

TM & HM MOVES

No.	Name	Type	Kind	Pow.	Acc.	PP	Range
TM05	Roar	Normal	Status	—	—	20	Normal
TM06	Toxic	Poison	Status	—	90	10	Normal
TM10	Hidden Power	Normal	Special	60	100	15	Normal
TM11	Sunny Day	Fire	Status	—	—	5	Both Sides
TM15	Hyper Beam	Normal	Special	150	90	5	Normal
TM17	Protect	Normal	Status	—	—	10	Self
TM18	Rain Dance	Water	Status	—	—	5	Both Sides
TM21	Frustration	Normal	Physical	—	100	20	Normal
TM24	Thunderbolt	Electric	Special	90	100	15	Normal
TM25	Thunder	Electric	Special	110	70	10	Normal
TM27	Return	Normal	Physical	—	100	20	Normal
TM28	Dig	Ground	Physical	80	100	10	Normal
TM30	Shadow Ball	Ghost	Special	80	100	15	Normal
TM32	Double Team	Normal	Status	—	—	15	Self
TM39	Rock Tomb	Rock	Physical	60	95	15	Normal
TM40	Aerial Ace	Flying	Physical	60	—	20	Normal
TM42	Facade	Normal	Physical	70	100	20	Normal
TM44	Rest	Psychic	Status	—	—	10	Self
TM45	Attract	Normal	Status	—	100	15	Normal
TM48	Round	Normal	Special	60	100	15	Normal
TM66	Payback	Dark	Physical	50	100	10	Normal
TM67	Retaliate	Normal	Physical	70	100	5	Normal
TM68	Giga Impact	Normal	Physical	150	90	5	Normal
TM73	Thunder Wave	Electric	Status	—	100	20	Normal
TM87	Swagger	Normal	Status	—	90	15	Normal
TM88	Sleep Talk	Normal	Status	—	—	10	Self
TM90	Substitute	Normal	Status	—	—	10	Self
TM93	Wild Charge	Electric	Physical	90	100	15	Normal
TM94	Secret Power	Normal	Physical	70	100	20	Normal
TM95	Snarl	Dark	Special	55	95	15	Many Others
TM100	Confide	Normal	Status	—	—	20	Normal
HM03	Surf	Water	Special	90	100	15	Adjacent
HM04	Strength	Normal	Physical	80	100	15	Normal
HM06	Rock Smash	Fighting	Physical	40	100	15	Normal

MOVES LEARNED IN EXCHANGE FOR BP

Name	Type	Kind	Pow.	Acc.	PP	Range
Covet	Normal	Physical	60	100	25	Normal
Iron Head	Steel	Physical	80	100	15	Normal
Uproar	Normal	Special	90	100	10	1 Random
Last Resort	Normal	Physical	140	100	5	Normal
Superpower	Fighting	Physical	120	100	5	Normal
Hyper Voice	Normal	Special	90	100	10	Many Others
Snore	Normal	Special	50	100	15	Normal
Shock Wave	Electric	Special	60	—	20	Normal
After You	Normal	Status	—	—	15	Normal
Helping Hand	Normal	Status	—	—	20	1 Ally

MOVES TAUGHT BY PEOPLE

Name	Type	Kind	Pow.	Acc.	PP	Range

National Pokédex **509** Hoenn Pokédex —

Purrloin

Devious Pokémon

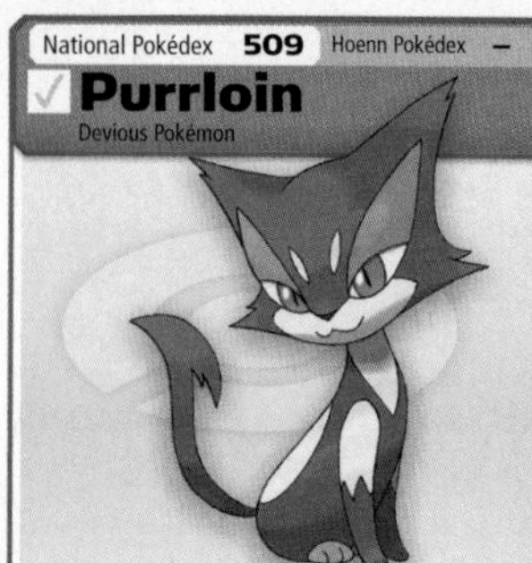

Dark

HEIGHT: 1'04" WEIGHT: 22.3 lbs.

Same form for ♂ / ♀

Ω Its cute act is a ruse. When victims let down their guard, they find their items taken. It attacks with sharp claws.

α They steal from people for fun, but their victims can't help but forgive them. Their deceptively cute act is perfect.

ABILITIES
Limber
Unburden

HIDDEN ABILITY
Prankster

EGG GROUPS
Field

STAT GROWTH RATES
HP
Attack
Defense
Sp. Atk
Sp. Def
Speed

ITEMS SOMETIMES HELD BY WILD POKÉMON
—

EVOLUTION

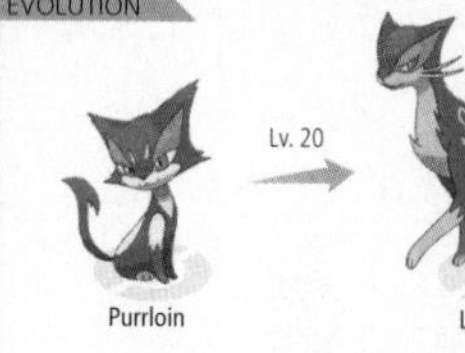

MAIN WAY TO REGISTER IN THE NATIONAL POKÉDEX

Leave a Liepard obtained via Link Trade or the GTS at a Pokémon Day Care, then hatch the Pokémon Egg that is found.

Damage taken in normal battles

Type		Type	
Normal	×1	Flying	×1
Fire	×1	Psychic	×0
Water	×1	Bug	×2
Grass	×1	Rock	×1
Electric	×1	Ghost	×0.5
Ice	×1	Dragon	×1
Fighting	×2	Dark	×0.5
Poison	×1	Steel	×1
Ground	×1	Fairy	×2

Damage taken in Inverse battles

Type		Type	
Normal	×1	Flying	×1
Fire	×1	Psychic	×2
Water	×1	Bug	×0.5
Grass	×1	Rock	×1
Electric	×1	Ghost	×2
Ice	×1	Dragon	×1
Fighting	×0.5	Dark	×2
Poison	×1	Steel	×1
Ground	×1	Fairy	×0.5

Can be used in
Inverse Battle
Battle Institute
Battle Maison
Random Matchup (Free Battle)
Random Matchup (Others)

LEVEL-UP MOVES

Lv.	Name	Type	Kind	Pow.	Acc.	PP	Range
1	Scratch	Normal	Physical	40	100	35	Normal
3	Growl	Normal	Status	—	100	40	Many Others
6	Assist	Normal	Status	—	—	20	Self
10	Sand Attack	Ground	Status	—	100	15	Normal
12	Fury Swipes	Normal	Physical	18	80	15	Normal
15	Pursuit	Dark	Physical	40	100	20	Normal
19	Torment	Dark	Status	—	100	15	Normal
21	Fake Out	Normal	Physical	40	100	10	Normal
24	Hone Claws	Dark	Status	—	—	15	Self
28	Assurance	Dark	Physical	60	100	10	Normal
30	Slash	Normal	Physical	70	100	20	Normal
33	Captivate	Normal	Status	—	100	20	Many Others
37	Night Slash	Dark	Physical	70	100	15	Normal
39	Snatch	Dark	Status	—	—	10	Self
42	Nasty Plot	Dark	Status	—	—	20	Self
46	Sucker Punch	Dark	Physical	80	100	5	Normal
49	Play Rough	Fairy	Physical	90	90	10	Normal

TM & HM MOVES

No.	Name	Type	Kind	Pow.	Acc.	PP	Range
TM01	Hone Claws	Dark	Status	—	—	15	Self
TM06	Toxic	Poison	Status	—	90	10	Normal
TM10	Hidden Power	Normal	Special	60	100	15	Normal
TM11	Sunny Day	Fire	Status	—	—	5	Both Sides
TM12	Taunt	Dark	Status	—	100	20	Normal
TM17	Protect	Normal	Status	—	—	10	Self
TM18	Rain Dance	Water	Status	—	—	5	Both Sides
TM21	Frustration	Normal	Physical	—	100	20	Normal
TM27	Return	Normal	Physical	—	100	20	Normal
TM30	Shadow Ball	Ghost	Special	80	100	15	Normal
TM32	Double Team	Normal	Status	—	—	15	Self
TM40	Aerial Ace	Flying	Physical	60	—	20	Normal
TM41	Torment	Dark	Status	—	100	15	Normal
TM42	Facade	Normal	Physical	70	100	20	Normal
TM44	Rest	Psychic	Status	—	—	10	Self
TM45	Attract	Normal	Status	—	100	15	Normal
TM46	Thief	Dark	Physical	60	100	25	Normal
TM48	Round	Normal	Special	60	100	15	Normal
TM49	Echoed Voice	Normal	Special	40	100	15	Normal
TM63	Embargo	Dark	Status	—	100	15	Normal
TM65	Shadow Claw	Ghost	Physical	70	100	15	Normal
TM66	Payback	Dark	Physical	50	100	10	Normal
TM73	Thunder Wave	Electric	Status	—	100	20	Normal
TM77	Psych Up	Normal	Status	—	—	10	Normal
TM85	Dream Eater	Psychic	Special	100	100	15	Normal
TM86	Grass Knot	Grass	Special	—	100	20	Normal
TM87	Swagger	Normal	Status	—	90	15	Normal
TM88	Sleep Talk	Normal	Status	—	—	10	Self
TM89	U-turn	Bug	Physical	70	100	20	Normal
TM90	Substitute	Normal	Status	—	—	10	Self
TM94	Secret Power	Normal	Physical	70	100	20	Normal
TM95	Snarl	Dark	Special	55	95	15	Many Others
TM97	Dark Pulse	Dark	Special	80	100	15	Normal
TM100	Confide	Normal	Status	—	—	20	Normal
HM01	Cut	Normal	Physical	50	95	30	Normal

MOVES LEARNED IN EXCHANGE FOR BP

Name	Type	Kind	Pow.	Acc.	PP	Range
Covet	Normal	Physical	60	100	25	Normal
Seed Bomb	Grass	Physical	80	100	15	Normal
Gunk Shot	Poison	Physical	120	80	5	Normal
Foul Play	Dark	Physical	95	100	15	Normal
Hyper Voice	Normal	Special	90	100	10	Many Others
Iron Tail	Steel	Physical	100	75	15	Normal
Snore	Normal	Special	50	100	15	Normal
Knock Off	Dark	Physical	65	100	20	Normal
Role Play	Psychic	Status	—	—	10	Normal
Spite	Ghost	Status	—	100	10	Normal
Trick	Psychic	Status	—	100	10	Normal
Snatch	Dark	Status	—	—	10	Self

MOVES TAUGHT BY PEOPLE

Name	Type	Kind	Pow.	Acc.	PP	Range

EGG MOVES

Name	Type	Kind	Pow.	Acc.	PP	Range
Pay Day	Normal	Physical	40	100	20	Normal
Foul Play	Dark	Physical	95	100	15	Normal
Feint Attack	Dark	Physical	60	—	20	Normal
Fake Tears	Dark	Status	—	100	20	Normal
Charm	Fairy	Status	—	100	20	Normal
Encore	Normal	Status	—	100	5	Normal
Yawn	Normal	Status	—	—	10	Normal
Covet	Normal	Physical	60	100	25	Normal
Copycat	Normal	Status	—	—	20	Self

National Pokédex **510** Hoenn Pokédex —

Liepard

Cruel Pokémon

Dark

HEIGHT: 3'07" WEIGHT: 82.7 lbs.

Same form for ♂ / ♀

Ω Their beautiful form comes from the muscles they have developed. They run silently in the night.

α Stealthily, it sneaks up on its target, striking from behind before its victim has a chance to react.

ABILITIES
Limber
Unburden

HIDDEN ABILITY
Prankster

EGG GROUPS
Field

STAT GROWTH RATES
HP
Attack
Defense
Sp. Atk
Sp. Def
Speed

ITEMS SOMETIMES HELD BY WILD POKÉMON
—

EVOLUTION

MAIN WAY TO REGISTER IN THE NATIONAL POKÉDEX

Appears in *Pokémon Y*. Bring it to your game using Link Trade or the GTS.

Damage taken in normal battles

Type		Type	
Normal	×1	Flying	×1
Fire	×1	Psychic	×0
Water	×1	Bug	×2
Grass	×1	Rock	×1
Electric	×1	Ghost	×0.5
Ice	×1	Dragon	×1
Fighting	×2	Dark	×0.5
Poison	×1	Steel	×1
Ground	×1	Fairy	×2

Damage taken in Inverse battles

Type		Type	
Normal	×1	Flying	×1
Fire	×1	Psychic	×2
Water	×1	Bug	×0.5
Grass	×1	Rock	×1
Electric	×1	Ghost	×2
Ice	×1	Dragon	×1
Fighting	×0.5	Dark	×2
Poison	×1	Steel	×1
Ground	×1	Fairy	×0.5

Can be used in
Inverse Battle
Battle Institute
Battle Maison
Random Matchup (Free Battle)
Random Matchup (Others)

LEVEL-UP MOVES

Lv.	Name	Type	Kind	Pow.	Acc.	PP	Range
1	Scratch	Normal	Physical	40	100	35	Normal
1	Growl	Normal	Status	—	100	40	Many Others
1	Assist	Normal	Status	—	—	20	Self
1	Sand Attack	Ground	Status	—	100	15	Normal
3	Growl	Normal	Status	—	100	40	Many Others
6	Assist	Normal	Status	—	—	20	Self
10	Sand Attack	Ground	Status	—	100	15	Normal
12	Fury Swipes	Normal	Physical	18	80	15	Normal
15	Pursuit	Dark	Physical	40	100	20	Normal
19	Torment	Dark	Status	—	100	15	Normal
22	Fake Out	Normal	Physical	40	100	10	Normal
26	Hone Claws	Dark	Status	—	—	15	Self
31	Assurance	Dark	Physical	60	100	10	Normal
34	Slash	Normal	Physical	70	100	20	Normal
38	Taunt	Dark	Status	—	100	20	Normal
43	Night Slash	Dark	Physical	70	100	15	Normal
47	Snatch	Dark	Status	—	—	10	Self
50	Nasty Plot	Dark	Status	—	—	20	Self
55	Sucker Punch	Dark	Physical	80	100	5	Normal
58	Play Rough	Fairy	Physical	90	90	10	Normal

TM & HM MOVES

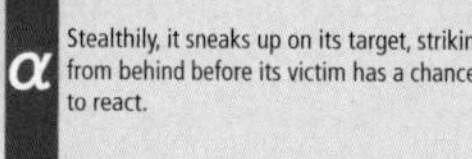

No.	Name	Type	Kind	Pow.	Acc.	PP	Range
TM01	Hone Claws	Dark	Status	—	—	15	Self
TM06	Toxic	Poison	Status	—	90	10	Normal
TM10	Hidden Power	Normal	Special	60	100	15	Normal
TM11	Sunny Day	Fire	Status	—	—	5	Both Sides
TM12	Taunt	Dark	Status	—	100	20	Normal
TM15	Hyper Beam	Normal	Special	150	90	5	Normal
TM17	Protect	Normal	Status	—	—	10	Self
TM18	Rain Dance	Water	Status	—	—	5	Both Sides
TM21	Frustration	Normal	Physical	—	100	20	Normal
TM27	Return	Normal	Physical	—	100	20	Normal
TM30	Shadow Ball	Ghost	Special	80	100	15	Normal
TM32	Double Team	Normal	Status	—	—	15	Self
TM40	Aerial Ace	Flying	Physical	60	—	20	Normal
TM41	Torment	Dark	Status	—	100	15	Normal
TM42	Facade	Normal	Physical	70	100	20	Normal
TM44	Rest	Psychic	Status	—	—	10	Self
TM45	Attract	Normal	Status	—	100	15	Normal
TM46	Thief	Dark	Physical	60	100	25	Normal
TM48	Round	Normal	Special	60	100	15	Normal
TM49	Echoed Voice	Normal	Special	40	100	15	Normal
TM63	Embargo	Dark	Status	—	100	15	Normal
TM65	Shadow Claw	Ghost	Physical	70	100	15	Normal
TM66	Payback	Dark	Physical	50	100	10	Normal
TM68	Giga Impact	Normal	Physical	150	90	5	Normal
TM73	Thunder Wave	Electric	Status	—	100	20	Normal
TM77	Psych Up	Normal	Status	—	—	10	Normal
TM85	Dream Eater	Psychic	Special	100	100	15	Normal
TM86	Grass Knot	Grass	Special	—	100	20	Normal
TM87	Swagger	Normal	Status	—	90	15	Normal
TM88	Sleep Talk	Normal	Status	—	—	10	Self
TM89	U-turn	Bug	Physical	70	100	20	Normal
TM90	Substitute	Normal	Status	—	—	10	Self
TM94	Secret Power	Normal	Physical	70	100	20	Normal
TM95	Snarl	Dark	Special	55	95	15	Many Others
TM97	Dark Pulse	Dark	Special	80	100	15	Normal
TM100	Confide	Normal	Status	—	—	20	Normal
HM01	Cut	Normal	Physical	50	95	30	Normal
HM06	Rock Smash	Fighting	Physical	40	100	15	Normal

MOVES LEARNED IN EXCHANGE FOR BP

Name	Type	Kind	Pow.	Acc.	PP	Range
Covet	Normal	Physical	60	100	25	Normal
Seed Bomb	Grass	Physical	80	100	15	Normal
Gunk Shot	Poison	Physical	120	80	5	Normal
Foul Play	Dark	Physical	95	100	15	Normal
Hyper Voice	Normal	Special	90	100	10	Many Others
Iron Tail	Steel	Physical	100	75	15	Normal
Snore	Normal	Special	50	100	15	Normal
Knock Off	Dark	Physical	65	100	20	Normal
Role Play	Psychic	Status	—	—	10	Normal
Spite	Ghost	Status	—	100	10	Normal
Trick	Psychic	Status	—	100	10	Normal
Snatch	Dark	Status	—	—	10	Self

MOVES TAUGHT BY PEOPLE

Name	Type	Kind	Pow.	Acc.	PP	Range

National Pokédex **511** Hoenn Pokédex —

Pansage

Grass Monkey Pokémon

Grass

HEIGHT: 2'00" WEIGHT: 23.1 lbs.

Same form for ♂ / ♀

Ω It shares the leaf on its head with weary-looking Pokémon. These leaves are known to relieve stress.

α It's good at finding berries and gathers them from all over. It's kind enough to share them with friends.

ABILITY: Gluttony

HIDDEN ABILITY: Overgrow

EGG GROUPS: Field

STAT GROWTH RATES: HP, Attack, Defense, Sp. Atk, Sp. Def, Speed

ITEMS SOMETIMES HELD BY WILD POKÉMON: —

EVOLUTION

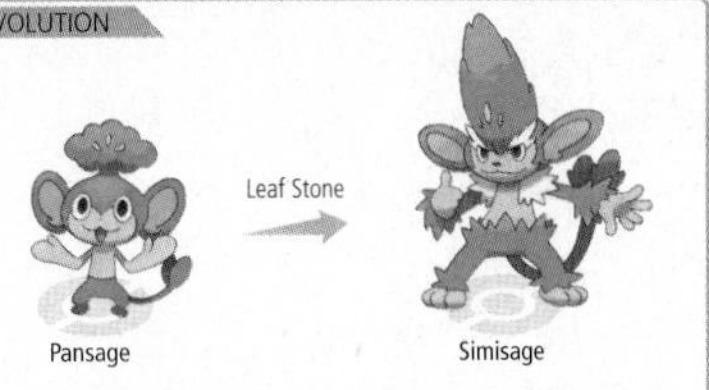

MAIN WAY TO REGISTER IN THE NATIONAL POKÉDEX

Appears in *Pokémon X* and *Pokémon Y*. Bring it to your game using Link Trade or the GTS.

Damage taken in normal battles

Type		Type	
Normal	×1	Flying	×2
Fire	×2	Psychic	×1
Water	×0.5	Bug	×2
Grass	×0.5	Rock	×1
Electric	×0.5	Ghost	×1
Ice	×2	Dragon	×1
Fighting	×1	Dark	×1
Poison	×2	Steel	×1
Ground	×0.5	Fairy	×1

Damage taken in Inverse battles

Type		Type	
Normal	×1	Flying	×0.5
Fire	×0.5	Psychic	×1
Water	×2	Bug	×0.5
Grass	×2	Rock	×1
Electric	×2	Ghost	×1
Ice	×0.5	Dragon	×1
Fighting	×1	Dark	×1
Poison	×0.5	Steel	×1
Ground	×2	Fairy	×1

Can be used in

- Inverse Battle
- Battle Institute
- Battle Maison
- Random Matchup (Free Battle)
- Random Matchup (Others)

LEVEL-UP MOVES

Lv.	Name	Type	Kind	Pow.	Acc.	PP	Range
1	Scratch	Normal	Physical	40	100	35	Normal
1	Play Nice	Normal	Status	—	—	20	Normal
4	Leer	Normal	Status	—	100	30	Many Others
7	Lick	Ghost	Physical	30	100	30	Normal
10	Vine Whip	Grass	Physical	45	100	25	Normal
13	Fury Swipes	Normal	Physical	18	80	15	Normal
16	Leech Seed	Grass	Status	—	90	10	Normal
19	Bite	Dark	Physical	60	100	25	Normal
22	Seed Bomb	Grass	Physical	80	100	15	Normal
25	Torment	Dark	Status	—	100	15	Normal
28	Fling	Dark	Physical	—	100	10	Normal
31	Acrobatics	Flying	Physical	55	100	15	Normal
34	Grass Knot	Grass	Special	—	100	20	Normal
37	Recycle	Normal	Status	—	—	10	Self
40	Natural Gift	Normal	Physical	—	100	15	Normal
43	Crunch	Dark	Physical	80	100	15	Normal

TM & HM MOVES

No.	Name	Type	Kind	Pow.	Acc.	PP	Range
TM01	Hone Claws	Dark	Status	—	—	15	Self
TM06	Toxic	Poison	Status	—	90	10	Normal
TM10	Hidden Power	Normal	Special	60	100	15	Normal
TM11	Sunny Day	Fire	Status	—	—	5	Both Sides
TM12	Taunt	Dark	Status	—	100	20	Normal
TM17	Protect	Normal	Status	—	—	10	Self
TM21	Frustration	Normal	Physical	—	100	20	Normal
TM22	Solar Beam	Grass	Special	120	100	10	Normal
TM27	Return	Normal	Physical	—	100	20	Normal
TM28	Dig	Ground	Physical	80	100	10	Normal
TM32	Double Team	Normal	Status	—	—	15	Self
TM39	Rock Tomb	Rock	Physical	60	95	15	Normal
TM41	Torment	Dark	Status	—	100	15	Normal
TM42	Facade	Normal	Physical	70	100	20	Normal
TM44	Rest	Psychic	Status	—	—	10	Self
TM45	Attract	Normal	Status	—	100	15	Normal
TM46	Thief	Dark	Physical	60	100	25	Normal
TM47	Low Sweep	Fighting	Physical	65	100	20	Normal
TM48	Round	Normal	Special	60	100	15	Normal
TM53	Energy Ball	Grass	Special	90	100	10	Normal
TM56	Fling	Dark	Physical	—	100	10	Normal
TM62	Acrobatics	Flying	Physical	55	100	15	Normal
TM65	Shadow Claw	Ghost	Physical	70	100	15	Normal
TM66	Payback	Dark	Physical	50	100	10	Normal
TM70	Flash	Normal	Status	—	100	20	Normal
TM86	Grass Knot	Grass	Special	—	100	20	Normal
TM87	Swagger	Normal	Status	—	90	15	Normal
TM88	Sleep Talk	Normal	Status	—	—	10	Self
TM90	Substitute	Normal	Status	—	—	10	Self
TM94	Secret Power	Normal	Physical	70	100	20	Normal
TM96	Nature Power	Normal	Status	—	—	20	Normal
TM100	Confide	Normal	Status	—	—	20	Normal
HM01	Cut	Normal	Physical	50	95	30	Normal
HM06	Rock Smash	Fighting	Physical	40	100	15	Normal

MOVES LEARNED IN EXCHANGE FOR BP

Name	Type	Kind	Pow.	Acc.	PP	Range
Covet	Normal	Physical	60	100	25	Normal
Seed Bomb	Grass	Physical	80	100	15	Normal
Low Kick	Fighting	Physical	—	100	20	Normal
Gunk Shot	Poison	Physical	120	80	5	Normal
Uproar	Normal	Special	90	100	10	1 Random
Iron Tail	Steel	Physical	100	75	15	Normal
Snore	Normal	Special	50	100	15	Normal
Knock Off	Dark	Physical	65	100	20	Normal
Synthesis	Grass	Status	—	—	5	Self
Role Play	Psychic	Status	—	—	10	Normal
Giga Drain	Grass	Special	75	100	10	Normal
Focus Punch	Fighting	Physical	150	100	20	Normal
Gastro Acid	Poison	Status	—	100	10	Normal
Worry Seed	Grass	Status	—	100	10	Normal
Helping Hand	Normal	Status	—	—	20	1 Ally
Endeavor	Normal	Physical	—	100	5	Normal
Recycle	Normal	Status	—	—	10	Self

MOVES TAUGHT BY PEOPLE

Name	Type	Kind	Pow.	Acc.	PP	Range

EGG MOVES

Name	Type	Kind	Pow.	Acc.	PP	Range
Covet	Normal	Physical	60	100	25	Normal
Low Kick	Fighting	Physical	—	100	20	Normal
Tickle	Normal	Status	—	100	20	Normal
Nasty Plot	Dark	Status	—	—	20	Self
Role Play	Psychic	Status	—	—	10	Normal
Astonish	Ghost	Physical	30	100	15	Normal
Grass Whistle	Grass	Status	—	55	15	Normal
Magical Leaf	Grass	Special	60	—	20	Normal
Bullet Seed	Grass	Physical	25	100	30	Normal
Leaf Storm	Grass	Special	130	90	5	Normal
Disarming Voice	Fairy	Special	40	—	15	Many Others

National Pokédex **512** Hoenn Pokédex —

Simisage

Thorn Monkey Pokémon

Grass

HEIGHT: 3'07" WEIGHT: 67.2 lbs.

Same form for ♂ / ♀

Ω It attacks enemies with strikes of its thorn-covered tail. This Pokémon is wild tempered.

α Ill tempered, it fights by swinging its barbed tail around wildly. The leaf growing on its head is very bitter.

ABILITY: Gluttony

HIDDEN ABILITY: Overgrow

EGG GROUPS: Field

STAT GROWTH RATES: HP, Attack, Defense, Sp. Atk, Sp. Def, Speed

ITEMS SOMETIMES HELD BY WILD POKÉMON: —

EVOLUTION

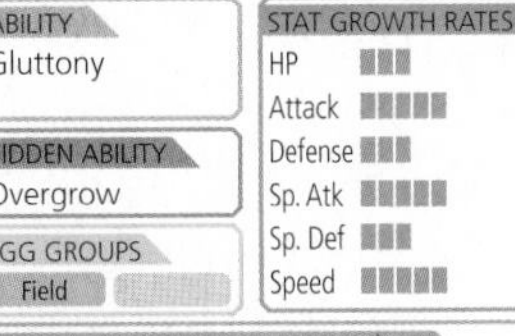

MAIN WAY TO REGISTER IN THE NATIONAL POKÉDEX

Use a Leaf Stone on a Pansage obtained via Link Trade or the GTS.

Damage taken in normal battles

Type		Type	
Normal	×1	Flying	×2
Fire	×2	Psychic	×1
Water	×0.5	Bug	×2
Grass	×0.5	Rock	×1
Electric	×0.5	Ghost	×1
Ice	×2	Dragon	×1
Fighting	×1	Dark	×1
Poison	×2	Steel	×1
Ground	×0.5	Fairy	×1

Damage taken in Inverse battles

Type		Type	
Normal	×1	Flying	×0.5
Fire	×0.5	Psychic	×1
Water	×2	Bug	×0.5
Grass	×2	Rock	×1
Electric	×2	Ghost	×1
Ice	×0.5	Dragon	×1
Fighting	×1	Dark	×1
Poison	×0.5	Steel	×1
Ground	×2	Fairy	×1

Can be used in

- Inverse Battle
- Battle Institute
- Battle Maison
- Random Matchup (Free Battle)
- Random Matchup (Others)

LEVEL-UP MOVES

Lv.	Name	Type	Kind	Pow.	Acc.	PP	Range
1	Leer	Normal	Status	—	100	30	Many Others
1	Lick	Ghost	Physical	30	100	30	Normal
1	Fury Swipes	Normal	Physical	18	80	15	Normal
1	Seed Bomb	Grass	Physical	80	100	15	Normal

TM & HM MOVES

No.	Name	Type	Kind	Pow.	Acc.	PP	Range
TM01	Hone Claws	Dark	Status	—	—	15	Self
TM06	Toxic	Poison	Status	—	90	10	Normal
TM10	Hidden Power	Normal	Special	60	100	15	Normal
TM11	Sunny Day	Fire	Status	—	—	5	Both Sides
TM12	Taunt	Dark	Status	—	100	20	Normal
TM15	Hyper Beam	Normal	Special	150	90	5	Normal
TM17	Protect	Normal	Status	—	—	10	Self
TM21	Frustration	Normal	Physical	—	100	20	Normal
TM22	Solar Beam	Grass	Special	120	100	10	Normal
TM27	Return	Normal	Physical	—	100	20	Normal
TM28	Dig	Ground	Physical	80	100	10	Normal
TM31	Brick Break	Fighting	Physical	75	100	15	Normal
TM32	Double Team	Normal	Status	—	—	15	Self
TM39	Rock Tomb	Rock	Physical	60	95	15	Normal
TM41	Torment	Dark	Status	—	100	15	Normal
TM42	Facade	Normal	Physical	70	100	20	Normal
TM44	Rest	Psychic	Status	—	—	10	Self
TM45	Attract	Normal	Status	—	100	15	Normal
TM46	Thief	Dark	Physical	60	100	25	Normal
TM47	Low Sweep	Fighting	Physical	65	100	20	Normal
TM48	Round	Normal	Special	60	100	15	Normal
TM52	Focus Blast	Fighting	Special	120	70	5	Normal
TM53	Energy Ball	Grass	Special	90	100	10	Normal
TM56	Fling	Dark	Physical	—	100	10	Normal
TM62	Acrobatics	Flying	Physical	55	100	15	Normal
TM65	Shadow Claw	Ghost	Physical	70	100	15	Normal
TM66	Payback	Dark	Physical	50	100	10	Normal
TM68	Giga Impact	Normal	Physical	150	90	5	Normal
TM70	Flash	Normal	Status	—	100	20	Normal
TM80	Rock Slide	Rock	Physical	75	90	10	Many Others
TM86	Grass Knot	Grass	Special	—	100	20	Normal
TM87	Swagger	Normal	Status	—	90	15	Normal
TM88	Sleep Talk	Normal	Status	—	—	10	Self
TM90	Substitute	Normal	Status	—	—	10	Self
TM94	Secret Power	Normal	Physical	70	100	20	Normal
TM96	Nature Power	Normal	Status	—	—	20	Normal
TM98	Power-Up Punch	Fighting	Physical	40	100	20	Normal
TM100	Confide	Normal	Status	—	—	20	Normal
HM01	Cut	Normal	Physical	50	95	30	Normal
HM06	Rock Smash	Fighting	Physical	40	100	15	Normal

MOVES LEARNED IN EXCHANGE FOR BP

Name	Type	Kind	Pow.	Acc.	PP	Range
Covet	Normal	Physical	60	100	25	Normal
Seed Bomb	Grass	Physical	80	100	15	Normal
Low Kick	Fighting	Physical	—	100	20	Normal
Gunk Shot	Poison	Physical	120	80	5	Normal
Uproar	Normal	Special	90	100	10	1 Random
Superpower	Fighting	Physical	120	100	5	Normal
Iron Tail	Steel	Physical	100	75	15	Normal
Snore	Normal	Special	50	100	15	Normal
Knock Off	Dark	Physical	65	100	20	Normal
Synthesis	Grass	Status	—	—	5	Self
Role Play	Psychic	Status	—	—	10	Normal
Giga Drain	Grass	Special	75	100	10	Normal
Focus Punch	Fighting	Physical	150	100	20	Normal
Gastro Acid	Poison	Status	—	100	10	Normal
Worry Seed	Grass	Status	—	100	10	Normal
Helping Hand	Normal	Status	—	—	20	1 Ally
Endeavor	Normal	Physical	—	100	5	Normal
Recycle	Normal	Status	—	—	10	Self

MOVES TAUGHT BY PEOPLE

Name	Type	Kind	Pow.	Acc.	PP	Range

National Pokédex **513** Hoenn Pokédex —

Pansear

High Temp Pokémon

Fire

HEIGHT: 2'00" WEIGHT: 24.3 lbs.

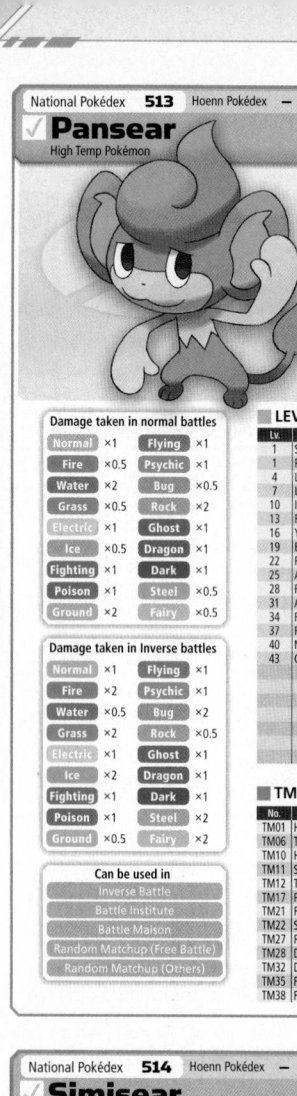

Same form for ♂ / ♀

Ω Very intelligent, it roasts berries before eating them. It likes to help people.

α This Pokémon lives in caves in volcanoes. The fire within the tuft on its head can reach 600 degrees Fahrenheit.

ABILITY
Gluttony

HIDDEN ABILITY
Blaze

EGG GROUPS
Field

STAT GROWTH RATES
HP ■■
Attack ■■■
Defense ■■
Sp. Atk ■■■
Sp. Def ■■
Speed ■■■■

ITEMS SOMETIMES HELD BY WILD POKÉMON
—

EVOLUTION

MAIN WAY TO REGISTER IN THE NATIONAL POKÉDEX

Appears in *Pokémon X* and *Pokémon Y*. Bring it to your game using Link Trade or the GTS.

Damage taken in normal battles

Type		Type	
Normal	×1	Flying	×1
Fire	×0.5	Psychic	×1
Water	×2	Bug	×0.5
Grass	×0.5	Rock	×2
Electric	×1	Ghost	×1
Ice	×0.5	Dragon	×1
Fighting	×1	Dark	×1
Poison	×1	Steel	×0.5
Ground	×2	Fairy	×0.5

Damage taken in Inverse battles

Type		Type	
Normal	×1	Flying	×1
Fire	×2	Psychic	×1
Water	×0.5	Bug	×2
Grass	×2	Rock	×0.5
Electric	×1	Ghost	×1
Ice	×2	Dragon	×1
Fighting	×1	Dark	×1
Poison	×1	Steel	×2
Ground	×0.5	Fairy	×2

Can be used in
- Inverse Battle
- Battle Institute
- Battle Maison
- Random Matchup (Free Battle)
- Random Matchup (Others)

LEVEL-UP MOVES

Lv.	Name	Type	Kind	Pow.	Acc.	PP	Range
1	Scratch	Normal	Physical	40	100	35	Normal
1	Play Nice	Normal	Status	—	—	20	Normal
4	Leer	Normal	Status	—	100	30	Many Others
7	Lick	Ghost	Physical	30	100	30	Normal
10	Incinerate	Fire	Special	60	100	15	Many Others
13	Fury Swipes	Normal	Physical	18	80	15	Normal
16	Yawn	Normal	Status	—	—	10	Normal
19	Bite	Dark	Physical	60	100	25	Normal
22	Flame Burst	Fire	Special	70	100	15	Normal
25	Amnesia	Psychic	Status	—	—	20	Self
28	Fling	Dark	Physical	—	100	10	Normal
31	Acrobatics	Flying	Physical	55	100	15	Normal
34	Fire Blast	Fire	Special	110	85	5	Normal
37	Recycle	Normal	Status	—	—	10	Self
40	Natural Gift	Normal	Physical	—	100	15	Normal
43	Crunch	Dark	Physical	80	100	15	Normal

TM & HM MOVES

No.	Name	Type	Kind	Pow.	Acc.	PP	Range
TM01	Hone Claws	Dark	Status	—	—	15	Self
TM06	Toxic	Poison	Status	—	90	10	Normal
TM10	Hidden Power	Normal	Special	60	100	15	Normal
TM11	Sunny Day	Fire	Status	—	—	5	Both Sides
TM12	Taunt	Dark	Status	—	100	20	Normal
TM17	Protect	Normal	Status	—	—	10	Self
TM21	Frustration	Normal	Physical	—	100	20	Normal
TM22	Solar Beam	Grass	Special	120	100	10	Normal
TM27	Return	Normal	Physical	—	100	20	Normal
TM28	Dig	Ground	Physical	80	100	10	Normal
TM32	Double Team	Normal	Status	—	—	15	Self
TM35	Flamethrower	Fire	Special	90	100	15	Normal
TM38	Fire Blast	Fire	Special	110	85	5	Normal
TM39	Rock Tomb	Rock	Physical	60	95	15	Normal
TM41	Torment	Dark	Status	—	100	15	Normal
TM42	Facade	Normal	Physical	70	100	20	Normal
TM43	Flame Charge	Fire	Physical	50	100	20	Normal
TM44	Rest	Psychic	Status	—	—	10	Self
TM45	Attract	Normal	Status	—	100	15	Normal
TM46	Thief	Dark	Physical	60	100	25	Normal
TM47	Low Sweep	Fighting	Physical	65	100	20	Normal
TM48	Round	Normal	Special	60	100	15	Normal
TM50	Overheat	Fire	Special	130	90	5	Normal
TM56	Fling	Dark	Physical	—	100	10	Normal
TM59	Incinerate	Fire	Special	60	100	15	Many Others
TM61	Will-O-Wisp	Fire	Status	—	85	15	Normal
TM62	Acrobatics	Flying	Physical	55	100	15	Normal
TM65	Shadow Claw	Ghost	Physical	70	100	15	Normal
TM66	Payback	Dark	Physical	50	100	10	Normal
TM86	Grass Knot	Grass	Special	—	100	20	Normal
TM87	Swagger	Normal	Status	—	90	15	Normal
TM88	Sleep Talk	Normal	Status	—	—	10	Self
TM90	Substitute	Normal	Status	—	—	10	Self
TM94	Secret Power	Normal	Physical	70	100	20	Normal
TM100	Confide	Normal	Status	—	—	20	Normal
HM01	Cut	Normal	Physical	50	95	30	Normal
HM06	Rock Smash	Fighting	Physical	40	100	15	Normal

MOVES LEARNED IN EXCHANGE FOR BP

Name	Type	Kind	Pow.	Acc.	PP	Range
Covet	Normal	Physical	60	100	25	Normal
Low Kick	Fighting	Physical	—	100	20	Normal
Gunk Shot	Poison	Physical	120	80	5	Normal
Uproar	Normal	Special	90	100	10	1 Random
Fire Punch	Fire	Physical	75	100	15	Normal
Iron Tail	Steel	Physical	100	75	15	Normal
Snore	Normal	Special	50	100	15	Normal
Knock Off	Dark	Physical	65	100	20	Normal
Heat Wave	Fire	Special	95	90	10	Many Others
Role Play	Psychic	Status	—	—	10	Normal
Focus Punch	Fighting	Physical	150	100	20	Normal
Gastro Acid	Poison	Status	—	100	10	Normal
Helping Hand	Normal	Status	—	—	20	1 Ally
Endeavor	Normal	Physical	—	100	5	Normal
Recycle	Normal	Status	—	—	10	Self

MOVES TAUGHT BY PEOPLE

Name	Type	Kind	Pow.	Acc.	PP	Range

EGG MOVES

Name	Type	Kind	Pow.	Acc.	PP	Range
Covet	Normal	Physical	60	100	25	Normal
Low Kick	Fighting	Physical	—	100	20	Normal
Tickle	Normal	Status	—	100	20	Normal
Nasty Plot	Dark	Status	—	—	20	Self
Role Play	Psychic	Status	—	—	10	Normal
Astonish	Ghost	Physical	30	100	15	Normal
Sleep Talk	Normal	Status	—	—	10	Self
Fire Spin	Fire	Special	35	85	15	Normal
Fire Punch	Fire	Physical	75	100	15	Normal
Heat Wave	Fire	Special	95	90	10	Many Others
Disarming Voice	Fairy	Special	40	—	15	Many Others

National Pokédex **514** Hoenn Pokédex —

Simisear

Ember Pokémon

Fire

HEIGHT: 3'03" WEIGHT: 61.7 lbs.

Same form for ♂ / ♀

Ω A flame burns inside its body. It scatters embers from its head and tail to sear its opponents.

α When it gets excited, embers rise from its head and tail and it gets hot. For some reason, it loves sweets.

ABILITY
Gluttony

HIDDEN ABILITY
Blaze

EGG GROUPS
Field

STAT GROWTH RATES
HP ■■■
Attack ■■■■■
Defense ■■■
Sp. Atk ■■■■■
Sp. Def ■■■
Speed ■■■■■

ITEMS SOMETIMES HELD BY WILD POKÉMON
—

EVOLUTION

MAIN WAY TO REGISTER IN THE NATIONAL POKÉDEX

Use a Fire Stone on a Pansear obtained via Link Trade or the GTS.

Damage taken in normal battles

Type		Type	
Normal	×1	Flying	×1
Fire	×0.5	Psychic	×1
Water	×2	Bug	×0.5
Grass	×0.5	Rock	×2
Electric	×1	Ghost	×1
Ice	×0.5	Dragon	×1
Fighting	×1	Dark	×1
Poison	×1	Steel	×0.5
Ground	×2	Fairy	×0.5

Damage taken in Inverse battles

Type		Type	
Normal	×1	Flying	×1
Fire	×2	Psychic	×1
Water	×0.5	Bug	×2
Grass	×2	Rock	×0.5
Electric	×1	Ghost	×1
Ice	×2	Dragon	×1
Fighting	×1	Dark	×1
Poison	×1	Steel	×2
Ground	×0.5	Fairy	×2

Can be used in
- Inverse Battle
- Battle Institute
- Battle Maison
- Random Matchup (Free Battle)
- Random Matchup (Others)

LEVEL-UP MOVES

Lv.	Name	Type	Kind	Pow.	Acc.	PP	Range
1	Leer	Normal	Status	—	100	30	Many Others
1	Lick	Ghost	Physical	30	100	30	Normal
1	Fury Swipes	Normal	Physical	18	80	15	Normal
1	Flame Burst	Fire	Special	70	100	15	Normal

TM & HM MOVES

No.	Name	Type	Kind	Pow.	Acc.	PP	Range
TM01	Hone Claws	Dark	Status	—	—	15	Self
TM06	Toxic	Poison	Status	—	90	10	Normal
TM10	Hidden Power	Normal	Special	60	100	15	Normal
TM11	Sunny Day	Fire	Status	—	—	5	Both Sides
TM12	Taunt	Dark	Status	—	100	20	Normal
TM15	Hyper Beam	Normal	Special	150	90	5	Normal
TM17	Protect	Normal	Status	—	—	10	Self
TM21	Frustration	Normal	Physical	—	100	20	Normal
TM22	Solar Beam	Grass	Special	120	100	10	Normal
TM27	Return	Normal	Physical	—	100	20	Normal
TM28	Dig	Ground	Physical	80	100	10	Normal
TM31	Brick Break	Fighting	Physical	75	100	15	Normal
TM32	Double Team	Normal	Status	—	—	15	Self
TM35	Flamethrower	Fire	Special	90	100	15	Normal
TM38	Fire Blast	Fire	Special	110	85	5	Normal
TM39	Rock Tomb	Rock	Physical	60	95	15	Normal
TM41	Torment	Dark	Status	—	100	15	Normal
TM42	Facade	Normal	Physical	70	100	20	Normal
TM43	Flame Charge	Fire	Physical	50	100	20	Normal
TM44	Rest	Psychic	Status	—	—	10	Self
TM45	Attract	Normal	Status	—	100	15	Normal
TM46	Thief	Dark	Physical	60	100	25	Normal
TM47	Low Sweep	Fighting	Physical	65	100	20	Normal
TM48	Round	Normal	Special	60	100	15	Normal
TM50	Overheat	Fire	Special	130	90	5	Normal
TM52	Focus Blast	Fighting	Special	120	70	5	Normal
TM56	Fling	Dark	Physical	—	100	10	Normal
TM59	Incinerate	Fire	Special	60	100	15	Many Others
TM61	Will-O-Wisp	Fire	Status	—	85	15	Normal
TM62	Acrobatics	Flying	Physical	55	100	15	Normal
TM65	Shadow Claw	Ghost	Physical	70	100	15	Normal
TM66	Payback	Dark	Physical	50	100	10	Normal
TM68	Giga Impact	Normal	Physical	150	90	5	Normal
TM80	Rock Slide	Rock	Physical	75	90	10	Many Others
TM86	Grass Knot	Grass	Special	—	100	20	Normal
TM87	Swagger	Normal	Status	—	90	15	Normal
TM88	Sleep Talk	Normal	Status	—	—	10	Self
TM90	Substitute	Normal	Status	—	—	10	Self
TM94	Secret Power	Normal	Physical	70	100	20	Normal
TM98	Power-Up Punch	Fighting	Physical	40	100	20	Normal
TM100	Confide	Normal	Status	—	—	20	Normal
HM01	Cut	Normal	Physical	50	95	30	Normal
HM06	Rock Smash	Fighting	Physical	40	100	15	Normal

MOVES LEARNED IN EXCHANGE FOR BP

Name	Type	Kind	Pow.	Acc.	PP	Range
Covet	Normal	Physical	60	100	25	Normal
Low Kick	Fighting	Physical	—	100	20	Normal
Gunk Shot	Poison	Physical	120	80	5	Normal
Uproar	Normal	Special	90	100	10	1 Random
Fire Punch	Fire	Physical	75	100	15	Normal
Superpower	Fighting	Physical	120	100	5	Normal
Iron Tail	Steel	Physical	100	75	15	Normal
Snore	Normal	Special	50	100	15	Normal
Knock Off	Dark	Physical	65	100	20	Normal
Heat Wave	Fire	Special	95	90	10	Many Others
Role Play	Psychic	Status	—	—	10	Normal
Focus Punch	Fighting	Physical	150	100	20	Normal
Gastro Acid	Poison	Status	—	100	10	Normal
Helping Hand	Normal	Status	—	—	20	1 Ally
Endeavor	Normal	Physical	—	100	5	Normal
Recycle	Normal	Status	—	—	10	Self

MOVES TAUGHT BY PEOPLE

Name	Type	Kind	Pow.	Acc.	PP	Range

National Pokédex **515** Hoenn Pokédex —

Panpour

Spray Pokémon

Water

HEIGHT: 2'00" WEIGHT: 29.8 lbs.

Same form for ♂ / ♀

Ω The water stored inside the tuft on its head is full of nutrients. It waters plants with it using its tail.

α The water stored inside the tuft on its head is full of nutrients. Plants that receive its water grow large.

ABILITY: Gluttony

HIDDEN ABILITY: Torrent

EGG GROUPS: Field

STAT GROWTH RATES: HP, Attack, Defense, Sp. Atk, Sp. Def, Speed

ITEMS SOMETIMES HELD BY WILD POKÉMON: —

EVOLUTION

MAIN WAY TO REGISTER IN THE NATIONAL POKÉDEX

Appears in *Pokémon X* and *Pokémon Y*. Bring it to your game using Link Trade or the GTS.

Damage taken in normal battles

Type		Type	
Normal	×1	Flying	×1
Fire	×0.5	Psychic	×1
Water	×0.5	Bug	×1
Grass	×2	Rock	×1
Electric	×2	Ghost	×1
Ice	×0.5	Dragon	×1
Fighting	×1	Dark	×1
Poison	×1	Steel	×0.5
Ground	×1	Fairy	×1

Damage taken in Inverse battles

Type		Type	
Normal	×1	Flying	×1
Fire	×2	Psychic	×1
Water	×2	Bug	×1
Grass	×0.5	Rock	×1
Electric	×0.5	Ghost	×1
Ice	×2	Dragon	×1
Fighting	×1	Dark	×1
Poison	×1	Steel	×2
Ground	×1	Fairy	×1

Can be used in

- Inverse Battle
- Battle Institute
- Battle Maison
- Random Matchup (Free Battle)
- Random Matchup (Others)

LEVEL-UP MOVES

Lv.	Name	Type	Kind	Pow.	Acc.	PP	Range
1	Scratch	Normal	Physical	40	100	35	Normal
1	Play Nice	Normal	Status	—	—	20	Normal
4	Leer	Normal	Status	—	100	30	Many Others
7	Lick	Ghost	Physical	30	100	30	Normal
10	Water Gun	Water	Special	40	100	25	Normal
13	Fury Swipes	Normal	Physical	18	80	15	Normal
16	Water Sport	Water	Status	—	—	15	Both Sides
19	Bite	Dark	Physical	60	100	25	Normal
22	Scald	Water	Special	80	100	15	Normal
25	Taunt	Dark	Status	—	100	20	Normal
28	Fling	Dark	Physical	—	100	10	Normal
31	Acrobatics	Flying	Physical	55	100	15	Normal
34	Brine	Water	Special	65	100	10	Normal
37	Recycle	Normal	Status	—	—	10	Self
40	Natural Gift	Normal	Physical	—	100	15	Normal
43	Crunch	Dark	Physical	80	100	15	Normal

TM & HM MOVES

No.	Name	Type	Kind	Pow.	Acc.	PP	Range
TM01	Hone Claws	Dark	Status	—	—	15	Self
TM06	Toxic	Poison	Status	—	90	10	Normal
TM07	Hail	Ice	Status	—	—	10	Both Sides
TM10	Hidden Power	Normal	Special	60	100	15	Normal
TM12	Taunt	Dark	Status	—	100	20	Normal
TM13	Ice Beam	Ice	Special	90	100	10	Normal
TM14	Blizzard	Ice	Special	110	70	5	Many Others
TM17	Protect	Normal	Status	—	—	10	Self
TM18	Rain Dance	Water	Status	—	—	5	Both Sides
TM21	Frustration	Normal	Physical	—	100	20	Normal
TM27	Return	Normal	Physical	—	100	20	Normal
TM28	Dig	Ground	Physical	80	100	10	Normal
TM32	Double Team	Normal	Status	—	—	15	Self
TM39	Rock Tomb	Rock	Physical	60	95	15	Normal
TM41	Torment	Dark	Status	—	100	15	Normal
TM42	Facade	Normal	Physical	70	100	20	Normal
TM44	Rest	Psychic	Status	—	—	10	Self
TM45	Attract	Normal	Status	—	100	15	Normal
TM46	Thief	Dark	Physical	60	100	25	Normal
TM47	Low Sweep	Fighting	Physical	65	100	20	Normal
TM48	Round	Normal	Special	60	100	15	Normal
TM55	Scald	Water	Special	80	100	15	Normal
TM56	Fling	Dark	Physical	—	100	10	Normal
TM62	Acrobatics	Flying	Physical	55	100	15	Normal
TM65	Shadow Claw	Ghost	Physical	70	100	15	Normal
TM66	Payback	Dark	Physical	50	100	10	Normal
TM86	Grass Knot	Grass	Special	—	100	20	Normal
TM87	Swagger	Normal	Status	—	90	15	Normal
TM88	Sleep Talk	Normal	Status	—	—	10	Self
TM90	Substitute	Normal	Status	—	—	10	Self
TM94	Secret Power	Normal	Physical	70	100	20	Normal
TM100	Confide	Normal	Status	—	—	20	Normal
HM01	Cut	Normal	Physical	50	95	30	Normal
HM03	Surf	Water	Special	90	100	15	Adjacent
HM05	Waterfall	Water	Physical	80	100	15	Normal
HM06	Rock Smash	Fighting	Physical	40	100	15	Normal
HM07	Dive	Water	Physical	80	100	10	Normal

MOVES LEARNED IN EXCHANGE FOR BP

Name	Type	Kind	Pow.	Acc.	PP	Range
Covet	Normal	Physical	60	100	25	Normal
Low Kick	Fighting	Physical	—	100	20	Normal
Gunk Shot	Poison	Physical	120	80	5	Normal
Uproar	Normal	Special	90	100	10	1 Random
Ice Punch	Ice	Physical	75	100	15	Normal
Icy Wind	Ice	Special	55	95	15	Many Others
Aqua Tail	Water	Physical	90	90	10	Normal
Iron Tail	Steel	Physical	100	75	15	Normal
Snore	Normal	Special	50	100	15	Normal
Knock Off	Dark	Physical	65	100	20	Normal
Role Play	Psychic	Status	—	—	10	Normal
Focus Punch	Fighting	Physical	150	100	20	Normal
Water Pulse	Water	Special	60	100	20	Normal
Gastro Acid	Poison	Status	—	100	10	Normal
Helping Hand	Normal	Status	—	—	20	1 Ally
Endeavor	Normal	Physical	—	100	5	Normal
Recycle	Normal	Status	—	—	10	Self

MOVES TAUGHT BY PEOPLE

Name	Type	Kind	Pow.	Acc.	PP	Range

EGG MOVES

Name	Type	Kind	Pow.	Acc.	PP	Range
Covet	Normal	Physical	60	100	25	Normal
Low Kick	Fighting	Physical	—	100	20	Normal
Tickle	Normal	Status	—	100	20	Normal
Nasty Plot	Dark	Status	—	—	20	Self
Role Play	Psychic	Status	—	—	10	Normal
Astonish	Ghost	Physical	30	100	15	Normal
Aqua Ring	Water	Status	—	—	20	Self
Aqua Tail	Water	Physical	90	90	10	Normal
Mud Sport	Ground	Status	—	—	15	Both Sides
Hydro Pump	Water	Special	110	80	5	Normal
Disarming Voice	Fairy	Special	40	—	15	Many Others

National Pokédex **516** Hoenn Pokédex —

Simipour

Geyser Pokémon

Water

HEIGHT: 3'03" WEIGHT: 63.9 lbs.

Same form for ♂ / ♀

Ω The high-pressure water expelled from its tail is so powerful, it can destroy a concrete wall.

α It prefers places with clean water. When its tuft runs low, it replenishes it by siphoning up water with its tail.

ABILITY: Gluttony

HIDDEN ABILITY: Torrent

EGG GROUPS: Field

STAT GROWTH RATES: HP, Attack, Defense, Sp. Atk, Sp. Def, Speed

ITEMS SOMETIMES HELD BY WILD POKÉMON: —

EVOLUTION

Water Stone

Panpour → Simipour

MAIN WAY TO REGISTER IN THE NATIONAL POKÉDEX

Use a Water Stone on a Panpour obtained via Link Trade or the GTS.

Damage taken in normal battles

Type		Type	
Normal	×1	Flying	×1
Fire	×0.5	Psychic	×1
Water	×0.5	Bug	×1
Grass	×2	Rock	×1
Electric	×2	Ghost	×1
Ice	×0.5	Dragon	×1
Fighting	×1	Dark	×1
Poison	×1	Steel	×0.5
Ground	×1	Fairy	×1

Damage taken in Inverse battles

Type		Type	
Normal	×1	Flying	×1
Fire	×2	Psychic	×1
Water	×2	Bug	×1
Grass	×0.5	Rock	×1
Electric	×0.5	Ghost	×1
Ice	×2	Dragon	×1
Fighting	×1	Dark	×1
Poison	×1	Steel	×2
Ground	×1	Fairy	×1

Can be used in

- Inverse Battle
- Battle Institute
- Battle Maison
- Random Matchup (Free Battle)
- Random Matchup (Others)

LEVEL-UP MOVES

Lv.	Name	Type	Kind	Pow.	Acc.	PP	Range
1	Leer	Normal	Status	—	100	30	Many Others
1	Lick	Ghost	Physical	30	100	30	Normal
1	Fury Swipes	Normal	Physical	18	80	15	Normal
1	Scald	Water	Special	80	100	15	Normal

TM & HM MOVES

No.	Name	Type	Kind	Pow.	Acc.	PP	Range
TM01	Hone Claws	Dark	Status	—	—	15	Self
TM06	Toxic	Poison	Status	—	90	10	Normal
TM07	Hail	Ice	Status	—	—	10	Both Sides
TM10	Hidden Power	Normal	Special	60	100	15	Normal
TM12	Taunt	Dark	Status	—	100	20	Normal
TM13	Ice Beam	Ice	Special	90	100	10	Normal
TM14	Blizzard	Ice	Special	110	70	5	Many Others
TM15	Hyper Beam	Normal	Special	150	90	5	Normal
TM17	Protect	Normal	Status	—	—	10	Self
TM18	Rain Dance	Water	Status	—	—	5	Both Sides
TM21	Frustration	Normal	Physical	—	100	20	Normal
TM27	Return	Normal	Physical	—	100	20	Normal
TM28	Dig	Ground	Physical	80	100	10	Normal
TM31	Brick Break	Fighting	Physical	75	100	15	Normal
TM32	Double Team	Normal	Status	—	—	15	Self
TM39	Rock Tomb	Rock	Physical	60	95	15	Normal
TM41	Torment	Dark	Status	—	100	15	Normal
TM42	Facade	Normal	Physical	70	100	20	Normal
TM44	Rest	Psychic	Status	—	—	10	Self
TM45	Attract	Normal	Status	—	100	15	Normal
TM46	Thief	Dark	Physical	60	100	25	Normal
TM47	Low Sweep	Fighting	Physical	65	100	20	Normal
TM48	Round	Normal	Special	60	100	15	Normal
TM52	Focus Blast	Fighting	Special	120	70	5	Normal
TM55	Scald	Water	Special	80	100	15	Normal
TM56	Fling	Dark	Physical	—	100	10	Normal
TM62	Acrobatics	Flying	Physical	55	100	15	Normal
TM65	Shadow Claw	Ghost	Physical	70	100	15	Normal
TM66	Payback	Dark	Physical	50	100	10	Normal
TM68	Giga Impact	Normal	Physical	150	90	5	Normal
TM80	Rock Slide	Rock	Physical	75	90	10	Many Others
TM86	Grass Knot	Grass	Special	—	100	20	Normal
TM87	Swagger	Normal	Status	—	90	15	Normal
TM88	Sleep Talk	Normal	Status	—	—	10	Self
TM90	Substitute	Normal	Status	—	—	10	Self
TM94	Secret Power	Normal	Physical	70	100	20	Normal
TM98	Power-Up Punch	Fighting	Physical	40	100	20	Normal
TM100	Confide	Normal	Status	—	—	20	Normal
HM01	Cut	Normal	Physical	50	95	30	Normal
HM03	Surf	Water	Special	90	100	15	Adjacent
HM05	Waterfall	Water	Physical	80	100	15	Normal
HM06	Rock Smash	Fighting	Physical	40	100	15	Normal
HM07	Dive	Water	Physical	80	100	10	Normal

MOVES LEARNED IN EXCHANGE FOR BP

Name	Type	Kind	Pow.	Acc.	PP	Range
Covet	Normal	Physical	60	100	25	Normal
Low Kick	Fighting	Physical	—	100	20	Normal
Gunk Shot	Poison	Physical	120	80	5	Normal
Uproar	Normal	Special	90	100	10	1 Random
Ice Punch	Ice	Physical	75	100	15	Normal
Superpower	Fighting	Physical	120	100	5	Normal
Icy Wind	Ice	Special	55	95	15	Many Others
Aqua Tail	Water	Physical	90	90	10	Normal
Iron Tail	Steel	Physical	100	75	15	Normal
Snore	Normal	Special	50	100	15	Normal
Knock Off	Dark	Physical	65	100	20	Normal
Role Play	Psychic	Status	—	—	10	Normal
Focus Punch	Fighting	Physical	150	100	20	Normal
Water Pulse	Water	Special	60	100	20	Normal
Gastro Acid	Poison	Status	—	100	10	Normal
Helping Hand	Normal	Status	—	—	20	1 Ally
Endeavor	Normal	Physical	—	100	5	Normal
Recycle	Normal	Status	—	—	10	Self

MOVES TAUGHT BY PEOPLE

Name	Type	Kind	Pow.	Acc.	PP	Range

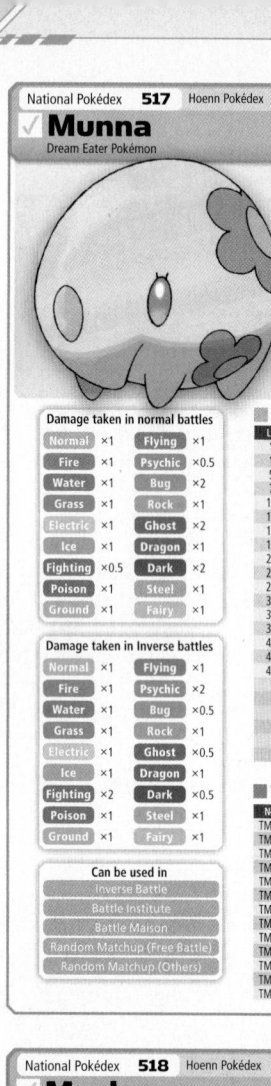

National Pokédex **517** Hoenn Pokédex —

Munna

Dream Eater Pokémon

Psychic

HEIGHT: 2'00" WEIGHT: 51.4 lbs.

Same form for ♂ / ♀

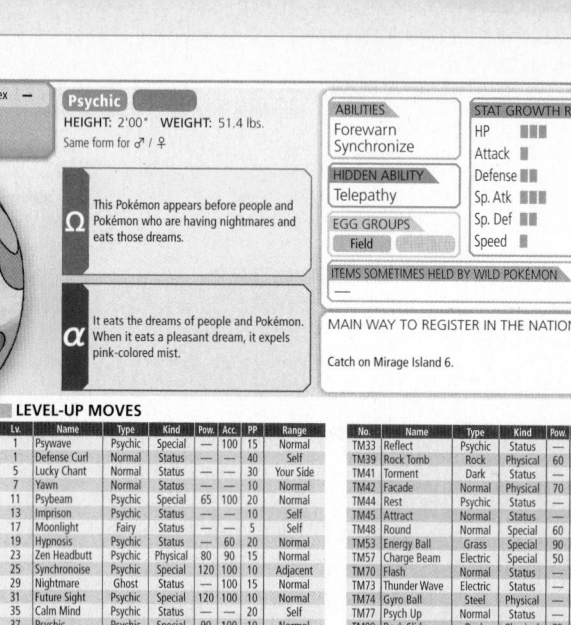

Ω This Pokémon appears before people and Pokémon who are having nightmares and eats those dreams.

α It eats the dreams of people and Pokémon. When it eats a pleasant dream, it expels pink-colored mist.

ABILITIES
Forewarn
Synchronize

HIDDEN ABILITY
Telepathy

EGG GROUPS
Field

STAT GROWTH RATES
HP
Attack
Defense
Sp. Atk
Sp. Def
Speed

ITEMS SOMETIMES HELD BY WILD POKÉMON
—

EVOLUTION
Munna → Moon Stone → Musharna

MAIN WAY TO REGISTER IN THE NATIONAL POKÉDEX

Catch on Mirage Island 6.

Damage taken in normal battles

Type		Type	
Normal	×1	Flying	×1
Fire	×1	Psychic	×0.5
Water	×1	Bug	×2
Grass	×1	Rock	×1
Electric	×1	Ghost	×2
Ice	×1	Dragon	×1
Fighting	×0.5	Dark	×2
Poison	×1	Steel	×1
Ground	×1	Fairy	×1

Damage taken in Inverse battles

Type		Type	
Normal	×1	Flying	×1
Fire	×1	Psychic	×2
Water	×1	Bug	×0.5
Grass	×1	Rock	×1
Electric	×1	Ghost	×0.5
Ice	×1	Dragon	×1
Fighting	×2	Dark	×0.5
Poison	×1	Steel	×1
Ground	×1	Fairy	×1

Can be used in
Inverse Battle
Battle Institute
Battle Maison
Random Matchup (Free Battle)
Random Matchup (Others)

LEVEL-UP MOVES

Lv.	Name	Type	Kind	Pow.	Acc.	PP	Range
1	Psywave	Psychic	Special	—	100	15	Normal
1	Defense Curl	Normal	Status	—	—	40	Self
5	Lucky Chant	Normal	Status	—	—	30	Your Side
7	Yawn	Normal	Status	—	—	10	Normal
11	Psybeam	Psychic	Special	65	100	20	Normal
13	Imprison	Psychic	Status	—	—	10	Self
17	Moonlight	Fairy	Status	—	—	5	Self
19	Hypnosis	Psychic	Status	—	60	20	Normal
23	Zen Headbutt	Psychic	Physical	80	90	15	Normal
25	Synchronoise	Psychic	Special	120	100	10	Adjacent
29	Nightmare	Ghost	Status	—	100	15	Normal
31	Future Sight	Psychic	Special	120	100	10	Normal
35	Calm Mind	Psychic	Status	—	—	20	Self
37	Psychic	Psychic	Special	90	100	10	Normal
41	Dream Eater	Psychic	Special	100	100	15	Normal
43	Telekinesis	Psychic	Status	—	—	15	Normal
47	Stored Power	Psychic	Special	20	100	10	Normal

TM & HM MOVES

No.	Name	Type	Kind	Pow.	Acc.	PP	Range
TM03	Psyshock	Psychic	Special	80	100	10	Normal
TM04	Calm Mind	Psychic	Status	—	—	20	Self
TM06	Toxic	Poison	Status	—	90	10	Normal
TM10	Hidden Power	Normal	Special	60	100	15	Normal
TM16	Light Screen	Psychic	Status	—	—	30	Your Side
TM17	Protect	Normal	Status	—	—	10	Self
TM18	Rain Dance	Water	Status	—	—	5	Both Sides
TM20	Safeguard	Normal	Status	—	—	25	Your Side
TM21	Frustration	Normal	Physical	—	100	20	Normal
TM27	Return	Normal	Physical	—	100	20	Normal
TM29	Psychic	Psychic	Special	90	100	10	Normal
TM30	Shadow Ball	Ghost	Special	80	100	15	Normal
TM32	Double Team	Normal	Status	—	—	15	Self
TM33	Reflect	Psychic	Status	—	—	20	Your Side
TM39	Rock Tomb	Rock	Physical	60	95	15	Normal
TM41	Torment	Dark	Status	—	100	15	Normal
TM42	Facade	Normal	Physical	70	100	20	Normal
TM44	Rest	Psychic	Status	—	—	10	Self
TM45	Attract	Normal	Status	—	100	15	Normal
TM48	Round	Normal	Special	60	100	15	Normal
TM53	Energy Ball	Grass	Special	90	100	10	Normal
TM57	Charge Beam	Electric	Special	50	90	10	Normal
TM70	Flash	Normal	Status	—	100	20	Normal
TM73	Thunder Wave	Electric	Status	—	100	20	Normal
TM74	Gyro Ball	Steel	Physical	—	100	5	Normal
TM77	Psych Up	Normal	Status	—	—	10	Normal
TM80	Rock Slide	Rock	Physical	75	90	10	Many Others
TM85	Dream Eater	Psychic	Special	100	100	15	Normal
TM87	Swagger	Normal	Status	—	90	15	Normal
TM88	Sleep Talk	Normal	Status	—	—	10	Self
TM90	Substitute	Normal	Status	—	—	10	Self
TM92	Trick Room	Psychic	Status	—	—	5	Both Sides
TM94	Secret Power	Normal	Physical	70	100	20	Normal
TM99	Dazzling Gleam	Fairy	Special	80	100	10	Many Others
TM100	Confide	Normal	Status	—	—	20	Normal

MOVES LEARNED IN EXCHANGE FOR BP

Name	Type	Kind	Pow.	Acc.	PP	Range
Signal Beam	Bug	Special	75	100	15	Normal
Magic Coat	Psychic	Status	—	—	15	Self
Gravity	Psychic	Status	—	—	5	Both Sides
Zen Headbutt	Psychic	Physical	80	90	15	Normal
Snore	Normal	Special	50	100	15	Normal
Heal Bell	Normal	Status	—	—	5	Your Party
Pain Split	Normal	Status	—	—	20	Normal
Shock Wave	Electric	Special	60	—	20	Normal
Worry Seed	Grass	Status	—	100	10	Normal
After You	Normal	Status	—	—	15	Normal
Helping Hand	Normal	Status	—	—	20	1 Ally
Trick	Psychic	Status	—	100	10	Normal
Wonder Room	Psychic	Status	—	—	10	Both Sides
Skill Swap	Psychic	Status	—	—	10	Normal

MOVES TAUGHT BY PEOPLE

Name	Type	Kind	Pow.	Acc.	PP	Range

EGG MOVES

Name	Type	Kind	Pow.	Acc.	PP	Range
Sleep Talk	Normal	Status	—	—	10	Self
Secret Power	Normal	Physical	70	100	20	Normal
Barrier	Psychic	Status	—	—	20	Self
Magic Coat	Psychic	Status	—	—	15	Self
Helping Hand	Normal	Status	—	—	20	1 Ally
Baton Pass	Normal	Status	—	—	40	Self
Swift	Normal	Special	60	—	20	Many Others
Curse	Ghost	Status	—	—	10	Varies
Sonic Boom	Normal	Special	—	90	20	Normal
Healing Wish	Psychic	Status	—	—	10	Self

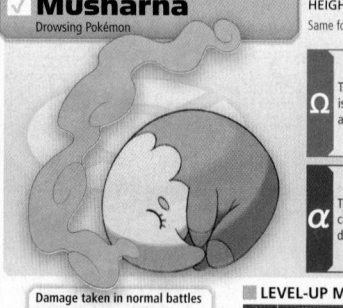

National Pokédex **518** Hoenn Pokédex —

Musharna

Drowsing Pokémon

Psychic

HEIGHT: 3'07" WEIGHT: 133.4 lbs.

Same form for ♂ / ♀

Ω The mist emanating from their foreheads is packed with the dreams of people and Pokémon.

α The dream mist coming from its forehead changes into many different colors depending on the dream that was eaten.

ABILITIES
Forewarn
Synchronize

HIDDEN ABILITY
Telepathy

EGG GROUPS
Field

STAT GROWTH RATES
HP
Attack
Defense
Sp. Atk
Sp. Def
Speed

ITEMS SOMETIMES HELD BY WILD POKÉMON
—

EVOLUTION
Munna → Moon Stone → Musharna

MAIN WAY TO REGISTER IN THE NATIONAL POKÉDEX

Use a Moon Stone on Munna.

Damage taken in normal battles

Type		Type	
Normal	×1	Flying	×1
Fire	×1	Psychic	×0.5
Water	×1	Bug	×2
Grass	×1	Rock	×1
Electric	×1	Ghost	×2
Ice	×1	Dragon	×1
Fighting	×0.5	Dark	×2
Poison	×1	Steel	×1
Ground	×1	Fairy	×1

Damage taken in Inverse battles

Type		Type	
Normal	×1	Flying	×1
Fire	×1	Psychic	×2
Water	×1	Bug	×0.5
Grass	×1	Rock	×1
Electric	×1	Ghost	×0.5
Ice	×1	Dragon	×1
Fighting	×2	Dark	×0.5
Poison	×1	Steel	×1
Ground	×1	Fairy	×1

Can be used in
Inverse Battle
Battle Institute
Battle Maison
Random Matchup (Free Battle)
Random Matchup (Others)

LEVEL-UP MOVES

Lv.	Name	Type	Kind	Pow.	Acc.	PP	Range
1	Defense Curl	Normal	Status	—	—	40	Self
1	Lucky Chant	Normal	Status	—	—	30	Your Side
1	Psybeam	Psychic	Special	65	100	20	Normal
1	Hypnosis	Psychic	Status	—	60	20	Normal

TM & HM MOVES

No.	Name	Type	Kind	Pow.	Acc.	PP	Range
TM03	Psyshock	Psychic	Special	80	100	10	Normal
TM04	Calm Mind	Psychic	Status	—	—	20	Self
TM06	Toxic	Poison	Status	—	90	10	Normal
TM10	Hidden Power	Normal	Special	60	100	15	Normal
TM15	Hyper Beam	Normal	Special	150	90	5	Normal
TM16	Light Screen	Psychic	Status	—	—	30	Your Side
TM17	Protect	Normal	Status	—	—	10	Self
TM18	Rain Dance	Water	Status	—	—	5	Both Sides
TM20	Safeguard	Normal	Status	—	—	25	Your Side
TM21	Frustration	Normal	Physical	—	100	20	Normal
TM27	Return	Normal	Physical	—	100	20	Normal
TM29	Psychic	Psychic	Special	90	100	10	Normal
TM30	Shadow Ball	Ghost	Special	80	100	15	Normal
TM32	Double Team	Normal	Status	—	—	15	Self
TM33	Reflect	Psychic	Status	—	—	20	Your Side
TM39	Rock Tomb	Rock	Physical	60	95	15	Normal
TM41	Torment	Dark	Status	—	100	15	Normal
TM42	Facade	Normal	Physical	70	100	20	Normal
TM44	Rest	Psychic	Status	—	—	10	Self
TM45	Attract	Normal	Status	—	100	15	Normal
TM48	Round	Normal	Special	60	100	15	Normal
TM53	Energy Ball	Grass	Special	90	100	10	Normal
TM57	Charge Beam	Electric	Special	50	90	10	Normal
TM68	Giga Impact	Normal	Physical	150	90	5	Normal
TM70	Flash	Normal	Status	—	100	20	Normal
TM73	Thunder Wave	Electric	Status	—	100	20	Normal
TM74	Gyro Ball	Steel	Physical	—	100	5	Normal
TM77	Psych Up	Normal	Status	—	—	10	Normal
TM80	Rock Slide	Rock	Physical	75	90	10	Many Others
TM85	Dream Eater	Psychic	Special	100	100	15	Normal
TM87	Swagger	Normal	Status	—	90	15	Normal
TM88	Sleep Talk	Normal	Status	—	—	10	Self
TM90	Substitute	Normal	Status	—	—	10	Self
TM92	Trick Room	Psychic	Status	—	—	5	Both Sides
TM94	Secret Power	Normal	Physical	70	100	20	Normal
TM99	Dazzling Gleam	Fairy	Special	80	100	10	Many Others
TM100	Confide	Normal	Status	—	—	20	Normal

MOVES LEARNED IN EXCHANGE FOR BP

Name	Type	Kind	Pow.	Acc.	PP	Range
Signal Beam	Bug	Special	75	100	15	Normal
Magic Coat	Psychic	Status	—	—	15	Self
Gravity	Psychic	Status	—	—	5	Both Sides
Zen Headbutt	Psychic	Physical	80	90	15	Normal
Snore	Normal	Special	50	100	15	Normal
Heal Bell	Normal	Status	—	—	5	Your Party
Pain Split	Normal	Status	—	—	20	Normal
Shock Wave	Electric	Special	60	—	20	Normal
Worry Seed	Grass	Status	—	100	10	Normal
After You	Normal	Status	—	—	15	Normal
Helping Hand	Normal	Status	—	—	20	1 Ally
Trick	Psychic	Status	—	100	10	Normal
Wonder Room	Psychic	Status	—	—	10	Both Sides
Skill Swap	Psychic	Status	—	—	10	Normal

MOVES TAUGHT BY PEOPLE

Name	Type	Kind	Pow.	Acc.	PP	Range

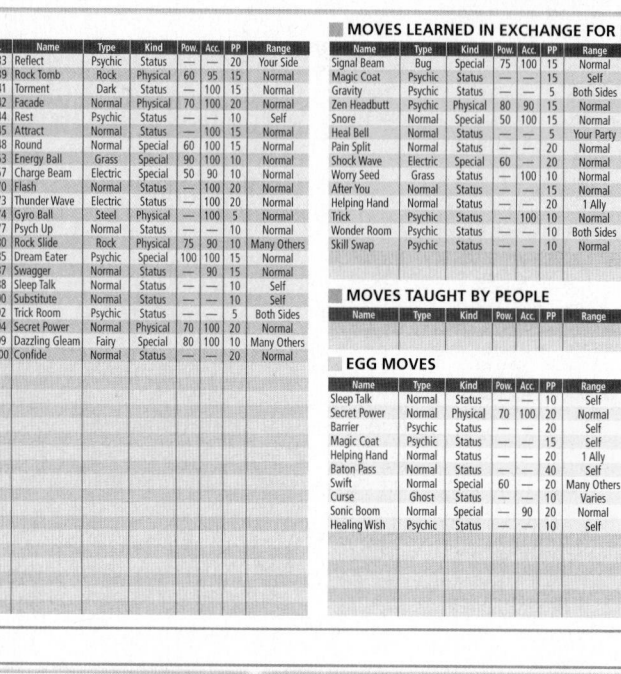

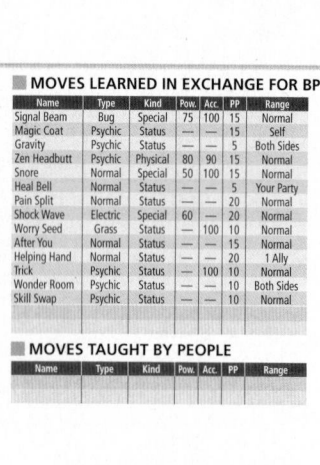

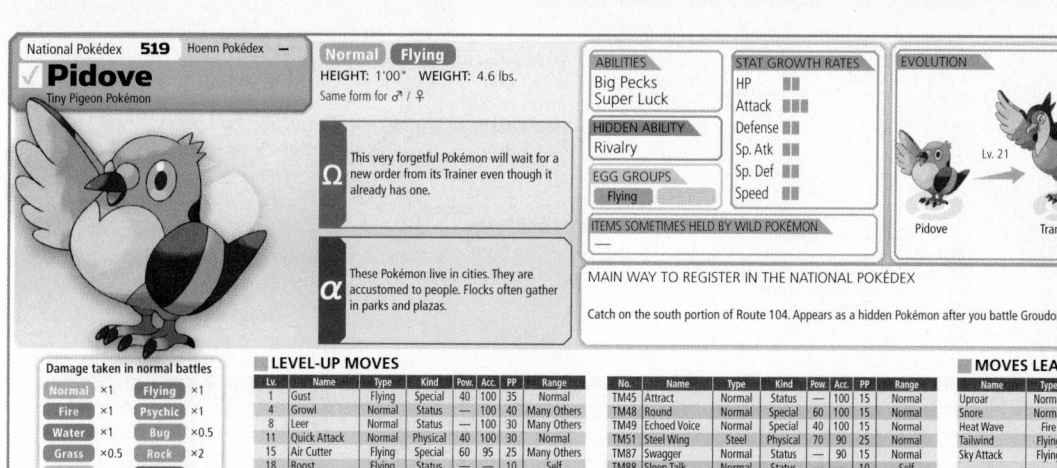

National Pokédex **519** Hoenn Pokédex —

Pidove

Tiny Pigeon Pokémon

Normal Flying

HEIGHT: 1'00" WEIGHT: 4.6 lbs.

Same form for ♂ / ♀

Ω This very forgetful Pokémon will wait for a new order from its Trainer even though it already has one.

α These Pokémon live in cities. They are accustomed to people. Flocks often gather in parks and plazas.

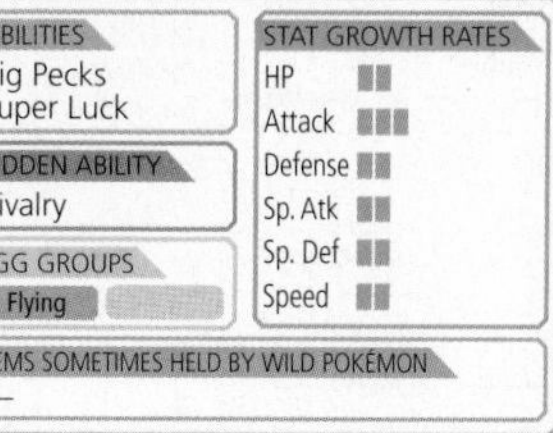

ABILITIES
Big Pecks
Super Luck

HIDDEN ABILITY
Rivalry

EGG GROUPS
Flying

STAT GROWTH RATES
HP
Attack
Defense
Sp. Atk
Sp. Def
Speed

ITEMS SOMETIMES HELD BY WILD POKÉMON
—

EVOLUTION

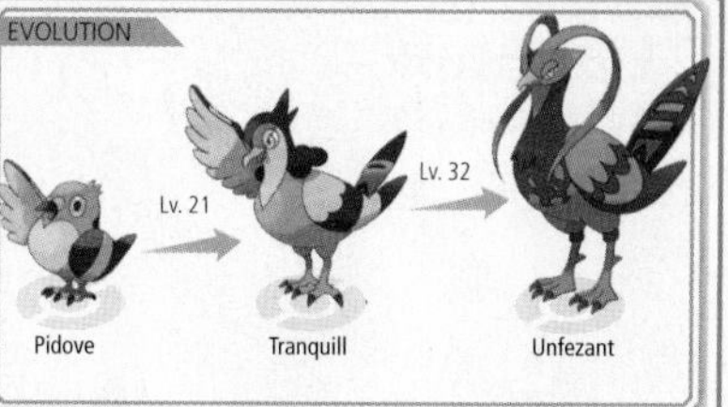

MAIN WAY TO REGISTER IN THE NATIONAL POKÉDEX

Catch on the south portion of Route 104. Appears as a hidden Pokémon after you battle Groudon or Kyogre.

Damage taken in normal battles

Type		Type	
Normal	×1	Flying	×1
Fire	×1	Psychic	×1
Water	×1	Bug	×0.5
Grass	×0.5	Rock	×2
Electric	×2	Ghost	×0
Ice	×2	Dragon	×1
Fighting	×1	Dark	×1
Poison	×1	Steel	×1
Ground	×0	Fairy	×1

Damage taken in Inverse battles

Type		Type	
Normal	×1	Flying	×1
Fire	×1	Psychic	×1
Water	×1	Bug	×2
Grass	×2	Rock	×0.5
Electric	×0.5	Ghost	×2
Ice	×0.5	Dragon	×1
Fighting	×1	Dark	×1
Poison	×1	Steel	×1
Ground	×2	Fairy	×1

Can be used in

Inverse Battle
Battle Institute
Battle Maison
Random Matchup (Free Battle)
Random Matchup (Others)

LEVEL-UP MOVES

Lv.	Name	Type	Kind	Pow.	Acc.	PP	Range
1	Gust	Flying	Special	40	100	35	Normal
4	Growl	Normal	Status	—	100	40	Many Others
8	Leer	Normal	Status	—	100	30	Many Others
11	Quick Attack	Normal	Physical	40	100	30	Normal
15	Air Cutter	Flying	Special	60	95	25	Many Others
18	Roost	Flying	Status	—	—	10	Self
22	Detect	Fighting	Status	—	—	5	Self
25	Taunt	Dark	Status	—	100	20	Normal
29	Air Slash	Flying	Special	75	95	15	Normal
32	Razor Wind	Normal	Special	80	100	10	Many Others
36	Feather Dance	Flying	Status	—	100	15	Normal
39	Swagger	Normal	Status	—	90	15	Normal
43	Facade	Normal	Physical	70	100	20	Normal
46	Tailwind	Flying	Status	—	—	15	Your Side
50	Sky Attack	Flying	Physical	140	90	5	Normal

TM & HM MOVES

No.	Name	Type	Kind	Pow.	Acc.	PP	Range
TM06	Toxic	Poison	Status	—	90	10	Normal
TM10	Hidden Power	Normal	Special	60	100	15	Normal
TM11	Sunny Day	Fire	Status	—	—	5	Both Sides
TM12	Taunt	Dark	Status	—	100	20	Normal
TM17	Protect	Normal	Status	—	—	10	Self
TM18	Rain Dance	Water	Status	—	—	5	Both Sides
TM19	Roost	Flying	Status	—	—	10	Self
TM21	Frustration	Normal	Physical	—	100	20	Normal
TM27	Return	Normal	Physical	—	100	20	Normal
TM32	Double Team	Normal	Status	—	—	15	Self
TM40	Aerial Ace	Flying	Physical	60	—	20	Normal
TM42	Facade	Normal	Physical	70	100	20	Normal
TM44	Rest	Psychic	Status	—	—	10	Self
TM45	Attract	Normal	Status	—	100	15	Normal
TM48	Round	Normal	Special	60	100	15	Normal
TM49	Echoed Voice	Normal	Special	40	100	15	Normal
TM51	Steel Wing	Steel	Physical	70	90	25	Normal
TM87	Swagger	Normal	Status	—	90	15	Normal
TM88	Sleep Talk	Normal	Status	—	—	10	Self
TM89	U-turn	Bug	Physical	70	100	20	Normal
TM90	Substitute	Normal	Status	—	—	10	Self
TM94	Secret Power	Normal	Physical	70	100	20	Normal
TM100	Confide	Normal	Status	—	—	20	Normal
HM02	Fly	Flying	Physical	90	95	15	Normal

MOVES LEARNED IN EXCHANGE FOR BP

Name	Type	Kind	Pow.	Acc.	PP	Range
Uproar	Normal	Special	90	100	10	1 Random
Snore	Normal	Special	50	100	15	Normal
Heat Wave	Fire	Special	95	90	10	Many Others
Tailwind	Flying	Status	—	—	15	Your Side
Sky Attack	Flying	Physical	140	90	5	Normal

MOVES TAUGHT BY PEOPLE

Name	Type	Kind	Pow.	Acc.	PP	Range

EGG MOVES

Name	Type	Kind	Pow.	Acc.	PP	Range
Steel Wing	Steel	Physical	70	90	25	Normal
Hypnosis	Psychic	Status	—	60	20	Normal
Uproar	Normal	Special	90	100	10	1 Random
Bestow	Normal	Status	—	—	15	Normal
Wish	Normal	Status	—	—	10	Self
Morning Sun	Normal	Status	—	—	5	Self
Lucky Chant	Normal	Status	—	—	30	Your Side
Night Slash	Dark	Physical	70	100	15	Normal

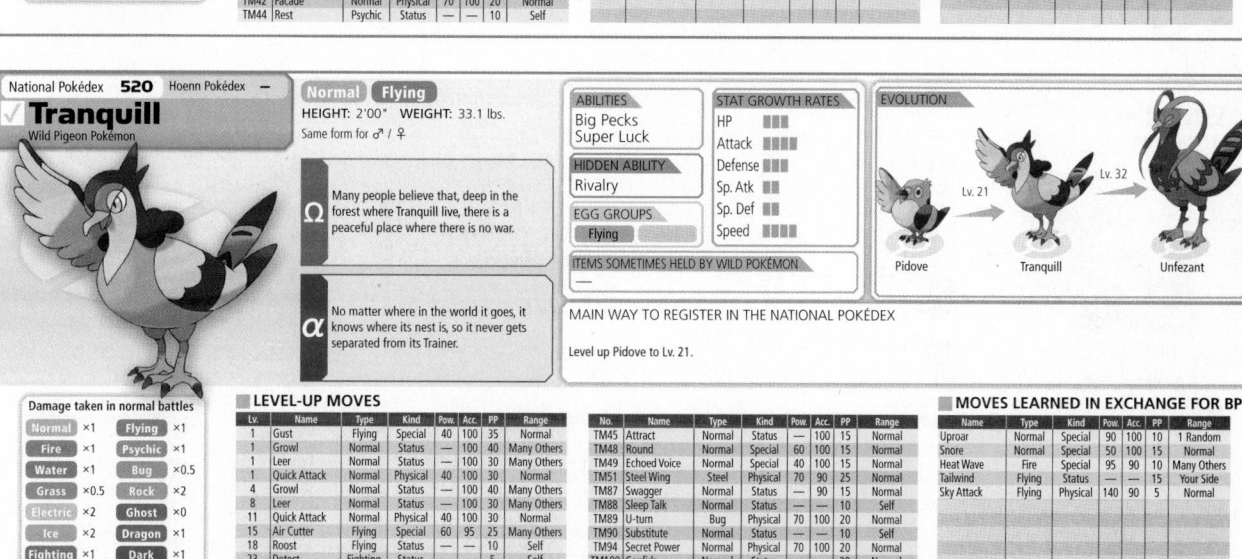

National Pokédex **520** Hoenn Pokédex —

Tranquill

Wild Pigeon Pokémon

Normal Flying

HEIGHT: 2'00" WEIGHT: 33.1 lbs.

Same form for ♂ / ♀

Ω Many people believe that, deep in the forest where Tranquill live, there is a peaceful place where there is no war.

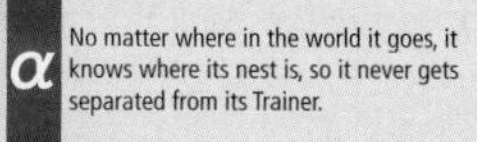

α No matter where in the world it goes, it knows where its nest is, so it never gets separated from its Trainer.

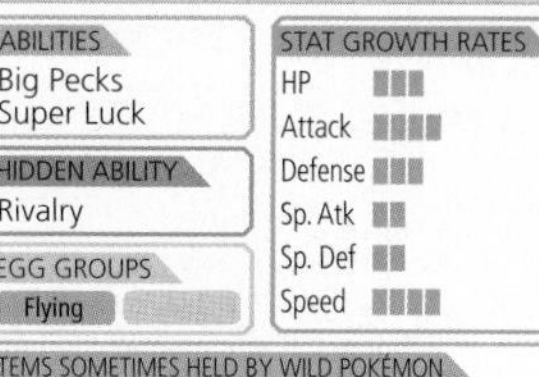

ABILITIES
Big Pecks
Super Luck

HIDDEN ABILITY
Rivalry

EGG GROUPS
Flying

STAT GROWTH RATES
HP
Attack
Defense
Sp. Atk
Sp. Def
Speed

ITEMS SOMETIMES HELD BY WILD POKÉMON
—

EVOLUTION

MAIN WAY TO REGISTER IN THE NATIONAL POKÉDEX

Level up Pidove to Lv. 21.

Damage taken in normal battles

Type		Type	
Normal	×1	Flying	×1
Fire	×1	Psychic	×1
Water	×1	Bug	×0.5
Grass	×0.5	Rock	×2
Electric	×2	Ghost	×0
Ice	×2	Dragon	×1
Fighting	×1	Dark	×1
Poison	×1	Steel	×1
Ground	×0	Fairy	×1

Damage taken in Inverse battles

Type		Type	
Normal	×1	Flying	×1
Fire	×1	Psychic	×1
Water	×1	Bug	×2
Grass	×2	Rock	×0.5
Electric	×0.5	Ghost	×2
Ice	×0.5	Dragon	×1
Fighting	×1	Dark	×1
Poison	×1	Steel	×1
Ground	×2	Fairy	×1

Can be used in

Inverse Battle
Battle Institute
Battle Maison
Random Matchup (Free Battle)
Random Matchup (Others)

LEVEL-UP MOVES

Lv.	Name	Type	Kind	Pow.	Acc.	PP	Range
1	Gust	Flying	Special	40	100	35	Normal
1	Growl	Normal	Status	—	100	40	Many Others
1	Leer	Normal	Status	—	100	30	Many Others
1	Quick Attack	Normal	Physical	40	100	30	Normal
4	Growl	Normal	Status	—	100	40	Many Others
8	Leer	Normal	Status	—	100	30	Many Others
11	Quick Attack	Normal	Physical	40	100	30	Normal
15	Air Cutter	Flying	Special	60	95	25	Many Others
18	Roost	Flying	Status	—	—	10	Self
23	Detect	Fighting	Status	—	—	5	Self
27	Taunt	Dark	Status	—	100	20	Normal
32	Air Slash	Flying	Special	75	95	15	Normal
36	Razor Wind	Normal	Special	80	100	10	Many Others
41	Feather Dance	Flying	Status	—	100	15	Normal
45	Swagger	Normal	Status	—	90	15	Normal
50	Facade	Normal	Physical	70	100	20	Normal
54	Tailwind	Flying	Status	—	—	15	Your Side
59	Sky Attack	Flying	Physical	140	90	5	Normal

TM & HM MOVES

No.	Name	Type	Kind	Pow.	Acc.	PP	Range
TM06	Toxic	Poison	Status	—	90	10	Normal
TM10	Hidden Power	Normal	Special	60	100	15	Normal
TM11	Sunny Day	Fire	Status	—	—	5	Both Sides
TM12	Taunt	Dark	Status	—	100	20	Normal
TM17	Protect	Normal	Status	—	—	10	Self
TM18	Rain Dance	Water	Status	—	—	5	Both Sides
TM19	Roost	Flying	Status	—	—	10	Self
TM21	Frustration	Normal	Physical	—	100	20	Normal
TM27	Return	Normal	Physical	—	100	20	Normal
TM32	Double Team	Normal	Status	—	—	15	Self
TM40	Aerial Ace	Flying	Physical	60	—	20	Normal
TM42	Facade	Normal	Physical	70	100	20	Normal
TM44	Rest	Psychic	Status	—	—	10	Self
TM45	Attract	Normal	Status	—	100	15	Normal
TM48	Round	Normal	Special	60	100	15	Normal
TM49	Echoed Voice	Normal	Special	40	100	15	Normal
TM51	Steel Wing	Steel	Physical	70	90	25	Normal
TM87	Swagger	Normal	Status	—	90	15	Normal
TM88	Sleep Talk	Normal	Status	—	—	10	Self
TM89	U-turn	Bug	Physical	70	100	20	Normal
TM90	Substitute	Normal	Status	—	—	10	Self
TM94	Secret Power	Normal	Physical	70	100	20	Normal
TM100	Confide	Normal	Status	—	—	20	Normal
HM02	Fly	Flying	Physical	90	95	15	Normal

MOVES LEARNED IN EXCHANGE FOR BP

Name	Type	Kind	Pow.	Acc.	PP	Range
Uproar	Normal	Special	90	100	10	1 Random
Snore	Normal	Special	50	100	15	Normal
Heat Wave	Fire	Special	95	90	10	Many Others
Tailwind	Flying	Status	—	—	15	Your Side
Sky Attack	Flying	Physical	140	90	5	Normal

MOVES TAUGHT BY PEOPLE

Name	Type	Kind	Pow.	Acc.	PP	Range

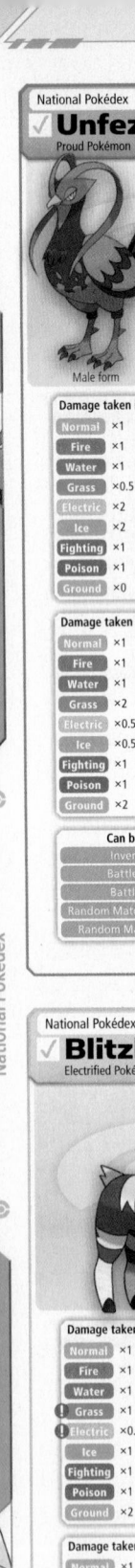

National Pokédex **521** Hoenn Pokédex —

Unfezant

Proud Pokémon

Normal Flying

HEIGHT: 3'11" WEIGHT: 63.9 lbs.

The male has a mask-like plumage and a green pattern on its belly. The female has a brown pattern on its belly.

Male form Female form

Ω Males swing their head plumage to threaten opponents. The females' flying abilities surpass those of the males.

α Males have plumage on their heads. They will never let themselves feel close to anyone other than their Trainers.

ABILITIES
Big Pecks
Super Luck

HIDDEN ABILITY
Rivalry

EGG GROUPS
Flying

ITEMS SOMETIMES HELD BY WILD POKÉMON
—

STAT GROWTH RATES
HP
Attack
Defense
Sp. Atk
Sp. Def
Speed

EVOLUTION

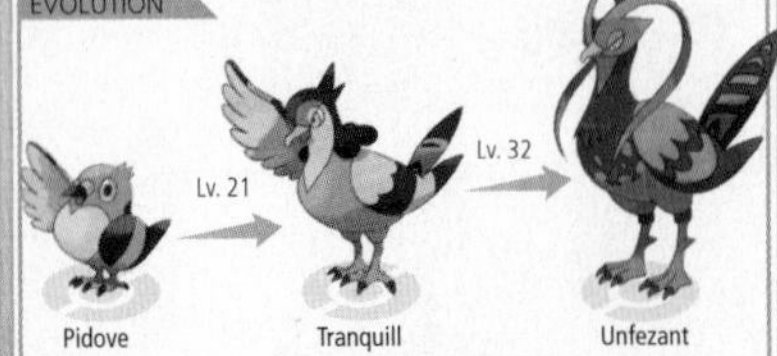

MAIN WAY TO REGISTER IN THE NATIONAL POKÉDEX

Level up Tranquill to Lv. 32.

Damage taken in normal battles

Type		Type	
Normal	×1	Flying	×1
Fire	×1	Psychic	×1
Water	×1	Bug	×0.5
Grass	×0.5	Rock	×2
Electric	×2	Ghost	×0
Ice	×2	Dragon	×1
Fighting	×1	Dark	×1
Poison	×1	Steel	×1
Ground	×0	Fairy	×1

Damage taken in Inverse battles

Type		Type	
Normal	×1	Flying	×1
Fire	×1	Psychic	×1
Water	×1	Bug	×2
Grass	×2	Rock	×0.5
Electric	×0.5	Ghost	×2
Ice	×0.5	Dragon	×1
Fighting	×1	Dark	×1
Poison	×1	Steel	×1
Ground	×2	Fairy	×1

Can be used in
Inverse Battle
Battle Institute
Battle Maison
Random Matchup (Free Battle)
Random Matchup (Others)

LEVEL-UP MOVES

Lv.	Name	Type	Kind	Pow.	Acc.	PP	Range
1	Gust	Flying	Special	40	100	35	Normal
1	Growl	Normal	Status	—	100	40	Many Others
1	Leer	Normal	Status	—	100	30	Many Others
1	Quick Attack	Normal	Physical	40	100	30	Normal
4	Growl	Normal	Status	—	100	40	Many Others
8	Leer	Normal	Status	—	100	30	Many Others
11	Quick Attack	Normal	Physical	40	100	30	Normal
15	Air Cutter	Flying	Special	60	95	25	Many Others
18	Roost	Flying	Status	—	—	10	Self
23	Detect	Fighting	Status	—	—	5	Self
27	Taunt	Dark	Status	—	100	20	Normal
33	Air Slash	Flying	Special	75	95	15	Normal
38	Razor Wind	Normal	Special	80	100	10	Many Others
44	Feather Dance	Flying	Status	—	100	15	Normal
49	Swagger	Normal	Status	—	90	15	Normal
55	Facade	Normal	Physical	70	100	20	Normal
60	Tailwind	Flying	Status	—	—	15	Your Side
66	Sky Attack	Flying	Physical	140	90	5	Normal

TM & HM MOVES

No.	Name	Type	Kind	Pow.	Acc.	PP	Range
TM06	Toxic	Poison	Status	—	90	10	Normal
TM10	Hidden Power	Normal	Special	60	100	15	Normal
TM11	Sunny Day	Fire	Status	—	—	5	Both Sides
TM12	Taunt	Dark	Status	—	100	20	Normal
TM15	Hyper Beam	Normal	Special	150	90	5	Normal
TM17	Protect	Normal	Status	—	—	10	Self
TM18	Rain Dance	Water	Status	—	—	5	Both Sides
TM19	Roost	Flying	Status	—	—	10	Self
TM21	Frustration	Normal	Physical	—	100	20	Normal
TM27	Return	Normal	Physical	—	100	20	Normal
TM32	Double Team	Normal	Status	—	—	15	Self
TM40	Aerial Ace	Flying	Physical	60	—	20	Normal
TM42	Facade	Normal	Physical	70	100	20	Normal
TM44	Rest	Psychic	Status	—	—	10	Self
TM45	Attract	Normal	Status	—	100	15	Normal
TM48	Round	Normal	Special	60	100	15	Normal
TM49	Echoed Voice	Normal	Special	40	100	15	Normal
TM51	Steel Wing	Steel	Physical	70	90	25	Normal
TM68	Giga Impact	Normal	Physical	150	90	5	Normal
TM77	Psych Up	Normal	Status	—	—	10	Normal
TM87	Swagger	Normal	Status	—	90	15	Normal
TM88	Sleep Talk	Normal	Status	—	—	10	Self
TM89	U-turn	Bug	Physical	70	100	20	Normal
TM90	Substitute	Normal	Status	—	—	10	Self
TM94	Secret Power	Normal	Physical	70	100	20	Normal
TM100	Confide	Normal	Status	—	—	20	Normal
HM02	Fly	Flying	Physical	90	95	15	Normal

MOVES LEARNED IN EXCHANGE FOR BP

Name	Type	Kind	Pow.	Acc.	PP	Range
Uproar	Normal	Special	90	100	10	1 Random
Snore	Normal	Special	50	100	15	Normal
Heat Wave	Fire	Special	95	90	10	Many Others
Tailwind	Flying	Status	—	—	15	Your Side
Sky Attack	Flying	Physical	140	90	5	Normal

MOVES TAUGHT BY PEOPLE

Name	Type	Kind	Pow.	Acc.	PP	Range

National Pokédex **522** Hoenn Pokédex —

Blitzle

Electrified Pokémon

Electric

HEIGHT: 2'07" WEIGHT: 65.7 lbs.

Same form for ♂ / ♀

Ω When thunderclouds cover the sky, it will appear. It can catch lightning with its mane and store the electricity.

α Its mane shines when it discharges electricity. They use the frequency and rhythm of these flashes to communicate.

ABILITIES
Lightning Rod
Motor Drive

HIDDEN ABILITY
Sap Sipper

EGG GROUPS
Field

ITEMS SOMETIMES HELD BY WILD POKÉMON
—

STAT GROWTH RATES
HP
Attack
Defense
Sp. Atk
Sp. Def
Speed

EVOLUTION

MAIN WAY TO REGISTER IN THE NATIONAL POKÉDEX

Leave a Zebstrika at a Pokémon Day Care, then hatch the Pokémon Egg that is found.

Damage taken in normal battles

Type		Type	
Normal	×1	Flying	×0.5
Fire	×1	Psychic	×1
Water	×1	Bug	×1
Grass	×1	Rock	×1
Electric	×0.5	Ghost	×1
Ice	×1	Dragon	×1
Fighting	×1	Dark	×1
Poison	×1	Steel	×0.5
Ground	×2	Fairy	×1

Damage taken in Inverse battles

Type		Type	
Normal	×1	Flying	×2
Fire	×1	Psychic	×1
Water	×1	Bug	×1
Grass	×1	Rock	×1
Electric	×2	Ghost	×1
Ice	×1	Dragon	×1
Fighting	×1	Dark	×1
Poison	×1	Steel	×2
Ground	×0.5	Fairy	×1

Can be used in
Inverse Battle
Battle Institute
Battle Maison
Random Matchup (Free Battle)
Random Matchup (Others)

LEVEL-UP MOVES

Lv.	Name	Type	Kind	Pow.	Acc.	PP	Range
1	Quick Attack	Normal	Physical	40	100	30	Normal
4	Tail Whip	Normal	Status	—	100	30	Many Others
8	Charge	Electric	Status	—	—	20	Self
11	Shock Wave	Electric	Special	60	—	20	Normal
15	Thunder Wave	Electric	Status	—	100	20	Normal
18	Flame Charge	Fire	Physical	50	100	20	Normal
22	Pursuit	Dark	Physical	40	100	20	Normal
25	Spark	Electric	Physical	65	100	20	Normal
29	Stomp	Normal	Physical	65	100	20	Normal
32	Discharge	Electric	Special	80	100	15	Adjacent
36	Agility	Psychic	Status	—	—	30	Self
39	Wild Charge	Electric	Physical	90	100	15	Normal
43	Thrash	Normal	Physical	120	100	10	1 Random

TM & HM MOVES

No.	Name	Type	Kind	Pow.	Acc.	PP	Range
TM06	Toxic	Poison	Status	—	90	10	Normal
TM10	Hidden Power	Normal	Special	60	100	15	Normal
TM16	Light Screen	Psychic	Status	—	—	30	Your Side
TM17	Protect	Normal	Status	—	—	10	Self
TM18	Rain Dance	Water	Status	—	—	5	Both Sides
TM21	Frustration	Normal	Physical	—	100	20	Normal
TM24	Thunderbolt	Electric	Special	90	100	15	Normal
TM25	Thunder	Electric	Special	110	70	10	Normal
TM27	Return	Normal	Physical	—	100	20	Normal
TM32	Double Team	Normal	Status	—	—	15	Self
TM42	Facade	Normal	Physical	70	100	20	Normal
TM43	Flame Charge	Fire	Physical	50	100	20	Normal
TM44	Rest	Psychic	Status	—	—	10	Self
TM45	Attract	Normal	Status	—	100	15	Normal
TM48	Round	Normal	Special	60	100	15	Normal
TM57	Charge Beam	Electric	Special	50	90	10	Normal
TM70	Flash	Normal	Status	—	100	20	Normal
TM72	Volt Switch	Electric	Special	70	100	20	Normal
TM73	Thunder Wave	Electric	Status	—	100	20	Normal
TM87	Swagger	Normal	Status	—	90	15	Normal
TM88	Sleep Talk	Normal	Status	—	—	10	Self
TM90	Substitute	Normal	Status	—	—	10	Self
TM93	Wild Charge	Electric	Physical	90	100	15	Normal
TM94	Secret Power	Normal	Physical	70	100	20	Normal
TM100	Confide	Normal	Status	—	—	20	Normal

MOVES LEARNED IN EXCHANGE FOR BP

Name	Type	Kind	Pow.	Acc.	PP	Range
Signal Beam	Bug	Special	75	100	15	Normal
Bounce	Flying	Physical	85	85	5	Normal
Magnet Rise	Electric	Status	—	—	10	Self
Snore	Normal	Special	50	100	15	Normal
Shock Wave	Electric	Special	60	—	20	Normal
Snatch	Dark	Status	—	—	10	Self

MOVES TAUGHT BY PEOPLE

Name	Type	Kind	Pow.	Acc.	PP	Range

EGG MOVES

Name	Type	Kind	Pow.	Acc.	PP	Range
Me First	Normal	Status	—	—	20	Varies
Take Down	Normal	Physical	90	85	20	Normal
Sand Attack	Ground	Status	—	100	15	Normal
Double Kick	Fighting	Physical	30	100	30	Normal
Screech	Normal	Status	—	85	40	Normal
Rage	Normal	Physical	20	100	20	Normal
Endure	Normal	Status	—	—	10	Self
Double-Edge	Normal	Physical	120	100	15	Normal
Shock Wave	Electric	Special	60	—	20	Normal
Snatch	Dark	Status	—	—	10	Self

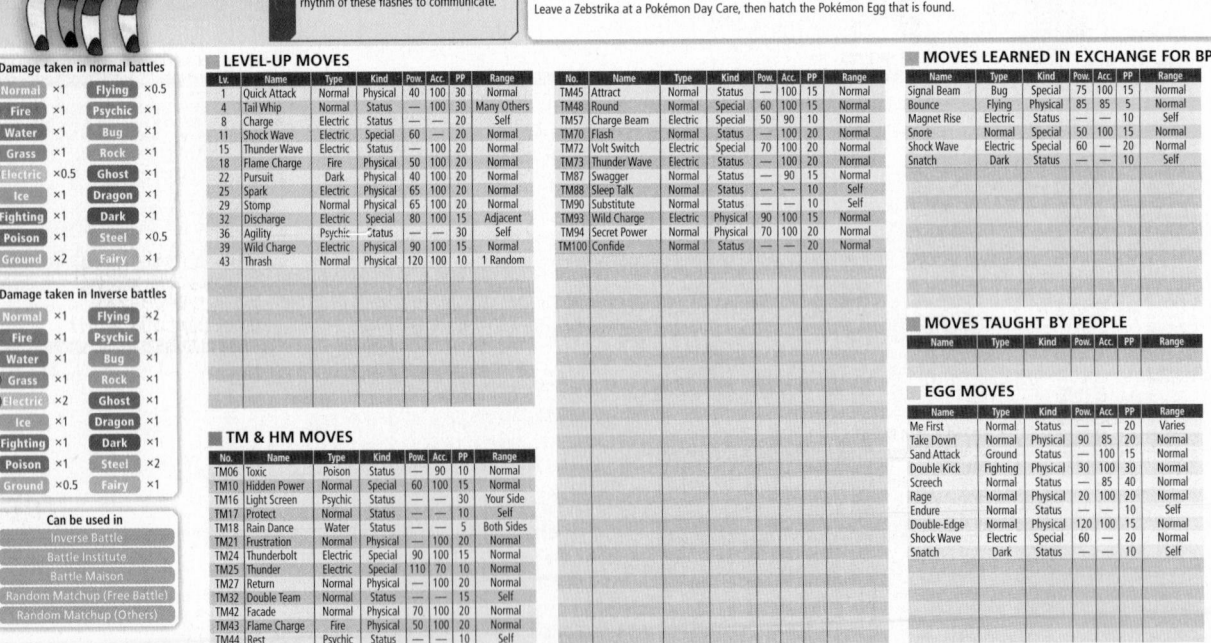

National Pokédex **523** Hoenn Pokédex —

Zebstrika

Thunderbolt Pokémon

Electric

HEIGHT: 5'03" WEIGHT: 175.3 lbs.

Same form for ♂ / ♀

Ω When this ill-tempered Pokémon runs wild, it shoots lightning from its mane in all directions.

α They have lightning-like movements. When Zebstrika run at full speed, the sound of thunder reverberates.

ABILITIES
Lightning Rod
Motor Drive

HIDDEN ABILITY
Sap Sipper

EGG GROUPS
Field

STAT GROWTH RATES
HP
Attack
Defense
Sp. Atk
Sp. Def
Speed

ITEMS SOMETIMES HELD BY WILD POKÉMON
—

EVOLUTION

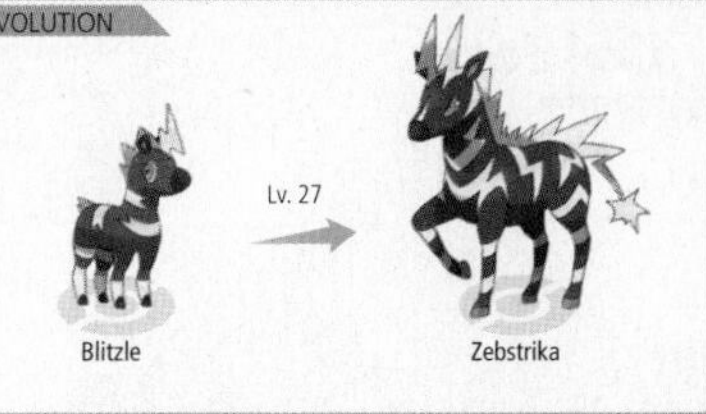

MAIN WAY TO REGISTER IN THE NATIONAL POKÉDEX

Catch on Mirage Mountain 6.

Damage taken in normal battles

Type		Type	
Normal	×1	Flying	×0.5
Fire	×1	Psychic	×1
Water	×1	Bug	×1
Grass	×1	Rock	×1
Electric	×0.5	Ghost	×1
Ice	×1	Dragon	×1
Fighting	×1	Dark	×1
Poison	×1	Steel	×0.5
Ground	×2	Fairy	×1

Damage taken in Inverse battles

Type		Type	
Normal	×1	Flying	×2
Fire	×1	Psychic	×1
Water	×1	Bug	×1
Grass	×1	Rock	×1
Electric	×2	Ghost	×1
Ice	×1	Dragon	×1
Fighting	×1	Dark	×1
Poison	×1	Steel	×2
Ground	×0.5	Fairy	×1

Can be used in
Inverse Battle
Battle Institute
Battle Maison
Random Matchup (Free Battle)
Random Matchup (Others)

LEVEL-UP MOVES

Lv.	Name	Type	Kind	Pow.	Acc.	PP	Range
1	Ion Deluge	Electric	Status	—	—	25	Both Sides
1	Quick Attack	Normal	Physical	40	100	30	Normal
1	Tail Whip	Normal	Status	—	100	30	Many Others
1	Charge	Electric	Status	—	—	20	Self
1	Thunder Wave	Electric	Status	—	100	20	Normal
4	Tail Whip	Normal	Status	—	100	30	Many Others
8	Charge	Electric	Status	—	—	20	Self
11	Shock Wave	Electric	Special	60	—	20	Normal
15	Thunder Wave	Electric	Status	—	100	20	Normal
18	Flame Charge	Fire	Physical	50	100	20	Normal
22	Pursuit	Dark	Physical	40	100	20	Normal
25	Spark	Electric	Physical	65	100	20	Normal
31	Stomp	Normal	Physical	65	100	20	Normal
36	Discharge	Electric	Special	80	100	15	Adjacent
42	Agility	Psychic	Status	—	—	30	Self
47	Wild Charge	Electric	Physical	90	100	15	Normal
53	Thrash	Normal	Physical	120	100	10	1 Random
58	Ion Deluge	Electric	Status	—	—	25	Both Sides

TM & HM MOVES

No.	Name	Type	Kind	Pow.	Acc.	PP	Range
TM06	Toxic	Poison	Status	—	90	10	Normal
TM10	Hidden Power	Normal	Special	60	100	15	Normal
TM15	Hyper Beam	Normal	Special	150	90	5	Normal
TM16	Light Screen	Psychic	Status	—	—	30	Your Side
TM17	Protect	Normal	Status	—	—	10	Self
TM18	Rain Dance	Water	Status	—	—	5	Both Sides
TM21	Frustration	Normal	Physical	—	100	20	Normal
TM24	Thunderbolt	Electric	Special	90	100	15	Normal
TM25	Thunder	Electric	Special	110	70	10	Normal
TM27	Return	Normal	Physical	—	100	20	Normal
TM32	Double Team	Normal	Status	—	—	15	Self
TM42	Facade	Normal	Physical	70	100	20	Normal
TM43	Flame Charge	Fire	Physical	50	100	20	Normal
TM44	Rest	Psychic	Status	—	—	10	Self
TM45	Attract	Normal	Status	—	100	15	Normal
TM48	Round	Normal	Special	60	100	15	Normal
TM50	Overheat	Fire	Special	130	90	5	Normal
TM57	Charge Beam	Electric	Special	50	90	10	Normal
TM68	Giga Impact	Normal	Physical	150	90	5	Normal
TM70	Flash	Normal	Status	—	100	20	Normal
TM72	Volt Switch	Electric	Special	70	100	20	Normal
TM73	Thunder Wave	Electric	Status	—	100	20	Normal
TM87	Swagger	Normal	Status	—	90	15	Normal
TM88	Sleep Talk	Normal	Status	—	—	10	Self
TM90	Substitute	Normal	Status	—	—	10	Self
TM93	Wild Charge	Electric	Physical	90	100	15	Normal
TM94	Secret Power	Normal	Physical	70	100	20	Normal
TM100	Confide	Normal	Status	—	—	20	Normal
HM06	Rock Smash	Fighting	Physical	40	100	15	Normal

MOVES LEARNED IN EXCHANGE FOR BP

Name	Type	Kind	Pow.	Acc.	PP	Range
Signal Beam	Bug	Special	75	100	15	Normal
Bounce	Flying	Physical	85	85	5	Normal
Magnet Rise	Electric	Status	—	—	10	Self
Snore	Normal	Special	50	100	15	Normal
Shock Wave	Electric	Special	60	—	20	Normal
Snatch	Dark	Status	—	—	10	Self

MOVES TAUGHT BY PEOPLE

Name	Type	Kind	Pow.	Acc.	PP	Range

National Pokédex **524** Hoenn Pokédex —

Roggenrola

Mantle Pokémon

Rock

HEIGHT: 1'04" WEIGHT: 39.7 lbs.

Same form for ♂ / ♀

Ω Its ear is hexagonal in shape. Compressed underground, its body is as hard as steel.

α They were discovered a hundred years ago in an earthquake fissure. Inside each one is an energy core.

ABILITY
Sturdy

HIDDEN ABILITY
Sand Force

EGG GROUPS
Mineral

STAT GROWTH RATES
HP
Attack
Defense
Sp. Atk
Sp. Def
Speed

ITEMS SOMETIMES HELD BY WILD POKÉMON
Everstone / Hard Stone

EVOLUTION

Roggenrola → Lv. 25 → Boldore → Link Trade → Gigalith

MAIN WAY TO REGISTER IN THE NATIONAL POKÉDEX

Catch on the Fiery Path. Appears as a hidden Pokémon after you battle Groudon or Kyogre.

Damage taken in normal battles

Type		Type	
Normal	×0.5	Flying	×0.5
Fire	×0.5	Psychic	×1
Water	×2	Bug	×1
Grass	×2	Rock	×1
Electric	×1	Ghost	×1
Ice	×1	Dragon	×1
Fighting	×2	Dark	×1
Poison	×0.5	Steel	×2
Ground	×2	Fairy	×1

Damage taken in Inverse battles

Type		Type	
Normal	×2	Flying	×2
Fire	×2	Psychic	×1
Water	×0.5	Bug	×1
Grass	×0.5	Rock	×1
Electric	×1	Ghost	×1
Ice	×1	Dragon	×1
Fighting	×0.5	Dark	×1
Poison	×2	Steel	×0.5
Ground	×0.5	Fairy	×1

Can be used in
Inverse Battle
Battle Institute
Battle Maison
Random Matchup (Free Battle)
Random Matchup (Others)

LEVEL-UP MOVES

Lv.	Name	Type	Kind	Pow.	Acc.	PP	Range
1	Tackle	Normal	Physical	50	100	35	Normal
4	Harden	Normal	Status	—	—	30	Self
7	Sand Attack	Ground	Status	—	100	15	Normal
10	Headbutt	Normal	Physical	70	100	15	Normal
14	Rock Blast	Rock	Physical	25	90	10	Normal
17	Mud-Slap	Ground	Special	20	100	10	Normal
20	Iron Defense	Steel	Status	—	—	15	Self
23	Smack Down	Rock	Physical	50	100	15	Normal
27	Rock Slide	Rock	Physical	75	90	10	Many Others
30	Stealth Rock	Rock	Status	—	—	20	Other Side
33	Sandstorm	Rock	Status	—	—	10	Both Sides
36	Stone Edge	Rock	Physical	100	80	5	Normal
40	Explosion	Normal	Physical	250	100	5	Adjacent

TM & HM MOVES

No.	Name	Type	Kind	Pow.	Acc.	PP	Range
TM06	Toxic	Poison	Status	—	90	10	Normal
TM10	Hidden Power	Normal	Special	60	100	15	Normal
TM17	Protect	Normal	Status	—	—	10	Self
TM21	Frustration	Normal	Physical	—	100	20	Normal
TM23	Smack Down	Rock	Physical	50	100	15	Normal
TM26	Earthquake	Ground	Physical	100	100	10	Adjacent
TM27	Return	Normal	Physical	—	100	20	Normal
TM32	Double Team	Normal	Status	—	—	15	Self
TM37	Sandstorm	Rock	Status	—	—	10	Both Sides
TM39	Rock Tomb	Rock	Physical	60	95	15	Normal
TM42	Facade	Normal	Physical	70	100	20	Normal
TM44	Rest	Psychic	Status	—	—	10	Self
TM45	Attract	Normal	Status	—	100	15	Normal
TM48	Round	Normal	Special	60	100	15	Normal
TM64	Explosion	Normal	Physical	250	100	5	Adjacent
TM69	Rock Polish	Rock	Status	—	—	20	Self
TM71	Stone Edge	Rock	Physical	100	80	5	Normal
TM78	Bulldoze	Ground	Physical	60	100	20	Adjacent
TM80	Rock Slide	Rock	Physical	75	90	10	Many Others
TM87	Swagger	Normal	Status	—	90	15	Normal
TM88	Sleep Talk	Normal	Status	—	—	10	Self
TM90	Substitute	Normal	Status	—	—	10	Self
TM91	Flash Cannon	Steel	Special	80	100	10	Normal
TM94	Secret Power	Normal	Physical	70	100	20	Normal
TM96	Nature Power	Normal	Status	—	—	20	Normal
TM100	Confide	Normal	Status	—	—	20	Normal
HM04	Strength	Normal	Physical	80	100	15	Normal
HM06	Rock Smash	Fighting	Physical	40	100	15	Normal

MOVES LEARNED IN EXCHANGE FOR BP

Name	Type	Kind	Pow.	Acc.	PP	Range
Block	Normal	Status	—	—	5	Normal
Earth Power	Ground	Special	90	100	10	Normal
Gravity	Psychic	Status	—	—	5	Both Sides
Iron Defense	Steel	Status	—	—	15	Self
Snore	Normal	Special	50	100	15	Normal
Stealth Rock	Rock	Status	—	—	20	Other Side

MOVES TAUGHT BY PEOPLE

Name	Type	Kind	Pow.	Acc.	PP	Range

EGG MOVES

Name	Type	Kind	Pow.	Acc.	PP	Range
Magnitude	Ground	Physical	—	100	30	Adjacent
Curse	Ghost	Status	—	—	10	Varies
Autotomize	Steel	Status	—	—	15	Self
Rock Tomb	Rock	Physical	60	95	15	Normal
Lock-On	Normal	Status	—	—	5	Normal
Heavy Slam	Steel	Physical	—	100	10	Normal
Take Down	Normal	Physical	90	85	20	Normal
Gravity	Psychic	Status	—	—	5	Both Sides
Wide Guard	Rock	Status	—	—	10	Your Side

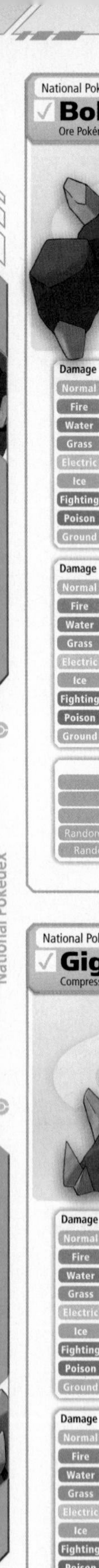

National Pokédex **525** Hoenn Pokédex —

Boldore

Ore Pokémon

Rock

HEIGHT: 2'11" WEIGHT: 224.9 lbs.

Same form for ♂ / ♀

Ω Because its energy was too great to be contained, the energy leaked and formed orange crystals.

α When it is healthy, its core sticks out. Always facing the same way, it swiftly moves front to back and left to right.

ABILITY
Sturdy

HIDDEN ABILITY
Sand Force

EGG GROUPS
Mineral

STAT GROWTH RATES
HP ■■■
Attack ■■■■■
Defense ■■■■■
Sp. Atk ■■
Sp. Def ■■
Speed ■

ITEMS SOMETIMES HELD BY WILD POKÉMON
Everstone / Hard Stone

EVOLUTION 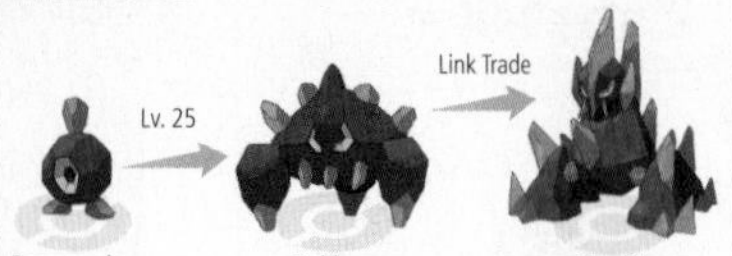
Roggenrola → Lv. 25 → Boldore → Link Trade → Gigalith

MAIN WAY TO REGISTER IN THE NATIONAL POKÉDEX

Catch when it appears from a cracked rock in Mirage Cave 1 (using Rock Smash).

Damage taken in normal battles

Type		Type	
Normal	×0.5	Flying	×0.5
Fire	×0.5	Psychic	×1
Water	×2	Bug	×1
Grass	×2	Rock	×1
Electric	×1	Ghost	×1
Ice	×1	Dragon	×1
Fighting	×2	Dark	×1
Poison	×0.5	Steel	×2
Ground	×2	Fairy	×1

Damage taken in Inverse battles

Type		Type	
Normal	×2	Flying	×2
Fire	×2	Psychic	×1
Water	×0.5	Bug	×1
Grass	×0.5	Rock	×1
Electric	×1	Ghost	×1
Ice	×1	Dragon	×1
Fighting	×0.5	Dark	×1
Poison	×2	Steel	×0.5
Ground	×0.5	Fairy	×1

Can be used in
Inverse Battle
Battle Institute
Battle Maison
Random Matchup (Free Battle)
Random Matchup (Others)

LEVEL-UP MOVES

Lv.	Name	Type	Kind	Pow.	Acc.	PP	Range
1	Tackle	Normal	Physical	50	100	35	Normal
1	Harden	Normal	Status	—	—	30	Self
1	Sand Attack	Ground	Status	—	100	15	Normal
1	Headbutt	Normal	Physical	70	100	15	Normal
4	Harden	Normal	Status	—	—	30	Self
7	Sand Attack	Ground	Status	—	100	15	Normal
10	Headbutt	Normal	Physical	70	100	15	Normal
14	Rock Blast	Rock	Physical	25	90	10	Normal
17	Mud-Slap	Ground	Special	20	100	10	Normal
20	Iron Defense	Steel	Status	—	—	15	Self
23	Smack Down	Rock	Physical	50	100	15	Normal
25	Power Gem	Rock	Special	80	100	20	Normal
30	Rock Slide	Rock	Physical	75	90	10	Many Others
36	Stealth Rock	Rock	Status	—	—	20	Other Side
42	Sandstorm	Rock	Status	—	—	10	Both Sides
48	Stone Edge	Rock	Physical	100	80	5	Normal
55	Explosion	Normal	Physical	250	100	5	Adjacent

TM & HM MOVES

No.	Name	Type	Kind	Pow.	Acc.	PP	Range
TM06	Toxic	Poison	Status	—	90	10	Normal
TM10	Hidden Power	Normal	Special	60	100	15	Normal
TM17	Protect	Normal	Status	—	—	10	Self
TM21	Frustration	Normal	Physical	—	100	20	Normal
TM23	Smack Down	Rock	Physical	50	100	15	Normal
TM26	Earthquake	Ground	Physical	100	100	10	Adjacent
TM27	Return	Normal	Physical	—	100	20	Normal
TM32	Double Team	Normal	Status	—	—	15	Self
TM37	Sandstorm	Rock	Status	—	—	10	Both Sides
TM39	Rock Tomb	Rock	Physical	60	95	15	Normal
TM42	Facade	Normal	Physical	70	100	20	Normal
TM44	Rest	Psychic	Status	—	—	10	Self
TM45	Attract	Normal	Status	—	100	15	Normal
TM48	Round	Normal	Special	60	100	15	Normal
TM64	Explosion	Normal	Physical	250	100	5	Adjacent
TM69	Rock Polish	Rock	Status	—	—	20	Self
TM71	Stone Edge	Rock	Physical	100	80	5	Normal
TM78	Bulldoze	Ground	Physical	60	100	20	Adjacent
TM80	Rock Slide	Rock	Physical	75	90	10	Many Others
TM87	Swagger	Normal	Status	—	90	15	Normal
TM88	Sleep Talk	Normal	Status	—	—	10	Self
TM90	Substitute	Normal	Status	—	—	10	Self
TM91	Flash Cannon	Steel	Special	80	100	10	Normal
TM94	Secret Power	Normal	Physical	70	100	20	Normal
TM96	Nature Power	Normal	Status	—	—	20	Normal
TM100	Confide	Normal	Status	—	—	20	Normal
HM04	Strength	Normal	Physical	80	100	15	Normal
HM06	Rock Smash	Fighting	Physical	40	100	15	Normal

MOVES LEARNED IN EXCHANGE FOR BP

Name	Type	Kind	Pow.	Acc.	PP	Range
Block	Normal	Status	—	—	5	Normal
Earth Power	Ground	Special	90	100	10	Normal
Gravity	Psychic	Status	—	—	5	Both Sides
Iron Defense	Steel	Status	—	—	15	Self
Snore	Normal	Special	50	100	15	Normal
Stealth Rock	Rock	Status	—	—	20	Other Side

MOVES TAUGHT BY PEOPLE

Name	Type	Kind	Pow.	Acc.	PP	Range

National Pokédex **526** Hoenn Pokédex —

Gigalith

Compressed Pokémon

Rock

HEIGHT: 5'07" WEIGHT: 573.2 lbs.

Same form for ♂ / ♀

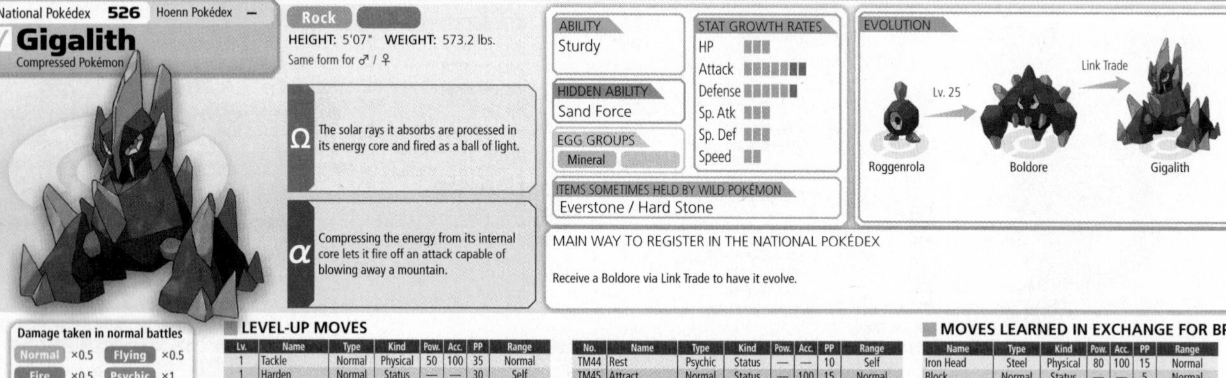

Ω The solar rays it absorbs are processed in its energy core and fired as a ball of light.

α Compressing the energy from its internal core lets it fire off an attack capable of blowing away a mountain.

ABILITY
Sturdy

HIDDEN ABILITY
Sand Force

EGG GROUPS
Mineral

STAT GROWTH RATES
HP ■■■
Attack ■■■■■■■
Defense ■■■■■■
Sp. Atk ■■■
Sp. Def ■■■
Speed ■■

ITEMS SOMETIMES HELD BY WILD POKÉMON
Everstone / Hard Stone

EVOLUTION
Roggenrola → Lv. 25 → Boldore → Link Trade → Gigalith

MAIN WAY TO REGISTER IN THE NATIONAL POKÉDEX

Receive a Boldore via Link Trade to have it evolve.

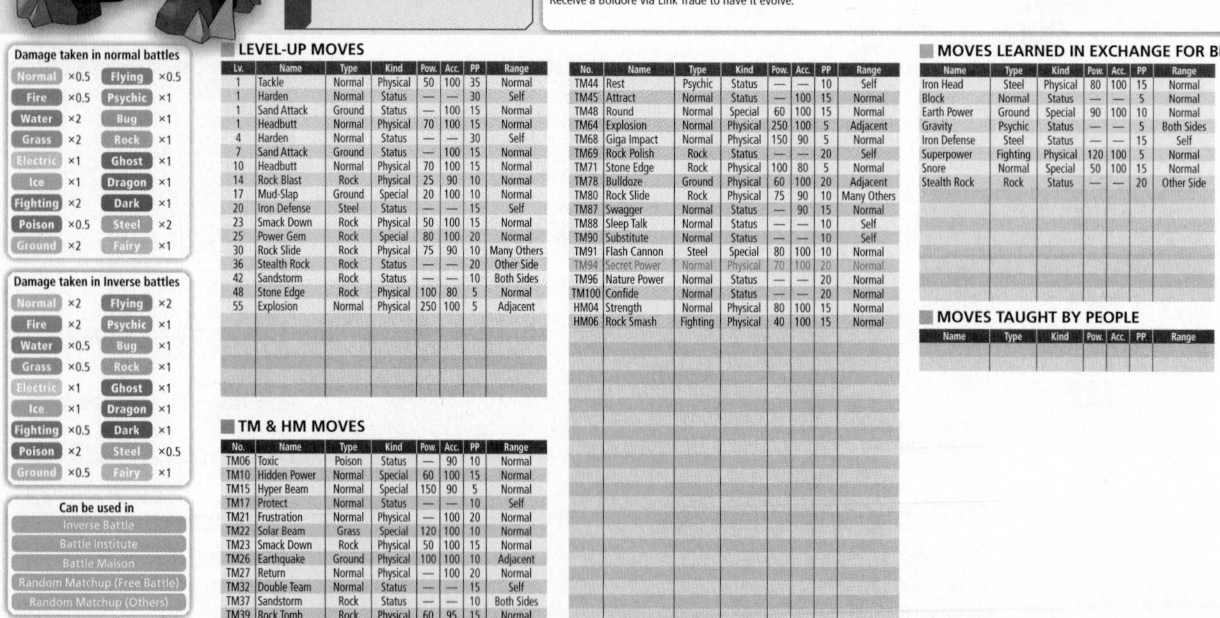

Damage taken in normal battles

Type		Type	
Normal	×0.5	Flying	×0.5
Fire	×0.5	Psychic	×1
Water	×2	Bug	×1
Grass	×2	Rock	×1
Electric	×1	Ghost	×1
Ice	×1	Dragon	×1
Fighting	×2	Dark	×1
Poison	×0.5	Steel	×2
Ground	×2	Fairy	×1

Damage taken in Inverse battles

Type		Type	
Normal	×2	Flying	×2
Fire	×2	Psychic	×1
Water	×0.5	Bug	×1
Grass	×0.5	Rock	×1
Electric	×1	Ghost	×1
Ice	×1	Dragon	×1
Fighting	×0.5	Dark	×1
Poison	×2	Steel	×0.5
Ground	×0.5	Fairy	×1

Can be used in
Inverse Battle
Battle Institute
Battle Maison
Random Matchup (Free Battle)
Random Matchup (Others)

LEVEL-UP MOVES

Lv.	Name	Type	Kind	Pow.	Acc.	PP	Range
1	Tackle	Normal	Physical	50	100	35	Normal
1	Harden	Normal	Status	—	—	30	Self
1	Sand Attack	Ground	Status	—	100	15	Normal
1	Headbutt	Normal	Physical	70	100	15	Normal
4	Harden	Normal	Status	—	—	30	Self
7	Sand Attack	Ground	Status	—	100	15	Normal
10	Headbutt	Normal	Physical	70	100	15	Normal
14	Rock Blast	Rock	Physical	25	90	10	Normal
17	Mud-Slap	Ground	Special	20	100	10	Normal
20	Iron Defense	Steel	Status	—	—	15	Self
23	Smack Down	Rock	Physical	50	100	15	Normal
25	Power Gem	Rock	Special	80	100	20	Normal
30	Rock Slide	Rock	Physical	75	90	10	Many Others
36	Stealth Rock	Rock	Status	—	—	20	Other Side
42	Sandstorm	Rock	Status	—	—	10	Both Sides
48	Stone Edge	Rock	Physical	100	80	5	Normal
55	Explosion	Normal	Physical	250	100	5	Adjacent

TM & HM MOVES

No.	Name	Type	Kind	Pow.	Acc.	PP	Range
TM06	Toxic	Poison	Status	—	90	10	Normal
TM10	Hidden Power	Normal	Special	60	100	15	Normal
TM15	Hyper Beam	Normal	Special	150	90	5	Normal
TM17	Protect	Normal	Status	—	—	10	Self
TM21	Frustration	Normal	Physical	—	100	20	Normal
TM22	Solar Beam	Grass	Special	120	100	10	Normal
TM23	Smack Down	Rock	Physical	50	100	15	Normal
TM26	Earthquake	Ground	Physical	100	100	10	Adjacent
TM27	Return	Normal	Physical	—	100	20	Normal
TM32	Double Team	Normal	Status	—	—	15	Self
TM37	Sandstorm	Rock	Status	—	—	10	Both Sides
TM39	Rock Tomb	Rock	Physical	60	95	15	Normal
TM42	Facade	Normal	Physical	70	100	20	Normal
TM44	Rest	Psychic	Status	—	—	10	Self
TM45	Attract	Normal	Status	—	100	15	Normal
TM48	Round	Normal	Special	60	100	15	Normal
TM64	Explosion	Normal	Physical	250	100	5	Adjacent
TM68	Giga Impact	Normal	Physical	150	90	5	Normal
TM69	Rock Polish	Rock	Status	—	—	20	Self
TM71	Stone Edge	Rock	Physical	100	80	5	Normal
TM78	Bulldoze	Ground	Physical	60	100	20	Adjacent
TM80	Rock Slide	Rock	Physical	75	90	10	Many Others
TM87	Swagger	Normal	Status	—	90	15	Normal
TM88	Sleep Talk	Normal	Status	—	—	10	Self
TM90	Substitute	Normal	Status	—	—	10	Self
TM91	Flash Cannon	Steel	Special	80	100	10	Normal
TM94	Secret Power	Normal	Physical	70	100	20	Normal
TM96	Nature Power	Normal	Status	—	—	20	Normal
TM100	Confide	Normal	Status	—	—	20	Normal
HM04	Strength	Normal	Physical	80	100	15	Normal
HM06	Rock Smash	Fighting	Physical	40	100	15	Normal

MOVES LEARNED IN EXCHANGE FOR BP

Name	Type	Kind	Pow.	Acc.	PP	Range
Iron Head	Steel	Physical	80	100	15	Normal
Block	Normal	Status	—	—	5	Normal
Earth Power	Ground	Special	90	100	10	Normal
Gravity	Psychic	Status	—	—	5	Both Sides
Iron Defense	Steel	Status	—	—	15	Self
Superpower	Fighting	Physical	120	100	5	Normal
Snore	Normal	Special	50	100	15	Normal
Stealth Rock	Rock	Status	—	—	20	Other Side

MOVES TAUGHT BY PEOPLE

Name	Type	Kind	Pow.	Acc.	PP	Range

National Pokédex **527** Hoenn Pokédex —

Woobat

Bat Pokémon

Psychic | Flying

HEIGHT: 1'04" WEIGHT: 4.6 lbs.

Same form for ♂ / ♀

Ω Its habitat is dark forests and caves. It emits ultrasonic waves from its nose to learn about its surroundings.

α The heart-shaped mark left on a body after a Woobat has been attached to it is said to bring good fortune.

ABILITIES
Unaware
Klutz

HIDDEN ABILITY
Simple

EGG GROUPS
Field | Flying

STAT GROWTH RATES

HP	■■
Attack	■■
Defense	■■
Sp. Atk	■■■
Sp. Def	■■
Speed	■■■■

ITEMS SOMETIMES HELD BY WILD POKÉMON
—

EVOLUTION
Woobat → Level up with high friendship → Swoobat

MAIN WAY TO REGISTER IN THE NATIONAL POKÉDEX

Appears in *Pokémon X* and *Pokémon Y*. Bring it to your game using Link Trade or the GTS.

Damage taken in normal battles

Type		Type	
Normal	×1	Flying	×1
Fire	×1	Psychic	×0.5
Water	×1	Bug	×1
Grass	×0.5	Rock	×2
Electric	×2	Ghost	×2
Ice	×2	Dragon	×1
Fighting	×0.25	Dark	×2
Poison	×1	Steel	×1
Ground	×0	Fairy	×1

Damage taken in Inverse battles

Type		Type	
Normal	×1	Flying	×1
Fire	×1	Psychic	×2
Water	×1	Bug	×1
Grass	×2	Rock	×0.5
Electric	×0.5	Ghost	×0.5
Ice	×0.5	Dragon	×1
Fighting	×4	Dark	×0.5
Poison	×1	Steel	×1
Ground	×2	Fairy	×1

Can be used in
Inverse Battle
Battle Institute
Battle Maison
Random Matchup (Free Battle)
Random Matchup (Others)

LEVEL-UP MOVES

Lv.	Name	Type	Kind	Pow.	Acc.	PP	Range
1	Confusion	Psychic	Special	50	100	25	Normal
4	Odor Sleuth	Normal	Status	—	—	40	Normal
8	Gust	Flying	Special	40	100	35	Normal
12	Assurance	Dark	Physical	60	100	10	Normal
15	Heart Stamp	Psychic	Physical	60	100	25	Normal
19	Imprison	Psychic	Status	—	—	10	Self
21	Air Cutter	Flying	Special	60	95	25	Many Others
25	Attract	Normal	Status	—	100	15	Normal
29	Amnesia	Psychic	Status	—	—	20	Self
29	Calm Mind	Psychic	Status	—	—	20	Self
32	Air Slash	Flying	Special	75	95	15	Normal
36	Future Sight	Psychic	Special	120	100	10	Normal
41	Psychic	Psychic	Special	90	100	10	Normal
47	Endeavor	Normal	Physical	—	100	5	Normal

TM & HM MOVES

No.	Name	Type	Kind	Pow.	Acc.	PP	Range
TM03	Psyshock	Psychic	Special	80	100	10	Normal
TM04	Calm Mind	Psychic	Status	—	—	20	Self
TM06	Toxic	Poison	Status	—	90	10	Normal
TM10	Hidden Power	Normal	Special	60	100	15	Normal
TM12	Taunt	Dark	Status	—	100	20	Normal
TM16	Light Screen	Psychic	Status	—	—	30	Your Side
TM17	Protect	Normal	Status	—	—	10	Self
TM18	Rain Dance	Water	Status	—	—	5	Both Sides
TM19	Roost	Flying	Status	—	—	10	Self
TM20	Safeguard	Normal	Status	—	—	25	Your Side
TM21	Frustration	Normal	Physical	—	100	20	Normal
TM27	Return	Normal	Physical	—	100	20	Normal
TM29	Psychic	Psychic	Special	90	100	10	Normal
TM30	Shadow Ball	Ghost	Special	80	100	15	Normal
TM32	Double Team	Normal	Status	—	—	15	Self
TM33	Reflect	Psychic	Status	—	—	20	Your Side
TM40	Aerial Ace	Flying	Physical	60	—	20	Normal
TM41	Torment	Dark	Status	—	100	15	Normal
TM42	Facade	Normal	Physical	70	100	20	Normal
TM44	Rest	Psychic	Status	—	—	10	Self
TM45	Attract	Normal	Status	—	100	15	Normal
TM46	Thief	Dark	Physical	60	100	25	Normal
TM48	Round	Normal	Special	60	100	15	Normal
TM51	Steel Wing	Steel	Physical	70	90	25	Normal
TM53	Energy Ball	Grass	Special	90	100	10	Normal
TM57	Charge Beam	Electric	Special	50	90	10	Normal
TM62	Acrobatics	Flying	Physical	55	100	15	Normal
TM63	Embargo	Dark	Status	—	100	15	Normal
TM70	Flash	Normal	Status	—	100	20	Normal
TM73	Thunder Wave	Electric	Status	—	100	20	Normal
TM74	Gyro Ball	Steel	Physical	—	100	5	Normal
TM77	Psych Up	Normal	Status	—	—	10	Normal
TM85	Dream Eater	Psychic	Special	100	100	15	Normal
TM87	Swagger	Normal	Status	—	90	15	Normal
TM88	Sleep Talk	Normal	Status	—	—	10	Self
TM89	U-turn	Bug	Physical	70	100	20	Normal
TM90	Substitute	Normal	Status	—	—	10	Self
TM92	Trick Room	Psychic	Status	—	—	5	Both Sides
TM94	Secret Power	Normal	Physical	70	100	20	Normal
TM100	Confide	Normal	Status	—	—	20	Normal
HM02	Fly	Flying	Physical	90	95	15	Normal

MOVES LEARNED IN EXCHANGE FOR BP

Name	Type	Kind	Pow.	Acc.	PP	Range
Super Fang	Normal	Physical	—	90	10	Normal
Signal Beam	Bug	Special	75	100	15	Normal
Uproar	Normal	Special	90	100	10	1 Random
Magic Coat	Psychic	Status	—	—	15	Self
Zen Headbutt	Psychic	Physical	80	90	15	Normal
Snore	Normal	Special	50	100	15	Normal
Knock Off	Dark	Physical	65	100	20	Normal
Heat Wave	Fire	Special	95	90	10	Many Others
Tailwind	Flying	Status	—	—	15	Your Side
Giga Drain	Grass	Special	75	100	10	Normal
Shock Wave	Electric	Special	60	—	20	Normal
After You	Normal	Status	—	—	15	Normal
Helping Hand	Normal	Status	—	—	20	1 Ally
Trick	Psychic	Status	—	100	10	Normal
Endeavor	Normal	Physical	—	100	5	Normal
Skill Swap	Psychic	Status	—	—	10	Normal

MOVES TAUGHT BY PEOPLE

Name	Type	Kind	Pow.	Acc.	PP	Range

EGG MOVES

Name	Type	Kind	Pow.	Acc.	PP	Range
Charm	Fairy	Status	—	100	20	Normal
Knock Off	Dark	Physical	65	100	20	Normal
Fake Tears	Dark	Status	—	100	20	Normal
Supersonic	Normal	Status	—	55	20	Normal
Synchronoise	Psychic	Special	120	100	10	Adjacent
Stored Power	Psychic	Special	20	100	10	Normal
Roost	Flying	Status	—	—	10	Self
Flatter	Dark	Status	—	100	15	Normal
Helping Hand	Normal	Status	—	—	20	1 Ally
Captivate	Normal	Status	—	100	20	Many Others
Venom Drench	Poison	Status	—	100	20	Many Others
Psycho Shift	Psychic	Status	—	100	10	Normal

National Pokédex **528** Hoenn Pokédex —

Swoobat

Courting Pokémon

Psychic | Flying

HEIGHT: 2'11" WEIGHT: 23.1 lbs.

Same form for ♂ / ♀

Ω Its habitat is dark forests and caves. It emits ultrasonic waves from its nose to learn about its surroundings.

α The heart-shaped mark left on a body after a Woobat has been attached to it is said to bring good fortune.

ABILITIES
Unaware
Klutz

HIDDEN ABILITY
Simple

EGG GROUPS
Field | Flying

STAT GROWTH RATES

HP	■■■
Attack	■■■
Defense	■■■
Sp. Atk	■■■■
Sp. Def	■■
Speed	■■■■■■

ITEMS SOMETIMES HELD BY WILD POKÉMON
—

EVOLUTION
Woobat → Level up with high friendship → Swoobat

MAIN WAY TO REGISTER IN THE NATIONAL POKÉDEX

Appears in *Pokémon X* and *Pokémon Y*. Bring it to your game using Link Trade or the GTS.

Damage taken in normal battles

Type		Type	
Normal	×1	Flying	×1
Fire	×1	Psychic	×0.5
Water	×1	Bug	×1
Grass	×0.5	Rock	×2
Electric	×2	Ghost	×2
Ice	×2	Dragon	×1
Fighting	×0.25	Dark	×2
Poison	×1	Steel	×1
Ground	×0	Fairy	×1

Damage taken in Inverse battles

Type		Type	
Normal	×1	Flying	×1
Fire	×1	Psychic	×2
Water	×1	Bug	×1
Grass	×2	Rock	×0.5
Electric	×0.5	Ghost	×0.5
Ice	×0.5	Dragon	×1
Fighting	×4	Dark	×0.5
Poison	×1	Steel	×1
Ground	×2	Fairy	×1

Can be used in
Inverse Battle
Battle Institute
Battle Maison
Random Matchup (Free Battle)
Random Matchup (Others)

LEVEL-UP MOVES

Lv.	Name	Type	Kind	Pow.	Acc.	PP	Range
1	Confusion	Psychic	Special	50	100	25	Normal
1	Odor Sleuth	Normal	Status	—	—	40	Normal
1	Gust	Flying	Special	40	100	35	Normal
1	Assurance	Dark	Physical	60	100	10	Normal
4	Odor Sleuth	Normal	Status	—	—	40	Normal
8	Gust	Flying	Special	40	100	35	Normal
12	Assurance	Dark	Physical	60	100	10	Normal
15	Heart Stamp	Psychic	Physical	60	100	25	Normal
19	Imprison	Psychic	Status	—	—	10	Self
21	Air Cutter	Flying	Special	60	95	25	Many Others
25	Attract	Normal	Status	—	100	15	Normal
29	Amnesia	Psychic	Status	—	—	20	Self
29	Calm Mind	Psychic	Status	—	—	20	Self
32	Air Slash	Flying	Special	75	95	15	Normal
36	Future Sight	Psychic	Special	120	100	10	Normal
41	Psychic	Psychic	Special	90	100	10	Normal
47	Endeavor	Normal	Physical	—	100	5	Normal

TM & HM MOVES

No.	Name	Type	Kind	Pow.	Acc.	PP	Range
TM03	Psyshock	Psychic	Special	80	100	10	Normal
TM04	Calm Mind	Psychic	Status	—	—	20	Self
TM06	Toxic	Poison	Status	—	90	10	Normal
TM10	Hidden Power	Normal	Special	60	100	15	Normal
TM12	Taunt	Dark	Status	—	100	20	Normal
TM15	Hyper Beam	Normal	Special	150	90	5	Normal
TM16	Light Screen	Psychic	Status	—	—	30	Your Side
TM17	Protect	Normal	Status	—	—	10	Self
TM18	Rain Dance	Water	Status	—	—	5	Both Sides
TM19	Roost	Flying	Status	—	—	10	Self
TM20	Safeguard	Normal	Status	—	—	25	Your Side
TM21	Frustration	Normal	Physical	—	100	20	Normal
TM27	Return	Normal	Physical	—	100	20	Normal
TM29	Psychic	Psychic	Special	90	100	10	Normal
TM30	Shadow Ball	Ghost	Special	80	100	15	Normal
TM32	Double Team	Normal	Status	—	—	15	Self
TM33	Reflect	Psychic	Status	—	—	20	Your Side
TM40	Aerial Ace	Flying	Physical	60	—	20	Normal
TM41	Torment	Dark	Status	—	100	15	Normal
TM42	Facade	Normal	Physical	70	100	20	Normal
TM44	Rest	Psychic	Status	—	—	10	Self
TM45	Attract	Normal	Status	—	100	15	Normal
TM46	Thief	Dark	Physical	60	100	25	Normal
TM48	Round	Normal	Special	60	100	15	Normal
TM51	Steel Wing	Steel	Physical	70	90	25	Normal
TM53	Energy Ball	Grass	Special	90	100	10	Normal
TM57	Charge Beam	Electric	Special	50	90	10	Normal
TM62	Acrobatics	Flying	Physical	55	100	15	Normal
TM63	Embargo	Dark	Status	—	100	15	Normal
TM68	Giga Impact	Normal	Physical	150	90	5	Normal
TM70	Flash	Normal	Status	—	100	20	Normal
TM73	Thunder Wave	Electric	Status	—	100	20	Normal
TM74	Gyro Ball	Steel	Physical	—	100	5	Normal
TM77	Psych Up	Normal	Status	—	—	10	Normal
TM85	Dream Eater	Psychic	Special	100	100	15	Normal
TM87	Swagger	Normal	Status	—	90	15	Normal
TM88	Sleep Talk	Normal	Status	—	—	10	Self
TM89	U-turn	Bug	Physical	70	100	20	Normal
TM90	Substitute	Normal	Status	—	—	10	Self
TM92	Trick Room	Psychic	Status	—	—	5	Both Sides
TM94	Secret Power	Normal	Physical	70	100	20	Normal
TM100	Confide	Normal	Status	—	—	20	Normal
HM02	Fly	Flying	Physical	90	95	15	Normal

MOVES LEARNED IN EXCHANGE FOR BP

Name	Type	Kind	Pow.	Acc.	PP	Range
Super Fang	Normal	Physical	—	90	10	Normal
Signal Beam	Bug	Special	75	100	15	Normal
Uproar	Normal	Special	90	100	10	1 Random
Magic Coat	Psychic	Status	—	—	15	Self
Zen Headbutt	Psychic	Physical	80	90	15	Normal
Snore	Normal	Special	50	100	15	Normal
Knock Off	Dark	Physical	65	100	20	Normal
Heat Wave	Fire	Special	95	90	10	Many Others
Tailwind	Flying	Status	—	—	15	Your Side
Sky Attack	Flying	Physical	140	90	5	Normal
Giga Drain	Grass	Special	75	100	10	Normal
Shock Wave	Electric	Special	60	—	20	Normal
After You	Normal	Status	—	—	15	Normal
Helping Hand	Normal	Status	—	—	20	1 Ally
Trick	Psychic	Status	—	100	10	Normal
Endeavor	Normal	Physical	—	100	5	Normal
Skill Swap	Psychic	Status	—	—	10	Normal

MOVES TAUGHT BY PEOPLE

Name	Type	Kind	Pow.	Acc.	PP	Range

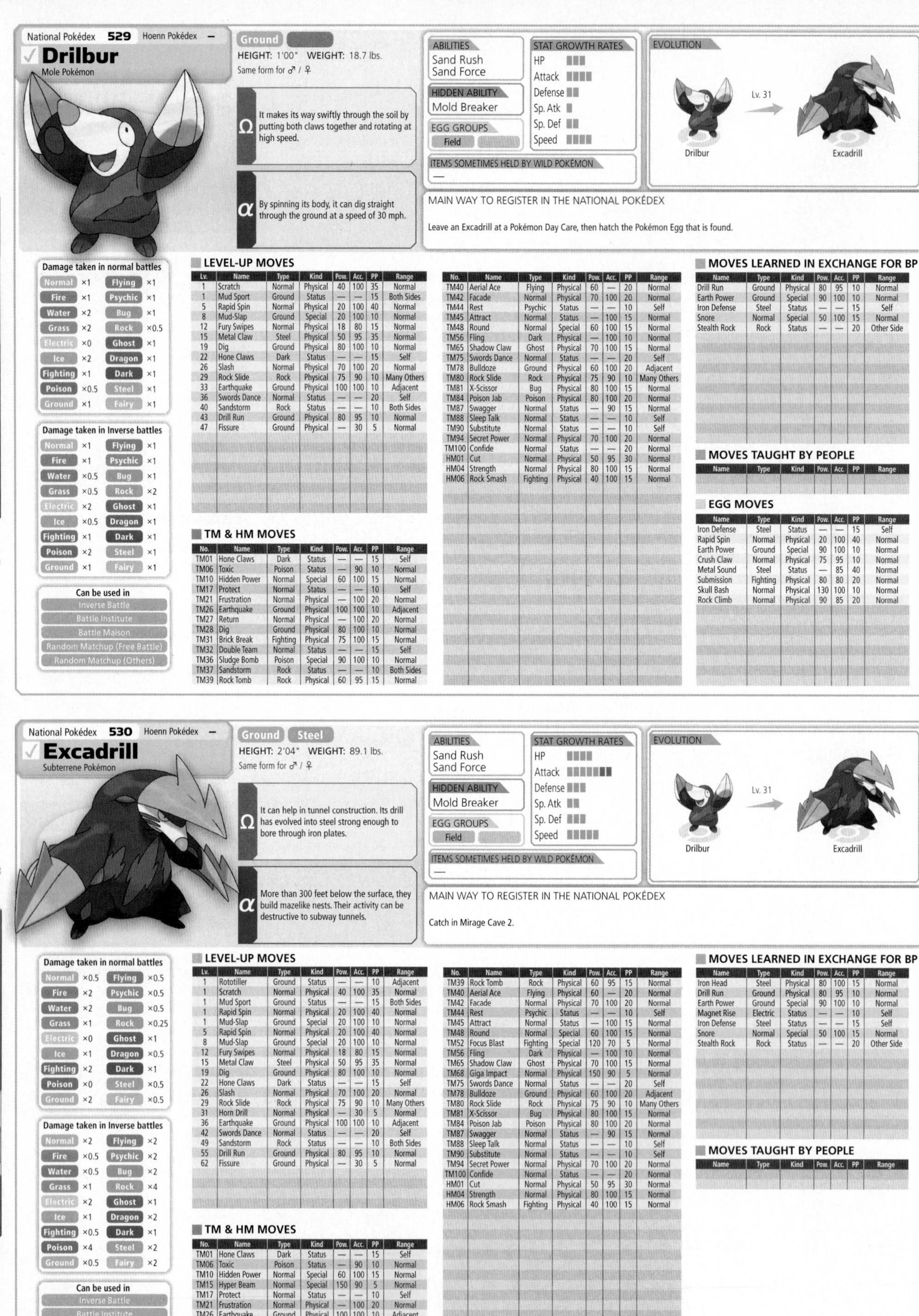

National Pokédex **529** Hoenn Pokédex —

Drilbur

Mole Pokémon

Ground

HEIGHT: 1'00" WEIGHT: 18.7 lbs.

Same form for ♂ / ♀

Ω It makes its way swiftly through the soil by putting both claws together and rotating at high speed.

α By spinning its body, it can dig straight through the ground at a speed of 30 mph.

ABILITIES
Sand Rush
Sand Force

HIDDEN ABILITY
Mold Breaker

EGG GROUPS
Field

STAT GROWTH RATES
HP
Attack
Defense
Sp. Atk
Sp. Def
Speed

ITEMS SOMETIMES HELD BY WILD POKÉMON
—

EVOLUTION
Drilbur → Lv. 31 → Excadrill

MAIN WAY TO REGISTER IN THE NATIONAL POKÉDEX

Leave an Excadrill at a Pokémon Day Care, then hatch the Pokémon Egg that is found.

Damage taken in normal battles

Type		Type	
Normal	×1	Flying	×1
Fire	×1	Psychic	×1
Water	×2	Bug	×1
Grass	×2	Rock	×0.5
Electric	×0	Ghost	×1
Ice	×2	Dragon	×1
Fighting	×1	Dark	×1
Poison	×0.5	Steel	×1
Ground	×1	Fairy	×1

Damage taken in Inverse battles

Type		Type	
Normal	×1	Flying	×1
Fire	×1	Psychic	×1
Water	×0.5	Bug	×1
Grass	×0.5	Rock	×2
Electric	×2	Ghost	×1
Ice	×0.5	Dragon	×1
Fighting	×1	Dark	×1
Poison	×2	Steel	×1
Ground	×1	Fairy	×1

Can be used in
Inverse Battle
Battle Institute
Battle Maison
Random Matchup (Free Battle)
Random Matchup (Others)

LEVEL-UP MOVES

Lv.	Name	Type	Kind	Pow.	Acc.	PP	Range
1	Scratch	Normal	Physical	40	100	35	Normal
1	Mud Sport	Ground	Status	—	—	15	Both Sides
5	Rapid Spin	Normal	Physical	20	100	40	Normal
8	Mud-Slap	Ground	Special	20	100	10	Normal
12	Fury Swipes	Normal	Physical	18	80	15	Normal
15	Metal Claw	Steel	Physical	50	95	35	Normal
19	Dig	Ground	Physical	80	100	10	Normal
22	Hone Claws	Dark	Status	—	—	15	Self
26	Slash	Normal	Physical	70	100	20	Normal
29	Rock Slide	Rock	Physical	75	90	10	Many Others
33	Earthquake	Ground	Physical	100	100	10	Adjacent
36	Swords Dance	Normal	Status	—	—	20	Self
40	Sandstorm	Rock	Status	—	—	10	Both Sides
43	Drill Run	Ground	Physical	80	95	10	Normal
47	Fissure	Ground	Physical	—	30	5	Normal

TM & HM MOVES

No.	Name	Type	Kind	Pow.	Acc.	PP	Range
TM01	Hone Claws	Dark	Status	—	—	15	Self
TM06	Toxic	Poison	Status	—	90	10	Normal
TM10	Hidden Power	Normal	Special	60	100	15	Normal
TM17	Protect	Normal	Status	—	—	10	Self
TM21	Frustration	Normal	Physical	—	100	20	Normal
TM26	Earthquake	Ground	Physical	100	100	10	Adjacent
TM27	Return	Normal	Physical	—	100	20	Normal
TM28	Dig	Ground	Physical	80	100	10	Normal
TM31	Brick Break	Fighting	Physical	75	100	15	Normal
TM32	Double Team	Normal	Status	—	—	15	Self
TM36	Sludge Bomb	Poison	Special	90	100	10	Normal
TM37	Sandstorm	Rock	Status	—	—	10	Both Sides
TM39	Rock Tomb	Rock	Physical	60	95	15	Normal
TM40	Aerial Ace	Flying	Physical	60	—	20	Normal
TM42	Facade	Normal	Physical	70	100	20	Normal
TM44	Rest	Psychic	Status	—	—	10	Self
TM45	Attract	Normal	Status	—	100	15	Normal
TM48	Round	Normal	Special	60	100	15	Normal
TM56	Fling	Dark	Physical	—	100	10	Normal
TM65	Shadow Claw	Ghost	Physical	70	100	15	Normal
TM75	Swords Dance	Normal	Status	—	—	20	Self
TM78	Bulldoze	Ground	Physical	60	100	20	Adjacent
TM80	Rock Slide	Rock	Physical	75	90	10	Many Others
TM81	X-Scissor	Bug	Physical	80	100	15	Normal
TM84	Poison Jab	Poison	Physical	80	100	20	Normal
TM87	Swagger	Normal	Status	—	90	15	Normal
TM88	Sleep Talk	Normal	Status	—	—	10	Self
TM90	Substitute	Normal	Status	—	—	10	Self
TM94	Secret Power	Normal	Physical	70	100	20	Normal
TM100	Confide	Normal	Status	—	—	20	Normal
HM01	Cut	Normal	Physical	50	95	30	Normal
HM04	Strength	Normal	Physical	80	100	15	Normal
HM06	Rock Smash	Fighting	Physical	40	100	15	Normal

MOVES LEARNED IN EXCHANGE FOR BP

Name	Type	Kind	Pow.	Acc.	PP	Range
Drill Run	Ground	Physical	80	95	10	Normal
Earth Power	Ground	Special	90	100	10	Normal
Iron Defense	Steel	Status	—	—	15	Self
Snore	Normal	Special	50	100	15	Normal
Stealth Rock	Rock	Status	—	—	20	Other Side

MOVES TAUGHT BY PEOPLE

Name	Type	Kind	Pow.	Acc.	PP	Range

EGG MOVES

Name	Type	Kind	Pow.	Acc.	PP	Range
Iron Defense	Steel	Status	—	—	15	Self
Rapid Spin	Normal	Physical	20	100	40	Normal
Earth Power	Ground	Special	90	100	10	Normal
Crush Claw	Normal	Physical	75	95	10	Normal
Metal Sound	Steel	Status	—	85	40	Normal
Submission	Fighting	Physical	80	80	20	Normal
Skull Bash	Normal	Physical	130	100	10	Normal
Rock Climb	Normal	Physical	90	85	20	Normal

National Pokédex **530** Hoenn Pokédex —

Excadrill

Subterrene Pokémon

Ground Steel

HEIGHT: 2'04" WEIGHT: 89.1 lbs.

Same form for ♂ / ♀

Ω It can help in tunnel construction. Its drill has evolved into steel strong enough to bore through iron plates.

α More than 300 feet below the surface, they build mazelike nests. Their activity can be destructive to subway tunnels.

ABILITIES
Sand Rush
Sand Force

HIDDEN ABILITY
Mold Breaker

EGG GROUPS
Field

STAT GROWTH RATES
HP
Attack
Defense
Sp. Atk
Sp. Def
Speed

ITEMS SOMETIMES HELD BY WILD POKÉMON
—

EVOLUTION
Drilbur → Lv. 31 → Excadrill

MAIN WAY TO REGISTER IN THE NATIONAL POKÉDEX

Catch in Mirage Cave 2.

Damage taken in normal battles

Type		Type	
Normal	×0.5	Flying	×0.5
Fire	×2	Psychic	×0.5
Water	×2	Bug	×0.5
Grass	×1	Rock	×0.25
Electric	×0	Ghost	×1
Ice	×1	Dragon	×0.5
Fighting	×2	Dark	×1
Poison	×0	Steel	×0.5
Ground	×2	Fairy	×0.5

Damage taken in Inverse battles

Type		Type	
Normal	×2	Flying	×2
Fire	×0.5	Psychic	×2
Water	×0.5	Bug	×2
Grass	×1	Rock	×4
Electric	×2	Ghost	×1
Ice	×1	Dragon	×2
Fighting	×0.5	Dark	×1
Poison	×4	Steel	×2
Ground	×0.5	Fairy	×2

Can be used in
Inverse Battle
Battle Institute
Battle Maison
Random Matchup (Free Battle)
Random Matchup (Others)

LEVEL-UP MOVES

Lv.	Name	Type	Kind	Pow.	Acc.	PP	Range
1	Rototiller	Ground	Status	—	—	10	Adjacent
1	Scratch	Normal	Physical	40	100	35	Normal
1	Mud Sport	Ground	Status	—	—	15	Both Sides
1	Rapid Spin	Normal	Physical	20	100	40	Normal
1	Mud-Slap	Ground	Special	20	100	10	Normal
5	Rapid Spin	Normal	Physical	20	100	40	Normal
8	Mud-Slap	Ground	Special	20	100	10	Normal
12	Fury Swipes	Normal	Physical	18	80	15	Normal
15	Metal Claw	Steel	Physical	50	95	35	Normal
19	Dig	Ground	Physical	80	100	10	Normal
22	Hone Claws	Dark	Status	—	—	15	Self
26	Slash	Normal	Physical	70	100	20	Normal
29	Rock Slide	Rock	Physical	75	90	10	Many Others
31	Horn Drill	Normal	Physical	—	30	5	Normal
36	Earthquake	Ground	Physical	100	100	10	Adjacent
42	Swords Dance	Normal	Status	—	—	20	Self
49	Sandstorm	Rock	Status	—	—	10	Both Sides
55	Drill Run	Ground	Physical	80	95	10	Normal
62	Fissure	Ground	Physical	—	30	5	Normal

TM & HM MOVES

No.	Name	Type	Kind	Pow.	Acc.	PP	Range
TM01	Hone Claws	Dark	Status	—	—	15	Self
TM06	Toxic	Poison	Status	—	90	10	Normal
TM10	Hidden Power	Normal	Special	60	100	15	Normal
TM15	Hyper Beam	Normal	Special	150	90	5	Normal
TM17	Protect	Normal	Status	—	—	10	Self
TM21	Frustration	Normal	Physical	—	100	20	Normal
TM26	Earthquake	Ground	Physical	100	100	10	Adjacent
TM27	Return	Normal	Physical	—	100	20	Normal
TM28	Dig	Ground	Physical	80	100	10	Normal
TM31	Brick Break	Fighting	Physical	75	100	15	Normal
TM32	Double Team	Normal	Status	—	—	15	Self
TM36	Sludge Bomb	Poison	Special	90	100	10	Normal
TM37	Sandstorm	Rock	Status	—	—	10	Both Sides
TM39	Rock Tomb	Rock	Physical	60	95	15	Normal
TM40	Aerial Ace	Flying	Physical	60	—	20	Normal
TM42	Facade	Normal	Physical	70	100	20	Normal
TM44	Rest	Psychic	Status	—	—	10	Self
TM45	Attract	Normal	Status	—	100	15	Normal
TM48	Round	Normal	Special	60	100	15	Normal
TM52	Focus Blast	Fighting	Special	120	70	5	Normal
TM56	Fling	Dark	Physical	—	100	10	Normal
TM65	Shadow Claw	Ghost	Physical	70	100	15	Normal
TM68	Giga Impact	Normal	Physical	150	90	5	Normal
TM75	Swords Dance	Normal	Status	—	—	20	Self
TM78	Bulldoze	Ground	Physical	60	100	20	Adjacent
TM80	Rock Slide	Rock	Physical	75	90	10	Many Others
TM81	X-Scissor	Bug	Physical	80	100	15	Normal
TM84	Poison Jab	Poison	Physical	80	100	20	Normal
TM87	Swagger	Normal	Status	—	90	15	Normal
TM88	Sleep Talk	Normal	Status	—	—	10	Self
TM90	Substitute	Normal	Status	—	—	10	Self
TM94	Secret Power	Normal	Physical	70	100	20	Normal
TM100	Confide	Normal	Status	—	—	20	Normal
HM01	Cut	Normal	Physical	50	95	30	Normal
HM04	Strength	Normal	Physical	80	100	15	Normal
HM06	Rock Smash	Fighting	Physical	40	100	15	Normal

MOVES LEARNED IN EXCHANGE FOR BP

Name	Type	Kind	Pow.	Acc.	PP	Range
Iron Head	Steel	Physical	80	100	15	Normal
Drill Run	Ground	Physical	80	95	10	Normal
Earth Power	Ground	Special	90	100	10	Normal
Magnet Rise	Electric	Status	—	—	10	Self
Iron Defense	Steel	Status	—	—	15	Self
Snore	Normal	Special	50	100	15	Normal
Stealth Rock	Rock	Status	—	—	20	Other Side

MOVES TAUGHT BY PEOPLE

Name	Type	Kind	Pow.	Acc.	PP	Range

National Pokédex **531** Hoenn Pokédex **—**

Audino

Hearing Pokémon

Normal

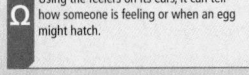

HEIGHT: 3'07" WEIGHT: 68.3 lbs.

Same form for ♂ / ♀

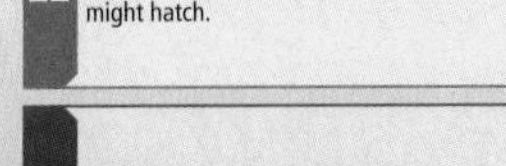

Ω Using the feelers on its ears, it can tell how someone is feeling or when an egg might hatch.

α It touches others with the feelers on its ears, using the sound of their heartbeats to tell how they are feeling.

ABILITIES
Healer
Regenerator

HIDDEN ABILITY
Klutz

EGG GROUPS
Fairy

STAT GROWTH RATES
HP
Attack
Defense
Sp. Atk
Sp. Def
Speed

ITEMS SOMETIMES HELD BY WILD POKÉMON
Oran Berry / Sitrus Berry

EVOLUTION

Does not evolve

MAIN WAY TO REGISTER IN THE NATIONAL POKÉDEX

Catch in Mirage Forest 7.

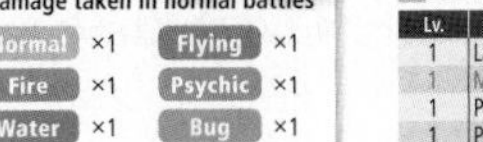

Damage taken in normal battles

Type		Type	
Normal	×1	Flying	×1
Fire	×1	Psychic	×1
Water	×1	Bug	×1
Grass	×1	Rock	×1
Electric	×1	Ghost	×0
Ice	×1	Dragon	×1
Fighting	×2	Dark	×1
Poison	×1	Steel	×1
Ground	×1	Fairy	×1

Damage taken in Inverse battles

Type		Type	
Normal	×1	Flying	×1
Fire	×1	Psychic	×1
Water	×1	Bug	×1
Grass	×1	Rock	×1
Electric	×1	Ghost	×2
Ice	×1	Dragon	×1
Fighting	×0.5	Dark	×1
Poison	×1	Steel	×1
Ground	×1	Fairy	×1

Can be used in
Inverse Battle
Battle Institute
Battle Maison
Random Matchup (Free Battle)
Random Matchup (Others)

LEVEL-UP MOVES

Lv.	Name	Type	Kind	Pow.	Acc.	PP	Range
1	Last Resort	Normal	Physical	140	100	5	Normal
1	Misty Terrain	Fairy	Status	—	—	10	Both Sides
1	Play Nice	Normal	Status	—	—	20	Normal
1	Pound	Normal	Physical	40	100	35	Normal
1	Growl	Normal	Status	—	100	40	Many Others
1	Helping Hand	Normal	Status	—	—	20	1 Ally
5	Baby-Doll Eyes	Fairy	Status	—	100	30	Normal
9	Refresh	Normal	Status	—	—	20	Self
13	Disarming Voice	Fairy	Special	40	—	15	Many Others
17	Double Slap	Normal	Physical	15	85	10	Normal
21	Attract	Normal	Status	—	100	15	Normal
25	Secret Power	Normal	Physical	70	100	20	Normal
29	Entrainment	Normal	Status	—	100	15	Normal
33	Take Down	Normal	Physical	90	85	20	Normal
37	Heal Pulse	Psychic	Status	—	—	10	Normal
41	After You	Normal	Status	—	—	15	Normal
45	Simple Beam	Normal	Status	—	100	15	Normal
49	Double-Edge	Normal	Physical	120	100	15	Normal
53	Last Resort	Normal	Physical	140	100	5	Normal

TM & HM MOVES

No.	Name	Type	Kind	Pow.	Acc.	PP	Range
TM03	Psyshock	Psychic	Special	80	100	10	Normal
TM04	Calm Mind	Psychic	Status	—	—	20	Self
TM06	Toxic	Poison	Status	—	90	10	Normal
TM10	Hidden Power	Normal	Special	60	100	15	Normal
TM11	Sunny Day	Fire	Status	—	—	5	Both Sides
TM13	Ice Beam	Ice	Special	90	100	10	Normal
TM14	Blizzard	Ice	Special	110	70	5	Many Others
TM15	Hyper Beam	Normal	Special	150	90	5	Normal
TM16	Light Screen	Psychic	Status	—	—	30	Your Side
TM17	Protect	Normal	Status	—	—	10	Self
TM18	Rain Dance	Water	Status	—	—	5	Both Sides
TM20	Safeguard	Normal	Status	—	—	25	Your Side
TM21	Frustration	Normal	Physical	—	100	20	Normal
TM22	Solar Beam	Grass	Special	120	100	10	Normal
TM24	Thunderbolt	Electric	Special	90	100	15	Normal
TM25	Thunder	Electric	Special	110	70	10	Normal
TM27	Return	Normal	Physical	—	100	20	Normal
TM28	Dig	Ground	Physical	80	100	10	Normal
TM29	Psychic	Psychic	Special	90	100	10	Normal
TM30	Shadow Ball	Ghost	Special	80	100	15	Normal
TM32	Double Team	Normal	Status	—	—	15	Self
TM33	Reflect	Psychic	Status	—	—	20	Your Side
TM35	Flamethrower	Fire	Special	90	100	15	Normal
TM38	Fire Blast	Fire	Special	110	85	5	Normal
TM42	Facade	Normal	Physical	70	100	20	Normal
TM44	Rest	Psychic	Status	—	—	10	Self
TM45	Attract	Normal	Status	—	100	15	Normal
TM48	Round	Normal	Special	60	100	15	Normal
TM49	Echoed Voice	Normal	Special	40	100	15	Normal
TM56	Fling	Dark	Physical	—	100	10	Normal
TM57	Charge Beam	Electric	Special	50	90	10	Normal
TM59	Incinerate	Fire	Special	60	100	15	Many Others
TM67	Retaliate	Normal	Physical	70	100	5	Normal
TM70	Flash	Normal	Status	—	100	20	Normal
TM73	Thunder Wave	Electric	Status	—	100	20	Normal
TM77	Psych Up	Normal	Status	—	—	10	Normal
TM85	Dream Eater	Psychic	Special	100	100	15	Normal
TM86	Grass Knot	Grass	Special	—	100	20	Normal
TM87	Swagger	Normal	Status	—	90	15	Normal
TM88	Sleep Talk	Normal	Status	—	—	10	Self
TM90	Substitute	Normal	Status	—	—	10	Self
TM92	Trick Room	Psychic	Status	—	—	5	Both Sides
TM93	Wild Charge	Electric	Physical	90	100	15	Normal
TM94	Secret Power	Normal	Physical	70	100	20	Normal
TM98	Power-Up Punch	Fighting	Physical	40	100	20	Normal
TM99	Dazzling Gleam	Fairy	Special	80	100	10	Many Others
TM100	Confide	Normal	Status	—	—	20	Normal
HM03	Surf	Water	Special	90	100	15	Adjacent

MOVES LEARNED IN EXCHANGE FOR BP

Name	Type	Kind	Pow.	Acc.	PP	Range
Covet	Normal	Physical	60	100	25	Normal
Signal Beam	Bug	Special	75	100	15	Normal
Low Kick	Fighting	Physical	—	100	20	Normal
Uproar	Normal	Special	90	100	10	1 Random
Thunder Punch	Electric	Physical	75	100	15	Normal
Fire Punch	Fire	Physical	75	100	15	Normal
Ice Punch	Ice	Physical	75	100	15	Normal
Magic Coat	Psychic	Status	—	—	15	Self
Gravity	Psychic	Status	—	—	5	Both Sides
Last Resort	Normal	Physical	140	100	5	Normal
Icy Wind	Ice	Special	55	95	15	Many Others
Zen Headbutt	Psychic	Physical	80	90	15	Normal
Hyper Voice	Normal	Special	90	100	10	Many Others
Iron Tail	Steel	Physical	100	75	15	Normal
Snore	Normal	Special	50	100	15	Normal
Knock Off	Dark	Physical	65	100	20	Normal
Role Play	Psychic	Status	—	—	10	Normal
Heal Bell	Normal	Status	—	—	5	Your Party
Pain Split	Normal	Status	—	—	20	Normal
Drain Punch	Fighting	Physical	75	100	10	Normal
Focus Punch	Fighting	Physical	150	100	20	Normal
After You	Normal	Status	—	—	15	Normal
Helping Hand	Normal	Status	—	—	20	1 Ally
Snatch	Dark	Status	—	—	10	Self
Skill Swap	Psychic	Status	—	—	10	Normal

MOVES TAUGHT BY PEOPLE

Name	Type	Kind	Pow.	Acc.	PP	Range

EGG MOVES

Name	Type	Kind	Pow.	Acc.	PP	Range
Wish	Normal	Status	—	—	10	Self
Heal Bell	Normal	Status	—	—	5	Your Party
Lucky Chant	Normal	Status	—	—	30	Your Side
Encore	Normal	Status	—	100	5	Normal
Bestow	Normal	Status	—	—	15	Normal
Sweet Kiss	Fairy	Status	—	75	10	Normal
Yawn	Normal	Status	—	—	10	Normal
Sleep Talk	Normal	Status	—	—	10	Self
Healing Wish	Psychic	Status	—	—	10	Self
Amnesia	Psychic	Status	—	—	20	Self
Draining Kiss	Fairy	Special	50	100	10	Normal

Mega Evolution

Mega Audino

Hearing Pokémon

Normal Fairy

HEIGHT: 4'11" WEIGHT: 70.5 lbs.

Same form for ♂ / ♀

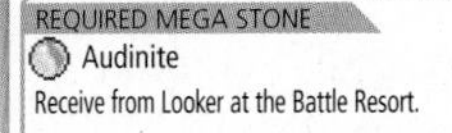

REQUIRED MEGA STONE
Audinite
Receive from Looker at the Battle Resort.

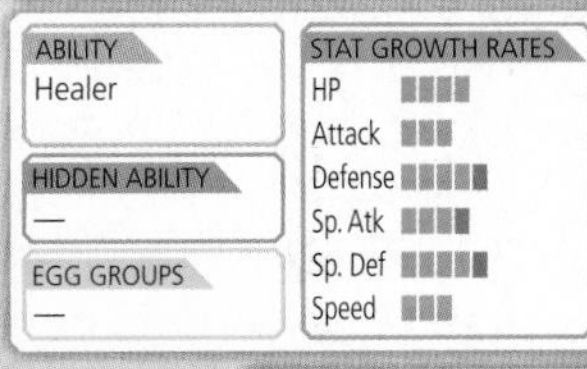

ABILITY
Healer

HIDDEN ABILITY
—

EGG GROUPS
—

STAT GROWTH RATES
HP
Attack
Defense
Sp. Atk
Sp. Def
Speed

Damage taken in normal battles

Type		Type	
Normal	×1	Flying	×1
Fire	×1	Psychic	×1
Water	×1	Bug	×0.5
Grass	×1	Rock	×1
Electric	×1	Ghost	×0
Ice	×1	Dragon	×0
Fighting	×1	Dark	×0.5
Poison	×2	Steel	×2
Ground	×1	Fairy	×1

Damage taken in Inverse battles

Type		Type	
Normal	×1	Flying	×1
Fire	×1	Psychic	×1
Water	×1	Bug	×2
Grass	×1	Rock	×1
Electric	×1	Ghost	×2
Ice	×1	Dragon	×2
Fighting	×1	Dark	×2
Poison	×0.5	Steel	×0.5
Ground	×1	Fairy	×1

Can be used in
Inverse Battle
Battle Institute
Battle Maison
Random Matchup (Free Battle)
Random Matchup (Others)

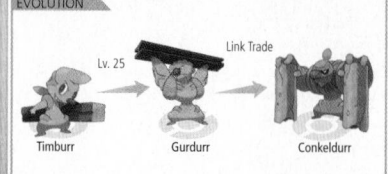

National Pokédex **532** Hoenn Pokédex —

Timburr

Muscular Pokémon

Fighting

HEIGHT: 2'00" WEIGHT: 27.6 lbs.

Same form for ♂ / ♀

Ω These Pokémon appear at building sites and help out with construction. They always carry squared logs.

α Always carrying squared logs, they help out with construction. As they grow, they carry bigger logs.

ABILITIES
Guts
Sheer Force

HIDDEN ABILITY
Iron Fist

EGG GROUPS
Human-Like

STAT GROWTH RATES
HP ■■■
Attack ■■■■
Defense ■■■
Sp. Atk ■
Sp. Def ■■
Speed ■■

ITEMS SOMETIMES HELD BY WILD POKÉMON
—

EVOLUTION
Timburr → Lv. 25 → Gurdurr → Link Trade → Conkeldurr

MAIN WAY TO REGISTER IN THE NATIONAL POKÉDEX

Catch in Granite Cave (1F). Appears as a hidden Pokémon after you battle Groudon or Kyogre.

Damage taken in normal battles

Type		Type	
Normal	×1	Flying	×2
Fire	×1	Psychic	×2
Water	×1	Bug	×0.5
Grass	×1	Rock	×0.5
Electric	×1	Ghost	×1
Ice	×1	Dragon	×1
Fighting	×1	Dark	×0.5
Poison	×1	Steel	×1
Ground	×1	Fairy	×2

Damage taken in Inverse battles

Type		Type	
Normal	×1	Flying	×0.5
Fire	×1	Psychic	×0.5
Water	×1	Bug	×2
Grass	×1	Rock	×2
Electric	×1	Ghost	×1
Ice	×1	Dragon	×1
Fighting	×1	Dark	×2
Poison	×1	Steel	×1
Ground	×1	Fairy	×0.5

Can be used in
Inverse Battle
Battle Institute
Battle Maison
Random Matchup (Free Battle)
Random Matchup (Others)

LEVEL-UP MOVES

Lv.	Name	Type	Kind	Pow.	Acc.	PP	Range
1	Pound	Normal	Physical	40	100	35	Normal
1	Leer	Normal	Status	—	100	30	Many Others
4	Focus Energy	Normal	Status	—	—	30	Self
8	Bide	Normal	Physical	—	—	10	Self
12	Low Kick	Fighting	Physical	—	100	20	Normal
16	Rock Throw	Rock	Physical	50	90	15	Normal
20	Wake-Up Slap	Fighting	Physical	70	100	10	Normal
24	Chip Away	Normal	Physical	70	100	20	Normal
28	Bulk Up	Fighting	Status	—	—	20	Self
31	Rock Slide	Rock	Physical	75	90	10	Many Others
34	Dynamic Punch	Fighting	Physical	100	50	5	Normal
37	Scary Face	Normal	Status	—	100	10	Normal
40	Hammer Arm	Fighting	Physical	100	90	10	Normal
43	Stone Edge	Rock	Physical	100	80	5	Normal
46	Focus Punch	Fighting	Physical	150	100	20	Normal
49	Superpower	Fighting	Physical	120	100	5	Normal

TM & HM MOVES

No.	Name	Type	Kind	Pow.	Acc.	PP	Range
TM06	Toxic	Poison	Status	—	90	10	Normal
TM08	Bulk Up	Fighting	Status	—	—	20	Self
TM10	Hidden Power	Normal	Special	60	100	15	Normal
TM11	Sunny Day	Fire	Status	—	—	5	Both Sides
TM12	Taunt	Dark	Status	—	100	20	Normal
TM17	Protect	Normal	Status	—	—	10	Self
TM18	Rain Dance	Water	Status	—	—	5	Both Sides
TM21	Frustration	Normal	Physical	—	100	20	Normal
TM23	Smack Down	Rock	Physical	50	100	15	Normal
TM27	Return	Normal	Physical	—	100	20	Normal
TM28	Dig	Ground	Physical	80	100	10	Normal
TM31	Brick Break	Fighting	Physical	75	100	15	Normal
TM32	Double Team	Normal	Status	—	—	15	Self
TM39	Rock Tomb	Rock	Physical	60	95	15	Normal
TM42	Facade	Normal	Physical	70	100	20	Normal
TM44	Rest	Psychic	Status	—	—	10	Self
TM45	Attract	Normal	Status	—	100	15	Normal
TM47	Low Sweep	Fighting	Physical	65	100	20	Normal
TM48	Round	Normal	Special	60	100	15	Normal
TM52	Focus Blast	Fighting	Special	120	70	5	Normal
TM56	Fling	Dark	Physical	—	100	10	Normal
TM66	Payback	Dark	Physical	50	100	10	Normal
TM67	Retaliate	Normal	Physical	70	100	5	Normal
TM71	Stone Edge	Rock	Physical	100	80	5	Normal
TM80	Rock Slide	Rock	Physical	75	90	10	Many Others
TM84	Poison Jab	Poison	Physical	80	100	20	Normal
TM86	Grass Knot	Grass	Special	—	100	20	Normal
TM87	Swagger	Normal	Status	—	90	15	Normal
TM88	Sleep Talk	Normal	Status	—	—	10	Self
TM90	Substitute	Normal	Status	—	—	10	Self
TM94	Secret Power	Normal	Physical	70	100	20	Normal
TM98	Power-Up Punch	Fighting	Physical	40	100	20	Normal
TM100	Confide	Normal	Status	—	—	20	Normal
HM04	Strength	Normal	Physical	80	100	15	Normal
HM06	Rock Smash	Fighting	Physical	40	100	15	Normal

MOVES LEARNED IN EXCHANGE FOR BP

Name	Type	Kind	Pow.	Acc.	PP	Range
Low Kick	Fighting	Physical	—	100	20	Normal
Thunder Punch	Electric	Physical	75	100	15	Normal
Fire Punch	Fire	Physical	75	100	15	Normal
Ice Punch	Ice	Physical	75	100	15	Normal
Block	Normal	Status	—	—	5	Normal
Superpower	Fighting	Physical	120	100	5	Normal
Snore	Normal	Special	50	100	15	Normal
Knock Off	Dark	Physical	65	100	20	Normal
Drain Punch	Fighting	Physical	75	100	10	Normal
Focus Punch	Fighting	Physical	150	100	20	Normal
Helping Hand	Normal	Status	—	—	20	1 Ally

MOVES TAUGHT BY PEOPLE

Name	Type	Kind	Pow.	Acc.	PP	Range

EGG MOVES

Name	Type	Kind	Pow.	Acc.	PP	Range
Drain Punch	Fighting	Physical	75	100	10	Normal
Endure	Normal	Status	—	—	10	Self
Counter	Fighting	Physical	—	100	20	Varies
Comet Punch	Normal	Physical	18	85	15	Normal
Foresight	Normal	Status	—	—	40	Normal
Smelling Salts	Normal	Physical	70	100	10	Normal
Detect	Fighting	Status	—	—	5	Self
Wide Guard	Rock	Status	—	—	10	Your Side
Force Palm	Fighting	Physical	60	100	10	Normal
Reversal	Fighting	Physical	—	100	15	Normal
Mach Punch	Fighting	Physical	40	100	30	Normal

National Pokédex **533** Hoenn Pokédex —

Gurdurr

Muscular Pokémon

Fighting

HEIGHT: 3'11" WEIGHT: 88.2 lbs.

Same form for ♂ / ♀

Ω With strengthened bodies, they skillfully wield steel beams to take down buildings.

α This Pokémon is so muscular and strongly built that even a group of wrestlers could not make it budge an inch.

ABILITIES
Guts
Sheer Force

HIDDEN ABILITY
Iron Fist

EGG GROUPS
Human-Like

STAT GROWTH RATES
HP ■■■
Attack ■■■■■
Defense ■■■■
Sp. Atk ■■
Sp. Def ■■
Speed ■■

ITEMS SOMETIMES HELD BY WILD POKÉMON
—

EVOLUTION
Timburr → Lv. 25 → Gurdurr → Link Trade → Conkeldurr

MAIN WAY TO REGISTER IN THE NATIONAL POKÉDEX

Level up Timburr to Lv. 25.

Damage taken in normal battles

Type		Type	
Normal	×1	Flying	×2
Fire	×1	Psychic	×2
Water	×1	Bug	×0.5
Grass	×1	Rock	×0.5
Electric	×1	Ghost	×1
Ice	×1	Dragon	×1
Fighting	×1	Dark	×0.5
Poison	×1	Steel	×1
Ground	×1	Fairy	×2

Damage taken in Inverse battles

Type		Type	
Normal	×1	Flying	×0.5
Fire	×1	Psychic	×0.5
Water	×1	Bug	×2
Grass	×1	Rock	×2
Electric	×1	Ghost	×1
Ice	×1	Dragon	×1
Fighting	×1	Dark	×2
Poison	×1	Steel	×1
Ground	×1	Fairy	×0.5

Can be used in
Inverse Battle
Battle Institute
Battle Maison
Random Matchup (Free Battle)
Random Matchup (Others)

LEVEL-UP MOVES

Lv.	Name	Type	Kind	Pow.	Acc.	PP	Range
1	Pound	Normal	Physical	40	100	35	Normal
1	Leer	Normal	Status	—	100	30	Many Others
1	Focus Energy	Normal	Status	—	—	30	Self
1	Bide	Normal	Physical	—	—	10	Self
4	Focus Energy	Normal	Status	—	—	30	Self
8	Bide	Normal	Physical	—	—	10	Self
12	Low Kick	Fighting	Physical	—	100	20	Normal
16	Rock Throw	Rock	Physical	50	90	15	Normal
20	Wake-Up Slap	Fighting	Physical	70	100	10	Normal
24	Chip Away	Normal	Physical	70	100	20	Normal
29	Bulk Up	Fighting	Status	—	—	20	Self
33	Rock Slide	Rock	Physical	75	90	10	Many Others
37	Dynamic Punch	Fighting	Physical	100	50	5	Normal
41	Scary Face	Normal	Status	—	100	10	Normal
45	Hammer Arm	Fighting	Physical	100	90	10	Normal
49	Stone Edge	Rock	Physical	100	80	5	Normal
53	Focus Punch	Fighting	Physical	150	100	20	Normal
57	Superpower	Fighting	Physical	120	100	5	Normal

TM & HM MOVES

No.	Name	Type	Kind	Pow.	Acc.	PP	Range
TM06	Toxic	Poison	Status	—	90	10	Normal
TM08	Bulk Up	Fighting	Status	—	—	20	Self
TM10	Hidden Power	Normal	Special	60	100	15	Normal
TM11	Sunny Day	Fire	Status	—	—	5	Both Sides
TM12	Taunt	Dark	Status	—	100	20	Normal
TM17	Protect	Normal	Status	—	—	10	Self
TM18	Rain Dance	Water	Status	—	—	5	Both Sides
TM21	Frustration	Normal	Physical	—	100	20	Normal
TM23	Smack Down	Rock	Physical	50	100	15	Normal
TM27	Return	Normal	Physical	—	100	20	Normal
TM28	Dig	Ground	Physical	80	100	10	Normal
TM31	Brick Break	Fighting	Physical	75	100	15	Normal
TM32	Double Team	Normal	Status	—	—	15	Self
TM39	Rock Tomb	Rock	Physical	60	95	15	Normal
TM42	Facade	Normal	Physical	70	100	20	Normal
TM44	Rest	Psychic	Status	—	—	10	Self
TM45	Attract	Normal	Status	—	100	15	Normal
TM47	Low Sweep	Fighting	Physical	65	100	20	Normal
TM48	Round	Normal	Special	60	100	15	Normal
TM52	Focus Blast	Fighting	Special	120	70	5	Normal
TM56	Fling	Dark	Physical	—	100	10	Normal
TM66	Payback	Dark	Physical	50	100	10	Normal
TM67	Retaliate	Normal	Physical	70	100	5	Normal
TM71	Stone Edge	Rock	Physical	100	80	5	Normal
TM80	Rock Slide	Rock	Physical	75	90	10	Many Others
TM84	Poison Jab	Poison	Physical	80	100	20	Normal
TM86	Grass Knot	Grass	Special	—	100	20	Normal
TM87	Swagger	Normal	Status	—	90	15	Normal
TM88	Sleep Talk	Normal	Status	—	—	10	Self
TM90	Substitute	Normal	Status	—	—	10	Self
TM94	Secret Power	Normal	Physical	70	100	20	Normal
TM98	Power-Up Punch	Fighting	Physical	40	100	20	Normal
TM100	Confide	Normal	Status	—	—	20	Normal
HM04	Strength	Normal	Physical	80	100	15	Normal
HM06	Rock Smash	Fighting	Physical	40	100	15	Normal

MOVES LEARNED IN EXCHANGE FOR BP

Name	Type	Kind	Pow.	Acc.	PP	Range
Low Kick	Fighting	Physical	—	100	20	Normal
Thunder Punch	Electric	Physical	75	100	15	Normal
Fire Punch	Fire	Physical	75	100	15	Normal
Ice Punch	Ice	Physical	75	100	15	Normal
Block	Normal	Status	—	—	5	Normal
Superpower	Fighting	Physical	120	100	5	Normal
Snore	Normal	Special	50	100	15	Normal
Knock Off	Dark	Physical	65	100	20	Normal
Drain Punch	Fighting	Physical	75	100	10	Normal
Focus Punch	Fighting	Physical	150	100	20	Normal
Helping Hand	Normal	Status	—	—	20	1 Ally

MOVES TAUGHT BY PEOPLE

Name	Type	Kind	Pow.	Acc.	PP	Range

National Pokédex **534** Hoenn Pokédex —

Conkeldurr

Muscular Pokémon

Fighting

HEIGHT: 4'07" WEIGHT: 191.8 lbs.

Same form for ♂ / ♀

Ω It is thought that Conkeldurr taught humans how to make concrete more than 2,000 years ago.

α Rather than rely on force, they master moves that utilize the centrifugal force of spinning concrete.

ABILITIES
Guts
Sheer Force

HIDDEN ABILITY
Iron Fist

EGG GROUPS
Human-Like

STAT GROWTH RATES
HP ■■■■
Attack ■■■■■■■■
Defense ■■■■
Sp. Atk ■■■
Sp. Def ■■■
Speed ■■■

ITEMS SOMETIMES HELD BY WILD POKÉMON
—

EVOLUTION

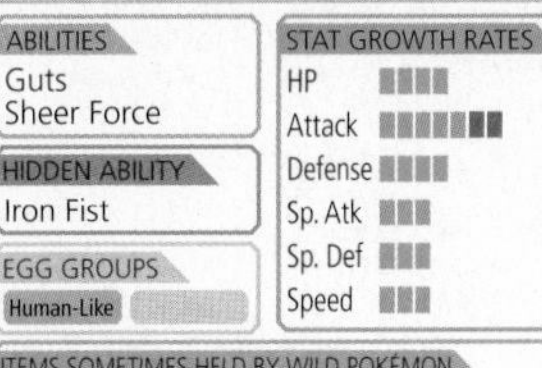

Timburr → Lv. 25 → Gurdurr → Link Trade → Conkeldurr

MAIN WAY TO REGISTER IN THE NATIONAL POKÉDEX

Receive a Gurdurr via Link Trade to have it evolve.

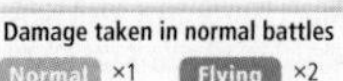

Damage taken in normal battles

Type		Type	
Normal	×1	Flying	×2
Fire	×1	Psychic	×2
Water	×1	Bug	×0.5
Grass	×1	Rock	×0.5
Electric	×1	Ghost	×1
Ice	×1	Dragon	×1
Fighting	×1	Dark	×0.5
Poison	×1	Steel	×1
Ground	×1	Fairy	×2

Damage taken in Inverse battles

Type		Type	
Normal	×1	Flying	×0.5
Fire	×1	Psychic	×0.5
Water	×1	Bug	×2
Grass	×1	Rock	×2
Electric	×1	Ghost	×1
Ice	×1	Dragon	×1
Fighting	×1	Dark	×2
Poison	×1	Steel	×1
Ground	×1	Fairy	×0.5

Can be used in
Inverse Battle
Battle Institute
Battle Maison
Random Matchup (Free Battle)
Random Matchup (Others)

LEVEL-UP MOVES

Lv.	Name	Type	Kind	Pow.	Acc.	PP	Range
1	Pound	Normal	Physical	40	100	35	Normal
1	Leer	Normal	Status	—	100	30	Many Others
1	Focus Energy	Normal	Status	—	—	30	Self
1	Bide	Normal	Physical	—	—	10	Self
4	Focus Energy	Normal	Status	—	—	30	Self
8	Bide	Normal	Physical	—	—	10	Self
12	Low Kick	Fighting	Physical	—	100	20	Normal
16	Rock Throw	Rock	Physical	50	90	15	Normal
20	Wake-Up Slap	Fighting	Physical	70	100	10	Normal
24	Chip Away	Normal	Physical	70	100	20	Normal
29	Bulk Up	Fighting	Status	—	—	20	Self
33	Rock Slide	Rock	Physical	75	90	10	Many Others
37	Dynamic Punch	Fighting	Physical	100	50	5	Normal
41	Scary Face	Normal	Status	—	100	10	Normal
45	Hammer Arm	Fighting	Physical	100	90	10	Normal
49	Stone Edge	Rock	Physical	100	80	5	Normal
53	Focus Punch	Fighting	Physical	150	100	20	Normal
57	Superpower	Fighting	Physical	120	100	5	Normal

TM & HM MOVES

No.	Name	Type	Kind	Pow.	Acc.	PP	Range
TM06	Toxic	Poison	Status	—	90	10	Normal
TM08	Bulk Up	Fighting	Status	—	—	20	Self
TM10	Hidden Power	Normal	Special	60	100	15	Normal
TM11	Sunny Day	Fire	Status	—	—	5	Both Sides
TM12	Taunt	Dark	Status	—	100	20	Normal
TM15	Hyper Beam	Normal	Special	150	90	5	Normal
TM17	Protect	Normal	Status	—	—	10	Self
TM18	Rain Dance	Water	Status	—	—	5	Both Sides
TM21	Frustration	Normal	Physical	—	100	20	Normal
TM23	Smack Down	Rock	Physical	50	100	15	Normal
TM26	Earthquake	Ground	Physical	100	100	10	Adjacent
TM27	Return	Normal	Physical	—	100	20	Normal
TM28	Dig	Ground	Physical	80	100	10	Normal
TM31	Brick Break	Fighting	Physical	75	100	15	Normal
TM32	Double Team	Normal	Status	—	—	15	Self
TM39	Rock Tomb	Rock	Physical	60	95	15	Normal
TM42	Facade	Normal	Physical	70	100	20	Normal
TM44	Rest	Psychic	Status	—	—	10	Self
TM45	Attract	Normal	Status	—	100	15	Normal
TM47	Low Sweep	Fighting	Physical	65	100	20	Normal
TM48	Round	Normal	Special	60	100	15	Normal
TM52	Focus Blast	Fighting	Special	120	70	5	Normal
TM56	Fling	Dark	Physical	—	100	10	Normal
TM66	Payback	Dark	Physical	50	100	10	Normal
TM67	Retaliate	Normal	Physical	70	100	5	Normal
TM68	Giga Impact	Normal	Physical	150	90	5	Normal
TM71	Stone Edge	Rock	Physical	100	80	5	Normal
TM78	Bulldoze	Ground	Physical	60	100	20	Adjacent
TM80	Rock Slide	Rock	Physical	75	90	10	Many Others
TM84	Poison Jab	Poison	Physical	80	100	20	Normal
TM86	Grass Knot	Grass	Special	—	100	20	Normal
TM87	Swagger	Normal	Status	—	90	15	Normal
TM88	Sleep Talk	Normal	Status	—	—	10	Self
TM90	Substitute	Normal	Status	—	—	10	Self
TM94	Secret Power	Normal	Physical	70	100	20	Normal
TM98	Power-Up Punch	Fighting	Physical	40	100	20	Normal
TM100	Confide	Normal	Status	—	—	20	Normal
HM04	Strength	Normal	Physical	80	100	15	Normal
HM06	Rock Smash	Fighting	Physical	40	100	15	Normal

MOVES LEARNED IN EXCHANGE FOR BP

Name	Type	Kind	Pow.	Acc.	PP	Range
Low Kick	Fighting	Physical	—	100	20	Normal
Thunder Punch	Electric	Physical	75	100	15	Normal
Fire Punch	Fire	Physical	75	100	15	Normal
Ice Punch	Ice	Physical	75	100	15	Normal
Block	Normal	Status	—	—	5	Normal
Superpower	Fighting	Physical	120	100	5	Normal
Snore	Normal	Special	50	100	15	Normal
Knock Off	Dark	Physical	65	100	20	Normal
Drain Punch	Fighting	Physical	75	100	10	Normal
Focus Punch	Fighting	Physical	150	100	20	Normal
Helping Hand	Normal	Status	—	—	20	1 Ally

MOVES TAUGHT BY PEOPLE

Name	Type	Kind	Pow.	Acc.	PP	Range

National Pokédex **535** Hoenn Pokédex —

Tympole

Tadpole Pokémon

Water

HEIGHT: 1'08" WEIGHT: 9.9 lbs.

Same form for ♂ / ♀

Ω By vibrating its cheeks, it emits sound waves imperceptible to humans and warns others of danger.

α By vibrating its cheeks, it emits sound waves imperceptible to humans. It uses the rhythm of these sounds to talk.

ABILITIES
Swift Swim
Hydration

HIDDEN ABILITY
Water Absorb

EGG GROUPS
Water 1

STAT GROWTH RATES
HP ■■
Attack ■■■
Defense ■■
Sp. Atk ■■
Sp. Def ■■
Speed ■■■■

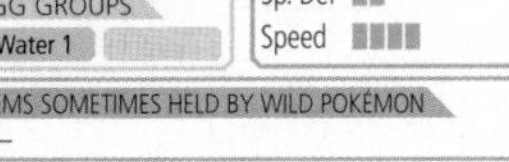

ITEMS SOMETIMES HELD BY WILD POKÉMON
—

EVOLUTION

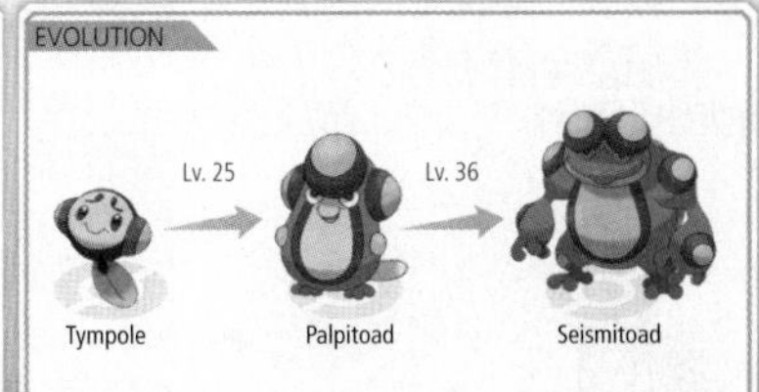

Tympole → Lv. 25 → Palpitoad → Lv. 36 → Seismitoad

MAIN WAY TO REGISTER IN THE NATIONAL POKÉDEX

Catch on Route 102. Appears as a hidden Pokémon after you battle Groudon or Kyogre.

Damage taken in normal battles

Type		Type	
Normal	×1	Flying	×1
Fire	×0.5	Psychic	×1
! Water	×0.5	Bug	×1
Grass	×2	Rock	×1
Electric	×2	Ghost	×1
Ice	×0.5	Dragon	×1
Fighting	×1	Dark	×1
Poison	×1	Steel	×0.5
Ground	×1	Fairy	×1

Damage taken in Inverse battles

Type		Type	
Normal	×1	Flying	×1
Fire	×2	Psychic	×1
! Water	×2	Bug	×1
Grass	×0.5	Rock	×1
Electric	×0.5	Ghost	×1
Ice	×2	Dragon	×1
Fighting	×1	Dark	×1
Poison	×1	Steel	×2
Ground	×1	Fairy	×1

Can be used in
Inverse Battle
Battle Institute
Battle Maison
Random Matchup (Free Battle)
Random Matchup (Others)

LEVEL-UP MOVES

Lv.	Name	Type	Kind	Pow.	Acc.	PP	Range
1	Bubble	Water	Special	40	100	30	Many Others
1	Growl	Normal	Status	—	100	40	Many Others
5	Supersonic	Normal	Status	—	55	20	Normal
9	Round	Normal	Special	60	100	15	Normal
12	Bubble Beam	Water	Special	65	100	20	Normal
16	Mud Shot	Ground	Special	55	95	15	Normal
20	Aqua Ring	Water	Status	—	—	20	Self
23	Uproar	Normal	Special	90	100	10	1 Random
27	Muddy Water	Water	Special	90	85	10	Many Others
31	Rain Dance	Water	Status	—	—	5	Both Sides
34	Flail	Normal	Physical	—	100	15	Normal
38	Echoed Voice	Normal	Special	40	100	15	Normal
42	Hydro Pump	Water	Special	110	80	5	Normal
45	Hyper Voice	Normal	Special	90	100	10	Many Others

TM & HM MOVES

No.	Name	Type	Kind	Pow.	Acc.	PP	Range
TM06	Toxic	Poison	Status	—	90	10	Normal
TM07	Hail	Ice	Status	—	—	10	Both Sides
TM10	Hidden Power	Normal	Special	60	100	15	Normal
TM17	Protect	Normal	Status	—	—	10	Self
TM18	Rain Dance	Water	Status	—	—	5	Both Sides
TM21	Frustration	Normal	Physical	—	100	20	Normal
TM27	Return	Normal	Physical	—	100	20	Normal
TM32	Double Team	Normal	Status	—	—	15	Self
TM34	Sludge Wave	Poison	Special	95	100	10	Adjacent
TM36	Sludge Bomb	Poison	Special	90	100	10	Normal
TM42	Facade	Normal	Physical	70	100	20	Normal
TM44	Rest	Psychic	Status	—	—	10	Self
TM45	Attract	Normal	Status	—	100	15	Normal
TM48	Round	Normal	Special	60	100	15	Normal
TM49	Echoed Voice	Normal	Special	40	100	15	Normal
TM55	Scald	Water	Special	80	100	15	Normal
TM83	Infestation	Bug	Special	20	100	20	Normal
TM87	Swagger	Normal	Status	—	90	15	Normal
TM88	Sleep Talk	Normal	Status	—	—	10	Self
TM90	Substitute	Normal	Status	—	—	10	Self
TM94	Secret Power	Normal	Physical	70	100	20	Normal
TM100	Confide	Normal	Status	—	—	20	Normal
HM03	Surf	Water	Special	90	100	15	Adjacent

MOVES LEARNED IN EXCHANGE FOR BP

Name	Type	Kind	Pow.	Acc.	PP	Range
Bounce	Flying	Physical	85	85	5	Normal
Uproar	Normal	Special	90	100	10	1 Random
Earth Power	Ground	Special	90	100	10	Normal
Icy Wind	Ice	Special	55	95	15	Many Others
Hyper Voice	Normal	Special	90	100	10	Many Others
Snore	Normal	Special	50	100	15	Normal
Water Pulse	Water	Special	60	100	20	Normal
After You	Normal	Status	—	—	15	Normal
Endeavor	Normal	Physical	—	100	5	Normal

MOVES TAUGHT BY PEOPLE

Name	Type	Kind	Pow.	Acc.	PP	Range

EGG MOVES

Name	Type	Kind	Pow.	Acc.	PP	Range
Water Pulse	Water	Special	60	100	20	Normal
Refresh	Normal	Status	—	—	20	Self
Mud Sport	Ground	Status	—	—	15	Both Sides
Mud Bomb	Ground	Special	65	85	10	Normal
Sleep Talk	Normal	Status	—	—	10	Self
Snore	Normal	Special	50	100	15	Normal
Mist	Ice	Status	—	—	30	Your Side
Earth Power	Ground	Special	90	100	10	Normal
After You	Normal	Status	—	—	15	Normal

National Pokédex **536** Hoenn Pokédex —

Palpitoad

Vibration Pokémon

Water Ground

HEIGHT: 2'07" WEIGHT: 37.5 lbs.

Same form for ♂ / ♀

Ω When they vibrate the bumps on their heads, they can make waves in water or earthquake-like vibrations on land.

α It lives in the water and on land. It uses its long, sticky tongue to immobilize its opponents.

ABILITIES
Swift Swim
Hydration

HIDDEN ABILITY
Water Absorb

EGG GROUPS
Water 1

STAT GROWTH RATES
HP
Attack
Defense
Sp. Atk
Sp. Def
Speed

ITEMS SOMETIMES HELD BY WILD POKÉMON
—

EVOLUTION

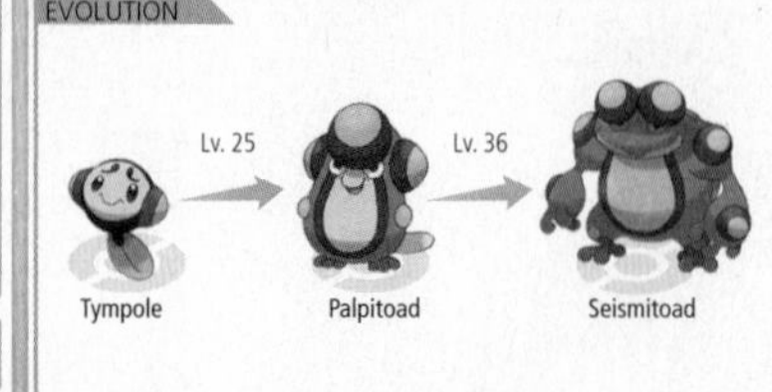

MAIN WAY TO REGISTER IN THE NATIONAL POKÉDEX

Level up Tympole to Lv. 25.

Damage taken in normal battles

Type		Type	
Normal	×1	Flying	×1
Fire	×0.5	Psychic	×1
Water	×1	Bug	×1
Grass	×4	Rock	×0.5
Electric	×0	Ghost	×1
Ice	×1	Dragon	×1
Fighting	×1	Dark	×1
Poison	×0.5	Steel	×0.5
Ground	×1	Fairy	×1

Damage taken in Inverse battles

Type		Type	
Normal	×1	Flying	×1
Fire	×2	Psychic	×1
Water	×1	Bug	×1
Grass	×0.25	Rock	×2
Electric	×1	Ghost	×1
Ice	×1	Dragon	×1
Fighting	×1	Dark	×1
Poison	×2	Steel	×2
Ground	×1	Fairy	×1

Can be used in
Inverse Battle
Battle Institute
Battle Maison
Random Matchup (Free Battle)
Random Matchup (Others)

LEVEL-UP MOVES

Lv.	Name	Type	Kind	Pow.	Acc.	PP	Range
1	Bubble	Water	Special	40	100	30	Many Others
1	Growl	Normal	Status	—	100	40	Many Others
1	Supersonic	Normal	Status	—	55	20	Normal
1	Round	Normal	Special	60	100	15	Normal
5	Supersonic	Normal	Status	—	55	20	Normal
9	Round	Normal	Special	60	100	15	Normal
12	Bubble Beam	Water	Special	65	100	20	Normal
16	Mud Shot	Ground	Special	55	95	15	Normal
20	Aqua Ring	Water	Status	—	—	20	Self
23	Uproar	Normal	Special	90	100	10	1 Random
28	Muddy Water	Water	Special	90	85	10	Many Others
33	Rain Dance	Water	Status	—	—	5	Both Sides
37	Flail	Normal	Physical	—	100	15	Normal
42	Echoed Voice	Normal	Special	40	100	15	Normal
47	Hydro Pump	Water	Special	110	80	5	Normal
51	Hyper Voice	Normal	Special	90	100	10	Many Others

TM & HM MOVES

No.	Name	Type	Kind	Pow.	Acc.	PP	Range
TM06	Toxic	Poison	Status	—	90	10	Normal
TM07	Hail	Ice	Status	—	—	10	Both Sides
TM10	Hidden Power	Normal	Special	60	100	15	Normal
TM17	Protect	Normal	Status	—	—	10	Self
TM18	Rain Dance	Water	Status	—	—	5	Both Sides
TM21	Frustration	Normal	Physical	—	100	20	Normal
TM27	Return	Normal	Physical	—	100	20	Normal
TM32	Double Team	Normal	Status	—	—	15	Self
TM34	Sludge Wave	Poison	Special	95	100	10	Adjacent
TM36	Sludge Bomb	Poison	Special	90	100	10	Normal
TM42	Facade	Normal	Physical	70	100	20	Normal
TM44	Rest	Psychic	Status	—	—	10	Self
TM45	Attract	Normal	Status	—	100	15	Normal
TM48	Round	Normal	Special	60	100	15	Normal
TM49	Echoed Voice	Normal	Special	40	100	15	Normal
TM55	Scald	Water	Special	80	100	15	Normal
TM78	Bulldoze	Ground	Physical	60	100	20	Adjacent
TM83	Infestation	Bug	Special	20	100	20	Normal
TM87	Swagger	Normal	Status	—	90	15	Normal
TM88	Sleep Talk	Normal	Status	—	—	10	Self
TM90	Substitute	Normal	Status	—	—	10	Self
TM94	Secret Power	Normal	Physical	70	100	20	Normal
TM100	Confide	Normal	Status	—	—	20	Normal
HM03	Surf	Water	Special	90	100	15	Adjacent
HM06	Rock Smash	Fighting	Physical	40	100	15	Normal

MOVES LEARNED IN EXCHANGE FOR BP

Name	Type	Kind	Pow.	Acc.	PP	Range
Bounce	Flying	Physical	85	85	5	Normal
Uproar	Normal	Special	90	100	10	1 Random
Earth Power	Ground	Special	90	100	10	Normal
Icy Wind	Ice	Special	55	95	15	Many Others
Hyper Voice	Normal	Special	90	100	10	Many Others
Snore	Normal	Special	50	100	15	Normal
Focus Punch	Fighting	Physical	150	100	20	Normal
Water Pulse	Water	Special	60	100	20	Normal
Gastro Acid	Poison	Status	—	100	10	Normal
After You	Normal	Status	—	—	15	Normal
Endeavor	Normal	Physical	—	100	5	Normal
Stealth Rock	Rock	Status	—	—	20	Other Side

MOVES TAUGHT BY PEOPLE

Name	Type	Kind	Pow.	Acc.	PP	Range

National Pokédex **537** Hoenn Pokédex —

Seismitoad

Vibration Pokémon

Water Ground

HEIGHT: 4'11" WEIGHT: 136.7 lbs.

Same form for ♂ / ♀

Ω It increases the power of its punches by vibrating the bumps on its fists. It can turn a boulder to rubble with one punch.

α They shoot paralyzing liquid from their head bumps. They use vibration to hurt their opponents.

ABILITIES
Swift Swim
Poison Touch

HIDDEN ABILITY
Water Absorb

EGG GROUPS
Water 1

STAT GROWTH RATES
HP
Attack
Defense
Sp. Atk
Sp. Def
Speed

ITEMS SOMETIMES HELD BY WILD POKÉMON
—

EVOLUTION

Lv. 25 Lv. 36
Tympole Palpitoad Seismitoad

MAIN WAY TO REGISTER IN THE NATIONAL POKÉDEX

Level up Palpitoad to Lv. 36.

Damage taken in normal battles

Type		Type	
Normal	×1	Flying	×1
Fire	×0.5	Psychic	×1
Water	×1	Bug	×1
Grass	×4	Rock	×0.5
Electric	×0	Ghost	×1
Ice	×1	Dragon	×1
Fighting	×1	Dark	×1
Poison	×0.5	Steel	×0.5
Ground	×1	Fairy	×1

Damage taken in Inverse battles

Type		Type	
Normal	×1	Flying	×1
Fire	×2	Psychic	×1
Water	×1	Bug	×1
Grass	×0.25	Rock	×2
Electric	×1	Ghost	×1
Ice	×1	Dragon	×1
Fighting	×1	Dark	×1
Poison	×2	Steel	×2
Ground	×1	Fairy	×1

Can be used in
Inverse Battle
Battle Institute
Battle Maison
Random Matchup (Free Battle)
Random Matchup (Others)

LEVEL-UP MOVES

Lv.	Name	Type	Kind	Pow.	Acc.	PP	Range
1	Bubble	Water	Special	40	100	30	Many Others
1	Growl	Normal	Status	—	100	40	Many Others
1	Supersonic	Normal	Status	—	55	20	Normal
1	Round	Normal	Special	60	100	15	Normal
5	Supersonic	Normal	Status	—	55	20	Normal
9	Round	Normal	Special	60	100	15	Normal
12	Bubble Beam	Water	Special	65	100	20	Normal
16	Mud Shot	Ground	Special	55	95	15	Normal
20	Aqua Ring	Water	Status	—	—	20	Self
23	Uproar	Normal	Special	90	100	10	1 Random
28	Muddy Water	Water	Special	90	85	10	Many Others
33	Rain Dance	Water	Status	—	—	5	Both Sides
36	Acid	Poison	Special	40	100	30	Many Others
39	Flail	Normal	Physical	—	100	15	Normal
44	Drain Punch	Fighting	Physical	75	100	10	Normal
49	Echoed Voice	Normal	Special	40	100	15	Normal
53	Hydro Pump	Water	Special	110	80	5	Normal
59	Hyper Voice	Normal	Special	90	100	10	Many Others

TM & HM MOVES

No.	Name	Type	Kind	Pow.	Acc.	PP	Range
TM06	Toxic	Poison	Status	—	90	10	Normal
TM07	Hail	Ice	Status	—	—	10	Both Sides
TM09	Venoshock	Poison	Special	65	100	10	Normal
TM10	Hidden Power	Normal	Special	60	100	15	Normal
TM15	Hyper Beam	Normal	Special	150	90	5	Normal
TM17	Protect	Normal	Status	—	—	10	Self
TM18	Rain Dance	Water	Status	—	—	5	Both Sides
TM21	Frustration	Normal	Physical	—	100	20	Normal
TM26	Earthquake	Ground	Physical	100	100	10	Adjacent
TM27	Return	Normal	Physical	—	100	20	Normal
TM28	Dig	Ground	Physical	80	100	10	Normal
TM31	Brick Break	Fighting	Physical	75	100	15	Normal
TM32	Double Team	Normal	Status	—	—	15	Self
TM34	Sludge Wave	Poison	Special	95	100	10	Adjacent
TM36	Sludge Bomb	Poison	Special	90	100	10	Normal
TM39	Rock Tomb	Rock	Physical	60	95	15	Normal
TM42	Facade	Normal	Physical	70	100	20	Normal
TM44	Rest	Psychic	Status	—	—	10	Self
TM45	Attract	Normal	Status	—	100	15	Normal
TM48	Round	Normal	Special	60	100	15	Normal
TM49	Echoed Voice	Normal	Special	40	100	15	Normal
TM52	Focus Blast	Fighting	Special	120	70	5	Normal
TM55	Scald	Water	Special	80	100	15	Normal
TM56	Fling	Dark	Physical	—	100	10	Normal
TM66	Payback	Dark	Physical	50	100	10	Normal
TM68	Giga Impact	Normal	Physical	150	90	5	Normal
TM78	Bulldoze	Ground	Physical	60	100	20	Adjacent
TM80	Rock Slide	Rock	Physical	75	90	10	Many Others
TM83	Infestation	Bug	Special	20	100	20	Normal
TM84	Poison Jab	Poison	Physical	80	100	20	Normal
TM86	Grass Knot	Grass	Special	—	100	20	Normal
TM87	Swagger	Normal	Status	—	90	15	Normal
TM88	Sleep Talk	Normal	Status	—	—	10	Self
TM90	Substitute	Normal	Status	—	—	10	Self
TM94	Secret Power	Normal	Physical	70	100	20	Normal
TM98	Power-Up Punch	Fighting	Physical	40	100	20	Normal
TM100	Confide	Normal	Status	—	—	20	Normal
HM03	Surf	Water	Special	90	100	15	Adjacent
HM04	Strength	Normal	Physical	80	100	15	Normal
HM06	Rock Smash	Fighting	Physical	40	100	15	Normal

MOVES LEARNED IN EXCHANGE FOR BP

Name	Type	Kind	Pow.	Acc.	PP	Range
Bounce	Flying	Physical	85	85	5	Normal
Low Kick	Fighting	Physical	—	100	20	Normal
Uproar	Normal	Special	90	100	10	1 Random
Ice Punch	Ice	Physical	75	100	15	Normal
Earth Power	Ground	Special	90	100	10	Normal
Icy Wind	Ice	Special	55	95	15	Many Others
Hyper Voice	Normal	Special	90	100	10	Many Others
Snore	Normal	Special	50	100	15	Normal
Knock Off	Dark	Physical	65	100	20	Normal
Drain Punch	Fighting	Physical	75	100	10	Normal
Focus Punch	Fighting	Physical	150	100	20	Normal
Water Pulse	Water	Special	60	100	20	Normal
Gastro Acid	Poison	Status	—	100	10	Normal
After You	Normal	Status	—	—	15	Normal
Endeavor	Normal	Physical	—	100	5	Normal
Stealth Rock	Rock	Status	—	—	20	Other Side

MOVES TAUGHT BY PEOPLE

Name	Type	Kind	Pow.	Acc.	PP	Range

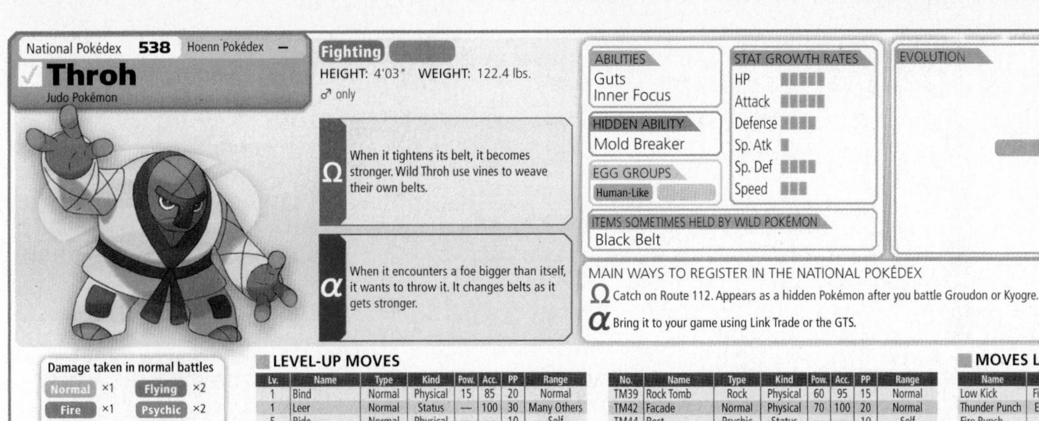

National Pokédex **538** Hoenn Pokédex —

Throh

Judo Pokémon

Fighting

HEIGHT: 4'03" WEIGHT: 122.4 lbs.

♂ only

Ω When it tightens its belt, it becomes stronger. Wild Throh use vines to weave their own belts.

α When it encounters a foe bigger than itself, it wants to throw it. It changes belts as it gets stronger.

ABILITIES
Guts
Inner Focus

HIDDEN ABILITY
Mold Breaker

EGG GROUPS
Human-Like

STAT GROWTH RATES
HP ■■■■■
Attack ■■■■■
Defense ■■■■
Sp. Atk ■
Sp. Def ■■■■
Speed ■■■

ITEMS SOMETIMES HELD BY WILD POKÉMON
Black Belt

EVOLUTION
Does not evolve

MAIN WAYS TO REGISTER IN THE NATIONAL POKÉDEX

Ω Catch on Route 112. Appears as a hidden Pokémon after you battle Groudon or Kyogre.

α Bring it to your game using Link Trade or the GTS.

Damage taken in normal battles

Type		Type	
Normal	×1	Flying	×2
Fire	×1	Psychic	×2
Water	×1	Bug	×0.5
Grass	×1	Rock	×0.5
Electric	×1	Ghost	×1
Ice	×1	Dragon	×1
Fighting	×1	Dark	×0.5
Poison	×1	Steel	×1
Ground	×1	Fairy	×2

Damage taken in Inverse battles

Type		Type	
Normal	×1	Flying	×0.5
Fire	×1	Psychic	×0.5
Water	×1	Bug	×2
Grass	×1	Rock	×2
Electric	×1	Ghost	×1
Ice	×1	Dragon	×1
Fighting	×1	Dark	×2
Poison	×1	Steel	×1
Ground	×1	Fairy	×0.5

Can be used in
Inverse Battle
Battle Institute
Battle Maison
Random Matchup (Free Battle)
Random Matchup (Others)

LEVEL-UP MOVES

Lv.	Name	Type	Kind	Pow.	Acc.	PP	Range
1	Bind	Normal	Physical	15	85	20	Normal
1	Leer	Normal	Status	—	100	30	Many Others
5	Bide	Normal	Physical	—	—	10	Self
9	Focus Energy	Normal	Status	—	—	30	Self
13	Seismic Toss	Fighting	Physical	—	100	20	Normal
17	Vital Throw	Fighting	Physical	70	—	10	Normal
21	Revenge	Fighting	Physical	60	100	10	Normal
25	Storm Throw	Fighting	Physical	60	100	10	Normal
29	Body Slam	Normal	Physical	85	100	15	Normal
33	Bulk Up	Fighting	Status	—	—	20	Self
37	Circle Throw	Fighting	Physical	60	90	10	Normal
41	Endure	Normal	Status	—	—	10	Self
45	Wide Guard	Rock	Status	—	—	10	Your Side
48	Superpower	Fighting	Physical	120	100	5	Normal
50	Reversal	Fighting	Physical	—	100	15	Normal

TM & HM MOVES

No.	Name	Type	Kind	Pow.	Acc.	PP	Range
TM06	Toxic	Poison	Status	—	90	10	Normal
TM08	Bulk Up	Fighting	Status	—	—	20	Self
TM10	Hidden Power	Normal	Special	60	100	15	Normal
TM11	Sunny Day	Fire	Status	—	—	5	Both Sides
TM12	Taunt	Dark	Status	—	100	20	Normal
TM17	Protect	Normal	Status	—	—	10	Self
TM18	Rain Dance	Water	Status	—	—	5	Both Sides
TM21	Frustration	Normal	Physical	—	100	20	Normal
TM26	Earthquake	Ground	Physical	100	100	10	Adjacent
TM27	Return	Normal	Physical	—	100	20	Normal
TM28	Dig	Ground	Physical	80	100	10	Normal
TM31	Brick Break	Fighting	Physical	75	100	15	Normal
TM32	Double Team	Normal	Status	—	—	15	Self
TM39	Rock Tomb	Rock	Physical	60	95	15	Normal
TM42	Facade	Normal	Physical	70	100	20	Normal
TM44	Rest	Psychic	Status	—	—	10	Self
TM45	Attract	Normal	Status	—	100	15	Normal
TM47	Low Sweep	Fighting	Physical	65	100	20	Normal
TM48	Round	Normal	Special	60	100	15	Normal
TM52	Focus Blast	Fighting	Special	120	70	5	Normal
TM56	Fling	Dark	Physical	—	100	10	Normal
TM66	Payback	Dark	Physical	50	100	10	Normal
TM67	Retaliate	Normal	Physical	70	100	5	Normal
TM68	Giga Impact	Normal	Physical	150	90	5	Normal
TM71	Stone Edge	Rock	Physical	100	80	5	Normal
TM78	Bulldoze	Ground	Physical	60	100	20	Adjacent
TM80	Rock Slide	Rock	Physical	75	90	10	Many Others
TM84	Poison Jab	Poison	Physical	80	100	20	Normal
TM86	Grass Knot	Grass	Special	—	100	20	Normal
TM87	Swagger	Normal	Status	—	90	15	Normal
TM88	Sleep Talk	Normal	Status	—	—	10	Self
TM90	Substitute	Normal	Status	—	—	10	Self
TM94	Secret Power	Normal	Physical	70	100	20	Normal
TM98	Power-Up Punch	Fighting	Physical	40	100	20	Normal
TM100	Confide	Normal	Status	—	—	20	Normal
HM04	Strength	Normal	Physical	80	100	15	Normal
HM06	Rock Smash	Fighting	Physical	40	100	15	Normal

MOVES LEARNED IN EXCHANGE FOR BP

Name	Type	Kind	Pow.	Acc.	PP	Range
Low Kick	Fighting	Physical	—	100	20	Normal
Thunder Punch	Electric	Physical	75	100	15	Normal
Fire Punch	Fire	Physical	75	100	15	Normal
Ice Punch	Ice	Physical	75	100	15	Normal
Block	Normal	Status	—	—	5	Normal
Superpower	Fighting	Physical	120	100	5	Normal
Zen Headbutt	Psychic	Physical	80	90	15	Normal
Bind	Normal	Physical	15	85	20	Normal
Snore	Normal	Special	50	100	15	Normal
Knock Off	Dark	Physical	65	100	20	Normal
Pain Split	Normal	Status	—	—	20	Normal
Focus Punch	Fighting	Physical	150	100	20	Normal
Helping Hand	Normal	Status	—	—	20	1 Ally

MOVES TAUGHT BY PEOPLE

Name	Type	Kind	Pow.	Acc.	PP	Range

National Pokédex **539** Hoenn Pokédex —

Sawk

Karate Pokémon

Fighting

HEIGHT: 4'07" WEIGHT: 112.4 lbs.

♂ only

Ω Desiring the strongest karate chop, they seclude themselves in mountains and train without sleeping.

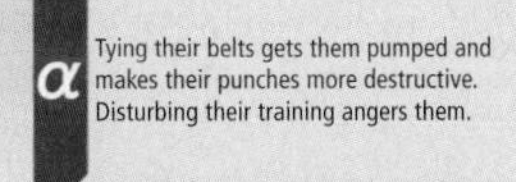

α Tying their belts gets them pumped and makes their punches more destructive. Disturbing their training angers them.

ABILITIES
Sturdy
Inner Focus

HIDDEN ABILITY
Mold Breaker

EGG GROUPS
Human-Like

STAT GROWTH RATES
HP ■■■
Attack ■■■■■■
Defense ■■■
Sp. Atk ■
Sp. Def ■■■
Speed ■■■■■

ITEMS SOMETIMES HELD BY WILD POKÉMON
Black Belt

EVOLUTION
Does not evolve

MAIN WAYS TO REGISTER IN THE NATIONAL POKÉDEX

Ω Bring it to your game using Link Trade or the GTS.

α Catch on Route 112. Appears as a hidden Pokémon after you battle Groudon or Kyogre.

Damage taken in normal battles

Type		Type	
Normal	×1	Flying	×2
Fire	×1	Psychic	×2
Water	×1	Bug	×0.5
Grass	×1	Rock	×0.5
Electric	×1	Ghost	×1
Ice	×1	Dragon	×1
Fighting	×1	Dark	×0.5
Poison	×1	Steel	×1
Ground	×1	Fairy	×2

Damage taken in Inverse battles

Type		Type	
Normal	×1	Flying	×0.5
Fire	×1	Psychic	×0.5
Water	×1	Bug	×2
Grass	×1	Rock	×2
Electric	×1	Ghost	×1
Ice	×1	Dragon	×1
Fighting	×1	Dark	×2
Poison	×1	Steel	×1
Ground	×1	Fairy	×0.5

Can be used in
Inverse Battle
Battle Institute
Battle Maison
Random Matchup (Free Battle)
Random Matchup (Others)

LEVEL-UP MOVES

Lv.	Name	Type	Kind	Pow.	Acc.	PP	Range
1	Rock Smash	Fighting	Physical	40	100	15	Normal
1	Leer	Normal	Status	—	100	30	Many Others
5	Bide	Normal	Physical	—	—	10	Self
9	Focus Energy	Normal	Status	—	—	30	Self
13	Double Kick	Fighting	Physical	30	100	30	Normal
17	Low Sweep	Fighting	Physical	65	100	20	Normal
21	Counter	Fighting	Physical	—	100	20	Varies
25	Karate Chop	Fighting	Physical	50	100	25	Normal
29	Brick Break	Fighting	Physical	75	100	15	Normal
33	Bulk Up	Fighting	Status	—	—	20	Self
37	Retaliate	Normal	Physical	70	100	5	Normal
41	Endure	Normal	Status	—	—	10	Self
45	Quick Guard	Fighting	Status	—	—	15	Your Side
48	Close Combat	Fighting	Physical	120	100	5	Normal
50	Reversal	Fighting	Physical	—	100	15	Normal

TM & HM MOVES

No.	Name	Type	Kind	Pow.	Acc.	PP	Range
TM06	Toxic	Poison	Status	—	90	10	Normal
TM08	Bulk Up	Fighting	Status	—	—	20	Self
TM10	Hidden Power	Normal	Special	60	100	15	Normal
TM11	Sunny Day	Fire	Status	—	—	5	Both Sides
TM12	Taunt	Dark	Status	—	100	20	Normal
TM17	Protect	Normal	Status	—	—	10	Self
TM18	Rain Dance	Water	Status	—	—	5	Both Sides
TM21	Frustration	Normal	Physical	—	100	20	Normal
TM26	Earthquake	Ground	Physical	100	100	10	Adjacent
TM27	Return	Normal	Physical	—	100	20	Normal
TM28	Dig	Ground	Physical	80	100	10	Normal
TM31	Brick Break	Fighting	Physical	75	100	15	Normal
TM32	Double Team	Normal	Status	—	—	15	Self
TM39	Rock Tomb	Rock	Physical	60	95	15	Normal
TM42	Facade	Normal	Physical	70	100	20	Normal
TM44	Rest	Psychic	Status	—	—	10	Self
TM45	Attract	Normal	Status	—	100	15	Normal
TM47	Low Sweep	Fighting	Physical	65	100	20	Normal
TM48	Round	Normal	Special	60	100	15	Normal
TM52	Focus Blast	Fighting	Special	120	70	5	Normal
TM56	Fling	Dark	Physical	—	100	10	Normal
TM66	Payback	Dark	Physical	50	100	10	Normal
TM67	Retaliate	Normal	Physical	70	100	5	Normal
TM68	Giga Impact	Normal	Physical	150	90	5	Normal
TM71	Stone Edge	Rock	Physical	100	80	5	Normal
TM78	Bulldoze	Ground	Physical	60	100	20	Adjacent
TM80	Rock Slide	Rock	Physical	75	90	10	Many Others
TM84	Poison Jab	Poison	Physical	80	100	20	Normal
TM86	Grass Knot	Grass	Special	—	100	20	Normal
TM87	Swagger	Normal	Status	—	90	15	Normal
TM88	Sleep Talk	Normal	Status	—	—	10	Self
TM90	Substitute	Normal	Status	—	—	10	Self
TM94	Secret Power	Normal	Physical	70	100	20	Normal
TM98	Power-Up Punch	Fighting	Physical	40	100	20	Normal
TM100	Confide	Normal	Status	—	—	20	Normal
HM04	Strength	Normal	Physical	80	100	15	Normal
HM06	Rock Smash	Fighting	Physical	40	100	15	Normal

MOVES LEARNED IN EXCHANGE FOR BP

Name	Type	Kind	Pow.	Acc.	PP	Range
Dual Chop	Dragon	Physical	40	90	15	Normal
Low Kick	Fighting	Physical	—	100	20	Normal
Thunder Punch	Electric	Physical	75	100	15	Normal
Fire Punch	Fire	Physical	75	100	15	Normal
Ice Punch	Ice	Physical	75	100	15	Normal
Block	Normal	Status	—	—	5	Normal
Superpower	Fighting	Physical	120	100	5	Normal
Zen Headbutt	Psychic	Physical	80	90	15	Normal
Snore	Normal	Special	50	100	15	Normal
Knock Off	Dark	Physical	65	100	20	Normal
Pain Split	Normal	Status	—	—	20	Normal
Focus Punch	Fighting	Physical	150	100	20	Normal
Helping Hand	Normal	Status	—	—	20	1 Ally

MOVES TAUGHT BY PEOPLE

Name	Type	Kind	Pow.	Acc.	PP	Range

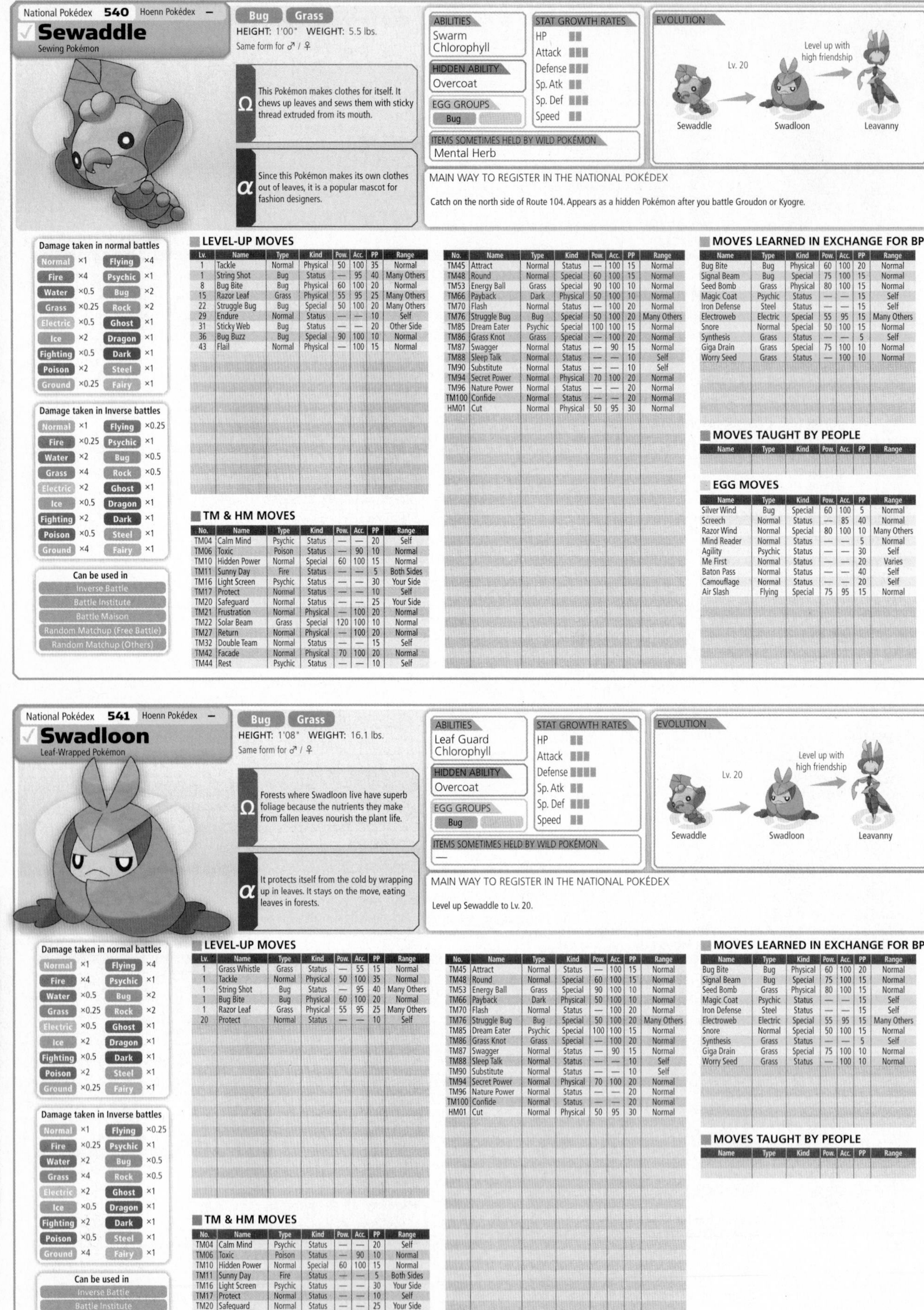

National Pokédex **540** Hoenn Pokédex —

Sewaddle

Sewing Pokémon

Bug / Grass

HEIGHT: 1'00" WEIGHT: 5.5 lbs.

Same form for ♂ / ♀

Ω This Pokémon makes clothes for itself. It chews up leaves and sews them with sticky thread extruded from its mouth.

α Since this Pokémon makes its own clothes out of leaves, it is a popular mascot for fashion designers.

ABILITIES
Swarm
Chlorophyll

HIDDEN ABILITY
Overcoat

EGG GROUPS
Bug

STAT GROWTH RATES
HP
Attack
Defense
Sp. Atk
Sp. Def
Speed

ITEMS SOMETIMES HELD BY WILD POKÉMON
Mental Herb

EVOLUTION
Sewaddle → Lv. 20 → Swadloon → Level up with high friendship → Leavanny

MAIN WAY TO REGISTER IN THE NATIONAL POKÉDEX

Catch on the north side of Route 104. Appears as a hidden Pokémon after you battle Groudon or Kyogre.

Damage taken in normal battles

Type		Type	
Normal	×1	Flying	×4
Fire	×4	Psychic	×1
Water	×0.5	Bug	×2
Grass	×0.25	Rock	×2
Electric	×0.5	Ghost	×1
Ice	×2	Dragon	×1
Fighting	×0.5	Dark	×1
Poison	×2	Steel	×1
Ground	×0.25	Fairy	×1

Damage taken in Inverse battles

Type		Type	
Normal	×1	Flying	×0.25
Fire	×0.25	Psychic	×1
Water	×2	Bug	×0.5
Grass	×4	Rock	×0.5
Electric	×2	Ghost	×1
Ice	×0.5	Dragon	×1
Fighting	×2	Dark	×1
Poison	×0.5	Steel	×1
Ground	×4	Fairy	×1

Can be used in
Inverse Battle
Battle Institute
Battle Maison
Random Matchup (Free Battle)
Random Matchup (Others)

LEVEL-UP MOVES

Lv.	Name	Type	Kind	Pow.	Acc.	PP	Range
1	Tackle	Normal	Physical	50	100	35	Normal
1	String Shot	Bug	Status	—	95	40	Many Others
8	Bug Bite	Bug	Physical	60	100	20	Normal
15	Razor Leaf	Grass	Physical	55	95	25	Many Others
22	Struggle Bug	Bug	Special	50	100	20	Many Others
29	Endure	Normal	Status	—	—	10	Self
31	Sticky Web	Bug	Status	—	—	20	Other Side
36	Bug Buzz	Bug	Special	90	100	10	Normal
43	Flail	Normal	Physical	—	100	15	Normal

TM & HM MOVES

No.	Name	Type	Kind	Pow.	Acc.	PP	Range
TM04	Calm Mind	Psychic	Status	—	—	20	Self
TM06	Toxic	Poison	Status	—	90	10	Normal
TM10	Hidden Power	Normal	Special	60	100	15	Normal
TM11	Sunny Day	Fire	Status	—	—	5	Both Sides
TM16	Light Screen	Psychic	Status	—	—	30	Your Side
TM17	Protect	Normal	Status	—	—	10	Self
TM20	Safeguard	Normal	Status	—	—	25	Your Side
TM21	Frustration	Normal	Physical	—	100	20	Normal
TM22	Solar Beam	Grass	Special	120	100	10	Normal
TM27	Return	Normal	Physical	—	100	20	Normal
TM32	Double Team	Normal	Status	—	—	15	Self
TM42	Facade	Normal	Physical	70	100	20	Normal
TM44	Rest	Psychic	Status	—	—	10	Self
TM45	Attract	Normal	Status	—	100	15	Normal
TM48	Round	Normal	Special	60	100	15	Normal
TM53	Energy Ball	Grass	Special	90	100	10	Normal
TM66	Payback	Dark	Physical	50	100	10	Normal
TM70	Flash	Normal	Status	—	100	20	Normal
TM76	Struggle Bug	Bug	Special	50	100	20	Many Others
TM85	Dream Eater	Psychic	Special	100	100	15	Normal
TM86	Grass Knot	Grass	Special	—	100	20	Normal
TM87	Swagger	Normal	Status	—	90	15	Normal
TM88	Sleep Talk	Normal	Status	—	—	10	Self
TM90	Substitute	Normal	Status	—	—	10	Self
TM94	Secret Power	Normal	Physical	70	100	20	Normal
TM96	Nature Power	Normal	Status	—	—	20	Normal
TM100	Confide	Normal	Status	—	—	20	Normal
HM01	Cut	Normal	Physical	50	95	30	Normal

MOVES LEARNED IN EXCHANGE FOR BP

Name	Type	Kind	Pow.	Acc.	PP	Range
Bug Bite	Bug	Physical	60	100	20	Normal
Signal Beam	Bug	Special	75	100	15	Normal
Seed Bomb	Grass	Physical	80	100	15	Normal
Magic Coat	Psychic	Status	—	—	15	Self
Iron Defense	Steel	Status	—	—	15	Self
Electroweb	Electric	Special	55	95	15	Many Others
Snore	Normal	Special	50	100	15	Normal
Synthesis	Grass	Status	—	—	5	Self
Giga Drain	Grass	Special	75	100	10	Normal
Worry Seed	Grass	Status	—	100	10	Normal

MOVES TAUGHT BY PEOPLE

Name	Type	Kind	Pow.	Acc.	PP	Range

EGG MOVES

Name	Type	Kind	Pow.	Acc.	PP	Range
Silver Wind	Bug	Special	60	100	5	Normal
Screech	Normal	Status	—	85	40	Normal
Razor Wind	Normal	Special	80	100	10	Many Others
Mind Reader	Normal	Status	—	—	5	Normal
Agility	Psychic	Status	—	—	30	Self
Me First	Normal	Status	—	—	20	Varies
Baton Pass	Normal	Status	—	—	40	Self
Camouflage	Normal	Status	—	—	20	Self
Air Slash	Flying	Special	75	95	15	Normal

National Pokédex **541** Hoenn Pokédex —

Swadloon

Leaf-Wrapped Pokémon

Bug / Grass

HEIGHT: 1'08" WEIGHT: 16.1 lbs.

Same form for ♂ / ♀

Ω Forests where Swadloon live have superb foliage because the nutrients they make from fallen leaves nourish the plant life.

α It protects itself from the cold by wrapping up in leaves. It stays on the move, eating leaves in forests.

ABILITIES
Leaf Guard
Chlorophyll

HIDDEN ABILITY
Overcoat

EGG GROUPS
Bug

STAT GROWTH RATES
HP
Attack
Defense
Sp. Atk
Sp. Def
Speed

ITEMS SOMETIMES HELD BY WILD POKÉMON
—

EVOLUTION
Sewaddle → Lv. 20 → Swadloon → Level up with high friendship → Leavanny

MAIN WAY TO REGISTER IN THE NATIONAL POKÉDEX

Level up Sewaddle to Lv. 20.

Damage taken in normal battles

Type		Type	
Normal	×1	Flying	×4
Fire	×4	Psychic	×1
Water	×0.5	Bug	×2
Grass	×0.25	Rock	×2
Electric	×0.5	Ghost	×1
Ice	×2	Dragon	×1
Fighting	×0.5	Dark	×1
Poison	×2	Steel	×1
Ground	×0.25	Fairy	×1

Damage taken in Inverse battles

Type		Type	
Normal	×1	Flying	×0.25
Fire	×0.25	Psychic	×1
Water	×2	Bug	×0.5
Grass	×4	Rock	×0.5
Electric	×2	Ghost	×1
Ice	×0.5	Dragon	×1
Fighting	×2	Dark	×1
Poison	×0.5	Steel	×1
Ground	×4	Fairy	×1

Can be used in
Inverse Battle
Battle Institute
Battle Maison
Random Matchup (Free Battle)
Random Matchup (Others)

LEVEL-UP MOVES

Lv.	Name	Type	Kind	Pow.	Acc.	PP	Range
1	Grass Whistle	Grass	Status	—	55	15	Normal
1	Tackle	Normal	Physical	50	100	35	Normal
1	String Shot	Bug	Status	—	95	40	Many Others
1	Bug Bite	Bug	Physical	60	100	20	Normal
1	Razor Leaf	Grass	Physical	55	95	25	Many Others
20	Protect	Normal	Status	—	—	10	Self

TM & HM MOVES

No.	Name	Type	Kind	Pow.	Acc.	PP	Range
TM04	Calm Mind	Psychic	Status	—	—	20	Self
TM06	Toxic	Poison	Status	—	90	10	Normal
TM10	Hidden Power	Normal	Special	60	100	15	Normal
TM11	Sunny Day	Fire	Status	—	—	5	Both Sides
TM16	Light Screen	Psychic	Status	—	—	30	Your Side
TM17	Protect	Normal	Status	—	—	10	Self
TM20	Safeguard	Normal	Status	—	—	25	Your Side
TM21	Frustration	Normal	Physical	—	100	20	Normal
TM22	Solar Beam	Grass	Special	120	100	10	Normal
TM27	Return	Normal	Physical	—	100	20	Normal
TM32	Double Team	Normal	Status	—	—	15	Self
TM42	Facade	Normal	Physical	70	100	20	Normal
TM44	Rest	Psychic	Status	—	—	10	Self
TM45	Attract	Normal	Status	—	100	15	Normal
TM48	Round	Normal	Special	60	100	15	Normal
TM53	Energy Ball	Grass	Special	90	100	10	Normal
TM66	Payback	Dark	Physical	50	100	10	Normal
TM70	Flash	Normal	Status	—	100	20	Normal
TM76	Struggle Bug	Bug	Special	50	100	20	Many Others
TM85	Dream Eater	Psychic	Special	100	100	15	Normal
TM86	Grass Knot	Grass	Special	—	100	20	Normal
TM87	Swagger	Normal	Status	—	90	15	Normal
TM88	Sleep Talk	Normal	Status	—	—	10	Self
TM90	Substitute	Normal	Status	—	—	10	Self
TM94	Secret Power	Normal	Physical	70	100	20	Normal
TM96	Nature Power	Normal	Status	—	—	20	Normal
TM100	Confide	Normal	Status	—	—	20	Normal
HM01	Cut	Normal	Physical	50	95	30	Normal

MOVES LEARNED IN EXCHANGE FOR BP

Name	Type	Kind	Pow.	Acc.	PP	Range
Bug Bite	Bug	Physical	60	100	20	Normal
Signal Beam	Bug	Special	75	100	15	Normal
Seed Bomb	Grass	Physical	80	100	15	Normal
Magic Coat	Psychic	Status	—	—	15	Self
Iron Defense	Steel	Status	—	—	15	Self
Electroweb	Electric	Special	55	95	15	Many Others
Snore	Normal	Special	50	100	15	Normal
Synthesis	Grass	Status	—	—	5	Self
Giga Drain	Grass	Special	75	100	10	Normal
Worry Seed	Grass	Status	—	100	10	Normal

MOVES TAUGHT BY PEOPLE

Name	Type	Kind	Pow.	Acc.	PP	Range

National Pokédex **542** Hoenn Pokédex —

Leavanny

Nurturing Pokémon

Bug **Grass**

HEIGHT: 3'11" WEIGHT: 45.2 lbs.

Same form for ♂ / ♀

Ω Upon finding a small Pokémon, it weaves clothing for it from leaves by using the sticky silk secreted from its mouth.

α It keeps its eggs warm with heat from fermenting leaves. It also uses leaves to make warm wrappings for Sewaddle.

ABILITIES

Swarm
Chlorophyll

HIDDEN ABILITY

Overcoat

EGG GROUPS

Bug

STAT GROWTH RATES

HP
Attack
Defense
Sp. Atk
Sp. Def
Speed

ITEMS SOMETIMES HELD BY WILD POKÉMON

—

EVOLUTION

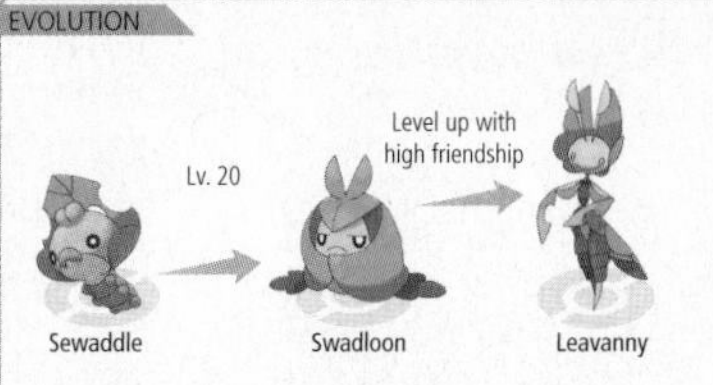

MAIN WAY TO REGISTER IN THE NATIONAL POKÉDEX

Level up Swadloon with high friendship.

Damage taken in normal battles

Type		Type	
Normal	×1	Flying	×4
Fire	×4	Psychic	×1
Water	×0.5	Bug	×2
Grass	×0.25	Rock	×2
Electric	×0.5	Ghost	×1
Ice	×2	Dragon	×1
Fighting	×0.5	Dark	×1
Poison	×2	Steel	×1
Ground	×0.25	Fairy	×1

Damage taken in Inverse battles

Type		Type	
Normal	×1	Flying	×0.25
Fire	×0.25	Psychic	×1
Water	×2	Bug	×0.5
Grass	×4	Rock	×0.5
Electric	×2	Ghost	×1
Ice	×0.5	Dragon	×1
Fighting	×2	Dark	×1
Poison	×0.5	Steel	×1
Ground	×4	Fairy	×1

Can be used in

Inverse Battle
Battle Institute
Battle Maison
Random Matchup (Free Battle)
Random Matchup (Others)

LEVEL-UP MOVES

Lv.	Name	Type	Kind	Pow.	Acc.	PP	Range
1	False Swipe	Normal	Physical	40	100	40	Normal
1	Tackle	Normal	Physical	50	100	35	Normal
1	String Shot	Bug	Status	—	95	40	Many Others
1	Bug Bite	Bug	Physical	60	100	20	Normal
1	Razor Leaf	Grass	Physical	55	95	25	Many Others
8	Bug Bite	Bug	Physical	60	100	20	Normal
15	Razor Leaf	Grass	Physical	55	95	25	Many Others
22	Struggle Bug	Bug	Special	50	100	20	Many Others
29	Slash	Normal	Physical	70	100	20	Normal
32	Helping Hand	Normal	Status	—	—	20	1 Ally
34	Fell Stinger	Bug	Physical	30	100	25	Normal
36	Leaf Blade	Grass	Physical	90	100	15	Normal
39	X-Scissor	Bug	Physical	80	100	15	Normal
43	Entrainment	Normal	Status	—	100	15	Normal
46	Swords Dance	Normal	Status	—	—	20	Self
50	Leaf Storm	Grass	Special	130	90	5	Normal

TM & HM MOVES

No.	Name	Type	Kind	Pow.	Acc.	PP	Range
TM01	Hone Claws	Dark	Status	—	—	15	Self
TM04	Calm Mind	Psychic	Status	—	—	20	Self
TM06	Toxic	Poison	Status	—	90	10	Normal
TM10	Hidden Power	Normal	Special	60	100	15	Normal
TM11	Sunny Day	Fire	Status	—	—	5	Both Sides
TM15	Hyper Beam	Normal	Special	150	90	5	Normal
TM16	Light Screen	Psychic	Status	—	—	30	Your Side
TM17	Protect	Normal	Status	—	—	10	Self
TM20	Safeguard	Normal	Status	—	—	25	Your Side
TM21	Frustration	Normal	Physical	—	100	20	Normal
TM22	Solar Beam	Grass	Special	120	100	10	Normal
TM27	Return	Normal	Physical	—	100	20	Normal
TM32	Double Team	Normal	Status	—	—	15	Self
TM33	Reflect	Psychic	Status	—	—	20	Your Side
TM40	Aerial Ace	Flying	Physical	60	—	20	Normal
TM42	Facade	Normal	Physical	70	100	20	Normal
TM44	Rest	Psychic	Status	—	—	10	Self
TM45	Attract	Normal	Status	—	100	15	Normal
TM48	Round	Normal	Special	60	100	15	Normal
TM51	Steel Wing	Steel	Physical	70	90	25	Normal
TM53	Energy Ball	Grass	Special	90	100	10	Normal
TM54	False Swipe	Normal	Physical	40	100	40	Normal
TM65	Shadow Claw	Ghost	Physical	70	100	15	Normal
TM66	Payback	Dark	Physical	50	100	10	Normal
TM67	Retaliate	Normal	Physical	70	100	5	Normal
TM68	Giga Impact	Normal	Physical	150	90	5	Normal
TM70	Flash	Normal	Status	—	100	20	Normal
TM75	Swords Dance	Normal	Status	—	—	20	Self
TM76	Struggle Bug	Bug	Special	50	100	20	Many Others
TM81	X-Scissor	Bug	Physical	80	100	15	Normal
TM84	Poison Jab	Poison	Physical	80	100	20	Normal
TM85	Dream Eater	Psychic	Special	100	100	15	Normal
TM86	Grass Knot	Grass	Special	—	100	20	Normal
TM87	Swagger	Normal	Status	—	90	15	Normal
TM88	Sleep Talk	Normal	Status	—	—	10	Self
TM90	Substitute	Normal	Status	—	—	10	Self
TM94	Secret Power	Normal	Physical	70	100	20	Normal
TM96	Nature Power	Normal	Status	—	—	20	Normal
TM100	Confide	Normal	Status	—	—	20	Normal
HM01	Cut	Normal	Physical	50	95	30	Normal

MOVES LEARNED IN EXCHANGE FOR BP

Name	Type	Kind	Pow.	Acc.	PP	Range
Bug Bite	Bug	Physical	60	100	20	Normal
Signal Beam	Bug	Special	75	100	15	Normal
Seed Bomb	Grass	Physical	80	100	15	Normal
Magic Coat	Psychic	Status	—	—	15	Self
Iron Defense	Steel	Status	—	—	15	Self
Electroweb	Electric	Special	55	95	15	Many Others
Snore	Normal	Special	50	100	15	Normal
Knock Off	Dark	Physical	65	100	20	Normal
Synthesis	Grass	Status	—	—	5	Self
Heal Bell	Normal	Status	—	—	5	Your Party
Giga Drain	Grass	Special	75	100	10	Normal
Worry Seed	Grass	Status	—	100	10	Normal
Helping Hand	Normal	Status	—	—	20	1 Ally

MOVES TAUGHT BY PEOPLE

Name	Type	Kind	Pow.	Acc.	PP	Range

National Pokédex **543** Hoenn Pokédex —

Venipede

Centipede Pokémon

Bug **Poison**

HEIGHT: 1'04" WEIGHT: 11.7 lbs.

Same form for ♂ / ♀

Ω It discovers what is going on around it by using the feelers on its head and tail. It is brutally aggressive.

α Its bite injects a potent poison, enough to paralyze large bird Pokémon that try to prey on it.

ABILITIES

Poison Point
Swarm

HIDDEN ABILITY

Speed Boost

EGG GROUPS

Bug

STAT GROWTH RATES

HP
Attack
Defense
Sp. Atk
Sp. Def
Speed

ITEMS SOMETIMES HELD BY WILD POKÉMON

—

EVOLUTION

Lv. 22
Lv. 30
Venipede
Whirlipede
Scolipede

MAIN WAY TO REGISTER IN THE NATIONAL POKÉDEX

Appears in *Pokémon X* and *Pokémon Y.* Bring it to your game using Link Trade or the GTS.

Damage taken in normal battles

Type		Type	
Normal	×1	Flying	×2
Fire	×2	Psychic	×2
Water	×1	Bug	×0.5
Grass	×0.25	Rock	×2
Electric	×1	Ghost	×1
Ice	×1	Dragon	×1
Fighting	×0.25	Dark	×1
Poison	×0.5	Steel	×1
Ground	×1	Fairy	×0.5

Damage taken in Inverse battles

Type		Type	
Normal	×1	Flying	×0.5
Fire	×0.5	Psychic	×0.5
Water	×1	Bug	×2
Grass	×4	Rock	×0.5
Electric	×1	Ghost	×1
Ice	×1	Dragon	×1
Fighting	×4	Dark	×1
Poison	×2	Steel	×1
Ground	×1	Fairy	×2

Can be used in

Inverse Battle
Battle Institute
Battle Maison
Random Matchup (Free Battle)
Random Matchup (Others)

LEVEL-UP MOVES

Lv.	Name	Type	Kind	Pow.	Acc.	PP	Range
1	Defense Curl	Normal	Status	—	—	40	Self
1	Rollout	Rock	Physical	30	90	20	Normal
5	Poison Sting	Poison	Physical	15	100	35	Normal
8	Screech	Normal	Status	—	85	40	Normal
12	Pursuit	Dark	Physical	40	100	20	Normal
15	Protect	Normal	Status	—	—	10	Self
19	Poison Tail	Poison	Physical	50	100	25	Normal
22	Bug Bite	Bug	Physical	60	100	20	Normal
26	Venoshock	Poison	Special	65	100	10	Normal
29	Agility	Psychic	Status	—	—	30	Self
33	Steamroller	Bug	Physical	65	100	20	Normal
36	Toxic	Poison	Status	—	90	10	Normal
38	Venoshock	Poison	Special	65	100	10	Normal
40	Rock Climb	Normal	Physical	90	85	20	Normal
43	Double-Edge	Normal	Physical	120	100	15	Normal

TM & HM MOVES

No.	Name	Type	Kind	Pow.	Acc.	PP	Range
TM06	Toxic	Poison	Status	—	90	10	Normal
TM09	Venoshock	Poison	Special	65	100	10	Normal
TM10	Hidden Power	Normal	Special	60	100	15	Normal
TM11	Sunny Day	Fire	Status	—	—	5	Both Sides
TM17	Protect	Normal	Status	—	—	10	Self
TM21	Frustration	Normal	Physical	—	100	20	Normal
TM22	Solar Beam	Grass	Special	120	100	10	Normal
TM27	Return	Normal	Physical	—	100	20	Normal
TM32	Double Team	Normal	Status	—	—	15	Self
TM36	Sludge Bomb	Poison	Special	90	100	10	Normal
TM42	Facade	Normal	Physical	70	100	20	Normal
TM44	Rest	Psychic	Status	—	—	10	Self
TM45	Attract	Normal	Status	—	100	15	Normal
TM48	Round	Normal	Special	60	100	15	Normal
TM66	Payback	Dark	Physical	50	100	10	Normal
TM74	Gyro Ball	Steel	Physical	—	100	5	Normal
TM76	Struggle Bug	Bug	Special	50	100	20	Many Others
TM83	Infestation	Bug	Special	20	100	20	Normal
TM84	Poison Jab	Poison	Physical	80	100	20	Normal
TM87	Swagger	Normal	Status	—	90	15	Normal
TM88	Sleep Talk	Normal	Status	—	—	10	Self
TM90	Substitute	Normal	Status	—	—	10	Self
TM94	Secret Power	Normal	Physical	70	100	20	Normal
TM100	Confide	Normal	Status	—	—	20	Normal
HM06	Rock Smash	Fighting	Physical	40	100	15	Normal

MOVES LEARNED IN EXCHANGE FOR BP

Name	Type	Kind	Pow.	Acc.	PP	Range
Bug Bite	Bug	Physical	60	100	20	Normal
Signal Beam	Bug	Special	75	100	15	Normal
Iron Defense	Steel	Status	—	—	15	Self
Snore	Normal	Special	50	100	15	Normal
Endeavor	Normal	Physical	—	100	5	Normal

MOVES TAUGHT BY PEOPLE

Name	Type	Kind	Pow.	Acc.	PP	Range

EGG MOVES

Name	Type	Kind	Pow.	Acc.	PP	Range
Twineedle	Bug	Physical	25	100	20	Normal
Pin Missile	Bug	Physical	25	95	20	Normal
Toxic Spikes	Poison	Status	—	—	20	Other Side
Spikes	Ground	Status	—	—	20	Other Side
Take Down	Normal	Physical	90	85	20	Normal
Rock Climb	Normal	Physical	90	85	20	Normal

National Pokédex **544** Hoenn Pokédex —

Whirlipede

Curlipede Pokémon

Bug Poison

HEIGHT: 3'11" WEIGHT: 129 lbs.

Same form for ♂ / ♀

Ω Protected by a hard shell, it spins its body like a wheel and crashes furiously into its enemies.

α It is usually motionless, but when attacked, it rotates at high speed and then crashes into its opponent.

ABILITIES
Poison Point
Swarm

HIDDEN ABILITY
Speed Boost

EGG GROUPS
Bug

STAT GROWTH RATES
HP ■■
Attack ■■■
Defense ■■■■
Sp. Atk ■■
Sp. Def ■■■
Speed ■■■

ITEMS SOMETIMES HELD BY WILD POKÉMON
—

EVOLUTION

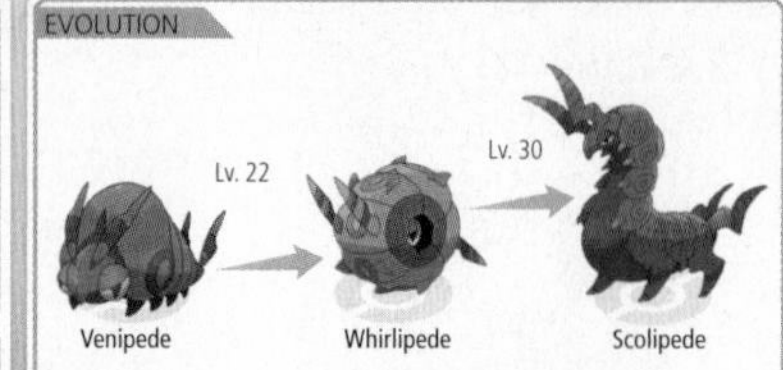

MAIN WAY TO REGISTER IN THE NATIONAL POKÉDEX

Level up a Venipede obtained via Link Trade or the GTS to Lv. 22.

Damage taken in normal battles

Type		Type	
Normal	×1	Flying	×2
Fire	×2	Psychic	×2
Water	×1	Bug	×0.5
Grass	×0.25	Rock	×2
Electric	×1	Ghost	×1
Ice	×1	Dragon	×1
Fighting	×0.25	Dark	×1
Poison	×0.5	Steel	×1
Ground	×1	Fairy	×0.5

Damage taken in Inverse battles

Type		Type	
Normal	×1	Flying	×0.5
Fire	×0.5	Psychic	×0.5
Water	×1	Bug	×2
Grass	×4	Rock	×0.5
Electric	×1	Ghost	×1
Ice	×1	Dragon	×1
Fighting	×4	Dark	×1
Poison	×2	Steel	×1
Ground	×1	Fairy	×2

Can be used in
Inverse Battle
Battle Institute
Battle Maison
Random Matchup (Free Battle)
Random Matchup (Others)

LEVEL-UP MOVES

Lv.	Name	Type	Kind	Pow.	Acc.	PP	Range
1	Defense Curl	Normal	Status	—	—	40	Self
1	Rollout	Rock	Physical	30	90	20	Normal
1	Poison Sting	Poison	Physical	15	100	35	Normal
1	Screech	Normal	Status	—	85	40	Normal
5	Poison Sting	Poison	Physical	15	100	35	Normal
8	Screech	Normal	Status	—	85	40	Normal
12	Pursuit	Dark	Physical	40	100	20	Normal
15	Protect	Normal	Status	—	—	10	Self
19	Poison Tail	Poison	Physical	50	100	25	Normal
22	Iron Defense	Steel	Status	—	—	15	Self
23	Bug Bite	Bug	Physical	60	100	20	Normal
28	Venoshock	Poison	Special	65	100	10	Normal
32	Agility	Psychic	Status	—	—	30	Self
37	Steamroller	Bug	Physical	65	100	20	Normal
41	Toxic	Poison	Status	—	90	10	Normal
43	Venom Drench	Poison	Status	—	100	20	Many Others
46	Rock Climb	Normal	Physical	90	85	20	Normal
50	Double-Edge	Normal	Physical	120	100	15	Normal

TM & HM MOVES

No.	Name	Type	Kind	Pow.	Acc.	PP	Range
TM06	Toxic	Poison	Status	—	90	10	Normal
TM09	Venoshock	Poison	Special	65	100	10	Normal
TM10	Hidden Power	Normal	Special	60	100	15	Normal
TM11	Sunny Day	Fire	Status	—	—	5	Both Sides
TM17	Protect	Normal	Status	—	—	10	Self
TM21	Frustration	Normal	Physical	—	100	20	Normal
TM22	Solar Beam	Grass	Special	120	100	10	Normal
TM27	Return	Normal	Physical	—	100	20	Normal
TM32	Double Team	Normal	Status	—	—	15	Self
TM36	Sludge Bomb	Poison	Special	90	100	10	Normal
TM42	Facade	Normal	Physical	70	100	20	Normal
TM44	Rest	Psychic	Status	—	—	10	Self
TM45	Attract	Normal	Status	—	100	15	Normal
TM48	Round	Normal	Special	60	100	15	Normal
TM66	Payback	Dark	Physical	50	100	10	Normal
TM74	Gyro Ball	Steel	Physical	—	100	5	Normal
TM76	Struggle Bug	Bug	Special	50	100	20	Many Others
TM83	Infestation	Bug	Special	20	100	20	Normal
TM84	Poison Jab	Poison	Physical	80	100	20	Normal
TM87	Swagger	Normal	Status	—	90	15	Normal
TM88	Sleep Talk	Normal	Status	—	—	10	Self
TM90	Substitute	Normal	Status	—	—	10	Self
TM94	Secret Power	Normal	Physical	70	100	20	Normal
TM100	Confide	Normal	Status	—	—	20	Normal
HM06	Rock Smash	Fighting	Physical	40	100	15	Normal

MOVES LEARNED IN EXCHANGE FOR BP

Name	Type	Kind	Pow.	Acc.	PP	Range
Bug Bite	Bug	Physical	60	100	20	Normal
Signal Beam	Bug	Special	75	100	15	Normal
Iron Defense	Steel	Status	—	—	15	Self
Snore	Normal	Special	50	100	15	Normal
Endeavor	Normal	Physical	—	100	5	Normal

MOVES TAUGHT BY PEOPLE

Name	Type	Kind	Pow.	Acc.	PP	Range

National Pokédex **545** Hoenn Pokédex —

Scolipede

Megapede Pokémon

Bug Poison

HEIGHT: 8'02" WEIGHT: 442 lbs.

Same form for ♂ / ♀

Ω It clasps its prey with the claws on its neck until it stops moving. Then it finishes it off with deadly poison.

α With quick movements, it chases down its foes, attacking relentlessly with its horns until it prevails.

ABILITIES
Poison Point
Swarm

HIDDEN ABILITY
Speed Boost

EGG GROUPS
Bug

STAT GROWTH RATES
HP ■■■
Attack ■■■■■
Defense ■■■■
Sp. Atk ■■■
Sp. Def ■■■
Speed ■■■■■■

ITEMS SOMETIMES HELD BY WILD POKÉMON
—

EVOLUTION

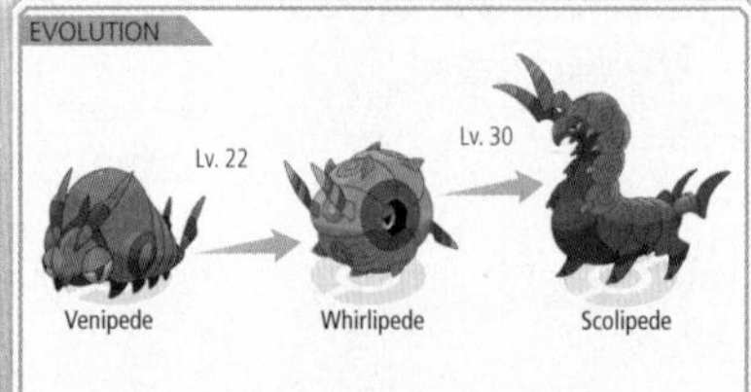

MAIN WAY TO REGISTER IN THE NATIONAL POKÉDEX

Level up a Whirlipede obtained via Link Trade or the GTS to Lv. 30.

Damage taken in normal battles

Type		Type	
Normal	×1	Flying	×2
Fire	×2	Psychic	×2
Water	×1	Bug	×0.5
Grass	×0.25	Rock	×2
Electric	×1	Ghost	×1
Ice	×1	Dragon	×1
Fighting	×0.25	Dark	×1
Poison	×0.5	Steel	×1
Ground	×1	Fairy	×0.5

Damage taken in Inverse battles

Type		Type	
Normal	×1	Flying	×0.5
Fire	×0.5	Psychic	×0.5
Water	×1	Bug	×2
Grass	×4	Rock	×0.5
Electric	×1	Ghost	×1
Ice	×1	Dragon	×1
Fighting	×4	Dark	×1
Poison	×2	Steel	×1
Ground	×1	Fairy	×2

Can be used in
Inverse Battle
Battle Institute
Battle Maison
Random Matchup (Free Battle)
Random Matchup (Others)

LEVEL-UP MOVES

Lv.	Name	Type	Kind	Pow.	Acc.	PP	Range
1	Megahorn	Bug	Physical	120	85	10	Normal
1	Defense Curl	Normal	Status	—	—	40	Self
1	Rollout	Rock	Physical	30	90	20	Normal
1	Poison Sting	Poison	Physical	15	100	35	Normal
1	Screech	Normal	Status	—	85	40	Normal
5	Poison Sting	Poison	Physical	15	100	35	Normal
8	Screech	Normal	Status	—	85	40	Normal
12	Pursuit	Dark	Physical	40	100	20	Normal
15	Protect	Normal	Status	—	—	10	Self
19	Poison Tail	Poison	Physical	50	100	25	Normal
23	Bug Bite	Bug	Physical	60	100	20	Normal
28	Venoshock	Poison	Special	65	100	10	Normal
30	Baton Pass	Normal	Status	—	—	40	Self
33	Agility	Psychic	Status	—	—	30	Self
39	Steamroller	Bug	Physical	65	100	20	Normal
44	Toxic	Poison	Status	—	90	10	Normal
47	Venom Drench	Poison	Status	—	100	20	Many Others
50	Rock Climb	Normal	Physical	90	85	20	Normal
55	Double-Edge	Normal	Physical	120	100	15	Normal
65	Megahorn	Bug	Physical	120	85	10	Normal

TM & HM MOVES

No.	Name	Type	Kind	Pow.	Acc.	PP	Range
TM06	Toxic	Poison	Status	—	90	10	Normal
TM09	Venoshock	Poison	Special	65	100	10	Normal
TM10	Hidden Power	Normal	Special	60	100	15	Normal
TM11	Sunny Day	Fire	Status	—	—	5	Both Sides
TM15	Hyper Beam	Normal	Special	150	90	5	Normal
TM17	Protect	Normal	Status	—	—	10	Self
TM21	Frustration	Normal	Physical	—	100	20	Normal
TM22	Solar Beam	Grass	Special	120	100	10	Normal
TM26	Earthquake	Ground	Physical	100	100	10	Adjacent
TM27	Return	Normal	Physical	—	100	20	Normal
TM28	Dig	Ground	Physical	80	100	10	Normal
TM32	Double Team	Normal	Status	—	—	15	Self
TM36	Sludge Bomb	Poison	Special	90	100	10	Normal
TM39	Rock Tomb	Rock	Physical	60	95	15	Normal
TM42	Facade	Normal	Physical	70	100	20	Normal
TM44	Rest	Psychic	Status	—	—	10	Self
TM45	Attract	Normal	Status	—	100	15	Normal
TM48	Round	Normal	Special	60	100	15	Normal
TM66	Payback	Dark	Physical	50	100	10	Normal
TM68	Giga Impact	Normal	Physical	150	90	5	Normal
TM74	Gyro Ball	Steel	Physical	—	100	5	Normal
TM75	Swords Dance	Normal	Status	—	—	20	Self
TM76	Struggle Bug	Bug	Special	50	100	20	Many Others
TM78	Bulldoze	Ground	Physical	60	100	20	Adjacent
TM80	Rock Slide	Rock	Physical	75	90	10	Many Others
TM81	X-Scissor	Bug	Physical	80	100	15	Normal
TM83	Infestation	Bug	Special	20	100	20	Normal
TM84	Poison Jab	Poison	Physical	80	100	20	Normal
TM87	Swagger	Normal	Status	—	90	15	Normal
TM88	Sleep Talk	Normal	Status	—	—	10	Self
TM90	Substitute	Normal	Status	—	—	10	Self
TM94	Secret Power	Normal	Physical	70	100	20	Normal
TM100	Confide	Normal	Status	—	—	20	Normal
HM01	Cut	Normal	Physical	50	95	30	Normal
HM04	Strength	Normal	Physical	80	100	15	Normal
HM06	Rock Smash	Fighting	Physical	40	100	15	Normal

MOVES LEARNED IN EXCHANGE FOR BP

Name	Type	Kind	Pow.	Acc.	PP	Range
Bug Bite	Bug	Physical	60	100	20	Normal
Signal Beam	Bug	Special	75	100	15	Normal
Iron Defense	Steel	Status	—	—	15	Self
Superpower	Fighting	Physical	120	100	5	Normal
Aqua Tail	Water	Physical	90	90	10	Normal
Iron Tail	Steel	Physical	100	75	15	Normal
Snore	Normal	Special	50	100	15	Normal
Endeavor	Normal	Physical	—	100	5	Normal
Snatch	Dark	Status	—	—	10	Self

MOVES TAUGHT BY PEOPLE

Name	Type	Kind	Pow.	Acc.	PP	Range

National Pokédex **546** Hoenn Pokédex —

Cottonee

Cotton Puff Pokémon

Grass Fairy

HEIGHT: 1'00" WEIGHT: 1.3 lbs.

Same form for ♂ / ♀

Ω When attacked, it escapes by shooting cotton from its body. The cotton serves as a decoy to distract the attacker.

α Perhaps because they feel more at ease in a group, they stick to others they find. They end up looking like a cloud.

ABILITIES
Prankster
Infiltrator

HIDDEN ABILITY
Chlorophyll

EGG GROUPS
Grass / Fairy

STAT GROWTH RATES
HP ▮▮
Attack ▮▮
Defense ▮▮▮
Sp. Atk ▮▮
Sp. Def ▮▮
Speed ▮▮▮▮

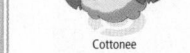

ITEMS SOMETIMES HELD BY WILD POKÉMON
—

EVOLUTION
Cottonee → (Sun Stone) → Whimsicott

MAIN WAY TO REGISTER IN THE NATIONAL POKÉDEX

Catch in Petalburg Woods. Appears as a hidden Pokémon after you battle Groudon or Kyogre.

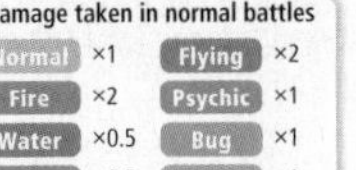

Damage taken in normal battles

Normal	×1	Flying	×2
Fire	×2	Psychic	×1
Water	×0.5	Bug	×1
Grass	×0.5	Rock	×1
Electric	×0.5	Ghost	×1
Ice	×2	Dragon	×0
Fighting	×0.5	Dark	×0.5
Poison	×4	Steel	×2
Ground	×0.5	Fairy	×1

Damage taken in Inverse battles

Normal	×1	Flying	×0.5
Fire	×0.5	Psychic	×1
Water	×2	Bug	×1
Grass	×2	Rock	×1
Electric	×2	Ghost	×1
Ice	×0.5	Dragon	×2
Fighting	×2	Dark	×2
Poison	×0.25	Steel	×0.5
Ground	×2	Fairy	×1

Can be used in
Inverse Battle
Battle Institute
Battle Maison
Random Matchup (Free Battle)
Random Matchup (Others)

LEVEL-UP MOVES

Lv.	Name	Type	Kind	Pow.	Acc.	PP	Range
1	Absorb	Grass	Special	20	100	25	Normal
1	Fairy Wind	Fairy	Special	40	100	30	Normal
4	Growth	Normal	Status	—	—	20	Self
8	Leech Seed	Grass	Status	—	90	10	Normal
10	Stun Spore	Grass	Status	—	75	30	Normal
13	Mega Drain	Grass	Special	40	100	15	Normal
17	Cotton Spore	Grass	Status	—	100	40	Many Others
19	Razor Leaf	Grass	Physical	55	95	25	Many Others
22	Poison Powder	Poison	Status	—	75	35	Normal
26	Giga Drain	Grass	Special	75	100	10	Normal
28	Charm	Fairy	Status	—	100	20	Normal
31	Helping Hand	Normal	Status	—	—	20	1 Ally
35	Energy Ball	Grass	Special	90	100	10	Normal
37	Cotton Guard	Grass	Status	—	—	10	Self
40	Sunny Day	Fire	Status	—	—	5	Both Sides
44	Endeavor	Normal	Physical	—	100	5	Normal
46	Solar Beam	Grass	Special	120	100	10	Normal

TM & HM MOVES

No.	Name	Type	Kind	Pow.	Acc.	PP	Range
TM06	Toxic	Poison	Status	—	90	10	Normal
TM10	Hidden Power	Normal	Special	60	100	15	Normal
TM11	Sunny Day	Fire	Status	—	—	5	Both Sides
TM12	Taunt	Dark	Status	—	100	20	Normal
TM17	Protect	Normal	Status	—	—	10	Self
TM20	Safeguard	Normal	Status	—	—	25	Your Side
TM21	Frustration	Normal	Physical	—	100	20	Normal
TM22	Solar Beam	Grass	Special	120	100	10	Normal
TM27	Return	Normal	Physical	—	100	20	Normal
TM32	Double Team	Normal	Status	—	—	15	Self
TM42	Facade	Normal	Physical	70	100	20	Normal
TM44	Rest	Psychic	Status	—	—	10	Self
TM45	Attract	Normal	Status	—	100	15	Normal
TM48	Round	Normal	Special	60	100	15	Normal
TM53	Energy Ball	Grass	Special	90	100	10	Normal
TM70	Flash	Normal	Status	—	100	20	Normal
TM85	Dream Eater	Psychic	Special	100	100	15	Normal
TM86	Grass Knot	Grass	Special	—	100	20	Normal
TM87	Swagger	Normal	Status	—	90	15	Normal
TM88	Sleep Talk	Normal	Status	—	—	10	Self
TM90	Substitute	Normal	Status	—	—	10	Self
TM94	Secret Power	Normal	Physical	70	100	20	Normal
TM96	Nature Power	Normal	Status	—	—	20	Normal
TM99	Dazzling Gleam	Fairy	Special	80	100	10	Many Others
TM100	Confide	Normal	Status	—	—	20	Normal

MOVES LEARNED IN EXCHANGE FOR BP

Name	Type	Kind	Pow.	Acc.	PP	Range
Covet	Normal	Physical	60	100	25	Normal
Seed Bomb	Grass	Physical	80	100	15	Normal
Snore	Normal	Special	50	100	15	Normal
Knock Off	Dark	Physical	65	100	20	Normal
Tailwind	Flying	Status	—	—	15	Your Side
Giga Drain	Grass	Special	75	100	10	Normal
Worry Seed	Grass	Status	—	100	10	Normal
Helping Hand	Normal	Status	—	—	20	1 Ally
Endeavor	Normal	Physical	—	100	5	Normal

MOVES TAUGHT BY PEOPLE

Name	Type	Kind	Pow.	Acc.	PP	Range

EGG MOVES

Name	Type	Kind	Pow.	Acc.	PP	Range
Natural Gift	Normal	Physical	—	100	15	Normal
Encore	Normal	Status	—	100	5	Normal
Tickle	Normal	Status	—	100	20	Normal
Fake Tears	Dark	Status	—	100	20	Normal
Grass Whistle	Grass	Status	—	55	15	Normal
Memento	Dark	Status	—	100	10	Normal
Beat Up	Dark	Physical	—	100	10	Normal
Switcheroo	Dark	Status	—	100	10	Normal
Worry Seed	Grass	Status	—	100	10	Normal
Captivate	Normal	Status	—	100	20	Many Others

National Pokédex **547** Hoenn Pokédex —

Whimsicott

Windveiled Pokémon

Grass Fairy

HEIGHT: 2'04" WEIGHT: 14.6 lbs.

Same form for ♂ / ♀

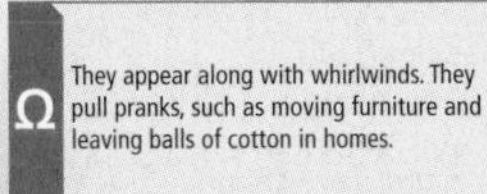

Ω They appear along with whirlwinds. They pull pranks, such as moving furniture and leaving balls of cotton in homes.

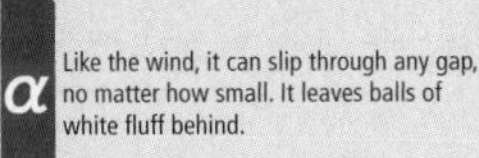

α Like the wind, it can slip through any gap, no matter how small. It leaves balls of white fluff behind.

ABILITIES
Prankster
Infiltrator

HIDDEN ABILITY
Chlorophyll

EGG GROUPS
Grass / Fairy

STAT GROWTH RATES
HP ▮▮▮
Attack ▮▮▮▮
Defense ▮▮▮▮
Sp. Atk ▮▮▮▮
Sp. Def ▮▮▮
Speed ▮▮▮▮▮▮

ITEMS SOMETIMES HELD BY WILD POKÉMON
—

EVOLUTION
Cottonee → (Sun Stone) → Whimsicott

MAIN WAY TO REGISTER IN THE NATIONAL POKÉDEX

Use a Sun Stone on Cottonee.

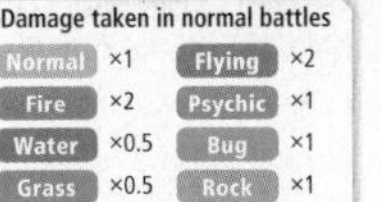

Damage taken in normal battles

Normal	×1	Flying	×2
Fire	×2	Psychic	×1
Water	×0.5	Bug	×1
Grass	×0.5	Rock	×1
Electric	×0.5	Ghost	×1
Ice	×2	Dragon	×0
Fighting	×0.5	Dark	×0.5
Poison	×4	Steel	×2
Ground	×0.5	Fairy	×1

Damage taken in Inverse battles

Normal	×1	Flying	×0.5
Fire	×0.5	Psychic	×1
Water	×2	Bug	×1
Grass	×2	Rock	×1
Electric	×2	Ghost	×1
Ice	×0.5	Dragon	×2
Fighting	×2	Dark	×2
Poison	×0.25	Steel	×0.5
Ground	×2	Fairy	×1

Can be used in
Inverse Battle
Battle Institute
Battle Maison
Random Matchup (Free Battle)
Random Matchup (Others)

LEVEL-UP MOVES

Lv.	Name	Type	Kind	Pow.	Acc.	PP	Range
1	Growth	Normal	Status	—	—	20	Self
1	Leech Seed	Grass	Status	—	90	10	Normal
1	Mega Drain	Grass	Special	40	100	15	Normal
1	Cotton Spore	Grass	Status	—	100	40	Many Others
10	Gust	Flying	Special	40	100	35	Normal
28	Tailwind	Flying	Status	—	—	15	Your Side
46	Hurricane	Flying	Special	110	70	10	Normal
50	Moonblast	Fairy	Special	95	100	15	Normal

TM & HM MOVES

No.	Name	Type	Kind	Pow.	Acc.	PP	Range
TM06	Toxic	Poison	Status	—	90	10	Normal
TM10	Hidden Power	Normal	Special	60	100	15	Normal
TM11	Sunny Day	Fire	Status	—	—	5	Both Sides
TM12	Taunt	Dark	Status	—	100	20	Normal
TM15	Hyper Beam	Normal	Special	150	90	5	Normal
TM16	Light Screen	Psychic	Status	—	—	30	Your Side
TM17	Protect	Normal	Status	—	—	10	Self
TM20	Safeguard	Normal	Status	—	—	25	Your Side
TM21	Frustration	Normal	Physical	—	100	20	Normal
TM22	Solar Beam	Grass	Special	120	100	10	Normal
TM27	Return	Normal	Physical	—	100	20	Normal
TM29	Psychic	Psychic	Special	90	100	10	Normal
TM30	Shadow Ball	Ghost	Special	80	100	15	Normal
TM32	Double Team	Normal	Status	—	—	15	Self
TM42	Facade	Normal	Physical	70	100	20	Normal
TM44	Rest	Psychic	Status	—	—	10	Self
TM45	Attract	Normal	Status	—	100	15	Normal
TM46	Thief	Dark	Physical	60	100	25	Normal
TM48	Round	Normal	Special	60	100	15	Normal
TM53	Energy Ball	Grass	Special	90	100	10	Normal
TM56	Fling	Dark	Physical	—	100	10	Normal
TM68	Giga Impact	Normal	Physical	150	90	5	Normal
TM70	Flash	Normal	Status	—	100	20	Normal
TM85	Dream Eater	Psychic	Special	100	100	15	Normal
TM86	Grass Knot	Grass	Special	—	100	20	Normal
TM87	Swagger	Normal	Status	—	90	15	Normal
TM88	Sleep Talk	Normal	Status	—	—	10	Self
TM89	U-turn	Bug	Physical	70	100	20	Normal
TM90	Substitute	Normal	Status	—	—	10	Self
TM92	Trick Room	Psychic	Status	—	—	5	Both Sides
TM94	Secret Power	Normal	Physical	70	100	20	Normal
TM96	Nature Power	Normal	Status	—	—	20	Normal
TM99	Dazzling Gleam	Fairy	Special	80	100	10	Many Others
TM100	Confide	Normal	Status	—	—	20	Normal

MOVES LEARNED IN EXCHANGE FOR BP

Name	Type	Kind	Pow.	Acc.	PP	Range
Covet	Normal	Physical	60	100	25	Normal
Seed Bomb	Grass	Physical	80	100	15	Normal
Snore	Normal	Special	50	100	15	Normal
Knock Off	Dark	Physical	65	100	20	Normal
Tailwind	Flying	Status	—	—	15	Your Side
Giga Drain	Grass	Special	75	100	10	Normal
Worry Seed	Grass	Status	—	100	10	Normal
Helping Hand	Normal	Status	—	—	20	1 Ally
Endeavor	Normal	Physical	—	100	5	Normal

MOVES TAUGHT BY PEOPLE

Name	Type	Kind	Pow.	Acc.	PP	Range

National Pokédex **548** Hoenn Pokédex —

Petilil
Bulb Pokémon

Grass

HEIGHT: 1'08" WEIGHT: 14.6 lbs.
♀ only

Ω The leaves on its head are very bitter. Eating one of these leaves is known to refresh a tired body.

α Since they prefer moist, nutrient-rich soil, the areas where Petilil live are known to be good for growing plants.

ABILITIES
Chlorophyll
Own Tempo

HIDDEN ABILITY
Leaf Guard

EGG GROUPS
Grass

STAT GROWTH RATES
HP
Attack
Defense
Sp. Atk
Sp. Def
Speed

ITEMS SOMETIMES HELD BY WILD POKÉMON
—

EVOLUTION

MAIN WAY TO REGISTER IN THE NATIONAL POKÉDEX

Catch in Mirage Forest 5.

Damage taken in normal battles

Normal	×1	Flying	×2
Fire	×2	Psychic	×1
Water	×0.5	Bug	×2
Grass	×0.5	Rock	×1
Electric	×0.5	Ghost	×1
Ice	×2	Dragon	×1
Fighting	×1	Dark	×1
Poison	×2	Steel	×1
Ground	×0.5	Fairy	×1

Damage taken in Inverse battles

Normal	×1	Flying	×0.5
Fire	×0.5	Psychic	×1
Water	×2	Bug	×0.5
Grass	×2	Rock	×1
Electric	×2	Ghost	×1
Ice	×0.5	Dragon	×1
Fighting	×1	Dark	×1
Poison	×0.5	Steel	×1
Ground	×2	Fairy	×1

Can be used in
Inverse Battle
Battle Institute
Battle Maison
Random Matchup (Free Battle)
Random Matchup (Others)

LEVEL-UP MOVES

Lv.	Name	Type	Kind	Pow.	Acc.	PP	Range
1	Absorb	Grass	Special	20	100	25	Normal
4	Growth	Normal	Status	—	—	20	Self
8	Leech Seed	Grass	Status	—	90	10	Normal
10	Sleep Powder	Grass	Status	—	75	15	Normal
13	Mega Drain	Grass	Special	40	100	15	Normal
17	Synthesis	Grass	Status	—	—	5	Self
19	Magical Leaf	Grass	Special	60	—	20	Normal
22	Stun Spore	Grass	Status	—	75	30	Normal
26	Giga Drain	Grass	Special	75	100	10	Normal
28	Aromatherapy	Grass	Status	—	—	5	Your Party
31	Helping Hand	Normal	Status	—	—	20	1 Ally
35	Energy Ball	Grass	Special	90	100	10	Normal
37	Entrainment	Normal	Status	—	100	15	Normal
40	Sunny Day	Fire	Status	—	—	5	Both Sides
44	After You	Normal	Status	—	—	15	Normal
46	Leaf Storm	Grass	Special	130	90	5	Normal

TM & HM MOVES

No.	Name	Type	Kind	Pow.	Acc.	PP	Range
TM06	Toxic	Poison	Status	—	90	10	Normal
TM10	Hidden Power	Normal	Special	60	100	15	Normal
TM11	Sunny Day	Fire	Status	—	—	5	Both Sides
TM17	Protect	Normal	Status	—	—	10	Self
TM20	Safeguard	Normal	Status	—	—	25	Your Side
TM21	Frustration	Normal	Physical	—	100	20	Normal
TM22	Solar Beam	Grass	Special	120	100	10	Normal
TM27	Return	Normal	Physical	—	100	20	Normal
TM32	Double Team	Normal	Status	—	—	15	Self
TM42	Facade	Normal	Physical	70	100	20	Normal
TM44	Rest	Psychic	Status	—	—	10	Self
TM45	Attract	Normal	Status	—	100	15	Normal
TM48	Round	Normal	Special	60	100	15	Normal
TM53	Energy Ball	Grass	Special	90	100	10	Normal
TM70	Flash	Normal	Status	—	100	20	Normal
TM85	Dream Eater	Psychic	Special	100	100	15	Normal
TM86	Grass Knot	Grass	Special	—	100	20	Normal
TM87	Swagger	Normal	Status	—	90	15	Normal
TM88	Sleep Talk	Normal	Status	—	—	10	Self
TM90	Substitute	Normal	Status	—	—	10	Self
TM94	Secret Power	Normal	Physical	70	100	20	Normal
TM96	Nature Power	Normal	Status	—	—	20	Normal
TM100	Confide	Normal	Status	—	—	20	Normal
HM01	Cut	Normal	Physical	50	95	30	Normal

MOVES LEARNED IN EXCHANGE FOR BP

Name	Type	Kind	Pow.	Acc.	PP	Range
Covet	Normal	Physical	60	100	25	Normal
Seed Bomb	Grass	Physical	80	100	15	Normal
Snore	Normal	Special	50	100	15	Normal
Synthesis	Grass	Status	—	—	5	Self
Heal Bell	Normal	Status	—	—	5	Your Party
Giga Drain	Grass	Special	75	100	10	Normal
Worry Seed	Grass	Status	—	100	10	Normal
After You	Normal	Status	—	—	15	Normal
Helping Hand	Normal	Status	—	—	20	1 Ally

MOVES TAUGHT BY PEOPLE

Name	Type	Kind	Pow.	Acc.	PP	Range

EGG MOVES

Name	Type	Kind	Pow.	Acc.	PP	Range
Natural Gift	Normal	Physical	—	100	15	Normal
Charm	Fairy	Status	—	100	20	Normal
Endure	Normal	Status	—	—	10	Self
Ingrain	Grass	Status	—	—	20	Self
Worry Seed	Grass	Status	—	100	10	Normal
Grass Whistle	Grass	Status	—	55	15	Normal
Sweet Scent	Normal	Status	—	100	20	Many Others
Bide	Normal	Physical	—	—	10	Self
Healing Wish	Psychic	Status	—	—	10	Self

National Pokédex **549** Hoenn Pokédex —

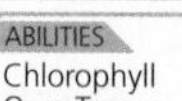

Lilligant
Flowering Pokémon

Grass

HEIGHT: 3'07" WEIGHT: 35.9 lbs.
♀ only

Ω The fragrance of the garland on its head has a relaxing effect. It withers if a Trainer does not take good care of it.

α Even veteran Trainers face a challenge in getting its beautiful flower to bloom. This Pokémon is popular with celebrities.

ABILITIES
Chlorophyll
Own Tempo

HIDDEN ABILITY
Leaf Guard

EGG GROUPS
Grass

STAT GROWTH RATES
HP
Attack
Defense
Sp. Atk
Sp. Def
Speed

ITEMS SOMETIMES HELD BY WILD POKÉMON
—

EVOLUTION

Sun Stone
Petilil
Lilligant

MAIN WAY TO REGISTER IN THE NATIONAL POKÉDEX

Use a Sun Stone on Petilil.

Damage taken in normal battles

Normal	×1	Flying	×2
Fire	×2	Psychic	×1
Water	×0.5	Bug	×2
Grass	×0.5	Rock	×1
Electric	×0.5	Ghost	×1
Ice	×2	Dragon	×1
Fighting	×1	Dark	×1
Poison	×2	Steel	×1
Ground	×0.5	Fairy	×1

Damage taken in Inverse battles

Normal	×1	Flying	×0.5
Fire	×0.5	Psychic	×1
Water	×2	Bug	×0.5
Grass	×2	Rock	×1
Electric	×2	Ghost	×1
Ice	×0.5	Dragon	×1
Fighting	×1	Dark	×1
Poison	×0.5	Steel	×1
Ground	×2	Fairy	×1

Can be used in
Inverse Battle
Battle Institute
Battle Maison
Random Matchup (Free Battle)
Random Matchup (Others)

LEVEL-UP MOVES

Lv.	Name	Type	Kind	Pow.	Acc.	PP	Range
1	Growth	Normal	Status	—	—	20	Self
1	Leech Seed	Grass	Status	—	90	10	Normal
1	Mega Drain	Grass	Special	40	100	15	Normal
1	Synthesis	Grass	Status	—	—	5	Self
10	Teeter Dance	Normal	Status	—	100	20	Adjacent
28	Quiver Dance	Bug	Status	—	—	20	Self
46	Petal Dance	Grass	Special	120	100	10	1 Random
50	Petal Blizzard	Grass	Physical	90	100	15	Adjacent

TM & HM MOVES

No.	Name	Type	Kind	Pow.	Acc.	PP	Range
TM06	Toxic	Poison	Status	—	90	10	Normal
TM10	Hidden Power	Normal	Special	60	100	15	Normal
TM11	Sunny Day	Fire	Status	—	—	5	Both Sides
TM15	Hyper Beam	Normal	Special	150	90	5	Normal
TM16	Light Screen	Psychic	Status	—	—	30	Your Side
TM17	Protect	Normal	Status	—	—	10	Self
TM20	Safeguard	Normal	Status	—	—	25	Your Side
TM21	Frustration	Normal	Physical	—	100	20	Normal
TM22	Solar Beam	Grass	Special	120	100	10	Normal
TM27	Return	Normal	Physical	—	100	20	Normal
TM32	Double Team	Normal	Status	—	—	15	Self
TM42	Facade	Normal	Physical	70	100	20	Normal
TM44	Rest	Psychic	Status	—	—	10	Self
TM45	Attract	Normal	Status	—	100	15	Normal
TM48	Round	Normal	Special	60	100	15	Normal
TM53	Energy Ball	Grass	Special	90	100	10	Normal
TM68	Giga Impact	Normal	Physical	150	90	5	Normal
TM70	Flash	Normal	Status	—	100	20	Normal
TM75	Swords Dance	Normal	Status	—	—	20	Self
TM85	Dream Eater	Psychic	Special	100	100	15	Normal
TM86	Grass Knot	Grass	Special	—	100	20	Normal
TM87	Swagger	Normal	Status	—	90	15	Normal
TM88	Sleep Talk	Normal	Status	—	—	10	Self
TM90	Substitute	Normal	Status	—	—	10	Self
TM94	Secret Power	Normal	Physical	70	100	20	Normal
TM96	Nature Power	Normal	Status	—	—	20	Normal
TM100	Confide	Normal	Status	—	—	20	Normal
HM01	Cut	Normal	Physical	50	95	30	Normal

MOVES LEARNED IN EXCHANGE FOR BP

Name	Type	Kind	Pow.	Acc.	PP	Range
Covet	Normal	Physical	60	100	25	Normal
Seed Bomb	Grass	Physical	80	100	15	Normal
Snore	Normal	Special	50	100	15	Normal
Synthesis	Grass	Status	—	—	5	Self
Role Play	Psychic	Status	—	—	10	Normal
Heal Bell	Normal	Status	—	—	5	Your Party
Giga Drain	Grass	Special	75	100	10	Normal
Worry Seed	Grass	Status	—	100	10	Normal
After You	Normal	Status	—	—	15	Normal
Helping Hand	Normal	Status	—	—	20	1 Ally

MOVES TAUGHT BY PEOPLE

Name	Type	Kind	Pow.	Acc.	PP	Range

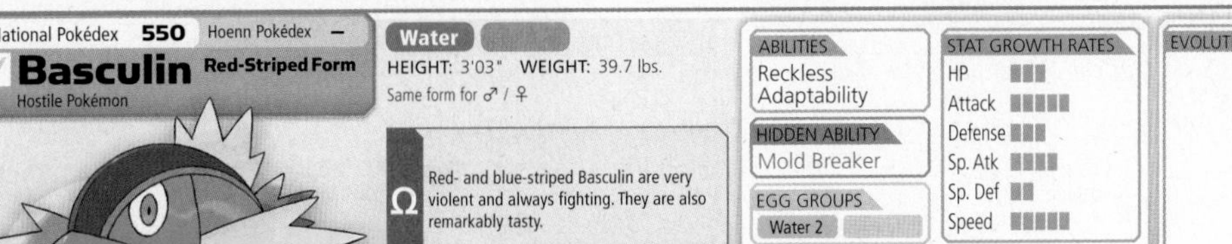

National Pokédex **550** Hoenn Pokédex —

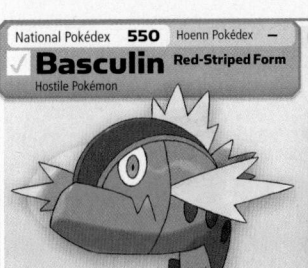

Basculin Red-Striped Form

Hostile Pokémon

Water

HEIGHT: 3'03" WEIGHT: 39.7 lbs.

Same form for ♂ / ♀

Ω Red- and blue-striped Basculin are very violent and always fighting. They are also remarkably tasty.

α Red and blue Basculin usually do not get along, but sometimes members of one school mingle with the other's school.

ABILITIES
Reckless
Adaptability

HIDDEN ABILITY
Mold Breaker

EGG GROUPS
Water 2

STAT GROWTH RATES

HP	■■■
Attack	■■■■■
Defense	■■■
Sp. Atk	■■■■
Sp. Def	■■
Speed	■■■■■

ITEMS SOMETIMES HELD BY WILD POKÉMON
—

EVOLUTION
Does not evolve

MAIN WAY TO REGISTER IN THE NATIONAL POKÉDEX

Appears in Pokémon X and *Pokémon Y*. Bring it to your game using Link Trade or the GTS.

Damage taken in normal battles

Type		Type	
Normal	×1	Flying	×1
Fire	×0.5	Psychic	×1
Water	×0.5	Bug	×1
Grass	×2	Rock	×1
Electric	×2	Ghost	×1
Ice	×0.5	Dragon	×1
Fighting	×1	Dark	×1
Poison	×1	Steel	×0.5
Ground	×1	Fairy	×1

Damage taken in Inverse battles

Type		Type	
Normal	×1	Flying	×1
Fire	×2	Psychic	×1
Water	×2	Bug	×1
Grass	×0.5	Rock	×1
Electric	×0.5	Ghost	×1
Ice	×2	Dragon	×1
Fighting	×1	Dark	×1
Poison	×1	Steel	×2
Ground	×1	Fairy	×1

Can be used in
Inverse Battle
Battle Institute
Battle Maison
Random Matchup (Free Battle)
Random Matchup (Others)

LEVEL-UP MOVES

Lv.	Name	Type	Kind	Pow.	Acc.	PP	Range
1	Thrash	Normal	Physical	120	100	10	1 Random
1	Flail	Normal	Physical	—	100	15	Normal
1	Tail Whip	Normal	Status	—	100	30	Many Others
1	Tackle	Normal	Physical	50	100	35	Normal
1	Water Gun	Water	Special	40	100	25	Normal
4	Uproar	Normal	Special	90	100	10	1 Random
7	Headbutt	Normal	Physical	70	100	15	Normal
10	Bite	Dark	Physical	60	100	25	Normal
13	Aqua Jet	Water	Physical	40	100	20	Normal
16	Chip Away	Normal	Physical	70	100	20	Normal
20	Take Down	Normal	Physical	90	85	20	Normal
24	Crunch	Dark	Physical	80	100	15	Normal
28	Aqua Tail	Water	Physical	90	90	10	Normal
32	Soak	Water	Status	—	100	20	Normal
36	Double-Edge	Normal	Physical	120	100	15	Normal
41	Scary Face	Normal	Status	—	100	10	Normal
46	Flail	Normal	Physical	—	100	15	Normal
50	Final Gambit	Fighting	Special	—	100	5	Normal
56	Thrash	Normal	Physical	120	100	10	1 Random

TM & HM MOVES

No.	Name	Type	Kind	Pow.	Acc.	PP	Range
TM06	Toxic	Poison	Status	—	90	10	Normal
TM07	Hail	Ice	Status	—	—	10	Both Sides
TM10	Hidden Power	Normal	Special	60	100	15	Normal
TM12	Taunt	Dark	Status	—	100	20	Normal
TM13	Ice Beam	Ice	Special	90	100	10	Normal
TM17	Protect	Normal	Status	—	—	10	Self
TM18	Rain Dance	Water	Status	—	—	5	Both Sides
TM21	Frustration	Normal	Physical	—	100	20	Normal
TM27	Return	Normal	Physical	—	100	20	Normal
TM32	Double Team	Normal	Status	—	—	15	Self
TM42	Facade	Normal	Physical	70	100	20	Normal
TM44	Rest	Psychic	Status	—	—	10	Self
TM45	Attract	Normal	Status	—	100	15	Normal
TM48	Round	Normal	Special	60	100	15	Normal
TM55	Scald	Water	Special	80	100	15	Normal
TM87	Swagger	Normal	Status	—	90	15	Normal
TM88	Sleep Talk	Normal	Status	—	—	10	Self
TM90	Substitute	Normal	Status	—	—	10	Self
TM94	Secret Power	Normal	Physical	70	100	20	Normal
TM100	Confide	Normal	Status	—	—	20	Normal
HM01	Cut	Normal	Physical	50	95	30	Normal
HM03	Surf	Water	Special	90	100	15	Adjacent
HM05	Waterfall	Water	Physical	80	100	15	Normal
HM07	Dive	Water	Physical	80	100	10	Normal

MOVES LEARNED IN EXCHANGE FOR BP

Name	Type	Kind	Pow.	Acc.	PP	Range
Bounce	Flying	Physical	85	85	5	Normal
Uproar	Normal	Special	90	100	10	1 Random
Superpower	Fighting	Physical	120	100	5	Normal
Icy Wind	Ice	Special	55	95	15	Many Others
Aqua Tail	Water	Physical	90	90	10	Normal
Zen Headbutt	Psychic	Physical	80	90	15	Normal
Snore	Normal	Special	50	100	15	Normal
Endeavor	Normal	Physical	—	100	5	Normal

MOVES TAUGHT BY PEOPLE

Name	Type	Kind	Pow.	Acc.	PP	Range

EGG MOVES

Name	Type	Kind	Pow.	Acc.	PP	Range
Swift	Normal	Special	60	—	20	Many Others
Bubble Beam	Water	Special	65	100	20	Normal
Mud Shot	Ground	Special	55	95	15	Normal
Muddy Water	Water	Special	90	85	10	Many Others
Agility	Psychic	Status	—	—	30	Self
Whirlpool	Water	Special	35	85	15	Normal
Rage	Normal	Physical	20	100	20	Normal
Brine	Water	Special	65	100	10	Normal
Revenge	Fighting	Physical	60	100	10	Normal

National Pokédex **550** Hoenn Pokédex —

Basculin Blue-Striped Form

Hostile Pokémon

Water

HEIGHT: 3'03" WEIGHT: 39.7 lbs.

Same form for ♂ / ♀

Ω Red- and blue-striped Basculin are very violent and always fighting. They are also remarkably tasty.

α Red and blue Basculin usually do not get along, but sometimes members of one school mingle with the other's school.

ABILITIES
Rock Head
Adaptability

HIDDEN ABILITY
Mold Breaker

EGG GROUPS
Water 2

STAT GROWTH RATES

HP	■■■
Attack	■■■■■
Defense	■■■
Sp. Atk	■■■■
Sp. Def	■■
Speed	■■■■■

ITEMS SOMETIMES HELD BY WILD POKÉMON
—

EVOLUTION
Does not evolve

MAIN WAY TO REGISTER IN THE NATIONAL POKÉDEX

Appears in *Pokémon X* and *Pokémon Y*. Bring it to your game using Link Trade or the GTS.

Damage taken in normal battles

Type		Type	
Normal	×1	Flying	×1
Fire	×0.5	Psychic	×1
Water	×0.5	Bug	×1
Grass	×2	Rock	×1
Electric	×2	Ghost	×1
Ice	×0.5	Dragon	×1
Fighting	×1	Dark	×1
Poison	×1	Steel	×0.5
Ground	×1	Fairy	×1

Damage taken in Inverse battles

Type		Type	
Normal	×1	Flying	×1
Fire	×2	Psychic	×1
Water	×2	Bug	×1
Grass	×0.5	Rock	×1
Electric	×0.5	Ghost	×1
Ice	×2	Dragon	×1
Fighting	×1	Dark	×1
Poison	×1	Steel	×2
Ground	×1	Fairy	×1

Can be used in
Inverse Battle
Battle Institute
Battle Maison
Random Matchup (Free Battle)
Random Matchup (Others)

LEVEL-UP MOVES

Lv.	Name	Type	Kind	Pow.	Acc.	PP	Range
1	Thrash	Normal	Physical	120	100	10	1 Random
1	Flail	Normal	Physical	—	100	15	Normal
1	Tail Whip	Normal	Status	—	100	30	Many Others
1	Tackle	Normal	Physical	50	100	35	Normal
1	Water Gun	Water	Special	40	100	25	Normal
4	Uproar	Normal	Special	90	100	10	1 Random
7	Headbutt	Normal	Physical	70	100	15	Normal
10	Bite	Dark	Physical	60	100	25	Normal
13	Aqua Jet	Water	Physical	40	100	20	Normal
16	Chip Away	Normal	Physical	70	100	20	Normal
20	Take Down	Normal	Physical	90	85	20	Normal
24	Crunch	Dark	Physical	80	100	15	Normal
28	Aqua Tail	Water	Physical	90	90	10	Normal
32	Soak	Water	Status	—	100	20	Normal
36	Double-Edge	Normal	Physical	120	100	15	Normal
41	Scary Face	Normal	Status	—	100	10	Normal
46	Flail	Normal	Physical	—	100	15	Normal
50	Final Gambit	Fighting	Special	—	100	5	Normal
56	Thrash	Normal	Physical	120	100	10	1 Random

TM & HM MOVES

No.	Name	Type	Kind	Pow.	Acc.	PP	Range
TM06	Toxic	Poison	Status	—	90	10	Normal
TM07	Hail	Ice	Status	—	—	10	Both Sides
TM10	Hidden Power	Normal	Special	60	100	15	Normal
TM12	Taunt	Dark	Status	—	100	20	Normal
TM13	Ice Beam	Ice	Special	90	100	10	Normal
TM17	Protect	Normal	Status	—	—	10	Self
TM18	Rain Dance	Water	Status	—	—	5	Both Sides
TM21	Frustration	Normal	Physical	—	100	20	Normal
TM27	Return	Normal	Physical	—	100	20	Normal
TM32	Double Team	Normal	Status	—	—	15	Self
TM42	Facade	Normal	Physical	70	100	20	Normal
TM44	Rest	Psychic	Status	—	—	10	Self
TM45	Attract	Normal	Status	—	100	15	Normal
TM48	Round	Normal	Special	60	100	15	Normal
TM55	Scald	Water	Special	80	100	15	Normal
TM87	Swagger	Normal	Status	—	90	15	Normal
TM88	Sleep Talk	Normal	Status	—	—	10	Self
TM90	Substitute	Normal	Status	—	—	10	Self
TM94	Secret Power	Normal	Physical	70	100	20	Normal
TM100	Confide	Normal	Status	—	—	20	Normal
HM01	Cut	Normal	Physical	50	95	30	Normal
HM03	Surf	Water	Special	90	100	15	Adjacent
HM05	Waterfall	Water	Physical	80	100	15	Normal
HM07	Dive	Water	Physical	80	100	10	Normal

MOVES LEARNED IN EXCHANGE FOR BP

Name	Type	Kind	Pow.	Acc.	PP	Range
Bounce	Flying	Physical	85	85	5	Normal
Uproar	Normal	Special	90	100	10	1 Random
Superpower	Fighting	Physical	120	100	5	Normal
Icy Wind	Ice	Special	55	95	15	Many Others
Aqua Tail	Water	Physical	90	90	10	Normal
Zen Headbutt	Psychic	Physical	80	90	15	Normal
Snore	Normal	Special	50	100	15	Normal
Endeavor	Normal	Physical	—	100	5	Normal

MOVES TAUGHT BY PEOPLE

Name	Type	Kind	Pow.	Acc.	PP	Range

EGG MOVES

Name	Type	Kind	Pow.	Acc.	PP	Range
Swift	Normal	Special	60	—	20	Many Others
Bubble Beam	Water	Special	65	100	20	Normal
Mud Shot	Ground	Special	55	95	15	Normal
Muddy Water	Water	Special	90	85	10	Many Others
Agility	Psychic	Status	—	—	30	Self
Whirlpool	Water	Special	35	85	15	Normal
Rage	Normal	Physical	20	100	20	Normal
Brine	Water	Special	65	100	10	Normal
Revenge	Fighting	Physical	60	100	10	Normal

National Pokédex **551** Hoenn Pokédex —

Sandile

Desert Croc Pokémon

Ground | Dark

HEIGHT: 2'04" WEIGHT: 33.5 lbs.

Same form for ♂ / ♀

Ω It moves along below the sand's surface, except for its nose and eyes. A dark membrane shields its eyes from the sun.

α They live buried in the sands of the desert. The sun-warmed sands prevent their body temperature from dropping.

ABILITIES
Intimidate
Moxie

HIDDEN ABILITY
Anger Point

EGG GROUPS
Field

STAT GROWTH RATES
HP ■■
Attack ■■■■
Defense ■■
Sp. Atk ■■
Sp. Def ■■
Speed ■■■■

ITEMS SOMETIMES HELD BY WILD POKÉMON
—

EVOLUTION

MAIN WAY TO REGISTER IN THE NATIONAL POKÉDEX

Catch in the desert on Route 111. Appears as a hidden Pokémon after you battle Groudon or Kyogre.

Damage taken in normal battles

Type		Type	
Normal	×1	Flying	×1
Fire	×1	Psychic	×0
Water	×2	Bug	×2
Grass	×2	Rock	×0.5
Electric	×0	Ghost	×0.5
Ice	×2	Dragon	×1
Fighting	×2	Dark	×0.5
Poison	×0.5	Steel	×1
Ground	×1	Fairy	×2

Damage taken in Inverse battles

Type		Type	
Normal	×1	Flying	×1
Fire	×1	Psychic	×2
Water	×0.5	Bug	×0.5
Grass	×0.5	Rock	×2
Electric	×2	Ghost	×2
Ice	×0.5	Dragon	×1
Fighting	×0.5	Dark	×2
Poison	×2	Steel	×1
Ground	×1	Fairy	×0.5

Can be used in
Inverse Battle
Battle Institute
Battle Maison
Random Matchup (Free Battle)
Random Matchup (Others)

LEVEL-UP MOVES

Lv.	Name	Type	Kind	Pow.	Acc.	PP	Range
1	Leer	Normal	Status	—	100	30	Many Others
1	Rage	Normal	Physical	20	100	20	Normal
4	Bite	Dark	Physical	60	100	25	Normal
7	Sand Attack	Ground	Status	—	100	15	Normal
10	Torment	Dark	Status	—	100	15	Normal
13	Sand Tomb	Ground	Physical	35	85	15	Normal
16	Assurance	Dark	Physical	60	100	10	Normal
19	Mud-Slap	Ground	Special	20	100	10	Normal
22	Embargo	Dark	Status	—	100	15	Normal
25	Swagger	Normal	Status	—	90	15	Normal
28	Crunch	Dark	Physical	80	100	15	Normal
31	Dig	Ground	Physical	80	100	10	Normal
34	Scary Face	Normal	Status	—	100	10	Normal
37	Foul Play	Dark	Physical	95	100	15	Normal
40	Sandstorm	Rock	Status	—	—	10	Both Sides
43	Earthquake	Ground	Physical	100	100	10	Adjacent
46	Thrash	Normal	Physical	120	100	10	1 Random

TM & HM MOVES

No.	Name	Type	Kind	Pow.	Acc.	PP	Range
TM01	Hone Claws	Dark	Status	—	—	15	Self
TM05	Roar	Normal	Status	—	—	20	Normal
TM06	Toxic	Poison	Status	—	90	10	Normal
TM10	Hidden Power	Normal	Special	60	100	15	Normal
TM12	Taunt	Dark	Status	—	100	20	Normal
TM17	Protect	Normal	Status	—	—	10	Self
TM21	Frustration	Normal	Physical	—	100	20	Normal
TM26	Earthquake	Ground	Physical	100	100	10	Adjacent
TM27	Return	Normal	Physical	—	100	20	Normal
TM28	Dig	Ground	Physical	80	100	10	Normal
TM32	Double Team	Normal	Status	—	—	15	Self
TM36	Sludge Bomb	Poison	Special	90	100	10	Normal
TM37	Sandstorm	Rock	Status	—	—	10	Both Sides
TM39	Rock Tomb	Rock	Physical	60	95	15	Normal
TM41	Torment	Dark	Status	—	100	15	Normal
TM42	Facade	Normal	Physical	70	100	20	Normal
TM44	Rest	Psychic	Status	—	—	10	Self
TM45	Attract	Normal	Status	—	100	15	Normal
TM46	Thief	Dark	Physical	60	100	25	Normal
TM48	Round	Normal	Special	60	100	15	Normal
TM59	Incinerate	Fire	Special	60	100	15	Many Others
TM63	Embargo	Dark	Status	—	100	15	Normal
TM66	Payback	Dark	Physical	50	100	10	Normal
TM67	Retaliate	Normal	Physical	70	100	5	Normal
TM71	Stone Edge	Rock	Physical	100	80	5	Normal
TM78	Bulldoze	Ground	Physical	60	100	20	Adjacent
TM80	Rock Slide	Rock	Physical	75	90	10	Many Others
TM87	Swagger	Normal	Status	—	90	15	Normal
TM88	Sleep Talk	Normal	Status	—	—	10	Self
TM90	Substitute	Normal	Status	—	—	10	Self
TM94	Secret Power	Normal	Physical	70	100	20	Normal
TM95	Snarl	Dark	Special	55	95	15	Many Others
TM97	Dark Pulse	Dark	Special	80	100	15	Normal
TM100	Confide	Normal	Status	—	—	20	Normal
HM01	Cut	Normal	Physical	50	95	30	Normal

MOVES LEARNED IN EXCHANGE FOR BP

Name	Type	Kind	Pow.	Acc.	PP	Range
Uproar	Normal	Special	90	100	10	1 Random
Earth Power	Ground	Special	90	100	10	Normal
Foul Play	Dark	Physical	95	100	15	Normal
Aqua Tail	Water	Physical	90	90	10	Normal
Iron Tail	Steel	Physical	100	75	15	Normal
Snore	Normal	Special	50	100	15	Normal
Spite	Ghost	Status	—	100	10	Normal
Snatch	Dark	Status	—	—	10	Self
Stealth Rock	Rock	Status	—	—	20	Other Side

MOVES TAUGHT BY PEOPLE

Name	Type	Kind	Pow.	Acc.	PP	Range

EGG MOVES

Name	Type	Kind	Pow.	Acc.	PP	Range
Double-Edge	Normal	Physical	120	100	15	Normal
Rock Climb	Normal	Physical	90	85	20	Normal
Pursuit	Dark	Physical	40	100	20	Normal
Uproar	Normal	Special	90	100	10	1 Random
Fire Fang	Fire	Physical	65	95	15	Normal
Thunder Fang	Electric	Physical	65	95	15	Normal
Beat Up	Dark	Physical	—	100	10	Normal
Focus Energy	Normal	Status	—	—	30	Self
Counter	Fighting	Physical	—	100	20	Varies
Mean Look	Normal	Status	—	—	5	Normal
Me First	Normal	Status	—	—	20	Varies

National Pokédex **552** Hoenn Pokédex —

Krokorok

Desert Croc Pokémon

Ground | Dark

HEIGHT: 3'03" WEIGHT: 73.6 lbs.

Same form for ♂ / ♀

Ω They live in groups of a few individuals. Protective membranes shield their eyes from sandstorms.

α The special membrane covering its eyes can sense the heat of objects, so it can see its surroundings even in darkness.

ABILITIES
Intimidate
Moxie

HIDDEN ABILITY
Anger Point

EGG GROUPS
Field

STAT GROWTH RATES
HP ■■■
Attack ■■■■
Defense ■■
Sp. Atk ■■
Sp. Def ■■
Speed ■■■■

ITEMS SOMETIMES HELD BY WILD POKÉMON
—

EVOLUTION

Lv. 29 Lv. 40
Sandile Krokorok Krookodile

MAIN WAY TO REGISTER IN THE NATIONAL POKÉDEX

Level up Sandile to Lv. 29.

Damage taken in normal battles

Type		Type	
Normal	×1	Flying	×1
Fire	×1	Psychic	×0
Water	×2	Bug	×2
Grass	×2	Rock	×0.5
Electric	×0	Ghost	×0.5
Ice	×2	Dragon	×1
Fighting	×2	Dark	×0.5
Poison	×0.5	Steel	×1
Ground	×1	Fairy	×2

Damage taken in Inverse battles

Type		Type	
Normal	×1	Flying	×1
Fire	×1	Psychic	×2
Water	×0.5	Bug	×0.5
Grass	×0.5	Rock	×2
Electric	×2	Ghost	×2
Ice	×0.5	Dragon	×1
Fighting	×0.5	Dark	×2
Poison	×2	Steel	×1
Ground	×1	Fairy	×0.5

Can be used in
Inverse Battle
Battle Institute
Battle Maison
Random Matchup (Free Battle)
Random Matchup (Others)

LEVEL-UP MOVES

Lv.	Name	Type	Kind	Pow.	Acc.	PP	Range
1	Leer	Normal	Status	—	100	30	Many Others
1	Rage	Normal	Physical	20	100	20	Normal
1	Bite	Dark	Physical	60	100	25	Normal
1	Sand Attack	Ground	Status	—	100	15	Normal
4	Bite	Dark	Physical	60	100	25	Normal
7	Sand Attack	Ground	Status	—	100	15	Normal
10	Torment	Dark	Status	—	100	15	Normal
13	Sand Tomb	Ground	Physical	35	85	15	Normal
16	Assurance	Dark	Physical	60	100	10	Normal
19	Mud-Slap	Ground	Special	20	100	10	Normal
22	Embargo	Dark	Status	—	100	15	Normal
25	Swagger	Normal	Status	—	90	15	Normal
28	Crunch	Dark	Physical	80	100	15	Normal
32	Dig	Ground	Physical	80	100	10	Normal
36	Scary Face	Normal	Status	—	100	10	Normal
40	Foul Play	Dark	Physical	95	100	15	Normal
44	Sandstorm	Rock	Status	—	—	10	Both Sides
48	Earthquake	Ground	Physical	100	100	10	Adjacent
52	Thrash	Normal	Physical	120	100	10	1 Random

TM & HM MOVES

No.	Name	Type	Kind	Pow.	Acc.	PP	Range
TM01	Hone Claws	Dark	Status	—	—	15	Self
TM05	Roar	Normal	Status	—	—	20	Normal
TM06	Toxic	Poison	Status	—	90	10	Normal
TM10	Hidden Power	Normal	Special	60	100	15	Normal
TM12	Taunt	Dark	Status	—	100	20	Normal
TM17	Protect	Normal	Status	—	—	10	Self
TM21	Frustration	Normal	Physical	—	100	20	Normal
TM26	Earthquake	Ground	Physical	100	100	10	Adjacent
TM27	Return	Normal	Physical	—	100	20	Normal
TM28	Dig	Ground	Physical	80	100	10	Normal
TM31	Brick Break	Fighting	Physical	75	100	15	Normal
TM32	Double Team	Normal	Status	—	—	15	Self
TM36	Sludge Bomb	Poison	Special	90	100	10	Normal
TM37	Sandstorm	Rock	Status	—	—	10	Both Sides
TM39	Rock Tomb	Rock	Physical	60	95	15	Normal
TM41	Torment	Dark	Status	—	100	15	Normal
TM42	Facade	Normal	Physical	70	100	20	Normal
TM44	Rest	Psychic	Status	—	—	10	Self
TM45	Attract	Normal	Status	—	100	15	Normal
TM46	Thief	Dark	Physical	60	100	25	Normal
TM47	Low Sweep	Fighting	Physical	65	100	20	Normal
TM48	Round	Normal	Special	60	100	15	Normal
TM56	Fling	Dark	Physical	—	100	10	Normal
TM59	Incinerate	Fire	Special	60	100	15	Many Others
TM63	Embargo	Dark	Status	—	100	15	Normal
TM65	Shadow Claw	Ghost	Physical	70	100	15	Normal
TM66	Payback	Dark	Physical	50	100	10	Normal
TM67	Retaliate	Normal	Physical	70	100	5	Normal
TM71	Stone Edge	Rock	Physical	100	80	5	Normal
TM78	Bulldoze	Ground	Physical	60	100	20	Adjacent
TM80	Rock Slide	Rock	Physical	75	90	10	Many Others
TM86	Grass Knot	Grass	Special	—	100	20	Normal
TM87	Swagger	Normal	Status	—	90	15	Normal
TM88	Sleep Talk	Normal	Status	—	—	10	Self
TM90	Substitute	Normal	Status	—	—	10	Self
TM94	Secret Power	Normal	Physical	70	100	20	Normal
TM95	Snarl	Dark	Special	55	95	15	Many Others
TM97	Dark Pulse	Dark	Special	80	100	15	Normal
TM98	Power-Up Punch	Fighting	Physical	40	100	20	Normal
TM100	Confide	Normal	Status	—	—	20	Normal
HM01	Cut	Normal	Physical	50	95	30	Normal
HM04	Strength	Normal	Physical	80	100	15	Normal
HM06	Rock Smash	Fighting	Physical	40	100	15	Normal

MOVES LEARNED IN EXCHANGE FOR BP

Name	Type	Kind	Pow.	Acc.	PP	Range
Low Kick	Fighting	Physical	—	100	20	Normal
Uproar	Normal	Special	90	100	10	1 Random
Earth Power	Ground	Special	90	100	10	Normal
Foul Play	Dark	Physical	95	100	15	Normal
Aqua Tail	Water	Physical	90	90	10	Normal
Iron Tail	Steel	Physical	100	75	15	Normal
Snore	Normal	Special	50	100	15	Normal
Knock Off	Dark	Physical	65	100	20	Normal
Focus Punch	Fighting	Physical	150	100	20	Normal
Spite	Ghost	Status	—	100	10	Normal
Snatch	Dark	Status	—	—	10	Self
Stealth Rock	Rock	Status	—	—	20	Other Side

MOVES TAUGHT BY PEOPLE

Name	Type	Kind	Pow.	Acc.	PP	Range

National Pokédex **553** Hoenn Pokédex —

Krookodile

Intimidation Pokémon

Ground | Dark

HEIGHT: 4'11" WEIGHT: 212.3 lbs.

Same form for ♂ / ♀

Ω Very violent Pokémon, they try to clamp down on anything that moves in front of their eyes.

α They never allow prey to escape. Their jaws are so powerful, they can crush the body of an automobile.

ABILITIES
Intimidate
Moxie

HIDDEN ABILITY
Anger Point

EGG GROUPS
Field

STAT GROWTH RATES
HP
Attack
Defense
Sp. Atk
Sp. Def
Speed

ITEMS SOMETIMES HELD BY WILD POKÉMON
—

EVOLUTION

MAIN WAY TO REGISTER IN THE NATIONAL POKÉDEX

Level up Krokorok to Lv. 40.

Damage taken in normal battles

Type		Type	
Normal	×1	Flying	×1
Fire	×1	Psychic	×0
Water	×2	Bug	×2
Grass	×2	Rock	×0.5
Electric	×0	Ghost	×0.5
Ice	×2	Dragon	×1
Fighting	×2	Dark	×0.5
Poison	×0.5	Steel	×1
Ground	×1	Fairy	×2

Damage taken in Inverse battles

Type		Type	
Normal	×1	Flying	×1
Fire	×1	Psychic	×2
Water	×0.5	Bug	×0.5
Grass	×0.5	Rock	×2
Electric	×2	Ghost	×2
Ice	×0.5	Dragon	×1
Fighting	×0.5	Dark	×2
Poison	×2	Steel	×1
Ground	×1	Fairy	×0.5

Can be used in
Inverse Battle
Battle Institute
Battle Maison
Random Matchup (Free Battle)
Random Matchup (Others)

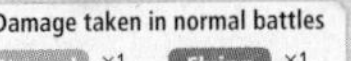

LEVEL-UP MOVES

Lv.	Name	Type	Kind	Pow.	Acc.	PP	Range
1	Outrage	Dragon	Physical	120	100	10	1 Random
1	Leer	Normal	Status	—	100	30	Many Others
1	Rage	Normal	Physical	20	100	20	Normal
1	Bite	Dark	Physical	60	100	25	Normal
1	Sand Attack	Ground	Status	—	100	15	Normal
4	Bite	Dark	Physical	60	100	25	Normal
7	Sand Attack	Ground	Status	—	100	15	Normal
10	Torment	Dark	Status	—	100	15	Normal
13	Sand Tomb	Ground	Physical	35	85	15	Normal
16	Assurance	Dark	Physical	60	100	10	Normal
19	Mud-Slap	Ground	Special	20	100	10	Normal
22	Embargo	Dark	Status	—	100	15	Normal
25	Swagger	Normal	Status	—	90	15	Normal
28	Crunch	Dark	Physical	80	100	15	Normal
32	Dig	Ground	Physical	80	100	10	Normal
36	Scary Face	Normal	Status	—	100	10	Normal
42	Foul Play	Dark	Physical	95	100	15	Normal
48	Sandstorm	Rock	Status	—	—	10	Both Sides
54	Earthquake	Ground	Physical	100	100	10	Adjacent
60	Outrage	Dragon	Physical	120	100	10	1 Random

TM & HM MOVES

No.	Name	Type	Kind	Pow.	Acc.	PP	Range
TM01	Hone Claws	Dark	Status	—	—	15	Self
TM02	Dragon Claw	Dragon	Physical	80	100	15	Normal
TM05	Roar	Normal	Status	—	—	20	Normal
TM06	Toxic	Poison	Status	—	90	10	Normal
TM08	Bulk Up	Fighting	Status	—	—	20	Self
TM10	Hidden Power	Normal	Special	60	100	15	Normal
TM12	Taunt	Dark	Status	—	100	20	Normal
TM15	Hyper Beam	Normal	Special	150	90	5	Normal
TM17	Protect	Normal	Status	—	—	10	Self
TM21	Frustration	Normal	Physical	—	100	20	Normal
TM23	Smack Down	Rock	Physical	50	100	15	Normal
TM26	Earthquake	Ground	Physical	100	100	10	Adjacent
TM27	Return	Normal	Physical	—	100	20	Normal
TM28	Dig	Ground	Physical	80	100	10	Normal
TM31	Brick Break	Fighting	Physical	75	100	15	Normal
TM32	Double Team	Normal	Status	—	—	15	Self
TM36	Sludge Bomb	Poison	Special	90	100	10	Normal
TM37	Sandstorm	Rock	Status	—	—	10	Both Sides
TM39	Rock Tomb	Rock	Physical	60	95	15	Normal
TM40	Aerial Ace	Flying	Physical	60	—	20	Normal
TM41	Torment	Dark	Status	—	100	15	Normal
TM42	Facade	Normal	Physical	70	100	20	Normal
TM44	Rest	Psychic	Status	—	—	10	Self
TM45	Attract	Normal	Status	—	100	15	Normal
TM46	Thief	Dark	Physical	60	100	25	Normal
TM47	Low Sweep	Fighting	Physical	65	100	20	Normal
TM48	Round	Normal	Special	60	100	15	Normal
TM52	Focus Blast	Fighting	Special	120	70	5	Normal
TM56	Fling	Dark	Physical	—	100	10	Normal
TM59	Incinerate	Fire	Special	60	100	15	Many Others
TM63	Embargo	Dark	Status	—	100	15	Normal
TM65	Shadow Claw	Ghost	Physical	70	100	15	Normal
TM66	Payback	Dark	Physical	50	100	10	Normal
TM67	Retaliate	Normal	Physical	70	100	5	Normal
TM68	Giga Impact	Normal	Physical	150	90	5	Normal
TM71	Stone Edge	Rock	Physical	100	80	5	Normal
TM78	Bulldoze	Ground	Physical	60	100	20	Adjacent
TM80	Rock Slide	Rock	Physical	75	90	10	Many Others
TM82	Dragon Tail	Dragon	Physical	60	90	10	Normal
TM86	Grass Knot	Grass	Special	—	100	20	Normal
TM87	Swagger	Normal	Status	—	90	15	Normal
TM88	Sleep Talk	Normal	Status	—	—	10	Self
TM90	Substitute	Normal	Status	—	—	10	Self
TM94	Secret Power	Normal	Physical	70	100	20	Normal
TM95	Snarl	Dark	Special	55	95	15	Many Others
TM97	Dark Pulse	Dark	Special	80	100	15	Normal
TM98	Power-Up Punch	Fighting	Physical	40	100	20	Normal
TM100	Confide	Normal	Status	—	—	20	Normal
HM01	Cut	Normal	Physical	50	95	30	Normal
HM04	Strength	Normal	Physical	80	100	15	Normal
HM06	Rock Smash	Fighting	Physical	40	100	15	Normal

MOVES LEARNED IN EXCHANGE FOR BP

Name	Type	Kind	Pow.	Acc.	PP	Range
Low Kick	Fighting	Physical	—	100	20	Normal
Uproar	Normal	Special	90	100	10	1 Random
Block	Normal	Status	—	—	5	Normal
Earth Power	Ground	Special	90	100	10	Normal
Foul Play	Dark	Physical	95	100	15	Normal
Superpower	Fighting	Physical	120	100	5	Normal
Aqua Tail	Water	Physical	90	90	10	Normal
Dragon Pulse	Dragon	Special	85	100	10	Normal
Iron Tail	Steel	Physical	100	75	15	Normal
Snore	Normal	Special	50	100	15	Normal
Knock Off	Dark	Physical	65	100	20	Normal
Focus Punch	Fighting	Physical	150	100	20	Normal
Spite	Ghost	Status	—	100	10	Normal
Outrage	Dragon	Physical	120	100	10	1 Random
Snatch	Dark	Status	—	—	10	Self
Stealth Rock	Rock	Status	—	—	20	Other Side

MOVES TAUGHT BY PEOPLE

Name	Type	Kind	Pow.	Acc.	PP	Range

National Pokédex **554** Hoenn Pokédex —

Darumaka

Zen Charm Pokémon

Fire

HEIGHT: 2'00" WEIGHT: 82.7 lbs.

Same form for ♂ / ♀

Ω Darumaka's droppings are hot, so people used to put them in their clothes to keep themselves warm.

α When it sleeps, it pulls its limbs into its body and its internal fire goes down to 1,100 degrees Fahrenheit.

ABILITY
Hustle

HIDDEN ABILITY
Inner Focus

EGG GROUPS
Field

STAT GROWTH RATES
HP
Attack
Defense
Sp. Atk
Sp. Def
Speed

ITEMS SOMETIMES HELD BY WILD POKÉMON
—

EVOLUTION

MAIN WAY TO REGISTER IN THE NATIONAL POKÉDEX

Leave a Darmanitan at a Pokémon Day Care, then hatch the Pokémon Egg that is found.

Damage taken in normal battles

Type		Type	
Normal	×1	Flying	×1
Fire	×0.5	Psychic	×1
Water	×2	Bug	×0.5
Grass	×0.5	Rock	×2
Electric	×1	Ghost	×1
Ice	×0.5	Dragon	×1
Fighting	×1	Dark	×1
Poison	×1	Steel	×0.5
Ground	×2	Fairy	×0.5

Damage taken in Inverse battles

Type		Type	
Normal	×1	Flying	×1
Fire	×2	Psychic	×1
Water	×0.5	Bug	×2
Grass	×2	Rock	×0.5
Electric	×1	Ghost	×1
Ice	×2	Dragon	×1
Fighting	×1	Dark	×1
Poison	×1	Steel	×2
Ground	×0.5	Fairy	×2

Can be used in
Inverse Battle
Battle Institute
Battle Maison
Random Matchup (Free Battle)
Random Matchup (Others)

LEVEL-UP MOVES

Lv.	Name	Type	Kind	Pow.	Acc.	PP	Range
1	Tackle	Normal	Physical	50	100	35	Normal
3	Rollout	Rock	Physical	30	90	20	Normal
6	Incinerate	Fire	Special	60	100	15	Many Others
9	Rage	Normal	Physical	20	100	20	Normal
11	Fire Fang	Fire	Physical	65	95	15	Normal
14	Headbutt	Normal	Physical	70	100	15	Normal
17	Uproar	Normal	Special	90	100	10	1 Random
19	Facade	Normal	Physical	70	100	20	Normal
22	Fire Punch	Fire	Physical	75	100	15	Normal
25	Work Up	Normal	Status	—	—	30	Self
27	Thrash	Normal	Physical	120	100	10	1 Random
30	Belly Drum	Normal	Status	—	—	10	Self
33	Flare Blitz	Fire	Physical	120	100	15	Normal
35	Taunt	Dark	Status	—	100	20	Normal
39	Superpower	Fighting	Physical	120	100	5	Normal
42	Overheat	Fire	Special	130	90	5	Normal

TM & HM MOVES

No.	Name	Type	Kind	Pow.	Acc.	PP	Range
TM05	Roar	Normal	Status	—	—	20	Normal
TM06	Toxic	Poison	Status	—	90	10	Normal
TM10	Hidden Power	Normal	Special	60	100	15	Normal
TM11	Sunny Day	Fire	Status	—	—	5	Both Sides
TM12	Taunt	Dark	Status	—	100	20	Normal
TM17	Protect	Normal	Status	—	—	10	Self
TM21	Frustration	Normal	Physical	—	100	20	Normal
TM22	Solar Beam	Grass	Special	120	100	10	Normal
TM27	Return	Normal	Physical	—	100	20	Normal
TM28	Dig	Ground	Physical	80	100	10	Normal
TM31	Brick Break	Fighting	Physical	75	100	15	Normal
TM32	Double Team	Normal	Status	—	—	15	Self
TM35	Flamethrower	Fire	Special	90	100	15	Normal
TM38	Fire Blast	Fire	Special	110	85	5	Normal
TM39	Rock Tomb	Rock	Physical	60	95	15	Normal
TM42	Facade	Normal	Physical	70	100	20	Normal
TM43	Flame Charge	Fire	Physical	50	100	20	Normal
TM44	Rest	Psychic	Status	—	—	10	Self
TM45	Attract	Normal	Status	—	100	15	Normal
TM46	Thief	Dark	Physical	60	100	25	Normal
TM48	Round	Normal	Special	60	100	15	Normal
TM50	Overheat	Fire	Special	130	90	5	Normal
TM56	Fling	Dark	Physical	—	100	10	Normal
TM59	Incinerate	Fire	Special	60	100	15	Many Others
TM61	Will-O-Wisp	Fire	Status	—	85	15	Normal
TM74	Gyro Ball	Steel	Physical	—	100	5	Normal
TM80	Rock Slide	Rock	Physical	75	90	10	Many Others
TM86	Grass Knot	Grass	Special	—	100	20	Normal
TM87	Swagger	Normal	Status	—	90	15	Normal
TM88	Sleep Talk	Normal	Status	—	—	10	Self
TM89	U-turn	Bug	Physical	70	100	20	Normal
TM90	Substitute	Normal	Status	—	—	10	Self
TM94	Secret Power	Normal	Physical	70	100	20	Normal
TM98	Power-Up Punch	Fighting	Physical	40	100	20	Normal
TM100	Confide	Normal	Status	—	—	20	Normal
HM04	Strength	Normal	Physical	80	100	15	Normal
HM06	Rock Smash	Fighting	Physical	40	100	15	Normal

MOVES LEARNED IN EXCHANGE FOR BP

Name	Type	Kind	Pow.	Acc.	PP	Range
Uproar	Normal	Special	90	100	10	1 Random
Fire Punch	Fire	Physical	75	100	15	Normal
Superpower	Fighting	Physical	120	100	5	Normal
Zen Headbutt	Psychic	Physical	80	90	15	Normal
Snore	Normal	Special	50	100	15	Normal
Heat Wave	Fire	Special	95	90	10	Many Others
Focus Punch	Fighting	Physical	150	100	20	Normal
Endeavor	Normal	Physical	—	100	5	Normal
Snatch	Dark	Status	—	—	10	Self

MOVES TAUGHT BY PEOPLE

Name	Type	Kind	Pow.	Acc.	PP	Range

EGG MOVES

Name	Type	Kind	Pow.	Acc.	PP	Range
Sleep Talk	Normal	Status	—	—	10	Self
Focus Punch	Fighting	Physical	150	100	20	Normal
Focus Energy	Normal	Status	—	—	30	Self
Endure	Normal	Status	—	—	10	Self
Hammer Arm	Fighting	Physical	100	90	10	Normal
Take Down	Normal	Physical	90	85	20	Normal
Flame Wheel	Fire	Physical	60	100	25	Normal
Encore	Normal	Status	—	100	5	Normal
Yawn	Normal	Status	—	—	10	Normal
Snatch	Dark	Status	—	—	10	Self

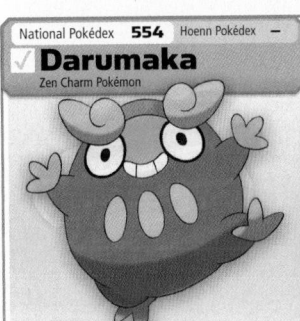

National Pokédex **555** Hoenn Pokédex —

Darmanitan Standard Mode

Blazing Pokémon

Fire

HEIGHT: 4'03" WEIGHT: 204.8 lbs.

Same form for ♂ / ♀

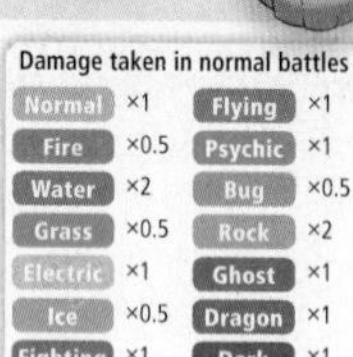

Ω When one is injured in a fierce battle, it hardens into a stone-like form. Then it meditates and sharpens its mind.

α Its internal fire burns at 2,500 degrees Fahrenheit, making enough power that it can destroy a dump truck with one punch.

ABILITY
Sheer Force

HIDDEN ABILITY
Zen Mode

EGG GROUPS
Field

STAT GROWTH RATES
HP
Attack
Defense
Sp. Atk
Sp. Def
Speed

ITEMS SOMETIMES HELD BY WILD POKÉMON
—

EVOLUTION

MAIN WAY TO REGISTER IN THE NATIONAL POKÉDEX

Catch on Mirage Island 7.

Damage taken in normal battles

Normal	×1	Flying	×1
Fire	×0.5	Psychic	×1
Water	×2	Bug	×0.5
Grass	×0.5	Rock	×2
Electric	×1	Ghost	×1
Ice	×0.5	Dragon	×1
Fighting	×1	Dark	×1
Poison	×1	Steel	×0.5
Ground	×2	Fairy	×0.5

Damage taken in Inverse battles

Normal	×1	Flying	×1
Fire	×2	Psychic	×1
Water	×0.5	Bug	×2
Grass	×2	Rock	×0.5
Electric	×1	Ghost	×1
Ice	×2	Dragon	×1
Fighting	×1	Dark	×1
Poison	×1	Steel	×2
Ground	×0.5	Fairy	×2

Can be used in

- Inverse Battle
- Battle Institute
- Battle Maison
- Random Matchup (Free Battle)
- Random Matchup (Others)

LEVEL-UP MOVES

Lv.	Name	Type	Kind	Pow.	Acc.	PP	Range
1	Tackle	Normal	Physical	50	100	35	Normal
1	Rollout	Rock	Physical	30	90	20	Normal
1	Incinerate	Fire	Special	60	100	15	Many Others
1	Rage	Normal	Physical	20	100	20	Normal
3	Rollout	Rock	Physical	30	90	20	Normal
6	Incinerate	Fire	Special	60	100	15	Many Others
9	Rage	Normal	Physical	20	100	20	Normal
11	Fire Fang	Fire	Physical	65	95	15	Normal
14	Headbutt	Normal	Physical	70	100	15	Normal
17	Swagger	Normal	Status	—	90	15	Normal
19	Facade	Normal	Physical	70	100	20	Normal
22	Fire Punch	Fire	Physical	75	100	15	Normal
25	Work Up	Normal	Status	—	—	30	Self
27	Thrash	Normal	Physical	120	100	10	1 Random
30	Belly Drum	Normal	Status	—	—	10	Self
33	Flare Blitz	Fire	Physical	120	100	15	Normal
35	Hammer Arm	Fighting	Physical	100	90	10	Normal
39	Taunt	Dark	Status	—	100	20	Normal
47	Superpower	Fighting	Physical	120	100	5	Normal
54	Overheat	Fire	Special	130	90	5	Normal

TM & HM MOVES

No.	Name	Type	Kind	Pow.	Acc.	PP	Range
TM05	Roar	Normal	Status	—	—	20	Normal
TM06	Toxic	Poison	Status	—	90	10	Normal
TM08	Bulk Up	Fighting	Status	—	—	20	Self
TM10	Hidden Power	Normal	Special	60	100	15	Normal
TM11	Sunny Day	Fire	Status	—	—	5	Both Sides
TM12	Taunt	Dark	Status	—	100	20	Normal
TM15	Hyper Beam	Normal	Special	150	90	5	Normal
TM17	Protect	Normal	Status	—	—	10	Self
TM21	Frustration	Normal	Physical	—	100	20	Normal
TM22	Solar Beam	Grass	Special	120	100	10	Normal
TM23	Smack Down	Rock	Physical	50	100	15	Normal
TM26	Earthquake	Ground	Physical	100	100	10	Adjacent
TM27	Return	Normal	Physical	—	100	20	Normal
TM28	Dig	Ground	Physical	80	100	10	Normal
TM29	Psychic	Psychic	Special	90	100	10	Normal
TM31	Brick Break	Fighting	Physical	75	100	15	Normal
TM32	Double Team	Normal	Status	—	—	15	Self
TM35	Flamethrower	Fire	Special	90	100	15	Normal
TM38	Fire Blast	Fire	Special	110	85	5	Normal
TM39	Rock Tomb	Rock	Physical	60	95	15	Normal
TM41	Torment	Dark	Status	—	100	15	Normal
TM42	Facade	Normal	Physical	70	100	20	Normal
TM43	Flame Charge	Fire	Physical	50	100	20	Normal
TM44	Rest	Psychic	Status	—	—	10	Self
TM45	Attract	Normal	Status	—	100	15	Normal
TM46	Thief	Dark	Physical	60	100	25	Normal
TM48	Round	Normal	Special	60	100	15	Normal
TM50	Overheat	Fire	Special	130	90	5	Normal
TM52	Focus Blast	Fighting	Special	120	70	5	Normal
TM56	Fling	Dark	Physical	—	100	10	Normal
TM59	Incinerate	Fire	Special	60	100	15	Many Others
TM61	Will-O-Wisp	Fire	Status	—	85	15	Normal
TM66	Payback	Dark	Physical	50	100	10	Normal
TM68	Giga Impact	Normal	Physical	150	90	5	Normal
TM71	Stone Edge	Rock	Physical	100	80	5	Normal
TM74	Gyro Ball	Steel	Physical	—	100	5	Normal
TM78	Bulldoze	Ground	Physical	60	100	20	Adjacent
TM80	Rock Slide	Rock	Physical	75	90	10	Many Others
TM86	Grass Knot	Grass	Special	—	100	20	Normal
TM87	Swagger	Normal	Status	—	90	15	Normal
TM88	Sleep Talk	Normal	Status	—	—	10	Self
TM89	U-turn	Bug	Physical	70	100	20	Normal
TM90	Substitute	Normal	Status	—	—	10	Self
TM94	Secret Power	Normal	Physical	70	100	20	Normal
TM98	Power-Up Punch	Fighting	Physical	40	100	20	Normal
TM100	Confide	Normal	Status	—	—	20	Normal
HM04	Strength	Normal	Physical	80	100	15	Normal
HM06	Rock Smash	Fighting	Physical	40	100	15	Normal

MOVES LEARNED IN EXCHANGE FOR BP

Name	Type	Kind	Pow.	Acc.	PP	Range
Uproar	Normal	Special	90	100	10	1 Random
Fire Punch	Fire	Physical	75	100	15	Normal
Superpower	Fighting	Physical	120	100	5	Normal
Zen Headbutt	Psychic	Physical	80	90	15	Normal
Snore	Normal	Special	50	100	15	Normal
Heat Wave	Fire	Special	95	90	10	Many Others
Focus Punch	Fighting	Physical	150	100	20	Normal
Endeavor	Normal	Physical	—	100	5	Normal
Snatch	Dark	Status	—	—	10	Self

MOVES TAUGHT BY PEOPLE

Name	Type	Kind	Pow.	Acc.	PP	Range

National Pokédex **555** Hoenn Pokédex —

Darmanitan Zen Mode

Blazing Pokémon

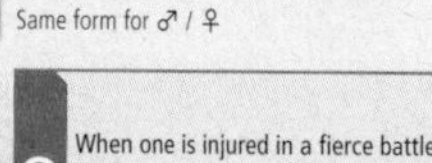

Fire Psychic

HEIGHT: 4'03" WEIGHT: 204.8 lbs.

Same form for ♂ / ♀

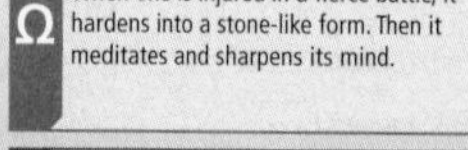

This Pokémon art is from in-game data.

Ω When one is injured in a fierce battle, it hardens into a stone-like form. Then it meditates and sharpens its mind.

α Its internal fire burns at 2,500 degrees Fahrenheit, making enough power that it can destroy a dump truck with one punch.

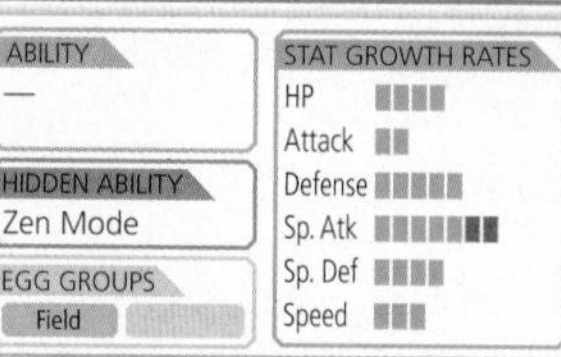

ABILITY
—

HIDDEN ABILITY
Zen Mode

EGG GROUPS
Field

STAT GROWTH RATES
HP
Attack
Defense
Sp. Atk
Sp. Def
Speed

ITEMS SOMETIMES HELD BY WILD POKÉMON
—

EVOLUTION

MAIN WAY TO REGISTER IN THE NATIONAL POKÉDEX

Catch on Mirage Island 7.

Damage taken in normal battles

Normal	×1	Flying	×1
Fire	×0.5	Psychic	×0.5
Water	×2	Bug	×1
Grass	×0.5	Rock	×2
Electric	×1	Ghost	×2
Ice	×0.5	Dragon	×1
Fighting	×0.5	Dark	×2
Poison	×1	Steel	×0.5
Ground	×2	Fairy	×0.5

Damage taken in Inverse battles

Normal	×1	Flying	×1
Fire	×2	Psychic	×2
Water	×0.5	Bug	×1
Grass	×2	Rock	×0.5
Electric	×1	Ghost	×0.5
Ice	×2	Dragon	×1
Fighting	×2	Dark	×0.5
Poison	×1	Steel	×2
Ground	×0.5	Fairy	×2

Can be used in

- Inverse Battle
- Battle Institute
- Battle Maison
- Random Matchup (Free Battle)
- Random Matchup (Others)

LEVEL-UP MOVES

Lv.	Name	Type	Kind	Pow.	Acc.	PP	Range
1	Tackle	Normal	Physical	50	100	35	Normal
1	Rollout	Rock	Physical	30	90	20	Normal
1	Incinerate	Fire	Special	60	100	15	Many Others
1	Rage	Normal	Physical	20	100	20	Normal
3	Rollout	Rock	Physical	30	90	20	Normal
6	Incinerate	Fire	Special	60	100	15	Many Others
9	Rage	Normal	Physical	20	100	20	Normal
11	Fire Fang	Fire	Physical	65	95	15	Normal
14	Headbutt	Normal	Physical	70	100	15	Normal
17	Swagger	Normal	Status	—	90	15	Normal
19	Facade	Normal	Physical	70	100	20	Normal
22	Fire Punch	Fire	Physical	75	100	15	Normal
25	Work Up	Normal	Status	—	—	30	Self
27	Thrash	Normal	Physical	120	100	10	1 Random
30	Belly Drum	Normal	Status	—	—	10	Self
33	Flare Blitz	Fire	Physical	120	100	15	Normal
35	Hammer Arm	Fighting	Physical	100	90	10	Normal
39	Taunt	Dark	Status	—	100	20	Normal
47	Superpower	Fighting	Physical	120	100	5	Normal
54	Overheat	Fire	Special	130	90	5	Normal

TM & HM MOVES

No.	Name	Type	Kind	Pow.	Acc.	PP	Range
TM05	Roar	Normal	Status	—	—	20	Normal
TM06	Toxic	Poison	Status	—	90	10	Normal
TM08	Bulk Up	Fighting	Status	—	—	20	Self
TM10	Hidden Power	Normal	Special	60	100	15	Normal
TM11	Sunny Day	Fire	Status	—	—	5	Both Sides
TM12	Taunt	Dark	Status	—	100	20	Normal
TM15	Hyper Beam	Normal	Special	150	90	5	Normal
TM17	Protect	Normal	Status	—	—	10	Self
TM21	Frustration	Normal	Physical	—	100	20	Normal
TM22	Solar Beam	Grass	Special	120	100	10	Normal
TM23	Smack Down	Rock	Physical	50	100	15	Normal
TM26	Earthquake	Ground	Physical	100	100	10	Adjacent
TM27	Return	Normal	Physical	—	100	20	Normal
TM28	Dig	Ground	Physical	80	100	10	Normal
TM29	Psychic	Psychic	Special	90	100	10	Normal
TM31	Brick Break	Fighting	Physical	75	100	15	Normal
TM32	Double Team	Normal	Status	—	—	15	Self
TM35	Flamethrower	Fire	Special	90	100	15	Normal
TM38	Fire Blast	Fire	Special	110	85	5	Normal
TM39	Rock Tomb	Rock	Physical	60	95	15	Normal
TM41	Torment	Dark	Status	—	100	15	Normal
TM42	Facade	Normal	Physical	70	100	20	Normal
TM43	Flame Charge	Fire	Physical	50	100	20	Normal
TM44	Rest	Psychic	Status	—	—	10	Self
TM45	Attract	Normal	Status	—	100	15	Normal
TM46	Thief	Dark	Physical	60	100	25	Normal
TM48	Round	Normal	Special	60	100	15	Normal
TM50	Overheat	Fire	Special	130	90	5	Normal
TM52	Focus Blast	Fighting	Special	120	70	5	Normal
TM56	Fling	Dark	Physical	—	100	10	Normal
TM59	Incinerate	Fire	Special	60	100	15	Many Others
TM61	Will-O-Wisp	Fire	Status	—	85	15	Normal
TM66	Payback	Dark	Physical	50	100	10	Normal
TM68	Giga Impact	Normal	Physical	150	90	5	Normal
TM71	Stone Edge	Rock	Physical	100	80	5	Normal
TM74	Gyro Ball	Steel	Physical	—	100	5	Normal
TM78	Bulldoze	Ground	Physical	60	100	20	Adjacent
TM80	Rock Slide	Rock	Physical	75	90	10	Many Others
TM86	Grass Knot	Grass	Special	—	100	20	Normal
TM87	Swagger	Normal	Status	—	90	15	Normal
TM88	Sleep Talk	Normal	Status	—	—	10	Self
TM89	U-turn	Bug	Physical	70	100	20	Normal
TM90	Substitute	Normal	Status	—	—	10	Self
TM94	Secret Power	Normal	Physical	70	100	20	Normal
TM98	Power-Up Punch	Fighting	Physical	40	100	20	Normal
TM100	Confide	Normal	Status	—	—	20	Normal
HM04	Strength	Normal	Physical	80	100	15	Normal
HM06	Rock Smash	Fighting	Physical	40	100	15	Normal

MOVES LEARNED IN EXCHANGE FOR BP

Name	Type	Kind	Pow.	Acc.	PP	Range
Uproar	Normal	Special	90	100	10	1 Random
Fire Punch	Fire	Physical	75	100	15	Normal
Superpower	Fighting	Physical	120	100	5	Normal
Zen Headbutt	Psychic	Physical	80	90	15	Normal
Snore	Normal	Special	50	100	15	Normal
Heat Wave	Fire	Special	95	90	10	Many Others
Focus Punch	Fighting	Physical	150	100	20	Normal
Endeavor	Normal	Physical	—	100	5	Normal
Snatch	Dark	Status	—	—	10	Self

MOVES TAUGHT BY PEOPLE

Name	Type	Kind	Pow.	Acc.	PP	Range

◆ A Darmanitan with the Zen Mode Hidden Ability can change to Zen Mode in battle if its HP drops to half or less of its maximum value.

National Pokédex **556** Hoenn Pokédex –

Maractus

Cactus Pokémon

Grass

HEIGHT: 3'03" WEIGHT: 61.7 lbs.

Same form for ♂ / ♀

Ω It uses an up-tempo song and dance to drive away the bird Pokémon that prey on its flower seeds.

α Arid regions are their habitat. They move rhythmically, making a sound similar to maracas.

ABILITIES
Water Absorb
Chlorophyll

HIDDEN ABILITY
Storm Drain

EGG GROUPS
Grass

STAT GROWTH RATES
HP ■■■
Attack ■■■■
Defense ■■■
Sp. Atk ■■■■■
Sp. Def ■■■
Speed ■■■

ITEMS SOMETIMES HELD BY WILD POKÉMON
Miracle Seed

EVOLUTION
Does not evolve

MAIN WAY TO REGISTER IN THE NATIONAL POKÉDEX
Catch on Mirage Island 2.

Damage taken in normal battles

Type		Type	
Normal	×1	Flying	×2
Fire	×2	Psychic	×1
Water	×0.5	Bug	×2
Grass	×0.5	Rock	×1
Electric	×0.5	Ghost	×1
Ice	×2	Dragon	×1
Fighting	×1	Dark	×1
Poison	×2	Steel	×1
Ground	×0.5	Fairy	×1

Damage taken in Inverse battles

Type		Type	
Normal	×1	Flying	×0.5
Fire	×0.5	Psychic	×1
Water	×2	Bug	×0.5
Grass	×2	Rock	×1
Electric	×2	Ghost	×1
Ice	×0.5	Dragon	×1
Fighting	×1	Dark	×1
Poison	×0.5	Steel	×1
Ground	×2	Fairy	×1

Can be used in
Inverse Battle
Battle Institute
Battle Maison
Random Matchup (Free Battle)
Random Matchup (Others)

LEVEL-UP MOVES

Lv.	Name	Type	Kind	Pow.	Acc.	PP	Range
1	Spiky Shield	Grass	Status	—	—	10	Self
1	Cotton Guard	Grass	Status	—	—	10	Self
1	After You	Normal	Status	—	—	15	Normal
1	Peck	Flying	Physical	35	100	35	Normal
1	Absorb	Grass	Special	20	100	25	Normal
3	Sweet Scent	Normal	Status	—	100	20	Many Others
6	Growth	Normal	Status	—	—	20	Self
10	Pin Missile	Bug	Physical	25	95	20	Normal
13	Mega Drain	Grass	Special	40	100	15	Normal
15	Synthesis	Grass	Status	—	—	5	Self
18	Cotton Spore	Grass	Status	—	100	40	Many Others
22	Needle Arm	Grass	Physical	60	100	15	Normal
26	Giga Drain	Grass	Special	75	100	10	Normal
29	Acupressure	Normal	Status	—	—	30	Self/Ally
33	Ingrain	Grass	Status	—	—	20	Self
38	Petal Dance	Grass	Special	120	100	10	1 Random
42	Sucker Punch	Dark	Physical	80	100	5	Normal
45	Sunny Day	Fire	Status	—	—	5	Both Sides
48	Petal Blizzard	Grass	Physical	90	100	15	Adjacent
50	Solar Beam	Grass	Special	120	100	10	Normal
55	Cotton Guard	Grass	Status	—	—	10	Self
57	After You	Normal	Status	—	—	15	Normal

TM & HM MOVES

No.	Name	Type	Kind	Pow.	Acc.	PP	Range
TM06	Toxic	Poison	Status	—	90	10	Normal
TM10	Hidden Power	Normal	Special	60	100	15	Normal
TM11	Sunny Day	Fire	Status	—	—	5	Both Sides
TM17	Protect	Normal	Status	—	—	10	Self
TM20	Safeguard	Normal	Status	—	—	25	Your Side
TM21	Frustration	Normal	Physical	—	100	20	Normal
TM22	Solar Beam	Grass	Special	120	100	10	Normal
TM27	Return	Normal	Physical	—	100	20	Normal
TM32	Double Team	Normal	Status	—	—	15	Self
TM40	Aerial Ace	Flying	Physical	60	—	20	Normal
TM42	Facade	Normal	Physical	70	100	20	Normal
TM44	Rest	Psychic	Status	—	—	10	Self
TM45	Attract	Normal	Status	—	100	15	Normal
TM48	Round	Normal	Special	60	100	15	Normal
TM53	Energy Ball	Grass	Special	90	100	10	Normal
TM84	Poison Jab	Poison	Physical	80	100	20	Normal
TM86	Grass Knot	Grass	Special	—	100	20	Normal
TM87	Swagger	Normal	Status	—	90	15	Normal
TM88	Sleep Talk	Normal	Status	—	—	10	Self
TM90	Substitute	Normal	Status	—	—	10	Self
TM94	Secret Power	Normal	Physical	70	100	20	Normal
TM96	Nature Power	Normal	Status	—	—	20	Normal
TM100	Confide	Normal	Status	—	—	20	Normal

MOVES LEARNED IN EXCHANGE FOR BP

Name	Type	Kind	Pow.	Acc.	PP	Range
Seed Bomb	Grass	Physical	80	100	15	Normal
Bounce	Flying	Physical	85	85	5	Normal
Uproar	Normal	Special	90	100	10	1 Random
Hyper Voice	Normal	Special	90	100	10	Many Others
Snore	Normal	Special	50	100	15	Normal
Knock Off	Dark	Physical	65	100	20	Normal
Synthesis	Grass	Status	—	—	5	Self
Giga Drain	Grass	Special	75	100	10	Normal
Drain Punch	Fighting	Physical	75	100	10	Normal
Worry Seed	Grass	Status	—	100	10	Normal
After You	Normal	Status	—	—	15	Normal
Helping Hand	Normal	Status	—	—	20	1 Ally
Endeavor	Normal	Physical	—	100	5	Normal

MOVES TAUGHT BY PEOPLE

Name	Type	Kind	Pow.	Acc.	PP	Range

EGG MOVES

Name	Type	Kind	Pow.	Acc.	PP	Range
Bullet Seed	Grass	Physical	25	100	30	Normal
Bounce	Flying	Physical	85	85	5	Normal
Worry Seed	Grass	Status	—	100	10	Normal
Leech Seed	Grass	Status	—	90	10	Normal
Seed Bomb	Grass	Physical	80	100	15	Normal
Wood Hammer	Grass	Physical	120	100	15	Normal
Spikes	Ground	Status	—	—	20	Other Side
Grass Whistle	Grass	Status	—	55	15	Normal
Grassy Terrain	Grass	Status	—	—	10	Both Sides

National Pokédex **557** Hoenn Pokédex –

Dwebble

Rock Inn Pokémon

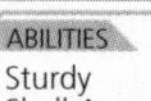

Bug Rock

HEIGHT: 1'00" WEIGHT: 32 lbs.

Same form for ♂ / ♀

Ω It makes a hole in a suitable rock. If that rock breaks, the Pokémon remains agitated until it locates a replacement.

α When it finds a stone of a suitable size, it secretes a liquid from its mouth to open up a hole to crawl into.

ABILITIES
Sturdy
Shell Armor

HIDDEN ABILITY
Weak Armor

EGG GROUPS
Bug Mineral

STAT GROWTH RATES
HP ■■
Attack ■■■
Defense ■■■■
Sp. Atk ■■
Sp. Def ■■
Speed ■■■

ITEMS SOMETIMES HELD BY WILD POKÉMON
Hard Stone

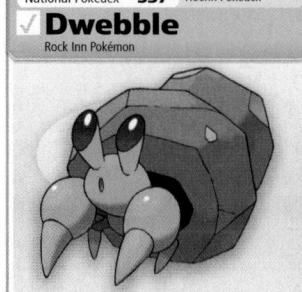

EVOLUTION
Dwebble → Lv. 34 → Crustle

MAIN WAY TO REGISTER IN THE NATIONAL POKÉDEX
Catch in the desert on Route 111. Appears as a hidden Pokémon after you battle Groudon or Kyogre.

Damage taken in normal battles

Type		Type	
Normal	×0.5	Flying	×1
Fire	×1	Psychic	×1
Water	×2	Bug	×1
Grass	×1	Rock	×2
Electric	×1	Ghost	×1
Ice	×1	Dragon	×1
Fighting	×1	Dark	×1
Poison	×0.5	Steel	×2
Ground	×1	Fairy	×1

Damage taken in Inverse battles

Type		Type	
Normal	×2	Flying	×1
Fire	×1	Psychic	×1
Water	×0.5	Bug	×1
Grass	×1	Rock	×0.5
Electric	×1	Ghost	×1
Ice	×1	Dragon	×1
Fighting	×1	Dark	×1
Poison	×2	Steel	×0.5
Ground	×1	Fairy	×1

Can be used in
Inverse Battle
Battle Institute
Battle Maison
Random Matchup (Free Battle)
Random Matchup (Others)

LEVEL-UP MOVES

Lv.	Name	Type	Kind	Pow.	Acc.	PP	Range
1	Fury Cutter	Bug	Physical	40	95	20	Normal
5	Rock Blast	Rock	Physical	25	90	10	Normal
7	Withdraw	Water	Status	—	—	40	Self
11	Sand Attack	Ground	Status	—	100	15	Normal
13	Feint Attack	Dark	Physical	60	—	20	Normal
17	Smack Down	Rock	Physical	50	100	15	Normal
19	Rock Polish	Rock	Status	—	—	20	Self
23	Bug Bite	Bug	Physical	60	100	20	Normal
24	Stealth Rock	Rock	Status	—	—	20	Other Side
29	Rock Slide	Rock	Physical	75	90	10	Many Others
31	Slash	Normal	Physical	70	100	20	Normal
35	X-Scissor	Bug	Physical	80	100	15	Normal
37	Shell Smash	Normal	Status	—	—	15	Self
41	Flail	Normal	Physical	—	100	15	Normal
43	Rock Wrecker	Rock	Physical	150	90	5	Normal

TM & HM MOVES

No.	Name	Type	Kind	Pow.	Acc.	PP	Range
TM01	Hone Claws	Dark	Status	—	—	15	Self
TM06	Toxic	Poison	Status	—	90	10	Normal
TM10	Hidden Power	Normal	Special	60	100	15	Normal
TM17	Protect	Normal	Status	—	—	10	Self
TM21	Frustration	Normal	Physical	—	100	20	Normal
TM22	Solar Beam	Grass	Special	120	100	10	Normal
TM23	Smack Down	Rock	Physical	50	100	15	Normal
TM26	Earthquake	Ground	Physical	100	100	10	Adjacent
TM27	Return	Normal	Physical	—	100	20	Normal
TM28	Dig	Ground	Physical	80	100	10	Normal
TM32	Double Team	Normal	Status	—	—	15	Self
TM37	Sandstorm	Rock	Status	—	—	10	Both Sides
TM39	Rock Tomb	Rock	Physical	60	95	15	Normal
TM40	Aerial Ace	Flying	Physical	60	—	20	Normal
TM42	Facade	Normal	Physical	70	100	20	Normal
TM44	Rest	Psychic	Status	—	—	10	Self
TM45	Attract	Normal	Status	—	100	15	Normal
TM48	Round	Normal	Special	60	100	15	Normal
TM65	Shadow Claw	Ghost	Physical	70	100	15	Normal
TM69	Rock Polish	Rock	Status	—	—	20	Self
TM71	Stone Edge	Rock	Physical	100	80	5	Normal
TM75	Swords Dance	Normal	Status	—	—	20	Self
TM76	Struggle Bug	Bug	Special	50	100	20	Many Others
TM78	Bulldoze	Ground	Physical	60	100	20	Adjacent
TM80	Rock Slide	Rock	Physical	75	90	10	Many Others
TM81	X-Scissor	Bug	Physical	80	100	15	Normal
TM84	Poison Jab	Poison	Physical	80	100	20	Normal
TM87	Swagger	Normal	Status	—	90	15	Normal
TM88	Sleep Talk	Normal	Status	—	—	10	Self
TM90	Substitute	Normal	Status	—	—	10	Self
TM94	Secret Power	Normal	Physical	70	100	20	Normal
TM96	Nature Power	Normal	Status	—	—	20	Normal
TM100	Confide	Normal	Status	—	—	20	Normal
HM01	Cut	Normal	Physical	50	95	30	Normal
HM04	Strength	Normal	Physical	80	100	15	Normal
HM06	Rock Smash	Fighting	Physical	40	100	15	Normal

MOVES LEARNED IN EXCHANGE FOR BP

Name	Type	Kind	Pow.	Acc.	PP	Range
Bug Bite	Bug	Physical	60	100	20	Normal
Block	Normal	Status	—	—	5	Normal
Iron Defense	Steel	Status	—	—	15	Self
Snore	Normal	Special	50	100	15	Normal
Knock Off	Dark	Physical	65	100	20	Normal
Stealth Rock	Rock	Status	—	—	20	Other Side

MOVES TAUGHT BY PEOPLE

Name	Type	Kind	Pow.	Acc.	PP	Range

EGG MOVES

Name	Type	Kind	Pow.	Acc.	PP	Range
Endure	Normal	Status	—	—	10	Self
Iron Defense	Steel	Status	—	—	15	Self
Night Slash	Dark	Physical	70	100	15	Normal
Sand Tomb	Ground	Physical	35	85	15	Normal
Counter	Fighting	Physical	—	100	20	Varies
Curse	Ghost	Status	—	—	10	Varies
Spikes	Ground	Status	—	—	20	Other Side
Block	Normal	Status	—	—	5	Normal
Wide Guard	Rock	Status	—	—	10	Your Side
Rototiller	Ground	Status	—	—	10	Adjacent

National Pokédex **558** Hoenn Pokédex —

Crustle

Stone Home Pokémon

Bug | Rock

HEIGHT: 4'07" WEIGHT: 440.9 lbs.

Same form for ♂ / ♀

Ω It possesses legs of enormous strength, enabling it to carry heavy slabs for many days, even when crossing arid land.

α Competing for territory, Crustle fight viciously. The one whose boulder is broken is the loser of the battle.

ABILITIES
Sturdy
Shell Armor

HIDDEN ABILITY
Weak Armor

EGG GROUPS
Bug | Mineral

STAT GROWTH RATES
HP
Attack
Defense
Sp. Atk
Sp. Def
Speed

ITEMS SOMETIMES HELD BY WILD POKÉMON
Hard Stone

EVOLUTION

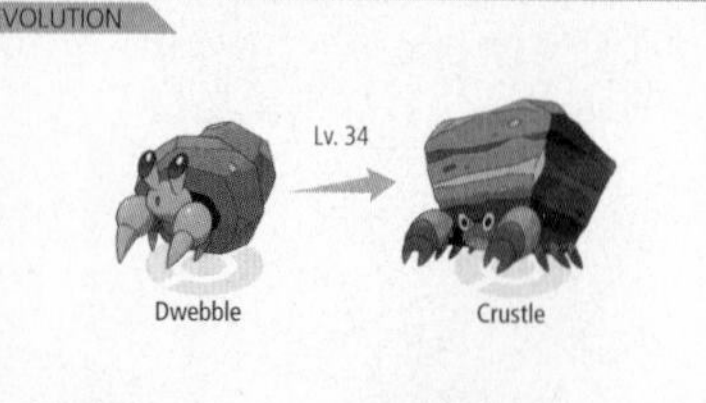

MAIN WAY TO REGISTER IN THE NATIONAL POKÉDEX

Catch when it appears from a cracked rock in Mirage Mountain 7 (using Rock Smash).

Damage taken in normal battles

Normal	×0.5	Flying	×1
Fire	×1	Psychic	×1
Water	×2	Bug	×1
Grass	×1	Rock	×2
Electric	×1	Ghost	×1
Ice	×1	Dragon	×1
Fighting	×1	Dark	×1
Poison	×0.5	Steel	×2
Ground	×1	Fairy	×1

Damage taken in Inverse battles

Normal	×2	Flying	×1
Fire	×1	Psychic	×1
Water	×0.5	Bug	×1
Grass	×1	Rock	×0.5
Electric	×1	Ghost	×1
Ice	×1	Dragon	×1
Fighting	×1	Dark	×1
Poison	×2	Steel	×0.5
Ground	×1	Fairy	×1

Can be used in
Inverse Battle
Battle Institute
Battle Maison
Random Matchup (Free Battle)
Random Matchup (Others)

LEVEL-UP MOVES

Lv.	Name	Type	Kind	Pow.	Acc.	PP	Range
1	Shell Smash	Normal	Status	—	—	15	Self
1	Rock Blast	Rock	Physical	25	90	10	Normal
1	Withdraw	Water	Status	—	—	40	Self
1	Sand Attack	Ground	Status	—	100	15	Normal
5	Rock Blast	Rock	Physical	25	90	10	Normal
7	Withdraw	Water	Status	—	—	40	Self
11	Sand Attack	Ground	Status	—	100	15	Normal
13	Feint Attack	Dark	Physical	60	—	20	Normal
17	Smack Down	Rock	Physical	50	100	15	Normal
19	Rock Polish	Rock	Status	—	—	20	Self
23	Bug Bite	Bug	Physical	60	100	20	Normal
24	Stealth Rock	Rock	Status	—	—	20	Other Side
29	Rock Slide	Rock	Physical	75	90	10	Many Others
31	Slash	Normal	Physical	70	100	20	Normal
38	X-Scissor	Bug	Physical	80	100	15	Normal
43	Shell Smash	Normal	Status	—	—	15	Self
50	Flail	Normal	Physical	—	100	15	Normal
55	Rock Wrecker	Rock	Physical	150	90	5	Normal

TM & HM MOVES

No.	Name	Type	Kind	Pow.	Acc.	PP	Range
TM01	Hone Claws	Dark	Status	—	—	15	Self
TM06	Toxic	Poison	Status	—	90	10	Normal
TM10	Hidden Power	Normal	Special	60	100	15	Normal
TM15	Hyper Beam	Normal	Special	150	90	5	Normal
TM17	Protect	Normal	Status	—	—	10	Self
TM21	Frustration	Normal	Physical	—	100	20	Normal
TM22	Solar Beam	Grass	Special	120	100	10	Normal
TM23	Smack Down	Rock	Physical	50	100	15	Normal
TM26	Earthquake	Ground	Physical	100	100	10	Adjacent
TM27	Return	Normal	Physical	—	100	20	Normal
TM28	Dig	Ground	Physical	80	100	10	Normal
TM32	Double Team	Normal	Status	—	—	15	Self
TM37	Sandstorm	Rock	Status	—	—	10	Both Sides
TM39	Rock Tomb	Rock	Physical	60	95	15	Normal
TM40	Aerial Ace	Flying	Physical	60	—	20	Normal
TM42	Facade	Normal	Physical	70	100	20	Normal
TM44	Rest	Psychic	Status	—	—	10	Self
TM45	Attract	Normal	Status	—	100	15	Normal
TM48	Round	Normal	Special	60	100	15	Normal
TM65	Shadow Claw	Ghost	Physical	70	100	15	Normal
TM68	Giga Impact	Normal	Physical	150	90	5	Normal
TM69	Rock Polish	Rock	Status	—	—	20	Self
TM71	Stone Edge	Rock	Physical	100	80	5	Normal
TM75	Swords Dance	Normal	Status	—	—	20	Self
TM76	Struggle Bug	Bug	Special	50	100	20	Many Others
TM78	Bulldoze	Ground	Physical	60	100	20	Adjacent
TM80	Rock Slide	Rock	Physical	75	90	10	Many Others
TM81	X-Scissor	Bug	Physical	80	100	15	Normal
TM84	Poison Jab	Poison	Physical	80	100	20	Normal
TM87	Swagger	Normal	Status	—	90	15	Normal
TM88	Sleep Talk	Normal	Status	—	—	10	Self
TM90	Substitute	Normal	Status	—	—	10	Self
TM94	Secret Power	Normal	Physical	70	100	20	Normal
TM96	Nature Power	Normal	Status	—	—	20	Normal
TM100	Confide	Normal	Status	—	—	20	Normal
HM01	Cut	Normal	Physical	50	95	30	Normal
HM04	Strength	Normal	Physical	80	100	15	Normal
HM06	Rock Smash	Fighting	Physical	40	100	15	Normal

MOVES LEARNED IN EXCHANGE FOR BP

Name	Type	Kind	Pow.	Acc.	PP	Range
Bug Bite	Bug	Physical	60	100	20	Normal
Block	Normal	Status	—	—	5	Normal
Iron Defense	Steel	Status	—	—	15	Self
Snore	Normal	Special	50	100	15	Normal
Knock Off	Dark	Physical	65	100	20	Normal
Stealth Rock	Rock	Status	—	—	20	Other Side

MOVES TAUGHT BY PEOPLE

Name	Type	Kind	Pow.	Acc.	PP	Range

National Pokédex **559** Hoenn Pokédex —

Scraggy

Shedding Pokémon

Dark | Fighting

HEIGHT: 2'00" WEIGHT: 26 lbs.

Same form for ♂ / ♀

Ω Its skin has a rubbery elasticity, so it can reduce damage by defensively pulling its skin up to its neck.

α Proud of its sturdy skull, it suddenly headbutts everything, but its weight makes it unstable, too.

ABILITIES
Shed Skin
Moxie

HIDDEN ABILITY
Intimidate

EGG GROUPS
Field | Dragon

STAT GROWTH RATES
HP
Attack
Defense
Sp. Atk
Sp. Def
Speed

ITEMS SOMETIMES HELD BY WILD POKÉMON
Shed Shell

EVOLUTION

MAIN WAY TO REGISTER IN THE NATIONAL POKÉDEX

Catch on Route 113. Appears as a hidden Pokémon after you battle Groudon or Kyogre.

Damage taken in normal battles

Normal	×1	Flying	×2
Fire	×1	Psychic	×0
Water	×1	Bug	×1
Grass	×1	Rock	×0.5
Electric	×1	Ghost	×0.5
Ice	×1	Dragon	×1
Fighting	×2	Dark	×0.25
Poison	×1	Steel	×1
Ground	×1	Fairy	×4

Damage taken in Inverse battles

Normal	×1	Flying	×0.5
Fire	×1	Psychic	×1
Water	×1	Bug	×1
Grass	×1	Rock	×2
Electric	×1	Ghost	×2
Ice	×1	Dragon	×1
Fighting	×0.5	Dark	×4
Poison	×1	Steel	×1
Ground	×1	Fairy	×0.25

Can be used in
Inverse Battle
Battle Institute
Battle Maison
Random Matchup (Free Battle)
Random Matchup (Others)

LEVEL-UP MOVES

Lv.	Name	Type	Kind	Pow.	Acc.	PP	Range
1	Leer	Normal	Status	—	100	30	Many Others
1	Low Kick	Fighting	Physical	—	100	20	Normal
5	Sand Attack	Ground	Status	—	100	15	Normal
9	Feint Attack	Dark	Physical	60	—	20	Normal
12	Headbutt	Normal	Physical	70	100	15	Normal
16	Swagger	Normal	Status	—	90	15	Normal
20	Brick Break	Fighting	Physical	75	100	15	Normal
23	Payback	Dark	Physical	50	100	10	Normal
27	Chip Away	Normal	Physical	70	100	20	Normal
31	High Jump Kick	Fighting	Physical	130	90	10	Normal
34	Scary Face	Normal	Status	—	100	10	Normal
38	Crunch	Dark	Physical	80	100	15	Normal
42	Facade	Normal	Physical	70	100	20	Normal
45	Rock Climb	Normal	Physical	90	85	20	Normal
48	Focus Punch	Fighting	Physical	150	100	20	Normal
50	Head Smash	Rock	Physical	150	80	5	Normal

TM & HM MOVES

No.	Name	Type	Kind	Pow.	Acc.	PP	Range
TM02	Dragon Claw	Dragon	Physical	80	100	15	Normal
TM05	Roar	Normal	Status	—	—	20	Normal
TM06	Toxic	Poison	Status	—	90	10	Normal
TM08	Bulk Up	Fighting	Status	—	—	20	Self
TM10	Hidden Power	Normal	Special	60	100	15	Normal
TM11	Sunny Day	Fire	Status	—	—	5	Both Sides
TM12	Taunt	Dark	Status	—	100	20	Normal
TM17	Protect	Normal	Status	—	—	10	Self
TM18	Rain Dance	Water	Status	—	—	5	Both Sides
TM21	Frustration	Normal	Physical	—	100	20	Normal
TM23	Smack Down	Rock	Physical	50	100	15	Normal
TM27	Return	Normal	Physical	—	100	20	Normal
TM28	Dig	Ground	Physical	80	100	10	Normal
TM31	Brick Break	Fighting	Physical	75	100	15	Normal
TM32	Double Team	Normal	Status	—	—	15	Self
TM36	Sludge Bomb	Poison	Special	90	100	10	Normal
TM39	Rock Tomb	Rock	Physical	60	95	15	Normal
TM41	Torment	Dark	Status	—	100	15	Normal
TM42	Facade	Normal	Physical	70	100	20	Normal
TM44	Rest	Psychic	Status	—	—	10	Self
TM45	Attract	Normal	Status	—	100	15	Normal
TM47	Low Sweep	Fighting	Physical	65	100	20	Normal
TM48	Round	Normal	Special	60	100	15	Normal
TM52	Focus Blast	Fighting	Special	120	70	5	Normal
TM56	Fling	Dark	Physical	—	100	10	Normal
TM59	Incinerate	Fire	Special	60	100	15	Many Others
TM66	Payback	Dark	Physical	50	100	10	Normal
TM67	Retaliate	Normal	Physical	70	100	5	Normal
TM71	Stone Edge	Rock	Physical	100	80	5	Normal
TM80	Rock Slide	Rock	Physical	75	90	10	Many Others
TM82	Dragon Tail	Dragon	Physical	60	90	10	Normal
TM84	Poison Jab	Poison	Physical	80	100	20	Normal
TM86	Grass Knot	Grass	Special	—	100	20	Normal
TM87	Swagger	Normal	Status	—	90	15	Normal
TM88	Sleep Talk	Normal	Status	—	—	10	Self
TM90	Substitute	Normal	Status	—	—	10	Self
TM94	Secret Power	Normal	Physical	70	100	20	Normal
TM95	Snarl	Dark	Special	55	95	15	Many Others
TM97	Dark Pulse	Dark	Special	80	100	15	Normal
TM98	Power-Up Punch	Fighting	Physical	40	100	20	Normal
TM100	Confide	Normal	Status	—	—	20	Normal
HM04	Strength	Normal	Physical	80	100	15	Normal
HM06	Rock Smash	Fighting	Physical	40	100	15	Normal

MOVES LEARNED IN EXCHANGE FOR BP

Name	Type	Kind	Pow.	Acc.	PP	Range
Super Fang	Normal	Physical	—	90	10	Normal
Dual Chop	Dragon	Physical	40	90	15	Normal
Iron Head	Steel	Physical	80	100	15	Normal
Low Kick	Fighting	Physical	—	100	20	Normal
Thunder Punch	Electric	Physical	75	100	15	Normal
Fire Punch	Fire	Physical	75	100	15	Normal
Ice Punch	Ice	Physical	75	100	15	Normal
Foul Play	Dark	Physical	95	100	15	Normal
Iron Defense	Steel	Status	—	—	15	Self
Zen Headbutt	Psychic	Physical	80	90	15	Normal
Dragon Pulse	Dragon	Special	85	100	10	Normal
Iron Tail	Steel	Physical	100	75	15	Normal
Snore	Normal	Special	50	100	15	Normal
Knock Off	Dark	Physical	65	100	20	Normal
Drain Punch	Fighting	Physical	75	100	10	Normal
Focus Punch	Fighting	Physical	150	100	20	Normal
Spite	Ghost	Status	—	100	10	Normal
Snatch	Dark	Status	—	—	10	Self

MOVES TAUGHT BY PEOPLE

Name	Type	Kind	Pow.	Acc.	PP	Range

EGG MOVES

Name	Type	Kind	Pow.	Acc.	PP	Range
Drain Punch	Fighting	Physical	75	100	10	Normal
Counter	Fighting	Physical	—	100	20	Varies
Dragon Dance	Dragon	Status	—	—	20	Self
Detect	Fighting	Status	—	—	5	Self
Fake Out	Normal	Physical	40	100	10	Normal
Fire Punch	Fire	Physical	75	100	15	Normal
Ice Punch	Ice	Physical	75	100	15	Normal
Thunder Punch	Electric	Physical	75	100	15	Normal
Amnesia	Psychic	Status	—	—	20	Self
Feint Attack	Dark	Physical	60	—	20	Normal
Zen Headbutt	Psychic	Physical	80	90	15	Normal
Quick Guard	Fighting	Status	—	—	15	Your Side

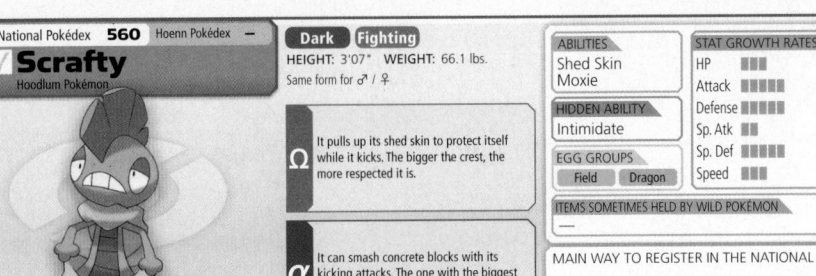

National Pokédex **560** Hoenn Pokédex —

Scrafty

Hoodlum Pokémon

Dark | Fighting

HEIGHT: 3'07" WEIGHT: 66.1 lbs.

Same form for ♂ / ♀

Ω It pulls up its shed skin to protect itself while it kicks. The bigger the crest, the more respected it is.

α It can smash concrete blocks with its kicking attacks. The one with the biggest crest is the group leader.

ABILITIES
Shed Skin
Moxie

HIDDEN ABILITY
Intimidate

EGG GROUPS
Field | Dragon

STAT GROWTH RATES
HP ■■■
Attack ■■■■■
Defense ■■■■■
Sp. Atk ■■
Sp. Def ■■■■■
Speed ■■■

ITEMS SOMETIMES HELD BY WILD POKÉMON
—

EVOLUTION

MAIN WAY TO REGISTER IN THE NATIONAL POKÉDEX

Level up Scraggy to Lv. 39.

Damage taken in normal battles

Type		Type	
Normal	×1	Flying	×2
Fire	×1	Psychic	×0
Water	×1	Bug	×1
Grass	×1	Rock	×0.5
Electric	×1	Ghost	×0.5
Ice	×1	Dragon	×1
Fighting	×2	Dark	×0.25
Poison	×1	Steel	×1
Ground	×1	Fairy	×4

Damage taken in Inverse battles

Type		Type	
Normal	×1	Flying	×0.5
Fire	×1	Psychic	×1
Water	×1	Bug	×1
Grass	×1	Rock	×2
Electric	×1	Ghost	×2
Ice	×1	Dragon	×1
Fighting	×0.5	Dark	×4
Poison	×1	Steel	×1
Ground	×1	Fairy	×0.25

Can be used in
Inverse Battle
Battle Institute
Battle Maison
Random Matchup (Free Battle)
Random Matchup (Others)

LEVEL-UP MOVES

Lv.	Name	Type	Kind	Pow.	Acc.	PP	Range
1	Leer	Normal	Status	—	100	30	Many Others
1	Low Kick	Fighting	Physical	—	100	20	Normal
1	Sand Attack	Ground	Status	—	100	15	Normal
1	Feint Attack	Dark	Physical	60	—	20	Normal
5	Sand Attack	Ground	Status	—	100	15	Normal
9	Feint Attack	Dark	Physical	60	—	20	Normal
12	Headbutt	Normal	Physical	70	100	15	Normal
16	Swagger	Normal	Status	—	90	15	Normal
20	Brick Break	Fighting	Physical	75	100	15	Normal
23	Payback	Dark	Physical	50	100	10	Normal
27	Chip Away	Normal	Physical	70	100	20	Normal
31	High Jump Kick	Fighting	Physical	130	90	10	Normal
34	Scary Face	Normal	Status	—	100	10	Normal
38	Crunch	Dark	Physical	80	100	15	Normal
45	Facade	Normal	Physical	70	100	20	Normal
51	Rock Climb	Normal	Physical	90	85	20	Normal
58	Focus Punch	Fighting	Physical	150	100	20	Normal
65	Head Smash	Rock	Physical	150	80	5	Normal

TM & HM MOVES

No.	Name	Type	Kind	Pow.	Acc.	PP	Range
TM02	Dragon Claw	Dragon	Physical	80	100	15	Normal
TM05	Roar	Normal	Status	—	—	20	Normal
TM06	Toxic	Poison	Status	—	90	10	Normal
TM08	Bulk Up	Fighting	Status	—	—	20	Self
TM10	Hidden Power	Normal	Special	60	100	15	Normal
TM11	Sunny Day	Fire	Status	—	—	5	Both Sides
TM12	Taunt	Dark	Status	—	100	20	Normal
TM15	Hyper Beam	Normal	Special	150	90	5	Normal
TM17	Protect	Normal	Status	—	—	10	Self
TM18	Rain Dance	Water	Status	—	—	5	Both Sides
TM21	Frustration	Normal	Physical	—	100	20	Normal
TM23	Smack Down	Rock	Physical	50	100	15	Normal
TM27	Return	Normal	Physical	—	100	20	Normal
TM28	Dig	Ground	Physical	80	100	10	Normal
TM31	Brick Break	Fighting	Physical	75	100	15	Normal
TM32	Double Team	Normal	Status	—	—	15	Self
TM36	Sludge Bomb	Poison	Special	90	100	10	Normal
TM39	Rock Tomb	Rock	Physical	60	95	15	Normal
TM41	Torment	Dark	Status	—	100	15	Normal
TM42	Facade	Normal	Physical	70	100	20	Normal
TM44	Rest	Psychic	Status	—	—	10	Self
TM45	Attract	Normal	Status	—	100	15	Normal
TM46	Thief	Dark	Physical	60	100	25	Normal
TM47	Low Sweep	Fighting	Physical	65	100	20	Normal
TM48	Round	Normal	Special	60	100	15	Normal
TM52	Focus Blast	Fighting	Special	120	70	5	Normal
TM56	Fling	Dark	Physical	—	100	10	Normal
TM59	Incinerate	Fire	Special	60	100	15	Many Others
TM66	Payback	Dark	Physical	50	100	10	Normal
TM67	Retaliate	Normal	Physical	70	100	5	Normal
TM68	Giga Impact	Normal	Physical	150	90	5	Normal
TM71	Stone Edge	Rock	Physical	100	80	5	Normal
TM80	Rock Slide	Rock	Physical	75	90	10	Many Others
TM82	Dragon Tail	Dragon	Physical	60	90	10	Normal
TM84	Poison Jab	Poison	Physical	80	100	20	Normal
TM86	Grass Knot	Grass	Special	—	100	20	Normal
TM87	Swagger	Normal	Status	—	90	15	Normal
TM88	Sleep Talk	Normal	Status	—	—	10	Self
TM90	Substitute	Normal	Status	—	—	10	Self
TM94	Secret Power	Normal	Physical	70	100	20	Normal
TM95	Snarl	Dark	Special	55	95	15	Many Others
TM97	Dark Pulse	Dark	Special	80	100	15	Normal
TM98	Power-Up Punch	Fighting	Physical	40	100	20	Normal
TM100	Confide	Normal	Status	—	—	20	Normal
HM04	Strength	Normal	Physical	80	100	15	Normal
HM06	Rock Smash	Fighting	Physical	40	100	15	Normal

MOVES LEARNED IN EXCHANGE FOR BP

Name	Type	Kind	Pow.	Acc.	PP	Range
Super Fang	Normal	Physical	—	90	10	Normal
Dual Chop	Dragon	Physical	40	90	15	Normal
Iron Head	Steel	Physical	80	100	15	Normal
Low Kick	Fighting	Physical	—	100	20	Normal
Thunder Punch	Electric	Physical	75	100	15	Normal
Fire Punch	Fire	Physical	75	100	15	Normal
Ice Punch	Ice	Physical	75	100	15	Normal
Foul Play	Dark	Physical	95	100	15	Normal
Iron Defense	Steel	Status	—	—	15	Self
Zen Headbutt	Psychic	Physical	80	90	15	Normal
Dragon Pulse	Dragon	Special	85	100	10	Normal
Iron Tail	Steel	Physical	100	75	15	Normal
Snore	Normal	Special	50	100	15	Normal
Knock Off	Dark	Physical	65	100	20	Normal
Drain Punch	Fighting	Physical	75	100	10	Normal
Focus Punch	Fighting	Physical	150	100	20	Normal
Spite	Ghost	Status	—	100	10	Normal
Outrage	Dragon	Physical	120	100	10	1 Random
Snatch	Dark	Status	—	—	10	Self

MOVES TAUGHT BY PEOPLE

Name	Type	Kind	Pow.	Acc.	PP	Range

National Pokédex **561** Hoenn Pokédex —

Sigilyph

Avianoid Pokémon

Psychic | Flying

HEIGHT: 4'07" WEIGHT: 30.9 lbs.

Same form for ♂ / ♀

Ω The guardians of an ancient city, they use their psychic power to attack enemies that invade their territory.

α The guardians of an ancient city, they always fly the same route while keeping watch for invaders.

ABILITIES
Wonder Skin
Magic Guard

HIDDEN ABILITY
Tinted Lens

EGG GROUPS
Flying

STAT GROWTH RATES
HP ■■■
Attack ■■■
Defense ■■■■
Sp. Atk ■■■■■
Sp. Def ■■■
Speed ■■■■■

ITEMS SOMETIMES HELD BY WILD POKÉMON
—

EVOLUTION

Does not evolve

MAIN WAY TO REGISTER IN THE NATIONAL POKÉDEX

Appears in *Pokémon X* and *Pokémon Y*. Bring it to your game using Link Trade or the GTS.

Damage taken in normal battles

Type		Type	
Normal	×1	Flying	×1
Fire	×1	Psychic	×0.5
Water	×1	Bug	×1
Grass	×0.5	Rock	×2
Electric	×2	Ghost	×2
Ice	×2	Dragon	×1
Fighting	×0.25	Dark	×2
Poison	×1	Steel	×1
Ground	×0	Fairy	×1

Damage taken in Inverse battles

Type		Type	
Normal	×1	Flying	×1
Fire	×1	Psychic	×2
Water	×1	Bug	×1
Grass	×2	Rock	×0.5
Electric	×0.5	Ghost	×0.5
Ice	×0.5	Dragon	×1
Fighting	×4	Dark	×0.5
Poison	×1	Steel	×1
Ground	×2	Fairy	×1

Can be used in
Inverse Battle
Battle Institute
Battle Maison
Random Matchup (Free Battle)
Random Matchup (Others)

LEVEL-UP MOVES

Lv.	Name	Type	Kind	Pow.	Acc.	PP	Range
1	Gust	Flying	Special	40	100	35	Normal
1	Miracle Eye	Psychic	Status	—	—	40	Normal
4	Hypnosis	Psychic	Status	—	60	20	Normal
8	Psywave	Psychic	Special	—	100	15	Normal
11	Tailwind	Flying	Status	—	—	15	Your Side
14	Whirlwind	Normal	Status	—	—	20	Normal
18	Psybeam	Psychic	Special	65	100	20	Normal
21	Air Cutter	Flying	Special	60	95	25	Many Others
24	Light Screen	Psychic	Status	—	—	30	Your Side
28	Reflect	Psychic	Status	—	—	20	Your Side
31	Synchronoise	Psychic	Special	120	100	10	Adjacent
34	Mirror Move	Flying	Status	—	—	20	Normal
38	Gravity	Psychic	Status	—	—	5	Both Sides
41	Air Slash	Flying	Special	75	95	15	Normal
44	Psychic	Psychic	Special	90	100	10	Normal
48	Cosmic Power	Psychic	Status	—	—	20	Self
50	Sky Attack	Flying	Physical	140	90	5	Normal

TM & HM MOVES

No.	Name	Type	Kind	Pow.	Acc.	PP	Range
TM03	Psyshock	Psychic	Special	80	100	10	Normal
TM04	Calm Mind	Psychic	Status	—	—	20	Self
TM06	Toxic	Poison	Status	—	90	10	Normal
TM10	Hidden Power	Normal	Special	60	100	15	Normal
TM13	Ice Beam	Ice	Special	90	100	10	Normal
TM15	Hyper Beam	Normal	Special	150	90	5	Normal
TM16	Light Screen	Psychic	Status	—	—	30	Your Side
TM17	Protect	Normal	Status	—	—	10	Self
TM18	Rain Dance	Water	Status	—	—	5	Both Sides
TM19	Roost	Flying	Status	—	—	10	Self
TM20	Safeguard	Normal	Status	—	—	25	Your Side
TM21	Frustration	Normal	Physical	—	100	20	Normal
TM22	Solar Beam	Grass	Special	120	100	10	Normal
TM23	Smack Down	Rock	Physical	50	100	15	Normal
TM27	Return	Normal	Physical	—	100	20	Normal
TM29	Psychic	Psychic	Special	90	100	10	Normal
TM30	Shadow Ball	Ghost	Special	80	100	15	Normal
TM32	Double Team	Normal	Status	—	—	15	Self
TM33	Reflect	Psychic	Status	—	—	20	Your Side
TM40	Aerial Ace	Flying	Physical	60	—	20	Normal
TM42	Facade	Normal	Physical	70	100	20	Normal
TM44	Rest	Psychic	Status	—	—	10	Self
TM45	Attract	Normal	Status	—	100	15	Normal
TM46	Thief	Dark	Physical	60	100	25	Normal
TM48	Round	Normal	Special	60	100	15	Normal
TM51	Steel Wing	Steel	Physical	70	90	25	Normal
TM53	Energy Ball	Grass	Special	90	100	10	Normal
TM57	Charge Beam	Electric	Special	50	90	10	Normal
TM70	Flash	Normal	Status	—	100	20	Normal
TM73	Thunder Wave	Electric	Status	—	100	20	Normal
TM77	Psych Up	Normal	Status	—	—	10	Normal
TM85	Dream Eater	Psychic	Special	100	100	15	Normal
TM87	Swagger	Normal	Status	—	90	15	Normal
TM88	Sleep Talk	Normal	Status	—	—	10	Self
TM90	Substitute	Normal	Status	—	—	10	Self
TM91	Flash Cannon	Steel	Special	80	100	10	Normal
TM92	Trick Room	Psychic	Status	—	—	5	Both Sides
TM94	Secret Power	Normal	Physical	70	100	20	Normal
TM97	Dark Pulse	Dark	Special	80	100	15	Normal
TM99	Dazzling Gleam	Fairy	Special	80	100	10	Many Others
TM100	Confide	Normal	Status	—	—	20	Normal
HM02	Fly	Flying	Physical	90	95	15	Normal

MOVES LEARNED IN EXCHANGE FOR BP

Name	Type	Kind	Pow.	Acc.	PP	Range
Signal Beam	Bug	Special	75	100	15	Normal
Magic Coat	Psychic	Status	—	—	15	Self
Gravity	Psychic	Status	—	—	5	Both Sides
Icy Wind	Ice	Special	55	95	15	Many Others
Zen Headbutt	Psychic	Physical	80	90	15	Normal
Snore	Normal	Special	50	100	15	Normal
Heat Wave	Fire	Special	95	90	10	Many Others
Tailwind	Flying	Status	—	—	15	Your Side
Sky Attack	Flying	Physical	140	90	5	Normal
Shock Wave	Electric	Special	60	—	20	Normal
Trick	Psychic	Status	—	100	10	Normal
Magic Room	Psychic	Status	—	—	10	Both Sides
Skill Swap	Psychic	Status	—	—	10	Normal

MOVES TAUGHT BY PEOPLE

Name	Type	Kind	Pow.	Acc.	PP	Range

EGG MOVES

Name	Type	Kind	Pow.	Acc.	PP	Range
Stored Power	Psychic	Special	20	100	10	Normal
Psycho Shift	Psychic	Status	—	100	10	Normal
Ancient Power	Rock	Special	60	100	5	Normal
Steel Wing	Steel	Physical	70	90	25	Normal
Roost	Flying	Status	—	—	10	Self
Skill Swap	Psychic	Status	—	—	10	Normal
Future Sight	Psychic	Special	120	100	10	Normal

National Pokédex **562** Hoenn Pokédex —

Yamask

Spirit Pokémon

Ghost

HEIGHT: 1'08" WEIGHT: 3.3 lbs.

Same form for ♂ / ♀

Ω These Pokémon arose from the spirits of people interred in graves. Each retains memories of its former life.

α Each of them carries a mask that used to be its face when it was human. Sometimes they look at it and cry.

ABILITY
Mummy

HIDDEN ABILITY
—

EGG GROUPS
Mineral / Amorphous

STAT GROWTH RATES
HP / Attack / Defense / Sp. Atk / Sp. Def / Speed

ITEMS SOMETIMES HELD BY WILD POKÉMON
—

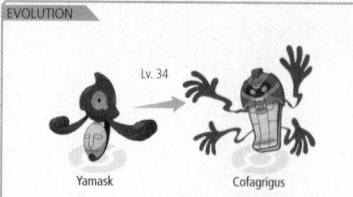

EVOLUTION
Yamask → Lv. 34 → Cofagrigus

MAIN WAY TO REGISTER IN THE NATIONAL POKÉDEX

Leave a Cofagrigus at a Pokémon Day Care, then hatch the Pokémon Egg that is found.

Damage taken in normal battles

Type	×	Type	×
Normal	×0	Flying	×1
Fire	×1	Psychic	×1
Water	×1	Bug	×0.5
Grass	×1	Rock	×1
Electric	×1	Ghost	×2
Ice	×1	Dragon	×1
Fighting	×0	Dark	×2
Poison	×0.5	Steel	×1
Ground	×1	Fairy	×1

Damage taken in Inverse battles

Type	×	Type	×
Normal	×2	Flying	×1
Fire	×1	Psychic	×1
Water	×1	Bug	×2
Grass	×1	Rock	×1
Electric	×1	Ghost	×0.5
Ice	×1	Dragon	×1
Fighting	×2	Dark	×0.5
Poison	×2	Steel	×1
Ground	×1	Fairy	×1

Can be used in
- Inverse Battle
- Battle Institute
- Battle Maison
- Random Matchup (Free Battle)
- Random Matchup (Others)

LEVEL-UP MOVES

Lv.	Name	Type	Kind	Pow.	Acc.	PP	Range
1	Astonish	Ghost	Physical	30	100	15	Normal
1	Protect	Normal	Status	—	—	10	Self
5	Disable	Normal	Status	—	100	20	Normal
9	Haze	Ice	Status	—	—	30	Both Sides
13	Night Shade	Ghost	Special	—	100	15	Normal
17	Hex	Ghost	Special	65	100	10	Normal
21	Will-O-Wisp	Fire	Status	—	85	15	Normal
25	Ominous Wind	Ghost	Special	60	100	5	Normal
29	Curse	Ghost	Status	—	—	10	Varies
33	Power Split	Psychic	Status	—	—	10	Normal
33	Guard Split	Psychic	Status	—	—	10	Normal
37	Shadow Ball	Ghost	Special	80	100	15	Normal
41	Grudge	Ghost	Status	—	—	5	Self
45	Mean Look	Normal	Status	—	—	5	Normal
49	Destiny Bond	Ghost	Status	—	—	5	Self

TM & HM MOVES

No.	Name	Type	Kind	Pow.	Acc.	PP	Range
TM04	Calm Mind	Psychic	Status	—	—	20	Self
TM06	Toxic	Poison	Status	—	90	10	Normal
TM10	Hidden Power	Normal	Special	60	100	15	Normal
TM17	Protect	Normal	Status	—	—	10	Self
TM18	Rain Dance	Water	Status	—	—	5	Both Sides
TM20	Safeguard	Normal	Status	—	—	25	Your Side
TM21	Frustration	Normal	Physical	—	100	20	Normal
TM27	Return	Normal	Physical	—	100	20	Normal
TM29	Psychic	Psychic	Special	90	100	10	Normal
TM30	Shadow Ball	Ghost	Special	80	100	15	Normal
TM32	Double Team	Normal	Status	—	—	15	Self
TM42	Facade	Normal	Physical	70	100	20	Normal
TM44	Rest	Psychic	Status	—	—	10	Self
TM45	Attract	Normal	Status	—	100	15	Normal
TM46	Thief	Dark	Physical	60	100	25	Normal
TM48	Round	Normal	Special	60	100	15	Normal
TM53	Energy Ball	Grass	Special	90	100	10	Normal
TM61	Will-O-Wisp	Fire	Status	—	85	15	Normal
TM63	Embargo	Dark	Status	—	100	15	Normal
TM66	Payback	Dark	Physical	50	100	10	Normal
TM70	Flash	Normal	Status	—	100	20	Normal
TM77	Psych Up	Normal	Status	—	—	10	Normal
TM83	Infestation	Bug	Special	20	100	20	Normal
TM85	Dream Eater	Psychic	Special	100	100	15	Normal
TM87	Swagger	Normal	Status	—	90	15	Normal
TM88	Sleep Talk	Normal	Status	—	—	10	Self
TM90	Substitute	Normal	Status	—	—	10	Self
TM92	Trick Room	Psychic	Status	—	—	5	Both Sides
TM94	Secret Power	Normal	Physical	70	100	20	Normal
TM97	Dark Pulse	Dark	Special	80	100	15	Normal
TM100	Confide	Normal	Status	—	—	20	Normal

MOVES LEARNED IN EXCHANGE FOR BP

Name	Type	Kind	Pow.	Acc.	PP	Range
Magic Coat	Psychic	Status	—	—	15	Self
Block	Normal	Status	—	—	5	Normal
Iron Defense	Steel	Status	—	—	15	Self
Zen Headbutt	Psychic	Physical	80	90	15	Normal
Snore	Normal	Special	50	100	15	Normal
Knock Off	Dark	Physical	65	100	20	Normal
Role Play	Psychic	Status	—	—	10	Normal
Pain Split	Normal	Status	—	—	20	Normal
Shock Wave	Electric	Special	60	—	20	Normal
Spite	Ghost	Status	—	100	10	Normal
After You	Normal	Status	—	—	15	Normal
Trick	Psychic	Status	—	100	10	Normal
Wonder Room	Psychic	Status	—	—	10	Both Sides
Snatch	Dark	Status	—	—	10	Self
Skill Swap	Psychic	Status	—	—	10	Normal

MOVES TAUGHT BY PEOPLE

Name	Type	Kind	Pow.	Acc.	PP	Range

EGG MOVES

Name	Type	Kind	Pow.	Acc.	PP	Range
Memento	Dark	Status	—	100	10	Normal
Fake Tears	Dark	Status	—	100	20	Normal
Nasty Plot	Dark	Status	—	—	20	Self
Endure	Normal	Status	—	—	10	Self
Heal Block	Psychic	Status	—	100	15	Many Others
Imprison	Psychic	Status	—	—	10	Self
Nightmare	Ghost	Status	—	100	15	Normal
Disable	Normal	Status	—	100	20	Normal
Ally Switch	Psychic	Status	—	—	15	Self
Toxic Spikes	Poison	Status	—	—	20	Other Side

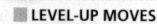

National Pokédex **563** Hoenn Pokédex —

Cofagrigus

Coffin Pokémon

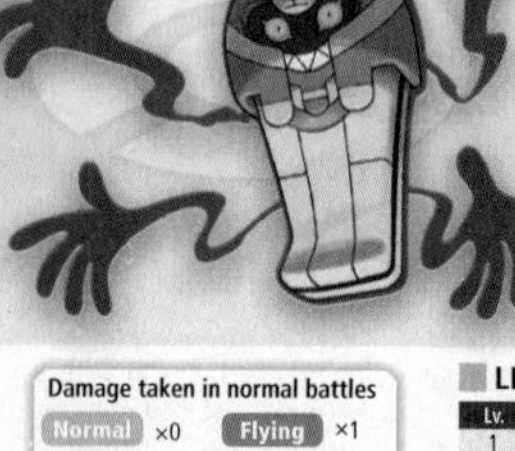

Ghost

HEIGHT: 5'07" WEIGHT: 168.7 lbs.

Same form for ♂ / ♀

Ω It has been said that they swallow those who get too close and turn them into mummies. They like to eat gold nuggets.

α Grave robbers who mistake them for real coffins and get too close end up trapped inside their bodies.

ABILITY
Mummy

HIDDEN ABILITY
—

EGG GROUPS
Mineral / Amorphous

STAT GROWTH RATES
HP / Attack / Defense / Sp. Atk / Sp. Def / Speed

ITEMS SOMETIMES HELD BY WILD POKÉMON
Spell Tag

EVOLUTION
Yamask → Lv. 34 → Cofagrigus

MAIN WAY TO REGISTER IN THE NATIONAL POKÉDEX

Catch in Mirage Cave 5.

Damage taken in normal battles

Type	×	Type	×
Normal	×0	Flying	×1
Fire	×1	Psychic	×1
Water	×1	Bug	×0.5
Grass	×1	Rock	×1
Electric	×1	Ghost	×2
Ice	×1	Dragon	×1
Fighting	×0	Dark	×2
Poison	×0.5	Steel	×1
Ground	×1	Fairy	×1

Damage taken in Inverse battles

Type	×	Type	×
Normal	×2	Flying	×1
Fire	×1	Psychic	×1
Water	×1	Bug	×2
Grass	×1	Rock	×1
Electric	×1	Ghost	×0.5
Ice	×1	Dragon	×1
Fighting	×2	Dark	×0.5
Poison	×2	Steel	×1
Ground	×1	Fairy	×1

Can be used in
- Inverse Battle
- Battle Institute
- Battle Maison
- Random Matchup (Free Battle)
- Random Matchup (Others)

LEVEL-UP MOVES

Lv.	Name	Type	Kind	Pow.	Acc.	PP	Range
1	Astonish	Ghost	Physical	30	100	15	Normal
1	Protect	Normal	Status	—	—	10	Self
1	Disable	Normal	Status	—	100	20	Normal
1	Haze	Ice	Status	—	—	30	Both Sides
5	Disable	Normal	Status	—	100	20	Normal
9	Haze	Ice	Status	—	—	30	Both Sides
13	Night Shade	Ghost	Special	—	100	15	Normal
17	Hex	Ghost	Special	65	100	10	Normal
21	Will-O-Wisp	Fire	Status	—	85	15	Normal
25	Ominous Wind	Ghost	Special	60	100	5	Normal
29	Curse	Ghost	Status	—	—	10	Varies
33	Power Split	Psychic	Status	—	—	10	Normal
33	Guard Split	Psychic	Status	—	—	10	Normal
34	Scary Face	Normal	Status	—	100	10	Normal
39	Shadow Ball	Ghost	Special	80	100	15	Normal
45	Grudge	Ghost	Status	—	—	5	Self
51	Mean Look	Normal	Status	—	—	5	Normal
57	Destiny Bond	Ghost	Status	—	—	5	Self

TM & HM MOVES

No.	Name	Type	Kind	Pow.	Acc.	PP	Range
TM04	Calm Mind	Psychic	Status	—	—	20	Self
TM06	Toxic	Poison	Status	—	90	10	Normal
TM10	Hidden Power	Normal	Special	60	100	15	Normal
TM15	Hyper Beam	Normal	Special	150	90	5	Normal
TM17	Protect	Normal	Status	—	—	10	Self
TM18	Rain Dance	Water	Status	—	—	5	Both Sides
TM20	Safeguard	Normal	Status	—	—	25	Your Side
TM21	Frustration	Normal	Physical	—	100	20	Normal
TM27	Return	Normal	Physical	—	100	20	Normal
TM29	Psychic	Psychic	Special	90	100	10	Normal
TM30	Shadow Ball	Ghost	Special	80	100	15	Normal
TM32	Double Team	Normal	Status	—	—	15	Self
TM42	Facade	Normal	Physical	70	100	20	Normal
TM44	Rest	Psychic	Status	—	—	10	Self
TM45	Attract	Normal	Status	—	100	15	Normal
TM46	Thief	Dark	Physical	60	100	25	Normal
TM48	Round	Normal	Special	60	100	15	Normal
TM53	Energy Ball	Grass	Special	90	100	10	Normal
TM61	Will-O-Wisp	Fire	Status	—	85	15	Normal
TM63	Embargo	Dark	Status	—	100	15	Normal
TM66	Payback	Dark	Physical	50	100	10	Normal
TM68	Giga Impact	Normal	Physical	150	90	5	Normal
TM70	Flash	Normal	Status	—	100	20	Normal
TM77	Psych Up	Normal	Status	—	—	10	Normal
TM83	Infestation	Bug	Special	20	100	20	Normal
TM85	Dream Eater	Psychic	Special	100	100	15	Normal
TM86	Grass Knot	Grass	Special	—	100	20	Normal
TM87	Swagger	Normal	Status	—	90	15	Normal
TM88	Sleep Talk	Normal	Status	—	—	10	Self
TM90	Substitute	Normal	Status	—	—	10	Self
TM92	Trick Room	Psychic	Status	—	—	5	Both Sides
TM94	Secret Power	Normal	Physical	70	100	20	Normal
TM97	Dark Pulse	Dark	Special	80	100	15	Normal
TM100	Confide	Normal	Status	—	—	20	Normal

MOVES LEARNED IN EXCHANGE FOR BP

Name	Type	Kind	Pow.	Acc.	PP	Range
Magic Coat	Psychic	Status	—	—	15	Self
Block	Normal	Status	—	—	5	Normal
Iron Defense	Steel	Status	—	—	15	Self
Zen Headbutt	Psychic	Physical	80	90	15	Normal
Snore	Normal	Special	50	100	15	Normal
Knock Off	Dark	Physical	65	100	20	Normal
Role Play	Psychic	Status	—	—	10	Normal
Pain Split	Normal	Status	—	—	20	Normal
Shock Wave	Electric	Special	60	—	20	Normal
Spite	Ghost	Status	—	100	10	Normal
After You	Normal	Status	—	—	15	Normal
Trick	Psychic	Status	—	100	10	Normal
Wonder Room	Psychic	Status	—	—	10	Both Sides
Snatch	Dark	Status	—	—	10	Self
Skill Swap	Psychic	Status	—	—	10	Normal

MOVES TAUGHT BY PEOPLE

Name	Type	Kind	Pow.	Acc.	PP	Range

National Pokédex **564** Hoenn Pokédex —

Tirtouga

Prototurtle Pokémon

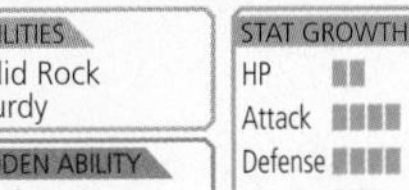

Water Rock

HEIGHT: 2'04" WEIGHT: 36.4 lbs.

Same form for ♂ / ♀

Ω About 100 million years ago, these Pokémon swam in oceans. It is thought they also went on land to attack prey.

α Restored from a fossil, this Pokémon can dive to depths beyond half a mile.

ABILITIES
Solid Rock
Sturdy

HIDDEN ABILITY
Swift Swim

EGG GROUPS
Water 1 | Water 3

STAT GROWTH RATES
HP
Attack
Defense
Sp. Atk
Sp. Def
Speed

ITEMS SOMETIMES HELD BY WILD POKÉMON
—

EVOLUTION

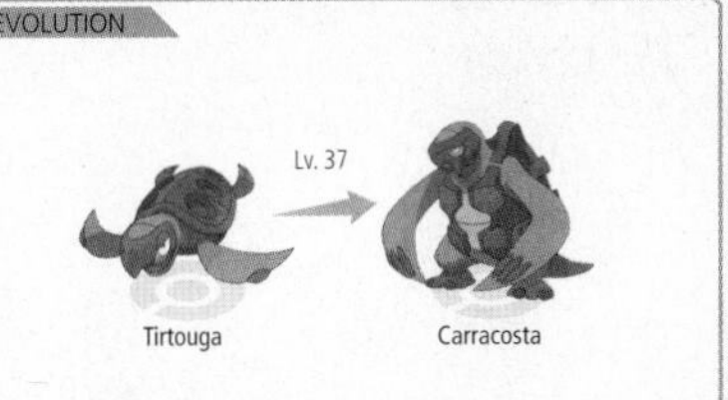

MAIN WAYS TO REGISTER IN THE NATIONAL POKÉDEX

Ω Bring it to your game using Link Trade or the GTS.

α Obtain a Cover Fossil from a cracked rock in a Mirage spot by using Rock Smash, then have it restored at the Devon Corporation (2F) in Rustboro City.

Damage taken in normal battles

Type	×	Type	×
Normal	×0.5	Flying	×0.5
Fire	×0.25	Psychic	×1
Water	×1	Bug	×1
Grass	×4	Rock	×1
Electric	×2	Ghost	×1
Ice	×0.5	Dragon	×1
Fighting	×2	Dark	×1
Poison	×0.5	Steel	×1
Ground	×2	Fairy	×1

Damage taken in Inverse battles

Type	×	Type	×
Normal	×2	Flying	×2
Fire	×4	Psychic	×1
Water	×1	Bug	×1
Grass	×0.25	Rock	×1
Electric	×0.5	Ghost	×1
Ice	×2	Dragon	×1
Fighting	×0.5	Dark	×1
Poison	×2	Steel	×1
Ground	×0.5	Fairy	×1

Can be used in
Inverse Battle
Battle Institute
Battle Maison
Random Matchup (Free Battle)
Random Matchup (Others)

LEVEL-UP MOVES

Lv.	Name	Type	Kind	Pow.	Acc.	PP	Range
1	Bide	Normal	Physical	—	—	10	Self
1	Withdraw	Water	Status	—	—	40	Self
1	Water Gun	Water	Special	40	100	25	Normal
5	Rollout	Rock	Physical	30	90	20	Normal
8	Bite	Dark	Physical	60	100	25	Normal
11	Protect	Normal	Status	—	—	10	Self
15	Aqua Jet	Water	Physical	40	100	20	Normal
18	Ancient Power	Rock	Special	60	100	5	Normal
21	Crunch	Dark	Physical	80	100	15	Normal
25	Wide Guard	Rock	Status	—	—	10	Your Side
28	Brine	Water	Special	65	100	10	Normal
31	Smack Down	Rock	Physical	50	100	15	Normal
35	Curse	Ghost	Status	—	—	10	Varies
38	Shell Smash	Normal	Status	—	—	15	Self
41	Aqua Tail	Water	Physical	90	90	10	Normal
45	Rock Slide	Rock	Physical	75	90	10	Many Others
48	Rain Dance	Water	Status	—	—	5	Both Sides
50	Hydro Pump	Water	Special	110	80	5	Normal

TM & HM MOVES

No.	Name	Type	Kind	Pow.	Acc.	PP	Range
TM06	Toxic	Poison	Status	—	90	10	Normal
TM10	Hidden Power	Normal	Special	60	100	15	Normal
TM13	Ice Beam	Ice	Special	90	100	10	Normal
TM14	Blizzard	Ice	Special	110	70	5	Many Others
TM17	Protect	Normal	Status	—	—	10	Self
TM18	Rain Dance	Water	Status	—	—	5	Both Sides
TM21	Frustration	Normal	Physical	—	100	20	Normal
TM23	Smack Down	Rock	Physical	50	100	15	Normal
TM26	Earthquake	Ground	Physical	100	100	10	Adjacent
TM27	Return	Normal	Physical	—	100	20	Normal
TM28	Dig	Ground	Physical	80	100	10	Normal
TM32	Double Team	Normal	Status	—	—	15	Self
TM37	Sandstorm	Rock	Status	—	—	10	Both Sides
TM39	Rock Tomb	Rock	Physical	60	95	15	Normal
TM42	Facade	Normal	Physical	70	100	20	Normal
TM44	Rest	Psychic	Status	—	—	10	Self
TM45	Attract	Normal	Status	—	100	15	Normal
TM48	Round	Normal	Special	60	100	15	Normal
TM55	Scald	Water	Special	80	100	15	Normal
TM69	Rock Polish	Rock	Status	—	—	20	Self
TM71	Stone Edge	Rock	Physical	100	80	5	Normal
TM78	Bulldoze	Ground	Physical	60	100	20	Adjacent
TM80	Rock Slide	Rock	Physical	75	90	10	Many Others
TM87	Swagger	Normal	Status	—	90	15	Normal
TM88	Sleep Talk	Normal	Status	—	—	10	Self
TM90	Substitute	Normal	Status	—	—	10	Self
TM94	Secret Power	Normal	Physical	70	100	20	Normal
TM100	Confide	Normal	Status	—	—	20	Normal
HM03	Surf	Water	Special	90	100	15	Adjacent
HM04	Strength	Normal	Physical	80	100	15	Normal
HM05	Waterfall	Water	Physical	80	100	15	Normal
HM06	Rock Smash	Fighting	Physical	40	100	15	Normal
HM07	Dive	Water	Physical	80	100	10	Normal

MOVES LEARNED IN EXCHANGE FOR BP

Name	Type	Kind	Pow.	Acc.	PP	Range
Block	Normal	Status	—	—	5	Normal
Earth Power	Ground	Special	90	100	10	Normal
Iron Defense	Steel	Status	—	—	15	Self
Icy Wind	Ice	Special	55	95	15	Many Others
Aqua Tail	Water	Physical	90	90	10	Normal
Zen Headbutt	Psychic	Physical	80	90	15	Normal
Iron Tail	Steel	Physical	100	75	15	Normal
Snore	Normal	Special	50	100	15	Normal
Knock Off	Dark	Physical	65	100	20	Normal
Water Pulse	Water	Special	60	100	20	Normal
Stealth Rock	Rock	Status	—	—	20	Other Side

MOVES TAUGHT BY PEOPLE

Name	Type	Kind	Pow.	Acc.	PP	Range

EGG MOVES

Name	Type	Kind	Pow.	Acc.	PP	Range
Water Pulse	Water	Special	60	100	20	Normal
Knock Off	Dark	Physical	65	100	20	Normal
Rock Throw	Rock	Physical	50	90	15	Normal
Slam	Normal	Physical	80	75	20	Normal
Iron Defense	Steel	Status	—	—	15	Self
Flail	Normal	Physical	—	100	15	Normal
Whirlpool	Water	Special	35	85	15	Normal
Body Slam	Normal	Physical	85	100	15	Normal
Bide	Normal	Physical	—	—	10	Self
Guard Swap	Psychic	Status	—	—	10	Normal

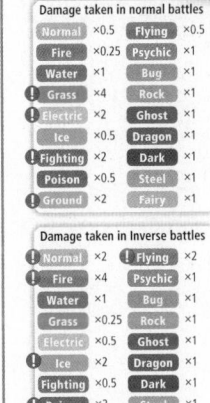

National Pokédex **565** Hoenn Pokédex —

Carracosta

Prototurtle Pokémon

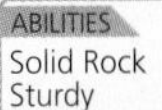

Water Rock

HEIGHT: 3'11" WEIGHT: 178.6 lbs.

Same form for ♂ / ♀

Ω They can live both in the ocean and on land. A slap from one of them is enough to open a hole in the bottom of a tanker.

α It could knock out a foe with a slap from one of its developed front appendages and chew it up, shell or bones and all.

ABILITIES
Solid Rock
Sturdy

HIDDEN ABILITY
Swift Swim

EGG GROUPS
Water 1 | Water 3

STAT GROWTH RATES
HP
Attack
Defense
Sp. Atk
Sp. Def
Speed

ITEMS SOMETIMES HELD BY WILD POKÉMON
—

EVOLUTION

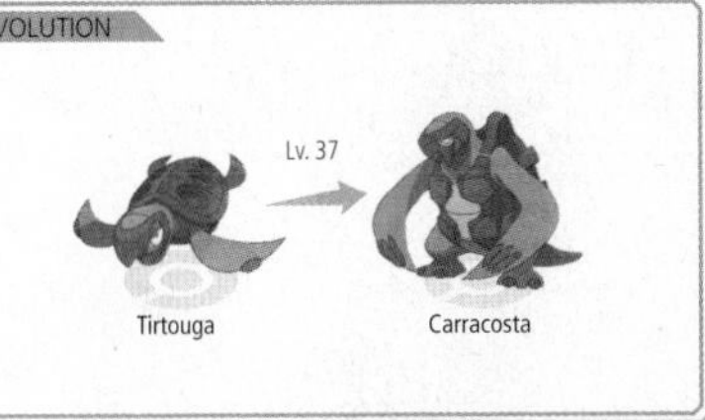

MAIN WAYS TO REGISTER IN THE NATIONAL POKÉDEX

Ω Bring it to your game using Link Trade or the GTS.

α Level up Tirtouga to Lv. 37.

Damage taken in normal battles

Type	×	Type	×
Normal	×0.5	Flying	×0.5
Fire	×0.25	Psychic	×1
Water	×1	Bug	×1
Grass	×4	Rock	×1
Electric	×2	Ghost	×1
Ice	×0.5	Dragon	×1
Fighting	×2	Dark	×1
Poison	×0.5	Steel	×1
Ground	×2	Fairy	×1

Damage taken in Inverse battles

Type	×	Type	×
Normal	×2	Flying	×2
Fire	×4	Psychic	×1
Water	×1	Bug	×1
Grass	×0.25	Rock	×1
Electric	×0.5	Ghost	×1
Ice	×2	Dragon	×1
Fighting	×0.5	Dark	×1
Poison	×2	Steel	×1
Ground	×0.5	Fairy	×1

Can be used in
Inverse Battle
Battle Institute
Battle Maison
Random Matchup (Free Battle)
Random Matchup (Others)

LEVEL-UP MOVES

Lv.	Name	Type	Kind	Pow.	Acc.	PP	Range
1	Bide	Normal	Physical	—	—	10	Self
1	Withdraw	Water	Status	—	—	40	Self
1	Water Gun	Water	Special	40	100	25	Normal
1	Rollout	Rock	Physical	30	90	20	Normal
5	Rollout	Rock	Physical	30	90	20	Normal
8	Bite	Dark	Physical	60	100	25	Normal
11	Protect	Normal	Status	—	—	10	Self
15	Aqua Jet	Water	Physical	40	100	20	Normal
18	Ancient Power	Rock	Special	60	100	5	Normal
21	Crunch	Dark	Physical	80	100	15	Normal
25	Wide Guard	Rock	Status	—	—	10	Your Side
28	Brine	Water	Special	65	100	10	Normal
31	Smack Down	Rock	Physical	50	100	15	Normal
35	Curse	Ghost	Status	—	—	10	Varies
40	Shell Smash	Normal	Status	—	—	15	Self
45	Aqua Tail	Water	Physical	90	90	10	Normal
51	Rock Slide	Rock	Physical	75	90	10	Many Others
56	Rain Dance	Water	Status	—	—	5	Both Sides
61	Hydro Pump	Water	Special	110	80	5	Normal

TM & HM MOVES

No.	Name	Type	Kind	Pow.	Acc.	PP	Range
TM06	Toxic	Poison	Status	—	90	10	Normal
TM10	Hidden Power	Normal	Special	60	100	15	Normal
TM13	Ice Beam	Ice	Special	90	100	10	Normal
TM14	Blizzard	Ice	Special	110	70	5	Many Others
TM15	Hyper Beam	Normal	Special	150	90	5	Normal
TM17	Protect	Normal	Status	—	—	10	Self
TM18	Rain Dance	Water	Status	—	—	5	Both Sides
TM21	Frustration	Normal	Physical	—	100	20	Normal
TM23	Smack Down	Rock	Physical	50	100	15	Normal
TM26	Earthquake	Ground	Physical	100	100	10	Adjacent
TM27	Return	Normal	Physical	—	100	20	Normal
TM28	Dig	Ground	Physical	80	100	10	Normal
TM32	Double Team	Normal	Status	—	—	15	Self
TM37	Sandstorm	Rock	Status	—	—	10	Both Sides
TM39	Rock Tomb	Rock	Physical	60	95	15	Normal
TM42	Facade	Normal	Physical	70	100	20	Normal
TM44	Rest	Psychic	Status	—	—	10	Self
TM45	Attract	Normal	Status	—	100	15	Normal
TM48	Round	Normal	Special	60	100	15	Normal
TM52	Focus Blast	Fighting	Special	120	70	5	Normal
TM55	Scald	Water	Special	80	100	15	Normal
TM68	Giga Impact	Normal	Physical	150	90	5	Normal
TM69	Rock Polish	Rock	Status	—	—	20	Self
TM71	Stone Edge	Rock	Physical	100	80	5	Normal
TM78	Bulldoze	Ground	Physical	60	100	20	Adjacent
TM80	Rock Slide	Rock	Physical	75	90	10	Many Others
TM87	Swagger	Normal	Status	—	90	15	Normal
TM88	Sleep Talk	Normal	Status	—	—	10	Self
TM90	Substitute	Normal	Status	—	—	10	Self
TM94	Secret Power	Normal	Physical	70	100	20	Normal
TM100	Confide	Normal	Status	—	—	20	Normal
HM03	Surf	Water	Special	90	100	15	Adjacent
HM04	Strength	Normal	Physical	80	100	15	Normal
HM05	Waterfall	Water	Physical	80	100	15	Normal
HM06	Rock Smash	Fighting	Physical	40	100	15	Normal
HM07	Dive	Water	Physical	80	100	10	Normal

MOVES LEARNED IN EXCHANGE FOR BP

Name	Type	Kind	Pow.	Acc.	PP	Range
Iron Head	Steel	Physical	80	100	15	Normal
Low Kick	Fighting	Physical	—	100	20	Normal
Block	Normal	Status	—	—	5	Normal
Earth Power	Ground	Special	90	100	10	Normal
Iron Defense	Steel	Status	—	—	15	Self
Superpower	Fighting	Physical	120	100	5	Normal
Icy Wind	Ice	Special	55	95	15	Many Others
Aqua Tail	Water	Physical	90	90	10	Normal
Zen Headbutt	Psychic	Physical	80	90	15	Normal
Iron Tail	Steel	Physical	100	75	15	Normal
Snore	Normal	Special	50	100	15	Normal
Knock Off	Dark	Physical	65	100	20	Normal
Water Pulse	Water	Special	60	100	20	Normal
Stealth Rock	Rock	Status	—	—	20	Other Side

MOVES TAUGHT BY PEOPLE

Name	Type	Kind	Pow.	Acc.	PP	Range

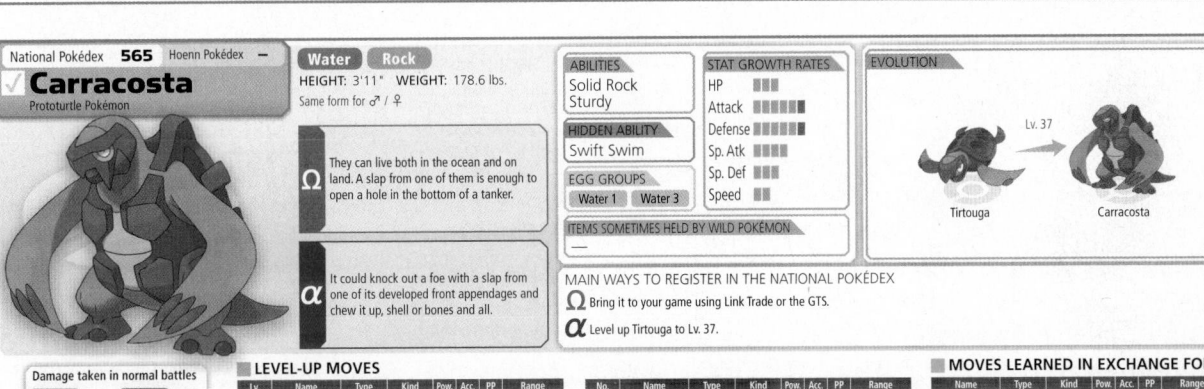

National Pokédex **566** Hoenn Pokédex —

Archen

First Bird Pokémon

Rock | Flying

HEIGHT: 1'08" WEIGHT: 20.9 lbs.

Same form for ♂ / ♀

Ω Revived from a fossil, this Pokémon is thought to be the ancestor of all bird Pokémon.

α Said to be an ancestor of bird Pokémon, they were unable to fly and moved about by hopping from one branch to another.

ABILITY
Defeatist

HIDDEN ABILITY
—

EGG GROUPS
Flying | Water 3

STAT GROWTH RATES
HP
Attack
Defense
Sp. Atk
Sp. Def
Speed

ITEMS SOMETIMES HELD BY WILD POKÉMON
—

EVOLUTION

MAIN WAYS TO REGISTER IN THE NATIONAL POKÉDEX

Ω Obtain a Plume Fossil from a cracked rock in a Mirage spot by using Rock Smash, then have it restored at the Devon Corporation (2F) in Rustboro City.

α Bring it to your game using Link Trade or the GTS.

Damage taken in normal battles

Type		Type	
Normal	×0.5	Flying	×0.5
Fire	×0.5	Psychic	×1
Water	×2	Bug	×0.5
Grass	×1	Rock	×2
Electric	×2	Ghost	×1
Ice	×2	Dragon	×1
Fighting	×1	Dark	×1
Poison	×0.5	Steel	×2
Ground	×0	Fairy	×1

Damage taken in Inverse battles

Type		Type	
Normal	×2	Flying	×2
Fire	×2	Psychic	×1
Water	×0.5	Bug	×2
Grass	×1	Rock	×0.5
Electric	×0.5	Ghost	×1
Ice	×0.5	Dragon	×1
Fighting	×1	Dark	×1
Poison	×2	Steel	×0.5
Ground	×1	Fairy	×1

Can be used in
- Inverse Battle
- Battle Institute
- Battle Maison
- Random Matchup (Free Battle)
- Random Matchup (Others)

LEVEL-UP MOVES

Lv.	Name	Type	Kind	Pow.	Acc.	PP	Range
1	Quick Attack	Normal	Physical	40	100	30	Normal
1	Leer	Normal	Status	—	100	30	Many Others
1	Wing Attack	Flying	Physical	60	100	35	Normal
5	Rock Throw	Rock	Physical	50	90	15	Normal
8	Double Team	Normal	Status	—	—	15	Self
11	Scary Face	Normal	Status	—	100	10	Normal
15	Pluck	Flying	Physical	60	100	20	Normal
18	Ancient Power	Rock	Special	60	100	5	Normal
21	Agility	Psychic	Status	—	—	30	Self
25	Quick Guard	Fighting	Status	—	—	15	Your Side
28	Acrobatics	Flying	Physical	55	100	15	Normal
31	Dragon Breath	Dragon	Special	60	100	20	Normal
35	Crunch	Dark	Physical	80	100	15	Normal
38	Endeavor	Normal	Physical	—	100	5	Normal
41	U-turn	Bug	Physical	70	100	20	Normal
45	Rock Slide	Rock	Physical	75	90	10	Many Others
48	Dragon Claw	Dragon	Physical	80	100	15	Normal
50	Thrash	Normal	Physical	120	100	10	1 Random

TM & HM MOVES

No.	Name	Type	Kind	Pow.	Acc.	PP	Range
TM01	Hone Claws	Dark	Status	—	—	15	Self
TM02	Dragon Claw	Dragon	Physical	80	100	15	Normal
TM05	Roar	Normal	Status	—	—	20	Normal
TM06	Toxic	Poison	Status	—	90	10	Normal
TM10	Hidden Power	Normal	Special	60	100	15	Normal
TM12	Taunt	Dark	Status	—	100	20	Normal
TM17	Protect	Normal	Status	—	—	10	Self
TM19	Roost	Flying	Status	—	—	10	Self
TM21	Frustration	Normal	Physical	—	100	20	Normal
TM23	Smack Down	Rock	Physical	50	100	15	Normal
TM26	Earthquake	Ground	Physical	100	100	10	Adjacent
TM27	Return	Normal	Physical	—	100	20	Normal
TM28	Dig	Ground	Physical	80	100	10	Normal
TM32	Double Team	Normal	Status	—	—	15	Self
TM37	Sandstorm	Rock	Status	—	—	10	Both Sides
TM39	Rock Tomb	Rock	Physical	60	95	15	Normal
TM40	Aerial Ace	Flying	Physical	60	—	20	Normal
TM41	Torment	Dark	Status	—	100	15	Normal
TM42	Facade	Normal	Physical	70	100	20	Normal
TM44	Rest	Psychic	Status	—	—	10	Self
TM45	Attract	Normal	Status	—	100	15	Normal
TM48	Round	Normal	Special	60	100	15	Normal
TM51	Steel Wing	Steel	Physical	70	90	25	Normal
TM62	Acrobatics	Flying	Physical	55	100	15	Normal
TM65	Shadow Claw	Ghost	Physical	70	100	15	Normal
TM69	Rock Polish	Rock	Status	—	—	20	Self
TM71	Stone Edge	Rock	Physical	100	80	5	Normal
TM78	Bulldoze	Ground	Physical	60	100	20	Adjacent
TM80	Rock Slide	Rock	Physical	75	90	10	Many Others
TM87	Swagger	Normal	Status	—	90	15	Normal
TM88	Sleep Talk	Normal	Status	—	—	10	Self
TM89	U-turn	Bug	Physical	70	100	20	Normal
TM90	Substitute	Normal	Status	—	—	10	Self
TM94	Secret Power	Normal	Physical	70	100	20	Normal
TM100	Confide	Normal	Status	—	—	20	Normal
HM01	Cut	Normal	Physical	50	95	30	Normal
HM06	Rock Smash	Fighting	Physical	40	100	15	Normal

MOVES LEARNED IN EXCHANGE FOR BP

Name	Type	Kind	Pow.	Acc.	PP	Range
Bounce	Flying	Physical	85	85	5	Normal
Uproar	Normal	Special	90	100	10	1 Random
Earth Power	Ground	Special	90	100	10	Normal
Iron Defense	Steel	Status	—	—	15	Self
Aqua Tail	Water	Physical	90	90	10	Normal
Zen Headbutt	Psychic	Physical	80	90	15	Normal
Dragon Pulse	Dragon	Special	85	100	10	Normal
Iron Tail	Steel	Physical	100	75	15	Normal
Snore	Normal	Special	50	100	15	Normal
Knock Off	Dark	Physical	65	100	20	Normal
Heat Wave	Fire	Special	95	90	10	Many Others
Tailwind	Flying	Status	—	—	15	Your Side
Endeavor	Normal	Physical	—	100	5	Normal
Stealth Rock	Rock	Status	—	—	20	Other Side

MOVES TAUGHT BY PEOPLE

Name	Type	Kind	Pow.	Acc.	PP	Range

EGG MOVES

Name	Type	Kind	Pow.	Acc.	PP	Range
Steel Wing	Steel	Physical	70	90	25	Normal
Defog	Flying	Status	—	—	15	Normal
Dragon Pulse	Dragon	Special	85	100	10	Normal
Head Smash	Rock	Physical	150	80	5	Normal
Knock Off	Dark	Physical	65	100	20	Normal
Earth Power	Ground	Special	90	100	10	Normal
Bite	Dark	Physical	60	100	25	Normal
Ally Switch	Psychic	Status	—	—	15	Self
Switcheroo	Dark	Status	—	100	10	Normal

National Pokédex **567** Hoenn Pokédex —

Archeops

First Bird Pokémon

Rock | Flying

HEIGHT: 4'07" WEIGHT: 70.5 lbs.

Same form for ♂ / ♀

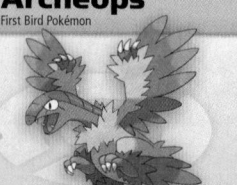

Ω They are intelligent and will cooperate to catch prey. From the ground, they use a running start to take flight.

α It runs better than it flies. It takes off into the sky by running at a speed of 25 mph.

ABILITY
Defeatist

HIDDEN ABILITY
—

EGG GROUPS
Flying | Water 3

STAT GROWTH RATES
HP
Attack
Defense
Sp. Atk
Sp. Def
Speed

ITEMS SOMETIMES HELD BY WILD POKÉMON
—

EVOLUTION

Lv. 37
Archen
Archeops

MAIN WAYS TO REGISTER IN THE NATIONAL POKÉDEX

Ω Level up Archen to Lv. 37.

α Bring it to your game using Link Trade or the GTS.

Damage taken in normal battles

Type		Type	
Normal	×0.5	Flying	×0.5
Fire	×0.5	Psychic	×1
Water	×2	Bug	×0.5
Grass	×1	Rock	×2
Electric	×2	Ghost	×1
Ice	×2	Dragon	×1
Fighting	×1	Dark	×1
Poison	×0.5	Steel	×2
Ground	×0	Fairy	×1

Damage taken in Inverse battles

Type		Type	
Normal	×2	Flying	×2
Fire	×2	Psychic	×1
Water	×0.5	Bug	×2
Grass	×1	Rock	×0.5
Electric	×0.5	Ghost	×1
Ice	×0.5	Dragon	×1
Fighting	×1	Dark	×1
Poison	×2	Steel	×0.5
Ground	×1	Fairy	×1

Can be used in
- Inverse Battle
- Battle Institute
- Battle Maison
- Random Matchup (Free Battle)
- Random Matchup (Others)

LEVEL-UP MOVES

Lv.	Name	Type	Kind	Pow.	Acc.	PP	Range
1	Quick Attack	Normal	Physical	40	100	30	Normal
1	Leer	Normal	Status	—	100	30	Many Others
1	Wing Attack	Flying	Physical	60	100	35	Normal
1	Rock Throw	Rock	Physical	50	90	15	Normal
5	Rock Throw	Rock	Physical	50	90	15	Normal
8	Double Team	Normal	Status	—	—	15	Self
11	Scary Face	Normal	Status	—	100	10	Normal
15	Pluck	Flying	Physical	60	100	20	Normal
18	Ancient Power	Rock	Special	60	100	5	Normal
21	Agility	Psychic	Status	—	—	30	Self
25	Quick Guard	Fighting	Status	—	—	15	Your Side
28	Acrobatics	Flying	Physical	55	100	15	Normal
31	Dragon Breath	Dragon	Special	60	100	20	Normal
35	Crunch	Dark	Physical	80	100	15	Normal
40	Endeavor	Normal	Physical	—	100	5	Normal
45	U-turn	Bug	Physical	70	100	20	Normal
51	Rock Slide	Rock	Physical	75	90	10	Many Others
56	Dragon Claw	Dragon	Physical	80	100	15	Normal
61	Thrash	Normal	Physical	120	100	10	1 Random

TM & HM MOVES

No.	Name	Type	Kind	Pow.	Acc.	PP	Range
TM01	Hone Claws	Dark	Status	—	—	15	Self
TM02	Dragon Claw	Dragon	Physical	80	100	15	Normal
TM05	Roar	Normal	Status	—	—	20	Normal
TM06	Toxic	Poison	Status	—	90	10	Normal
TM10	Hidden Power	Normal	Special	60	100	15	Normal
TM12	Taunt	Dark	Status	—	100	20	Normal
TM15	Hyper Beam	Normal	Special	150	90	5	Normal
TM17	Protect	Normal	Status	—	—	10	Self
TM19	Roost	Flying	Status	—	—	10	Self
TM21	Frustration	Normal	Physical	—	100	20	Normal
TM23	Smack Down	Rock	Physical	50	100	15	Normal
TM26	Earthquake	Ground	Physical	100	100	10	Adjacent
TM27	Return	Normal	Physical	—	100	20	Normal
TM28	Dig	Ground	Physical	80	100	10	Normal
TM32	Double Team	Normal	Status	—	—	15	Self
TM37	Sandstorm	Rock	Status	—	—	10	Both Sides
TM39	Rock Tomb	Rock	Physical	60	95	15	Normal
TM40	Aerial Ace	Flying	Physical	60	—	20	Normal
TM41	Torment	Dark	Status	—	100	15	Normal
TM42	Facade	Normal	Physical	70	100	20	Normal
TM44	Rest	Psychic	Status	—	—	10	Self
TM45	Attract	Normal	Status	—	100	15	Normal
TM48	Round	Normal	Special	60	100	15	Normal
TM51	Steel Wing	Steel	Physical	70	90	25	Normal
TM52	Focus Blast	Fighting	Special	120	70	5	Normal
TM62	Acrobatics	Flying	Physical	55	100	15	Normal
TM65	Shadow Claw	Ghost	Physical	70	100	15	Normal
TM68	Giga Impact	Normal	Physical	150	90	5	Normal
TM69	Rock Polish	Rock	Status	—	—	20	Self
TM71	Stone Edge	Rock	Physical	100	80	5	Normal
TM78	Bulldoze	Ground	Physical	60	100	20	Adjacent
TM80	Rock Slide	Rock	Physical	75	90	10	Many Others
TM82	Dragon Tail	Dragon	Physical	60	90	10	Normal
TM87	Swagger	Normal	Status	—	90	15	Normal
TM88	Sleep Talk	Normal	Status	—	—	10	Self
TM89	U-turn	Bug	Physical	70	100	20	Normal
TM90	Substitute	Normal	Status	—	—	10	Self
TM94	Secret Power	Normal	Physical	70	100	20	Normal
TM100	Confide	Normal	Status	—	—	20	Normal
HM01	Cut	Normal	Physical	50	95	30	Normal
HM02	Fly	Flying	Physical	90	95	15	Normal
HM06	Rock Smash	Fighting	Physical	40	100	15	Normal

MOVES LEARNED IN EXCHANGE FOR BP

Name	Type	Kind	Pow.	Acc.	PP	Range
Bounce	Flying	Physical	85	85	5	Normal
Uproar	Normal	Special	90	100	10	1 Random
Earth Power	Ground	Special	90	100	10	Normal
Iron Defense	Steel	Status	—	—	15	Self
Aqua Tail	Water	Physical	90	90	10	Normal
Zen Headbutt	Psychic	Physical	80	90	15	Normal
Dragon Pulse	Dragon	Special	85	100	10	Normal
Iron Tail	Steel	Physical	100	75	15	Normal
Snore	Normal	Special	50	100	15	Normal
Knock Off	Dark	Physical	65	100	20	Normal
Heat Wave	Fire	Special	95	90	10	Many Others
Tailwind	Flying	Status	—	—	15	Your Side
Sky Attack	Flying	Physical	140	90	5	Normal
Endeavor	Normal	Physical	—	100	5	Normal
Outrage	Dragon	Physical	120	100	10	1 Random
Stealth Rock	Rock	Status	—	—	20	Other Side

MOVES TAUGHT BY PEOPLE

Name	Type	Kind	Pow.	Acc.	PP	Range

National Pokédex 568 Hoenn Pokédex —

Trubbish

Trash Bag Pokémon

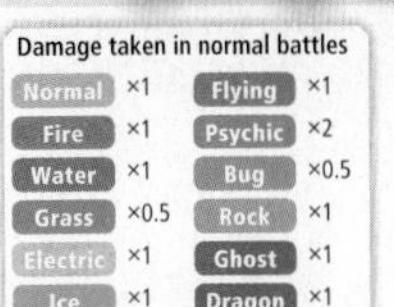

Poison

HEIGHT: 2'00" WEIGHT: 68.3 lbs.

Same form for ♂ / ♀

Ω The combination of garbage bags and industrial waste caused the chemical reaction that created this Pokémon.

α Inhaling the gas they belch will make you sleep for a week. They prefer unsanitary places.

ABILITIES
Stench
Sticky Hold

HIDDEN ABILITY
Aftermath

EGG GROUPS
Mineral

STAT GROWTH RATES
HP ■■
Attack ■■■
Defense ■■■
Sp. Atk ■■
Sp. Def ■■■
Speed ■■■■

ITEMS SOMETIMES HELD BY WILD POKÉMON
Black Sludge

EVOLUTION
Trubbish → Lv. 36 → Garbodor

MAIN WAY TO REGISTER IN THE NATIONAL POKÉDEX

Catch on Route 110. Appears as a hidden Pokémon after you battle Groudon or Kyogre.

Damage taken in normal battles

Type		Type	
Normal	×1	Flying	×1
Fire	×1	Psychic	×2
Water	×1	Bug	×0.5
Grass	×0.5	Rock	×1
Electric	×1	Ghost	×1
Ice	×1	Dragon	×1
Fighting	×0.5	Dark	×1
Poison	×0.5	Steel	×1
Ground	×2	Fairy	×0.5

Damage taken in Inverse battles

Type		Type	
Normal	×1	Flying	×1
Fire	×1	Psychic	×0.5
Water	×1	Bug	×2
Grass	×2	Rock	×1
Electric	×1	Ghost	×1
Ice	×1	Dragon	×1
Fighting	×2	Dark	×1
Poison	×2	Steel	×1
Ground	×0.5	Fairy	×2

Can be used in
Inverse Battle
Battle Institute
Battle Maison
Random Matchup (Free Battle)
Random Matchup (Others)

LEVEL-UP MOVES

Lv.	Name	Type	Kind	Pow.	Acc.	PP	Range
1	Pound	Normal	Physical	40	100	35	Normal
1	Poison Gas	Poison	Status	—	90	40	Many Others
3	Recycle	Normal	Status	—	—	10	Self
7	Toxic Spikes	Poison	Status	—	—	20	Other Side
12	Acid Spray	Poison	Special	40	100	20	Normal
14	Double Slap	Normal	Physical	15	85	10	Normal
18	Sludge	Poison	Special	65	100	20	Normal
23	Stockpile	Normal	Status	—	—	20	Self
23	Swallow	Normal	Status	—	—	10	Self
25	Take Down	Normal	Physical	90	85	20	Normal
29	Sludge Bomb	Poison	Special	90	100	10	Normal
34	Clear Smog	Poison	Special	50	—	15	Normal
36	Toxic	Poison	Status	—	90	10	Normal
40	Amnesia	Psychic	Status	—	—	20	Self
42	Belch	Poison	Special	120	90	10	Normal
45	Gunk Shot	Poison	Physical	120	80	5	Normal
47	Explosion	Normal	Physical	250	100	5	Adjacent

TM & HM MOVES

No.	Name	Type	Kind	Pow.	Acc.	PP	Range
TM06	Toxic	Poison	Status	—	90	10	Normal
TM09	Venoshock	Poison	Special	65	100	10	Normal
TM10	Hidden Power	Normal	Special	60	100	15	Normal
TM11	Sunny Day	Fire	Status	—	—	5	Both Sides
TM17	Protect	Normal	Status	—	—	10	Self
TM18	Rain Dance	Water	Status	—	—	5	Both Sides
TM21	Frustration	Normal	Physical	—	100	20	Normal
TM27	Return	Normal	Physical	—	100	20	Normal
TM32	Double Team	Normal	Status	—	—	15	Self
TM34	Sludge Wave	Poison	Special	95	100	10	Adjacent
TM36	Sludge Bomb	Poison	Special	90	100	10	Normal
TM42	Facade	Normal	Physical	70	100	20	Normal
TM44	Rest	Psychic	Status	—	—	10	Self
TM45	Attract	Normal	Status	—	100	15	Normal
TM46	Thief	Dark	Physical	60	100	25	Normal
TM48	Round	Normal	Special	60	100	15	Normal
TM64	Explosion	Normal	Physical	250	100	5	Adjacent
TM66	Payback	Dark	Physical	50	100	10	Normal
TM83	Infestation	Bug	Special	20	100	20	Normal
TM87	Swagger	Normal	Status	—	90	15	Normal
TM88	Sleep Talk	Normal	Status	—	—	10	Self
TM90	Substitute	Normal	Status	—	—	10	Self
TM94	Secret Power	Normal	Physical	70	100	20	Normal
TM97	Dark Pulse	Dark	Special	80	100	15	Normal
TM100	Confide	Normal	Status	—	—	20	Normal

MOVES LEARNED IN EXCHANGE FOR BP

Name	Type	Kind	Pow.	Acc.	PP	Range
Seed Bomb	Grass	Physical	80	100	15	Normal
Gunk Shot	Poison	Physical	120	80	5	Normal
Snore	Normal	Special	50	100	15	Normal
Pain Split	Normal	Status	—	—	20	Normal
Giga Drain	Grass	Special	75	100	10	Normal
Drain Punch	Fighting	Physical	75	100	10	Normal
Spite	Ghost	Status	—	100	10	Normal
Recycle	Normal	Status	—	—	10	Self

MOVES TAUGHT BY PEOPLE

Name	Type	Kind	Pow.	Acc.	PP	Range

EGG MOVES

Name	Type	Kind	Pow.	Acc.	PP	Range
Spikes	Ground	Status	—	—	20	Other Side
Rollout	Rock	Physical	30	90	20	Normal
Haze	Ice	Status	—	—	30	Both Sides
Curse	Ghost	Status	—	—	10	Varies
Rock Blast	Rock	Physical	25	90	10	Normal
Sand Attack	Ground	Status	—	100	15	Normal
Mud Sport	Ground	Status	—	—	15	Both Sides
Self-Destruct	Normal	Physical	200	100	5	Adjacent

National Pokédex 569 Hoenn Pokédex —

Garbodor

Trash Heap Pokémon

Poison

HEIGHT: 6'03" WEIGHT: 236.6 lbs.

Same form for ♂ / ♀

Ω It clenches opponents with its left arm and finishes them off with foul-smelling poison gas belched from its mouth.

α Consuming garbage makes new kinds of poison gases and liquids inside their bodies.

ABILITIES
Stench
Weak Armor

HIDDEN ABILITY
Aftermath

EGG GROUPS
Mineral

STAT GROWTH RATES
HP ■■■
Attack ■■■■■
Defense ■■■■
Sp. Atk ■■■
Sp. Def ■■■■
Speed ■■■■

ITEMS SOMETIMES HELD BY WILD POKÉMON
—

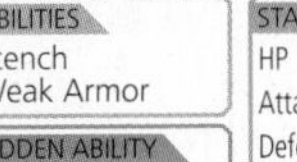

EVOLUTION
Trubbish → Lv. 36 → Garbodor

MAIN WAY TO REGISTER IN THE NATIONAL POKÉDEX

Level up Trubbish to Lv. 36.

Damage taken in normal battles

Type		Type	
Normal	×1	Flying	×1
Fire	×1	Psychic	×2
Water	×1	Bug	×0.5
Grass	×0.5	Rock	×1
Electric	×1	Ghost	×1
Ice	×1	Dragon	×1
Fighting	×0.5	Dark	×1
Poison	×0.5	Steel	×1
Ground	×2	Fairy	×0.5

Damage taken in Inverse battles

Type		Type	
Normal	×1	Flying	×1
Fire	×1	Psychic	×0.5
Water	×1	Bug	×2
Grass	×2	Rock	×1
Electric	×1	Ghost	×1
Ice	×1	Dragon	×1
Fighting	×2	Dark	×1
Poison	×2	Steel	×1
Ground	×0.5	Fairy	×2

Can be used in
Inverse Battle
Battle Institute
Battle Maison
Random Matchup (Free Battle)
Random Matchup (Others)

LEVEL-UP MOVES

Lv.	Name	Type	Kind	Pow.	Acc.	PP	Range
1	Pound	Normal	Physical	40	100	35	Normal
1	Poison Gas	Poison	Status	—	90	40	Many Others
1	Recycle	Normal	Status	—	—	10	Self
1	Toxic Spikes	Poison	Status	—	—	20	Other Side
3	Recycle	Normal	Status	—	—	10	Self
7	Toxic Spikes	Poison	Status	—	—	20	Other Side
12	Acid Spray	Poison	Special	40	100	20	Normal
14	Double Slap	Normal	Physical	15	85	10	Normal
18	Sludge	Poison	Special	65	100	20	Normal
23	Stockpile	Normal	Status	—	—	20	Self
23	Swallow	Normal	Status	—	—	10	Self
25	Body Slam	Normal	Physical	85	100	15	Normal
29	Sludge Bomb	Poison	Special	90	100	10	Normal
34	Clear Smog	Poison	Special	50	—	15	Normal
39	Toxic	Poison	Status	—	90	10	Normal
46	Amnesia	Psychic	Status	—	—	20	Self
49	Belch	Poison	Special	120	90	10	Normal
54	Gunk Shot	Poison	Physical	120	80	5	Normal
59	Explosion	Normal	Physical	250	100	5	Adjacent

TM & HM MOVES

No.	Name	Type	Kind	Pow.	Acc.	PP	Range
TM06	Toxic	Poison	Status	—	90	10	Normal
TM09	Venoshock	Poison	Special	65	100	10	Normal
TM10	Hidden Power	Normal	Special	60	100	15	Normal
TM11	Sunny Day	Fire	Status	—	—	5	Both Sides
TM15	Hyper Beam	Normal	Special	150	90	5	Normal
TM17	Protect	Normal	Status	—	—	10	Self
TM18	Rain Dance	Water	Status	—	—	5	Both Sides
TM21	Frustration	Normal	Physical	—	100	20	Normal
TM22	Solar Beam	Grass	Special	120	100	10	Normal
TM23	Smack Down	Rock	Physical	50	100	15	Normal
TM24	Thunderbolt	Electric	Special	90	100	15	Normal
TM27	Return	Normal	Physical	—	100	20	Normal
TM29	Psychic	Psychic	Special	90	100	10	Normal
TM32	Double Team	Normal	Status	—	—	15	Self
TM34	Sludge Wave	Poison	Special	95	100	10	Adjacent
TM36	Sludge Bomb	Poison	Special	90	100	10	Normal
TM42	Facade	Normal	Physical	70	100	20	Normal
TM44	Rest	Psychic	Status	—	—	10	Self
TM45	Attract	Normal	Status	—	100	15	Normal
TM46	Thief	Dark	Physical	60	100	25	Normal
TM48	Round	Normal	Special	60	100	15	Normal
TM52	Focus Blast	Fighting	Special	120	70	5	Normal
TM56	Fling	Dark	Physical	—	100	10	Normal
TM64	Explosion	Normal	Physical	250	100	5	Adjacent
TM66	Payback	Dark	Physical	50	100	10	Normal
TM68	Giga Impact	Normal	Physical	150	90	5	Normal
TM69	Rock Polish	Rock	Status	—	—	20	Self
TM83	Infestation	Bug	Special	20	100	20	Normal
TM87	Swagger	Normal	Status	—	90	15	Normal
TM88	Sleep Talk	Normal	Status	—	—	10	Self
TM90	Substitute	Normal	Status	—	—	10	Self
TM94	Secret Power	Normal	Physical	70	100	20	Normal
TM97	Dark Pulse	Dark	Special	80	100	15	Normal
TM100	Confide	Normal	Status	—	—	20	Normal

MOVES LEARNED IN EXCHANGE FOR BP

Name	Type	Kind	Pow.	Acc.	PP	Range
Seed Bomb	Grass	Physical	80	100	15	Normal
Gunk Shot	Poison	Physical	120	80	5	Normal
Snore	Normal	Special	50	100	15	Normal
Pain Split	Normal	Status	—	—	20	Normal
Giga Drain	Grass	Special	75	100	10	Normal
Drain Punch	Fighting	Physical	75	100	10	Normal
Spite	Ghost	Status	—	100	10	Normal
Recycle	Normal	Status	—	—	10	Self

MOVES TAUGHT BY PEOPLE

Name	Type	Kind	Pow.	Acc.	PP	Range

National Pokédex **570** Hoenn Pokédex —

Zorua

Tricky Fox Pokémon

Dark

HEIGHT: 2'04" WEIGHT: 27.6 lbs.

Same form for ♂ / ♀

Ω It changes so it looks just like its foe, tricks it, and then uses that opportunity to flee.

α To protect themselves from danger, they hide their true identities by transforming into people and Pokémon.

ABILITY: Illusion

HIDDEN ABILITY: —

EGG GROUPS: Field

STAT GROWTH RATES: HP, Attack, Defense, Sp. Atk, Sp. Def, Speed

ITEMS SOMETIMES HELD BY WILD POKÉMON: —

EVOLUTION: Zorua → Lv. 30 → Zoroark

MAIN WAY TO REGISTER IN THE NATIONAL POKÉDEX

Catch on Route 101. Appears as a hidden Pokémon after you battle Groudon or Kyogre.

Damage taken in normal battles

Type		Type	
Normal	×1	Flying	×1
Fire	×1	Psychic	×0
Water	×1	Bug	×2
Grass	×1	Rock	×1
Electric	×1	Ghost	×0.5
Ice	×1	Dragon	×1
Fighting	×2	Dark	×0.5
Poison	×1	Steel	×1
Ground	×1	Fairy	×2

Damage taken in Inverse battles

Type		Type	
Normal	×1	Flying	×1
Fire	×1	Psychic	×2
Water	×1	Bug	×0.5
Grass	×1	Rock	×1
Electric	×1	Ghost	×2
Ice	×1	Dragon	×1
Fighting	×0.5	Dark	×2
Poison	×1	Steel	×1
Ground	×1	Fairy	×0.5

Can be used in

- Inverse Battle
- Battle Institute
- Battle Maison
- Random Matchup (Free Battle)
- Random Matchup (Others)

LEVEL-UP MOVES

Lv.	Name	Type	Kind	Pow.	Acc.	PP	Range
1	Scratch	Normal	Physical	40	100	35	Normal
1	Leer	Normal	Status	—	100	30	Many Others
5	Pursuit	Dark	Physical	40	100	20	Normal
9	Fake Tears	Dark	Status	—	100	20	Normal
13	Fury Swipes	Normal	Physical	18	80	15	Normal
17	Feint Attack	Dark	Physical	60	—	20	Normal
21	Scary Face	Normal	Status	—	100	10	Normal
25	Taunt	Dark	Status	—	100	20	Normal
29	Foul Play	Dark	Physical	95	100	15	Normal
33	Torment	Dark	Status	—	100	15	Normal
37	Agility	Psychic	Status	—	—	30	Self
41	Embargo	Dark	Status	—	100	15	Normal
45	Punishment	Dark	Physical	—	100	5	Normal
49	Nasty Plot	Dark	Status	—	—	20	Self
53	Imprison	Psychic	Status	—	—	10	Self
57	Night Daze	Dark	Special	85	95	10	Normal

TM & HM MOVES

No.	Name	Type	Kind	Pow.	Acc.	PP	Range
TM01	Hone Claws	Dark	Status	—	—	15	Self
TM04	Calm Mind	Psychic	Status	—	—	20	Self
TM05	Roar	Normal	Status	—	—	20	Normal
TM06	Toxic	Poison	Status	—	90	10	Normal
TM10	Hidden Power	Normal	Special	60	100	15	Normal
TM11	Sunny Day	Fire	Status	—	—	5	Both Sides
TM12	Taunt	Dark	Status	—	100	20	Normal
TM17	Protect	Normal	Status	—	—	10	Self
TM18	Rain Dance	Water	Status	—	—	5	Both Sides
TM21	Frustration	Normal	Physical	—	100	20	Normal
TM27	Return	Normal	Physical	—	100	20	Normal
TM28	Dig	Ground	Physical	80	100	10	Normal
TM30	Shadow Ball	Ghost	Special	80	100	15	Normal
TM32	Double Team	Normal	Status	—	—	15	Self
TM40	Aerial Ace	Flying	Physical	60	—	20	Normal
TM41	Torment	Dark	Status	—	100	15	Normal
TM42	Facade	Normal	Physical	70	100	20	Normal
TM44	Rest	Psychic	Status	—	—	10	Self
TM45	Attract	Normal	Status	—	100	15	Normal
TM46	Thief	Dark	Physical	60	100	25	Normal
TM48	Round	Normal	Special	60	100	15	Normal
TM56	Fling	Dark	Physical	—	100	10	Normal
TM59	Incinerate	Fire	Special	60	100	15	Many Others
TM63	Embargo	Dark	Status	—	100	15	Normal
TM66	Payback	Dark	Physical	50	100	10	Normal
TM67	Retaliate	Normal	Physical	70	100	5	Normal
TM75	Swords Dance	Normal	Status	—	—	20	Self
TM77	Psych Up	Normal	Status	—	—	10	Normal
TM86	Grass Knot	Grass	Special	—	100	20	Normal
TM87	Swagger	Normal	Status	—	90	15	Normal
TM88	Sleep Talk	Normal	Status	—	—	10	Self
TM89	U-turn	Bug	Physical	70	100	20	Normal
TM90	Substitute	Normal	Status	—	—	10	Self
TM94	Secret Power	Normal	Physical	70	100	20	Normal
TM95	Snarl	Dark	Special	55	95	15	Many Others
TM97	Dark Pulse	Dark	Special	80	100	15	Normal
TM100	Confide	Normal	Status	—	—	20	Normal
HM01	Cut	Normal	Physical	50	95	30	Normal

MOVES LEARNED IN EXCHANGE FOR BP

Name	Type	Kind	Pow.	Acc.	PP	Range
Covet	Normal	Physical	60	100	25	Normal
Bounce	Flying	Physical	85	85	5	Normal
Uproar	Normal	Special	90	100	10	1 Random
Foul Play	Dark	Physical	95	100	15	Normal
Hyper Voice	Normal	Special	90	100	10	Many Others
Snore	Normal	Special	50	100	15	Normal
Knock Off	Dark	Physical	65	100	20	Normal
Spite	Ghost	Status	—	100	10	Normal
Trick	Psychic	Status	—	100	10	Normal
Snatch	Dark	Status	—	—	10	Self

MOVES TAUGHT BY PEOPLE

Name	Type	Kind	Pow.	Acc.	PP	Range

EGG MOVES

Name	Type	Kind	Pow.	Acc.	PP	Range
Detect	Fighting	Status	—	—	5	Self
Captivate	Normal	Status	—	100	20	Many Others
Dark Pulse	Dark	Special	80	100	15	Normal
Snatch	Dark	Status	—	—	10	Self
Memento	Dark	Status	—	100	10	Normal
Sucker Punch	Dark	Physical	80	100	5	Normal
Extrasensory	Psychic	Special	80	100	20	Normal
Counter	Fighting	Physical	—	100	20	Varies
Copycat	Normal	Status	—	—	20	Self

National Pokédex **571** Hoenn Pokédex —

Zoroark

Illusion Fox Pokémon

Dark

HEIGHT: 5'03" WEIGHT: 178.8 lbs.

Same form for ♂ / ♀

Ω Each has the ability to fool a large group of people simultaneously. They protect their lair with illusory scenery.

α Bonds between these Pokémon are very strong. It protects the safety of its pack by tricking its opponents.

ABILITY: Illusion

HIDDEN ABILITY: —

EGG GROUPS: Field

STAT GROWTH RATES: HP, Attack, Defense, Sp. Atk, Sp. Def, Speed

ITEMS SOMETIMES HELD BY WILD POKÉMON: —

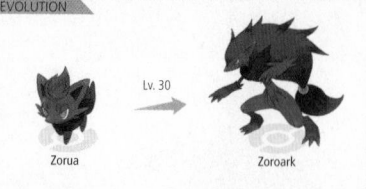

EVOLUTION: Zorua → Lv. 30 → Zoroark

MAIN WAY TO REGISTER IN THE NATIONAL POKÉDEX

Level up Zorua to Lv. 30.

Damage taken in normal battles

Type		Type	
Normal	×1	Flying	×1
Fire	×1	Psychic	×0
Water	×1	Bug	×2
Grass	×1	Rock	×1
Electric	×1	Ghost	×0.5
Ice	×1	Dragon	×1
Fighting	×2	Dark	×0.5
Poison	×1	Steel	×1
Ground	×1	Fairy	×2

Damage taken in Inverse battles

Type		Type	
Normal	×1	Flying	×1
Fire	×1	Psychic	×2
Water	×1	Bug	×0.5
Grass	×1	Rock	×1
Electric	×1	Ghost	×2
Ice	×1	Dragon	×1
Fighting	×0.5	Dark	×2
Poison	×1	Steel	×1
Ground	×1	Fairy	×0.5

Can be used in

- Inverse Battle
- Battle Institute
- Battle Maison
- Random Matchup (Free Battle)
- Random Matchup (Others)

LEVEL-UP MOVES

Lv.	Name	Type	Kind	Pow.	Acc.	PP	Range
1	Night Daze	Dark	Special	85	95	10	Normal
1	Imprison	Psychic	Status	—	—	10	Self
1	U-turn	Bug	Physical	70	100	20	Normal
1	Scratch	Normal	Physical	40	100	35	Normal
1	Leer	Normal	Status	—	100	30	Many Others
1	Pursuit	Dark	Physical	40	100	20	Normal
1	Hone Claws	Dark	Status	—	—	15	Self
5	Pursuit	Dark	Physical	40	100	20	Normal
9	Hone Claws	Dark	Status	—	—	15	Self
13	Fury Swipes	Normal	Physical	18	80	15	Normal
17	Feint Attack	Dark	Physical	60	—	20	Normal
21	Scary Face	Normal	Status	—	100	10	Normal
25	Taunt	Dark	Status	—	100	20	Normal
29	Foul Play	Dark	Physical	95	100	15	Normal
30	Night Slash	Dark	Physical	70	100	15	Normal
34	Torment	Dark	Status	—	100	15	Normal
39	Agility	Psychic	Status	—	—	30	Self
44	Embargo	Dark	Status	—	100	15	Normal
49	Punishment	Dark	Physical	—	100	5	Normal
54	Nasty Plot	Dark	Status	—	—	20	Self
59	Imprison	Psychic	Status	—	—	10	Self
64	Night Daze	Dark	Special	85	95	10	Normal

TM & HM MOVES

No.	Name	Type	Kind	Pow.	Acc.	PP	Range
TM01	Hone Claws	Dark	Status	—	—	15	Self
TM04	Calm Mind	Psychic	Status	—	—	20	Self
TM05	Roar	Normal	Status	—	—	20	Normal
TM06	Toxic	Poison	Status	—	90	10	Normal
TM10	Hidden Power	Normal	Special	60	100	15	Normal
TM11	Sunny Day	Fire	Status	—	—	5	Both Sides
TM12	Taunt	Dark	Status	—	100	20	Normal
TM15	Hyper Beam	Normal	Special	150	90	5	Normal
TM17	Protect	Normal	Status	—	—	10	Self
TM18	Rain Dance	Water	Status	—	—	5	Both Sides
TM21	Frustration	Normal	Physical	—	100	20	Normal
TM27	Return	Normal	Physical	—	100	20	Normal
TM28	Dig	Ground	Physical	80	100	10	Normal
TM30	Shadow Ball	Ghost	Special	80	100	15	Normal
TM32	Double Team	Normal	Status	—	—	15	Self
TM35	Flamethrower	Fire	Special	90	100	15	Normal
TM40	Aerial Ace	Flying	Physical	60	—	20	Normal
TM41	Torment	Dark	Status	—	100	15	Normal
TM42	Facade	Normal	Physical	70	100	20	Normal
TM44	Rest	Psychic	Status	—	—	10	Self
TM45	Attract	Normal	Status	—	100	15	Normal
TM46	Thief	Dark	Physical	60	100	25	Normal
TM47	Low Sweep	Fighting	Physical	65	100	20	Normal
TM48	Round	Normal	Special	60	100	15	Normal
TM52	Focus Blast	Fighting	Special	120	70	5	Normal
TM56	Fling	Dark	Physical	—	100	10	Normal
TM59	Incinerate	Fire	Special	60	100	15	Many Others
TM63	Embargo	Dark	Status	—	100	15	Normal
TM65	Shadow Claw	Ghost	Physical	70	100	15	Normal
TM66	Payback	Dark	Physical	50	100	10	Normal
TM67	Retaliate	Normal	Physical	70	100	5	Normal
TM68	Giga Impact	Normal	Physical	150	90	5	Normal
TM75	Swords Dance	Normal	Status	—	—	20	Self
TM77	Psych Up	Normal	Status	—	—	10	Normal
TM86	Grass Knot	Grass	Special	—	100	20	Normal
TM87	Swagger	Normal	Status	—	90	15	Normal
TM88	Sleep Talk	Normal	Status	—	—	10	Self
TM89	U-turn	Bug	Physical	70	100	20	Normal
TM90	Substitute	Normal	Status	—	—	10	Self
TM94	Secret Power	Normal	Physical	70	100	20	Normal
TM95	Snarl	Dark	Special	55	95	15	Many Others
TM97	Dark Pulse	Dark	Special	80	100	15	Normal
TM100	Confide	Normal	Status	—	—	20	Normal
HM01	Cut	Normal	Physical	50	95	30	Normal
HM06	Rock Smash	Fighting	Physical	40	100	15	Normal

MOVES LEARNED IN EXCHANGE FOR BP

Name	Type	Kind	Pow.	Acc.	PP	Range
Covet	Normal	Physical	60	100	25	Normal
Bounce	Flying	Physical	85	85	5	Normal
Low Kick	Fighting	Physical	—	100	20	Normal
Uproar	Normal	Special	90	100	10	1 Random
Foul Play	Dark	Physical	95	100	15	Normal
Hyper Voice	Normal	Special	90	100	10	Many Others
Snore	Normal	Special	50	100	15	Normal
Knock Off	Dark	Physical	65	100	20	Normal
Spite	Ghost	Status	—	100	10	Normal
Trick	Psychic	Status	—	100	10	Normal
Snatch	Dark	Status	—	—	10	Self

MOVES TAUGHT BY PEOPLE

Name	Type	Kind	Pow.	Acc.	PP	Range

National Pokédex **572** Hoenn Pokédex –

Minccino

Chinchilla Pokémon

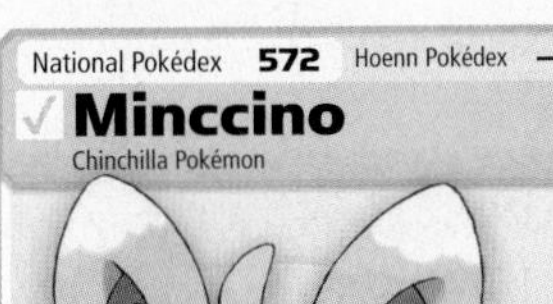

Normal

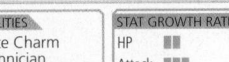

HEIGHT: 1'04" WEIGHT: 12.8 lbs.

Same form for ♂ / ♀

Ω Minccino greet each other by grooming one another thoroughly with their tails.

α These Pokémon prefer a tidy habitat. They are always sweeping and dusting, using their tails as brooms.

ABILITIES
Cute Charm
Technician

HIDDEN ABILITY
Skill Link

EGG GROUPS
Field

STAT GROWTH RATES

HP	■■
Attack	■■■
Defense	■■
Sp. Atk	■■
Sp. Def	■■
Speed	■■■■

ITEMS SOMETIMES HELD BY WILD POKÉMON
—

EVOLUTION

MAIN WAY TO REGISTER IN THE NATIONAL POKÉDEX

Catch in Mirage Forest 1.

Damage taken in normal battles

Normal	×1	Flying	×1
Fire	×1	Psychic	×1
Water	×1	Bug	×1
Grass	×1	Rock	×1
Electric	×1	Ghost	×0
Ice	×1	Dragon	×1
Fighting	×2	Dark	×1
Poison	×1	Steel	×1
Ground	×1	Fairy	×1

Damage taken in Inverse battles

Normal	×1	Flying	×1
Fire	×1	Psychic	×1
Water	×1	Bug	×1
Grass	×1	Rock	×1
Electric	×1	Ghost	×2
Ice	×1	Dragon	×1
Fighting	×0.5	Dark	×1
Poison	×1	Steel	×1
Ground	×1	Fairy	×1

Can be used in
Inverse Battle
Battle Institute
Battle Maison
Random Matchup (Free Battle)
Random Matchup (Others)

LEVEL-UP MOVES

Lv.	Name	Type	Kind	Pow.	Acc.	PP	Range
1	Pound	Normal	Physical	40	100	35	Normal
3	Baby-Doll Eyes	Fairy	Status	—	100	30	Normal
7	Helping Hand	Normal	Status	—	—	20	1 Ally
9	Tickle	Normal	Status	—	100	20	Normal
13	Double Slap	Normal	Physical	15	85	10	Normal
15	Encore	Normal	Status	—	100	5	Normal
19	Swift	Normal	Special	60	—	20	Many Others
21	Sing	Normal	Status	—	55	15	Normal
25	Tail Slap	Normal	Physical	25	85	10	Normal
27	Charm	Fairy	Status	—	100	20	Normal
31	Wake-Up Slap	Fighting	Physical	70	100	10	Normal
33	Echoed Voice	Normal	Special	40	100	15	Normal
37	Slam	Normal	Physical	80	75	20	Normal
39	Captivate	Normal	Status	—	100	20	Many Others
43	Hyper Voice	Normal	Special	90	100	10	Many Others
45	Last Resort	Normal	Physical	140	100	5	Normal
49	After You	Normal	Status	—	—	15	Normal

TM & HM MOVES

No.	Name	Type	Kind	Pow.	Acc.	PP	Range
TM04	Calm Mind	Psychic	Status	—	—	20	Self
TM06	Toxic	Poison	Status	—	90	10	Normal
TM10	Hidden Power	Normal	Special	60	100	15	Normal
TM11	Sunny Day	Fire	Status	—	—	5	Both Sides
TM17	Protect	Normal	Status	—	—	10	Self
TM18	Rain Dance	Water	Status	—	—	5	Both Sides
TM20	Safeguard	Normal	Status	—	—	25	Your Side
TM21	Frustration	Normal	Physical	—	100	20	Normal
TM24	Thunderbolt	Electric	Special	90	100	15	Normal
TM27	Return	Normal	Physical	—	100	20	Normal
TM28	Dig	Ground	Physical	80	100	10	Normal
TM32	Double Team	Normal	Status	—	—	15	Self
TM42	Facade	Normal	Physical	70	100	20	Normal
TM44	Rest	Psychic	Status	—	—	10	Self
TM45	Attract	Normal	Status	—	100	15	Normal
TM46	Thief	Dark	Physical	60	100	25	Normal
TM48	Round	Normal	Special	60	100	15	Normal
TM49	Echoed Voice	Normal	Special	40	100	15	Normal
TM56	Fling	Dark	Physical	—	100	10	Normal
TM67	Retaliate	Normal	Physical	70	100	5	Normal
TM73	Thunder Wave	Electric	Status	—	100	20	Normal
TM86	Grass Knot	Grass	Special	—	100	20	Normal
TM87	Swagger	Normal	Status	—	90	15	Normal
TM88	Sleep Talk	Normal	Status	—	—	10	Self
TM89	U-turn	Bug	Physical	70	100	20	Normal
TM90	Substitute	Normal	Status	—	—	10	Self
TM94	Secret Power	Normal	Physical	70	100	20	Normal
TM99	Dazzling Gleam	Fairy	Special	80	100	10	Many Others
TM100	Confide	Normal	Status	—	—	20	Normal

MOVES LEARNED IN EXCHANGE FOR BP

Name	Type	Kind	Pow.	Acc.	PP	Range
Covet	Normal	Physical	60	100	25	Normal
Seed Bomb	Grass	Physical	80	100	15	Normal
Gunk Shot	Poison	Physical	120	80	5	Normal
Uproar	Normal	Special	90	100	10	1 Random
Last Resort	Normal	Physical	140	100	5	Normal
Aqua Tail	Water	Physical	90	90	10	Normal
Hyper Voice	Normal	Special	90	100	10	Many Others
Iron Tail	Steel	Physical	100	75	15	Normal
Snore	Normal	Special	50	100	15	Normal
Knock Off	Dark	Physical	65	100	20	Normal
Shock Wave	Electric	Special	60	—	20	Normal
After You	Normal	Status	—	—	15	Normal
Helping Hand	Normal	Status	—	—	20	1 Ally

MOVES TAUGHT BY PEOPLE

Name	Type	Kind	Pow.	Acc.	PP	Range

EGG MOVES

Name	Type	Kind	Pow.	Acc.	PP	Range
Iron Tail	Steel	Physical	100	75	15	Normal
Tail Whip	Normal	Status	—	100	30	Many Others
Aqua Tail	Water	Physical	90	90	10	Normal
Mud-Slap	Ground	Special	20	100	10	Normal
Knock Off	Dark	Physical	65	100	20	Normal
Fake Tears	Dark	Status	—	100	20	Normal
Sleep Talk	Normal	Status	—	—	10	Self
Endure	Normal	Status	—	—	10	Self
Flail	Normal	Physical	—	100	15	Normal

National Pokédex **573** Hoenn Pokédex –

Cinccino

Scarf Pokémon

Normal

HEIGHT: 1'08" WEIGHT: 16.5 lbs.

Same form for ♂ / ♀

Ω Their white fur feels amazing to touch. Their fur repels dust and prevents static electricity from building up.

α Cinccino's body is coated in a special oil that helps it deflect attacks, such as punches.

ABILITIES
Cute Charm
Technician

HIDDEN ABILITY
Skill Link

EGG GROUPS
Field

STAT GROWTH RATES

HP	■■■
Attack	■■■■■
Defense	■■■
Sp. Atk	■■■
Sp. Def	■■■
Speed	■■■■■■

ITEMS SOMETIMES HELD BY WILD POKÉMON
—

EVOLUTION

Minccino → Shiny Stone → Cinccino

MAIN WAY TO REGISTER IN THE NATIONAL POKÉDEX

Use a Shiny Stone on Minccino.

Damage taken in normal battles

Normal	×1	Flying	×1
Fire	×1	Psychic	×1
Water	×1	Bug	×1
Grass	×1	Rock	×1
Electric	×1	Ghost	×0
Ice	×1	Dragon	×1
Fighting	×2	Dark	×1
Poison	×1	Steel	×1
Ground	×1	Fairy	×1

Damage taken in Inverse battles

Normal	×1	Flying	×1
Fire	×1	Psychic	×1
Water	×1	Bug	×1
Grass	×1	Rock	×1
Electric	×1	Ghost	×2
Ice	×1	Dragon	×1
Fighting	×0.5	Dark	×1
Poison	×1	Steel	×1
Ground	×1	Fairy	×1

Can be used in
Inverse Battle
Battle Institute
Battle Maison
Random Matchup (Free Battle)
Random Matchup (Others)

LEVEL-UP MOVES

Lv.	Name	Type	Kind	Pow.	Acc.	PP	Range
1	Bullet Seed	Grass	Physical	25	100	30	Normal
1	Rock Blast	Rock	Physical	25	90	10	Normal
1	Helping Hand	Normal	Status	—	—	20	1 Ally
1	Tickle	Normal	Status	—	100	20	Normal
1	Sing	Normal	Status	—	55	15	Normal
1	Tail Slap	Normal	Physical	25	85	10	Normal

TM & HM MOVES

No.	Name	Type	Kind	Pow.	Acc.	PP	Range
TM04	Calm Mind	Psychic	Status	—	—	20	Self
TM06	Toxic	Poison	Status	—	90	10	Normal
TM10	Hidden Power	Normal	Special	60	100	15	Normal
TM11	Sunny Day	Fire	Status	—	—	5	Both Sides
TM15	Hyper Beam	Normal	Special	150	90	5	Normal
TM16	Light Screen	Psychic	Status	—	—	30	Your Side
TM17	Protect	Normal	Status	—	—	10	Self
TM18	Rain Dance	Water	Status	—	—	5	Both Sides
TM20	Safeguard	Normal	Status	—	—	25	Your Side
TM21	Frustration	Normal	Physical	—	100	20	Normal
TM24	Thunderbolt	Electric	Special	90	100	15	Normal
TM25	Thunder	Electric	Special	110	70	10	Normal
TM27	Return	Normal	Physical	—	100	20	Normal
TM28	Dig	Ground	Physical	80	100	10	Normal
TM32	Double Team	Normal	Status	—	—	15	Self
TM42	Facade	Normal	Physical	70	100	20	Normal
TM44	Rest	Psychic	Status	—	—	10	Self
TM45	Attract	Normal	Status	—	100	15	Normal
TM46	Thief	Dark	Physical	60	100	25	Normal
TM48	Round	Normal	Special	60	100	15	Normal
TM49	Echoed Voice	Normal	Special	40	100	15	Normal
TM52	Focus Blast	Fighting	Special	120	70	5	Normal
TM56	Fling	Dark	Physical	—	100	10	Normal
TM67	Retaliate	Normal	Physical	70	100	5	Normal
TM68	Giga Impact	Normal	Physical	150	90	5	Normal
TM73	Thunder Wave	Electric	Status	—	100	20	Normal
TM86	Grass Knot	Grass	Special	—	100	20	Normal
TM87	Swagger	Normal	Status	—	90	15	Normal
TM88	Sleep Talk	Normal	Status	—	—	10	Self
TM89	U-turn	Bug	Physical	70	100	20	Normal
TM90	Substitute	Normal	Status	—	—	10	Self
TM94	Secret Power	Normal	Physical	70	100	20	Normal
TM99	Dazzling Gleam	Fairy	Special	80	100	10	Many Others
TM100	Confide	Normal	Status	—	—	20	Normal

MOVES LEARNED IN EXCHANGE FOR BP

Name	Type	Kind	Pow.	Acc.	PP	Range
Covet	Normal	Physical	60	100	25	Normal
Seed Bomb	Grass	Physical	80	100	15	Normal
Gunk Shot	Poison	Physical	120	80	5	Normal
Uproar	Normal	Special	90	100	10	1 Random
Last Resort	Normal	Physical	140	100	5	Normal
Aqua Tail	Water	Physical	90	90	10	Normal
Hyper Voice	Normal	Special	90	100	10	Many Others
Iron Tail	Steel	Physical	100	75	15	Normal
Snore	Normal	Special	50	100	15	Normal
Knock Off	Dark	Physical	65	100	20	Normal
Shock Wave	Electric	Special	60	—	20	Normal
After You	Normal	Status	—	—	15	Normal
Helping Hand	Normal	Status	—	—	20	1 Ally

MOVES TAUGHT BY PEOPLE

Name	Type	Kind	Pow.	Acc.	PP	Range

National Pokédex **574** Hoenn Pokédex —

Gothita

Fixation Pokémon

Psychic

HEIGHT: 1'04" WEIGHT: 12.8 lbs.

Same form for ♂ / ♀

Ω Their ribbonlike feelers increase their psychic power. They are always staring at something.

α They intently observe both Trainers and Pokémon. Apparently, they are looking at something that only Gothita can see.

ABILITIES
Frisk
Competitive

HIDDEN ABILITY
Shadow Tag

EGG GROUPS
Human-Like

STAT GROWTH RATES
HP
Attack
Defense
Sp. Atk
Sp. Def
Speed

ITEMS SOMETIMES HELD BY WILD POKÉMON
—

EVOLUTION

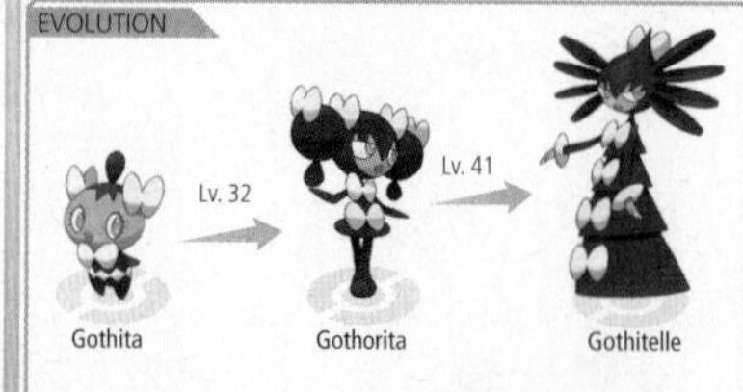

Gothita → Gothorita → Gothitelle

MAIN WAY TO REGISTER IN THE NATIONAL POKÉDEX

Catch on Route 102. Appears as a hidden Pokémon after you battle Groudon or Kyogre.

Damage taken in normal battles

Type		Type	
Normal	×1	Flying	×1
Fire	×1	Psychic	×0.5
Water	×1	Bug	×2
Grass	×1	Rock	×1
Electric	×1	Ghost	×2
Ice	×1	Dragon	×1
Fighting	×0.5	Dark	×2
Poison	×1	Steel	×1
Ground	×1	Fairy	×1

Damage taken in Inverse battles

Type		Type	
Normal	×1	Flying	×1
Fire	×1	Psychic	×2
Water	×1	Bug	×0.5
Grass	×1	Rock	×1
Electric	×1	Ghost	×0.5
Ice	×1	Dragon	×1
Fighting	×2	Dark	×0.5
Poison	×1	Steel	×1
Ground	×1	Fairy	×1

Can be used in
Inverse Battle
Battle Institute
Battle Maison
Random Matchup (Free Battle)
Random Matchup (Others)

LEVEL-UP MOVES

Lv.	Name	Type	Kind	Pow.	Acc.	PP	Range
1	Pound	Normal	Physical	40	100	35	Normal
3	Confusion	Psychic	Special	50	100	25	Normal
7	Tickle	Normal	Status	—	100	20	Normal
8	Play Nice	Normal	Status	—	—	20	Normal
10	Fake Tears	Dark	Status	—	100	20	Normal
14	Double Slap	Normal	Physical	15	85	10	Normal
16	Psybeam	Psychic	Special	65	100	20	Normal
19	Embargo	Dark	Status	—	100	15	Normal
24	Feint Attack	Dark	Physical	60	—	20	Normal
25	Psyshock	Psychic	Special	80	100	10	Normal
28	Flatter	Dark	Status	—	100	15	Normal
31	Future Sight	Psychic	Special	120	100	10	Normal
33	Heal Block	Psychic	Status	—	100	15	Many Others
37	Psychic	Psychic	Special	90	100	10	Normal
40	Telekinesis	Psychic	Status	—	—	15	Normal
46	Charm	Fairy	Status	—	100	20	Normal
48	Magic Room	Psychic	Status	—	—	10	Both Sides

TM & HM MOVES

No.	Name	Type	Kind	Pow.	Acc.	PP	Range
TM03	Psyshock	Psychic	Special	80	100	10	Normal
TM04	Calm Mind	Psychic	Status	—	—	20	Self
TM06	Toxic	Poison	Status	—	90	10	Normal
TM10	Hidden Power	Normal	Special	60	100	15	Normal
TM12	Taunt	Dark	Status	—	100	20	Normal
TM16	Light Screen	Psychic	Status	—	—	30	Your Side
TM17	Protect	Normal	Status	—	—	10	Self
TM18	Rain Dance	Water	Status	—	—	5	Both Sides
TM20	Safeguard	Normal	Status	—	—	25	Your Side
TM21	Frustration	Normal	Physical	—	100	20	Normal
TM24	Thunderbolt	Electric	Special	90	100	15	Normal
TM27	Return	Normal	Physical	—	100	20	Normal
TM29	Psychic	Psychic	Special	90	100	10	Normal
TM30	Shadow Ball	Ghost	Special	80	100	15	Normal
TM32	Double Team	Normal	Status	—	—	15	Self
TM33	Reflect	Psychic	Status	—	—	20	Your Side
TM39	Rock Tomb	Rock	Physical	60	95	15	Normal
TM41	Torment	Dark	Status	—	100	15	Normal
TM42	Facade	Normal	Physical	70	100	20	Normal
TM44	Rest	Psychic	Status	—	—	10	Self
TM45	Attract	Normal	Status	—	100	15	Normal
TM46	Thief	Dark	Physical	60	100	25	Normal
TM48	Round	Normal	Special	60	100	15	Normal
TM53	Energy Ball	Grass	Special	90	100	10	Normal
TM56	Fling	Dark	Physical	—	100	10	Normal
TM57	Charge Beam	Electric	Special	50	90	10	Normal
TM63	Embargo	Dark	Status	—	100	15	Normal
TM66	Payback	Dark	Physical	50	100	10	Normal
TM70	Flash	Normal	Status	—	100	20	Normal
TM73	Thunder Wave	Electric	Status	—	100	20	Normal
TM77	Psych Up	Normal	Status	—	—	10	Normal
TM80	Rock Slide	Rock	Physical	75	90	10	Many Others
TM85	Dream Eater	Psychic	Special	100	100	15	Normal
TM86	Grass Knot	Grass	Special	—	100	20	Normal
TM87	Swagger	Normal	Status	—	90	15	Normal
TM88	Sleep Talk	Normal	Status	—	—	10	Self
TM90	Substitute	Normal	Status	—	—	10	Self
TM92	Trick Room	Psychic	Status	—	—	5	Both Sides
TM94	Secret Power	Normal	Physical	70	100	20	Normal
TM97	Dark Pulse	Dark	Special	80	100	15	Normal
TM100	Confide	Normal	Status	—	—	20	Normal

MOVES LEARNED IN EXCHANGE FOR BP

Name	Type	Kind	Pow.	Acc.	PP	Range
Covet	Normal	Physical	60	100	25	Normal
Signal Beam	Bug	Special	75	100	15	Normal
Uproar	Normal	Special	90	100	10	1 Random
Magic Coat	Psychic	Status	—	—	15	Self
Foul Play	Dark	Physical	95	100	15	Normal
Gravity	Psychic	Status	—	—	5	Both Sides
Zen Headbutt	Psychic	Physical	80	90	15	Normal
Snore	Normal	Special	50	100	15	Normal
Role Play	Psychic	Status	—	—	10	Normal
Trick	Psychic	Status	—	100	10	Normal
Heal Bell	Normal	Status	—	—	5	Your Party
Shock Wave	Electric	Special	60	—	20	Normal
Helping Hand	Normal	Status	—	—	20	1 Ally
Magic Room	Psychic	Status	—	—	10	Both Sides
Recycle	Normal	Status	—	—	10	Self
Snatch	Dark	Status	—	—	10	Self
Skill Swap	Psychic	Status	—	—	10	Normal

MOVES TAUGHT BY PEOPLE

Name	Type	Kind	Pow.	Acc.	PP	Range

EGG MOVES

Name	Type	Kind	Pow.	Acc.	PP	Range
Mirror Coat	Psychic	Special	—	100	20	Varies
Uproar	Normal	Special	90	100	10	1 Random
Miracle Eye	Psychic	Status	—	—	40	Normal
Captivate	Normal	Status	—	100	20	Many Others
Mean Look	Normal	Status	—	—	5	Normal
Dark Pulse	Dark	Special	80	100	15	Normal
Heal Pulse	Psychic	Status	—	—	10	Normal

National Pokédex **575** Hoenn Pokédex —

Gothorita

Manipulate Pokémon

Psychic

HEIGHT: 2'04" WEIGHT: 39.7 lbs.

Same form for ♂ / ♀

Ω Starlight is the source of their power. At night, they mark star positions by using psychic power to float stones.

α According to many old tales, it creates friends for itself by controlling sleeping children on starry nights.

ABILITIES
Frisk
Competitive

HIDDEN ABILITY
Shadow Tag

EGG GROUPS
Human-Like

STAT GROWTH RATES
HP
Attack
Defense
Sp. Atk
Sp. Def
Speed

ITEMS SOMETIMES HELD BY WILD POKÉMON
—

EVOLUTION

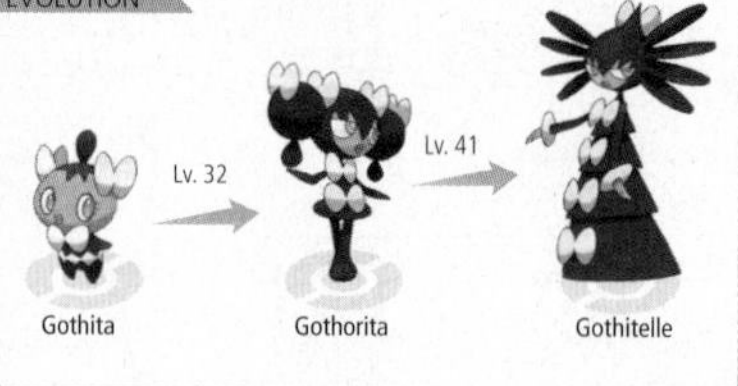

Gothita → Gothorita → Gothitelle

MAIN WAY TO REGISTER IN THE NATIONAL POKÉDEX

Level up Gothita to Lv. 32.

Damage taken in normal battles

Type		Type	
Normal	×1	Flying	×1
Fire	×1	Psychic	×0.5
Water	×1	Bug	×2
Grass	×1	Rock	×1
Electric	×1	Ghost	×2
Ice	×1	Dragon	×1
Fighting	×0.5	Dark	×2
Poison	×1	Steel	×1
Ground	×1	Fairy	×1

Damage taken in Inverse battles

Type		Type	
Normal	×1	Flying	×1
Fire	×1	Psychic	×2
Water	×1	Bug	×0.5
Grass	×1	Rock	×1
Electric	×1	Ghost	×0.5
Ice	×1	Dragon	×1
Fighting	×2	Dark	×0.5
Poison	×1	Steel	×1
Ground	×1	Fairy	×1

Can be used in
Inverse Battle
Battle Institute
Battle Maison
Random Matchup (Free Battle)
Random Matchup (Others)

LEVEL-UP MOVES

Lv.	Name	Type	Kind	Pow.	Acc.	PP	Range
1	Pound	Normal	Physical	40	100	35	Normal
1	Confusion	Psychic	Special	50	100	25	Normal
1	Tickle	Normal	Status	—	100	20	Normal
1	Play Nice	Normal	Status	—	—	20	Normal
3	Confusion	Psychic	Special	50	100	25	Normal
7	Tickle	Normal	Status	—	100	20	Normal
10	Fake Tears	Dark	Status	—	100	20	Normal
14	Double Slap	Normal	Physical	15	85	10	Normal
16	Psybeam	Psychic	Special	65	100	20	Normal
19	Embargo	Dark	Status	—	100	15	Normal
24	Feint Attack	Dark	Physical	60	—	20	Normal
25	Psyshock	Psychic	Special	80	100	10	Normal
28	Flatter	Dark	Status	—	100	15	Normal
31	Future Sight	Psychic	Special	120	100	10	Normal
34	Heal Block	Psychic	Status	—	100	15	Many Others
39	Psychic	Psychic	Special	90	100	10	Normal
43	Telekinesis	Psychic	Status	—	—	15	Normal
50	Charm	Fairy	Status	—	100	20	Normal
53	Magic Room	Psychic	Status	—	—	10	Both Sides

TM & HM MOVES

No.	Name	Type	Kind	Pow.	Acc.	PP	Range
TM03	Psyshock	Psychic	Special	80	100	10	Normal
TM04	Calm Mind	Psychic	Status	—	—	20	Self
TM06	Toxic	Poison	Status	—	90	10	Normal
TM10	Hidden Power	Normal	Special	60	100	15	Normal
TM12	Taunt	Dark	Status	—	100	20	Normal
TM16	Light Screen	Psychic	Status	—	—	30	Your Side
TM17	Protect	Normal	Status	—	—	10	Self
TM18	Rain Dance	Water	Status	—	—	5	Both Sides
TM20	Safeguard	Normal	Status	—	—	25	Your Side
TM21	Frustration	Normal	Physical	—	100	20	Normal
TM24	Thunderbolt	Electric	Special	90	100	15	Normal
TM27	Return	Normal	Physical	—	100	20	Normal
TM29	Psychic	Psychic	Special	90	100	10	Normal
TM30	Shadow Ball	Ghost	Special	80	100	15	Normal
TM32	Double Team	Normal	Status	—	—	15	Self
TM33	Reflect	Psychic	Status	—	—	20	Your Side
TM39	Rock Tomb	Rock	Physical	60	95	15	Normal
TM41	Torment	Dark	Status	—	100	15	Normal
TM42	Facade	Normal	Physical	70	100	20	Normal
TM44	Rest	Psychic	Status	—	—	10	Self
TM45	Attract	Normal	Status	—	100	15	Normal
TM46	Thief	Dark	Physical	60	100	25	Normal
TM48	Round	Normal	Special	60	100	15	Normal
TM53	Energy Ball	Grass	Special	90	100	10	Normal
TM56	Fling	Dark	Physical	—	100	10	Normal
TM57	Charge Beam	Electric	Special	50	90	10	Normal
TM63	Embargo	Dark	Status	—	100	15	Normal
TM66	Payback	Dark	Physical	50	100	10	Normal
TM70	Flash	Normal	Status	—	100	20	Normal
TM73	Thunder Wave	Electric	Status	—	100	20	Normal
TM77	Psych Up	Normal	Status	—	—	10	Normal
TM80	Rock Slide	Rock	Physical	75	90	10	Many Others
TM85	Dream Eater	Psychic	Special	100	100	15	Normal
TM86	Grass Knot	Grass	Special	—	100	20	Normal
TM87	Swagger	Normal	Status	—	90	15	Normal
TM88	Sleep Talk	Normal	Status	—	—	10	Self
TM90	Substitute	Normal	Status	—	—	10	Self
TM92	Trick Room	Psychic	Status	—	—	5	Both Sides
TM94	Secret Power	Normal	Physical	70	100	20	Normal
TM97	Dark Pulse	Dark	Special	80	100	15	Normal
TM100	Confide	Normal	Status	—	—	20	Normal

MOVES LEARNED IN EXCHANGE FOR BP

Name	Type	Kind	Pow.	Acc.	PP	Range
Covet	Normal	Physical	60	100	25	Normal
Signal Beam	Bug	Special	75	100	15	Normal
Uproar	Normal	Special	90	100	10	1 Random
Magic Coat	Psychic	Status	—	—	15	Self
Foul Play	Dark	Physical	95	100	15	Normal
Gravity	Psychic	Status	—	—	5	Both Sides
Zen Headbutt	Psychic	Physical	80	90	15	Normal
Snore	Normal	Special	50	100	15	Normal
Role Play	Psychic	Status	—	—	10	Normal
Heal Bell	Normal	Status	—	—	5	Your Party
Shock Wave	Electric	Special	60	—	20	Normal
Helping Hand	Normal	Status	—	—	20	1 Ally
Trick	Psychic	Status	—	100	10	Normal
Magic Room	Psychic	Status	—	—	10	Both Sides
Recycle	Normal	Status	—	—	10	Self
Snatch	Dark	Status	—	—	10	Self
Skill Swap	Psychic	Status	—	—	10	Normal

MOVES TAUGHT BY PEOPLE

Name	Type	Kind	Pow.	Acc.	PP	Range

National Pokédex **576** Hoenn Pokédex —

Gothitelle

Astral Body Pokémon

Psychic

HEIGHT: 4'11" WEIGHT: 97 lbs.

Same form for ♂ / ♀

Ω Starry skies thousands of light-years away are visible in the space distorted by their intense psychic power.

α They can predict the future from the placement and movement of the stars. They can see Trainers' life spans.

ABILITIES
Frisk
Competitive

HIDDEN ABILITY
Shadow Tag

EGG GROUPS
Human-Like

STAT GROWTH RATES
HP
Attack
Defense
Sp. Atk
Sp. Def
Speed

ITEMS SOMETIMES HELD BY WILD POKÉMON
—

EVOLUTION
Gothita → Lv. 32 → Gothorita → Lv. 41 → Gothitelle

MAIN WAY TO REGISTER IN THE NATIONAL POKÉDEX

Level up Gothorita to Lv. 41.

Damage taken in normal battles

Type		Type	
Normal	×1	Flying	×1
Fire	×1	Psychic	×0.5
Water	×1	Bug	×2
Grass	×1	Rock	×1
Electric	×1	Ghost	×2
Ice	×1	Dragon	×1
Fighting	×0.5	Dark	×2
Poison	×1	Steel	×1
Ground	×1	Fairy	×1

Damage taken in Inverse battles

Type		Type	
Normal	×1	Flying	×1
Fire	×1	Psychic	×2
Water	×1	Bug	×0.5
Grass	×1	Rock	×1
Electric	×1	Ghost	×0.5
Ice	×1	Dragon	×1
Fighting	×2	Dark	×0.5
Poison	×1	Steel	×1
Ground	×1	Fairy	×1

Can be used in
Inverse Battle
Battle Institute
Battle Maison
Random Matchup (Free Battle)
Random Matchup (Others)

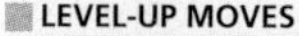

LEVEL-UP MOVES

Lv.	Name	Type	Kind	Pow.	Acc.	PP	Range
1	Pound	Normal	Physical	40	100	35	Normal
1	Confusion	Psychic	Special	50	100	25	Normal
1	Tickle	Normal	Status	—	100	20	Normal
1	Play Nice	Normal	Status	—	—	20	Normal
3	Confusion	Psychic	Special	50	100	25	Normal
7	Tickle	Normal	Status	—	100	20	Normal
10	Fake Tears	Dark	Status	—	100	20	Normal
14	Double Slap	Normal	Physical	15	85	10	Normal
16	Psybeam	Psychic	Special	65	100	20	Normal
19	Embargo	Dark	Status	—	100	15	Normal
24	Feint Attack	Dark	Physical	60	—	20	Normal
25	Psyshock	Psychic	Special	80	100	10	Normal
28	Flatter	Dark	Status	—	100	15	Normal
31	Future Sight	Psychic	Special	120	100	10	Normal
34	Heal Block	Psychic	Status	—	100	15	Many Others
39	Psychic	Psychic	Special	90	100	10	Normal
45	Telekinesis	Psychic	Status	—	—	15	Normal
54	Charm	Fairy	Status	—	100	20	Normal
59	Magic Room	Psychic	Status	—	—	10	Both Sides

TM & HM MOVES

No.	Name	Type	Kind	Pow.	Acc.	PP	Range
TM03	Psyshock	Psychic	Special	80	100	10	Normal
TM04	Calm Mind	Psychic	Status	—	—	20	Self
TM06	Toxic	Poison	Status	—	90	10	Normal
TM10	Hidden Power	Normal	Special	60	100	15	Normal
TM12	Taunt	Dark	Status	—	100	20	Normal
TM15	Hyper Beam	Normal	Special	150	90	5	Normal
TM16	Light Screen	Psychic	Status	—	—	30	Your Side
TM17	Protect	Normal	Status	—	—	10	Self
TM18	Rain Dance	Water	Status	—	—	5	Both Sides
TM20	Safeguard	Normal	Status	—	—	25	Your Side
TM21	Frustration	Normal	Physical	—	100	20	Normal
TM24	Thunderbolt	Electric	Special	90	100	15	Normal
TM27	Return	Normal	Physical	—	100	20	Normal
TM29	Psychic	Psychic	Special	90	100	10	Normal
TM30	Shadow Ball	Ghost	Special	80	100	15	Normal
TM31	Brick Break	Fighting	Physical	75	100	15	Normal
TM32	Double Team	Normal	Status	—	—	15	Self
TM33	Reflect	Psychic	Status	—	—	20	Your Side
TM39	Rock Tomb	Rock	Physical	60	95	15	Normal
TM41	Torment	Dark	Status	—	100	15	Normal
TM42	Facade	Normal	Physical	70	100	20	Normal
TM44	Rest	Psychic	Status	—	—	10	Self
TM45	Attract	Normal	Status	—	100	15	Normal
TM46	Thief	Dark	Physical	60	100	25	Normal
TM47	Low Sweep	Fighting	Physical	65	100	20	Normal
TM48	Round	Normal	Special	60	100	15	Normal
TM53	Energy Ball	Grass	Special	90	100	10	Normal
TM56	Fling	Dark	Physical	—	100	10	Normal
TM57	Charge Beam	Electric	Special	50	90	10	Normal
TM63	Embargo	Dark	Status	—	100	15	Normal
TM66	Payback	Dark	Physical	50	100	10	Normal
TM68	Giga Impact	Normal	Physical	150	90	5	Normal
TM70	Flash	Normal	Status	—	100	20	Normal
TM73	Thunder Wave	Electric	Status	—	100	20	Normal
TM77	Psych Up	Normal	Status	—	—	10	Normal
TM80	Rock Slide	Rock	Physical	75	90	10	Many Others
TM85	Dream Eater	Psychic	Special	100	100	15	Normal
TM86	Grass Knot	Grass	Special	—	100	20	Normal
TM87	Swagger	Normal	Status	—	90	15	Normal
TM88	Sleep Talk	Normal	Status	—	—	10	Self
TM90	Substitute	Normal	Status	—	—	10	Self
TM92	Trick Room	Psychic	Status	—	—	5	Both Sides
TM94	Secret Power	Normal	Physical	70	100	20	Normal
TM97	Dark Pulse	Dark	Special	80	100	15	Normal
TM98	Power-Up Punch	Fighting	Physical	40	100	20	Normal
TM100	Confide	Normal	Status	—	—	20	Normal

MOVES LEARNED IN EXCHANGE FOR BP

Name	Type	Kind	Pow.	Acc.	PP	Range
Covet	Normal	Physical	60	100	25	Normal
Signal Beam	Bug	Special	75	100	15	Normal
Uproar	Normal	Special	90	100	10	1 Random
Magic Coat	Psychic	Status	—	—	15	Self
Foul Play	Dark	Physical	95	100	15	Normal
Gravity	Psychic	Status	—	—	5	Both Sides
Zen Headbutt	Psychic	Physical	80	90	15	Normal
Snore	Normal	Special	50	100	15	Normal
Role Play	Psychic	Status	—	—	10	Normal
Heal Bell	Normal	Status	—	—	5	Your Party
Shock Wave	Electric	Special	60	—	20	Normal
Helping Hand	Normal	Status	—	—	20	1 Ally
Trick	Psychic	Status	—	100	10	Normal
Magic Room	Psychic	Status	—	—	10	Both Sides
Recycle	Normal	Status	—	—	10	Self
Snatch	Dark	Status	—	—	10	Self
Skill Swap	Psychic	Status	—	—	10	Normal

MOVES TAUGHT BY PEOPLE

Name	Type	Kind	Pow.	Acc.	PP	Range

National Pokédex **577** Hoenn Pokédex —

Solosis

Cell Pokémon

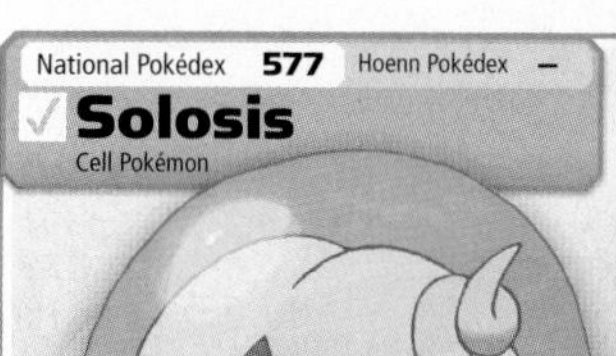

Psychic

HEIGHT: 1'00" WEIGHT: 2.2 lbs.

Same form for ♂ / ♀

Ω Because their bodies are enveloped in a special liquid, they are fine in any environment, no matter how severe.

α They drive away attackers by unleashing psychic power. They can use telepathy to talk with others.

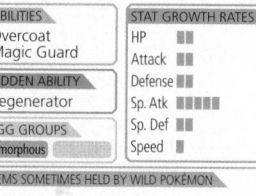

ABILITIES
Overcoat
Magic Guard

HIDDEN ABILITY
Regenerator

EGG GROUPS
Amorphous

STAT GROWTH RATES
HP
Attack
Defense
Sp. Atk
Sp. Def
Speed

ITEMS SOMETIMES HELD BY WILD POKÉMON
—

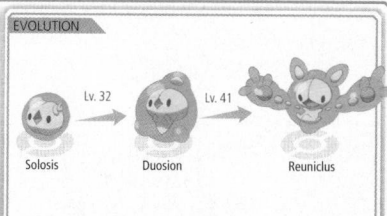

EVOLUTION
Solosis → Lv. 32 → Duosion → Lv. 41 → Reuniclus

MAIN WAY TO REGISTER IN THE NATIONAL POKÉDEX

Appears in *Pokémon X* and *Pokémon Y*. Bring it to your game using Link Trade or the GTS.

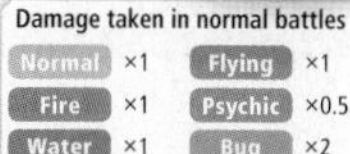

Damage taken in normal battles

Type		Type	
Normal	×1	Flying	×1
Fire	×1	Psychic	×0.5
Water	×1	Bug	×2
Grass	×1	Rock	×1
Electric	×1	Ghost	×2
Ice	×1	Dragon	×1
Fighting	×0.5	Dark	×2
Poison	×1	Steel	×1
Ground	×1	Fairy	×1

Damage taken in Inverse battles

Type		Type	
Normal	×1	Flying	×1
Fire	×1	Psychic	×2
Water	×1	Bug	×0.5
Grass	×1	Rock	×1
Electric	×1	Ghost	×0.5
Ice	×1	Dragon	×1
Fighting	×2	Dark	×0.5
Poison	×1	Steel	×1
Ground	×1	Fairy	×1

Can be used in
Inverse Battle
Battle Institute
Battle Maison
Random Matchup (Free Battle)
Random Matchup (Others)

LEVEL-UP MOVES

Lv.	Name	Type	Kind	Pow.	Acc.	PP	Range
1	Psywave	Psychic	Special	—	100	15	Normal
3	Reflect	Psychic	Status	—	—	20	Your Side
7	Rollout	Rock	Physical	30	90	20	Normal
10	Snatch	Dark	Status	—	—	10	Self
14	Hidden Power	Normal	Special	60	100	15	Normal
16	Light Screen	Psychic	Status	—	—	30	Your Side
19	Charm	Fairy	Status	—	100	20	Normal
24	Recover	Normal	Status	—	—	10	Self
25	Psyshock	Psychic	Special	80	100	10	Normal
28	Endeavor	Normal	Physical	—	100	5	Normal
31	Future Sight	Psychic	Special	120	100	10	Normal
33	Pain Split	Normal	Status	—	—	20	Normal
37	Psychic	Psychic	Special	90	100	10	Normal
40	Skill Swap	Psychic	Status	—	—	10	Normal
46	Heal Block	Psychic	Status	—	100	15	Many Others
48	Wonder Room	Psychic	Status	—	—	10	Both Sides

TM & HM MOVES

No.	Name	Type	Kind	Pow.	Acc.	PP	Range
TM03	Psyshock	Psychic	Special	80	100	10	Normal
TM04	Calm Mind	Psychic	Status	—	—	20	Self
TM06	Toxic	Poison	Status	—	90	10	Normal
TM10	Hidden Power	Normal	Special	60	100	15	Normal
TM16	Light Screen	Psychic	Status	—	—	30	Your Side
TM17	Protect	Normal	Status	—	—	10	Self
TM18	Rain Dance	Water	Status	—	—	5	Both Sides
TM20	Safeguard	Normal	Status	—	—	25	Your Side
TM21	Frustration	Normal	Physical	—	100	20	Normal
TM25	Thunder	Electric	Special	110	70	10	Normal
TM27	Return	Normal	Physical	—	100	20	Normal
TM29	Psychic	Psychic	Special	90	100	10	Normal
TM30	Shadow Ball	Ghost	Special	80	100	15	Normal
TM32	Double Team	Normal	Status	—	—	15	Self
TM33	Reflect	Psychic	Status	—	—	20	Your Side
TM39	Rock Tomb	Rock	Physical	60	95	15	Normal
TM42	Facade	Normal	Physical	70	100	20	Normal
TM44	Rest	Psychic	Status	—	—	10	Self
TM45	Attract	Normal	Status	—	100	15	Normal
TM48	Round	Normal	Special	60	100	15	Normal
TM53	Energy Ball	Grass	Special	90	100	10	Normal
TM63	Embargo	Dark	Status	—	100	15	Normal
TM64	Explosion	Normal	Physical	250	100	5	Adjacent
TM70	Flash	Normal	Status	—	100	20	Normal
TM73	Thunder Wave	Electric	Status	—	100	20	Normal
TM74	Gyro Ball	Steel	Physical	—	100	5	Normal
TM77	Psych Up	Normal	Status	—	—	10	Normal
TM80	Rock Slide	Rock	Physical	75	90	10	Many Others
TM83	Infestation	Bug	Special	20	100	20	Normal
TM85	Dream Eater	Psychic	Special	100	100	15	Normal
TM87	Swagger	Normal	Status	—	90	15	Normal
TM88	Sleep Talk	Normal	Status	—	—	10	Self
TM90	Substitute	Normal	Status	—	—	10	Self
TM91	Flash Cannon	Steel	Special	80	100	10	Normal
TM92	Trick Room	Psychic	Status	—	—	5	Both Sides
TM94	Secret Power	Normal	Physical	70	100	20	Normal
TM100	Confide	Normal	Status	—	—	20	Normal

MOVES LEARNED IN EXCHANGE FOR BP

Name	Type	Kind	Pow.	Acc.	PP	Range
Signal Beam	Bug	Special	75	100	15	Normal
Magic Coat	Psychic	Status	—	—	15	Self
Gravity	Psychic	Status	—	—	5	Both Sides
Iron Defense	Steel	Status	—	—	15	Self
Zen Headbutt	Psychic	Physical	80	90	15	Normal
Snore	Normal	Special	50	100	15	Normal
Role Play	Psychic	Status	—	—	10	Normal
Pain Split	Normal	Status	—	—	20	Normal
Shock Wave	Electric	Special	60	—	20	Normal
After You	Normal	Status	—	—	15	Normal
Helping Hand	Normal	Status	—	—	20	1 Ally
Trick	Psychic	Status	—	100	10	Normal
Wonder Room	Psychic	Status	—	—	10	Both Sides
Endeavor	Normal	Physical	—	100	5	Normal
Snatch	Dark	Status	—	—	10	Self
Skill Swap	Psychic	Status	—	—	10	Normal

MOVES TAUGHT BY PEOPLE

Name	Type	Kind	Pow.	Acc.	PP	Range

EGG MOVES

Name	Type	Kind	Pow.	Acc.	PP	Range
Night Shade	Ghost	Special	—	100	15	Normal
Astonish	Ghost	Physical	30	100	15	Normal
Confuse Ray	Ghost	Status	—	100	10	Normal
Acid Armor	Poison	Status	—	—	20	Self
Trick	Psychic	Status	—	100	10	Normal
Imprison	Psychic	Status	—	—	10	Self
Secret Power	Normal	Physical	70	100	20	Normal
Helping Hand	Normal	Status	—	—	20	1 Ally

National Pokédex **578** Hoenn Pokédex —

Duosion

Mitosis Pokémon

Psychic

HEIGHT: 2'00" WEIGHT: 17.6 lbs.

Same form for ♂ / ♀

Ω Since they have two divided brains, at times they suddenly try to take two different actions at once.

α When their two divided brains think the same thoughts, their psychic power is maximized.

ABILITIES
Overcoat
Magic Guard

HIDDEN ABILITY
Regenerator

EGG GROUPS
Amorphous

STAT GROWTH RATES
HP
Attack
Defense
Sp. Atk
Sp. Def
Speed

EVOLUTION
Solosis → Lv. 32 → Duosion → Lv. 41 → Reuniclus

ITEMS SOMETIMES HELD BY WILD POKÉMON
—

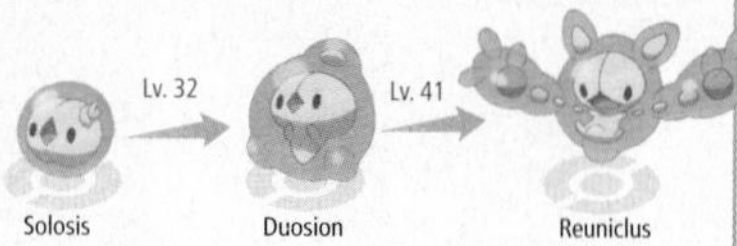

MAIN WAY TO REGISTER IN THE NATIONAL POKÉDEX

Level up a Solosis obtained via Link Trade or the GTS to Lv. 32.

Damage taken in normal battles

Type		Type	
Normal	×1	Flying	×1
Fire	×1	Psychic	×0.5
Water	×1	Bug	×2
Grass	×1	Rock	×1
Electric	×1	Ghost	×2
Ice	×1	Dragon	×1
Fighting	×0.5	Dark	×2
Poison	×1	Steel	×1
Ground	×1	Fairy	×1

Damage taken in Inverse battles

Type		Type	
Normal	×1	Flying	×1
Fire	×1	Psychic	×2
Water	×1	Bug	×0.5
Grass	×1	Rock	×1
Electric	×1	Ghost	×0.5
Ice	×1	Dragon	×1
Fighting	×2	Dark	×0.5
Poison	×1	Steel	×1
Ground	×1	Fairy	×1

Can be used in
Inverse Battle
Battle Institute
Battle Maison
Random Matchup (Free Battle)
Random Matchup (Others)

LEVEL-UP MOVES

Lv.	Name	Type	Kind	Pow.	Acc.	PP	Range
1	Psywave	Psychic	Special	—	100	15	Normal
1	Reflect	Psychic	Status	—	—	20	Your Side
1	Rollout	Rock	Physical	30	90	20	Normal
1	Snatch	Dark	Status	—	—	10	Self
3	Reflect	Psychic	Status	—	—	20	Your Side
7	Rollout	Rock	Physical	30	90	20	Normal
10	Snatch	Dark	Status	—	—	10	Self
14	Hidden Power	Normal	Special	60	100	15	Normal
16	Light Screen	Psychic	Status	—	—	30	Your Side
19	Charm	Fairy	Status	—	100	20	Normal
24	Recover	Normal	Status	—	—	10	Self
25	Psyshock	Psychic	Special	80	100	10	Normal
28	Endeavor	Normal	Physical	—	100	5	Normal
31	Future Sight	Psychic	Special	120	100	10	Normal
34	Pain Split	Normal	Status	—	—	20	Normal
39	Psychic	Psychic	Special	90	100	10	Normal
43	Skill Swap	Psychic	Status	—	—	10	Normal
50	Heal Block	Psychic	Status	—	100	15	Many Others
53	Wonder Room	Psychic	Status	—	—	10	Both Sides

TM & HM MOVES

No.	Name	Type	Kind	Pow.	Acc.	PP	Range
TM03	Psyshock	Psychic	Special	80	100	10	Normal
TM04	Calm Mind	Psychic	Status	—	—	20	Self
TM06	Toxic	Poison	Status	—	90	10	Normal
TM10	Hidden Power	Normal	Special	60	100	15	Normal
TM16	Light Screen	Psychic	Status	—	—	30	Your Side
TM17	Protect	Normal	Status	—	—	10	Self
TM18	Rain Dance	Water	Status	—	—	5	Both Sides
TM20	Safeguard	Normal	Status	—	—	25	Your Side
TM21	Frustration	Normal	Physical	—	100	20	Normal
TM25	Thunder	Electric	Special	110	70	10	Normal
TM27	Return	Normal	Physical	—	100	20	Normal
TM29	Psychic	Psychic	Special	90	100	10	Normal
TM30	Shadow Ball	Ghost	Special	80	100	15	Normal
TM32	Double Team	Normal	Status	—	—	15	Self
TM33	Reflect	Psychic	Status	—	—	20	Your Side
TM39	Rock Tomb	Rock	Physical	60	95	15	Normal
TM42	Facade	Normal	Physical	70	100	20	Normal
TM44	Rest	Psychic	Status	—	—	10	Self
TM45	Attract	Normal	Status	—	100	15	Normal
TM48	Round	Normal	Special	60	100	15	Normal
TM53	Energy Ball	Grass	Special	90	100	10	Normal
TM63	Embargo	Dark	Status	—	100	15	Normal
TM64	Explosion	Normal	Physical	250	100	5	Adjacent
TM70	Flash	Normal	Status	—	100	20	Normal
TM73	Thunder Wave	Electric	Status	—	100	20	Normal
TM74	Gyro Ball	Steel	Physical	—	100	5	Normal
TM77	Psych Up	Normal	Status	—	—	10	Normal
TM80	Rock Slide	Rock	Physical	75	90	10	Many Others
TM83	Infestation	Bug	Special	20	100	20	Normal
TM85	Dream Eater	Psychic	Special	100	100	15	Normal
TM87	Swagger	Normal	Status	—	90	15	Normal
TM88	Sleep Talk	Normal	Status	—	—	10	Self
TM90	Substitute	Normal	Status	—	—	10	Self
TM91	Flash Cannon	Steel	Special	80	100	10	Normal
TM92	Trick Room	Psychic	Status	—	—	5	Both Sides
TM94	Secret Power	Normal	Physical	70	100	20	Normal
TM100	Confide	Normal	Status	—	—	20	Normal

MOVES LEARNED IN EXCHANGE FOR BP

Name	Type	Kind	Pow.	Acc.	PP	Range
Signal Beam	Bug	Special	75	100	15	Normal
Magic Coat	Psychic	Status	—	—	15	Self
Gravity	Psychic	Status	—	—	5	Both Sides
Iron Defense	Steel	Status	—	—	15	Self
Zen Headbutt	Psychic	Physical	80	90	15	Normal
Snore	Normal	Special	50	100	15	Normal
Role Play	Psychic	Status	—	—	10	Normal
Pain Split	Normal	Status	—	—	20	Normal
Shock Wave	Electric	Special	60	—	20	Normal
After You	Normal	Status	—	—	15	Normal
Helping Hand	Normal	Status	—	—	20	1 Ally
Trick	Psychic	Status	—	100	10	Normal
Wonder Room	Psychic	Status	—	—	10	Both Sides
Endeavor	Normal	Physical	—	100	5	Normal
Snatch	Dark	Status	—	—	10	Self
Skill Swap	Psychic	Status	—	—	10	Normal

MOVES TAUGHT BY PEOPLE

Name	Type	Kind	Pow.	Acc.	PP	Range

National Pokédex **579** Hoenn Pokédex —

Reuniclus

Multiplying Pokémon

Psychic

HEIGHT: 3'03" WEIGHT: 44.3 lbs.

Same form for ♂ / ♀

Ω They use psychic power to control their arms, which are made of a special liquid. They can crush boulders psychically.

α When Reuniclus shake hands, a network forms between their brains, increasing their psychic power.

ABILITIES
Overcoat
Magic Guard

HIDDEN ABILITY
Regenerator

EGG GROUPS
Amorphous

STAT GROWTH RATES
HP
Attack
Defense
Sp. Atk
Sp. Def
Speed

EVOLUTION
Solosis → Lv. 32 → Duosion → Lv. 41 → Reuniclus

ITEMS SOMETIMES HELD BY WILD POKÉMON
—

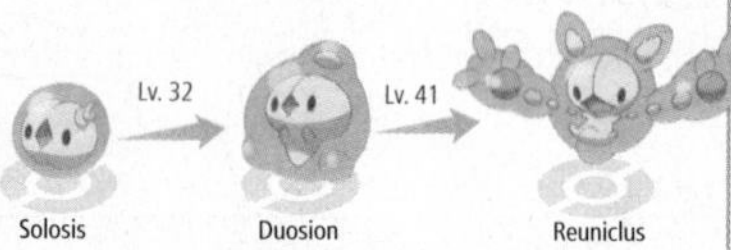

MAIN WAY TO REGISTER IN THE NATIONAL POKÉDEX

Level up a Duosion obtained via Link Trade or the GTS to Lv. 41.

Damage taken in normal battles

Type		Type	
Normal	×1	Flying	×1
Fire	×1	Psychic	×0.5
Water	×1	Bug	×2
Grass	×1	Rock	×1
Electric	×1	Ghost	×2
Ice	×1	Dragon	×1
Fighting	×0.5	Dark	×2
Poison	×1	Steel	×1
Ground	×1	Fairy	×1

Damage taken in Inverse battles

Type		Type	
Normal	×1	Flying	×1
Fire	×1	Psychic	×2
Water	×1	Bug	×0.5
Grass	×1	Rock	×1
Electric	×1	Ghost	×0.5
Ice	×1	Dragon	×1
Fighting	×2	Dark	×0.5
Poison	×1	Steel	×1
Ground	×1	Fairy	×1

Can be used in
Inverse Battle
Battle Institute
Battle Maison
Random Matchup (Free Battle)
Random Matchup (Others)

LEVEL-UP MOVES

Lv.	Name	Type	Kind	Pow.	Acc.	PP	Range
1	Psywave	Psychic	Special	—	100	15	Normal
1	Reflect	Psychic	Status	—	—	20	Your Side
1	Rollout	Rock	Physical	30	90	20	Normal
1	Snatch	Dark	Status	—	—	10	Self
3	Reflect	Psychic	Status	—	—	20	Your Side
7	Rollout	Rock	Physical	30	90	20	Normal
10	Snatch	Dark	Status	—	—	10	Self
14	Hidden Power	Normal	Special	60	100	15	Normal
16	Light Screen	Psychic	Status	—	—	30	Your Side
19	Charm	Fairy	Status	—	100	20	Normal
24	Recover	Normal	Status	—	—	10	Self
25	Psyshock	Psychic	Special	80	100	10	Normal
28	Endeavor	Normal	Physical	—	100	5	Normal
31	Future Sight	Psychic	Special	120	100	10	Normal
34	Pain Split	Normal	Status	—	—	20	Normal
39	Psychic	Psychic	Special	90	100	10	Normal
41	Dizzy Punch	Normal	Physical	70	100	10	Normal
45	Skill Swap	Psychic	Status	—	—	10	Normal
54	Heal Block	Psychic	Status	—	100	15	Many Others
59	Wonder Room	Psychic	Status	—	—	10	Both Sides

TM & HM MOVES

No.	Name	Type	Kind	Pow.	Acc.	PP	Range
TM03	Psyshock	Psychic	Special	80	100	10	Normal
TM04	Calm Mind	Psychic	Status	—	—	20	Self
TM06	Toxic	Poison	Status	—	90	10	Normal
TM10	Hidden Power	Normal	Special	60	100	15	Normal
TM15	Hyper Beam	Normal	Special	150	90	5	Normal
TM16	Light Screen	Psychic	Status	—	—	30	Your Side
TM17	Protect	Normal	Status	—	—	10	Self
TM18	Rain Dance	Water	Status	—	—	5	Both Sides
TM20	Safeguard	Normal	Status	—	—	25	Your Side
TM21	Frustration	Normal	Physical	—	100	20	Normal
TM25	Thunder	Electric	Special	110	70	10	Normal
TM27	Return	Normal	Physical	—	100	20	Normal
TM29	Psychic	Psychic	Special	90	100	10	Normal
TM30	Shadow Ball	Ghost	Special	80	100	15	Normal
TM32	Double Team	Normal	Status	—	—	15	Self
TM33	Reflect	Psychic	Status	—	—	20	Your Side
TM39	Rock Tomb	Rock	Physical	60	95	15	Normal
TM42	Facade	Normal	Physical	70	100	20	Normal
TM44	Rest	Psychic	Status	—	—	10	Self
TM45	Attract	Normal	Status	—	100	15	Normal
TM48	Round	Normal	Special	60	100	15	Normal
TM52	Focus Blast	Fighting	Special	120	70	5	Normal
TM53	Energy Ball	Grass	Special	90	100	10	Normal
TM56	Fling	Dark	Physical	—	100	10	Normal
TM63	Embargo	Dark	Status	—	100	15	Normal
TM64	Explosion	Normal	Physical	250	100	5	Adjacent
TM68	Giga Impact	Normal	Physical	150	90	5	Normal
TM70	Flash	Normal	Status	—	100	20	Normal
TM73	Thunder Wave	Electric	Status	—	100	20	Normal
TM74	Gyro Ball	Steel	Physical	—	100	5	Normal
TM77	Psych Up	Normal	Status	—	—	10	Normal
TM80	Rock Slide	Rock	Physical	75	90	10	Many Others
TM83	Infestation	Bug	Special	20	100	20	Normal
TM85	Dream Eater	Psychic	Special	100	100	15	Normal
TM86	Grass Knot	Grass	Special	—	100	20	Normal
TM87	Swagger	Normal	Status	—	90	15	Normal
TM88	Sleep Talk	Normal	Status	—	—	10	Self
TM90	Substitute	Normal	Status	—	—	10	Self
TM91	Flash Cannon	Steel	Special	80	100	10	Normal
TM92	Trick Room	Psychic	Status	—	—	5	Both Sides
TM94	Secret Power	Normal	Physical	70	100	20	Normal
TM98	Power-Up Punch	Fighting	Physical	40	100	20	Normal
TM100	Confide	Normal	Status	—	—	20	Normal
HM04	Strength	Normal	Physical	80	100	15	Normal
HM06	Rock Smash	Fighting	Physical	40	100	15	Normal

MOVES LEARNED IN EXCHANGE FOR BP

Name	Type	Kind	Pow.	Acc.	PP	Range
Signal Beam	Bug	Special	75	100	15	Normal
Thunder Punch	Electric	Physical	75	100	15	Normal
Fire Punch	Fire	Physical	75	100	15	Normal
Ice Punch	Ice	Physical	75	100	15	Normal
Magic Coat	Psychic	Status	—	—	15	Self
Gravity	Psychic	Status	—	—	5	Both Sides
Iron Defense	Steel	Status	—	—	15	Self
Superpower	Fighting	Physical	120	100	5	Normal
Zen Headbutt	Psychic	Physical	80	90	15	Normal
Snore	Normal	Special	50	100	15	Normal
Knock Off	Dark	Physical	65	100	20	Normal
Role Play	Psychic	Status	—	—	10	Normal
Pain Split	Normal	Status	—	—	20	Normal
Drain Punch	Fighting	Physical	75	100	10	Normal
Focus Punch	Fighting	Physical	150	100	20	Normal
Shock Wave	Electric	Special	60	—	20	Normal
After You	Normal	Status	—	—	15	Normal
Helping Hand	Normal	Status	—	—	20	1 Ally
Trick	Psychic	Status	—	100	10	Normal
Wonder Room	Psychic	Status	—	—	10	Both Sides
Endeavor	Normal	Physical	—	100	5	Normal
Snatch	Dark	Status	—	—	10	Self
Skill Swap	Psychic	Status	—	—	10	Normal

MOVES TAUGHT BY PEOPLE

Name	Type	Kind	Pow.	Acc.	PP	Range

National Pokédex **580** Hoenn Pokédex —

Ducklett

Water Bird Pokémon

Water **Flying**

HEIGHT: 1'08" WEIGHT: 12.1 lbs.

Same form for ♂ / ♀

Ω When attacked, it uses its feathers to splash water, escaping under cover of the spray.

α They are better at swimming than flying, and they happily eat their favorite food, peat moss, as they dive underwater.

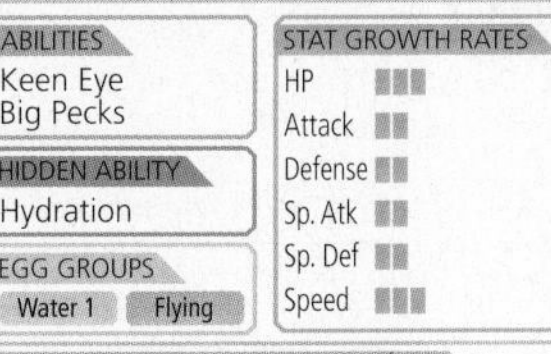

ABILITIES
Keen Eye
Big Pecks

HIDDEN ABILITY
Hydration

EGG GROUPS
Water 1 | Flying

STAT GROWTH RATES
HP ■■■
Attack ■■
Defense ■■
Sp. Atk ■■
Sp. Def ■■
Speed ■■■

ITEMS SOMETIMES HELD BY WILD POKÉMON
—

EVOLUTION

MAIN WAY TO REGISTER IN THE NATIONAL POKÉDEX

Appears in *Pokémon X* and *Pokémon Y*. Bring it to your game using Link Trade or the GTS.

Damage taken in normal battles

Type		Type	
Normal	×1	Flying	×1
Fire	×0.5	Psychic	×1
Water	×0.5	Bug	×0.5
Grass	×1	Rock	×2
Electric	×4	Ghost	×1
Ice	×1	Dragon	×1
Fighting	×0.5	Dark	×1
Poison	×1	Steel	×0.5
Ground	×0	Fairy	×1

Damage taken in Inverse battles

Type		Type	
Normal	×1	Flying	×1
Fire	×2	Psychic	×1
Water	×2	Bug	×2
Grass	×1	Rock	×0.5
Electric	×0.25	Ghost	×1
Ice	×1	Dragon	×1
Fighting	×2	Dark	×1
Poison	×1	Steel	×2
Ground	×2	Fairy	×1

Can be used in
- Inverse Battle
- Battle Institute
- Battle Maison
- Random Matchup (Free Battle)
- Random Matchup (Others)

LEVEL-UP MOVES

Lv.	Name	Type	Kind	Pow.	Acc.	PP	Range
1	Water Gun	Water	Special	40	100	25	Normal
3	Water Sport	Water	Status	—	—	15	Both Sides
6	Defog	Flying	Status	—	—	15	Normal
9	Wing Attack	Flying	Physical	60	100	35	Normal
13	Water Pulse	Water	Special	60	100	20	Normal
15	Aerial Ace	Flying	Physical	60	—	20	Normal
19	Bubble Beam	Water	Special	65	100	20	Normal
21	Feather Dance	Flying	Status	—	100	15	Normal
24	Aqua Ring	Water	Status	—	—	20	Self
27	Air Slash	Flying	Special	75	95	15	Normal
30	Roost	Flying	Status	—	—	10	Self
34	Rain Dance	Water	Status	—	—	5	Both Sides
37	Tailwind	Flying	Status	—	—	15	Your Side
41	Brave Bird	Flying	Physical	120	100	15	Normal
46	Hurricane	Flying	Special	110	70	10	Normal

TM & HM MOVES

No.	Name	Type	Kind	Pow.	Acc.	PP	Range
TM06	Toxic	Poison	Status	—	90	10	Normal
TM07	Hail	Ice	Status	—	—	10	Both Sides
TM10	Hidden Power	Normal	Special	60	100	15	Normal
TM13	Ice Beam	Ice	Special	90	100	10	Normal
TM17	Protect	Normal	Status	—	—	10	Self
TM18	Rain Dance	Water	Status	—	—	5	Both Sides
TM19	Roost	Flying	Status	—	—	10	Self
TM21	Frustration	Normal	Physical	—	100	20	Normal
TM27	Return	Normal	Physical	—	100	20	Normal
TM32	Double Team	Normal	Status	—	—	15	Self
TM40	Aerial Ace	Flying	Physical	60	—	20	Normal
TM42	Facade	Normal	Physical	70	100	20	Normal
TM44	Rest	Psychic	Status	—	—	10	Self
TM45	Attract	Normal	Status	—	100	15	Normal
TM48	Round	Normal	Special	60	100	15	Normal
TM51	Steel Wing	Steel	Physical	70	90	25	Normal
TM55	Scald	Water	Special	80	100	15	Normal
TM87	Swagger	Normal	Status	—	90	15	Normal
TM88	Sleep Talk	Normal	Status	—	—	10	Self
TM90	Substitute	Normal	Status	—	—	10	Self
TM94	Secret Power	Normal	Physical	70	100	20	Normal
TM100	Confide	Normal	Status	—	—	20	Normal
HM02	Fly	Flying	Physical	90	95	15	Normal
HM03	Surf	Water	Special	90	100	15	Adjacent
HM07	Dive	Water	Physical	80	100	10	Normal

MOVES LEARNED IN EXCHANGE FOR BP

Name	Type	Kind	Pow.	Acc.	PP	Range
Uproar	Normal	Special	90	100	10	1 Random
Icy Wind	Ice	Special	55	95	15	Many Others
Snore	Normal	Special	50	100	15	Normal
Tailwind	Flying	Status	—	—	15	Your Side
Water Pulse	Water	Special	60	100	20	Normal
Endeavor	Normal	Physical	—	100	5	Normal

MOVES TAUGHT BY PEOPLE

Name	Type	Kind	Pow.	Acc.	PP	Range

EGG MOVES

Name	Type	Kind	Pow.	Acc.	PP	Range
Steel Wing	Steel	Physical	70	90	25	Normal
Brine	Water	Special	65	100	10	Normal
Gust	Flying	Special	40	100	35	Normal
Air Cutter	Flying	Special	60	95	25	Many Others
Mirror Move	Flying	Status	—	—	20	Normal
Me First	Normal	Status	—	—	20	Varies
Lucky Chant	Normal	Status	—	—	30	Your Side
Mud Sport	Ground	Status	—	—	15	Both Sides

National Pokédex **581** Hoenn Pokédex —

Swanna

White Bird Pokémon

Water **Flying**

HEIGHT: 4'03" WEIGHT: 53.4 lbs.

Same form for ♂ / ♀

Ω Despite their elegant appearance, they can flap their wings strongly and fly for thousands of miles.

α Swanna start to dance at dusk. The one dancing in the middle is the leader of the flock.

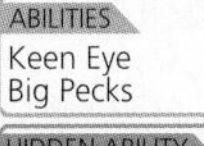

ABILITIES
Keen Eye
Big Pecks

HIDDEN ABILITY
Hydration

EGG GROUPS
Water 1 | Flying

STAT GROWTH RATES
HP ■■■
Attack ■■■■
Defense ■■■
Sp. Atk ■■■■
Sp. Def ■■■
Speed ■■■■■

ITEMS SOMETIMES HELD BY WILD POKÉMON
—

EVOLUTION

Ducklett → Lv. 35 → Swanna

MAIN WAY TO REGISTER IN THE NATIONAL POKÉDEX

Level up a Ducklett obtained via Link Trade or the GTS to Lv. 35.

Damage taken in normal battles

Type		Type	
Normal	×1	Flying	×1
Fire	×0.5	Psychic	×1
Water	×0.5	Bug	×0.5
Grass	×1	Rock	×2
Electric	×4	Ghost	×1
Ice	×1	Dragon	×1
Fighting	×0.5	Dark	×1
Poison	×1	Steel	×0.5
Ground	×0	Fairy	×1

Damage taken in Inverse battles

Type		Type	
Normal	×1	Flying	×1
Fire	×2	Psychic	×1
Water	×2	Bug	×2
Grass	×1	Rock	×0.5
Electric	×0.25	Ghost	×1
Ice	×1	Dragon	×1
Fighting	×2	Dark	×1
Poison	×1	Steel	×2
Ground	×2	Fairy	×1

Can be used in
- Inverse Battle
- Battle Institute
- Battle Maison
- Random Matchup (Free Battle)
- Random Matchup (Others)

LEVEL-UP MOVES

Lv.	Name	Type	Kind	Pow.	Acc.	PP	Range
1	Water Gun	Water	Special	40	100	25	Normal
1	Water Sport	Water	Status	—	—	15	Both Sides
1	Defog	Flying	Status	—	—	15	Normal
1	Wing Attack	Flying	Physical	60	100	35	Normal
3	Water Sport	Water	Status	—	—	15	Both Sides
6	Defog	Flying	Status	—	—	15	Normal
9	Wing Attack	Flying	Physical	60	100	35	Normal
13	Water Pulse	Water	Special	60	100	20	Normal
15	Aerial Ace	Flying	Physical	60	—	20	Normal
19	Bubble Beam	Water	Special	65	100	20	Normal
21	Feather Dance	Flying	Status	—	100	15	Normal
24	Aqua Ring	Water	Status	—	—	20	Self
27	Air Slash	Flying	Special	75	95	15	Normal
30	Roost	Flying	Status	—	—	10	Self
34	Rain Dance	Water	Status	—	—	5	Both Sides
40	Tailwind	Flying	Status	—	—	15	Your Side
47	Brave Bird	Flying	Physical	120	100	15	Normal
55	Hurricane	Flying	Special	110	70	10	Normal

TM & HM MOVES

No.	Name	Type	Kind	Pow.	Acc.	PP	Range
TM06	Toxic	Poison	Status	—	90	10	Normal
TM07	Hail	Ice	Status	—	—	10	Both Sides
TM10	Hidden Power	Normal	Special	60	100	15	Normal
TM13	Ice Beam	Ice	Special	90	100	10	Normal
TM15	Hyper Beam	Normal	Special	150	90	5	Normal
TM17	Protect	Normal	Status	—	—	10	Self
TM18	Rain Dance	Water	Status	—	—	5	Both Sides
TM19	Roost	Flying	Status	—	—	10	Self
TM21	Frustration	Normal	Physical	—	100	20	Normal
TM27	Return	Normal	Physical	—	100	20	Normal
TM32	Double Team	Normal	Status	—	—	15	Self
TM40	Aerial Ace	Flying	Physical	60	—	20	Normal
TM42	Facade	Normal	Physical	70	100	20	Normal
TM44	Rest	Psychic	Status	—	—	10	Self
TM45	Attract	Normal	Status	—	100	15	Normal
TM48	Round	Normal	Special	60	100	15	Normal
TM51	Steel Wing	Steel	Physical	70	90	25	Normal
TM55	Scald	Water	Special	80	100	15	Normal
TM68	Giga Impact	Normal	Physical	150	90	5	Normal
TM87	Swagger	Normal	Status	—	90	15	Normal
TM88	Sleep Talk	Normal	Status	—	—	10	Self
TM90	Substitute	Normal	Status	—	—	10	Self
TM94	Secret Power	Normal	Physical	70	100	20	Normal
TM100	Confide	Normal	Status	—	—	20	Normal
HM02	Fly	Flying	Physical	90	95	15	Normal
HM03	Surf	Water	Special	90	100	15	Adjacent
HM07	Dive	Water	Physical	80	100	10	Normal

MOVES LEARNED IN EXCHANGE FOR BP

Name	Type	Kind	Pow.	Acc.	PP	Range
Uproar	Normal	Special	90	100	10	1 Random
Icy Wind	Ice	Special	55	95	15	Many Others
Snore	Normal	Special	50	100	15	Normal
Tailwind	Flying	Status	—	—	15	Your Side
Sky Attack	Flying	Physical	140	90	5	Normal
Water Pulse	Water	Special	60	100	20	Normal
Endeavor	Normal	Physical	—	100	5	Normal

MOVES TAUGHT BY PEOPLE

Name	Type	Kind	Pow.	Acc.	PP	Range

National Pokédex **582** Hoenn Pokédex —

Vanillite

Fresh Snow Pokémon

Ice

HEIGHT: 1'04" WEIGHT: 12.6 lbs.

Same form for ♂ / ♀

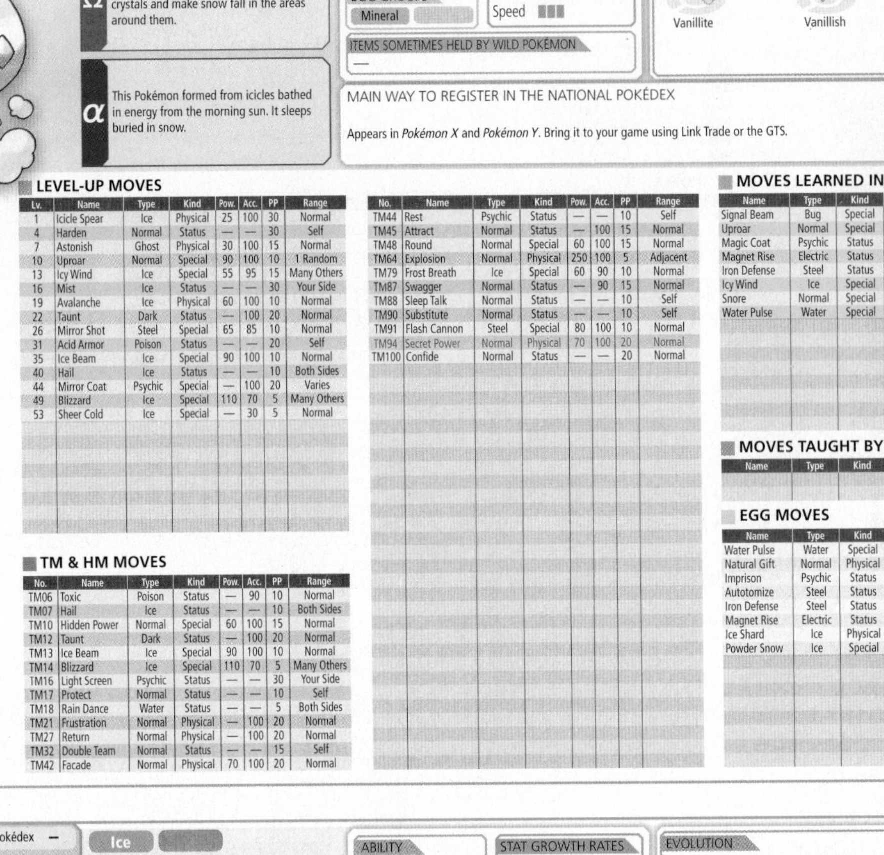

Ω The temperature of their breath is -58 degrees Fahrenheit. They create snow crystals and make snow fall in the areas around them.

α This Pokémon formed from icicles bathed in energy from the morning sun. It sleeps buried in snow.

ABILITY
Ice Body

HIDDEN ABILITY
Weak Armor

EGG GROUPS
Mineral

STAT GROWTH RATES
HP ▮▮
Attack ▮▮▮
Defense ▮▮
Sp. Atk ▮▮▮
Sp. Def ▮▮▮
Speed ▮▮▮

ITEMS SOMETIMES HELD BY WILD POKÉMON
—

EVOLUTION
Vanillite → Lv. 35 → Vanillish → Lv. 47 → Vanilluxe

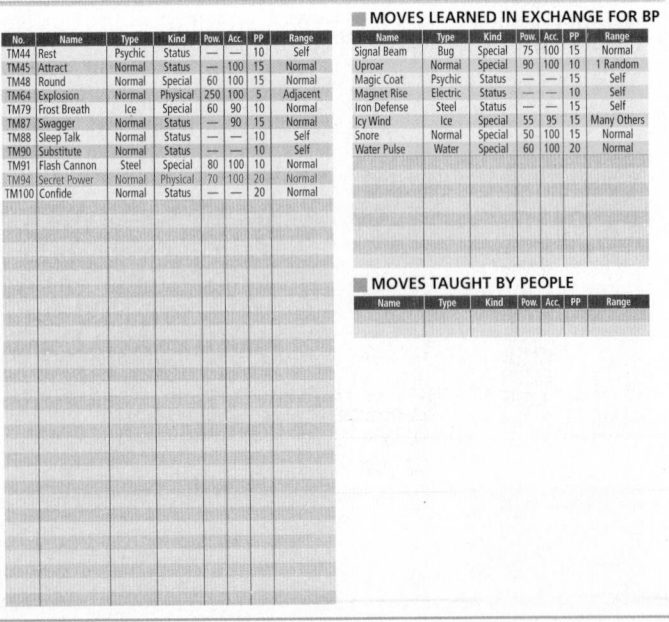

MAIN WAY TO REGISTER IN THE NATIONAL POKÉDEX

Appears in *Pokémon X* and *Pokémon Y*. Bring it to your game using Link Trade or the GTS.

Damage taken in normal battles

Type		Type	
Normal	×1	Flying	×1
Fire	×2	Psychic	×1
Water	×1	Bug	×1
Grass	×1	Rock	×2
Electric	×1	Ghost	×1
Ice	×0.5	Dragon	×1
Fighting	×2	Dark	×1
Poison	×1	Steel	×2
Ground	×1	Fairy	×1

Damage taken in Inverse battles

Type		Type	
Normal	×1	Flying	×1
Fire	×0.5	Psychic	×1
Water	×1	Bug	×1
Grass	×1	Rock	×0.5
Electric	×1	Ghost	×1
Ice	×2	Dragon	×1
Fighting	×0.5	Dark	×1
Poison	×1	Steel	×0.5
Ground	×1	Fairy	×1

Can be used in
Inverse Battle
Battle Institute
Battle Maison
Random Matchup (Free Battle)
Random Matchup (Others)

LEVEL-UP MOVES

Lv.	Name	Type	Kind	Pow.	Acc.	PP	Range
1	Icicle Spear	Ice	Physical	25	100	30	Normal
4	Harden	Normal	Status	—	—	30	Self
7	Astonish	Ghost	Physical	30	100	15	Normal
10	Uproar	Normal	Special	90	100	10	1 Random
13	Icy Wind	Ice	Special	55	95	15	Many Others
16	Mist	Ice	Status	—	—	30	Your Side
19	Avalanche	Ice	Physical	60	100	10	Normal
22	Taunt	Dark	Status	—	100	20	Normal
26	Mirror Shot	Steel	Special	65	85	10	Normal
31	Acid Armor	Poison	Status	—	—	20	Self
35	Ice Beam	Ice	Special	90	100	10	Normal
40	Hail	Ice	Status	—	—	10	Both Sides
44	Mirror Coat	Psychic	Special	—	100	20	Varies
49	Blizzard	Ice	Special	110	70	5	Many Others
53	Sheer Cold	Ice	Special	—	30	5	Normal

TM & HM MOVES

No.	Name	Type	Kind	Pow.	Acc.	PP	Range
TM06	Toxic	Poison	Status	—	90	10	Normal
TM07	Hail	Ice	Status	—	—	10	Both Sides
TM10	Hidden Power	Normal	Special	60	100	15	Normal
TM12	Taunt	Dark	Status	—	100	20	Normal
TM13	Ice Beam	Ice	Special	90	100	10	Normal
TM14	Blizzard	Ice	Special	110	70	5	Many Others
TM16	Light Screen	Psychic	Status	—	—	30	Your Side
TM17	Protect	Normal	Status	—	—	10	Self
TM18	Rain Dance	Water	Status	—	—	5	Both Sides
TM21	Frustration	Normal	Physical	—	100	20	Normal
TM27	Return	Normal	Physical	—	100	20	Normal
TM32	Double Team	Normal	Status	—	—	15	Self
TM42	Facade	Normal	Physical	70	100	20	Normal
TM44	Rest	Psychic	Status	—	—	10	Self
TM45	Attract	Normal	Status	—	100	15	Normal
TM48	Round	Normal	Special	60	100	15	Normal
TM64	Explosion	Normal	Physical	250	100	5	Adjacent
TM79	Frost Breath	Ice	Special	60	90	10	Normal
TM87	Swagger	Normal	Status	—	90	15	Normal
TM88	Sleep Talk	Normal	Status	—	—	10	Self
TM90	Substitute	Normal	Status	—	—	10	Self
TM91	Flash Cannon	Steel	Special	80	100	10	Normal
TM94	Secret Power	Normal	Physical	70	100	20	Normal
TM100	Confide	Normal	Status	—	—	20	Normal

MOVES LEARNED IN EXCHANGE FOR BP

Name	Type	Kind	Pow.	Acc.	PP	Range
Signal Beam	Bug	Special	75	100	15	Normal
Uproar	Normal	Special	90	100	10	1 Random
Magic Coat	Psychic	Status	—	—	15	Self
Magnet Rise	Electric	Status	—	—	10	Self
Iron Defense	Steel	Status	—	—	15	Self
Icy Wind	Ice	Special	55	95	15	Many Others
Snore	Normal	Special	50	100	15	Normal
Water Pulse	Water	Special	60	100	20	Normal

MOVES TAUGHT BY PEOPLE

Name	Type	Kind	Pow.	Acc.	PP	Range

EGG MOVES

Name	Type	Kind	Pow.	Acc.	PP	Range
Water Pulse	Water	Special	60	100	20	Normal
Natural Gift	Normal	Physical	—	100	15	Normal
Imprison	Psychic	Status	—	—	10	Self
Autotomize	Steel	Status	—	—	15	Self
Iron Defense	Steel	Status	—	—	15	Self
Magnet Rise	Electric	Status	—	—	10	Self
Ice Shard	Ice	Physical	40	100	30	Normal
Powder Snow	Ice	Special	40	100	25	Many Others

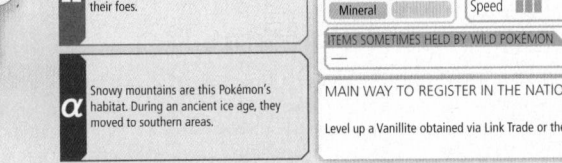

National Pokédex **583** Hoenn Pokédex —

Vanillish

Icy Snow Pokémon

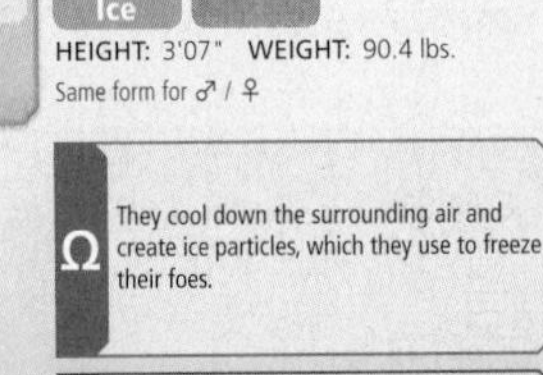

Ice

HEIGHT: 3'07" WEIGHT: 90.4 lbs.

Same form for ♂ / ♀

Ω They cool down the surrounding air and create ice particles, which they use to freeze their foes.

α Snowy mountains are this Pokémon's habitat. During an ancient ice age, they moved to southern areas.

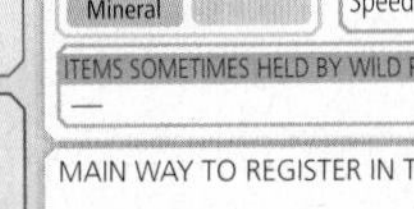

ABILITY
Ice Body

HIDDEN ABILITY
Weak Armor

EGG GROUPS
Mineral

STAT GROWTH RATES
HP ▮▮
Attack ▮▮▮
Defense ▮▮▮
Sp. Atk ▮▮▮▮
Sp. Def ▮▮▮
Speed ▮▮▮

ITEMS SOMETIMES HELD BY WILD POKÉMON
—

EVOLUTION

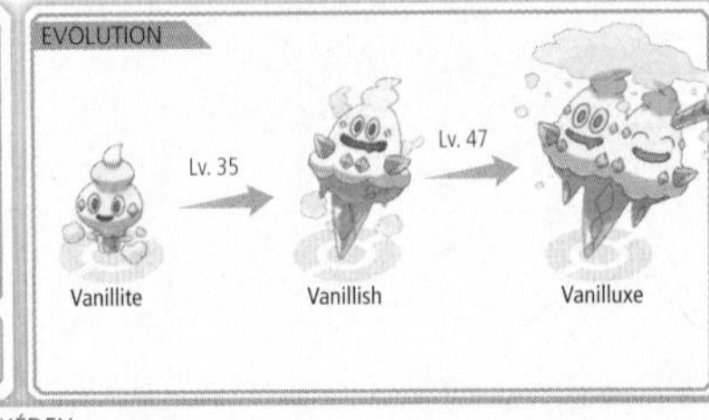
Vanillite → Lv. 35 → Vanillish → Lv. 47 → Vanilluxe

MAIN WAY TO REGISTER IN THE NATIONAL POKÉDEX

Level up a Vanillite obtained via Link Trade or the GTS to Lv. 35.

Damage taken in normal battles

Type		Type	
Normal	×1	Flying	×1
Fire	×2	Psychic	×1
Water	×1	Bug	×1
Grass	×1	Rock	×2
Electric	×1	Ghost	×1
Ice	×0.5	Dragon	×1
Fighting	×2	Dark	×1
Poison	×1	Steel	×2
Ground	×1	Fairy	×1

Damage taken in Inverse battles

Type		Type	
Normal	×1	Flying	×1
Fire	×0.5	Psychic	×1
Water	×1	Bug	×1
Grass	×1	Rock	×0.5
Electric	×1	Ghost	×1
Ice	×2	Dragon	×1
Fighting	×0.5	Dark	×1
Poison	×1	Steel	×0.5
Ground	×1	Fairy	×1

Can be used in
Inverse Battle
Battle Institute
Battle Maison
Random Matchup (Free Battle)
Random Matchup (Others)

LEVEL-UP MOVES

Lv.	Name	Type	Kind	Pow.	Acc.	PP	Range
1	Icicle Spear	Ice	Physical	25	100	30	Normal
1	Harden	Normal	Status	—	—	30	Self
1	Astonish	Ghost	Physical	30	100	15	Normal
1	Uproar	Normal	Special	90	100	10	1 Random
4	Harden	Normal	Status	—	—	30	Self
7	Astonish	Ghost	Physical	30	100	15	Normal
10	Uproar	Normal	Special	90	100	10	1 Random
13	Icy Wind	Ice	Special	55	95	15	Many Others
16	Mist	Ice	Status	—	—	30	Your Side
19	Avalanche	Ice	Physical	60	100	10	Normal
22	Taunt	Dark	Status	—	100	20	Normal
26	Mirror Shot	Steel	Special	65	85	10	Normal
31	Acid Armor	Poison	Status	—	—	20	Self
36	Ice Beam	Ice	Special	90	100	10	Normal
42	Hail	Ice	Status	—	—	10	Both Sides
47	Mirror Coat	Psychic	Special	—	100	20	Varies
53	Blizzard	Ice	Special	110	70	5	Many Others
58	Sheer Cold	Ice	Special	—	30	5	Normal

TM & HM MOVES

No.	Name	Type	Kind	Pow.	Acc.	PP	Range
TM06	Toxic	Poison	Status	—	90	10	Normal
TM07	Hail	Ice	Status	—	—	10	Both Sides
TM10	Hidden Power	Normal	Special	60	100	15	Normal
TM12	Taunt	Dark	Status	—	100	20	Normal
TM13	Ice Beam	Ice	Special	90	100	10	Normal
TM14	Blizzard	Ice	Special	110	70	5	Many Others
TM16	Light Screen	Psychic	Status	—	—	30	Your Side
TM17	Protect	Normal	Status	—	—	10	Self
TM18	Rain Dance	Water	Status	—	—	5	Both Sides
TM21	Frustration	Normal	Physical	—	100	20	Normal
TM27	Return	Normal	Physical	—	100	20	Normal
TM32	Double Team	Normal	Status	—	—	15	Self
TM42	Facade	Normal	Physical	70	100	20	Normal
TM44	Rest	Psychic	Status	—	—	10	Self
TM45	Attract	Normal	Status	—	100	15	Normal
TM48	Round	Normal	Special	60	100	15	Normal
TM64	Explosion	Normal	Physical	250	100	5	Adjacent
TM79	Frost Breath	Ice	Special	60	90	10	Normal
TM87	Swagger	Normal	Status	—	90	15	Normal
TM88	Sleep Talk	Normal	Status	—	—	10	Self
TM90	Substitute	Normal	Status	—	—	10	Self
TM91	Flash Cannon	Steel	Special	80	100	10	Normal
TM94	Secret Power	Normal	Physical	70	100	20	Normal
TM100	Confide	Normal	Status	—	—	20	Normal

MOVES LEARNED IN EXCHANGE FOR BP

Name	Type	Kind	Pow.	Acc.	PP	Range
Signal Beam	Bug	Special	75	100	15	Normal
Uproar	Normal	Special	90	100	10	1 Random
Magic Coat	Psychic	Status	—	—	15	Self
Magnet Rise	Electric	Status	—	—	10	Self
Iron Defense	Steel	Status	—	—	15	Self
Icy Wind	Ice	Special	55	95	15	Many Others
Snore	Normal	Special	50	100	15	Normal
Water Pulse	Water	Special	60	100	20	Normal

MOVES TAUGHT BY PEOPLE

Name	Type	Kind	Pow.	Acc.	PP	Range

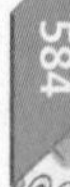

National Pokédex **584** Hoenn Pokédex —

Vanilluxe

Snowstorm Pokémon

Ice

HEIGHT: 4'03" WEIGHT: 126.8 lbs.

Same form for ♂ / ♀

Ω If both heads get angry simultaneously, this Pokémon expels a blizzard, burying everything in snow.

α Swallowing large amounts of water, they make snow clouds inside their bodies and, when angry, cause violent blizzards.

ABILITY
Ice Body

HIDDEN ABILITY
Weak Armor

EGG GROUPS
Mineral

STAT GROWTH RATES
HP ■■■
Attack ■■■■■
Defense ■■■■
Sp. Atk ■■■■■
Sp. Def ■■■■
Speed ■■■■

ITEMS SOMETIMES HELD BY WILD POKÉMON
—

EVOLUTION
Vanillite → Lv. 35 → Vanillish → Lv. 47 → Vanilluxe

MAIN WAY TO REGISTER IN THE NATIONAL POKÉDEX

Level up a Vanillish obtained via Link Trade or the GTS to Lv. 47.

Damage taken in normal battles

Type	×	Type	×
Normal	×1	Flying	×1
Fire	×2	Psychic	×1
Water	×1	Bug	×1
Grass	×1	Rock	×2
Electric	×1	Ghost	×1
Ice	×0.5	Dragon	×1
Fighting	×2	Dark	×1
Poison	×1	Steel	×2
Ground	×1	Fairy	×1

Damage taken in Inverse battles

Type	×	Type	×
Normal	×1	Flying	×1
Fire	×0.5	Psychic	×1
Water	×1	Bug	×1
Grass	×1	Rock	×0.5
Electric	×1	Ghost	×1
Ice	×2	Dragon	×1
Fighting	×0.5	Dark	×1
Poison	×1	Steel	×0.5
Ground	×1	Fairy	×1

Can be used in
Inverse Battle
Battle Institute
Battle Maison
Random Matchup (Free Battle)
Random Matchup (Others)

LEVEL-UP MOVES

Lv.	Name	Type	Kind	Pow.	Acc.	PP	Range
1	Sheer Cold	Ice	Special	—	30	5	Normal
1	Freeze-Dry	Ice	Special	70	100	20	Normal
1	Weather Ball	Normal	Special	50	100	10	Normal
1	Icicle Spear	Ice	Physical	25	100	30	Normal
1	Harden	Normal	Status	—	—	30	Self
1	Astonish	Ghost	Physical	30	100	15	Normal
1	Uproar	Normal	Special	90	100	10	1 Random
4	Harden	Normal	Status	—	—	30	Self
7	Astonish	Ghost	Physical	30	100	15	Normal
10	Uproar	Normal	Special	90	100	10	1 Random
13	Icy Wind	Ice	Special	55	95	15	Many Others
16	Mist	Ice	Status	—	—	30	Your Side
19	Avalanche	Ice	Physical	60	100	10	Normal
22	Taunt	Dark	Status	—	100	20	Normal
26	Mirror Shot	Steel	Special	65	85	10	Normal
31	Acid Armor	Poison	Status	—	—	20	Self
36	Ice Beam	Ice	Special	90	100	10	Normal
42	Hail	Ice	Status	—	—	10	Both Sides
50	Mirror Coat	Psychic	Special	—	100	20	Varies
59	Blizzard	Ice	Special	110	70	5	Many Others
67	Sheer Cold	Ice	Special	—	30	5	Normal

TM & HM MOVES

No.	Name	Type	Kind	Pow.	Acc.	PP	Range
TM06	Toxic	Poison	Status	—	90	10	Normal
TM07	Hail	Ice	Status	—	—	10	Both Sides
TM10	Hidden Power	Normal	Special	60	100	15	Normal
TM12	Taunt	Dark	Status	—	100	20	Normal
TM13	Ice Beam	Ice	Special	90	100	10	Normal
TM14	Blizzard	Ice	Special	110	70	5	Many Others
TM15	Hyper Beam	Normal	Special	150	90	5	Normal
TM16	Light Screen	Psychic	Status	—	—	30	Your Side
TM17	Protect	Normal	Status	—	—	10	Self
TM18	Rain Dance	Water	Status	—	—	5	Both Sides
TM21	Frustration	Normal	Physical	—	100	20	Normal
TM27	Return	Normal	Physical	—	100	20	Normal
TM32	Double Team	Normal	Status	—	—	15	Self
TM42	Facade	Normal	Physical	70	100	20	Normal
TM44	Rest	Psychic	Status	—	—	10	Self
TM45	Attract	Normal	Status	—	100	15	Normal
TM48	Round	Normal	Special	60	100	15	Normal
TM64	Explosion	Normal	Physical	250	100	5	Adjacent
TM68	Giga Impact	Normal	Physical	150	90	5	Normal
TM79	Frost Breath	Ice	Special	60	90	10	Normal
TM87	Swagger	Normal	Status	—	90	15	Normal
TM88	Sleep Talk	Normal	Status	—	—	10	Self
TM90	Substitute	Normal	Status	—	—	10	Self
TM91	Flash Cannon	Steel	Special	80	100	10	Normal
TM94	Secret Power	Normal	Physical	70	100	20	Normal
TM100	Confide	Normal	Status	—	—	20	Normal

MOVES LEARNED IN EXCHANGE FOR BP

Name	Type	Kind	Pow.	Acc.	PP	Range
Signal Beam	Bug	Special	75	100	15	Normal
Uproar	Normal	Special	90	100	10	1 Random
Magic Coat	Psychic	Status	—	—	15	Self
Magnet Rise	Electric	Status	—	—	10	Self
Iron Defense	Steel	Status	—	—	15	Self
Icy Wind	Ice	Special	55	95	15	Many Others
Snore	Normal	Special	50	100	15	Normal
Water Pulse	Water	Special	60	100	20	Normal

MOVES TAUGHT BY PEOPLE

Name	Type	Kind	Pow.	Acc.	PP	Range

National Pokédex **585** Hoenn Pokédex —

Deerling

Season Pokémon

Normal Grass

HEIGHT: 2'00" WEIGHT: 43 lbs.

Same form for ♂ / ♀

Spring Form Summer Form Autumn Form Winter Form

Ω Their coloring changes according to the seasons and can be slightly affected by the temperature and humidity as well.

α The turning of the seasons changes the color and scent of this Pokémon's fur. People use it to mark the seasons.

ABILITIES
Chlorophyll
Sap Sipper

HIDDEN ABILITY
Serene Grace

EGG GROUPS
Field

STAT GROWTH RATES
HP ■■■
Attack ■■■
Defense ■■
Sp. Atk ■■
Sp. Def ■■
Speed ■■■■

ITEMS SOMETIMES HELD BY WILD POKÉMON
—

EVOLUTION
Deerling → Lv. 34 → Sawsbuck

MAIN WAY TO REGISTER IN THE NATIONAL POKÉDEX

Catch on Route 117 (only appears in its Spring Form). Appears as a hidden Pokémon after you battle Groudon or Kyogre.

Damage taken in normal battles

Type	×	Type	×
Normal	×1	Flying	×2
Fire	×2	Psychic	×1
Water	×0.5	Bug	×2
Grass	×0.5	Rock	×1
Electric	×0.5	Ghost	×0
Ice	×2	Dragon	×1
Fighting	×2	Dark	×1
Poison	×2	Steel	×1
Ground	×0.5	Fairy	×1

Damage taken in Inverse battles

Type	×	Type	×
Normal	×1	Flying	×0.5
Fire	×0.5	Psychic	×1
Water	×2	Bug	×0.5
Grass	×2	Rock	×1
Electric	×2	Ghost	×2
Ice	×0.5	Dragon	×1
Fighting	×0.5	Dark	×1
Poison	×0.5	Steel	×1
Ground	×2	Fairy	×1

Can be used in
Inverse Battle
Battle Institute
Battle Maison
Random Matchup (Free Battle)
Random Matchup (Others)

LEVEL-UP MOVES

Lv.	Name	Type	Kind	Pow.	Acc.	PP	Range
1	Tackle	Normal	Physical	50	100	35	Normal
1	Camouflage	Normal	Status	—	—	20	Self
4	Growl	Normal	Status	—	100	40	Many Others
7	Sand Attack	Ground	Status	—	100	15	Normal
10	Double Kick	Fighting	Physical	30	100	30	Normal
13	Leech Seed	Grass	Status	—	90	10	Normal
16	Feint Attack	Dark	Physical	60	—	20	Normal
20	Take Down	Normal	Physical	90	85	20	Normal
24	Jump Kick	Fighting	Physical	100	95	10	Normal
28	Aromatherapy	Grass	Status	—	—	5	Your Party
32	Energy Ball	Grass	Special	90	100	10	Normal
36	Charm	Fairy	Status	—	100	20	Normal
41	Nature Power	Normal	Status	—	—	20	Normal
46	Double-Edge	Normal	Physical	120	100	15	Normal
51	Solar Beam	Grass	Special	120	100	10	Normal

TM & HM MOVES

No.	Name	Type	Kind	Pow.	Acc.	PP	Range
TM06	Toxic	Poison	Status	—	90	10	Normal
TM10	Hidden Power	Normal	Special	60	100	15	Normal
TM11	Sunny Day	Fire	Status	—	—	5	Both Sides
TM16	Light Screen	Psychic	Status	—	—	30	Your Side
TM17	Protect	Normal	Status	—	—	10	Self
TM18	Rain Dance	Water	Status	—	—	5	Both Sides
TM20	Safeguard	Normal	Status	—	—	25	Your Side
TM21	Frustration	Normal	Physical	—	100	20	Normal
TM22	Solar Beam	Grass	Special	120	100	10	Normal
TM27	Return	Normal	Physical	—	100	20	Normal
TM30	Shadow Ball	Ghost	Special	80	100	15	Normal
TM32	Double Team	Normal	Status	—	—	15	Self
TM42	Facade	Normal	Physical	70	100	20	Normal
TM44	Rest	Psychic	Status	—	—	10	Self
TM45	Attract	Normal	Status	—	100	15	Normal
TM48	Round	Normal	Special	60	100	15	Normal
TM49	Echoed Voice	Normal	Special	40	100	15	Normal
TM53	Energy Ball	Grass	Special	90	100	10	Normal
TM67	Retaliate	Normal	Physical	70	100	5	Normal
TM70	Flash	Normal	Status	—	100	20	Normal
TM73	Thunder Wave	Electric	Status	—	100	20	Normal
TM86	Grass Knot	Grass	Special	—	100	20	Normal
TM87	Swagger	Normal	Status	—	90	15	Normal
TM88	Sleep Talk	Normal	Status	—	—	10	Self
TM90	Substitute	Normal	Status	—	—	10	Self
TM93	Wild Charge	Electric	Physical	90	100	15	Normal
TM94	Secret Power	Normal	Physical	70	100	20	Normal
TM96	Nature Power	Normal	Status	—	—	20	Normal
TM100	Confide	Normal	Status	—	—	20	Normal

MOVES LEARNED IN EXCHANGE FOR BP

Name	Type	Kind	Pow.	Acc.	PP	Range
Seed Bomb	Grass	Physical	80	100	15	Normal
Bounce	Flying	Physical	85	85	5	Normal
Last Resort	Normal	Physical	140	100	5	Normal
Snore	Normal	Special	50	100	15	Normal
Synthesis	Grass	Status	—	—	5	Self
Giga Drain	Grass	Special	75	100	10	Normal
Worry Seed	Grass	Status	—	100	10	Normal

MOVES TAUGHT BY PEOPLE

Name	Type	Kind	Pow.	Acc.	PP	Range

EGG MOVES

Name	Type	Kind	Pow.	Acc.	PP	Range
Fake Tears	Dark	Status	—	100	20	Normal
Natural Gift	Normal	Physical	—	100	15	Normal
Synthesis	Grass	Status	—	—	5	Self
Worry Seed	Grass	Status	—	100	10	Normal
Odor Sleuth	Normal	Status	—	—	40	Normal
Agility	Psychic	Status	—	—	30	Self
Sleep Talk	Normal	Status	—	—	10	Self
Baton Pass	Normal	Status	—	—	40	Self
Grass Whistle	Grass	Status	—	55	15	Normal

◆ There are four forms in all, but in *Pokémon Omega Ruby* and *Pokémon Alpha Sapphire*, you'll encounter Deerling with the Spring Form.

National Pokédex **586** Hoenn Pokédex —

Sawsbuck

Season Pokémon

Normal Grass

HEIGHT: 6'03" WEIGHT: 203.9 lbs.

Same form for ♂ / ♀

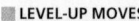

Spring Form | Summer Form | Autumn Form | Winter Form

Ω They migrate according to the seasons. People can tell the season by looking at Sawsbuck's horns.

α They migrate according to the seasons, so some people call Sawsbuck the harbingers of spring.

ABILITIES
Chlorophyll
Sap Sipper

HIDDEN ABILITY
Serene Grace

EGG GROUPS
Field

STAT GROWTH RATES
HP ■■■
Attack ■■■■■
Defense ■■■
Sp. Atk ■■■
Sp. Def ■■■
Speed ■■■■■

ITEMS SOMETIMES HELD BY WILD POKÉMON
—

EVOLUTION 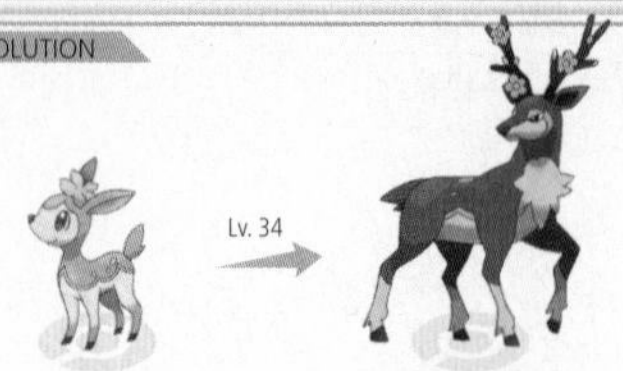
Deerling → Lv. 34 → Sawsbuck

MAIN WAY TO REGISTER IN THE NATIONAL POKÉDEX

Level up Deerling to Lv. 34.

Damage taken in normal battles

Normal	×1	Flying	×2
Fire	×2	Psychic	×1
Water	×0.5	Bug	×2
! Grass	×0.5	Rock	×1
Electric	×0.5	Ghost	×0
Ice	×2	Dragon	×1
Fighting	×2	Dark	×1
Poison	×2	Steel	×1
Ground	×0.5	Fairy	×1

Damage taken in Inverse battles

Normal	×1	Flying	×0.5
Fire	×0.5	Psychic	×1
Water	×2	Bug	×0.5
! Grass	×2	Rock	×1
Electric	×2	Ghost	×2
Ice	×0.5	Dragon	×1
Fighting	×0.5	Dark	×1
Poison	×0.5	Steel	×1
Ground	×2	Fairy	×1

Can be used in
Inverse Battle
Battle Institute
Battle Maison
Random Matchup (Free Battle)
Random Matchup (Others)

LEVEL-UP MOVES

Lv.	Name	Type	Kind	Pow.	Acc.	PP	Range
1	Megahorn	Bug	Physical	120	85	10	Normal
1	Tackle	Normal	Physical	50	100	35	Normal
1	Camouflage	Normal	Status	—	—	20	Self
1	Growl	Normal	Status	—	100	40	Many Others
1	Sand Attack	Ground	Status	—	100	15	Normal
4	Growl	Normal	Status	—	100	40	Many Others
7	Sand Attack	Ground	Status	—	100	15	Normal
10	Double Kick	Fighting	Physical	30	100	30	Normal
13	Leech Seed	Grass	Status	—	90	10	Normal
16	Feint Attack	Dark	Physical	60	—	20	Normal
20	Take Down	Normal	Physical	90	85	20	Normal
24	Jump Kick	Fighting	Physical	100	95	10	Normal
28	Aromatherapy	Grass	Status	—	—	5	Your Party
32	Energy Ball	Grass	Special	90	100	10	Normal
36	Charm	Fairy	Status	—	100	20	Normal
37	Horn Leech	Grass	Physical	75	100	10	Normal
44	Nature Power	Normal	Status	—	—	20	Normal
52	Double-Edge	Normal	Physical	120	100	15	Normal
60	Solar Beam	Grass	Special	120	100	10	Normal

TM & HM MOVES

No.	Name	Type	Kind	Pow.	Acc.	PP	Range
TM06	Toxic	Poison	Status	—	90	10	Normal
TM10	Hidden Power	Normal	Special	60	100	15	Normal
TM11	Sunny Day	Fire	Status	—	—	5	Both Sides
TM15	Hyper Beam	Normal	Special	150	90	5	Normal
TM16	Light Screen	Psychic	Status	—	—	30	Your Side
TM17	Protect	Normal	Status	—	—	10	Self
TM18	Rain Dance	Water	Status	—	—	5	Both Sides
TM20	Safeguard	Normal	Status	—	—	25	Your Side
TM21	Frustration	Normal	Physical	—	100	20	Normal
TM22	Solar Beam	Grass	Special	120	100	10	Normal
TM27	Return	Normal	Physical	—	100	20	Normal
TM30	Shadow Ball	Ghost	Special	80	100	15	Normal
TM32	Double Team	Normal	Status	—	—	15	Self
TM42	Facade	Normal	Physical	70	100	20	Normal
TM44	Rest	Psychic	Status	—	—	10	Self
TM45	Attract	Normal	Status	—	100	15	Normal
TM48	Round	Normal	Special	60	100	15	Normal
TM49	Echoed Voice	Normal	Special	40	100	15	Normal
TM53	Energy Ball	Grass	Special	90	100	10	Normal
TM67	Retaliate	Normal	Physical	70	100	5	Normal
TM68	Giga Impact	Normal	Physical	150	90	5	Normal
TM70	Flash	Normal	Status	—	100	20	Normal
TM73	Thunder Wave	Electric	Status	—	100	20	Normal
TM75	Swords Dance	Normal	Status	—	—	20	Self
TM86	Grass Knot	Grass	Special	—	100	20	Normal
TM87	Swagger	Normal	Status	—	90	15	Normal
TM88	Sleep Talk	Normal	Status	—	—	10	Self
TM90	Substitute	Normal	Status	—	—	10	Self
TM93	Wild Charge	Electric	Physical	90	100	15	Normal
TM94	Secret Power	Normal	Physical	70	100	20	Normal
TM96	Nature Power	Normal	Status	—	—	20	Normal
TM100	Confide	Normal	Status	—	—	20	Normal
HM01	Cut	Normal	Physical	50	95	30	Normal
HM06	Rock Smash	Fighting	Physical	40	100	15	Normal

MOVES LEARNED IN EXCHANGE FOR BP

Name	Type	Kind	Pow.	Acc.	PP	Range
Seed Bomb	Grass	Physical	80	100	15	Normal
Bounce	Flying	Physical	85	85	5	Normal
Last Resort	Normal	Physical	140	100	5	Normal
Snore	Normal	Special	50	100	15	Normal
Synthesis	Grass	Status	—	—	5	Self
Giga Drain	Grass	Special	75	100	10	Normal
Worry Seed	Grass	Status	—	100	10	Normal

MOVES TAUGHT BY PEOPLE

Name	Type	Kind	Pow.	Acc.	PP	Range

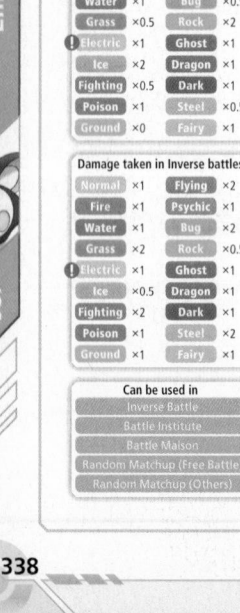

National Pokédex **587** Hoenn Pokédex —

Emolga

Sky Squirrel Pokémon

Electric Flying

HEIGHT: 1'04" WEIGHT: 11 lbs.

Same form for ♂ / ♀

Ω They live on treetops and glide using the inside of a cape-like membrane while discharging electricity.

α The energy made in its cheeks' electric pouches is stored inside its membrane and released while it is gliding.

ABILITY
Static

HIDDEN ABILITY
Motor Drive

EGG GROUPS
Field

STAT GROWTH RATES
HP ■■
Attack ■■■■
Defense ■■■
Sp. Atk ■■■■
Sp. Def ■■■
Speed ■■■■■■

ITEMS SOMETIMES HELD BY WILD POKÉMON
—

EVOLUTION
Does not evolve

MAIN WAY TO REGISTER IN THE NATIONAL POKÉDEX

Appears in *Pokémon X* and *Pokémon Y*. Bring it to your game using Link Trade or the GTS.

Damage taken in normal battles

Normal	×1	Flying	×0.5
Fire	×1	Psychic	×1
Water	×1	Bug	×0.5
Grass	×0.5	Rock	×2
! Electric	×1	Ghost	×1
Ice	×2	Dragon	×1
Fighting	×0.5	Dark	×1
Poison	×1	Steel	×0.5
Ground	×0	Fairy	×1

Damage taken in Inverse battles

Normal	×1	Flying	×2
Fire	×1	Psychic	×1
Water	×1	Bug	×2
Grass	×2	Rock	×0.5
! Electric	×1	Ghost	×1
Ice	×0.5	Dragon	×1
Fighting	×2	Dark	×1
Poison	×1	Steel	×2
Ground	×1	Fairy	×1

Can be used in
Inverse Battle
Battle Institute
Battle Maison
Random Matchup (Free Battle)
Random Matchup (Others)

LEVEL-UP MOVES

Lv.	Name	Type	Kind	Pow.	Acc.	PP	Range
1	Thunder Shock	Electric	Special	40	100	30	Normal
4	Quick Attack	Normal	Physical	40	100	30	Normal
7	Tail Whip	Normal	Status	—	100	30	Many Others
10	Charge	Electric	Status	—	—	20	Self
13	Spark	Electric	Physical	65	100	20	Normal
15	Nuzzle	Electric	Physical	20	100	20	Normal
16	Pursuit	Dark	Physical	40	100	20	Normal
19	Double Team	Normal	Status	—	—	15	Self
22	Shock Wave	Electric	Special	60	—	20	Normal
26	Electro Ball	Electric	Special	—	100	10	Normal
30	Acrobatics	Flying	Physical	55	100	15	Normal
34	Light Screen	Psychic	Status	—	—	30	Your Side
38	Encore	Normal	Status	—	100	5	Normal
42	Volt Switch	Electric	Special	70	100	20	Normal
46	Agility	Psychic	Status	—	—	30	Self
50	Discharge	Electric	Special	80	100	15	Adjacent

TM & HM MOVES

No.	Name	Type	Kind	Pow.	Acc.	PP	Range
TM06	Toxic	Poison	Status	—	90	10	Normal
TM10	Hidden Power	Normal	Special	60	100	15	Normal
TM12	Taunt	Dark	Status	—	100	20	Normal
TM16	Light Screen	Psychic	Status	—	—	30	Your Side
TM17	Protect	Normal	Status	—	—	10	Self
TM18	Rain Dance	Water	Status	—	—	5	Both Sides
TM19	Roost	Flying	Status	—	—	10	Self
TM21	Frustration	Normal	Physical	—	100	20	Normal
TM24	Thunderbolt	Electric	Special	90	100	15	Normal
TM25	Thunder	Electric	Special	110	70	10	Normal
TM27	Return	Normal	Physical	—	100	20	Normal
TM32	Double Team	Normal	Status	—	—	15	Self
TM40	Aerial Ace	Flying	Physical	60	—	20	Normal
TM42	Facade	Normal	Physical	70	100	20	Normal
TM44	Rest	Psychic	Status	—	—	10	Self
TM45	Attract	Normal	Status	—	100	15	Normal
TM48	Round	Normal	Special	60	100	15	Normal
TM56	Fling	Dark	Physical	—	100	10	Normal
TM57	Charge Beam	Electric	Special	50	90	10	Normal
TM62	Acrobatics	Flying	Physical	55	100	15	Normal
TM70	Flash	Normal	Status	—	100	20	Normal
TM72	Volt Switch	Electric	Special	70	100	20	Normal
TM73	Thunder Wave	Electric	Status	—	100	20	Normal
TM87	Swagger	Normal	Status	—	90	15	Normal
TM88	Sleep Talk	Normal	Status	—	—	10	Self
TM89	U-turn	Bug	Physical	70	100	20	Normal
TM90	Substitute	Normal	Status	—	—	10	Self
TM93	Wild Charge	Electric	Physical	90	100	15	Normal
TM94	Secret Power	Normal	Physical	70	100	20	Normal
TM100	Confide	Normal	Status	—	—	20	Normal
HM01	Cut	Normal	Physical	50	95	30	Normal

MOVES LEARNED IN EXCHANGE FOR BP

Name	Type	Kind	Pow.	Acc.	PP	Range
Covet	Normal	Physical	60	100	25	Normal
Signal Beam	Bug	Special	75	100	15	Normal
Last Resort	Normal	Physical	140	100	5	Normal
Electroweb	Electric	Special	55	95	15	Many Others
Iron Tail	Steel	Physical	100	75	15	Normal
Snore	Normal	Special	50	100	15	Normal
Knock Off	Dark	Physical	65	100	20	Normal
Tailwind	Flying	Status	—	—	15	Your Side
Shock Wave	Electric	Special	60	—	20	Normal
Helping Hand	Normal	Status	—	—	20	1 Ally

MOVES TAUGHT BY PEOPLE

Name	Type	Kind	Pow.	Acc.	PP	Range

EGG MOVES

Name	Type	Kind	Pow.	Acc.	PP	Range
Roost	Flying	Status	—	—	10	Self
Iron Tail	Steel	Physical	100	75	15	Normal
Astonish	Ghost	Physical	30	100	15	Normal
Air Slash	Flying	Special	75	95	15	Normal
Shock Wave	Electric	Special	60	—	20	Normal
Charm	Fairy	Status	—	100	20	Normal
Covet	Normal	Physical	60	100	25	Normal
Tickle	Normal	Status	—	100	20	Normal
Baton Pass	Normal	Status	—	—	40	Self
Ion Deluge	Electric	Status	—	—	25	Both Sides

National Pokédex **588** Hoenn Pokédex —

Karrablast

Clamping Pokémon

Bug

HEIGHT: 1'08" WEIGHT: 13 lbs.

Same form for ♂ / ♀

Ω These mysterious Pokémon evolve when they receive electrical stimulation while they are in the same place as Shelmet.

α For some reason they evolve when they receive electrical energy while they are attacking Shelmet.

ABILITIES
Swarm
Shed Skin

HIDDEN ABILITY
No Guard

EGG GROUPS
Bug

STAT GROWTH RATES
HP
Attack
Defense
Sp. Atk
Sp. Def
Speed

ITEMS SOMETIMES HELD BY WILD POKÉMON
—

EVOLUTION

MAIN WAY TO REGISTER IN THE NATIONAL POKÉDEX

Appears in *Pokémon X* and *Pokémon Y*. Bring it to your game using Link Trade or the GTS.

Damage taken in normal battles

Type		Type	
Normal	×1	Flying	×2
Fire	×2	Psychic	×1
Water	×1	Bug	×1
Grass	×0.5	Rock	×2
Electric	×1	Ghost	×1
Ice	×1	Dragon	×1
Fighting	×0.5	Dark	×1
Poison	×1	Steel	×1
Ground	×0.5	Fairy	×1

Damage taken in Inverse battles

Type		Type	
Normal	×1	Flying	×0.5
Fire	×0.5	Psychic	×1
Water	×1	Bug	×1
Grass	×2	Rock	×0.5
Electric	×1	Ghost	×1
Ice	×1	Dragon	×1
Fighting	×2	Dark	×1
Poison	×1	Steel	×1
Ground	×2	Fairy	×1

Can be used in
Inverse Battle
Battle Institute
Battle Maison
Random Matchup (Free Battle)
Random Matchup (Others)

LEVEL-UP MOVES

Lv.	Name	Type	Kind	Pow.	Acc.	PP	Range
1	Peck	Flying	Physical	35	100	35	Normal
4	Leer	Normal	Status	—	100	30	Many Others
8	Endure	Normal	Status	—	—	10	Self
13	Fury Cutter	Bug	Physical	40	95	20	Normal
16	Fury Attack	Normal	Physical	15	85	20	Normal
20	Headbutt	Normal	Physical	70	100	15	Normal
25	False Swipe	Normal	Physical	40	100	40	Normal
28	Bug Buzz	Bug	Special	90	100	10	Normal
32	Slash	Normal	Physical	70	100	20	Normal
37	Take Down	Normal	Physical	90	85	20	Normal
40	Scary Face	Normal	Status	—	100	10	Normal
44	X-Scissor	Bug	Physical	80	100	15	Normal
49	Flail	Normal	Physical	—	100	15	Normal
52	Swords Dance	Normal	Status	—	—	20	Self
56	Double-Edge	Normal	Physical	120	100	15	Normal

TM & HM MOVES

No.	Name	Type	Kind	Pow.	Acc.	PP	Range
TM06	Toxic	Poison	Status	—	90	10	Normal
TM10	Hidden Power	Normal	Special	60	100	15	Normal
TM17	Protect	Normal	Status	—	—	10	Self
TM18	Rain Dance	Water	Status	—	—	5	Both Sides
TM21	Frustration	Normal	Physical	—	100	20	Normal
TM27	Return	Normal	Physical	—	100	20	Normal
TM32	Double Team	Normal	Status	—	—	15	Self
TM40	Aerial Ace	Flying	Physical	60	—	20	Normal
TM42	Facade	Normal	Physical	70	100	20	Normal
TM44	Rest	Psychic	Status	—	—	10	Self
TM45	Attract	Normal	Status	—	100	15	Normal
TM48	Round	Normal	Special	60	100	15	Normal
TM53	Energy Ball	Grass	Special	90	100	10	Normal
TM54	False Swipe	Normal	Physical	40	100	40	Normal
TM75	Swords Dance	Normal	Status	—	—	20	Self
TM76	Struggle Bug	Bug	Special	50	100	20	Many Others
TM81	X-Scissor	Bug	Physical	80	100	15	Normal
TM83	Infestation	Bug	Special	20	100	20	Normal
TM84	Poison Jab	Poison	Physical	80	100	20	Normal
TM87	Swagger	Normal	Status	—	90	15	Normal
TM88	Sleep Talk	Normal	Status	—	—	10	Self
TM90	Substitute	Normal	Status	—	—	10	Self
TM94	Secret Power	Normal	Physical	70	100	20	Normal
TM100	Confide	Normal	Status	—	—	20	Normal
HM01	Cut	Normal	Physical	50	95	30	Normal

MOVES LEARNED IN EXCHANGE FOR BP

Name	Type	Kind	Pow.	Acc.	PP	Range
Bug Bite	Bug	Physical	60	100	20	Normal
Signal Beam	Bug	Special	75	100	15	Normal
Drill Run	Ground	Physical	80	95	10	Normal
Iron Defense	Steel	Status	—	—	15	Self
Snore	Normal	Special	50	100	15	Normal
Knock Off	Dark	Physical	65	100	20	Normal
Giga Drain	Grass	Special	75	100	10	Normal

MOVES TAUGHT BY PEOPLE

Name	Type	Kind	Pow.	Acc.	PP	Range

EGG MOVES

Name	Type	Kind	Pow.	Acc.	PP	Range
Megahorn	Bug	Physical	120	85	10	Normal
Pursuit	Dark	Physical	40	100	20	Normal
Counter	Fighting	Physical	—	100	20	Varies
Horn Attack	Normal	Physical	65	100	25	Normal
Feint Attack	Dark	Physical	60	—	20	Normal
Bug Bite	Bug	Physical	60	100	20	Normal
Screech	Normal	Status	—	85	40	Normal
Knock Off	Dark	Physical	65	100	20	Normal
Drill Run	Ground	Physical	80	95	10	Normal

National Pokédex **589** Hoenn Pokédex —

Escavalier

Cavalry Pokémon

Bug Steel

HEIGHT: 3'03" WEIGHT: 72.8 lbs.

Same form for ♂ / ♀

Ω Wearing the shell covering they stole from Shelmet, they defend themselves and attack with two lances.

α These Pokémon evolve by wearing the shell covering of a Shelmet. The steel armor protects their whole body.

ABILITIES
Swarm
Shell Armor

HIDDEN ABILITY
Overcoat

EGG GROUPS
Bug

STAT GROWTH RATES
HP
Attack
Defense
Sp. Atk
Sp. Def
Speed

ITEMS SOMETIMES HELD BY WILD POKÉMON
—

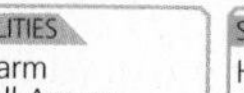

EVOLUTION

MAIN WAY TO REGISTER IN THE NATIONAL POKÉDEX

Link Trade a Shelmet for a Karrablast to have it evolve into Escavalier.

Damage taken in normal battles

Type		Type	
Normal	×0.5	Flying	×1
Fire	×4	Psychic	×0.5
Water	×1	Bug	×0.5
Grass	×0.25	Rock	×1
Electric	×1	Ghost	×1
Ice	×0.5	Dragon	×0.5
Fighting	×1	Dark	×1
Poison	×0	Steel	×0.5
Ground	×1	Fairy	×0.5

Damage taken in Inverse battles

Type		Type	
Normal	×2	Flying	×1
Fire	×0.25	Psychic	×2
Water	×1	Bug	×2
Grass	×4	Rock	×1
Electric	×1	Ghost	×1
Ice	×2	Dragon	×2
Fighting	×1	Dark	×1
Poison	×2	Steel	×2
Ground	×1	Fairy	×2

Can be used in
Inverse Battle
Battle Institute
Battle Maison
Random Matchup (Free Battle)
Random Matchup (Others)

LEVEL-UP MOVES

Lv.	Name	Type	Kind	Pow.	Acc.	PP	Range
1	Double-Edge	Normal	Physical	120	100	15	Normal
1	Fell Stinger	Bug	Physical	30	100	25	Normal
1	Peck	Flying	Physical	35	100	35	Normal
1	Leer	Normal	Status	—	100	30	Many Others
1	Quick Guard	Fighting	Status	—	—	15	Your Side
1	Twineedle	Bug	Physical	25	100	20	Normal
4	Leer	Normal	Status	—	100	30	Many Others
8	Quick Guard	Fighting	Status	—	—	15	Your Side
13	Twineedle	Bug	Physical	25	100	20	Normal
16	Fury Attack	Normal	Physical	15	85	20	Normal
20	Headbutt	Normal	Physical	70	100	15	Normal
25	False Swipe	Normal	Physical	40	100	40	Normal
28	Bug Buzz	Bug	Special	90	100	10	Normal
32	Slash	Normal	Physical	70	100	20	Normal
37	Iron Head	Steel	Physical	80	100	15	Normal
40	Iron Defense	Steel	Status	—	—	15	Self
44	X-Scissor	Bug	Physical	80	100	15	Normal
49	Reversal	Fighting	Physical	—	100	15	Normal
52	Swords Dance	Normal	Status	—	—	20	Self
56	Giga Impact	Normal	Physical	150	90	5	Normal
60	Fell Stinger	Bug	Physical	30	100	25	Normal

TM & HM MOVES

No.	Name	Type	Kind	Pow.	Acc.	PP	Range
TM06	Toxic	Poison	Status	—	90	10	Normal
TM10	Hidden Power	Normal	Special	60	100	15	Normal
TM15	Hyper Beam	Normal	Special	150	90	5	Normal
TM17	Protect	Normal	Status	—	—	10	Self
TM18	Rain Dance	Water	Status	—	—	5	Both Sides
TM21	Frustration	Normal	Physical	—	100	20	Normal
TM27	Return	Normal	Physical	—	100	20	Normal
TM32	Double Team	Normal	Status	—	—	15	Self
TM40	Aerial Ace	Flying	Physical	60	—	20	Normal
TM42	Facade	Normal	Physical	70	100	20	Normal
TM44	Rest	Psychic	Status	—	—	10	Self
TM45	Attract	Normal	Status	—	100	15	Normal
TM48	Round	Normal	Special	60	100	15	Normal
TM52	Focus Blast	Fighting	Special	120	70	5	Normal
TM53	Energy Ball	Grass	Special	90	100	10	Normal
TM54	False Swipe	Normal	Physical	40	100	40	Normal
TM68	Giga Impact	Normal	Physical	150	90	5	Normal
TM75	Swords Dance	Normal	Status	—	—	20	Self
TM76	Struggle Bug	Bug	Special	50	100	20	Many Others
TM81	X-Scissor	Bug	Physical	80	100	15	Normal
TM83	Infestation	Bug	Special	20	100	20	Normal
TM84	Poison Jab	Poison	Physical	80	100	20	Normal
TM87	Swagger	Normal	Status	—	90	15	Normal
TM88	Sleep Talk	Normal	Status	—	—	10	Self
TM90	Substitute	Normal	Status	—	—	10	Self
TM94	Secret Power	Normal	Physical	70	100	20	Normal
TM100	Confide	Normal	Status	—	—	20	Normal
HM01	Cut	Normal	Physical	50	95	30	Normal
HM06	Rock Smash	Fighting	Physical	40	100	15	Normal

MOVES LEARNED IN EXCHANGE FOR BP

Name	Type	Kind	Pow.	Acc.	PP	Range
Bug Bite	Bug	Physical	60	100	20	Normal
Signal Beam	Bug	Special	75	100	15	Normal
Iron Head	Steel	Physical	80	100	15	Normal
Drill Run	Ground	Physical	80	95	10	Normal
Iron Defense	Steel	Status	—	—	15	Self
Snore	Normal	Special	50	100	15	Normal
Knock Off	Dark	Physical	65	100	20	Normal
Giga Drain	Grass	Special	75	100	10	Normal

MOVES TAUGHT BY PEOPLE

Name	Type	Kind	Pow.	Acc.	PP	Range

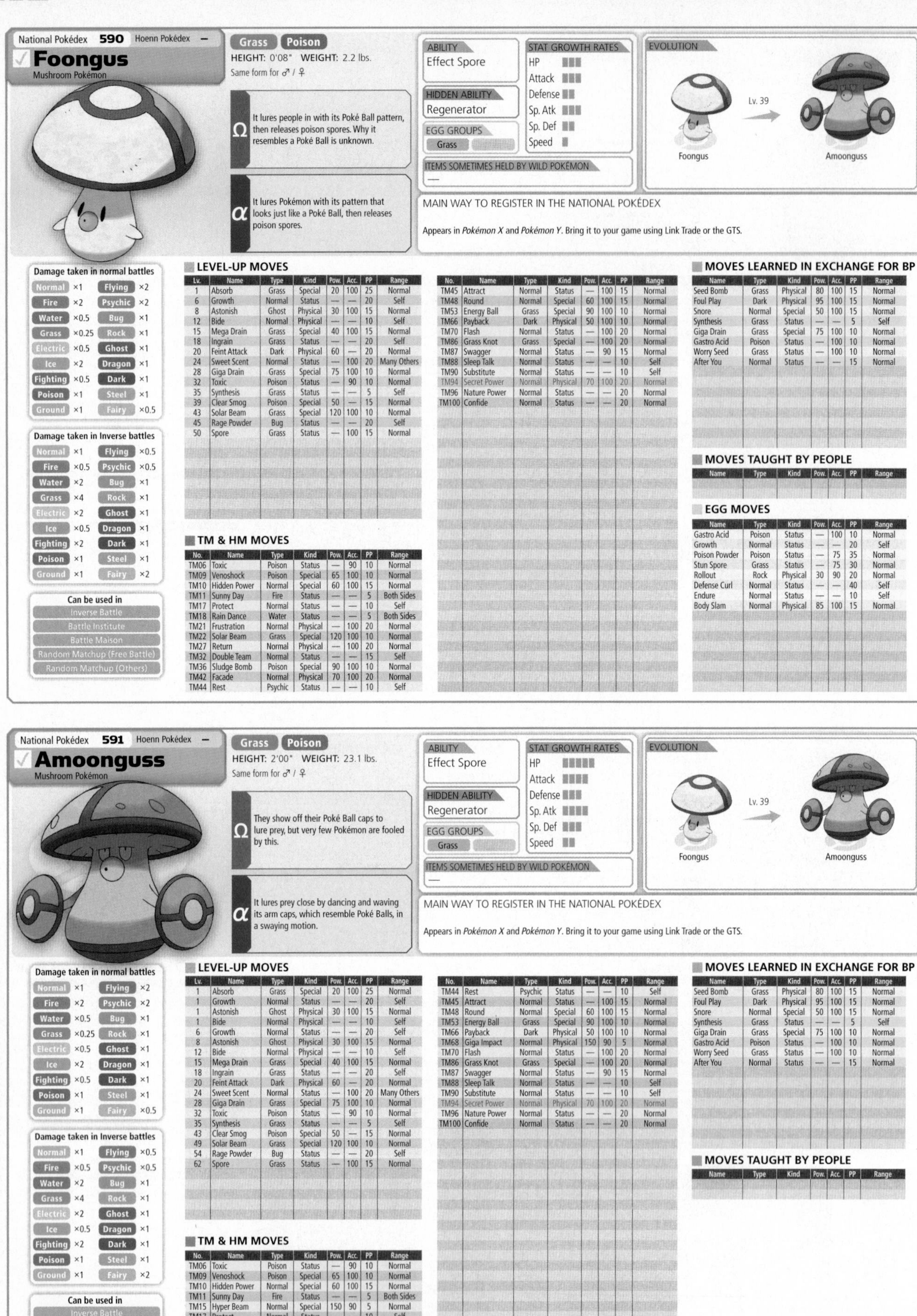

National Pokédex **590** Hoenn Pokédex —

Foongus

Mushroom Pokémon

Grass Poison

HEIGHT: 0'08" WEIGHT: 2.2 lbs.

Same form for ♂ / ♀

Ω It lures people in with its Poké Ball pattern, then releases poison spores. Why it resembles a Poké Ball is unknown.

α It lures Pokémon with its pattern that looks just like a Poké Ball, then releases poison spores.

ABILITY
Effect Spore

HIDDEN ABILITY
Regenerator

EGG GROUPS
Grass

STAT GROWTH RATES
HP
Attack
Defense
Sp. Atk
Sp. Def
Speed

ITEMS SOMETIMES HELD BY WILD POKÉMON
—

EVOLUTION
Foongus → Lv. 39 → Amoonguss

MAIN WAY TO REGISTER IN THE NATIONAL POKÉDEX

Appears in *Pokémon X* and *Pokémon Y*. Bring it to your game using Link Trade or the GTS.

Damage taken in normal battles

Type	×	Type	×
Normal	×1	Flying	×2
Fire	×2	Psychic	×2
Water	×0.5	Bug	×1
Grass	×0.25	Rock	×1
Electric	×0.5	Ghost	×1
Ice	×2	Dragon	×1
Fighting	×0.5	Dark	×1
Poison	×1	Steel	×1
Ground	×1	Fairy	×0.5

Damage taken in Inverse battles

Type	×	Type	×
Normal	×1	Flying	×0.5
Fire	×0.5	Psychic	×0.5
Water	×2	Bug	×1
Grass	×4	Rock	×1
Electric	×2	Ghost	×1
Ice	×0.5	Dragon	×1
Fighting	×2	Dark	×1
Poison	×1	Steel	×1
Ground	×1	Fairy	×2

Can be used in
Inverse Battle
Battle Institute
Battle Maison
Random Matchup (Free Battle)
Random Matchup (Others)

LEVEL-UP MOVES

Lv.	Name	Type	Kind	Pow.	Acc.	PP	Range
1	Absorb	Grass	Special	20	100	25	Normal
6	Growth	Normal	Status	—	—	20	Self
8	Astonish	Ghost	Physical	30	100	15	Normal
12	Bide	Normal	Physical	—	—	10	Self
15	Mega Drain	Grass	Special	40	100	15	Normal
18	Ingrain	Grass	Status	—	—	20	Self
20	Feint Attack	Dark	Physical	60	—	20	Normal
24	Sweet Scent	Normal	Status	—	100	20	Many Others
28	Giga Drain	Grass	Special	75	100	10	Normal
32	Toxic	Poison	Status	—	90	10	Normal
35	Synthesis	Grass	Status	—	—	5	Self
39	Clear Smog	Poison	Special	50	—	15	Normal
43	Solar Beam	Grass	Special	120	100	10	Normal
45	Rage Powder	Bug	Status	—	—	20	Self
50	Spore	Grass	Status	—	100	15	Normal

TM & HM MOVES

No.	Name	Type	Kind	Pow.	Acc.	PP	Range
TM06	Toxic	Poison	Status	—	90	10	Normal
TM09	Venoshock	Poison	Special	65	100	10	Normal
TM10	Hidden Power	Normal	Special	60	100	15	Normal
TM11	Sunny Day	Fire	Status	—	—	5	Both Sides
TM17	Protect	Normal	Status	—	—	10	Self
TM18	Rain Dance	Water	Status	—	—	5	Both Sides
TM21	Frustration	Normal	Physical	—	100	20	Normal
TM22	Solar Beam	Grass	Special	120	100	10	Normal
TM27	Return	Normal	Physical	—	100	20	Normal
TM32	Double Team	Normal	Status	—	—	15	Self
TM36	Sludge Bomb	Poison	Special	90	100	10	Normal
TM42	Facade	Normal	Physical	70	100	20	Normal
TM44	Rest	Psychic	Status	—	—	10	Self
TM45	Attract	Normal	Status	—	100	15	Normal
TM48	Round	Normal	Special	60	100	15	Normal
TM53	Energy Ball	Grass	Special	90	100	10	Normal
TM66	Payback	Dark	Physical	50	100	10	Normal
TM70	Flash	Normal	Status	—	100	20	Normal
TM86	Grass Knot	Grass	Special	—	100	20	Normal
TM87	Swagger	Normal	Status	—	90	15	Normal
TM88	Sleep Talk	Normal	Status	—	—	10	Self
TM90	Substitute	Normal	Status	—	—	10	Self
TM94	Secret Power	Normal	Physical	70	100	20	Normal
TM96	Nature Power	Normal	Status	—	—	20	Normal
TM100	Confide	Normal	Status	—	—	20	Normal

MOVES LEARNED IN EXCHANGE FOR BP

Name	Type	Kind	Pow.	Acc.	PP	Range
Seed Bomb	Grass	Physical	80	100	15	Normal
Foul Play	Dark	Physical	95	100	15	Normal
Snore	Normal	Special	50	100	15	Normal
Synthesis	Grass	Status	—	—	5	Self
Giga Drain	Grass	Special	75	100	10	Normal
Gastro Acid	Poison	Status	—	100	10	Normal
Worry Seed	Grass	Status	—	100	10	Normal
After You	Normal	Status	—	—	15	Normal

MOVES TAUGHT BY PEOPLE

Name	Type	Kind	Pow.	Acc.	PP	Range

EGG MOVES

Name	Type	Kind	Pow.	Acc.	PP	Range
Gastro Acid	Poison	Status	—	100	10	Normal
Growth	Normal	Status	—	—	20	Self
Poison Powder	Poison	Status	—	75	35	Normal
Stun Spore	Grass	Status	—	75	30	Normal
Rollout	Rock	Physical	30	90	20	Normal
Defense Curl	Normal	Status	—	—	40	Self
Endure	Normal	Status	—	—	10	Self
Body Slam	Normal	Physical	85	100	15	Normal

National Pokédex **591** Hoenn Pokédex —

Amoonguss

Mushroom Pokémon

Grass Poison

HEIGHT: 2'00" WEIGHT: 23.1 lbs.

Same form for ♂ / ♀

Ω They show off their Poké Ball caps to lure prey, but very few Pokémon are fooled by this.

α It lures prey close by dancing and waving its arm caps, which resemble Poké Balls, in a swaying motion.

ABILITY
Effect Spore

HIDDEN ABILITY
Regenerator

EGG GROUPS
Grass

STAT GROWTH RATES
HP
Attack
Defense
Sp. Atk
Sp. Def
Speed

ITEMS SOMETIMES HELD BY WILD POKÉMON
—

EVOLUTION
Foongus → Lv. 39 → Amoonguss

MAIN WAY TO REGISTER IN THE NATIONAL POKÉDEX

Appears in *Pokémon X* and *Pokémon Y*. Bring it to your game using Link Trade or the GTS.

Damage taken in normal battles

Type	×	Type	×
Normal	×1	Flying	×2
Fire	×2	Psychic	×2
Water	×0.5	Bug	×1
Grass	×0.25	Rock	×1
Electric	×0.5	Ghost	×1
Ice	×2	Dragon	×1
Fighting	×0.5	Dark	×1
Poison	×1	Steel	×1
Ground	×1	Fairy	×0.5

Damage taken in Inverse battles

Type	×	Type	×
Normal	×1	Flying	×0.5
Fire	×0.5	Psychic	×0.5
Water	×2	Bug	×1
Grass	×4	Rock	×1
Electric	×2	Ghost	×1
Ice	×0.5	Dragon	×1
Fighting	×2	Dark	×1
Poison	×1	Steel	×1
Ground	×1	Fairy	×2

Can be used in
Inverse Battle
Battle Institute
Battle Maison
Random Matchup (Free Battle)
Random Matchup (Others)

LEVEL-UP MOVES

Lv.	Name	Type	Kind	Pow.	Acc.	PP	Range
1	Absorb	Grass	Special	20	100	25	Normal
1	Growth	Normal	Status	—	—	20	Self
1	Astonish	Ghost	Physical	30	100	15	Normal
1	Bide	Normal	Physical	—	—	10	Self
6	Growth	Normal	Status	—	—	20	Self
8	Astonish	Ghost	Physical	30	100	15	Normal
12	Bide	Normal	Physical	—	—	10	Self
15	Mega Drain	Grass	Special	40	100	15	Normal
18	Ingrain	Grass	Status	—	—	20	Self
20	Feint Attack	Dark	Physical	60	—	20	Normal
24	Sweet Scent	Normal	Status	—	100	20	Many Others
28	Giga Drain	Grass	Special	75	100	10	Normal
32	Toxic	Poison	Status	—	90	10	Normal
35	Synthesis	Grass	Status	—	—	5	Self
43	Clear Smog	Poison	Special	50	—	15	Normal
49	Solar Beam	Grass	Special	120	100	10	Normal
54	Rage Powder	Bug	Status	—	—	20	Self
62	Spore	Grass	Status	—	100	15	Normal

TM & HM MOVES

No.	Name	Type	Kind	Pow.	Acc.	PP	Range
TM06	Toxic	Poison	Status	—	90	10	Normal
TM09	Venoshock	Poison	Special	65	100	10	Normal
TM10	Hidden Power	Normal	Special	60	100	15	Normal
TM11	Sunny Day	Fire	Status	—	—	5	Both Sides
TM15	Hyper Beam	Normal	Special	150	90	5	Normal
TM17	Protect	Normal	Status	—	—	10	Self
TM18	Rain Dance	Water	Status	—	—	5	Both Sides
TM21	Frustration	Normal	Physical	—	100	20	Normal
TM22	Solar Beam	Grass	Special	120	100	10	Normal
TM27	Return	Normal	Physical	—	100	20	Normal
TM32	Double Team	Normal	Status	—	—	15	Self
TM36	Sludge Bomb	Poison	Special	90	100	10	Normal
TM42	Facade	Normal	Physical	70	100	20	Normal
TM44	Rest	Psychic	Status	—	—	10	Self
TM45	Attract	Normal	Status	—	100	15	Normal
TM48	Round	Normal	Special	60	100	15	Normal
TM53	Energy Ball	Grass	Special	90	100	10	Normal
TM66	Payback	Dark	Physical	50	100	10	Normal
TM68	Giga Impact	Normal	Physical	150	90	5	Normal
TM70	Flash	Normal	Status	—	100	20	Normal
TM86	Grass Knot	Grass	Special	—	100	20	Normal
TM87	Swagger	Normal	Status	—	90	15	Normal
TM88	Sleep Talk	Normal	Status	—	—	10	Self
TM90	Substitute	Normal	Status	—	—	10	Self
TM94	Secret Power	Normal	Physical	70	100	20	Normal
TM96	Nature Power	Normal	Status	—	—	20	Normal
TM100	Confide	Normal	Status	—	—	20	Normal

MOVES LEARNED IN EXCHANGE FOR BP

Name	Type	Kind	Pow.	Acc.	PP	Range
Seed Bomb	Grass	Physical	80	100	15	Normal
Foul Play	Dark	Physical	95	100	15	Normal
Snore	Normal	Special	50	100	15	Normal
Synthesis	Grass	Status	—	—	5	Self
Giga Drain	Grass	Special	75	100	10	Normal
Gastro Acid	Poison	Status	—	100	10	Normal
Worry Seed	Grass	Status	—	100	10	Normal
After You	Normal	Status	—	—	15	Normal

MOVES TAUGHT BY PEOPLE

Name	Type	Kind	Pow.	Acc.	PP	Range

National Pokédex **592** Hoenn Pokédex —

Frillish

Floating Pokémon

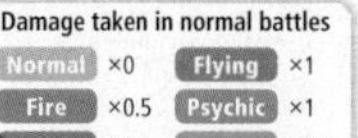

Male form

Female form

Water **Ghost**

HEIGHT: 3'11" WEIGHT: 72.8 lbs.

The male is blue while the female is pink.

Ω They paralyze prey with poison, then drag them down to their lairs, five miles below the surface.

α If its veil-like arms stun and wrap a foe, that foe will be dragged miles below the surface, never to return.

ABILITIES
Water Absorb
Cursed Body

HIDDEN ABILITY
Damp

EGG GROUPS
Amorphous

STAT GROWTH RATES
HP
Attack
Defense
Sp. Atk
Sp. Def
Speed

EVOLUTION

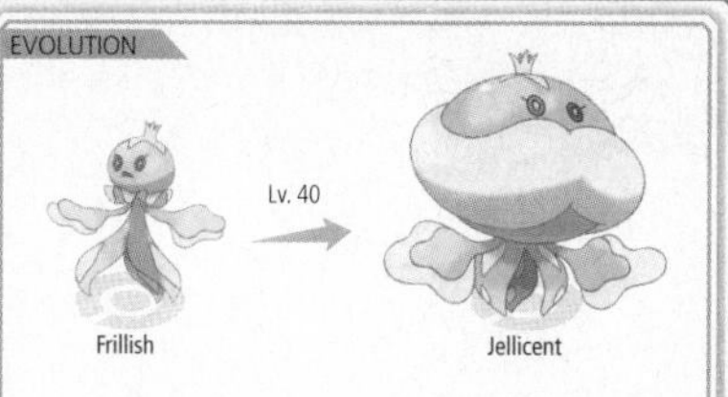

Frillish → Jellicent

ITEMS SOMETIMES HELD BY WILD POKÉMON
—

MAIN WAY TO REGISTER IN THE NATIONAL POKÉDEX

Catch on the water surface on Route 105. Appears as a hidden Pokémon after you battle Groudon or Kyogre.

Damage taken in normal battles

Type		Type	
Normal	×0	Flying	×1
Fire	×0.5	Psychic	×1
Water	×0.5	Bug	×0.5
Grass	×2	Rock	×1
Electric	×2	Ghost	×2
Ice	×0.5	Dragon	×1
Fighting	×0	Dark	×2
Poison	×0.5	Steel	×0.5
Ground	×1	Fairy	×1

Damage taken in Inverse battles

Type		Type	
Normal	×2	Flying	×1
Fire	×2	Psychic	×1
Water	×2	Bug	×2
Grass	×0.5	Rock	×1
Electric	×0.5	Ghost	×0.5
Ice	×2	Dragon	×1
Fighting	×2	Dark	×0.5
Poison	×2	Steel	×2
Ground	×1	Fairy	×1

Can be used in
Inverse Battle
Battle Institute
Battle Maison
Random Matchup (Free Battle)
Random Matchup (Others)

LEVEL-UP MOVES

Lv.	Name	Type	Kind	Pow.	Acc.	PP	Range
1	Bubble	Water	Special	40	100	30	Many Others
1	Water Sport	Water	Status	—	—	15	Both Sides
5	Absorb	Grass	Special	20	100	25	Normal
9	Night Shade	Ghost	Special	—	100	15	Normal
13	Bubble Beam	Water	Special	65	100	20	Normal
17	Recover	Normal	Status	—	—	10	Self
22	Water Pulse	Water	Special	60	100	20	Normal
27	Ominous Wind	Ghost	Special	60	100	5	Normal
32	Brine	Water	Special	65	100	10	Normal
37	Rain Dance	Water	Status	—	—	5	Both Sides
43	Hex	Ghost	Special	65	100	10	Normal
49	Hydro Pump	Water	Special	110	80	5	Normal
55	Wring Out	Normal	Special	—	100	5	Normal
61	Water Spout	Water	Special	150	100	5	Many Others

TM & HM MOVES

No.	Name	Type	Kind	Pow.	Acc.	PP	Range
TM06	Toxic	Poison	Status	—	90	10	Normal
TM07	Hail	Ice	Status	—	—	10	Both Sides
TM10	Hidden Power	Normal	Special	60	100	15	Normal
TM12	Taunt	Dark	Status	—	100	20	Normal
TM13	Ice Beam	Ice	Special	90	100	10	Normal
TM14	Blizzard	Ice	Special	110	70	5	Many Others
TM17	Protect	Normal	Status	—	—	10	Self
TM18	Rain Dance	Water	Status	—	—	5	Both Sides
TM20	Safeguard	Normal	Status	—	—	25	Your Side
TM21	Frustration	Normal	Physical	—	100	20	Normal
TM27	Return	Normal	Physical	—	100	20	Normal
TM29	Psychic	Psychic	Special	90	100	10	Normal
TM30	Shadow Ball	Ghost	Special	80	100	15	Normal
TM32	Double Team	Normal	Status	—	—	15	Self
TM34	Sludge Wave	Poison	Special	95	100	10	Adjacent
TM36	Sludge Bomb	Poison	Special	90	100	10	Normal
TM42	Facade	Normal	Physical	70	100	20	Normal
TM44	Rest	Psychic	Status	—	—	10	Self
TM45	Attract	Normal	Status	—	100	15	Normal
TM48	Round	Normal	Special	60	100	15	Normal
TM53	Energy Ball	Grass	Special	90	100	10	Normal
TM55	Scald	Water	Special	80	100	15	Normal
TM61	Will-O-Wisp	Fire	Status	—	85	15	Normal
TM70	Flash	Normal	Status	—	100	20	Normal
TM77	Psych Up	Normal	Status	—	—	10	Normal
TM85	Dream Eater	Psychic	Special	100	100	15	Normal
TM87	Swagger	Normal	Status	—	90	15	Normal
TM88	Sleep Talk	Normal	Status	—	—	10	Self
TM90	Substitute	Normal	Status	—	—	10	Self
TM92	Trick Room	Psychic	Status	—	—	5	Both Sides
TM94	Secret Power	Normal	Physical	70	100	20	Normal
TM97	Dark Pulse	Dark	Special	80	100	15	Normal
TM99	Dazzling Gleam	Fairy	Special	80	100	10	Many Others
TM100	Confide	Normal	Status	—	—	20	Normal
HM03	Surf	Water	Special	90	100	15	Adjacent
HM05	Waterfall	Water	Physical	80	100	15	Normal
HM07	Dive	Water	Physical	80	100	10	Normal

MOVES LEARNED IN EXCHANGE FOR BP

Name	Type	Kind	Pow.	Acc.	PP	Range
Magic Coat	Psychic	Status	—	—	15	Self
Icy Wind	Ice	Special	55	95	15	Many Others
Bind	Normal	Physical	15	85	20	Normal
Snore	Normal	Special	50	100	15	Normal
Pain Split	Normal	Status	—	—	20	Normal
Giga Drain	Grass	Special	75	100	10	Normal
Shock Wave	Electric	Special	60	—	20	Normal
Water Pulse	Water	Special	60	100	20	Normal
Spite	Ghost	Status	—	100	10	Normal
Trick	Psychic	Status	—	100	10	Normal

MOVES TAUGHT BY PEOPLE

Name	Type	Kind	Pow.	Acc.	PP	Range

EGG MOVES

Name	Type	Kind	Pow.	Acc.	PP	Range
Acid Armor	Poison	Status	—	—	20	Self
Confuse Ray	Ghost	Status	—	100	10	Normal
Pain Split	Normal	Status	—	—	20	Normal
Mist	Ice	Status	—	—	30	Your Side
Recover	Normal	Status	—	—	10	Self
Constrict	Normal	Physical	10	100	35	Normal

National Pokédex **593** Hoenn Pokédex —

Jellicent

Floating Pokémon

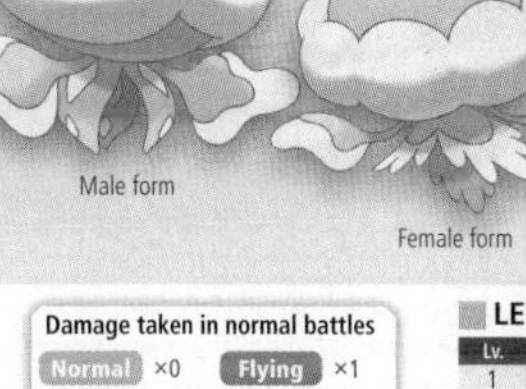

Male form

Female form

Water **Ghost**

HEIGHT: 7'03" WEIGHT: 297.6 lbs.

The male is blue while the female is pink.

Ω Its body is mostly seawater. It's said there's a castle of ships Jellicent have sunk on the seafloor.

α The fate of the ships and crew that wander into Jellicent's habitat: all sunken, all lost, all vanished.

ABILITIES
Water Absorb
Cursed Body

HIDDEN ABILITY
Damp

EGG GROUPS
Amorphous

STAT GROWTH RATES
HP
Attack
Defense
Sp. Atk
Sp. Def
Speed

EVOLUTION

Lv. 40

Frillish → Jellicent

ITEMS SOMETIMES HELD BY WILD POKÉMON
—

MAIN WAY TO REGISTER IN THE NATIONAL POKÉDEX

Level up Frillish to Lv. 40.

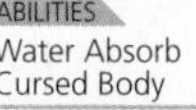

Damage taken in normal battles

Type		Type	
Normal	×0	Flying	×1
Fire	×0.5	Psychic	×1
Water	×0.5	Bug	×0.5
Grass	×2	Rock	×1
Electric	×2	Ghost	×2
Ice	×0.5	Dragon	×1
Fighting	×0	Dark	×2
Poison	×0.5	Steel	×0.5
Ground	×1	Fairy	×1

Damage taken in Inverse battles

Type		Type	
Normal	×2	Flying	×1
Fire	×2	Psychic	×1
Water	×2	Bug	×2
Grass	×0.5	Rock	×1
Electric	×0.5	Ghost	×0.5
Ice	×2	Dragon	×1
Fighting	×2	Dark	×0.5
Poison	×2	Steel	×2
Ground	×1	Fairy	×1

Can be used in
Inverse Battle
Battle Institute
Battle Maison
Random Matchup (Free Battle)
Random Matchup (Others)

LEVEL-UP MOVES

Lv.	Name	Type	Kind	Pow.	Acc.	PP	Range
1	Water Spout	Water	Special	150	100	5	Many Others
1	Wring Out	Normal	Special	—	100	5	Normal
1	Bubble	Water	Special	40	100	30	Many Others
1	Water Sport	Water	Status	—	—	15	Both Sides
1	Absorb	Grass	Special	20	100	25	Normal
1	Night Shade	Ghost	Special	—	100	15	Normal
5	Absorb	Grass	Special	20	100	25	Normal
9	Night Shade	Ghost	Special	—	100	15	Normal
13	Bubble Beam	Water	Special	65	100	20	Normal
17	Recover	Normal	Status	—	—	10	Self
22	Water Pulse	Water	Special	60	100	20	Normal
27	Ominous Wind	Ghost	Special	60	100	5	Normal
32	Brine	Water	Special	65	100	10	Normal
37	Rain Dance	Water	Status	—	—	5	Both Sides
45	Hex	Ghost	Special	65	100	10	Normal
53	Hydro Pump	Water	Special	110	80	5	Normal
61	Wring Out	Normal	Special	—	100	5	Normal
69	Water Spout	Water	Special	150	100	5	Many Others

TM & HM MOVES

No.	Name	Type	Kind	Pow.	Acc.	PP	Range
TM06	Toxic	Poison	Status	—	90	10	Normal
TM07	Hail	Ice	Status	—	—	10	Both Sides
TM10	Hidden Power	Normal	Special	60	100	15	Normal
TM12	Taunt	Dark	Status	—	100	20	Normal
TM13	Ice Beam	Ice	Special	90	100	10	Normal
TM14	Blizzard	Ice	Special	110	70	5	Many Others
TM15	Hyper Beam	Normal	Special	150	90	5	Normal
TM17	Protect	Normal	Status	—	—	10	Self
TM18	Rain Dance	Water	Status	—	—	5	Both Sides
TM20	Safeguard	Normal	Status	—	—	25	Your Side
TM21	Frustration	Normal	Physical	—	100	20	Normal
TM27	Return	Normal	Physical	—	100	20	Normal
TM29	Psychic	Psychic	Special	90	100	10	Normal
TM30	Shadow Ball	Ghost	Special	80	100	15	Normal
TM32	Double Team	Normal	Status	—	—	15	Self
TM34	Sludge Wave	Poison	Special	95	100	10	Adjacent
TM36	Sludge Bomb	Poison	Special	90	100	10	Normal
TM42	Facade	Normal	Physical	70	100	20	Normal
TM44	Rest	Psychic	Status	—	—	10	Self
TM45	Attract	Normal	Status	—	100	15	Normal
TM48	Round	Normal	Special	60	100	15	Normal
TM53	Energy Ball	Grass	Special	90	100	10	Normal
TM55	Scald	Water	Special	80	100	15	Normal
TM61	Will-O-Wisp	Fire	Status	—	85	15	Normal
TM68	Giga Impact	Normal	Physical	150	90	5	Normal
TM70	Flash	Normal	Status	—	100	20	Normal
TM77	Psych Up	Normal	Status	—	—	10	Normal
TM85	Dream Eater	Psychic	Special	100	100	15	Normal
TM87	Swagger	Normal	Status	—	90	15	Normal
TM88	Sleep Talk	Normal	Status	—	—	10	Self
TM90	Substitute	Normal	Status	—	—	10	Self
TM92	Trick Room	Psychic	Status	—	—	5	Both Sides
TM94	Secret Power	Normal	Physical	70	100	20	Normal
TM97	Dark Pulse	Dark	Special	80	100	15	Normal
TM99	Dazzling Gleam	Fairy	Special	80	100	10	Many Others
TM100	Confide	Normal	Status	—	—	20	Normal
HM03	Surf	Water	Special	90	100	15	Adjacent
HM05	Waterfall	Water	Physical	80	100	15	Normal
HM07	Dive	Water	Physical	80	100	10	Normal

MOVES LEARNED IN EXCHANGE FOR BP

Name	Type	Kind	Pow.	Acc.	PP	Range
Magic Coat	Psychic	Status	—	—	15	Self
Icy Wind	Ice	Special	55	95	15	Many Others
Bind	Normal	Physical	15	85	20	Normal
Snore	Normal	Special	50	100	15	Normal
Pain Split	Normal	Status	—	—	20	Normal
Giga Drain	Grass	Special	75	100	10	Normal
Shock Wave	Electric	Special	60	—	20	Normal
Water Pulse	Water	Special	60	100	20	Normal
Spite	Ghost	Status	—	100	10	Normal
Trick	Psychic	Status	—	100	10	Normal

MOVES TAUGHT BY PEOPLE

Name	Type	Kind	Pow.	Acc.	PP	Range

National Pokédex **594** Hoenn Pokédex —

Alomomola

Caring Pokémon

Water

HEIGHT: 3'11" WEIGHT: 69.7 lbs.

Same form for ♂ / ♀

Ω Floating in the open sea is how they live. When they find a wounded Pokémon, they embrace it and bring it to shore.

α It gently holds injured and weak Pokémon in its fins. Its special membrane heals their wounds.

ABILITIES
Healer
Hydration

HIDDEN ABILITY
Regenerator

EGG GROUPS
Water 1 Water 2

STAT GROWTH RATES
HP
Attack
Defense
Sp. Atk
Sp. Def
Speed

ITEMS SOMETIMES HELD BY WILD POKÉMON
—

EVOLUTION
Does not evolve

MAIN WAY TO REGISTER IN THE NATIONAL POKÉDEX

Catch on the water surface on Route 122. Appears as a hidden Pokémon after you battle Groudon or Kyogre.

Damage taken in normal battles

Normal	×1	Flying	×1
Fire	×0.5	Psychic	×1
Water	×0.5	Bug	×1
Grass	×2	Rock	×1
Electric	×2	Ghost	×1
Ice	×0.5	Dragon	×1
Fighting	×1	Dark	×1
Poison	×1	Steel	×0.5
Ground	×1	Fairy	×1

Damage taken in Inverse battles

Normal	×1	Flying	×1
Fire	×2	Psychic	×1
Water	×2	Bug	×1
Grass	×0.5	Rock	×1
Electric	×0.5	Ghost	×1
Ice	×2	Dragon	×1
Fighting	×1	Dark	×1
Poison	×1	Steel	×2
Ground	×1	Fairy	×1

Can be used in
Inverse Battle
Battle Institute
Battle Maison
Random Matchup (Free Battle)
Random Matchup (Others)

LEVEL-UP MOVES

Lv.	Name	Type	Kind	Pow.	Acc.	PP	Range
1	Hydro Pump	Water	Special	110	80	5	Normal
1	Wide Guard	Rock	Status	—	—	10	Your Side
1	Healing Wish	Psychic	Status	—	—	10	Self
1	Pound	Normal	Physical	40	100	35	Normal
1	Water Sport	Water	Status	—	—	15	Both Sides
5	Aqua Ring	Water	Status	—	—	20	Self
9	Aqua Jet	Water	Physical	40	100	20	Normal
13	Double Slap	Normal	Physical	15	85	10	Normal
17	Heal Pulse	Psychic	Status	—	—	10	Normal
21	Protect	Normal	Status	—	—	10	Self
25	Water Pulse	Water	Special	60	100	20	Normal
29	Wake-Up Slap	Fighting	Physical	70	100	10	Normal
33	Soak	Water	Status	—	100	20	Normal
37	Wish	Normal	Status	—	—	10	Self
41	Brine	Water	Special	65	100	10	Normal
45	Safeguard	Normal	Status	—	—	25	Your Side
49	Helping Hand	Normal	Status	—	—	20	1 Ally
53	Wide Guard	Rock	Status	—	—	10	Your Side
57	Healing Wish	Psychic	Status	—	—	10	Self
61	Hydro Pump	Water	Special	110	80	5	Normal

TM & HM MOVES

No.	Name	Type	Kind	Pow.	Acc.	PP	Range
TM04	Calm Mind	Psychic	Status	—	—	20	Self
TM06	Toxic	Poison	Status	—	90	10	Normal
TM07	Hail	Ice	Status	—	—	10	Both Sides
TM10	Hidden Power	Normal	Special	60	100	15	Normal
TM13	Ice Beam	Ice	Special	90	100	10	Normal
TM14	Blizzard	Ice	Special	110	70	5	Many Others
TM16	Light Screen	Psychic	Status	—	—	30	Your Side
TM17	Protect	Normal	Status	—	—	10	Self
TM18	Rain Dance	Water	Status	—	—	5	Both Sides
TM20	Safeguard	Normal	Status	—	—	25	Your Side
TM21	Frustration	Normal	Physical	—	100	20	Normal
TM27	Return	Normal	Physical	—	100	20	Normal
TM29	Psychic	Psychic	Special	90	100	10	Normal
TM30	Shadow Ball	Ghost	Special	80	100	15	Normal
TM32	Double Team	Normal	Status	—	—	15	Self
TM42	Facade	Normal	Physical	70	100	20	Normal
TM44	Rest	Psychic	Status	—	—	10	Self
TM45	Attract	Normal	Status	—	100	15	Normal
TM48	Round	Normal	Special	60	100	15	Normal
TM55	Scald	Water	Special	80	100	15	Normal
TM77	Psych Up	Normal	Status	—	—	10	Normal
TM87	Swagger	Normal	Status	—	90	15	Normal
TM88	Sleep Talk	Normal	Status	—	—	10	Self
TM90	Substitute	Normal	Status	—	—	10	Self
TM94	Secret Power	Normal	Physical	70	100	20	Normal
TM100	Confide	Normal	Status	—	—	20	Normal
HM03	Surf	Water	Special	90	100	15	Adjacent
HM05	Waterfall	Water	Physical	80	100	15	Normal
HM07	Dive	Water	Physical	80	100	10	Normal

MOVES LEARNED IN EXCHANGE FOR BP

Name	Type	Kind	Pow.	Acc.	PP	Range
Bounce	Flying	Physical	85	85	5	Normal
Magic Coat	Psychic	Status	—	—	15	Self
Icy Wind	Ice	Special	55	95	15	Many Others
Snore	Normal	Special	50	100	15	Normal
Knock Off	Dark	Physical	65	100	20	Normal
Pain Split	Normal	Status	—	—	20	Normal
Water Pulse	Water	Special	60	100	20	Normal
Helping Hand	Normal	Status	—	—	20	1 Ally

MOVES TAUGHT BY PEOPLE

Name	Type	Kind	Pow.	Acc.	PP	Range

EGG MOVES

Name	Type	Kind	Pow.	Acc.	PP	Range
Pain Split	Normal	Status	—	—	20	Normal
Refresh	Normal	Status	—	—	20	Self
Tickle	Normal	Status	—	100	20	Normal
Mirror Coat	Psychic	Special	—	100	20	Varies
Mist	Ice	Status	—	—	30	Your Side
Endure	Normal	Status	—	—	10	Self

National Pokédex **595** Hoenn Pokédex —

Joltik

Attaching Pokémon

Bug Electric

HEIGHT: 0'04" WEIGHT: 1.3 lbs.

Same form for ♂ / ♀

Ω Since it can't generate its own electricity, it sticks onto large-bodied Pokémon and absorbs static electricity.

α They attach themselves to large-bodied Pokémon and absorb static electricity, which they store in an electric pouch.

ABILITIES
Compound Eyes
Unnerve

HIDDEN ABILITY
Swarm

EGG GROUPS
Bug

STAT GROWTH RATES
HP
Attack
Defense
Sp. Atk
Sp. Def
Speed

ITEMS SOMETIMES HELD BY WILD POKÉMON
—

EVOLUTION 
Joltik → Lv. 36 → Galvantula

MAIN WAY TO REGISTER IN THE NATIONAL POKÉDEX

Catch on Route 116. Appears as a hidden Pokémon after you battle Groudon or Kyogre.

Damage taken in normal battles

Normal	×1	Flying	×1
Fire	×2	Psychic	×1
Water	×1	Bug	×1
Grass	×0.5	Rock	×2
Electric	×0.5	Ghost	×1
Ice	×1	Dragon	×1
Fighting	×0.5	Dark	×1
Poison	×1	Steel	×0.5
Ground	×1	Fairy	×1

Damage taken in Inverse battles

Normal	×1	Flying	×1
Fire	×0.5	Psychic	×1
Water	×1	Bug	×1
Grass	×2	Rock	×0.5
Electric	×2	Ghost	×1
Ice	×1	Dragon	×1
Fighting	×2	Dark	×1
Poison	×1	Steel	×2
Ground	×1	Fairy	×1

Can be used in
Inverse Battle
Battle Institute
Battle Maison
Random Matchup (Free Battle)
Random Matchup (Others)

LEVEL-UP MOVES

Lv.	Name	Type	Kind	Pow.	Acc.	PP	Range
1	String Shot	Bug	Status	—	95	40	Many Others
1	Leech Life	Bug	Physical	20	100	15	Normal
1	Spider Web	Bug	Status	—	—	10	Normal
4	Thunder Wave	Electric	Status	—	100	20	Normal
7	Screech	Normal	Status	—	85	40	Normal
12	Fury Cutter	Bug	Physical	40	95	20	Normal
15	Electroweb	Electric	Special	55	95	15	Many Others
18	Bug Bite	Bug	Physical	60	100	20	Normal
23	Gastro Acid	Poison	Status	—	100	10	Normal
26	Slash	Normal	Physical	70	100	20	Normal
29	Electro Ball	Electric	Special	—	100	10	Normal
34	Signal Beam	Bug	Special	75	100	15	Normal
37	Agility	Psychic	Status	—	—	30	Self
40	Sucker Punch	Dark	Physical	80	100	5	Normal
45	Discharge	Electric	Special	80	100	15	Adjacent
48	Bug Buzz	Bug	Special	90	100	10	Normal

TM & HM MOVES

No.	Name	Type	Kind	Pow.	Acc.	PP	Range
TM06	Toxic	Poison	Status	—	90	10	Normal
TM10	Hidden Power	Normal	Special	60	100	15	Normal
TM16	Light Screen	Psychic	Status	—	—	30	Your Side
TM17	Protect	Normal	Status	—	—	10	Self
TM18	Rain Dance	Water	Status	—	—	5	Both Sides
TM21	Frustration	Normal	Physical	—	100	20	Normal
TM24	Thunderbolt	Electric	Special	90	100	15	Normal
TM27	Return	Normal	Physical	—	100	20	Normal
TM32	Double Team	Normal	Status	—	—	15	Self
TM42	Facade	Normal	Physical	70	100	20	Normal
TM44	Rest	Psychic	Status	—	—	10	Self
TM45	Attract	Normal	Status	—	100	15	Normal
TM46	Thief	Dark	Physical	60	100	25	Normal
TM48	Round	Normal	Special	60	100	15	Normal
TM53	Energy Ball	Grass	Special	90	100	10	Normal
TM57	Charge Beam	Electric	Special	50	90	10	Normal
TM70	Flash	Normal	Status	—	100	20	Normal
TM72	Volt Switch	Electric	Special	70	100	20	Normal
TM73	Thunder Wave	Electric	Status	—	100	20	Normal
TM76	Struggle Bug	Bug	Special	50	100	20	Many Others
TM81	X-Scissor	Bug	Physical	80	100	15	Normal
TM83	Infestation	Bug	Special	20	100	20	Normal
TM84	Poison Jab	Poison	Physical	80	100	20	Normal
TM87	Swagger	Normal	Status	—	90	15	Normal
TM88	Sleep Talk	Normal	Status	—	—	10	Self
TM90	Substitute	Normal	Status	—	—	10	Self
TM93	Wild Charge	Electric	Physical	90	100	15	Normal
TM94	Secret Power	Normal	Physical	70	100	20	Normal
TM100	Confide	Normal	Status	—	—	20	Normal
HM01	Cut	Normal	Physical	50	95	30	Normal

MOVES LEARNED IN EXCHANGE FOR BP

Name	Type	Kind	Pow.	Acc.	PP	Range
Bug Bite	Bug	Physical	60	100	20	Normal
Signal Beam	Bug	Special	75	100	15	Normal
Bounce	Flying	Physical	85	85	5	Normal
Magnet Rise	Electric	Status	—	—	10	Self
Electroweb	Electric	Special	55	95	15	Many Others
Snore	Normal	Special	50	100	15	Normal
Giga Drain	Grass	Special	75	100	10	Normal
Shock Wave	Electric	Special	60	—	20	Normal
Gastro Acid	Poison	Status	—	100	10	Normal

MOVES TAUGHT BY PEOPLE

Name	Type	Kind	Pow.	Acc.	PP	Range

EGG MOVES

Name	Type	Kind	Pow.	Acc.	PP	Range
Pin Missile	Bug	Physical	25	95	20	Normal
Poison Sting	Poison	Physical	15	100	35	Normal
Cross Poison	Poison	Physical	70	100	20	Normal
Rock Climb	Normal	Physical	90	85	20	Normal
Pursuit	Dark	Physical	40	100	20	Normal
Disable	Normal	Status	—	100	20	Normal
Feint Attack	Dark	Physical	60	—	20	Normal
Camouflage	Normal	Status	—	—	20	Self

National Pokédex **596** Hoenn Pokédex —

Galvantula

EleSpider Pokémon

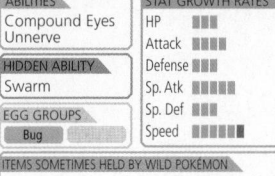

Bug Electric

HEIGHT: 2'07" WEIGHT: 31.5 lbs.

Same form for ♂ / ♀

Ω They employ an electrically charged web to trap their prey. While it is immobilized by shock, they leisurely consume it.

α When attacked, they create an electric barrier by spitting out many electrically charged threads.

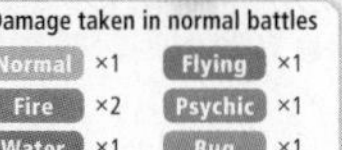

ABILITIES
Compound Eyes
Unnerve

HIDDEN ABILITY
Swarm

EGG GROUPS
Bug

STAT GROWTH RATES
HP
Attack
Defense
Sp. Atk
Sp. Def
Speed

ITEMS SOMETIMES HELD BY WILD POKÉMON
—

EVOLUTION

Joltik → Lv. 36 → Galvantula

MAIN WAY TO REGISTER IN THE NATIONAL POKÉDEX

Level up Joltik to Lv. 36.

Damage taken in normal battles

Type	×	Type	×
Normal	×1	Flying	×1
Fire	×2	Psychic	×1
Water	×1	Bug	×1
Grass	×0.5	Rock	×2
Electric	×0.5	Ghost	×1
Ice	×1	Dragon	×1
Fighting	×0.5	Dark	×1
Poison	×1	Steel	×0.5
Ground	×1	Fairy	×1

Damage taken in Inverse battles

Type	×	Type	×
Normal	×1	Flying	×1
Fire	×0.5	Psychic	×1
Water	×1	Bug	×1
Grass	×2	Rock	×0.5
Electric	×2	Ghost	×1
Ice	×1	Dragon	×1
Fighting	×2	Dark	×1
Poison	×1	Steel	×2
Ground	×1	Fairy	×1

Can be used in
- Inverse Battle
- Battle Institute
- Battle Maison
- Random Matchup (Free Battle)
- Random Matchup (Others)

LEVEL-UP MOVES

Lv.	Name	Type	Kind	Pow.	Acc.	PP	Range
1	Sticky Web	Bug	Status	—	—	20	Other Side
1	String Shot	Bug	Status	—	95	40	Many Others
1	Leech Life	Bug	Physical	20	100	15	Normal
1	Spider Web	Bug	Status	—	—	10	Normal
1	Thunder Wave	Electric	Status	—	100	20	Normal
4	Thunder Wave	Electric	Status	—	100	20	Normal
7	Screech	Normal	Status	—	85	40	Normal
12	Fury Cutter	Bug	Physical	40	95	20	Normal
15	Electroweb	Electric	Special	55	95	15	Many Others
18	Bug Bite	Bug	Physical	60	100	20	Normal
23	Gastro Acid	Poison	Status	—	100	10	Normal
26	Slash	Normal	Physical	70	100	20	Normal
29	Electro Ball	Electric	Special	—	100	10	Normal
34	Signal Beam	Bug	Special	75	100	15	Normal
40	Agility	Psychic	Status	—	—	30	Self
46	Sucker Punch	Dark	Physical	80	100	5	Normal
54	Discharge	Electric	Special	80	100	15	Adjacent
60	Bug Buzz	Bug	Special	90	100	10	Normal
65	Sticky Web	Bug	Status	—	—	20	Other Side

TM & HM MOVES

No.	Name	Type	Kind	Pow.	Acc.	PP	Range
TM06	Toxic	Poison	Status	—	90	10	Normal
TM10	Hidden Power	Normal	Special	60	100	15	Normal
TM15	Hyper Beam	Normal	Special	150	90	5	Normal
TM16	Light Screen	Psychic	Status	—	—	30	Your Side
TM17	Protect	Normal	Status	—	—	10	Self
TM18	Rain Dance	Water	Status	—	—	5	Both Sides
TM21	Frustration	Normal	Physical	—	100	20	Normal
TM24	Thunderbolt	Electric	Special	90	100	15	Normal
TM25	Thunder	Electric	Special	110	70	10	Normal
TM27	Return	Normal	Physical	—	100	20	Normal
TM32	Double Team	Normal	Status	—	—	15	Self
TM42	Facade	Normal	Physical	70	100	20	Normal
TM44	Rest	Psychic	Status	—	—	10	Self
TM45	Attract	Normal	Status	—	100	15	Normal
TM46	Thief	Dark	Physical	60	100	25	Normal
TM48	Round	Normal	Special	60	100	15	Normal
TM53	Energy Ball	Grass	Special	90	100	10	Normal
TM57	Charge Beam	Electric	Special	50	90	10	Normal
TM68	Giga Impact	Normal	Physical	150	90	5	Normal
TM70	Flash	Normal	Status	—	100	20	Normal
TM72	Volt Switch	Electric	Special	70	100	20	Normal
TM73	Thunder Wave	Electric	Status	—	100	20	Normal
TM76	Struggle Bug	Bug	Special	50	100	20	Many Others
TM81	X-Scissor	Bug	Physical	80	100	15	Normal
TM83	Infestation	Bug	Special	20	100	20	Normal
TM84	Poison Jab	Poison	Physical	80	100	20	Normal
TM87	Swagger	Normal	Status	—	90	15	Normal
TM88	Sleep Talk	Normal	Status	—	—	10	Self
TM90	Substitute	Normal	Status	—	—	10	Self
TM93	Wild Charge	Electric	Physical	90	100	15	Normal
TM94	Secret Power	Normal	Physical	70	100	20	Normal
TM100	Confide	Normal	Status	—	—	20	Normal
HM01	Cut	Normal	Physical	50	95	30	Normal

MOVES LEARNED IN EXCHANGE FOR BP

Name	Type	Kind	Pow.	Acc.	PP	Range
Bug Bite	Bug	Physical	60	100	20	Normal
Signal Beam	Bug	Special	75	100	15	Normal
Bounce	Flying	Physical	85	85	5	Normal
Magnet Rise	Electric	Status	—	—	10	Self
Electroweb	Electric	Special	55	95	15	Many Others
Snore	Normal	Special	50	100	15	Normal
Giga Drain	Grass	Special	75	100	10	Normal
Shock Wave	Electric	Special	60	—	20	Normal
Gastro Acid	Poison	Status	—	100	10	Normal

MOVES TAUGHT BY PEOPLE

Name	Type	Kind	Pow.	Acc.	PP	Range

National Pokédex **597** Hoenn Pokédex —

Ferroseed

Thorn Seed Pokémon

Grass Steel

HEIGHT: 2'00" WEIGHT: 41.4 lbs.

Same form for ♂ / ♀

Ω When threatened, it attacks by shooting a barrage of spikes, which gives it a chance to escape by rolling away.

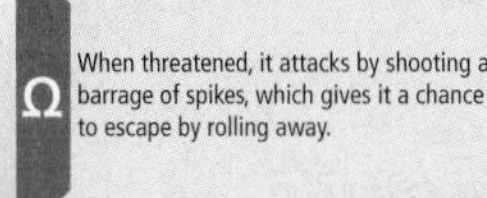

α It absorbs the iron it finds in the rock while clinging to the ceiling. It shoots spikes when in danger.

ABILITY
Iron Barbs

HIDDEN ABILITY
—

EGG GROUPS
Grass Mineral

STAT GROWTH RATES
HP
Attack
Defense
Sp. Atk
Sp. Def
Speed

ITEMS SOMETIMES HELD BY WILD POKÉMON
—

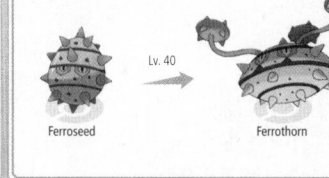

EVOLUTION

Ferroseed → Lv. 40 → Ferrothorn

MAIN WAY TO REGISTER IN THE NATIONAL POKÉDEX

Appears in *Pokémon X* and *Pokémon Y*. Bring it to your game using Link Trade or the GTS.

Damage taken in normal battles

Type	×	Type	×
Normal	×0.5	Flying	×1
Fire	×4	Psychic	×0.5
Water	×0.5	Bug	×1
Grass	×0.25	Rock	×0.5
Electric	×0.5	Ghost	×1
Ice	×1	Dragon	×0.5
Fighting	×2	Dark	×1
Poison	×0	Steel	×0.5
Ground	×1	Fairy	×0.5

Damage taken in Inverse battles

Type	×	Type	×
Normal	×2	Flying	×1
Fire	×0.25	Psychic	×2
Water	×2	Bug	×1
Grass	×4	Rock	×2
Electric	×2	Ghost	×1
Ice	×1	Dragon	×2
Fighting	×0.5	Dark	×1
Poison	×1	Steel	×2
Ground	×1	Fairy	×2

Can be used in
- Inverse Battle
- Battle Institute
- Battle Maison
- Random Matchup (Free Battle)
- Random Matchup (Others)

LEVEL-UP MOVES

Lv.	Name	Type	Kind	Pow.	Acc.	PP	Range
1	Tackle	Normal	Physical	50	100	35	Normal
1	Harden	Normal	Status	—	—	30	Self
6	Rollout	Rock	Physical	30	90	20	Normal
9	Curse	Ghost	Status	—	—	10	Varies
14	Metal Claw	Steel	Physical	50	95	35	Normal
18	Pin Missile	Bug	Physical	25	95	20	Normal
21	Gyro Ball	Steel	Physical	—	100	5	Normal
26	Iron Defense	Steel	Status	—	—	15	Self
30	Mirror Shot	Steel	Special	65	85	10	Normal
35	Ingrain	Grass	Status	—	—	20	Self
38	Self-Destruct	Normal	Physical	200	100	5	Adjacent
43	Iron Head	Steel	Physical	80	100	15	Normal
47	Payback	Dark	Physical	50	100	10	Normal
52	Flash Cannon	Steel	Special	80	100	10	Normal
55	Explosion	Normal	Physical	250	100	5	Adjacent

TM & HM MOVES

No.	Name	Type	Kind	Pow.	Acc.	PP	Range
TM01	Hone Claws	Dark	Status	—	—	15	Self
TM06	Toxic	Poison	Status	—	90	10	Normal
TM10	Hidden Power	Normal	Special	60	100	15	Normal
TM11	Sunny Day	Fire	Status	—	—	5	Both Sides
TM17	Protect	Normal	Status	—	—	10	Self
TM21	Frustration	Normal	Physical	—	100	20	Normal
TM22	Solar Beam	Grass	Special	120	100	10	Normal
TM24	Thunderbolt	Electric	Special	90	100	15	Normal
TM27	Return	Normal	Physical	—	100	20	Normal
TM32	Double Team	Normal	Status	—	—	15	Self
TM42	Facade	Normal	Physical	70	100	20	Normal
TM44	Rest	Psychic	Status	—	—	10	Self
TM48	Round	Normal	Special	60	100	15	Normal
TM53	Energy Ball	Grass	Special	90	100	10	Normal
TM64	Explosion	Normal	Physical	250	100	5	Adjacent
TM66	Payback	Dark	Physical	50	100	10	Normal
TM69	Rock Polish	Rock	Status	—	—	20	Self
TM70	Flash	Normal	Status	—	100	20	Normal
TM73	Thunder Wave	Electric	Status	—	100	20	Normal
TM74	Gyro Ball	Steel	Physical	—	100	5	Normal
TM84	Poison Jab	Poison	Physical	80	100	20	Normal
TM87	Swagger	Normal	Status	—	90	15	Normal
TM88	Sleep Talk	Normal	Status	—	—	10	Self
TM90	Substitute	Normal	Status	—	—	10	Self
TM91	Flash Cannon	Steel	Special	80	100	10	Normal
TM94	Secret Power	Normal	Physical	70	100	20	Normal
TM96	Nature Power	Normal	Status	—	—	20	Normal
TM100	Confide	Normal	Status	—	—	20	Normal
HM06	Rock Smash	Fighting	Physical	40	100	15	Normal

MOVES LEARNED IN EXCHANGE FOR BP

Name	Type	Kind	Pow.	Acc.	PP	Range
Iron Head	Steel	Physical	80	100	15	Normal
Seed Bomb	Grass	Physical	80	100	15	Normal
Gravity	Psychic	Status	—	—	5	Both Sides
Magnet Rise	Electric	Status	—	—	10	Self
Iron Defense	Steel	Status	—	—	15	Self
Snore	Normal	Special	50	100	15	Normal
Knock Off	Dark	Physical	65	100	20	Normal
Giga Drain	Grass	Special	75	100	10	Normal
Worry Seed	Grass	Status	—	100	10	Normal
Endeavor	Normal	Physical	—	100	5	Normal
Stealth Rock	Rock	Status	—	—	20	Other Side

MOVES TAUGHT BY PEOPLE

Name	Type	Kind	Pow.	Acc.	PP	Range

EGG MOVES

Name	Type	Kind	Pow.	Acc.	PP	Range
Bullet Seed	Grass	Physical	25	100	30	Normal
Leech Seed	Grass	Status	—	90	10	Normal
Spikes	Ground	Status	—	—	20	Other Side
Worry Seed	Grass	Status	—	100	10	Normal
Seed Bomb	Grass	Physical	80	100	15	Normal
Gravity	Psychic	Status	—	—	5	Both Sides
Rock Climb	Normal	Physical	90	85	20	Normal
Stealth Rock	Rock	Status	—	—	20	Other Side
Acid Spray	Poison	Special	40	100	20	Normal

National Pokédex **598** Hoenn Pokédex —

Ferrothorn

Thorn Pod Pokémon

Grass | Steel

HEIGHT: 3'03" WEIGHT: 242.5 lbs.

Same form for ♂ / ♀

Ω By swinging around its three spiky feelers and shooting spikes, it can obliterate an opponent.

α They attach themselves to cave ceilings, firing steel spikes at targets passing beneath them.

ABILITY
Iron Barbs

HIDDEN ABILITY
Anticipation

EGG GROUPS
Grass | Mineral

STAT GROWTH RATES
HP ■■■
Attack ■■■■■
Defense ■■■■■■
Sp. Atk ■■■
Sp. Def ■■■■■
Speed ■

ITEMS SOMETIMES HELD BY WILD POKÉMON
—

EVOLUTION
Ferroseed → Lv. 40 → Ferrothorn

MAIN WAY TO REGISTER IN THE NATIONAL POKÉDEX

Level up a Ferroseed obtained via Link Trade or the GTS to Lv. 40.

Damage taken in normal battles

Normal	×0.5	Flying	×1
Fire	×4	Psychic	×0.5
Water	×0.5	Bug	×1
Grass	×0.25	Rock	×0.5
Electric	×0.5	Ghost	×1
Ice	×1	Dragon	×0.5
Fighting	×2	Dark	×1
Poison	×0	Steel	×0.5
Ground	×1	Fairy	×0.5

Damage taken in Inverse battles

Normal	×2	Flying	×1
Fire	×0.25	Psychic	×2
Water	×2	Bug	×1
Grass	×4	Rock	×2
Electric	×2	Ghost	×1
Ice	×1	Dragon	×2
Fighting	×0.5	Dark	×1
Poison	×1	Steel	×2
Ground	×1	Fairy	×2

Can be used in
Inverse Battle
Battle Institute
Battle Maison
Random Matchup (Free Battle)
Random Matchup (Others)

LEVEL-UP MOVES

Lv.	Name	Type	Kind	Pow.	Acc.	PP	Range
1	Rock Climb	Normal	Physical	90	85	20	Normal
1	Tackle	Normal	Physical	50	100	35	Normal
1	Harden	Normal	Status	—	—	30	Self
1	Rollout	Rock	Physical	30	90	20	Normal
1	Curse	Ghost	Status	—	—	10	Varies
6	Rollout	Rock	Physical	30	90	20	Normal
9	Curse	Ghost	Status	—	—	10	Varies
14	Metal Claw	Steel	Physical	50	95	35	Normal
18	Pin Missile	Bug	Physical	25	95	20	Normal
21	Gyro Ball	Steel	Physical	—	100	5	Normal
26	Iron Defense	Steel	Status	—	—	15	Self
30	Mirror Shot	Steel	Special	65	85	10	Normal
35	Ingrain	Grass	Status	—	—	20	Self
38	Self-Destruct	Normal	Physical	200	100	5	Adjacent
40	Power Whip	Grass	Physical	120	85	10	Normal
46	Iron Head	Steel	Physical	80	100	15	Normal
53	Payback	Dark	Physical	50	100	10	Normal
61	Flash Cannon	Steel	Special	80	100	10	Normal
67	Explosion	Normal	Physical	250	100	5	Adjacent

TM & HM MOVES

No.	Name	Type	Kind	Pow.	Acc.	PP	Range
TM01	Hone Claws	Dark	Status	—	—	15	Self
TM06	Toxic	Poison	Status	—	90	10	Normal
TM10	Hidden Power	Normal	Special	60	100	15	Normal
TM11	Sunny Day	Fire	Status	—	—	5	Both Sides
TM15	Hyper Beam	Normal	Special	150	90	5	Normal
TM17	Protect	Normal	Status	—	—	10	Self
TM21	Frustration	Normal	Physical	—	100	20	Normal
TM22	Solar Beam	Grass	Special	120	100	10	Normal
TM24	Thunderbolt	Electric	Special	90	100	15	Normal
TM25	Thunder	Electric	Special	110	70	10	Normal
TM27	Return	Normal	Physical	—	100	20	Normal
TM32	Double Team	Normal	Status	—	—	15	Self
TM37	Sandstorm	Rock	Status	—	—	10	Both Sides
TM40	Aerial Ace	Flying	Physical	60	—	20	Normal
TM42	Facade	Normal	Physical	70	100	20	Normal
TM44	Rest	Psychic	Status	—	—	10	Self
TM48	Round	Normal	Special	60	100	15	Normal
TM53	Energy Ball	Grass	Special	90	100	10	Normal
TM64	Explosion	Normal	Physical	250	100	5	Adjacent
TM65	Shadow Claw	Ghost	Physical	70	100	15	Normal
TM66	Payback	Dark	Physical	50	100	10	Normal
TM68	Giga Impact	Normal	Physical	150	90	5	Normal
TM69	Rock Polish	Rock	Status	—	—	20	Self
TM70	Flash	Normal	Status	—	100	20	Normal
TM73	Thunder Wave	Electric	Status	—	100	20	Normal
TM74	Gyro Ball	Steel	Physical	—	100	5	Normal
TM75	Swords Dance	Normal	Status	—	—	20	Self
TM78	Bulldoze	Ground	Physical	60	100	20	Adjacent
TM84	Poison Jab	Poison	Physical	80	100	20	Normal
TM86	Grass Knot	Grass	Special	—	100	20	Normal
TM87	Swagger	Normal	Status	—	90	15	Normal
TM88	Sleep Talk	Normal	Status	—	—	10	Self
TM90	Substitute	Normal	Status	—	—	10	Self
TM91	Flash Cannon	Steel	Special	80	100	10	Normal
TM94	Secret Power	Normal	Physical	70	100	20	Normal
TM96	Nature Power	Normal	Status	—	—	20	Normal
TM100	Confide	Normal	Status	—	—	20	Normal
HM01	Cut	Normal	Physical	50	95	30	Normal
HM04	Strength	Normal	Physical	80	100	15	Normal
HM06	Rock Smash	Fighting	Physical	40	100	15	Normal

MOVES LEARNED IN EXCHANGE FOR BP

Name	Type	Kind	Pow.	Acc.	PP	Range
Iron Head	Steel	Physical	80	100	15	Normal
Seed Bomb	Grass	Physical	80	100	15	Normal
Block	Normal	Status	—	—	5	Normal
Gravity	Psychic	Status	—	—	5	Both Sides
Magnet Rise	Electric	Status	—	—	10	Self
Iron Defense	Steel	Status	—	—	15	Self
Snore	Normal	Special	50	100	15	Normal
Knock Off	Dark	Physical	65	100	20	Normal
Giga Drain	Grass	Special	75	100	10	Normal
Worry Seed	Grass	Status	—	100	10	Normal
Endeavor	Normal	Physical	—	100	5	Normal
Stealth Rock	Rock	Status	—	—	20	Other Side

MOVES TAUGHT BY PEOPLE

Name	Type	Kind	Pow.	Acc.	PP	Range

National Pokédex **599** Hoenn Pokédex —

Klink

Gear Pokémon

Steel

HEIGHT: 1'00" WEIGHT: 46.3 lbs.

Gender unknown

Ω Interlocking two bodies and spinning around generates the energy they need to live.

α The two minigears that mesh together are predetermined. Each will rebound from other minigears without meshing.

ABILITIES
Plus
Minus

HIDDEN ABILITY
Clear Body

EGG GROUPS
Mineral

STAT GROWTH RATES
HP ■■
Attack ■■■
Defense ■■■
Sp. Atk ■■
Sp. Def ■■■
Speed ■■

ITEMS SOMETIMES HELD BY WILD POKÉMON
—

EVOLUTION
Klink → Lv. 38 → Klang → Lv. 49 → Klinklang

MAIN WAY TO REGISTER IN THE NATIONAL POKÉDEX

Catch in Mirage Cave 1.

Damage taken in normal battles

Normal	×0.5	Flying	×0.5
Fire	×2	Psychic	×0.5
Water	×1	Bug	×0.5
Grass	×0.5	Rock	×0.5
Electric	×1	Ghost	×1
Ice	×0.5	Dragon	×0.5
Fighting	×2	Dark	×1
Poison	×0	Steel	×0.5
Ground	×2	Fairy	×0.5

Damage taken in Inverse battles

Normal	×2	Flying	×2
Fire	×0.5	Psychic	×2
Water	×1	Bug	×2
Grass	×2	Rock	×2
Electric	×1	Ghost	×1
Ice	×2	Dragon	×2
Fighting	×0.5	Dark	×1
Poison	×2	Steel	×2
Ground	×0.5	Fairy	×2

Can be used in
Inverse Battle
Battle Institute
Battle Maison
Random Matchup (Free Battle)
Random Matchup (Others)

LEVEL-UP MOVES

Lv.	Name	Type	Kind	Pow.	Acc.	PP	Range
1	Vice Grip	Normal	Physical	55	100	30	Normal
6	Charge	Electric	Status	—	—	20	Self
11	Thunder Shock	Electric	Special	40	100	30	Normal
16	Gear Grind	Steel	Physical	50	85	15	Normal
21	Bind	Normal	Physical	15	85	20	Normal
26	Charge Beam	Electric	Special	50	90	10	Normal
31	Autotomize	Steel	Status	—	—	15	Self
36	Mirror Shot	Steel	Special	65	85	10	Normal
39	Screech	Normal	Status	—	85	40	Normal
42	Discharge	Electric	Special	80	100	15	Adjacent
45	Metal Sound	Steel	Status	—	85	40	Normal
48	Shift Gear	Steel	Status	—	—	10	Self
50	Lock-On	Normal	Status	—	—	5	Normal
54	Zap Cannon	Electric	Special	120	50	5	Normal
57	Hyper Beam	Normal	Special	150	90	5	Normal

TM & HM MOVES

No.	Name	Type	Kind	Pow.	Acc.	PP	Range
TM06	Toxic	Poison	Status	—	90	10	Normal
TM10	Hidden Power	Normal	Special	60	100	15	Normal
TM15	Hyper Beam	Normal	Special	150	90	5	Normal
TM17	Protect	Normal	Status	—	—	10	Self
TM21	Frustration	Normal	Physical	—	100	20	Normal
TM24	Thunderbolt	Electric	Special	90	100	15	Normal
TM27	Return	Normal	Physical	—	100	20	Normal
TM32	Double Team	Normal	Status	—	—	15	Self
TM37	Sandstorm	Rock	Status	—	—	10	Both Sides
TM42	Facade	Normal	Physical	70	100	20	Normal
TM44	Rest	Psychic	Status	—	—	10	Self
TM48	Round	Normal	Special	60	100	15	Normal
TM57	Charge Beam	Electric	Special	50	90	10	Normal
TM69	Rock Polish	Rock	Status	—	—	20	Self
TM72	Volt Switch	Electric	Special	70	100	20	Normal
TM73	Thunder Wave	Electric	Status	—	100	20	Normal
TM87	Swagger	Normal	Status	—	90	15	Normal
TM88	Sleep Talk	Normal	Status	—	—	10	Self
TM90	Substitute	Normal	Status	—	—	10	Self
TM91	Flash Cannon	Steel	Special	80	100	10	Normal
TM93	Wild Charge	Electric	Physical	90	100	15	Normal
TM94	Secret Power	Normal	Physical	70	100	20	Normal
TM100	Confide	Normal	Status	—	—	20	Normal
HM06	Rock Smash	Fighting	Physical	40	100	15	Normal

MOVES LEARNED IN EXCHANGE FOR BP

Name	Type	Kind	Pow.	Acc.	PP	Range
Signal Beam	Bug	Special	75	100	15	Normal
Uproar	Normal	Special	90	100	10	1 Random
Magic Coat	Psychic	Status	—	—	15	Self
Gravity	Psychic	Status	—	—	5	Both Sides
Magnet Rise	Electric	Status	—	—	10	Self
Iron Defense	Steel	Status	—	—	15	Self
Bind	Normal	Physical	15	85	20	Normal
Snore	Normal	Special	50	100	15	Normal
Shock Wave	Electric	Special	60	—	20	Normal
Recycle	Normal	Status	—	—	10	Self

MOVES TAUGHT BY PEOPLE

Name	Type	Kind	Pow.	Acc.	PP	Range

National Pokédex **600** Hoenn Pokédex —

Klang

Gear Pokémon

Steel

HEIGHT: 2'00" WEIGHT: 112.4 lbs.
Gender unknown

Ω By changing the direction in which it rotates, it communicates its feelings to others. When angry, it rotates faster.

α A minigear and big gear comprise its body. If the minigear it launches at a foe doesn't return, it will die.

ABILITIES
Plus
Minus

HIDDEN ABILITY
Clear Body

EGG GROUPS
Mineral

STAT GROWTH RATES
HP ■■■
Attack ■■■■
Defense ■■■■
Sp. Atk ■■■
Sp. Def ■■■■
Speed ■■■

ITEMS SOMETIMES HELD BY WILD POKÉMON
—

EVOLUTION

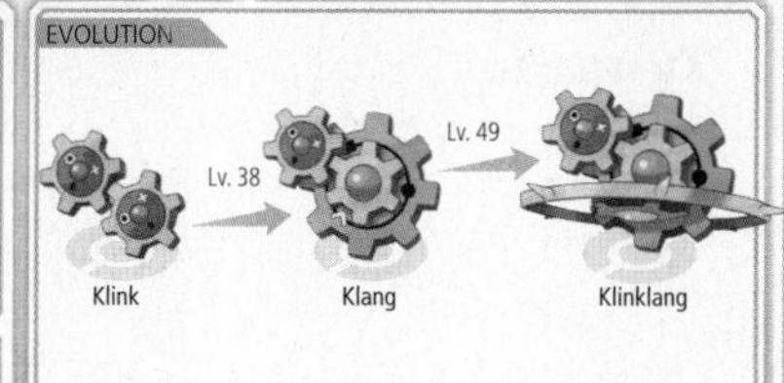

MAIN WAY TO REGISTER IN THE NATIONAL POKÉDEX

Level up Klink to Lv. 38.

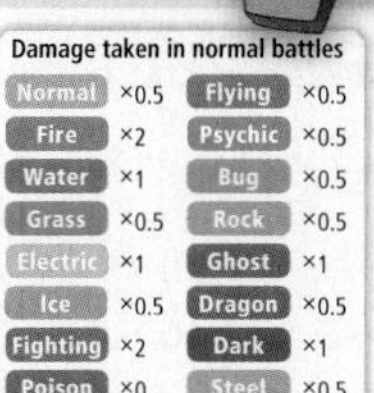

Damage taken in normal battles

Type		Type	
Normal	×0.5	Flying	×0.5
Fire	×2	Psychic	×0.5
Water	×1	Bug	×0.5
Grass	×0.5	Rock	×0.5
Electric	×1	Ghost	×1
Ice	×0.5	Dragon	×0.5
Fighting	×2	Dark	×1
Poison	×0	Steel	×0.5
Ground	×2	Fairy	×0.5

Damage taken in Inverse battles

Type		Type	
Normal	×2	Flying	×2
Fire	×0.5	Psychic	×2
Water	×1	Bug	×2
Grass	×2	Rock	×2
Electric	×1	Ghost	×1
Ice	×2	Dragon	×2
Fighting	×0.5	Dark	×1
Poison	×2	Steel	×2
Ground	×0.5	Fairy	×2

Can be used in
Inverse Battle
Battle Institute
Battle Maison
Random Matchup (Free Battle)
Random Matchup (Others)

LEVEL-UP MOVES

Lv.	Name	Type	Kind	Pow.	Acc.	PP	Range
1	Vice Grip	Normal	Physical	55	100	30	Normal
1	Charge	Electric	Status	—	—	20	Self
1	Thunder Shock	Electric	Special	40	100	30	Normal
1	Gear Grind	Steel	Physical	50	85	15	Normal
6	Charge	Electric	Status	—	—	20	Self
11	Thunder Shock	Electric	Special	40	100	30	Normal
16	Gear Grind	Steel	Physical	50	85	15	Normal
21	Bind	Normal	Physical	15	85	20	Normal
26	Charge Beam	Electric	Special	50	90	10	Normal
31	Autotomize	Steel	Status	—	—	15	Self
36	Mirror Shot	Steel	Special	65	85	10	Normal
40	Screech	Normal	Status	—	85	40	Normal
44	Discharge	Electric	Special	80	100	15	Adjacent
48	Metal Sound	Steel	Status	—	85	40	Normal
52	Shift Gear	Steel	Status	—	—	10	Self
56	Lock-On	Normal	Status	—	—	5	Normal
60	Zap Cannon	Electric	Special	120	50	5	Normal
64	Hyper Beam	Normal	Special	150	90	5	Normal

TM & HM MOVES

No.	Name	Type	Kind	Pow.	Acc.	PP	Range
TM06	Toxic	Poison	Status	—	90	10	Normal
TM10	Hidden Power	Normal	Special	60	100	15	Normal
TM15	Hyper Beam	Normal	Special	150	90	5	Normal
TM17	Protect	Normal	Status	—	—	10	Self
TM21	Frustration	Normal	Physical	—	100	20	Normal
TM24	Thunderbolt	Electric	Special	90	100	15	Normal
TM27	Return	Normal	Physical	—	100	20	Normal
TM32	Double Team	Normal	Status	—	—	15	Self
TM37	Sandstorm	Rock	Status	—	—	10	Both Sides
TM42	Facade	Normal	Physical	70	100	20	Normal
TM44	Rest	Psychic	Status	—	—	10	Self
TM48	Round	Normal	Special	60	100	15	Normal
TM57	Charge Beam	Electric	Special	50	90	10	Normal
TM69	Rock Polish	Rock	Status	—	—	20	Self
TM72	Volt Switch	Electric	Special	70	100	20	Normal
TM73	Thunder Wave	Electric	Status	—	100	20	Normal
TM87	Swagger	Normal	Status	—	90	15	Normal
TM88	Sleep Talk	Normal	Status	—	—	10	Self
TM90	Substitute	Normal	Status	—	—	10	Self
TM91	Flash Cannon	Steel	Special	80	100	10	Normal
TM93	Wild Charge	Electric	Physical	90	100	15	Normal
TM94	Secret Power	Normal	Physical	70	100	20	Normal
TM100	Confide	Normal	Status	—	—	20	Normal
HM06	Rock Smash	Fighting	Physical	40	100	15	Normal

MOVES LEARNED IN EXCHANGE FOR BP

Name	Type	Kind	Pow.	Acc.	PP	Range
Signal Beam	Bug	Special	75	100	15	Normal
Uproar	Normal	Special	90	100	10	1 Random
Magic Coat	Psychic	Status	—	—	15	Self
Gravity	Psychic	Status	—	—	5	Both Sides
Magnet Rise	Electric	Status	—	—	10	Self
Iron Defense	Steel	Status	—	—	15	Self
Bind	Normal	Physical	15	85	20	Normal
Snore	Normal	Special	50	100	15	Normal
Shock Wave	Electric	Special	60	—	20	Normal
Recycle	Normal	Status	—	—	10	Self

MOVES TAUGHT BY PEOPLE

Name	Type	Kind	Pow.	Acc.	PP	Range

600 Klang

National Pokédex

National Pokédex **601** Hoenn Pokédex —

Klinklang

Gear Pokémon

Steel

HEIGHT: 2'00" WEIGHT: 178.6 lbs.
Gender unknown

Ω The gear with the red core is rotated at high speed for a rapid energy charge.

α Its red core functions as an energy tank. It fires the charged energy through its spikes into an area.

ABILITIES
Plus
Minus

HIDDEN ABILITY
Clear Body

EGG GROUPS
Mineral

STAT GROWTH RATES
HP ■■■
Attack ■■■■■
Defense ■■■■■
Sp. Atk ■■■
Sp. Def ■■■■
Speed ■■■■■

ITEMS SOMETIMES HELD BY WILD POKÉMON
—

EVOLUTION

Lv. 38 Lv. 49
Klink Klang Klinklang

MAIN WAY TO REGISTER IN THE NATIONAL POKÉDEX

Level up Klang to Lv. 49.

Damage taken in normal battles

Type		Type	
Normal	×0.5	Flying	×0.5
Fire	×2	Psychic	×0.5
Water	×1	Bug	×0.5
Grass	×0.5	Rock	×0.5
Electric	×1	Ghost	×1
Ice	×0.5	Dragon	×0.5
Fighting	×2	Dark	×1
Poison	×0	Steel	×0.5
Ground	×2	Fairy	×0.5

Damage taken in Inverse battles

Type		Type	
Normal	×2	Flying	×2
Fire	×0.5	Psychic	×2
Water	×1	Bug	×2
Grass	×2	Rock	×2
Electric	×1	Ghost	×1
Ice	×2	Dragon	×2
Fighting	×0.5	Dark	×1
Poison	×2	Steel	×2
Ground	×0.5	Fairy	×2

Can be used in
Inverse Battle
Battle Institute
Battle Maison
Random Matchup (Free Battle)
Random Matchup (Others)

LEVEL-UP MOVES

Lv.	Name	Type	Kind	Pow.	Acc.	PP	Range
1	Magnetic Flux	Electric	Status	—	—	20	Your Party
1	Zap Cannon	Electric	Special	120	50	5	Normal
1	Vice Grip	Normal	Physical	55	100	30	Normal
1	Charge	Electric	Status	—	—	20	Self
1	Thunder Shock	Electric	Special	40	100	30	Normal
1	Gear Grind	Steel	Physical	50	85	15	Normal
6	Charge	Electric	Status	—	—	20	Self
11	Thunder Shock	Electric	Special	40	100	30	Normal
16	Gear Grind	Steel	Physical	50	85	15	Normal
21	Bind	Normal	Physical	15	85	20	Normal
25	Charge Beam	Electric	Special	50	90	10	Normal
31	Autotomize	Steel	Status	—	—	15	Self
36	Mirror Shot	Steel	Special	65	85	10	Normal
40	Screech	Normal	Status	—	85	40	Normal
44	Discharge	Electric	Special	80	100	15	Adjacent
48	Metal Sound	Steel	Status	—	85	40	Normal
54	Shift Gear	Steel	Status	—	—	10	Self
60	Lock-On	Normal	Status	—	—	5	Normal
66	Zap Cannon	Electric	Special	120	50	5	Normal
72	Hyper Beam	Normal	Special	150	90	5	Normal
76	Magnetic Flux	Electric	Status	—	—	20	Your Party

TM & HM MOVES

No.	Name	Type	Kind	Pow.	Acc.	PP	Range
TM06	Toxic	Poison	Status	—	90	10	Normal
TM10	Hidden Power	Normal	Special	60	100	15	Normal
TM15	Hyper Beam	Normal	Special	150	90	5	Normal
TM17	Protect	Normal	Status	—	—	10	Self
TM21	Frustration	Normal	Physical	—	100	20	Normal
TM24	Thunderbolt	Electric	Special	90	100	15	Normal
TM25	Thunder	Electric	Special	110	70	10	Normal
TM27	Return	Normal	Physical	—	100	20	Normal
TM32	Double Team	Normal	Status	—	—	15	Self
TM37	Sandstorm	Rock	Status	—	—	10	Both Sides
TM42	Facade	Normal	Physical	70	100	20	Normal
TM44	Rest	Psychic	Status	—	—	10	Self
TM48	Round	Normal	Special	60	100	15	Normal
TM57	Charge Beam	Electric	Special	50	90	10	Normal
TM68	Giga Impact	Normal	Physical	150	90	5	Normal
TM69	Rock Polish	Rock	Status	—	—	20	Self
TM72	Volt Switch	Electric	Special	70	100	20	Normal
TM73	Thunder Wave	Electric	Status	—	100	20	Normal
TM87	Swagger	Normal	Status	—	90	15	Normal
TM88	Sleep Talk	Normal	Status	—	—	10	Self
TM90	Substitute	Normal	Status	—	—	10	Self
TM91	Flash Cannon	Steel	Special	80	100	10	Normal
TM92	Trick Room	Psychic	Status	—	—	5	Both Sides
TM93	Wild Charge	Electric	Physical	90	100	15	Normal
TM94	Secret Power	Normal	Physical	70	100	20	Normal
TM100	Confide	Normal	Status	—	—	20	Normal
HM06	Rock Smash	Fighting	Physical	40	100	15	Normal

MOVES LEARNED IN EXCHANGE FOR BP

Name	Type	Kind	Pow.	Acc.	PP	Range
Signal Beam	Bug	Special	75	100	15	Normal
Uproar	Normal	Special	90	100	10	1 Random
Magic Coat	Psychic	Status	—	—	15	Self
Gravity	Psychic	Status	—	—	5	Both Sides
Magnet Rise	Electric	Status	—	—	10	Self
Iron Defense	Steel	Status	—	—	15	Self
Bind	Normal	Physical	15	85	20	Normal
Snore	Normal	Special	50	100	15	Normal
Shock Wave	Electric	Special	60	—	20	Normal
Recycle	Normal	Status	—	—	10	Self

MOVES TAUGHT BY PEOPLE

Name	Type	Kind	Pow.	Acc.	PP	Range

Klinklang 601

National Pokédex **602** Hoenn Pokédex —

Tynamo

EleFish Pokémon

Electric

HEIGHT: 0'08" WEIGHT: 0.7 lbs.

Same form for ♂ / ♀

Ω While one alone doesn't have much power, a chain of many Tynamo can be as powerful as lightning.

α One alone can emit only a trickle of electricity, so a group of them gathers to unleash a powerful electric shock.

ABILITY
Levitate

HIDDEN ABILITY
—

EGG GROUPS
Amorphous

STAT GROWTH RATES
HP
Attack
Defense
Sp. Atk
Sp. Def
Speed

ITEMS SOMETIMES HELD BY WILD POKÉMON
—

EVOLUTION

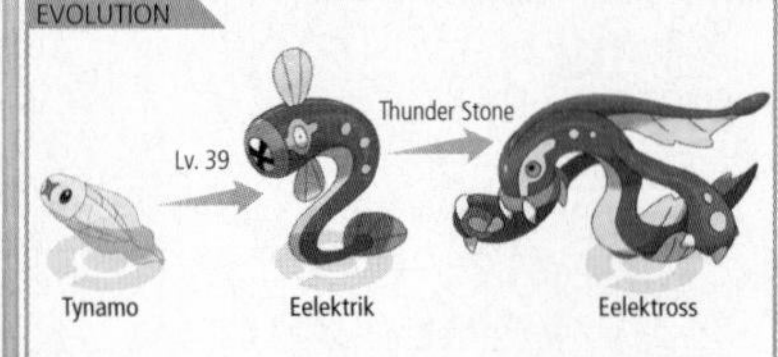

MAIN WAY TO REGISTER IN THE NATIONAL POKÉDEX

Catch in Mirage Cave 1.

Damage taken in normal battles

Type		Type	
Normal	×1	Flying	×0.5
Fire	×1	Psychic	×1
Water	×1	Bug	×1
Grass	×1	Rock	×1
Electric	×0.5	Ghost	×1
Ice	×1	Dragon	×1
Fighting	×1	Dark	×1
Poison	×1	Steel	×0.5
! Ground	×2	Fairy	×1

Damage taken in Inverse battles

Type		Type	
Normal	×1	Flying	×2
Fire	×1	Psychic	×1
Water	×1	Bug	×1
Grass	×1	Rock	×1
Electric	×2	Ghost	×1
Ice	×1	Dragon	×1
Fighting	×1	Dark	×1
Poison	×1	Steel	×2
! Ground	×0.5	Fairy	×1

Can be used in
Inverse Battle
Battle Institute
Battle Maison
Random Matchup (Free Battle)
Random Matchup (Others)

LEVEL-UP MOVES

Lv.	Name	Type	Kind	Pow.	Acc.	PP	Range
1	Tackle	Normal	Physical	50	100	35	Normal
1	Thunder Wave	Electric	Status	—	100	20	Normal
1	Spark	Electric	Physical	65	100	20	Normal
1	Charge Beam	Electric	Special	50	90	10	Normal

TM & HM MOVES

No.	Name	Type	Kind	Pow.	Acc.	PP	Range
TM57	Charge Beam	Electric	Special	50	90	10	Normal
TM73	Thunder Wave	Electric	Status	—	100	20	Normal

MOVES LEARNED IN EXCHANGE FOR BP

Name	Type	Kind	Pow.	Acc.	PP	Range
Magnet Rise	Electric	Status	—	—	10	Self

MOVES TAUGHT BY PEOPLE

Name	Type	Kind	Pow.	Acc.	PP	Range

National Pokédex **603** Hoenn Pokédex —

Eelektrik

EleFish Pokémon

Electric

HEIGHT: 3'11" WEIGHT: 48.5 lbs.

Same form for ♂ / ♀

Ω It wraps itself around its prey and paralyzes it with electricity from the round spots on its sides. Then it chomps.

α These Pokémon have a big appetite. When they spot their prey, they attack it and paralyze it with electricity.

ABILITY
Levitate

HIDDEN ABILITY
—

EGG GROUPS
Amorphous

STAT GROWTH RATES
HP
Attack
Defense
Sp. Atk
Sp. Def
Speed

ITEMS SOMETIMES HELD BY WILD POKÉMON
—

EVOLUTION

Lv. 39
Thunder Stone
Tynamo
Eelektrik
Eelektross

MAIN WAY TO REGISTER IN THE NATIONAL POKÉDEX

Level up Tynamo to Lv. 39.

Damage taken in normal battles

Type		Type	
Normal	×1	Flying	×0.5
Fire	×1	Psychic	×1
Water	×1	Bug	×1
Grass	×1	Rock	×1
Electric	×0.5	Ghost	×1
Ice	×1	Dragon	×1
Fighting	×1	Dark	×1
Poison	×1	Steel	×0.5
! Ground	×2	Fairy	×1

Damage taken in Inverse battles

Type		Type	
Normal	×1	Flying	×2
Fire	×1	Psychic	×1
Water	×1	Bug	×1
Grass	×1	Rock	×1
Electric	×2	Ghost	×1
Ice	×1	Dragon	×1
Fighting	×1	Dark	×1
Poison	×1	Steel	×2
! Ground	×0.5	Fairy	×1

Can be used in
Inverse Battle
Battle Institute
Battle Maison
Random Matchup (Free Battle)
Random Matchup (Others)

LEVEL-UP MOVES

Lv.	Name	Type	Kind	Pow.	Acc.	PP	Range
1	Headbutt	Normal	Physical	70	100	15	Normal
1	Thunder Wave	Electric	Status	—	100	20	Normal
1	Spark	Electric	Physical	65	100	20	Normal
1	Charge Beam	Electric	Special	50	90	10	Normal
9	Bind	Normal	Physical	15	85	20	Normal
19	Acid	Poison	Special	40	100	30	Many Others
29	Discharge	Electric	Special	80	100	15	Adjacent
39	Crunch	Dark	Physical	80	100	15	Normal
44	Thunderbolt	Electric	Special	90	100	15	Normal
49	Acid Spray	Poison	Special	40	100	20	Normal
54	Coil	Poison	Status	—	—	20	Self
59	Wild Charge	Electric	Physical	90	100	15	Normal
64	Gastro Acid	Poison	Status	—	100	10	Normal
69	Zap Cannon	Electric	Special	120	50	5	Normal
74	Thrash	Normal	Physical	120	100	10	1 Random

TM & HM MOVES

No.	Name	Type	Kind	Pow.	Acc.	PP	Range
TM06	Toxic	Poison	Status	—	90	10	Normal
TM10	Hidden Power	Normal	Special	60	100	15	Normal
TM16	Light Screen	Psychic	Status	—	—	30	Your Side
TM17	Protect	Normal	Status	—	—	10	Self
TM18	Rain Dance	Water	Status	—	—	5	Both Sides
TM21	Frustration	Normal	Physical	—	100	20	Normal
TM24	Thunderbolt	Electric	Special	90	100	15	Normal
TM25	Thunder	Electric	Special	110	70	10	Normal
TM27	Return	Normal	Physical	—	100	20	Normal
TM32	Double Team	Normal	Status	—	—	15	Self
TM42	Facade	Normal	Physical	70	100	20	Normal
TM44	Rest	Psychic	Status	—	—	10	Self
TM45	Attract	Normal	Status	—	100	15	Normal
TM48	Round	Normal	Special	60	100	15	Normal
TM57	Charge Beam	Electric	Special	50	90	10	Normal
TM62	Acrobatics	Flying	Physical	55	100	15	Normal
TM70	Flash	Normal	Status	—	100	20	Normal
TM72	Volt Switch	Electric	Special	70	100	20	Normal
TM73	Thunder Wave	Electric	Status	—	100	20	Normal
TM87	Swagger	Normal	Status	—	90	15	Normal
TM88	Sleep Talk	Normal	Status	—	—	10	Self
TM89	U-turn	Bug	Physical	70	100	20	Normal
TM90	Substitute	Normal	Status	—	—	10	Self
TM91	Flash Cannon	Steel	Special	80	100	10	Normal
TM93	Wild Charge	Electric	Physical	90	100	15	Normal
TM94	Secret Power	Normal	Physical	70	100	20	Normal
TM100	Confide	Normal	Status	—	—	20	Normal

MOVES LEARNED IN EXCHANGE FOR BP

Name	Type	Kind	Pow.	Acc.	PP	Range
Super Fang	Normal	Physical	—	90	10	Normal
Signal Beam	Bug	Special	75	100	15	Normal
Bounce	Flying	Physical	85	85	5	Normal
Magnet Rise	Electric	Status	—	—	10	Self
Aqua Tail	Water	Physical	90	90	10	Normal
Iron Tail	Steel	Physical	100	75	15	Normal
Bind	Normal	Physical	15	85	20	Normal
Snore	Normal	Special	50	100	15	Normal
Knock Off	Dark	Physical	65	100	20	Normal
Giga Drain	Grass	Special	75	100	10	Normal
Shock Wave	Electric	Special	60	—	20	Normal
Gastro Acid	Poison	Status	—	100	10	Normal

MOVES TAUGHT BY PEOPLE

Name	Type	Kind	Pow.	Acc.	PP	Range

National Pokédex **604** Hoenn Pokédex —

Eelektross

EleFish Pokémon

Electric

HEIGHT: 6'11" WEIGHT: V 177.5 lbs.

Same form for ♂ / ♀

Ω With their sucker mouths, they suck in prey. Then they use their fangs to shock the prey with electricity.

α They crawl out of the ocean using their arms. They will attack prey on shore and immediately drag it into the ocean.

ABILITY
Levitate

HIDDEN ABILITY
—

EGG GROUPS
Amorphous

STAT GROWTH RATES
HP ▮▮▮
Attack ▮▮▮▮▮▮
Defense ▮▮▮▮
Sp. Atk ▮▮▮▮▮
Sp. Def ▮▮▮▮
Speed ▮▮▮

ITEMS SOMETIMES HELD BY WILD POKÉMON
—

EVOLUTION
Tynamo → Lv. 39 → Eelektrik → Thunder Stone → Eelektross

MAIN WAY TO REGISTER IN THE NATIONAL POKÉDEX

Use a Thunder Stone on Eelektrik.

Damage taken in normal battles

Type		Type	
Normal	×1	Flying	×0.5
Fire	×1	Psychic	×1
Water	×1	Bug	×1
Grass	×1	Rock	×1
Electric	×0.5	Ghost	×1
Ice	×1	Dragon	×1
Fighting	×1	Dark	×1
Poison	×1	Steel	×0.5
! Ground	×2	Fairy	×1

Damage taken in Inverse battles

Type		Type	
Normal	×1	Flying	×2
Fire	×1	Psychic	×1
Water	×1	Bug	×1
Grass	×1	Rock	×1
Electric	×2	Ghost	×1
Ice	×1	Dragon	×1
Fighting	×1	Dark	×1
Poison	×1	Steel	×2
! Ground	×0.5	Fairy	×1

Can be used in
Inverse Battle
Battle Institute
Battle Maison
Random Matchup (Free Battle)
Random Matchup (Others)

LEVEL-UP MOVES

Lv.	Name	Type	Kind	Pow.	Acc.	PP	Range
1	Thrash	Normal	Physical	120	100	10	1 Random
1	Zap Cannon	Electric	Special	120	50	5	Normal
1	Gastro Acid	Poison	Status	—	100	10	Normal
1	Coil	Poison	Status	—	—	20	Self
1	Ion Deluge	Electric	Status	—	—	25	Both Sides
1	Crush Claw	Normal	Physical	75	95	10	Normal
1	Headbutt	Normal	Physical	70	100	15	Normal
1	Acid	Poison	Special	40	100	30	Many Others
1	Discharge	Electric	Special	80	100	15	Adjacent
1	Crunch	Dark	Physical	80	100	15	Normal

TM & HM MOVES

No.	Name	Type	Kind	Pow.	Acc.	PP	Range
TM01	Hone Claws	Dark	Status	—	—	15	Self
TM02	Dragon Claw	Dragon	Physical	80	100	15	Normal
TM05	Roar	Normal	Status	—	—	20	Normal
TM06	Toxic	Poison	Status	—	90	10	Normal
TM10	Hidden Power	Normal	Special	60	100	15	Normal
TM15	Hyper Beam	Normal	Special	150	90	5	Normal
TM16	Light Screen	Psychic	Status	—	—	30	Your Side
TM17	Protect	Normal	Status	—	—	10	Self
TM18	Rain Dance	Water	Status	—	—	5	Both Sides
TM21	Frustration	Normal	Physical	—	100	20	Normal
TM24	Thunderbolt	Electric	Special	90	100	15	Normal
TM25	Thunder	Electric	Special	110	70	10	Normal
TM27	Return	Normal	Physical	—	100	20	Normal
TM31	Brick Break	Fighting	Physical	75	100	15	Normal
TM32	Double Team	Normal	Status	—	—	15	Self
TM35	Flamethrower	Fire	Special	90	100	15	Normal
TM39	Rock Tomb	Rock	Physical	60	95	15	Normal
TM42	Facade	Normal	Physical	70	100	20	Normal
TM44	Rest	Psychic	Status	—	—	10	Self
TM45	Attract	Normal	Status	—	100	15	Normal
TM48	Round	Normal	Special	60	100	15	Normal
TM57	Charge Beam	Electric	Special	50	90	10	Normal
TM62	Acrobatics	Flying	Physical	55	100	15	Normal
TM68	Giga Impact	Normal	Physical	150	90	5	Normal
TM70	Flash	Normal	Status	—	100	20	Normal
TM72	Volt Switch	Electric	Special	70	100	20	Normal
TM73	Thunder Wave	Electric	Status	—	100	20	Normal
TM80	Rock Slide	Rock	Physical	75	90	10	Many Others
TM82	Dragon Tail	Dragon	Physical	60	90	10	Normal
TM86	Grass Knot	Grass	Special	—	100	20	Normal
TM87	Swagger	Normal	Status	—	90	15	Normal
TM88	Sleep Talk	Normal	Status	—	—	10	Self
TM89	U-turn	Bug	Physical	70	100	20	Normal
TM90	Substitute	Normal	Status	—	—	10	Self
TM91	Flash Cannon	Steel	Special	80	100	10	Normal
TM93	Wild Charge	Electric	Physical	90	100	15	Normal
TM94	Secret Power	Normal	Physical	70	100	20	Normal
TM98	Power-Up Punch	Fighting	Physical	40	100	20	Normal
TM100	Confide	Normal	Status	—	—	20	Normal
HM01	Cut	Normal	Physical	50	95	30	Normal
HM04	Strength	Normal	Physical	80	100	15	Normal
HM06	Rock Smash	Fighting	Physical	40	100	15	Normal

MOVES LEARNED IN EXCHANGE FOR BP

Name	Type	Kind	Pow.	Acc.	PP	Range
Super Fang	Normal	Physical	—	90	10	Normal
Signal Beam	Bug	Special	75	100	15	Normal
Bounce	Flying	Physical	85	85	5	Normal
Thunder Punch	Electric	Physical	75	100	15	Normal
Fire Punch	Fire	Physical	75	100	15	Normal
Magnet Rise	Electric	Status	—	—	10	Self
Superpower	Fighting	Physical	120	100	5	Normal
Aqua Tail	Water	Physical	90	90	10	Normal
Dragon Pulse	Dragon	Special	85	100	10	Normal
Iron Tail	Steel	Physical	100	75	15	Normal
Bind	Normal	Physical	15	85	20	Normal
Snore	Normal	Special	50	100	15	Normal
Knock Off	Dark	Physical	65	100	20	Normal
Giga Drain	Grass	Special	75	100	10	Normal
Drain Punch	Fighting	Physical	75	100	10	Normal
Focus Punch	Fighting	Physical	150	100	20	Normal
Shock Wave	Electric	Special	60	—	20	Normal
Gastro Acid	Poison	Status	—	100	10	Normal
Outrage	Dragon	Physical	120	100	10	1 Random

MOVES TAUGHT BY PEOPLE

Name	Type	Kind	Pow.	Acc.	PP	Range

National Pokédex **605** Hoenn Pokédex —

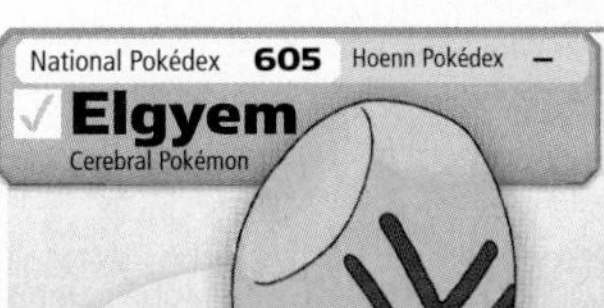

Elgyem

Cerebral Pokémon

Psychic

HEIGHT: 1'08" WEIGHT: 19.8 lbs.

Same form for ♂ / ♀

Ω It uses its strong psychic power to squeeze its opponent's brain, causing unendurable headaches.

α Rumors of its origin are linked to a UFO crash site in the desert 50 years ago.

ABILITIES
Telepathy
Synchronize

HIDDEN ABILITY
Analytic

EGG GROUPS
Human-Like

STAT GROWTH RATES
HP ▮▮
Attack ▮▮▮
Defense ▮▮▮
Sp. Atk ▮▮▮▮
Sp. Def ▮▮▮
Speed ▮▮

ITEMS SOMETIMES HELD BY WILD POKÉMON
—

EVOLUTION
Elgyem → Lv. 42 → Beheeyem

MAIN WAY TO REGISTER IN THE NATIONAL POKÉDEX

Catch on Route 121. Appears as a hidden Pokémon after you battle Groudon or Kyogre.

Damage taken in normal battles

Type		Type	
Normal	×1	Flying	×1
Fire	×1	Psychic	×0.5
Water	×1	Bug	×2
Grass	×1	Rock	×1
Electric	×1	Ghost	×2
Ice	×1	Dragon	×1
Fighting	×0.5	Dark	×2
Poison	×1	Steel	×1
Ground	×1	Fairy	×1

Damage taken in Inverse battles

Type		Type	
Normal	×1	Flying	×1
Fire	×1	Psychic	×2
Water	×1	Bug	×0.5
Grass	×1	Rock	×1
Electric	×1	Ghost	×0.5
Ice	×1	Dragon	×1
Fighting	×2	Dark	×0.5
Poison	×1	Steel	×1
Ground	×1	Fairy	×1

Can be used in
Inverse Battle
Battle Institute
Battle Maison
Random Matchup (Free Battle)
Random Matchup (Others)

LEVEL-UP MOVES

Lv.	Name	Type	Kind	Pow.	Acc.	PP	Range
1	Confusion	Psychic	Special	50	100	25	Normal
4	Growl	Normal	Status	—	100	40	Many Others
8	Heal Block	Psychic	Status	—	100	15	Many Others
11	Miracle Eye	Psychic	Status	—	—	40	Normal
15	Psybeam	Psychic	Special	65	100	20	Normal
18	Headbutt	Normal	Physical	70	100	15	Normal
22	Hidden Power	Normal	Special	60	100	15	Normal
25	Imprison	Psychic	Status	—	—	10	Self
29	Simple Beam	Normal	Status	—	100	15	Normal
32	Zen Headbutt	Psychic	Physical	80	90	15	Normal
36	Psych Up	Normal	Status	—	—	10	Normal
39	Psychic	Psychic	Special	90	100	10	Normal
43	Calm Mind	Psychic	Status	—	—	20	Self
46	Recover	Normal	Status	—	—	10	Self
50	Guard Split	Psychic	Status	—	—	10	Normal
50	Power Split	Psychic	Status	—	—	10	Normal
53	Synchronoise	Psychic	Special	120	100	10	Adjacent
56	Wonder Room	Psychic	Status	—	—	10	Both Sides

TM & HM MOVES

No.	Name	Type	Kind	Pow.	Acc.	PP	Range
TM03	Psyshock	Psychic	Special	80	100	10	Normal
TM04	Calm Mind	Psychic	Status	—	—	20	Self
TM06	Toxic	Poison	Status	—	90	10	Normal
TM10	Hidden Power	Normal	Special	60	100	15	Normal
TM16	Light Screen	Psychic	Status	—	—	30	Your Side
TM17	Protect	Normal	Status	—	—	10	Self
TM18	Rain Dance	Water	Status	—	—	5	Both Sides
TM20	Safeguard	Normal	Status	—	—	25	Your Side
TM21	Frustration	Normal	Physical	—	100	20	Normal
TM24	Thunderbolt	Electric	Special	90	100	15	Normal
TM27	Return	Normal	Physical	—	100	20	Normal
TM29	Psychic	Psychic	Special	90	100	10	Normal
TM30	Shadow Ball	Ghost	Special	80	100	15	Normal
TM32	Double Team	Normal	Status	—	—	15	Self
TM33	Reflect	Psychic	Status	—	—	20	Your Side
TM39	Rock Tomb	Rock	Physical	60	95	15	Normal
TM42	Facade	Normal	Physical	70	100	20	Normal
TM44	Rest	Psychic	Status	—	—	10	Self
TM45	Attract	Normal	Status	—	100	15	Normal
TM46	Thief	Dark	Physical	60	100	25	Normal
TM48	Round	Normal	Special	60	100	15	Normal
TM49	Echoed Voice	Normal	Special	40	100	15	Normal
TM51	Steel Wing	Steel	Physical	70	90	25	Normal
TM53	Energy Ball	Grass	Special	90	100	10	Normal
TM57	Charge Beam	Electric	Special	50	90	10	Normal
TM63	Embargo	Dark	Status	—	100	15	Normal
TM70	Flash	Normal	Status	—	100	20	Normal
TM73	Thunder Wave	Electric	Status	—	100	20	Normal
TM77	Psych Up	Normal	Status	—	—	10	Normal
TM80	Rock Slide	Rock	Physical	75	90	10	Many Others
TM85	Dream Eater	Psychic	Special	100	100	15	Normal
TM87	Swagger	Normal	Status	—	90	15	Normal
TM88	Sleep Talk	Normal	Status	—	—	10	Self
TM90	Substitute	Normal	Status	—	—	10	Self
TM92	Trick Room	Psychic	Status	—	—	5	Both Sides
TM94	Secret Power	Normal	Physical	70	100	20	Normal
TM97	Dark Pulse	Dark	Special	80	100	15	Normal
TM100	Confide	Normal	Status	—	—	20	Normal

MOVES LEARNED IN EXCHANGE FOR BP

Name	Type	Kind	Pow.	Acc.	PP	Range
Signal Beam	Bug	Special	75	100	15	Normal
Uproar	Normal	Special	90	100	10	1 Random
Magic Coat	Psychic	Status	—	—	15	Self
Gravity	Psychic	Status	—	—	5	Both Sides
Zen Headbutt	Psychic	Physical	80	90	15	Normal
Snore	Normal	Special	50	100	15	Normal
Role Play	Psychic	Status	—	—	10	Normal
Pain Split	Normal	Status	—	—	20	Normal
Shock Wave	Electric	Special	60	—	20	Normal
After You	Normal	Status	—	—	15	Normal
Trick	Psychic	Status	—	100	10	Normal
Wonder Room	Psychic	Status	—	—	10	Both Sides
Recycle	Normal	Status	—	—	10	Self
Snatch	Dark	Status	—	—	10	Self
Skill Swap	Psychic	Status	—	—	10	Normal

MOVES TAUGHT BY PEOPLE

Name	Type	Kind	Pow.	Acc.	PP	Range

EGG MOVES

Name	Type	Kind	Pow.	Acc.	PP	Range
Teleport	Psychic	Status	—	—	20	Self
Disable	Normal	Status	—	100	20	Normal
Astonish	Ghost	Physical	30	100	15	Normal
Power Swap	Psychic	Status	—	—	10	Normal
Guard Swap	Psychic	Status	—	—	10	Normal
Barrier	Psychic	Status	—	—	20	Self
Nasty Plot	Dark	Status	—	—	20	Self
Skill Swap	Psychic	Status	—	—	10	Normal
Cosmic Power	Psychic	Status	—	—	20	Self
Ally Switch	Psychic	Status	—	—	15	Self

National Pokédex **606** Hoenn Pokédex —

Beheeyem

Cerebral Pokémon

Psychic

HEIGHT: 3'03" WEIGHT: 76.1 lbs.

Same form for ♂ / ♀

Ω Apparently, it communicates by flashing its three fingers, but those patterns haven't been decoded.

α It uses psychic power to control an opponent's brain and tamper with its memories.

ABILITIES
Telepathy
Synchronize

HIDDEN ABILITY
Analytic

EGG GROUPS
Human-Like

STAT GROWTH RATES
HP
Attack
Defense
Sp. Atk
Sp. Def
Speed

ITEMS SOMETIMES HELD BY WILD POKÉMON
—

EVOLUTION

Elgyem

Lv. 42

Beheeyem

MAIN WAY TO REGISTER IN THE NATIONAL POKÉDEX

Level up Elgyem to Lv. 42.

Damage taken in normal battles

Type		Type	
Normal	×1	Flying	×1
Fire	×1	Psychic	×0.5
Water	×1	Bug	×2
Grass	×1	Rock	×1
Electric	×1	Ghost	×2
Ice	×1	Dragon	×1
Fighting	×0.5	Dark	×2
Poison	×1	Steel	×1
Ground	×1	Fairy	×1

Damage taken in Inverse battles

Type		Type	
Normal	×1	Flying	×1
Fire	×1	Psychic	×2
Water	×1	Bug	×0.5
Grass	×1	Rock	×1
Electric	×1	Ghost	×0.5
Ice	×1	Dragon	×1
Fighting	×2	Dark	×0.5
Poison	×1	Steel	×1
Ground	×1	Fairy	×1

Can be used in
Inverse Battle
Battle Institute
Battle Maison
Random Matchup (Free Battle)
Random Matchup (Others)

LEVEL-UP MOVES

Lv.	Name	Type	Kind	Pow.	Acc.	PP	Range
1	Wonder Room	Psychic	Status	—	—	10	Both Sides
1	Synchronoise	Psychic	Special	120	100	10	Adjacent
1	Confusion	Psychic	Special	50	100	25	Normal
1	Growl	Normal	Status	—	100	40	Many Others
1	Heal Block	Psychic	Status	—	100	15	Many Others
1	Miracle Eye	Psychic	Status	—	—	40	Normal
4	Growl	Normal	Status	—	100	40	Many Others
8	Heal Block	Psychic	Status	—	100	15	Many Others
11	Miracle Eye	Psychic	Status	—	—	40	Normal
15	Psybeam	Psychic	Special	65	100	20	Normal
18	Headbutt	Normal	Physical	70	100	15	Normal
22	Hidden Power	Normal	Special	60	100	15	Normal
25	Imprison	Psychic	Status	—	—	10	Self
29	Simple Beam	Normal	Status	—	100	15	Normal
32	Zen Headbutt	Psychic	Physical	80	90	15	Normal
36	Psych Up	Normal	Status	—	—	10	Normal
39	Psychic	Psychic	Special	90	100	10	Normal
45	Calm Mind	Psychic	Status	—	—	20	Self
50	Recover	Normal	Status	—	—	10	Self
56	Guard Split	Psychic	Status	—	—	10	Normal
58	Power Split	Psychic	Status	—	—	10	Normal
63	Synchronoise	Psychic	Special	120	100	10	Adjacent
68	Wonder Room	Psychic	Status	—	—	10	Both Sides

TM & HM MOVES

No.	Name	Type	Kind	Pow.	Acc.	PP	Range
TM03	Psyshock	Psychic	Special	80	100	10	Normal
TM04	Calm Mind	Psychic	Status	—	—	20	Self
TM06	Toxic	Poison	Status	—	90	10	Normal
TM10	Hidden Power	Normal	Special	60	100	15	Normal
TM15	Hyper Beam	Normal	Special	150	90	5	Normal
TM16	Light Screen	Psychic	Status	—	—	30	Your Side
TM17	Protect	Normal	Status	—	—	10	Self
TM18	Rain Dance	Water	Status	—	—	5	Both Sides
TM20	Safeguard	Normal	Status	—	—	25	Your Side
TM21	Frustration	Normal	Physical	—	100	20	Normal
TM24	Thunderbolt	Electric	Special	90	100	15	Normal
TM27	Return	Normal	Physical	—	100	20	Normal
TM29	Psychic	Psychic	Special	90	100	10	Normal
TM30	Shadow Ball	Ghost	Special	80	100	15	Normal
TM32	Double Team	Normal	Status	—	—	15	Self
TM33	Reflect	Psychic	Status	—	—	20	Your Side
TM39	Rock Tomb	Rock	Physical	60	95	15	Normal
TM42	Facade	Normal	Physical	70	100	20	Normal
TM44	Rest	Psychic	Status	—	—	10	Self
TM45	Attract	Normal	Status	—	100	15	Normal
TM46	Thief	Dark	Physical	60	100	25	Normal
TM48	Round	Normal	Special	60	100	15	Normal
TM49	Echoed Voice	Normal	Special	40	100	15	Normal
TM51	Steel Wing	Steel	Physical	70	90	25	Normal
TM53	Energy Ball	Grass	Special	90	100	10	Normal
TM57	Charge Beam	Electric	Special	50	90	10	Normal
TM63	Embargo	Dark	Status	—	100	15	Normal
TM68	Giga Impact	Normal	Physical	150	90	5	Normal
TM70	Flash	Normal	Status	—	100	20	Normal
TM73	Thunder Wave	Electric	Status	—	100	20	Normal
TM77	Psych Up	Normal	Status	—	—	10	Normal
TM80	Rock Slide	Rock	Physical	75	90	10	Many Others
TM85	Dream Eater	Psychic	Special	100	100	15	Normal
TM87	Swagger	Normal	Status	—	90	15	Normal
TM88	Sleep Talk	Normal	Status	—	—	10	Self
TM90	Substitute	Normal	Status	—	—	10	Self
TM92	Trick Room	Psychic	Status	—	—	5	Both Sides
TM94	Secret Power	Normal	Physical	70	100	20	Normal
TM97	Dark Pulse	Dark	Special	80	100	15	Normal
TM100	Confide	Normal	Status	—	—	20	Normal

MOVES LEARNED IN EXCHANGE FOR BP

Name	Type	Kind	Pow.	Acc.	PP	Range
Signal Beam	Bug	Special	75	100	15	Normal
Uproar	Normal	Special	90	100	10	1 Random
Magic Coat	Psychic	Status	—	—	15	Self
Gravity	Psychic	Status	—	—	5	Both Sides
Zen Headbutt	Psychic	Physical	80	90	15	Normal
Snore	Normal	Special	50	100	15	Normal
Role Play	Psychic	Status	—	—	10	Normal
Pain Split	Normal	Status	—	—	20	Normal
Shock Wave	Electric	Special	60	—	20	Normal
After You	Normal	Status	—	—	15	Normal
Trick	Psychic	Status	—	100	10	Normal
Wonder Room	Psychic	Status	—	—	10	Both Sides
Recycle	Normal	Status	—	—	10	Self
Snatch	Dark	Status	—	—	10	Self
Skill Swap	Psychic	Status	—	—	10	Normal

MOVES TAUGHT BY PEOPLE

Name	Type	Kind	Pow.	Acc.	PP	Range

National Pokédex **607** Hoenn Pokédex —

Litwick

Candle Pokémon

Ghost **Fire**

HEIGHT: 1'00" WEIGHT: 6.8 lbs.

Same form for ♂ / ♀

Ω While shining a light and pretending to be a guide, it leeches off the life force of any who follow it.

α Litwick shines a light that absorbs the life energy of people and Pokémon, which becomes the fuel that it burns.

ABILITIES
Flash Fire
Flame Body

HIDDEN ABILITY
Infiltrator

EGG GROUPS
Amorphous

STAT GROWTH RATES
HP
Attack
Defense
Sp. Atk
Sp. Def
Speed

ITEMS SOMETIMES HELD BY WILD POKÉMON
—

EVOLUTION

Litwick → Lv. 41 → Lampent → Dusk Stone → Chandelure

MAIN WAY TO REGISTER IN THE NATIONAL POKÉDEX

Appears in *Pokémon X* and *Pokémon Y*. Bring it to your game using Link Trade or the GTS.

Damage taken in normal battles

Type		Type	
Normal	×0	Flying	×1
Fire	×0.5	Psychic	×1
Water	×2	Bug	×0.25
Grass	×0.5	Rock	×2
Electric	×1	Ghost	×2
Ice	×0.5	Dragon	×1
Fighting	×0	Dark	×2
Poison	×0.5	Steel	×0.5
Ground	×2	Fairy	×0.5

Damage taken in Inverse battles

Type		Type	
Normal	×2	Flying	×1
Fire	×2	Psychic	×1
Water	×0.5	Bug	×4
Grass	×2	Rock	×0.5
Electric	×1	Ghost	×0.5
Ice	×2	Dragon	×1
Fighting	×2	Dark	×0.5
Poison	×2	Steel	×2
Ground	×0.5	Fairy	×2

Can be used in
Inverse Battle
Battle Institute
Battle Maison
Random Matchup (Free Battle)
Random Matchup (Others)

LEVEL-UP MOVES

Lv.	Name	Type	Kind	Pow.	Acc.	PP	Range
1	Ember	Fire	Special	40	100	25	Normal
1	Astonish	Ghost	Physical	30	100	15	Normal
3	Minimize	Normal	Status	—	—	10	Self
5	Smog	Poison	Special	30	70	20	Normal
7	Fire Spin	Fire	Special	35	85	15	Normal
10	Confuse Ray	Ghost	Status	—	100	10	Normal
13	Night Shade	Ghost	Special	—	100	15	Normal
16	Will-O-Wisp	Fire	Status	—	85	15	Normal
20	Flame Burst	Fire	Special	70	100	15	Normal
24	Imprison	Psychic	Status	—	—	10	Self
28	Hex	Ghost	Special	65	100	10	Normal
33	Memento	Dark	Status	—	100	10	Normal
38	Inferno	Fire	Special	100	50	5	Normal
43	Curse	Ghost	Status	—	—	10	Varies
49	Shadow Ball	Ghost	Special	80	100	15	Normal
55	Pain Split	Normal	Status	—	—	20	Normal
61	Overheat	Fire	Special	130	90	5	Normal

TM & HM MOVES

No.	Name	Type	Kind	Pow.	Acc.	PP	Range
TM04	Calm Mind	Psychic	Status	—	—	20	Self
TM06	Toxic	Poison	Status	—	90	10	Normal
TM10	Hidden Power	Normal	Special	60	100	15	Normal
TM11	Sunny Day	Fire	Status	—	—	5	Both Sides
TM12	Taunt	Dark	Status	—	100	20	Normal
TM17	Protect	Normal	Status	—	—	10	Self
TM20	Safeguard	Normal	Status	—	—	25	Your Side
TM21	Frustration	Normal	Physical	—	100	20	Normal
TM22	Solar Beam	Grass	Special	120	100	10	Normal
TM27	Return	Normal	Physical	—	100	20	Normal
TM29	Psychic	Psychic	Special	90	100	10	Normal
TM30	Shadow Ball	Ghost	Special	80	100	15	Normal
TM32	Double Team	Normal	Status	—	—	15	Self
TM35	Flamethrower	Fire	Special	90	100	15	Normal
TM38	Fire Blast	Fire	Special	110	85	5	Normal
TM42	Facade	Normal	Physical	70	100	20	Normal
TM43	Flame Charge	Fire	Physical	50	100	20	Normal
TM44	Rest	Psychic	Status	—	—	10	Self
TM45	Attract	Normal	Status	—	100	15	Normal
TM46	Thief	Dark	Physical	60	100	25	Normal
TM48	Round	Normal	Special	60	100	15	Normal
TM50	Overheat	Fire	Special	130	90	5	Normal
TM53	Energy Ball	Grass	Special	90	100	10	Normal
TM59	Incinerate	Fire	Special	60	100	15	Many Others
TM61	Will-O-Wisp	Fire	Status	—	85	15	Normal
TM63	Embargo	Dark	Status	—	100	15	Normal
TM66	Payback	Dark	Physical	50	100	10	Normal
TM70	Flash	Normal	Status	—	100	20	Normal
TM77	Psych Up	Normal	Status	—	—	10	Normal
TM85	Dream Eater	Psychic	Special	100	100	15	Normal
TM87	Swagger	Normal	Status	—	90	15	Normal
TM88	Sleep Talk	Normal	Status	—	—	10	Self
TM90	Substitute	Normal	Status	—	—	10	Self
TM92	Trick Room	Psychic	Status	—	—	5	Both Sides
TM94	Secret Power	Normal	Physical	70	100	20	Normal
TM97	Dark Pulse	Dark	Special	80	100	15	Normal
TM100	Confide	Normal	Status	—	—	20	Normal

MOVES LEARNED IN EXCHANGE FOR BP

Name	Type	Kind	Pow.	Acc.	PP	Range
Snore	Normal	Special	50	100	15	Normal
Heat Wave	Fire	Special	95	90	10	Many Others
Pain Split	Normal	Status	—	—	20	Normal
Shock Wave	Electric	Special	60	—	20	Normal
Spite	Ghost	Status	—	100	10	Normal
Trick	Psychic	Status	—	100	10	Normal

MOVES TAUGHT BY PEOPLE

Name	Type	Kind	Pow.	Acc.	PP	Range

EGG MOVES

Name	Type	Kind	Pow.	Acc.	PP	Range
Acid Armor	Poison	Status	—	—	20	Self
Heat Wave	Fire	Special	95	90	10	Many Others
Haze	Ice	Status	—	—	30	Both Sides
Endure	Normal	Status	—	—	10	Self
Captivate	Normal	Status	—	100	20	Many Others
Acid	Poison	Special	40	100	30	Many Others
Clear Smog	Poison	Special	50	—	15	Normal
Power Split	Psychic	Status	—	—	10	Normal

National Pokédex **608** Hoenn Pokédex —

✓ Lampent

Lamp Pokémon

Ghost | Fire

HEIGHT: 2'00" WEIGHT: 28.7 lbs.

Same form for ♂ / ♀

Ω The spirits it absorbs fuel its baleful fire. It hangs around hospitals waiting for people to pass on.

α It arrives near the moment of death and steals spirit from the body.

ABILITIES
Flash Fire
Flame Body

HIDDEN ABILITY
Infiltrator

EGG GROUPS
Amorphous

STAT GROWTH RATES
HP
Attack
Defense
Sp. Atk
Sp. Def
Speed

ITEMS SOMETIMES HELD BY WILD POKÉMON
—

EVOLUTION

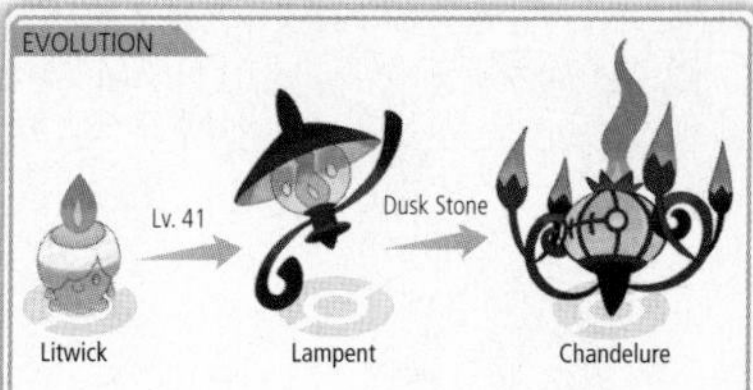

MAIN WAY TO REGISTER IN THE NATIONAL POKÉDEX

Level up a Litwick obtained via Link Trade or the GTS to Lv. 41.

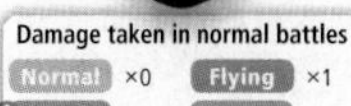

Damage taken in normal battles

Type		Type	
Normal	×0	Flying	×1
Fire	×0.5	Psychic	×1
Water	×2	Bug	×0.25
Grass	×0.5	Rock	×2
Electric	×1	Ghost	×2
Ice	×0.5	Dragon	×1
Fighting	×0	Dark	×2
Poison	×0.5	Steel	×0.5
Ground	×2	Fairy	×0.5

Damage taken in Inverse battles

Type		Type	
Normal	×2	Flying	×1
Fire	×2	Psychic	×1
Water	×0.5	Bug	×4
Grass	×2	Rock	×0.5
Electric	×1	Ghost	×0.5
Ice	×2	Dragon	×1
Fighting	×2	Dark	×0.5
Poison	×2	Steel	×2
Ground	×0.5	Fairy	×2

Can be used in
Inverse Battle
Battle Institute
Battle Maison
Random Matchup (Free Battle)
Random Matchup (Others)

LEVEL-UP MOVES

Lv.	Name	Type	Kind	Pow.	Acc.	PP	Range
1	Ember	Fire	Special	40	100	25	Normal
1	Astonish	Ghost	Physical	30	100	15	Normal
1	Minimize	Normal	Status	—	—	10	Self
1	Smog	Poison	Special	30	70	20	Normal
3	Minimize	Normal	Status	—	—	10	Self
5	Smog	Poison	Special	30	70	20	Normal
7	Fire Spin	Fire	Special	35	85	15	Normal
10	Confuse Ray	Ghost	Status	—	100	10	Normal
13	Night Shade	Ghost	Special	—	100	15	Normal
16	Will-O-Wisp	Fire	Status	—	85	15	Normal
20	Flame Burst	Fire	Special	70	100	15	Normal
24	Imprison	Psychic	Status	—	—	10	Self
28	Hex	Ghost	Special	65	100	10	Normal
33	Memento	Dark	Status	—	100	10	Normal
38	Inferno	Fire	Special	100	50	5	Normal
45	Curse	Ghost	Status	—	—	10	Varies
53	Shadow Ball	Ghost	Special	80	100	15	Normal
61	Pain Split	Normal	Status	—	—	20	Normal
69	Overheat	Fire	Special	130	90	5	Normal

TM & HM MOVES

No.	Name	Type	Kind	Pow.	Acc.	PP	Range
TM04	Calm Mind	Psychic	Status	—	—	20	Self
TM06	Toxic	Poison	Status	—	90	10	Normal
TM10	Hidden Power	Normal	Special	60	100	15	Normal
TM11	Sunny Day	Fire	Status	—	—	5	Both Sides
TM12	Taunt	Dark	Status	—	100	20	Normal
TM17	Protect	Normal	Status	—	—	10	Self
TM20	Safeguard	Normal	Status	—	—	25	Your Side
TM21	Frustration	Normal	Physical	—	100	20	Normal
TM22	Solar Beam	Grass	Special	120	100	10	Normal
TM27	Return	Normal	Physical	—	100	20	Normal
TM29	Psychic	Psychic	Special	90	100	10	Normal
TM30	Shadow Ball	Ghost	Special	80	100	15	Normal
TM32	Double Team	Normal	Status	—	—	15	Self
TM35	Flamethrower	Fire	Special	90	100	15	Normal
TM38	Fire Blast	Fire	Special	110	85	5	Normal
TM42	Facade	Normal	Physical	70	100	20	Normal
TM43	Flame Charge	Fire	Physical	50	100	20	Normal
TM44	Rest	Psychic	Status	—	—	10	Self
TM45	Attract	Normal	Status	—	100	15	Normal
TM46	Thief	Dark	Physical	60	100	25	Normal
TM48	Round	Normal	Special	60	100	15	Normal
TM50	Overheat	Fire	Special	130	90	5	Normal
TM53	Energy Ball	Grass	Special	90	100	10	Normal
TM59	Incinerate	Fire	Special	60	100	15	Many Others
TM61	Will-O-Wisp	Fire	Status	—	85	15	Normal
TM63	Embargo	Dark	Status	—	100	15	Normal
TM66	Payback	Dark	Physical	50	100	10	Normal
TM70	Flash	Normal	Status	—	100	20	Normal
TM77	Psych Up	Normal	Status	—	—	10	Normal
TM85	Dream Eater	Psychic	Special	100	100	15	Normal
TM87	Swagger	Normal	Status	—	90	15	Normal
TM88	Sleep Talk	Normal	Status	—	—	10	Self
TM90	Substitute	Normal	Status	—	—	10	Self
TM92	Trick Room	Psychic	Status	—	—	5	Both Sides
TM94	Secret Power	Normal	Physical	70	100	20	Normal
TM97	Dark Pulse	Dark	Special	80	100	15	Normal
TM100	Confide	Normal	Status	—	—	20	Normal

MOVES LEARNED IN EXCHANGE FOR BP

Name	Type	Kind	Pow.	Acc.	PP	Range
Snore	Normal	Special	50	100	15	Normal
Heat Wave	Fire	Special	95	90	10	Many Others
Pain Split	Normal	Status	—	—	20	Normal
Shock Wave	Electric	Special	60	—	20	Normal
Spite	Ghost	Status	—	100	10	Normal
Trick	Psychic	Status	—	100	10	Normal

MOVES TAUGHT BY PEOPLE

Name	Type	Kind	Pow.	Acc.	PP	Range

National Pokédex **609** Hoenn Pokédex —

✓ Chandelure

Luring Pokémon

Ghost | Fire

HEIGHT: 3'03" WEIGHT: 75.6 lbs.

Same form for ♂ / ♀

Ω Being consumed in Chandelure's flame burns up the spirit, leaving the body behind.

α The spirits burned up in its ominous flame lose their way and wander this world forever.

ABILITIES
Flash Fire
Flame Body

HIDDEN ABILITY
Infiltrator

EGG GROUPS
Amorphous

STAT GROWTH RATES
HP
Attack
Defense
Sp. Atk
Sp. Def
Speed

ITEMS SOMETIMES HELD BY WILD POKÉMON
—

EVOLUTION

Litwick
Lv. 41
Lampent
Dusk Stone
Chandelure

MAIN WAY TO REGISTER IN THE NATIONAL POKÉDEX

Use a Dusk Stone on a Lampent obtained via Link Trade or the GTS.

Damage taken in normal battles

Type		Type	
Normal	×0	Flying	×1
Fire	×0.5	Psychic	×1
Water	×2	Bug	×0.25
Grass	×0.5	Rock	×2
Electric	×1	Ghost	×2
Ice	×0.5	Dragon	×1
Fighting	×0	Dark	×2
Poison	×0.5	Steel	×0.5
Ground	×2	Fairy	×0.5

Damage taken in Inverse battles

Type		Type	
Normal	×2	Flying	×1
Fire	×2	Psychic	×1
Water	×0.5	Bug	×4
Grass	×2	Rock	×0.5
Electric	×1	Ghost	×0.5
Ice	×2	Dragon	×1
Fighting	×2	Dark	×0.5
Poison	×2	Steel	×2
Ground	×0.5	Fairy	×2

Can be used in
Inverse Battle
Battle Institute
Battle Maison
Random Matchup (Free Battle)
Random Matchup (Others)

LEVEL-UP MOVES

Lv.	Name	Type	Kind	Pow.	Acc.	PP	Range
1	Pain Split	Normal	Status	—	—	20	Normal
1	Smog	Poison	Special	30	70	20	Normal
1	Confuse Ray	Ghost	Status	—	100	10	Normal
1	Flame Burst	Fire	Special	70	100	15	Normal
1	Hex	Ghost	Special	65	100	10	Normal

TM & HM MOVES

No.	Name	Type	Kind	Pow.	Acc.	PP	Range
TM04	Calm Mind	Psychic	Status	—	—	20	Self
TM06	Toxic	Poison	Status	—	90	10	Normal
TM10	Hidden Power	Normal	Special	60	100	15	Normal
TM11	Sunny Day	Fire	Status	—	—	5	Both Sides
TM12	Taunt	Dark	Status	—	100	20	Normal
TM15	Hyper Beam	Normal	Special	150	90	5	Normal
TM17	Protect	Normal	Status	—	—	10	Self
TM20	Safeguard	Normal	Status	—	—	25	Your Side
TM21	Frustration	Normal	Physical	—	100	20	Normal
TM22	Solar Beam	Grass	Special	120	100	10	Normal
TM27	Return	Normal	Physical	—	100	20	Normal
TM29	Psychic	Psychic	Special	90	100	10	Normal
TM30	Shadow Ball	Ghost	Special	80	100	15	Normal
TM32	Double Team	Normal	Status	—	—	15	Self
TM35	Flamethrower	Fire	Special	90	100	15	Normal
TM38	Fire Blast	Fire	Special	110	85	5	Normal
TM42	Facade	Normal	Physical	70	100	20	Normal
TM43	Flame Charge	Fire	Physical	50	100	20	Normal
TM44	Rest	Psychic	Status	—	—	10	Self
TM45	Attract	Normal	Status	—	100	15	Normal
TM46	Thief	Dark	Physical	60	100	25	Normal
TM48	Round	Normal	Special	60	100	15	Normal
TM50	Overheat	Fire	Special	130	90	5	Normal
TM53	Energy Ball	Grass	Special	90	100	10	Normal
TM59	Incinerate	Fire	Special	60	100	15	Many Others
TM61	Will-O-Wisp	Fire	Status	—	85	15	Normal
TM63	Embargo	Dark	Status	—	100	15	Normal
TM66	Payback	Dark	Physical	50	100	10	Normal
TM68	Giga Impact	Normal	Physical	150	90	5	Normal
TM70	Flash	Normal	Status	—	100	20	Normal
TM77	Psych Up	Normal	Status	—	—	10	Normal
TM85	Dream Eater	Psychic	Special	100	100	15	Normal
TM87	Swagger	Normal	Status	—	90	15	Normal
TM88	Sleep Talk	Normal	Status	—	—	10	Self
TM90	Substitute	Normal	Status	—	—	10	Self
TM92	Trick Room	Psychic	Status	—	—	5	Both Sides
TM94	Secret Power	Normal	Physical	70	100	20	Normal
TM97	Dark Pulse	Dark	Special	80	100	15	Normal
TM100	Confide	Normal	Status	—	—	20	Normal

MOVES LEARNED IN EXCHANGE FOR BP

Name	Type	Kind	Pow.	Acc.	PP	Range
Snore	Normal	Special	50	100	15	Normal
Heat Wave	Fire	Special	95	90	10	Many Others
Pain Split	Normal	Status	—	—	20	Normal
Shock Wave	Electric	Special	60	—	20	Normal
Spite	Ghost	Status	—	100	10	Normal
Trick	Psychic	Status	—	100	10	Normal

MOVES TAUGHT BY PEOPLE

Name	Type	Kind	Pow.	Acc.	PP	Range

National Pokédex **610** Hoenn Pokédex —

Axew

Tusk Pokémon

Dragon

HEIGHT: 2'00" WEIGHT: 39.7 lbs.

Same form for ♂ / ♀

Ω They use their tusks to crush the berries they eat. Repeated regrowth makes their tusks strong and sharp.

α They mark their territory by leaving gashes in trees with their tusks. If a tusk breaks, a new one grows in quickly.

ABILITIES
Rivalry
Mold Breaker

HIDDEN ABILITY
Unnerve

EGG GROUPS
Monster / Dragon

STAT GROWTH RATES
HP
Attack
Defense
Sp. Atk
Sp. Def
Speed

ITEMS SOMETIMES HELD BY WILD POKÉMON
—

EVOLUTION

MAIN WAY TO REGISTER IN THE NATIONAL POKÉDEX

Catch in Granite Cave (1F). Appears as a hidden Pokémon after you battle Groudon or Kyogre.

Damage taken in normal battles

Type		Type	
Normal	×1	Flying	×1
Fire	×0.5	Psychic	×1
Water	×0.5	Bug	×1
Grass	×0.5	Rock	×1
Electric	×0.5	Ghost	×1
Ice	×2	Dragon	×2
Fighting	×1	Dark	×1
Poison	×1	Steel	×1
Ground	×1	Fairy	×2

Damage taken in Inverse battles

Type		Type	
Normal	×1	Flying	×1
Fire	×2	Psychic	×1
Water	×2	Bug	×1
Grass	×2	Rock	×1
Electric	×2	Ghost	×1
Ice	×0.5	Dragon	×0.5
Fighting	×1	Dark	×1
Poison	×1	Steel	×1
Ground	×1	Fairy	×0.5

Can be used in
Inverse Battle
Battle Institute
Battle Maison
Random Matchup (Free Battle)
Random Matchup (Others)

LEVEL-UP MOVES

Lv.	Name	Type	Kind	Pow.	Acc.	PP	Range
1	Scratch	Normal	Physical	40	100	35	Normal
4	Leer	Normal	Status	—	100	30	Many Others
7	Assurance	Dark	Physical	60	100	10	Normal
10	Dragon Rage	Dragon	Special	—	100	10	Normal
13	Dual Chop	Dragon	Physical	40	90	15	Normal
16	Scary Face	Normal	Status	—	100	10	Normal
20	Slash	Normal	Physical	70	100	20	Normal
24	False Swipe	Normal	Physical	40	100	40	Normal
28	Dragon Claw	Dragon	Physical	80	100	15	Normal
32	Dragon Dance	Dragon	Status	—	—	20	Self
36	Taunt	Dark	Status	—	100	20	Normal
41	Dragon Pulse	Dragon	Special	85	100	10	Normal
46	Swords Dance	Normal	Status	—	—	20	Self
50	Guillotine	Normal	Physical	—	30	5	Normal
56	Outrage	Dragon	Physical	120	100	10	1 Random
61	Giga Impact	Normal	Physical	150	90	5	Normal

TM & HM MOVES

No.	Name	Type	Kind	Pow.	Acc.	PP	Range
TM01	Hone Claws	Dark	Status	—	—	15	Self
TM02	Dragon Claw	Dragon	Physical	80	100	15	Normal
TM05	Roar	Normal	Status	—	—	20	Normal
TM06	Toxic	Poison	Status	—	90	10	Normal
TM10	Hidden Power	Normal	Special	60	100	15	Normal
TM11	Sunny Day	Fire	Status	—	—	5	Both Sides
TM12	Taunt	Dark	Status	—	100	20	Normal
TM17	Protect	Normal	Status	—	—	10	Self
TM18	Rain Dance	Water	Status	—	—	5	Both Sides
TM21	Frustration	Normal	Physical	—	100	20	Normal
TM27	Return	Normal	Physical	—	100	20	Normal
TM28	Dig	Ground	Physical	80	100	10	Normal
TM32	Double Team	Normal	Status	—	—	15	Self
TM39	Rock Tomb	Rock	Physical	60	95	15	Normal
TM40	Aerial Ace	Flying	Physical	60	—	20	Normal
TM42	Facade	Normal	Physical	70	100	20	Normal
TM44	Rest	Psychic	Status	—	—	10	Self
TM45	Attract	Normal	Status	—	100	15	Normal
TM48	Round	Normal	Special	60	100	15	Normal
TM54	False Swipe	Normal	Physical	40	100	40	Normal
TM56	Fling	Dark	Physical	—	100	10	Normal
TM59	Incinerate	Fire	Special	60	100	15	Many Others
TM66	Payback	Dark	Physical	50	100	10	Normal
TM68	Giga Impact	Normal	Physical	150	90	5	Normal
TM75	Swords Dance	Normal	Status	—	—	20	Self
TM81	X-Scissor	Bug	Physical	80	100	15	Normal
TM84	Poison Jab	Poison	Physical	80	100	20	Normal
TM87	Swagger	Normal	Status	—	90	15	Normal
TM88	Sleep Talk	Normal	Status	—	—	10	Self
TM90	Substitute	Normal	Status	—	—	10	Self
TM94	Secret Power	Normal	Physical	70	100	20	Normal
TM100	Confide	Normal	Status	—	—	20	Normal
HM01	Cut	Normal	Physical	50	95	30	Normal
HM04	Strength	Normal	Physical	80	100	15	Normal
HM06	Rock Smash	Fighting	Physical	40	100	15	Normal

MOVES LEARNED IN EXCHANGE FOR BP

Name	Type	Kind	Pow.	Acc.	PP	Range
Dual Chop	Dragon	Physical	40	90	15	Normal
Superpower	Fighting	Physical	120	100	5	Normal
Aqua Tail	Water	Physical	90	90	10	Normal
Dragon Pulse	Dragon	Special	85	100	10	Normal
Iron Tail	Steel	Physical	100	75	15	Normal
Snore	Normal	Special	50	100	15	Normal
Shock Wave	Electric	Special	60	—	20	Normal
Endeavor	Normal	Physical	—	100	5	Normal
Outrage	Dragon	Physical	120	100	10	1 Random

MOVES TAUGHT BY PEOPLE

Name	Type	Kind	Pow.	Acc.	PP	Range
Draco Meteor	Dragon	Special	130	90	5	Normal

EGG MOVES

Name	Type	Kind	Pow.	Acc.	PP	Range
Counter	Fighting	Physical	—	100	20	Varies
Focus Energy	Normal	Status	—	—	30	Self
Reversal	Fighting	Physical	—	100	15	Normal
Endure	Normal	Status	—	—	10	Self
Razor Wind	Normal	Special	80	100	10	Many Others
Night Slash	Dark	Physical	70	100	15	Normal
Endeavor	Normal	Physical	—	100	5	Normal
Iron Tail	Steel	Physical	100	75	15	Normal
Dragon Pulse	Dragon	Special	85	100	10	Normal
Harden	Normal	Status	—	—	30	Self

National Pokédex **611** Hoenn Pokédex —

Fraxure

Axe Jaw Pokémon

Dragon

HEIGHT: 3'03" WEIGHT: 79.4 lbs.

Same form for ♂ / ♀

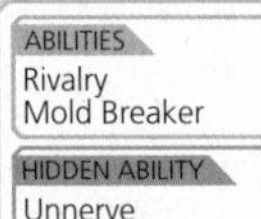

Ω Their tusks can shatter rocks. Territory battles between Fraxure can be intensely violent.

α A broken tusk will not grow back, so it diligently sharpens its tusks on river rocks after the end of a battle.

ABILITIES
Rivalry
Mold Breaker

HIDDEN ABILITY
Unnerve

EGG GROUPS
Monster / Dragon

STAT GROWTH RATES
HP
Attack
Defense
Sp. Atk
Sp. Def
Speed

ITEMS SOMETIMES HELD BY WILD POKÉMON
—

EVOLUTION

Lv. 38
Lv. 48
Axew
Fraxure
Haxorus

MAIN WAY TO REGISTER IN THE NATIONAL POKÉDEX

Level up Axew to Lv. 38.

Damage taken in normal battles

Type		Type	
Normal	×1	Flying	×1
Fire	×0.5	Psychic	×1
Water	×0.5	Bug	×1
Grass	×0.5	Rock	×1
Electric	×0.5	Ghost	×1
Ice	×2	Dragon	×2
Fighting	×1	Dark	×1
Poison	×1	Steel	×1
Ground	×1	Fairy	×2

Damage taken in Inverse battles

Type		Type	
Normal	×1	Flying	×1
Fire	×2	Psychic	×1
Water	×2	Bug	×1
Grass	×2	Rock	×1
Electric	×2	Ghost	×1
Ice	×0.5	Dragon	×0.5
Fighting	×1	Dark	×1
Poison	×1	Steel	×1
Ground	×1	Fairy	×0.5

Can be used in
Inverse Battle
Battle Institute
Battle Maison
Random Matchup (Free Battle)
Random Matchup (Others)

LEVEL-UP MOVES

Lv.	Name	Type	Kind	Pow.	Acc.	PP	Range
1	Scratch	Normal	Physical	40	100	35	Normal
1	Leer	Normal	Status	—	100	30	Many Others
1	Assurance	Dark	Physical	60	100	10	Normal
1	Dragon Rage	Dragon	Special	—	100	10	Normal
4	Leer	Normal	Status	—	100	30	Many Others
7	Assurance	Dark	Physical	60	100	10	Normal
10	Dragon Rage	Dragon	Special	—	100	10	Normal
13	Dual Chop	Dragon	Physical	40	90	15	Normal
16	Scary Face	Normal	Status	—	100	10	Normal
20	Slash	Normal	Physical	70	100	20	Normal
24	False Swipe	Normal	Physical	40	100	40	Normal
28	Dragon Claw	Dragon	Physical	80	100	15	Normal
32	Dragon Dance	Dragon	Status	—	—	20	Self
36	Taunt	Dark	Status	—	100	20	Normal
42	Dragon Pulse	Dragon	Special	85	100	10	Normal
48	Swords Dance	Normal	Status	—	—	20	Self
54	Guillotine	Normal	Physical	—	30	5	Normal
60	Outrage	Dragon	Physical	120	100	10	1 Random
66	Giga Impact	Normal	Physical	150	90	5	Normal

TM & HM MOVES

No.	Name	Type	Kind	Pow.	Acc.	PP	Range
TM01	Hone Claws	Dark	Status	—	—	15	Self
TM02	Dragon Claw	Dragon	Physical	80	100	15	Normal
TM05	Roar	Normal	Status	—	—	20	Normal
TM06	Toxic	Poison	Status	—	90	10	Normal
TM10	Hidden Power	Normal	Special	60	100	15	Normal
TM11	Sunny Day	Fire	Status	—	—	5	Both Sides
TM12	Taunt	Dark	Status	—	100	20	Normal
TM17	Protect	Normal	Status	—	—	10	Self
TM18	Rain Dance	Water	Status	—	—	5	Both Sides
TM21	Frustration	Normal	Physical	—	100	20	Normal
TM27	Return	Normal	Physical	—	100	20	Normal
TM28	Dig	Ground	Physical	80	100	10	Normal
TM32	Double Team	Normal	Status	—	—	15	Self
TM39	Rock Tomb	Rock	Physical	60	95	15	Normal
TM40	Aerial Ace	Flying	Physical	60	—	20	Normal
TM42	Facade	Normal	Physical	70	100	20	Normal
TM44	Rest	Psychic	Status	—	—	10	Self
TM45	Attract	Normal	Status	—	100	15	Normal
TM48	Round	Normal	Special	60	100	15	Normal
TM54	False Swipe	Normal	Physical	40	100	40	Normal
TM56	Fling	Dark	Physical	—	100	10	Normal
TM59	Incinerate	Fire	Special	60	100	15	Many Others
TM65	Shadow Claw	Ghost	Physical	70	100	15	Normal
TM66	Payback	Dark	Physical	50	100	10	Normal
TM68	Giga Impact	Normal	Physical	150	90	5	Normal
TM75	Swords Dance	Normal	Status	—	—	20	Self
TM81	X-Scissor	Bug	Physical	80	100	15	Normal
TM82	Dragon Tail	Dragon	Physical	60	90	10	Normal
TM84	Poison Jab	Poison	Physical	80	100	20	Normal
TM87	Swagger	Normal	Status	—	90	15	Normal
TM88	Sleep Talk	Normal	Status	—	—	10	Self
TM90	Substitute	Normal	Status	—	—	10	Self
TM94	Secret Power	Normal	Physical	70	100	20	Normal
TM100	Confide	Normal	Status	—	—	20	Normal
HM01	Cut	Normal	Physical	50	95	30	Normal
HM04	Strength	Normal	Physical	80	100	15	Normal
HM06	Rock Smash	Fighting	Physical	40	100	15	Normal

MOVES LEARNED IN EXCHANGE FOR BP

Name	Type	Kind	Pow.	Acc.	PP	Range
Dual Chop	Dragon	Physical	40	90	15	Normal
Low Kick	Fighting	Physical	—	100	20	Normal
Superpower	Fighting	Physical	120	100	5	Normal
Aqua Tail	Water	Physical	90	90	10	Normal
Dragon Pulse	Dragon	Special	85	100	10	Normal
Iron Tail	Steel	Physical	100	75	15	Normal
Snore	Normal	Special	50	100	15	Normal
Shock Wave	Electric	Special	60	—	20	Normal
Endeavor	Normal	Physical	—	100	5	Normal
Outrage	Dragon	Physical	120	100	10	1 Random

MOVES TAUGHT BY PEOPLE

Name	Type	Kind	Pow.	Acc.	PP	Range
Draco Meteor	Dragon	Special	130	90	5	Normal

National Pokédex **612** Hoenn Pokédex —

Haxorus

Axe Jaw Pokémon

Dragon

HEIGHT: 5'11" WEIGHT: 232.6 lbs.

Same form for ♂ / ♀

Ω They are kind but can be relentless when defending territory. They challenge foes with tusks that can cut steel.

α Their sturdy tusks will stay sharp even if used to cut steel beams. These Pokémon are covered in hard armor.

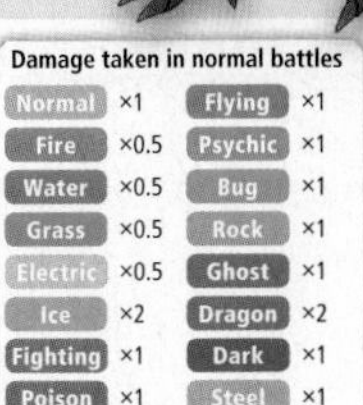

ABILITIES
Rivalry
Mold Breaker

HIDDEN ABILITY
Unnerve

EGG GROUPS
Monster / Dragon

STAT GROWTH RATES
HP ▮▮▮
Attack ▮▮▮▮▮▮▮
Defense ▮▮▮▮
Sp. Atk ▮▮▮
Sp. Def ▮▮▮
Speed ▮▮▮▮▮

ITEMS SOMETIMES HELD BY WILD POKÉMON
—

EVOLUTION

MAIN WAY TO REGISTER IN THE NATIONAL POKÉDEX

Level up Fraxure to Lv. 48.

Damage taken in normal battles

Normal	×1	Flying	×1
Fire	×0.5	Psychic	×1
Water	×0.5	Bug	×1
Grass	×0.5	Rock	×1
Electric	×0.5	Ghost	×1
Ice	×2	Dragon	×2
Fighting	×1	Dark	×1
Poison	×1	Steel	×1
Ground	×1	Fairy	×2

Damage taken in Inverse battles

Normal	×1	Flying	×1
Fire	×2	Psychic	×1
Water	×2	Bug	×1
Grass	×2	Rock	×1
Electric	×2	Ghost	×1
Ice	×0.5	Dragon	×0.5
Fighting	×1	Dark	×1
Poison	×1	Steel	×1
Ground	×1	Fairy	×0.5

Can be used in
Inverse Battle
Battle Institute
Battle Maison
Random Matchup (Free Battle)
Random Matchup (Others)

LEVEL-UP MOVES

Lv.	Name	Type	Kind	Pow.	Acc.	PP	Range
1	Outrage	Dragon	Physical	120	100	10	1 Random
1	Scratch	Normal	Physical	40	100	35	Normal
1	Leer	Normal	Status	—	100	30	Many Others
1	Assurance	Dark	Physical	60	100	10	Normal
1	Dragon Rage	Dragon	Special	—	100	10	Normal
4	Leer	Normal	Status	—	100	30	Many Others
7	Assurance	Dark	Physical	60	100	10	Normal
10	Dragon Rage	Dragon	Special	—	100	10	Normal
13	Dual Chop	Dragon	Physical	40	90	15	Normal
16	Scary Face	Normal	Status	—	100	10	Normal
20	Slash	Normal	Physical	70	100	20	Normal
24	False Swipe	Normal	Physical	40	100	40	Normal
28	Dragon Claw	Dragon	Physical	80	100	15	Normal
32	Dragon Dance	Dragon	Status	—	—	20	Self
36	Taunt	Dark	Status	—	100	20	Normal
42	Dragon Pulse	Dragon	Special	85	100	10	Normal
50	Swords Dance	Normal	Status	—	—	20	Self
58	Guillotine	Normal	Physical	—	30	5	Normal
66	Outrage	Dragon	Physical	120	100	10	1 Random
74	Giga Impact	Normal	Physical	150	90	5	Normal

TM & HM MOVES

No.	Name	Type	Kind	Pow.	Acc.	PP	Range
TM01	Hone Claws	Dark	Status	—	—	15	Self
TM02	Dragon Claw	Dragon	Physical	80	100	15	Normal
TM05	Roar	Normal	Status	—	—	20	Normal
TM06	Toxic	Poison	Status	—	90	10	Normal
TM10	Hidden Power	Normal	Special	60	100	15	Normal
TM11	Sunny Day	Fire	Status	—	—	5	Both Sides
TM12	Taunt	Dark	Status	—	100	20	Normal
TM15	Hyper Beam	Normal	Special	150	90	5	Normal
TM17	Protect	Normal	Status	—	—	10	Self
TM18	Rain Dance	Water	Status	—	—	5	Both Sides
TM21	Frustration	Normal	Physical	—	100	20	Normal
TM26	Earthquake	Ground	Physical	100	100	10	Adjacent
TM27	Return	Normal	Physical	—	100	20	Normal
TM28	Dig	Ground	Physical	80	100	10	Normal
TM31	Brick Break	Fighting	Physical	75	100	15	Normal
TM32	Double Team	Normal	Status	—	—	15	Self
TM39	Rock Tomb	Rock	Physical	60	95	15	Normal
TM40	Aerial Ace	Flying	Physical	60	—	20	Normal
TM42	Facade	Normal	Physical	70	100	20	Normal
TM44	Rest	Psychic	Status	—	—	10	Self
TM45	Attract	Normal	Status	—	100	15	Normal
TM48	Round	Normal	Special	60	100	15	Normal
TM52	Focus Blast	Fighting	Special	120	70	5	Normal
TM54	False Swipe	Normal	Physical	40	100	40	Normal
TM56	Fling	Dark	Physical	—	100	10	Normal
TM59	Incinerate	Fire	Special	60	100	15	Many Others
TM65	Shadow Claw	Ghost	Physical	70	100	15	Normal
TM66	Payback	Dark	Physical	50	100	10	Normal
TM68	Giga Impact	Normal	Physical	150	90	5	Normal
TM75	Swords Dance	Normal	Status	—	—	20	Self
TM78	Bulldoze	Ground	Physical	60	100	20	Adjacent
TM80	Rock Slide	Rock	Physical	75	90	10	Many Others
TM81	X-Scissor	Bug	Physical	80	100	15	Normal
TM82	Dragon Tail	Dragon	Physical	60	90	10	Normal
TM84	Poison Jab	Poison	Physical	80	100	20	Normal
TM86	Grass Knot	Grass	Special	—	100	20	Normal
TM87	Swagger	Normal	Status	—	90	15	Normal
TM88	Sleep Talk	Normal	Status	—	—	10	Self
TM90	Substitute	Normal	Status	—	—	10	Self
TM94	Secret Power	Normal	Physical	70	100	20	Normal
TM100	Confide	Normal	Status	—	—	20	Normal
HM01	Cut	Normal	Physical	50	95	30	Normal
HM03	Surf	Water	Special	90	100	15	Adjacent
HM04	Strength	Normal	Physical	80	100	15	Normal
HM06	Rock Smash	Fighting	Physical	40	100	15	Normal

MOVES LEARNED IN EXCHANGE FOR BP

Name	Type	Kind	Pow.	Acc.	PP	Range
Dual Chop	Dragon	Physical	40	90	15	Normal
Low Kick	Fighting	Physical	—	100	20	Normal
Superpower	Fighting	Physical	120	100	5	Normal
Aqua Tail	Water	Physical	90	90	10	Normal
Dragon Pulse	Dragon	Special	85	100	10	Normal
Iron Tail	Steel	Physical	100	75	15	Normal
Snore	Normal	Special	50	100	15	Normal
Shock Wave	Electric	Special	60	—	20	Normal
Endeavor	Normal	Physical	—	100	5	Normal
Outrage	Dragon	Physical	120	100	10	1 Random

MOVES TAUGHT BY PEOPLE

Name	Type	Kind	Pow.	Acc.	PP	Range
Draco Meteor	Dragon	Special	130	90	5	Normal

National Pokédex **613** Hoenn Pokédex —

Cubchoo

Chill Pokémon

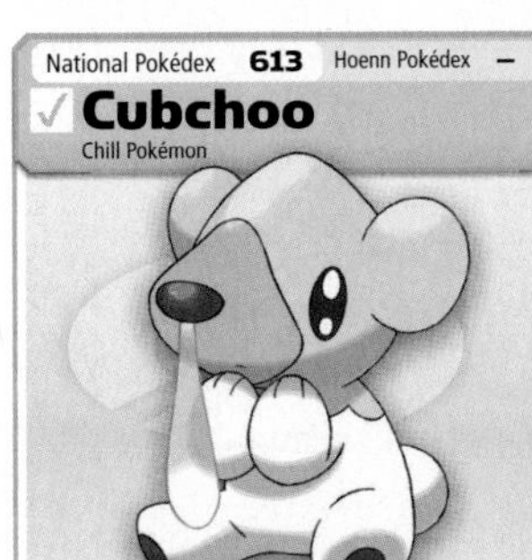

Ice

HEIGHT: 1'08" WEIGHT: 18.7 lbs.

Same form for ♂ / ♀

Ω Its nose is always running. It sniffs the snot back up because the mucus provides the raw material for its moves.

α Their snot is a barometer of health. When healthy, their snot is sticky and the power of their ice moves increases.

ABILITY
Snow Cloak

HIDDEN ABILITY
Rattled

EGG GROUPS
Field

STAT GROWTH RATES
HP ▮▮
Attack ▮▮▮▮
Defense ▮▮
Sp. Atk ▮▮▮
Sp. Def ▮▮
Speed ▮▮

ITEMS SOMETIMES HELD BY WILD POKÉMON
—

EVOLUTION

Cubchoo → Lv. 37 → Beartic

MAIN WAY TO REGISTER IN THE NATIONAL POKÉDEX

Catch in Shoal Cave. Appears as a hidden Pokémon after you battle Groudon or Kyogre.

Damage taken in normal battles

Normal	×1	Flying	×1
Fire	×2	Psychic	×1
Water	×1	Bug	×1
Grass	×1	Rock	×2
Electric	×1	Ghost	×1
Ice	×0.5	Dragon	×1
Fighting	×2	Dark	×1
Poison	×1	Steel	×2
Ground	×1	Fairy	×1

Damage taken in Inverse battles

Normal	×1	Flying	×1
Fire	×0.5	Psychic	×1
Water	×1	Bug	×1
Grass	×1	Rock	×0.5
Electric	×1	Ghost	×1
Ice	×2	Dragon	×1
Fighting	×0.5	Dark	×1
Poison	×1	Steel	×0.5
Ground	×1	Fairy	×1

Can be used in
Inverse Battle
Battle Institute
Battle Maison
Random Matchup (Free Battle)
Random Matchup (Others)

LEVEL-UP MOVES

Lv.	Name	Type	Kind	Pow.	Acc.	PP	Range
1	Growl	Normal	Status	—	100	40	Many Others
5	Powder Snow	Ice	Special	40	100	25	Many Others
9	Bide	Normal	Physical	—	—	10	Self
13	Icy Wind	Ice	Special	55	95	15	Many Others
15	Play Nice	Normal	Status	—	—	20	Normal
17	Fury Swipes	Normal	Physical	18	80	15	Normal
21	Brine	Water	Special	65	100	10	Normal
25	Endure	Normal	Status	—	—	10	Self
29	Charm	Fairy	Status	—	100	20	Normal
33	Slash	Normal	Physical	70	100	20	Normal
36	Flail	Normal	Physical	—	100	15	Normal
41	Rest	Psychic	Status	—	—	10	Self
45	Blizzard	Ice	Special	110	70	5	Many Others
49	Hail	Ice	Status	—	—	10	Both Sides
53	Thrash	Normal	Physical	120	100	10	1 Random
57	Sheer Cold	Ice	Special	—	30	5	Normal

TM & HM MOVES

No.	Name	Type	Kind	Pow.	Acc.	PP	Range
TM01	Hone Claws	Dark	Status	—	—	15	Self
TM06	Toxic	Poison	Status	—	90	10	Normal
TM07	Hail	Ice	Status	—	—	10	Both Sides
TM10	Hidden Power	Normal	Special	60	100	15	Normal
TM13	Ice Beam	Ice	Special	90	100	10	Normal
TM14	Blizzard	Ice	Special	110	70	5	Many Others
TM17	Protect	Normal	Status	—	—	10	Self
TM18	Rain Dance	Water	Status	—	—	5	Both Sides
TM21	Frustration	Normal	Physical	—	100	20	Normal
TM27	Return	Normal	Physical	—	100	20	Normal
TM28	Dig	Ground	Physical	80	100	10	Normal
TM32	Double Team	Normal	Status	—	—	15	Self
TM39	Rock Tomb	Rock	Physical	60	95	15	Normal
TM40	Aerial Ace	Flying	Physical	60	—	20	Normal
TM42	Facade	Normal	Physical	70	100	20	Normal
TM44	Rest	Psychic	Status	—	—	10	Self
TM45	Attract	Normal	Status	—	100	15	Normal
TM48	Round	Normal	Special	60	100	15	Normal
TM49	Echoed Voice	Normal	Special	40	100	15	Normal
TM56	Fling	Dark	Physical	—	100	10	Normal
TM65	Shadow Claw	Ghost	Physical	70	100	15	Normal
TM79	Frost Breath	Ice	Special	60	90	10	Normal
TM86	Grass Knot	Grass	Special	—	100	20	Normal
TM87	Swagger	Normal	Status	—	90	15	Normal
TM88	Sleep Talk	Normal	Status	—	—	10	Self
TM90	Substitute	Normal	Status	—	—	10	Self
TM94	Secret Power	Normal	Physical	70	100	20	Normal
TM98	Power-Up Punch	Fighting	Physical	40	100	20	Normal
TM100	Confide	Normal	Status	—	—	20	Normal
HM01	Cut	Normal	Physical	50	95	30	Normal
HM03	Surf	Water	Special	90	100	15	Adjacent
HM04	Strength	Normal	Physical	80	100	15	Normal
HM06	Rock Smash	Fighting	Physical	40	100	15	Normal

MOVES LEARNED IN EXCHANGE FOR BP

Name	Type	Kind	Pow.	Acc.	PP	Range
Covet	Normal	Physical	60	100	25	Normal
Low Kick	Fighting	Physical	—	100	20	Normal
Ice Punch	Ice	Physical	75	100	15	Normal
Superpower	Fighting	Physical	120	100	5	Normal
Icy Wind	Ice	Special	55	95	15	Many Others
Snore	Normal	Special	50	100	15	Normal
Focus Punch	Fighting	Physical	150	100	20	Normal
Water Pulse	Water	Special	60	100	20	Normal

MOVES TAUGHT BY PEOPLE

Name	Type	Kind	Pow.	Acc.	PP	Range

EGG MOVES

Name	Type	Kind	Pow.	Acc.	PP	Range
Yawn	Normal	Status	—	—	10	Normal
Avalanche	Ice	Physical	60	100	10	Normal
Encore	Normal	Status	—	100	5	Normal
Ice Punch	Ice	Physical	75	100	15	Normal
Night Slash	Dark	Physical	70	100	15	Normal
Assurance	Dark	Physical	60	100	10	Normal
Sleep Talk	Normal	Status	—	—	10	Self
Focus Punch	Fighting	Physical	150	100	20	Normal
Play Rough	Fairy	Physical	90	90	10	Normal

National Pokédex **614** Hoenn Pokédex —

✓ Beartic

Freezing Pokémon

Ice

HEIGHT: 8'06" WEIGHT: 573.2 lbs.

Same form for ♂ / ♀

Ω They love the cold seas of the north. They create pathways across the ocean waters by freezing their own breath.

α It freezes its breath to create fangs and claws of ice to fight with. Cold northern areas are its habitat.

ABILITY
Snow Cloak

HIDDEN ABILITY
Swift Swim

EGG GROUPS
Field

STAT GROWTH RATES
HP ■■■■
Attack ■■■■■■
Defense ■■■■
Sp. Atk ■■■
Sp. Def ■■■
Speed ■■■

ITEMS SOMETIMES HELD BY WILD POKÉMON
—

EVOLUTION

MAIN WAY TO REGISTER IN THE NATIONAL POKÉDEX

Level up Cubchoo to Lv. 37.

Damage taken in normal battles

Type		Type	
Normal	×1	Flying	×1
Fire	×2	Psychic	×1
Water	×1	Bug	×1
Grass	×1	Rock	×2
Electric	×1	Ghost	×1
Ice	×0.5	Dragon	×1
Fighting	×2	Dark	×1
Poison	×1	Steel	×2
Ground	×1	Fairy	×1

Damage taken in Inverse battles

Type		Type	
Normal	×1	Flying	×1
Fire	×0.5	Psychic	×1
Water	×1	Bug	×1
Grass	×1	Rock	×0.5
Electric	×1	Ghost	×1
Ice	×2	Dragon	×1
Fighting	×0.5	Dark	×1
Poison	×1	Steel	×0.5
Ground	×1	Fairy	×1

Can be used in
- Inverse Battle
- Battle Institute
- Battle Maison
- Random Matchup (Free Battle)
- Random Matchup (Others)

LEVEL-UP MOVES

Lv.	Name	Type	Kind	Pow.	Acc.	PP	Range
1	Sheer Cold	Ice	Special	—	30	5	Normal
1	Thrash	Normal	Physical	120	100	10	1 Random
1	Superpower	Fighting	Physical	120	100	5	Normal
1	Aqua Jet	Water	Physical	40	100	20	Normal
1	Growl	Normal	Status	—	100	40	Many Others
1	Powder Snow	Ice	Special	40	100	25	Many Others
1	Bide	Normal	Physical	—	—	10	Self
1	Icy Wind	Ice	Special	55	95	15	Many Others
9	Play Nice	Normal	Status	—	—	20	Normal
13	Icy Wind	Ice	Special	55	95	15	Many Others
17	Fury Swipes	Normal	Physical	18	80	15	Normal
21	Brine	Water	Special	65	100	10	Normal
25	Endure	Normal	Status	—	—	10	Self
29	Swagger	Normal	Status	—	90	15	Normal
33	Slash	Normal	Physical	70	100	20	Normal
36	Flail	Normal	Physical	—	100	15	Normal
37	Icicle Crash	Ice	Physical	85	90	10	Normal
41	Rest	Psychic	Status	—	—	10	Self
45	Blizzard	Ice	Special	110	70	5	Many Others
53	Hail	Ice	Status	—	—	10	Both Sides
59	Thrash	Normal	Physical	120	100	10	1 Random
66	Sheer Cold	Ice	Special	—	30	5	Normal

TM & HM MOVES

No.	Name	Type	Kind	Pow.	Acc.	PP	Range
TM01	Hone Claws	Dark	Status	—	—	15	Self
TM05	Roar	Normal	Status	—	—	20	Normal
TM06	Toxic	Poison	Status	—	90	10	Normal
TM07	Hail	Ice	Status	—	—	10	Both Sides
TM08	Bulk Up	Fighting	Status	—	—	20	Self
TM10	Hidden Power	Normal	Special	60	100	15	Normal
TM12	Taunt	Dark	Status	—	100	20	Normal
TM13	Ice Beam	Ice	Special	90	100	10	Normal
TM14	Blizzard	Ice	Special	110	70	5	Many Others
TM15	Hyper Beam	Normal	Special	150	90	5	Normal
TM17	Protect	Normal	Status	—	—	10	Self
TM18	Rain Dance	Water	Status	—	—	5	Both Sides
TM21	Frustration	Normal	Physical	—	100	20	Normal
TM27	Return	Normal	Physical	—	100	20	Normal
TM28	Dig	Ground	Physical	80	100	10	Normal
TM31	Brick Break	Fighting	Physical	75	100	15	Normal
TM32	Double Team	Normal	Status	—	—	15	Self
TM39	Rock Tomb	Rock	Physical	60	95	15	Normal
TM40	Aerial Ace	Flying	Physical	60	—	20	Normal
TM42	Facade	Normal	Physical	70	100	20	Normal
TM44	Rest	Psychic	Status	—	—	10	Self
TM45	Attract	Normal	Status	—	100	15	Normal
TM48	Round	Normal	Special	60	100	15	Normal
TM49	Echoed Voice	Normal	Special	40	100	15	Normal
TM52	Focus Blast	Fighting	Special	120	70	5	Normal
TM56	Fling	Dark	Physical	—	100	10	Normal
TM65	Shadow Claw	Ghost	Physical	70	100	15	Normal
TM68	Giga Impact	Normal	Physical	150	90	5	Normal
TM71	Stone Edge	Rock	Physical	100	80	5	Normal
TM75	Swords Dance	Normal	Status	—	—	20	Self
TM78	Bulldoze	Ground	Physical	60	100	20	Adjacent
TM79	Frost Breath	Ice	Special	60	90	10	Normal
TM80	Rock Slide	Rock	Physical	75	90	10	Many Others
TM86	Grass Knot	Grass	Special	—	100	20	Normal
TM87	Swagger	Normal	Status	—	90	15	Normal
TM88	Sleep Talk	Normal	Status	—	—	10	Self
TM90	Substitute	Normal	Status	—	—	10	Self
TM94	Secret Power	Normal	Physical	70	100	20	Normal
TM98	Power-Up Punch	Fighting	Physical	40	100	20	Normal
TM100	Confide	Normal	Status	—	—	20	Normal
HM01	Cut	Normal	Physical	50	95	30	Normal
HM03	Surf	Water	Special	90	100	15	Adjacent
HM04	Strength	Normal	Physical	80	100	15	Normal
HM06	Rock Smash	Fighting	Physical	40	100	15	Normal
HM07	Dive	Water	Physical	80	100	10	Normal

MOVES LEARNED IN EXCHANGE FOR BP

Name	Type	Kind	Pow.	Acc.	PP	Range
Covet	Normal	Physical	60	100	25	Normal
Low Kick	Fighting	Physical	—	100	20	Normal
Ice Punch	Ice	Physical	75	100	15	Normal
Superpower	Fighting	Physical	120	100	5	Normal
Icy Wind	Ice	Special	55	95	15	Many Others
Snore	Normal	Special	50	100	15	Normal
Focus Punch	Fighting	Physical	150	100	20	Normal
Water Pulse	Water	Special	60	100	20	Normal

MOVES TAUGHT BY PEOPLE

Name	Type	Kind	Pow.	Acc.	PP	Range

National Pokédex **615** Hoenn Pokédex —

✓ Cryogonal

Crystallizing Pokémon

Ice

HEIGHT: 3'07" WEIGHT: 326.3 lbs.

Gender unknown

Ω They are born in snow clouds. They use chains made of ice crystals to capture prey.

α They are composed of ice crystals. They capture prey with chains of ice, freezing the prey at -148 degrees Fahrenheit.

ABILITY
Levitate

HIDDEN ABILITY
—

EGG GROUPS
Mineral

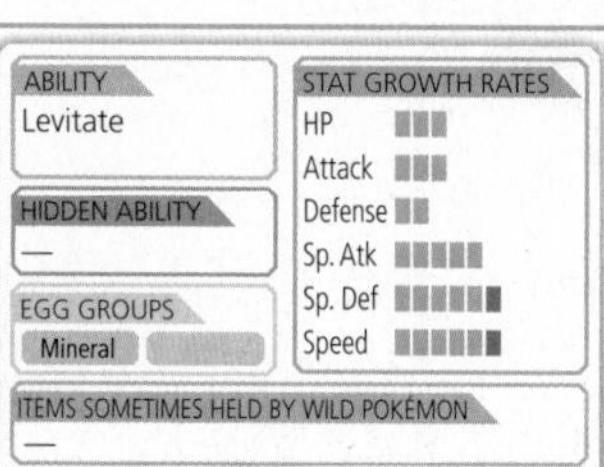

STAT GROWTH RATES
HP ■■■
Attack ■■■
Defense ■■
Sp. Atk ■■■■■
Sp. Def ■■■■■■
Speed ■■■■■■

ITEMS SOMETIMES HELD BY WILD POKÉMON
—

EVOLUTION

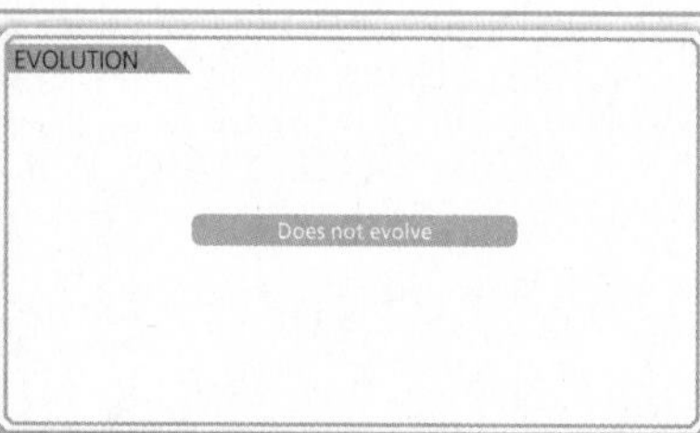

MAIN WAY TO REGISTER IN THE NATIONAL POKÉDEX

Appears in *Pokémon X* and *Pokémon Y*. Bring it to your game using Link Trade or the GTS.

Damage taken in normal battles

Type		Type	
Normal	×1	Flying	×1
Fire	×2	Psychic	×1
Water	×1	Bug	×1
Grass	×1	Rock	×2
Electric	×1	Ghost	×1
Ice	×0.5	Dragon	×1
Fighting	×2	Dark	×1
Poison	×1	Steel	×2
! Ground	×1	Fairy	×1

Damage taken in Inverse battles

Type		Type	
Normal	×1	Flying	×1
Fire	×0.5	Psychic	×1
Water	×1	Bug	×1
Grass	×1	Rock	×0.5
Electric	×1	Ghost	×1
Ice	×2	Dragon	×1
Fighting	×0.5	Dark	×1
Poison	×1	Steel	×0.5
! Ground	×1	Fairy	×1

Can be used in
- Inverse Battle
- Battle Institute
- Battle Maison
- Random Matchup (Free Battle)
- Random Matchup (Others)

LEVEL-UP MOVES

Lv.	Name	Type	Kind	Pow.	Acc.	PP	Range
1	Sheer Cold	Ice	Special	—	30	5	Normal
1	Night Slash	Dark	Physical	70	100	15	Normal
1	Ice Shard	Ice	Physical	40	100	30	Normal
1	Mist	Ice	Status	—	—	30	Your Side
1	Haze	Ice	Status	—	—	30	Both Sides
1	Bind	Normal	Physical	15	85	20	Normal
5	Ice Shard	Ice	Physical	40	100	30	Normal
9	Sharpen	Normal	Status	—	—	30	Self
13	Rapid Spin	Normal	Physical	20	100	40	Normal
17	Icy Wind	Ice	Special	55	95	15	Many Others
21	Mist	Ice	Status	—	—	30	Your Side
21	Haze	Ice	Status	—	—	30	Both Sides
25	Aurora Beam	Ice	Special	65	100	20	Normal
29	Acid Armor	Poison	Status	—	—	20	Self
33	Ice Beam	Ice	Special	90	100	10	Normal
37	Light Screen	Psychic	Status	—	—	30	Your Side
37	Reflect	Psychic	Status	—	—	20	Your Side
41	Slash	Normal	Physical	70	100	20	Normal
45	Confuse Ray	Ghost	Status	—	100	10	Normal
49	Recover	Normal	Status	—	—	10	Self
50	Freeze-Dry	Ice	Special	70	100	20	Normal
53	Solar Beam	Grass	Special	120	100	10	Normal
57	Night Slash	Dark	Physical	70	100	15	Normal
61	Sheer Cold	Ice	Special	—	30	5	Normal

TM & HM MOVES

No.	Name	Type	Kind	Pow.	Acc.	PP	Range
TM06	Toxic	Poison	Status	—	90	10	Normal
TM07	Hail	Ice	Status	—	—	10	Both Sides
TM10	Hidden Power	Normal	Special	60	100	15	Normal
TM13	Ice Beam	Ice	Special	90	100	10	Normal
TM14	Blizzard	Ice	Special	110	70	5	Many Others
TM15	Hyper Beam	Normal	Special	150	90	5	Normal
TM16	Light Screen	Psychic	Status	—	—	30	Your Side
TM17	Protect	Normal	Status	—	—	10	Self
TM18	Rain Dance	Water	Status	—	—	5	Both Sides
TM21	Frustration	Normal	Physical	—	100	20	Normal
TM22	Solar Beam	Grass	Special	120	100	10	Normal
TM27	Return	Normal	Physical	—	100	20	Normal
TM32	Double Team	Normal	Status	—	—	15	Self
TM33	Reflect	Psychic	Status	—	—	20	Your Side
TM42	Facade	Normal	Physical	70	100	20	Normal
TM44	Rest	Psychic	Status	—	—	10	Self
TM45	Attract	Normal	Status	—	100	15	Normal
TM48	Round	Normal	Special	60	100	15	Normal
TM62	Acrobatics	Flying	Physical	55	100	15	Normal
TM64	Explosion	Normal	Physical	250	100	5	Adjacent
TM79	Frost Breath	Ice	Special	60	90	10	Normal
TM84	Poison Jab	Poison	Physical	80	100	20	Normal
TM87	Swagger	Normal	Status	—	90	15	Normal
TM88	Sleep Talk	Normal	Status	—	—	10	Self
TM90	Substitute	Normal	Status	—	—	10	Self
TM91	Flash Cannon	Steel	Special	80	100	10	Normal
TM94	Secret Power	Normal	Physical	70	100	20	Normal
TM100	Confide	Normal	Status	—	—	20	Normal

MOVES LEARNED IN EXCHANGE FOR BP

Name	Type	Kind	Pow.	Acc.	PP	Range
Signal Beam	Bug	Special	75	100	15	Normal
Magic Coat	Psychic	Status	—	—	15	Self
Iron Defense	Steel	Status	—	—	15	Self
Icy Wind	Ice	Special	55	95	15	Many Others
Bind	Normal	Physical	15	85	20	Normal
Snore	Normal	Special	50	100	15	Normal
Knock Off	Dark	Physical	65	100	20	Normal
Water Pulse	Water	Special	60	100	20	Normal

MOVES TAUGHT BY PEOPLE

Name	Type	Kind	Pow.	Acc.	PP	Range

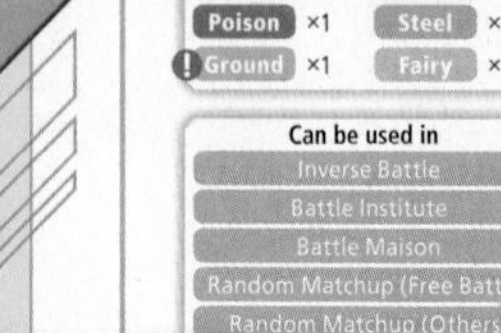

National Pokédex **616** Hoenn Pokédex —

Shelmet

Snail Pokémon

Bug

HEIGHT: 1'04" WEIGHT: 17 lbs.

Same form for ♂ / ♀

Ω When it and Karrablast are together, and both receive electrical stimulation, they both evolve.

α It evolves when bathed in an electric-like energy along with Karrablast. The reason is still unknown.

ABILITIES
Hydration
Shell Armor

HIDDEN ABILITY
Overcoat

EGG GROUPS
Bug

STAT GROWTH RATES

HP	■■
Attack	■■
Defense	■■■■
Sp. Atk	■■
Sp. Def	■■■
Speed	■■

ITEMS SOMETIMES HELD BY WILD POKÉMON
—

EVOLUTION

Shelmet → Link Trade for Karrablast → Accelgor

MAIN WAY TO REGISTER IN THE NATIONAL POKÉDEX

Appears in *Pokémon X* and *Pokémon Y*. Bring it to your game using Link Trade or the GTS.

Damage taken in normal battles

Type		Type	
Normal	×1	Flying	×2
Fire	×2	Psychic	×1
Water	×1	Bug	×1
Grass	×0.5	Rock	×2
Electric	×1	Ghost	×1
Ice	×1	Dragon	×1
Fighting	×0.5	Dark	×1
Poison	×1	Steel	×1
Ground	×0.5	Fairy	×1

Damage taken in Inverse battles

Type		Type	
Normal	×1	Flying	×0.5
Fire	×0.5	Psychic	×1
Water	×1	Bug	×1
Grass	×2	Rock	×0.5
Electric	×1	Ghost	×1
Ice	×1	Dragon	×1
Fighting	×2	Dark	×1
Poison	×1	Steel	×1
Ground	×2	Fairy	×1

Can be used in
Inverse Battle
Battle Institute
Battle Maison
Random Matchup (Free Battle)
Random Matchup (Others)

LEVEL-UP MOVES

Lv.	Name	Type	Kind	Pow.	Acc.	PP	Range
1	Leech Life	Bug	Physical	20	100	15	Normal
4	Acid	Poison	Special	40	100	30	Many Others
8	Bide	Normal	Physical	—	—	10	Self
13	Curse	Ghost	Status	—	—	10	Varies
16	Struggle Bug	Bug	Special	50	100	20	Many Others
20	Mega Drain	Grass	Special	40	100	15	Normal
25	Yawn	Normal	Status	—	—	10	Normal
28	Protect	Normal	Status	—	—	10	Self
32	Acid Armor	Poison	Status	—	—	20	Self
37	Giga Drain	Grass	Special	75	100	10	Normal
40	Body Slam	Normal	Physical	85	100	15	Normal
44	Bug Buzz	Bug	Special	90	100	10	Normal
49	Recover	Normal	Status	—	—	10	Self
50	Guard Swap	Psychic	Status	—	—	10	Normal
56	Final Gambit	Fighting	Special	—	100	5	Normal

TM & HM MOVES

No.	Name	Type	Kind	Pow.	Acc.	PP	Range
TM06	Toxic	Poison	Status	—	90	10	Normal
TM09	Venoshock	Poison	Special	65	100	10	Normal
TM10	Hidden Power	Normal	Special	60	100	15	Normal
TM17	Protect	Normal	Status	—	—	10	Self
TM18	Rain Dance	Water	Status	—	—	5	Both Sides
TM21	Frustration	Normal	Physical	—	100	20	Normal
TM27	Return	Normal	Physical	—	100	20	Normal
TM32	Double Team	Normal	Status	—	—	15	Self
TM36	Sludge Bomb	Poison	Special	90	100	10	Normal
TM42	Facade	Normal	Physical	70	100	20	Normal
TM44	Rest	Psychic	Status	—	—	10	Self
TM45	Attract	Normal	Status	—	100	15	Normal
TM48	Round	Normal	Special	60	100	15	Normal
TM53	Energy Ball	Grass	Special	90	100	10	Normal
TM76	Struggle Bug	Bug	Special	50	100	20	Many Others
TM83	Infestation	Bug	Special	20	100	20	Normal
TM87	Swagger	Normal	Status	—	90	15	Normal
TM88	Sleep Talk	Normal	Status	—	—	10	Self
TM90	Substitute	Normal	Status	—	—	10	Self
TM94	Secret Power	Normal	Physical	70	100	20	Normal
TM100	Confide	Normal	Status	—	—	20	Normal

MOVES LEARNED IN EXCHANGE FOR BP

Name	Type	Kind	Pow.	Acc.	PP	Range
Bug Bite	Bug	Physical	60	100	20	Normal
Signal Beam	Bug	Special	75	100	15	Normal
Snore	Normal	Special	50	100	15	Normal
Giga Drain	Grass	Special	75	100	10	Normal
Gastro Acid	Poison	Status	—	100	10	Normal

MOVES TAUGHT BY PEOPLE

Name	Type	Kind	Pow.	Acc.	PP	Range

EGG MOVES

Name	Type	Kind	Pow.	Acc.	PP	Range
Endure	Normal	Status	—	—	10	Self
Baton Pass	Normal	Status	—	—	40	Self
Double-Edge	Normal	Physical	120	100	15	Normal
Encore	Normal	Status	—	100	5	Normal
Guard Split	Psychic	Status	—	—	10	Normal
Mind Reader	Normal	Status	—	—	5	Normal
Mud-Slap	Ground	Special	20	100	10	Normal
Spikes	Ground	Status	—	—	20	Other Side
Feint	Normal	Physical	30	100	10	Normal
Pursuit	Dark	Physical	40	100	20	Normal

National Pokédex **617** Hoenn Pokédex —

Accelgor

Shell Out Pokémon

Bug

HEIGHT: 2'07" WEIGHT: 55.8 lbs.

Same form for ♂ / ♀

Ω Having removed its heavy shell, it becomes very light and can fight with ninja-like movements.

α When its body dries out, it weakens. So, to prevent dehydration, it wraps itself in many layers of thin membrane.

ABILITIES
Hydration
Sticky Hold

HIDDEN ABILITY
Unburden

EGG GROUPS
Bug

STAT GROWTH RATES

HP	■■■
Attack	■■■■
Defense	■■
Sp. Atk	■■■■■
Sp. Def	■■■
Speed	■■■■■■■■

ITEMS SOMETIMES HELD BY WILD POKÉMON
—

EVOLUTION

Shelmet → Link Trade for Karrablast → Accelgor

MAIN WAY TO REGISTER IN THE NATIONAL POKÉDEX

Link Trade your Karrablast for a Shelmet, and have the Shelmet evolve.

Damage taken in normal battles

Type		Type	
Normal	×1	Flying	×2
Fire	×2	Psychic	×1
Water	×1	Bug	×1
Grass	×0.5	Rock	×2
Electric	×1	Ghost	×1
Ice	×1	Dragon	×1
Fighting	×0.5	Dark	×1
Poison	×1	Steel	×1
Ground	×0.5	Fairy	×1

Damage taken in Inverse battles

Type		Type	
Normal	×1	Flying	×0.5
Fire	×0.5	Psychic	×1
Water	×1	Bug	×1
Grass	×2	Rock	×0.5
Electric	×1	Ghost	×1
Ice	×1	Dragon	×1
Fighting	×2	Dark	×1
Poison	×1	Steel	×1
Ground	×2	Fairy	×1

Can be used in
Inverse Battle
Battle Institute
Battle Maison
Random Matchup (Free Battle)
Random Matchup (Others)

LEVEL-UP MOVES

Lv.	Name	Type	Kind	Pow.	Acc.	PP	Range
1	Water Shuriken	Water	Physical	15	100	20	Normal
1	Final Gambit	Fighting	Special	—	100	5	Normal
1	Power Swap	Psychic	Status	—	—	10	Normal
1	Leech Life	Bug	Physical	20	100	15	Normal
1	Acid Spray	Poison	Special	40	100	20	Normal
1	Double Team	Normal	Status	—	—	15	Self
1	Quick Attack	Normal	Physical	40	100	30	Normal
4	Acid Spray	Poison	Special	40	100	20	Normal
8	Double Team	Normal	Status	—	—	15	Self
13	Quick Attack	Normal	Physical	40	100	30	Normal
16	Struggle Bug	Bug	Special	50	100	20	Many Others
20	Mega Drain	Grass	Special	40	100	15	Normal
25	Swift	Normal	Special	60	—	20	Many Others
28	Me First	Normal	Status	—	—	20	Varies
32	Agility	Psychic	Status	—	—	30	Self
37	Giga Drain	Grass	Special	75	100	10	Normal
40	U-turn	Bug	Physical	70	100	20	Normal
44	Bug Buzz	Bug	Special	90	100	10	Normal
49	Recover	Normal	Status	—	—	10	Self
52	Power Swap	Psychic	Status	—	—	10	Normal
56	Final Gambit	Fighting	Special	—	100	5	Normal

TM & HM MOVES

No.	Name	Type	Kind	Pow.	Acc.	PP	Range
TM06	Toxic	Poison	Status	—	90	10	Normal
TM09	Venoshock	Poison	Special	65	100	10	Normal
TM10	Hidden Power	Normal	Special	60	100	15	Normal
TM15	Hyper Beam	Normal	Special	150	90	5	Normal
TM17	Protect	Normal	Status	—	—	10	Self
TM18	Rain Dance	Water	Status	—	—	5	Both Sides
TM21	Frustration	Normal	Physical	—	100	20	Normal
TM27	Return	Normal	Physical	—	100	20	Normal
TM32	Double Team	Normal	Status	—	—	15	Self
TM36	Sludge Bomb	Poison	Special	90	100	10	Normal
TM37	Sandstorm	Rock	Status	—	—	10	Both Sides
TM42	Facade	Normal	Physical	70	100	20	Normal
TM44	Rest	Psychic	Status	—	—	10	Self
TM45	Attract	Normal	Status	—	100	15	Normal
TM48	Round	Normal	Special	60	100	15	Normal
TM52	Focus Blast	Fighting	Special	120	70	5	Normal
TM53	Energy Ball	Grass	Special	90	100	10	Normal
TM68	Giga Impact	Normal	Physical	150	90	5	Normal
TM76	Struggle Bug	Bug	Special	50	100	20	Many Others
TM83	Infestation	Bug	Special	20	100	20	Normal
TM87	Swagger	Normal	Status	—	90	15	Normal
TM88	Sleep Talk	Normal	Status	—	—	10	Self
TM89	U-turn	Bug	Physical	70	100	20	Normal
TM90	Substitute	Normal	Status	—	—	10	Self
TM94	Secret Power	Normal	Physical	70	100	20	Normal
TM100	Confide	Normal	Status	—	—	20	Normal

MOVES LEARNED IN EXCHANGE FOR BP

Name	Type	Kind	Pow.	Acc.	PP	Range
Bug Bite	Bug	Physical	60	100	20	Normal
Signal Beam	Bug	Special	75	100	15	Normal
Snore	Normal	Special	50	100	15	Normal
Knock Off	Dark	Physical	65	100	20	Normal
Giga Drain	Grass	Special	75	100	10	Normal
Gastro Acid	Poison	Status	—	100	10	Normal

MOVES TAUGHT BY PEOPLE

Name	Type	Kind	Pow.	Acc.	PP	Range

National Pokédex **618** Hoenn Pokédex —

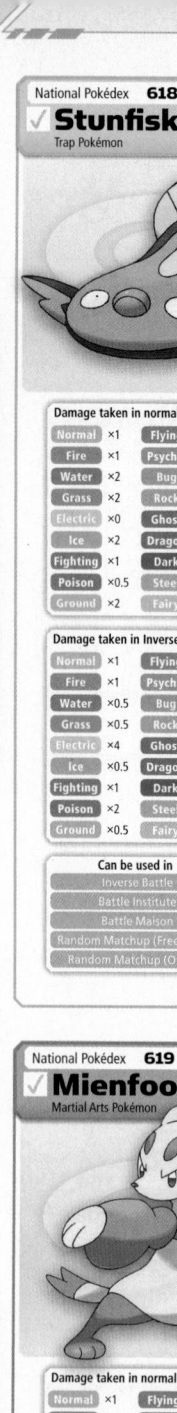

Stunfisk

Trap Pokémon

Ground / Electric

HEIGHT: 2'04" WEIGHT: 24.3 lbs.

Same form for ♂ / ♀

Ω It's skin is very hard, so it is unhurt even if stepped on by sumo wrestlers. It smiles when transmitting electricity.

α It conceals itself in the mud of the seashore. Then it waits. When prey touch it, it delivers a jolt of electricity.

ABILITIES
Static
Limber

HIDDEN ABILITY
Sand Veil

EGG GROUPS
Water 1 / Amorphous

STAT GROWTH RATES
HP
Attack
Defense
Sp. Atk
Sp. Def
Speed

ITEMS SOMETIMES HELD BY WILD POKÉMON
—

EVOLUTION

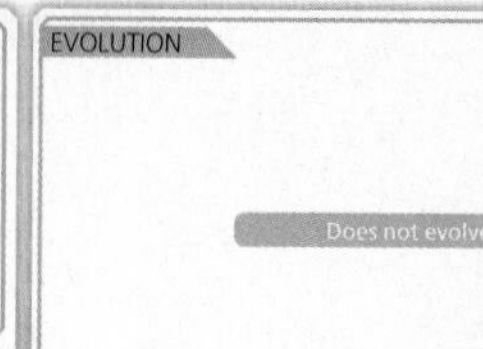

Does not evolve

MAIN WAY TO REGISTER IN THE NATIONAL POKÉDEX

Appears in *Pokémon X* and *Pokémon Y*. Bring it to your game using Link Trade or the GTS.

Damage taken in normal battles

Type		Type	
Normal	×1	Flying	×0.5
Fire	×1	Psychic	×1
Water	×2	Bug	×1
Grass	×2	Rock	×0.5
Electric	×0	Ghost	×1
Ice	×2	Dragon	×1
Fighting	×1	Dark	×1
Poison	×0.5	Steel	×0.5
Ground	×2	Fairy	×1

Damage taken in Inverse battles

Type		Type	
Normal	×1	Flying	×2
Fire	×1	Psychic	×1
Water	×0.5	Bug	×1
Grass	×0.5	Rock	×2
Electric	×4	Ghost	×1
Ice	×0.5	Dragon	×1
Fighting	×1	Dark	×1
Poison	×2	Steel	×2
Ground	×0.5	Fairy	×1

Can be used in
Inverse Battle
Battle Institute
Battle Maison
Random Matchup (Free Battle)
Random Matchup (Others)

LEVEL-UP MOVES

Lv.	Name	Type	Kind	Pow.	Acc.	PP	Range
1	Fissure	Ground	Physical	—	30	5	Normal
1	Flail	Normal	Physical	—	100	15	Normal
1	Tackle	Normal	Physical	50	100	35	Normal
1	Water Gun	Water	Special	40	100	25	Normal
1	Mud-Slap	Ground	Special	20	100	10	Normal
1	Mud Sport	Ground	Status	—	—	15	Both Sides
5	Bide	Normal	Physical	—	—	10	Self
9	Thunder Shock	Electric	Special	40	100	30	Normal
13	Mud Shot	Ground	Special	55	95	15	Normal
17	Camouflage	Normal	Status	—	—	20	Self
21	Mud Bomb	Ground	Special	65	85	10	Normal
25	Discharge	Electric	Special	80	100	15	Adjacent
30	Endure	Normal	Status	—	—	10	Self
35	Bounce	Flying	Physical	85	85	5	Normal
40	Muddy Water	Water	Special	90	85	10	Many Others
45	Thunderbolt	Electric	Special	90	100	15	Normal
50	Revenge	Fighting	Physical	60	100	10	Normal
55	Flail	Normal	Physical	—	100	15	Normal
61	Fissure	Ground	Physical	—	30	5	Normal

TM & HM MOVES

No.	Name	Type	Kind	Pow.	Acc.	PP	Range
TM06	Toxic	Poison	Status	—	90	10	Normal
TM10	Hidden Power	Normal	Special	60	100	15	Normal
TM17	Protect	Normal	Status	—	—	10	Self
TM18	Rain Dance	Water	Status	—	—	5	Both Sides
TM21	Frustration	Normal	Physical	—	100	20	Normal
TM24	Thunderbolt	Electric	Special	90	100	15	Normal
TM25	Thunder	Electric	Special	110	70	10	Normal
TM26	Earthquake	Ground	Physical	100	100	10	Adjacent
TM27	Return	Normal	Physical	—	100	20	Normal
TM28	Dig	Ground	Physical	80	100	10	Normal
TM32	Double Team	Normal	Status	—	—	15	Self
TM34	Sludge Wave	Poison	Special	95	100	10	Adjacent
TM36	Sludge Bomb	Poison	Special	90	100	10	Normal
TM37	Sandstorm	Rock	Status	—	—	10	Both Sides
TM39	Rock Tomb	Rock	Physical	60	95	15	Normal
TM42	Facade	Normal	Physical	70	100	20	Normal
TM44	Rest	Psychic	Status	—	—	10	Self
TM45	Attract	Normal	Status	—	100	15	Normal
TM48	Round	Normal	Special	60	100	15	Normal
TM55	Scald	Water	Special	80	100	15	Normal
TM66	Payback	Dark	Physical	50	100	10	Normal
TM70	Flash	Normal	Status	—	100	20	Normal
TM71	Stone Edge	Rock	Physical	100	80	5	Normal
TM73	Thunder Wave	Electric	Status	—	100	20	Normal
TM78	Bulldoze	Ground	Physical	60	100	20	Adjacent
TM80	Rock Slide	Rock	Physical	75	90	10	Many Others
TM83	Infestation	Bug	Special	20	100	20	Normal
TM87	Swagger	Normal	Status	—	90	15	Normal
TM88	Sleep Talk	Normal	Status	—	—	10	Self
TM90	Substitute	Normal	Status	—	—	10	Self
TM94	Secret Power	Normal	Physical	70	100	20	Normal
TM100	Confide	Normal	Status	—	—	20	Normal
HM03	Surf	Water	Special	90	100	15	Adjacent

MOVES LEARNED IN EXCHANGE FOR BP

Name	Type	Kind	Pow.	Acc.	PP	Range
Bounce	Flying	Physical	85	85	5	Normal
Uproar	Normal	Special	90	100	10	1 Random
Earth Power	Ground	Special	90	100	10	Normal
Foul Play	Dark	Physical	95	100	15	Normal
Magnet Rise	Electric	Status	—	—	10	Self
Electroweb	Electric	Special	55	95	15	Many Others
Aqua Tail	Water	Physical	90	90	10	Normal
Snore	Normal	Special	50	100	15	Normal
Pain Split	Normal	Status	—	—	20	Normal
Shock Wave	Electric	Special	60	—	20	Normal
Water Pulse	Water	Special	60	100	20	Normal
Spite	Ghost	Status	—	100	10	Normal
Endeavor	Normal	Physical	—	100	5	Normal
Stealth Rock	Rock	Status	—	—	20	Other Side

MOVES TAUGHT BY PEOPLE

Name	Type	Kind	Pow.	Acc.	PP	Range

EGG MOVES

Name	Type	Kind	Pow.	Acc.	PP	Range
Shock Wave	Electric	Special	60	—	20	Normal
Earth Power	Ground	Special	90	100	10	Normal
Yawn	Normal	Status	—	—	10	Normal
Sleep Talk	Normal	Status	—	—	10	Self
Astonish	Ghost	Physical	30	100	15	Normal
Curse	Ghost	Status	—	—	10	Varies
Spite	Ghost	Status	—	100	10	Normal
Spark	Electric	Physical	65	100	20	Normal
Pain Split	Normal	Status	—	—	20	Normal
Eerie Impulse	Electric	Status	—	100	15	Normal
Reflect Type	Normal	Status	—	—	15	Normal
Me First	Normal	Status	—	—	20	Varies

National Pokédex **619** Hoenn Pokédex —

Mienfoo

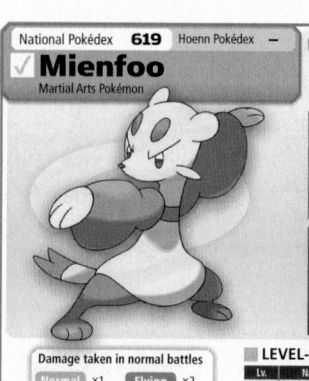

Martial Arts Pokémon

Fighting

HEIGHT: 2'11" WEIGHT: 44.1 lbs.

Same form for ♂ / ♀

Ω It takes pride in the speed at which it can use moves. What it loses in power, it makes up for in quantity.

α In fights, they dominate with onslaughts of flowing, continuous attacks. With their sharp claws, they cut enemies.

ABILITIES
Inner Focus
Regenerator

HIDDEN ABILITY
Reckless

EGG GROUPS
Field / Human-Like

STAT GROWTH RATES
HP
Attack
Defense
Sp. Atk
Sp. Def
Speed

ITEMS SOMETIMES HELD BY WILD POKÉMON
—

EVOLUTION

MAIN WAY TO REGISTER IN THE NATIONAL POKÉDEX

Appears in *Pokémon X* and *Pokémon Y*. Bring it to your game using Link Trade or the GTS.

Damage taken in normal battles

Type		Type	
Normal	×1	Flying	×2
Fire	×1	Psychic	×2
Water	×1	Bug	×0.5
Grass	×1	Rock	×0.5
Electric	×1	Ghost	×1
Ice	×1	Dragon	×1
Fighting	×1	Dark	×0.5
Poison	×1	Steel	×1
Ground	×1	Fairy	×2

Damage taken in Inverse battles

Type		Type	
Normal	×1	Flying	×0.5
Fire	×1	Psychic	×0.5
Water	×1	Bug	×2
Grass	×1	Rock	×2
Electric	×1	Ghost	×1
Ice	×1	Dragon	×1
Fighting	×1	Dark	×2
Poison	×1	Steel	×1
Ground	×1	Fairy	×0.5

Can be used in
Inverse Battle
Battle Institute
Battle Maison
Random Matchup (Free Battle)
Random Matchup (Others)

LEVEL-UP MOVES

Lv.	Name	Type	Kind	Pow.	Acc.	PP	Range
1	Pound	Normal	Physical	40	100	35	Normal
5	Meditate	Psychic	Status	—	—	40	Self
9	Detect	Fighting	Status	—	—	5	Self
13	Fake Out	Normal	Physical	40	100	10	Normal
17	Double Slap	Normal	Physical	15	85	10	Normal
21	Swift	Normal	Special	60	—	20	Many Others
25	Calm Mind	Psychic	Status	—	—	20	Self
29	Force Palm	Fighting	Physical	60	100	10	Normal
33	Drain Punch	Fighting	Physical	75	100	10	Normal
37	Jump Kick	Fighting	Physical	100	95	10	Normal
41	U-turn	Bug	Physical	70	100	20	Normal
45	Quick Guard	Fighting	Status	—	—	15	Your Side
49	Bounce	Flying	Physical	85	85	5	Normal
50	High Jump Kick	Fighting	Physical	130	90	10	Normal
57	Reversal	Fighting	Physical	—	100	15	Normal
61	Aura Sphere	Fighting	Special	80	—	20	Normal

TM & HM MOVES

No.	Name	Type	Kind	Pow.	Acc.	PP	Range
TM04	Calm Mind	Psychic	Status	—	—	20	Self
TM06	Toxic	Poison	Status	—	90	10	Normal
TM08	Bulk Up	Fighting	Status	—	—	20	Self
TM10	Hidden Power	Normal	Special	60	100	15	Normal
TM11	Sunny Day	Fire	Status	—	—	5	Both Sides
TM12	Taunt	Dark	Status	—	100	20	Normal
TM17	Protect	Normal	Status	—	—	10	Self
TM18	Rain Dance	Water	Status	—	—	5	Both Sides
TM21	Frustration	Normal	Physical	—	100	20	Normal
TM27	Return	Normal	Physical	—	100	20	Normal
TM28	Dig	Ground	Physical	80	100	10	Normal
TM31	Brick Break	Fighting	Physical	75	100	15	Normal
TM32	Double Team	Normal	Status	—	—	15	Self
TM33	Reflect	Psychic	Status	—	—	20	Your Side
TM39	Rock Tomb	Rock	Physical	60	95	15	Normal
TM40	Aerial Ace	Flying	Physical	60	—	20	Normal
TM42	Facade	Normal	Physical	70	100	20	Normal
TM44	Rest	Psychic	Status	—	—	10	Self
TM45	Attract	Normal	Status	—	100	15	Normal
TM47	Low Sweep	Fighting	Physical	65	100	20	Normal
TM48	Round	Normal	Special	60	100	15	Normal
TM52	Focus Blast	Fighting	Special	120	70	5	Normal
TM56	Fling	Dark	Physical	—	100	10	Normal
TM62	Acrobatics	Flying	Physical	55	100	15	Normal
TM66	Payback	Dark	Physical	50	100	10	Normal
TM67	Retaliate	Normal	Physical	70	100	5	Normal
TM71	Stone Edge	Rock	Physical	100	80	5	Normal
TM75	Swords Dance	Normal	Status	—	—	20	Self
TM77	Psych Up	Normal	Status	—	—	10	Normal
TM80	Rock Slide	Rock	Physical	75	90	10	Many Others
TM84	Poison Jab	Poison	Physical	80	100	20	Normal
TM86	Grass Knot	Grass	Special	—	100	20	Normal
TM87	Swagger	Normal	Status	—	90	15	Normal
TM88	Sleep Talk	Normal	Status	—	—	10	Self
TM89	U-turn	Bug	Physical	70	100	20	Normal
TM90	Substitute	Normal	Status	—	—	10	Self
TM94	Secret Power	Normal	Physical	70	100	20	Normal
TM98	Power-Up Punch	Fighting	Physical	40	100	20	Normal
TM100	Confide	Normal	Status	—	—	20	Normal
HM04	Strength	Normal	Physical	80	100	15	Normal
HM06	Rock Smash	Fighting	Physical	40	100	15	Normal

MOVES LEARNED IN EXCHANGE FOR BP

Name	Type	Kind	Pow.	Acc.	PP	Range
Dual Chop	Dragon	Physical	40	90	15	Normal
Bounce	Flying	Physical	85	85	5	Normal
Low Kick	Fighting	Physical	—	100	20	Normal
Snore	Normal	Special	50	100	15	Normal
Knock Off	Dark	Physical	65	100	20	Normal
Role Play	Psychic	Status	—	—	10	Normal
Drain Punch	Fighting	Physical	75	100	10	Normal
Focus Punch	Fighting	Physical	150	100	20	Normal
Helping Hand	Normal	Status	—	—	20	1 Ally

MOVES TAUGHT BY PEOPLE

Name	Type	Kind	Pow.	Acc.	PP	Range

EGG MOVES

Name	Type	Kind	Pow.	Acc.	PP	Range
Endure	Normal	Status	—	—	10	Self
Vital Throw	Fighting	Physical	70	—	10	Normal
Baton Pass	Normal	Status	—	—	40	Self
Smelling Salts	Normal	Physical	70	100	10	Normal
Low Kick	Fighting	Physical	—	100	20	Normal
Feint	Normal	Physical	30	100	10	Normal
Me First	Normal	Status	—	—	20	Varies
Knock Off	Dark	Physical	65	100	20	Normal
Ally Switch	Psychic	Status	—	—	15	Self

National Pokédex **620** Hoenn Pokédex —

Mienshao

Martial Arts Pokémon

Fighting

HEIGHT: 4'07" WEIGHT: 78.3 lbs.

Same form for ♂ / ♀

Ω It wields the fur on its arms like a whip. Its arm attacks come with such rapidity that they cannot even be seen.

α Using the long fur on its arms like whips, it launches into combo attacks that, once started, no one can stop.

ABILITIES
Inner Focus
Regenerator

HIDDEN ABILITY
Reckless

EGG GROUPS
Field / Human-Like

STAT GROWTH RATES
HP
Attack
Defense
Sp. Atk
Sp. Def
Speed

ITEMS SOMETIMES HELD BY WILD POKÉMON
—

EVOLUTION
Mienfoo → Lv. 50 → Mienshao

MAIN WAY TO REGISTER IN THE NATIONAL POKÉDEX

Level up a Mienfoo obtained via Link Trade or the GTS to Lv. 50.

Damage taken in normal battles

Normal	×1	Flying	×2
Fire	×1	Psychic	×2
Water	×1	Bug	×0.5
Grass	×1	Rock	×0.5
Electric	×1	Ghost	×1
Ice	×1	Dragon	×1
Fighting	×1	Dark	×0.5
Poison	×1	Steel	×1
Ground	×1	Fairy	×2

Damage taken in Inverse battles

Normal	×1	Flying	×0.5
Fire	×1	Psychic	×0.5
Water	×1	Bug	×2
Grass	×1	Rock	×2
Electric	×1	Ghost	×1
Ice	×1	Dragon	×1
Fighting	×1	Dark	×2
Poison	×1	Steel	×1
Ground	×1	Fairy	×0.5

Can be used in
Inverse Battle
Battle Institute
Battle Maison
Random Matchup (Free Battle)
Random Matchup (Others)

LEVEL-UP MOVES

Lv.	Name	Type	Kind	Pow.	Acc.	PP	Range
1	Aura Sphere	Fighting	Special	80	—	20	Normal
1	Reversal	Fighting	Physical	—	100	15	Normal
1	Pound	Normal	Physical	40	100	35	Normal
1	Meditate	Psychic	Status	—	—	40	Self
1	Detect	Fighting	Status	—	—	5	Self
1	Fake Out	Normal	Physical	40	100	10	Normal
5	Meditate	Psychic	Status	—	—	40	Self
9	Detect	Fighting	Status	—	—	5	Self
13	Fake Out	Normal	Physical	40	100	10	Normal
17	Double Slap	Normal	Physical	15	85	10	Normal
21	Swift	Normal	Special	60	—	20	Many Others
25	Calm Mind	Psychic	Status	—	—	20	Self
29	Force Palm	Fighting	Physical	60	100	10	Normal
33	Drain Punch	Fighting	Physical	75	100	10	Normal
37	Jump Kick	Fighting	Physical	100	95	10	Normal
41	U-turn	Bug	Physical	70	100	20	Normal
45	Wide Guard	Rock	Status	—	—	10	Your Side
49	Bounce	Flying	Physical	85	85	5	Normal
56	High Jump Kick	Fighting	Physical	130	90	10	Normal
63	Reversal	Fighting	Physical	—	100	15	Normal
70	Aura Sphere	Fighting	Special	80	—	20	Normal

TM & HM MOVES

No.	Name	Type	Kind	Pow.	Acc.	PP	Range
TM04	Calm Mind	Psychic	Status	—	—	20	Self
TM06	Toxic	Poison	Status	—	90	10	Normal
TM08	Bulk Up	Fighting	Status	—	—	20	Self
TM10	Hidden Power	Normal	Special	60	100	15	Normal
TM11	Sunny Day	Fire	Status	—	—	5	Both Sides
TM12	Taunt	Dark	Status	—	100	20	Normal
TM15	Hyper Beam	Normal	Special	150	90	5	Normal
TM17	Protect	Normal	Status	—	—	10	Self
TM18	Rain Dance	Water	Status	—	—	5	Both Sides
TM21	Frustration	Normal	Physical	—	100	20	Normal
TM27	Return	Normal	Physical	—	100	20	Normal
TM28	Dig	Ground	Physical	80	100	10	Normal
TM31	Brick Break	Fighting	Physical	75	100	15	Normal
TM32	Double Team	Normal	Status	—	—	15	Self
TM33	Reflect	Psychic	Status	—	—	20	Your Side
TM39	Rock Tomb	Rock	Physical	60	95	15	Normal
TM40	Aerial Ace	Flying	Physical	60	—	20	Normal
TM42	Facade	Normal	Physical	70	100	20	Normal
TM44	Rest	Psychic	Status	—	—	10	Self
TM45	Attract	Normal	Status	—	100	15	Normal
TM47	Low Sweep	Fighting	Physical	65	100	20	Normal
TM48	Round	Normal	Special	60	100	15	Normal
TM52	Focus Blast	Fighting	Special	120	70	5	Normal
TM56	Fling	Dark	Physical	—	100	10	Normal
TM62	Acrobatics	Flying	Physical	55	100	15	Normal
TM66	Payback	Dark	Physical	50	100	10	Normal
TM67	Retaliate	Normal	Physical	70	100	5	Normal
TM68	Giga Impact	Normal	Physical	150	90	5	Normal
TM71	Stone Edge	Rock	Physical	100	80	5	Normal
TM75	Swords Dance	Normal	Status	—	—	20	Self
TM77	Psych Up	Normal	Status	—	—	10	Normal
TM80	Rock Slide	Rock	Physical	75	90	10	Many Others
TM84	Poison Jab	Poison	Physical	80	100	20	Normal
TM86	Grass Knot	Grass	Special	—	100	20	Normal
TM87	Swagger	Normal	Status	—	90	15	Normal
TM88	Sleep Talk	Normal	Status	—	—	10	Self
TM89	U-turn	Bug	Physical	70	100	20	Normal
TM90	Substitute	Normal	Status	—	—	10	Self
TM94	Secret Power	Normal	Physical	70	100	20	Normal
TM98	Power-Up Punch	Fighting	Physical	40	100	20	Normal
TM100	Confide	Normal	Status	—	—	20	Normal
HM04	Strength	Normal	Physical	80	100	15	Normal
HM06	Rock Smash	Fighting	Physical	40	100	15	Normal

MOVES LEARNED IN EXCHANGE FOR BP

Name	Type	Kind	Pow.	Acc.	PP	Range
Dual Chop	Dragon	Physical	40	90	15	Normal
Bounce	Flying	Physical	85	85	5	Normal
Low Kick	Fighting	Physical	—	100	20	Normal
Snore	Normal	Special	50	100	15	Normal
Knock Off	Dark	Physical	65	100	20	Normal
Role Play	Psychic	Status	—	—	10	Normal
Drain Punch	Fighting	Physical	75	100	10	Normal
Focus Punch	Fighting	Physical	150	100	20	Normal
Helping Hand	Normal	Status	—	—	20	1 Ally

MOVES TAUGHT BY PEOPLE

Name	Type	Kind	Pow.	Acc.	PP	Range

National Pokédex **621** Hoenn Pokédex —

Druddigon

Cave Pokémon

Dragon

HEIGHT: 5'03" WEIGHT: 306.4 lbs.

Same form for ♂ / ♀

Ω It races through narrow caves, using its sharp claws to catch prey. The skin on its face is harder than a rock.

α It warms its body by absorbing sunlight with its wings. When its body temperature falls, it can no longer move.

ABILITIES
Rough Skin
Sheer Force

HIDDEN ABILITY
Mold Breaker

EGG GROUPS
Dragon / Monster

STAT GROWTH RATES
HP
Attack
Defense
Sp. Atk
Sp. Def
Speed

ITEMS SOMETIMES HELD BY WILD POKÉMON
Dragon Fang

EVOLUTION
Does not evolve

MAIN WAY TO REGISTER IN THE NATIONAL POKÉDEX

Catch in the Meteor Falls entrance. Appears as a hidden Pokémon after you battle Groudon or Kyogre.

Damage taken in normal battles

Normal	×1	Flying	×1
Fire	×0.5	Psychic	×1
Water	×0.5	Bug	×1
Grass	×0.5	Rock	×1
Electric	×0.5	Ghost	×1
Ice	×2	Dragon	×2
Fighting	×1	Dark	×1
Poison	×1	Steel	×1
Ground	×1	Fairy	×2

Damage taken in Inverse battles

Normal	×1	Flying	×1
Fire	×2	Psychic	×1
Water	×2	Bug	×1
Grass	×2	Rock	×1
Electric	×2	Ghost	×1
Ice	×0.5	Dragon	×0.5
Fighting	×1	Dark	×1
Poison	×1	Steel	×1
Ground	×1	Fairy	×0.5

Can be used in
Inverse Battle
Battle Institute
Battle Maison
Random Matchup (Free Battle)
Random Matchup (Others)

LEVEL-UP MOVES

Lv.	Name	Type	Kind	Pow.	Acc.	PP	Range
1	Leer	Normal	Status	—	100	30	Many Others
1	Scratch	Normal	Physical	40	100	35	Normal
5	Hone Claws	Dark	Status	—	—	15	Self
9	Bite	Dark	Physical	60	100	25	Normal
13	Scary Face	Normal	Status	—	100	10	Normal
18	Dragon Rage	Dragon	Special	—	100	10	Normal
21	Slash	Normal	Physical	70	100	20	Normal
25	Crunch	Dark	Physical	80	100	15	Normal
27	Dragon Claw	Dragon	Physical	80	100	15	Normal
31	Chip Away	Normal	Physical	70	100	20	Normal
35	Revenge	Fighting	Physical	60	100	10	Normal
40	Night Slash	Dark	Physical	70	100	15	Normal
45	Dragon Tail	Dragon	Physical	60	90	10	Normal
49	Rock Climb	Normal	Physical	90	85	20	Normal
55	Superpower	Fighting	Physical	120	100	5	Normal
62	Outrage	Dragon	Physical	120	100	10	1 Random

TM & HM MOVES

No.	Name	Type	Kind	Pow.	Acc.	PP	Range
TM01	Hone Claws	Dark	Status	—	—	15	Self
TM02	Dragon Claw	Dragon	Physical	80	100	15	Normal
TM05	Roar	Normal	Status	—	—	20	Normal
TM06	Toxic	Poison	Status	—	90	10	Normal
TM10	Hidden Power	Normal	Special	60	100	15	Normal
TM11	Sunny Day	Fire	Status	—	—	5	Both Sides
TM12	Taunt	Dark	Status	—	100	20	Normal
TM15	Hyper Beam	Normal	Special	150	90	5	Normal
TM17	Protect	Normal	Status	—	—	10	Self
TM18	Rain Dance	Water	Status	—	—	5	Both Sides
TM21	Frustration	Normal	Physical	—	100	20	Normal
TM23	Smack Down	Rock	Physical	50	100	15	Normal
TM26	Earthquake	Ground	Physical	100	100	10	Adjacent
TM27	Return	Normal	Physical	—	100	20	Normal
TM28	Dig	Ground	Physical	80	100	10	Normal
TM32	Double Team	Normal	Status	—	—	15	Self
TM35	Flamethrow	Fire	Special	90	100	15	Normal
TM36	Sludge Bomb	Poison	Special	90	100	10	Normal
TM39	Rock Tomb	Rock	Physical	60	95	15	Normal
TM40	Aerial Ace	Flying	Physical	60	—	20	Normal
TM41	Torment	Dark	Status	—	100	15	Normal
TM42	Facade	Normal	Physical	70	100	20	Normal
TM44	Rest	Psychic	Status	—	—	10	Self
TM45	Attract	Normal	Status	—	100	15	Normal
TM48	Round	Normal	Special	60	100	15	Normal
TM52	Focus Blast	Fighting	Special	120	70	5	Normal
TM56	Fling	Dark	Physical	—	100	10	Normal
TM57	Charge Beam	Electric	Special	50	90	10	Normal
TM59	Incinerate	Fire	Special	60	100	15	Many Others
TM65	Shadow Claw	Ghost	Physical	70	100	15	Normal
TM66	Payback	Dark	Physical	50	100	10	Normal
TM67	Retaliate	Normal	Physical	70	100	5	Normal
TM68	Giga Impact	Normal	Physical	150	90	5	Normal
TM78	Bulldoze	Ground	Physical	60	100	20	Adjacent
TM80	Rock Slide	Rock	Physical	75	90	10	Many Others
TM82	Dragon Tail	Dragon	Physical	60	90	10	Normal
TM87	Swagger	Normal	Status	—	90	15	Normal
TM88	Sleep Talk	Normal	Status	—	—	10	Self
TM90	Substitute	Normal	Status	—	—	10	Self
TM91	Flash Cannon	Steel	Special	80	100	10	Normal
TM94	Secret Power	Normal	Physical	70	100	20	Normal
TM95	Snarl	Dark	Special	55	95	15	Many Others
TM97	Dark Pulse	Dark	Special	80	100	15	Normal
TM98	Power-Up Punch	Fighting	Physical	40	100	20	Normal
TM100	Confide	Normal	Status	—	—	20	Normal
HM01	Cut	Normal	Physical	50	95	30	Normal
HM03	Surf	Water	Special	90	100	15	Adjacent
HM04	Strength	Normal	Physical	80	100	15	Normal
HM06	Rock Smash	Fighting	Physical	40	100	15	Normal

MOVES LEARNED IN EXCHANGE FOR BP

Name	Type	Kind	Pow.	Acc.	PP	Range
Iron Head	Steel	Physical	80	100	15	Normal
Gunk Shot	Poison	Physical	120	80	5	Normal
Thunder Punch	Electric	Physical	75	100	15	Normal
Fire Punch	Fire	Physical	75	100	15	Normal
Superpower	Fighting	Physical	120	100	5	Normal
Aqua Tail	Water	Physical	90	90	10	Normal
Dragon Pulse	Dragon	Special	85	100	10	Normal
Iron Tail	Steel	Physical	100	75	15	Normal
Snore	Normal	Special	50	100	15	Normal
Heat Wave	Fire	Special	95	90	10	Many Others
Shock Wave	Electric	Special	60	—	20	Normal
Outrage	Dragon	Physical	120	100	10	1 Random
Snatch	Dark	Status	—	—	10	Self
Stealth Rock	Rock	Status	—	—	20	Other Side

MOVES TAUGHT BY PEOPLE

Name	Type	Kind	Pow.	Acc.	PP	Range
Draco Meteor	Dragon	Special	130	90	5	Normal

EGG MOVES

Name	Type	Kind	Pow.	Acc.	PP	Range
Fire Fang	Fire	Physical	65	95	15	Normal
Thunder Fang	Electric	Physical	65	95	15	Normal
Crush Claw	Normal	Physical	75	95	10	Normal
Feint Attack	Dark	Physical	60	—	20	Normal
Pursuit	Dark	Physical	40	100	20	Normal
Iron Tail	Steel	Physical	100	75	15	Normal
Poison Tail	Poison	Physical	50	100	25	Normal
Snatch	Dark	Status	—	—	10	Self
Metal Claw	Steel	Physical	50	95	35	Normal
Glare	Normal	Status	—	100	30	Normal
Sucker Punch	Dark	Physical	80	100	5	Normal

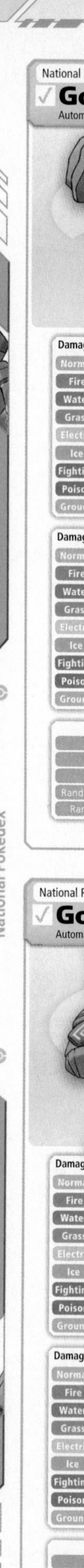

National Pokédex **622** Hoenn Pokédex —

√ Golett

Automaton Pokémon

Ground | Ghost

HEIGHT: 3'03" WEIGHT: 202.8 lbs.

Gender unknown

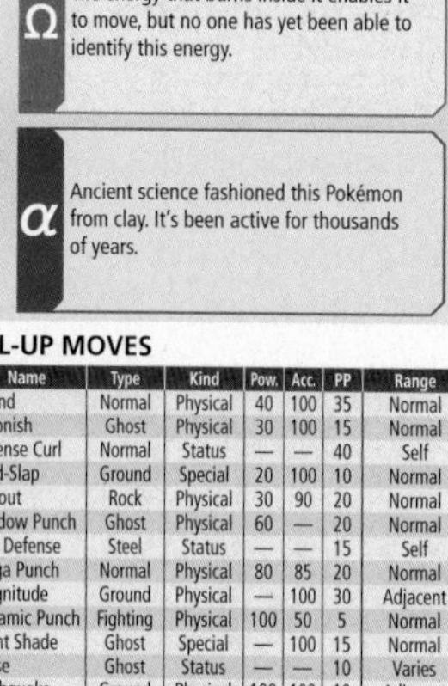

Ω The energy that burns inside it enables it to move, but no one has yet been able to identify this energy.

α Ancient science fashioned this Pokémon from clay. It's been active for thousands of years.

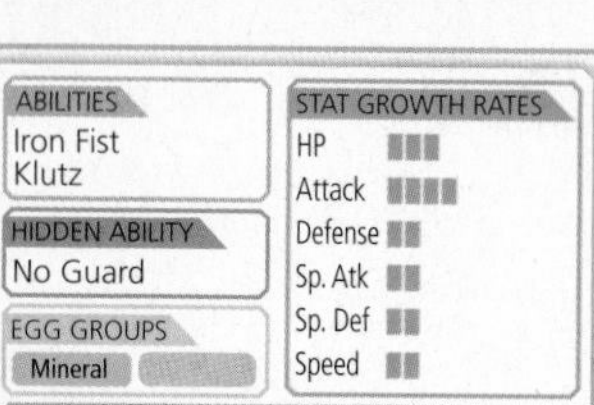

ABILITIES
Iron Fist
Klutz

HIDDEN ABILITY
No Guard

EGG GROUPS
Mineral

STAT GROWTH RATES
HP
Attack
Defense
Sp. Atk
Sp. Def
Speed

ITEMS SOMETIMES HELD BY WILD POKÉMON
—

EVOLUTION

MAIN WAY TO REGISTER IN THE NATIONAL POKÉDEX

Appears in *Pokémon X* and *Pokémon Y*. Bring it to your game using Link Trade or the GTS.

Damage taken in normal battles

Type		Type	
Normal	×0	Flying	×1
Fire	×1	Psychic	×1
Water	×2	Bug	×0.5
Grass	×2	Rock	×0.5
Electric	×0	Ghost	×2
Ice	×2	Dragon	×1
Fighting	×0	Dark	×2
Poison	×0.25	Steel	×1
Ground	×1	Fairy	×1

Damage taken in Inverse battles

Type		Type	
Normal	×2	Flying	×1
Fire	×1	Psychic	×1
Water	×0.5	Bug	×2
Grass	×0.5	Rock	×2
Electric	×2	Ghost	×0.5
Ice	×0.5	Dragon	×1
Fighting	×2	Dark	×0.5
Poison	×4	Steel	×1
Ground	×1	Fairy	×1

Can be used in
Inverse Battle
Battle Institute
Battle Maison
Random Matchup (Free Battle)
Random Matchup (Others)

LEVEL-UP MOVES

Lv.	Name	Type	Kind	Pow.	Acc.	PP	Range
1	Pound	Normal	Physical	40	100	35	Normal
1	Astonish	Ghost	Physical	30	100	15	Normal
1	Defense Curl	Normal	Status	—	—	40	Self
5	Mud-Slap	Ground	Special	20	100	10	Normal
9	Rollout	Rock	Physical	30	90	20	Normal
13	Shadow Punch	Ghost	Physical	60	—	20	Normal
17	Iron Defense	Steel	Status	—	—	15	Self
21	Mega Punch	Normal	Physical	80	85	20	Normal
25	Magnitude	Ground	Physical	—	100	30	Adjacent
30	Dynamic Punch	Fighting	Physical	100	50	5	Normal
35	Night Shade	Ghost	Special	—	100	15	Normal
40	Curse	Ghost	Status	—	—	10	Varies
45	Earthquake	Ground	Physical	100	100	10	Adjacent
50	Hammer Arm	Fighting	Physical	100	90	10	Normal
55	Focus Punch	Fighting	Physical	150	100	20	Normal

TM & HM MOVES

No.	Name	Type	Kind	Pow.	Acc.	PP	Range
TM06	Toxic	Poison	Status	—	90	10	Normal
TM10	Hidden Power	Normal	Special	60	100	15	Normal
TM13	Ice Beam	Ice	Special	90	100	10	Normal
TM17	Protect	Normal	Status	—	—	10	Self
TM18	Rain Dance	Water	Status	—	—	5	Both Sides
TM20	Safeguard	Normal	Status	—	—	25	Your Side
TM21	Frustration	Normal	Physical	—	100	20	Normal
TM26	Earthquake	Ground	Physical	100	100	10	Adjacent
TM27	Return	Normal	Physical	—	100	20	Normal
TM29	Psychic	Psychic	Special	90	100	10	Normal
TM30	Shadow Ball	Ghost	Special	80	100	15	Normal
TM31	Brick Break	Fighting	Physical	75	100	15	Normal
TM32	Double Team	Normal	Status	—	—	15	Self
TM39	Rock Tomb	Rock	Physical	60	95	15	Normal
TM42	Facade	Normal	Physical	70	100	20	Normal
TM44	Rest	Psychic	Status	—	—	10	Self
TM46	Thief	Dark	Physical	60	100	25	Normal
TM47	Low Sweep	Fighting	Physical	65	100	20	Normal
TM48	Round	Normal	Special	60	100	15	Normal
TM52	Focus Blast	Fighting	Special	120	70	5	Normal
TM56	Fling	Dark	Physical	—	100	10	Normal
TM69	Rock Polish	Rock	Status	—	—	20	Self
TM70	Flash	Normal	Status	—	100	20	Normal
TM74	Gyro Ball	Steel	Physical	—	100	5	Normal
TM78	Bulldoze	Ground	Physical	60	100	20	Adjacent
TM80	Rock Slide	Rock	Physical	75	90	10	Many Others
TM86	Grass Knot	Grass	Special	—	100	20	Normal
TM87	Swagger	Normal	Status	—	90	15	Normal
TM88	Sleep Talk	Normal	Status	—	—	10	Self
TM90	Substitute	Normal	Status	—	—	10	Self
TM94	Secret Power	Normal	Physical	70	100	20	Normal
TM98	Power-Up Punch	Fighting	Physical	40	100	20	Normal
TM100	Confide	Normal	Status	—	—	20	Normal
HM04	Strength	Normal	Physical	80	100	15	Normal
HM06	Rock Smash	Fighting	Physical	40	100	15	Normal

MOVES LEARNED IN EXCHANGE FOR BP

Name	Type	Kind	Pow.	Acc.	PP	Range
Signal Beam	Bug	Special	75	100	15	Normal
Low Kick	Fighting	Physical	—	100	20	Normal
Thunder Punch	Electric	Physical	75	100	15	Normal
Fire Punch	Fire	Physical	75	100	15	Normal
Ice Punch	Ice	Physical	75	100	15	Normal
Magic Coat	Psychic	Status	—	—	15	Self
Block	Normal	Status	—	—	5	Normal
Earth Power	Ground	Special	90	100	10	Normal
Gravity	Psychic	Status	—	—	5	Both Sides
Iron Defense	Steel	Status	—	—	15	Self
Superpower	Fighting	Physical	120	100	5	Normal
Icy Wind	Ice	Special	55	95	15	Many Others
Snore	Normal	Special	50	100	15	Normal
Drain Punch	Fighting	Physical	75	100	10	Normal
Focus Punch	Fighting	Physical	150	100	20	Normal
Shock Wave	Electric	Special	60	—	20	Normal
Stealth Rock	Rock	Status	—	—	20	Other Side

MOVES TAUGHT BY PEOPLE

Name	Type	Kind	Pow.	Acc.	PP	Range

National Pokédex **623** Hoenn Pokédex —

√ Golurk

Automaton Pokémon

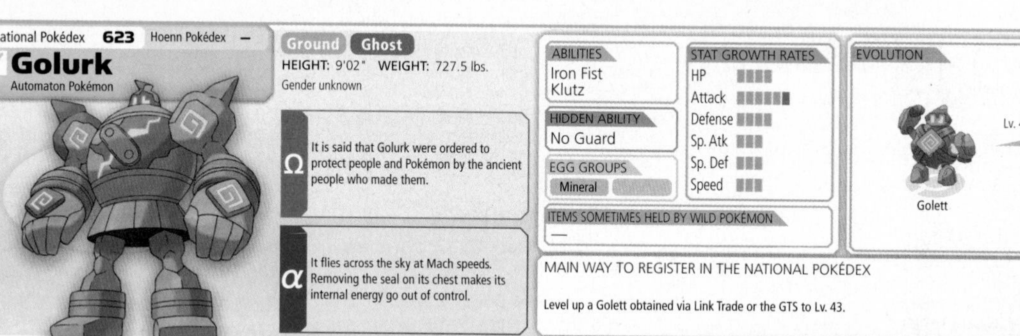

Ground | Ghost

HEIGHT: 9'02" WEIGHT: 727.5 lbs.

Gender unknown

Ω It is said that Golurk were ordered to protect people and Pokémon by the ancient people who made them.

α It flies across the sky at Mach speeds. Removing the seal on its chest makes its internal energy go out of control.

ABILITIES
Iron Fist
Klutz

HIDDEN ABILITY
No Guard

EGG GROUPS
Mineral

STAT GROWTH RATES
HP
Attack
Defense
Sp. Atk
Sp. Def
Speed

ITEMS SOMETIMES HELD BY WILD POKÉMON
—

EVOLUTION

Golett → Lv. 43 → Golurk

MAIN WAY TO REGISTER IN THE NATIONAL POKÉDEX

Level up a Golett obtained via Link Trade or the GTS to Lv. 43.

Damage taken in normal battles

Type		Type	
Normal	×0	Flying	×1
Fire	×1	Psychic	×1
Water	×2	Bug	×0.5
Grass	×2	Rock	×0.5
Electric	×0	Ghost	×2
Ice	×2	Dragon	×1
Fighting	×0	Dark	×2
Poison	×0.25	Steel	×1
Ground	×1	Fairy	×1

Damage taken in Inverse battles

Type		Type	
Normal	×2	Flying	×1
Fire	×1	Psychic	×1
Water	×0.5	Bug	×2
Grass	×0.5	Rock	×2
Electric	×2	Ghost	×0.5
Ice	×0.5	Dragon	×1
Fighting	×2	Dark	×0.5
Poison	×4	Steel	×1
Ground	×1	Fairy	×1

Can be used in
Inverse Battle
Battle Institute
Battle Maison
Random Matchup (Free Battle)
Random Matchup (Others)

LEVEL-UP MOVES

Lv.	Name	Type	Kind	Pow.	Acc.	PP	Range
1	Phantom Force	Ghost	Physical	90	100	10	Normal
1	Focus Punch	Fighting	Physical	150	100	20	Normal
1	Pound	Normal	Physical	40	100	35	Normal
1	Astonish	Ghost	Physical	30	100	15	Normal
1	Defense Curl	Normal	Status	—	—	40	Self
1	Mud-Slap	Ground	Special	20	100	10	Normal
5	Mud-Slap	Ground	Special	20	100	10	Normal
9	Rollout	Rock	Physical	30	90	20	Normal
13	Shadow Punch	Ghost	Physical	60	—	20	Normal
17	Iron Defense	Steel	Status	—	—	15	Self
21	Mega Punch	Normal	Physical	80	85	20	Normal
25	Magnitude	Ground	Physical	—	100	30	Adjacent
30	Dynamic Punch	Fighting	Physical	100	50	5	Normal
35	Night Shade	Ghost	Special	—	100	15	Normal
40	Curse	Ghost	Status	—	—	10	Varies
43	Heavy Slam	Steel	Physical	—	100	10	Normal
50	Earthquake	Ground	Physical	100	100	10	Adjacent
60	Hammer Arm	Fighting	Physical	100	90	10	Normal
70	Focus Punch	Fighting	Physical	150	100	20	Normal
75	Phantom Force	Ghost	Physical	90	100	10	Normal

TM & HM MOVES

No.	Name	Type	Kind	Pow.	Acc.	PP	Range
TM06	Toxic	Poison	Status	—	90	10	Normal
TM10	Hidden Power	Normal	Special	60	100	15	Normal
TM13	Ice Beam	Ice	Special	90	100	10	Normal
TM15	Hyper Beam	Normal	Special	150	90	5	Normal
TM17	Protect	Normal	Status	—	—	10	Self
TM18	Rain Dance	Water	Status	—	—	5	Both Sides
TM20	Safeguard	Normal	Status	—	—	25	Your Side
TM21	Frustration	Normal	Physical	—	100	20	Normal
TM22	Solar Beam	Grass	Special	120	100	10	Normal
TM24	Thunderbolt	Electric	Special	90	100	15	Normal
TM26	Earthquake	Ground	Physical	100	100	10	Adjacent
TM27	Return	Normal	Physical	—	100	20	Normal
TM29	Psychic	Psychic	Special	90	100	10	Normal
TM30	Shadow Ball	Ghost	Special	80	100	15	Normal
TM31	Brick Break	Fighting	Physical	75	100	15	Normal
TM32	Double Team	Normal	Status	—	—	15	Self
TM39	Rock Tomb	Rock	Physical	60	95	15	Normal
TM42	Facade	Normal	Physical	70	100	20	Normal
TM44	Rest	Psychic	Status	—	—	10	Self
TM46	Thief	Dark	Physical	60	100	25	Normal
TM47	Low Sweep	Fighting	Physical	65	100	20	Normal
TM48	Round	Normal	Special	60	100	15	Normal
TM52	Focus Blast	Fighting	Special	120	70	5	Normal
TM56	Fling	Dark	Physical	—	100	10	Normal
TM57	Charge Beam	Electric	Special	50	90	10	Normal
TM68	Giga Impact	Normal	Physical	150	90	5	Normal
TM69	Rock Polish	Rock	Status	—	—	20	Self
TM70	Flash	Normal	Status	—	100	20	Normal
TM71	Stone Edge	Rock	Physical	100	80	5	Normal
TM74	Gyro Ball	Steel	Physical	—	100	5	Normal
TM78	Bulldoze	Ground	Physical	60	100	20	Adjacent
TM80	Rock Slide	Rock	Physical	75	90	10	Many Others
TM86	Grass Knot	Grass	Special	—	100	20	Normal
TM87	Swagger	Normal	Status	—	90	15	Normal
TM88	Sleep Talk	Normal	Status	—	—	10	Self
TM90	Substitute	Normal	Status	—	—	10	Self
TM91	Flash Cannon	Steel	Special	80	100	10	Normal
TM94	Secret Power	Normal	Physical	70	100	20	Normal
TM98	Power-Up Punch	Fighting	Physical	40	100	20	Normal
TM100	Confide	Normal	Status	—	—	20	Normal
HM02	Fly	Flying	Physical	90	95	15	Normal
HM04	Strength	Normal	Physical	80	100	15	Normal
HM06	Rock Smash	Fighting	Physical	40	100	15	Normal

MOVES LEARNED IN EXCHANGE FOR BP

Name	Type	Kind	Pow.	Acc.	PP	Range
Signal Beam	Bug	Special	75	100	15	Normal
Low Kick	Fighting	Physical	—	100	20	Normal
Thunder Punch	Electric	Physical	75	100	15	Normal
Fire Punch	Fire	Physical	75	100	15	Normal
Ice Punch	Ice	Physical	75	100	15	Normal
Magic Coat	Psychic	Status	—	—	15	Self
Block	Normal	Status	—	—	5	Normal
Earth Power	Ground	Special	90	100	10	Normal
Gravity	Psychic	Status	—	—	5	Both Sides
Iron Defense	Steel	Status	—	—	15	Self
Superpower	Fighting	Physical	120	100	5	Normal
Icy Wind	Ice	Special	55	95	15	Many Others
Zen Headbutt	Psychic	Physical	80	90	15	Normal
Snore	Normal	Special	50	100	15	Normal
Drain Punch	Fighting	Physical	75	100	10	Normal
Focus Punch	Fighting	Physical	150	100	20	Normal
Shock Wave	Electric	Special	60	—	20	Normal
Stealth Rock	Rock	Status	—	—	20	Other Side

MOVES TAUGHT BY PEOPLE

Name	Type	Kind	Pow.	Acc.	PP	Range

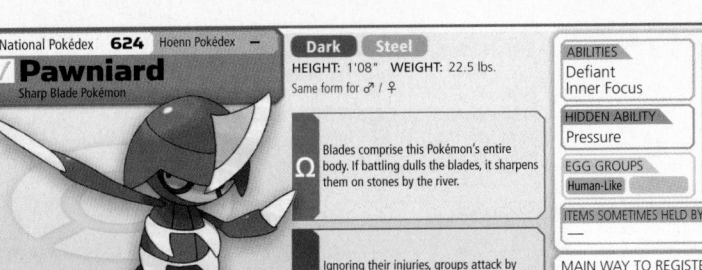

National Pokédex 624 — Hoenn Pokédex —

Pawniard

Sharp Blade Pokémon

Dark **Steel**

HEIGHT: 1'08" WEIGHT: 22.5 lbs.

Same form for ♂ / ♀

Ω Blades comprise this Pokémon's entire body. If battling dulls the blades, it sharpens them on stones by the river.

α Ignoring their injuries, groups attack by sinking the blades that cover their bodies into their prey.

ABILITIES
Defiant
Inner Focus

HIDDEN ABILITY
Pressure

EGG GROUPS
Human-Like

STAT GROWTH RATES
HP
Attack
Defense
Sp. Atk
Sp. Def
Speed

ITEMS SOMETIMES HELD BY WILD POKÉMON
—

EVOLUTION

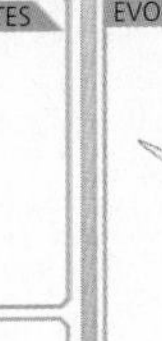
Pawniard

Lv. 52

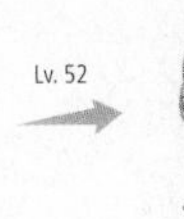
Bisharp

MAIN WAY TO REGISTER IN THE NATIONAL POKÉDEX

Appears in *Pokémon X* and *Pokémon Y*. Bring it to your game using Link Trade or the GTS.

Damage taken in normal battles

Type		Type	
Normal	×0.5	Flying	×0.5
Fire	×2	Psychic	×0
Water	×1	Bug	×1
Grass	×0.5	Rock	×0.5
Electric	×1	Ghost	×0.5
Ice	×0.5	Dragon	×0.5
Fighting	×4	Dark	×0.5
Poison	×0	Steel	×0.5
Ground	×2	Fairy	×1

Damage taken in Inverse battles

Type		Type	
Normal	×2	Flying	×2
Fire	×0.5	Psychic	×4
Water	×1	Bug	×1
Grass	×2	Rock	×2
Electric	×1	Ghost	×2
Ice	×2	Dragon	×2
Fighting	×0.25	Dark	×2
Poison	×2	Steel	×2
Ground	×0.5	Fairy	×1

Can be used in

Inverse Battle
Battle Institute
Battle Maison
Random Matchup (Free Battle)
Random Matchup (Others)

LEVEL-UP MOVES

Lv.	Name	Type	Kind	Pow.	Acc.	PP	Range
1	Scratch	Normal	Physical	40	100	35	Normal
6	Leer	Normal	Status	—	100	30	Many Others
9	Fury Cutter	Bug	Physical	40	95	20	Normal
14	Torment	Dark	Status	—	100	15	Normal
17	Feint Attack	Dark	Physical	60	—	20	Normal
22	Scary Face	Normal	Status	—	100	10	Normal
25	Metal Claw	Steel	Physical	50	95	35	Normal
30	Slash	Normal	Physical	70	100	20	Normal
33	Assurance	Dark	Physical	60	100	10	Normal
38	Metal Sound	Steel	Status	—	85	40	Normal
41	Embargo	Dark	Status	—	100	15	Normal
46	Iron Defense	Steel	Status	—	—	15	Self
49	Night Slash	Dark	Physical	70	100	15	Normal
54	Iron Head	Steel	Physical	80	100	15	Normal
57	Swords Dance	Normal	Status	—	—	20	Self
62	Guillotine	Normal	Physical	—	30	5	Normal

TM & HM MOVES

No.	Name	Type	Kind	Pow.	Acc.	PP	Range
TM01	Hone Claws	Dark	Status	—	—	15	Self
TM06	Toxic	Poison	Status	—	90	10	Normal
TM10	Hidden Power	Normal	Special	60	100	15	Normal
TM12	Taunt	Dark	Status	—	100	20	Normal
TM17	Protect	Normal	Status	—	—	10	Self
TM18	Rain Dance	Water	Status	—	—	5	Both Sides
TM21	Frustration	Normal	Physical	—	100	20	Normal
TM27	Return	Normal	Physical	—	100	20	Normal
TM28	Dig	Ground	Physical	80	100	10	Normal
TM31	Brick Break	Fighting	Physical	75	100	15	Normal
TM32	Double Team	Normal	Status	—	—	15	Self
TM37	Sandstorm	Rock	Status	—	—	10	Both Sides
TM39	Rock Tomb	Rock	Physical	60	95	15	Normal
TM40	Aerial Ace	Flying	Physical	60	—	20	Normal
TM41	Torment	Dark	Status	—	100	15	Normal
TM42	Facade	Normal	Physical	70	100	20	Normal
TM44	Rest	Psychic	Status	—	—	10	Self
TM45	Attract	Normal	Status	—	100	15	Normal
TM46	Thief	Dark	Physical	60	100	25	Normal
TM47	Low Sweep	Fighting	Physical	65	100	20	Normal
TM48	Round	Normal	Special	60	100	15	Normal
TM54	False Swipe	Normal	Physical	40	100	40	Normal
TM56	Fling	Dark	Physical	—	100	10	Normal
TM63	Embargo	Dark	Status	—	100	15	Normal
TM65	Shadow Claw	Ghost	Physical	70	100	15	Normal
TM66	Payback	Dark	Physical	50	100	10	Normal
TM67	Retaliate	Normal	Physical	70	100	5	Normal
TM69	Rock Polish	Rock	Status	—	—	20	Self
TM73	Thunder Wave	Electric	Status	—	100	20	Normal
TM75	Swords Dance	Normal	Status	—	—	20	Self
TM81	X-Scissor	Bug	Physical	80	100	15	Normal
TM84	Poison Jab	Poison	Physical	80	100	20	Normal
TM86	Grass Knot	Grass	Special	—	100	20	Normal
TM87	Swagger	Normal	Status	—	90	15	Normal
TM88	Sleep Talk	Normal	Status	—	—	10	Self
TM90	Substitute	Normal	Status	—	—	10	Self
TM94	Secret Power	Normal	Physical	70	100	20	Normal
TM95	Snarl	Dark	Special	55	95	15	Many Others
TM97	Dark Pulse	Dark	Special	80	100	15	Normal
TM98	Power-Up Punch	Fighting	Physical	40	100	20	Normal
TM100	Confide	Normal	Status	—	—	20	Normal
HM01	Cut	Normal	Physical	50	95	30	Normal
HM06	Rock Smash	Fighting	Physical	40	100	15	Normal

MOVES LEARNED IN EXCHANGE FOR BP

Name	Type	Kind	Pow.	Acc.	PP	Range
Dual Chop	Dragon	Physical	40	90	15	Normal
Iron Head	Steel	Physical	80	100	15	Normal
Low Kick	Fighting	Physical	—	100	20	Normal
Foul Play	Dark	Physical	95	100	15	Normal
Magnet Rise	Electric	Status	—	—	10	Self
Iron Defense	Steel	Status	—	—	15	Self
Snore	Normal	Special	50	100	15	Normal
Knock Off	Dark	Physical	65	100	20	Normal
Role Play	Psychic	Status	—	—	10	Normal
Spite	Ghost	Status	—	100	10	Normal
Snatch	Dark	Status	—	—	10	Self
Stealth Rock	Rock	Status	—	—	20	Other Side

MOVES TAUGHT BY PEOPLE

Name	Type	Kind	Pow.	Acc.	PP	Range

EGG MOVES

Name	Type	Kind	Pow.	Acc.	PP	Range
Revenge	Fighting	Physical	60	100	10	Normal
Sucker Punch	Dark	Physical	80	100	5	Normal
Pursuit	Dark	Physical	40	100	20	Normal
Headbutt	Normal	Physical	70	100	15	Normal
Stealth Rock	Rock	Status	—	—	20	Other Side
Psycho Cut	Psychic	Physical	70	100	20	Normal
Mean Look	Normal	Status	—	—	5	Normal
Quick Guard	Fighting	Status	—	—	15	Your Side

National Pokédex 625 — Hoenn Pokédex —

Bisharp

Sword Blade Pokémon

Dark **Steel**

HEIGHT: 5'03" WEIGHT: 154.3 lbs.

Same form for ♂ / ♀

Ω This pitiless Pokémon commands a group of Pawniard to hound prey into immobility. It then moves in to finish the prey off.

α Bisharp pursues prey in the company of a large group of Pawniard. Then Bisharp finishes off the prey.

ABILITIES
Defiant
Inner Focus

HIDDEN ABILITY
Pressure

EGG GROUPS
Human-Like

STAT GROWTH RATES
HP
Attack
Defense
Sp. Atk
Sp. Def
Speed

ITEMS SOMETIMES HELD BY WILD POKÉMON
—

EVOLUTION

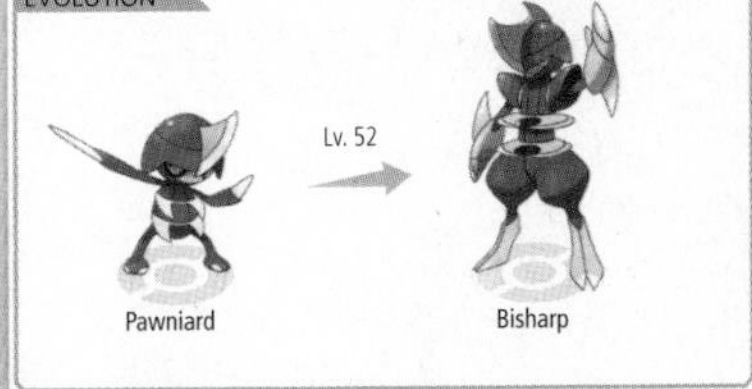

Pawniard Bisharp

MAIN WAY TO REGISTER IN THE NATIONAL POKÉDEX

Obtain in *Pokémon X* or *Pokémon Y*. Bring it to your game using Link Trade or the GTS.

Damage taken in normal battles

Type		Type	
Normal	×0.5	Flying	×0.5
Fire	×2	Psychic	×0
Water	×1	Bug	×1
Grass	×0.5	Rock	×0.5
Electric	×1	Ghost	×0.5
Ice	×0.5	Dragon	×0.5
Fighting	×4	Dark	×0.5
Poison	×0	Steel	×0.5
Ground	×2	Fairy	×1

Damage taken in Inverse battles

Type		Type	
Normal	×2	Flying	×2
Fire	×0.5	Psychic	×4
Water	×1	Bug	×1
Grass	×2	Rock	×2
Electric	×1	Ghost	×2
Ice	×2	Dragon	×2
Fighting	×0.25	Dark	×2
Poison	×2	Steel	×2
Ground	×0.5	Fairy	×1

Can be used in

Inverse Battle
Battle Institute
Battle Maison
Random Matchup (Free Battle)
Random Matchup (Others)

LEVEL-UP MOVES

Lv.	Name	Type	Kind	Pow.	Acc.	PP*	Range
1	Guillotine	Normal	Physical	—	30	5	Normal
1	Iron Head	Steel	Physical	80	100	15	Normal
1	Metal Burst	Steel	Physical	—	100	10	Varies
1	Scratch	Normal	Physical	40	100	35	Normal
1	Leer	Normal	Status	—	100	30	Many Others
1	Fury Cutter	Bug	Physical	40	95	20	Normal
1	Torment	Dark	Status	—	100	15	Normal
6	Leer	Normal	Status	—	100	30	Many Others
9	Fury Cutter	Bug	Physical	40	95	20	Normal
14	Torment	Dark	Status	—	100	15	Normal
17	Feint Attack	Dark	Physical	60	—	20	Normal
22	Scary Face	Normal	Status	—	100	10	Normal
25	Metal Claw	Steel	Physical	50	95	35	Normal
30	Slash	Normal	Physical	70	100	20	Normal
33	Assurance	Dark	Physical	60	100	10	Normal
38	Metal Sound	Steel	Status	—	85	40	Normal
41	Embargo	Dark	Status	—	100	15	Normal
46	Iron Defense	Steel	Status	—	—	15	Self
49	Night Slash	Dark	Physical	70	100	15	Normal
57	Iron Head	Steel	Physical	80	100	15	Normal
63	Swords Dance	Normal	Status	—	—	20	Self
71	Guillotine	Normal	Physical	—	30	5	Normal

TM & HM MOVES

No.	Name	Type	Kind	Pow.	Acc.	PP	Range
TM01	Hone Claws	Dark	Status	—	—	15	Self
TM06	Toxic	Poison	Status	—	90	10	Normal
TM10	Hidden Power	Normal	Special	60	100	15	Normal
TM12	Taunt	Dark	Status	—	100	20	Normal
TM15	Hyper Beam	Normal	Special	150	90	5	Normal
TM17	Protect	Normal	Status	—	—	10	Self
TM18	Rain Dance	Water	Status	—	—	5	Both Sides
TM21	Frustration	Normal	Physical	—	100	20	Normal
TM27	Return	Normal	Physical	—	100	20	Normal
TM28	Dig	Ground	Physical	80	100	10	Normal
TM31	Brick Break	Fighting	Physical	75	100	15	Normal
TM32	Double Team	Normal	Status	—	—	15	Self
TM37	Sandstorm	Rock	Status	—	—	10	Both Sides
TM39	Rock Tomb	Rock	Physical	60	95	15	Normal
TM40	Aerial Ace	Flying	Physical	60	—	20	Normal
TM41	Torment	Dark	Status	—	100	15	Normal
TM42	Facade	Normal	Physical	70	100	20	Normal
TM44	Rest	Psychic	Status	—	—	10	Self
TM45	Attract	Normal	Status	—	100	15	Normal
TM46	Thief	Dark	Physical	60	100	25	Normal
TM47	Low Sweep	Fighting	Physical	65	100	20	Normal
TM48	Round	Normal	Special	60	100	15	Normal
TM52	Focus Blast	Fighting	Special	120	70	5	Normal
TM54	False Swipe	Normal	Physical	40	100	40	Normal
TM56	Fling	Dark	Physical	—	100	10	Normal
TM63	Embargo	Dark	Status	—	100	15	Normal
TM65	Shadow Claw	Ghost	Physical	70	100	15	Normal
TM66	Payback	Dark	Physical	50	100	10	Normal
TM67	Retaliate	Normal	Physical	70	100	5	Normal
TM68	Giga Impact	Normal	Physical	150	90	5	Normal
TM69	Rock Polish	Rock	Status	—	—	20	Self
TM71	Stone Edge	Rock	Physical	100	80	5	Normal
TM73	Thunder Wave	Electric	Status	—	100	20	Normal
TM75	Swords Dance	Normal	Status	—	—	20	Self
TM81	X-Scissor	Bug	Physical	80	100	15	Normal
TM84	Poison Jab	Poison	Physical	80	100	20	Normal
TM86	Grass Knot	Grass	Special	—	100	20	Normal
TM87	Swagger	Normal	Status	—	90	15	Normal
TM88	Sleep Talk	Normal	Status	—	—	10	Self
TM90	Substitute	Normal	Status	—	—	10	Self
TM94	Secret Power	Normal	Physical	70	100	20	Normal
TM95	Snarl	Dark	Special	55	95	15	Many Others
TM97	Dark Pulse	Dark	Special	80	100	15	Normal
TM98	Power-Up Punch	Fighting	Physical	40	100	20	Normal
TM100	Confide	Normal	Status	—	—	20	Normal
HM01	Cut	Normal	Physical	50	95	30	Normal
HM06	Rock Smash	Fighting	Physical	40	100	15	Normal

MOVES LEARNED IN EXCHANGE FOR BP

Name	Type	Kind	Pow.	Acc.	PP	Range
Dual Chop	Dragon	Physical	40	90	15	Normal
Iron Head	Steel	Physical	80	100	15	Normal
Low Kick	Fighting	Physical	—	100	20	Normal
Foul Play	Dark	Physical	95	100	15	Normal
Magnet Rise	Electric	Status	—	—	10	Self
Iron Defense	Steel	Status	—	—	15	Self
Snore	Normal	Special	50	100	15	Normal
Knock Off	Dark	Physical	65	100	20	Normal
Role Play	Psychic	Status	—	—	10	Normal
Spite	Ghost	Status	—	100	10	Normal
Snatch	Dark	Status	—	—	10	Self
Stealth Rock	Rock	Status	—	—	20	Other Side

MOVES TAUGHT BY PEOPLE

Name	Type	Kind	Pow.	Acc.	PP	Range

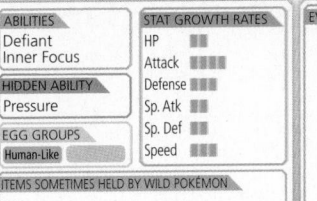

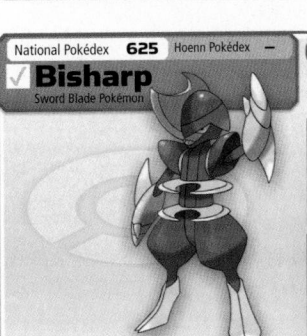

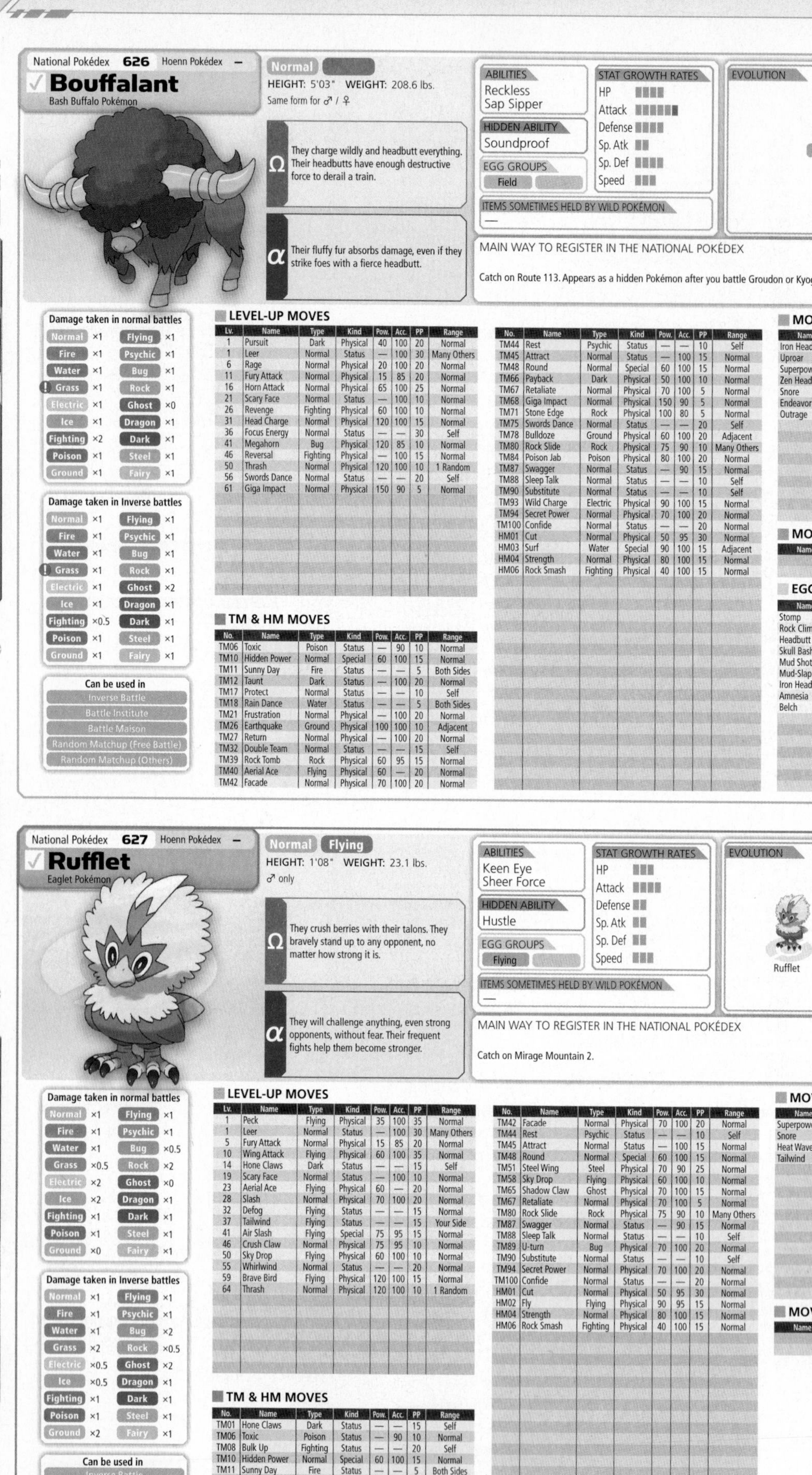

National Pokédex **626** Hoenn Pokédex —

Bouffalant

Bash Buffalo Pokémon

Normal

HEIGHT: 5'03" WEIGHT: 208.6 lbs.

Same form for ♂ / ♀

Ω They charge wildly and headbutt everything. Their headbutts have enough destructive force to derail a train.

α Their fluffy fur absorbs damage, even if they strike foes with a fierce headbutt.

ABILITIES
Reckless
Sap Sipper

HIDDEN ABILITY
Soundproof

EGG GROUPS
Field

STAT GROWTH RATES
HP
Attack
Defense
Sp. Atk
Sp. Def
Speed

ITEMS SOMETIMES HELD BY WILD POKÉMON
—

EVOLUTION
Does not evolve

MAIN WAY TO REGISTER IN THE NATIONAL POKÉDEX
Catch on Route 113. Appears as a hidden Pokémon after you battle Groudon or Kyogre.

Damage taken in normal battles

Type		Type	
Normal	×1	Flying	×1
Fire	×1	Psychic	×1
Water	×1	Bug	×1
Grass	×1	Rock	×1
Electric	×1	Ghost	×0
Ice	×1	Dragon	×1
Fighting	×2	Dark	×1
Poison	×1	Steel	×1
Ground	×1	Fairy	×1

Damage taken in Inverse battles

Type		Type	
Normal	×1	Flying	×1
Fire	×1	Psychic	×1
Water	×1	Bug	×1
Grass	×1	Rock	×1
Electric	×1	Ghost	×2
Ice	×1	Dragon	×1
Fighting	×0.5	Dark	×1
Poison	×1	Steel	×1
Ground	×1	Fairy	×1

Can be used in
Inverse Battle
Battle Institute
Battle Maison
Random Matchup (Free Battle)
Random Matchup (Others)

LEVEL-UP MOVES

Lv.	Name	Type	Kind	Pow.	Acc.	PP	Range
1	Pursuit	Dark	Physical	40	100	20	Normal
1	Leer	Normal	Status	—	100	30	Many Others
6	Rage	Normal	Physical	20	100	20	Normal
11	Fury Attack	Normal	Physical	15	85	20	Normal
16	Horn Attack	Normal	Physical	65	100	25	Normal
21	Scary Face	Normal	Status	—	100	10	Normal
26	Revenge	Fighting	Physical	60	100	10	Normal
31	Head Charge	Normal	Physical	120	100	15	Normal
36	Focus Energy	Normal	Status	—	—	30	Self
41	Megahorn	Bug	Physical	120	85	10	Normal
46	Reversal	Fighting	Physical	—	100	15	Normal
50	Thrash	Normal	Physical	120	100	10	1 Random
56	Swords Dance	Normal	Status	—	—	20	Self
61	Giga Impact	Normal	Physical	150	90	5	Normal

TM & HM MOVES

No.	Name	Type	Kind	Pow.	Acc.	PP	Range
TM06	Toxic	Poison	Status	—	90	10	Normal
TM10	Hidden Power	Normal	Special	60	100	15	Normal
TM11	Sunny Day	Fire	Status	—	—	5	Both Sides
TM12	Taunt	Dark	Status	—	100	20	Normal
TM17	Protect	Normal	Status	—	—	10	Self
TM18	Rain Dance	Water	Status	—	—	5	Both Sides
TM21	Frustration	Normal	Physical	—	100	20	Normal
TM26	Earthquake	Ground	Physical	100	100	10	Adjacent
TM27	Return	Normal	Physical	—	100	20	Normal
TM32	Double Team	Normal	Status	—	—	15	Self
TM39	Rock Tomb	Rock	Physical	60	95	15	Normal
TM40	Aerial Ace	Flying	Physical	60	—	20	Normal
TM42	Facade	Normal	Physical	70	100	20	Normal
TM44	Rest	Psychic	Status	—	—	10	Self
TM45	Attract	Normal	Status	—	100	15	Normal
TM48	Round	Normal	Special	60	100	15	Normal
TM66	Payback	Dark	Physical	50	100	10	Normal
TM67	Retaliate	Normal	Physical	70	100	5	Normal
TM68	Giga Impact	Normal	Physical	150	90	5	Normal
TM71	Stone Edge	Rock	Physical	100	80	5	Normal
TM75	Swords Dance	Normal	Status	—	—	20	Self
TM78	Bulldoze	Ground	Physical	60	100	20	Adjacent
TM80	Rock Slide	Rock	Physical	75	90	10	Many Others
TM84	Poison Jab	Poison	Physical	80	100	20	Normal
TM87	Swagger	Normal	Status	—	90	15	Normal
TM88	Sleep Talk	Normal	Status	—	—	10	Self
TM90	Substitute	Normal	Status	—	—	10	Self
TM93	Wild Charge	Electric	Physical	90	100	15	Normal
TM94	Secret Power	Normal	Physical	70	100	20	Normal
TM100	Confide	Normal	Status	—	—	20	Normal
HM01	Cut	Normal	Physical	50	95	30	Normal
HM03	Surf	Water	Special	90	100	15	Adjacent
HM04	Strength	Normal	Physical	80	100	15	Normal
HM06	Rock Smash	Fighting	Physical	40	100	15	Normal

MOVES LEARNED IN EXCHANGE FOR BP

Name	Type	Kind	Pow.	Acc.	PP	Range
Iron Head	Steel	Physical	80	100	15	Normal
Uproar	Normal	Special	90	100	10	1 Random
Superpower	Fighting	Physical	120	100	5	Normal
Zen Headbutt	Psychic	Physical	80	90	15	Normal
Snore	Normal	Special	50	100	15	Normal
Endeavor	Normal	Physical	—	100	5	Normal
Outrage	Dragon	Physical	120	100	10	1 Random

MOVES TAUGHT BY PEOPLE

Name	Type	Kind	Pow.	Acc.	PP	Range

EGG MOVES

Name	Type	Kind	Pow.	Acc.	PP	Range
Stomp	Normal	Physical	65	100	20	Normal
Rock Climb	Normal	Physical	90	85	20	Normal
Headbutt	Normal	Physical	70	100	15	Normal
Skull Bash	Normal	Physical	130	100	10	Normal
Mud Shot	Ground	Special	55	95	15	Normal
Mud-Slap	Ground	Special	20	100	10	Normal
Iron Head	Steel	Physical	80	100	15	Normal
Amnesia	Psychic	Status	—	—	20	Self
Belch	Poison	Special	120	90	10	Normal

National Pokédex **627** Hoenn Pokédex —

Rufflet

Eaglet Pokémon

Normal Flying

HEIGHT: 1'08" WEIGHT: 23.1 lbs.

♂ only

Ω They crush berries with their talons. They bravely stand up to any opponent, no matter how strong it is.

α They will challenge anything, even strong opponents, without fear. Their frequent fights help them become stronger.

ABILITIES
Keen Eye
Sheer Force

HIDDEN ABILITY
Hustle

EGG GROUPS
Flying

STAT GROWTH RATES
HP
Attack
Defense
Sp. Atk
Sp. Def
Speed

ITEMS SOMETIMES HELD BY WILD POKÉMON
—

EVOLUTION
Rufflet → Lv. 54 → Braviary

MAIN WAY TO REGISTER IN THE NATIONAL POKÉDEX
Catch on Mirage Mountain 2.

Damage taken in normal battles

Type		Type	
Normal	×1	Flying	×1
Fire	×1	Psychic	×1
Water	×1	Bug	×0.5
Grass	×0.5	Rock	×2
Electric	×2	Ghost	×0
Ice	×2	Dragon	×1
Fighting	×1	Dark	×1
Poison	×1	Steel	×1
Ground	×0	Fairy	×1

Damage taken in Inverse battles

Type		Type	
Normal	×1	Flying	×1
Fire	×1	Psychic	×1
Water	×1	Bug	×2
Grass	×2	Rock	×0.5
Electric	×0.5	Ghost	×2
Ice	×0.5	Dragon	×1
Fighting	×1	Dark	×1
Poison	×1	Steel	×1
Ground	×2	Fairy	×1

Can be used in
Inverse Battle
Battle Institute
Battle Maison
Random Matchup (Free Battle)
Random Matchup (Others)

LEVEL-UP MOVES

Lv.	Name	Type	Kind	Pow.	Acc.	PP	Range
1	Peck	Flying	Physical	35	100	35	Normal
1	Leer	Normal	Status	—	100	30	Many Others
5	Fury Attack	Normal	Physical	15	85	20	Normal
10	Wing Attack	Flying	Physical	60	100	35	Normal
14	Hone Claws	Dark	Status	—	—	15	Self
19	Scary Face	Normal	Status	—	100	10	Normal
23	Aerial Ace	Flying	Physical	60	—	20	Normal
28	Slash	Normal	Physical	70	100	20	Normal
32	Defog	Flying	Status	—	—	15	Normal
37	Tailwind	Flying	Status	—	—	15	Your Side
41	Air Slash	Flying	Special	75	95	15	Normal
46	Crush Claw	Normal	Physical	75	95	10	Normal
50	Sky Drop	Flying	Physical	60	100	10	Normal
55	Whirlwind	Normal	Status	—	—	20	Normal
59	Brave Bird	Flying	Physical	120	100	15	Normal
64	Thrash	Normal	Physical	120	100	10	1 Random

TM & HM MOVES

No.	Name	Type	Kind	Pow.	Acc.	PP	Range
TM01	Hone Claws	Dark	Status	—	—	15	Self
TM06	Toxic	Poison	Status	—	90	10	Normal
TM08	Bulk Up	Fighting	Status	—	—	20	Self
TM10	Hidden Power	Normal	Special	60	100	15	Normal
TM11	Sunny Day	Fire	Status	—	—	5	Both Sides
TM17	Protect	Normal	Status	—	—	10	Self
TM18	Rain Dance	Water	Status	—	—	5	Both Sides
TM19	Roost	Flying	Status	—	—	10	Self
TM21	Frustration	Normal	Physical	—	100	20	Normal
TM27	Return	Normal	Physical	—	100	20	Normal
TM32	Double Team	Normal	Status	—	—	15	Self
TM39	Rock Tomb	Rock	Physical	60	95	15	Normal
TM40	Aerial Ace	Flying	Physical	60	—	20	Normal
TM42	Facade	Normal	Physical	70	100	20	Normal
TM44	Rest	Psychic	Status	—	—	10	Self
TM45	Attract	Normal	Status	—	100	15	Normal
TM48	Round	Normal	Special	60	100	15	Normal
TM51	Steel Wing	Steel	Physical	70	90	25	Normal
TM58	Sky Drop	Flying	Physical	60	100	10	Normal
TM65	Shadow Claw	Ghost	Physical	70	100	15	Normal
TM67	Retaliate	Normal	Physical	70	100	5	Normal
TM80	Rock Slide	Rock	Physical	75	90	10	Many Others
TM87	Swagger	Normal	Status	—	90	15	Normal
TM88	Sleep Talk	Normal	Status	—	—	10	Self
TM89	U-turn	Bug	Physical	70	100	20	Normal
TM90	Substitute	Normal	Status	—	—	10	Self
TM94	Secret Power	Normal	Physical	70	100	20	Normal
TM100	Confide	Normal	Status	—	—	20	Normal
HM01	Cut	Normal	Physical	50	95	30	Normal
HM02	Fly	Flying	Physical	90	95	15	Normal
HM04	Strength	Normal	Physical	80	100	15	Normal
HM06	Rock Smash	Fighting	Physical	40	100	15	Normal

MOVES LEARNED IN EXCHANGE FOR BP

Name	Type	Kind	Pow.	Acc.	PP	Range
Superpower	Fighting	Physical	120	100	5	Normal
Snore	Normal	Special	50	100	15	Normal
Heat Wave	Fire	Special	95	90	10	Many Others
Tailwind	Flying	Status	—	—	15	Your Side

MOVES TAUGHT BY PEOPLE

Name	Type	Kind	Pow.	Acc.	PP	Range

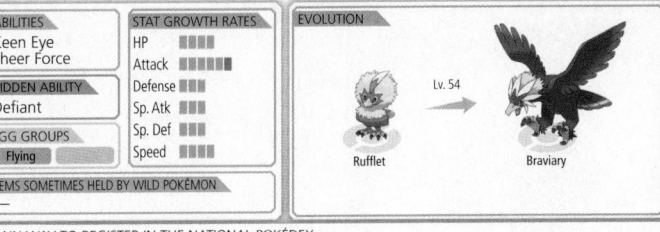

National Pokédex **628** Hoenn Pokédex —

Braviary

Valiant Pokémon

Normal | Flying

HEIGHT: 4'11" WEIGHT: 90.4 lbs.

♂ only

Ω For the sake of its friends, this brave warrior of the sky will not stop battling, even if injured.

α They fight for their friends without any thought about danger to themselves. One can carry a car while flying.

ABILITIES
Keen Eye
Sheer Force

HIDDEN ABILITY
Defiant

EGG GROUPS
Flying

STAT GROWTH RATES
HP
Attack
Defense
Sp. Atk
Sp. Def
Speed

ITEMS SOMETIMES HELD BY WILD POKÉMON
—

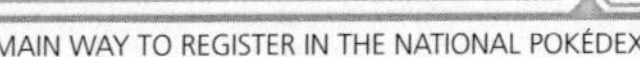

EVOLUTION
Rufflet → Lv. 54 → Braviary

MAIN WAY TO REGISTER IN THE NATIONAL POKÉDEX

While Soaring in the sky, approach the shadows of flying Pokémon, and catch it when it appears.

Damage taken in normal battles

Type		Type	
Normal	×1	Flying	×1
Fire	×1	Psychic	×1
Water	×1	Bug	×0.5
Grass	×0.5	Rock	×2
Electric	×2	Ghost	×0
Ice	×2	Dragon	×1
Fighting	×1	Dark	×1
Poison	×1	Steel	×1
Ground	×0	Fairy	×1

Damage taken in Inverse battles

Type		Type	
Normal	×1	Flying	×1
Fire	×1	Psychic	×1
Water	×1	Bug	×2
Grass	×2	Rock	×0.5
Electric	×0.5	Ghost	×2
Ice	×0.5	Dragon	×1
Fighting	×1	Dark	×1
Poison	×1	Steel	×1
Ground	×2	Fairy	×1

Can be used in
Inverse Battle
Battle Institute
Battle Maison
Random Matchup (Free Battle)
Random Matchup (Others)

LEVEL-UP MOVES

Lv.	Name	Type	Kind	Pow.	Acc.	PP	Range
1	Thrash	Normal	Physical	120	100	10	1 Random
1	Brave Bird	Flying	Physical	120	100	15	Normal
1	Whirlwind	Normal	Status	—	—	20	Normal
1	Superpower	Fighting	Physical	120	100	5	Normal
1	Peck	Flying	Physical	35	100	35	Normal
1	Leer	Normal	Status	—	100	30	Many Others
1	Fury Attack	Normal	Physical	15	85	20	Normal
1	Wing Attack	Flying	Physical	60	100	35	Normal
5	Fury Attack	Normal	Physical	15	85	20	Normal
10	Wing Attack	Flying	Physical	60	100	35	Normal
14	Hone Claws	Dark	Status	—	—	15	Self
19	Scary Face	Normal	Status	—	100	10	Normal
23	Aerial Ace	Flying	Physical	60	—	20	Normal
28	Slash	Normal	Physical	70	100	20	Normal
32	Defog	Flying	Status	—	—	15	Normal
37	Tailwind	Flying	Status	—	—	15	Your Side
41	Air Slash	Flying	Special	75	95	15	Normal
46	Crush Claw	Normal	Physical	75	95	10	Normal
50	Sky Drop	Flying	Physical	60	100	10	Normal
51	Superpower	Fighting	Physical	120	100	5	Normal
57	Whirlwind	Normal	Status	—	—	20	Normal
63	Brave Bird	Flying	Physical	120	100	15	Normal
70	Thrash	Normal	Physical	120	100	10	1 Random

TM & HM MOVES

No.	Name	Type	Kind	Pow.	Acc.	PP	Range
TM01	Hone Claws	Dark	Status	—	—	15	Self
TM06	Toxic	Poison	Status	—	90	10	Normal
TM08	Bulk Up	Fighting	Status	—	—	20	Self
TM10	Hidden Power	Normal	Special	60	100	15	Normal
TM11	Sunny Day	Fire	Status	—	—	5	Both Sides
TM15	Hyper Beam	Normal	Special	150	90	5	Normal
TM17	Protect	Normal	Status	—	—	10	Self
TM18	Rain Dance	Water	Status	—	—	5	Both Sides
TM19	Roost	Flying	Status	—	—	10	Self
TM21	Frustration	Normal	Physical	—	100	20	Normal
TM27	Return	Normal	Physical	—	100	20	Normal
TM32	Double Team	Normal	Status	—	—	15	Self
TM39	Rock Tomb	Rock	Physical	60	95	15	Normal
TM40	Aerial Ace	Flying	Physical	60	—	20	Normal
TM42	Facade	Normal	Physical	70	100	20	Normal
TM44	Rest	Psychic	Status	—	—	10	Self
TM45	Attract	Normal	Status	—	100	15	Normal
TM48	Round	Normal	Special	60	100	15	Normal
TM51	Steel Wing	Steel	Physical	70	90	25	Normal
TM58	Sky Drop	Flying	Physical	60	100	10	Normal
TM65	Shadow Claw	Ghost	Physical	70	100	15	Normal
TM67	Retaliate	Normal	Physical	70	100	5	Normal
TM68	Giga Impact	Normal	Physical	150	90	5	Normal
TM80	Rock Slide	Rock	Physical	75	90	10	Many Others
TM87	Swagger	Normal	Status	—	90	15	Normal
TM88	Sleep Talk	Normal	Status	—	—	10	Self
TM89	U-turn	Bug	Physical	70	100	20	Normal
TM90	Substitute	Normal	Status	—	—	10	Self
TM94	Secret Power	Normal	Physical	70	100	20	Normal
TM100	Confide	Normal	Status	—	—	20	Normal
HM01	Cut	Normal	Physical	50	95	30	Normal
HM02	Fly	Flying	Physical	90	95	15	Normal
HM04	Strength	Normal	Physical	80	100	15	Normal
HM06	Rock Smash	Fighting	Physical	40	100	15	Normal

MOVES LEARNED IN EXCHANGE FOR BP

Name	Type	Kind	Pow.	Acc.	PP	Range
Superpower	Fighting	Physical	120	100	5	Normal
Zen Headbutt	Psychic	Physical	80	90	15	Normal
Snore	Normal	Special	50	100	15	Normal
Heat Wave	Fire	Special	95	90	10	Many Others
Tailwind	Flying	Status	—	—	15	Your Side
Sky Attack	Flying	Physical	140	90	5	Normal

MOVES TAUGHT BY PEOPLE

Name	Type	Kind	Pow.	Acc.	PP	Range

National Pokédex **629** Hoenn Pokédex —

Vullaby

Diapered Pokémon

Dark | Flying

HEIGHT: 1'08" WEIGHT: 19.8 lbs.

♀ only

Ω Its wings are too tiny to allow it to fly. As the time approaches for it to evolve, it discards the bones it was wearing.

α Their wings are too tiny to allow them to fly. They guard their posteriors with bones that were gathered by Mandibuzz.

ABILITIES
Big Pecks
Overcoat

HIDDEN ABILITY
Weak Armor

EGG GROUPS
Flying

STAT GROWTH RATES
HP
Attack
Defense
Sp. Atk
Sp. Def
Speed

ITEMS SOMETIMES HELD BY WILD POKÉMON
—

EVOLUTION
Vullaby → Lv. 54 → Mandibuzz

MAIN WAY TO REGISTER IN THE NATIONAL POKÉDEX

Catch on Mirage Mountain 3.

Damage taken in normal battles

Type		Type	
Normal	×1	Flying	×1
Fire	×1	Psychic	×0
Water	×1	Bug	×1
Grass	×0.5	Rock	×2
Electric	×2	Ghost	×0.5
Ice	×2	Dragon	×1
Fighting	×1	Dark	×0.5
Poison	×1	Steel	×1
Ground	×0	Fairy	×2

Damage taken in Inverse battles

Type		Type	
Normal	×1	Flying	×1
Fire	×1	Psychic	×2
Water	×1	Bug	×1
Grass	×2	Rock	×0.5
Electric	×0.5	Ghost	×2
Ice	×0.5	Dragon	×1
Fighting	×1	Dark	×2
Poison	×1	Steel	×1
Ground	×2	Fairy	×0.5

Can be used in
Inverse Battle
Battle Institute
Battle Maison
Random Matchup (Free Battle)
Random Matchup (Others)

LEVEL-UP MOVES

Lv.	Name	Type	Kind	Pow.	Acc.	PP	Range
1	Gust	Flying	Special	40	100	35	Normal
1	Leer	Normal	Status	—	100	30	Many Others
5	Fury Attack	Normal	Physical	15	85	20	Normal
10	Pluck	Flying	Physical	60	100	20	Normal
14	Nasty Plot	Dark	Status	—	—	20	Self
19	Flatter	Dark	Status	—	100	15	Normal
23	Feint Attack	Dark	Physical	60	—	20	Normal
28	Punishment	Dark	Physical	—	100	5	Normal
32	Defog	Flying	Status	—	—	15	Normal
37	Tailwind	Flying	Status	—	—	15	Your Side
41	Air Slash	Flying	Special	75	95	15	Normal
46	Dark Pulse	Dark	Special	80	100	15	Normal
50	Embargo	Dark	Status	—	100	15	Normal
55	Whirlwind	Normal	Status	—	—	20	Normal
59	Brave Bird	Flying	Physical	120	100	15	Normal
64	Mirror Move	Flying	Status	—	—	20	Normal

TM & HM MOVES

No.	Name	Type	Kind	Pow.	Acc.	PP	Range
TM06	Toxic	Poison	Status	—	90	10	Normal
TM10	Hidden Power	Normal	Special	60	100	15	Normal
TM11	Sunny Day	Fire	Status	—	—	5	Both Sides
TM12	Taunt	Dark	Status	—	100	20	Normal
TM17	Protect	Normal	Status	—	—	10	Self
TM18	Rain Dance	Water	Status	—	—	5	Both Sides
TM19	Roost	Flying	Status	—	—	10	Self
TM21	Frustration	Normal	Physical	—	100	20	Normal
TM27	Return	Normal	Physical	—	100	20	Normal
TM30	Shadow Ball	Ghost	Special	80	100	15	Normal
TM32	Double Team	Normal	Status	—	—	15	Self
TM39	Rock Tomb	Rock	Physical	60	95	15	Normal
TM40	Aerial Ace	Flying	Physical	60	—	20	Normal
TM41	Torment	Dark	Status	—	100	15	Normal
TM42	Facade	Normal	Physical	70	100	20	Normal
TM44	Rest	Psychic	Status	—	—	10	Self
TM45	Attract	Normal	Status	—	100	15	Normal
TM46	Thief	Dark	Physical	60	100	25	Normal
TM48	Round	Normal	Special	60	100	15	Normal
TM51	Steel Wing	Steel	Physical	70	90	25	Normal
TM59	Incinerate	Fire	Special	60	100	15	Many Others
TM63	Embargo	Dark	Status	—	100	15	Normal
TM66	Payback	Dark	Physical	50	100	10	Normal
TM67	Retaliate	Normal	Physical	70	100	5	Normal
TM77	Psych Up	Normal	Status	—	—	10	Normal
TM87	Swagger	Normal	Status	—	90	15	Normal
TM88	Sleep Talk	Normal	Status	—	—	10	Self
TM89	U-turn	Bug	Physical	70	100	20	Normal
TM90	Substitute	Normal	Status	—	—	10	Self
TM94	Secret Power	Normal	Physical	70	100	20	Normal
TM95	Snarl	Dark	Special	55	95	15	Many Others
TM97	Dark Pulse	Dark	Special	80	100	15	Normal
TM100	Confide	Normal	Status	—	—	20	Normal
HM01	Cut	Normal	Physical	50	95	30	Normal
HM02	Fly	Flying	Physical	90	95	15	Normal
HM06	Rock Smash	Fighting	Physical	40	100	15	Normal

MOVES LEARNED IN EXCHANGE FOR BP

Name	Type	Kind	Pow.	Acc.	PP	Range
Block	Normal	Status	—	—	5	Normal
Foul Play	Dark	Physical	95	100	15	Normal
Snore	Normal	Special	50	100	15	Normal
Knock Off	Dark	Physical	65	100	20	Normal
Heat Wave	Fire	Special	95	90	10	Many Others
Tailwind	Flying	Status	—	—	15	Your Side
Snatch	Dark	Status	—	—	10	Self

MOVES TAUGHT BY PEOPLE

Name	Type	Kind	Pow.	Acc.	PP	Range

EGG MOVES

Name	Type	Kind	Pow.	Acc.	PP	Range
Steel Wing	Steel	Physical	70	90	25	Normal
Mean Look	Normal	Status	—	—	5	Normal
Roost	Flying	Status	—	—	10	Self
Scary Face	Normal	Status	—	100	10	Normal
Knock Off	Dark	Physical	65	100	20	Normal
Fake Tears	Dark	Status	—	100	20	Normal
Foul Play	Dark	Physical	95	100	15	Normal

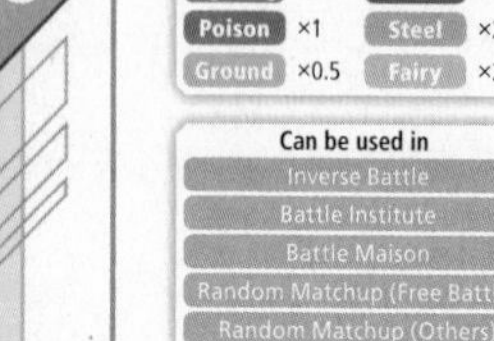

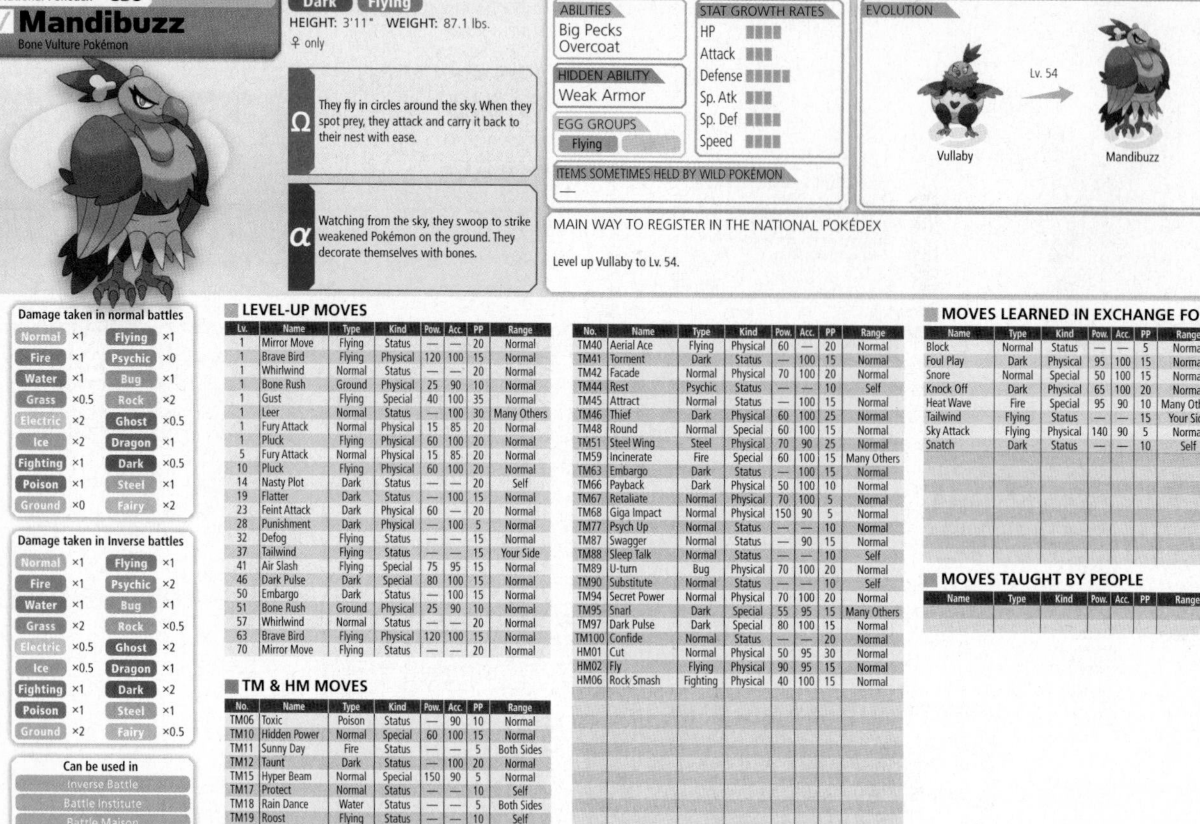

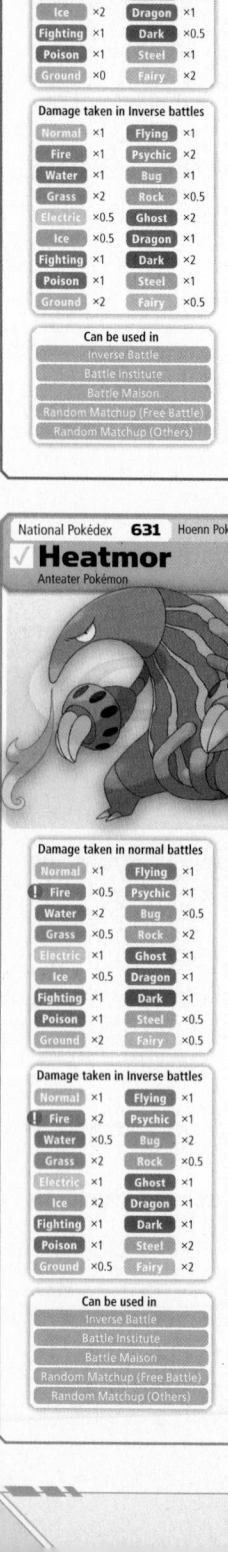

National Pokédex **630** Hoenn Pokédex —

✓ Mandibuzz

Bone Vulture Pokémon

Dark | Flying

HEIGHT: 3'11" WEIGHT: 87.1 lbs.

♀ only

Ω They fly in circles around the sky. When they spot prey, they attack and carry it back to their nest with ease.

α Watching from the sky, they swoop to strike weakened Pokémon on the ground. They decorate themselves with bones.

ABILITIES
Big Pecks
Overcoat

HIDDEN ABILITY
Weak Armor

EGG GROUPS
Flying

STAT GROWTH RATES
HP
Attack
Defense
Sp. Atk
Sp. Def
Speed

ITEMS SOMETIMES HELD BY WILD POKÉMON
—

EVOLUTION
Vullaby → Lv. 54 → Mandibuzz

MAIN WAY TO REGISTER IN THE NATIONAL POKÉDEX

Level up Vullaby to Lv. 54.

Damage taken in normal battles

Type		Type	
Normal	×1	Flying	×1
Fire	×1	Psychic	×0
Water	×1	Bug	×1
Grass	×0.5	Rock	×2
Electric	×2	Ghost	×0.5
Ice	×2	Dragon	×1
Fighting	×1	Dark	×0.5
Poison	×1	Steel	×1
Ground	×0	Fairy	×2

Damage taken in Inverse battles

Type		Type	
Normal	×1	Flying	×1
Fire	×1	Psychic	×2
Water	×1	Bug	×1
Grass	×2	Rock	×0.5
Electric	×0.5	Ghost	×2
Ice	×0.5	Dragon	×1
Fighting	×1	Dark	×2
Poison	×1	Steel	×1
Ground	×2	Fairy	×0.5

Can be used in
Inverse Battle
Battle Institute
Battle Maison
Random Matchup (Free Battle)
Random Matchup (Others)

LEVEL-UP MOVES

Lv.	Name	Type	Kind	Pow.	Acc.	PP	Range
1	Mirror Move	Flying	Status	—	—	20	Normal
1	Brave Bird	Flying	Physical	120	100	15	Normal
1	Whirlwind	Normal	Status	—	—	20	Normal
1	Bone Rush	Ground	Physical	25	90	10	Normal
1	Gust	Flying	Special	40	100	35	Normal
1	Leer	Normal	Status	—	100	30	Many Others
1	Fury Attack	Normal	Physical	15	85	20	Normal
1	Pluck	Flying	Physical	60	100	20	Normal
5	Fury Attack	Normal	Physical	15	85	20	Normal
10	Pluck	Flying	Physical	60	100	20	Normal
14	Nasty Plot	Dark	Status	—	—	20	Self
19	Flatter	Dark	Status	—	100	15	Normal
23	Feint Attack	Dark	Physical	60	—	20	Normal
28	Punishment	Dark	Physical	—	100	5	Normal
32	Defog	Flying	Status	—	—	15	Normal
37	Tailwind	Flying	Status	—	—	15	Your Side
41	Air Slash	Flying	Special	75	95	15	Normal
46	Dark Pulse	Dark	Special	80	100	15	Normal
50	Embargo	Dark	Status	—	100	15	Normal
51	Bone Rush	Ground	Physical	25	90	10	Normal
57	Whirlwind	Normal	Status	—	—	20	Normal
63	Brave Bird	Flying	Physical	120	100	15	Normal
70	Mirror Move	Flying	Status	—	—	20	Normal

TM & HM MOVES

No.	Name	Type	Kind	Pow.	Acc.	PP	Range
TM06	Toxic	Poison	Status	—	90	10	Normal
TM10	Hidden Power	Normal	Special	60	100	15	Normal
TM11	Sunny Day	Fire	Status	—	—	5	Both Sides
TM12	Taunt	Dark	Status	—	100	20	Normal
TM15	Hyper Beam	Normal	Special	150	90	5	Normal
TM17	Protect	Normal	Status	—	—	10	Self
TM18	Rain Dance	Water	Status	—	—	5	Both Sides
TM19	Roost	Flying	Status	—	—	10	Self
TM21	Frustration	Normal	Physical	—	100	20	Normal
TM27	Return	Normal	Physical	—	100	20	Normal
TM30	Shadow Ball	Ghost	Special	80	100	15	Normal
TM32	Double Team	Normal	Status	—	—	15	Self
TM39	Rock Tomb	Rock	Physical	60	95	15	Normal
TM40	Aerial Ace	Flying	Physical	60	—	20	Normal
TM41	Torment	Dark	Status	—	100	15	Normal
TM42	Facade	Normal	Physical	70	100	20	Normal
TM44	Rest	Psychic	Status	—	—	10	Self
TM45	Attract	Normal	Status	—	100	15	Normal
TM46	Thief	Dark	Physical	60	100	25	Normal
TM48	Round	Normal	Special	60	100	15	Normal
TM51	Steel Wing	Steel	Physical	70	90	25	Normal
TM59	Incinerate	Fire	Special	60	100	15	Many Others
TM63	Embargo	Dark	Status	—	100	15	Normal
TM66	Payback	Dark	Physical	50	100	10	Normal
TM67	Retaliate	Normal	Physical	70	100	5	Normal
TM68	Giga Impact	Normal	Physical	150	90	5	Normal
TM77	Psych Up	Normal	Status	—	—	10	Normal
TM87	Swagger	Normal	Status	—	90	15	Normal
TM88	Sleep Talk	Normal	Status	—	—	10	Self
TM89	U-turn	Bug	Physical	70	100	20	Normal
TM90	Substitute	Normal	Status	—	—	10	Self
TM94	Secret Power	Normal	Physical	70	100	20	Normal
TM95	Snarl	Dark	Special	55	95	15	Many Others
TM97	Dark Pulse	Dark	Special	80	100	15	Normal
TM100	Confide	Normal	Status	—	—	20	Normal
HM01	Cut	Normal	Physical	50	95	30	Normal
HM02	Fly	Flying	Physical	90	95	15	Normal
HM06	Rock Smash	Fighting	Physical	40	100	15	Normal

MOVES LEARNED IN EXCHANGE FOR BP

Name	Type	Kind	Pow.	Acc.	PP	Range
Block	Normal	Status	—	—	5	Normal
Foul Play	Dark	Physical	95	100	15	Normal
Snore	Normal	Special	50	100	15	Normal
Knock Off	Dark	Physical	65	100	20	Normal
Heat Wave	Fire	Special	95	90	10	Many Others
Tailwind	Flying	Status	—	—	15	Your Side
Sky Attack	Flying	Physical	140	90	5	Normal
Snatch	Dark	Status	—	—	10	Self

MOVES TAUGHT BY PEOPLE

Name	Type	Kind	Pow.	Acc.	PP	Range

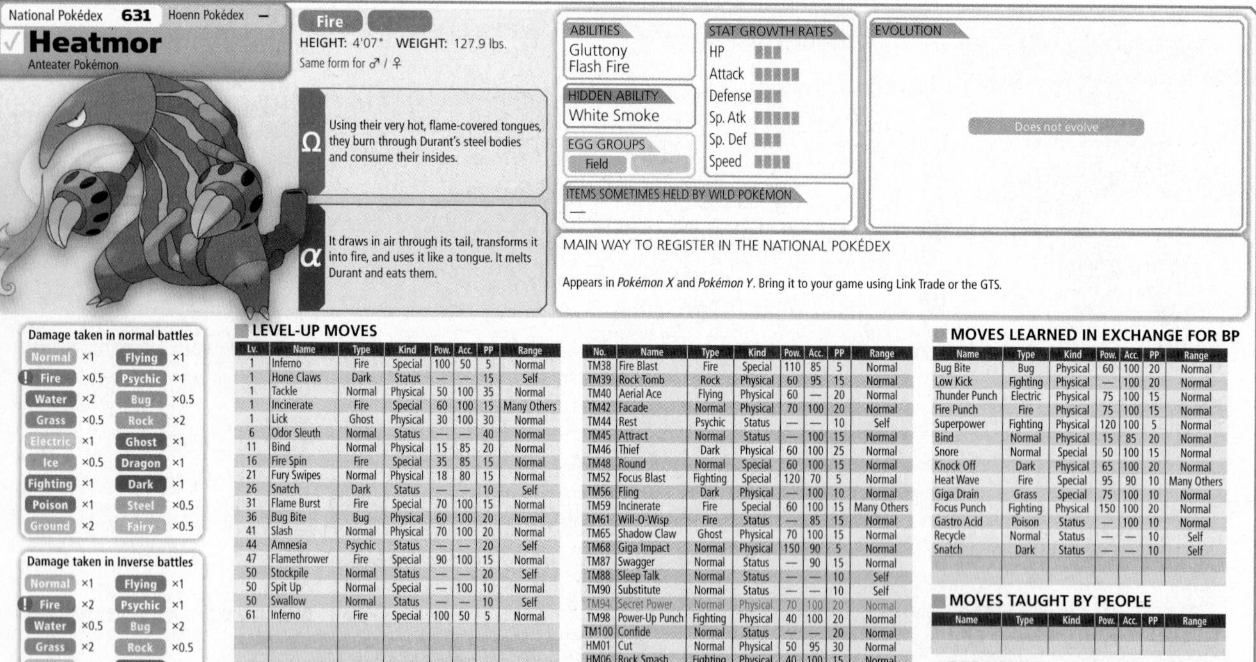

National Pokédex **631** Hoenn Pokédex —

✓ Heatmor

Anteater Pokémon

Fire

HEIGHT: 4'07" WEIGHT: 127.9 lbs.

Same form for ♂ / ♀

Ω Using their very hot, flame-covered tongues, they burn through Durant's steel bodies and consume their insides.

α It draws in air through its tail, transforms it into fire, and uses it like a tongue. It melts Durant and eats them.

ABILITIES
Gluttony
Flash Fire

HIDDEN ABILITY
White Smoke

EGG GROUPS
Field

STAT GROWTH RATES
HP
Attack
Defense
Sp. Atk
Sp. Def
Speed

ITEMS SOMETIMES HELD BY WILD POKÉMON
—

EVOLUTION
Does not evolve

MAIN WAY TO REGISTER IN THE NATIONAL POKÉDEX

Appears in *Pokémon X* and *Pokémon Y*. Bring it to your game using Link Trade or the GTS.

Damage taken in normal battles

Type		Type	
Normal	×1	Flying	×1
! Fire	×0.5	Psychic	×1
Water	×2	Bug	×0.5
Grass	×0.5	Rock	×2
Electric	×1	Ghost	×1
Ice	×0.5	Dragon	×1
Fighting	×1	Dark	×1
Poison	×1	Steel	×0.5
Ground	×2	Fairy	×0.5

Damage taken in Inverse battles

Type		Type	
Normal	×1	Flying	×1
! Fire	×2	Psychic	×1
Water	×0.5	Bug	×2
Grass	×2	Rock	×0.5
Electric	×1	Ghost	×1
Ice	×2	Dragon	×1
Fighting	×1	Dark	×1
Poison	×1	Steel	×2
Ground	×0.5	Fairy	×2

Can be used in
Inverse Battle
Battle Institute
Battle Maison
Random Matchup (Free Battle)
Random Matchup (Others)

LEVEL-UP MOVES

Lv.	Name	Type	Kind	Pow.	Acc.	PP	Range
1	Inferno	Fire	Special	100	50	5	Normal
1	Hone Claws	Dark	Status	—	—	15	Self
1	Tackle	Normal	Physical	50	100	35	Normal
1	Incinerate	Fire	Special	60	100	15	Many Others
1	Lick	Ghost	Physical	30	100	30	Normal
6	Odor Sleuth	Normal	Status	—	—	40	Normal
11	Bind	Normal	Physical	15	85	20	Normal
16	Fire Spin	Fire	Special	35	85	15	Normal
21	Fury Swipes	Normal	Physical	18	80	15	Normal
26	Snatch	Dark	Status	—	—	10	Self
31	Flame Burst	Fire	Special	70	100	15	Normal
36	Bug Bite	Bug	Physical	60	100	20	Normal
41	Slash	Normal	Physical	70	100	20	Normal
44	Amnesia	Psychic	Status	—	—	20	Self
47	Flamethrower	Fire	Special	90	100	15	Normal
50	Stockpile	Normal	Status	—	—	20	Self
50	Spit Up	Normal	Special	—	100	10	Normal
50	Swallow	Normal	Status	—	—	10	Self
61	Inferno	Fire	Special	100	50	5	Normal

TM & HM MOVES

No.	Name	Type	Kind	Pow.	Acc.	PP	Range
TM01	Hone Claws	Dark	Status	—	—	15	Self
TM06	Toxic	Poison	Status	—	90	10	Normal
TM10	Hidden Power	Normal	Special	60	100	15	Normal
TM11	Sunny Day	Fire	Status	—	—	5	Both Sides
TM12	Taunt	Dark	Status	—	100	20	Normal
TM17	Protect	Normal	Status	—	—	10	Self
TM18	Rain Dance	Water	Status	—	—	5	Both Sides
TM21	Frustration	Normal	Physical	—	100	20	Normal
TM22	Solar Beam	Grass	Special	120	100	10	Normal
TM27	Return	Normal	Physical	—	100	20	Normal
TM28	Dig	Ground	Physical	80	100	10	Normal
TM32	Double Team	Normal	Status	—	—	15	Self
TM35	Flamethrower	Fire	Special	90	100	15	Normal
TM38	Fire Blast	Fire	Special	110	85	5	Normal
TM39	Rock Tomb	Rock	Physical	60	95	15	Normal
TM40	Aerial Ace	Flying	Physical	60	—	20	Normal
TM42	Facade	Normal	Physical	70	100	20	Normal
TM44	Rest	Psychic	Status	—	—	10	Self
TM45	Attract	Normal	Status	—	100	15	Normal
TM46	Thief	Dark	Physical	60	100	25	Normal
TM48	Round	Normal	Special	60	100	15	Normal
TM52	Focus Blast	Fighting	Special	120	70	5	Normal
TM56	Fling	Dark	Physical	—	100	10	Normal
TM59	Incinerate	Fire	Special	60	100	15	Many Others
TM61	Will-O-Wisp	Fire	Status	—	85	15	Normal
TM65	Shadow Claw	Ghost	Physical	70	100	15	Normal
TM68	Giga Impact	Normal	Physical	150	90	5	Normal
TM87	Swagger	Normal	Status	—	90	15	Normal
TM88	Sleep Talk	Normal	Status	—	—	10	Self
TM90	Substitute	Normal	Status	—	—	10	Self
TM94	Secret Power	Normal	Physical	70	100	20	Normal
TM98	Power-Up Punch	Fighting	Physical	40	100	20	Normal
TM100	Confide	Normal	Status	—	—	20	Normal
HM01	Cut	Normal	Physical	50	95	30	Normal
HM06	Rock Smash	Fighting	Physical	40	100	15	Normal

MOVES LEARNED IN EXCHANGE FOR BP

Name	Type	Kind	Pow.	Acc.	PP	Range
Bug Bite	Bug	Physical	60	100	20	Normal
Low Kick	Fighting	Physical	—	100	20	Normal
Thunder Punch	Electric	Physical	75	100	15	Normal
Fire Punch	Fire	Physical	75	100	15	Normal
Superpower	Fighting	Physical	120	100	5	Normal
Bind	Normal	Physical	15	85	20	Normal
Snore	Normal	Special	50	100	15	Normal
Knock Off	Dark	Physical	65	100	20	Normal
Heat Wave	Fire	Special	95	90	10	Many Others
Giga Drain	Grass	Special	75	100	10	Normal
Focus Punch	Fighting	Physical	150	100	20	Normal
Gastro Acid	Poison	Status	—	100	10	Normal
Recycle	Normal	Status	—	—	10	Self
Snatch	Dark	Status	—	—	10	Self

MOVES TAUGHT BY PEOPLE

Name	Type	Kind	Pow.	Acc.	PP	Range

EGG MOVES

Name	Type	Kind	Pow.	Acc.	PP	Range
Pursuit	Dark	Physical	40	100	20	Normal
Wrap	Normal	Physical	15	90	20	Normal
Night Slash	Dark	Physical	70	100	15	Normal
Curse	Ghost	Status	—	—	10	Varies
Body Slam	Normal	Physical	85	100	15	Normal
Heat Wave	Fire	Special	95	90	10	Many Others
Feint Attack	Dark	Physical	60	—	20	Normal
Sucker Punch	Dark	Physical	80	100	5	Normal
Tickle	Normal	Status	—	100	20	Normal
Sleep Talk	Normal	Status	—	—	10	Self
Belch	Poison	Special	120	90	10	Normal

National Pokédex **632** Hoenn Pokédex —

Durant

Iron Ant Pokémon

Bug | Steel

HEIGHT: 1'00" WEIGHT: 72.8 lbs.

Same form for ♂ / ♀

Ω Individuals each play different roles in driving Heatmor, their natural predator, away from their colony.

α They attack in groups, covering themselves in steel armor to protect themselves from Heatmor.

ABILITIES
Swarm
Hustle

HIDDEN ABILITY
Truant

EGG GROUPS
Bug

STAT GROWTH RATES
HP ■■■
Attack ■■■■■■
Defense ■■■■■
Sp. Atk ■■
Sp. Def ■■
Speed ■■■■■■

ITEMS SOMETIMES HELD BY WILD POKÉMON
—

EVOLUTION
Does not evolve

MAIN WAY TO REGISTER IN THE NATIONAL POKÉDEX

Appears in *Pokémon X* and *Pokémon Y*. Bring it to your game using Link Trade or the GTS.

Damage taken in normal battles

Type		Type	
Normal	×0.5	Flying	×1
Fire	×4	Psychic	×0.5
Water	×1	Bug	×0.5
Grass	×0.25	Rock	×1
Electric	×1	Ghost	×1
Ice	×0.5	Dragon	×0.5
Fighting	×1	Dark	×1
Poison	×0	Steel	×0.5
Ground	×1	Fairy	×0.5

Damage taken in Inverse battles

Type		Type	
Normal	×2	Flying	×1
Fire	×0.25	Psychic	×2
Water	×1	Bug	×2
Grass	×4	Rock	×1
Electric	×1	Ghost	×1
Ice	×2	Dragon	×2
Fighting	×1	Dark	×1
Poison	×2	Steel	×2
Ground	×1	Fairy	×2

Can be used in
Inverse Battle
Battle Institute
Battle Maison
Random Matchup (Free Battle)
Random Matchup (Others)

LEVEL-UP MOVES

Lv.	Name	Type	Kind	Pow.	Acc.	PP	Range
1	Guillotine	Normal	Physical	—	30	5	Normal
1	Iron Defense	Steel	Status	—	—	15	Self
1	Metal Sound	Steel	Status	—	85	40	Normal
1	Vice Grip	Normal	Physical	55	100	30	Normal
1	Sand Attack	Ground	Status	—	100	15	Normal
6	Fury Cutter	Bug	Physical	40	95	20	Normal
11	Bite	Dark	Physical	60	100	25	Normal
16	Agility	Psychic	Status	—	—	30	Self
21	Metal Claw	Steel	Physical	50	95	35	Normal
26	Bug Bite	Bug	Physical	60	100	20	Normal
31	Crunch	Dark	Physical	80	100	15	Normal
36	Iron Head	Steel	Physical	80	100	15	Normal
41	Dig	Ground	Physical	80	100	10	Normal
46	Entrainment	Normal	Status	—	100	15	Normal
51	X-Scissor	Bug	Physical	80	100	15	Normal
56	Iron Defense	Steel	Status	—	—	15	Self
61	Guillotine	Normal	Physical	—	30	5	Normal
66	Metal Sound	Steel	Status	—	85	40	Normal

TM & HM MOVES

No.	Name	Type	Kind	Pow.	Acc.	PP	Range
TM01	Hone Claws	Dark	Status	—	—	15	Self
TM06	Toxic	Poison	Status	—	90	10	Normal
TM10	Hidden Power	Normal	Special	60	100	15	Normal
TM17	Protect	Normal	Status	—	—	10	Self
TM21	Frustration	Normal	Physical	—	100	20	Normal
TM27	Return	Normal	Physical	—	100	20	Normal
TM28	Dig	Ground	Physical	80	100	10	Normal
TM32	Double Team	Normal	Status	—	—	15	Self
TM37	Sandstorm	Rock	Status	—	—	10	Both Sides
TM39	Rock Tomb	Rock	Physical	60	95	15	Normal
TM40	Aerial Ace	Flying	Physical	60	—	20	Normal
TM42	Facade	Normal	Physical	70	100	20	Normal
TM44	Rest	Psychic	Status	—	—	10	Self
TM45	Attract	Normal	Status	—	100	15	Normal
TM48	Round	Normal	Special	60	100	15	Normal
TM53	Energy Ball	Grass	Special	90	100	10	Normal
TM65	Shadow Claw	Ghost	Physical	70	100	15	Normal
TM67	Retaliate	Normal	Physical	70	100	5	Normal
TM68	Giga Impact	Normal	Physical	150	90	5	Normal
TM69	Rock Polish	Rock	Status	—	—	20	Self
TM71	Stone Edge	Rock	Physical	100	80	5	Normal
TM73	Thunder Wave	Electric	Status	—	100	20	Normal
TM76	Struggle Bug	Bug	Special	50	100	20	Many Others
TM80	Rock Slide	Rock	Physical	75	90	10	Many Others
TM81	X-Scissor	Bug	Physical	80	100	15	Normal
TM87	Swagger	Normal	Status	—	90	15	Normal
TM88	Sleep Talk	Normal	Status	—	—	10	Self
TM90	Substitute	Normal	Status	—	—	10	Self
TM91	Flash Cannon	Steel	Special	80	100	10	Normal
TM94	Secret Power	Normal	Physical	70	100	20	Normal
TM100	Confide	Normal	Status	—	—	20	Normal
HM01	Cut	Normal	Physical	50	95	30	Normal
HM04	Strength	Normal	Physical	80	100	15	Normal
HM06	Rock Smash	Fighting	Physical	40	100	15	Normal

MOVES LEARNED IN EXCHANGE FOR BP

Name	Type	Kind	Pow.	Acc.	PP	Range
Bug Bite	Bug	Physical	60	100	20	Normal
Iron Head	Steel	Physical	80	100	15	Normal
Iron Defense	Steel	Status	—	—	15	Self
Superpower	Fighting	Physical	120	100	5	Normal
Snore	Normal	Special	50	100	15	Normal
Endeavor	Normal	Physical	—	100	5	Normal

MOVES TAUGHT BY PEOPLE

Name	Type	Kind	Pow.	Acc.	PP	Range

EGG MOVES

Name	Type	Kind	Pow.	Acc.	PP	Range
Screech	Normal	Status	—	85	40	Normal
Endure	Normal	Status	—	—	10	Self
Rock Climb	Normal	Physical	90	85	20	Normal
Baton Pass	Normal	Status	—	—	40	Self
Thunder Fang	Electric	Physical	65	95	15	Normal
Feint Attack	Dark	Physical	60	—	20	Normal

National Pokédex **633** Hoenn Pokédex —

Deino

Irate Pokémon

Dark | Dragon

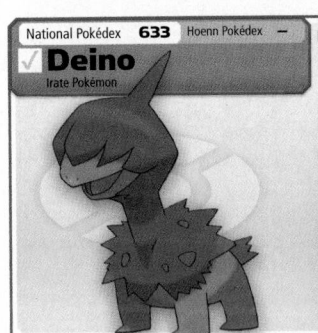

HEIGHT: 2'07" WEIGHT: 38.1 lbs.

Same form for ♂ / ♀

Ω They cannot see, so they tackle and bite to learn about their surroundings. Their bodies are covered in wounds.

α Lacking sight, it's unaware of its surroundings, so it bumps into things and eats anything that moves.

ABILITY
Hustle

HIDDEN ABILITY
—

EGG GROUPS
Dragon

STAT GROWTH RATES
HP ■■
Attack ■■■
Defense ■■
Sp. Atk ■■
Sp. Def ■■
Speed ■■

ITEMS SOMETIMES HELD BY WILD POKÉMON
—

EVOLUTION
Deino → Lv. 50 → Zweilous → Lv. 64 → Hydreigon

MAIN WAY TO REGISTER IN THE NATIONAL POKÉDEX

Catch in the Meteor Falls entrance. Appears as a hidden Pokémon after you battle Groudon or Kyogre.

Damage taken in normal battles

Type		Type	
Normal	×1	Flying	×1
Fire	×0.5	Psychic	×0
Water	×0.5	Bug	×2
Grass	×0.5	Rock	×1
Electric	×0.5	Ghost	×0.5
Ice	×2	Dragon	×2
Fighting	×2	Dark	×0.5
Poison	×1	Steel	×1
Ground	×1	Fairy	×4

Damage taken in Inverse battles

Type		Type	
Normal	×1	Flying	×1
Fire	×2	Psychic	×2
Water	×2	Bug	×0.5
Grass	×2	Rock	×1
Electric	×2	Ghost	×2
Ice	×0.5	Dragon	×0.5
Fighting	×0.5	Dark	×2
Poison	×1	Steel	×1
Ground	×1	Fairy	×0.25

Can be used in
Inverse Battle
Battle Institute
Battle Maison
Random Matchup (Free Battle)
Random Matchup (Others)

LEVEL-UP MOVES

Lv.	Name	Type	Kind	Pow.	Acc.	PP	Range
1	Tackle	Normal	Physical	50	100	35	Normal
1	Dragon Rage	Dragon	Special	—	100	10	Normal
4	Focus Energy	Normal	Status	—	—	30	Self
9	Bite	Dark	Physical	60	100	25	Normal
12	Headbutt	Normal	Physical	70	100	15	Normal
17	Dragon Breath	Dragon	Special	60	100	20	Normal
20	Roar	Normal	Status	—	—	20	Normal
25	Crunch	Dark	Physical	80	100	15	Normal
28	Slam	Normal	Physical	80	75	20	Normal
32	Dragon Pulse	Dragon	Special	85	100	10	Normal
38	Work Up	Normal	Status	—	—	30	Self
42	Dragon Rush	Dragon	Physical	100	75	10	Normal
48	Body Slam	Normal	Physical	85	100	15	Normal
50	Scary Face	Normal	Status	—	100	10	Normal
58	Hyper Voice	Normal	Special	90	100	10	Many Others
62	Outrage	Dragon	Physical	120	100	10	1 Random

TM & HM MOVES

No.	Name	Type	Kind	Pow.	Acc.	PP	Range
TM05	Roar	Normal	Status	—	—	20	Normal
TM06	Toxic	Poison	Status	—	90	10	Normal
TM10	Hidden Power	Normal	Special	60	100	15	Normal
TM11	Sunny Day	Fire	Status	—	—	5	Both Sides
TM12	Taunt	Dark	Status	—	100	20	Normal
TM17	Protect	Normal	Status	—	—	10	Self
TM18	Rain Dance	Water	Status	—	—	5	Both Sides
TM21	Frustration	Normal	Physical	—	100	20	Normal
TM27	Return	Normal	Physical	—	100	20	Normal
TM32	Double Team	Normal	Status	—	—	15	Self
TM41	Torment	Dark	Status	—	100	15	Normal
TM42	Facade	Normal	Physical	70	100	20	Normal
TM44	Rest	Psychic	Status	—	—	10	Self
TM45	Attract	Normal	Status	—	100	15	Normal
TM46	Thief	Dark	Physical	60	100	25	Normal
TM48	Round	Normal	Special	60	100	15	Normal
TM59	Incinerate	Fire	Special	60	100	15	Many Others
TM73	Thunder Wave	Electric	Status	—	100	20	Normal
TM77	Psych Up	Normal	Status	—	—	10	Normal
TM82	Dragon Tail	Dragon	Physical	60	90	10	Normal
TM87	Swagger	Normal	Status	—	90	15	Normal
TM88	Sleep Talk	Normal	Status	—	—	10	Self
TM90	Substitute	Normal	Status	—	—	10	Self
TM94	Secret Power	Normal	Physical	70	100	20	Normal
TM97	Dark Pulse	Dark	Special	80	100	15	Normal
TM100	Confide	Normal	Status	—	—	20	Normal
HM04	Strength	Normal	Physical	80	100	15	Normal
HM06	Rock Smash	Fighting	Physical	40	100	15	Normal

MOVES LEARNED IN EXCHANGE FOR BP

Name	Type	Kind	Pow.	Acc.	PP	Range
Uproar	Normal	Special	90	100	10	1 Random
Earth Power	Ground	Special	90	100	10	Normal
Superpower	Fighting	Physical	120	100	5	Normal
Aqua Tail	Water	Physical	90	90	10	Normal
Zen Headbutt	Psychic	Physical	80	90	15	Normal
Dragon Pulse	Dragon	Special	85	100	10	Normal
Hyper Voice	Normal	Special	90	100	10	Many Others
Snore	Normal	Special	50	100	15	Normal
Shock Wave	Electric	Special	60	—	20	Normal
Spite	Ghost	Status	—	100	10	Normal
Outrage	Dragon	Physical	120	100	10	1 Random

MOVES TAUGHT BY PEOPLE

Name	Type	Kind	Pow.	Acc.	PP	Range
Draco Meteor	Dragon	Special	130	90	5	Normal

EGG MOVES

Name	Type	Kind	Pow.	Acc.	PP	Range
Fire Fang	Fire	Physical	65	95	15	Normal
Thunder Fang	Electric	Physical	65	95	15	Normal
Ice Fang	Ice	Physical	65	95	15	Normal
Double Hit	Normal	Physical	35	90	10	Normal
Astonish	Ghost	Physical	30	100	15	Normal
Earth Power	Ground	Special	90	100	10	Normal
Screech	Normal	Status	—	85	40	Normal
Head Smash	Rock	Physical	150	80	5	Normal
Assurance	Dark	Physical	60	100	10	Normal
Dark Pulse	Dark	Special	80	100	15	Normal

National Pokédex **634** Hoenn Pokédex —

Zweilous

Hostile Pokémon

Dark Dragon

HEIGHT: 4'07" WEIGHT: 110.2 lbs.

Same form for ♂ / ♀

Ω The two heads do not get along. Whichever head eats more than the other gets to be the leader.

α After it has eaten up all the food in its territory, it moves to another area. Its two heads do not get along.

ABILITY
Hustle

HIDDEN ABILITY
—

EGG GROUPS
Dragon

STAT GROWTH RATES

HP	■■■
Attack	■■■■
Defense	■■■
Sp. Atk	■■■
Sp. Def	■■■
Speed	■■■

ITEMS SOMETIMES HELD BY WILD POKÉMON
—

EVOLUTION

MAIN WAY TO REGISTER IN THE NATIONAL POKÉDEX

Level up Deino to Lv. 50.

Damage taken in normal battles

Type	×	Type	×
Normal	×1	Flying	×1
Fire	×0.5	Psychic	×0
Water	×0.5	Bug	×2
Grass	×0.5	Rock	×1
Electric	×0.5	Ghost	×0.5
Ice	×2	Dragon	×2
Fighting	×2	Dark	×0.5
Poison	×1	Steel	×1
Ground	×1	Fairy	×4

Damage taken in Inverse battles

Type	×	Type	×
Normal	×1	Flying	×1
Fire	×2	Psychic	×2
Water	×2	Bug	×0.5
Grass	×2	Rock	×1
Electric	×2	Ghost	×2
Ice	×0.5	Dragon	×0.5
Fighting	×0.5	Dark	×2
Poison	×1	Steel	×1
Ground	×1	Fairy	×0.25

Can be used in
Inverse Battle
Battle Institute
Battle Maison
Random Matchup (Free Battle)
Random Matchup (Others)

LEVEL-UP MOVES

Lv.	Name	Type	Kind	Pow.	Acc.	PP	Range
1	Double Hit	Normal	Physical	35	90	10	Normal
1	Dragon Rage	Dragon	Special	—	100	10	Normal
1	Focus Energy	Normal	Status	—	—	30	Self
1	Bite	Dark	Physical	60	100	25	Normal
4	Focus Energy	Normal	Status	—	—	30	Self
9	Bite	Dark	Physical	60	100	25	Normal
12	Headbutt	Normal	Physical	70	100	15	Normal
17	Dragon Breath	Dragon	Special	60	100	20	Normal
20	Roar	Normal	Status	—	—	20	Normal
25	Crunch	Dark	Physical	80	100	15	Normal
28	Slam	Normal	Physical	80	75	20	Normal
32	Dragon Pulse	Dragon	Special	85	100	10	Normal
38	Work Up	Normal	Status	—	—	30	Self
42	Dragon Rush	Dragon	Physical	100	75	10	Normal
48	Body Slam	Normal	Physical	85	100	15	Normal
55	Scary Face	Normal	Status	—	100	10	Normal
64	Hyper Voice	Normal	Special	90	100	10	Many Others
71	Outrage	Dragon	Physical	120	100	10	1 Random

TM & HM MOVES

No.	Name	Type	Kind	Pow.	Acc.	PP	Range
TM05	Roar	Normal	Status	—	—	20	Normal
TM06	Toxic	Poison	Status	—	90	10	Normal
TM10	Hidden Power	Normal	Special	60	100	15	Normal
TM11	Sunny Day	Fire	Status	—	—	5	Both Sides
TM12	Taunt	Dark	Status	—	100	20	Normal
TM17	Protect	Normal	Status	—	—	10	Self
TM18	Rain Dance	Water	Status	—	—	5	Both Sides
TM21	Frustration	Normal	Physical	—	100	20	Normal
TM27	Return	Normal	Physical	—	100	20	Normal
TM32	Double Team	Normal	Status	—	—	15	Self
TM41	Torment	Dark	Status	—	100	15	Normal
TM42	Facade	Normal	Physical	70	100	20	Normal
TM44	Rest	Psychic	Status	—	—	10	Self
TM45	Attract	Normal	Status	—	100	15	Normal
TM46	Thief	Dark	Physical	60	100	25	Normal
TM48	Round	Normal	Special	60	100	15	Normal
TM59	Incinerate	Fire	Special	60	100	15	Many Others
TM73	Thunder Wave	Electric	Status	—	100	20	Normal
TM77	Psych Up	Normal	Status	—	—	10	Normal
TM82	Dragon Tail	Dragon	Physical	60	90	10	Normal
TM87	Swagger	Normal	Status	—	90	15	Normal
TM88	Sleep Talk	Normal	Status	—	—	10	Self
TM90	Substitute	Normal	Status	—	—	10	Self
TM94	Secret Power	Normal	Physical	70	100	20	Normal
TM97	Dark Pulse	Dark	Special	80	100	15	Normal
TM100	Confide	Normal	Status	—	—	20	Normal
HM04	Strength	Normal	Physical	80	100	15	Normal
HM06	Rock Smash	Fighting	Physical	40	100	15	Normal

MOVES LEARNED IN EXCHANGE FOR BP

Name	Type	Kind	Pow.	Acc.	PP	Range
Uproar	Normal	Special	90	100	10	1 Random
Earth Power	Ground	Special	90	100	10	Normal
Superpower	Fighting	Physical	120	100	5	Normal
Aqua Tail	Water	Physical	90	90	10	Normal
Zen Headbutt	Psychic	Physical	80	90	15	Normal
Dragon Pulse	Dragon	Special	85	100	10	Normal
Hyper Voice	Normal	Special	90	100	10	Many Others
Snore	Normal	Special	50	100	15	Normal
Shock Wave	Electric	Special	60	—	20	Normal
Spite	Ghost	Status	—	100	10	Normal
Outrage	Dragon	Physical	120	100	10	1 Random

MOVES TAUGHT BY PEOPLE

Name	Type	Kind	Pow.	Acc.	PP	Range
Draco Meteor	Dragon	Special	130	90	5	Normal

National Pokédex **635** Hoenn Pokédex —

Hydreigon

Brutal Pokémon

Dark Dragon

HEIGHT: 5'11" WEIGHT: 352.7 lbs.

Same form for ♂ / ♀

Ω The heads on their arms do not have brains. They use all three heads to consume and destroy everything.

α It responds to movement by attacking. This scary, three-headed Pokémon devours everything in its path!

ABILITY
Levitate

HIDDEN ABILITY
—

EGG GROUPS
Dragon

STAT GROWTH RATES

HP	■■■■
Attack	■■■■■
Defense	■■■■
Sp. Atk	■■■■■■
Sp. Def	■■■■
Speed	■■■■■

ITEMS SOMETIMES HELD BY WILD POKÉMON
—

EVOLUTION

Lv. 50 Lv. 64

Deino Zweilous Hydreigon

MAIN WAY TO REGISTER IN THE NATIONAL POKÉDEX

Level up Zweilous to Lv. 64.

Damage taken in normal battles

Type	×	Type	×
Normal	×1	Flying	×1
Fire	×0.5	Psychic	×0
Water	×0.5	Bug	×2
Grass	×0.5	Rock	×1
Electric	×0.5	Ghost	×0.5
Ice	×2	Dragon	×2
Fighting	×2	Dark	×0.5
Poison	×1	Steel	×1
! Ground	×1	Fairy	×4

Damage taken in Inverse battles

Type	×	Type	×
Normal	×1	Flying	×1
Fire	×2	Psychic	×2
Water	×2	Bug	×0.5
Grass	×2	Rock	×1
Electric	×2	Ghost	×2
Ice	×0.5	Dragon	×0.5
Fighting	×0.5	Dark	×2
Poison	×1	Steel	×1
! Ground	×1	Fairy	×0.25

Can be used in
Inverse Battle
Battle Institute
Battle Maison
Random Matchup (Free Battle)
Random Matchup (Others)

LEVEL-UP MOVES

Lv.	Name	Type	Kind	Pow.	Acc.	PP	Range
1	Outrage	Dragon	Physical	120	100	10	1 Random
1	Hyper Voice	Normal	Special	90	100	10	Many Others
1	Tri Attack	Normal	Special	80	100	10	Normal
1	Dragon Rage	Dragon	Special	—	100	10	Normal
1	Focus Energy	Normal	Status	—	—	30	Self
1	Bite	Dark	Physical	60	100	25	Normal
4	Focus Energy	Normal	Status	—	—	30	Self
9	Bite	Dark	Physical	60	100	25	Normal
12	Headbutt	Normal	Physical	70	100	15	Normal
17	Dragon Breath	Dragon	Special	60	100	20	Normal
20	Roar	Normal	Status	—	—	20	Normal
25	Crunch	Dark	Physical	80	100	15	Normal
28	Slam	Normal	Physical	80	75	20	Normal
32	Dragon Pulse	Dragon	Special	85	100	10	Normal
38	Work Up	Normal	Status	—	—	30	Self
42	Dragon Rush	Dragon	Physical	100	75	10	Normal
48	Body Slam	Normal	Physical	85	100	15	Normal
55	Scary Face	Normal	Status	—	100	10	Normal
68	Hyper Voice	Normal	Special	90	100	10	Many Others
79	Outrage	Dragon	Physical	120	100	10	1 Random

TM & HM MOVES

No.	Name	Type	Kind	Pow.	Acc.	PP	Range
TM05	Roar	Normal	Status	—	—	20	Normal
TM06	Toxic	Poison	Status	—	90	10	Normal
TM10	Hidden Power	Normal	Special	60	100	15	Normal
TM11	Sunny Day	Fire	Status	—	—	5	Both Sides
TM12	Taunt	Dark	Status	—	100	20	Normal
TM15	Hyper Beam	Normal	Special	150	90	5	Normal
TM17	Protect	Normal	Status	—	—	10	Self
TM18	Rain Dance	Water	Status	—	—	5	Both Sides
TM19	Roost	Flying	Status	—	—	10	Self
TM21	Frustration	Normal	Physical	—	100	20	Normal
TM26	Earthquake	Ground	Physical	100	100	10	Adjacent
TM27	Return	Normal	Physical	—	100	20	Normal
TM32	Double Team	Normal	Status	—	—	15	Self
TM33	Reflect	Psychic	Status	—	—	20	Your Side
TM35	Flamethrower	Fire	Special	90	100	15	Normal
TM38	Fire Blast	Fire	Special	110	85	5	Normal
TM39	Rock Tomb	Rock	Physical	60	95	15	Normal
TM41	Torment	Dark	Status	—	100	15	Normal
TM42	Facade	Normal	Physical	70	100	20	Normal
TM44	Rest	Psychic	Status	—	—	10	Self
TM45	Attract	Normal	Status	—	100	15	Normal
TM46	Thief	Dark	Physical	60	100	25	Normal
TM48	Round	Normal	Special	60	100	15	Normal
TM49	Echoed Voice	Normal	Special	40	100	15	Normal
TM51	Steel Wing	Steel	Physical	70	90	25	Normal
TM52	Focus Blast	Fighting	Special	120	70	5	Normal
TM57	Charge Beam	Electric	Special	50	90	10	Normal
TM59	Incinerate	Fire	Special	60	100	15	Many Others
TM62	Acrobatics	Flying	Physical	55	100	15	Normal
TM66	Payback	Dark	Physical	50	100	10	Normal
TM68	Giga Impact	Normal	Physical	150	90	5	Normal
TM71	Stone Edge	Rock	Physical	100	80	5	Normal
TM73	Thunder Wave	Electric	Status	—	100	20	Normal
TM77	Psych Up	Normal	Status	—	—	10	Normal
TM78	Bulldoze	Ground	Physical	60	100	20	Adjacent
TM80	Rock Slide	Rock	Physical	75	90	10	Many Others
TM82	Dragon Tail	Dragon	Physical	60	90	10	Normal
TM87	Swagger	Normal	Status	—	90	15	Normal
TM88	Sleep Talk	Normal	Status	—	—	10	Self
TM89	U-turn	Bug	Physical	70	100	20	Normal
TM90	Substitute	Normal	Status	—	—	10	Self
TM91	Flash Cannon	Steel	Special	80	100	10	Normal
TM94	Secret Power	Normal	Physical	70	100	20	Normal
TM97	Dark Pulse	Dark	Special	80	100	15	Normal
TM100	Confide	Normal	Status	—	—	20	Normal
HM02	Fly	Flying	Physical	90	95	15	Normal
HM03	Surf	Water	Special	90	100	15	Adjacent
HM04	Strength	Normal	Physical	80	100	15	Normal
HM06	Rock Smash	Fighting	Physical	40	100	15	Normal

MOVES LEARNED IN EXCHANGE FOR BP

Name	Type	Kind	Pow.	Acc.	PP	Range
Signal Beam	Bug	Special	75	100	15	Normal
Uproar	Normal	Special	90	100	10	1 Random
Earth Power	Ground	Special	90	100	10	Normal
Superpower	Fighting	Physical	120	100	5	Normal
Aqua Tail	Water	Physical	90	90	10	Normal
Zen Headbutt	Psychic	Physical	80	90	15	Normal
Dragon Pulse	Dragon	Special	85	100	10	Normal
Hyper Voice	Normal	Special	90	100	10	Many Others
Iron Tail	Steel	Physical	100	75	15	Normal
Snore	Normal	Special	50	100	15	Normal
Heat Wave	Fire	Special	95	90	10	Many Others
Tailwind	Flying	Status	—	—	15	Your Side
Shock Wave	Electric	Special	60	—	20	Normal
Spite	Ghost	Status	—	100	10	Normal
Outrage	Dragon	Physical	120	100	10	1 Random

MOVES TAUGHT BY PEOPLE

Name	Type	Kind	Pow.	Acc.	PP	Range
Draco Meteor	Dragon	Special	130	90	5	Normal

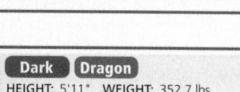

National Pokédex **636** Hoenn Pokédex —

Larvesta

Torch Pokémon

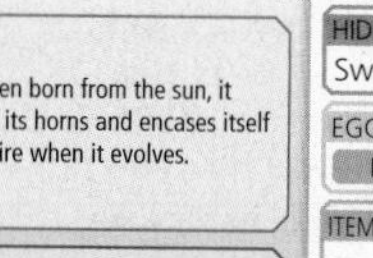

Bug / Fire

HEIGHT: 3'07" WEIGHT: 63.5 lbs.

Same form for ♂ / ♀

Ω Said to have been born from the sun, it spews fire from its horns and encases itself in a cocoon of fire when it evolves.

α The base of volcanoes is where they make their homes. They shoot fire from their five horns to repel attacking enemies.

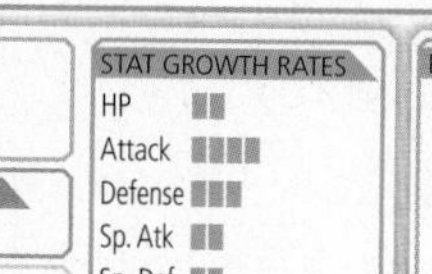

ABILITY
Flame Body

HIDDEN ABILITY
Swarm

EGG GROUPS
Bug

STAT GROWTH RATES
HP
Attack
Defense
Sp. Atk
Sp. Def
Speed

ITEMS SOMETIMES HELD BY WILD POKÉMON
—

EVOLUTION

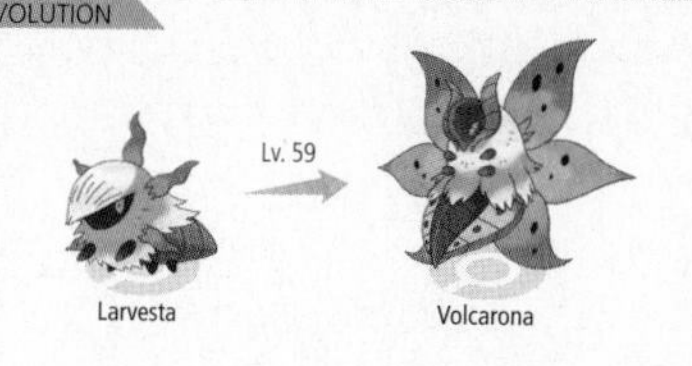

MAIN WAY TO REGISTER IN THE NATIONAL POKÉDEX

Catch in Mirage Forest 8.

Damage taken in normal battles

Type		Type	
Normal	×1	Flying	×2
Fire	×1	Psychic	×1
Water	×2	Bug	×0.5
Grass	×0.25	Rock	×4
Electric	×1	Ghost	×1
Ice	×0.5	Dragon	×1
Fighting	×0.5	Dark	×1
Poison	×1	Steel	×0.5
Ground	×1	Fairy	×0.5

Damage taken in Inverse battles

Type		Type	
Normal	×1	Flying	×0.5
Fire	×1	Psychic	×1
Water	×0.5	Bug	×2
Grass	×4	Rock	×0.25
Electric	×1	Ghost	×1
Ice	×2	Dragon	×1
Fighting	×2	Dark	×1
Poison	×1	Steel	×2
Ground	×1	Fairy	×2

Can be used in
- Inverse Battle
- Battle Institute
- Battle Maison
- Random Matchup (Free Battle)
- Random Matchup (Others)

LEVEL-UP MOVES

Lv.	Name	Type	Kind	Pow.	Acc.	PP	Range
1	Ember	Fire	Special	40	100	25	Normal
1	String Shot	Bug	Status	—	95	40	Many Others
10	Leech Life	Bug	Physical	20	100	15	Normal
20	Take Down	Normal	Physical	90	85	20	Normal
30	Flame Charge	Fire	Physical	50	100	20	Normal
40	Bug Bite	Bug	Physical	60	100	20	Normal
50	Double-Edge	Normal	Physical	120	100	15	Normal
60	Flame Wheel	Fire	Physical	60	100	25	Normal
70	Bug Buzz	Bug	Special	90	100	10	Normal
80	Amnesia	Psychic	Status	—	—	20	Self
90	Thrash	Normal	Physical	120	100	10	1 Random
100	Flare Blitz	Fire	Physical	120	100	15	Normal

TM & HM MOVES

No.	Name	Type	Kind	Pow.	Acc.	PP	Range
TM04	Calm Mind	Psychic	Status	—	—	20	Self
TM06	Toxic	Poison	Status	—	90	10	Normal
TM10	Hidden Power	Normal	Special	60	100	15	Normal
TM11	Sunny Day	Fire	Status	—	—	5	Both Sides
TM16	Light Screen	Psychic	Status	—	—	30	Your Side
TM17	Protect	Normal	Status	—	—	10	Self
TM20	Safeguard	Normal	Status	—	—	25	Your Side
TM21	Frustration	Normal	Physical	—	100	20	Normal
TM22	Solar Beam	Grass	Special	120	100	10	Normal
TM27	Return	Normal	Physical	—	100	20	Normal
TM29	Psychic	Psychic	Special	90	100	10	Normal
TM32	Double Team	Normal	Status	—	—	15	Self
TM35	Flamethrower	Fire	Special	90	100	15	Normal
TM38	Fire Blast	Fire	Special	110	85	5	Normal
TM42	Facade	Normal	Physical	70	100	20	Normal
TM43	Flame Charge	Fire	Physical	50	100	20	Normal
TM44	Rest	Psychic	Status	—	—	10	Self
TM48	Round	Normal	Special	60	100	15	Normal
TM50	Overheat	Fire	Special	130	90	5	Normal
TM59	Incinerate	Fire	Special	60	100	15	Many Others
TM61	Will-O-Wisp	Fire	Status	—	85	15	Normal
TM62	Acrobatics	Flying	Physical	55	100	15	Normal
TM76	Struggle Bug	Bug	Special	50	100	20	Many Others
TM87	Swagger	Normal	Status	—	90	15	Normal
TM88	Sleep Talk	Normal	Status	—	—	10	Self
TM89	U-turn	Bug	Physical	70	100	20	Normal
TM90	Substitute	Normal	Status	—	—	10	Self
TM93	Wild Charge	Electric	Physical	90	100	15	Normal
TM94	Secret Power	Normal	Physical	70	100	20	Normal
TM100	Confide	Normal	Status	—	—	20	Normal

MOVES LEARNED IN EXCHANGE FOR BP

Name	Type	Kind	Pow.	Acc.	PP	Range
Bug Bite	Bug	Physical	60	100	20	Normal
Signal Beam	Bug	Special	75	100	15	Normal
Magnet Rise	Electric	Status	—	—	10	Self
Zen Headbutt	Psychic	Physical	80	90	15	Normal
Snore	Normal	Special	50	100	15	Normal
Heat Wave	Fire	Special	95	90	10	Many Others
Giga Drain	Grass	Special	75	100	10	Normal

MOVES TAUGHT BY PEOPLE

Name	Type	Kind	Pow.	Acc.	PP	Range

EGG MOVES

Name	Type	Kind	Pow.	Acc.	PP	Range
String Shot	Bug	Status	—	95	40	Many Others
Harden	Normal	Status	—	—	30	Self
Foresight	Normal	Status	—	—	40	Normal
Endure	Normal	Status	—	—	10	Self
Zen Headbutt	Psychic	Physical	80	90	15	Normal
Morning Sun	Normal	Status	—	—	5	Self
Magnet Rise	Electric	Status	—	—	10	Self

National Pokédex **637** Hoenn Pokédex —

Volcarona

Sun Pokémon

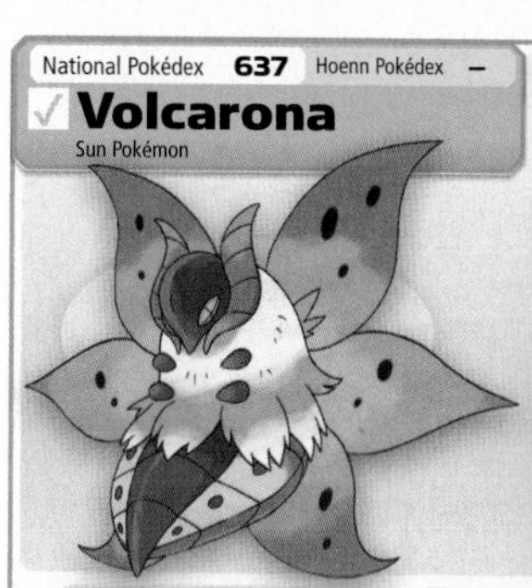

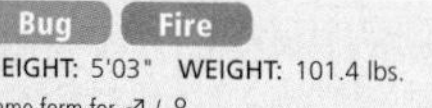

Bug / Fire

HEIGHT: 5'03" WEIGHT: 101.4 lbs.

Same form for ♂ / ♀

Ω A sea of fire engulfs the surroundings of their battles, since they use their six wings to scatter their ember scales.

α When volcanic ash darkened the atmosphere, it is said that Volcarona's fire provided a replacement for the sun.

ABILITY
Flame Body

HIDDEN ABILITY
Swarm

EGG GROUPS
Bug

STAT GROWTH RATES
HP
Attack
Defense
Sp. Atk
Sp. Def
Speed

ITEMS SOMETIMES HELD BY WILD POKÉMON
—

EVOLUTION

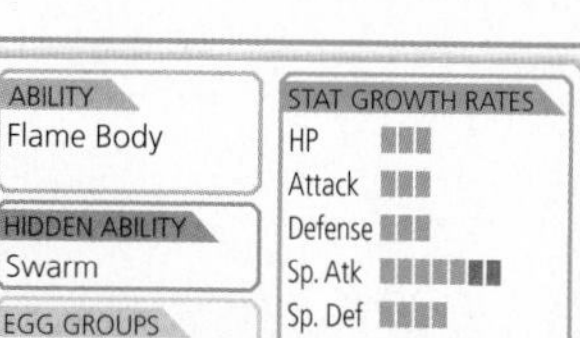

MAIN WAY TO REGISTER IN THE NATIONAL POKÉDEX

Level up Larvesta to Lv. 59.

Damage taken in normal battles

Type		Type	
Normal	×1	Flying	×2
Fire	×1	Psychic	×1
Water	×2	Bug	×0.5
Grass	×0.25	Rock	×4
Electric	×1	Ghost	×1
Ice	×0.5	Dragon	×1
Fighting	×0.5	Dark	×1
Poison	×1	Steel	×0.5
Ground	×1	Fairy	×0.5

Damage taken in Inverse battles

Type		Type	
Normal	×1	Flying	×0.5
Fire	×1	Psychic	×1
Water	×0.5	Bug	×2
Grass	×4	Rock	×0.25
Electric	×1	Ghost	×1
Ice	×2	Dragon	×1
Fighting	×2	Dark	×1
Poison	×1	Steel	×2
Ground	×1	Fairy	×2

Can be used in
- Inverse Battle
- Battle Institute
- Battle Maison
- Random Matchup (Free Battle)
- Random Matchup (Others)

LEVEL-UP MOVES

Lv.	Name	Type	Kind	Pow.	Acc.	PP	Range
1	Fiery Dance	Fire	Special	80	100	10	Normal
1	Hurricane	Flying	Special	110	70	10	Normal
1	Rage Powder	Bug	Status	—	—	20	Self
1	Heat Wave	Fire	Special	95	90	10	Many Others
1	Quiver Dance	Bug	Status	—	—	20	Self
1	Flare Blitz	Fire	Physical	120	100	15	Normal
1	Thrash	Normal	Physical	120	100	10	1 Random
1	Amnesia	Psychic	Status	—	—	20	Self
1	Bug Buzz	Bug	Special	90	100	10	Normal
1	Flame Wheel	Fire	Physical	60	100	25	Normal
1	Ember	Fire	Special	40	100	25	Normal
1	String Shot	Bug	Status	—	95	40	Many Others
1	Leech Life	Bug	Physical	20	100	15	Normal
1	Gust	Flying	Special	40	100	35	Normal
10	Leech Life	Bug	Physical	20	100	15	Normal
20	Gust	Flying	Special	40	100	35	Normal
30	Fire Spin	Fire	Special	35	85	15	Normal
40	Whirlwind	Normal	Status	—	—	20	Normal
50	Silver Wind	Bug	Special	60	100	5	Normal
59	Quiver Dance	Bug	Status	—	—	20	Self
60	Heat Wave	Fire	Special	95	90	10	Many Others
70	Bug Buzz	Bug	Special	90	100	10	Normal
80	Rage Powder	Bug	Status	—	—	20	Self
90	Hurricane	Flying	Special	110	70	10	Normal
100	Fiery Dance	Fire	Special	80	100	10	Normal

TM & HM MOVES

No.	Name	Type	Kind	Pow.	Acc.	PP	Range
TM04	Calm Mind	Psychic	Status	—	—	20	Self
TM06	Toxic	Poison	Status	—	90	10	Normal
TM10	Hidden Power	Normal	Special	60	100	15	Normal
TM11	Sunny Day	Fire	Status	—	—	5	Both Sides
TM15	Hyper Beam	Normal	Special	150	90	5	Normal
TM16	Light Screen	Psychic	Status	—	—	30	Your Side
TM17	Protect	Normal	Status	—	—	10	Self
TM19	Roost	Flying	Status	—	—	10	Self
TM20	Safeguard	Normal	Status	—	—	25	Your Side
TM21	Frustration	Normal	Physical	—	100	20	Normal
TM22	Solar Beam	Grass	Special	120	100	10	Normal
TM27	Return	Normal	Physical	—	100	20	Normal
TM29	Psychic	Psychic	Special	90	100	10	Normal
TM32	Double Team	Normal	Status	—	—	15	Self
TM35	Flamethrower	Fire	Special	90	100	15	Normal
TM38	Fire Blast	Fire	Special	110	85	5	Normal
TM40	Aerial Ace	Flying	Physical	60	—	20	Normal
TM42	Facade	Normal	Physical	70	100	20	Normal
TM43	Flame Charge	Fire	Physical	50	100	20	Normal
TM44	Rest	Psychic	Status	—	—	10	Self
TM48	Round	Normal	Special	60	100	15	Normal
TM50	Overheat	Fire	Special	130	90	5	Normal
TM59	Incinerate	Fire	Special	60	100	15	Many Others
TM61	Will-O-Wisp	Fire	Status	—	85	15	Normal
TM62	Acrobatics	Flying	Physical	55	100	15	Normal
TM68	Giga Impact	Normal	Physical	150	90	5	Normal
TM76	Struggle Bug	Bug	Special	50	100	20	Many Others
TM84	Poison Jab	Poison	Physical	80	100	20	Normal
TM87	Swagger	Normal	Status	—	90	15	Normal
TM88	Sleep Talk	Normal	Status	—	—	10	Self
TM89	U-turn	Bug	Physical	70	100	20	Normal
TM90	Substitute	Normal	Status	—	—	10	Self
TM93	Wild Charge	Electric	Physical	90	100	15	Normal
TM94	Secret Power	Normal	Physical	70	100	20	Normal
TM100	Confide	Normal	Status	—	—	20	Normal
HM02	Fly	Flying	Physical	90	95	15	Normal

MOVES LEARNED IN EXCHANGE FOR BP

Name	Type	Kind	Pow.	Acc.	PP	Range
Bug Bite	Bug	Physical	60	100	20	Normal
Signal Beam	Bug	Special	75	100	15	Normal
Magnet Rise	Electric	Status	—	—	10	Self
Zen Headbutt	Psychic	Physical	80	90	15	Normal
Snore	Normal	Special	50	100	15	Normal
Heat Wave	Fire	Special	95	90	10	Many Others
Tailwind	Flying	Status	—	—	15	Your Side
Giga Drain	Grass	Special	75	100	10	Normal

MOVES TAUGHT BY PEOPLE

Name	Type	Kind	Pow.	Acc.	PP	Range

National Pokédex **638** Hoenn Pokédex —

Cobalion

Iron Will Pokémon

Steel Fighting

HEIGHT: 6'11" WEIGHT: 551.2 lbs.

Gender unknown

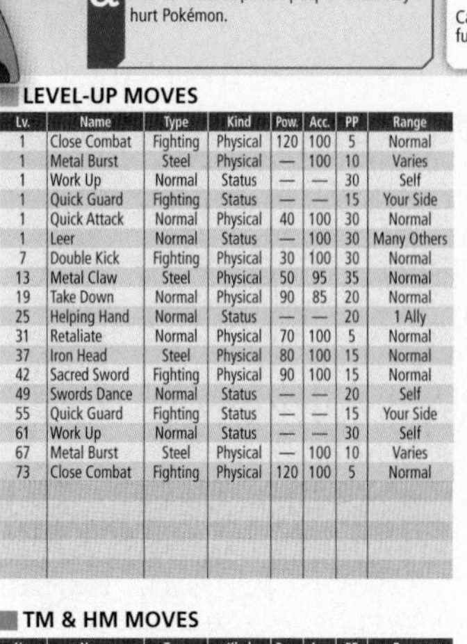

Ω It has a body and heart of steel. Its glare is sufficient to make even an unruly Pokémon obey it.

α It has a body and heart of steel. It worked with its allies to punish people when they hurt Pokémon.

ABILITY
Justified

HIDDEN ABILITY
—

EGG GROUPS
No Eggs Discovered

STAT GROWTH RATES
HP
Attack
Defense
Sp. Atk
Sp. Def
Speed

ITEMS SOMETIMES HELD BY WILD POKÉMON
—

EVOLUTION

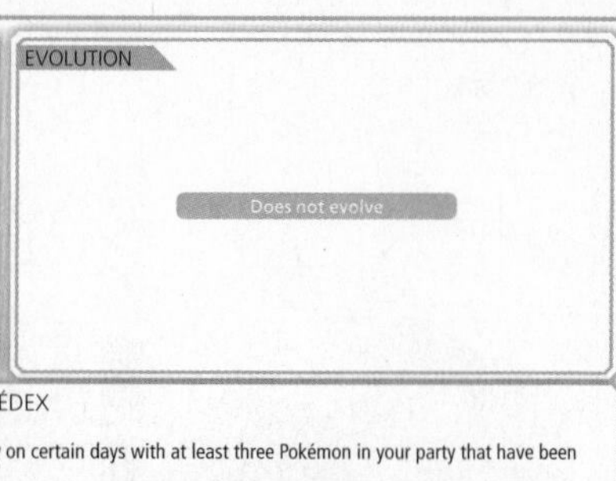

Does not evolve

MAIN WAY TO REGISTER IN THE NATIONAL POKÉDEX

Catch in the Pathless Plain Mirage spot by Soaring in the sky on certain days with at least three Pokémon in your party that have been fully trained in Super Training.

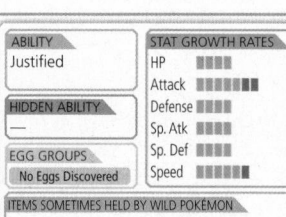

Damage taken in normal battles

Type		Type	
Normal	×0.5	Flying	×1
Fire	×2	Psychic	×1
Water	×1	Bug	×0.25
Grass	×0.5	Rock	×0.25
Electric	×1	Ghost	×1
Ice	×0.5	Dragon	×0.5
Fighting	×2	Dark	×0.5
Poison	×0	Steel	×0.5
Ground	×2	Fairy	×1

Damage taken in Inverse battles

Type		Type	
Normal	×2	Flying	×1
Fire	×0.5	Psychic	×1
Water	×1	Bug	×4
Grass	×2	Rock	×4
Electric	×1	Ghost	×1
Ice	×2	Dragon	×2
Fighting	×0.5	Dark	×2
Poison	×2	Steel	×2
Ground	×0.5	Fairy	×1

Can be used in

- Inverse Battle
- Battle Institute
- Battle Maison
- Random Matchup (Free Battle)
- Random Matchup (Others)

LEVEL-UP MOVES

Lv.	Name	Type	Kind	Pow.	Acc.	PP	Range
1	Close Combat	Fighting	Physical	120	100	5	Normal
1	Metal Burst	Steel	Physical	—	100	10	Varies
1	Work Up	Normal	Status	—	—	30	Self
1	Quick Guard	Fighting	Status	—	—	15	Your Side
1	Quick Attack	Normal	Physical	40	100	30	Normal
1	Leer	Normal	Status	—	100	30	Many Others
7	Double Kick	Fighting	Physical	30	100	30	Normal
13	Metal Claw	Steel	Physical	50	95	35	Normal
19	Take Down	Normal	Physical	90	85	20	Normal
25	Helping Hand	Normal	Status	—	—	20	1 Ally
31	Retaliate	Normal	Physical	70	100	5	Normal
37	Iron Head	Steel	Physical	80	100	15	Normal
42	Sacred Sword	Fighting	Physical	90	100	15	Normal
49	Swords Dance	Normal	Status	—	—	20	Self
55	Quick Guard	Fighting	Status	—	—	15	Your Side
61	Work Up	Normal	Status	—	—	30	Self
67	Metal Burst	Steel	Physical	—	100	10	Varies
73	Close Combat	Fighting	Physical	120	100	5	Normal

TM & HM MOVES

No.	Name	Type	Kind	Pow.	Acc.	PP	Range
TM01	Hone Claws	Dark	Status	—	—	15	Self
TM04	Calm Mind	Psychic	Status	—	—	20	Self
TM05	Roar	Normal	Status	—	—	20	Normal
TM06	Toxic	Poison	Status	—	90	10	Normal
TM10	Hidden Power	Normal	Special	60	100	15	Normal
TM12	Taunt	Dark	Status	—	100	20	Normal
TM15	Hyper Beam	Normal	Special	150	90	5	Normal
TM17	Protect	Normal	Status	—	—	10	Self
TM20	Safeguard	Normal	Status	—	—	25	Your Side
TM21	Frustration	Normal	Physical	—	100	20	Normal
TM27	Return	Normal	Physical	—	100	20	Normal
TM32	Double Team	Normal	Status	—	—	15	Self
TM33	Reflect	Psychic	Status	—	—	20	Your Side
TM37	Sandstorm	Rock	Status	—	—	10	Both Sides
TM40	Aerial Ace	Flying	Physical	60	—	20	Normal
TM42	Facade	Normal	Physical	70	100	20	Normal
TM44	Rest	Psychic	Status	—	—	10	Self
TM48	Round	Normal	Special	60	100	15	Normal
TM52	Focus Blast	Fighting	Special	120	70	5	Normal
TM54	False Swipe	Normal	Physical	40	100	40	Normal
TM67	Retaliate	Normal	Physical	70	100	5	Normal
TM68	Giga Impact	Normal	Physical	150	90	5	Normal
TM69	Rock Polish	Rock	Status	—	—	20	Self
TM71	Stone Edge	Rock	Physical	100	80	5	Normal
TM72	Volt Switch	Electric	Special	70	100	20	Normal
TM73	Thunder Wave	Electric	Status	—	100	20	Normal
TM75	Swords Dance	Normal	Status	—	—	20	Self
TM77	Psych Up	Normal	Status	—	—	10	Normal
TM81	X-Scissor	Bug	Physical	80	100	15	Normal
TM84	Poison Jab	Poison	Physical	80	100	20	Normal
TM87	Swagger	Normal	Status	—	90	15	Normal
TM88	Sleep Talk	Normal	Status	—	—	10	Self
TM90	Substitute	Normal	Status	—	—	10	Self
TM91	Flash Cannon	Steel	Special	80	100	10	Normal
TM94	Secret Power	Normal	Physical	70	100	20	Normal
TM100	Confide	Normal	Status	—	—	20	Normal
HM01	Cut	Normal	Physical	50	95	30	Normal
HM04	Strength	Normal	Physical	80	100	15	Normal
HM06	Rock Smash	Fighting	Physical	40	100	15	Normal

MOVES LEARNED IN EXCHANGE FOR BP

Name	Type	Kind	Pow.	Acc.	PP	Range
Iron Head	Steel	Physical	80	100	15	Normal
Bounce	Flying	Physical	85	85	5	Normal
Block	Normal	Status	—	—	5	Normal
Magnet Rise	Electric	Status	—	—	10	Self
Iron Defense	Steel	Status	—	—	15	Self
Superpower	Fighting	Physical	120	100	5	Normal
Zen Headbutt	Psychic	Physical	80	90	15	Normal
Snore	Normal	Special	50	100	15	Normal
Helping Hand	Normal	Status	—	—	20	1 Ally
Stealth Rock	Rock	Status	—	—	20	Other Side

MOVES TAUGHT BY PEOPLE

Name	Type	Kind	Pow.	Acc.	PP	Range

National Pokédex **639** Hoenn Pokédex —

Terrakion

Cavern Pokémon

Rock Fighting

HEIGHT: 6'03" WEIGHT: 573.2 lbs.

Gender unknown

Ω Its charge is strong enough to break through a giant castle wall in one blow. This Pokémon is spoken of in legends.

α Spoken of in legend, this Pokémon used its phenomenal power to destroy a castle in its effort to protect Pokémon.

ABILITY
Justified

HIDDEN ABILITY
—

EGG GROUPS
No Eggs Discovered

STAT GROWTH RATES
HP
Attack
Defense
Sp. Atk
Sp. Def
Speed

ITEMS SOMETIMES HELD BY WILD POKÉMON
—

EVOLUTION

Does not evolve

MAIN WAY TO REGISTER IN THE NATIONAL POKÉDEX

Catch in the Pathless Plain Mirage spot by Soaring in the sky on certain days with at least three Pokémon in your party that have been fully trained in Super Training.

Damage taken in normal battles

Type		Type	
Normal	×0.5	Flying	×1
Fire	×0.5	Psychic	×2
Water	×2	Bug	×0.5
Grass	×2	Rock	×0.5
Electric	×1	Ghost	×1
Ice	×1	Dragon	×1
Fighting	×2	Dark	×0.5
Poison	×0.5	Steel	×2
Ground	×2	Fairy	×2

Damage taken in Inverse battles

Type		Type	
Normal	×2	Flying	×1
Fire	×2	Psychic	×0.5
Water	×0.5	Bug	×2
Grass	×0.5	Rock	×2
Electric	×1	Ghost	×1
Ice	×1	Dragon	×1
Fighting	×0.5	Dark	×2
Poison	×2	Steel	×0.5
Ground	×0.5	Fairy	×0.5

Can be used in

- Inverse Battle
- Battle Institute
- Battle Maison
- Random Matchup (Free Battle)
- Random Matchup (Others)

LEVEL-UP MOVES

Lv.	Name	Type	Kind	Pow.	Acc.	PP	Range
1	Close Combat	Fighting	Physical	120	100	5	Normal
1	Work Up	Normal	Status	—	—	30	Self
1	Quick Guard	Fighting	Status	—	—	15	Your Side
1	Quick Attack	Normal	Physical	40	100	30	Normal
1	Leer	Normal	Status	—	100	30	Many Others
7	Double Kick	Fighting	Physical	30	100	30	Normal
13	Smack Down	Rock	Physical	50	100	15	Normal
19	Take Down	Normal	Physical	90	85	20	Normal
25	Helping Hand	Normal	Status	—	—	20	1 Ally
31	Retaliate	Normal	Physical	70	100	5	Normal
37	Rock Slide	Rock	Physical	75	90	10	Many Others
42	Sacred Sword	Fighting	Physical	90	100	15	Normal
49	Swords Dance	Normal	Status	—	—	20	Self
55	Quick Guard	Fighting	Status	—	—	15	Your Side
61	Work Up	Normal	Status	—	—	30	Self
67	Stone Edge	Rock	Physical	100	80	5	Normal
73	Close Combat	Fighting	Physical	120	100	5	Normal

TM & HM MOVES

No.	Name	Type	Kind	Pow.	Acc.	PP	Range
TM04	Calm Mind	Psychic	Status	—	—	20	Self
TM05	Roar	Normal	Status	—	—	20	Normal
TM06	Toxic	Poison	Status	—	90	10	Normal
TM10	Hidden Power	Normal	Special	60	100	15	Normal
TM12	Taunt	Dark	Status	—	100	20	Normal
TM15	Hyper Beam	Normal	Special	150	90	5	Normal
TM17	Protect	Normal	Status	—	—	10	Self
TM20	Safeguard	Normal	Status	—	—	25	Your Side
TM21	Frustration	Normal	Physical	—	100	20	Normal
TM23	Smack Down	Rock	Physical	50	100	15	Normal
TM26	Earthquake	Ground	Physical	100	100	10	Adjacent
TM27	Return	Normal	Physical	—	100	20	Normal
TM32	Double Team	Normal	Status	—	—	15	Self
TM33	Reflect	Psychic	Status	—	—	20	Your Side
TM37	Sandstorm	Rock	Status	—	—	10	Both Sides
TM39	Rock Tomb	Rock	Physical	60	95	15	Normal
TM40	Aerial Ace	Flying	Physical	60	—	20	Normal
TM42	Facade	Normal	Physical	70	100	20	Normal
TM44	Rest	Psychic	Status	—	—	10	Self
TM48	Round	Normal	Special	60	100	15	Normal
TM52	Focus Blast	Fighting	Special	120	70	5	Normal
TM54	False Swipe	Normal	Physical	40	100	40	Normal
TM67	Retaliate	Normal	Physical	70	100	5	Normal
TM68	Giga Impact	Normal	Physical	150	90	5	Normal
TM69	Rock Polish	Rock	Status	—	—	20	Self
TM71	Stone Edge	Rock	Physical	100	80	5	Normal
TM75	Swords Dance	Normal	Status	—	—	20	Self
TM77	Psych Up	Normal	Status	—	—	10	Normal
TM78	Bulldoze	Ground	Physical	60	100	20	Adjacent
TM80	Rock Slide	Rock	Physical	75	90	10	Many Others
TM81	X-Scissor	Bug	Physical	80	100	15	Normal
TM84	Poison Jab	Poison	Physical	80	100	20	Normal
TM87	Swagger	Normal	Status	—	90	15	Normal
TM88	Sleep Talk	Normal	Status	—	—	10	Self
TM90	Substitute	Normal	Status	—	—	10	Self
TM94	Secret Power	Normal	Physical	70	100	20	Normal
TM100	Confide	Normal	Status	—	—	20	Normal
HM01	Cut	Normal	Physical	50	95	30	Normal
HM04	Strength	Normal	Physical	80	100	15	Normal
HM06	Rock Smash	Fighting	Physical	40	100	15	Normal

MOVES LEARNED IN EXCHANGE FOR BP

Name	Type	Kind	Pow.	Acc.	PP	Range
Iron Head	Steel	Physical	80	100	15	Normal
Block	Normal	Status	—	—	5	Normal
Earth Power	Ground	Special	90	100	10	Normal
Superpower	Fighting	Physical	120	100	5	Normal
Zen Headbutt	Psychic	Physical	80	90	15	Normal
Snore	Normal	Special	50	100	15	Normal
Helping Hand	Normal	Status	—	—	20	1 Ally
Stealth Rock	Rock	Status	—	—	20	Other Side

MOVES TAUGHT BY PEOPLE

Name	Type	Kind	Pow.	Acc.	PP	Range

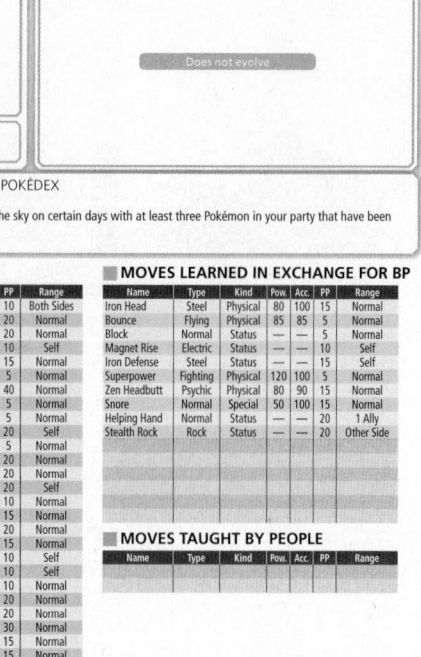

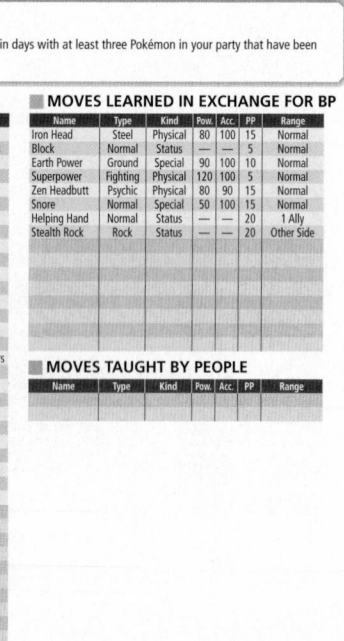

National Pokédex **640** Hoenn Pokédex —

✓ Virizion

Grassland Pokémon

Grass / Fighting

HEIGHT: 6'07" WEIGHT: 440.9 lbs.

Gender unknown

Ω Its head sprouts horns as sharp as blades. Using whirlwind-like movements, it confounds and swiftly cuts opponents.

α Legends say this Pokémon confounded opponents with its swift movements.

ABILITY
Justified

HIDDEN ABILITY
—

EGG GROUPS
No Eggs Discovered

STAT GROWTH RATES
HP
Attack
Defense
Sp. Atk
Sp. Def
Speed

ITEMS SOMETIMES HELD BY WILD POKÉMON
—

EVOLUTION
Does not evolve

MAIN WAY TO REGISTER IN THE NATIONAL POKÉDEX

Catch in the Pathless Plain Mirage spot by Soaring in the sky on certain days with at least three Pokémon in your party that have been fully trained in Super Training.

Damage taken in normal battles

Type	×	Type	×
Normal	×1	Flying	×4
Fire	×2	Psychic	×2
Water	×0.5	Bug	×1
Grass	×0.5	Rock	×0.5
Electric	×0.5	Ghost	×1
Ice	×2	Dragon	×1
Fighting	×1	Dark	×0.5
Poison	×2	Steel	×1
Ground	×0.5	Fairy	×2

Damage taken in Inverse battles

Type	×	Type	×
Normal	×1	Flying	×0.25
Fire	×0.5	Psychic	×0.5
Water	×2	Bug	×1
Grass	×2	Rock	×2
Electric	×2	Ghost	×1
Ice	×0.5	Dragon	×1
Fighting	×1	Dark	×2
Poison	×0.5	Steel	×1
Ground	×2	Fairy	×0.5

Can be used in
Inverse Battle
Battle Institute
Battle Maison
Random Matchup (Free Battle)
Random Matchup (Others)

LEVEL-UP MOVES

Lv.	Name	Type	Kind	Pow.	Acc.	PP	Range
1	Close Combat	Fighting	Physical	120	100	5	Normal
1	Leaf Blade	Grass	Physical	90	100	15	Normal
1	Work Up	Normal	Status	—	—	30	Self
1	Quick Guard	Fighting	Status	—	—	15	Your Side
1	Quick Attack	Normal	Physical	40	100	30	Normal
1	Leer	Normal	Status	—	100	30	Many Others
7	Double Kick	Fighting	Physical	30	100	30	Normal
13	Magical Leaf	Grass	Special	60	—	20	Normal
19	Take Down	Normal	Physical	90	85	20	Normal
25	Helping Hand	Normal	Status	—	—	20	1 Ally
31	Retaliate	Normal	Physical	70	100	5	Normal
37	Giga Drain	Grass	Special	75	100	10	Normal
42	Sacred Sword	Fighting	Physical	90	100	15	Normal
49	Swords Dance	Normal	Status	—	—	20	Self
55	Quick Guard	Fighting	Status	—	—	15	Your Side
61	Work Up	Normal	Status	—	—	30	Self
67	Leaf Blade	Grass	Physical	90	100	15	Normal
73	Close Combat	Fighting	Physical	120	100	5	Normal

TM & HM MOVES

No.	Name	Type	Kind	Pow.	Acc.	PP	Range
TM04	Calm Mind	Psychic	Status	—	—	20	Self
TM05	Roar	Normal	Status	—	—	20	Normal
TM06	Toxic	Poison	Status	—	90	10	Normal
TM10	Hidden Power	Normal	Special	60	100	15	Normal
TM11	Sunny Day	Fire	Status	—	—	5	Both Sides
TM12	Taunt	Dark	Status	—	100	20	Normal
TM15	Hyper Beam	Normal	Special	150	90	5	Normal
TM16	Light Screen	Psychic	Status	—	—	30	Your Side
TM17	Protect	Normal	Status	—	—	10	Self
TM20	Safeguard	Normal	Status	—	—	25	Your Side
TM21	Frustration	Normal	Physical	—	100	20	Normal
TM22	Solar Beam	Grass	Special	120	100	10	Normal
TM27	Return	Normal	Physical	—	100	20	Normal
TM32	Double Team	Normal	Status	—	—	15	Self
TM33	Reflect	Psychic	Status	—	—	20	Your Side
TM40	Aerial Ace	Flying	Physical	60	—	20	Normal
TM42	Facade	Normal	Physical	70	100	20	Normal
TM44	Rest	Psychic	Status	—	—	10	Self
TM48	Round	Normal	Special	60	100	15	Normal
TM52	Focus Blast	Fighting	Special	120	70	5	Normal
TM53	Energy Ball	Grass	Special	90	100	10	Normal
TM54	False Swipe	Normal	Physical	40	100	40	Normal
TM67	Retaliate	Normal	Physical	70	100	5	Normal
TM68	Giga Impact	Normal	Physical	150	90	5	Normal
TM70	Flash	Normal	Status	—	100	20	Normal
TM71	Stone Edge	Rock	Physical	100	80	5	Normal
TM75	Swords Dance	Normal	Status	—	—	20	Self
TM77	Psych Up	Normal	Status	—	—	10	Normal
TM81	X-Scissor	Bug	Physical	80	100	15	Normal
TM86	Grass Knot	Grass	Special	—	100	20	Normal
TM87	Swagger	Normal	Status	—	90	15	Normal
TM88	Sleep Talk	Normal	Status	—	—	10	Self
TM90	Substitute	Normal	Status	—	—	10	Self
TM94	Secret Power	Normal	Physical	70	100	20	Normal
TM96	Nature Power	Normal	Status	—	—	20	Normal
TM100	Confide	Normal	Status	—	—	20	Normal
HM01	Cut	Normal	Physical	50	95	30	Normal
HM04	Strength	Normal	Physical	80	100	15	Normal
HM06	Rock Smash	Fighting	Physical	40	100	15	Normal

MOVES LEARNED IN EXCHANGE FOR BP

Name	Type	Kind	Pow.	Acc.	PP	Range
Seed Bomb	Grass	Physical	80	100	15	Normal
Bounce	Flying	Physical	85	85	5	Normal
Block	Normal	Status	—	—	5	Normal
Superpower	Fighting	Physical	120	100	5	Normal
Zen Headbutt	Psychic	Physical	80	90	15	Normal
Snore	Normal	Special	50	100	15	Normal
Synthesis	Grass	Status	—	—	5	Self
Giga Drain	Grass	Special	75	100	10	Normal
Worry Seed	Grass	Status	—	100	10	Normal
Helping Hand	Normal	Status	—	—	20	1 Ally

MOVES TAUGHT BY PEOPLE

Name	Type	Kind	Pow.	Acc.	PP	Range

640

Virizion

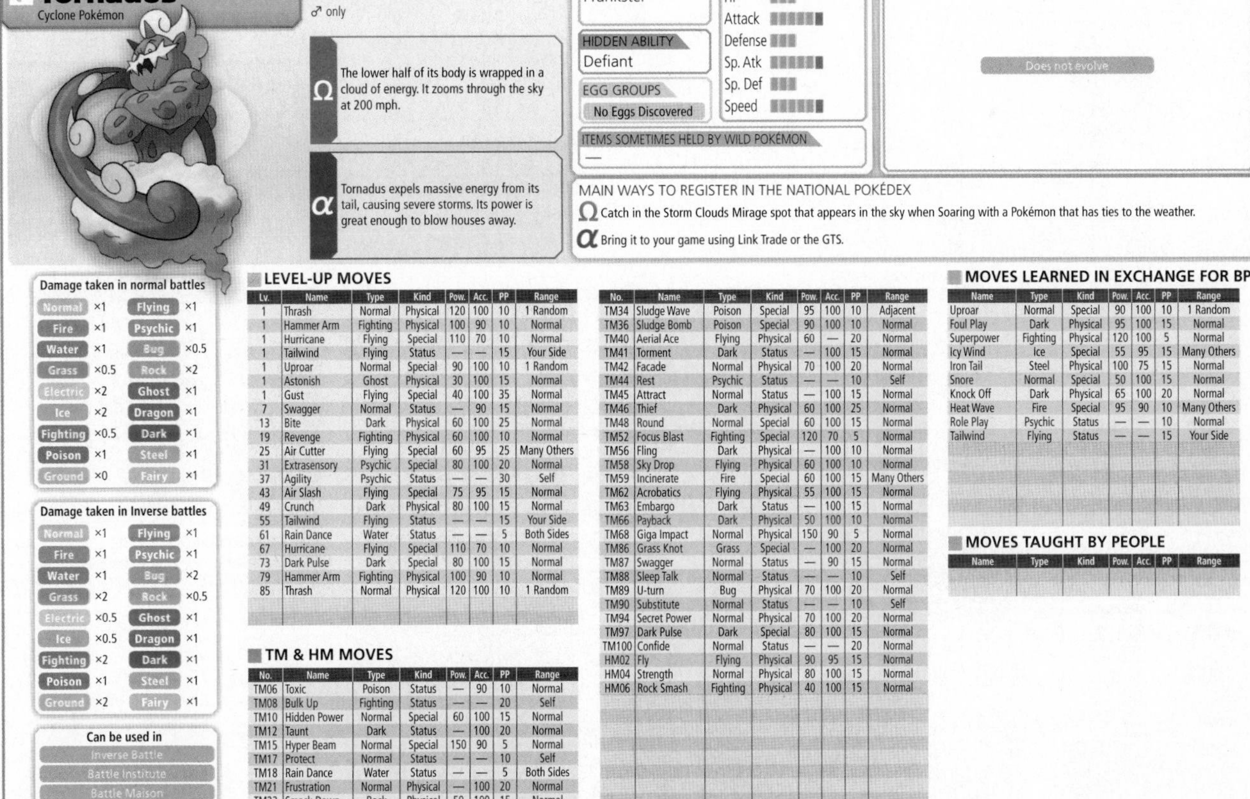

National Pokédex **641** Hoenn Pokédex —

✓ Tornadus Incarnate Forme

Cyclone Pokémon

Flying

HEIGHT: 4'11" WEIGHT: 138.9 lbs.

♂ only

Ω The lower half of its body is wrapped in a cloud of energy. It zooms through the sky at 200 mph.

α Tornadus expels massive energy from its tail, causing severe storms. Its power is great enough to blow houses away.

ABILITY
Prankster

HIDDEN ABILITY
Defiant

EGG GROUPS
No Eggs Discovered

STAT GROWTH RATES
HP
Attack
Defense
Sp. Atk
Sp. Def
Speed

ITEMS SOMETIMES HELD BY WILD POKÉMON
—

EVOLUTION
Does not evolve

MAIN WAYS TO REGISTER IN THE NATIONAL POKÉDEX

Ω Catch in the Storm Clouds Mirage spot that appears in the sky when Soaring with a Pokémon that has ties to the weather.

α Bring it to your game using Link Trade or the GTS.

Damage taken in normal battles

Type	×	Type	×
Normal	×1	Flying	×1
Fire	×1	Psychic	×1
Water	×1	Bug	×0.5
Grass	×0.5	Rock	×2
Electric	×2	Ghost	×1
Ice	×2	Dragon	×1
Fighting	×0.5	Dark	×1
Poison	×1	Steel	×1
Ground	×0	Fairy	×1

Damage taken in Inverse battles

Type	×	Type	×
Normal	×1	Flying	×1
Fire	×1	Psychic	×1
Water	×1	Bug	×2
Grass	×2	Rock	×0.5
Electric	×0.5	Ghost	×1
Ice	×0.5	Dragon	×1
Fighting	×2	Dark	×1
Poison	×1	Steel	×1
Ground	×2	Fairy	×1

Can be used in
Inverse Battle
Battle Institute
Battle Maison
Random Matchup (Free Battle)
Random Matchup (Others)

LEVEL-UP MOVES

Lv.	Name	Type	Kind	Pow.	Acc.	PP	Range
1	Thrash	Normal	Physical	120	100	10	1 Random
1	Hammer Arm	Fighting	Physical	100	90	10	Normal
1	Hurricane	Flying	Special	110	70	10	Normal
1	Tailwind	Flying	Status	—	—	15	Your Side
1	Uproar	Normal	Special	90	100	10	1 Random
1	Astonish	Ghost	Physical	30	100	15	Normal
1	Gust	Flying	Special	40	100	35	Normal
7	Swagger	Normal	Status	—	90	15	Normal
13	Bite	Dark	Physical	60	100	25	Normal
19	Revenge	Fighting	Physical	60	100	10	Normal
25	Air Cutter	Flying	Special	60	95	25	Many Others
31	Extrasensory	Psychic	Special	80	100	20	Normal
37	Agility	Psychic	Status	—	—	30	Self
43	Air Slash	Flying	Special	75	95	15	Normal
49	Crunch	Dark	Physical	80	100	15	Normal
55	Tailwind	Flying	Status	—	—	15	Your Side
61	Rain Dance	Water	Status	—	—	5	Both Sides
67	Hurricane	Flying	Special	110	70	10	Normal
73	Dark Pulse	Dark	Special	80	100	15	Normal
79	Hammer Arm	Fighting	Physical	100	90	10	Normal
85	Thrash	Normal	Physical	120	100	10	1 Random

TM & HM MOVES

No.	Name	Type	Kind	Pow.	Acc.	PP	Range
TM06	Toxic	Poison	Status	—	90	10	Normal
TM08	Bulk Up	Fighting	Status	—	—	20	Self
TM10	Hidden Power	Normal	Special	60	100	15	Normal
TM12	Taunt	Dark	Status	—	100	20	Normal
TM15	Hyper Beam	Normal	Special	150	90	5	Normal
TM17	Protect	Normal	Status	—	—	10	Self
TM18	Rain Dance	Water	Status	—	—	5	Both Sides
TM21	Frustration	Normal	Physical	—	100	20	Normal
TM23	Smack Down	Rock	Physical	50	100	15	Normal
TM27	Return	Normal	Physical	—	100	20	Normal
TM29	Psychic	Psychic	Special	90	100	10	Normal
TM31	Brick Break	Fighting	Physical	75	100	15	Normal
TM32	Double Team	Normal	Status	—	—	15	Self
TM34	Sludge Wave	Poison	Special	95	100	10	Adjacent
TM36	Sludge Bomb	Poison	Special	90	100	10	Normal
TM40	Aerial Ace	Flying	Physical	60	—	20	Normal
TM41	Torment	Dark	Status	—	100	15	Normal
TM42	Facade	Normal	Physical	70	100	20	Normal
TM44	Rest	Psychic	Status	—	—	10	Self
TM45	Attract	Normal	Status	—	100	15	Normal
TM46	Thief	Dark	Physical	60	100	25	Normal
TM48	Round	Normal	Special	60	100	15	Normal
TM52	Focus Blast	Fighting	Special	120	70	5	Normal
TM56	Fling	Dark	Physical	—	100	10	Normal
TM58	Sky Drop	Flying	Physical	60	100	10	Normal
TM59	Incinerate	Fire	Special	60	100	15	Many Others
TM62	Acrobatics	Flying	Physical	55	100	15	Normal
TM63	Embargo	Dark	Status	—	100	15	Normal
TM66	Payback	Dark	Physical	50	100	10	Normal
TM68	Giga Impact	Normal	Physical	150	90	5	Normal
TM86	Grass Knot	Grass	Special	—	100	20	Normal
TM87	Swagger	Normal	Status	—	90	15	Normal
TM88	Sleep Talk	Normal	Status	—	—	10	Self
TM89	U-turn	Bug	Physical	70	100	20	Normal
TM90	Substitute	Normal	Status	—	—	10	Self
TM94	Secret Power	Normal	Physical	70	100	20	Normal
TM97	Dark Pulse	Dark	Special	80	100	15	Normal
TM100	Confide	Normal	Status	—	—	20	Normal
HM02	Fly	Flying	Physical	90	95	15	Normal
HM04	Strength	Normal	Physical	80	100	15	Normal
HM06	Rock Smash	Fighting	Physical	40	100	15	Normal

MOVES LEARNED IN EXCHANGE FOR BP

Name	Type	Kind	Pow.	Acc.	PP	Range
Uproar	Normal	Special	90	100	10	1 Random
Foul Play	Dark	Physical	95	100	15	Normal
Superpower	Fighting	Physical	120	100	5	Normal
Icy Wind	Ice	Special	55	95	15	Many Others
Iron Tail	Steel	Physical	100	75	15	Normal
Snore	Normal	Special	50	100	15	Normal
Knock Off	Dark	Physical	65	100	20	Normal
Heat Wave	Fire	Special	95	90	10	Many Others
Role Play	Psychic	Status	—	—	10	Normal
Tailwind	Flying	Status	—	—	15	Your Side

MOVES TAUGHT BY PEOPLE

Name	Type	Kind	Pow.	Acc.	PP	Range

Tornadus

641

National Pokédex

641
Tornadus
National Pokédex
Thundurus
642

National Pokédex **641** Hoenn Pokédex —

Tornadus Therian Forme

Cyclone Pokémon

Flying

HEIGHT: 4'07" WEIGHT: 138.9 lbs.

♂ only

Ω The lower half of its body is wrapped in a cloud of energy. It zooms through the sky at 200 mph.

α Tornadus expels massive energy from its tail, causing severe storms. Its power is great enough to blow houses away.

ABILITY
Regenerator

HIDDEN ABILITY
—

EGG GROUPS
No Eggs Discovered

STAT GROWTH RATES
HP
Attack
Defense
Sp. Atk
Sp. Def
Speed

ITEMS SOMETIMES HELD BY WILD POKÉMON
—

EVOLUTION
Does not evolve

MAIN WAY TO REGISTER IN THE NATIONAL POKÉDEX
Use a Reveal Glass on Tornadus (Incarnate Forme).

Damage taken in normal battles

Type		Type	
Normal	×1	Flying	×1
Fire	×1	Psychic	×1
Water	×1	Bug	×0.5
Grass	×0.5	Rock	×2
Electric	×2	Ghost	×1
Ice	×2	Dragon	×1
Fighting	×0.5	Dark	×1
Poison	×1	Steel	×1
Ground	×0	Fairy	×1

Damage taken in Inverse battles

Type		Type	
Normal	×1	Flying	×1
Fire	×1	Psychic	×1
Water	×1	Bug	×2
Grass	×2	Rock	×0.5
Electric	×0.5	Ghost	×1
Ice	×0.5	Dragon	×1
Fighting	×2	Dark	×1
Poison	×1	Steel	×1
Ground	×2	Fairy	×1

Can be used in
Inverse Battle
Battle Institute
Battle Maison
Random Matchup (Free Battle)
Random Matchup (Others)

LEVEL-UP MOVES

Lv.	Name	Type	Kind	Pow.	Acc.	PP	Range
1	Thrash	Normal	Physical	120	100	10	1 Random
1	Hammer Arm	Fighting	Physical	100	90	10	Normal
1	Hurricane	Flying	Special	110	70	10	Normal
1	Tailwind	Flying	Status	—	—	15	Your Side
1	Uproar	Normal	Special	90	100	10	1 Random
1	Astonish	Ghost	Physical	30	100	15	Normal
1	Gust	Flying	Special	40	100	35	Normal
7	Swagger	Normal	Status	—	90	15	Normal
13	Bite	Dark	Physical	60	100	25	Normal
19	Revenge	Fighting	Physical	60	100	10	Normal
25	Air Cutter	Flying	Special	60	95	25	Many Others
31	Extrasensory	Psychic	Special	80	100	20	Normal
37	Agility	Psychic	Status	—	—	30	Self
43	Air Slash	Flying	Special	75	95	15	Normal
49	Crunch	Dark	Physical	80	100	15	Normal
55	Tailwind	Flying	Status	—	—	15	Your Side
61	Rain Dance	Water	Status	—	—	5	Both Sides
67	Hurricane	Flying	Special	110	70	10	Normal
73	Dark Pulse	Dark	Special	80	100	15	Normal
79	Hammer Arm	Fighting	Physical	100	90	10	Normal
85	Thrash	Normal	Physical	120	100	10	1 Random

TM & HM MOVES

No.	Name	Type	Kind	Pow.	Acc.	PP	Range
TM06	Toxic	Poison	Status	—	90	10	Normal
TM08	Bulk Up	Fighting	Status	—	—	20	Self
TM10	Hidden Power	Normal	Special	60	100	15	Normal
TM12	Taunt	Dark	Status	—	100	20	Normal
TM15	Hyper Beam	Normal	Special	150	90	5	Normal
TM17	Protect	Normal	Status	—	—	10	Self
TM18	Rain Dance	Water	Status	—	—	5	Both Sides
TM21	Frustration	Normal	Physical	—	100	20	Normal
TM23	Smack Down	Rock	Physical	50	100	15	Normal
TM27	Return	Normal	Physical	—	100	20	Normal
TM29	Psychic	Psychic	Special	90	100	10	Normal
TM31	Brick Break	Fighting	Physical	75	100	15	Normal
TM32	Double Team	Normal	Status	—	—	15	Self
TM34	Sludge Wave	Poison	Special	95	100	10	Adjacent
TM36	Sludge Bomb	Poison	Special	90	100	10	Normal
TM40	Aerial Ace	Flying	Physical	60	—	20	Normal
TM41	Torment	Dark	Status	—	100	15	Normal
TM42	Facade	Normal	Physical	70	100	20	Normal
TM44	Rest	Psychic	Status	—	—	10	Self
TM45	Attract	Normal	Status	—	100	15	Normal
TM46	Thief	Dark	Physical	60	100	25	Normal
TM48	Round	Normal	Special	60	100	15	Normal
TM52	Focus Blast	Fighting	Special	120	70	5	Normal
TM56	Fling	Dark	Physical	—	100	10	Normal
TM58	Sky Drop	Flying	Physical	60	100	10	Normal
TM59	Incinerate	Fire	Special	60	100	15	Many Others
TM62	Acrobatics	Flying	Physical	55	100	15	Normal
TM63	Embargo	Dark	Status	—	100	15	Normal
TM66	Payback	Dark	Physical	50	100	10	Normal
TM68	Giga Impact	Normal	Physical	150	90	5	Normal
TM86	Grass Knot	Grass	Special	—	100	20	Normal
TM87	Swagger	Normal	Status	—	90	15	Normal
TM88	Sleep Talk	Normal	Status	—	—	10	Self
TM89	U-turn	Bug	Physical	70	100	20	Normal
TM90	Substitute	Normal	Status	—	—	10	Self
TM94	Secret Power	Normal	Physical	70	100	20	Normal
TM97	Dark Pulse	Dark	Special	80	100	15	Normal
TM100	Confide	Normal	Status	—	—	20	Normal
HM02	Fly	Flying	Physical	90	95	15	Normal
HM04	Strength	Normal	Physical	80	100	15	Normal
HM06	Rock Smash	Fighting	Physical	40	100	15	Normal

MOVES LEARNED IN EXCHANGE FOR BP

Name	Type	Kind	Pow.	Acc.	PP	Range
Uproar	Normal	Special	90	100	10	1 Random
Foul Play	Dark	Physical	95	100	15	Normal
Superpower	Fighting	Physical	120	100	5	Normal
Icy Wind	Ice	Special	55	95	15	Many Others
Iron Tail	Steel	Physical	100	75	15	Normal
Snore	Normal	Special	50	100	15	Normal
Knock Off	Dark	Physical	65	100	20	Normal
Heat Wave	Fire	Special	95	90	10	Many Others
Role Play	Psychic	Status	—	—	10	Normal
Tailwind	Flying	Status	—	—	15	Your Side

MOVES TAUGHT BY PEOPLE

Name	Type	Kind	Pow.	Acc.	PP	Range

National Pokédex **642** Hoenn Pokédex —

Thundurus Incarnate Forme

Bolt Strike Pokémon

Electric Flying

HEIGHT: 4'11" WEIGHT: 134.5 lbs.

♂ only

Ω The spikes on its tail discharge immense bolts of lightning. It flies around the Unova region firing off lightning bolts.

α As it flies around, it shoots lightning all over the place and causes forest fires. It is therefore disliked.

ABILITY
Prankster

HIDDEN ABILITY
Defiant

EGG GROUPS
No Eggs Discovered

STAT GROWTH RATES
HP
Attack
Defense
Sp. Atk
Sp. Def
Speed

ITEMS SOMETIMES HELD BY WILD POKÉMON
—

EVOLUTION
Does not evolve

MAIN WAYS TO REGISTER IN THE NATIONAL POKÉDEX
Ω Bring it to your game using Link Trade or the GTS.
α Catch in the Storm Clouds Mirage spot that appears in the sky when Soaring with a Pokémon that has ties to the weather.

Damage taken in normal battles

Type		Type	
Normal	×1	Flying	×0.5
Fire	×1	Psychic	×1
Water	×1	Bug	×0.5
Grass	×0.5	Rock	×2
Electric	×1	Ghost	×1
Ice	×2	Dragon	×1
Fighting	×0.5	Dark	×1
Poison	×1	Steel	×0.5
Ground	×0	Fairy	×1

Damage taken in Inverse battles

Type		Type	
Normal	×1	Flying	×2
Fire	×1	Psychic	×1
Water	×1	Bug	×2
Grass	×2	Rock	×0.5
Electric	×1	Ghost	×1
Ice	×0.5	Dragon	×1
Fighting	×2	Dark	×1
Poison	×1	Steel	×2
Ground	×1	Fairy	×1

Can be used in
Inverse Battle
Battle Institute
Battle Maison
Random Matchup (Free Battle)
Random Matchup (Others)

LEVEL-UP MOVES

Lv.	Name	Type	Kind	Pow.	Acc.	PP	Range
1	Thrash	Normal	Physical	120	100	10	1 Random
1	Hammer Arm	Fighting	Physical	100	90	10	Normal
1	Nasty Plot	Dark	Status	—	—	20	Self
1	Charge	Electric	Status	—	—	20	Self
1	Uproar	Normal	Special	90	100	10	1 Random
1	Astonish	Ghost	Physical	30	100	15	Normal
1	Thunder Shock	Electric	Special	40	100	30	Normal
7	Swagger	Normal	Status	—	90	15	Normal
13	Bite	Dark	Physical	60	100	25	Normal
19	Revenge	Fighting	Physical	60	100	10	Normal
25	Shock Wave	Electric	Special	60	—	20	Normal
31	Heal Block	Psychic	Status	—	100	15	Many Others
37	Agility	Psychic	Status	—	—	30	Self
43	Discharge	Electric	Special	80	100	15	Adjacent
49	Crunch	Dark	Physical	80	100	15	Normal
55	Charge	Electric	Status	—	—	20	Self
61	Nasty Plot	Dark	Status	—	—	20	Self
67	Thunder	Electric	Special	110	70	10	Normal
73	Dark Pulse	Dark	Special	80	100	15	Normal
79	Hammer Arm	Fighting	Physical	100	90	10	Normal
85	Thrash	Normal	Physical	120	100	10	1 Random

TM & HM MOVES

No.	Name	Type	Kind	Pow.	Acc.	PP	Range
TM06	Toxic	Poison	Status	—	90	10	Normal
TM08	Bulk Up	Fighting	Status	—	—	20	Self
TM10	Hidden Power	Normal	Special	60	100	15	Normal
TM12	Taunt	Dark	Status	—	100	20	Normal
TM15	Hyper Beam	Normal	Special	150	90	5	Normal
TM17	Protect	Normal	Status	—	—	10	Self
TM18	Rain Dance	Water	Status	—	—	5	Both Sides
TM21	Frustration	Normal	Physical	—	100	20	Normal
TM23	Smack Down	Rock	Physical	50	100	15	Normal
TM24	Thunderbolt	Electric	Special	90	100	15	Normal
TM25	Thunder	Electric	Special	110	70	10	Normal
TM27	Return	Normal	Physical	—	100	20	Normal
TM29	Psychic	Psychic	Special	90	100	10	Normal
TM31	Brick Break	Fighting	Physical	75	100	15	Normal
TM32	Double Team	Normal	Status	—	—	15	Self
TM34	Sludge Wave	Poison	Special	95	100	10	Adjacent
TM36	Sludge Bomb	Poison	Special	90	100	10	Normal
TM41	Torment	Dark	Status	—	100	15	Normal
TM42	Facade	Normal	Physical	70	100	20	Normal
TM44	Rest	Psychic	Status	—	—	10	Self
TM45	Attract	Normal	Status	—	100	15	Normal
TM46	Thief	Dark	Physical	60	100	25	Normal
TM48	Round	Normal	Special	60	100	15	Normal
TM52	Focus Blast	Fighting	Special	120	70	5	Normal
TM56	Fling	Dark	Physical	—	100	10	Normal
TM57	Charge Beam	Electric	Special	50	90	10	Normal
TM58	Sky Drop	Flying	Physical	60	100	10	Normal
TM59	Incinerate	Fire	Special	60	100	15	Many Others
TM63	Embargo	Dark	Status	—	100	15	Normal
TM66	Payback	Dark	Physical	50	100	10	Normal
TM68	Giga Impact	Normal	Physical	150	90	5	Normal
TM72	Volt Switch	Electric	Special	70	100	20	Normal
TM73	Thunder Wave	Electric	Status	—	100	20	Normal
TM86	Grass Knot	Grass	Special	—	100	20	Normal
TM87	Swagger	Normal	Status	—	90	15	Normal
TM88	Sleep Talk	Normal	Status	—	—	10	Self
TM89	U-turn	Bug	Physical	70	100	20	Normal
TM90	Substitute	Normal	Status	—	—	10	Self
TM91	Flash Cannon	Steel	Special	80	100	10	Normal
TM93	Wild Charge	Electric	Physical	90	100	15	Normal
TM94	Secret Power	Normal	Physical	70	100	20	Normal
TM97	Dark Pulse	Dark	Special	80	100	15	Normal
TM100	Confide	Normal	Status	—	—	20	Normal
HM02	Fly	Flying	Physical	90	95	15	Normal
HM04	Strength	Normal	Physical	80	100	15	Normal
HM06	Rock Smash	Fighting	Physical	40	100	15	Normal

MOVES LEARNED IN EXCHANGE FOR BP

Name	Type	Kind	Pow.	Acc.	PP	Range
Uproar	Normal	Special	90	100	10	1 Random
Thunder Punch	Electric	Physical	75	100	15	Normal
Foul Play	Dark	Physical	95	100	15	Normal
Superpower	Fighting	Physical	120	100	5	Normal
Electroweb	Electric	Special	55	95	15	Many Others
Iron Tail	Steel	Physical	100	75	15	Normal
Snore	Normal	Special	50	100	15	Normal
Knock Off	Dark	Physical	65	100	20	Normal
Role Play	Psychic	Status	—	—	10	Normal
Shock Wave	Electric	Special	60	—	20	Normal

MOVES TAUGHT BY PEOPLE

Name	Type	Kind	Pow.	Acc.	PP	Range

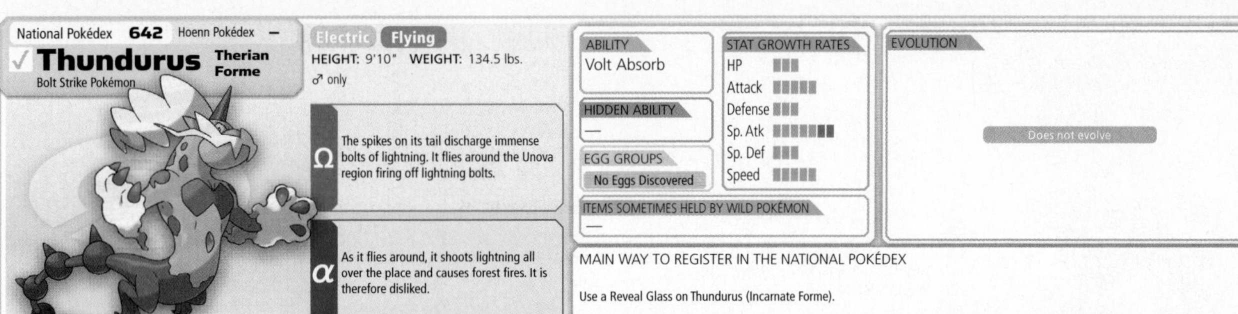

National Pokédex **642** Hoenn Pokédex —

✓ Thundurus Therian Forme

Bolt Strike Pokémon

Electric | Flying

HEIGHT: 9'10" WEIGHT: 134.5 lbs.

♂ only

Ω The spikes on its tail discharge immense bolts of lightning. It flies around the Unova region firing off lightning bolts.

α As it flies around, it shoots lightning all over the place and causes forest fires. It is therefore disliked.

ABILITY
Volt Absorb

HIDDEN ABILITY
—

EGG GROUPS
No Eggs Discovered

STAT GROWTH RATES
HP
Attack
Defense
Sp. Atk
Sp. Def
Speed

ITEMS SOMETIMES HELD BY WILD POKÉMON
—

EVOLUTION
Does not evolve

MAIN WAY TO REGISTER IN THE NATIONAL POKÉDEX

Use a Reveal Glass on Thundurus (Incarnate Forme).

Damage taken in normal battles

Normal	×1	Flying	×0.5
Fire	×1	Psychic	×1
Water	×1	Bug	×0.5
Grass	×0.5	Rock	×2
Electric	×1	Ghost	×1
Ice	×2	Dragon	×1
Fighting	×0.5	Dark	×1
Poison	×1	Steel	×0.5
Ground	×0	Fairy	×1

Damage taken in Inverse battles

Normal	×1	Flying	×2
Fire	×1	Psychic	×1
Water	×1	Bug	×2
Grass	×2	Rock	×0.5
Electric	×1	Ghost	×1
Ice	×0.5	Dragon	×1
Fighting	×2	Dark	×1
Poison	×1	Steel	×2
Ground	×1	Fairy	×1

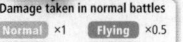

Can be used in
Inverse Battle
Battle Institute
Battle Maison
Random Matchup (Free Battle)
Random Matchup (Others)

LEVEL-UP MOVES

Lv.	Name	Type	Kind	Pow.	Acc.	PP	Range
1	Thrash	Normal	Physical	120	100	10	1 Random
1	Hammer Arm	Fighting	Physical	100	90	10	Normal
1	Nasty Plot	Dark	Status	—	—	20	Self
1	Charge	Electric	Status	—	—	20	Self
1	Uproar	Normal	Special	90	100	10	1 Random
1	Astonish	Ghost	Physical	30	100	15	Normal
1	Thunder Shock	Electric	Special	40	100	30	Normal
7	Swagger	Normal	Status	—	90	15	Normal
13	Bite	Dark	Physical	60	100	25	Normal
19	Revenge	Fighting	Physical	60	100	10	Normal
25	Shock Wave	Electric	Special	60	—	20	Normal
31	Heal Block	Psychic	Status	—	100	15	Many Others
37	Agility	Psychic	Status	—	—	30	Self
43	Discharge	Electric	Special	80	100	15	Adjacent
49	Crunch	Dark	Physical	80	100	15	Normal
55	Charge	Electric	Status	—	—	20	Self
61	Nasty Plot	Dark	Status	—	—	20	Self
67	Thunder	Electric	Special	110	70	10	Normal
73	Dark Pulse	Dark	Special	80	100	15	Normal
79	Hammer Arm	Fighting	Physical	100	90	10	Normal
85	Thrash	Normal	Physical	120	100	10	1 Random

TM & HM MOVES

No.	Name	Type	Kind	Pow.	Acc.	PP	Range
TM06	Toxic	Poison	Status	—	90	10	Normal
TM08	Bulk Up	Fighting	Status	—	—	20	Self
TM10	Hidden Power	Normal	Special	60	100	15	Normal
TM12	Taunt	Dark	Status	—	100	20	Normal
TM15	Hyper Beam	Normal	Special	150	90	5	Normal
TM17	Protect	Normal	Status	—	—	10	Self
TM18	Rain Dance	Water	Status	—	—	5	Both Sides
TM21	Frustration	Normal	Physical	—	100	20	Normal
TM23	Smack Down	Rock	Physical	50	100	15	Normal
TM24	Thunderbolt	Electric	Special	90	100	15	Normal
TM25	Thunder	Electric	Special	110	70	10	Normal
TM27	Return	Normal	Physical	—	100	20	Normal
TM29	Psychic	Psychic	Special	90	100	10	Normal
TM31	Brick Break	Fighting	Physical	75	100	15	Normal
TM32	Double Team	Normal	Status	—	—	15	Self
TM34	Sludge Wave	Poison	Special	95	100	10	Adjacent
TM36	Sludge Bomb	Poison	Special	90	100	10	Normal
TM41	Torment	Dark	Status	—	100	15	Normal
TM42	Facade	Normal	Physical	70	100	20	Normal
TM44	Rest	Psychic	Status	—	—	10	Self
TM45	Attract	Normal	Status	—	100	15	Normal
TM46	Thief	Dark	Physical	60	100	25	Normal
TM48	Round	Normal	Special	60	100	15	Normal
TM52	Focus Blast	Fighting	Special	120	70	5	Normal
TM56	Fling	Dark	Physical	—	100	10	Normal
TM57	Charge Beam	Electric	Special	50	90	10	Normal
TM58	Sky Drop	Flying	Physical	60	100	10	Normal
TM59	Incinerate	Fire	Special	60	100	15	Many Others
TM63	Embargo	Dark	Status	—	100	15	Normal
TM66	Payback	Dark	Physical	50	100	10	Normal
TM68	Giga Impact	Normal	Physical	150	90	5	Normal
TM72	Volt Switch	Electric	Special	70	100	20	Normal
TM73	Thunder Wave	Electric	Status	—	100	20	Normal
TM86	Grass Knot	Grass	Special	—	100	20	Normal
TM87	Swagger	Normal	Status	—	90	15	Normal
TM88	Sleep Talk	Normal	Status	—	—	10	Self
TM89	U-turn	Bug	Physical	70	100	20	Normal
TM90	Substitute	Normal	Status	—	—	10	Self
TM91	Flash Cannon	Steel	Special	80	100	10	Normal
TM93	Wild Charge	Electric	Physical	90	100	15	Normal
TM94	Secret Power	Normal	Physical	70	100	20	Normal
TM97	Dark Pulse	Dark	Special	80	100	15	Normal
TM100	Confide	Normal	Status	—	—	20	Normal
HM02	Fly	Flying	Physical	90	95	15	Normal
HM04	Strength	Normal	Physical	80	100	15	Normal
HM06	Rock Smash	Fighting	Physical	40	100	15	Normal

MOVES LEARNED IN EXCHANGE FOR BP

Name	Type	Kind	Pow.	Acc.	PP	Range
Uproar	Normal	Special	90	100	10	1 Random
Thunder Punch	Electric	Physical	75	100	15	Normal
Foul Play	Dark	Physical	95	100	15	Normal
Superpower	Fighting	Physical	120	100	5	Normal
Electroweb	Electric	Special	55	95	15	Many Others
Iron Tail	Steel	Physical	100	75	15	Normal
Snore	Normal	Special	50	100	15	Normal
Knock Off	Dark	Physical	65	100	20	Normal
Role Play	Psychic	Status	—	—	10	Normal
Shock Wave	Electric	Special	60	—	20	Normal

MOVES TAUGHT BY PEOPLE

Name	Type	Kind	Pow.	Acc.	PP	Range

National Pokédex **643** Hoenn Pokédex —

✓ Reshiram

Vast White Pokémon

Dragon | Fire

HEIGHT: 10'06" WEIGHT: 727.5 lbs.

Gender unknown

Ω This legendary Pokémon can scorch the world with fire. It helps those who want to build a world of truth.

α When Reshiram's tail flares, the heat energy moves the atmosphere and changes the world's weather.

ABILITY
Turboblaze

HIDDEN ABILITY
—

EGG GROUPS
No Eggs Discovered

STAT GROWTH RATES
HP
Attack
Defense
Sp. Atk
Sp. Def
Speed

ITEMS SOMETIMES HELD BY WILD POKÉMON
—

EVOLUTION
Does not evolve

MAIN WAYS TO REGISTER IN THE NATIONAL POKÉDEX

Ω Catch in the Fabled Cave Mirage spot by Soaring in the sky with a very high-level Pokémon in your party.

α Bring it to your game using Link Trade or the GTS.

Damage taken in normal battles

Normal	×1	Flying	×1
Fire	×0.25	Psychic	×1
Water	×1	Bug	×0.5
Grass	×0.25	Rock	×2
Electric	×0.5	Ghost	×1
Ice	×1	Dragon	×2
Fighting	×1	Dark	×1
Poison	×1	Steel	×0.5
Ground	×2	Fairy	×1

Damage taken in Inverse battles

Normal	×1	Flying	×1
Fire	×4	Psychic	×1
Water	×1	Bug	×2
Grass	×4	Rock	×0.5
Electric	×2	Ghost	×1
Ice	×1	Dragon	×0.5
Fighting	×1	Dark	×1
Poison	×1	Steel	×2
Ground	×0.5	Fairy	×1

Can be used in
Inverse Battle
Battle Institute
Battle Maison
Random Matchup (Free Battle)
Random Matchup (Others)

LEVEL-UP MOVES

Lv.	Name	Type	Kind	Pow.	Acc.	PP	Range
1	Fire Fang	Fire	Physical	65	95	15	Normal
1	Dragon Rage	Dragon	Special	—	100	10	Normal
8	Imprison	Psychic	Status	—	—	10	Self
15	Ancient Power	Rock	Special	60	100	5	Normal
22	Flamethrower	Fire	Special	90	100	15	Normal
29	Dragon Breath	Dragon	Special	60	100	20	Normal
36	Slash	Normal	Physical	70	100	20	Normal
43	Extrasensory	Psychic	Special	80	100	20	Normal
50	Fusion Flare	Fire	Special	100	100	5	Normal
54	Dragon Pulse	Dragon	Special	85	100	10	Normal
64	Imprison	Psychic	Status	—	—	10	Self
71	Crunch	Dark	Physical	80	100	15	Normal
78	Fire Blast	Fire	Special	110	85	5	Normal
85	Outrage	Dragon	Physical	120	100	10	1 Random
92	Hyper Voice	Normal	Special	90	100	10	Many Others
100	Blue Flare	Fire	Special	130	85	5	Normal

TM & HM MOVES

No.	Name	Type	Kind	Pow.	Acc.	PP	Range
TM01	Hone Claws	Dark	Status	—	—	15	Self
TM02	Dragon Claw	Dragon	Physical	80	100	15	Normal
TM06	Toxic	Poison	Status	—	90	10	Normal
TM10	Hidden Power	Normal	Special	60	100	15	Normal
TM11	Sunny Day	Fire	Status	—	—	5	Both Sides
TM15	Hyper Beam	Normal	Special	150	90	5	Normal
TM16	Light Screen	Psychic	Status	—	—	30	Your Side
TM17	Protect	Normal	Status	—	—	10	Self
TM19	Roost	Flying	Status	—	—	10	Self
TM20	Safeguard	Normal	Status	—	—	25	Your Side
TM21	Frustration	Normal	Physical	—	100	20	Normal
TM22	Solar Beam	Grass	Special	120	100	10	Normal
TM27	Return	Normal	Physical	—	100	20	Normal
TM29	Psychic	Psychic	Special	90	100	10	Normal
TM30	Shadow Ball	Ghost	Special	80	100	15	Normal
TM32	Double Team	Normal	Status	—	—	15	Self
TM33	Reflect	Psychic	Status	—	—	20	Your Side
TM35	Flamethrower	Fire	Special	90	100	15	Normal
TM38	Fire Blast	Fire	Special	110	85	5	Normal
TM39	Rock Tomb	Rock	Physical	60	95	15	Normal
TM42	Facade	Normal	Physical	70	100	20	Normal
TM43	Flame Charge	Fire	Physical	50	100	20	Normal
TM44	Rest	Psychic	Status	—	—	10	Self
TM48	Round	Normal	Special	60	100	15	Normal
TM49	Echoed Voice	Normal	Special	40	100	15	Normal
TM50	Overheat	Fire	Special	130	90	5	Normal
TM51	Steel Wing	Steel	Physical	70	90	25	Normal
TM52	Focus Blast	Fighting	Special	120	70	5	Normal
TM56	Fling	Dark	Physical	—	100	10	Normal
TM59	Incinerate	Fire	Special	60	100	15	Many Others
TM61	Will-O-Wisp	Fire	Status	—	85	15	Normal
TM65	Shadow Claw	Ghost	Physical	70	100	15	Normal
TM66	Payback	Dark	Physical	50	100	10	Normal
TM68	Giga Impact	Normal	Physical	150	90	5	Normal
TM71	Stone Edge	Rock	Physical	100	80	5	Normal
TM80	Rock Slide	Rock	Physical	75	90	10	Many Others
TM82	Dragon Tail	Dragon	Physical	60	90	10	Normal
TM87	Swagger	Normal	Status	—	90	15	Normal
TM88	Sleep Talk	Normal	Status	—	—	10	Self
TM90	Substitute	Normal	Status	—	—	10	Self
TM94	Secret Power	Normal	Physical	70	100	20	Normal
TM100	Confide	Normal	Status	—	—	20	Normal
HM01	Cut	Normal	Physical	50	95	30	Normal
HM02	Fly	Flying	Physical	90	95	15	Normal
HM04	Strength	Normal	Physical	80	100	15	Normal
HM06	Rock Smash	Fighting	Physical	40	100	15	Normal

MOVES LEARNED IN EXCHANGE FOR BP

Name	Type	Kind	Pow.	Acc.	PP	Range
Earth Power	Ground	Special	90	100	10	Normal
Zen Headbutt	Psychic	Physical	80	90	15	Normal
Dragon Pulse	Dragon	Special	85	100	10	Normal
Hyper Voice	Normal	Special	90	100	10	Many Others
Snore	Normal	Special	50	100	15	Normal
Heat Wave	Fire	Special	95	90	10	Many Others
Tailwind	Flying	Status	—	—	15	Your Side
Outrage	Dragon	Physical	120	100	10	1 Random

MOVES TAUGHT BY PEOPLE

Name	Type	Kind	Pow.	Acc.	PP	Range
Draco Meteor	Dragon	Special	130	90	5	Normal

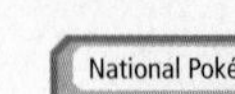

National Pokédex **644** Hoenn Pokédex —

✓ Zekrom

Deep Black Pokémon

Dragon Electric

HEIGHT: 9'06" WEIGHT: 760.6 lbs.

Gender unknown

Ω This legendary Pokémon can scorch the world with lightning. It assists those who want to build an ideal world.

α Concealing itself in lightning clouds, it flies throughout the Unova region. It creates electricity in its tail.

ABILITY
Teravolt

HIDDEN ABILITY
—

EGG GROUPS
No Eggs Discovered

STAT GROWTH RATES
HP
Attack
Defense
Sp. Atk
Sp. Def
Speed

ITEMS SOMETIMES HELD BY WILD POKÉMON
—

EVOLUTION
Does not evolve

MAIN WAYS TO REGISTER IN THE NATIONAL POKÉDEX

Ω Bring it to your game using Link Trade or the GTS.

α Catch in the Fabled Cave Mirage spot by Soaring in the sky with a very high-level Pokémon in your party.

Damage taken in normal battles

Normal	×1	Flying	×0.5
Fire	×0.5	Psychic	×1
Water	×0.5	Bug	×1
Grass	×0.5	Rock	×1
Electric	×0.25	Ghost	×1
Ice	×2	Dragon	×2
Fighting	×1	Dark	×1
Poison	×1	Steel	×0.5
Ground	×2	Fairy	×2

Damage taken in Inverse battles

Normal	×1	Flying	×2
Fire	×2	Psychic	×1
Water	×2	Bug	×1
Grass	×2	Rock	×1
Electric	×4	Ghost	×1
Ice	×0.5	Dragon	×0.5
Fighting	×1	Dark	×1
Poison	×1	Steel	×2
Ground	×0.5	Fairy	×0.5

Can be used in

Inverse Battle
Battle Institute
Battle Maison
Random Matchup (Free Battle)
Random Matchup (Others)

LEVEL-UP MOVES

Lv.	Name	Type	Kind	Pow.	Acc.	PP	Range
1	Thunder Fang	Electric	Physical	65	95	15	Normal
1	Dragon Rage	Dragon	Special	—	100	10	Normal
8	Imprison	Psychic	Status	—	—	10	Self
15	Ancient Power	Rock	Special	60	100	5	Normal
22	Thunderbolt	Electric	Special	90	100	15	Normal
29	Dragon Breath	Dragon	Special	60	100	20	Normal
36	Slash	Normal	Physical	70	100	20	Normal
43	Zen Headbutt	Psychic	Physical	80	90	15	Normal
50	Fusion Bolt	Electric	Physical	100	100	5	Normal
54	Dragon Claw	Dragon	Physical	80	100	15	Normal
64	Imprison	Psychic	Status	—	—	10	Self
71	Crunch	Dark	Physical	80	100	15	Normal
78	Thunder	Electric	Special	110	70	10	Normal
85	Outrage	Dragon	Physical	120	100	10	1 Random
92	Hyper Voice	Normal	Special	90	100	10	Many Others
100	Bolt Strike	Electric	Physical	130	85	5	Normal

TM & HM MOVES

No.	Name	Type	Kind	Pow.	Acc.	PP	Range
TM01	Hone Claws	Dark	Status	—	—	15	Self
TM02	Dragon Claw	Dragon	Physical	80	100	15	Normal
TM06	Toxic	Poison	Status	—	90	10	Normal
TM10	Hidden Power	Normal	Special	60	100	15	Normal
TM15	Hyper Beam	Normal	Special	150	90	5	Normal
TM16	Light Screen	Psychic	Status	—	—	30	Your Side
TM17	Protect	Normal	Status	—	—	10	Self
TM18	Rain Dance	Water	Status	—	—	5	Both Sides
TM19	Roost	Flying	Status	—	—	10	Self
TM20	Safeguard	Normal	Status	—	—	25	Your Side
TM21	Frustration	Normal	Physical	—	100	20	Normal
TM24	Thunderbolt	Electric	Special	90	100	15	Normal
TM25	Thunder	Electric	Special	110	70	10	Normal
TM27	Return	Normal	Physical	—	100	20	Normal
TM29	Psychic	Psychic	Special	90	100	10	Normal
TM30	Shadow Ball	Ghost	Special	80	100	15	Normal
TM32	Double Team	Normal	Status	—	—	15	Self
TM33	Reflect	Psychic	Status	—	—	20	Your Side
TM39	Rock Tomb	Rock	Physical	60	95	15	Normal
TM42	Facade	Normal	Physical	70	100	20	Normal
TM44	Rest	Psychic	Status	—	—	10	Self
TM48	Round	Normal	Special	60	100	15	Normal
TM49	Echoed Voice	Normal	Special	40	100	15	Normal
TM51	Steel Wing	Steel	Physical	70	90	25	Normal
TM52	Focus Blast	Fighting	Special	120	70	5	Normal
TM56	Fling	Dark	Physical	—	100	10	Normal
TM57	Charge Beam	Electric	Special	50	90	10	Normal
TM65	Shadow Claw	Ghost	Physical	70	100	15	Normal
TM66	Payback	Dark	Physical	50	100	10	Normal
TM68	Giga Impact	Normal	Physical	150	90	5	Normal
TM70	Flash	Normal	Status	—	100	20	Normal
TM71	Stone Edge	Rock	Physical	100	80	5	Normal
TM72	Volt Switch	Electric	Special	70	100	20	Normal
TM73	Thunder Wave	Electric	Status	—	100	20	Normal
TM80	Rock Slide	Rock	Physical	75	90	10	Many Others
TM82	Dragon Tail	Dragon	Physical	60	90	10	Normal
TM87	Swagger	Normal	Status	—	90	15	Normal
TM88	Sleep Talk	Normal	Status	—	—	10	Self
TM90	Substitute	Normal	Status	—	—	10	Self
TM91	Flash Cannon	Steel	Special	80	100	10	Normal
TM93	Wild Charge	Electric	Physical	90	100	15	Normal
TM94	Secret Power	Normal	Physical	70	100	20	Normal
TM100	Confide	Normal	Status	—	—	20	Normal
HM01	Cut	Normal	Physical	50	95	30	Normal
HM02	Fly	Flying	Physical	90	95	15	Normal
HM04	Strength	Normal	Physical	80	100	15	Normal
HM06	Rock Smash	Fighting	Physical	40	100	15	Normal

MOVES LEARNED IN EXCHANGE FOR BP

Name	Type	Kind	Pow.	Acc.	PP	Range
Signal Beam	Bug	Special	75	100	15	Normal
Thunder Punch	Electric	Physical	75	100	15	Normal
Earth Power	Ground	Special	90	100	10	Normal
Magnet Rise	Electric	Status	—	—	10	Self
Zen Headbutt	Psychic	Physical	80	90	15	Normal
Dragon Pulse	Dragon	Special	85	100	10	Normal
Hyper Voice	Normal	Special	90	100	10	Many Others
Snore	Normal	Special	50	100	15	Normal
Tailwind	Flying	Status	—	—	15	Your Side
Shock Wave	Electric	Special	60	—	20	Normal
Outrage	Dragon	Physical	120	100	10	1 Random

MOVES TAUGHT BY PEOPLE

Name	Type	Kind	Pow.	Acc.	PP	Range
Draco Meteor	Dragon	Special	130	90	5	Normal

National Pokédex **645** Hoenn Pokédex —

✓ Landorus Incarnate Forme

Abundance Pokémon

Ground Flying

HEIGHT: 4'11" WEIGHT: 149.9 lbs.

♂ only

Ω Lands visited by Landorus grant such bountiful crops that it has been hailed as "The Guardian of the Fields."

α From the forces of lightning and wind, it creates energy to give nutrients to the soil and make the land abundant.

ABILITY
Sand Force

HIDDEN ABILITY
Sheer Force

EGG GROUPS
No Eggs Discovered

STAT GROWTH RATES
HP
Attack
Defense
Sp. Atk
Sp. Def
Speed

ITEMS SOMETIMES HELD BY WILD POKÉMON
—

EVOLUTION
Does not evolve

MAIN WAY TO REGISTER IN THE NATIONAL POKÉDEX

Catch in the Storm Clouds Mirage spot that appears in the sky when Soaring with a specific pair of similar Legendary Pokémon in your party.

Damage taken in normal battles

Normal	×1	Flying	×1
Fire	×1	Psychic	×1
Water	×2	Bug	×0.5
Grass	×1	Rock	×1
Electric	×0	Ghost	×1
Ice	×4	Dragon	×1
Fighting	×0.5	Dark	×1
Poison	×0.5	Steel	×1
Ground	×0	Fairy	×1

Damage taken in Inverse battles

Normal	×1	Flying	×1
Fire	×1	Psychic	×1
Water	×0.5	Bug	×2
Grass	×1	Rock	×1
Electric	×1	Ghost	×1
Ice	×0.25	Dragon	×1
Fighting	×2	Dark	×1
Poison	×2	Steel	×1
Ground	×2	Fairy	×1

Can be used in

Inverse Battle
Battle Institute
Battle Maison
Random Matchup (Free Battle)
Random Matchup (Others)

LEVEL-UP MOVES

Lv.	Name	Type	Kind	Pow.	Acc.	PP	Range
1	Outrage	Dragon	Physical	120	100	10	1 Random
1	Hammer Arm	Fighting	Physical	100	90	10	Normal
1	Fissure	Ground	Physical	—	30	5	Normal
1	Block	Normal	Status	—	—	5	Normal
1	Mud Shot	Ground	Special	55	95	15	Normal
1	Rock Tomb	Rock	Physical	60	95	15	Normal
7	Imprison	Psychic	Status	—	—	10	Self
13	Punishment	Dark	Physical	—	100	5	Normal
19	Bulldoze	Ground	Physical	60	100	20	Adjacent
25	Rock Throw	Rock	Physical	50	90	15	Normal
31	Extrasensory	Psychic	Special	80	100	20	Normal
37	Swords Dance	Normal	Status	—	—	20	Self
43	Earth Power	Ground	Special	90	100	10	Normal
49	Rock Slide	Rock	Physical	75	90	10	Many Others
55	Earthquake	Ground	Physical	100	100	10	Adjacent
61	Sandstorm	Rock	Status	—	—	10	Both Sides
67	Fissure	Ground	Physical	—	30	5	Normal
73	Stone Edge	Rock	Physical	100	80	5	Normal
79	Hammer Arm	Fighting	Physical	100	90	10	Normal
85	Outrage	Dragon	Physical	120	100	10	1 Random

TM & HM MOVES

No.	Name	Type	Kind	Pow.	Acc.	PP	Range
TM04	Calm Mind	Psychic	Status	—	—	20	Self
TM06	Toxic	Poison	Status	—	90	10	Normal
TM08	Bulk Up	Fighting	Status	—	—	20	Self
TM10	Hidden Power	Normal	Special	60	100	15	Normal
TM15	Hyper Beam	Normal	Special	150	90	5	Normal
TM17	Protect	Normal	Status	—	—	10	Self
TM21	Frustration	Normal	Physical	—	100	20	Normal
TM23	Smack Down	Rock	Physical	50	100	15	Normal
TM26	Earthquake	Ground	Physical	100	100	10	Adjacent
TM27	Return	Normal	Physical	—	100	20	Normal
TM28	Dig	Ground	Physical	80	100	10	Normal
TM29	Psychic	Psychic	Special	90	100	10	Normal
TM31	Brick Break	Fighting	Physical	75	100	15	Normal
TM32	Double Team	Normal	Status	—	—	15	Self
TM34	Sludge Wave	Poison	Special	95	100	10	Adjacent
TM36	Sludge Bomb	Poison	Special	90	100	10	Normal
TM37	Sandstorm	Rock	Status	—	—	10	Both Sides
TM39	Rock Tomb	Rock	Physical	60	95	15	Normal
TM42	Facade	Normal	Physical	70	100	20	Normal
TM44	Rest	Psychic	Status	—	—	10	Self
TM45	Attract	Normal	Status	—	100	15	Normal
TM48	Round	Normal	Special	60	100	15	Normal
TM52	Focus Blast	Fighting	Special	120	70	5	Normal
TM56	Fling	Dark	Physical	—	100	10	Normal
TM64	Explosion	Normal	Physical	250	100	5	Adjacent
TM66	Payback	Dark	Physical	50	100	10	Normal
TM68	Giga Impact	Normal	Physical	150	90	5	Normal
TM69	Rock Polish	Rock	Status	—	—	20	Self
TM71	Stone Edge	Rock	Physical	100	80	5	Normal
TM75	Swords Dance	Normal	Status	—	—	20	Self
TM78	Bulldoze	Ground	Physical	60	100	20	Adjacent
TM80	Rock Slide	Rock	Physical	75	90	10	Many Others
TM86	Grass Knot	Grass	Special	—	100	20	Normal
TM87	Swagger	Normal	Status	—	90	15	Normal
TM88	Sleep Talk	Normal	Status	—	—	10	Self
TM89	U-turn	Bug	Physical	70	100	20	Normal
TM90	Substitute	Normal	Status	—	—	10	Self
TM94	Secret Power	Normal	Physical	70	100	20	Normal
TM100	Confide	Normal	Status	—	—	20	Normal
HM02	Fly	Flying	Physical	90	95	15	Normal
HM04	Strength	Normal	Physical	80	100	15	Normal
HM06	Rock Smash	Fighting	Physical	40	100	15	Normal

MOVES LEARNED IN EXCHANGE FOR BP

Name	Type	Kind	Pow.	Acc.	PP	Range
Block	Normal	Status	—	—	5	Normal
Earth Power	Ground	Special	90	100	10	Normal
Gravity	Psychic	Status	—	—	5	Both Sides
Superpower	Fighting	Physical	120	100	5	Normal
Iron Tail	Steel	Physical	100	75	15	Normal
Snore	Normal	Special	50	100	15	Normal
Knock Off	Dark	Physical	65	100	20	Normal
Role Play	Psychic	Status	—	—	10	Normal
Outrage	Dragon	Physical	120	100	10	1 Random
Stealth Rock	Rock	Status	—	—	20	Other Side

MOVES TAUGHT BY PEOPLE

Name	Type	Kind	Pow.	Acc.	PP	Range

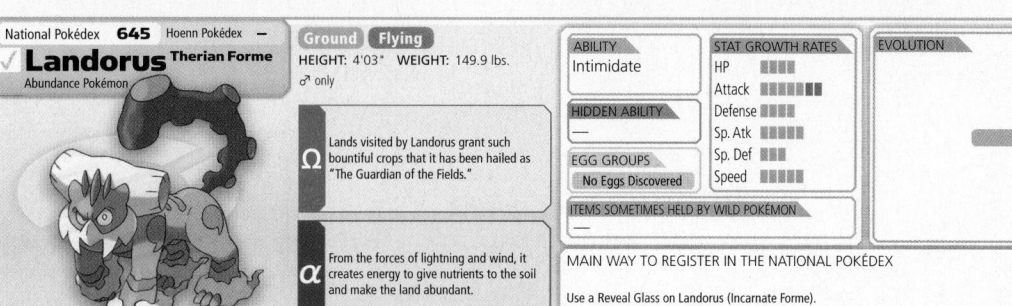

National Pokédex **645** Hoenn Pokédex —

Landorus Therian Forme

Abundance Pokémon

Ground Flying

HEIGHT: 4'03" WEIGHT: 149.9 lbs.

♂ only

Ω Lands visited by Landorus grant such bountiful crops that it has been hailed as "The Guardian of the Fields."

α From the forces of lightning and wind, it creates energy to give nutrients to the soil and make the land abundant.

ABILITY
Intimidate

HIDDEN ABILITY
—

EGG GROUPS
No Eggs Discovered

STAT GROWTH RATES
HP
Attack
Defense
Sp. Atk
Sp. Def
Speed

ITEMS SOMETIMES HELD BY WILD POKÉMON
—

EVOLUTION
Does not evolve

MAIN WAY TO REGISTER IN THE NATIONAL POKÉDEX

Use a Reveal Glass on Landorus (Incarnate Forme).

Damage taken in normal battles

Normal	×1	Flying	×1
Fire	×1	Psychic	×1
Water	×2	Bug	×0.5
Grass	×1	Rock	×1
Electric	×0	Ghost	×1
Ice	×4	Dragon	×1
Fighting	×0.5	Dark	×1
Poison	×0.5	Steel	×1
Ground	×0	Fairy	×1

Damage taken in Inverse battles

Normal	×1	Flying	×1
Fire	×1	Psychic	×1
Water	×0.5	Bug	×2
Grass	×1	Rock	×1
Electric	×1	Ghost	×1
Ice	×0.25	Dragon	×1
Fighting	×2	Dark	×1
Poison	×2	Steel	×1
Ground	×2	Fairy	×1

Can be used in
- Inverse Battle
- Battle Institute
- Battle Maison
- Random Matchup (Free Battle)
- Random Matchup (Others)

LEVEL-UP MOVES

Lv.	Name	Type	Kind	Pow.	Acc.	PP	Range
1	Outrage	Dragon	Physical	120	100	10	1 Random
1	Hammer Arm	Fighting	Physical	100	90	10	Normal
1	Fissure	Ground	Physical	—	30	5	Normal
1	Block	Normal	Status	—	—	5	Normal
1	Mud Shot	Ground	Special	55	95	15	Normal
1	Rock Tomb	Rock	Physical	60	95	15	Normal
7	Imprison	Psychic	Status	—	—	10	Self
13	Punishment	Dark	Physical	—	100	5	Normal
19	Bulldoze	Ground	Physical	60	100	20	Adjacent
25	Rock Throw	Rock	Physical	50	90	15	Normal
31	Extrasensory	Psychic	Special	80	100	20	Normal
37	Swords Dance	Normal	Status	—	—	20	Self
43	Earth Power	Ground	Special	90	100	10	Normal
49	Rock Slide	Rock	Physical	75	90	10	Many Others
55	Earthquake	Ground	Physical	100	100	10	Adjacent
61	Sandstorm	Rock	Status	—	—	10	Both Sides
67	Fissure	Ground	Physical	—	30	5	Normal
73	Stone Edge	Rock	Physical	100	80	5	Normal
79	Hammer Arm	Fighting	Physical	100	90	10	Normal
85	Outrage	Dragon	Physical	120	100	10	1 Random

TM & HM MOVES

No.	Name	Type	Kind	Pow.	Acc.	PP	Range
TM04	Calm Mind	Psychic	Status	—	—	20	Self
TM06	Toxic	Poison	Status	—	90	10	Normal
TM08	Bulk Up	Fighting	Status	—	—	20	Self
TM10	Hidden Power	Normal	Special	60	100	15	Normal
TM15	Hyper Beam	Normal	Special	150	90	5	Normal
TM17	Protect	Normal	Status	—	—	10	Self
TM21	Frustration	Normal	Physical	—	100	20	Normal
TM23	Smack Down	Rock	Physical	50	100	15	Normal
TM26	Earthquake	Ground	Physical	100	100	10	Adjacent
TM27	Return	Normal	Physical	—	100	20	Normal
TM28	Dig	Ground	Physical	80	100	10	Normal
TM29	Psychic	Psychic	Special	90	100	10	Normal
TM31	Brick Break	Fighting	Physical	75	100	15	Normal
TM32	Double Team	Normal	Status	—	—	15	Self
TM34	Sludge Wave	Poison	Special	95	100	10	Adjacent
TM36	Sludge Bomb	Poison	Special	90	100	10	Normal
TM37	Sandstorm	Rock	Status	—	—	10	Both Sides
TM39	Rock Tomb	Rock	Physical	60	95	15	Normal
TM42	Facade	Normal	Physical	70	100	20	Normal
TM44	Rest	Psychic	Status	—	—	10	Self
TM45	Attract	Normal	Status	—	100	15	Normal
TM48	Round	Normal	Special	60	100	15	Normal
TM52	Focus Blast	Fighting	Special	120	70	5	Normal
TM56	Fling	Dark	Physical	—	100	10	Normal
TM64	Explosion	Normal	Physical	250	100	5	Adjacent
TM66	Payback	Dark	Physical	50	100	10	Normal
TM68	Giga Impact	Normal	Physical	150	90	5	Normal
TM69	Rock Polish	Rock	Status	—	—	20	Self
TM71	Stone Edge	Rock	Physical	100	80	5	Normal
TM75	Swords Dance	Normal	Status	—	—	20	Self
TM78	Bulldoze	Ground	Physical	60	100	20	Adjacent
TM80	Rock Slide	Rock	Physical	75	90	10	Many Others
TM86	Grass Knot	Grass	Special	—	100	20	Normal
TM87	Swagger	Normal	Status	—	90	15	Normal
TM88	Sleep Talk	Normal	Status	—	—	10	Self
TM89	U-turn	Bug	Physical	70	100	20	Normal
TM90	Substitute	Normal	Status	—	—	10	Self
TM94	Secret Power	Normal	Physical	70	100	20	Normal
TM100	Confide	Normal	Status	—	—	20	Normal
HM02	Fly	Flying	Physical	90	95	15	Normal
HM04	Strength	Normal	Physical	80	100	15	Normal
HM06	Rock Smash	Fighting	Physical	40	100	15	Normal

MOVES LEARNED IN EXCHANGE FOR BP

Name	Type	Kind	Pow.	Acc.	PP	Range
Block	Normal	Status	—	—	5	Normal
Earth Power	Ground	Special	90	100	10	Normal
Gravity	Psychic	Status	—	—	5	Both Sides
Superpower	Fighting	Physical	120	100	5	Normal
Iron Tail	Steel	Physical	100	75	15	Normal
Snore	Normal	Special	50	100	15	Normal
Knock Off	Dark	Physical	65	100	20	Normal
Role Play	Psychic	Status	—	—	10	Normal
Outrage	Dragon	Physical	120	100	10	1 Random
Stealth Rock	Rock	Status	—	—	20	Other Side

MOVES TAUGHT BY PEOPLE

Name	Type	Kind	Pow.	Acc.	PP	Range

National Pokédex **646** Hoenn Pokédex —

Kyurem

Boundary Pokémon

Dragon Ice

HEIGHT: 9'10" WEIGHT: 716.5 lbs.

Gender unknown

Ω This legendary ice Pokémon waits for a hero to fill in the missing parts of its body with truth or ideals.

α It generates a powerful, freezing energy inside itself, but its body became frozen when the energy leaked out.

ABILITY
Pressure

HIDDEN ABILITY
—

EGG GROUPS
No Eggs Discovered

STAT GROWTH RATES
HP
Attack
Defense
Sp. Atk
Sp. Def
Speed

ITEMS SOMETIMES HELD BY WILD POKÉMON
—

EVOLUTION
Does not evolve

MAIN WAY TO REGISTER IN THE NATIONAL POKÉDEX

Catch in the Gnarled Den Mirage spot that appears in the sky when Soaring with a certain black and white pair of Legendary Pokémon in your party.

Damage taken in normal battles

Normal	×1	Flying	×1
Fire	×1	Psychic	×1
Water	×0.5	Bug	×1
Grass	×0.5	Rock	×2
Electric	×0.5	Ghost	×1
Ice	×1	Dragon	×2
Fighting	×2	Dark	×1
Poison	×1	Steel	×2
Ground	×1	Fairy	×2

Damage taken in Inverse battles

Normal	×1	Flying	×1
Fire	×1	Psychic	×1
Water	×2	Bug	×1
Grass	×2	Rock	×0.5
Electric	×2	Ghost	×1
Ice	×1	Dragon	×0.5
Fighting	×0.5	Dark	×1
Poison	×1	Steel	×0.5
Ground	×1	Fairy	×0.5

Can be used in
- Inverse Battle
- Battle Institute
- Battle Maison
- Random Matchup (Free Battle)
- Random Matchup (Others)

LEVEL-UP MOVES

Lv.	Name	Type	Kind	Pow.	Acc.	PP	Range
1	Icy Wind	Ice	Special	55	95	15	Many Others
1	Dragon Rage	Dragon	Special	—	100	10	Normal
8	Imprison	Psychic	Status	—	—	10	Self
15	Ancient Power	Rock	Special	60	100	5	Normal
22	Ice Beam	Ice	Special	90	100	10	Normal
29	Dragon Breath	Dragon	Special	60	100	20	Normal
36	Slash	Normal	Physical	70	100	20	Normal
43	Scary Face	Normal	Status	—	100	10	Normal
50	Glaciate	Ice	Special	65	95	10	Many Others
57	Dragon Pulse	Dragon	Special	85	100	10	Normal
64	Imprison	Psychic	Status	—	—	10	Self
71	Endeavor	Normal	Physical	—	100	5	Normal
78	Blizzard	Ice	Special	110	70	5	Many Others
85	Outrage	Dragon	Physical	120	100	10	1 Random
92	Hyper Voice	Normal	Special	90	100	10	Many Others

TM & HM MOVES

No.	Name	Type	Kind	Pow.	Acc.	PP	Range
TM01	Hone Claws	Dark	Status	—	—	15	Self
TM02	Dragon Claw	Dragon	Physical	80	100	15	Normal
TM06	Toxic	Poison	Status	—	90	10	Normal
TM07	Hail	Ice	Status	—	—	10	Both Sides
TM10	Hidden Power	Normal	Special	60	100	15	Normal
TM11	Sunny Day	Fire	Status	—	—	5	Both Sides
TM13	Ice Beam	Ice	Special	90	100	10	Normal
TM14	Blizzard	Ice	Special	110	70	5	Many Others
TM15	Hyper Beam	Normal	Special	150	90	5	Normal
TM16	Light Screen	Psychic	Status	—	—	30	Your Side
TM17	Protect	Normal	Status	—	—	10	Self
TM18	Rain Dance	Water	Status	—	—	5	Both Sides
TM19	Roost	Flying	Status	—	—	10	Self
TM20	Safeguard	Normal	Status	—	—	25	Your Side
TM21	Frustration	Normal	Physical	—	100	20	Normal
TM27	Return	Normal	Physical	—	100	20	Normal
TM29	Psychic	Psychic	Special	90	100	10	Normal
TM30	Shadow Ball	Ghost	Special	80	100	15	Normal
TM32	Double Team	Normal	Status	—	—	15	Self
TM33	Reflect	Psychic	Status	—	—	20	Your Side
TM39	Rock Tomb	Rock	Physical	60	95	15	Normal
TM42	Facade	Normal	Physical	70	100	20	Normal
TM44	Rest	Psychic	Status	—	—	10	Self
TM48	Round	Normal	Special	60	100	15	Normal
TM49	Echoed Voice	Normal	Special	40	100	15	Normal
TM51	Steel Wing	Steel	Physical	70	90	25	Normal
TM52	Focus Blast	Fighting	Special	120	70	5	Normal
TM56	Fling	Dark	Physical	—	100	10	Normal
TM65	Shadow Claw	Ghost	Physical	70	100	15	Normal
TM66	Payback	Dark	Physical	50	100	10	Normal
TM68	Giga Impact	Normal	Physical	150	90	5	Normal
TM71	Stone Edge	Rock	Physical	100	80	5	Normal
TM80	Rock Slide	Rock	Physical	75	90	10	Many Others
TM82	Dragon Tail	Dragon	Physical	60	90	10	Normal
TM87	Swagger	Normal	Status	—	90	15	Normal
TM88	Sleep Talk	Normal	Status	—	—	10	Self
TM90	Substitute	Normal	Status	—	—	10	Self
TM91	Flash Cannon	Steel	Special	80	100	10	Normal
TM94	Secret Power	Normal	Physical	70	100	20	Normal
TM100	Confide	Normal	Status	—	—	20	Normal
HM01	Cut	Normal	Physical	50	95	30	Normal
HM02	Fly	Flying	Physical	90	95	15	Normal
HM04	Strength	Normal	Physical	80	100	15	Normal
HM06	Rock Smash	Fighting	Physical	40	100	15	Normal

MOVES LEARNED IN EXCHANGE FOR BP

Name	Type	Kind	Pow.	Acc.	PP	Range
Signal Beam	Bug	Special	75	100	15	Normal
Iron Head	Steel	Physical	80	100	15	Normal
Earth Power	Ground	Special	90	100	10	Normal
Icy Wind	Ice	Special	55	95	15	Many Others
Zen Headbutt	Psychic	Physical	80	90	15	Normal
Dragon Pulse	Dragon	Special	85	100	10	Normal
Hyper Voice	Normal	Special	90	100	10	Many Others
Snore	Normal	Special	50	100	15	Normal
Endeavor	Normal	Physical	—	100	5	Normal
Outrage	Dragon	Physical	120	100	10	1 Random

MOVES TAUGHT BY PEOPLE

Name	Type	Kind	Pow.	Acc.	PP	Range
Draco Meteor	Dragon	Special	130	90	5	Normal

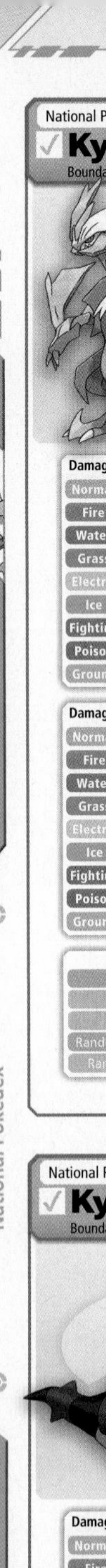

National Pokédex **646** Hoenn Pokédex **—**

✓ Kyurem

White Kyurem

Boundary Pokémon

Dragon **Ice**

HEIGHT: 11'10" WEIGHT: 716.5 lbs.

Gender unknown

Ω This legendary ice Pokémon waits for a hero to fill in the missing parts of its body with truth or ideals.

α It generates a powerful, freezing energy inside itself, but its body became frozen when the energy leaked out.

ABILITY
Turboblaze

HIDDEN ABILITY
—

EGG GROUPS
No Eggs Discovered

STAT GROWTH RATES
HP
Attack
Defense
Sp. Atk
Sp. Def
Speed

ITEMS SOMETIMES HELD BY WILD POKÉMON
—

EVOLUTION
Does not evolve

MAIN WAY TO REGISTER IN THE NATIONAL POKÉDEX

Use the DNA Splicers on Kyurem to have it fuse with Reshiram.

Damage taken in normal battles

Type		Type	
Normal	×1	Flying	×1
Fire	×1	Psychic	×1
Water	×0.5	Bug	×1
Grass	×0.5	Rock	×2
Electric	×0.5	Ghost	×1
Ice	×1	Dragon	×2
Fighting	×2	Dark	×1
Poison	×1	Steel	×2
Ground	×1	Fairy	×2

Damage taken in Inverse battles

Type		Type	
Normal	×1	Flying	×1
Fire	×1	Psychic	×1
Water	×2	Bug	×1
Grass	×2	Rock	×0.5
Electric	×2	Ghost	×1
Ice	×1	Dragon	×0.5
Fighting	×0.5	Dark	×1
Poison	×1	Steel	×0.5
Ground	×1	Fairy	×0.5

Can be used in

Inverse Battle
Battle Institute
Battle Maison
Random Matchup (Free Battle)
Random Matchup (Others)

LEVEL-UP MOVES

Lv.	Name	Type	Kind	Pow.	Acc.	PP	Range
1	Icy Wind	Ice	Special	55	95	15	Many Others
1	Dragon Rage	Dragon	Special	—	100	10	Normal
8	Imprison	Psychic	Status	—	—	10	Self
15	Ancient Power	Rock	Special	60	100	5	Normal
22	Ice Beam	Ice	Special	90	100	10	Normal
29	Dragon Breath	Dragon	Special	60	100	20	Normal
36	Slash	Normal	Physical	70	100	20	Normal
43	Fusion Flare	Fire	Special	100	100	5	Normal
50	Ice Burn	Ice	Special	140	90	5	Normal
57	Dragon Pulse	Dragon	Special	85	100	10	Normal
64	Imprison	Psychic	Status	—	—	10	Self
71	Endeavor	Normal	Physical	—	100	5	Normal
78	Blizzard	Ice	Special	110	70	5	Many Others
85	Outrage	Dragon	Physical	120	100	10	1 Random
92	Hyper Voice	Normal	Special	90	100	10	Many Others

TM & HM MOVES

No.	Name	Type	Kind	Pow.	Acc.	PP	Range
TM01	Hone Claws	Dark	Status	—	—	15	Self
TM02	Dragon Claw	Dragon	Physical	80	100	15	Normal
TM06	Toxic	Poison	Status	—	90	10	Normal
TM07	Hail	Ice	Status	—	—	10	Both Sides
TM10	Hidden Power	Normal	Special	60	100	15	Normal
TM11	Sunny Day	Fire	Status	—	—	5	Both Sides
TM13	Ice Beam	Ice	Special	90	100	10	Normal
TM14	Blizzard	Ice	Special	110	70	5	Many Others
TM15	Hyper Beam	Normal	Special	150	90	5	Normal
TM16	Light Screen	Psychic	Status	—	—	30	Your Side
TM17	Protect	Normal	Status	—	—	10	Self
TM18	Rain Dance	Water	Status	—	—	5	Both Sides
TM19	Roost	Flying	Status	—	—	10	Self
TM20	Safeguard	Normal	Status	—	—	25	Your Side
TM21	Frustration	Normal	Physical	—	100	20	Normal
TM27	Return	Normal	Physical	—	100	20	Normal
TM29	Psychic	Psychic	Special	90	100	10	Normal
TM30	Shadow Ball	Ghost	Special	80	100	15	Normal
TM32	Double Team	Normal	Status	—	—	15	Self
TM33	Reflect	Psychic	Status	—	—	20	Your Side
TM39	Rock Tomb	Rock	Physical	60	95	15	Normal
TM42	Facade	Normal	Physical	70	100	20	Normal
TM44	Rest	Psychic	Status	—	—	10	Self
TM48	Round	Normal	Special	60	100	15	Normal
TM49	Echoed Voice	Normal	Special	40	100	15	Normal
TM51	Steel Wing	Steel	Physical	70	90	25	Normal
TM52	Focus Blast	Fighting	Special	120	70	5	Normal
TM56	Fling	Dark	Physical	—	100	10	Normal
TM65	Shadow Claw	Ghost	Physical	70	100	15	Normal
TM66	Payback	Dark	Physical	50	100	10	Normal
TM68	Giga Impact	Normal	Physical	150	90	5	Normal
TM71	Stone Edge	Rock	Physical	100	80	5	Normal
TM80	Rock Slide	Rock	Physical	75	90	10	Many Others
TM82	Dragon Tail	Dragon	Physical	60	90	10	Normal
TM87	Swagger	Normal	Status	—	90	15	Normal
TM88	Sleep Talk	Normal	Status	—	—	10	Self
TM90	Substitute	Normal	Status	—	—	10	Self
TM91	Flash Cannon	Steel	Special	80	100	10	Normal
TM94	Secret Power	Normal	Physical	70	100	20	Normal
TM100	Confide	Normal	Status	—	—	20	Normal
HM01	Cut	Normal	Physical	50	95	30	Normal
HM02	Fly	Flying	Physical	90	95	15	Normal
HM04	Strength	Normal	Physical	80	100	15	Normal
HM06	Rock Smash	Fighting	Physical	40	100	15	Normal

MOVES LEARNED IN EXCHANGE FOR BP

Name	Type	Kind	Pow.	Acc.	PP	Range
Signal Beam	Bug	Special	75	100	15	Normal
Iron Head	Steel	Physical	80	100	15	Normal
Earth Power	Ground	Special	90	100	10	Normal
Icy Wind	Ice	Special	55	95	15	Many Others
Zen Headbutt	Psychic	Physical	80	90	15	Normal
Dragon Pulse	Dragon	Special	85	100	10	Normal
Hyper Voice	Normal	Special	90	100	10	Many Others
Snore	Normal	Special	50	100	15	Normal
Endeavor	Normal	Physical	—	100	5	Normal
Outrage	Dragon	Physical	120	100	10	1 Random

MOVES TAUGHT BY PEOPLE

Name	Type	Kind	Pow.	Acc.	PP	Range
Draco Meteor	Dragon	Special	130	90	5	Normal

National Pokédex **646** Hoenn Pokédex **—**

✓ Kyurem

Black Kyurem

Boundary Pokémon

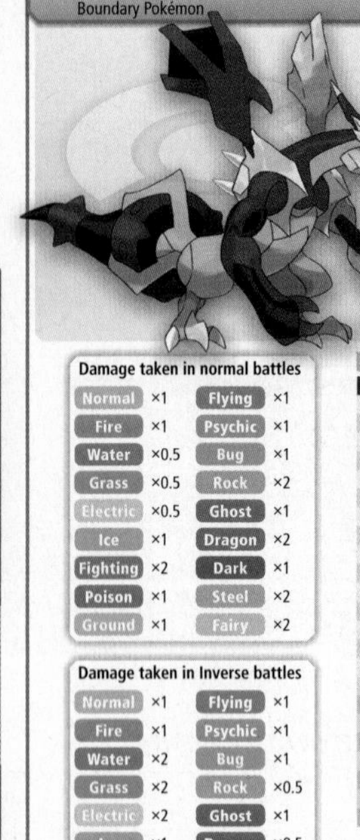

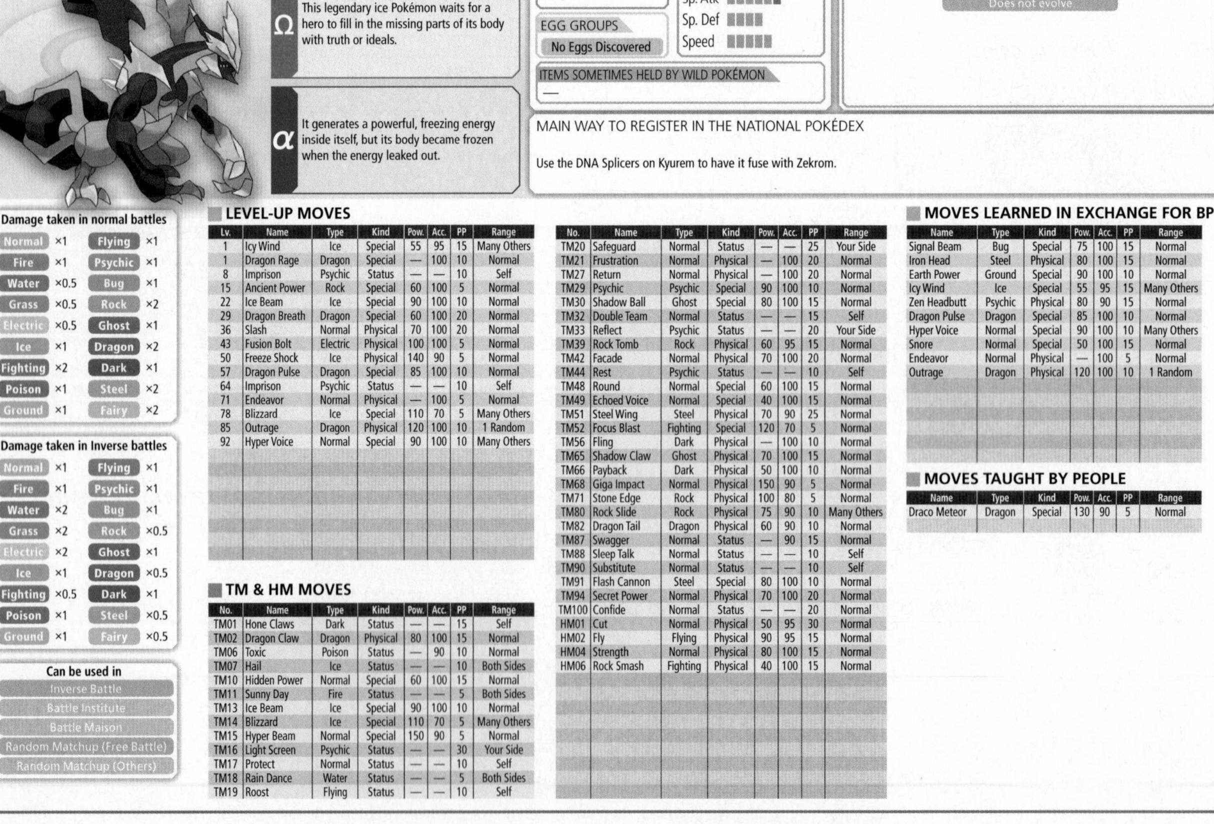

Dragon **Ice**

HEIGHT: 10'10" WEIGHT: 716.5 lbs.

Gender unknown

Ω This legendary ice Pokémon waits for a hero to fill in the missing parts of its body with truth or ideals.

α It generates a powerful, freezing energy inside itself, but its body became frozen when the energy leaked out.

ABILITY
Teravolt

HIDDEN ABILITY
—

EGG GROUPS
No Eggs Discovered

STAT GROWTH RATES
HP
Attack
Defense
Sp. Atk
Sp. Def
Speed

ITEMS SOMETIMES HELD BY WILD POKÉMON
—

EVOLUTION
Does not evolve

MAIN WAY TO REGISTER IN THE NATIONAL POKÉDEX

Use the DNA Splicers on Kyurem to have it fuse with Zekrom.

Damage taken in normal battles

Type		Type	
Normal	×1	Flying	×1
Fire	×1	Psychic	×1
Water	×0.5	Bug	×1
Grass	×0.5	Rock	×2
Electric	×0.5	Ghost	×1
Ice	×1	Dragon	×2
Fighting	×2	Dark	×1
Poison	×1	Steel	×2
Ground	×1	Fairy	×2

Damage taken in Inverse battles

Type		Type	
Normal	×1	Flying	×1
Fire	×1	Psychic	×1
Water	×2	Bug	×1
Grass	×2	Rock	×0.5
Electric	×2	Ghost	×1
Ice	×1	Dragon	×0.5
Fighting	×0.5	Dark	×1
Poison	×1	Steel	×0.5
Ground	×1	Fairy	×0.5

Can be used in

Inverse Battle
Battle Institute
Battle Maison
Random Matchup (Free Battle)
Random Matchup (Others)

LEVEL-UP MOVES

Lv.	Name	Type	Kind	Pow.	Acc.	PP	Range
1	Icy Wind	Ice	Special	55	95	15	Many Others
1	Dragon Rage	Dragon	Special	—	100	10	Normal
8	Imprison	Psychic	Status	—	—	10	Self
15	Ancient Power	Rock	Special	60	100	5	Normal
22	Ice Beam	Ice	Special	90	100	10	Normal
29	Dragon Breath	Dragon	Special	60	100	20	Normal
36	Slash	Normal	Physical	70	100	20	Normal
43	Fusion Bolt	Electric	Physical	100	100	5	Normal
50	Freeze Shock	Ice	Physical	140	90	5	Normal
57	Dragon Pulse	Dragon	Special	85	100	10	Normal
64	Imprison	Psychic	Status	—	—	10	Self
71	Endeavor	Normal	Physical	—	100	5	Normal
78	Blizzard	Ice	Special	110	70	5	Many Others
85	Outrage	Dragon	Physical	120	100	10	1 Random
92	Hyper Voice	Normal	Special	90	100	10	Many Others

TM & HM MOVES

No.	Name	Type	Kind	Pow.	Acc.	PP	Range
TM01	Hone Claws	Dark	Status	—	—	15	Self
TM02	Dragon Claw	Dragon	Physical	80	100	15	Normal
TM06	Toxic	Poison	Status	—	90	10	Normal
TM07	Hail	Ice	Status	—	—	10	Both Sides
TM10	Hidden Power	Normal	Special	60	100	15	Normal
TM11	Sunny Day	Fire	Status	—	—	5	Both Sides
TM13	Ice Beam	Ice	Special	90	100	10	Normal
TM14	Blizzard	Ice	Special	110	70	5	Many Others
TM15	Hyper Beam	Normal	Special	150	90	5	Normal
TM16	Light Screen	Psychic	Status	—	—	30	Your Side
TM17	Protect	Normal	Status	—	—	10	Self
TM18	Rain Dance	Water	Status	—	—	5	Both Sides
TM19	Roost	Flying	Status	—	—	10	Self
TM20	Safeguard	Normal	Status	—	—	25	Your Side
TM21	Frustration	Normal	Physical	—	100	20	Normal
TM27	Return	Normal	Physical	—	100	20	Normal
TM29	Psychic	Psychic	Special	90	100	10	Normal
TM30	Shadow Ball	Ghost	Special	80	100	15	Normal
TM32	Double Team	Normal	Status	—	—	15	Self
TM33	Reflect	Psychic	Status	—	—	20	Your Side
TM39	Rock Tomb	Rock	Physical	60	95	15	Normal
TM42	Facade	Normal	Physical	70	100	20	Normal
TM44	Rest	Psychic	Status	—	—	10	Self
TM48	Round	Normal	Special	60	100	15	Normal
TM49	Echoed Voice	Normal	Special	40	100	15	Normal
TM51	Steel Wing	Steel	Physical	70	90	25	Normal
TM52	Focus Blast	Fighting	Special	120	70	5	Normal
TM56	Fling	Dark	Physical	—	100	10	Normal
TM65	Shadow Claw	Ghost	Physical	70	100	15	Normal
TM66	Payback	Dark	Physical	50	100	10	Normal
TM68	Giga Impact	Normal	Physical	150	90	5	Normal
TM71	Stone Edge	Rock	Physical	100	80	5	Normal
TM80	Rock Slide	Rock	Physical	75	90	10	Many Others
TM82	Dragon Tail	Dragon	Physical	60	90	10	Normal
TM87	Swagger	Normal	Status	—	90	15	Normal
TM88	Sleep Talk	Normal	Status	—	—	10	Self
TM90	Substitute	Normal	Status	—	—	10	Self
TM91	Flash Cannon	Steel	Special	80	100	10	Normal
TM94	Secret Power	Normal	Physical	70	100	20	Normal
TM100	Confide	Normal	Status	—	—	20	Normal
HM01	Cut	Normal	Physical	50	95	30	Normal
HM02	Fly	Flying	Physical	90	95	15	Normal
HM04	Strength	Normal	Physical	80	100	15	Normal
HM06	Rock Smash	Fighting	Physical	40	100	15	Normal

MOVES LEARNED IN EXCHANGE FOR BP

Name	Type	Kind	Pow.	Acc.	PP	Range
Signal Beam	Bug	Special	75	100	15	Normal
Iron Head	Steel	Physical	80	100	15	Normal
Earth Power	Ground	Special	90	100	10	Normal
Icy Wind	Ice	Special	55	95	15	Many Others
Zen Headbutt	Psychic	Physical	80	90	15	Normal
Dragon Pulse	Dragon	Special	85	100	10	Normal
Hyper Voice	Normal	Special	90	100	10	Many Others
Snore	Normal	Special	50	100	15	Normal
Endeavor	Normal	Physical	—	100	5	Normal
Outrage	Dragon	Physical	120	100	10	1 Random

MOVES TAUGHT BY PEOPLE

Name	Type	Kind	Pow.	Acc.	PP	Range
Draco Meteor	Dragon	Special	130	90	5	Normal

National Pokédex **647** Hoenn Pokédex —

Keldeo Ordinary Form

Colt Pokémon

Water Fighting

HEIGHT: 4'07" WEIGHT: 106.9 lbs.

Gender unknown

Ω It crosses the world, running over the surfaces of oceans and rivers. It appears at scenic waterfronts.

α When it is resolute, its body fills with power and it becomes swifter. Its jumps are then too fast to follow.

ABILITY: Justified

HIDDEN ABILITY: —

EGG GROUPS: No Eggs Discovered

STAT GROWTH RATES: HP ▮▮▮▮ / Attack ▮▮▮▮ / Defense ▮▮▮▮ / Sp. Atk ▮▮▮▮▮▮ / Sp. Def ▮▮▮▮ / Speed ▮▮▮▮▮▮

ITEMS SOMETIMES HELD BY WILD POKÉMON: —

EVOLUTION: Does not evolve

MAIN WAY TO REGISTER IN THE NATIONAL POKÉDEX

Previously obtainable through a special distribution. There may be more announcements to come regarding future opportunities to obtain it, so keep checking the official Pokémon website.

Damage taken in normal battles

Type		Type	
Normal	×1	Flying	×2
Fire	×0.5	Psychic	×2
Water	×0.5	Bug	×0.5
Grass	×2	Rock	×0.5
Electric	×2	Ghost	×1
Ice	×0.5	Dragon	×1
Fighting	×1	Dark	×0.5
Poison	×1	Steel	×0.5
Ground	×1	Fairy	×2

Damage taken in Inverse battles

Type		Type	
Normal	×1	Flying	×0.5
Fire	×2	Psychic	×0.5
Water	×2	Bug	×2
Grass	×0.5	Rock	×2
Electric	×0.5	Ghost	×1
Ice	×2	Dragon	×1
Fighting	×1	Dark	×2
Poison	×1	Steel	×2
Ground	×1	Fairy	×0.5

Can be used in: Inverse Battle / Battle Institute / Battle Maison / Random Matchup (Free Battle) / Random Matchup (Others)

LEVEL-UP MOVES

Lv.	Name	Type	Kind	Pow.	Acc.	PP	Range
1	Aqua Jet	Water	Physical	40	100	20	Normal
1	Leer	Normal	Status	—	100	30	Many Others
7	Double Kick	Fighting	Physical	30	100	30	Normal
13	Bubble Beam	Water	Special	65	100	20	Normal
19	Take Down	Normal	Physical	90	85	20	Normal
25	Helping Hand	Normal	Status	—	—	20	1 Ally
31	Retaliate	Normal	Physical	70	100	5	Normal
37	Aqua Tail	Water	Physical	90	90	10	Normal
43	Sacred Sword	Fighting	Physical	90	100	15	Normal
49	Swords Dance	Normal	Status	—	—	20	Self
55	Quick Guard	Fighting	Status	—	—	15	Your Side
61	Work Up	Normal	Status	—	—	30	Self
67	Hydro Pump	Water	Special	110	80	5	Normal
73	Close Combat	Fighting	Physical	120	100	5	Normal

TM & HM MOVES

No.	Name	Type	Kind	Pow.	Acc.	PP	Range
TM04	Calm Mind	Psychic	Status	—	—	20	Self
TM05	Roar	Normal	Status	—	—	20	Normal
TM06	Toxic	Poison	Status	—	90	10	Normal
TM07	Hail	Ice	Status	—	—	10	Both Sides
TM10	Hidden Power	Normal	Special	60	100	15	Normal
TM12	Taunt	Dark	Status	—	100	20	Normal
TM15	Hyper Beam	Normal	Special	150	90	5	Normal
TM17	Protect	Normal	Status	—	—	10	Self
TM18	Rain Dance	Water	Status	—	—	5	Both Sides
TM20	Safeguard	Normal	Status	—	—	25	Your Side
TM21	Frustration	Normal	Physical	—	100	20	Normal
TM27	Return	Normal	Physical	—	100	20	Normal
TM32	Double Team	Normal	Status	—	—	15	Self
TM33	Reflect	Psychic	Status	—	—	20	Your Side
TM40	Aerial Ace	Flying	Physical	60	—	20	Normal
TM42	Facade	Normal	Physical	70	100	20	Normal
TM44	Rest	Psychic	Status	—	—	10	Self
TM48	Round	Normal	Special	60	100	15	Normal
TM52	Focus Blast	Fighting	Special	120	70	5	Normal
TM54	False Swipe	Normal	Physical	40	100	40	Normal
TM55	Scald	Water	Special	80	100	15	Normal
TM67	Retaliate	Normal	Physical	70	100	5	Normal
TM68	Giga Impact	Normal	Physical	150	90	5	Normal
TM71	Stone Edge	Rock	Physical	100	80	5	Normal
TM75	Swords Dance	Normal	Status	—	—	20	Self
TM77	Psych Up	Normal	Status	—	—	10	Normal
TM81	X-Scissor	Bug	Physical	80	100	15	Normal
TM84	Poison Jab	Poison	Physical	80	100	20	Normal
TM87	Swagger	Normal	Status	—	90	15	Normal
TM88	Sleep Talk	Normal	Status	—	—	10	Self
TM90	Substitute	Normal	Status	—	—	10	Self
TM94	Secret Power	Normal	Physical	70	100	20	Normal
TM100	Confide	Normal	Status	—	—	20	Normal
HM01	Cut	Normal	Physical	50	95	30	Normal
HM03	Surf	Water	Special	90	100	15	Adjacent
HM04	Strength	Normal	Physical	80	100	15	Normal
HM06	Rock Smash	Fighting	Physical	40	100	15	Normal

MOVES LEARNED IN EXCHANGE FOR BP

Name	Type	Kind	Pow.	Acc.	PP	Range
Covet	Normal	Physical	60	100	25	Normal
Bounce	Flying	Physical	85	85	5	Normal
Last Resort	Normal	Physical	140	100	5	Normal
Superpower	Fighting	Physical	120	100	5	Normal
Icy Wind	Ice	Special	55	95	15	Many Others
Aqua Tail	Water	Physical	90	90	10	Normal
Snore	Normal	Special	50	100	15	Normal
Water Pulse	Water	Special	60	100	20	Normal
Helping Hand	Normal	Status	—	—	20	1 Ally
Endeavor	Normal	Physical	—	100	5	Normal

MOVES TAUGHT BY PEOPLE

Name	Type	Kind	Pow.	Acc.	PP	Range
Secret Sword	Fighting	Special	85	100	10	Normal

National Pokédex **647** Hoenn Pokédex —

Keldeo Resolute Form

Colt Pokémon

Water Fighting

HEIGHT: 4'07" WEIGHT: 106.9 lbs.

Gender unknown

Ω It crosses the world, running over the surfaces of oceans and rivers. It appears at scenic waterfronts.

α When it is resolute, its body fills with power and it becomes swifter. Its jumps are then too fast to follow.

ABILITY: Justified

HIDDEN ABILITY: —

EGG GROUPS: No Eggs Discovered

STAT GROWTH RATES: HP ▮▮▮▮ / Attack ▮▮▮▮ / Defense ▮▮▮▮ / Sp. Atk ▮▮▮▮▮▮ / Sp. Def ▮▮▮▮ / Speed ▮▮▮▮▮▮

ITEMS SOMETIMES HELD BY WILD POKÉMON: —

EVOLUTION: Does not evolve

MAIN WAY TO REGISTER IN THE NATIONAL POKÉDEX

Talk to the old man in Mauville City's Crooner's Café and have him teach Keldeo the move Secret Sword. Alternatively, talk to the old man with a Keldeo which already knows Secret Sword.

Damage taken in normal battles

Type		Type	
Normal	×1	Flying	×2
Fire	×0.5	Psychic	×2
Water	×0.5	Bug	×0.5
Grass	×2	Rock	×0.5
Electric	×2	Ghost	×1
Ice	×0.5	Dragon	×1
Fighting	×1	Dark	×0.5
Poison	×1	Steel	×0.5
Ground	×1	Fairy	×2

Damage taken in Inverse battles

Type		Type	
Normal	×1	Flying	×0.5
Fire	×2	Psychic	×0.5
Water	×2	Bug	×2
Grass	×0.5	Rock	×2
Electric	×0.5	Ghost	×1
Ice	×2	Dragon	×1
Fighting	×1	Dark	×2
Poison	×1	Steel	×2
Ground	×1	Fairy	×0.5

Can be used in: Inverse Battle / Battle Institute / Battle Maison / Random Matchup (Free Battle) / Random Matchup (Others)

LEVEL-UP MOVES

Lv.	Name	Type	Kind	Pow.	Acc.	PP	Range
1	Aqua Jet	Water	Physical	40	100	20	Normal
1	Leer	Normal	Status	—	100	30	Many Others
7	Double Kick	Fighting	Physical	30	100	30	Normal
13	Bubble Beam	Water	Special	65	100	20	Normal
19	Take Down	Normal	Physical	90	85	20	Normal
25	Helping Hand	Normal	Status	—	—	20	1 Ally
31	Retaliate	Normal	Physical	70	100	5	Normal
37	Aqua Tail	Water	Physical	90	90	10	Normal
43	Sacred Sword	Fighting	Physical	90	100	15	Normal
49	Swords Dance	Normal	Status	—	—	20	Self
55	Quick Guard	Fighting	Status	—	—	15	Your Side
61	Work Up	Normal	Status	—	—	30	Self
67	Hydro Pump	Water	Special	110	80	5	Normal
73	Close Combat	Fighting	Physical	120	100	5	Normal

TM & HM MOVES

No.	Name	Type	Kind	Pow.	Acc.	PP	Range
TM04	Calm Mind	Psychic	Status	—	—	20	Self
TM05	Roar	Normal	Status	—	—	20	Normal
TM06	Toxic	Poison	Status	—	90	10	Normal
TM07	Hail	Ice	Status	—	—	10	Both Sides
TM10	Hidden Power	Normal	Special	60	100	15	Normal
TM12	Taunt	Dark	Status	—	100	20	Normal
TM15	Hyper Beam	Normal	Special	150	90	5	Normal
TM17	Protect	Normal	Status	—	—	10	Self
TM18	Rain Dance	Water	Status	—	—	5	Both Sides
TM20	Safeguard	Normal	Status	—	—	25	Your Side
TM21	Frustration	Normal	Physical	—	100	20	Normal
TM27	Return	Normal	Physical	—	100	20	Normal
TM32	Double Team	Normal	Status	—	—	15	Self
TM33	Reflect	Psychic	Status	—	—	20	Your Side
TM40	Aerial Ace	Flying	Physical	60	—	20	Normal
TM42	Facade	Normal	Physical	70	100	20	Normal
TM44	Rest	Psychic	Status	—	—	10	Self
TM48	Round	Normal	Special	60	100	15	Normal
TM52	Focus Blast	Fighting	Special	120	70	5	Normal
TM54	False Swipe	Normal	Physical	40	100	40	Normal
TM55	Scald	Water	Special	80	100	15	Normal
TM67	Retaliate	Normal	Physical	70	100	5	Normal
TM68	Giga Impact	Normal	Physical	150	90	5	Normal
TM71	Stone Edge	Rock	Physical	100	80	5	Normal
TM75	Swords Dance	Normal	Status	—	—	20	Self
TM77	Psych Up	Normal	Status	—	—	10	Normal
TM81	X-Scissor	Bug	Physical	80	100	15	Normal
TM84	Poison Jab	Poison	Physical	80	100	20	Normal
TM87	Swagger	Normal	Status	—	90	15	Normal
TM88	Sleep Talk	Normal	Status	—	—	10	Self
TM90	Substitute	Normal	Status	—	—	10	Self
TM94	Secret Power	Normal	Physical	70	100	20	Normal
TM100	Confide	Normal	Status	—	—	20	Normal
HM01	Cut	Normal	Physical	50	95	30	Normal
HM03	Surf	Water	Special	90	100	15	Adjacent
HM04	Strength	Normal	Physical	80	100	15	Normal
HM06	Rock Smash	Fighting	Physical	40	100	15	Normal

MOVES LEARNED IN EXCHANGE FOR BP

Name	Type	Kind	Pow.	Acc.	PP	Range
Covet	Normal	Physical	60	100	25	Normal
Bounce	Flying	Physical	85	85	5	Normal
Last Resort	Normal	Physical	140	100	5	Normal
Superpower	Fighting	Physical	120	100	5	Normal
Icy Wind	Ice	Special	55	95	15	Many Others
Aqua Tail	Water	Physical	90	90	10	Normal
Snore	Normal	Special	50	100	15	Normal
Water Pulse	Water	Special	60	100	20	Normal
Helping Hand	Normal	Status	—	—	20	1 Ally
Endeavor	Normal	Physical	—	100	5	Normal

MOVES TAUGHT BY PEOPLE

Name	Type	Kind	Pow.	Acc.	PP	Range
Secret Sword	Fighting	Special	85	100	10	Normal

National Pokédex **648** Hoenn Pokédex —

Meloetta Aria Forme

Melody Pokémon

Normal Psychic

HEIGHT: 2'00" WEIGHT: 14.3 lbs.

Gender unknown

Ω The melodies sung by Meloetta have the power to make Pokémon that hear them happy or sad.

α Its melodies are sung with a special vocalization method that can control the feelings of those who hear it.

ABILITY
Serene Grace

HIDDEN ABILITY
—

EGG GROUPS
No Eggs Discovered

STAT GROWTH RATES
HP
Attack
Defense
Sp. Atk
Sp. Def
Speed

ITEMS SOMETIMES HELD BY WILD POKÉMON
—

EVOLUTION
Does not evolve

MAIN WAY TO REGISTER IN THE NATIONAL POKÉDEX

Previously obtainable through a special distribution. There may be more announcements to come regarding future opportunities to obtain it, so keep checking the official Pokémon website.

Damage taken in normal battles

Type		Type	
Normal	×1	Flying	×1
Fire	×1	Psychic	×0.5
Water	×1	Bug	×2
Grass	×1	Rock	×1
Electric	×1	Ghost	×0
Ice	×1	Dragon	×1
Fighting	×1	Dark	×2
Poison	×1	Steel	×1
Ground	×1	Fairy	×1

Damage taken in Inverse battles

Type		Type	
Normal	×1	Flying	×1
Fire	×1	Psychic	×2
Water	×1	Bug	×0.5
Grass	×1	Rock	×1
Electric	×1	Ghost	×1
Ice	×1	Dragon	×1
Fighting	×1	Dark	×0.5
Poison	×1	Steel	×1
Ground	×1	Fairy	×1

Can be used in
- Inverse Battle
- Battle Institute
- Battle Maison
- Random Matchup (Free Battle)
- Random Matchup (Others)

LEVEL-UP MOVES

Lv.	Name	Type	Kind	Pow.	Acc.	PP	Range
1	Round	Normal	Special	60	100	15	Normal
6	Quick Attack	Normal	Physical	40	100	30	Normal
11	Confusion	Psychic	Special	50	100	25	Normal
16	Sing	Normal	Status	—	55	15	Normal
21	Teeter Dance	Normal	Status	—	100	20	Adjacent
26	Acrobatics	Flying	Physical	55	100	15	Normal
31	Psybeam	Psychic	Special	65	100	20	Normal
36	Echoed Voice	Normal	Special	40	100	15	Normal
43	U-turn	Bug	Physical	70	100	20	Normal
50	Wake-Up Slap	Fighting	Physical	70	100	10	Normal
57	Psychic	Psychic	Special	90	100	10	Normal
64	Hyper Voice	Normal	Special	90	100	10	Many Others
71	Role Play	Psychic	Status	—	—	10	Normal
78	Close Combat	Fighting	Physical	120	100	5	Normal
85	Perish Song	Normal	Status	—	—	5	Adjacent

TM & HM MOVES

No.	Name	Type	Kind	Pow.	Acc.	PP	Range
TM01	Hone Claws	Dark	Status	—	—	15	Self
TM03	Psyshock	Psychic	Special	80	100	10	Normal
TM04	Calm Mind	Psychic	Status	—	—	20	Self
TM06	Toxic	Poison	Status	—	90	10	Normal
TM10	Hidden Power	Normal	Special	60	100	15	Normal
TM11	Sunny Day	Fire	Status	—	—	5	Both Sides
TM15	Hyper Beam	Normal	Special	150	90	5	Normal
TM16	Light Screen	Psychic	Status	—	—	30	Your Side
TM17	Protect	Normal	Status	—	—	10	Self
TM18	Rain Dance	Water	Status	—	—	5	Both Sides
TM20	Safeguard	Normal	Status	—	—	25	Your Side
TM21	Frustration	Normal	Physical	—	100	20	Normal
TM24	Thunderbolt	Electric	Special	90	100	15	Normal
TM25	Thunder	Electric	Special	110	70	10	Normal
TM27	Return	Normal	Physical	—	100	20	Normal
TM29	Psychic	Psychic	Special	90	100	10	Normal
TM30	Shadow Ball	Ghost	Special	80	100	15	Normal
TM31	Brick Break	Fighting	Physical	75	100	15	Normal
TM32	Double Team	Normal	Status	—	—	15	Self
TM42	Facade	Normal	Physical	70	100	20	Normal
TM44	Rest	Psychic	Status	—	—	10	Self
TM47	Low Sweep	Fighting	Physical	65	100	20	Normal
TM48	Round	Normal	Special	60	100	15	Normal
TM49	Echoed Voice	Normal	Special	40	100	15	Normal
TM52	Focus Blast	Fighting	Special	120	70	5	Normal
TM53	Energy Ball	Grass	Special	90	100	10	Normal
TM56	Fling	Dark	Physical	—	100	10	Normal
TM57	Charge Beam	Electric	Special	50	90	10	Normal
TM62	Acrobatics	Flying	Physical	55	100	15	Normal
TM63	Embargo	Dark	Status	—	100	15	Normal
TM65	Shadow Claw	Ghost	Physical	70	100	15	Normal
TM66	Payback	Dark	Physical	50	100	10	Normal
TM67	Retaliate	Normal	Physical	70	100	5	Normal
TM68	Giga Impact	Normal	Physical	150	90	5	Normal
TM70	Flash	Normal	Status	—	100	20	Normal
TM71	Stone Edge	Rock	Physical	100	80	5	Normal
TM73	Thunder Wave	Electric	Status	—	100	20	Normal
TM77	Psych Up	Normal	Status	—	—	10	Normal
TM85	Dream Eater	Psychic	Special	100	100	15	Normal
TM86	Grass Knot	Grass	Special	—	100	20	Normal
TM87	Swagger	Normal	Status	—	90	15	Normal
TM88	Sleep Talk	Normal	Status	—	—	10	Self
TM89	U-turn	Bug	Physical	70	100	20	Normal
TM90	Substitute	Normal	Status	—	—	10	Self
TM92	Trick Room	Psychic	Status	—	—	5	Both Sides
TM94	Secret Power	Normal	Physical	70	100	20	Normal
TM98	Power-Up Punch	Fighting	Physical	40	100	20	Normal
TM99	Dazzling Gleam	Fairy	Special	80	100	10	Many Others
TM100	Confide	Normal	Status	—	—	20	Normal
HM04	Strength	Normal	Physical	80	100	15	Normal
HM06	Rock Smash	Fighting	Physical	40	100	15	Normal

MOVES LEARNED IN EXCHANGE FOR BP

Name	Type	Kind	Pow.	Acc.	PP	Range
Covet	Normal	Physical	60	100	25	Normal
Dual Chop	Dragon	Physical	40	90	15	Normal
Signal Beam	Bug	Special	75	100	15	Normal
Low Kick	Fighting	Physical	—	100	20	Normal
Uproar	Normal	Special	90	100	10	1 Random
Thunder Punch	Electric	Physical	75	100	15	Normal
Fire Punch	Fire	Physical	75	100	15	Normal
Ice Punch	Ice	Physical	75	100	15	Normal
Magic Coat	Psychic	Status	—	—	15	Self
Gravity	Psychic	Status	—	—	5	Both Sides
Last Resort	Normal	Physical	140	100	5	Normal
Zen Headbutt	Psychic	Physical	80	90	15	Normal
Hyper Voice	Normal	Special	90	100	10	Many Others
Snore	Normal	Special	50	100	15	Normal
Knock Off	Dark	Physical	65	100	20	Normal
Role Play	Psychic	Status	—	—	10	Normal
Heal Bell	Normal	Status	—	—	5	Your Party
Drain Punch	Fighting	Physical	75	100	10	Normal
Focus Punch	Fighting	Physical	150	100	20	Normal
Shock Wave	Electric	Special	60	—	20	Normal
Helping Hand	Normal	Status	—	—	20	1 Ally
Trick	Psychic	Status	—	100	10	Normal
Magic Room	Psychic	Status	—	—	10	Both Sides
Wonder Room	Psychic	Status	—	—	10	Both Sides
Recycle	Normal	Status	—	—	10	Self
Snatch	Dark	Status	—	—	10	Self
Skill Swap	Psychic	Status	—	—	10	Normal

MOVES TAUGHT BY PEOPLE

Name	Type	Kind	Pow.	Acc.	PP	Range
Relic Song	Normal	Special	75	100	10	Many Others

National Pokédex **648** Hoenn Pokédex —

Meloetta Pirouette Forme

Melody Pokémon

Normal Fighting

HEIGHT: 2'00" WEIGHT: 14.3 lbs.

Gender unknown

Ω The melodies sung by Meloetta have the power to make Pokémon that hear them happy or sad.

α Its melodies are sung with a special vocalization method that can control the feelings of those who hear it.

ABILITY
Serene Grace

HIDDEN ABILITY
—

EGG GROUPS
No Eggs Discovered

STAT GROWTH RATES
HP
Attack
Defense
Sp. Atk
Sp. Def
Speed

ITEMS SOMETIMES HELD BY WILD POKÉMON
—

EVOLUTION
Does not evolve

MAIN WAY TO REGISTER IN THE NATIONAL POKÉDEX

Use the Relic Song move during battle. (Talk to the old man in Mauville City's Crooner's Café and have him teach Meloetta the move Relic Song.)

Damage taken in normal battles

Type		Type	
Normal	×1	Flying	×2
Fire	×1	Psychic	×2
Water	×1	Bug	×0.5
Grass	×1	Rock	×0.5
Electric	×1	Ghost	×0
Ice	×1	Dragon	×1
Fighting	×2	Dark	×0.5
Poison	×1	Steel	×1
Ground	×1	Fairy	×2

Damage taken in Inverse battles

Type		Type	
Normal	×1	Flying	×0.5
Fire	×1	Psychic	×0.5
Water	×1	Bug	×2
Grass	×1	Rock	×2
Electric	×1	Ghost	×2
Ice	×1	Dragon	×1
Fighting	×0.5	Dark	×2
Poison	×1	Steel	×1
Ground	×1	Fairy	×0.5

Can be used in
- Inverse Battle
- Battle Institute
- Battle Maison
- Random Matchup (Free Battle)
- Random Matchup (Others)

LEVEL-UP MOVES

Lv.	Name	Type	Kind	Pow.	Acc.	PP	Range
1	Round	Normal	Special	60	100	15	Normal
6	Quick Attack	Normal	Physical	40	100	30	Normal
11	Confusion	Psychic	Special	50	100	25	Normal
16	Sing	Normal	Status	—	55	15	Normal
21	Teeter Dance	Normal	Status	—	100	20	Adjacent
26	Acrobatics	Flying	Physical	55	100	15	Normal
31	Psybeam	Psychic	Special	65	100	20	Normal
36	Echoed Voice	Normal	Special	40	100	15	Normal
43	U-turn	Bug	Physical	70	100	20	Normal
50	Wake-Up Slap	Fighting	Physical	70	100	10	Normal
57	Psychic	Psychic	Special	90	100	10	Normal
64	Hyper Voice	Normal	Special	90	100	10	Many Others
71	Role Play	Psychic	Status	—	—	10	Normal
78	Close Combat	Fighting	Physical	120	100	5	Normal
85	Perish Song	Normal	Status	—	—	5	Adjacent

TM & HM MOVES

No.	Name	Type	Kind	Pow.	Acc.	PP	Range
TM01	Hone Claws	Dark	Status	—	—	15	Self
TM03	Psyshock	Psychic	Special	80	100	10	Normal
TM04	Calm Mind	Psychic	Status	—	—	20	Self
TM06	Toxic	Poison	Status	—	90	10	Normal
TM10	Hidden Power	Normal	Special	60	100	15	Normal
TM11	Sunny Day	Fire	Status	—	—	5	Both Sides
TM15	Hyper Beam	Normal	Special	150	90	5	Normal
TM16	Light Screen	Psychic	Status	—	—	30	Your Side
TM17	Protect	Normal	Status	—	—	10	Self
TM18	Rain Dance	Water	Status	—	—	5	Both Sides
TM20	Safeguard	Normal	Status	—	—	25	Your Side
TM21	Frustration	Normal	Physical	—	100	20	Normal
TM24	Thunderbolt	Electric	Special	90	100	15	Normal
TM25	Thunder	Electric	Special	110	70	10	Normal
TM27	Return	Normal	Physical	—	100	20	Normal
TM29	Psychic	Psychic	Special	90	100	10	Normal
TM30	Shadow Ball	Ghost	Special	80	100	15	Normal
TM31	Brick Break	Fighting	Physical	75	100	15	Normal
TM32	Double Team	Normal	Status	—	—	15	Self
TM42	Facade	Normal	Physical	70	100	20	Normal
TM44	Rest	Psychic	Status	—	—	10	Self
TM47	Low Sweep	Fighting	Physical	65	100	20	Normal
TM48	Round	Normal	Special	60	100	15	Normal
TM49	Echoed Voice	Normal	Special	40	100	15	Normal
TM52	Focus Blast	Fighting	Special	120	70	5	Normal
TM53	Energy Ball	Grass	Special	90	100	10	Normal
TM56	Fling	Dark	Physical	—	100	10	Normal
TM57	Charge Beam	Electric	Special	50	90	10	Normal
TM62	Acrobatics	Flying	Physical	55	100	15	Normal
TM63	Embargo	Dark	Status	—	100	15	Normal
TM65	Shadow Claw	Ghost	Physical	70	100	15	Normal
TM66	Payback	Dark	Physical	50	100	10	Normal
TM67	Retaliate	Normal	Physical	70	100	5	Normal
TM68	Giga Impact	Normal	Physical	150	90	5	Normal
TM70	Flash	Normal	Status	—	100	20	Normal
TM71	Stone Edge	Rock	Physical	100	80	5	Normal
TM73	Thunder Wave	Electric	Status	—	100	20	Normal
TM77	Psych Up	Normal	Status	—	—	10	Normal
TM85	Dream Eater	Psychic	Special	100	100	15	Normal
TM86	Grass Knot	Grass	Special	—	100	20	Normal
TM87	Swagger	Normal	Status	—	90	15	Normal
TM88	Sleep Talk	Normal	Status	—	—	10	Self
TM89	U-turn	Bug	Physical	70	100	20	Normal
TM90	Substitute	Normal	Status	—	—	10	Self
TM92	Trick Room	Psychic	Status	—	—	5	Both Sides
TM94	Secret Power	Normal	Physical	70	100	20	Normal
TM98	Power-Up Punch	Fighting	Physical	40	100	20	Normal
TM99	Dazzling Gleam	Fairy	Special	80	100	10	Many Others
TM100	Confide	Normal	Status	—	—	20	Normal
HM04	Strength	Normal	Physical	80	100	15	Normal
HM06	Rock Smash	Fighting	Physical	40	100	15	Normal

MOVES LEARNED IN EXCHANGE FOR BP

Name	Type	Kind	Pow.	Acc.	PP	Range
Covet	Normal	Physical	60	100	25	Normal
Dual Chop	Dragon	Physical	40	90	15	Normal
Signal Beam	Bug	Special	75	100	15	Normal
Low Kick	Fighting	Physical	—	100	20	Normal
Uproar	Normal	Special	90	100	10	1 Random
Thunder Punch	Electric	Physical	75	100	15	Normal
Fire Punch	Fire	Physical	75	100	15	Normal
Ice Punch	Ice	Physical	75	100	15	Normal
Magic Coat	Psychic	Status	—	—	15	Self
Gravity	Psychic	Status	—	—	5	Both Sides
Last Resort	Normal	Physical	140	100	5	Normal
Zen Headbutt	Psychic	Physical	80	90	15	Normal
Hyper Voice	Normal	Special	90	100	10	Many Others
Snore	Normal	Special	50	100	15	Normal
Knock Off	Dark	Physical	65	100	20	Normal
Role Play	Psychic	Status	—	—	10	Normal
Heal Bell	Normal	Status	—	—	5	Your Party
Drain Punch	Fighting	Physical	75	100	10	Normal
Focus Punch	Fighting	Physical	150	100	20	Normal
Shock Wave	Electric	Special	60	—	20	Normal
Helping Hand	Normal	Status	—	—	20	1 Ally
Trick	Psychic	Status	—	100	10	Normal
Magic Room	Psychic	Status	—	—	10	Both Sides
Wonder Room	Psychic	Status	—	—	10	Both Sides
Recycle	Normal	Status	—	—	10	Self
Snatch	Dark	Status	—	—	10	Self
Skill Swap	Psychic	Status	—	—	10	Normal

MOVES TAUGHT BY PEOPLE

Name	Type	Kind	Pow.	Acc.	PP	Range
Relic Song	Normal	Special	75	100	10	Many Others

National Pokédex **649** Hoenn Pokédex —

Genesect

Paleozoic Pokémon

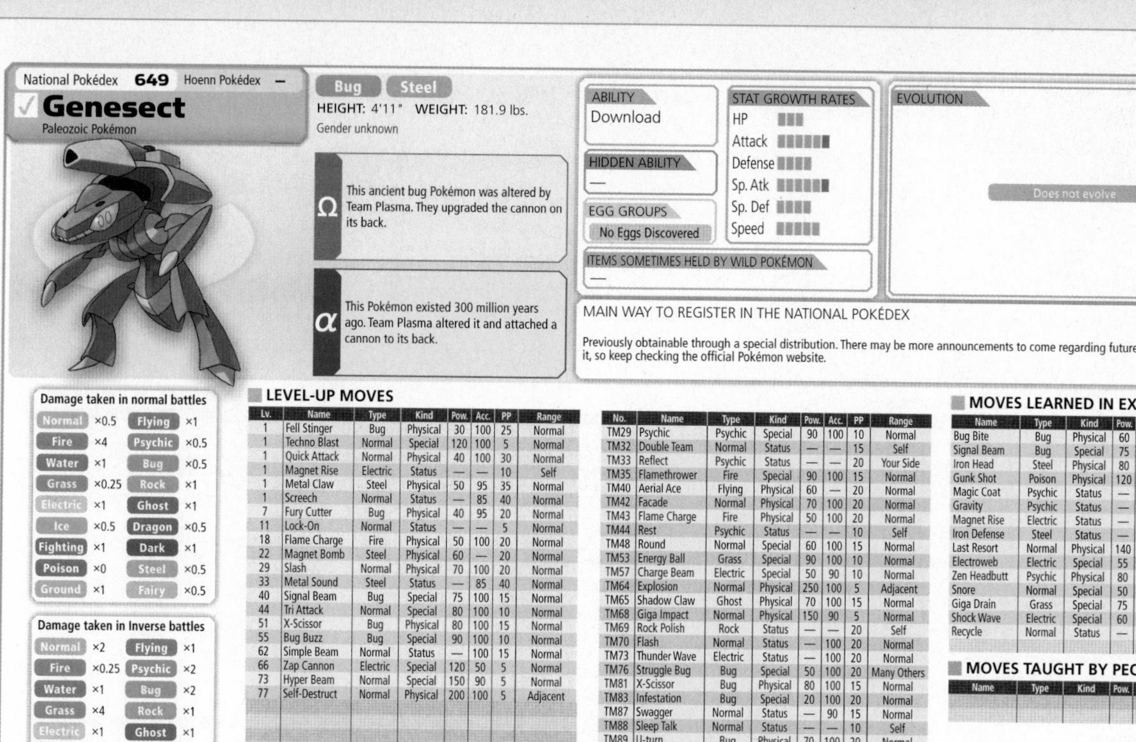

Bug | Steel

HEIGHT: 4'11" WEIGHT: 181.9 lbs.

Gender unknown

Ω This ancient bug Pokémon was altered by Team Plasma. They upgraded the cannon on its back.

α This Pokémon existed 300 million years ago. Team Plasma altered it and attached a cannon to its back.

ABILITY
Download

HIDDEN ABILITY
—

EGG GROUPS
No Eggs Discovered

STAT GROWTH RATES
HP, Attack, Defense, Sp. Atk, Sp. Def, Speed

ITEMS SOMETIMES HELD BY WILD POKÉMON
—

EVOLUTION
Does not evolve

MAIN WAY TO REGISTER IN THE NATIONAL POKÉDEX

Previously obtainable through a special distribution. There may be more announcements to come regarding future opportunities to obtain it, so keep checking the official Pokémon website.

Damage taken in normal battles

Normal	×0.5	Flying	×1
Fire	×4	Psychic	×0.5
Water	×1	Bug	×0.5
Grass	×0.25	Rock	×1
Electric	×1	Ghost	×1
Ice	×0.5	Dragon	×0.5
Fighting	×1	Dark	×1
Poison	×0	Steel	×0.5
Ground	×1	Fairy	×0.5

Damage taken in Inverse battles

Normal	×2	Flying	×1
Fire	×0.25	Psychic	×2
Water	×1	Bug	×2
Grass	×4	Rock	×1
Electric	×1	Ghost	×1
Ice	×2	Dragon	×2
Fighting	×1	Dark	×1
Poison	×2	Steel	×2
Ground	×1	Fairy	×2

Can be used in
Inverse Battle
Battle Institute
Battle Maison
Random Matchup (Free Battle)
Random Matchup (Others)

LEVEL-UP MOVES

Lv.	Name	Type	Kind	Pow.	Acc.	PP	Range
1	Fell Stinger	Bug	Physical	30	100	25	Normal
1	Techno Blast	Normal	Special	120	100	5	Normal
1	Quick Attack	Normal	Physical	40	100	30	Normal
1	Magnet Rise	Electric	Status	—	—	10	Self
1	Metal Claw	Steel	Physical	50	95	35	Normal
1	Screech	Normal	Status	—	85	40	Normal
7	Fury Cutter	Bug	Physical	40	95	20	Normal
11	Lock-On	Normal	Status	—	—	5	Normal
18	Flame Charge	Fire	Physical	50	100	20	Normal
22	Magnet Bomb	Steel	Physical	60	—	20	Normal
29	Slash	Normal	Physical	70	100	20	Normal
33	Metal Sound	Steel	Status	—	85	40	Normal
40	Signal Beam	Bug	Special	75	100	15	Normal
44	Tri Attack	Normal	Special	80	100	10	Normal
51	X-Scissor	Bug	Physical	80	100	15	Normal
55	Bug Buzz	Bug	Special	90	100	10	Normal
62	Simple Beam	Normal	Status	—	100	15	Normal
66	Zap Cannon	Electric	Special	120	50	5	Normal
73	Hyper Beam	Normal	Special	150	90	5	Normal
77	Self-Destruct	Normal	Physical	200	100	5	Adjacent

TM & HM MOVES

No.	Name	Type	Kind	Pow.	Acc.	PP	Range
TM01	Hone Claws	Dark	Status	—	—	15	Self
TM06	Toxic	Poison	Status	—	90	10	Normal
TM10	Hidden Power	Normal	Special	60	100	15	Normal
TM13	Ice Beam	Ice	Special	90	100	10	Normal
TM14	Blizzard	Ice	Special	110	70	5	Many Others
TM15	Hyper Beam	Normal	Special	150	90	5	Normal
TM16	Light Screen	Psychic	Status	—	—	30	Your Side
TM17	Protect	Normal	Status	—	—	10	Self
TM21	Frustration	Normal	Physical	—	100	20	Normal
TM22	Solar Beam	Grass	Special	120	100	10	Normal
TM24	Thunderbolt	Electric	Special	90	100	15	Normal
TM25	Thunder	Electric	Special	110	70	10	Normal
TM27	Return	Normal	Physical	—	100	20	Normal
TM29	Psychic	Psychic	Special	90	100	10	Normal
TM32	Double Team	Normal	Status	—	—	15	Self
TM33	Reflect	Psychic	Status	—	—	20	Your Side
TM35	Flamethrower	Fire	Special	90	100	15	Normal
TM40	Aerial Ace	Flying	Physical	60	—	20	Normal
TM42	Facade	Normal	Physical	70	100	20	Normal
TM43	Flame Charge	Fire	Physical	50	100	20	Normal
TM44	Rest	Psychic	Status	—	—	10	Self
TM48	Round	Normal	Special	60	100	15	Normal
TM53	Energy Ball	Grass	Special	90	100	10	Normal
TM57	Charge Beam	Electric	Special	50	90	10	Normal
TM64	Explosion	Normal	Physical	250	100	5	Adjacent
TM65	Shadow Claw	Ghost	Physical	70	100	15	Normal
TM68	Giga Impact	Normal	Physical	150	90	5	Normal
TM69	Rock Polish	Rock	Status	—	—	20	Self
TM70	Flash	Normal	Status	—	100	20	Normal
TM73	Thunder Wave	Electric	Status	—	100	20	Normal
TM76	Struggle Bug	Bug	Special	50	100	20	Many Others
TM81	X-Scissor	Bug	Physical	80	100	15	Normal
TM83	Infestation	Bug	Special	20	100	20	Normal
TM87	Swagger	Normal	Status	—	90	15	Normal
TM88	Sleep Talk	Normal	Status	—	—	10	Self
TM89	U-turn	Bug	Physical	70	100	20	Normal
TM90	Substitute	Normal	Status	—	—	10	Self
TM91	Flash Cannon	Steel	Special	80	100	10	Normal
TM94	Secret Power	Normal	Physical	70	100	20	Normal
TM97	Dark Pulse	Dark	Special	80	100	15	Normal
TM100	Confide	Normal	Status	—	—	20	Normal
HM02	Fly	Flying	Physical	90	95	15	Normal

MOVES LEARNED IN EXCHANGE FOR BP

Name	Type	Kind	Pow.	Acc.	PP	Range
Bug Bite	Bug	Physical	60	100	20	Normal
Signal Beam	Bug	Special	75	100	15	Normal
Iron Head	Steel	Physical	80	100	15	Normal
Gunk Shot	Poison	Physical	120	80	5	Normal
Magic Coat	Psychic	Status	—	—	15	Self
Gravity	Psychic	Status	—	—	5	Both Sides
Magnet Rise	Electric	Status	—	—	10	Self
Iron Defense	Steel	Status	—	—	15	Self
Last Resort	Normal	Physical	140	100	5	Normal
Electroweb	Electric	Special	55	95	15	Many Others
Zen Headbutt	Psychic	Physical	80	90	15	Normal
Snore	Normal	Special	50	100	15	Normal
Giga Drain	Grass	Special	75	100	10	Normal
Shock Wave	Electric	Special	60	—	20	Normal
Recycle	Normal	Status	—	—	10	Self

MOVES TAUGHT BY PEOPLE

Name	Type	Kind	Pow.	Acc.	PP	Range

◆ Genesect can hold four different drives, which will change the color of part of its body as well as the type of its Techno Blast move. Drives can be obtained from a man in Mauville City.

National Pokédex **650** Hoenn Pokédex —

Chespin

Spiny Nut Pokémon

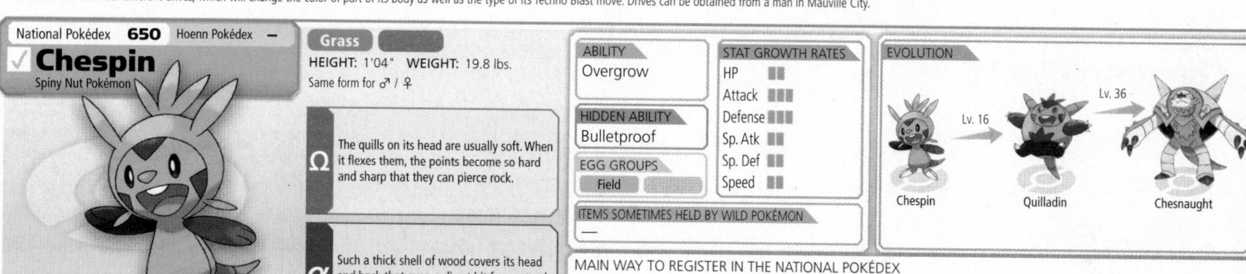

Grass

HEIGHT: 1'04" WEIGHT: 19.8 lbs.

Same form for ♂ / ♀

Ω The quills on its head are usually soft. When it flexes them, the points become so hard and sharp that they can pierce rock.

α Such a thick shell of wood covers its head and back that even a direct hit from a truck wouldn't faze it.

ABILITY
Overgrow

HIDDEN ABILITY
Bulletproof

EGG GROUPS
Field

STAT GROWTH RATES
HP, Attack, Defense, Sp. Atk, Sp. Def, Speed

ITEMS SOMETIMES HELD BY WILD POKÉMON
—

EVOLUTION

MAIN WAY TO REGISTER IN THE NATIONAL POKÉDEX

Obtain in *Pokémon X* or *Pokémon Y*. Bring it to your game using Link Trade or the GTS.

Damage taken in normal battles

Normal	×1	Flying	×2
Fire	×2	Psychic	×1
Water	×0.5	Bug	×2
Grass	×0.5	Rock	×1
Electric	×0.5	Ghost	×1
Ice	×2	Dragon	×1
Fighting	×1	Dark	×1
Poison	×2	Steel	×1
Ground	×0.5	Fairy	×1

Damage taken in Inverse battles

Normal	×1	Flying	×0.5
Fire	×0.5	Psychic	×1
Water	×2	Bug	×0.5
Grass	×2	Rock	×1
Electric	×2	Ghost	×1
Ice	×0.5	Dragon	×1
Fighting	×1	Dark	×1
Poison	×0.5	Steel	×1
Ground	×2	Fairy	×1

Can be used in
Inverse Battle
Battle Institute
Battle Maison
Random Matchup (Free Battle)
Random Matchup (Others)

LEVEL-UP MOVES

Lv.	Name	Type	Kind	Pow.	Acc.	PP	Range
1	Tackle	Normal	Physical	50	100	35	Normal
1	Growl	Normal	Status	—	100	40	Many Others
5	Vine Whip	Grass	Physical	45	100	25	Normal
8	Rollout	Rock	Physical	30	90	20	Normal
11	Bite	Dark	Physical	60	100	25	Normal
15	Leech Seed	Grass	Status	—	90	10	Normal
18	Pin Missile	Bug	Physical	25	95	20	Normal
27	Take Down	Normal	Physical	90	85	20	Normal
32	Seed Bomb	Grass	Physical	80	100	15	Normal
35	Mud Shot	Ground	Special	55	95	15	Normal
39	Bulk Up	Fighting	Status	—	—	20	Self
42	Body Slam	Normal	Physical	85	100	15	Normal
45	Pain Split	Normal	Status	—	—	20	Normal
48	Wood Hammer	Grass	Physical	120	100	15	Normal

TM & HM MOVES

No.	Name	Type	Kind	Pow.	Acc.	PP	Range
TM05	Roar	Normal	Status	—	—	20	Normal
TM06	Toxic	Poison	Status	—	90	10	Normal
TM08	Bulk Up	Fighting	Status	—	—	20	Self
TM10	Hidden Power	Normal	Special	60	100	15	Normal
TM11	Sunny Day	Fire	Status	—	—	5	Both Sides
TM12	Taunt	Dark	Status	—	100	20	Normal
TM17	Protect	Normal	Status	—	—	10	Self
TM21	Frustration	Normal	Physical	—	100	20	Normal
TM22	Solar Beam	Grass	Special	120	100	10	Normal
TM23	Smack Down	Rock	Physical	50	100	15	Normal
TM27	Return	Normal	Physical	—	100	20	Normal
TM28	Dig	Ground	Physical	80	100	10	Normal
TM31	Brick Break	Fighting	Physical	75	100	15	Normal
TM32	Double Team	Normal	Status	—	—	15	Self
TM33	Reflect	Psychic	Status	—	—	20	Your Side
TM36	Sludge Bomb	Poison	Special	90	100	10	Normal
TM39	Rock Tomb	Rock	Physical	60	95	15	Normal
TM40	Aerial Ace	Flying	Physical	60	—	20	Normal
TM42	Facade	Normal	Physical	70	100	20	Normal
TM44	Rest	Psychic	Status	—	—	10	Self
TM45	Attract	Normal	Status	—	100	15	Normal
TM47	Low Sweep	Fighting	Physical	65	100	20	Normal
TM48	Round	Normal	Special	60	100	15	Normal
TM53	Energy Ball	Grass	Special	90	100	10	Normal
TM56	Fling	Dark	Physical	—	100	10	Normal
TM65	Shadow Claw	Ghost	Physical	70	100	15	Normal
TM66	Payback	Dark	Physical	50	100	10	Normal
TM67	Retaliate	Normal	Physical	70	100	5	Normal
TM70	Flash	Normal	Status	—	100	20	Normal
TM71	Stone Edge	Rock	Physical	100	80	5	Normal
TM74	Gyro Ball	Steel	Physical	—	100	5	Normal
TM75	Swords Dance	Normal	Status	—	—	20	Self
TM78	Bulldoze	Ground	Physical	60	100	20	Adjacent
TM80	Rock Slide	Rock	Physical	75	90	10	Many Others
TM84	Poison Jab	Poison	Physical	80	100	20	Normal
TM86	Grass Knot	Grass	Special	—	100	20	Normal
TM87	Swagger	Normal	Status	—	90	15	Normal
TM88	Sleep Talk	Normal	Status	—	—	10	Self
TM90	Substitute	Normal	Status	—	—	10	Self
TM94	Secret Power	Normal	Physical	70	100	20	Normal
TM96	Nature Power	Normal	Status	—	—	20	Normal
TM98	Power-Up Punch	Fighting	Physical	40	100	20	Normal
TM100	Confide	Normal	Status	—	—	20	Normal
HM01	Cut	Normal	Physical	50	95	30	Normal
HM04	Strength	Normal	Physical	80	100	15	Normal
HM06	Rock Smash	Fighting	Physical	40	100	15	Normal

MOVES LEARNED IN EXCHANGE FOR BP

Name	Type	Kind	Pow.	Acc.	PP	Range
Super Fang	Normal	Physical	—	90	10	Normal
Dual Chop	Dragon	Physical	40	90	15	Normal
Iron Head	Steel	Physical	80	100	15	Normal
Seed Bomb	Grass	Physical	80	100	15	Normal
Low Kick	Fighting	Physical	—	100	20	Normal
Thunder Punch	Electric	Physical	75	100	15	Normal
Iron Defense	Steel	Status	—	—	15	Self
Superpower	Fighting	Physical	120	100	5	Normal
Zen Headbutt	Psychic	Physical	80	90	15	Normal
Iron Tail	Steel	Physical	100	75	15	Normal
Snore	Normal	Special	50	100	15	Normal
Synthesis	Grass	Status	—	—	5	Self
Pain Split	Normal	Status	—	—	20	Normal
Giga Drain	Grass	Special	75	100	10	Normal
Drain Punch	Fighting	Physical	75	100	10	Normal
Focus Punch	Fighting	Physical	150	100	20	Normal
Worry Seed	Grass	Status	—	100	10	Normal
Helping Hand	Normal	Status	—	—	20	1 Ally
Endeavor	Normal	Physical	—	100	5	Normal

MOVES TAUGHT BY PEOPLE

Name	Type	Kind	Pow.	Acc.	PP	Range
Grass Pledge	Grass	Special	80	100	10	Normal

EGG MOVES

Name	Type	Kind	Pow.	Acc.	PP	Range
Synthesis	Grass	Status	—	—	5	Self
Belly Drum	Normal	Status	—	—	10	Self
Curse	Ghost	Status	—	—	10	Varies
Quick Guard	Fighting	Status	—	—	15	Your Side
Spikes	Ground	Status	—	—	20	Other Side
Defense Curl	Normal	Status	—	—	40	Self
Rollout	Rock	Physical	30	90	20	Normal

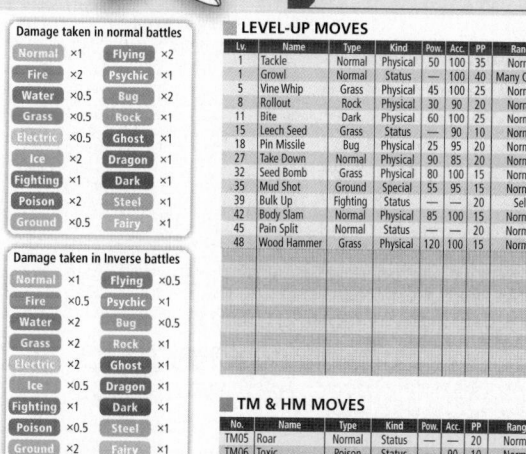

National Pokédex **651** Hoenn Pokédex —

Quilladin

Spiny Armor Pokémon

Grass

HEIGHT: 2'04" WEIGHT: 63.9 lbs.

Same form for ♂ / ♀

Ω It relies on its sturdy shell to deflect predators' attacks. It counterattacks with its sharp quills.

α They strengthen their lower bodies by running into one another. They are very kind and won't start fights.

ABILITY: Overgrow

HIDDEN ABILITY: Bulletproof

EGG GROUPS: Field

STAT GROWTH RATES: HP, Attack, Defense, Sp. Atk, Sp. Def, Speed

ITEMS SOMETIMES HELD BY WILD POKÉMON: —

EVOLUTION

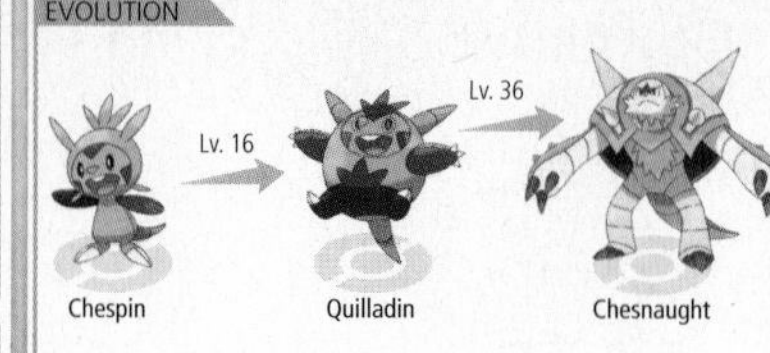

MAIN WAY TO REGISTER IN THE NATIONAL POKÉDEX

Level up a Chespin obtained via Link Trade or the GTS to Lv. 16.

Damage taken in normal battles

Normal	×1	Flying	×2
Fire	×2	Psychic	×1
Water	×0.5	Bug	×2
Grass	×0.5	Rock	×1
Electric	×0.5	Ghost	×1
Ice	×2	Dragon	×1
Fighting	×1	Dark	×1
Poison	×2	Steel	×1
Ground	×0.5	Fairy	×1

Damage taken in Inverse battles

Normal	×1	Flying	×0.5
Fire	×0.5	Psychic	×1
Water	×2	Bug	×0.5
Grass	×2	Rock	×1
Electric	×2	Ghost	×1
Ice	×0.5	Dragon	×1
Fighting	×1	Dark	×1
Poison	×0.5	Steel	×1
Ground	×2	Fairy	×1

Can be used in

- Inverse Battle
- Battle Institute
- Battle Maison
- Random Matchup (Free Battle)
- Random Matchup (Others)

LEVEL-UP MOVES

Lv.	Name	Type	Kind	Pow.	Acc.	PP	Range
1	Tackle	Normal	Physical	50	100	35	Normal
1	Growl	Normal	Status	—	100	40	Many Others
5	Vine Whip	Grass	Physical	45	100	25	Normal
8	Rollout	Rock	Physical	30	90	20	Normal
11	Bite	Dark	Physical	60	100	25	Normal
15	Leech Seed	Grass	Status	—	90	10	Normal
20	Pin Missile	Bug	Physical	25	95	20	Normal
26	Needle Arm	Grass	Physical	60	100	15	Normal
30	Take Down	Normal	Physical	90	85	20	Normal
35	Seed Bomb	Grass	Physical	80	100	15	Normal
39	Mud Shot	Ground	Special	55	95	15	Normal
44	Bulk Up	Fighting	Status	—	—	20	Self
48	Body Slam	Normal	Physical	85	100	15	Normal
52	Pain Split	Normal	Status	—	—	20	Normal
55	Wood Hammer	Grass	Physical	120	100	15	Normal

TM & HM MOVES

No.	Name	Type	Kind	Pow.	Acc.	PP	Range
TM01	Hone Claws	Dark	Status	—	—	15	Self
TM05	Roar	Normal	Status	—	—	20	Normal
TM06	Toxic	Poison	Status	—	90	10	Normal
TM08	Bulk Up	Fighting	Status	—	—	20	Self
TM10	Hidden Power	Normal	Special	60	100	15	Normal
TM11	Sunny Day	Fire	Status	—	—	5	Both Sides
TM12	Taunt	Dark	Status	—	100	20	Normal
TM17	Protect	Normal	Status	—	—	10	Self
TM21	Frustration	Normal	Physical	—	100	20	Normal
TM22	Solar Beam	Grass	Special	120	100	10	Normal
TM23	Smack Down	Rock	Physical	50	100	15	Normal
TM27	Return	Normal	Physical	—	100	20	Normal
TM28	Dig	Ground	Physical	80	100	10	Normal
TM31	Brick Break	Fighting	Physical	75	100	15	Normal
TM32	Double Team	Normal	Status	—	—	15	Self
TM33	Reflect	Psychic	Status	—	—	20	Your Side
TM36	Sludge Bomb	Poison	Special	90	100	10	Normal
TM39	Rock Tomb	Rock	Physical	60	95	15	Normal
TM40	Aerial Ace	Flying	Physical	60	—	20	Normal
TM42	Facade	Normal	Physical	70	100	20	Normal
TM44	Rest	Psychic	Status	—	—	10	Self
TM45	Attract	Normal	Status	—	100	15	Normal
TM47	Low Sweep	Fighting	Physical	65	100	20	Normal
TM48	Round	Normal	Special	60	100	15	Normal
TM53	Energy Ball	Grass	Special	90	100	10	Normal
TM56	Fling	Dark	Physical	—	100	10	Normal
TM65	Shadow Claw	Ghost	Physical	70	100	15	Normal
TM66	Payback	Dark	Physical	50	100	10	Normal
TM67	Retaliate	Normal	Physical	70	100	5	Normal
TM70	Flash	Normal	Status	—	100	20	Normal
TM71	Stone Edge	Rock	Physical	100	80	5	Normal
TM74	Gyro Ball	Steel	Physical	—	100	5	Normal
TM75	Swords Dance	Normal	Status	—	—	20	Self
TM78	Bulldoze	Ground	Physical	60	100	20	Adjacent
TM80	Rock Slide	Rock	Physical	75	90	10	Many Others
TM84	Poison Jab	Poison	Physical	80	100	20	Normal
TM86	Grass Knot	Grass	Special	—	100	20	Normal
TM87	Swagger	Normal	Status	—	90	15	Normal
TM88	Sleep Talk	Normal	Status	—	—	10	Self
TM90	Substitute	Normal	Status	—	—	10	Self
TM94	Secret Power	Normal	Physical	70	100	20	Normal
TM96	Nature Power	Normal	Status	—	—	20	Normal
TM98	Power-Up Punch	Fighting	Physical	40	100	20	Normal
TM100	Confide	Normal	Status	—	—	20	Normal
HM01	Cut	Normal	Physical	50	95	30	Normal
HM04	Strength	Normal	Physical	80	100	15	Normal
HM06	Rock Smash	Fighting	Physical	40	100	15	Normal

MOVES LEARNED IN EXCHANGE FOR BP

Name	Type	Kind	Pow.	Acc.	PP	Range
Super Fang	Normal	Physical	—	90	10	Normal
Dual Chop	Dragon	Physical	40	90	15	Normal
Iron Head	Steel	Physical	80	100	15	Normal
Seed Bomb	Grass	Physical	80	100	15	Normal
Low Kick	Fighting	Physical	—	100	20	Normal
Thunder Punch	Electric	Physical	75	100	15	Normal
Iron Defense	Steel	Status	—	—	15	Self
Superpower	Fighting	Physical	120	100	5	Normal
Zen Headbutt	Psychic	Physical	80	90	15	Normal
Iron Tail	Steel	Physical	100	75	15	Normal
Snore	Normal	Special	50	100	15	Normal
Synthesis	Grass	Status	—	—	5	Self
Pain Split	Normal	Status	—	—	20	Normal
Giga Drain	Grass	Special	75	100	10	Normal
Drain Punch	Fighting	Physical	75	100	10	Normal
Focus Punch	Fighting	Physical	150	100	20	Normal
Worry Seed	Grass	Status	—	100	10	Normal
Helping Hand	Normal	Status	—	—	20	1 Ally
Endeavor	Normal	Physical	—	100	5	Normal

MOVES TAUGHT BY PEOPLE

Name	Type	Kind	Pow.	Acc.	PP	Range
Grass Pledge	Grass	Special	80	100	10	Normal

National Pokédex **652** Hoenn Pokédex —

Chesnaught

Spiny Armor Pokémon

Grass Fighting

HEIGHT: 5'03" WEIGHT: 198.4 lbs.

Same form for ♂ / ♀

Ω Its Tackle is forceful enough to flip a 50-ton tank. It shields its allies from danger with its own body.

α When it takes a defensive posture with its fists guarding its face, it could withstand a bomb blast.

ABILITY: Overgrow

HIDDEN ABILITY: Bulletproof

EGG GROUPS: Field

STAT GROWTH RATES: HP, Attack, Defense, Sp. Atk, Sp. Def, Speed

ITEMS SOMETIMES HELD BY WILD POKÉMON: —

EVOLUTION

Chespin → Lv. 16 → Quilladin → Lv. 36 → Chesnaught

MAIN WAY TO REGISTER IN THE NATIONAL POKÉDEX

Level up a Quilladin obtained via Link Trade or the GTS to Lv. 36.

Damage taken in normal battles

Normal	×1	Flying	×4
Fire	×2	Psychic	×2
Water	×0.5	Bug	×1
Grass	×0.5	Rock	×0.5
Electric	×0.5	Ghost	×1
Ice	×2	Dragon	×1
Fighting	×1	Dark	×0.5
Poison	×2	Steel	×1
Ground	×0.5	Fairy	×2

Damage taken in Inverse battles

Normal	×1	Flying	×0.25
Fire	×0.5	Psychic	×0.5
Water	×2	Bug	×1
Grass	×2	Rock	×2
Electric	×2	Ghost	×1
Ice	×0.5	Dragon	×1
Fighting	×1	Dark	×2
Poison	×0.5	Steel	×1
Ground	×2	Fairy	×0.5

Can be used in

- Inverse Battle
- Battle Institute
- Battle Maison
- Random Matchup (Free Battle)
- Random Matchup (Others)

LEVEL-UP MOVES

Lv.	Name	Type	Kind	Pow.	Acc.	PP	Range
1	Feint	Normal	Physical	30	100	10	Normal
1	Hammer Arm	Fighting	Physical	100	90	10	Normal
1	Belly Drum	Normal	Status	—	—	10	Self
1	Tackle	Normal	Physical	50	100	35	Normal
1	Growl	Normal	Status	—	100	40	Many Others
5	Vine Whip	Grass	Physical	45	100	25	Normal
8	Rollout	Rock	Physical	30	90	20	Normal
11	Bite	Dark	Physical	60	100	25	Normal
15	Leech Seed	Grass	Status	—	90	10	Normal
20	Pin Missile	Bug	Physical	25	95	20	Normal
26	Needle Arm	Grass	Physical	60	100	15	Normal
30	Take Down	Normal	Physical	90	85	20	Normal
35	Seed Bomb	Grass	Physical	80	100	15	Normal
36	Spiky Shield	Grass	Status	—	—	10	Self
41	Mud Shot	Ground	Special	55	95	15	Normal
44	Bulk Up	Fighting	Status	—	—	20	Self
48	Body Slam	Normal	Physical	85	100	15	Normal
52	Pain Split	Normal	Status	—	—	20	Normal
55	Wood Hammer	Grass	Physical	120	100	15	Normal
60	Hammer Arm	Fighting	Physical	100	90	10	Normal
70	Giga Impact	Normal	Physical	150	90	5	Normal
75	Spiky Shield	Grass	Status	—	—	10	Self

TM & HM MOVES

No.	Name	Type	Kind	Pow.	Acc.	PP	Range
TM01	Hone Claws	Dark	Status	—	—	15	Self
TM02	Dragon Claw	Dragon	Physical	80	100	15	Normal
TM05	Roar	Normal	Status	—	—	20	Normal
TM06	Toxic	Poison	Status	—	90	10	Normal
TM08	Bulk Up	Fighting	Status	—	—	20	Self
TM10	Hidden Power	Normal	Special	60	100	15	Normal
TM11	Sunny Day	Fire	Status	—	—	5	Both Sides
TM12	Taunt	Dark	Status	—	100	20	Normal
TM15	Hyper Beam	Normal	Special	150	90	5	Normal
TM17	Protect	Normal	Status	—	—	10	Self
TM21	Frustration	Normal	Physical	—	100	20	Normal
TM22	Solar Beam	Grass	Special	120	100	10	Normal
TM23	Smack Down	Rock	Physical	50	100	15	Normal
TM26	Earthquake	Ground	Physical	100	100	10	Adjacent
TM27	Return	Normal	Physical	—	100	20	Normal
TM28	Dig	Ground	Physical	80	100	10	Normal
TM31	Brick Break	Fighting	Physical	75	100	15	Normal
TM32	Double Team	Normal	Status	—	—	15	Self
TM33	Reflect	Psychic	Status	—	—	20	Your Side
TM36	Sludge Bomb	Poison	Special	90	100	10	Normal
TM39	Rock Tomb	Rock	Physical	60	95	15	Normal
TM40	Aerial Ace	Flying	Physical	60	—	20	Normal
TM42	Facade	Normal	Physical	70	100	20	Normal
TM44	Rest	Psychic	Status	—	—	10	Self
TM45	Attract	Normal	Status	—	100	15	Normal
TM47	Low Sweep	Fighting	Physical	65	100	20	Normal
TM48	Round	Normal	Special	60	100	15	Normal
TM52	Focus Blast	Fighting	Special	120	70	5	Normal
TM53	Energy Ball	Grass	Special	90	100	10	Normal
TM56	Fling	Dark	Physical	—	100	10	Normal
TM65	Shadow Claw	Ghost	Physical	70	100	15	Normal
TM66	Payback	Dark	Physical	50	100	10	Normal
TM67	Retaliate	Normal	Physical	70	100	5	Normal
TM68	Giga Impact	Normal	Physical	150	90	5	Normal
TM70	Flash	Normal	Status	—	100	20	Normal
TM71	Stone Edge	Rock	Physical	100	80	5	Normal
TM74	Gyro Ball	Steel	Physical	—	100	5	Normal
TM75	Swords Dance	Normal	Status	—	—	20	Self
TM78	Bulldoze	Ground	Physical	60	100	20	Adjacent
TM80	Rock Slide	Rock	Physical	75	90	10	Many Others
TM84	Poison Jab	Poison	Physical	80	100	20	Normal
TM86	Grass Knot	Grass	Special	—	100	20	Normal
TM87	Swagger	Normal	Status	—	90	15	Normal
TM88	Sleep Talk	Normal	Status	—	—	10	Self
TM90	Substitute	Normal	Status	—	—	10	Self
TM94	Secret Power	Normal	Physical	70	100	20	Normal
TM96	Nature Power	Normal	Status	—	—	20	Normal
TM98	Power-Up Punch	Fighting	Physical	40	100	20	Normal
TM100	Confide	Normal	Status	—	—	20	Normal
HM01	Cut	Normal	Physical	50	95	30	Normal
HM04	Strength	Normal	Physical	80	100	15	Normal
HM06	Rock Smash	Fighting	Physical	40	100	15	Normal

MOVES LEARNED IN EXCHANGE FOR BP

Name	Type	Kind	Pow.	Acc.	PP	Range
Super Fang	Normal	Physical	—	90	10	Normal
Dual Chop	Dragon	Physical	40	90	15	Normal
Iron Head	Steel	Physical	80	100	15	Normal
Seed Bomb	Grass	Physical	80	100	15	Normal
Low Kick	Fighting	Physical	—	100	20	Normal
Thunder Punch	Electric	Physical	75	100	15	Normal
Block	Normal	Status	—	—	5	Normal
Iron Defense	Steel	Status	—	—	15	Self
Superpower	Fighting	Physical	120	100	5	Normal
Zen Headbutt	Psychic	Physical	80	90	15	Normal
Iron Tail	Steel	Physical	100	75	15	Normal
Snore	Normal	Special	50	100	15	Normal
Synthesis	Grass	Status	—	—	5	Self
Pain Split	Normal	Status	—	—	20	Normal
Giga Drain	Grass	Special	75	100	10	Normal
Drain Punch	Fighting	Physical	75	100	10	Normal
Focus Punch	Fighting	Physical	150	100	20	Normal
Worry Seed	Grass	Status	—	100	10	Normal
Helping Hand	Normal	Status	—	—	20	1 Ally
Endeavor	Normal	Physical	—	100	5	Normal

MOVES TAUGHT BY PEOPLE

Name	Type	Kind	Pow.	Acc.	PP	Range
Grass Pledge	Grass	Special	80	100	10	Normal
Frenzy Plant	Grass	Special	150	90	5	Normal

National Pokédex **653** Hoenn Pokédex —

Fennekin

Fox Pokémon

Fire

HEIGHT: 1'04" WEIGHT: 20.7 lbs.

Same form for ♂ / ♀

Ω Eating a twig fills it with energy, and its roomy ears give vent to air hotter than 390 degrees Fahrenheit.

α As it walks, it munches on a twig in place of a snack. It intimidates opponents by puffing hot air out of its ears.

ABILITY
Blaze

HIDDEN ABILITY
Magician

EGG GROUPS
Field

STAT GROWTH RATES

HP	■■
Attack	■■
Defense	■■
Sp. Atk	■■■
Sp. Def	■■■
Speed	■■■

ITEMS SOMETIMES HELD BY WILD POKÉMON
—

EVOLUTION

Fennekin → Lv. 16 → Braixen → Lv. 36 → Delphox

MAIN WAY TO REGISTER IN THE NATIONAL POKÉDEX

Obtain in *Pokémon X* or *Pokémon Y*. Bring it to your game using Link Trade or the GTS.

Damage taken in normal battles

Type		Type	
Normal	×1	Flying	×1
Fire	×0.5	Psychic	×1
Water	×2	Bug	×0.5
Grass	×0.5	Rock	×2
Electric	×1	Ghost	×1
Ice	×0.5	Dragon	×1
Fighting	×1	Dark	×1
Poison	×1	Steel	×0.5
Ground	×2	Fairy	×0.5

Damage taken in Inverse battles

Type		Type	
Normal	×1	Flying	×1
Fire	×2	Psychic	×1
Water	×0.5	Bug	×2
Grass	×2	Rock	×0.5
Electric	×1	Ghost	×1
Ice	×2	Dragon	×1
Fighting	×1	Dark	×1
Poison	×1	Steel	×2
Ground	×0.5	Fairy	×2

Can be used in
Inverse Battle
Battle Institute
Battle Maison
Random Matchup (Free Battle)
Random Matchup (Others)

LEVEL-UP MOVES

Lv.	Name	Type	Kind	Pow.	Acc.	PP	Range
1	Scratch	Normal	Physical	40	100	35	Normal
1	Tail Whip	Normal	Status	—	100	30	Many Others
5	Ember	Fire	Special	40	100	25	Normal
11	Howl	Normal	Status	—	—	40	Self
14	Flame Charge	Fire	Physical	50	100	20	Normal
17	Psybeam	Psychic	Special	65	100	20	Normal
20	Fire Spin	Fire	Special	35	85	15	Normal
25	Lucky Chant	Normal	Status	—	—	30	Your Side
27	Light Screen	Psychic	Status	—	—	30	Your Side
31	Psyshock	Psychic	Special	80	100	10	Normal
35	Flamethrower	Fire	Special	90	100	15	Normal
38	Will-O-Wisp	Fire	Status	—	85	15	Normal
41	Psychic	Psychic	Special	90	100	10	Normal
43	Sunny Day	Fire	Status	—	—	5	Both Sides
46	Magic Room	Psychic	Status	—	—	10	Both Sides
48	Fire Blast	Fire	Special	110	85	5	Normal

TM & HM MOVES

No.	Name	Type	Kind	Pow.	Acc.	PP	Range
TM03	Psyshock	Psychic	Special	80	100	10	Normal
TM06	Toxic	Poison	Status	—	90	10	Normal
TM10	Hidden Power	Normal	Special	60	100	15	Normal
TM11	Sunny Day	Fire	Status	—	—	5	Both Sides
TM16	Light Screen	Psychic	Status	—	—	30	Your Side
TM17	Protect	Normal	Status	—	—	10	Self
TM18	Rain Dance	Water	Status	—	—	5	Both Sides
TM20	Safeguard	Normal	Status	—	—	25	Your Side
TM21	Frustration	Normal	Physical	—	100	20	Normal
TM22	Solar Beam	Grass	Special	120	100	10	Normal
TM27	Return	Normal	Physical	—	100	20	Normal
TM29	Psychic	Psychic	Special	90	100	10	Normal
TM32	Double Team	Normal	Status	—	—	15	Self
TM35	Flamethrower	Fire	Special	90	100	15	Normal
TM38	Fire Blast	Fire	Special	110	85	5	Normal
TM42	Facade	Normal	Physical	70	100	20	Normal
TM43	Flame Charge	Fire	Physical	50	100	20	Normal
TM44	Rest	Psychic	Status	—	—	10	Self
TM45	Attract	Normal	Status	—	100	15	Normal
TM46	Thief	Dark	Physical	60	100	25	Normal
TM48	Round	Normal	Special	60	100	15	Normal
TM49	Echoed Voice	Normal	Special	40	100	15	Normal
TM50	Overheat	Fire	Special	130	90	5	Normal
TM59	Incinerate	Fire	Special	60	100	15	Many Others
TM61	Will-O-Wisp	Fire	Status	—	85	15	Normal
TM63	Embargo	Dark	Status	—	100	15	Normal
TM77	Psych Up	Normal	Status	—	—	10	Normal
TM85	Dream Eater	Psychic	Special	100	100	15	Normal
TM86	Grass Knot	Grass	Special	—	100	20	Normal
TM87	Swagger	Normal	Status	—	90	15	Normal
TM88	Sleep Talk	Normal	Status	—	—	10	Self
TM90	Substitute	Normal	Status	—	—	10	Self
TM94	Secret Power	Normal	Physical	70	100	20	Normal
TM98	Power-Up Punch	Fighting	Physical	40	100	20	Normal
TM100	Confide	Normal	Status	—	—	20	Normal
HM01	Cut	Normal	Physical	50	95	30	Normal

MOVES LEARNED IN EXCHANGE FOR BP

Name	Type	Kind	Pow.	Acc.	PP	Range
Covet	Normal	Physical	60	100	25	Normal
Magic Coat	Psychic	Status	—	—	15	Self
Foul Play	Dark	Physical	95	100	15	Normal
Iron Tail	Steel	Physical	100	75	15	Normal
Snore	Normal	Special	50	100	15	Normal
Heat Wave	Fire	Special	95	90	10	Many Others
Magic Room	Psychic	Status	—	—	10	Both Sides

MOVES TAUGHT BY PEOPLE

Name	Type	Kind	Pow.	Acc.	PP	Range
Fire Pledge	Fire	Special	80	100	10	Normal

EGG MOVES

Name	Type	Kind	Pow.	Acc.	PP	Range
Wish	Normal	Status	—	—	10	Self
Hypnosis	Psychic	Status	—	60	20	Normal
Heat Wave	Fire	Special	95	90	10	Many Others
Magic Coat	Psychic	Status	—	—	15	Self

National Pokédex **654** Hoenn Pokédex —

Braixen

Fox Pokémon

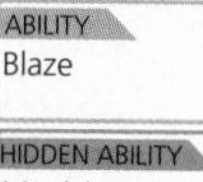

Fire

HEIGHT: 3'03" WEIGHT: 32 lbs.

Same form for ♂ / ♀

Ω It has a twig stuck in its tail. With friction from its tail fur, it sets the twig on fire and launches into battle.

α When the twig is plucked from its tail, friction sets the twig alight. The flame is used to send signals to its allies.

ABILITY
Blaze

HIDDEN ABILITY
Magician

EGG GROUPS
Field

STAT GROWTH RATES

HP	■■■
Attack	■■■
Defense	■■■
Sp. Atk	■■■■
Sp. Def	■■■
Speed	■■■■

ITEMS SOMETIMES HELD BY WILD POKÉMON
—

EVOLUTION

Fennekin → Lv. 16 → Braixen → Lv. 36 → Delphox

MAIN WAY TO REGISTER IN THE NATIONAL POKÉDEX

Level up a Fennekin obtained via Link Trade or the GTS to Lv. 16.

Damage taken in normal battles

Type		Type	
Normal	×1	Flying	×1
Fire	×0.5	Psychic	×1
Water	×2	Bug	×0.5
Grass	×0.5	Rock	×2
Electric	×1	Ghost	×1
Ice	×0.5	Dragon	×1
Fighting	×1	Dark	×1
Poison	×1	Steel	×0.5
Ground	×2	Fairy	×0.5

Damage taken in Inverse battles

Type		Type	
Normal	×1	Flying	×1
Fire	×2	Psychic	×1
Water	×0.5	Bug	×2
Grass	×2	Rock	×0.5
Electric	×1	Ghost	×1
Ice	×2	Dragon	×1
Fighting	×1	Dark	×1
Poison	×1	Steel	×2
Ground	×0.5	Fairy	×2

Can be used in
Inverse Battle
Battle Institute
Battle Maison
Random Matchup (Free Battle)
Random Matchup (Others)

LEVEL-UP MOVES

Lv.	Name	Type	Kind	Pow.	Acc.	PP	Range
1	Scratch	Normal	Physical	40	100	35	Normal
1	Tail Whip	Normal	Status	—	100	30	Many Others
5	Ember	Fire	Special	40	100	25	Normal
11	Howl	Normal	Status	—	—	40	Self
14	Flame Charge	Fire	Physical	50	100	20	Normal
18	Psybeam	Psychic	Special	65	100	20	Normal
22	Fire Spin	Fire	Special	35	85	15	Normal
27	Lucky Chant	Normal	Status	—	—	30	Your Side
30	Light Screen	Psychic	Status	—	—	30	Your Side
34	Psyshock	Psychic	Special	80	100	10	Normal
41	Flamethrower	Fire	Special	90	100	15	Normal
45	Will-O-Wisp	Fire	Status	—	85	15	Normal
48	Psychic	Psychic	Special	90	100	10	Normal
51	Sunny Day	Fire	Status	—	—	5	Both Sides
53	Magic Room	Psychic	Status	—	—	10	Both Sides
55	Fire Blast	Fire	Special	110	85	5	Normal

TM & HM MOVES

No.	Name	Type	Kind	Pow.	Acc.	PP	Range
TM03	Psyshock	Psychic	Special	80	100	10	Normal
TM06	Toxic	Poison	Status	—	90	10	Normal
TM10	Hidden Power	Normal	Special	60	100	15	Normal
TM11	Sunny Day	Fire	Status	—	—	5	Both Sides
TM16	Light Screen	Psychic	Status	—	—	30	Your Side
TM17	Protect	Normal	Status	—	—	10	Self
TM18	Rain Dance	Water	Status	—	—	5	Both Sides
TM20	Safeguard	Normal	Status	—	—	25	Your Side
TM21	Frustration	Normal	Physical	—	100	20	Normal
TM22	Solar Beam	Grass	Special	120	100	10	Normal
TM27	Return	Normal	Physical	—	100	20	Normal
TM29	Psychic	Psychic	Special	90	100	10	Normal
TM32	Double Team	Normal	Status	—	—	15	Self
TM35	Flamethrower	Fire	Special	90	100	15	Normal
TM38	Fire Blast	Fire	Special	110	85	5	Normal
TM42	Facade	Normal	Physical	70	100	20	Normal
TM43	Flame Charge	Fire	Physical	50	100	20	Normal
TM44	Rest	Psychic	Status	—	—	10	Self
TM45	Attract	Normal	Status	—	100	15	Normal
TM46	Thief	Dark	Physical	60	100	25	Normal
TM48	Round	Normal	Special	60	100	15	Normal
TM49	Echoed Voice	Normal	Special	40	100	15	Normal
TM50	Overheat	Fire	Special	130	90	5	Normal
TM59	Incinerate	Fire	Special	60	100	15	Many Others
TM61	Will-O-Wisp	Fire	Status	—	85	15	Normal
TM63	Embargo	Dark	Status	—	100	15	Normal
TM77	Psych Up	Normal	Status	—	—	10	Normal
TM85	Dream Eater	Psychic	Special	100	100	15	Normal
TM86	Grass Knot	Grass	Special	—	100	20	Normal
TM87	Swagger	Normal	Status	—	90	15	Normal
TM88	Sleep Talk	Normal	Status	—	—	10	Self
TM90	Substitute	Normal	Status	—	—	10	Self
TM94	Secret Power	Normal	Physical	70	100	20	Normal
TM98	Power-Up Punch	Fighting	Physical	40	100	20	Normal
TM100	Confide	Normal	Status	—	—	20	Normal
HM01	Cut	Normal	Physical	50	95	30	Normal

MOVES LEARNED IN EXCHANGE FOR BP

Name	Type	Kind	Pow.	Acc.	PP	Range
Covet	Normal	Physical	60	100	25	Normal
Low Kick	Fighting	Physical	—	100	20	Normal
Thunder Punch	Electric	Physical	75	100	15	Normal
Fire Punch	Fire	Physical	75	100	15	Normal
Magic Coat	Psychic	Status	—	—	15	Self
Foul Play	Dark	Physical	95	100	15	Normal
Zen Headbutt	Psychic	Physical	80	90	15	Normal
Iron Tail	Steel	Physical	100	75	15	Normal
Snore	Normal	Special	50	100	15	Normal
Heat Wave	Fire	Special	95	90	10	Many Others
Shock Wave	Electric	Special	60	—	20	Normal
Trick	Psychic	Status	—	100	10	Normal
Magic Room	Psychic	Status	—	—	10	Both Sides
Wonder Room	Psychic	Status	—	—	10	Both Sides
Recycle	Normal	Status	—	—	10	Self
Snatch	Dark	Status	—	—	10	Self
Skill Swap	Psychic	Status	—	—	10	Normal

MOVES TAUGHT BY PEOPLE

Name	Type	Kind	Pow.	Acc.	PP	Range
Fire Pledge	Fire	Special	80	100	10	Normal

National Pokédex **655** Hoenn Pokédex —

Delphox

Fox Pokémon

Fire | Psychic

HEIGHT: 4'11" WEIGHT: 86 lbs.

Same form for ♂ / ♀

Ω It gazes into the flame at the tip of its branch to achieve a focused state, which allows it to see into the future.

α Using psychic power, it generates a fiery vortex of 5,400 degrees Fahrenheit, incinerating foes swept into this whirl of flame.

ABILITY: Blaze

HIDDEN ABILITY: Magician

EGG GROUPS: Field

STAT GROWTH RATES: HP, Attack, Defense, Sp. Atk, Sp. Def, Speed

ITEMS SOMETIMES HELD BY WILD POKÉMON: —

EVOLUTION: Fennekin → Lv. 16 → Braixen → Lv. 36 → Delphox

MAIN WAY TO REGISTER IN THE NATIONAL POKÉDEX

Level up a Braixen obtained via Link Trade or the GTS to Lv. 36.

Damage taken in normal battles

Type		Type	
Normal	×1	Flying	×1
Fire	×0.5	Psychic	×0.5
Water	×2	Bug	×1
Grass	×0.5	Rock	×2
Electric	×1	Ghost	×2
Ice	×0.5	Dragon	×1
Fighting	×0.5	Dark	×2
Poison	×1	Steel	×0.5
Ground	×2	Fairy	×0.5

Damage taken in Inverse battles

Type		Type	
Normal	×1	Flying	×1
Fire	×2	Psychic	×2
Water	×0.5	Bug	×1
Grass	×2	Rock	×0.5
Electric	×1	Ghost	×0.5
Ice	×2	Dragon	×1
Fighting	×2	Dark	×0.5
Poison	×1	Steel	×2
Ground	×0.5	Fairy	×2

Can be used in

Inverse Battle
Battle Institute
Battle Maison
Random Matchup (Free Battle)
Random Matchup (Others)

LEVEL-UP MOVES

Lv.	Name	Type	Kind	Pow.	Acc.	PP	Range
1	Future Sight	Psychic	Special	120	100	10	Normal
1	Role Play	Psychic	Status	—	—	10	Normal
1	Switcheroo	Dark	Status	—	100	10	Normal
1	Shadow Ball	Ghost	Special	80	100	15	Normal
1	Scratch	Normal	Physical	40	100	35	Normal
1	Tail Whip	Normal	Status	—	100	30	Many Others
5	Ember	Fire	Special	40	100	25	Normal
11	Howl	Normal	Status	—	—	40	Self
14	Flame Charge	Fire	Physical	50	100	20	Normal
18	Psybeam	Psychic	Special	65	100	20	Normal
22	Fire Spin	Fire	Special	35	85	15	Normal
27	Lucky Chant	Normal	Status	—	—	30	Your Side
30	Light Screen	Psychic	Status	—	—	30	Your Side
34	Psyshock	Psychic	Special	80	100	10	Normal
36	Mystical Fire	Fire	Special	65	100	10	Normal
42	Flamethrower	Fire	Special	90	100	15	Normal
47	Will-O-Wisp	Fire	Status	—	85	15	Normal
51	Psychic	Psychic	Special	90	100	10	Normal
55	Sunny Day	Fire	Status	—	—	5	Both Sides
58	Magic Room	Psychic	Status	—	—	10	Both Sides
61	Fire Blast	Fire	Special	110	85	5	Normal
69	Future Sight	Psychic	Special	120	100	10	Normal
75	Mystical Fire	Fire	Special	65	100	10	Normal

TM & HM MOVES

No.	Name	Type	Kind	Pow.	Acc.	PP	Range
TM03	Psyshock	Psychic	Special	80	100	10	Normal
TM04	Calm Mind	Psychic	Status	—	—	20	Self
TM06	Toxic	Poison	Status	—	90	10	Normal
TM10	Hidden Power	Normal	Special	60	100	15	Normal
TM11	Sunny Day	Fire	Status	—	—	5	Both Sides
TM15	Hyper Beam	Normal	Special	150	90	5	Normal
TM16	Light Screen	Psychic	Status	—	—	30	Your Side
TM17	Protect	Normal	Status	—	—	10	Self
TM18	Rain Dance	Water	Status	—	—	5	Both Sides
TM20	Safeguard	Normal	Status	—	—	25	Your Side
TM21	Frustration	Normal	Physical	—	100	20	Normal
TM22	Solar Beam	Grass	Special	120	100	10	Normal
TM32	Double Team	Normal	Status	—	—	15	Self
TM27	Return	Normal	Physical	—	100	20	Normal
TM29	Psychic	Psychic	Special	90	100	10	Normal
TM30	Shadow Ball	Ghost	Special	80	100	15	Normal
TM32	Double Team	Normal	Status	—	—	15	Self
TM35	Flamethrower	Fire	Special	90	100	15	Normal
TM38	Fire Blast	Fire	Special	110	85	5	Normal
TM42	Facade	Normal	Physical	70	100	20	Normal
TM43	Flame Charge	Fire	Physical	50	100	20	Normal
TM44	Rest	Psychic	Status	—	—	10	Self
TM45	Attract	Normal	Status	—	100	15	Normal
TM46	Thief	Dark	Physical	60	100	25	Normal
TM48	Round	Normal	Special	60	100	15	Normal
TM49	Echoed Voice	Normal	Special	40	100	15	Normal
TM50	Overheat	Fire	Special	130	90	5	Normal
TM59	Incinerate	Fire	Special	60	100	15	Many Others
TM61	Will-O-Wisp	Fire	Status	—	85	15	Normal
TM63	Embargo	Dark	Status	—	100	15	Normal
TM68	Giga Impact	Normal	Physical	150	90	5	Normal
TM77	Psych Up	Normal	Status	—	—	10	Normal
TM85	Dream Eater	Psychic	Special	100	100	15	Normal
TM86	Grass Knot	Grass	Special	—	100	20	Normal
TM87	Swagger	Normal	Status	—	90	15	Normal
TM88	Sleep Talk	Normal	Status	—	—	10	Self
TM90	Substitute	Normal	Status	—	—	10	Self
TM92	Trick Room	Psychic	Status	—	—	5	Both Sides
TM94	Secret Power	Normal	Physical	70	100	20	Normal
TM98	Power-Up Punch	Fighting	Physical	40	100	20	Normal
TM99	Dazzling Gleam	Fairy	Special	80	100	10	Many Others
TM100	Confide	Normal	Status	—	—	20	Normal
HM01	Cut	Normal	Physical	50	95	30	Normal

MOVES LEARNED IN EXCHANGE FOR BP

Name	Type	Kind	Pow.	Acc.	PP	Range
Covet	Normal	Physical	60	100	25	Normal
Signal Beam	Bug	Special	75	100	15	Normal
Low Kick	Fighting	Physical	—	100	20	Normal
Thunder Punch	Electric	Physical	75	100	15	Normal
Fire Punch	Fire	Physical	75	100	15	Normal
Magic Coat	Psychic	Status	—	—	15	Self
Foul Play	Dark	Physical	95	100	15	Normal
Zen Headbutt	Psychic	Physical	80	90	15	Normal
Iron Tail	Steel	Physical	100	75	15	Normal
Snore	Normal	Special	50	100	15	Normal
Heat Wave	Fire	Special	95	90	10	Many Others
Role Play	Psychic	Status	—	—	10	Normal
Shock Wave	Electric	Special	60	—	20	Normal
Trick	Psychic	Status	—	100	10	Normal
Magic Room	Psychic	Status	—	—	10	Both Sides
Wonder Room	Psychic	Status	—	—	10	Both Sides
Recycle	Normal	Status	—	—	10	Self
Snatch	Dark	Status	—	—	10	Self
Skill Swap	Psychic	Status	—	—	10	Normal

MOVES TAUGHT BY PEOPLE

Name	Type	Kind	Pow.	Acc.	PP	Range
Fire Pledge	Fire	Special	80	100	10	Normal
Blast Burn	Fire	Special	150	90	5	Normal

National Pokédex **656** Hoenn Pokédex —

Froakie

Bubble Frog Pokémon

Water

HEIGHT: 1'00" WEIGHT: 15.4 lbs.

Same form for ♂ / ♀

Ω It secretes flexible bubbles from its chest and back. The bubbles reduce the damage it would otherwise take when attacked.

α It protects its skin by covering its body in delicate bubbles. Beneath its happy-go-lucky air, it keeps a watchful eye on its surroundings.

ABILITY: Torrent

HIDDEN ABILITY: Protean

EGG GROUPS: Water 1

STAT GROWTH RATES: HP, Attack, Defense, Sp. Atk, Sp. Def, Speed

ITEMS SOMETIMES HELD BY WILD POKÉMON: —

EVOLUTION: Froakie → Lv. 16 → Frogadier → Lv. 36 → Greninja

MAIN WAY TO REGISTER IN THE NATIONAL POKÉDEX

Obtain in *Pokémon X* or *Pokémon Y*. Bring it to your game using Link Trade or the GTS.

Damage taken in normal battles

Type		Type	
Normal	×1	Flying	×1
Fire	×0.5	Psychic	×1
Water	×0.5	Bug	×1
Grass	×2	Rock	×1
Electric	×2	Ghost	×1
Ice	×0.5	Dragon	×1
Fighting	×1	Dark	×1
Poison	×1	Steel	×0.5
Ground	×1	Fairy	×1

Damage taken in Inverse battles

Type		Type	
Normal	×1	Flying	×1
Fire	×2	Psychic	×1
Water	×2	Bug	×1
Grass	×0.5	Rock	×1
Electric	×0.5	Ghost	×1
Ice	×2	Dragon	×1
Fighting	×1	Dark	×1
Poison	×1	Steel	×2
Ground	×1	Fairy	×1

Can be used in

Inverse Battle
Battle Institute
Battle Maison
Random Matchup (Free Battle)
Random Matchup (Others)

LEVEL-UP MOVES

Lv.	Name	Type	Kind	Pow.	Acc.	PP	Range
1	Pound	Normal	Physical	40	100	35	Normal
1	Growl	Normal	Status	—	100	40	Many Others
5	Bubble	Water	Special	40	100	30	Many Others
8	Quick Attack	Normal	Physical	40	100	30	Normal
10	Lick	Ghost	Physical	30	100	30	Normal
14	Water Pulse	Water	Special	60	100	20	Normal
18	Smokescreen	Normal	Status	—	100	20	Normal
21	Round	Normal	Special	60	100	15	Normal
25	Fling	Dark	Physical	—	100	10	Normal
29	Smack Down	Rock	Physical	50	100	15	Normal
35	Substitute	Normal	Status	—	—	10	Self
39	Bounce	Flying	Physical	85	85	5	Normal
43	Double Team	Normal	Status	—	—	15	Self
48	Hydro Pump	Water	Special	110	80	5	Normal

TM & HM MOVES

No.	Name	Type	Kind	Pow.	Acc.	PP	Range
TM06	Toxic	Poison	Status	—	90	10	Normal
TM10	Hidden Power	Normal	Special	60	100	15	Normal
TM12	Taunt	Dark	Status	—	100	20	Normal
TM13	Ice Beam	Ice	Special	90	100	10	Normal
TM14	Blizzard	Ice	Special	110	70	5	Many Others
TM17	Protect	Normal	Status	—	—	10	Self
TM18	Rain Dance	Water	Status	—	—	5	Both Sides
TM21	Frustration	Normal	Physical	—	100	20	Normal
TM23	Smack Down	Rock	Physical	50	100	15	Normal
TM27	Return	Normal	Physical	—	100	20	Normal
TM28	Dig	Ground	Physical	80	100	10	Normal
TM32	Double Team	Normal	Status	—	—	15	Self
TM39	Rock Tomb	Rock	Physical	60	95	15	Normal
TM40	Aerial Ace	Flying	Physical	60	—	20	Normal
TM42	Facade	Normal	Physical	70	100	20	Normal
TM44	Rest	Psychic	Status	—	—	10	Self
TM45	Attract	Normal	Status	—	100	15	Normal
TM46	Thief	Dark	Physical	60	100	25	Normal
TM48	Round	Normal	Special	60	100	15	Normal
TM49	Echoed Voice	Normal	Special	40	100	15	Normal
TM55	Scald	Water	Special	80	100	15	Normal
TM56	Fling	Dark	Physical	—	100	10	Normal
TM62	Acrobatics	Flying	Physical	55	100	15	Normal
TM80	Rock Slide	Rock	Physical	75	90	10	Many Others
TM86	Grass Knot	Grass	Special	—	100	20	Normal
TM87	Swagger	Normal	Status	—	90	15	Normal
TM88	Sleep Talk	Normal	Status	—	—	10	Self
TM89	U-turn	Bug	Physical	70	100	20	Normal
TM90	Substitute	Normal	Status	—	—	10	Self
TM94	Secret Power	Normal	Physical	70	100	20	Normal
TM98	Power-Up Punch	Fighting	Physical	40	100	20	Normal
TM100	Confide	Normal	Status	—	—	20	Normal
HM01	Cut	Normal	Physical	50	95	30	Normal
HM03	Surf	Water	Special	90	100	15	Adjacent
HM04	Strength	Normal	Physical	80	100	15	Normal
HM05	Waterfall	Water	Physical	80	100	15	Normal
HM06	Rock Smash	Fighting	Physical	40	100	15	Normal
HM07	Dive	Water	Physical	80	100	10	Normal

MOVES LEARNED IN EXCHANGE FOR BP

Name	Type	Kind	Pow.	Acc.	PP	Range
Bounce	Flying	Physical	85	85	5	Normal
Icy Wind	Ice	Special	55	95	15	Many Others
Snore	Normal	Special	50	100	15	Normal
Role Play	Psychic	Status	—	—	10	Normal
Water Pulse	Water	Special	60	100	20	Normal
Spite	Ghost	Status	—	100	10	Normal
Snatch	Dark	Status	—	—	10	Self

MOVES TAUGHT BY PEOPLE

Name	Type	Kind	Pow.	Acc.	PP	Range
Water Pledge	Water	Special	80	100	10	Normal

EGG MOVES

Name	Type	Kind	Pow.	Acc.	PP	Range
Bestow	Normal	Status	—	—	15	Normal
Mind Reader	Normal	Status	—	—	5	Normal
Toxic Spikes	Poison	Status	—	—	20	Other Side
Mud Sport	Ground	Status	—	—	15	Both Sides
Camouflage	Normal	Status	—	—	20	Self
Water Sport	Water	Status	—	—	15	Both Sides

National Pokédex **657** Hoenn Pokédex —

Frogadier

Bubble Frog Pokémon

Water

HEIGHT: 2'00" WEIGHT: 24 lbs.

Same form for ♂ / ♀

Ω It can throw bubble-covered pebbles with precise control, hitting empty cans up to a hundred feet away.

α Its swiftness is unparalleled. It can scale a tower of more than 2,000 feet in a minute's time.

ABILITY

Torrent

HIDDEN ABILITY

Protean

EGG GROUPS

Water 1

STAT GROWTH RATES

HP

Attack

Defense

Sp. Atk

Sp. Def

Speed

ITEMS SOMETIMES HELD BY WILD POKÉMON

—

EVOLUTION

MAIN WAY TO REGISTER IN THE NATIONAL POKÉDEX

Level up a Froakie obtained via Link Trade or the GTS to Lv. 16.

Damage taken in normal battles

Type		Type	
Normal	×1	Flying	×1
Fire	×0.5	Psychic	×1
Water	×0.5	Bug	×1
Grass	×2	Rock	×1
Electric	×2	Ghost	×1
Ice	×0.5	Dragon	×1
Fighting	×1	Dark	×1
Poison	×1	Steel	×0.5
Ground	×1	Fairy	×1

Damage taken in Inverse battles

Type		Type	
Normal	×1	Flying	×1
Fire	×2	Psychic	×1
Water	×2	Bug	×1
Grass	×0.5	Rock	×1
Electric	×0.5	Ghost	×1
Ice	×2	Dragon	×1
Fighting	×1	Dark	×1
Poison	×1	Steel	×2
Ground	×1	Fairy	×1

Can be used in

- Inverse Battle
- Battle Institute
- Battle Maison
- Random Matchup (Free Battle)
- Random Matchup (Others)

LEVEL-UP MOVES

Lv.	Name	Type	Kind	Pow.	Acc.	PP	Range
1	Pound	Normal	Physical	40	100	35	Normal
1	Growl	Normal	Status	—	100	40	Many Others
5	Bubble	Water	Special	40	100	30	Many Others
8	Quick Attack	Normal	Physical	40	100	30	Normal
10	Lick	Ghost	Physical	30	100	30	Normal
14	Water Pulse	Water	Special	60	100	20	Normal
20	Smokescreen	Normal	Status	—	100	20	Normal
23	Round	Normal	Special	60	100	15	Normal
28	Fling	Dark	Physical	—	100	10	Normal
33	Smack Down	Rock	Physical	50	100	15	Normal
38	Substitute	Normal	Status	—	—	10	Self
44	Bounce	Flying	Physical	85	85	5	Normal
48	Double Team	Normal	Status	—	—	15	Self
55	Hydro Pump	Water	Special	110	80	5	Normal

TM & HM MOVES

No.	Name	Type	Kind	Pow.	Acc.	PP	Range
TM06	Toxic	Poison	Status	—	90	10	Normal
TM10	Hidden Power	Normal	Special	60	100	15	Normal
TM12	Taunt	Dark	Status	—	100	20	Normal
TM13	Ice Beam	Ice	Special	90	100	10	Normal
TM14	Blizzard	Ice	Special	110	70	5	Many Others
TM17	Protect	Normal	Status	—	—	10	Self
TM18	Rain Dance	Water	Status	—	—	5	Both Sides
TM21	Frustration	Normal	Physical	—	100	20	Normal
TM23	Smack Down	Rock	Physical	50	100	15	Normal
TM27	Return	Normal	Physical	—	100	20	Normal
TM28	Dig	Ground	Physical	80	100	10	Normal
TM32	Double Team	Normal	Status	—	—	15	Self
TM39	Rock Tomb	Rock	Physical	60	95	15	Normal
TM40	Aerial Ace	Flying	Physical	60	—	20	Normal
TM42	Facade	Normal	Physical	70	100	20	Normal
TM44	Rest	Psychic	Status	—	—	10	Self
TM45	Attract	Normal	Status	—	100	15	Normal
TM46	Thief	Dark	Physical	60	100	25	Normal
TM48	Round	Normal	Special	60	100	15	Normal
TM49	Echoed Voice	Normal	Special	40	100	15	Normal
TM55	Scald	Water	Special	80	100	15	Normal
TM56	Fling	Dark	Physical	—	100	10	Normal
TM62	Acrobatics	Flying	Physical	55	100	15	Normal
TM80	Rock Slide	Rock	Physical	75	90	10	Many Others
TM86	Grass Knot	Grass	Special	—	100	20	Normal
TM87	Swagger	Normal	Status	—	90	15	Normal
TM88	Sleep Talk	Normal	Status	—	—	10	Self
TM89	U-turn	Bug	Physical	70	100	20	Normal
TM90	Substitute	Normal	Status	—	—	10	Self
TM94	Secret Power	Normal	Physical	70	100	20	Normal
TM97	Dark Pulse	Dark	Special	80	100	15	Normal
TM98	Power-Up Punch	Fighting	Physical	40	100	20	Normal
TM100	Confide	Normal	Status	—	—	20	Normal
HM01	Cut	Normal	Physical	50	95	30	Normal
HM03	Surf	Water	Special	90	100	15	Adjacent
HM04	Strength	Normal	Physical	80	100	15	Normal
HM05	Waterfall	Water	Physical	80	100	15	Normal
HM06	Rock Smash	Fighting	Physical	40	100	15	Normal
HM07	Dive	Water	Physical	80	100	10	Normal

MOVES LEARNED IN EXCHANGE FOR BP

Name	Type	Kind	Pow.	Acc.	PP	Range
Bounce	Flying	Physical	85	85	5	Normal
Low Kick	Fighting	Physical	—	100	20	Normal
Gunk Shot	Poison	Physical	120	80	5	Normal
Ice Punch	Ice	Physical	75	100	15	Normal
Icy Wind	Ice	Special	55	95	15	Many Others
Snore	Normal	Special	50	100	15	Normal
Role Play	Psychic	Status	—	—	10	Normal
Water Pulse	Water	Special	60	100	20	Normal
Spite	Ghost	Status	—	100	10	Normal
Snatch	Dark	Status	—	—	10	Self

MOVES TAUGHT BY PEOPLE

Name	Type	Kind	Pow.	Acc.	PP	Range
Water Pledge	Water	Special	80	100	10	Normal

National Pokédex **658** Hoenn Pokédex —

Greninja

Ninja Pokémon

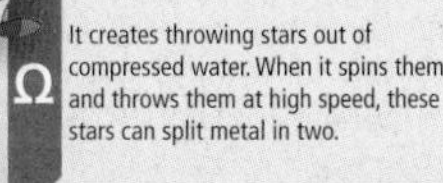

Water Dark

HEIGHT: 4'11" WEIGHT: 88.2 lbs.

Same form for ♂ / ♀

Ω It creates throwing stars out of compressed water. When it spins them and throws them at high speed, these stars can split metal in two.

α It appears and vanishes with a ninja's grace. It toys with its enemies using swift movements, while slicing them with throwing stars of sharpest water.

ABILITY

Torrent

HIDDEN ABILITY

Protean

EGG GROUPS

Water 1

STAT GROWTH RATES

HP

Attack

Defense

Sp. Atk

Sp. Def

Speed

ITEMS SOMETIMES HELD BY WILD POKÉMON

—

EVOLUTION

Froakie — Lv. 16 → Frogadier — Lv. 36 → Greninja

MAIN WAY TO REGISTER IN THE NATIONAL POKÉDEX

Level up a Frogadier obtained via Link Trade or the GTS to Lv. 36.

Damage taken in normal battles

Type		Type	
Normal	×1	Flying	×1
Fire	×0.5	Psychic	×0
Water	×0.5	Bug	×2
Grass	×2	Rock	×1
Electric	×2	Ghost	×0.5
Ice	×0.5	Dragon	×1
Fighting	×2	Dark	×0.5
Poison	×1	Steel	×0.5
Ground	×1	Fairy	×2

Damage taken in Inverse battles

Type		Type	
Normal	×1	Flying	×1
Fire	×2	Psychic	×2
Water	×2	Bug	×0.5
Grass	×0.5	Rock	×1
Electric	×0.5	Ghost	×2
Ice	×2	Dragon	×1
Fighting	×0.5	Dark	×2
Poison	×1	Steel	×2
Ground	×1	Fairy	×0.5

Can be used in

- Inverse Battle
- Battle Institute
- Battle Maison
- Random Matchup (Free Battle)
- Random Matchup (Others)

LEVEL-UP MOVES

Lv.	Name	Type	Kind	Pow.	Acc.	PP	Range
1	Night Slash	Dark	Physical	70	100	15	Normal
1	Role Play	Psychic	Status	—	—	10	Normal
1	Mat Block	Fighting	Status	—	—	10	Your Side
1	Pound	Normal	Physical	40	100	35	Normal
1	Growl	Normal	Status	—	100	40	Many Others
5	Bubble	Water	Special	40	100	30	Many Others
8	Quick Attack	Normal	Physical	40	100	30	Normal
10	Lick	Ghost	Physical	30	100	30	Normal
14	Water Pulse	Water	Special	60	100	20	Normal
20	Smokescreen	Normal	Status	—	100	20	Normal
23	Shadow Sneak	Ghost	Physical	40	100	30	Normal
28	Spikes	Ground	Status	—	—	20	Other Side
33	Feint Attack	Dark	Physical	60	—	20	Normal
36	Water Shuriken	Water	Physical	15	100	20	Normal
43	Substitute	Normal	Status	—	—	10	Self
49	Extrasensory	Psychic	Special	80	100	20	Normal
52	Double Team	Normal	Status	—	—	15	Self
56	Haze	Ice	Status	—	—	30	Both Sides
60	Hydro Pump	Water	Special	110	80	5	Normal
70	Night Slash	Dark	Physical	70	100	15	Normal
75	Water Shuriken	Water	Physical	15	100	20	Normal

TM & HM MOVES

No.	Name	Type	Kind	Pow.	Acc.	PP	Range
TM06	Toxic	Poison	Status	—	90	10	Normal
TM10	Hidden Power	Normal	Special	60	100	15	Normal
TM12	Taunt	Dark	Status	—	100	20	Normal
TM13	Ice Beam	Ice	Special	90	100	10	Normal
TM14	Blizzard	Ice	Special	110	70	5	Many Others
TM15	Hyper Beam	Normal	Special	150	90	5	Normal
TM17	Protect	Normal	Status	—	—	10	Self
TM18	Rain Dance	Water	Status	—	—	5	Both Sides
TM21	Frustration	Normal	Physical	—	100	20	Normal
TM23	Smack Down	Rock	Physical	50	100	15	Normal
TM27	Return	Normal	Physical	—	100	20	Normal
TM28	Dig	Ground	Physical	80	100	10	Normal
TM32	Double Team	Normal	Status	—	—	15	Self
TM39	Rock Tomb	Rock	Physical	60	95	15	Normal
TM40	Aerial Ace	Flying	Physical	60	—	20	Normal
TM42	Facade	Normal	Physical	70	100	20	Normal
TM44	Rest	Psychic	Status	—	—	10	Self
TM45	Attract	Normal	Status	—	100	15	Normal
TM46	Thief	Dark	Physical	60	100	25	Normal
TM48	Round	Normal	Special	60	100	15	Normal
TM49	Echoed Voice	Normal	Special	40	100	15	Normal
TM55	Scald	Water	Special	80	100	15	Normal
TM56	Fling	Dark	Physical	—	100	10	Normal
TM62	Acrobatics	Flying	Physical	55	100	15	Normal
TM68	Giga Impact	Normal	Physical	150	90	5	Normal
TM80	Rock Slide	Rock	Physical	75	90	10	Many Others
TM86	Grass Knot	Grass	Special	—	100	20	Normal
TM87	Swagger	Normal	Status	—	90	15	Normal
TM88	Sleep Talk	Normal	Status	—	—	10	Self
TM89	U-turn	Bug	Physical	70	100	20	Normal
TM90	Substitute	Normal	Status	—	—	10	Self
TM94	Secret Power	Normal	Physical	70	100	20	Normal
TM97	Dark Pulse	Dark	Special	80	100	15	Normal
TM98	Power-Up Punch	Fighting	Physical	40	100	20	Normal
TM100	Confide	Normal	Status	—	—	20	Normal
HM01	Cut	Normal	Physical	50	95	30	Normal
HM03	Surf	Water	Special	90	100	15	Adjacent
HM04	Strength	Normal	Physical	80	100	15	Normal
HM05	Waterfall	Water	Physical	80	100	15	Normal
HM06	Rock Smash	Fighting	Physical	40	100	15	Normal
HM07	Dive	Water	Physical	80	100	10	Normal

MOVES LEARNED IN EXCHANGE FOR BP

Name	Type	Kind	Pow.	Acc.	PP	Range
Bounce	Flying	Physical	85	85	5	Normal
Low Kick	Fighting	Physical	—	100	20	Normal
Gunk Shot	Poison	Physical	120	80	5	Normal
Ice Punch	Ice	Physical	75	100	15	Normal
Icy Wind	Ice	Special	55	95	15	Many Others
Snore	Normal	Special	50	100	15	Normal
Role Play	Psychic	Status	—	—	10	Normal
Water Pulse	Water	Special	60	100	20	Normal
Spite	Ghost	Status	—	100	10	Normal
Snatch	Dark	Status	—	—	10	Self

MOVES TAUGHT BY PEOPLE

Name	Type	Kind	Pow.	Acc.	PP	Range
Water Pledge	Water	Special	80	100	10	Normal
Hydro Cannon	Water	Special	150	90	5	Normal

National Pokédex **659** Hoenn Pokédex —

Bunnelby

Digging Pokémon

Normal

HEIGHT: 1'04" WEIGHT: 11 lbs.

Same form for ♂ / ♀

Ω They use their large ears to dig burrows. They will dig the whole night through.

α It has ears like shovels. Digging holes strengthens its ears so much that they can sever thick roots effortlessly.

ABILITIES
Pickup
Cheek Pouch

HIDDEN ABILITY
Huge Power

EGG GROUPS
Field

STAT GROWTH RATES

HP	■■
Attack	■■
Defense	■■
Sp. Atk	■■
Sp. Def	■■
Speed	■■■

ITEMS SOMETIMES HELD BY WILD POKÉMON
—

EVOLUTION

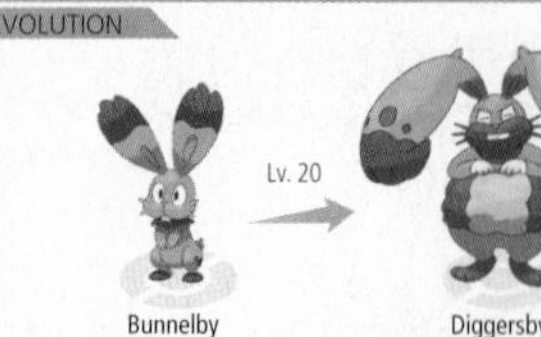

MAIN WAY TO REGISTER IN THE NATIONAL POKÉDEX

Appears in *Pokémon X* and *Pokémon Y*. Bring it to your game using Link Trade or the GTS.

Damage taken in normal battles

Type		Type	
Normal	×1	Flying	×1
Fire	×1	Psychic	×1
Water	×1	Bug	×1
Grass	×1	Rock	×1
Electric	×1	Ghost	×0
Ice	×1	Dragon	×1
Fighting	×2	Dark	×1
Poison	×1	Steel	×1
Ground	×1	Fairy	×1

Damage taken in Inverse battles

Type		Type	
Normal	×1	Flying	×1
Fire	×1	Psychic	×1
Water	×1	Bug	×1
Grass	×1	Rock	×1
Electric	×1	Ghost	×2
Ice	×1	Dragon	×1
Fighting	×0.5	Dark	×1
Poison	×1	Steel	×1
Ground	×1	Fairy	×1

Can be used in
Inverse Battle
Battle Institute
Battle Maison
Random Matchup (Free Battle)
Random Matchup (Others)

LEVEL-UP MOVES

Lv.	Name	Type	Kind	Pow.	Acc.	PP	Range
1	Tackle	Normal	Physical	50	100	35	Normal
1	Agility	Psychic	Status	—	—	30	Self
1	Leer	Normal	Status	—	100	30	Many Others
7	Quick Attack	Normal	Physical	40	100	30	Normal
10	Double Slap	Normal	Physical	15	85	10	Normal
13	Mud-Slap	Ground	Special	20	100	10	Normal
15	Take Down	Normal	Physical	90	85	20	Normal
18	Mud Shot	Ground	Special	55	95	15	Normal
20	Double Kick	Fighting	Physical	30	100	30	Normal
25	Odor Sleuth	Normal	Status	—	—	40	Normal
29	Flail	Normal	Physical	—	100	15	Normal
33	Dig	Ground	Physical	80	100	10	Normal
38	Bounce	Flying	Physical	85	85	5	Normal
42	Super Fang	Normal	Physical	—	90	10	Normal
47	Facade	Normal	Physical	70	100	20	Normal
49	Earthquake	Ground	Physical	100	100	10	Adjacent

TM & HM MOVES

No.	Name	Type	Kind	Pow.	Acc.	PP	Range
TM06	Toxic	Poison	Status	—	90	10	Normal
TM08	Bulk Up	Fighting	Status	—	—	20	Self
TM10	Hidden Power	Normal	Special	60	100	15	Normal
TM17	Protect	Normal	Status	—	—	10	Self
TM21	Frustration	Normal	Physical	—	100	20	Normal
TM23	Smack Down	Rock	Physical	50	100	15	Normal
TM26	Earthquake	Ground	Physical	100	100	10	Adjacent
TM27	Return	Normal	Physical	—	100	20	Normal
TM28	Dig	Ground	Physical	80	100	10	Normal
TM31	Brick Break	Fighting	Physical	75	100	15	Normal
TM32	Double Team	Normal	Status	—	—	15	Self
TM36	Sludge Bomb	Poison	Special	90	100	10	Normal
TM37	Sandstorm	Rock	Status	—	—	10	Both Sides
TM39	Rock Tomb	Rock	Physical	60	95	15	Normal
TM41	Torment	Dark	Status	—	100	15	Normal
TM42	Facade	Normal	Physical	70	100	20	Normal
TM44	Rest	Psychic	Status	—	—	10	Self
TM45	Attract	Normal	Status	—	100	15	Normal
TM46	Thief	Dark	Physical	60	100	25	Normal
TM48	Round	Normal	Special	60	100	15	Normal
TM56	Fling	Dark	Physical	—	100	10	Normal
TM66	Payback	Dark	Physical	50	100	10	Normal
TM71	Stone Edge	Rock	Physical	100	80	5	Normal
TM78	Bulldoze	Ground	Physical	60	100	20	Adjacent
TM80	Rock Slide	Rock	Physical	75	90	10	Many Others
TM86	Grass Knot	Grass	Special	—	100	20	Normal
TM87	Swagger	Normal	Status	—	90	15	Normal
TM88	Sleep Talk	Normal	Status	—	—	10	Self
TM89	U-turn	Bug	Physical	70	100	20	Normal
TM90	Substitute	Normal	Status	—	—	10	Self
TM93	Wild Charge	Electric	Physical	90	100	15	Normal
TM94	Secret Power	Normal	Physical	70	100	20	Normal
TM96	Nature Power	Normal	Status	—	—	20	Normal
TM98	Power-Up Punch	Fighting	Physical	40	100	20	Normal
TM100	Confide	Normal	Status	—	—	20	Normal
HM01	Cut	Normal	Physical	50	95	30	Normal
HM03	Surf	Water	Special	90	100	15	Adjacent
HM04	Strength	Normal	Physical	80	100	15	Normal
HM06	Rock Smash	Fighting	Physical	40	100	15	Normal

MOVES LEARNED IN EXCHANGE FOR BP

Name	Type	Kind	Pow.	Acc.	PP	Range
Super Fang	Normal	Physical	—	90	10	Normal
Iron Head	Steel	Physical	80	100	15	Normal
Bounce	Flying	Physical	85	85	5	Normal
Last Resort	Normal	Physical	140	100	5	Normal
Iron Tail	Steel	Physical	100	75	15	Normal
Snore	Normal	Special	50	100	15	Normal
Endeavor	Normal	Physical	—	100	5	Normal
Recycle	Normal	Status	—	—	10	Self

MOVES TAUGHT BY PEOPLE

Name	Type	Kind	Pow.	Acc.	PP	Range

EGG MOVES

Name	Type	Kind	Pow.	Acc.	PP	Range
Spikes	Ground	Status	—	—	20	Other Side
Defense Curl	Normal	Status	—	—	40	Self
Rollout	Rock	Physical	30	90	20	Normal

National Pokédex **660** Hoenn Pokédex —

Diggersby

Digging Pokémon

Normal Ground

HEIGHT: 3'03" WEIGHT: 93.5 lbs.

Same form for ♂ / ♀

Ω With their powerful ears, they can heft boulders of a ton or more with ease. They can be a big help at construction sites.

α As powerful as an excavator, its ears can reduce dense bedrock to rubble. When it's finished digging, it lounges lazily.

ABILITIES
Pickup
Cheek Pouch

HIDDEN ABILITY
Huge Power

EGG GROUPS
Field

STAT GROWTH RATES

HP	■■■
Attack	■■■
Defense	■■■
Sp. Atk	■■
Sp. Def	■■■
Speed	■■■■

ITEMS SOMETIMES HELD BY WILD POKÉMON
—

EVOLUTION

Lv. 20
Bunnelby
Diggersby

MAIN WAY TO REGISTER IN THE NATIONAL POKÉDEX

Level up a Bunnelby obtained via Link Trade or the GTS to Lv. 20.

Damage taken in normal battles

Type		Type	
Normal	×1	Flying	×1
Fire	×1	Psychic	×1
Water	×2	Bug	×1
Grass	×2	Rock	×0.5
Electric	×0	Ghost	×0
Ice	×2	Dragon	×1
Fighting	×2	Dark	×1
Poison	×0.5	Steel	×1
Ground	×1	Fairy	×1

Damage taken in Inverse battles

Type		Type	
Normal	×1	Flying	×1
Fire	×1	Psychic	×1
Water	×0.5	Bug	×1
Grass	×0.5	Rock	×2
Electric	×2	Ghost	×2
Ice	×0.5	Dragon	×1
Fighting	×0.5	Dark	×1
Poison	×2	Steel	×1
Ground	×1	Fairy	×1

Can be used in
Inverse Battle
Battle Institute
Battle Maison
Random Matchup (Free Battle)
Random Matchup (Others)

LEVEL-UP MOVES

Lv.	Name	Type	Kind	Pow.	Acc.	PP	Range
1	Hammer Arm	Fighting	Physical	100	90	10	Normal
1	Rototiller	Ground	Status	—	—	10	Adjacent
1	Bulldoze	Ground	Physical	60	100	20	Adjacent
1	Swords Dance	Normal	Status	—	—	20	Self
1	Tackle	Normal	Physical	50	100	35	Normal
1	Agility	Psychic	Status	—	—	30	Self
1	Leer	Normal	Status	—	100	30	Many Others
7	Quick Attack	Normal	Physical	40	100	30	Normal
13	Mud-Slap	Ground	Special	20	100	10	Normal
15	Take Down	Normal	Physical	90	85	20	Normal
18	Mud Shot	Ground	Special	55	95	15	Normal
20	Double Kick	Fighting	Physical	30	100	30	Normal
26	Odor Sleuth	Normal	Status	—	—	40	Normal
31	Flail	Normal	Physical	—	100	15	Normal
37	Dig	Ground	Physical	80	100	10	Normal
42	Bounce	Flying	Physical	85	85	5	Normal
48	Super Fang	Normal	Physical	—	90	10	Normal
53	Facade	Normal	Physical	70	100	20	Normal
57	Earthquake	Ground	Physical	100	100	10	Adjacent
60	Hammer Arm	Fighting	Physical	100	90	10	Normal

TM & HM MOVES

No.	Name	Type	Kind	Pow.	Acc.	PP	Range
TM06	Toxic	Poison	Status	—	90	10	Normal
TM08	Bulk Up	Fighting	Status	—	—	20	Self
TM10	Hidden Power	Normal	Special	60	100	15	Normal
TM15	Hyper Beam	Normal	Special	150	90	5	Normal
TM17	Protect	Normal	Status	—	—	10	Self
TM21	Frustration	Normal	Physical	—	100	20	Normal
TM23	Smack Down	Rock	Physical	50	100	15	Normal
TM26	Earthquake	Ground	Physical	100	100	10	Adjacent
TM27	Return	Normal	Physical	—	100	20	Normal
TM28	Dig	Ground	Physical	80	100	10	Normal
TM31	Brick Break	Fighting	Physical	75	100	15	Normal
TM32	Double Team	Normal	Status	—	—	15	Self
TM36	Sludge Bomb	Poison	Special	90	100	10	Normal
TM37	Sandstorm	Rock	Status	—	—	10	Both Sides
TM39	Rock Tomb	Rock	Physical	60	95	15	Normal
TM41	Torment	Dark	Status	—	100	15	Normal
TM42	Facade	Normal	Physical	70	100	20	Normal
TM44	Rest	Psychic	Status	—	—	10	Self
TM45	Attract	Normal	Status	—	100	15	Normal
TM46	Thief	Dark	Physical	60	100	25	Normal
TM48	Round	Normal	Special	60	100	15	Normal
TM56	Fling	Dark	Physical	—	100	10	Normal
TM66	Payback	Dark	Physical	50	100	10	Normal
TM68	Giga Impact	Normal	Physical	150	90	5	Normal
TM71	Stone Edge	Rock	Physical	100	80	5	Normal
TM75	Swords Dance	Normal	Status	—	—	20	Self
TM78	Bulldoze	Ground	Physical	60	100	20	Adjacent
TM80	Rock Slide	Rock	Physical	75	90	10	Many Others
TM86	Grass Knot	Grass	Special	—	100	20	Normal
TM87	Swagger	Normal	Status	—	90	15	Normal
TM88	Sleep Talk	Normal	Status	—	—	10	Self
TM89	U-turn	Bug	Physical	70	100	20	Normal
TM90	Substitute	Normal	Status	—	—	10	Self
TM93	Wild Charge	Electric	Physical	90	100	15	Normal
TM94	Secret Power	Normal	Physical	70	100	20	Normal
TM96	Nature Power	Normal	Status	—	—	20	Normal
TM98	Power-Up Punch	Fighting	Physical	40	100	20	Normal
TM100	Confide	Normal	Status	—	—	20	Normal
HM01	Cut	Normal	Physical	50	95	30	Normal
HM03	Surf	Water	Special	90	100	15	Adjacent
HM04	Strength	Normal	Physical	80	100	15	Normal
HM06	Rock Smash	Fighting	Physical	40	100	15	Normal

MOVES LEARNED IN EXCHANGE FOR BP

Name	Type	Kind	Pow.	Acc.	PP	Range
Super Fang	Normal	Physical	—	90	10	Normal
Iron Head	Steel	Physical	80	100	15	Normal
Bounce	Flying	Physical	85	85	5	Normal
Low Kick	Fighting	Physical	—	100	20	Normal
Gunk Shot	Poison	Physical	120	80	5	Normal
Uproar	Normal	Special	90	100	10	1 Random
Thunder Punch	Electric	Physical	75	100	15	Normal
Fire Punch	Fire	Physical	75	100	15	Normal
Ice Punch	Ice	Physical	75	100	15	Normal
Earth Power	Ground	Special	90	100	10	Normal
Foul Play	Dark	Physical	95	100	15	Normal
Last Resort	Normal	Physical	140	100	5	Normal
Superpower	Fighting	Physical	120	100	5	Normal
Iron Tail	Steel	Physical	100	75	15	Normal
Snore	Normal	Special	50	100	15	Normal
Knock Off	Dark	Physical	65	100	20	Normal
Focus Punch	Fighting	Physical	150	100	20	Normal
Gastro Acid	Poison	Status	—	100	10	Normal
Endeavor	Normal	Physical	—	100	5	Normal
Recycle	Normal	Status	—	—	10	Self
Snatch	Dark	Status	—	—	10	Self

MOVES TAUGHT BY PEOPLE

Name	Type	Kind	Pow.	Acc.	PP	Range

National Pokédex **661** Hoenn Pokédex –

Fletchling

Tiny Robin Pokémon

Normal | Flying

HEIGHT: 1'00" WEIGHT: 3.7 lbs.

Same form for ♂ / ♀

Ω These friendly Pokémon send signals to one another with beautiful chirps and tail-feather movements.

α Despite the beauty of its lilting voice, it's merciless to intruders that enter its territory.

ABILITY
Big Pecks

HIDDEN ABILITY
Gale Wings

EGG GROUPS
Flying

STAT GROWTH RATES

HP	■■
Attack	■■■
Defense	■■
Sp. Atk	■■
Sp. Def	■■
Speed	■■■

ITEMS SOMETIMES HELD BY WILD POKÉMON
—

EVOLUTION

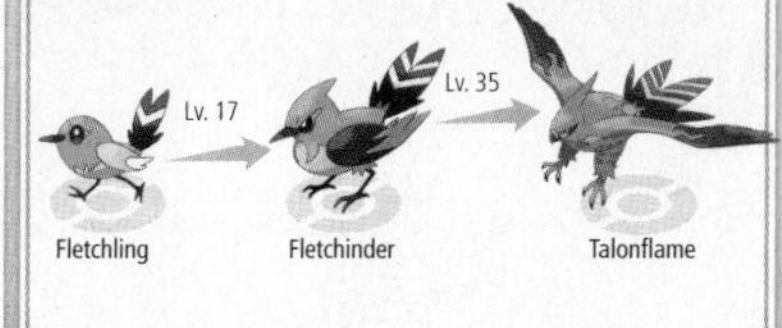

MAIN WAY TO REGISTER IN THE NATIONAL POKÉDEX

Appears in *Pokémon X* and *Pokémon Y*. Bring it to your game using Link Trade or the GTS.

Damage taken in normal battles

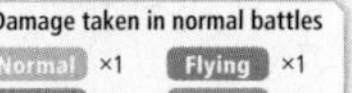

Type		Type	
Normal	×1	Flying	×1
Fire	×1	Psychic	×1
Water	×1	Bug	×0.5
Grass	×0.5	Rock	×2
Electric	×2	Ghost	×0
Ice	×2	Dragon	×1
Fighting	×1	Dark	×1
Poison	×1	Steel	×1
Ground	×0	Fairy	×1

Damage taken in Inverse battles

Type		Type	
Normal	×1	Flying	×1
Fire	×1	Psychic	×1
Water	×1	Bug	×2
Grass	×2	Rock	×0.5
Electric	×0.5	Ghost	×2
Ice	×0.5	Dragon	×1
Fighting	×1	Dark	×1
Poison	×1	Steel	×1
Ground	×2	Fairy	×1

Can be used in
- Inverse Battle
- Battle Institute
- Battle Maison
- Random Matchup (Free Battle)
- Random Matchup (Others)

LEVEL-UP MOVES

Lv.	Name	Type	Kind	Pow.	Acc.	PP	Range
1	Tackle	Normal	Physical	50	100	35	Normal
1	Growl	Normal	Status	—	100	40	Many Others
6	Quick Attack	Normal	Physical	40	100	30	Normal
10	Peck	Flying	Physical	35	100	35	Normal
13	Agility	Psychic	Status	—	—	30	Self
16	Flail	Normal	Physical	—	100	15	Normal
21	Roost	Flying	Status	—	—	10	Self
25	Razor Wind	Normal	Special	80	100	10	Many Others
29	Natural Gift	Normal	Physical	—	100	15	Normal
34	Flame Charge	Fire	Physical	50	100	20	Normal
39	Acrobatics	Flying	Physical	55	100	15	Normal
41	Me First	Normal	Status	—	—	20	Varies
45	Tailwind	Flying	Status	—	—	15	Your Side
48	Steel Wing	Steel	Physical	70	90	25	Normal

TM & HM MOVES

No.	Name	Type	Kind	Pow.	Acc.	PP	Range
TM06	Toxic	Poison	Status	—	90	10	Normal
TM10	Hidden Power	Normal	Special	60	100	15	Normal
TM11	Sunny Day	Fire	Status	—	—	5	Both Sides
TM12	Taunt	Dark	Status	—	100	20	Normal
TM17	Protect	Normal	Status	—	—	10	Self
TM19	Roost	Flying	Status	—	—	10	Self
TM21	Frustration	Normal	Physical	—	100	20	Normal
TM27	Return	Normal	Physical	—	100	20	Normal
TM32	Double Team	Normal	Status	—	—	15	Self
TM40	Aerial Ace	Flying	Physical	60	—	20	Normal
TM42	Facade	Normal	Physical	70	100	20	Normal
TM43	Flame Charge	Fire	Physical	50	100	20	Normal
TM44	Rest	Psychic	Status	—	—	10	Self
TM45	Attract	Normal	Status	—	100	15	Normal
TM46	Thief	Dark	Physical	60	100	25	Normal
TM48	Round	Normal	Special	60	100	15	Normal
TM50	Overheat	Fire	Special	130	90	5	Normal
TM51	Steel Wing	Steel	Physical	70	90	25	Normal
TM62	Acrobatics	Flying	Physical	55	100	15	Normal
TM75	Swords Dance	Normal	Status	—	—	20	Self
TM87	Swagger	Normal	Status	—	90	15	Normal
TM88	Sleep Talk	Normal	Status	—	—	10	Self
TM89	U-turn	Bug	Physical	70	100	20	Normal
TM90	Substitute	Normal	Status	—	—	10	Self
TM94	Secret Power	Normal	Physical	70	100	20	Normal
TM100	Confide	Normal	Status	—	—	20	Normal
HM02	Fly	Flying	Physical	90	95	15	Normal

MOVES LEARNED IN EXCHANGE FOR BP

Name	Type	Kind	Pow.	Acc.	PP	Range
Snore	Normal	Special	50	100	15	Normal
Heat Wave	Fire	Special	95	90	10	Many Others
Tailwind	Flying	Status	—	—	15	Your Side
Snatch	Dark	Status	—	—	10	Self

MOVES TAUGHT BY PEOPLE

Name	Type	Kind	Pow.	Acc.	PP	Range

EGG MOVES

Name	Type	Kind	Pow.	Acc.	PP	Range
Tailwind	Flying	Status	—	—	15	Your Side
Snatch	Dark	Status	—	—	10	Self
Quick Guard	Fighting	Status	—	—	15	Your Side

National Pokédex **662** Hoenn Pokédex –

Fletchinder

Ember Pokémon

Fire | Flying

HEIGHT: 2'04" WEIGHT: 35.3 lbs.

Same form for ♂ / ♀

Ω From its beak, it expels embers that set the tall grass on fire. Then it pounces on the bewildered prey that pop out of the grass.

α The hotter the flame sac on its belly, the faster it can fly, but it takes some time to get the fire going.

ABILITY
Flame Body

HIDDEN ABILITY
Gale Wings

EGG GROUPS
Flying

STAT GROWTH RATES

HP	■■■
Attack	■■■■
Defense	■■■
Sp. Atk	■■■
Sp. Def	■■
Speed	■■■■■

ITEMS SOMETIMES HELD BY WILD POKÉMON
—

EVOLUTION

Lv. 17
Lv. 35
Fletchling
Fletchinder
Talonflame

MAIN WAY TO REGISTER IN THE NATIONAL POKÉDEX

Level up a Fletchling obtained via Link Trade or the GTS to Lv. 17.

Damage taken in normal battles

Type		Type	
Normal	×1	Flying	×1
Fire	×0.5	Psychic	×1
Water	×2	Bug	×0.25
Grass	×0.25	Rock	×4
Electric	×2	Ghost	×1
Ice	×1	Dragon	×1
Fighting	×0.5	Dark	×1
Poison	×1	Steel	×0.5
Ground	×0	Fairy	×0.5

Damage taken in Inverse battles

Type		Type	
Normal	×1	Flying	×1
Fire	×2	Psychic	×1
Water	×0.5	Bug	×4
Grass	×4	Rock	×0.25
Electric	×0.5	Ghost	×1
Ice	×1	Dragon	×1
Fighting	×2	Dark	×1
Poison	×1	Steel	×2
Ground	×1	Fairy	×2

Can be used in
- Inverse Battle
- Battle Institute
- Battle Maison
- Random Matchup (Free Battle)
- Random Matchup (Others)

LEVEL-UP MOVES

Lv.	Name	Type	Kind	Pow.	Acc.	PP	Range
1	Tackle	Normal	Physical	50	100	35	Normal
1	Growl	Normal	Status	—	100	40	Many Others
6	Quick Attack	Normal	Physical	40	100	30	Normal
10	Peck	Flying	Physical	35	100	35	Normal
13	Agility	Psychic	Status	—	—	30	Self
16	Flail	Normal	Physical	—	100	15	Normal
17	Ember	Fire	Special	40	100	25	Normal
25	Roost	Flying	Status	—	—	10	Self
27	Razor Wind	Normal	Special	80	100	10	Many Others
31	Natural Gift	Normal	Physical	—	100	15	Normal
38	Flame Charge	Fire	Physical	50	100	20	Normal
42	Acrobatics	Flying	Physical	55	100	15	Normal
46	Me First	Normal	Status	—	—	20	Varies
51	Tailwind	Flying	Status	—	—	15	Your Side
55	Steel Wing	Steel	Physical	70	90	25	Normal

TM & HM MOVES

No.	Name	Type	Kind	Pow.	Acc.	PP	Range
TM06	Toxic	Poison	Status	—	90	10	Normal
TM10	Hidden Power	Normal	Special	60	100	15	Normal
TM11	Sunny Day	Fire	Status	—	—	5	Both Sides
TM12	Taunt	Dark	Status	—	100	20	Normal
TM17	Protect	Normal	Status	—	—	10	Self
TM19	Roost	Flying	Status	—	—	10	Self
TM21	Frustration	Normal	Physical	—	100	20	Normal
TM27	Return	Normal	Physical	—	100	20	Normal
TM32	Double Team	Normal	Status	—	—	15	Self
TM35	Flamethrower	Fire	Special	90	100	15	Normal
TM38	Fire Blast	Fire	Special	110	85	5	Normal
TM40	Aerial Ace	Flying	Physical	60	—	20	Normal
TM42	Facade	Normal	Physical	70	100	20	Normal
TM43	Flame Charge	Fire	Physical	50	100	20	Normal
TM44	Rest	Psychic	Status	—	—	10	Self
TM45	Attract	Normal	Status	—	100	15	Normal
TM46	Thief	Dark	Physical	60	100	25	Normal
TM48	Round	Normal	Special	60	100	15	Normal
TM50	Overheat	Fire	Special	130	90	5	Normal
TM51	Steel Wing	Steel	Physical	70	90	25	Normal
TM59	Incinerate	Fire	Special	60	100	15	Many Others
TM61	Will-O-Wisp	Fire	Status	—	85	15	Normal
TM62	Acrobatics	Flying	Physical	55	100	15	Normal
TM75	Swords Dance	Normal	Status	—	—	20	Self
TM87	Swagger	Normal	Status	—	90	15	Normal
TM88	Sleep Talk	Normal	Status	—	—	10	Self
TM89	U-turn	Bug	Physical	70	100	20	Normal
TM90	Substitute	Normal	Status	—	—	10	Self
TM94	Secret Power	Normal	Physical	70	100	20	Normal
TM100	Confide	Normal	Status	—	—	20	Normal
HM02	Fly	Flying	Physical	90	95	15	Normal

MOVES LEARNED IN EXCHANGE FOR BP

Name	Type	Kind	Pow.	Acc.	PP	Range
Snore	Normal	Special	50	100	15	Normal
Heat Wave	Fire	Special	95	90	10	Many Others
Tailwind	Flying	Status	—	—	15	Your Side
Snatch	Dark	Status	—	—	10	Self

MOVES TAUGHT BY PEOPLE

Name	Type	Kind	Pow.	Acc.	PP	Range

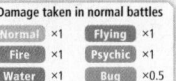

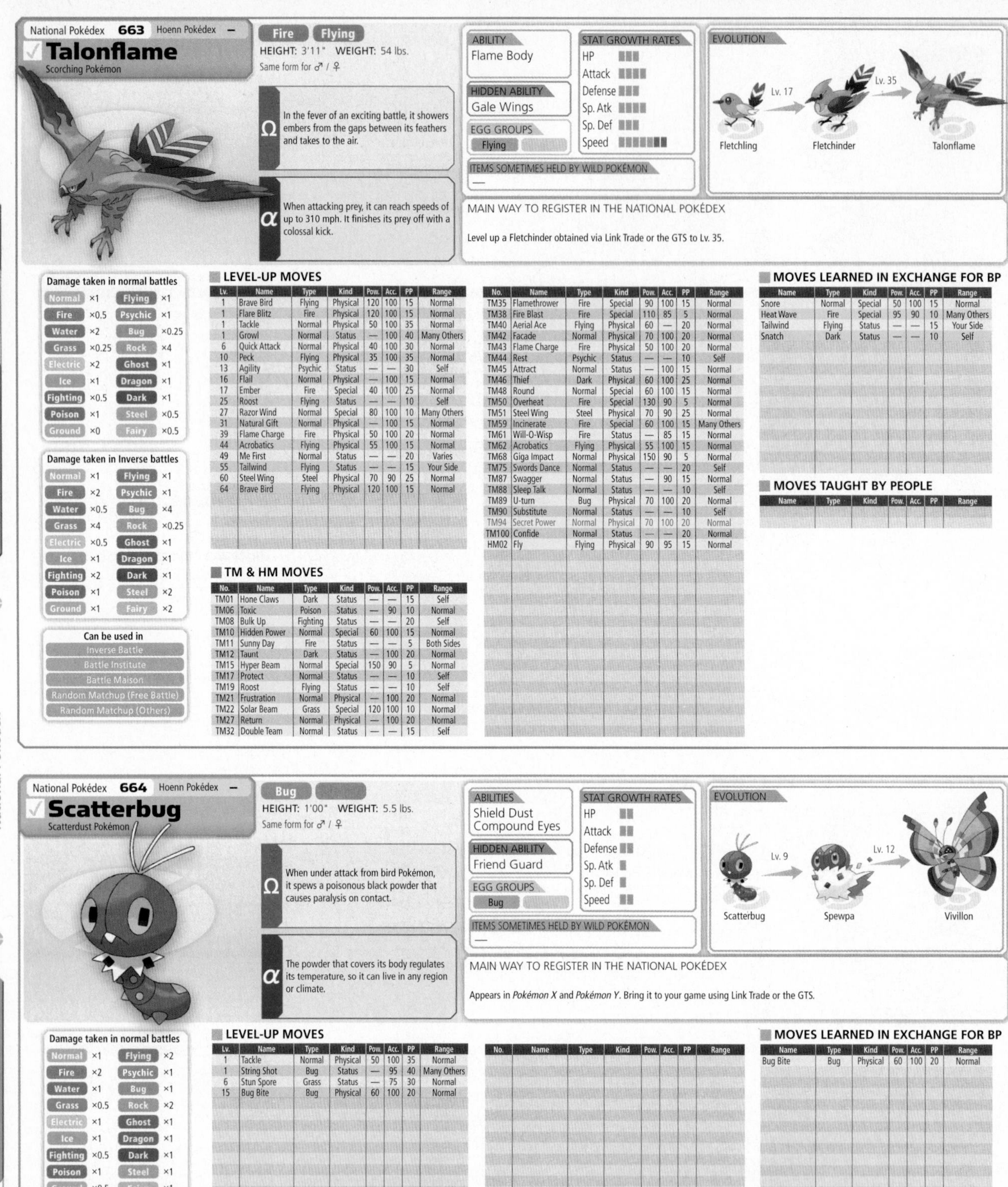

National Pokédex **663** Hoenn Pokédex —

Talonflame

Scorching Pokémon

Fire | Flying

HEIGHT: 3'11" WEIGHT: 54 lbs.

Same form for ♂ / ♀

Ω In the fever of an exciting battle, it showers embers from the gaps between its feathers and takes to the air.

α When attacking prey, it can reach speeds of up to 310 mph. It finishes its prey off with a colossal kick.

ABILITY
Flame Body

HIDDEN ABILITY
Gale Wings

EGG GROUPS
Flying

STAT GROWTH RATES
HP
Attack
Defense
Sp. Atk
Sp. Def
Speed

ITEMS SOMETIMES HELD BY WILD POKÉMON
—

EVOLUTION
Fletchling → Lv. 17 → Fletchinder → Lv. 35 → Talonflame

MAIN WAY TO REGISTER IN THE NATIONAL POKÉDEX

Level up a Fletchinder obtained via Link Trade or the GTS to Lv. 35.

Damage taken in normal battles

Type		Type	
Normal	×1	Flying	×1
Fire	×0.5	Psychic	×1
Water	×2	Bug	×0.25
Grass	×0.25	Rock	×4
Electric	×2	Ghost	×1
Ice	×1	Dragon	×1
Fighting	×0.5	Dark	×1
Poison	×1	Steel	×0.5
Ground	×0	Fairy	×0.5

Damage taken in Inverse battles

Type		Type	
Normal	×1	Flying	×1
Fire	×2	Psychic	×1
Water	×0.5	Bug	×4
Grass	×4	Rock	×0.25
Electric	×0.5	Ghost	×1
Ice	×1	Dragon	×1
Fighting	×2	Dark	×1
Poison	×1	Steel	×2
Ground	×1	Fairy	×2

Can be used in

Inverse Battle
Battle Institute
Battle Maison
Random Matchup (Free Battle)
Random Matchup (Others)

LEVEL-UP MOVES

Lv.	Name	Type	Kind	Pow.	Acc.	PP	Range
1	Brave Bird	Flying	Physical	120	100	15	Normal
1	Flare Blitz	Fire	Physical	120	100	15	Normal
1	Tackle	Normal	Physical	50	100	35	Normal
1	Growl	Normal	Status	—	100	40	Many Others
6	Quick Attack	Normal	Physical	40	100	30	Normal
10	Peck	Flying	Physical	35	100	35	Normal
13	Agility	Psychic	Status	—	—	30	Self
16	Flail	Normal	Physical	—	100	15	Normal
17	Ember	Fire	Special	40	100	25	Normal
25	Roost	Flying	Status	—	—	10	Self
27	Razor Wind	Normal	Special	80	100	10	Many Others
31	Natural Gift	Normal	Physical	—	100	15	Normal
39	Flame Charge	Fire	Physical	50	100	20	Normal
44	Acrobatics	Flying	Physical	55	100	15	Normal
49	Me First	Normal	Status	—	—	20	Varies
55	Tailwind	Flying	Status	—	—	15	Your Side
60	Steel Wing	Steel	Physical	70	90	25	Normal
64	Brave Bird	Flying	Physical	120	100	15	Normal

TM & HM MOVES

No.	Name	Type	Kind	Pow.	Acc.	PP	Range
TM01	Hone Claws	Dark	Status	—	—	15	Self
TM06	Toxic	Poison	Status	—	90	10	Normal
TM08	Bulk Up	Fighting	Status	—	—	20	Self
TM10	Hidden Power	Normal	Special	60	100	15	Normal
TM11	Sunny Day	Fire	Status	—	—	5	Both Sides
TM12	Taunt	Dark	Status	—	100	20	Normal
TM15	Hyper Beam	Normal	Special	150	90	5	Normal
TM17	Protect	Normal	Status	—	—	10	Self
TM19	Roost	Flying	Status	—	—	10	Self
TM21	Frustration	Normal	Physical	—	100	20	Normal
TM22	Solar Beam	Grass	Special	120	100	10	Normal
TM27	Return	Normal	Physical	—	100	20	Normal
TM32	Double Team	Normal	Status	—	—	15	Self
TM35	Flamethrower	Fire	Special	90	100	15	Normal
TM38	Fire Blast	Fire	Special	110	85	5	Normal
TM40	Aerial Ace	Flying	Physical	60	—	20	Normal
TM42	Facade	Normal	Physical	70	100	20	Normal
TM43	Flame Charge	Fire	Physical	50	100	20	Normal
TM44	Rest	Psychic	Status	—	—	10	Self
TM45	Attract	Normal	Status	—	100	15	Normal
TM46	Thief	Dark	Physical	60	100	25	Normal
TM48	Round	Normal	Special	60	100	15	Normal
TM50	Overheat	Fire	Special	130	90	5	Normal
TM51	Steel Wing	Steel	Physical	70	90	25	Normal
TM59	Incinerate	Fire	Special	60	100	15	Many Others
TM61	Will-O-Wisp	Fire	Status	—	85	15	Normal
TM62	Acrobatics	Flying	Physical	55	100	15	Normal
TM68	Giga Impact	Normal	Physical	150	90	5	Normal
TM75	Swords Dance	Normal	Status	—	—	20	Self
TM87	Swagger	Normal	Status	—	90	15	Normal
TM88	Sleep Talk	Normal	Status	—	—	10	Self
TM89	U-turn	Bug	Physical	70	100	20	Normal
TM90	Substitute	Normal	Status	—	—	10	Self
TM94	Secret Power	Normal	Physical	70	100	20	Normal
TM100	Confide	Normal	Status	—	—	20	Normal
HM02	Fly	Flying	Physical	90	95	15	Normal

MOVES LEARNED IN EXCHANGE FOR BP

Name	Type	Kind	Pow.	Acc.	PP	Range
Snore	Normal	Special	50	100	15	Normal
Heat Wave	Fire	Special	95	90	10	Many Others
Tailwind	Flying	Status	—	—	15	Your Side
Snatch	Dark	Status	—	—	10	Self

MOVES TAUGHT BY PEOPLE

Name	Type	Kind	Pow.	Acc.	PP	Range

National Pokédex **664** Hoenn Pokédex —

Scatterbug

Scatterdust Pokémon

Bug

HEIGHT: 1'00" WEIGHT: 5.5 lbs.

Same form for ♂ / ♀

Ω When under attack from bird Pokémon, it spews a poisonous black powder that causes paralysis on contact.

α The powder that covers its body regulates its temperature, so it can live in any region or climate.

ABILITIES
Shield Dust
Compound Eyes

HIDDEN ABILITY
Friend Guard

EGG GROUPS
Bug

STAT GROWTH RATES
HP
Attack
Defense
Sp. Atk
Sp. Def
Speed

ITEMS SOMETIMES HELD BY WILD POKÉMON
—

EVOLUTION
Scatterbug → Lv. 9 → Spewpa → Lv. 12 → Vivillon

MAIN WAY TO REGISTER IN THE NATIONAL POKÉDEX

Appears in *Pokémon X* and *Pokémon Y*. Bring it to your game using Link Trade or the GTS.

Damage taken in normal battles

Type		Type	
Normal	×1	Flying	×2
Fire	×2	Psychic	×1
Water	×1	Bug	×1
Grass	×0.5	Rock	×2
Electric	×1	Ghost	×1
Ice	×1	Dragon	×1
Fighting	×0.5	Dark	×1
Poison	×1	Steel	×1
Ground	×0.5	Fairy	×1

Damage taken in Inverse battles

Type		Type	
Normal	×1	Flying	×0.5
Fire	×0.5	Psychic	×1
Water	×1	Bug	×1
Grass	×2	Rock	×0.5
Electric	×1	Ghost	×1
Ice	×1	Dragon	×1
Fighting	×2	Dark	×1
Poison	×1	Steel	×1
Ground	×2	Fairy	×1

Can be used in

Inverse Battle
Battle Institute
Battle Maison
Random Matchup (Free Battle)
Random Matchup (Others)

LEVEL-UP MOVES

Lv.	Name	Type	Kind	Pow.	Acc.	PP	Range
1	Tackle	Normal	Physical	50	100	35	Normal
1	String Shot	Bug	Status	—	95	40	Many Others
6	Stun Spore	Grass	Status	—	75	30	Normal
15	Bug Bite	Bug	Physical	60	100	20	Normal

TM & HM MOVES

No.	Name	Type	Kind	Pow.	Acc.	PP	Range

MOVES LEARNED IN EXCHANGE FOR BP

Name	Type	Kind	Pow.	Acc.	PP	Range
Bug Bite	Bug	Physical	60	100	20	Normal

MOVES TAUGHT BY PEOPLE

Name	Type	Kind	Pow.	Acc.	PP	Range

EGG MOVES

Name	Type	Kind	Pow.	Acc.	PP	Range
Stun Spore	Grass	Status	—	75	30	Normal
Poison Powder	Poison	Status	—	75	35	Normal
Rage Powder	Bug	Status	—	—	20	Self

National Pokédex **665** Hoenn Pokédex —

Spewpa

Scatterdust Pokémon

Bug

HEIGHT: 1'00" WEIGHT: 18.5 lbs.

Same form for ♂ / ♀

Ω It lives hidden within thicket shadows. When predators attack, it quickly bristles the fur covering its body in an effort to threaten them.

α The beaks of bird Pokémon can't begin to scratch its stalwart body. To defend itself, it spews powder.

ABILITY
Shed Skin

HIDDEN ABILITY
Friend Guard

EGG GROUPS
Bug

STAT GROWTH RATES
HP ■■
Attack ■
Defense ■■■
Sp. Atk ■
Sp. Def ■
Speed ■■

ITEMS SOMETIMES HELD BY WILD POKÉMON
—

EVOLUTION

Scatterbug → Lv. 9 → Spewpa → Lv. 12 → Vivillon

MAIN WAY TO REGISTER IN THE NATIONAL POKÉDEX

Level up a Scatterbug obtained via Link Trade or the GTS to Lv. 9.

Damage taken in normal battles

Type		Type	
Normal	×1	Flying	×2
Fire	×2	Psychic	×1
Water	×1	Bug	×1
Grass	×0.5	Rock	×2
Electric	×1	Ghost	×1
Ice	×1	Dragon	×1
Fighting	×0.5	Dark	×1
Poison	×1	Steel	×1
Ground	×0.5	Fairy	×1

Damage taken in Inverse battles

Type		Type	
Normal	×1	Flying	×0.5
Fire	×0.5	Psychic	×1
Water	×1	Bug	×1
Grass	×2	Rock	×0.5
Electric	×1	Ghost	×1
Ice	×1	Dragon	×1
Fighting	×2	Dark	×1
Poison	×1	Steel	×1
Ground	×2	Fairy	×1

Can be used in
Inverse Battle
Battle Institute
Battle Maison
Random Matchup (Free Battle)
Random Matchup (Others)

LEVEL-UP MOVES

Lv.	Name	Type	Kind	Pow.	Acc.	PP	Range
1	Harden	Normal	Status	—	—	30	Self
9	Protect	Normal	Status	—	—	10	Self

TM & HM MOVES

No.	Name	Type	Kind	Pow.	Acc.	PP	Range
TM17	Protect	Normal	Status	—	—	10	Self

MOVES LEARNED IN EXCHANGE FOR BP

Name	Type	Kind	Pow.	Acc.	PP	Range
Bug Bite	Bug	Physical	60	100	20	Normal
Iron Defense	Steel	Status	—	—	15	Self
Electroweb	Electric	Special	55	95	15	Many Others

MOVES TAUGHT BY PEOPLE

Name	Type	Kind	Pow.	Acc.	PP	Range

National Pokédex **666** Hoenn Pokédex —

Vivillon

Scale Pokémon

Bug Flying

HEIGHT: 3'11" WEIGHT: 37.5 lbs.

Same form for ♂ / ♀

Ω Vivillon with many different patterns are found all over the world. These patterns are affected by the climate of their habitat.

α The patterns on this Pokémon's wings depend on the climate and topography of its habitat. It scatters colorful scales.

ABILITIES
Shield Dust
Compound Eyes

HIDDEN ABILITY
Friend Guard

EGG GROUPS
Bug

STAT GROWTH RATES
HP ■■■
Attack ■■■
Defense ■■
Sp. Atk ■■■■
Sp. Def ■■
Speed ■■■■■

ITEMS SOMETIMES HELD BY WILD POKÉMON
—

EVOLUTION

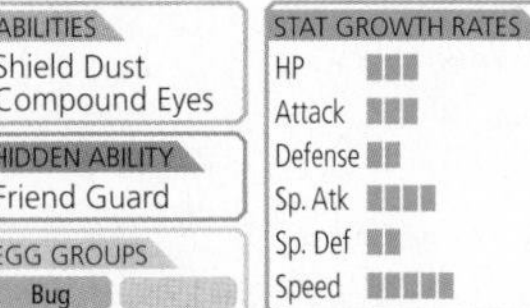

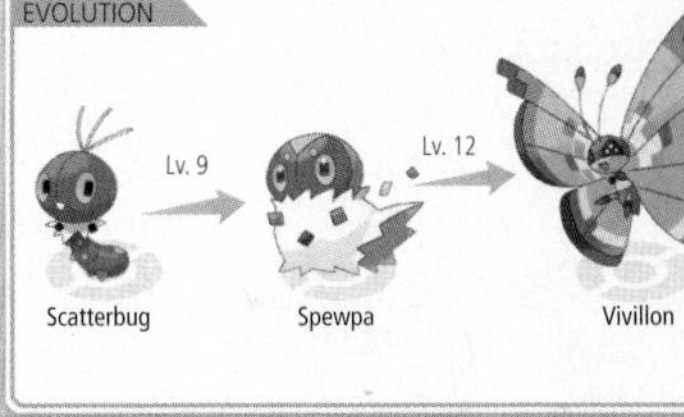

Scatterbug → Lv. 9 → Spewpa → Lv. 12 → Vivillon

MAIN WAY TO REGISTER IN THE NATIONAL POKÉDEX

Level up a Spewpa obtained via Link Trade or the GTS to Lv. 12.

Damage taken in normal battles

Type		Type	
Normal	×1	Flying	×2
Fire	×2	Psychic	×1
Water	×1	Bug	×0.5
Grass	×0.25	Rock	×4
Electric	×2	Ghost	×1
Ice	×2	Dragon	×1
Fighting	×0.25	Dark	×1
Poison	×1	Steel	×1
Ground	×0	Fairy	×1

Damage taken in Inverse battles

Type		Type	
Normal	×1	Flying	×0.5
Fire	×0.5	Psychic	×1
Water	×1	Bug	×2
Grass	×4	Rock	×0.25
Electric	×0.5	Ghost	×1
Ice	×0.5	Dragon	×1
Fighting	×4	Dark	×1
Poison	×1	Steel	×1
Ground	×4	Fairy	×1

Can be used in
Inverse Battle
Battle Institute
Battle Maison
Random Matchup (Free Battle)
Random Matchup (Others)

LEVEL-UP MOVES

Lv.	Name	Type	Kind	Pow.	Acc.	PP	Range
1	Powder	Bug	Status	—	100	20	Normal
1	Sleep Powder	Grass	Status	—	75	15	Normal
1	Poison Powder	Poison	Status	—	75	35	Normal
1	Stun Spore	Grass	Status	—	75	30	Normal
1	Gust	Flying	Special	40	100	35	Normal
1	Light Screen	Psychic	Status	—	—	30	Your Side
12	Struggle Bug	Bug	Special	50	100	20	Many Others
17	Psybeam	Psychic	Special	65	100	20	Normal
21	Supersonic	Normal	Status	—	55	20	Normal
25	Draining Kiss	Fairy	Special	50	100	10	Normal
31	Aromatherapy	Grass	Status	—	—	5	Your Party
35	Bug Buzz	Bug	Special	90	100	10	Normal
41	Safeguard	Normal	Status	—	—	25	Your Side
45	Quiver Dance	Bug	Status	—	—	20	Self
50	Hurricane	Flying	Special	110	70	10	Normal
55	Powder	Bug	Status	—	100	20	Normal

TM & HM MOVES

No.	Name	Type	Kind	Pow.	Acc.	PP	Range
TM04	Calm Mind	Psychic	Status	—	—	20	Self
TM06	Toxic	Poison	Status	—	90	10	Normal
TM10	Hidden Power	Normal	Special	60	100	15	Normal
TM11	Sunny Day	Fire	Status	—	—	5	Both Sides
TM15	Hyper Beam	Normal	Special	150	90	5	Normal
TM16	Light Screen	Psychic	Status	—	—	30	Your Side
TM17	Protect	Normal	Status	—	—	10	Self
TM18	Rain Dance	Water	Status	—	—	5	Both Sides
TM19	Roost	Flying	Status	—	—	10	Self
TM20	Safeguard	Normal	Status	—	—	25	Your Side
TM21	Frustration	Normal	Physical	—	100	20	Normal
TM22	Solar Beam	Grass	Special	120	100	10	Normal
TM27	Return	Normal	Physical	—	100	20	Normal
TM29	Psychic	Psychic	Special	90	100	10	Normal
TM32	Double Team	Normal	Status	—	—	15	Self
TM40	Aerial Ace	Flying	Physical	60	—	20	Normal
TM42	Facade	Normal	Physical	70	100	20	Normal
TM44	Rest	Psychic	Status	—	—	10	Self
TM45	Attract	Normal	Status	—	100	15	Normal
TM46	Thief	Dark	Physical	60	100	25	Normal
TM48	Round	Normal	Special	60	100	15	Normal
TM53	Energy Ball	Grass	Special	90	100	10	Normal
TM62	Acrobatics	Flying	Physical	55	100	15	Normal
TM68	Giga Impact	Normal	Physical	150	90	5	Normal
TM70	Flash	Normal	Status	—	100	20	Normal
TM76	Struggle Bug	Bug	Special	50	100	20	Many Others
TM77	Psych Up	Normal	Status	—	—	10	Normal
TM83	Infestation	Bug	Special	20	100	20	Normal
TM85	Dream Eater	Psychic	Special	100	100	15	Normal
TM87	Swagger	Normal	Status	—	90	15	Normal
TM88	Sleep Talk	Normal	Status	—	—	10	Self
TM89	U-turn	Bug	Physical	70	100	20	Normal
TM90	Substitute	Normal	Status	—	—	10	Self
TM94	Secret Power	Normal	Physical	70	100	20	Normal
TM100	Confide	Normal	Status	—	—	20	Normal

MOVES LEARNED IN EXCHANGE FOR BP

Name	Type	Kind	Pow.	Acc.	PP	Range
Bug Bite	Bug	Physical	60	100	20	Normal
Signal Beam	Bug	Special	75	100	15	Normal
Electroweb	Electric	Special	55	95	15	Many Others
Snore	Normal	Special	50	100	15	Normal
Tailwind	Flying	Status	—	—	15	Your Side
Giga Drain	Grass	Special	75	100	10	Normal
Endeavor	Normal	Physical	—	100	5	Normal

MOVES TAUGHT BY PEOPLE

Name	Type	Kind	Pow.	Acc.	PP	Range

◆ The colors and patterns of Vivillon's wings are different depending on the areas where players playing the game are from.

National Pokédex **667** Hoenn Pokédex —

Litleo

Lion Cub Pokémon

Fire Normal

HEIGHT: 2'00" WEIGHT: 29.8 lbs.

Same form for ♂ / ♀

Ω The stronger the opponent it faces, the more heat surges from its mane and the more power flows through its body.

α They set off on their own from their pride and live by themselves to become stronger. These hot-blooded Pokémon are quick to fight.

ABILITIES
Rivalry
Unnerve

HIDDEN ABILITY
Moxie

EGG GROUPS
Field

STAT GROWTH RATES
HP
Attack
Defense
Sp. Atk
Sp. Def
Speed

ITEMS SOMETIMES HELD BY WILD POKÉMON
—

EVOLUTION
Litleo
Level up Litleo ♂ to Lv. 35 → Pyroar ♂
Level up Litleo ♀ to Lv. 35 → Pyroar ♀

MAIN WAY TO REGISTER IN THE NATIONAL POKÉDEX

Appears in *Pokémon X* and *Pokémon Y*. Bring it to your game using Link Trade or the GTS.

Damage taken in normal battles

Type		Type	
Normal	×1	Flying	×1
Fire	×0.5	Psychic	×1
Water	×2	Bug	×0.5
Grass	×0.5	Rock	×2
Electric	×1	Ghost	×0
Ice	×0.5	Dragon	×1
Fighting	×2	Dark	×1
Poison	×1	Steel	×0.5
Ground	×2	Fairy	×0.5

Damage taken in Inverse battles

Type		Type	
Normal	×1	Flying	×1
Fire	×2	Psychic	×1
Water	×0.5	Bug	×2
Grass	×2	Rock	×0.5
Electric	×1	Ghost	×2
Ice	×2	Dragon	×1
Fighting	×0.5	Dark	×1
Poison	×1	Steel	×2
Ground	×0.5	Fairy	×2

Can be used in
Inverse Battle
Battle Institute
Battle Maison
Random Matchup (Free Battle)
Random Matchup (Others)

LEVEL-UP MOVES

Lv.	Name	Type	Kind	Pow.	Acc.	PP	Range
1	Tackle	Normal	Physical	50	100	35	Normal
1	Leer	Normal	Status	—	100	30	Many Others
5	Ember	Fire	Special	40	100	25	Normal
8	Work Up	Normal	Status	—	—	30	Self
11	Headbutt	Normal	Physical	70	100	15	Normal
15	Noble Roar	Normal	Status	—	100	30	Normal
20	Take Down	Normal	Physical	90	85	20	Normal
23	Fire Fang	Fire	Physical	65	95	15	Normal
28	Endeavor	Normal	Physical	—	100	5	Normal
33	Echoed Voice	Normal	Special	40	100	15	Normal
36	Flamethrower	Fire	Special	90	100	15	Normal
39	Crunch	Dark	Physical	80	100	15	Normal
43	Hyper Voice	Normal	Special	90	100	10	Many Others
46	Incinerate	Fire	Special	60	100	15	Many Others
50	Overheat	Fire	Special	130	90	5	Normal

TM & HM MOVES

No.	Name	Type	Kind	Pow.	Acc.	PP	Range
TM05	Roar	Normal	Status	—	—	20	Normal
TM06	Toxic	Poison	Status	—	90	10	Normal
TM10	Hidden Power	Normal	Special	60	100	15	Normal
TM11	Sunny Day	Fire	Status	—	—	5	Both Sides
TM12	Taunt	Dark	Status	—	100	20	Normal
TM17	Protect	Normal	Status	—	—	10	Self
TM18	Rain Dance	Water	Status	—	—	5	Both Sides
TM21	Frustration	Normal	Physical	—	100	20	Normal
TM22	Solar Beam	Grass	Special	120	100	10	Normal
TM27	Return	Normal	Physical	—	100	20	Normal
TM28	Dig	Ground	Physical	80	100	10	Normal
TM32	Double Team	Normal	Status	—	—	15	Self
TM35	Flamethrower	Fire	Special	90	100	15	Normal
TM38	Fire Blast	Fire	Special	110	85	5	Normal
TM42	Facade	Normal	Physical	70	100	20	Normal
TM43	Flame Charge	Fire	Physical	50	100	20	Normal
TM44	Rest	Psychic	Status	—	—	10	Self
TM45	Attract	Normal	Status	—	100	15	Normal
TM46	Thief	Dark	Physical	60	100	25	Normal
TM48	Round	Normal	Special	60	100	15	Normal
TM49	Echoed Voice	Normal	Special	40	100	15	Normal
TM50	Overheat	Fire	Special	130	90	5	Normal
TM59	Incinerate	Fire	Special	60	100	15	Many Others
TM61	Will-O-Wisp	Fire	Status	—	85	15	Normal
TM66	Payback	Dark	Physical	50	100	10	Normal
TM67	Retaliate	Normal	Physical	70	100	5	Normal
TM78	Bulldoze	Ground	Physical	60	100	20	Adjacent
TM87	Swagger	Normal	Status	—	90	15	Normal
TM88	Sleep Talk	Normal	Status	—	—	10	Self
TM90	Substitute	Normal	Status	—	—	10	Self
TM93	Wild Charge	Electric	Physical	90	100	15	Normal
TM94	Secret Power	Normal	Physical	70	100	20	Normal
TM95	Snarl	Dark	Special	55	95	15	Many Others
TM97	Dark Pulse	Dark	Special	80	100	15	Normal
TM100	Confide	Normal	Status	—	—	20	Normal
HM04	Strength	Normal	Physical	80	100	15	Normal
HM06	Rock Smash	Fighting	Physical	40	100	15	Normal

MOVES LEARNED IN EXCHANGE FOR BP

Name	Type	Kind	Pow.	Acc.	PP	Range
Hyper Voice	Normal	Special	90	100	10	Many Others
Iron Tail	Steel	Physical	100	75	15	Normal
Snore	Normal	Special	50	100	15	Normal
Heat Wave	Fire	Special	95	90	10	Many Others
Helping Hand	Normal	Status	—	—	20	1 Ally
Endeavor	Normal	Physical	—	100	5	Normal
Snatch	Dark	Status	—	—	10	Self

MOVES TAUGHT BY PEOPLE

Name	Type	Kind	Pow.	Acc.	PP	Range

EGG MOVES

Name	Type	Kind	Pow.	Acc.	PP	Range
Entrainment	Normal	Status	—	100	15	Normal
Yawn	Normal	Status	—	—	10	Normal
Snatch	Dark	Status	—	—	10	Self
Fire Spin	Fire	Special	35	85	15	Normal

National Pokédex **668** Hoenn Pokédex —

Pyroar

Royal Pokémon

Fire Normal

HEIGHT: 4'11" WEIGHT: 179.7 lbs.

The male has a mane around its face.
The female has a mane on its head.

Male form Female form

Ω The male with the largest mane of fire is the leader of the pride.

α With fiery breath of more than 10,000 degrees Fahrenheit, they viciously threaten any challenger. The females protect the pride's cubs.

ABILITIES
Rivalry
Unnerve

HIDDEN ABILITY
Moxie

EGG GROUPS
Field

STAT GROWTH RATES
HP
Attack
Defense
Sp. Atk
Sp. Def
Speed

ITEMS SOMETIMES HELD BY WILD POKÉMON
—

EVOLUTION
Litleo
Level up Litleo ♂ to Lv. 35 → Pyroar ♂
Level up Litleo ♀ to Lv. 35 → Pyroar ♀

MAIN WAY TO REGISTER IN THE NATIONAL POKÉDEX

Level up a Litleo obtained via Link Trade or the GTS to Lv. 35.

Damage taken in normal battles

Type		Type	
Normal	×1	Flying	×1
Fire	×0.5	Psychic	×1
Water	×2	Bug	×0.5
Grass	×0.5	Rock	×2
Electric	×1	Ghost	×0
Ice	×0.5	Dragon	×1
Fighting	×2	Dark	×1
Poison	×1	Steel	×0.5
Ground	×2	Fairy	×0.5

Damage taken in Inverse battles

Type		Type	
Normal	×1	Flying	×1
Fire	×2	Psychic	×1
Water	×0.5	Bug	×2
Grass	×2	Rock	×0.5
Electric	×1	Ghost	×2
Ice	×2	Dragon	×1
Fighting	×0.5	Dark	×1
Poison	×1	Steel	×2
Ground	×0.5	Fairy	×2

Can be used in
Inverse Battle
Battle Institute
Battle Maison
Random Matchup (Free Battle)
Random Matchup (Others)

LEVEL-UP MOVES

Lv.	Name	Type	Kind	Pow.	Acc.	PP	Range
1	Hyper Beam	Normal	Special	150	90	5	Normal
1	Tackle	Normal	Physical	50	100	35	Normal
1	Leer	Normal	Status	—	100	30	Many Others
5	Ember	Fire	Special	40	100	25	Normal
8	Work Up	Normal	Status	—	—	30	Self
11	Headbutt	Normal	Physical	70	100	15	Normal
15	Noble Roar	Normal	Status	—	100	30	Normal
20	Take Down	Normal	Physical	90	85	20	Normal
23	Fire Fang	Fire	Physical	65	95	15	Normal
28	Endeavor	Normal	Physical	—	100	5	Normal
33	Echoed Voice	Normal	Special	40	100	15	Normal
38	Flamethrower	Fire	Special	90	100	15	Normal
42	Crunch	Dark	Physical	80	100	15	Normal
48	Hyper Voice	Normal	Special	90	100	10	Many Others
51	Incinerate	Fire	Special	60	100	15	Many Others
57	Overheat	Fire	Special	130	90	5	Normal

TM & HM MOVES

No.	Name	Type	Kind	Pow.	Acc.	PP	Range
TM05	Roar	Normal	Status	—	—	20	Normal
TM06	Toxic	Poison	Status	—	90	10	Normal
TM10	Hidden Power	Normal	Special	60	100	15	Normal
TM11	Sunny Day	Fire	Status	—	—	5	Both Sides
TM12	Taunt	Dark	Status	—	100	20	Normal
TM15	Hyper Beam	Normal	Special	150	90	5	Normal
TM17	Protect	Normal	Status	—	—	10	Self
TM18	Rain Dance	Water	Status	—	—	5	Both Sides
TM21	Frustration	Normal	Physical	—	100	20	Normal
TM22	Solar Beam	Grass	Special	120	100	10	Normal
TM27	Return	Normal	Physical	—	100	20	Normal
TM28	Dig	Ground	Physical	80	100	10	Normal
TM32	Double Team	Normal	Status	—	—	15	Self
TM35	Flamethrower	Fire	Special	90	100	15	Normal
TM38	Fire Blast	Fire	Special	110	85	5	Normal
TM42	Facade	Normal	Physical	70	100	20	Normal
TM43	Flame Charge	Fire	Physical	50	100	20	Normal
TM44	Rest	Psychic	Status	—	—	10	Self
TM45	Attract	Normal	Status	—	100	15	Normal
TM46	Thief	Dark	Physical	60	100	25	Normal
TM48	Round	Normal	Special	60	100	15	Normal
TM49	Echoed Voice	Normal	Special	40	100	15	Normal
TM50	Overheat	Fire	Special	130	90	5	Normal
TM59	Incinerate	Fire	Special	60	100	15	Many Others
TM61	Will-O-Wisp	Fire	Status	—	85	15	Normal
TM66	Payback	Dark	Physical	50	100	10	Normal
TM67	Retaliate	Normal	Physical	70	100	5	Normal
TM68	Giga Impact	Normal	Physical	150	90	5	Normal
TM78	Bulldoze	Ground	Physical	60	100	20	Adjacent
TM87	Swagger	Normal	Status	—	90	15	Normal
TM88	Sleep Talk	Normal	Status	—	—	10	Self
TM90	Substitute	Normal	Status	—	—	10	Self
TM93	Wild Charge	Electric	Physical	90	100	15	Normal
TM94	Secret Power	Normal	Physical	70	100	20	Normal
TM95	Snarl	Dark	Special	55	95	15	Many Others
TM97	Dark Pulse	Dark	Special	80	100	15	Normal
TM100	Confide	Normal	Status	—	—	20	Normal
HM04	Strength	Normal	Physical	80	100	15	Normal
HM06	Rock Smash	Fighting	Physical	40	100	15	Normal

MOVES LEARNED IN EXCHANGE FOR BP

Name	Type	Kind	Pow.	Acc.	PP	Range
Bounce	Flying	Physical	85	85	5	Normal
Hyper Voice	Normal	Special	90	100	10	Many Others
Iron Tail	Steel	Physical	100	75	15	Normal
Snore	Normal	Special	50	100	15	Normal
Heat Wave	Fire	Special	95	90	10	Many Others
Helping Hand	Normal	Status	—	—	20	1 Ally
Endeavor	Normal	Physical	—	100	5	Normal
Snatch	Dark	Status	—	—	10	Self

MOVES TAUGHT BY PEOPLE

Name	Type	Kind	Pow.	Acc.	PP	Range

National Pokédex **669** Hoenn Pokédex —

Flabébé

Single Bloom Pokémon

Fairy

HEIGHT: 0'04" WEIGHT: 0.2 lbs.

♀ only

Ω It draws out and controls the hidden power of flowers. The flower Flabébé holds is most likely part of its body.

α When it finds a flower it likes, it dwells on that flower its whole life long. It floats in the wind's embrace with an untroubled heart.

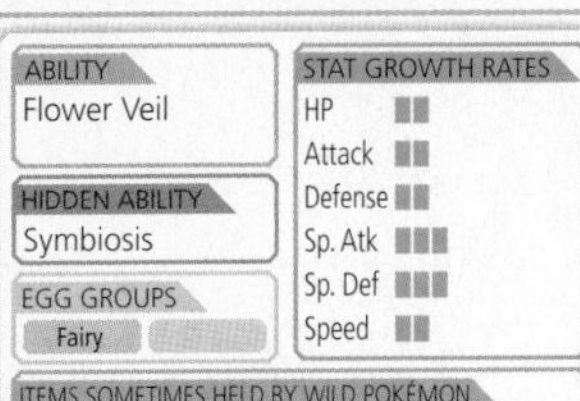

ABILITY: Flower Veil

HIDDEN ABILITY: Symbiosis

EGG GROUPS: Fairy

STAT GROWTH RATES

- HP ■■
- Attack ■■
- Defense ■■
- Sp. Atk ■■■
- Sp. Def ■■■
- Speed ■■

ITEMS SOMETIMES HELD BY WILD POKÉMON: —

EVOLUTION

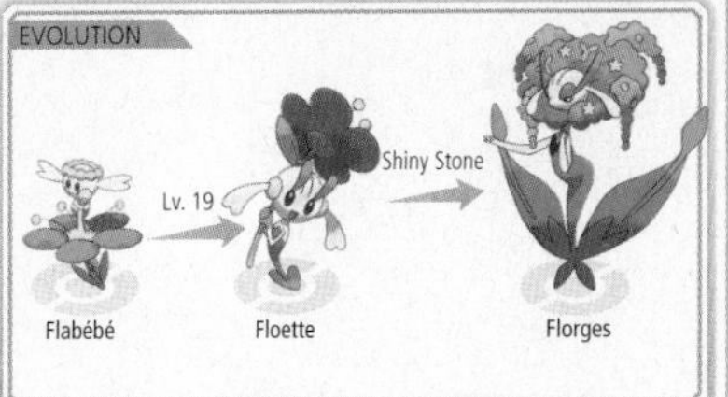

MAIN WAY TO REGISTER IN THE NATIONAL POKÉDEX

Appears in *Pokémon X* and *Pokémon Y*. Bring it to your game using Link Trade or the GTS.

Damage taken in normal battles

Type		Type	
Normal	×1	Flying	×1
Fire	×1	Psychic	×1
Water	×1	Bug	×0.5
Grass	×1	Rock	×1
Electric	×1	Ghost	×1
Ice	×1	Dragon	×0
Fighting	×0.5	Dark	×0.5
Poison	×2	Steel	×2
Ground	×1	Fairy	×1

Damage taken in Inverse battles

Type		Type	
Normal	×1	Flying	×1
Fire	×1	Psychic	×1
Water	×1	Bug	×2
Grass	×1	Rock	×1
Electric	×1	Ghost	×1
Ice	×1	Dragon	×2
Fighting	×2	Dark	×2
Poison	×0.5	Steel	×0.5
Ground	×1	Fairy	×1

Can be used in

- Inverse Battle
- Battle Institute
- Battle Maison
- Random Matchup (Free Battle)
- Random Matchup (Others)

LEVEL-UP MOVES

Lv.	Name	Type	Kind	Pow.	Acc.	PP	Range
1	Tackle	Normal	Physical	50	100	35	Normal
1	Vine Whip	Grass	Physical	45	100	25	Normal
6	Fairy Wind	Fairy	Special	40	100	30	Normal
10	Lucky Chant	Normal	Status	—	—	30	Your Side
15	Razor Leaf	Grass	Physical	55	95	25	Many Others
20	Wish	Normal	Status	—	—	10	Self
22	Magical Leaf	Grass	Special	60	—	20	Normal
24	Grassy Terrain	Grass	Status	—	—	10	Both Sides
28	Petal Blizzard	Grass	Physical	90	100	15	Adjacent
33	Aromatherapy	Grass	Status	—	—	5	Your Party
37	Misty Terrain	Fairy	Status	—	—	10	Both Sides
41	Moonblast	Fairy	Special	95	100	15	Normal
45	Petal Dance	Grass	Special	120	100	10	1 Random
48	Solar Beam	Grass	Special	120	100	10	Normal

TM & HM MOVES

No.	Name	Type	Kind	Pow.	Acc.	PP	Range
TM04	Calm Mind	Psychic	Status	—	—	20	Self
TM06	Toxic	Poison	Status	—	90	10	Normal
TM10	Hidden Power	Normal	Special	60	100	15	Normal
TM11	Sunny Day	Fire	Status	—	—	5	Both Sides
TM17	Protect	Normal	Status	—	—	10	Self
TM18	Rain Dance	Water	Status	—	—	5	Both Sides
TM20	Safeguard	Normal	Status	—	—	25	Your Side
TM21	Frustration	Normal	Physical	—	100	20	Normal
TM22	Solar Beam	Grass	Special	120	100	10	Normal
TM27	Return	Normal	Physical	—	100	20	Normal
TM29	Psychic	Psychic	Special	90	100	10	Normal
TM32	Double Team	Normal	Status	—	—	15	Self
TM42	Facade	Normal	Physical	70	100	20	Normal
TM44	Rest	Psychic	Status	—	—	10	Self
TM45	Attract	Normal	Status	—	100	15	Normal
TM48	Round	Normal	Special	60	100	15	Normal
TM49	Echoed Voice	Normal	Special	40	100	15	Normal
TM53	Energy Ball	Grass	Special	90	100	10	Normal
TM70	Flash	Normal	Status	—	100	20	Normal
TM86	Grass Knot	Grass	Special	—	100	20	Normal
TM87	Swagger	Normal	Status	—	90	15	Normal
TM88	Sleep Talk	Normal	Status	—	—	10	Self
TM90	Substitute	Normal	Status	—	—	10	Self
TM94	Secret Power	Normal	Physical	70	100	20	Normal
TM96	Nature Power	Normal	Status	—	—	20	Normal
TM99	Dazzling Gleam	Fairy	Special	80	100	10	Many Others
TM100	Confide	Normal	Status	—	—	20	Normal

MOVES LEARNED IN EXCHANGE FOR BP

Name	Type	Kind	Pow.	Acc.	PP	Range
Covet	Normal	Physical	60	100	25	Normal
Seed Bomb	Grass	Physical	80	100	15	Normal
Magic Coat	Psychic	Status	—	—	15	Self
Snore	Normal	Special	50	100	15	Normal
Synthesis	Grass	Status	—	—	5	Self
Heal Bell	Normal	Status	—	—	5	Your Party
Giga Drain	Grass	Special	75	100	10	Normal
Worry Seed	Grass	Status	—	100	10	Normal
After You	Normal	Status	—	—	15	Normal
Helping Hand	Normal	Status	—	—	20	1 Ally
Endeavor	Normal	Physical	—	100	5	Normal

MOVES TAUGHT BY PEOPLE

Name	Type	Kind	Pow.	Acc.	PP	Range

EGG MOVES

Name	Type	Kind	Pow.	Acc.	PP	Range
Copycat	Normal	Status	—	—	20	Self
Captivate	Normal	Status	—	100	20	Many Others
Camouflage	Normal	Status	—	—	20	Self

◆ There are five different colors of flowers that Flabébé hold: red, yellow, orange, blue, and white.

National Pokédex **670** Hoenn Pokédex —

Floette

Single Bloom Pokémon

Fairy

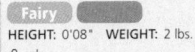

HEIGHT: 0'08" WEIGHT: 2 lbs.

♀ only

Ω It flutters around fields of flowers and cares for flowers that are starting to wilt. It draws out the hidden power of flowers to battle.

α When the flowers of a well-tended flower bed bloom, it appears and celebrates with an elegant dance.

ABILITY: Flower Veil

HIDDEN ABILITY: Symbiosis

EGG GROUPS: Fairy

STAT GROWTH RATES

- HP ■■
- Attack ■■
- Defense ■■
- Sp. Atk ■■■■
- Sp. Def ■■■■
- Speed ■■■

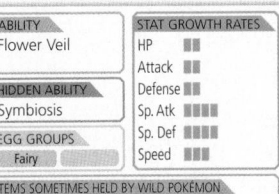

ITEMS SOMETIMES HELD BY WILD POKÉMON: —

EVOLUTION

Flabébé → Lv. 19 → Floette → Shiny Stone → Florges

MAIN WAY TO REGISTER IN THE NATIONAL POKÉDEX

Level up a Flabébé obtained via Link Trade or the GTS to Lv. 19.

Damage taken in normal battles

Type		Type	
Normal	×1	Flying	×1
Fire	×1	Psychic	×1
Water	×1	Bug	×0.5
Grass	×1	Rock	×1
Electric	×1	Ghost	×1
Ice	×1	Dragon	×0
Fighting	×0.5	Dark	×0.5
Poison	×2	Steel	×2
Ground	×1	Fairy	×1

Damage taken in Inverse battles

Type		Type	
Normal	×1	Flying	×1
Fire	×1	Psychic	×1
Water	×1	Bug	×2
Grass	×1	Rock	×1
Electric	×1	Ghost	×1
Ice	×1	Dragon	×2
Fighting	×2	Dark	×2
Poison	×0.5	Steel	×0.5
Ground	×1	Fairy	×1

Can be used in

- Inverse Battle
- Battle Institute
- Battle Maison
- Random Matchup (Free Battle)
- Random Matchup (Others)

LEVEL-UP MOVES

Lv.	Name	Type	Kind	Pow.	Acc.	PP	Range
1	Tackle	Normal	Physical	50	100	35	Normal
1	Vine Whip	Grass	Physical	45	100	25	Normal
6	Fairy Wind	Fairy	Special	40	100	30	Normal
10	Lucky Chant	Normal	Status	—	—	30	Your Side
15	Razor Leaf	Grass	Physical	55	95	25	Many Others
20	Wish	Normal	Status	—	—	10	Self
25	Magical Leaf	Grass	Special	60	—	20	Normal
27	Grassy Terrain	Grass	Status	—	—	10	Both Sides
33	Petal Blizzard	Grass	Physical	90	100	15	Adjacent
38	Aromatherapy	Grass	Status	—	—	5	Your Party
43	Misty Terrain	Fairy	Status	—	—	10	Both Sides
46	Moonblast	Fairy	Special	95	100	15	Normal
51	Petal Dance	Grass	Special	120	100	10	1 Random
58	Solar Beam	Grass	Special	120	100	10	Normal

TM & HM MOVES

No.	Name	Type	Kind	Pow.	Acc.	PP	Range
TM04	Calm Mind	Psychic	Status	—	—	20	Self
TM06	Toxic	Poison	Status	—	90	10	Normal
TM10	Hidden Power	Normal	Special	60	100	15	Normal
TM11	Sunny Day	Fire	Status	—	—	5	Both Sides
TM17	Protect	Normal	Status	—	—	10	Self
TM18	Rain Dance	Water	Status	—	—	5	Both Sides
TM20	Safeguard	Normal	Status	—	—	25	Your Side
TM21	Frustration	Normal	Physical	—	100	20	Normal
TM22	Solar Beam	Grass	Special	120	100	10	Normal
TM27	Return	Normal	Physical	—	100	20	Normal
TM29	Psychic	Psychic	Special	90	100	10	Normal
TM32	Double Team	Normal	Status	—	—	15	Self
TM42	Facade	Normal	Physical	70	100	20	Normal
TM44	Rest	Psychic	Status	—	—	10	Self
TM45	Attract	Normal	Status	—	100	15	Normal
TM48	Round	Normal	Special	60	100	15	Normal
TM49	Echoed Voice	Normal	Special	40	100	15	Normal
TM53	Energy Ball	Grass	Special	90	100	10	Normal
TM70	Flash	Normal	Status	—	100	20	Normal
TM86	Grass Knot	Grass	Special	—	100	20	Normal
TM87	Swagger	Normal	Status	—	90	15	Normal
TM88	Sleep Talk	Normal	Status	—	—	10	Self
TM90	Substitute	Normal	Status	—	—	10	Self
TM94	Secret Power	Normal	Physical	70	100	20	Normal
TM96	Nature Power	Normal	Status	—	—	20	Normal
TM99	Dazzling Gleam	Fairy	Special	80	100	10	Many Others
TM100	Confide	Normal	Status	—	—	20	Normal

MOVES LEARNED IN EXCHANGE FOR BP

Name	Type	Kind	Pow.	Acc.	PP	Range
Covet	Normal	Physical	60	100	25	Normal
Seed Bomb	Grass	Physical	80	100	15	Normal
Magic Coat	Psychic	Status	—	—	15	Self
Snore	Normal	Special	50	100	15	Normal
Synthesis	Grass	Status	—	—	5	Self
Heal Bell	Normal	Status	—	—	5	Your Party
Giga Drain	Grass	Special	75	100	10	Normal
Worry Seed	Grass	Status	—	100	10	Normal
After You	Normal	Status	—	—	15	Normal
Helping Hand	Normal	Status	—	—	20	1 Ally
Endeavor	Normal	Physical	—	100	5	Normal

MOVES TAUGHT BY PEOPLE

Name	Type	Kind	Pow.	Acc.	PP	Range

◆ There are five different colors of flowers that Floette hold: red, yellow, orange, blue, and white.

National Pokédex **671** Hoenn Pokédex —

Florges

Garden Pokémon

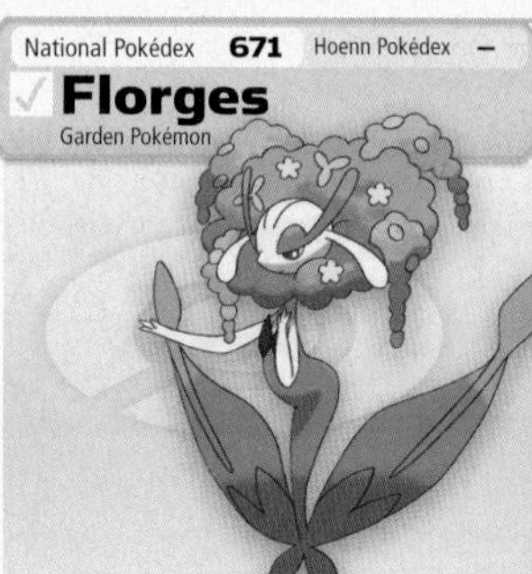

Fairy

HEIGHT: 3'07" WEIGHT: 22 lbs.

♀ only

Ω It claims exquisite flower gardens as its territory, and it obtains power from basking in the energy emitted by flowering plants.

α In times long past, governors of castles would invite Florges to create flower gardens to embellish the castle domains.

ABILITY
Flower Veil

HIDDEN ABILITY
Symbiosis

EGG GROUPS
Fairy

STAT GROWTH RATES
HP ■■■
Attack ■■■
Defense ■■■
Sp. Atk ■■■■■
Sp. Def ■■■■■■
Speed ■■■■

ITEMS SOMETIMES HELD BY WILD POKÉMON
—

EVOLUTION
Flabébé → Lv. 19 → Floette → Shiny Stone → Florges

MAIN WAY TO REGISTER IN THE NATIONAL POKÉDEX

Use a Shiny Stone on a Floette obtained via Link Trade or the GTS.

Damage taken in normal battles

Type		Type	
Normal	×1	Flying	×1
Fire	×1	Psychic	×1
Water	×1	Bug	×0.5
Grass	×1	Rock	×1
Electric	×1	Ghost	×1
Ice	×1	Dragon	×0
Fighting	×0.5	Dark	×0.5
Poison	×2	Steel	×2
Ground	×1	Fairy	×1

Damage taken in Inverse battles

Type		Type	
Normal	×1	Flying	×1
Fire	×1	Psychic	×1
Water	×1	Bug	×2
Grass	×1	Rock	×1
Electric	×1	Ghost	×1
Ice	×1	Dragon	×2
Fighting	×2	Dark	×2
Poison	×0.5	Steel	×0.5
Ground	×1	Fairy	×1

Can be used in
Inverse Battle
Battle Institute
Battle Maison
Random Matchup (Free Battle)
Random Matchup (Others)

LEVEL-UP MOVES

Lv.	Name	Type	Kind	Pow.	Acc.	PP	Range
1	Disarming Voice	Fairy	Special	40	—	15	Many Others
1	Lucky Chant	Normal	Status	—	—	30	Your Side
1	Wish	Normal	Status	—	—	10	Self
1	Magical Leaf	Grass	Special	60	—	20	Normal
1	Flower Shield	Fairy	Status	—	—	10	Adjacent
1	Grass Knot	Grass	Special	—	100	20	Normal
1	Grassy Terrain	Grass	Status	—	—	10	Both Sides
1	Petal Blizzard	Grass	Physical	90	100	15	Adjacent
1	Misty Terrain	Fairy	Status	—	—	10	Both Sides
1	Moonblast	Fairy	Special	95	100	15	Normal
1	Petal Dance	Grass	Special	120	100	10	1 Random
1	Aromatherapy	Grass	Status	—	—	5	Your Party

TM & HM MOVES

No.	Name	Type	Kind	Pow.	Acc.	PP	Range
TM04	Calm Mind	Psychic	Status	—	—	20	Self
TM06	Toxic	Poison	Status	—	90	10	Normal
TM10	Hidden Power	Normal	Special	60	100	15	Normal
TM11	Sunny Day	Fire	Status	—	—	5	Both Sides
TM15	Hyper Beam	Normal	Special	150	90	5	Normal
TM16	Light Screen	Psychic	Status	—	—	30	Your Side
TM17	Protect	Normal	Status	—	—	10	Self
TM18	Rain Dance	Water	Status	—	—	5	Both Sides
TM20	Safeguard	Normal	Status	—	—	25	Your Side
TM21	Frustration	Normal	Physical	—	100	20	Normal
TM22	Solar Beam	Grass	Special	120	100	10	Normal
TM27	Return	Normal	Physical	—	100	20	Normal
TM29	Psychic	Psychic	Special	90	100	10	Normal
TM32	Double Team	Normal	Status	—	—	15	Self
TM42	Facade	Normal	Physical	70	100	20	Normal
TM44	Rest	Psychic	Status	—	—	10	Self
TM45	Attract	Normal	Status	—	100	15	Normal
TM48	Round	Normal	Special	60	100	15	Normal
TM49	Echoed Voice	Normal	Special	40	100	15	Normal
TM53	Energy Ball	Grass	Special	90	100	10	Normal
TM68	Giga Impact	Normal	Physical	150	90	5	Normal
TM70	Flash	Normal	Status	—	100	20	Normal
TM86	Grass Knot	Grass	Special	—	100	20	Normal
TM87	Swagger	Normal	Status	—	90	15	Normal
TM88	Sleep Talk	Normal	Status	—	—	10	Self
TM90	Substitute	Normal	Status	—	—	10	Self
TM94	Secret Power	Normal	Physical	70	100	20	Normal
TM96	Nature Power	Normal	Status	—	—	20	Normal
TM99	Dazzling Gleam	Fairy	Special	80	100	10	Many Others
TM100	Confide	Normal	Status	—	—	20	Normal

MOVES LEARNED IN EXCHANGE FOR BP

Name	Type	Kind	Pow.	Acc.	PP	Range
Covet	Normal	Physical	60	100	25	Normal
Seed Bomb	Grass	Physical	80	100	15	Normal
Magic Coat	Psychic	Status	—	—	15	Self
Snore	Normal	Special	50	100	15	Normal
Synthesis	Grass	Status	—	—	5	Self
Heal Bell	Normal	Status	—	—	5	Your Party
Giga Drain	Grass	Special	75	100	10	Normal
Worry Seed	Grass	Status	—	100	10	Normal
After You	Normal	Status	—	—	15	Normal
Helping Hand	Normal	Status	—	—	20	1 Ally
Endeavor	Normal	Physical	—	100	5	Normal

MOVES TAUGHT BY PEOPLE

Name	Type	Kind	Pow.	Acc.	PP	Range

◆ There are five different colors of flowers that Florges hold: red, yellow, orange, blue, and white.

National Pokédex **672** Hoenn Pokédex —

Skiddo

Mount Pokémon

Grass

HEIGHT: 2'11" WEIGHT: 68.3 lbs.

Same form for ♂ / ♀

Ω Thought to be one of the first Pokémon to live in harmony with humans, it has a placid disposition.

α If it has sunshine and water, it doesn't need to eat, because it can generate energy from the leaves on its back.

ABILITY
Sap Sipper

HIDDEN ABILITY
Grass Pelt

EGG GROUPS
Field

STAT GROWTH RATES
HP ■■■
Attack ■■■
Defense ■■
Sp. Atk ■■■
Sp. Def ■■
Speed ■■■

ITEMS SOMETIMES HELD BY WILD POKÉMON
—

EVOLUTION
Skiddo → Lv. 32 → Gogoat

MAIN WAY TO REGISTER IN THE NATIONAL POKÉDEX

Appears in *Pokémon X* and *Pokémon Y*. Bring it to your game using Link Trade or the GTS.

Damage taken in normal battles

Type		Type	
Normal	×1	Flying	×2
Fire	×2	Psychic	×1
Water	×0.5	Bug	×2
! Grass	×0.5	Rock	×1
Electric	×0.5	Ghost	×1
Ice	×2	Dragon	×1
Fighting	×1	Dark	×1
Poison	×2	Steel	×1
Ground	×0.5	Fairy	×1

Damage taken in Inverse battles

Type		Type	
Normal	×1	Flying	×0.5
Fire	×0.5	Psychic	×1
Water	×2	Bug	×0.5
! Grass	×2	Rock	×1
Electric	×2	Ghost	×1
Ice	×0.5	Dragon	×1
Fighting	×1	Dark	×1
Poison	×0.5	Steel	×1
Ground	×2	Fairy	×1

Can be used in
Inverse Battle
Battle Institute
Battle Maison
Random Matchup (Free Battle)
Random Matchup (Others)

LEVEL-UP MOVES

Lv.	Name	Type	Kind	Pow.	Acc.	PP	Range
1	Tackle	Normal	Physical	50	100	35	Normal
1	Growth	Normal	Status	—	—	20	Self
7	Vine Whip	Grass	Physical	45	100	25	Normal
9	Tail Whip	Normal	Status	—	100	30	Many Others
12	Leech Seed	Grass	Status	—	90	10	Normal
13	Razor Leaf	Grass	Physical	55	95	25	Many Others
16	Worry Seed	Grass	Status	—	100	10	Normal
20	Synthesis	Grass	Status	—	—	5	Self
22	Take Down	Normal	Physical	90	85	20	Normal
26	Bulldoze	Ground	Physical	60	100	20	Adjacent
30	Seed Bomb	Grass	Physical	80	100	15	Normal
34	Bulk Up	Fighting	Status	—	—	20	Self
38	Double-Edge	Normal	Physical	120	100	15	Normal
42	Horn Leech	Grass	Physical	75	100	10	Normal
45	Leaf Blade	Grass	Physical	90	100	15	Normal
50	Milk Drink	Normal	Status	—	—	10	Self

TM & HM MOVES

No.	Name	Type	Kind	Pow.	Acc.	PP	Range
TM05	Roar	Normal	Status	—	—	20	Normal
TM06	Toxic	Poison	Status	—	90	10	Normal
TM08	Bulk Up	Fighting	Status	—	—	20	Self
TM10	Hidden Power	Normal	Special	60	100	15	Normal
TM11	Sunny Day	Fire	Status	—	—	5	Both Sides
TM17	Protect	Normal	Status	—	—	10	Self
TM18	Rain Dance	Water	Status	—	—	5	Both Sides
TM21	Frustration	Normal	Physical	—	100	20	Normal
TM22	Solar Beam	Grass	Special	120	100	10	Normal
TM27	Return	Normal	Physical	—	100	20	Normal
TM28	Dig	Ground	Physical	80	100	10	Normal
TM31	Brick Break	Fighting	Physical	75	100	15	Normal
TM32	Double Team	Normal	Status	—	—	15	Self
TM42	Facade	Normal	Physical	70	100	20	Normal
TM44	Rest	Psychic	Status	—	—	10	Self
TM45	Attract	Normal	Status	—	100	15	Normal
TM48	Round	Normal	Special	60	100	15	Normal
TM53	Energy Ball	Grass	Special	90	100	10	Normal
TM66	Payback	Dark	Physical	50	100	10	Normal
TM67	Retaliate	Normal	Physical	70	100	5	Normal
TM78	Bulldoze	Ground	Physical	60	100	20	Adjacent
TM80	Rock Slide	Rock	Physical	75	90	10	Many Others
TM86	Grass Knot	Grass	Special	—	100	20	Normal
TM87	Swagger	Normal	Status	—	90	15	Normal
TM88	Sleep Talk	Normal	Status	—	—	10	Self
TM90	Substitute	Normal	Status	—	—	10	Self
TM93	Wild Charge	Electric	Physical	90	100	15	Normal
TM94	Secret Power	Normal	Physical	70	100	20	Normal
TM96	Nature Power	Normal	Status	—	—	20	Normal
TM100	Confide	Normal	Status	—	—	20	Normal
HM03	Surf	Water	Special	90	100	15	Adjacent
HM04	Strength	Normal	Physical	80	100	15	Normal
HM06	Rock Smash	Fighting	Physical	40	100	15	Normal

MOVES LEARNED IN EXCHANGE FOR BP

Name	Type	Kind	Pow.	Acc.	PP	Range
Seed Bomb	Grass	Physical	80	100	15	Normal
Zen Headbutt	Psychic	Physical	80	90	15	Normal
Iron Tail	Steel	Physical	100	75	15	Normal
Snore	Normal	Special	50	100	15	Normal
Synthesis	Grass	Status	—	—	5	Self
Giga Drain	Grass	Special	75	100	10	Normal
Worry Seed	Grass	Status	—	100	10	Normal

MOVES TAUGHT BY PEOPLE

Name	Type	Kind	Pow.	Acc.	PP	Range

EGG MOVES

Name	Type	Kind	Pow.	Acc.	PP	Range
Defense Curl	Normal	Status	—	—	40	Self
Rollout	Rock	Physical	30	90	20	Normal
Milk Drink	Normal	Status	—	—	10	Self

National Pokédex **673** Hoenn Pokédex —

Gogoat

Mount Pokémon

Grass

HEIGHT: 5'07" WEIGHT: 200.6 lbs.

Same form for ♂ / ♀

Ω It can tell how its Trainer is feeling by subtle shifts in the grip on its horns. This empathic sense lets them run as if one being.

α They inhabit mountainous regions. The leader of the herd is decided by a battle of clashing horns.

ABILITY
Sap Sipper

HIDDEN ABILITY
Grass Pelt

EGG GROUPS
Field

STAT GROWTH RATES
HP ■■■■■
Attack ■■■■■
Defense ■■■
Sp. Atk ■■■■■
Sp. Def ■■■
Speed ■■■■

ITEMS SOMETIMES HELD BY WILD POKÉMON
—

EVOLUTION
Skiddo → Lv. 32 → Gogoat

MAIN WAY TO REGISTER IN THE NATIONAL POKÉDEX

Level up a Skiddo obtained via Link Trade or the GTS to Lv. 32.

Damage taken in normal battles

Type		Type	
Normal	×1	Flying	×2
Fire	×2	Psychic	×1
Water	×0.5	Bug	×2
Grass	×0.5	Rock	×1
Electric	×0.5	Ghost	×1
Ice	×2	Dragon	×1
Fighting	×1	Dark	×1
Poison	×2	Steel	×1
Ground	×0.5	Fairy	×1

Damage taken in Inverse battles

Type		Type	
Normal	×1	Flying	×0.5
Fire	×0.5	Psychic	×1
Water	×2	Bug	×0.5
Grass	×2	Rock	×1
Electric	×2	Ghost	×1
Ice	×0.5	Dragon	×1
Fighting	×1	Dark	×1
Poison	×0.5	Steel	×1
Ground	×2	Fairy	×1

Can be used in
Inverse Battle
Battle Institute
Battle Maison
Random Matchup (Free Battle)
Random Matchup (Others)

LEVEL-UP MOVES

Lv.	Name	Type	Kind	Pow.	Acc.	PP	Range
1	Aerial Ace	Flying	Physical	60	—	20	Normal
1	Tackle	Normal	Physical	50	100	35	Normal
1	Growth	Normal	Status	—	—	20	Self
7	Vine Whip	Grass	Physical	45	100	25	Normal
9	Tail Whip	Normal	Status	—	100	30	Many Others
12	Leech Seed	Grass	Status	—	90	10	Normal
13	Razor Leaf	Grass	Physical	55	95	25	Many Others
16	Worry Seed	Grass	Status	—	100	10	Normal
20	Synthesis	Grass	Status	—	—	5	Self
22	Take Down	Normal	Physical	90	85	20	Normal
26	Bulldoze	Ground	Physical	60	100	20	Adjacent
30	Seed Bomb	Grass	Physical	80	100	15	Normal
34	Bulk Up	Fighting	Status	—	—	20	Self
40	Double-Edge	Normal	Physical	120	100	15	Normal
47	Horn Leech	Grass	Physical	75	100	10	Normal
55	Leaf Blade	Grass	Physical	90	100	15	Normal
58	Milk Drink	Normal	Status	—	—	10	Self
60	Earthquake	Ground	Physical	100	100	10	Adjacent
65	Aerial Ace	Flying	Physical	60	—	20	Normal

TM & HM MOVES

No.	Name	Type	Kind	Pow.	Acc.	PP	Range
TM05	Roar	Normal	Status	—	—	20	Normal
TM06	Toxic	Poison	Status	—	90	10	Normal
TM08	Bulk Up	Fighting	Status	—	—	20	Self
TM10	Hidden Power	Normal	Special	60	100	15	Normal
TM11	Sunny Day	Fire	Status	—	—	5	Both Sides
TM15	Hyper Beam	Normal	Special	150	90	5	Normal
TM17	Protect	Normal	Status	—	—	10	Self
TM18	Rain Dance	Water	Status	—	—	5	Both Sides
TM21	Frustration	Normal	Physical	—	100	20	Normal
TM22	Solar Beam	Grass	Special	120	100	10	Normal
TM26	Earthquake	Ground	Physical	100	100	10	Adjacent
TM27	Return	Normal	Physical	—	100	20	Normal
TM28	Dig	Ground	Physical	80	100	10	Normal
TM31	Brick Break	Fighting	Physical	75	100	15	Normal
TM32	Double Team	Normal	Status	—	—	15	Self
TM40	Aerial Ace	Flying	Physical	60	—	20	Normal
TM42	Facade	Normal	Physical	70	100	20	Normal
TM44	Rest	Psychic	Status	—	—	10	Self
TM45	Attract	Normal	Status	—	100	15	Normal
TM48	Round	Normal	Special	60	100	15	Normal
TM53	Energy Ball	Grass	Special	90	100	10	Normal
TM66	Payback	Dark	Physical	50	100	10	Normal
TM67	Retaliate	Normal	Physical	70	100	5	Normal
TM68	Giga Impact	Normal	Physical	150	90	5	Normal
TM78	Bulldoze	Ground	Physical	60	100	20	Adjacent
TM80	Rock Slide	Rock	Physical	75	90	10	Many Others
TM86	Grass Knot	Grass	Special	—	100	20	Normal
TM87	Swagger	Normal	Status	—	90	15	Normal
TM88	Sleep Talk	Normal	Status	—	—	10	Self
TM90	Substitute	Normal	Status	—	—	10	Self
TM93	Wild Charge	Electric	Physical	90	100	15	Normal
TM94	Secret Power	Normal	Physical	70	100	20	Normal
TM96	Nature Power	Normal	Status	—	—	20	Normal
TM100	Confide	Normal	Status	—	—	20	Normal
HM03	Surf	Water	Special	90	100	15	Adjacent
HM04	Strength	Normal	Physical	80	100	15	Normal
HM06	Rock Smash	Fighting	Physical	40	100	15	Normal

MOVES LEARNED IN EXCHANGE FOR BP

Name	Type	Kind	Pow.	Acc.	PP	Range
Seed Bomb	Grass	Physical	80	100	15	Normal
Bounce	Flying	Physical	85	85	5	Normal
Superpower	Fighting	Physical	120	100	5	Normal
Zen Headbutt	Psychic	Physical	80	90	15	Normal
Iron Tail	Steel	Physical	100	75	15	Normal
Snore	Normal	Special	50	100	15	Normal
Synthesis	Grass	Status	—	—	5	Self
Giga Drain	Grass	Special	75	100	10	Normal
Worry Seed	Grass	Status	—	100	10	Normal

MOVES TAUGHT BY PEOPLE

Name	Type	Kind	Pow.	Acc.	PP	Range

National Pokédex **674** Hoenn Pokédex —

Pancham

Playful Pokémon

Fighting

HEIGHT: 2'00" WEIGHT: 17.6 lbs.

Same form for ♂ / ♀

Ω It does its best to be taken seriously by its enemies, but its glare is not sufficiently intimidating. Chewing on a leaf is its trademark.

α It does its level best to glare and pull a scary face, but it can't help grinning if anyone pats its head.

ABILITIES
Iron Fist
Mold Breaker

HIDDEN ABILITY
Scrappy

EGG GROUPS
Field | Human-Like

STAT GROWTH RATES
HP ■■■
Attack ■■■■
Defense ■■■
Sp. Atk ■■
Sp. Def ■■
Speed ■■

ITEMS SOMETIMES HELD BY WILD POKÉMON
—

EVOLUTION
Pancham → Lv. 32 with a Dark-type → Pangoro

MAIN WAY TO REGISTER IN THE NATIONAL POKÉDEX

Appears in *Pokémon X* and *Pokémon Y*. Bring it to your game using Link Trade or the GTS.

Damage taken in normal battles

Type		Type	
Normal	×1	Flying	×2
Fire	×1	Psychic	×2
Water	×1	Bug	×0.5
Grass	×1	Rock	×0.5
Electric	×1	Ghost	×1
Ice	×1	Dragon	×1
Fighting	×1	Dark	×0.5
Poison	×1	Steel	×1
Ground	×1	Fairy	×2

Damage taken in Inverse battles

Type		Type	
Normal	×1	Flying	×0.5
Fire	×1	Psychic	×0.5
Water	×1	Bug	×2
Grass	×1	Rock	×2
Electric	×1	Ghost	×1
Ice	×1	Dragon	×1
Fighting	×1	Dark	×2
Poison	×1	Steel	×1
Ground	×1	Fairy	×0.5

Can be used in
Inverse Battle
Battle Institute
Battle Maison
Random Matchup (Free Battle)
Random Matchup (Others)

LEVEL-UP MOVES

Lv.	Name	Type	Kind	Pow.	Acc.	PP	Range
1	Tackle	Normal	Physical	50	100	35	Normal
1	Leer	Normal	Status	—	100	30	Many Others
7	Arm Thrust	Fighting	Physical	15	100	20	Normal
10	Work Up	Normal	Status	—	—	30	Self
12	Karate Chop	Fighting	Physical	50	100	25	Normal
15	Comet Punch	Normal	Physical	18	85	15	Normal
20	Slash	Normal	Physical	70	100	20	Normal
25	Circle Throw	Fighting	Physical	60	90	10	Normal
27	Vital Throw	Fighting	Physical	70	—	10	Normal
33	Body Slam	Normal	Physical	85	100	15	Normal
39	Crunch	Dark	Physical	80	100	15	Normal
42	Entrainment	Normal	Status	—	100	15	Normal
45	Parting Shot	Dark	Status	—	100	20	Normal
48	Sky Uppercut	Fighting	Physical	85	90	15	Normal

TM & HM MOVES

No.	Name	Type	Kind	Pow.	Acc.	PP	Range
TM05	Roar	Normal	Status	—	—	20	Normal
TM06	Toxic	Poison	Status	—	90	10	Normal
TM08	Bulk Up	Fighting	Status	—	—	20	Self
TM10	Hidden Power	Normal	Special	60	100	15	Normal
TM11	Sunny Day	Fire	Status	—	—	5	Both Sides
TM17	Protect	Normal	Status	—	—	10	Self
TM18	Rain Dance	Water	Status	—	—	5	Both Sides
TM21	Frustration	Normal	Physical	—	100	20	Normal
TM27	Return	Normal	Physical	—	100	20	Normal
TM28	Dig	Ground	Physical	80	100	10	Normal
TM31	Brick Break	Fighting	Physical	75	100	15	Normal
TM32	Double Team	Normal	Status	—	—	15	Self
TM36	Sludge Bomb	Poison	Special	90	100	10	Normal
TM39	Rock Tomb	Rock	Physical	60	95	15	Normal
TM40	Aerial Ace	Flying	Physical	60	—	20	Normal
TM41	Torment	Dark	Status	—	100	15	Normal
TM42	Facade	Normal	Physical	70	100	20	Normal
TM44	Rest	Psychic	Status	—	—	10	Self
TM45	Attract	Normal	Status	—	100	15	Normal
TM47	Low Sweep	Fighting	Physical	65	100	20	Normal
TM48	Round	Normal	Special	60	100	15	Normal
TM49	Echoed Voice	Normal	Special	40	100	15	Normal
TM54	False Swipe	Normal	Physical	40	100	40	Normal
TM56	Fling	Dark	Physical	—	100	10	Normal
TM65	Shadow Claw	Ghost	Physical	70	100	15	Normal
TM66	Payback	Dark	Physical	50	100	10	Normal
TM67	Retaliate	Normal	Physical	70	100	5	Normal
TM71	Stone Edge	Rock	Physical	100	80	5	Normal
TM75	Swords Dance	Normal	Status	—	—	20	Self
TM78	Bulldoze	Ground	Physical	60	100	20	Adjacent
TM80	Rock Slide	Rock	Physical	75	90	10	Many Others
TM86	Grass Knot	Grass	Special	—	100	20	Normal
TM87	Swagger	Normal	Status	—	90	15	Normal
TM88	Sleep Talk	Normal	Status	—	—	10	Self
TM90	Substitute	Normal	Status	—	—	10	Self
TM94	Secret Power	Normal	Physical	70	100	20	Normal
TM97	Dark Pulse	Dark	Special	80	100	15	Normal
TM98	Power-Up Punch	Fighting	Physical	40	100	20	Normal
TM100	Confide	Normal	Status	—	—	20	Normal
HM01	Cut	Normal	Physical	50	95	30	Normal
HM03	Surf	Water	Special	90	100	15	Adjacent
HM04	Strength	Normal	Physical	80	100	15	Normal
HM06	Rock Smash	Fighting	Physical	40	100	15	Normal

MOVES LEARNED IN EXCHANGE FOR BP

Name	Type	Kind	Pow.	Acc.	PP	Range
Covet	Normal	Physical	60	100	25	Normal
Dual Chop	Dragon	Physical	40	90	15	Normal
Iron Head	Steel	Physical	80	100	15	Normal
Low Kick	Fighting	Physical	—	100	20	Normal
Gunk Shot	Poison	Physical	120	80	5	Normal
Uproar	Normal	Special	90	100	10	1 Random
Thunder Punch	Electric	Physical	75	100	15	Normal
Fire Punch	Fire	Physical	75	100	15	Normal
Ice Punch	Ice	Physical	75	100	15	Normal
Block	Normal	Status	—	—	5	Normal
Foul Play	Dark	Physical	95	100	15	Normal
Superpower	Fighting	Physical	120	100	5	Normal
Zen Headbutt	Psychic	Physical	80	90	15	Normal
Hyper Voice	Normal	Special	90	100	10	Many Others
Snore	Normal	Special	50	100	15	Normal
Knock Off	Dark	Physical	65	100	20	Normal
Drain Punch	Fighting	Physical	75	100	10	Normal
Focus Punch	Fighting	Physical	150	100	20	Normal
Spite	Ghost	Status	—	100	10	Normal
Helping Hand	Normal	Status	—	—	20	1 Ally
Endeavor	Normal	Physical	—	100	5	Normal
Snatch	Dark	Status	—	—	10	Self

MOVES TAUGHT BY PEOPLE

Name	Type	Kind	Pow.	Acc.	PP	Range

EGG MOVES

Name	Type	Kind	Pow.	Acc.	PP	Range
Quash	Dark	Status	—	100	15	Normal
Me First	Normal	Status	—	—	20	Varies
Quick Guard	Fighting	Status	—	—	15	Your Side
Foul Play	Dark	Physical	95	100	15	Normal
Storm Throw	Fighting	Physical	60	100	10	Normal

National Pokédex **675** Hoenn Pokédex —

Pangoro

Daunting Pokémon

Fighting | Dark

HEIGHT: 6'11" WEIGHT: 299.8 lbs.

Same form for ♂ / ♀

Ω Although it possesses a violent temperament, it won't put up with bullying. It uses the leaf in its mouth to sense the movements of its enemies.

α It charges ahead and bashes its opponents like a berserker, uncaring about any hits it might take. Its arms are mighty enough to snap a telephone pole.

ABILITIES
Iron Fist
Mold Breaker

HIDDEN ABILITY
Scrappy

EGG GROUPS
Field | Human-Like

STAT GROWTH RATES
HP
Attack
Defense
Sp. Atk
Sp. Def
Speed

ITEMS SOMETIMES HELD BY WILD POKÉMON
—

EVOLUTION

Pancham

Lv. 32 with a Dark-type

Pangoro

MAIN WAY TO REGISTER IN THE NATIONAL POKÉDEX

Level up a Pancham obtained via Link Trade or the GTS to Lv. 32 while you have a Dark-type Pokémon in your party.

Damage taken in normal battles

Type		Type	
Normal	×1	Flying	×2
Fire	×1	Psychic	×0
Water	×1	Bug	×1
Grass	×1	Rock	×0.5
Electric	×1	Ghost	×0.5
Ice	×1	Dragon	×1
Fighting	×2	Dark	×0.25
Poison	×1	Steel	×1
Ground	×1	Fairy	×4

Damage taken in Inverse battles

Type		Type	
Normal	×1	Flying	×0.5
Fire	×1	Psychic	×1
Water	×1	Bug	×1
Grass	×1	Rock	×2
Electric	×1	Ghost	×2
Ice	×1	Dragon	×1
Fighting	×0.5	Dark	×4
Poison	×1	Steel	×1
Ground	×1	Fairy	×0.25

Can be used in
Inverse Battle
Battle Institute
Battle Maison
Random Matchup (Free Battle)
Random Matchup (Others)

LEVEL-UP MOVES

Lv.	Name	Type	Kind	Pow.	Acc.	PP	Range
1	Entrainment	Normal	Status	—	100	15	Normal
1	Hammer Arm	Fighting	Physical	100	90	10	Normal
1	Tackle	Normal	Physical	50	100	35	Normal
1	Leer	Normal	Status	—	100	30	Many Others
7	Arm Thrust	Fighting	Physical	15	100	20	Normal
10	Work Up	Normal	Status	—	—	30	Self
12	Karate Chop	Fighting	Physical	50	100	25	Normal
15	Comet Punch	Normal	Physical	18	85	15	Normal
20	Slash	Normal	Physical	70	100	20	Normal
25	Circle Throw	Fighting	Physical	60	90	10	Normal
27	Vital Throw	Fighting	Physical	70	—	10	Normal
35	Body Slam	Normal	Physical	85	100	15	Normal
42	Crunch	Dark	Physical	80	100	15	Normal
45	Entrainment	Normal	Status	—	100	15	Normal
48	Parting Shot	Dark	Status	—	100	20	Normal
52	Sky Uppercut	Fighting	Physical	85	90	15	Normal
57	Hammer Arm	Fighting	Physical	100	90	10	Normal
65	Taunt	Dark	Status	—	100	20	Normal
70	Low Sweep	Fighting	Physical	65	100	20	Normal

TM & HM MOVES

No.	Name	Type	Kind	Pow.	Acc.	PP	Range
TM01	Hone Claws	Dark	Status	—	—	15	Self
TM02	Dragon Claw	Dragon	Physical	80	100	15	Normal
TM05	Roar	Normal	Status	—	—	20	Normal
TM06	Toxic	Poison	Status	—	90	10	Normal
TM08	Bulk Up	Fighting	Status	—	—	20	Self
TM10	Hidden Power	Normal	Special	60	100	15	Normal
TM11	Sunny Day	Fire	Status	—	—	5	Both Sides
TM12	Taunt	Dark	Status	—	100	20	Normal
TM15	Hyper Beam	Normal	Special	150	90	5	Normal
TM17	Protect	Normal	Status	—	—	10	Self
TM18	Rain Dance	Water	Status	—	—	5	Both Sides
TM21	Frustration	Normal	Physical	—	100	20	Normal
TM26	Earthquake	Ground	Physical	100	100	10	Adjacent
TM27	Return	Normal	Physical	—	100	20	Normal
TM28	Dig	Ground	Physical	80	100	10	Normal
TM31	Brick Break	Fighting	Physical	75	100	15	Normal
TM32	Double Team	Normal	Status	—	—	15	Self
TM36	Sludge Bomb	Poison	Special	90	100	10	Normal

No.	Name	Type	Kind	Pow.	Acc.	PP	Range
TM32	Double Team	Normal	Status	—	—	15	Self
TM36	Sludge Bomb	Poison	Special	90	100	10	Normal
TM39	Rock Tomb	Rock	Physical	60	95	15	Normal
TM40	Aerial Ace	Flying	Physical	60	—	20	Normal
TM41	Torment	Dark	Status	—	100	15	Normal
TM42	Facade	Normal	Physical	70	100	20	Normal
TM44	Rest	Psychic	Status	—	—	10	Self
TM45	Attract	Normal	Status	—	100	15	Normal
TM46	Thief	Dark	Physical	60	100	25	Normal
TM47	Low Sweep	Fighting	Physical	65	100	20	Normal
TM48	Round	Normal	Special	60	100	15	Normal
TM49	Echoed Voice	Normal	Special	40	100	15	Normal
TM52	Focus Blast	Fighting	Special	120	70	5	Normal
TM54	False Swipe	Normal	Physical	40	100	40	Normal
TM56	Fling	Dark	Physical	—	100	10	Normal
TM60	Quash	Dark	Status	—	100	15	Normal
TM63	Embargo	Dark	Status	—	100	15	Normal
TM65	Shadow Claw	Ghost	Physical	70	100	15	Normal
TM66	Payback	Dark	Physical	50	100	10	Normal
TM67	Retaliate	Normal	Physical	70	100	5	Normal
TM68	Giga Impact	Normal	Physical	150	90	5	Normal
TM71	Stone Edge	Rock	Physical	100	80	5	Normal
TM75	Swords Dance	Normal	Status	—	—	20	Self
TM78	Bulldoze	Ground	Physical	60	100	20	Adjacent
TM80	Rock Slide	Rock	Physical	75	90	10	Many Others
TM81	X-Scissor	Bug	Physical	80	100	15	Normal
TM83	Infestation	Bug	Special	20	100	20	Normal
TM84	Poison Jab	Poison	Physical	80	100	20	Normal
TM86	Grass Knot	Grass	Special	—	100	20	Normal
TM87	Swagger	Normal	Status	—	90	15	Normal
TM88	Sleep Talk	Normal	Status	—	—	10	Self
TM90	Substitute	Normal	Status	—	—	10	Self
TM94	Secret Power	Normal	Physical	70	100	20	Normal
TM95	Snarl	Dark	Special	55	95	15	Many Others
TM97	Dark Pulse	Dark	Special	80	100	15	Normal
TM98	Power-Up Punch	Fighting	Physical	40	100	20	Normal
TM100	Confide	Normal	Status	—	—	20	Normal
HM01	Cut	Normal	Physical	50	95	30	Normal
HM03	Surf	Water	Special	90	100	15	Adjacent
HM04	Strength	Normal	Physical	80	100	15	Normal
HM06	Rock Smash	Fighting	Physical	40	100	15	Normal

MOVES LEARNED IN EXCHANGE FOR BP

Name	Type	Kind	Pow.	Acc.	PP	Range
Covet	Normal	Physical	60	100	25	Normal
Dual Chop	Dragon	Physical	40	90	15	Normal
Iron Head	Steel	Physical	80	100	15	Normal
Low Kick	Fighting	Physical	—	100	20	Normal
Gunk Shot	Poison	Physical	120	80	5	Normal
Uproar	Normal	Special	90	100	10	1 Random
Thunder Punch	Electric	Physical	75	100	15	Normal
Fire Punch	Fire	Physical	75	100	15	Normal
Ice Punch	Ice	Physical	75	100	15	Normal
Block	Normal	Status	—	—	5	Normal
Foul Play	Dark	Physical	95	100	15	Normal
Superpower	Fighting	Physical	120	100	5	Normal
Zen Headbutt	Psychic	Physical	80	90	15	Normal
Hyper Voice	Normal	Special	90	100	10	Many Others
Snore	Normal	Special	50	100	15	Normal
Knock Off	Dark	Physical	65	100	20	Normal
Drain Punch	Fighting	Physical	75	100	10	Normal
Focus Punch	Fighting	Physical	150	100	20	Normal
Spite	Ghost	Status	—	100	10	Normal
Helping Hand	Normal	Status	—	—	20	1 Ally
Endeavor	Normal	Physical	—	100	5	Normal
Outrage	Dragon	Physical	120	100	10	1 Random
Snatch	Dark	Status	—	—	10	Self

MOVES TAUGHT BY PEOPLE

Name	Type	Kind	Pow.	Acc.	PP	Range

National Pokédex **676** Hoenn Pokédex —

Furfrou

Poodle Pokémon

Normal

HEIGHT: 3'11" WEIGHT: 61.7 lbs.

Same form for ♂ / ♀

Ω Trimming its fluffy fur not only makes it more elegant but also increases the swiftness of its movements.

α Historically, in the Kalos region, these Pokémon were the designated guardians of the king.

ABILITY
Fur Coat

HIDDEN ABILITY
—

EGG GROUPS
Field

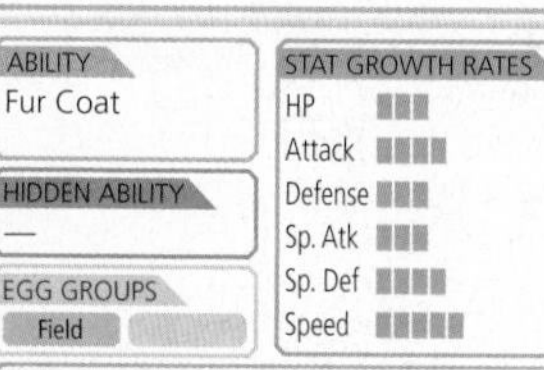

STAT GROWTH RATES
HP
Attack
Defense
Sp. Atk
Sp. Def
Speed

ITEMS SOMETIMES HELD BY WILD POKÉMON
—

EVOLUTION

Does not evolve

MAIN WAY TO REGISTER IN THE NATIONAL POKÉDEX

Appears in *Pokémon X* and *Pokémon Y*. Bring it to your game using Link Trade or the GTS.

Damage taken in normal battles

Type		Type	
Normal	×1	Flying	×1
Fire	×1	Psychic	×1
Water	×1	Bug	×1
Grass	×1	Rock	×1
Electric	×1	Ghost	×0
Ice	×1	Dragon	×1
Fighting	×2	Dark	×1
Poison	×1	Steel	×1
Ground	×1	Fairy	×1

Damage taken in Inverse battles

Type		Type	
Normal	×1	Flying	×1
Fire	×1	Psychic	×1
Water	×1	Bug	×1
Grass	×1	Rock	×1
Electric	×1	Ghost	×2
Ice	×1	Dragon	×1
Fighting	×0.5	Dark	×1
Poison	×1	Steel	×1
Ground	×1	Fairy	×1

Can be used in
Inverse Battle
Battle Institute
Battle Maison
Random Matchup (Free Battle)
Random Matchup (Others)

LEVEL-UP MOVES

Lv.	Name	Type	Kind	Pow.	Acc.	PP	Range
1	Tackle	Normal	Physical	50	100	35	Normal
1	Growl	Normal	Status	—	100	40	Many Others
5	Sand Attack	Ground	Status	—	100	15	Normal
9	Baby-Doll Eyes	Fairy	Status	—	100	30	Normal
12	Headbutt	Normal	Physical	70	100	15	Normal
15	Tail Whip	Normal	Status	—	100	30	Many Others
22	Bite	Dark	Physical	60	100	25	Normal
27	Odor Sleuth	Normal	Status	—	—	40	Normal
33	Retaliate	Normal	Physical	70	100	5	Normal
35	Take Down	Normal	Physical	90	85	20	Normal
38	Charm	Fairy	Status	—	100	20	Normal
42	Sucker Punch	Dark	Physical	80	100	5	Normal
48	Cotton Guard	Grass	Status	—	—	10	Self

TM & HM MOVES

No.	Name	Type	Kind	Pow.	Acc.	PP	Range
TM05	Roar	Normal	Status	—	—	20	Normal
TM06	Toxic	Poison	Status	—	90	10	Normal
TM10	Hidden Power	Normal	Special	60	100	15	Normal
TM11	Sunny Day	Fire	Status	—	—	5	Both Sides
TM17	Protect	Normal	Status	—	—	10	Self
TM18	Rain Dance	Water	Status	—	—	5	Both Sides
TM21	Frustration	Normal	Physical	—	100	20	Normal
TM27	Return	Normal	Physical	—	100	20	Normal
TM28	Dig	Ground	Physical	80	100	10	Normal
TM32	Double Team	Normal	Status	—	—	15	Self
TM42	Facade	Normal	Physical	70	100	20	Normal
TM44	Rest	Psychic	Status	—	—	10	Self
TM45	Attract	Normal	Status	—	100	15	Normal

No.	Name	Type	Kind	Pow.	Acc.	PP	Range
TM48	Round	Normal	Special	60	100	15	Normal
TM49	Echoed Voice	Normal	Special	40	100	15	Normal
TM57	Charge Beam	Electric	Special	50	90	10	Normal
TM67	Retaliate	Normal	Physical	70	100	5	Normal
TM68	Giga Impact	Normal	Physical	150	90	5	Normal
TM70	Flash	Normal	Status	—	100	20	Normal
TM73	Thunder Wave	Electric	Status	—	100	20	Normal
TM86	Grass Knot	Grass	Special	—	100	20	Normal
TM87	Swagger	Normal	Status	—	90	15	Normal
TM88	Sleep Talk	Normal	Status	—	—	10	Self
TM89	U-turn	Bug	Physical	70	100	20	Normal
TM90	Substitute	Normal	Status	—	—	10	Self
TM93	Wild Charge	Electric	Physical	90	100	15	Normal
TM94	Secret Power	Normal	Physical	70	100	20	Normal
TM95	Snarl	Dark	Special	55	95	15	Many Others
TM97	Dark Pulse	Dark	Special	80	100	15	Normal
TM100	Confide	Normal	Status	—	—	20	Normal
HM03	Surf	Water	Special	90	100	15	Adjacent
HM06	Rock Smash	Fighting	Physical	40	100	15	Normal

MOVES LEARNED IN EXCHANGE FOR BP

Name	Type	Kind	Pow.	Acc.	PP	Range
Uproar	Normal	Special	90	100	10	1 Random
Last Resort	Normal	Physical	140	100	5	Normal
Zen Headbutt	Psychic	Physical	80	90	15	Normal
Hyper Voice	Normal	Special	90	100	10	Many Others
Iron Tail	Steel	Physical	100	75	15	Normal
Snore	Normal	Special	50	100	15	Normal
Role Play	Psychic	Status	—	—	10	Normal
Helping Hand	Normal	Status	—	—	20	1 Ally
Endeavor	Normal	Physical	—	100	5	Normal

MOVES TAUGHT BY PEOPLE

Name	Type	Kind	Pow.	Acc.	PP	Range

EGG MOVES

Name	Type	Kind	Pow.	Acc.	PP	Range
Role Play	Psychic	Status	—	—	10	Normal
Work Up	Normal	Status	—	—	30	Self
Mimic	Normal	Status	—	—	10	Normal
Captivate	Normal	Status	—	100	20	Many Others
Refresh	Normal	Status	—	—	20	Self

◆ If you put Furfrou in your party and talk to the woman in Slateport City's Pokémon Fan Club, she can groom it into one of nine different trims.

National Pokédex **677** Hoenn Pokédex —

Espurr

Restraint Pokémon

Psychic

HEIGHT: 1'00" WEIGHT: 7.7 lbs.

Same form for ♂ / ♀

Ω The organ that emits its intense psychic power is sheltered by its ears to keep power from leaking out.

α It has enough psychic energy to blast everything within 300 feet of itself, but it has no control over its power.

ABILITIES
Keen Eye
Infiltrator

HIDDEN ABILITY
Own Tempo

EGG GROUPS
Field

STAT GROWTH RATES
HP ▮▮▮
Attack ▮▮▮
Defense ▮▮
Sp. Atk ▮▮▮
Sp. Def ▮▮▮
Speed ▮▮▮▮

ITEMS SOMETIMES HELD BY WILD POKÉMON
—

EVOLUTION

MAIN WAY TO REGISTER IN THE NATIONAL POKÉDEX

Appears in *Pokémon X* and *Pokémon Y*. Bring it to your game using Link Trade or the GTS.

Damage taken in normal battles

Type		Type	
Normal	×1	Flying	×1
Fire	×1	Psychic	×0.5
Water	×1	Bug	×2
Grass	×1	Rock	×1
Electric	×1	Ghost	×2
Ice	×1	Dragon	×1
Fighting	×0.5	Dark	×2
Poison	×1	Steel	×1
Ground	×1	Fairy	×1

Damage taken in Inverse battles

Type		Type	
Normal	×1	Flying	×1
Fire	×1	Psychic	×2
Water	×1	Bug	×0.5
Grass	×1	Rock	×1
Electric	×1	Ghost	×0.5
Ice	×1	Dragon	×1
Fighting	×2	Dark	×0.5
Poison	×1	Steel	×1
Ground	×1	Fairy	×1

Can be used in
Inverse Battle
Battle Institute
Battle Maison
Random Matchup (Free Battle)
Random Matchup (Others)

LEVEL-UP MOVES

Lv.	Name	Type	Kind	Pow.	Acc.	PP	Range
1	Scratch	Normal	Physical	40	100	35	Normal
1	Leer	Normal	Status	—	100	30	Many Others
5	Covet	Normal	Physical	60	100	25	Normal
9	Confusion	Psychic	Special	50	100	25	Normal
13	Light Screen	Psychic	Status	—	—	30	Your Side
17	Psybeam	Psychic	Special	65	100	20	Normal
19	Fake Out	Normal	Physical	40	100	10	Normal
22	Disarming Voice	Fairy	Special	40	—	15	Many Others
25	Psyshock	Psychic	Special	80	100	10	Normal

TM & HM MOVES

No.	Name	Type	Kind	Pow.	Acc.	PP	Range
TM03	Psyshock	Psychic	Special	80	100	10	Normal
TM04	Calm Mind	Psychic	Status	—	—	20	Self
TM06	Toxic	Poison	Status	—	90	10	Normal
TM10	Hidden Power	Normal	Special	60	100	15	Normal
TM11	Sunny Day	Fire	Status	—	—	5	Both Sides
TM16	Light Screen	Psychic	Status	—	—	30	Your Side
TM17	Protect	Normal	Status	—	—	10	Self
TM18	Rain Dance	Water	Status	—	—	5	Both Sides
TM20	Safeguard	Normal	Status	—	—	25	Your Side
TM21	Frustration	Normal	Physical	—	100	20	Normal
TM24	Thunderbolt	Electric	Special	90	100	15	Normal
TM27	Return	Normal	Physical	—	100	20	Normal
TM29	Psychic	Psychic	Special	90	100	10	Normal
TM32	Double Team	Normal	Status	—	—	15	Self
TM33	Reflect	Psychic	Status	—	—	20	Your Side
TM41	Torment	Dark	Status	—	100	15	Normal
TM42	Facade	Normal	Physical	70	100	20	Normal
TM44	Rest	Psychic	Status	—	—	10	Self
TM45	Attract	Normal	Status	—	100	15	Normal
TM48	Round	Normal	Special	60	100	15	Normal
TM49	Echoed Voice	Normal	Special	40	100	15	Normal
TM53	Energy Ball	Grass	Special	90	100	10	Normal
TM57	Charge Beam	Electric	Special	50	90	10	Normal
TM66	Payback	Dark	Physical	50	100	10	Normal
TM70	Flash	Normal	Status	—	100	20	Normal
TM73	Thunder Wave	Electric	Status	—	100	20	Normal
TM77	Psych Up	Normal	Status	—	—	10	Normal
TM85	Dream Eater	Psychic	Special	100	100	15	Normal
TM87	Swagger	Normal	Status	—	90	15	Normal
TM88	Sleep Talk	Normal	Status	—	—	10	Self
TM90	Substitute	Normal	Status	—	—	10	Self
TM92	Trick Room	Psychic	Status	—	—	5	Both Sides
TM94	Secret Power	Normal	Physical	70	100	20	Normal
TM97	Dark Pulse	Dark	Special	80	100	15	Normal
TM100	Confide	Normal	Status	—	—	20	Normal
HM01	Cut	Normal	Physical	50	95	30	Normal

MOVES LEARNED IN EXCHANGE FOR BP

Name	Type	Kind	Pow.	Acc.	PP	Range
Covet	Normal	Physical	60	100	25	Normal
Signal Beam	Bug	Special	75	100	15	Normal
Magic Coat	Psychic	Status	—	—	15	Self
Gravity	Psychic	Status	—	—	5	Both Sides
Zen Headbutt	Psychic	Physical	80	90	15	Normal
Iron Tail	Steel	Physical	100	75	15	Normal
Snore	Normal	Special	50	100	15	Normal
Role Play	Psychic	Status	—	—	10	Normal
Heal Bell	Normal	Status	—	—	5	Your Party
Shock Wave	Electric	Special	60	—	20	Normal
Helping Hand	Normal	Status	—	—	20	1 Ally
Trick	Psychic	Status	—	100	10	Normal
Magic Room	Psychic	Status	—	—	10	Both Sides
Wonder Room	Psychic	Status	—	—	10	Both Sides
Recycle	Normal	Status	—	—	10	Self
Snatch	Dark	Status	—	—	10	Self

MOVES TAUGHT BY PEOPLE

Name	Type	Kind	Pow.	Acc.	PP	Range

EGG MOVES

Name	Type	Kind	Pow.	Acc.	PP	Range
Trick	Psychic	Status	—	100	10	Normal
Yawn	Normal	Status	—	—	10	Normal
Assist	Normal	Status	—	—	20	Self
Barrier	Psychic	Status	—	—	20	Self

National Pokédex **678** Hoenn Pokédex —

Meowstic

Constraint Pokémon

Psychic

HEIGHT: 2'00" WEIGHT: 18.7 lbs.

♂ only

The male's fur is predominately blue.

Ω When in danger, it raises its ears and releases enough psychic power to grind a 10-ton truck into dust.

α The eyeball patterns on the interior of its ears emit psychic energy. It keeps the patterns tightly covered because that power is too immense.

ABILITIES
Keen Eye
Infiltrator

HIDDEN ABILITY
Prankster

EGG GROUPS
Field

STAT GROWTH RATES
HP ▮▮▮
Attack ▮▮▮
Defense ▮▮▮
Sp. Atk ▮▮▮▮
Sp. Def ▮▮▮
Speed ▮▮▮▮▮

ITEMS SOMETIMES HELD BY WILD POKÉMON
—

EVOLUTION

Espurr ♂ → Lv. 25 → Meowstic ♂

MAIN WAY TO REGISTER IN THE NATIONAL POKÉDEX

Level up a male Espurr obtained via Link Trade or the GTS to Lv. 25.

Damage taken in normal battles

Type		Type	
Normal	×1	Flying	×1
Fire	×1	Psychic	×0.5
Water	×1	Bug	×2
Grass	×1	Rock	×1
Electric	×1	Ghost	×2
Ice	×1	Dragon	×1
Fighting	×0.5	Dark	×2
Poison	×1	Steel	×1
Ground	×1	Fairy	×1

Damage taken in Inverse battles

Type		Type	
Normal	×1	Flying	×1
Fire	×1	Psychic	×2
Water	×1	Bug	×0.5
Grass	×1	Rock	×1
Electric	×1	Ghost	×0.5
Ice	×1	Dragon	×1
Fighting	×2	Dark	×0.5
Poison	×1	Steel	×1
Ground	×1	Fairy	×1

Can be used in
Inverse Battle
Battle Institute
Battle Maison
Random Matchup (Free Battle)
Random Matchup (Others)

LEVEL-UP MOVES

Lv.	Name	Type	Kind	Pow.	Acc.	PP	Range
1	Quick Guard	Fighting	Status	—	—	15	Your Side
1	Mean Look	Normal	Status	—	—	5	Normal
1	Helping Hand	Normal	Status	—	—	20	1 Ally
1	Scratch	Normal	Physical	40	100	35	Normal
1	Leer	Normal	Status	—	100	30	Many Others
5	Covet	Normal	Physical	60	100	25	Normal
9	Confusion	Psychic	Special	50	100	25	Normal
13	Light Screen	Psychic	Status	—	—	30	Your Side
17	Psybeam	Psychic	Special	65	100	20	Normal
19	Fake Out	Normal	Physical	40	100	10	Normal
22	Disarming Voice	Fairy	Special	40	—	15	Many Others
25	Psyshock	Psychic	Special	80	100	10	Normal
28	Charm	Fairy	Status	—	100	20	Normal
31	Miracle Eye	Psychic	Status	—	—	40	Normal
35	Reflect	Psychic	Status	—	—	20	Your Side
40	Psychic	Psychic	Special	90	100	10	Normal
43	Role Play	Psychic	Status	—	—	10	Normal
45	Imprison	Psychic	Status	—	—	10	Self
48	Sucker Punch	Dark	Physical	80	100	5	Normal
50	Misty Terrain	Fairy	Status	—	—	10	Both Sides
53	Quick Guard	Fighting	Status	—	—	15	Your Side

TM & HM MOVES

No.	Name	Type	Kind	Pow.	Acc.	PP	Range
TM03	Psyshock	Psychic	Special	80	100	10	Normal
TM04	Calm Mind	Psychic	Status	—	—	20	Self
TM06	Toxic	Poison	Status	—	90	10	Normal
TM10	Hidden Power	Normal	Special	60	100	15	Normal
TM11	Sunny Day	Fire	Status	—	—	5	Both Sides
TM15	Hyper Beam	Normal	Special	150	90	5	Normal
TM16	Light Screen	Psychic	Status	—	—	30	Your Side
TM17	Protect	Normal	Status	—	—	10	Self
TM18	Rain Dance	Water	Status	—	—	5	Both Sides
TM20	Safeguard	Normal	Status	—	—	25	Your Side
TM21	Frustration	Normal	Physical	—	100	20	Normal
TM24	Thunderbolt	Electric	Special	90	100	15	Normal
TM27	Return	Normal	Physical	—	100	20	Normal
TM28	Dig	Ground	Physical	80	100	10	Normal
TM29	Psychic	Psychic	Special	90	100	10	Normal
TM30	Shadow Ball	Ghost	Special	80	100	15	Normal
TM32	Double Team	Normal	Status	—	—	15	Self
TM33	Reflect	Psychic	Status	—	—	20	Your Side
TM41	Torment	Dark	Status	—	100	15	Normal
TM42	Facade	Normal	Physical	70	100	20	Normal
TM44	Rest	Psychic	Status	—	—	10	Self
TM45	Attract	Normal	Status	—	100	15	Normal
TM48	Round	Normal	Special	60	100	15	Normal
TM49	Echoed Voice	Normal	Special	40	100	15	Normal
TM53	Energy Ball	Grass	Special	90	100	10	Normal
TM57	Charge Beam	Electric	Special	50	90	10	Normal
TM66	Payback	Dark	Physical	50	100	10	Normal
TM68	Giga Impact	Normal	Physical	150	90	5	Normal
TM70	Flash	Normal	Status	—	100	20	Normal
TM73	Thunder Wave	Electric	Status	—	100	20	Normal
TM77	Psych Up	Normal	Status	—	—	10	Normal
TM85	Dream Eater	Psychic	Special	100	100	15	Normal
TM87	Swagger	Normal	Status	—	90	15	Normal
TM88	Sleep Talk	Normal	Status	—	—	10	Self
TM90	Substitute	Normal	Status	—	—	10	Self
TM92	Trick Room	Psychic	Status	—	—	5	Both Sides
TM94	Secret Power	Normal	Physical	70	100	20	Normal
TM97	Dark Pulse	Dark	Special	80	100	15	Normal
TM98	Power-Up Punch	Fighting	Physical	40	100	20	Normal
TM100	Confide	Normal	Status	—	—	20	Normal
HM01	Cut	Normal	Physical	50	95	30	Normal

MOVES LEARNED IN EXCHANGE FOR BP

Name	Type	Kind	Pow.	Acc.	PP	Range
Covet	Normal	Physical	60	100	25	Normal
Signal Beam	Bug	Special	75	100	15	Normal
Magic Coat	Psychic	Status	—	—	15	Self
Gravity	Psychic	Status	—	—	5	Both Sides
Zen Headbutt	Psychic	Physical	80	90	15	Normal
Iron Tail	Steel	Physical	100	75	15	Normal
Snore	Normal	Special	50	100	15	Normal
Role Play	Psychic	Status	—	—	10	Normal
Heal Bell	Normal	Status	—	—	5	Your Party
Shock Wave	Electric	Special	60	—	20	Normal
Helping Hand	Normal	Status	—	—	20	1 Ally
Trick	Psychic	Status	—	100	10	Normal
Magic Room	Psychic	Status	—	—	10	Both Sides
Wonder Room	Psychic	Status	—	—	10	Both Sides
Recycle	Normal	Status	—	—	10	Self
Snatch	Dark	Status	—	—	10	Self

MOVES TAUGHT BY PEOPLE

Name	Type	Kind	Pow.	Acc.	PP	Range

National Pokédex **678** Hoenn Pokédex —

Meowstic

Constraint Pokémon

Psychic

HEIGHT: 2'00" WEIGHT: 18.7 lbs.

♀ only

The female's fur is predominately white.

Ω When in danger, it raises its ears and releases enough psychic power to grind a 10-ton truck into dust.

α The eyeball patterns on the interior of its ears emit psychic energy. It keeps the patterns tightly covered because that power is too immense.

ABILITIES
Keen Eye
Infiltrator

HIDDEN ABILITY
Competitive

EGG GROUPS
Field

STAT GROWTH RATES
HP
Attack
Defense
Sp. Atk
Sp. Def
Speed

ITEMS SOMETIMES HELD BY WILD POKÉMON
—

EVOLUTION

Espurr ♀

Lv. 25

Meowstic ♀

MAIN WAY TO REGISTER IN THE NATIONAL POKÉDEX

Level up a female Espurr obtained via Link Trade or the GTS to Lv. 25.

Damage taken in normal battles

Type		Type	
Normal	×1	Flying	×1
Fire	×1	Psychic	×0.5
Water	×1	Bug	×2
Grass	×1	Rock	×1
Electric	×1	Ghost	×2
Ice	×1	Dragon	×1
Fighting	×0.5	Dark	×2
Poison	×1	Steel	×1
Ground	×1	Fairy	×1

Damage taken in Inverse battles

Type		Type	
Normal	×1	Flying	×1
Fire	×1	Psychic	×2
Water	×1	Bug	×0.5
Grass	×1	Rock	×1
Electric	×1	Ghost	×0.5
Ice	×1	Dragon	×1
Fighting	×2	Dark	×0.5
Poison	×1	Steel	×1
Ground	×1	Fairy	×1

Can be used in
Inverse Battle
Battle Institute
Battle Maison
Random Matchup (Free Battle)
Random Matchup (Others)

LEVEL-UP MOVES

Lv.	Name	Type	Kind	Pow.	Acc.	PP	Range
1	Stored Power	Psychic	Special	20	100	10	Normal
1	Me First	Normal	Status	—	—	20	Varies
1	Magical Leaf	Grass	Special	60	—	20	Normal
1	Scratch	Normal	Physical	40	100	35	Normal
1	Leer	Normal	Status	—	100	30	Many Others
5	Covet	Normal	Physical	60	100	25	Normal
9	Confusion	Psychic	Special	50	100	25	Normal
13	Light Screen	Psychic	Status	—	—	30	Your Side
17	Psybeam	Psychic	Special	65	100	20	Normal
19	Fake Out	Normal	Physical	40	100	10	Normal
22	Disarming Voice	Fairy	Special	40	—	15	Many Others
25	Psyshock	Psychic	Special	80	100	10	Normal
28	Charge Beam	Electric	Special	50	90	10	Normal
31	Shadow Ball	Ghost	Special	80	100	15	Normal
35	Extrasensory	Psychic	Special	80	100	20	Normal
40	Psychic	Psychic	Special	90	100	10	Normal
43	Role Play	Psychic	Status	—	—	10	Normal
45	Signal Beam	Bug	Special	75	100	15	Normal
48	Sucker Punch	Dark	Physical	80	100	5	Normal
50	Future Sight	Psychic	Special	120	100	10	Normal
53	Stored Power	Psychic	Special	20	100	10	Normal

TM & HM MOVES

No.	Name	Type	Kind	Pow.	Acc.	PP	Range
TM03	Psyshock	Psychic	Special	80	100	10	Normal
TM04	Calm Mind	Psychic	Status	—	—	20	Self
TM06	Toxic	Poison	Status	—	90	10	Normal
TM10	Hidden Power	Normal	Special	60	100	15	Normal
TM11	Sunny Day	Fire	Status	—	—	5	Both Sides
TM15	Hyper Beam	Normal	Special	150	90	5	Normal
TM16	Light Screen	Psychic	Status	—	—	30	Your Side
TM17	Protect	Normal	Status	—	—	10	Self
TM18	Rain Dance	Water	Status	—	—	5	Both Sides
TM20	Safeguard	Normal	Status	—	—	25	Your Side
TM21	Frustration	Normal	Physical	—	100	20	Normal
TM24	Thunderbolt	Electric	Special	90	100	15	Normal
TM27	Return	Normal	Physical	—	100	20	Normal
TM28	Dig	Ground	Physical	80	100	10	Normal
TM29	Psychic	Psychic	Special	90	100	10	Normal
TM30	Shadow Ball	Ghost	Special	80	100	15	Normal
TM32	Double Team	Normal	Status	—	—	15	Self
TM33	Reflect	Psychic	Status	—	—	20	Your Side
TM41	Torment	Dark	Status	—	100	15	Normal
TM42	Facade	Normal	Physical	70	100	20	Normal
TM44	Rest	Psychic	Status	—	—	10	Self
TM45	Attract	Normal	Status	—	100	15	Normal
TM48	Round	Normal	Special	60	100	15	Normal
TM49	Echoed Voice	Normal	Special	40	100	15	Normal
TM53	Energy Ball	Grass	Special	90	100	10	Normal
TM57	Charge Beam	Electric	Special	50	90	10	Normal
TM66	Payback	Dark	Physical	50	100	10	Normal
TM68	Giga Impact	Normal	Physical	150	90	5	Normal
TM70	Flash	Normal	Status	—	100	20	Normal
TM73	Thunder Wave	Electric	Status	—	100	20	Normal
TM77	Psych Up	Normal	Status	—	—	10	Normal
TM85	Dream Eater	Psychic	Special	100	100	15	Normal
TM87	Swagger	Normal	Status	—	90	15	Normal
TM88	Sleep Talk	Normal	Status	—	—	10	Self
TM90	Substitute	Normal	Status	—	—	10	Self
TM92	Trick Room	Psychic	Status	—	—	5	Both Sides
TM94	Secret Power	Normal	Physical	70	100	20	Normal
TM97	Dark Pulse	Dark	Special	80	100	15	Normal
TM98	Power-Up Punch	Fighting	Physical	40	100	20	Normal
TM100	Confide	Normal	Status	—	—	20	Normal
HM01	Cut	Normal	Physical	50	95	30	Normal

MOVES LEARNED IN EXCHANGE FOR BP

Name	Type	Kind	Pow.	Acc.	PP	Range
Covet	Normal	Physical	60	100	25	Normal
Signal Beam	Bug	Special	75	100	15	Normal
Magic Coat	Psychic	Status	—	—	15	Self
Gravity	Psychic	Status	—	—	5	Both Sides
Zen Headbutt	Psychic	Physical	80	90	15	Normal
Iron Tail	Steel	Physical	100	75	15	Normal
Snore	Normal	Special	50	100	15	Normal
Role Play	Psychic	Status	—	—	10	Normal
Heal Bell	Normal	Status	—	—	5	Your Party
Shock Wave	Electric	Special	60	—	20	Normal
Trick	Psychic	Status	—	100	10	Normal
Magic Room	Psychic	Status	—	—	10	Both Sides
Wonder Room	Psychic	Status	—	—	10	Both Sides
Recycle	Normal	Status	—	—	10	Self
Snatch	Dark	Status	—	—	10	Self

MOVES TAUGHT BY PEOPLE

Name	Type	Kind	Pow.	Acc.	PP	Range

National Pokédex **679** Hoenn Pokédex —

Honedge

Sword Pokémon

Steel **Ghost**

HEIGHT: 2'07" WEIGHT: 4.4 lbs.

Same form for ♂ / ♀

Ω Apparently this Pokémon is born when a departed spirit inhabits a sword. It attaches itself to people and drinks their life force.

α If anyone dares to grab its hilt, it wraps a blue cloth around that person's arm and drains that person's life energy completely.

ABILITY
No Guard

HIDDEN ABILITY
—

EGG GROUPS
Mineral

STAT GROWTH RATES
HP
Attack
Defense
Sp. Atk
Sp. Def
Speed

ITEMS SOMETIMES HELD BY WILD POKÉMON
—

EVOLUTION

Honedge → Lv. 35 → Doublade → Dusk Stone → Aegislash Shield Forme

MAIN WAY TO REGISTER IN THE NATIONAL POKÉDEX

Appears in *Pokémon X* and *Pokémon Y*. Bring it to your game using Link Trade or the GTS.

Damage taken in normal battles

Type		Type	
Normal	×0	Flying	×0.5
Fire	×2	Psychic	×0.5
Water	×1	Bug	×0.25
Grass	×0.5	Rock	×0.5
Electric	×1	Ghost	×2
Ice	×0.5	Dragon	×0.5
Fighting	×0	Dark	×2
Poison	×0	Steel	×0.5
Ground	×2	Fairy	×0.5

Damage taken in Inverse battles

Type		Type	
Normal	×4	Flying	×2
Fire	×0.5	Psychic	×2
Water	×1	Bug	×4
Grass	×2	Rock	×2
Electric	×1	Ghost	×0.5
Ice	×2	Dragon	×2
Fighting	×1	Dark	×0.5
Poison	×4	Steel	×2
Ground	×0.5	Fairy	×2

Can be used in
Inverse Battle
Battle Institute
Battle Maison
Random Matchup (Free Battle)
Random Matchup (Others)

LEVEL-UP MOVES

Lv.	Name	Type	Kind	Pow.	Acc.	PP	Range
1	Tackle	Normal	Physical	50	100	35	Normal
1	Swords Dance	Normal	Status	—	—	20	Self
5	Fury Cutter	Bug	Physical	40	95	20	Normal
8	Metal Sound	Steel	Status	—	85	40	Normal
13	Pursuit	Dark	Physical	40	100	20	Normal
18	Autotomize	Steel	Status	—	—	15	Self
20	Shadow Sneak	Ghost	Physical	40	100	30	Normal
22	Aerial Ace	Flying	Physical	60	—	20	Normal
26	Retaliate	Normal	Physical	70	100	5	Normal
29	Slash	Normal	Physical	70	100	20	Normal
32	Iron Defense	Steel	Status	—	—	15	Self
35	Night Slash	Dark	Physical	70	100	15	Normal
39	Power Trick	Psychic	Status	—	—	10	Self
42	Iron Head	Steel	Physical	80	100	15	Normal
47	Sacred Sword	Fighting	Physical	90	100	15	Normal

TM & HM MOVES

No.	Name	Type	Kind	Pow.	Acc.	PP	Range
TM06	Toxic	Poison	Status	—	90	10	Normal
TM10	Hidden Power	Normal	Special	60	100	15	Normal
TM17	Protect	Normal	Status	—	—	10	Self
TM18	Rain Dance	Water	Status	—	—	5	Both Sides
TM21	Frustration	Normal	Physical	—	100	20	Normal
TM27	Return	Normal	Physical	—	100	20	Normal
TM31	Brick Break	Fighting	Physical	75	100	15	Normal
TM32	Double Team	Normal	Status	—	—	15	Self
TM33	Reflect	Psychic	Status	—	—	20	Your Side
TM40	Aerial Ace	Flying	Physical	60	—	20	Normal
TM42	Facade	Normal	Physical	70	100	20	Normal
TM44	Rest	Psychic	Status	—	—	10	Self
TM45	Attract	Normal	Status	—	100	15	Normal
TM54	False Swipe	Normal	Physical	40	100	40	Normal
TM65	Shadow Claw	Ghost	Physical	70	100	15	Normal
TM67	Retaliate	Normal	Physical	70	100	5	Normal
TM74	Gyro Ball	Steel	Physical	—	100	5	Normal
TM75	Swords Dance	Normal	Status	—	—	20	Self
TM80	Rock Slide	Rock	Physical	75	90	10	Many Others
TM87	Swagger	Normal	Status	—	90	15	Normal
TM88	Sleep Talk	Normal	Status	—	—	10	Self
TM90	Substitute	Normal	Status	—	—	10	Self
TM91	Flash Cannon	Steel	Special	80	100	10	Normal
TM94	Secret Power	Normal	Physical	70	100	20	Normal
TM100	Confide	Normal	Status	—	—	20	Normal
HM01	Cut	Normal	Physical	50	95	30	Normal
HM06	Rock Smash	Fighting	Physical	40	100	15	Normal

MOVES LEARNED IN EXCHANGE FOR BP

Name	Type	Kind	Pow.	Acc.	PP	Range
Iron Head	Steel	Physical	80	100	15	Normal
Magnet Rise	Electric	Status	—	—	10	Self
Iron Defense	Steel	Status	—	—	15	Self
Snore	Normal	Special	50	100	15	Normal
Shock Wave	Electric	Special	60	—	20	Normal
Spite	Ghost	Status	—	100	10	Normal
After You	Normal	Status	—	—	15	Normal

MOVES TAUGHT BY PEOPLE

Name	Type	Kind	Pow.	Acc.	PP	Range

EGG MOVES

Name	Type	Kind	Pow.	Acc.	PP	Range
Metal Sound	Steel	Status	—	85	40	Normal
Shadow Sneak	Ghost	Physical	40	100	30	Normal
Destiny Bond	Ghost	Status	—	—	5	Self
Wide Guard	Rock	Status	—	—	10	Your Side

National Pokédex **680** Hoenn Pokédex —

Doublade

Sword Pokémon

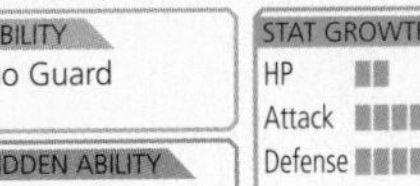

HEIGHT: 2'07" WEIGHT: 9.9 lbs.

Same form for ♂ / ♀

Ω When Honedge evolves, it divides into two swords, which cooperate via telepathy to coordinate attacks and slash their enemies to ribbons.

α The complex attack patterns of its two swords are unstoppable, even for an opponent greatly accomplished at swordplay.

ABILITY
No Guard

HIDDEN ABILITY
—

EGG GROUPS
Mineral

STAT GROWTH RATES
HP
Attack
Defense
Sp. Atk
Sp. Def
Speed

ITEMS SOMETIMES HELD BY WILD POKÉMON
—

EVOLUTION

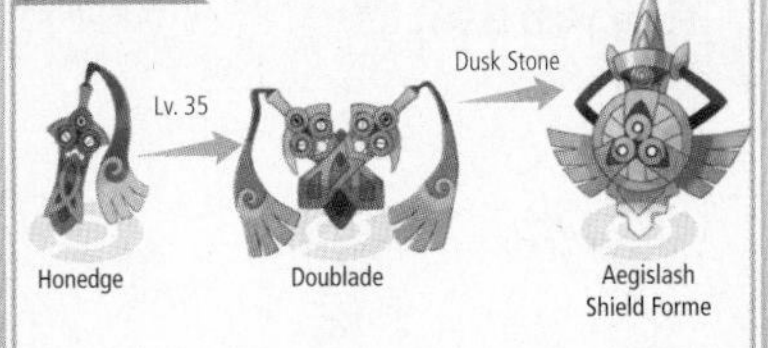

MAIN WAY TO REGISTER IN THE NATIONAL POKÉDEX

Level up an Honedge obtained via Link Trade or the GTS to Lv. 35.

Damage taken in normal battles

Type		Type	
Normal	×0	Flying	×0.5
Fire	×2	Psychic	×0.5
Water	×1	Bug	×0.25
Grass	×0.5	Rock	×0.5
Electric	×1	Ghost	×2
Ice	×0.5	Dragon	×0.5
Fighting	×0	Dark	×2
Poison	×0	Steel	×0.5
Ground	×2	Fairy	×0.5

Damage taken in Inverse battles

Type		Type	
Normal	×4	Flying	×2
Fire	×0.5	Psychic	×2
Water	×1	Bug	×4
Grass	×2	Rock	×2
Electric	×1	Ghost	×0.5
Ice	×2	Dragon	×2
Fighting	×1	Dark	×0.5
Poison	×4	Steel	×2
Ground	×0.5	Fairy	×2

Can be used in
- Inverse Battle
- Battle Institute
- Battle Maison
- Random Matchup (Free Battle)
- Random Matchup (Others)

LEVEL-UP MOVES

Lv.	Name	Type	Kind	Pow.	Acc.	PP	Range
1	Tackle	Normal	Physical	50	100	35	Normal
1	Swords Dance	Normal	Status	—	—	20	Self
5	Fury Cutter	Bug	Physical	40	95	20	Normal
8	Metal Sound	Steel	Status	—	85	40	Normal
13	Pursuit	Dark	Physical	40	100	20	Normal
18	Autotomize	Steel	Status	—	—	15	Self
20	Shadow Sneak	Ghost	Physical	40	100	30	Normal
22	Aerial Ace	Flying	Physical	60	—	20	Normal
26	Retaliate	Normal	Physical	70	100	5	Normal
29	Slash	Normal	Physical	70	100	20	Normal
32	Iron Defense	Steel	Status	—	—	15	Self
36	Night Slash	Dark	Physical	70	100	15	Normal
41	Power Trick	Psychic	Status	—	—	10	Self
45	Iron Head	Steel	Physical	80	100	15	Normal
51	Sacred Sword	Fighting	Physical	90	100	15	Normal

TM & HM MOVES

No.	Name	Type	Kind	Pow.	Acc.	PP	Range
TM06	Toxic	Poison	Status	—	90	10	Normal
TM10	Hidden Power	Normal	Special	60	100	15	Normal
TM17	Protect	Normal	Status	—	—	10	Self
TM18	Rain Dance	Water	Status	—	—	5	Both Sides
TM21	Frustration	Normal	Physical	—	100	20	Normal
TM27	Return	Normal	Physical	—	100	20	Normal
TM31	Brick Break	Fighting	Physical	75	100	15	Normal
TM32	Double Team	Normal	Status	—	—	15	Self
TM33	Reflect	Psychic	Status	—	—	20	Your Side
TM40	Aerial Ace	Flying	Physical	60	—	20	Normal
TM42	Facade	Normal	Physical	70	100	20	Normal
TM44	Rest	Psychic	Status	—	—	10	Self
TM45	Attract	Normal	Status	—	100	15	Normal
TM54	False Swipe	Normal	Physical	40	100	40	Normal
TM65	Shadow Claw	Ghost	Physical	70	100	15	Normal
TM67	Retaliate	Normal	Physical	70	100	5	Normal
TM74	Gyro Ball	Steel	Physical	—	100	5	Normal
TM75	Swords Dance	Normal	Status	—	—	20	Self
TM80	Rock Slide	Rock	Physical	75	90	10	Many Others
TM87	Swagger	Normal	Status	—	90	15	Normal
TM88	Sleep Talk	Normal	Status	—	—	10	Self
TM90	Substitute	Normal	Status	—	—	10	Self
TM91	Flash Cannon	Steel	Special	80	100	10	Normal
TM94	Secret Power	Normal	Physical	70	100	20	Normal
TM100	Confide	Normal	Status	—	—	20	Normal
HM01	Cut	Normal	Physical	50	95	30	Normal
HM06	Rock Smash	Fighting	Physical	40	100	15	Normal

MOVES LEARNED IN EXCHANGE FOR BP

Name	Type	Kind	Pow.	Acc.	PP	Range
Iron Head	Steel	Physical	80	100	15	Normal
Magnet Rise	Electric	Status	—	—	10	Self
Iron Defense	Steel	Status	—	—	15	Self
Snore	Normal	Special	50	100	15	Normal
Shock Wave	Electric	Special	60	—	20	Normal
Spite	Ghost	Status	—	100	10	Normal
After You	Normal	Status	—	—	15	Normal

MOVES TAUGHT BY PEOPLE

Name	Type	Kind	Pow.	Acc.	PP	Range

National Pokédex **681** Hoenn Pokédex —

Aegislash Shield Forme

Royal Sword Pokémon

HEIGHT: 5'07" WEIGHT: 116.8 lbs.

Same form for ♂ / ♀

Ω Generations of kings were attended by these Pokémon, which used their spectral power to manipulate and control people and Pokémon.

α Apparently, it can detect the innate qualities of leadership. According to legend, whoever it recognizes is destined to become king.

ABILITY
Stance Change

HIDDEN ABILITY
—

EGG GROUPS
Mineral

STAT GROWTH RATES
HP
Attack
Defense
Sp. Atk
Sp. Def
Speed

ITEMS SOMETIMES HELD BY WILD POKÉMON
—

EVOLUTION

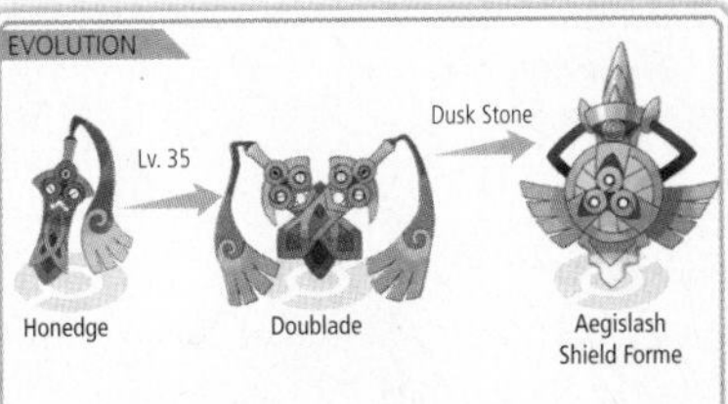

MAIN WAY TO REGISTER IN THE NATIONAL POKÉDEX

Use a Dusk Stone on a Doublade obtained via Link Trade or the GTS.

Damage taken in normal battles

Type		Type	
Normal	×0	Flying	×0.5
Fire	×2	Psychic	×0.5
Water	×1	Bug	×0.25
Grass	×0.5	Rock	×0.5
Electric	×1	Ghost	×2
Ice	×0.5	Dragon	×0.5
Fighting	×0	Dark	×2
Poison	×0	Steel	×0.5
Ground	×2	Fairy	×0.5

Damage taken in Inverse battles

Type		Type	
Normal	×4	Flying	×2
Fire	×0.5	Psychic	×2
Water	×1	Bug	×4
Grass	×2	Rock	×2
Electric	×1	Ghost	×0.5
Ice	×2	Dragon	×2
Fighting	×1	Dark	×0.5
Poison	×4	Steel	×2
Ground	×0.5	Fairy	×2

Can be used in
- Inverse Battle
- Battle Institute
- Battle Maison
- Random Matchup (Free Battle)
- Random Matchup (Others)

LEVEL-UP MOVES

Lv.	Name	Type	Kind	Pow.	Acc.	PP	Range
1	Fury Cutter	Bug	Physical	40	95	20	Normal
1	Pursuit	Dark	Physical	40	100	20	Normal
1	Autotomize	Steel	Status	—	—	15	Self
1	Shadow Sneak	Ghost	Physical	40	100	30	Normal
1	Slash	Normal	Physical	70	100	20	Normal
1	Iron Defense	Steel	Status	—	—	15	Self
1	Night Slash	Dark	Physical	70	100	15	Normal
1	Power Trick	Psychic	Status	—	—	10	Self
1	Iron Head	Steel	Physical	80	100	15	Normal
1	Head Smash	Rock	Physical	150	80	5	Normal
1	Swords Dance	Normal	Status	—	—	20	Self
1	Aerial Ace	Flying	Physical	60	—	20	Normal
1	King's Shield	Steel	Status	—	—	10	Self
1	Sacred Sword	Fighting	Physical	90	100	15	Normal

TM & HM MOVES

No.	Name	Type	Kind	Pow.	Acc.	PP	Range
TM06	Toxic	Poison	Status	—	90	10	Normal
TM10	Hidden Power	Normal	Special	60	100	15	Normal
TM11	Sunny Day	Fire	Status	—	—	5	Both Sides
TM15	Hyper Beam	Normal	Special	150	90	5	Normal
TM17	Protect	Normal	Status	—	—	10	Self
TM18	Rain Dance	Water	Status	—	—	5	Both Sides
TM21	Frustration	Normal	Physical	—	100	20	Normal
TM27	Return	Normal	Physical	—	100	20	Normal
TM30	Shadow Ball	Ghost	Special	80	100	15	Normal
TM31	Brick Break	Fighting	Physical	75	100	15	Normal
TM32	Double Team	Normal	Status	—	—	15	Self
TM33	Reflect	Psychic	Status	—	—	20	Your Side
TM40	Aerial Ace	Flying	Physical	60	—	20	Normal
TM42	Facade	Normal	Physical	70	100	20	Normal
TM44	Rest	Psychic	Status	—	—	10	Self
TM45	Attract	Normal	Status	—	100	15	Normal
TM48	Round	Normal	Special	60	100	15	Normal
TM54	False Swipe	Normal	Physical	40	100	40	Normal
TM65	Shadow Claw	Ghost	Physical	70	100	15	Normal
TM67	Retaliate	Normal	Physical	70	100	5	Normal
TM68	Giga Impact	Normal	Physical	150	90	5	Normal
TM74	Gyro Ball	Steel	Physical	—	100	5	Normal
TM75	Swords Dance	Normal	Status	—	—	20	Self
TM80	Rock Slide	Rock	Physical	75	90	10	Many Others
TM87	Swagger	Normal	Status	—	90	15	Normal
TM88	Sleep Talk	Normal	Status	—	—	10	Self
TM90	Substitute	Normal	Status	—	—	10	Self
TM91	Flash Cannon	Steel	Special	80	100	10	Normal
TM94	Secret Power	Normal	Physical	70	100	20	Normal
TM100	Confide	Normal	Status	—	—	20	Normal
HM01	Cut	Normal	Physical	50	95	30	Normal
HM06	Rock Smash	Fighting	Physical	40	100	15	Normal

MOVES LEARNED IN EXCHANGE FOR BP

Name	Type	Kind	Pow.	Acc.	PP	Range
Iron Head	Steel	Physical	80	100	15	Normal
Block	Normal	Status	—	—	5	Normal
Magnet Rise	Electric	Status	—	—	10	Self
Iron Defense	Steel	Status	—	—	15	Self
Snore	Normal	Special	50	100	15	Normal
Shock Wave	Electric	Special	60	—	20	Normal
Spite	Ghost	Status	—	100	10	Normal
After You	Normal	Status	—	—	15	Normal

MOVES TAUGHT BY PEOPLE

Name	Type	Kind	Pow.	Acc.	PP	Range

National Pokédex **681** Hoenn Pokédex –

Aegislash Blade Forme

Royal Sword Pokémon

Steel | Ghost

HEIGHT: 5'07" WEIGHT: 116.8 lbs.

Same form for ♂ / ♀

Ω Generations of kings were attended by these Pokémon, which used their spectral power to manipulate and control people and Pokémon.

α Apparently, it can detect the innate qualities of leadership. According to legend, whoever it recognizes is destined to become king.

ABILITY
Stance Change

HIDDEN ABILITY
—

EGG GROUPS
Mineral

STAT GROWTH RATES
HP ▮▮▮
Attack ▮▮▮▮▮▮▮▮
Defense ▮▮
Sp. Atk ▮▮▮▮▮▮▮
Sp. Def ▮▮
Speed ▮▮▮

ITEMS SOMETIMES HELD BY WILD POKÉMON
—

EVOLUTION

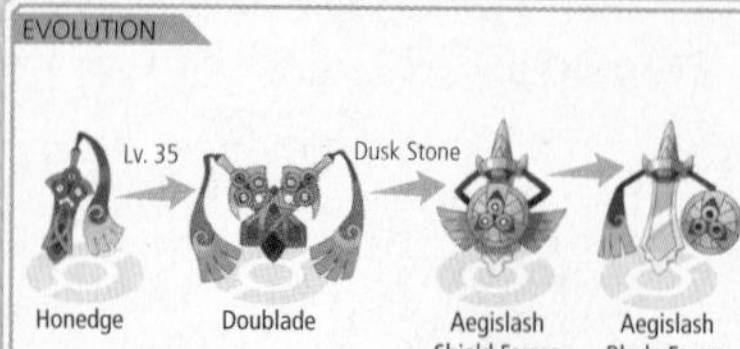

MAIN WAY TO REGISTER IN THE NATIONAL POKÉDEX

Use a physical or special move with Aegislash Shield Forme to make it change into its Blade Forme. Use the move King's Shield to return it to its Shield Forme.

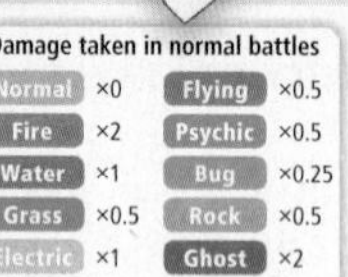

Damage taken in normal battles

Normal	×0	Flying	×0.5
Fire	×2	Psychic	×0.5
Water	×1	Bug	×0.25
Grass	×0.5	Rock	×0.5
Electric	×1	Ghost	×2
Ice	×0.5	Dragon	×0.5
Fighting	×0	Dark	×2
Poison	×0	Steel	×0.5
Ground	×2	Fairy	×0.5

Damage taken in Inverse battles

Normal	×4	Flying	×2
Fire	×0.5	Psychic	×2
Water	×1	Bug	×4
Grass	×2	Rock	×2
Electric	×1	Ghost	×0.5
Ice	×2	Dragon	×2
Fighting	×1	Dark	×0.5
Poison	×4	Steel	×2
Ground	×0.5	Fairy	×2

Can be used in
- Inverse Battle
- Battle Institute
- Battle Maison
- Random Matchup (Free Battle)
- Random Matchup (Others)

LEVEL-UP MOVES

Lv.	Name	Type	Kind	Pow.	Acc.	PP	Range
1	Fury Cutter	Bug	Physical	40	95	20	Normal
1	Pursuit	Dark	Physical	40	100	20	Normal
1	Autotomize	Steel	Status	—	—	15	Self
1	Shadow Sneak	Ghost	Physical	40	100	30	Normal
1	Slash	Normal	Physical	70	100	20	Normal
1	Iron Defense	Steel	Status	—	—	15	Self
1	Night Slash	Dark	Physical	70	100	15	Normal
1	Power Trick	Psychic	Status	—	—	10	Self
1	Iron Head	Steel	Physical	80	100	15	Normal
1	Head Smash	Rock	Physical	150	80	5	Normal
1	Swords Dance	Normal	Status	—	—	20	Self
1	Aerial Ace	Flying	Physical	60	—	20	Normal
1	King's Shield	Steel	Status	—	—	10	Self
1	Sacred Sword	Fighting	Physical	90	100	15	Normal

TM & HM MOVES

No.	Name	Type	Kind	Pow.	Acc.	PP	Range
TM06	Toxic	Poison	Status	—	90	10	Normal
TM10	Hidden Power	Normal	Special	60	100	15	Normal
TM11	Sunny Day	Fire	Status	—	—	5	Both Sides
TM15	Hyper Beam	Normal	Special	150	90	5	Normal
TM17	Protect	Normal	Status	—	—	10	Self
TM18	Rain Dance	Water	Status	—	—	5	Both Sides
TM21	Frustration	Normal	Physical	—	100	20	Normal
TM27	Return	Normal	Physical	—	100	20	Normal
TM30	Shadow Ball	Ghost	Special	80	100	15	Normal
TM31	Brick Break	Fighting	Physical	75	100	15	Normal
TM32	Double Team	Normal	Status	—	—	15	Self
TM33	Reflect	Psychic	Status	—	—	20	Your Side
TM40	Aerial Ace	Flying	Physical	60	—	20	Normal
TM42	Facade	Normal	Physical	70	100	20	Normal
TM44	Rest	Psychic	Status	—	—	10	Self
TM45	Attract	Normal	Status	—	100	15	Normal
TM48	Round	Normal	Special	60	100	15	Normal
TM54	False Swipe	Normal	Physical	40	100	40	Normal
TM65	Shadow Claw	Ghost	Physical	70	100	15	Normal
TM67	Retaliate	Normal	Physical	70	100	5	Normal
TM68	Giga Impact	Normal	Physical	150	90	5	Normal
TM74	Gyro Ball	Steel	Physical	—	100	5	Normal
TM75	Swords Dance	Normal	Status	—	—	20	Self
TM80	Rock Slide	Rock	Physical	75	90	10	Many Others
TM87	Swagger	Normal	Status	—	90	15	Normal
TM88	Sleep Talk	Normal	Status	—	—	10	Self
TM90	Substitute	Normal	Status	—	—	10	Self
TM91	Flash Cannon	Steel	Special	80	100	10	Normal
TM94	Secret Power	Normal	Physical	70	100	20	Normal
TM100	Confide	Normal	Status	—	—	20	Normal
HM01	Cut	Normal	Physical	50	95	30	Normal
HM06	Rock Smash	Fighting	Physical	40	100	15	Normal

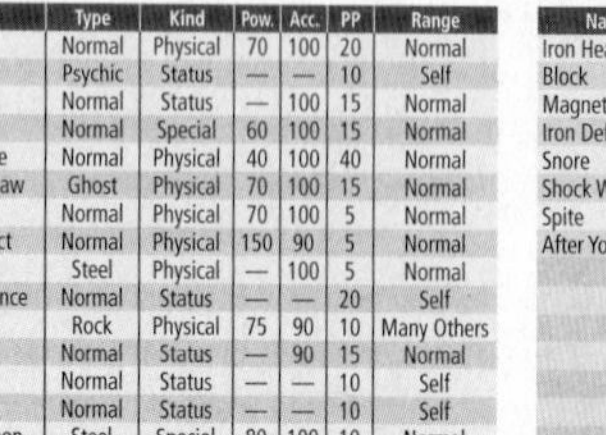

MOVES LEARNED IN EXCHANGE FOR BP

Name	Type	Kind	Pow.	Acc.	PP	Range
Iron Head	Steel	Physical	80	100	15	Normal
Block	Normal	Status	—	—	5	Normal
Magnet Rise	Electric	Status	—	—	10	Self
Iron Defense	Steel	Status	—	—	15	Self
Snore	Normal	Special	50	100	15	Normal
Shock Wave	Electric	Special	60	—	20	Normal
Spite	Ghost	Status	—	100	10	Normal
After You	Normal	Status	—	—	15	Normal

MOVES TAUGHT BY PEOPLE

Name	Type	Kind	Pow.	Acc.	PP	Range

National Pokédex **682** Hoenn Pokédex –

Spritzee

Perfume Pokémon

Fairy

HEIGHT: 0'08" WEIGHT: 1.1 lbs.

Same form for ♂ / ♀

Ω It emits a scent that enraptures those who smell it. This fragrance changes depending on what it has eaten.

α In the past, rather than using perfume, royal ladies carried a Spritzee that would waft a fragrance they liked.

ABILITY
Healer

HIDDEN ABILITY
Aroma Veil

EGG GROUPS
Fairy

STAT GROWTH RATES
HP ▮▮▮
Attack ▮▮▮
Defense ▮▮▮
Sp. Atk ▮▮▮
Sp. Def ▮▮▮
Speed ▮

ITEMS SOMETIMES HELD BY WILD POKÉMON
—

EVOLUTION

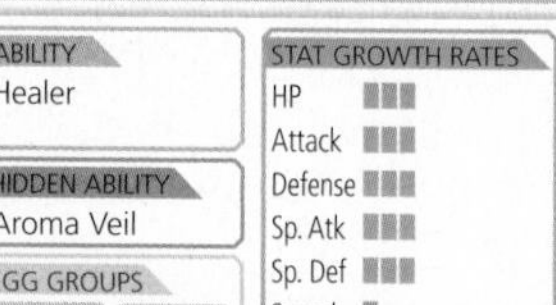

MAIN WAY TO REGISTER IN THE NATIONAL POKÉDEX

Appears in *Pokémon Y*. Bring it to your game using Link Trade or the GTS.

Damage taken in normal battles

Normal	×1	Flying	×1
Fire	×1	Psychic	×1
Water	×1	Bug	×0.5
Grass	×1	Rock	×1
Electric	×1	Ghost	×1
Ice	×1	Dragon	×0
Fighting	×0.5	Dark	×0.5
Poison	×2	Steel	×2
Ground	×1	Fairy	×1

Damage taken in Inverse battles

Normal	×1	Flying	×1
Fire	×1	Psychic	×1
Water	×1	Bug	×2
Grass	×1	Rock	×1
Electric	×1	Ghost	×1
Ice	×1	Dragon	×2
Fighting	×2	Dark	×2
Poison	×0.5	Steel	×0.5
Ground	×1	Fairy	×1

Can be used in
- Inverse Battle
- Battle Institute
- Battle Maison
- Random Matchup (Free Battle)
- Random Matchup (Others)

LEVEL-UP MOVES

Lv.	Name	Type	Kind	Pow.	Acc.	PP	Range
1	Sweet Scent	Normal	Status	—	100	20	Many Others
1	Fairy Wind	Fairy	Special	40	100	30	Normal
6	Sweet Kiss	Fairy	Status	—	75	10	Normal
8	Odor Sleuth	Normal	Status	—	—	40	Normal
13	Echoed Voice	Normal	Special	40	100	15	Normal
17	Calm Mind	Psychic	Status	—	—	20	Self
21	Draining Kiss	Fairy	Special	50	100	10	Normal
25	Aromatherapy	Grass	Status	—	—	5	Your Party
29	Attract	Normal	Status	—	100	15	Normal
31	Moonblast	Fairy	Special	95	100	15	Normal
35	Charm	Fairy	Status	—	100	20	Normal
38	Flail	Normal	Physical	—	100	15	Normal
42	Misty Terrain	Fairy	Status	—	—	10	Both Sides
44	Skill Swap	Psychic	Status	—	—	10	Normal
48	Psychic	Psychic	Special	90	100	10	Normal
50	Disarming Voice	Fairy	Special	40	—	15	Many Others

TM & HM MOVES

No.	Name	Type	Kind	Pow.	Acc.	PP	Range
TM04	Calm Mind	Psychic	Status	—	—	20	Self
TM06	Toxic	Poison	Status	—	90	10	Normal
TM10	Hidden Power	Normal	Special	60	100	15	Normal
TM11	Sunny Day	Fire	Status	—	—	5	Both Sides
TM16	Light Screen	Psychic	Status	—	—	30	Your Side
TM17	Protect	Normal	Status	—	—	10	Self
TM18	Rain Dance	Water	Status	—	—	5	Both Sides
TM21	Frustration	Normal	Physical	—	100	20	Normal
TM24	Thunderbolt	Electric	Special	90	100	15	Normal
TM27	Return	Normal	Physical	—	100	20	Normal
TM29	Psychic	Psychic	Special	90	100	10	Normal
TM32	Double Team	Normal	Status	—	—	15	Self
TM33	Reflect	Psychic	Status	—	—	20	Your Side
TM41	Torment	Dark	Status	—	100	15	Normal
TM42	Facade	Normal	Physical	70	100	20	Normal
TM44	Rest	Psychic	Status	—	—	10	Self
TM45	Attract	Normal	Status	—	100	15	Normal
TM48	Round	Normal	Special	60	100	15	Normal
TM49	Echoed Voice	Normal	Special	40	100	15	Normal
TM53	Energy Ball	Grass	Special	90	100	10	Normal
TM57	Charge Beam	Electric	Special	50	90	10	Normal
TM70	Flash	Normal	Status	—	100	20	Normal
TM74	Gyro Ball	Steel	Physical	—	100	5	Normal
TM77	Psych Up	Normal	Status	—	—	10	Normal
TM85	Dream Eater	Psychic	Special	100	100	15	Normal
TM87	Swagger	Normal	Status	—	90	15	Normal
TM88	Sleep Talk	Normal	Status	—	—	10	Self
TM90	Substitute	Normal	Status	—	—	10	Self
TM91	Flash Cannon	Steel	Special	80	100	10	Normal
TM92	Trick Room	Psychic	Status	—	—	5	Both Sides
TM94	Secret Power	Normal	Physical	70	100	20	Normal
TM99	Dazzling Gleam	Fairy	Special	80	100	10	Many Others
TM100	Confide	Normal	Status	—	—	20	Normal

MOVES LEARNED IN EXCHANGE FOR BP

Name	Type	Kind	Pow.	Acc.	PP	Range
Covet	Normal	Physical	60	100	25	Normal
Magic Coat	Psychic	Status	—	—	15	Self
Snore	Normal	Special	50	100	15	Normal
Heal Bell	Normal	Status	—	—	5	Your Party
After You	Normal	Status	—	—	15	Normal
Helping Hand	Normal	Status	—	—	20	1 Ally
Endeavor	Normal	Physical	—	100	5	Normal
Skill Swap	Psychic	Status	—	—	10	Normal

MOVES TAUGHT BY PEOPLE

Name	Type	Kind	Pow.	Acc.	PP	Range

EGG MOVES

Name	Type	Kind	Pow.	Acc.	PP	Range
Disable	Normal	Status	—	100	20	Normal
Wish	Normal	Status	—	—	10	Self
Captivate	Normal	Status	—	100	20	Many Others
Refresh	Normal	Status	—	—	20	Self

National Pokédex **683** Hoenn Pokédex —

Aromatisse

Fragrance Pokémon

Fairy

HEIGHT: 2'07" WEIGHT: 34.2 lbs.

Same form for ♂ / ♀

Ω It devises various scents, pleasant and unpleasant, and emits scents that its enemies dislike in order to gain an edge in battle.

α Its scent is so overpowering that, unless a Trainer happens to really enjoy the smell, he or she will have a hard time walking alongside it.

ABILITY
Healer

HIDDEN ABILITY
Aroma Veil

EGG GROUPS
Fairy

STAT GROWTH RATES

HP	■■■■
Attack	■■■■
Defense	■■■
Sp. Atk	■■■■■
Sp. Def	■■■■
Speed	■■

ITEMS SOMETIMES HELD BY WILD POKÉMON
—

EVOLUTION

Spritzee → Link Trade with Sachet → Aromatisse

MAIN WAY TO REGISTER IN THE NATIONAL POKÉDEX

Receive a Spritzee that is holding a Sachet via Link Trade to have it evolve.

Damage taken in normal battles

Type	×	Type	×
Normal	×1	Flying	×1
Fire	×1	Psychic	×1
Water	×1	Bug	×0.5
Grass	×1	Rock	×1
Electric	×1	Ghost	×1
Ice	×1	Dragon	×0
Fighting	×0.5	Dark	×0.5
Poison	×2	Steel	×2
Ground	×1	Fairy	×1

Damage taken in Inverse battles

Type	×	Type	×
Normal	×1	Flying	×1
Fire	×1	Psychic	×1
Water	×1	Bug	×2
Grass	×1	Rock	×1
Electric	×1	Ghost	×1
Ice	×1	Dragon	×2
Fighting	×2	Dark	×2
Poison	×0.5	Steel	×0.5
Ground	×1	Fairy	×1

Can be used in
Inverse Battle
Battle Institute
Battle Maison
Random Matchup (Free Battle)
Random Matchup (Others)

LEVEL-UP MOVES

Lv.	Name	Type	Kind	Pow.	Acc.	PP	Range
1	Aromatic Mist	Fairy	Status	—	—	20	1 Ally
1	Heal Pulse	Psychic	Status	—	—	10	Normal
1	Sweet Scent	Normal	Status	—	100	20	Many Others
1	Fairy Wind	Fairy	Special	40	100	30	Normal
6	Sweet Kiss	Fairy	Status	—	75	10	Normal
8	Odor Sleuth	Normal	Status	—	—	40	Normal
13	Echoed Voice	Normal	Special	40	100	15	Normal
17	Calm Mind	Psychic	Status	—	—	20	Self
21	Draining Kiss	Fairy	Special	50	100	10	Normal
25	Aromatherapy	Grass	Status	—	—	5	Your Party
29	Attract	Normal	Status	—	100	15	Normal
31	Moonblast	Fairy	Special	95	100	15	Normal
35	Charm	Fairy	Status	—	100	20	Normal
38	Flail	Normal	Physical	—	100	15	Normal
42	Misty Terrain	Fairy	Status	—	—	10	Both Sides
44	Skill Swap	Psychic	Status	—	—	10	Normal
48	Psychic	Psychic	Special	90	100	10	Normal
53	Disarming Voice	Fairy	Special	40	—	15	Many Others
57	Reflect	Psychic	Status	—	—	20	Your Side
64	Psych Up	Normal	Status	—	—	10	Normal

TM & HM MOVES

No.	Name	Type	Kind	Pow.	Acc.	PP	Range
TM03	Psyshock	Psychic	Special	80	100	10	Normal
TM04	Calm Mind	Psychic	Status	—	—	20	Self
TM06	Toxic	Poison	Status	—	90	10	Normal
TM10	Hidden Power	Normal	Special	60	100	15	Normal
TM11	Sunny Day	Fire	Status	—	—	5	Both Sides
TM15	Hyper Beam	Normal	Special	150	90	5	Normal
TM16	Light Screen	Psychic	Status	—	—	30	Your Side
TM17	Protect	Normal	Status	—	—	10	Self
TM18	Rain Dance	Water	Status	—	—	5	Both Sides
TM21	Frustration	Normal	Physical	—	100	20	Normal
TM24	Thunderbolt	Electric	Special	90	100	15	Normal
TM25	Thunder	Electric	Special	110	70	10	Normal
TM27	Return	Normal	Physical	—	100	20	Normal
TM29	Psychic	Psychic	Special	90	100	10	Normal
TM32	Double Team	Normal	Status	—	—	15	Self
TM33	Reflect	Psychic	Status	—	—	20	Your Side
TM41	Torment	Dark	Status	—	100	15	Normal
TM42	Facade	Normal	Physical	70	100	20	Normal
TM44	Rest	Psychic	Status	—	—	10	Self
TM45	Attract	Normal	Status	—	100	15	Normal
TM48	Round	Normal	Special	60	100	15	Normal
TM49	Echoed Voice	Normal	Special	40	100	15	Normal
TM53	Energy Ball	Grass	Special	90	100	10	Normal
TM57	Charge Beam	Electric	Special	50	90	10	Normal
TM68	Giga Impact	Normal	Physical	150	90	5	Normal
TM70	Flash	Normal	Status	—	100	20	Normal
TM74	Gyro Ball	Steel	Physical	—	100	5	Normal
TM77	Psych Up	Normal	Status	—	—	10	Normal
TM85	Dream Eater	Psychic	Special	100	100	15	Normal
TM87	Swagger	Normal	Status	—	90	15	Normal
TM88	Sleep Talk	Normal	Status	—	—	10	Self
TM90	Substitute	Normal	Status	—	—	10	Self
TM91	Flash Cannon	Steel	Special	80	100	10	Normal
TM92	Trick Room	Psychic	Status	—	—	5	Both Sides
TM94	Secret Power	Normal	Physical	70	100	20	Normal
TM99	Dazzling Gleam	Fairy	Special	80	100	10	Many Others
TM100	Confide	Normal	Status	—	—	20	Normal

MOVES LEARNED IN EXCHANGE FOR BP

Name	Type	Kind	Pow.	Acc.	PP	Range
Covet	Normal	Physical	60	100	25	Normal
Magic Coat	Psychic	Status	—	—	15	Self
Snore	Normal	Special	50	100	15	Normal
Heal Bell	Normal	Status	—	—	5	Your Party
Drain Punch	Fighting	Physical	75	100	10	Normal
After You	Normal	Status	—	—	15	Normal
Helping Hand	Normal	Status	—	—	20	1 Ally
Endeavor	Normal	Physical	—	100	5	Normal
Skill Swap	Psychic	Status	—	—	10	Normal

MOVES TAUGHT BY PEOPLE

Name	Type	Kind	Pow.	Acc.	PP	Range

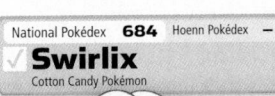

National Pokédex **684** Hoenn Pokédex —

Swirlix

Cotton Candy Pokémon

Fairy

HEIGHT: 1'04" WEIGHT: 7.7 lbs.

Same form for ♂ / ♀

Ω To entangle its opponents in battle, it extrudes white threads as sweet and sticky as cotton candy.

α Because it eats nothing but sweets, its fur is as sticky sweet as cotton candy.

ABILITY
Sweet Veil

HIDDEN ABILITY
Unburden

EGG GROUPS
Fairy

STAT GROWTH RATES

HP	■■■
Attack	■■■
Defense	■■■
Sp. Atk	■■■
Sp. Def	■■
Speed	■■■

ITEMS SOMETIMES HELD BY WILD POKÉMON
—

EVOLUTION

Swirlix → Link Trade with Whipped Dream → Slurpuff

MAIN WAY TO REGISTER IN THE NATIONAL POKÉDEX

Appears in *Pokémon X*. Bring it to your game using Link Trade or the GTS.

Damage taken in normal battles

Type	×	Type	×
Normal	×1	Flying	×1
Fire	×1	Psychic	×1
Water	×1	Bug	×0.5
Grass	×1	Rock	×1
Electric	×1	Ghost	×1
Ice	×1	Dragon	×0
Fighting	×0.5	Dark	×0.5
Poison	×2	Steel	×2
Ground	×1	Fairy	×1

Damage taken in Inverse battles

Type	×	Type	×
Normal	×1	Flying	×1
Fire	×1	Psychic	×1
Water	×1	Bug	×2
Grass	×1	Rock	×1
Electric	×1	Ghost	×1
Ice	×1	Dragon	×2
Fighting	×2	Dark	×2
Poison	×0.5	Steel	×0.5
Ground	×1	Fairy	×1

Can be used in
Inverse Battle
Battle Institute
Battle Maison
Random Matchup (Free Battle)
Random Matchup (Others)

LEVEL-UP MOVES

Lv.	Name	Type	Kind	Pow.	Acc.	PP	Range
1	Sweet Scent	Normal	Status	—	100	20	Many Others
1	Tackle	Normal	Physical	50	100	35	Normal
5	Fairy Wind	Fairy	Special	40	100	30	Normal
8	Play Nice	Normal	Status	—	—	20	Normal
10	Fake Tears	Dark	Status	—	100	20	Normal
13	Round	Normal	Special	60	100	15	Normal
17	Cotton Spore	Grass	Status	—	100	40	Many Others
21	Endeavor	Normal	Physical	—	100	5	Normal
26	Aromatherapy	Grass	Status	—	—	5	Your Party
31	Draining Kiss	Fairy	Special	50	100	10	Normal
36	Energy Ball	Grass	Special	90	100	10	Normal
41	Cotton Guard	Grass	Status	—	—	10	Self
45	Wish	Normal	Status	—	—	10	Self
49	Play Rough	Fairy	Physical	90	90	10	Normal
58	Light Screen	Psychic	Status	—	—	30	Your Side
67	Safeguard	Normal	Status	—	—	25	Your Side

TM & HM MOVES

No.	Name	Type	Kind	Pow.	Acc.	PP	Range
TM04	Calm Mind	Psychic	Status	—	—	20	Self
TM06	Toxic	Poison	Status	—	90	10	Normal
TM10	Hidden Power	Normal	Special	60	100	15	Normal
TM11	Sunny Day	Fire	Status	—	—	5	Both Sides
TM16	Light Screen	Psychic	Status	—	—	30	Your Side
TM17	Protect	Normal	Status	—	—	10	Self
TM18	Rain Dance	Water	Status	—	—	5	Both Sides
TM20	Safeguard	Normal	Status	—	—	25	Your Side
TM21	Frustration	Normal	Physical	—	100	20	Normal
TM24	Thunderbolt	Electric	Special	90	100	15	Normal
TM27	Return	Normal	Physical	—	100	20	Normal
TM29	Psychic	Psychic	Special	90	100	10	Normal
TM32	Double Team	Normal	Status	—	—	15	Self
TM35	Flamethrower	Fire	Special	90	100	15	Normal
TM42	Facade	Normal	Physical	70	100	20	Normal
TM44	Rest	Psychic	Status	—	—	10	Self
TM45	Attract	Normal	Status	—	100	15	Normal
TM46	Thief	Dark	Physical	60	100	25	Normal
TM48	Round	Normal	Special	60	100	15	Normal
TM53	Energy Ball	Grass	Special	90	100	10	Normal
TM70	Flash	Normal	Status	—	100	20	Normal
TM77	Psych Up	Normal	Status	—	—	10	Normal
TM85	Dream Eater	Psychic	Special	100	100	15	Normal
TM87	Swagger	Normal	Status	—	90	15	Normal
TM88	Sleep Talk	Normal	Status	—	—	10	Self
TM90	Substitute	Normal	Status	—	—	10	Self
TM94	Secret Power	Normal	Physical	70	100	20	Normal
TM99	Dazzling Gleam	Fairy	Special	80	100	10	Many Others
TM100	Confide	Normal	Status	—	—	20	Normal
HM03	Surf	Water	Special	90	100	15	Adjacent

MOVES LEARNED IN EXCHANGE FOR BP

Name	Type	Kind	Pow.	Acc.	PP	Range
Covet	Normal	Physical	60	100	25	Normal
Magic Coat	Psychic	Status	—	—	15	Self
Snore	Normal	Special	50	100	15	Normal
Heal Bell	Normal	Status	—	—	5	Your Party
Gastro Acid	Poison	Status	—	100	10	Normal
After You	Normal	Status	—	—	15	Normal
Helping Hand	Normal	Status	—	—	20	1 Ally
Endeavor	Normal	Physical	—	100	5	Normal

MOVES TAUGHT BY PEOPLE

Name	Type	Kind	Pow.	Acc.	PP	Range

EGG MOVES

Name	Type	Kind	Pow.	Acc.	PP	Range
After You	Normal	Status	—	—	15	Normal
Yawn	Normal	Status	—	—	10	Normal
Belly Drum	Normal	Status	—	—	10	Self
Copycat	Normal	Status	—	—	20	Self

685
Slurpuff

National Pokédex **685** Hoenn Pokédex —

Slurpuff

Meringue Pokémon

Fairy

HEIGHT: 2'07" WEIGHT: 11 lbs.

Same form for ♂ / ♀

Ω It can distinguish the faintest of scents. It puts its sensitive sense of smell to use by helping pastry chefs in their work.

α Its sense of smell is 100 million times better than a human's, so even the faintest scent tells it about everything in the area. It's like it can see with its nose!

ABILITY
Sweet Veil

HIDDEN ABILITY
Unburden

EGG GROUPS
Fairy

STAT GROWTH RATES
HP
Attack
Defense
Sp. Atk
Sp. Def
Speed

ITEMS SOMETIMES HELD BY WILD POKÉMON
—

EVOLUTION

Swirlix → Link Trade with Whipped Dream → Slurpuff

MAIN WAY TO REGISTER IN THE NATIONAL POKÉDEX

Receive a Swirlix that is holding a Whipped Dream via Link Trade to have it evolve.

Damage taken in normal battles

Type		Type	
Normal	×1	Flying	×1
Fire	×1	Psychic	×1
Water	×1	Bug	×0.5
Grass	×1	Rock	×1
Electric	×1	Ghost	×1
Ice	×1	Dragon	×0
Fighting	×0.5	Dark	×0.5
Poison	×2	Steel	×2
Ground	×1	Fairy	×1

Damage taken in Inverse battles

Type		Type	
Normal	×1	Flying	×1
Fire	×1	Psychic	×1
Water	×1	Bug	×2
Grass	×1	Rock	×1
Electric	×1	Ghost	×1
Ice	×1	Dragon	×2
Fighting	×2	Dark	×2
Poison	×0.5	Steel	×0.5
Ground	×1	Fairy	×1

Can be used in
- Inverse Battle
- Battle Institute
- Battle Maison
- Random Matchup (Free Battle)
- Random Matchup (Others)

LEVEL-UP MOVES

Lv.	Name	Type	Kind	Pow.	Acc.	PP	Range
1	Sweet Scent	Normal	Status	—	100	20	Many Others
1	Tackle	Normal	Physical	50	100	35	Normal
5	Fairy Wind	Fairy	Special	40	100	30	Normal
8	Play Nice	Normal	Status	—	—	20	Normal
10	Fake Tears	Dark	Status	—	100	20	Normal
13	Round	Normal	Special	60	100	15	Normal
17	Cotton Spore	Grass	Status	—	100	40	Many Others
21	Endeavor	Normal	Physical	—	100	5	Normal
26	Aromatherapy	Grass	Status	—	—	5	Your Party
31	Draining Kiss	Fairy	Special	50	100	10	Normal
36	Energy Ball	Grass	Special	90	100	10	Normal
41	Cotton Guard	Grass	Status	—	—	10	Self
45	Wish	Normal	Status	—	—	10	Self
49	Play Rough	Fairy	Physical	90	90	10	Normal
58	Light Screen	Psychic	Status	—	—	30	Your Side
67	Safeguard	Normal	Status	—	—	25	Your Side

TM & HM MOVES

No.	Name	Type	Kind	Pow.	Acc.	PP	Range
TM04	Calm Mind	Psychic	Status	—	—	20	Self
TM06	Toxic	Poison	Status	—	90	10	Normal
TM10	Hidden Power	Normal	Special	60	100	15	Normal
TM11	Sunny Day	Fire	Status	—	—	5	Both Sides
TM15	Hyper Beam	Normal	Special	150	90	5	Normal
TM16	Light Screen	Psychic	Status	—	—	30	Your Side
TM17	Protect	Normal	Status	—	—	10	Self
TM18	Rain Dance	Water	Status	—	—	5	Both Sides
TM20	Safeguard	Normal	Status	—	—	25	Your Side
TM21	Frustration	Normal	Physical	—	100	20	Normal
TM24	Thunderbolt	Electric	Special	90	100	15	Normal
TM27	Return	Normal	Physical	—	100	20	Normal
TM29	Psychic	Psychic	Special	90	100	10	Normal
TM32	Double Team	Normal	Status	—	—	15	Self
TM35	Flamethrower	Fire	Special	90	100	15	Normal
TM42	Facade	Normal	Physical	70	100	20	Normal
TM44	Rest	Psychic	Status	—	—	10	Self
TM45	Attract	Normal	Status	—	100	15	Normal
TM46	Thief	Dark	Physical	60	100	25	Normal
TM48	Round	Normal	Special	60	100	15	Normal
TM53	Energy Ball	Grass	Special	90	100	10	Normal
TM68	Giga Impact	Normal	Physical	150	90	5	Normal
TM70	Flash	Normal	Status	—	100	20	Normal
TM77	Psych Up	Normal	Status	—	—	10	Normal
TM85	Dream Eater	Psychic	Special	100	100	15	Normal
TM87	Swagger	Normal	Status	—	90	15	Normal
TM88	Sleep Talk	Normal	Status	—	—	10	Self
TM90	Substitute	Normal	Status	—	—	10	Self
TM94	Secret Power	Normal	Physical	70	100	20	Normal
TM99	Dazzling Gleam	Fairy	Special	80	100	10	Many Others
TM100	Confide	Normal	Status	—	—	20	Normal
HM03	Surf	Water	Special	90	100	15	Adjacent

MOVES LEARNED IN EXCHANGE FOR BP

Name	Type	Kind	Pow.	Acc.	PP	Range
Covet	Normal	Physical	60	100	25	Normal
Magic Coat	Psychic	Status	—	—	15	Self
Snore	Normal	Special	50	100	15	Normal
Heal Bell	Normal	Status	—	—	5	Your Party
Drain Punch	Fighting	Physical	75	100	10	Normal
Gastro Acid	Poison	Status	—	100	10	Normal
After You	Normal	Status	—	—	15	Normal
Helping Hand	Normal	Status	—	—	20	1 Ally
Endeavor	Normal	Physical	—	100	5	Normal

MOVES TAUGHT BY PEOPLE

Name	Type	Kind	Pow.	Acc.	PP	Range

National Pokédex

Inkay

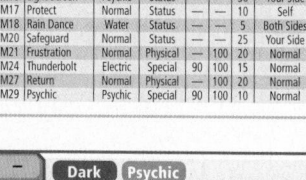

686

National Pokédex **686** Hoenn Pokédex —

Inkay

Revolving Pokémon

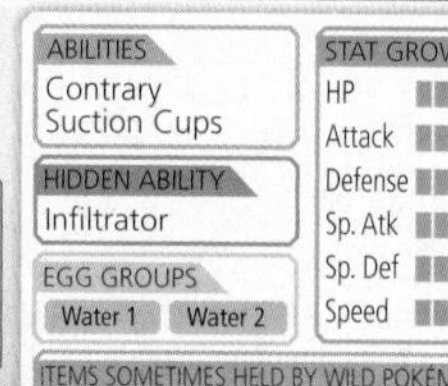

Dark Psychic

HEIGHT: 1'04" WEIGHT: 7.7 lbs.

Same form for ♂ / ♀

Ω Opponents who stare at the flashing of the light-emitting spots on its body become dazed and lose their will to fight.

α It flashes the light-emitting spots on its body, which drains its opponent's will to fight. It takes the opportunity to scuttle away and hide.

ABILITIES
Contrary
Suction Cups

HIDDEN ABILITY
Infiltrator

EGG GROUPS
Water 1 Water 2

STAT GROWTH RATES
HP
Attack
Defense
Sp. Atk
Sp. Def
Speed

ITEMS SOMETIMES HELD BY WILD POKÉMON
—

EVOLUTION

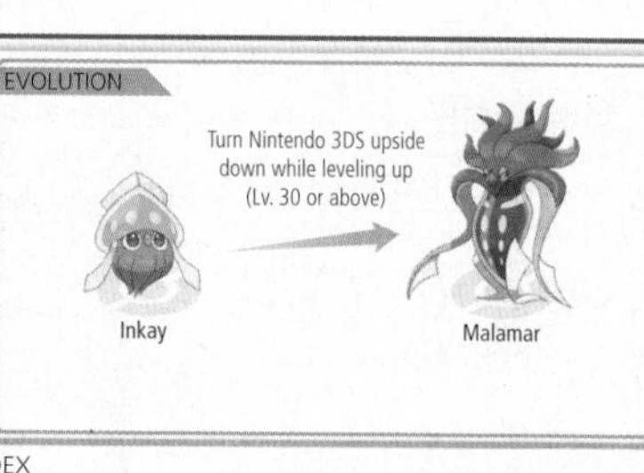

MAIN WAY TO REGISTER IN THE NATIONAL POKÉDEX

Appears in *Pokémon X* and *Pokémon Y*. Bring it to your game using Link Trade or the GTS.

Damage taken in normal battles

Type		Type	
Normal	×1	Flying	×1
Fire	×1	Psychic	×0
Water	×1	Bug	×4
Grass	×1	Rock	×1
Electric	×1	Ghost	×1
Ice	×1	Dragon	×1
Fighting	×1	Dark	×1
Poison	×1	Steel	×1
Ground	×1	Fairy	×2

Damage taken in Inverse battles

Type		Type	
Normal	×1	Flying	×1
Fire	×1	Psychic	×4
Water	×1	Bug	×0.25
Grass	×1	Rock	×1
Electric	×1	Ghost	×1
Ice	×1	Dragon	×1
Fighting	×1	Dark	×1
Poison	×1	Steel	×1
Ground	×1	Fairy	×0.5

Can be used in
- Inverse Battle
- Battle Institute
- Battle Maison
- Random Matchup (Free Battle)
- Random Matchup (Others)

LEVEL-UP MOVES

Lv.	Name	Type	Kind	Pow.	Acc.	PP	Range
1	Tackle	Normal	Physical	50	100	35	Normal
1	Peck	Flying	Physical	35	100	35	Normal
1	Constrict	Normal	Physical	10	100	35	Normal
4	Reflect	Psychic	Status	—	—	20	Your Side
8	Foul Play	Dark	Physical	95	100	15	Normal
12	Swagger	Normal	Status	—	90	15	Normal
13	Psywave	Psychic	Special	—	100	15	Normal
15	Topsy-Turvy	Dark	Status	—	—	20	Normal
18	Hypnosis	Psychic	Status	—	60	20	Normal
21	Psybeam	Psychic	Special	65	100	20	Normal
23	Switcheroo	Dark	Status	—	100	10	Normal
27	Payback	Dark	Physical	50	100	10	Normal
31	Light Screen	Psychic	Status	—	—	30	Your Side
35	Pluck	Flying	Physical	60	100	20	Normal
39	Psycho Cut	Psychic	Physical	70	100	20	Normal
43	Slash	Normal	Physical	70	100	20	Normal
46	Night Slash	Dark	Physical	70	100	15	Normal
48	Superpower	Fighting	Physical	120	100	5	Normal

TM & HM MOVES

No.	Name	Type	Kind	Pow.	Acc.	PP	Range
TM04	Calm Mind	Psychic	Status	—	—	20	Self
TM06	Toxic	Poison	Status	—	90	10	Normal
TM10	Hidden Power	Normal	Special	60	100	15	Normal
TM11	Sunny Day	Fire	Status	—	—	5	Both Sides
TM12	Taunt	Dark	Status	—	100	20	Normal
TM16	Light Screen	Psychic	Status	—	—	30	Your Side
TM17	Protect	Normal	Status	—	—	10	Self
TM18	Rain Dance	Water	Status	—	—	5	Both Sides
TM21	Frustration	Normal	Physical	—	100	20	Normal
TM24	Thunderbolt	Electric	Special	90	100	15	Normal
TM27	Return	Normal	Physical	—	100	20	Normal
TM29	Psychic	Psychic	Special	90	100	10	Normal
TM32	Double Team	Normal	Status	—	—	15	Self
TM33	Reflect	Psychic	Status	—	—	20	Your Side
TM35	Flamethrower	Fire	Special	90	100	15	Normal
TM40	Aerial Ace	Flying	Physical	60	—	20	Normal
TM41	Torment	Dark	Status	—	100	15	Normal
TM42	Facade	Normal	Physical	70	100	20	Normal
TM44	Rest	Psychic	Status	—	—	10	Self
TM45	Attract	Normal	Status	—	100	15	Normal
TM46	Thief	Dark	Physical	60	100	25	Normal
TM48	Round	Normal	Special	60	100	15	Normal
TM56	Fling	Dark	Physical	—	100	10	Normal
TM63	Embargo	Dark	Status	—	100	15	Normal
TM66	Payback	Dark	Physical	50	100	10	Normal
TM67	Retaliate	Normal	Physical	70	100	5	Normal
TM70	Flash	Normal	Status	—	100	20	Normal
TM77	Psych Up	Normal	Status	—	—	10	Normal
TM80	Rock Slide	Rock	Physical	75	90	10	Many Others
TM87	Swagger	Normal	Status	—	90	15	Normal
TM88	Sleep Talk	Normal	Status	—	—	10	Self
TM90	Substitute	Normal	Status	—	—	10	Self
TM92	Trick Room	Psychic	Status	—	—	5	Both Sides
TM94	Secret Power	Normal	Physical	70	100	20	Normal
TM97	Dark Pulse	Dark	Special	80	100	15	Normal
TM100	Confide	Normal	Status	—	—	20	Normal
HM01	Cut	Normal	Physical	50	95	30	Normal

MOVES LEARNED IN EXCHANGE FOR BP

Name	Type	Kind	Pow.	Acc.	PP	Range
Foul Play	Dark	Physical	95	100	15	Normal
Superpower	Fighting	Physical	120	100	5	Normal
Bind	Normal	Physical	15	85	20	Normal
Snore	Normal	Special	50	100	15	Normal
Knock Off	Dark	Physical	65	100	20	Normal
Role Play	Psychic	Status	—	—	10	Normal
Spite	Ghost	Status	—	100	10	Normal
Snatch	Dark	Status	—	—	10	Self

MOVES TAUGHT BY PEOPLE

Name	Type	Kind	Pow.	Acc.	PP	Range

EGG MOVES

Name	Type	Kind	Pow.	Acc.	PP	Range
Simple Beam	Normal	Status	—	100	15	Normal
Power Split	Psychic	Status	—	—	10	Normal
Camouflage	Normal	Status	—	—	20	Self
Flatter	Dark	Status	—	100	15	Normal
Destiny Bond	Ghost	Status	—	—	5	Self

National Pokédex **687** Hoenn Pokédex —

Malamar

Overturning Pokémon

Dark **Psychic**

HEIGHT: 4'11" WEIGHT: 103.6 lbs.

Same form for ♂ / ♀

Ω It wields the most compelling hypnotic powers of any Pokémon, and it forces others to do whatever it wants.

α It lures its prey close with hypnotic motions, then wraps its tentacles around it before finishing it off with digestive fluids.

ABILITIES
Contrary
Suction Cups

HIDDEN ABILITY
Infiltrator

EGG GROUPS
Water 1 | Water 2

STAT GROWTH RATES
HP
Attack
Defense
Sp. Atk
Sp. Def
Speed

ITEMS SOMETIMES HELD BY WILD POKÉMON
—

EVOLUTION

Inkay → Turn Nintendo 3DS upside down while leveling up (Lv. 30 or above) → Malamar

MAIN WAY TO REGISTER IN THE NATIONAL POKÉDEX

Level up an Inkay obtained via Link Trade or the GTS to Lv. 30 or above, while holding your Nintendo 3DS upside down.

Damage taken in normal battles

Type		Type	
Normal	×1	Flying	×1
Fire	×1	Psychic	×0
Water	×1	Bug	×4
Grass	×1	Rock	×1
Electric	×1	Ghost	×1
Ice	×1	Dragon	×1
Fighting	×1	Dark	×1
Poison	×1	Steel	×1
Ground	×1	Fairy	×2

Damage taken in Inverse battles

Type		Type	
Normal	×1	Flying	×1
Fire	×1	Psychic	×4
Water	×1	Bug	×0.25
Grass	×1	Rock	×1
Electric	×1	Ghost	×1
Ice	×1	Dragon	×1
Fighting	×1	Dark	×1
Poison	×1	Steel	×1
Ground	×1	Fairy	×0.5

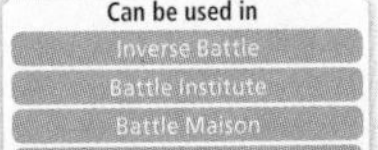

Can be used in
Inverse Battle
Battle Institute
Battle Maison
Random Matchup (Free Battle)
Random Matchup (Others)

LEVEL-UP MOVES

Lv.	Name	Type	Kind	Pow.	Acc.	PP	Range
1	Superpower	Fighting	Physical	120	100	5	Normal
1	Reversal	Fighting	Physical	—	100	15	Normal
1	Tackle	Normal	Physical	50	100	35	Normal
1	Peck	Flying	Physical	35	100	35	Normal
1	Constrict	Normal	Physical	10	100	35	Normal
4	Reflect	Psychic	Status	—	—	20	Your Side
8	Foul Play	Dark	Physical	95	100	15	Normal
12	Swagger	Normal	Status	—	90	15	Normal
13	Psywave	Psychic	Special	—	100	15	Normal
15	Topsy-Turvy	Dark	Status	—	—	20	Normal
18	Hypnosis	Psychic	Status	—	60	20	Normal
21	Psybeam	Psychic	Special	65	100	20	Normal
23	Switcheroo	Dark	Status	—	100	10	Normal
27	Payback	Dark	Physical	50	100	10	Normal
31	Light Screen	Psychic	Status	—	—	30	Your Side
35	Pluck	Flying	Physical	60	100	20	Normal
39	Psycho Cut	Psychic	Physical	70	100	20	Normal
43	Slash	Normal	Physical	70	100	20	Normal
46	Night Slash	Dark	Physical	70	100	15	Normal
48	Superpower	Fighting	Physical	120	100	5	Normal

TM & HM MOVES

No.	Name	Type	Kind	Pow.	Acc.	PP	Range
TM03	Psyshock	Psychic	Special	80	100	10	Normal
TM04	Calm Mind	Psychic	Status	—	—	20	Self
TM06	Toxic	Poison	Status	—	90	10	Normal
TM10	Hidden Power	Normal	Special	60	100	15	Normal
TM11	Sunny Day	Fire	Status	—	—	5	Both Sides
TM12	Taunt	Dark	Status	—	100	20	Normal
TM15	Hyper Beam	Normal	Special	150	90	5	Normal
TM16	Light Screen	Psychic	Status	—	—	30	Your Side
TM17	Protect	Normal	Status	—	—	10	Self
TM18	Rain Dance	Water	Status	—	—	5	Both Sides
TM21	Frustration	Normal	Physical	—	100	20	Normal
TM24	Thunderbolt	Electric	Special	90	100	15	Normal
TM27	Return	Normal	Physical	—	100	20	Normal
TM29	Psychic	Psychic	Special	90	100	10	Normal
TM32	Double Team	Normal	Status	—	—	15	Self
TM33	Reflect	Psychic	Status	—	—	20	Your Side
TM35	Flamethrower	Fire	Special	90	100	15	Normal
TM40	Aerial Ace	Flying	Physical	60	—	20	Normal
TM41	Torment	Dark	Status	—	100	15	Normal
TM42	Facade	Normal	Physical	70	100	20	Normal
TM44	Rest	Psychic	Status	—	—	10	Self
TM45	Attract	Normal	Status	—	100	15	Normal
TM46	Thief	Dark	Physical	60	100	25	Normal
TM48	Round	Normal	Special	60	100	15	Normal
TM56	Fling	Dark	Physical	—	100	10	Normal
TM63	Embargo	Dark	Status	—	100	15	Normal
TM66	Payback	Dark	Physical	50	100	10	Normal
TM67	Retaliate	Normal	Physical	70	100	5	Normal
TM68	Giga Impact	Normal	Physical	150	90	5	Normal
TM70	Flash	Normal	Status	—	100	20	Normal
TM77	Psych Up	Normal	Status	—	—	10	Normal
TM80	Rock Slide	Rock	Physical	75	90	10	Many Others
TM87	Swagger	Normal	Status	—	90	15	Normal
TM88	Sleep Talk	Normal	Status	—	—	10	Self
TM90	Substitute	Normal	Status	—	—	10	Self
TM92	Trick Room	Psychic	Status	—	—	5	Both Sides
TM94	Secret Power	Normal	Physical	70	100	20	Normal
TM97	Dark Pulse	Dark	Special	80	100	15	Normal
TM100	Confide	Normal	Status	—	—	20	Normal
HM01	Cut	Normal	Physical	50	95	30	Normal

MOVES LEARNED IN EXCHANGE FOR BP

Name	Type	Kind	Pow.	Acc.	PP	Range
Signal Beam	Bug	Special	75	100	15	Normal
Block	Normal	Status	—	—	5	Normal
Foul Play	Dark	Physical	95	100	15	Normal
Superpower	Fighting	Physical	120	100	5	Normal
Bind	Normal	Physical	15	85	20	Normal
Snore	Normal	Special	50	100	15	Normal
Knock Off	Dark	Physical	65	100	20	Normal
Role Play	Psychic	Status	—	—	10	Normal
Spite	Ghost	Status	—	100	10	Normal
Snatch	Dark	Status	—	—	10	Self

MOVES TAUGHT BY PEOPLE

Name	Type	Kind	Pow.	Acc.	PP	Range

National Pokédex **688** Hoenn Pokédex —

Binacle

Two-Handed Pokémon

Rock **Water**

HEIGHT: 1'08" WEIGHT: 68.3 lbs.

Same form for ♂ / ♀

Ω Two Binacle live together on one rock. When they fight, one of them will move to a different rock.

α They stretch and then contract, yanking their rocks along with them in bold hops. They eat seaweed that washes up on the shoreline.

ABILITIES
Tough Claws
Sniper

HIDDEN ABILITY
Pickpocket

EGG GROUPS
Water 3

STAT GROWTH RATES
HP
Attack
Defense
Sp. Atk
Sp. Def
Speed

ITEMS SOMETIMES HELD BY WILD POKÉMON
—

EVOLUTION

Binacle → Lv. 39 → Barbaracle

MAIN WAY TO REGISTER IN THE NATIONAL POKÉDEX

Catch when it appears from a cracked rock on Mirage Island 2 (using Rock Smash).

Damage taken in normal battles

Type		Type	
Normal	×0.5	Flying	×0.5
Fire	×0.25	Psychic	×1
Water	×1	Bug	×1
Grass	×4	Rock	×1
Electric	×2	Ghost	×1
Ice	×0.5	Dragon	×1
Fighting	×2	Dark	×1
Poison	×0.5	Steel	×1
Ground	×2	Fairy	×1

Damage taken in Inverse battles

Type		Type	
Normal	×2	Flying	×2
Fire	×4	Psychic	×1
Water	×1	Bug	×1
Grass	×0.25	Rock	×1
Electric	×0.5	Ghost	×1
Ice	×2	Dragon	×1
Fighting	×0.5	Dark	×1
Poison	×2	Steel	×1
Ground	×0.5	Fairy	×1

Can be used in
Inverse Battle
Battle Institute
Battle Maison
Random Matchup (Free Battle)
Random Matchup (Others)

LEVEL-UP MOVES

Lv.	Name	Type	Kind	Pow.	Acc.	PP	Range
1	Shell Smash	Normal	Status	—	—	15	Self
1	Scratch	Normal	Physical	40	100	35	Normal
1	Sand Attack	Ground	Status	—	100	15	Normal
4	Water Gun	Water	Special	40	100	25	Normal
7	Withdraw	Water	Status	—	—	40	Self
10	Fury Swipes	Normal	Physical	18	80	15	Normal
13	Slash	Normal	Physical	70	100	20	Normal
18	Mud-Slap	Ground	Special	20	100	10	Normal
20	Clamp	Water	Physical	35	85	15	Normal
24	Rock Polish	Rock	Status	—	—	20	Self
28	Ancient Power	Rock	Special	60	100	5	Normal
32	Hone Claws	Dark	Status	—	—	15	Self
37	Fury Cutter	Bug	Physical	40	95	20	Normal
41	Night Slash	Dark	Physical	70	100	15	Normal
45	Razor Shell	Water	Physical	75	95	10	Normal
49	Cross Chop	Fighting	Physical	100	80	5	Normal

TM & HM MOVES

No.	Name	Type	Kind	Pow.	Acc.	PP	Range
TM01	Hone Claws	Dark	Status	—	—	15	Self
TM06	Toxic	Poison	Status	—	90	10	Normal
TM10	Hidden Power	Normal	Special	60	100	15	Normal
TM12	Taunt	Dark	Status	—	100	20	Normal
TM13	Ice Beam	Ice	Special	90	100	10	Normal
TM14	Blizzard	Ice	Special	110	70	5	Many Others
TM17	Protect	Normal	Status	—	—	10	Self
TM18	Rain Dance	Water	Status	—	—	5	Both Sides
TM20	Safeguard	Normal	Status	—	—	25	Your Side
TM21	Frustration	Normal	Physical	—	100	20	Normal
TM23	Smack Down	Rock	Physical	50	100	15	Normal
TM26	Earthquake	Ground	Physical	100	100	10	Adjacent
TM27	Return	Normal	Physical	—	100	20	Normal
TM28	Dig	Ground	Physical	80	100	10	Normal
TM31	Brick Break	Fighting	Physical	75	100	15	Normal
TM32	Double Team	Normal	Status	—	—	15	Self
TM34	Sludge Wave	Poison	Special	95	100	10	Adjacent
TM36	Sludge Bomb	Poison	Special	90	100	10	Normal
TM37	Sandstorm	Rock	Status	—	—	10	Both Sides
TM39	Rock Tomb	Rock	Physical	60	95	15	Normal
TM40	Aerial Ace	Flying	Physical	60	—	20	Normal
TM41	Torment	Dark	Status	—	100	15	Normal
TM42	Facade	Normal	Physical	70	100	20	Normal
TM44	Rest	Psychic	Status	—	—	10	Self
TM45	Attract	Normal	Status	—	100	15	Normal
TM46	Thief	Dark	Physical	60	100	25	Normal
TM48	Round	Normal	Special	60	100	15	Normal
TM54	False Swipe	Normal	Physical	40	100	40	Normal
TM55	Scald	Water	Special	80	100	15	Normal
TM56	Fling	Dark	Physical	—	100	10	Normal
TM63	Embargo	Dark	Status	—	100	15	Normal
TM65	Shadow Claw	Ghost	Physical	70	100	15	Normal
TM66	Payback	Dark	Physical	50	100	10	Normal
TM69	Rock Polish	Rock	Status	—	—	20	Self
TM71	Stone Edge	Rock	Physical	100	80	5	Normal
TM75	Swords Dance	Normal	Status	—	—	20	Self
TM78	Bulldoze	Ground	Physical	60	100	20	Adjacent
TM80	Rock Slide	Rock	Physical	75	90	10	Many Others
TM81	X-Scissor	Bug	Physical	80	100	15	Normal
TM83	Infestation	Bug	Special	20	100	20	Normal
TM84	Poison Jab	Poison	Physical	80	100	20	Normal
TM86	Grass Knot	Grass	Special	—	100	20	Normal
TM87	Swagger	Normal	Status	—	90	15	Normal
TM88	Sleep Talk	Normal	Status	—	—	10	Self
TM90	Substitute	Normal	Status	—	—	10	Self
TM94	Secret Power	Normal	Physical	70	100	20	Normal
TM96	Nature Power	Normal	Status	—	—	20	Normal
TM98	Power-Up Punch	Fighting	Physical	40	100	20	Normal
TM100	Confide	Normal	Status	—	—	20	Normal
HM01	Cut	Normal	Physical	50	95	30	Normal
HM03	Surf	Water	Special	90	100	15	Adjacent
HM04	Strength	Normal	Physical	80	100	15	Normal
HM06	Rock Smash	Fighting	Physical	40	100	15	Normal

MOVES LEARNED IN EXCHANGE FOR BP

Name	Type	Kind	Pow.	Acc.	PP	Range
Dual Chop	Dragon	Physical	40	90	15	Normal
Iron Defense	Steel	Status	—	—	15	Self
Icy Wind	Ice	Special	55	95	15	Many Others
Snore	Normal	Special	50	100	15	Normal
Water Pulse	Water	Special	60	100	20	Normal
Helping Hand	Normal	Status	—	—	20	1 Ally
Endeavor	Normal	Physical	—	100	5	Normal
Stealth Rock	Rock	Status	—	—	20	Other Side

MOVES TAUGHT BY PEOPLE

Name	Type	Kind	Pow.	Acc.	PP	Range

EGG MOVES

Name	Type	Kind	Pow.	Acc.	PP	Range
Tickle	Normal	Status	—	100	20	Normal
Switcheroo	Dark	Status	—	100	10	Normal
Helping Hand	Normal	Status	—	—	20	1 Ally
Water Sport	Water	Status	—	—	15	Both Sides

National Pokédex **689** Hoenn Pokédex —

Barbaracle

Collective Pokémon

Rock Water

HEIGHT: 4'03" WEIGHT: 211.6 lbs.

Same form for ♂ / ♀

Ω When they evolve, two Binacle multiply into seven. They fight with the power of seven Binacle.

α Barbaracle's legs and hands have minds of their own, and they will move independently. But they usually follow the head's orders.

ABILITIES
Tough Claws
Sniper

HIDDEN ABILITY
Pickpocket

EGG GROUPS
Water 3

STAT GROWTH RATES

HP	■■■
Attack	■■■■■
Defense	■■■■■
Sp. Atk	■■■
Sp. Def	■■■■
Speed	■■■■

ITEMS SOMETIMES HELD BY WILD POKÉMON
—

EVOLUTION

MAIN WAY TO REGISTER IN THE NATIONAL POKÉDEX

Level up Binacle to Lv. 39.

Damage taken in normal battles

Type	×	Type	×
Normal	×0.5	Flying	×0.5
Fire	×0.25	Psychic	×1
Water	×1	Bug	×1
Grass	×4	Rock	×1
Electric	×2	Ghost	×1
Ice	×0.5	Dragon	×1
Fighting	×2	Dark	×1
Poison	×0.5	Steel	×1
Ground	×2	Fairy	×1

Damage taken in Inverse battles

Type	×	Type	×
Normal	×2	Flying	×2
Fire	×4	Psychic	×1
Water	×1	Bug	×1
Grass	×0.25	Rock	×1
Electric	×0.5	Ghost	×1
Ice	×2	Dragon	×1
Fighting	×0.5	Dark	×1
Poison	×2	Steel	×1
Ground	×0.5	Fairy	×1

Can be used in
Inverse Battle
Battle Institute
Battle Maison
Random Matchup (Free Battle)
Random Matchup (Others)

LEVEL-UP MOVES

Lv.	Name	Type	Kind	Pow.	Acc.	PP	Range
1	Stone Edge	Rock	Physical	100	80	5	Normal
1	Skull Bash	Normal	Physical	130	100	10	Normal
1	Shell Smash	Normal	Status	—	—	15	Self
1	Scratch	Normal	Physical	40	100	35	Normal
1	Sand Attack	Ground	Status	—	100	15	Normal
4	Water Gun	Water	Special	40	100	25	Normal
7	Withdraw	Water	Status	—	—	40	Self
10	Fury Swipes	Normal	Physical	18	80	15	Normal
13	Slash	Normal	Physical	70	100	20	Normal
18	Mud-Slap	Ground	Special	20	100	10	Normal
20	Clamp	Water	Physical	35	85	15	Normal
24	Rock Polish	Rock	Status	—	—	20	Self
28	Ancient Power	Rock	Special	60	100	5	Normal
32	Hone Claws	Dark	Status	—	—	15	Self
37	Fury Cutter	Bug	Physical	40	95	20	Normal
44	Night Slash	Dark	Physical	70	100	15	Normal
48	Razor Shell	Water	Physical	75	95	10	Normal
55	Cross Chop	Fighting	Physical	100	80	5	Normal
60	Stone Edge	Rock	Physical	100	80	5	Normal
65	Skull Bash	Normal	Physical	130	100	10	Normal

TM & HM MOVES

No.	Name	Type	Kind	Pow.	Acc.	PP	Range
TM01	Hone Claws	Dark	Status	—	—	15	Self
TM02	Dragon Claw	Dragon	Physical	80	100	15	Normal
TM06	Toxic	Poison	Status	—	90	10	Normal
TM08	Bulk Up	Fighting	Status	—	—	20	Self
TM10	Hidden Power	Normal	Special	60	100	15	Normal
TM12	Taunt	Dark	Status	—	100	20	Normal
TM13	Ice Beam	Ice	Special	90	100	10	Normal
TM14	Blizzard	Ice	Special	110	70	5	Many Others
TM15	Hyper Beam	Normal	Special	150	90	5	Normal
TM17	Protect	Normal	Status	—	—	10	Self
TM18	Rain Dance	Water	Status	—	—	5	Both Sides
TM20	Safeguard	Normal	Status	—	—	25	Your Side
TM21	Frustration	Normal	Physical	—	100	20	Normal
TM23	Smack Down	Rock	Physical	50	100	15	Normal
TM26	Earthquake	Ground	Physical	100	100	10	Adjacent
TM27	Return	Normal	Physical	—	100	20	Normal
TM28	Dig	Ground	Physical	80	100	10	Normal
TM31	Brick Break	Fighting	Physical	75	100	15	Normal
TM32	Double Team	Normal	Status	—	—	15	Self
TM34	Sludge Wave	Poison	Special	95	100	10	Adjacent
TM36	Sludge Bomb	Poison	Special	90	100	10	Normal
TM37	Sandstorm	Rock	Status	—	—	10	Both Sides
TM39	Rock Tomb	Rock	Physical	60	95	15	Normal
TM40	Aerial Ace	Flying	Physical	60	—	20	Normal
TM41	Torment	Dark	Status	—	100	15	Normal
TM42	Facade	Normal	Physical	70	100	20	Normal
TM44	Rest	Psychic	Status	—	—	10	Self
TM45	Attract	Normal	Status	—	100	15	Normal
TM46	Thief	Dark	Physical	60	100	25	Normal
TM48	Round	Normal	Special	60	100	15	Normal
TM52	Focus Blast	Fighting	Special	120	70	5	Normal
TM54	False Swipe	Normal	Physical	40	100	40	Normal
TM55	Scald	Water	Special	80	100	15	Normal
TM56	Fling	Dark	Physical	—	100	10	Normal
TM63	Embargo	Dark	Status	—	100	15	Normal
TM65	Shadow Claw	Ghost	Physical	70	100	15	Normal
TM66	Payback	Dark	Physical	50	100	10	Normal
TM68	Giga Impact	Normal	Physical	150	90	5	Normal
TM69	Rock Polish	Rock	Status	—	—	20	Self
TM71	Stone Edge	Rock	Physical	100	80	5	Normal
TM75	Swords Dance	Normal	Status	—	—	20	Self
TM78	Bulldoze	Ground	Physical	60	100	20	Adjacent
TM80	Rock Slide	Rock	Physical	75	90	10	Many Others
TM81	X-Scissor	Bug	Physical	80	100	15	Normal
TM83	Infestation	Bug	Special	20	100	20	Normal
TM84	Poison Jab	Poison	Physical	80	100	20	Normal
TM86	Grass Knot	Grass	Special	—	100	20	Normal
TM87	Swagger	Normal	Status	—	90	15	Normal
TM88	Sleep Talk	Normal	Status	—	—	10	Self
TM90	Substitute	Normal	Status	—	—	10	Self
TM94	Secret Power	Normal	Physical	70	100	20	Normal
TM96	Nature Power	Normal	Status	—	—	20	Normal
TM98	Power-Up Punch	Fighting	Physical	40	100	20	Normal
TM100	Confide	Normal	Status	—	—	20	Normal
HM01	Cut	Normal	Physical	50	95	30	Normal
HM03	Surf	Water	Special	90	100	15	Adjacent
HM04	Strength	Normal	Physical	80	100	15	Normal
HM06	Rock Smash	Fighting	Physical	40	100	15	Normal

MOVES LEARNED IN EXCHANGE FOR BP

Name	Type	Kind	Pow.	Acc.	PP	Range
Dual Chop	Dragon	Physical	40	90	15	Normal
Low Kick	Fighting	Physical	—	100	20	Normal
Earth Power	Ground	Special	90	100	10	Normal
Iron Defense	Steel	Status	—	—	15	Self
Superpower	Fighting	Physical	120	100	5	Normal
Icy Wind	Ice	Special	55	95	15	Many Others
Snore	Normal	Special	50	100	15	Normal
Water Pulse	Water	Special	60	100	20	Normal
Helping Hand	Normal	Status	—	—	20	1 Ally
Endeavor	Normal	Physical	—	100	5	Normal
Stealth Rock	Rock	Status	—	—	20	Other Side

MOVES TAUGHT BY PEOPLE

Name	Type	Kind	Pow.	Acc.	PP	Range

National Pokédex **690** Hoenn Pokédex —

Skrelp

Mock Kelp Pokémon

Poison Water

HEIGHT: 1'08" WEIGHT: 16.1 lbs.

Same form for ♂ / ♀

Ω Camouflaged as rotten kelp, they spray liquid poison on prey that approaches unawares and then finish it off.

α It looks just like rotten kelp. It hides from foes while storing up power for its evolution.

ABILITIES
Poison Point
Poison Touch

HIDDEN ABILITY
Adaptability

EGG GROUPS
Water 1 Dragon

STAT GROWTH RATES

HP	■■
Attack	■■■
Defense	■■■
Sp. Atk	■■■
Sp. Def	■■■
Speed	■■

ITEMS SOMETIMES HELD BY WILD POKÉMON
—

EVOLUTION

Skrelp → Lv. 48 → Dragalge

MAIN WAYS TO REGISTER IN THE NATIONAL POKÉDEX

Ω Catch on the water surface on Route 105. Appears as a hidden Pokémon after you battle Groudon or Kyogre.

α Bring it to your game using Link Trade or the GTS.

Damage taken in normal battles

Type	×	Type	×
Normal	×1	Flying	×1
Fire	×0.5	Psychic	×2
Water	×0.5	Bug	×0.5
Grass	×1	Rock	×1
Electric	×2	Ghost	×1
Ice	×0.5	Dragon	×1
Fighting	×0.5	Dark	×1
Poison	×0.5	Steel	×0.5
Ground	×2	Fairy	×0.5

Damage taken in Inverse battles

Type	×	Type	×
Normal	×1	Flying	×1
Fire	×2	Psychic	×0.5
Water	×2	Bug	×2
Grass	×1	Rock	×1
Electric	×0.5	Ghost	×1
Ice	×2	Dragon	×1
Fighting	×2	Dark	×1
Poison	×2	Steel	×2
Ground	×0.5	Fairy	×2

Can be used in
Inverse Battle
Battle Institute
Battle Maison
Random Matchup (Free Battle)
Random Matchup (Others)

LEVEL-UP MOVES

Lv.	Name	Type	Kind	Pow.	Acc.	PP	Range
1	Tackle	Normal	Physical	50	100	35	Normal
1	Smokescreen	Normal	Status	—	100	20	Normal
1	Water Gun	Water	Special	40	100	25	Normal
5	Feint Attack	Dark	Physical	60	—	20	Normal
9	Tail Whip	Normal	Status	—	100	30	Many Others
12	Bubble	Water	Special	40	100	30	Many Others
15	Acid	Poison	Special	40	100	30	Many Others
19	Camouflage	Normal	Status	—	—	20	Self
23	Poison Tail	Poison	Physical	50	100	25	Normal
25	Water Pulse	Water	Special	60	100	20	Normal
28	Double Team	Normal	Status	—	—	15	Self
32	Toxic	Poison	Status	—	90	10	Normal
35	Aqua Tail	Water	Physical	90	90	10	Normal
38	Sludge Bomb	Poison	Special	90	100	10	Normal
42	Hydro Pump	Water	Special	110	80	5	Normal
49	Dragon Pulse	Dragon	Special	85	100	10	Normal

TM & HM MOVES

No.	Name	Type	Kind	Pow.	Acc.	PP	Range
TM06	Toxic	Poison	Status	—	90	10	Normal
TM07	Hail	Ice	Status	—	—	10	Both Sides
TM09	Venoshock	Poison	Special	65	100	10	Normal
TM10	Hidden Power	Normal	Special	60	100	15	Normal
TM17	Protect	Normal	Status	—	—	10	Self
TM18	Rain Dance	Water	Status	—	—	5	Both Sides
TM21	Frustration	Normal	Physical	—	100	20	Normal
TM24	Thunderbolt	Electric	Special	90	100	15	Normal
TM27	Return	Normal	Physical	—	100	20	Normal
TM30	Shadow Ball	Ghost	Special	80	100	15	Normal
TM32	Double Team	Normal	Status	—	—	15	Self
TM34	Sludge Wave	Poison	Special	95	100	10	Adjacent
TM36	Sludge Bomb	Poison	Special	90	100	10	Normal
TM42	Facade	Normal	Physical	70	100	20	Normal
TM44	Rest	Psychic	Status	—	—	10	Self
TM45	Attract	Normal	Status	—	100	15	Normal
TM48	Round	Normal	Special	60	100	15	Normal
TM55	Scald	Water	Special	80	100	15	Normal
TM87	Swagger	Normal	Status	—	90	15	Normal
TM88	Sleep Talk	Normal	Status	—	—	10	Self
TM90	Substitute	Normal	Status	—	—	10	Self
TM94	Secret Power	Normal	Physical	70	100	20	Normal
TM100	Confide	Normal	Status	—	—	20	Normal
HM03	Surf	Water	Special	90	100	15	Adjacent
HM05	Waterfall	Water	Physical	80	100	15	Normal
HM07	Dive	Water	Physical	80	100	10	Normal

MOVES LEARNED IN EXCHANGE FOR BP

Name	Type	Kind	Pow.	Acc.	PP	Range
Bounce	Flying	Physical	85	85	5	Normal
Gunk Shot	Poison	Physical	120	80	5	Normal
Icy Wind	Ice	Special	55	95	15	Many Others
Aqua Tail	Water	Physical	90	90	10	Normal
Dragon Pulse	Dragon	Special	85	100	10	Normal
Iron Tail	Steel	Physical	100	75	15	Normal
Snore	Normal	Special	50	100	15	Normal
Shock Wave	Electric	Special	60	—	20	Normal
Water Pulse	Water	Special	60	100	20	Normal
Outrage	Dragon	Physical	120	100	10	1 Random

MOVES TAUGHT BY PEOPLE

Name	Type	Kind	Pow.	Acc.	PP	Range

EGG MOVES

Name	Type	Kind	Pow.	Acc.	PP	Range
Toxic Spikes	Poison	Status	—	—	20	Other Side
Play Rough	Fairy	Physical	90	90	10	Normal
Haze	Ice	Status	—	—	30	Both Sides
Acid Armor	Poison	Status	—	—	20	Self
Venom Drench	Poison	Status	—	100	20	Many Others

National Pokédex **691** Hoenn Pokédex —

Dragalge

Mock Kelp Pokémon

Poison **Dragon**

HEIGHT: 5'11" WEIGHT: 179.7 lbs.

Same form for ♂ / ♀

Ω Their poison is strong enough to eat through the hull of a tanker, and they spit it indiscriminately at anything that enters their territory.

α Tales are told of ships that wander into seas where Dragalge live, never to return.

ABILITIES
Poison Point
Poison Touch

HIDDEN ABILITY
Adaptability

EGG GROUPS
Water 1 | Dragon

STAT GROWTH RATES
HP ■■■
Attack ■■■■
Defense ■■■■
Sp. Atk ■■■■■
Sp. Def ■■■■■
Speed ■■■

ITEMS SOMETIMES HELD BY WILD POKÉMON
—

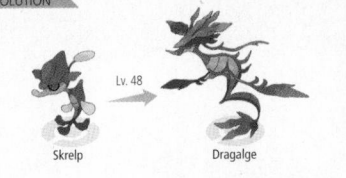

EVOLUTION
Skrelp → Lv. 48 → Dragalge

MAIN WAYS TO REGISTER IN THE NATIONAL POKÉDEX
Ω Level up Skrelp to Lv. 48.
α Bring it to your game using Link Trade or the GTS.

Damage taken in normal battles

Type		Type	
Normal	×1	Flying	×1
Fire	×0.5	Psychic	×2
Water	×0.5	Bug	×0.5
Grass	×0.25	Rock	×1
Electric	×0.5	Ghost	×1
Ice	×2	Dragon	×2
Fighting	×0.5	Dark	×1
Poison	×0.5	Steel	×1
Ground	×2	Fairy	×1

Damage taken in Inverse battles

Type		Type	
Normal	×1	Flying	×1
Fire	×2	Psychic	×0.5
Water	×2	Bug	×2
Grass	×4	Rock	×1
Electric	×2	Ghost	×1
Ice	×0.5	Dragon	×0.5
Fighting	×2	Dark	×1
Poison	×2	Steel	×1
Ground	×0.5	Fairy	×1

Can be used in
Inverse Battle
Battle Institute
Battle Maison
Random Matchup (Free Battle)
Random Matchup (Others)

LEVEL-UP MOVES

Lv.	Name	Type	Kind	Pow.	Acc.	PP	Range
1	Dragon Tail	Dragon	Physical	60	90	10	Normal
1	Twister	Dragon	Special	40	100	20	Many Others
1	Tackle	Normal	Physical	50	100	35	Normal
1	Smokescreen	Normal	Status	—	100	20	Normal
1	Water Gun	Water	Special	40	100	25	Normal
5	Feint Attack	Dark	Physical	60	—	20	Normal
9	Tail Whip	Normal	Status	—	100	30	Many Others
12	Bubble	Water	Special	40	100	30	Many Others
15	Acid	Poison	Special	40	100	30	Many Others
19	Camouflage	Normal	Status	—	—	20	Self
23	Poison Tail	Poison	Physical	50	100	25	Normal
25	Water Pulse	Water	Special	60	100	20	Normal
28	Double Team	Normal	Status	—	—	15	Self
32	Toxic	Poison	Status	—	90	10	Normal
35	Aqua Tail	Water	Physical	90	90	10	Normal
38	Sludge Bomb	Poison	Special	90	100	10	Normal
42	Hydro Pump	Water	Special	110	80	5	Normal
53	Dragon Pulse	Dragon	Special	85	100	10	Normal
59	Dragon Tail	Dragon	Physical	60	90	10	Normal
67	Twister	Dragon	Special	40	100	20	Many Others

TM & HM MOVES

No.	Name	Type	Kind	Pow.	Acc.	PP	Range
TM06	Toxic	Poison	Status	—	90	10	Normal
TM07	Hail	Ice	Status	—	—	10	Both Sides
TM09	Venoshock	Poison	Special	65	100	10	Normal
TM10	Hidden Power	Normal	Special	60	100	15	Normal
TM15	Hyper Beam	Normal	Special	150	90	5	Normal
TM17	Protect	Normal	Status	—	—	10	Self
TM18	Rain Dance	Water	Status	—	—	5	Both Sides
TM21	Frustration	Normal	Physical	—	100	20	Normal
TM24	Thunderbolt	Electric	Special	90	100	15	Normal
TM25	Thunder	Electric	Special	110	70	10	Normal
TM27	Return	Normal	Physical	—	100	20	Normal
TM30	Shadow Ball	Ghost	Special	80	100	15	Normal
TM32	Double Team	Normal	Status	—	—	15	Self
TM34	Sludge Wave	Poison	Special	95	100	10	Adjacent
TM36	Sludge Bomb	Poison	Special	90	100	10	Normal
TM42	Facade	Normal	Physical	70	100	20	Normal
TM44	Rest	Psychic	Status	—	—	10	Self
TM45	Attract	Normal	Status	—	100	15	Normal
TM48	Round	Normal	Special	60	100	15	Normal
TM52	Focus Blast	Fighting	Special	120	70	5	Normal
TM55	Scald	Water	Special	80	100	15	Normal
TM68	Giga Impact	Normal	Physical	150	90	5	Normal
TM82	Dragon Tail	Dragon	Physical	60	90	10	Normal
TM87	Swagger	Normal	Status	—	90	15	Normal
TM88	Sleep Talk	Normal	Status	—	—	10	Self
TM90	Substitute	Normal	Status	—	—	10	Self
TM94	Secret Power	Normal	Physical	70	100	20	Normal
TM100	Confide	Normal	Status	—	—	20	Normal
HM03	Surf	Water	Special	90	100	15	Adjacent
HM05	Waterfall	Water	Physical	80	100	15	Normal
HM07	Dive	Water	Physical	80	100	10	Normal

MOVES LEARNED IN EXCHANGE FOR BP

Name	Type	Kind	Pow.	Acc.	PP	Range
Bounce	Flying	Physical	85	85	5	Normal
Gunk Shot	Poison	Physical	120	80	5	Normal
Icy Wind	Ice	Special	55	95	15	Many Others
Aqua Tail	Water	Physical	90	90	10	Normal
Dragon Pulse	Dragon	Special	85	100	10	Normal
Iron Tail	Steel	Physical	100	75	15	Normal
Snore	Normal	Special	50	100	15	Normal
Shock Wave	Electric	Special	60	—	20	Normal
Water Pulse	Water	Special	60	100	20	Normal
Outrage	Dragon	Physical	120	100	10	1 Random

MOVES TAUGHT BY PEOPLE

Name	Type	Kind	Pow.	Acc.	PP	Range
Draco Meteor	Dragon	Special	130	90	5	Normal

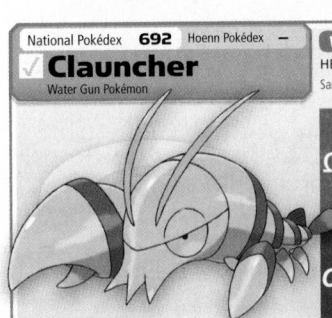

National Pokédex **692** Hoenn Pokédex —

Clauncher

Water Gun Pokémon

Water 

HEIGHT: 1'08" WEIGHT: 18.3 lbs.

Same form for ♂ / ♀

Ω They knock down flying prey by firing compressed water from their massive claws like shooting a pistol.

α Through controlled explosions of internal gas, it can expel water like a pistol shot. At close distances, it can shatter rock.

ABILITY
Mega Launcher

HIDDEN ABILITY
—

EGG GROUPS
Water 1 | Water 3

STAT GROWTH RATES
HP ■■
Attack ■■■
Defense ■■■
Sp. Atk ■■■
Sp. Def ■■■
Speed ■■■

ITEMS SOMETIMES HELD BY WILD POKÉMON
—

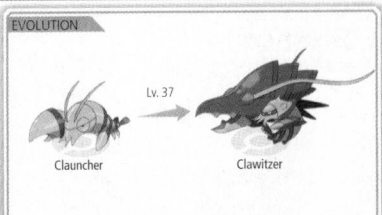

EVOLUTION
Clauncher → Lv. 37 → Clawitzer

MAIN WAYS TO REGISTER IN THE NATIONAL POKÉDEX
Ω Bring it to your game using Link Trade or the GTS.
α Catch on the water surface on Route 105. Appears as a hidden Pokémon after you battle Groudon or Kyogre.

Damage taken in normal battles

Type		Type	
Normal	×1	Flying	×1
Fire	×0.5	Psychic	×1
Water	×0.5	Bug	×1
Grass	×2	Rock	×1
Electric	×2	Ghost	×1
Ice	×0.5	Dragon	×1
Fighting	×1	Dark	×1
Poison	×1	Steel	×0.5
Ground	×1	Fairy	×1

Damage taken in Inverse battles

Type		Type	
Normal	×1	Flying	×1
Fire	×2	Psychic	×1
Water	×2	Bug	×1
Grass	×0.5	Rock	×1
Electric	×0.5	Ghost	×1
Ice	×2	Dragon	×1
Fighting	×1	Dark	×1
Poison	×1	Steel	×2
Ground	×1	Fairy	×1

Can be used in
Inverse Battle
Battle Institute
Battle Maison
Random Matchup (Free Battle)
Random Matchup (Others)

LEVEL-UP MOVES

Lv.	Name	Type	Kind	Pow.	Acc.	PP	Range
1	Splash	Normal	Status	—	—	40	Self
1	Water Gun	Water	Special	40	100	25	Normal
7	Water Sport	Water	Status	—	—	15	Both Sides
9	Vice Grip	Normal	Physical	55	100	30	Normal
12	Bubble	Water	Special	40	100	30	Many Others
16	Flail	Normal	Physical	—	100	15	Normal
20	Bubble Beam	Water	Special	65	100	20	Normal
25	Swords Dance	Normal	Status	—	—	20	Self
30	Crabhammer	Water	Physical	100	90	10	Normal
34	Water Pulse	Water	Special	60	100	20	Normal
39	Smack Down	Rock	Physical	50	100	15	Normal
43	Aqua Jet	Water	Physical	40	100	20	Normal
48	Muddy Water	Water	Special	90	85	10	Many Others

TM & HM MOVES

No.	Name	Type	Kind	Pow.	Acc.	PP	Range
TM06	Toxic	Poison	Status	—	90	10	Normal
TM09	Venoshock	Poison	Special	65	100	10	Normal
TM10	Hidden Power	Normal	Special	60	100	15	Normal
TM13	Ice Beam	Ice	Special	90	100	10	Normal
TM17	Protect	Normal	Status	—	—	10	Self
TM18	Rain Dance	Water	Status	—	—	5	Both Sides
TM21	Frustration	Normal	Physical	—	100	20	Normal
TM23	Smack Down	Rock	Physical	50	100	15	Normal
TM27	Return	Normal	Physical	—	100	20	Normal
TM32	Double Team	Normal	Status	—	—	15	Self
TM34	Sludge Wave	Poison	Special	95	100	10	Adjacent
TM36	Sludge Bomb	Poison	Special	90	100	10	Normal
TM42	Facade	Normal	Physical	70	100	20	Normal
TM44	Rest	Psychic	Status	—	—	10	Self
TM45	Attract	Normal	Status	—	100	15	Normal
TM48	Round	Normal	Special	60	100	15	Normal
TM55	Scald	Water	Special	80	100	15	Normal
TM75	Swords Dance	Normal	Status	—	—	20	Self
TM80	Rock Slide	Rock	Physical	75	90	10	Many Others
TM87	Swagger	Normal	Status	—	90	15	Normal
TM88	Sleep Talk	Normal	Status	—	—	10	Self
TM89	U-turn	Bug	Physical	70	100	20	Normal
TM90	Substitute	Normal	Status	—	—	10	Self
TM91	Flash Cannon	Steel	Special	80	100	10	Normal
TM94	Secret Power	Normal	Physical	70	100	20	Normal
TM100	Confide	Normal	Status	—	—	20	Normal
HM01	Cut	Normal	Physical	50	95	30	Normal
HM03	Surf	Water	Special	90	100	15	Adjacent
HM05	Waterfall	Water	Physical	80	100	15	Normal
HM07	Dive	Water	Physical	80	100	10	Normal

MOVES LEARNED IN EXCHANGE FOR BP

Name	Type	Kind	Pow.	Acc.	PP	Range
Bounce	Flying	Physical	85	85	5	Normal
Icy Wind	Ice	Special	55	95	15	Many Others
Aqua Tail	Water	Physical	90	90	10	Normal
Dragon Pulse	Dragon	Special	85	100	10	Normal
Iron Tail	Steel	Physical	100	75	15	Normal
Snore	Normal	Special	50	100	15	Normal
Water Pulse	Water	Special	60	100	20	Normal
Helping Hand	Normal	Status	—	—	20	1 Ally

MOVES TAUGHT BY PEOPLE

Name	Type	Kind	Pow.	Acc.	PP	Range

EGG MOVES

Name	Type	Kind	Pow.	Acc.	PP	Range
Aqua Jet	Water	Physical	40	100	20	Normal
Entrainment	Normal	Status	—	100	15	Normal
Endure	Normal	Status	—	—	10	Self
Crabhammer	Water	Physical	100	90	10	Normal
Helping Hand	Normal	Status	—	—	20	1 Ally

National Pokédex 693 Hoenn Pokédex —

Clawitzer

Howitzer Pokémon

Water

HEIGHT: 4'03" WEIGHT: 77.8 lbs.

Same form for ♂ / ♀

Ω Their enormous claws launch cannonballs of water powerful enough to pierce tanker hulls.

α By expelling water from the nozzle in the back of its claw, it can move at a speed of 60 knots.

ABILITY
Mega Launcher

HIDDEN ABILITY
—

EGG GROUPS
Water 1 Water 3

STAT GROWTH RATES
HP
Attack
Defense
Sp. Atk
Sp. Def
Speed

EVOLUTION
Clauncher → Lv. 37 → Clawitzer

ITEMS SOMETIMES HELD BY WILD POKÉMON
—

MAIN WAYS TO REGISTER IN THE NATIONAL POKÉDEX
Ω Bring it to your game using Link Trade or the GTS.
α Level up Clauncher to Lv. 37.

Damage taken in normal battles

Type		Type	
Normal	×1	Flying	×1
Fire	×0.5	Psychic	×1
Water	×0.5	Bug	×1
Grass	×2	Rock	×1
Electric	×2	Ghost	×1
Ice	×0.5	Dragon	×1
Fighting	×1	Dark	×1
Poison	×1	Steel	×0.5
Ground	×1	Fairy	×1

Damage taken in Inverse battles

Type		Type	
Normal	×1	Flying	×1
Fire	×2	Psychic	×1
Water	×2	Bug	×1
Grass	×0.5	Rock	×1
Electric	×0.5	Ghost	×1
Ice	×2	Dragon	×1
Fighting	×1	Dark	×1
Poison	×1	Steel	×2
Ground	×1	Fairy	×1

Can be used in
Inverse Battle
Battle Institute
Battle Maison
Random Matchup (Free Battle)
Random Matchup (Others)

LEVEL-UP MOVES

Lv.	Name	Type	Kind	Pow.	Acc.	PP	Range
1	Heal Pulse	Psychic	Status	—	—	10	Normal
1	Dark Pulse	Dark	Special	80	100	15	Normal
1	Dragon Pulse	Dragon	Special	85	100	10	Normal
1	Aura Sphere	Fighting	Special	80	—	20	Normal
1	Splash	Normal	Status	—	—	40	Self
1	Water Gun	Water	Special	40	100	25	Normal
7	Water Sport	Water	Status	—	—	15	Both Sides
9	Vice Grip	Normal	Physical	55	100	30	Normal
12	Bubble	Water	Special	40	100	30	Many Others
16	Flail	Normal	Physical	—	100	15	Normal
20	Bubble Beam	Water	Special	65	100	20	Normal
25	Swords Dance	Normal	Status	—	—	20	Self
30	Crabhammer	Water	Physical	100	90	10	Normal
34	Water Pulse	Water	Special	60	100	20	Normal
42	Smack Down	Rock	Physical	50	100	15	Normal
47	Aqua Jet	Water	Physical	40	100	20	Normal
53	Muddy Water	Water	Special	90	85	10	Many Others
57	Dark Pulse	Dark	Special	80	100	15	Normal
63	Dragon Pulse	Dragon	Special	85	100	10	Normal
67	Aura Sphere	Fighting	Special	80	—	20	Normal

TM & HM MOVES

No.	Name	Type	Kind	Pow.	Acc.	PP	Range
TM06	Toxic	Poison	Status	—	90	10	Normal
TM09	Venoshock	Poison	Special	65	100	10	Normal
TM10	Hidden Power	Normal	Special	60	100	15	Normal
TM13	Ice Beam	Ice	Special	90	100	10	Normal
TM15	Hyper Beam	Normal	Special	150	90	5	Normal
TM17	Protect	Normal	Status	—	—	10	Self
TM18	Rain Dance	Water	Status	—	—	5	Both Sides
TM21	Frustration	Normal	Physical	—	100	20	Normal
TM23	Smack Down	Rock	Physical	50	100	15	Normal
TM27	Return	Normal	Physical	—	100	20	Normal
TM30	Shadow Ball	Ghost	Special	80	100	15	Normal
TM32	Double Team	Normal	Status	—	—	15	Self
TM34	Sludge Wave	Poison	Special	95	100	10	Adjacent
TM36	Sludge Bomb	Poison	Special	90	100	10	Normal
TM42	Facade	Normal	Physical	70	100	20	Normal
TM44	Rest	Psychic	Status	—	—	10	Self
TM45	Attract	Normal	Status	—	100	15	Normal
TM48	Round	Normal	Special	60	100	15	Normal
TM52	Focus Blast	Fighting	Special	120	70	5	Normal
TM55	Scald	Water	Special	80	100	15	Normal
TM68	Giga Impact	Normal	Physical	150	90	5	Normal
TM75	Swords Dance	Normal	Status	—	—	20	Self
TM80	Rock Slide	Rock	Physical	75	90	10	Many Others
TM87	Swagger	Normal	Status	—	90	15	Normal
TM88	Sleep Talk	Normal	Status	—	—	10	Self
TM89	U-turn	Bug	Physical	70	100	20	Normal
TM90	Substitute	Normal	Status	—	—	10	Self
TM91	Flash Cannon	Steel	Special	80	100	10	Normal
TM94	Secret Power	Normal	Physical	70	100	20	Normal
TM97	Dark Pulse	Dark	Special	80	100	15	Normal
TM100	Confide	Normal	Status	—	—	20	Normal
HM01	Cut	Normal	Physical	50	95	30	Normal
HM03	Surf	Water	Special	90	100	15	Adjacent
HM05	Waterfall	Water	Physical	80	100	15	Normal
HM07	Dive	Water	Physical	80	100	10	Normal

MOVES LEARNED IN EXCHANGE FOR BP

Name	Type	Kind	Pow.	Acc.	PP	Range
Bounce	Flying	Physical	85	85	5	Normal
Icy Wind	Ice	Special	55	95	15	Many Others
Aqua Tail	Water	Physical	90	90	10	Normal
Dragon Pulse	Dragon	Special	85	100	10	Normal
Iron Tail	Steel	Physical	100	75	15	Normal
Snore	Normal	Special	50	100	15	Normal
Water Pulse	Water	Special	60	100	20	Normal
Helping Hand	Normal	Status	—	—	20	1 Ally

MOVES TAUGHT BY PEOPLE

Name	Type	Kind	Pow.	Acc.	PP	Range

National Pokédex 694 Hoenn Pokédex —

Helioptile

Generator Pokémon

Electric Normal

HEIGHT: 1'08" WEIGHT: 13.2 lbs.

Same form for ♂ / ♀

Ω They make their home in deserts. They can generate their energy from basking in the sun, so eating food is not a requirement.

α The frills on either side of its head have cells that generate electricity when exposed to sunlight.

ABILITIES
Dry Skin
Sand Veil

HIDDEN ABILITY
Solar Power

EGG GROUPS
Monster Dragon

STAT GROWTH RATES
HP
Attack
Defense
Sp. Atk
Sp. Def
Speed

EVOLUTION
Helioptile → Sun Stone → Heliolisk

ITEMS SOMETIMES HELD BY WILD POKÉMON
—

MAIN WAY TO REGISTER IN THE NATIONAL POKÉDEX
Appears in *Pokémon X* and *Pokémon Y*. Bring it to your game using Link Trade or the GTS.

Damage taken in normal battles

Type		Type	
Normal	×1	Flying	×0.5
Fire	×1	Psychic	×1
Water	×1	Bug	×1
Grass	×1	Rock	×1
Electric	×0.5	Ghost	×0
Ice	×1	Dragon	×1
Fighting	×2	Dark	×1
Poison	×1	Steel	×0.5
Ground	×2	Fairy	×1

Damage taken in Inverse battles

Type		Type	
Normal	×1	Flying	×2
Fire	×1	Psychic	×1
Water	×1	Bug	×1
Grass	×1	Rock	×1
Electric	×2	Ghost	×2
Ice	×1	Dragon	×1
Fighting	×0.5	Dark	×1
Poison	×1	Steel	×2
Ground	×0.5	Fairy	×1

Can be used in
Inverse Battle
Battle Institute
Battle Maison
Random Matchup (Free Battle)
Random Matchup (Others)

LEVEL-UP MOVES

Lv.	Name	Type	Kind	Pow.	Acc.	PP	Range
1	Pound	Normal	Physical	40	100	35	Normal
1	Tail Whip	Normal	Status	—	100	30	Many Others
6	Thunder Shock	Electric	Special	40	100	30	Normal
11	Charge	Electric	Status	—	—	20	Self
13	Mud-Slap	Ground	Special	20	100	10	Normal
17	Quick Attack	Normal	Physical	40	100	30	Normal
22	Razor Wind	Normal	Special	80	100	10	Many Others
25	Parabolic Charge	Electric	Special	50	100	20	Adjacent
31	Thunder Wave	Electric	Status	—	100	20	Normal
35	Bulldoze	Ground	Physical	60	100	20	Adjacent
40	Volt Switch	Electric	Special	70	100	20	Normal
45	Electrify	Electric	Status	—	—	20	Normal
49	Thunderbolt	Electric	Special	90	100	15	Normal

TM & HM MOVES

No.	Name	Type	Kind	Pow.	Acc.	PP	Range
TM06	Toxic	Poison	Status	—	90	10	Normal
TM10	Hidden Power	Normal	Special	60	100	15	Normal
TM16	Light Screen	Psychic	Status	—	—	30	Your Side
TM17	Protect	Normal	Status	—	—	10	Self
TM18	Rain Dance	Water	Status	—	—	5	Both Sides
TM21	Frustration	Normal	Physical	—	100	20	Normal
TM24	Thunderbolt	Electric	Special	90	100	15	Normal
TM25	Thunder	Electric	Special	110	70	10	Normal
TM27	Return	Normal	Physical	—	100	20	Normal
TM28	Dig	Ground	Physical	80	100	10	Normal
TM32	Double Team	Normal	Status	—	—	15	Self
TM37	Sandstorm	Rock	Status	—	—	10	Both Sides
TM39	Rock Tomb	Rock	Physical	60	95	15	Normal
TM42	Facade	Normal	Physical	70	100	20	Normal
TM44	Rest	Psychic	Status	—	—	10	Self
TM45	Attract	Normal	Status	—	100	15	Normal
TM47	Low Sweep	Fighting	Physical	65	100	20	Normal
TM48	Round	Normal	Special	60	100	15	Normal
TM57	Charge Beam	Electric	Special	50	90	10	Normal
TM70	Flash	Normal	Status	—	100	20	Normal
TM72	Volt Switch	Electric	Special	70	100	20	Normal
TM73	Thunder Wave	Electric	Status	—	100	20	Normal
TM77	Psych Up	Normal	Status	—	—	10	Normal
TM78	Bulldoze	Ground	Physical	60	100	20	Adjacent
TM80	Rock Slide	Rock	Physical	75	90	10	Many Others
TM82	Dragon Tail	Dragon	Physical	60	90	10	Normal
TM86	Grass Knot	Grass	Special	—	100	20	Normal
TM87	Swagger	Normal	Status	—	90	15	Normal
TM88	Sleep Talk	Normal	Status	—	—	10	Self
TM89	U-turn	Bug	Physical	70	100	20	Normal
TM90	Substitute	Normal	Status	—	—	10	Self
TM93	Wild Charge	Electric	Physical	90	100	15	Normal
TM94	Secret Power	Normal	Physical	70	100	20	Normal
TM97	Dark Pulse	Dark	Special	80	100	15	Normal
TM100	Confide	Normal	Status	—	—	20	Normal
HM01	Cut	Normal	Physical	50	95	30	Normal
HM03	Surf	Water	Special	90	100	15	Adjacent

MOVES LEARNED IN EXCHANGE FOR BP

Name	Type	Kind	Pow.	Acc.	PP	Range
Signal Beam	Bug	Special	75	100	15	Normal
Magnet Rise	Electric	Status	—	—	10	Self
Electroweb	Electric	Special	55	95	15	Many Others
Iron Tail	Steel	Physical	100	75	15	Normal
Snore	Normal	Special	50	100	15	Normal
Shock Wave	Electric	Special	60	—	20	Normal

MOVES TAUGHT BY PEOPLE

Name	Type	Kind	Pow.	Acc.	PP	Range

EGG MOVES

Name	Type	Kind	Pow.	Acc.	PP	Range
Agility	Psychic	Status	—	—	30	Self
Glare	Normal	Status	—	100	30	Normal
Camouflage	Normal	Status	—	—	20	Self
Electric Terrain	Electric	Status	—	—	10	Both Sides

National Pokédex **695** Hoenn Pokédex —

Heliolisk

Generator Pokémon

Electric / Normal

HEIGHT: 3'03" WEIGHT: 46.3 lbs.

Same form for ♂ / ♀

Ω They flare their frills and generate energy. A single Heliolisk can generate sufficient electricity to power a skyscraper.

α It stimulates its muscles with electricity, boosting the strength in its legs and enabling it to run 100 yards in five seconds.

ABILITIES
Dry Skin
Sand Veil

HIDDEN ABILITY
Solar Power

EGG GROUPS
Monster / Dragon

STAT GROWTH RATES
HP
Attack
Defense
Sp. Atk
Sp. Def
Speed

ITEMS SOMETIMES HELD BY WILD POKÉMON
—

EVOLUTION

MAIN WAY TO REGISTER IN THE NATIONAL POKÉDEX

Use a Sun Stone on a Helioptile obtained via Link Trade or the GTS.

Damage taken in normal battles

Type		Type	
Normal	×1	Flying	×0.5
Fire	×1	Psychic	×1
Water	×1	Bug	×1
Grass	×1	Rock	×1
Electric	×0.5	Ghost	×0
Ice	×1	Dragon	×1
Fighting	×2	Dark	×1
Poison	×1	Steel	×0.5
Ground	×2	Fairy	×1

Damage taken in Inverse battles

Type		Type	
Normal	×1	Flying	×2
Fire	×1	Psychic	×1
Water	×1	Bug	×1
Grass	×1	Rock	×1
Electric	×2	Ghost	×2
Ice	×1	Dragon	×1
Fighting	×0.5	Dark	×1
Poison	×1	Steel	×2
Ground	×0.5	Fairy	×1

Can be used in
Inverse Battle
Battle Institute
Battle Maison
Random Matchup (Free Battle)
Random Matchup (Others)

LEVEL-UP MOVES

Lv.	Name	Type	Kind	Pow.	Acc.	PP	Range
1	Eerie Impulse	Electric	Status	—	100	15	Normal
1	Electrify	Electric	Status	—	—	20	Normal
1	Razor Wind	Normal	Special	80	100	10	Many Others
1	Quick Attack	Normal	Physical	40	100	30	Normal
1	Thunder	Electric	Special	110	70	10	Normal
1	Charge	Electric	Status	—	—	20	Self
1	Parabolic Charge	Electric	Special	50	100	20	Adjacent

TM & HM MOVES

No.	Name	Type	Kind	Pow.	Acc.	PP	Range
TM06	Toxic	Poison	Status	—	90	10	Normal
TM10	Hidden Power	Normal	Special	60	100	15	Normal
TM15	Hyper Beam	Normal	Special	150	90	5	Normal
TM16	Light Screen	Psychic	Status	—	—	30	Your Side
TM17	Protect	Normal	Status	—	—	10	Self
TM18	Rain Dance	Water	Status	—	—	5	Both Sides
TM21	Frustration	Normal	Physical	—	100	20	Normal
TM24	Thunderbolt	Electric	Special	90	100	15	Normal
TM25	Thunder	Electric	Special	110	70	10	Normal
TM27	Return	Normal	Physical	—	100	20	Normal
TM28	Dig	Ground	Physical	80	100	10	Normal
TM32	Double Team	Normal	Status	—	—	15	Self
TM37	Sandstorm	Rock	Status	—	—	10	Both Sides
TM39	Rock Tomb	Rock	Physical	60	95	15	Normal
TM42	Facade	Normal	Physical	70	100	20	Normal
TM44	Rest	Psychic	Status	—	—	10	Self
TM45	Attract	Normal	Status	—	100	15	Normal
TM47	Low Sweep	Fighting	Physical	65	100	20	Normal
TM48	Round	Normal	Special	60	100	15	Normal
TM52	Focus Blast	Fighting	Special	120	70	5	Normal
TM57	Charge Beam	Electric	Special	50	90	10	Normal
TM68	Giga Impact	Normal	Physical	150	90	5	Normal
TM70	Flash	Normal	Status	—	100	20	Normal
TM72	Volt Switch	Electric	Special	70	100	20	Normal
TM73	Thunder Wave	Electric	Status	—	100	20	Normal
TM77	Psych Up	Normal	Status	—	—	10	Normal
TM78	Bulldoze	Ground	Physical	60	100	20	Adjacent
TM80	Rock Slide	Rock	Physical	75	90	10	Many Others
TM82	Dragon Tail	Dragon	Physical	60	90	10	Normal
TM86	Grass Knot	Grass	Special	—	100	20	Normal
TM87	Swagger	Normal	Status	—	90	15	Normal
TM88	Sleep Talk	Normal	Status	—	—	10	Self
TM89	U-turn	Bug	Physical	70	100	20	Normal
TM90	Substitute	Normal	Status	—	—	10	Self
TM93	Wild Charge	Electric	Physical	90	100	15	Normal
TM94	Secret Power	Normal	Physical	70	100	20	Normal
TM97	Dark Pulse	Dark	Special	80	100	15	Normal
TM100	Confide	Normal	Status	—	—	20	Normal
HM01	Cut	Normal	Physical	50	95	30	Normal
HM03	Surf	Water	Special	90	100	15	Adjacent

MOVES LEARNED IN EXCHANGE FOR BP

Name	Type	Kind	Pow.	Acc.	PP	Range
Signal Beam	Bug	Special	75	100	15	Normal
Low Kick	Fighting	Physical	—	100	20	Normal
Thunder Punch	Electric	Physical	75	100	15	Normal
Fire Punch	Fire	Physical	75	100	15	Normal
Magnet Rise	Electric	Status	—	—	10	Self
Electroweb	Electric	Special	55	95	15	Many Others
Dragon Pulse	Dragon	Special	85	100	10	Normal
Hyper Voice	Normal	Special	90	100	10	Many Others
Iron Tail	Steel	Physical	100	75	15	Normal
Snore	Normal	Special	50	100	15	Normal
Shock Wave	Electric	Special	60	—	20	Normal

MOVES TAUGHT BY PEOPLE

Name	Type	Kind	Pow.	Acc.	PP	Range

National Pokédex **696** Hoenn Pokédex —

Tyrunt

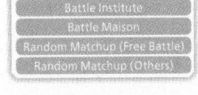

Royal Heir Pokémon

Rock / Dragon

HEIGHT: 2'07" WEIGHT: 57.3 lbs.

Same form for ♂ / ♀

Ω This Pokémon was restored from a fossil. If something happens that it doesn't like, it throws a tantrum and runs wild.

α Its immense jaws have enough destructive force that it can chew up an automobile. It lived 100 million years ago.

ABILITY
Strong Jaw

HIDDEN ABILITY
Sturdy

EGG GROUPS
Monster / Dragon

STAT GROWTH RATES
HP
Attack
Defense
Sp. Atk
Sp. Def
Speed

ITEMS SOMETIMES HELD BY WILD POKÉMON
—

EVOLUTION

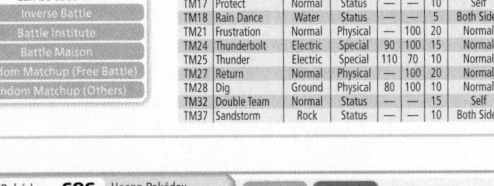

Tyrunt → Lv. 39 between 4 A.M. and 7:59 P.M. → Tyrantrum

MAIN WAY TO REGISTER IN THE NATIONAL POKÉDEX

Obtain in *Pokémon X* or *Pokémon Y*. Bring it to your game using Link Trade or the GTS.

Damage taken in normal battles

Type		Type	
Normal	×0.5	Flying	×0.5
Fire	×0.25	Psychic	×1
Water	×1	Bug	×1
Grass	×1	Rock	×1
Electric	×0.5	Ghost	×1
Ice	×2	Dragon	×2
Fighting	×2	Dark	×1
Poison	×0.5	Steel	×2
Ground	×2	Fairy	×2

Damage taken in Inverse battles

Type		Type	
Normal	×2	Flying	×2
Fire	×4	Psychic	×1
Water	×1	Bug	×1
Grass	×1	Rock	×1
Electric	×2	Ghost	×1
Ice	×0.5	Dragon	×0.5
Fighting	×0.5	Dark	×1
Poison	×2	Steel	×0.5
Ground	×0.5	Fairy	×0.5

Can be used in
Inverse Battle
Battle Institute
Battle Maison
Random Matchup (Free Battle)
Random Matchup (Others)

LEVEL-UP MOVES

Lv.	Name	Type	Kind	Pow.	Acc.	PP	Range
1	Tail Whip	Normal	Status	—	100	30	Many Others
1	Tackle	Normal	Physical	50	100	35	Normal
6	Roar	Normal	Status	—	—	20	Normal
10	Stomp	Normal	Physical	65	100	20	Normal
12	Bide	Normal	Physical	—	—	10	Self
15	Stealth Rock	Rock	Status	—	—	20	Other Side
17	Bite	Dark	Physical	60	100	25	Normal
20	Charm	Fairy	Status	—	100	20	Normal
26	Ancient Power	Rock	Special	60	100	5	Normal
30	Dragon Tail	Dragon	Physical	60	90	10	Normal
34	Crunch	Dark	Physical	80	100	15	Normal
37	Dragon Claw	Dragon	Physical	80	100	15	Normal
40	Thrash	Normal	Physical	120	100	10	1 Random
44	Earthquake	Ground	Physical	100	100	10	Adjacent
49	Horn Drill	Normal	Physical	—	30	5	Normal

TM & HM MOVES

No.	Name	Type	Kind	Pow.	Acc.	PP	Range
TM01	Hone Claws	Dark	Status	—	—	15	Self
TM02	Dragon Claw	Dragon	Physical	80	100	15	Normal
TM05	Roar	Normal	Status	—	—	20	Normal
TM06	Toxic	Poison	Status	—	90	10	Normal
TM10	Hidden Power	Normal	Special	60	100	15	Normal
TM11	Sunny Day	Fire	Status	—	—	5	Both Sides
TM17	Protect	Normal	Status	—	—	10	Self
TM21	Frustration	Normal	Physical	—	100	20	Normal
TM26	Earthquake	Ground	Physical	100	100	10	Adjacent
TM27	Return	Normal	Physical	—	100	20	Normal
TM28	Dig	Ground	Physical	80	100	10	Normal
TM31	Brick Break	Fighting	Physical	75	100	15	Normal
TM32	Double Team	Normal	Status	—	—	15	Self
TM37	Sandstorm	Rock	Status	—	—	10	Both Sides
TM39	Rock Tomb	Rock	Physical	60	95	15	Normal
TM40	Aerial Ace	Flying	Physical	60	—	20	Normal
TM42	Facade	Normal	Physical	70	100	20	Normal
TM44	Rest	Psychic	Status	—	—	10	Self
TM45	Attract	Normal	Status	—	100	15	Normal
TM48	Round	Normal	Special	60	100	15	Normal
TM69	Rock Polish	Rock	Status	—	—	20	Self
TM71	Stone Edge	Rock	Physical	100	80	5	Normal
TM78	Bulldoze	Ground	Physical	60	100	20	Adjacent
TM80	Rock Slide	Rock	Physical	75	90	10	Many Others
TM82	Dragon Tail	Dragon	Physical	60	90	10	Normal
TM87	Swagger	Normal	Status	—	90	15	Normal
TM88	Sleep Talk	Normal	Status	—	—	10	Self
TM90	Substitute	Normal	Status	—	—	10	Self
TM94	Secret Power	Normal	Physical	70	100	20	Normal
TM97	Dark Pulse	Dark	Special	80	100	15	Normal
TM100	Confide	Normal	Status	—	—	20	Normal
HM04	Strength	Normal	Physical	80	100	15	Normal
HM06	Rock Smash	Fighting	Physical	40	100	15	Normal

MOVES LEARNED IN EXCHANGE FOR BP

Name	Type	Kind	Pow.	Acc.	PP	Range
Iron Head	Steel	Physical	80	100	15	Normal
Block	Normal	Status	—	—	5	Normal
Earth Power	Ground	Special	90	100	10	Normal
Iron Defense	Steel	Status	—	—	15	Self
Superpower	Fighting	Physical	120	100	5	Normal
Zen Headbutt	Psychic	Physical	80	90	15	Normal
Dragon Pulse	Dragon	Special	85	100	10	Normal
Hyper Voice	Normal	Special	90	100	10	Many Others
Iron Tail	Steel	Physical	100	75	15	Normal
Snore	Normal	Special	50	100	15	Normal
Outrage	Dragon	Physical	120	100	10	1 Random
Stealth Rock	Rock	Status	—	—	20	Other Side

MOVES TAUGHT BY PEOPLE

Name	Type	Kind	Pow.	Acc.	PP	Range
Draco Meteor	Dragon	Special	130	90	5	Normal

EGG MOVES

Name	Type	Kind	Pow.	Acc.	PP	Range
Dragon Dance	Dragon	Status	—	—	20	Self
Thunder Fang	Electric	Physical	65	95	15	Normal
Ice Fang	Ice	Physical	65	95	15	Normal
Poison Fang	Poison	Physical	50	100	15	Normal
Rock Polish	Rock	Status	—	—	20	Self
Fire Fang	Fire	Physical	65	95	15	Normal
Curse	Ghost	Status	—	—	10	Varies

National Pokédex **697** Hoenn Pokédex —

Tyrantrum

Despot Pokémon

Rock / Dragon

HEIGHT: 8'02" WEIGHT: 595.2 lbs.

Same form for ♂ / ♀

Ω Thanks to its gargantuan jaws, which could shred thick metal plates as if they were paper, it was invincible in the ancient world it once inhabited.

α Nothing could stop this Pokémon 100 million years ago, so it behaved like a king.

ABILITY: Strong Jaw

HIDDEN ABILITY: Rock Head

EGG GROUPS: Monster, Dragon

STAT GROWTH RATES: HP, Attack, Defense, Sp. Atk, Sp. Def, Speed

ITEMS SOMETIMES HELD BY WILD POKÉMON: —

EVOLUTION

MAIN WAY TO REGISTER IN THE NATIONAL POKÉDEX

Level up a Tyrunt obtained via Link Trade or the GTS to Lv. 39 between 4:00 A.M. and 7:59 P.M.

Damage taken in normal battles

Normal	×0.5	Flying	×0.5
Fire	×0.25	Psychic	×1
Water	×1	Bug	×1
Grass	×1	Rock	×1
Electric	×0.5	Ghost	×1
Ice	×2	Dragon	×2
Fighting	×2	Dark	×1
Poison	×0.5	Steel	×2
Ground	×2	Fairy	×2

Damage taken in Inverse battles

Normal	×2	Flying	×2
Fire	×4	Psychic	×1
Water	×1	Bug	×1
Grass	×1	Rock	×1
Electric	×2	Ghost	×1
Ice	×0.5	Dragon	×0.5
Fighting	×0.5	Dark	×1
Poison	×2	Steel	×0.5
Ground	×0.5	Fairy	×0.5

Can be used in

- Inverse Battle
- Battle Institute
- Battle Maison
- Random Matchup (Free Battle)
- Random Matchup (Others)

LEVEL-UP MOVES

Lv.	Name	Type	Kind	Pow.	Acc.	PP	Range
1	Head Smash	Rock	Physical	150	80	5	Normal
1	Tail Whip	Normal	Status	—	100	30	Many Others
1	Tackle	Normal	Physical	50	100	35	Normal
6	Roar	Normal	Status	—	—	20	Normal
10	Stomp	Normal	Physical	65	100	20	Normal
12	Bide	Normal	Physical	—	—	10	Self
15	Stealth Rock	Rock	Status	—	—	20	Other Side
17	Bite	Dark	Physical	60	100	25	Normal
20	Charm	Fairy	Status	—	100	20	Normal
26	Ancient Power	Rock	Special	60	100	5	Normal
30	Dragon Tail	Dragon	Physical	60	90	10	Normal
34	Crunch	Dark	Physical	80	100	15	Normal
37	Dragon Claw	Dragon	Physical	80	100	15	Normal
42	Thrash	Normal	Physical	120	100	10	1 Random
47	Earthquake	Ground	Physical	100	100	10	Adjacent
53	Horn Drill	Normal	Physical	—	30	5	Normal
58	Head Smash	Rock	Physical	150	80	5	Normal
68	Rock Slide	Rock	Physical	75	90	10	Many Others
75	Giga Impact	Normal	Physical	150	90	5	Normal

TM & HM MOVES

No.	Name	Type	Kind	Pow.	Acc.	PP	Range
TM01	Hone Claws	Dark	Status	—	—	15	Self
TM02	Dragon Claw	Dragon	Physical	80	100	15	Normal
TM05	Roar	Normal	Status	—	—	20	Normal
TM06	Toxic	Poison	Status	—	90	10	Normal
TM10	Hidden Power	Normal	Special	60	100	15	Normal
TM11	Sunny Day	Fire	Status	—	—	5	Both Sides
TM15	Hyper Beam	Normal	Special	150	90	5	Normal
TM17	Protect	Normal	Status	—	—	10	Self
TM21	Frustration	Normal	Physical	—	100	20	Normal
TM26	Earthquake	Ground	Physical	100	100	10	Adjacent
TM27	Return	Normal	Physical	—	100	20	Normal
TM28	Dig	Ground	Physical	80	100	10	Normal
TM31	Brick Break	Fighting	Physical	75	100	15	Normal
TM32	Double Team	Normal	Status	—	—	15	Self
TM37	Sandstorm	Rock	Status	—	—	10	Both Sides
TM39	Rock Tomb	Rock	Physical	60	95	15	Normal
TM40	Aerial Ace	Flying	Physical	60	—	20	Normal
TM42	Facade	Normal	Physical	70	100	20	Normal
TM44	Rest	Psychic	Status	—	—	10	Self
TM45	Attract	Normal	Status	—	100	15	Normal
TM48	Round	Normal	Special	60	100	15	Normal
TM68	Giga Impact	Normal	Physical	150	90	5	Normal
TM69	Rock Polish	Rock	Status	—	—	20	Self
TM71	Stone Edge	Rock	Physical	100	80	5	Normal
TM78	Bulldoze	Ground	Physical	60	100	20	Adjacent
TM80	Rock Slide	Rock	Physical	75	90	10	Many Others
TM82	Dragon Tail	Dragon	Physical	60	90	10	Normal
TM87	Swagger	Normal	Status	—	90	15	Normal
TM88	Sleep Talk	Normal	Status	—	—	10	Self
TM90	Substitute	Normal	Status	—	—	10	Self
TM94	Secret Power	Normal	Physical	70	100	20	Normal
TM97	Dark Pulse	Dark	Special	80	100	15	Normal
TM100	Confide	Normal	Status	—	—	20	Normal
HM04	Strength	Normal	Physical	80	100	15	Normal
HM06	Rock Smash	Fighting	Physical	40	100	15	Normal

MOVES LEARNED IN EXCHANGE FOR BP

Name	Type	Kind	Pow.	Acc.	PP	Range
Iron Head	Steel	Physical	80	100	15	Normal
Block	Normal	Status	—	—	5	Normal
Earth Power	Ground	Special	90	100	10	Normal
Iron Defense	Steel	Status	—	—	15	Self
Superpower	Fighting	Physical	120	100	5	Normal
Zen Headbutt	Psychic	Physical	80	90	15	Normal
Dragon Pulse	Dragon	Special	85	100	10	Normal
Hyper Voice	Normal	Special	90	100	10	Many Others
Iron Tail	Steel	Physical	100	75	15	Normal
Snore	Normal	Special	50	100	15	Normal
Outrage	Dragon	Physical	120	100	10	1 Random
Stealth Rock	Rock	Status	—	—	20	Other Side

MOVES TAUGHT BY PEOPLE

Name	Type	Kind	Pow.	Acc.	PP	Range
Draco Meteor	Dragon	Special	130	90	5	Normal

National Pokédex **698** Hoenn Pokédex —

Amaura

Tundra Pokémon

Rock / Ice

HEIGHT: 4'03" WEIGHT: 55.6 lbs.

Same form for ♂ / ♀

Ω This ancient Pokémon was restored from part of its body that had been frozen in ice for over 100 million years.

α This calm Pokémon lived in a cold land where there were no violent predators like Tyrantrum.

ABILITY: Refrigerate

HIDDEN ABILITY: —

EGG GROUPS: Monster

STAT GROWTH RATES: HP, Attack, Defense, Sp. Atk, Sp. Def, Speed

ITEMS SOMETIMES HELD BY WILD POKÉMON: —

EVOLUTION

Lv. 39 between 8 P.M. and 3:59 A.M.

Amaura → Aurorus

MAIN WAY TO REGISTER IN THE NATIONAL POKÉDEX

Obtain in *Pokémon X* or *Pokémon Y*. Bring it to your game using Link Trade or the GTS.

Damage taken in normal battles

Normal	×0.5	Flying	×0.5
Fire	×1	Psychic	×1
Water	×2	Bug	×1
Grass	×2	Rock	×2
Electric	×1	Ghost	×1
Ice	×0.5	Dragon	×1
Fighting	×4	Dark	×1
Poison	×0.5	Steel	×4
Ground	×2	Fairy	×1

Damage taken in Inverse battles

Normal	×2	Flying	×2
Fire	×1	Psychic	×1
Water	×0.5	Bug	×1
Grass	×0.5	Rock	×0.5
Electric	×1	Ghost	×1
Ice	×2	Dragon	×1
Fighting	×0.25	Dark	×1
Poison	×2	Steel	×0.25
Ground	×0.5	Fairy	×1

Can be used in

- Inverse Battle
- Battle Institute
- Battle Maison
- Random Matchup (Free Battle)
- Random Matchup (Others)

LEVEL-UP MOVES

Lv.	Name	Type	Kind	Pow.	Acc.	PP	Range
1	Growl	Normal	Status	—	100	40	Many Others
1	Powder Snow	Ice	Special	40	100	25	Many Others
5	Thunder Wave	Electric	Status	—	100	20	Normal
10	Rock Throw	Rock	Physical	50	90	15	Normal
13	Icy Wind	Ice	Special	55	95	15	Many Others
15	Take Down	Normal	Physical	90	85	20	Normal
18	Mist	Ice	Status	—	—	30	Your Side
20	Aurora Beam	Ice	Special	65	100	20	Normal
26	Ancient Power	Rock	Special	60	100	5	Normal
30	Round	Normal	Special	60	100	15	Normal
34	Avalanche	Ice	Physical	60	100	10	Normal
38	Hail	Ice	Status	—	—	10	Both Sides
41	Nature Power	Normal	Status	—	—	20	Normal
44	Encore	Normal	Status	—	100	5	Normal
47	Light Screen	Psychic	Status	—	—	30	Your Side
50	Ice Beam	Ice	Special	90	100	10	Normal
57	Hyper Beam	Normal	Special	150	90	5	Normal
65	Blizzard	Ice	Special	110	70	5	Many Others

TM & HM MOVES

No.	Name	Type	Kind	Pow.	Acc.	PP	Range
TM04	Calm Mind	Psychic	Status	—	—	20	Self
TM05	Roar	Normal	Status	—	—	20	Normal
TM06	Toxic	Poison	Status	—	90	10	Normal
TM07	Hail	Ice	Status	—	—	10	Both Sides
TM10	Hidden Power	Normal	Special	60	100	15	Normal
TM13	Ice Beam	Ice	Special	90	100	10	Normal
TM14	Blizzard	Ice	Special	110	70	5	Many Others
TM15	Hyper Beam	Normal	Special	150	90	5	Normal
TM16	Light Screen	Psychic	Status	—	—	30	Your Side
TM17	Protect	Normal	Status	—	—	10	Self
TM18	Rain Dance	Water	Status	—	—	5	Both Sides
TM20	Safeguard	Normal	Status	—	—	25	Your Side
TM21	Frustration	Normal	Physical	—	100	20	Normal
TM24	Thunderbolt	Electric	Special	90	100	15	Normal
TM27	Return	Normal	Physical	—	100	20	Normal
TM32	Double Team	Normal	Status	—	—	15	Self
TM33	Reflect	Psychic	Status	—	—	20	Your Side
TM37	Sandstorm	Rock	Status	—	—	10	Both Sides
TM39	Rock Tomb	Rock	Physical	60	95	15	Normal
TM42	Facade	Normal	Physical	70	100	20	Normal
TM44	Rest	Psychic	Status	—	—	10	Self
TM45	Attract	Normal	Status	—	100	15	Normal
TM48	Round	Normal	Special	60	100	15	Normal
TM49	Echoed Voice	Normal	Special	40	100	15	Normal
TM57	Charge Beam	Electric	Special	50	90	10	Normal
TM69	Rock Polish	Rock	Status	—	—	20	Self
TM70	Flash	Normal	Status	—	100	20	Normal
TM71	Stone Edge	Rock	Physical	100	80	5	Normal
TM73	Thunder Wave	Electric	Status	—	100	20	Normal
TM77	Psych Up	Normal	Status	—	—	10	Normal
TM78	Bulldoze	Ground	Physical	60	100	20	Adjacent
TM79	Frost Breath	Ice	Special	60	90	10	Normal
TM80	Rock Slide	Rock	Physical	75	90	10	Many Others
TM82	Dragon Tail	Dragon	Physical	60	90	10	Normal
TM85	Dream Eater	Psychic	Special	100	100	15	Normal
TM87	Swagger	Normal	Status	—	90	15	Normal
TM88	Sleep Talk	Normal	Status	—	—	10	Self
TM90	Substitute	Normal	Status	—	—	10	Self
TM91	Flash Cannon	Steel	Special	80	100	10	Normal
TM94	Secret Power	Normal	Physical	70	100	20	Normal
TM96	Nature Power	Normal	Status	—	—	20	Normal
TM97	Dark Pulse	Dark	Special	80	100	15	Normal
TM100	Confide	Normal	Status	—	—	20	Normal
HM06	Rock Smash	Fighting	Physical	40	100	15	Normal

MOVES LEARNED IN EXCHANGE FOR BP

Name	Type	Kind	Pow.	Acc.	PP	Range
Iron Head	Steel	Physical	80	100	15	Normal
Earth Power	Ground	Special	90	100	10	Normal
Magnet Rise	Electric	Status	—	—	10	Self
Iron Defense	Steel	Status	—	—	15	Self
Icy Wind	Ice	Special	55	95	15	Many Others
Aqua Tail	Water	Physical	90	90	10	Normal
Zen Headbutt	Psychic	Physical	80	90	15	Normal
Hyper Voice	Normal	Special	90	100	10	Many Others
Iron Tail	Steel	Physical	100	75	15	Normal
Snore	Normal	Special	50	100	15	Normal
Water Pulse	Water	Special	60	100	20	Normal
Outrage	Dragon	Physical	120	100	10	1 Random
Stealth Rock	Rock	Status	—	—	20	Other Side

MOVES TAUGHT BY PEOPLE

Name	Type	Kind	Pow.	Acc.	PP	Range

EGG MOVES

Name	Type	Kind	Pow.	Acc.	PP	Range
Haze	Ice	Status	—	—	30	Both Sides
Barrier	Psychic	Status	—	—	20	Self
Mirror Coat	Psychic	Special	—	100	20	Varies
Magnet Rise	Electric	Status	—	—	10	Self
Discharge	Electric	Special	80	100	15	Adjacent

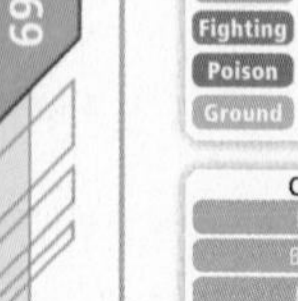

National Pokédex **699** Hoenn Pokédex —

Aurorus

Tundra Pokémon

Rock | Ice

HEIGHT: 8'10" WEIGHT: 496 lbs.

Same form for ♂ / ♀

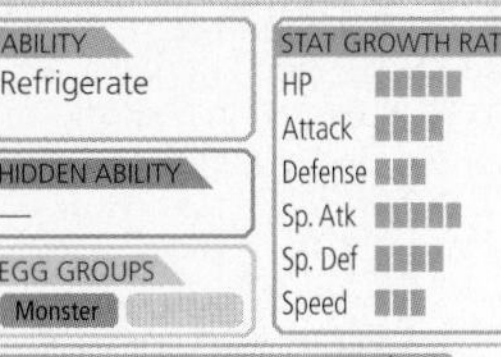

Ω The diamond-shaped crystals on its body expel air as cold as -240 degrees Fahrenheit, surrounding its enemies and encasing them in ice.

α Using its diamond-shaped crystals, it can instantly create a wall of ice to block an opponent's attack.

ABILITY
Refrigerate

HIDDEN ABILITY
—

EGG GROUPS
Monster

STAT GROWTH RATES
HP
Attack
Defense
Sp. Atk
Sp. Def
Speed

ITEMS SOMETIMES HELD BY WILD POKÉMON
—

EVOLUTION

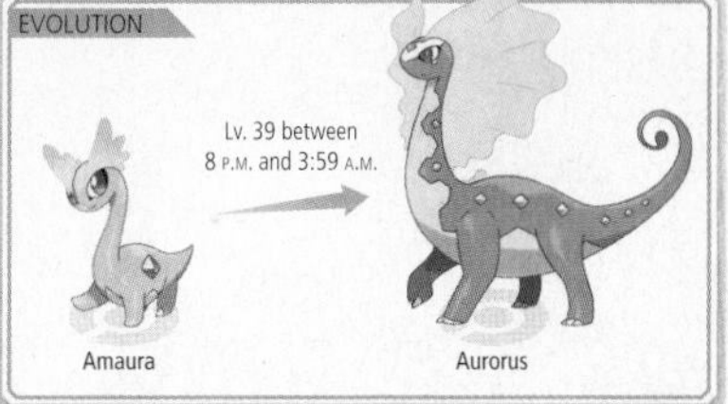

MAIN WAY TO REGISTER IN THE NATIONAL POKÉDEX

Level up a Amaura obtained via Link Trade or the GTS to Lv. 39 between 8:00 P.M. and 3:59 A.M.

Damage taken in normal battles

Type		Type	
Normal	×0.5	Flying	×0.5
Fire	×1	Psychic	×1
Water	×2	Bug	×1
Grass	×2	Rock	×2
Electric	×1	Ghost	×1
Ice	×0.5	Dragon	×1
Fighting	×4	Dark	×1
Poison	×0.5	Steel	×4
Ground	×2	Fairy	×1

Damage taken in Inverse battles

Type		Type	
Normal	×2	Flying	×2
Fire	×1	Psychic	×1
Water	×0.5	Bug	×1
Grass	×0.5	Rock	×0.5
Electric	×1	Ghost	×1
Ice	×2	Dragon	×1
Fighting	×0.25	Dark	×1
Poison	×2	Steel	×0.25
Ground	×0.5	Fairy	×1

Can be used in

Inverse Battle
Battle Institute
Battle Maison
Random Matchup (Free Battle)
Random Matchup (Others)

LEVEL-UP MOVES

Lv.	Name	Type	Kind	Pow.	Acc.	PP	Range
1	Freeze-Dry	Ice	Special	70	100	20	Normal
1	Growl	Normal	Status	—	100	40	Many Others
1	Powder Snow	Ice	Special	40	100	25	Many Others
5	Thunder Wave	Electric	Status	—	100	20	Normal
10	Rock Throw	Rock	Physical	50	90	15	Normal
13	Icy Wind	Ice	Special	55	95	15	Many Others
15	Take Down	Normal	Physical	90	85	20	Normal
18	Mist	Ice	Status	—	—	30	Your Side
20	Aurora Beam	Ice	Special	65	100	20	Normal
26	Ancient Power	Rock	Special	60	100	5	Normal
30	Round	Normal	Special	60	100	15	Normal
34	Avalanche	Ice	Physical	60	100	10	Normal
38	Hail	Ice	Status	—	—	10	Both Sides
43	Nature Power	Normal	Status	—	—	20	Normal
46	Encore	Normal	Status	—	100	5	Normal
50	Light Screen	Psychic	Status	—	—	30	Your Side
56	Ice Beam	Ice	Special	90	100	10	Normal
63	Hyper Beam	Normal	Special	150	90	5	Normal
74	Blizzard	Ice	Special	110	70	5	Many Others
77	Freeze-Dry	Ice	Special	70	100	20	Normal

TM & HM MOVES

No.	Name	Type	Kind	Pow.	Acc.	PP	Range
TM04	Calm Mind	Psychic	Status	—	—	20	Self
TM05	Roar	Normal	Status	—	—	20	Normal
TM06	Toxic	Poison	Status	—	90	10	Normal
TM07	Hail	Ice	Status	—	—	10	Both Sides
TM10	Hidden Power	Normal	Special	60	100	15	Normal
TM13	Ice Beam	Ice	Special	90	100	10	Normal
TM14	Blizzard	Ice	Special	110	70	5	Many Others
TM15	Hyper Beam	Normal	Special	150	90	5	Normal
TM16	Light Screen	Psychic	Status	—	—	30	Your Side
TM17	Protect	Normal	Status	—	—	10	Self
TM18	Rain Dance	Water	Status	—	—	5	Both Sides
TM20	Safeguard	Normal	Status	—	—	25	Your Side
TM21	Frustration	Normal	Physical	—	100	20	Normal
TM24	Thunderbolt	Electric	Special	90	100	15	Normal
TM25	Thunder	Electric	Special	110	70	10	Normal
TM26	Earthquake	Ground	Physical	100	100	10	Adjacent
TM27	Return	Normal	Physical	—	100	20	Normal
TM29	Psychic	Psychic	Special	90	100	10	Normal
TM32	Double Team	Normal	Status	—	—	15	Self
TM33	Reflect	Psychic	Status	—	—	20	Your Side
TM37	Sandstorm	Rock	Status	—	—	10	Both Sides
TM39	Rock Tomb	Rock	Physical	60	95	15	Normal
TM42	Facade	Normal	Physical	70	100	20	Normal
TM44	Rest	Psychic	Status	—	—	10	Self
TM45	Attract	Normal	Status	—	100	15	Normal
TM48	Round	Normal	Special	60	100	15	Normal
TM49	Echoed Voice	Normal	Special	40	100	15	Normal
TM57	Charge Beam	Electric	Special	50	90	10	Normal
TM68	Giga Impact	Normal	Physical	150	90	5	Normal
TM69	Rock Polish	Rock	Status	—	—	20	Self
TM70	Flash	Normal	Status	—	100	20	Normal
TM71	Stone Edge	Rock	Physical	100	80	5	Normal
TM73	Thunder Wave	Electric	Status	—	100	20	Normal
TM77	Psych Up	Normal	Status	—	—	10	Normal
TM78	Bulldoze	Ground	Physical	60	100	20	Adjacent
TM79	Frost Breath	Ice	Special	60	90	10	Normal
TM80	Rock Slide	Rock	Physical	75	90	10	Many Others
TM82	Dragon Tail	Dragon	Physical	60	90	10	Normal
TM85	Dream Eater	Psychic	Special	100	100	15	Normal
TM87	Swagger	Normal	Status	—	90	15	Normal
TM88	Sleep Talk	Normal	Status	—	—	10	Self
TM90	Substitute	Normal	Status	—	—	10	Self
TM91	Flash Cannon	Steel	Special	80	100	10	Normal
TM94	Secret Power	Normal	Physical	70	100	20	Normal
TM96	Nature Power	Normal	Status	—	—	20	Normal
TM97	Dark Pulse	Dark	Special	80	100	15	Normal
TM100	Confide	Normal	Status	—	—	20	Normal
HM06	Rock Smash	Fighting	Physical	40	100	15	Normal

MOVES LEARNED IN EXCHANGE FOR BP

Name	Type	Kind	Pow.	Acc.	PP	Range
Iron Head	Steel	Physical	80	100	15	Normal
Earth Power	Ground	Special	90	100	10	Normal
Magnet Rise	Electric	Status	—	—	10	Self
Iron Defense	Steel	Status	—	—	15	Self
Icy Wind	Ice	Special	55	95	15	Many Others
Aqua Tail	Water	Physical	90	90	10	Normal
Zen Headbutt	Psychic	Physical	80	90	15	Normal
Hyper Voice	Normal	Special	90	100	10	Many Others
Iron Tail	Steel	Physical	100	75	15	Normal
Snore	Normal	Special	50	100	15	Normal
Water Pulse	Water	Special	60	100	20	Normal
Outrage	Dragon	Physical	120	100	10	1 Random
Stealth Rock	Rock	Status	—	—	20	Other Side

MOVES TAUGHT BY PEOPLE

Name	Type	Kind	Pow.	Acc.	PP	Range

National Pokédex **700** Hoenn Pokédex —

Sylveon

Intertwining Pokémon

Fairy

HEIGHT: 3'03" WEIGHT: 51.8 lbs.

Same form for ♂ / ♀

Ω It sends a soothing aura from its ribbonlike feelers to calm fights.

α It wraps its ribbonlike feelers around the arm of its beloved Trainer and walks with him or her.

ABILITY
Cute Charm

HIDDEN ABILITY
Pixilate

EGG GROUPS
Field

STAT GROWTH RATES
HP
Attack
Defense
Sp. Atk
Sp. Def
Speed

ITEMS SOMETIMES HELD BY WILD POKÉMON
—

EVOLUTION

High affection with a Fairy-type move

Eevee → Sylveon

MAIN WAY TO REGISTER IN THE NATIONAL POKÉDEX

Level up an Eevee with high affection from playing in Pokémon-Amie, then have it learn a Fairy-type move. Alternatively, teach it a Fairy-type move first, then level it up after ensuring that it is very affectionate.

Damage taken in normal battles

Type		Type	
Normal	×1	Flying	×1
Fire	×1	Psychic	×1
Water	×1	Bug	×0.5
Grass	×1	Rock	×1
Electric	×1	Ghost	×1
Ice	×1	Dragon	×0
Fighting	×0.5	Dark	×0.5
Poison	×2	Steel	×2
Ground	×1	Fairy	×1

Damage taken in Inverse battles

Type		Type	
Normal	×1	Flying	×1
Fire	×1	Psychic	×1
Water	×1	Bug	×2
Grass	×1	Rock	×1
Electric	×1	Ghost	×1
Ice	×1	Dragon	×2
Fighting	×2	Dark	×2
Poison	×0.5	Steel	×0.5
Ground	×1	Fairy	×1

Can be used in

Inverse Battle
Battle Institute
Battle Maison
Random Matchup (Free Battle)
Random Matchup (Others)

LEVEL-UP MOVES

Lv.	Name	Type	Kind	Pow.	Acc.	PP	Range
1	Disarming Voice	Fairy	Special	40	—	15	Many Others
1	Tail Whip	Normal	Status	—	100	30	Many Others
1	Tackle	Normal	Physical	50	100	35	Normal
1	Helping Hand	Normal	Status	—	—	20	1 Ally
5	Sand Attack	Ground	Status	—	100	15	Normal
9	Fairy Wind	Fairy	Special	40	100	30	Normal
13	Quick Attack	Normal	Physical	40	100	30	Normal
17	Swift	Normal	Special	60	—	20	Many Others
20	Draining Kiss	Fairy	Special	50	100	10	Normal
25	Skill Swap	Psychic	Status	—	—	10	Normal
29	Misty Terrain	Fairy	Status	—	—	10	Both Sides
33	Light Screen	Psychic	Status	—	—	30	Your Side
37	Moonblast	Fairy	Special	95	100	15	Normal
41	Last Resort	Normal	Physical	140	100	5	Normal
45	Psych Up	Normal	Status	—	—	10	Normal

TM & HM MOVES

No.	Name	Type	Kind	Pow.	Acc.	PP	Range
TM03	Psyshock	Psychic	Special	80	100	10	Normal
TM04	Calm Mind	Psychic	Status	—	—	20	Self
TM06	Toxic	Poison	Status	—	90	10	Normal
TM10	Hidden Power	Normal	Special	60	100	15	Normal
TM11	Sunny Day	Fire	Status	—	—	5	Both Sides
TM15	Hyper Beam	Normal	Special	150	90	5	Normal
TM16	Light Screen	Psychic	Status	—	—	30	Your Side
TM17	Protect	Normal	Status	—	—	10	Self
TM18	Rain Dance	Water	Status	—	—	5	Both Sides
TM20	Safeguard	Normal	Status	—	—	25	Your Side
TM21	Frustration	Normal	Physical	—	100	20	Normal
TM27	Return	Normal	Physical	—	100	20	Normal
TM28	Dig	Ground	Physical	80	100	10	Normal
TM30	Shadow Ball	Ghost	Special	80	100	15	Normal
TM32	Double Team	Normal	Status	—	—	15	Self
TM33	Reflect	Psychic	Status	—	—	20	Your Side
TM42	Facade	Normal	Physical	70	100	20	Normal
TM44	Rest	Psychic	Status	—	—	10	Self
TM45	Attract	Normal	Status	—	100	15	Normal
TM48	Round	Normal	Special	60	100	15	Normal
TM49	Echoed Voice	Normal	Special	40	100	15	Normal
TM67	Retaliate	Normal	Physical	70	100	5	Normal
TM68	Giga Impact	Normal	Physical	150	90	5	Normal
TM70	Flash	Normal	Status	—	100	20	Normal
TM77	Psych Up	Normal	Status	—	—	10	Normal
TM87	Swagger	Normal	Status	—	90	15	Normal
TM88	Sleep Talk	Normal	Status	—	—	10	Self
TM90	Substitute	Normal	Status	—	—	10	Self
TM94	Secret Power	Normal	Physical	70	100	20	Normal
TM99	Dazzling Gleam	Fairy	Special	80	100	10	Many Others
TM100	Confide	Normal	Status	—	—	20	Normal
HM01	Cut	Normal	Physical	50	95	30	Normal

MOVES LEARNED IN EXCHANGE FOR BP

Name	Type	Kind	Pow.	Acc.	PP	Range
Covet	Normal	Physical	60	100	25	Normal
Magic Coat	Psychic	Status	—	—	15	Self
Last Resort	Normal	Physical	140	100	5	Normal
Hyper Voice	Normal	Special	90	100	10	Many Others
Iron Tail	Steel	Physical	100	75	15	Normal
Snore	Normal	Special	50	100	15	Normal
Heal Bell	Normal	Status	—	—	5	Your Party
Helping Hand	Normal	Status	—	—	20	1 Ally
Skill Swap	Psychic	Status	—	—	10	Normal

MOVES TAUGHT BY PEOPLE

Name	Type	Kind	Pow.	Acc.	PP	Range

National Pokédex **701** Hoenn Pokédex —

Hawlucha

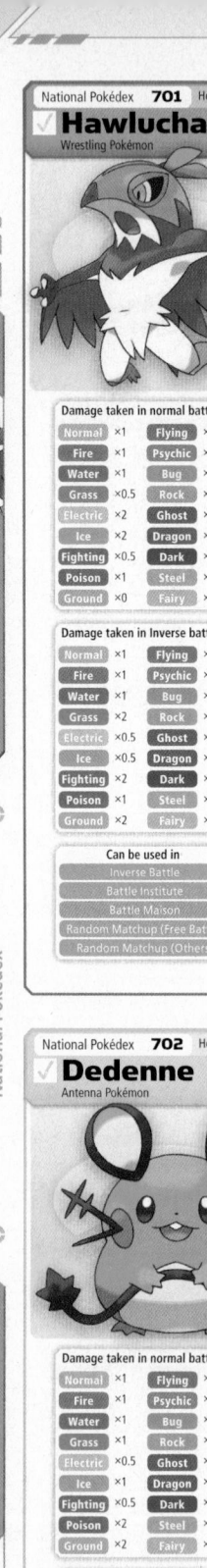

Wrestling Pokémon

Fighting Flying

HEIGHT: 2'07" WEIGHT: 47.4 lbs.

Same form for ♂ / ♀

Ω Although its body is small, its proficient fighting skills enable it to keep up with big bruisers like Machamp and Hariyama.

α With its wings, it controls its position in the air. It likes to attack from above, a maneuver that is difficult to defend against.

ABILITIES
Limber
Unburden

HIDDEN ABILITY
Mold Breaker

EGG GROUPS
Human-Like

STAT GROWTH RATES
HP
Attack
Defense
Sp. Atk
Sp. Def
Speed

ITEMS SOMETIMES HELD BY WILD POKÉMON
—

EVOLUTION
Does not evolve

MAIN WAY TO REGISTER IN THE NATIONAL POKÉDEX

Appears in *Pokémon X* and *Pokémon Y*. Bring it to your game using Link Trade or the GTS.

Damage taken in normal battles

Normal	×1	Flying	×2
Fire	×1	Psychic	×2
Water	×1	Bug	×0.25
Grass	×0.5	Rock	×1
Electric	×2	Ghost	×1
Ice	×2	Dragon	×1
Fighting	×0.5	Dark	×0.5
Poison	×1	Steel	×1
Ground	×0	Fairy	×2

Damage taken in Inverse battles

Normal	×1	Flying	×0.5
Fire	×1	Psychic	×0.5
Water	×1	Bug	×4
Grass	×2	Rock	×1
Electric	×0.5	Ghost	×1
Ice	×0.5	Dragon	×1
Fighting	×2	Dark	×2
Poison	×1	Steel	×1
Ground	×2	Fairy	×0.5

Can be used in
Inverse Battle
Battle Institute
Battle Maison
Random Matchup (Free Battle)
Random Matchup (Others)

LEVEL-UP MOVES

Lv.	Name	Type	Kind	Pow.	Acc.	PP	Range
1	Detect	Fighting	Status	—	—	5	Self
1	Tackle	Normal	Physical	50	100	35	Normal
1	Hone Claws	Dark	Status	—	—	15	Self
4	Karate Chop	Fighting	Physical	50	100	25	Normal
8	Wing Attack	Flying	Physical	60	100	35	Normal
12	Roost	Flying	Status	—	—	10	Self
16	Aerial Ace	Flying	Physical	60	—	20	Normal
20	Encore	Normal	Status	—	100	5	Normal
24	Fling	Dark	Physical	—	100	10	Normal
28	Flying Press	Fighting	Physical	80	95	10	Normal
32	Bounce	Flying	Physical	85	85	5	Normal
36	Endeavor	Normal	Physical	—	100	5	Normal
40	Feather Dance	Flying	Status	—	100	15	Normal
44	High Jump Kick	Fighting	Physical	130	90	10	Normal
48	Sky Attack	Flying	Physical	140	90	5	Normal
55	Sky Drop	Flying	Physical	60	100	10	Normal
60	Swords Dance	Normal	Status	—	—	20	Self

TM & HM MOVES

No.	Name	Type	Kind	Pow.	Acc.	PP	Range
TM01	Hone Claws	Dark	Status	—	—	15	Self
TM06	Toxic	Poison	Status	—	90	10	Normal
TM08	Bulk Up	Fighting	Status	—	—	20	Self
TM10	Hidden Power	Normal	Special	60	100	15	Normal
TM11	Sunny Day	Fire	Status	—	—	5	Both Sides
TM12	Taunt	Dark	Status	—	100	20	Normal
TM17	Protect	Normal	Status	—	—	10	Self
TM18	Rain Dance	Water	Status	—	—	5	Both Sides
TM19	Roost	Flying	Status	—	—	10	Self
TM21	Frustration	Normal	Physical	—	100	20	Normal
TM27	Return	Normal	Physical	—	100	20	Normal
TM28	Dig	Ground	Physical	80	100	10	Normal
TM31	Brick Break	Fighting	Physical	75	100	15	Normal
TM32	Double Team	Normal	Status	—	—	15	Self
TM39	Rock Tomb	Rock	Physical	60	95	15	Normal
TM40	Aerial Ace	Flying	Physical	60	—	20	Normal
TM41	Torment	Dark	Status	—	100	15	Normal
TM42	Facade	Normal	Physical	70	100	20	Normal
TM44	Rest	Psychic	Status	—	—	10	Self
TM45	Attract	Normal	Status	—	100	15	Normal
TM47	Low Sweep	Fighting	Physical	65	100	20	Normal
TM48	Round	Normal	Special	60	100	15	Normal
TM51	Steel Wing	Steel	Physical	70	90	25	Normal
TM52	Focus Blast	Fighting	Special	120	70	5	Normal
TM54	False Swipe	Normal	Physical	40	100	40	Normal
TM56	Fling	Dark	Physical	—	100	10	Normal
TM58	Sky Drop	Flying	Physical	60	100	10	Normal
TM62	Acrobatics	Flying	Physical	55	100	15	Normal
TM66	Payback	Dark	Physical	50	100	10	Normal
TM67	Retaliate	Normal	Physical	70	100	5	Normal
TM68	Giga Impact	Normal	Physical	150	90	5	Normal
TM71	Stone Edge	Rock	Physical	100	80	5	Normal
TM75	Swords Dance	Normal	Status	—	—	20	Self
TM80	Rock Slide	Rock	Physical	75	90	10	Many Others
TM81	X-Scissor	Bug	Physical	80	100	15	Normal
TM84	Poison Jab	Poison	Physical	80	100	20	Normal
TM86	Grass Knot	Grass	Special	—	100	20	Normal
TM87	Swagger	Normal	Status	—	90	15	Normal
TM88	Sleep Talk	Normal	Status	—	—	10	Self
TM89	U-turn	Bug	Physical	70	100	20	Normal
TM90	Substitute	Normal	Status	—	—	10	Self
TM94	Secret Power	Normal	Physical	70	100	20	Normal
TM98	Power-Up Punch	Fighting	Physical	40	100	20	Normal
TM100	Confide	Normal	Status	—	—	20	Normal
HM01	Cut	Normal	Physical	50	95	30	Normal
HM02	Fly	Flying	Physical	90	95	15	Normal
HM04	Strength	Normal	Physical	80	100	15	Normal
HM06	Rock Smash	Fighting	Physical	40	100	15	Normal

MOVES LEARNED IN EXCHANGE FOR BP

Name	Type	Kind	Pow.	Acc.	PP	Range
Dual Chop	Dragon	Physical	40	90	15	Normal
Iron Head	Steel	Physical	80	100	15	Normal
Bounce	Flying	Physical	85	85	5	Normal
Low Kick	Fighting	Physical	—	100	20	Normal
Thunder Punch	Electric	Physical	75	100	15	Normal
Fire Punch	Fire	Physical	75	100	15	Normal
Last Resort	Normal	Physical	140	100	5	Normal
Superpower	Fighting	Physical	120	100	5	Normal
Zen Headbutt	Psychic	Physical	80	90	15	Normal
Snore	Normal	Special	50	100	15	Normal
Tailwind	Flying	Status	—	—	15	Your Side
Sky Attack	Flying	Physical	140	90	5	Normal
Drain Punch	Fighting	Physical	75	100	10	Normal
Focus Punch	Fighting	Physical	150	100	20	Normal
Helping Hand	Normal	Status	—	—	20	1 Ally
Endeavor	Normal	Physical	—	100	5	Normal

MOVES TAUGHT BY PEOPLE

Name	Type	Kind	Pow.	Acc.	PP	Range

EGG MOVES

Name	Type	Kind	Pow.	Acc.	PP	Range
Agility	Psychic	Status	—	—	30	Self
Me First	Normal	Status	—	—	20	Varies
Ally Switch	Psychic	Status	—	—	15	Self
Entrainment	Normal	Status	—	100	15	Normal
Mud Sport	Ground	Status	—	—	15	Both Sides
Baton Pass	Normal	Status	—	—	40	Self
Quick Guard	Fighting	Status	—	—	15	Your Side

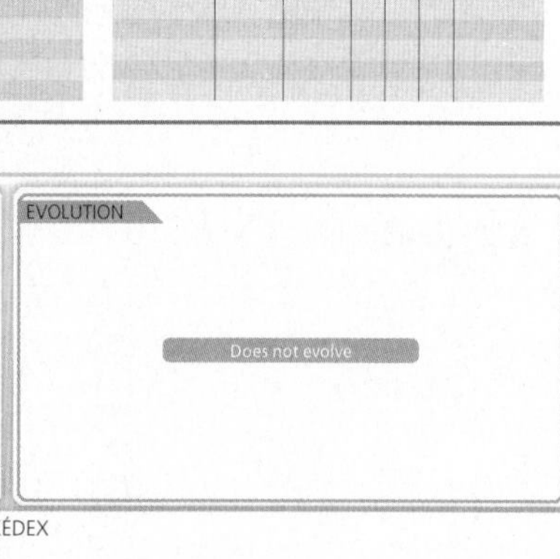

National Pokédex **702** Hoenn Pokédex —

Dedenne

Antenna Pokémon

Electric Fairy

HEIGHT: 0'08" WEIGHT: 4.9 lbs.

Same form for ♂ / ♀

Ω Its whiskers serve as antennas. By sending and receiving electrical waves, it can communicate with others over vast distances.

α It uses its tail to absorb electricity from power plants or from outlets in houses, and then it fires the electricity from its whiskers.

ABILITIES
Cheek Pouch
Pickup

HIDDEN ABILITY
Plus

EGG GROUPS
Field Fairy

STAT GROWTH RATES
HP
Attack
Defense
Sp. Atk
Sp. Def
Speed

ITEMS SOMETIMES HELD BY WILD POKÉMON
—

EVOLUTION
Does not evolve

MAIN WAY TO REGISTER IN THE NATIONAL POKÉDEX

Appears in *Pokémon X* and *Pokémon Y*. Bring it to your game using Link Trade or the GTS.

Damage taken in normal battles

Normal	×1	Flying	×0.5
Fire	×1	Psychic	×1
Water	×1	Bug	×0.5
Grass	×1	Rock	×1
Electric	×0.5	Ghost	×1
Ice	×1	Dragon	×0
Fighting	×0.5	Dark	×0.5
Poison	×2	Steel	×1
Ground	×2	Fairy	×1

Damage taken in Inverse battles

Normal	×1	Flying	×2
Fire	×1	Psychic	×1
Water	×1	Bug	×2
Grass	×1	Rock	×1
Electric	×2	Ghost	×1
Ice	×1	Dragon	×2
Fighting	×2	Dark	×2
Poison	×0.5	Steel	×1
Ground	×0.5	Fairy	×1

Can be used in
Inverse Battle
Battle Institute
Battle Maison
Random Matchup (Free Battle)
Random Matchup (Others)

LEVEL-UP MOVES

Lv.	Name	Type	Kind	Pow.	Acc.	PP	Range
1	Tackle	Normal	Physical	50	100	35	Normal
1	Tail Whip	Normal	Status	—	100	30	Many Others
7	Thunder Shock	Electric	Special	40	100	30	Normal
11	Charge	Electric	Status	—	—	20	Self
14	Charm	Fairy	Status	—	100	20	Normal
17	Parabolic Charge	Electric	Special	50	100	20	Adjacent
20	Nuzzle	Electric	Physical	20	100	20	Normal
23	Thunder Wave	Electric	Status	—	100	20	Normal
26	Volt Switch	Electric	Special	70	100	20	Normal
30	Rest	Psychic	Status	—	—	10	Self
31	Snore	Normal	Special	50	100	15	Normal
34	Charge Beam	Electric	Special	50	90	10	Normal
39	Entrainment	Normal	Status	—	100	15	Normal
42	Play Rough	Fairy	Physical	90	90	10	Normal
45	Thunder	Electric	Special	110	70	10	Normal
50	Discharge	Electric	Special	80	100	15	Adjacent

TM & HM MOVES

No.	Name	Type	Kind	Pow.	Acc.	PP	Range
TM06	Toxic	Poison	Status	—	90	10	Normal
TM10	Hidden Power	Normal	Special	60	100	15	Normal
TM11	Sunny Day	Fire	Status	—	—	5	Both Sides
TM17	Protect	Normal	Status	—	—	10	Self
TM18	Rain Dance	Water	Status	—	—	5	Both Sides
TM21	Frustration	Normal	Physical	—	100	20	Normal
TM24	Thunderbolt	Electric	Special	90	100	15	Normal
TM25	Thunder	Electric	Special	110	70	10	Normal
TM27	Return	Normal	Physical	—	100	20	Normal
TM28	Dig	Ground	Physical	80	100	10	Normal
TM32	Double Team	Normal	Status	—	—	15	Self
TM40	Aerial Ace	Flying	Physical	60	—	20	Normal
TM42	Facade	Normal	Physical	70	100	20	Normal
TM44	Rest	Psychic	Status	—	—	10	Self
TM45	Attract	Normal	Status	—	100	15	Normal
TM46	Thief	Dark	Physical	60	100	25	Normal
TM48	Round	Normal	Special	60	100	15	Normal
TM56	Fling	Dark	Physical	—	100	10	Normal
TM57	Charge Beam	Electric	Special	50	90	10	Normal
TM67	Retaliate	Normal	Physical	70	100	5	Normal
TM68	Giga Impact	Normal	Physical	150	90	5	Normal
TM70	Flash	Normal	Status	—	100	20	Normal
TM72	Volt Switch	Electric	Special	70	100	20	Normal
TM73	Thunder Wave	Electric	Status	—	100	20	Normal
TM86	Grass Knot	Grass	Special	—	100	20	Normal
TM87	Swagger	Normal	Status	—	90	15	Normal
TM88	Sleep Talk	Normal	Status	—	—	10	Self
TM89	U-turn	Bug	Physical	70	100	20	Normal
TM90	Substitute	Normal	Status	—	—	10	Self
TM93	Wild Charge	Electric	Physical	90	100	15	Normal
TM94	Secret Power	Normal	Physical	70	100	20	Normal
TM100	Confide	Normal	Status	—	—	20	Normal
HM01	Cut	Normal	Physical	50	95	30	Normal

MOVES LEARNED IN EXCHANGE FOR BP

Name	Type	Kind	Pow.	Acc.	PP	Range
Covet	Normal	Physical	60	100	25	Normal
Super Fang	Normal	Physical	—	90	10	Normal
Signal Beam	Bug	Special	75	100	15	Normal
Thunder Punch	Electric	Physical	75	100	15	Normal
Magnet Rise	Electric	Status	—	—	10	Self
Last Resort	Normal	Physical	140	100	5	Normal
Electroweb	Electric	Special	55	95	15	Many Others
Iron Tail	Steel	Physical	100	75	15	Normal
Snore	Normal	Special	50	100	15	Normal
Shock Wave	Electric	Special	60	—	20	Normal
Helping Hand	Normal	Status	—	—	20	1 Ally
Recycle	Normal	Status	—	—	10	Self

MOVES TAUGHT BY PEOPLE

Name	Type	Kind	Pow.	Acc.	PP	Range

EGG MOVES

Name	Type	Kind	Pow.	Acc.	PP	Range
Eerie Impulse	Electric	Status	—	100	15	Normal
Covet	Normal	Physical	60	100	25	Normal
Helping Hand	Normal	Status	—	—	20	1 Ally
Natural Gift	Normal	Physical	—	100	15	Normal

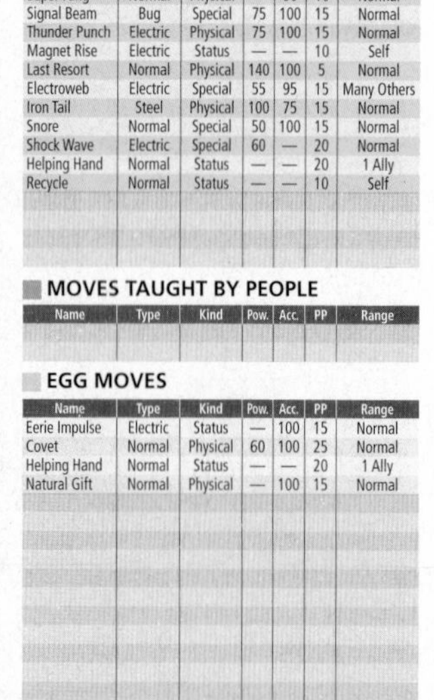

National Pokédex **703** Hoenn Pokédex —

Carbink

Jewel Pokémon

Rock / Fairy

HEIGHT: 1'00" WEIGHT: 12.6 lbs.

Gender unknown

Ω Born from the temperatures and pressures deep underground, it fires beams from the stone in its head.

α It has slept underground for hundreds of millions of years since its birth. It's occasionally found during the excavation of caves.

ABILITY
Clear Body

HIDDEN ABILITY
Sturdy

EGG GROUPS
Fairy / Mineral

STAT GROWTH RATES

Stat	Rate
HP	■■
Attack	■■■
Defense	■■■■■■
Sp. Atk	■■
Sp. Def	■■■■■■
Speed	■■■

ITEMS SOMETIMES HELD BY WILD POKÉMON
—

EVOLUTION
Does not evolve

MAIN WAY TO REGISTER IN THE NATIONAL POKÉDEX

Appears in *Pokémon X* and *Pokémon Y*. Bring it to your game using Link Trade or the GTS.

Damage taken in normal battles

Type	Damage	Type	Damage
Normal	×0.5	Flying	×0.5
Fire	×0.5	Psychic	×1
Water	×2	Bug	×0.5
Grass	×2	Rock	×1
Electric	×1	Ghost	×1
Ice	×1	Dragon	×0
Fighting	×1	Dark	×0.5
Poison	×1	Steel	×4
Ground	×2	Fairy	×1

Damage taken in Inverse battles

Type	Damage	Type	Damage
Normal	×2	Flying	×2
Fire	×2	Psychic	×1
Water	×0.5	Bug	×2
Grass	×0.5	Rock	×1
Electric	×1	Ghost	×1
Ice	×1	Dragon	×2
Fighting	×1	Dark	×2
Poison	×1	Steel	×0.25
Ground	×0.5	Fairy	×1

Can be used in
- Inverse Battle
- Battle Institute
- Battle Maison
- Random Matchup (Free Battle)
- Random Matchup (Others)

LEVEL-UP MOVES

Lv.	Name	Type	Kind	Pow.	Acc.	PP	Range
1	Tackle	Normal	Physical	50	100	35	Normal
1	Harden	Normal	Status	—	—	30	Self
5	Rock Throw	Rock	Physical	50	90	15	Normal
8	Sharpen	Normal	Status	—	—	30	Self
12	Smack Down	Rock	Physical	50	100	15	Normal
18	Reflect	Psychic	Status	—	—	20	Your Side
21	Stealth Rock	Rock	Status	—	—	20	Other Side
27	Guard Split	Psychic	Status	—	—	10	Normal
31	Ancient Power	Rock	Special	60	100	5	Normal
35	Flail	Normal	Physical	—	100	15	Normal
40	Skill Swap	Psychic	Status	—	—	10	Normal
46	Power Gem	Rock	Special	80	100	20	Normal
49	Stone Edge	Rock	Physical	100	80	5	Normal
50	Moonblast	Fairy	Special	95	100	15	Normal
60	Light Screen	Psychic	Status	—	—	30	Your Side
70	Safeguard	Normal	Status	—	—	25	Your Side

TM & HM MOVES

No.	Name	Type	Kind	Pow.	Acc.	PP	Range
TM04	Calm Mind	Psychic	Status	—	—	20	Self
TM06	Toxic	Poison	Status	—	90	10	Normal
TM07	Hail	Ice	Status	—	—	10	Both Sides
TM10	Hidden Power	Normal	Special	60	100	15	Normal
TM11	Sunny Day	Fire	Status	—	—	5	Both Sides
TM16	Light Screen	Psychic	Status	—	—	30	Your Side
TM17	Protect	Normal	Status	—	—	10	Self
TM20	Safeguard	Normal	Status	—	—	25	Your Side
TM21	Frustration	Normal	Physical	—	100	20	Normal
TM23	Smack Down	Rock	Physical	50	100	15	Normal
TM27	Return	Normal	Physical	—	100	20	Normal
TM29	Psychic	Psychic	Special	90	100	10	Normal
TM32	Double Team	Normal	Status	—	—	15	Self
TM33	Reflect	Psychic	Status	—	—	20	Your Side
TM37	Sandstorm	Rock	Status	—	—	10	Both Sides
TM39	Rock Tomb	Rock	Physical	60	95	15	Normal
TM42	Facade	Normal	Physical	70	100	20	Normal
TM44	Rest	Psychic	Status	—	—	10	Self
TM48	Round	Normal	Special	60	100	15	Normal
TM64	Explosion	Normal	Physical	250	100	5	Adjacent
TM69	Rock Polish	Rock	Status	—	—	20	Self
TM70	Flash	Normal	Status	—	100	20	Normal
TM71	Stone Edge	Rock	Physical	100	80	5	Normal
TM74	Gyro Ball	Steel	Physical	—	100	5	Normal
TM77	Psych Up	Normal	Status	—	—	10	Normal
TM80	Rock Slide	Rock	Physical	75	90	10	Many Others
TM87	Swagger	Normal	Status	—	90	15	Normal
TM88	Sleep Talk	Normal	Status	—	—	10	Self
TM90	Substitute	Normal	Status	—	—	10	Self
TM92	Trick Room	Psychic	Status	—	—	5	Both Sides
TM94	Secret Power	Normal	Physical	70	100	20	Normal
TM96	Nature Power	Normal	Status	—	—	20	Normal
TM99	Dazzling Gleam	Fairy	Special	80	100	10	Many Others
TM100	Confide	Normal	Status	—	—	20	Normal

MOVES LEARNED IN EXCHANGE FOR BP

Name	Type	Kind	Pow.	Acc.	PP	Range
Covet	Normal	Physical	60	100	25	Normal
Magic Coat	Psychic	Status	—	—	15	Self
Earth Power	Ground	Special	90	100	10	Normal
Gravity	Psychic	Status	—	—	5	Both Sides
Magnet Rise	Electric	Status	—	—	10	Self
Iron Defense	Steel	Status	—	—	15	Self
Snore	Normal	Special	50	100	15	Normal
After You	Normal	Status	—	—	15	Normal
Wonder Room	Psychic	Status	—	—	10	Both Sides
Stealth Rock	Rock	Status	—	—	20	Other Side
Skill Swap	Psychic	Status	—	—	10	Normal

MOVES TAUGHT BY PEOPLE

Name	Type	Kind	Pow.	Acc.	PP	Range

National Pokédex **704** Hoenn Pokédex —

Goomy

Soft Tissue Pokémon

Dragon

HEIGHT: 1'00" WEIGHT: 6.2 lbs.

Same form for ♂ / ♀

Ω The weakest Dragon-type Pokémon, it lives in damp, shady places, so its body doesn't dry out.

α It's covered in a slimy membrane that makes any punches or kicks slide off it harmlessly.

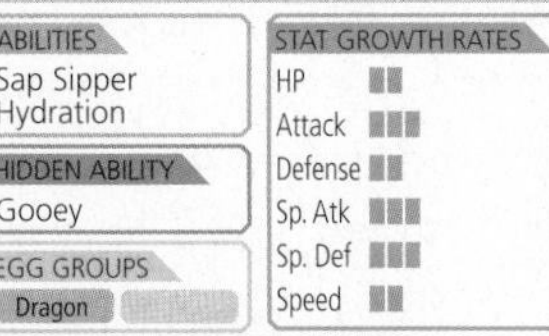

ABILITIES
Sap Sipper
Hydration

HIDDEN ABILITY
Gooey

EGG GROUPS
Dragon

STAT GROWTH RATES

Stat	Rate
HP	■■
Attack	■■■
Defense	■■
Sp. Atk	■■■
Sp. Def	■■■
Speed	■■

ITEMS SOMETIMES HELD BY WILD POKÉMON
—

EVOLUTION

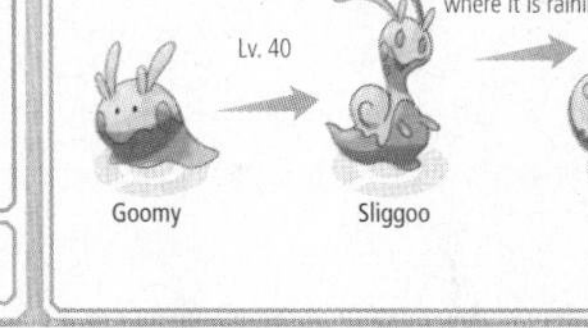

MAIN WAY TO REGISTER IN THE NATIONAL POKÉDEX

Appears in *Pokémon X* and *Pokémon Y*. Bring it to your game using Link Trade or the GTS.

Damage taken in normal battles

Type	Damage	Type	Damage
Normal	×1	Flying	×1
Fire	×0.5	Psychic	×1
Water	×0.5	Bug	×1
Grass	×0.5	Rock	×1
Electric	×0.5	Ghost	×1
Ice	×2	Dragon	×2
Fighting	×1	Dark	×1
Poison	×1	Steel	×1
Ground	×1	Fairy	×2

Damage taken in Inverse battles

Type	Damage	Type	Damage
Normal	×1	Flying	×1
Fire	×2	Psychic	×1
Water	×2	Bug	×1
Grass	×2	Rock	×1
Electric	×2	Ghost	×1
Ice	×0.5	Dragon	×0.5
Fighting	×1	Dark	×1
Poison	×1	Steel	×1
Ground	×1	Fairy	×0.5

Can be used in
- Inverse Battle
- Battle Institute
- Battle Maison
- Random Matchup (Free Battle)
- Random Matchup (Others)

LEVEL-UP MOVES

Lv.	Name	Type	Kind	Pow.	Acc.	PP	Range
1	Tackle	Normal	Physical	50	100	35	Normal
1	Bubble	Water	Special	40	100	30	Many Others
5	Absorb	Grass	Special	20	100	25	Normal
9	Protect	Normal	Status	—	—	10	Self
13	Bide	Normal	Physical	—	—	10	Self
18	Dragon Breath	Dragon	Special	60	100	20	Normal
25	Rain Dance	Water	Status	—	—	5	Both Sides
28	Flail	Normal	Physical	—	100	15	Normal
32	Body Slam	Normal	Physical	85	100	15	Normal
38	Muddy Water	Water	Special	90	85	10	Many Others
42	Dragon Pulse	Dragon	Special	85	100	10	Normal

TM & HM MOVES

No.	Name	Type	Kind	Pow.	Acc.	PP	Range
TM06	Toxic	Poison	Status	—	90	10	Normal
TM10	Hidden Power	Normal	Special	60	100	15	Normal
TM11	Sunny Day	Fire	Status	—	—	5	Both Sides
TM17	Protect	Normal	Status	—	—	10	Self
TM18	Rain Dance	Water	Status	—	—	5	Both Sides
TM21	Frustration	Normal	Physical	—	100	20	Normal
TM24	Thunderbolt	Electric	Special	90	100	15	Normal
TM27	Return	Normal	Physical	—	100	20	Normal
TM32	Double Team	Normal	Status	—	—	15	Self
TM34	Sludge Wave	Poison	Special	95	100	10	Adjacent
TM36	Sludge Bomb	Poison	Special	90	100	10	Normal
TM42	Facade	Normal	Physical	70	100	20	Normal
TM44	Rest	Psychic	Status	—	—	10	Self
TM45	Attract	Normal	Status	—	100	15	Normal
TM48	Round	Normal	Special	60	100	15	Normal
TM80	Rock Slide	Rock	Physical	75	90	10	Many Others
TM83	Infestation	Bug	Special	20	100	20	Normal
TM87	Swagger	Normal	Status	—	90	15	Normal
TM88	Sleep Talk	Normal	Status	—	—	10	Self
TM90	Substitute	Normal	Status	—	—	10	Self
TM94	Secret Power	Normal	Physical	70	100	20	Normal
TM100	Confide	Normal	Status	—	—	20	Normal

MOVES LEARNED IN EXCHANGE FOR BP

Name	Type	Kind	Pow.	Acc.	PP	Range
Dragon Pulse	Dragon	Special	85	100	10	Normal
Iron Tail	Steel	Physical	100	75	15	Normal
Snore	Normal	Special	50	100	15	Normal
Shock Wave	Electric	Special	60	—	20	Normal
Water Pulse	Water	Special	60	100	20	Normal
Outrage	Dragon	Physical	120	100	10	1 Random

MOVES TAUGHT BY PEOPLE

Name	Type	Kind	Pow.	Acc.	PP	Range
Draco Meteor	Dragon	Special	130	90	5	Normal

EGG MOVES

Name	Type	Kind	Pow.	Acc.	PP	Range
Acid Armor	Poison	Status	—	—	20	Self
Curse	Ghost	Status	—	—	10	Varies
Iron Tail	Steel	Physical	100	75	15	Normal
Poison Tail	Poison	Physical	50	100	25	Normal
Counter	Fighting	Physical	—	100	20	Varies
Endure	Normal	Status	—	—	10	Self

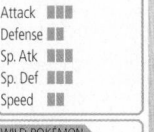

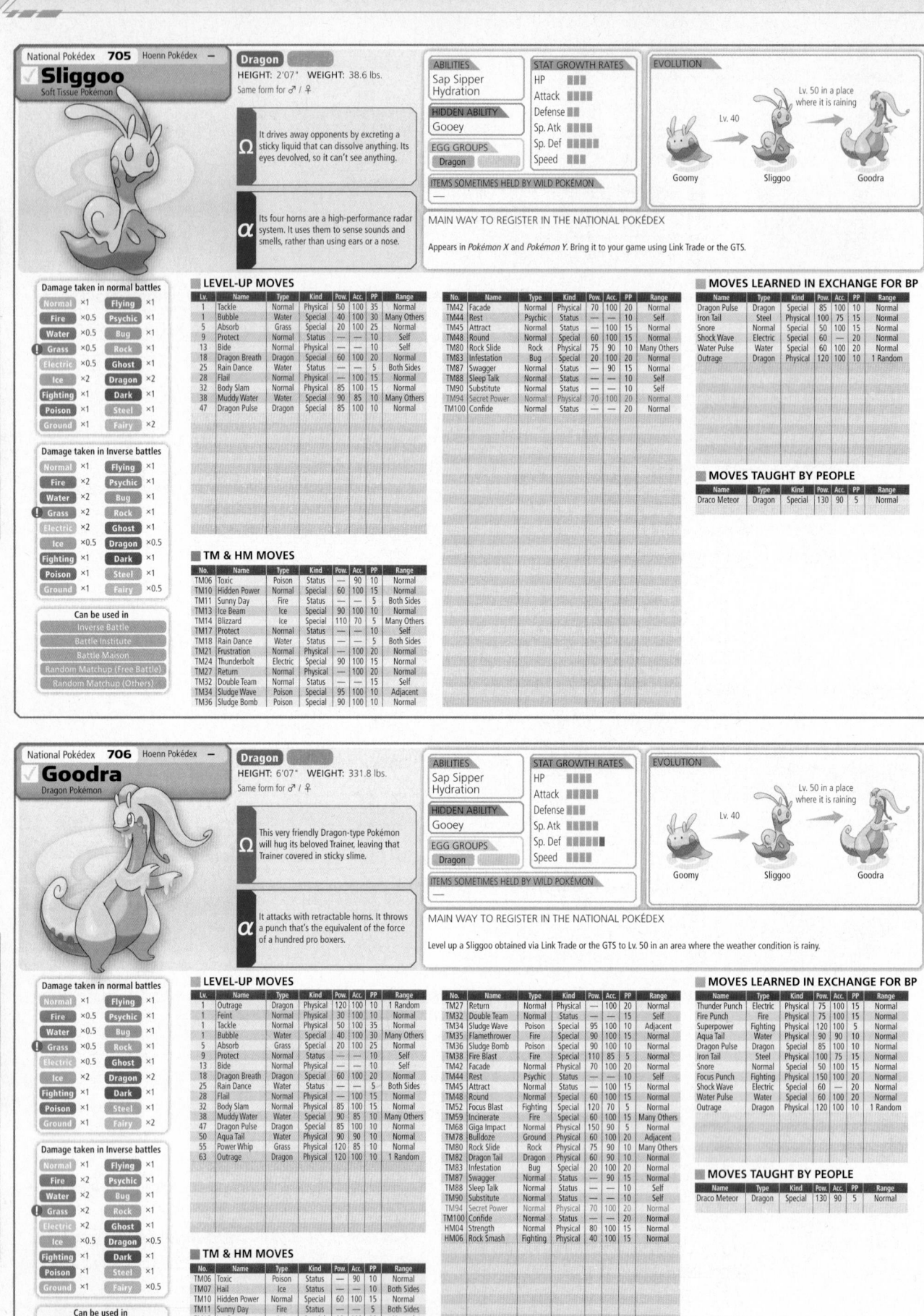

National Pokédex **705** Hoenn Pokédex —

Sliggoo

Soft Tissue Pokémon

Dragon

HEIGHT: 2'07" WEIGHT: 38.6 lbs.

Same form for ♂ / ♀

Ω It drives away opponents by excreting a sticky liquid that can dissolve anything. Its eyes devolved, so it can't see anything.

α Its four horns are a high-performance radar system. It uses them to sense sounds and smells, rather than using ears or a nose.

ABILITIES
Sap Sipper
Hydration

HIDDEN ABILITY
Gooey

EGG GROUPS
Dragon

STAT GROWTH RATES
HP
Attack
Defense
Sp. Atk
Sp. Def
Speed

ITEMS SOMETIMES HELD BY WILD POKÉMON
—

EVOLUTION

Goomy → Lv. 40 → Sliggoo → Lv. 50 in a place where it is raining → Goodra

MAIN WAY TO REGISTER IN THE NATIONAL POKÉDEX

Appears in *Pokémon X* and *Pokémon Y*. Bring it to your game using Link Trade or the GTS.

Damage taken in normal battles

Type		Type	
Normal	×1	Flying	×1
Fire	×0.5	Psychic	×1
Water	×0.5	Bug	×1
Grass	×0.5	Rock	×1
Electric	×0.5	Ghost	×1
Ice	×2	Dragon	×2
Fighting	×1	Dark	×1
Poison	×1	Steel	×1
Ground	×1	Fairy	×2

Damage taken in Inverse battles

Type		Type	
Normal	×1	Flying	×1
Fire	×2	Psychic	×1
Water	×2	Bug	×1
Grass	×2	Rock	×1
Electric	×2	Ghost	×1
Ice	×0.5	Dragon	×0.5
Fighting	×1	Dark	×1
Poison	×1	Steel	×1
Ground	×1	Fairy	×0.5

Can be used in
Inverse Battle
Battle Institute
Battle Maison
Random Matchup (Free Battle)
Random Matchup (Others)

LEVEL-UP MOVES

Lv.	Name	Type	Kind	Pow.	Acc.	PP	Range
1	Tackle	Normal	Physical	50	100	35	Normal
1	Bubble	Water	Special	40	100	30	Many Others
5	Absorb	Grass	Special	20	100	25	Normal
9	Protect	Normal	Status	—	—	10	Self
13	Bide	Normal	Physical	—	—	10	Self
18	Dragon Breath	Dragon	Special	60	100	20	Normal
25	Rain Dance	Water	Status	—	—	5	Both Sides
28	Flail	Normal	Physical	—	100	15	Normal
32	Body Slam	Normal	Physical	85	100	15	Normal
38	Muddy Water	Water	Special	90	85	10	Many Others
47	Dragon Pulse	Dragon	Special	85	100	10	Normal

TM & HM MOVES

No.	Name	Type	Kind	Pow.	Acc.	PP	Range
TM06	Toxic	Poison	Status	—	90	10	Normal
TM10	Hidden Power	Normal	Special	60	100	15	Normal
TM11	Sunny Day	Fire	Status	—	—	5	Both Sides
TM13	Ice Beam	Ice	Special	90	100	10	Normal
TM14	Blizzard	Ice	Special	110	70	5	Many Others
TM17	Protect	Normal	Status	—	—	10	Self
TM18	Rain Dance	Water	Status	—	—	5	Both Sides
TM21	Frustration	Normal	Physical	—	100	20	Normal
TM24	Thunderbolt	Electric	Special	90	100	15	Normal
TM27	Return	Normal	Physical	—	100	20	Normal
TM32	Double Team	Normal	Status	—	—	15	Self
TM34	Sludge Wave	Poison	Special	95	100	10	Adjacent
TM36	Sludge Bomb	Poison	Special	90	100	10	Normal
TM42	Facade	Normal	Physical	70	100	20	Normal
TM44	Rest	Psychic	Status	—	—	10	Self
TM45	Attract	Normal	Status	—	100	15	Normal
TM48	Round	Normal	Special	60	100	15	Normal
TM80	Rock Slide	Rock	Physical	75	90	10	Many Others
TM83	Infestation	Bug	Special	20	100	20	Normal
TM87	Swagger	Normal	Status	—	90	15	Normal
TM88	Sleep Talk	Normal	Status	—	—	10	Self
TM90	Substitute	Normal	Status	—	—	10	Self
TM94	Secret Power	Normal	Physical	70	100	20	Normal
TM100	Confide	Normal	Status	—	—	20	Normal

MOVES LEARNED IN EXCHANGE FOR BP

Name	Type	Kind	Pow.	Acc.	PP	Range
Dragon Pulse	Dragon	Special	85	100	10	Normal
Iron Tail	Steel	Physical	100	75	15	Normal
Snore	Normal	Special	50	100	15	Normal
Shock Wave	Electric	Special	60	—	20	Normal
Water Pulse	Water	Special	60	100	20	Normal
Outrage	Dragon	Physical	120	100	10	1 Random

MOVES TAUGHT BY PEOPLE

Name	Type	Kind	Pow.	Acc.	PP	Range
Draco Meteor	Dragon	Special	130	90	5	Normal

National Pokédex **706** Hoenn Pokédex —

Goodra

Dragon Pokémon

Dragon

HEIGHT: 6'07" WEIGHT: 331.8 lbs.

Same form for ♂ / ♀

Ω This very friendly Dragon-type Pokémon will hug its beloved Trainer, leaving that Trainer covered in sticky slime.

α It attacks with retractable horns. It throws a punch that's the equivalent of the force of a hundred pro boxers.

ABILITIES
Sap Sipper
Hydration

HIDDEN ABILITY
Gooey

EGG GROUPS
Dragon

STAT GROWTH RATES
HP
Attack
Defense
Sp. Atk
Sp. Def
Speed

ITEMS SOMETIMES HELD BY WILD POKÉMON
—

EVOLUTION

Goomy → Lv. 40 → Sliggoo → Lv. 50 in a place where it is raining → Goodra

MAIN WAY TO REGISTER IN THE NATIONAL POKÉDEX

Level up a Sliggoo obtained via Link Trade or the GTS to Lv. 50 in an area where the weather condition is rainy.

Damage taken in normal battles

Type		Type	
Normal	×1	Flying	×1
Fire	×0.5	Psychic	×1
Water	×0.5	Bug	×1
Grass	×0.5	Rock	×1
Electric	×0.5	Ghost	×1
Ice	×2	Dragon	×2
Fighting	×1	Dark	×1
Poison	×1	Steel	×1
Ground	×1	Fairy	×2

Damage taken in Inverse battles

Type		Type	
Normal	×1	Flying	×1
Fire	×2	Psychic	×1
Water	×2	Bug	×1
Grass	×2	Rock	×1
Electric	×2	Ghost	×1
Ice	×0.5	Dragon	×0.5
Fighting	×1	Dark	×1
Poison	×1	Steel	×1
Ground	×1	Fairy	×0.5

Can be used in
Inverse Battle
Battle Institute
Battle Maison
Random Matchup (Free Battle)
Random Matchup (Others)

LEVEL-UP MOVES

Lv.	Name	Type	Kind	Pow.	Acc.	PP	Range
1	Outrage	Dragon	Physical	120	100	10	1 Random
1	Feint	Normal	Physical	30	100	10	Normal
1	Tackle	Normal	Physical	50	100	35	Normal
1	Bubble	Water	Special	40	100	30	Many Others
5	Absorb	Grass	Special	20	100	25	Normal
9	Protect	Normal	Status	—	—	10	Self
13	Bide	Normal	Physical	—	—	10	Self
18	Dragon Breath	Dragon	Special	60	100	20	Normal
25	Rain Dance	Water	Status	—	—	5	Both Sides
28	Flail	Normal	Physical	—	100	15	Normal
32	Body Slam	Normal	Physical	85	100	15	Normal
38	Muddy Water	Water	Special	90	85	10	Many Others
47	Dragon Pulse	Dragon	Special	85	100	10	Normal
50	Aqua Tail	Water	Physical	90	90	10	Normal
55	Power Whip	Grass	Physical	120	85	10	Normal
63	Outrage	Dragon	Physical	120	100	10	1 Random

TM & HM MOVES

No.	Name	Type	Kind	Pow.	Acc.	PP	Range
TM06	Toxic	Poison	Status	—	90	10	Normal
TM07	Hail	Ice	Status	—	—	10	Both Sides
TM10	Hidden Power	Normal	Special	60	100	15	Normal
TM11	Sunny Day	Fire	Status	—	—	5	Both Sides
TM13	Ice Beam	Ice	Special	90	100	10	Normal
TM14	Blizzard	Ice	Special	110	70	5	Many Others
TM15	Hyper Beam	Normal	Special	150	90	5	Normal
TM17	Protect	Normal	Status	—	—	10	Self
TM18	Rain Dance	Water	Status	—	—	5	Both Sides
TM21	Frustration	Normal	Physical	—	100	20	Normal
TM24	Thunderbolt	Electric	Special	90	100	15	Normal
TM25	Thunder	Electric	Special	110	70	10	Normal
TM26	Earthquake	Ground	Physical	100	100	10	Adjacent
TM27	Return	Normal	Physical	—	100	20	Normal
TM32	Double Team	Normal	Status	—	—	15	Self
TM34	Sludge Wave	Poison	Special	95	100	10	Adjacent
TM35	Flamethrower	Fire	Special	90	100	15	Normal
TM36	Sludge Bomb	Poison	Special	90	100	10	Normal
TM38	Fire Blast	Fire	Special	110	85	5	Normal
TM42	Facade	Normal	Physical	70	100	20	Normal
TM44	Rest	Psychic	Status	—	—	10	Self
TM45	Attract	Normal	Status	—	100	15	Normal
TM48	Round	Normal	Special	60	100	15	Normal
TM52	Focus Blast	Fighting	Special	120	70	5	Normal
TM59	Incinerate	Fire	Special	60	100	15	Many Others
TM68	Giga Impact	Normal	Physical	150	90	5	Normal
TM78	Bulldoze	Ground	Physical	60	100	20	Adjacent
TM80	Rock Slide	Rock	Physical	75	90	10	Many Others
TM82	Dragon Tail	Dragon	Physical	60	90	10	Normal
TM83	Infestation	Bug	Special	20	100	20	Normal
TM87	Swagger	Normal	Status	—	90	15	Normal
TM88	Sleep Talk	Normal	Status	—	—	10	Self
TM90	Substitute	Normal	Status	—	—	10	Self
TM94	Secret Power	Normal	Physical	70	100	20	Normal
TM100	Confide	Normal	Status	—	—	20	Normal
HM04	Strength	Normal	Physical	80	100	15	Normal
HM06	Rock Smash	Fighting	Physical	40	100	15	Normal

MOVES LEARNED IN EXCHANGE FOR BP

Name	Type	Kind	Pow.	Acc.	PP	Range
Thunder Punch	Electric	Physical	75	100	15	Normal
Fire Punch	Fire	Physical	75	100	15	Normal
Superpower	Fighting	Physical	120	100	5	Normal
Aqua Tail	Water	Physical	90	90	10	Normal
Dragon Pulse	Dragon	Special	85	100	10	Normal
Iron Tail	Steel	Physical	100	75	15	Normal
Snore	Normal	Special	50	100	15	Normal
Focus Punch	Fighting	Physical	150	100	20	Normal
Shock Wave	Electric	Special	60	—	20	Normal
Water Pulse	Water	Special	60	100	20	Normal
Outrage	Dragon	Physical	120	100	10	1 Random

MOVES TAUGHT BY PEOPLE

Name	Type	Kind	Pow.	Acc.	PP	Range
Draco Meteor	Dragon	Special	130	90	5	Normal

National Pokédex **707** Hoenn Pokédex —

Klefki

Key Ring Pokémon

Steel **Fairy**

HEIGHT: 0'08" WEIGHT: 6.6 lbs.

Same form for ♂ / ♀

Ω These key collectors threaten any attackers by fiercely jingling their keys at them.

α It never lets go of a key that it likes, so people give it the keys to vaults and safes as a way to prevent crime.

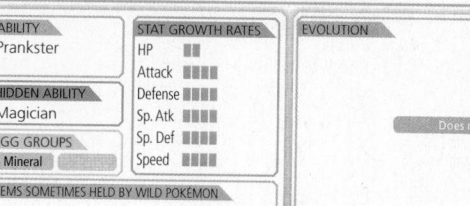

ABILITY
Prankster

HIDDEN ABILITY
Magician

EGG GROUPS
Mineral

STAT GROWTH RATES
HP ■■
Attack ■■■■
Defense ■■■■
Sp. Atk ■■■■
Sp. Def ■■■■
Speed ■■■■

EVOLUTION
Does not evolve

ITEMS SOMETIMES HELD BY WILD POKÉMON
—

MAIN WAY TO REGISTER IN THE NATIONAL POKÉDEX

Catch on Route 113. Appears as a hidden Pokémon after you battle Groudon or Kyogre.

Damage taken in normal battles

Normal	×0.5	Flying	×0.5
Fire	×2	Psychic	×0.5
Water	×1	Bug	×0.25
Grass	×0.5	Rock	×0.5
Electric	×1	Ghost	×1
Ice	×0.5	Dragon	×0
Fighting	×1	Dark	×0.5
Poison	×0	Steel	×1
Ground	×2	Fairy	×0.5

Damage taken in Inverse battles

Normal	×2	Flying	×2
Fire	×0.5	Psychic	×2
Water	×1	Bug	×4
Grass	×2	Rock	×2
Electric	×1	Ghost	×1
Ice	×2	Dragon	×4
Fighting	×1	Dark	×2
Poison	×1	Steel	×1
Ground	×0.5	Fairy	×2

Can be used in
Inverse Battle
Battle Institute
Battle Maison
Random Matchup (Free Battle)
Random Matchup (Others)

LEVEL-UP MOVES

Lv.	Name	Type	Kind	Pow.	Acc.	PP	Range
1	Fairy Lock	Fairy	Status	—	—	10	Both Sides
1	Tackle	Normal	Physical	50	100	35	Normal
5	Fairy Wind	Fairy	Special	40	100	30	Normal
8	Astonish	Ghost	Physical	30	100	15	Normal
12	Metal Sound	Steel	Status	—	85	40	Normal
15	Spikes	Ground	Status	—	—	20	Other Side
18	Draining Kiss	Fairy	Special	50	100	10	Normal
23	Crafty Shield	Fairy	Status	—	—	10	Your Side
27	Foul Play	Dark	Physical	95	100	15	Normal
32	Torment	Dark	Status	—	100	15	Normal
34	Mirror Shot	Steel	Special	65	85	10	Normal
36	Imprison	Psychic	Status	—	—	10	Self
40	Recycle	Normal	Status	—	—	10	Self
43	Play Rough	Fairy	Physical	90	90	10	Normal
44	Magic Room	Psychic	Status	—	—	10	Both Sides
50	Heal Block	Psychic	Status	—	100	15	Many Others

TM & HM MOVES

No.	Name	Type	Kind	Pow.	Acc.	PP	Range
TM03	Psyshock	Psychic	Special	80	100	10	Normal
TM04	Calm Mind	Psychic	Status	—	—	20	Self
TM06	Toxic	Poison	Status	—	90	10	Normal
TM10	Hidden Power	Normal	Special	60	100	15	Normal
TM11	Sunny Day	Fire	Status	—	—	5	Both Sides
TM15	Hyper Beam	Normal	Special	150	90	5	Normal
TM16	Light Screen	Psychic	Status	—	—	30	Your Side
TM17	Protect	Normal	Status	—	—	10	Self
TM18	Rain Dance	Water	Status	—	—	5	Both Sides
TM20	Safeguard	Normal	Status	—	—	25	Your Side
TM21	Frustration	Normal	Physical	—	100	20	Normal
TM27	Return	Normal	Physical	—	100	20	Normal
TM29	Psychic	Psychic	Special	90	100	10	Normal
TM32	Double Team	Normal	Status	—	—	15	Self
TM33	Reflect	Psychic	Status	—	—	20	Your Side
TM41	Torment	Dark	Status	—	100	15	Normal
TM42	Facade	Normal	Physical	70	100	20	Normal
TM44	Rest	Psychic	Status	—	—	10	Self
TM45	Attract	Normal	Status	—	100	15	Normal
TM46	Thief	Dark	Physical	60	100	25	Normal
TM48	Round	Normal	Special	60	100	15	Normal
TM68	Giga Impact	Normal	Physical	150	90	5	Normal
TM73	Thunder Wave	Electric	Status	—	100	20	Normal
TM77	Psych Up	Normal	Status	—	—	10	Normal
TM87	Swagger	Normal	Status	—	90	15	Normal
TM88	Sleep Talk	Normal	Status	—	—	10	Self
TM90	Substitute	Normal	Status	—	—	10	Self
TM91	Flash Cannon	Steel	Special	80	100	10	Normal
TM94	Secret Power	Normal	Physical	70	100	20	Normal
TM99	Dazzling Gleam	Fairy	Special	80	100	10	Many Others
TM100	Confide	Normal	Status	—	—	20	Normal
HM01	Cut	Normal	Physical	50	95	30	Normal

MOVES LEARNED IN EXCHANGE FOR BP

Name	Type	Kind	Pow.	Acc.	PP	Range
Covet	Normal	Physical	60	100	25	Normal
Magic Coat	Psychic	Status	—	—	15	Self
Foul Play	Dark	Physical	95	100	15	Normal
Magnet Rise	Electric	Status	—	—	10	Self
Iron Defense	Steel	Status	—	—	15	Self
Last Resort	Normal	Physical	140	100	5	Normal
Snore	Normal	Special	50	100	15	Normal
Magic Room	Psychic	Status	—	—	10	Both Sides
Recycle	Normal	Status	—	—	10	Self

MOVES TAUGHT BY PEOPLE

Name	Type	Kind	Pow.	Acc.	PP	Range

EGG MOVES

Name	Type	Kind	Pow.	Acc.	PP	Range
Switcheroo	Dark	Status	—	100	10	Normal
Thief	Dark	Physical	60	100	25	Normal
Lock-On	Normal	Status	—	—	5	Normal
Iron Defense	Steel	Status	—	—	15	Self

National Pokédex **708** Hoenn Pokédex —

Phantump

Stump Pokémon

Ghost **Grass**

HEIGHT: 1'04" WEIGHT: 15.4 lbs.

Same form for ♂ / ♀

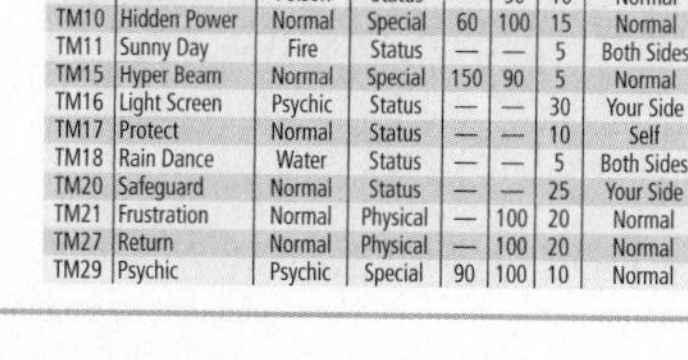

Ω These Pokémon are created when spirits possess rotten tree stumps. They prefer to live in abandoned forests.

α According to old tales, these Pokémon are stumps possessed by the spirits of children who died while lost in the forest.

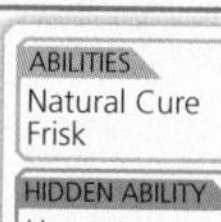

ABILITIES
Natural Cure
Frisk

HIDDEN ABILITY
Harvest

EGG GROUPS
Grass
Amorphous

STAT GROWTH RATES
HP ■■
Attack ■■■■
Defense ■■
Sp. Atk ■■
Sp. Def ■■■
Speed ■■

EVOLUTION

ITEMS SOMETIMES HELD BY WILD POKÉMON
—

MAIN WAY TO REGISTER IN THE NATIONAL POKÉDEX

Catch in the Petalburg Woods. Appears as a hidden Pokémon after you battle Groudon or Kyogre.

Damage taken in normal battles

Normal	×0	Flying	×2
Fire	×2	Psychic	×1
Water	×0.5	Bug	×0.5
Grass	×0.5	Rock	×1
Electric	×0.5	Ghost	×2
Ice	×2	Dragon	×1
Fighting	×0	Dark	×2
Poison	×1	Steel	×1
Ground	×0.5	Fairy	×1

Damage taken in Inverse battles

Normal	×2	Flying	×0.5
Fire	×0.5	Psychic	×1
Water	×2	Bug	×1
Grass	×2	Rock	×1
Electric	×2	Ghost	×0.5
Ice	×0.5	Dragon	×1
Fighting	×2	Dark	×0.5
Poison	×1	Steel	×1
Ground	×2	Fairy	×1

Can be used in
Inverse Battle
Battle Institute
Battle Maison
Random Matchup (Free Battle)
Random Matchup (Others)

LEVEL-UP MOVES

Lv.	Name	Type	Kind	Pow.	Acc.	PP	Range
1	Tackle	Normal	Physical	50	100	35	Normal
1	Confuse Ray	Ghost	Status	—	100	10	Normal
5	Astonish	Ghost	Physical	30	100	15	Normal
8	Growth	Normal	Status	—	—	20	Self
13	Ingrain	Grass	Status	—	—	20	Self
19	Feint Attack	Dark	Physical	60	—	20	Normal
23	Leech Seed	Grass	Status	—	90	10	Normal
28	Curse	Ghost	Status	—	—	10	Varies
31	Will-O-Wisp	Fire	Status	—	85	15	Normal
35	Forest's Curse	Grass	Status	—	100	20	Normal
39	Destiny Bond	Ghost	Status	—	—	5	Self
45	Phantom Force	Ghost	Physical	90	100	10	Normal
49	Wood Hammer	Grass	Physical	120	100	15	Normal
54	Horn Leech	Grass	Physical	75	100	10	Normal

TM & HM MOVES

No.	Name	Type	Kind	Pow.	Acc.	PP	Range
TM06	Toxic	Poison	Status	—	90	10	Normal
TM10	Hidden Power	Normal	Special	60	100	15	Normal
TM11	Sunny Day	Fire	Status	—	—	5	Both Sides
TM17	Protect	Normal	Status	—	—	10	Self
TM20	Safeguard	Normal	Status	—	—	25	Your Side
TM21	Frustration	Normal	Physical	—	100	20	Normal
TM22	Solar Beam	Grass	Special	120	100	10	Normal
TM27	Return	Normal	Physical	—	100	20	Normal
TM28	Dig	Ground	Physical	80	100	10	Normal
TM29	Psychic	Psychic	Special	90	100	10	Normal
TM30	Shadow Ball	Ghost	Special	80	100	15	Normal
TM32	Double Team	Normal	Status	—	—	15	Self
TM33	Reflect	Psychic	Status	—	—	20	Your Side
TM42	Facade	Normal	Physical	70	100	20	Normal
TM44	Rest	Psychic	Status	—	—	10	Self
TM45	Attract	Normal	Status	—	100	15	Normal
TM46	Thief	Dark	Physical	60	100	25	Normal
TM48	Round	Normal	Special	60	100	15	Normal
TM53	Energy Ball	Grass	Special	90	100	10	Normal
TM61	Will-O-Wisp	Fire	Status	—	85	15	Normal
TM65	Shadow Claw	Ghost	Physical	70	100	15	Normal
TM78	Bulldoze	Ground	Physical	60	100	20	Adjacent
TM80	Rock Slide	Rock	Physical	75	90	10	Many Others
TM84	Poison Jab	Poison	Physical	80	100	20	Normal
TM85	Dream Eater	Psychic	Special	100	100	15	Normal
TM86	Grass Knot	Grass	Special	—	100	20	Normal
TM87	Swagger	Normal	Status	—	90	15	Normal
TM88	Sleep Talk	Normal	Status	—	—	10	Self
TM90	Substitute	Normal	Status	—	—	10	Self
TM92	Trick Room	Psychic	Status	—	—	5	Both Sides
TM94	Secret Power	Normal	Physical	70	100	20	Normal
TM96	Nature Power	Normal	Status	—	—	20	Normal
TM97	Dark Pulse	Dark	Special	80	100	15	Normal
TM100	Confide	Normal	Status	—	—	20	Normal
HM01	Cut	Normal	Physical	50	95	30	Normal
HM04	Strength	Normal	Physical	80	100	15	Normal
HM06	Rock Smash	Fighting	Physical	40	100	15	Normal

MOVES LEARNED IN EXCHANGE FOR BP

Name	Type	Kind	Pow.	Acc.	PP	Range
Seed Bomb	Grass	Physical	80	100	15	Normal
Magic Coat	Psychic	Status	—	—	15	Self
Foul Play	Dark	Physical	95	100	15	Normal
Snore	Normal	Special	50	100	15	Normal
Role Play	Psychic	Status	—	—	10	Normal
Pain Split	Normal	Status	—	—	20	Normal
Giga Drain	Grass	Special	75	100	10	Normal
Worry Seed	Grass	Status	—	100	10	Normal
Spite	Ghost	Status	—	100	10	Normal
Trick	Psychic	Status	—	100	10	Normal
Skill Swap	Psychic	Status	—	—	10	Normal

MOVES TAUGHT BY PEOPLE

Name	Type	Kind	Pow.	Acc.	PP	Range

EGG MOVES

Name	Type	Kind	Pow.	Acc.	PP	Range
Grudge	Ghost	Status	—	—	5	Self
Bestow	Normal	Status	—	—	15	Normal
Imprison	Psychic	Status	—	—	10	Self
Venom Drench	Poison	Status	—	100	20	Many Others

National Pokédex **709** Hoenn Pokédex —

Trevenant

Elder Tree Pokémon

Ghost Grass

HEIGHT: 4'11" WEIGHT: 156.5 lbs.

Same form for ♂ / ♀

Ω It can control trees at will. It will trap people who harm the forest, so they can never leave.

α Using its roots as a nervous system, it controls the trees in the forest. It's kind to the Pokémon that reside in its body.

ABILITIES
Natural Cure
Frisk

HIDDEN ABILITY
Harvest

EGG GROUPS
Grass, Amorphous

STAT GROWTH RATES
HP
Attack
Defense
Sp. Atk
Sp. Def
Speed

ITEMS SOMETIMES HELD BY WILD POKÉMON
—

EVOLUTION
Phantump → Link Trade → Trevenant

MAIN WAY TO REGISTER IN THE NATIONAL POKÉDEX

Receive a Phantump via Link Trade to have it evolve.

Damage taken in normal battles

Type		Type	
Normal	×0	Flying	×2
Fire	×2	Psychic	×1
Water	×0.5	Bug	×1
Grass	×0.5	Rock	×1
Electric	×0.5	Ghost	×2
Ice	×2	Dragon	×1
Fighting	×0	Dark	×2
Poison	×1	Steel	×1
Ground	×0.5	Fairy	×1

Damage taken in Inverse battles

Type		Type	
Normal	×2	Flying	×0.5
Fire	×0.5	Psychic	×1
Water	×2	Bug	×1
Grass	×2	Rock	×1
Electric	×2	Ghost	×0.5
Ice	×0.5	Dragon	×1
Fighting	×2	Dark	×0.5
Poison	×1	Steel	×1
Ground	×2	Fairy	×1

Can be used in
Inverse Battle
Battle Institute
Battle Maison
Random Matchup (Free Battle)
Random Matchup (Others)

LEVEL-UP MOVES

Lv.	Name	Type	Kind	Pow.	Acc.	PP	Range
1	Horn Leech	Grass	Physical	75	100	10	Normal
1	Tackle	Normal	Physical	50	100	35	Normal
1	Confuse Ray	Ghost	Status	—	100	10	Normal
5	Astonish	Ghost	Physical	30	100	15	Normal
8	Growth	Normal	Status	—	—	20	Self
13	Ingrain	Grass	Status	—	—	20	Self
19	Feint Attack	Dark	Physical	60	—	20	Normal
23	Leech Seed	Grass	Status	—	90	10	Normal
28	Curse	Ghost	Status	—	—	10	Varies
31	Will-O-Wisp	Fire	Status	—	85	15	Normal
35	Forest's Curse	Grass	Status	—	100	20	Normal
39	Destiny Bond	Ghost	Status	—	—	5	Self
45	Phantom Force	Ghost	Physical	90	100	10	Normal
49	Wood Hammer	Grass	Physical	120	100	15	Normal
55	Shadow Claw	Ghost	Physical	70	100	15	Normal
62	Horn Leech	Grass	Physical	75	100	10	Normal

TM & HM MOVES

No.	Name	Type	Kind	Pow.	Acc.	PP	Range
TM01	Hone Claws	Dark	Status	—	—	15	Self
TM04	Calm Mind	Psychic	Status	—	—	20	Self
TM06	Toxic	Poison	Status	—	90	10	Normal
TM10	Hidden Power	Normal	Special	60	100	15	Normal
TM11	Sunny Day	Fire	Status	—	—	5	Both Sides
TM15	Hyper Beam	Normal	Special	150	90	5	Normal
TM17	Protect	Normal	Status	—	—	10	Self
TM20	Safeguard	Normal	Status	—	—	25	Your Side
TM21	Frustration	Normal	Physical	—	100	20	Normal
TM22	Solar Beam	Grass	Special	120	100	10	Normal
TM26	Earthquake	Ground	Physical	100	100	10	Adjacent
TM27	Return	Normal	Physical	—	100	20	Normal
TM28	Dig	Ground	Physical	80	100	10	Normal
TM29	Psychic	Psychic	Special	90	100	10	Normal
TM30	Shadow Ball	Ghost	Special	80	100	15	Normal
TM32	Double Team	Normal	Status	—	—	15	Self
TM33	Reflect	Psychic	Status	—	—	20	Your Side
TM42	Facade	Normal	Physical	70	100	20	Normal
TM44	Rest	Psychic	Status	—	—	10	Self
TM45	Attract	Normal	Status	—	100	15	Normal
TM46	Thief	Dark	Physical	60	100	25	Normal
TM48	Round	Normal	Special	60	100	15	Normal
TM52	Focus Blast	Fighting	Special	120	70	5	Normal
TM53	Energy Ball	Grass	Special	90	100	10	Normal
TM61	Will-O-Wisp	Fire	Status	—	85	15	Normal
TM65	Shadow Claw	Ghost	Physical	70	100	15	Normal
TM68	Giga Impact	Normal	Physical	150	90	5	Normal
TM78	Bulldoze	Ground	Physical	60	100	20	Adjacent
TM80	Rock Slide	Rock	Physical	75	90	10	Many Others
TM81	X-Scissor	Bug	Physical	80	100	15	Normal
TM84	Poison Jab	Poison	Physical	80	100	20	Normal
TM85	Dream Eater	Psychic	Special	100	100	15	Normal
TM86	Grass Knot	Grass	Special	—	100	20	Normal
TM87	Swagger	Normal	Status	—	90	15	Normal
TM88	Sleep Talk	Normal	Status	—	—	10	Self
TM90	Substitute	Normal	Status	—	—	10	Self
TM92	Trick Room	Psychic	Status	—	—	5	Both Sides
TM94	Secret Power	Normal	Physical	70	100	20	Normal
TM96	Nature Power	Normal	Status	—	—	20	Normal
TM97	Dark Pulse	Dark	Special	80	100	15	Normal
TM98	Power-Up Punch	Fighting	Physical	40	100	20	Normal
TM100	Confide	Normal	Status	—	—	20	Normal
HM01	Cut	Normal	Physical	50	95	30	Normal
HM04	Strength	Normal	Physical	80	100	15	Normal
HM06	Rock Smash	Fighting	Physical	40	100	15	Normal

MOVES LEARNED IN EXCHANGE FOR BP

Name	Type	Kind	Pow.	Acc.	PP	Range
Seed Bomb	Grass	Physical	80	100	15	Normal
Magic Coat	Psychic	Status	—	—	15	Self
Block	Normal	Status	—	—	5	Normal
Foul Play	Dark	Physical	95	100	15	Normal
Snore	Normal	Special	50	100	15	Normal
Role Play	Psychic	Status	—	—	10	Normal
Pain Split	Normal	Status	—	—	20	Normal
Giga Drain	Grass	Special	75	100	10	Normal
Drain Punch	Fighting	Physical	75	100	10	Normal
Worry Seed	Grass	Status	—	100	10	Normal
Spite	Ghost	Status	—	100	10	Normal
Trick	Psychic	Status	—	100	10	Normal
Skill Swap	Psychic	Status	—	—	10	Normal

MOVES TAUGHT BY PEOPLE

Name	Type	Kind	Pow.	Acc.	PP	Range

National Pokédex **710** Hoenn Pokédex —

Pumpkaboo Average Size

Pumpkin Pokémon

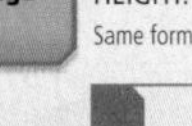

Ghost Grass

HEIGHT: 1'04" WEIGHT: 11 lbs.

Same form for ♂ / ♀

Ω The pumpkin body is inhabited by a spirit trapped in this world. As the sun sets, it becomes restless and active.

α It is said to carry wandering spirits to the place where they belong so they can move on.

ABILITIES
Pickup
Frisk

HIDDEN ABILITY
Insomnia

EGG GROUPS
Amorphous

STAT GROWTH RATES
HP
Attack
Defense
Sp. Atk
Sp. Def
Speed

ITEMS SOMETIMES HELD BY WILD POKÉMON
—

EVOLUTION
Pumpkaboo → Link Trade → Gourgeist

MAIN WAY TO REGISTER IN THE NATIONAL POKÉDEX

Appears in *Pokémon X* and *Pokémon Y*. Bring it to your game using Link Trade or the GTS.

Damage taken in normal battles

Type		Type	
Normal	×0	Flying	×2
Fire	×2	Psychic	×1
Water	×0.5	Bug	×1
Grass	×0.5	Rock	×1
Electric	×0.5	Ghost	×2
Ice	×2	Dragon	×1
Fighting	×0	Dark	×2
Poison	×1	Steel	×1
Ground	×0.5	Fairy	×1

Damage taken in Inverse battles

Type		Type	
Normal	×2	Flying	×0.5
Fire	×0.5	Psychic	×1
Water	×2	Bug	×1
Grass	×2	Rock	×1
Electric	×2	Ghost	×0.5
Ice	×0.5	Dragon	×1
Fighting	×2	Dark	×0.5
Poison	×1	Steel	×1
Ground	×2	Fairy	×1

Can be used in
Inverse Battle
Battle Institute
Battle Maison
Random Matchup (Free Battle)
Random Matchup (Others)

LEVEL-UP MOVES

Lv.	Name	Type	Kind	Pow.	Acc.	PP	Range
1	Trick	Psychic	Status	—	100	10	Normal
1	Astonish	Ghost	Physical	30	100	15	Normal
1	Confuse Ray	Ghost	Status	—	100	10	Normal
4	Scary Face	Normal	Status	—	100	10	Normal
6	Trick-or-Treat	Ghost	Status	—	100	20	Normal
11	Worry Seed	Grass	Status	—	100	10	Normal
16	Razor Leaf	Grass	Physical	55	95	25	Many Others
20	Leech Seed	Grass	Status	—	90	10	Normal
23	Trick-or-Treat	Ghost	Status	—	100	20	Normal
26	Bullet Seed	Grass	Physical	25	100	30	Normal
30	Shadow Sneak	Ghost	Physical	40	100	30	Normal
36	Shadow Ball	Ghost	Special	80	100	15	Normal
40	Trick-or-Treat	Ghost	Status	—	100	20	Normal
42	Pain Split	Normal	Status	—	—	20	Normal
48	Seed Bomb	Grass	Physical	80	100	15	Normal

TM & HM MOVES

No.	Name	Type	Kind	Pow.	Acc.	PP	Range
TM06	Toxic	Poison	Status	—	90	10	Normal
TM10	Hidden Power	Normal	Special	60	100	15	Normal
TM11	Sunny Day	Fire	Status	—	—	5	Both Sides
TM16	Light Screen	Psychic	Status	—	—	30	Your Side
TM17	Protect	Normal	Status	—	—	10	Self
TM20	Safeguard	Normal	Status	—	—	25	Your Side
TM21	Frustration	Normal	Physical	—	100	20	Normal
TM22	Solar Beam	Grass	Special	120	100	10	Normal
TM27	Return	Normal	Physical	—	100	20	Normal
TM29	Psychic	Psychic	Special	90	100	10	Normal
TM30	Shadow Ball	Ghost	Special	80	100	15	Normal
TM32	Double Team	Normal	Status	—	—	15	Self
TM35	Flamethrower	Fire	Special	90	100	15	Normal
TM36	Sludge Bomb	Poison	Special	90	100	10	Normal
TM38	Fire Blast	Fire	Special	110	85	5	Normal
TM42	Facade	Normal	Physical	70	100	20	Normal
TM43	Flame Charge	Fire	Physical	50	100	20	Normal
TM44	Rest	Psychic	Status	—	—	10	Self
TM45	Attract	Normal	Status	—	100	15	Normal
TM46	Thief	Dark	Physical	60	100	25	Normal
TM48	Round	Normal	Special	60	100	15	Normal
TM53	Energy Ball	Grass	Special	90	100	10	Normal
TM57	Charge Beam	Electric	Special	50	90	10	Normal
TM59	Incinerate	Fire	Special	60	100	15	Many Others
TM61	Will-O-Wisp	Fire	Status	—	85	15	Normal
TM64	Explosion	Normal	Physical	250	100	5	Adjacent
TM70	Flash	Normal	Status	—	100	20	Normal
TM74	Gyro Ball	Steel	Physical	—	100	5	Normal
TM80	Rock Slide	Rock	Physical	75	90	10	Many Others
TM85	Dream Eater	Psychic	Special	100	100	15	Normal
TM86	Grass Knot	Grass	Special	—	100	20	Normal
TM87	Swagger	Normal	Status	—	90	15	Normal
TM88	Sleep Talk	Normal	Status	—	—	10	Self
TM90	Substitute	Normal	Status	—	—	10	Self
TM92	Trick Room	Psychic	Status	—	—	5	Both Sides
TM94	Secret Power	Normal	Physical	70	100	20	Normal
TM96	Nature Power	Normal	Status	—	—	20	Normal
TM97	Dark Pulse	Dark	Special	80	100	15	Normal
TM100	Confide	Normal	Status	—	—	20	Normal
HM06	Rock Smash	Fighting	Physical	40	100	15	Normal

MOVES LEARNED IN EXCHANGE FOR BP

Name	Type	Kind	Pow.	Acc.	PP	Range
Seed Bomb	Grass	Physical	80	100	15	Normal
Magic Coat	Psychic	Status	—	—	15	Self
Foul Play	Dark	Physical	95	100	15	Normal
Synthesis	Grass	Status	—	—	5	Self
Role Play	Psychic	Status	—	—	10	Normal
Pain Split	Normal	Status	—	—	20	Normal
Giga Drain	Grass	Special	75	100	10	Normal
Worry Seed	Grass	Status	—	100	10	Normal
Spite	Ghost	Status	—	100	10	Normal
Trick	Psychic	Status	—	100	10	Normal
Skill Swap	Psychic	Status	—	—	10	Normal

MOVES TAUGHT BY PEOPLE

Name	Type	Kind	Pow.	Acc.	PP	Range

EGG MOVES

Name	Type	Kind	Pow.	Acc.	PP	Range
Disable	Normal	Status	—	100	20	Normal
Bestow	Normal	Status	—	—	15	Normal
Destiny Bond	Ghost	Status	—	—	5	Self

National Pokédex 710 Hoenn Pokédex —

Pumpkaboo Small Size

Pumpkin Pokémon

Ghost Grass

HEIGHT: 1'00" WEIGHT: 7.7 lbs.

Same form for ♂ / ♀

Ω The pumpkin body is inhabited by a spirit trapped in this world. As the sun sets, it becomes restless and active.

α It is said to carry wandering spirits to the place where they belong so they can move on.

ABILITIES
Pickup
Frisk

HIDDEN ABILITY
Insomnia

EGG GROUPS
Amorphous

STAT GROWTH RATES
HP
Attack
Defense
Sp. Atk
Sp. Def
Speed

ITEMS SOMETIMES HELD BY WILD POKÉMON
—

EVOLUTION

MAIN WAY TO REGISTER IN THE NATIONAL POKÉDEX

Appears in *Pokémon X* and *Pokémon Y*. Bring it to your game using Link Trade or the GTS.

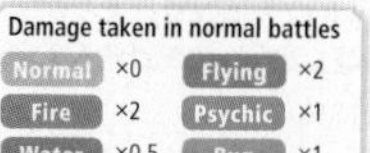

Damage taken in normal battles

Type		Type	
Normal	×0	Flying	×2
Fire	×2	Psychic	×1
Water	×0.5	Bug	×1
Grass	×0.5	Rock	×1
Electric	×0.5	Ghost	×2
Ice	×2	Dragon	×1
Fighting	×0	Dark	×2
Poison	×1	Steel	×1
Ground	×0.5	Fairy	×1

Damage taken in Inverse battles

Type		Type	
Normal	×2	Flying	×0.5
Fire	×0.5	Psychic	×1
Water	×2	Bug	×1
Grass	×2	Rock	×1
Electric	×2	Ghost	×0.5
Ice	×0.5	Dragon	×1
Fighting	×2	Dark	×0.5
Poison	×1	Steel	×1
Ground	×2	Fairy	×1

Can be used in
- Inverse Battle
- Battle Institute
- Battle Maison
- Random Matchup (Free Battle)
- Random Matchup (Others)

LEVEL-UP MOVES

Lv.	Name	Type	Kind	Pow.	Acc.	PP	Range
1	Trick	Psychic	Status	—	100	10	Normal
1	Astonish	Ghost	Physical	30	100	15	Normal
1	Confuse Ray	Ghost	Status	—	100	10	Normal
4	Scary Face	Normal	Status	—	100	10	Normal
6	Trick-or-Treat	Ghost	Status	—	100	20	Normal
11	Worry Seed	Grass	Status	—	100	10	Normal
16	Razor Leaf	Grass	Physical	55	95	25	Many Others
20	Leech Seed	Grass	Status	—	90	10	Normal
23	Trick-or-Treat	Ghost	Status	—	100	20	Normal
26	Bullet Seed	Grass	Physical	25	100	30	Normal
30	Shadow Sneak	Ghost	Physical	40	100	30	Normal
36	Shadow Ball	Ghost	Special	80	100	15	Normal
40	Trick-or-Treat	Ghost	Status	—	100	20	Normal
42	Pain Split	Normal	Status	—	—	20	Normal
48	Seed Bomb	Grass	Physical	80	100	15	Normal

TM & HM MOVES

No.	Name	Type	Kind	Pow.	Acc.	PP	Range
TM06	Toxic	Poison	Status	—	90	10	Normal
TM10	Hidden Power	Normal	Special	60	100	15	Normal
TM11	Sunny Day	Fire	Status	—	—	5	Both Sides
TM16	Light Screen	Psychic	Status	—	—	30	Your Side
TM17	Protect	Normal	Status	—	—	10	Self
TM20	Safeguard	Normal	Status	—	—	25	Your Side
TM21	Frustration	Normal	Physical	—	100	20	Normal
TM22	Solar Beam	Grass	Special	120	100	10	Normal
TM27	Return	Normal	Physical	—	100	20	Normal
TM29	Psychic	Psychic	Special	90	100	10	Normal
TM30	Shadow Ball	Ghost	Special	80	100	15	Normal
TM32	Double Team	Normal	Status	—	—	15	Self
TM35	Flamethrower	Fire	Special	90	100	15	Normal
TM36	Sludge Bomb	Poison	Special	90	100	10	Normal
TM38	Fire Blast	Fire	Special	110	85	5	Normal
TM42	Facade	Normal	Physical	70	100	20	Normal
TM43	Flame Charge	Fire	Physical	50	100	20	Normal
TM44	Rest	Psychic	Status	—	—	10	Self
TM45	Attract	Normal	Status	—	100	15	Normal
TM46	Thief	Dark	Physical	60	100	25	Normal
TM48	Round	Normal	Special	60	100	15	Normal
TM53	Energy Ball	Grass	Special	90	100	10	Normal
TM57	Charge Beam	Electric	Special	50	90	10	Normal
TM59	Incinerate	Fire	Special	60	100	15	Many Others
TM61	Will-O-Wisp	Fire	Status	—	85	15	Normal
TM64	Explosion	Normal	Physical	250	100	5	Adjacent
TM70	Flash	Normal	Status	—	100	20	Normal
TM74	Gyro Ball	Steel	Physical	—	100	5	Normal
TM80	Rock Slide	Rock	Physical	75	90	10	Many Others
TM85	Dream Eater	Psychic	Special	100	100	15	Normal
TM86	Grass Knot	Grass	Special	—	100	20	Normal
TM87	Swagger	Normal	Status	—	90	15	Normal
TM88	Sleep Talk	Normal	Status	—	—	10	Self
TM90	Substitute	Normal	Status	—	—	10	Self
TM92	Trick Room	Psychic	Status	—	—	5	Both Sides
TM94	Secret Power	Normal	Physical	70	100	20	Normal
TM96	Nature Power	Normal	Status	—	—	20	Normal
TM97	Dark Pulse	Dark	Special	80	100	15	Normal
TM100	Confide	Normal	Status	—	—	20	Normal
HM06	Rock Smash	Fighting	Physical	40	100	15	Normal

MOVES LEARNED IN EXCHANGE FOR BP

Name	Type	Kind	Pow.	Acc.	PP	Range
Seed Bomb	Grass	Physical	80	100	15	Normal
Magic Coat	Psychic	Status	—	—	15	Self
Foul Play	Dark	Physical	95	100	15	Normal
Synthesis	Grass	Status	—	—	5	Self
Role Play	Psychic	Status	—	—	10	Normal
Pain Split	Normal	Status	—	—	20	Normal
Giga Drain	Grass	Special	75	100	10	Normal
Worry Seed	Grass	Status	—	100	10	Normal
Spite	Ghost	Status	—	100	10	Normal
Trick	Psychic	Status	—	100	10	Normal
Skill Swap	Psychic	Status	—	—	10	Normal

MOVES TAUGHT BY PEOPLE

Name	Type	Kind	Pow.	Acc.	PP	Range

EGG MOVES

Name	Type	Kind	Pow.	Acc.	PP	Range
Disable	Normal	Status	—	100	20	Normal
Bestow	Normal	Status	—	—	15	Normal
Destiny Bond	Ghost	Status	—	—	5	Self

National Pokédex 710 Hoenn Pokédex —

Pumpkaboo Large Size

Pumpkin Pokémon

Ghost Grass

HEIGHT: 1'08" WEIGHT: 16.5 lbs.

Same form for ♂ / ♀

Ω The pumpkin body is inhabited by a spirit trapped in this world. As the sun sets, it becomes restless and active.

α It is said to carry wandering spirits to the place where they belong so they can move on.

ABILITIES
Pickup
Frisk

HIDDEN ABILITY
Insomnia

EGG GROUPS
Amorphous

STAT GROWTH RATES
HP
Attack
Defense
Sp. Atk
Sp. Def
Speed

ITEMS SOMETIMES HELD BY WILD POKÉMON
—

EVOLUTION

Link Trade
Pumpkaboo
Gourgeist

MAIN WAY TO REGISTER IN THE NATIONAL POKÉDEX

Appears in *Pokémon X* and *Pokémon Y*. Bring it to your game using Link Trade or the GTS.

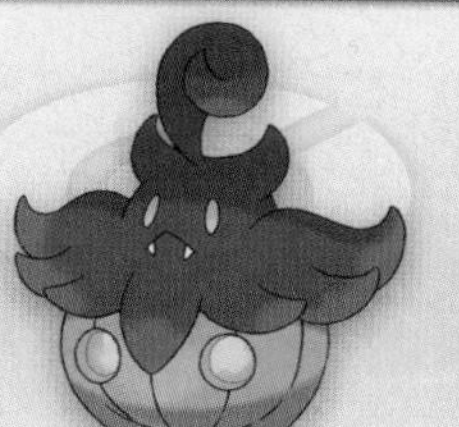

Damage taken in normal battles

Type		Type	
Normal	×0	Flying	×2
Fire	×2	Psychic	×1
Water	×0.5	Bug	×1
Grass	×0.5	Rock	×1
Electric	×0.5	Ghost	×2
Ice	×2	Dragon	×1
Fighting	×0	Dark	×2
Poison	×1	Steel	×1
Ground	×0.5	Fairy	×1

Damage taken in Inverse battles

Type		Type	
Normal	×2	Flying	×0.5
Fire	×0.5	Psychic	×1
Water	×2	Bug	×1
Grass	×2	Rock	×1
Electric	×2	Ghost	×0.5
Ice	×0.5	Dragon	×1
Fighting	×2	Dark	×0.5
Poison	×1	Steel	×1
Ground	×2	Fairy	×1

Can be used in
- Inverse Battle
- Battle Institute
- Battle Maison
- Random Matchup (Free Battle)
- Random Matchup (Others)

LEVEL-UP MOVES

Lv.	Name	Type	Kind	Pow.	Acc.	PP	Range
1	Trick	Psychic	Status	—	100	10	Normal
1	Astonish	Ghost	Physical	30	100	15	Normal
1	Confuse Ray	Ghost	Status	—	100	10	Normal
4	Scary Face	Normal	Status	—	100	10	Normal
6	Trick-or-Treat	Ghost	Status	—	100	20	Normal
11	Worry Seed	Grass	Status	—	100	10	Normal
16	Razor Leaf	Grass	Physical	55	95	25	Many Others
20	Leech Seed	Grass	Status	—	90	10	Normal
23	Trick-or-Treat	Ghost	Status	—	100	20	Normal
26	Bullet Seed	Grass	Physical	25	100	30	Normal
30	Shadow Sneak	Ghost	Physical	40	100	30	Normal
36	Shadow Ball	Ghost	Special	80	100	15	Normal
40	Trick-or-Treat	Ghost	Status	—	100	20	Normal
42	Pain Split	Normal	Status	—	—	20	Normal
48	Seed Bomb	Grass	Physical	80	100	15	Normal

TM & HM MOVES

No.	Name	Type	Kind	Pow.	Acc.	PP	Range
TM06	Toxic	Poison	Status	—	90	10	Normal
TM10	Hidden Power	Normal	Special	60	100	15	Normal
TM11	Sunny Day	Fire	Status	—	—	5	Both Sides
TM16	Light Screen	Psychic	Status	—	—	30	Your Side
TM17	Protect	Normal	Status	—	—	10	Self
TM20	Safeguard	Normal	Status	—	—	25	Your Side
TM21	Frustration	Normal	Physical	—	100	20	Normal
TM22	Solar Beam	Grass	Special	120	100	10	Normal
TM27	Return	Normal	Physical	—	100	20	Normal
TM29	Psychic	Psychic	Special	90	100	10	Normal
TM30	Shadow Ball	Ghost	Special	80	100	15	Normal
TM32	Double Team	Normal	Status	—	—	15	Self
TM35	Flamethrower	Fire	Special	90	100	15	Normal
TM36	Sludge Bomb	Poison	Special	90	100	10	Normal
TM38	Fire Blast	Fire	Special	110	85	5	Normal
TM42	Facade	Normal	Physical	70	100	20	Normal
TM43	Flame Charge	Fire	Physical	50	100	20	Normal
TM44	Rest	Psychic	Status	—	—	10	Self
TM45	Attract	Normal	Status	—	100	15	Normal
TM46	Thief	Dark	Physical	60	100	25	Normal
TM48	Round	Normal	Special	60	100	15	Normal
TM53	Energy Ball	Grass	Special	90	100	10	Normal
TM57	Charge Beam	Electric	Special	50	90	10	Normal
TM59	Incinerate	Fire	Special	60	100	15	Many Others
TM61	Will-O-Wisp	Fire	Status	—	85	15	Normal
TM64	Explosion	Normal	Physical	250	100	5	Adjacent
TM70	Flash	Normal	Status	—	100	20	Normal
TM74	Gyro Ball	Steel	Physical	—	100	5	Normal
TM80	Rock Slide	Rock	Physical	75	90	10	Many Others
TM85	Dream Eater	Psychic	Special	100	100	15	Normal
TM86	Grass Knot	Grass	Special	—	100	20	Normal
TM87	Swagger	Normal	Status	—	90	15	Normal
TM88	Sleep Talk	Normal	Status	—	—	10	Self
TM90	Substitute	Normal	Status	—	—	10	Self
TM92	Trick Room	Psychic	Status	—	—	5	Both Sides
TM94	Secret Power	Normal	Physical	70	100	20	Normal
TM96	Nature Power	Normal	Status	—	—	20	Normal
TM97	Dark Pulse	Dark	Special	80	100	15	Normal
TM100	Confide	Normal	Status	—	—	20	Normal
HM06	Rock Smash	Fighting	Physical	40	100	15	Normal

MOVES LEARNED IN EXCHANGE FOR BP

Name	Type	Kind	Pow.	Acc.	PP	Range
Seed Bomb	Grass	Physical	80	100	15	Normal
Magic Coat	Psychic	Status	—	—	15	Self
Foul Play	Dark	Physical	95	100	15	Normal
Synthesis	Grass	Status	—	—	5	Self
Role Play	Psychic	Status	—	—	10	Normal
Pain Split	Normal	Status	—	—	20	Normal
Giga Drain	Grass	Special	75	100	10	Normal
Worry Seed	Grass	Status	—	100	10	Normal
Spite	Ghost	Status	—	100	10	Normal
Trick	Psychic	Status	—	100	10	Normal
Skill Swap	Psychic	Status	—	—	10	Normal

MOVES TAUGHT BY PEOPLE

Name	Type	Kind	Pow.	Acc.	PP	Range

EGG MOVES

Name	Type	Kind	Pow.	Acc.	PP	Range
Disable	Normal	Status	—	100	20	Normal
Bestow	Normal	Status	—	—	15	Normal
Destiny Bond	Ghost	Status	—	—	5	Self

National Pokédex **710** Hoenn Pokédex —

Pumpkaboo Super Size

Pumpkin Pokémon

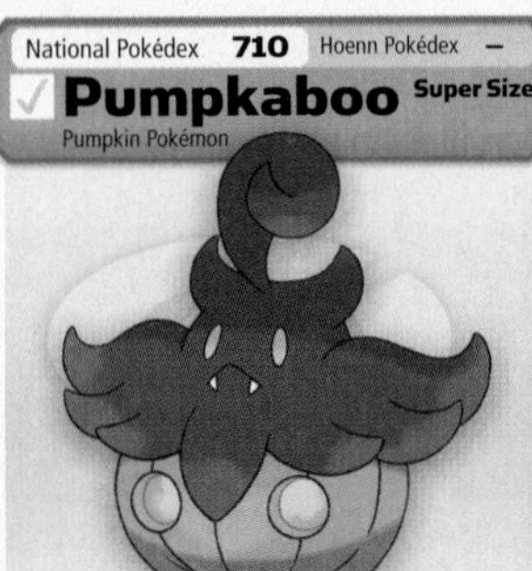

Ghost Grass

HEIGHT: 2'07" WEIGHT: 33.1 lbs.

Same form for ♂ / ♀

Ω The pumpkin body is inhabited by a spirit trapped in this world. As the sun sets, it becomes restless and active.

α It is said to carry wandering spirits to the place where they belong so they can move on.

ABILITIES
Pickup
Frisk

HIDDEN ABILITY
Insomnia

EGG GROUPS
Amorphous

STAT GROWTH RATES
HP ■■■
Attack ■■■
Defense ■■■
Sp. Atk ■■
Sp. Def ■■
Speed ■■

ITEMS SOMETIMES HELD BY WILD POKÉMON
—

EVOLUTION
Pumpkaboo → Link Trade → Gourgeist

MAIN WAY TO REGISTER IN THE NATIONAL POKÉDEX

Appears in *Pokémon X* and *Pokémon Y*. Bring it to your game using Link Trade or the GTS.

Damage taken in normal battles

Type	×	Type	×
Normal	×0	Flying	×2
Fire	×2	Psychic	×1
Water	×0.5	Bug	×1
Grass	×0.5	Rock	×1
Electric	×0.5	Ghost	×2
Ice	×2	Dragon	×1
Fighting	×0	Dark	×2
Poison	×1	Steel	×1
Ground	×0.5	Fairy	×1

Damage taken in Inverse battles

Type	×	Type	×
Normal	×2	Flying	×0.5
Fire	×0.5	Psychic	×1
Water	×2	Bug	×1
Grass	×2	Rock	×1
Electric	×2	Ghost	×0.5
Ice	×0.5	Dragon	×1
Fighting	×2	Dark	×0.5
Poison	×1	Steel	×1
Ground	×2	Fairy	×1

Can be used in
Inverse Battle
Battle Institute
Battle Maison
Random Matchup (Free Battle)
Random Matchup (Others)

LEVEL-UP MOVES

Lv.	Name	Type	Kind	Pow.	Acc.	PP	Range
1	Trick	Psychic	Status	—	100	10	Normal
1	Astonish	Ghost	Physical	30	100	15	Normal
1	Confuse Ray	Ghost	Status	—	100	10	Normal
4	Scary Face	Normal	Status	—	100	10	Normal
6	Trick-or-Treat	Ghost	Status	—	100	20	Normal
11	Worry Seed	Grass	Status	—	100	10	Normal
16	Razor Leaf	Grass	Physical	55	95	25	Many Others
20	Leech Seed	Grass	Status	—	90	10	Normal
23	Trick-or-Treat	Ghost	Status	—	100	20	Normal
26	Bullet Seed	Grass	Physical	25	100	30	Normal
30	Shadow Sneak	Ghost	Physical	40	100	30	Normal
36	Shadow Ball	Ghost	Special	80	100	15	Normal
40	Trick-or-Treat	Ghost	Status	—	100	20	Normal
42	Pain Split	Normal	Status	—	—	20	Normal
48	Seed Bomb	Grass	Physical	80	100	15	Normal

TM & HM MOVES

No.	Name	Type	Kind	Pow.	Acc.	PP	Range
TM06	Toxic	Poison	Status	—	90	10	Normal
TM10	Hidden Power	Normal	Special	60	100	15	Normal
TM11	Sunny Day	Fire	Status	—	—	5	Both Sides
TM16	Light Screen	Psychic	Status	—	—	30	Your Side
TM17	Protect	Normal	Status	—	—	10	Self
TM20	Safeguard	Normal	Status	—	—	25	Your Side
TM21	Frustration	Normal	Physical	—	100	20	Normal
TM22	Solar Beam	Grass	Special	120	100	10	Normal
TM27	Return	Normal	Physical	—	100	20	Normal
TM29	Psychic	Psychic	Special	90	100	10	Normal
TM30	Shadow Ball	Ghost	Special	80	100	15	Normal
TM32	Double Team	Normal	Status	—	—	15	Self
TM35	Flamethrower	Fire	Special	90	100	15	Normal
TM36	Sludge Bomb	Poison	Special	90	100	10	Normal
TM38	Fire Blast	Fire	Special	110	85	5	Normal
TM42	Facade	Normal	Physical	70	100	20	Normal
TM43	Flame Charge	Fire	Physical	50	100	20	Normal
TM44	Rest	Psychic	Status	—	—	10	Self
TM45	Attract	Normal	Status	—	100	15	Normal
TM46	Thief	Dark	Physical	60	100	25	Normal
TM48	Round	Normal	Special	60	100	15	Normal
TM53	Energy Ball	Grass	Special	90	100	10	Normal
TM57	Charge Beam	Electric	Special	50	90	10	Normal
TM59	Incinerate	Fire	Special	60	100	15	Many Others
TM61	Will-O-Wisp	Fire	Status	—	85	15	Normal
TM64	Explosion	Normal	Physical	250	100	5	Adjacent
TM70	Flash	Normal	Status	—	100	20	Normal
TM74	Gyro Ball	Steel	Physical	—	100	5	Normal
TM80	Rock Slide	Rock	Physical	75	90	10	Many Others
TM85	Dream Eater	Psychic	Special	100	100	15	Normal
TM86	Grass Knot	Grass	Special	—	100	20	Normal
TM87	Swagger	Normal	Status	—	90	15	Normal
TM88	Sleep Talk	Normal	Status	—	—	10	Self
TM90	Substitute	Normal	Status	—	—	10	Self
TM92	Trick Room	Psychic	Status	—	—	5	Both Sides
TM94	Secret Power	Normal	Physical	70	100	20	Normal
TM96	Nature Power	Normal	Status	—	—	20	Normal
TM97	Dark Pulse	Dark	Special	80	100	15	Normal
TM100	Confide	Normal	Status	—	—	20	Normal
HM06	Rock Smash	Fighting	Physical	40	100	15	Normal

MOVES LEARNED IN EXCHANGE FOR BP

Name	Type	Kind	Pow.	Acc.	PP	Range
Seed Bomb	Grass	Physical	80	100	15	Normal
Magic Coat	Psychic	Status	—	—	15	Self
Foul Play	Dark	Physical	95	100	15	Normal
Synthesis	Grass	Status	—	—	5	Self
Role Play	Psychic	Status	—	—	10	Normal
Pain Split	Normal	Status	—	—	20	Normal
Giga Drain	Grass	Special	75	100	10	Normal
Worry Seed	Grass	Status	—	100	10	Normal
Spite	Ghost	Status	—	100	10	Normal
Trick	Psychic	Status	—	100	10	Normal
Skill Swap	Psychic	Status	—	—	10	Normal

MOVES TAUGHT BY PEOPLE

Name	Type	Kind	Pow.	Acc.	PP	Range

EGG MOVES

Name	Type	Kind	Pow.	Acc.	PP	Range
Disable	Normal	Status	—	100	20	Normal
Bestow	Normal	Status	—	—	15	Normal
Destiny Bond	Ghost	Status	—	—	5	Self

National Pokédex **711** Hoenn Pokédex —

Gourgeist Average Size

Pumpkin Pokémon

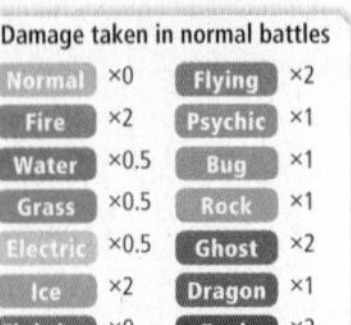

Ghost Grass

HEIGHT: 2'11" WEIGHT: 27.6 lbs.

Same form for ♂ / ♀

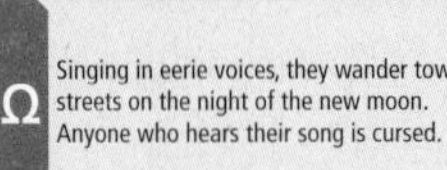

Ω Singing in eerie voices, they wander town streets on the night of the new moon. Anyone who hears their song is cursed.

α It enwraps its prey in its hairlike arms. It sings joyfully as it observes the suffering of its prey.

ABILITIES
Pickup
Frisk

HIDDEN ABILITY
Insomnia

EGG GROUPS
Amorphous

STAT GROWTH RATES
HP ■■■
Attack ■■■■■
Defense ■■■■■
Sp. Atk ■■■
Sp. Def ■■■
Speed ■■■■■

ITEMS SOMETIMES HELD BY WILD POKÉMON
—

EVOLUTION

MAIN WAY TO REGISTER IN THE NATIONAL POKÉDEX

Receive a Pumpkaboo via Link Trade to have it evolve.

Damage taken in normal battles

Type	×	Type	×
Normal	×0	Flying	×2
Fire	×2	Psychic	×1
Water	×0.5	Bug	×1
Grass	×0.5	Rock	×1
Electric	×0.5	Ghost	×2
Ice	×2	Dragon	×1
Fighting	×0	Dark	×2
Poison	×1	Steel	×1
Ground	×0.5	Fairy	×1

Damage taken in Inverse battles

Type	×	Type	×
Normal	×2	Flying	×0.5
Fire	×0.5	Psychic	×1
Water	×2	Bug	×1
Grass	×2	Rock	×1
Electric	×2	Ghost	×0.5
Ice	×0.5	Dragon	×1
Fighting	×2	Dark	×0.5
Poison	×1	Steel	×1
Ground	×2	Fairy	×1

Can be used in
Inverse Battle
Battle Institute
Battle Maison
Random Matchup (Free Battle)
Random Matchup (Others)

LEVEL-UP MOVES

Lv.	Name	Type	Kind	Pow.	Acc.	PP	Range
1	Explosion	Normal	Physical	250	100	5	Adjacent
1	Phantom Force	Ghost	Physical	90	100	10	Normal
1	Trick	Psychic	Status	—	100	10	Normal
1	Astonish	Ghost	Physical	30	100	15	Normal
1	Confuse Ray	Ghost	Status	—	100	10	Normal
4	Scary Face	Normal	Status	—	100	10	Normal
6	Trick-or-Treat	Ghost	Status	—	100	20	Normal
11	Worry Seed	Grass	Status	—	100	10	Normal
16	Razor Leaf	Grass	Physical	55	95	25	Many Others
20	Leech Seed	Grass	Status	—	90	10	Normal
23	Trick-or-Treat	Ghost	Status	—	100	20	Normal
26	Bullet Seed	Grass	Physical	25	100	30	Normal
30	Shadow Sneak	Ghost	Physical	40	100	30	Normal
36	Shadow Ball	Ghost	Special	80	100	15	Normal
40	Trick-or-Treat	Ghost	Status	—	100	20	Normal
42	Pain Split	Normal	Status	—	—	20	Normal
48	Seed Bomb	Grass	Physical	80	100	15	Normal
57	Phantom Force	Ghost	Physical	90	100	10	Normal
63	Trick-or-Treat	Ghost	Status	—	100	20	Normal
70	Shadow Ball	Ghost	Special	80	100	15	Normal
75	Explosion	Normal	Physical	250	100	5	Adjacent

TM & HM MOVES

No.	Name	Type	Kind	Pow.	Acc.	PP	Range
TM06	Toxic	Poison	Status	—	90	10	Normal
TM10	Hidden Power	Normal	Special	60	100	15	Normal
TM11	Sunny Day	Fire	Status	—	—	5	Both Sides
TM15	Hyper Beam	Normal	Special	150	90	5	Normal
TM16	Light Screen	Psychic	Status	—	—	30	Your Side
TM17	Protect	Normal	Status	—	—	10	Self
TM20	Safeguard	Normal	Status	—	—	25	Your Side
TM21	Frustration	Normal	Physical	—	100	20	Normal
TM22	Solar Beam	Grass	Special	120	100	10	Normal
TM27	Return	Normal	Physical	—	100	20	Normal
TM29	Psychic	Psychic	Special	90	100	10	Normal
TM30	Shadow Ball	Ghost	Special	80	100	15	Normal
TM32	Double Team	Normal	Status	—	—	15	Self
TM35	Flamethrower	Fire	Special	90	100	15	Normal
TM36	Sludge Bomb	Poison	Special	90	100	10	Normal
TM38	Fire Blast	Fire	Special	110	85	5	Normal
TM42	Facade	Normal	Physical	70	100	20	Normal
TM43	Flame Charge	Fire	Physical	50	100	20	Normal
TM44	Rest	Psychic	Status	—	—	10	Self
TM45	Attract	Normal	Status	—	100	15	Normal
TM46	Thief	Dark	Physical	60	100	25	Normal
TM48	Round	Normal	Special	60	100	15	Normal
TM52	Focus Blast	Fighting	Special	120	70	5	Normal
TM53	Energy Ball	Grass	Special	90	100	10	Normal
TM57	Charge Beam	Electric	Special	50	90	10	Normal
TM59	Incinerate	Fire	Special	60	100	15	Many Others
TM61	Will-O-Wisp	Fire	Status	—	85	15	Normal
TM64	Explosion	Normal	Physical	250	100	5	Adjacent
TM68	Giga Impact	Normal	Physical	150	90	5	Normal
TM70	Flash	Normal	Status	—	100	20	Normal
TM74	Gyro Ball	Steel	Physical	—	100	5	Normal
TM80	Rock Slide	Rock	Physical	75	90	10	Many Others
TM85	Dream Eater	Psychic	Special	100	100	15	Normal
TM86	Grass Knot	Grass	Special	—	100	20	Normal
TM87	Swagger	Normal	Status	—	90	15	Normal
TM88	Sleep Talk	Normal	Status	—	—	10	Self
TM90	Substitute	Normal	Status	—	—	10	Self
TM92	Trick Room	Psychic	Status	—	—	5	Both Sides
TM94	Secret Power	Normal	Physical	70	100	20	Normal
TM96	Nature Power	Normal	Status	—	—	20	Normal
TM97	Dark Pulse	Dark	Special	80	100	15	Normal
TM100	Confide	Normal	Status	—	—	20	Normal
HM06	Rock Smash	Fighting	Physical	40	100	15	Normal

MOVES LEARNED IN EXCHANGE FOR BP

Name	Type	Kind	Pow.	Acc.	PP	Range
Seed Bomb	Grass	Physical	80	100	15	Normal
Magic Coat	Psychic	Status	—	—	15	Self
Foul Play	Dark	Physical	95	100	15	Normal
Synthesis	Grass	Status	—	—	5	Self
Role Play	Psychic	Status	—	—	10	Normal
Pain Split	Normal	Status	—	—	20	Normal
Giga Drain	Grass	Special	75	100	10	Normal
Worry Seed	Grass	Status	—	100	10	Normal
Spite	Ghost	Status	—	100	10	Normal
Trick	Psychic	Status	—	100	10	Normal
Skill Swap	Psychic	Status	—	—	10	Normal

MOVES TAUGHT BY PEOPLE

Name	Type	Kind	Pow.	Acc.	PP	Range

National Pokédex **711** Hoenn Pokédex —

Gourgeist Small Size

Pumpkin Pokémon

Ghost Grass

HEIGHT: 2'04" WEIGHT: 20.9 lbs.

Same form for ♂ / ♀

Ω Singing in eerie voices, they wander town streets on the night of the new moon. Anyone who hears their song is cursed.

α It enwraps its prey in its hairlike arms. It sings joyfully as it observes the suffering of its prey.

ABILITIES
Pickup
Frisk

HIDDEN ABILITY
Insomnia

EGG GROUPS
Amorphous

STAT GROWTH RATES

HP	■■
Attack	■■■■
Defense	■■■■■
Sp. Atk	■■■
Sp. Def	■■■
Speed	■■■■■

ITEMS SOMETIMES HELD BY WILD POKÉMON
—

EVOLUTION

Pumpkaboo → Gourgeist

MAIN WAY TO REGISTER IN THE NATIONAL POKÉDEX

Receive a Pumpkaboo via Link Trade to have it evolve.

Damage taken in normal battles

Type	×	Type	×
Normal	×0	Flying	×2
Fire	×2	Psychic	×1
Water	×0.5	Bug	×1
Grass	×0.5	Rock	×1
Electric	×0.5	Ghost	×2
Ice	×2	Dragon	×1
Fighting	×0	Dark	×2
Poison	×1	Steel	×1
Ground	×0.5	Fairy	×1

Damage taken in Inverse battles

Type	×	Type	×
Normal	×2	Flying	×0.5
Fire	×0.5	Psychic	×1
Water	×2	Bug	×1
Grass	×2	Rock	×1
Electric	×2	Ghost	×0.5
Ice	×0.5	Dragon	×1
Fighting	×2	Dark	×0.5
Poison	×1	Steel	×1
Ground	×2	Fairy	×1

Can be used in
- Inverse Battle
- Battle Institute
- Battle Maison
- Random Matchup (Free Battle)
- Random Matchup (Others)

LEVEL-UP MOVES

Lv.	Name	Type	Kind	Pow.	Acc.	PP	Range
1	Explosion	Normal	Physical	250	100	5	Adjacent
1	Phantom Force	Ghost	Physical	90	100	10	Normal
1	Trick	Psychic	Status	—	100	10	Normal
1	Astonish	Ghost	Physical	30	100	15	Normal
1	Confuse Ray	Ghost	Status	—	100	10	Normal
4	Scary Face	Normal	Status	—	100	10	Normal
6	Trick-or-Treat	Ghost	Status	—	100	20	Normal
11	Worry Seed	Grass	Status	—	100	10	Normal
16	Razor Leaf	Grass	Physical	55	95	25	Many Others
20	Leech Seed	Grass	Status	—	90	10	Normal
23	Trick-or-Treat	Ghost	Status	—	100	20	Normal
26	Bullet Seed	Grass	Physical	25	100	30	Normal
30	Shadow Sneak	Ghost	Physical	40	100	30	Normal
36	Shadow Ball	Ghost	Special	80	100	15	Normal
40	Trick-or-Treat	Ghost	Status	—	100	20	Normal
42	Pain Split	Normal	Status	—	—	20	Normal
48	Seed Bomb	Grass	Physical	80	100	15	Normal
57	Phantom Force	Ghost	Physical	90	100	10	Normal
63	Trick-or-Treat	Ghost	Status	—	100	20	Normal
70	Shadow Ball	Ghost	Special	80	100	15	Normal
75	Explosion	Normal	Physical	250	100	5	Adjacent

TM & HM MOVES

No.	Name	Type	Kind	Pow.	Acc.	PP	Range
TM06	Toxic	Poison	Status	—	90	10	Normal
TM10	Hidden Power	Normal	Special	60	100	15	Normal
TM11	Sunny Day	Fire	Status	—	—	5	Both Sides
TM15	Hyper Beam	Normal	Special	150	90	5	Normal
TM16	Light Screen	Psychic	Status	—	—	30	Your Side
TM17	Protect	Normal	Status	—	—	10	Self
TM20	Safeguard	Normal	Status	—	—	25	Your Side
TM21	Frustration	Normal	Physical	—	100	20	Normal
TM22	Solar Beam	Grass	Special	120	100	10	Normal
TM27	Return	Normal	Physical	—	100	20	Normal
TM29	Psychic	Psychic	Special	90	100	10	Normal
TM30	Shadow Ball	Ghost	Special	80	100	15	Normal
TM32	Double Team	Normal	Status	—	—	15	Self
TM35	Flamethrower	Fire	Special	90	100	15	Normal
TM36	Sludge Bomb	Poison	Special	90	100	10	Normal
TM38	Fire Blast	Fire	Special	110	85	5	Normal
TM42	Facade	Normal	Physical	70	100	20	Normal
TM43	Flame Charge	Fire	Physical	50	100	20	Normal
TM44	Rest	Psychic	Status	—	—	10	Self
TM45	Attract	Normal	Status	—	100	15	Normal
TM46	Thief	Dark	Physical	60	100	25	Normal
TM48	Round	Normal	Special	60	100	15	Normal
TM52	Focus Blast	Fighting	Special	120	70	5	Normal
TM53	Energy Ball	Grass	Special	90	100	10	Normal
TM57	Charge Beam	Electric	Special	50	90	10	Normal
TM59	Incinerate	Fire	Special	60	100	15	Many Others
TM61	Will-O-Wisp	Fire	Status	—	85	15	Normal
TM64	Explosion	Normal	Physical	250	100	5	Adjacent
TM68	Giga Impact	Normal	Physical	150	90	5	Normal
TM70	Flash	Normal	Status	—	100	20	Normal
TM74	Gyro Ball	Steel	Physical	—	100	5	Normal
TM80	Rock Slide	Rock	Physical	75	90	10	Many Others
TM85	Dream Eater	Psychic	Special	100	100	15	Normal
TM86	Grass Knot	Grass	Special	—	100	20	Normal
TM87	Swagger	Normal	Status	—	90	15	Normal
TM88	Sleep Talk	Normal	Status	—	—	10	Self
TM90	Substitute	Normal	Status	—	—	10	Self
TM92	Trick Room	Psychic	Status	—	—	5	Both Sides
TM94	Secret Power	Normal	Physical	70	100	20	Normal
TM96	Nature Power	Normal	Status	—	—	20	Normal
TM97	Dark Pulse	Dark	Special	80	100	15	Normal
TM100	Confide	Normal	Status	—	—	20	Normal
HM06	Rock Smash	Fighting	Physical	40	100	15	Normal

MOVES LEARNED IN EXCHANGE FOR BP

Name	Type	Kind	Pow.	Acc.	PP	Range
Seed Bomb	Grass	Physical	80	100	15	Normal
Magic Coat	Psychic	Status	—	—	15	Self
Foul Play	Dark	Physical	95	100	15	Normal
Synthesis	Grass	Status	—	—	5	Self
Role Play	Psychic	Status	—	—	10	Normal
Pain Split	Normal	Status	—	—	20	Normal
Giga Drain	Grass	Special	75	100	10	Normal
Worry Seed	Grass	Status	—	100	10	Normal
Spite	Ghost	Status	—	100	10	Normal
Trick	Psychic	Status	—	100	10	Normal
Skill Swap	Psychic	Status	—	—	10	Normal

MOVES TAUGHT BY PEOPLE

Name	Type	Kind	Pow.	Acc.	PP	Range

National Pokédex **711** Hoenn Pokédex —

Gourgeist Large Size

Pumpkin Pokémon

Ghost Grass

HEIGHT: 3'07" WEIGHT: 30.9 lbs.

Same form for ♂ / ♀

Ω Singing in eerie voices, they wander town streets on the night of the new moon. Anyone who hears their song is cursed.

α It enwraps its prey in its hairlike arms. It sings joyfully as it observes the suffering of its prey.

ABILITIES
Pickup
Frisk

HIDDEN ABILITY
Insomnia

EGG GROUPS
Amorphous

STAT GROWTH RATES

HP	■■■
Attack	■■■■■
Defense	■■■■■
Sp. Atk	■■■
Sp. Def	■■■
Speed	■■■■

ITEMS SOMETIMES HELD BY WILD POKÉMON
—

EVOLUTION

Link Trade

Pumpkaboo → Gourgeist

MAIN WAY TO REGISTER IN THE NATIONAL POKÉDEX

Receive a Pumpkaboo via Link Trade to have it evolve.

Damage taken in normal battles

Type	×	Type	×
Normal	×0	Flying	×2
Fire	×2	Psychic	×1
Water	×0.5	Bug	×1
Grass	×0.5	Rock	×1
Electric	×0.5	Ghost	×2
Ice	×2	Dragon	×1
Fighting	×0	Dark	×2
Poison	×1	Steel	×1
Ground	×0.5	Fairy	×1

Damage taken in Inverse battles

Type	×	Type	×
Normal	×2	Flying	×0.5
Fire	×0.5	Psychic	×1
Water	×2	Bug	×1
Grass	×2	Rock	×1
Electric	×2	Ghost	×0.5
Ice	×0.5	Dragon	×1
Fighting	×2	Dark	×0.5
Poison	×1	Steel	×1
Ground	×2	Fairy	×1

Can be used in
- Inverse Battle
- Battle Institute
- Battle Maison
- Random Matchup (Free Battle)
- Random Matchup (Others)

LEVEL-UP MOVES

Lv.	Name	Type	Kind	Pow.	Acc.	PP	Range
1	Explosion	Normal	Physical	250	100	5	Adjacent
1	Phantom Force	Ghost	Physical	90	100	10	Normal
1	Trick	Psychic	Status	—	100	10	Normal
1	Astonish	Ghost	Physical	30	100	15	Normal
1	Confuse Ray	Ghost	Status	—	100	10	Normal
4	Scary Face	Normal	Status	—	100	10	Normal
6	Trick-or-Treat	Ghost	Status	—	100	20	Normal
11	Worry Seed	Grass	Status	—	100	10	Normal
16	Razor Leaf	Grass	Physical	55	95	25	Many Others
20	Leech Seed	Grass	Status	—	90	10	Normal
23	Trick-or-Treat	Ghost	Status	—	100	20	Normal
26	Bullet Seed	Grass	Physical	25	100	30	Normal
30	Shadow Sneak	Ghost	Physical	40	100	30	Normal
36	Shadow Ball	Ghost	Special	80	100	15	Normal
40	Trick-or-Treat	Ghost	Status	—	100	20	Normal
42	Pain Split	Normal	Status	—	—	20	Normal
48	Seed Bomb	Grass	Physical	80	100	15	Normal
57	Phantom Force	Ghost	Physical	90	100	10	Normal
63	Trick-or-Treat	Ghost	Status	—	100	20	Normal
70	Shadow Ball	Ghost	Special	80	100	15	Normal
75	Explosion	Normal	Physical	250	100	5	Adjacent

TM & HM MOVES

No.	Name	Type	Kind	Pow.	Acc.	PP	Range
TM06	Toxic	Poison	Status	—	90	10	Normal
TM10	Hidden Power	Normal	Special	60	100	15	Normal
TM11	Sunny Day	Fire	Status	—	—	5	Both Sides
TM15	Hyper Beam	Normal	Special	150	90	5	Normal
TM16	Light Screen	Psychic	Status	—	—	30	Your Side
TM17	Protect	Normal	Status	—	—	10	Self
TM20	Safeguard	Normal	Status	—	—	25	Your Side
TM21	Frustration	Normal	Physical	—	100	20	Normal
TM22	Solar Beam	Grass	Special	120	100	10	Normal
TM27	Return	Normal	Physical	—	100	20	Normal
TM29	Psychic	Psychic	Special	90	100	10	Normal
TM30	Shadow Ball	Ghost	Special	80	100	15	Normal
TM32	Double Team	Normal	Status	—	—	15	Self
TM35	Flamethrower	Fire	Special	90	100	15	Normal
TM36	Sludge Bomb	Poison	Special	90	100	10	Normal
TM38	Fire Blast	Fire	Special	110	85	5	Normal
TM42	Facade	Normal	Physical	70	100	20	Normal
TM43	Flame Charge	Fire	Physical	50	100	20	Normal
TM44	Rest	Psychic	Status	—	—	10	Self
TM45	Attract	Normal	Status	—	100	15	Normal
TM46	Thief	Dark	Physical	60	100	25	Normal
TM48	Round	Normal	Special	60	100	15	Normal
TM52	Focus Blast	Fighting	Special	120	70	5	Normal
TM53	Energy Ball	Grass	Special	90	100	10	Normal
TM57	Charge Beam	Electric	Special	50	90	10	Normal
TM59	Incinerate	Fire	Special	60	100	15	Many Others
TM61	Will-O-Wisp	Fire	Status	—	85	15	Normal
TM64	Explosion	Normal	Physical	250	100	5	Adjacent
TM68	Giga Impact	Normal	Physical	150	90	5	Normal
TM70	Flash	Normal	Status	—	100	20	Normal
TM74	Gyro Ball	Steel	Physical	—	100	5	Normal
TM80	Rock Slide	Rock	Physical	75	90	10	Many Others
TM85	Dream Eater	Psychic	Special	100	100	15	Normal
TM86	Grass Knot	Grass	Special	—	100	20	Normal
TM87	Swagger	Normal	Status	—	90	15	Normal
TM88	Sleep Talk	Normal	Status	—	—	10	Self
TM90	Substitute	Normal	Status	—	—	10	Self
TM92	Trick Room	Psychic	Status	—	—	5	Both Sides
TM94	Secret Power	Normal	Physical	70	100	20	Normal
TM96	Nature Power	Normal	Status	—	—	20	Normal
TM97	Dark Pulse	Dark	Special	80	100	15	Normal
TM100	Confide	Normal	Status	—	—	20	Normal
HM06	Rock Smash	Fighting	Physical	40	100	15	Normal

MOVES LEARNED IN EXCHANGE FOR BP

Name	Type	Kind	Pow.	Acc.	PP	Range
Seed Bomb	Grass	Physical	80	100	15	Normal
Magic Coat	Psychic	Status	—	—	15	Self
Foul Play	Dark	Physical	95	100	15	Normal
Synthesis	Grass	Status	—	—	5	Self
Role Play	Psychic	Status	—	—	10	Normal
Pain Split	Normal	Status	—	—	20	Normal
Giga Drain	Grass	Special	75	100	10	Normal
Worry Seed	Grass	Status	—	100	10	Normal
Spite	Ghost	Status	—	100	10	Normal
Trick	Psychic	Status	—	100	10	Normal
Skill Swap	Psychic	Status	—	—	10	Normal

MOVES TAUGHT BY PEOPLE

Name	Type	Kind	Pow.	Acc.	PP	Range

National Pokédex **711** Hoenn Pokédex —

Gourgeist Super Size

Pumpkin Pokémon

Ghost Grass

HEIGHT: 5'07" WEIGHT: 86 lbs.

Same form for ♂ / ♀

Ω Singing in eerie voices, they wander town streets on the night of the new moon. Anyone who hears their song is cursed.

α It enwraps its prey in its hairlike arms. It sings joyfully as it observes the suffering of its prey.

ABILITIES
Pickup
Frisk

HIDDEN ABILITY
Insomnia

EGG GROUPS
Amorphous

STAT GROWTH RATES
HP ■■■
Attack ■■■■■
Defense ■■■■■
Sp. Atk ■■■
Sp. Def ■■■
Speed ■■■

ITEMS SOMETIMES HELD BY WILD POKÉMON
—

EVOLUTION
Pumpkaboo → Link Trade → Gourgeist

MAIN WAY TO REGISTER IN THE NATIONAL POKÉDEX

Receive a Pumpkaboo via Link Trade to have it evolve.

Damage taken in normal battles

Type		Type	
Normal	×0	Flying	×2
Fire	×2	Psychic	×1
Water	×0.5	Bug	×1
Grass	×0.5	Rock	×1
Electric	×0.5	Ghost	×2
Ice	×2	Dragon	×1
Fighting	×0	Dark	×2
Poison	×1	Steel	×1
Ground	×0.5	Fairy	×1

Damage taken in Inverse battles

Type		Type	
Normal	×2	Flying	×0.5
Fire	×0.5	Psychic	×1
Water	×2	Bug	×1
Grass	×2	Rock	×1
Electric	×2	Ghost	×0.5
Ice	×0.5	Dragon	×1
Fighting	×2	Dark	×0.5
Poison	×1	Steel	×1
Ground	×2	Fairy	×1

Can be used in
- Inverse Battle
- Battle Institute
- Battle Maison
- Random Matchup (Free Battle)
- Random Matchup (Others)

LEVEL-UP MOVES

Lv.	Name	Type	Kind	Pow.	Acc.	PP	Range
1	Explosion	Normal	Physical	250	100	5	Adjacent
1	Phantom Force	Ghost	Physical	90	100	10	Normal
1	Trick	Psychic	Status	—	100	10	Normal
1	Astonish	Ghost	Physical	30	100	15	Normal
1	Confuse Ray	Ghost	Status	—	100	10	Normal
4	Scary Face	Normal	Status	—	100	10	Normal
6	Trick-or-Treat	Ghost	Status	—	100	20	Normal
11	Worry Seed	Grass	Status	—	100	10	Normal
16	Razor Leaf	Grass	Physical	55	95	25	Many Others
20	Leech Seed	Grass	Status	—	90	10	Normal
23	Trick-or-Treat	Ghost	Status	—	100	20	Normal
26	Bullet Seed	Grass	Physical	25	100	30	Normal
30	Shadow Sneak	Ghost	Physical	40	100	30	Normal
36	Shadow Ball	Ghost	Special	80	100	15	Normal
40	Trick-or-Treat	Ghost	Status	—	100	20	Normal
42	Pain Split	Normal	Status	—	—	20	Normal
48	Seed Bomb	Grass	Physical	80	100	15	Normal
57	Phantom Force	Ghost	Physical	90	100	10	Normal
63	Trick-or-Treat	Ghost	Status	—	100	20	Normal
70	Shadow Ball	Ghost	Special	80	100	15	Normal
75	Explosion	Normal	Physical	250	100	5	Adjacent

TM & HM MOVES

No.	Name	Type	Kind	Pow.	Acc.	PP	Range
TM06	Toxic	Poison	Status	—	90	10	Normal
TM10	Hidden Power	Normal	Special	60	100	15	Normal
TM11	Sunny Day	Fire	Status	—	—	5	Both Sides
TM15	Hyper Beam	Normal	Special	150	90	5	Normal
TM16	Light Screen	Psychic	Status	—	—	30	Your Side
TM17	Protect	Normal	Status	—	—	10	Self
TM20	Safeguard	Normal	Status	—	—	25	Your Side
TM21	Frustration	Normal	Physical	—	100	20	Normal
TM22	Solar Beam	Grass	Special	120	100	10	Normal
TM27	Return	Normal	Physical	—	100	20	Normal
TM29	Psychic	Psychic	Special	90	100	10	Normal
TM30	Shadow Ball	Ghost	Special	80	100	15	Normal
TM32	Double Team	Normal	Status	—	—	15	Self
TM35	Flamethrower	Fire	Special	90	100	15	Normal
TM36	Sludge Bomb	Poison	Special	90	100	10	Normal
TM38	Fire Blast	Fire	Special	110	85	5	Normal
TM42	Facade	Normal	Physical	70	100	20	Normal
TM43	Flame Charge	Fire	Physical	50	100	20	Normal
TM44	Rest	Psychic	Status	—	—	10	Self
TM45	Attract	Normal	Status	—	100	15	Normal
TM46	Thief	Dark	Physical	60	100	25	Normal
TM48	Round	Normal	Special	60	100	15	Normal
TM52	Focus Blast	Fighting	Special	120	70	5	Normal
TM53	Energy Ball	Grass	Special	90	100	10	Normal
TM57	Charge Beam	Electric	Special	50	90	10	Normal
TM59	Incinerate	Fire	Special	60	100	15	Many Others
TM61	Will-O-Wisp	Fire	Status	—	85	15	Normal
TM64	Explosion	Normal	Physical	250	100	5	Adjacent
TM68	Giga Impact	Normal	Physical	150	90	5	Normal
TM70	Flash	Normal	Status	—	100	20	Normal
TM74	Gyro Ball	Steel	Physical	—	100	5	Normal
TM80	Rock Slide	Rock	Physical	75	90	10	Many Others
TM85	Dream Eater	Psychic	Special	100	100	15	Normal
TM86	Grass Knot	Grass	Special	—	100	20	Normal
TM87	Swagger	Normal	Status	—	90	15	Normal
TM88	Sleep Talk	Normal	Status	—	—	10	Self
TM90	Substitute	Normal	Status	—	—	10	Self
TM92	Trick Room	Psychic	Status	—	—	5	Both Sides
TM94	Secret Power	Normal	Physical	70	100	20	Normal
TM96	Nature Power	Normal	Status	—	—	20	Normal
TM97	Dark Pulse	Dark	Special	80	100	15	Normal
TM100	Confide	Normal	Status	—	—	20	Normal
HM06	Rock Smash	Fighting	Physical	40	100	15	Normal

MOVES LEARNED IN EXCHANGE FOR BP

Name	Type	Kind	Pow.	Acc.	PP	Range
Seed Bomb	Grass	Physical	80	100	15	Normal
Magic Coat	Psychic	Status	—	—	15	Self
Foul Play	Dark	Physical	95	100	15	Normal
Synthesis	Grass	Status	—	—	5	Self
Role Play	Psychic	Status	—	—	10	Normal
Pain Split	Normal	Status	—	—	20	Normal
Giga Drain	Grass	Special	75	100	10	Normal
Worry Seed	Grass	Status	—	100	10	Normal
Spite	Ghost	Status	—	100	10	Normal
Trick	Psychic	Status	—	100	10	Normal
Skill Swap	Psychic	Status	—	—	10	Normal

MOVES TAUGHT BY PEOPLE

Name	Type	Kind	Pow.	Acc.	PP	Range

National Pokédex **712** Hoenn Pokédex —

Bergmite

Ice Chunk Pokémon

Ice

HEIGHT: 3'03" WEIGHT: 219.4 lbs.

Same form for ♂ / ♀

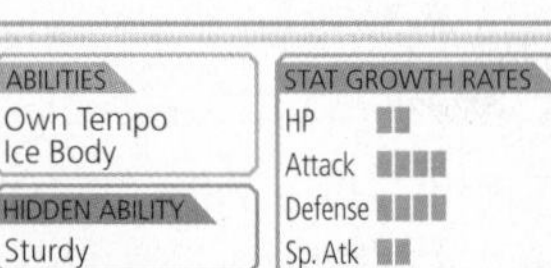

Ω It blocks opponents' attacks with the ice that shields its body. It uses cold air to repair any cracks with new ice.

α Using air of -150 degrees Fahrenheit, they freeze opponents solid. They live in herds above the snow line on mountains.

ABILITIES
Own Tempo
Ice Body

HIDDEN ABILITY
Sturdy

EGG GROUPS
Monster

STAT GROWTH RATES
HP ■■
Attack ■■■■
Defense ■■■■
Sp. Atk ■■
Sp. Def ■■
Speed ■■

ITEMS SOMETIMES HELD BY WILD POKÉMON
—

EVOLUTION

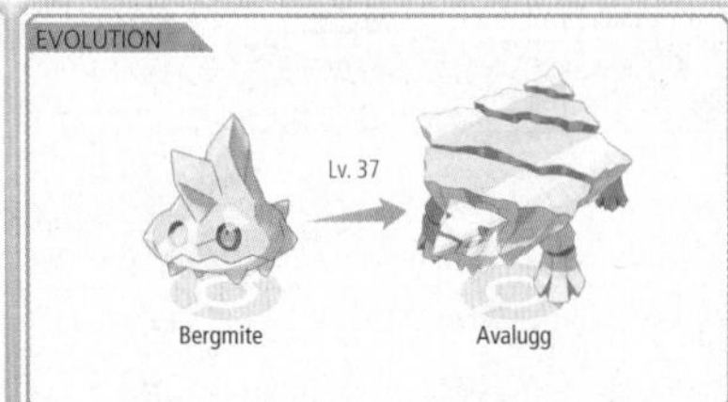

MAIN WAY TO REGISTER IN THE NATIONAL POKÉDEX

Appears in *Pokémon X* and *Pokémon Y*. Bring it to your game using Link Trade or the GTS.

Damage taken in normal battles

Type		Type	
Normal	×1	Flying	×1
Fire	×2	Psychic	×1
Water	×1	Bug	×1
Grass	×1	Rock	×2
Electric	×1	Ghost	×1
Ice	×0.5	Dragon	×1
Fighting	×2	Dark	×1
Poison	×1	Steel	×2
Ground	×1	Fairy	×1

Damage taken in Inverse battles

Type		Type	
Normal	×1	Flying	×1
Fire	×0.5	Psychic	×1
Water	×1	Bug	×1
Grass	×1	Rock	×0.5
Electric	×1	Ghost	×1
Ice	×2	Dragon	×1
Fighting	×0.5	Dark	×1
Poison	×1	Steel	×0.5
Ground	×1	Fairy	×1

Can be used in
- Inverse Battle
- Battle Institute
- Battle Maison
- Random Matchup (Free Battle)
- Random Matchup (Others)

LEVEL-UP MOVES

Lv.	Name	Type	Kind	Pow.	Acc.	PP	Range
1	Tackle	Normal	Physical	50	100	35	Normal
1	Bite	Dark	Physical	60	100	25	Normal
1	Harden	Normal	Status	—	—	30	Self
5	Powder Snow	Ice	Special	40	100	25	Many Others
10	Icy Wind	Ice	Special	55	95	15	Many Others
15	Take Down	Normal	Physical	90	85	20	Normal
20	Sharpen	Normal	Status	—	—	30	Self
22	Curse	Ghost	Status	—	—	10	Varies
26	Ice Fang	Ice	Physical	65	95	15	Normal
30	Ice Ball	Ice	Physical	30	90	20	Normal
35	Rapid Spin	Normal	Physical	20	100	40	Normal
39	Avalanche	Ice	Physical	60	100	10	Normal
43	Blizzard	Ice	Special	110	70	5	Many Others
47	Recover	Normal	Status	—	—	10	Self
49	Double-Edge	Normal	Physical	120	100	15	Normal

TM & HM MOVES

No.	Name	Type	Kind	Pow.	Acc.	PP	Range
TM06	Toxic	Poison	Status	—	90	10	Normal
TM07	Hail	Ice	Status	—	—	10	Both Sides
TM10	Hidden Power	Normal	Special	60	100	15	Normal
TM13	Ice Beam	Ice	Special	90	100	10	Normal
TM14	Blizzard	Ice	Special	110	70	5	Many Others
TM17	Protect	Normal	Status	—	—	10	Self
TM18	Rain Dance	Water	Status	—	—	5	Both Sides
TM20	Safeguard	Normal	Status	—	—	25	Your Side
TM21	Frustration	Normal	Physical	—	100	20	Normal
TM27	Return	Normal	Physical	—	100	20	Normal
TM32	Double Team	Normal	Status	—	—	15	Self
TM39	Rock Tomb	Rock	Physical	60	95	15	Normal
TM42	Facade	Normal	Physical	70	100	20	Normal
TM44	Rest	Psychic	Status	—	—	10	Self
TM45	Attract	Normal	Status	—	100	15	Normal
TM48	Round	Normal	Special	60	100	15	Normal
TM69	Rock Polish	Rock	Status	—	—	20	Self
TM70	Flash	Normal	Status	—	100	20	Normal
TM71	Stone Edge	Rock	Physical	100	80	5	Normal
TM74	Gyro Ball	Steel	Physical	—	100	5	Normal
TM79	Frost Breath	Ice	Special	60	90	10	Normal
TM80	Rock Slide	Rock	Physical	75	90	10	Many Others
TM87	Swagger	Normal	Status	—	90	15	Normal
TM88	Sleep Talk	Normal	Status	—	—	10	Self
TM90	Substitute	Normal	Status	—	—	10	Self
TM91	Flash Cannon	Steel	Special	80	100	10	Normal
TM94	Secret Power	Normal	Physical	70	100	20	Normal
TM100	Confide	Normal	Status	—	—	20	Normal
HM03	Surf	Water	Special	90	100	15	Adjacent
HM04	Strength	Normal	Physical	80	100	15	Normal
HM06	Rock Smash	Fighting	Physical	40	100	15	Normal

MOVES LEARNED IN EXCHANGE FOR BP

Name	Type	Kind	Pow.	Acc.	PP	Range
Iron Defense	Steel	Status	—	—	15	Self
Icy Wind	Ice	Special	55	95	15	Many Others
Snore	Normal	Special	50	100	15	Normal
Water Pulse	Water	Special	60	100	20	Normal
After You	Normal	Status	—	—	15	Normal

MOVES TAUGHT BY PEOPLE

Name	Type	Kind	Pow.	Acc.	PP	Range

EGG MOVES

Name	Type	Kind	Pow.	Acc.	PP	Range
Recover	Normal	Status	—	—	10	Self
Mist	Ice	Status	—	—	30	Your Side
Barrier	Psychic	Status	—	—	20	Self
Mirror Coat	Psychic	Special	—	100	20	Varies

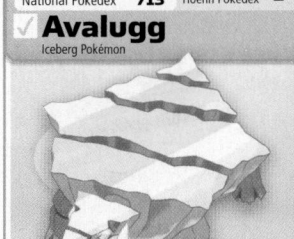

National Pokédex **713** Hoenn Pokédex –

Avalugg

Iceberg Pokémon

Ice

HEIGHT: 6'07" WEIGHT: 1113.3 lbs.

Same form for ♂ / ♀

Ω Its ice-covered body is as hard as steel. Its cumbersome frame crushes anything that stands in its way.

α The way several Bergmite huddle on its back makes it look like an aircraft carrier made of ice.

ABILITIES
Own Tempo
Ice Body

HIDDEN ABILITY
Sturdy

EGG GROUPS
Monster

STAT GROWTH RATES
HP
Attack
Defense
Sp. Atk
Sp. Def
Speed

ITEMS SOMETIMES HELD BY WILD POKÉMON
—

EVOLUTION

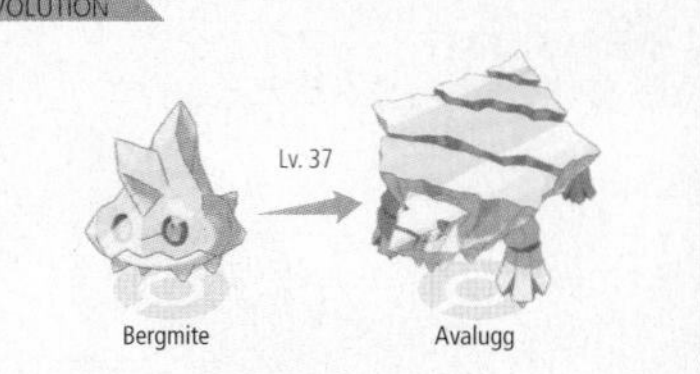

MAIN WAY TO REGISTER IN THE NATIONAL POKÉDEX

Level up a Bergmite obtained via Link Trade or the GTS to Lv. 37.

Damage taken in normal battles

Type		Type	
Normal	×1	Flying	×1
Fire	×2	Psychic	×1
Water	×1	Bug	×1
Grass	×1	Rock	×2
Electric	×1	Ghost	×1
Ice	×0.5	Dragon	×1
Fighting	×2	Dark	×1
Poison	×1	Steel	×2
Ground	×1	Fairy	×1

Damage taken in Inverse battles

Type		Type	
Normal	×1	Flying	×1
Fire	×0.5	Psychic	×1
Water	×1	Bug	×1
Grass	×1	Rock	×0.5
Electric	×1	Ghost	×1
Ice	×2	Dragon	×1
Fighting	×0.5	Dark	×1
Poison	×1	Steel	×0.5
Ground	×1	Fairy	×1

Can be used in
Inverse Battle
Battle Institute
Battle Maison
Random Matchup (Free Battle)
Random Matchup (Others)

LEVEL-UP MOVES

Lv.	Name	Type	Kind	Pow.	Acc.	PP	Range
1	Iron Defense	Steel	Status	—	—	15	Self
1	Crunch	Dark	Physical	80	100	15	Normal
1	Skull Bash	Normal	Physical	130	100	10	Normal
1	Tackle	Normal	Physical	50	100	35	Normal
1	Bite	Dark	Physical	60	100	25	Normal
1	Harden	Normal	Status	—	—	30	Self
5	Powder Snow	Ice	Special	40	100	25	Many Others
10	Icy Wind	Ice	Special	55	95	15	Many Others
15	Take Down	Normal	Physical	90	85	20	Normal
20	Sharpen	Normal	Status	—	—	30	Self
22	Curse	Ghost	Status	—	—	10	Varies
26	Ice Fang	Ice	Physical	65	95	15	Normal
30	Ice Ball	Ice	Physical	30	90	20	Normal
35	Rapid Spin	Normal	Physical	20	100	40	Normal
42	Avalanche	Ice	Physical	60	100	10	Normal
46	Blizzard	Ice	Special	110	70	5	Many Others
51	Recover	Normal	Status	—	—	10	Self
56	Double-Edge	Normal	Physical	120	100	15	Normal
60	Skull Bash	Normal	Physical	130	100	10	Normal
65	Crunch	Dark	Physical	80	100	15	Normal

TM & HM MOVES

No.	Name	Type	Kind	Pow.	Acc.	PP	Range
TM05	Roar	Normal	Status	—	—	20	Normal
TM06	Toxic	Poison	Status	—	90	10	Normal
TM07	Hail	Ice	Status	—	—	10	Both Sides
TM10	Hidden Power	Normal	Special	60	100	15	Normal
TM13	Ice Beam	Ice	Special	90	100	10	Normal
TM14	Blizzard	Ice	Special	110	70	5	Many Others
TM15	Hyper Beam	Normal	Special	150	90	5	Normal
TM17	Protect	Normal	Status	—	—	10	Self
TM18	Rain Dance	Water	Status	—	—	5	Both Sides
TM20	Safeguard	Normal	Status	—	—	25	Your Side
TM21	Frustration	Normal	Physical	—	100	20	Normal
TM26	Earthquake	Ground	Physical	100	100	10	Adjacent
TM27	Return	Normal	Physical	—	100	20	Normal
TM32	Double Team	Normal	Status	—	—	15	Self
TM39	Rock Tomb	Rock	Physical	60	95	15	Normal
TM42	Facade	Normal	Physical	70	100	20	Normal
TM44	Rest	Psychic	Status	—	—	10	Self
TM45	Attract	Normal	Status	—	100	15	Normal
TM48	Round	Normal	Special	60	100	15	Normal
TM68	Giga Impact	Normal	Physical	150	90	5	Normal
TM69	Rock Polish	Rock	Status	—	—	20	Self
TM70	Flash	Normal	Status	—	100	20	Normal
TM71	Stone Edge	Rock	Physical	100	80	5	Normal
TM74	Gyro Ball	Steel	Physical	—	100	5	Normal
TM78	Bulldoze	Ground	Physical	60	100	20	Adjacent
TM79	Frost Breath	Ice	Special	60	90	10	Normal
TM80	Rock Slide	Rock	Physical	75	90	10	Many Others
TM87	Swagger	Normal	Status	—	90	15	Normal
TM88	Sleep Talk	Normal	Status	—	—	10	Self
TM90	Substitute	Normal	Status	—	—	10	Self
TM91	Flash Cannon	Steel	Special	80	100	10	Normal
TM94	Secret Power	Normal	Physical	70	100	20	Normal
TM100	Confide	Normal	Status	—	—	20	Normal
HM03	Surf	Water	Special	90	100	15	Adjacent
HM04	Strength	Normal	Physical	80	100	15	Normal
HM06	Rock Smash	Fighting	Physical	40	100	15	Normal

MOVES LEARNED IN EXCHANGE FOR BP

Name	Type	Kind	Pow.	Acc.	PP	Range
Iron Head	Steel	Physical	80	100	15	Normal
Block	Normal	Status	—	—	5	Normal
Iron Defense	Steel	Status	—	—	15	Self
Superpower	Fighting	Physical	120	100	5	Normal
Icy Wind	Ice	Special	55	95	15	Many Others
Snore	Normal	Special	50	100	15	Normal
Water Pulse	Water	Special	60	100	20	Normal
After You	Normal	Status	—	—	15	Normal

MOVES TAUGHT BY PEOPLE

Name	Type	Kind	Pow.	Acc.	PP	Range

National Pokédex **714** Hoenn Pokédex –

Noibat

Sound Wave Pokémon

Flying Dragon

HEIGHT: 1'08" WEIGHT: 17.6 lbs.

Same form for ♂ / ♀

Ω They live in pitch-black caves. Their enormous ears can emit ultrasonic waves of 200,000 hertz.

α Even a robust wrestler will become dizzy and unable to stand when exposed to its 200,000-hertz ultrasonic waves.

ABILITIES
Frisk
Infiltrator

HIDDEN ABILITY
Telepathy

EGG GROUPS
Flying

STAT GROWTH RATES
HP
Attack
Defense
Sp. Atk
Sp. Def
Speed

ITEMS SOMETIMES HELD BY WILD POKÉMON
—

EVOLUTION

Lv. 48
Noibat
Noivern

MAIN WAY TO REGISTER IN THE NATIONAL POKÉDEX

Appears in *Pokémon X* and *Pokémon Y.* Bring it to your game using Link Trade or the GTS.

Damage taken in normal battles

Type		Type	
Normal	×1	Flying	×1
Fire	×0.5	Psychic	×1
Water	×0.5	Bug	×0.5
Grass	×0.25	Rock	×2
Electric	×1	Ghost	×1
Ice	×4	Dragon	×2
Fighting	×0.5	Dark	×1
Poison	×1	Steel	×1
Ground	×0	Fairy	×2

Damage taken in Inverse battles

Type		Type	
Normal	×1	Flying	×1
Fire	×2	Psychic	×1
Water	×2	Bug	×2
Grass	×4	Rock	×0.5
Electric	×1	Ghost	×1
Ice	×0.25	Dragon	×0.5
Fighting	×2	Dark	×1
Poison	×1	Steel	×1
Ground	×2	Fairy	×0.5

Can be used in
Inverse Battle
Battle Institute
Battle Maison
Random Matchup (Free Battle)
Random Matchup (Others)

LEVEL-UP MOVES

Lv.	Name	Type	Kind	Pow.	Acc.	PP	Range
1	Screech	Normal	Status	—	85	40	Normal
1	Supersonic	Normal	Status	—	55	20	Normal
1	Tackle	Normal	Physical	50	100	35	Normal
5	Leech Life	Bug	Physical	20	100	15	Normal
11	Gust	Flying	Special	40	100	35	Normal
13	Bite	Dark	Physical	60	100	25	Normal
16	Wing Attack	Flying	Physical	60	100	35	Normal
18	Agility	Psychic	Status	—	—	30	Self
23	Air Cutter	Flying	Special	60	95	25	Many Others
27	Roost	Flying	Status	—	—	10	Self
31	Razor Wind	Normal	Special	80	100	10	Many Others
35	Tailwind	Flying	Status	—	—	15	Your Side
40	Whirlwind	Normal	Status	—	—	20	Normal
43	Super Fang	Normal	Physical	—	90	10	Normal
48	Air Slash	Flying	Special	75	95	15	Normal
58	Hurricane	Flying	Special	110	70	10	Normal

TM & HM MOVES

No.	Name	Type	Kind	Pow.	Acc.	PP	Range
TM06	Toxic	Poison	Status	—	90	10	Normal
TM10	Hidden Power	Normal	Special	60	100	15	Normal
TM11	Sunny Day	Fire	Status	—	—	5	Both Sides
TM12	Taunt	Dark	Status	—	100	20	Normal
TM17	Protect	Normal	Status	—	—	10	Self
TM19	Roost	Flying	Status	—	—	10	Self
TM21	Frustration	Normal	Physical	—	100	20	Normal
TM22	Solar Beam	Grass	Special	120	100	10	Normal
TM27	Return	Normal	Physical	—	100	20	Normal
TM29	Psychic	Psychic	Special	90	100	10	Normal
TM30	Shadow Ball	Ghost	Special	80	100	15	Normal
TM31	Brick Break	Fighting	Physical	75	100	15	Normal
TM32	Double Team	Normal	Status	—	—	15	Self
TM40	Aerial Ace	Flying	Physical	60	—	20	Normal
TM41	Torment	Dark	Status	—	100	15	Normal
TM42	Facade	Normal	Physical	70	100	20	Normal
TM44	Rest	Psychic	Status	—	—	10	Self
TM45	Attract	Normal	Status	—	100	15	Normal
TM46	Thief	Dark	Physical	60	100	25	Normal
TM48	Round	Normal	Special	60	100	15	Normal
TM49	Echoed Voice	Normal	Special	40	100	15	Normal
TM51	Steel Wing	Steel	Physical	70	90	25	Normal
TM62	Acrobatics	Flying	Physical	55	100	15	Normal
TM65	Shadow Claw	Ghost	Physical	70	100	15	Normal
TM81	X-Scissor	Bug	Physical	80	100	15	Normal
TM85	Dream Eater	Psychic	Special	100	100	15	Normal
TM87	Swagger	Normal	Status	—	90	15	Normal
TM88	Sleep Talk	Normal	Status	—	—	10	Self
TM89	U-turn	Bug	Physical	70	100	20	Normal
TM90	Substitute	Normal	Status	—	—	10	Self
TM93	Wild Charge	Electric	Physical	90	100	15	Normal
TM94	Secret Power	Normal	Physical	70	100	20	Normal
TM97	Dark Pulse	Dark	Special	80	100	15	Normal
TM100	Confide	Normal	Status	—	—	20	Normal
HM01	Cut	Normal	Physical	50	95	30	Normal
HM02	Fly	Flying	Physical	90	95	15	Normal

MOVES LEARNED IN EXCHANGE FOR BP

Name	Type	Kind	Pow.	Acc.	PP	Range
Super Fang	Normal	Physical	—	90	10	Normal
Uproar	Normal	Special	90	100	10	1 Random
Dragon Pulse	Dragon	Special	85	100	10	Normal
Hyper Voice	Normal	Special	90	100	10	Many Others
Iron Tail	Steel	Physical	100	75	15	Normal
Snore	Normal	Special	50	100	15	Normal
Heat Wave	Fire	Special	95	90	10	Many Others
Tailwind	Flying	Status	—	—	15	Your Side
Sky Attack	Flying	Physical	140	90	5	Normal
Water Pulse	Water	Special	60	100	20	Normal
Outrage	Dragon	Physical	120	100	10	1 Random
Snatch	Dark	Status	—	—	10	Self

MOVES TAUGHT BY PEOPLE

Name	Type	Kind	Pow.	Acc.	PP	Range
Draco Meteor	Dragon	Special	130	90	5	Normal

EGG MOVES

Name	Type	Kind	Pow.	Acc.	PP	Range
Switcheroo	Dark	Status	—	100	10	Normal
Snatch	Dark	Status	—	—	10	Self
Outrage	Dragon	Physical	120	100	10	1 Random
Tailwind	Flying	Status	—	—	15	Your Side

National Pokédex **715** Hoenn Pokédex —

Noivern

Sound Wave Pokémon

Flying / Dragon

HEIGHT: 4'11" WEIGHT: 187.4 lbs.

Same form for ♂ / ♀

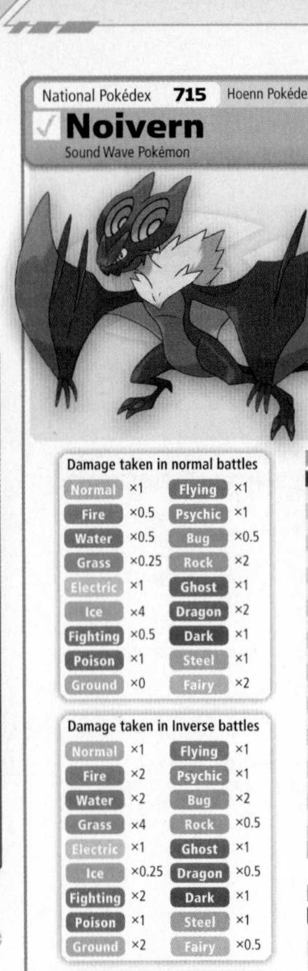

Ω They fly around on moonless nights and attack careless prey. Nothing can beat them in a battle in the dark.

α The ultrasonic waves it emits from its ears can reduce a large boulder to pebbles. It swoops out of the dark to attack.

ABILITIES
Frisk
Infiltrator

HIDDEN ABILITY
Telepathy

EGG GROUPS
Flying

STAT GROWTH RATES
HP
Attack
Defense
Sp. Atk
Sp. Def
Speed

ITEMS SOMETIMES HELD BY WILD POKÉMON
—

EVOLUTION

MAIN WAY TO REGISTER IN THE NATIONAL POKÉDEX

Level up a Noibat obtained via Link Trade or the GTS to Lv. 48.

Damage taken in normal battles

Type		Type	
Normal	×1	Flying	×1
Fire	×0.5	Psychic	×1
Water	×0.5	Bug	×0.5
Grass	×0.25	Rock	×2
Electric	×1	Ghost	×1
Ice	×4	Dragon	×2
Fighting	×0.5	Dark	×1
Poison	×1	Steel	×1
Ground	×0	Fairy	×2

Damage taken in Inverse battles

Type		Type	
Normal	×1	Flying	×1
Fire	×2	Psychic	×1
Water	×2	Bug	×2
Grass	×4	Rock	×0.5
Electric	×1	Ghost	×1
Ice	×0.25	Dragon	×0.5
Fighting	×2	Dark	×1
Poison	×1	Steel	×1
Ground	×2	Fairy	×0.5

Can be used in
Inverse Battle
Battle Institute
Battle Maison
Random Matchup (Free Battle)
Random Matchup (Others)

LEVEL-UP MOVES

Lv.	Name	Type	Kind	Pow.	Acc.	PP	Range
1	Moonlight	Fairy	Status	—	—	5	Self
1	Boomburst	Normal	Special	140	100	10	Adjacent
1	Dragon Pulse	Dragon	Special	85	100	10	Normal
1	Hurricane	Flying	Special	110	70	10	Normal
1	Screech	Normal	Status	—	85	40	Normal
1	Supersonic	Normal	Status	—	55	20	Normal
1	Tackle	Normal	Physical	50	100	35	Normal
5	Leech Life	Bug	Physical	20	100	15	Normal
11	Gust	Flying	Special	40	100	35	Normal
13	Bite	Dark	Physical	60	100	25	Normal
16	Wing Attack	Flying	Physical	60	100	35	Normal
18	Agility	Psychic	Status	—	—	30	Self
23	Air Cutter	Flying	Special	60	95	25	Many Others
27	Roost	Flying	Status	—	—	10	Self
31	Razor Wind	Normal	Special	80	100	10	Many Others
35	Tailwind	Flying	Status	—	—	15	Your Side
40	Whirlwind	Normal	Status	—	—	20	Normal
43	Super Fang	Normal	Physical	—	90	10	Normal
53	Air Slash	Flying	Special	75	95	15	Normal
62	Hurricane	Flying	Special	110	70	10	Normal
70	Dragon Pulse	Dragon	Special	85	100	10	Normal
75	Boomburst	Normal	Special	140	100	10	Adjacent

TM & HM MOVES

No.	Name	Type	Kind	Pow.	Acc.	PP	Range
TM01	Hone Claws	Dark	Status	—	—	15	Self
TM02	Dragon Claw	Dragon	Physical	80	100	15	Normal
TM06	Toxic	Poison	Status	—	90	10	Normal
TM10	Hidden Power	Normal	Special	60	100	15	Normal
TM11	Sunny Day	Fire	Status	—	—	5	Both Sides
TM12	Taunt	Dark	Status	—	100	20	Normal
TM15	Hyper Beam	Normal	Special	150	90	5	Normal
TM17	Protect	Normal	Status	—	—	10	Self
TM19	Roost	Flying	Status	—	—	10	Self
TM21	Frustration	Normal	Physical	—	100	20	Normal
TM22	Solar Beam	Grass	Special	120	100	10	Normal
TM27	Return	Normal	Physical	—	100	20	Normal
TM29	Psychic	Psychic	Special	90	100	10	Normal
TM30	Shadow Ball	Ghost	Special	80	100	15	Normal
TM31	Brick Break	Fighting	Physical	75	100	15	Normal
TM32	Double Team	Normal	Status	—	—	15	Self
TM35	Flamethrower	Fire	Special	90	100	15	Normal
TM40	Aerial Ace	Flying	Physical	60	—	20	Normal
TM41	Torment	Dark	Status	—	100	15	Normal
TM42	Facade	Normal	Physical	70	100	20	Normal
TM44	Rest	Psychic	Status	—	—	10	Self
TM45	Attract	Normal	Status	—	100	15	Normal
TM46	Thief	Dark	Physical	60	100	25	Normal
TM48	Round	Normal	Special	60	100	15	Normal
TM49	Echoed Voice	Normal	Special	40	100	15	Normal
TM51	Steel Wing	Steel	Physical	70	90	25	Normal
TM52	Focus Blast	Fighting	Special	120	70	5	Normal
TM62	Acrobatics	Flying	Physical	55	100	15	Normal
TM65	Shadow Claw	Ghost	Physical	70	100	15	Normal
TM68	Giga Impact	Normal	Physical	150	90	5	Normal
TM81	X-Scissor	Bug	Physical	80	100	15	Normal
TM85	Dream Eater	Psychic	Special	100	100	15	Normal
TM87	Swagger	Normal	Status	—	90	15	Normal
TM88	Sleep Talk	Normal	Status	—	—	10	Self
TM89	U-turn	Bug	Physical	70	100	20	Normal
TM90	Substitute	Normal	Status	—	—	10	Self
TM93	Wild Charge	Electric	Physical	90	100	15	Normal
TM94	Secret Power	Normal	Physical	70	100	20	Normal
TM97	Dark Pulse	Dark	Special	80	100	15	Normal
TM100	Confide	Normal	Status	—	—	20	Normal
HM01	Cut	Normal	Physical	50	95	30	Normal
HM02	Fly	Flying	Physical	90	95	15	Normal

MOVES LEARNED IN EXCHANGE FOR BP

Name	Type	Kind	Pow.	Acc.	PP	Range
Super Fang	Normal	Physical	—	90	10	Normal
Uproar	Normal	Special	90	100	10	1 Random
Dragon Pulse	Dragon	Special	85	100	10	Normal
Hyper Voice	Normal	Special	90	100	10	Many Others
Iron Tail	Steel	Physical	100	75	15	Normal
Snore	Normal	Special	50	100	15	Normal
Heat Wave	Fire	Special	95	90	10	Many Others
Tailwind	Flying	Status	—	—	15	Your Side
Sky Attack	Flying	Physical	140	90	5	Normal
Water Pulse	Water	Special	60	100	20	Normal
Outrage	Dragon	Physical	120	100	10	1 Random
Snatch	Dark	Status	—	—	10	Self

MOVES TAUGHT BY PEOPLE

Name	Type	Kind	Pow.	Acc.	PP	Range
Draco Meteor	Dragon	Special	130	90	5	Normal

National Pokédex **716** Hoenn Pokédex —

Xerneas

Life Pokémon

Fairy

HEIGHT: 9'10" WEIGHT: 474 lbs.

Gender unknown

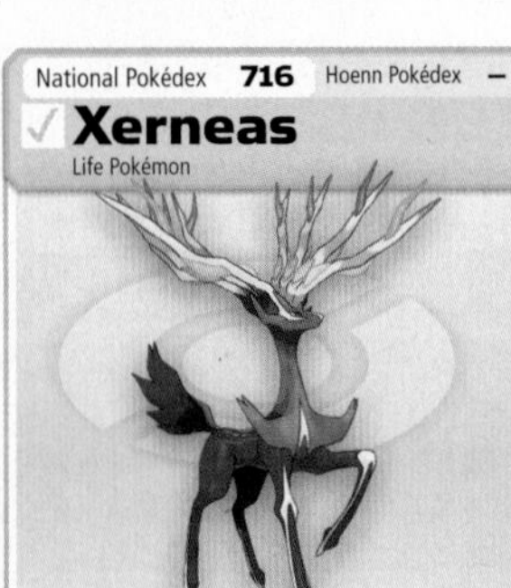

Ω Legends say it can share eternal life. It slept for a thousand years in the form of a tree before its revival.

α When the horns on its head shine in seven colors, it is said to be sharing everlasting life.

ABILITY
Fairy Aura

HIDDEN ABILITY
—

EGG GROUPS
No Eggs Discovered

STAT GROWTH RATES
HP
Attack
Defense
Sp. Atk
Sp. Def
Speed

ITEMS SOMETIMES HELD BY WILD POKÉMON
—

EVOLUTION

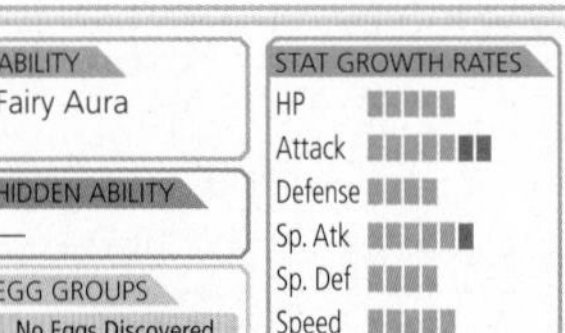

MAIN WAY TO REGISTER IN THE NATIONAL POKÉDEX

Appears in *Pokémon X*. Bring it to your game using Link Trade or the GTS.

Damage taken in normal battles

Type		Type	
Normal	×1	Flying	×1
Fire	×1	Psychic	×1
Water	×1	Bug	×0.5
Grass	×1	Rock	×1
Electric	×1	Ghost	×1
Ice	×1	Dragon	×0
Fighting	×0.5	Dark	×0.5
Poison	×2	Steel	×2
Ground	×1	Fairy	×1

Damage taken in Inverse battles

Type		Type	
Normal	×1	Flying	×1
Fire	×1	Psychic	×1
Water	×1	Bug	×2
Grass	×1	Rock	×1
Electric	×1	Ghost	×1
Ice	×1	Dragon	×2
Fighting	×2	Dark	×2
Poison	×0.5	Steel	×0.5
Ground	×1	Fairy	×1

Can be used in
Inverse Battle
Battle Institute
Battle Maison
Random Matchup (Free Battle)
Random Matchup (Others)

LEVEL-UP MOVES

Lv.	Name	Type	Kind	Pow.	Acc.	PP	Range
1	Heal Pulse	Psychic	Status	—	—	10	Normal
1	Aromatherapy	Grass	Status	—	—	5	Your Party
1	Ingrain	Grass	Status	—	—	20	Self
1	Take Down	Normal	Physical	90	85	20	Normal
5	Light Screen	Psychic	Status	—	—	30	Your Side
10	Aurora Beam	Ice	Special	65	100	20	Normal
18	Gravity	Psychic	Status	—	—	5	Both Sides
26	Geomancy	Fairy	Status	—	—	10	Self
35	Moonblast	Fairy	Special	95	100	15	Normal
44	Megahorn	Bug	Physical	120	85	10	Normal
51	Night Slash	Dark	Physical	70	100	15	Normal
55	Horn Leech	Grass	Physical	75	100	10	Normal
59	Psych Up	Normal	Status	—	—	10	Normal
63	Misty Terrain	Fairy	Status	—	—	10	Both Sides
72	Nature Power	Normal	Status	—	—	20	Normal
80	Close Combat	Fighting	Physical	120	100	5	Normal
88	Giga Impact	Normal	Physical	150	90	5	Normal
93	Outrage	Dragon	Physical	120	100	10	1 Random

TM & HM MOVES

No.	Name	Type	Kind	Pow.	Acc.	PP	Range
TM03	Psyshock	Psychic	Special	80	100	10	Normal
TM04	Calm Mind	Psychic	Status	—	—	20	Self
TM05	Roar	Normal	Status	—	—	20	Normal
TM06	Toxic	Poison	Status	—	90	10	Normal
TM07	Hail	Ice	Status	—	—	10	Both Sides
TM10	Hidden Power	Normal	Special	60	100	15	Normal
TM11	Sunny Day	Fire	Status	—	—	5	Both Sides
TM15	Hyper Beam	Normal	Special	150	90	5	Normal
TM16	Light Screen	Psychic	Status	—	—	30	Your Side
TM17	Protect	Normal	Status	—	—	10	Self
TM18	Rain Dance	Water	Status	—	—	5	Both Sides
TM21	Frustration	Normal	Physical	—	100	20	Normal
TM24	Thunderbolt	Electric	Special	90	100	15	Normal
TM25	Thunder	Electric	Special	110	70	10	Normal
TM27	Return	Normal	Physical	—	100	20	Normal
TM29	Psychic	Psychic	Special	90	100	10	Normal
TM32	Double Team	Normal	Status	—	—	15	Self
TM33	Reflect	Psychic	Status	—	—	20	Your Side
TM42	Facade	Normal	Physical	70	100	20	Normal
TM44	Rest	Psychic	Status	—	—	10	Self
TM48	Round	Normal	Special	60	100	15	Normal
TM49	Echoed Voice	Normal	Special	40	100	15	Normal
TM52	Focus Blast	Fighting	Special	120	70	5	Normal
TM68	Giga Impact	Normal	Physical	150	90	5	Normal
TM70	Flash	Normal	Status	—	100	20	Normal
TM73	Thunder Wave	Electric	Status	—	100	20	Normal
TM77	Psych Up	Normal	Status	—	—	10	Normal
TM80	Rock Slide	Rock	Physical	75	90	10	Many Others
TM86	Grass Knot	Grass	Special	—	100	20	Normal
TM87	Swagger	Normal	Status	—	90	15	Normal
TM88	Sleep Talk	Normal	Status	—	—	10	Self
TM90	Substitute	Normal	Status	—	—	10	Self
TM91	Flash Cannon	Steel	Special	80	100	10	Normal
TM94	Secret Power	Normal	Physical	70	100	20	Normal
TM96	Nature Power	Normal	Status	—	—	20	Normal
TM99	Dazzling Gleam	Fairy	Special	80	100	10	Many Others
TM100	Confide	Normal	Status	—	—	20	Normal
HM01	Cut	Normal	Physical	50	95	30	Normal

MOVES LEARNED IN EXCHANGE FOR BP

Name	Type	Kind	Pow.	Acc.	PP	Range
Block	Normal	Status	—	—	5	Normal
Gravity	Psychic	Status	—	—	5	Both Sides
Zen Headbutt	Psychic	Physical	80	90	15	Normal
Hyper Voice	Normal	Special	90	100	10	Many Others
Snore	Normal	Special	50	100	15	Normal
Wonder Room	Psychic	Status	—	—	10	Both Sides
Endeavor	Normal	Physical	—	100	5	Normal
Outrage	Dragon	Physical	120	100	10	1 Random

MOVES TAUGHT BY PEOPLE

Name	Type	Kind	Pow.	Acc.	PP	Range

National Pokédex **717** Hoenn Pokédex –

Yveltal

Destruction Pokémon

Dark **Flying**

HEIGHT: 19'00" WEIGHT: 447.5 lbs.

Gender unknown

Ω When this legendary Pokémon's wings and tail feathers spread wide and glow red, it absorbs the life force of living creatures.

α When its life comes to an end, it absorbs the life energy of every living thing and turns into a cocoon once more.

ABILITY
Dark Aura

HIDDEN ABILITY
—

EGG GROUPS
No Eggs Discovered

STAT GROWTH RATES
HP
Attack
Defense
Sp. Atk
Sp. Def
Speed

ITEMS SOMETIMES HELD BY WILD POKÉMON
—

EVOLUTION
Does not evolve

MAIN WAY TO REGISTER IN THE NATIONAL POKÉDEX

Appears in *Pokémon Y*. Bring it to your game using Link Trade or the GTS.

Damage taken in normal battles

Type		Type	
Normal	×1	Flying	×1
Fire	×1	Psychic	×0
Water	×1	Bug	×1
Grass	×0.5	Rock	×2
Electric	×2	Ghost	×0.5
Ice	×2	Dragon	×1
Fighting	×1	Dark	×0.5
Poison	×1	Steel	×1
Ground	×0	Fairy	×2

Damage taken in Inverse battles

Type		Type	
Normal	×1	Flying	×1
Fire	×1	Psychic	×2
Water	×1	Bug	×1
Grass	×2	Rock	×0.5
Electric	×0.5	Ghost	×2
Ice	×0.5	Dragon	×1
Fighting	×1	Dark	×2
Poison	×1	Steel	×1
Ground	×2	Fairy	×0.5

Can be used in
Inverse Battle
Battle Institute
Battle Maison
Random Matchup (Free Battle)
Random Matchup (Others)

LEVEL-UP MOVES

Lv.	Name	Type	Kind	Pow.	Acc.	PP	Range
1	Hurricane	Flying	Special	110	70	10	Normal
1	Razor Wind	Normal	Special	80	100	10	Many Others
1	Taunt	Dark	Status	—	100	20	Normal
1	Roost	Flying	Status	—	—	10	Self
5	Double Team	Normal	Status	—	—	15	Self
10	Air Slash	Flying	Special	75	95	15	Normal
18	Snarl	Dark	Special	55	95	15	Many Others
26	Oblivion Wing	Flying	Special	80	100	10	Normal
35	Disable	Normal	Status	—	100	20	Normal
44	Dark Pulse	Dark	Special	80	100	15	Normal
51	Foul Play	Dark	Physical	95	100	15	Normal
55	Phantom Force	Ghost	Physical	90	100	10	Normal
59	Psychic	Psychic	Special	90	100	10	Normal
63	Dragon Rush	Dragon	Physical	100	75	10	Normal
72	Focus Blast	Fighting	Special	120	70	5	Normal
80	Sucker Punch	Dark	Physical	80	100	5	Normal
88	Hyper Beam	Normal	Special	150	90	5	Normal
93	Sky Attack	Flying	Physical	140	90	5	Normal

TM & HM MOVES

No.	Name	Type	Kind	Pow.	Acc.	PP	Range
TM01	Hone Claws	Dark	Status	—	—	15	Self
TM02	Dragon Claw	Dragon	Physical	80	100	15	Normal
TM06	Toxic	Poison	Status	—	90	10	Normal
TM10	Hidden Power	Normal	Special	60	100	15	Normal
TM11	Sunny Day	Fire	Status	—	—	5	Both Sides
TM12	Taunt	Dark	Status	—	100	20	Normal
TM15	Hyper Beam	Normal	Special	150	90	5	Normal
TM17	Protect	Normal	Status	—	—	10	Self
TM18	Rain Dance	Water	Status	—	—	5	Both Sides
TM19	Roost	Flying	Status	—	—	10	Self
TM21	Frustration	Normal	Physical	—	100	20	Normal
TM27	Return	Normal	Physical	—	100	20	Normal
TM29	Psychic	Psychic	Special	90	100	10	Normal
TM30	Shadow Ball	Ghost	Special	80	100	15	Normal
TM32	Double Team	Normal	Status	—	—	15	Self
TM40	Aerial Ace	Flying	Physical	60	—	20	Normal
TM41	Torment	Dark	Status	—	100	15	Normal
TM42	Facade	Normal	Physical	70	100	20	Normal
TM44	Rest	Psychic	Status	—	—	10	Self
TM46	Thief	Dark	Physical	60	100	25	Normal
TM48	Round	Normal	Special	60	100	15	Normal
TM51	Steel Wing	Steel	Physical	70	90	25	Normal
TM52	Focus Blast	Fighting	Special	120	70	5	Normal
TM58	Sky Drop	Flying	Physical	60	100	10	Normal
TM62	Acrobatics	Flying	Physical	55	100	15	Normal
TM63	Embargo	Dark	Status	—	100	15	Normal
TM65	Shadow Claw	Ghost	Physical	70	100	15	Normal
TM68	Giga Impact	Normal	Physical	150	90	5	Normal
TM80	Rock Slide	Rock	Physical	75	90	10	Many Others
TM85	Dream Eater	Psychic	Special	100	100	15	Normal
TM87	Swagger	Normal	Status	—	90	15	Normal
TM88	Sleep Talk	Normal	Status	—	—	10	Self
TM89	U-turn	Bug	Physical	70	100	20	Normal
TM90	Substitute	Normal	Status	—	—	10	Self
TM94	Secret Power	Normal	Physical	70	100	20	Normal
TM95	Snarl	Dark	Special	55	95	15	Many Others
TM97	Dark Pulse	Dark	Special	80	100	15	Normal
TM100	Confide	Normal	Status	—	—	20	Normal
HM01	Cut	Normal	Physical	50	95	30	Normal
HM02	Fly	Flying	Physical	90	95	15	Normal

MOVES LEARNED IN EXCHANGE FOR BP

Name	Type	Kind	Pow.	Acc.	PP	Range
Block	Normal	Status	—	—	5	Normal
Foul Play	Dark	Physical	95	100	15	Normal
Zen Headbutt	Psychic	Physical	80	90	15	Normal
Hyper Voice	Normal	Special	90	100	10	Many Others
Snore	Normal	Special	50	100	15	Normal
Knock Off	Dark	Physical	65	100	20	Normal
Heat Wave	Fire	Special	95	90	10	Many Others
Tailwind	Flying	Status	—	—	15	Your Side
Sky Attack	Flying	Physical	140	90	5	Normal

MOVES TAUGHT BY PEOPLE

Name	Type	Kind	Pow.	Acc.	PP	Range

National Pokédex **718** Hoenn Pokédex –

Zygarde

Order Pokémon

Dragon **Ground**

HEIGHT: 16'05" WEIGHT: 672.4 lbs.

Gender unknown

Ω When the Kalos region's ecosystem falls into disarray, it appears and reveals its secret power.

α It's hypothesized that it's monitoring those who destroy the ecosystem from deep in the cave where it lives.

ABILITY
Aura Break

HIDDEN ABILITY
—

EGG GROUPS
No Eggs Discovered

STAT GROWTH RATES
HP
Attack
Defense
Sp. Atk
Sp. Def
Speed

ITEMS SOMETIMES HELD BY WILD POKÉMON
—

EVOLUTION
Does not evolve

MAIN WAY TO REGISTER IN THE NATIONAL POKÉDEX

Appears in *Pokémon X* and *Pokémon Y*. Bring it to your game using Link Trade or the GTS.

Damage taken in normal battles

Type		Type	
Normal	×1	Flying	×1
Fire	×0.5	Psychic	×1
Water	×1	Bug	×1
Grass	×1	Rock	×0.5
Electric	×0	Ghost	×1
Ice	×4	Dragon	×2
Fighting	×1	Dark	×1
Poison	×0.5	Steel	×1
Ground	×1	Fairy	×2

Damage taken in Inverse battles

Type		Type	
Normal	×1	Flying	×1
Fire	×2	Psychic	×1
Water	×1	Bug	×1
Grass	×1	Rock	×2
Electric	×2	Ghost	×1
Ice	×0.25	Dragon	×0.5
Fighting	×1	Dark	×1
Poison	×2	Steel	×1
Ground	×1	Fairy	×0.5

Can be used in
Inverse Battle
Battle Institute
Battle Maison
Random Matchup (Free Battle)
Random Matchup (Others)

LEVEL-UP MOVES

Lv.	Name	Type	Kind	Pow.	Acc.	PP	Range
1	Glare	Normal	Status	—	100	30	Normal
1	Bulldoze	Ground	Physical	60	100	20	Adjacent
1	Dragon Breath	Dragon	Special	60	100	20	Normal
1	Bite	Dark	Physical	60	100	25	Normal
5	Safeguard	Normal	Status	—	—	25	Your Side
10	Dig	Ground	Physical	80	100	10	Normal
18	Bind	Normal	Physical	15	85	20	Normal
26	Land's Wrath	Ground	Physical	90	100	10	Many Others
35	Sandstorm	Rock	Status	—	—	10	Both Sides
44	Haze	Ice	Status	—	—	30	Both Sides
51	Crunch	Dark	Physical	80	100	15	Normal
55	Earthquake	Ground	Physical	100	100	10	Adjacent
59	Camouflage	Normal	Status	—	—	20	Self
63	Dragon Pulse	Dragon	Special	85	100	10	Normal
72	Dragon Dance	Dragon	Status	—	—	20	Self
80	Coil	Poison	Status	—	—	20	Self
88	Extreme Speed	Normal	Physical	80	100	5	Normal
93	Outrage	Dragon	Physical	120	100	10	1 Random

TM & HM MOVES

No.	Name	Type	Kind	Pow.	Acc.	PP	Range
TM06	Toxic	Poison	Status	—	90	10	Normal
TM10	Hidden Power	Normal	Special	60	100	15	Normal
TM11	Sunny Day	Fire	Status	—	—	5	Both Sides
TM15	Hyper Beam	Normal	Special	150	90	5	Normal
TM17	Protect	Normal	Status	—	—	10	Self
TM20	Safeguard	Normal	Status	—	—	25	Your Side
TM21	Frustration	Normal	Physical	—	100	20	Normal
TM26	Earthquake	Ground	Physical	100	100	10	Adjacent
TM27	Return	Normal	Physical	—	100	20	Normal
TM28	Dig	Ground	Physical	80	100	10	Normal
TM31	Brick Break	Fighting	Physical	75	100	15	Normal
TM32	Double Team	Normal	Status	—	—	15	Self
TM34	Sludge Wave	Poison	Special	95	100	10	Adjacent
TM37	Sandstorm	Rock	Status	—	—	10	Both Sides
TM42	Facade	Normal	Physical	70	100	20	Normal
TM44	Rest	Psychic	Status	—	—	10	Self
TM48	Round	Normal	Special	60	100	15	Normal
TM52	Focus Blast	Fighting	Special	120	70	5	Normal
TM68	Giga Impact	Normal	Physical	150	90	5	Normal
TM71	Stone Edge	Rock	Physical	100	80	5	Normal
TM78	Bulldoze	Ground	Physical	60	100	20	Adjacent
TM80	Rock Slide	Rock	Physical	75	90	10	Many Others
TM82	Dragon Tail	Dragon	Physical	60	90	10	Normal
TM86	Grass Knot	Grass	Special	—	100	20	Normal
TM87	Swagger	Normal	Status	—	90	15	Normal
TM88	Sleep Talk	Normal	Status	—	—	10	Self
TM90	Substitute	Normal	Status	—	—	10	Self
TM94	Secret Power	Normal	Physical	70	100	20	Normal
TM100	Confide	Normal	Status	—	—	20	Normal
HM04	Strength	Normal	Physical	80	100	15	Normal
HM06	Rock Smash	Fighting	Physical	40	100	15	Normal

MOVES LEARNED IN EXCHANGE FOR BP

Name	Type	Kind	Pow.	Acc.	PP	Range
Block	Normal	Status	—	—	5	Normal
Earth Power	Ground	Special	90	100	10	Normal
Superpower	Fighting	Physical	120	100	5	Normal
Zen Headbutt	Psychic	Physical	80	90	15	Normal
Dragon Pulse	Dragon	Special	85	100	10	Normal
Hyper Voice	Normal	Special	90	100	10	Many Others
Iron Tail	Steel	Physical	100	75	15	Normal
Bind	Normal	Physical	15	85	20	Normal
Snore	Normal	Special	50	100	15	Normal
Pain Split	Normal	Status	—	—	20	Normal
Shock Wave	Electric	Special	60	—	20	Normal
Spite	Ghost	Status	—	100	10	Normal
Outrage	Dragon	Physical	120	100	10	1 Random

MOVES TAUGHT BY PEOPLE

Name	Type	Kind	Pow.	Acc.	PP	Range
Draco Meteor	Dragon	Special	130	90	5	Normal

National Pokédex **719** Hoenn Pokédex **—**

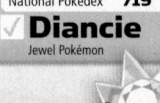

Diancie

Jewel Pokémon

Rock / Fairy

HEIGHT: 2'04" WEIGHT: 19.4 lbs.

Gender unknown

Ω A sudden transformation of Carbink, its pink, glimmering body is said to be the loveliest sight in the whole world.

α It can instantly create many diamonds by compressing the carbon in the air between its hands.

ABILITY
Clear Body

HIDDEN ABILITY
—

EGG GROUPS
No Eggs Discovered

STAT GROWTH RATES
HP ■■
Attack ■■■■■
Defense ■■■■■■
Sp. Atk ■■■■■
Sp. Def ■■■■■■
Speed ■■■

ITEMS SOMETIMES HELD BY WILD POKÉMON
—

EVOLUTION
Does not evolve

MAIN WAY TO REGISTER IN THE NATIONAL POKÉDEX

Diancie was gifted to *Pokémon X* and *Pokémon Y* players between October 27 and November 16, 2014. There may be more announcements to come regarding future opportunities to obtain it, so keep checking the official Pokémon website.

Damage taken in normal battles

Normal	×0.5	Flying	×0.5
Fire	×0.5	Psychic	×1
Water	×2	Bug	×0.5
Grass	×2	Rock	×1
Electric	×1	Ghost	×1
Ice	×1	Dragon	×0
Fighting	×1	Dark	×0.5
Poison	×1	Steel	×4
Ground	×2	Fairy	×1

Damage taken in Inverse battles

Normal	×2	Flying	×2
Fire	×2	Psychic	×1
Water	×0.5	Bug	×2
Grass	×0.5	Rock	×1
Electric	×1	Ghost	×1
Ice	×1	Dragon	×2
Fighting	×1	Dark	×2
Poison	×1	Steel	×0.25
Ground	×0.5	Fairy	×1

Can be used in
Inverse Battle
Battle Institute
Battle Maison
Random Matchup (Free Battle)
Random Matchup (Others)

LEVEL-UP MOVES

Lv.	Name	Type	Kind	Pow.	Acc.	PP	Range
1	Tackle	Normal	Physical	50	100	35	Normal
1	Harden	Normal	Status	—	—	30	Self
5	Rock Throw	Rock	Physical	50	90	15	Normal
8	Sharpen	Normal	Status	—	—	30	Self
12	Smack Down	Rock	Physical	50	100	15	Normal
18	Reflect	Psychic	Status	—	—	20	Your Side
21	Stealth Rock	Rock	Status	—	—	20	Other Side
27	Guard Split	Psychic	Status	—	—	10	Normal
31	Ancient Power	Rock	Special	60	100	5	Normal
35	Flail	Normal	Physical	—	100	15	Normal
40	Skill Swap	Psychic	Status	—	—	10	Normal
46	Trick Room	Psychic	Status	—	—	5	Both Sides
49	Stone Edge	Rock	Physical	100	80	5	Normal
50	Moonblast	Fairy	Special	95	100	15	Normal
50	Diamond Storm	Rock	Physical	100	95	5	Many Others
60	Light Screen	Psychic	Status	—	—	30	Your Side
70	Safeguard	Normal	Status	—	—	25	Your Side

TM & HM MOVES

No.	Name	Type	Kind	Pow.	Acc.	PP	Range
TM03	Psyshock	Psychic	Special	80	100	10	Normal
TM04	Calm Mind	Psychic	Status	—	—	20	Self
TM06	Toxic	Poison	Status	—	90	10	Normal
TM07	Hail	Ice	Status	—	—	10	Both Sides
TM10	Hidden Power	Normal	Special	60	100	15	Normal
TM11	Sunny Day	Fire	Status	—	—	5	Both Sides
TM15	Hyper Beam	Normal	Special	150	90	5	Normal
TM16	Light Screen	Psychic	Status	—	—	30	Your Side
TM17	Protect	Normal	Status	—	—	10	Self
TM20	Safeguard	Normal	Status	—	—	25	Your Side
TM21	Frustration	Normal	Physical	—	100	20	Normal
TM23	Smack Down	Rock	Physical	50	100	15	Normal
TM27	Return	Normal	Physical	—	100	20	Normal
TM29	Psychic	Psychic	Special	90	100	10	Normal
TM32	Double Team	Normal	Status	—	—	15	Self
TM33	Reflect	Psychic	Status	—	—	20	Your Side
TM37	Sandstorm	Rock	Status	—	—	10	Both Sides
TM39	Rock Tomb	Rock	Physical	60	95	15	Normal
TM42	Facade	Normal	Physical	70	100	20	Normal
TM44	Rest	Psychic	Status	—	—	10	Self
TM48	Round	Normal	Special	60	100	15	Normal
TM64	Explosion	Normal	Physical	250	100	5	Adjacent
TM68	Giga Impact	Normal	Physical	150	90	5	Normal
TM69	Rock Polish	Rock	Status	—	—	20	Self
TM70	Flash	Normal	Status	—	100	20	Normal
TM71	Stone Edge	Rock	Physical	100	80	5	Normal
TM74	Gyro Ball	Steel	Physical	—	100	5	Normal
TM77	Psych Up	Normal	Status	—	—	10	Normal
TM80	Rock Slide	Rock	Physical	75	90	10	Many Others
TM87	Swagger	Normal	Status	—	90	15	Normal
TM88	Sleep Talk	Normal	Status	—	—	10	Self
TM90	Substitute	Normal	Status	—	—	10	Self
TM92	Trick Room	Psychic	Status	—	—	5	Both Sides
TM94	Secret Power	Normal	Physical	70	100	20	Normal
TM96	Nature Power	Normal	Status	—	—	20	Normal
TM99	Dazzling Gleam	Fairy	Special	80	100	10	Many Others
TM100	Confide	Normal	Status	—	—	20	Normal

MOVES LEARNED IN EXCHANGE FOR BP

Name	Type	Kind	Pow.	Acc.	PP	Range
Covet	Normal	Physical	60	100	25	Normal
Earth Power	Ground	Special	90	100	10	Normal
Gravity	Psychic	Status	—	—	5	Both Sides
Magnet Rise	Electric	Status	—	—	10	Self
Iron Defense	Steel	Status	—	—	15	Self
Last Resort	Normal	Physical	140	100	5	Normal
Snore	Normal	Special	50	100	15	Normal
Heal Bell	Normal	Status	—	—	5	Your Party
After You	Normal	Status	—	—	15	Normal
Helping Hand	Normal	Status	—	—	20	1 Ally
Wonder Room	Psychic	Status	—	—	10	Both Sides
Endeavor	Normal	Physical	—	100	5	Normal
Stealth Rock	Rock	Status	—	—	20	Other Side
Skill Swap	Psychic	Status	—	—	10	Normal

MOVES TAUGHT BY PEOPLE

Name	Type	Kind	Pow.	Acc.	PP	Range

Mega Evolution

Mega Diancie

Jewel Pokémon

Rock / Fairy

HEIGHT: 3'07" WEIGHT: 61.3 lbs.

Gender unknown

REQUIRED MEGA STONE
Diancite

Bring a Diancie that you obtained through a past distribution to *Pokémon Omega Ruby* or *Pokémon Alpha Sapphire*, and enter a Pokémon Center with it in your party.

ABILITY
Magic Bounce

HIDDEN ABILITY
—

EGG GROUPS
—

STAT GROWTH RATES
HP ■■
Attack ■■■■■■■■
Defense ■■■■■
Sp. Atk ■■■■■■■■
Sp. Def ■■■■■
Speed ■■■■■■

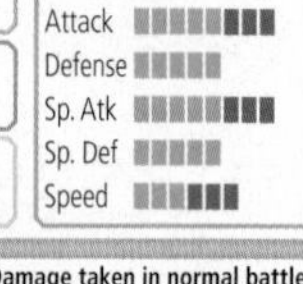

Damage taken in normal battles

Type	Damage	Type	Damage
Normal	×0.5	Flying	×0.5
Fire	×0.5	Psychic	×1
Water	×2	Bug	×0.5
Grass	×2	Rock	×1
Electric	×1	Ghost	×1
Ice	×1	Dragon	×0
Fighting	×1	Dark	×0.5
Poison	×1	Steel	×4
Ground	×2	Fairy	×1

Damage taken in Inverse battles

Type	Damage	Type	Damage
Normal	×2	Flying	×2
Fire	×2	Psychic	×1
Water	×0.5	Bug	×2
Grass	×0.5	Rock	×1
Electric	×1	Ghost	×1
Ice	×1	Dragon	×2
Fighting	×1	Dark	×2
Poison	×1	Steel	×0.25
Ground	×0.5	Fairy	×1

Can be used in
Inverse Battle
Battle Institute
Battle Maison
Random Matchup (Free Battle)
Random Matchup (Others)

Learn All There Is to Know about Pokémon That Change Form

Among Pokémon, there are some specimens that exist in different forms or can change forms even within a species. Read on to learn about these Pokémon as they appear in the National Pokédex!

National Pokédex 025
Pikachu

When Cosplay Pikachu dresses up, it learns special moves!

This special Pikachu, which you can receive after taking part in a Contest Spectacular, likes to cosplay, of all things! You can help it change costumes by talking to the Pokémon Breeder standing near the wardrobe in the green room or by examining the wardrobe yourself. When Cosplay Pikachu changes its costume, it learns a different move.

Pikachu's costumes

Pikachu Rock Star
Electric
Move learned:
● Meteor Mash

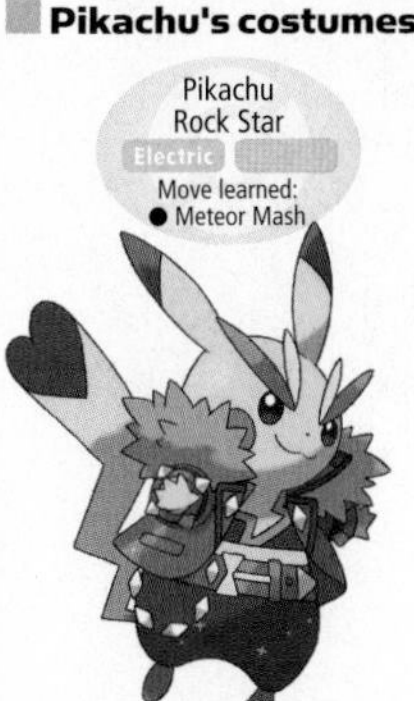

Pikachu Belle
Electric
Move learned:
● Icicle Crash

Pikachu Pop Star
Electric
Move learned:
● Draining Kiss

Pikachu, Ph.D.
Electric
Move learned:
● Electric Terrain

Pikachu Libre
Electric
Move learned:
● Flying Press

About Cosplay Pikachu

1. Have Cosplay Pikachu change in the green room in any Pokémon Contest Spectacular Hall around the Hoenn region.
2. Cosplay Pikachu has a black heart pattern at the edge of its tail.
3. When Cosplay Pikachu changes costumes, its appearance changes and it learns a move suited to its new look.
4. Cosplay Pikachu can be used in contests and also in battles.
5. You can use Pokémon-Amie to bond with it or Super Training to train it up.
6. Cosplay Pikachu cannot evolve into Raichu, even if you try to use a Thunder Stone on it.
7. An Egg cannot be found, even if you leave it at a Pokémon Day Care.

National Pokédex 201
Unown

A Pokémon with 28 alphabet-like forms

Unown is a Pokémon that possesses 28 different forms which bear a resemblance to the alphabet's letters and symbols. Unown appear in Mirage Cave 4, one of the Mirage spots you can reach when you Soar on Mega Latios or Mega Latias. Consider using tools like Repeat Balls to try to catch all of their forms!

Unown
Psychic

Unown's different forms

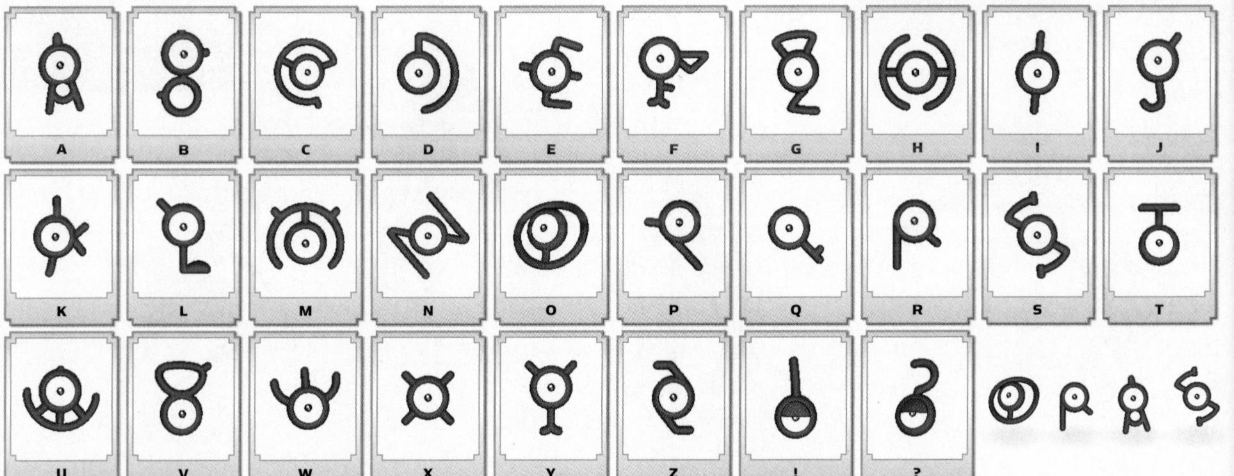

National Pokédex 327
Spinda

The pattern on their faces differ

The pattern on each Spinda's face differs slightly. It is said that no two Spinda exist that are completely identical. Spinda appear in the wild on Route 113. Use Repeat Balls or other tools to catch several and observe the differences in their markings for yourself!

Spinda's different appearances

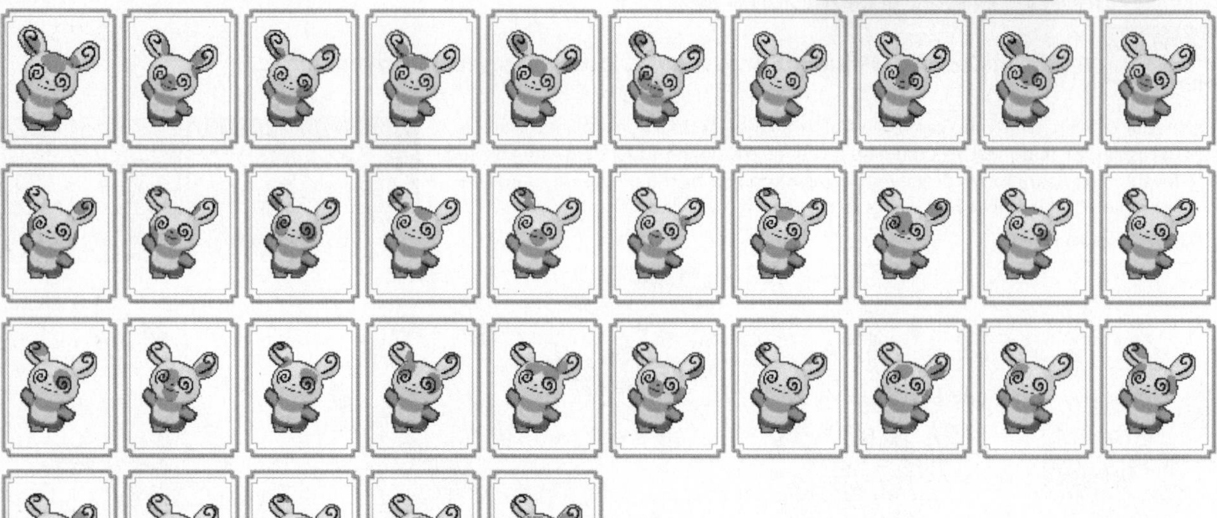

National Pokédex 351
Castform

Its appearance and type change based on the weather

Castform can changes its appearance and type based on the weather in battle. It can also learn moves that can change the weather, so try to use that in battle! You can receive one at the Weather Institute on Route 119.

Castform's different forms

National Pokédex 386
Deoxys

It changes Formes with the meteorite

Deoxys can change between its Normal, Attack, Defense, and Speed Forme. To make it change, have Deoxys in your party and examine the meteorite in Professor Cozmo's lab in Fallarbor Town. Each time that you examine the meteorite, Deoxys will change Forme.

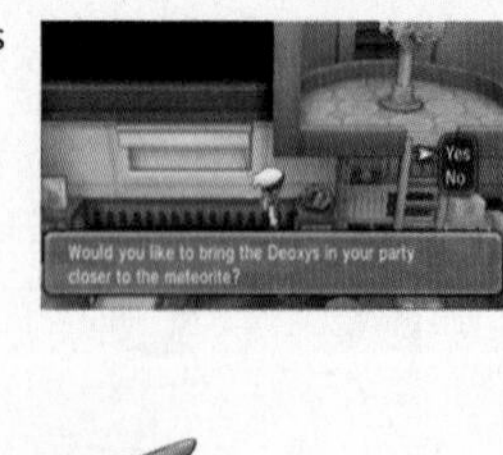

Deoxys's Forme changes

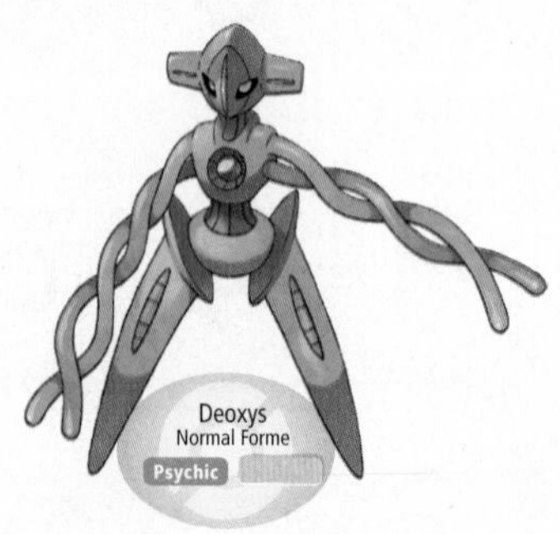

National Pokédex 412
Burmy

It changes appearance after battle based on the location

Burmy changes its form after the battle based on where the battle took place. When you battle in tall grass, it will don its Plant Cloak form; in a cave or desert, it will don its Sandy Cloak form; and when you battle in a building, it will don its Trash Cloak form. Burmy appears in *Pokémon X* and *Pokémon Y*. Use the PSS to bring it to *Pokémon Omega Ruby* and *Pokémon Alpha Sapphire*.

Burmy's different forms

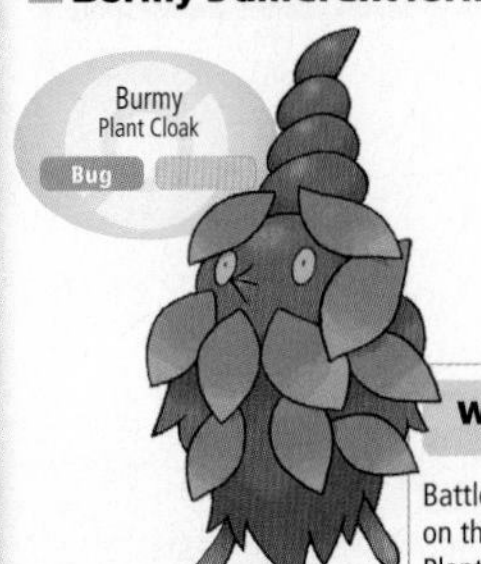

Where to change form

Battle in the tall grass, in forests, or on the water surface, and it dons its Plant Cloak form.

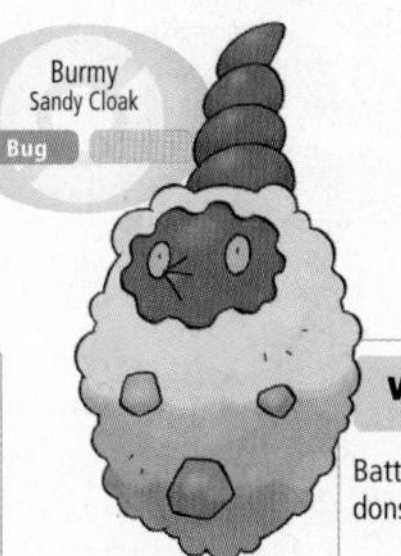

Where to change form

Battle in a cave or a desert, and it dons its Sandy Cloak form.

Where to change form

Battle in a building, and it dons its Trash Cloak form.

National Pokédex 421
Cherrim

It changes its form if the weather is sunny

Cherrim will change from its Overcast Form to its Sunshine Form when the weather is sunny or extremely harsh sunlight during battle. This does not change its type or its stats. It appears in Mirage Forest 4.

Cherrim's form change

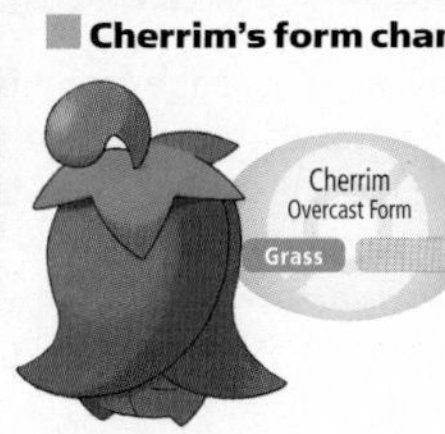

National Pokédex 422
Shellos

Form differs based on the game

Shellos appear on Routes 103 and 110, and exist in two forms with different colors and body types. The West Sea form appears in *Pokémon Omega Ruby*, and the East Sea form appears in *Pokémon Alpha Sapphire*.

Shellos's different forms

National Pokédex 479
Rotom

Check out the boxes in the Pokémon Lab to change forms

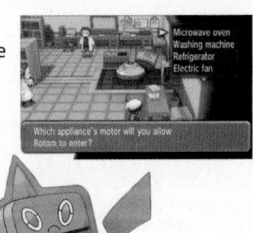

Rotom has a total of six different forms. Have Rotom in your party and check out the cardboard boxes in Littleroot Town's Pokémon Lab to have it change forms and learn different moves. If you check the microwave oven, it will transform into Heat Rotom; the washing machine, to Wash Rotom; the refrigerator, to Frost Rotom; the electric fan, to Fan Rotom; and the lawnmower, to Mow Rotom. Rotom appears in *Pokémon X* and *Pokémon Y*. Use the PSS to bring it to *Pokémon Omega Ruby* and *Pokémon Alpha* Sapphire.

Rotom's form changes

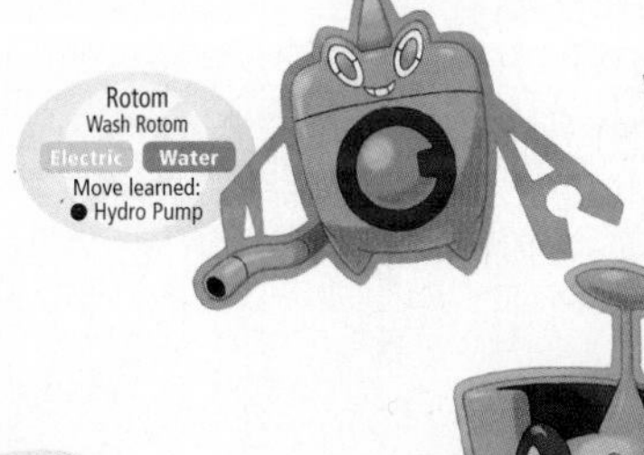

Rotom
Fan Rotom
Electric Flying
Move learned:
● Air Slash

Rotom
Mow Rotom
Electric Grass
Move learned:
● Leaf Storm

National Pokédex 487
Giratina

Give it the Griseous Orb to change it to Origin Forme

Giratina is normally in its Altered Forme, but have it hold a Griseous Orb and it will change to its Origin Forme. When it changes, it doesn't change types but its Ability changes from Pressure to Levitate and its stats change a great deal. The Griseous Orb can be discovered in the underwater trench beneath Route 130.

Orlando found a Griseous Orb!

Giratina's Forme change

Griseous Orb

Find it at the bottom of the sea beneath Route 130.

National Pokédex 492
Shaymin

Use the Gracidea flower to change it to its Sky Forme

If Shaymin uses the Gracidea flower, it will change from its Land Forme to its Sky Forme. When it changes Formes, its type changes from Grass type to Grass and Flying type, its Ability changes from Natural Cure to Serene Grace, and its stats change a lot.

Orlando obtained the Gracidea!

Ways to return Shaymin to the Land Forme

- Deposit it in the PC
- Wait until night or late at night in the game
- Let it be Frozen
- Drop it off at a Pokémon Day Care
- Link Trade it
- Deposit it in the GTS

Gracidea

Have Shaymin in your party and visit the Berry Master's house on Route 123. Talk to the younger man inside.

Shaymin's Forme change

How to obtain: Previously obtainable through a special distribution. There may be more announcements to come regarding future opportunities to obtain it, so keep checking the Pokémon official website, www.pokemon.com.

National Pokédex 493
Arceus

Give it a plate to change its type

Arceus shifts between types freely. Its default type is Normal type, but there are 17 plates you can have it hold to change to the type linked to that plate. Since *Pokémon X* and *Pokémon Y*, it has become able to Type Shift to the Fairy type by holding the Pixie Plate.

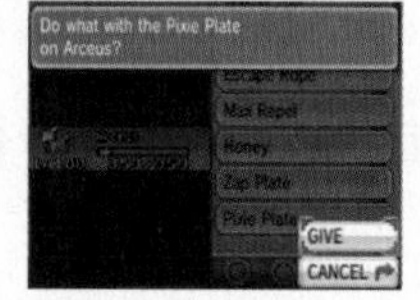

Do what with the Pixie Plate on Arceus?
GIVE
CANCEL

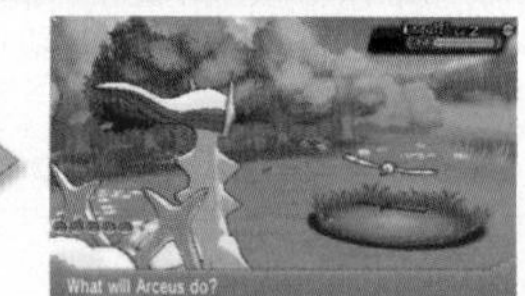

What will Arceus do?

Arceus's types

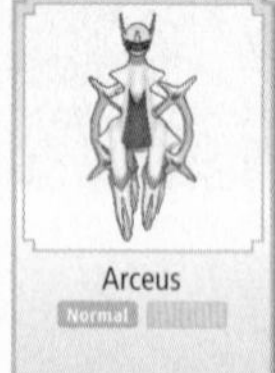

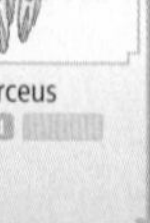

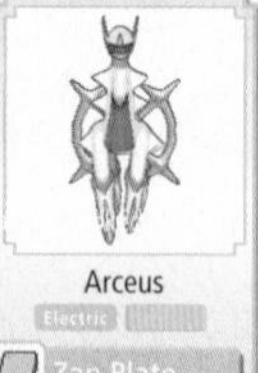

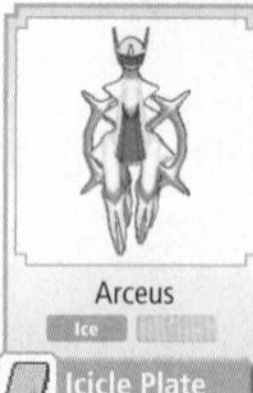

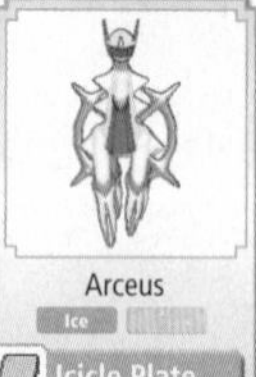

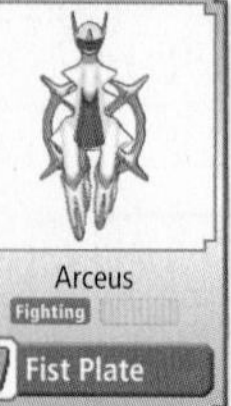

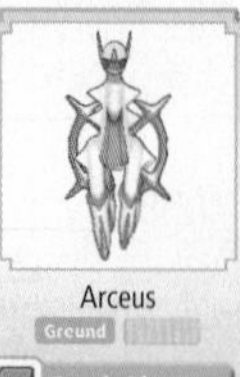

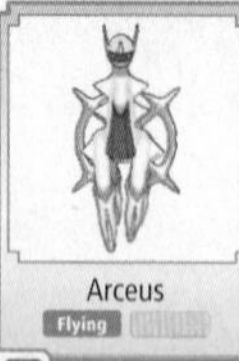

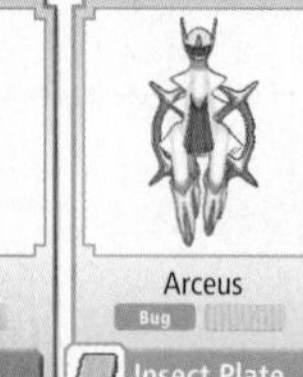

How to obtain: Previously obtainable through a special distribution. There may be more announcements to come regarding future opportunities to obtain it, so keep checking the Pokémon official website, www.pokemon.com.

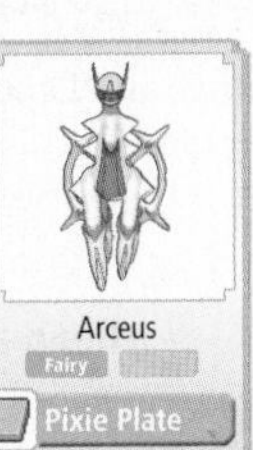

Learn where to get Arceus's plates to Type Shift

Most plates can be found in the underwater trenches that lie beneath Routes 107, 124, and 126–130. Be sure to investigate the deep sea thoroughly! The Iron Plate is held by the Beldum that you can receive at Steven's house after clearing the Delta Episode.

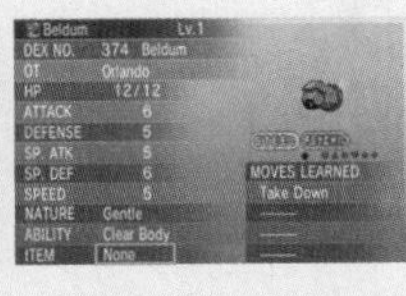
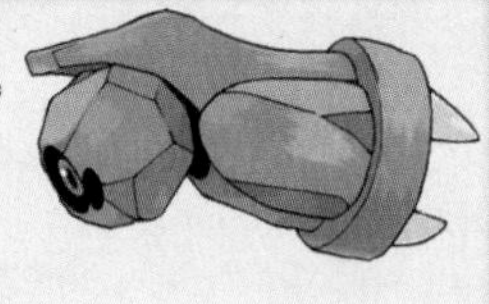

National Pokédex 550
Basculin

Its Abilities, stripes, and fins are different

Basculin can appear in a Red- or Blue-Striped Form. They have different coloration and fin shapes and appear in *Pokémon X* and *Pokémon Y*. Use the PSS to bring them to *Pokémon Omega Ruby* and *Pokémon Alpha Sapphire*.

Basculin's different forms

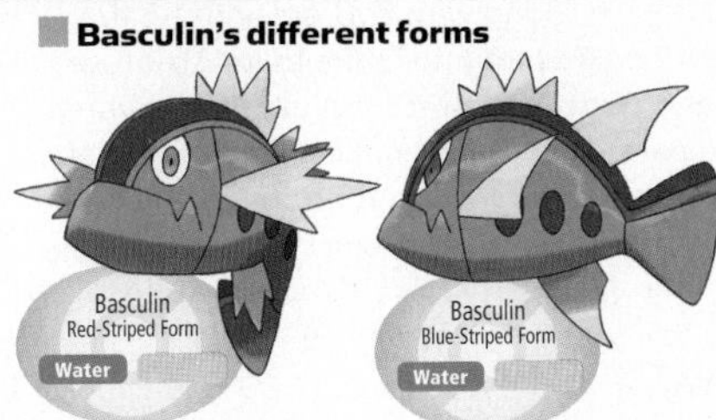

National Pokédex 555
Darmanitan

It changes form when its HP drops below half

A Darmanitan with the Zen Mode Hidden Ability can change to Zen Mode in battle if its HP drops to half or less of its maximum value. When it switches to Zen Mode, its type changes to Fire and Psychic, and its stats change dramatically. This change only happens during battle, and when the battle ends, it returns to its standard form. It appears on Mirage Island 1 and 7 and on Mirage Mountain 5.

Darmanitan's different forms

National Pokédex 585
Deerling

Deerling appears in Spring Form

Deerling is a Pokémon that changes form based on the season. In *Pokémon Omega Ruby* and *Pokémon Alpha Sapphire*, it will only appear in Spring Form. The form will stay the same even after it evolves into Sawsbuck.

Deerling in *Pokémon Omega Ruby* and *Pokémon Alpha Sapphire*

1. Can be found on Route 117 (Spring Form only).
2. Bring it from *Pokémon Black, Pokémon White, Pokémon Black 2*, or *Pokémon White 2*, and it will stay in that form.
3. Leave a female Deerling or Sawsbuck at the Pokémon Day Care and the Pokémon Eggs found will inherit its form.

National Pokédex 641 **Tornadus** | National Pokédex 642 **Thundurus** | National Pokédex 645 **Landorus**

They change Formes with the Reveal Glass

Using the Reveal Glass on Tornadus, Thundurus, and Landorus will change them from their Incarnate Formes to their Therian Formes. When they change, their Abilities change, as do their stats.

Reveal Glass

Have either Tornadus, Thundurus, or Landorus in your party and talk to the woman at the Narcissus Mirror Shop in Mauville City to obtain it.

Tornadus's Forme change

Thundurus's Forme change

Landorus's Forme change

National Pokédex 646 **Kyurem**

It changes form when it Absofuses with Reshiram or Zekrom

Have Reshiram or Zekrom in your party along with Kyurem and use the DNA Splicers. Select Kyurem and then Reshiram to make them Absofuse into White Kyurem or Kyurem and Zekrom to Absofuse into Black Kyurem. Use the DNA Splicers again to separate Kyurem from Reshiram or Zekrom, but make sure you have enough space in your team for both of them.

DNA Splicers

Can be found with the Dowsing Machine in the Gnarled Den Mirage spot.

Kyurem and Zekrom's Absofusion

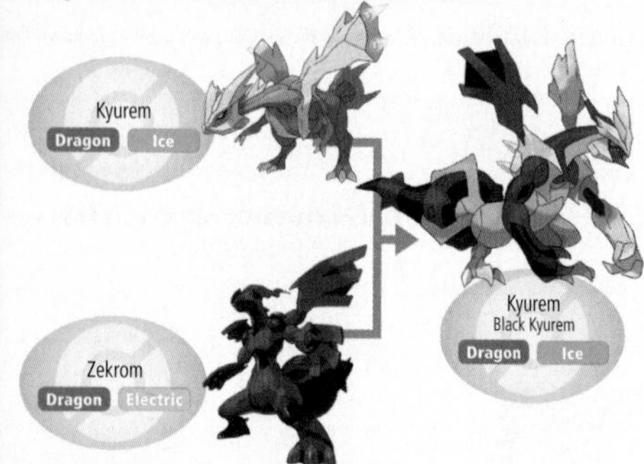

Kyurem and Reshiram's Absofusion

National Pokédex 647 **Keldeo**

Learn the move Secret Sword to change form

Keldeo can change between its Ordinary and Resolute Forms. Have Keldeo in your party when you talk to the old man in Mauville City's Crooner's Café and he will teach it Secret Sword, transforming Keldeo into its Resolute Form. If it forgets Secret Sword, it will return to its Ordinary Form.

How to obtain: Previously obtainable through a special distribution. There may be more announcements to come regarding future opportunities to obtain it, so keep checking the Pokémon official website, www.pokemon.com.

Keldeo's form change

National Pokédex 648
Meloetta

The Relic Song move changes its Forme

Meloetta can change from Aria to Pirouette Forme. Have Meloetta in your party when you talk to the old man in Mauville City's Crooner's Café and he will teach it Relic Song. If Meloetta uses Relic Song in battle, it will change Forme. After the battle ends, it will return to normal.

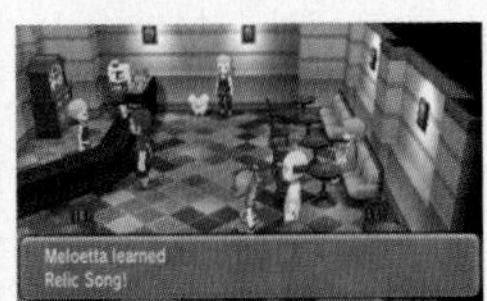

How to obtain: Previously obtainable through a special distribution. There may be more announcements to come regarding future opportunities to obtain it, so keep checking the Pokémon official website, www.pokemon.com.

Meloetta's Forme change

National Pokédex 649
Genesect

Give it a drive for some extra color

Genesect can hold four different drives, which will change the color of part of its body. But that's not all: the type of drive it holds will also change its Techno Blast move to Water, Electric, Ice, or Fire type. You can obtain these drives by having Genesect in your party and talking to the man hanging out in one of the Mauville City stairwells that leads up to the roof.

How to obtain: Previously obtainable through a special distribution. There may be more announcements to come regarding future opportunities to obtain it, so keep checking the Pokémon official website, www.pokemon.com.

Genesect's different forms

Genesect
Douse Drive

National Pokédex 666
Vivillon

Their wing patterns and colors vary by area

Vivillon appears in *Pokémon X* and *Pokémon Y*, and its coloration varies based on where a player lives. If you leave Vivillon at a Pokémon Day Care and find a Pokémon Egg, any Vivillon that hatches from that Egg will have the pattern native to your region. Use the PSS to bring Vivillon to *Pokémon Omega Ruby* and *Pokémon Alpha Sapphire* and communicate with other players from around the world to try to collect them all.

Vivillon
Bug
Flying

Vivillon's different colors and patterns

Areas where Icy Snow Pattern Vivillon appear

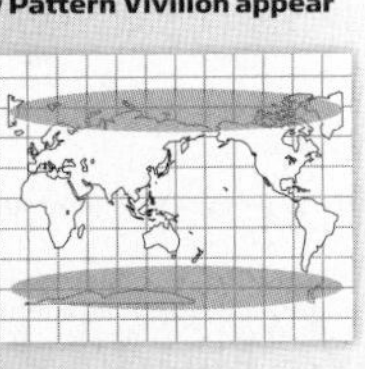

Areas where Tundra Pattern Vivillon appear

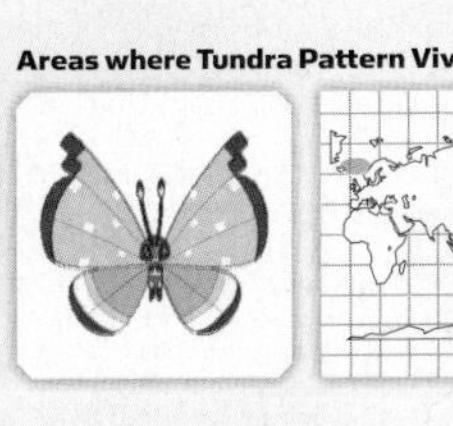

Areas where Polar Pattern Vivillon appear

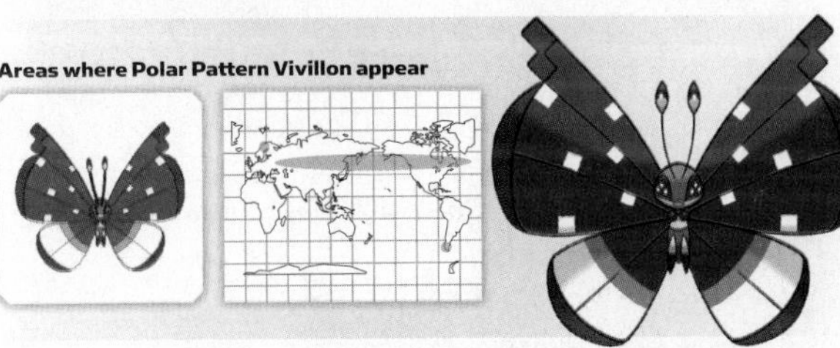

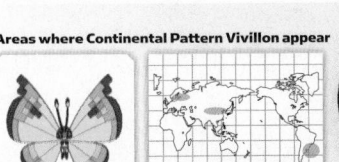

Areas where Continental Pattern Vivillon appear

National Pokédex 666

Vivillon

Areas where Garden Pattern Vivillon appear

Areas where Sandstorm Pattern Vivillon appear

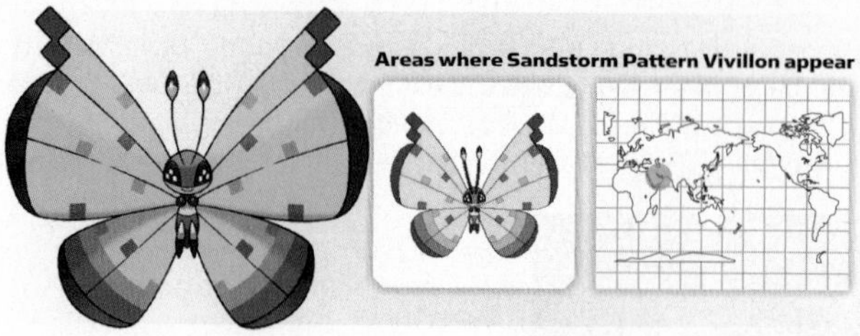

Areas where Elegant Pattern Vivillon appear

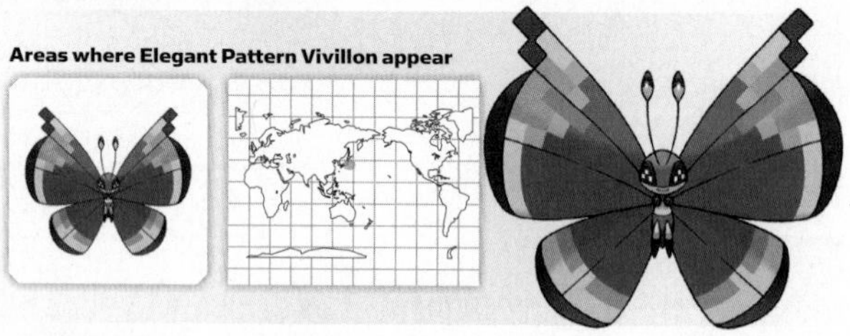

Areas where River Pattern Vivillon appear

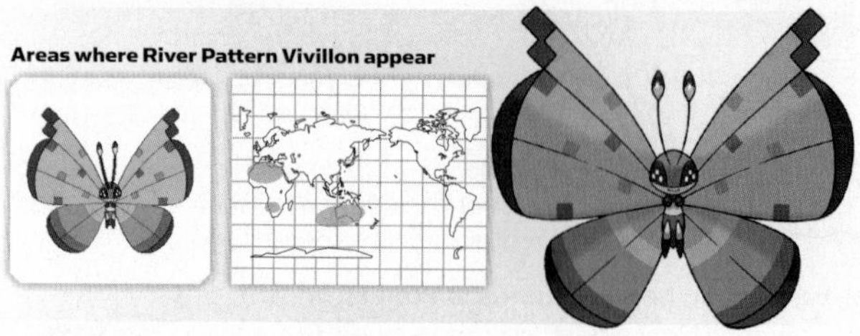

Areas where Meadow Pattern Vivillon appear

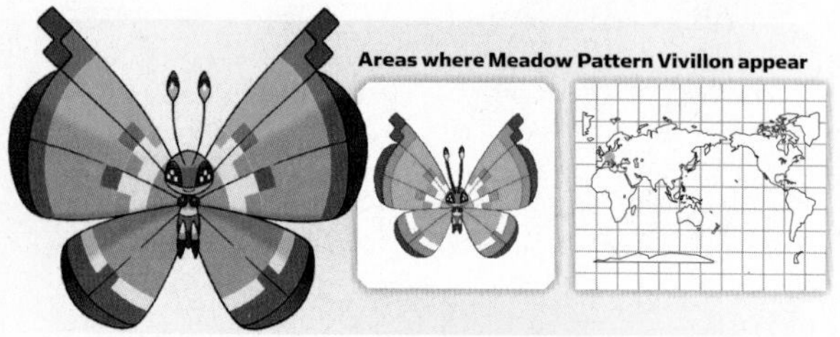

Areas where Monsoon Pattern Vivillon appear

Areas where Modern Pattern Vivillon appear

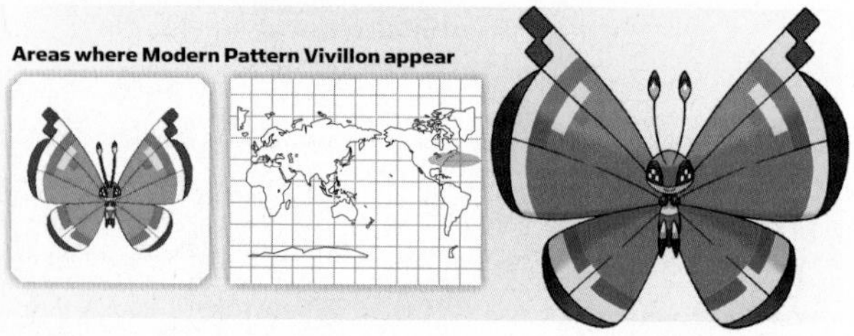

Areas where Savanna Pattern Vivillon appear

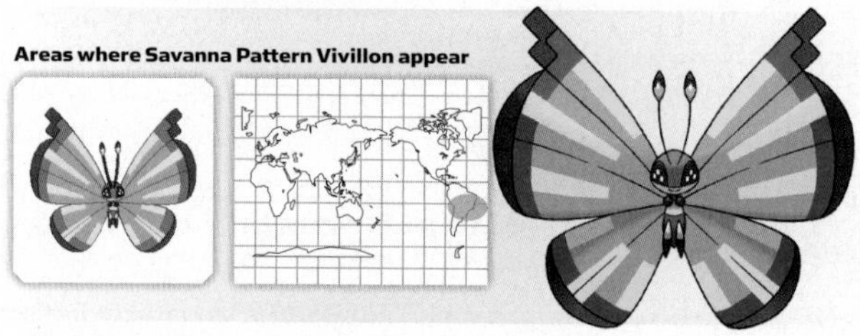

Areas where Marine Pattern Vivillon appear

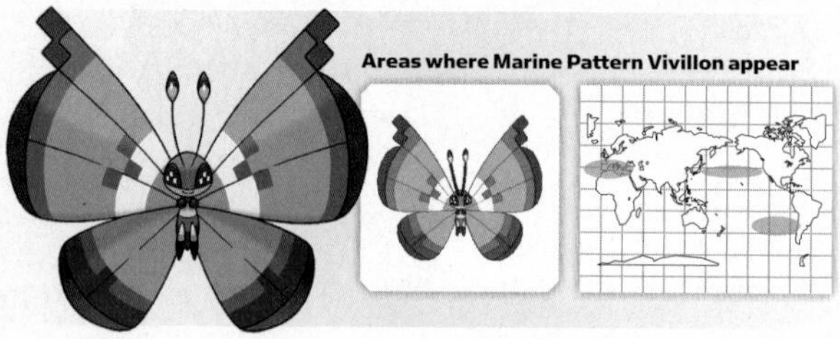

Areas where Sun Pattern Vivillon appear

Areas where Archipelago Pattern Vivillon appear

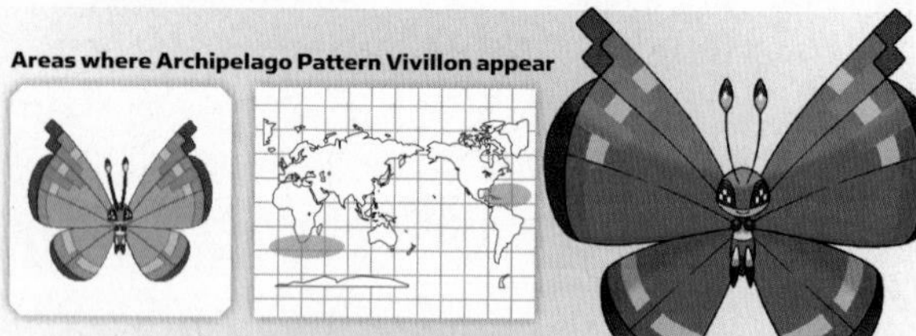

Areas where Ocean Pattern Vivillon appear

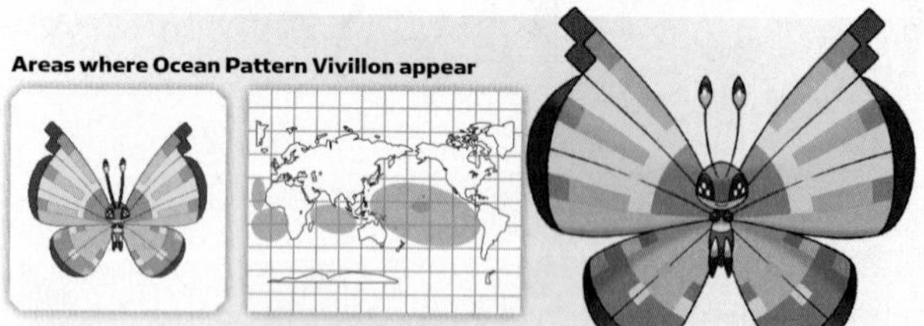

Areas where High Plains Pattern Vivillon appear

Areas where Jungle Pattern Vivillon appear

National Pokédex 666
Vivillon

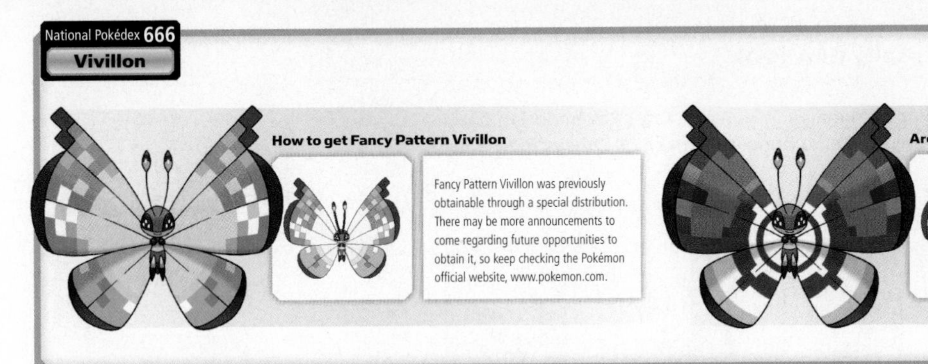

How to get Fancy Pattern Vivillon

Fancy Pattern Vivillon was previously obtainable through a special distribution. There may be more announcements to come regarding future opportunities to obtain it, so keep checking the Pokémon official website, www.pokemon.com.

Areas where Poké Ball Pattern Vivillon appear

Poké Ball Pattern Vivillon was previously obtainable through a special distribution. There may be more announcements to come regarding future opportunities to obtain it, so keep checking the Pokémon official website, www.pokemon.com.

National Pokédex 669 **Flabébé** | National Pokédex 670 **Floette** | National Pokédex 671 **Florges**

Different varieties have different colored flowers

Flabébé appears in *Pokémon X* and *Pokémon Y* and can be found holding one of five different flowers. It has a peculiar biology in which its habitat determines the color of flower it chooses. When Flabébé evolves into Floette and Florges, the color of its flower will remain the same. Use the PSS to bring them to *Pokémon Omega Ruby* and *Pokémon Alpha Sapphire*.

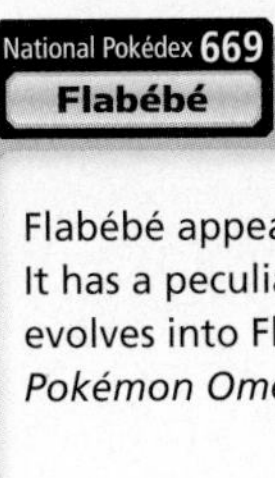

Flabébé
Fairy

Floette
Fairy

Florges
Fairy

Flabébé's different flower colors

Flabébé
Red Flower

Flabébé
Yellow Flower

Flabébé
Orange Flower

Flabébé
Blue Flower

Flabébé
White Flower

Floette's different flower colors

Floette
Red Flower

Floette
Yellow Flower

Floette
Orange Flower

Floette
Blue Flower

Floette
White Flower

Florges' different flower colors

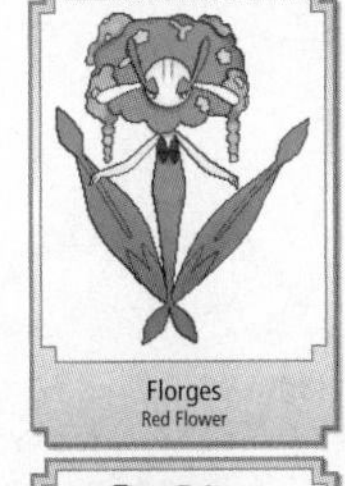

Florges
Red Flower

Florges
Yellow Flower

Florges
Orange Flower

Florges
Blue Flower

Florges
White Flower

National Pokédex 676
Furfrou

Get a trim for a totally new look

If you put Furfrou in your party and talk to the woman in Slateport City's Pokémon Fan Club, she can groom it into a different form. Use the PSS to bring it to *Pokémon Omega Ruby* and *Pokémon Alpha Sapphire*.

Furfrou's different forms

National Pokédex 681
Aegislash

Using a move in battle changes its Forme

Aegislash can change from its Shield Forme to its Blade Forme. When it changes, it gains a different appearance and different stats. Using a physical or special move to attack an opponent during battle will change Aegislash into its Blade Forme. Using the King's Shield move in battle or swapping it out of battle will return it to its Shield Forme.

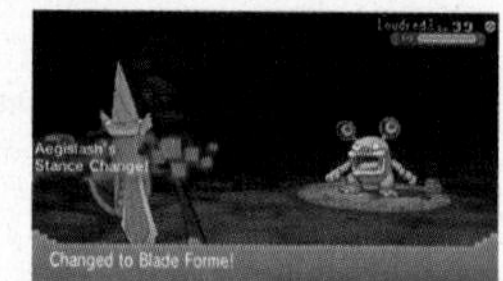

Aegislash's Forme change

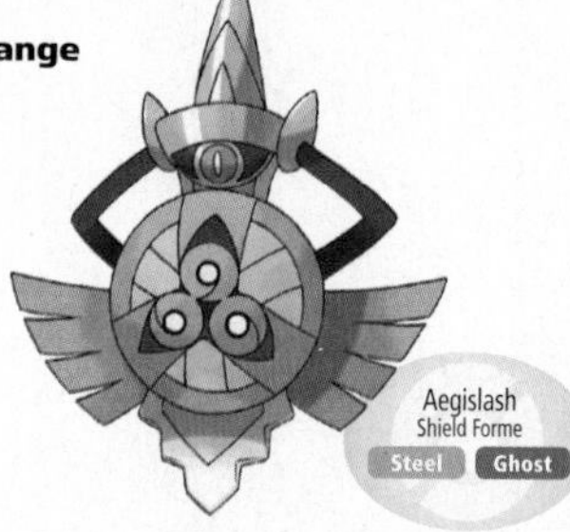

National Pokédex 710 **Pumpkaboo** National Pokédex 711 **Gourgeist**

Their size and stats vary

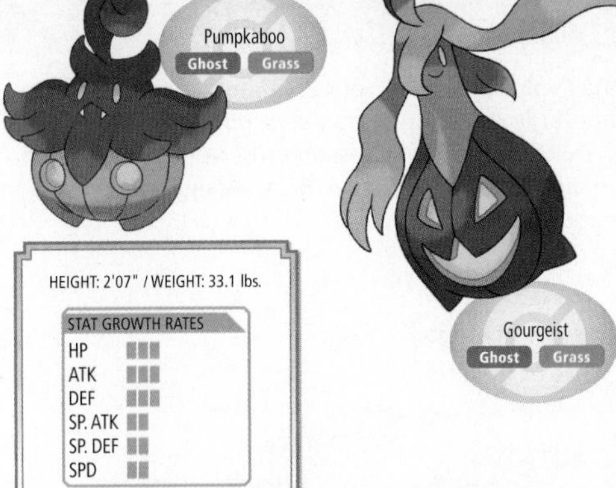

Pumpkaboo can come in four different sizes. The size of its body will have a great effect on its stats. When Pumpkaboo evolves into Gourgeist, its body size will be inherited. Use the PSS to bring Pumpkaboo from *Pokémon X* and *Pokémon Y* to *Pokémon Omega Ruby* and *Pokémon Alpha Sapphire*.

Pumpkaboo's differing sizes and stat growth rates

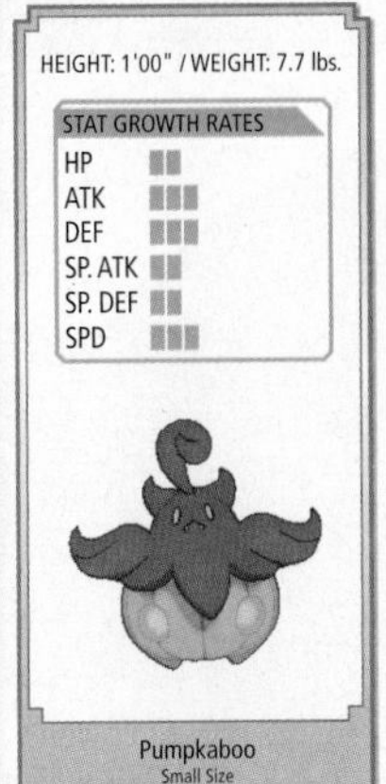

HEIGHT: 1'00" / WEIGHT: 7.7 lbs.
STAT GROWTH RATES
HP
ATK
DEF
SP. ATK
SP. DEF
SPD

Pumpkaboo
Small Size

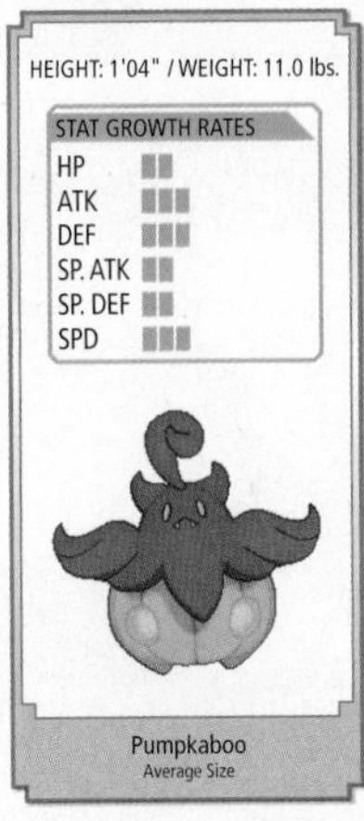

HEIGHT: 1'04" / WEIGHT: 11.0 lbs.
STAT GROWTH RATES
HP
ATK
DEF
SP. ATK
SP. DEF
SPD

Pumpkaboo
Average Size

HEIGHT: 1'08" / WEIGHT: 16.5 lbs.
STAT GROWTH RATES
HP
ATK
DEF
SP. ATK
SP. DEF
SPD

Pumpkaboo
Large Size

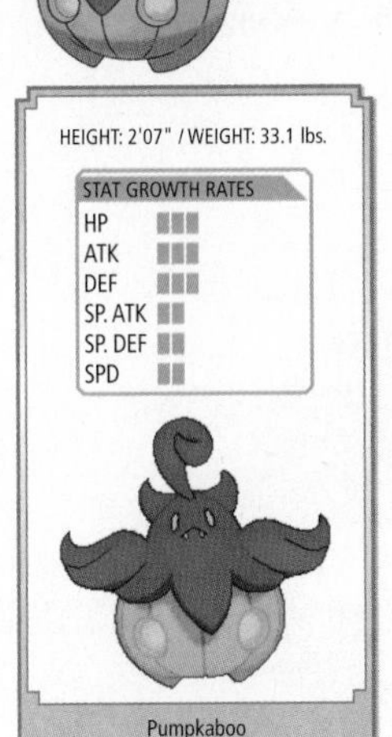

HEIGHT: 2'07" / WEIGHT: 33.1 lbs.
STAT GROWTH RATES
HP
ATK
DEF
SP. ATK
SP. DEF
SPD

Pumpkaboo
Super Size

Gourgeist's differing sizes and stat growth rates

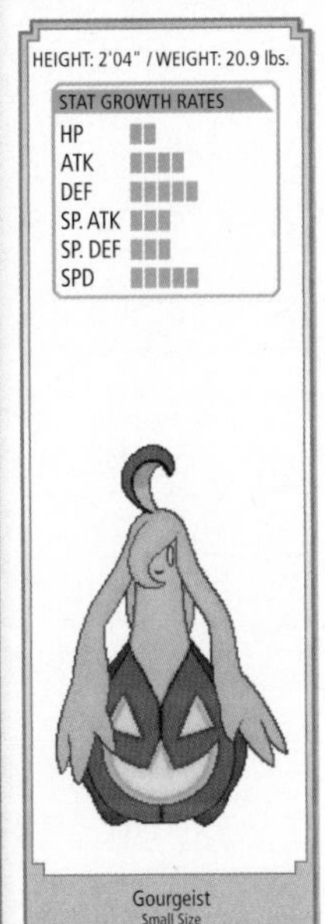

HEIGHT: 2'04" / WEIGHT: 20.9 lbs.
STAT GROWTH RATES
HP
ATK
DEF
SP. ATK
SP. DEF
SPD

Gourgeist
Small Size

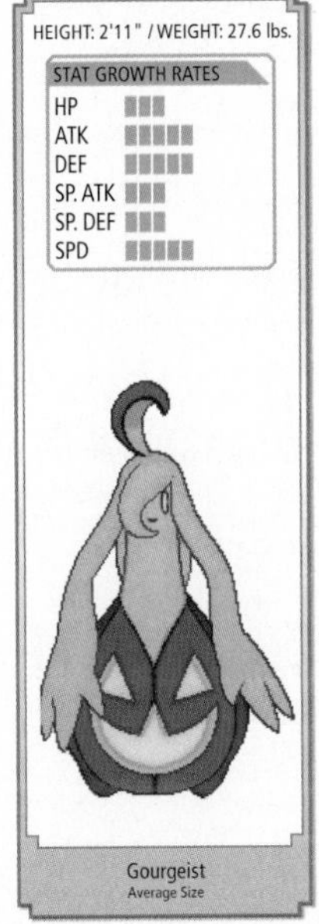

Gourgeist
Average Size

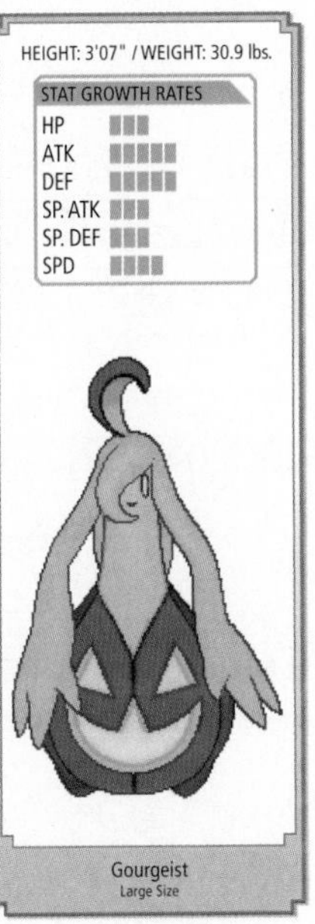

Gourgeist
Large Size

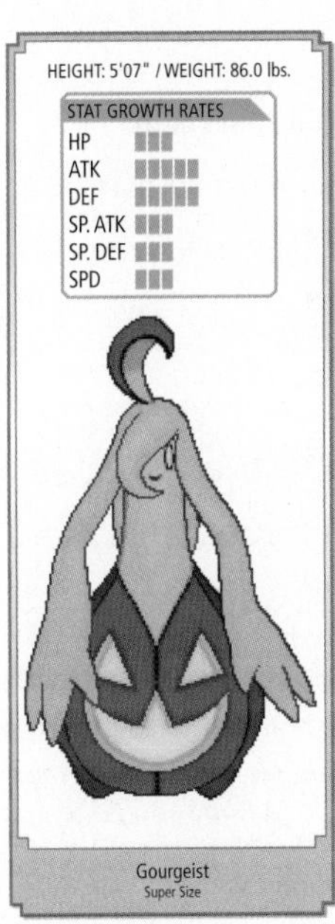

Gourgeist
Super Size

Have Your Pokémon Mega Evolve!

Mega Evolution allows your Pokémon to further evolve during battle, temporarily releasing the powers within them. Pokémon Trainers must hold a Key Stone, and their Pokémon must hold a Mega Stone. There is also Primal Reversion, a transformation in the Hoenn region that only Groudon and Kyogre can trigger.

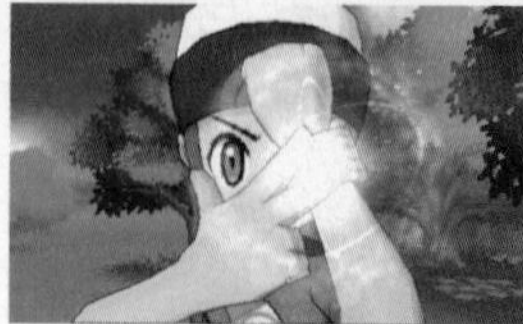

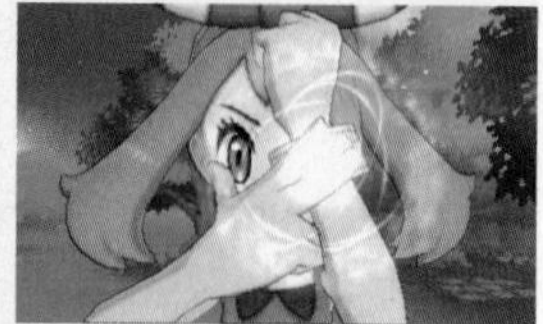

Example of Mega Evolution

Salamence

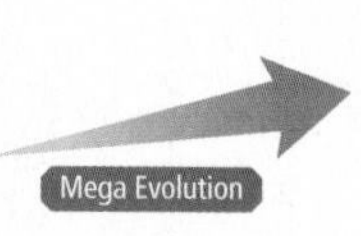

Mega Salamence

Major features of Mega-Evolved Pokémon

1. When a Pokémon Mega Evolves, there may be changes in its Ability, types, or stats.
2. You can only Mega Evolve one Pokémon on your team during each battle.
3. When the battle ends, your Pokémon will return to its normal state.

Triggering Primal Reversion

1. Have Groudon hold the Red Orb or have Kyogre hold the Blue Orb, and send it into battle. That is all that's necessary to trigger Primal Reversion.

National Pokédex **719**
Diancie

Bring Diancie to your game and have it Mega Evolve into Mega Diancie

Diancie was distributed for *Pokémon X* and *Pokémon Y*. Bring Diancie to *Pokémon Omega Ruby* and *Pokémon Alpha Sapphire* and have it Mega Evolve by putting Diancie in your party and taking it to a Pokémon Center. A boy there will give you a Diancite.

How to obtain: Previously obtainable through a special distribution. There may be more announcements to come regarding future opportunities to obtain it, so keep checking the Pokémon official website, www.pokemon.com.

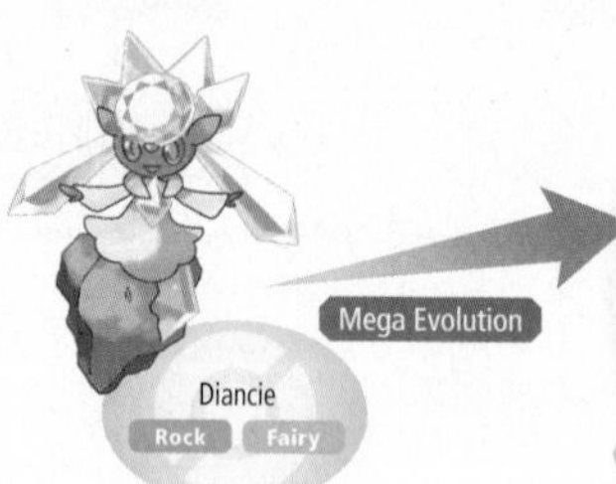

Mega-Evolved Pokémon
Mega Diancie
Type: Rock, Fairy
● HEIGHT: 3'07" ● WEIGHT: 61.3 lbs.
● Gender unknown

Mega Evolution and Primal Reversion in the Hoenn Region

In the rich Hoenn region, abundant in natural resources, you can find a large number of Mega Stones. Along with the Mega Stones that you were able to obtain in *Pokémon X* and *Pokémon Y*, you'll discover additional new Mega Stones to collect!

Mega Venusaur

Mega Stone: Venusaurite

Can be found on Route 119 after battling Groudon or Kyogre.

Mega Beedrill

Mega Stone: Beedrillite

Find it in Sea Mauville's storage hold.

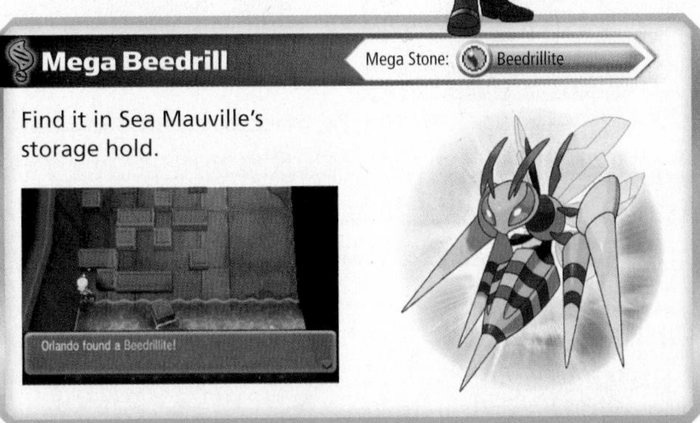

Mega Charizard X

Mega Stone: Charizardite X

Can be found on the Fiery Path after battling Groudon or Kyogre.

Mega Pidgeot

Mega Stone: Pidgeotite

After obtaining the Intriguing Stone in Verdanturf Town, take it to Rustboro City's Devon Corporation and talk to President Stone.

Mega Charizard

Mega Stone: Charizardite Y

Can be found on Route 120's Scorched Slab (B2F) after battling Groudon or Kyogre.

Mega Alakazam

Mega Stone: Alakazite

Can be found in the Slateport Market.

Mega Blastoise

Mega Stone: Blastoisinite

Can be found on the deck of the *S.S. Tidal*, which you can take from Slateport City or Lilycove City after completing the Delta Episode.

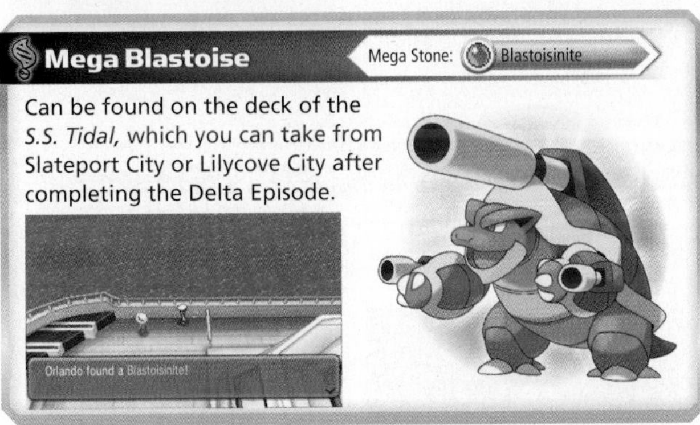

Mega Slowbro

Mega Stone: Slowbronite

Find four Shoal Salts and four Shoal Shells in Shoal Cave and give them to the old man. He will give you a Shell Bell and a Slowbronite.

Mega Gengar

Mega Stone: Gengarite

Can be found in the custodian's hut at the Battle Resort after entering the Hall of Fame.

Orlando found a Gengarite!

Mega Mewtwo X

Mega Stone: Mewtwonite X

Can be found in Littleroot Town after battling Groudon or Kyogre.

Orlando found a Mewtwonite X!

Mega Kangaskhan

Mega Stone: Kangaskhanite

Can be found in Pacifidlog Town after battling Groudon or Kyogre.

Orlando found a Kangaskhanite!

Mega Mewtwo Y

Mega Stone: Mewtwonite Y

Can be found near the entrance of the Pokémon League after battling Groudon or Kyogre.

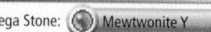

Orlando found a Mewtwonite Y!

Mega Pinsir

Mega Stone: Pinsirite

Can be found on Route 124.

Orlando found a Pinsirite!

Mega Ampharos

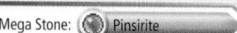

Mega Stone: Ampharosite

Can be found in New Mauville after battling Groudon or Kyogre.

Orlando found an Ampharosite!

Mega Gyarados

Mega Stone: Gyaradosite

Talk to the Poochyena at 123 Go Fish on Route 123 and select "Yes."

Yes
No
Could you give it a little scratch?

Mega Steelix

Mega Stone: Steelixite

Can be found on the second basement floor of Granite Cave.

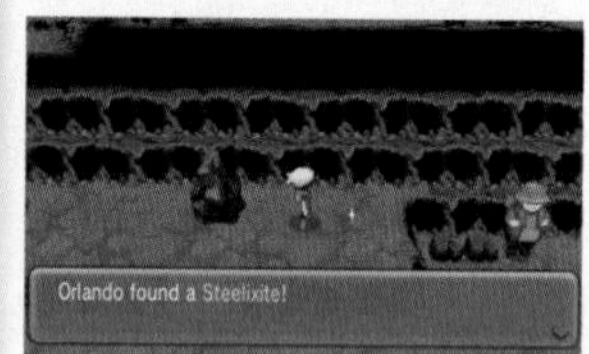
Orlando found a Steelixite!

Mega Aerodactyl

Mega Stone: Aerodactylite

Can be found in Meteor Falls (Back chamber) after battling Groudon or Kyogre.

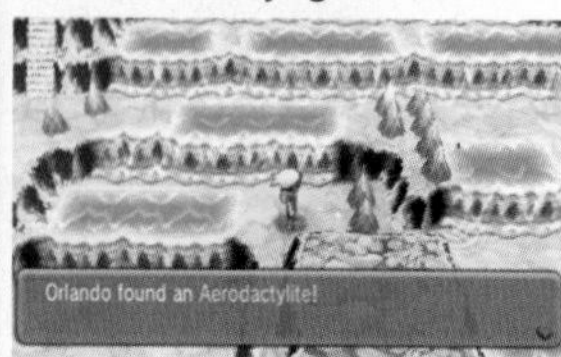
Orlando found an Aerodactylite!

Mega Scizor

Mega Stone: Scizorite

Can be found in Petalburg Woods after battling Groudon or Kyogre.

Orlando found a Scizorite!

Mega Heracross

Mega Stone: Heracronite

Can be found on Route 127.

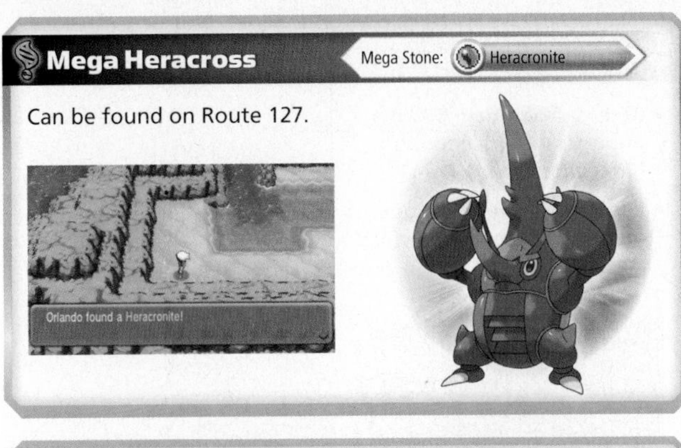
Orlando found a Heracronite!

Mega Houndoom

Mega Stone: Houndoominite

Can be found in Lavaridge Town after battling Groudon or Kyogre.

Orlando found a Houndoominite!

Mega Tyranitar

Mega Stone: Tyranitarite

Can be found on Jagged Pass after battling Groudon or Kyogre.

Orlando found a Tyranitarite!

Mega Sceptile

Mega Stone: Sceptilite

Can be received from Steven on Route 120 if you chose Treecko at the beginning of the game.

Orlando obtained a Sceptilite!

Mega Blaziken

Mega Stone: Blazikenite

Can be received from Steven on Route 120 if you chose Torchic at the beginning of the game.

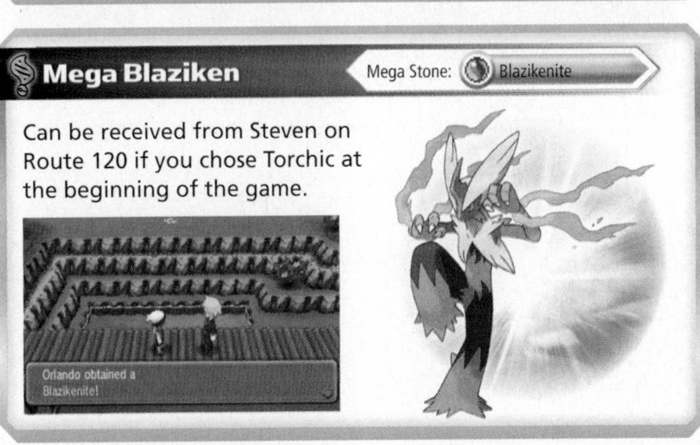
Orlando obtained a Blazikenite!

Mega Swampert

Mega Stone: Swampertite

Can be received from Steven on Route 120 if you chose Mudkip at the beginning of the game.

Orlando obtained a Swampertite!

Mega Gardevoir

Mega Stone: Gardevoirite

Can be received from Wanda at her house in Verdanturf Town after battling Groudon or Kyogre.

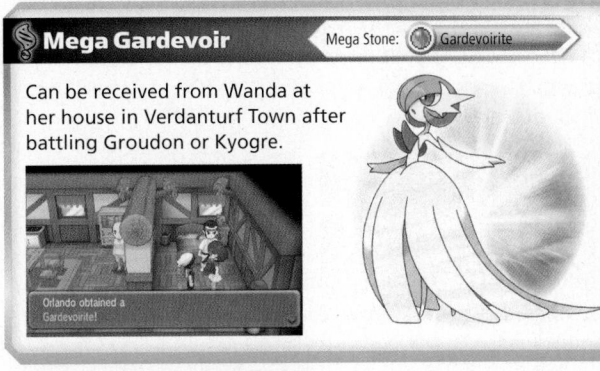

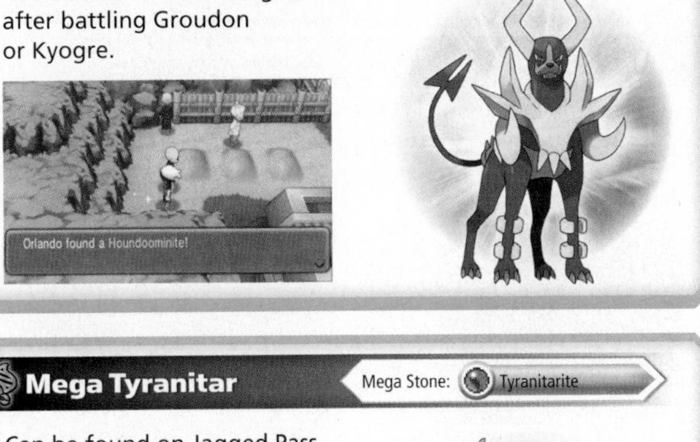
Orlando obtained a Gardevoirite!

Mega Sableye

Mega Stone: Sablenite

Can be found outside the Cave of Origin in Sootopolis City.

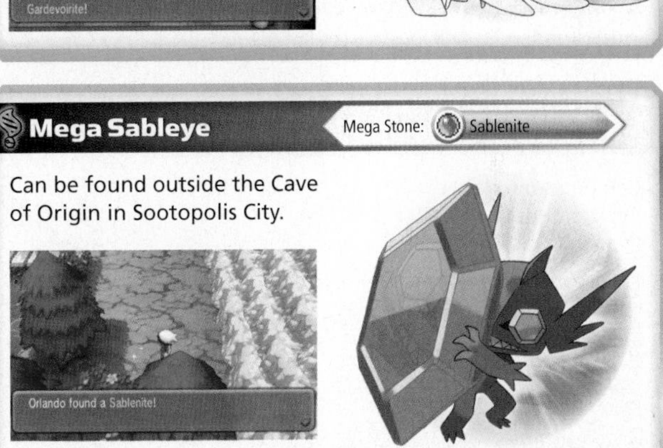
Orlando found a Sablenite!

Mega Mawile

Mega Stone: Mawilite

Can be found on the east side of Verdanturf Town, accessible from Route 117.

Orlando found a Mawilite!

- You can also buy Sceptilite, Blazikenite, and Swampertite from a stone seller who appears on Route 114 after battling Groudon and Kyogre (you can buy the Mega Stone for the two Pokémon you didn't choose at the beginning of the game). The seller will offer them under different names (Withered Tree, Fading Fire, and Ebb Tide).

Mega Aggron

Mega Stone: Aggronite

Receive from a Black Belt after unblocking Rusturf Tunnel.

Orlando obtained an Aggronite!

Mega Medicham

Mega Stone: Medichamite

Can be found on the fourth floor of Mt. Pyre.

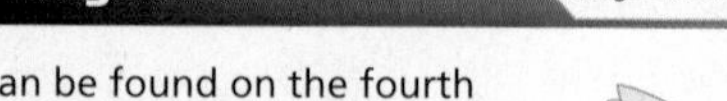

Orlando found a Medichamite!

Mega Manectric

Mega Stone: Manectite

Can be found near the Cycling Road on Route 110 after obtaining the Mach Bike or Acro Bike.

Orlando found a Manectite!

Mega Sharpedo

Mega Stone: Sharpedonite

- Receive from Team Aqua at the Battle Resort (*Pokémon Omega Ruby*).
- Receive from Team Aqua during the Delta Episode (*Pokémon Alpha Sapphire*).

Orlando obtained a Sharpedonite!

Mega Camerupt

Mega Stone: Cameruptite

- Receive from Team Magma during the Delta Episode (*Pokémon Omega Ruby*).
- Receive from Team Magma at the Battle Resort (*Pokémon Alpha Sapphire*).

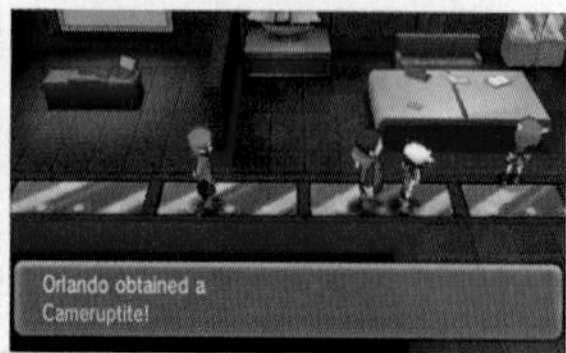
Orlando obtained a Cameruptite!

Mega Altaria

Mega Stone: Altarianite

Receive from a man in Lilycove City if you answer his question with "Altaria" and have an Altaria in your party.

Orlando obtained an Altarianite!

Mega Banette

Mega Stone: Banettite

Can be found on the peak of Mt. Pyre.

Orlando found a Banettite!

Mega Absol

Mega Stone: Absolite

Can be found in the Safari Zone.

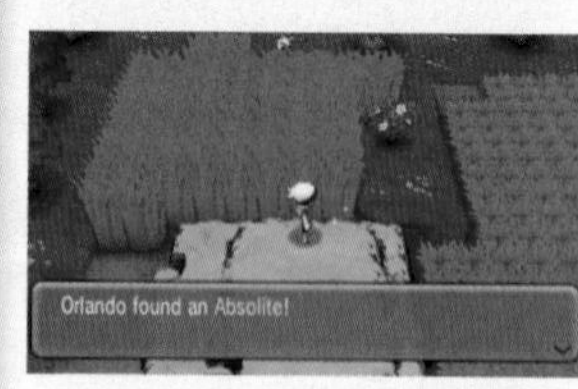
Orlando found an Absolite!

Mega Glalie

Mega Stone: Glalitite

Can be found in Shoal Cave's ice cavern at low tide (3–8:59 A.M. and 3–8:59 P.M.).

Orlando found a Glalitite!

Mega Salamence

Mega Stone: Salamencite

Receive from the old Draconid woman at Meteor Falls after completing the Delta Episode.

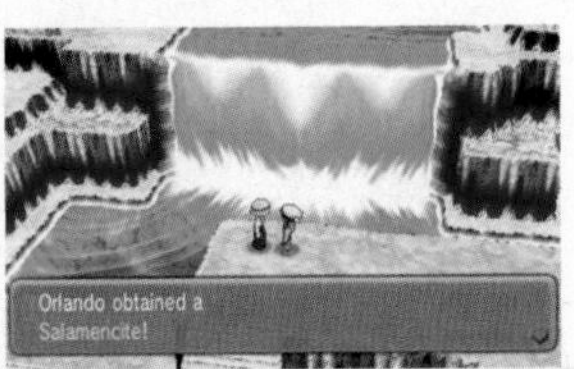
Orlando obtained a Salamencite!

Mega Metagross

Mega Stone: Metagrossite

Receive from Steven after completing the Delta Episode, challenging the Pokémon League again, and defeating Steven once again.

Orlando obtained a Metagrossite!

Mega Latias

Mega Stone: Latiasite

- Receive from your mom after completing the Delta Episode *(Pokémon Omega Ruby)*.
- Obtain on Southern Island (*Pokémon Alpha Sapphire*).

Latias is carrying a piece of Latiasite!

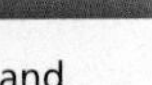

Mega Latios

Mega Stone: Latiosite

- Obtain on Southern Island *(Pokémon Omega Ruby)*.
- Receive from your mom after completing the Delta Episode *(Pokémon Alpha Sapphire)*.

Latios is carrying a piece of Latiosite!

Primal Kyogre

Item: Blue Orb

- Receive from the old lady at the peak of Mt. Pyre *(Pokémon Omega Ruby)*.
- Receive from Archie near the Cave of Origin *(Pokémon Alpha Sapphire)*.

Orlando obtained a Blue Orb!

Primal Groudon

Item: Red Orb

- Receive from Maxie near the Cave of Origin *(Pokémon Omega Ruby)*.
- Receive from the old lady at the peak of Mt. Pyre (*Pokémon Alpha Sapphire*).

Orlando obtained a Red Orb!

Mega Rayquaza

Move: Dragon Ascent

Catch Rayquaza and have it learn Dragon Ascent during the Delta Episode.

Rayquaza succeeded to the power of Dragon Ascent!

Orlando obtained a Lopunnite!

Mega Lopunny

Mega Stone: Lopunnite

Talk to the man wearing sunglasses and standing in front of Apt. 12 in Mauville Hills two times.

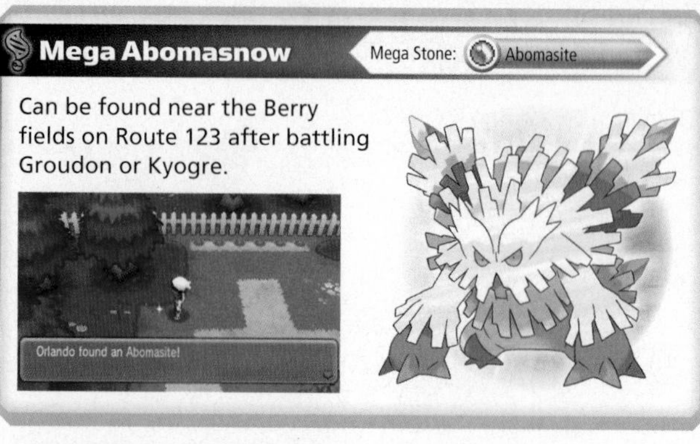
Orlando found an Abomasite!

Mega Abomasnow

Mega Stone: Abomasite

Can be found near the Berry fields on Route 123 after battling Groudon or Kyogre.

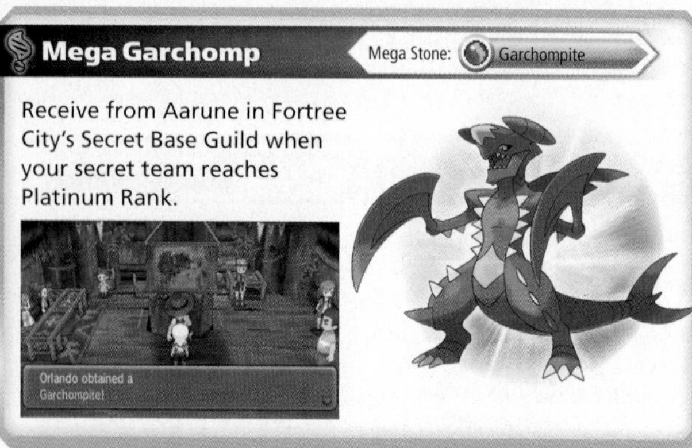
Orlando obtained a Garchompite!

Mega Garchomp

Mega Stone: Garchompite

Receive from Aarune in Fortree City's Secret Base Guild when your secret team reaches Platinum Rank.

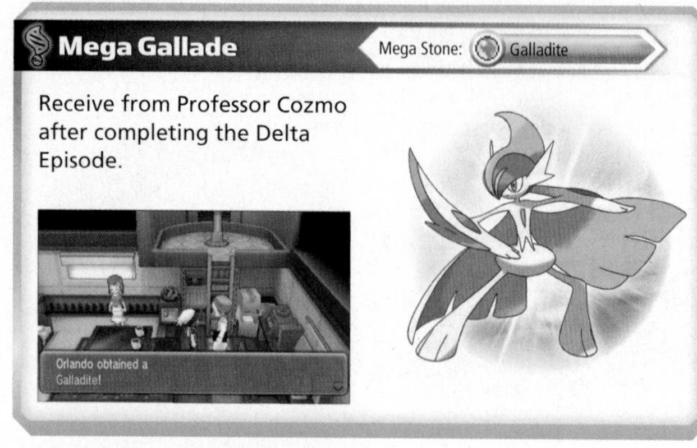
Orlando obtained a Galladite!

Mega Gallade

Mega Stone: Galladite

Receive from Professor Cozmo after completing the Delta Episode.

Orlando obtained a Lucarionite!

Mega Lucario

Mega Stone: Lucarionite

Receive from Chaz after you win Master Rank contests in all five contest conditions and then defeat Lisia at the Master Rank.

Orlando obtained an Audinite!

Mega Audino

Mega Stone: Audinite

Receive from Looker in a cottage at the Battle Resort.

Explanations of the Move List

Move............The move's name
Type ....The move's type
Kind ....Physical moves deal more damage when a Pokémon's Attack is high. Special moves deal more damage when a Pokémon's Sp. Atk is high. Status moves cause effects, such as status conditions.
Pow. ....The move's attack power
Acc. ....The move's accuracy
PP...................How many times the move can be used
Range...........The number and types of targets the move affects
DA..................Moves that make direct contact with the target
Long..............Moves that can target the Pokémon on the other side during Triple Battles

Range Guide

Normal: The move affects the selected target.
Self: The move affects only the user.
1 Ally: The move affects an adjacent ally in Double, Triple, and Multi Battles.
Self/Ally: The move affects the user or one of its allies.
Your Party: The move affects your entire party, including party Pokémon that are still in their Poké Balls.
1 Random: The move affects one of the opposing Pokémon at random.
Many Others: The move affects multiple Pokémon at the same time.
Adjacent: The move affects the surrounding Pokémon at the same time.
Your Side: The move affects the side of the field where your Pokémon are.
Other Side: The move affects the opponent's side of the field.
Both Sides: The move affects the entire playing field without regard to opposing and ally Pokémon.
Varies: The move is influenced by things like the opposing Pokémon's move or the user's type, so the effect and range are not fixed.

A

Move	Type	Kind	Pow.	Acc.	PP	Range	DA	Long	Effect
Absorb	Grass	Special	20	100	25	Normal	—	—	Restores HP by up to half of the damage dealt to the target.
Acid	Poison	Special	40	100	30	Many Others	—	—	A 10% chance of lowering the targets' Sp. Def by 1. Its power is reduced by 25% when it hits multiple Pokémon.
Acid Armor	Poison	Status	—	—	20	Self	—	—	Raises the user's Defense by 2.
Acid Spray	Poison	Special	40	100	20	Normal	—	—	Lowers the target's Sp. Def by 2.
Acrobatics	Flying	Physical	55	100	15	Normal	○	○	This move's power is doubled if the user isn't holding an item.
Acupressure	Normal	Status	—	—	30	Self/Ally	—	—	Raises a random stat by 2.
Aerial Ace	Flying	Physical	60	—	20	Normal	○	○	A sure hit.
After You	Normal	Status	—	—	15	Normal	—	—	The user helps the target and makes it use its move right after the user, regardless of its Speed. It fails if the target was going to use its move right after anyway, or if the target has already used its move this turn.
Agility	Psychic	Status	—	—	30	Self	—	—	Raises the user's Speed by 2.
Air Cutter	Flying	Special	60	95	25	Many Others	—	—	Critical hits land more easily. Its power is reduced by 25% when it hits multiple Pokémon.
Air Slash	Flying	Special	75	95	15	Normal	—	○	A 30% chance of making the target flinch (unable to use moves on that turn).
Ally Switch	Psychic	Status	—	—	15	Self	—	—	The user switches places with an ally. It fails if the user or target is in the middle (works only when the target is on the other end).
Amnesia	Psychic	Status	—	—	20	Self	—	—	Raises the user's Sp. Def by 2.
Ancient Power	Rock	Special	60	100	5	Normal	—	—	A 10% chance of raising the user's Attack, Defense, Speed, Sp. Atk, and Sp. Def stats by 1.
Aqua Jet	Water	Physical	40	100	20	Normal	○	—	Always strikes first. The user with the higher Speed goes first if similar moves are used.
Aqua Ring	Water	Status	—	—	20	Self	—	—	Restores 1/16 of max HP every turn.
Aqua Tail	Water	Physical	90	90	10	Normal	○	—	A regular attack.
Arm Thrust	Fighting	Physical	15	100	20	Normal	○	—	Attacks 2–5 times in a row in a single turn.
Aromatherapy	Grass	Status	—	—	5	Your Party	—	○	Heals status conditions of all your Pokémon, including those in your party.
Aromatic Mist	Fairy	Status	—	—	20	1 Ally	—	—	Raises one ally's Sp. Def by 1.
Assist	Normal	Status	—	—	20	Self	—	—	Uses a random move from one of the Pokémon in your party that is not in battle.
Assurance	Dark	Physical	60	100	10	Normal	○	—	Move's power is doubled if the target has already taken some damage in the same turn.
Astonish	Ghost	Physical	30	100	15	Normal	○	—	A 30% chance of making the target flinch (unable to use moves on that turn).
Attack Order	Bug	Physical	90	100	15	Normal	—	—	Critical hits land more easily.
Attract	Normal	Status	—	100	15	Normal	—	—	Leaves the target unable to attack 50% of the time. Only works if the user and the target are of different genders.
Aura Sphere	Fighting	Special	80	—	20	Normal	—	○	A sure hit.
Aurora Beam	Ice	Special	65	100	20	Normal	—	—	A 10% chance of lowering the target's Attack by 1.
Autotomize	Steel	Status	—	—	15	Self	—	—	Raises the user's Speed by 2 and lowers its weight by 220 lbs.
Avalanche	Ice	Physical	60	100	10	Normal	○	—	Always strikes last. This move's power is doubled if the user has taken damage from the target that turn.

B

Move	Type	Kind	Pow.	Acc.	PP	Range	DA	Long	Effect
Baby-Doll Eyes	Fairy	Status	—	100	30	Normal	—	—	Always strikes first. Lowers the target's Attack by 1.
Barrage	Normal	Physical	15	85	20	Normal	—	—	Attacks 2–5 times in a row in a single turn.

Move	Type	Kind	Pow.	Acc.	PP	Range	DA	Long	Effect
Barrier	Psychic	Status	—	—	20	Self	—	—	Raises the user's Defense by 2.
Baton Pass	Normal	Status	—	—	40	Self	—	—	User swaps out with an ally Pokémon and passes along any stat changes.
Beat Up	Dark	Physical	—	100	10	Normal	—	—	Attacks once for each Pokémon in your party, including the user. Does not count Pokémon that have fainted or have status conditions.
Belch	Poison	Special	120	90	10	Normal	—	—	Cannot be used without first eating a Berry.
Belly Drum	Normal	Status	—	—	10	Self	—	—	The user loses half of its maximum HP but raises its Attack to the maximum.
Bestow	Normal	Status	—	—	15	Normal	—	—	If the target is not holding an item and the user is, the user can give that item to the target. Fails if the user is not holding an item or the target is holding an item.
Bide	Normal	Physical	—	—	10	Self	○	—	Inflicts twice the damage received during the next 2 turns. Cannot choose moves during those 2 turns.
Bind	Normal	Physical	15	85	20	Normal	○	—	Inflicts damage equal to 1/8 the target's max HP for 4–5 turns. The target cannot flee during that time.
Bite	Dark	Physical	60	100	25	Normal	○	—	A 30% chance of making the target flinch (unable to use moves on that turn).
Blast Burn	Fire	Special	150	90	5	Normal	—	—	The user can't move during the next turn. If the target is Frozen, it will be thawed.
Blaze Kick	Fire	Physical	85	90	10	Normal	○	—	A 10% chance of inflicting the Burned status condition on the target. Critical hits land more easily. If the target is Frozen, it will be thawed.
Blizzard	Ice	Special	110	70	5	Many Others	—	—	A 10% chance of inflicting the Frozen status condition on the targets. Is 100% accurate in the hail weather condition. Its power is reduced by 25% when it hits multiple Pokémon.
Block	Normal	Status	—	—	5	Normal	—	—	The target cannot escape. If used during a Trainer battle, the opposing Trainer cannot switch Pokémon. Has no effect on Ghost-type Pokémon.
Body Slam	Normal	Physical	85	100	15	Normal	○	—	A 30% chance of inflicting the Paralysis status condition on the target. If the target has used Minimize, this move will be a sure hit and its power will be doubled.
Bone Club	Ground	Physical	65	85	20	Normal	—	—	A 10% chance of making the target flinch (unable to use moves on that turn).
Bone Rush	Ground	Physical	25	90	10	Normal	—	—	Attacks 2–5 times in a row in a single turn.
Bonemerang	Ground	Physical	50	90	10	Normal	—	—	Attacks twice in a row in a single turn.
Boomburst	Normal	Special	140	100	10	Adjacent	—	—	Its power is reduced by 25% when it hits multiple Pokémon. Strikes the target even if it is using Substitute.
Bounce	Flying	Physical	85	85	5	Normal	○	○	The user flies into the air on the first turn and attacks on the second. A 30% chance of the target.
Brave Bird	Flying	Physical	120	100	15	Normal	○	○	The user takes 1/3 of the damage inflicted.
Brick Break	Fighting	Physical	75	100	15	Normal	○	—	This move is not affected by Reflect. It removes the effect of Reflect and Light Screen.
Brine	Water	Special	65	100	10	Normal	—	—	This move's power is doubled if the target's HP is at half or below.
Bubble	Water	Special	40	100	30	Many Others	—	—	A 10% chance of lowering the targets' Speed by 1. Its power is reduced by 25% when it hits multiple Pokémon.
Bubble Beam	Water	Special	65	100	20	Normal	—	—	A 10% chance of lowering the target's Speed by 1.
Bug Bite	Bug	Physical	60	100	20	Normal	○	—	If the target is holding a Berry with a battle effect, the user eats that Berry and uses its effect.
Bug Buzz	Bug	Special	90	100	10	Normal	—	—	A 10% chance of lowering the target's Sp. Def by 1. Strikes the target even if it is using Substitute.
Bulk Up	Fighting	Status	—	—	20	Self	—	—	Raises the user's Attack and Defense by 1.
Bulldoze	Ground	Physical	60	100	20	Adjacent	—	—	Lowers the targets' Speed by 1. Its power is reduced by 25% when it hits multiple Pokémon.
Bullet Punch	Steel	Physical	40	100	30	Normal	○	—	Always strikes first. The user with the higher Speed goes first if similar moves are used.
Bullet Seed	Grass	Physical	25	100	30	Normal	—	—	Attacks 2–5 times in a row in a single turn.

C

Move	Type	Kind	Pow.	Acc.	PP	Range	DA	Long	Effect
Calm Mind	Psychic	Status	—	—	20	Self	—	—	Raises the user's Sp. Atk and Sp. Def by 1.
Camouflage	Normal	Status	—	—	20	Self	—	—	Changes the user's type to match the environment: Cave: Rock type. Dirt/Sand/Swamp: Ground type. Electric Terrain: Electric type. Grass / Grassy Terrain: Grass type. Indoors / Link: Normal type. Misty Terrain: Fairy type. Snow/Ice: Ice type. Water Surface / Puddle / Shoal: Water type
Captivate	Normal	Status	—	100	20	Many Others	—	—	Lowers the target's Sp. Atk by 2. Only works if the user and the target are of different genders.
Charge	Electric	Status	—	—	20	Self	—	—	Doubles the attack power of an Electric-type move used the next turn. Raises the user's Sp. Def by 1.
Charge Beam	Electric	Special	50	90	10	Normal	—	—	A 70% chance of raising the user's Sp. Atk by 1.
Charm	Fairy	Status	—	100	20	Normal	—	—	Lowers the target's Attack by 2.
Chatter	Flying	Special	65	100	20	Normal	—	○	When the user is Chatot, this move also inflicts the Confused status condition on the target. Strikes the target even if it is using Substitute.
Chip Away	Normal	Physical	70	100	20	Normal	○	—	Damage dealt is not affected by the opposing Pokémon's stat changes.
Circle Throw	Fighting	Physical	60	90	10	Normal	○	—	Always strikes last. Ends wild Pokémon battles after attacking. When battling multiple wild Pokémon or if the wild Pokémon's level is higher than the user's, no additional effect takes place. In a battle with a Trainer, this move forces another Pokémon to switch in. If there is no Pokémon to switch in, no additional effect takes place.
Clamp	Water	Physical	35	85	15	Normal	○	—	Inflicts damage equal to 1/8 the target's max HP for 4–5 turns. The target cannot flee during that time.
Clear Smog	Poison	Special	50	—	15	Normal	—	—	Eliminates every stat change of the target.
Close Combat	Fighting	Physical	120	100	5	Normal	○	—	Lowers the user's Defense and Sp. Def by 1.
Coil	Poison	Status	—	—	20	Self	—	—	Raises the user's Attack, Defense, and accuracy by 1.
Comet Punch	Normal	Physical	18	85	15	Normal	○	—	Attacks 2–5 times in a row in a single turn.

Move	Type	Kind	Pow.	Acc.	PP	Range	DA	Long	Effect
Confide	Normal	Status	—	—	20	Normal	—	—	A sure hit. Lowers the target's Sp. Atk by 1. Strikes the target even if it is using Detect, King's Shield, Mat Block, Protect, Spiky Shield, or Substitute.
Confuse Ray	Ghost	Status	—	100	10	Normal	—	—	Inflicts the Confused status condition on the target.
Confusion	Psychic	Special	50	100	25	Normal	—	—	A 10% chance of inflicting the Confused status condition on the target.
Constrict	Normal	Physical	10	100	35	Normal	○	—	A 10% chance of lowering the target's Speed by 1.
Copycat	Normal	Status	—	—	20	Self	—	—	Uses the last move used.
Cosmic Power	Psychic	Status	—	—	20	Self	—	—	Raises the user's Defense and Sp. Def by 1.
Cotton Guard	Grass	Status	—	—	10	Self	—	—	Raises the user's Defense by 3.
Cotton Spore	Grass	Status	—	100	40	Many Others	—	—	Lowers the targets' Speed by 2. Has no effect on Grass-type Pokémon.
Counter	Fighting	Physical	—	100	20	Varies	○	—	If the user is attacked physically, this move inflicts twice the damage done to the user. Always strikes last.
Covet	Normal	Physical	60	100	25	Normal	○	—	When the target is holding an item and the user is not, the user can steal that item. A regular attack if the target is not holding an item.
Crabhammer	Water	Physical	100	90	10	Normal	○	—	Critical hits land more easily.
Crafty Shield	Fairy	Status	—	—	10	Your Side	—	—	Protects the user and allies from status moves used in the same turn. Does not protect against damage-dealing moves.
Cross Chop	Fighting	Physical	100	80	5	Normal	○	—	Critical hits land more easily.
Cross Poison	Poison	Physical	70	100	20	Normal	○	—	Critical hits land more easily. A 10% chance of inflicting the Poison status condition on the target.
Crunch	Dark	Physical	80	100	15	Normal	○	—	A 20% chance of lowering the target's Defense by 1.
Crush Claw	Normal	Physical	75	95	10	Normal	○	—	A 50% chance of lowering the target's Defense by 1.
Curse	Ghost	Status	—	—	10	Varies	—	—	Lowers the user's Speed by 1 and raises its Attack and Defense by 1. If used by a Ghost-type Pokémon, the user loses half of its maximum HP, but the move lowers the target's HP by 1/4 of its maximum every turn.
Cut	Normal	Physical	50	95	30	Normal	○	—	A regular attack.

D

Move	Type	Kind	Pow.	Acc.	PP	Range	DA	Long	Effect
Dark Pulse	Dark	Special	80	100	15	Normal	—	○	Has a 20% chance of making the target flinch (unable to use moves on that turn).
Dazzling Gleam	Fairy	Special	80	100	10	Many Others	—	—	Its power is reduced by 25% when it hits multiple Pokémon.
Defend Order	Bug	Status	—	—	10	Self	—	—	Raises the user's Defense and Sp. Def by 1.
Defense Curl	Normal	Status	—	—	40	Self	—	—	Raises the user's Defense by 1.
Defog	Flying	Status	—	—	15	Normal	—	—	Lowers the target's evasion by 1. Nullifies the effects of Light Screen, Reflect, Safeguard, Mist, Spikes, Toxic Spikes, and Stealth Rock on the target's side.
Destiny Bond	Ghost	Status	—	—	5	Self	—	—	If the user faints due to damage from a Pokémon, that Pokémon faints as well.
Detect	Fighting	Status	—	—	5	Self	—	—	The user evades all moves that turn. If used in succession, its chance of failing rises.
Diamond Storm	Rock	Physical	100	95	5	Many Others	—	—	A 50% chance of raising the user's Defense by 1. Its power is reduced by 25% when it hits multiple Pokémon.
Dig	Ground	Physical	80	100	10	Normal	○	—	The user burrows underground on the first turn and attacks on the second.
Disable	Normal	Status	—	100	20	Normal	—	—	The target can't use the move it just used for 4 turns.
Disarming Voice	Fairy	Special	40	—	15	Many Others	—	—	A sure hit. Strikes the target even if it is using Substitute. Its power is reduced by 25% when it hits multiple Pokémon.
Discharge	Electric	Special	80	100	15	Adjacent	—	—	A 30% chance of inflicting the Paralysis status condition on the targets. Its power is reduced by 25% when it hits multiple Pokémon.
Dive	Water	Physical	80	100	10	Normal	○	—	The user dives deep on the first turn and attacks on the second.
Dizzy Punch	Normal	Physical	70	100	10	Normal	○	—	A 20% chance of inflicting the Confused status condition on the target.
Double Hit	Normal	Physical	35	90	10	Normal	○	—	Attacks twice in a row in a single turn.
Double Kick	Fighting	Physical	30	100	30	Normal	○	—	Attacks twice in a row in a single turn.
Double Slap	Normal	Physical	15	85	10	Normal	○	—	Attacks 2–5 times in a row in a single turn.
Double Team	Normal	Status	—	—	15	Self	—	—	Raises the user's evasion by 1.
Double-Edge	Normal	Physical	120	100	15	Normal	○	—	The user takes 1/3 of the damage inflicted.
Draco Meteor	Dragon	Special	130	90	5	Normal	—	—	Lowers the user's Sp. Atk by 2.
Dragon Ascent	Flying	Physical	120	100	5	Normal	○	○	Lowers the user's Defense and Sp. Def by 1.
Dragon Breath	Dragon	Special	60	100	20	Normal	—	—	A 30% chance of inflicting the Paralysis status condition on the target.
Dragon Claw	Dragon	Physical	80	100	15	Normal	○	—	A regular attack.
Dragon Dance	Dragon	Status	—	—	20	Self	—	—	Raises the user's Attack and Speed by 1.
Dragon Pulse	Dragon	Special	85	100	10	Normal	—	○	A regular attack.
Dragon Rage	Dragon	Special	—	100	10	Normal	—	—	Deals a fixed 40 points of damage.
Dragon Rush	Dragon	Physical	100	75	10	Normal	○	—	A 20% chance of making the target flinch (unable to use moves on that turn). If the target has used Minimize, this move will be a sure hit and its power will be doubled.

Move	Type	Kind	Pow.	Acc.	PP	Range	DA	Long	Effect
Dragon Tail	Dragon	Physical	60	90	10	Normal	○	—	Attacks last. Ends wild Pokémon battles after attacking. When battling multiple wild Pokémon or if the wild Pokémon's level is higher than the user's, no additional effect takes place. In a battle with a Trainer, this move forces another Pokémon to switch in. If there is no Pokémon to switch in, no additional effect takes place.
Drain Punch	Fighting	Physical	75	100	10	Normal	○	—	Restores HP by up to half of the damage dealt to the target.
Draining Kiss	Fairy	Special	50	100	10	Normal	○	—	Restores HP by up to 3/4 of the damage dealt to the target.
Dream Eater	Psychic	Special	100	100	15	Normal	—	—	Only works when the target is asleep. Restores HP by up to half of the damage dealt to the target.
Drill Peck	Flying	Physical	80	100	20	Normal	○	○	A regular attack.
Drill Run	Ground	Physical	80	95	10	Normal	○	—	Critical hits land more easily.
Dual Chop	Dragon	Physical	40	90	15	Normal	○	—	Attacks twice in a row in a single turn.
Dynamic Punch	Fighting	Physical	100	50	5	Normal	○	—	Inflicts the Confused status condition on the target.

E

Move	Type	Kind	Pow.	Acc.	PP	Range	DA	Long	Effect
Earth Power	Ground	Special	90	100	10	Normal	—	—	A 10% chance of lowering the target's Sp. Def by 1.
Earthquake	Ground	Physical	100	100	10	Adjacent	—	—	Does twice the damage if targets are underground due to using Dig. Its power is reduced by 25% when it hits multiple Pokémon.
Echoed Voice	Normal	Special	40	100	15	Normal	—	—	If this move is used every turn, no matter which Pokémon uses it, its power increases (max 200). If no Pokémon uses it in a turn, the power returns to normal. Strikes the target even if it is using Substitute.
Eerie Impulse	Electric	Status	—	100	15	Normal	—	—	Lowers the target's Sp. Atk by 2.
Egg Bomb	Normal	Physical	100	75	10	Normal	—	—	A regular attack.
Electric Terrain	Electric	Status	—	—	10	Both Sides	—	—	Electrifies the field for 5 turns. During that time, Pokémon on the ground will be able to do 50% more damage with Electric-type moves and cannot fall asleep.
Electrify	Electric	Status	—	—	20	Normal	—	—	Changes any attack used by the target in the same turn into an Electric-type move.
Electro Ball	Electric	Special	—	100	10	Normal	—	—	The faster the user is than the target, the greater the move's power (max 150).
Electroweb	Electric	Special	55	95	15	Many Others	—	—	Lowers the targets' Speed by 1. Its power is reduced by 25% when it hits multiple Pokémon.
Embargo	Dark	Status	—	100	15	Normal	—	—	The target can't use items for 5 turns. The Trainer also can't use items on that Pokémon.
Ember	Fire	Special	40	100	25	Normal	—	—	A 10% chance of inflicting the Burned status condition on the target. If the target is Frozen, it will be thawed.
Encore	Normal	Status	—	100	5	Normal	—	—	The target is forced to keep using the last move it used. This effect lasts 3 turns.
Endeavor	Normal	Physical	—	100	5	Normal	○	—	Inflicts damage equal to the target's HP minus the user's HP.
Endure	Normal	Status	—	—	10	Self	—	—	Leaves the user with 1 HP when hit by a move that would KO it. If used in succession, its chance of failing rises.
Energy Ball	Grass	Special	90	100	10	Normal	—	—	A 10% chance of lowering the target's Sp. Def by 1.
Entrainment	Normal	Status	—	100	15	Normal	—	—	Makes the target's Ability the same as the user's. Fails with certain Abilities, however.
Eruption	Fire	Special	150	100	5	Many Others	—	—	If the user's HP is low, this move has lower attack power. If the targets are Frozen, they will be thawed. Its power is reduced by 25% when it hits multiple Pokémon.
Explosion	Normal	Physical	250	100	5	Adjacent	—	—	The user faints after using it. Its power is reduced by 25% when it hits multiple Pokémon.
Extrasensory	Psychic	Special	80	100	20	Normal	—	—	A 10% chance of making the target flinch (unable to use moves on that turn).
Extreme Speed	Normal	Physical	80	100	5	Normal	○	—	Always strikes first. Faster than other moves that strike first, except for Fake Out. (If two Pokémon use this move, the one with the higher Speed goes first.)

F

Move	Type	Kind	Pow.	Acc.	PP	Range	DA	Long	Effect
Facade	Normal	Physical	70	100	20	Normal	○	—	This move's power is doubled if the user has a Paralysis, Poison, or Burned status condition.
Fairy Lock	Fairy	Status	—	—	10	Both Sides	—	—	The target cannot escape during the next turn. If used during a Trainer battle, the opposing Trainer cannot switch Pokémon. Has no effect on Ghost-type Pokémon.
Fairy Wind	Fairy	Special	40	100	30	Normal	—	—	A regular attack.
Fake Out	Normal	Physical	40	100	10	Normal	○	—	Always strikes first and makes the target flinch (unable to use moves on that turn). Only works on the first turn after the user is sent out. Faster than other moves that strike first.
Fake Tears	Dark	Status	—	100	20	Normal	—	—	Lowers the target's Sp. Def by 2.
False Swipe	Normal	Physical	40	100	40	Normal	○	—	Always leaves 1 HP, even if the damage would have made the target faint.
Feather Dance	Flying	Status	—	100	15	Normal	—	—	Lowers the target's Attack by 2.
Feint	Normal	Physical	30	100	10	Normal	—	—	Always strikes first. Faster than other moves that strike first, except Fake Out. If two Pokémon use this move, or if the other Pokémon uses the move Extreme Speed, the one with the higher Speed goes first. Strikes the target even if it is using Detect, King's Shield, Mat Block, Protect, Quick Guard, Spiky Shield, or Wide Guard, and eliminates the effects of those moves.
Feint Attack	Dark	Physical	60	—	20	Normal	○	—	A sure hit.
Fell Stinger	Bug	Physical	30	100	25	Normal	○	—	When the Pokémon knocks out an opponent with this move, its Attack goes up 2.
Final Gambit	Fighting	Special	—	100	5	Normal	○	—	Does damage to the target equal to the user's remaining HP. If the move lands, the user faints. If the move does not land, the user will not faint.
Fire Blast	Fire	Special	110	85	5	Normal	—	—	A 10% chance of inflicting the Burned status condition on the target. If the target is Frozen, it will be thawed.

Move	Type	Kind	Pow.	Acc.	PP	Range	DA	Long	Effect
Fire Fang	Fire	Physical	65	95	15	Normal	○	—	A 10% chance of inflicting the Burned status condition or making the target flinch (unable to use moves on that turn). If the target is Frozen, it will be thawed.
Fire Pledge	Fire	Special	80	100	10	Normal	—	—	When combined with Water Pledge or Grass Pledge, the power and effect change. If combined with Water Pledge, the power is 150 and it becomes a Water-type move. This makes it more likely that your team's moves will have additional effects for 4 turns. If combined with Grass Pledge, the power is 150 and it remains a Fire-type move. This damages opposing Pokémon, except Fire types, for 4 turns. If the target is Frozen, it will be thawed.
Fire Punch	Fire	Physical	75	100	15	Normal	○	—	A 10% chance of inflicting the Burned status condition on the target. If the target is Frozen, it will be thawed.
Fire Spin	Fire	Special	35	85	15	Normal	—	—	Inflicts damage equal to 1/8 the target's max HP for 4–5 turns. The target cannot flee during that time. If the target is Frozen, it will be thawed.
Fissure	Ground	Physical	—	30	5	Normal	—	—	The target faints with one hit if the user's level is equal to or greater than the target's level. The higher the user's level is compared to the target's, the more accurate the move is.
Flail	Normal	Physical	—	100	15	Normal	○	—	The lower the user's HP is, the greater the move's power becomes (max 200).
Flame Burst	Fire	Special	70	100	15	Normal	—	—	It deals damage equal to 1/16 of the max HP of any Pokémon next to the target during Double or Triple Battles. If the target is Frozen, it will be thawed.
Flame Charge	Fire	Physical	50	100	20	Normal	○	—	Raises the user's Speed by 1. If the target is Frozen, it will be thawed.
Flame Wheel	Fire	Physical	60	100	25	Normal	○	—	A 10% chance of inflicting the Burned status condition on the target. If the target is Frozen, it will be thawed. This move can be used even if the user is Frozen. If the user is Frozen, this also thaws the user.
Flamethrower	Fire	Special	90	100	15	Normal	—	—	A 10% chance of inflicting the Burned status condition on the target. If the target is Frozen, it will be thawed.
Flare Blitz	Fire	Physical	120	100	15	Normal	○	—	User takes 1/3 of the damage done to the target. A 10% chance of inflicting the Burned status condition on the target. If the target is Frozen, it will be thawed. This move can be used even if the user is Frozen. If the user is Frozen, this also thaws the user.
Flash	Normal	Status	—	100	20	Normal	—	—	Lowers the target's accuracy by 1.
Flash Cannon	Steel	Special	80	100	10	Normal	—	—	A 10% chance of lowering the target's Sp. Def by 1.
Flatter	Dark	Status	—	100	15	Normal	—	—	Inflicts the Confused status condition on the target, but also raises its Sp. Atk by 1.
Fling	Dark	Physical	—	100	10	Normal	—	—	The user attacks by throwing its held item at the target. Power and effect vary depending on the item.
Flower Shield	Fairy	Status	—	—	10	Adjacent	—	○	Raises the Defense of any Grass-type Pokémon by 1.
Fly	Flying	Physical	90	95	15	Normal	○	○	The user flies into the air on the first turn and attacks on the second.
Flying Press	Fighting	Physical	80	95	10	Normal	○	○	This move is both Fighting type and Flying type. If the target has used Minimize, it will be a sure hit and its power will be doubled.
Focus Blast	Fighting	Special	120	70	5	Normal	—	—	A 10% chance of lowering the target's Sp. Def by 1.
Focus Energy	Normal	Status	—	—	30	Self	—	—	Heightens the critical-hit ratio of the user's subsequent moves.
Focus Punch	Fighting	Physical	150	100	20	Normal	○	—	Always strikes last. The move misses if the user is hit before this move lands.
Follow Me	Normal	Status	—	—	20	Self	—	—	This move goes first. Opposing Pokémon aim only at the user.
Force Palm	Fighting	Physical	60	100	10	Normal	○	—	A 30% chance of inflicting the Paralysis status condition on the target.
Foresight	Normal	Status	—	—	40	Normal	—	—	Attacks land easily regardless of the target's evasion. Makes Ghost-type Pokémon vulnerable to Normal- and Fighting-type moves.
Forest's Curse	Grass	Status	—	100	20	Normal	—	—	Gives the target the Grass type.
Foul Play	Dark	Physical	95	100	15	Normal	○	—	The user turns the target's power against it. Damage varies depending on the target's Attack and Defense.
Freeze-Dry	Ice	Special	70	100	20	Normal	—	—	Super effective even against Water-type Pokémon. A 10% chance of inflicting the Frozen status condition.
Frenzy Plant	Grass	Special	150	90	5	Normal	—	—	The user can't move during the next turn.
Frost Breath	Ice	Special	60	90	10	Normal	—	—	Always delivers a critical hit.
Frustration	Normal	Physical	—	100	20	Normal	○	—	The lower the user's friendship, the greater this move's power (max 102).
Fury Attack	Normal	Physical	15	85	20	Normal	○	—	Attacks 2–5 times in a row in a single turn.
Fury Cutter	Bug	Physical	40	95	20	Normal	○	—	This move doubles in power with every successful hit (max 120). Power returns to normal once it misses.
Fury Swipes	Normal	Physical	18	80	15	Normal	○	—	Attacks 2–5 times in a row in a single turn.
Future Sight	Psychic	Special	120	100	10	Normal	—	—	Attacks the target after 2 turns. This move is affected by the target's type.

G

Move	Type	Kind	Pow.	Acc.	PP	Range	DA	Long	Effect
Gastro Acid	Poison	Status	—	100	10	Normal	—	—	Disables the target's Ability.
Geomancy	Fairy	Status	—	—	10	Self	—	—	Builds power on the first turn and increases the user's Sp. Atk, Sp. Def, and Speed by 2 on the second.
Giga Drain	Grass	Special	75	100	10	Normal	—	—	Restores HP by up to half of the damage dealt to the target.
Giga Impact	Normal	Physical	150	90	5	Normal	○	—	The user can't move during the next turn.
Glare	Normal	Status	—	100	30	Normal	—	—	Inflicts the Paralysis status condition on the target.
Grass Knot	Grass	Special	—	100	20	Normal	○	—	The heavier the target is compared to the user, the greater the move's power becomes (max 120).
Grass Pledge	Grass	Special	80	100	10	Normal	—	—	When combined with Water Pledge or Fire Pledge, the power and effect change. If combined with Water Pledge, the power is 150 and it remains a Grass-type move. This lowers the Speed of opposing Pokémon for 4 turns. If combined with Fire Pledge, the power is 150 and it becomes a Fire-type move. This damages all non-Fire types for 4 turns. If the target is Frozen, it will be thawed.
Grass Whistle	Grass	Status	—	55	15	Normal	—	—	Inflicts the Sleep status condition on the target. Strikes the target even if it is using Substitute.

Move	Type	Kind	Pow.	Acc.	PP	Range	DA	Long	Effect
Grassy Terrain	Grass	Status	—	—	10	Both Sides	—	—	Covers the field with grass for 5 turns. During that time, Pokémon on the ground will be able to do 50% more damage with Grass-type moves and will recover 1/16 of the Pokémon's maximum HP each turn.
Gravity	Psychic	Status	—	—	5	Both Sides	—	—	Raises the accuracy of all Pokémon in battle for 5 turns. Ground-type moves will now hit a Pokémon with the Levitate Ability or a Flying-type Pokémon. Prevents the use of Bounce, Fly, High Jump Kick, Jump Kick, Magnet Rise, Sky Drop, Splash, and Telekinesis. Pulls any airborne Pokémon to the ground.
Growl	Normal	Status	—	100	40	Many Others	—	—	Lowers the target's Attack by 1. Strikes the target even if it is using Substitute.
Growth	Normal	Status	—	—	20	Self	—	—	Raises the user's Attack and Sp. Atk by 1. Raises them by 2 when the weather condition is sunny or extremely harsh sunlight.
Grudge	Ghost	Status	—	—	5	Self	—	—	Any move that causes the user to faint will have its PP dropped to 0.
Guard Split	Psychic	Status	—	—	10	Normal	—	—	The user and the target's Defense and Sp. Def are added, then divided equally between them.
Guard Swap	Psychic	Status	—	—	10	Normal	—	—	Swaps Defense and Sp. Def changes between the user and the target.
Guillotine	Normal	Physical	—	30	5	Normal	○	—	The target faints with one hit if the user's level is equal to or greater than the target's level. The higher the user's level is compared to the target's, the more accurate the move is.
Gunk Shot	Poison	Physical	120	80	5	Normal	—	—	A 30% chance of inflicting the Poison status condition on the target.
Gust	Flying	Special	40	100	35	Normal	—	○	It even hits Pokémon that are in the sky due to using moves such as Fly and Bounce, dealing them twice the usual damage.
Gyro Ball	Steel	Physical	—	100	5	Normal	○	—	The slower the user is than the target, the greater the move's power becomes (max 150).

H·I

Move	Type	Kind	Pow.	Acc.	PP	Range	DA	Long	Effect
Hail	Ice	Status	—	—	10	Both Sides	—	—	Changes the weather condition to hail for 5 turns, dealing damage every turn equal to 1/16 of its max HP to each Pokémon in the field that is not an Ice type.
Hammer Arm	Fighting	Physical	100	90	10	Normal	○	—	Lowers the user's Speed by 1.
Harden	Normal	Status	—	—	30	Self	—	—	Raises the user's Defense by 1.
Haze	Ice	Status	—	—	30	Both Sides	—	—	Eliminates every stat change of the targets.
Head Smash	Rock	Physical	150	80	5	Normal	○	—	The user takes 1/2 of the damage inflicted.
Headbutt	Normal	Physical	70	100	15	Normal	○	—	A 30% chance of making the target flinch (unable to use moves on that turn).
Heal Bell	Normal	Status	—	—	5	Your Party	—	○	Heals status conditions of all your Pokémon, including those in your party. Affects the target even if it is using Substitute.
Heal Block	Psychic	Status	—	100	15	Many Others	—	—	Targets cannot have HP restored by moves, Abilities, or held items for 5 turns.
Heal Order	Bug	Status	—	—	10	Self	—	—	Restores HP by up to half of the user's maximum HP.
Heal Pulse	Psychic	Status	—	—	10	Normal	—	○	Restores the target's HP by up to half of its maximum HP.
Healing Wish	Psychic	Status	—	—	10	Self	—	—	The user faints, but fully heals the next Pokémon's HP and status conditions.
Heart Stamp	Psychic	Physical	60	100	25	Normal	○	—	A 30% chance of making the target flinch (unable to use moves on that turn).
Heat Wave	Fire	Special	95	90	10	Many Others	—	—	A 10% chance of inflicting the Burned status condition on the targets. If the targets are Frozen, they will be thawed. Its power is reduced by 25% when it hits multiple Pokémon.
Heavy Slam	Steel	Physical	—	100	10	Normal	○	—	The heavier the user is compared to the target, the greater the move's power becomes (max 120).
Helping Hand	Normal	Status	—	—	20	1 Ally	—	—	Always strikes first. Strengthens the attack power of one ally's moves by 50%.
Hex	Ghost	Special	65	100	10	Normal	—	—	Deals twice the usual damage to a target affected by status conditions.
Hidden Power	Normal	Special	60	100	15	Normal	—	—	Type changes depending on the user.
High Jump Kick	Fighting	Physical	130	90	10	Normal	○	—	If this move misses, the user loses half of its maximum HP.
Hone Claws	Dark	Status	—	—	15	Self	—	—	Raises Attack and accuracy by 1.
Horn Attack	Normal	Physical	65	100	25	Normal	○	—	A regular attack.
Horn Drill	Normal	Physical	—	30	5	Normal	○	—	The target faints with one hit if the user's level is equal to or greater than the target's level. The higher the user's level is compared to the target's, the more accurate the move is.
Horn Leech	Grass	Physical	75	100	10	Normal	○	—	Restores HP by up to half of the damage dealt to the target.
Howl	Normal	Status	—	—	40	Self	—	—	Raises the user's Attack by 1.
Hurricane	Flying	Special	110	70	10	Normal	—	○	A 30% chance of inflicting the Confused status condition on the target. Is 100% accurate in the rain / heavy rain weather conditions and 50% accurate in the sunny / extremely harsh sunlight weather conditions. It can hit Pokémon that are in the sky due to using moves such as Fly and Bounce.
Hydro Cannon	Water	Special	150	90	5	Normal	—	—	The user can't move during the next turn.
Hydro Pump	Water	Special	110	80	5	Normal	—	—	A regular attack.
Hyper Beam	Normal	Special	150	90	5	Normal	—	—	The user can't move during the next turn.
Hyper Fang	Normal	Physical	80	90	15	Normal	○	—	A 10% chance of making the target flinch (unable to use moves on that turn).
Hyper Voice	Normal	Special	90	100	10	Many Others	—	—	Strikes the target even if it is using Substitute. Its power is reduced by 25% when it hits multiple Pokémon.
Hypnosis	Psychic	Status	—	60	20	Normal	—	—	Inflicts the Sleep status condition on the target.
Ice Ball	Ice	Physical	30	90	20	Normal	○	—	Attacks consecutively over 5 turns or until it misses. Cannot choose other moves during this time. Damage dealt doubles with each successful hit (max 480). Its power is doubled if used after Defense Curl.
Ice Beam	Ice	Special	90	100	10	Normal	—	—	A 10% chance of inflicting the Frozen status condition on the target.
Ice Fang	Ice	Physical	65	95	15	Normal	○	—	A 10% chance of inflicting the Frozen status condition or making the target flinch (unable to use moves on that turn).

Move	Type	Kind	Pow.	Acc.	PP	Range	DA	Long	Effect
Ice Punch	Ice	Physical	75	100	15	Normal	○	—	A 10% chance of inflicting the Frozen status condition on the target.
Ice Shard	Ice	Physical	40	100	30	Normal	—	—	Always strikes first. The user with the higher Speed goes first if similar moves are used.
Icicle Crash	Ice	Physical	85	90	10	Normal	—	—	A 30% chance of making the target flinch (unable to use moves on that turn).
Icicle Spear	Ice	Physical	25	100	30	Normal	—	—	Attacks 2–5 times in a row in a single turn.
Icy Wind	Ice	Special	55	95	15	Many Others	—	—	Lowers the targets' Speed by 1. Its power is reduced by 25% when it hits multiple Pokémon.
Imprison	Psychic	Status	—	—	10	Self	—	—	Opposing Pokémon cannot use a move if the user knows that move as well.
Incinerate	Fire	Special	60	100	15	Many Others	—	—	Burns up the Berry or Gem being held by each of the targets, which makes them unusable. If the targets are Frozen, they will be thawed. Its power is reduced by 25% when it hits multiple Pokémon.
Inferno	Fire	Special	100	50	5	Normal	—	—	Inflicts the Burned status condition on the target. If the target is Frozen, it will be thawed.
Infestation	Bug	Special	20	100	20	Normal	○	—	Inflicts damage equal to 1/8 the target's max HP for 4–5 turns. The target cannot flee during that time.
Ingrain	Grass	Status	—	—	20	Self	—	—	Restores 1/16 of max HP every turn. The user cannot be switched out after using this move. Ground-type moves will now hit the user even if it is a Flying-type Pokémon or has the Levitate Ability.
Ion Deluge	Electric	Status	—	—	25	Both Sides	—	—	Attacks first. Changes any Normal-type moves used in the same turn into Electric-type moves.
Iron Defense	Steel	Status	—	—	15	Self	—	—	Raises the user's Defense by 2.
Iron Head	Steel	Physical	80	100	15	Normal	○	—	A 30% chance of making the target flinch (unable to use moves on that turn).
Iron Tail	Steel	Physical	100	75	15	Normal	○	—	A 30% chance of lowering the target's Defense by 1.

J·K·L

Move	Type	Kind	Pow.	Acc.	PP	Range	DA	Long	Effect
Jump Kick	Fighting	Physical	100	95	10	Normal	○	—	If this move misses, the user loses half of its maximum HP.
Karate Chop	Fighting	Physical	50	100	25	Normal	○	—	Critical hits land more easily.
Kinesis	Psychic	Status	—	80	15	Normal	—	—	Lowers the target's accuracy by 1.
King's Shield	Steel	Status	—	—	10	Self	—	—	The user evades all attacks that turn. If an opposing Pokémon uses a move that makes direct contact, its Attack will be lowered by 2. Fails more easily when used repeatedly.
Knock Off	Dark	Physical	65	100	20	Normal	○	—	The target drops its held item. It gets the item back after the battle. This move does 50% more damage to opponents holding items.
Land's Wrath	Ground	Physical	90	100	10	Many Others	—	—	Its power is reduced by 25% when it hits multiple Pokémon.
Last Resort	Normal	Physical	140	100	5	Normal	○	—	Fails unless the user has used each of its other moves at least once.
Lava Plume	Fire	Special	80	100	15	Adjacent	—	—	A 30% chance of inflicting the Burned status condition on the targets. If the targets are Frozen, they will be thawed. Its power is reduced by 25% when it hits multiple Pokémon.
Leaf Blade	Grass	Physical	90	100	15	Normal	○	—	Critical hits land more easily.
Leaf Storm	Grass	Special	130	90	5	Normal	—	—	Lowers the user's Sp. Atk by 2.
Leaf Tornado	Grass	Special	65	90	10	Normal	—	—	A 50% chance of lowering the target's accuracy by 1.
Leech Life	Bug	Physical	20	100	15	Normal	○	—	Restores HP by up to half of the damage dealt to the target.
Leech Seed	Grass	Status	—	90	10	Normal	—	—	Steals 1/8 of the target's max HP every turn and absorbs it to restore the user. Keeps working even after the user switches out. Does not work on Grass types.
Leer	Normal	Status	—	100	30	Many Others	—	—	Lowers the targets' Defense by 1.
Lick	Ghost	Physical	30	100	30	Normal	○	—	A 30% chance of inflicting the Paralysis status condition on the target.
Light Screen	Psychic	Status	—	—	30	Your Side	—	—	Halves the damage to the Pokémon on your side from special moves. Effect lasts 5 turns even if the user is switched out. Effect is weaker in Double and Triple Battles.
Lock-On	Normal	Status	—	—	5	Normal	—	—	The user's next move will be a sure hit.
Lovely Kiss	Normal	Status	—	75	10	Normal	—	—	Inflicts the Sleep status condition on the target.
Low Kick	Fighting	Physical	—	100	20	Normal	○	—	The heavier the target is compared to the user, the greater the move's power becomes (max 120).
Low Sweep	Fighting	Physical	65	100	20	Normal	○	—	Lowers the target's Speed by 1.
Lucky Chant	Normal	Status	—	—	30	Your Side	—	—	The Pokémon on your side take no critical hits for 5 turns.
Luster Purge	Psychic	Special	70	100	5	Normal	—	—	Has a 50% chance of lowering the target's Sp. Def by 1.

M

Move	Type	Kind	Pow.	Acc.	PP	Range	DA	Long	Effect
Mach Punch	Fighting	Physical	40	100	30	Normal	○	—	Always strikes first. The user with the higher Speed goes first if similar moves are used.
Magic Coat	Psychic	Status	—	—	15	Self	—	—	Always strikes first. Reflects moves with effects like Leech Seed or those that inflict status conditions such as Sleep, Poison, Paralysis, or Confused.
Magic Room	Psychic	Status	—	—	10	Both Sides	—	—	Always strikes last. No held items will have any effect for 5 turns. Fling cannot be used to throw items while Magic Room is in effect. The effect ends if the move is used again.
Magical Leaf	Grass	Special	60	—	20	Normal	—	—	A sure hit.
Magnet Bomb	Steel	Physical	60	—	20	Normal	—	—	A sure hit.
Magnet Rise	Electric	Status	—	—	10	Self	—	—	Nullifies Ground-type moves for 5 turns.

Move	Type	Kind	Pow.	Acc.	PP	Range	DA	Long	Effect
Magnetic Flux	Electric	Status	—	—	20	Your Party	—	○	Raises the Defense and Sp. Def of allies with either the Plus or Minus Abilities.
Magnitude	Ground	Physical	—	100	30	Adjacent	—	—	This move's power varies among 10, 30, 50, 70, 90, 110, and 150. Does twice the damage if targets are underground due to using Dig. Its power is reduced by 25% when it hits multiple Pokémon.
Mat Block	Fighting	Status	—	—	10	Your Side	—	—	Protects the user and allies from damage-dealing moves used in the same turn. Does not protect against status moves.
Me First	Normal	Status	—	—	20	Varies	—	—	Copies the target's chosen move and uses it with 50% greater power. Fails if it does not strike first.
Mean Look	Normal	Status	—	—	5	Normal	—	—	The target cannot escape. If used during a Trainer battle, the opposing Trainer cannot switch Pokémon. Has no effect on Ghost-type Pokémon.
Meditate	Psychic	Status	—	—	40	Self	—	—	Raises the user's Attack by 1.
Mega Drain	Grass	Special	40	100	15	Normal	—	—	Restores HP by up to half of the damage dealt to the target.
Mega Punch	Normal	Physical	80	85	20	Normal	○	—	A regular attack.
Megahorn	Bug	Physical	120	85	10	Normal	○	—	A regular attack.
Memento	Dark	Status	—	100	10	Normal	—	—	The user faints, but the target's Attack and Sp. Atk are lowered by 2.
Metal Burst	Steel	Physical	—	100	10	Varies	—	—	Targets the Pokémon that most recently damaged the user with a move. Inflicts 1.5 times the damage taken.
Metal Claw	Steel	Physical	50	95	35	Normal	○	—	A 10% chance of raising the user's Attack by 1.
Metal Sound	Steel	Status	—	85	40	Normal	—	—	Lowers the target's Sp. Def by 2. Strikes the target even if it is using Substitute.
Meteor Mash	Steel	Physical	90	90	10	Normal	—	○	Has a 20% chance of raising the user's Attack by 1.
Metronome	Normal	Status	—	—	10	Self	—	—	Uses one move randomly chosen from all possible moves.
Milk Drink	Normal	Status	—	—	10	Self	—	—	Restores HP by up to half of the user's maximum HP.
Mimic	Normal	Status	—	—	10	Normal	—	—	Copies the target's last-used move (copied move has a PP of 5). Fails if used before the opposing Pokémon uses a move.
Mind Reader	Normal	Status	—	—	5	Normal	—	—	The user's next move will be a sure hit.
Minimize	Normal	Status	—	—	10	Self	—	—	Raises the user's evasion by 2.
Miracle Eye	Psychic	Status	—	—	40	Normal	—	—	Attacks land easily regardless of the target's evasion. Makes Dark-type Pokémon vulnerable to Psychic-type moves.
Mirror Coat	Psychic	Special	—	100	20	Varies	—	—	If the user is attacked with a special move, this move inflicts twice the damage done to the user. Always strikes last.
Mirror Move	Flying	Status	—	—	20	Normal	—	—	Uses the last move that the target used.
Mirror Shot	Steel	Special	65	85	10	Normal	—	—	A 30% chance of lowering the target's accuracy by 1.
Mist	Ice	Status	—	—	30	Your Side	—	—	Protects against stat-lowering moves and additional effects for 5 turns.
Mist Ball	Psychic	Special	70	100	5	Normal	—	—	Has a 50% chance of reducing the target's Sp. Atk by 1.
Misty Terrain	Fairy	Status	—	—	10	Both Sides	—	—	Covers the field with mist for 5 turns. During that time, Pokémon on the ground take half damage from Dragon-type moves and cannot be afflicted with new status conditions.
Moonblast	Fairy	Special	95	100	15	Normal	—	—	A 30% chance of lowering the target's Sp. Atk by 1.
Moonlight	Fairy	Status	—	—	5	Self	—	—	Recovers 1/2 of the user's maximum HP in normal weather conditions. Recovers 2/3 of the user's maximum HP in sunny or extremely harsh sunlight weather conditions. Recovers 1/4 of the user's maximum HP in rain/heavy rain/sandstorm/hail weather conditions.
Morning Sun	Normal	Status	—	—	5	Self	—	—	Recovers 1/2 of the user's maximum HP in normal weather conditions. Recovers 2/3 of the user's maximum HP in sunny or extremely harsh sunlight weather conditions. Recovers 1/4 of the user's maximum HP in rain/heavy rain/sandstorm/hail weather conditions.
Mud Bomb	Ground	Special	65	85	10	Normal	—	—	A 30% chance of lowering the target's accuracy by 1.
Mud Shot	Ground	Special	55	95	15	Normal	—	—	Lowers the target's Speed by 1.
Mud Sport	Ground	Status	—	—	15	Both Sides	—	—	Lowers the power of Electric-type moves to 1/3 of normal for 5 turns.
Muddy Water	Water	Special	90	85	10	Many Others	—	—	A 30% chance of lowering the targets' accuracy by 1. Its power is reduced by 25% when it hits multiple Pokémon.
Mud-Slap	Ground	Special	20	100	10	Normal	—	—	Lowers the target's accuracy by 1.
Mystical Fire	Fire	Special	65	100	10	Normal	—	—	Lowers the target's Sp. Atk by 1.

N·O

Move	Type	Kind	Pow.	Acc.	PP	Range	DA	Long	Effect
Nasty Plot	Dark	Status	—	—	20	Self	—	—	Raises the user's Sp. Atk by 2.
Natural Gift	Normal	Physical	—	100	15	Normal	—	—	This move's type and power change according to the Berry held by the user. The Berry is consumed when this move is used. This move fails if the user is not holding a Berry.
Nature Power	Normal	Status	—	—	20	Normal	—	—	This move varies depending on the environment: Cave: Power Gem. Dirt/Sand: Earth Power. Grass / Grassy Terrain: Energy Ball. Electric Terrain: Thunderbolt. Ice: Ice Beam. Indoors / Link Battle: Tri Attack. Misty Terrain: Moonblast. Snow: Frost Breath. Swamp: Mud Bomb. Water Surface / Puddles / Shoals: Hydro Pump.
Needle Arm	Grass	Physical	60	100	15	Normal	○	—	A 30% chance of making the target flinch (unable to use moves on that turn).
Night Daze	Dark	Special	85	95	10	Normal	—	—	A 40% chance of lowering the target's accuracy by 1.
Night Shade	Ghost	Special	—	100	15	Normal	—	—	Deals a fixed amount of damage equal to the user's level.
Night Slash	Dark	Physical	70	100	15	Normal	○	—	Critical hits land more easily.
Nightmare	Ghost	Status	—	100	15	Normal	—	—	Lowers the target's HP by 1/4 of maximum after each turn. Fails if the target is not asleep.
Noble Roar	Normal	Status	—	100	30	Normal	—	—	Lowers the target's Attack and Sp. Atk by 1. Strikes the target even if it is using Substitute.
Nuzzle	Electric	Physical	20	100	20	Normal	○	—	Inflicts the Paralysis status condition on the target.

Move	Type	Kind	Pow.	Acc.	PP	Range	DA	Long	Effect
Oblivion Wing	Flying	Special	80	100	10	Normal	—	○	Restores HP by up to 3/4 of the damage dealt to the target.
Octazooka	Water	Special	65	85	10	Normal	—	—	A 50% chance of lowering the target's accuracy by 1.
Odor Sleuth	Normal	Status	—	—	40	Normal	—	—	Attacks land easily regardless of the target's evasion. Makes Ghost-type Pokémon vulnerable to Normal- and Fighting-type moves.
Ominous Wind	Ghost	Special	60	100	5	Normal	—	—	A 10% chance of raising the user's Attack, Defense, Speed, Sp. Atk, and Sp. Def stats by 1.
Origin Pulse	Water	Special	110	85	10	Many Others	—	—	Its power is reduced by 25% when it hits multiple Pokémon.
Outrage	Dragon	Physical	120	100	10	1 Random	○	—	Attacks consecutively over 2–3 turns. Cannot choose other moves during this time. The user becomes Confused after using this move.
Overheat	Fire	Special	130	90	5	Normal	—	—	Lowers the user's Sp. Atk by 2. If the target is Frozen, it will be thawed.

P

Move	Type	Kind	Pow.	Acc.	PP	Range	DA	Long	Effect
Pain Split	Normal	Status	—	—	20	Normal	—	—	The user and target's HP are added, then divided equally between them.
Parabolic Charge	Electric	Special	50	100	20	Adjacent	—	—	Restores HP by up to half of the damage dealt to the target. Its power is reduced by 25% when it hits multiple Pokémon.
Parting Shot	Dark	Status	—	100	20	Normal	—	—	Lowers the target's Attack and Sp. Atk. After attacking, user switches out with another Pokémon in the party. Strikes the target even if it is using Substitute.
Pay Day	Normal	Physical	40	100	20	Normal	—	—	Increases the amount of prize money received after battle (the user's level, multiplied by the number of attacks, multiplied by 5).
Payback	Dark	Physical	50	100	10	Normal	○	—	This move's power is doubled if the user strikes after the target.
Peck	Flying	Physical	35	100	35	Normal	○	○	A regular attack.
Perish Song	Normal	Status	—	—	5	Adjacent	—	○	All adjacent Pokémon in battle will faint after 3 turns, unless switched out. Strikes the target even if it is using Substitute.
Petal Blizzard	Grass	Physical	90	100	15	Adjacent	—	—	Its power is reduced by 25% when it hits multiple Pokémon.
Petal Dance	Grass	Special	120	100	10	1 Random	○	—	Attacks consecutively over 2–3 turns. Cannot choose other moves during this time. The user becomes Confused after using this move.
Phantom Force	Ghost	Physical	90	100	10	Normal	○	—	User disappears on the first turn and attacks on the second. Strikes the target even if it is using Detect, King's Shield, Mat Block, Protect, or Spiky Shield. If the target has used Minimize, it will be a sure hit and its power will be doubled.
Pin Missile	Bug	Physical	25	95	20	Normal	—	—	Attacks 2–5 times in a row in a single turn.
Play Nice	Normal	Status	—	—	20	Normal	—	—	A sure hit. Lowers the target's Attack by 1. Strikes the target even if it is using Detect, King's Shield, Mat Block, Protect, Spiky Shield, or Substitute.
Play Rough	Fairy	Physical	90	90	10	Normal	○	—	A 10% chance of lowering the target's Attack by 1.
Pluck	Flying	Physical	60	100	20	Normal	○	○	If the target is holding a Berry with a battle effect, the user eats that Berry and uses its effect.
Poison Fang	Poison	Physical	50	100	15	Normal	○	—	A 50% chance of inflicting the Badly Poisoned status condition on the target. Damage from being Badly Poisoned increases with every turn.
Poison Gas	Poison	Status	—	90	40	Many Others	—	—	Inflicts the Poison status condition on the targets.
Poison Jab	Poison	Physical	80	100	20	Normal	○	—	A 30% chance of inflicting the Poison status condition on the target.
Poison Powder	Poison	Status	—	75	35	Normal	—	—	Inflicts the Poison status condition on the targets. Has no effect on Grass-type Pokémon.
Poison Sting	Poison	Physical	15	100	35	Normal	—	—	A 30% chance of inflicting the Poison status condition on the target.
Poison Tail	Poison	Physical	50	100	25	Normal	○	—	A 10% chance of inflicting the Poison status condition on the target. Critical hits land more easily.
Pound	Normal	Physical	40	100	35	Normal	○	—	A regular attack.
Powder	Bug	Status	—	100	20	Normal	—	—	Always attacks first. Has no effect on Grass-type Pokémon. Deals damage equal to 1/4 of max HP if the target uses a Fire-type move in the same turn.
Powder Snow	Ice	Special	40	100	25	Many Others	—	—	A 10% chance of inflicting the Frozen status condition on the targets. Its power is reduced by 25% when it hits multiple Pokémon.
Power Gem	Rock	Special	80	100	20	Normal	—	—	A regular attack.
Power Split	Psychic	Status	—	—	10	Normal	—	—	The user and the target's Attack and Sp. Atk are added, then divided equally between them.
Power Swap	Psychic	Status	—	—	10	Normal	—	—	Swaps Attack and Sp. Atk changes between the user and the target.
Power Trick	Psychic	Status	—	—	10	Self	—	—	Swaps original Attack and Defense stats (does not swap stat changes).
Power Whip	Grass	Physical	120	85	10	Normal	○	—	A regular attack.
Power-Up Punch	Fighting	Physical	40	100	20	Normal	○	—	Raises the user's Attack by 1.
Precipice Blades	Ground	Physical	120	85	10	Many Others	—	—	Its power is reduced by 25% when it hits multiple Pokémon.
Present	Normal	Physical	—	90	15	Normal	—	—	This move's power varies among 40 (40% chance), 80 (30% chance), and 120 (10% chance). It also has a 20% chance of healing the target by 1/4 of its maximum HP.
Protect	Normal	Status	—	—	10	Self	—	—	The user evades all moves that turn. If used in succession, its chance of failing rises.
Psybeam	Psychic	Special	65	100	20	Normal	—	—	A 10% chance of inflicting the Confused status condition on the target.
Psych Up	Normal	Status	—	—	10	Normal	—	—	Copies the target's stat changes to the user.
Psychic	Psychic	Special	90	100	10	Normal	—	—	A 10% chance of lowering the target's Sp. Def by 1.
Psycho Cut	Psychic	Physical	70	100	20	Normal	—	—	Critical hits land more easily.
Psycho Shift	Psychic	Status	—	100	10	Normal	—	—	Shifts the user's Paralysis, Poison, Badly Poisoned, Burned, or Sleep status conditions to the target and heals the user.

Move	Type	Kind	Pow.	Acc.	PP	Range	DA	Long	Effect
Psyshock	Psychic	Special	80	100	10	Normal	—	—	Damage depends on the user's Sp. Atk and the target's Defense.
Psystrike	Psychic	Special	100	100	10	Normal	—	—	Damage depends on the user's Sp. Atk and the target's Defense.
Psywave	Psychic	Special	—	100	15	Normal	—	—	Inflicts damage equal to the user's level multiplied by a random value between 0.5 and 1.5.
Punishment	Dark	Physical	—	100	5	Normal	○	—	With each level that the target's stats increase, the move's power becomes greater (max 200).
Pursuit	Dark	Physical	40	100	20	Normal	○	—	Does twice the usual damage if the target is switching out.

Q·R

Move	Type	Kind	Pow.	Acc.	PP	Range	DA	Long	Effect
Quash	Dark	Status	—	100	15	Normal	—	—	The user suppresses the target and makes it move last that turn. Fails if the target has already used its move that turn.
Quick Attack	Normal	Physical	40	100	30	Normal	○	—	Always strikes first. The user with the higher Speed goes first if similar moves are used.
Quick Guard	Fighting	Status	—	—	15	Your Side	—	—	Protects the user and its allies from first-strike moves.
Quiver Dance	Bug	Status	—	—	20	Self	—	—	Raises the user's Sp. Atk, Sp. Def, and Speed by 1.
Rage	Normal	Physical	20	100	20	Normal	○	—	Attack rises by 1 with each hit the user takes.
Rage Powder	Bug	Status	—	—	20	Self	—	—	This move goes first. Opposing Pokémon aim only at the user. Has no effect on Grass-type Pokémon.
Rain Dance	Water	Status	—	—	5	Both Sides	—	—	Changes the weather condition to rain for 5 turns, strengthening Water-type moves by 50% and reducing the power of Fire-type moves by 50%.
Rapid Spin	Normal	Physical	20	100	40	Normal	○	—	Releases the user from moves such as Bind, Leech Seed, Spikes, and Wrap.
Razor Leaf	Grass	Physical	55	95	25	Many Others	—	—	Critical hits land more easily. Its power is reduced by 25% when it hits multiple Pokémon.
Razor Shell	Water	Physical	75	95	10	Normal	○	—	A 50% chance of lowering the target's Defense by 1.
Razor Wind	Normal	Special	80	100	10	Many Others	—	—	The user stores power on the first turn and attacks on the second. Critical hits land more easily. Its power is reduced by 25% when it hits multiple Pokémon.
Recover	Normal	Status	—	—	10	Self	—	—	Restores HP by up to half of the user's maximum HP.
Recycle	Normal	Status	—	—	10	Self	—	—	A held item that has been used can be used again.
Reflect	Psychic	Status	—	—	20	Your Side	—	—	Halves the damage to the Pokémon on your side from physical moves. Effect lasts 5 turns even if the user is switched out. Effect is weaker in Double and Triple Battles.
Reflect Type	Normal	Status	—	—	15	Normal	—	—	The user becomes the same type as the target.
Refresh	Normal	Status	—	—	20	Self	—	—	Heals Poison, Badly Poisoned, Paralysis, and Burned conditions.
Rest	Psychic	Status	—	—	10	Self	—	—	Fully restores HP, but makes the user sleep for 2 turns.
Retaliate	Normal	Physical	70	100	5	Normal	○	—	This move's power is doubled if an ally fainted in the previous turn.
Return	Normal	Physical	—	100	20	Normal	○	—	This move's power is affected by friendship. The higher the user's friendship, the greater the move's power (max 102).
Revenge	Fighting	Physical	60	100	10	Normal	○	—	Attacks last. This move's power is doubled if the user has taken damage from the target that turn.
Reversal	Fighting	Physical	—	100	15	Normal	○	—	The lower the user's HP is, the greater the move's power becomes (max 200).
Roar	Normal	Status	—	—	20	Normal	—	—	Attacks last. Ends wild Pokémon battles. If the opposing Pokémon's level is higher than the user's, this move fails. In a Double Battle with wild Pokémon, this move fails. In a battle with a Trainer, this move forces the opposing Trainer to switch Pokémon. When there is no Pokémon to switch in, this move fails. Strikes the target even if it is using Detect, King's Shield, Mat Block, Protect, Spiky Shield, or Substitute.
Rock Blast	Rock	Physical	25	90	10	Normal	—	—	Attacks 2–5 times in a row in a single turn.
Rock Climb	Normal	Physical	90	85	20	Normal	○	—	A 20% chance of inflicting the Confused status condition on the target.
Rock Polish	Rock	Status	—	—	20	Self	—	—	Raises the user's Speed by 2.
Rock Slide	Rock	Physical	75	90	10	Many Others	—	—	A 30% chance of making the targets flinch (unable to use moves on that turn). Its power is reduced by 25% when it hits multiple Pokémon.
Rock Smash	Fighting	Physical	40	100	15	Normal	○	—	A 50% chance of lowering the target's Defense by 1.
Rock Throw	Rock	Physical	50	90	15	Normal	—	—	A regular attack.
Rock Tomb	Rock	Physical	60	95	15	Normal	—	—	Lowers the target's Speed by 1.
Rock Wrecker	Rock	Physical	150	90	5	Normal	—	—	The user can't move during the next turn.
Role Play	Psychic	Status	—	—	10	Normal	—	—	Copies the target's Ability. Fails with certain Abilities, however.
Rolling Kick	Fighting	Physical	60	85	15	Normal	○	—	A 30% chance of making the target flinch (unable to use moves on that turn).
Rollout	Rock	Physical	30	90	20	Normal	○	—	Attacks consecutively over 5 turns or until it misses. Cannot choose other moves during this time. Damage dealt doubles with every successful hit (max 480). Does twice the damage if used after Defense Curl.
Roost	Flying	Status	—	—	10	Self	—	—	Restores HP by up to half of the user's maximum HP, but takes away the Flying type from the user for that turn.
Rototiller	Ground	Status	—	—	10	Adjacent	—	○	Raises the Attack and Sp. Atk of Grass-type Pokémon by 1.
Round	Normal	Special	60	100	15	Normal	—	—	When multiple Pokémon use this move in a turn, the first one to use it is followed immediately by the others. Attack's power is doubled when following another Pokémon using the same move. Strikes the target even if it is using Substitute.

S

Move	Type	Kind	Pow.	Acc.	PP	Range	DA	Long	Effect
Sacred Sword	Fighting	Physical	90	100	15	Normal	○	—	Ignores the stat changes of the opposing Pokémon, except for Speed.
Safeguard	Normal	Status	—	—	25	Your Side	—	—	Protects the Pokémon on your side from status conditions and confusion for 5 turns. Effects last even if the user switches out.
Sand Attack	Ground	Status	—	100	15	Normal	—	—	Lowers the target's accuracy by 1.
Sand Tomb	Ground	Physical	35	85	15	Normal	—	—	Inflicts damage equal to 1/8 the target's max HP for 4–5 turns. The target cannot flee during that time.
Sandstorm	Rock	Status	—	—	10	Both Sides	—	—	Changes the weather condition to sandstorm for 5 turns. Raises the Sp. Def of Rock-type Pokémon by 50% for the length of the sandstorm. All Pokémon other than Rock, Steel, and Ground types take damage each turn equal to 1/16 of their max HP.
Scald	Water	Special	80	100	15	Normal	—	—	A 30% chance of inflicting the Burned status condition on the target. This move can be used even when the user is Frozen. Using this move will thaw the user, relieving the Frozen status condition.
Scary Face	Normal	Status	—	100	10	Normal	—	—	Lowers the targets' Speed by 2.
Scratch	Normal	Physical	40	100	35	Normal	○	—	A regular attack.
Screech	Normal	Status	—	85	40	Normal	—	—	Lowers the target's Defense by 2. Strikes the target even if it is using Substitute.
Secret Power	Normal	Physical	70	100	20	Normal	—	—	A 30% chance of one of the following additional effects, depending on the environment: Cave: Target flinches. Dirt/Sand: Lowers accuracy by 1. Grass / Grassy Terrain: Sleep status condition. Indoors / Electric Terrain / Link Battle: Inflicts Paralysis status condition. Misty Terrain: Lowers Sp. Atk by 1. Snow/Ice: Inflicts Frozen status condition. Swamp: Lowers Speed by 1. Water Surface / Puddles / Shoals: Lowers Attack by 1
Seed Bomb	Grass	Physical	80	100	15	Normal	—	—	A regular attack.
Seismic Toss	Fighting	Physical	—	100	20	Normal	○	—	Deals a fixed amount of damage equal to the user's level.
Self-Destruct	Normal	Physical	200	100	5	Adjacent	—	—	The user faints after using it. Its power is reduced by 25% when it hits multiple Pokémon.
Shadow Ball	Ghost	Special	80	100	15	Normal	—	—	A 20% chance of lowering the target's Sp. Def by 1.
Shadow Claw	Ghost	Physical	70	100	15	Normal	○	—	Critical hits land more easily.
Shadow Punch	Ghost	Physical	60	—	20	Normal	○	—	A sure hit.
Shadow Sneak	Ghost	Physical	40	100	30	Normal	○	—	Always strikes first. The user with the higher Speed goes first if similar moves are used.
Sharpen	Normal	Status	—	—	30	Self	—	—	Raises the user's Attack by 1.
Sheer Cold	Ice	Special	—	30	5	Normal	—	—	The target faints with one hit if the user's level is equal to or greater than the target's level. The higher the user's level is compared to the target's, the more accurate the move is.
Shell Smash	Normal	Status	—	—	15	Self	—	—	Lowers the user's Defense and Sp. Def by 1 and raises the user's Attack, Sp. Atk, and Speed by 2.
Shock Wave	Electric	Special	60	—	20	Normal	—	—	A sure hit.
Signal Beam	Bug	Special	75	100	15	Normal	—	—	A 10% chance of inflicting the Confused status condition on the target.
Silver Wind	Bug	Special	60	100	5	Normal	—	—	A 10% chance of raising the user's Attack, Defense, Speed, Sp. Atk, and Sp. Def stats by 1.
Simple Beam	Normal	Status	—	100	15	Normal	—	—	Changes the target's Ability to Simple. Fails with certain Abilities, however.
Sing	Normal	Status	—	55	15	Normal	—	—	Inflicts the Sleep status condition on the target. Strikes the target even if it is using Substitute.
Sketch	Normal	Status	—	—	1	Normal	—	—	Copies the last move used by the target. The user then forgets Sketch and learns the new move.
Skill Swap	Psychic	Status	—	—	10	Normal	—	—	Swaps Abilities between the user and target. Fails with certain Abilities, however.
Skull Bash	Normal	Physical	130	100	10	Normal	○	—	Builds power on the first turn and attacks on the second. It raises the user's Defense stat by 1 on the first turn.
Sky Attack	Flying	Physical	140	90	5	Normal	—	○	Builds power on the first turn and attacks on the second. Critical hits land more easily. A 30% chance of making the target flinch (unable to use moves on that turn).
Sky Drop	Flying	Physical	60	100	10	Normal	○	○	The user takes the target into the sky, and then damages it by dropping it during the next turn. Does not damage Flying-type Pokémon. Pokémon weighing over 440.9 lbs. cannot be lifted.
Sky Uppercut	Fighting	Physical	85	90	15	Normal	○	—	It even hits Pokémon that are in the sky due to having used moves such as Fly and Bounce.
Slack Off	Normal	Status	—	—	10	Self	—	—	Restores HP by up to half of the user's maximum HP.
Slam	Normal	Physical	80	75	20	Normal	○	—	A regular attack.
Slash	Normal	Physical	70	100	20	Normal	○	—	Critical hits land more easily.
Sleep Powder	Grass	Status	—	75	15	Normal	—	—	Inflicts the Sleep status condition on the target. Has no effect on Grass-type Pokémon.
Sleep Talk	Normal	Status	—	—	10	Self	—	—	Only works when the user is asleep. Randomly uses one of the user's moves.
Sludge	Poison	Special	65	100	20	Normal	—	—	A 30% chance of inflicting the Poison status condition on the target.
Sludge Bomb	Poison	Special	90	100	10	Normal	—	—	A 30% chance of inflicting the Poison status condition on the target.
Sludge Wave	Poison	Special	95	100	10	Adjacent	—	—	A 10% chance of inflicting the Poison status condition on the targets. Its power is reduced by 25% when it hits multiple Pokémon.
Smack Down	Rock	Physical	50	100	15	Normal	—	—	Ground-type moves will now hit a Pokémon with the Levitate Ability or a Flying-type Pokémon. They will also hit a Pokémon that is in the sky due to using a move such as Fly or Bounce.
Smelling Salts	Normal	Physical	70	100	10	Normal	○	—	Deals twice the usual damage to targets with Paralysis, but heals that status condition.
Smog	Poison	Special	30	70	20	Normal	—	—	A 40% chance of inflicting the Poison status condition on the target.
Smokescreen	Normal	Status	—	100	20	Normal	—	—	Lowers the target's accuracy by 1.
Snarl	Dark	Special	55	95	15	Many Others	—	—	Lowers the targets' Sp. Atk by 1. Its power is reduced by 25% when it hits multiple Pokémon. Strikes the target even if it is using Substitute.
Snatch	Dark	Status	—	—	10	Self	—	—	Steals the effects of recovery or stat-changing moves used by the target on that turn and applies them to the user.

Move	Type	Kind	Pow.	Acc.	PP	Range	DA	Long	Effect
Snore	Normal	Special	50	100	15	Normal	—	—	Only works when the user is asleep. A 30% chance of making the target flinch (unable to use moves on that turn). Strikes the target even if it is using Substitute.
Soak	Water	Status	—	100	20	Normal	—	—	Changes the target's type to Water.
Solar Beam	Grass	Special	120	100	10	Normal	—	—	Builds power on the first turn and attacks on the second. In sunny or extremely harsh sunlight weather conditions, attacks on first turn. In rain/heavy rain/sandstorm/hail weather conditions, the power is halved.
Sonic Boom	Normal	Special	—	90	20	Normal	—	—	Deals a fixed 20 points of damage.
Spark	Electric	Physical	65	100	20	Normal	○	—	A 30% chance of inflicting the Paralysis status condition on the target.
Spider Web	Bug	Status	—	—	10	Normal	—	—	The target cannot escape. If used during a Trainer battle, the opposing Trainer cannot switch Pokémon. Has no effect on Ghost-type Pokémon.
Spike Cannon	Normal	Physical	20	100	15	Normal	—	—	Attacks 2–5 times in a row in a single turn.
Spikes	Ground	Status	—	—	20	Other Side	—	—	Damages Pokémon as they are sent out to the opposing side. Power rises with each use, up to 3 times (1st time: 1/8 of maximum HP; 2nd time: 1/6 of maximum HP; 3rd time: 1/4 of maximum HP). Ineffective against Flying-type Pokémon and Pokémon with the Levitate Ability.
Spiky Shield	Grass	Status	—	—	10	Self	—	—	The user takes no damage in the same turn this move is used. If an opposing Pokémon uses a move that makes direct contact, the attacker will be damaged for 1/8 of its maximum HP.
Spit Up	Normal	Special	—	100	10	Normal	—	—	The more times the user has used Stockpile, the greater the move's power becomes (max 300). Fails if the user has not used Stockpile first. Nullifies Defense and Sp. Def stat increases caused by Stockpile.
Spite	Ghost	Status	—	100	10	Normal	—	—	Takes 4 points from the PP of the target's last used move.
Splash	Normal	Status	—	—	40	Self	—	—	No effect.
Spore	Grass	Status	—	100	15	Normal	—	—	Inflicts the Sleep status condition on the target. Has no effect on Grass-type Pokémon.
Stealth Rock	Rock	Status	—	—	20	Other Side	—	—	Damages Pokémon as they are sent out to the opposing side. Damage is subject to type matchups.
Steamroller	Bug	Physical	65	100	20	Normal	○	—	A 30% chance of making the targets flinch (unable to use moves on that turn). If the target has used Minimize, this move will be a sure hit and its power will be doubled.
Steel Wing	Steel	Physical	70	90	25	Normal	○	—	A 10% chance of raising the user's Defense by 1.
Sticky Web	Bug	Status	—	—	20	Other Side	—	—	Lowers the Speed of any Pokémon sent out to the opposing side by 1.
Stockpile	Normal	Status	—	—	20	Self	—	—	Raises the user's Defense and Sp. Def by 1. Can be used up to 3 times.
Stomp	Normal	Physical	65	100	20	Normal	○	—	A 30% chance of making the targets flinch (unable to use moves on that turn). If the target has used Minimize, this move will be a sure hit and its power will be doubled.
Stone Edge	Rock	Physical	100	80	5	Normal	—	—	Critical hits land more easily.
Stored Power	Psychic	Special	20	100	10	Normal	—	—	With each level that the user's stats increase, the move's power increases by 20 (max 860).
Storm Throw	Fighting	Physical	60	100	10	Normal	○	—	Always delivers a critical hit.
Strength	Normal	Physical	80	100	15	Normal	○	—	A regular attack.
String Shot	Bug	Status	—	95	40	Many Others	—	—	Lowers the targets' Speed by 2.
Struggle	Normal	Physical	50	—	1	Normal	○	—	This move becomes available when all other moves are out of PP. The user takes damage equal to 1/4 of its maximum HP. Inflicts damage regardless of type matchup.
Struggle Bug	Bug	Special	50	100	20	Many Others	—	—	Lowers the targets' Sp. Atk by 1. Its power is reduced by 25% when it hits multiple Pokémon.
Stun Spore	Grass	Status	—	75	30	Normal	—	—	Inflicts the Paralysis status condition on the target. Has no effect on Grass-type Pokémon.
Submission	Fighting	Physical	80	80	20	Normal	○	—	The user takes 1/4 of the damage inflicted.
Substitute	Normal	Status	—	—	10	Self	—	—	Uses 1/4 of maximum HP to create a copy of the user.
Sucker Punch	Dark	Physical	80	100	5	Normal	○	—	This move attacks first and deals damage only if the target's chosen move is an attack move.
Sunny Day	Fire	Status	—	—	5	Both Sides	—	—	Changes the weather condition to sunny for 5 turns, strengthening Fire-type moves by 50% and reducing the power of Water-type moves by 50%.
Super Fang	Normal	Physical	—	90	10	Normal	○	—	Halves the target's HP.
Superpower	Fighting	Physical	120	100	5	Normal	○	—	Lowers the user's Attack and Defense by 1.
Supersonic	Normal	Status	—	55	20	Normal	—	—	Inflicts the Confused status condition on the target. Strikes the target even if it is using Substitute.
Surf	Water	Special	90	100	15	Adjacent	—	—	Does twice the damage if the target is using Dive when attacked. Its power is weaker when it hits multiple Pokémon.
Swagger	Normal	Status	—	90	15	Normal	—	—	Inflicts the Confused status condition on the target, but also raises its Attack by 2.
Swallow	Normal	Status	—	—	10	Self	—	—	Restores HP, the amount of which is determined by how many times the user has used Stockpile. Fails if the user has not used Stockpile first. Nullifies Defense and Sp. Def stat increases caused by Stockpile.
Sweet Kiss	Fairy	Status	—	75	10	Normal	—	—	Inflicts the Confused status condition on the target.
Sweet Scent	Normal	Status	—	100	20	Many Others	—	—	Lowers the targets' evasion by 2.
Swift	Normal	Special	60	—	20	Many Others	—	—	A sure hit. Its power is reduced by 25% when it hits multiple Pokémon.
Switcheroo	Dark	Status	—	100	10	Normal	—	—	Swaps items between the user and the target.
Swords Dance	Normal	Status	—	—	20	Self	—	—	Raises the user's Attack by 2.
Synchronoise	Psychic	Special	120	100	10	Adjacent	—	—	Inflicts damage on any Pokémon of the same type as the user. Its power is weaker when it hits multiple Pokémon.
Synthesis	Grass	Status	—	—	5	Self	—	—	Recovers 1/2 of the user's maximum HP in normal weather conditions. Recovers 2/3 of the user's maximum HP in sunny or extremely harsh sunlight weather conditions. Recovers 1/4 of the user's maximum HP in rain/heavy rain/sandstorm/hail weather conditions.

T

Move	Type	Kind	Pow.	Acc.	PP	Range	DA	Long	Effect
Tackle	Normal	Physical	50	100	35	Normal	○	—	A regular attack.
Tail Glow	Bug	Status	—	—	20	Self	—	—	Raises the user's Sp. Atk by 3.
Tail Slap	Normal	Physical	25	85	10	Normal	○	—	Attacks 2–5 times in a row in a single turn.
Tail Whip	Normal	Status	—	100	30	Many Others	—	—	Lowers the targets' Defense by 1.
Tailwind	Flying	Status	—	—	15	Your Side	—	—	Doubles the Speed of the Pokémon on your side for 4 turns.
Take Down	Normal	Physical	90	85	20	Normal	○	—	The user takes 1/4 of the damage inflicted.
Taunt	Dark	Status	—	100	20	Normal	—	—	Prevents the target from using anything other than attack moves for 3 turns.
Teeter Dance	Normal	Status	—	100	20	Adjacent	—	—	Inflicts the Confused status condition on the target.
Telekinesis	Psychic	Status	—	—	15	Normal	—	—	Makes the target float for 3 turns. All moves land regardless of their accuracy except for Ground-type moves and one-hit KO moves such as Fissure, Guillotine, Horn Drill, and Sheer Cold.
Teleport	Psychic	Status	—	—	20	Self	—	—	Ends wild Pokémon battles.
Thief	Dark	Physical	60	100	25	Normal	○	—	When the target is holding an item and the user is not, the user can steal that item. When the target is not holding an item, this move will function as a normal attack.
Thrash	Normal	Physical	120	100	10	1 Random	○	—	Attacks consecutively over 2–3 turns. Cannot choose other moves during this time. The user becomes Confused after using this move.
Thunder	Electric	Special	110	70	10	Normal	—	—	A 30% chance of inflicting the Paralysis status condition on the target. Is 100% accurate in the rain or heavy rain weather condition and 50% accurate in the sunny or extremely harsh sunlight weather condition. It hits even Pokémon that are in the sky due to using moves such as Fly and Bounce.
Thunder Fang	Electric	Physical	65	95	15	Normal	○	—	A 10% chance of inflicting the Paralysis status condition or making the target flinch (unable to use moves on that turn).
Thunder Punch	Electric	Physical	75	100	15	Normal	○	—	A 10% chance of inflicting the Paralysis status condition on the target.
Thunder Shock	Electric	Special	40	100	30	Normal	—	—	A 10% chance of inflicting the Paralysis status condition on the target.
Thunder Wave	Electric	Status	—	100	20	Normal	—	—	Inflicts the Paralysis status condition on the target. Does not work on Ground types.
Thunderbolt	Electric	Special	90	100	15	Normal	—	—	A 10% chance of inflicting the Paralysis status condition on the target.
Tickle	Normal	Status	—	100	20	Normal	—	—	Lowers the target's Attack and Defense by 1.
Topsy-Turvy	Dark	Status	—	—	20	Normal	—	—	Reverses the effects of any stat changes affecting the target.
Torment	Dark	Status	—	100	15	Normal	—	—	Makes the target unable to use the same move twice in a row.
Toxic	Poison	Status	—	90	10	Normal	—	—	Inflicts the Badly Poisoned status condition on the target. Damage from being Badly Poisoned increases with every turn. It never misses if used by a Poison-type Pokémon.
Toxic Spikes	Poison	Status	—	—	20	Other Side	—	—	Lays a trap of poison spikes on the opposing side that inflict the Poison status condition on Pokémon that switch into battle. Using Toxic Spikes twice inflicts the Badly Poisoned condition. The damage from the Badly Poisoned condition increases every turn. Toxic Spikes' effects end when a Poison-type Pokémon switches into battle. Ineffective against Flying-type Pokémon and Pokémon with the Levitate Ability.
Transform	Normal	Status	—	—	10	Normal	—	—	The user transforms into the target. The user has the same moves and Ability as the target (all moves have 5 PP).
Tri Attack	Normal	Special	80	100	10	Normal	—	—	A 20% chance of inflicting the Paralysis, Burned, or Frozen status condition on the target.
Trick	Psychic	Status	—	100	10	Normal	—	—	Swaps items between the user and the target.
Trick Room	Psychic	Status	—	—	5	Both Sides	—	—	Always strikes last. For 5 turns, Pokémon with lower Speed go first. First-strike moves still go first. Self-canceling if used again while Trick Room is still in effect.
Trick-or-Treat	Ghost	Status	—	100	20	Normal	—	—	Gives the target the Ghost type in addition to its original type(s).
Trump Card	Normal	Special	—	—	5	Normal	○	—	A sure hit. The lower the user's PP is, the greater the move's power becomes (max 200).
Twineedle	Bug	Physical	25	100	20	Normal	—	—	Attacks twice in a row in a single turn. A 20% chance of inflicting the Poison status condition on the target.
Twister	Dragon	Special	40	100	20	Many Others	—	—	A 20% chance of making the targets flinch (unable to use moves on that turn). Does twice the damage if the targets are in the sky due to moves such as Fly or Bounce. Its power is reduced by 25% when it hits multiple Pokémon.

U·V

Move	Type	Kind	Pow.	Acc.	PP	Range	DA	Long	Effect
Uproar	Normal	Special	90	100	10	1 Random	—	—	The user makes an uproar for 3 turns. During that time, no Pokémon can fall asleep. Strikes the target even if it is using Substitute.
U-turn	Bug	Physical	70	100	20	Normal	○	—	After attacking, the user switches out with another Pokémon in the party.
Vacuum Wave	Fighting	Special	40	100	30	Normal	—	—	Always strikes first. The user with the higher Speed goes first if similar moves are used.
Venom Drench	Poison	Status	—	100	20	Many Others	—	—	Lowers the Attack, Sp. Atk, and Speed of opposing Pokémon afflicted with Poison or Badly Poisoned status conditions by 1.
Venoshock	Poison	Special	65	100	10	Normal	—	—	Does twice the damage to a target that has the Poison or Badly Poisoned status condition.
Vice Grip	Normal	Physical	55	100	30	Normal	○	—	A regular attack.
Vine Whip	Grass	Physical	45	100	25	Normal	○	—	A regular attack.
Vital Throw	Fighting	Physical	70	—	10	Normal	○	—	Always strikes later than normal, but has perfect accuracy.
Volt Switch	Electric	Special	70	100	20	Normal	—	—	After attacking, the user switches out with another Pokémon in the party.
Volt Tackle	Electric	Physical	120	100	15	Normal	○	—	The user takes 1/3 of the damage inflicted. A 10% chance of inflicting the Paralysis status condition on the target.

W

Move	Type	Kind	Pow.	Acc.	PP	Range	DA	Long	Effect
Wake-Up Slap	Fighting	Physical	70	100	10	Normal	○	—	Does twice the usual damage to a sleeping target, but heals that status condition.
Water Gun	Water	Special	40	100	25	Normal	—	—	A regular attack.
Water Pledge	Water	Special	80	100	10	Normal	—	—	When combined with Fire Pledge or Grass Pledge, the power and effect change. If combined with Fire Pledge, the power is 150 and it remains a Water-type move. This makes it more likely that your team's moves will have additional effects for 4 turns. If combined with Grass Pledge, the power is 150 and it becomes a Grass-type move. This lowers the Speed of opposing Pokémon for 4 turns.
Water Pulse	Water	Special	60	100	20	Normal	—	○	A 20% chance of inflicting the Confused status condition on the target.
Water Shuriken	Water	Physical	15	100	20	Normal	—	—	Always strikes first. The user with the higher Speed goes first if similar moves are used. Attacks 2–5 times in a row in a single turn.
Water Sport	Water	Status	—	—	15	Both Sides	—	—	Lowers the power of Fire-type moves to 1/3 of normal for 5 turns.
Water Spout	Water	Special	150	100	5	Many Others	—	—	If the user's HP is low, this move has lower power. Its power is reduced by 25% when it hits multiple Pokémon.
Waterfall	Water	Physical	80	100	15	Normal	○	—	A 20% chance of making the target flinch (unable to use moves on that turn).
Weather Ball	Normal	Special	50	100	10	Normal	—	—	In special weather conditions, this move's type changes and its attack power doubles. Sunny / extremely harsh sunlight weather condition: Fire type. Rain / heavy rain weather condition: Water type. Hail weather condition: Ice type. Sandstorm weather condition: Rock type.
Whirlpool	Water	Special	35	85	15	Normal	—	—	Inflicts damage equal to 1/8 the target's max HP for 4–5 turns. The target cannot flee during that time. Does twice the damage if the target is using Dive when attacked.
Whirlwind	Normal	Status	—	—	20	Normal	—	—	Ends wild Pokémon battles. If the opposing Pokémon's level is higher than the user's, this move fails. In a Double Battle with wild Pokémon, this move fails. Strikes the target even if it is using Substitute. In a battle with a Trainer, this move forces the opposing Trainer to switch Pokémon. When there are no Pokémon to switch in, this move fails. Strikes the target even if it is using Detect, King's Shield, Mat Block, Protect, or Spiky Shield.
Wide Guard	Rock	Status	—	—	10	Your Side	—	—	Protects your side from any moves used that turn that target multiple Pokémon.
Wild Charge	Electric	Physical	90	100	15	Normal	○	—	The user takes 1/4 of the damage inflicted.
Will-O-Wisp	Fire	Status	—	85	15	Normal	—	—	Inflicts the Burned status condition on the target.
Wing Attack	Flying	Physical	60	100	35	Normal	○	○	A regular attack.
Wish	Normal	Status	—	—	10	Self	—	—	Restores 1/2 of maximum HP at the end of the next turn. Works even if the user has switched out.
Withdraw	Water	Status	—	—	40	Self	—	—	Raises the user's Defense by 1.
Wonder Room	Psychic	Status	—	—	10	Both Sides	—	—	Always strikes last. Each Pokémon's Defense and Sp. Def stats are swapped for 5 turns. The effect ends if the move is used again.
Wood Hammer	Grass	Physical	120	100	15	Normal	○	—	The user takes 1/3 of the damage inflicted.
Work Up	Normal	Status	—	—	30	Self	—	—	Raises the user's Attack and Sp. Atk by 1.
Worry Seed	Grass	Status	—	100	10	Normal	—	—	Changes the target's Ability to Insomnia. Fails with certain Abilities, however.
Wrap	Normal	Physical	15	90	20	Normal	○	—	Inflicts damage equal to 1/8 the target's max HP for 4–5 turns. The target cannot flee during that time.
Wring Out	Normal	Special	—	100	5	Normal	○	—	The more HP the target has left, the greater the move's power becomes (max 120).

X·Y·Z

Move	Type	Kind	Pow.	Acc.	PP	Range	DA	Long	Effect
X-Scissor	Bug	Physical	80	100	15	Normal	○	—	A regular attack.
Yawn	Normal	Status	—	—	10	Normal	—	—	Inflicts the Sleep status condition on the target at the end of the next turn unless the target switches out.
Zap Cannon	Electric	Special	120	50	5	Normal	—	—	Inflicts the Paralysis status condition on the target.
Zen Headbutt	Psychic	Physical	80	90	15	Normal	○	—	A 20% chance of making the target flinch (unable to use moves on that turn).

Field Moves

Move	Effects in the field
Cut	Cuts down thorny trees so your party may pass.
Dig	Pulls you out of spaces like caves, returning you to the last entrance you went through.
Dive	Lets you move underwater.
Flash	Enables you to see farther and makes you less likely to encounter wild Pokémon in caves. The effect lasts until you exit the cave.
Fly	Whisks you instantly to a town or city you've visited before.
Milk Drink	Distributes part of the user's own HP among teammates.
Rock Smash	Smashes cracked rocks and walls so your party may pass. Smashed rocks may contain items or wild Pokémon.
Secret Power	Allows you to open suspicious-looking trees, bushes, and caves up to use as a Secret Base.
Soar	Lets you fly around freely, allowing access to previously inaccessible areas.
Soft-Boiled	Distributes part of the user's own HP among teammates.
Strength	Allows you to move large rocks and push them into holes to create new paths.
Surf	Allows you to move across the surface of a body of water.
Sweet Scent	Attracts wild Pokémon and makes them attack. If you are in an area prone to Horde Encounters, a horde of Pokémon will definitely appear.
Teleport	Transports you to the last Pokémon Center you used (cannot be used in caves or similar locations).
Waterfall	Allows you to climb up and down waterfalls.

How to Obtain TMs

No.	Move	How to Obtain	Price
TM01	Hone Claws	Buy at a stall in the Slateport Market	5,000
TM02	Dragon Claw	Find in Meteor Falls (need Surf and Waterfall)	—
TM03	Psyshock	Get in a house in Pacifidlog Town	—
TM04	Calm Mind	Defeat Gym Leaders Liza & Tate in Mossdeep City	—
TM05	Roar	Get from a Gentleman on Route 114	—
TM06	Toxic	Find on the Fiery Path (need Strength)	—
TM07	Hail	Find in Shoal Cave on Route 125 at low tide (need Surf)	—
TM08	Bulk Up	Defeat Gym Leader Brawly in Dewford Town	—
TM09	Venoshock	Buy from the upper clerk at the Mauville Poké Mart	10,000
TM10	Hidden Power	Get from an old woman in Fortree City	—
TM11	Sunny Day	Find in Scorched Slab on Route 120 (need Surf)	—
TM12	Taunt	Get as a reward in the Trick House	—
TM13	Ice Beam	Find in Sea Mauville on Route 108 (need Surf and Dive)	—
TM14	Blizzard	Buy in the Lilycove Department Store (4F)	30,000
TM15	Hyper Beam	Buy in the Lilycove Department Store (4F)	50,000
TM16	Light Screen	Buy in the Lilycove Department Store (4F)	10,000
TM17	Protect	Buy in the Lilycove Department Store (4F)	10,000
TM18	Rain Dance	Find in Sea Mauville on Route 108 (need Surf and Dive)	—
TM19	Roost	Defeat Gym Leader Winona in Fortree City	—
TM20	Safeguard	Buy in the Lilycove Department Store (4F)	10,000
TM21	Frustration	Get in a house in Pacifidlog Town (with an unfriendly Pokémon in lead position)	—
TM22	Solar Beam	Find in the Safari Zone (need Surf and Bikes)	—
TM23	Smack Down	Get from Professor Cozmo after rescuing him from Team Magma / Team Aqua	—
TM24	Thunderbolt	Get from Gym Leader Wattson in his apartment after helping sort out New Mauville	—
TM25	Thunder	Buy in the Lilycove Department Store (4F)	30,000
TM26	Earthquake	Find in the Seafloor Cavern on Route 128 (need Surf and Dive)	—
TM27	Return	Get in a house in Pacifidlog Town (with a friendly Pokémon in lead position)	—
TM28	Dig	Get from the Fossil Maniac's little brother in their home on Route 114	—
TM29	Psychic	Find in Ever Grande City (from Victory Road)	—
TM30	Shadow Ball	Find on Mt. Pyre	—
TM31	Brick Break	Get in a house in Sootopolis City	—
TM32	Double Team	Find on Route 113	—
TM33	Reflect	Buy in the Lilycove Department Store (4F)	10,000
TM34	Sludge Wave	Find on a shoal on Route 132	—
TM35	Flamethrower	Find on Victory Road	—
TM36	Sludge Bomb	Get from a Collector in Dewford Hall (after entering the Hall of Fame)	—
TM37	Sandstorm	Find in the desert on Route 111 (need Go-Goggles)	—
TM38	Fire Blast	Buy in the Lilycove Department Store (4F)	30,000
TM39	Rock Tomb	Defeat Gym Leader Roxanne in Rustboro City	—
TM40	Aerial Ace	Buy from the upper clerk at the Mauville Poké Mart	10,000
TM41	Torment	Get from Sailor in Slateport's Contest Spectacular Hall	—
TM42	Facade	Buy from the upper clerk at the Mauville Poké Mart	10,000
TM43	Flame Charge	Find on Jagged Pass (need Acro Bike)	—
TM44	Rest	Get in a house in Lilycove City	—

No.	Move	How to Obtain	Price
TM45	Attract	Get from girl in Verdanturf's Contest Spectacular Hall	—
TM46	Thief	Get from Team Magma / Team Aqua Grunt in Slateport's Oceanic Museum	—
TM47	Low Sweep	Buy from the upper clerk at the Mauville Poké Mart	10,000
TM48	Round	Get in Crooner's Café on the west side of Mauville City	—
TM49	Echoed Voice	Get from a boy on Route 104	—
TM50	Overheat	Defeat Gym Leader Flannery in Lavaridge Town	—
TM51	Steel Wing	Get from Steven in Granite Cave	—
TM52	Focus Blast	Buy in the Lilycove Department Store (4F)	30,000
TM53	Energy Ball	Find in Safari Zone (need Surf and Bikes)	—
TM54	False Swipe	Get from man in Rustboro's Poké Mart	—
TM55	Scald	Find in Seafloor Cavern on Route 128 (need Surf and Dive)	—
TM56	Fling	Get in a house in Pacifidlog Town	—
TM57	Charge Beam	Buy from the upper clerk at the Mauville Poké Mart	10,000
TM58	Sky Drop	Get from a Delinquent in Mauville's Poké Mart	—
TM59	Incinerate	Find on Mt. Chimney	—
TM60	Quash	Get from a girl in the Mossdeep Poké Mart	—
TM61	Will-O-Wisp	Find on Mt. Pyre	—
TM62	Acrobatics	Find on Route 119 (need Surf and Waterfall)	—
TM63	Embargo	Receive from a Bug Maniac on the *S.S. Tidal*	—
TM64	Explosion	Find in the Sky Pillar (need Surf)	—
TM65	Shadow Claw	Find in Granite Cave's lower levels (need Acro Bike)	—
TM66	Payback	Find on Mirage Island #2	—
TM67	Retaliate	Defeat Gym Leader Norman in Petalburg City	—
TM68	Giga Impact	Buy in the Lilycove Department Store (4F)	50,000
TM69	Rock Polish	Find on Jagged Pass (need Acro Bike)	—
TM70	Flash	Get from a Hiker in Granite Cave	—
TM71	Stone Edge	Buy in the Lilycove Department Store (4F)	30,000
TM72	Volt Switch	Defeat Gym Leader Wattson in Mauville City	—
TM73	Thunder Wave	Buy at a stall in the Slateport Market	5,000
TM74	Gyro Ball	Find in Mirage Forest #8	—
TM75	Swords Dance	Get from a Black Belt in Lavaridge Town	—
TM76	Struggle Bug	Buy at a stall in the Slateport Market	5,000
TM77	Psych Up	Get from a Psychic on the upper part of Route 133	—
TM78	Bulldoze	Buy from the upper clerk at the Mauville Poké Mart	10,000
TM79	Frost Breath	Find in Shoal Cave on Route 125 at low tide (need Surf)	—
TM80	Rock Slide	Find on a shoal on Route 134	—
TM81	X-Scissor	Find on Victory Road	—
TM82	Dragon Tail	Buy from the upper clerk at the Mauville Poké Mart	10,000
TM83	Infestation	Get from Lisia's fan in Sootopolis	—
TM84	Poison Jab	Find on Mirage Mountain #2 (need Acro Bike)	—
TM85	Dream Eater	Get from a man in the entrance hall of the Safari Zone	—
TM86	Grass Knot	Find in Fortree City (need Devon Scope)	—
TM87	Swagger	Receive from a Lady in the Battle Resort's Pokémon Day Care in return for a loan	—
TM88	Sleep Talk	Get in a house in Lilycove City	—
TM89	U-turn	Find in Mauville Hills (need Rain Badge)	—

No.	Move	How to Obtain	Price
TM90	Substitute	Find on Mirage Island #5	—
TM91	Flash Cannon	Find on Mirage Island #8	—
TM92	Trick Room	Get as a reward in the Trick House	—
TM93	Wild Charge	Find in the Safari Zone (need Surf and Bikes)	—
TM94	Secret Power	Get from Aarune on Route 111	—
TM95	Snarl	Find in Mirage Cave #8	—
TM96	Nature Power	Get from Aarune in the Fiery Path (need the Heat Badge)	—
TM97	Dark Pulse	Find in Team Magma / Team Aqua Hideout (need Surf)	—
TM98	Power-Up Punch	Buy from the upper clerk at the Mauville Poké Mart	10,000
TM99	Dazzling Gleam	Get from a Fairy Tale Girl on Route 123	—
TM100	Confide	Buy at a stall in the Slateport Market	5,000

How to Obtain HMs

No.	Move	How to Obtain	Price
HM01	Cut	Get from a man in the Cutter's House in Rustboro City	—
HM02	Fly	Get from May/Brendan on Route 119	—
HM03	Surf	Get from Wally's father (need the Balance Badge)	—
HM04	Strength	Get from May/Brendan on Route 112	—
HM05	Waterfall	Defeat Gym Leader Wallace in Sootopolis City	—
HM06	Rock Smash	Get from Wally's uncle in Mauville City	—
HM07	Dive	Get from Steven in Mossdeep City (need the Mind Badge)	—

MOVE TUTORS

Other Places to Learn Moves around Hoenn

Location	Move	Restrictions
Move Reminder (Fallarbor Town)	Can teach Pokémon any move they can naturally learn by leveling up	Must have a Heart Scale to exchange
Pledge Move Dojo (Mauville City)	Fire Pledge / Grass Pledge / Water Pledge	Pokémon must be one that can be received from a professor and be friendly toward you
Song and Sword Move Academy (Mauville City)	Relic Song / Secret Sword	Relic Song can only be taught to Meloetta. Secret Sword can only be taught to Keldeo.
Ultimate Move Studio (Mauville City)	Blast Burn / Frenzy Plant / Hydro Cannon	Pokémon must be the final Evolution of one that can be received from a professor and be friendly toward you
Dragon-type Move Tutor (Sootopolis City)	Draco Meteor	Pokémon must be a Dragon type and be friendly toward you
Draconid Elder (Meteor Falls)	Dragon Ascent	Can only be taught to Rayquaza (must have completed Delta Episode)
Stand #1 at the Battle Resort	Electroweb / Gravity / Heal Bell / Magic Room / Stealth Rock / Tailwind / Wonder Room	Must enter Hall of Fame and have 8 BP to exchange
	Icy Wind	Must enter Hall of Fame and have 12 BP to exchange
Stand #2 at the Battle Resort	After You / Block / Gastro Acid / Helping Hand / Iron Defense / Magic Coat / Magnet Rise / Pain Split / Recycle / Role Play / Skill Swap / Snatch / Spite / Synthesis / Trick / Worry Seed	Must enter Hall of Fame and have 8 BP to exchange
Stand #3 at the Battle Resort	Bounce / Drill Run / Iron Head / Iron Tail / Uproar / Zen Headbutt	Must enter Hall of Fame and have 8 BP to exchange
	Aqua Tail / Dragon Pulse / Earth Power / Foul Play / Heat Wave / Hyper Voice / Last Resort / Seed Bomb	Must enter Hall of Fame and have 12 BP to exchange
	Focus Punch / Gunk Shot / Outrage / Sky Attack / Superpower	Must enter Hall of Fame and have 16 BP to exchange
Stand #4 at the Battle Resort	Bind / Bug Bite / Covet / Shock Wave / Snore / Water Pulse	Must enter Hall of Fame and have 4 BP to exchange
	Drain Punch / Fire Punch / Giga Drain / Ice Punch / Low Kick / Signal Beam / Thunder Punch	Must enter Hall of Fame and have 8 BP to exchange
	Dual Chop / Knock Off / Super Fang	Must enter Hall of Fame and have 12 BP to exchange
	Endeavor	Must enter Hall of Fame and have 16 BP to exchange

Where to Forget Moves in Hoenn

Location	Move	Restrictions
Move Deleter (Lilycove City)	Can delete any move, including HMs	—

A

Ability	Effect in Battle	Effect when the Pokémon is the lead in your party
Adaptability	The power boost received by using a move of the same type as the Pokémon will be 100% instead of 50%.	—
Aerilate	Changes Normal-type moves to Flying type and increases their power by 30%.	—
Aftermath	Knocks off 1/4 of the attacking Pokémon's maximum HP when a direct attack causes the Pokémon to faint.	—
Air Lock	Eliminates effects of weather on Pokémon.	—
Analytic	The power of its move is increased by 30% when the Pokémon moves last.	—
Anger Point	Raises the Pokémon's Attack to the maximum when hit by a critical hit.	—
Anticipation	Warns if your opponent's Pokémon has supereffective moves or one-hit KO moves when the Pokémon enters battle.	—
Arena Trap	Prevents the opponent's Pokémon from fleeing or switching out. Ineffective against Flying-type Pokémon and Pokémon with the Levitate Ability.	Makes it easier to encounter wild Pokémon.
Aroma Veil	Protects the team from Attract, Disable, Encore, Heal Block, Taunt, and Torment.	—
Aura Break	Reverses the effects of the Fairy Aura Ability and lowers the power of Fairy-type moves by 25%. Reverses the Dark Aura Ability and lowers the power of Dark-type moves by 25%.	—

B

Ability	Effect in Battle	Effect when the Pokémon is the lead in your party
Bad Dreams	Lowers the HP of sleeping Pokémon by 1/8 of their maximum HP every turn.	—
Battle Armor	Opposing Pokémon's moves will not hit critically.	—
Big Pecks	Prevents Defense from being lowered.	—
Blaze	Raises the power of Fire-type moves by 50% when the Pokémon's HP drops to 1/3 or less.	—
Bulletproof	Protects against Acid Spray, Aura Sphere, Barrage, Bullet Seed, Egg Bomb, Electro Ball, Energy Ball, Focus Blast, Gyro Ball, Ice Ball, Magnet Bomb, Mist Ball, Mud Bomb, Octazooka, Rock Wrecker, Searing Shot, Seed Bomb, Shadow Ball, Sludge Bomb, Weather Ball, and Zap Cannon.	—

C

Ability	Effect in Battle	Effect when the Pokémon is the lead in your party
Cheek Pouch	Eating a Berry not only grants its usual benefits, but also restores 1/3 of the Pokémon's maximum HP.	—
Chlorophyll	Doubles Speed in the sunny or extremely harsh weather conditions.	—
Clear Body	Protects against stat-lowering moves and Abilities.	—
Cloud Nine	Eliminates effects of weather on Pokémon.	—
Color Change	Changes the Pokémon's type into the type of the move that just hit it.	—
Competitive	When an opponent's move or Ability lowers the Pokémon's stats, the Pokémon's Sp. Atk rises by 2.	—
Compound Eyes	Raises accuracy by 30%.	Raises encounter rate with wild Pokémon holding items.
Contrary	Makes stat changes have an opposite effect (increase instead of decrease and vice versa).	—
Cursed Body	Provides a 30% chance of inflicting Disable on the move the opponent used to hit the Pokémon. (Cannot use that move for three turns.)	—
Cute Charm	Provides a 30% chance of causing infatuation when hit with a direct attack.	Raises encounter rate of wild Pokémon of the opposite gender.

D

Ability	Effect in Battle	Effect when the Pokémon is the lead in your party
Damp	Prevents Pokémon on either side from using Explosion or Self-Destruct. Nullifies the Aftermath Ability.	—
Dark Aura	Raises the power of Dark-type moves by 1/3. Affects all Pokémon in the field.	—
Defeatist	The Pokémon's Attack and Sp. Atk gets halved when HP becomes half or less.	—
Defiant	When an opponent's move or Ability lowers the Pokémon's stats, the Pokémon's Attack rises by 2.	—
Delta Stream	Makes the weather strong winds when the Pokémon enters battle. This weather makes Flying-type Pokémon receive half the damage from supereffective moves against them.	—
Desolate Land	Makes the weather extremely harsh sunlight when the Pokémon enters battle. This weather raises the power of Fire-type moves by 50%, reduces that of Water-type moves to zero, and prevents the Frozen status condition.	—
Download	When the Pokémon enters battle, this Ability raises its Attack by 1 if the opposing Pokémon's Defense is lower than its Sp. Def, and raises its Sp. Atk by 1 if the opposing Pokémon's Sp. Def is lower than its Defense. If the opponent's Defense and Sp. Def are the same, this Ability raises its Sp. Atk by 1.	—
Drizzle	Makes the weather rain for five turns when the Pokémon enters battle. Does nothing when the weather is extremely harsh sunlight, heavy rain, or strong winds.	—
Drought	Makes the weather sunny for five turns when the Pokémon enters battle. Does nothing when the weather is extremely harsh sunlight, heavy rain, or strong winds.	—

Ability	Effect in Battle	Effect when the Pokémon is the lead in your party
Dry Skin	Restores HP by 1/4 of the Pokémon's maximum HP when the Pokémon is hit by a Water-type move. Restores HP by 1/8 of its maximum HP at the end of every turn in the rain or heavy rain weather condition. However, the damage the Pokémon receives from Fire-type moves increases by 25%. Takes damage of 1/8 of its maximum HP at the end of every turn in the sunny or extremely harsh sunlight weather condition.	—

E

Ability	Effect in Battle	Effect when the Pokémon is the lead in your party
Early Bird	Causes the Pokémon to wake quickly from the Sleep status condition.	—
Effect Spore	Provides a 30% chance of inflicting the Poison, Paralysis, or Sleep status conditions when hit with a direct attack. Grass-type Pokémon are immune to this effect.	—

F

Ability	Effect in Battle	Effect when the Pokémon is the lead in your party
Fairy Aura	Raises the power of Fairy-type moves by 1/3. Affects all Pokémon in the field.	—
Filter	Decreases the damage received from supereffective moves by 25%.	—
Flame Body	Provides a 30% chance of inflicting the Burned status condition when hit with a direct attack.	Facilitates hatching Eggs in your party.
Flare Boost	Increases the power of special moves by 50% when Burned.	—
Flash Fire	When the Pokémon is hit by a Fire-type move, rather than taking damage, its Fire-type moves increase power by 50%.	—
Flower Gift	Raises Attack and Sp. Def of the Pokémon and its allies by 50% in the sunny or extremely harsh sunlight weather condition.	—
Flower Veil	Grass-type allies cannot have their stats lowered, and they are protected from being inflicted with status conditions.	—
Forecast	Changes Castform's form and type. Sunny or extremely harsh sunlight weather conditions: changes to Fire type. Rain or heavy rain weather conditions: changes to Water type. Hail weather conditions: changes to Ice type.	—
Forewarn	Reveals a move an opponent knows when the Pokémon enters battle. Damaging moves with high power are prioritized.	—
Friend Guard	Reduces damage done to allies by 25%.	—
Frisk	Checks an opponent's held item when the Pokémon enters battle.	—
Fur Coat	Halves the damage taken from physical moves.	—

G

Ability	Effect in Battle	Effect when the Pokémon is the lead in your party
Gale Wings	Gives priority to Flying-type moves.	—
Gluttony	Allows the Pokémon to use its held Berry sooner when it has low HP.	—
Gooey	Lowers by 1 the Speed of an attacker who makes direct contact.	—
Grass Pelt	Raises Defense by 50% when the field is affected by Grassy Terrain.	—
Guts	Attack stat rises by 50% when the Pokémon is affected by a status condition.	—

H

Ability	Effect in Battle	Effect when the Pokémon is the lead in your party
Harvest	Provides at every turn end a 50% chance of restoring the Berry the Pokémon used, and a 100% chance when the weather conditions is sunny or extremely harsh sunlight.	—
Healer	At the end of every turn, it provides a 33% chance that an ally Pokémon's status condition will be healed.	—
Heatproof	Halves damage from Fire-type moves and from the Burned status condition.	—
Heavy Metal	Doubles the Pokémon's weight.	—
Honey Gather	If the Pokémon isn't holding an item, it will sometimes be left holding Honey after a battle (even if it didn't participate). Its chance of finding Honey increases with its level.	—
Huge Power	Doubles Attack.	—
Hustle	Raises Attack by 50%, but lowers the accuracy of the Pokémon's physical moves by 20%.	Makes it easier to encounter high-level wild Pokémon.
Hydration	Cures status conditions at the end of each turn during the rain or heavy rain weather conditions.	—
Hyper Cutter	Prevents Attack from being lowered.	—

I

Ability	Effect in Battle	Effect when the Pokémon is the lead in your party
Ice Body	Restores HP by 1/16 of the Pokémon's maximum HP at the end of every turn in the hail weather conditions rather than taking damage.	—
Illuminate	No effect.	Makes it easier to encounter wild Pokémon.
Illusion	Appears in battle disguised as the last Pokémon in the party.	—
Immunity	Protects against the Poison status condition.	—
Imposter	Transforms itself into the Pokémon it is facing as it enters battle.	—
Infiltrator	Moves can hit ignoring the effects of Light Screen, Mist, Reflect, Safeguard, or Substitute.	—
Inner Focus	The Pokémon doesn't flinch as an additional effect of a move.	—
Insomnia	Protects against the Sleep status condition.	—
Intimidate	When this Pokémon enters battle, it lowers the opposing Pokémon's Attack by 1.	Lowers encounter rate with low-level wild Pokémon.
Iron Barbs	Reduces the HP of an opponent that hits the Pokémon with a direct attack by 1/8 of its maximum HP.	—
Iron Fist	Increases the power of Bullet Punch, Comet Punch, Dizzy Punch, Drain Punch, Dynamic Punch, Fire Punch, Focus Punch, Hammer Arm, Ice Punch, Mach Punch, Mega Punch, Meteor Mash, Power-Up Punch, Shadow Punch, Sky Uppercut, and Thunder Punch by 20%.	—

J

Ability	Effect in Battle	Effect when the Pokémon is the lead in your party
Justified	When the Pokémon is hit by a Dark-type move, Attack goes up by 1.	—

K

Ability	Effect in Battle	Effect when the Pokémon is the lead in your party
Keen Eye	Prevents accuracy from being lowered. Ignores evasiveness-raising moves.	Lowers encounter rate with low-level wild Pokémon.
Klutz	The Pokémon's held item has no effect.	—

L

Ability	Effect in Battle	Effect when the Pokémon is the lead in your party
Leaf Guard	Protects the Pokémon from status conditions when in the sunny or extremely harsh weather conditions.	—
Levitate	Gives full immunity from all Ground-type moves.	—
Light Metal	Halves the Pokémon's weight.	—
Lightning Rod	Draws all Electric-type moves to the Pokémon. When the Pokémon is hit by an Electric-type move, rather than taking damage, its Sp. Atk goes up by 1.	—
Limber	Protects against the Paralysis status condition.	—
Liquid Ooze	When an opposing Pokémon uses an HP-draining move, it damages the user instead.	—

M

Ability	Effect in Battle	Effect when the Pokémon is the lead in your party
Magic Bounce	Reflects status moves that lower stats or inflict status conditions.	—
Magic Guard	The Pokémon will not take damage from anything other than indirect damage. Nullifies the Aftermath, Bad Dreams, Iron Barbs, Liquid Ooze, and Rough Skin Abilities, the hail and sandstorm weather conditions, and the Burned, Poison, and Badly Poisoned status conditions. The effects of Bind, Clamp, Curse, Fire Pledge, Fire Spin, Flame Burst, Infestation, Leech Seed, Magma Storm, Nightmare, Sand Tomb, Spikes, Stealth Rock, Whirlpool, and Wrap are negated, as are the item effects from Black Sludge, Life Orb, Rocky Helmet, and Sticky Barb. The Pokémon also receives no recoil or move-failure damage from attacks. Receives no damage from attacking a Pokémon that has used the Spiky Shield move or damage from using a Fire-type move after the Powder move has been used.	—
Magician	The Pokémon seizes the item of an opponent it hits with a move. Fails if the Pokémon is already holding an item.	—
Magma Armor	Prevents the Frozen status condition.	Facilitates hatching Eggs in your party.
Magnet Pull	Prevents Steel-type opponents from fleeing or switching out.	Raises encounter rate with wild Steel-type Pokémon.
Marvel Scale	Defense stat increases by 50% when the Pokémon is affected by a status condition.	—
Mega Launcher	Raises the power of Aura Sphere, Dark Pulse, Dragon Pulse, Origin Pulse, and Water Pulse by 50%. Heal Pulse will restore 75% of the target's maximum HP.	—
Minus	Raises Sp. Atk by 50% when another ally has the Ability Plus or Minus.	—
Mold Breaker	Allows the Pokémon to use moves on targets regardless of their Abilities. Does not nullify Abilities that have effects after an attack. For example, the Pokémon can score a critical hit against a target with Battle Armor, but it will still take damage from Rough Skin.	—

Ability	Effect in Battle	Effect when the Pokémon is the lead in your party
Moody	Raises one stat by 2 and lowers another by 1 at the end of every turn.	—
Motor Drive	When the Pokémon is hit by an Electric-type move, its Speed goes up by 1 and damage and effects of the move are nullified.	—
Moxie	When the Pokémon knocks out an opponent with a move, Attack goes up 1.	—
Multiscale	Halves damage when HP is full.	—
Multitype	Type changes according to the Plate Arceus is holding.	—
Mummy	Changes the Ability of the opponent that hits the Pokémon with a direct attack to Mummy.	—

N

Ability	Effect in Battle	Effect when the Pokémon is the lead in your party
Natural Cure	Cures the Pokémon's status conditions when it switches out.	—
No Guard	Moves used by or against the Pokémon always strike their targets.	Makes it easier to encounter wild Pokémon.
Normalize	Changes all of the Pokémon's moves to Normal-type.	—

O

Ability	Effect in Battle	Effect when the Pokémon is the lead in your party
Oblivious	Protects against infatuation. Immune to Captivate and Taunt.	—
Overcoat	Protects the Pokémon from weather damage, such as hail and sandstorm. Protects it from Cotton Spore, Poison Powder, Powder, Rage Powder, Sleep Powder, Spore, and Stun Spore. Immune to the Effect Spore Ability.	—
Overgrow	Raises the power of Grass-type moves by 50% when the Pokémon's HP drops to 1/3 or less.	—
Own Tempo	Protects against confusion.	—

P

Ability	Effect in Battle	Effect when the Pokémon is the lead in your party
Parental Bond	Causes attacks to strike twice, with the second hit dealing only half the normal damage. Does not affect moves that naturally strike multiple times or moves that strike multiple targets.	—
Pickpocket	Steals an item when hit with a direct attack. It fails if the Pokémon is already holding an item.	—
Pickup	At the end of every turn, the Pokémon picks up the item that the opposing Pokémon used that turn. Fails if the Pokémon is already holding an item.	If the Pokémon has no held item, it sometimes picks one up after battle (even if it didn't participate). It picks up different items depending on its level.
Pixilate	Changes Normal-type moves to Fairy type and increases their power by 30%.	—
Plus	Raises Sp. Atk by 50% when another ally has the Ability Plus or Minus.	—
Poison Heal	Restores 1/8 of the Pokémon's maximum HP at the end of every turn if the Pokémon has the Poison or Badly Poisoned status condition rather than taking damage.	—
Poison Point	Provides a 30% chance of inflicting the Poison status condition when the Pokémon is hit by a direct attack.	—
Poison Touch	Provides a 30% chance of inflicting the Poison status condition when the Pokémon uses a direct attack.	—
Prankster	Gives priority to status moves.	—
Pressure	When the Pokémon is hit by an opponent's move, it depletes 1 additional PP from that move.	Makes it easier to encounter high-level wild Pokémon.
Primordial Sea	Makes the weather heavy rain when the Pokémon enters battle. This weather raises the power of Water-type moves by 50% and reduces that of Fire-type moves to zero.	—
Protean	Changes the Pokémon's type to the same type as the move it has just used.	—
Pure Power	Doubles its Attack stat.	—

Q

Ability	Effect in Battle	Effect when the Pokémon is the lead in your party
Quick Feet	Increases Speed by 50% when the Pokémon is affected by status conditions.	Lowers wild Pokémon encounter rate.

R

Ability	Effect in Battle	Effect when the Pokémon is the lead in your party
Rain Dish	Restores HP by 1/16 of the Pokémon's maximum HP at the end of every turn in the rain or heavy rain weather conditions.	—
Rattled	When the Pokémon is hit by a Ghost-, Dark-, or Bug-type move, Speed goes up by 1.	—
Reckless	Raises the power of moves by 20% with recoil damage.	—
Refrigerate	Changes Normal-type moves to Ice type and increases their power by 30%.	—

Ability	Effect in Battle	Effect when the Pokémon is the lead in your party
Regenerator	Restores 1/3 its maximum HP when withdrawn from battle.	—
Rivalry	If the target is the same gender, the Pokémon's Attack goes up by 25%. If the target is of the opposite gender, its Attack goes down by 25%. No effect when the gender is unknown.	
Rock Head	No recoil damage from moves like Take Down and Double-Edge.	—
Rough Skin	Knocks off 1/8 of the attacking Pokémon's maximum HP when the Pokémon makes a direct attack.	—
Run Away	Allows the Pokémon to always escape from a battle with a wild Pokémon.	—

S

Ability	Effect in Battle	Effect when the Pokémon is the lead in your party
Sand Force	Raises the power of Ground-, Rock-, and Steel-type moves by 30% in the sandstorm weather conditions. Sandstorm does not damage the Pokémon.	—
Sand Rush	Doubles Speed in the sandstorm weather conditions. Sandstorm does not damage the Pokémon.	—
Sand Stream	Makes the weather sandstorm for five turns when the Pokémon enters battle. Rock-type Pokémon's Sp. Def increases by 50% and Pokémon other than Rock, Steel, and Ground types take damage of 1/16 of the Pokémon's maximum HP during the weather sandstorm. Does nothing when the weather is extremely harsh sunlight, heavy rain, or strong winds.	—
Sand Veil	The accuracy of the opposing Pokémon's move decreases by 20% in the sandstorm weather conditions. Sandstorm does not damage the Pokémon with this Ability.	Lowers encounter rate with wild Pokémon in the sandstorm weather conditions.
Sap Sipper	When the Pokémon is hit by a Grass-type move, rather than taking damage, its Attack goes up by 1.	—
Scrappy	Allows the Pokémon to hit Ghost-type Pokémon with Normal- and Fighting-type moves. (The type matchup changes from "It's not very effective..." to normal.)	—
Serene Grace	Doubles chances of moves inflicting additional effects.	—
Shadow Tag	Prevents the opposing Pokémon from fleeing or switching out. If both your and the opposing Pokémon have this Ability, the effect is canceled. Does not affect Ghost types.	—
Shed Skin	At the end of every turn, provides a 33% chance of curing the Pokémon's status conditions.	—
Sheer Force	When moves with an additional effect are used, power increases by 30%, but the additional effect is lost.	—
Shell Armor	Opposing Pokémon's moves will not hit critically.	—
Shield Dust	Protects the Pokémon from additional effects of moves.	—
Simple	Doubles the effects of stat changes.	—
Skill Link	Moves that strike successively strike the maximum number of times (2-5 times means it always strikes 5 times).	—
Slow Start	Halves Attack and Speed for 5 turns after the Pokémon enters battle.	—
Sniper	Moves that deliver a critical hit deal 125% more damage.	—
Snow Cloak	The accuracy of the opposing Pokémon's move decreases by 20% in the hail weather conditions. Hail does not damage Pokémon with this Ability.	Lowers encounter rate with wild Pokémon in the hail weather conditions.
Snow Warning	Makes the weather hail for five turns when the Pokémon enters battle. Pokémon other than Ice types take damage of 1/16 of the Pokémon's maximum HP during the weather hail. Does nothing when the weather is extremely harsh sunlight, heavy rain, or strong winds.	—
Solar Power	Raises Sp. Atk by 50%, but takes damage of 1/8 of the Pokémon's maximum HP at the end of every turn in the sunny or extremely harsh weather conditions.	—
Solid Rock	Decreases the damage received from supereffective moves by 25%.	—
Soundproof	Protects the Pokémon from sound-based moves: Boomburst, Bug Buzz, Chatter, Confide, Disarming Voice, Echoed Voice, Grass Whistle, Growl, Heal Bell, Hyper Voice, Metal Sound, Noble Roar, Parting Shot, Perish Song, Roar, Round, Screech, Sing, Snarl, Snore, Supersonic, and Uproar.	—
Speed Boost	Raises Speed by 1 at the end of every turn.	—
Stall	The Pokémon's moves are used last in the turn.	—
Stance Change	Changes from Shield Forme to Blade Forme when an attack move is used. Changes from Blade Forme to Shield Forme when King's Shield is used.	—
Static	A 30% chance of inflicting the Paralysis status condition when hit with a direct attack.	Raises encounter rate with wild Electric-type Pokémon.
Steadfast	Raises Speed by 1 every time the Pokémon flinches.	—
Stench	Has a 10% chance of making the target flinch when the Pokémon uses a move to deal damage.	Lowers wild Pokémon encounter rate.
Sticky Hold	Prevents the Pokémon's held item from being stolen.	Makes Pokémon bite more often when fishing.
Storm Drain	Draws all Water-type moves to the Pokémon. When the Pokémon is hit by a Water-type move, rather than taking damage, Sp. Atk goes up by 1.	—
Strong Jaw	Raises the power of Bite, Crunch, Fire Fang, Hyper Fang, Ice Fang, Poison Fang, and Thunder Fang by 50%.	—
Sturdy	Protects the Pokémon against one-hit KO moves like Horn Drill and Sheer Cold. Leaves the Pokémon with 1 HP if hit by a move that would knock it out when its HP is full.	—
Suction Cups	Nullifies moves like Dragon Tail, Roar, and Whirlwind, which would force Pokémon to switch out.	Makes Pokémon bite more often when fishing.
Super Luck	Heightens the critical-hit ratio of the Pokémon's moves.	—

Ability	Effect in Battle	Effect when the Pokémon is the lead in your party
Swarm	Raises the power of Bug-type moves by 50% when the Pokémon's HP drops to 1/3 or less.	—
Sweet Veil	Protects the team against the Sleep status condition.	—
Swift Swim	Doubles Speed in the rain or heavy rain weather conditions.	—
Symbiosis	When an ally uses its item, the Pokémon gives its own item to that ally.	—
Synchronize	When the Pokémon receives the Poison, Paralysis, or Burned status condition, this inflicts the same condition.	Raises encounter rate with wild Pokémon with the same Nature.

T

Ability	Effect in Battle	Effect when the Pokémon is the lead in your party
Tangled Feet	Raises evasion when the Pokémon has the Confused status condition.	—
Technician	If the move's power is 60 or less, its power will increase by 50%. Also takes effect if a move's power is altered by itself or by another move.	—
Telepathy	Prevents damage from allies.	—
Teravolt	Use moves on targets regardless of their Abilities. Does not nullify Abilities that have effects after an attack. For example, the Pokémon can score a critical hit against the target with Battle Armor, but it will still take damage from Rough Skin.	—
Thick Fat	Halves damage from Fire- and Ice-type moves.	—
Tinted Lens	Nullifies the type disadvantage of the Pokémon's not-very-effective moves: 1/2 damage turns into regular damage, 1/4 damage turns into 1/2 damage.	—
Torrent	Raises the power of Water-type moves by 50% when the Pokémon's HP drops to 1/3 or less.	—
Tough Claws	Raises the power of direct attacks by 30%.	—
Toxic Boost	Increases the power of physical moves by 50% when it has the Poison or Badly Poisoned status condition.	—
Trace	Makes the Pokémon's Ability the same as the opponent's, except for certain Abilities like Trace.	—
Truant	Allows the Pokémon to use a move only once every other turn.	—
Turboblaze	Use moves on targets regardless of their Abilities. Does not nullify Abilities that have effects after an attack. For example, the Pokémon can score a critical hit against the target with Battle Armor, but it will still take damage from Rough Skin.	—

U

Ability	Effect in Battle	Effect when the Pokémon is the lead in your party
Unaware	Ignores the stat changes of the opposing Pokémon, except Speed.	—
Unburden	Doubles Speed if the Pokémon loses or consumes a held item. Its Speed returns to normal if the Pokémon holds another item. No effect if the Pokémon starts out with no held item.	—
Unnerve	Prevent the opposing Pokémon from eating Berries.	—

V

Ability	Effect in Battle	Effect when the Pokémon is the lead in your party
Victory Star	The accuracy of the Pokémon and its allies is 10% higher.	—
Vital Spirit	Protects against the Sleep status condition.	Makes it easier to encounter high-level wild Pokémon.
Volt Absorb	When the Pokémon is hit by an Electric-type move, HP is restored by 25% of its maximum HP rather than taking damage.	—

W

Ability	Effect in Battle	Effect when the Pokémon is the lead in your party
Water Absorb	When the Pokémon is hit by a Water-type move, HP is restored by 25% of its maximum HP rather than taking damage.	—
Water Veil	Prevents the Burned status condition.	—
Weak Armor	When the Pokémon is hit by a physical attack, Defense goes down by 1, but Speed goes up by 1.	—
White Smoke	Protects against stat-lowering moves and Abilities.	Lowers wild Pokémon encounter rate.
Wonder Guard	Protects the Pokémon against all moves except supereffective ones.	—
Wonder Skin	Makes status moves more likely to miss.	—

Z

Ability	Effect in Battle	Effect when the Pokémon is the lead in your party
Zen Mode	When over half its HP is lost, the Pokémon changes form.	—

Pokémon's Natures

Each individual Pokémon has a Nature, which affects how its stats grow when it levels up. Most Natures will cause one stat to increase more quickly and one stat to increase more slowly than others. A few Natures, however, provide no benefit and no liability.

Nature	ATK	DEF	SP. ATK	SP. DEF	SPD
Adamant	○		▲		
Bashful					
Bold	▲	○			
Brave	○				▲
Calm	▲			○	
Careful			▲	○	
Docile					
Gentle		▲		○	
Hardy					
Hasty		▲			○
Impish		○	▲		
Jolly			▲		○
Lax		○		▲	
Lonely	○	▲			
Mild		▲	○		
Modest	▲		○		
Naive				▲	○
Naughty	○			▲	
Quiet			○		▲
Quirky					
Rash			○	▲	
Relaxed		○			▲
Sassy				○	▲
Serious					
Timid	▲				○

○ Gains more upon leveling up

▲ Gains less upon leveling up

Pokémon's Characteristics

On top of having a Nature, each individual Pokémon has a Characteristic. This also affects how the Pokémon's stats grow when it levels up. Every Characteristic will make one stat increase more quickly than average.

Stat that grows easily	Characteristic
HP	Loves to eat.
	Takes plenty of siestas.
	Nods off a lot.
	Scatters things often.
	Likes to relax.
ATTACK	Proud of its power.
	Likes to thrash about.
	A little quick tempered.
	Likes to fight.
	Quick tempered.
DEFENSE	Sturdy body.
	Capable of taking hits.
	Highly persistent.
	Good endurance.
	Good perseverance.
SP. ATK	Highly curious.
	Mischievous.
	Thoroughly cunning.
	Often lost in thought.
	Very finicky.
SP. DEF	Strong willed.
	Somewhat vain.
	Strongly defiant.
	Hates to lose.
	Somewhat stubborn.
SPEED	Likes to run.
	Alert to sounds.
	Impetuous and silly.
	Somewhat of a clown.
	Quick to flee.

National Pokédex No.	Hoenn Pokédex No.	Pokémon	HP	ATTACK	DEFENSE	SP. ATK	SP. DEF	SPEED
14	—	Kakuna	—	—	○	—	—	—
17	—	Pidgeotto	—	—	—	—	—	○
19	—	Rattata	—	—	—	—	—	○
20	—	Raticate	—	—	—	—	—	○
25	163	Pikachu	—	—	—	—	—	○
27	117	Sandshrew	—	—	○	—	—	—
35	—	Clefairy	○	—	—	—	—	—
37	160	Vulpix	—	—	—	—	—	○
39	143	Jigglypuff	○	—	—	—	—	—
41	65	Zubat	—	—	—	—	—	○
42	66	Golbat	—	—	—	—	—	○
43	91	Oddish	—	—	—	○	—	—
44	92	Gloom	—	—	—	○	—	—
46	—	Paras	—	○	—	—	—	—
49	—	Venomoth	—	—	—	○	—	○
50	—	Diglett	—	—	—	—	—	○
53	—	Persian	—	—	—	—	—	○
54	165	Psyduck	—	—	—	○	—	—
56	—	Mankey	—	○	—	—	—	—
58	—	Growlithe	—	○	—	—	—	—
63	40	Abra	—	—	—	○	—	—
66	75	Machop	—	○	—	—	—	—
72	68	Tentacool	—	—	—	—	○	—
73	69	Tentacruel	—	—	—	—	○	—
74	58	Geodude	—	—	○	—	—	—
75	59	Graveler	—	—	○	—	—	—
77	—	Ponyta	—	—	—	—	—	○
79	—	Slowpoke	○	—	—	—	—	—
81	84	Magnemite	—	—	—	○	—	—
84	95	Doduo	—	○	—	—	—	—
86	—	Seel	—	—	—	—	○	—
87	—	Dewgong	—	—	—	—	○	—
88	111	Grimer	○	—	—	—	—	—
95	—	Onix	—	—	○	—	—	—
97	—	Hypno	—	—	—	—	○	—
98	—	Krabby	—	○	—	—	—	—
100	87	Voltorb	—	—	—	—	—	○
109	113	Koffing	—	—	○	—	—	—
111	176	Rhyhorn	—	—	○	—	—	—
114	—	Tangela	—	—	○	—	—	—
116	193	Horsea	—	—	—	○	—	—
117	194	Seadra	—	—	○	○	—	—
118	51	Goldeen	—	○	—	—	—	—
119	52	Seaking	—	○	—	—	—	—
120	148	Staryu	—	—	—	—	—	○
127	174	Pinsir	—	○	—	—	—	—
129	53	Magikarp	—	—	—	—	—	○
130	54	Gyarados	—	○	—	—	—	—
132	—	Ditto	○	—	—	—	—	—
133	—	Eevee	—	—	—	—	○	—
137	—	Porygon	—	—	—	○	—	—
168	—	Ariados	—	○	—	—	—	—
170	190	Chinchou	○	—	—	—	—	—
171	191	Lanturn	○	—	—	—	—	—
178	170	Xatu	—	—	—	○	—	○
183	56	Marill	○	—	—	—	—	—
184	57	Azumarill	○	—	—	—	—	—
190	—	Aipom	—	—	—	—	—	○
191	—	Sunkern	—	—	—	○	—	—
198	—	Murkrow	—	—	—	—	—	○
200	—	Misdreavus	—	—	—	—	○	—
201	—	Unown	—	○	—	○	—	—
202	168	Wobbuffet	○	—	—	—	—	—
203	171	Girafarig	—	—	—	○	—	—
205	—	Forretress	—	—	○	—	—	—
214	175	Heracross	—	○	—	—	—	—
218	108	Slugma	—	—	—	○	—	—
222	189	Corsola	—	—	○	—	○	—
223	—	Remoraid	—	—	—	○	—	—
224	—	Octillery	—	○	—	○	—	—
225	—	Delibird	—	—	—	—	—	○
226	—	Mantine	—	—	—	—	○	—
227	120	Skarmory	—	—	○	—	—	—
232	173	Donphan	—	○	○	—	—	—
234	—	Stantler	—	○	—	—	—	—
236	—	Tyrogue	—	○	—	—	—	—
239	—	Elekid	—	—	—	—	—	○
240	—	Magby	—	—	—	—	—	○
261	10	Poochyena	—	○	—	—	—	—
263	12	Zigzagoon	—	—	—	—	—	○
264	13	Linoone	—	—	—	—	—	○
265	14	Wurmple	○	—	—	—	—	—
266	15	Silcoon	—	—	○	—	—	—
268	17	Cascoon	—	—	○	—	—	—
270	19	Lotad	—	—	—	—	○	—
271	20	Lombre	—	—	—	—	○	—
273	22	Seedot	—	—	○	—	—	—
274	23	Nuzleaf	—	○	—	—	—	—
276	25	Taillow	—	—	—	—	—	○
278	27	Wingull	—	—	—	—	—	○
279	28	Pelipper	—	—	○	—	—	—
280	29	Ralts	—	—	—	○	—	—
283	33	Surskit	—	—	—	—	—	○
284	34	Masquerain	—	—	—	○	○	—
285	35	Shroomish	○	—	—	—	—	—
287	37	Slakoth	○	—	—	—	—	—
290	43	Nincada	—	—	○	—	—	—
293	46	Whismur	○	—	—	—	—	—
294	47	Loudred	○	—	—	—	—	—
296	49	Makuhita	○	—	—	—	—	—
297	50	Hariyama	○	—	—	—	—	—
299	61	Nosepass	—	—	○	—	—	—
300	63	Skitty	—	—	—	—	—	○
302	70	Sableye	—	○	○	—	—	—
303	71	Mawile	—	○	○	—	—	—
304	72	Aron	—	—	○	—	—	—
305	73	Lairon	—	—	○	—	—	—
307	78	Meditite	—	—	—	—	—	○
308	79	Medicham	—	—	—	—	—	○
309	80	Electrike	—	—	—	—	—	○
311	82	Plusle	—	—	—	—	—	○
312	83	Minun	—	—	—	—	—	○
313	89	Volbeat	—	—	—	—	—	○
314	90	Illumise	—	—	—	—	—	○
315	98	Roselia	—	—	—	○	—	—
316	100	Gulpin	○	—	—	—	—	—
318	102	Carvanha	—	○	—	—	—	—
319	103	Sharpedo	—	○	—	—	—	—
320	104	Wailmer	○	—	—	—	—	—
322	106	Numel	—	—	—	○	—	—
324	110	Torkoal	—	—	○	—	—	—
325	115	Spoink	—	—	—	—	○	—
327	119	Spinda	—	—	—	○	—	—
328	121	Trapinch	—	○	—	—	—	—
331	124	Cacnea	—	—	—	○	—	—
333	126	Swablu	—	—	—	—	○	—
335	128	Zangoose	—	○	—	—	—	—
336	129	Seviper	—	○	—	○	—	—
337	130	Lunatone	—	—	—	○	—	—
338	131	Solrock	—	○	—	—	—	—
339	132	Barboach	○	—	—	—	—	—
340	133	Whiscash	○	—	—	—	—	—
341	134	Corphish	—	○	—	—	—	—
342	135	Crawdaunt	—	○	—	—	—	—
343	136	Baltoy	—	—	—	—	○	—
344	137	Claydol	—	—	—	—	○	—
349	145	Feebas	—	—	—	—	—	○
352	150	Kecleon	—	—	—	—	○	—
353	151	Shuppet	—	○	—	—	—	—
355	153	Duskull	—	—	—	—	○	—

National Pokédex No.	Hoenn Pokédex No.	Pokémon	HP	ATTACK	DEFENSE	SP. ATK	SP. DEF	SPEED
357	156	Tropius	○	—	—	—	—	—
358	158	Chimecho	—	—	—	○	○	—
359	159	Absol	—	○	—	—	—	—
361	179	Snorunt	○	—	—	—	—	—
363	182	Spheal	○	—	—	—	—	—
364	183	Sealeo	○	—	—	—	—	—
366	185	Clamperl	—	—	○	—	—	—
369	188	Relicanth	○	—	○	—	—	—
370	192	Luvdisc	—	—	—	—	—	○
371	196	Bagon	—	○	—	—	—	—
402	—	Kricketune	—	○	—	—	—	—
404	—	Luxio	—	○	—	—	—	—
421	—	Cherrim	—	—	—	○	—	—
422	—	Shellos	○	—	—	—	—	—
425	—	Drifloon	○	—	—	—	—	—
427	—	Buneary	—	—	—	—	—	○
431	—	Glameow	—	—	—	—	—	○
432	—	Purugly	—	—	—	—	—	○
436	—	Bronzor	—	—	○	—	—	—
440	—	Happiny	○	—	—	—	—	—
441	—	Chatot	—	○	—	—	—	—
443	—	Gible	—	○	—	—	—	—
451	—	Skorupi	—	—	○	—	—	—
456	—	Finneon	—	—	—	—	—	○
458	—	Mantyke	—	—	—	—	○	—
506	—	Lillipup	—	○	—	—	—	—
517	—	Munna	○	—	—	—	—	—
519	—	Pidove	—	○	—	—	—	—
523	—	Zebstrika	—	—	—	—	—	○
524	—	Roggenrola	—	—	○	—	—	—
525	—	Boldore	—	○	○	—	—	—
530	—	Excadrill	—	○	—	—	—	—
531	—	Audino	○	—	—	—	—	—
532	—	Timburr	—	○	—	—	—	—
535	—	Tympole	—	—	—	—	—	○
538	—	Throh	○	—	—	—	—	—
539	—	Sawk	—	○	—	—	—	—
540	—	Sewaddle	—	—	○	—	—	—
546	—	Cottonee	—	—	—	—	—	○
548	—	Petilil	—	—	—	○	—	—
551	—	Sandile	—	○	—	—	—	—
555	—	Darmanitan	—	○	—	—	—	—
556	—	Maractus	—	—	—	○	—	—
557	—	Dwebble	—	—	○	—	—	—
558	—	Crustle	—	—	○	—	—	—
559	—	Scraggy	—	○	—	—	—	—
563	—	Cofagrigus	—	—	○	—	—	—
568	—	Trubbish	—	—	—	—	—	○
570	—	Zorua	—	—	—	○	—	—
572	—	Minccino	—	—	—	—	—	○
574	—	Gothita	—	—	—	—	○	—
585	—	Deerling	—	—	—	—	—	○
592	—	Frillish	—	—	—	—	○	—
594	—	Alomomola	○	—	—	—	—	—
595	—	Joltik	—	—	—	—	—	○
599	—	Klink	—	—	○	—	—	—
602	—	Tynamo	—	—	—	—	—	○
605	—	Elgyem	—	—	—	○	—	—
610	—	Axew	—	○	—	—	—	—
613	—	Cubchoo	—	○	—	—	—	—
621	—	Druddigon	—	○	—	—	—	—
626	—	Bouffalant	—	○	—	—	—	—
627	—	Rufflet	—	○	—	—	—	—
628	—	Braviary	—	○	—	—	—	—
629	—	Vullaby	—	—	○	—	—	—
633	—	Deino	—	○	—	—	—	—
636	—	Larvesta	—	○	—	—	—	—
688	—	Binacle	—	○	—	—	—	—
690	—	Skrelp	—	—	—	—	○	—
692	—	Clauncher	—	—	—	○	—	—
707	—	Klefki	—	—	○	—	—	—
708	—	Phantump	—	○	—	—	—	—

Suggestions of Hordes of Pokémon to Battle for Great Base Stat Increases

If you want to raise your base stats most efficiently through wild Pokémon encounters, use the Sweet Scent move (or the item Honey) to attract Hordes of Pokémon that raise the base stat you are most interested in. Below are suggestions of Pokémon that appear commonly in hordes, and where they horde, for quick 5× base stat gains!

Base Stat	Pokémon	Where they appear in Hordes
HP	Whismur	Rusturf Tunnel
Attack	Shuppet	Mt. Pyre
Defense	Sandshrew	Route 111 (Central Desert)
Sp. Atk	Oddish	Route 119
Sp. Def	Swablu	Route 114 / Route 115
Speed	Zubat	Meteor Falls

ITEMS

A

Item	Description	How to obtain	Price
Ability Capsule	Allows a Pokémon with two Abilities (excluding Hidden Abilities) to switch between these Abilities.	Get for 200 BP in the Battle Maison in the Battle Resort	—
Abomasite	When held, it allows Abomasnow to Mega Evolve into Mega Abomasnow during battle.	Berry fields on Route 123 after obtaining the National Pokédex	—
Absolite	When held, it allows Absol to Mega Evolve into Mega Absol during battle.	Safari Zone	—
Absorb Bulb	Raises the holder's Sp. Atk by 1 when it is hit by a Water-type move. It goes away after use.	Get for 32 BP in the Battle Maison in the Battle Resort / Sometimes held by wild Gloom or Oddish	—
Adamant Orb	When held by Dialga, it boosts the power of Dragon-and Steel-type moves by 20%.	Route 128 (Underwater)	—
Aerodactylite	When held, it allows Aerodactyl to Mega Evolve into Mega Aerodactyl during battle.	Meteor Falls (Back chamber) after battling Groudon or Kyogre	—
Aggronite	When held, it allows Aggron to Mega Evolve into Mega Aggron during battle.	Receive from Wanda's boyfriend after smashing rocks in Rusturf Tunnel	—
Air Balloon	The holder floats and Ground-type moves will no longer hit the holder. The balloon pops when the holder is hit by an attack.	Get for 48 BP in the Battle Maison in the Battle Resort	—
Alakazite	When held, it allows Alakazam to Mega Evolve into Mega Alakazam during battle.	Slateport Market in Slateport	—
Altarianite	When held, it allows Altaria to Mega Evolve into Mega Altaria during battle.	Receive from a man in Lilycove City by answering "Altaria" when you have Altaria in your party	—
Ampharosite	When held, it allows Ampharos to Mega Evolve into Mega Ampharos during battle.	New Mauville after obtaining the National Pokédex	—
Amulet Coin	Doubles the prize money from a battle if the Pokémon holding it joins in.	Receive from your mom in your house after obtaining the Petalburg Gym Badge	—
Antidote	Cures the Poison status condition.	Buy at Poké Marts after receiving Poké Balls from May/Brendan in Littleroot Town	100
Armor Fossil	A Pokémon Fossil. When restored, it becomes Shieldon.	Can be obtained by breaking cracked rocks using Rock Smash in Mirage spots (*Pokémon Omega Ruby*)	—
Assault Vest	Raises Sp. Def when held by 50%, but prevents the use of status moves.	Get for 48 BP in the Battle Maison in the Battle Resort	—
Audinite	When held, it allows Audino to Mega Evolve into Mega Audino during battle.	Receive from Looker in the Battle Resort	—
Awakening	Cures the Sleep status condition.	Buy at Poké Marts (after obtaining first Gym Badge)	250

B

Item	Description	How to obtain	Price
Balm Mushroom	A fragrant mushroom. It can be sold at shops for 6,250.	Petalburg Woods (using Dowsing Machine)	—
Banettite	When held, it allows Banette to Mega Evolve into Mega Banette during battle.	The summit of Mt. Pyre	—
Beedrillite	When held, it allows Beedrill to Mega Evolve into Mega Beedrill during battle.	Sea Mauville (Storage)	—
Berry Juice	Restores the HP of one Pokémon by 20 points.	Get for 10 Poké Miles at the PokéMileage Center in Mauville City	—
Big Mushroom	A big mushroom. It can be sold at shops for 2,500.	Win the Whismur Show in Battle Resort / Sometimes held by wild Paras or Shroomish	—
Big Nugget	A big nugget of pure gold. It can be sold at shops for 10,000.	Sea Mauville (Storage) / Win in the Mauville Food Court when you order Mauville Ramen Bowl	—
Big Pearl	A big pearl. It can be sold at shops for 3,750.	Route 109 / Safari Zone / Route 125 / Shoal Cave at high tide / Sometimes held by wild Clamperl	—
Big Root	When the holder uses an HP-draining move, it increases the amount of HP recovered by 30%.	Receive from a girl on Route 123 when you have a Grass-type Pokémon in your party	—
Binding Band	When held, the damage done to a target by moves like Bind or Wrap will be 1/6 of the target's maximum HP every turn.	Get for 48 BP in the Battle Maison in the Battle Resort	—
Black Belt	When held by a Pokémon, it boosts the power of Fighting-type moves by 20%.	Sometimes held by wild Makuhita, Sawk, or Throh	—
Black Flute	Makes it easier to encounter strong Pokémon.	Receive from a guy in the Glass Workshop on Route 113 in exchange for collected ash (1,000g)	—
Black Glasses	When held by a Pokémon, it boosts the power of Dark-type moves by 20%.	Route 116 (using the Dowsing Machine) and speak to a man who's looking for glasses	—
Black Sludge	If the holder is a Poison-type Pokémon, it restores 1/16 of its maximum HP every turn. If the holder is any other type, it loses 1/8 of its maximum HP every turn.	Sometimes held by wild Grimer or Trubbish	—
Blastoisinite	When held, it allows Blastoise to Mega Evolve into Mega Blastoise during battle.	*S.S. Tidal*	—
Blazikenite	When held, it allows Blaziken to Mega Evolve into Mega Blaziken during battle.	Receive from Steven on Route 120 if you chose Torchic as your first Pokémon / Buy the stone titled "Fading Fire" on Route 114	1,500
Blue Flute	Awakens sleeping Pokémon.	Receive from a guy in the Glass Workshop on Route 113 in exchange for collected ash (250g)	—
Blue Orb	A shiny blue orb that is said to have a legend tied to it. It's known to have a deep connection with the Hoenn region.	Receive from an old woman at the summit of Mt. Pyre (*Pokémon Omega Ruby*) / Receive from Archie in the Cave of Origin (*Pokémon Alpha Sapphire*)	—
Blue Scarf	When held by a Pokémon, it raises the Beauty aspect of the Pokémon in a Contest Spectacular.	Receive from the chairman of the Pokémon Fan Club in Slateport City when your lead Pokémon has the max Beauty stat	—

Item	Description	How to obtain	Price
Blue Shard	A Shard you can trade for a Water Stone with the Treasure Hunter on Route 124.	Route 124	—
Bright Powder	Boosts the holder's evasion.	Sometimes held by wild Illumise, Volbeat, or Wurmple / Get for 48 BP in the Battle Maison in the Battle Resort	—
Burn Drive	When held by Genesect, it changes Genesect's Techno Blast move so it becomes Fire type.	Receive from a Street Thug standing near the stairs to the top of Mauville City when you have Genesect in your party	—
Burn Heal	Cures the Burned status condition.	Buy at Poké Marts (after obtaining first Gym Badge)	250

C

Item	Description	How to obtain	Price
Calcium	Raises the base Sp. Atk stat of a Pokémon.	Buy from the Energy Guru in Slateport Market / Lilycove Department Store (3F)	9,800
Cameruptite	When held, it allows Camerupt to Mega Evolve into Mega Camerupt during battle.	Receive from Team Magma during the Delta Episode (*Pokémon Omega Ruby*) / Receive from Team Magma in the Battle Resort (*Pokémon Alpha Sapphire*)	—
Carbos	Raises the base Speed stat of a Pokémon.	Buy from the Energy Guru in Slateport Market / Lilycove Department Store (3F)	9,800
Casteliacone	Heals all the status problems and confusion of a single Pokémon.	4th maze in the Trick House on Route 110 / Buy from a girl in Apt. 14 in Mauville Hills when you have Regice in your party	200
Cell Battery	Increases Attack by 1 when the holder is hit with Electric-type moves. It goes away after use.	Sometimes held by wild Minun or Plusle / Get for 32 BP in the Battle Maison in the Battle Resort	—
Charcoal	When held by a Pokémon, it boosts the power of Fire-type moves by 20%.	Receive from an old man in the Pokémon Herb Shop in Lavaridge Town / Sometimes held by wild Torkoal or Vulpix	—
Charizardite X	When held, it allows Charizard to Mega Evolve into Mega Charizard X during battle.	Fiery Path after obtaining the National Pokédex	—
Charizardite Y	When held, it allows Charizard to Mega Evolve into Mega Charizard Y during battle.	Scorched Slab (B2F) on Route 120 after obtaining the National Pokédex	—
Chill Drive	When held by Genesect, it changes Genesect's Techno Blast move so it becomes Ice type.	Receive from a Street Thug standing near the stairs to the top of Mauville City when you have Genesect in your party	—
Choice Band	The holder can use only one of its moves, but the power of physical moves increases by 50%.	Get for 48 BP in the Battle Maison in the Battle Resort	—
Choice Scarf	The holder can use only one of its moves, but Speed increases by 50%.	Get for 48 BP in the Battle Maison in the Battle Resort	—
Choice Specs	The holder can use only one of its moves, but the power of special moves increases by 50%.	Get for 48 BP in the Battle Maison in the Battle Resort	—
Claw Fossil	A Pokémon Fossil. When restored, it becomes Anorith.	Route 111 (Select either Root Fossil or Claw Fossil)	—
Cleanse Tag	Helps keep wild Pokémon away if the holder is the first one in the party.	Receive from an old woman on Mt. Pyre (1F) / Sometimes held by wild Chimecho	—
Clever Wing	Slightly increases the base Sp. Def stat of a single Pokémon. It can be used until the max of base stats.	Can be won by reaching Beginner Rank, Novice Rank, or Normal Rank in the Battle Institute in Mauville City	—
Comet Shard	A shard that fell to the ground when a comet approached. It can be sold at shops for 15,000.	Route 114 using Dowsing Machine / Receive from your fan in the Trainer Fan Club	—
Cover Fossil	A Pokémon Fossil. When restored, it becomes Tirtouga.	Can be obtained by breaking cracked rocks using Rock Smash in Mirage spots (*Pokémon Alpha Sapphire*)	—

D

Item	Description	How to obtain	Price
Damp Rock	Extends the duration of the rainy weather by three turns when held.	Receive from the receptionist in the Weather Institute on Route 119	—
Dawn Stone	It can evolve male Kirlia and female Snorunt.	Receive from Wally on Victory Road / Can be obtained by winning an Inverse Battle at the Inverse Battle Stop in Mauville City	—
Deep Sea Scale	When held by Clamperl, it doubles Sp. Def. Link Trade Clamperl while it holds the Deep Sea Scale to evolve it into Gorebyss.	Sometimes held by wild Chinchou, Lanturn, or Relicanth	—
Deep Sea Tooth	When held by Clamperl, it doubles Sp. Atk. Link Trade Clamperl while it holds the Deep Sea Tooth to evolve it into Huntail.	Sometimes held by wild Carvanha or Sharpedo	—
Destiny Knot	When a Pokémon holding it is inflicted with Infatuation, the Pokémon shares the condition with its attacker.	Sometimes picked up by a Pokémon with the Pickup Ability	—
Diancite	When held, it allows Diancie to Mega Evolve into Mega Diancie during battle.	Visit a Pokémon Center when you have Diancie distributed through past special events in your party	—
Dire Hit	Significantly raises the critical-hit ratio of the Pokémon on which it is used. It can be used only once and wears off if the Pokémon is withdrawn.	Buy from the Poké Mart in Slateport City / Lilycove Department Store (3F)	650
Dome Fossil	A Pokémon Fossil. When restored, it becomes Kabuto.	Can be obtained by breaking cracked rocks using Rock Smash in Mirage spots (*Pokémon Omega Ruby*)	—
Douse Drive	When held by Genesect, it changes Genesect's Techno Blast move so it becomes Water type.	Receive from a Street Thug standing near the stairs to the top of Mauville City when you have Genesect in your party	—
Draco Plate	When held by a Pokémon, it boosts the power of Dragon-type moves by 20%. (When held by Arceus, it shifts Arceus's type to Dragon type.)	Route 128 (Underwater)	—
Dragon Fang	When held by a Pokémon, it boosts the power of Dragon-type moves by 20%.	Sometimes held by wild Bagon or Druddigon	—
Dragon Scale	Link Trade Seadra while it holds the Dragon Scale to evolve it into Kingdra.	Sky Pillar (2F) / Sometimes held by wild Horsea or Seadra	—

Item	Description	How to obtain	Price
Dread Plate	When held by a Pokémon, it boosts the power of Dark-type moves by 20%. (When held by Arceus, it shifts Arceus's type to Dark type.)	Route 127 (Underwater)	—
Dubious Disc	Link Trade Porygon2 while it holds the Dubious Disc to evolve it into Porygon-Z.	Get for 32 BP in the Battle Maison in the Battle Resort	—
Dusk Stone	It can evolve Doublade, Lampent, Misdreavus, and Murkrow.	Can be obtained by winning an Inverse Battle at the Inverse Battle Stop in Mauville City	—

E

Item	Description	How to obtain	Price
Earth Plate	When held by a Pokémon, it boosts the power of Ground-type moves by 20%. (When held by Arceus, it shifts Arceus's type to Ground type.)	Route 130 (Underwater)	—
Eject Button	If the holder is hit by an attack, it switches places with a party Pokémon. It goes away after use.	Get for 32 BP in the Battle Maison in the Battle Resort	—
Electirizer	Link Trade Electabuzz while it holds the Electirizer to evolve it into Electivire.	Sometimes held by wild Elekid / Get for 32 BP in the Battle Maison in the Battle Resort	—
Elixir	Restores the PP of all of a Pokémon's moves by 10 points.	Route 110 / Route 111 / Route 119 / Route 123	—
Energy Powder	Restores the HP of one Pokémon by 50 points. Very bitter (lowers a Pokémon's friendship).	Buy at Pokémon Herb Shop in Lavaridge Town	500
Energy Root	Restores the HP of one Pokémon by 200 points. Very bitter (lowers a Pokémon's friendship).	Buy at Pokémon Herb Shop in Lavaridge Town	800
Escape Rope	Use it to escape instantly from a cave or a dungeon.	Buy at Poké Marts (after obtaining second Gym Badge)	550
Ether	Restores the PP of a Pokémon's move by 10 points.	Petalburg City / Petalburg Woods / Route 116	—
Everstone	Prevents the Pokémon that holds it from evolving.	Sometimes held by Geodude or Graveler / Often held by wild Boldore or Roggenrola	—
Eviolite	Raises Defense and Sp. Def by 50% when held by a Pokémon that can still evolve.	Receive from a Fisherman at 123 Go Fish on Route 123 after answering "Magikarp" to his question	—
Expert Belt	Raises the power of supereffective moves by 20%.	Trick Master's room in the Trick House on Route 110 / Get for 48 BP in the Battle Maison in the Battle Resort	—

F

Item	Description	How to obtain	Price
Fire Stone	It can evolve Eevee, Growlithe, Pansear, and Vulpix.	Fiery Path / Receive from the Treasure Hunter on Route 124 in exchange for a Red Shard	—
Fist Plate	When held by a Pokémon, it boosts the power of Fighting-type moves by 20%. (When held by Arceus, it shifts Arceus's type to Fighting type.)	Route 130 (Underwater)	—
Flame Orb	Inflicts the Burned status condition on the holder during battle.	Get for 16 BP in the Battle Maison in the Battle Resort	—
Flame Plate	When held by a Pokémon, it boosts the power of Fire-type moves by 20%. (When held by Arceus, it shifts Arceus's type to Fire type.)	Route 107 (Underwater)	—
Float Stone	Halves the holder's weight.	Receive from a guy on the second floor of the Devon company dormitory in Rustboro City	—
Fluffy Tail	Guarantees escape from any battle with wild Pokémon.	Buy at Lilycove Department Store (2F)	1,000
Focus Band	Has a 10% chance of leaving the holder with 1 HP when it receives damage that would cause it to faint.	Receive from a Black Belt in Shoal Cave (B1F) at low tide / Sometimes held by wild Machop / Get for 48 BP in the Battle Maison in the Battle Resort	—
Focus Sash	A holder with full HP is left with 1 HP when it is hit by a move that would cause it to faint. Then the item disappears.	Get for 48 BP in the Battle Maison in the Battle Resort	—
Fresh Water	Restores the HP of one Pokémon by 50 points.	Buy at a vending machine	200
Full Heal	Cures all status conditions and confusion.	Buy at Poké Marts (after obtaining third Gym Badge)	600
Full Incense	When held by a Pokémon, it makes the holder move later.	Buy from the Incense shop in Slateport Market	9,600
Full Restore	Restore the HP of a Pokémon and cures status conditions and confusion.	Buy at Poké Marts (after obtaining fifth Gym Badge)	3,000

G

Item	Description	How to obtain	Price
Galladite	When held, it allows Gallade to Mega Evolve into Mega Gallade during battle.	Talk to Professor Cozmo in Fallarbor Town (after clearing the Delta Episode)	—
Garchompite	When held, it allows Garchomp to Mega Evolve into Mega Garchomp during battle.	Receive from Aarune in the Secret Base Guild in Fortree City as a reward that your team reached Platinum Rank	—
Gardevoirite	When held, it allows Gardevoir to Mega Evolve into Mega Gardevoir during battle.	Receive from Wanda in her house in Verdanturf Town after battling Groudon or Kyogre	—
Gengarite	When held, it allows Gengar to Mega Evolve into Mega Gengar during battle.	A house in the Battle Resort after entering the Hall of Fame	—
Genius Wing	Slightly increases the base Sp. Atk stat of a single Pokémon. It can be used until the base stat reaches its maximum value.	Can be won by reaching Beginner Rank, Novice Rank, or Normal Rank in the Battle Institute in Mauville City	—
Glalitite	When held, it allows Glalie to Mega Evolve into Mega Glalie during battle.	Shoal Cave at low tide (ice cavern)	—

H

Item	Description	How to obtain	Price
Hard Stone	When held by a Pokémon, it boosts the power of Rock-type moves by 20%.	Receive from the Trick Master as a reward (Challenge 2) / Sometimes held by wild Aron	—
Heal Powder	Cures all status conditions and confusion. Very bitter (lowers a Pokémon's friendship).	Buy at Pokémon Herb Shop in Lavaridge Town	450
Health Wing	Slightly increases the base HP of a single Pokémon. It can be used until the max of base stats.	Can be won by reaching Beginner Rank, Novice Rank, or Normal Rank in the Battle Institute in Mauville City	—
Heart Scale	Give one to Move Maniac in Fallarbor Town, and he will have your Pokémon remember a move it has forgotten.	Route 134 (using Dowsing Machine) / Held by the Corsola you can get by trade in a house in Pacifidlog Town / Often held by wild Luvdisc	—
Heat Rock	When held by a Pokémon, it extends the duration of the sunny weather by three turns.	Receive from the receptionist in the Weather Institute on Route 119	—
Helix Fossil	A Pokémon Fossil. When restored, it becomes Omanyte.	Can be obtained by breaking cracked rocks using Rock Smash in Mirage spots (*Pokémon Alpha Sapphire*)	—
Heracronite	When held, it allows Heracross to Mega Evolve into Mega Heracross during battle.	Route 127	—
Honey	Attracts wild Pokémon where wild Pokémon can appear, and causes a Horde Encounter.	Receive from a Bug Maniac in the Pokémon Center in Fallarbor Town / Often held by wild Surskit	—
Houndoominite	When held, it allows Houndoom to Mega Evolve into Mega Houndoom during battle.	Lavaridge Town after obtaining the National Pokédex	—
HP Up	Raises the base HP of a Pokémon.	Buy from the Energy Guru in Slateport Market / Lilycove Department Store (3F)	9,800
Hyper Potion	Restores the HP of one Pokémon by 200 points.	Buy at Poké Marts (after obtaining second Gym Badge)	1,200

I

Item	Description	How to obtain	Price
Ice Heal	Cures the Frozen status condition.	Buy at Poké Marts (after obtaining first Gym Badge)	250
Icicle Plate	When held by a Pokémon, it boosts the power of Ice-type moves by 20%. (When held by Arceus, it shifts Arceus's type to Ice type.)	Route 130 (Underwater)	—
Icy Rock	Extends the duration of the hail by three turns when held.	Receive from the receptionist in the Weather Institute on Route 119	—
Insect Plate	When held by a Pokémon, it boosts the power of Bug-type moves by 20%. (When held by Arceus, it shifts Arceus's type to Bug type.)	Route 127 (Underwater)	—
Iron	Raises the base Defense stat of a Pokémon.	Buy from the Energy Guru in Slateport Market / Lilycove Department Store (3F)	9,800
Iron Ball	Halves the holder's Speed. If the holder has the Levitate Ability or is a Flying-type Pokémon, Ground-type moves can hit it.	Sometimes held by wild Mawile / Get for 48 BP in the Battle Maison in the Battle Resort	—
Iron Plate	When held by a Pokémon, it boosts the power of Steel-type moves by 20%. (When held by Arceus, it shifts Arceus's type to Steel type.)	Held by the Beldum you obtain in Steven's house in Mossdeep City after clearing the Delta Episode	—

J

Item	Description	How to obtain	Price
Jaw Fossil	A Pokémon Fossil. When restored, it becomes Tyrunt.	Can be obtained in *Pokémon X* and *Pokémon Y*	—

K

Item	Description	How to obtain	Price
Kangaskhanite	When held, it allows Kangaskhan to Mega Evolve into Mega Kangaskhan during battle.	Pacifidlog Town after receiving the National Pokédex	—
King's Rock	When the holder successfully inflicts damage, the target may also flinch. Link Trade Poliwhirl or Slowpoke while they hold a King's Rock to evolve them.	Receive from a guy in Mossdeep City / Sometimes held by wild Hariyama	—

L

Item	Description	How to obtain	Price
Lagging Tail	When held by a Pokémon, it makes it move later.	Sometimes held by wild Slowpoke	—
Latiasite	When held, it allows Latias to Mega Evolve into Mega Latias during battle.	Receive from your mom in Littleroot Town after the Delta Episode (*Pokémon Omega Ruby*) / Southern Island (*Pokémon Alpha Sapphire*)	—
Latiosite	When held, it allows Latios to Mega Evolve into Mega Latios during battle.	Southern Island (*Pokémon Omega Ruby*) / Receive from your mom in Littleroot Town after the Delta Episode (*Pokémon Alpha Sapphire*)	—
Lava Cookie	Lavaridge Town's famous specialty. Cures all status conditions and confusion.	Buy from an old woman at the summit of Mt. Chimney (after visiting Lavaridge Challenge 1 maze in the Trick House on Route 110)	200
Lax Incense	Boosts the holder's evasion.	Buy from the Incense shop in Slateport Market	9,600
Leaf Stone	It can evolve Exeggcute, Gloom, Nuzleaf, Pansage, and Weepinbell.	Route 119 / Receive from the Treasure Hunter on Route 124 in exchange for a Green Shard	—
Leftovers	It restores 1/16 of the holder's maximum HP every turn.	*S.S. Tidal* (Storage)	—

Item	Description	How to obtain	Price
Lemonade	Restores the HP of one Pokémon by 80 points.	Buy at a vending machine	350
Life Orb	Lowers the holder's HP each time it attacks, but raises the power of moves by 30%.	Sometimes held by wild Absol / Get for 48 BP in the Battle Maison in the Battle Resort	—
Light Ball	Doubles the power of both physical and special moves when held by Pikachu.	Route 120 / Sometimes held by wild Pikachu	—
Light Clay	Extends the duration of moves like Reflect and Light Screen by three turns.	Sometimes held by wild Baltoy or Claydol	—
Lopunnite	When held, it allows Lopunny to Mega Evolve into Mega Lopunny during battle.	Receive from a guy in front of Apt. 12 in Mauville Hills (speak to him twice)	—
Lucarionite	When held, it allows Lucario to Mega Evolve into Mega Lucario during battle.	Receive from Chaz after defeating Lisia in Master Rank contest	—
Luck Incense	Doubles prize money from a battle if the holding Pokémon joins in.	Buy from the Incense shop in Slateport Market	9,600
Lucky Egg	Increases the number of Experience Points received from battle by 50%.	Sometimes held by wild Happiny or Pelipper	—
Lucky Punch	It is a pair of gloves that boosts Chansey's critical-hit ratio.	Can be obtained in *Pokémon X* and *Pokémon Y*	—
Luminous Moss	Increases Sp. Def by 1 when the holder is hit with Water-type moves. It goes away after use.	Sometimes held by wild Corsola / Get for 32 BP in the Battle Maison in the Battle Resort	—
Lumiose Galette	A popular pastry sold in Lumiose City. Cures all status conditions and confusion for one Pokémon.	Challenge 3 maze in the Trick House on Route 110	—
Lustrous Orb	When held by Palkia, it boosts the power of Dragon- and Water-type moves by 20%.	Route 129 (Underwater)	—

M

Item	Description	How to obtain	Price
Macho Brace	Halves Speed, but makes it easier to raise base stats.	Receive from Victoria after defeating four members of the Winstrate family on Route 111	—
Magmarizer	Link Trade Magmar while it holds the Magmarizer to evolve it into Magmortar.	Sometimes held by wild Magby / Get for 32 BP in the Battle Maison in the Battle Resort	—
Magnet	When held by a Pokémon, it boosts the power of Electric-type moves by 20%.	Receive from the Trick Master as a reward (Challenge 5)	—
Manectite	When held, it allows Manectric to Mega Evolve into Mega Manectric during battle.	Route 110	—
Mawilite	When held, it allows Mawile to Mega Evolve into Mega Mawile during battle.	Verdanturf Town	—
Max Elixir	Completely restores the PP of all of a Pokémon's moves.	Team Magma Hideout (*Pokémon Omega Ruby*) / Team Aqua Hideout (*Pokémon Alpha Sapphire*) / Receive from brothers by showing affectionate Barboach or Shroomish in Sootopolis City	—
Max Ether	Completely restores the PP of a Pokémon's move.	Rusturf Tunnel / Route 113	—
Max Potion	Completely restores the HP of a single Pokémon.	Buy at Poké Marts (after obtaining fourth Gym Badge)	2,500
Max Repel	Prevents weak wild Pokémon from appearing for 250 steps after its use.	Buy at Poké Marts (after obtaining third Gym Badge)	700
Max Revive	Revives a fainted Pokémon and fully restores its HP.	Safari Zone / Team Magma Hideout (*Pokémon Omega Ruby*) / Team Aqua Hideout (*Pokémon Alpha Sapphire*) / Route 133	—
Meadow Plate	When held by a Pokémon, it boosts the power of Grass-type moves by 20%. (When held by Arceus, it shifts Arceus's type to Grass type.)	Route 130 (Underwater)	—
Medichamite	When held, it allows Medicham to Mega Evolve into Mega Medicham during battle.	Mt. Pyre (4F)	—
Mental Herb	The holder shakes off the effects of Attract, Disable, Encore, Heal Block, Taunt, and Torment. It goes away after use.	Receive from a man in a house in Fortree City after speaking to a woman in a house in Mossdeep City / Sometimes held by wild Lotad, Lombre, or Sewaddle	—
Metagrossite	When held, it allows Metagross to Mega Evolve into Mega Metagross during battle.	Defeat Steven once again in the Pokémon League after the Delta Episode	—
Metal Coat	When held by a Pokémon, it boosts the power of Steel-type moves by 20%. Link Trade Onix or Scyther while they hold a Metal Coat to evolve them.	New Mauville / Sometimes held by wild Bronzor, Magnemite, or Skarmory	—
Metal Powder	When held by Ditto, Defense doubles.	Sometimes held by wild Ditto / Win perfectly at the Mauville Food Court when you order Magnemite Croquettes	—
Metronome	When held, it raises the power of a move used consecutively by that Pokémon (up to a maximum increase of 100%)	Buy from a guy on the top of Mauville City / Sometimes held by wild Chatot or Kricketune	1,000
Mewtwonite X	When held, it allows Mewtwo to Mega Evolve into Mega Mewtwo X during battle.	Littleroot Town after obtaining the National Pokédex	—
Mewtwonite Y	When held, it allows Mewtwo to Mega Evolve into Mega Mewtwo Y during battle.	Pokémon League	—
Mind Plate	When held by a Pokémon, it boosts the power of Psychic-type moves by 20%. (When held by Arceus, it shifts Arceus's type to Psychic type.)	Route 126 (Underwater)	—
Miracle Seed	When held by a Pokémon, it boosts the power of Grass-type moves by 20%.	Receive from a girl in Petalburg Woods / Sometimes held by wild Cherrim or Maractus	—
Moomoo Milk	Restores the HP of one Pokémon by 100 points.	Buy from a woman in the Pokémon Center in Lavaridge Town	500
Moon Stone	It can evolve Clefairy, Jigglypuff, Munna, Nidorina, Nidorino, and Skitty.	Meteor Falls (Entrance) / Sometimes held by wild Clefairy or Lunatone	—
Muscle Band	When held by a Pokémon, it boosts the power of physical moves by 10%.	Get for 48 BP in the Battle Maison in the Battle Resort	—

Item	Description	How to obtain	Price
Muscle Wing	Slightly increases the base Attack stat of a single Pokémon. It can be used until the max of base stats.	Can be won by reaching Beginner Rank, Novice Rank, or Normal Rank in the Battle Institute in Mauville City	—
Mystic Water	When held by a Pokémon, it boosts the power of Water-type moves by 20%.	Held by the Castform you can receive at the Weather Institute on Route 119 / Sometimes held by wild Goldeen or Seaking	—

N

Item	Description	How to obtain	Price
Never-Melt Ice	When held by a Pokémon, it boosts the power of Ice-type moves by 20%.	Shoal Cave at low tide (ice cavern)	—
Normal Gem	When held by a Normal-type Pokémon, it boosts the power of a Normal-type move by 30% one time. It goes away after use.	Can be obtained by breaking cracked rocks using Rock Smash	—
Nugget	A nugget of pure gold. It can be sold at shops for 5,000.	Win in the Mauville Food Court when you order the Village Sub Combo / Receive from a man on the top of Mauville City / Route 112 / Route 120	—

O

Item	Description	How to obtain	Price
Odd Incense	When held by a Pokémon, it boosts the power of Psychic-type moves by 20%.	Buy from the Incense shop in Slateport Market	9,600
Old Amber	A piece of amber that contains genetic material. When restored, it becomes Aerodactyl.	Can be obtained by breaking cracked rocks using Rock Smash in Mirage spots	—
Old Gateau	The Old Chateau's hidden specialty. It can heal all the status conditions and confusion.	Challenge 5 mazes in the Trick House on Route 110	—
Oval Stone	Level up Happiny between 4 A.M. and 7:59 P.M. while it holds the Oval Stone to evolve it into Chansey.	Often held by wild Happiny	—

P

Item	Description	How to obtain	Price
Paralyze Heal	Cures the Paralysis status condition.	Buy at Poké Marts (after obtaining first Gym Badge)	200
Pearl	A pretty pearl. It can be sold at shops for 700.	Often held by wild Clamperl / Can be obtained by breaking cracked rocks using Rock Smash / Receive from the Treasure Hunter in Secret Base	—
Pearl String	Very large pearls that sparkle in a pretty silver collar. It can be sold at shops for 7,500.	Win in the Mauville Food Court when you order Magnemite Croquettes / Receive from the Treasure Hunter in Secret Base	—
Pidgeotite	When held, it allows Pidgeot to Mega Evolve into Mega Pidgeot during battle.	Show the Intriguing Stone to Mr. Stone in Rustboro City after obtaining it in Verdanturf Town	—
Pink Scarf	When held by a Pokémon, it raises the Cuteness aspect of the Pokémon in Contest Spectacular.	Receive from the chairman of the Pokémon Fan Club in Slateport City when your lead Pokémon has the max Cuteness stat	—
Pinsirite	When held, it allows Pinsir to Mega Evolve into Mega Pinsir during battle.	Route 124	—
Pixie Plate	When held by a Pokémon, it boosts the power of Fairy-type moves by 20%. (When held by Arceus, it shifts Arceus's type to Fairy type.)	Route 128 (Underwater)	—
Plume Fossil	A Pokémon Fossil. When restored, it becomes Archen.	Can be obtained by breaking cracked rocks using Rock Smash in Mirage spots (*Pokémon Omega Ruby*)	—
Poison Barb	When held by a Pokémon, it boosts the power of Poison-type moves by 20%.	Sometimes held by wild Skorupi, Roselia, Tentacool, or Tentacruel	—
Poké Doll	Ensures that the holder can successfully run from a wild Pokémon encounter.	Buy at Lilycove Department Store (2F)	1,000
Poké Toy	Ensures that the holder can successfully run from a wild Pokémon encounter.	Buy at Lilycove Department Store (2F)	1,000
Potion	Restores the HP of one Pokémon by 20 points.	Buy at Poké Marts (from the start)	300
Power Anklet	Halves the holder's Speed, but makes the Speed base stat easier to raise.	Get for 16 BP in the Battle Maison in the Battle Resort	—
Power Band	Halves the holder's Speed, but makes the Sp. Def base stat easier to raise.	Get for 16 BP in the Battle Maison in the Battle Resort	—
Power Belt	Halves the holder's Speed, but makes the Defense base stat easier to raise.	Get for 16 BP in the Battle Maison in the Battle Resort	—
Power Bracer	Halves the holder's Speed, but makes the Attack base stat easier to raise.	Get for 16 BP in the Battle Maison in the Battle Resort	—
Power Herb	The holder can immediately use a move that requires a one-turn charge. It goes away after use.	Sometimes held by wild Nuzleaf or Seedot / Get for 32 BP in the Battle Maison in the Battle Resort	—
Power Lens	Halves the holder's Speed, but makes the Sp. Atk base stat easier to raise.	Get for 16 BP in the Battle Maison in the Battle Resort	—
Power Weight	Halves the holder's Speed, but makes the HP base stat easier to raise.	Get for 16 BP in the Battle Maison in the Battle Resort	—
PP Max	Increases the max number of PP as high as it will go.	Route 119 / Team Magma Hideout (*Pokémon Omega Ruby*) / Team Aqua Hideout (*Pokémon Alpha Sapphire*) / Meteor Falls Entrance	—
PP Up	Increases the max number of PP by one level.	Route 104 / Route 109 / Route 115 / Route 123 / Victory Road	—
Pretty Wing	A beautiful feather. It can be sold at shops for 100.	Often held by wild Wingull or Pelipper	—

Item	Description	How to obtain	Price
Protector	Link Trade Rhydon while it holds the Protector to evolve it into Rhyperior.	Get for 32 BP in the Battle Maison in the Battle Resort	—
Protein	Raises the base Attack stat of a Pokémon.	Buy from the Energy Guru in Slateport Market / Lilycove Department Store (3F)	9,800
Pure Incense	Helps keep wild Pokémon away if the holder is the first one in the party.	Buy from the Incense shop in Slateport Market	9,600

Q

Item	Description	How to obtain	Price
Quick Claw	Allows the holder to strike first sometimes.	Receive from the teacher in the Trainers' School in Rustboro City / Sometimes held by wild Persian or Zangoose	—
Quick Powder	When held by Ditto, Speed doubles.	Often held by wild Ditto	—

R

Item	Description	How to obtain	Price
Rage Candy Bar	Mahogany Town's famous snack. Restores the HP of one Pokémon by 20.	Challenge 2 maze in the Trick House on Route 110	—
Rare Bone	A rare bone. It can be sold at shops for 5,000.	Route 114 (using Dowsing Machine) / Receive from the Treasure Hunter in Secret Base	—
Rare Candy	Raises a Pokémon's level by 1.	Granite Cave (B2F) / Route 110 / Route 114 / Route 119	—
Razor Claw	Boosts the holder's critical-hit ratio. ●	Get for 48 BP in the Battle Maison in the Battle Resort	—
Razor Fang	When the holder hits a target with an attack, there is a 10% chance the target will flinch. ★	Get for 48 BP in the Battle Maison in the Battle Resort	—
Reaper Cloth	Link Trade Dusclops while it holds the Reaper Cloth to evolve it into Dusknoir.	Get for 32 BP in the Battle Maison in the Battle Resort	—
Red Card	If the holder is hit by an attack that makes direct contact, the opposing Trainer is forced to switch out the attacking Pokémon. It goes away after use.	Get for 32 BP in the Battle Maison in the Battle Resort	—
Red Flute	Snaps Pokémon out of infatuation.	Receive from a guy in the Glass Workshop on Route 113 in exchange for collected ash (500g)	—
Red Orb	A shiny red orb that is said to have a legend tied to it. It's known to have a deep connection with the Hoenn region.	Receive from Maxie in the Cave of Origin (*Pokémon Omega Ruby*) / Receive from an old woman at the summit of Mt. Pyre (*Pokémon Alpha Sapphire*)	—
Red Scarf	When held by a Pokémon, it raises the Coolness aspect of the Pokémon in Contest Spectacular.	Receive from the chairman of the Pokémon Fan Club in Slateport City when your lead Pokémon has the max Coolness stat	—
Red Shard	A Shard you can trade for a Fire Stone with the Treasure Hunter on Route 124.	Route 124	—
Repel	Prevents weak wild Pokémon from appearing for 100 steps after its use.	Buy at Poké Marts (after obtaining first Gym Badge)	350
Resist Wing	Slightly increases the base Defense stat of a single Pokémon. It can be used until the max of base stats.	Can be won by reaching Beginner Rank, Novice Rank, or Normal Rank in the Battle Institute in Mauville City	—
Revival Herb	Revives a fainted Pokémon. Very bitter (lowers a Pokémon's friendship).	Buy at Pokémon Herb Shop in Lavaridge Town	2,800
Revive	Revives a fainted Pokémon and restores half of its HP.	Buy at Poké Marts (after obtaining second Gym Badge)	1,500
Ring Target	Moves that would otherwise have no effect will hit the holder.	Get for 32 BP in the Battle Maison in the Battle Resort	—
Rock Incense	When held by a Pokémon, it boosts the power of Rock-type moves by 20%.	Buy from the Incense shop in Slateport Market	9,600
Rocky Helmet	When the bearer is hit with an attack that makes direct contact, it damages the attacker for 1/6 of its maximum HP.	Receive from the assistant in the Weather Institute on Route 119	—
Root Fossil	A Pokémon Fossil. When restored, it becomes Lileep.	Route 111 (select either Root Fossil or Claw Fossil)	—
Rose Incense	When held by a Pokémon, it boosts the power of Grass-type moves by 20%.	Buy from the Incense shop in Slateport Market	9,600

S

Item	Description	How to obtain	Price
Sablenite	When held, it allows Sableye to Mega Evolve into Mega Sableye during battle.	In front of the Cave of Origin in Sootopolis City	—
Sachet	Link Trade Spritzee while it holds the Sachet to evolve it into Aromatisse.	Get for 32 BP in the Battle Maison in the Battle Resort	—
Sacred Ash	Revives fainted Pokémon in a party and fully restores their HP.	Held by Ho-Oh you meet in Sea Mauville (*Pokémon Omega Ruby*)	—
Safety Goggles	Protect the holder from weather-related damage, from certain moves ◆ and from the Effect Spore Ability.	Receive from a guy in the desert on Route 111 / Get for 48 BP in the Battle Maison in the Battle Resort	—

● If you give Sneasel the Razor Claw to hold and level it up between 8 P.M. and 3:59 A.M., it will evolve into Weavile.
★ If you give Gligar the Razor Fang to hold and level it up between 8 P.M. and 3:59 A.M., it will evolve into Gliscor.
◆ Safety Goggles protect from Cotton Spore, Poison Powder, Powder, Rage Powder, Sleep Powder, Spore, and Stun Spore.

Item	Description	How to obtain	Price
Sail Fossil	A Pokémon Fossil. When restored, it becomes Amaura.	Can be obtained in *Pokémon X* and *Pokémon Y*	—
Salamencite	When held, it allows Salamence to Mega Evolve into Mega Salamence during battle.	Receive from an old woman in Meteor Falls after the Delta Episode	—
Sceptilite	When held, it allows Sceptile to Mega Evolve into Mega Sceptile during battle.	Receive from Steven on Route 120 if you chose Treecko as your first Pokémon / Buy the stone titled "Withered Tree" on Route 114	1,500
Scizorite	When held, it allows Scizor to Mega Evolve into Mega Scizor during battle.	Petalburg Woods after obtaining the National Pokédex	—
Scope Lens	Boosts the holder's critical-hit ratio.	Get for 48 BP in the Battle Maison in the Battle Resort	—
Sea Incense	When held by a Pokémon, it boosts the power of Water-type moves by 20%.	Buy from the Incense shop in Slateport Market	9,600
Shalour Sable	Shalour City's famous shortbread. It can be used once to heal all the status conditions and confusion of a Pokémon.	Challenge 6 maze in the Trick House on Route 110	—
Sharp Beak	When held by a Pokémon, it boosts the power of Flying-type moves by 20%.	Receive from a guy from Unova in the storage of *S.S. Tidal* / Sometimes held by wild Doduo	—
Sharpedonite	When held, it allows Sharpedo to Mega Evolve into Mega Sharpedo during battle.	Receive from Team Aqua in the Battle Resort (*Pokémon Omega Ruby*) / Receive from Team Aqua during the Delta Episode (*Pokémon Alpha Sapphire*)	—
Shed Shell	Always allows the holder to be switched out.	Sometimes held by wild Scraggy, Seviper, or Venomoth	—
Shell Bell	Restores the holder's HP by up to 1/8th of the damage dealt to the target.	Receive from an old guy in Shoal Cave on Route 125 in exchange for 4 Shoal Salts and 4 Shoal Shells	—
Shiny Stone	It can evolve Floette, Minccino, Togetic, and Roselia.	Route 121 / Can be obtained by winning an Inverse Battle at the Inverse Battle Stop in Mauville City	—
Shoal Salt	Salt that is one of the ingredients for a Shell Bell.	Shoal Cave on Route 125 at low tide	—
Shoal Shell	A seashell that is one of the ingredients for a Shell Bell.	Shoal Cave on Route 125 at high tide	—
Shock Drive	When held by Genesect, it changes Genesect's Techno Blast move so it becomes Electric type.	Receive from a Street Thug standing near the stairs to the top of Mauville City when you have Genesect in your party	—
Silk Scarf	When held by a Pokémon, it boosts the power of Normal-type moves by 20%.	Receive from a guy in a house in Dewford Town	—
Silver Powder	When held by a Pokémon, it boosts the power of Bug-type moves by 20%.	Sometimes held by wild Masquerain	—
Skull Fossil	A Pokémon Fossil. When restored, it becomes Cranidos.	Can be obtained by breaking cracked rocks using Rock Smash in Mirage spots (*Pokémon Alpha Sapphire*)	—
Sky Plate	When held by a Pokémon, it boosts the power of Flying-type moves by 20%. (When held by Arceus, it shifts Arceus's type to Flying type.)	Route 124 (Underwater)	—
Slowbronite	When held, it allows Slowbro to Mega Evolve into Mega Slowbro during battle.	Receive from a guy in Shoal Cave when you have a Shell Bell made for the first time	—
Smoke Ball	Allows the holder to successfully run away from wild Pokémon.	Receive from the Trick Master as a reward (Challenge 4) / Sometimes held by wild Koffing	—
Smooth Rock	Extends the duration of the sandstorm weather by three turns when held.	Receive from the receptionist in the Weather Institute on Route 119	—
Snowball	Increases Attack by 1 when the holder is hit with Ice-type moves. It goes away after use.	Sometimes held by wild Snorunt / Get for 32 BP in the Battle Maison in the Battle Resort	—
Soda Pop	Restores the HP of one Pokémon by 60 points.	Buy at a vending machine / Buy at a Seashore House on Route 109 after defeating every Trainer in the house	300
Soft Sand	When held by a Pokémon, it boosts the power of Ground-type moves by 20%.	Receive from a girl on Route 109 / Sometimes held by wild Diglett, Nincada, or Trapinch	—
Soothe Bell	The holder's friendship improves more quickly.	Receive from a Poké Fan in Slateport City when you are with a friendly lead Pokémon	—
Spell Tag	When held by a Pokémon, it boosts the power of Ghost-type moves by 20%.	Sometimes held by wild Cofagrigus, Duskull, or Shuppet	—
Splash Plate	When held by a Pokémon, it boosts the power of Water-type moves by 20%. (When held by Arceus, it shifts Arceus's type to Water type.)	Route 129 (Underwater)	—
Spooky Plate	When held by a Pokémon, it boosts the power of Ghost-type moves by 20%. (When held by Arceus, it shifts Arceus's type to Ghost type.)	Route 127 (Underwater)	—
Star Piece	A red gem. It can be sold at shops for 4,900.	Route 108 / Route 133 / Route 134 / Sometimes held by wild Staryu	—
Stardust	Lovely, red-colored sand. It can be sold at shops for 1,000.	Route 111 / Often held by wild Lunatone, Staryu, or Solrock	—
Steelixite	When held, it allows Steelix to Mega Evolve into Mega Steelix during battle.	Granite Cave (B2F)	—
Stick	When held by Farfetch'd, it raises the critical-hit ratio of its moves.	Can be obtained in *Pokémon X* and *Pokémon Y*	—
Sticky Barb	Damages the holder by 1/8 of its maximum HP every turn. It latches on to the attacker that touches the holder if the attacker doesn't have an item.	Sometimes held by wild Cacnea	—
Stone Plate	When held by a Pokémon, it boosts the power of Rock-type moves by 20%. (When held by Arceus, it shifts Arceus's type to Rock type.)	Route 128 (Underwater)	—
Sun Stone	It can evolve to Cottonee, Gloom, Helioptile, Petilil, and Sunkern.	Receive from a person at the Space Center in Mossdeep City / Sometimes held by wild Solrock	—
Super Potion	Restores the HP of one Pokémon by 50 points.	Buy at Poké Marts (after obtaining first Gym Badge)	700
Super Repel	Prevents weak wild Pokémon from appearing for 200 steps after its use.	Buy at Poké Marts (after obtaining second Gym Badge)	500

Item	Description	How to obtain	Price
Swampertite	When held, it allows Swampert to Mega Evolve into Mega Swampert during battle.	Receive from Steven on Route 120 if you chose Mudkip as your first Pokémon / Buy the stone titled "Ebb Tide" on Route 114	1,500
Sweet Heart	Restores the HP of one Pokémon by 20 points.	Sometimes given by your fan after you've participated in a contest	—
Swift Wing	Slightly increases the base Speed stat of a single Pokémon. It can be used until the max of base stats.	Can be won by reaching Beginner Rank, Novice Rank, or Normal Rank in the Battle Institute in Mauville City	—

T

Item	Description	How to obtain	Price
Thick Club	When held by Cubone or Marowak, the power of Physical Moves is doubled.	Can be obtained in *Pokémon X* and *Pokémon Y*	—
Thunder Stone	It can evolve Eelektrik, Eevee, and Pikachu.	New Mauville / Receive from the Treasure Hunter on Route 124 in exchange for a Yellow Shard	—
Tiny Mushroom	A tiny mushroom. It can be sold at shops for 250.	Often held by wild Paras or Shroomish	—
Toxic Orb	Inflicts the Badly Poisoned status condition on the holder during battle.	Get for 16 BP in the Battle Maison in the Battle Resort	—
Toxic Plate	When held by a Pokémon, it boosts the power of Poison-type moves by 20%. (When held by Arceus, it shifts Arceus's type to Poison type.)	Route 129 (Underwater)	—
Twisted Spoon	When held by a Pokémon, it boosts the power of Psychic-type moves by 20%.	Sometimes held by wild Abra	—
Tyranitarite	When held, it allows Tyranitar to Mega Evolve into Mega Tyranitar during battle.	Jagged Pass after obtaining the National Pokédex	—

U•V•W

Item	Description	How to obtain	Price
Up-Grade	Link Trade Porygon while it holds the Up-Grade to evolve it into Porygon2.	Get for 32 BP in the Battle Maison in the Battle Resort	—
Venusaurite	When held, it allows Venusaur to Mega Evolve into Mega Venusaur during battle.	Route 119 after obtaining the National Pokédex	—
Water Stone	It can evolve Eevee, Lombre, Panpour, Poliwhirl, Shellder, and Staryu.	Receive from the Treasure Hunter on Route 124 in exchange for a Blue Shard	—
Wave Incense	When held by a Pokémon, it boosts the power of Water-type moves by 20%.	Buy from the Incense shop in Slateport Market	9,600
Weakness Policy	Increases Attack and Sp. Atk by 2 if the holder is hit with a move that it's weak to.	Get for 32 BP in the Battle Maison in the Battle Resort	—
Whipped Dream	Link Trade Swirlix while it holds a Whipped Dream to evolve it into Slurpuff.	Get for 32 BP in the Battle Maison in the Battle Resort	—
White Flute	Makes it easier to encounter weak Pokémon.	Receive from a guy in the Glass Workshop on Route 113 in exchange for collected ash (1,000g)	—
White Herb	Restores lowered stats. It goes away after use.	Sea Mauville / Get for 32 BP in the Battle Maison in the Battle Resort / Get from a girl on Route 104 after talking with the eldest sister of the flower shop owner and obtaining the Petalburg City Gym Badge	—
Wide Lens	Raises the holder's accuracy by 10%.	Route 123 / Sometimes held by wild Sableye / Get for 48 BP in the Battle Maison in the Battle Resort	—
Wise Glasses	When held by a Pokémon, it boosts the power of special moves by 10%.	Get for 48 BP in the Battle Maison in the Battle Resort	—

X

Item	Description	How to obtain	Price
X Accuracy	Raises the accuracy of a Pokémon on which it is used during battle.	Buy from the Poké Mart in Slateport City / Lilycove Department Store (3F)	950
X Attack	Raises the Attack stat of a Pokémon by 1 during battle.	Buy from the Poké Mart in Slateport City / Lilycove Department Store (3F)	500
X Defense	Raises the Defense stat of a Pokémon by 1 during battle.	Buy from the Poké Mart in Slateport City / Lilycove Department Store (3F)	550
X Sp. Atk	Raises the Sp. Atk stat of a Pokémon by 1 during battle.	Buy from the Poké Mart in Slateport City / Lilycove Department Store (3F)	350
X Sp. Def	Raises the Sp. Def stat of a Pokémon by 1 during battle.	Buy from the Poké Mart in Slateport City / Lilycove Department Store (3F)	350
X Speed	Raises the Speed of a Pokémon by 1 during battle.	Buy from the Poké Mart in Slateport City / Lilycove Department Store (3F)	350
Yellow Flute	Snaps Pokémon out of confusion.	Receive from a guy in the Glass Workshop on Route 113 in exchange for collected ash (500g)	—

Item	Description	How to obtain	Price
Yellow Scarf	When held by a Pokémon, it raises the Toughness aspect of the Pokémon in Contest Spectacular.	Receive from the chairman of the Pokémon Fan Club in Slateport City when your lead Pokémon has the max Toughness stat	—
Yellow Shard	A Shard you can trade for a Thunder Stone with the Treasure Hunter on Route 124.	Route 124	—
Zap Plate	When held by a Pokémon, it boosts the power of Electric-type moves by 20%. (When held by Arceus, it shifts Arceus's type to Electric type.)	Route 129 (Underwater)	—

Z

Item	Description	How to obtain	Price
Zinc	Raises the base Sp. Def stat of a Pokémon.	Buy from the Energy Guru in Slateport Market / Lilycove Department Store (3F)	9,800
Zoom Lens	Raises the holder's accuracy by 20% when it moves after the opposing Pokémon.	Get for 48 BP in the Battle Maison in the Battle Resort	—

Key Items

Item	Description	How to obtain	Price
Acro Bike	A folding Bike that allows you to perform actions such as wheelies and bunny hops.	Receive from Rydel at Rydel's Cycles in Mauville City	—
Aqua Suit	A suit made with the collective technological know-how of Team Aqua. It can withstand any impact.	Receive from Archie in Sootopolis City (*Pokémon Alpha Sapphire*)	—
Clear Bell	A very old-fashioned bell that makes a gentle ringing sound. It allows you to meet Ho-Oh.	Receive from Captain Stern in Slateport City after finding the Scanner (*Pokémon Omega Ruby*)	—
Contest Costume	A very cool suit to be worn during the Contest Spectacular.	Receive from Lisia in Slateport City (if you chose the boy character)	—
Contest Costume	A very pretty suit to be worn during the Contest Spectacular.	Receive from Lisia in Slateport City (if you chose the girl character)	—
Contest Pass	A pass required for entering Pokémon Contests. It has a drawing of an award ribbon on its front.	Receive from Lisia in Slateport City	—
Devon Parts	A case that contains mechanical parts of some sort made by the Devon Corporation.	Get back from Team Magma/Aqua Grunt in Rusturf Tunnel	—
Devon Scope	A special device made by Devon Corporation that signals the presence of any unseen Pokémon.	Receive from Steven on Route 120	—
Devon Scuba Gear	A device made by Devon Corporation that provides oxygen to users during the use of Dive.	Receive from Steven in his house in Mossdeep City	—
DNA Splicers	A pair of splicers that fuse Kyurem and Zekrom or Reshiram.	Gnarled Den (using the Dowsing Machine)	—
Dowsing Machine	It searches for hidden items in the area and emits different lights and sounds when it detects something.	Receive from May / Brendan on Route 110	—
Eon Flute	A flute that can be used to summon Latios or Latias no matter where you are.	Receive from Steven in Sootopolis City	—
Exp. Share	When it is switched to ON, all of the Pokémon in your party will receive Exp. Points, even if they themselves do not battle.	Receive from a Devon researcher in Petalburg Woods	—
Go-Goggles	Nifty goggles to protect eyes from desert sandstorms.	Receive from May/Brendan in Lavaridge Town	—
Good Rod	A nice, new fishing rod. You can use it to fish for Pokémon from the waterside.	Receive from a Fisherman on Route 118	—
Gracidea	A flower to convey gratitude. Shaymin will change its Forme if Gracidea is used on it (except at night).	Receive from a man in Berry Master's House on Route 123 when you have Shaymin in your party	—
Intriguing Stone	A rather curious stone that might appear valuable to some.	Find the lost Shroomish in Verdanturf Town and speak to the girl who lost Shroomish	—
Key to Room 1	A key that opens a door inside Sea Mauville.	Receive from a Tuber girl in Sea Mauville	—
Key to Room 2	A key that opens a door inside Sea Mauville.	Check a file cabinet in Room 1 in Sea Mauville	—
Key to Room 4	A key that opens a door inside Sea Mauville.	Receive from a Fisherman on the beach by Sea Mauville (after speaking to the Fisherman, choose "You caught anything?")	—
Key to Room 6	A key that opens a door inside Sea Mauville.	Receive from a school girl in Room 2 in Sea Mauville	—
Letter	A letter entrusted to you by the President of Devon Corporation.	Receive from the president on the third floor of the Devon Corporation in Rustboro City	—
Mach Bike	A folding Bike that can double your movement speed.	Receive from Rydel at Rydel's Cycles in Mauville City	—
Magma Suit	A suit made with the collective technological know-how of Team Magma. It can withstand any impact.	Receive from Maxie in Sootopolis City (*Pokémon Omega Ruby*)	—
Mega Bracelet	The cuff that contains an untold power that somehow enables Pokémon carrying a Mega Stone to Mega Evolve in battle.	Receive from Steven on Southern Island	—

Item		Description	How to obtain	Price
	Meteorite	A meteorite originally found at Meteor Falls.	Receive from Maxie/Archie at the summit of Mt. Chimney	—
	Meteorite Shard	One of the fragments of a meteorite from Granite Cave. It's faintly warm to the touch.	Receive during the Delta Episode	—
	Old Rod	An old and beat-up fishing rod. You can use it to fish for Pokémon from the waterside.	Receive from a Fisherman in Dewford Town	—
	Oval Charm	An oval charm said to increase the chance of Pokémon Eggs being found at the Day Care.	Receive from Professor Birch in his lab in Littleroot Town after completing the Hoenn Pokédex	—
	Pair of Tickets	Tickets for two to the astronomical show being held at the Mossdeep Space Center.	Receive from Norman after entering the Hall of Fame	—
	Pokéblock Kit	A set containing a Berry Blender for making Pokéblocks and a Pokéblock Case for storing Pokéblocks.	Receive from Lisia in Slateport City	—
	Reveal Glass	A looking glass necessary to change Tornadus, Thundurus, and Landorus from Incarnate Forme into Therian Forme.	Receive from the shop keeper at Narcissus Mirror Shop in Mauville City when you have Tornadus, Thundurus, or Landorus in your party	—
	S.S. Ticket	A ticket required for sailing on the ferry *S.S. Tidal.*	Receive from Norman in Littleroot Town after clearing the Delta Episode	—
	Scanner	A device needed by Captain Stern for some research.	Sea Mauville after obtaining the National Pokédex	—
	Shiny Charm	A shiny charm said to increase the change of finding a Shiny Pokémon in the wild.	Receive from Professor Birch in his lab in Littleroot Town after completing the National Pokédex	—
	Soot Sack	A sack used to gather and hold volcanic ash.	Receive from a guy in the Glass Workshop on Route 113	—
	Storage Key	A key that opens the storage hold inside Sea Mauville.	Find in Room 4 in Sea Mauville	—
	Super Rod	An awesome, high-tech fishing rod. You can use it to fish for Pokémon from the waterside.	Receive from a Fisherman in a house in Mossdeep City	—
	Tidal Bell	A very old-fashioned bell that makes a gentle ringing sound. It allows you to meet Lugia.	Receive from Captain Stern in Slateport City after finding the Scanner (*Pokémon Alpha Sapphire*)	—
	Vs. Recorder	An amazing device that can record a battle between friends or the battles at certain special battle facilities.	Receive from a guy in the Battle Institute in Mauville City	—
	Wailmer Pail	A tool for watering Berries you planted to make them grow more quickly.	Receive from a woman in the Pretty Petal Flower Shop on Route 104	—

Poké Balls

Item		Description	How to obtain	Price
	Poké Ball	A device for catching wild Pokémon.	Buy at Poké Marts (after receiving Poké Balls from May / Brendan in Littleroot Town)	200
	Great Ball	A Poké Ball that provides a higher Pokémon catch rate than a standard Poké Ball can.	Buy at Poké Marts (after obtaining first Gym Badge)	600
	Ultra Ball	A Poké Ball that provides a higher Pokémon catch rate than a Great Ball can.	Buy at Poké Marts (after obtaining third Gym Badge)	1,200
	Master Ball	A Poké Ball that will catch any wild Pokémon without fail.	Find at Team Magma Hideout (B3F) (*Pokémon Omega Ruby*) / Team Aqua Hideout (B3F) (*Pokémon Alpha Sapphire*)	—
	Premier Ball	A rare Poké Ball made to celebrate an event of some sort.	Buy 10 or more Poké Balls at a time	—
	Dive Ball	A Poké Ball that works especially well when catching Pokémon that live underwater.	Buy at the Poké Mart in Fallarbor Town	1,000
	Dusk Ball	A Poké Ball that makes it easier to catch wild Pokémon in caves or at night (between 8 P.M. and 3:59 A.M.).	Buy at the Poké Mart in Fallarbor Town	1,000
	Heal Ball	A remedial Poké Ball that restores the HP of a Pokémon caught with it and eliminates any status conditions.	Buy at the Poké Mart in Verdanturf Town	300
	Luxury Ball	A Poké Ball that makes a wild Pokémon quickly grow friendlier after being caught.	Buy at the Poké Mart in Verdanturf Town	1,000
	Nest Ball	A Poké Ball that becomes more effective the lower the level of the wild Pokémon.	Buy at the Poké Mart in Verdanturf Town	1,000
	Net Ball	A Poké Ball that is more effective when attempting to catch Water- or Bug-type Pokémon.	Buy at the Poké Mart in Rustboro City (after opening Rusturf Tunnel and talking to the Scientist outside)	1,000
	Quick Ball	A Poké Ball that has a more successful catch rate if used at the start of a wild encounter.	Buy at the Poké Mart in Fallarbor Town	1,000
	Repeat Ball	A Poké Ball that works especially well on a Pokémon species that has been caught before.	Buy at the Poké Mart in Rustboro City (after opening Rusturf Tunnel and talking to the Scientist outside)	1,000
	Timer Ball	A Poké Ball that becomes progressively more effective the more turns that are taken in battle.	Buy at the Poké Mart in Rustboro City (after opening Rusturf Tunnel and talking to the Scientist outside)	1,000

National Pokédex No.	Hoenn Pokédex No.	Pokémon	Often holding	Sometimes holding
25	163	Pikachu	—	Light Ball
27	117	Sandshrew	—	Grip Claw
35	—	Clefairy	—	Moon Stone
37	160	Vulpix	—	Charcoal
43	91	Oddish	—	Absorb Bulb
44	92	Gloom	—	Absorb Bulb
46	—	Paras	Tiny Mushroom	Big Mushroom
49	—	Venomoth	—	Shed Shell
50	—	Diglett	—	Soft Sand
53	—	Persian	—	Quick Claw
63	40	Abra	—	Twisted Spoon
66	75	Machop	—	Focus Band
72	68	Tentacool	—	Poison Barb
73	69	Tentacruel	—	Poison Barb
74	58	Geodude	—	Everstone
75	59	Graveler	—	Everstone
79	—	Slowpoke	—	Lagging Tail
81	84	Magnemite	—	Metal Coat
84	95	Doduo	—	Sharp Beak
88	111	Grimer	—	Black Sludge
109	113	Koffing	—	Smoke Ball
116	193	Horsea	—	Dragon Scale
117	194	Seadra	—	Dragon Scale
118	51	Goldeen	—	Mystic Water
119	52	Seaking	—	Mystic Water
120	148	Staryu	Stardust	Star Piece
132	—	Ditto	Quick Powder	Metal Powder
170	190	Chinchou	—	Deep Sea Scale
171	191	Lanturn	—	Deep Sea Scale
222	189	Corsola	—	Luminous Moss
227	120	Skarmory	—	Metal Coat
239	—	Elekid	—	Electirizer
240	—	Magby	—	Magmarizer
263	12	Zigzagoon	Potion	Revive
264	13	Linoone	Potion	Max Revive
265	14	Wurmple	Pecha Berry	Bright Powder
270	19	Lotad	—	Mental Herb
271	20	Lombre	—	Mental Herb
273	22	Seedot	—	Power Herb
274	23	Nuzleaf	—	Power Herb
278	27	Wingull	Pretty Wing	—
279	28	Pelipper	Pretty Wing	Lucky Egg
283	33	Surskit	Honey	—
284	34	Masquerain	—	Silver Powder
285	35	Shroomish	Tiny Mushroom	Big Mushroom
290	43	Nincada	—	Soft Sand
296	49	Makuhita	—	Black Belt
297	50	Hariyama	—	King's Rock
299	61	Nosepass	—	Hard Stone

National Pokédex No.	Hoenn Pokédex No.	Pokémon	Often holding	Sometimes holding
302	70	Sableye	—	Wide Lens
303	71	Mawile	—	Iron Ball
304	72	Aron	—	Hard Stone
305	73	Lairon	—	Hard Stone
311	82	Plusle	—	Cell Battery
312	83	Minun	—	Cell Battery
313	89	Volbeat	—	Bright Powder
314	90	Illumise	—	Bright Powder
315	98	Roselia	—	Poison Barb
316	100	Gulpin	Oran Berry	Sitrus Berry
318	102	Carvanha	—	Deep Sea Tooth
319	103	Sharpedo	—	Deep Sea Tooth
324	110	Torkoal	—	Charcoal
328	121	Trapinch	—	Soft Sand
331	124	Cacnea	—	Sticky Barb
335	128	Zangoose	—	Quick Claw
336	129	Seviper	—	Shed Shell
337	130	Lunatone	Stardust	Moon Stone
338	131	Solrock	Stardust	Sun Stone
343	136	Baltoy	—	Light Clay
344	137	Claydol	—	Light Clay
353	151	Shuppet	—	Spell Tag
355	153	Duskull	—	Spell Tag
358	158	Chimecho	—	Cleanse Tag
359	159	Absol	—	Life Orb
361	179	Snorunt	—	Snowball
366	185	Clamperl	Pearl	Big Pearl
369	188	Relicanth	—	Deep Sea Scale
370	192	Luvdisc	Heart Scale	—
371	196	Bagon	—	Dragon Fang
402	—	Kricketune	—	Metronome
421	—	Cherrim	—	Miracle Seed
436	—	Bronzor	—	Metal Coat
440	—	Happiny	Oval Stone	Lucky Egg
441	—	Chatot	—	Metronome
451	—	Skorupi	—	Poison Barb
524	—	Roggenrola	Everstone	Hard Stone
525	—	Boldore	Everstone	Hard Stone
531	—	Audino	Oran Berry	Sitrus Berry
538	—	Throh	—	Black Belt
539	—	Sawk	—	Black Belt
540	—	Sewaddle	—	Mental Herb
556	—	Maractus	—	Miracle Seed
557	—	Dwebble	—	Hard Stone
558	—	Crustle	—	Hard Stone
559	—	Scraggy	—	Shed Shell
563	—	Cofagrigus	—	Spell Tag
568	—	Trubbish	—	Black Sludge
621	—	Druddigon	—	Dragon Fang

HOW AND WHERE TO MEET SPECIAL POKÉMON

Pokémon	Level	Location	How to meet it again if you defeat it in battle or run from battle
Regirock	Lv. 40	Desert Ruins in the central desert on Route 111 (after unlocking the mysteries of the Sealed Chamber)	Defeat the Elite Four and the Champion at the Pokémon League. It comes back until you catch it.
Regice	Lv. 40	Island Cave on Route 105 (after unlocking the mysteries of the Sealed Chamber)	Defeat the Elite Four and the Champion at the Pokémon League. It comes back until you catch it.
Registeel	Lv. 40	Ancient Tomb on Route 120 (after unlocking the mysteries of the Sealed Chamber)	Defeat the Elite Four and the Champion at the Pokémon League. It comes back until you catch it.
Groudon	Lv. 45	Deepest part of the Cave of Origin (*Pokémon Omega Ruby*)	Defeat the Elite Four and the Champion at the Pokémon League. It comes back until you catch it.
Kyogre	Lv. 45	Deepest part of the Cave of Origin (*Pokémon Alpha Sapphire*)	Defeat the Elite Four and the Champion at the Pokémon League. It comes back until you catch it.
Rayquaza	Lv. 70	Top of Sky Pillar	It comes back until you catch it.
Deoxys	Lv. 80	In the stratosphere (during the Delta Episode)	Defeat the Elite Four and the Champion at the Pokémon League. It comes back until you catch it.
Lugia	Lv. 50	Sea Mauville (after obtaining the Tidal Bell in *Pokémon Alpha Sapphire*)	Defeat the Elite Four and the Champion at the Pokémon League. It comes back until you catch it.
Ho-Oh	Lv. 50	Sea Mauville (after obtaining the Clear Bell in *Pokémon Omega Ruby*)	Defeat the Elite Four and the Champion at the Pokémon League. It comes back until you catch it.
Raikou	Lv. 50	Trackless Forest Mirage spot (Soar at a certain time with either Ho-Oh or Lugia in your party)	Defeat the Elite Four and the Champion at the Pokémon League. It comes back until you catch it.
Entei	Lv. 50	Trackless Forest Mirage spot (Soar at a certain time with either Ho-Oh or Lugia in your party)	Defeat the Elite Four and the Champion at the Pokémon League. It comes back until you catch it.
Suicune	Lv. 50	Trackless Forest Mirage spot (Soar at a certain time with either Ho-Oh or Lugia in your party)	Defeat the Elite Four and the Champion at the Pokémon League. It comes back until you catch it.
Spiritomb	Lv. 50	Sea Mauville (stand in front of a bookcase in an eastern room on the first floor and press X to open the menu, then select "Pokémon," "Pokédex," or "Bag" to change the screen)	Defeat the Elite Four and the Champion at the Pokémon League. It comes back until you catch it.
Uxie	Lv. 50	Nameless Cavern Mirage spot (Soar at a certain time with three or more Pokémon in your party that have maximum friendship levels)	Defeat the Elite Four and the Champion at the Pokémon League. It comes back until you catch it.
Mesprit	Lv. 50	Nameless Cavern Mirage spot (Soar at a certain time with three or more Pokémon in your party that have maximum friendship levels)	Defeat the Elite Four and the Champion at the Pokémon League. It comes back until you catch it.
Azelf	Lv. 50	Nameless Cavern Mirage spot (Soar at a certain time with three or more Pokémon in your party that have maximum friendship levels)	Defeat the Elite Four and the Champion at the Pokémon League. It comes back until you catch it.

Pokémon	Level	Location	How to meet it again if you defeat it in battle or run from battle
Dialga	Lv. 50	Dimensional Rift Mirage spot in the sky (Soar with a specific Psychic trio of Legendary Pokémon in your party in *Pokémon Alpha Sapphire*)	Return to the ground and use the Eon Flute again to Soar.
Palkia	Lv. 50	Dimensional Rift Mirage spot in the sky (Soar with a specific Psychic trio of Legendary Pokémon in your party in *Pokémon Omega Ruby*)	Return to the ground and use the Eon Flute again to Soar.
Heatran	Lv. 50	Third basement floor of the Scorched Slab on Route 120 (after battling Groudon or Kyogre)	Defeat the Elite Four and the Champion at the Pokémon League. It comes back until you catch it.
Regigigas	Lv. 50	Island Cave on Route 105 (with Regirock, Regice, and Registeel in your party and after battling Groudon or Kyogre and following the hints you get at the house in Pacifidlog Town)	Defeat the Elite Four and the Champion at the Pokémon League. It comes back until you catch it.
Giratina (Altered Forme)	Lv. 50	Dimensional Rift Mirage spot in the sky (Soar with a certain pair of temporal and spatial Legendary Pokémon in your party)	Return to the ground and use the Eon Flute again to Soar.
Cresselia	Lv. 50	Crescent Isle Mirage spot	Defeat the Elite Four and the Champion at the Pokémon League. It comes back until you catch it.
Cobalion	Lv. 50	Pathless Plain Mirage spot (Soar on a certain day of the week with three Pokémon that have been fully trained in Super Training)	Defeat the Elite Four and the Champion at the Pokémon League. It comes back until you catch it.
Terrakion	Lv. 50	Pathless Plain Mirage spot (Soar on a certain day of the week with three Pokémon that have been fully trained in Super Training)	Defeat the Elite Four and the Champion at the Pokémon League. It comes back until you catch it.
Virizion	Lv. 50	Pathless Plain Mirage spot (Soar on a certain day of the week with three Pokémon that have been fully trained in Super Training)	Defeat the Elite Four and the Champion at the Pokémon League. It comes back until you catch it.
Tornadus (Incarnate Forme)	Lv. 50	Storm Clouds Mirage spot in the sky (Soar with a Pokémon that has something to do with weather in *Pokémon Omega Ruby*)	Return to the ground and use the Eon Flute again to Soar.
Thundurus (Incarnate Forme)	Lv. 50	Storm Clouds Mirage spot in the sky (Soar with a Pokémon that has something to do with weather in *Pokémon Alpha Sapphire*)	Return to the ground and use the Eon Flute again to Soar.
Reshiram	Lv. 50	Fabled Cave Mirage spot (Soar with a high level Pokémon in your party in *Pokémon Omega Ruby*)	Defeat the Elite Four and the Champion at the Pokémon League. It comes back until you catch it.
Zekrom	Lv. 50	Fabled Cave Mirage spot (Soar with a high level Pokémon in your party in *Pokémon Alpha Sapphire*)	Defeat the Elite Four and the Champion at the Pokémon League. It comes back until you catch it.
Landorus (Incarnate Forme)	Lv. 50	Storm Clouds Mirage spot in the sky (Soar with a specific pair of similar Legendary Pokémon in your party)	Return to the ground and use the Eon Flute again to Soar.
Kyurem	Lv. 50	Gnarled Den Mirage spot (Soar with a certain black and white Legendary Pokémon duo in your party)	Defeat the Elite Four and the Champion at the Pokémon League. It comes back until you catch it.

POKÉMON MOVES REVERSE LOOKUP

The number in the brackets is the level at which the Pokémon learns the move. [E] is an Egg Move, [TM] is a Technical Machine move, [HM] is a Hidden Machine move, [T] is a move that someone teaches the Pokémon, and [BP] is a move for which you need Battle Points. Form(e) names of Deoxys, Giratina, Kyurem, Meowstic, Shaymin, Rotom, and Wormadam are in parentheses.

A

	Move	Pokémon that can learn it						
Grass	Absorb	591 Amoonguss [1]	267 Beautifly [12]	286 Breloom [1]	406 Budew [1]	331 Cacnea [4]	332 Cacturne [1, 4]	546 Cottonee [1]
		590 Foongus [1]	592 Frillish [5]	044 Gloom [1]	706 Goodra [5]	704 Goomy [5]	388 Grotle [9]	253 Grovyle [1, 5]
		593 Jellicent [1, 5]	140 Kabuto [6]	141 Kabutops [1, 6]	271 Lombre [6]	270 Lotad [6]	556 Maractus [1]	043 Oddish [1]
		548 Petilil [1]	315 Roselia [1]	254 Sceptile [1, 5]	285 Shroomish [1]	705 Sliggoo [5]	192 Sunflora [1]	191 Sunkern [1]
		114 Tangela [10]	465 Tangrowth [10]	389 Torterra [1, 9]	252 Treecko [5]	387 Turtwig [9]		
Poison	Acid	024 Arbok [20]	069 Bellsprout [23]	331 Cacnea [E]	346 Cradily [1, 5]	691 Dragalge [15]	603 Eelektrik [19]	604 Eelektross [1]
		023 Ekans [20]	044 Gloom [1, 9]	345 Lileep [5]	607 Litwick [E]	043 Oddish [9]	537 Seismitoad [36]	616 Shelmet [4]
		213 Shuckle [E]	690 Skrelp [15]	072 Tentacool [10]	073 Tentacruel [1, 10]	070 Weepinbell [23]		
	Acid Armor	615 Cryogonal [29]	592 Frillish [E]	704 Goomy [E]	088 Grimer [43]	316 Gulpin [E]	607 Litwick [E]	490 Manaphy [31]
		089 Muk [46]	489 Phione [31]	422 Shellos [E]	616 Shelmet [32]	690 Skrelp [E]	218 Slugma [E]	577 Solosis [E]
		583 Vanillish [31]	582 Vanillite [31]	584 Vanilluxe [31]	134 Vaporeon [29]			
	Acid Spray	617 Accelgor [1, 4]	024 Arbok [32]	069 Bellsprout [E]	603 Eelektrik [49]	023 Ekans [28]	597 Ferroseed [E]	569 Garbodor [12]
		088 Grimer [E]	316 Gulpin [17]	211 Qwilfish [E]	223 Remoraid [E]	435 Skuntank [32]	434 Stunky [32]	317 Swalot [17]
		072 Tentacool [22]	073 Tentacruel [22]	568 Trubbish [12]	194 Wooper [E]			
Flying	Acrobatics (TM62)	190 Aipom [TM]	424 Ambipom [TM]	566 Archen [28, TM]	567 Archeops [28, TM]	482 Azelf [TM]	267 Beautifly [TM]	015 Beedrill [TM]
		257 Blaziken [TM]	012 Butterfree [TM]	390 Chimchar [39, TM]	169 Crobat [35, TM]	615 Cryogonal [TM]	426 Drifblim [TM]	425 Drifloon [TM]
		269 Dustox [TM]	603 Eelektrik [TM]	604 Eelektross [TM]	587 Emolga [30, TM]	083 Farfetch'd [37, TM]	662 Fletchinder [42, TM]	661 Fletchling [39, TM]
		656 Froakie [TM]	657 Frogadier [TM]	207 Gligar [22, TM]	472 Gliscor [22, TM]	042 Golbat [35, TM]	658 Greninja [TM]	253 Grovyle [TM]
		701 Hawlucha [TM]	187 Hoppip [28, TM]	635 Hydreigon [TM]	314 Illumise [TM]	392 Infernape [52, TM]	189 Jumpluff [34, TM]	636 Larvesta [TM]
		166 Ledian [TM]	165 Ledyba [TM]	337 Lunatone [TM]	056 Mankey [TM]	226 Mantine [TM]	458 Mantyke [TM]	648 Meloetta [26, TM]
		481 Mesprit [TM]	151 Mew [TM]	619 Mienfoo [TM]	620 Mienshao [TM]	391 Monferno [46, TM]	414 Mothim [TM]	714 Noibat [TM]
		715 Noivern [TM]	515 Panpour [31, TM]	511 Pansage [31, TM]	513 Pansear [31, TM]	057 Primeape [TM]	254 Sceptile [TM]	212 Scizor [TM]
		516 Simipour [TM]	512 Simisage [TM]	514 Simisear [TM]	188 Skiploom [32, TM]	338 Solrock [TM]	528 Swoobat [TM]	663 Talonflame [44, TM]
		641 Tornadus [TM]	252 Treecko [TM]	480 Uxie [TM]	049 Venomoth [TM]	416 Vespiquen [TM]	666 Vivillon [TM]	313 Volbeat [TM]
		637 Volcarona [TM]	527 Woobat [TM]	717 Yveltal [TM]	041 Zubat [31, TM]			
Normal	Acupressure	453 Croagunk [E]	085 Dodrio [29]	084 Doduo [29]	452 Drapion [13]	556 Maractus [29]	308 Medicham [33]	307 Meditite [33]
		213 Shuckle [E]	451 Skorupi [13]	072 Tentacool [E]				
Flying	Aerial Ace (TM40)	359 Absol [TM]	681 Aegislash [1, TM]	142 Aerodactyl [TM]	306 Aggron [TM]	190 Aipom [TM]	334 Altaria [TM]	424 Ambipom [TM]
		347 Anorith [TM]	059 Arcanine [TM]	493 Arceus [TM]	566 Archen [TM]	567 Archeops [TM]	348 Armaldo [TM]	304 Aron [TM]
		144 Articuno [TM]	610 Axew [TM]	371 Bagon [TM]	689 Barbaracle [TM]	614 Beartic [TM]	267 Beautifly [TM]	015 Beedrill [TM]
		688 Binacle [TM]	625 Bisharp [TM]	257 Blaziken [TM]	626 Bouffalant [TM]	628 Braviary [23, TM]	012 Butterfree [TM]	251 Celebi [TM]
		006 Charizard [TM]	004 Charmander [TM]	005 Charmeleon [TM]	441 Chatot [TM]	652 Chesnaught [TM]	650 Chespin [TM]	390 Chimchar [TM]
		638 Cobalion [TM]	256 Combusken [TM]	341 Corphish [TM]	342 Crawdaunt [TM]	169 Crobat [TM]	159 Croconaw [TM]	558 Crustle [TM]
		613 Cubchoo [TM]	104 Cubone [TM]	155 Cyndaquil [TM]	491 Darkrai [TM]	702 Dedenne [TM]	225 Delibird [TM]	386 Deoxys (Atk) [TM]
		386 Deoxys (Def) [TM]	386 Deoxys (Nor) [TM]	386 Deoxys (Spd) [TM]	502 Dewott [TM]	483 Dialga [TM]	050 Diglett [TM]	085 Dodrio [TM]
		084 Doduo [TM]	680 Doublade [22, TM]	149 Dragonite [TM]	452 Drapion [TM]	529 Drilbur [TM]	621 Druddigon [TM]	580 Ducklett [15, TM]
		051 Dugtrio [TM]	632 Durant [TM]	269 Dustox [TM]	557 Dwebble [TM]	587 Emolga [TM]	395 Empoleon [TM]	589 Escavalier [TM]
		530 Excadrill [TM]	083 Farfetch'd [9, TM]	022 Fearow [17, TM]	160 Feraligatr [TM]	598 Ferrothorn [TM]	662 Fletchinder [TM]	661 Fletchling [TM]
		330 Flygon [TM]	611 Fraxure [TM]	656 Froakie [TM]	657 Frogadier [TM]	444 Gabite [TM]	475 Gallade [TM]	445 Garchomp [TM]
		649 Genesect [TM]	443 Gible [TM]	487 Giratina (Alt) [TM]	487 Giratina (Ori) [TM]	431 Glameow [TM]	207 Gligar [TM]	472 Gliscor [TM]
		673 Gogoat [1, 65, TM]	042 Golbat [TM]	055 Golduck [TM]	658 Greninja [TM]	383 Groudon [TM]	253 Grovyle [TM]	058 Growlithe [TM]
		701 Hawlucha [16, TM]	612 Haxorus [TM]	631 Heatmor [TM]	214 Heracross [10, TM]	507 Herdier [TM]	237 Hitmontop [TM]	430 Honchkrow [TM]
		679 Honedge [22, TM]	250 Ho-Oh [TM]	163 Hoothoot [TM]	187 Hoppip [TM]	314 Illumise [TM]	392 Infernape [TM]	686 Inkay [TM]
		385 Jirachi [TM]	189 Jumpluff [TM]	140 Kabuto [TM]	141 Kabutops [TM]	115 Kangaskhan [TM]	588 Karrablast [TM]	352 Kecleon [TM]
		647 Keldeo [TM]	402 Kricketune [TM]	553 Krookodile [TM]	305 Lairon [TM]	380 Latias [TM]	381 Latios [TM]	470 Leafeon [TM]
		542 Leavanny [TM]	166 Ledian [TM]	165 Ledyba [TM]	510 Liepard [TM]	506 Lillipup [TM]	249 Lugia [TM]	687 Malamar [TM]
		630 Mandibuzz [TM]	056 Mankey [TM]	226 Mantine [TM]	458 Mantyke [TM]	556 Maractus [TM]	105 Marowak [TM]	284 Masquerain [TM]
		052 Meowth [TM]	376 Metagross [TM]	375 Metang [TM]	151 Mew [TM]	150 Mewtwo [TM]	619 Mienfoo [TM]	620 Mienshao [TM]
		200 Misdreavus [TM]	429 Mismagius [TM]	146 Moltres [TM]	391 Monferno [TM]	414 Mothim [TM]	122 Mr. Mime [TM]	198 Murkrow [TM]
		177 Natu [TM]	031 Nidoqueen [TM]	029 Nidoran ♀ [TM]	030 Nidorina [TM]	290 Nincada [TM]	291 Ninjask [TM]	164 Noctowl [TM]
		714 Noibat [TM]	715 Noivern [TM]	501 Oshawott [TM]	484 Palkia [TM]	674 Pancham [TM]	675 Pangoro [TM]	046 Paras [TM]
		047 Parasect [TM]	624 Pawniard [TM]	279 Pelipper [TM]	053 Persian [TM]	018 Pidgeot [TM]	017 Pidgeotto [TM]	016 Pidgey [TM]
		519 Pidove [TM]	393 Piplup [TM]	137 Porygon [TM]	233 Porygon2 [TM]	474 Porygon-Z [TM]	057 Primeape [TM]	394 Prinplup [TM]
		054 Psyduck [TM]	509 Purrloin [TM]	432 Purugly [TM]	156 Quilava [TM]	651 Quilladin [TM]	384 Rayquaza [TM]	486 Regigigas [TM]
		379 Registeel [TM]	627 Rufflet [23, TM]	302 Sableye [TM]	373 Salamence [TM]	503 Samurott [TM]	027 Sandshrew [TM]	028 Sandslash [TM]
		254 Sceptile [TM]	212 Scizor [TM]	123 Scyther [TM]	497 Serperior [TM]	496 Servine [TM]	292 Shedinja [TM]	372 Shelgon [TM]
		275 Shiftry [TM]	561 Sigilyph [TM]	227 Skarmory [TM]	188 Skiploom [TM]	451 Skorupi [TM]	289 Slaking [TM]	287 Slakoth [TM]
		080 Slowbro [TM]	215 Sneasel [TM]	495 Snivy [TM]	021 Spearow [17, TM]	398 Staraptor [28, TM]	397 Staravia [28, TM]	396 Starly [25, TM]
		508 Stoutland [TM]	333 Swablu [TM]	581 Swanna [15, TM]	277 Swellow [21, TM]	528 Swoobat [TM]	276 Taillow [21, TM]	663 Talonflame [TM]
		465 Tangrowth [TM]	216 Teddiursa [TM]	639 Terrakion [TM]	468 Togekiss [TM]	176 Togetic [TM]	255 Torchic [TM]	641 Tornadus [TM]
		158 Totodile [TM]	520 Tranquill [TM]	252 Treecko [TM]	357 Tropius [TM]	157 Typhlosion [TM]	248 Tyranitar [TM]	697 Tyrantrum [TM]
		696 Tyrunt [TM]	521 Unfezant [TM]	217 Ursaring [TM]	049 Venomoth [TM]	416 Vespiquen [TM]	288 Vigoroth [TM]	640 Virizion [TM]

Type	Move	Pokémon that can learn it						
Flying	Aerial Ace (TM40)	666 Vivillon [TM]	313 Volbeat [TM]	637 Volcarona [TM]	629 Vullaby [TM]	461 Weavile [TM]	278 Wingull [29, TM]	527 Woobat [TM]
		178 Xatu [TM]	193 Yanma [TM]	469 Yanmega [TM]	717 Yveltal [TM]	335 Zangoose [TM]	145 Zapdos [TM]	571 Zoroark [TM]
		570 Zorua [TM]	041 Zubat [TM]					
	Aeroblast	249 Lugia [43]						
Normal	After You	681 Aegislash [BP]	591 Amoonguss [BP]	181 Ampharos [BP]	683 Aromatisse [BP]	531 Audino [41, BP]	713 Avalugg [BP]	606 Beheeyem [BP]
		182 Bellossom [BP]	712 Bergmite [BP]	438 Bonsly [BP]	427 Buneary [43, BP]	323 Camerupt [BP]	703 Carbink [BP]	573 Cinccino [BP]
		036 Clefable [BP]	035 Clefairy [1, 58, BP]	173 Cleffa [BP]	563 Cofagrigus [BP]	719 Diancie [BP]	680 Doublade [BP]	578 Duosion [BP]
		605 Elgyem [BP]	180 Flaaffy [BP]	669 Flabébé [BP]	670 Floette [BP]	671 Florges [BP]	590 Foongus [BP]	044 Gloom [BP]
		507 Herdier [BP]	679 Honedge [BP]	352 Kecleon [BP]	549 Lilligant [BP]	506 Lillipup [BP, E]	428 Lopunny [43, BP]	219 Magcargo [BP]
		556 Maractus [1, 57, BP]	179 Mareep [BP, E]	151 Mew [BP]	241 Miltank [BP]	572 Minccino [49, BP]	446 Munchlax [BP, E]	517 Munna [BP]
		518 Musharna [BP]	322 Numel [BP]	043 Oddish [BP, E]	536 Palpitoad [BP]	046 Paras [BP]	047 Parasect [BP]	504 Patrat [23, BP]
		548 Petilil [44, BP]	195 Quagsire [BP]	579 Reuniclus [BP]	537 Seismitoad [BP]	213 Shuckle [BP]	289 Slaking [BP]	287 Slakoth [BP, E]
		080 Slowbro [BP]	199 Slowking [BP]	079 Slowpoke [BP]	218 Slugma [BP]	685 Slurpuff [BP]	143 Snorlax [BP, E]	577 Solosis [BP]
		682 Spritzee [BP]	508 Stoutland [BP]	185 Sudowoodo [BP]	192 Sunflora [BP]	191 Sunkern [BP]	684 Swirlix [BP, E]	528 Swoobat [BP]
		468 Togekiss [1, BP]	175 Togepi [53, BP]	176 Togetic [53, BP]	324 Torkoal [BP]	535 Tympole [BP, E]	288 Vigoroth [BP]	045 Vileplume [BP]
		505 Watchog [25, BP]	527 Woobat [BP]	194 Wooper [BP, E]	562 Yamask [BP]			
Psychic	Agility	617 Accelgor [32]	142 Aerodactyl [17]	190 Aipom [29, E]	424 Ambipom [29]	566 Archen [21]	567 Archeops [21]	168 Ariados [37]
		144 Articuno [36]	550 Basculin [E]	015 Beedrill [31]	522 Blitzle [36]	418 Buizel [41]	427 Buneary [33]	659 Bunnelby [1]
		318 Carvanha [39]	441 Chatot [E]	170 Chinchou [E]	585 Deerling [E]	386 Deoxys (Spd) [55]	660 Diggersby [1]	085 Dodrio [35]
		084 Doduo [33]	148 Dragonair [25]	149 Dragonite [25]	147 Dratini [25]	206 Dunsparce [E]	632 Durant [16]	587 Emolga [46]
		083 Farfetch'd [31]	022 Fearow [29]	160 Feraligatr [30]	456 Finneon [E]	662 Fletchinder [13]	661 Fletchling [13]	419 Floatzel [51]
		596 Galvantula [40]	203 Girafarig [23]	207 Gligar [E]	118 Goldeen [29]	368 Gorebyss [9]	253 Grovyle [28]	058 Growlithe [30]
		701 Hawlucha [E]	694 Helioptile [E]	107 Hitmonchan [6]	237 Hitmontop [37]	163 Hoothoot [E]	116 Horsea [36]	135 Jolteon [29]
		595 Joltik [37]	230 Kingdra [38]	098 Krabby [E]	166 Ledian [36]	165 Ledyba [30]	428 Lopunny [33]	370 Luvdisc [7]
		226 Mantine [32]	458 Mantyke [32]	179 Mareep [E]	376 Metagross [41]	375 Metang [41]	312 Minun [37]	146 Moltres [15]
		291 Ninjask [17]	714 Noibat [18]	715 Noivern [18]	046 Paras [E]	018 Pidgeot [32]	017 Pidgeotto [32]	016 Pidgey [29]
		025 Pikachu [45]	393 Piplup [E]	311 Plusle [37]	077 Ponyta [37]	137 Porygon [12]	233 Porygon2 [12]	474 Porygon-Z [12]
		078 Rapidash [37]	447 Riolu [E]	254 Sceptile [28]	212 Scizor [17]	545 Scolipede [33]	123 Scyther [17]	117 Seadra [38]
		119 Seaking [29]	540 Sewaddle [E]	319 Sharpedo [45]	227 Skarmory [31]	451 Skorupi [E]	215 Sneasel [20]	021 Spearow [25]
		167 Spinarak [33]	398 Staraptor [41]	397 Staravia [38]	396 Starly [33]	283 Surskit [22]	333 Swablu [E]	277 Swellow [33]
		276 Taillow [29]	663 Talonflame [13]	642 Thundurus [37]	255 Torchic [E]	641 Tornadus [37]	252 Treecko [25]	543 Venipede [29]
		048 Venonat [E]	544 Whirlipede [32]	278 Wingull [36, E]	145 Zapdos [43]	523 Zebstrika [42]	571 Zoroark [39]	570 Zorua [37]
Flying	Air Cutter	267 Beautifly [20]	004 Charmander [E]	441 Chatot [E]	169 Crobat [19]	580 Ducklett [E]	083 Farfetch'd [21]	042 Golbat [19]
		284 Masquerain [22]	714 Noibat [23]	715 Noivern [23]	016 Pidgey [E]	519 Pidove [15]	561 Sigilyph [21]	227 Skarmory [12]
		528 Swoobat [21]	641 Tornadus [25]	520 Tranquill [15]	521 Unfezant [15]	278 Wingull [22]	527 Woobat [21]	041 Zubat [19]
	Air Slash	628 Braviary [41]	006 Charizard [1]	169 Crobat [48]	580 Ducklett [27]	587 Emolga [E]	083 Farfetch'd [49]	042 Golbat [48]
		163 Hoothoot [33]	630 Mandibuzz [41]	226 Mantine [36]	458 Mantyke [36]	284 Masquerain [38]	146 Moltres [50]	414 Mothim [41]
		164 Noctowl [37]	714 Noibat [48]	715 Noivern [53]	501 Oshawott [E]	018 Pidgeot [62]	017 Pidgeotto [57]	016 Pidgey [49, E]
		519 Pidove [29]	384 Rayquaza [30]	479 Rotom (Fan) ◆	627 Rufflet [41]	123 Scyther [50]	540 Sewaddle [E]	492 Shaymin (Sky) [64]
		561 Sigilyph [41]	227 Skarmory [45]	581 Swanna [27]	277 Swellow [1, 45]	528 Swoobat [32]	276 Taillow [33]	468 Togekiss [1]
		641 Tornadus [43]	520 Tranquill [32]	357 Tropius [36]	521 Unfezant [33]	416 Vespiquen [37]	629 Vullaby [41]	278 Wingull [40]
		527 Woobat [32]	178 Xatu [25]	193 Yanma [54]	469 Yanmega [1, 54]	717 Yveltal [10]	041 Zubat [41]	
	Ally Switch	063 Abra [E]	065 Alakazam [36]	566 Archen [E]	605 Elgyem [E]	701 Hawlucha [E]	064 Kadabra [36]	098 Krabby [E]
		619 Mienfoo [E]	177 Natu [E]	077 Ponyta [E]	280 Ralts [E]	562 Yamask [E]		
Psychic	Amnesia	531 Audino [E]	339 Barboach [15]	400 Bibarel [33]	399 Bidoof [29]	626 Bouffalant [E]	001 Bulbasaur [E]	323 Camerupt [19]
		351 Castform [E]	170 Chinchou [E]	173 Cleffa [E]	222 Corsola [E]	346 Cradily [36]	386 Deoxys (Def) [55]	426 Drifblim [46]
		425 Drifloon [40]	162 Furret [42]	569 Garbodor [46]	203 Girafarig [E]	055 Golduck [49]	368 Gorebyss [16]	316 Gulpin [12]
		631 Heatmor [44]	187 Hoppip [E]	098 Krabby [E]	636 Larvesta [80]	108 Lickitung [E]	345 Lileep [36]	219 Magcargo [36]
		226 Mantine [E]	458 Mantyke [E]	183 Marill [E]	052 Meowth [E]	151 Mew [60]	150 Mewtwo [79]	446 Munchlax [9]
		032 Nidoran ♂ [E]	322 Numel [19]	513 Pansear [25]	221 Piloswine [58]	054 Psyduck [43]	195 Quagsire [24]	378 Regice [37]
		379 Registeel [37]	369 Relicanth [E]	559 Scraggy [E]	273 Seedot [E]	161 Sentret [36]	422 Shellos [E]	289 Slaking [17]
		287 Slakoth [17]	080 Slowbro [43]	079 Slowpoke [41]	218 Slugma [36]	143 Snorlax [9]	325 Spoink [E]	317 Swalot [12]
		220 Swinub [48]	528 Swoobat [29]	114 Tangela [E]	324 Torkoal [40]	568 Trubbish [40]	387 Turtwig [E]	480 Uxie [46]
		637 Volcarona [1]	320 Wailmer [37]	321 Wailord [37]	340 Whiscash [15]	527 Woobat [29]	194 Wooper [23]	
Rock	Ancient Power	142 Aerodactyl [25]	698 Amaura [26]	347 Anorith [21]	566 Archen [18]	567 Archeops [18]	348 Armaldo [21]	144 Articuno [29]
		699 Aurorus [26]	343 Baltoy [19]	689 Barbaracle [28]	411 Bastiodon [28]	688 Binacle [28]	703 Carbink [31]	565 Carracosta [18]
		318 Carvanha [E]	251 Celebi [28]	004 Charmander [E]	152 Chikorita [E]	344 Claydol [19]	341 Corphish [E]	222 Corsola [17]
		346 Cradily [17]	408 Cranidos [33]	104 Cubone [E]	483 Dialga [10]	719 Diancie [31]	050 Diglett [E]	206 Dunsparce [19, E]
		102 Exeggcute [E]	487 Giratina (Alt) [10]	487 Giratina (Ori) [10]	383 Groudon [1]	485 Heatran [1]	250 Ho-Oh [57]	140 Kabuto [46]
		141 Kabutops [54]	352 Kecleon [21]	098 Krabby [E]	382 Kyogre [1]	646 Kyurem (Blk) [15]	646 Kyurem (Wht) [15]	646 Kyurem [15]
		131 Lapras [E]	246 Larvitar [E]	345 Lileep [17]	249 Lugia [57]	219 Magcargo [22]	473 Mamoswine [1]	303 Mawile [E]
		151 Mew [50]	146 Moltres [29]	258 Mudkip [E]	322 Numel [E]	138 Omanyte [37]	139 Omastar [37]	484 Palkia [10]
		231 Phanpy [E]	221 Piloswine [1]	409 Rampardos [36]	384 Rayquaza [15]	378 Regice [31]	377 Regirock [31]	379 Registeel [31]
		369 Relicanth [21]	643 Reshiram [15]	410 Shieldon [28]	561 Sigilyph [E]	218 Slugma [22]	220 Swinub [E]	114 Tangela [38]
		465 Tangrowth [40]	564 Tirtouga [18]	175 Togepi [33]	176 Togetic [33]	158 Totodile [E]	697 Tyrantrum [26]	696 Tyrunt [26]
		194 Wooper [E]	193 Yanma [33]	469 Yanmega [33]	145 Zapdos [29]	644 Zekrom [15]		

◆ When Rotom becomes Fan Rotom, it learns the move Air Slash. When it changes back to Rotom, it forgets the move.

Type	Move	Pokémon that can learn it						
Water	Aqua Jet	594 Alomomola [9]	347 Anorith [E]	550 Basculin [13]	614 Beartic [1]	418 Buizel [24]	565 Carracosta [15]	318 Carvanha [11]
		692 Clauncher [43, E]	693 Clawitzer [47]	341 Corphish [E]	087 Dewgong [31]	502 Dewott [33]	147 Dratini [E]	395 Empoleon [36]
		419 Floatzel [24]	055 Golduck [1]	140 Kabuto [31]	141 Kabutops [31]	647 Keldeo [1]	370 Luvdisc [E]	183 Marill [E]
		501 Oshawott [29]	211 Qwilfish [E]	503 Samurott [33]	086 Seel [31]	319 Sharpedo [11]	007 Squirtle [E]	283 Surskit [30, E]
		564 Tirtouga [15]	158 Totodile [E]					
	Aqua Ring	594 Alomomola [5]	184 Azumarill [31]	418 Buizel [E]	170 Chinchou [42]	366 Clamperl [E]	222 Corsola [38, E]	087 Dewgong [23]
		580 Ducklett [24]	456 Finneon [33]	118 Goldeen [21]	368 Gorebyss [19]	382 Kyogre [30]	171 Lanturn [47]	457 Lumineon [35]
		370 Luvdisc [40, E]	490 Manaphy [54]	226 Mantine [39]	458 Mantyke [39]	183 Marill [28]	350 Milotic [21]	536 Palpitoad [20]
		515 Panpour [E]	489 Phione [54]	393 Piplup [E]	119 Seaking [21]	086 Seel [23]	537 Seismitoad [20]	090 Shellder [E]
		363 Spheal [E]	007 Squirtle [E]	581 Swanna [24]	072 Tentacool [E]	535 Tympole [20]	134 Vaporeon [25]	320 Wailmer [E]
		278 Wingull [E]						
	Aqua Tail	142 Aerodactyl [BP]	306 Aggron [BP]	698 Amaura [BP]	024 Arbok [BP]	493 Arceus [BP]	566 Archen [BP]	567 Archeops [BP]
		348 Armaldo [BP]	699 Aurorus [BP]	610 Axew [BP]	184 Azumarill [21, BP]	339 Barboach [28, BP]	550 Basculin [28, BP]	400 Bibarel [BP]
		399 Bidoof [BP, E]	009 Blastoise [32, BP]	418 Buizel [38, BP, E]	565 Carracosta [45, BP]	573 Cinccino [BP]	692 Clauncher [BP]	693 Clawitzer [BP]
		159 Croconaw [51, BP]	633 Deino [BP]	087 Dewgong [49, BP]	502 Dewott [41, BP]	691 Dragalge [35, BP]	148 Dragonair [39, BP]	149 Dragonite [39, BP]
		452 Drapion [BP]	147 Dratini [35, BP]	621 Druddigon [BP]	206 Dunsparce [BP]	603 Eelektrik [BP]	604 Eelektross [BP]	023 Ekans [BP]
		160 Feraligatr [63, BP]	456 Finneon [BP, E]	419 Floatzel [46, BP]	611 Fraxure [BP]	162 Furret [BP]	445 Garchomp [BP]	487 Giratina (Alt) [BP]
		487 Giratina (Ori) [BP]	471 Glaceon [BP]	207 Gligar [BP]	472 Gliscor [BP]	118 Goldeen [BP, E]	055 Golduck [32, BP]	706 Goodra [50, BP]
		368 Gorebyss [39, BP]	130 Gyarados [35, BP]	612 Haxorus [BP]	367 Huntail [39, BP]	635 Hydreigon [BP]	141 Kabutops [BP]	115 Kangaskhan [BP]
		352 Kecleon [BP]	647 Keldeo [37, BP]	552 Krokorok [BP]	553 Krookodile [BP]	382 Kyogre [15, BP]	171 Lanturn [BP]	131 Lapras [BP]
		463 Lickilicky [BP]	108 Lickitung [BP]	249 Lugia [BP]	457 Lumineon [BP]	226 Mantine [BP]	183 Marill [20, BP]	259 Marshtomp [BP]
		151 Mew [BP]	150 Mewtwo [BP]	350 Milotic [34, BP]	572 Minccino [BP, E]	258 Mudkip [BP]	034 Nidoking [BP]	031 Nidoqueen [BP]
		501 Oshawott [35, BP]	484 Palkia [24, 42, BP]	515 Panpour [BP, E]	504 Patrat [BP]	054 Psyduck [29, BP]	195 Quagsire [BP]	211 Qwilfish [45, BP]
		384 Rayquaza [BP]	369 Relicanth [BP, E]	112 Rhydon [BP]	111 Rhyhorn [BP]	464 Rhyperior [BP]	373 Salamence [BP]	503 Samurott [45, BP]
		551 Sandile [BP]	545 Scolipede [BP]	119 Seaking [BP]	364 Sealeo [BP]	086 Seel [43, BP]	161 Sentret [BP]	497 Serperior [BP]
		496 Servine [BP]	336 Seviper [BP]	516 Simipour [BP]	451 Skorupi [BP]	690 Skrelp [35, BP]	080 Slowbro [BP]	199 Slowking [BP]
		079 Slowpoke [BP]	495 Snivy [BP]	363 Spheal [BP]	007 Squirtle [28, BP]	208 Steelix [BP]	618 Stunfisk [BP]	260 Swampert [BP]
		564 Tirtouga [41, BP]	158 Totodile [43, BP]	248 Tyranitar [BP]	134 Vaporeon [BP]	365 Walrein [BP]	008 Wartortle [32, BP]	505 Watchog [BP]
		340 Whiscash [28, BP]	194 Wooper [BP]	634 Zweilous [BP]				
Fighting	Arm Thrust	500 Emboar [17]	297 Hariyama [1, 7]	214 Heracross [1]	296 Makuhita [7]	674 Pancham [7]	675 Pangoro [7]	499 Pignite [17]
Grass	Aromatherapy	683 Aromatisse [25]	153 Bayleef [50]	113 Chansey [E]	420 Cherubi [E]	152 Chikorita [42, E]	173 Cleffa [E]	585 Deerling [28]
		669 Flabébé [33]	670 Floette [38]	671 Florges [1]	440 Happiny [E]	187 Hoppip [E]	154 Meganium [60]	046 Paras [43]
		047 Parasect [51]	548 Petilil [28]	315 Roselia [43]	586 Sawsbuck [28]	492 Shaymin (Land) [64]	685 Slurpuff [26]	682 Spritzee [25]
		684 Swirlix [26]	045 Vileplume [1]	666 Vivillon [31]	716 Xerneas [1]			
Fairy	Aromatic Mist	683 Aromatisse [1]						
Normal	Assist	390 Chimchar [E]	096 Drowzee [E]	677 Espurr [E]	431 Glameow [29]	510 Liepard [1, 6]	052 Meowth [E]	509 Purrloin [6]
		432 Purugly [29]	161 Sentret [E]	300 Skitty [31]	215 Sneasel [E]	327 Spinda [E]		
Dark	Assurance	359 Absol [E]	142 Aerodactyl [E]	610 Axew [7]	015 Beedrill [34]	625 Bisharp [33]	318 Carvanha [15]	408 Cranidos [24]
		613 Cubchoo [E]	633 Deino [E]	084 Doduo [E]	232 Donphan [15]	500 Emboar [38]	022 Fearow [35]	611 Fraxure [1, 7]
		203 Girafarig [10]	431 Glameow [E]	612 Haxorus [1, 7]	109 Koffing [12]	552 Krokorok [16]	553 Krookodile [16]	246 Larvitar [E]
		510 Liepard [31]	056 Mankey [25]	052 Meowth [41]	262 Mightyena [24]	198 Murkrow [25, E]	501 Oshawott [E]	504 Patrat [E]
		624 Pawniard [33]	053 Persian [49]	499 Pignite [36]	261 Poochyena [22]	057 Primeape [25]	509 Purrloin [28]	409 Rampardos [24]
		020 Raticate [29]	019 Rattata [25]	551 Sandile [16]	336 Seviper [E]	319 Sharpedo [15]	227 Skarmory [E]	021 Spearow [29]
		528 Swoobat [1, 12]	498 Tepig [31]	197 Umbreon [25]	461 Weavile [1]	110 Weezing [12]	527 Woobat [12]	
Ghost	Astonish	190 Aipom [8]	334 Altaria [1, 3]	424 Ambipom [1, 8]	591 Amoonguss [1, 8]	358 Chimecho [1, 7]	433 Chingling [7]	563 Cofagrigus [1]
		346 Cradily [1]	453 Croagunk [1]	169 Crobat [1, 7]	633 Deino [E]	050 Diglett [7, E]	426 Drifblim [1, 4]	425 Drifloon [4]
		051 Dugtrio [7]	206 Dunsparce [E]	356 Dusclops [1, 9]	477 Dusknoir [1, 9]	355 Duskull [9]	605 Elgyem [E]	587 Emolga [E]
		295 Exploud [1, 9]	590 Foongus [8]	478 Froslass [19]	092 Gastly [E]	203 Girafarig [1]	042 Golbat [1, 7]	622 Golett [1]
		623 Golurk [1]	711 Gourgeist [1]	430 Honchkrow [1]	352 Kecleon [1]	707 Klefki [8]	608 Lampent [1]	345 Lileep [1]
		607 Litwick [1]	271 Lombre [1]	270 Lotad [1]	294 Loudred [1, 9]	272 Ludicolo [1]	303 Mawile [1]	200 Misdreavus [10]
		429 Mismagius [1]	198 Murkrow [1]	515 Panpour [E]	511 Pansage [E]	513 Pansear [E]	708 Phantump [5]	261 Poochyena [E]
		710 Pumpkaboo [1]	211 Qwilfish [E]	479 Rotom (Fan) [1]	479 Rotom (Frost) [1]	479 Rotom (Heat) [1]	479 Rotom (Mow) [1]	479 Rotom (Wash) [1]
		479 Rotom [1]	302 Sableye [9]	353 Shuppet [E]	577 Solosis [E]	021 Spearow [E]	234 Stantler [7]	396 Starly [E]
		618 Stunfisk [E]	434 Stunky [E]	333 Swablu [3]	642 Thundurus [1]	641 Tornadus [1]	454 Toxicroak [1]	709 Trevenant [5]
		583 Vanillish [1, 7]	582 Vanillite [7]	584 Vanilluxe [1, 7]	320 Wailmer [16]	321 Wailord [16]	293 Whismur [8]	562 Yamask [1]
		041 Zubat [7]						
Bug	Attack Order	416 Vespiquen [45]						
Normal	Attract (TM45)	460 Abomasnow [TM]	063 Abra [TM]	359 Absol [TM]	617 Accelgor [TM]	681 Aegislash [TM]	142 Aerodactyl [TM]	306 Aggron [TM]
		190 Aipom [TM]	065 Alakazam [TM]	594 Alomomola [TM]	334 Altaria [TM]	698 Amaura [TM]	424 Ambipom [TM]	591 Amoonguss [TM]
		181 Ampharos [TM]	347 Anorith [TM]	024 Arbok [TM]	059 Arcanine [TM]	566 Archen [TM]	567 Archeops [TM]	168 Ariados [TM]
		348 Armaldo [TM]	683 Aromatisse [29, TM]	304 Aron [TM]	531 Audino [21, TM]	699 Aurorus [TM]	713 Avalugg [TM]	610 Axew [TM]
		184 Azumarill [TM]	298 Azurill [TM]	371 Bagon [TM]	354 Banette [TM]	689 Barbaracle [TM]	339 Barboach [TM]	550 Basculin [TM]
		411 Bastiodon [TM]	153 Bayleef [TM]	614 Beartic [TM]	267 Beautifly [27, TM]	015 Beedrill [TM]	606 Beheeyem [TM]	182 Bellossom [TM]
		069 Bellsprout [TM]	712 Bergmite [TM]	400 Bibarel [TM]	399 Bidoof [TM]	688 Binacle [TM]	625 Bisharp [TM]	009 Blastoise [TM]

Type	Move	Pokémon that can learn it						
Normal	Attract (TM45)	257 Blaziken [TM]	242 Blissey [TM]	522 Blitzle [TM]	525 Boldore [TM]	438 Bonsly [TM]	626 Bouffalant [TM]	654 Braixen [TM]
		628 Braviary [TM]	286 Breloom [TM]	406 Budew [TM]	418 Buizel [TM]	001 Bulbasaur [TM]	427 Buneary [TM]	659 Bunnelby [TM]
		012 Butterfree [TM]	331 Cacnea [TM]	332 Cacturne [TM]	323 Camerupt [TM]	455 Carnivine [TM]	565 Carracosta [TM]	318 Carvanha [TM]
		351 Castform [TM]	609 Chandelure [TM]	113 Chansey [TM]	006 Charizard [TM]	004 Charmander [TM]	005 Charmeleon [TM]	441 Chatot [TM]
		421 Cherrim [TM]	420 Cherubi [TM]	652 Chesnaught [TM]	650 Chespin [TM]	152 Chikorita [TM]	390 Chimchar [TM]	358 Chimecho [TM]
		170 Chinchou [TM]	433 Chingling [TM]	573 Cinccino [TM]	366 Clamperl [TM]	692 Clauncher [TM]	693 Clawitzer [TM]	036 Clefable [TM]
		035 Clefairy [TM]	173 Cleffa [TM]	091 Cloyster [TM]	563 Cofagrigus [TM]	256 Combusken [TM]	534 Conkeldurr [TM]	341 Corphish [TM]
		222 Corsola [TM]	546 Cottonee [TM]	346 Cradily [TM]	408 Cranidos [TM]	342 Crawdaunt [TM]	488 Cresselia [TM]	453 Croagunk [TM]
		169 Crobat [TM]	159 Croconaw [TM]	558 Crustle [TM]	615 Cryogonal [TM]	613 Cubchoo [TM]	104 Cubone [TM]	155 Cyndaquil [TM]
		555 Darmanitan [TM]	554 Darumaka [TM]	702 Dedenne [TM]	585 Deerling [TM]	633 Deino [TM]	301 Delcatty [1, TM]	225 Delibird [TM]
		655 Delphox [TM]	087 Dewgong [TM]	502 Dewott [TM]	660 Diggersby [TM]	050 Diglett [TM]	085 Dodrio [TM]	084 Doduo [TM]
		232 Donphan [TM]	680 Doublade [TM]	691 Dragalge [TM]	148 Dragonair [TM]	149 Dragonite [TM]	452 Drapion [TM]	147 Dratini [TM]
		426 Drifblim [TM]	425 Drifloon [TM]	529 Drilbur [TM]	096 Drowzee [TM]	621 Druddigon [TM]	580 Ducklett [TM]	051 Dugtrio [TM]
		206 Dunsparce [TM]	578 Duosion [TM]	632 Durant [TM]	356 Dusclops [TM]	477 Dusknoir [TM]	355 Duskull [TM]	269 Dustox [TM]
		557 Dwebble [TM]	603 Eelektrik [TM]	604 Eelektross [TM]	133 Eevee [TM]	023 Ekans [TM]	125 Electabuzz [TM]	466 Electivire [TM]
		309 Electrike [TM]	239 Elekid [TM]	605 Elgyem [TM]	500 Emboar [TM]	587 Emolga [TM]	395 Empoleon [TM]	589 Escavalier [TM]
		196 Espeon [TM]	677 Espurr [TM]	530 Excadrill [TM]	102 Exeggcute [TM]	103 Exeggutor [TM]	295 Exploud [TM]	083 Farfetch'd [TM]
		022 Fearow [TM]	349 Feebas [TM]	653 Fennekin [TM]	160 Feraligatr [TM]	456 Finneon [10, TM]	180 Flaaffy [TM]	669 Flabébé [TM]
		136 Flareon [TM]	662 Fletchinder [TM]	661 Fletchling [TM]	419 Floatzel [TM]	670 Floette [TM]	671 Florges [TM]	330 Flygon [TM]
		590 Foongus [TM]	205 Forretress [TM]	611 Fraxure [TM]	592 Frillish [TM]	656 Froakie [TM]	657 Frogadier [TM]	478 Froslass [TM]
		676 Furfrou [TM]	162 Furret [TM]	444 Gabite [TM]	475 Gallade [TM]	596 Galvantula [TM]	569 Garbodor [TM]	445 Garchomp [TM]
		282 Gardevoir [TM]	092 Gastly [TM]	423 Gastrodon [TM]	094 Gengar [TM]	074 Geodude [TM]	443 Gible [TM]	526 Gigalith [TM]
		203 Girafarig [TM]	471 Glaceon [TM]	362 Glalie [TM]	431 Glameow [44, TM]	207 Gligar [TM]	472 Gliscor [TM]	044 Gloom [TM]
		673 Gogoat [TM]	042 Golbat [TM]	118 Goldeen [TM]	055 Golduck [TM]	076 Golem [TM]	706 Goodra [TM]	704 Goomy [TM]
		368 Gorebyss [TM]	574 Gothita [TM]	576 Gothitelle [TM]	575 Gothorita [TM]	711 Gourgeist [TM]	210 Granbull [TM]	075 Graveler [TM]
		658 Greninja [TM]	088 Grimer [TM]	388 Grotle [TM]	253 Grovyle [TM]	058 Growlithe [TM]	326 Grumpig [TM]	316 Gulpin [TM]
		533 Gurdurr [TM]	130 Gyarados [TM]	440 Happiny [TM]	297 Hariyama [TM]	093 Haunter [TM]	701 Hawlucha [TM]	612 Haxorus [TM]
		631 Heatmor [TM]	485 Heatran [TM]	695 Heliolisk [TM]	694 Helioptile [TM]	214 Heracross [TM]	507 Herdier [TM]	449 Hippopotas [TM]
		450 Hippowdon [TM]	107 Hitmonchan [TM]	106 Hitmonlee [TM]	237 Hitmontop [TM]	430 Honchkrow [TM]	679 Honedge [TM]	163 Hoothoot [TM]
		187 Hoppip [TM]	116 Horsea [TM]	229 Houndoom [TM]	228 Houndour [TM]	367 Huntail [TM]	635 Hydreigon [TM]	097 Hypno [TM]
		174 Igglybuff [TM]	314 Illumise [TM]	392 Infernape [TM]	686 Inkay [TM]	002 Ivysaur [TM]	593 Jellicent [TM]	039 Jigglypuff [TM]
		135 Jolteon [TM]	595 Joltik [TM]	189 Jumpluff [TM]	124 Jynx [TM]	140 Kabuto [TM]	141 Kabutops [TM]	064 Kadabra [TM]
		115 Kangaskhan [TM]	588 Karrablast [TM]	352 Kecleon [TM]	230 Kingdra [TM]	099 Kingler [TM]	281 Kirlia [TM]	707 Klefki [TM]
		109 Koffing [TM]	098 Krabby [TM]	402 Kricketune [TM]	552 Krokorok [TM]	553 Krookodile [TM]	305 Lairon [TM]	608 Lampent [TM]
		645 Landorus [TM]	171 Lanturn [TM]	131 Lapras [TM]	246 Larvitar [TM]	380 Latias [TM]	381 Latios [TM]	470 Leafeon [TM]
		542 Leavanny [TM]	166 Ledian [TM]	165 Ledyba [TM]	463 Lickilicky [TM]	108 Lickitung [TM]	510 Liepard [TM]	345 Lileep [TM]
		549 Lilligant [TM]	506 Lillipup [TM]	264 Linoone [TM]	667 Litleo [TM]	607 Litwick [TM]	271 Lombre [TM]	428 Lopunny [TM]
		270 Lotad [TM]	294 Loudred [TM]	448 Lucario [TM]	272 Ludicolo [TM]	457 Lumineon [1, 10, TM]	370 Luvdisc [22, TM]	404 Luxio [TM]
		405 Luxray [TM]	068 Machamp [TM]	067 Machoke [TM]	066 Machop [TM]	240 Magby [TM]	219 Magcargo [TM]	126 Magmar [TM]
		467 Magmortar [TM]	296 Makuhita [TM]	687 Malamar [TM]	473 Mamoswine [TM]	630 Mandibuzz [TM]	310 Manectric [TM]	056 Mankey [TM]
		226 Mantine [TM]	458 Mantyke [TM]	556 Maractus [TM]	179 Mareep [TM]	183 Marill [TM]	105 Marowak [TM]	259 Marshtomp [TM]
		284 Masquerain [TM]	303 Mawile [TM]	308 Medicham [TM]	307 Meditite [TM]	154 Meganium [TM]	678 Meowstic (F) [TM]	678 Meowstic (M) [TM]
		052 Meowth [TM]	151 Mew [TM]	619 Mienfoo [TM]	620 Mienshao [TM]	262 Mightyena [TM]	350 Milotic [37, TM]	241 Miltank [TM]
		439 Mime Jr. [TM]	572 Minccino [TM]	312 Minun [TM]	200 Misdreavus [TM]	429 Mismagius [TM]	391 Monferno [TM]	414 Mothim [TM]
		122 Mr. Mime [TM]	258 Mudkip [TM]	089 Muk [TM]	446 Munchlax [TM]	517 Munna [TM]	198 Murkrow [TM]	518 Musharna [TM]
		177 Natu [TM]	034 Nidoking [TM]	031 Nidoqueen [TM]	029 Nidoran ♀ [TM]	032 Nidoran ♂ [TM]	030 Nidorina [TM]	033 Nidorino [TM]
		038 Ninetales [TM]	291 Ninjask [TM]	164 Noctowl [TM]	714 Noibat [TM]	715 Noivern [TM]	299 Nosepass [TM]	322 Numel [TM]
		274 Nuzleaf [TM]	224 Octillery [TM]	043 Oddish [TM]	138 Omanyte [TM]	139 Omastar [TM]	095 Onix [TM]	501 Oshawott [TM]
		417 Pachirisu [TM]	536 Palpitoad [TM]	674 Pancham [TM]	675 Pangoro [TM]	515 Panpour [TM]	511 Pansage [TM]	513 Pansear [TM]
		046 Paras [TM]	047 Parasect [TM]	504 Patrat [TM]	624 Pawniard [TM]	279 Pelipper [TM]	053 Persian [TM]	548 Petilil [TM]
		231 Phanpy [TM]	708 Phantump [TM]	172 Pichu [TM]	018 Pidgeot [TM]	017 Pidgeotto [TM]	016 Pidgey [TM]	519 Pidove [TM]
		499 Pignite [TM]	025 Pikachu [TM]	221 Piloswine [TM]	204 Pineco [TM]	127 Pinsir [TM]	393 Piplup [TM]	311 Plusle [TM]
		186 Politoed [TM]	060 Poliwag [TM]	061 Poliwhirl [TM]	062 Poliwrath [TM]	077 Ponyta [TM]	261 Poochyena [TM]	057 Primeape [TM]
		394 Prinplup [TM]	476 Probopass [TM]	054 Psyduck [TM]	710 Pumpkaboo [TM]	247 Pupitar [TM]	509 Purrloin [TM]	432 Purugly [52, TM]
		668 Pyroar [TM]	195 Quagsire [TM]	156 Quilava [TM]	651 Quilladin [TM]	211 Qwilfish [TM]	026 Raichu [TM]	280 Ralts [TM]
		409 Rampardos [TM]	078 Rapidash [TM]	020 Raticate [TM]	019 Rattata [TM]	369 Relicanth [TM]	223 Remoraid [TM]	579 Reuniclus [TM]
		112 Rhydon [TM]	111 Rhyhorn [TM]	464 Rhyperior [TM]	447 Riolu [TM]	524 Roggenrola [TM]	315 Roselia [TM]	407 Roserade [TM]
		627 Rufflet [TM]	302 Sableye [TM]	373 Salamence [TM]	503 Samurott [TM]	551 Sandile [TM]	027 Sandshrew [TM]	028 Sandslash [TM]
		539 Sawk [TM]	586 Sawsbuck [TM]	254 Sceptile [TM]	212 Scizor [TM]	545 Scolipede [TM]	560 Scrafty [TM]	559 Scraggy [TM]
		123 Scyther [TM]	117 Seadra [TM]	119 Seaking [TM]	364 Sealeo [TM]	273 Seedot [TM]	086 Seel [TM]	537 Seismitoad [TM]
		161 Sentret [TM]	497 Serperior [TM]	496 Servine [TM]	336 Seviper [TM]	540 Sewaddle [TM]	319 Sharpedo [TM]	372 Shelgon [TM]
		090 Shellder [TM]	422 Shellos [TM]	616 Shelmet [TM]	410 Shieldon [TM]	275 Shiftry [TM]	403 Shinx [TM]	285 Shroomish [TM]
		213 Shuckle [TM]	353 Shuppet [TM]	561 Sigilyph [TM]	516 Simipour [TM]	512 Simisage [TM]	514 Simisear [TM]	227 Skarmory [TM]
		672 Skiddo [TM]	188 Skiploom [TM]	300 Skitty [10, TM]	451 Skorupi [TM]	690 Skrelp [TM]	435 Skuntank [TM]	289 Slaking [TM]
		287 Slakoth [TM]	705 Sliggoo [TM]	080 Slowbro [TM]	199 Slowking [TM]	079 Slowpoke [TM]	218 Slugma [TM]	685 Slurpuff [TM]
		238 Smoochum [TM]	215 Sneasel [TM]	495 Snivy [TM]	143 Snorlax [TM]	361 Snorunt [TM]	459 Snover [TM]	209 Snubbull [TM]

Type	Move	Pokémon that can learn it						
Normal	Attract (TM45)	577 Solosis [TM]	021 Spearow [TM]	363 Spheal [TM]	167 Spinarak [TM]	327 Spinda [TM]	442 Spiritomb [TM]	325 Spoink [TM]
		682 Spritzee [29, TM]	007 Squirtle [TM]	234 Stantler [TM]	398 Staraptor [TM]	397 Staravia [TM]	396 Starly [TM]	208 Steelix [TM]
		508 Stoutland [TM]	618 Stunfisk [TM]	434 Stunky [TM]	185 Sudowoodo [TM]	192 Sunflora [TM]	191 Sunkern [TM]	283 Surskit [TM]
		333 Swablu [TM]	541 Swadloon [TM]	317 Swalot [TM]	260 Swampert [TM]	581 Swanna [TM]	277 Swellow [TM]	220 Swinub [TM]
		684 Swirlix [TM]	528 Swoobat [25, TM]	700 Sylveon [TM]	276 Taillow [TM]	663 Talonflame [TM]	114 Tangela [TM]	465 Tangrowth [TM]
		128 Tauros [TM]	216 Teddiursa [TM]	072 Tentacool [TM]	073 Tentacruel [TM]	498 Tepig [TM]	538 Throh [TM]	642 Thundurus [TM]
		532 Timburr [TM]	564 Tirtouga [TM]	468 Togekiss [TM]	175 Togepi [TM]	176 Togetic [TM]	255 Torchic [TM]	324 Torkoal [TM]
		641 Tornadus [TM]	389 Torterra [TM]	158 Totodile [TM]	454 Toxicroak [TM]	520 Tranquill [TM]	328 Trapinch [TM]	252 Treecko [TM]
		709 Trevenant [TM]	357 Tropius [TM]	568 Trubbish [TM]	387 Turtwig [TM]	535 Tympole [TM]	157 Typhlosion [TM]	248 Tyranitar [TM]
		697 Tyrantrum [TM]	236 Tyrogue [TM]	696 Tyrunt [TM]	197 Umbreon [TM]	521 Unfezant [TM]	217 Ursaring [TM]	583 Vanillish [TM]
		582 Vanillite [TM]	584 Vanilluxe [TM]	134 Vaporeon [TM]	543 Venipede [TM]	049 Venomoth [TM]	048 Venonat [TM]	003 Venusaur [TM]
		416 Vespiquen [TM]	329 Vibrava [TM]	071 Victreebel [TM]	288 Vigoroth [TM]	045 Vileplume [TM]	666 Vivillon [TM]	313 Volbeat [TM]
		629 Vullaby [TM]	037 Vulpix [TM]	320 Wailmer [TM]	321 Wailord [TM]	365 Walrein [TM]	008 Wartortle [TM]	505 Watchog [TM]
		461 Weavile [TM]	070 Weepinbell [TM]	110 Weezing [TM]	547 Whimsicott [TM]	544 Whirlipede [TM]	340 Whiscash [TM]	293 Whismur [TM]
		040 Wigglytuff [TM]	278 Wingull [TM]	527 Woobat [25, TM]	194 Wooper [TM]	413 Wormadam (Plant) [41, TM]	413 Wormadam (Sand) [41, TM]	413 Wormadam (Trash) [41, TM]
		178 Xatu [TM]	562 Yamask [TM]	193 Yanma [TM]	469 Yanmega [TM]	335 Zangoose [TM]	523 Zebstrika [TM]	263 Zigzagoon [TM]
		571 Zoroark [TM]	570 Zorua [TM]	041 Zubat [TM]	634 Zweilous [TM]			
Fighting	Aura Sphere	693 Clawitzer [1, 67]	483 Dialga [37]	487 Giratina (Alt) [37]	487 Giratina (Ori) [37]	448 Lucario [1, 42]	151 Mew [100]	150 Mewtwo [70]
		619 Mienfoo [61]	620 Mienshao [1, 70]	484 Palkia [37]	007 Squirtle [E]	468 Togekiss [1]		
Ice	Aurora Beam	698 Amaura [20]	699 Aurorus [20]	091 Cloyster [1]	488 Cresselia [29]	615 Cryogonal [25]	225 Delibird [E]	087 Dewgong [27]
		456 Finneon [E]	116 Horsea [E]	140 Kabuto [E]	224 Octillery [1, 14]	138 Omanyte [E]	223 Remoraid [14, E]	364 Sealeo [21]
		086 Seel [27]	090 Shellder [37]	363 Spheal [21]	245 Suicune [29]	072 Tentacool [E]	134 Vaporeon [20]	365 Walrein [19]
		716 Xerneas [10]						
Steel	Autotomize	681 Aegislash [1]	306 Aggron [51]	304 Aron [43]	680 Doublade [18]	205 Forretress [32]	074 Geodude [E]	679 Honedge [18]
		600 Klang [31]	599 Klink [31]	601 Klinklang [31]	305 Lairon [47]	524 Roggenrola [E]	227 Skarmory [50]	208 Steelix [19]
		582 Vanillite [E]						
Ice	Avalanche	698 Amaura [34]	699 Aurorus [34]	713 Avalugg [42]	712 Bergmite [39]	613 Cubchoo [E]	124 Jynx [39]	131 Lapras [E]
		258 Mudkip [E]	090 Shellder [E]	238 Smoochum [35]	215 Sneasel [E]	361 Snorunt [E]	459 Snover [E]	220 Swinub [E]
		583 Vanillish [19]	582 Vanillite [19]	584 Vanilluxe [19]				

B

Type	Move	Pokémon that can learn it						
Fairy	Baby-Doll Eyes	531 Audino [5]	427 Buneary [10]	133 Eevee [9]	676 Furfrou [9]	506 Lillipup [10]	572 Minccino [3]	403 Shinx [11]
		216 Teddiursa [1]	037 Vulpix [9]	263 Zigzagoon [12]				
Normal	Barrage	102 Exeggcute [1]	103 Exeggutor [1]					
Psychic	Barrier	063 Abra [E]	698 Amaura [E]	712 Bergmite [E]	366 Clamperl [E]	222 Corsola [E]	096 Drowzee [E]	239 Elekid [E]
		605 Elgyem [E]	677 Espurr [E]	471 Glaceon [29]	345 Lileep [E]	240 Magby [E]	462 Magnezone [1]	151 Mew [40]
		150 Mewtwo [64]	439 Mime Jr. [1]	122 Mr. Mime [1]	258 Mudkip [E]	517 Munna [E]	090 Shellder [E]	072 Tentacool [28]
		073 Tentacruel [28]						
Normal	Baton Pass	359 Absol [E]	190 Aipom [11]	424 Ambipom [11]	418 Buizel [E]	427 Buneary [26]	251 Celebi [37]	585 Deerling [E]
		426 Drifblim [52]	425 Drifloon [44]	632 Durant [E]	133 Eevee [33]	587 Emolga [E]	162 Furret [46]	203 Girafarig [41]
		207 Gligar [E]	368 Gorebyss [29]	701 Hawlucha [E]	367 Huntail [29]	314 Illumise [E]	166 Ledian [24]	165 Ledyba [22]
		428 Lopunny [26]	303 Mawile [25]	307 Meditite [E]	151 Mew [80]	619 Mienfoo [E]	439 Mime Jr. [46]	312 Minun [34]
		122 Mr. Mime [46]	517 Munna [E]	291 Ninjask [35]	504 Patrat [33]	311 Plusle [34]	545 Scolipede [30]	123 Scyther [E]
		161 Sentret [39]	540 Sewaddle [E]	616 Shelmet [E]	300 Skitty [E]	167 Spinarak [E]	327 Spinda [E]	283 Surskit [35]
		175 Togepi [41]	176 Togetic [41]	255 Torchic [E]	048 Venonat [E]	313 Volbeat [E]	505 Watchog [39]	
Dark	Beat Up	190 Aipom [E]	004 Charmander [E]	546 Cottonee [E]	050 Diglett [E]	023 Ekans [E]	203 Girafarig [E]	229 Houndoom [26]
		228 Houndour [25, E]	056 Mankey [E]	029 Nidoran ♀ [E]	032 Nidoran ♂ [E]	551 Sandile [E]	273 Seedot [E]	215 Sneasel [28]
Poison	Belch	024 Arbok [48]	069 Bellsprout [E]	626 Bouffalant [E]	331 Cacnea [E]	453 Croagunk [47]	023 Ekans [38]	569 Garbodor [49]
		088 Grimer [46]	316 Gulpin [41]	631 Heatmor [E]	109 Koffing [42]	108 Lickitung [E]	240 Magby [E]	241 Miltank [E]
		089 Muk [52]	446 Munchlax [E]	086 Seel [E]	336 Seviper [43]	435 Skuntank [56]	079 Slowpoke [E]	143 Snorlax [E]
		434 Stunky [46]	317 Swalot [49]	454 Toxicroak [58]	568 Trubbish [42]	110 Weezing [51]		
Normal	Belly Drum	004 Charmander [E]	652 Chesnaught [1]	650 Chespin [E]	173 Cleffa [E]	104 Cubone [E]	555 Darmanitan [30]	554 Darumaka [30]
		297 Hariyama [26]	108 Lickitung [E]	264 Linoone [43]	240 Magby [E]	296 Makuhita [25]	183 Marill [E]	446 Munchlax [44]
		060 Poliwag [31]	061 Poliwhirl [37]	079 Slowpoke [E]	143 Snorlax [44]	363 Spheal [E]	684 Swirlix [E]	216 Teddiursa [E]
		263 Zigzagoon [37]						
Normal	Bestow	531 Audino [E]	242 Blissey [20]	113 Chansey [20]	035 Clefairy [19]	225 Delibird [E]	102 Exeggcute [50]	656 Froakie [E]
		264 Linoone [27]	417 Pachirisu [E]	708 Phantump [E]	172 Pichu [E]	519 Pidove [E]	311 Plusle [13]	710 Pumpkaboo [E]
		175 Togepi [25]	176 Togetic [25]	357 Tropius [46]	263 Zigzagoon [25]			
	Bide	591 Amoonguss [1, 12]	614 Beartic [1]	565 Carracosta [1]	534 Conkeldurr [1, 8]	222 Corsola [E]	613 Cubchoo [9]	206 Dunsparce [E]
		330 Flygon [1]	590 Foongus [12]	205 Forretress [20]	706 Goodra [13]	704 Goomy [13]	533 Gurdurr [1, 8]	214 Heracross [E]
		098 Krabby [E]	401 Kricketot [1]	402 Kricketune [1]	165 Ledyba [E]	259 Marshtomp [18]	308 Medicham [1]	307 Meditite [1]
		241 Miltank [15]	258 Mudkip [17]	290 Nincada [29]	138 Omanyte [E]	417 Pachirisu [1]	504 Patrat [8]	548 Petilil [E]
		172 Pichu [E]	204 Pineco [20]	393 Piplup [22, E]	394 Prinplup [24]	539 Sawk [5]	273 Seedot [1]	616 Shelmet [8]

	Move	Pokémon that can learn it						
Normal	Bide	213 Shuckle [1]	705 Sliggoo [13]	361 Snorunt [E]	618 Stunfisk [5]	191 Sunkern [E]	260 Swampert [18]	538 Throh [5]
		532 Timburr [8]	564 Tirtouga [1, E]	328 Trapinch [1]	697 Tyrantrum [12]	696 Tyrunt [12]	329 Vibrava [1]	505 Watchog [8]
	Bind	024 Arbok [BP]	069 Bellsprout [BP]	001 Bulbasaur [BP]	455 Carnivine [1, BP]	358 Chimecho [BP]	433 Chingling [BP]	346 Cradily [BP]
		615 Cryogonal [1, BP]	386 Deoxys (Atk) [BP]	386 Deoxys (Def) [BP]	386 Deoxys (Nor) [BP]	386 Deoxys (Spd) [BP]	148 Dragonair [BP]	149 Dragonite [BP]
		147 Dratini [BP]	426 Drifblim [BP]	425 Drifloon [BP]	206 Dunsparce [BP]	356 Dusclops [1, BP]	477 Dusknoir [1, BP]	603 Eelektrik [9, BP]
		604 Eelektross [BP]	023 Ekans [BP]	592 Frillish [BP]	368 Gorebyss [BP]	631 Heatmor [11, BP]	367 Huntail [BP]	686 Inkay [BP]
		002 Ivysaur [BP]	593 Jellicent [BP]	352 Kecleon [4, BP]	600 Klang [21, BP]	599 Klink [21, BP]	601 Klinklang [21, BP]	463 Lickilicky [BP]
		108 Lickitung [BP]	345 Lileep [BP]	687 Malamar [BP]	151 Mew [BP]	350 Milotic [BP]	224 Octillery [BP]	138 Omanyte [BP]
		139 Omastar [BP]	095 Onix [1, BP]	127 Pinsir [4, BP]	384 Rayquaza [BP]	497 Serperior [BP]	496 Servine [BP]	336 Seviper [BP]
		213 Shuckle [BP]	495 Snivy [BP]	208 Steelix [1, BP]	114 Tangela [17, BP]	465 Tangrowth [17, BP]	072 Tentacool [BP]	073 Tentacruel [BP]
		538 Throh [1, BP]	003 Venusaur [BP]	071 Victreebel [BP]	070 Weepinbell [BP]	718 Zygarde [18, BP]		
Dark	Bite	359 Absol [16]	142 Aerodactyl [1]	024 Arbok [1, 9]	059 Arcanine [1]	566 Archen [E]	713 Avalugg [1]	371 Bagon [10]
		550 Basculin [10]	712 Bergmite [1]	009 Blastoise [16]	455 Carnivine [7]	565 Carracosta [8]	318 Carvanha [1]	004 Charmander [E]
		652 Chesnaught [11]	650 Chespin [11]	169 Crobat [1, 11]	159 Croconaw [13]	633 Deino [9]	452 Drapion [1]	621 Druddigon [9]
		206 Dunsparce [E]	632 Durant [11]	133 Eevee [17]	023 Ekans [9]	309 Electrike [24]	244 Entei [1]	295 Exploud [20]
		160 Feraligatr [13]	136 Flareon [17]	676 Furfrou [22]	471 Glaceon [17]	362 Glalie [19]	431 Glameow [E]	042 Golbat [1, 11]
		210 Granbull [7]	388 Grotle [22]	058 Growlithe [1]	130 Gyarados [20]	507 Herdier [1, 8]	449 Hippopotas [7]	450 Hippowdon [1, 7]
		229 Houndoom [16]	228 Houndour [16]	367 Huntail [1]	635 Hydreigon [1, 9]	115 Kangaskhan [13]	552 Krokorok [1, 4]	553 Krookodile [1, 4]
		246 Larvitar [1]	506 Lillipup [8]	294 Loudred [20]	404 Luxio [18]	405 Luxray [18]	310 Manectric [24]	303 Mawile [9]
		052 Meowth [6]	262 Mightyena [1, 10]	258 Mudkip [E]	029 Nidoran ♀ [21]	030 Nidorina [23]	714 Noibat [13]	715 Noivern [13]
		138 Omanyte [7]	139 Omastar [1, 7]	417 Pachirisu [E]	515 Panpour [19]	511 Pansage [19]	513 Pansear [19]	504 Patrat [6]
		053 Persian [1, 6]	261 Poochyena [10]	247 Pupitar [1]	651 Quilladin [11]	243 Raikou [1]	020 Raticate [10]	019 Rattata [10, E]
		447 Riolu [E]	373 Salamence [1, 10]	551 Sandile [4]	336 Seviper [4]	319 Sharpedo [1]	372 Shelgon [1, 10]	403 Shinx [17]
		451 Skorupi [1]	215 Sneasel [E]	361 Snorunt [19]	209 Snubbull [7]	007 Squirtle [16]	234 Stantler [E]	508 Stoutland [1, 8]
		245 Suicune [1]	220 Swinub [E]	642 Thundurus [13]	564 Tirtouga [8]	641 Tornadus [13]	389 Torterra [22]	158 Totodile [13]
		328 Trapinch [1]	387 Turtwig [21]	248 Tyranitar [1]	697 Tyrantrum [17]	696 Tyrunt [17]	008 Wartortle [16]	505 Watchog [1, 6]
		041 Zubat [11]	634 Zweilous [1, 9]	718 Zygarde [1]				
Fire	Blast Burn	257 Blaziken [T]	006 Charizard [T]	655 Delphox [T]	500 Emboar [T]	392 Infernape [T]	157 Typhlosion [T]	
	Blaze Kick	257 Blaziken [36]	390 Chimchar [E]	106 Hitmonlee [45]	447 Riolu [E]			
Ice	Blizzard (TM14)	460 Abomasnow [47, TM]	359 Absol [TM]	306 Aggron [TM]	594 Alomomola [TM]	698 Amaura [65, TM]	493 Arceus [TM]	144 Articuno [71, TM]
		531 Audino [TM]	699 Aurorus [74, TM]	713 Avalugg [46, TM]	184 Azumarill [TM]	298 Azurill [TM]	689 Barbaracle [TM]	339 Barboach [TM]
		411 Bastiodon [TM]	614 Beartic [45, TM]	712 Bergmite [43, TM]	400 Bibarel [TM]	399 Bidoof [TM]	688 Binacle [TM]	009 Blastoise [TM]
		242 Blissey [TM]	418 Buizel [TM]	565 Carracosta [TM]	318 Carvanha [TM]	351 Castform [35, TM]	113 Chansey [TM]	170 Chinchou [TM]
		366 Clamperl [TM]	036 Clefable [TM]	035 Clefairy [TM]	091 Cloyster [TM]	341 Corphish [TM]	222 Corsola [TM]	408 Cranidos [TM]
		342 Crawdaunt [TM]	159 Croconaw [TM]	615 Cryogonal [TM]	613 Cubchoo [45, TM]	104 Cubone [TM]	491 Darkrai [TM]	301 Delcatty [TM]
		225 Delibird [TM]	087 Dewgong [TM]	502 Dewott [TM]	483 Dialga [TM]	148 Dragonair [TM]	149 Dragonite [TM]	147 Dratini [TM]
		206 Dunsparce [TM]	356 Dusclops [TM]	477 Dusknoir [TM]	355 Duskull [TM]	395 Empoleon [TM]	295 Exploud [TM]	349 Feebas [TM]
		160 Feraligatr [TM]	456 Finneon [TM]	419 Floatzel [TM]	592 Frillish [TM]	656 Froakie [TM]	657 Frogadier [TM]	478 Froslass [48, TM]
		162 Furret [TM]	423 Gastrodon [TM]	649 Genesect [TM]	471 Glaceon [45, TM]	362 Glalie [48, TM]	118 Goldeen [TM]	055 Golduck [TM]
		706 Goodra [TM]	368 Gorebyss [TM]	658 Greninja [TM]	130 Gyarados [TM]	116 Horsea [TM]	367 Huntail [TM]	593 Jellicent [TM]
		039 Jigglypuff [TM]	124 Jynx [60, TM]	140 Kabuto [TM]	141 Kabutops [TM]	115 Kangaskhan [TM]	352 Kecleon [TM]	230 Kingdra [TM]
		099 Kingler [TM]	098 Krabby [TM]	382 Kyogre [TM]	646 Kyurem (Blk) [78, TM]	646 Kyurem (Wht) [78, TM]	646 Kyurem [78, TM]	171 Lanturn [TM]
		131 Lapras [TM]	463 Lickilicky [TM]	108 Lickitung [TM]	264 Linoone [TM]	271 Lombre [TM]	428 Lopunny [TM]	270 Lotad [TM]
		294 Loudred [TM]	272 Ludicolo [TM]	249 Lugia [TM]	457 Lumineon [TM]	337 Lunatone [TM]	370 Luvdisc [TM]	473 Mamoswine [52, TM]
		490 Manaphy [TM]	226 Mantine [TM]	458 Mantyke [TM]	183 Marill [TM]	105 Marowak [TM]	259 Marshtomp [TM]	284 Masquerain [TM]
		481 Mesprit [TM]	151 Mew [TM]	150 Mewtwo [TM]	350 Milotic [TM]	241 Miltank [TM]	258 Mudkip [TM]	446 Munchlax [TM]
		034 Nidoking [TM]	031 Nidoqueen [TM]	029 Nidoran ♀ [TM]	032 Nidoran ♂ [TM]	030 Nidorina [TM]	033 Nidorino [TM]	224 Octillery [TM]
		138 Omanyte [TM]	139 Omastar [TM]	501 Oshawott [TM]	484 Palkia [TM]	515 Panpour [TM]	279 Pelipper [TM]	489 Phione [TM]
		221 Piloswine [52, TM]	393 Piplup [TM]	186 Politoed [TM]	060 Poliwag [TM]	061 Poliwhirl [TM]	062 Poliwrath [TM]	137 Porygon [TM]
		233 Porygon2 [TM]	474 Porygon-Z [TM]	394 Prinplup [TM]	054 Psyduck [TM]	195 Quagsire [TM]	211 Qwilfish [TM]	409 Rampardos [TM]
		020 Raticate [TM]	019 Rattata [TM]	384 Rayquaza [TM]	378 Regice [TM]	369 Relicanth [TM]	223 Remoraid [TM]	112 Rhydon [TM]
		111 Rhyhorn [TM]	464 Rhyperior [TM]	479 Rotom (Frost) ◆	503 Samurott [TM]	117 Seadra [TM]	119 Seaking [TM]	364 Sealeo [45, TM]
		086 Seel [TM]	319 Sharpedo [TM]	090 Shellder [TM]	422 Shellos [TM]	410 Shieldon [TM]	516 Simipour [TM]	300 Skitty [TM]
		289 Slaking [TM]	287 Slakoth [TM]	705 Sliggoo [TM]	080 Slowbro [TM]	199 Slowking [TM]	079 Slowpoke [TM]	238 Smoochum [48, TM]
		215 Sneasel [TM]	143 Snorlax [TM]	361 Snorunt [46, TM]	459 Snover [41, TM]	363 Spheal [41, TM]	007 Squirtle [TM]	121 Starmie [TM]
		120 Staryu [TM]	245 Suicune [85, TM]	283 Surskit [TM]	260 Swampert [TM]	220 Swinub [44, TM]	128 Tauros [TM]	072 Tentacool [TM]
		073 Tentacruel [TM]	564 Tirtouga [TM]	158 Totodile [TM]	248 Tyranitar [TM]	583 Vanillish [53, TM]	582 Vanillite [49, TM]	584 Vanilluxe [59, TM]
		134 Vaporeon [TM]	288 Vigoroth [TM]	320 Wailmer [TM]	321 Wailord [TM]	365 Walrein [49, TM]	008 Wartortle [TM]	461 Weavile [TM]
		340 Whiscash [TM]	293 Whismur [TM]	040 Wigglytuff [TM]	278 Wingull [TM]	194 Wooper [TM]	335 Zangoose [TM]	263 Zigzagoon [TM]

◆ When Rotom becomes Frost Rotom, it learns the move Blizzard. When it changes back to Rotom, it forgets the move.

Type	Move	Pokémon that can learn it						
Normal	Block	460 Abomasnow [BP]	681 Aegislash [BP]	306 Aggron [BP]	348 Armaldo [BP]	713 Avalugg [BP]	411 Bastiodon [30, BP]	242 Blissey [BP]
		525 Boldore [BP]	438 Bonsly [26, BP]	437 Bronzong [33, BP]	331 Cacnea [BP, E]	332 Cacturne [BP]	565 Carracosta [BP]	652 Chesnaught [BP]
		638 Cobalion [BP]	563 Cofagrigus [BP]	534 Conkeldurr [BP]	346 Cradily [BP]	159 Croconaw [BP]	558 Crustle [BP]	232 Donphan [BP]
		557 Dwebble [BP, E]	500 Emboar [BP]	102 Exeggcute [BP, E]	103 Exeggutor [BP]	160 Feraligatr [BP]	598 Ferrothorn [BP]	205 Forretress [BP]
		478 Froslass [BP]	423 Gastrodon [BP]	074 Geodude [BP, E]	526 Gigalith [BP]	362 Glalie [BP]	076 Golem [BP]	622 Golett [BP]
		623 Golurk [BP]	075 Graveler [BP]	383 Groudon [BP]	533 Gurdurr [BP]	553 Krookodile [BP]	382 Kyogre [BP]	645 Landorus [1, BP]
		131 Lapras [BP]	463 Lickilicky [BP]	687 Malamar [BP]	473 Mamoswine [BP]	630 Mandibuzz [BP]	376 Metagross [BP]	151 Mew [BP]
		241 Miltank [BP]	089 Muk [BP]	299 Nosepass [7, BP, E]	095 Onix [BP, E]	674 Pancham [BP]	675 Pangoro [BP]	476 Probopass [1, 7, BP]
		378 Regice [BP]	486 Regigigas [BP]	377 Regirock [BP]	379 Registeel [BP]	112 Rhydon [BP]	464 Rhyperior [BP]	524 Roggenrola [BP]
		503 Samurott [BP]	539 Sawk [BP]	289 Slaking [BP]	080 Slowbro [BP]	199 Slowking [BP]	079 Slowpoke [BP, E]	143 Snorlax [41, BP]
		361 Snorunt [BP, E]	208 Steelix [BP]	185 Sudowoodo [26, BP]	317 Swalot [BP]	465 Tangrowth [1, 56, BP]	639 Terrakion [BP]	538 Throh [BP]
		532 Timburr [BP]	564 Tirtouga [BP]	389 Torterra [BP]	158 Totodile [BP, E]	709 Trevenant [BP]	248 Tyranitar [BP]	697 Tyrantrum [BP]
		696 Tyrunt [BP]	003 Venusaur [BP]	640 Virizion [BP]	629 Vullaby [BP]	321 Wailord [BP]	365 Walrein [BP]	716 Xerneas [BP]
		562 Yamask [BP]	717 Yveltal [BP]	718 Zygarde [BP]				
Fire	Blue Flare	643 Reshiram [100]						
Normal	Body Slam	304 Aron [E]	298 Azurill [E]	153 Bayleef [40]	652 Chesnaught [48]	650 Chespin [42]	152 Chikorita [34, E]	366 Clamperl [E]
		035 Clefairy [40]	341 Corphish [E]	633 Deino [48]	425 Drifloon [E]	590 Foongus [E]	569 Garbodor [25]	423 Gastrodon [29]
		443 Gible [E]	118 Goldeen [E]	706 Goodra [32]	704 Goomy [32]	058 Growlithe [E]	631 Heatmor [E]	449 Hippopotas [E]
		635 Hydreigon [48]	039 Jigglypuff [35]	124 Jynx [44]	382 Kyogre [20]	131 Lapras [18]	108 Lickitung [E]	219 Magcargo [43]
		179 Mareep [E]	183 Marill [E]	154 Meganium [46]	241 Miltank [24]	446 Munchlax [25]	031 Nidoqueen [35]	322 Numel [E]
		674 Pancham [33]	675 Pangoro [35]	231 Phanpy [E]	060 Poliwag [21]	061 Poliwhirl [21]	432 Purugly [45]	651 Quilladin [48]
		364 Sealeo [26]	336 Seviper [E]	422 Shellos [29]	616 Shelmet [40]	410 Shieldon [E]	287 Slakoth [E]	705 Sliggoo [32]
		218 Slugma [41]	143 Snorlax [25]	363 Spheal [26]	317 Swalot [26]	220 Swinub [E]	498 Tepig [E]	538 Throh [29]
		564 Tirtouga [E]	324 Torkoal [27]	357 Tropius [41]	387 Turtwig [E]	320 Wailmer [E]	365 Walrein [25]	194 Wooper [E]
		634 Zweilous [48]						
Electric	Bolt Strike	644 Zekrom [100]						
Ground	Bone Club	104 Cubone [7]	105 Marowak [1, 7]					
	Bone Rush	104 Cubone [37]	448 Lucario [29]	630 Mandibuzz [1, 51]	105 Marowak [43]			
	Bonemerang	104 Cubone [21]	105 Marowak [21]					
Normal	Boomburst	441 Chatot [E]	295 Exploud [1, 58]	715 Noivern [1, 75]	276 Taillow [E]	329 Vibrava [47]		
Flying	Bounce	359 Absol [BP]	190 Aipom [BP, E]	594 Alomomola [BP]	424 Ambipom [BP]	566 Archen [BP]	567 Archeops [BP]	168 Ariados [BP]
		184 Azumarill [BP]	298 Azurill [23, BP]	339 Barboach [BP]	550 Basculin [BP]	257 Blaziken [BP]	522 Blitzle [BP]	427 Buneary [56, BP]
		659 Bunnelby [38, BP]	318 Carvanha [BP]	170 Chinchou [BP]	692 Clauncher [BP]	693 Clawitzer [BP]	036 Clefable [BP]	035 Clefairy [BP]
		638 Cobalion [BP]	256 Combusken [BP]	453 Croagunk [BP]	585 Deerling [BP]	225 Delibird [BP]	660 Diggersby [42, BP]	232 Donphan [BP]
		691 Dragalge [BP]	603 Eelektrik [BP]	604 Eelektross [BP]	456 Finneon [45, BP]	656 Froakie [39, BP]	657 Frogadier [44, BP]	596 Galvantula [BP]
		673 Gogoat [BP]	118 Goldeen [BP]	368 Gorebyss [BP]	658 Greninja [BP]	326 Grumpig [60, BP]	130 Gyarados [BP]	701 Hawlucha [32, BP]
		106 Hitmonlee [BP]	187 Hoppip [46, BP]	116 Horsea [BP]	367 Huntail [BP]	174 Igglybuff [BP]	039 Jigglypuff [BP]	595 Joltik [BP]
		189 Jumpluff [64, BP]	647 Keldeo [BP]	230 Kingdra [BP]	171 Lanturn [BP]	428 Lopunny [1, 56, BP]	457 Lumineon [53, BP]	370 Luvdisc [BP]
		129 Magikarp [BP]	490 Manaphy [BP]	226 Mantine [46, BP]	458 Mantyke [46, BP]	556 Maractus [BP, E]	183 Marill [BP]	151 Mew [BP]
		619 Mienfoo [49, BP]	620 Mienshao [49, BP]	224 Octillery [BP]	536 Palpitoad [BP]	489 Phione [BP]	186 Politoed [37, BP]	077 Ponyta [45, BP]
		668 Pyroar [BP]	211 Qwilfish [BP]	078 Rapidash [45, BP]	369 Relicanth [BP]	223 Remoraid [BP]	586 Sawsbuck [BP]	117 Seadra [BP]
		119 Seaking [BP]	537 Seismitoad [BP]	319 Sharpedo [BP]	275 Shiftry [BP]	188 Skiploom [56, BP]	690 Skrelp [BP]	167 Spinarak [BP]
		325 Spoink [50, BP]	234 Stantler [BP]	618 Stunfisk [35, BP]	255 Torchic [BP]	454 Toxicroak [BP]	535 Tympole [BP]	494 Victini [BP]
		640 Virizion [BP]	320 Wailmer [45, BP]	321 Wailord [51, BP]	340 Whiscash [BP]	040 Wigglytuff [BP]	523 Zebstrika [BP]	571 Zoroark [BP]
		570 Zorua [BP]						
	Brave Bird	257 Blaziken [50]	628 Braviary [1, 63]	084 Doduo [E]	580 Ducklett [41]	083 Farfetch'd [1, 55]	250 Ho-Oh [15]	630 Mandibuzz [1, 63]
		198 Murkrow [E]	016 Pidgey [E]	627 Rufflet [59]	227 Skarmory [E]	398 Staraptor [49]	397 Staravia [43]	396 Starly [37]
		581 Swanna [47]	277 Swellow [1, 51]	276 Taillow [41, E]	663 Talonflame [1, 64]	629 Vullaby [59]	041 Zubat [E]	
Fighting	Brick Break (TM31)	460 Abomasnow [TM]	681 Aegislash [TM]	306 Aggron [TM]	190 Aipom [TM]	424 Ambipom [TM]	181 Ampharos [TM]	347 Anorith [TM]
		493 Arceus [TM]	348 Armaldo [TM]	184 Azumarill [TM]	371 Bagon [TM]	689 Barbaracle [TM]	614 Beartic [TM]	015 Beedrill [TM]
		688 Binacle [TM]	625 Bisharp [TM]	009 Blastoise [TM]	257 Blaziken [TM]	242 Blissey [TM]	438 Bonsly [TM]	286 Breloom [TM]
		418 Buizel [TM]	659 Bunnelby [TM]	331 Cacnea [TM]	332 Cacturne [TM]	113 Chansey [TM]	006 Charizard [TM]	004 Charmander [TM]
		005 Charmeleon [TM]	652 Chesnaught [TM]	650 Chespin [TM]	390 Chimchar [TM]	036 Clefable [TM]	035 Clefairy [TM]	256 Combusken [TM]
		534 Conkeldurr [TM]	341 Corphish [TM]	342 Crawdaunt [TM]	453 Croagunk [TM]	159 Croconaw [TM]	104 Cubone [TM]	491 Darkrai [TM]
		555 Darmanitan [TM]	554 Darumaka [TM]	225 Delibird [TM]	386 Deoxys (Atk) [TM]	386 Deoxys (Def) [TM]	386 Deoxys (Nor) [TM]	386 Deoxys (Spd) [TM]
		483 Dialga [TM]	660 Diggersby [TM]	680 Doublade [TM]	149 Dragonite [TM]	452 Drapion [TM]	529 Drilbur [TM]	096 Drowzee [TM]
		356 Dusclops [TM]	477 Dusknoir [TM]	604 Eelektross [TM]	125 Electabuzz [TM]	466 Electivire [TM]	239 Elekid [TM]	500 Emboar [TM]
		395 Empoleon [TM]	530 Excadrill [TM]	295 Exploud [TM]	160 Feraligatr [TM]	180 Flaaffy [TM]	419 Floatzel [TM]	162 Furret [TM]
		475 Gallade [TM]	445 Garchomp [TM]	094 Gengar [TM]	074 Geodude [TM]	207 Gligar [TM]	472 Gliscor [TM]	673 Gogoat [TM]
		055 Golduck [TM]	076 Golem [TM]	622 Golett [TM]	623 Golurk [TM]	576 Gothitelle [TM]	210 Granbull [TM]	075 Graveler [TM]
		383 Groudon [TM]	253 Grovyle [TM]	326 Grumpig [TM]	533 Gurdurr [TM]	297 Hariyama [TM]	701 Hawlucha [TM]	612 Haxorus [TM]
		214 Heracross [28, TM]	107 Hitmonchan [TM]	106 Hitmonlee [17, TM]	237 Hitmontop [TM]	679 Honedge [TM]	097 Hypno [TM]	314 Illumise [TM]
		392 Infernape [TM]	039 Jigglypuff [TM]	124 Jynx [TM]	141 Kabutops [TM]	115 Kangaskhan [TM]	352 Kecleon [TM]	099 Kingler [TM]

ADVENTURE DATA

Type	Move	Pokémon that can learn it						
Fighting	Brick Break (TM31)	098 Krabby [TM]	402 Kricketune [TM]	552 Krokorok [TM]	553 Krookodile [TM]	382 Kyogre [TM]	645 Landorus [TM]	246 Larvitar [TM]
		166 Ledian [TM]	165 Ledyba [TM]	463 Lickilicky [TM]	108 Lickitung [TM]	271 Lombre [TM]	294 Loudred [TM]	448 Lucario [TM]
		272 Ludicolo [TM]	068 Machamp [TM]	067 Machoke [TM]	066 Machop [TM]	240 Magby [TM]	126 Magmar [TM]	467 Magmortar [TM]
		296 Makuhita [TM]	056 Mankey [TM]	183 Marill [TM]	105 Marowak [TM]	259 Marshtomp [TM]	303 Mawile [TM]	308 Medicham [TM]
		307 Meditite [TM]	648 Meloetta [TM]	376 Metagross [TM]	375 Metang [TM]	151 Mew [TM]	150 Mewtwo [TM]	619 Mienfoo [TM]
		620 Mienshao [TM]	241 Miltank [TM]	439 Mime Jr. [TM]	391 Monferno [TM]	122 Mr. Mime [TM]	089 Muk [TM]	446 Munchlax [TM]
		034 Nidoking [TM]	031 Nidoqueen [TM]	714 Noibat [TM]	715 Noivern [TM]	274 Nuzleaf [TM]	484 Palkia [TM]	674 Pancham [TM]
		675 Pangoro [TM]	046 Paras [TM]	047 Parasect [TM]	624 Pawniard [TM]	499 Pignite [TM]	025 Pikachu [TM]	127 Pinsir [26, TM]
		393 Piplup [TM]	186 Politoed [TM]	061 Poliwhirl [TM]	062 Poliwrath [TM]	057 Primeape [TM]	394 Prinplup [TM]	054 Psyduck [TM]
		247 Pupitar [TM]	195 Quagsire [TM]	156 Quilava [TM]	651 Quilladin [TM]	026 Raichu [TM]	409 Rampardos [TM]	384 Rayquaza [TM]
		378 Regice [TM]	486 Regigigas [TM]	377 Regirock [TM]	379 Registeel [TM]	112 Rhydon [TM]	464 Rhyperior [TM]	447 Riolu [TM]
		302 Sableye [TM]	373 Salamence [TM]	027 Sandshrew [TM]	028 Sandslash [TM]	539 Sawk [29, TM]	254 Sceptile [TM]	212 Scizor [TM]
		560 Scrafty [20, TM]	559 Scraggy [20, TM]	123 Scyther [TM]	537 Seismitoad [TM]	161 Sentret [TM]	372 Shelgon [TM]	275 Shiftry [TM]
		516 Simipour [TM]	512 Simisage [TM]	514 Simisear [TM]	672 Skiddo [TM]	451 Skorupi [TM]	289 Slaking [TM]	287 Slakoth [TM]
		080 Slowbro [TM]	199 Slowking [TM]	215 Sneasel [TM]	143 Snorlax [TM]	209 Snubbull [TM]	327 Spinda [TM]	007 Squirtle [TM]
		185 Sudowoodo [TM]	260 Swampert [TM]	465 Tangrowth [TM]	216 Teddiursa [TM]	538 Throh [TM]	642 Thundurus [TM]	532 Timburr [TM]
		468 Togekiss [TM]	176 Togetic [TM]	641 Tornadus [TM]	158 Totodile [TM]	454 Toxicroak [TM]	252 Treecko [TM]	157 Typhlosion [TM]
		248 Tyranitar [TM]	697 Tyrantrum [TM]	236 Tyrogue [TM]	696 Tyrunt [TM]	217 Ursaring [TM]	494 Victini [TM]	288 Vigoroth [TM]
		313 Volbeat [TM]	008 Wartortle [TM]	461 Weavile [TM]	040 Wigglytuff [TM]	335 Zangoose [TM]	718 Zygarde [TM]	
Water	Brine	594 Alomomola [41]	347 Anorith [29]	348 Armaldo [29]	550 Basculin [E]	614 Beartic [21]	565 Carracosta [28]	318 Carvanha [E]
		170 Chinchou [E]	366 Clamperl [E]	222 Corsola [27]	346 Cradily [21]	613 Cubchoo [21]	087 Dewgong [33]	580 Ducklett [E]
		395 Empoleon [33]	349 Feebas [E]	456 Finneon [E]	592 Frillish [32]	297 Hariyama [1]	116 Horsea [31]	367 Huntail [19]
		593 Jellicent [32]	230 Kingdra [31]	099 Kingler [51]	098 Krabby [39]	131 Lapras [37]	345 Lileep [21]	370 Luvdisc [E]
		138 Omanyte [28]	139 Omastar [28]	501 Oshawott [E]	515 Panpour [34]	279 Pelipper [28]	393 Piplup [29]	394 Prinplup [33]
		211 Qwilfish [33, E]	369 Relicanth [E]	117 Seadra [31]	364 Sealeo [17]	086 Seel [33]	090 Shellder [44]	422 Shellos [E]
		363 Spheal [17]	007 Squirtle [E]	120 Staryu [28]	072 Tentacool [34]	073 Tentacruel [36]	564 Tirtouga [28]	320 Wailmer [25]
		321 Wailord [29]	365 Walrein [19]	278 Wingull [E]				
	Bubble	184 Azumarill [7]	298 Azurill [7]	009 Blastoise [13]	170 Chinchou [1]	692 Clauncher [12]	693 Clawitzer [12]	341 Corphish [1]
		222 Corsola [4]	342 Crawdaunt [1]	691 Dragalge [12]	395 Empoleon [1, 8]	592 Frillish [1]	656 Froakie [5]	657 Frogadier [5]
		706 Goodra [1]	704 Goomy [1]	658 Greninja [5]	116 Horsea [1]	593 Jellicent [1]	230 Kingdra [1]	099 Kingler [1]
		098 Krabby [1]	171 Lanturn [1]	271 Lombre [9]	270 Lotad [9]	490 Manaphy [1]	226 Mantine [1]	458 Mantyke [1]
		183 Marill [7]	284 Masquerain [1]	536 Palpitoad [1]	489 Phione [1]	393 Piplup [8]	060 Poliwag [11]	061 Poliwhirl [11]
		394 Prinplup [8]	211 Qwilfish [13]	117 Seadra [1]	537 Seismitoad [1]	690 Skrelp [12]	705 Sliggoo [1]	007 Squirtle [13]
		283 Surskit [1]	072 Tentacool [E]	535 Tympole [1]	008 Wartortle [13]			
	Bubble Beam	184 Azumarill [13]	298 Azurill [13]	550 Basculin [E]	170 Chinchou [20]	692 Clauncher [20]	693 Clawitzer [20]	341 Corphish [14]
		222 Corsola [10]	342 Crawdaunt [14]	580 Ducklett [19]	395 Empoleon [19]	592 Frillish [13]	116 Horsea [21]	593 Jellicent [13]
		140 Kabuto [E]	647 Keldeo [13]	230 Kingdra [21]	099 Kingler [15]	098 Krabby [15]	171 Lanturn [20]	271 Lombre [24]
		270 Lotad [21]	490 Manaphy [24]	226 Mantine [1, 7]	458 Mantyke [7]	183 Marill [13]	224 Octillery [18]	138 Omanyte [E]
		536 Palpitoad [12]	489 Phione [24]	393 Piplup [18]	186 Politoed [1]	060 Poliwag [25, E]	061 Poliwhirl [27]	062 Poliwrath [1]
		394 Prinplup [19]	211 Qwilfish [E]	223 Remoraid [18]	117 Seadra [21]	537 Seismitoad [12]	090 Shellder [E]	120 Staryu [18]
		245 Suicune [8]	283 Surskit [17]	581 Swanna [19]	072 Tentacool [25]	073 Tentacruel [25]	535 Tympole [12]	
Bug	Bug Bite	617 Accelgor [BP]	347 Anorith [25, BP]	168 Ariados [1, BP]	348 Armaldo [BP]	267 Beautifly [BP]	015 Beedrill [BP]	412 Burmy [15, BP]
		012 Butterfree [BP]	455 Carnivine [BP]	268 Cascoon [BP]	010 Caterpie [15, BP]	415 Combee [13, BP]	558 Crustle [23, BP]	452 Drapion [20, BP]
		632 Durant [26, BP]	269 Dustox [BP]	557 Dwebble [23, BP]	589 Escavalier [BP]	330 Flygon [BP]	205 Forretress [1, BP]	596 Galvantula [18, BP]
		649 Genesect [BP]	207 Gligar [BP]	472 Gliscor [BP]	631 Heatmor [36, BP]	485 Heatran [BP]	214 Heracross [BP]	314 Illumise [BP]
		595 Joltik [18, BP]	014 Kakuna [BP]	588 Karrablast [BP, E]	401 Kricketot [16, BP]	402 Kricketune [BP]	636 Larvesta [40, BP]	542 Leavanny [1, 8, BP]
		166 Ledian [BP]	165 Ledyba [BP, E]	284 Masquerain [BP]	011 Metapod [BP]	151 Mew [BP]	414 Mothim [15, BP]	290 Nincada [BP, E]
		291 Ninjask [1, BP]	046 Paras [BP, E]	047 Parasect [BP]	204 Pineco [9, BP]	127 Pinsir [BP, E]	664 Scatterbug [15, BP]	212 Scizor [BP]
		545 Scolipede [23, BP]	123 Scyther [BP]	540 Sewaddle [8, BP]	292 Shedinja [BP]	616 Shelmet [BP]	213 Shuckle [42, BP]	266 Silcoon [BP]
		451 Skorupi [20, BP]	665 Spewpa [BP]	167 Spinarak [BP]	283 Surskit [BP, E]	541 Swadloon [1, BP]	328 Trapinch [BP, E]	543 Venipede [22, BP]
		049 Venomoth [BP]	048 Venonat [BP, E]	416 Vespiquen [BP]	329 Vibrava [BP]	666 Vivillon [BP]	313 Volbeat [BP]	637 Volcarona [BP]
		013 Weedle [15, BP]	544 Whirlipede [23, BP]	413 Wormadam (Plant) [15, BP]	413 Wormadam (Sand) [15, BP]	413 Wormadam (Trash) [15, BP]	265 Wurmple [15, BP]	193 Yanma [BP]
		469 Yanmega [1, BP]						
	Bug Buzz	617 Accelgor [44]	267 Beautifly [35]	012 Butterfree [42]	415 Combee [29]	269 Dustox [35]	589 Escavalier [28]	596 Galvantula [60]
		649 Genesect [55]	314 Illumise [40, E]	595 Joltik [48]	588 Karrablast [28]	402 Kricketune [46]	636 Larvesta [70]	166 Ledian [53]
		165 Ledyba [41, E]	284 Masquerain [1, 42]	414 Mothim [47]	290 Nincada [E]	123 Scyther [E]	540 Sewaddle [36]	616 Shelmet [44]
		049 Venomoth [1, 59]	329 Vibrava [29]	666 Vivillon [35]	313 Volbeat [40, E]	637 Volcarona [1, 70]	193 Yanma [57]	469 Yanmega [1, 57]

	Move	Pokémon that can learn it						
Fighting	Bulk Up (TM08)	689 Barbaracle [TM]	614 Beartic [TM]	257 Blaziken [31, TM]	628 Braviary [TM]	286 Breloom [TM]	418 Buizel [TM]	659 Bunnelby [TM]
		652 Chesnaught [44, TM]	650 Chespin [39, TM]	390 Chimchar [TM]	256 Combusken [31, TM]	534 Conkeldurr [29, TM]	453 Croagunk [TM]	555 Darmanitan [TM]
		483 Dialga [TM]	660 Diggersby [TM]	500 Emboar [TM]	419 Floatzel [TM]	475 Gallade [TM]	673 Gogoat [34, TM]	210 Granbull [TM]
		383 Groudon [50, TM]	533 Gurdurr [29, TM]	297 Hariyama [TM]	701 Hawlucha [TM]	214 Heracross [TM]	107 Hitmonchan [TM]	106 Hitmonlee [TM]
		237 Hitmontop [TM]	392 Infernape [TM]	553 Krookodile [TM]	645 Landorus [TM]	448 Lucario [TM]	068 Machamp [43, TM]	067 Machoke [43, TM]
		066 Machop [37, TM]	296 Makuhita [TM]	056 Mankey [TM]	308 Medicham [TM]	307 Meditite [TM]	151 Mew [TM]	150 Mewtwo [TM]
		619 Mienfoo [TM]	620 Mienshao [TM]	391 Monferno [TM]	484 Palkia [TM]	674 Pancham [TM]	675 Pangoro [TM]	127 Pinsir [TM]
		062 Poliwrath [TM]	057 Primeape [TM]	651 Quilladin [44, TM]	384 Rayquaza [TM]	447 Riolu [TM]	627 Rufflet [TM]	539 Sawk [33, TM]
		560 Scrafty [TM]	559 Scraggy [TM]	672 Skiddo [34, TM]	289 Slaking [TM]	287 Slakoth [TM]	209 Snubbull [TM]	663 Talonflame [TM]
		216 Teddiursa [TM]	538 Throh [33, TM]	642 Thundurus [TM]	532 Timburr [28, TM]	641 Tornadus [TM]	454 Toxicroak [TM]	236 Tyrogue [TM]
		217 Ursaring [TM]	288 Vigoroth [TM]					
Ground	Bulldoze (TM78)	460 Abomasnow [TM]	142 Aerodactyl [TM]	306 Aggron [TM]	334 Altaria [TM]	698 Amaura [TM]	181 Ampharos [TM]	024 Arbok [TM]
		059 Arcanine [TM]	493 Arceus [TM]	566 Archen [TM]	567 Archeops [TM]	348 Armaldo [TM]	304 Aron [TM]	699 Aurorus [TM]
		713 Avalugg [TM]	184 Azumarill [TM]	343 Baltoy [TM]	689 Barbaracle [TM]	339 Barboach [TM]	411 Bastiodon [TM]	614 Beartic [TM]
		400 Bibarel [TM]	688 Binacle [TM]	009 Blastoise [TM]	257 Blaziken [TM]	242 Blissey [TM]	525 Boldore [TM]	626 Bouffalant [TM]
		437 Bronzong [TM]	436 Bronzor [TM]	659 Bunnelby [TM]	323 Camerupt [TM]	565 Carracosta [TM]	113 Chansey [TM]	006 Charizard [TM]
		652 Chesnaught [TM]	650 Chespin [TM]	344 Claydol [TM]	534 Conkeldurr [TM]	222 Corsola [TM]	346 Cradily [TM]	408 Cranidos [TM]
		453 Croagunk [TM]	558 Crustle [TM]	104 Cubone [TM]	555 Darmanitan [TM]	483 Dialga [TM]	660 Diggersby [1, TM]	050 Diglett [18, TM]
		232 Donphan [1, TM]	149 Dragonite [TM]	452 Drapion [TM]	529 Drilbur [TM]	621 Druddigon [TM]	051 Dugtrio [18, TM]	206 Dunsparce [TM]
		356 Dusclops [TM]	477 Dusknoir [TM]	557 Dwebble [TM]	023 Ekans [TM]	466 Electivire [TM]	500 Emboar [TM]	395 Empoleon [TM]
		244 Entei [TM]	530 Excadrill [TM]	295 Exploud [TM]	160 Feraligatr [TM]	598 Ferrothorn [TM]	330 Flygon [8, TM]	205 Forretress [TM]
		444 Gabite [TM]	475 Gallade [TM]	445 Garchomp [TM]	423 Gastrodon [TM]	074 Geodude [22, TM]	443 Gible [TM]	526 Gigalith [TM]
		203 Girafarig [TM]	487 Giratina (Alt) [TM]	487 Giratina (Ori) [TM]	362 Glalie [TM]	207 Gligar [TM]	472 Gliscor [TM]	673 Gogoat [26, TM]
		076 Golem [22, TM]	622 Golett [TM]	623 Golurk [TM]	706 Goodra [TM]	210 Granbull [TM]	075 Graveler [22, TM]	383 Groudon [TM]
		326 Grumpig [TM]	130 Gyarados [TM]	297 Hariyama [TM]	612 Haxorus [TM]	485 Heatran [TM]	695 Heliolisk [TM]	694 Helioptile [35, TM]
		214 Heracross [TM]	449 Hippopotas [TM]	450 Hippowdon [TM]	107 Hitmonchan [TM]	106 Hitmonlee [TM]	237 Hitmontop [TM]	250 Ho-Oh [TM]
		635 Hydreigon [TM]	392 Infernape [TM]	115 Kangaskhan [TM]	552 Krokorok [TM]	553 Krookodile [TM]	382 Kyogre [TM]	305 Lairon [TM]
		645 Landorus [19, TM]	131 Lapras [TM]	246 Larvitar [TM]	380 Latias [TM]	381 Latios [TM]	463 Lickilicky [TM]	108 Lickitung [TM]
		667 Litleo [TM]	294 Loudred [TM]	448 Lucario [TM]	249 Lugia [TM]	337 Lunatone [TM]	068 Machamp [TM]	067 Machoke [TM]
		066 Machop [TM]	219 Magcargo [TM]	467 Magmortar [TM]	296 Makuhita [TM]	473 Mamoswine [TM]	056 Mankey [TM]	226 Mantine [TM]
		458 Mantyke [TM]	105 Marowak [TM]	259 Marshtomp [TM]	154 Meganium [TM]	376 Metagross [TM]	375 Metang [TM]	151 Mew [TM]
		150 Mewtwo [TM]	350 Milotic [TM]	241 Miltank [TM]	446 Munchlax [TM]	034 Nidoking [TM]	031 Nidoqueen [TM]	299 Nosepass [TM]
		322 Numel [TM]	095 Onix [TM]	484 Palkia [TM]	536 Palpitoad [TM]	674 Pancham [TM]	675 Pangoro [TM]	231 Phanpy [TM]
		708 Phantump [TM]	499 Pignite [TM]	221 Piloswine [TM]	204 Pineco [TM]	127 Pinsir [TM]	186 Politoed [TM]	061 Poliwhirl [TM]
		062 Poliwrath [TM]	057 Primeape [TM]	476 Probopass [TM]	247 Pupitar [TM]	432 Purugly [TM]	668 Pyroar [TM]	195 Quagsire [TM]
		651 Quilladin [TM]	243 Raikou [TM]	409 Rampardos [TM]	384 Rayquaza [TM]	378 Regice [1, 19, TM]	486 Regigigas [TM]	377 Regirock [1, 19, TM]
		379 Registeel [1, 19, TM]	369 Relicanth [TM]	112 Rhydon [21, TM]	111 Rhyhorn [21, TM]	464 Rhyperior [21, TM]	447 Riolu [TM]	524 Roggenrola [TM]
		373 Salamence [TM]	551 Sandile [TM]	027 Sandshrew [TM]	028 Sandslash [TM]	539 Sawk [TM]	254 Sceptile [TM]	545 Scolipede [TM]
		364 Sealeo [TM]	537 Seismitoad [TM]	336 Seviper [TM]	319 Sharpedo [TM]	410 Shieldon [TM]	213 Shuckle [TM]	672 Skiddo [26, TM]
		289 Slaking [TM]	080 Slowbro [TM]	199 Slowking [TM]	079 Slowpoke [TM]	143 Snorlax [TM]	209 Snubbull [TM]	338 Solrock [TM]
		363 Spheal [TM]	234 Stantler [TM]	208 Steelix [TM]	618 Stunfisk [TM]	185 Sudowoodo [TM]	245 Suicune [TM]	317 Swalot [TM]
		260 Swampert [TM]	220 Swinub [TM]	465 Tangrowth [TM]	128 Tauros [TM]	216 Teddiursa [TM]	639 Terrakion [TM]	538 Throh [TM]
		564 Tirtouga [TM]	324 Torkoal [TM]	389 Torterra [TM]	454 Toxicroak [TM]	328 Trapinch [8, TM]	709 Trevenant [TM]	357 Tropius [TM]
		157 Typhlosion [TM]	248 Tyranitar [TM]	697 Tyrantrum [TM]	236 Tyrogue [TM]	696 Tyrunt [TM]	217 Ursaring [TM]	003 Venusaur [TM]
		329 Vibrava [8, TM]	288 Vigoroth [TM]	320 Wailmer [TM]	321 Wailord [TM]	365 Walrein [TM]	340 Whiscash [TM]	194 Wooper [TM]
		413 Wormadam (Sand) [TM]	718 Zygarde [1, TM]					
Steel	Bullet Punch	453 Croagunk [E]	107 Hitmonchan [16]	066 Machop [E]	296 Makuhita [E]	307 Meditite [E]	376 Metagross [26]	375 Metang [26]
		447 Riolu [E]	212 Scizor [1]	236 Tyrogue [E]				
Grass	Bullet Seed	069 Bellsprout [E]	573 Cinccino [1]	102 Exeggcute [17]	597 Ferroseed [E]	711 Gourgeist [26]	214 Heracross [1]	187 Hoppip [19]
		189 Jumpluff [20]	226 Mantine [1]	556 Maractus [E]	224 Octillery [46]	511 Pansage [E]	710 Pumpkaboo [26]	223 Remoraid [38]
		315 Roselia [E]	273 Seedot [E]	285 Shroomish [E]	188 Skiploom [20]	459 Snover [E]	192 Sunflora [25]	252 Treecko [E]
		357 Tropius [E]						

C

	Move	Pokémon that can learn it						
Psychic	Calm Mind (TM04)	063 Abra [TM]	359 Absol [TM]	065 Alakazam [41, TM]	594 Alomomola [TM]	698 Amaura [TM]	493 Arceus [TM]	683 Aromatisse [17, TM]
		531 Audino [TM]	699 Aurorus [TM]	482 Azelf [TM]	343 Baltoy [TM]	354 Banette [TM]	606 Beheeyem [45, TM]	242 Blissey [TM]
		438 Bonsly [TM]	437 Bronzong [TM]	436 Bronzor [TM]	703 Carbink [TM]	251 Celebi [TM]	609 Chandelure [TM]	113 Chansey [TM]
		358 Chimecho [TM]	433 Chingling [TM]	573 Cinccino [TM]	344 Claydol [TM]	036 Clefable [TM]	035 Clefairy [TM]	638 Cobalion [TM]
		563 Cofagrigus [TM]	222 Corsola [TM]	488 Cresselia [TM]	491 Darkrai [TM]	301 Delcatty [TM]	655 Delphox [TM]	386 Deoxys (Atk) [TM]
		386 Deoxys (Def) [TM]	386 Deoxys (Nor) [TM]	386 Deoxys (Spd) [TM]	719 Diancie [TM]	426 Drifblim [TM]	425 Drifloon [TM]	096 Drowzee [TM]
		206 Dunsparce [TM]	578 Duosion [TM]	356 Dusclops [TM]	477 Dusknoir [TM]	355 Duskull [TM]	605 Elgyem [43, TM]	244 Entei [78, TM]
		196 Espeon [TM]	677 Espurr [TM]	669 Flabébé [TM]	670 Floette [TM]	671 Florges [TM]	475 Gallade [TM]	282 Gardevoir [26, TM]
		203 Girafarig [TM]	487 Giratina (Alt) [TM]	487 Giratina (Ori) [TM]	055 Golduck [TM]	574 Gothita [TM]	576 Gothitelle [TM]	575 Gothorita [TM]
		326 Grumpig [TM]	430 Honchkrow [TM]	250 Ho-Oh [93, TM]	097 Hypno [TM]	392 Infernape [58, TM]	686 Inkay [TM]	385 Jirachi [TM]
		124 Jynx [TM]	064 Kadabra [TM]	647 Keldeo [TM]	281 Kirlia [26, TM]	707 Klefki [TM]	382 Kyogre [50, TM]	608 Lampent [TM]
		645 Landorus [TM]	636 Larvesta [TM]	380 Latias [TM]	381 Latios [TM]	542 Leavanny [TM]	607 Litwick [TM]	448 Lucario [47, TM]
		249 Lugia [93, TM]	337 Lunatone [TM]	687 Malamar [TM]	490 Manaphy [TM]	308 Medicham [23, TM]	307 Meditite [23, TM]	648 Meloetta [TM]
		678 Meowstic (F) [TM]	678 Meowstic (M) [TM]	481 Mesprit [TM]	151 Mew [TM]	150 Mewtwo [TM]	619 Mienfoo [25, TM]	620 Mienshao [25, TM]
		439 Mime Jr. [TM]	572 Minccino [TM]	200 Misdreavus [TM]	429 Mismagius [TM]	122 Mr. Mime [TM]	517 Munna [35, TM]	198 Murkrow [TM]
		518 Musharna [TM]	177 Natu [TM]	038 Ninetales [TM]	054 Psyduck [TM]	243 Raikou [78, TM]	280 Ralts [24, TM]	369 Relicanth [TM]
		579 Reuniclus [TM]	302 Sableye [TM]	497 Serperior [TM]	496 Servine [TM]	540 Sewaddle [TM]	353 Shuppet [TM]	561 Sigilyph [TM]
		300 Skitty [TM]	080 Slowbro [TM]	199 Slowking [TM]	079 Slowpoke [TM]	685 Slurpuff [TM]	238 Smoochum [TM]	215 Sneasel [TM]
		495 Snivy [TM]	577 Solosis [TM]	338 Solrock [TM]	327 Spinda [TM]	442 Spiritomb [TM]	325 Spoink [TM]	682 Spritzee [17, TM]
		234 Stantler [27, TM]	185 Sudowoodo [TM]	245 Suicune [78, TM]	541 Swadloon [TM]	684 Swirlix [TM]	528 Swoobat [29, TM]	700 Sylveon [TM]
		639 Terrakion [TM]	709 Trevenant [TM]	480 Uxie [TM]	640 Virizion [TM]	666 Vivillon [TM]	637 Volcarona [TM]	461 Weavile [TM]
		527 Woobat [29, TM]	178 Xatu [TM]	716 Xerneas [TM]	562 Yamask [TM]	571 Zoroark [TM]	570 Zorua [TM]	
Normal	Camouflage	298 Azurill [E]	222 Corsola [E]	585 Deerling [1]	691 Dragalge [19]	669 Flabébé [E]	656 Froakie [E]	694 Helioptile [E]
		686 Inkay [E]	595 Joltik [E]	352 Kecleon [30, E]	183 Marill [E]	414 Mothim [35]	586 Sawsbuck [1]	540 Sewaddle [E]
		690 Skrelp [19]	120 Staryu [22]	618 Stunfisk [17]	718 Zygarde [59]			
	Captivate	012 Butterfree [40]	546 Cottonee [E]	133 Eevee [E]	349 Feebas [E]	456 Finneon [26]	669 Flabébé [E]	478 Froslass [41]
		676 Furfrou [E]	282 Gardevoir [44]	431 Glameow [32]	368 Gorebyss [23]	574 Gothita [E]	174 Igglybuff [E]	314 Illumise [E]
		607 Litwick [E]	457 Lumineon [26]	370 Luvdisc [46, E]	303 Mawile [E]	052 Meowth [46]	350 Milotic [24]	241 Miltank [35]
		572 Minccino [39]	029 Nidoran ♀ [43]	032 Nidoran ♂ [43]	030 Nidorina [50]	033 Nidorino [50]	053 Persian [56]	077 Ponyta [E]
		509 Purrloin [33]	432 Purugly [32]	302 Sableye [E]	161 Sentret [E]	300 Skitty [43, E]	238 Smoochum [E]	495 Snivy [E]
		442 Spiritomb [E]	682 Spritzee [E]	234 Stantler [50]	416 Vespiquen [41]	037 Vulpix [47, E]	527 Woobat [E]	413 Wormadam (Plant) [35]
		413 Wormadam (Sand) [35]	413 Wormadam (Trash) [35]	570 Zorua [E]				
Electric	Charge	181 Ampharos [16]	522 Blitzle [8]	170 Chinchou [50]	702 Dedenne [11]	309 Electrike [44]	101 Electrode [1]	587 Emolga [10]
		180 Flaaffy [16]	695 Heliolisk [1]	694 Helioptile [11]	600 Klang [1, 6]	599 Klink [6]	601 Klinklang [1, 6]	171 Lanturn [58]
		404 Luxio [9]	405 Luxray [1, 9]	310 Manectric [48]	179 Mareep [15, E]	312 Minun [28]	417 Pachirisu [E]	172 Pichu [E]
		311 Plusle [28]	479 Rotom (Fan) [1, 57]	479 Rotom (Frost) [1, 57]	479 Rotom (Heat) [1, 57]	479 Rotom (Mow) [1, 57]	479 Rotom (Wash) [1, 57]	479 Rotom [1, 57]
		403 Shinx [9]	642 Thundurus [1, 55]	100 Voltorb [1]	145 Zapdos [36]	523 Zebstrika [1, 8]		
	Charge Beam (TM57)	063 Abra [TM]	359 Absol [TM]	065 Alakazam [TM]	698 Amaura [TM]	181 Ampharos [TM]	493 Arceus [TM]	683 Aromatisse [TM]
		531 Audino [TM]	699 Aurorus [TM]	482 Azelf [TM]	343 Baltoy [TM]	354 Banette [TM]	606 Beheeyem [TM]	400 Bibarel [TM]
		399 Bidoof [TM]	242 Blissey [TM]	522 Blitzle [TM]	437 Bronzong [TM]	436 Bronzor [TM]	427 Buneary [TM]	251 Celebi [TM]
		113 Chansey [TM]	358 Chimecho [TM]	170 Chinchou [TM]	433 Chingling [TM]	344 Claydol [TM]	036 Clefable [TM]	035 Clefairy [TM]
		488 Cresselia [TM]	491 Darkrai [TM]	702 Dedenne [34, TM]	301 Delcatty [TM]	386 Deoxys (Atk) [TM]	386 Deoxys (Def) [TM]	386 Deoxys (Nor) [TM]
		386 Deoxys (Spd) [TM]	426 Drifblim [TM]	425 Drifloon [TM]	621 Druddigon [TM]	206 Dunsparce [TM]	356 Dusclops [TM]	477 Dusknoir [TM]
		355 Duskull [TM]	603 Eelektrik [1, TM]	604 Eelektross [TM]	125 Electabuzz [TM]	466 Electivire [TM]	309 Electrike [TM]	101 Electrode [16, TM]
		239 Elekid [TM]	605 Elgyem [TM]	587 Emolga [TM]	677 Espurr [TM]	180 Flaaffy [TM]	676 Furfrou [TM]	162 Furret [TM]
		475 Gallade [TM]	596 Galvantula [TM]	282 Gardevoir [TM]	649 Genesect [TM]	203 Girafarig [TM]	487 Giratina (Alt) [TM]	487 Giratina (Ori) [TM]
		623 Golurk [TM]	574 Gothita [TM]	576 Gothitelle [TM]	575 Gothorita [TM]	711 Gourgeist [TM]	326 Grumpig [TM]	695 Heliolisk [TM]
		694 Helioptile [TM]	250 Ho-Oh [TM]	635 Hydreigon [TM]	314 Illumise [TM]	039 Jigglypuff [TM]	385 Jirachi [TM]	135 Jolteon [TM]
		595 Joltik [TM]	064 Kadabra [TM]	352 Kecleon [TM]	281 Kirlia [TM]	600 Klang [26, TM]	599 Klink [26, TM]	601 Klinklang [25, TM]
		171 Lanturn [TM]	380 Latias [TM]	381 Latios [TM]	264 Linoone [TM]	428 Lopunny [TM]	249 Lugia [TM]	337 Lunatone [TM]
		404 Luxio [TM]	405 Luxray [TM]	081 Magnemite [TM]	082 Magneton [TM]	462 Magnezone [TM]	310 Manectric [TM]	179 Mareep [TM]
		303 Mawile [TM]	648 Meloetta [TM]	678 Meowstic (F) [28, TM]	678 Meowstic (M) [TM]	481 Mesprit [TM]	151 Mew [TM]	150 Mewtwo [TM]
		439 Mime Jr. [TM]	312 Minun [TM]	200 Misdreavus [TM]	429 Mismagius [TM]	122 Mr. Mime [TM]	517 Munna [TM]	518 Musharna [TM]
		224 Octillery [TM]	417 Pachirisu [TM]	172 Pichu [TM]	025 Pikachu [TM]	311 Plusle [TM]	137 Porygon [TM]	233 Porygon2 [TM]
		474 Porygon-Z [TM]	710 Pumpkaboo [TM]	026 Raichu [TM]	243 Raikou [TM]	280 Ralts [TM]	020 Raticate [TM]	019 Rattata [TM]
		378 Regice [1, 13, TM]	377 Regirock [1, 13, TM]	379 Registeel [1, 13, TM]	223 Remoraid [TM]	479 Rotom (Fan) [TM]	479 Rotom (Frost) [TM]	479 Rotom (Heat) [TM]
		479 Rotom (Mow) [TM]	479 Rotom (Wash) [TM]	479 Rotom [TM]	161 Sentret [TM]	403 Shinx [TM]	353 Shuppet [TM]	561 Sigilyph [TM]
		300 Skitty [TM]	338 Solrock [TM]	325 Spoink [TM]	682 Spritzee [TM]	234 Stantler [TM]	528 Swoobat [TM]	642 Thundurus [TM]
		602 Tynamo [1, TM]	480 Uxie [TM]	494 Victini [TM]	313 Volbeat [TM]	100 Voltorb [16, TM]	040 Wigglytuff [TM]	527 Woobat [TM]
		145 Zapdos [TM]	523 Zebstrika [TM]	644 Zekrom [TM]	263 Zigzagoon [TM]			

Type	Move	Pokémon that can learn it						
Fairy	Charm	683 Aromatisse [35]	298 Azurill [10]	001 Bulbasaur [E]	427 Buneary [46]	173 Cleffa [1]	546 Cottonee [28]	613 Cubchoo [29]
		702 Dedenne [14]	585 Deerling [36]	578 Duosion [19]	133 Eevee [29, E]	587 Emolga [E]	456 Finneon [E]	676 Furfrou [38]
		431 Glameow [25]	574 Gothita [46]	576 Gothitelle [54]	575 Gothorita [50]	210 Granbull [1]	440 Happiny [1]	174 Igglybuff [1]
		314 Illumise [9]	281 Kirlia [40]	380 Latias [7]	506 Lillipup [E]	428 Lopunny [46]	370 Luvdisc [1]	490 Manaphy [9]
		678 Meowstic (M) [28]	052 Meowth [E]	481 Mesprit [46]	439 Mime Jr. [E]	572 Minccino [27]	312 Minun [E]	446 Munchlax [E]
		029 Nidoran ♀ [E]	043 Oddish [E]	417 Pachirisu [9]	548 Petilil [E]	231 Phanpy [33]	489 Phione [9]	172 Pichu [1]
		311 Plusle [25, E]	077 Ponyta [E]	509 Purrloin [E]	432 Purugly [25]	280 Ralts [34]	579 Reuniclus [19]	586 Sawsbuck [36]
		161 Sentret [E]	285 Shroomish [E]	300 Skitty [25]	143 Snorlax [E]	209 Snubbull [1]	577 Solosis [19]	682 Spritzee [35]
		216 Teddiursa [36]	175 Togepi [1]	176 Togetic [1]	697 Tyrantrum [20]	696 Tyrunt [20]	527 Woobat [E]	360 Wynaut [1]
		263 Zigzagoon [E]						
Flying	Chatter	441 Chatot [1, 21]						
Normal	Chip Away	550 Basculin [16]	534 Conkeldurr [24]	341 Corphish [E]	408 Cranidos [28]	159 Croconaw [33]	104 Cubone [E]	621 Druddigon [31]
		160 Feraligatr [37]	533 Gurdurr [24]	214 Heracross [16]	115 Kangaskhan [31]	098 Krabby [E]	246 Larvitar [14]	463 Lickilicky [37]
		108 Lickitung [37]	296 Makuhita [E]	446 Munchlax [17]	034 Nidoking [23]	031 Nidoqueen [23]	029 Nidoran ♀ [E]	032 Nidoran ♂ [E]
		247 Pupitar [14]	409 Rampardos [28]	112 Rhydon [25]	111 Rhyhorn [25]	464 Rhyperior [25]	027 Sandshrew [E]	560 Scrafty [27]
		559 Scraggy [27]	289 Slaking [27]	287 Slakoth [25]	143 Snorlax [17]	216 Teddiursa [E]	532 Timburr [24]	158 Totodile [29]
		248 Tyranitar [14]	288 Vigoroth [27]					
Fighting	Circle Throw	427 Buneary [E]	115 Kangaskhan [E]	674 Pancham [25]	675 Pangoro [25]	062 Poliwrath [1, 53]	447 Riolu [E]	538 Throh [37]
		293 Whismur [E]						
Water	Clamp	689 Barbaracle [20]	688 Binacle [20]	366 Clamperl [1]	090 Shellder [25]			
Poison	Clear Smog	591 Amoonguss [43]	069 Bellsprout [E]	351 Castform [E]	425 Drifloon [E]	590 Foongus [39]	569 Garbodor [34]	092 Gastly [E]
		116 Horsea [E]	109 Koffing [15]	607 Litwick [E]	240 Magby [19]	219 Magcargo [20]	126 Magmar [19]	467 Magmortar [19]
		054 Psyduck [E]	422 Shellos [E]	218 Slugma [20]	324 Torkoal [E]	568 Trubbish [34]	320 Wailmer [E]	110 Weezing [15]
Fighting	Close Combat	638 Cobalion [1, 73]	475 Gallade [1, 53]	058 Growlithe [E]	297 Hariyama [46]	214 Heracross [43]	107 Hitmonchan [1, 66]	106 Hitmonlee [1, 57]
		237 Hitmontop [1, 55]	392 Infernape [36]	647 Keldeo [73]	448 Lucario [1, 55]	066 Machop [E]	296 Makuhita [40]	056 Mankey [49, E]
		648 Meloetta [78]	391 Monferno [36]	127 Pinsir [E]	057 Primeape [59]	539 Sawk [48]	209 Snubbull [E]	398 Staraptor [34]
		216 Teddiursa [E]	639 Terrakion [1, 73]	640 Virizion [1, 73]	716 Xerneas [80]	335 Zangoose [50]		
Poison	Coil	024 Arbok [56]	206 Dunsparce [37]	603 Eelektrik [54]	604 Eelektross [1]	023 Ekans [44]	368 Gorebyss [45]	367 Huntail [45]
		350 Milotic [44]	497 Serperior [38]	496 Servine [36]	336 Seviper [46]	495 Snivy [31]	718 Zygarde [80]	
Normal	Comet Punch	107 Hitmonchan [1]	115 Kangaskhan [1]	166 Ledian [1, 9]	165 Ledyba [9]	674 Pancham [15]	675 Pangoro [15]	532 Timburr [E]
Normal	Confide (TM100)	460 Abomasnow [TM]	063 Abra [TM]	359 Absol [TM]	617 Accelgor [TM]	681 Aegislash [TM]	142 Aerodactyl [TM]	306 Aggron [TM]
		190 Aipom [TM]	065 Alakazam [TM]	594 Alomomola [TM]	334 Altaria [TM]	698 Amaura [TM]	424 Ambipom [TM]	591 Amoonguss [TM]
		181 Ampharos [TM]	347 Anorith [TM]	024 Arbok [TM]	059 Arcanine [TM]	493 Arceus [TM]	566 Archen [TM]	567 Archeops [TM]
		168 Ariados [TM]	348 Armaldo [TM]	683 Aromatisse [TM]	304 Aron [TM]	144 Articuno [TM]	531 Audino [TM]	699 Aurorus [TM]
		713 Avalugg [TM]	610 Axew [TM]	482 Azelf [TM]	184 Azumarill [TM]	298 Azurill [TM]	371 Bagon [TM]	343 Baltoy [TM]
		354 Banette [TM]	689 Barbaracle [TM]	339 Barboach [TM]	550 Basculin [TM]	411 Bastiodon [TM]	153 Bayleef [TM]	614 Beartic [TM]
		267 Beautifly [TM]	015 Beedrill [TM]	606 Beheeyem [TM]	182 Bellossom [TM]	069 Bellsprout [TM]	712 Bergmite [TM]	400 Bibarel [TM]
		399 Bidoof [TM]	688 Binacle [TM]	625 Bisharp [TM]	009 Blastoise [TM]	257 Blaziken [TM]	242 Blissey [TM]	522 Blitzle [TM]
		525 Boldore [TM]	438 Bonsly [TM]	626 Bouffalant [TM]	654 Braixen [TM]	628 Braviary [TM]	286 Breloom [TM]	437 Bronzong [TM]
		436 Bronzor [TM]	406 Budew [TM]	418 Buizel [TM]	001 Bulbasaur [TM]	427 Buneary [TM]	659 Bunnelby [TM]	012 Butterfree [TM]
		331 Cacnea [TM]	332 Cacturne [TM]	323 Camerupt [TM]	703 Carbink [TM]	455 Carnivine [TM]	565 Carracosta [TM]	318 Carvanha [TM]
		351 Castform [TM]	251 Celebi [TM]	609 Chandelure [TM]	113 Chansey [TM]	006 Charizard [TM]	004 Charmander [TM]	005 Charmeleon [TM]
		441 Chatot [1, TM]	421 Cherrim [TM]	420 Cherubi [TM]	652 Chesnaught [TM]	650 Chespin [TM]	152 Chikorita [TM]	390 Chimchar [TM]
		358 Chimecho [TM]	170 Chinchou [TM]	433 Chingling [TM]	573 Cinccino [TM]	366 Clamperl [TM]	692 Clauncher [TM]	693 Clawitzer [TM]
		344 Claydol [TM]	036 Clefable [TM]	035 Clefairy [TM]	173 Cleffa [TM]	091 Cloyster [TM]	638 Cobalion [TM]	563 Cofagrigus [TM]
		256 Combusken [TM]	534 Conkeldurr [TM]	341 Corphish [TM]	222 Corsola [TM]	546 Cottonee [TM]	346 Cradily [TM]	408 Cranidos [TM]
		342 Crawdaunt [TM]	488 Cresselia [TM]	453 Croagunk [TM]	169 Crobat [TM]	159 Croconaw [TM]	558 Crustle [TM]	615 Cryogonal [TM]
		613 Cubchoo [TM]	104 Cubone [TM]	155 Cyndaquil [TM]	491 Darkrai [TM]	555 Darmanitan [TM]	554 Darumaka [TM]	702 Dedenne [TM]
		585 Deerling [TM]	633 Deino [TM]	301 Delcatty [TM]	225 Delibird [TM]	655 Delphox [TM]	386 Deoxys (Atk) [TM]	386 Deoxys (Def) [TM]
		386 Deoxys (Nor) [TM]	386 Deoxys (Spd) [TM]	087 Dewgong [TM]	502 Dewott [TM]	483 Dialga [TM]	719 Diancie [TM]	660 Diggersby [TM]
		050 Diglett [TM]	085 Dodrio [TM]	084 Doduo [TM]	232 Donphan [TM]	680 Doublade [TM]	691 Dragalge [TM]	148 Dragonair [TM]
		149 Dragonite [TM]	452 Drapion [TM]	147 Dratini [TM]	426 Drifblim [TM]	425 Drifloon [TM]	529 Drilbur [TM]	096 Drowzee [TM]
		621 Druddigon [TM]	580 Ducklett [TM]	051 Dugtrio [TM]	206 Dunsparce [TM]	578 Duosion [TM]	632 Durant [TM]	356 Dusclops [TM]
		477 Dusknoir [TM]	355 Duskull [TM]	269 Dustox [TM]	557 Dwebble [TM]	603 Eelektrik [TM]	604 Eelektross [TM]	133 Eevee [TM]
		023 Ekans [TM]	125 Electabuzz [TM]	466 Electivire [TM]	309 Electrike [TM]	101 Electrode [TM]	239 Elekid [TM]	605 Elgyem [TM]
		500 Emboar [TM]	587 Emolga [TM]	395 Empoleon [TM]	244 Entei [TM]	589 Escavalier [TM]	196 Espeon [TM]	677 Espurr [TM]
		530 Excadrill [TM]	102 Exeggcute [TM]	103 Exeggutor [TM]	295 Exploud [TM]	083 Farfetch'd [TM]	022 Fearow [TM]	349 Feebas [TM]
		653 Fennekin [TM]	160 Feraligatr [TM]	597 Ferroseed [TM]	598 Ferrothorn [TM]	456 Finneon [TM]	180 Flaaffy [TM]	669 Flabébé [TM]
		136 Flareon [TM]	662 Fletchinder [TM]	661 Fletchling [TM]	419 Floatzel [TM]	670 Floette [TM]	671 Florges [TM]	330 Flygon [TM]
		590 Foongus [TM]	205 Forretress [TM]	611 Fraxure [TM]	592 Frillish [TM]	656 Froakie [TM]	657 Frogadier [TM]	478 Froslass [TM]
		676 Furfrou [TM]	162 Furret [TM]	444 Gabite [TM]	475 Gallade [TM]	596 Galvantula [TM]	569 Garbodor [TM]	445 Garchomp [TM]
		282 Gardevoir [TM]	092 Gastly [TM]	423 Gastrodon [TM]	649 Genesect [TM]	094 Gengar [TM]	074 Geodude [TM]	443 Gible [TM]
		526 Gigalith [TM]	203 Girafarig [TM]	487 Giratina (Alt) [TM]	487 Giratina (Ori) [TM]	471 Glaceon [TM]	362 Glalie [TM]	431 Glameow [TM]
		207 Gligar [TM]	472 Gliscor [TM]	044 Gloom [TM]	673 Gogoat [TM]	042 Golbat [TM]	118 Goldeen [TM]	055 Golduck [TM]

	Move	Pokémon that can learn it						
Normal	Confide (TM100)	076 Golem [TM]	622 Golett [TM]	623 Golurk [TM]	706 Goodra [TM]	704 Goomy [TM]	368 Gorebyss [TM]	574 Gothita [TM]
		576 Gothitelle [TM]	575 Gothorita [TM]	711 Gourgeist [TM]	210 Granbull [TM]	075 Graveler [TM]	658 Greninja [TM]	088 Grimer [TM]
		388 Grotle [TM]	383 Groudon [TM]	253 Grovyle [TM]	058 Growlithe [TM]	326 Grumpig [TM]	316 Gulpin [TM]	533 Gurdurr [TM]
		130 Gyarados [TM]	440 Happiny [TM]	297 Hariyama [TM]	093 Haunter [TM]	701 Hawlucha [TM]	612 Haxorus [TM]	631 Heatmor [TM]
		485 Heatran [TM]	695 Heliolisk [TM]	694 Helioptile [TM]	214 Heracross [TM]	507 Herdier [TM]	449 Hippopotas [TM]	450 Hippowdon [TM]
		107 Hitmonchan [TM]	106 Hitmonlee [TM]	237 Hitmontop [TM]	430 Honchkrow [TM]	679 Honedge [TM]	250 Ho-Oh [TM]	163 Hoothoot [TM]
		187 Hoppip [TM]	116 Horsea [TM]	229 Houndoom [TM]	228 Houndour [TM]	367 Huntail [TM]	635 Hydreigon [TM]	097 Hypno [TM]
		174 Igglybuff [TM]	314 Illumise [TM]	392 Infernape [TM]	686 Inkay [TM]	002 Ivysaur [TM]	593 Jellicent [TM]	039 Jigglypuff [TM]
		385 Jirachi [TM]	135 Jolteon [TM]	595 Joltik [TM]	189 Jumpluff [TM]	124 Jynx [TM]	140 Kabuto [TM]	141 Kabutops [TM]
		064 Kadabra [TM]	115 Kangaskhan [TM]	588 Karrablast [TM]	352 Kecleon [TM]	647 Keldeo [TM]	230 Kingdra [TM]	099 Kingler [TM]
		281 Kirlia [TM]	600 Klang [TM]	707 Klefki [TM]	599 Klink [TM]	601 Klinklang [TM]	109 Koffing [TM]	098 Krabby [TM]
		402 Kricketune [TM]	552 Krokorok [TM]	553 Krookodile [TM]	382 Kyogre [TM]	646 Kyurem (Blk) [TM]	646 Kyurem (Wht) [TM]	646 Kyurem [TM]
		305 Lairon [TM]	608 Lampent [TM]	645 Landorus [TM]	171 Lanturn [TM]	131 Lapras [TM]	636 Larvesta [TM]	246 Larvitar [TM]
		380 Latias [TM]	381 Latios [TM]	470 Leafeon [TM]	542 Leavanny [TM]	166 Ledian [TM]	165 Ledyba [TM]	463 Lickilicky [TM]
		108 Lickitung [TM]	510 Liepard [TM]	345 Lileep [TM]	549 Lilligant [TM]	506 Lillipup [TM]	264 Linoone [TM]	667 Litleo [TM]
		607 Litwick [TM]	271 Lombre [TM]	428 Lopunny [TM]	270 Lotad [TM]	294 Loudred [TM]	448 Lucario [TM]	272 Ludicolo [TM]
		249 Lugia [TM]	457 Lumineon [TM]	337 Lunatone [TM]	370 Luvdisc [TM]	404 Luxio [TM]	405 Luxray [TM]	068 Machamp [TM]
		067 Machoke [TM]	066 Machop [TM]	240 Magby [TM]	219 Magcargo [TM]	126 Magmar [TM]	467 Magmortar [TM]	081 Magnemite [TM]
		082 Magneton [TM]	462 Magnezone [TM]	296 Makuhita [TM]	687 Malamar [TM]	473 Mamoswine [TM]	490 Manaphy [TM]	630 Mandibuzz [TM]
		310 Manectric [TM]	056 Mankey [TM]	226 Mantine [TM]	458 Mantyke [TM]	556 Maractus [TM]	179 Mareep [TM]	183 Marill [TM]
		105 Marowak [TM]	259 Marshtomp [TM]	284 Masquerain [TM]	303 Mawile [TM]	308 Medicham [TM]	307 Meditite [TM]	154 Meganium [TM]
		648 Meloetta [TM]	678 Meowstic (F) [TM]	678 Meowstic (M) [TM]	052 Meowth [TM]	481 Mesprit [TM]	376 Metagross [TM]	375 Metang [TM]
		151 Mew [TM]	150 Mewtwo [TM]	619 Mienfoo [TM]	620 Mienshao [TM]	262 Mightyena [TM]	350 Milotic [TM]	241 Miltank [TM]
		439 Mime Jr. [TM]	572 Minccino [TM]	312 Minun [TM]	200 Misdreavus [TM]	429 Mismagius [TM]	146 Moltres [TM]	391 Monferno [TM]
		414 Mothim [TM]	122 Mr. Mime [TM]	258 Mudkip [TM]	089 Muk [TM]	446 Munchlax [TM]	517 Munna [TM]	198 Murkrow [TM]
		518 Musharna [TM]	177 Natu [TM]	034 Nidoking [TM]	031 Nidoqueen [TM]	029 Nidoran ♀ [TM]	032 Nidoran ♂ [TM]	030 Nidorina [TM]
		033 Nidorino [TM]	290 Nincada [TM]	038 Ninetales [TM]	291 Ninjask [TM]	164 Noctowl [TM]	714 Noibat [TM]	715 Noivern [TM]
		299 Nosepass [TM]	322 Numel [TM]	274 Nuzleaf [TM]	224 Octillery [TM]	043 Oddish [TM]	138 Omanyte [TM]	139 Omastar [TM]
		095 Onix [TM]	501 Oshawott [TM]	417 Pachirisu [TM]	484 Palkia [TM]	536 Palpitoad [TM]	674 Pancham [TM]	675 Pangoro [TM]
		515 Panpour [TM]	511 Pansage [TM]	513 Pansear [TM]	046 Paras [TM]	047 Parasect [TM]	504 Patrat [TM]	624 Pawniard [TM]
		279 Pelipper [TM]	053 Persian [TM]	548 Petilil [TM]	231 Phanpy [TM]	708 Phantump [TM]	489 Phione [TM]	172 Pichu [TM]
		018 Pidgeot [TM]	017 Pidgeotto [TM]	016 Pidgey [TM]	519 Pidove [TM]	499 Pignite [TM]	025 Pikachu [TM]	221 Piloswine [TM]
		204 Pineco [TM]	127 Pinsir [TM]	393 Piplup [TM]	311 Plusle [TM]	186 Politoed [TM]	060 Poliwag [TM]	061 Poliwhirl [TM]
		062 Poliwrath [TM]	077 Ponyta [TM]	261 Poochyena [TM]	137 Porygon [TM]	233 Porygon2 [TM]	474 Porygon-Z [TM]	057 Primeape [TM]
		394 Prinplup [TM]	476 Probopass [TM]	054 Psyduck [TM]	710 Pumpkaboo [TM]	247 Pupitar [TM]	509 Purrloin [TM]	432 Purugly [TM]
		668 Pyroar [TM]	195 Quagsire [TM]	156 Quilava [TM]	651 Quilladin [TM]	211 Qwilfish [TM]	026 Raichu [TM]	243 Raikou [TM]
		280 Ralts [TM]	409 Rampardos [TM]	078 Rapidash [TM]	020 Raticate [TM]	019 Rattata [TM]	384 Rayquaza [TM]	378 Regice [TM]
		486 Regigigas [TM]	377 Regirock [TM]	379 Registeel [TM]	369 Relicanth [TM]	223 Remoraid [TM]	643 Reshiram [TM]	579 Reuniclus [TM]
		112 Rhydon [TM]	111 Rhyhorn [TM]	464 Rhyperior [TM]	447 Riolu [TM]	524 Roggenrola [TM]	315 Roselia [TM]	407 Roserade [TM]
		479 Rotom (Fan) [TM]	479 Rotom (Frost) [TM]	479 Rotom (Heat) [TM]	479 Rotom (Mow) [TM]	479 Rotom (Wash) [TM]	479 Rotom [TM]	627 Rufflet [TM]
		302 Sableye [TM]	373 Salamence [TM]	503 Samurott [TM]	551 Sandile [TM]	027 Sandshrew [TM]	028 Sandslash [TM]	539 Sawk [TM]
		586 Sawsbuck [TM]	254 Sceptile [TM]	212 Scizor [TM]	545 Scolipede [TM]	560 Scrafty [TM]	559 Scraggy [TM]	123 Scyther [TM]
		117 Seadra [TM]	119 Seaking [TM]	364 Sealeo [TM]	273 Seedot [TM]	086 Seel [TM]	537 Seismitoad [TM]	161 Sentret [TM]
		497 Serperior [TM]	496 Servine [TM]	336 Seviper [TM]	540 Sewaddle [TM]	319 Sharpedo [TM]	492 Shaymin (Land) [TM]	492 Shaymin (Sky) [TM]
		292 Shedinja [TM]	372 Shelgon [TM]	090 Shellder [TM]	422 Shellos [TM]	616 Shelmet [TM]	410 Shieldon [TM]	275 Shiftry [TM]
		403 Shinx [TM]	285 Shroomish [TM]	213 Shuckle [TM]	353 Shuppet [TM]	561 Sigilyph [TM]	516 Simipour [TM]	512 Simisage [TM]
		514 Simisear [TM]	227 Skarmory [TM]	672 Skiddo [TM]	188 Skiploom [TM]	300 Skitty [TM]	451 Skorupi [TM]	690 Skrelp [TM]
		435 Skuntank [TM]	289 Slaking [TM]	287 Slakoth [TM]	705 Sliggoo [TM]	080 Slowbro [TM]	199 Slowking [TM]	079 Slowpoke [TM]
		218 Slugma [TM]	685 Slurpuff [TM]	238 Smoochum [TM]	215 Sneasel [TM]	495 Snivy [TM]	143 Snorlax [TM]	361 Snorunt [TM]
		459 Snover [TM]	209 Snubbull [TM]	577 Solosis [TM]	338 Solrock [TM]	021 Spearow [TM]	363 Spheal [TM]	167 Spinarak [TM]
		327 Spinda [TM]	442 Spiritomb [TM]	325 Spoink [TM]	682 Spritzee [TM]	007 Squirtle [TM]	234 Stantler [TM]	398 Staraptor [TM]
		397 Staravia [TM]	396 Starly [TM]	121 Starmie [TM]	120 Staryu [TM]	208 Steelix [TM]	508 Stoutland [TM]	618 Stunfisk [TM]
		434 Stunky [TM]	185 Sudowoodo [TM]	245 Suicune [TM]	192 Sunflora [TM]	191 Sunkern [TM]	283 Surskit [TM]	333 Swablu [TM]
		541 Swadloon [TM]	317 Swalot [TM]	260 Swampert [TM]	581 Swanna [TM]	277 Swellow [TM]	220 Swinub [TM]	684 Swirlix [TM]
		528 Swoobat [TM]	700 Sylveon [TM]	276 Taillow [TM]	663 Talonflame [TM]	114 Tangela [TM]	465 Tangrowth [TM]	128 Tauros [TM]
		216 Teddiursa [TM]	072 Tentacool [TM]	073 Tentacruel [TM]	498 Tepig [TM]	639 Terrakion [TM]	538 Throh [TM]	642 Thundurus [TM]
		532 Timburr [TM]	564 Tirtouga [TM]	468 Togekiss [TM]	175 Togepi [TM]	176 Togetic [TM]	255 Torchic [TM]	324 Torkoal [TM]
		641 Tornadus [TM]	389 Torterra [TM]	158 Totodile [TM]	454 Toxicroak [TM]	520 Tranquill [TM]	328 Trapinch [TM]	252 Treecko [TM]
		709 Trevenant [TM]	357 Tropius [TM]	568 Trubbish [TM]	387 Turtwig [TM]	535 Tympole [TM]	157 Typhlosion [TM]	248 Tyranitar [TM]
		697 Tyrantrum [TM]	236 Tyrogue [TM]	696 Tyrunt [TM]	197 Umbreon [TM]	521 Unfezant [TM]	217 Ursaring [TM]	480 Uxie [TM]
		583 Vanillish [TM]	582 Vanillite [TM]	584 Vanilluxe [TM]	134 Vaporeon [TM]	543 Venipede [TM]	049 Venomoth [TM]	048 Venonat [TM]
		003 Venusaur [TM]	416 Vespiquen [TM]	329 Vibrava [TM]	494 Victini [TM]	071 Victreebel [TM]	288 Vigoroth [TM]	045 Vileplume [TM]
		640 Virizion [TM]	666 Vivillon [TM]	313 Volbeat [TM]	637 Volcarona [TM]	100 Voltorb [TM]	629 Vullaby [TM]	037 Vulpix [TM]
		320 Wailmer [TM]	321 Wailord [TM]	365 Walrein [TM]	008 Wartortle [TM]	505 Watchog [TM]	461 Weavile [TM]	070 Weepinbell [TM]
		110 Weezing [TM]	547 Whimsicott [TM]	544 Whirlipede [TM]	340 Whiscash [TM]	293 Whismur [TM]	040 Wigglytuff [TM]	278 Wingull [TM]

	Move	Pokémon that can learn it						
Normal	Confide (TM100)	527 Woobat [TM]	194 Wooper [TM]	413 Wormadam (Plant) [TM]	413 Wormadam (Sand) [TM]	413 Wormadam (Trash) [TM]	178 Xatu [TM]	716 Xerneas [TM]
		562 Yamask [TM]	193 Yanma [TM]	469 Yanmega [TM]	717 Yveltal [TM]	335 Zangoose [TM]	145 Zapdos [TM]	523 Zebstrika [TM]
		644 Zekrom [TM]	263 Zigzagoon [TM]	571 Zoroark [TM]	570 Zorua [TM]	041 Zubat [TM]	634 Zweilous [TM]	718 Zygarde [TM]
Ghost	Confuse Ray	181 Ampharos [29]	437 Bronzong [11]	436 Bronzor [11]	609 Chandelure [1]	170 Chinchou [17]	366 Clamperl [E]	222 Corsola [E]
		346 Cradily [13]	169 Crobat [17]	615 Cryogonal [45]	356 Dusclops [30]	477 Dusknoir [30]	355 Duskull [30]	349 Feebas [E]
		180 Flaaffy [29]	592 Frillish [E]	478 Froslass [32]	092 Gastly [19]	094 Gengar [19]	042 Golbat [17]	711 Gourgeist [1]
		326 Grumpig [18]	093 Haunter [19]	314 Illumise [E]	140 Kabuto [E]	608 Lampent [10]	171 Lanturn [17]	131 Lapras [7]
		345 Lileep [13]	607 Litwick [10]	240 Magby [26]	126 Magmar [26]	467 Magmortar [26]	226 Mantine [11]	458 Mantyke [11]
		179 Mareep [25]	439 Mime Jr. [E]	200 Misdreavus [14]	122 Mr. Mime [E]	198 Murkrow [E]	177 Natu [23]	038 Ninetales [1]
		708 Phantump [1]	054 Psyduck [E]	710 Pumpkaboo [1]	280 Ralts [E]	486 Regigigas [1]	479 Rotom (Fan) [1]	479 Rotom (Frost) [1]
		479 Rotom (Heat) [1]	479 Rotom (Mow) [1]	479 Rotom (Wash) [1]	479 Rotom [1]	302 Sableye [31]	292 Shedinja [29]	353 Shuppet [E]
		451 Skorupi [E]	577 Solosis [E]	442 Spiritomb [1]	325 Spoink [18]	234 Stantler [23]	121 Starmie [40]	120 Staryu [40]
		072 Tentacool [E]	709 Trevenant [1]	197 Umbreon [17]	416 Vespiquen [1]	313 Volbeat [8]	037 Vulpix [12]	505 Watchog [20]
		178 Xatu [23]	041 Zubat [17]					
Psychic	Confusion	065 Alakazam [1, 16]	482 Azelf [1]	343 Baltoy [1]	606 Beheeyem [1]	437 Bronzong [1]	436 Bronzor [1]	012 Butterfree [1, 10]
		251 Celebi [1]	358 Chimecho [1, 10]	433 Chingling [10]	344 Claydol [1]	488 Cresselia [1]	096 Drowzee [9]	269 Dustox [12]
		605 Elgyem [1]	196 Espeon [9]	677 Espurr [9]	102 Exeggcute [27]	103 Exeggutor [1]	475 Gallade [1, 4]	282 Gardevoir [1, 4]
		203 Girafarig [1]	055 Golduck [11]	368 Gorebyss [1]	574 Gothita [3]	576 Gothitelle [1, 3]	575 Gothorita [1, 3]	163 Hoothoot [21]
		187 Hoppip [E]	097 Hypno [1, 9]	385 Jirachi [1]	064 Kadabra [1, 16]	281 Kirlia [1, 4]	337 Lunatone [1]	308 Medicham [1, 7]
		307 Meditite [7]	648 Meloetta [11]	678 Meowstic (F) [9]	678 Meowstic (M) [9]	481 Mesprit [1]	376 Metagross [1, 20]	375 Metang [1, 20]
		150 Mewtwo [1]	439 Mime Jr. [1]	414 Mothim [23]	122 Mr. Mime [1]	032 Nidoran ♂ [E]	164 Noctowl [22]	054 Psyduck [11]
		280 Ralts [4]	080 Slowbro [14]	199 Slowking [14]	079 Slowpoke [14]	238 Smoochum [15]	338 Solrock [1]	528 Swoobat [1]
		114 Tangela [E]	480 Uxie [1]	049 Venomoth [11]	048 Venonat [11]	494 Victini [1]	527 Woobat [1]	413 Wormadam (Plant) [23]
		413 Wormadam (Sand) [23]	413 Wormadam (Trash) [23]					
Normal	Constrict	168 Ariados [1, 8]	346 Cradily [1]	426 Drifblim [1]	425 Drifloon [1]	592 Frillish [E]	686 Inkay [1]	345 Lileep [1]
		687 Malamar [1]	224 Octillery [1, 6]	138 Omanyte [1]	139 Omastar [1]	213 Shuckle [1]	167 Spinarak [8]	114 Tangela [1]
		465 Tangrowth [1]	072 Tentacool [7]	073 Tentacruel [1, 7]				
	Conversion	137 Porygon [1]	233 Porygon2 [1]	474 Porygon-Z [1]				
	Conversion 2	137 Porygon [1]	233 Porygon2 [1]	474 Porygon-Z [1]				
	Copycat	298 Azurill [E]	438 Bonsly [1]	427 Buneary [E]	173 Cleffa [13]	669 Flabébé [E]	440 Happiny [5]	174 Igglybuff [11]
		481 Mesprit [1, 61]	439 Mime Jr. [4]	312 Minun [22]	122 Mr. Mime [4]	501 Oshawott [E]	311 Plusle [22]	509 Purrloin [E]
		447 Riolu [19]	300 Skitty [19]	238 Smoochum [41]	327 Spinda [5]	185 Sudowoodo [1]	684 Swirlix [E]	570 Zorua [E]
Psychic	Cosmic Power	493 Arceus [1]	343 Baltoy [22]	427 Buneary [E]	351 Castform [E]	358 Chimecho [E]	433 Chingling [E]	344 Claydol [22]
		035 Clefairy [34]	386 Deoxys (Atk) [55]	386 Deoxys (Nor) [55]	605 Elgyem [E]	385 Jirachi [60]	337 Lunatone [25]	561 Sigilyph [48]
		300 Skitty [E]	338 Solrock [25]	120 Staryu [49]				
Grass	Cotton Guard	334 Altaria [34]	181 Ampharos [46]	546 Cottonee [37]	180 Flaaffy [43]	676 Furfrou [48]	187 Hoppip [E]	556 Maractus [1, 55]
		179 Mareep [36]	685 Slurpuff [41]	333 Swablu [34]	684 Swirlix [41]			
	Cotton Spore	181 Ampharos [11]	406 Budew [E]	331 Cacnea [46]	332 Cacturne [49]	546 Cottonee [17]	180 Flaaffy [11]	187 Hoppip [34]
		189 Jumpluff [44]	556 Maractus [18]	179 Mareep [11]	315 Roselia [E]	188 Skiploom [40]	685 Slurpuff [17]	684 Swirlix [17]
		547 Whimsicott [1]						
Fighting	Counter	190 Aipom [E]	610 Axew [E]	438 Bonsly [33]	286 Breloom [22]	331 Cacnea [E]	113 Chansey [E]	004 Charmander [E]
		152 Chikorita [E]	390 Chimchar [E]	453 Croagunk [E]	386 Deoxys (Def) [73]	557 Dwebble [E]	207 Gligar [E]	704 Goomy [E]
		440 Happiny [E]	214 Heracross [19]	107 Hitmonchan [1, 61]	237 Hitmontop [28]	228 Houndour [E]	115 Kangaskhan [E]	588 Karrablast [E]
		270 Lotad [E]	448 Lucario [6]	066 Machop [E]	296 Makuhita [E]	056 Mankey [E]	308 Medicham [53]	307 Meditite [44]
		258 Mudkip [E]	446 Munchlax [E]	029 Nidoran ♀ [E]	032 Nidoran ♂ [E]	046 Paras [E]	231 Phanpy [E]	204 Pineco [E]
		019 Rattata [E]	111 Rhyhorn [E]	447 Riolu [6]	551 Sandile [E]	027 Sandshrew [E]	539 Sawk [21]	559 Scraggy [E]
		123 Scyther [E]	422 Shellos [E]	410 Shieldon [E]	289 Slaking [33]	287 Slakoth [30]	215 Sneasel [E]	143 Snorlax [E]
		185 Sudowoodo [33]	216 Teddiursa [E]	532 Timburr [E]	255 Torchic [E]	236 Tyrogue [E]	288 Vigoroth [33]	202 Wobbuffet [1]
		194 Wooper [E]	360 Wynaut [15]	335 Zangoose [E]	570 Zorua [E]			
Normal	Covet	190 Aipom [BP, E]	424 Ambipom [BP]	059 Arcanine [BP]	683 Aromatisse [BP]	531 Audino [BP]	184 Azumarill [BP]	298 Azurill [BP]
		614 Beartic [BP]	400 Bibarel [BP]	399 Bidoof [BP]	242 Blissey [BP]	438 Bonsly [BP]	654 Braixen [BP]	406 Budew [BP]
		427 Buneary [BP]	703 Carbink [BP]	113 Chansey [BP]	390 Chimchar [BP]	573 Cinccino [BP]	036 Clefable [BP]	035 Clefairy [BP]
		173 Cleffa [BP, E]	546 Cottonee [BP]	613 Cubchoo [BP]	155 Cyndaquil [BP, E]	702 Dedenne [BP, E]	301 Delcatty [BP]	655 Delphox [BP]
		502 Dewott [BP]	719 Diancie [BP]	133 Eevee [23, BP, E]	125 Electabuzz [BP]	466 Electivire [BP]	239 Elekid [BP]	500 Emboar [BP]
		587 Emolga [BP, E]	395 Empoleon [BP]	196 Espeon [BP]	677 Espurr [5, BP]	083 Farfetch'd [BP, E]	653 Fennekin [BP]	669 Flabébé [BP]
		136 Flareon [BP]	670 Floette [BP]	671 Florges [BP]	162 Furret [BP]	471 Glaceon [BP]	431 Glameow [BP]	574 Gothita [BP]
		576 Gothitelle [BP]	575 Gothorita [BP]	210 Granbull [BP]	058 Growlithe [BP, E]	326 Grumpig [BP]	440 Happiny [BP]	507 Herdier [BP]
		107 Hitmonchan [BP]	106 Hitmonlee [BP]	237 Hitmontop [BP]	174 Igglybuff [BP, E]	314 Illumise [47, BP]	392 Infernape [BP]	039 Jigglypuff [BP]
		135 Jolteon [BP]	124 Jynx [BP]	115 Kangaskhan [BP]	647 Keldeo [BP]	707 Klefki [BP]	380 Latias [BP]	470 Leafeon [BP]
		510 Liepard [BP]	549 Lilligant [BP]	506 Lillipup [BP]	264 Linoone [24, BP]	428 Lopunny [BP]	240 Magby [BP]	126 Magmar [BP]
		467 Magmortar [BP]	490 Manaphy [BP]	056 Mankey [1, BP]	183 Marill [BP]	648 Meloetta [BP]	678 Meowstic (F) [5, BP]	678 Meowstic (M) [5, BP]
		052 Meowth [BP]	151 Mew [BP]	262 Mightyena [BP]	439 Mime Jr. [BP]	572 Minccino [BP]	391 Monferno [BP]	122 Mr. Mime [BP]
		446 Munchlax [BP]	038 Ninetales [BP]	501 Oshawott [BP]	417 Pachirisu [BP, E]	674 Pancham [BP]	675 Pangoro [BP]	515 Panpour [BP, E]
		511 Pansage [BP, E]	513 Pansear [BP, E]	504 Patrat [BP]	053 Persian [BP]	548 Petilil [BP]	489 Phione [BP]	172 Pichu [BP]

Type	Move	Pokémon that can learn it						
Normal	Covet	499 Pignite [BP]	025 Pikachu [BP]	393 Piplup [BP]	261 Poochyena [BP, E]	057 Primeape [BP]	394 Prinplup [BP]	509 Purrloin [BP, E]
		432 Purugly [BP]	156 Quilava [BP]	026 Raichu [BP]	020 Raticate [BP]	019 Rattata [BP]	315 Roselia [BP]	407 Roserade [BP]
		503 Samurott [BP]	027 Sandshrew [BP]	028 Sandslash [BP]	161 Sentret [BP, E]	492 Shaymin (Land) [BP]	492 Shaymin (Sky) [BP]	516 Simipour [BP]
		512 Simisage [BP]	514 Simisear [BP]	300 Skitty [34, BP]	289 Slaking [23, BP]	287 Slakoth [22, BP]	685 Slurpuff [BP]	238 Smoochum [BP]
		143 Snorlax [BP]	209 Snubbull [BP]	327 Spinda [BP]	325 Spoink [BP]	682 Spritzee [BP]	508 Stoutland [BP]	185 Sudowoodo [BP]
		684 Swirlix [BP]	700 Sylveon [BP]	216 Teddiursa [1, BP]	498 Tepig [BP, E]	468 Togekiss [BP]	175 Togepi [BP]	176 Togetic [BP]
		157 Typhlosion [BP]	236 Tyrogue [BP]	197 Umbreon [BP]	217 Ursaring [1, BP]	134 Vaporeon [BP]	288 Vigoroth [BP]	037 Vulpix [BP]
		505 Watchog [BP]	547 Whimsicott [BP]	040 Wigglytuff [BP]	263 Zigzagoon [23, BP]	571 Zoroark [BP]	570 Zorua [BP]	
Water	Crabhammer	692 Clauncher [30, E]	693 Clawitzer [30]	341 Corphish [43]	342 Crawdaunt [48]	099 Kingler [56]	098 Krabby [41]	
Fairy	Crafty Shield	707 Klefki [23]						
Fighting	Cross Chop	689 Barbaracle [55]	688 Binacle [49]	453 Croagunk [E]	239 Elekid [E]	068 Machamp [47]	067 Machoke [47]	066 Machop [39]
		240 Magby [E]	296 Makuhita [E]	056 Mankey [37]	057 Primeape [41]	054 Psyduck [E]	447 Riolu [E]	216 Teddiursa [E]
Poison	Cross Poison	347 Anorith [E]	168 Ariados [55]	169 Crobat [1]	452 Drapion [57]	207 Gligar [E]	595 Joltik [E]	046 Paras [E]
		047 Parasect [1]	451 Skorupi [49]	167 Spinarak [47]				
Dark	Crunch	142 Aerodactyl [33]	024 Arbok [22]	566 Archen [35]	567 Archeops [35]	713 Avalugg [1, 65]	371 Bagon [25]	550 Basculin [24]
		455 Carnivine [41]	565 Carracosta [21]	318 Carvanha [36]	004 Charmander [E]	341 Corphish [39]	408 Cranidos [E]	342 Crawdaunt [43]
		159 Croconaw [30]	633 Deino [25]	452 Drapion [49]	621 Druddigon [25]	632 Durant [31]	603 Eelektrik [39]	604 Eelektross [1]
		309 Electrike [E]	295 Exploud [40]	160 Feraligatr [32]	419 Floatzel [1]	445 Garchomp [48]	203 Girafarig [37]	362 Glalie [41]
		210 Granbull [59]	388 Grotle [42]	058 Growlithe [39, E]	130 Gyarados [41]	485 Heatran [33]	507 Herdier [24]	449 Hippopotas [31]
		450 Hippowdon [31]	229 Houndoom [56]	228 Houndour [49]	367 Huntail [34]	635 Hydreigon [25]	115 Kangaskhan [37]	552 Krokorok [28]
		553 Krookodile [28]	246 Larvitar [41]	506 Lillipup [22]	667 Litleo [39]	404 Luxio [38]	405 Luxray [42]	303 Mawile [29]
		262 Mightyena [1, 44]	029 Nidoran ♀ [37]	030 Nidorina [43]	674 Pancham [39]	675 Pangoro [42]	515 Panpour [43]	511 Pansage [43]
		513 Pansear [43]	504 Patrat [16]	261 Poochyena [37]	247 Pupitar [47]	668 Pyroar [42]	243 Raikou [43]	020 Raticate [24]
		019 Rattata [22]	384 Rayquaza [20]	643 Reshiram [71]	111 Rhyhorn [E]	447 Riolu [E]	373 Salamence [25]	551 Sandile [28]
		560 Scrafty [38]	559 Scraggy [38]	336 Seviper [40]	319 Sharpedo [40]	372 Shelgon [25]	403 Shinx [33]	451 Skorupi [45]
		143 Snorlax [49]	361 Snorunt [41]	209 Snubbull [49, E]	208 Steelix [37]	508 Stoutland [24]	434 Stunky [E]	216 Teddiursa [E]
		642 Thundurus [49]	564 Tirtouga [21]	641 Tornadus [49]	389 Torterra [45]	158 Totodile [27, E]	328 Trapinch [22]	252 Treecko [E]
		387 Turtwig [37]	248 Tyranitar [47]	697 Tyrantrum [34]	696 Tyrunt [34]	365 Walrein [1]	505 Watchog [16]	644 Zekrom [71]
		634 Zweilous [25]	718 Zygarde [51]					
Normal	Crush Claw	347 Anorith [39]	348 Armaldo [39]	628 Braviary [46]	155 Cyndaquil [E]	529 Drilbur [E]	621 Druddigon [E]	604 Eelektross [1]
		115 Kangaskhan [E]	111 Rhyhorn [E]	627 Rufflet [46]	027 Sandshrew [E]	028 Sandslash [22]	287 Slakoth [E]	215 Sneasel [E]
		255 Torchic [E]	252 Treecko [E]	335 Zangoose [26]				
	Crush Grip	486 Regigigas [1, 75]						
Ghost	Curse	359 Absol [E]	142 Aerodactyl [E]	347 Anorith [E]	304 Aron [E]	713 Avalugg [22]	354 Banette [26]	712 Bergmite [22]
		400 Bibarel [53]	399 Bidoof [45]	438 Bonsly [E]	001 Bulbasaur [E]	323 Camerupt [29]	565 Carracosta [35]	650 Chespin [E]
		358 Chimecho [E]	433 Chingling [E]	563 Cofagrigus [29]	222 Corsola [E]	408 Cranidos [E]	206 Dunsparce [E]	356 Dusclops [33]
		477 Dusknoir [33]	355 Duskull [33]	557 Dwebble [E]	133 Eevee [E]	309 Electrike [E]	102 Exeggcute [E]	083 Farfetch'd [E]
		597 Ferroseed [9]	598 Ferrothorn [1, 9]	092 Gastly [12]	094 Gengar [12]	074 Geodude [E]	622 Golett [40]	623 Golurk [40]
		704 Goomy [E]	088 Grimer [E]	388 Grotle [17]	316 Gulpin [E]	093 Haunter [12]	631 Heatmor [E]	449 Hippopotas [E]
		109 Koffing [E]	608 Lampent [45]	131 Lapras [E]	246 Larvitar [E]	108 Lickitung [E]	345 Lileep [E]	607 Litwick [43]
		241 Miltank [E]	200 Misdreavus [E]	258 Mudkip [E]	446 Munchlax [E]	517 Munna [E]	322 Numel [29]	095 Onix [4]
		708 Phantump [28]	378 Regice [25]	377 Regirock [25]	379 Registeel [25]	111 Rhyhorn [E]	524 Roggenrola [E]	422 Shellos [E]
		616 Shelmet [13]	410 Shieldon [E]	353 Shuppet [26]	227 Skarmory [E]	287 Slakoth [E]	080 Slowbro [1]	199 Slowking [1]
		079 Slowpoke [1]	218 Slugma [E]	143 Snorlax [E]	363 Spheal [E]	442 Spiritomb [1]	208 Steelix [4]	618 Stunfisk [E]
		185 Sudowoodo [E]	191 Sunkern [E]	220 Swinub [E]	498 Tepig [E]	564 Tirtouga [35]	255 Torchic [E]	324 Torkoal [22]
		389 Torterra [17]	709 Trevenant [28]	357 Tropius [E]	568 Trubbish [E]	387 Turtwig [17]	696 Tyrunt [E]	320 Wailmer [E]
		194 Wooper [E]	562 Yamask [29]	335 Zangoose [E]	041 Zubat [E]			
Normal	Cut (HM01)	359 Absol [HM]	681 Aegislash [HM]	306 Aggron [HM]	190 Aipom [HM]	424 Ambipom [HM]	347 Anorith [HM]	493 Arceus [HM]
		566 Archen [HM]	567 Archeops [HM]	348 Armaldo [HM]	304 Aron [HM]	610 Axew [HM]	371 Bagon [HM]	689 Barbaracle [HM]
		550 Basculin [HM]	153 Bayleef [HM]	614 Beartic [HM]	015 Beedrill [HM]	182 Bellossom [HM]	069 Bellsprout [HM]	400 Bibarel [HM]
		399 Bidoof [HM]	688 Binacle [HM]	625 Bisharp [HM]	257 Blaziken [HM]	626 Bouffalant [HM]	654 Braixen [HM]	628 Braviary [HM]
		286 Breloom [HM]	406 Budew [HM]	001 Bulbasaur [HM]	427 Buneary [HM]	659 Bunnelby [HM]	331 Cacnea [HM]	332 Cacturne [HM]
		455 Carnivine [HM]	251 Celebi [HM]	006 Charizard [HM]	004 Charmander [HM]	005 Charmeleon [HM]	652 Chesnaught [HM]	650 Chespin [HM]
		152 Chikorita [HM]	390 Chimchar [HM]	692 Clauncher [HM]	693 Clawitzer [HM]	638 Cobalion [HM]	256 Combusken [HM]	341 Corphish [HM]
		342 Crawdaunt [HM]	159 Croconaw [HM]	558 Crustle [HM]	613 Cubchoo [HM]	155 Cyndaquil [HM]	491 Darkrai [HM]	702 Dedenne [HM]
		655 Delphox [HM]	386 Deoxys (Atk) [HM]	386 Deoxys (Def) [HM]	386 Deoxys (Nor) [HM]	386 Deoxys (Spd) [HM]	502 Dewott [HM]	483 Dialga [HM]
		660 Diggersby [HM]	050 Diglett [HM]	680 Doublade [HM]	149 Dragonite [HM]	452 Drapion [HM]	426 Drifblim [HM]	425 Drifloon [HM]
		529 Drilbur [HM]	621 Druddigon [HM]	051 Dugtrio [HM]	632 Durant [HM]	557 Dwebble [HM]	604 Eelektross [HM]	587 Emolga [HM]
		395 Empoleon [HM]	244 Entei [HM]	589 Escavalier [HM]	196 Espeon [HM]	677 Espurr [HM]	530 Excadrill [HM]	083 Farfetch'd [HM]
		653 Fennekin [HM]	160 Feraligatr [HM]	598 Ferrothorn [HM]	611 Fraxure [HM]	656 Froakie [HM]	657 Frogadier [HM]	162 Furret [HM]
		444 Gabite [HM]	475 Gallade [HM]	596 Galvantula [HM]	445 Garchomp [HM]	443 Gible [HM]	487 Giratina (Alt) [HM]	487 Giratina (Ori) [HM]
		431 Glameow [HM]	207 Gligar [HM]	472 Gliscor [HM]	044 Gloom [HM]	658 Greninja [HM]	388 Grotle [HM]	383 Groudon [HM]
		253 Grovyle [HM]	701 Hawlucha [HM]	612 Haxorus [HM]	631 Heatmor [HM]	695 Heliolisk [HM]	694 Helioptile [HM]	214 Heracross [HM]
		679 Honedge [HM]	392 Infernape [HM]	686 Inkay [HM]	002 Ivysaur [HM]	595 Joltik [HM]	141 Kabutops [HM]	115 Kangaskhan [HM]

	Move	Pokémon that can learn it						
Normal	Cut (HM01)	588 Karrablast [HM]	352 Kecleon [HM]	647 Keldeo [HM]	099 Kingler [HM]	707 Klefki [HM]	098 Krabby [HM]	402 Kricketune [HM]
		552 Krokorok [HM]	553 Krookodile [HM]	646 Kyurem (Blk) [HM]	646 Kyurem (Wht) [HM]	646 Kyurem [HM]	305 Lairon [HM]	380 Latias [HM]
		381 Latios [HM]	542 Leavanny [HM]	463 Lickilicky [HM]	108 Lickitung [HM]	510 Liepard [HM]	549 Lilligant [HM]	264 Linoone [HM]
		428 Lopunny [HM]	687 Malamar [HM]	630 Mandibuzz [HM]	154 Meganium [HM]	678 Meowstic (F) [HM]	678 Meowstic (M) [HM]	052 Meowth [HM]
		376 Metagross [HM]	375 Metang [HM]	151 Mew [HM]	391 Monferno [HM]	034 Nidoking [HM]	031 Nidoqueen [HM]	029 Nidoran ♀ [HM]
		032 Nidoran ♂ [HM]	030 Nidorina [HM]	033 Nidorino [HM]	290 Nincada [HM]	291 Ninjask [HM]	714 Noibat [HM]	715 Noivern [HM]
		274 Nuzleaf [HM]	043 Oddish [HM]	501 Oshawott [HM]	417 Pachirisu [HM]	484 Palkia [HM]	674 Pancham [HM]	675 Pangoro [HM]
		515 Panpour [HM]	511 Pansage [HM]	513 Pansear [HM]	046 Paras [HM]	047 Parasect [HM]	504 Patrat [HM]	624 Pawniard [HM]
		053 Persian [HM]	548 Petilil [HM]	708 Phantump [HM]	127 Pinsir [HM]	393 Piplup [HM]	394 Prinplup [HM]	509 Purrloin [HM]
		432 Purugly [HM]	156 Quilava [HM]	651 Quilladin [HM]	243 Raikou [HM]	409 Rampardos [HM]	020 Raticate [HM]	019 Rattata [HM]
		643 Reshiram [HM]	112 Rhydon [HM]	464 Rhyperior [HM]	315 Roselia [HM]	407 Roserade [HM]	627 Rufflet [HM]	302 Sableye [HM]
		373 Salamence [HM]	503 Samurott [HM]	551 Sandile [HM]	027 Sandshrew [HM]	028 Sandslash [HM]	586 Sawsbuck [HM]	254 Sceptile [HM]
		212 Scizor [HM]	545 Scolipede [HM]	123 Scyther [HM]	161 Sentret [HM]	497 Serperior [HM]	496 Servine [HM]	540 Sewaddle [HM]
		292 Shedinja [HM]	372 Shelgon [HM]	275 Shiftry [HM]	516 Simipour [HM]	512 Simisage [HM]	514 Simisear [HM]	227 Skarmory [HM]
		451 Skorupi [HM]	435 Skuntank [HM]	289 Slaking [HM]	287 Slakoth [HM]	215 Sneasel [HM]	495 Snivy [HM]	208 Steelix [HM]
		434 Stunky [HM]	245 Suicune [HM]	192 Sunflora [HM]	191 Sunkern [HM]	541 Swadloon [HM]	700 Sylveon [HM]	114 Tangela [HM]
		465 Tangrowth [HM]	216 Teddiursa [HM]	072 Tentacool [HM]	073 Tentacruel [HM]	639 Terrakion [HM]	255 Torchic [HM]	389 Torterra [HM]
		158 Totodile [HM]	454 Toxicroak [HM]	252 Treecko [HM]	709 Trevenant [HM]	357 Tropius [HM]	387 Turtwig [HM]	157 Typhlosion [HM]
		248 Tyranitar [HM]	197 Umbreon [HM]	217 Ursaring [HM]	003 Venusaur [HM]	416 Vespiquen [HM]	071 Victreebel [HM]	288 Vigoroth [HM]
		045 Vileplume [HM]	640 Virizion [HM]	629 Vullaby [HM]	505 Watchog [HM]	461 Weavile [HM]	070 Weepinbell [HM]	716 Xerneas [HM]
		717 Yveltal [HM]	644 Zekrom [HM]	263 Zigzagoon [HM]	571 Zoroark [HM]	570 Zorua [HM]		

D

	Move	Pokémon that can learn it						
Dark	Dark Pulse (TM97)	359 Absol [TM]	306 Aggron [TM]	698 Amaura [TM]	024 Arbok [TM]	493 Arceus [TM]	699 Aurorus [TM]	354 Banette [TM]
		606 Beheeyem [TM]	625 Bisharp [TM]	009 Blastoise [TM]	331 Cacnea [TM]	332 Cacturne [TM]	318 Carvanha [TM]	609 Chandelure [TM]
		693 Clawitzer [1, 57, TM]	563 Cofagrigus [TM]	342 Crawdaunt [TM]	453 Croagunk [TM]	169 Crobat [TM]	491 Darkrai [93, TM]	633 Deino [TM, E]
		386 Deoxys (Atk) [TM]	386 Deoxys (Def) [TM]	386 Deoxys (Nor) [TM]	386 Deoxys (Spd) [TM]	452 Drapion [TM]	621 Druddigon [TM]	356 Dusclops [TM]
		477 Dusknoir [TM]	355 Duskull [TM, E]	023 Ekans [TM]	605 Elgyem [TM]	677 Espurr [TM]	592 Frillish [TM]	657 Frogadier [TM]
		676 Furfrou [TM]	569 Garbodor [TM]	092 Gastly [36, TM]	649 Genesect [TM]	094 Gengar [44, TM]	487 Giratina (Alt) [TM]	487 Giratina (Ori) [TM]
		362 Glalie [TM]	207 Gligar [TM]	472 Gliscor [TM]	574 Gothita [TM, E]	576 Gothitelle [TM]	575 Gothorita [TM]	711 Gourgeist [TM]
		658 Greninja [TM]	130 Gyarados [TM]	093 Haunter [44, TM]	485 Heatran [TM]	695 Heliolisk [TM]	694 Helioptile [TM]	430 Honchkrow [75, TM]
		229 Houndoom [TM]	228 Houndour [TM]	635 Hydreigon [TM]	686 Inkay [TM]	593 Jellicent [TM]	109 Koffing [TM]	552 Krokorok [TM]
		553 Krookodile [TM]	608 Lampent [TM]	246 Larvitar [32, TM]	510 Liepard [TM]	667 Litleo [TM]	607 Litwick [TM]	448 Lucario [TM]
		687 Malamar [TM]	630 Mandibuzz [46, TM]	303 Mawile [TM]	678 Meowstic (F) [TM]	678 Meowstic (M) [TM]	052 Meowth [TM]	151 Mew [TM]
		262 Mightyena [TM]	200 Misdreavus [TM]	429 Mismagius [TM]	089 Muk [TM]	198 Murkrow [TM]	038 Ninetales [TM]	714 Noibat [TM]
		715 Noivern [TM]	274 Nuzleaf [TM]	674 Pancham [TM]	675 Pangoro [TM]	624 Pawniard [TM]	053 Persian [TM]	708 Phantump [TM]
		261 Poochyena [TM]	474 Porygon-Z [TM]	710 Pumpkaboo [TM]	247 Pupitar [34, TM]	509 Purrloin [TM]	668 Pyroar [TM]	479 Rotom (Fan) [TM]
		479 Rotom (Frost) [TM]	479 Rotom (Heat) [TM]	479 Rotom (Mow) [TM]	479 Rotom (Wash) [TM]	479 Rotom [TM]	302 Sableye [TM]	551 Sandile [TM]
		560 Scrafty [TM]	559 Scraggy [TM]	336 Seviper [TM]	319 Sharpedo [TM]	275 Shiftry [TM]	353 Shuppet [TM]	561 Sigilyph [TM]
		227 Skarmory [TM]	451 Skorupi [TM]	435 Skuntank [TM]	215 Sneasel [TM]	442 Spiritomb [49, TM]	208 Steelix [TM]	434 Stunky [TM]
		642 Thundurus [73, TM]	641 Tornadus [73, TM]	454 Toxicroak [TM]	709 Trevenant [TM]	568 Trubbish [TM]	248 Tyranitar [34, TM]	697 Tyrantrum [TM]
		696 Tyrunt [TM]	197 Umbreon [TM]	629 Vullaby [46, TM]	037 Vulpix [TM]	461 Weavile [47, TM]	110 Weezing [TM]	562 Yamask [TM]
		717 Yveltal [44, TM]	571 Zoroark [TM]	570 Zorua [TM, E]	634 Zweilous [TM]			
	Dark Void	491 Darkrai [66]						
Fairy	Dazzling Gleam (TM99)	063 Abra [TM]	065 Alakazam [TM]	334 Altaria [TM]	683 Aromatisse [TM]	531 Audino [TM]	482 Azelf [TM]	343 Baltoy [TM]
		354 Banette [TM]	182 Bellossom [TM]	242 Blissey [TM]	406 Budew [TM]	703 Carbink [TM]	251 Celebi [TM]	113 Chansey [TM]
		421 Cherrim [TM]	420 Cherubi [TM]	358 Chimecho [TM]	170 Chinchou [TM]	433 Chingling [TM]	573 Cinccino [TM]	344 Claydol [TM]
		036 Clefable [TM]	035 Clefairy [TM]	546 Cottonee [TM]	655 Delphox [TM]	719 Diancie [TM]	096 Drowzee [TM]	196 Espeon [TM]
		669 Flabébé [TM]	670 Floette [TM]	671 Florges [TM]	592 Frillish [TM]	475 Gallade [TM]	282 Gardevoir [TM]	092 Gastly [TM]
		094 Gengar [TM]	203 Girafarig [TM]	044 Gloom [TM]	210 Granbull [TM]	093 Haunter [TM]	187 Hoppip [TM]	097 Hypno [TM]
		314 Illumise [TM]	593 Jellicent [TM]	039 Jigglypuff [TM]	385 Jirachi [TM]	189 Jumpluff [TM]	064 Kadabra [TM]	281 Kirlia [TM]
		707 Klefki [TM]	171 Lanturn [TM]	490 Manaphy [TM]	648 Meloetta [TM]	481 Mesprit [TM]	151 Mew [TM]	572 Minccino [TM]
		200 Misdreavus [TM]	429 Mismagius [TM]	122 Mr. Mime [TM]	517 Munna [TM]	518 Musharna [TM]	177 Natu [TM]	299 Nosepass [TM]
		043 Oddish [TM]	489 Phione [TM]	476 Probopass [TM]	280 Ralts [TM]	315 Roselia [TM]	407 Roserade [TM]	302 Sableye [TM]
		492 Shaymin (Land) [TM]	492 Shaymin (Sky) [TM]	353 Shuppet [TM]	561 Sigilyph [TM]	188 Skiploom [TM]	685 Slurpuff [TM]	209 Snubbull [TM]
		682 Spritzee [TM]	121 Starmie [TM]	120 Staryu [TM]	333 Swablu [TM]	684 Swirlix [TM]	700 Sylveon [TM]	072 Tentacool [TM]
		073 Tentacruel [TM]	468 Togekiss [TM]	175 Togepi [TM]	176 Togetic [TM]	480 Uxie [TM]	494 Victini [TM]	045 Vileplume [TM]
		313 Volbeat [TM]	547 Whimsicott [TM]	040 Wigglytuff [TM]	178 Xatu [TM]	716 Xerneas [TM]		
Bug	Defend Order	416 Vespiquen [17]						

	Move	Pokémon that can learn it						
Normal	Defense Curl	184 Azumarill [10]	371 Bagon [E]	400 Bibarel [9]	399 Bidoof [9, E]	242 Blissey [1]	438 Bonsly [E]	427 Buneary [1]
		659 Bunnelby [E]	113 Chansey [1]	420 Cherubi [E]	650 Chespin [E]	035 Clefairy [13]	155 Cyndaquil [22]	232 Donphan [1]
		206 Dunsparce [1]	500 Emboar [13]	590 Foongus [E]	162 Furret [1, 4]	074 Geodude [1]	076 Golem [1]	622 Golett [1]
		623 Golurk [1]	075 Graveler [1]	174 Igglybuff [3]	039 Jigglypuff [3]	463 Lickilicky [9]	108 Lickitung [9]	428 Lopunny [1]
		183 Marill [10]	241 Miltank [5]	446 Munchlax [4]	517 Munna [1]	518 Musharna [1]	322 Numel [E]	095 Onix [E]
		417 Pachirisu [E]	231 Phanpy [1]	499 Pignite [13]	233 Porygon2 [1]	156 Quilava [24]	027 Sandshrew [1]	028 Sandslash [1]
		545 Scolipede [1]	364 Sealeo [1]	161 Sentret [4]	672 Skiddo [E]	143 Snorlax [4]	363 Spheal [1]	185 Sudowoodo [E]
		498 Tepig [13]	157 Typhlosion [24]	543 Venipede [1]	320 Wailmer [E]	365 Walrein [1]	544 Whirlipede [1]	040 Wigglytuff [1]
Flying	Defog	566 Archen [E]	628 Braviary [32]	441 Chatot [E]	425 Drifloon [E]	580 Ducklett [6]	163 Hoothoot [E]	630 Mandibuzz [32]
		016 Pidgey [E]	627 Rufflet [32]	123 Scyther [E]	273 Seedot [E]	581 Swanna [1, 6]	276 Taillow [E]	629 Vullaby [32]
		041 Zubat [E]						
Ghost	Destiny Bond	331 Cacnea [54]	332 Cacturne [1, 59]	318 Carvanha [E]	563 Cofagrigus [57]	225 Delibird [E]	425 Drifloon [E]	355 Duskull [E]
		478 Froslass [1, 61]	092 Gastly [40]	094 Gengar [50]	487 Giratina (Alt) [24]	487 Giratina (Ori) [24]	316 Gulpin [E]	093 Haunter [50]
		679 Honedge [E]	228 Houndour [E]	686 Inkay [E]	109 Koffing [40, E]	200 Misdreavus [E]	708 Phantump [39]	710 Pumpkaboo [E]
		211 Qwilfish [1, 53]	280 Ralts [E]	353 Shuppet [E]	442 Spiritomb [E]	709 Trevenant [39]	416 Vespiquen [1, 53]	110 Weezing [46]
		202 Wobbuffet [1]	360 Wynaut [15]	562 Yamask [49]				
Fighting	Detect	359 Absol [33]	482 Azelf [16]	104 Cubone [E]	133 Eevee [E]	253 Grovyle [38]	701 Hawlucha [1]	107 Hitmonchan [50]
		237 Hitmontop [50]	448 Lucario [1]	296 Makuhita [E]	308 Medicham [1, 9]	307 Meditite [9]	619 Mienfoo [9]	620 Mienshao [1, 9]
		501 Oshawott [E]	504 Patrat [11]	519 Pidove [22]	447 Riolu [E]	302 Sableye [14]	254 Sceptile [39]	559 Scraggy [E]
		396 Starly [E]	532 Timburr [E]	520 Tranquill [23]	252 Treecko [33]	521 Unfezant [23]	505 Watchog [11]	193 Yanma [17]
		469 Yanmega [17]	335 Zangoose [36]	145 Zapdos [15]	570 Zorua [E]			
Rock	Diamond Storm	719 Diancie [50]						
Ground	Dig (TM28)	306 Aggron [TM]	190 Aipom [TM]	424 Ambipom [TM]	347 Anorith [TM]	024 Arbok [TM]	059 Arcanine [TM]	566 Archen [TM]
		567 Archeops [TM]	168 Ariados [TM]	348 Armaldo [TM]	304 Aron [TM]	531 Audino [TM]	610 Axew [TM]	184 Azumarill [TM]
		343 Baltoy [TM]	689 Barbaracle [TM]	411 Bastiodon [TM]	614 Beartic [TM]	400 Bibarel [TM]	399 Bidoof [TM]	688 Binacle [TM]
		625 Bisharp [TM]	009 Blastoise [TM]	257 Blaziken [TM]	438 Bonsly [TM]	418 Buizel [TM]	427 Buneary [TM]	659 Bunnelby [33, TM]
		323 Camerupt [TM]	565 Carracosta [TM]	006 Charizard [TM]	004 Charmander [TM]	005 Charmeleon [TM]	652 Chesnaught [TM]	650 Chespin [TM]
		390 Chimchar [TM]	573 Cinccino [TM]	344 Claydol [TM]	036 Clefable [TM]	035 Clefairy [TM]	173 Cleffa [TM]	256 Combusken [TM]
		534 Conkeldurr [TM]	341 Corphish [TM]	222 Corsola [TM]	408 Cranidos [TM]	342 Crawdaunt [TM]	453 Croagunk [TM]	159 Croconaw [TM]
		558 Crustle [TM]	613 Cubchoo [TM]	104 Cubone [TM]	155 Cyndaquil [TM]	555 Darmanitan [TM]	554 Darumaka [TM]	702 Dedenne [TM]
		301 Delcatty [TM]	502 Dewott [TM]	660 Diggersby [37, TM]	050 Diglett [34, TM]	452 Drapion [TM]	529 Drilbur [19, TM]	621 Druddigon [TM]
		051 Dugtrio [40, TM]	206 Dunsparce [31, TM]	632 Durant [41, TM]	557 Dwebble [TM]	133 Eevee [TM]	023 Ekans [TM]	466 Electivire [TM]
		395 Empoleon [TM]	244 Entei [TM]	196 Espeon [TM]	530 Excadrill [19, TM]	160 Feraligatr [TM]	136 Flareon [TM]	419 Floatzel [TM]
		330 Flygon [TM]	205 Forretress [TM]	611 Fraxure [TM]	656 Froakie [TM]	657 Frogadier [TM]	676 Furfrou [TM]	162 Furret [TM]
		444 Gabite [40, TM]	445 Garchomp [40, TM]	423 Gastrodon [TM]	074 Geodude [TM]	443 Gible [31, TM]	471 Glaceon [TM]	431 Glameow [TM]
		207 Gligar [TM]	472 Gliscor [TM]	673 Gogoat [TM]	055 Golduck [TM]	076 Golem [TM]	210 Granbull [TM]	075 Graveler [TM]
		658 Greninja [TM]	088 Grimer [TM]	383 Groudon [TM]	253 Grovyle [TM]	058 Growlithe [TM]	533 Gurdurr [TM]	297 Hariyama [TM]
		701 Hawlucha [TM]	612 Haxorus [TM]	631 Heatmor [TM]	485 Heatran [TM]	695 Heliolisk [TM]	694 Helioptile [TM]	214 Heracross [TM]
		507 Herdier [TM]	449 Hippopotas [19, TM]	450 Hippowdon [19, TM]	237 Hitmontop [TM]	174 Igglybuff [TM]	392 Infernape [TM]	039 Jigglypuff [TM]
		135 Jolteon [TM]	140 Kabuto [TM]	141 Kabutops [TM]	115 Kangaskhan [TM]	352 Kecleon [TM]	099 Kingler [TM]	098 Krabby [TM]
		552 Krokorok [32, TM]	553 Krookodile [32, TM]	305 Lairon [TM]	645 Landorus [TM]	246 Larvitar [TM]	470 Leafeon [TM]	166 Ledian [TM]
		165 Ledyba [TM]	463 Lickilicky [TM]	108 Lickitung [TM]	506 Lillipup [TM]	264 Linoone [TM]	667 Litleo [TM]	428 Lopunny [TM]
		448 Lucario [TM]	068 Machamp [TM]	067 Machoke [TM]	066 Machop [TM]	296 Makuhita [TM]	473 Mamoswine [TM]	056 Mankey [TM]
		183 Marill [TM]	105 Marowak [TM]	259 Marshtomp [TM]	678 Meowstic (F) [TM]	678 Meowstic (M) [TM]	052 Meowth [TM]	151 Mew [TM]
		619 Mienfoo [TM]	620 Mienshao [TM]	262 Mightyena [TM]	572 Minccino [TM]	391 Monferno [TM]	258 Mudkip [TM]	089 Muk [TM]
		034 Nidoking [TM]	031 Nidoqueen [TM]	029 Nidoran ♀ [TM]	032 Nidoran ♂ [TM]	030 Nidorina [TM]	033 Nidorino [TM]	290 Nincada [37, TM]
		038 Ninetales [TM]	291 Ninjask [TM]	322 Numel [TM]	274 Nuzleaf [TM]	095 Onix [43, TM]	501 Oshawott [TM]	417 Pachirisu [TM]
		674 Pancham [TM]	675 Pangoro [TM]	515 Panpour [TM]	511 Pansage [TM]	513 Pansear [TM]	046 Paras [TM]	047 Parasect [TM]
		504 Patrat [TM]	624 Pawniard [TM]	053 Persian [TM]	708 Phantump [TM]	025 Pikachu [TM]	221 Piloswine [TM]	204 Pineco [TM]
		127 Pinsir [TM]	393 Piplup [TM]	186 Politoed [TM]	060 Poliwag [TM]	061 Poliwhirl [TM]	062 Poliwrath [TM]	261 Poochyena [TM]
		057 Primeape [TM]	394 Prinplup [TM]	054 Psyduck [TM]	247 Pupitar [TM]	432 Purugly [TM]	668 Pyroar [TM]	195 Quagsire [TM]
		156 Quilava [TM]	651 Quilladin [TM]	026 Raichu [TM]	243 Raikou [TM]	409 Rampardos [TM]	020 Raticate [TM]	019 Rattata [TM]
		377 Regirock [TM]	112 Rhydon [TM]	111 Rhyhorn [TM]	464 Rhyperior [TM]	447 Riolu [TM]	302 Sableye [TM]	503 Samurott [TM]
		551 Sandile [31, TM]	027 Sandshrew [30, TM]	028 Sandslash [33, TM]	539 Sawk [TM]	254 Sceptile [TM]	545 Scolipede [TM]	560 Scrafty [TM]
		559 Scraggy [TM]	273 Seedot [TM]	537 Seismitoad [TM]	161 Sentret [TM]	336 Seviper [TM]	292 Shedinja [TM]	410 Shieldon [TM]
		275 Shiftry [TM]	213 Shuckle [TM]	516 Simipour [TM]	512 Simisage [TM]	514 Simisear [TM]	672 Skiddo [TM]	300 Skitty [TM]
		451 Skorupi [TM]	435 Skuntank [TM]	080 Slowbro [TM]	199 Slowking [TM]	079 Slowpoke [TM]	215 Sneasel [TM]	209 Snubbull [TM]
		167 Spinarak [TM]	327 Spinda [TM]	007 Squirtle [TM]	208 Steelix [43, TM]	508 Stoutland [TM]	618 Stunfisk [TM]	434 Stunky [TM]
		185 Sudowoodo [TM]	245 Suicune [TM]	260 Swampert [TM]	220 Swinub [TM]	700 Sylveon [TM]	216 Teddiursa [TM]	538 Throh [TM]
		532 Timburr [TM]	564 Tirtouga [TM]	255 Torchic [TM]	158 Totodile [TM]	454 Toxicroak [TM]	328 Trapinch [19, TM]	252 Treecko [TM]
		709 Trevenant [TM]	157 Typhlosion [TM]	248 Tyranitar [TM]	697 Tyrantrum [TM]	696 Tyrunt [TM]	197 Umbreon [TM]	217 Ursaring [TM]
		134 Vaporeon [TM]	329 Vibrava [TM]	037 Vulpix [TM]	008 Wartortle [TM]	505 Watchog [TM]	461 Weavile [TM]	040 Wigglytuff [TM]
		194 Wooper [TM]	413 Wormadam (Sand) [TM]	335 Zangoose [TM]	263 Zigzagoon [TM]	571 Zoroark [TM]	570 Zorua [TM]	718 Zygarde [10, TM]

	Move	Pokémon that can learn it						
Normal	Disable	065 Alakazam [18]	331 Cacnea [E]	351 Castform [E]	358 Chimecho [E]	433 Chingling [E]	563 Cofagrigus [1, 5]	491 Darkrai [1]
		425 Drifloon [E]	096 Drowzee [5]	356 Dusclops [1, 6]	477 Dusknoir [1, 6]	355 Duskull [6]	023 Ekans [E]	605 Elgyem [E]
		092 Gastly [E]	055 Golduck [22]	088 Grimer [12]	116 Horsea [E]	097 Hypno [1, 5]	039 Jigglypuff [15]	595 Joltik [E]
		064 Kadabra [18]	115 Kangaskhan [E]	352 Kecleon [E]	463 Lickilicky [25]	108 Lickitung [25]	150 Mewtwo [1]	089 Muk [12]
		029 Nidoran ♀ [E]	032 Nidoran ♂ [E]	054 Psyduck [22]	710 Pumpkaboo [E]	280 Ralts [E]	086 Seel [E]	353 Shuppet [E]
		080 Slowbro [19]	199 Slowking [19]	079 Slowpoke [19]	361 Snorunt [E]	167 Spinarak [E]	327 Spinda [E]	682 Spritzee [E]
		234 Stantler [E]	049 Venomoth [1]	048 Venonat [1]	037 Vulpix [E]	040 Wigglytuff [1]	562 Yamask [5, E]	717 Yveltal [35]
		335 Zangoose [E]						
Fairy	Disarming Voice	334 Altaria [11]	683 Aromatisse [53]	531 Audino [13]	036 Clefable [1]	035 Clefairy [1]	677 Espurr [22]	671 Florges [1]
		282 Gardevoir [11]	039 Jigglypuff [11]	281 Kirlia [11]	678 Meowstic (F) [22]	678 Meowstic (M) [22]	350 Milotic [11]	515 Panpour [E]
		511 Pansage [E]	513 Pansear [E]	172 Pichu [E]	280 Ralts [11]	300 Skitty [13]	682 Spritzee [50]	333 Swablu [11]
		700 Sylveon [1]	293 Whismur [E]					
Electric	Discharge	698 Amaura [E]	181 Ampharos [40]	522 Blitzle [32]	170 Chinchou [34]	702 Dedenne [50]	603 Eelektrik [29]	604 Eelektross [1]
		125 Electabuzz [36]	466 Electivire [36]	309 Electrike [29, E]	101 Electrode [41]	239 Elekid [33]	587 Emolga [50]	180 Flaaffy [38]
		596 Galvantula [54]	135 Jolteon [37]	595 Joltik [45]	600 Klang [44]	599 Klink [42]	601 Klinklang [44]	171 Lanturn [37]
		404 Luxio [48]	405 Luxray [56]	081 Magnemite [37]	082 Magneton [43]	462 Magnezone [43]	310 Manectric [30]	179 Mareep [32]
		312 Minun [31, E]	299 Nosepass [31]	417 Pachirisu [41]	025 Pikachu [34]	311 Plusle [31, E]	137 Porygon [40]	233 Porygon2 [40]
		474 Porygon-Z [40]	476 Probopass [31]	243 Raikou [1, 57]	479 Rotom (Fan) [1, 64]	479 Rotom (Frost) [1, 64]	479 Rotom (Heat) [1, 64]	479 Rotom (Mow) [1, 64]
		479 Rotom (Wash) [1, 64]	479 Rotom [1, 64]	403 Shinx [41]	618 Stunfisk [25]	642 Thundurus [43]	100 Voltorb [37]	145 Zapdos [50]
		523 Zebstrika [36]						
Water	Dive (HM07)	594 Alomomola [HM]	493 Arceus [HM]	184 Azumarill [HM]	339 Barboach [HM]	550 Basculin [HM]	614 Beartic [HM]	400 Bibarel [HM]
		009 Blastoise [HM]	418 Buizel [HM]	565 Carracosta [HM]	318 Carvanha [HM]	170 Chinchou [HM]	366 Clamperl [HM]	692 Clauncher [HM]
		693 Clawitzer [HM]	091 Cloyster [HM]	342 Crawdaunt [HM]	159 Croconaw [HM]	087 Dewgong [45, HM]	502 Dewott [HM]	691 Dragalge [HM]
		149 Dragonite [HM]	580 Ducklett [HM]	395 Empoleon [HM]	349 Feebas [HM]	160 Feraligatr [HM]	456 Finneon [HM]	419 Floatzel [HM]
		592 Frillish [HM]	656 Froakie [HM]	657 Frogadier [HM]	423 Gastrodon [HM]	118 Goldeen [HM]	055 Golduck [HM]	368 Gorebyss [26, HM]
		658 Greninja [HM]	130 Gyarados [HM]	116 Horsea [HM]	367 Huntail [26, HM]	593 Jellicent [HM]	141 Kabutops [HM]	230 Kingdra [HM]
		099 Kingler [HM]	098 Krabby [HM]	382 Kyogre [HM]	171 Lanturn [HM]	131 Lapras [HM]	380 Latias [HM]	381 Latios [HM]
		271 Lombre [HM]	272 Ludicolo [HM]	249 Lugia [HM]	457 Lumineon [HM]	370 Luvdisc [HM]	490 Manaphy [61, HM]	226 Mantine [HM]
		458 Mantyke [HM]	183 Marill [HM]	259 Marshtomp [HM]	151 Mew [HM]	150 Mewtwo [HM]	350 Milotic [HM]	258 Mudkip [HM]
		224 Octillery [HM]	138 Omanyte [HM]	139 Omastar [HM]	501 Oshawott [HM]	484 Palkia [HM]	515 Panpour [HM]	489 Phione [61, HM]
		393 Piplup [HM]	186 Politoed [HM]	060 Poliwag [HM]	061 Poliwhirl [HM]	062 Poliwrath [HM]	394 Prinplup [HM]	054 Psyduck [HM]
		195 Quagsire [HM]	211 Qwilfish [HM]	384 Rayquaza [HM]	369 Relicanth [26, HM]	223 Remoraid [HM]	503 Samurott [HM]	117 Seadra [HM]
		119 Seaking [HM]	364 Sealeo [HM]	086 Seel [41, HM]	319 Sharpedo [HM]	090 Shellder [HM]	422 Shellos [HM]	516 Simipour [HM]
		690 Skrelp [HM]	080 Slowbro [HM]	199 Slowking [HM]	079 Slowpoke [HM]	363 Spheal [HM]	007 Squirtle [HM]	121 Starmie [HM]
		120 Staryu [HM]	245 Suicune [HM]	260 Swampert [HM]	581 Swanna [HM]	072 Tentacool [HM]	073 Tentacruel [HM]	564 Tirtouga [HM]
		158 Totodile [HM]	134 Vaporeon [HM]	320 Wailmer [33, HM]	321 Wailord [44, HM]	365 Walrein [HM]	008 Wartortle [HM]	340 Whiscash [HM]
		194 Wooper [HM]						
Normal	Dizzy Punch	427 Buneary [36]	115 Kangaskhan [34]	352 Kecleon [E]	165 Ledyba [E]	428 Lopunny [36]	241 Miltank [E]	486 Regigigas [1]
		579 Reuniclus [41]	327 Spinda [23]	313 Volbeat [E]				
Steel	Doom Desire	385 Jirachi [70]						
Normal	Double Hit	190 Aipom [32]	424 Ambipom [32]	418 Buizel [27]	427 Buneary [E]	341 Corphish [20]	342 Crawdaunt [20]	633 Deino [E]
		084 Doduo [25]	419 Floatzel [29]	203 Girafarig [28]	115 Kangaskhan [19]	473 Mamoswine [33]	127 Pinsir [22]	393 Piplup [E]
		212 Scizor [49]	123 Scyther [49]	215 Sneasel [E]	110 Weezing [29]	335 Zangoose [E]	634 Zweilous [1]	
Fighting	Double Kick	257 Blaziken [16]	522 Blitzle [E]	659 Bunnelby [20]	390 Chimchar [E]	638 Cobalion [7]	256 Combusken [16]	104 Cubone [E]
		155 Cyndaquil [E]	585 Deerling [10]	660 Diggersby [20]	203 Girafarig [E]	058 Growlithe [E]	106 Hitmonlee [1]	135 Jolteon [17]
		647 Keldeo [7]	034 Nidoking [1]	031 Nidoqueen [1]	029 Nidoran ♀ [9]	032 Nidoran ♂ [9]	030 Nidorina [9]	033 Nidorino [9]
		077 Ponyta [E]	539 Sawk [13]	586 Sawsbuck [10]	403 Shinx [E]	234 Stantler [E]	639 Terrakion [7]	252 Treecko [E]
		640 Virizion [7]	194 Wooper [E]	335 Zangoose [E]				
Normal	Double Slap	190 Aipom [E]	594 Alomomola [13]	531 Audino [17]	242 Blissey [12]	418 Buizel [E]	659 Bunnelby [10]	113 Chansey [12]
		036 Clefable [1]	035 Clefairy [10]	301 Delcatty [1]	569 Garbodor [14]	574 Gothita [14]	576 Gothitelle [14]	575 Gothorita [14]
		039 Jigglypuff [18]	124 Jynx [15]	619 Mienfoo [17]	620 Mienshao [17]	439 Mime Jr. [11]	572 Minccino [13]	122 Mr. Mime [11]
		172 Pichu [E]	186 Politoed [1]	060 Poliwag [15]	061 Poliwhirl [15]	062 Poliwrath [1]	300 Skitty [16]	568 Trubbish [14]
		040 Wigglytuff [1]						
Normal	Double Team (TM32)	460 Abomasnow [TM]	063 Abra [TM]	359 Absol [19, TM]	617 Accelgor [1, 8, TM]	681 Aegislash [TM]	142 Aerodactyl [TM]	306 Aggron [TM]
		190 Aipom [TM]	065 Alakazam [TM]	594 Alomomola [TM]	334 Altaria [TM]	698 Amaura [TM]	424 Ambipom [TM]	591 Amoonguss [TM]
		181 Ampharos [TM]	347 Anorith [TM]	024 Arbok [TM]	059 Arcanine [TM]	493 Arceus [TM]	566 Archen [8, TM]	567 Archeops [8, TM]
		168 Ariados [TM]	348 Armaldo [TM]	683 Aromatisse [TM]	304 Aron [TM]	144 Articuno [TM]	531 Audino [TM]	699 Aurorus [TM]
		713 Avalugg [TM]	610 Axew [TM]	482 Azelf [TM]	184 Azumarill [TM]	298 Azurill [TM]	371 Bagon [TM]	343 Baltoy [TM]
		354 Banette [TM]	689 Barbaracle [TM]	339 Barboach [TM]	550 Basculin [TM]	411 Bastiodon [TM]	153 Bayleef [TM]	614 Beartic [TM]
		267 Beautifly [TM]	015 Beedrill [TM]	606 Beheeyem [TM]	182 Bellossom [TM]	069 Bellsprout [TM]	712 Bergmite [TM]	400 Bibarel [TM]
		399 Bidoof [TM]	688 Binacle [TM]	625 Bisharp [TM]	009 Blastoise [TM]	257 Blaziken [TM]	242 Blissey [TM]	522 Blitzle [TM]
		525 Boldore [TM]	438 Bonsly [TM]	626 Bouffalant [TM]	654 Braixen [TM]	628 Braviary [TM]	286 Breloom [TM]	437 Bronzong [TM]
		436 Bronzor [TM]	406 Budew [TM]	418 Buizel [TM]	001 Bulbasaur [TM]	427 Buneary [TM]	659 Bunnelby [TM]	012 Butterfree [TM]
		331 Cacnea [TM]	332 Cacturne [TM]	323 Camerupt [TM]	703 Carbink [TM]	455 Carnivine [TM]	565 Carracosta [TM]	318 Carvanha [TM]

	Move	Pokémon that can learn it						
Normal	Double Team (TM32)	351 Castform [TM]	251 Celebi [TM]	609 Chandelure [TM]	113 Chansey [TM]	006 Charizard [TM]	004 Charmander [TM]	005 Charmeleon [TM]
		441 Chatot [TM]	421 Cherrim [TM]	420 Cherubi [TM]	652 Chesnaught [TM]	650 Chespin [TM]	152 Chikorita [TM]	390 Chimchar [TM]
		358 Chimecho [TM]	170 Chinchou [TM]	433 Chingling [TM]	573 Cinccino [TM]	366 Clamperl [TM]	692 Clauncher [TM]	693 Clawitzer [TM]
		344 Claydol [TM]	036 Clefable [TM]	035 Clefairy [TM]	173 Cleffa [TM]	091 Cloyster [TM]	638 Cobalion [TM]	563 Cofagrigus [TM]
		256 Combusken [TM]	534 Conkeldurr [TM]	341 Corphish [TM]	222 Corsola [TM]	546 Cottonee [TM]	346 Cradily [TM]	408 Cranidos [TM]
		342 Crawdaunt [TM]	488 Cresselia [1, TM]	453 Croagunk [TM]	169 Crobat [TM]	159 Croconaw [TM]	558 Crustle [TM]	615 Cryogonal [TM]
		613 Cubchoo [TM]	104 Cubone [TM]	155 Cyndaquil [TM]	491 Darkrai [47, TM]	555 Darmanitan [TM]	554 Darumaka [TM]	702 Dedenne [TM]
		585 Deerling [TM]	633 Deino [TM]	301 Delcatty [TM]	225 Delibird [TM]	655 Delphox [TM]	386 Deoxys (Atk) [TM]	386 Deoxys (Def) [TM]
		386 Deoxys (Nor) [TM]	386 Deoxys (Spd) [13, TM]	087 Dewgong [TM]	502 Dewott [TM]	483 Dialga [TM]	719 Diancie [TM]	660 Diggersby [TM]
		050 Diglett [TM]	085 Dodrio [TM]	084 Doduo [TM]	232 Donphan [TM]	680 Doublade [TM]	691 Dragalge [28, TM]	148 Dragonair [TM]
		149 Dragonite [TM]	452 Drapion [TM]	147 Dratini [TM]	426 Drifblim [TM]	425 Drifloon [TM]	529 Drilbur [TM]	096 Drowzee [TM]
		621 Druddigon [TM]	580 Ducklett [TM]	051 Dugtrio [TM]	206 Dunsparce [TM]	578 Duosion [TM]	632 Durant [TM]	356 Dusclops [TM]
		477 Dusknoir [TM]	355 Duskull [TM]	269 Dustox [TM]	557 Dwebble [TM]	603 Eelektrik [TM]	604 Eelektross [TM]	133 Eevee [TM]
		023 Ekans [TM]	125 Electabuzz [TM]	466 Electivire [TM]	309 Electrike [TM]	101 Electrode [TM]	239 Elekid [TM]	605 Elgyem [TM]
		500 Emboar [TM]	587 Emolga [19, TM]	395 Empoleon [TM]	244 Entei [TM]	589 Escavalier [TM]	196 Espeon [TM]	677 Espurr [TM]
		530 Excadrill [TM]	102 Exeggcute [TM]	103 Exeggutor [TM]	295 Exploud [TM]	083 Farfetch'd [TM]	022 Fearow [TM]	349 Feebas [TM]
		653 Fennekin [TM]	160 Feraligatr [TM]	597 Ferroseed [TM]	598 Ferrothorn [TM]	456 Finneon [TM]	180 Flaaffy [TM]	669 Flabébé [TM]
		136 Flareon [TM]	662 Fletchinder [TM]	661 Fletchling [TM]	419 Floatzel [TM]	670 Floette [TM]	671 Florges [TM]	330 Flygon [TM]
		590 Foongus [TM]	205 Forretress [TM]	611 Fraxure [TM]	592 Frillish [TM]	656 Froakie [43, TM]	657 Frogadier [48, TM]	478 Froslass [1, 5, TM]
		676 Furfrou [TM]	162 Furret [TM]	444 Gabite [TM]	475 Gallade [1, 6, TM]	596 Galvantula [TM]	569 Garbodor [TM]	445 Garchomp [TM]
		282 Gardevoir [1, 6, TM]	092 Gastly [TM]	423 Gastrodon [TM]	649 Genesect [TM]	094 Gengar [TM]	074 Geodude [TM]	443 Gible [TM]
		526 Gigalith [TM]	203 Girafarig [TM]	487 Giratina (Alt) [TM]	487 Giratina (Ori) [TM]	471 Glaceon [TM]	362 Glalie [1, 5, TM]	431 Glameow [TM]
		207 Gligar [TM]	472 Gliscor [TM]	044 Gloom [TM]	673 Gogoat [TM]	042 Golbat [TM]	118 Goldeen [TM]	055 Golduck [TM]
		076 Golem [TM]	622 Golett [TM]	623 Golurk [TM]	706 Goodra [TM]	704 Goomy [TM]	368 Gorebyss [TM]	574 Gothita [TM]
		576 Gothitelle [TM]	575 Gothorita [TM]	711 Gourgeist [TM]	210 Granbull [TM]	075 Graveler [TM]	658 Greninja [52, TM]	088 Grimer [TM]
		388 Grotle [TM]	383 Groudon [TM]	253 Grovyle [TM]	058 Growlithe [TM]	326 Grumpig [TM]	316 Gulpin [TM]	533 Gurdurr [TM]
		130 Gyarados [TM]	440 Happiny [TM]	297 Hariyama [TM]	093 Haunter [TM]	701 Hawlucha [TM]	612 Haxorus [TM]	631 Heatmor [TM]
		485 Heatran [TM]	695 Heliolisk [TM]	694 Helioptile [TM]	214 Heracross [TM]	507 Herdier [TM]	449 Hippopotas [TM]	450 Hippowdon [TM]
		107 Hitmonchan [TM]	106 Hitmonlee [TM]	237 Hitmontop [TM]	430 Honchkrow [TM]	679 Honedge [TM]	250 Ho-Oh [TM]	163 Hoothoot [TM]
		187 Hoppip [TM]	116 Horsea [TM]	229 Houndoom [TM]	228 Houndour [TM]	367 Huntail [TM]	635 Hydreigon [TM]	097 Hypno [TM]
		174 Igglybuff [TM]	314 Illumise [TM]	392 Infernape [TM]	686 Inkay [TM]	002 Ivysaur [TM]	593 Jellicent [TM]	039 Jigglypuff [TM]
		385 Jirachi [TM]	135 Jolteon [TM]	595 Joltik [TM]	189 Jumpluff [TM]	124 Jynx [TM]	140 Kabuto [TM]	141 Kabutops [TM]
		064 Kadabra [TM]	115 Kangaskhan [TM]	588 Karrablast [TM]	352 Kecleon [TM]	647 Keldeo [TM]	230 Kingdra [TM]	099 Kingler [TM]
		281 Kirlia [1, 6, TM]	600 Klang [TM]	707 Klefki [TM]	599 Klink [TM]	601 Klinklang [TM]	109 Koffing [TM]	098 Krabby [TM]
		402 Kricketune [TM]	552 Krokorok [TM]	553 Krookodile [TM]	382 Kyogre [TM]	646 Kyurem (Blk) [TM]	646 Kyurem (Wht) [TM]	646 Kyurem [TM]
		305 Lairon [TM]	608 Lampent [TM]	645 Landorus [TM]	171 Lanturn [TM]	131 Lapras [TM]	636 Larvesta [TM]	246 Larvitar [TM]
		380 Latias [TM]	381 Latios [TM]	470 Leafeon [TM]	542 Leavanny [TM]	166 Ledian [TM]	165 Ledyba [TM]	463 Lickilicky [TM]
		108 Lickitung [TM]	510 Liepard [TM]	345 Lileep [TM]	549 Lilligant [TM]	506 Lillipup [TM]	264 Linoone [TM]	667 Litleo [TM]
		607 Litwick [TM]	271 Lombre [TM]	428 Lopunny [TM]	270 Lotad [TM]	294 Loudred [TM]	448 Lucario [TM]	272 Ludicolo [TM]
		249 Lugia [TM]	457 Lumineon [TM]	337 Lunatone [TM]	370 Luvdisc [TM]	404 Luxio [TM]	405 Luxray [TM]	068 Machamp [TM]
		067 Machoke [TM]	066 Machop [TM]	240 Magby [TM]	219 Magcargo [TM]	126 Magmar [TM]	467 Magmortar [TM]	081 Magnemite [TM]
		082 Magneton [TM]	462 Magnezone [TM]	296 Makuhita [TM]	687 Malamar [TM]	473 Mamoswine [TM]	490 Manaphy [TM]	630 Mandibuzz [TM]
		310 Manectric [TM]	056 Mankey [TM]	226 Mantine [TM]	458 Mantyke [TM]	556 Maractus [TM]	179 Mareep [TM]	183 Marill [TM]
		105 Marowak [TM]	259 Marshtomp [TM]	284 Masquerain [TM]	303 Mawile [TM]	308 Medicham [TM]	307 Meditite [TM]	154 Meganium [TM]
		648 Meloetta [TM]	678 Meowstic (F) [TM]	678 Meowstic (M) [TM]	052 Meowth [TM]	481 Mesprit [TM]	376 Metagross [TM]	375 Metang [TM]
		151 Mew [TM]	150 Mewtwo [TM]	619 Mienfoo [TM]	620 Mienshao [TM]	262 Mightyena [TM]	350 Milotic [TM]	241 Miltank [TM]
		439 Mime Jr. [TM]	572 Minccino [TM]	312 Minun [TM]	200 Misdreavus [TM]	429 Mismagius [TM]	146 Moltres [TM]	391 Monferno [TM]
		414 Mothim [TM]	122 Mr. Mime [TM]	258 Mudkip [TM]	089 Muk [TM]	446 Munchlax [TM]	517 Munna [TM]	198 Murkrow [TM]
		518 Musharna [TM]	177 Natu [TM]	034 Nidoking [TM]	031 Nidoqueen [TM]	029 Nidoran ♀ [TM]	032 Nidoran ♂ [TM]	030 Nidorina [TM]
		033 Nidorino [TM]	290 Nincada [TM]	038 Ninetales [TM]	291 Ninjask [20, TM]	164 Noctowl [TM]	714 Noibat [TM]	715 Noivern [TM]
		299 Nosepass [TM]	322 Numel [TM]	274 Nuzleaf [TM]	224 Octillery [TM]	043 Oddish [TM]	138 Omanyte [TM]	139 Omastar [TM]
		095 Onix [TM]	501 Oshawott [TM]	417 Pachirisu [TM]	484 Palkia [TM]	536 Palpitoad [TM]	674 Pancham [TM]	675 Pangoro [TM]
		515 Panpour [TM]	511 Pansage [TM]	513 Pansear [TM]	046 Paras [TM]	047 Parasect [TM]	504 Patrat [TM]	624 Pawniard [TM]
		279 Pelipper [TM]	053 Persian [TM]	548 Petilil [TM]	231 Phanpy [TM]	708 Phantump [TM]	489 Phione [TM]	172 Pichu [TM]
		018 Pidgeot [TM]	017 Pidgeotto [TM]	016 Pidgey [TM]	519 Pidove [TM]	499 Pignite [TM]	025 Pikachu [23, TM]	221 Piloswine [TM]
		204 Pineco [TM]	127 Pinsir [TM]	393 Piplup [TM]	311 Plusle [TM]	186 Politoed [TM]	060 Poliwag [TM]	061 Poliwhirl [TM]
		062 Poliwrath [TM]	077 Ponyta [TM]	261 Poochyena [TM]	137 Porygon [TM]	233 Porygon2 [TM]	474 Porygon-Z [TM]	057 Primeape [TM]
		394 Prinplup [TM]	476 Probopass [TM]	054 Psyduck [TM]	710 Pumpkaboo [TM]	247 Pupitar [TM]	509 Purrloin [TM]	432 Purugly [TM]
		668 Pyroar [TM]	195 Quagsire [TM]	156 Quilava [TM]	651 Quilladin [TM]	211 Qwilfish [TM]	026 Raichu [TM]	243 Raikou [TM]
		280 Ralts [6, TM]	409 Rampardos [TM]	078 Rapidash [TM]	020 Raticate [TM]	019 Rattata [TM]	384 Rayquaza [TM]	378 Regice [TM]
		486 Regigigas [TM]	377 Regirock [TM]	379 Registeel [TM]	369 Relicanth [TM]	223 Remoraid [TM]	643 Reshiram [TM]	579 Reuniclus [TM]
		112 Rhydon [TM]	111 Rhyhorn [TM]	464 Rhyperior [TM]	447 Riolu [TM]	524 Roggenrola [TM]	315 Roselia [TM]	407 Roserade [TM]
		479 Rotom (Fan) [15, TM]	479 Rotom (Frost) [15, TM]	479 Rotom (Heat) [15, TM]	479 Rotom (Mow) [15, TM]	479 Rotom (Wash) [15, TM]	479 Rotom [15, TM]	627 Rufflet [TM]
		302 Sableye [TM]	373 Salamence [TM]	503 Samurott [TM]	551 Sandile [TM]	027 Sandshrew [TM]	028 Sandslash [TM]	539 Sawk [TM]
		586 Sawsbuck [TM]	254 Sceptile [TM]	212 Scizor [TM]	545 Scolipede [TM]	560 Scrafty [TM]	559 Scraggy [TM]	123 Scyther [37, TM]

	Move	Pokémon that can learn it						
Normal	Double Team (TM32)	117 Seadra [TM]	119 Seaking [TM]	364 Sealeo [TM]	273 Seedot [TM]	086 Seel [TM]	537 Seismitoad [TM]	161 Sentret [TM]
		497 Serperior [TM]	496 Servine [TM]	336 Seviper [TM]	540 Sewaddle [TM]	319 Sharpedo [TM]	492 Shaymin (Land) [TM]	492 Shaymin (Sky) [TM]
		292 Shedinja [TM]	372 Shelgon [TM]	090 Shellder [TM]	422 Shellos [TM]	616 Shelmet [TM]	410 Shieldon [TM]	275 Shiftry [TM]
		403 Shinx [TM]	285 Shroomish [TM]	213 Shuckle [TM]	353 Shuppet [TM]	561 Sigilyph [TM]	516 Simipour [TM]	512 Simisage [TM]
		514 Simisear [TM]	227 Skarmory [TM]	672 Skiddo [TM]	188 Skiploom [TM]	300 Skitty [TM]	451 Skorupi [TM]	690 Skrelp [28, TM]
		435 Skuntank [TM]	289 Slaking [TM]	287 Slakoth [TM]	705 Sliggoo [TM]	080 Slowbro [TM]	199 Slowking [TM]	079 Slowpoke [TM]
		218 Slugma [TM]	685 Slurpuff [TM]	238 Smoochum [TM]	215 Sneasel [TM]	495 Snivy [TM]	143 Snorlax [TM]	361 Snorunt [5, TM]
		459 Snover [TM]	209 Snubbull [TM]	577 Solosis [TM]	338 Solrock [TM]	021 Spearow [TM]	363 Spheal [TM]	167 Spinarak [TM]
		327 Spinda [TM]	442 Spiritomb [TM]	325 Spoink [TM]	682 Spritzee [TM]	007 Squirtle [TM]	234 Stantler [TM]	398 Staraptor [13, TM]
		397 Staravia [13, TM]	396 Starly [13, TM]	121 Starmie [TM]	120 Staryu [TM]	208 Steelix [TM]	508 Stoutland [TM]	618 Stunfisk [TM]
		434 Stunky [TM]	185 Sudowoodo [TM]	245 Suicune [TM]	192 Sunflora [TM]	191 Sunkern [TM]	283 Surskit [TM]	333 Swablu [TM]
		541 Swadloon [TM]	317 Swalot [TM]	260 Swampert [TM]	581 Swanna [TM]	277 Swellow [17, TM]	220 Swinub [TM]	684 Swirlix [TM]
		528 Swoobat [TM]	700 Sylveon [TM]	276 Taillow [17, TM]	663 Talonflame [TM]	114 Tangela [TM]	465 Tangrowth [TM]	128 Tauros [TM]
		216 Teddiursa [TM]	072 Tentacool [TM]	073 Tentacruel [TM]	498 Tepig [TM]	639 Terrakion [TM]	538 Throh [TM]	642 Thundurus [TM]
		532 Timburr [TM]	564 Tirtouga [TM]	468 Togekiss [TM]	175 Togepi [TM]	176 Togetic [TM]	255 Torchic [TM]	324 Torkoal [TM]
		641 Tornadus [TM]	389 Torterra [TM]	158 Totodile [TM]	454 Toxicroak [TM]	520 Tranquill [TM]	328 Trapinch [TM]	252 Treecko [TM]
		709 Trevenant [TM]	357 Tropius [TM]	568 Trubbish [TM]	387 Turtwig [TM]	535 Tympole [TM]	157 Typhlosion [TM]	248 Tyranitar [TM]
		697 Tyrantrum [TM]	236 Tyrogue [TM]	696 Tyrunt [TM]	197 Umbreon [TM]	521 Unfezant [TM]	217 Ursaring [TM]	480 Uxie [TM]
		583 Vanillish [TM]	582 Vanillite [TM]	584 Vanilluxe [TM]	134 Vaporeon [TM]	543 Venipede [TM]	049 Venomoth [TM]	048 Venonat [TM]
		003 Venusaur [TM]	416 Vespiquen [TM]	329 Vibrava [TM]	494 Victini [TM]	071 Victreebel [TM]	288 Vigoroth [TM]	045 Vileplume [TM]
		640 Virizion [TM]	666 Vivillon [TM]	313 Volbeat [5, TM]	637 Volcarona [TM]	100 Voltorb [TM]	629 Vullaby [TM]	037 Vulpix [TM]
		320 Wailmer [TM]	321 Wailord [TM]	365 Walrein [TM]	008 Wartortle [TM]	505 Watchog [TM]	461 Weavile [TM]	070 Weepinbell [TM]
		110 Weezing [TM]	547 Whimsicott [TM]	544 Whirlipede [TM]	340 Whiscash [TM]	293 Whismur [TM]	040 Wigglytuff [TM]	278 Wingull [TM]
		527 Woobat [TM]	194 Wooper [TM]	413 Wormadam (Plant) [TM]	413 Wormadam (Sand) [TM]	413 Wormadam (Trash) [TM]	178 Xatu [TM]	716 Xerneas [TM]
		562 Yamask [TM]	193 Yanma [11, TM]	469 Yanmega [1, 11, TM]	717 Yveltal [5, TM]	335 Zangoose [TM]	145 Zapdos [TM]	523 Zebstrika [TM]
		644 Zekrom [TM]	263 Zigzagoon [TM]	571 Zoroark [TM]	570 Zorua [TM]	041 Zubat [TM]	634 Zweilous [TM]	718 Zygarde [TM]
	Double-Edge	359 Absol [E]	306 Aggron [45]	304 Aron [40]	531 Audino [49]	713 Avalugg [56]	184 Azumarill [42]	371 Bagon [49]
		550 Basculin [36]	712 Bergmite [49]	399 Bidoof [E]	242 Blissey [1, 54]	522 Blitzle [E]	438 Bonsly [40]	001 Bulbasaur [27]
		318 Carvanha [E]	113 Chansey [1, 54]	358 Chimecho [42]	341 Corphish [E]	408 Cranidos [E]	104 Cubone [43]	155 Cyndaquil [55, E]
		585 Deerling [46]	206 Dunsparce [34]	133 Eevee [37]	589 Escavalier [1]	205 Forretress [56]	074 Geodude [40]	443 Gible [E]
		207 Gligar [E]	673 Gogoat [40]	076 Golem [50]	075 Graveler [50]	058 Growlithe [E]	214 Heracross [E]	449 Hippopotas [44]
		450 Hippowdon [50]	187 Hoppip [E]	002 Ivysaur [31]	039 Jigglypuff [49]	385 Jirachi [40]	115 Kangaskhan [E]	588 Karrablast [56]
		382 Kyogre [80]	305 Lairon [43]	636 Larvesta [50]	166 Ledian [48]	165 Ledyba [38]	264 Linoone [35]	183 Marill [37]
		105 Marowak [53]	241 Miltank [E]	258 Mudkip [E]	446 Munchlax [E]	299 Nosepass [E]	322 Numel [47]	095 Onix [49]
		231 Phanpy [42]	204 Pineco [45, E]	077 Ponyta [E]	156 Quilava [64]	020 Raticate [39]	019 Rattata [31]	369 Relicanth [50]
		373 Salamence [63]	551 Sandile [E]	586 Sawsbuck [52]	545 Scolipede [55]	161 Sentret [E]	372 Shelgon [56]	616 Shelmet [E]
		410 Shieldon [E]	672 Skiddo [38]	300 Skitty [40]	143 Snorlax [E]	459 Snover [E]	209 Snubbull [E]	327 Spinda [46]
		396 Starly [E]	208 Steelix [49]	434 Stunky [E]	185 Sudowoodo [40]	192 Sunflora [37]	191 Sunkern [37]	220 Swinub [E]
		216 Teddiursa [E]	175 Togepi [45]	176 Togetic [45]	387 Turtwig [E]	157 Typhlosion [1, 69]	543 Venipede [43]	003 Venusaur [31]
		494 Victini [65]	313 Volbeat [47]	320 Wailmer [E]	544 Whirlipede [50]	040 Wigglytuff [1]	193 Yanma [E]	
Dragon	Draco Meteor	334 Altaria [T]	493 Arceus [T]	610 Axew [T]	371 Bagon [T]	633 Deino [T]	483 Dialga [T]	691 Dragalge [T]
		148 Dragonair [T]	149 Dragonite [T]	147 Dratini [T]	621 Druddigon [T]	330 Flygon [T]	611 Fraxure [T]	444 Gabite [T]
		445 Garchomp [T]	443 Gible [T]	487 Giratina (Alt) [T]	487 Giratina (Ori) [T]	706 Goodra [T]	704 Goomy [T]	612 Haxorus [T]
		635 Hydreigon [T]	230 Kingdra [T]	646 Kyurem (Blk) [T]	646 Kyurem (Wht) [T]	646 Kyurem [T]	380 Latias [T]	381 Latios [T]
		714 Noibat [T]	715 Noivern [T]	484 Palkia [T]	384 Rayquaza [T]	643 Reshiram [T]	373 Salamence [T]	372 Shelgon [T]
		705 Sliggoo [T]	697 Tyrantrum [T]	696 Tyrunt [T]	329 Vibrava [T]	644 Zekrom [T]	634 Zweilous [T]	718 Zygarde [T]
Flying	Dragon Ascent	384 Rayquaza [T]						
Dragon	Dragon Breath	142 Aerodactyl [E]	334 Altaria [35]	566 Archen [31]	567 Archeops [31]	371 Bagon [13]	633 Deino [17]	483 Dialga [1]
		147 Dratini [E]	349 Feebas [E]	330 Flygon [35]	443 Gible [E]	487 Giratina (Alt) [1]	487 Giratina (Ori) [1]	706 Goodra [18]
		704 Goomy [18]	116 Horsea [E]	635 Hydreigon [17]	646 Kyurem (Blk) [29]	646 Kyurem (Wht) [29]	646 Kyurem [29]	380 Latias [20]
		381 Latios [20]	095 Onix [25]	484 Palkia [1]	643 Reshiram [29]	373 Salamence [13]	372 Shelgon [13]	705 Sliggoo [18]
		208 Steelix [25]	252 Treecko [E]	329 Vibrava [35]	644 Zekrom [29]	634 Zweilous [17]	718 Zygarde [1]	
	Dragon Claw (TM02)	142 Aerodactyl [TM]	306 Aggron [TM]	334 Altaria [TM]	493 Arceus [TM]	566 Archen [48, TM]	567 Archeops [56, TM]	610 Axew [28, TM]
		371 Bagon [29, TM]	689 Barbaracle [TM]	006 Charizard [1, TM]	004 Charmander [TM]	005 Charmeleon [TM]	652 Chesnaught [TM]	159 Croconaw [TM]
		483 Dialga [28, TM]	149 Dragonite [TM]	621 Druddigon [27, TM]	604 Eelektross [TM]	160 Feraligatr [TM]	330 Flygon [45, TM]	611 Fraxure [28, TM]
		444 Gabite [33, TM]	445 Garchomp [33, TM]	443 Gible [27, TM]	487 Giratina (Alt) [28, TM]	487 Giratina (Ori) [28, TM]	383 Groudon [TM]	612 Haxorus [28, TM]
		553 Krookodile [TM]	646 Kyurem (Blk) [TM]	646 Kyurem (Wht) [TM]	646 Kyurem [TM]	380 Latias [TM]	381 Latios [TM]	151 Mew [TM]
		715 Noivern [TM]	484 Palkia [28, TM]	675 Pangoro [TM]	384 Rayquaza [TM]	643 Reshiram [TM]	373 Salamence [29, TM]	254 Sceptile [TM]
		560 Scrafty [TM]	559 Scraggy [TM]	372 Shelgon [29, TM]	158 Totodile [TM]	248 Tyranitar [TM]	697 Tyrantrum [37, TM]	696 Tyrunt [37, TM]
		717 Yveltal [TM]	644 Zekrom [54, TM]					
	Dragon Dance	334 Altaria [30]	610 Axew [32]	371 Bagon [E]	339 Barboach [E]	004 Charmander [E]	341 Corphish [E]	148 Dragonair [61]
		149 Dragonite [61]	147 Dratini [51, E]	611 Fraxure [32]	130 Gyarados [47]	612 Haxorus [32]	116 Horsea [46]	230 Kingdra [52]
		131 Lapras [E]	246 Larvitar [E]	381 Latios [7]	384 Rayquaza [60]	559 Scraggy [E]	117 Seadra [52]	158 Totodile [E]
		357 Tropius [E]	696 Tyrunt [E]	718 Zygarde [72]				

Type	Move	Pokémon that can learn it						
Dragon	Dragon Pulse	142 Aerodactyl [BP]	306 Aggron [BP]	334 Altaria [40, BP]	181 Ampharos [1, 65, BP]	059 Arcanine [BP]	493 Arceus [BP]	566 Archen [BP, E]
		567 Archeops [BP]	610 Axew [41, BP, E]	371 Bagon [BP, E]	009 Blastoise [BP]	006 Charizard [BP]	004 Charmander [BP, E]	005 Charmeleon [BP]
		692 Clauncher [BP]	693 Clawitzer [1, 63, BP]	408 Cranidos [BP]	633 Deino [32, BP]	483 Dialga [BP]	691 Dragalge [53, BP]	148 Dragonair [BP]
		149 Dragonite [BP]	147 Dratini [BP, E]	621 Druddigon [BP]	604 Eelektross [BP]	349 Feebas [BP, E]	160 Feraligatr [BP]	330 Flygon [BP]
		611 Fraxure [42, BP]	444 Gabite [BP]	445 Garchomp [BP]	443 Gible [BP]	487 Giratina (Alt) [BP]	487 Giratina (Ori) [BP]	706 Goodra [47, BP]
		704 Goomy [42, BP]	383 Groudon [BP]	130 Gyarados [BP]	612 Haxorus [42, BP]	485 Heatran [BP]	695 Heliolisk [BP]	116 Horsea [41, BP]
		635 Hydreigon [32, BP]	230 Kingdra [45, BP]	553 Krookodile [BP]	646 Kyurem (Blk) [57, BP]	646 Kyurem (Wht) [57, BP]	646 Kyurem [57, BP]	131 Lapras [BP, E]
		380 Latias [56, BP]	381 Latios [56, BP]	448 Lucario [1, 60, BP]	249 Lugia [BP]	151 Mew [BP]	350 Milotic [BP]	034 Nidoking [BP]
		031 Nidoqueen [BP]	714 Noibat [BP]	715 Noivern [1, 70, BP]	095 Onix [BP]	484 Palkia [BP]	409 Rampardos [BP]	384 Rayquaza [50, BP]
		643 Reshiram [54, BP]	112 Rhydon [BP]	111 Rhyhorn [BP]	464 Rhyperior [BP]	373 Salamence [BP]	254 Sceptile [BP]	560 Scrafty [BP]
		559 Scraggy [BP]	117 Seadra [45, BP]	497 Serperior [BP]	372 Shelgon [BP]	690 Skrelp [49, BP]	705 Sliggoo [47, BP]	007 Squirtle [BP, E]
		208 Steelix [BP]	333 Swablu [38, BP]	357 Tropius [BP]	248 Tyranitar [BP]	697 Tyrantrum [BP]	696 Tyrunt [BP]	329 Vibrava [BP]
		008 Wartortle [BP]	644 Zekrom [BP]	634 Zweilous [32, BP]	718 Zygarde [63, BP]			
	Dragon Rage	610 Axew [10]	371 Bagon [E]	006 Charizard [17]	004 Charmander [16]	005 Charmeleon [17]	633 Deino [1]	148 Dragonair [15]
		149 Dragonite [15]	147 Dratini [15]	621 Druddigon [18]	611 Fraxure [1, 10]	444 Gabite [7]	445 Garchomp [1, 7]	443 Gible [7]
		130 Gyarados [23]	612 Haxorus [1, 10]	116 Horsea [E]	635 Hydreigon [1]	646 Kyurem (Blk) [1]	646 Kyurem (Wht) [1]	646 Kyurem [1]
		643 Reshiram [1]	644 Zekrom [1]	634 Zweilous [1]				
	Dragon Rush	304 Aron [E]	371 Bagon [E]	004 Charmander [E]	633 Deino [42]	148 Dragonair [47]	149 Dragonite [47]	147 Dratini [41, E]
		330 Flygon [47]	444 Gabite [49]	445 Garchomp [55]	443 Gible [37]	635 Hydreigon [42]	249 Lugia [15]	111 Rhyhorn [E]
		333 Swablu [E]	717 Yveltal [63]	634 Zweilous [42]				
	Dragon Tail (TM82)	306 Aggron [TM]	698 Amaura [TM]	024 Arbok [TM]	567 Archeops [TM]	699 Aurorus [TM]	009 Blastoise [TM]	006 Charizard [TM]
		633 Deino [TM]	483 Dialga [TM]	691 Dragalge [1, 59, TM]	148 Dragonair [33, TM]	149 Dragonite [33, TM]	147 Dratini [31, TM]	621 Druddigon [45, TM]
		604 Eelektross [TM]	160 Feraligatr [TM]	330 Flygon [29, TM]	611 Fraxure [TM]	445 Garchomp [TM]	487 Giratina (Alt) [TM]	487 Giratina (Ori) [TM]
		706 Goodra [TM]	383 Groudon [TM]	130 Gyarados [TM]	612 Haxorus [TM]	695 Heliolisk [TM]	694 Helioptile [TM]	635 Hydreigon [TM]
		553 Krookodile [TM]	646 Kyurem (Blk) [TM]	646 Kyurem (Wht) [TM]	646 Kyurem [TM]	463 Lickilicky [TM]	108 Lickitung [TM]	249 Lugia [TM]
		154 Meganium [TM]	151 Mew [TM]	350 Milotic [27, TM]	034 Nidoking [TM]	031 Nidoqueen [TM]	095 Onix [TM]	484 Palkia [TM]
		409 Rampardos [TM]	384 Rayquaza [TM]	643 Reshiram [TM]	112 Rhydon [TM]	464 Rhyperior [TM]	373 Salamence [1, TM]	503 Samurott [TM]
		560 Scrafty [TM]	559 Scraggy [TM]	497 Serperior [TM]	336 Seviper [TM]	199 Slowking [TM]	208 Steelix [TM]	248 Tyranitar [TM]
		697 Tyrantrum [30, TM]	696 Tyrunt [30, TM]	644 Zekrom [TM]	634 Zweilous [TM]	718 Zygarde [TM]		
Fighting	Drain Punch	063 Abra [BP]	065 Alakazam [BP]	683 Aromatisse [BP]	531 Audino [BP]	182 Bellossom [BP]	242 Blissey [BP]	286 Breloom [BP]
		427 Buneary [BP]	331 Cacnea [BP]	332 Cacturne [BP]	113 Chansey [BP]	652 Chesnaught [BP]	650 Chespin [BP]	036 Clefable [BP]
		035 Clefairy [BP]	534 Conkeldurr [BP]	453 Croagunk [BP, E]	491 Darkrai [BP]	386 Deoxys (Atk) [BP]	386 Deoxys (Def) [BP]	386 Deoxys (Nor) [BP]
		386 Deoxys (Spd) [BP]	096 Drowzee [BP]	604 Eelektross [BP]	475 Gallade [BP]	569 Garbodor [BP]	094 Gengar [BP]	044 Gloom [BP]
		622 Golett [BP]	623 Golurk [BP]	253 Grovyle [BP]	326 Grumpig [BP]	533 Gurdurr [BP]	440 Happiny [BP]	701 Hawlucha [BP]
		107 Hitmonchan [BP]	097 Hypno [BP]	039 Jigglypuff [BP]	385 Jirachi [BP]	124 Jynx [BP]	064 Kadabra [BP]	115 Kangaskhan [BP]
		352 Kecleon [BP]	166 Ledian [BP]	165 Ledyba [BP, E]	271 Lombre [BP]	428 Lopunny [BP]	448 Lucario [BP]	272 Ludicolo [BP]
		556 Maractus [BP]	308 Medicham [BP]	307 Meditite [BP, E]	648 Meloetta [BP]	151 Mew [BP]	150 Mewtwo [BP]	619 Mienfoo [33, BP]
		620 Mienshao [33, BP]	439 Mime Jr. [BP]	122 Mr. Mime [BP]	674 Pancham [BP]	675 Pangoro [BP]	651 Quilladin [BP]	486 Regigigas [BP]
		377 Regirock [BP]	579 Reuniclus [BP]	447 Riolu [BP]	254 Sceptile [BP]	560 Scrafty [BP]	559 Scraggy [BP, E]	537 Seismitoad [44, BP]
		285 Shroomish [BP, E]	080 Slowbro [BP]	199 Slowking [BP]	685 Slurpuff [BP]	327 Spinda [BP]	532 Timburr [BP, E]	468 Togekiss [BP]
		176 Togetic [BP]	454 Toxicroak [BP]	252 Treecko [BP]	709 Trevenant [BP]	568 Trubbish [BP]	045 Vileplume [BP]	040 Wigglytuff [BP]
Fairy	Draining Kiss	683 Aromatisse [21]	531 Audino [E]	478 Froslass [23]	282 Gardevoir [23]	368 Gorebyss [11]	124 Jynx [1]	281 Kirlia [23]
		707 Klefki [18]	370 Luvdisc [9]	025 Pikachu ◆	280 Ralts [22]	685 Slurpuff [31]	682 Spritzee [21]	684 Swirlix [31]
		700 Sylveon [20]	666 Vivillon [25]					
Psychic	Dream Eater (TM85)	063 Abra [TM]	359 Absol [TM]	190 Aipom [TM]	065 Alakazam [TM]	334 Altaria [TM]	698 Amaura [TM]	424 Ambipom [TM]
		493 Arceus [TM]	683 Aromatisse [TM]	531 Audino [TM]	699 Aurorus [TM]	482 Azelf [TM]	343 Baltoy [TM]	354 Banette [TM]
		606 Beheeyem [TM]	242 Blissey [TM]	654 Braixen [TM]	437 Bronzong [TM]	436 Bronzor [TM]	012 Butterfree [TM]	251 Celebi [TM]
		609 Chandelure [TM]	113 Chansey [TM]	358 Chimecho [TM]	433 Chingling [TM]	344 Claydol [TM]	036 Clefable [TM]	035 Clefairy [TM]
		173 Cleffa [TM]	563 Cofagrigus [TM]	546 Cottonee [TM]	488 Cresselia [TM]	491 Darkrai [84, TM]	301 Delcatty [TM]	655 Delphox [TM]
		386 Deoxys (Atk) [TM]	386 Deoxys (Def) [TM]	386 Deoxys (Nor) [TM]	386 Deoxys (Spd) [TM]	426 Drifblim [TM]	425 Drifloon [TM]	096 Drowzee [TM]
		206 Dunsparce [TM]	578 Duosion [TM]	356 Dusclops [TM]	477 Dusknoir [TM]	355 Duskull [TM]	605 Elgyem [TM]	196 Espeon [TM]
		677 Espurr [TM]	102 Exeggcute [TM]	103 Exeggutor [TM]	653 Fennekin [TM]	592 Frillish [TM]	478 Froslass [TM]	475 Gallade [TM]
		282 Gardevoir [53, TM]	092 Gastly [33, TM]	094 Gengar [39, TM]	203 Girafarig [TM]	487 Giratina (Alt) [TM]	487 Giratina (Ori) [TM]	431 Glameow [TM]
		574 Gothita [TM]	576 Gothitelle [TM]	575 Gothorita [TM]	711 Gourgeist [TM]	326 Grumpig [TM]	316 Gulpin [TM]	440 Happiny [TM]
		093 Haunter [39, TM]	430 Honchkrow [TM]	250 Ho-Oh [TM]	163 Hoothoot [57, TM]	229 Houndoom [TM]	228 Houndour [TM]	097 Hypno [TM]
		174 Igglybuff [TM]	593 Jellicent [TM]	039 Jigglypuff [TM]	385 Jirachi [TM]	124 Jynx [TM]	064 Kadabra [TM]	281 Kirlia [47, TM]
		608 Lampent [TM]	131 Lapras [TM]	380 Latias [TM]	381 Latios [TM]	542 Leavanny [TM]	463 Lickilicky [TM]	108 Lickitung [TM]
		510 Liepard [TM]	549 Lilligant [TM]	607 Litwick [TM]	249 Lugia [TM]	337 Lunatone [TM]	308 Medicham [TM]	307 Meditite [TM]
		648 Meloetta [TM]	678 Meowstic (F) [TM]	678 Meowstic (M) [TM]	052 Meowth [TM]	481 Mesprit [TM]	151 Mew [TM]	150 Mewtwo [TM]
		439 Mime Jr. [TM]	200 Misdreavus [TM]	429 Mismagius [TM]	414 Mothim [TM]	122 Mr. Mime [TM]	517 Munna [41, TM]	198 Murkrow [TM]
		518 Musharna [TM]	177 Natu [TM]	038 Ninetales [TM]	164 Noctowl [1, 67, TM]	714 Noibat [TM]	715 Noivern [TM]	053 Persian [TM]
		548 Petilil [TM]	708 Phantump [TM]	137 Porygon [TM]	233 Porygon2 [TM]	474 Porygon-Z [TM]	710 Pumpkaboo [TM]	509 Purrloin [TM]
		432 Purugly [TM]	280 Ralts [39, TM]	579 Reuniclus [TM]	479 Rotom (Fan) [TM]	479 Rotom (Frost) [TM]	479 Rotom (Heat) [TM]	479 Rotom (Mow) [TM]
		479 Rotom (Wash) [TM]	479 Rotom [TM]	302 Sableye [TM]	540 Sewaddle [TM]	292 Shedinja [TM]	353 Shuppet [TM]	561 Sigilyph [TM]
		300 Skitty [TM]	080 Slowbro [TM]	199 Slowking [TM]	079 Slowpoke [TM]	685 Slurpuff [TM]	238 Smoochum [TM]	215 Sneasel [TM]

◆ When Cosplay Pikachu becomes Pikachu Pop Star, it learns the move Draining Kiss. When it changes back to Cosplay Pikachu or wears other costumes, it forgets the move.

Type	Move	Pokémon that can learn it						
Psychic	Dream Eater (TM85)	577 Solosis [TM]	338 Solrock [TM]	327 Spinda [TM]	442 Spiritomb [19, TM]	325 Spoink [TM]	682 Spritzee [TM]	234 Stantler [TM]
		121 Starmie [TM]	333 Swablu [TM]	541 Swadloon [TM]	317 Swalot [TM]	684 Swirlix [TM]	528 Swoobat [TM]	468 Togekiss [TM]
		175 Togepi [TM]	176 Togetic [TM]	709 Trevenant [TM]	197 Umbreon [TM]	480 Uxie [TM]	666 Vivillon [TM]	505 Watchog [TM]
		461 Weavile [TM]	547 Whimsicott [TM]	040 Wigglytuff [TM]	527 Woobat [TM]	413 Wormadam (Plant) [TM]	413 Wormadam (Sand) [TM]	413 Wormadam (Trash) [TM]
		178 Xatu [TM]	562 Yamask [TM]	193 Yanma [TM]	469 Yanmega [TM]	717 Yveltal [TM]		
Flying	Drill Peck	085 Dodrio [41]	084 Doduo [37]	395 Empoleon [52]	022 Fearow [47]	198 Murkrow [E]	177 Natu [E]	393 Piplup [39]
		394 Prinplup [46]	227 Skarmory [E]	021 Spearow [37]	145 Zapdos [1, 71]			
Ground	Drill Run	343 Baltoy [BP]	015 Beedrill [BP]	344 Claydol [BP]	087 Dewgong [BP]	529 Drilbur [43, BP]	206 Dunsparce [43, BP]	589 Escavalier [BP]
		530 Excadrill [55, BP]	022 Fearow [1, 53, BP]	205 Forretress [BP]	118 Goldeen [BP]	588 Karrablast [BP, E]	131 Lapras [BP]	151 Mew [BP]
		034 Nidoking [BP]	031 Nidoqueen [BP]	032 Nidoran ♂ [BP]	033 Nidorino [BP]	204 Pineco [BP]	078 Rapidash [BP]	112 Rhydon [33, BP]
		111 Rhyhorn [33, BP]	464 Rhyperior [33, BP]	119 Seaking [BP]	086 Seel [BP]	021 Spearow [BP]		
Dragon	Dual Chop	610 Axew [13, BP]	689 Barbaracle [BP]	688 Binacle [BP]	625 Bisharp [BP]	257 Blaziken [BP]	652 Chesnaught [BP]	650 Chespin [BP]
		256 Combusken [BP]	453 Croagunk [BP]	125 Electabuzz [BP]	466 Electivire [BP]	239 Elekid [BP]	611 Fraxure [13, BP]	444 Gabite [24, BP]
		475 Gallade [BP]	445 Garchomp [24, BP]	701 Hawlucha [BP]	612 Haxorus [13, BP]	392 Infernape [BP]	448 Lucario [BP]	068 Machamp [33, BP]
		067 Machoke [33, BP]	066 Machop [31, BP]	240 Magby [BP]	126 Magmar [BP]	467 Magmortar [BP]	056 Mankey [BP]	648 Meloetta [BP]
		151 Mew [BP]	619 Mienfoo [BP]	620 Mienshao [BP]	391 Monferno [BP]	674 Pancham [BP]	675 Pangoro [BP]	624 Pawniard [BP]
		057 Primeape [BP]	651 Quilladin [BP]	447 Riolu [BP]	539 Sawk [BP]	254 Sceptile [36, BP]	560 Scrafty [BP]	559 Scraggy [BP]
		454 Toxicroak [BP]						
Fighting	Dynamic Punch	286 Breloom [50]	331 Cacnea [E]	534 Conkeldurr [37]	453 Croagunk [E]	239 Elekid [E]	622 Golett [30]	623 Golurk [30]
		533 Gurdurr [37]	068 Machamp [57]	067 Machoke [57]	066 Machop [45]	240 Magby [E]	296 Makuhita [E]	307 Meditite [E]
		062 Poliwrath [32]	532 Timburr [34]					

E

Type	Move	Pokémon that can learn it						
Ground	Earth Power	142 Aerodactyl [BP]	306 Aggron [BP]	698 Amaura [BP]	347 Anorith [BP]	493 Arceus [20, BP]	566 Archen [BP, E]	567 Archeops [BP]
		348 Armaldo [BP]	304 Aron [BP]	699 Aurorus [BP]	343 Baltoy [37, BP]	689 Barbaracle [BP]	339 Barboach [BP, E]	411 Bastiodon [BP]
		525 Boldore [BP]	438 Bonsly [BP]	323 Camerupt [26, BP]	703 Carbink [BP]	565 Carracosta [BP]	251 Celebi [BP]	344 Claydol [40, BP]
		222 Corsola [47, BP]	346 Cradily [BP]	408 Cranidos [BP]	104 Cubone [BP]	633 Deino [BP, E]	483 Dialga [33, BP]	719 Diancie [BP]
		660 Diggersby [BP]	050 Diglett [29, BP]	232 Donphan [BP]	529 Drilbur [BP, E]	051 Dugtrio [33, BP]	530 Excadrill [BP]	330 Flygon [26, BP]
		444 Gabite [BP]	445 Garchomp [BP]	423 Gastrodon [BP]	074 Geodude [BP]	443 Gible [BP]	526 Gigalith [BP]	487 Giratina (Alt) [33, BP]
		487 Giratina (Ori) [33, BP]	207 Gligar [BP]	472 Gliscor [BP]	076 Golem [BP]	622 Golett [BP]	623 Golurk [BP]	075 Graveler [BP]
		388 Grotle [BP]	383 Groudon [15, BP]	485 Heatran [1, 73, BP]	449 Hippopotas [BP]	450 Hippowdon [BP]	250 Ho-Oh [BP]	635 Hydreigon [BP]
		140 Kabuto [BP]	141 Kabutops [BP]	552 Krokorok [BP]	553 Krookodile [BP]	646 Kyurem (Blk) [BP]	646 Kyurem (Wht) [BP]	646 Kyurem [BP]
		305 Lairon [BP]	645 Landorus [43, BP]	246 Larvitar [BP]	345 Lileep [BP]	249 Lugia [BP]	337 Lunatone [BP]	219 Magcargo [1, 58, BP]
		473 Mamoswine [BP]	105 Marowak [BP]	259 Marshtomp [BP]	151 Mew [BP]	258 Mudkip [BP]	034 Nidoking [43, BP]	031 Nidoqueen [43, BP]
		299 Nosepass [37, BP]	322 Numel [26, BP]	138 Omanyte [BP]	139 Omastar [BP]	095 Onix [BP]	484 Palkia [33, BP]	536 Palpitoad [BP]
		231 Phanpy [BP]	221 Piloswine [BP]	476 Probopass [37, BP]	247 Pupitar [BP]	195 Quagsire [BP]	409 Rampardos [BP]	384 Rayquaza [BP]
		486 Regigigas [BP]	377 Regirock [BP]	369 Relicanth [BP]	643 Reshiram [BP]	112 Rhydon [BP]	111 Rhyhorn [BP]	464 Rhyperior [BP]
		524 Roggenrola [BP]	551 Sandile [BP]	027 Sandshrew [BP]	028 Sandslash [BP]	537 Seismitoad [BP]	492 Shaymin (Land) [BP]	422 Shellos [BP]
		410 Shieldon [BP]	213 Shuckle [BP]	218 Slugma [50, BP, E]	338 Solrock [BP]	208 Steelix [BP]	618 Stunfisk [BP, E]	185 Sudowoodo [BP]
		192 Sunflora [BP]	191 Sunkern [BP]	260 Swampert [BP]	220 Swinub [BP]	639 Terrakion [BP]	564 Tirtouga [BP]	324 Torkoal [BP]
		389 Torterra [BP]	328 Trapinch [26, BP, E]	387 Turtwig [BP, E]	535 Tympole [BP, E]	248 Tyranitar [BP]	697 Tyrantrum [BP]	696 Tyrunt [BP]
		329 Vibrava [26, BP]	340 Whiscash [BP]	194 Wooper [BP]	413 Wormadam (Sand) [BP]	644 Zekrom [BP]	634 Zweilous [BP]	718 Zygarde [BP]
	Earthquake (TM26)	460 Abomasnow [TM]	142 Aerodactyl [TM]	306 Aggron [TM]	334 Altaria [TM]	024 Arbok [TM]	493 Arceus [TM]	566 Archen [TM]
		567 Archeops [TM]	348 Armaldo [TM]	304 Aron [TM]	699 Aurorus [TM]	713 Avalugg [TM]	343 Baltoy [TM]	689 Barbaracle [TM]
		339 Barboach [32, TM]	411 Bastiodon [TM]	688 Binacle [TM]	009 Blastoise [TM]	257 Blaziken [TM]	242 Blissey [TM]	525 Boldore [TM]
		626 Bouffalant [TM]	437 Bronzong [TM]	436 Bronzor [TM]	659 Bunnelby [49, TM]	323 Camerupt [46, TM]	565 Carracosta [TM]	113 Chansey [TM]
		006 Charizard [TM]	652 Chesnaught [TM]	344 Claydol [TM]	534 Conkeldurr [TM]	222 Corsola [TM]	346 Cradily [TM]	408 Cranidos [TM]
		453 Croagunk [TM]	558 Crustle [TM]	104 Cubone [TM]	555 Darmanitan [TM]	483 Dialga [TM]	660 Diggersby [57, TM]	050 Diglett [40, TM]
		232 Donphan [43, TM]	149 Dragonite [TM]	452 Drapion [TM]	529 Drilbur [33, TM]	621 Druddigon [TM]	051 Dugtrio [50, TM]	206 Dunsparce [TM]
		356 Dusclops [TM]	477 Dusknoir [TM]	557 Dwebble [TM]	023 Ekans [TM]	466 Electivire [TM]	500 Emboar [TM]	395 Empoleon [TM]
		530 Excadrill [36, TM]	295 Exploud [TM]	160 Feraligatr [TM]	330 Flygon [33, TM]	205 Forretress [TM]	444 Gabite [TM]	475 Gallade [TM]
		445 Garchomp [TM]	423 Gastrodon [TM]	074 Geodude [34, TM]	443 Gible [TM]	526 Gigalith [TM]	203 Girafarig [TM]	487 Giratina (Alt) [TM]
		487 Giratina (Ori) [TM]	362 Glalie [TM]	207 Gligar [TM]	472 Gliscor [TM]	673 Gogoat [60, TM]	076 Golem [40, TM]	622 Golett [45, TM]
		623 Golurk [50, TM]	706 Goodra [TM]	210 Granbull [TM]	075 Graveler [40, TM]	383 Groudon [35, TM]	130 Gyarados [TM]	297 Hariyama [TM]
		612 Haxorus [TM]	485 Heatran [TM]	214 Heracross [TM]	449 Hippopotas [37, TM]	450 Hippowdon [40, TM]	107 Hitmonchan [TM]	106 Hitmonlee [TM]
		237 Hitmontop [TM]	250 Ho-Oh [TM]	635 Hydreigon [TM]	392 Infernape [TM]	115 Kangaskhan [TM]	552 Krokorok [48, TM]	553 Krookodile [54, TM]
		382 Kyogre [TM]	305 Lairon [TM]	645 Landorus [55, TM]	246 Larvitar [46, TM]	380 Latias [TM]	381 Latios [TM]	463 Lickilicky [TM]
		108 Lickitung [TM]	294 Loudred [TM]	448 Lucario [TM]	249 Lugia [TM]	337 Lunatone [TM]	068 Machamp [TM]	067 Machoke [TM]
		066 Machop [TM]	219 Magcargo [TM]	467 Magmortar [TM]	296 Makuhita [TM]	473 Mamoswine [46, TM]	056 Mankey [TM]	226 Mantine [TM]

Type	Move	Pokémon that can learn it						
Ground	Earthquake (TM26)	458 Mantyke [TM]	105 Marowak [TM]	259 Marshtomp [48, TM]	154 Meganium [TM]	376 Metagross [TM]	375 Metang [TM]	151 Mew [TM]
		150 Mewtwo [TM]	241 Miltank [TM]	446 Munchlax [TM]	034 Nidoking [TM]	031 Nidoqueen [TM]	299 Nosepass [TM]	322 Numel [40, TM]
		095 Onix [TM]	484 Palkia [TM]	675 Pangoro [TM]	231 Phanpy [TM]	221 Piloswine [46, TM]	204 Pineco [TM]	127 Pinsir [TM]
		186 Politoed [TM]	061 Poliwhirl [TM]	062 Poliwrath [TM]	057 Primeape [TM]	476 Probopass [TM]	247 Pupitar [54, TM]	195 Quagsire [36, TM]
		409 Rampardos [TM]	384 Rayquaza [TM]	378 Regice [TM]	486 Regigigas [TM]	377 Regirock [TM]	379 Registeel [TM]	369 Relicanth [TM]
		112 Rhydon [48, TM]	111 Rhyhorn [45, TM]	464 Rhyperior [48, TM]	447 Riolu [TM]	524 Roggenrola [TM]	373 Salamence [TM]	551 Sandile [43, TM]
		027 Sandshrew [46, TM]	028 Sandslash [53, TM]	539 Sawk [TM]	254 Sceptile [TM]	545 Scolipede [TM]	364 Sealeo [TM]	537 Seismitoad [TM]
		336 Seviper [TM]	319 Sharpedo [TM]	410 Shieldon [TM]	213 Shuckle [TM]	289 Slaking [TM]	080 Slowbro [TM]	199 Slowking [TM]
		079 Slowpoke [TM]	143 Snorlax [TM]	209 Snubbull [TM]	338 Solrock [TM]	363 Spheal [TM]	234 Stantler [TM]	208 Steelix [TM]
		618 Stunfisk [TM]	185 Sudowoodo [TM]	317 Swalot [TM]	260 Swampert [51, TM]	220 Swinub [37, TM]	465 Tangrowth [TM]	128 Tauros [TM]
		216 Teddiursa [TM]	639 Terrakion [TM]	538 Throh [TM]	564 Tirtouga [TM]	324 Torkoal [TM]	389 Torterra [32, TM]	454 Toxicroak [TM]
		328 Trapinch [33, TM]	709 Trevenant [TM]	357 Tropius [TM]	157 Typhlosion [TM]	248 Tyranitar [54, TM]	697 Tyrantrum [47, TM]	236 Tyrogue [TM]
		696 Tyrunt [44, TM]	217 Ursaring [TM]	003 Venusaur [TM]	329 Vibrava [33, TM]	288 Vigoroth [TM]	320 Wailmer [TM]	321 Wailord [TM]
		365 Walrein [TM]	340 Whiscash [34, TM]	194 Wooper [33, TM]	413 Wormadam (Sand) [TM]	718 Zygarde [55, TM]		
Normal	Echoed Voice (TM49)	359 Absol [TM]	334 Altaria [TM]	698 Amaura [TM]	181 Ampharos [TM]	493 Arceus [TM]	683 Aromatisse [13, TM]	531 Audino [TM]
		699 Aurorus [TM]	153 Bayleef [TM]	614 Beartic [TM]	606 Beheeyem [TM]	400 Bibarel [TM]	399 Bidoof [TM]	257 Blaziken [TM]
		242 Blissey [TM]	654 Braixen [TM]	418 Buizel [TM]	001 Bulbasaur [TM]	323 Camerupt [TM]	251 Celebi [TM]	113 Chansey [TM]
		006 Charizard [TM]	004 Charmander [TM]	005 Charmeleon [TM]	441 Chatot [37, TM]	152 Chikorita [TM]	358 Chimecho [TM]	433 Chingling [TM]
		573 Cinccino [TM]	036 Clefable [TM]	035 Clefairy [TM]	173 Cleffa [TM]	256 Combusken [TM]	613 Cubchoo [TM]	104 Cubone [TM]
		585 Deerling [TM]	301 Delcatty [TM]	655 Delphox [TM]	087 Dewgong [TM]	483 Dialga [TM]	050 Diglett [TM]	085 Dodrio [TM]
		084 Doduo [TM]	232 Donphan [TM]	051 Dugtrio [TM]	133 Eevee [TM]	605 Elgyem [TM]	500 Emboar [TM]	395 Empoleon [TM]
		196 Espeon [TM]	677 Espurr [TM]	295 Exploud [1, 4, TM]	022 Fearow [TM]	653 Fennekin [TM]	180 Flaaffy [TM]	669 Flabébé [TM]
		136 Flareon [TM]	419 Floatzel [TM]	670 Floette [TM]	671 Florges [TM]	656 Froakie [TM]	657 Frogadier [TM]	676 Furfrou [TM]
		162 Furret [TM]	475 Gallade [TM]	282 Gardevoir [TM]	203 Girafarig [TM]	487 Giratina (Alt) [TM]	487 Giratina (Ori) [TM]	471 Glaceon [TM]
		431 Glameow [TM]	658 Greninja [TM]	440 Happiny [TM]	250 Ho-Oh [TM]	163 Hoothoot [25, TM]	635 Hydreigon [TM]	174 Igglybuff [TM]
		002 Ivysaur [TM]	039 Jigglypuff [TM]	135 Jolteon [TM]	124 Jynx [TM]	281 Kirlia [TM]	402 Kricketune [TM]	646 Kyurem (Blk) [TM]
		646 Kyurem (Wht) [TM]	646 Kyurem [TM]	131 Lapras [TM]	470 Leafeon [TM]	510 Liepard [TM]	264 Linoone [TM]	667 Litleo [33, TM]
		271 Lombre [TM]	270 Lotad [TM]	294 Loudred [1, 4, TM]	272 Ludicolo [TM]	249 Lugia [TM]	179 Mareep [TM]	105 Marowak [TM]
		259 Marshtomp [TM]	154 Meganium [TM]	648 Meloetta [36, TM]	678 Meowstic (F) [TM]	678 Meowstic (M) [TM]	052 Meowth [TM]	151 Mew [TM]
		241 Miltank [TM]	572 Minccino [33, TM]	312 Minun [TM]	200 Misdreavus [TM]	429 Mismagius [TM]	258 Mudkip [TM]	034 Nidoking [TM]
		031 Nidoqueen [TM]	029 Nidoran ♀ [TM]	032 Nidoran ♂ [TM]	030 Nidorina [TM]	033 Nidorino [TM]	164 Noctowl [27, TM]	714 Noibat [TM]
		715 Noivern [TM]	322 Numel [TM]	417 Pachirisu [TM]	484 Palkia [TM]	536 Palpitoad [42, TM]	674 Pancham [TM]	675 Pangoro [TM]
		279 Pelipper [TM]	053 Persian [TM]	231 Phanpy [TM]	172 Pichu [TM]	519 Pidove [TM]	499 Pignite [TM]	025 Pikachu [TM]
		393 Piplup [TM]	311 Plusle [TM]	186 Politoed [TM]	077 Ponyta [TM]	394 Prinplup [TM]	509 Purrloin [TM]	432 Purugly [TM]
		668 Pyroar [33, TM]	026 Raichu [TM]	280 Ralts [TM]	078 Rapidash [TM]	384 Rayquaza [TM]	643 Reshiram [TM]	586 Sawsbuck [TM]
		364 Sealeo [TM]	086 Seel [TM]	537 Seismitoad [49, TM]	161 Sentret [TM]	300 Skitty [TM]	080 Slowbro [TM]	199 Slowking [TM]
		079 Slowpoke [TM]	238 Smoochum [TM]	021 Spearow [TM]	363 Spheal [TM]	682 Spritzee [13, TM]	398 Staraptor [TM]	397 Staravia [TM]
		396 Starly [TM]	333 Swablu [TM]	260 Swampert [TM]	277 Swellow [TM]	700 Sylveon [TM]	276 Taillow [TM]	498 Tepig [TM]
		468 Togekiss [TM]	175 Togepi [TM]	176 Togetic [TM]	255 Torchic [TM]	520 Tranquill [TM]	535 Tympole [38, TM]	197 Umbreon [TM]
		521 Unfezant [TM]	134 Vaporeon [TM]	003 Venusaur [TM]	320 Wailmer [TM]	321 Wailord [TM]	365 Walrein [TM]	293 Whismur [4, TM]
		040 Wigglytuff [TM]	278 Wingull [TM]	716 Xerneas [TM]	644 Zekrom [TM]	263 Zigzagoon [TM]		
Electric	Eerie Impulse	702 Dedenne [E]	309 Electrike [E]	101 Electrode [6]	695 Heliolisk [1]	171 Lanturn [1]	179 Mareep [E]	403 Shinx [E]
		618 Stunfisk [E]	100 Voltorb [6]	194 Wooper [E]				
Normal	Egg Bomb	242 Blissey [42]	113 Chansey [42]	103 Exeggutor [27]				
Electric	Electric Terrain	466 Electivire [1, 65]	694 Helioptile [E]	405 Luxray [1, 67]	082 Magneton [1]	462 Magnezone [1]	310 Manectric [1, 60]	179 Mareep [E]
		025 Pikachu ◆						
	Electrify	695 Heliolisk [1]	694 Helioptile [45]					
	Electro Ball	181 Ampharos [25]	170 Chinchou [9]	125 Electabuzz [22]	466 Electivire [22]	309 Electrike [E]	101 Electrode [22]	239 Elekid [22]
		587 Emolga [26]	180 Flaaffy [25]	596 Galvantula [29]	595 Joltik [29]	171 Lanturn [1, 9]	081 Magnemite [29]	082 Magneton [29]
		462 Magnezone [29]	179 Mareep [22]	312 Minun [19]	417 Pachirisu [25]	025 Pikachu [13]	311 Plusle [19]	479 Rotom (Fan) [43]
		479 Rotom (Frost) [43]	479 Rotom (Heat) [43]	479 Rotom (Mow) [43]	479 Rotom (Wash) [43]	479 Rotom [43]	100 Voltorb [22]	
	Electroweb	181 Ampharos [BP]	168 Ariados [BP]	267 Beautifly [BP]	015 Beedrill [BP]	412 Burmy [BP]	012 Butterfree [BP]	268 Cascoon [BP]
		010 Caterpie [BP]	702 Dedenne [BP]	269 Dustox [BP]	125 Electabuzz [BP]	466 Electivire [BP]	239 Elekid [BP]	587 Emolga [BP]
		180 Flaaffy [BP]	596 Galvantula [15, BP]	649 Genesect [BP]	695 Heliolisk [BP]	694 Helioptile [BP]	595 Joltik [15, BP]	014 Kakuna [BP]
		542 Leavanny [BP]	081 Magnemite [BP]	082 Magneton [BP]	462 Magnezone [BP]	179 Mareep [BP]	011 Metapod [BP]	151 Mew [BP]
		312 Minun [BP]	414 Mothim [BP]	417 Pachirisu [BP]	172 Pichu [BP]	025 Pikachu [BP]	311 Plusle [BP]	137 Porygon [BP]
		233 Porygon2 [BP]	474 Porygon-Z [BP]	026 Raichu [BP]	479 Rotom (Fan) [BP]	479 Rotom (Frost) [BP]	479 Rotom (Heat) [BP]	479 Rotom (Mow) [BP]
		479 Rotom (Wash) [BP]	479 Rotom [BP]	540 Sewaddle [BP]	266 Silcoon [BP]	665 Spewpa [BP]	167 Spinarak [BP, E]	618 Stunfisk [BP]
		541 Swadloon [BP]	642 Thundurus [BP]	666 Vivillon [BP]	013 Weedle [BP]	413 Wormadam (Plant) [BP]	413 Wormadam (Sand) [BP]	413 Wormadam (Trash) [BP]
		265 Wurmple [BP]						

◆ When Cosplay Pikachu becomes Pikachu, Ph.D., it learns the move Electric Terrain. When it changes back to Cosplay Pikachu or wears other costumes, it forgets the move.

	Move	Pokémon that can learn it						
Dark	Embargo (TM63)	063 Abra [TM]	065 Alakazam [TM]	354 Banette [34, TM]	689 Barbaracle [TM]	606 Beheeyem [TM]	688 Binacle [TM]	625 Bisharp [41, TM]
		654 Braixen [TM]	332 Cacturne [TM]	609 Chandelure [TM]	563 Cofagrigus [TM]	453 Croagunk [TM]	491 Darkrai [TM]	655 Delphox [TM]
		426 Drifblim [TM]	425 Drifloon [TM]	578 Duosion [TM]	356 Dusclops [TM]	477 Dusknoir [TM]	355 Duskull [TM]	605 Elgyem [TM]
		653 Fennekin [TM]	478 Froslass [TM]	092 Gastly [TM]	094 Gengar [TM]	574 Gothita [19, TM]	576 Gothitelle [19, TM]	575 Gothorita [19, TM]
		093 Haunter [TM]	430 Honchkrow [TM]	229 Houndoom [41, TM]	228 Houndour [37, TM]	686 Inkay [TM]	064 Kadabra [TM]	552 Krokorok [22, TM]
		553 Krookodile [22, TM]	608 Lampent [TM]	510 Liepard [TM]	607 Litwick [TM]	337 Lunatone [17, TM]	687 Malamar [TM]	630 Mandibuzz [50, TM]
		303 Mawile [TM]	648 Meloetta [TM]	151 Mew [TM]	150 Mewtwo [TM]	262 Mightyena [32, TM]	200 Misdreavus [TM]	429 Mismagius [TM]
		198 Murkrow [TM]	274 Nuzleaf [TM]	675 Pangoro [TM]	624 Pawniard [41, TM]	053 Persian [TM]	261 Poochyena [28, TM]	474 Porygon-Z [34, TM]
		509 Purrloin [TM]	579 Reuniclus [TM]	302 Sableye [TM]	551 Sandile [22, TM]	275 Shiftry [TM]	353 Shuppet [34, TM]	215 Sneasel [TM]
		577 Solosis [TM]	338 Solrock [17, TM]	442 Spiritomb [TM]	528 Swoobat [TM]	642 Thundurus [TM]	641 Tornadus [TM]	454 Toxicroak [TM]
		494 Victini [TM]	629 Vullaby [50, TM]	461 Weavile [1, TM]	527 Woobat [TM]	562 Yamask [TM]	717 Yveltal [TM]	335 Zangoose [33, TM]
		571 Zoroark [44, TM]	570 Zorua [41, TM]					
Fire	Ember	371 Bagon [4]	257 Blaziken [1, 5]	654 Braixen [5]	323 Camerupt [1, 5]	351 Castform [10]	006 Charizard [1, 7]	004 Charmander [7]
		005 Charmeleon [1, 7]	390 Chimchar [7]	256 Combusken [1, 5]	155 Cyndaquil [10]	655 Delphox [5]	500 Emboar [1, 7]	244 Entei [8]
		653 Fennekin [5]	136 Flareon [9]	662 Fletchinder [17]	058 Growlithe [6]	229 Houndoom [1]	228 Houndour [1]	392 Infernape [1, 7]
		608 Lampent [1]	636 Larvesta [1]	667 Litleo [5]	607 Litwick [1]	240 Magby [5]	219 Magcargo [1, 6]	126 Magmar [1, 5]
		467 Magmortar [1, 5]	146 Moltres [1]	391 Monferno [1, 7]	322 Numel [5]	499 Pignite [1, 7]	077 Ponyta [9]	668 Pyroar [5]
		156 Quilava [10]	078 Rapidash [1, 9]	373 Salamence [1, 4]	372 Shelgon [1, 4]	218 Slugma [6]	663 Talonflame [17]	498 Tepig [7]
		255 Torchic [5]	324 Torkoal [1]	157 Typhlosion [1, 10]	637 Volcarona [1]	037 Vulpix [1]		
Normal	Encore	063 Abra [E]	698 Amaura [44]	531 Audino [E]	699 Aurorus [46]	298 Azurill [E]	069 Bellsprout [E]	427 Buneary [E]
		441 Chatot [E]	390 Chimchar [E]	035 Clefairy [1]	173 Cleffa [4]	546 Cottonee [E]	613 Cubchoo [E]	554 Darumaka [E]
		087 Dewgong [13]	502 Dewott [36]	587 Emolga [38]	316 Gulpin [20]	701 Hawlucha [20]	187 Hoppip [E]	314 Illumise [26, E]
		165 Ledyba [E]	066 Machop [E]	056 Mankey [E]	439 Mime Jr. [18]	572 Minccino [15]	312 Minun [10]	122 Mr. Mime [18]
		501 Oshawott [31]	172 Pichu [E]	311 Plusle [10]	060 Poliwag [E]	054 Psyduck [E]	509 Purrloin [E]	280 Ralts [E]
		503 Samurott [38]	364 Sealeo [9]	086 Seel [13, E]	616 Shelmet [E]	213 Shuckle [5]	289 Slaking [1, 6]	287 Slakoth [6]
		363 Spheal [9]	327 Spinda [E]	191 Sunkern [E]	317 Swalot [20]	175 Togepi [17]	176 Togetic [17]	288 Vigoroth [1, 6]
		313 Volbeat [E]	365 Walrein [7]	194 Wooper [E]	360 Wynaut [1]			
	Endeavor	306 Aggron [BP]	566 Archen [38, BP]	567 Archeops [40, BP]	683 Aromatisse [BP]	304 Aron [BP, E]	610 Axew [BP, E]	689 Barbaracle [BP]
		550 Basculin [BP]	015 Beedrill [40, BP]	688 Binacle [BP]	242 Blissey [BP]	626 Bouffalant [BP]	427 Buneary [BP]	659 Bunnelby [BP]
		113 Chansey [BP]	652 Chesnaught [BP]	650 Chespin [BP]	390 Chimchar [BP]	036 Clefable [BP]	035 Clefairy [BP]	173 Cleffa [BP]
		415 Combee [BP]	341 Corphish [BP, E]	222 Corsola [BP]	546 Cottonee [44, BP]	408 Cranidos [BP]	342 Crawdaunt [BP]	104 Cubone [41, BP]
		555 Darmanitan [BP]	554 Darumaka [BP]	719 Diancie [BP]	660 Diggersby [BP]	085 Dodrio [53, BP]	084 Doduo [45, BP, E]	232 Donphan [BP]
		580 Ducklett [BP]	206 Dunsparce [46, BP]	578 Duosion [28, BP]	632 Durant [BP]	500 Emboar [BP]	295 Exploud [BP]	597 Ferroseed [BP]
		598 Ferrothorn [BP]	669 Flabébé [BP]	670 Floette [BP]	671 Florges [BP]	611 Fraxure [BP]	676 Furfrou [BP]	253 Grovyle [BP]
		440 Happiny [BP]	701 Hawlucha [36, BP]	612 Haxorus [BP]	237 Hitmontop [1, 60, BP]	174 Igglybuff [BP]	392 Infernape [BP]	039 Jigglypuff [BP]
		115 Kangaskhan [BP, E]	647 Keldeo [BP]	401 Kricketot [BP]	402 Kricketune [BP]	646 Kyurem (Blk) [71, BP]	646 Kyurem (Wht) [71, BP]	646 Kyurem [71, BP]
		305 Lairon [BP]	667 Litleo [28, BP]	428 Lopunny [BP]	294 Loudred [BP]	473 Mamoswine [BP]	056 Mankey [BP]	556 Maractus [BP]
		105 Marowak [49, BP]	259 Marshtomp [52, BP]	151 Mew [BP]	391 Monferno [BP]	258 Mudkip [44, BP]	536 Palpitoad [BP]	674 Pancham [BP]
		675 Pangoro [BP]	515 Panpour [BP]	511 Pansage [BP]	513 Pansear [BP]	504 Patrat [BP]	231 Phanpy [BP, E]	499 Pignite [BP]
		221 Piloswine [BP]	186 Politoed [BP]	060 Poliwag [BP, E]	061 Poliwhirl [BP]	062 Poliwrath [BP]	057 Primeape [BP]	668 Pyroar [28, BP]
		651 Quilladin [BP]	409 Rampardos [30, BP]	020 Raticate [44, BP]	019 Rattata [34, BP]	579 Reuniclus [28, BP]	112 Rhydon [BP]	111 Rhyhorn [BP]
		464 Rhyperior [BP]	254 Sceptile [BP]	545 Scolipede [BP]	537 Seismitoad [BP]	492 Shaymin (Land) [BP]	516 Simipour [BP]	512 Simisage [BP]
		514 Simisear [BP]	685 Slurpuff [21, BP]	577 Solosis [28, BP]	682 Spritzee [BP]	398 Staraptor [18, BP]	397 Staravia [18, BP]	396 Starly [17, BP]
		618 Stunfisk [BP]	192 Sunflora [BP]	191 Sunkern [25, BP]	260 Swampert [56, BP]	581 Swanna [BP]	277 Swellow [39, BP]	220 Swinub [BP]
		684 Swirlix [21, BP]	528 Swoobat [47, BP]	276 Taillow [37, BP]	114 Tangela [BP, E]	465 Tangrowth [BP]	128 Tauros [BP]	498 Tepig [BP, E]
		468 Togekiss [BP]	175 Togepi [BP]	176 Togetic [BP]	252 Treecko [45, BP, E]	535 Tympole [BP]	543 Venipede [BP]	416 Vespiquen [BP]
		666 Vivillon [BP]	505 Watchog [BP]	547 Whimsicott [BP]	544 Whirlipede [BP]	293 Whismur [BP, E]	040 Wigglytuff [BP]	527 Woobat [47, BP]
		413 Wormadam (Plant) [BP]	413 Wormadam (Sand) [BP]	413 Wormadam (Trash) [BP]	716 Xerneas [BP]	335 Zangoose [BP]		
	Endure	594 Alomomola [E]	610 Axew [E]	371 Bagon [E]	411 Bastiodon [36]	614 Beartic [25]	399 Bidoof [E]	522 Blitzle [E]
		438 Bonsly [E]	001 Bulbasaur [E]	427 Buneary [6]	113 Chansey [E]	366 Clamperl [E]	692 Clauncher [E]	222 Corsola [35]
		613 Cubchoo [25]	104 Cubone [E]	554 Darumaka [E]	050 Diglett [E]	206 Dunsparce [40]	632 Durant [E]	557 Dwebble [E]
		133 Eevee [E]	590 Foongus [E]	074 Geodude [E]	704 Goomy [E]	440 Happiny [E]	297 Hariyama [42]	214 Heracross [1]
		106 Hitmonlee [49]	187 Hoppip [E]	140 Kabuto [26]	141 Kabutops [26]	115 Kangaskhan [43]	588 Karrablast [8]	098 Krabby [E]
		636 Larvesta [E]	345 Lileep [E]	506 Lillipup [E]	607 Litwick [E]	428 Lopunny [6]	296 Makuhita [37]	473 Mamoswine [14]
		308 Medicham [12]	307 Meditite [12]	619 Mienfoo [E]	241 Miltank [E]	572 Minccino [E]	146 Moltres [22]	029 Nidoran ♀ [E]
		032 Nidoran ♂ [E]	290 Nincada [E]	299 Nosepass [E]	322 Numel [E]	417 Pachirisu [17]	046 Paras [E]	548 Petilil [E]
		231 Phanpy [19]	172 Pichu [E]	221 Piloswine [14]	204 Pineco [E]	060 Poliwag [E]	447 Riolu [1]	027 Sandshrew [E]
		539 Sawk [41]	123 Scyther [E]	540 Sewaddle [29]	616 Shelmet [E]	410 Shieldon [33]	227 Skarmory [E]	325 Spoink [E]
		618 Stunfisk [30]	185 Sudowoodo [E]	191 Sunkern [E]	283 Surskit [E]	220 Swinub [14]	538 Throh [41]	532 Timburr [E]
		255 Torchic [E]	324 Torkoal [E]	328 Trapinch [E]	236 Tyrogue [E]	480 Uxie [16]	494 Victini [9]	288 Vigoroth [17]
		562 Yamask [E]						

Type	Move	Pokémon that can learn it						
Grass	Energy Ball (TM53)	460 Abomasnow [TM]	063 Abra [TM]	617 Accelgor [TM]	065 Alakazam [TM]	591 Amoonguss [TM]	493 Arceus [TM]	683 Aromatisse [TM]
		482 Azelf [TM]	153 Bayleef [TM]	267 Beautifly [TM]	606 Beheeyem [TM]	182 Bellossom [TM]	069 Bellsprout [TM]	286 Breloom [TM]
		406 Budew [TM]	001 Bulbasaur [TM]	012 Butterfree [TM]	331 Cacnea [42, TM]	332 Cacturne [44, TM]	455 Carnivine [TM]	351 Castform [TM]
		251 Celebi [TM]	609 Chandelure [TM]	421 Cherrim [TM]	420 Cherubi [TM]	652 Chesnaught [TM]	650 Chespin [TM]	152 Chikorita [TM]
		358 Chimecho [TM]	563 Cofagrigus [TM]	546 Cottonee [35, TM]	346 Cradily [44, TM]	488 Cresselia [TM]	585 Deerling [32, TM]	386 Deoxys (Atk) [TM]
		386 Deoxys (Def) [TM]	386 Deoxys (Nor) [TM]	386 Deoxys (Spd) [TM]	578 Duosion [TM]	632 Durant [TM]	269 Dustox [TM]	605 Elgyem [TM]
		589 Escavalier [TM]	677 Espurr [TM]	102 Exeggcute [TM]	103 Exeggutor [TM]	597 Ferroseed [TM]	598 Ferrothorn [TM]	669 Flabébé [TM]
		670 Floette [TM]	671 Florges [TM]	590 Foongus [TM]	592 Frillish [TM]	596 Galvantula [TM]	282 Gardevoir [TM]	092 Gastly [TM]
		649 Genesect [TM]	094 Gengar [TM]	203 Girafarig [TM]	487 Giratina (Alt) [TM]	487 Giratina (Ori) [TM]	044 Gloom [TM]	673 Gogoat [TM]
		574 Gothita [TM]	576 Gothitelle [TM]	575 Gothorita [TM]	711 Gourgeist [TM]	388 Grotle [TM]	253 Grovyle [TM]	326 Grumpig [TM]
		093 Haunter [TM]	187 Hoppip [TM]	002 Ivysaur [TM]	593 Jellicent [TM]	385 Jirachi [TM]	595 Joltik [TM]	189 Jumpluff [TM]
		124 Jynx [TM]	064 Kadabra [TM]	588 Karrablast [TM]	608 Lampent [TM]	380 Latias [TM]	381 Latios [TM]	470 Leafeon [TM]
		542 Leavanny [TM]	345 Lileep [41, TM]	549 Lilligant [TM]	607 Litwick [TM]	271 Lombre [TM]	270 Lotad [36, TM]	272 Ludicolo [TM]
		490 Manaphy [TM]	556 Maractus [TM]	284 Masquerain [TM]	308 Medicham [TM]	154 Meganium [TM]	648 Meloetta [TM]	678 Meowstic (F) [TM]
		678 Meowstic (M) [TM]	481 Mesprit [TM]	151 Mew [TM]	150 Mewtwo [TM]	429 Mismagius [TM]	414 Mothim [TM]	122 Mr. Mime [TM]
		517 Munna [TM]	518 Musharna [TM]	038 Ninetales [TM]	274 Nuzleaf [TM]	224 Octillery [TM]	043 Oddish [TM]	511 Pansage [TM]
		046 Paras [TM]	047 Parasect [TM]	548 Petilil [35, TM]	708 Phantump [TM]	710 Pumpkaboo [TM]	651 Quilladin [TM]	384 Rayquaza [TM]
		579 Reuniclus [TM]	315 Roselia [TM]	407 Roserade [TM]	586 Sawsbuck [32, TM]	254 Sceptile [TM]	273 Seedot [TM]	497 Serperior [TM]
		496 Servine [TM]	540 Sewaddle [TM]	492 Shaymin (Land) [73, TM]	492 Shaymin (Sky) [73, TM]	616 Shelmet [TM]	275 Shiftry [TM]	285 Shroomish [TM]
		561 Sigilyph [TM]	512 Simisage [TM]	672 Skiddo [TM]	188 Skiploom [TM]	685 Slurpuff [36, TM]	495 Snivy [TM]	459 Snover [TM]
		577 Solosis [TM]	682 Spritzee [TM]	234 Stantler [TM]	192 Sunflora [TM]	191 Sunkern [TM]	541 Swadloon [TM]	684 Swirlix [36, TM]
		528 Swoobat [TM]	114 Tangela [TM]	465 Tangrowth [TM]	389 Torterra [TM]	252 Treecko [37, TM]	709 Trevenant [TM]	357 Tropius [TM]
		387 Turtwig [TM]	480 Uxie [TM]	049 Venomoth [TM]	003 Venusaur [TM]	494 Victini [TM]	071 Victreebel [TM]	045 Vileplume [TM]
		640 Virizion [TM]	666 Vivillon [TM]	037 Vulpix [TM]	070 Weepinbell [TM]	547 Whimsicott [TM]	527 Woobat [TM]	413 Wormadam (Plant) [TM]
		562 Yamask [TM]						
Normal	Entrainment	531 Audino [29]	427 Buneary [50]	433 Chingling [19]	692 Clauncher [E]	702 Dedenne [39]	632 Durant [46]	701 Hawlucha [E]
		542 Leavanny [43]	667 Litleo [E]	428 Lopunny [53]	370 Luvdisc [E]	312 Minun [49]	674 Pancham [42]	675 Pangoro [1, 45]
		548 Petilil [37]	311 Plusle [49]	223 Remoraid [E]	086 Seel [E]			
Fire	Eruption	323 Camerupt [1, 52]	155 Cyndaquil [58]	244 Entei [1, 85]	383 Groudon [90]	156 Quilava [68]	324 Torkoal [E]	157 Typhlosion [1, 74]
Normal	Explosion (TM64)	482 Azelf [76, TM]	343 Baltoy [46, TM]	525 Boldore [55, TM]	438 Bonsly [TM]	437 Bronzong [TM]	323 Camerupt [TM]	703 Carbink [TM]
		344 Claydol [58, TM]	091 Cloyster [TM]	222 Corsola [TM]	615 Cryogonal [TM]	719 Diancie [TM]	426 Drifblim [60, TM]	425 Drifloon [50, TM]
		578 Duosion [TM]	101 Electrode [47, TM]	102 Exeggcute [TM]	103 Exeggutor [TM]	597 Ferroseed [55, TM]	598 Ferrothorn [67, TM]	205 Forretress [42, TM]
		569 Garbodor [59, TM]	092 Gastly [TM]	649 Genesect [TM]	094 Gengar [TM]	074 Geodude [36, TM]	526 Gigalith [55, TM]	362 Glalie [TM]
		076 Golem [44, TM]	711 Gourgeist [1, 75, TM]	075 Graveler [44, TM]	088 Grimer [TM]	316 Gulpin [TM]	093 Haunter [TM]	485 Heatran [TM]
		109 Koffing [37, TM]	645 Landorus [TM]	463 Lickilicky [TM]	337 Lunatone [45, TM]	219 Magcargo [TM]	081 Magnemite [TM]	082 Magneton [TM]
		462 Magnezone [TM]	376 Metagross [TM]	375 Metang [TM]	151 Mew [TM]	089 Muk [TM]	299 Nosepass [TM]	274 Nuzleaf [TM]
		095 Onix [TM]	204 Pineco [34, TM]	476 Probopass [TM]	710 Pumpkaboo [TM]	211 Qwilfish [TM]	378 Regice [1, TM]	377 Regirock [1, TM]
		379 Registeel [1, TM]	579 Reuniclus [TM]	524 Roggenrola [40, TM]	273 Seedot [33, TM]	090 Shellder [TM]	275 Shiftry [TM]	435 Skuntank [61, TM]
		577 Solosis [TM]	338 Solrock [45, TM]	208 Steelix [TM]	434 Stunky [49, TM]	185 Sudowoodo [TM]	317 Swalot [TM]	324 Torkoal [TM]
		568 Trubbish [47, TM]	583 Vanillish [TM]	582 Vanillite [TM]	584 Vanilluxe [TM]	100 Voltorb [41, TM]	110 Weezing [40, TM]	
Psychic	Extrasensory	482 Azelf [50]	343 Baltoy [31]	437 Bronzong [42]	436 Bronzor [39]	406 Budew [E]	358 Chimecho [22]	344 Claydol [31]
		155 Cyndaquil [E]	244 Entei [1, 64]	102 Exeggcute [47]	658 Greninja [49]	250 Ho-Oh [23]	163 Hoothoot [45]	645 Landorus [31]
		249 Lugia [23]	678 Meowstic (F) [35]	481 Mesprit [50]	164 Noctowl [52]	274 Nuzleaf [36]	243 Raikou [1, 64]	643 Reshiram [43]
		325 Spoink [E]	234 Stantler [E]	245 Suicune [1, 64]	175 Togepi [E]	641 Tornadus [31]	480 Uxie [50]	037 Vulpix [31, E]
		293 Whismur [E]	570 Zorua [E]					
Normal	Extreme Speed	059 Arcanine [34]	493 Arceus [40]	386 Deoxys (Spd) [73]	147 Dratini [E]	448 Lucario [1, 65]	384 Rayquaza [45]	468 Togekiss [1]
		718 Zygarde [88]						

F

Type	Move	Pokémon that can learn it						
Normal	Facade (TM42)	460 Abomasnow [TM]	063 Abra [TM]	359 Absol [TM]	617 Accelgor [TM]	681 Aegislash [TM]	142 Aerodactyl [TM]	306 Aggron [TM]
		190 Aipom [TM]	065 Alakazam [TM]	594 Alomomola [TM]	334 Altaria [TM]	698 Amaura [TM]	424 Ambipom [TM]	591 Amoonguss [TM]
		181 Ampharos [TM]	347 Anorith [TM]	024 Arbok [TM]	059 Arcanine [TM]	493 Arceus [TM]	566 Archen [TM]	567 Archeops [TM]
		168 Ariados [TM]	348 Armaldo [TM]	683 Aromatisse [TM]	304 Aron [TM]	144 Articuno [TM]	531 Audino [TM]	699 Aurorus [TM]
		713 Avalugg [TM]	610 Axew [TM]	482 Azelf [TM]	184 Azumarill [TM]	298 Azurill [TM]	371 Bagon [TM]	343 Baltoy [TM]
		354 Banette [TM]	689 Barbaracle [TM]	339 Barboach [TM]	550 Basculin [TM]	411 Bastiodon [TM]	153 Bayleef [TM]	614 Beartic [TM]
		267 Beautifly [TM]	015 Beedrill [TM]	606 Beheeyem [TM]	182 Bellossom [TM]	069 Bellsprout [TM]	712 Bergmite [TM]	400 Bibarel [TM]
		399 Bidoof [TM]	688 Binacle [TM]	625 Bisharp [TM]	009 Blastoise [TM]	257 Blaziken [TM]	242 Blissey [TM]	522 Blitzle [TM]
		525 Boldore [TM]	438 Bonsly [TM]	626 Bouffalant [TM]	654 Braixen [TM]	628 Braviary [TM]	286 Breloom [TM]	437 Bronzong [TM]
		436 Bronzor [TM]	406 Budew [TM]	418 Buizel [TM]	001 Bulbasaur [TM]	427 Buneary [TM]	659 Bunnelby [47, TM]	012 Butterfree [TM]
		331 Cacnea [TM]	332 Cacturne [TM]	323 Camerupt [TM]	703 Carbink [TM]	455 Carnivine [TM]	565 Carracosta [TM]	318 Carvanha [TM]
		351 Castform [TM]	251 Celebi [TM]	609 Chandelure [TM]	113 Chansey [TM]	006 Charizard [TM]	004 Charmander [TM]	005 Charmeleon [TM]
		441 Chatot [TM]	421 Cherrim [TM]	420 Cherubi [TM]	652 Chesnaught [TM]	650 Chespin [TM]	152 Chikorita [TM]	390 Chimchar [31, TM]

	Move	Pokémon that can learn it						
Normal	Facade (TM42)	358 Chimecho [TM]	170 Chinchou [TM]	433 Chingling [TM]	573 Cinccino [TM]	366 Clamperl [TM]	692 Clauncher [TM]	693 Clawitzer [TM]
		344 Claydol [TM]	036 Clefable [TM]	035 Clefairy [TM]	173 Cleffa [TM]	091 Cloyster [TM]	638 Cobalion [TM]	563 Cofagrigus [TM]
		256 Combusken [TM]	534 Conkeldurr [TM]	341 Corphish [TM]	222 Corsola [TM]	546 Cottonee [TM]	346 Cradily [TM]	408 Cranidos [TM]
		342 Crawdaunt [TM]	488 Cresselia [TM]	453 Croagunk [TM]	169 Crobat [TM]	159 Croconaw [TM]	558 Crustle [TM]	615 Cryogonal [TM]
		613 Cubchoo [TM]	104 Cubone [TM]	155 Cyndaquil [TM]	491 Darkrai [TM]	555 Darmanitan [19, TM]	554 Darumaka [19, TM]	702 Dedenne [TM]
		585 Deerling [TM]	633 Deino [TM]	301 Delcatty [TM]	225 Delibird [TM]	655 Delphox [TM]	386 Deoxys (Atk) [TM]	386 Deoxys (Def) [TM]
		386 Deoxys (Nor) [TM]	386 Deoxys (Spd) [TM]	087 Dewgong [TM]	502 Dewott [TM]	483 Dialga [TM]	719 Diancie [TM]	660 Diggersby [53, TM]
		050 Diglett [TM]	085 Dodrio [TM]	084 Doduo [TM]	232 Donphan [TM]	680 Doublade [TM]	691 Dragalge [TM]	148 Dragonair [TM]
		149 Dragonite [TM]	452 Drapion [TM]	147 Dratini [TM]	426 Drifblim [TM]	425 Drifloon [TM]	529 Drilbur [TM]	096 Drowzee [TM]
		621 Druddigon [TM]	580 Ducklett [TM]	051 Dugtrio [TM]	206 Dunsparce [TM]	578 Duosion [TM]	632 Durant [TM]	356 Dusclops [TM]
		477 Dusknoir [TM]	355 Duskull [TM]	269 Dustox [TM]	557 Dwebble [TM]	603 Eelektrik [TM]	604 Eelektross [TM]	133 Eevee [TM]
		023 Ekans [TM]	125 Electabuzz [TM]	466 Electivire [TM]	309 Electrike [TM]	101 Electrode [TM]	239 Elekid [TM]	605 Elgyem [TM]
		500 Emboar [TM]	587 Emolga [TM]	395 Empoleon [TM]	244 Entei [TM]	589 Escavalier [TM]	196 Espeon [TM]	677 Espurr [TM]
		530 Excadrill [TM]	102 Exeggcute [TM]	103 Exeggutor [TM]	295 Exploud [TM]	083 Farfetch'd [TM]	022 Fearow [TM]	349 Feebas [TM]
		653 Fennekin [TM]	160 Feraligatr [TM]	597 Ferroseed [TM]	598 Ferrothorn [TM]	456 Finneon [TM]	180 Flaaffy [TM]	669 Flabébé [TM]
		136 Flareon [TM]	662 Fletchinder [TM]	661 Fletchling [TM]	419 Floatzel [TM]	670 Floette [TM]	671 Florges [TM]	330 Flygon [TM]
		590 Foongus [TM]	205 Forretress [TM]	611 Fraxure [TM]	592 Frillish [TM]	656 Froakie [TM]	657 Frogadier [TM]	478 Froslass [TM]
		676 Furfrou [TM]	162 Furret [TM]	444 Gabite [TM]	475 Gallade [TM]	596 Galvantula [TM]	569 Garbodor [TM]	445 Garchomp [TM]
		282 Gardevoir [TM]	092 Gastly [TM]	423 Gastrodon [TM]	649 Genesect [TM]	094 Gengar [TM]	074 Geodude [TM]	443 Gible [TM]
		526 Gigalith [TM]	203 Girafarig [TM]	487 Giratina (Alt) [TM]	487 Giratina (Ori) [TM]	471 Glaceon [TM]	362 Glalie [TM]	431 Glameow [TM]
		207 Gligar [TM]	472 Gliscor [TM]	044 Gloom [TM]	673 Gogoat [TM]	042 Golbat [TM]	118 Goldeen [TM]	055 Golduck [TM]
		076 Golem [TM]	622 Golett [TM]	623 Golurk [TM]	706 Goodra [TM]	704 Goomy [TM]	368 Gorebyss [TM]	574 Gothita [TM]
		576 Gothitelle [TM]	575 Gothorita [TM]	711 Gourgeist [TM]	210 Granbull [TM]	075 Graveler [TM]	658 Greninja [TM]	088 Grimer [TM]
		388 Grotle [TM]	383 Groudon [TM]	253 Grovyle [TM]	058 Growlithe [TM]	326 Grumpig [TM]	316 Gulpin [TM]	533 Gurdurr [TM]
		130 Gyarados [TM]	440 Happiny [TM]	297 Hariyama [TM]	093 Haunter [TM]	701 Hawlucha [TM]	612 Haxorus [TM]	631 Heatmor [TM]
		485 Heatran [TM]	695 Heliolisk [TM]	694 Helioptile [TM]	214 Heracross [TM]	507 Herdier [TM]	449 Hippopotas [TM]	450 Hippowdon [TM]
		107 Hitmonchan [TM]	106 Hitmonlee [TM]	237 Hitmontop [TM]	430 Honchkrow [TM]	679 Honedge [TM]	250 Ho-Oh [TM]	163 Hoothoot [TM]
		187 Hoppip [TM]	116 Horsea [TM]	229 Houndoom [TM]	228 Houndour [TM]	367 Huntail [TM]	635 Hydreigon [TM]	097 Hypno [TM]
		174 Igglybuff [TM]	314 Illumise [TM]	392 Infernape [TM]	686 Inkay [TM]	002 Ivysaur [TM]	593 Jellicent [TM]	039 Jigglypuff [TM]
		385 Jirachi [TM]	135 Jolteon [TM]	595 Joltik [TM]	189 Jumpluff [TM]	124 Jynx [TM]	140 Kabuto [TM]	141 Kabutops [TM]
		064 Kadabra [TM]	115 Kangaskhan [TM]	588 Karrablast [TM]	352 Kecleon [TM]	647 Keldeo [TM]	230 Kingdra [TM]	099 Kingler [TM]
		281 Kirlia [TM]	600 Klang [TM]	707 Klefki [TM]	599 Klink [TM]	601 Klinklang [TM]	109 Koffing [TM]	098 Krabby [TM]
		402 Kricketune [TM]	552 Krokorok [TM]	553 Krookodile [TM]	382 Kyogre [TM]	646 Kyurem (Blk) [TM]	646 Kyurem (Wht) [TM]	646 Kyurem [TM]
		305 Lairon [TM]	608 Lampent [TM]	645 Landorus [TM]	171 Lanturn [TM]	131 Lapras [TM]	636 Larvesta [TM]	246 Larvitar [TM]
		380 Latias [TM]	381 Latios [TM]	470 Leafeon [TM]	542 Leavanny [TM]	166 Ledian [TM]	165 Ledyba [TM]	463 Lickilicky [TM]
		108 Lickitung [TM]	510 Liepard [TM]	345 Lileep [TM]	549 Lilligant [TM]	506 Lillipup [TM]	264 Linoone [TM]	667 Litleo [TM]
		607 Litwick [TM]	271 Lombre [TM]	428 Lopunny [TM]	270 Lotad [TM]	294 Loudred [TM]	448 Lucario [TM]	272 Ludicolo [TM]
		249 Lugia [TM]	457 Lumineon [TM]	337 Lunatone [TM]	370 Luvdisc [TM]	404 Luxio [TM]	405 Luxray [TM]	068 Machamp [TM]
		067 Machoke [TM]	066 Machop [TM]	240 Magby [TM]	219 Magcargo [TM]	126 Magmar [TM]	467 Magmortar [TM]	081 Magnemite [TM]
		082 Magneton [TM]	462 Magnezone [TM]	296 Makuhita [TM]	687 Malamar [TM]	473 Mamoswine [TM]	490 Manaphy [TM]	630 Mandibuzz [TM]
		310 Manectric [TM]	056 Mankey [TM]	226 Mantine [TM]	458 Mantyke [TM]	556 Maractus [TM]	179 Mareep [TM]	183 Marill [TM]
		105 Marowak [TM]	259 Marshtomp [TM]	284 Masquerain [TM]	303 Mawile [TM]	308 Medicham [TM]	307 Meditite [TM]	154 Meganium [TM]
		648 Meloetta [TM]	678 Meowstic (F) [TM]	678 Meowstic (M) [TM]	052 Meowth [TM]	481 Mesprit [TM]	376 Metagross [TM]	375 Metang [TM]
		151 Mew [TM]	150 Mewtwo [TM]	619 Mienfoo [TM]	620 Mienshao [TM]	262 Mightyena [TM]	350 Milotic [TM]	241 Miltank [TM]
		439 Mime Jr. [TM]	572 Minccino [TM]	312 Minun [TM]	200 Misdreavus [TM]	429 Mismagius [TM]	146 Moltres [TM]	391 Monferno [TM]
		414 Mothim [TM]	122 Mr. Mime [TM]	258 Mudkip [TM]	089 Muk [TM]	446 Munchlax [TM]	517 Munna [TM]	198 Murkrow [TM]
		518 Musharna [TM]	177 Natu [TM]	034 Nidoking [TM]	031 Nidoqueen [TM]	029 Nidoran ♀ [TM]	032 Nidoran ♂ [TM]	030 Nidorina [TM]
		033 Nidorino [TM]	290 Nincada [TM]	038 Ninetales [TM]	291 Ninjask [TM]	164 Noctowl [TM]	714 Noibat [TM]	715 Noivern [TM]
		299 Nosepass [TM]	322 Numel [TM]	274 Nuzleaf [TM]	224 Octillery [TM]	043 Oddish [TM]	138 Omanyte [TM]	139 Omastar [TM]
		095 Onix [TM]	501 Oshawott [TM]	417 Pachirisu [TM]	484 Palkia [TM]	536 Palpitoad [TM]	674 Pancham [TM]	675 Pangoro [TM]
		515 Panpour [TM]	511 Pansage [TM]	513 Pansear [TM]	046 Paras [TM]	047 Parasect [TM]	504 Patrat [TM]	624 Pawniard [TM]
		279 Pelipper [TM]	053 Persian [TM]	548 Petilil [TM]	231 Phanpy [TM]	708 Phantump [TM]	489 Phione [TM]	172 Pichu [TM]
		018 Pidgeot [TM]	017 Pidgeotto [TM]	016 Pidgey [TM]	519 Pidove [43, TM]	499 Pignite [TM]	025 Pikachu [TM]	221 Piloswine [TM]
		204 Pineco [TM]	127 Pinsir [TM]	393 Piplup [TM]	311 Plusle [TM]	186 Politoed [TM]	060 Poliwag [TM]	061 Poliwhirl [TM]
		062 Poliwrath [TM]	077 Ponyta [TM]	261 Poochyena [TM]	137 Porygon [TM]	233 Porygon2 [TM]	474 Porygon-Z [TM]	057 Primeape [TM]
		394 Prinplup [TM]	476 Probopass [TM]	054 Psyduck [TM]	710 Pumpkaboo [TM]	247 Pupitar [TM]	509 Purrloin [TM]	432 Purugly [TM]
		668 Pyroar [TM]	195 Quagsire [TM]	156 Quilava [TM]	651 Quilladin [TM]	211 Qwilfish [TM]	026 Raichu [TM]	243 Raikou [TM]
		280 Ralts [TM]	409 Rampardos [TM]	078 Rapidash [TM]	020 Raticate [TM]	019 Rattata [TM]	384 Rayquaza [TM]	378 Regice [TM]
		486 Regigigas [TM]	377 Regirock [TM]	379 Registeel [TM]	369 Relicanth [TM]	223 Remoraid [TM]	643 Reshiram [TM]	579 Reuniclus [TM]
		112 Rhydon [TM]	111 Rhyhorn [TM]	464 Rhyperior [TM]	447 Riolu [TM]	524 Roggenrola [TM]	315 Roselia [TM]	407 Roserade [TM]
		479 Rotom (Fan) [TM]	479 Rotom (Frost) [TM]	479 Rotom (Heat) [TM]	479 Rotom (Mow) [TM]	479 Rotom (Wash) [TM]	479 Rotom [TM]	627 Rufflet [TM]
		302 Sableye [TM]	373 Salamence [TM]	503 Samurott [TM]	551 Sandile [TM]	027 Sandshrew [TM]	028 Sandslash [TM]	539 Sawk [TM]
		586 Sawsbuck [TM]	254 Sceptile [TM]	212 Scizor [TM]	545 Scolipede [TM]	560 Scrafty [45, TM]	559 Scraggy [42, TM]	123 Scyther [TM]
		117 Seadra [TM]	119 Seaking [TM]	364 Sealeo [TM]	273 Seedot [TM]	086 Seel [TM]	537 Seismitoad [TM]	161 Sentret [TM]
		497 Serperior [TM]	496 Servine [TM]	336 Seviper [TM]	540 Sewaddle [TM]	319 Sharpedo [TM]	492 Shaymin (Land) [TM]	492 Shaymin (Sky) [TM]
		292 Shedinja [TM]	372 Shelgon [TM]	090 Shellder [TM]	422 Shellos [TM]	616 Shelmet [TM]	410 Shieldon [TM]	275 Shiftry [TM]

Type	Move	Pokémon that can learn it						
Normal	Facade (TM42)	403 Shinx [TM]	285 Shroomish [TM]	213 Shuckle [TM]	353 Shuppet [TM]	561 Sigilyph [TM]	516 Simipour [TM]	512 Simisage [TM]
		514 Simisear [TM]	227 Skarmory [TM]	672 Skiddo [TM]	188 Skiploom [TM]	300 Skitty [TM]	451 Skorupi [TM]	690 Skrelp [TM]
		435 Skuntank [TM]	289 Slaking [TM]	287 Slakoth [TM]	705 Sliggoo [TM]	080 Slowbro [TM]	199 Slowking [TM]	079 Slowpoke [TM]
		218 Slugma [TM]	685 Slurpuff [TM]	238 Smoochum [TM]	215 Sneasel [TM]	495 Snivy [TM]	143 Snorlax [TM]	361 Snorunt [TM]
		459 Snover [TM]	209 Snubbull [TM]	577 Solosis [TM]	338 Solrock [TM]	021 Spearow [TM]	363 Spheal [TM]	167 Spinarak [TM]
		327 Spinda [TM]	442 Spiritomb [TM]	325 Spoink [TM]	682 Spritzee [TM]	007 Squirtle [TM]	234 Stantler [TM]	398 Staraptor [TM]
		397 Staravia [TM]	396 Starly [TM]	121 Starmie [TM]	120 Staryu [TM]	208 Steelix [TM]	508 Stoutland [TM]	618 Stunfisk [TM]
		434 Stunky [TM]	185 Sudowoodo [TM]	245 Suicune [TM]	192 Sunflora [TM]	191 Sunkern [TM]	283 Surskit [TM]	333 Swablu [TM]
		541 Swadloon [TM]	317 Swalot [TM]	260 Swampert [TM]	581 Swanna [TM]	277 Swellow [TM]	220 Swinub [TM]	684 Swirlix [TM]
		528 Swoobat [TM]	700 Sylveon [TM]	276 Taillow [TM]	663 Talonflame [TM]	114 Tangela [TM]	465 Tangrowth [TM]	128 Tauros [TM]
		216 Teddiursa [TM]	072 Tentacool [TM]	073 Tentacruel [TM]	498 Tepig [TM]	639 Terrakion [TM]	538 Throh [TM]	642 Thundurus [TM]
		532 Timburr [TM]	564 Tirtouga [TM]	468 Togekiss [TM]	175 Togepi [TM]	176 Togetic [TM]	255 Torchic [TM]	324 Torkoal [TM]
		641 Tornadus [TM]	389 Torterra [TM]	158 Totodile [TM]	454 Toxicroak [TM]	520 Tranquill [50, TM]	328 Trapinch [TM]	252 Treecko [TM]
		709 Trevenant [TM]	357 Tropius [TM]	568 Trubbish [TM]	387 Turtwig [TM]	535 Tympole [TM]	157 Typhlosion [TM]	248 Tyranitar [TM]
		697 Tyrantrum [TM]	236 Tyrogue [TM]	696 Tyrunt [TM]	197 Umbreon [TM]	521 Unfezant [55, TM]	217 Ursaring [TM]	480 Uxie [TM]
		583 Vanillish [TM]	582 Vanillite [TM]	584 Vanilluxe [TM]	134 Vaporeon [TM]	543 Venipede [TM]	049 Venomoth [TM]	048 Venonat [TM]
		003 Venusaur [TM]	416 Vespiquen [TM]	329 Vibrava [TM]	494 Victini [TM]	071 Victreebel [TM]	288 Vigoroth [TM]	045 Vileplume [TM]
		640 Virizion [TM]	666 Vivillon [TM]	313 Volbeat [TM]	637 Volcarona [TM]	100 Voltorb [TM]	629 Vullaby [TM]	037 Vulpix [TM]
		320 Wailmer [TM]	321 Wailord [TM]	365 Walrein [TM]	008 Wartortle [TM]	505 Watchog [TM]	461 Weavile [TM]	070 Weepinbell [TM]
		110 Weezing [TM]	547 Whimsicott [TM]	544 Whirlipede [TM]	340 Whiscash [TM]	293 Whismur [TM]	040 Wigglytuff [TM]	278 Wingull [TM]
		527 Woobat [TM]	194 Wooper [TM]	413 Wormadam (Plant) [TM]	413 Wormadam (Sand) [TM]	413 Wormadam (Trash) [TM]	178 Xatu [TM]	716 Xerneas [TM]
		562 Yamask [TM]	193 Yanma [TM]	469 Yanmega [TM]	717 Yveltal [TM]	335 Zangoose [TM]	145 Zapdos [TM]	523 Zebstrika [TM]
		644 Zekrom [TM]	263 Zigzagoon [TM]	571 Zoroark [TM]	570 Zorua [TM]	041 Zubat [TM]	634 Zweilous [TM]	718 Zygarde [TM]
Fairy	Fairy Lock	707 Klefki [1]						
	Fairy Wind	683 Aromatisse [1]	546 Cottonee [1]	669 Flabébé [6]	670 Floette [6]	187 Hoppip [10]	189 Jumpluff [10]	707 Klefki [5]
		303 Mawile [1]	188 Skiploom [10]	685 Slurpuff [5]	682 Spritzee [1]	684 Swirlix [5]	700 Sylveon [9]	176 Togetic [14]
Normal	Fake Out	190 Aipom [E]	427 Buneary [E]	390 Chimchar [E]	453 Croagunk [E]	301 Delcatty [1]	225 Delibird [E]	677 Espurr [19]
		431 Glameow [1]	297 Hariyama [10]	115 Kangaskhan [7]	352 Kecleon [E]	510 Liepard [22]	271 Lombre [16]	296 Makuhita [10]
		307 Meditite [E]	678 Meowstic (F) [19]	678 Meowstic (M) [19]	052 Meowth [9]	619 Mienfoo [13]	620 Mienshao [1, 13]	439 Mime Jr. [E]
		122 Mr. Mime [E]	274 Nuzleaf [12]	053 Persian [1, 9]	172 Pichu [E]	509 Purrloin [21]	432 Purugly [1]	302 Sableye [21]
		559 Scraggy [E]	086 Seel [E]	300 Skitty [1, E]	238 Smoochum [E]	215 Sneasel [E]	327 Spinda [E]	007 Squirtle [E]
		236 Tyrogue [1]						
Dark	Fake Tears	298 Azurill [E]	438 Bonsly [1]	427 Buneary [E]	173 Cleffa [E]	546 Cottonee [E]	585 Deerling [E]	133 Eevee [E]
		431 Glameow [E]	574 Gothita [10]	576 Gothitelle [10]	575 Gothorita [10]	174 Igglybuff [E]	314 Illumise [E]	124 Jynx [28]
		303 Mawile [5]	572 Minccino [E]	312 Minun [25, E]	417 Pachirisu [E]	311 Plusle [E]	509 Purrloin [E]	403 Shinx [E]
		285 Shroomish [E]	300 Skitty [E]	685 Slurpuff [10]	238 Smoochum [28]	361 Snorunt [E]	209 Snubbull [E]	327 Spinda [E]
		684 Swirlix [10]	216 Teddiursa [1, E]	158 Totodile [E]	217 Ursaring [1]	629 Vullaby [E]	293 Whismur [E]	527 Woobat [E]
		562 Yamask [E]	570 Zorua [9]					
Normal	False Swipe (TM54)	359 Absol [TM]	681 Aegislash [TM]	347 Anorith [TM]	348 Armaldo [TM]	610 Axew [24, TM]	689 Barbaracle [TM]	015 Beedrill [TM]
		688 Binacle [TM]	625 Bisharp [TM]	286 Breloom [TM]	638 Cobalion [TM]	341 Corphish [TM]	342 Crawdaunt [TM]	104 Cubone [27, TM]
		502 Dewott [TM]	680 Doublade [TM]	452 Drapion [TM]	589 Escavalier [25, TM]	083 Farfetch'd [45, TM]	022 Fearow [TM]	611 Fraxure [24, TM]
		475 Gallade [44, TM]	445 Garchomp [TM]	207 Gligar [TM]	472 Gliscor [TM]	253 Grovyle [48, TM]	701 Hawlucha [TM]	612 Haxorus [24, TM]
		214 Heracross [TM]	679 Honedge [TM]	588 Karrablast [25, TM]	647 Keldeo [TM]	099 Kingler [TM]	098 Krabby [TM]	402 Kricketune [TM]
		542 Leavanny [1, TM]	105 Marowak [27, TM]	303 Mawile [TM]	151 Mew [TM]	290 Nincada [33, TM]	291 Ninjask [TM]	274 Nuzleaf [TM]
		501 Oshawott [TM]	674 Pancham [TM]	675 Pangoro [TM]	046 Paras [TM]	047 Parasect [TM]	624 Pawniard [TM]	127 Pinsir [TM]
		503 Samurott [TM]	254 Sceptile [51, TM]	212 Scizor [13, TM]	123 Scyther [13, TM]	273 Seedot [TM]	292 Shedinja [TM]	275 Shiftry [TM]
		285 Shroomish [TM]	451 Skorupi [TM]	215 Sneasel [TM]	021 Spearow [TM]	639 Terrakion [TM]	640 Virizion [TM]	461 Weavile [TM]
		335 Zangoose [29, TM]						
Flying	Feather Dance	441 Chatot [50]	580 Ducklett [21]	083 Farfetch'd [E]	701 Hawlucha [40]	163 Hoothoot [E]	198 Murkrow [E]	177 Natu [E]
		018 Pidgeot [27]	017 Pidgeotto [27]	016 Pidgey [25]	519 Pidove [36]	393 Piplup [E]	021 Spearow [E]	396 Starly [E]
		333 Swablu [E]	581 Swanna [21]	255 Torchic [E]	520 Tranquill [41]	521 Unfezant [44]		
Normal	Feint	359 Absol [1]	286 Breloom [19]	652 Chesnaught [1]	453 Croagunk [E]	239 Elekid [E]	083 Farfetch'd [43]	475 Gallade [40]
		207 Gligar [E]	706 Goodra [1]	214 Heracross [7]	107 Hitmonchan [21]	106 Hitmonlee [25]	237 Hitmontop [33]	228 Houndour [E]
		392 Infernape [26]	141 Kabutops [1]	352 Kecleon [10]	448 Lucario [11]	296 Makuhita [E]	308 Medicham [15]	307 Meditite [15]
		052 Meowth [50]	619 Mienfoo [E]	391 Monferno [26]	053 Persian [65]	025 Pikachu [21]	127 Pinsir [E]	447 Riolu [11]
		302 Sableye [E]	212 Scizor [1, 61]	123 Scyther [61]	319 Sharpedo [1]	616 Shelmet [E]	227 Skarmory [20]	435 Skuntank [18]
		215 Sneasel [E]	434 Stunky [18]	255 Torchic [E]	328 Trapinch [29]	236 Tyrogue [E]	193 Yanma [E]	469 Yanmega [38]
		335 Zangoose [E]						
Dark	Feint Attack	359 Absol [E]	591 Amoonguss [20]	354 Banette [19]	625 Bisharp [17]	438 Bonsly [19]	437 Bronzong [21]	436 Bronzor [21]
		331 Cacnea [19]	332 Cacturne [19]	455 Carnivine [27]	453 Croagunk [17]	558 Crustle [13]	491 Darkrai [29]	585 Deerling [16]
		050 Diglett [E]	084 Doduo [E]	691 Dragalge [5]	621 Druddigon [E]	632 Durant [E]	355 Duskull [E]	557 Dwebble [13]
		330 Flygon [1]	590 Foongus [20]	431 Glameow [17]	207 Gligar [19]	472 Gliscor [19]	574 Gothita [24]	576 Gothitelle [24]
		575 Gothorita [24]	658 Greninja [33]	631 Heatmor [E]	163 Hoothoot [E]	229 Houndoom [35]	228 Houndour [32]	367 Huntail [11]
		174 Igglybuff [E]	595 Joltik [E]	588 Karrablast [E]	352 Kecleon [16]	240 Magby [12]	126 Magmar [12]	467 Magmortar [12]
		296 Makuhita [E]	630 Mandibuzz [23]	303 Mawile [21]	052 Meowth [22]	198 Murkrow [35, E]	177 Natu [E]	290 Nincada [E]

ADVENTURE DATA

	Move	Pokémon that can learn it						
Dark	Feint Attack	274 Nuzleaf [24]	624 Pawniard [17]	053 Persian [22]	708 Phantump [19]	016 Pidgey [E]	127 Pinsir [E]	509 Purrloin [E]
		432 Purugly [17]	302 Sableye [19]	586 Sawsbuck [16]	560 Scrafty [1, 9]	559 Scraggy [9, E]	275 Shiftry [1]	353 Shuppet [19]
		300 Skitty [22]	451 Skorupi [E]	690 Skrelp [5]	289 Slaking [14]	287 Slakoth [14]	215 Sneasel [10]	209 Snubbull [E]
		021 Spearow [E]	327 Spinda [10]	442 Spiritomb [7]	185 Sudowoodo [19]	216 Teddiursa [15]	454 Toxicroak [17]	328 Trapinch [1]
		709 Trevenant [19]	197 Umbreon [20]	217 Ursaring [15]	329 Vibrava [1]	629 Vullaby [23]	037 Vulpix [23, E]	461 Weavile [10]
		193 Yanma [E]	571 Zoroark [17]	570 Zorua [17]	041 Zubat [E]			
Bug	Fell Stinger	168 Ariados [1]	015 Beedrill [45]	331 Cacnea [E]	452 Drapion [53]	589 Escavalier [1, 60]	649 Genesect [1]	402 Kricketune [36]
		542 Leavanny [34]	046 Paras [E]	211 Qwilfish [1, 60]	451 Skorupi [47]	283 Surskit [E]	416 Vespiquen [1, 57]	
Fire	Fiery Dance	637 Volcarona [1, 100]						
Fighting	Final Gambit	617 Accelgor [1, 56]	550 Basculin [50]	050 Diglett [E]	056 Mankey [53]	290 Nincada [E]	057 Primeape [1, 63]	019 Rattata [E]
		447 Riolu [50]	336 Seviper [E]	616 Shelmet [56]	213 Shuckle [E]	398 Staraptor [57]	397 Staravia [48]	396 Starly [41]
		494 Victini [81]	335 Zangoose [E]					
Fire	Fire Blast (TM38)	359 Absol [TM]	142 Aerodactyl [TM]	306 Aggron [TM]	334 Altaria [TM]	059 Arcanine [TM]	493 Arceus [TM]	531 Audino [TM]
		482 Azelf [TM]	371 Bagon [TM]	411 Bastiodon [TM]	257 Blaziken [TM]	242 Blissey [TM]	654 Braixen [55, TM]	323 Camerupt [TM]
		351 Castform [35, TM]	609 Chandelure [TM]	113 Chansey [TM]	006 Charizard [TM]	004 Charmander [TM]	005 Charmeleon [TM]	390 Chimchar [TM]
		036 Clefable [TM]	035 Clefairy [TM]	173 Cleffa [TM]	256 Combusken [TM]	408 Cranidos [TM]	104 Cubone [TM]	155 Cyndaquil [TM]
		555 Darmanitan [TM]	554 Darumaka [TM]	655 Delphox [61, TM]	483 Dialga [TM]	148 Dragonair [TM]	149 Dragonite [TM]	147 Dratini [TM]
		206 Dunsparce [TM]	500 Emboar [TM]	244 Entei [71, TM]	295 Exploud [TM]	653 Fennekin [48, TM]	136 Flareon [TM]	662 Fletchinder [TM]
		330 Flygon [TM]	444 Gabite [TM]	445 Garchomp [TM]	074 Geodude [TM]	443 Gible [TM]	076 Golem [TM]	706 Goodra [TM]
		711 Gourgeist [TM]	210 Granbull [TM]	075 Graveler [TM]	088 Grimer [TM]	383 Groudon [75, TM]	058 Growlithe [TM]	130 Gyarados [TM]
		440 Happiny [TM]	631 Heatmor [TM]	485 Heatran [TM]	250 Ho-Oh [37, TM]	229 Houndoom [TM]	228 Houndour [TM]	635 Hydreigon [TM]
		174 Igglybuff [TM]	392 Infernape [TM]	039 Jigglypuff [TM]	115 Kangaskhan [TM]	352 Kecleon [TM]	109 Koffing [TM]	608 Lampent [TM]
		636 Larvesta [TM]	463 Lickilicky [TM]	108 Lickitung [TM]	667 Litleo [TM]	607 Litwick [TM]	294 Loudred [TM]	068 Machamp [TM]
		067 Machoke [TM]	066 Machop [TM]	240 Magby [43, TM]	219 Magcargo [TM]	126 Magmar [55, TM]	467 Magmortar [55, TM]	105 Marowak [TM]
		303 Mawile [TM]	151 Mew [TM]	150 Mewtwo [TM]	146 Moltres [TM]	391 Monferno [TM]	089 Muk [TM]	446 Munchlax [TM]
		034 Nidoking [TM]	031 Nidoqueen [TM]	038 Ninetales [TM]	322 Numel [TM]	224 Octillery [TM]	484 Palkia [TM]	513 Pansear [34, TM]
		499 Pignite [TM]	077 Ponyta [41, TM]	710 Pumpkaboo [TM]	668 Pyroar [TM]	156 Quilava [TM]	409 Rampardos [TM]	078 Rapidash [41, TM]
		384 Rayquaza [TM]	223 Remoraid [TM]	643 Reshiram [78, TM]	112 Rhydon [TM]	111 Rhyhorn [TM]	464 Rhyperior [TM]	373 Salamence [TM]
		372 Shelgon [TM]	410 Shieldon [TM]	514 Simisear [TM]	435 Skuntank [TM]	289 Slaking [TM]	287 Slakoth [TM]	080 Slowbro [TM]
		199 Slowking [TM]	079 Slowpoke [TM]	218 Slugma [TM]	143 Snorlax [TM]	209 Snubbull [TM]	338 Solrock [TM]	434 Stunky [TM]
		663 Talonflame [TM]	128 Tauros [TM]	498 Tepig [TM]	468 Togekiss [TM]	175 Togepi [TM]	176 Togetic [TM]	255 Torchic [TM]
		324 Torkoal [TM]	157 Typhlosion [TM]	248 Tyranitar [TM]	494 Victini [TM]	288 Vigoroth [TM]	637 Volcarona [TM]	037 Vulpix [42, TM]
		110 Weezing [TM]	293 Whismur [TM]	040 Wigglytuff [TM]	335 Zangoose [TM]			
	Fire Fang	142 Aerodactyl [1]	024 Arbok [1]	059 Arcanine [1]	371 Bagon [E]	006 Charizard [28]	004 Charmander [25]	005 Charmeleon [28]
		555 Darmanitan [11]	554 Darumaka [11]	633 Deino [E]	232 Donphan [1]	452 Drapion [1]	621 Druddigon [E]	309 Electrike [E]
		244 Entei [50]	295 Exploud [1]	136 Flareon [20]	445 Garchomp [1]	472 Gliscor [1]	210 Granbull [1]	058 Growlithe [21]
		485 Heatran [17]	450 Hippowdon [1]	229 Houndoom [30]	228 Houndour [28, E]	506 Lillipup [E]	667 Litleo [23]	310 Manectric [1]
		303 Mawile [E]	261 Poochyena [E]	668 Pyroar [23]	643 Reshiram [1]	111 Rhyhorn [E]	373 Salamence [1]	551 Sandile [E]
		403 Shinx [E]	209 Snubbull [1, E]	208 Steelix [1]	508 Stoutland [1]	248 Tyranitar [1]	696 Tyrunt [E]	
	Fire Pledge	257 Blaziken [T]	654 Braixen [T]	006 Charizard [T]	004 Charmander [T]	005 Charmeleon [T]	390 Chimchar [T]	256 Combusken [T]
		155 Cyndaquil [T]	655 Delphox [T]	500 Emboar [T]	653 Fennekin [T]	392 Infernape [T]	391 Monferno [T]	499 Pignite [T]
		156 Quilava [T]	498 Tepig [T]	255 Torchic [T]	157 Typhlosion [T]			
	Fire Punch	063 Abra [BP, E]	306 Aggron [BP]	190 Aipom [BP]	065 Alakazam [BP]	424 Ambipom [BP]	181 Ampharos [1, BP]	531 Audino [BP]
		482 Azelf [BP]	257 Blaziken [1, BP]	242 Blissey [BP]	654 Braixen [BP]	427 Buneary [BP, E]	113 Chansey [BP]	006 Charizard [BP]
		004 Charmander [BP]	005 Charmeleon [BP]	390 Chimchar [BP, E]	036 Clefable [BP]	035 Clefairy [BP]	256 Combusken [BP]	534 Conkeldurr [BP]
		408 Cranidos [BP]	104 Cubone [BP]	555 Darmanitan [22, BP]	554 Darumaka [22, BP]	655 Delphox [BP]	386 Deoxys (Nor) [BP]	386 Deoxys (Spd) [BP]
		660 Diggersby [BP]	149 Dragonite [1, BP]	096 Drowzee [BP, E]	621 Druddigon [BP]	356 Dusclops [1, BP]	477 Dusknoir [1, BP]	604 Eelektross [BP]
		125 Electabuzz [BP]	466 Electivire [1, BP]	239 Elekid [BP, E]	500 Emboar [BP]	295 Exploud [BP]	180 Flaaffy [BP]	330 Flygon [BP]
		162 Furret [BP]	475 Gallade [BP]	282 Gardevoir [BP]	092 Gastly [BP, E]	094 Gengar [BP]	074 Geodude [BP]	076 Golem [BP]
		622 Golett [BP]	623 Golurk [BP]	706 Goodra [BP]	210 Granbull [BP]	075 Graveler [BP]	088 Grimer [BP]	383 Groudon [BP]
		326 Grumpig [BP]	316 Gulpin [BP]	533 Gurdurr [BP]	297 Hariyama [BP]	093 Haunter [BP]	701 Hawlucha [BP]	631 Heatmor [BP]
		695 Heliolisk [BP]	107 Hitmonchan [36, BP]	097 Hypno [BP]	392 Infernape [BP]	039 Jigglypuff [BP]	385 Jirachi [BP]	064 Kadabra [BP]
		115 Kangaskhan [BP]	352 Kecleon [BP]	281 Kirlia [BP]	463 Lickilicky [BP]	108 Lickitung [BP]	271 Lombre [BP]	428 Lopunny [BP]
		294 Loudred [BP]	272 Ludicolo [BP]	068 Machamp [BP]	067 Machoke [BP]	066 Machop [BP, E]	240 Magby [29, BP]	126 Magmar [29, BP]
		467 Magmortar [29, BP]	296 Makuhita [BP]	056 Mankey [BP]	105 Marowak [BP]	308 Medicham [1, BP]	307 Meditite [BP, E]	648 Meloetta [BP]
		481 Mesprit [BP]	151 Mew [BP]	150 Mewtwo [BP]	241 Miltank [BP]	391 Monferno [BP]	122 Mr. Mime [BP]	089 Muk [BP]
		446 Munchlax [BP]	034 Nidoking [BP]	031 Nidoqueen [BP]	299 Nosepass [BP]	674 Pancham [BP]	675 Pangoro [BP]	513 Pansear [BP, E]
		499 Pignite [BP]	057 Primeape [BP]	476 Probopass [BP]	280 Ralts [BP]	409 Rampardos [BP]	486 Regigigas [1, BP]	377 Regirock [BP]
		579 Reuniclus [BP]	112 Rhydon [BP]	464 Rhyperior [BP]	302 Sableye [BP]	539 Sawk [BP]	560 Scrafty [BP]	559 Scraggy [BP, E]
		161 Sentret [BP]	514 Simisear [BP]	289 Slaking [BP]	287 Slakoth [BP]	143 Snorlax [BP]	209 Snubbull [BP]	327 Spinda [BP]
		185 Sudowoodo [BP]	317 Swalot [BP]	216 Teddiursa [BP]	538 Throh [BP]	532 Timburr [BP]	157 Typhlosion [BP]	248 Tyranitar [BP]
		217 Ursaring [BP]	480 Uxie [BP]	494 Victini [BP]	288 Vigoroth [BP]	505 Watchog [BP]	293 Whismur [BP]	040 Wigglytuff [BP]
		335 Zangoose [BP]						

ADVENTURE DATA

Type	Move	Pokémon that can learn it						
Fire	Fire Spin	654 Braixen [22]	006 Charizard [56]	004 Charmander [43]	005 Charmeleon [50]	390 Chimchar [33]	655 Delphox [22]	244 Entei [22]
		653 Fennekin [20]	136 Flareon [25]	058 Growlithe [E]	631 Heatmor [16]	485 Heatran [1, 57]	228 Houndour [E]	392 Infernape [42]
		608 Lampent [7]	667 Litleo [E]	607 Litwick [7]	240 Magby [15]	126 Magmar [15]	467 Magmortar [15]	146 Moltres [8]
		391 Monferno [39]	513 Pansear [E]	077 Ponyta [25]	078 Rapidash [25]	338 Solrock [5]	255 Torchic [19]	324 Torkoal [13]
		637 Volcarona [30]	037 Vulpix [15]					
Ground	Fissure	339 Barboach [44]	323 Camerupt [1, 59]	050 Diglett [45]	529 Drilbur [47]	051 Dugtrio [57]	530 Excadrill [62]	383 Groudon [65]
		449 Hippopotas [50]	450 Hippowdon [60]	645 Landorus [1, 67]	131 Lapras [E]	231 Phanpy [E]	422 Shellos [E]	410 Shieldon [E]
		143 Snorlax [E]	363 Spheal [E]	618 Stunfisk [1, 61]	220 Swinub [E]	324 Torkoal [E]	328 Trapinch [47]	320 Wailmer [E]
		340 Whiscash [52]	413 Wormadam (Sand) [47]					
Normal	Flail	683 Aromatisse [38]	339 Barboach [E]	550 Basculin [1, 46]	614 Beartic [36]	438 Bonsly [5]	427 Buneary [E]	659 Bunnelby [29]
		703 Carbink [35]	152 Chikorita [E]	170 Chinchou [31, E]	692 Clauncher [16]	693 Clawitzer [16]	222 Corsola [50]	159 Croconaw [24]
		558 Crustle [50]	613 Cubchoo [36]	719 Diancie [35]	660 Diggersby [31]	084 Doduo [E]	206 Dunsparce [49]	557 Dwebble [41]
		133 Eevee [E]	083 Farfetch'd [E]	349 Feebas [30]	160 Feraligatr [24]	456 Finneon [E]	662 Fletchinder [16]	661 Fletchling [16]
		074 Geodude [E]	431 Glameow [E]	118 Goldeen [13]	706 Goodra [28]	704 Goomy [28]	214 Heracross [E]	116 Horsea [E]
		140 Kabuto [E]	588 Karrablast [49]	099 Kingler [63]	098 Krabby [45, E]	171 Lanturn [33]	270 Lotad [E]	370 Luvdisc [27]
		129 Magikarp [30]	052 Meowth [E]	572 Minccino [E]	043 Oddish [E]	095 Onix [E]	417 Pachirisu [E]	536 Palpitoad [37]
		046 Paras [E]	504 Patrat [E]	231 Phanpy [6]	172 Pichu [E]	204 Pineco [E]	127 Pinsir [E]	393 Piplup [E]
		211 Qwilfish [E]	223 Remoraid [E]	027 Sandshrew [E]	119 Seaking [13]	537 Seismitoad [39]	540 Sewaddle [43]	289 Slaking [39]
		287 Slakoth [33]	705 Sliggoo [28]	327 Spinda [50]	682 Spritzee [38]	007 Squirtle [E]	618 Stunfisk [1, 55]	185 Sudowoodo [1, 5]
		220 Swinub [40]	663 Talonflame [16]	114 Tangela [E]	564 Tirtouga [E]	324 Torkoal [42]	158 Totodile [22]	328 Trapinch [E]
		535 Tympole [34]	480 Uxie [1, 61]	037 Vulpix [E]	413 Wormadam (Plant) [38]	413 Wormadam (Sand) [38]	413 Wormadam (Trash) [38]	335 Zangoose [E]
		263 Zigzagoon [29]						
Fire	Flame Burst	323 Camerupt [15]	609 Chandelure [1]	006 Charizard [32]	004 Charmander [28]	005 Charmeleon [32]	155 Cyndaquil [E]	309 Electrike [E]
		058 Growlithe [28]	631 Heatmor [31]	608 Lampent [20]	607 Litwick [20]	240 Magby [22]	219 Magcargo [27]	126 Magmar [22]
		467 Magmortar [22]	322 Numel [15]	513 Pansear [22]	514 Simisear [1]	218 Slugma [27]	434 Stunky [E]	255 Torchic [28, E]
		324 Torkoal [E]	494 Victini [41]	037 Vulpix [28]				
	Flame Charge (TM43)	059 Arcanine [TM]	257 Blaziken [20, TM]	522 Blitzle [18, TM]	654 Braixen [14, TM]	323 Camerupt [TM]	609 Chandelure [TM]	006 Charizard [TM]
		004 Charmander [TM]	005 Charmeleon [TM]	390 Chimchar [TM]	256 Combusken [20, TM]	155 Cyndaquil [28, TM]	555 Darmanitan [TM]	554 Darumaka [TM]
		655 Delphox [14, TM]	500 Emboar [15, TM]	244 Entei [TM]	653 Fennekin [14, TM]	136 Flareon [TM]	662 Fletchinder [38, TM]	661 Fletchling [34, TM]
		649 Genesect [18, TM]	711 Gourgeist [TM]	058 Growlithe [TM]	485 Heatran [TM]	250 Ho-Oh [TM]	229 Houndoom [TM]	228 Houndour [TM]
		392 Infernape [TM]	608 Lampent [TM]	636 Larvesta [30, TM]	667 Litleo [TM]	607 Litwick [TM]	240 Magby [TM]	219 Magcargo [TM]
		126 Magmar [TM]	467 Magmortar [TM]	151 Mew [TM]	146 Moltres [TM]	391 Monferno [TM]	038 Ninetales [TM]	322 Numel [TM]
		513 Pansear [TM]	499 Pignite [15, TM]	077 Ponyta [21, TM]	710 Pumpkaboo [TM]	668 Pyroar [TM]	156 Quilava [35, TM]	078 Rapidash [21, TM]
		643 Reshiram [TM]	514 Simisear [TM]	218 Slugma [TM]	663 Talonflame [39, TM]	498 Tepig [15, TM]	255 Torchic [TM]	324 Torkoal [TM]
		157 Typhlosion [35, TM]	494 Victini [25, TM]	637 Volcarona [TM]	037 Vulpix [TM]	523 Zebstrika [18, TM]		
	Flame Wheel	390 Chimchar [17]	155 Cyndaquil [19]	554 Darumaka [E]	058 Growlithe [17]	392 Infernape [19]	636 Larvesta [60]	391 Monferno [19]
		077 Ponyta [13, E]	156 Quilava [20]	078 Rapidash [13]	019 Rattata [E]	324 Torkoal [18]	157 Typhlosion [20]	637 Volcarona [1]
	Flamethrower (TM35)	359 Absol [TM]	142 Aerodactyl [TM]	306 Aggron [TM]	334 Altaria [TM]	059 Arcanine [TM]	493 Arceus [TM]	531 Audino [TM]
		482 Azelf [TM]	371 Bagon [44, TM]	411 Bastiodon [TM]	257 Blaziken [TM]	242 Blissey [TM]	654 Braixen [41, TM]	323 Camerupt [TM]
		351 Castform [TM]	609 Chandelure [TM]	113 Chansey [TM]	006 Charizard [47, TM]	004 Charmander [37, TM]	005 Charmeleon [43, TM]	390 Chimchar [47, TM]
		036 Clefable [TM]	035 Clefairy [TM]	173 Cleffa [TM]	256 Combusken [TM]	408 Cranidos [TM]	104 Cubone [TM]	155 Cyndaquil [40, TM]
		555 Darmanitan [TM]	554 Darumaka [TM]	655 Delphox [42, TM]	483 Dialga [TM]	148 Dragonair [TM]	149 Dragonite [TM]	147 Dratini [TM]
		621 Druddigon [TM]	206 Dunsparce [TM]	604 Eelektross [TM]	466 Electivire [TM]	309 Electrike [TM]	500 Emboar [43, TM]	244 Entei [36, TM]
		295 Exploud [TM]	653 Fennekin [35, TM]	136 Flareon [TM]	662 Fletchinder [TM]	330 Flygon [TM]	162 Furret [TM]	444 Gabite [TM]
		445 Garchomp [TM]	649 Genesect [TM]	074 Geodude [TM]	443 Gible [TM]	076 Golem [TM]	706 Goodra [TM]	711 Gourgeist [TM]
		210 Granbull [TM]	075 Graveler [TM]	088 Grimer [TM]	383 Groudon [TM]	058 Growlithe [34, TM]	130 Gyarados [TM]	440 Happiny [TM]
		631 Heatmor [47, TM]	485 Heatran [TM]	250 Ho-Oh [TM]	229 Houndoom [50, TM]	228 Houndour [44, TM]	635 Hydreigon [TM]	174 Igglybuff [TM]
		392 Infernape [TM]	686 Inkay [TM]	039 Jigglypuff [TM]	115 Kangaskhan [TM]	352 Kecleon [TM]	109 Koffing [TM]	608 Lampent [TM]
		636 Larvesta [TM]	463 Lickilicky [TM]	108 Lickitung [TM]	667 Litleo [36, TM]	607 Litwick [TM]	294 Loudred [TM]	068 Machamp [TM]
		067 Machoke [TM]	066 Machop [TM]	240 Magby [40, TM]	219 Magcargo [54, TM]	126 Magmar [49, TM]	467 Magmortar [49, TM]	687 Malamar [TM]
		310 Manectric [TM]	105 Marowak [TM]	303 Mawile [TM]	151 Mew [TM]	150 Mewtwo [TM]	146 Moltres [36, TM]	391 Monferno [TM]
		089 Muk [TM]	446 Munchlax [TM]	034 Nidoking [TM]	031 Nidoqueen [TM]	038 Ninetales [1, TM]	715 Noivern [TM]	322 Numel [43, TM]
		224 Octillery [TM]	484 Palkia [TM]	513 Pansear [TM]	499 Pignite [39, TM]	077 Ponyta [TM]	710 Pumpkaboo [TM]	668 Pyroar [38, TM]
		156 Quilava [46, TM]	409 Rampardos [TM]	078 Rapidash [TM]	384 Rayquaza [TM]	223 Remoraid [TM]	643 Reshiram [22, TM]	112 Rhydon [TM]
		111 Rhyhorn [TM]	464 Rhyperior [TM]	373 Salamence [49, TM]	161 Sentret [TM]	336 Seviper [TM]	372 Shelgon [49, TM]	410 Shieldon [TM]
		514 Simisear [TM]	435 Skuntank [34, TM]	289 Slaking [TM]	287 Slakoth [TM]	080 Slowbro [TM]	199 Slowking [TM]	079 Slowpoke [TM]
		218 Slugma [48, TM]	685 Slurpuff [TM]	143 Snorlax [TM]	209 Snubbull [TM]	338 Solrock [TM]	434 Stunky [TM]	684 Swirlix [TM]
		663 Talonflame [TM]	128 Tauros [TM]	498 Tepig [33, TM]	468 Togekiss [TM]	175 Togepi [TM]	176 Togetic [TM]	255 Torchic [46, TM]
		324 Torkoal [34, TM]	157 Typhlosion [48, TM]	248 Tyranitar [TM]	494 Victini [TM]	288 Vigoroth [TM]	637 Volcarona [TM]	037 Vulpix [36, TM]
		505 Watchog [TM]	110 Weezing [TM]	293 Whismur [TM]	040 Wigglytuff [TM]	335 Zangoose [TM]	571 Zoroark [TM]	

ADVENTURE DATA

	Move	Pokémon that can learn it						
Fire	Flare Blitz	257 Blaziken [1, 63]	006 Charizard [1, 77]	004 Charmander [E]	256 Combusken [58]	155 Cyndaquil [E]	555 Darmanitan [33]	554 Darumaka [33]
		500 Emboar [62]	136 Flareon [45]	058 Growlithe [45, E]	392 Infernape [1, 68]	636 Larvesta [100]	240 Magby [E]	391 Monferno [56]
		499 Pignite [52]	077 Ponyta [49]	078 Rapidash [49]	663 Talonflame [1]	498 Tepig [43]	494 Victini [73]	637 Volcarona [1]
		037 Vulpix [E]						
Normal	Flash (TM70)	460 Abomasnow [TM]	063 Abra [TM]	359 Absol [TM]	065 Alakazam [TM]	698 Amaura [TM]	591 Amoonguss [TM]	181 Ampharos [TM]
		493 Arceus [TM]	168 Ariados [TM]	683 Aromatisse [TM]	531 Audino [TM]	699 Aurorus [TM]	713 Avalugg [TM]	482 Azelf [TM]
		343 Baltoy [TM]	354 Banette [TM]	153 Bayleef [TM]	267 Beautifly [TM]	015 Beedrill [TM]	606 Beheeyem [TM]	182 Bellossom [TM]
		069 Bellsprout [TM]	712 Bergmite [TM]	242 Blissey [TM]	522 Blitzle [TM]	286 Breloom [TM]	437 Bronzong [TM]	436 Bronzor [TM]
		406 Budew [TM]	001 Bulbasaur [TM]	012 Butterfree [TM]	331 Cacnea [TM]	332 Cacturne [TM]	703 Carbink [TM]	455 Carnivine [TM]
		351 Castform [TM]	251 Celebi [TM]	609 Chandelure [TM]	113 Chansey [TM]	421 Cherrim [TM]	420 Cherubi [TM]	652 Chesnaught [TM]
		650 Chespin [TM]	152 Chikorita [TM]	358 Chimecho [TM]	170 Chinchou [TM]	433 Chingling [TM]	344 Claydol [TM]	036 Clefable [TM]
		035 Clefairy [TM]	173 Cleffa [TM]	563 Cofagrigus [TM]	546 Cottonee [TM]	346 Cradily [TM]	488 Cresselia [TM]	491 Darkrai [TM]
		702 Dedenne [TM]	585 Deerling [TM]	301 Delcatty [TM]	386 Deoxys (Atk) [TM]	386 Deoxys (Def) [TM]	386 Deoxys (Nor) [TM]	386 Deoxys (Spd) [TM]
		483 Dialga [TM]	719 Diancie [TM]	452 Drapion [TM]	426 Drifblim [TM]	425 Drifloon [TM]	096 Drowzee [TM]	578 Duosion [TM]
		356 Dusclops [TM]	477 Dusknoir [TM]	355 Duskull [TM]	269 Dustox [TM]	603 Eelektrik [TM]	604 Eelektross [TM]	125 Electabuzz [TM]
		466 Electivire [TM]	309 Electrike [TM]	101 Electrode [TM]	239 Elekid [TM]	605 Elgyem [TM]	587 Emolga [TM]	244 Entei [TM]
		196 Espeon [TM]	677 Espurr [TM]	102 Exeggcute [TM]	103 Exeggutor [TM]	597 Ferroseed [TM]	598 Ferrothorn [TM]	456 Finneon [TM]
		180 Flaaffy [TM]	669 Flabébé [TM]	670 Floette [TM]	671 Florges [TM]	590 Foongus [TM]	592 Frillish [TM]	478 Froslass [TM]
		676 Furfrou [TM]	475 Gallade [TM]	596 Galvantula [TM]	282 Gardevoir [TM]	423 Gastrodon [TM]	649 Genesect [TM]	203 Girafarig [TM]
		362 Glalie [TM]	431 Glameow [TM]	044 Gloom [TM]	055 Golduck [TM]	622 Golett [TM]	623 Golurk [TM]	574 Gothita [TM]
		576 Gothitelle [TM]	575 Gothorita [TM]	711 Gourgeist [TM]	388 Grotle [TM]	253 Grovyle [TM]	326 Grumpig [TM]	440 Happiny [TM]
		695 Heliolisk [TM]	694 Helioptile [TM]	250 Ho-Oh [TM]	187 Hoppip [TM]	097 Hypno [TM]	174 Igglybuff [TM]	314 Illumise [TM]
		686 Inkay [TM]	002 Ivysaur [TM]	593 Jellicent [TM]	039 Jigglypuff [TM]	385 Jirachi [TM]	135 Jolteon [TM]	595 Joltik [TM]
		189 Jumpluff [TM]	124 Jynx [TM]	064 Kadabra [TM]	352 Kecleon [TM]	281 Kirlia [TM]	109 Koffing [TM]	402 Kricketune [TM]
		608 Lampent [TM]	171 Lanturn [TM]	380 Latias [TM]	381 Latios [TM]	470 Leafeon [TM]	542 Leavanny [TM]	166 Ledian [TM]
		165 Ledyba [TM]	345 Lileep [TM]	549 Lilligant [TM]	607 Litwick [TM]	271 Lombre [TM]	270 Lotad [TM]	272 Ludicolo [TM]
		249 Lugia [TM]	457 Lumineon [TM]	337 Lunatone [TM]	404 Luxio [TM]	405 Luxray [TM]	081 Magnemite [TM]	082 Magneton [TM]
		462 Magnezone [TM]	687 Malamar [TM]	490 Manaphy [TM]	310 Manectric [TM]	179 Mareep [TM]	284 Masquerain [TM]	308 Medicham [TM]
		307 Meditite [TM]	154 Meganium [TM]	648 Meloetta [TM]	678 Meowstic (F) [TM]	678 Meowstic (M) [TM]	052 Meowth [TM]	481 Mesprit [TM]
		376 Metagross [TM]	375 Metang [TM]	151 Mew [TM]	150 Mewtwo [TM]	439 Mime Jr. [TM]	312 Minun [TM]	200 Misdreavus [TM]
		429 Mismagius [TM]	414 Mothim [TM]	122 Mr. Mime [TM]	517 Munna [TM]	518 Musharna [TM]	177 Natu [TM]	290 Nincada [TM]
		291 Ninjask [TM]	274 Nuzleaf [TM]	043 Oddish [TM]	417 Pachirisu [TM]	511 Pansage [TM]	046 Paras [TM]	047 Parasect [TM]
		053 Persian [TM]	548 Petilil [TM]	172 Pichu [TM]	025 Pikachu [TM]	311 Plusle [TM]	137 Porygon [TM]	233 Porygon2 [TM]
		474 Porygon-Z [TM]	054 Psyduck [TM]	710 Pumpkaboo [TM]	432 Purugly [TM]	195 Quagsire [TM]	651 Quilladin [TM]	026 Raichu [TM]
		243 Raikou [TM]	280 Ralts [TM]	579 Reuniclus [TM]	315 Roselia [TM]	407 Roserade [TM]	479 Rotom (Fan) [TM]	479 Rotom (Frost) [TM]
		479 Rotom (Heat) [TM]	479 Rotom (Mow) [TM]	479 Rotom (Wash) [TM]	479 Rotom [TM]	302 Sableye [TM]	586 Sawsbuck [TM]	254 Sceptile [TM]
		273 Seedot [TM]	497 Serperior [TM]	496 Servine [TM]	540 Sewaddle [TM]	492 Shaymin (Land) [TM]	492 Shaymin (Sky) [TM]	292 Shedinja [TM]
		275 Shiftry [TM]	403 Shinx [TM]	285 Shroomish [TM]	213 Shuckle [TM]	353 Shuppet [TM]	561 Sigilyph [TM]	512 Simisage [TM]
		227 Skarmory [TM]	188 Skiploom [TM]	300 Skitty [TM]	451 Skorupi [TM]	080 Slowbro [TM]	199 Slowking [TM]	079 Slowpoke [TM]
		685 Slurpuff [TM]	238 Smoochum [TM]	495 Snivy [TM]	361 Snorunt [TM]	459 Snover [TM]	577 Solosis [TM]	338 Solrock [TM]
		167 Spinarak [TM]	327 Spinda [TM]	442 Spiritomb [TM]	325 Spoink [TM]	682 Spritzee [TM]	234 Stantler [TM]	121 Starmie [TM]
		120 Staryu [TM]	618 Stunfisk [TM]	192 Sunflora [TM]	191 Sunkern [TM]	283 Surskit [TM]	541 Swadloon [TM]	684 Swirlix [TM]
		528 Swoobat [TM]	700 Sylveon [TM]	114 Tangela [TM]	465 Tangrowth [TM]	468 Togekiss [TM]	175 Togepi [TM]	176 Togetic [TM]
		389 Torterra [TM]	252 Treecko [TM]	357 Tropius [TM]	387 Turtwig [TM]	197 Umbreon [TM]	480 Uxie [TM]	049 Venomoth [TM]
		048 Venonat [TM]	003 Venusaur [TM]	416 Vespiquen [TM]	494 Victini [TM]	071 Victreebel [TM]	045 Vileplume [TM]	640 Virizion [TM]
		666 Vivillon [TM]	313 Volbeat [1, TM]	100 Voltorb [TM]	505 Watchog [TM]	070 Weepinbell [TM]	110 Weezing [TM]	547 Whimsicott [TM]
		040 Wigglytuff [TM]	527 Woobat [TM]	194 Wooper [TM]	413 Wormadam (Plant) [TM]	413 Wormadam (Sand) [TM]	413 Wormadam (Trash) [TM]	178 Xatu [TM]
		716 Xerneas [TM]	562 Yamask [TM]	193 Yanma [TM]	469 Yanmega [TM]	145 Zapdos [TM]	523 Zebstrika [TM]	644 Zekrom [TM]
Steel	Flash Cannon (TM91)	681 Aegislash [TM]	306 Aggron [TM]	698 Amaura [TM]	493 Arceus [TM]	348 Armaldo [TM]	683 Aromatisse [TM]	699 Aurorus [TM]
		713 Avalugg [TM]	411 Bastiodon [TM]	712 Bergmite [TM]	009 Blastoise [1, TM]	525 Boldore [TM]	437 Bronzong [TM]	436 Bronzor [TM]
		323 Camerupt [TM]	692 Clauncher [TM]	693 Clawitzer [TM]	638 Cobalion [TM]	615 Cryogonal [TM]	386 Deoxys (Atk) [TM]	386 Deoxys (Def) [TM]
		386 Deoxys (Nor) [TM]	386 Deoxys (Spd) [TM]	483 Dialga [50, TM]	680 Doublade [TM]	621 Druddigon [TM]	578 Duosion [TM]	632 Durant [TM]
		603 Eelektrik [TM]	604 Eelektross [TM]	395 Empoleon [TM]	597 Ferroseed [52, TM]	598 Ferrothorn [61, TM]	205 Forretress [TM]	649 Genesect [TM]
		526 Gigalith [TM]	623 Golurk [TM]	485 Heatran [TM]	679 Honedge [TM]	116 Horsea [TM]	635 Hydreigon [TM]	385 Jirachi [TM]
		230 Kingdra [TM]	600 Klang [TM]	707 Klefki [TM]	599 Klink [TM]	601 Klinklang [TM]	646 Kyurem (Blk) [TM]	646 Kyurem (Wht) [TM]
		646 Kyurem [TM]	448 Lucario [TM]	081 Magnemite [31, TM]	082 Magneton [33, TM]	462 Magnezone [33, TM]	303 Mawile [TM]	376 Metagross [TM]
		375 Metang [TM]	151 Mew [TM]	224 Octillery [TM]	095 Onix [TM]	476 Probopass [TM]	378 Regice [TM]	379 Registeel [43, TM]
		579 Reuniclus [TM]	464 Rhyperior [TM]	524 Roggenrola [TM]	212 Scizor [TM]	117 Seadra [TM]	410 Shieldon [TM]	561 Sigilyph [TM]
		227 Skarmory [TM]	577 Solosis [TM]	682 Spritzee [TM]	121 Starmie [TM]	120 Staryu [TM]	208 Steelix [TM]	642 Thundurus [TM]
		583 Vanillish [TM]	582 Vanillite [TM]	584 Vanilluxe [TM]	413 Wormadam (Trash) [TM]	716 Xerneas [TM]	644 Zekrom [TM]	
Dark	Flatter	453 Croagunk [50]	096 Drowzee [E]	574 Gothita [28]	576 Gothitelle [28]	575 Gothorita [28]	314 Illumise [29]	686 Inkay [E]
		630 Mandibuzz [19]	179 Mareep [E]	198 Murkrow [E]	029 Nidoran ♀ [33]	032 Nidoran ♂ [33]	030 Nidorina [38]	033 Nidorino [38]
		417 Pachirisu [E]	302 Sableye [E]	158 Totodile [E]	454 Toxicroak [62]	629 Vullaby [19]	527 Woobat [E]	

	Move	Pokémon that can learn it						
Dark	Fling (TM56)	460 Abomasnow [TM]	063 Abra [TM]	306 Aggron [TM]	190 Aipom [36, TM]	065 Alakazam [TM]	424 Ambipom [36, TM]	181 Ampharos [TM]
		531 Audino [TM]	610 Axew [TM]	482 Azelf [TM]	184 Azumarill [TM]	354 Banette [TM]	689 Barbaracle [TM]	614 Beartic [TM]
		182 Bellossom [TM]	400 Bibarel [TM]	688 Binacle [TM]	625 Bisharp [TM]	009 Blastoise [TM]	257 Blaziken [TM]	242 Blissey [34, TM]
		286 Breloom [TM]	427 Buneary [TM]	659 Bunnelby [TM]	331 Cacnea [TM]	332 Cacturne [TM]	455 Carnivine [TM]	251 Celebi [TM]
		113 Chansey [34, TM]	006 Charizard [TM]	004 Charmander [TM]	005 Charmeleon [TM]	652 Chesnaught [TM]	650 Chespin [TM]	390 Chimchar [TM]
		573 Cinccino [TM]	036 Clefable [TM]	035 Clefairy [TM]	173 Cleffa [TM]	256 Combusken [TM]	534 Conkeldurr [TM]	341 Corphish [TM]
		408 Cranidos [TM]	342 Crawdaunt [TM]	453 Croagunk [TM]	159 Croconaw [TM]	613 Cubchoo [TM]	104 Cubone [33, TM]	491 Darkrai [TM]
		555 Darmanitan [TM]	554 Darumaka [TM]	702 Dedenne [TM]	225 Delibird [TM]	386 Deoxys (Atk) [TM]	386 Deoxys (Def) [TM]	386 Deoxys (Nor) [TM]
		386 Deoxys (Spd) [TM]	087 Dewgong [TM]	502 Dewott [TM]	660 Diggersby [TM]	149 Dragonite [TM]	452 Drapion [TM]	529 Drilbur [TM]
		096 Drowzee [TM]	621 Druddigon [TM]	356 Dusclops [TM]	477 Dusknoir [TM]	355 Duskull [TM]	125 Electabuzz [TM]	466 Electivire [TM]
		239 Elekid [TM]	500 Emboar [TM]	587 Emolga [TM]	395 Empoleon [TM]	530 Excadrill [TM]	295 Exploud [TM]	160 Feraligatr [TM]
		180 Flaaffy [TM]	611 Fraxure [TM]	656 Froakie [25, TM]	657 Frogadier [28, TM]	478 Froslass [TM]	162 Furret [TM]	475 Gallade [TM]
		569 Garbodor [TM]	445 Garchomp [TM]	282 Gardevoir [TM]	094 Gengar [TM]	074 Geodude [TM]	207 Gligar [TM]	472 Gliscor [TM]
		044 Gloom [TM]	055 Golduck [TM]	076 Golem [TM]	622 Golett [TM]	623 Golurk [TM]	574 Gothita [TM]	576 Gothitelle [TM]
		575 Gothorita [TM]	210 Granbull [TM]	075 Graveler [TM]	658 Greninja [TM]	088 Grimer [26, TM]	383 Groudon [TM]	253 Grovyle [TM]
		326 Grumpig [TM]	533 Gurdurr [TM]	440 Happiny [TM]	297 Hariyama [TM]	093 Haunter [TM]	701 Hawlucha [24, TM]	612 Haxorus [TM]
		631 Heatmor [TM]	214 Heracross [TM]	107 Hitmonchan [TM]	106 Hitmonlee [TM]	097 Hypno [TM]	174 Igglybuff [TM]	314 Illumise [TM]
		392 Infernape [TM]	686 Inkay [TM]	039 Jigglypuff [TM]	385 Jirachi [TM]	124 Jynx [TM]	064 Kadabra [TM]	115 Kangaskhan [TM]
		352 Kecleon [TM]	099 Kingler [TM]	281 Kirlia [TM]	098 Krabby [TM]	552 Krokorok [TM]	553 Krookodile [TM]	646 Kyurem (Blk) [TM]
		646 Kyurem (Wht) [TM]	646 Kyurem [TM]	645 Landorus [TM]	166 Ledian [TM]	165 Ledyba [TM]	463 Lickilicky [TM]	108 Lickitung [TM]
		264 Linoone [48, TM]	271 Lombre [TM]	428 Lopunny [TM]	294 Loudred [TM]	448 Lucario [TM]	272 Ludicolo [TM]	068 Machamp [TM]
		067 Machoke [TM]	066 Machop [TM]	240 Magby [TM]	126 Magmar [TM]	467 Magmortar [TM]	296 Makuhita [TM]	687 Malamar [TM]
		490 Manaphy [TM]	056 Mankey [TM]	183 Marill [TM]	105 Marowak [37, TM]	259 Marshtomp [TM]	303 Mawile [TM]	308 Medicham [TM]
		307 Meditite [TM]	648 Meloetta [TM]	481 Mesprit [TM]	151 Mew [TM]	150 Mewtwo [TM]	619 Mienfoo [TM]	620 Mienshao [TM]
		241 Miltank [TM]	439 Mime Jr. [TM]	572 Minccino [TM]	312 Minun [TM]	391 Monferno [TM]	122 Mr. Mime [TM]	089 Muk [26, TM]
		446 Munchlax [41, TM]	034 Nidoking [TM]	031 Nidoqueen [TM]	274 Nuzleaf [TM]	501 Oshawott [TM]	417 Pachirisu [TM]	484 Palkia [TM]
		674 Pancham [TM]	675 Pangoro [TM]	515 Panpour [28, TM]	511 Pansage [28, TM]	513 Pansear [28, TM]	504 Patrat [TM]	624 Pawniard [TM]
		279 Pelipper [39, TM]	489 Phione [TM]	172 Pichu [TM]	499 Pignite [TM]	025 Pikachu [TM]	127 Pinsir [TM]	393 Piplup [TM]
		311 Plusle [TM]	186 Politoed [TM]	061 Poliwhirl [TM]	062 Poliwrath [TM]	057 Primeape [1, TM]	394 Prinplup [TM]	054 Psyduck [TM]
		195 Quagsire [TM]	651 Quilladin [TM]	026 Raichu [TM]	280 Ralts [TM]	409 Rampardos [TM]	384 Rayquaza [TM]	378 Regice [TM]
		486 Regigigas [TM]	377 Regirock [TM]	379 Registeel [TM]	643 Reshiram [TM]	579 Reuniclus [TM]	112 Rhydon [TM]	464 Rhyperior [TM]
		447 Riolu [TM]	302 Sableye [TM]	503 Samurott [TM]	027 Sandshrew [TM]	028 Sandslash [TM]	539 Sawk [TM]	254 Sceptile [TM]
		212 Scizor [TM]	560 Scrafty [TM]	559 Scraggy [TM]	086 Seel [TM]	537 Seismitoad [TM]	161 Sentret [TM]	275 Shiftry [TM]
		516 Simipour [TM]	512 Simisage [TM]	514 Simisear [TM]	451 Skorupi [TM]	289 Slaking [1, 47, TM]	287 Slakoth [TM]	080 Slowbro [TM]
		199 Slowking [TM]	238 Smoochum [TM]	215 Sneasel [TM]	143 Snorlax [TM]	209 Snubbull [TM]	327 Spinda [TM]	007 Squirtle [TM]
		185 Sudowoodo [TM]	260 Swampert [TM]	465 Tangrowth [TM]	216 Teddiursa [1, 57, TM]	538 Throh [TM]	642 Thundurus [TM]	532 Timburr [TM]
		468 Togekiss [TM]	175 Togepi [TM]	176 Togetic [TM]	641 Tornadus [TM]	158 Totodile [TM]	454 Toxicroak [TM]	252 Treecko [TM]
		157 Typhlosion [TM]	248 Tyranitar [TM]	217 Ursaring [TM]	480 Uxie [TM]	416 Vespiquen [TM]	494 Victini [TM]	288 Vigoroth [TM]
		045 Vileplume [TM]	313 Volbeat [TM]	008 Wartortle [TM]	505 Watchog [TM]	461 Weavile [28, TM]	547 Whimsicott [TM]	293 Whismur [TM]
		040 Wigglytuff [TM]	335 Zangoose [TM]	644 Zekrom [TM]	263 Zigzagoon [41, TM]	571 Zoroark [TM]	570 Zorua [TM]	
Fairy	Flower Shield	420 Cherubi [E]	671 Florges [1]	192 Sunflora [1]				
Flying	Fly (HM02)	142 Aerodactyl [HM]	334 Altaria [HM]	493 Arceus [HM]	567 Archeops [HM]	144 Articuno [HM]	628 Braviary [HM]	006 Charizard [HM]
		441 Chatot [HM]	169 Crobat [HM]	225 Delibird [HM]	085 Dodrio [HM]	084 Doduo [HM]	149 Dragonite [HM]	426 Drifblim [HM]
		580 Ducklett [HM]	083 Farfetch'd [HM]	022 Fearow [HM]	662 Fletchinder [HM]	661 Fletchling [HM]	330 Flygon [HM]	649 Genesect [HM]
		487 Giratina (Alt) [HM]	487 Giratina (Ori) [HM]	042 Golbat [HM]	623 Golurk [HM]	701 Hawlucha [HM]	430 Honchkrow [HM]	250 Ho-Oh [HM]
		163 Hoothoot [HM]	635 Hydreigon [HM]	646 Kyurem (Blk) [HM]	646 Kyurem (Wht) [HM]	646 Kyurem [HM]	645 Landorus [HM]	380 Latias [HM]
		381 Latios [HM]	249 Lugia [HM]	630 Mandibuzz [HM]	151 Mew [HM]	146 Moltres [HM]	198 Murkrow [HM]	164 Noctowl [HM]
		714 Noibat [HM]	715 Noivern [HM]	279 Pelipper [HM]	018 Pidgeot [HM]	017 Pidgeotto [HM]	016 Pidgey [HM]	519 Pidove [HM]
		384 Rayquaza [65, HM]	643 Reshiram [HM]	627 Rufflet [HM]	373 Salamence [50, HM]	561 Sigilyph [HM]	227 Skarmory [HM]	021 Spearow [HM]
		398 Staraptor [HM]	397 Staravia [HM]	396 Starly [HM]	333 Swablu [HM]	581 Swanna [HM]	277 Swellow [HM]	528 Swoobat [HM]
		276 Taillow [HM]	663 Talonflame [HM]	642 Thundurus [HM]	468 Togekiss [HM]	176 Togetic [HM]	641 Tornadus [HM]	520 Tranquill [HM]
		357 Tropius [HM]	521 Unfezant [HM]	329 Vibrava [HM]	637 Volcarona [HM]	629 Vullaby [HM]	278 Wingull [HM]	527 Woobat [HM]
		178 Xatu [HM]	717 Yveltal [HM]	145 Zapdos [HM]	644 Zekrom [HM]	041 Zubat [HM]		
Fighting	Flying Press	701 Hawlucha [28]	025 Pikachu ◆					
	Focus Blast (TM52)	460 Abomasnow [TM]	617 Accelgor [TM]	306 Aggron [TM]	065 Alakazam [TM]	181 Ampharos [TM]	493 Arceus [TM]	567 Archeops [TM]
		184 Azumarill [TM]	689 Barbaracle [TM]	614 Beartic [TM]	625 Bisharp [TM]	009 Blastoise [TM]	257 Blaziken [TM]	242 Blissey [TM]
		286 Breloom [TM]	332 Cacturne [TM]	565 Carracosta [TM]	006 Charizard [TM]	652 Chesnaught [TM]	573 Cinccino [TM]	693 Clawitzer [TM]
		036 Clefable [TM]	638 Cobalion [TM]	256 Combusken [TM]	534 Conkeldurr [TM]	453 Croagunk [TM]	491 Darkrai [TM]	555 Darmanitan [TM]
		386 Deoxys (Atk) [TM]	386 Deoxys (Def) [TM]	386 Deoxys (Nor) [TM]	386 Deoxys (Spd) [TM]	691 Dragalge [TM]	149 Dragonite [TM]	621 Druddigon [TM]
		477 Dusknoir [TM]	125 Electabuzz [TM]	466 Electivire [TM]	500 Emboar [TM]	589 Escavalier [TM]	530 Excadrill [TM]	295 Exploud [TM]
		160 Feraligatr [TM]	419 Floatzel [TM]	162 Furret [TM]	475 Gallade [TM]	569 Garbodor [TM]	282 Gardevoir [TM]	094 Gengar [TM]
		055 Golduck [TM]	076 Golem [TM]	622 Golett [TM]	623 Golurk [TM]	706 Goodra [TM]	711 Gourgeist [TM]	210 Granbull [TM]
		383 Groudon [TM]	326 Grumpig [TM]	533 Gurdurr [TM]	297 Hariyama [TM]	701 Hawlucha [TM]	612 Haxorus [TM]	631 Heatmor [TM]
		695 Heliolisk [TM]	214 Heracross [TM]	107 Hitmonchan [TM]	106 Hitmonlee [TM]	635 Hydreigon [TM]	097 Hypno [TM]	392 Infernape [TM]
		124 Jynx [TM]	115 Kangaskhan [TM]	647 Keldeo [TM]	553 Krookodile [TM]	646 Kyurem (Blk) [TM]	646 Kyurem (Wht) [TM]	646 Kyurem [TM]

◆ When Cosplay Pikachu becomes Pikachu Libre, it learns the move Flying Press. When it changes back to Cosplay Pikachu or wears other costumes, it forgets the move.

	Move	Pokémon that can learn it						
Fighting	Focus Blast (TM52)	645 Landorus [TM]	166 Ledian [TM]	463 Lickilicky [TM]	428 Lopunny [TM]	448 Lucario [TM]	272 Ludicolo [TM]	068 Machamp [TM]
		067 Machoke [TM]	066 Machop [TM]	126 Magmar [TM]	467 Magmortar [TM]	296 Makuhita [TM]	056 Mankey [TM]	105 Marowak [TM]
		303 Mawile [TM]	308 Medicham [TM]	307 Meditite [TM]	648 Meloetta [TM]	151 Mew [TM]	150 Mewtwo [TM]	619 Mienfoo [TM]
		620 Mienshao [TM]	241 Miltank [TM]	391 Monferno [TM]	122 Mr. Mime [TM]	089 Muk [TM]	034 Nidoking [TM]	031 Nidoqueen [TM]
		715 Noivern [TM]	484 Palkia [TM]	675 Pangoro [TM]	499 Pignite [TM]	127 Pinsir [TM]	186 Politoed [TM]	062 Poliwrath [TM]
		057 Primeape [TM]	195 Quagsire [TM]	026 Raichu [TM]	409 Rampardos [TM]	384 Rayquaza [TM]	378 Regice [TM]	486 Regigigas [TM]
		377 Regirock [TM]	379 Registeel [TM]	643 Reshiram [TM]	579 Reuniclus [TM]	112 Rhydon [TM]	464 Rhyperior [TM]	447 Riolu [TM]
		028 Sandslash [TM]	539 Sawk [TM]	254 Sceptile [TM]	560 Scrafty [TM]	559 Scraggy [TM]	537 Seismitoad [TM]	275 Shiftry [TM]
		516 Simipour [TM]	512 Simisage [TM]	514 Simisear [TM]	289 Slaking [TM]	080 Slowbro [TM]	199 Slowking [TM]	143 Snorlax [TM]
		260 Swampert [TM]	465 Tangrowth [TM]	639 Terrakion [TM]	538 Throh [TM]	642 Thundurus [TM]	532 Timburr [TM]	641 Tornadus [TM]
		454 Toxicroak [TM]	709 Trevenant [TM]	157 Typhlosion [TM]	248 Tyranitar [TM]	217 Ursaring [TM]	494 Victini [TM]	288 Vigoroth [TM]
		640 Virizion [TM]	505 Watchog [TM]	461 Weavile [TM]	040 Wigglytuff [TM]	716 Xerneas [TM]	717 Yveltal [72, TM]	335 Zangoose [TM]
		644 Zekrom [TM]	571 Zoroark [TM]	718 Zygarde [TM]				
Normal	Focus Energy	610 Axew [E]	371 Bagon [21]	015 Beedrill [13]	257 Blaziken [37]	626 Bouffalant [36]	323 Camerupt [1, 8]	318 Carvanha [8]
		390 Chimchar [E]	256 Combusken [36]	534 Conkeldurr [1, 4]	408 Cranidos [6]	104 Cubone [17]	554 Darumaka [E]	633 Deino [4]
		502 Dewott [13]	426 Drifblim [13]	425 Drifloon [13]	533 Gurdurr [1, 4]	297 Hariyama [1]	106 Hitmonlee [21]	237 Hitmontop [6]
		116 Horsea [26]	635 Hydreigon [1, 4]	115 Kangaskhan [E]	230 Kingdra [26]	402 Kricketune [22]	246 Larvitar [E]	068 Machamp [1, 3]
		067 Machoke [1, 3]	066 Machop [3]	240 Magby [E]	296 Makuhita [1]	056 Mankey [1]	105 Marowak [17]	034 Nidoking [1]
		029 Nidoran ♀ [E]	032 Nidoran ♂ [7]	033 Nidorino [7]	322 Numel [8]	224 Octillery [22]	501 Oshawott [13]	231 Phanpy [E]
		127 Pinsir [1]	057 Primeape [1]	409 Rampardos [6]	020 Raticate [1, 7]	019 Rattata [7]	223 Remoraid [22]	373 Salamence [21]
		503 Samurott [13]	551 Sandile [E]	539 Sawk [9]	212 Scizor [5]	123 Scyther [5]	117 Seadra [26]	161 Sentret [E]
		319 Sharpedo [1, 8]	372 Shelgon [21]	410 Shieldon [E]	435 Skuntank [1]	434 Stunky [1]	277 Swellow [1, 5]	276 Taillow [5]
		538 Throh [9]	532 Timburr [4]	255 Torchic [32]	328 Trapinch [E]	494 Victini [1]	288 Vigoroth [1]	634 Zweilous [1, 4]
Fighting	Focus Punch	460 Abomasnow [BP]	063 Abra [BP]	306 Aggron [BP]	190 Aipom [BP]	065 Alakazam [BP]	424 Ambipom [BP]	181 Ampharos [BP]
		531 Audino [BP]	184 Azumarill [BP]	614 Beartic [BP]	400 Bibarel [BP]	009 Blastoise [BP]	257 Blaziken [BP]	242 Blissey [BP]
		286 Breloom [BP]	418 Buizel [BP]	427 Buneary [BP, E]	331 Cacnea [BP]	332 Cacturne [BP]	113 Chansey [BP]	006 Charizard [BP]
		004 Charmander [BP, E]	005 Charmeleon [BP]	652 Chesnaught [BP]	650 Chespin [BP]	390 Chimchar [BP, E]	036 Clefable [BP]	035 Clefairy [BP]
		256 Combusken [BP]	534 Conkeldurr [53, BP]	453 Croagunk [BP]	159 Croconaw [BP]	613 Cubchoo [BP, E]	104 Cubone [BP]	491 Darkrai [BP]
		555 Darmanitan [BP]	554 Darumaka [BP, E]	225 Delibird [BP]	386 Deoxys (Atk) [BP]	386 Deoxys (Def) [BP]	386 Deoxys (Nor) [BP]	386 Deoxys (Spd) [BP]
		660 Diggersby [BP]	149 Dragonite [BP]	096 Drowzee [BP]	356 Dusclops [BP]	477 Dusknoir [BP]	604 Eelektross [BP]	125 Electabuzz [BP]
		466 Electivire [BP]	239 Elekid [BP, E]	500 Emboar [BP]	160 Feraligatr [BP]	180 Flaaffy [BP]	419 Floatzel [BP]	162 Furret [BP]
		475 Gallade [BP]	094 Gengar [BP]	074 Geodude [BP, E]	055 Golduck [BP]	076 Golem [BP]	622 Golett [55, BP]	623 Golurk [1, 70, BP]
		706 Goodra [BP]	210 Granbull [BP]	075 Graveler [BP]	253 Grovyle [BP]	326 Grumpig [BP]	533 Gurdurr [53, BP]	297 Hariyama [BP]
		701 Hawlucha [BP]	631 Heatmor [BP]	214 Heracross [BP, E]	107 Hitmonchan [1, 56, BP]	106 Hitmonlee [BP]	097 Hypno [BP]	314 Illumise [BP]
		392 Infernape [BP]	039 Jigglypuff [BP]	124 Jynx [BP]	064 Kadabra [BP]	115 Kangaskhan [BP, E]	352 Kecleon [BP]	552 Krokorok [BP]
		553 Krookodile [BP]	166 Ledian [BP]	165 Ledyba [BP, E]	463 Lickilicky [BP]	108 Lickitung [BP]	428 Lopunny [BP]	448 Lucario [BP]
		272 Ludicolo [BP]	068 Machamp [BP]	067 Machoke [BP]	066 Machop [BP]	240 Magby [BP]	126 Magmar [BP]	467 Magmortar [BP]
		296 Makuhita [BP, E]	056 Mankey [BP, E]	183 Marill [BP]	105 Marowak [BP]	303 Mawile [BP]	308 Medicham [BP]	307 Meditite [BP]
		648 Meloetta [BP]	151 Mew [BP]	150 Mewtwo [BP]	619 Mienfoo [BP]	620 Mienshao [BP]	241 Miltank [BP]	439 Mime Jr. [BP]
		391 Monferno [BP]	122 Mr. Mime [BP]	089 Muk [BP]	446 Munchlax [BP]	034 Nidoking [BP]	031 Nidoqueen [BP]	484 Palkia [BP]
		536 Palpitoad [BP]	674 Pancham [BP]	675 Pangoro [BP]	515 Panpour [BP]	511 Pansage [BP]	513 Pansear [BP]	499 Pignite [BP]
		025 Pikachu [BP]	127 Pinsir [BP]	186 Politoed [BP]	061 Poliwhirl [BP]	062 Poliwrath [BP]	057 Primeape [BP]	054 Psyduck [BP]
		195 Quagsire [BP]	156 Quilava [BP]	651 Quilladin [BP]	026 Raichu [BP]	409 Rampardos [BP]	378 Regice [BP]	486 Regigigas [BP]
		377 Regirock [BP]	379 Registeel [BP]	579 Reuniclus [BP]	112 Rhydon [BP]	464 Rhyperior [BP]	447 Riolu [BP]	302 Sableye [BP]
		027 Sandshrew [BP]	028 Sandslash [BP]	539 Sawk [BP]	254 Sceptile [BP]	560 Scrafty [58, BP]	559 Scraggy [48, BP]	537 Seismitoad [BP]
		161 Sentret [BP]	285 Shroomish [BP, E]	516 Simipour [BP]	512 Simisage [BP]	514 Simisear [BP]	289 Slaking [BP]	287 Slakoth [BP]
		080 Slowbro [BP]	199 Slowking [BP]	215 Sneasel [BP]	143 Snorlax [BP]	209 Snubbull [BP, E]	327 Spinda [BP]	007 Squirtle [BP]
		185 Sudowoodo [BP]	260 Swampert [BP]	216 Teddiursa [BP]	538 Throh [BP]	532 Timburr [46, BP]	468 Togekiss [BP]	176 Togetic [BP]
		158 Totodile [BP]	454 Toxicroak [BP]	252 Treecko [BP]	157 Typhlosion [BP]	248 Tyranitar [BP]	217 Ursaring [BP]	288 Vigoroth [37, BP]
		313 Volbeat [BP]	008 Wartortle [BP]	505 Watchog [BP]	461 Weavile [BP]	040 Wigglytuff [BP]	335 Zangoose [BP]	
Normal	Follow Me	035 Clefairy [16]	162 Furret [21]	417 Pachirisu [E]	447 Riolu [E]	161 Sentret [19]	175 Togepi [21]	176 Togetic [21]
Fighting	Force Palm	286 Breloom [28]	297 Hariyama [13]	296 Makuhita [13]	308 Medicham [17]	307 Meditite [17]	619 Mienfoo [29]	620 Mienshao [29]
		447 Riolu [15]	532 Timburr [E]					
Normal	Foresight	142 Aerodactyl [E]	427 Buneary [1]	155 Cyndaquil [E]	356 Dusclops [14]	477 Dusknoir [14]	355 Duskull [14]	083 Farfetch'd [E]
		162 Furret [1]	203 Girafarig [E]	106 Hitmonlee [37]	163 Hoothoot [1]	140 Kabuto [E]	115 Kangaskhan [E]	131 Lapras [E]
		636 Larvesta [E]	428 Lopunny [1]	448 Lucario [1]	068 Machamp [9]	067 Machoke [9]	066 Machop [9]	296 Makuhita [E]
		056 Mankey [E]	259 Marshtomp [12]	307 Meditite [E]	258 Mudkip [12]	164 Noctowl [1]	504 Patrat [E]	016 Pidgey [E]
		054 Psyduck [E]	486 Regigigas [1]	447 Riolu [1]	302 Sableye [4]	161 Sentret [1]	353 Shuppet [E]	300 Skitty [4]
		215 Sneasel [E]	007 Squirtle [E]	396 Starly [E]	283 Surskit [E]	260 Swampert [12]	532 Timburr [E]	175 Togepi [E]
		236 Tyrogue [1]	049 Venomoth [1]	048 Venonat [1]	193 Yanmega [1]	469 Yanmega [1]		
Grass	Forest's Curse	708 Phantump [35]	709 Trevenant [35]					

ADVENTURE DATA

Type	Move	Pokémon that can learn it						
Dark	Foul Play	063 Abra [BP]	359 Absol [BP]	190 Aipom [BP]	065 Alakazam [BP]	424 Ambipom [BP]	591 Amoonguss [BP]	168 Ariados [BP]
		354 Banette [BP]	625 Bisharp [BP]	438 Bonsly [BP]	654 Braixen [BP]	332 Cacturne [BP]	453 Croagunk [BP]	491 Darkrai [BP]
		655 Delphox [BP]	660 Diggersby [BP]	096 Drowzee [BP]	101 Electrode [BP]	653 Fennekin [BP]	590 Foongus [BP]	092 Gastly [BP]
		094 Gengar [BP]	203 Girafarig [BP]	431 Glameow [BP]	574 Gothita [BP]	576 Gothitelle [BP]	575 Gothorita [BP]	711 Gourgeist [BP]
		093 Haunter [BP]	430 Honchkrow [45, BP]	229 Houndoom [45, BP]	228 Houndour [40, BP]	097 Hypno [BP]	686 Inkay [8, BP]	064 Kadabra [BP]
		352 Kecleon [BP, E]	707 Klefki [27, BP]	552 Krokorok [40, BP]	553 Krookodile [42, BP]	510 Liepard [BP]	687 Malamar [8, BP]	630 Mandibuzz [BP]
		303 Mawile [BP]	052 Meowth [BP, E]	151 Mew [BP]	150 Mewtwo [BP]	262 Mightyena [BP]	200 Misdreavus [BP]	429 Mismagius [BP]
		122 Mr. Mime [BP]	198 Murkrow [45, BP]	038 Ninetales [BP]	274 Nuzleaf [BP]	674 Pancham [BP, E]	675 Pangoro [BP]	624 Pawniard [BP]
		053 Persian [BP]	708 Phantump [BP]	261 Poochyena [BP]	137 Porygon [BP]	233 Porygon2 [BP]	474 Porygon-Z [BP]	710 Pumpkaboo [BP]
		509 Purrloin [BP, E]	432 Purugly [BP]	479 Rotom (Fan) [BP]	479 Rotom (Frost) [BP]	479 Rotom (Heat) [BP]	479 Rotom (Mow) [BP]	479 Rotom (Wash) [BP]
		479 Rotom [BP]	302 Sableye [41, BP]	551 Sandile [37, BP]	560 Scrafty [BP]	559 Scraggy [BP]	273 Seedot [BP, E]	275 Shiftry [BP]
		353 Shuppet [BP]	435 Skuntank [BP]	080 Slowbro [BP]	199 Slowking [BP]	215 Sneasel [BP]	167 Spinarak [BP]	442 Spiritomb [BP, E]
		618 Stunfisk [BP]	434 Stunky [BP, E]	185 Sudowoodo [BP]	642 Thundurus [BP]	641 Tornadus [BP]	454 Toxicroak [BP]	709 Trevenant [BP]
		248 Tyranitar [BP]	197 Umbreon [BP]	480 Uxie [BP]	100 Voltorb [BP]	629 Vullaby [BP, E]	037 Vulpix [BP]	461 Weavile [BP]
		178 Xatu [BP]	717 Yveltal [51, BP]	571 Zoroark [29, BP]	570 Zorua [29, BP]			
Ice	Freeze Shock	646 Kyurem (Blk) [50]						
	Freeze-Dry	144 Articuno [1]	699 Aurorus [1, 77]	615 Cryogonal [50]	225 Delibird [E]	362 Glalie [42]	131 Lapras [E]	220 Swinub [E]
		584 Vanilluxe [1]						
Grass	Frenzy Plant	652 Chesnaught [T]	154 Meganium [T]	254 Sceptile [T]	497 Serperior [T]	389 Torterra [T]	003 Venusaur [T]	
Ice	Frost Breath (TM79)	460 Abomasnow [TM]	698 Amaura [TM]	144 Articuno [TM]	699 Aurorus [TM]	713 Avalugg [TM]	614 Beartic [TM]	712 Bergmite [TM]
		091 Cloyster [TM]	615 Cryogonal [TM]	613 Cubchoo [TM]	225 Delibird [TM]	087 Dewgong [TM]	478 Froslass [TM]	471 Glaceon [TM]
		362 Glalie [37, TM]	124 Jynx [TM]	131 Lapras [TM]	151 Mew [TM]	378 Regice [TM]	364 Sealeo [TM]	238 Smoochum [TM]
		361 Snorunt [37, TM]	459 Snover [TM]	363 Spheal [TM]	583 Vanillish [TM]	582 Vanillite [TM]	584 Vanilluxe [TM]	365 Walrein [TM]
Normal	Frustration (TM21)	460 Abomasnow [TM]	063 Abra [TM]	359 Absol [TM]	617 Accelgor [TM]	681 Aegislash [TM]	142 Aerodactyl [TM]	306 Aggron [TM]
		190 Aipom [TM]	065 Alakazam [TM]	594 Alomomola [TM]	334 Altaria [TM]	698 Amaura [TM]	424 Ambipom [TM]	591 Amoonguss [TM]
		181 Ampharos [TM]	347 Anorith [TM]	024 Arbok [TM]	059 Arcanine [TM]	493 Arceus [TM]	566 Archen [TM]	567 Archeops [TM]
		168 Ariados [TM]	348 Armaldo [TM]	683 Aromatisse [TM]	304 Aron [TM]	144 Articuno [TM]	531 Audino [TM]	699 Aurorus [TM]
		713 Avalugg [TM]	610 Axew [TM]	482 Azelf [TM]	184 Azumarill [TM]	298 Azurill [TM]	371 Bagon [TM]	343 Baltoy [TM]
		354 Banette [TM]	689 Barbaracle [TM]	339 Barboach [TM]	550 Basculin [TM]	411 Bastiodon [TM]	153 Bayleef [TM]	614 Beartic [TM]
		267 Beautifly [TM]	015 Beedrill [TM]	606 Beheeyem [TM]	182 Bellossom [TM]	069 Bellsprout [TM]	712 Bergmite [TM]	400 Bibarel [TM]
		399 Bidoof [TM]	688 Binacle [TM]	625 Bisharp [TM]	009 Blastoise [TM]	257 Blaziken [TM]	242 Blissey [TM]	522 Blitzle [TM]
		525 Boldore [TM]	438 Bonsly [TM]	626 Bouffalant [TM]	654 Braixen [TM]	628 Braviary [TM]	286 Breloom [TM]	437 Bronzong [TM]
		436 Bronzor [TM]	406 Budew [TM]	418 Buizel [TM]	001 Bulbasaur [TM]	427 Buneary [13, TM]	659 Bunnelby [TM]	012 Butterfree [TM]
		331 Cacnea [TM]	332 Cacturne [TM]	323 Camerupt [TM]	703 Carbink [TM]	455 Carnivine [TM]	565 Carracosta [TM]	318 Carvanha [TM]
		351 Castform [TM]	251 Celebi [TM]	609 Chandelure [TM]	113 Chansey [TM]	006 Charizard [TM]	004 Charmander [TM]	005 Charmeleon [TM]
		441 Chatot [TM]	421 Cherrim [TM]	420 Cherubi [TM]	652 Chesnaught [TM]	650 Chespin [TM]	152 Chikorita [TM]	390 Chimchar [TM]
		358 Chimecho [TM]	170 Chinchou [TM]	433 Chingling [TM]	573 Cinccino [TM]	366 Clamperl [TM]	692 Clauncher [TM]	693 Clawitzer [TM]
		344 Claydol [TM]	036 Clefable [TM]	035 Clefairy [TM]	173 Cleffa [TM]	091 Cloyster [TM]	638 Cobalion [TM]	563 Cofagrigus [TM]
		256 Combusken [TM]	534 Conkeldurr [TM]	341 Corphish [TM]	222 Corsola [TM]	546 Cottonee [TM]	346 Cradily [TM]	408 Cranidos [TM]
		342 Crawdaunt [TM]	488 Cresselia [TM]	453 Croagunk [TM]	169 Crobat [TM]	159 Croconaw [TM]	558 Crustle [TM]	615 Cryogonal [TM]
		613 Cubchoo [TM]	104 Cubone [TM]	155 Cyndaquil [TM]	491 Darkrai [TM]	555 Darmanitan [TM]	554 Darumaka [TM]	702 Dedenne [TM]
		585 Deerling [TM]	633 Deino [TM]	301 Delcatty [TM]	225 Delibird [TM]	655 Delphox [TM]	386 Deoxys (Atk) [TM]	386 Deoxys (Def) [TM]
		386 Deoxys (Nor) [TM]	386 Deoxys (Spd) [TM]	087 Dewgong [TM]	502 Dewott [TM]	483 Dialga [TM]	719 Diancie [TM]	660 Diggersby [TM]
		050 Diglett [TM]	085 Dodrio [TM]	084 Doduo [TM]	232 Donphan [TM]	680 Doublade [TM]	691 Dragalge [TM]	148 Dragonair [TM]
		149 Dragonite [TM]	452 Drapion [TM]	147 Dratini [TM]	426 Drifblim [TM]	425 Drifloon [TM]	529 Drilbur [TM]	096 Drowzee [TM]
		621 Druddigon [TM]	580 Ducklett [TM]	051 Dugtrio [TM]	206 Dunsparce [TM]	578 Duosion [TM]	632 Durant [TM]	356 Dusclops [TM]
		477 Dusknoir [TM]	355 Duskull [TM]	269 Dustox [TM]	557 Dwebble [TM]	603 Eelektrik [TM]	604 Eelektross [TM]	133 Eevee [TM]
		023 Ekans [TM]	125 Electabuzz [TM]	466 Electivire [TM]	309 Electrike [TM]	101 Electrode [TM]	239 Elekid [TM]	605 Elgyem [TM]
		500 Emboar [TM]	587 Emolga [TM]	395 Empoleon [TM]	244 Entei [TM]	589 Escavalier [TM]	196 Espeon [TM]	677 Espurr [TM]
		530 Excadrill [TM]	102 Exeggcute [TM]	103 Exeggutor [TM]	295 Exploud [TM]	083 Farfetch'd [TM]	022 Fearow [TM]	349 Feebas [TM]
		653 Fennekin [TM]	160 Feraligatr [TM]	597 Ferroseed [TM]	598 Ferrothorn [TM]	456 Finneon [TM]	180 Flaaffy [TM]	669 Flabébé [TM]
		136 Flareon [TM]	662 Fletchinder [TM]	661 Fletchling [TM]	419 Floatzel [TM]	670 Floette [TM]	671 Florges [TM]	330 Flygon [TM]
		590 Foongus [TM]	205 Forretress [TM]	611 Fraxure [TM]	592 Frillish [TM]	656 Froakie [TM]	657 Frogadier [TM]	478 Froslass [TM]
		676 Furfrou [TM]	162 Furret [TM]	444 Gabite [TM]	475 Gallade [TM]	596 Galvantula [TM]	569 Garbodor [TM]	445 Garchomp [TM]
		282 Gardevoir [TM]	092 Gastly [TM]	423 Gastrodon [TM]	649 Genesect [TM]	094 Gengar [TM]	074 Geodude [TM]	443 Gible [TM]
		526 Gigalith [TM]	203 Girafarig [TM]	487 Giratina (Alt) [TM]	487 Giratina (Ori) [TM]	471 Glaceon [TM]	362 Glalie [TM]	431 Glameow [TM]
		207 Gligar [TM]	472 Gliscor [TM]	044 Gloom [TM]	673 Gogoat [TM]	042 Golbat [TM]	118 Goldeen [TM]	055 Golduck [TM]
		076 Golem [TM]	622 Golett [TM]	623 Golurk [TM]	706 Goodra [TM]	704 Goomy [TM]	368 Gorebyss [TM]	574 Gothita [TM]
		576 Gothitelle [TM]	575 Gothorita [TM]	711 Gourgeist [TM]	210 Granbull [TM]	075 Graveler [TM]	658 Greninja [TM]	088 Grimer [TM]
		388 Grotle [TM]	383 Groudon [TM]	253 Grovyle [TM]	058 Growlithe [TM]	326 Grumpig [TM]	316 Gulpin [TM]	533 Gurdurr [TM]
		130 Gyarados [TM]	440 Happiny [TM]	297 Hariyama [TM]	093 Haunter [TM]	701 Hawlucha [TM]	612 Haxorus [TM]	631 Heatmor [TM]
		485 Heatran [TM]	695 Heliolisk [TM]	694 Helioptile [TM]	214 Heracross [TM]	507 Herdier [TM]	449 Hippopotas [TM]	450 Hippowdon [TM]
		107 Hitmonchan [TM]	106 Hitmonlee [TM]	237 Hitmontop [TM]	430 Honchkrow [TM]	679 Honedge [TM]	250 Ho-Oh [TM]	163 Hoothoot [TM]
		187 Hoppip [TM]	116 Horsea [TM]	229 Houndoom [TM]	228 Houndour [TM]	367 Huntail [TM]	635 Hydreigon [TM]	097 Hypno [TM]
		174 Igglybuff [TM]	314 Illumise [TM]	392 Infernape [TM]	686 Inkay [TM]	002 Ivysaur [TM]	593 Jellicent [TM]	039 Jigglypuff [TM]

	Move	Pokémon that can learn it						
Normal	Frustration (TM21)	385 Jirachi [TM]	135 Jolteon [TM]	595 Joltik [TM]	189 Jumpluff [TM]	124 Jynx [TM]	140 Kabuto [TM]	141 Kabutops [TM]
		064 Kadabra [TM]	115 Kangaskhan [TM]	588 Karrablast [TM]	352 Kecleon [TM]	647 Keldeo [TM]	230 Kingdra [TM]	099 Kingler [TM]
		281 Kirlia [TM]	600 Klang [TM]	707 Klefki [TM]	599 Klink [TM]	601 Klinklang [TM]	109 Koffing [TM]	098 Krabby [TM]
		402 Kricketune [TM]	552 Krokorok [TM]	553 Krookodile [TM]	382 Kyogre [TM]	646 Kyurem (Blk) [TM]	646 Kyurem (Wht) [TM]	646 Kyurem [TM]
		305 Lairon [TM]	608 Lampent [TM]	645 Landorus [TM]	171 Lanturn [TM]	131 Lapras [TM]	636 Larvesta [TM]	246 Larvitar [TM]
		380 Latias [TM]	381 Latios [TM]	470 Leafeon [TM]	542 Leavanny [TM]	166 Ledian [TM]	165 Ledyba [TM]	463 Lickilicky [TM]
		108 Lickitung [TM]	510 Liepard [TM]	345 Lileep [TM]	549 Lilligant [TM]	506 Lillipup [TM]	264 Linoone [TM]	667 Litleo [TM]
		607 Litwick [TM]	271 Lombre [TM]	428 Lopunny [TM]	270 Lotad [TM]	294 Loudred [TM]	448 Lucario [TM]	272 Ludicolo [TM]
		249 Lugia [TM]	457 Lumineon [TM]	337 Lunatone [TM]	370 Luvdisc [TM]	404 Luxio [TM]	405 Luxray [TM]	068 Machamp [TM]
		067 Machoke [TM]	066 Machop [TM]	240 Magby [TM]	219 Magcargo [TM]	126 Magmar [TM]	467 Magmortar [TM]	081 Magnemite [TM]
		082 Magneton [TM]	462 Magnezone [TM]	296 Makuhita [TM]	687 Malamar [TM]	473 Mamoswine [TM]	490 Manaphy [TM]	630 Mandibuzz [TM]
		310 Manectric [TM]	056 Mankey [TM]	226 Mantine [TM]	458 Mantyke [TM]	556 Maractus [TM]	179 Mareep [TM]	183 Marill [TM]
		105 Marowak [TM]	259 Marshtomp [TM]	284 Masquerain [TM]	303 Mawile [TM]	308 Medicham [TM]	307 Meditite [TM]	154 Meganium [TM]
		648 Meloetta [TM]	678 Meowstic (F) [TM]	678 Meowstic (M) [TM]	052 Meowth [TM]	481 Mesprit [TM]	376 Metagross [TM]	375 Metang [TM]
		151 Mew [TM]	150 Mewtwo [TM]	619 Mienfoo [TM]	620 Mienshao [TM]	262 Mightyena [TM]	350 Milotic [TM]	241 Miltank [TM]
		439 Mime Jr. [TM]	572 Minccino [TM]	312 Minun [TM]	200 Misdreavus [TM]	429 Mismagius [TM]	146 Moltres [TM]	391 Monferno [TM]
		414 Mothim [TM]	122 Mr. Mime [TM]	258 Mudkip [TM]	089 Muk [TM]	446 Munchlax [TM]	517 Munna [TM]	198 Murkrow [TM]
		518 Musharna [TM]	177 Natu [TM]	034 Nidoking [TM]	031 Nidoqueen [TM]	029 Nidoran ♀ [TM]	032 Nidoran ♂ [TM]	030 Nidorina [TM]
		033 Nidorino [TM]	290 Nincada [TM]	038 Ninetales [TM]	291 Ninjask [TM]	164 Noctowl [TM]	714 Noibat [TM]	715 Noivern [TM]
		299 Nosepass [TM]	322 Numel [TM]	274 Nuzleaf [TM]	224 Octillery [TM]	043 Oddish [TM]	138 Omanyte [TM]	139 Omastar [TM]
		095 Onix [TM]	501 Oshawott [TM]	417 Pachirisu [TM]	484 Palkia [TM]	536 Palpitoad [TM]	674 Pancham [TM]	675 Pangoro [TM]
		515 Panpour [TM]	511 Pansage [TM]	513 Pansear [TM]	046 Paras [TM]	047 Parasect [TM]	504 Patrat [TM]	624 Pawniard [TM]
		279 Pelipper [TM]	053 Persian [TM]	548 Petilil [TM]	231 Phanpy [TM]	708 Phantump [TM]	489 Phione [TM]	172 Pichu [TM]
		018 Pidgeot [TM]	017 Pidgeotto [TM]	016 Pidgey [TM]	519 Pidove [TM]	499 Pignite [TM]	025 Pikachu [TM]	221 Piloswine [TM]
		204 Pineco [TM]	127 Pinsir [TM]	393 Piplup [TM]	311 Plusle [TM]	186 Politoed [TM]	060 Poliwag [TM]	061 Poliwhirl [TM]
		062 Poliwrath [TM]	077 Ponyta [TM]	261 Poochyena [TM]	137 Porygon [TM]	233 Porygon2 [TM]	474 Porygon-Z [TM]	057 Primeape [TM]
		394 Prinplup [TM]	476 Probopass [TM]	054 Psyduck [TM]	710 Pumpkaboo [TM]	247 Pupitar [TM]	509 Purrloin [TM]	432 Purugly [TM]
		668 Pyroar [TM]	195 Quagsire [TM]	156 Quilava [TM]	651 Quilladin [TM]	211 Qwilfish [TM]	026 Raichu [TM]	243 Raikou [TM]
		280 Ralts [TM]	409 Rampardos [TM]	078 Rapidash [TM]	020 Raticate [TM]	019 Rattata [TM]	384 Rayquaza [TM]	378 Regice [TM]
		486 Regigigas [TM]	377 Regirock [TM]	379 Registeel [TM]	369 Relicanth [TM]	223 Remoraid [TM]	643 Reshiram [TM]	579 Reuniclus [TM]
		112 Rhydon [TM]	111 Rhyhorn [TM]	464 Rhyperior [TM]	447 Riolu [TM]	524 Roggenrola [TM]	315 Roselia [TM]	407 Roserade [TM]
		479 Rotom (Fan) [TM]	479 Rotom (Frost) [TM]	479 Rotom (Heat) [TM]	479 Rotom (Mow) [TM]	479 Rotom (Wash) [TM]	479 Rotom [TM]	627 Rufflet [TM]
		302 Sableye [TM]	373 Salamence [TM]	503 Samurott [TM]	551 Sandile [TM]	027 Sandshrew [TM]	028 Sandslash [TM]	539 Sawk [TM]
		586 Sawsbuck [TM]	254 Sceptile [TM]	212 Scizor [TM]	545 Scolipede [TM]	560 Scrafty [TM]	559 Scraggy [TM]	123 Scyther [TM]
		117 Seadra [TM]	119 Seaking [TM]	364 Sealeo [TM]	273 Seedot [TM]	086 Seel [TM]	537 Seismitoad [TM]	161 Sentret [TM]
		497 Serperior [TM]	496 Servine [TM]	336 Seviper [TM]	540 Sewaddle [TM]	319 Sharpedo [TM]	492 Shaymin (Land) [TM]	492 Shaymin (Sky) [TM]
		292 Shedinja [TM]	372 Shelgon [TM]	090 Shellder [TM]	422 Shellos [TM]	616 Shelmet [TM]	410 Shieldon [TM]	275 Shiftry [TM]
		403 Shinx [TM]	285 Shroomish [TM]	213 Shuckle [TM]	353 Shuppet [TM]	561 Sigilyph [TM]	516 Simipour [TM]	512 Simisage [TM]
		514 Simisear [TM]	227 Skarmory [TM]	672 Skiddo [TM]	188 Skiploom [TM]	300 Skitty [TM]	451 Skorupi [TM]	690 Skrelp [TM]
		435 Skuntank [TM]	289 Slaking [TM]	287 Slakoth [TM]	705 Sliggoo [TM]	080 Slowbro [TM]	199 Slowking [TM]	079 Slowpoke [TM]
		218 Slugma [TM]	685 Slurpuff [TM]	238 Smoochum [TM]	215 Sneasel [TM]	495 Snivy [TM]	143 Snorlax [TM]	361 Snorunt [TM]
		459 Snover [TM]	209 Snubbull [TM]	577 Solosis [TM]	338 Solrock [TM]	021 Spearow [TM]	363 Spheal [TM]	167 Spinarak [TM]
		327 Spinda [TM]	442 Spiritomb [TM]	325 Spoink [TM]	682 Spritzee [TM]	007 Squirtle [TM]	234 Stantler [TM]	398 Staraptor [TM]
		397 Staravia [TM]	396 Starly [TM]	121 Starmie [TM]	120 Staryu [TM]	208 Steelix [TM]	508 Stoutland [TM]	618 Stunfisk [TM]
		434 Stunky [TM]	185 Sudowoodo [TM]	245 Suicune [TM]	192 Sunflora [TM]	191 Sunkern [TM]	283 Surskit [TM]	333 Swablu [TM]
		541 Swadloon [TM]	317 Swalot [TM]	260 Swampert [TM]	581 Swanna [TM]	277 Swellow [TM]	220 Swinub [TM]	684 Swirlix [TM]
		528 Swoobat [TM]	700 Sylveon [TM]	276 Taillow [TM]	663 Talonflame [TM]	114 Tangela [TM]	465 Tangrowth [TM]	128 Tauros [TM]
		216 Teddiursa [TM]	072 Tentacool [TM]	073 Tentacruel [TM]	498 Tepig [TM]	639 Terrakion [TM]	538 Throh [TM]	642 Thundurus [TM]
		532 Timburr [TM]	564 Tirtouga [TM]	468 Togekiss [TM]	175 Togepi [TM]	176 Togetic [TM]	255 Torchic [TM]	324 Torkoal [TM]
		641 Tornadus [TM]	389 Torterra [TM]	158 Totodile [TM]	454 Toxicroak [TM]	520 Tranquill [TM]	328 Trapinch [TM]	252 Treecko [TM]
		709 Trevenant [TM]	357 Tropius [TM]	568 Trubbish [TM]	387 Turtwig [TM]	535 Tympole [TM]	157 Typhlosion [TM]	248 Tyranitar [TM]
		697 Tyrantrum [TM]	236 Tyrogue [TM]	696 Tyrunt [TM]	197 Umbreon [TM]	521 Unfezant [TM]	217 Ursaring [TM]	480 Uxie [TM]
		583 Vanillish [TM]	582 Vanillite [TM]	584 Vanilluxe [TM]	134 Vaporeon [TM]	543 Venipede [TM]	049 Venomoth [TM]	048 Venonat [TM]
		003 Venusaur [TM]	416 Vespiquen [TM]	329 Vibrava [TM]	494 Victini [TM]	071 Victreebel [TM]	288 Vigoroth [TM]	045 Vileplume [TM]
		640 Virizion [TM]	666 Vivillon [TM]	313 Volbeat [TM]	637 Volcarona [TM]	100 Voltorb [TM]	629 Vullaby [TM]	037 Vulpix [TM]
		320 Wailmer [TM]	321 Wailord [TM]	365 Walrein [TM]	008 Wartortle [TM]	505 Watchog [TM]	461 Weavile [TM]	070 Weepinbell [TM]
		110 Weezing [TM]	547 Whimsicott [TM]	544 Whirlipede [TM]	340 Whiscash [TM]	293 Whismur [TM]	040 Wigglytuff [TM]	278 Wingull [TM]
		527 Woobat [TM]	194 Wooper [TM]	413 Wormadam (Plant) [TM]	413 Wormadam (Sand) [TM]	413 Wormadam (Trash) [TM]	178 Xatu [TM]	716 Xerneas [TM]
		562 Yamask [TM]	193 Yanma [TM]	469 Yanmega [TM]	717 Yveltal [TM]	335 Zangoose [TM]	145 Zapdos [TM]	523 Zebstrika [TM]
		644 Zekrom [TM]	263 Zigzagoon [TM]	571 Zoroark [TM]	570 Zorua [TM]	041 Zubat [TM]	634 Zweilous [TM]	718 Zygarde [TM]
	Fury Attack	334 Altaria [7]	015 Beedrill [1, 10]	626 Bouffalant [11]	628 Braviary [1, 5]	441 Chatot [17]	085 Dodrio [13]	084 Doduo [13]
		232 Donphan [25]	395 Empoleon [28]	589 Escavalier [16]	083 Farfetch'd [7]	022 Fearow [1, 9]	118 Goldeen [24]	214 Heracross [25]
		588 Karrablast [16]	630 Mandibuzz [1, 5]	032 Nidoran ♂ [19]	033 Nidorino [20]	221 Piloswine [33]	127 Pinsir [E]	393 Piplup [25]
		394 Prinplup [28]	078 Rapidash [40]	112 Rhydon [1, 5]	111 Rhyhorn [5]	464 Rhyperior [1, 5]	627 Rufflet [5]	119 Seaking [24]
		227 Skarmory [17]	021 Spearow [9]	396 Starly [E]	333 Swablu [7]	629 Vullaby [5]		

Type	Move	Pokémon that can learn it						
Bug	Fury Cutter	681 Aegislash [1]	347 Anorith [10]	348 Armaldo [10]	689 Barbaracle [37]	688 Binacle [37]	625 Bisharp [1, 9]	418 Buizel [E]
		502 Dewott [20]	680 Doublade [5]	632 Durant [6]	557 Dwebble [1]	083 Farfetch'd [1]	475 Gallade [14]	596 Galvantula [12]
		649 Genesect [7]	207 Gligar [16]	472 Gliscor [16]	253 Grovyle [16]	679 Honedge [5]	595 Joltik [12]	588 Karrablast [13]
		402 Kricketune [10]	291 Ninjask [20]	501 Oshawott [19]	046 Paras [17]	047 Parasect [17]	624 Pawniard [9]	503 Samurott [20]
		027 Sandshrew [11]	028 Sandslash [11]	254 Sceptile [16]	212 Scizor [25]	123 Scyther [25]	328 Trapinch [E]	416 Vespiquen [5]
		335 Zangoose [8]						
Normal	Fury Swipes	190 Aipom [18]	424 Ambipom [18]	168 Ariados [23]	689 Barbaracle [10]	614 Beartic [17]	399 Bidoof [E]	688 Binacle [10]
		418 Buizel [E]	390 Chimchar [15]	613 Cubchoo [17]	155 Cyndaquil [E]	529 Drilbur [12]	530 Excadrill [12]	162 Furret [13]
		431 Glameow [20]	055 Golduck [15]	631 Heatmor [21]	392 Infernape [16]	352 Kecleon [13]	510 Liepard [12]	264 Linoone [19]
		271 Lombre [12]	056 Mankey [9]	052 Meowth [14]	391 Monferno [16]	029 Nidoran ♀ [19]	030 Nidorina [20]	290 Nincada [13]
		291 Ninjask [13]	515 Panpour [13]	511 Pansage [13]	513 Pansear [13]	053 Persian [14]	057 Primeape [9]	054 Psyduck [15]
		509 Purrloin [12]	432 Purugly [20]	019 Rattata [E]	302 Sableye [11]	027 Sandshrew [20]	028 Sandslash [20]	161 Sentret [13]
		292 Shedinja [13]	516 Simipour [1]	512 Simisage [1]	514 Simisear [1]	435 Skuntank [10]	215 Sneasel [16]	167 Spinarak [22]
		434 Stunky [10]	216 Teddiursa [8]	217 Ursaring [8]	416 Vespiquen [13]	288 Vigoroth [14]	461 Weavile [16]	335 Zangoose [E]
		571 Zoroark [13]	570 Zorua [13]					
Electric	Fusion Bolt	646 Kyurem (Blk) [43]	644 Zekrom [50]					
Fire	Fusion Flare	646 Kyurem (Wht) [43]	643 Reshiram [50]					
Psychic	Future Sight	359 Absol [1, 53]	065 Alakazam [43]	493 Arceus [60]	482 Azelf [36]	339 Barboach [39]	437 Bronzong [29]	436 Bronzor [29]
		351 Castform [E]	251 Celebi [64]	358 Chimecho [E]	433 Chingling [E]	488 Cresselia [38]	225 Delibird [E]	655 Delphox [1, 69]
		096 Drowzee [61]	578 Duosion [31]	356 Dusclops [1, 64]	477 Dusknoir [1, 64]	355 Duskull [54]	196 Espeon [25]	282 Gardevoir [40]
		203 Girafarig [E]	574 Gothita [31]	576 Gothitelle [31]	575 Gothorita [31]	250 Ho-Oh [79]	097 Hypno [1, 61]	385 Jirachi [55]
		064 Kadabra [43]	281 Kirlia [37]	131 Lapras [E]	249 Lugia [79]	337 Lunatone [41]	183 Marill [E]	678 Meowstic (F) [50]
		481 Mesprit [36]	150 Mewtwo [15]	439 Mime Jr. [E]	122 Mr. Mime [E]	517 Munna [31]	177 Natu [44]	054 Psyduck [E]
		280 Ralts [32]	579 Reuniclus [31]	561 Sigilyph [E]	079 Slowpoke [E]	577 Solosis [31]	325 Spoink [E]	528 Swoobat [36]
		175 Togepi [E]	480 Uxie [36]	340 Whiscash [45]	527 Woobat [36]	178 Xatu [49]		

G

Type	Move	Pokémon that can learn it						
Poison	Gastro Acid	617 Accelgor [BP]	591 Amoonguss [BP]	024 Arbok [44, BP]	182 Bellossom [BP]	069 Bellsprout [35, BP]	455 Carnivine [BP]	346 Cradily [31, BP]
		660 Diggersby [BP]	603 Eelektrik [64, BP]	604 Eelektross [1, BP]	023 Ekans [36, BP]	590 Foongus [BP, E]	596 Galvantula [23, BP]	044 Gloom [BP]
		316 Gulpin [36, BP]	631 Heatmor [BP]	595 Joltik [23, BP]	345 Lileep [31, BP]	151 Mew [BP]	043 Oddish [BP]	536 Palpitoad [BP]
		515 Panpour [BP]	511 Pansage [BP]	513 Pansear [BP]	537 Seismitoad [BP]	497 Serperior [56, BP]	496 Servine [48, BP]	336 Seviper [31, BP]
		616 Shelmet [BP]	213 Shuckle [27, BP]	516 Simipour [BP]	512 Simisage [BP]	514 Simisear [BP]	685 Slurpuff [BP]	495 Snivy [40, BP]
		317 Swalot [42, BP]	684 Swirlix [BP]	071 Victreebel [BP]	045 Vileplume [BP]	070 Weepinbell [35, BP]		
Steel	Gear Grind	600 Klang [1, 16]	599 Klink [16]	601 Klinklang [1, 16]				
Fairy	Geomancy	716 Xerneas [26]						
Grass	Giga Drain	460 Abomasnow [BP]	617 Accelgor [37, BP]	591 Amoonguss [28, BP]	024 Arbok [BP]	493 Arceus [BP]	168 Ariados [BP]	153 Bayleef [BP]
		267 Beautifly [32, BP]	015 Beedrill [BP]	182 Bellossom [BP]	069 Bellsprout [BP, E]	286 Breloom [BP]	406 Budew [BP, E]	001 Bulbasaur [BP, E]
		012 Butterfree [BP]	331 Cacnea [BP]	332 Cacturne [BP]	455 Carnivine [BP, E]	251 Celebi [BP]	421 Cherrim [BP]	420 Cherubi [BP]
		652 Chesnaught [BP]	650 Chespin [BP]	152 Chikorita [BP]	546 Cottonee [26, BP]	346 Cradily [26, BP]	169 Crobat [BP]	585 Deerling [BP]
		269 Dustox [BP]	603 Eelektrik [BP]	604 Eelektross [BP]	023 Ekans [BP]	589 Escavalier [BP]	102 Exeggcute [BP, E]	103 Exeggutor [BP]
		597 Ferroseed [BP]	598 Ferrothorn [BP]	669 Flabébé [BP]	670 Floette [BP]	671 Florges [BP]	330 Flygon [BP]	590 Foongus [28, BP]
		205 Forretress [BP]	592 Frillish [BP]	596 Galvantula [BP]	569 Garbodor [BP]	092 Gastly [BP]	649 Genesect [BP]	094 Gengar [BP]
		044 Gloom [34, BP]	673 Gogoat [BP]	042 Golbat [BP]	711 Gourgeist [BP]	088 Grimer [BP]	388 Grotle [47, BP]	253 Grovyle [BP]
		316 Gulpin [BP]	093 Haunter [BP]	631 Heatmor [BP]	250 Ho-Oh [BP]	187 Hoppip [43, BP]	314 Illumise [BP]	002 Ivysaur [BP]
		593 Jellicent [BP]	595 Joltik [BP]	189 Jumpluff [59, BP]	140 Kabuto [BP, E]	141 Kabutops [BP]	588 Karrablast [BP]	636 Larvesta [BP]
		470 Leafeon [25, BP]	542 Leavanny [BP]	166 Ledian [BP]	165 Ledyba [BP]	345 Lileep [26, BP]	549 Lilligant [BP]	271 Lombre [BP]
		270 Lotad [30, BP, E]	272 Ludicolo [BP]	249 Lugia [BP]	556 Maractus [26, BP]	284 Masquerain [BP]	154 Meganium [BP]	151 Mew [BP]
		414 Mothim [BP]	089 Muk [BP]	177 Natu [BP]	290 Nincada [BP]	291 Ninjask [BP]	274 Nuzleaf [BP]	043 Oddish [31, BP]
		511 Pansage [BP]	046 Paras [38, BP]	047 Parasect [44, BP]	548 Petilil [26, BP]	708 Phantump [BP]	204 Pineco [BP]	710 Pumpkaboo [BP]
		651 Quilladin [BP]	315 Roselia [25, BP, E]	407 Roserade [BP]	586 Sawsbuck [BP]	254 Sceptile [BP]	273 Seedot [BP]	497 Serperior [44, BP]
		496 Servine [40, BP]	336 Seviper [BP]	540 Sewaddle [BP]	492 Shaymin (Land) [BP]	492 Shaymin (Sky) [BP]	292 Shedinja [BP]	616 Shelmet [37, BP]
		275 Shiftry [BP]	285 Shroomish [26, BP]	512 Simisage [BP]	672 Skiddo [BP]	188 Skiploom [52, BP]	495 Snivy [34, BP]	459 Snover [BP]
		167 Spinarak [BP]	192 Sunflora [22, BP]	191 Sunkern [22, BP]	283 Surskit [BP]	541 Swadloon [BP]	317 Swalot [BP]	528 Swoobat [BP]
		114 Tangela [36, BP, E]	465 Tangrowth [36, BP]	072 Tentacool [BP]	073 Tentacruel [BP]	389 Torterra [51, BP]	328 Trapinch [BP]	252 Treecko [21, BP]
		709 Trevenant [BP]	357 Tropius [BP]	568 Trubbish [BP]	387 Turtwig [41, BP]	480 Uxie [BP]	049 Venomoth [BP]	048 Venonat [BP, E]
		003 Venusaur [BP]	329 Vibrava [BP]	071 Victreebel [BP]	045 Vileplume [BP]	640 Virizion [37, BP]	666 Vivillon [BP]	313 Volbeat [BP]
		637 Volcarona [BP]	070 Weepinbell [BP]	547 Whimsicott [BP]	527 Woobat [BP]	413 Wormadam (Plant) [BP]	178 Xatu [BP]	193 Yanma [BP]
		469 Yanmega [BP]	335 Zangoose [BP]	041 Zubat [BP, E]				

	Move	Pokémon that can learn it						
Normal	Giga Impact (TM68)	460 Abomasnow [TM]	359 Absol [TM]	617 Accelgor [TM]	681 Aegislash [TM]	142 Aerodactyl [81, TM]	306 Aggron [TM]	065 Alakazam [TM]
		334 Altaria [TM]	424 Ambipom [TM]	591 Amoonguss [TM]	181 Ampharos [TM]	024 Arbok [TM]	059 Arcanine [TM]	493 Arceus [TM]
		567 Archeops [TM]	168 Ariados [TM]	348 Armaldo [TM]	683 Aromatisse [TM]	144 Articuno [TM]	699 Aurorus [TM]	713 Avalugg [TM]
		610 Axew [61, TM]	482 Azelf [TM]	184 Azumarill [TM]	354 Banette [TM]	689 Barbaracle [TM]	411 Bastiodon [TM]	614 Beartic [TM]
		267 Beautifly [TM]	015 Beedrill [TM]	606 Beheeyem [TM]	182 Bellossom [TM]	400 Bibarel [TM]	625 Bisharp [TM]	009 Blastoise [TM]
		257 Blaziken [TM]	242 Blissey [TM]	626 Bouffalant [61, TM]	628 Braviary [TM]	286 Breloom [TM]	437 Bronzong [TM]	012 Butterfree [TM]
		332 Cacturne [TM]	323 Camerupt [TM]	455 Carnivine [TM]	565 Carracosta [TM]	251 Celebi [TM]	609 Chandelure [TM]	113 Chansey [TM]
		006 Charizard [TM]	421 Cherrim [TM]	652 Chesnaught [70, TM]	573 Cinccino [TM]	693 Clawitzer [TM]	344 Claydol [TM]	036 Clefable [TM]
		091 Cloyster [TM]	638 Cobalion [TM]	563 Cofagrigus [TM]	534 Conkeldurr [TM]	346 Cradily [TM]	342 Crawdaunt [TM]	488 Cresselia [TM]
		169 Crobat [TM]	558 Crustle [TM]	491 Darkrai [TM]	555 Darmanitan [TM]	702 Dedenne [TM]	301 Delcatty [TM]	655 Delphox [TM]
		386 Deoxys (Atk) [TM]	386 Deoxys (Def) [TM]	386 Deoxys (Nor) [TM]	386 Deoxys (Spd) [TM]	087 Dewgong [TM]	483 Dialga [TM]	719 Diancie [TM]
		660 Diggersby [TM]	085 Dodrio [TM]	232 Donphan [50, TM]	691 Dragalge [TM]	149 Dragonite [TM]	452 Drapion [TM]	426 Drifblim [TM]
		621 Druddigon [TM]	051 Dugtrio [TM]	632 Durant [TM]	356 Dusclops [TM]	477 Dusknoir [TM]	269 Dustox [TM]	604 Eelektross [TM]
		125 Electabuzz [TM]	466 Electivire [62, TM]	101 Electrode [TM]	500 Emboar [TM]	395 Empoleon [TM]	244 Entei [TM]	589 Escavalier [56, TM]
		196 Espeon [TM]	530 Excadrill [TM]	103 Exeggutor [TM]	295 Exploud [TM]	022 Fearow [TM]	160 Feraligatr [TM]	598 Ferrothorn [TM]
		136 Flareon [TM]	419 Floatzel [TM]	671 Florges [TM]	330 Flygon [TM]	205 Forretress [TM]	611 Fraxure [66, TM]	478 Froslass [TM]
		676 Furfrou [TM]	162 Furret [TM]	475 Gallade [TM]	596 Galvantula [TM]	569 Garbodor [TM]	445 Garchomp [TM]	282 Gardevoir [TM]
		423 Gastrodon [TM]	649 Genesect [TM]	094 Gengar [TM]	526 Gigalith [TM]	487 Giratina (Alt) [TM]	487 Giratina (Ori) [TM]	471 Glaceon [TM]
		362 Glalie [TM]	472 Gliscor [TM]	673 Gogoat [TM]	042 Golbat [TM]	055 Golduck [TM]	076 Golem [TM]	623 Golurk [TM]
		706 Goodra [TM]	368 Gorebyss [TM]	576 Gothitelle [TM]	711 Gourgeist [TM]	210 Granbull [TM]	658 Greninja [TM]	383 Groudon [TM]
		326 Grumpig [TM]	130 Gyarados [TM]	297 Hariyama [TM]	701 Hawlucha [TM]	612 Haxorus [74, TM]	631 Heatmor [TM]	485 Heatran [TM]
		695 Heliolisk [TM]	214 Heracross [TM]	507 Herdier [47, TM]	450 Hippowdon [TM]	430 Honchkrow [TM]	250 Ho-Oh [TM]	229 Houndoom [TM]
		367 Huntail [TM]	635 Hydreigon [TM]	097 Hypno [TM]	392 Infernape [TM]	593 Jellicent [TM]	385 Jirachi [TM]	135 Jolteon [TM]
		189 Jumpluff [TM]	124 Jynx [TM]	141 Kabutops [TM]	115 Kangaskhan [TM]	647 Keldeo [TM]	230 Kingdra [TM]	099 Kingler [TM]
		707 Klefki [TM]	601 Klinklang [TM]	402 Kricketune [TM]	553 Krookodile [TM]	382 Kyogre [TM]	646 Kyurem (Blk) [TM]	646 Kyurem (Wht) [TM]
		646 Kyurem [TM]	645 Landorus [TM]	171 Lanturn [TM]	131 Lapras [TM]	380 Latias [TM]	381 Latios [TM]	470 Leafeon [TM]
		542 Leavanny [TM]	166 Ledian [TM]	463 Lickilicky [TM]	108 Lickitung [TM]	510 Liepard [TM]	549 Lilligant [TM]	506 Lillipup [40, TM]
		264 Linoone [TM]	428 Lopunny [TM]	448 Lucario [TM]	272 Ludicolo [TM]	249 Lugia [TM]	457 Lumineon [TM]	337 Lunatone [TM]
		405 Luxray [TM]	068 Machamp [TM]	219 Magcargo [TM]	126 Magmar [TM]	467 Magmortar [TM]	082 Magneton [TM]	462 Magnezone [TM]
		687 Malamar [TM]	473 Mamoswine [TM]	490 Manaphy [TM]	630 Mandibuzz [TM]	310 Manectric [TM]	226 Mantine [TM]	105 Marowak [TM]
		284 Masquerain [TM]	303 Mawile [TM]	308 Medicham [TM]	154 Meganium [TM]	648 Meloetta [TM]	678 Meowstic (F) [TM]	678 Meowstic (M) [TM]
		481 Mesprit [TM]	376 Metagross [TM]	151 Mew [TM]	150 Mewtwo [TM]	620 Mienshao [TM]	262 Mightyena [TM]	350 Milotic [TM]
		241 Miltank [TM]	429 Mismagius [TM]	146 Moltres [TM]	414 Mothim [TM]	122 Mr. Mime [TM]	089 Muk [TM]	518 Musharna [TM]
		034 Nidoking [TM]	031 Nidoqueen [TM]	038 Ninetales [TM]	291 Ninjask [TM]	164 Noctowl [TM]	715 Noivern [TM]	224 Octillery [TM]
		139 Omastar [TM]	484 Palkia [TM]	675 Pangoro [TM]	047 Parasect [TM]	279 Pelipper [TM]	053 Persian [TM]	018 Pidgeot [TM]
		221 Piloswine [TM]	127 Pinsir [TM]	186 Politoed [TM]	062 Poliwrath [TM]	137 Porygon [TM]	233 Porygon2 [TM]	474 Porygon-Z [TM]
		057 Primeape [TM]	476 Probopass [TM]	432 Purugly [TM]	668 Pyroar [TM]	195 Quagsire [TM]	026 Raichu [TM]	243 Raikou [TM]
		409 Rampardos [TM]	078 Rapidash [TM]	020 Raticate [TM]	384 Rayquaza [TM]	378 Regice [TM]	486 Regigigas [100, TM]	377 Regirock [TM]
		379 Registeel [TM]	369 Relicanth [TM]	643 Reshiram [TM]	579 Reuniclus [TM]	112 Rhydon [TM]	464 Rhyperior [TM]	407 Roserade [TM]
		373 Salamence [TM]	503 Samurott [TM]	028 Sandslash [TM]	539 Sawk [TM]	586 Sawsbuck [TM]	254 Sceptile [TM]	212 Scizor [TM]
		545 Scolipede [TM]	560 Scrafty [TM]	123 Scyther [TM]	117 Seadra [TM]	119 Seaking [TM]	537 Seismitoad [TM]	497 Serperior [TM]
		319 Sharpedo [TM]	492 Shaymin (Land) [TM]	492 Shaymin (Sky) [TM]	292 Shedinja [TM]	275 Shiftry [TM]	516 Simipour [TM]	512 Simisage [TM]
		514 Simisear [TM]	435 Skuntank [TM]	289 Slaking [TM]	080 Slowbro [TM]	199 Slowking [TM]	685 Slurpuff [TM]	143 Snorlax [57, TM]
		338 Solrock [TM]	442 Spiritomb [TM]	234 Stantler [TM]	398 Staraptor [TM]	121 Starmie [TM]	208 Steelix [TM]	508 Stoutland [59, TM]
		245 Suicune [TM]	192 Sunflora [TM]	317 Swalot [TM]	260 Swampert [TM]	581 Swanna [TM]	277 Swellow [TM]	528 Swoobat [TM]
		700 Sylveon [TM]	663 Talonflame [TM]	114 Tangela [TM]	465 Tangrowth [TM]	128 Tauros [63, TM]	073 Tentacruel [TM]	639 Terrakion [TM]
		538 Throh [TM]	642 Thundurus [TM]	468 Togekiss [TM]	176 Togetic [TM]	324 Torkoal [TM]	641 Tornadus [TM]	389 Torterra [TM]
		454 Toxicroak [TM]	709 Trevenant [TM]	357 Tropius [TM]	157 Typhlosion [TM]	248 Tyranitar [82, TM]	697 Tyrantrum [75, TM]	197 Umbreon [TM]
		521 Unfezant [TM]	217 Ursaring [TM]	480 Uxie [TM]	584 Vanilluxe [TM]	134 Vaporeon [TM]	049 Venomoth [TM]	003 Venusaur [TM]
		416 Vespiquen [TM]	494 Victini [TM]	071 Victreebel [TM]	045 Vileplume [TM]	640 Virizion [TM]	666 Vivillon [TM]	637 Volcarona [TM]
		321 Wailord [TM]	365 Walrein [TM]	505 Watchog [TM]	461 Weavile [TM]	110 Weezing [TM]	547 Whimsicott [TM]	340 Whiscash [TM]
		040 Wigglytuff [TM]	413 Wormadam (Plant) [TM]	413 Wormadam (Sand) [TM]	413 Wormadam (Trash) [TM]	178 Xatu [TM]	716 Xerneas [88, TM]	469 Yanmega [TM]
		717 Yveltal [TM]	145 Zapdos [TM]	523 Zebstrika [TM]	644 Zekrom [TM]	571 Zoroark [TM]	718 Zygarde [TM]	
Ice	Glaciate	646 Kyurem [50]						
Normal	Glare	024 Arbok [12]	621 Druddigon [E]	206 Dunsparce [28]	023 Ekans [12]	694 Helioptile [E]	336 Seviper [19]	495 Snivy [E]
		718 Zygarde [1]						
Grass	Grass Knot (TM86)	460 Abomasnow [TM]	063 Abra [TM]	190 Aipom [TM]	065 Alakazam [TM]	424 Ambipom [TM]	591 Amoonguss [TM]	493 Arceus [TM]
		531 Audino [TM]	482 Azelf [TM]	184 Azumarill [TM]	343 Baltoy [TM]	689 Barbaracle [TM]	153 Bayleef [TM]	614 Beartic [TM]
		182 Bellossom [TM]	069 Bellsprout [TM]	400 Bibarel [TM]	399 Bidoof [TM]	688 Binacle [TM]	625 Bisharp [TM]	242 Blissey [TM]
		654 Braixen [TM]	286 Breloom [TM]	437 Bronzong [TM]	436 Bronzor [TM]	406 Budew [TM]	001 Bulbasaur [TM]	427 Buneary [TM]
		659 Bunnelby [TM]	331 Cacnea [TM]	332 Cacturne [TM]	455 Carnivine [TM]	251 Celebi [TM]	113 Chansey [TM]	421 Cherrim [TM]
		420 Cherubi [TM]	652 Chesnaught [TM]	650 Chespin [TM]	152 Chikorita [TM]	390 Chimchar [TM]	358 Chimecho [TM]	433 Chingling [TM]
		573 Cinccino [TM]	344 Claydol [TM]	036 Clefable [TM]	035 Clefairy [TM]	173 Cleffa [TM]	563 Cofagrigus [TM]	534 Conkeldurr [TM]
		546 Cottonee [TM]	346 Cradily [TM]	488 Cresselia [TM]	613 Cubchoo [TM]	555 Darmanitan [TM]	554 Darumaka [TM]	702 Dedenne [TM]

	Move	Pokémon that can learn it						
Grass	Grass Knot (TM86)	585 Deerling [TM]	301 Delcatty [TM]	655 Delphox [TM]	386 Deoxys (Atk) [TM]	386 Deoxys (Def) [TM]	386 Deoxys (Nor) [TM]	386 Deoxys (Spd) [TM]
		502 Dewott [TM]	660 Diggersby [TM]	096 Drowzee [TM]	604 Eelektross [TM]	500 Emboar [TM]	395 Empoleon [TM]	196 Espeon [TM]
		102 Exeggcute [TM]	103 Exeggutor [TM]	653 Fennekin [TM]	598 Ferrothorn [TM]	669 Flabébé [TM]	670 Floette [TM]	671 Florges [1, TM]
		590 Foongus [TM]	656 Froakie [TM]	657 Frogadier [TM]	676 Furfrou [TM]	162 Furret [TM]	475 Gallade [TM]	282 Gardevoir [TM]
		203 Girafarig [TM]	044 Gloom [TM]	673 Gogoat [TM]	622 Golett [TM]	623 Golurk [TM]	574 Gothita [TM]	576 Gothitelle [TM]
		575 Gothorita [TM]	711 Gourgeist [TM]	658 Greninja [TM]	388 Grotle [TM]	253 Grovyle [TM]	326 Grumpig [TM]	533 Gurdurr [TM]
		440 Happiny [TM]	701 Hawlucha [TM]	612 Haxorus [TM]	695 Heliolisk [TM]	694 Helioptile [TM]	187 Hoppip [TM]	097 Hypno [TM]
		174 Igglybuff [TM]	392 Infernape [TM]	002 Ivysaur [TM]	039 Jigglypuff [TM]	385 Jirachi [TM]	189 Jumpluff [TM]	124 Jynx [TM]
		064 Kadabra [TM]	352 Kecleon [TM]	281 Kirlia [TM]	552 Krokorok [TM]	553 Krookodile [TM]	645 Landorus [TM]	380 Latias [TM]
		381 Latios [TM]	470 Leafeon [TM]	542 Leavanny [TM]	510 Liepard [TM]	345 Lileep [TM]	549 Lilligant [TM]	264 Linoone [TM]
		271 Lombre [TM]	428 Lopunny [TM]	270 Lotad [TM]	272 Ludicolo [TM]	337 Lunatone [TM]	490 Manaphy [TM]	556 Maractus [TM]
		183 Marill [TM]	303 Mawile [TM]	308 Medicham [TM]	307 Meditite [TM]	154 Meganium [TM]	648 Meloetta [TM]	481 Mesprit [TM]
		376 Metagross [TM]	375 Metang [TM]	151 Mew [TM]	150 Mewtwo [TM]	619 Mienfoo [TM]	620 Mienshao [TM]	439 Mime Jr. [TM]
		572 Minccino [TM]	312 Minun [TM]	391 Monferno [TM]	122 Mr. Mime [TM]	177 Natu [TM]	274 Nuzleaf [TM]	043 Oddish [TM]
		501 Oshawott [TM]	417 Pachirisu [TM]	674 Pancham [TM]	675 Pangoro [TM]	515 Panpour [TM]	511 Pansage [34, TM]	513 Pansear [TM]
		046 Paras [TM]	047 Parasect [TM]	504 Patrat [TM]	624 Pawniard [TM]	548 Petilil [TM]	708 Phantump [TM]	489 Phione [TM]
		172 Pichu [TM]	499 Pignite [TM]	025 Pikachu [TM]	393 Piplup [TM]	311 Plusle [TM]	394 Prinplup [TM]	710 Pumpkaboo [TM]
		509 Purrloin [TM]	651 Quilladin [TM]	026 Raichu [TM]	280 Ralts [TM]	020 Raticate [TM]	019 Rattata [TM]	579 Reuniclus [TM]
		315 Roselia [TM]	407 Roserade [TM]	503 Samurott [TM]	539 Sawk [TM]	586 Sawsbuck [TM]	254 Sceptile [TM]	560 Scrafty [TM]
		559 Scraggy [TM]	273 Seedot [TM]	537 Seismitoad [TM]	161 Sentret [TM]	497 Serperior [TM]	496 Servine [TM]	540 Sewaddle [TM]
		492 Shaymin (Land) [TM]	492 Shaymin (Sky) [TM]	275 Shiftry [TM]	285 Shroomish [TM]	516 Simipour [TM]	512 Simisage [TM]	514 Simisear [TM]
		672 Skiddo [TM]	188 Skiploom [TM]	300 Skitty [TM]	080 Slowbro [TM]	199 Slowking [TM]	079 Slowpoke [TM]	238 Smoochum [TM]
		495 Snivy [TM]	459 Snover [TM]	338 Solrock [TM]	325 Spoink [TM]	121 Starmie [TM]	192 Sunflora [TM]	191 Sunkern [TM]
		541 Swadloon [TM]	114 Tangela [TM]	465 Tangrowth [TM]	498 Tepig [TM]	538 Throh [TM]	642 Thundurus [TM]	532 Timburr [TM]
		468 Togekiss [TM]	175 Togepi [TM]	176 Togetic [TM]	641 Tornadus [TM]	389 Torterra [TM]	252 Treecko [TM]	709 Trevenant [TM]
		357 Tropius [TM]	387 Turtwig [TM]	480 Uxie [TM]	003 Venusaur [TM]	494 Victini [TM]	071 Victreebel [TM]	045 Vileplume [TM]
		640 Virizion [TM]	505 Watchog [TM]	070 Weepinbell [TM]	547 Whimsicott [TM]	040 Wigglytuff [TM]	413 Wormadam (Plant) [TM]	178 Xatu [TM]
		716 Xerneas [TM]	263 Zigzagoon [TM]	571 Zoroark [TM]	570 Zorua [TM]	718 Zygarde [TM]		
	Grass Pledge	153 Bayleef [T]	001 Bulbasaur [T]	652 Chesnaught [T]	650 Chespin [T]	152 Chikorita [T]	388 Grotle [T]	253 Grovyle [T]
		002 Ivysaur [T]	154 Meganium [T]	651 Quilladin [T]	254 Sceptile [T]	497 Serperior [T]	496 Servine [T]	495 Snivy [T]
		389 Torterra [T]	252 Treecko [T]	387 Turtwig [T]	003 Venusaur [T]			
	Grass Whistle	460 Abomasnow [13]	406 Budew [E]	001 Bulbasaur [E]	331 Cacnea [E]	455 Carnivine [E]	420 Cherubi [E]	152 Chikorita [E]
		546 Cottonee [E]	585 Deerling [E]	470 Leafeon [17]	556 Maractus [E]	511 Pansage [E]	548 Petilil [E]	315 Roselia [22, E]
		459 Snover [13]	192 Sunflora [7]	191 Sunkern [7, E]	541 Swadloon [1]	252 Treecko [E]		
	Grassy Terrain	001 Bulbasaur [E]	152 Chikorita [E]	102 Exeggcute [E]	669 Flabébé [24]	670 Floette [27]	671 Florges [1]	044 Gloom [54]
		187 Hoppip [E]	556 Maractus [E]	043 Oddish [47]	407 Roserade [1]	273 Seedot [E]	495 Snivy [E]	191 Sunkern [E]
		114 Tangela [48]	465 Tangrowth [50]	252 Treecko [E]	387 Turtwig [E]			
Psychic	Gravity	063 Abra [BP]	065 Alakazam [BP]	493 Arceus [10, BP]	531 Audino [BP]	343 Baltoy [BP]	606 Beheeyem [BP]	242 Blissey [BP]
		525 Boldore [BP]	437 Bronzong [BP]	436 Bronzor [BP]	703 Carbink [BP]	113 Chansey [BP, E]	358 Chimecho [BP]	433 Chingling [BP]
		344 Claydol [BP]	036 Clefable [BP]	035 Clefairy [49, BP]	173 Cleffa [BP]	488 Cresselia [BP]	386 Deoxys (Atk) [BP]	386 Deoxys (Def) [BP]
		386 Deoxys (Nor) [BP]	386 Deoxys (Spd) [BP]	483 Dialga [BP]	719 Diancie [BP]	578 Duosion [BP]	356 Dusclops [1, BP]	477 Dusknoir [1, BP]
		355 Duskull [BP]	605 Elgyem [BP]	677 Espurr [BP]	102 Exeggcute [BP]	103 Exeggutor [BP]	597 Ferroseed [BP, E]	598 Ferrothorn [BP]
		205 Forretress [BP]	649 Genesect [BP]	526 Gigalith [BP]	203 Girafarig [BP]	487 Giratina (Alt) [BP]	487 Giratina (Ori) [BP]	622 Golett [BP]
		623 Golurk [BP]	574 Gothita [BP]	576 Gothitelle [BP]	575 Gothorita [BP]	440 Happiny [BP, E]	174 Igglybuff [BP, E]	039 Jigglypuff [BP]
		385 Jirachi [45, BP]	064 Kadabra [BP]	600 Klang [BP]	599 Klink [BP]	601 Klinklang [BP]	645 Landorus [BP]	337 Lunatone [BP]
		081 Magnemite [BP]	082 Magneton [BP]	462 Magnezone [BP]	308 Medicham [BP]	307 Meditite [BP]	648 Meloetta [BP]	678 Meowstic (F) [BP]
		678 Meowstic (M) [BP]	376 Metagross [BP]	375 Metang [BP]	151 Mew [BP]	150 Mewtwo [BP]	517 Munna [BP]	518 Musharna [BP]
		299 Nosepass [BP]	484 Palkia [BP]	204 Pineco [BP]	137 Porygon [BP]	233 Porygon2 [BP]	474 Porygon-Z [BP]	476 Probopass [1, BP]
		378 Regice [BP]	486 Regigigas [BP]	377 Regirock [BP]	379 Registeel [BP]	579 Reuniclus [BP]	524 Roggenrola [BP, E]	302 Sableye [BP]
		561 Sigilyph [38, BP]	577 Solosis [BP]	338 Solrock [BP]	234 Stantler [BP]	121 Starmie [BP]	120 Staryu [BP]	040 Wigglytuff [BP]
		716 Xerneas [18, BP]						
Normal	Growl	334 Altaria [1]	698 Amaura [1]	181 Ampharos [1]	531 Audino [1]	699 Aurorus [1]	153 Bayleef [1]	614 Beartic [1]
		606 Beheeyem [1, 4]	400 Bibarel [1, 5]	399 Bidoof [5]	257 Blaziken [1]	242 Blissey [1]	418 Buizel [4]	001 Bulbasaur [3]
		323 Camerupt [1]	113 Chansey [1]	006 Charizard [1]	004 Charmander [1]	005 Charmeleon [1]	441 Chatot [5]	652 Chesnaught [1]
		650 Chespin [1]	152 Chikorita [1]	358 Chimecho [1, 4]	433 Chingling [4]	035 Clefairy [1]	256 Combusken [1]	613 Cubchoo [1]
		104 Cubone [1]	585 Deerling [4]	087 Dewgong [1, 3]	050 Diglett [4]	085 Dodrio [1]	084 Doduo [1]	232 Donphan [1]
		051 Dugtrio [1, 4]	133 Eevee [1]	605 Elgyem [4]	395 Empoleon [1, 4]	022 Fearow [1]	180 Flaaffy [1]	662 Fletchinder [1]
		661 Fletchling [1]	419 Floatzel [1, 4]	656 Froakie [1]	657 Frogadier [1]	676 Furfrou [1]	282 Gardevoir [1]	203 Girafarig [1]
		431 Glameow [8]	658 Greninja [1]	163 Hoothoot [1]	002 Ivysaur [1, 3]	281 Kirlia [1]	401 Kricketot [1]	402 Kricketune [1]
		131 Lapras [1]	510 Liepard [1, 3]	264 Linoone [1]	271 Lombre [3]	270 Lotad [3]	272 Ludicolo [1]	179 Mareep [1]
		105 Marowak [1]	259 Marshtomp [1]	303 Mawile [1]	154 Meganium [1]	052 Meowth [1]	241 Miltank [3]	312 Minun [1]
		200 Misdreavus [1]	429 Mismagius [1]	258 Mudkip [1]	029 Nidoran ♀ [1]	030 Nidorina [1]	164 Noctowl [1]	322 Numel [1]
		417 Pachirisu [1]	536 Palpitoad [1]	279 Pelipper [1]	053 Persian [1]	231 Phanpy [1]	519 Pidove [4]	025 Pikachu [5]
		393 Piplup [4]	311 Plusle [1]	077 Ponyta [1]	394 Prinplup [1, 4]	509 Purrloin [3]	432 Purugly [1, 8]	651 Quilladin [1]
		280 Ralts [1]	078 Rapidash [1]	586 Sawsbuck [1, 4]	364 Sealeo [1]	086 Seel [3]	537 Seismitoad [1]	300 Skitty [1]

Type	Move	Pokémon that can learn it						
Normal	Growl	080 Slowbro [1, 5]	199 Slowking [5]	079 Slowpoke [5]	021 Spearow [1]	363 Spheal [1]	398 Staraptor [1]	397 Staravia [1]
		396 Starly [1]	333 Swablu [1]	260 Swampert [1]	277 Swellow [1]	276 Taillow [1]	663 Talonflame [1]	175 Togepi [1]
		176 Togetic [1]	255 Torchic [1]	520 Tranquill [1, 4]	535 Tympole [1]	521 Unfezant [1, 4]	003 Venusaur [1, 3]	320 Wailmer [4]
		321 Wailord [1, 4]	365 Walrein [1]	278 Wingull [1]	263 Zigzagoon [1]			
	Growth	591 Amoonguss [1, 6]	069 Bellsprout [7]	406 Budew [4]	001 Bulbasaur [25]	331 Cacnea [7]	332 Cacturne [1, 7]	455 Carnivine [1]
		421 Cherrim [1, 7]	420 Cherubi [7]	546 Cottonee [4]	590 Foongus [6, E]	673 Gogoat [1]	314 Illumise [E]	002 Ivysaur [28]
		549 Lilligant [1]	556 Maractus [6]	322 Numel [E]	274 Nuzleaf [6]	046 Paras [33]	047 Parasect [37]	548 Petilil [4]
		708 Phantump [8]	315 Roselia [4]	273 Seedot [9]	497 Serperior [13]	496 Servine [13]	492 Shaymin (Land) [1]	492 Shaymin (Sky) [1]
		285 Shroomish [29]	672 Skiddo [1]	495 Snivy [13]	459 Snover [E]	192 Sunflora [1]	191 Sunkern [1]	114 Tangela [20]
		465 Tangrowth [20]	709 Trevenant [8]	357 Tropius [1]	387 Turtwig [E]	003 Venusaur [28]	070 Weepinbell [1, 7]	547 Whimsicott [1]
		413 Wormadam (Plant) [29]						
Ghost	Grudge	354 Banette [52]	563 Cofagrigus [45]	355 Duskull [E]	092 Gastly [E]	109 Koffing [E]	200 Misdreavus [50]	708 Phantump [E]
		280 Ralts [E]	292 Shedinja [37]	353 Shuppet [46]	442 Spiritomb [E]	037 Vulpix [44]	562 Yamask [41]	
Psychic	Guard Split	063 Abra [E]	343 Baltoy [34]	606 Beheeyem [56]	703 Carbink [27]	344 Claydol [34]	563 Cofagrigus [33]	719 Diancie [27]
		605 Elgyem [50]	380 Latias [46]	111 Rhyhorn [E]	616 Shelmet [E]	410 Shieldon [E]	213 Shuckle [45]	327 Spinda [E]
		562 Yamask [33]						
	Guard Swap	063 Abra [E]	351 Castform [E]	096 Drowzee [E]	605 Elgyem [E]	203 Girafarig [1]	303 Mawile [E]	307 Meditite [E]
		150 Mewtwo [43]	122 Mr. Mime [1]	177 Natu [47]	616 Shelmet [50]	227 Skarmory [E]	218 Slugma [E]	564 Tirtouga [E]
		197 Umbreon [45]	194 Wooper [E]	178 Xatu [53]				
Normal	Guillotine	610 Axew [50]	625 Bisharp [1, 71]	341 Corphish [48]	342 Crawdaunt [54]	632 Durant [1, 61]	611 Fraxure [54]	207 Gligar [55]
		472 Gliscor [1, 55]	612 Haxorus [58]	099 Kingler [37]	098 Krabby [31]	624 Pawniard [62]	127 Pinsir [50]	
Poison	Gunk Shot	190 Aipom [BP]	424 Ambipom [BP]	024 Arbok [63, BP]	390 Chimchar [BP]	573 Cinccino [BP]	453 Croagunk [BP]	225 Delibird [BP]
		660 Diggersby [BP]	232 Donphan [BP]	691 Dragalge [BP]	621 Druddigon [BP]	023 Ekans [49, BP]	657 Frogadier [BP]	569 Garbodor [54, BP]
		649 Genesect [BP]	658 Greninja [BP]	088 Grimer [40, BP]	316 Gulpin [49, BP, E]	392 Infernape [BP]	510 Liepard [BP]	264 Linoone [BP]
		056 Mankey [BP]	226 Mantine [BP]	052 Meowth [BP]	151 Mew [BP]	572 Minccino [BP]	391 Monferno [BP]	089 Muk [40, BP]
		446 Munchlax [BP]	224 Octillery [1, BP]	417 Pachirisu [BP]	674 Pancham [BP]	675 Pangoro [BP]	515 Panpour [BP]	511 Pansage [BP]
		513 Pansear [BP]	504 Patrat [BP]	279 Pelipper [BP]	053 Persian [BP]	231 Phanpy [BP]	057 Primeape [BP]	509 Purrloin [BP]
		223 Remoraid [BP]	353 Shuppet [E]	516 Simipour [BP]	512 Simisage [BP]	514 Simisear [BP]	690 Skrelp [BP]	289 Slaking [BP]
		287 Slakoth [BP]	143 Snorlax [BP]	317 Swalot [1, 61, BP]	216 Teddiursa [BP]	454 Toxicroak [BP]	568 Trubbish [45, BP]	217 Ursaring [BP]
		288 Vigoroth [BP]	505 Watchog [BP]	413 Wormadam (Trash) [BP]	263 Zigzagoon [BP]			
Flying	Gust	144 Articuno [1]	267 Beautifly [1, 10]	012 Butterfree [16]	415 Combee [1]	426 Drifblim [1, 8]	425 Drifloon [8]	580 Ducklett [E]
		269 Dustox [1, 10]	083 Farfetch'd [E]	456 Finneon [17]	250 Ho-Oh [9]	249 Lugia [9]	457 Lumineon [1, 17]	630 Mandibuzz [1]
		284 Masquerain [17]	414 Mothim [26]	290 Nincada [E]	714 Noibat [11]	715 Noivern [11]	018 Pidgeot [1, 9]	017 Pidgeotto [1, 9]
		016 Pidgey [9]	519 Pidove [1]	561 Sigilyph [1]	245 Suicune [22]	528 Swoobat [1, 8]	641 Tornadus [1]	520 Tranquill [1]
		328 Trapinch [E]	357 Tropius [1]	521 Unfezant [1]	049 Venomoth [31]	416 Vespiquen [1]	666 Vivillon [1]	637 Volcarona [1, 20]
		629 Vullaby [1]	547 Whimsicott [10]	278 Wingull [E]	527 Woobat [8]	041 Zubat [E]		
Steel	Gyro Ball (TM74)	681 Aegislash [TM]	683 Aromatisse [TM]	713 Avalugg [TM]	343 Baltoy [TM]	712 Bergmite [TM]	009 Blastoise [TM]	437 Bronzong [36, TM]
		436 Bronzor [35, TM]	703 Carbink [TM]	652 Chesnaught [TM]	650 Chespin [TM]	344 Claydol [TM]	555 Darmanitan [TM]	554 Darumaka [TM]
		719 Diancie [TM]	232 Donphan [TM]	680 Doublade [TM]	426 Drifblim [TM]	425 Drifloon [TM]	206 Dunsparce [TM]	578 Duosion [TM]
		101 Electrode [54, TM]	500 Emboar [TM]	597 Ferroseed [21, TM]	598 Ferrothorn [21, TM]	205 Forretress [50, TM]	074 Geodude [TM]	362 Glalie [TM]
		076 Golem [TM]	622 Golett [TM]	623 Golurk [TM]	711 Gourgeist [TM]	075 Graveler [TM]	237 Hitmontop [42, TM]	679 Honedge [TM]
		039 Jigglypuff [40, TM]	109 Koffing [29, TM]	463 Lickilicky [61, TM]	337 Lunatone [TM]	219 Magcargo [TM]	081 Magnemite [47, TM]	082 Magneton [59, TM]
		462 Magnezone [59, TM]	376 Metagross [TM]	375 Metang [TM]	151 Mew [TM]	241 Miltank [41, TM]	517 Munna [TM]	518 Musharna [TM]
		138 Omanyte [TM]	139 Omastar [TM]	095 Onix [20, TM]	499 Pignite [TM]	204 Pineco [42, TM]	710 Pumpkaboo [TM]	651 Quilladin [TM]
		211 Qwilfish [TM]	384 Rayquaza [TM]	579 Reuniclus [TM]	027 Sandshrew [34, TM]	028 Sandslash [38, TM]	545 Scolipede [TM]	213 Shuckle [TM]
		577 Solosis [TM]	338 Solrock [TM]	682 Spritzee [TM]	007 Squirtle [TM]	121 Starmie [TM]	120 Staryu [24, TM]	208 Steelix [20, TM]
		528 Swoobat [TM]	498 Tepig [TM]	324 Torkoal [TM]	157 Typhlosion [1, TM]	543 Venipede [TM]	100 Voltorb [46, TM]	008 Wartortle [TM]
		110 Weezing [TM]	544 Whirlipede [TM]	040 Wigglytuff [TM]	527 Woobat [TM]	413 Wormadam (Trash) [TM]		

H

Type	Move	Pokémon that can learn it						
Ice	Hail (TM07)	460 Abomasnow [TM]	359 Absol [TM]	594 Alomomola [TM]	698 Amaura [38, TM]	493 Arceus [TM]	144 Articuno [57, TM]	699 Aurorus [38, TM]
		713 Avalugg [TM]	184 Azumarill [TM]	298 Azurill [TM]	339 Barboach [TM]	550 Basculin [TM]	614 Beartic [53, TM]	712 Bergmite [TM]
		009 Blastoise [TM]	242 Blissey [TM]	418 Buizel [TM]	703 Carbink [TM]	318 Carvanha [TM]	351 Castform [20, TM]	113 Chansey [TM]
		170 Chinchou [TM]	366 Clamperl [TM]	091 Cloyster [TM]	341 Corphish [TM]	222 Corsola [TM]	342 Crawdaunt [TM]	159 Croconaw [TM]
		615 Cryogonal [TM]	613 Cubchoo [49, TM]	225 Delibird [TM]	087 Dewgong [65, TM]	502 Dewott [TM]	719 Diancie [TM]	691 Dragalge [TM]
		148 Dragonair [TM]	149 Dragonite [TM]	147 Dratini [TM]	580 Ducklett [TM]	395 Empoleon [TM]	349 Feebas [TM]	160 Feraligatr [TM]
		456 Finneon [TM]	419 Floatzel [TM]	592 Frillish [TM]	478 Froslass [54, TM]	423 Gastrodon [TM]	471 Glaceon [37, TM]	362 Glalie [54, TM]
		118 Goldeen [TM]	055 Golduck [TM]	706 Goodra [TM]	368 Gorebyss [TM]	130 Gyarados [TM]	440 Happiny [TM]	116 Horsea [TM]
		367 Huntail [TM]	593 Jellicent [TM]	124 Jynx [TM]	140 Kabuto [TM]	141 Kabutops [TM]	115 Kangaskhan [TM]	647 Keldeo [TM]
		230 Kingdra [TM]	099 Kingler [TM]	098 Krabby [TM]	382 Kyogre [TM]	646 Kyurem (Blk) [TM]	646 Kyurem (Wht) [TM]	646 Kyurem [TM]
		171 Lanturn [TM]	131 Lapras [TM]	271 Lombre [TM]	270 Lotad [TM]	272 Ludicolo [TM]	249 Lugia [TM]	457 Lumineon [TM]

	Move	Pokémon that can learn it						
Ice	Hail (TM07)	370 Luvdisc [TM]	473 Mamoswine [21, TM]	490 Manaphy [TM]	226 Mantine [TM]	458 Mantyke [TM]	183 Marill [TM]	259 Marshtomp [TM]
		151 Mew [TM]	150 Mewtwo [TM]	350 Milotic [TM]	258 Mudkip [TM]	138 Omanyte [TM]	139 Omastar [TM]	501 Oshawott [TM]
		484 Palkia [TM]	536 Palpitoad [TM]	515 Panpour [TM]	279 Pelipper [TM]	489 Phione [TM]	221 Piloswine [TM]	393 Piplup [TM]
		186 Politoed [TM]	060 Poliwag [TM]	061 Poliwhirl [TM]	062 Poliwrath [TM]	394 Prinplup [TM]	054 Psyduck [TM]	195 Quagsire [TM]
		211 Qwilfish [TM]	378 Regice [TM]	369 Relicanth [TM]	503 Samurott [TM]	117 Seadra [TM]	119 Seaking [TM]	364 Sealeo [38, TM]
		086 Seel [53, TM]	537 Seismitoad [TM]	319 Sharpedo [TM]	090 Shellder [TM]	422 Shellos [TM]	516 Simipour [TM]	690 Skrelp [TM]
		080 Slowbro [TM]	199 Slowking [TM]	079 Slowpoke [TM]	238 Smoochum [TM]	215 Sneasel [TM]	361 Snorunt [50, TM]	459 Snover [TM]
		363 Spheal [36, TM]	007 Squirtle [TM]	121 Starmie [TM]	120 Staryu [TM]	245 Suicune [TM]	260 Swampert [TM]	581 Swanna [TM]
		220 Swinub [TM]	072 Tentacool [TM]	073 Tentacruel [TM]	158 Totodile [TM]	535 Tympole [TM]	583 Vanillish [42, TM]	582 Vanillite [40, TM]
		584 Vanilluxe [42, TM]	134 Vaporeon [TM]	320 Wailmer [TM]	321 Wailord [TM]	365 Walrein [38, TM]	008 Wartortle [TM]	461 Weavile [TM]
		340 Whiscash [TM]	278 Wingull [TM]	194 Wooper [TM]	716 Xerneas [TM]			
Fighting	Hammer Arm	652 Chesnaught [1, 60]	534 Conkeldurr [45]	408 Cranidos [E]	555 Darmanitan [35]	554 Darumaka [E]	660 Diggersby [1, 60]	239 Elekid [E]
		500 Emboar [1]	074 Geodude [E]	622 Golett [50]	623 Golurk [60]	383 Groudon [80]	533 Gurdurr [45]	115 Kangaskhan [E]
		645 Landorus [1, 79]	108 Lickitung [E]	376 Metagross [45]	241 Miltank [E]	675 Pangoro [1, 57]	378 Regice [49]	377 Regirock [49]
		379 Registeel [49]	112 Rhydon [42]	464 Rhyperior [42]	289 Slaking [1, 61]	287 Slakoth [E]	185 Sudowoodo [47]	260 Swampert [1, 63]
		642 Thundurus [1, 79]	532 Timburr [40]	641 Tornadus [1, 79]	217 Ursaring [1, 67]	293 Whismur [E]		
Normal	Harden	306 Aggron [1]	347 Anorith [1]	348 Armaldo [1]	304 Aron [1]	713 Avalugg [1]	610 Axew [E]	343 Baltoy [1]
		712 Bergmite [1]	525 Boldore [1, 4]	438 Bonsly [E]	703 Carbink [1]	268 Cascoon [1, 7]	344 Claydol [1]	341 Corphish [5]
		222 Corsola [1]	342 Crawdaunt [1, 5]	719 Diancie [1]	597 Ferroseed [1]	598 Ferrothorn [1]	423 Gastrodon [1, 4]	526 Gigalith [1, 4]
		207 Gligar [7]	472 Gliscor [1, 7]	088 Grimer [4]	214 Heracross [E]	140 Kabuto [1]	141 Kabutops [1]	014 Kakuna [1, 7]
		099 Kingler [11]	098 Krabby [11]	305 Lairon [1]	636 Larvesta [E]	337 Lunatone [1]	219 Magcargo [13]	011 Metapod [1, 7]
		089 Muk [1, 4]	290 Nincada [1]	291 Ninjask [1]	299 Nosepass [4]	274 Nuzleaf [3]	095 Onix [1]	127 Pinsir [11]
		211 Qwilfish [9]	369 Relicanth [1]	524 Roggenrola [4]	273 Seedot [3]	292 Shedinja [1]	422 Shellos [4]	266 Silcoon [1, 7]
		218 Slugma [13]	338 Solrock [1]	665 Spewpa [1]	120 Staryu [1]	208 Steelix [1]	185 Sudowoodo [E]	583 Vanillish [1, 4]
		582 Vanillite [4]	584 Vanilluxe [1, 4]	413 Wormadam (Sand) [29]				
Ice	Haze	698 Amaura [E]	024 Arbok [51]	563 Cofagrigus [1, 9]	169 Crobat [40]	615 Cryogonal [1, 21]	491 Darkrai [57]	084 Doduo [E]
		147 Dratini [E]	425 Drifloon [E]	355 Duskull [E]	023 Ekans [41]	349 Feebas [E]	092 Gastly [E]	042 Golbat [40]
		118 Goldeen [E]	658 Greninja [56]	088 Grimer [E]	430 Honchkrow [1]	109 Koffing [26]	098 Krabby [E]	607 Litwick [E]
		226 Mantine [E]	458 Mantyke [E]	198 Murkrow [11]	177 Natu [E]	138 Omanyte [E]	060 Poliwag [E]	195 Quagsire [48]
		211 Qwilfish [E]	223 Remoraid [E]	336 Seviper [37]	690 Skrelp [E]	007 Squirtle [E]	434 Stunky [E]	283 Surskit [25]
		333 Swablu [E]	072 Tentacool [E]	568 Trubbish [E]	134 Vaporeon [33]	110 Weezing [26]	194 Wooper [43]	562 Yamask [9]
		041 Zubat [35]	718 Zygarde [44]					
Normal	Head Charge	626 Bouffalant [31]						
Rock	Head Smash	681 Aegislash [1]	566 Archen [E]	304 Aron [E]	222 Corsola [E]	408 Cranidos [46]	633 Deino [E]	500 Emboar [50]
		032 Nidoran ♂ [E]	231 Phanpy [E]	499 Pignite [44]	409 Rampardos [58]	369 Relicanth [1, 56]	560 Scrafty [65]	559 Scraggy [50]
		498 Tepig [37]	697 Tyrantrum [1, 58]					
Normal	Headbutt	306 Aggron [1, 7]	304 Aron [7]	371 Bagon [17]	550 Basculin [7]	606 Beheeyem [18]	400 Bibarel [18]	399 Bidoof [17]
		525 Boldore [1, 10]	438 Bonsly [E]	626 Bouffalant [E]	286 Breloom [15]	418 Buizel [E]	351 Castform [15]	408 Cranidos [1]
		453 Croagunk [E]	104 Cubone [11]	555 Darmanitan [14]	554 Darumaka [14]	633 Deino [12]	087 Dewgong [1]	050 Diglett [E]
		096 Drowzee [13, 29]	206 Dunsparce [E]	603 Eelektrik [1]	604 Eelektross [1]	309 Electrike [E]	605 Elgyem [18]	589 Escavalier [20]
		676 Furfrou [12]	526 Gigalith [1, 10]	362 Glalie [28]	210 Granbull [19]	635 Hydreigon [12]	097 Hypno [13, 29]	588 Karrablast [20]
		305 Lairon [1, 7]	264 Linoone [11]	667 Litleo [11]	226 Mantine [16]	458 Mantyke [16]	105 Marowak [1, 11]	624 Pawniard [E]
		668 Pyroar [11]	409 Rampardos [1]	524 Roggenrola [10]	373 Salamence [17]	560 Scrafty [12]	559 Scraggy [12]	086 Seel [1]
		372 Shelgon [17]	410 Shieldon [E]	285 Shroomish [15]	080 Slowbro [23]	199 Slowking [23]	079 Slowpoke [23]	361 Snorunt [28]
		209 Snubbull [19]	185 Sudowoodo [E]	357 Tropius [E]	494 Victini [17]	263 Zigzagoon [11]	634 Zweilous [12]	
Normal	Heal Bell	334 Altaria [BP]	181 Ampharos [BP]	683 Aromatisse [BP]	531 Audino [BP, E]	242 Blissey [BP]	427 Buneary [BP]	251 Celebi [1, BP]
		113 Chansey [BP, E]	358 Chimecho [27, BP]	170 Chinchou [BP]	433 Chingling [BP]	036 Clefable [BP]	035 Clefairy [BP]	301 Delcatty [BP]
		719 Diancie [BP]	133 Eevee [BP]	196 Espeon [BP]	677 Espurr [BP]	180 Flaaffy [BP]	669 Flabébé [BP]	136 Flareon [BP]
		670 Floette [BP]	671 Florges [BP]	282 Gardevoir [BP]	471 Glaceon [BP]	574 Gothita [BP]	576 Gothitelle [BP]	575 Gothorita [BP]
		210 Granbull [BP]	326 Grumpig [BP]	440 Happiny [BP, E]	174 Igglybuff [BP]	039 Jigglypuff [BP]	135 Jolteon [BP]	124 Jynx [BP]
		402 Kricketune [BP]	171 Lanturn [BP]	131 Lapras [BP]	470 Leafeon [BP]	542 Leavanny [BP]	549 Lilligant [BP]	428 Lopunny [BP]
		490 Manaphy [BP]	179 Mareep [BP]	648 Meloetta [BP]	678 Meowstic (F) [BP]	678 Meowstic (M) [BP]	151 Mew [BP]	241 Miltank [48, BP]
		200 Misdreavus [BP]	429 Mismagius [BP]	517 Munna [BP]	518 Musharna [BP]	548 Petilil [BP]	489 Phione [BP]	300 Skitty [37, BP]
		685 Slurpuff [BP]	238 Smoochum [BP]	209 Snubbull [BP, E]	325 Spoink [BP]	682 Spritzee [BP]	333 Swablu [BP]	684 Swirlix [BP]
		700 Sylveon [BP]	468 Togekiss [BP]	175 Togepi [BP]	176 Togetic [BP]	197 Umbreon [BP]	480 Uxie [BP]	134 Vaporeon [BP]
		040 Wigglytuff [BP]						
Psychic	Heal Block	343 Baltoy [10]	606 Beheeyem [1, 8]	437 Bronzong [52]	436 Bronzor [45]	251 Celebi [55]	344 Claydol [10]	578 Duosion [50]
		605 Elgyem [8]	574 Gothita [33]	576 Gothitelle [34]	575 Gothorita [34]	707 Klefki [50]	381 Latios [1]	337 Lunatone [33]
		579 Reuniclus [54]	292 Shedinja [41]	577 Solosis [46]	338 Solrock [33]	642 Thundurus [31]	562 Yamask [E]	
Bug	Heal Order	416 Vespiquen [29]						
Psychic	Heal Pulse	594 Alomomola [17]	683 Aromatisse [1]	531 Audino [37]	242 Blissey [38]	113 Chansey [38]	420 Cherubi [E]	152 Chikorita [E]
		358 Chimecho [47]	693 Clawitzer [1]	173 Cleffa [E]	475 Gallade [19]	282 Gardevoir [19]	574 Gothita [E]	174 Igglybuff [E]
		281 Kirlia [19]	380 Latias [16]	381 Latios [16]	448 Lucario [51]	370 Luvdisc [E]	280 Ralts [19]	080 Slowbro [1, 68]
		199 Slowking [1, 58]	079 Slowpoke [58]	716 Xerneas [1]				

	Move	Pokémon that can learn it						
Psychic	Healing Wish	594 Alomomola [1, 57]	531 Audino [E]	242 Blissey [50]	427 Buneary [63]	251 Celebi [73]	113 Chansey [50]	420 Cherubi [E]
		358 Chimecho [1, 57]	035 Clefairy [1, 55]	282 Gardevoir [1]	385 Jirachi [50]	380 Latias [1, 61]	428 Lopunny [1, 63]	481 Mesprit [1, 76]
		439 Mime Jr. [E]	517 Munna [E]	548 Petilil [E]	492 Shaymin (Land) [91]			
	Heart Stamp	124 Jynx [21]	241 Miltank [E]	238 Smoochum [21]	528 Swoobat [15]	527 Woobat [15]		
	Heart Swap	490 Manaphy [76]						
Fire	Heat Crash	500 Emboar [31]	499 Pignite [31]	498 Tepig [27]				
	Heat Wave	142 Aerodactyl [BP]	334 Altaria [BP]	059 Arcanine [BP]	493 Arceus [BP]	566 Archen [BP]	567 Archeops [BP]	257 Blaziken [BP]
		654 Braixen [BP]	628 Braviary [BP]	323 Camerupt [BP]	609 Chandelure [BP]	006 Charizard [1, 71, BP]	004 Charmander [BP]	005 Charmeleon [BP]
		441 Chatot [BP]	390 Chimchar [BP, E]	256 Combusken [BP]	169 Crobat [BP]	155 Cyndaquil [BP]	555 Darmanitan [BP]	554 Darumaka [BP]
		655 Delphox [BP]	149 Dragonite [BP]	621 Druddigon [BP]	500 Emboar [BP]	244 Entei [BP]	083 Farfetch'd [BP]	022 Fearow [BP]
		653 Fennekin [BP, E]	136 Flareon [BP]	662 Fletchinder [BP]	661 Fletchling [BP]	330 Flygon [BP]	042 Golbat [BP]	058 Growlithe [41, BP, E]
		631 Heatmor [BP, E]	485 Heatran [1, 81, BP]	430 Honchkrow [BP]	250 Ho-Oh [BP]	163 Hoothoot [BP]	229 Houndoom [BP]	228 Houndour [BP]
		635 Hydreigon [BP]	392 Infernape [BP]	608 Lampent [BP]	636 Larvesta [BP]	667 Litleo [BP]	607 Litwick [BP, E]	240 Magby [BP]
		219 Magcargo [BP]	126 Magmar [BP]	467 Magmortar [BP]	630 Mandibuzz [BP]	151 Mew [BP]	146 Moltres [1, 64, BP]	391 Monferno [BP]
		198 Murkrow [BP]	177 Natu [BP]	038 Ninetales [BP]	164 Noctowl [BP]	714 Noibat [BP]	715 Noivern [BP]	322 Numel [BP, E]
		513 Pansear [BP, E]	018 Pidgeot [BP]	017 Pidgeotto [BP]	016 Pidgey [BP]	519 Pidove [BP]	499 Pignite [BP]	077 Ponyta [BP]
		668 Pyroar [BP]	156 Quilava [BP]	078 Rapidash [BP]	643 Reshiram [BP]	627 Rufflet [BP]	373 Salamence [BP]	561 Sigilyph [BP]
		514 Simisear [BP]	218 Slugma [BP, E]	338 Solrock [BP]	021 Spearow [BP]	398 Staraptor [BP]	397 Staravia [BP]	396 Starly [BP]
		333 Swablu [BP]	277 Swellow [BP]	528 Swoobat [BP]	276 Taillow [BP]	663 Talonflame [BP]	498 Tepig [BP]	468 Togekiss [BP]
		176 Togetic [BP]	255 Torchic [BP]	324 Torkoal [45, BP]	641 Tornadus [BP]	520 Tranquill [BP]	157 Typhlosion [BP]	521 Unfezant [BP]
		329 Vibrava [BP]	494 Victini [BP]	637 Volcarona [1, 60, BP]	629 Vullaby [BP]	037 Vulpix [BP, E]	527 Woobat [BP]	178 Xatu [BP]
		717 Yveltal [BP]	145 Zapdos [BP]	041 Zubat [BP]				
Steel	Heavy Slam	306 Aggron [57]	304 Aron [46]	411 Bastiodon [58]	437 Bronzong [58]	436 Bronzor [49]	205 Forretress [1, 70]	076 Golem [1, 60]
		623 Golurk [43]	297 Hariyama [54]	305 Lairon [51]	066 Machop [E]	296 Makuhita [46]	095 Onix [E]	231 Phanpy [E]
		486 Regigigas [1, 90]	524 Roggenrola [E]	410 Shieldon [46]	143 Snorlax [50]	498 Tepig [E]	320 Wailmer [53]	321 Wailord [1, 65]
Normal	Helping Hand	594 Alomomola [49, BP]	059 Arcanine [BP]	683 Aromatisse [BP]	531 Audino [1, BP]	482 Azelf [BP]	184 Azumarill [16, BP]	298 Azurill [16, BP]
		689 Barbaracle [BP]	688 Binacle [BP, E]	257 Blaziken [BP]	242 Blissey [BP]	438 Bonsly [BP]	286 Breloom [BP]	427 Buneary [BP]
		251 Celebi [BP]	113 Chansey [BP, E]	421 Cherrim [13, BP]	420 Cherubi [13, BP]	652 Chesnaught [BP]	650 Chespin [BP]	390 Chimchar [BP, E]
		358 Chimecho [BP]	433 Chingling [BP]	573 Cinccino [1, BP]	692 Clauncher [BP, E]	693 Clawitzer [BP]	036 Clefable [BP]	035 Clefairy [BP]
		173 Cleffa [BP]	638 Cobalion [25, BP]	256 Combusken [BP]	534 Conkeldurr [BP]	546 Cottonee [31, BP]	488 Cresselia [BP]	453 Croagunk [BP]
		702 Dedenne [BP, E]	301 Delcatty [BP]	502 Dewott [BP]	719 Diancie [BP]	578 Duosion [BP]	133 Eevee [1, BP]	125 Electabuzz [BP]
		466 Electivire [BP]	239 Elekid [BP]	500 Emboar [BP]	587 Emolga [BP]	196 Espeon [1, BP]	677 Espurr [BP]	083 Farfetch'd [BP]
		669 Flabébé [BP]	136 Flareon [1, BP]	670 Floette [BP]	671 Florges [BP]	676 Furfrou [BP]	162 Furret [17, BP]	475 Gallade [35, BP]
		282 Gardevoir [BP]	471 Glaceon [1, BP]	574 Gothita [BP]	576 Gothitelle [BP]	575 Gothorita [BP]	058 Growlithe [12, BP]	533 Gurdurr [BP]
		440 Happiny [BP, E]	297 Hariyama [BP]	701 Hawlucha [BP]	214 Heracross [BP]	507 Herdier [12, BP]	107 Hitmonchan [BP]	106 Hitmonlee [BP]
		237 Hitmontop [BP]	187 Hoppip [BP, E]	174 Igglybuff [BP]	314 Illumise [36, BP]	392 Infernape [BP]	039 Jigglypuff [BP]	385 Jirachi [15, BP]
		135 Jolteon [1, BP]	189 Jumpluff [BP]	124 Jynx [BP]	115 Kangaskhan [BP]	647 Keldeo [25, BP]	281 Kirlia [BP]	380 Latias [1, BP]
		381 Latios [1, BP]	470 Leafeon [1, BP]	542 Leavanny [32, BP]	549 Lilligant [BP]	506 Lillipup [12, BP]	264 Linoone [BP]	667 Litleo [BP]
		428 Lopunny [BP]	448 Lucario [BP]	337 Lunatone [BP]	404 Luxio [BP]	405 Luxray [BP]	068 Machamp [BP]	067 Machoke [BP]
		066 Machop [BP]	240 Magby [BP]	126 Magmar [BP]	467 Magmortar [BP]	296 Makuhita [BP, E]	490 Manaphy [BP]	056 Mankey [BP]
		226 Mantine [BP]	458 Mantyke [BP]	556 Maractus [BP]	183 Marill [16, BP]	308 Medicham [BP]	307 Meditite [BP]	648 Meloetta [BP]
		678 Meowstic (M) [1, BP]	481 Mesprit [BP]	151 Mew [BP]	619 Mienfoo [BP]	620 Mienshao [BP]	241 Miltank [BP, E]	439 Mime Jr. [BP]
		572 Minccino [7, BP]	312 Minun [4, BP]	391 Monferno [BP]	122 Mr. Mime [BP]	517 Munna [BP, E]	518 Musharna [BP]	034 Nidoking [BP]
		031 Nidoqueen [BP]	029 Nidoran ♀ [25, BP]	032 Nidoran ♂ [25, BP]	030 Nidorina [28, BP]	033 Nidorino [28, BP]	501 Oshawott [BP]	417 Pachirisu [BP]
		674 Pancham [BP]	675 Pangoro [BP]	515 Panpour [BP]	511 Pansage [BP]	513 Pansear [BP]	504 Patrat [BP]	548 Petilil [31, BP]
		489 Phione [BP]	172 Pichu [BP]	499 Pignite [BP]	025 Pikachu [BP]	311 Plusle [4, BP]	186 Politoed [BP]	060 Poliwag [BP]
		061 Poliwhirl [BP]	062 Poliwrath [BP]	057 Primeape [BP]	668 Pyroar [BP]	651 Quilladin [BP]	026 Raichu [BP]	280 Ralts [BP]
		579 Reuniclus [BP]	447 Riolu [BP]	503 Samurott [BP]	539 Sawk [BP]	161 Sentret [16, BP]	403 Shinx [BP, E]	285 Shroomish [BP, E]
		213 Shuckle [BP, E]	516 Simipour [BP]	512 Simisage [BP]	514 Simisear [BP]	188 Skiploom [BP]	300 Skitty [BP, E]	685 Slurpuff [BP]
		238 Smoochum [BP]	577 Solosis [BP, E]	338 Solrock [BP]	327 Spinda [BP]	682 Spritzee [BP]	508 Stoutland [12, BP]	185 Sudowoodo [BP]
		192 Sunflora [BP]	191 Sunkern [BP, E]	684 Swirlix [BP]	528 Swoobat [BP]	700 Sylveon [1, BP]	128 Tauros [BP]	498 Tepig [BP]
		639 Terrakion [25, BP]	538 Throh [BP]	532 Timburr [BP]	255 Torchic [BP]	454 Toxicroak [BP]	236 Tyrogue [1, BP, E]	197 Umbreon [1, BP]
		480 Uxie [BP]	134 Vaporeon [1, BP]	494 Victini [BP]	640 Virizion [25, BP]	313 Volbeat [36, BP]	505 Watchog [BP]	547 Whimsicott [BP]
		040 Wigglytuff [BP]	527 Woobat [BP, E]	263 Zigzagoon [BP, E]				
Ghost	Hex	359 Absol [E]	354 Banette [22]	351 Castform [E]	609 Chandelure [1]	563 Cofagrigus [17]	426 Drifblim [27]	425 Drifloon [27]
		206 Dunsparce [E]	356 Dusclops [40]	477 Dusknoir [40]	355 Duskull [38]	592 Frillish [43]	092 Gastly [43]	094 Gengar [55]
		487 Giratina (Alt) [50]	487 Giratina (Ori) [50]	093 Haunter [55]	593 Jellicent [45]	608 Lampent [28]	607 Litwick [28]	200 Misdreavus [23]
		479 Rotom (Fan) [50]	479 Rotom (Frost) [50]	479 Rotom (Heat) [50]	479 Rotom (Mow) [50]	479 Rotom (Wash) [50]	479 Rotom [50]	353 Shuppet [22]
		361 Snorunt [E]	072 Tentacool [40]	073 Tentacruel [44]	037 Vulpix [26, E]	562 Yamask [17]		
Normal	Hidden Power (TM10)	460 Abomasnow [TM]	063 Abra [TM]	359 Absol [TM]	617 Accelgor [TM]	681 Aegislash [TM]	142 Aerodactyl [TM]	306 Aggron [TM]
		190 Aipom [TM]	065 Alakazam [TM]	594 Alomomola [TM]	334 Altaria [TM]	698 Amaura [TM]	424 Ambipom [TM]	591 Amoonguss [TM]
		181 Ampharos [TM]	347 Anorith [TM]	024 Arbok [TM]	059 Arcanine [TM]	493 Arceus [TM]	566 Archen [TM]	567 Archeops [TM]
		168 Ariados [TM]	348 Armaldo [TM]	683 Aromatisse [TM]	304 Aron [TM]	144 Articuno [TM]	531 Audino [TM]	699 Aurorus [TM]
		713 Avalugg [TM]	610 Axew [TM]	482 Azelf [TM]	184 Azumarill [TM]	298 Azurill [TM]	371 Bagon [TM]	343 Baltoy [TM]

	Move	Pokémon that can learn it						
Normal	Hidden Power (TM10)	354 Banette [TM]	689 Barbaracle [TM]	339 Barboach [TM]	550 Basculin [TM]	411 Bastiodon [TM]	153 Bayleef [TM]	614 Beartic [TM]
		267 Beautifly [TM]	015 Beedrill [TM]	606 Beheeyem [22, TM]	182 Bellossom [TM]	069 Bellsprout [TM]	712 Bergmite [TM]	400 Bibarel [TM]
		399 Bidoof [TM]	688 Binacle [TM]	625 Bisharp [TM]	009 Blastoise [TM]	257 Blaziken [TM]	242 Blissey [TM]	522 Blitzle [TM]
		525 Boldore [TM]	438 Bonsly [TM]	626 Bouffalant [TM]	654 Braixen [TM]	628 Braviary [TM]	286 Breloom [TM]	437 Bronzong [TM]
		436 Bronzor [TM]	406 Budew [TM]	418 Buizel [TM]	001 Bulbasaur [TM]	427 Buneary [TM]	659 Bunnelby [TM]	412 Burmy [20, TM]
		012 Butterfree [TM]	331 Cacnea [TM]	332 Cacturne [TM]	323 Camerupt [TM]	703 Carbink [TM]	455 Carnivine [TM]	565 Carracosta [TM]
		318 Carvanha [TM]	351 Castform [TM]	251 Celebi [TM]	609 Chandelure [TM]	113 Chansey [TM]	006 Charizard [TM]	004 Charmander [TM]
		005 Charmeleon [TM]	441 Chatot [TM]	421 Cherrim [TM]	420 Cherubi [TM]	652 Chesnaught [TM]	650 Chespin [TM]	152 Chikorita [TM]
		390 Chimchar [TM]	358 Chimecho [TM]	170 Chinchou [TM]	433 Chingling [TM]	573 Cinccino [TM]	366 Clamperl [TM]	692 Clauncher [TM]
		693 Clawitzer [TM]	344 Claydol [TM]	036 Clefable [TM]	035 Clefairy [TM]	173 Cleffa [TM]	091 Cloyster [TM]	638 Cobalion [TM]
		563 Cofagrigus [TM]	256 Combusken [TM]	534 Conkeldurr [TM]	341 Corphish [TM]	222 Corsola [TM]	546 Cottonee [TM]	346 Cradily [TM]
		408 Cranidos [TM]	342 Crawdaunt [TM]	488 Cresselia [TM]	453 Croagunk [TM]	169 Crobat [TM]	159 Croconaw [TM]	558 Crustle [TM]
		615 Cryogonal [TM]	613 Cubchoo [TM]	104 Cubone [TM]	155 Cyndaquil [TM]	491 Darkrai [TM]	555 Darmanitan [TM]	554 Darumaka [TM]
		702 Dedenne [TM]	585 Deerling [TM]	633 Deino [TM]	301 Delcatty [TM]	225 Delibird [TM]	655 Delphox [TM]	386 Deoxys (Atk) [TM]
		386 Deoxys (Def) [TM]	386 Deoxys (Nor) [TM]	386 Deoxys (Spd) [TM]	087 Dewgong [TM]	502 Dewott [TM]	483 Dialga [TM]	719 Diancie [TM]
		660 Diggersby [TM]	050 Diglett [TM]	085 Dodrio [TM]	084 Doduo [TM]	232 Donphan [TM]	680 Doublade [TM]	691 Dragalge [TM]
		148 Dragonair [TM]	149 Dragonite [TM]	452 Drapion [TM]	147 Dratini [TM]	426 Drifblim [TM]	425 Drifloon [TM]	529 Drilbur [TM]
		096 Drowzee [TM]	621 Druddigon [TM]	580 Ducklett [TM]	051 Dugtrio [TM]	206 Dunsparce [TM]	578 Duosion [14, TM]	632 Durant [TM]
		356 Dusclops [TM]	477 Dusknoir [TM]	355 Duskull [TM]	269 Dustox [TM]	557 Dwebble [TM]	603 Eelektrik [TM]	604 Eelektross [TM]
		133 Eevee [TM]	023 Ekans [TM]	125 Electabuzz [TM]	466 Electivire [TM]	309 Electrike [TM]	101 Electrode [TM]	239 Elekid [TM]
		605 Elgyem [22, TM]	500 Emboar [TM]	587 Emolga [TM]	395 Empoleon [TM]	244 Entei [TM]	589 Escavalier [TM]	196 Espeon [TM]
		677 Espurr [TM]	530 Excadrill [TM]	102 Exeggcute [TM]	103 Exeggutor [TM]	295 Exploud [TM]	083 Farfetch'd [TM]	022 Fearow [TM]
		349 Feebas [TM]	653 Fennekin [TM]	160 Feraligatr [TM]	597 Ferroseed [TM]	598 Ferrothorn [TM]	456 Finneon [TM]	180 Flaaffy [TM]
		669 Flabébé [TM]	136 Flareon [TM]	662 Fletchinder [TM]	661 Fletchling [TM]	419 Floatzel [TM]	670 Floette [TM]	671 Florges [TM]
		330 Flygon [TM]	590 Foongus [TM]	205 Forretress [TM]	611 Fraxure [TM]	592 Frillish [TM]	656 Froakie [TM]	657 Frogadier [TM]
		478 Froslass [TM]	676 Furfrou [TM]	162 Furret [TM]	444 Gabite [TM]	475 Gallade [TM]	596 Galvantula [TM]	569 Garbodor [TM]
		445 Garchomp [TM]	282 Gardevoir [TM]	092 Gastly [TM]	423 Gastrodon [16, TM]	649 Genesect [TM]	094 Gengar [TM]	074 Geodude [TM]
		443 Gible [TM]	526 Gigalith [TM]	203 Girafarig [TM]	487 Giratina (Alt) [TM]	487 Giratina (Ori) [TM]	471 Glaceon [TM]	362 Glalie [TM]
		431 Glameow [TM]	207 Gligar [TM]	472 Gliscor [TM]	044 Gloom [TM]	673 Gogoat [TM]	042 Golbat [TM]	118 Goldeen [TM]
		055 Golduck [TM]	076 Golem [TM]	622 Golett [TM]	623 Golurk [TM]	706 Goodra [TM]	704 Goomy [TM]	368 Gorebyss [TM]
		574 Gothita [TM]	576 Gothitelle [TM]	575 Gothorita [TM]	711 Gourgeist [TM]	210 Granbull [TM]	075 Graveler [TM]	658 Greninja [TM]
		088 Grimer [TM]	388 Grotle [TM]	383 Groudon [TM]	253 Grovyle [TM]	058 Growlithe [TM]	326 Grumpig [TM]	316 Gulpin [TM]
		533 Gurdurr [TM]	130 Gyarados [TM]	440 Happiny [TM]	297 Hariyama [TM]	093 Haunter [TM]	701 Hawlucha [TM]	612 Haxorus [TM]
		631 Heatmor [TM]	485 Heatran [TM]	695 Heliolisk [TM]	694 Helioptile [TM]	214 Heracross [TM]	507 Herdier [TM]	449 Hippopotas [TM]
		450 Hippowdon [TM]	107 Hitmonchan [TM]	106 Hitmonlee [TM]	237 Hitmontop [TM]	430 Honchkrow [TM]	679 Honedge [TM]	250 Ho-Oh [TM]
		163 Hoothoot [TM]	187 Hoppip [TM]	116 Horsea [TM]	229 Houndoom [TM]	228 Houndour [TM]	367 Huntail [TM]	635 Hydreigon [TM]
		097 Hypno [TM]	174 Igglybuff [TM]	314 Illumise [TM]	392 Infernape [TM]	686 Inkay [TM]	002 Ivysaur [TM]	593 Jellicent [TM]
		039 Jigglypuff [TM]	385 Jirachi [TM]	135 Jolteon [TM]	595 Joltik [TM]	189 Jumpluff [TM]	124 Jynx [TM]	140 Kabuto [TM]
		141 Kabutops [TM]	064 Kadabra [TM]	115 Kangaskhan [TM]	588 Karrablast [TM]	352 Kecleon [TM]	647 Keldeo [TM]	230 Kingdra [TM]
		099 Kingler [TM]	281 Kirlia [TM]	600 Klang [TM]	707 Klefki [TM]	599 Klink [TM]	601 Klinklang [TM]	109 Koffing [TM]
		098 Krabby [TM]	402 Kricketune [TM]	552 Krokorok [TM]	553 Krookodile [TM]	382 Kyogre [TM]	646 Kyurem (Blk) [TM]	646 Kyurem (Wht) [TM]
		646 Kyurem [TM]	305 Lairon [TM]	608 Lampent [TM]	645 Landorus [TM]	171 Lanturn [TM]	131 Lapras [TM]	636 Larvesta [TM]
		246 Larvitar [TM]	380 Latias [TM]	381 Latios [TM]	470 Leafeon [TM]	542 Leavanny [TM]	166 Ledian [TM]	165 Ledyba [TM]
		463 Lickilicky [TM]	108 Lickitung [TM]	510 Liepard [TM]	345 Lileep [TM]	549 Lilligant [TM]	506 Lillipup [TM]	264 Linoone [TM]
		667 Litleo [TM]	607 Litwick [TM]	271 Lombre [TM]	428 Lopunny [TM]	270 Lotad [TM]	294 Loudred [TM]	448 Lucario [TM]
		272 Ludicolo [TM]	249 Lugia [TM]	457 Lumineon [TM]	337 Lunatone [TM]	370 Luvdisc [TM]	404 Luxio [TM]	405 Luxray [TM]
		068 Machamp [TM]	067 Machoke [TM]	066 Machop [TM]	240 Magby [TM]	219 Magcargo [TM]	126 Magmar [TM]	467 Magmortar [TM]
		081 Magnemite [TM]	082 Magneton [TM]	462 Magnezone [TM]	296 Makuhita [TM]	687 Malamar [TM]	473 Mamoswine [TM]	490 Manaphy [TM]
		630 Mandibuzz [TM]	310 Manectric [TM]	056 Mankey [TM]	226 Mantine [TM]	458 Mantyke [TM]	556 Maractus [TM]	179 Mareep [TM]
		183 Marill [TM]	105 Marowak [TM]	259 Marshtomp [TM]	284 Masquerain [TM]	303 Mawile [TM]	308 Medicham [20, TM]	307 Meditite [20, TM]
		154 Meganium [TM]	648 Meloetta [TM]	678 Meowstic (F) [TM]	678 Meowstic (M) [TM]	052 Meowth [TM]	481 Mesprit [TM]	376 Metagross [TM]
		375 Metang [TM]	151 Mew [TM]	150 Mewtwo [TM]	619 Mienfoo [TM]	620 Mienshao [TM]	262 Mightyena [TM]	350 Milotic [TM]
		241 Miltank [TM]	439 Mime Jr. [TM]	572 Minccino [TM]	312 Minun [TM]	200 Misdreavus [TM]	429 Mismagius [TM]	146 Moltres [TM]
		391 Monferno [TM]	414 Mothim [20, TM]	122 Mr. Mime [TM]	258 Mudkip [TM]	089 Muk [TM]	446 Munchlax [TM]	517 Munna [TM]
		198 Murkrow [TM]	518 Musharna [TM]	177 Natu [TM]	034 Nidoking [TM]	031 Nidoqueen [TM]	029 Nidoran ♀ [TM]	032 Nidoran ♂ [TM]
		030 Nidorina [TM]	033 Nidorino [TM]	290 Nincada [TM]	038 Ninetales [TM]	291 Ninjask [TM]	164 Noctowl [TM]	714 Noibat [TM]
		715 Noivern [TM]	299 Nosepass [TM]	322 Numel [TM]	274 Nuzleaf [TM]	224 Octillery [TM]	043 Oddish [TM]	138 Omanyte [TM]
		139 Omastar [TM]	095 Onix [TM]	501 Oshawott [TM]	417 Pachirisu [TM]	484 Palkia [TM]	536 Palpitoad [TM]	674 Pancham [TM]
		675 Pangoro [TM]	515 Panpour [TM]	511 Pansage [TM]	513 Pansear [TM]	046 Paras [TM]	047 Parasect [TM]	504 Patrat [TM]
		624 Pawniard [TM]	279 Pelipper [TM]	053 Persian [TM]	548 Petilil [TM]	231 Phanpy [TM]	708 Phantump [TM]	489 Phione [TM]
		172 Pichu [TM]	018 Pidgeot [TM]	017 Pidgeotto [TM]	016 Pidgey [TM]	519 Pidove [TM]	499 Pignite [TM]	025 Pikachu [TM]
		221 Piloswine [TM]	204 Pineco [TM]	127 Pinsir [TM]	393 Piplup [TM]	311 Plusle [TM]	186 Politoed [TM]	060 Poliwag [TM]
		061 Poliwhirl [TM]	062 Poliwrath [TM]	077 Ponyta [TM]	261 Poochyena [TM]	137 Porygon [TM]	233 Porygon2 [TM]	474 Porygon-Z [TM]
		057 Primeape [TM]	394 Prinplup [TM]	476 Probopass [TM]	054 Psyduck [TM]	710 Pumpkaboo [TM]	247 Pupitar [TM]	509 Purrloin [TM]
		432 Purugly [TM]	668 Pyroar [TM]	195 Quagsire [TM]	156 Quilava [TM]	651 Quilladin [TM]	211 Qwilfish [TM]	026 Raichu [TM]

Type	Move	Pokémon that can learn it						
Normal	Hidden Power (TM10)	243 Raikou [TM]	280 Ralts [TM]	409 Rampardos [TM]	078 Rapidash [TM]	020 Raticate [TM]	019 Rattata [TM]	384 Rayquaza [TM]
		378 Regice [TM]	486 Regigigas [TM]	377 Regirock [TM]	379 Registeel [TM]	369 Relicanth [TM]	223 Remoraid [TM]	643 Reshiram [TM]
		579 Reuniclus [14, TM]	112 Rhydon [TM]	111 Rhyhorn [TM]	464 Rhyperior [TM]	447 Riolu [TM]	524 Roggenrola [TM]	315 Roselia [TM]
		407 Roserade [TM]	479 Rotom (Fan) [TM]	479 Rotom (Frost) [TM]	479 Rotom (Heat) [TM]	479 Rotom (Mow) [TM]	479 Rotom (Wash) [TM]	479 Rotom [TM]
		627 Rufflet [TM]	302 Sableye [TM]	373 Salamence [TM]	503 Samurott [TM]	551 Sandile [TM]	027 Sandshrew [TM]	028 Sandslash [TM]
		539 Sawk [TM]	586 Sawsbuck [TM]	254 Sceptile [TM]	212 Scizor [TM]	545 Scolipede [TM]	560 Scrafty [TM]	559 Scraggy [TM]
		123 Scyther [TM]	117 Seadra [TM]	119 Seaking [TM]	364 Sealeo [TM]	273 Seedot [TM]	086 Seel [TM]	537 Seismitoad [TM]
		161 Sentret [TM]	497 Serperior [TM]	496 Servine [TM]	336 Seviper [TM]	540 Sewaddle [TM]	319 Sharpedo [TM]	492 Shaymin (Land) [TM]
		492 Shaymin (Sky) [TM]	292 Shedinja [TM]	372 Shelgon [TM]	090 Shellder [TM]	422 Shellos [16, TM]	616 Shelmet [TM]	410 Shieldon [TM]
		275 Shiftry [TM]	403 Shinx [TM]	285 Shroomish [TM]	213 Shuckle [TM]	353 Shuppet [TM]	561 Sigilyph [TM]	516 Simipour [TM]
		512 Simisage [TM]	514 Simisear [TM]	227 Skarmory [TM]	672 Skiddo [TM]	188 Skiploom [TM]	300 Skitty [TM]	451 Skorupi [TM]
		690 Skrelp [TM]	435 Skuntank [TM]	289 Slaking [TM]	287 Slakoth [TM]	705 Sliggoo [TM]	080 Slowbro [TM]	199 Slowking [1, TM]
		079 Slowpoke [TM]	218 Slugma [TM]	685 Slurpuff [TM]	238 Smoochum [TM]	215 Sneasel [TM]	495 Snivy [TM]	143 Snorlax [TM]
		361 Snorunt [TM]	459 Snover [TM]	209 Snubbull [TM]	577 Solosis [14, TM]	338 Solrock [TM]	021 Spearow [TM]	363 Spheal [TM]
		167 Spinarak [TM]	327 Spinda [TM]	442 Spiritomb [TM]	325 Spoink [TM]	682 Spritzee [TM]	007 Squirtle [TM]	234 Stantler [TM]
		398 Staraptor [TM]	397 Staravia [TM]	396 Starly [TM]	121 Starmie [TM]	120 Staryu [TM]	208 Steelix [TM]	508 Stoutland [TM]
		618 Stunfisk [TM]	434 Stunky [TM]	185 Sudowoodo [TM]	245 Suicune [TM]	192 Sunflora [TM]	191 Sunkern [TM]	283 Surskit [TM]
		333 Swablu [TM]	541 Swadloon [TM]	317 Swalot [TM]	260 Swampert [TM]	581 Swanna [TM]	277 Swellow [TM]	220 Swinub [TM]
		684 Swirlix [TM]	528 Swoobat [TM]	700 Sylveon [TM]	276 Taillow [TM]	663 Talonflame [TM]	114 Tangela [TM]	465 Tangrowth [TM]
		128 Tauros [TM]	216 Teddiursa [TM]	072 Tentacool [TM]	073 Tentacruel [TM]	498 Tepig [TM]	639 Terrakion [TM]	538 Throh [TM]
		642 Thundurus [TM]	532 Timburr [TM]	564 Tirtouga [TM]	468 Togekiss [TM]	175 Togepi [TM]	176 Togetic [TM]	255 Torchic [TM]
		324 Torkoal [TM]	641 Tornadus [TM]	389 Torterra [TM]	158 Totodile [TM]	454 Toxicroak [TM]	520 Tranquill [TM]	328 Trapinch [TM]
		252 Treecko [TM]	709 Trevenant [TM]	357 Tropius [TM]	568 Trubbish [TM]	387 Turtwig [TM]	535 Tympole [TM]	157 Typhlosion [TM]
		248 Tyranitar [TM]	697 Tyrantrum [TM]	236 Tyrogue [TM]	696 Tyrunt [TM]	197 Umbreon [TM]	521 Unfezant [TM]	201 Unown [1, TM]
		217 Ursaring [TM]	480 Uxie [TM]	583 Vanillish [TM]	582 Vanillite [TM]	584 Vanilluxe [TM]	134 Vaporeon [TM]	543 Venipede [TM]
		049 Venomoth [TM]	048 Venonat [TM]	003 Venusaur [TM]	416 Vespiquen [TM]	329 Vibrava [TM]	494 Victini [TM]	071 Victreebel [TM]
		288 Vigoroth [TM]	045 Vileplume [TM]	640 Virizion [TM]	666 Vivillon [TM]	313 Volbeat [TM]	637 Volcarona [TM]	100 Voltorb [TM]
		629 Vullaby [TM]	037 Vulpix [TM]	320 Wailmer [TM]	321 Wailord [TM]	365 Walrein [TM]	008 Wartortle [TM]	505 Watchog [TM]
		461 Weavile [TM]	070 Weepinbell [TM]	110 Weezing [TM]	547 Whimsicott [TM]	544 Whirlipede [TM]	340 Whiscash [TM]	293 Whismur [TM]
		040 Wigglytuff [TM]	278 Wingull [TM]	527 Woobat [TM]	194 Wooper [TM]	413 Wormadam (Plant) [20, TM]	413 Wormadam (Sand) [20, TM]	413 Wormadam (Trash) [20, TM]
		178 Xatu [TM]	716 Xerneas [TM]	562 Yamask [TM]	193 Yanma [TM]	469 Yanmega [TM]	717 Yveltal [TM]	335 Zangoose [TM]
		145 Zapdos [TM]	523 Zebstrika [TM]	644 Zekrom [TM]	263 Zigzagoon [TM]	571 Zoroark [TM]	570 Zorua [TM]	041 Zubat [TM]
		634 Zweilous [TM]	718 Zygarde [TM]					
Fighting	High Jump Kick	257 Blaziken [1]	701 Hawlucha [44]	106 Hitmonlee [29]	428 Lopunny [66]	308 Medicham [28]	307 Meditite [28]	619 Mienfoo [50]
		620 Mienshao [56]	447 Riolu [E]	560 Scrafty [31]	559 Scraggy [31]	236 Tyrogue [E]		
Dark	Hone Claws (TM01)	359 Absol [TM]	142 Aerodactyl [TM]	306 Aggron [TM]	190 Aipom [TM]	334 Altaria [TM]	424 Ambipom [TM]	347 Anorith [TM]
		493 Arceus [TM]	566 Archen [TM]	567 Archeops [TM]	168 Ariados [TM]	348 Armaldo [TM]	304 Aron [TM]	610 Axew [TM]
		371 Bagon [TM]	689 Barbaracle [32, TM]	614 Beartic [TM]	688 Binacle [32, TM]	625 Bisharp [TM]	257 Blaziken [TM]	628 Braviary [14, TM]
		006 Charizard [TM]	004 Charmander [TM]	005 Charmeleon [TM]	652 Chesnaught [TM]	390 Chimchar [TM]	638 Cobalion [TM]	256 Combusken [TM]
		341 Corphish [TM]	342 Crawdaunt [TM]	159 Croconaw [TM]	558 Crustle [TM]	613 Cubchoo [TM]	483 Dialga [TM]	050 Diglett [TM]
		149 Dragonite [TM]	452 Drapion [30, TM]	529 Drilbur [22, TM]	621 Druddigon [5, TM]	051 Dugtrio [TM]	632 Durant [TM]	557 Dwebble [TM]
		604 Eelektross [TM]	395 Empoleon [TM]	530 Excadrill [22, TM]	160 Feraligatr [TM]	597 Ferroseed [TM]	598 Ferrothorn [TM]	330 Flygon [TM]
		611 Fraxure [TM]	162 Furret [TM]	444 Gabite [TM]	445 Garchomp [TM]	649 Genesect [TM]	443 Gible [TM]	487 Giratina (Alt) [TM]
		487 Giratina (Ori) [TM]	431 Glameow [48, TM]	207 Gligar [TM]	472 Gliscor [TM]	055 Golduck [TM]	383 Groudon [TM]	701 Hawlucha [1, TM]
		612 Haxorus [TM]	631 Heatmor [1, TM]	392 Infernape [TM]	140 Kabuto [TM]	141 Kabutops [TM]	352 Kecleon [TM]	099 Kingler [TM]
		098 Krabby [TM]	402 Kricketune [TM]	552 Krokorok [TM]	553 Krookodile [TM]	646 Kyurem (Blk) [TM]	646 Kyurem (Wht) [TM]	646 Kyurem [TM]
		305 Lairon [TM]	380 Latias [TM]	381 Latios [TM]	542 Leavanny [TM]	510 Liepard [26, TM]	264 Linoone [TM]	271 Lombre [TM]
		448 Lucario [TM]	272 Ludicolo [TM]	056 Mankey [TM]	648 Meloetta [TM]	052 Meowth [TM]	376 Metagross [TM]	375 Metang [TM]
		151 Mew [TM]	391 Monferno [TM]	034 Nidoking [TM]	031 Nidoqueen [TM]	029 Nidoran ♀ [TM]	032 Nidoran ♂ [TM]	030 Nidorina [TM]
		033 Nidorino [TM]	290 Nincada [TM]	291 Ninjask [TM]	715 Noivern [TM]	484 Palkia [TM]	675 Pangoro [TM]	515 Panpour [TM]
		511 Pansage [TM]	513 Pansear [TM]	046 Paras [TM]	047 Parasect [TM]	624 Pawniard [TM]	053 Persian [TM]	057 Primeape [TM]
		394 Prinplup [TM]	054 Psyduck [TM]	509 Purrloin [24, TM]	432 Purugly [60, TM]	651 Quilladin [TM]	384 Rayquaza [TM]	379 Registeel [TM]
		643 Reshiram [TM]	627 Rufflet [14, TM]	302 Sableye [TM]	373 Salamence [TM]	551 Sandile [TM]	027 Sandshrew [TM]	028 Sandslash [TM]
		254 Sceptile [TM]	161 Sentret [TM]	292 Shedinja [TM]	372 Shelgon [TM]	516 Simipour [TM]	512 Simisage [TM]	514 Simisear [TM]
		451 Skorupi [30, TM]	435 Skuntank [TM]	289 Slaking [TM]	287 Slakoth [TM]	215 Sneasel [25, TM]	167 Spinarak [TM]	434 Stunky [TM]
		663 Talonflame [TM]	216 Teddiursa [TM]	255 Torchic [TM]	158 Totodile [TM]	709 Trevenant [TM]	248 Tyranitar [TM]	697 Tyrantrum [TM]
		696 Tyrunt [TM]	217 Ursaring [TM]	416 Vespiquen [TM]	288 Vigoroth [TM]	461 Weavile [25, TM]	717 Yveltal [TM]	335 Zangoose [15, TM]
		644 Zekrom [TM]	263 Zigzagoon [TM]	571 Zoroark [1, 9, TM]	570 Zorua [TM]			
Normal	Horn Attack	626 Bouffalant [16]	232 Donphan [1]	118 Goldeen [8]	214 Heracross [1]	588 Karrablast [E]	032 Nidoran ♂ [21]	033 Nidorino [23]
		112 Rhydon [1]	111 Rhyhorn [1]	464 Rhyperior [1]	119 Seaking [8]	128 Tauros [8]		
Normal	Horn Drill	530 Excadrill [31]	118 Goldeen [37]	131 Lapras [E]	032 Nidoran ♂ [45]	033 Nidorino [58]	077 Ponyta [E]	112 Rhydon [1, 62]
		111 Rhyhorn [53]	464 Rhyperior [1, 62]	119 Seaking [40]	086 Seel [E]	697 Tyrantrum [53]	696 Tyrunt [49]	
Grass	Horn Leech	673 Gogoat [47]	708 Phantump [54]	586 Sawsbuck [37]	672 Skiddo [42]	709 Trevenant [1, 62]	716 Xerneas [55]	

	Move	Pokémon that can learn it						
Normal	Howl	654 Braixen [11]	155 Cyndaquil [E]	655 Delphox [11]	309 Electrike [7]	295 Exploud [1, 11]	653 Fennekin [11]	058 Growlithe [E]
		229 Houndoom [1, 4]	228 Houndour [4]	506 Lillipup [E]	294 Loudred [1, 11]	310 Manectric [1, 7]	262 Mightyena [1, 4]	322 Numel [E]
		261 Poochyena [4]	403 Shinx [E]	037 Vulpix [E]	293 Whismur [11]			
Flying	Hurricane	144 Articuno [1, 92]	351 Castform [45]	149 Dragonite [1, 81]	580 Ducklett [46]	146 Moltres [1, 92]	714 Noibat [58]	715 Noivern [1, 62]
		279 Pelipper [1, 55]	018 Pidgeot [1, 68]	017 Pidgeotto [62]	016 Pidgey [53]	275 Shiftry [32]	581 Swanna [55]	641 Tornadus [1, 67]
		666 Vivillon [50]	637 Volcarona [1, 90]	547 Whimsicott [46]	278 Wingull [43]	717 Yveltal [1]		
Water	Hydro Cannon	009 Blastoise [T]	395 Empoleon [T]	160 Feraligatr [T]	658 Greninja [T]	503 Samurott [T]	260 Swampert [T]	
	Hydro Pump	594 Alomomola [1, 61]	184 Azumarill [55]	371 Bagon [E]	339 Barboach [E]	009 Blastoise [60]	418 Buizel [45]	565 Carracosta [61]
		318 Carvanha [E]	351 Castform [35]	170 Chinchou [45]	091 Cloyster [1]	159 Croconaw [60]	502 Dewott [52]	691 Dragalge [42]
		395 Empoleon [59]	160 Feraligatr [76]	419 Floatzel [57]	592 Frillish [49]	656 Froakie [48]	657 Frogadier [55]	118 Goldeen [E]
		055 Golduck [54]	368 Gorebyss [50]	658 Greninja [60]	130 Gyarados [44]	116 Horsea [52]	367 Huntail [50]	593 Jellicent [53]
		647 Keldeo [67]	230 Kingdra [1, 60]	382 Kyogre [75]	171 Lanturn [51]	131 Lapras [47]	271 Lombre [44]	249 Lugia [37]
		370 Luvdisc [50]	226 Mantine [49, E]	458 Mantyke [49, E]	183 Marill [47]	350 Milotic [47]	258 Mudkip [41]	224 Octillery [52]
		138 Omanyte [55]	139 Omastar [1, 75]	501 Oshawott [43]	484 Palkia [50]	536 Palpitoad [47]	515 Panpour [E]	279 Pelipper [1, 50]
		393 Piplup [43, E]	060 Poliwag [38]	061 Poliwhirl [48]	394 Prinplup [50]	054 Psyduck [46]	211 Qwilfish [1, 57]	369 Relicanth [46]
		223 Remoraid [42]	479 Rotom (Wash) ◆	503 Samurott [62]	117 Seadra [1, 60]	537 Seismitoad [53]	090 Shellder [61]	690 Skrelp [42]
		007 Squirtle [40]	121 Starmie [1]	120 Staryu [53]	245 Suicune [1, 71]	283 Surskit [E]	072 Tentacool [46]	073 Tentacruel [52]
		564 Tirtouga [50]	158 Totodile [50, E]	535 Tympole [42]	134 Vaporeon [45]	320 Wailmer [49]	321 Wailord [58]	008 Wartortle [48]
Normal	Hyper Beam (TM15)	460 Abomasnow [TM]	359 Absol [TM]	617 Accelgor [TM]	681 Aegislash [TM]	142 Aerodactyl [65, TM]	306 Aggron [TM]	065 Alakazam [TM]
		334 Altaria [TM]	698 Amaura [57, TM]	424 Ambipom [TM]	591 Amoonguss [TM]	181 Ampharos [TM]	024 Arbok [TM]	059 Arcanine [TM]
		493 Arceus [80, TM]	567 Archeops [TM]	168 Ariados [TM]	348 Armaldo [TM]	683 Aromatisse [TM]	144 Articuno [TM]	531 Audino [TM]
		699 Aurorus [63, TM]	713 Avalugg [TM]	482 Azelf [TM]	184 Azumarill [TM]	354 Banette [TM]	689 Barbaracle [TM]	411 Bastiodon [TM]
		614 Beartic [TM]	267 Beautifly [TM]	015 Beedrill [TM]	606 Beheeyem [TM]	182 Bellossom [TM]	400 Bibarel [TM]	625 Bisharp [TM]
		009 Blastoise [TM]	257 Blaziken [TM]	242 Blissey [TM]	628 Braviary [TM]	286 Breloom [TM]	437 Bronzong [TM]	012 Butterfree [TM]
		332 Cacturne [TM]	323 Camerupt [TM]	455 Carnivine [TM]	565 Carracosta [TM]	251 Celebi [TM]	609 Chandelure [TM]	113 Chansey [TM]
		006 Charizard [TM]	421 Cherrim [TM]	652 Chesnaught [TM]	573 Cinccino [TM]	693 Clawitzer [TM]	344 Claydol [36, TM]	036 Clefable [TM]
		091 Cloyster [TM]	638 Cobalion [TM]	563 Cofagrigus [TM]	534 Conkeldurr [TM]	346 Cradily [TM]	342 Crawdaunt [TM]	488 Cresselia [TM]
		169 Crobat [TM]	558 Crustle [TM]	615 Cryogonal [TM]	491 Darkrai [TM]	555 Darmanitan [TM]	301 Delcatty [TM]	655 Delphox [TM]
		386 Deoxys (Atk) [73, TM]	386 Deoxys (Def) [TM]	386 Deoxys (Nor) [73, TM]	386 Deoxys (Spd) [TM]	087 Dewgong [TM]	483 Dialga [TM]	719 Diancie [TM]
		660 Diggersby [TM]	085 Dodrio [TM]	232 Donphan [TM]	691 Dragalge [TM]	148 Dragonair [75, TM]	149 Dragonite [75, TM]	452 Drapion [TM]
		147 Dratini [61, TM]	426 Drifblim [TM]	621 Druddigon [TM]	051 Dugtrio [TM]	356 Dusclops [TM]	477 Dusknoir [TM]	269 Dustox [TM]
		604 Eelektross [TM]	125 Electabuzz [TM]	466 Electivire [TM]	101 Electrode [TM]	500 Emboar [TM]	395 Empoleon [TM]	244 Entei [TM]
		589 Escavalier [TM]	196 Espeon [TM]	530 Excadrill [TM]	103 Exeggutor [TM]	295 Exploud [64, TM]	022 Fearow [TM]	160 Feraligatr [TM]
		598 Ferrothorn [TM]	136 Flareon [TM]	419 Floatzel [TM]	671 Florges [TM]	330 Flygon [43, TM]	205 Forretress [TM]	478 Froslass [TM]
		162 Furret [TM]	475 Gallade [TM]	596 Galvantula [TM]	569 Garbodor [TM]	445 Garchomp [TM]	282 Gardevoir [TM]	423 Gastrodon [TM]
		649 Genesect [73, TM]	094 Gengar [TM]	526 Gigalith [TM]	487 Giratina (Alt) [TM]	487 Giratina (Ori) [TM]	471 Glaceon [TM]	362 Glalie [TM]
		472 Gliscor [TM]	673 Gogoat [TM]	042 Golbat [TM]	055 Golduck [TM]	076 Golem [TM]	623 Golurk [TM]	706 Goodra [TM]
		368 Gorebyss [TM]	576 Gothitelle [TM]	711 Gourgeist [TM]	210 Granbull [TM]	658 Greninja [TM]	383 Groudon [TM]	326 Grumpig [TM]
		130 Gyarados [50, TM]	297 Hariyama [TM]	612 Haxorus [TM]	485 Heatran [TM]	695 Heliolisk [TM]	214 Heracross [TM]	450 Hippowdon [TM]
		430 Honchkrow [TM]	250 Ho-Oh [TM]	229 Houndoom [TM]	367 Huntail [TM]	635 Hydreigon [TM]	097 Hypno [TM]	392 Infernape [TM]
		593 Jellicent [TM]	385 Jirachi [TM]	135 Jolteon [TM]	189 Jumpluff [TM]	124 Jynx [TM]	141 Kabutops [TM]	115 Kangaskhan [TM]
		647 Keldeo [TM]	230 Kingdra [TM]	099 Kingler [TM]	600 Klang [64, TM]	707 Klefki [TM]	599 Klink [57, TM]	601 Klinklang [72, TM]
		402 Kricketune [TM]	553 Krookodile [TM]	382 Kyogre [TM]	646 Kyurem (Blk) [TM]	646 Kyurem (Wht) [TM]	646 Kyurem [TM]	645 Landorus [TM]
		171 Lanturn [TM]	131 Lapras [TM]	246 Larvitar [55, TM]	380 Latias [TM]	381 Latios [TM]	470 Leafeon [TM]	542 Leavanny [TM]
		166 Ledian [TM]	463 Lickilicky [TM]	108 Lickitung [TM]	510 Liepard [TM]	549 Lilligant [TM]	264 Linoone [TM]	428 Lopunny [TM]
		448 Lucario [TM]	272 Ludicolo [TM]	249 Lugia [TM]	457 Lumineon [TM]	337 Lunatone [TM]	405 Luxray [TM]	068 Machamp [TM]
		219 Magcargo [TM]	126 Magmar [TM]	467 Magmortar [62, TM]	082 Magneton [TM]	462 Magnezone [TM]	687 Malamar [TM]	473 Mamoswine [TM]
		490 Manaphy [TM]	630 Mandibuzz [TM]	310 Manectric [TM]	226 Mantine [TM]	105 Marowak [TM]	284 Masquerain [TM]	303 Mawile [TM]
		308 Medicham [TM]	154 Meganium [TM]	648 Meloetta [TM]	678 Meowstic (F) [TM]	678 Meowstic (M) [TM]	481 Mesprit [TM]	376 Metagross [60, TM]
		375 Metang [50, TM]	151 Mew [TM]	150 Mewtwo [TM]	620 Mienshao [TM]	262 Mightyena [TM]	350 Milotic [TM]	241 Miltank [TM]
		429 Mismagius [TM]	146 Moltres [TM]	414 Mothim [TM]	122 Mr. Mime [TM]	089 Muk [TM]	518 Musharna [TM]	034 Nidoking [TM]
		031 Nidoqueen [TM]	038 Ninetales [TM]	291 Ninjask [TM]	164 Noctowl [TM]	715 Noivern [TM]	274 Nuzleaf [TM]	224 Octillery [58, TM]
		139 Omastar [TM]	484 Palkia [TM]	675 Pangoro [TM]	047 Parasect [TM]	279 Pelipper [TM]	053 Persian [TM]	018 Pidgeot [TM]
		221 Piloswine [TM]	127 Pinsir [TM]	186 Politoed [TM]	062 Poliwrath [TM]	137 Porygon [TM]	233 Porygon2 [67, TM]	474 Porygon-Z [67, TM]
		057 Primeape [TM]	476 Probopass [TM]	247 Pupitar [67, TM]	432 Purugly [TM]	668 Pyroar [1, TM]	195 Quagsire [TM]	026 Raichu [TM]
		243 Raikou [TM]	409 Rampardos [TM]	078 Rapidash [TM]	020 Raticate [TM]	384 Rayquaza [90, TM]	378 Regice [67, TM]	486 Regigigas [TM]
		377 Regirock [67, TM]	379 Registeel [67, TM]	369 Relicanth [TM]	223 Remoraid [46, TM]	643 Reshiram [TM]	579 Reuniclus [TM]	112 Rhydon [TM]
		464 Rhyperior [TM]	407 Roserade [TM]	373 Salamence [TM]	503 Samurott [TM]	028 Sandslash [TM]	586 Sawsbuck [TM]	254 Sceptile [TM]
		212 Scizor [TM]	545 Scolipede [TM]	560 Scrafty [TM]	123 Scyther [TM]	117 Seadra [TM]	119 Seaking [TM]	537 Seismitoad [TM]
		497 Serperior [TM]	319 Sharpedo [TM]	492 Shaymin (Land) [TM]	492 Shaymin (Sky) [TM]	292 Shedinja [TM]	275 Shiftry [TM]	561 Sigilyph [TM]
		516 Simipour [TM]	512 Simisage [TM]	514 Simisear [TM]	435 Skuntank [TM]	289 Slaking [TM]	080 Slowbro [TM]	199 Slowking [TM]
		685 Slurpuff [TM]	143 Snorlax [TM]	338 Solrock [TM]	442 Spiritomb [TM]	398 Staraptor [TM]	121 Starmie [TM]	208 Steelix [TM]
		508 Stoutland [TM]	245 Suicune [TM]	192 Sunflora [TM]	317 Swalot [TM]	260 Swampert [TM]	581 Swanna [TM]	277 Swellow [TM]
		528 Swoobat [TM]	700 Sylveon [TM]	663 Talonflame [TM]	114 Tangela [TM]	465 Tangrowth [TM]	128 Tauros [TM]	073 Tentacruel [TM]

◆ When Rotom becomes Wash Rotom, it learns the move Hydro Pump. When it changes back to Rotom, it forgets the move.

Type	Move	Pokémon that can learn it						
Normal	Hyper Beam (TM15)	639 Terrakion [TM]	642 Thundurus [TM]	468 Togekiss [TM]	176 Togetic [TM]	324 Torkoal [TM]	641 Tornadus [TM]	389 Torterra [TM]
		454 Toxicroak [TM]	328 Trapinch [43, TM]	709 Trevenant [TM]	357 Tropius [TM]	157 Typhlosion [TM]	248 Tyranitar [73, TM]	697 Tyrantrum [TM]
		197 Umbreon [TM]	521 Unfezant [TM]	217 Ursaring [TM]	480 Uxie [TM]	584 Vanilluxe [TM]	134 Vaporeon [TM]	049 Venomoth [TM]
		003 Venusaur [TM]	416 Vespiquen [TM]	329 Vibrava [43, TM]	494 Victini [TM]	071 Victreebel [TM]	045 Vileplume [TM]	640 Virizion [TM]
		666 Vivillon [TM]	637 Volcarona [TM]	321 Wailord [TM]	365 Walrein [TM]	505 Watchog [TM]	461 Weavile [TM]	110 Weezing [TM]
		547 Whimsicott [TM]	340 Whiscash [TM]	040 Wigglytuff [TM]	413 Wormadam (Plant) [TM]	413 Wormadam (Sand) [TM]	413 Wormadam (Trash) [TM]	178 Xatu [TM]
		716 Xerneas [TM]	469 Yanmega [TM]	717 Yveltal [88, TM]	145 Zapdos [TM]	523 Zebstrika [TM]	644 Zekrom [TM]	571 Zoroark [TM]
		718 Zygarde [TM]						
	Hyper Fang	400 Bibarel [23]	399 Bidoof [21]	417 Pachirisu [49]	504 Patrat [28]	020 Raticate [16]	019 Rattata [16]	505 Watchog [32]
	Hyper Voice	334 Altaria [BP]	698 Amaura [BP]	493 Arceus [30, BP]	531 Audino [BP]	699 Aurorus [BP]	184 Azumarill [BP]	298 Azurill [BP]
		371 Bagon [BP]	242 Blissey [BP]	427 Buneary [BP]	113 Chansey [BP]	441 Chatot [1, 57, BP]	358 Chimecho [BP]	433 Chingling [BP]
		573 Cinccino [BP]	036 Clefable [BP]	035 Clefairy [BP]	173 Cleffa [BP]	633 Deino [58, BP]	301 Delcatty [BP]	483 Dialga [BP]
		232 Donphan [BP]	133 Eevee [BP]	196 Espeon [BP]	295 Exploud [47, BP]	136 Flareon [BP]	676 Furfrou [BP]	162 Furret [56, BP]
		475 Gallade [BP]	282 Gardevoir [BP]	203 Girafarig [BP]	487 Giratina (Alt) [BP]	487 Giratina (Ori) [BP]	471 Glaceon [BP]	431 Glameow [BP]
		210 Granbull [BP]	440 Happiny [BP]	695 Heliolisk [BP]	507 Herdier [BP]	250 Ho-Oh [BP]	163 Hoothoot [BP]	229 Houndoom [BP]
		228 Houndour [BP]	635 Hydreigon [1, 68, BP]	174 Igglybuff [BP]	039 Jigglypuff [44, BP]	135 Jolteon [BP]	124 Jynx [BP]	281 Kirlia [BP]
		402 Kricketune [BP]	646 Kyurem (Blk) [92, BP]	646 Kyurem (Wht) [92, BP]	646 Kyurem [92, BP]	131 Lapras [BP]	470 Leafeon [BP]	510 Liepard [BP]
		506 Lillipup [BP]	264 Linoone [BP]	667 Litleo [43, BP]	271 Lombre [BP]	428 Lopunny [BP]	294 Loudred [45, BP]	272 Ludicolo [BP]
		249 Lugia [BP]	556 Maractus [BP]	183 Marill [BP]	648 Meloetta [64, BP]	052 Meowth [BP]	151 Mew [BP]	262 Mightyena [BP]
		572 Minccino [43, BP]	200 Misdreavus [BP]	429 Mismagius [BP]	446 Munchlax [BP]	164 Noctowl [BP]	714 Noibat [BP]	715 Noivern [BP]
		484 Palkia [BP]	536 Palpitoad [51, BP]	674 Pancham [BP]	675 Pangoro [BP]	053 Persian [BP]	231 Phanpy [BP]	186 Politoed [48, BP]
		261 Poochyena [BP]	509 Purrloin [BP]	432 Purugly [BP]	668 Pyroar [48, BP]	280 Ralts [BP]	384 Rayquaza [75, BP]	643 Reshiram [92, BP]
		373 Salamence [BP]	537 Seismitoad [59, BP]	161 Sentret [47, BP]	372 Shelgon [BP]	300 Skitty [BP]	143 Snorlax [BP]	209 Snubbull [BP]
		327 Spinda [BP]	508 Stoutland [BP]	333 Swablu [BP, E]	700 Sylveon [BP]	216 Teddiursa [BP]	468 Togekiss [BP]	175 Togepi [BP]
		176 Togetic [BP]	535 Tympole [45, BP]	697 Tyrantrum [BP]	696 Tyrunt [BP]	197 Umbreon [BP]	217 Ursaring [BP]	134 Vaporeon [BP]
		320 Wailmer [BP]	321 Wailord [BP]	293 Whismur [39, BP]	040 Wigglytuff [BP]	716 Xerneas [BP]	717 Yveltal [BP]	644 Zekrom [92, BP]
		263 Zigzagoon [BP]	571 Zoroark [BP]	570 Zorua [BP]	634 Zweilous [64, BP]	718 Zygarde [BP]		
Psychic	Hypnosis	437 Bronzong [1, 5]	436 Bronzor [5]	358 Chimecho [E]	433 Chingling [E]	491 Darkrai [20]	425 Drifloon [E]	096 Drowzee [1]
		102 Exeggcute [1]	103 Exeggutor [1]	349 Feebas [E]	653 Fennekin [E]	282 Gardevoir [49]	092 Gastly [1]	094 Gengar [1]
		431 Glameow [13]	093 Haunter [1]	163 Hoothoot [5]	097 Hypno [1]	686 Inkay [18]	281 Kirlia [44]	337 Lunatone [5]
		687 Malamar [18]	052 Meowth [E]	439 Mime Jr. [E]	122 Mr. Mime [E]	517 Munna [19]	518 Musharna [1]	164 Noctowl [1, 5]
		504 Patrat [18]	519 Pidove [E]	186 Politoed [1]	060 Poliwag [8]	061 Poliwhirl [1, 8]	062 Poliwrath [1]	077 Ponyta [E]
		054 Psyduck [E]	432 Purugly [13]	280 Ralts [37]	561 Sigilyph [4]	327 Spinda [19]	442 Spiritomb [13]	234 Stantler [10]
		037 Vulpix [E]	505 Watchog [18]	193 Yanma [38]	041 Zubat [E]			

I

Type	Move	Pokémon that can learn it						
Ice	Ice Ball	713 Avalugg [30]	712 Bergmite [30]	225 Delibird [E]	258 Mudkip [E]	060 Poliwag [E]	364 Sealeo [13]	363 Spheal [13]
		365 Walrein [13]						
	Ice Beam (TM13)	460 Abomasnow [TM]	359 Absol [TM]	306 Aggron [TM]	594 Alomomola [TM]	334 Altaria [TM]	698 Amaura [50, TM]	493 Arceus [TM]
		144 Articuno [43, TM]	531 Audino [TM]	699 Aurorus [56, TM]	713 Avalugg [TM]	184 Azumarill [TM]	298 Azurill [TM]	343 Baltoy [TM]
		689 Barbaracle [TM]	339 Barboach [TM]	550 Basculin [TM]	411 Bastiodon [TM]	614 Beartic [TM]	712 Bergmite [TM]	400 Bibarel [TM]
		399 Bidoof [TM]	688 Binacle [TM]	009 Blastoise [TM]	242 Blissey [TM]	418 Buizel [TM]	427 Buneary [TM]	565 Carracosta [TM]
		318 Carvanha [TM]	351 Castform [TM]	113 Chansey [TM]	170 Chinchou [TM]	366 Clamperl [TM]	692 Clauncher [TM]	693 Clawitzer [TM]
		344 Claydol [TM]	036 Clefable [TM]	035 Clefairy [TM]	091 Cloyster [TM]	341 Corphish [TM]	222 Corsola [TM]	408 Cranidos [TM]
		342 Crawdaunt [TM]	488 Cresselia [TM]	159 Croconaw [TM]	615 Cryogonal [33, TM]	613 Cubchoo [TM]	104 Cubone [TM]	491 Darkrai [TM]
		301 Delcatty [TM]	225 Delibird [TM]	386 Deoxys (Atk) [TM]	386 Deoxys (Def) [TM]	386 Deoxys (Nor) [TM]	386 Deoxys (Spd) [TM]	087 Dewgong [55, TM]
		502 Dewott [TM]	483 Dialga [TM]	148 Dragonair [TM]	149 Dragonite [TM]	147 Dratini [TM]	580 Ducklett [TM]	206 Dunsparce [TM]
		356 Dusclops [TM]	477 Dusknoir [TM]	355 Duskull [TM]	395 Empoleon [TM]	295 Exploud [TM]	349 Feebas [TM]	160 Feraligatr [TM]
		456 Finneon [TM]	419 Floatzel [TM]	592 Frillish [TM]	656 Froakie [TM]	657 Frogadier [TM]	478 Froslass [TM]	162 Furret [TM]
		423 Gastrodon [TM]	649 Genesect [TM]	471 Glaceon [TM]	362 Glalie [TM]	118 Goldeen [TM]	055 Golduck [TM]	622 Golett [TM]
		623 Golurk [TM]	706 Goodra [TM]	368 Gorebyss [TM]	658 Greninja [TM]	316 Gulpin [TM]	130 Gyarados [TM]	116 Horsea [TM]
		367 Huntail [TM]	593 Jellicent [TM]	039 Jigglypuff [TM]	124 Jynx [TM]	140 Kabuto [TM]	141 Kabutops [TM]	115 Kangaskhan [TM]
		352 Kecleon [TM]	230 Kingdra [TM]	099 Kingler [TM]	098 Krabby [TM]	382 Kyogre [35, TM]	646 Kyurem (Blk) [22, TM]	646 Kyurem (Wht) [22, TM]
		646 Kyurem [22, TM]	171 Lanturn [TM]	131 Lapras [32, TM]	380 Latias [TM]	381 Latios [TM]	463 Lickilicky [TM]	108 Lickitung [TM]
		264 Linoone [TM]	271 Lombre [TM]	428 Lopunny [TM]	270 Lotad [TM]	294 Loudred [TM]	272 Ludicolo [TM]	249 Lugia [TM]
		457 Lumineon [TM]	337 Lunatone [TM]	370 Luvdisc [TM]	473 Mamoswine [TM]	490 Manaphy [TM]	226 Mantine [TM]	458 Mantyke [TM]
		183 Marill [TM]	105 Marowak [TM]	259 Marshtomp [TM]	284 Masquerain [TM]	303 Mawile [TM]	481 Mesprit [TM]	151 Mew [TM]
		150 Mewtwo [TM]	350 Milotic [TM]	241 Miltank [TM]	258 Mudkip [TM]	446 Munchlax [TM]	034 Nidoking [TM]	031 Nidoqueen [TM]
		029 Nidoran ♀ [TM]	032 Nidoran ♂ [TM]	030 Nidorina [TM]	033 Nidorino [TM]	224 Octillery [40, TM]	138 Omanyte [TM]	139 Omastar [TM]
		501 Oshawott [TM]	484 Palkia [TM]	515 Panpour [TM]	279 Pelipper [TM]	489 Phione [TM]	221 Piloswine [TM]	393 Piplup [TM]
		186 Politoed [TM]	060 Poliwag [TM]	061 Poliwhirl [TM]	062 Poliwrath [TM]	137 Porygon [TM]	233 Porygon2 [TM]	474 Porygon-Z [TM]
		394 Prinplup [TM]	054 Psyduck [TM]	195 Quagsire [TM]	211 Qwilfish [TM]	409 Rampardos [TM]	020 Raticate [TM]	019 Rattata [TM]

Type	Move	Pokémon that can learn it						
Ice	Ice Beam (TM13)	384 Rayquaza [TM]	378 Regice [43, TM]	369 Relicanth [TM]	223 Remoraid [34, TM]	112 Rhydon [TM]	111 Rhyhorn [TM]	464 Rhyperior [TM]
		503 Samurott [TM]	117 Seadra [TM]	119 Seaking [TM]	364 Sealeo [TM]	086 Seel [47, TM]	161 Sentret [TM]	319 Sharpedo [TM]
		090 Shellder [52, TM]	422 Shellos [TM]	410 Shieldon [TM]	561 Sigilyph [TM]	516 Simipour [TM]	300 Skitty [TM]	289 Slaking [TM]
		287 Slakoth [TM]	705 Sliggoo [TM]	080 Slowbro [TM]	199 Slowking [TM]	079 Slowpoke [TM]	238 Smoochum [TM]	215 Sneasel [TM]
		143 Snorlax [TM]	361 Snorunt [TM]	459 Snover [TM]	363 Spheal [TM]	007 Squirtle [TM]	121 Starmie [TM]	120 Staryu [TM]
		245 Suicune [TM]	283 Surskit [TM]	333 Swablu [TM]	317 Swalot [TM]	260 Swampert [TM]	581 Swanna [TM]	220 Swinub [TM]
		128 Tauros [TM]	072 Tentacool [TM]	073 Tentacruel [TM]	564 Tirtouga [TM]	158 Totodile [TM]	248 Tyranitar [TM]	583 Vanillish [36, TM]
		582 Vanillite [35, TM]	584 Vanilluxe [36, TM]	134 Vaporeon [TM]	288 Vigoroth [TM]	320 Wailmer [TM]	321 Wailord [TM]	365 Walrein [TM]
		008 Wartortle [TM]	461 Weavile [TM]	340 Whiscash [TM]	293 Whismur [TM]	040 Wigglytuff [TM]	278 Wingull [TM]	194 Wooper [TM]
		335 Zangoose [TM]	263 Zigzagoon [TM]					
	Ice Burn	646 Kyurem (Wht) [50]						
	Ice Fang	142 Aerodactyl [1]	024 Arbok [1]	713 Avalugg [26]	712 Bergmite [26]	318 Carvanha [25]	159 Croconaw [21]	633 Deino [E]
		452 Drapion [1]	309 Electrike [E]	295 Exploud [1]	160 Feraligatr [21]	419 Floatzel [1]	471 Glaceon [20]	362 Glalie [23]
		472 Gliscor [1]	210 Granbull [1]	130 Gyarados [32]	450 Hippowdon [1]	367 Huntail [16]	506 Lillipup [E]	473 Mamoswine [24]
		303 Mawile [E]	221 Piloswine [24]	261 Poochyena [E]	111 Rhyhorn [E]	319 Sharpedo [25]	403 Shinx [E]	361 Snorunt [23]
		209 Snubbull [1, E]	208 Steelix [1]	508 Stoutland [1]	245 Suicune [50]	158 Totodile [20]	248 Tyranitar [1]	696 Tyrunt [E]
		365 Walrein [44]						
	Ice Punch	460 Abomasnow [1, BP]	063 Abra [BP, E]	306 Aggron [BP]	190 Aipom [BP]	065 Alakazam [BP]	424 Ambipom [BP]	531 Audino [BP]
		482 Azelf [BP]	184 Azumarill [BP]	614 Beartic [BP]	009 Blastoise [BP]	242 Blissey [BP]	418 Buizel [BP]	427 Buneary [BP, E]
		113 Chansey [BP]	036 Clefable [BP]	035 Clefairy [BP]	534 Conkeldurr [BP]	453 Croagunk [BP]	159 Croconaw [BP]	613 Cubchoo [BP, E]
		225 Delibird [BP, E]	386 Deoxys (Nor) [BP]	386 Deoxys (Spd) [BP]	660 Diggersby [BP]	149 Dragonite [BP]	096 Drowzee [BP, E]	356 Dusclops [1, BP]
		477 Dusknoir [1, BP]	125 Electabuzz [BP]	466 Electivire [BP]	239 Elekid [BP, E]	295 Exploud [BP]	160 Feraligatr [BP]	419 Floatzel [BP]
		657 Frogadier [BP]	478 Froslass [BP]	162 Furret [BP]	475 Gallade [BP]	282 Gardevoir [BP]	092 Gastly [BP, E]	094 Gengar [BP]
		055 Golduck [BP]	622 Golett [BP]	623 Golurk [BP]	210 Granbull [BP]	658 Greninja [BP]	088 Grimer [BP]	326 Grumpig [BP]
		316 Gulpin [BP]	533 Gurdurr [BP]	297 Hariyama [BP]	093 Haunter [BP]	107 Hitmonchan [36, BP]	097 Hypno [BP]	314 Illumise [BP]
		039 Jigglypuff [BP]	385 Jirachi [BP]	124 Jynx [18, BP]	064 Kadabra [BP]	115 Kangaskhan [BP]	352 Kecleon [BP]	281 Kirlia [BP]
		166 Ledian [BP]	165 Ledyba [BP]	463 Lickilicky [BP]	108 Lickitung [BP]	271 Lombre [BP]	428 Lopunny [BP]	294 Loudred [BP]
		448 Lucario [BP]	272 Ludicolo [BP]	068 Machamp [BP]	067 Machoke [BP]	066 Machop [BP, E]	296 Makuhita [BP]	056 Mankey [BP]
		183 Marill [BP]	259 Marshtomp [BP]	303 Mawile [BP]	308 Medicham [1, BP]	307 Meditite [BP, E]	648 Meloetta [BP]	481 Mesprit [BP]
		376 Metagross [BP]	375 Metang [BP]	151 Mew [BP]	150 Mewtwo [BP]	241 Miltank [BP]	122 Mr. Mime [BP]	089 Muk [BP]
		446 Munchlax [BP]	034 Nidoking [BP]	031 Nidoqueen [BP]	299 Nosepass [BP]	674 Pancham [BP]	675 Pangoro [BP]	515 Panpour [BP]
		186 Politoed [BP]	061 Poliwhirl [BP]	062 Poliwrath [BP]	057 Primeape [BP]	476 Probopass [BP]	054 Psyduck [BP]	195 Quagsire [BP]
		280 Ralts [BP]	378 Regice [BP]	486 Regigigas [1, BP]	377 Regirock [BP]	379 Registeel [BP]	579 Reuniclus [BP]	112 Rhydon [BP]
		464 Rhyperior [BP]	447 Riolu [BP]	302 Sableye [BP]	539 Sawk [BP]	560 Scrafty [BP]	559 Scraggy [BP, E]	537 Seismitoad [BP]
		161 Sentret [BP]	516 Simipour [BP]	289 Slaking [BP]	287 Slakoth [BP]	080 Slowbro [BP]	199 Slowking [BP]	238 Smoochum [BP, E]
		215 Sneasel [BP, E]	143 Snorlax [BP]	459 Snover [BP]	209 Snubbull [BP]	327 Spinda [BP]	007 Squirtle [BP]	185 Sudowoodo [BP]
		317 Swalot [BP]	260 Swampert [BP]	216 Teddiursa [BP]	538 Throh [BP]	532 Timburr [BP]	158 Totodile [BP, E]	454 Toxicroak [BP]
		248 Tyranitar [BP]	217 Ursaring [BP]	480 Uxie [BP]	288 Vigoroth [BP]	313 Volbeat [BP]	008 Wartortle [BP]	505 Watchog [BP]
		461 Weavile [BP]	293 Whismur [BP]	040 Wigglytuff [BP]	194 Wooper [BP]	335 Zangoose [BP]		
	Ice Shard	460 Abomasnow [26]	144 Articuno [15]	615 Cryogonal [1, 5]	225 Delibird [E]	087 Dewgong [17]	478 Froslass [1, 10]	471 Glaceon [25]
		362 Glalie [1, 10]	131 Lapras [10]	231 Phanpy [E]	086 Seel [17]	090 Shellder [28]	215 Sneasel [47, E]	361 Snorunt [10]
		459 Snover [26]	220 Swinub [24]	582 Vanillite [E]				
	Icicle Crash	614 Beartic [37]	091 Cloyster [50]	025 Pikachu ◆	215 Sneasel [E]	220 Swinub [E]		
	Icicle Spear	222 Corsola [E]	086 Seel [E]	090 Shellder [13, E]	220 Swinub [E]	583 Vanillish [1]	582 Vanillite [1]	584 Vanilluxe [1]
	Icy Wind	460 Abomasnow [1, 9, BP]	359 Absol [BP]	306 Aggron [BP]	594 Alomomola [BP]	698 Amaura [13, BP]	493 Arceus [BP]	144 Articuno [BP]
		531 Audino [BP]	699 Aurorus [13, BP]	713 Avalugg [10, BP]	184 Azumarill [BP]	298 Azurill [BP]	354 Banette [BP]	689 Barbaracle [BP]
		339 Barboach [BP]	550 Basculin [BP]	614 Beartic [1, 13, BP]	712 Bergmite [10, BP]	400 Bibarel [BP]	399 Bidoof [BP]	688 Binacle [BP]
		009 Blastoise [BP]	242 Blissey [BP]	418 Buizel [BP]	565 Carracosta [BP]	318 Carvanha [BP]	351 Castform [BP]	113 Chansey [BP]
		358 Chimecho [BP]	170 Chinchou [BP]	433 Chingling [BP]	366 Clamperl [BP]	692 Clauncher [BP]	693 Clawitzer [BP]	036 Clefable [BP]
		035 Clefairy [BP]	173 Cleffa [BP]	091 Cloyster [BP]	341 Corphish [BP]	222 Corsola [BP]	342 Crawdaunt [BP]	488 Cresselia [BP]
		453 Croagunk [BP]	159 Croconaw [BP]	615 Cryogonal [17, BP]	613 Cubchoo [13, BP]	104 Cubone [BP]	491 Darkrai [BP]	301 Delcatty [BP]
		225 Delibird [BP, E]	386 Deoxys (Nor) [BP]	087 Dewgong [1, 11, BP]	502 Dewott [BP]	691 Dragalge [BP]	148 Dragonair [BP]	149 Dragonite [BP]
		147 Dratini [BP]	426 Drifblim [BP]	425 Drifloon [BP]	580 Ducklett [BP]	356 Dusclops [BP]	477 Dusknoir [BP]	355 Duskull [BP]
		395 Empoleon [BP]	295 Exploud [BP]	349 Feebas [BP]	160 Feraligatr [BP]	456 Finneon [BP]	419 Floatzel [BP]	592 Frillish [BP]
		656 Froakie [BP]	657 Frogadier [BP]	478 Froslass [14, BP]	282 Gardevoir [BP]	092 Gastly [BP]	423 Gastrodon [BP]	094 Gengar [BP]
		487 Giratina (Alt) [BP]	487 Giratina (Ori) [BP]	471 Glaceon [9, BP]	362 Glalie [14, BP]	118 Goldeen [BP]	055 Golduck [BP]	622 Golett [BP]
		623 Golurk [BP]	368 Gorebyss [BP]	658 Greninja [BP]	326 Grumpig [BP]	130 Gyarados [BP]	440 Happiny [BP]	093 Haunter [BP]
		430 Honchkrow [BP]	116 Horsea [BP]	367 Huntail [BP]	174 Igglybuff [BP]	593 Jellicent [BP]	039 Jigglypuff [BP]	385 Jirachi [BP]
		124 Jynx [BP]	140 Kabuto [BP, E]	141 Kabutops [BP]	115 Kangaskhan [BP]	352 Kecleon [BP]	647 Keldeo [BP]	230 Kingdra [BP]
		099 Kingler [BP]	281 Kirlia [BP]	098 Krabby [BP]	382 Kyogre [BP]	646 Kyurem (Blk) [1, BP]	646 Kyurem (Wht) [1, BP]	646 Kyurem [1, BP]
		171 Lanturn [BP]	131 Lapras [BP]	380 Latias [BP]	381 Latios [BP]	463 Lickilicky [BP]	108 Lickitung [BP]	264 Linoone [BP]
		271 Lombre [BP]	270 Lotad [BP]	294 Loudred [BP]	272 Ludicolo [BP]	249 Lugia [BP]	457 Lumineon [BP]	337 Lunatone [BP]
		370 Luvdisc [BP]	473 Mamoswine [BP]	490 Manaphy [BP]	226 Mantine [BP]	458 Mantyke [BP]	183 Marill [BP]	105 Marowak [BP]
		259 Marshtomp [BP]	284 Masquerain [BP]	303 Mawile [BP]	052 Meowth [BP]	376 Metagross [BP]	375 Metang [BP]	151 Mew [BP]

◆ When Cosplay Pikachu becomes Pikachu Belle, it learns the move Icicle Crash. When it changes back to Cosplay Pikachu or wears other costumes, it forgets the move.

Type	Move	Pokémon that can learn it						
Ice	Icy Wind	150 Mewtwo [BP]	350 Milotic [BP]	241 Miltank [BP]	439 Mime Jr. [BP, E]	200 Misdreavus [BP]	429 Mismagius [BP]	122 Mr. Mime [BP, E]
		258 Mudkip [BP]	446 Munchlax [BP]	198 Murkrow [BP]	034 Nidoking [BP]	031 Nidoqueen [BP]	224 Octillery [BP]	138 Omanyte [BP]
		139 Omastar [BP]	501 Oshawott [BP]	536 Palpitoad [BP]	515 Panpour [BP]	279 Pelipper [BP]	053 Persian [BP]	489 Phione [BP]
		221 Piloswine [21, BP]	393 Piplup [BP, E]	186 Politoed [BP]	060 Poliwag [BP]	061 Poliwhirl [BP]	062 Poliwrath [BP]	137 Porygon [BP]
		233 Porygon2 [BP]	474 Porygon-Z [BP]	394 Prinplup [BP]	054 Psyduck [BP]	195 Quagsire [BP]	211 Qwilfish [BP]	280 Ralts [BP]
		020 Raticate [BP]	019 Rattata [BP]	384 Rayquaza [BP]	378 Regice [1, 7, BP]	486 Regigigas [BP]	369 Relicanth [BP]	223 Remoraid [BP]
		112 Rhydon [BP]	111 Rhyhorn [BP]	464 Rhyperior [BP]	302 Sableye [BP]	503 Samurott [BP]	117 Seadra [BP]	119 Seaking [BP]
		364 Sealeo [BP]	086 Seel [11, BP]	537 Seismitoad [BP]	319 Sharpedo [BP]	090 Shellder [BP]	422 Shellos [BP]	275 Shiftry [BP]
		353 Shuppet [BP]	561 Sigilyph [BP]	516 Simipour [BP]	227 Skarmory [BP]	300 Skitty [BP]	690 Skrelp [BP]	289 Slaking [BP]
		287 Slakoth [BP]	080 Slowbro [BP]	199 Slowking [BP]	079 Slowpoke [BP]	238 Smoochum [BP]	215 Sneasel [14, BP]	143 Snorlax [BP]
		361 Snorunt [14, BP]	459 Snover [9, BP]	363 Spheal [BP]	327 Spinda [BP, E]	442 Spiritomb [BP]	325 Spoink [BP]	007 Squirtle [BP]
		121 Starmie [BP]	120 Staryu [BP]	245 Suicune [BP]	283 Surskit [BP]	260 Swampert [BP]	581 Swanna [BP]	220 Swinub [21, BP]
		128 Tauros [BP]	072 Tentacool [BP]	073 Tentacruel [BP]	564 Tirtouga [BP]	641 Tornadus [BP]	158 Totodile [BP]	454 Toxicroak [BP]
		535 Tympole [BP]	583 Vanillish [13, BP]	582 Vanillite [13, BP]	584 Vanilluxe [13, BP]	134 Vaporeon [BP]	288 Vigoroth [BP]	320 Wailmer [BP]
		321 Wailord [BP]	365 Walrein [BP]	008 Wartortle [BP]	461 Weavile [14, BP]	340 Whiscash [BP]	293 Whismur [BP]	040 Wigglytuff [BP]
		278 Wingull [BP]	194 Wooper [BP]	335 Zangoose [BP]	263 Zigzagoon [BP]			
Psychic	Imprison	482 Azelf [6]	343 Baltoy [43]	606 Beheeyem [25]	437 Bronzong [1, 9]	436 Bronzor [9]	344 Claydol [52]	355 Duskull [E]
		605 Elgyem [25]	282 Gardevoir [35]	088 Grimer [E]	281 Kirlia [33]	707 Klefki [36]	646 Kyurem (Blk) [64, 8]	646 Kyurem (Wht) [64, 8]
		646 Kyurem [64, 8]	608 Lampent [24]	645 Landorus [7]	607 Litwick [24]	678 Meowstic (M) [45]	481 Mesprit [6]	200 Misdreavus [E]
		517 Munna [13]	038 Ninetales [1]	708 Phantump [E]	280 Ralts [29]	643 Reshiram [64, 8]	302 Sableye [E]	353 Shuppet [E]
		577 Solosis [E]	442 Spiritomb [E]	234 Stantler [49]	528 Swoobat [19]	480 Uxie [6]	582 Vanillite [E]	037 Vulpix [39]
		527 Woobat [19]	562 Yamask [E]	644 Zekrom [64, 8]	571 Zoroark [1, 59]	570 Zorua [53]		
Fire	Incinerate (TM59)	359 Absol [TM]	142 Aerodactyl [TM]	306 Aggron [TM]	334 Altaria [TM]	059 Arcanine [TM]	493 Arceus [TM]	531 Audino [TM]
		610 Axew [TM]	482 Azelf [TM]	371 Bagon [TM]	411 Bastiodon [TM]	257 Blaziken [TM]	242 Blissey [TM]	654 Braixen [TM]
		323 Camerupt [TM]	351 Castform [TM]	609 Chandelure [TM]	113 Chansey [TM]	006 Charizard [TM]	004 Charmander [TM]	005 Charmeleon [TM]
		390 Chimchar [TM]	036 Clefable [TM]	035 Clefairy [TM]	173 Cleffa [TM]	256 Combusken [TM]	408 Cranidos [TM]	104 Cubone [TM]
		155 Cyndaquil [TM]	491 Darkrai [TM]	555 Darmanitan [1, 6, TM]	554 Darumaka [6, TM]	633 Deino [TM]	655 Delphox [TM]	483 Dialga [TM]
		148 Dragonair [TM]	149 Dragonite [TM]	147 Dratini [TM]	621 Druddigon [TM]	206 Dunsparce [TM]	500 Emboar [TM]	244 Entei [TM]
		295 Exploud [TM]	653 Fennekin [TM]	136 Flareon [TM]	662 Fletchinder [TM]	330 Flygon [TM]	611 Fraxure [TM]	444 Gabite [TM]
		445 Garchomp [TM]	074 Geodude [TM]	443 Gible [TM]	076 Golem [TM]	706 Goodra [TM]	711 Gourgeist [TM]	210 Granbull [TM]
		075 Graveler [TM]	088 Grimer [TM]	383 Groudon [TM]	058 Growlithe [TM]	130 Gyarados [TM]	440 Happiny [TM]	612 Haxorus [TM]
		631 Heatmor [1, TM]	485 Heatran [TM]	430 Honchkrow [TM]	250 Ho-Oh [TM]	229 Houndoom [TM]	228 Houndour [TM]	635 Hydreigon [TM]
		174 Igglybuff [TM]	392 Infernape [TM]	039 Jigglypuff [TM]	115 Kangaskhan [TM]	352 Kecleon [TM]	109 Koffing [TM]	552 Krokorok [TM]
		553 Krookodile [TM]	608 Lampent [TM]	636 Larvesta [TM]	463 Lickilicky [TM]	108 Lickitung [TM]	667 Litleo [46, TM]	607 Litwick [TM]
		294 Loudred [TM]	068 Machamp [TM]	067 Machoke [TM]	066 Machop [TM]	240 Magby [TM]	219 Magcargo [15, TM]	126 Magmar [TM]
		467 Magmortar [TM]	630 Mandibuzz [TM]	105 Marowak [TM]	303 Mawile [TM]	151 Mew [TM]	150 Mewtwo [TM]	262 Mightyena [TM]
		146 Moltres [TM]	391 Monferno [TM]	089 Muk [TM]	446 Munchlax [TM]	034 Nidoking [TM]	031 Nidoqueen [TM]	038 Ninetales [TM]
		322 Numel [TM]	224 Octillery [TM]	484 Palkia [TM]	513 Pansear [10, TM]	499 Pignite [TM]	077 Ponyta [TM]	261 Poochyena [TM]
		710 Pumpkaboo [TM]	668 Pyroar [51, TM]	156 Quilava [TM]	409 Rampardos [TM]	078 Rapidash [TM]	384 Rayquaza [TM]	223 Remoraid [TM]
		643 Reshiram [TM]	112 Rhydon [TM]	111 Rhyhorn [TM]	464 Rhyperior [TM]	302 Sableye [TM]	373 Salamence [TM]	551 Sandile [TM]
		560 Scrafty [TM]	559 Scraggy [TM]	372 Shelgon [TM]	410 Shieldon [TM]	514 Simisear [TM]	435 Skuntank [TM]	289 Slaking [TM]
		287 Slakoth [TM]	080 Slowbro [TM]	199 Slowking [TM]	079 Slowpoke [TM]	218 Slugma [15, TM]	143 Snorlax [TM]	209 Snubbull [TM]
		338 Solrock [TM]	434 Stunky [TM]	663 Talonflame [TM]	128 Tauros [TM]	498 Tepig [TM]	642 Thundurus [TM]	468 Togekiss [TM]
		175 Togepi [TM]	176 Togetic [TM]	255 Torchic [TM]	324 Torkoal [TM]	641 Tornadus [TM]	157 Typhlosion [TM]	248 Tyranitar [TM]
		494 Victini [1, TM]	288 Vigoroth [TM]	637 Volcarona [TM]	629 Vullaby [TM]	037 Vulpix [TM]	110 Weezing [TM]	293 Whismur [TM]
		040 Wigglytuff [TM]	335 Zangoose [TM]	571 Zoroark [TM]	570 Zorua [TM]	634 Zweilous [TM]		
	Inferno	006 Charizard [62]	004 Charmander [46]	005 Charmeleon [54]	155 Cyndaquil [46]	631 Heatmor [1, 61]	229 Houndoom [1, 65]	228 Houndour [56]
		608 Lampent [38]	607 Litwick [38]	077 Ponyta [33]	156 Quilava [53]	078 Rapidash [33]	218 Slugma [E]	324 Torkoal [50]
		157 Typhlosion [56]	494 Victini [57]	037 Vulpix [50]				
Bug	Infestation (TM83)	617 Accelgor [TM]	024 Arbok [TM]	168 Ariados [TM]	354 Banette [TM]	689 Barbaracle [TM]	267 Beautifly [TM]	015 Beedrill [TM]
		182 Bellossom [TM]	069 Bellsprout [TM]	688 Binacle [TM]	012 Butterfree [TM]	455 Carnivine [TM]	563 Cofagrigus [TM]	346 Cradily [TM]
		452 Drapion [TM]	578 Duosion [TM]	356 Dusclops [TM]	477 Dusknoir [TM]	355 Duskull [TM]	269 Dustox [TM]	023 Ekans [TM]
		589 Escavalier [TM]	102 Exeggcute [TM]	103 Exeggutor [TM]	596 Galvantula [TM]	569 Garbodor [TM]	092 Gastly [TM]	423 Gastrodon [TM]
		649 Genesect [TM]	094 Gengar [TM]	044 Gloom [TM]	706 Goodra [TM]	704 Goomy [TM]	368 Gorebyss [TM]	088 Grimer [TM]
		316 Gulpin [TM]	093 Haunter [TM]	187 Hoppip [TM]	367 Huntail [TM]	595 Joltik [TM]	189 Jumpluff [TM]	588 Karrablast [TM]
		109 Koffing [TM]	402 Kricketune [TM]	166 Ledian [TM]	165 Ledyba [TM]	345 Lileep [TM]	219 Magcargo [TM]	284 Masquerain [TM]
		151 Mew [TM]	439 Mime Jr. [TM]	414 Mothim [TM]	122 Mr. Mime [TM]	089 Muk [TM]	043 Oddish [TM]	536 Palpitoad [TM]
		675 Pangoro [TM]	195 Quagsire [TM]	579 Reuniclus [TM]	545 Scolipede [TM]	537 Seismitoad [TM]	336 Seviper [TM]	422 Shellos [TM]
		616 Shelmet [TM]	213 Shuckle [TM]	188 Skiploom [TM]	451 Skorupi [TM]	705 Sliggoo [TM]	218 Slugma [TM]	577 Solosis [TM]
		167 Spinarak [TM]	442 Spiritomb [TM]	618 Stunfisk [TM]	283 Surskit [TM]	317 Swalot [TM]	114 Tangela [TM]	465 Tangrowth [TM]
		072 Tentacool [TM]	073 Tentacruel [TM]	568 Trubbish [TM]	535 Tympole [TM]	543 Venipede [TM]	049 Venomoth [TM]	048 Venonat [TM]
		416 Vespiquen [TM]	071 Victreebel [TM]	045 Vileplume [TM]	666 Vivillon [TM]	070 Weepinbell [TM]	110 Weezing [TM]	544 Whirlipede [TM]
		194 Wooper [TM]	413 Wormadam (Plant) [TM]	413 Wormadam (Sand) [TM]	413 Wormadam (Trash) [TM]	562 Yamask [TM]		

	Move	Pokémon that can learn it						
Grass	Ingrain	460 Abomasnow [31]	591 Amoonguss [18]	069 Bellsprout [E]	001 Bulbasaur [E]	331 Cacnea [22]	332 Cacturne [22]	455 Carnivine [21]
		152 Chikorita [E]	222 Corsola [E]	346 Cradily [1, 9]	102 Exeggcute [E]	597 Ferroseed [35]	598 Ferrothorn [35]	590 Foongus [18]
		345 Lileep [9]	556 Maractus [33]	043 Oddish [E]	548 Petilil [E]	708 Phantump [13]	315 Roselia [34]	459 Snover [31]
		192 Sunflora [4]	191 Sunkern [4, E]	114 Tangela [1]	465 Tangrowth [1]	709 Trevenant [13]	716 Xerneas [1]	
Electric	Ion Deluge	181 Ampharos [1]	170 Chinchou [47]	604 Eelektross [1]	466 Electivire [1]	587 Emolga [E]	171 Lanturn [54]	417 Pachirisu [E]
		523 Zebstrika [1, 58]						
Steel	Iron Defense	681 Aegislash [1, BP]	306 Aggron [39, BP]	698 Amaura [BP]	347 Anorith [BP, E]	493 Arceus [BP]	566 Archen [BP]	567 Archeops [BP]
		348 Armaldo [BP]	304 Aron [37, BP]	699 Aurorus [BP]	713 Avalugg [1, BP]	689 Barbaracle [BP]	411 Bastiodon [19, BP]	374 Beldum [BP]
		712 Bergmite [BP]	688 Binacle [BP]	625 Bisharp [46, BP]	009 Blastoise [46, BP]	525 Boldore [20, BP]	437 Bronzong [19, BP]	436 Bronzor [19, BP]
		703 Carbink [BP]	565 Carracosta [BP]	268 Cascoon [BP]	652 Chesnaught [BP]	650 Chespin [BP]	366 Clamperl [1, BP]	091 Cloyster [BP]
		638 Cobalion [BP]	563 Cofagrigus [BP]	341 Corphish [BP]	222 Corsola [29, BP]	342 Crawdaunt [BP]	558 Crustle [BP]	615 Cryogonal [BP]
		104 Cubone [BP]	386 Deoxys (Def) [55, BP]	483 Dialga [BP]	719 Diancie [BP]	232 Donphan [BP]	680 Doublade [32, BP]	529 Drilbur [BP, E]
		578 Duosion [BP]	632 Durant [1, 56, BP]	557 Dwebble [BP, E]	395 Empoleon [BP]	589 Escavalier [40, BP]	530 Excadrill [BP]	597 Ferroseed [26, BP]
		598 Ferrothorn [26, BP]	205 Forretress [46, BP]	649 Genesect [BP]	074 Geodude [BP]	526 Gigalith [20, BP]	076 Golem [BP]	622 Golett [17, BP]
		623 Golurk [17, BP]	075 Graveler [BP]	485 Heatran [BP]	214 Heracross [BP]	679 Honedge [32, BP]	385 Jirachi [BP]	140 Kabuto [BP]
		141 Kabutops [BP]	014 Kakuna [BP]	588 Karrablast [BP]	099 Kingler [BP]	600 Klang [BP]	707 Klefki [BP, E]	599 Klink [BP]
		601 Klinklang [BP]	098 Krabby [BP]	305 Lairon [39, BP]	246 Larvitar [BP, E]	542 Leavanny [BP]	448 Lucario [BP]	219 Magcargo [BP]
		081 Magnemite [BP]	082 Magneton [BP]	462 Magnezone [BP]	105 Marowak [BP]	303 Mawile [33, BP]	376 Metagross [52, BP]	375 Metang [47, BP]
		011 Metapod [BP]	151 Mew [BP]	122 Mr. Mime [BP]	299 Nosepass [BP]	138 Omanyte [BP]	139 Omastar [BP]	624 Pawniard [46, BP]
		204 Pineco [39, BP]	127 Pinsir [BP]	476 Probopass [1, 4, BP]	247 Pupitar [BP]	651 Quilladin [BP]	377 Regirock [37, BP]	379 Registeel [37, BP]
		579 Reuniclus [BP]	447 Riolu [BP, E]	524 Roggenrola [20, BP]	212 Scizor [37, BP]	545 Scolipede [BP]	560 Scrafty [BP]	559 Scraggy [BP]
		540 Sewaddle [BP]	372 Shelgon [BP]	090 Shellder [49, BP]	410 Shieldon [19, BP]	266 Silcoon [BP]	227 Skarmory [BP]	080 Slowbro [BP]
		199 Slowking [BP]	218 Slugma [BP]	577 Solosis [BP]	338 Solrock [BP]	665 Spewpa [BP]	007 Squirtle [34, BP]	541 Swadloon [BP]
		564 Tirtouga [BP, E]	324 Torkoal [38, BP]	248 Tyranitar [BP]	697 Tyrantrum [BP]	696 Tyrunt [BP]	583 Vanillish [BP]	582 Vanillite [BP, E]
		584 Vanilluxe [BP]	543 Venipede [BP]	008 Wartortle [40, BP]	544 Whirlipede [22, BP]	413 Wormadam (Trash) [BP]	562 Yamask [BP]	
	Iron Head	681 Aegislash [1, BP]	142 Aerodactyl [1, 57, BP]	306 Aggron [22, BP]	698 Amaura [BP]	059 Arcanine [BP]	493 Arceus [BP]	304 Aron [22, BP, E]
		699 Aurorus [BP]	713 Avalugg [BP]	411 Bastiodon [51, BP]	374 Beldum [BP]	625 Bisharp [1, 57, BP]	626 Bouffalant [BP, E]	437 Bronzong [BP]
		659 Bunnelby [BP]	323 Camerupt [BP]	565 Carracosta [BP]	652 Chesnaught [BP]	650 Chespin [BP]	638 Cobalion [37, BP]	408 Cranidos [BP, E]
		104 Cubone [BP, E]	483 Dialga [BP]	660 Diggersby [BP]	680 Doublade [45, BP]	149 Dragonite [BP]	621 Druddigon [BP]	632 Durant [36, BP]
		500 Emboar [BP]	244 Entei [BP]	589 Escavalier [37, BP]	530 Excadrill [BP]	597 Ferroseed [43, BP]	598 Ferrothorn [46, BP]	444 Gabite [BP]
		445 Garchomp [BP]	649 Genesect [BP]	443 Gible [BP, E]	526 Gigalith [BP]	487 Giratina (Alt) [BP]	487 Giratina (Ori) [BP]	362 Glalie [BP]
		076 Golem [BP]	383 Groudon [BP]	130 Gyarados [BP]	297 Hariyama [BP]	701 Hawlucha [BP]	485 Heatran [1, 65, BP]	450 Hippowdon [BP]
		679 Honedge [42, BP]	250 Ho-Oh [BP]	385 Jirachi [BP]	230 Kingdra [BP]	382 Kyogre [BP]	646 Kyurem (Blk) [BP]	646 Kyurem (Wht) [BP]
		646 Kyurem [BP]	305 Lairon [22, BP]	131 Lapras [BP]	246 Larvitar [BP, E]	249 Lugia [BP]	337 Lunatone [BP]	462 Magnezone [BP]
		473 Mamoswine [BP]	226 Mantine [BP]	105 Marowak [BP]	303 Mawile [1, 45, BP]	376 Metagross [BP]	375 Metang [BP]	151 Mew [BP]
		350 Milotic [BP]	241 Miltank [BP]	322 Numel [BP, E]	095 Onix [BP]	674 Pancham [BP]	675 Pangoro [BP]	624 Pawniard [54, BP]
		476 Probopass [BP]	247 Pupitar [BP]	651 Quilladin [BP]	243 Raikou [BP]	409 Rampardos [BP]	384 Rayquaza [BP]	378 Regice [BP]
		486 Regigigas [BP]	377 Regirock [BP]	379 Registeel [43, BP]	464 Rhyperior [BP]	212 Scizor [50, BP]	560 Scrafty [BP]	559 Scraggy [BP]
		410 Shieldon [42, BP]	227 Skarmory [BP]	143 Snorlax [BP]	338 Solrock [BP]	208 Steelix [BP]	508 Stoutland [BP]	245 Suicune [BP]
		128 Tauros [BP]	639 Terrakion [BP]	389 Torterra [BP]	248 Tyranitar [BP]	697 Tyrantrum [BP]	696 Tyrunt [BP]	321 Wailord [BP]
		365 Walrein [BP]	413 Wormadam (Trash) [47, BP]					
	Iron Tail	460 Abomasnow [BP]	063 Abra [BP]	359 Absol [BP]	142 Aerodactyl [BP]	306 Aggron [35, BP]	190 Aipom [BP]	065 Alakazam [BP]
		334 Altaria [BP]	698 Amaura [BP]	424 Ambipom [BP]	181 Ampharos [BP]	024 Arbok [BP]	059 Arcanine [BP]	493 Arceus [BP]
		566 Archen [BP]	567 Archeops [BP]	348 Armaldo [BP]	304 Aron [34, BP]	531 Audino [BP]	699 Aurorus [BP]	610 Axew [BP, E]
		482 Azelf [BP]	184 Azumarill [BP]	298 Azurill [BP]	411 Bastiodon [BP]	153 Bayleef [BP]	400 Bibarel [BP]	399 Bidoof [BP]
		009 Blastoise [BP]	242 Blissey [BP]	654 Braixen [BP]	286 Breloom [BP]	418 Buizel [BP]	427 Buneary [BP]	659 Bunnelby [BP]
		565 Carracosta [BP]	113 Chansey [BP]	006 Charizard [BP]	004 Charmander [BP]	005 Charmeleon [BP]	652 Chesnaught [BP]	650 Chespin [BP]
		152 Chikorita [BP]	390 Chimchar [BP]	573 Cinccino [BP]	692 Clauncher [BP]	693 Clawitzer [BP]	036 Clefable [BP]	035 Clefairy [BP]
		173 Cleffa [BP]	408 Cranidos [BP, E]	159 Croconaw [BP]	104 Cubone [BP]	702 Dedenne [BP]	301 Delcatty [BP]	655 Delphox [BP]
		087 Dewgong [BP]	502 Dewott [BP]	483 Dialga [42, BP]	660 Diggersby [BP]	232 Donphan [BP]	691 Dragalge [BP]	148 Dragonair [BP]
		149 Dragonite [BP]	452 Drapion [BP]	147 Dratini [BP, E]	621 Druddigon [BP, E]	206 Dunsparce [BP]	603 Eelektrik [BP]	604 Eelektross [BP]
		133 Eevee [BP]	023 Ekans [BP, E]	125 Electabuzz [BP]	466 Electivire [BP]	309 Electrike [BP]	500 Emboar [BP]	587 Emolga [BP, E]
		244 Entei [BP]	196 Espeon [BP]	677 Espurr [BP]	083 Farfetch'd [BP]	349 Feebas [BP, E]	653 Fennekin [BP]	160 Feraligatr [BP]
		180 Flaaffy [BP]	136 Flareon [BP]	419 Floatzel [BP]	330 Flygon [BP]	611 Fraxure [BP]	676 Furfrou [BP]	162 Furret [BP]
		444 Gabite [BP]	445 Garchomp [BP]	443 Gible [BP, E]	203 Girafarig [BP]	487 Giratina (Alt) [BP]	487 Giratina (Ori) [BP]	471 Glaceon [BP]
		431 Glameow [BP]	207 Gligar [BP]	472 Gliscor [BP]	673 Gogoat [BP]	055 Golduck [BP]	706 Goodra [BP]	704 Goomy [BP, E]
		210 Granbull [BP]	388 Grotle [BP]	383 Groudon [BP]	253 Grovyle [BP]	058 Growlithe [BP, E]	326 Grumpig [BP]	130 Gyarados [BP]
		612 Haxorus [BP]	695 Heliolisk [BP]	694 Helioptile [BP]	449 Hippopotas [BP]	450 Hippowdon [BP]	229 Houndoom [BP]	228 Houndour [BP]
		635 Hydreigon [BP]	392 Infernape [BP]	135 Jolteon [BP]	064 Kadabra [BP]	115 Kangaskhan [BP]	352 Kecleon [BP]	552 Krokorok [BP]
		553 Krookodile [BP]	305 Lairon [35, BP]	645 Landorus [BP]	131 Lapras [BP]	246 Larvitar [BP, E]	470 Leafeon [BP]	463 Lickilicky [BP]
		108 Lickitung [BP]	510 Liepard [BP]	264 Linoone [BP]	667 Litleo [BP]	428 Lopunny [BP]	448 Lucario [BP]	249 Lugia [BP]
		404 Luxio [BP]	405 Luxray [BP]	240 Magby [BP, E]	126 Magmar [BP]	467 Magmortar [BP]	310 Manectric [BP]	056 Mankey [BP]
		179 Mareep [BP, E]	183 Marill [BP]	105 Marowak [BP]	259 Marshtomp [BP]	154 Meganium [BP]	678 Meowstic (F) [BP]	678 Meowstic (M) [BP]
		052 Meowth [BP, E]	481 Mesprit [BP]	151 Mew [BP]	150 Mewtwo [BP]	262 Mightyena [BP]	350 Milotic [BP]	241 Miltank [BP]

Type	Move	Pokémon that can learn it						
Steel	Iron Tail	572 Minccino [BP, E]	312 Minun [BP]	391 Monferno [BP]	258 Mudkip [BP]	034 Nidoking [BP]	031 Nidoqueen [BP]	029 Nidoran ♀ [BP, E]
		032 Nidoran ♂ [BP, E]	030 Nidorina [BP]	033 Nidorino [BP]	038 Ninetales [BP]	714 Noibat [BP]	715 Noivern [BP]	095 Onix [40, BP]
		501 Oshawott [BP]	417 Pachirisu [BP, E]	515 Panpour [BP]	511 Pansage [BP]	513 Pansear [BP]	504 Patrat [BP, E]	053 Persian [BP]
		231 Phanpy [BP]	172 Pichu [BP]	499 Pignite [BP]	025 Pikachu [BP]	311 Plusle [BP]	077 Ponyta [BP]	261 Poochyena [BP]
		137 Porygon [BP]	233 Porygon2 [BP]	474 Porygon-Z [BP]	057 Primeape [BP]	054 Psyduck [BP]	247 Pupitar [BP]	509 Purrloin [BP]
		432 Purugly [BP]	668 Pyroar [BP]	195 Quagsire [BP]	651 Quilladin [BP]	026 Raichu [BP]	243 Raikou [BP]	409 Rampardos [BP]
		078 Rapidash [BP]	020 Raticate [BP]	019 Rattata [BP]	384 Rayquaza [BP]	112 Rhydon [BP]	111 Rhyhorn [BP, E]	464 Rhyperior [BP]
		447 Riolu [BP]	373 Salamence [BP]	503 Samurott [BP]	551 Sandile [BP]	027 Sandshrew [BP]	028 Sandslash [BP]	254 Sceptile [BP]
		545 Scolipede [BP]	560 Scrafty [BP]	559 Scraggy [BP]	364 Sealeo [BP]	086 Seel [BP, E]	161 Sentret [BP, E]	497 Serperior [BP]
		496 Servine [BP]	336 Seviper [BP, E]	410 Shieldon [BP]	403 Shinx [BP]	516 Simipour [BP]	512 Simisage [BP]	514 Simisear [BP]
		672 Skiddo [BP]	300 Skitty [BP]	451 Skorupi [BP, E]	690 Skrelp [BP]	435 Skuntank [BP]	705 Sliggoo [BP]	080 Slowbro [BP]
		199 Slowking [BP]	079 Slowpoke [BP]	215 Sneasel [BP]	495 Snivy [BP, E]	459 Snover [BP]	363 Spheal [BP]	325 Spoink [BP]
		007 Squirtle [BP]	234 Stantler [BP]	208 Steelix [40, BP]	434 Stunky [BP, E]	245 Suicune [BP]	260 Swampert [BP]	700 Sylveon [BP]
		128 Tauros [BP]	498 Tepig [BP]	642 Thundurus [BP]	564 Tirtouga [BP]	324 Torkoal [BP]	641 Tornadus [BP]	389 Torterra [BP]
		158 Totodile [BP]	252 Treecko [BP]	387 Turtwig [BP]	248 Tyranitar [BP]	697 Tyrantrum [BP]	696 Tyrunt [BP]	197 Umbreon [BP]
		480 Uxie [BP]	134 Vaporeon [BP]	037 Vulpix [BP]	365 Walrein [BP]	008 Wartortle [BP]	505 Watchog [BP]	461 Weavile [BP]
		194 Wooper [BP]	335 Zangoose [BP, E]	263 Zigzagoon [BP]	718 Zygarde [BP]			

J·K

Type	Move	Pokémon that can learn it						
Normal	Judgment	493 Arceus [100]						
Fighting	Jump Kick	427 Buneary [23]	585 Deerling [24]	106 Hitmonlee [13]	428 Lopunny [23]	619 Mienfoo [37]	620 Mienshao [37]	586 Sawsbuck [24]
		234 Stantler [43]						
Fighting	Karate Chop	239 Elekid [E]	701 Hawlucha [4]	068 Machamp [1, 7]	067 Machoke [1, 7]	066 Machop [7]	240 Magby [E]	056 Mankey [13]
		674 Pancham [12]	675 Pangoro [12]	057 Primeape [13]	539 Sawk [25]			
Psychic	Kinesis	065 Alakazam [1]	064 Kadabra [1]					
Steel	King's Shield	681 Aegislash [1]						
Dark	Knock Off	063 Abra [BP, E]	359 Absol [BP]	617 Accelgor [BP]	190 Aipom [BP]	065 Alakazam [BP]	594 Alomomola [BP]	424 Ambipom [BP]
		347 Anorith [BP, E]	566 Archen [BP, E]	567 Archeops [BP]	348 Armaldo [BP]	531 Audino [BP]	482 Azelf [BP]	184 Azumarill [BP]
		298 Azurill [BP]	354 Banette [1, BP]	015 Beedrill [BP]	069 Bellsprout [27, BP]	625 Bisharp [BP]	257 Blaziken [BP]	001 Bulbasaur [BP]
		455 Carnivine [BP]	565 Carracosta [BP]	358 Chimecho [BP]	433 Chingling [BP]	573 Cinccino [BP]	036 Clefable [BP]	035 Clefairy [BP]
		563 Cofagrigus [BP]	534 Conkeldurr [BP]	341 Corphish [23, BP, E]	546 Cottonee [BP]	342 Crawdaunt [23, BP]	453 Croagunk [BP]	558 Crustle [BP]
		615 Cryogonal [BP]	104 Cubone [BP]	491 Darkrai [BP]	386 Deoxys (Def) [19, BP]	386 Deoxys (Nor) [19, BP]	386 Deoxys (Spd) [19, BP]	660 Diggersby [BP]
		085 Dodrio [BP]	084 Doduo [BP]	232 Donphan [19, BP]	452 Drapion [1, 5, BP]	426 Drifblim [BP]	425 Drifloon [BP]	557 Dwebble [BP]
		603 Eelektrik [BP]	604 Eelektross [BP]	587 Emolga [BP]	395 Empoleon [BP]	589 Escavalier [BP]	083 Farfetch'd [13, BP]	597 Ferroseed [BP]
		598 Ferrothorn [BP]	162 Furret [BP]	475 Gallade [BP]	092 Gastly [BP]	094 Gengar [BP]	431 Glameow [BP]	207 Gligar [10, BP]
		472 Gliscor [1, 10, BP]	118 Goldeen [BP]	533 Gurdurr [BP]	297 Hariyama [19, BP]	093 Haunter [BP]	631 Heatmor [BP]	214 Heracross [BP]
		106 Hitmonlee [BP]	686 Inkay [BP]	002 Ivysaur [BP]	039 Jigglypuff [BP]	140 Kabuto [BP, E]	141 Kabutops [BP]	064 Kadabra [BP]
		588 Karrablast [BP, E]	352 Kecleon [BP]	099 Kingler [BP]	098 Krabby [BP, E]	402 Kricketune [BP]	552 Krokorok [BP]	553 Krookodile [BP]
		645 Landorus [BP]	470 Leafeon [BP]	542 Leavanny [BP]	166 Ledian [BP]	165 Ledyba [BP, E]	463 Lickilicky [13, BP]	108 Lickitung [13, BP]
		510 Liepard [BP]	271 Lombre [36, BP]	272 Ludicolo [BP]	068 Machamp [21, BP]	067 Machoke [21, BP]	066 Machop [21, BP, E]	296 Makuhita [19, BP]
		687 Malamar [BP]	473 Mamoswine [BP]	490 Manaphy [BP]	630 Mandibuzz [BP]	556 Maractus [BP]	183 Marill [BP]	105 Marowak [BP]
		303 Mawile [BP]	648 Meloetta [BP]	052 Meowth [BP]	481 Mesprit [BP]	151 Mew [BP]	619 Mienfoo [BP, E]	620 Mienshao [BP]
		572 Minccino [BP, E]	138 Omanyte [BP, E]	139 Omastar [BP]	674 Pancham [BP]	675 Pangoro [BP]	515 Panpour [BP]	511 Pansage [BP]
		513 Pansear [BP]	046 Paras [BP]	047 Parasect [BP]	624 Pawniard [BP]	279 Pelipper [BP]	053 Persian [BP]	231 Phanpy [BP]
		489 Phione [BP]	025 Pikachu [BP]	127 Pinsir [BP]	509 Purrloin [BP]	432 Purugly [BP]	026 Raichu [BP]	486 Regigigas [1, BP]
		579 Reuniclus [BP]	302 Sableye [26, BP]	503 Samurott [BP]	027 Sandshrew [BP]	028 Sandslash [BP]	539 Sawk [BP]	212 Scizor [BP]
		560 Scrafty [BP]	559 Scraggy [BP]	123 Scyther [BP]	119 Seaking [BP]	537 Seismitoad [BP]	161 Sentret [BP]	497 Serperior [BP]
		496 Servine [BP]	336 Seviper [BP]	275 Shiftry [BP]	213 Shuckle [BP, E]	353 Shuppet [1, BP]	516 Simipour [BP]	512 Simisage [BP]
		514 Simisear [BP]	451 Skorupi [5, BP]	215 Sneasel [BP]	495 Snivy [BP]	528 Swoobat [BP]	114 Tangela [27, BP]	465 Tangrowth [27, BP]
		072 Tentacool [BP, E]	073 Tentacruel [BP]	538 Throh [BP]	642 Thundurus [BP]	532 Timburr [BP]	564 Tirtouga [BP, E]	641 Tornadus [BP]
		454 Toxicroak [BP]	480 Uxie [BP]	003 Venusaur [BP]	071 Victreebel [BP]	629 Vullaby [BP, E]	505 Watchog [BP]	461 Weavile [BP]
		070 Weepinbell [27, BP]	547 Whimsicott [BP]	040 Wigglytuff [BP]	278 Wingull [BP, E]	527 Woobat [BP, E]	562 Yamask [BP]	717 Yveltal [BP]
		335 Zangoose [BP]	571 Zoroark [BP]	570 Zorua [BP]				

L

Type	Move	Pokémon that can learn it						
Ground	Land's Wrath	718 Zygarde [26]						
Normal	Last Resort	190 Aipom [43, BP]	424 Ambipom [43, BP]	493 Arceus [BP]	531 Audino [1, 53, BP]	482 Azelf [1, 61, BP]	400 Bibarel [BP]	399 Bidoof [BP]
		257 Blaziken [BP]	242 Blissey [BP]	427 Buneary [BP]	659 Bunnelby [BP]	351 Castform [BP]	251 Celebi [BP]	113 Chansey [BP]
		358 Chimecho [BP]	433 Chingling [16, BP]	573 Cinccino [BP]	036 Clefable [BP]	035 Clefairy [BP]	173 Cleffa [BP]	256 Combusken [BP]
		491 Darkrai [BP]	702 Dedenne [BP]	585 Deerling [BP]	301 Delcatty [BP]	719 Diancie [BP]	660 Diggersby [BP]	232 Donphan [BP]
		206 Dunsparce [BP]	133 Eevee [41, BP]	587 Emolga [BP]	196 Espeon [41, BP]	083 Farfetch'd [BP]	136 Flareon [41, BP]	676 Furfrou [BP]
		162 Furret [BP]	649 Genesect [BP]	471 Glaceon [41, BP]	431 Glameow [BP, E]	210 Granbull [BP]	440 Happiny [BP, E]	701 Hawlucha [BP]
		507 Herdier [42, BP]	174 Igglybuff [BP, E]	039 Jigglypuff [BP]	385 Jirachi [65, BP]	135 Jolteon [41, BP]	352 Kecleon [BP]	647 Keldeo [BP]
		707 Klefki [BP]	380 Latias [BP]	381 Latios [BP]	470 Leafeon [41, BP]	506 Lillipup [36, BP]	264 Linoone [BP]	428 Lopunny [BP]
		490 Manaphy [BP]	303 Mawile [BP]	648 Meloetta [BP]	052 Meowth [BP, E]	151 Mew [BP]	572 Minccino [45, BP]	312 Minun [BP]
		446 Munchlax [1, 57, BP]	417 Pachirisu [45, BP]	504 Patrat [BP]	053 Persian [BP]	231 Phanpy [37, BP]	489 Phione [BP]	311 Plusle [40, BP]
		137 Porygon [BP]	233 Porygon2 [BP]	474 Porygon-Z [BP]	432 Purugly [BP]	020 Raticate [BP]	019 Rattata [BP, E]	586 Sawsbuck [BP]
		161 Sentret [BP, E]	492 Shaymin (Land) [BP]	492 Shaymin (Sky) [BP]	300 Skitty [BP, E]	143 Snorlax [BP]	209 Snubbull [BP]	327 Spinda [BP]
		234 Stantler [BP]	508 Stoutland [51, BP]	700 Sylveon [41, BP]	216 Teddiursa [BP]	468 Togekiss [BP]	175 Togepi [49, BP]	176 Togetic [49, BP]
		255 Torchic [BP, E]	197 Umbreon [41, BP]	217 Ursaring [BP]	134 Vaporeon [41, BP]	494 Victini [BP]	505 Watchog [BP]	040 Wigglytuff [BP]
		335 Zangoose [BP]	263 Zigzagoon [BP]					
Fire	Lava Plume	323 Camerupt [22]	155 Cyndaquil [37]	244 Entei [1, 57]	136 Flareon [37]	383 Groudon [20]	485 Heatran [49]	240 Magby [33]
		219 Magcargo [34]	126 Magmar [36]	467 Magmortar [36]	322 Numel [22]	156 Quilava [42]	218 Slugma [34]	324 Torkoal [25]
		157 Typhlosion [43]						
Grass	Leaf Blade	182 Bellossom [1]	083 Farfetch'd [E]	475 Gallade [1]	673 Gogoat [55]	253 Grovyle [23]	470 Leafeon [45]	542 Leavanny [36]
		274 Nuzleaf [28]	254 Sceptile [23]	497 Serperior [32]	496 Servine [32]	672 Skiddo [45]	495 Snivy [28]	357 Tropius [E]
		071 Victreebel [47]	640 Virizion [1, 67]					
	Leaf Storm	182 Bellossom [1, 64]	406 Budew [E]	001 Bulbasaur [E]	251 Celebi [82]	152 Chikorita [E]	102 Exeggcute [E]	103 Exeggutor [47]
		388 Grotle [52]	253 Grovyle [58]	542 Leavanny [50]	511 Pansage [E]	548 Petilil [46]	315 Roselia [E]	479 Rotom (Mow) ◆
		254 Sceptile [1, 63]	497 Serperior [62]	496 Servine [52]	492 Shaymin (Sky) [91]	275 Shiftry [44]	495 Snivy [43]	192 Sunflora [43]
		114 Tangela [E]	389 Torterra [57]	252 Treecko [E]	357 Tropius [1, 61, E]	387 Turtwig [45]	071 Victreebel [47]	413 Wormadam (Plant) [47]
	Leaf Tornado	455 Carnivine [31]	497 Serperior [16]	496 Servine [16]	275 Shiftry [20]	495 Snivy [16]	357 Tropius [26]	071 Victreebel [27]
Bug	Leech Life	617 Accelgor [1]	168 Ariados [12]	069 Bellsprout [E]	169 Crobat [1]	596 Galvantula [1]	042 Golbat [1]	595 Joltik [1]
		402 Kricketune [14]	636 Larvesta [10]	290 Nincada [5]	291 Ninjask [1, 5]	714 Noibat [5]	715 Noivern [5]	046 Paras [11]
		047 Parasect [1, 11]	292 Shedinja [5]	616 Shelmet [1]	167 Spinarak [12]	049 Venomoth [17]	048 Venonat [17]	637 Volcarona [1, 10]
		193 Yanma [E]	041 Zubat [1]					
Grass	Leech Seed	286 Breloom [1, 8]	001 Bulbasaur [7]	331 Cacnea [10]	332 Cacturne [10]	455 Carnivine [E]	251 Celebi [1]	421 Cherrim [10]
		420 Cherubi [10]	652 Chesnaught [15]	650 Chespin [15]	152 Chikorita [E]	546 Cottonee [8]	585 Deerling [13]	102 Exeggcute [11]
		597 Ferroseed [E]	673 Gogoat [12]	711 Gourgeist [20]	388 Grotle [32]	187 Hoppip [22]	002 Ivysaur [1, 7]	189 Jumpluff [24]
		549 Lilligant [1]	270 Lotad [E]	556 Maractus [E]	511 Pansage [16]	046 Paras [E]	548 Petilil [8]	708 Phantump [23]
		710 Pumpkaboo [20]	651 Quilladin [15]	315 Roselia [16]	586 Sawsbuck [13]	273 Seedot [E]	497 Serperior [20]	496 Servine [20]
		492 Shaymin (Land) [19]	492 Shaymin (Sky) [19]	285 Shroomish [8]	672 Skiddo [12]	188 Skiploom [24]	495 Snivy [19]	459 Snover [E]
		192 Sunflora [13]	191 Sunkern [13, E]	114 Tangela [E]	389 Torterra [33]	252 Treecko [E]	709 Trevenant [23]	357 Tropius [E]
		387 Turtwig [29]	003 Venusaur [1, 7]	547 Whimsicott [1]				
Normal	Leer	460 Abomasnow [1]	359 Absol [1, 4]	024 Arbok [1]	566 Archen [1]	567 Archeops [1]	610 Axew [4]	371 Bagon [7]
		625 Bisharp [1, 6]	626 Bouffalant [1]	628 Braviary [1]	659 Bunnelby [1]	331 Cacnea [1]	332 Cacturne [1]	318 Carvanha [1]
		390 Chimchar [1]	638 Cobalion [1]	534 Conkeldurr [1]	341 Corphish [10]	408 Cranidos [1, E]	342 Crawdaunt [1, 10]	159 Croconaw [1]
		104 Cubone [13]	155 Cyndaquil [1]	386 Deoxys (Atk) [1]	386 Deoxys (Def) [1]	386 Deoxys (Nor) [1]	386 Deoxys (Spd) [1]	660 Diggersby [1]
		148 Dragonair [1]	149 Dragonite [1]	452 Drapion [1]	147 Dratini [1]	621 Druddigon [1]	356 Dusclops [1]	477 Dusknoir [1]
		355 Duskull [1]	023 Ekans [1]	125 Electabuzz [1]	466 Electivire [1]	309 Electrike [4]	239 Elekid [1]	244 Entei [1]
		589 Escavalier [1, 4]	677 Espurr [1]	083 Farfetch'd [1]	022 Fearow [1, 5]	160 Feraligatr [1]	611 Fraxure [1, 4]	478 Froslass [1]
		475 Gallade [1]	362 Glalie [1]	253 Grovyle [1]	058 Growlithe [8]	533 Gurdurr [1]	130 Gyarados [26]	612 Haxorus [1, 4]
		485 Heatran [9]	214 Heracross [1]	507 Herdier [1]	116 Horsea [9]	229 Houndoom [1]	228 Houndour [1]	392 Infernape [1]
		140 Kabuto [11]	141 Kabutops [1, 11]	115 Kangaskhan [1]	588 Karrablast [4]	647 Keldeo [1]	230 Kingdra [1, 9]	099 Kingler [1, 9]
		098 Krabby [9]	552 Krokorok [1]	553 Krookodile [1]	246 Larvitar [1]	506 Lillipup [1]	667 Litleo [1]	404 Luxio [1, 5]
		405 Luxray [1, 5]	068 Machamp [1]	067 Machoke [1]	066 Machop [1]	240 Magby [1]	126 Magmar [1]	467 Magmortar [1]
		630 Mandibuzz [1]	310 Manectric [1, 4]	056 Mankey [1]	105 Marowak [13]	678 Meowstic (F) [1]	678 Meowstic (M) [1]	391 Monferno [1]
		177 Natu [1]	032 Nidoran ♂ [1]	033 Nidorino [1]	138 Omanyte [19]	139 Omastar [19]	674 Pancham [1]	675 Pangoro [1]
		515 Panpour [4]	511 Pansage [4]	513 Pansear [4]	504 Patrat [3]	624 Pawniard [6]	519 Pidove [8]	261 Poochyena [E]
		057 Primeape [1]	247 Pupitar [1]	668 Pyroar [1]	156 Quilava [1]	243 Raikou [1]	409 Rampardos [1]	627 Rufflet [1]
		302 Sableye [1]	373 Salamence [1, 7]	551 Sandile [1]	539 Sawk [1]	254 Sceptile [1]	212 Scizor [1]	560 Scrafty [1]
		559 Scraggy [1]	123 Scyther [1]	117 Seadra [1, 9]	497 Serperior [1, 4]	496 Servine [1, 4]	319 Sharpedo [1]	372 Shelgon [1, 7]
		090 Shellder [20]	403 Shinx [5]	516 Simipour [1]	512 Simisage [1]	514 Simisear [1]	227 Skarmory [1]	451 Skorupi [1]
		215 Sneasel [1]	495 Snivy [4]	361 Snorunt [1]	459 Snover [1]	021 Spearow [5]	234 Stantler [3]	508 Stoutland [1]
		434 Stunky [E]	245 Suicune [1]	639 Terrakion [1]	538 Throh [1]	532 Timburr [1]	158 Totodile [1]	520 Tranquill [1, 8]
		252 Treecko [1]	357 Tropius [1]	157 Typhlosion [1]	248 Tyranitar [1]	521 Unfezant [1, 8]	217 Ursaring [1]	640 Virizion [1]
		629 Vullaby [1]	505 Watchog [1, 3]	461 Weavile [1]	178 Xatu [1]	335 Zangoose [1]	571 Zoroark [1]	570 Zorua [1]

◆ When Rotom becomes Mow Rotom, it learns the move Leaf Storm. When it changes back to Rotom, it forgets the move.

Type	Move	Pokémon that can learn it						
Ghost	Lick	656 Froakie [10]	657 Frogadier [10]	092 Gastly [1]	094 Gengar [1]	210 Granbull [13]	658 Greninja [10]	088 Grimer [E]
		093 Haunter [1]	631 Heatmor [1]	124 Jynx [1, 5]	352 Kecleon [1]	463 Lickilicky [1]	108 Lickitung [1]	506 Lillipup [E]
		446 Munchlax [1, 12, E]	515 Panpour [7]	511 Pansage [7]	513 Pansear [7]	086 Seel [E]	336 Seviper [7]	516 Simipour [1]
		512 Simisage [1]	514 Simisear [1]	238 Smoochum [5]	143 Snorlax [12, E]	209 Snubbull [13]	216 Teddiursa [1]	217 Ursaring [1]
Psychic	Light Screen TM16)	460 Abomasnow [TM]	063 Abra [TM]	065 Alakazam [TM]	594 Alomomola [TM]	698 Amaura [47, TM]	181 Ampharos [57, TM]	493 Arceus [TM]
		683 Aromatisse [TM]	531 Audino [TM]	699 Aurorus [50, TM]	482 Azelf [TM]	184 Azumarill [TM]	298 Azurill [TM]	343 Baltoy [TM]
		153 Bayleef [36, TM]	606 Beheeyem [TM]	242 Blissey [46, TM]	522 Blitzle [TM]	654 Braixen [30, TM]	437 Bronzong [TM]	436 Bronzor [TM]
		001 Bulbasaur [TM]	703 Carbink [60, TM]	251 Celebi [TM]	113 Chansey [46, TM]	152 Chikorita [31, TM]	358 Chimecho [TM]	433 Chingling [TM]
		573 Cinccino [TM]	344 Claydol [TM]	036 Clefable [TM]	035 Clefairy [TM]	173 Cleffa [TM]	222 Corsola [TM]	488 Cresselia [TM]
		615 Cryogonal [37, TM]	585 Deerling [TM]	655 Delphox [30, TM]	386 Deoxys (Atk) [TM]	386 Deoxys (Def) [TM]	386 Deoxys (Nor) [TM]	386 Deoxys (Spd) [TM]
		719 Diancie [60, TM]	148 Dragonair [TM]	149 Dragonite [TM]	147 Dratini [TM]	096 Drowzee [TM]	578 Duosion [16, TM]	269 Dustox [27, TM]
		603 Eelektrik [TM]	604 Eelektross [TM]	125 Electabuzz [26, TM]	466 Electivire [26, TM]	309 Electrike [TM]	101 Electrode [29, TM]	239 Elekid [26, TM]
		605 Elgyem [TM]	587 Emolga [34, TM]	196 Espeon [TM]	677 Espurr [13, TM]	102 Exeggcute [TM]	103 Exeggutor [TM]	349 Feebas [TM]
		653 Fennekin [27, TM]	180 Flaaffy [52, TM]	671 Florges [TM]	205 Forretress [TM]	478 Froslass [TM]	475 Gallade [TM]	596 Galvantula [TM]
		282 Gardevoir [TM]	649 Genesect [TM]	203 Girafarig [TM]	362 Glalie [TM]	055 Golduck [TM]	574 Gothita [TM]	576 Gothitelle [TM]
		575 Gothorita [TM]	711 Gourgeist [TM]	388 Grotle [TM]	326 Grumpig [TM]	440 Happiny [TM]	695 Heliolisk [TM]	694 Helioptile [TM]
		250 Ho-Oh [TM]	097 Hypno [TM]	174 Igglybuff [TM]	314 Illumise [TM]	686 Inkay [31, TM]	002 Ivysaur [TM]	039 Jigglypuff [TM]
		385 Jirachi [TM]	135 Jolteon [TM]	595 Joltik [TM]	124 Jynx [TM]	064 Kadabra [TM]	281 Kirlia [TM]	707 Klefki [TM]
		646 Kyurem (Blk) [TM]	646 Kyurem (Wht) [TM]	646 Kyurem [TM]	636 Larvesta [TM]	380 Latias [TM]	381 Latios [TM]	542 Leavanny [TM]
		166 Ledian [14, TM]	165 Ledyba [14, TM]	549 Lilligant [TM]	249 Lugia [TM]	337 Lunatone [TM]	404 Luxio [TM]	405 Luxray [TM]
		068 Machamp [TM]	067 Machoke [TM]	066 Machop [TM]	219 Magcargo [TM]	081 Magnemite [TM]	082 Magneton [TM]	462 Magnezone [TM]
		687 Malamar [31, TM]	473 Mamoswine [TM]	490 Manaphy [TM]	310 Manectric [TM]	179 Mareep [43, TM]	183 Marill [TM]	308 Medicham [TM]
		307 Meditite [TM]	154 Meganium [40, TM]	648 Meloetta [TM]	678 Meowstic (F) [13, TM]	678 Meowstic (M) [13, TM]	481 Mesprit [TM]	376 Metagross [TM]
		375 Metang [TM]	151 Mew [TM]	150 Mewtwo [TM]	350 Milotic [TM]	439 Mime Jr. [22, TM]	312 Minun [TM]	122 Mr. Mime [22, TM]
		517 Munna [TM]	518 Musharna [TM]	177 Natu [TM]	417 Pachirisu [TM]	046 Paras [TM]	047 Parasect [TM]	172 Pichu [TM]
		025 Pikachu [53, TM]	221 Piloswine [TM]	204 Pineco [TM]	311 Plusle [TM]	054 Psyduck [TM]	710 Pumpkaboo [TM]	026 Raichu [TM]
		243 Raikou [TM]	280 Ralts [TM]	643 Reshiram [TM]	579 Reuniclus [16, TM]	479 Rotom (Fan) [TM]	479 Rotom (Frost) [TM]	479 Rotom (Heat) [TM]
		479 Rotom (Mow) [TM]	479 Rotom (Wash) [TM]	479 Rotom [TM]	586 Sawsbuck [TM]	212 Scizor [TM]	123 Scyther [TM]	497 Serperior [TM]
		496 Servine [TM]	540 Sewaddle [TM]	403 Shinx [TM]	561 Sigilyph [24, TM]	080 Slowbro [TM]	199 Slowking [TM]	079 Slowpoke [TM]
		218 Slugma [TM]	685 Slurpuff [58, TM]	238 Smoochum [TM]	495 Snivy [TM]	361 Snorunt [TM]	459 Snover [TM]	577 Solosis [16, TM]
		338 Solrock [TM]	325 Spoink [TM]	682 Spritzee [TM]	234 Stantler [TM]	121 Starmie [TM]	120 Staryu [46, TM]	192 Sunflora [TM]
		191 Sunkern [TM]	541 Swadloon [TM]	220 Swinub [TM]	684 Swirlix [58, TM]	528 Swoobat [TM]	700 Sylveon [33, TM]	468 Togekiss [TM]
		175 Togepi [TM]	176 Togetic [TM]	389 Torterra [TM]	387 Turtwig [TM]	480 Uxie [TM]	583 Vanillish [TM]	582 Vanillite [TM]
		584 Vanilluxe [TM]	003 Venusaur [TM]	494 Victini [TM]	640 Virizion [TM]	666 Vivillon [1, TM]	313 Volbeat [TM]	637 Volcarona [TM]
		100 Voltorb [29, TM]	505 Watchog [TM]	547 Whimsicott [TM]	040 Wigglytuff [TM]	527 Woobat [TM]	178 Xatu [TM]	716 Xerneas [5, TM]
		145 Zapdos [64, TM]	523 Zebstrika [TM]	644 Zekrom [TM]				
Normal	Lock-On	649 Genesect [11]	600 Klang [56]	707 Klefki [E]	599 Klink [50]	601 Klinklang [60]	081 Magnemite [41]	082 Magneton [49]
		462 Magnezone [49]	299 Nosepass [43]	137 Porygon [45]	233 Porygon2 [45]	474 Porygon-Z [45]	476 Probopass [43]	378 Regice [55]
		377 Regirock [55]	379 Registeel [55]	223 Remoraid [6]	524 Roggenrola [E]			
	Lovely Kiss	124 Jynx [1, 8]						
Fighting	Low Kick	306 Aggron [BP]	190 Aipom [BP]	424 Ambipom [BP]	348 Armaldo [BP]	531 Audino [BP]	689 Barbaracle [BP]	614 Beartic [BP]
		625 Bisharp [BP]	257 Blaziken [BP]	438 Bonsly [8, BP]	654 Braixen [BP]	427 Buneary [BP, E]	331 Cacnea [BP, E]	332 Cacturne [BP]
		565 Carracosta [BP]	652 Chesnaught [BP]	650 Chespin [BP]	390 Chimchar [BP]	256 Combusken [BP]	534 Conkeldurr [12, BP]	453 Croagunk [BP]
		159 Croconaw [BP]	613 Cubchoo [BP]	104 Cubone [BP]	655 Delphox [BP]	386 Deoxys (Atk) [BP]	386 Deoxys (Def) [BP]	386 Deoxys (Nor) [BP]
		386 Deoxys (Spd) [BP]	660 Diggersby [BP]	096 Drowzee [BP]	125 Electabuzz [8, BP]	466 Electivire [1, 8, BP]	239 Elekid [8, BP]	500 Emboar [BP]
		103 Exeggutor [BP]	295 Exploud [BP]	160 Feraligatr [BP]	419 Floatzel [BP]	611 Fraxure [BP]	657 Frogadier [BP]	475 Gallade [BP]
		055 Golduck [BP]	622 Golett [BP]	623 Golurk [BP]	210 Granbull [BP]	658 Greninja [BP]	253 Grovyle [BP]	533 Gurdurr [12, BP]
		297 Hariyama [BP]	701 Hawlucha [BP]	612 Haxorus [BP]	631 Heatmor [BP]	695 Heliolisk [BP]	214 Heracross [BP]	107 Hitmonchan [BP]
		106 Hitmonlee [BP]	237 Hitmontop [BP]	097 Hypno [BP]	392 Infernape [BP]	141 Kabutops [BP]	115 Kangaskhan [BP]	352 Kecleon [BP]
		552 Krokorok [BP]	553 Krookodile [BP]	428 Lopunny [BP]	294 Loudred [BP]	448 Lucario [BP]	068 Machamp [1, BP]	067 Machoke [1, BP]
		066 Machop [1, BP]	126 Magmar [BP]	467 Magmortar [BP]	296 Makuhita [BP]	056 Mankey [1, BP]	105 Marowak [BP]	259 Marshtomp [BP]
		308 Medicham [BP]	307 Meditite [BP]	648 Meloetta [BP]	151 Mew [BP]	150 Mewtwo [BP]	619 Mienfoo [BP, E]	620 Mienshao [BP]
		391 Monferno [BP]	258 Mudkip [BP]	274 Nuzleaf [BP]	674 Pancham [BP]	675 Pangoro [BP]	515 Panpour [BP, E]	511 Pansage [BP, E]
		513 Pansear [BP, E]	504 Patrat [BP]	624 Pawniard [BP]	499 Pignite [BP]	077 Ponyta [BP, E]	057 Primeape [1, BP]	651 Quilladin [BP]
		078 Rapidash [BP]	447 Riolu [BP, E]	302 Sableye [BP]	539 Sawk [BP]	254 Sceptile [BP]	560 Scrafty [1, BP]	559 Scraggy [1, BP]
		537 Seismitoad [BP]	275 Shiftry [BP]	516 Simipour [BP]	512 Simisage [BP]	514 Simisear [BP]	289 Slaking [BP]	215 Sneasel [BP]
		209 Snubbull [BP]	327 Spinda [BP]	185 Sudowoodo [1, 8, BP]	260 Swampert [BP]	538 Throh [BP]	532 Timburr [12, BP]	255 Torchic [BP, E]
		158 Totodile [BP]	454 Toxicroak [BP]	252 Treecko [BP]	157 Typhlosion [BP]	248 Tyranitar [BP]	236 Tyrogue [BP]	217 Ursaring [BP]
		288 Vigoroth [BP]	505 Watchog [1, BP]	461 Weavile [BP]	335 Zangoose [BP]	571 Zoroark [BP]		
	Low Sweep (TM47)	190 Aipom [TM]	424 Ambipom [TM]	625 Bisharp [TM]	257 Blaziken [TM]	286 Breloom [TM]	652 Chesnaught [TM]	650 Chespin [TM]
		390 Chimchar [TM]	256 Combusken [TM]	534 Conkeldurr [TM]	453 Croagunk [TM]	386 Deoxys (Atk) [TM]	386 Deoxys (Def) [TM]	386 Deoxys (Nor) [TM]
		386 Deoxys (Spd) [TM]	096 Drowzee [TM]	125 Electabuzz [TM]	466 Electivire [TM]	500 Emboar [TM]	475 Gallade [TM]	055 Golduck [TM]
		622 Golett [TM]	623 Golurk [TM]	576 Gothitelle [TM]	253 Grovyle [TM]	533 Gurdurr [TM]	297 Hariyama [TM]	701 Hawlucha [TM]
		695 Heliolisk [TM]	694 Helioptile [TM]	107 Hitmonchan [TM]	106 Hitmonlee [TM]	237 Hitmontop [TM]	097 Hypno [TM]	392 Infernape [TM]
		552 Krokorok [TM]	553 Krookodile [TM]	428 Lopunny [TM]	448 Lucario [TM]	068 Machamp [13, TM]	067 Machoke [13, TM]	066 Machop [13, TM]

	Move	Pokémon that can learn it						
Fighting	Low Sweep (TM47)	126 Magmar [TM]	467 Magmortar [TM]	296 Makuhita [TM]	056 Mankey [TM]	308 Medicham [TM]	307 Meditite [TM]	648 Meloetta [TM]
		151 Mew [TM]	150 Mewtwo [TM]	619 Mienfoo [TM]	620 Mienshao [TM]	391 Monferno [TM]	274 Nuzleaf [TM]	674 Pancham [TM]
		675 Pangoro [70, TM]	515 Panpour [TM]	511 Pansage [TM]	513 Pansear [TM]	624 Pawniard [TM]	499 Pignite [TM]	062 Poliwrath [TM]
		057 Primeape [TM]	651 Quilladin [TM]	447 Riolu [TM]	302 Sableye [TM]	539 Sawk [17, TM]	254 Sceptile [TM]	560 Scrafty [TM]
		559 Scraggy [TM]	275 Shiftry [TM]	516 Simipour [TM]	512 Simisage [TM]	514 Simisear [TM]	289 Slaking [TM]	215 Sneasel [TM]
		538 Throh [TM]	532 Timburr [TM]	454 Toxicroak [TM]	236 Tyrogue [TM]	288 Vigoroth [TM]	461 Weavile [TM]	571 Zoroark [TM]
Normal	Lucky Chant	531 Audino [E]	654 Braixen [27]	351 Castform [E]	421 Cherrim [48]	420 Cherubi [40]	035 Clefairy [37]	222 Corsola [23]
		655 Delphox [27]	580 Ducklett [E]	102 Exeggcute [E]	653 Fennekin [25]	669 Flabébé [10]	670 Floette [10]	671 Florges [1]
		044 Gloom [24]	281 Kirlia [14]	370 Luvdisc [14]	481 Mesprit [31]	312 Minun [E]	429 Mismagius [1]	517 Munna [5]
		518 Musharna [1]	177 Natu [12]	043 Oddish [23]	172 Pichu [E]	519 Pidove [E]	311 Plusle [E]	280 Ralts [14]
		238 Smoochum [31]	325 Spoink [E]	175 Togepi [E]	178 Xatu [12]			
Psychic	Lunar Dance	488 Cresselia [1, 84]						
Psychic	Luster Purge	381 Latios [24]						

M

	Move	Pokémon that can learn it						
Fighting	Mach Punch	286 Breloom [23]	107 Hitmonchan [16]	392 Infernape [14]	166 Ledian [17]	165 Ledyba [17]	240 Magby [E]	391 Monferno [14]
		532 Timburr [E]	236 Tyrogue [E]					
Psychic	Magic Coat	063 Abra [BP]	359 Absol [BP, E]	065 Alakazam [BP]	594 Alomomola [BP]	493 Arceus [BP]	683 Aromatisse [BP]	531 Audino [BP]
		482 Azelf [BP]	343 Baltoy [BP]	354 Banette [BP]	411 Bastiodon [BP]	153 Bayleef [BP]	606 Beheeyem [BP]	654 Braixen [BP]
		427 Buneary [BP]	703 Carbink [BP]	251 Celebi [BP]	152 Chikorita [BP]	358 Chimecho [BP]	433 Chingling [BP]	344 Claydol [BP]
		036 Clefable [BP]	035 Clefairy [BP]	173 Cleffa [BP]	563 Cofagrigus [BP]	222 Corsola [BP]	488 Cresselia [BP]	615 Cryogonal [BP]
		655 Delphox [BP]	386 Deoxys (Atk) [BP]	386 Deoxys (Def) [BP]	386 Deoxys (Nor) [BP]	386 Deoxys (Spd) [BP]	426 Drifblim [BP]	425 Drifloon [BP]
		096 Drowzee [BP]	206 Dunsparce [BP, E]	578 Duosion [BP]	101 Electrode [BP]	605 Elgyem [BP]	196 Espeon [BP]	677 Espurr [BP]
		653 Fennekin [BP, E]	669 Flabébé [BP]	670 Floette [BP]	671 Florges [BP]	592 Frillish [BP]	475 Gallade [BP]	282 Gardevoir [BP]
		649 Genesect [BP]	203 Girafarig [BP, E]	487 Giratina (Ori) [BP]	622 Golett [BP]	623 Golurk [BP]	574 Gothita [BP]	576 Gothitelle [BP]
		575 Gothorita [BP]	711 Gourgeist [BP]	326 Grumpig [21, BP]	163 Hoothoot [BP]	097 Hypno [BP]	174 Igglybuff [BP]	593 Jellicent [BP]
		039 Jigglypuff [BP]	385 Jirachi [BP]	124 Jynx [BP]	064 Kadabra [BP]	352 Kecleon [BP, E]	281 Kirlia [BP]	600 Klang [BP]
		707 Klefki [BP]	599 Klink [BP]	601 Klinklang [BP]	380 Latias [BP]	381 Latios [BP]	542 Leavanny [BP]	428 Lopunny [1, BP]
		337 Lunatone [BP]	081 Magnemite [BP]	082 Magneton [BP]	462 Magnezone [BP]	308 Medicham [BP]	307 Meditite [BP]	154 Meganium [BP]
		648 Meloetta [BP]	678 Meowstic (F) [BP]	678 Meowstic (M) [BP]	481 Mesprit [BP]	151 Mew [BP]	150 Mewtwo [BP]	350 Milotic [BP]
		439 Mime Jr. [BP]	200 Misdreavus [BP]	429 Mismagius [BP]	122 Mr. Mime [BP]	517 Munna [BP, E]	518 Musharna [BP]	177 Natu [BP]
		164 Noctowl [BP]	299 Nosepass [BP]	708 Phantump [BP]	137 Porygon [56, BP]	233 Porygon2 [1, 56, BP]	474 Porygon-Z [1, 56, BP]	476 Probopass [BP]
		710 Pumpkaboo [BP]	280 Ralts [BP]	579 Reuniclus [BP]	302 Sableye [BP]	540 Sewaddle [BP]	353 Shuppet [BP]	561 Sigilyph [BP]
		080 Slowbro [BP]	199 Slowking [BP]	079 Slowpoke [BP]	685 Slurpuff [BP]	238 Smoochum [BP]	577 Solosis [BP]	338 Solrock [BP]
		325 Spoink [21, BP]	682 Spritzee [BP]	121 Starmie [BP]	120 Staryu [BP]	541 Swadloon [BP]	684 Swirlix [BP]	528 Swoobat [BP]
		700 Sylveon [BP]	072 Tentacool [BP]	073 Tentacruel [BP]	468 Togekiss [BP]	175 Togepi [BP]	176 Togetic [BP]	709 Trevenant [BP]
		480 Uxie [BP]	583 Vanillish [BP]	582 Vanillite [BP]	584 Vanilluxe [BP]	494 Victini [BP]	100 Voltorb [BP]	040 Wigglytuff [BP]
		527 Woobat [BP]	178 Xatu [BP]	562 Yamask [BP]				
	Magic Room	063 Abra [BP]	065 Alakazam [BP]	482 Azelf [BP]	354 Banette [BP]	654 Braixen [53, BP]	251 Celebi [BP]	488 Cresselia [BP]
		655 Delphox [58, BP]	096 Drowzee [BP]	196 Espeon [BP]	677 Espurr [BP]	653 Fennekin [46, BP]	475 Gallade [BP]	282 Gardevoir [BP]
		574 Gothita [48, BP]	576 Gothitelle [59, BP]	575 Gothorita [53, BP]	097 Hypno [BP]	385 Jirachi [BP]	124 Jynx [BP]	064 Kadabra [BP]
		281 Kirlia [BP]	707 Klefki [44, BP]	380 Latias [BP]	337 Lunatone [49, BP]	648 Meloetta [BP]	678 Meowstic (F) [BP]	678 Meowstic (M) [BP]
		481 Mesprit [BP]	151 Mew [BP]	150 Mewtwo [BP]	439 Mime Jr. [BP, E]	200 Misdreavus [BP]	429 Mismagius [BP]	122 Mr. Mime [BP, E]
		177 Natu [BP]	280 Ralts [BP]	353 Shuppet [BP]	561 Sigilyph [BP]	238 Smoochum [BP]	234 Stantler [BP]	480 Uxie [BP]
		040 Wigglytuff [BP]	178 Xatu [BP]					
Grass	Magical Leaf	153 Bayleef [22]	182 Bellossom [24]	069 Bellsprout [E]	001 Bulbasaur [E]	331 Cacnea [E]	455 Carnivine [E]	251 Celebi [19]
		421 Cherrim [19]	420 Cherubi [19]	152 Chikorita [20]	173 Cleffa [16]	669 Flabébé [22]	670 Floette [25]	671 Florges [1]
		282 Gardevoir [17]	281 Kirlia [17]	470 Leafeon [20]	154 Meganium [22]	678 Meowstic (F) [1]	429 Mismagius [1]	122 Mr. Mime [1]
		511 Pansage [E]	548 Petilil [19]	280 Ralts [17]	315 Roselia [19]	407 Roserade [1]	492 Shaymin (Land) [10]	492 Shaymin (Sky) [10]
		495 Snivy [E]	459 Snover [E]	176 Togetic [1]	252 Treecko [E]	357 Tropius [16]	640 Virizion [13]	
Fire	Magma Storm	485 Heatran [1, 96]						
Steel	Magnet Bomb	649 Genesect [22]	081 Magnemite [17]	082 Magneton [17]	462 Magnezone [17]	476 Probopass [1, 10]		
Electric	Magnet Rise	681 Aegislash [BP]	306 Aggron [BP]	698 Amaura [BP, E]	181 Ampharos [BP]	304 Aron [BP]	699 Aurorus [BP]	411 Bastiodon [BP]
		625 Bisharp [BP]	522 Blitzle [BP]	703 Carbink [BP]	638 Cobalion [BP]	702 Dedenne [BP]	483 Dialga [BP]	719 Diancie [BP]
		680 Doublade [BP]	603 Eelektrik [BP]	604 Eelektross [BP]	125 Electabuzz [BP]	466 Electivire [BP]	309 Electrike [BP]	101 Electrode [36, BP]
		239 Elekid [BP]	530 Excadrill [BP]	597 Ferroseed [BP]	598 Ferrothorn [BP]	180 Flaaffy [BP]	205 Forretress [1, 60, BP]	596 Galvantula [BP]
		649 Genesect [1, BP]	695 Heliolisk [BP]	694 Helioptile [BP]	679 Honedge [BP]	135 Jolteon [BP]	595 Joltik [BP]	600 Klang [BP]
		707 Klefki [BP]	599 Klink [BP]	601 Klinklang [BP]	305 Lairon [BP]	636 Larvesta [BP, E]	448 Lucario [BP]	404 Luxio [BP]
		405 Luxray [BP]	081 Magnemite [43, BP]	082 Magneton [53, BP]	462 Magnezone [53, BP]	310 Manectric [BP]	179 Mareep [BP]	303 Mawile [BP]
		376 Metagross [1, BP]	375 Metang [1, BP]	151 Mew [BP]	312 Minun [BP]	299 Nosepass [BP]	417 Pachirisu [BP]	624 Pawniard [BP]
		172 Pichu [BP]	025 Pikachu [BP]	311 Plusle [BP]	137 Porygon [23, BP]	233 Porygon2 [23, BP]	474 Porygon-Z [23, BP]	476 Probopass [1, BP]

	Move	Pokémon that can learn it						
Electric	Magnet Rise	026 Raichu [BP]	243 Raikou [BP]	379 Registeel [BP]	447 Riolu [BP]	410 Shieldon [BP]	403 Shinx [BP]	208 Steelix [BP]
		618 Stunfisk [BP]	602 Tynamo [BP]	583 Vanillish [BP]	582 Vanillite [BP, E]	584 Vanilluxe [BP]	637 Volcarona [BP]	100 Voltorb [34, BP]
		413 Wormadam (Trash) [BP]	523 Zebstrika [BP]	644 Zekrom [BP]				
	Magnetic Flux	181 Ampharos [1]	101 Electrode [1]	601 Klinklang [1, 76]	462 Magnezone [1]			
Ground	Magnitude	339 Barboach [20]	323 Camerupt [12]	050 Diglett [15]	232 Donphan [30]	051 Dugtrio [15]	074 Geodude [12]	076 Golem [12]
		622 Golett [25]	623 Golurk [25]	075 Graveler [12]	108 Lickitung [E]	299 Nosepass [E]	322 Numel [12]	369 Relicanth [E]
		111 Rhyhorn [E]	524 Roggenrola [E]	027 Sandshrew [14]	028 Sandslash [14]	498 Tepig [E]	340 Whiscash [20]	
Fighting	Mat Block	658 Greninja [1]						
Normal	Me First	359 Absol [41, E]	617 Accelgor [28]	522 Blitzle [E]	418 Buizel [E]	453 Croagunk [E]	580 Ducklett [E]	662 Fletchinder [46]
		661 Fletchling [41]	162 Furret [50]	701 Hawlucha [E]	463 Lickilicky [41]	108 Lickitung [41]	448 Lucario [37]	678 Meowstic (F) [1]
		151 Mew [70]	150 Mewtwo [93]	619 Mienfoo [E]	200 Misdreavus [E]	177 Natu [50]	674 Pancham [E]	127 Pinsir [E]
		261 Poochyena [E]	019 Rattata [E]	551 Sandile [E]	161 Sentret [42]	540 Sewaddle [E]	079 Slowpoke [E]	234 Stantler [1, 55, E]
		618 Stunfisk [E]	663 Talonflame [49]	178 Xatu [57]				
	Mean Look	359 Absol [E]	563 Cofagrigus [51]	169 Crobat [32]	356 Dusclops [52]	477 Dusknoir [52]	355 Duskull [46]	092 Gastly [8]
		094 Gengar [8]	203 Girafarig [E]	042 Golbat [32]	574 Gothita [E]	088 Grimer [E]	093 Haunter [8]	124 Jynx [25]
		678 Meowstic (M) [1]	200 Misdreavus [19]	198 Murkrow [41]	504 Patrat [31]	624 Pawniard [E]	280 Ralts [E]	302 Sableye [46, E]
		551 Sandile [E]	238 Smoochum [25]	495 Snivy [E]	197 Umbreon [37]	629 Vullaby [E]	505 Watchog [36]	562 Yamask [45]
		041 Zubat [29]						
Psychic	Meditate	453 Croagunk [E]	096 Drowzee [21]	239 Elekid [E]	106 Hitmonlee [5]	097 Hypno [21]	066 Machop [E]	056 Mankey [E]
		308 Medicham [1, 4]	307 Meditite [4]	619 Mienfoo [5]	620 Mienshao [1, 5]	439 Mime Jr. [8]	122 Mr. Mime [8]	238 Smoochum [E]
Grass	Mega Drain	617 Accelgor [20]	591 Amoonguss [15]	267 Beautifly [22]	182 Bellossom [1]	286 Breloom [12]	406 Budew [13]	546 Cottonee [13]
		590 Foongus [15]	044 Gloom [19]	388 Grotle [27]	253 Grovyle [13]	187 Hoppip [25]	189 Jumpluff [29]	140 Kabuto [36]
		141 Kabutops [36]	345 Lileep [E]	549 Lilligant [1]	270 Lotad [18]	272 Ludicolo [1]	556 Maractus [13]	043 Oddish [19]
		548 Petilil [13]	315 Roselia [13]	407 Roserade [1]	254 Sceptile [13]	497 Serperior [24]	496 Servine [24]	616 Shelmet [20]
		285 Shroomish [12]	188 Skiploom [28]	495 Snivy [22]	192 Sunflora [10]	191 Sunkern [10]	114 Tangela [23, E]	465 Tangrowth [23]
		389 Torterra [27]	252 Treecko [13]	387 Turtwig [25]	045 Vileplume [1]	547 Whimsicott [1]		
Normal	Mega Kick	106 Hitmonlee [1, 53]						
	Mega Punch	074 Geodude [E]	622 Golett [21]	623 Golurk [21]	107 Hitmonchan [46]	115 Kangaskhan [25]	240 Magby [E]	151 Mew [10]
Bug	Megahorn	359 Absol [E]	626 Bouffalant [41]	118 Goldeen [45]	214 Heracross [37, E]	588 Karrablast [E]	034 Nidoking [1, 58]	078 Rapidash [1]
		112 Rhydon [55]	111 Rhyhorn [49]	464 Rhyperior [55]	503 Samurott [1]	586 Sawsbuck [1]	545 Scolipede [1, 65]	119 Seaking [1, 54]
		167 Spinarak [E]	234 Stantler [E]	716 Xerneas [44]				
Dark	Memento	546 Cottonee [E]	050 Diglett [E]	425 Drifloon [E]	355 Duskull [E]	088 Grimer [48]	187 Hoppip [49]	189 Jumpluff [69]
		109 Koffing [45]	608 Lampent [33]	381 Latios [1, 61]	607 Litwick [33]	200 Misdreavus [E]	089 Muk [57]	280 Ralts [E]
		422 Shellos [E]	188 Skiploom [60]	435 Skuntank [51]	218 Slugma [E]	442 Spiritomb [43]	434 Stunky [43]	480 Uxie [1, 76]
		110 Weezing [57]	562 Yamask [E]	570 Zorua [E]				
Steel	Metal Burst	306 Aggron [63]	304 Aron [49]	411 Bastiodon [43]	625 Bisharp [1]	638 Cobalion [1, 67]	483 Dialga [24]	305 Lairon [55]
		303 Mawile [E]	111 Rhyhorn [E]	302 Sableye [E]	410 Shieldon [37]			
	Metal Claw	306 Aggron [10]	347 Anorith [17]	348 Armaldo [17]	304 Aron [10]	625 Bisharp [25]	004 Charmander [E]	638 Cobalion [13]
		341 Corphish [E]	483 Dialga [6]	529 Drilbur [15]	621 Druddigon [E]	632 Durant [21]	395 Empoleon [16]	530 Excadrill [15]
		597 Ferroseed [14]	598 Ferrothorn [14]	649 Genesect [1]	443 Gible [E]	207 Gligar [E]	099 Kingler [21]	098 Krabby [21]
		305 Lairon [10]	448 Lucario [1]	376 Metagross [1, 20]	375 Metang [1, 20]	290 Nincada [21]	046 Paras [E]	624 Pawniard [25]
		394 Prinplup [16]	379 Registeel [1, 7]	027 Sandshrew [E]	212 Scizor [21]	227 Skarmory [9]	215 Sneasel [22]	216 Teddiursa [E]
		158 Totodile [E]	461 Weavile [22]	335 Zangoose [E]				
	Metal Sound	306 Aggron [31]	304 Aron [31]	411 Bastiodon [1, 10]	625 Bisharp [38]	437 Bronzong [31]	436 Bronzor [31]	680 Doublade [8]
		529 Drilbur [E]	632 Durant [1, 66]	649 Genesect [33]	485 Heatran [25]	679 Honedge [8, E]	140 Kabuto [41]	141 Kabutops [45]
		600 Klang [48]	707 Klefki [12]	599 Klink [45]	601 Klinklang [48]	305 Lairon [31]	448 Lucario [24]	081 Magnemite [25]
		082 Magneton [25]	462 Magnezone [25]	624 Pawniard [38]	410 Shieldon [10]	227 Skarmory [42]	413 Wormadam (Trash) [29]	
	Meteor Mash	035 Clefairy [50]	376 Metagross [44]	375 Metang [44]	025 Pikachu ◆			
Normal	Metronome	113 Chansey [E]	036 Clefable [1]	035 Clefairy [31]	173 Cleffa [E]	440 Happiny [E]	151 Mew [20]	446 Munchlax [1]
		209 Snubbull [E]	175 Togepi [5]	176 Togetic [1, 5]				
	Milk Drink	673 Gogoat [58]	241 Miltank [11]	672 Skiddo [50, E]				
	Mimic	438 Bonsly [15]	441 Chatot [33]	173 Cleffa [E]	676 Furfrou [E]	039 Jigglypuff [37]	439 Mime Jr. [15, E]	122 Mr. Mime [15, E]
		209 Snubbull [E]	185 Sudowoodo [15]					
	Mind Reader	144 Articuno [22]	286 Breloom [33]	406 Budew [E]	656 Froakie [E]	106 Hitmonlee [33]	308 Medicham [25]	307 Meditite [25]
		290 Nincada [25]	291 Ninjask [29]	060 Poliwag [E]	062 Poliwrath [43]	447 Riolu [E]	315 Roselia [E]	540 Sewaddle [E]
		292 Shedinja [25]	616 Shelmet [E]	283 Surskit [E]	236 Tyrogue [E]			
	Minimize	242 Blissey [23]	113 Chansey [23]	036 Clefable [1]	035 Clefairy [25]	426 Drifblim [1]	425 Drifloon [1]	088 Grimer [21]
		608 Lampent [1, 3]	607 Litwick [3]	089 Muk [21]	211 Qwilfish [9]	120 Staryu [31]		

◆ When Cosplay Pikachu becomes Pikachu Rock Star, it learns the move Meteor Mash. When it changes back to Cosplay Pikachu or wears other costumes, it forgets the move.

Type	Move	Pokémon that can learn it						
Psychic	Miracle Eye	065 Alakazam [23]	606 Beheeyem [1, 11]	605 Elgyem [11]	574 Gothita [E]	064 Kadabra [23]	678 Meowstic (M) [31]	376 Metagross [29]
		375 Metang [29]	150 Mewtwo [29]	177 Natu [36]	561 Sigilyph [1]	238 Smoochum [E]	178 Xatu [39]	
Psychic	Mirror Coat	594 Alomomola [E]	698 Amaura [E]	712 Bergmite [E]	222 Corsola [45]	386 Deoxys (Def) [73]	101 Electrode [58]	349 Feebas [E]
		203 Girafarig [E]	471 Glaceon [33]	574 Gothita [E]	345 Lileep [E]	428 Lopunny [1]	462 Magnezone [1]	226 Mantine [E]
		458 Mantyke [E]	258 Mudkip [E]	422 Shellos [E]	495 Snivy [E]	325 Spoink [E]	007 Squirtle [E]	245 Suicune [43]
		072 Tentacool [E]	583 Vanillish [47]	582 Vanillite [44]	584 Vanilluxe [50]	100 Voltorb [48]	202 Wobbuffet [1]	360 Wynaut [15]
Flying	Mirror Move	441 Chatot [9]	256 Combusken [47]	084 Doduo [E]	580 Ducklett [E]	083 Farfetch'd [E]	022 Fearow [23]	163 Hoothoot [E]
		630 Mandibuzz [1, 70]	198 Murkrow [E]	018 Pidgeot [56]	017 Pidgeotto [52]	016 Pidgey [45]	561 Sigilyph [34]	021 Spearow [21]
		396 Starly [E]	333 Swablu [30]	276 Taillow [E]	175 Togepi [E]	255 Torchic [41]	629 Vullaby [64]	
Steel	Mirror Shot	597 Ferroseed [30]	598 Ferrothorn [30]	205 Forretress [31]	600 Klang [36]	707 Klefki [34]	599 Klink [36]	601 Klinklang [36]
		081 Magnemite [23]	082 Magneton [23]	462 Magnezone [23]	583 Vanillish [26]	582 Vanillite [26]	584 Vanilluxe [26]	413 Wormadam (Trash) [26]
Ice	Mist	460 Abomasnow [21]	594 Alomomola [E]	334 Altaria [14]	698 Amaura [18]	144 Articuno [8]	699 Aurorus [18]	712 Bergmite [E]
		170 Chinchou [E]	222 Corsola [E]	488 Cresselia [20]	615 Cryogonal [1, 21]	147 Dratini [E]	395 Empoleon [46]	349 Feebas [E]
		592 Frillish [E]	131 Lapras [4]	270 Lotad [15]	473 Mamoswine [37]	150 Mewtwo [86]	279 Pelipper [12]	221 Piloswine [37]
		393 Piplup [36]	060 Poliwag [E]	394 Prinplup [42]	195 Quagsire [48]	422 Shellos [E]	459 Snover [21, E]	007 Squirtle [E]
		245 Suicune [36]	283 Surskit [25]	333 Swablu [14]	220 Swinub [35]	535 Tympole [E]	583 Vanillish [16]	582 Vanillite [16]
		584 Vanilluxe [16]	320 Wailmer [22]	321 Wailord [22]	278 Wingull [12, E]	194 Wooper [43]		
Psychic	Mist Ball	380 Latias [24]						
Fairy	Misty Terrain	683 Aromatisse [42]	531 Audino [1]	173 Cleffa [E]	669 Flabébé [37]	670 Floette [43]	671 Florges [1]	282 Gardevoir [1]
		174 Igglybuff [E]	303 Mawile [E]	678 Meowstic (M) [50]	122 Mr. Mime [1]	280 Ralts [E]	682 Spritzee [42]	700 Sylveon [29]
		716 Xerneas [63]						
Fairy	Moonblast	334 Altaria [52]	683 Aromatisse [31]	703 Carbink [50]	035 Clefairy [46]	488 Cresselia [99]	719 Diancie [50]	669 Flabébé [41]
		670 Floette [46]	671 Florges [1]	282 Gardevoir [1, 62]	337 Lunatone [1]	043 Oddish [43]	682 Spritzee [31]	333 Swablu [46]
		700 Sylveon [37]	547 Whimsicott [50]	716 Xerneas [35]				
Fairy	Moonlight	035 Clefairy [43]	488 Cresselia [1, 57]	269 Dustox [17]	102 Exeggcute [E]	044 Gloom [29]	314 Illumise [19]	517 Munna [17]
		715 Noivern [1]	043 Oddish [27]	302 Sableye [E]	197 Umbreon [33]	313 Volbeat [19]		
Normal	Morning Sun	267 Beautifly [17]	421 Cherrim [1]	420 Cherubi [1]	196 Espeon [33]	058 Growlithe [E]	636 Larvesta [E]	519 Pidove [E]
		077 Ponyta [E]	191 Sunkern [E]	175 Togepi [E]	048 Venonat [E]			
Ground	Mud Bomb	024 Arbok [39]	339 Barboach [13]	113 Chansey [E]	453 Croagunk [29]	050 Diglett [26, E]	051 Dugtrio [28]	023 Ekans [33]
		423 Gastrodon [11]	088 Grimer [18]	440 Happiny [E]	473 Mamoswine [18]	259 Marshtomp [22]	258 Mudkip [E]	089 Muk [18]
		322 Numel [E]	221 Piloswine [18]	060 Poliwag [41]	061 Poliwhirl [53]	054 Psyduck [E]	195 Quagsire [19]	422 Shellos [11]
		300 Skitty [E]	618 Stunfisk [21]	260 Swampert [22]	220 Swinub [18]	454 Toxicroak [29]	535 Tympole [E]	340 Whiscash [13]
		194 Wooper [19]						
Ground	Mud Shot	339 Barboach [E]	550 Basculin [E]	626 Bouffalant [E]	659 Bunnelby [18]	652 Chesnaught [41]	650 Chespin [35]	660 Diggersby [18]
		443 Gible [E]	118 Goldeen [E]	383 Groudon [1]	140 Kabuto [16, E]	141 Kabutops [16]	099 Kingler [19]	098 Krabby [19]
		645 Landorus [1]	259 Marshtomp [16]	138 Omanyte [25]	139 Omastar [25]	536 Palpitoad [16]	060 Poliwag [28, E]	061 Poliwhirl [32]
		195 Quagsire [9]	651 Quilladin [39]	369 Relicanth [E]	223 Remoraid [E]	027 Sandshrew [E]	537 Seismitoad [16]	090 Shellder [E]
		618 Stunfisk [13]	283 Surskit [E]	260 Swampert [16]	220 Swinub [E]	328 Trapinch [E]	535 Tympole [16]	194 Wooper [9]
Ground	Mud Sport	347 Anorith [4]	348 Armaldo [1, 4]	339 Barboach [6]	427 Buneary [E]	366 Clamperl [E]	341 Corphish [E]	529 Drilbur [1]
		580 Ducklett [E]	530 Excadrill [1]	349 Feebas [E]	656 Froakie [E]	423 Gastrodon [1, 2]	074 Geodude [4]	118 Goldeen [E]
		076 Golem [1, 4]	075 Graveler [1, 4]	701 Hawlucha [E]	099 Kingler [1]	098 Krabby [1]	264 Linoone [17]	370 Luvdisc [E]
		473 Mamoswine [1, 5]	226 Mantine [E]	458 Mantyke [E]	258 Mudkip [20]	095 Onix [1]	515 Panpour [E]	221 Piloswine [1, 5]
		393 Piplup [E]	195 Quagsire [1, 5]	369 Relicanth [1, 6]	422 Shellos [2]	079 Slowpoke [E]	007 Squirtle [E]	234 Stantler [E]
		208 Steelix [1]	618 Stunfisk [1]	220 Swinub [5]	158 Totodile [E]	252 Treecko [E]	568 Trubbish [E]	535 Tympole [E]
		340 Whiscash [1, 6]	194 Wooper [5, E]	263 Zigzagoon [17]				
Water	Muddy Water	298 Azurill [E]	339 Barboach [35, E]	550 Basculin [E]	366 Clamperl [E]	692 Clauncher [48]	693 Clawitzer [53]	423 Gastrodon [41]
		706 Goodra [38]	704 Goomy [38]	116 Horsea [E]	382 Kyogre [60]	108 Lickitung [E]	183 Marill [E]	259 Marshtomp [38]
		138 Omanyte [E]	536 Palpitoad [28]	195 Quagsire [53]	369 Relicanth [E]	537 Seismitoad [28]	422 Shellos [37]	705 Sliggoo [38]
		007 Squirtle [E]	618 Stunfisk [40]	260 Swampert [39]	072 Tentacool [E]	535 Tympole [27]	134 Vaporeon [37]	340 Whiscash [39]
		194 Wooper [47]						
Ground	Mud-Slap	306 Aggron [1, 4]	304 Aron [4]	343 Baltoy [7]	689 Barbaracle [18]	339 Barboach [1]	688 Binacle [18]	525 Boldore [17]
		626 Bouffalant [E]	418 Buizel [E]	659 Bunnelby [13]	344 Claydol [7]	453 Croagunk [3]	660 Diggersby [13]	050 Diglett [12]
		529 Drilbur [8]	051 Dugtrio [12]	530 Excadrill [1, 8]	083 Farfetch'd [E]	330 Flygon [5]	423 Gastrodon [1]	526 Gigalith [17]
		118 Goldeen [E]	622 Golett [5]	623 Golurk [1, 5]	088 Grimer [7]	316 Gulpin [E]	694 Helioptile [13]	552 Krokorok [19]
		553 Krookodile [19]	305 Lairon [1, 4]	506 Lillipup [E]	473 Mamoswine [11]	259 Marshtomp [1, 9]	572 Minccino [E]	258 Mudkip [9]
		089 Muk [1, 7]	290 Nincada [17]	231 Phanpy [E]	221 Piloswine [11]	393 Piplup [E]	369 Relicanth [E]	524 Roggenrola [17]
		551 Sandile [19]	422 Shellos [1]	616 Shelmet [E]	213 Shuckle [E]	618 Stunfisk [1]	260 Swampert [1, 9]	220 Swinub [11]
		454 Toxicroak [1, 3]	328 Trapinch [5]	329 Vibrava [5]	340 Whiscash [1]	263 Zigzagoon [E]		
Fire	Mystical Fire	655 Delphox [36, 75]	429 Mismagius [1]					

N

Type	Move	Pokémon that can learn it						
Dark	Nasty Plot	190 Aipom [39]	424 Ambipom [39]	482 Azelf [46]	331 Cacnea [E]	441 Chatot [E]	390 Chimchar [23]	453 Croagunk [38]
		491 Darkrai [75]	096 Drowzee [53, E]	605 Elgyem [E]	203 Girafarig [46]	430 Honchkrow [35]	229 Houndoom [1, 60]	228 Houndour [52, E]
		097 Hypno [1, 53]	352 Kecleon [E]	510 Liepard [50]	630 Mandibuzz [14]	052 Meowth [38]	151 Mew [90]	439 Mime Jr. [E]
		312 Minun [46]	200 Misdreavus [E]	122 Mr. Mime [E]	038 Ninetales [1]	515 Panpour [E]	511 Pansage [E]	513 Pansear [E]
		053 Persian [44]	172 Pichu [13]	311 Plusle [46]	474 Porygon-Z [1]	509 Purrloin [42]	447 Riolu [47]	302 Sableye [E]
		273 Seedot [E]	275 Shiftry [1]	199 Slowking [36]	238 Smoochum [E]	442 Spiritomb [37]	642 Thundurus [1, 61]	175 Togepi [E]
		454 Toxicroak [41]	629 Vullaby [14]	461 Weavile [20]	562 Yamask [E]	571 Zoroark [54]	570 Zorua [49]	041 Zubat [E]
Normal	Natural Gift	334 Altaria [20]	493 Arceus [1]	482 Azelf [1, 66]	153 Bayleef [26]	069 Bellsprout [E]	406 Budew [E]	251 Celebi [46]
		113 Chansey [E]	420 Cherubi [E]	152 Chikorita [23]	546 Cottonee [E]	702 Dedenne [E]	585 Deerling [E]	084 Doduo [E]
		133 Eevee [E]	102 Exeggcute [37, E]	662 Fletchinder [31]	661 Fletchling [29]	205 Forretress [23]	044 Gloom [44]	440 Happiny [E]
		250 Ho-Oh [85]	270 Lotad [12]	249 Lugia [85]	154 Meganium [26]	481 Mesprit [1, 66]	241 Miltank [E]	446 Munchlax [49, E]
		043 Oddish [39]	515 Panpour [40]	511 Pansage [40]	513 Pansear [40]	046 Paras [E]	548 Petilil [E]	231 Phanpy [15]
		204 Pineco [23]	315 Roselia [E]	161 Sentret [E]	492 Shaymin (Land) [46]	492 Shaymin (Sky) [46]	285 Shroomish [E]	495 Snivy [E]
		143 Snorlax [E]	459 Snover [E]	192 Sunflora [31]	191 Sunkern [31, E]	333 Swablu [20]	663 Talonflame [31]	114 Tangela [33, E]
		465 Tangrowth [33]	252 Treecko [E]	357 Tropius [30, E]	480 Uxie [1, 66]	582 Vanillite [E]		
	Nature Power (TM96)	698 Amaura [41, TM]	591 Amoonguss [TM]	699 Aurorus [43, TM]	689 Barbaracle [TM]	153 Bayleef [TM]	182 Bellossom [TM]	069 Bellsprout [TM]
		688 Binacle [TM]	525 Boldore [TM]	438 Bonsly [TM]	406 Budew [TM]	001 Bulbasaur [TM, E]	659 Bunnelby [TM]	331 Cacnea [TM]
		332 Cacturne [TM]	323 Camerupt [TM]	703 Carbink [TM]	455 Carnivine [TM]	251 Celebi [TM]	421 Cherrim [TM]	420 Cherubi [TM, E]
		652 Chesnaught [TM]	650 Chespin [TM]	152 Chikorita [TM, E]	222 Corsola [TM, E]	546 Cottonee [TM]	342 Crawdaunt [TM]	558 Crustle [TM]
		155 Cyndaquil [TM, E]	585 Deerling [41, TM]	719 Diancie [TM]	660 Diggersby [TM]	557 Dwebble [TM]	102 Exeggcute [TM, E]	103 Exeggutor [TM]
		597 Ferroseed [TM]	598 Ferrothorn [TM]	456 Finneon [TM]	669 Flabébé [TM]	670 Floette [TM]	671 Florges [TM]	590 Foongus [TM]
		074 Geodude [TM]	526 Gigalith [TM]	044 Gloom [TM]	673 Gogoat [TM]	076 Golem [TM]	711 Gourgeist [TM]	075 Graveler [TM]
		388 Grotle [TM]	253 Grovyle [TM]	485 Heatran [TM]	002 Ivysaur [TM]	141 Kabutops [TM]	470 Leafeon [TM]	542 Leavanny [TM]
		549 Lilligant [TM]	271 Lombre [28, TM]	270 Lotad [24, TM]	272 Ludicolo [1, TM]	219 Magcargo [TM]	556 Maractus [TM]	154 Meganium [TM]
		151 Mew [TM]	322 Numel [TM]	274 Nuzleaf [9, TM]	043 Oddish [TM, E]	095 Onix [TM]	511 Pansage [TM]	046 Paras [TM]
		047 Parasect [TM]	548 Petilil [TM]	708 Phantump [TM]	710 Pumpkaboo [TM]	156 Quilava [TM]	651 Quilladin [TM]	486 Regigigas [TM]
		524 Roggenrola [TM]	315 Roselia [TM]	407 Roserade [TM]	586 Sawsbuck [44, TM]	254 Sceptile [TM]	273 Seedot [15, TM]	497 Serperior [TM]
		496 Servine [TM]	540 Sewaddle [TM]	492 Shaymin (Land) [TM]	492 Shaymin (Sky) [TM]	275 Shiftry [TM]	512 Simisage [TM]	672 Skiddo [TM]
		218 Slugma [TM]	495 Snivy [TM]	208 Steelix [TM]	185 Sudowoodo [TM]	192 Sunflora [TM]	191 Sunkern [TM, E]	541 Swadloon [TM]
		114 Tangela [TM, E]	465 Tangrowth [TM]	324 Torkoal [TM]	389 Torterra [TM]	252 Treecko [TM]	709 Trevenant [TM]	357 Tropius [TM, E]
		387 Turtwig [TM]	157 Typhlosion [TM]	003 Venusaur [TM]	071 Victreebel [TM]	045 Vileplume [TM]	640 Virizion [TM]	070 Weepinbell [TM]
		547 Whimsicott [TM]	716 Xerneas [72, TM]					
Grass	Needle Arm	331 Cacnea [16]	332 Cacturne [16]	652 Chesnaught [26]	556 Maractus [22]	651 Quilladin [26]		
Dark	Night Daze	571 Zoroark [1, 64]	570 Zorua [57]					
Ghost	Night Shade	168 Ariados [15]	354 Banette [1, 7]	441 Chatot [E]	563 Cofagrigus [13]	386 Deoxys (Atk) [7]	386 Deoxys (Def) [7]	386 Deoxys (Nor) [7]
		386 Deoxys (Spd) [7]	356 Dusclops [1]	477 Dusknoir [1]	355 Duskull [1]	592 Frillish [9]	092 Gastly [15]	094 Gengar [15]
		622 Golett [35]	623 Golurk [35]	093 Haunter [15]	163 Hoothoot [E]	593 Jellicent [1, 9]	608 Lampent [13]	607 Litwick [13]
		198 Murkrow [21]	177 Natu [6]	302 Sableye [6]	353 Shuppet [7]	577 Solosis [E]	167 Spinarak [15]	178 Xatu [1, 6]
		562 Yamask [13]						
Dark	Night Slash	359 Absol [29]	681 Aegislash [1]	610 Axew [E]	689 Barbaracle [44]	688 Binacle [41]	625 Bisharp [49]	341 Corphish [26]
		342 Crawdaunt [26]	615 Cryogonal [1, 57]	613 Cubchoo [E]	680 Doublade [36]	452 Drapion [38]	621 Druddigon [40]	051 Dugtrio [1]
		557 Dwebble [E]	083 Farfetch'd [33, E]	475 Gallade [1]	207 Gligar [E]	472 Gliscor [27]	658 Greninja [1, 70]	631 Heatmor [E]
		214 Heracross [1]	430 Honchkrow [1, 55]	679 Honedge [35]	686 Inkay [46]	141 Kabutops [1, 72]	402 Kricketune [42]	510 Liepard [43]
		687 Malamar [46]	056 Mankey [E]	052 Meowth [49]	290 Nincada [E]	501 Oshawott [E]	624 Pawniard [49]	053 Persian [61]
		519 Pidove [E]	509 Purrloin [37]	027 Sandshrew [E]	254 Sceptile [1]	212 Scizor [45]	123 Scyther [45, E]	336 Seviper [28, E]
		319 Sharpedo [1, 62]	403 Shinx [E]	227 Skarmory [53]	451 Skorupi [38, E]	435 Skuntank [41]	287 Slakoth [E]	167 Spinarak [E]
		434 Stunky [37]	216 Teddiursa [E]	255 Torchic [E]	461 Weavile [35]	716 Xerneas [51]	469 Yanmega [1]	335 Zangoose [E]
		571 Zoroark [30]						
Ghost	Nightmare	491 Darkrai [38]	092 Gastly [47]	094 Gengar [61]	093 Haunter [61]	097 Hypno [1]	517 Munna [29]	442 Spiritomb [E]
		562 Yamask [E]						
Normal	Noble Roar	667 Litleo [15]	668 Pyroar [15]					
Electric	Nuzzle	702 Dedenne [20]	587 Emolga [15]	312 Minun [1]	417 Pachirisu [19]	025 Pikachu [29]	311 Plusle [1]	

O

Type	Move	Pokémon that can learn it						
Flying	Oblivion Wing	717 Yveltal [26]						
Water	Octazooka	116 Horsea [E]	224 Octillery [25]	223 Remoraid [E]				
Normal	Odor Sleuth	059 Arcanine [1]	683 Aromatisse [8]	399 Bidoof [E]	418 Buizel [E]	659 Bunnelby [25]	585 Deerling [E]	660 Diggersby [26]
		309 Electrike [16]	500 Emboar [1, 9]	676 Furfrou [27]	203 Girafarig [5]	058 Growlithe [10]	326 Grumpig [1, 10]	631 Heatmor [6]
		507 Herdier [1, 5]	229 Houndoom [20]	228 Houndour [20]	506 Lillipup [5]	264 Linoone [13]	473 Mamoswine [1]	310 Manectric [16]
		179 Mareep [E]	052 Meowth [E]	262 Mightyena [13]	446 Munchlax [1]	231 Phanpy [1]	499 Pignite [1, 9]	221 Piloswine [1]
		261 Poochyena [13]	325 Spoink [10]	682 Spritzee [8]	508 Stoutland [1, 5]	220 Swinub [1]	528 Swoobat [1, 4]	498 Tepig [9]
		527 Woobat [4]	263 Zigzagoon [13]					
Ghost	Ominous Wind	351 Castform [E]	563 Cofagrigus [25]	491 Darkrai [1]	426 Drifblim [20]	425 Drifloon [20]	355 Duskull [E]	592 Frillish [27]
		478 Froslass [28]	487 Giratina (Alt) [6]	487 Giratina (Ori) [6]	593 Jellicent [27]	284 Masquerain [1]	200 Misdreavus [E]	177 Natu [20]
		479 Rotom (Fan) [29]	479 Rotom (Frost) [29]	479 Rotom (Heat) [29]	479 Rotom (Mow) [29]	479 Rotom (Wash) [29]	479 Rotom [29]	353 Shuppet [E]
		442 Spiritomb [25]	178 Xatu [20]	562 Yamask [25]				
Water	Origin Pulse	382 Kyogre [45]						
Dragon	Outrage	460 Abomasnow [BP]	306 Aggron [BP]	334 Altaria [BP]	698 Amaura [BP]	181 Ampharos [BP]	059 Arcanine [BP]	493 Arceus [BP]
		567 Archeops [BP]	699 Aurorus [BP]	610 Axew [56, BP]	371 Bagon [BP]	411 Bastiodon [BP]	009 Blastoise [BP]	626 Bouffalant [BP]
		006 Charizard [BP]	004 Charmander [E]	633 Deino [62, BP]	483 Dialga [BP]	691 Dragalge [BP]	148 Dragonair [67, BP]	149 Dragonite [67, BP]
		147 Dratini [55, BP]	621 Druddigon [62, BP]	604 Eelektross [BP]	295 Exploud [BP]	160 Feraligatr [BP]	330 Flygon [BP]	611 Fraxure [60, BP]
		444 Gabite [BP]	445 Garchomp [BP]	443 Gible [BP, E]	487 Giratina (Alt) [BP]	487 Giratina (Ori) [BP]	706 Goodra [1, 63, BP]	704 Goomy [BP]
		210 Granbull [1, 67, BP]	058 Growlithe [43, BP]	130 Gyarados [BP]	612 Haxorus [1, 66, BP]	116 Horsea [BP, E]	635 Hydreigon [1, 79, BP]	115 Kangaskhan [46, BP]
		230 Kingdra [BP]	553 Krookodile [1, 60, BP]	646 Kyurem (Blk) [85, BP]	646 Kyurem (Wht) [85, BP]	646 Kyurem [85, BP]	645 Landorus [1, 85, BP]	131 Lapras [BP]
		246 Larvitar [BP, E]	380 Latias [BP]	381 Latios [BP]	056 Mankey [BP]	105 Marowak [BP]	154 Meganium [BP]	151 Mew [BP]
		034 Nidoking [BP]	031 Nidoqueen [BP]	714 Noibat [BP, E]	715 Noivern [BP]	484 Palkia [BP]	675 Pangoro [BP]	057 Primeape [BP]
		247 Pupitar [BP]	409 Rampardos [BP]	384 Rayquaza [80, BP]	643 Reshiram [85, BP]	112 Rhydon [BP]	464 Rhyperior [BP]	373 Salamence [BP]
		254 Sceptile [BP]	560 Scrafty [BP]	117 Seadra [BP]	497 Serperior [BP]	372 Shelgon [BP]	690 Skrelp [BP]	705 Sliggoo [BP]
		143 Snorlax [BP]	333 Swablu [BP]	260 Swampert [BP]	128 Tauros [BP]	389 Torterra [BP]	357 Tropius [BP]	248 Tyranitar [BP]
		697 Tyrantrum [BP]	696 Tyrunt [BP]	003 Venusaur [BP]	329 Vibrava [BP]	716 Xerneas [93, BP]	644 Zekrom [85, BP]	634 Zweilous [71, BP]
		718 Zygarde [93, BP]						
Fire	Overheat (TM50)	059 Arcanine [TM]	493 Arceus [TM]	257 Blaziken [TM]	654 Braixen [TM]	323 Camerupt [TM]	609 Chandelure [TM]	006 Charizard [TM]
		004 Charmander [TM]	005 Charmeleon [TM]	390 Chimchar [TM]	256 Combusken [TM]	155 Cyndaquil [TM]	555 Darmanitan [54, TM]	554 Darumaka [42, TM]
		655 Delphox [TM]	483 Dialga [TM]	500 Emboar [TM]	244 Entei [TM]	295 Exploud [TM]	653 Fennekin [TM]	136 Flareon [TM]
		662 Fletchinder [TM]	661 Fletchling [TM]	210 Granbull [TM]	383 Groudon [TM]	058 Growlithe [TM]	485 Heatran [TM]	250 Ho-Oh [TM]
		229 Houndoom [TM]	228 Houndour [TM]	392 Infernape [TM]	608 Lampent [69, TM]	636 Larvesta [TM]	667 Litleo [50, TM]	607 Litwick [61, TM]
		294 Loudred [TM]	240 Magby [TM]	219 Magcargo [TM]	126 Magmar [TM]	467 Magmortar [TM]	310 Manectric [TM]	056 Mankey [TM]
		151 Mew [TM]	146 Moltres [TM]	391 Monferno [TM]	038 Ninetales [TM]	322 Numel [TM]	513 Pansear [TM]	499 Pignite [TM]
		077 Ponyta [TM]	057 Primeape [TM]	668 Pyroar [57, TM]	156 Quilava [TM]	078 Rapidash [TM]	384 Rayquaza [TM]	643 Reshiram [TM]
		479 Rotom (Heat) ◆	514 Simisear [TM]	218 Slugma [TM]	209 Snubbull [TM]	338 Solrock [TM]	663 Talonflame [TM]	498 Tepig [TM]
		255 Torchic [TM]	324 Torkoal [TM]	157 Typhlosion [TM]	494 Victini [97, TM]	637 Volcarona [TM]	037 Vulpix [TM]	523 Zebstrika [TM]

P

Type	Move	Pokémon that can learn it						
Normal	Pain Split	594 Alomomola [BP, E]	531 Audino [BP]	354 Banette [BP]	606 Beheeyem [BP]	609 Chandelure [1, BP]	652 Chesnaught [52, BP]	650 Chespin [45, BP]
		563 Cofagrigus [BP]	346 Cradily [BP]	426 Drifblim [BP]	425 Drifloon [BP]	206 Dunsparce [BP]	578 Duosion [34, BP]	356 Dusclops [BP]
		477 Dusknoir [BP]	355 Duskull [BP, E]	605 Elgyem [BP]	205 Forretress [BP]	592 Frillish [BP, E]	478 Froslass [BP]	475 Gallade [BP]
		569 Garbodor [BP]	282 Gardevoir [BP]	092 Gastly [BP]	423 Gastrodon [BP]	094 Gengar [BP]	487 Giratina (Alt) [BP]	711 Gourgeist [42, BP]
		088 Grimer [BP]	316 Gulpin [BP, E]	093 Haunter [BP]	174 Igglybuff [BP]	593 Jellicent [BP]	039 Jigglypuff [BP]	281 Kirlia [BP]
		109 Koffing [BP, E]	608 Lampent [61, BP]	345 Lileep [BP]	607 Litwick [55, BP]	337 Lunatone [BP]	219 Magcargo [BP]	303 Mawile [BP]
		308 Medicham [BP]	307 Meditite [BP]	151 Mew [BP]	200 Misdreavus [32, BP]	429 Mismagius [BP]	089 Muk [BP]	517 Munna [BP]
		518 Musharna [BP]	177 Natu [BP]	038 Ninetales [BP]	299 Nosepass [BP]	708 Phantump [BP]	204 Pineco [BP]	137 Porygon [BP]
		233 Porygon2 [BP]	474 Porygon-Z [BP]	476 Probopass [BP]	710 Pumpkaboo [42, BP]	651 Quilladin [52, BP]	211 Qwilfish [BP]	280 Ralts [BP]
		409 Rampardos [BP]	579 Reuniclus [34, BP]	479 Rotom (Fan) [BP]	479 Rotom (Frost) [BP]	479 Rotom (Heat) [BP]	479 Rotom (Mow) [BP]	479 Rotom (Wash) [BP]
		479 Rotom [BP]	302 Sableye [BP]	539 Sawk [BP]	422 Shellos [BP]	353 Shuppet [BP]	218 Slugma [BP]	577 Solosis [33, BP]
		338 Solrock [BP]	442 Spiritomb [BP, E]	121 Starmie [BP]	120 Staryu [BP]	618 Stunfisk [BP, E]	317 Swalot [BP]	114 Tangela [BP]
		465 Tangrowth [BP]	538 Throh [BP]	709 Trevenant [BP]	568 Trubbish [BP]	037 Vulpix [BP]	110 Weezing [BP]	040 Wigglytuff [BP]
		178 Xatu [BP]	562 Yamask [BP]	718 Zygarde [BP]				
Electric	Parabolic Charge	702 Dedenne [17]	695 Heliolisk [1]	694 Helioptile [25]				
Dark	Parting Shot	674 Pancham [45]	675 Pangoro [48]					

◆ When Rotom becomes Heat Rotom, it learns the move Overheat. When it changes back to Rotom, it forgets the move.

	Move	Pokémon that can learn it						
Normal	Pay Day	052 Meowth [30]	509 Purrloin [E]					
Dark	Payback (TM66)	359 Absol [TM]	142 Aerodactyl [TM]	306 Aggron [TM]	190 Aipom [TM]	424 Ambipom [TM]	591 Amoonguss [TM]	024 Arbok [TM]
		493 Arceus [TM]	610 Axew [TM]	482 Azelf [TM]	354 Banette [TM]	689 Barbaracle [TM]	015 Beedrill [TM]	688 Binacle [TM]
		625 Bisharp [TM]	626 Bouffalant [TM]	437 Bronzong [46, TM]	436 Bronzor [41, TM]	659 Bunnelby [TM]	331 Cacnea [26, TM]	332 Cacturne [26, TM]
		455 Carnivine [TM]	318 Carvanha [TM]	609 Chandelure [TM]	652 Chesnaught [TM]	650 Chespin [TM]	091 Cloyster [TM]	563 Cofagrigus [TM]
		534 Conkeldurr [TM]	341 Corphish [TM]	408 Cranidos [TM]	342 Crawdaunt [TM]	453 Croagunk [TM]	169 Crobat [TM]	491 Darkrai [TM]
		555 Darmanitan [TM]	301 Delcatty [TM]	660 Diggersby [TM]	085 Dodrio [TM]	452 Drapion [TM]	426 Drifblim [16, TM]	425 Drifloon [16, TM]
		621 Druddigon [TM]	356 Dusclops [57, TM]	477 Dusknoir [57, TM]	355 Duskull [49, TM]	023 Ekans [TM]	677 Espurr [TM]	597 Ferroseed [47, TM]
		598 Ferrothorn [53, TM]	456 Finneon [TM]	419 Floatzel [TM]	590 Foongus [TM]	205 Forretress [36, TM]	611 Fraxure [TM]	478 Froslass [TM]
		569 Garbodor [TM]	092 Gastly [26, TM]	094 Gengar [28, TM]	487 Giratina (Alt) [TM]	487 Giratina (Ori) [TM]	362 Glalie [TM]	431 Glameow [TM]
		207 Gligar [TM]	472 Gliscor [TM]	673 Gogoat [TM]	042 Golbat [TM]	574 Gothita [TM]	576 Gothitelle [TM]	575 Gothorita [TM]
		210 Granbull [51, TM]	088 Grimer [TM]	326 Grumpig [46, TM]	533 Gurdurr [TM]	130 Gyarados [TM]	297 Hariyama [TM]	093 Haunter [28, TM]
		701 Hawlucha [TM]	612 Haxorus [TM]	485 Heatran [TM]	507 Herdier [TM]	430 Honchkrow [TM]	229 Houndoom [TM]	228 Houndour [TM]
		635 Hydreigon [TM]	686 Inkay [27, TM]	124 Jynx [TM]	109 Koffing [TM]	552 Krokorok [TM]	553 Krookodile [TM]	646 Kyurem (Blk) [TM]
		646 Kyurem (Wht) [TM]	646 Kyurem [TM]	608 Lampent [TM]	645 Landorus [TM]	246 Larvitar [37, TM]	542 Leavanny [TM]	510 Liepard [TM]
		667 Litleo [TM]	607 Litwick [TM]	448 Lucario [TM]	457 Lumineon [TM]	068 Machamp [TM]	067 Machoke [TM]	066 Machop [TM]
		687 Malamar [27, TM]	630 Mandibuzz [TM]	056 Mankey [TM]	303 Mawile [TM]	648 Meloetta [TM]	678 Meowstic (F) [TM]	678 Meowstic (M) [TM]
		052 Meowth [TM]	151 Mew [TM]	619 Mienfoo [TM]	620 Mienshao [TM]	262 Mightyena [TM]	200 Misdreavus [37, TM]	429 Mismagius [TM]
		122 Mr. Mime [TM]	089 Muk [TM]	198 Murkrow [TM]	038 Ninetales [TM]	274 Nuzleaf [TM]	224 Octillery [TM]	095 Onix [TM]
		674 Pancham [TM]	675 Pangoro [TM]	515 Panpour [TM]	511 Pansage [TM]	513 Pansear [TM]	624 Pawniard [TM]	279 Pelipper [19, TM]
		053 Persian [TM]	204 Pineco [31, TM]	186 Politoed [TM]	062 Poliwrath [TM]	261 Poochyena [TM]	057 Primeape [TM]	247 Pupitar [41, TM]
		509 Purrloin [TM]	432 Purugly [TM]	668 Pyroar [TM]	651 Quilladin [TM]	211 Qwilfish [TM]	409 Rampardos [TM]	486 Regigigas [65, TM]
		643 Reshiram [TM]	112 Rhydon [TM]	111 Rhyhorn [TM]	464 Rhyperior [TM]	447 Riolu [TM]	302 Sableye [TM]	551 Sandile [TM]
		539 Sawk [TM]	545 Scolipede [TM]	560 Scrafty [23, TM]	559 Scraggy [23, TM]	537 Seismitoad [TM]	336 Seviper [TM]	540 Sewaddle [TM]
		319 Sharpedo [TM]	090 Shellder [TM]	275 Shiftry [TM]	353 Shuppet [TM]	516 Simipour [TM]	512 Simisage [TM]	514 Simisear [TM]
		227 Skarmory [TM]	672 Skiddo [TM]	300 Skitty [TM]	451 Skorupi [TM]	435 Skuntank [TM]	238 Smoochum [TM]	215 Sneasel [TM]
		209 Snubbull [43, TM]	325 Spoink [40, TM]	208 Steelix [TM]	508 Stoutland [TM]	618 Stunfisk [TM]	434 Stunky [TM]	541 Swadloon [TM]
		465 Tangrowth [TM]	128 Tauros [24, TM]	216 Teddiursa [TM]	072 Tentacool [TM]	073 Tentacruel [TM]	538 Throh [TM]	642 Thundurus [TM]
		532 Timburr [TM]	641 Tornadus [TM]	454 Toxicroak [TM]	568 Trubbish [TM]	248 Tyranitar [41, TM]	197 Umbreon [TM]	217 Ursaring [TM]
		543 Venipede [TM]	629 Vullaby [TM]	037 Vulpix [18, TM]	461 Weavile [TM]	110 Weezing [TM]	544 Whirlipede [TM]	562 Yamask [TM]
		335 Zangoose [TM]	644 Zekrom [TM]	571 Zoroark [TM]	570 Zorua [TM]	041 Zubat [TM]		
Flying	Peck	334 Altaria [1]	257 Blaziken [14]	628 Braviary [1]	441 Chatot [1]	256 Combusken [14]	085 Dodrio [1]	084 Doduo [1]
		395 Empoleon [15]	589 Escavalier [1]	083 Farfetch'd [1]	022 Fearow [1]	662 Fletchinder [10]	661 Fletchling [10]	118 Goldeen [1]
		163 Hoothoot [9]	686 Inkay [1]	588 Karrablast [1]	687 Malamar [1]	473 Mamoswine [1]	556 Maractus [1]	198 Murkrow [1]
		177 Natu [1]	034 Nidoking [1]	032 Nidoran ♂ [1]	033 Nidorino [1]	164 Noctowl [9]	221 Piloswine [1]	393 Piplup [15]
		394 Prinplup [15]	627 Rufflet [1]	119 Seaking [1]	227 Skarmory [1]	021 Spearow [1]	333 Swablu [1]	277 Swellow [1]
		276 Taillow [1]	663 Talonflame [10]	175 Togepi [E]	255 Torchic [14]	178 Xatu [1]	145 Zapdos [1]	
Normal	Perish Song	359 Absol [1, 57, E]	334 Altaria [46]	493 Arceus [90]	251 Celebi [91]	104 Cubone [E]	092 Gastly [E]	174 Igglybuff [E]
		124 Jynx [1, 55]	402 Kricketune [50]	131 Lapras [27]	183 Marill [E]	648 Meloetta [85]	200 Misdreavus [46]	198 Murkrow [E]
		186 Politoed [1]	086 Seel [E]	238 Smoochum [45]	333 Swablu [42]			
Grass	Petal Blizzard	182 Bellossom [49]	421 Cherrim [50]	420 Cherubi [47]	669 Flabébé [28]	670 Floette [33]	671 Florges [1]	044 Gloom [49]
		549 Lilligant [50]	556 Maractus [48]	154 Meganium [1, 70]	315 Roselia [37]	192 Sunflora [50]	003 Venusaur [50]	045 Vileplume [49]
	Petal Dance	001 Bulbasaur [E]	421 Cherrim [25]	669 Flabébé [45]	670 Floette [51]	671 Florges [1]	044 Gloom [59]	549 Lilligant [46]
		556 Maractus [38]	154 Meganium [32]	043 Oddish [51]	315 Roselia [50]	192 Sunflora [28]	003 Venusaur [32]	045 Vileplume [59]
Ghost	Phantom Force	354 Banette [1, 64]	426 Drifblim [1, 65]	623 Golurk [1, 75]	711 Gourgeist [1, 57]	429 Mismagius [1]	708 Phantump [45]	292 Shedinja [45]
		353 Shuppet [54, E]	709 Trevenant [45]	717 Yveltal [55]				
Bug	Pin Missile	168 Ariados [41]	015 Beedrill [28]	406 Budew [E]	331 Cacnea [38]	332 Cacturne [38]	652 Chesnaught [20]	650 Chespin [18]
		452 Drapion [9]	597 Ferroseed [18]	598 Ferrothorn [18]	214 Heracross [31]	135 Jolteon [25]	595 Joltik [E]	556 Maractus [10]
		204 Pineco [E]	651 Quilladin [20]	211 Qwilfish [37]	315 Roselia [E]	451 Skorupi [9]	167 Spinarak [36]	543 Venipede [E]
		263 Zigzagoon [19]						
Normal	Play Nice	531 Audino [1]	614 Beartic [9]	613 Cubchoo [15]	574 Gothita [8]	576 Gothitelle [1]	575 Gothorita [1]	314 Illumise [1]
		039 Jigglypuff [8]	312 Minun [1]	515 Panpour [1]	511 Pansage [1]	513 Pansear [1]	025 Pikachu [7]	311 Plusle [1]
		685 Slurpuff [8]	684 Swirlix [8]	216 Teddiursa [25]	217 Ursaring [25]			
Fairy	Play Rough	359 Absol [E]	184 Azumarill [25]	613 Cubchoo [E]	702 Dedenne [42]	431 Glameow [50]	210 Granbull [43]	507 Herdier [52]
		314 Illumise [43]	707 Klefki [43]	510 Liepard [58]	506 Lillipup [45]	264 Linoone [1]	183 Marill [23]	303 Mawile [1, 49]
		053 Persian [1]	231 Phanpy [E]	261 Poochyena [E]	509 Purrloin [49]	300 Skitty [46]	690 Skrelp [E]	287 Slakoth [38]
		685 Slurpuff [49]	209 Snubbull [37]	508 Stoutland [63]	434 Stunky [E]	684 Swirlix [49]	216 Teddiursa [E]	313 Volbeat [43]
		040 Wigglytuff [1]						
Flying	Pluck	334 Altaria [1]	566 Archen [15]	567 Archeops [15]	085 Dodrio [21]	084 Doduo [21]	022 Fearow [1]	686 Inkay [35]
		687 Malamar [35]	630 Mandibuzz [1, 10]	277 Swellow [1]	629 Vullaby [10]	145 Zapdos [22]		
Poison	Poison Fang	318 Carvanha [32]	169 Crobat [27]	452 Drapion [23]	023 Ekans [E]	042 Golbat [27]	303 Mawile [E]	029 Nidoran ♀ [45]
		030 Nidorina [58]	261 Poochyena [E]	336 Seviper [22]	319 Sharpedo [34]	451 Skorupi [23]	696 Tyrunt [E]	049 Venomoth [47]
		048 Venonat [41]	041 Zubat [25]					
	Poison Gas	096 Drowzee [17]	569 Garbodor [1]	088 Grimer [1]	316 Gulpin [8]	097 Hypno [17]	109 Koffing [1]	089 Muk [1]
		435 Skuntank [1, 4]	434 Stunky [4]	317 Swalot [1, 8]	568 Trubbish [1]	110 Weezing [1]		

ADVENTURE DATA

Type	Move	Pokémon that can learn it						
Poison	Poison Jab (TM84)	024 Arbok [TM]	493 Arceus [TM]	168 Ariados [50, TM]	610 Axew [TM]	689 Barbaracle [TM]	015 Beedrill [37, TM]	688 Binacle [TM]
		625 Bisharp [TM]	257 Blaziken [TM]	626 Bouffalant [TM]	331 Cacnea [TM]	332 Cacturne [TM]	652 Chesnaught [TM]	650 Chespin [TM]
		091 Cloyster [TM]	638 Cobalion [TM]	256 Combusken [TM]	534 Conkeldurr [TM]	453 Croagunk [43, TM]	558 Crustle [TM]	615 Cryogonal [TM]
		491 Darkrai [TM]	386 Deoxys (Atk) [TM]	386 Deoxys (Def) [TM]	386 Deoxys (Nor) [TM]	386 Deoxys (Spd) [TM]	232 Donphan [TM]	452 Drapion [TM]
		529 Drilbur [TM]	206 Dunsparce [TM]	557 Dwebble [TM]	023 Ekans [TM]	500 Emboar [TM]	589 Escavalier [TM]	530 Excadrill [TM]
		083 Farfetch'd [1, TM]	597 Ferroseed [TM]	598 Ferrothorn [TM]	611 Fraxure [TM]	475 Gallade [TM]	596 Galvantula [TM]	445 Garchomp [TM]
		094 Gengar [TM]	207 Gligar [TM]	472 Gliscor [1, TM]	118 Goldeen [TM]	088 Grimer [TM]	533 Gurdurr [TM]	297 Hariyama [TM]
		093 Haunter [TM]	701 Hawlucha [TM]	612 Haxorus [TM]	106 Hitmonlee [TM]	392 Infernape [TM]	595 Joltik [TM]	588 Karrablast [TM]
		647 Keldeo [TM]	542 Leavanny [TM]	448 Lucario [TM]	068 Machamp [TM]	067 Machoke [TM]	066 Machop [TM]	296 Makuhita [TM]
		056 Mankey [TM]	556 Maractus [TM]	308 Medicham [TM]	307 Meditite [TM]	151 Mew [TM]	150 Mewtwo [TM]	619 Mienfoo [TM]
		620 Mienshao [TM]	391 Monferno [TM]	089 Muk [TM]	034 Nidoking [TM]	031 Nidoqueen [TM]	029 Nidoran ♀ [TM]	032 Nidoran ♂ [37, TM]
		030 Nidorina [TM]	033 Nidorino [43, TM]	675 Pangoro [TM]	624 Pawniard [TM]	708 Phantump [TM]	499 Pignite [TM]	062 Poliwrath [TM]
		057 Primeape [TM]	651 Quilladin [TM]	211 Qwilfish [49, TM]	078 Rapidash [1, TM]	112 Rhydon [TM]	111 Rhyhorn [TM]	464 Rhyperior [1, TM]
		447 Riolu [TM]	315 Roselia [TM]	407 Roserade [TM]	302 Sableye [TM]	027 Sandshrew [TM]	028 Sandslash [TM]	539 Sawk [TM]
		545 Scolipede [TM]	560 Scrafty [TM]	559 Scraggy [TM]	119 Seaking [1, TM]	537 Seismitoad [TM]	336 Seviper [34, TM]	319 Sharpedo [TM]
		451 Skorupi [TM]	435 Skuntank [TM]	215 Sneasel [TM]	167 Spinarak [43, TM]	465 Tangrowth [TM]	072 Tentacool [31, TM]	073 Tentacruel [32, TM]
		639 Terrakion [TM]	538 Throh [TM]	532 Timburr [TM]	454 Toxicroak [49, TM]	709 Trevenant [TM]	543 Venipede [TM]	637 Volcarona [TM]
		461 Weavile [TM]	544 Whirlipede [TM]	335 Zangoose [TM]				
	Poison Powder	153 Bayleef [1, 9]	069 Bellsprout [15]	001 Bulbasaur [13]	012 Butterfree [12]	152 Chikorita [9]	546 Cottonee [22]	269 Dustox [15]
		102 Exeggcute [21]	590 Foongus [E]	044 Gloom [13]	187 Hoppip [12]	002 Ivysaur [13]	189 Jumpluff [12]	154 Meganium [1, 9]
		414 Mothim [29]	043 Oddish [13]	046 Paras [6]	047 Parasect [1, 6]	664 Scatterbug [E]	285 Shroomish [19]	188 Skiploom [12]
		114 Tangela [14]	465 Tangrowth [14]	049 Venomoth [13]	048 Venonat [13]	003 Venusaur [13]	045 Vileplume [1]	666 Vivillon [1]
		070 Weepinbell [15]						
	Poison Sting	024 Arbok [1, 4]	168 Ariados [1]	331 Cacnea [1]	332 Cacturne [1]	453 Croagunk [8]	452 Drapion [1]	023 Ekans [4]
		207 Gligar [1]	595 Joltik [E]	034 Nidoking [1]	031 Nidoqueen [1]	029 Nidoran ♀ [13]	032 Nidoran ♂ [13]	030 Nidorina [13]
		033 Nidorino [13]	211 Qwilfish [1]	315 Roselia [7]	407 Roserade [1]	027 Sandshrew [5]	028 Sandslash [1, 5]	545 Scolipede [1, 5]
		451 Skorupi [1]	167 Spinarak [1]	072 Tentacool [1]	073 Tentacruel [1]	454 Toxicroak [1, 8]	543 Venipede [5]	416 Vespiquen [1]
		013 Weedle [1]	544 Whirlipede [1, 5]	265 Wurmple [5]				
	Poison Tail	691 Dragalge [23]	621 Druddigon [E]	023 Ekans [E]	207 Gligar [E]	704 Goomy [E]	029 Nidoran ♀ [E]	032 Nidoran ♂ [E]
		545 Scolipede [19]	336 Seviper [10]	451 Skorupi [E]	690 Skrelp [23]	543 Venipede [19]	544 Whirlipede [19]	
Normal	Pound	594 Alomomola [1]	531 Audino [1]	242 Blissey [1]	427 Buneary [1]	113 Chansey [1]	035 Clefairy [1]	173 Cleffa [1]
		534 Conkeldurr [1]	096 Drowzee [1]	295 Exploud [1]	456 Finneon [1]	656 Froakie [1]	657 Frogadier [1]	569 Garbodor [1]
		622 Golett [1]	623 Golurk [1]	574 Gothita [1]	576 Gothitelle [1]	575 Gothorita [1]	658 Greninja [1]	088 Grimer [1]
		253 Grovyle [1]	316 Gulpin [1]	533 Gurdurr [1]	440 Happiny [1]	694 Helioptile [1]	097 Hypno [1]	174 Igglybuff [5]
		039 Jigglypuff [5]	124 Jynx [1]	428 Lopunny [1]	294 Loudred [1]	457 Lumineon [1]	151 Mew [1]	619 Mienfoo [1]
		620 Mienshao [1]	572 Minccino [1]	089 Muk [1]	274 Nuzleaf [1]	393 Piplup [1]	254 Sceptile [1]	238 Smoochum [1]
		192 Sunflora [1]	317 Swalot [1]	532 Timburr [1]	252 Treecko [1]	568 Trubbish [1]	293 Whismur [1]	
Bug	Powder	666 Vivillon [1, 55]						
Ice	Powder Snow	460 Abomasnow [1]	698 Amaura [1]	144 Articuno [1]	699 Aurorus [1]	713 Avalugg [5]	614 Beartic [1]	712 Bergmite [5]
		351 Castform [10]	613 Cubchoo [5]	478 Froslass [1]	362 Glalie [1]	124 Jynx [1, 11]	473 Mamoswine [1, 8]	221 Piloswine [1, 8]
		364 Sealeo [1]	238 Smoochum [11]	361 Snorunt [1]	459 Snover [1]	363 Spheal [1]	220 Swinub [8]	582 Vanillite [E]
		365 Walrein [1]						
Rock	Power Gem	181 Ampharos [35]	525 Boldore [25]	703 Carbink [46]	222 Corsola [41]	483 Dialga [19]	180 Flaaffy [34]	526 Gigalith [25]
		326 Grumpig [29]	179 Mareep [29]	200 Misdreavus [55]	429 Mismagius [1]	299 Nosepass [25]	484 Palkia [19]	053 Persian [32]
		476 Probopass [25]	302 Sableye [36]	199 Slowking [1]	325 Spoink [29]	120 Staryu [37]	416 Vespiquen [25]	
Psychic	Power Split	343 Baltoy [34]	606 Beheeyem [58]	344 Claydol [34]	563 Cofagrigus [33]	605 Elgyem [50]	686 Inkay [E]	381 Latios [46]
		607 Litwick [E]	439 Mime Jr. [E]	122 Mr. Mime [E]	213 Shuckle [45]	283 Surskit [E]	562 Yamask [33]	
	Power Swap	617 Accelgor [1, 52]	605 Elgyem [E]	196 Espeon [45]	102 Exeggcute [E]	203 Girafarig [1]	240 Magby [E]	307 Meditite [E]
		150 Mewtwo [43]	122 Mr. Mime [1]	177 Natu [47]	273 Seedot [E]	333 Swablu [E]	114 Tangela [E]	037 Vulpix [E]
		178 Xatu [53]						
	Power Trick	063 Abra [E]	681 Aegislash [1]	343 Baltoy [25]	344 Claydol [25]	680 Doublade [41]	207 Gligar [E]	679 Honedge [39]
		066 Machop [E]	308 Medicham [36]	307 Meditite [36]	204 Pineco [E]	213 Shuckle [31]		
Grass	Power Whip	069 Bellsprout [E]	001 Bulbasaur [E]	455 Carnivine [50]	598 Ferrothorn [40]	706 Goodra [55]	463 Lickilicky [1, 53]	108 Lickitung [53]
		114 Tangela [50]	465 Tangrowth [53]					
Fighting	Power-Up Punch (TM98)	306 Aggron [TM]	190 Aipom [TM]	424 Ambipom [TM]	181 Ampharos [TM]	531 Audino [TM]	482 Azelf [TM]	184 Azumarill [TM]
		689 Barbaracle [TM]	614 Beartic [TM]	688 Binacle [TM]	625 Bisharp [TM]	009 Blastoise [TM]	257 Blaziken [TM]	242 Blissey [TM]
		654 Braixen [TM]	286 Breloom [TM]	418 Buizel [TM]	427 Buneary [TM]	659 Bunnelby [TM]	331 Cacnea [TM]	332 Cacturne [TM]
		113 Chansey [TM]	006 Charizard [TM]	004 Charmander [TM]	005 Charmeleon [TM]	652 Chesnaught [TM]	650 Chespin [TM]	390 Chimchar [TM]
		036 Clefable [TM]	035 Clefairy [TM]	256 Combusken [TM]	534 Conkeldurr [TM]	408 Cranidos [TM]	453 Croagunk [TM]	159 Croconaw [TM]
		613 Cubchoo [TM]	104 Cubone [TM]	491 Darkrai [TM]	555 Darmanitan [TM]	554 Darumaka [TM]	225 Delibird [TM]	655 Delphox [TM]
		386 Deoxys (Atk) [TM]	386 Deoxys (Def) [TM]	386 Deoxys (Nor) [TM]	386 Deoxys (Spd) [TM]	660 Diggersby [TM]	149 Dragonite [TM]	096 Drowzee [TM]
		621 Druddigon [TM]	356 Dusclops [TM]	477 Dusknoir [TM]	604 Eelektross [TM]	125 Electabuzz [TM]	466 Electivire [TM]	239 Elekid [TM]
		500 Emboar [TM]	295 Exploud [TM]	653 Fennekin [TM]	160 Feraligatr [TM]	180 Flaaffy [TM]	419 Floatzel [TM]	330 Flygon [TM]
		656 Froakie [TM]	657 Frogadier [TM]	162 Furret [TM]	475 Gallade [TM]	094 Gengar [TM]	074 Geodude [TM]	055 Golduck [TM]
		076 Golem [TM]	622 Golett [TM]	623 Golurk [TM]	576 Gothitelle [TM]	210 Granbull [TM]	075 Graveler [TM]	658 Greninja [TM]
		088 Grimer [TM]	383 Groudon [TM]	253 Grovyle [TM]	326 Grumpig [TM]	316 Gulpin [TM]	533 Gurdurr [TM]	297 Hariyama [TM]

ADVENTURE DATA

	Move	Pokémon that can learn it						
Fighting	Power-Up Punch (TM98)	701 Hawlucha [TM]	631 Heatmor [TM]	107 Hitmonchan [TM]	106 Hitmonlee [TM]	097 Hypno [TM]	314 Illumise [TM]	392 Infernape [TM]
		039 Jigglypuff [TM]	385 Jirachi [TM]	124 Jynx [TM]	115 Kangaskhan [TM]	352 Kecleon [TM]	402 Kricketune [TM]	552 Krokorok [TM]
		553 Krookodile [TM]	246 Larvitar [TM]	166 Ledian [TM]	165 Ledyba [TM]	463 Lickilicky [TM]	108 Lickitung [TM]	271 Lombre [TM]
		428 Lopunny [TM]	294 Loudred [TM]	448 Lucario [15, TM]	272 Ludicolo [TM]	068 Machamp [TM]	067 Machoke [TM]	066 Machop [TM]
		240 Magby [TM]	126 Magmar [TM]	467 Magmortar [TM]	296 Makuhita [TM]	056 Mankey [TM]	183 Marill [TM]	105 Marowak [TM]
		259 Marshtomp [TM]	303 Mawile [TM]	308 Medicham [TM]	307 Meditite [TM]	648 Meloetta [TM]	678 Meowstic (F) [TM]	678 Meowstic (M) [TM]
		481 Mesprit [TM]	376 Metagross [TM]	375 Metang [TM]	151 Mew [TM]	150 Mewtwo [TM]	619 Mienfoo [TM]	620 Mienshao [TM]
		241 Miltank [TM]	391 Monferno [TM]	122 Mr. Mime [TM]	089 Muk [TM]	446 Munchlax [TM]	034 Nidoking [TM]	031 Nidoqueen [TM]
		274 Nuzleaf [TM]	674 Pancham [TM]	675 Pangoro [TM]	624 Pawniard [TM]	499 Pignite [TM]	186 Politoed [TM]	061 Poliwhirl [TM]
		062 Poliwrath [TM]	057 Primeape [TM]	054 Psyduck [TM]	247 Pupitar [TM]	195 Quagsire [TM]	651 Quilladin [TM]	409 Rampardos [TM]
		378 Regice [TM]	486 Regigigas [TM]	377 Regirock [TM]	379 Registeel [TM]	579 Reuniclus [TM]	112 Rhydon [TM]	464 Rhyperior [TM]
		447 Riolu [TM]	302 Sableye [TM]	539 Sawk [TM]	254 Sceptile [TM]	560 Scrafty [TM]	559 Scraggy [TM]	537 Seismitoad [TM]
		161 Sentret [TM]	275 Shiftry [TM]	516 Simipour [TM]	512 Simisage [TM]	514 Simisear [TM]	289 Slaking [TM]	287 Slakoth [TM]
		199 Slowking [TM]	215 Sneasel [TM]	143 Snorlax [TM]	209 Snubbull [TM]	327 Spinda [TM]	007 Squirtle [TM]	185 Sudowoodo [TM]
		317 Swalot [TM]	260 Swampert [TM]	216 Teddiursa [TM]	538 Throh [TM]	532 Timburr [TM]	158 Totodile [TM]	454 Toxicroak [TM]
		252 Treecko [TM]	709 Trevenant [TM]	157 Typhlosion [TM]	248 Tyranitar [TM]	217 Ursaring [TM]	480 Uxie [TM]	494 Victini [TM]
		288 Vigoroth [TM]	313 Volbeat [TM]	008 Wartortle [TM]	505 Watchog [TM]	461 Weavile [TM]	040 Wigglytuff [TM]	335 Zangoose [TM]
Ground	Precipice Blades	383 Groudon [45]						
Normal	Present	113 Chansey [E]	173 Cleffa [E]	225 Delibird [1]	440 Happiny [E]	174 Igglybuff [E]	183 Marill [E]	241 Miltank [E]
		172 Pichu [E]	209 Snubbull [E]	175 Togepi [E]				
	Protect (TM17)	460 Abomasnow [TM]	063 Abra [TM]	359 Absol [TM]	617 Accelgor [TM]	681 Aegislash [TM]	142 Aerodactyl [TM]	306 Aggron [16, TM]
		190 Aipom [TM]	065 Alakazam [TM]	594 Alomomola [21, TM]	334 Altaria [TM]	698 Amaura [TM]	424 Ambipom [TM]	591 Amoonguss [TM]
		181 Ampharos [TM]	347 Anorith [49, TM]	024 Arbok [TM]	059 Arcanine [TM]	493 Arceus [TM]	566 Archen [TM]	567 Archeops [TM]
		168 Ariados [TM]	348 Armaldo [53, TM]	683 Aromatisse [TM]	304 Aron [16, TM]	144 Articuno [TM]	531 Audino [TM]	699 Aurorus [TM]
		713 Avalugg [TM]	610 Axew [TM]	482 Azelf [TM]	184 Azumarill [TM]	298 Azurill [TM]	371 Bagon [TM]	343 Baltoy [TM]
		354 Banette [TM]	689 Barbaracle [TM]	339 Barboach [TM]	550 Basculin [TM]	411 Bastiodon [1, TM]	153 Bayleef [TM]	614 Beartic [TM]
		267 Beautifly [TM]	015 Beedrill [TM]	606 Beheeyem [TM]	182 Bellossom [TM]	069 Bellsprout [TM]	712 Bergmite [TM]	400 Bibarel [TM]
		399 Bidoof [TM]	688 Binacle [TM]	625 Bisharp [TM]	009 Blastoise [24, TM]	257 Blaziken [TM]	242 Blissey [TM]	522 Blitzle [TM]
		525 Boldore [TM]	438 Bonsly [TM]	626 Bouffalant [TM]	654 Braixen [TM]	628 Braviary [TM]	286 Breloom [TM]	437 Bronzong [TM]
		436 Bronzor [TM]	406 Budew [TM]	418 Buizel [TM]	001 Bulbasaur [TM]	427 Buneary [TM]	659 Bunnelby [TM]	412 Burmy [1, TM]
		012 Butterfree [TM]	331 Cacnea [TM]	332 Cacturne [TM]	323 Camerupt [TM]	703 Carbink [TM]	455 Carnivine [TM]	565 Carracosta [11, TM]
		318 Carvanha [TM]	351 Castform [TM]	251 Celebi [TM]	609 Chandelure [TM]	113 Chansey [TM]	006 Charizard [TM]	004 Charmander [TM]
		005 Charmeleon [TM]	441 Chatot [TM]	421 Cherrim [TM]	420 Cherubi [TM]	652 Chesnaught [TM]	650 Chespin [TM]	152 Chikorita [TM]
		390 Chimchar [TM]	358 Chimecho [TM]	170 Chinchou [TM]	433 Chingling [TM]	573 Cinccino [TM]	366 Clamperl [TM]	692 Clauncher [TM]
		693 Clawitzer [TM]	344 Claydol [TM]	036 Clefable [TM]	035 Clefairy [TM]	173 Cleffa [TM]	091 Cloyster [1, TM]	638 Cobalion [TM]
		563 Cofagrigus [1, TM]	256 Combusken [TM]	534 Conkeldurr [TM]	341 Corphish [17, TM]	222 Corsola [TM]	546 Cottonee [TM]	346 Cradily [TM]
		408 Cranidos [TM]	342 Crawdaunt [17, TM]	488 Cresselia [TM]	453 Croagunk [TM]	169 Crobat [TM]	159 Croconaw [TM]	558 Crustle [TM]
		615 Cryogonal [TM]	613 Cubchoo [TM]	104 Cubone [TM]	155 Cyndaquil [TM]	491 Darkrai [TM]	555 Darmanitan [TM]	554 Darumaka [TM]
		702 Dedenne [TM]	585 Deerling [TM]	633 Deino [TM]	301 Delcatty [TM]	225 Delibird [TM]	655 Delphox [TM]	386 Deoxys (Atk) [TM]
		386 Deoxys (Def) [TM]	386 Deoxys (Nor) [TM]	386 Deoxys (Spd) [TM]	087 Dewgong [TM]	502 Dewott [TM]	483 Dialga [TM]	719 Diancie [TM]
		660 Diggersby [TM]	050 Diglett [TM]	085 Dodrio [TM]	084 Doduo [TM]	232 Donphan [TM]	680 Doublade [TM]	691 Dragalge [TM]
		148 Dragonair [TM]	149 Dragonite [TM]	452 Drapion [TM]	147 Dratini [TM]	426 Drifblim [TM]	425 Drifloon [TM]	529 Drilbur [TM]
		096 Drowzee [TM]	621 Druddigon [TM]	580 Ducklett [TM]	051 Dugtrio [TM]	206 Dunsparce [TM]	578 Duosion [TM]	632 Durant [TM]
		356 Dusclops [TM]	477 Dusknoir [TM]	355 Duskull [TM]	269 Dustox [37, TM]	557 Dwebble [TM]	603 Eelektrik [TM]	604 Eelektross [TM]
		133 Eevee [TM]	023 Ekans [TM]	125 Electabuzz [TM]	466 Electivire [TM]	309 Electrike [TM]	101 Electrode [TM]	239 Elekid [TM]
		605 Elgyem [TM]	500 Emboar [TM]	587 Emolga [TM]	395 Empoleon [TM]	244 Entei [TM]	589 Escavalier [TM]	196 Espeon [TM]
		677 Espurr [TM]	530 Excadrill [TM]	102 Exeggcute [TM]	103 Exeggutor [TM]	295 Exploud [TM]	083 Farfetch'd [TM]	022 Fearow [TM]
		349 Feebas [TM]	653 Fennekin [TM]	160 Feraligatr [TM]	597 Ferroseed [TM]	598 Ferrothorn [TM]	456 Finneon [TM]	180 Flaaffy [TM]
		669 Flabébé [TM]	136 Flareon [TM]	662 Fletchinder [TM]	661 Fletchling [TM]	419 Floatzel [TM]	670 Floette [TM]	671 Florges [TM]
		330 Flygon [TM]	590 Foongus [TM]	205 Forretress [1, TM]	611 Fraxure [TM]	592 Frillish [TM]	656 Froakie [TM]	657 Frogadier [TM]
		478 Froslass [TM]	676 Furfrou [TM]	162 Furret [TM]	444 Gabite [TM]	475 Gallade [49, TM]	596 Galvantula [TM]	569 Garbodor [TM]
		445 Garchomp [TM]	282 Gardevoir [TM]	092 Gastly [TM]	423 Gastrodon [TM]	649 Genesect [TM]	094 Gengar [TM]	074 Geodude [TM]
		443 Gible [TM]	526 Gigalith [TM]	203 Girafarig [TM]	487 Giratina (Alt) [TM]	487 Giratina (Ori) [TM]	471 Glaceon [TM]	362 Glalie [32, TM]
		431 Glameow [TM]	207 Gligar [TM]	472 Gliscor [TM]	044 Gloom [TM]	673 Gogoat [TM]	042 Golbat [TM]	118 Goldeen [TM]
		055 Golduck [TM]	076 Golem [TM]	622 Golett [TM]	623 Golurk [TM]	706 Goodra [9, TM]	704 Goomy [9, TM]	368 Gorebyss [TM]
		574 Gothita [TM]	576 Gothitelle [TM]	575 Gothorita [TM]	711 Gourgeist [TM]	210 Granbull [TM]	075 Graveler [TM]	658 Greninja [TM]
		088 Grimer [TM]	388 Grotle [TM]	383 Groudon [TM]	253 Grovyle [TM]	058 Growlithe [TM]	326 Grumpig [TM]	316 Gulpin [TM]
		533 Gurdurr [TM]	130 Gyarados [TM]	440 Happiny [TM]	297 Hariyama [TM]	093 Haunter [TM]	701 Hawlucha [TM]	612 Haxorus [TM]
		631 Heatmor [TM]	485 Heatran [TM]	695 Heliolisk [TM]	694 Helioptile [TM]	214 Heracross [TM]	507 Herdier [TM]	449 Hippopotas [TM]
		450 Hippowdon [TM]	107 Hitmonchan [TM]	106 Hitmonlee [TM]	237 Hitmontop [TM]	430 Honchkrow [TM]	679 Honedge [TM]	250 Ho-Oh [TM]
		163 Hoothoot [TM]	187 Hoppip [TM]	116 Horsea [TM]	229 Houndoom [TM]	228 Houndour [TM]	367 Huntail [TM]	635 Hydreigon [TM]
		097 Hypno [TM]	174 Igglybuff [TM]	314 Illumise [TM]	392 Infernape [TM]	686 Inkay [TM]	002 Ivysaur [TM]	593 Jellicent [TM]
		039 Jigglypuff [TM]	385 Jirachi [TM]	135 Jolteon [TM]	595 Joltik [TM]	189 Jumpluff [TM]	124 Jynx [TM]	140 Kabuto [TM]

ADVENTURE DATA

	Move	Pokémon that can learn it						
Normal	Protect (TM17)	141 Kabutops [TM]	064 Kadabra [TM]	115 Kangaskhan [TM]	588 Karrablast [TM]	352 Kecleon [TM]	647 Keldeo [TM]	230 Kingdra [TM]
		099 Kingler [32, TM]	281 Kirlia [TM]	600 Klang [TM]	707 Klefki [TM]	599 Klink [TM]	601 Klinklang [TM]	109 Koffing [TM]
		098 Krabby [29, TM]	402 Kricketune [TM]	552 Krokorok [TM]	553 Krookodile [TM]	382 Kyogre [TM]	646 Kyurem (Blk) [TM]	646 Kyurem (Wht) [TM]
		646 Kyurem [TM]	305 Lairon [16, TM]	608 Lampent [TM]	645 Landorus [TM]	171 Lanturn [TM]	131 Lapras [TM]	636 Larvesta [TM]
		246 Larvitar [TM]	380 Latias [TM]	381 Latios [4, TM]	470 Leafeon [TM]	542 Leavanny [TM]	166 Ledian [TM]	165 Ledyba [TM]
		463 Lickilicky [TM]	108 Lickitung [TM]	510 Liepard [TM]	345 Lileep [TM]	549 Lilligant [TM]	506 Lillipup [TM]	264 Linoone [TM]
		667 Litleo [TM]	607 Litwick [TM]	271 Lombre [TM]	428 Lopunny [TM]	270 Lotad [TM]	294 Loudred [TM]	448 Lucario [TM]
		272 Ludicolo [TM]	249 Lugia [TM]	457 Lumineon [TM]	337 Lunatone [TM]	370 Luvdisc [TM]	404 Luxio [TM]	405 Luxray [TM]
		068 Machamp [TM]	067 Machoke [TM]	066 Machop [TM]	240 Magby [TM]	219 Magcargo [TM]	126 Magmar [TM]	467 Magmortar [TM]
		081 Magnemite [TM]	082 Magneton [TM]	462 Magnezone [TM]	296 Makuhita [TM]	687 Malamar [TM]	473 Mamoswine [TM]	490 Manaphy [TM]
		630 Mandibuzz [TM]	310 Manectric [TM]	056 Mankey [TM]	226 Mantine [TM]	458 Mantyke [TM]	556 Maractus [TM]	179 Mareep [TM]
		183 Marill [TM]	105 Marowak [TM]	259 Marshtomp [32, TM]	284 Masquerain [TM]	303 Mawile [TM]	308 Medicham [TM]	307 Meditite [TM]
		154 Meganium [TM]	648 Meloetta [TM]	678 Meowstic (F) [TM]	678 Meowstic (M) [TM]	052 Meowth [TM]	481 Mesprit [16, TM]	376 Metagross [TM]
		375 Metang [TM]	151 Mew [TM]	150 Mewtwo [TM]	619 Mienfoo [TM]	620 Mienshao [TM]	262 Mightyena [TM]	350 Milotic [TM]
		241 Miltank [TM]	439 Mime Jr. [TM]	572 Minccino [TM]	312 Minun [TM]	200 Misdreavus [TM]	429 Mismagius [TM]	146 Moltres [TM]
		391 Monferno [TM]	414 Mothim [10, TM]	122 Mr. Mime [TM]	258 Mudkip [28, TM]	089 Muk [TM]	446 Munchlax [TM]	517 Munna [TM]
		198 Murkrow [TM]	518 Musharna [TM]	177 Natu [TM]	034 Nidoking [TM]	031 Nidoqueen [TM]	029 Nidoran ♀ [TM]	032 Nidoran ♂ [TM]
		030 Nidorina [TM]	033 Nidorino [TM]	290 Nincada [TM]	038 Ninetales [TM]	291 Ninjask [TM]	164 Noctowl [TM]	714 Noibat [TM]
		715 Noivern [TM]	299 Nosepass [TM]	322 Numel [TM]	274 Nuzleaf [TM]	224 Octillery [TM]	043 Oddish [TM]	138 Omanyte [34, TM]
		139 Omastar [34, TM]	095 Onix [TM]	501 Oshawott [TM]	417 Pachirisu [TM]	484 Palkia [TM]	536 Palpitoad [TM]	674 Pancham [TM]
		675 Pangoro [TM]	515 Panpour [TM]	511 Pansage [TM]	513 Pansear [TM]	046 Paras [TM]	047 Parasect [TM]	504 Patrat [TM]
		624 Pawniard [TM]	279 Pelipper [25, TM]	053 Persian [TM]	548 Petilil [TM]	231 Phanpy [TM]	708 Phantump [TM]	489 Phione [TM]
		172 Pichu [TM]	018 Pidgeot [TM]	017 Pidgeotto [TM]	016 Pidgey [TM]	519 Pidove [TM]	499 Pignite [TM]	025 Pikachu [TM]
		221 Piloswine [TM]	204 Pineco [1, TM]	127 Pinsir [TM]	393 Piplup [TM]	311 Plusle [TM]	186 Politoed [TM]	060 Poliwag [TM]
		061 Poliwhirl [TM]	062 Poliwrath [TM]	077 Ponyta [TM]	261 Poochyena [TM]	137 Porygon [TM]	233 Porygon2 [TM]	474 Porygon-Z [TM]
		057 Primeape [TM]	394 Prinplup [TM]	476 Probopass [TM]	054 Psyduck [TM]	710 Pumpkaboo [TM]	247 Pupitar [TM]	509 Purrloin [TM]
		432 Purugly [TM]	668 Pyroar [TM]	195 Quagsire [TM]	156 Quilava [TM]	651 Quilladin [TM]	211 Qwilfish [TM]	026 Raichu [TM]
		243 Raikou [TM]	280 Ralts [TM]	409 Rampardos [TM]	078 Rapidash [TM]	020 Raticate [TM]	019 Rattata [TM]	384 Rayquaza [TM]
		378 Regice [TM]	377 Regirock [TM]	379 Registeel [TM]	369 Relicanth [TM]	223 Remoraid [TM]	643 Reshiram [TM]	579 Reuniclus [TM]
		112 Rhydon [TM]	111 Rhyhorn [TM]	464 Rhyperior [TM]	447 Riolu [TM]	524 Roggenrola [TM]	315 Roselia [TM]	407 Roserade [TM]
		479 Rotom (Fan) [TM]	479 Rotom (Frost) [TM]	479 Rotom (Heat) [TM]	479 Rotom (Mow) [TM]	479 Rotom (Wash) [TM]	479 Rotom [TM]	627 Rufflet [TM]
		302 Sableye [TM]	373 Salamence [30, TM]	503 Samurott [TM]	551 Sandile [TM]	027 Sandshrew [TM]	028 Sandslash [TM]	539 Sawk [TM]
		586 Sawsbuck [TM]	254 Sceptile [TM]	212 Scizor [TM]	545 Scolipede [15, TM]	560 Scrafty [TM]	559 Scraggy [TM]	123 Scyther [TM]
		117 Seadra [TM]	119 Seaking [TM]	364 Sealeo [TM]	273 Seedot [TM]	086 Seel [TM]	537 Seismitoad [TM]	161 Sentret [TM]
		497 Serperior [TM]	496 Servine [TM]	336 Seviper [TM]	540 Sewaddle [TM]	319 Sharpedo [TM]	492 Shaymin (Land) [TM]	492 Shaymin (Sky) [TM]
		292 Shedinja [TM]	372 Shelgon [30, TM]	090 Shellder [16, TM]	422 Shellos [TM]	616 Shelmet [28, TM]	410 Shieldon [1, TM]	275 Shiftry [TM]
		403 Shinx [TM]	285 Shroomish [TM]	213 Shuckle [TM]	353 Shuppet [TM]	561 Sigilyph [TM]	516 Simipour [TM]	512 Simisage [TM]
		514 Simisear [TM]	227 Skarmory [TM]	672 Skiddo [TM]	188 Skiploom [TM]	300 Skitty [TM]	451 Skorupi [TM]	690 Skrelp [TM]
		435 Skuntank [TM]	289 Slaking [TM]	287 Slakoth [TM]	705 Sliggoo [9, TM]	080 Slowbro [TM]	199 Slowking [TM]	079 Slowpoke [TM]
		218 Slugma [TM]	685 Slurpuff [TM]	238 Smoochum [TM]	215 Sneasel [TM]	495 Snivy [TM]	143 Snorlax [TM]	361 Snorunt [32, TM]
		459 Snover [TM]	209 Snubbull [TM]	577 Solosis [TM]	338 Solrock [TM]	021 Spearow [TM]	665 Spewpa [9, TM]	363 Spheal [TM]
		167 Spinarak [TM]	327 Spinda [TM]	442 Spiritomb [TM]	325 Spoink [TM]	682 Spritzee [TM]	007 Squirtle [22, TM]	234 Stantler [TM]
		398 Staraptor [TM]	397 Staravia [TM]	396 Starly [TM]	121 Starmie [TM]	120 Staryu [TM]	208 Steelix [TM]	508 Stoutland [TM]
		618 Stunfisk [TM]	434 Stunky [TM]	185 Sudowoodo [TM]	245 Suicune [TM]	192 Sunflora [TM]	191 Sunkern [TM]	283 Surskit [TM]
		333 Swablu [TM]	541 Swadloon [20, TM]	317 Swalot [TM]	260 Swampert [32, TM]	581 Swanna [TM]	277 Swellow [TM]	220 Swinub [TM]
		684 Swirlix [TM]	528 Swoobat [TM]	700 Sylveon [TM]	276 Taillow [TM]	663 Talonflame [TM]	114 Tangela [TM]	465 Tangrowth [TM]
		128 Tauros [TM]	216 Teddiursa [TM]	072 Tentacool [TM]	073 Tentacruel [TM]	498 Tepig [TM]	639 Terrakion [TM]	538 Throh [TM]
		642 Thundurus [TM]	532 Timburr [TM]	564 Tirtouga [11, TM]	468 Togekiss [TM]	175 Togepi [TM]	176 Togetic [TM]	255 Torchic [TM]
		324 Torkoal [30, TM]	641 Tornadus [TM]	389 Torterra [TM]	158 Totodile [TM]	454 Toxicroak [TM]	520 Tranquill [TM]	328 Trapinch [TM]
		252 Treecko [TM]	709 Trevenant [TM]	357 Tropius [TM]	568 Trubbish [TM]	387 Turtwig [TM]	535 Tympole [TM]	157 Typhlosion [TM]
		248 Tyranitar [TM]	697 Tyrantrum [TM]	236 Tyrogue [TM]	696 Tyrunt [TM]	197 Umbreon [TM]	521 Unfezant [TM]	217 Ursaring [TM]
		480 Uxie [TM]	583 Vanillish [TM]	582 Vanillite [TM]	584 Vanilluxe [TM]	134 Vaporeon [TM]	543 Venipede [15, TM]	049 Venomoth [TM]
		048 Venonat [TM]	003 Venusaur [TM]	416 Vespiquen [TM]	329 Vibrava [TM]	494 Victini [TM]	071 Victreebel [TM]	288 Vigoroth [TM]
		045 Vileplume [TM]	640 Virizion [TM]	666 Vivillon [TM]	313 Volbeat [29, TM]	637 Volcarona [TM]	100 Voltorb [TM]	629 Vullaby [TM]
		037 Vulpix [TM]	320 Wailmer [TM]	321 Wailord [TM]	365 Walrein [TM]	008 Wartortle [24, TM]	505 Watchog [TM]	461 Weavile [TM]
		070 Weepinbell [TM]	110 Weezing [TM]	547 Whimsicott [TM]	544 Whirlipede [15, TM]	340 Whiscash [TM]	293 Whismur [TM]	040 Wigglytuff [TM]
		278 Wingull [TM]	527 Woobat [TM]	194 Wooper [TM]	413 Wormadam (Plant) [10, TM]	413 Wormadam (Sand) [10, TM]	413 Wormadam (Trash) [10, TM]	178 Xatu [TM]
		716 Xerneas [TM]	562 Yamask [1, TM]	193 Yanma [TM]	469 Yanmega [TM]	717 Yveltal [TM]	335 Zangoose [TM]	145 Zapdos [TM]
		523 Zebstrika [TM]	644 Zekrom [TM]	263 Zigzagoon [TM]	571 Zoroark [TM]	570 Zorua [TM]	041 Zubat [TM]	634 Zweilous [TM]
		718 Zygarde [TM]						

	Move	Pokémon that can learn it						
Psychic	Psybeam	065 Alakazam [21]	343 Baltoy [16]	606 Beheeyem [15]	654 Braixen [18]	012 Butterfree [24]	170 Chinchou [E]	344 Claydol [16]
		655 Delphox [18]	096 Drowzee [25]	269 Dustox [22]	605 Elgyem [15]	196 Espeon [20]	677 Espurr [17]	653 Fennekin [17]
		456 Finneon [E]	203 Girafarig [19]	118 Goldeen [E]	574 Gothita [16]	576 Gothitelle [16]	575 Gothorita [16]	326 Grumpig [1, 14]
		097 Hypno [25]	686 Inkay [21]	064 Kadabra [21]	352 Kecleon [18]	109 Koffing [E]	165 Ledyba [E]	687 Malamar [21]
		226 Mantine [1]	648 Meloetta [31]	678 Meowstic (F) [17]	678 Meowstic (M) [17]	439 Mime Jr. [25]	200 Misdreavus [28]	414 Mothim [32]
		122 Mr. Mime [25]	517 Munna [11]	518 Musharna [1]	224 Octillery [1, 10]	046 Paras [E]	137 Porygon [7]	233 Porygon2 [7]
		474 Porygon-Z [7]	054 Psyduck [E]	223 Remoraid [10]	561 Sigilyph [18]	167 Spinarak [E]	327 Spinda [14]	325 Spoink [14]
		283 Surskit [E]	049 Venomoth [25]	048 Venonat [25]	666 Vivillon [17]	413 Wormadam (Plant) [32]	413 Wormadam (Sand) [32]	413 Wormadam (Trash) [32]
Normal	Psych Up (TM77)	063 Abra [TM]	359 Absol [TM]	065 Alakazam [TM]	594 Alomomola [TM]	334 Altaria [TM]	698 Amaura [TM]	493 Arceus [TM]
		683 Aromatisse [64, TM]	531 Audino [TM]	699 Aurorus [TM]	482 Azelf [TM]	343 Baltoy [TM]	354 Banette [TM]	606 Beheeyem [36, TM]
		242 Blissey [TM]	438 Bonsly [TM]	654 Braixen [TM]	437 Bronzong [TM]	436 Bronzor [TM]	406 Budew [TM]	012 Butterfree [TM]
		703 Carbink [TM]	351 Castform [TM]	251 Celebi [TM]	609 Chandelure [TM]	113 Chansey [TM]	358 Chimecho [TM]	433 Chingling [TM]
		344 Claydol [TM]	036 Clefable [TM]	035 Clefairy [TM]	173 Cleffa [TM]	638 Cobalion [TM]	563 Cofagrigus [TM]	488 Cresselia [TM]
		491 Darkrai [TM]	633 Deino [TM]	301 Delcatty [TM]	655 Delphox [TM]	386 Deoxys (Atk) [TM]	386 Deoxys (Def) [TM]	386 Deoxys (Nor) [TM]
		386 Deoxys (Spd) [TM]	483 Dialga [TM]	719 Diancie [TM]	426 Drifblim [TM]	425 Drifloon [TM]	096 Drowzee [33, TM]	206 Dunsparce [TM]
		578 Duosion [TM]	356 Dusclops [TM]	477 Dusknoir [TM]	355 Duskull [TM]	605 Elgyem [36, TM]	244 Entei [TM]	196 Espeon [29, TM]
		677 Espurr [TM]	102 Exeggcute [TM]	103 Exeggutor [TM]	083 Farfetch'd [TM]	653 Fennekin [TM]	456 Finneon [TM]	592 Frillish [TM]
		478 Froslass [TM]	475 Gallade [TM]	282 Gardevoir [TM]	092 Gastly [TM]	094 Gengar [TM]	203 Girafarig [TM]	487 Giratina (Alt) [TM]
		487 Giratina (Ori) [TM]	431 Glameow [TM]	055 Golduck [43, TM]	368 Gorebyss [TM]	574 Gothita [TM]	576 Gothitelle [TM]	575 Gothorita [TM]
		383 Groudon [TM]	326 Grumpig [15, TM]	440 Happiny [TM]	093 Haunter [TM]	695 Heliolisk [TM]	694 Helioptile [TM]	430 Honchkrow [TM]
		250 Ho-Oh [TM]	163 Hoothoot [TM]	187 Hoppip [TM]	635 Hydreigon [TM]	097 Hypno [33, TM]	174 Igglybuff [TM]	314 Illumise [TM]
		686 Inkay [TM]	593 Jellicent [TM]	039 Jigglypuff [TM]	385 Jirachi [TM]	189 Jumpluff [TM]	124 Jynx [TM]	064 Kadabra [TM]
		352 Kecleon [TM]	647 Keldeo [TM]	281 Kirlia [TM]	707 Klefki [TM]	382 Kyogre [TM]	608 Lampent [TM]	380 Latias [TM]
		381 Latios [TM]	463 Lickilicky [TM]	108 Lickitung [TM]	510 Liepard [TM]	607 Litwick [TM]	249 Lugia [TM]	457 Lumineon [TM]
		337 Lunatone [TM]	370 Luvdisc [TM]	081 Magnemite [TM]	082 Magneton [TM]	462 Magnezone [TM]	687 Malamar [TM]	490 Manaphy [TM]
		630 Mandibuzz [TM]	284 Masquerain [TM]	303 Mawile [TM]	308 Medicham [31, TM]	307 Meditite [31, TM]	648 Meloetta [TM]	678 Meowstic (F) [TM]
		678 Meowstic (M) [TM]	052 Meowth [TM]	481 Mesprit [TM]	376 Metagross [TM]	375 Metang [TM]	151 Mew [TM]	150 Mewtwo [22, TM]
		619 Mienfoo [TM]	620 Mienshao [TM]	350 Milotic [TM]	241 Miltank [TM]	439 Mime Jr. [TM]	200 Misdreavus [TM]	429 Mismagius [TM]
		414 Mothim [TM]	122 Mr. Mime [TM]	517 Munna [TM]	198 Murkrow [TM]	518 Musharna [TM]	177 Natu [TM]	038 Ninetales [TM]
		164 Noctowl [TM]	274 Nuzleaf [TM]	095 Onix [TM]	484 Palkia [TM]	053 Persian [TM]	489 Phione [TM]	137 Porygon [TM]
		233 Porygon2 [TM]	474 Porygon-Z [TM]	054 Psyduck [39, TM]	509 Purrloin [TM]	432 Purugly [TM]	243 Raikou [TM]	280 Ralts [TM]
		384 Rayquaza [TM]	378 Regice [TM]	486 Regigigas [TM]	377 Regirock [TM]	379 Registeel [TM]	369 Relicanth [TM]	579 Reuniclus [TM]
		315 Roselia [TM]	407 Roserade [TM]	479 Rotom (Fan) [TM]	479 Rotom (Frost) [TM]	479 Rotom (Heat) [TM]	479 Rotom (Mow) [TM]	479 Rotom (Wash) [TM]
		479 Rotom [TM]	302 Sableye [TM]	492 Shaymin (Land) [TM]	492 Shaymin (Sky) [TM]	275 Shiftry [TM]	353 Shuppet [TM]	561 Sigilyph [TM]
		188 Skiploom [TM]	300 Skitty [TM]	080 Slowbro [62, TM]	199 Slowking [54, TM]	079 Slowpoke [54, TM]	685 Slurpuff [TM]	238 Smoochum [TM]
		215 Sneasel [TM]	577 Solosis [TM]	338 Solrock [TM]	327 Spinda [41, TM]	442 Spiritomb [TM]	325 Spoink [15, TM]	682 Spritzee [TM]
		234 Stantler [TM]	121 Starmie [TM]	120 Staryu [TM]	208 Steelix [TM]	185 Sudowoodo [TM]	245 Suicune [TM]	283 Surskit [TM]
		333 Swablu [TM]	684 Swirlix [TM]	528 Swoobat [TM]	700 Sylveon [45, TM]	114 Tangela [TM]	465 Tangrowth [TM]	639 Terrakion [TM]
		468 Togekiss [TM]	175 Togepi [TM]	176 Togetic [TM]	197 Umbreon [TM]	521 Unfezant [TM]	480 Uxie [TM]	494 Victini [TM]
		640 Virizion [TM]	666 Vivillon [TM]	313 Volbeat [TM]	629 Vullaby [TM]	037 Vulpix [TM]	505 Watchog [29, TM]	461 Weavile [TM]
		040 Wigglytuff [TM]	527 Woobat [TM]	413 Wormadam (Plant) [TM]	413 Wormadam (Sand) [TM]	413 Wormadam (Trash) [TM]	178 Xatu [TM]	716 Xerneas [59, TM]
		562 Yamask [TM]	469 Yanmega [TM]	571 Zoroark [TM]	570 Zorua [TM]	634 Zweilous [TM]		
Psychic	Psychic (TM29)	063 Abra [TM]	065 Alakazam [38, TM]	594 Alomomola [TM]	493 Arceus [TM]	168 Ariados [46, TM]	683 Aromatisse [48, TM]	531 Audino [TM]
		699 Aurorus [TM]	482 Azelf [TM]	343 Baltoy [TM]	354 Banette [TM]	267 Beautifly [TM]	606 Beheeyem [39, TM]	242 Blissey [TM]
		654 Braixen [48, TM]	437 Bronzong [TM]	436 Bronzor [TM]	012 Butterfree [TM]	703 Carbink [TM]	251 Celebi [TM]	609 Chandelure [TM]
		113 Chansey [TM]	358 Chimecho [TM]	433 Chingling [TM]	344 Claydol [TM]	036 Clefable [TM]	035 Clefairy [TM]	173 Cleffa [TM]
		563 Cofagrigus [TM]	222 Corsola [TM]	488 Cresselia [93, TM]	491 Darkrai [TM]	555 Darmanitan [TM]	655 Delphox [51, TM]	386 Deoxys (Atk) [31, TM]
		386 Deoxys (Def) [31, TM]	386 Deoxys (Nor) [31, TM]	386 Deoxys (Spd) [31, TM]	719 Diancie [TM]	426 Drifblim [TM]	425 Drifloon [TM]	096 Drowzee [49, TM]
		578 Duosion [39, TM]	356 Dusclops [TM]	477 Dusknoir [TM]	355 Duskull [TM]	269 Dustox [TM]	125 Electabuzz [TM]	466 Electivire [TM]
		239 Elekid [TM]	605 Elgyem [39, TM]	196 Espeon [37, TM]	677 Espurr [TM]	102 Exeggcute [TM]	103 Exeggutor [TM]	653 Fennekin [41, TM]
		669 Flabébé [TM]	670 Floette [TM]	671 Florges [TM]	592 Frillish [TM]	478 Froslass [TM]	475 Gallade [TM]	569 Garbodor [TM]
		282 Gardevoir [31, TM]	092 Gastly [TM]	649 Genesect [TM]	094 Gengar [TM]	203 Girafarig [50, TM]	487 Giratina (Alt) [TM]	487 Giratina (Ori) [TM]
		055 Golduck [TM]	622 Golett [TM]	623 Golurk [TM]	368 Gorebyss [34, TM]	574 Gothita [37, TM]	576 Gothitelle [39, TM]	575 Gothorita [39, TM]
		711 Gourgeist [TM]	326 Grumpig [52, TM]	440 Happiny [TM]	093 Haunter [TM]	430 Honchkrow [TM]	250 Ho-Oh [TM]	163 Hoothoot [TM]
		097 Hypno [49, TM]	174 Igglybuff [TM]	686 Inkay [TM]	593 Jellicent [TM]	039 Jigglypuff [TM]	385 Jirachi [20, TM]	124 Jynx [TM]
		064 Kadabra [38, TM]	281 Kirlia [30, TM]	707 Klefki [TM]	646 Kyurem (Blk) [TM]	646 Kyurem (Wht) [TM]	646 Kyurem [TM]	608 Lampent [TM]
		645 Landorus [TM]	131 Lapras [TM]	636 Larvesta [TM]	380 Latias [51, TM]	381 Latios [51, TM]	607 Litwick [TM]	448 Lucario [TM]
		249 Lugia [TM]	337 Lunatone [29, TM]	240 Magby [TM]	126 Magmar [TM]	467 Magmortar [TM]	687 Malamar [TM]	490 Manaphy [TM]
		308 Medicham [TM]	307 Meditite [TM]	648 Meloetta [57, TM]	678 Meowstic (F) [40, TM]	678 Meowstic (M) [40, TM]	481 Mesprit [TM]	376 Metagross [38, TM]
		375 Metang [38, TM]	151 Mew [30, TM]	150 Mewtwo [57, TM]	439 Mime Jr. [39, TM]	200 Misdreavus [TM]	429 Mismagius [TM]	414 Mothim [44, TM]
		122 Mr. Mime [39, TM]	446 Munchlax [TM]	517 Munna [37, TM]	198 Murkrow [TM]	518 Musharna [TM]	177 Natu [33, TM]	164 Noctowl [TM]

ADVENTURE DATA

Type	Move	Pokémon that can learn it						
Psychic	Psychic (TM29)	714 Noibat [TM]	715 Noivern [TM]	224 Octillery [TM]	708 Phantump [TM]	186 Politoed [TM]	060 Poliwag [TM]	061 Poliwhirl [TM]
		062 Poliwrath [TM]	137 Porygon [TM]	233 Porygon2 [TM]	474 Porygon-Z [TM]	054 Psyduck [TM]	710 Pumpkaboo [TM]	280 Ralts [27, TM]
		223 Remoraid [TM]	643 Reshiram [TM]	579 Reuniclus [39, TM]	302 Sableye [TM]	492 Shaymin (Land) [TM]	492 Shaymin (Sky) [TM]	353 Shuppet [TM]
		561 Sigilyph [44, TM]	080 Slowbro [49, TM]	199 Slowking [45, TM]	079 Slowpoke [45, TM]	685 Slurpuff [TM]	238 Smoochum [38, TM]	143 Snorlax [TM]
		577 Solosis [37, TM]	338 Solrock [29, TM]	167 Spinarak [40, TM]	327 Spinda [TM]	442 Spiritomb [TM]	325 Spoink [44, TM]	682 Spritzee [48, TM]
		234 Stantler [TM]	121 Starmie [TM]	120 Staryu [42, TM]	684 Swirlix [TM]	528 Swoobat [41, TM]	642 Thundurus [TM]	468 Togekiss [TM]
		175 Togepi [TM]	176 Togetic [TM]	641 Tornadus [TM]	709 Trevenant [TM]	197 Umbreon [TM]	480 Uxie [TM]	049 Venomoth [55, TM]
		048 Venonat [47, TM]	494 Victini [TM]	666 Vivillon [TM]	637 Volcarona [TM]	547 Whimsicott [TM]	040 Wigglytuff [TM]	527 Woobat [41, TM]
		413 Wormadam (Plant) [44, TM]	413 Wormadam (Sand) [44, TM]	413 Wormadam (Trash) [44, TM]	178 Xatu [35, TM]	716 Xerneas [TM]	562 Yamask [TM]	193 Yanma [TM]
		469 Yanmega [TM]	717 Yveltal [59, TM]	644 Zekrom [TM]				
	Psycho Boost	386 Deoxys (Atk) [67]	386 Deoxys (Def) [67]	386 Deoxys (Nor) [67]	386 Deoxys (Spd) [67]			
	Psycho Cut	359 Absol [37]	065 Alakazam [28]	488 Cresselia [1, 66]	096 Drowzee [E]	475 Gallade [31]	686 Inkay [39]	064 Kadabra [28]
		687 Malamar [39]	307 Meditite [E]	150 Mewtwo [36]	624 Pawniard [E]	327 Spinda [E]		
	Psycho Shift	063 Abra [E]	488 Cresselia [1, 75]	386 Deoxys (Atk) [43]	386 Deoxys (Def) [43]	386 Deoxys (Nor) [43]	386 Deoxys (Spd) [43]	163 Hoothoot [49]
		380 Latias [28]	381 Latios [28]	198 Murkrow [E]	177 Natu [39]	164 Noctowl [57]	561 Sigilyph [E]	327 Spinda [E]
		175 Togepi [E]	527 Woobat [E]	178 Xatu [43]				
	Psyshock (TM03)	063 Abra [TM]	065 Alakazam [TM]	493 Arceus [TM]	683 Aromatisse [TM]	531 Audino [TM]	482 Azelf [TM]	343 Baltoy [TM]
		606 Beheeyem [TM]	654 Braixen [34, TM]	437 Bronzong [TM]	436 Bronzor [TM]	358 Chimecho [TM]	433 Chingling [TM]	344 Claydol [TM]
		036 Clefable [TM]	035 Clefairy [TM]	173 Cleffa [TM]	488 Cresselia [TM]	655 Delphox [34, TM]	386 Deoxys (Atk) [TM]	386 Deoxys (Def) [TM]
		386 Deoxys (Nor) [TM]	386 Deoxys (Spd) [TM]	719 Diancie [TM]	096 Drowzee [57, TM]	578 Duosion [25, TM]	605 Elgyem [TM]	196 Espeon [TM]
		677 Espurr [25, TM]	103 Exeggutor [17, TM]	653 Fennekin [31, TM]	475 Gallade [TM]	282 Gardevoir [TM]	203 Girafarig [TM]	055 Golduck [TM]
		574 Gothita [25, TM]	576 Gothitelle [25, TM]	575 Gothorita [25, TM]	326 Grumpig [42, TM]	097 Hypno [57, TM]	385 Jirachi [TM]	124 Jynx [TM]
		064 Kadabra [TM]	281 Kirlia [TM]	707 Klefki [TM]	380 Latias [TM]	381 Latios [TM]	249 Lugia [TM]	337 Lunatone [TM]
		687 Malamar [TM]	308 Medicham [TM]	307 Meditite [TM]	648 Meloetta [TM]	678 Meowstic (F) [25, TM]	678 Meowstic (M) [25, TM]	481 Mesprit [TM]
		376 Metagross [TM]	375 Metang [TM]	151 Mew [TM]	150 Mewtwo [TM]	439 Mime Jr. [TM]	122 Mr. Mime [TM]	517 Munna [TM]
		518 Musharna [TM]	177 Natu [TM]	038 Ninetales [TM]	137 Porygon [TM]	233 Porygon2 [TM]	474 Porygon-Z [TM]	054 Psyduck [TM]
		280 Ralts [TM]	579 Reuniclus [25, TM]	561 Sigilyph [TM]	080 Slowbro [TM]	199 Slowking [TM]	079 Slowpoke [TM]	238 Smoochum [TM]
		577 Solosis [25, TM]	338 Solrock [TM]	325 Spoink [38, TM]	234 Stantler [TM]	121 Starmie [TM]	528 Swoobat [TM]	700 Sylveon [TM]
		468 Togekiss [TM]	175 Togepi [TM]	176 Togetic [TM]	480 Uxie [TM]	494 Victini [TM]	527 Woobat [TM]	178 Xatu [TM]
		716 Xerneas [TM]						
	Psystrike	150 Mewtwo [100]						
	Psywave	437 Bronzong [15]	436 Bronzor [15]	358 Chimecho [16]	578 Duosion [1]	092 Gastly [E]	326 Grumpig [1, 7]	686 Inkay [13]
		109 Koffing [E]	380 Latias [1]	381 Latios [1]	337 Lunatone [13]	687 Malamar [13]	200 Misdreavus [1]	429 Mismagius [1]
		122 Mr. Mime [15]	517 Munna [1]	579 Reuniclus [1]	561 Sigilyph [8]	577 Solosis [1]	338 Solrock [13]	325 Spoink [7]
		120 Staryu [13]						
Dark	Punishment	359 Absol [E]	493 Arceus [1]	250 Ho-Oh [50]	228 Houndour [E]	174 Igglybuff [E]	392 Infernape [29]	645 Landorus [13]
		249 Lugia [50]	630 Mandibuzz [28]	056 Mankey [45]	303 Mawile [E]	052 Meowth [E]	241 Miltank [E]	057 Primeape [53]
		302 Sableye [24]	336 Seviper [E]	289 Slaking [1, 53]	215 Sneasel [44, E]	434 Stunky [E]	629 Vullaby [28]	461 Weavile [44]
		571 Zoroark [49]	570 Zorua [45]					
	Pursuit	359 Absol [10]	681 Aegislash [1]	142 Aerodactyl [E]	190 Aipom [E]	015 Beedrill [22]	522 Blitzle [22]	626 Bouffalant [1]
		418 Buizel [18]	408 Cranidos [10]	453 Croagunk [15]	386 Deoxys (Atk) [25]	386 Deoxys (Nor) [25]	386 Deoxys (Spd) [25]	050 Diglett [E]
		085 Dodrio [17]	084 Doduo [17]	680 Doublade [13]	452 Drapion [16]	621 Druddigon [E]	206 Dunsparce [10]	356 Dusclops [22]
		477 Dusknoir [22]	355 Duskull [22]	023 Ekans [E]	587 Emolga [16]	022 Fearow [13]	419 Floatzel [18]	253 Grovyle [18]
		631 Heatmor [E]	214 Heracross [E]	107 Hitmonchan [11]	237 Hitmontop [10]	430 Honchkrow [1]	679 Honedge [13]	228 Houndour [E]
		595 Joltik [E]	588 Karrablast [E]	246 Larvitar [E]	510 Liepard [15]	506 Lillipup [E]	376 Metagross [23]	375 Metang [23]
		446 Munchlax [E]	198 Murkrow [5]	029 Nidoran ♀ [E]	046 Paras [E]	504 Patrat [E]	624 Pawniard [E]	016 Pidgey [E]
		509 Purrloin [15]	409 Rampardos [10]	020 Raticate [13]	019 Rattata [13]	551 Sandile [E]	254 Sceptile [18]	212 Scizor [9]
		545 Scolipede [12]	123 Scyther [9]	161 Sentret [E]	616 Shelmet [E]	353 Shuppet [E]	227 Skarmory [E]	451 Skorupi [16, E]
		287 Slakoth [E]	215 Sneasel [E]	495 Snivy [E]	143 Snorlax [E]	021 Spearow [13]	167 Spinarak [E]	442 Spiritomb [1]
		396 Starly [E]	434 Stunky [E]	333 Swablu [E]	276 Taillow [E]	128 Tauros [15]	454 Toxicroak [15]	252 Treecko [17]
		236 Tyrogue [E]	197 Umbreon [9]	543 Venipede [12]	416 Vespiquen [9]	544 Whirlipede [12]	278 Wingull [26]	193 Yanma [30, E]
		469 Yanmega [30]	335 Zangoose [12]	523 Zebstrika [22]	263 Zigzagoon [E]	571 Zoroark [1, 5]	570 Zorua [5]	041 Zubat [E]

Q•R

	Move	Pokémon that can learn it						
Dark	Quash (TM60)	493 Arceus [TM]	395 Empoleon [TM]	244 Entei [TM]	430 Honchkrow [65, TM]	230 Kingdra [TM]	099 Kingler [TM]	151 Mew [TM]
		198 Murkrow [65, TM]	034 Nidoking [TM]	031 Nidoqueen [TM]	674 Pancham [E]	675 Pangoro [TM]	393 Piplup [TM]	394 Prinplup [TM]
		243 Raikou [TM]	302 Sableye [44, TM]	289 Slaking [TM]	199 Slowking [TM]	442 Spiritomb [TM]	245 Suicune [TM]	416 Vespiquen [TM]
Normal	Quick Attack	359 Absol [1, 7]	617 Accelgor [1, 13]	566 Archen [1]	567 Archeops [1]	399 Bidoof [E]	257 Blaziken [25]	522 Blitzle [1]
		418 Buizel [11]	427 Buneary [16]	659 Bunnelby [7]	638 Cobalion [1]	256 Combusken [25]	155 Cyndaquil [13, E]	491 Darkrai [11]
		225 Delibird [E]	660 Diggersby [7]	085 Dodrio [1, 5]	084 Doduo [5, E]	133 Eevee [13]	125 Electabuzz [1]	466 Electivire [1]
		309 Electrike [10]	239 Elekid [1]	587 Emolga [4]	196 Espeon [13]	083 Farfetch'd [E]	136 Flareon [13]	662 Fletchinder [6]
		661 Fletchling [6]	419 Floatzel [1, 11]	656 Froakie [8]	657 Frogadier [8]	162 Furret [1, 7]	649 Genesect [1]	471 Glaceon [13]
		431 Glameow [E]	207 Gligar [13]	472 Gliscor [13]	658 Greninja [8]	253 Grovyle [1, 9]	695 Heliolisk [1]	694 Helioptile [17]
		237 Hitmontop [15]	314 Illumise [12]	135 Jolteon [13]	470 Leafeon [13]	428 Lopunny [16]	448 Lucario [1]	310 Manectric [10]
		284 Masquerain [1, 6]	648 Meloetta [6]	312 Minun [1]	177 Natu [E]	038 Ninetales [1]	417 Pachirisu [5]	018 Pidgeot [1, 13]
		017 Pidgeotto [13]	016 Pidgey [13]	519 Pidove [11]	025 Pikachu [10]	127 Pinsir [E]	311 Plusle [1]	156 Quilava [13]
		026 Raichu [1]	243 Raikou [22]	078 Rapidash [1]	020 Raticate [1, 4]	019 Rattata [4]	447 Riolu [1]	254 Sceptile [1, 9]
		212 Scizor [1]	123 Scyther [1]	273 Seedot [E]	161 Sentret [7]	492 Shaymin (Sky) [28]	403 Shinx [E]	215 Sneasel [8]
		021 Spearow [E]	398 Staraptor [1, 5]	397 Staravia [1, 5]	396 Starly [5]	283 Surskit [6]	277 Swellow [1, 9]	700 Sylveon [13]
		276 Taillow [9]	663 Talonflame [6]	639 Terrakion [1]	255 Torchic [23]	520 Tranquill [1, 11]	328 Trapinch [E]	252 Treecko [9]
		157 Typhlosion [13]	197 Umbreon [13]	521 Unfezant [1, 11]	134 Vaporeon [13]	494 Victini [1]	640 Virizion [1]	313 Volbeat [12]
		037 Vulpix [10]	461 Weavile [1, 8]	278 Wingull [19]	193 Yanma [6]	469 Yanmega [1, 6]	335 Zangoose [5]	523 Zebstrika [1]
		041 Zubat [E]						
Fighting	Quick Guard	190 Aipom [E]	566 Archen [25]	567 Archeops [25]	650 Chespin [E]	390 Chimchar [E]	638 Cobalion [1, 55]	453 Croagunk [E]
		169 Crobat [51]	589 Escavalier [1, 8]	661 Fletchling [E]	475 Gallade [11]	042 Golbat [51]	253 Grovyle [53]	701 Hawlucha [E]
		107 Hitmonchan [31]	237 Hitmontop [46]	647 Keldeo [55]	448 Lucario [33]	066 Machop [E]	307 Meditite [E]	678 Meowstic (M) [1, 53]
		619 Mienfoo [45]	122 Mr. Mime [1]	674 Pancham [E]	624 Pawniard [E]	539 Sawk [45]	254 Sceptile [57]	559 Scraggy [E]
		123 Scyther [E]	277 Swellow [27]	276 Taillow [25]	639 Terrakion [1, 55]	252 Treecko [41]	640 Virizion [1, 55]	335 Zangoose [E]
		041 Zubat [43]						
Bug	Quiver Dance	267 Beautifly [40]	012 Butterfree [46]	269 Dustox [40]	549 Lilligant [28]	284 Masquerain [1, 52]	414 Mothim [50]	049 Venomoth [1, 63]
		666 Vivillon [45]	637 Volcarona [1, 59]					
Normal	Rage	371 Bagon [1]	550 Basculin [E]	267 Beautifly [37]	015 Beedrill [19]	522 Blitzle [E]	626 Bouffalant [6]	318 Carvanha [4]
		159 Croconaw [8]	104 Cubone [23]	555 Darmanitan [1, 9]	554 Darumaka [9]	085 Dodrio [1, 9]	084 Doduo [9]	206 Dunsparce [1]
		160 Feraligatr [1, 8]	210 Granbull [35]	228 Houndour [E]	115 Kangaskhan [22]	552 Krokorok [1]	553 Krookodile [1]	105 Marowak [23]
		095 Onix [13]	057 Primeape [28]	373 Salamence [1]	551 Sandile [1]	319 Sharpedo [1, 4]	372 Shelgon [1]	209 Snubbull [31]
		234 Stantler [E]	208 Steelix [13]	333 Swablu [E]	276 Taillow [E]	128 Tauros [5]	158 Totodile [8]	
Bug	Rage Powder	591 Amoonguss [54]	012 Butterfree [34]	455 Carnivine [E]	590 Foongus [45]	187 Hoppip [31]	189 Jumpluff [39]	046 Paras [49]
		047 Parasect [59]	664 Scatterbug [E]	188 Skiploom [36]	167 Spinarak [E]	114 Tangela [E]	048 Venonat [E]	637 Volcarona [1, 80]
Water	Rain Dance (TM18)	460 Abomasnow [TM]	063 Abra [TM]	359 Absol [TM]	617 Accelgor [TM]	681 Aegislash [TM]	142 Aerodactyl [TM]	306 Aggron [TM]
		190 Aipom [TM]	065 Alakazam [TM]	594 Alomomola [TM]	334 Altaria [TM]	698 Amaura [TM]	424 Ambipom [TM]	591 Amoonguss [TM]
		181 Ampharos [TM]	024 Arbok [TM]	493 Arceus [TM]	683 Aromatisse [TM]	304 Aron [TM]	144 Articuno [TM]	531 Audino [TM]
		699 Aurorus [TM]	713 Avalugg [TM]	610 Axew [TM]	482 Azelf [TM]	184 Azumarill [35, TM]	298 Azurill [TM]	371 Bagon [TM]
		343 Baltoy [TM]	354 Banette [TM]	689 Barbaracle [TM]	339 Barboach [TM]	550 Basculin [TM]	411 Bastiodon [TM]	614 Beartic [TM]
		606 Beheeyem [TM]	712 Bergmite [TM]	400 Bibarel [TM]	399 Bidoof [TM]	688 Binacle [TM]	625 Bisharp [TM]	009 Blastoise [53, TM]
		242 Blissey [TM]	522 Blitzle [TM]	626 Bouffalant [TM]	654 Braixen [TM]	628 Braviary [TM]	437 Bronzong [1, TM]	436 Bronzor [TM]
		406 Budew [TM]	418 Buizel [TM]	427 Buneary [TM]	012 Butterfree [TM]	565 Carracosta [56, TM]	318 Carvanha [TM]	351 Castform [20, TM]
		251 Celebi [TM]	113 Chansey [TM]	441 Chatot [TM]	358 Chimecho [TM]	170 Chinchou [TM]	433 Chingling [TM]	573 Cinccino [TM]
		366 Clamperl [TM]	692 Clauncher [TM]	693 Clawitzer [TM]	344 Claydol [TM]	036 Clefable [TM]	035 Clefairy [TM]	173 Cleffa [TM]
		091 Cloyster [TM]	563 Cofagrigus [TM]	534 Conkeldurr [TM]	341 Corphish [TM]	222 Corsola [TM]	408 Cranidos [TM]	342 Crawdaunt [TM]
		488 Cresselia [TM]	453 Croagunk [TM]	169 Crobat [TM]	159 Croconaw [TM]	615 Cryogonal [TM]	613 Cubchoo [TM]	491 Darkrai [TM]
		702 Dedenne [TM]	585 Deerling [TM]	633 Deino [TM]	301 Delcatty [TM]	225 Delibird [TM]	655 Delphox [TM]	386 Deoxys (Atk) [TM]
		386 Deoxys (Def) [TM]	386 Deoxys (Nor) [TM]	386 Deoxys (Spd) [TM]	087 Dewgong [TM]	502 Dewott [TM]	483 Dialga [TM]	680 Doublade [TM]
		691 Dragalge [TM]	148 Dragonair [TM]	149 Dragonite [TM]	452 Drapion [TM]	147 Dratini [TM]	426 Drifblim [TM]	425 Drifloon [TM]
		096 Drowzee [TM]	621 Druddigon [TM]	580 Ducklett [34, TM]	206 Dunsparce [TM]	578 Duosion [TM]	356 Dusclops [TM]	477 Dusknoir [TM]
		355 Duskull [TM]	603 Eelektrik [TM]	604 Eelektross [TM]	133 Eevee [TM]	023 Ekans [TM]	125 Electabuzz [TM]	466 Electivire [TM]
		309 Electrike [TM]	101 Electrode [TM]	239 Elekid [TM]	605 Elgyem [TM]	587 Emolga [TM]	395 Empoleon [TM]	244 Entei [TM]
		589 Escavalier [TM]	196 Espeon [TM]	677 Espurr [TM]	295 Exploud [TM]	022 Fearow [TM]	349 Feebas [TM]	653 Fennekin [TM]
		160 Feraligatr [TM]	456 Finneon [13, TM]	180 Flaaffy [TM]	669 Flabébé [TM]	136 Flareon [TM]	419 Floatzel [TM]	670 Floette [TM]
		671 Florges [TM]	590 Foongus [TM]	611 Fraxure [TM]	592 Frillish [37, TM]	656 Froakie [TM]	657 Frogadier [TM]	478 Froslass [TM]
		676 Furfrou [TM]	162 Furret [TM]	444 Gabite [TM]	475 Gallade [TM]	596 Galvantula [TM]	569 Garbodor [TM]	445 Garchomp [TM]
		282 Gardevoir [TM]	092 Gastly [TM]	423 Gastrodon [22, TM]	094 Gengar [TM]	443 Gible [TM]	203 Girafarig [TM]	487 Giratina (Alt) [TM]
		487 Giratina (Ori) [TM]	471 Glaceon [TM]	362 Glalie [TM]	431 Glameow [TM]	207 Gligar [TM]	472 Gliscor [TM]	673 Gogoat [TM]
		042 Golbat [TM]	118 Goldeen [TM]	055 Golduck [TM]	622 Golett [TM]	623 Golurk [TM]	706 Goodra [25, TM]	704 Goomy [25, TM]
		368 Gorebyss [TM]	574 Gothita [TM]	576 Gothitelle [TM]	575 Gothorita [TM]	210 Granbull [TM]	658 Greninja [TM]	088 Grimer [TM]
		326 Grumpig [TM]	316 Gulpin [TM]	533 Gurdurr [TM]	130 Gyarados [38, TM]	440 Happiny [TM]	297 Hariyama [TM]	093 Haunter [TM]
		701 Hawlucha [TM]	612 Haxorus [TM]	631 Heatmor [TM]	695 Heliolisk [TM]	694 Helioptile [TM]	214 Heracross [TM]	507 Herdier [TM]
		107 Hitmonchan [TM]	106 Hitmonlee [TM]	237 Hitmontop [TM]	430 Honchkrow [TM]	679 Honedge [TM]	250 Ho-Oh [TM]	163 Hoothoot [TM]
		116 Horsea [TM]	367 Huntail [TM]	635 Hydreigon [TM]	097 Hypno [TM]	174 Igglybuff [TM]	314 Illumise [TM]	686 Inkay [TM]

ADVENTURE DATA

	Move	Pokémon that can learn it						
Water	Rain Dance (TM18)	593 Jellicent [37, TM]	039 Jigglypuff [TM]	385 Jirachi [TM]	135 Jolteon [TM]	595 Joltik [TM]	124 Jynx [TM]	140 Kabuto [TM]
		141 Kabutops [TM]	064 Kadabra [TM]	115 Kangaskhan [TM]	588 Karrablast [TM]	352 Kecleon [TM]	647 Keldeo [TM]	230 Kingdra [TM]
		099 Kingler [TM]	281 Kirlia [TM]	707 Klefki [TM]	109 Koffing [TM]	098 Krabby [TM]	402 Kricketune [TM]	382 Kyogre [TM]
		646 Kyurem (Blk) [TM]	646 Kyurem (Wht) [TM]	646 Kyurem [TM]	305 Lairon [TM]	171 Lanturn [TM]	131 Lapras [22, TM]	246 Larvitar [TM]
		380 Latias [TM]	381 Latios [TM]	470 Leafeon [TM]	463 Lickilicky [TM]	108 Lickitung [TM]	510 Liepard [TM]	506 Lillipup [TM]
		264 Linoone [TM]	667 Litleo [TM]	271 Lombre [TM]	428 Lopunny [TM]	270 Lotad [27, TM]	294 Loudred [TM]	448 Lucario [TM]
		272 Ludicolo [TM]	249 Lugia [29, TM]	457 Lumineon [13, TM]	337 Lunatone [TM]	370 Luvdisc [TM]	404 Luxio [TM]	405 Luxray [TM]
		068 Machamp [TM]	067 Machoke [TM]	066 Machop [TM]	081 Magnemite [TM]	082 Magneton [TM]	462 Magnezone [TM]	296 Makuhita [TM]
		687 Malamar [TM]	473 Mamoswine [TM]	490 Manaphy [69, TM]	630 Mandibuzz [TM]	310 Manectric [TM]	056 Mankey [TM]	226 Mantine [TM]
		458 Mantyke [TM]	179 Mareep [TM]	183 Marill [31, TM]	259 Marshtomp [TM]	284 Masquerain [TM]	303 Mawile [TM]	308 Medicham [TM]
		307 Meditite [TM]	648 Meloetta [TM]	678 Meowstic (F) [TM]	678 Meowstic (M) [TM]	052 Meowth [TM]	481 Mesprit [TM]	376 Metagross [TM]
		375 Metang [TM]	151 Mew [TM]	150 Mewtwo [TM]	619 Mienfoo [TM]	620 Mienshao [TM]	262 Mightyena [TM]	350 Milotic [51, TM]
		241 Miltank [TM]	439 Mime Jr. [TM]	572 Minccino [TM]	312 Minun [TM]	200 Misdreavus [TM]	429 Mismagius [TM]	146 Moltres [TM]
		414 Mothim [TM]	122 Mr. Mime [TM]	258 Mudkip [TM]	089 Muk [TM]	446 Munchlax [TM]	517 Munna [TM]	198 Murkrow [TM]
		518 Musharna [TM]	177 Natu [TM]	034 Nidoking [TM]	031 Nidoqueen [TM]	029 Nidoran ♀ [TM]	032 Nidoran ♂ [TM]	030 Nidorina [TM]
		033 Nidorino [TM]	164 Noctowl [TM]	224 Octillery [TM]	138 Omanyte [TM]	139 Omastar [TM]	501 Oshawott [TM]	417 Pachirisu [TM]
		484 Palkia [TM]	536 Palpitoad [33, TM]	674 Pancham [TM]	675 Pangoro [TM]	515 Panpour [TM]	504 Patrat [TM]	624 Pawniard [TM]
		279 Pelipper [TM]	053 Persian [TM]	489 Phione [69, TM]	172 Pichu [TM]	018 Pidgeot [TM]	017 Pidgeotto [TM]	016 Pidgey [TM]
		519 Pidove [TM]	025 Pikachu [TM]	221 Piloswine [TM]	127 Pinsir [TM]	393 Piplup [TM]	311 Plusle [TM]	186 Politoed [TM]
		060 Poliwag [18, TM]	061 Poliwhirl [18, TM]	062 Poliwrath [TM]	261 Poochyena [TM]	137 Porygon [TM]	233 Porygon2 [TM]	474 Porygon-Z [TM]
		057 Primeape [TM]	394 Prinplup [TM]	054 Psyduck [TM]	247 Pupitar [TM]	509 Purrloin [TM]	432 Purugly [TM]	668 Pyroar [TM]
		195 Quagsire [41, TM]	211 Qwilfish [TM]	026 Raichu [TM]	243 Raikou [71, TM]	280 Ralts [TM]	409 Rampardos [TM]	020 Raticate [TM]
		019 Rattata [TM]	384 Rayquaza [TM]	378 Regice [TM]	486 Regigigas [TM]	379 Registeel [TM]	369 Relicanth [TM]	223 Remoraid [TM]
		579 Reuniclus [TM]	112 Rhydon [TM]	111 Rhyhorn [TM]	464 Rhyperior [TM]	447 Riolu [TM]	315 Roselia [TM]	407 Roserade [TM]
		479 Rotom (Fan) [TM]	479 Rotom (Frost) [TM]	479 Rotom (Heat) [TM]	479 Rotom (Mow) [TM]	479 Rotom (Wash) [TM]	479 Rotom [TM]	627 Rufflet [TM]
		302 Sableye [TM]	373 Salamence [TM]	503 Samurott [TM]	539 Sawk [TM]	586 Sawsbuck [TM]	212 Scizor [TM]	560 Scrafty [TM]
		559 Scraggy [TM]	123 Scyther [TM]	117 Seadra [TM]	119 Seaking [TM]	364 Sealeo [TM]	086 Seel [TM]	537 Seismitoad [33, TM]
		161 Sentret [TM]	336 Seviper [TM]	319 Sharpedo [TM]	372 Shelgon [TM]	090 Shellder [TM]	422 Shellos [22, TM]	616 Shelmet [TM]
		410 Shieldon [TM]	403 Shinx [TM]	353 Shuppet [TM]	561 Sigilyph [TM]	516 Simipour [TM]	672 Skiddo [TM]	300 Skitty [TM]
		451 Skorupi [TM]	690 Skrelp [TM]	435 Skuntank [TM]	289 Slaking [TM]	287 Slakoth [TM]	705 Sliggoo [25, TM]	080 Slowbro [55, TM]
		199 Slowking [TM]	079 Slowpoke [49, TM]	685 Slurpuff [TM]	238 Smoochum [TM]	215 Sneasel [TM]	143 Snorlax [TM]	361 Snorunt [TM]
		459 Snover [TM]	209 Snubbull [TM]	577 Solosis [TM]	021 Spearow [TM]	363 Spheal [TM]	327 Spinda [TM]	442 Spiritomb [TM]
		325 Spoink [TM]	682 Spritzee [TM]	007 Squirtle [37, TM]	234 Stantler [TM]	398 Staraptor [TM]	397 Staravia [TM]	396 Starly [TM]
		121 Starmie [TM]	120 Staryu [TM]	508 Stoutland [TM]	618 Stunfisk [TM]	434 Stunky [TM]	245 Suicune [15, TM]	283 Surskit [TM]
		333 Swablu [TM]	317 Swalot [TM]	260 Swampert [TM]	581 Swanna [34, TM]	277 Swellow [TM]	220 Swinub [TM]	684 Swirlix [TM]
		528 Swoobat [TM]	700 Sylveon [TM]	276 Taillow [TM]	128 Tauros [TM]	216 Teddiursa [TM]	072 Tentacool [TM]	073 Tentacruel [TM]
		538 Throh [TM]	642 Thundurus [TM]	532 Timburr [TM]	564 Tirtouga [48, TM]	468 Togekiss [TM]	175 Togepi [TM]	176 Togetic [TM]
		641 Tornadus [61, TM]	158 Totodile [TM]	454 Toxicroak [TM]	520 Tranquill [TM]	568 Trubbish [TM]	535 Tympole [31, TM]	248 Tyranitar [TM]
		236 Tyrogue [TM]	197 Umbreon [TM]	521 Unfezant [TM]	217 Ursaring [TM]	480 Uxie [TM]	583 Vanillish [TM]	582 Vanillite [TM]
		584 Vanilluxe [TM]	134 Vaporeon [TM]	416 Vespiquen [TM]	288 Vigoroth [TM]	666 Vivillon [TM]	313 Volbeat [TM]	100 Voltorb [TM]
		629 Vullaby [TM]	320 Wailmer [TM]	321 Wailord [TM]	365 Walrein [TM]	008 Wartortle [44, TM]	505 Watchog [TM]	461 Weavile [TM]
		110 Weezing [TM]	340 Whiscash [TM]	293 Whismur [TM]	040 Wigglytuff [TM]	278 Wingull [TM]	527 Woobat [TM]	194 Wooper [37, TM]
		413 Wormadam (Plant) [TM]	413 Wormadam (Sand) [TM]	413 Wormadam (Trash) [TM]	178 Xatu [TM]	716 Xerneas [TM]	562 Yamask [TM]	717 Yveltal [TM]
		335 Zangoose [TM]	145 Zapdos [57, TM]	523 Zebstrika [TM]	644 Zekrom [TM]	263 Zigzagoon [TM]	571 Zoroark [TM]	570 Zorua [TM]
		041 Zubat [TM]	634 Zweilous [TM]					
Normal	Rapid Spin	347 Anorith [E]	713 Avalugg [35]	343 Baltoy [4]	712 Bergmite [35]	009 Blastoise [20]	344 Claydol [1, 4]	615 Cryogonal [13]
		225 Delibird [E]	232 Donphan [6]	529 Drilbur [5, E]	530 Excadrill [1, 5]	205 Forretress [17]	237 Hitmontop [24]	140 Kabuto [E]
		204 Pineco [17]	027 Sandshrew [9, E]	028 Sandslash [9]	090 Shellder [E]	327 Spinda [E]	007 Squirtle [19]	121 Starmie [1]
		120 Staryu [7]	072 Tentacool [E]	324 Torkoal [10]	236 Tyrogue [E]	008 Wartortle [20]		
Grass	Razor Leaf	460 Abomasnow [1, 5]	153 Bayleef [1, 6]	069 Bellsprout [39]	406 Budew [E]	001 Bulbasaur [19]	455 Carnivine [E]	420 Cherubi [E]
		152 Chikorita [6]	546 Cottonee [19]	669 Flabébé [15]	670 Floette [15]	673 Gogoat [13]	711 Gourgeist [16]	388 Grotle [13]
		002 Ivysaur [20]	470 Leafeon [9]	542 Leavanny [1, 15]	270 Lotad [E]	154 Meganium [1, 6]	274 Nuzleaf [14]	043 Oddish [E]
		710 Pumpkaboo [16]	315 Roselia [E]	540 Sewaddle [15]	275 Shiftry [1]	672 Skiddo [13]	459 Snover [5]	192 Sunflora [16]
		191 Sunkern [16]	541 Swadloon [1]	389 Torterra [1, 13]	357 Tropius [1]	387 Turtwig [13]	003 Venusaur [20]	071 Victreebel [1]
		070 Weepinbell [39]	413 Wormadam (Plant) [26]					
Water	Razor Shell	689 Barbaracle [48]	688 Binacle [45]	341 Corphish [31]	342 Crawdaunt [32]	502 Dewott [17]	501 Oshawott [17]	503 Samurott [17]
		090 Shellder [32]						
Normal	Razor Wind	359 Absol [49]	610 Axew [E]	418 Buizel [35]	662 Fletchinder [27]	661 Fletchling [25]	419 Floatzel [41]	203 Girafarig [E]
		207 Gligar [E]	695 Heliolisk [1]	694 Helioptile [22]	116 Horsea [E]	714 Noibat [31]	715 Noivern [31]	274 Nuzleaf [20]
		519 Pidove [32]	212 Scizor [33]	123 Scyther [33, E]	273 Seedot [E]	540 Sewaddle [E]	021 Spearow [E]	663 Talonflame [27]
		520 Tranquill [36]	252 Treecko [E]	357 Tropius [E]	521 Unfezant [38]	717 Yveltal [1]	335 Zangoose [E]	

Type	Move	Pokémon that can learn it						
Normal	Recover	617 Accelgor [49]	065 Alakazam [31]	493 Arceus [70]	713 Avalugg [51]	606 Beheeyem [50]	712 Bergmite [47, E]	251 Celebi [1]
		358 Chimecho [E]	433 Chingling [E]	222 Corsola [8]	615 Cryogonal [49]	386 Deoxys (Def) [61]	386 Deoxys (Nor) [61]	386 Deoxys (Spd) [61]
		578 Duosion [24]	605 Elgyem [46]	592 Frillish [17, E]	423 Gastrodon [54]	250 Ho-Oh [71]	593 Jellicent [17]	064 Kadabra [31]
		352 Kecleon [E]	380 Latias [32]	381 Latios [32]	345 Lileep [E]	249 Lugia [71]	219 Magcargo [47]	308 Medicham [47]
		307 Meditite [41]	150 Mewtwo [50]	350 Milotic [31]	137 Porygon [18]	233 Porygon2 [18]	474 Porygon-Z [18]	579 Reuniclus [24]
		302 Sableye [E]	422 Shellos [46]	616 Shelmet [49]	218 Slugma [43]	577 Solosis [24]	121 Starmie [1]	120 Staryu [10]
		194 Wooper [E]						
	Recycle	063 Abra [BP]	065 Alakazam [BP]	493 Arceus [BP]	482 Azelf [BP]	343 Baltoy [BP]	606 Beheeyem [BP]	242 Blissey [BP]
		654 Braixen [BP]	437 Bronzong [BP]	436 Bronzor [BP]	659 Bunnelby [BP]	113 Chansey [BP]	358 Chimecho [BP]	433 Chingling [BP]
		344 Claydol [BP]	036 Clefable [BP]	035 Clefairy [BP]	173 Cleffa [BP]	488 Cresselia [BP]	702 Dedenne [BP]	225 Delibird [BP]
		655 Delphox [BP]	386 Deoxys (Atk) [BP]	386 Deoxys (Def) [BP]	386 Deoxys (Nor) [BP]	386 Deoxys (Spd) [BP]	660 Diggersby [BP]	426 Drifblim [BP]
		425 Drifloon [BP]	096 Drowzee [BP]	605 Elgyem [BP]	677 Espurr [BP]	475 Gallade [BP]	569 Garbodor [1, 3, BP]	282 Gardevoir [BP]
		649 Genesect [BP]	203 Girafarig [BP]	574 Gothita [BP]	576 Gothitelle [BP]	575 Gothorita [BP]	326 Grumpig [BP]	440 Happiny [BP]
		631 Heatmor [BP]	163 Hoothoot [BP]	097 Hypno [BP]	174 Igglybuff [BP]	039 Jigglypuff [BP]	385 Jirachi [BP]	124 Jynx [BP]
		064 Kadabra [BP]	352 Kecleon [BP]	281 Kirlia [BP]	600 Klang [BP]	707 Klefki [40, BP]	599 Klink [BP]	601 Klinklang [BP]
		337 Lunatone [BP]	081 Magnemite [BP]	082 Magneton [BP]	462 Magnezone [BP]	308 Medicham [BP]	307 Meditite [BP]	648 Meloetta [BP]
		678 Meowstic (F) [BP]	678 Meowstic (M) [BP]	481 Mesprit [BP]	151 Mew [BP]	150 Mewtwo [BP]	439 Mime Jr. [32, BP]	122 Mr. Mime [32, BP]
		446 Munchlax [1, BP]	164 Noctowl [BP]	515 Panpour [37, BP]	511 Pansage [37, BP]	513 Pansear [37, BP]	137 Porygon [34, BP]	233 Porygon2 [34, BP]
		474 Porygon-Z [BP]	280 Ralts [BP]	516 Simipour [BP]	512 Simisage [BP]	514 Simisear [BP]	080 Slowbro [BP]	199 Slowking [BP]
		079 Slowpoke [BP]	238 Smoochum [BP]	143 Snorlax [BP]	338 Solrock [BP]	327 Spinda [BP]	325 Spoink [BP]	121 Starmie [BP]
		120 Staryu [BP]	568 Trubbish [3, BP]	480 Uxie [BP]	040 Wigglytuff [BP]			
Psychic	Reflect (TM33)	063 Abra [TM]	681 Aegislash [TM]	065 Alakazam [26, TM]	698 Amaura [TM]	493 Arceus [TM]	683 Aromatisse [57, TM]	144 Articuno [50, TM]
		531 Audino [TM]	699 Aurorus [TM]	482 Azelf [TM]	343 Baltoy [TM]	153 Bayleef [18, TM]	606 Beheeyem [TM]	069 Bellsprout [TM]
		437 Bronzong [TM]	436 Bronzor [TM]	703 Carbink [18, TM]	251 Celebi [TM]	652 Chesnaught [TM]	650 Chespin [TM]	152 Chikorita [17, TM]
		358 Chimecho [TM]	433 Chingling [TM]	344 Claydol [TM]	036 Clefable [TM]	035 Clefairy [TM]	173 Cleffa [TM]	638 Cobalion [TM]
		222 Corsola [TM]	488 Cresselia [TM]	615 Cryogonal [37, TM]	386 Deoxys (Atk) [TM]	386 Deoxys (Def) [TM]	386 Deoxys (Nor) [TM]	386 Deoxys (Spd) [TM]
		719 Diancie [18, TM]	680 Doublade [TM]	096 Drowzee [TM]	578 Duosion [1, 3, TM]	605 Elgyem [TM]	244 Entei [TM]	196 Espeon [TM]
		677 Espurr [TM]	102 Exeggcute [7, TM]	103 Exeggutor [TM]	205 Forretress [TM]	475 Gallade [TM]	282 Gardevoir [TM]	649 Genesect [TM]
		203 Girafarig [TM]	574 Gothita [TM]	576 Gothitelle [TM]	575 Gothorita [TM]	210 Granbull [TM]	388 Grotle [TM]	326 Grumpig [TM]
		679 Honedge [TM]	250 Ho-Oh [TM]	163 Hoothoot [17, TM]	187 Hoppip [TM]	635 Hydreigon [TM]	097 Hypno [TM]	174 Igglybuff [TM]
		686 Inkay [4, TM]	039 Jigglypuff [TM]	385 Jirachi [TM]	189 Jumpluff [TM]	124 Jynx [TM]	064 Kadabra [26, TM]	647 Keldeo [TM]
		281 Kirlia [TM]	707 Klefki [TM]	646 Kyurem (Blk) [TM]	646 Kyurem (Wht) [TM]	646 Kyurem [TM]	380 Latias [TM]	381 Latios [TM]
		542 Leavanny [TM]	166 Ledian [14, TM]	165 Ledyba [14, TM]	249 Lugia [TM]	337 Lunatone [TM]	219 Magcargo [TM]	081 Magnemite [TM]
		082 Magneton [TM]	462 Magnezone [TM]	687 Malamar [4, TM]	473 Mamoswine [TM]	490 Manaphy [TM]	308 Medicham [TM]	307 Meditite [TM]
		154 Meganium [18, TM]	678 Meowstic (F) [TM]	678 Meowstic (M) [35, TM]	481 Mesprit [TM]	376 Metagross [TM]	375 Metang [TM]	151 Mew [TM]
		150 Mewtwo [TM]	619 Mienfoo [TM]	620 Mienshao [TM]	439 Mime Jr. [22, TM]	122 Mr. Mime [22, TM]	517 Munna [TM]	518 Musharna [TM]
		177 Natu [TM]	164 Noctowl [17, TM]	708 Phantump [TM]	221 Piloswine [TM]	204 Pineco [TM]	651 Quilladin [TM]	243 Raikou [36, TM]
		280 Ralts [TM]	643 Reshiram [TM]	579 Reuniclus [1, 3, TM]	479 Rotom (Fan) [TM]	479 Rotom (Frost) [TM]	479 Rotom (Heat) [TM]	479 Rotom (Mow) [TM]
		479 Rotom (Wash) [TM]	479 Rotom [TM]	497 Serperior [TM]	496 Servine [TM]	561 Sigilyph [28, TM]	188 Skiploom [TM]	218 Slugma [TM]
		238 Smoochum [TM]	215 Sneasel [TM]	495 Snivy [TM]	209 Snubbull [TM]	577 Solosis [3, TM]	338 Solrock [TM]	325 Spoink [TM]
		682 Spritzee [TM]	234 Stantler [TM]	121 Starmie [TM]	120 Staryu [TM]	245 Suicune [TM]	220 Swinub [TM]	528 Swoobat [TM]
		700 Sylveon [TM]	114 Tangela [TM]	465 Tangrowth [TM]	639 Terrakion [TM]	468 Togekiss [TM]	175 Togepi [TM]	176 Togetic [TM]
		389 Torterra [TM]	709 Trevenant [TM]	387 Turtwig [TM]	480 Uxie [TM]	071 Victreebel [TM]	640 Virizion [TM]	461 Weavile [TM]
		070 Weepinbell [TM]	040 Wigglytuff [TM]	527 Woobat [TM]	178 Xatu [TM]	716 Xerneas [TM]	644 Zekrom [TM]	
	Reflect Type	351 Castform [E]	092 Gastly [E]	380 Latias [36]	151 Mew [1]	138 Omanyte [E]	120 Staryu [35]	618 Stunfisk [E]
		073 Tentacruel [1]						
Normal	Refresh	594 Alomomola [E]	334 Altaria [26]	493 Arceus [50]	531 Audino [9]	298 Azurill [E]	242 Blissey [9]	113 Chansey [9]
		152 Chikorita [E]	366 Clamperl [E]	222 Corsola [13]	133 Eevee [20]	676 Furfrou [E]	440 Happiny [9]	385 Jirachi [25]
		131 Lapras [E]	380 Latias [13]	381 Latios [13]	463 Lickilicky [45]	108 Lickitung [45]	183 Marill [E]	350 Milotic [7]
		258 Mudkip [E]	177 Natu [E]	060 Poliwag [E]	054 Psyduck [E]	682 Spritzee [E]	007 Squirtle [E]	333 Swablu [26]
		276 Taillow [E]	535 Tympole [E]					
	Relic Song	648 Meloetta [T]						
Psychic	Rest (TM44)	460 Abomasnow [TM]	063 Abra [TM]	359 Absol [TM]	617 Accelgor [TM]	681 Aegislash [TM]	142 Aerodactyl [TM]	306 Aggron [TM]
		190 Aipom [TM]	065 Alakazam [TM]	594 Alomomola [TM]	334 Altaria [TM]	698 Amaura [TM]	424 Ambipom [TM]	591 Amoonguss [TM]
		181 Ampharos [TM]	347 Anorith [TM]	024 Arbok [TM]	059 Arcanine [TM]	493 Arceus [TM]	566 Archen [TM]	567 Archeops [TM]
		168 Ariados [TM]	348 Armaldo [TM]	683 Aromatisse [TM]	304 Aron [TM]	144 Articuno [TM]	531 Audino [TM]	699 Aurorus [TM]
		713 Avalugg [TM]	610 Axew [TM]	482 Azelf [1, TM]	184 Azumarill [TM]	298 Azurill [TM]	371 Bagon [TM]	343 Baltoy [TM]
		354 Banette [TM]	689 Barbaracle [TM]	339 Barboach [25, TM]	550 Basculin [TM]	411 Bastiodon [TM]	153 Bayleef [TM]	614 Beartic [41, TM]
		267 Beautifly [TM]	015 Beedrill [TM]	606 Beheeyem [TM]	182 Bellossom [TM]	069 Bellsprout [TM]	712 Bergmite [TM]	400 Bibarel [TM]
		399 Bidoof [TM]	688 Binacle [TM]	625 Bisharp [TM]	009 Blastoise [TM]	257 Blaziken [TM]	242 Blissey [TM]	522 Blitzle [TM]
		525 Boldore [TM]	438 Bonsly [TM]	626 Bouffalant [TM]	654 Braixen [TM]	628 Braviary [TM]	286 Breloom [TM]	437 Bronzong [TM]
		436 Bronzor [TM]	406 Budew [TM]	418 Buizel [TM]	001 Bulbasaur [TM]	427 Buneary [TM]	659 Bunnelby [TM]	012 Butterfree [TM]
		331 Cacnea [TM]	332 Cacturne [TM]	323 Camerupt [TM]	703 Carbink [TM]	455 Carnivine [TM]	565 Carracosta [TM]	318 Carvanha [TM]
		351 Castform [TM]	251 Celebi [TM]	609 Chandelure [TM]	113 Chansey [TM]	006 Charizard [TM]	004 Charmander [TM]	005 Charmeleon [TM]
		441 Chatot [TM]	421 Cherrim [TM]	420 Cherubi [TM]	652 Chesnaught [TM]	650 Chespin [TM]	152 Chikorita [TM]	390 Chimchar [TM]
		358 Chimecho [TM]	170 Chinchou [TM]	433 Chingling [TM]	573 Cinccino [TM]	366 Clamperl [TM]	692 Clauncher [TM]	693 Clawitzer [TM]

ADVENTURE DATA

Type	Move	Pokémon that can learn it						
Psychic	Rest (TM44)	344 Claydol [TM]	036 Clefable [TM]	035 Clefairy [TM]	173 Cleffa [TM]	091 Cloyster [TM]	638 Cobalion [TM]	563 Cofagrigus [TM]
		256 Combusken [TM]	534 Conkeldurr [TM]	341 Corphish [TM]	222 Corsola [TM]	546 Cottonee [TM]	346 Cradily [TM]	408 Cranidos [TM]
		342 Crawdaunt [TM]	488 Cresselia [TM]	453 Croagunk [TM]	169 Crobat [TM]	159 Croconaw [TM]	558 Crustle [TM]	615 Cryogonal [TM]
		613 Cubchoo [41, TM]	104 Cubone [TM]	155 Cyndaquil [TM]	491 Darkrai [TM]	555 Darmanitan [TM]	554 Darumaka [TM]	702 Dedenne [30, TM]
		585 Deerling [TM]	633 Deino [TM]	301 Delcatty [TM]	225 Delibird [TM]	655 Delphox [TM]	386 Deoxys (Atk) [TM]	386 Deoxys (Def) [TM]
		386 Deoxys (Nor) [TM]	386 Deoxys (Spd) [TM]	087 Dewgong [21, TM]	502 Dewott [TM]	483 Dialga [TM]	719 Diancie [TM]	660 Diggersby [TM]
		050 Diglett [TM]	085 Dodrio [TM]	084 Doduo [TM]	232 Donphan [TM]	680 Doublade [TM]	691 Dragalge [TM]	148 Dragonair [TM]
		149 Dragonite [TM]	452 Drapion [TM]	147 Dratini [TM]	426 Drifblim [TM]	425 Drifloon [TM]	529 Drilbur [TM]	096 Drowzee [TM]
		621 Druddigon [TM]	580 Ducklett [TM]	051 Dugtrio [TM]	206 Dunsparce [TM]	578 Duosion [TM]	632 Durant [TM]	356 Dusclops [TM]
		477 Dusknoir [TM]	355 Duskull [TM]	269 Dustox [TM]	557 Dwebble [TM]	603 Eelektrik [TM]	604 Eelektross [TM]	133 Eevee [TM]
		023 Ekans [TM]	125 Electabuzz [TM]	466 Electivire [TM]	309 Electrike [TM]	101 Electrode [TM]	239 Elekid [TM]	605 Elgyem [TM]
		500 Emboar [TM]	587 Emolga [TM]	395 Empoleon [TM]	244 Entei [TM]	589 Escavalier [TM]	196 Espeon [TM]	677 Espurr [TM]
		530 Excadrill [TM]	102 Exeggcute [TM]	103 Exeggutor [TM]	295 Exploud [36, TM]	083 Farfetch'd [TM]	022 Fearow [TM]	349 Feebas [TM]
		653 Fennekin [TM]	160 Feraligatr [TM]	597 Ferroseed [TM]	598 Ferrothorn [TM]	456 Finneon [TM]	180 Flaaffy [TM]	669 Flabébé [TM]
		136 Flareon [TM]	662 Fletchinder [TM]	661 Fletchling [TM]	419 Floatzel [TM]	670 Floette [TM]	671 Florges [TM]	330 Flygon [TM]
		590 Foongus [TM]	205 Forretress [TM]	611 Fraxure [TM]	592 Frillish [TM]	656 Froakie [TM]	657 Frogadier [TM]	478 Froslass [TM]
		676 Furfrou [TM]	162 Furret [32, TM]	444 Gabite [TM]	475 Gallade [TM]	596 Galvantula [TM]	569 Garbodor [TM]	445 Garchomp [TM]
		282 Gardevoir [TM]	092 Gastly [TM]	423 Gastrodon [TM]	649 Genesect [TM]	094 Gengar [TM]	074 Geodude [TM]	443 Gible [TM]
		526 Gigalith [TM]	203 Girafarig [TM]	487 Giratina (Alt) [TM]	487 Giratina (Ori) [TM]	471 Glaceon [TM]	362 Glalie [TM]	431 Glameow [TM]
		207 Gligar [TM]	472 Gliscor [TM]	044 Gloom [TM]	673 Gogoat [TM]	042 Golbat [TM]	118 Goldeen [TM]	055 Golduck [TM]
		076 Golem [TM]	622 Golett [TM]	623 Golurk [TM]	706 Goodra [TM]	704 Goomy [TM]	368 Gorebyss [TM]	574 Gothita [TM]
		576 Gothitelle [TM]	575 Gothorita [TM]	711 Gourgeist [TM]	210 Granbull [TM]	075 Graveler [TM]	658 Greninja [TM]	088 Grimer [TM]
		388 Grotle [TM]	383 Groudon [30, TM]	253 Grovyle [TM]	058 Growlithe [TM]	326 Grumpig [35, TM]	316 Gulpin [TM]	533 Gurdurr [TM]
		130 Gyarados [TM]	440 Happiny [TM]	297 Hariyama [TM]	093 Haunter [TM]	701 Hawlucha [TM]	612 Haxorus [TM]	631 Heatmor [TM]
		485 Heatran [TM]	695 Heliolisk [TM]	694 Helioptile [TM]	214 Heracross [TM]	507 Herdier [TM]	449 Hippopotas [TM]	450 Hippowdon [TM]
		107 Hitmonchan [TM]	106 Hitmonlee [TM]	237 Hitmontop [TM]	430 Honchkrow [TM]	679 Honedge [TM]	250 Ho-Oh [TM]	163 Hoothoot [TM]
		187 Hoppip [TM]	116 Horsea [TM]	229 Houndoom [TM]	228 Houndour [TM]	367 Huntail [TM]	635 Hydreigon [TM]	097 Hypno [TM]
		174 Igglybuff [TM]	314 Illumise [TM]	392 Infernape [TM]	686 Inkay [TM]	002 Ivysaur [TM]	593 Jellicent [TM]	039 Jigglypuff [32, TM]
		385 Jirachi [5, 30, TM]	135 Jolteon [TM]	595 Joltik [TM]	189 Jumpluff [TM]	124 Jynx [TM]	140 Kabuto [TM]	141 Kabutops [TM]
		064 Kadabra [TM]	115 Kangaskhan [TM]	588 Karrablast [TM]	352 Kecleon [TM]	647 Keldeo [TM]	230 Kingdra [TM]	099 Kingler [TM]
		281 Kirlia [TM]	600 Klang [TM]	707 Klefki [TM]	599 Klink [TM]	601 Klinklang [TM]	109 Koffing [TM]	098 Krabby [TM]
		402 Kricketune [TM]	552 Krokorok [TM]	553 Krookodile [TM]	382 Kyogre [TM]	646 Kyurem (Blk) [TM]	646 Kyurem (Wht) [TM]	646 Kyurem [TM]
		305 Lairon [TM]	608 Lampent [TM]	645 Landorus [TM]	171 Lanturn [TM]	131 Lapras [TM]	636 Larvesta [TM]	246 Larvitar [TM]
		380 Latias [TM]	381 Latios [TM]	470 Leafeon [TM]	542 Leavanny [TM]	166 Ledian [TM]	165 Ledyba [TM]	463 Lickilicky [TM]
		108 Lickitung [TM]	510 Liepard [TM]	345 Lileep [TM]	549 Lilligant [TM]	506 Lillipup [TM]	264 Linoone [40, TM]	667 Litleo [TM]
		607 Litwick [TM]	271 Lombre [TM]	428 Lopunny [TM]	270 Lotad [TM]	294 Loudred [36, TM]	448 Lucario [TM]	272 Ludicolo [TM]
		249 Lugia [TM]	457 Lumineon [TM]	337 Lunatone [TM]	370 Luvdisc [TM]	404 Luxio [TM]	405 Luxray [TM]	068 Machamp [TM]
		067 Machoke [TM]	066 Machop [TM]	240 Magby [TM]	219 Magcargo [TM]	126 Magmar [TM]	467 Magmortar [TM]	081 Magnemite [TM]
		082 Magneton [TM]	462 Magnezone [TM]	296 Makuhita [TM]	687 Malamar [TM]	473 Mamoswine [TM]	490 Manaphy [TM]	630 Mandibuzz [TM]
		310 Manectric [TM]	056 Mankey [TM]	226 Mantine [TM]	458 Mantyke [TM]	556 Maractus [TM]	179 Mareep [TM]	183 Marill [TM]
		105 Marowak [TM]	259 Marshtomp [TM]	284 Masquerain [TM]	303 Mawile [TM]	308 Medicham [TM]	307 Meditite [TM]	154 Meganium [TM]
		648 Meloetta [TM]	678 Meowstic (F) [TM]	678 Meowstic (M) [TM]	052 Meowth [TM]	481 Mesprit [1, TM]	376 Metagross [TM]	375 Metang [TM]
		151 Mew [TM]	150 Mewtwo [TM]	619 Mienfoo [TM]	620 Mienshao [TM]	262 Mightyena [TM]	350 Milotic [TM]	241 Miltank [TM]
		439 Mime Jr. [TM]	572 Minccino [TM]	312 Minun [TM]	200 Misdreavus [TM]	429 Mismagius [TM]	146 Moltres [TM]	391 Monferno [TM]
		414 Mothim [TM]	122 Mr. Mime [TM]	258 Mudkip [TM]	089 Muk [TM]	446 Munchlax [TM]	517 Munna [TM]	198 Murkrow [TM]
		518 Musharna [TM]	177 Natu [TM]	034 Nidoking [TM]	031 Nidoqueen [TM]	029 Nidoran ♀ [TM]	032 Nidoran ♂ [TM]	030 Nidorina [TM]
		033 Nidorino [TM]	290 Nincada [TM]	038 Ninetales [TM]	291 Ninjask [TM]	164 Noctowl [TM]	714 Noibat [TM]	715 Noivern [TM]
		299 Nosepass [16, TM]	322 Numel [TM]	274 Nuzleaf [TM]	224 Octillery [TM]	043 Oddish [TM]	138 Omanyte [TM]	139 Omastar [TM]
		095 Onix [TM]	501 Oshawott [TM]	417 Pachirisu [TM]	484 Palkia [TM]	536 Palpitoad [TM]	674 Pancham [TM]	675 Pangoro [TM]
		515 Panpour [TM]	511 Pansage [TM]	513 Pansear [TM]	046 Paras [TM]	047 Parasect [TM]	504 Patrat [TM]	624 Pawniard [TM]
		279 Pelipper [TM]	053 Persian [TM]	548 Petilil [TM]	231 Phanpy [TM]	708 Phantump [TM]	489 Phione [TM]	172 Pichu [TM]
		018 Pidgeot [TM]	017 Pidgeotto [TM]	016 Pidgey [TM]	519 Pidove [TM]	499 Pignite [TM]	025 Pikachu [TM]	221 Piloswine [TM]
		204 Pineco [TM]	127 Pinsir [TM]	393 Piplup [TM]	311 Plusle [TM]	186 Politoed [TM]	060 Poliwag [TM]	061 Poliwhirl [TM]
		062 Poliwrath [TM]	077 Ponyta [TM]	261 Poochyena [TM]	137 Porygon [TM]	233 Porygon2 [TM]	474 Porygon-Z [TM]	057 Primeape [TM]
		394 Prinplup [TM]	476 Probopass [16, TM]	054 Psyduck [TM]	710 Pumpkaboo [TM]	247 Pupitar [TM]	509 Purrloin [TM]	432 Purugly [TM]
		668 Pyroar [TM]	195 Quagsire [TM]	156 Quilava [TM]	651 Quilladin [TM]	211 Qwilfish [TM]	026 Raichu [TM]	243 Raikou [TM]
		280 Ralts [TM]	409 Rampardos [TM]	078 Rapidash [TM]	020 Raticate [TM]	019 Rattata [TM]	384 Rayquaza [35, TM]	378 Regice [TM]
		377 Regirock [TM]	379 Registeel [TM]	369 Relicanth [41, TM]	223 Remoraid [TM]	643 Reshiram [TM]	579 Reuniclus [TM]	112 Rhydon [TM]
		111 Rhyhorn [TM]	464 Rhyperior [TM]	447 Riolu [TM]	524 Roggenrola [TM]	315 Roselia [TM]	407 Roserade [TM]	479 Rotom (Fan) [TM]
		479 Rotom (Frost) [TM]	479 Rotom (Heat) [TM]	479 Rotom (Mow) [TM]	479 Rotom (Wash) [TM]	479 Rotom [TM]	627 Rufflet [TM]	302 Sableye [TM]
		373 Salamence [TM]	503 Samurott [TM]	551 Sandile [TM]	027 Sandshrew [TM]	028 Sandslash [TM]	539 Sawk [TM]	586 Sawsbuck [TM]
		254 Sceptile [TM]	212 Scizor [TM]	545 Scolipede [TM]	560 Scrafty [TM]	559 Scraggy [TM]	123 Scyther [TM]	117 Seadra [TM]
		119 Seaking [TM]	364 Sealeo [31, TM]	273 Seedot [TM]	086 Seel [21, TM]	537 Seismitoad [TM]	161 Sentret [28, TM]	497 Serperior [TM]
		496 Servine [TM]	336 Seviper [TM]	540 Sewaddle [TM]	319 Sharpedo [TM]	492 Shaymin (Land) [TM]	492 Shaymin (Sky) [TM]	292 Shedinja [TM]
		372 Shelgon [TM]	090 Shellder [TM]	422 Shellos [TM]	616 Shelmet [TM]	410 Shieldon [TM]	275 Shiftry [TM]	403 Shinx [TM]
		285 Shroomish [TM]	213 Shuckle [20, TM]	353 Shuppet [TM]	561 Sigilyph [TM]	516 Simipour [TM]	512 Simisage [TM]	514 Simisear [TM]

	Move	Pokémon that can learn it						
Psychic	Rest (TM44)	227 Skarmory [TM]	672 Skiddo [TM]	188 Skiploom [TM]	300 Skitty [TM]	451 Skorupi [TM]	690 Skrelp [TM]	435 Skuntank [TM]
		289 Slaking [TM]	287 Slakoth [TM]	705 Sliggoo [TM]	080 Slowbro [TM]	199 Slowking [TM]	079 Slowpoke [TM]	218 Slugma [TM]
		685 Slurpuff [TM]	238 Smoochum [TM]	215 Sneasel [TM]	495 Snivy [TM]	143 Snorlax [28, TM]	361 Snorunt [TM]	459 Snover [TM]
		209 Snubbull [TM]	577 Solosis [TM]	338 Solrock [TM]	021 Spearow [TM]	363 Spheal [31, TM]	167 Spinarak [TM]	327 Spinda [TM]
		442 Spiritomb [TM]	325 Spoink [29, TM]	682 Spritzee [TM]	007 Squirtle [TM]	234 Stantler [TM]	398 Staraptor [TM]	397 Staravia [TM]
		396 Starly [TM]	121 Starmie [TM]	120 Staryu [TM]	208 Steelix [TM]	508 Stoutland [TM]	618 Stunfisk [TM]	434 Stunky [TM]
		185 Sudowoodo [TM]	245 Suicune [TM]	192 Sunflora [TM]	191 Sunkern [TM]	283 Surskit [TM]	333 Swablu [TM]	541 Swadloon [TM]
		317 Swalot [TM]	260 Swampert [TM]	581 Swanna [TM]	277 Swellow [TM]	220 Swinub [TM]	684 Swirlix [TM]	528 Swoobat [TM]
		700 Sylveon [TM]	276 Taillow [TM]	663 Talonflame [TM]	114 Tangela [TM]	465 Tangrowth [TM]	128 Tauros [19, TM]	216 Teddiursa [43, TM]
		072 Tentacool [TM]	073 Tentacruel [TM]	498 Tepig [TM]	639 Terrakion [TM]	538 Throh [TM]	642 Thundurus [TM]	532 Timburr [TM]
		564 Tirtouga [TM]	468 Togekiss [TM]	175 Togepi [TM]	176 Togetic [TM]	255 Torchic [TM]	324 Torkoal [TM]	641 Tornadus [TM]
		389 Torterra [TM]	158 Totodile [TM]	454 Toxicroak [TM]	520 Tranquill [TM]	328 Trapinch [TM]	252 Treecko [TM]	709 Trevenant [TM]
		357 Tropius [TM]	568 Trubbish [TM]	387 Turtwig [TM]	535 Tympole [TM]	157 Typhlosion [TM]	248 Tyranitar [TM]	697 Tyrantrum [TM]
		236 Tyrogue [TM]	696 Tyrunt [TM]	197 Umbreon [TM]	521 Unfezant [TM]	217 Ursaring [47, TM]	480 Uxie [1, TM]	583 Vanillish [TM]
		582 Vanillite [TM]	584 Vanilluxe [TM]	134 Vaporeon [TM]	543 Venipede [TM]	049 Venomoth [TM]	048 Venonat [TM]	003 Venusaur [TM]
		416 Vespiquen [TM]	329 Vibrava [TM]	494 Victini [TM]	071 Victreebel [TM]	288 Vigoroth [TM]	045 Vileplume [TM]	640 Virizion [TM]
		666 Vivillon [TM]	313 Volbeat [TM]	637 Volcarona [TM]	100 Voltorb [TM]	629 Vullaby [TM]	037 Vulpix [TM]	320 Wailmer [29, TM]
		321 Wailord [25, TM]	365 Walrein [31, TM]	008 Wartortle [TM]	505 Watchog [TM]	461 Weavile [TM]	070 Weepinbell [TM]	110 Weezing [TM]
		547 Whimsicott [TM]	544 Whirlipede [TM]	340 Whiscash [25, TM]	293 Whismur [32, TM]	040 Wigglytuff [TM]	278 Wingull [TM]	527 Woobat [TM]
		194 Wooper [TM]	413 Wormadam (Plant) [TM]	413 Wormadam (Sand) [TM]	413 Wormadam (Trash) [TM]	178 Xatu [TM]	716 Xerneas [TM]	562 Yamask [TM]
		193 Yanma [TM]	469 Yanmega [TM]	717 Yveltal [TM]	335 Zangoose [TM]	145 Zapdos [TM]	523 Zebstrika [TM]	644 Zekrom [TM]
		263 Zigzagoon [35, TM]	571 Zoroark [TM]	570 Zorua [TM]	041 Zubat [TM]	634 Zweilous [TM]	718 Zygarde [TM]	
Normal	Retaliate (TM67)	359 Absol [TM]	681 Aegislash [TM]	190 Aipom [TM]	424 Ambipom [TM]	059 Arcanine [TM]	493 Arceus [TM]	531 Audino [TM]
		400 Bibarel [TM]	399 Bidoof [TM]	625 Bisharp [TM]	242 Blissey [TM]	626 Bouffalant [TM]	628 Braviary [TM]	286 Breloom [TM]
		427 Buneary [TM]	332 Cacturne [TM]	318 Carvanha [TM]	351 Castform [TM]	113 Chansey [TM]	652 Chesnaught [TM]	650 Chespin [TM]
		573 Cinccino [TM]	036 Clefable [TM]	035 Clefairy [TM]	638 Cobalion [31, TM]	534 Conkeldurr [TM]	342 Crawdaunt [TM]	453 Croagunk [TM]
		104 Cubone [47, TM]	491 Darkrai [TM]	702 Dedenne [TM]	585 Deerling [TM]	301 Delcatty [TM]	502 Dewott [44, TM]	680 Doublade [26, TM]
		452 Drapion [TM]	621 Druddigon [TM]	206 Dunsparce [TM]	632 Durant [TM]	133 Eevee [TM]	196 Espeon [TM]	295 Exploud [TM]
		083 Farfetch'd [TM]	136 Flareon [TM]	676 Furfrou [33, TM]	162 Furret [TM]	475 Gallade [TM]	203 Girafarig [TM]	471 Glaceon [TM]
		431 Glameow [TM]	673 Gogoat [TM]	210 Granbull [TM]	058 Growlithe [32, TM]	533 Gurdurr [TM]	297 Hariyama [TM]	701 Hawlucha [TM]
		214 Heracross [TM]	507 Herdier [33, TM]	107 Hitmonchan [TM]	106 Hitmonlee [TM]	237 Hitmontop [TM]	430 Honchkrow [TM]	679 Honedge [26, TM]
		229 Houndoom [TM]	228 Houndour [TM]	392 Infernape [TM]	686 Inkay [TM]	039 Jigglypuff [TM]	135 Jolteon [TM]	115 Kangaskhan [TM]
		352 Kecleon [TM]	647 Keldeo [31, TM]	552 Krokorok [TM]	553 Krookodile [TM]	246 Larvitar [TM]	380 Latias [TM]	381 Latios [TM]
		470 Leafeon [TM]	542 Leavanny [TM]	463 Lickilicky [TM]	108 Lickitung [TM]	506 Lillipup [29, TM]	264 Linoone [TM]	667 Litleo [TM]
		428 Lopunny [TM]	294 Loudred [TM]	448 Lucario [TM]	068 Machamp [TM]	067 Machoke [TM]	066 Machop [TM]	296 Makuhita [TM]
		687 Malamar [TM]	630 Mandibuzz [TM]	056 Mankey [TM]	105 Marowak [59, TM]	308 Medicham [TM]	307 Meditite [TM]	648 Meloetta [TM]
		052 Meowth [TM]	151 Mew [TM]	619 Mienfoo [TM]	620 Mienshao [TM]	262 Mightyena [TM]	241 Miltank [TM]	572 Minccino [TM]
		391 Monferno [TM]	446 Munchlax [TM]	198 Murkrow [TM]	274 Nuzleaf [TM]	501 Oshawott [37, TM]	674 Pancham [TM]	675 Pangoro [TM]
		504 Patrat [TM]	624 Pawniard [TM]	053 Persian [TM]	261 Poochyena [TM]	057 Primeape [TM]	247 Pupitar [TM]	432 Purugly [TM]
		668 Pyroar [TM]	651 Quilladin [TM]	020 Raticate [TM]	019 Rattata [TM]	486 Regigigas [TM]	447 Riolu [TM]	627 Rufflet [TM]
		302 Sableye [TM]	503 Samurott [50, TM]	551 Sandile [TM]	539 Sawk [37, TM]	586 Sawsbuck [TM]	560 Scrafty [TM]	559 Scraggy [TM]
		273 Seedot [TM]	161 Sentret [TM]	336 Seviper [TM]	319 Sharpedo [TM]	275 Shiftry [TM]	672 Skiddo [TM]	300 Skitty [TM]
		289 Slaking [TM]	287 Slakoth [TM]	215 Sneasel [TM]	143 Snorlax [TM]	209 Snubbull [TM]	327 Spinda [TM]	442 Spiritomb [TM]
		234 Stantler [TM]	398 Staraptor [TM]	397 Staravia [TM]	508 Stoutland [36, TM]	700 Sylveon [TM]	128 Tauros [TM]	216 Teddiursa [TM]
		639 Terrakion [31, TM]	538 Throh [TM]	532 Timburr [TM]	468 Togekiss [TM]	176 Togetic [TM]	454 Toxicroak [TM]	248 Tyranitar [TM]
		236 Tyrogue [TM]	197 Umbreon [TM]	217 Ursaring [TM]	134 Vaporeon [TM]	288 Vigoroth [TM]	640 Virizion [31, TM]	629 Vullaby [TM]
		505 Watchog [TM]	461 Weavile [TM]	293 Whismur [TM]	040 Wigglytuff [TM]	335 Zangoose [TM]	263 Zigzagoon [TM]	571 Zoroark [TM]
		570 Zorua [TM]						
Normal	Return (TM27)	460 Abomasnow [TM]	063 Abra [TM]	359 Absol [TM]	617 Accelgor [TM]	681 Aegislash [TM]	142 Aerodactyl [TM]	306 Aggron [TM]
		190 Aipom [TM]	065 Alakazam [TM]	594 Alomomola [TM]	334 Altaria [TM]	698 Amaura [TM]	424 Ambipom [TM]	591 Amoonguss [TM]
		181 Ampharos [TM]	347 Anorith [TM]	024 Arbok [TM]	059 Arcanine [TM]	493 Arceus [TM]	566 Archen [TM]	567 Archeops [TM]
		168 Ariados [TM]	348 Armaldo [TM]	683 Aromatisse [TM]	304 Aron [TM]	144 Articuno [TM]	531 Audino [TM]	699 Aurorus [TM]
		713 Avalugg [TM]	610 Axew [TM]	482 Azelf [TM]	184 Azumarill [TM]	298 Azurill [TM]	371 Bagon [TM]	343 Baltoy [TM]
		354 Banette [TM]	689 Barbaracle [TM]	339 Barboach [TM]	550 Basculin [TM]	411 Bastiodon [TM]	153 Bayleef [TM]	614 Beartic [TM]
		267 Beautifly [TM]	015 Beedrill [TM]	606 Beheeyem [TM]	182 Bellossom [TM]	069 Bellsprout [TM]	712 Bergmite [TM]	400 Bibarel [TM]
		399 Bidoof [TM]	688 Binacle [TM]	625 Bisharp [TM]	009 Blastoise [TM]	257 Blaziken [TM]	242 Blissey [TM]	522 Blitzle [TM]
		525 Boldore [TM]	438 Bonsly [TM]	626 Bouffalant [TM]	654 Braixen [TM]	628 Braviary [TM]	286 Breloom [TM]	437 Bronzong [TM]
		436 Bronzor [TM]	406 Budew [TM]	418 Buizel [TM]	001 Bulbasaur [TM]	427 Buneary [TM]	659 Bunnelby [TM]	012 Butterfree [TM]
		331 Cacnea [TM]	332 Cacturne [TM]	323 Camerupt [TM]	703 Carbink [TM]	455 Carnivine [TM]	565 Carracosta [TM]	318 Carvanha [TM]
		351 Castform [TM]	251 Celebi [TM]	609 Chandelure [TM]	113 Chansey [TM]	006 Charizard [TM]	004 Charmander [TM]	005 Charmeleon [TM]
		441 Chatot [TM]	421 Cherrim [TM]	420 Cherubi [TM]	652 Chesnaught [TM]	650 Chespin [TM]	152 Chikorita [TM]	390 Chimchar [TM]
		358 Chimecho [TM]	170 Chinchou [TM]	433 Chingling [TM]	573 Cinccino [TM]	366 Clamperl [TM]	692 Clauncher [TM]	693 Clawitzer [TM]
		344 Claydol [TM]	036 Clefable [TM]	035 Clefairy [TM]	173 Cleffa [TM]	091 Cloyster [TM]	638 Cobalion [TM]	563 Cofagrigus [TM]
		256 Combusken [TM]	534 Conkeldurr [TM]	341 Corphish [TM]	222 Corsola [TM]	546 Cottonee [TM]	346 Cradily [TM]	408 Cranidos [TM]
		342 Crawdaunt [TM]	488 Cresselia [TM]	453 Croagunk [TM]	169 Crobat [TM]	159 Croconaw [TM]	558 Crustle [TM]	615 Cryogonal [TM]
		613 Cubchoo [TM]	104 Cubone [TM]	155 Cyndaquil [TM]	491 Darkrai [TM]	555 Darmanitan [TM]	554 Darumaka [TM]	702 Dedenne [TM]

	Move	Pokémon that can learn it						
Normal	Return (TM27)	585 Deerling [TM]	633 Deino [TM]	301 Delcatty [TM]	225 Delibird [TM]	655 Delphox [TM]	386 Deoxys (Atk) [TM]	386 Deoxys (Def) [TM]
		386 Deoxys (Nor) [TM]	386 Deoxys (Spd) [TM]	087 Dewgong [TM]	502 Dewott [TM]	483 Dialga [TM]	719 Diancie [TM]	660 Diggersby [TM]
		050 Diglett [TM]	085 Dodrio [TM]	084 Doduo [TM]	232 Donphan [TM]	680 Doublade [TM]	691 Dragalge [TM]	148 Dragonair [TM]
		149 Dragonite [TM]	452 Drapion [TM]	147 Dratini [TM]	426 Drifblim [TM]	425 Drifloon [TM]	529 Drilbur [TM]	096 Drowzee [TM]
		621 Druddigon [TM]	580 Ducklett [TM]	051 Dugtrio [TM]	206 Dunsparce [TM]	578 Duosion [TM]	632 Durant [TM]	356 Dusclops [TM]
		477 Dusknoir [TM]	355 Duskull [TM]	269 Dustox [TM]	557 Dwebble [TM]	603 Eelektrik [TM]	604 Eelektross [TM]	133 Eevee [TM]
		023 Ekans [TM]	125 Electabuzz [TM]	466 Electivire [TM]	309 Electrike [TM]	101 Electrode [TM]	239 Elekid [TM]	605 Elgyem [TM]
		500 Emboar [TM]	587 Emolga [TM]	395 Empoleon [TM]	244 Entei [TM]	589 Escavalier [TM]	196 Espeon [TM]	677 Espurr [TM]
		530 Excadrill [TM]	102 Exeggcute [TM]	103 Exeggutor [TM]	295 Exploud [TM]	083 Farfetch'd [TM]	022 Fearow [TM]	349 Feebas [TM]
		653 Fennekin [TM]	160 Feraligatr [TM]	597 Ferroseed [TM]	598 Ferrothorn [TM]	456 Finneon [TM]	180 Flaaffy [TM]	669 Flabébé [TM]
		136 Flareon [TM]	662 Fletchinder [TM]	661 Fletchling [TM]	419 Floatzel [TM]	670 Floette [TM]	671 Florges [TM]	330 Flygon [TM]
		590 Foongus [TM]	205 Forretress [TM]	611 Fraxure [TM]	592 Frillish [TM]	656 Froakie [TM]	657 Frogadier [TM]	478 Froslass [TM]
		676 Furfrou [TM]	162 Furret [TM]	444 Gabite [TM]	475 Gallade [TM]	596 Galvantula [TM]	569 Garbodor [TM]	445 Garchomp [TM]
		282 Gardevoir [TM]	092 Gastly [TM]	423 Gastrodon [TM]	649 Genesect [TM]	094 Gengar [TM]	074 Geodude [TM]	443 Gible [TM]
		526 Gigalith [TM]	203 Girafarig [TM]	487 Giratina (Alt) [TM]	487 Giratina (Ori) [TM]	471 Glaceon [TM]	362 Glalie [TM]	431 Glameow [TM]
		207 Gligar [TM]	472 Gliscor [TM]	044 Gloom [TM]	673 Gogoat [TM]	042 Golbat [TM]	118 Goldeen [TM]	055 Golduck [TM]
		076 Golem [TM]	622 Golett [TM]	623 Golurk [TM]	706 Goodra [TM]	704 Goomy [TM]	368 Gorebyss [TM]	574 Gothita [TM]
		576 Gothitelle [TM]	575 Gothorita [TM]	711 Gourgeist [TM]	210 Granbull [TM]	075 Graveler [TM]	658 Greninja [TM]	088 Grimer [TM]
		388 Grotle [TM]	383 Groudon [TM]	253 Grovyle [TM]	058 Growlithe [TM]	326 Grumpig [TM]	316 Gulpin [TM]	533 Gurdurr [TM]
		130 Gyarados [TM]	440 Happiny [TM]	297 Hariyama [TM]	093 Haunter [TM]	701 Hawlucha [TM]	612 Haxorus [TM]	631 Heatmor [TM]
		485 Heatran [TM]	695 Heliolisk [TM]	694 Helioptile [TM]	214 Heracross [TM]	507 Herdier [TM]	449 Hippopotas [TM]	450 Hippowdon [TM]
		107 Hitmonchan [TM]	106 Hitmonlee [TM]	237 Hitmontop [TM]	430 Honchkrow [TM]	679 Honedge [TM]	250 Ho-Oh [TM]	163 Hoothoot [TM]
		187 Hoppip [TM]	116 Horsea [TM]	229 Houndoom [TM]	228 Houndour [TM]	367 Huntail [TM]	635 Hydreigon [TM]	097 Hypno [TM]
		174 Igglybuff [TM]	314 Illumise [TM]	392 Infernape [TM]	686 Inkay [TM]	002 Ivysaur [TM]	593 Jellicent [TM]	039 Jigglypuff [TM]
		385 Jirachi [TM]	135 Jolteon [TM]	595 Joltik [TM]	189 Jumpluff [TM]	124 Jynx [TM]	140 Kabuto [TM]	141 Kabutops [TM]
		064 Kadabra [TM]	115 Kangaskhan [TM]	588 Karrablast [TM]	352 Kecleon [TM]	647 Keldeo [TM]	230 Kingdra [TM]	099 Kingler [TM]
		281 Kirlia [TM]	600 Klang [TM]	707 Klefki [TM]	599 Klink [TM]	601 Klinklang [TM]	109 Koffing [TM]	098 Krabby [TM]
		402 Kricketune [TM]	552 Krokorok [TM]	553 Krookodile [TM]	382 Kyogre [TM]	646 Kyurem (Blk) [TM]	646 Kyurem (Wht) [TM]	646 Kyurem [TM]
		305 Lairon [TM]	608 Lampent [TM]	645 Landorus [TM]	171 Lanturn [TM]	131 Lapras [TM]	636 Larvesta [TM]	246 Larvitar [TM]
		380 Latias [TM]	381 Latios [TM]	470 Leafeon [TM]	542 Leavanny [TM]	166 Ledian [TM]	165 Ledyba [TM]	463 Lickilicky [TM]
		108 Lickitung [TM]	510 Liepard [TM]	345 Lileep [TM]	549 Lilligant [TM]	506 Lillipup [TM]	264 Linoone [TM]	667 Litleo [TM]
		607 Litwick [TM]	271 Lombre [TM]	428 Lopunny [13, TM]	270 Lotad [TM]	294 Loudred [TM]	448 Lucario [TM]	272 Ludicolo [TM]
		249 Lugia [TM]	457 Lumineon [TM]	337 Lunatone [TM]	370 Luvdisc [TM]	404 Luxio [TM]	405 Luxray [TM]	068 Machamp [TM]
		067 Machoke [TM]	066 Machop [TM]	240 Magby [TM]	219 Magcargo [TM]	126 Magmar [TM]	467 Magmortar [TM]	081 Magnemite [TM]
		082 Magneton [TM]	462 Magnezone [TM]	296 Makuhita [TM]	687 Malamar [TM]	473 Mamoswine [TM]	490 Manaphy [TM]	630 Mandibuzz [TM]
		310 Manectric [TM]	056 Mankey [TM]	226 Mantine [TM]	458 Mantyke [TM]	556 Maractus [TM]	179 Mareep [TM]	183 Marill [TM]
		105 Marowak [TM]	259 Marshtomp [TM]	284 Masquerain [TM]	303 Mawile [TM]	308 Medicham [TM]	307 Meditite [TM]	154 Meganium [TM]
		648 Meloetta [TM]	678 Meowstic (F) [TM]	678 Meowstic (M) [TM]	052 Meowth [TM]	481 Mesprit [TM]	376 Metagross [TM]	375 Metang [TM]
		151 Mew [TM]	150 Mewtwo [TM]	619 Mienfoo [TM]	620 Mienshao [TM]	262 Mightyena [TM]	350 Milotic [TM]	241 Miltank [TM]
		439 Mime Jr. [TM]	572 Minccino [TM]	312 Minun [TM]	200 Misdreavus [TM]	429 Mismagius [TM]	146 Moltres [TM]	391 Monferno [TM]
		414 Mothim [TM]	122 Mr. Mime [TM]	258 Mudkip [TM]	089 Muk [TM]	446 Munchlax [TM]	517 Munna [TM]	198 Murkrow [TM]
		518 Musharna [TM]	177 Natu [TM]	034 Nidoking [TM]	031 Nidoqueen [TM]	029 Nidoran ♀ [TM]	032 Nidoran ♂ [TM]	030 Nidorina [TM]
		033 Nidorino [TM]	290 Nincada [TM]	038 Ninetales [TM]	291 Ninjask [TM]	164 Noctowl [TM]	714 Noibat [TM]	715 Noivern [TM]
		299 Nosepass [TM]	322 Numel [TM]	274 Nuzleaf [TM]	224 Octillery [TM]	043 Oddish [TM]	138 Omanyte [TM]	139 Omastar [TM]
		095 Onix [TM]	501 Oshawott [TM]	417 Pachirisu [TM]	484 Palkia [TM]	536 Palpitoad [TM]	674 Pancham [TM]	675 Pangoro [TM]
		515 Panpour [TM]	511 Pansage [TM]	513 Pansear [TM]	046 Paras [TM]	047 Parasect [TM]	504 Patrat [TM]	624 Pawniard [TM]
		279 Pelipper [TM]	053 Persian [TM]	548 Petilil [TM]	231 Phanpy [TM]	708 Phantump [TM]	489 Phione [TM]	172 Pichu [TM]
		018 Pidgeot [TM]	017 Pidgeotto [TM]	016 Pidgey [TM]	519 Pidove [TM]	499 Pignite [TM]	025 Pikachu [TM]	221 Piloswine [TM]
		204 Pineco [TM]	127 Pinsir [TM]	393 Piplup [TM]	311 Plusle [TM]	186 Politoed [TM]	060 Poliwag [TM]	061 Poliwhirl [TM]
		062 Poliwrath [TM]	077 Ponyta [TM]	261 Poochyena [TM]	137 Porygon [TM]	233 Porygon2 [TM]	474 Porygon-Z [TM]	057 Primeape [TM]
		394 Prinplup [TM]	476 Probopass [TM]	054 Psyduck [TM]	710 Pumpkaboo [TM]	247 Pupitar [TM]	509 Purrloin [TM]	432 Purugly [TM]
		668 Pyroar [TM]	195 Quagsire [TM]	156 Quilava [TM]	651 Quilladin [TM]	211 Qwilfish [TM]	026 Raichu [TM]	243 Raikou [TM]
		280 Ralts [TM]	409 Rampardos [TM]	078 Rapidash [TM]	020 Raticate [TM]	019 Rattata [TM]	384 Rayquaza [TM]	378 Regice [TM]
		486 Regigigas [TM]	377 Regirock [TM]	379 Registeel [TM]	369 Relicanth [TM]	223 Remoraid [TM]	643 Reshiram [TM]	579 Reuniclus [TM]
		112 Rhydon [TM]	111 Rhyhorn [TM]	464 Rhyperior [TM]	447 Riolu [TM]	524 Roggenrola [TM]	315 Roselia [TM]	407 Roserade [TM]
		479 Rotom (Fan) [TM]	479 Rotom (Frost) [TM]	479 Rotom (Heat) [TM]	479 Rotom (Mow) [TM]	479 Rotom (Wash) [TM]	479 Rotom [TM]	627 Rufflet [TM]
		302 Sableye [TM]	373 Salamence [TM]	503 Samurott [TM]	551 Sandile [TM]	027 Sandshrew [TM]	028 Sandslash [TM]	539 Sawk [TM]
		586 Sawsbuck [TM]	254 Sceptile [TM]	212 Scizor [TM]	545 Scolipede [TM]	560 Scrafty [TM]	559 Scraggy [TM]	123 Scyther [TM]
		117 Seadra [TM]	119 Seaking [TM]	364 Sealeo [TM]	273 Seedot [TM]	086 Seel [TM]	537 Seismitoad [TM]	161 Sentret [TM]
		497 Serperior [TM]	496 Servine [TM]	336 Seviper [TM]	540 Sewaddle [TM]	319 Sharpedo [TM]	492 Shaymin (Land) [TM]	492 Shaymin (Sky) [TM]
		292 Shedinja [TM]	372 Shelgon [TM]	090 Shellder [TM]	422 Shellos [TM]	616 Shelmet [TM]	410 Shieldon [TM]	275 Shiftry [TM]
		403 Shinx [TM]	285 Shroomish [TM]	213 Shuckle [TM]	353 Shuppet [TM]	561 Sigilyph [TM]	516 Simipour [TM]	512 Simisage [TM]
		514 Simisear [TM]	227 Skarmory [TM]	672 Skiddo [TM]	188 Skiploom [TM]	300 Skitty [TM]	451 Skorupi [TM]	690 Skrelp [TM]
		435 Skuntank [TM]	289 Slaking [TM]	287 Slakoth [TM]	705 Sliggoo [TM]	080 Slowbro [TM]	199 Slowking [TM]	079 Slowpoke [TM]
		218 Slugma [TM]	685 Slurpuff [TM]	238 Smoochum [TM]	215 Sneasel [TM]	495 Snivy [TM]	143 Snorlax [TM]	361 Snorunt [TM]
		459 Snover [TM]	209 Snubbull [TM]	577 Solosis [TM]	338 Solrock [TM]	021 Spearow [TM]	363 Spheal [TM]	167 Spinarak [TM]

	Move	Pokémon that can learn it						
Normal	Return (TM27)	327 Spinda [TM]	442 Spiritomb [TM]	325 Spoink [TM]	682 Spritzee [TM]	007 Squirtle [TM]	234 Stantler [TM]	398 Staraptor [TM]
		397 Staravia [TM]	396 Starly [TM]	121 Starmie [TM]	120 Staryu [TM]	208 Steelix [TM]	508 Stoutland [TM]	618 Stunfisk [TM]
		434 Stunky [TM]	185 Sudowoodo [TM]	245 Suicune [TM]	192 Sunflora [TM]	191 Sunkern [TM]	283 Surskit [TM]	333 Swablu [TM]
		541 Swadloon [TM]	317 Swalot [TM]	260 Swampert [TM]	581 Swanna [TM]	277 Swellow [TM]	220 Swinub [TM]	684 Swirlix [TM]
		528 Swoobat [TM]	700 Sylveon [TM]	276 Taillow [TM]	663 Talonflame [TM]	114 Tangela [TM]	465 Tangrowth [TM]	128 Tauros [TM]
		216 Teddiursa [TM]	072 Tentacool [TM]	073 Tentacruel [TM]	498 Tepig [TM]	639 Terrakion [TM]	538 Throh [TM]	642 Thundurus [TM]
		532 Timburr [TM]	564 Tirtouga [TM]	468 Togekiss [TM]	175 Togepi [TM]	176 Togetic [TM]	255 Torchic [TM]	324 Torkoal [TM]
		641 Tornadus [TM]	389 Torterra [TM]	158 Totodile [TM]	454 Toxicroak [TM]	520 Tranquill [TM]	328 Trapinch [TM]	252 Treecko [TM]
		709 Trevenant [TM]	357 Tropius [TM]	568 Trubbish [TM]	387 Turtwig [TM]	535 Tympole [TM]	157 Typhlosion [TM]	248 Tyranitar [TM]
		697 Tyrantrum [TM]	236 Tyrogue [TM]	696 Tyrunt [TM]	197 Umbreon [TM]	521 Unfezant [TM]	217 Ursaring [TM]	480 Uxie [TM]
		583 Vanillish [TM]	582 Vanillite [TM]	584 Vanilluxe [TM]	134 Vaporeon [TM]	543 Venipede [TM]	049 Venomoth [TM]	048 Venonat [TM]
		003 Venusaur [TM]	416 Vespiquen [TM]	329 Vibrava [TM]	494 Victini [TM]	071 Victreebel [TM]	288 Vigoroth [TM]	045 Vileplume [TM]
		640 Virizion [TM]	666 Vivillon [TM]	313 Volbeat [TM]	637 Volcarona [TM]	100 Voltorb [TM]	629 Vullaby [TM]	037 Vulpix [TM]
		320 Wailmer [TM]	321 Wailord [TM]	365 Walrein [TM]	008 Wartortle [TM]	505 Watchog [TM]	461 Weavile [TM]	070 Weepinbell [TM]
		110 Weezing [TM]	547 Whimsicott [TM]	544 Whirlipede [TM]	340 Whiscash [TM]	293 Whismur [TM]	040 Wigglytuff [TM]	278 Wingull [TM]
		527 Woobat [TM]	194 Wooper [TM]	413 Wormadam (Plant) [TM]	413 Wormadam (Sand) [TM]	413 Wormadam (Trash) [TM]	178 Xatu [TM]	716 Xerneas [TM]
		562 Yamask [TM]	193 Yanma [TM]	469 Yanmega [TM]	717 Yveltal [TM]	335 Zangoose [TM]	145 Zapdos [TM]	523 Zebstrika [TM]
		644 Zekrom [TM]	263 Zigzagoon [TM]	571 Zoroark [TM]	570 Zorua [TM]	041 Zubat [TM]	634 Zweilous [TM]	718 Zygarde [TM]
Fighting	Revenge	190 Aipom [E]	550 Basculin [E]	626 Bouffalant [26]	332 Cacturne [1]	453 Croagunk [22]	502 Dewott [28]	621 Druddigon [35]
		083 Farfetch'd [E]	214 Heracross [E]	449 Hippopotas [E]	107 Hitmonchan [1]	106 Hitmonlee [1]	237 Hitmontop [1]	068 Machamp [19]
		067 Machoke [19]	066 Machop [19]	296 Makuhita [E]	056 Mankey [E]	501 Oshawott [25]	504 Patrat [E]	624 Pawniard [E]
		204 Pineco [E]	127 Pinsir [15]	211 Qwilfish [29]	019 Rattata [E]	486 Regigigas [25]	503 Samurott [28]	396 Starly [E]
		618 Stunfisk [50]	538 Throh [21]	642 Thundurus [19]	641 Tornadus [19]	454 Toxicroak [22]	461 Weavile [1]	335 Zangoose [22]
	Reversal	304 Aron [E]	610 Axew [E]	626 Bouffalant [46]	155 Cyndaquil [E]	050 Diglett [E]	589 Escavalier [49]	058 Growlithe [19]
		297 Hariyama [50]	214 Heracross [46]	507 Herdier [38]	106 Hitmonlee [1, 61]	228 Houndour [E]	115 Kangaskhan [50]	506 Lillipup [33]
		296 Makuhita [43]	687 Malamar [1]	056 Mankey [E]	308 Medicham [42]	307 Meditite [39]	619 Mienfoo [57]	620 Mienshao [1, 63]
		241 Miltank [E]	172 Pichu [E]	019 Rattata [E]	111 Rhyhorn [E]	447 Riolu [29]	539 Sawk [50]	123 Scyther [E]
		161 Sentret [E]	508 Stoutland [42]	538 Throh [50]	532 Timburr [E]	255 Torchic [E]	494 Victini [33]	288 Vigoroth [1, 43]
		193 Yanma [E]						
Normal	Roar (TM05)	142 Aerodactyl [9, TM]	306 Aggron [19, TM]	334 Altaria [TM]	698 Amaura [TM]	059 Arcanine [1, TM]	493 Arceus [TM]	566 Archen [TM]
		567 Archeops [TM]	304 Aron [19, TM]	144 Articuno [TM]	699 Aurorus [TM]	713 Avalugg [TM]	610 Axew [TM]	371 Bagon [TM]
		411 Bastiodon [TM]	614 Beartic [TM]	009 Blastoise [TM]	257 Blaziken [TM]	323 Camerupt [TM]	006 Charizard [TM]	652 Chesnaught [TM]
		650 Chespin [TM]	638 Cobalion [TM]	408 Cranidos [TM]	159 Croconaw [TM]	555 Darmanitan [TM]	554 Darumaka [TM]	633 Deino [20, TM]
		483 Dialga [TM]	232 Donphan [TM]	149 Dragonite [TM]	452 Drapion [TM]	621 Druddigon [TM]	604 Eelektross [TM]	309 Electrike [34, TM]
		500 Emboar [55, TM]	395 Empoleon [TM]	244 Entei [15, TM]	295 Exploud [32, TM]	160 Feraligatr [TM]	136 Flareon [TM]	419 Floatzel [TM]
		611 Fraxure [TM]	676 Furfrou [TM]	444 Gabite [TM]	445 Garchomp [TM]	443 Gible [TM]	487 Giratina (Alt) [TM]	487 Giratina (Ori) [TM]
		471 Glaceon [TM]	673 Gogoat [TM]	076 Golem [TM]	210 Granbull [27, TM]	383 Groudon [TM]	058 Growlithe [1, TM]	130 Gyarados [TM]
		612 Haxorus [TM]	485 Heatran [TM]	507 Herdier [29, TM]	449 Hippopotas [TM]	450 Hippowdon [TM]	250 Ho-Oh [TM]	229 Houndoom [13, TM]
		228 Houndour [13, TM]	635 Hydreigon [20, TM]	392 Infernape [TM]	135 Jolteon [TM]	115 Kangaskhan [TM]	647 Keldeo [TM]	552 Krokorok [TM]
		553 Krookodile [TM]	382 Kyogre [TM]	305 Lairon [19, TM]	131 Lapras [TM]	380 Latias [TM]	381 Latios [TM]	470 Leafeon [TM]
		506 Lillipup [26, TM]	264 Linoone [TM]	667 Litleo [TM]	294 Loudred [32, TM]	448 Lucario [TM]	249 Lugia [TM]	404 Luxio [23, TM]
		405 Luxray [23, TM]	473 Mamoswine [TM]	310 Manectric [36, TM]	151 Mew [TM]	262 Mightyena [16, TM]	146 Moltres [TM]	034 Nidoking [TM]
		031 Nidoqueen [TM]	038 Ninetales [TM]	095 Onix [TM]	484 Palkia [TM]	674 Pancham [TM]	675 Pangoro [TM]	053 Persian [TM]
		231 Phanpy [TM]	499 Pignite [47, TM]	221 Piloswine [TM]	261 Poochyena [16, TM]	432 Purugly [TM]	668 Pyroar [TM]	156 Quilava [TM]
		651 Quilladin [TM]	243 Raikou [15, TM]	409 Rampardos [TM]	020 Raticate [TM]	384 Rayquaza [TM]	112 Rhydon [TM]	111 Rhyhorn [TM]
		464 Rhyperior [TM]	447 Riolu [TM]	373 Salamence [TM]	551 Sandile [TM]	254 Sceptile [TM]	560 Scrafty [TM]	559 Scraggy [TM]
		364 Sealeo [TM]	319 Sharpedo [TM]	372 Shelgon [TM]	410 Shieldon [TM]	403 Shinx [21, TM]	227 Skarmory [TM]	672 Skiddo [TM]
		435 Skuntank [TM]	289 Slaking [TM]	209 Snubbull [25, TM]	234 Stantler [TM]	208 Steelix [TM]	508 Stoutland [29, TM]	434 Stunky [TM]
		245 Suicune [TM]	260 Swampert [TM]	220 Swinub [TM]	216 Teddiursa [TM]	498 Tepig [39, TM]	639 Terrakion [TM]	389 Torterra [TM]
		357 Tropius [TM]	157 Typhlosion [TM]	248 Tyranitar [TM]	697 Tyrantrum [6, TM]	696 Tyrunt [6, TM]	217 Ursaring [TM]	134 Vaporeon [TM]
		003 Venusaur [TM]	288 Vigoroth [TM]	640 Virizion [TM]	037 Vulpix [7, TM]	320 Wailmer [TM]	321 Wailord [TM]	365 Walrein [TM]
		293 Whismur [29, TM]	716 Xerneas [TM]	335 Zangoose [TM]	145 Zapdos [TM]	571 Zoroark [TM]	570 Zorua [TM]	634 Zweilous [20, TM]
Dragon	Roar of Time	483 Dialga [46]						
Rock	Rock Blast	347 Anorith [55]	348 Armaldo [61]	525 Boldore [14]	573 Cinccino [1]	222 Corsola [31]	558 Crustle [1, 5]	557 Dwebble [5]
		074 Geodude [30]	526 Gigalith [14]	076 Golem [34]	075 Graveler [34]	214 Heracross [E]	299 Nosepass [28]	224 Octillery [1]
		138 Omanyte [46]	139 Omastar [56]	095 Onix [E]	476 Probopass [28]	223 Remoraid [E]	112 Rhydon [29]	111 Rhyhorn [29]
		464 Rhyperior [29]	524 Roggenrola [14]	090 Shellder [E]	410 Shieldon [E]	213 Shuckle [E]	568 Trubbish [E]	413 Wormadam (Sand) [26]
Normal	Rock Climb	399 Bidoof [E]	626 Bouffalant [E]	529 Drilbur [E]	621 Druddigon [49]	632 Durant [E]	597 Ferroseed [E]	598 Ferrothorn [1]
		074 Geodude [E]	443 Gible [E]	207 Gligar [E]	595 Joltik [E]	095 Onix [E]	111 Rhyhorn [E]	551 Sandile [E]
		027 Sandshrew [E]	545 Scolipede [50]	560 Scrafty [51]	559 Scraggy [45]	543 Venipede [40, E]	544 Whirlipede [46]	263 Zigzagoon [E]

	Move	Pokémon that can learn it						
Rock	Rock Polish (TM69)	142 Aerodactyl [TM]	306 Aggron [TM]	698 Amaura [TM]	347 Anorith [TM]	566 Archen [TM]	567 Archeops [TM]	348 Armaldo [TM]
		304 Aron [TM]	699 Aurorus [TM]	713 Avalugg [TM]	343 Baltoy [TM]	689 Barbaracle [24, TM]	411 Bastiodon [TM]	712 Bergmite [TM]
		688 Binacle [24, TM]	625 Bisharp [TM]	525 Boldore [TM]	438 Bonsly [TM]	437 Bronzong [TM]	436 Bronzor [TM]	323 Camerupt [TM]
		703 Carbink [TM]	565 Carracosta [TM]	344 Claydol [TM]	638 Cobalion [TM]	222 Corsola [TM]	346 Cradily [TM]	408 Cranidos [TM]
		558 Crustle [19, TM]	719 Diancie [TM]	232 Donphan [TM]	632 Durant [TM]	557 Dwebble [19, TM]	597 Ferroseed [TM]	598 Ferrothorn [TM]
		205 Forretress [TM]	569 Garbodor [TM]	649 Genesect [TM]	074 Geodude [6, TM]	526 Gigalith [TM]	207 Gligar [TM]	472 Gliscor [TM]
		076 Golem [1, 6, TM]	622 Golett [TM]	623 Golurk [TM]	075 Graveler [1, 6, TM]	383 Groudon [TM]	140 Kabuto [TM]	141 Kabutops [TM]
		600 Klang [TM]	599 Klink [TM]	601 Klinklang [TM]	305 Lairon [TM]	645 Landorus [TM]	246 Larvitar [TM]	345 Lileep [TM]
		337 Lunatone [9, TM]	219 Magcargo [TM]	376 Metagross [TM]	375 Metang [TM]	151 Mew [TM]	299 Nosepass [TM]	138 Omanyte [TM]
		139 Omastar [TM]	095 Onix [19, TM]	624 Pawniard [TM]	476 Probopass [TM]	247 Pupitar [TM]	409 Rampardos [TM]	378 Regice [TM]
		486 Regigigas [TM]	377 Regirock [TM]	379 Registeel [TM]	369 Relicanth [TM]	112 Rhydon [TM]	111 Rhyhorn [TM]	464 Rhyperior [TM]
		524 Roggenrola [TM]	410 Shieldon [TM]	213 Shuckle [TM]	338 Solrock [9, TM]	208 Steelix [TM]	185 Sudowoodo [TM]	639 Terrakion [TM]
		564 Tirtouga [TM]	389 Torterra [TM]	248 Tyranitar [TM]	697 Tyrantrum [TM]	696 Tyrunt [TM, E]		
	Rock Slide (TM80)	460 Abomasnow [TM]	359 Absol [TM]	681 Aegislash [TM]	142 Aerodactyl [73, TM]	306 Aggron [25, TM]	698 Amaura [TM]	347 Anorith [TM]
		024 Arbok [TM]	493 Arceus [TM]	566 Archen [45, TM]	567 Archeops [51, TM]	348 Armaldo [TM]	304 Aron [25, TM]	699 Aurorus [TM]
		713 Avalugg [TM]	371 Bagon [TM]	343 Baltoy [TM]	689 Barbaracle [TM]	411 Bastiodon [TM]	614 Beartic [TM]	606 Beheeyem [TM]
		712 Bergmite [TM]	688 Binacle [TM]	009 Blastoise [TM]	257 Blaziken [TM]	242 Blissey [TM]	525 Boldore [30, TM]	438 Bonsly [29, TM]
		626 Bouffalant [TM]	628 Braviary [TM]	286 Breloom [TM]	437 Bronzong [TM]	436 Bronzor [TM]	659 Bunnelby [TM]	323 Camerupt [33, TM]
		703 Carbink [TM]	565 Carracosta [51, TM]	113 Chansey [TM]	006 Charizard [TM]	004 Charmander [TM]	005 Charmeleon [TM]	652 Chesnaught [TM]
		650 Chespin [TM]	692 Clauncher [TM]	693 Clawitzer [TM]	344 Claydol [TM]	256 Combusken [TM]	534 Conkeldurr [33, TM]	341 Corphish [TM]
		222 Corsola [TM]	346 Cradily [TM]	408 Cranidos [TM]	342 Crawdaunt [TM]	453 Croagunk [TM]	159 Croconaw [TM]	558 Crustle [29, TM]
		104 Cubone [TM]	491 Darkrai [TM]	555 Darmanitan [TM]	554 Darumaka [TM]	386 Deoxys (Atk) [TM]	386 Deoxys (Def) [TM]	386 Deoxys (Nor) [TM]
		386 Deoxys (Spd) [TM]	483 Dialga [TM]	719 Diancie [TM]	660 Diggersby [TM]	050 Diglett [TM]	232 Donphan [TM]	680 Doublade [TM]
		149 Dragonite [TM]	452 Drapion [TM]	529 Drilbur [29, TM]	621 Druddigon [TM]	051 Dugtrio [TM]	206 Dunsparce [TM]	578 Duosion [TM]
		632 Durant [TM]	356 Dusclops [TM]	477 Dusknoir [TM]	557 Dwebble [29, TM]	604 Eelektross [TM]	023 Ekans [TM]	466 Electivire [TM]
		605 Elgyem [TM]	500 Emboar [TM]	395 Empoleon [TM]	530 Excadrill [29, TM]	295 Exploud [TM]	160 Feraligatr [TM]	330 Flygon [15, TM]
		205 Forretress [TM]	656 Froakie [TM]	657 Frogadier [TM]	444 Gabite [TM]	475 Gallade [TM]	445 Garchomp [TM]	423 Gastrodon [TM]
		074 Geodude [TM]	443 Gible [TM]	526 Gigalith [30, TM]	207 Gligar [TM]	472 Gliscor [TM]	673 Gogoat [TM]	076 Golem [TM]
		622 Golett [TM]	623 Golurk [TM]	706 Goodra [TM]	704 Goomy [TM]	574 Gothita [TM]	576 Gothitelle [TM]	575 Gothorita [TM]
		711 Gourgeist [TM]	210 Granbull [TM]	075 Graveler [TM]	658 Greninja [TM]	088 Grimer [TM]	383 Groudon [TM]	253 Grovyle [TM]
		533 Gurdurr [33, TM]	297 Hariyama [TM]	701 Hawlucha [TM]	612 Haxorus [TM]	485 Heatran [TM]	695 Heliolisk [TM]	694 Helioptile [TM]
		214 Heracross [TM]	449 Hippopotas [TM]	450 Hippowdon [TM]	107 Hitmonchan [TM]	106 Hitmonlee [TM]	237 Hitmontop [TM]	679 Honedge [TM]
		635 Hydreigon [TM]	392 Infernape [TM]	686 Inkay [TM]	140 Kabuto [TM]	141 Kabutops [TM]	115 Kangaskhan [TM]	352 Kecleon [TM]
		099 Kingler [TM]	098 Krabby [TM]	552 Krokorok [TM]	553 Krookodile [TM]	382 Kyogre [TM]	646 Kyurem (Blk) [TM]	646 Kyurem (Wht) [TM]
		646 Kyurem [TM]	305 Lairon [25, TM]	645 Landorus [49, TM]	246 Larvitar [19, TM]	463 Lickilicky [TM]	108 Lickitung [TM]	345 Lileep [TM]
		294 Loudred [TM]	448 Lucario [TM]	337 Lunatone [21, TM]	068 Machamp [TM]	067 Machoke [TM]	066 Machop [TM]	219 Magcargo [29, TM]
		467 Magmortar [TM]	296 Makuhita [TM]	687 Malamar [TM]	473 Mamoswine [TM]	056 Mankey [TM]	226 Mantine [TM]	458 Mantyke [TM]
		105 Marowak [TM]	259 Marshtomp [28, TM]	303 Mawile [TM]	308 Medicham [TM]	307 Meditite [TM]	376 Metagross [TM]	375 Metang [TM]
		151 Mew [TM]	150 Mewtwo [TM]	619 Mienfoo [TM]	620 Mienshao [TM]	241 Miltank [TM]	391 Monferno [TM]	258 Mudkip [TM]
		089 Muk [TM]	446 Munchlax [TM]	517 Munna [TM]	518 Musharna [TM]	034 Nidoking [TM]	031 Nidoqueen [TM]	299 Nosepass [22, TM]
		322 Numel [TM]	274 Nuzleaf [TM]	138 Omanyte [TM]	139 Omastar [TM]	095 Onix [34, TM]	484 Palkia [TM]	674 Pancham [TM]
		675 Pangoro [TM]	231 Phanpy [TM]	708 Phantump [TM]	499 Pignite [TM]	221 Piloswine [TM]	204 Pineco [TM]	127 Pinsir [TM]
		062 Poliwrath [TM]	057 Primeape [TM]	476 Probopass [22, TM]	710 Pumpkaboo [TM]	247 Pupitar [19, TM]	195 Quagsire [TM]	651 Quilladin [TM]
		409 Rampardos [TM]	384 Rayquaza [TM]	378 Regice [TM]	486 Regigigas [TM]	377 Regirock [TM]	379 Registeel [TM]	369 Relicanth [TM]
		643 Reshiram [TM]	579 Reuniclus [TM]	112 Rhydon [TM]	111 Rhyhorn [TM]	464 Rhyperior [TM]	447 Riolu [TM]	524 Roggenrola [27, TM]
		627 Rufflet [TM]	373 Salamence [TM]	551 Sandile [TM]	027 Sandshrew [TM]	028 Sandslash [TM]	539 Sawk [TM]	254 Sceptile [TM]
		545 Scolipede [TM]	560 Scrafty [TM]	559 Scraggy [TM]	364 Sealeo [TM]	537 Seismitoad [TM]	372 Shelgon [TM]	410 Shieldon [TM]
		275 Shiftry [TM]	213 Shuckle [38, TM]	516 Simipour [TM]	512 Simisage [TM]	514 Simisear [TM]	227 Skarmory [TM]	672 Skiddo [TM]
		289 Slaking [TM]	287 Slakoth [TM]	705 Sliggoo [TM]	218 Slugma [29, TM]	143 Snorlax [TM]	577 Solosis [TM]	338 Solrock [21, TM]
		363 Spheal [TM]	327 Spinda [TM]	208 Steelix [34, TM]	618 Stunfisk [TM]	185 Sudowoodo [29, TM]	260 Swampert [28, TM]	220 Swinub [TM]
		465 Tangrowth [TM]	128 Tauros [TM]	216 Teddiursa [TM]	639 Terrakion [37, TM]	538 Throh [TM]	532 Timburr [31, TM]	564 Tirtouga [45, TM]
		255 Torchic [TM]	324 Torkoal [TM]	389 Torterra [TM]	158 Totodile [TM]	454 Toxicroak [TM]	328 Trapinch [15, TM]	252 Treecko [TM]
		709 Trevenant [TM]	157 Typhlosion [TM]	248 Tyranitar [19, TM]	697 Tyrantrum [68, TM]	236 Tyrogue [TM]	696 Tyrunt [TM]	217 Ursaring [TM]
		329 Vibrava [15, TM]	288 Vigoroth [TM]	365 Walrein [TM]	340 Whiscash [TM]	716 Xerneas [TM]	717 Yveltal [TM]	335 Zangoose [TM]
		644 Zekrom [TM]	718 Zygarde [TM]					
Fighting	Rock Smash (HM06)	460 Abomasnow [HM]	359 Absol [HM]	681 Aegislash [HM]	142 Aerodactyl [HM]	306 Aggron [HM]	190 Aipom [HM]	334 Altaria [HM]
		698 Amaura [HM]	424 Ambipom [HM]	181 Ampharos [HM]	347 Anorith [HM]	059 Arcanine [HM]	493 Arceus [HM]	566 Archen [HM]
		567 Archeops [HM]	348 Armaldo [HM]	304 Aron [HM]	144 Articuno [HM]	699 Aurorus [HM]	713 Avalugg [HM]	610 Axew [HM]
		184 Azumarill [HM]	371 Bagon [HM]	689 Barbaracle [HM]	411 Bastiodon [HM]	153 Bayleef [HM]	614 Beartic [HM]	015 Beedrill [HM]
		712 Bergmite [HM]	400 Bibarel [HM]	399 Bidoof [HM]	688 Binacle [HM]	625 Bisharp [HM]	009 Blastoise [HM]	257 Blaziken [HM]
		242 Blissey [HM]	525 Boldore [HM]	626 Bouffalant [HM]	628 Braviary [HM]	286 Breloom [HM]	437 Bronzong [HM]	418 Buizel [HM]
		001 Bulbasaur [HM]	427 Buneary [HM]	659 Bunnelby [HM]	323 Camerupt [HM]	565 Carracosta [HM]	113 Chansey [HM]	006 Charizard [HM]
		004 Charmander [HM]	005 Charmeleon [HM]	652 Chesnaught [HM]	650 Chespin [HM]	390 Chimchar [HM]	344 Claydol [HM]	036 Clefable [HM]
		035 Clefairy [HM]	638 Cobalion [HM]	256 Combusken [HM]	534 Conkeldurr [HM]	341 Corphish [HM]	222 Corsola [HM]	346 Cradily [HM]

ADVENTURE DATA

Type	Move	Pokémon that can learn it						
Fighting	Rock Smash (HM06)	408 Cranidos [HM]	342 Crawdaunt [HM]	453 Croagunk [HM]	159 Croconaw [HM]	558 Crustle [HM]	613 Cubchoo [HM]	104 Cubone [HM]
		491 Darkrai [HM]	555 Darmanitan [HM]	554 Darumaka [HM]	633 Deino [HM]	301 Delcatty [HM]	386 Deoxys (Atk) [HM]	386 Deoxys (Def) [HM]
		386 Deoxys (Nor) [HM]	386 Deoxys (Spd) [HM]	502 Dewott [HM]	483 Dialga [HM]	660 Diggersby [HM]	050 Diglett [HM]	232 Donphan [HM]
		680 Doublade [HM]	149 Dragonite [HM]	452 Drapion [HM]	529 Drilbur [HM]	621 Druddigon [HM]	051 Dugtrio [HM]	206 Dunsparce [HM]
		632 Durant [HM]	356 Dusclops [HM]	477 Dusknoir [HM]	557 Dwebble [HM]	604 Eelektross [HM]	125 Electabuzz [HM]	466 Electivire [HM]
		239 Elekid [HM]	500 Emboar [HM]	395 Empoleon [HM]	244 Entei [HM]	589 Escavalier [HM]	530 Excadrill [HM]	295 Exploud [HM]
		160 Feraligatr [HM]	597 Ferroseed [HM]	598 Ferrothorn [HM]	180 Flaaffy [HM]	136 Flareon [HM]	419 Floatzel [HM]	330 Flygon [HM]
		205 Forretress [HM]	611 Fraxure [HM]	656 Froakie [HM]	657 Frogadier [HM]	676 Furfrou [HM]	162 Furret [HM]	444 Gabite [HM]
		475 Gallade [HM]	445 Garchomp [HM]	423 Gastrodon [HM]	094 Gengar [HM]	074 Geodude [HM]	443 Gible [HM]	526 Gigalith [HM]
		203 Girafarig [HM]	487 Giratina (Alt) [HM]	487 Giratina (Ori) [HM]	471 Glaceon [HM]	207 Gligar [HM]	472 Gliscor [HM]	673 Gogoat [HM]
		055 Golduck [HM]	076 Golem [HM]	622 Golett [HM]	623 Golurk [HM]	706 Goodra [HM]	711 Gourgeist [HM]	210 Granbull [HM]
		075 Graveler [HM]	658 Greninja [HM]	388 Grotle [HM]	383 Groudon [HM]	253 Grovyle [HM]	058 Growlithe [HM]	316 Gulpin [HM]
		533 Gurdurr [HM]	130 Gyarados [HM]	297 Hariyama [HM]	701 Hawlucha [HM]	612 Haxorus [HM]	631 Heatmor [HM]	485 Heatran [HM]
		214 Heracross [HM]	507 Herdier [HM]	449 Hippopotas [HM]	450 Hippowdon [HM]	107 Hitmonchan [HM]	106 Hitmonlee [HM]	237 Hitmontop [HM]
		679 Honedge [HM]	250 Ho-Oh [HM]	229 Houndoom [HM]	228 Houndour [HM]	635 Hydreigon [HM]	392 Infernape [HM]	002 Ivysaur [HM]
		135 Jolteon [HM]	140 Kabuto [HM]	141 Kabutops [HM]	115 Kangaskhan [HM]	352 Kecleon [HM]	647 Keldeo [HM]	099 Kingler [HM]
		600 Klang [HM]	599 Klink [HM]	601 Klinklang [HM]	098 Krabby [HM]	402 Kricketune [HM]	552 Krokorok [HM]	553 Krookodile [HM]
		382 Kyogre [HM]	646 Kyurem (Blk) [HM]	646 Kyurem (Wht) [HM]	646 Kyurem [HM]	305 Lairon [HM]	645 Landorus [HM]	131 Lapras [HM]
		246 Larvitar [HM]	470 Leafeon [HM]	166 Ledian [HM]	463 Lickilicky [HM]	108 Lickitung [HM]	510 Liepard [HM]	506 Lillipup [HM]
		264 Linoone [HM]	667 Litleo [HM]	271 Lombre [HM]	428 Lopunny [HM]	294 Loudred [HM]	448 Lucario [HM]	272 Ludicolo [HM]
		249 Lugia [HM]	068 Machamp [HM]	067 Machoke [HM]	066 Machop [HM]	240 Magby [HM]	219 Magcargo [HM]	126 Magmar [HM]
		467 Magmortar [HM]	296 Makuhita [HM]	473 Mamoswine [HM]	630 Mandibuzz [HM]	056 Mankey [HM]	183 Marill [HM]	105 Marowak [HM]
		259 Marshtomp [HM]	303 Mawile [HM]	308 Medicham [HM]	307 Meditite [HM]	154 Meganium [HM]	648 Meloetta [HM]	376 Metagross [HM]
		375 Metang [HM]	151 Mew [HM]	150 Mewtwo [HM]	619 Mienfoo [HM]	620 Mienshao [HM]	262 Mightyena [HM]	241 Miltank [HM]
		146 Moltres [HM]	391 Monferno [HM]	258 Mudkip [HM]	089 Muk [HM]	446 Munchlax [HM]	034 Nidoking [HM]	031 Nidoqueen [HM]
		029 Nidoran ♀ [HM]	032 Nidoran ♂ [HM]	030 Nidorina [HM]	033 Nidorino [HM]	299 Nosepass [HM]	322 Numel [HM]	274 Nuzleaf [HM]
		138 Omanyte [HM]	139 Omastar [HM]	095 Onix [HM]	501 Oshawott [HM]	484 Palkia [HM]	536 Palpitoad [HM]	674 Pancham [HM]
		675 Pangoro [HM]	515 Panpour [HM]	511 Pansage [HM]	513 Pansear [HM]	046 Paras [HM]	047 Parasect [HM]	624 Pawniard [HM]
		231 Phanpy [HM]	708 Phantump [HM]	499 Pignite [HM]	025 Pikachu [HM]	221 Piloswine [HM]	204 Pineco [HM]	127 Pinsir [HM]
		186 Politoed [HM]	061 Poliwhirl [HM]	062 Poliwrath [HM]	261 Poochyena [HM]	057 Primeape [HM]	394 Prinplup [HM]	476 Probopass [HM]
		054 Psyduck [HM]	710 Pumpkaboo [HM]	247 Pupitar [HM]	668 Pyroar [HM]	195 Quagsire [HM]	156 Quilava [HM]	651 Quilladin [HM]
		026 Raichu [HM]	243 Raikou [HM]	409 Rampardos [HM]	020 Raticate [HM]	019 Rattata [HM]	384 Rayquaza [HM]	378 Regice [HM]
		486 Regigigas [HM]	377 Regirock [HM]	379 Registeel [HM]	369 Relicanth [HM]	643 Reshiram [HM]	579 Reuniclus [HM]	112 Rhydon [HM]
		111 Rhyhorn [HM]	464 Rhyperior [HM]	447 Riolu [HM]	524 Roggenrola [HM]	627 Rufflet [HM]	302 Sableye [HM]	373 Salamence [HM]
		503 Samurott [HM]	027 Sandshrew [HM]	028 Sandslash [HM]	539 Sawk [1, HM]	586 Sawsbuck [HM]	254 Sceptile [HM]	212 Scizor [HM]
		545 Scolipede [HM]	560 Scrafty [HM]	559 Scraggy [HM]	123 Scyther [HM]	364 Sealeo [HM]	273 Seedot [HM]	537 Seismitoad [HM]
		497 Serperior [HM]	336 Seviper [HM]	319 Sharpedo [HM]	372 Shelgon [HM]	410 Shieldon [HM]	275 Shiftry [HM]	213 Shuckle [HM]
		516 Simipour [HM]	512 Simisage [HM]	514 Simisear [HM]	227 Skarmory [HM]	672 Skiddo [HM]	451 Skorupi [HM]	435 Skuntank [HM]
		289 Slaking [HM]	287 Slakoth [HM]	080 Slowbro [HM]	199 Slowking [HM]	218 Slugma [HM]	215 Sneasel [HM]	143 Snorlax [HM]
		209 Snubbull [HM]	363 Spheal [HM]	327 Spinda [HM]	007 Squirtle [HM]	208 Steelix [HM]	508 Stoutland [HM]	434 Stunky [HM]
		185 Sudowoodo [HM]	245 Suicune [HM]	317 Swalot [HM]	260 Swampert [HM]	220 Swinub [HM]	114 Tangela [HM]	465 Tangrowth [HM]
		128 Tauros [HM]	216 Teddiursa [HM]	498 Tepig [HM]	639 Terrakion [HM]	538 Throh [HM]	642 Thundurus [HM]	532 Timburr [HM]
		564 Tirtouga [HM]	468 Togekiss [HM]	175 Togepi [HM]	176 Togetic [HM]	255 Torchic [HM]	324 Torkoal [HM]	641 Tornadus [HM]
		389 Torterra [HM]	454 Toxicroak [HM]	328 Trapinch [HM]	252 Treecko [HM]	709 Trevenant [HM]	357 Tropius [HM]	387 Turtwig [HM]
		157 Typhlosion [HM]	248 Tyranitar [HM]	697 Tyrantrum [HM]	236 Tyrogue [HM]	696 Tyrunt [HM]	217 Ursaring [HM]	134 Vaporeon [HM]
		543 Venipede [HM]	003 Venusaur [HM]	329 Vibrava [HM]	494 Victini [HM]	288 Vigoroth [HM]	640 Virizion [HM]	629 Vullaby [HM]
		320 Wailmer [HM]	321 Wailord [HM]	365 Walrein [HM]	008 Wartortle [HM]	505 Watchog [HM]	461 Weavile [HM]	544 Whirlipede [HM]
		340 Whiscash [HM]	194 Wooper [HM]	335 Zangoose [HM]	145 Zapdos [HM]	523 Zebstrika [HM]	644 Zekrom [HM]	263 Zigzagoon [HM]
		571 Zoroark [HM]	634 Zweilous [HM]	718 Zygarde [HM]				
Rock	Rock Throw	698 Amaura [10]	566 Archen [5]	567 Archeops [1, 5]	699 Aurorus [10]	438 Bonsly [12]	703 Carbink [5]	534 Conkeldurr [16]
		719 Diancie [5]	074 Geodude [16]	076 Golem [16]	075 Graveler [16]	533 Gurdurr [16]	645 Landorus [25]	337 Lunatone [1]
		219 Magcargo [1, 8]	258 Mudkip [25]	299 Nosepass [10]	095 Onix [7]	377 Regirock [1, 7]	213 Shuckle [23]	218 Slugma [8]
		338 Solrock [1]	208 Steelix [7]	185 Sudowoodo [1, 12]	532 Timburr [16]	564 Tirtouga [E]		
	Rock Tomb (TM39)	460 Abomasnow [TM]	359 Absol [TM]	142 Aerodactyl [TM]	306 Aggron [13, TM]	698 Amaura [TM]	347 Anorith [TM]	024 Arbok [TM]
		493 Arceus [TM]	566 Archen [TM]	567 Archeops [TM]	348 Armaldo [TM]	304 Aron [13, TM]	699 Aurorus [TM]	713 Avalugg [TM]
		610 Axew [TM]	371 Bagon [TM]	343 Baltoy [13, TM]	689 Barbaracle [TM]	339 Barboach [TM]	411 Bastiodon [TM]	614 Beartic [TM]
		606 Beheeyem [TM]	712 Bergmite [TM]	688 Binacle [TM]	625 Bisharp [TM]	009 Blastoise [TM]	257 Blaziken [TM]	242 Blissey [TM]
		525 Boldore [TM]	438 Bonsly [22, TM]	626 Bouffalant [TM]	628 Braviary [TM]	286 Breloom [TM]	437 Bronzong [TM]	436 Bronzor [TM]
		418 Buizel [TM]	659 Bunnelby [TM]	323 Camerupt [TM]	703 Carbink [TM]	565 Carracosta [TM]	113 Chansey [TM]	006 Charizard [TM]
		004 Charmander [TM]	005 Charmeleon [TM]	652 Chesnaught [TM]	650 Chespin [TM]	344 Claydol [13, TM]	256 Combusken [TM]	534 Conkeldurr [TM]
		341 Corphish [TM]	222 Corsola [TM]	346 Cradily [TM]	408 Cranidos [TM]	342 Crawdaunt [TM]	453 Croagunk [TM]	159 Croconaw [TM]
		558 Crustle [TM]	613 Cubchoo [TM]	104 Cubone [TM]	491 Darkrai [TM]	555 Darmanitan [TM]	554 Darumaka [TM]	386 Deoxys (Atk) [TM]
		386 Deoxys (Def) [TM]	386 Deoxys (Nor) [TM]	386 Deoxys (Spd) [TM]	483 Dialga [TM]	719 Diancie [TM]	660 Diggersby [TM]	050 Diglett [TM]
		232 Donphan [TM]	149 Dragonite [TM]	452 Drapion [TM]	529 Drilbur [TM]	621 Druddigon [TM]	051 Dugtrio [TM]	206 Dunsparce [TM]
		578 Duosion [TM]	632 Durant [TM]	356 Dusclops [TM]	477 Dusknoir [TM]	557 Dwebble [TM]	604 Eelektross [TM]	023 Ekans [TM]
		466 Electivire [TM]	605 Elgyem [TM]	500 Emboar [TM]	395 Empoleon [TM]	530 Excadrill [TM]	295 Exploud [TM]	160 Feraligatr [TM]

	Move	Pokémon that can learn it						
Normal	Round (TM48)	337 Lunatone [TM]	370 Luvdisc [TM]	404 Luxio [TM]	405 Luxray [TM]	068 Machamp [TM]	067 Machoke [TM]	066 Machop [TM]
		240 Magby [TM]	219 Magcargo [TM]	126 Magmar [TM]	467 Magmortar [TM]	081 Magnemite [TM]	082 Magneton [TM]	462 Magnezone [TM]
		296 Makuhita [TM]	687 Malamar [TM]	473 Mamoswine [TM]	490 Manaphy [TM]	630 Mandibuzz [TM]	310 Manectric [TM]	056 Mankey [TM]
		226 Mantine [TM]	458 Mantyke [TM]	556 Maractus [TM]	179 Mareep [TM]	183 Marill [TM]	105 Marowak [TM]	259 Marshtomp [TM]
		284 Masquerain [TM]	303 Mawile [TM]	308 Medicham [TM]	307 Meditite [TM]	154 Meganium [TM]	648 Meloetta [1, TM]	678 Meowstic (F) [TM]
		678 Meowstic (M) [TM]	052 Meowth [TM]	481 Mesprit [TM]	376 Metagross [TM]	375 Metang [TM]	151 Mew [TM]	150 Mewtwo [TM]
		619 Mienfoo [TM]	620 Mienshao [TM]	262 Mightyena [TM]	350 Milotic [TM]	241 Miltank [TM]	439 Mime Jr. [TM]	572 Minccino [TM]
		312 Minun [TM]	200 Misdreavus [TM]	429 Mismagius [TM]	146 Moltres [TM]	391 Monferno [TM]	414 Mothim [TM]	122 Mr. Mime [TM]
		258 Mudkip [TM]	089 Muk [TM]	446 Munchlax [TM]	517 Munna [TM]	198 Murkrow [TM]	518 Musharna [TM]	177 Natu [TM]
		034 Nidoking [TM]	031 Nidoqueen [TM]	029 Nidoran ♀ [TM]	032 Nidoran ♂ [TM]	030 Nidorina [TM]	033 Nidorino [TM]	290 Nincada [TM]
		038 Ninetales [TM]	291 Ninjask [TM]	164 Noctowl [TM]	714 Noibat [TM]	715 Noivern [TM]	299 Nosepass [TM]	322 Numel [TM]
		274 Nuzleaf [TM]	224 Octillery [TM]	043 Oddish [TM]	138 Omanyte [TM]	139 Omastar [TM]	095 Onix [TM]	501 Oshawott [TM]
		417 Pachirisu [TM]	484 Palkia [TM]	536 Palpitoad [1, 9, TM]	674 Pancham [TM]	675 Pangoro [TM]	515 Panpour [TM]	511 Pansage [TM]
		513 Pansear [TM]	046 Paras [TM]	047 Parasect [TM]	504 Patrat [TM]	624 Pawniard [TM]	279 Pelipper [TM]	053 Persian [TM]
		548 Petilil [TM]	231 Phanpy [TM]	708 Phantump [TM]	489 Phione [TM]	172 Pichu [TM]	018 Pidgeot [TM]	017 Pidgeotto [TM]
		016 Pidgey [TM]	519 Pidove [TM]	499 Pignite [TM]	025 Pikachu [TM]	221 Piloswine [TM]	204 Pineco [TM]	127 Pinsir [TM]
		393 Piplup [TM]	311 Plusle [TM]	186 Politoed [TM]	060 Poliwag [TM]	061 Poliwhirl [TM]	062 Poliwrath [TM]	077 Ponyta [TM]
		261 Poochyena [TM]	137 Porygon [TM]	233 Porygon2 [TM]	474 Porygon-Z [TM]	057 Primeape [TM]	394 Prinplup [TM]	476 Probopass [TM]
		054 Psyduck [TM]	710 Pumpkaboo [TM]	247 Pupitar [TM]	509 Purrloin [TM]	432 Purugly [TM]	668 Pyroar [TM]	195 Quagsire [TM]
		156 Quilava [TM]	651 Quilladin [TM]	211 Qwilfish [TM]	026 Raichu [TM]	243 Raikou [TM]	280 Ralts [TM]	409 Rampardos [TM]
		078 Rapidash [TM]	020 Raticate [TM]	019 Rattata [TM]	384 Rayquaza [TM]	378 Regice [TM]	486 Regigigas [TM]	377 Regirock [TM]
		379 Registeel [TM]	369 Relicanth [TM]	223 Remoraid [TM]	643 Reshiram [TM]	579 Reuniclus [TM]	112 Rhydon [TM]	111 Rhyhorn [TM]
		464 Rhyperior [TM]	447 Riolu [TM]	524 Roggenrola [TM]	315 Roselia [TM]	407 Roserade [TM]	479 Rotom (Fan) [TM]	479 Rotom (Frost) [TM]
		479 Rotom (Heat) [TM]	479 Rotom (Mow) [TM]	479 Rotom (Wash) [TM]	479 Rotom [TM]	627 Rufflet [TM]	302 Sableye [TM]	373 Salamence [TM]
		503 Samurott [TM]	551 Sandile [TM]	027 Sandshrew [TM]	028 Sandslash [TM]	539 Sawk [TM]	586 Sawsbuck [TM]	254 Sceptile [TM]
		212 Scizor [TM]	545 Scolipede [TM]	560 Scrafty [TM]	559 Scraggy [TM]	123 Scyther [TM]	117 Seadra [TM]	119 Seaking [TM]
		364 Sealeo [TM]	273 Seedot [TM]	086 Seel [TM]	537 Seismitoad [1, 9, TM]	161 Sentret [TM]	497 Serperior [TM]	496 Servine [TM]
		336 Seviper [TM]	540 Sewaddle [TM]	319 Sharpedo [TM]	492 Shaymin (Land) [TM]	492 Shaymin (Sky) [TM]	292 Shedinja [TM]	372 Shelgon [TM]
		090 Shellder [TM]	422 Shellos [TM]	616 Shelmet [TM]	410 Shieldon [TM]	275 Shiftry [TM]	403 Shinx [TM]	285 Shroomish [TM]
		213 Shuckle [TM]	353 Shuppet [TM]	561 Sigilyph [TM]	516 Simipour [TM]	512 Simisage [TM]	514 Simisear [TM]	227 Skarmory [TM]
		672 Skiddo [TM]	188 Skiploom [TM]	300 Skitty [TM]	451 Skorupi [TM]	690 Skrelp [TM]	435 Skuntank [TM]	289 Slaking [TM]
		287 Slakoth [TM]	705 Sliggoo [TM]	080 Slowbro [TM]	199 Slowking [TM]	079 Slowpoke [TM]	218 Slugma [TM]	685 Slurpuff [13, TM]
		238 Smoochum [TM]	215 Sneasel [TM]	495 Snivy [TM]	143 Snorlax [TM]	361 Snorunt [TM]	459 Snover [TM]	209 Snubbull [TM]
		577 Solosis [TM]	338 Solrock [TM]	021 Spearow [TM]	363 Spheal [TM]	167 Spinarak [TM]	327 Spinda [TM]	442 Spiritomb [TM]
		325 Spoink [TM]	682 Spritzee [TM]	007 Squirtle [TM]	234 Stantler [TM]	398 Staraptor [TM]	397 Staravia [TM]	396 Starly [TM]
		121 Starmie [TM]	120 Staryu [TM]	208 Steelix [TM]	508 Stoutland [TM]	618 Stunfisk [TM]	434 Stunky [TM]	185 Sudowoodo [TM]
		245 Suicune [TM]	192 Sunflora [TM]	191 Sunkern [TM]	283 Surskit [TM]	333 Swablu [17, TM]	541 Swadloon [TM]	317 Swalot [TM]
		260 Swampert [TM]	581 Swanna [TM]	277 Swellow [TM]	220 Swinub [TM]	684 Swirlix [13, TM]	528 Swoobat [TM]	700 Sylveon [TM]
		276 Taillow [TM]	663 Talonflame [TM]	114 Tangela [TM]	465 Tangrowth [TM]	128 Tauros [TM]	216 Teddiursa [TM]	072 Tentacool [TM]
		073 Tentacruel [TM]	498 Tepig [TM]	639 Terrakion [TM]	538 Throh [TM]	642 Thundurus [TM]	532 Timburr [TM]	564 Tirtouga [TM]
		468 Togekiss [TM]	175 Togepi [TM]	176 Togetic [TM]	255 Torchic [TM]	324 Torkoal [TM]	641 Tornadus [TM]	389 Torterra [TM]
		158 Totodile [TM]	454 Toxicroak [TM]	520 Tranquill [TM]	328 Trapinch [TM]	252 Treecko [TM]	709 Trevenant [TM]	357 Tropius [TM]
		568 Trubbish [TM]	387 Turtwig [TM]	535 Tympole [9, TM]	157 Typhlosion [TM]	248 Tyranitar [TM]	697 Tyrantrum [TM]	236 Tyrogue [TM]
		696 Tyrunt [TM]	197 Umbreon [TM]	521 Unfezant [TM]	217 Ursaring [TM]	480 Uxie [TM]	583 Vanillish [TM]	582 Vanillite [TM]
		584 Vanilluxe [TM]	134 Vaporeon [TM]	543 Venipede [TM]	049 Venomoth [TM]	048 Venonat [TM]	003 Venusaur [TM]	416 Vespiquen [TM]
		329 Vibrava [TM]	494 Victini [TM]	071 Victreebel [TM]	288 Vigoroth [TM]	045 Vileplume [TM]	640 Virizion [TM]	666 Vivillon [TM]
		313 Volbeat [TM]	637 Volcarona [TM]	100 Voltorb [TM]	629 Vullaby [TM]	037 Vulpix [TM]	320 Wailmer [TM]	321 Wailord [TM]
		365 Walrein [TM]	008 Wartortle [TM]	505 Watchog [TM]	461 Weavile [TM]	070 Weepinbell [TM]	110 Weezing [TM]	547 Whimsicott [TM]
		544 Whirlipede [TM]	340 Whiscash [TM]	293 Whismur [TM]	040 Wigglytuff [TM]	278 Wingull [TM]	527 Woobat [TM]	194 Wooper [TM]
		413 Wormadam (Plant) [TM]	413 Wormadam (Sand) [TM]	413 Wormadam (Trash) [TM]	178 Xatu [TM]	716 Xerneas [TM]	562 Yamask [TM]	193 Yanma [TM]
		469 Yanmega [TM]	717 Yveltal [TM]	335 Zangoose [TM]	145 Zapdos [TM]	523 Zebstrika [TM]	644 Zekrom [TM]	263 Zigzagoon [TM]
		571 Zoroark [TM]	570 Zorua [TM]	041 Zubat [TM]	634 Zweilous [TM]	718 Zygarde [TM]		

S

	Move	Pokémon that can learn it						
Fire	Sacred Fire	244 Entei [1]	250 Ho-Oh [43]					
Fighting	Sacred Sword	681 Aegislash [1]	638 Cobalion [42]	680 Doublade [51]	679 Honedge [47]	647 Keldeo [43]	639 Terrakion [42]	640 Virizion [42]
Normal	Safeguard (TM20)	460 Abomasnow [TM]	063 Abra [TM]	065 Alakazam [TM]	594 Alomomola [45, TM]	334 Altaria [9, TM]	698 Amaura [TM]	181 Ampharos [TM]
		059 Arcanine [TM]	493 Arceus [TM]	531 Audino [TM]	699 Aurorus [TM]	713 Avalugg [TM]	482 Azelf [TM]	343 Baltoy [TM]
		689 Barbaracle [TM]	153 Bayleef [46, TM]	267 Beautifly [TM]	606 Beheeyem [TM]	182 Bellossom [TM]	712 Bergmite [TM]	688 Binacle [TM]
		242 Blissey [TM]	654 Braixen [TM]	286 Breloom [TM]	437 Bronzong [25, TM]	436 Bronzor [25, TM]	001 Bulbasaur [TM]	012 Butterfree [36, TM]
		703 Carbink [70, TM]	251 Celebi [10, TM]	609 Chandelure [TM]	113 Chansey [TM]	421 Cherrim [TM]	420 Cherubi [TM]	152 Chikorita [39, TM]
		358 Chimecho [37, TM]	433 Chingling [TM]	573 Cinccino [TM]	344 Claydol [TM]	036 Clefable [TM]	035 Clefairy [TM]	173 Cleffa [TM]

Type	Move	Pokémon that can learn it						
Normal	Safeguard (TM20)	638 Cobalion [TM]	563 Cofagrigus [TM]	222 Corsola [TM]	546 Cottonee [TM]	488 Cresselia [11, TM]	585 Deerling [TM]	301 Delcatty [TM]
		655 Delphox [TM]	386 Deoxys (Atk) [TM]	386 Deoxys (Def) [TM]	386 Deoxys (Nor) [TM]	386 Deoxys (Spd) [TM]	087 Dewgong [61, TM]	483 Dialga [TM]
		719 Diancie [70, TM]	148 Dragonair [53, TM]	149 Dragonite [53, TM]	147 Dratini [45, TM]	096 Drowzee [TM]	578 Duosion [TM]	605 Elgyem [TM]
		677 Espurr [TM]	653 Fennekin [TM]	456 Finneon [29, TM]	180 Flaaffy [TM]	669 Flabébé [TM]	670 Floette [TM]	671 Florges [TM]
		592 Frillish [TM]	478 Froslass [TM]	475 Gallade [TM]	282 Gardevoir [TM]	487 Giratina (Alt) [TM]	487 Giratina (Ori) [TM]	362 Glalie [TM]
		622 Golett [TM]	623 Golurk [TM]	368 Gorebyss [TM]	574 Gothita [TM]	576 Gothitelle [TM]	575 Gothorita [TM]	711 Gourgeist [TM]
		388 Grotle [TM]	383 Groudon [TM]	253 Grovyle [TM]	058 Growlithe [TM]	440 Happiny [TM]	250 Ho-Oh [65, TM]	097 Hypno [TM]
		174 Igglybuff [TM]	002 Ivysaur [TM]	593 Jellicent [TM]	039 Jigglypuff [TM]	385 Jirachi [TM]	064 Kadabra [TM]	115 Kangaskhan [TM]
		647 Keldeo [TM]	281 Kirlia [TM]	707 Klefki [TM]	382 Kyogre [TM]	646 Kyurem (Blk) [TM]	646 Kyurem (Wht) [TM]	646 Kyurem [TM]
		608 Lampent [TM]	131 Lapras [43, TM]	636 Larvesta [TM]	380 Latias [1, TM]	381 Latios [1, TM]	542 Leavanny [TM]	166 Ledian [14, TM]
		165 Ledyba [14, TM]	549 Lilligant [TM]	607 Litwick [TM]	249 Lugia [65, TM]	457 Lumineon [29, TM]	337 Lunatone [TM]	370 Luvdisc [55, TM]
		490 Manaphy [TM]	556 Maractus [TM]	179 Mareep [TM]	154 Meganium [54, TM]	648 Meloetta [TM]	678 Meowstic (F) [TM]	678 Meowstic (M) [TM]
		481 Mesprit [TM]	151 Mew [TM]	150 Mewtwo [1, TM]	350 Milotic [41, TM]	439 Mime Jr. [50, TM]	572 Minccino [TM]	146 Moltres [43, TM]
		414 Mothim [TM]	122 Mr. Mime [50, TM]	517 Munna [TM]	518 Musharna [TM]	038 Ninetales [1, TM]	484 Palkia [TM]	548 Petilil [TM]
		708 Phantump [TM]	489 Phione [TM]	710 Pumpkaboo [TM]	195 Quagsire [TM]	280 Ralts [TM]	378 Regice [TM]	486 Regigigas [TM]
		377 Regirock [TM]	379 Registeel [TM]	369 Relicanth [TM]	643 Reshiram [TM]	579 Reuniclus [TM]	027 Sandshrew [TM]	028 Sandslash [TM]
		586 Sawsbuck [TM]	254 Sceptile [TM]	212 Scizor [TM]	123 Scyther [TM]	086 Seel [51, TM]	497 Serperior [TM]	496 Servine [TM]
		540 Sewaddle [TM]	492 Shaymin (Land) [TM]	492 Shaymin (Sky) [TM]	285 Shroomish [TM]	213 Shuckle [16, TM]	561 Sigilyph [TM]	300 Skitty [TM]
		080 Slowbro [TM]	199 Slowking [TM]	079 Slowpoke [TM]	685 Slurpuff [67, TM]	495 Snivy [TM]	361 Snorunt [TM]	459 Snover [TM]
		577 Solosis [TM]	338 Solrock [TM]	327 Spinda [TM]	192 Sunflora [TM]	191 Sunkern [TM]	333 Swablu [9, TM]	541 Swadloon [TM]
		684 Swirlix [67, TM]	528 Swoobat [TM]	700 Sylveon [TM]	072 Tentacool [TM]	073 Tentacruel [TM]	639 Terrakion [TM]	468 Togekiss [TM]
		175 Togepi [37, TM]	176 Togetic [37, TM]	389 Torterra [TM]	252 Treecko [TM]	709 Trevenant [TM]	357 Tropius [TM]	387 Turtwig [TM]
		480 Uxie [TM]	003 Venusaur [TM]	494 Victini [TM]	045 Vileplume [TM]	640 Virizion [TM]	666 Vivillon [41, TM]	637 Volcarona [TM]
		037 Vulpix [34, TM]	547 Whimsicott [TM]	040 Wigglytuff [TM]	202 Wobbuffet [1, TM]	527 Woobat [TM]	194 Wooper [TM]	413 Wormadam (Plant) [TM]
		413 Wormadam (Sand) [TM]	413 Wormadam (Trash) [TM]	360 Wynaut [15, TM]	562 Yamask [TM]	644 Zekrom [TM]	718 Zygarde [5, TM]	
Ground	Sand Attack	190 Aipom [4]	424 Ambipom [1, 4]	347 Anorith [E]	689 Barbaracle [1]	688 Binacle [1]	257 Blaziken [1, 10]	522 Blitzle [E]
		525 Boldore [1, 7]	331 Cacnea [13]	332 Cacturne [13]	256 Combusken [1, 10]	558 Crustle [1, 11]	585 Deerling [7]	050 Diglett [1]
		051 Dugtrio [1]	632 Durant [1]	557 Dwebble [11]	133 Eevee [5]	196 Espeon [5]	083 Farfetch'd [1]	136 Flareon [5]
		330 Flygon [1]	676 Furfrou [5]	444 Gabite [1, 3]	445 Garchomp [1, 3]	443 Gible [3]	526 Gigalith [1, 7]	471 Glaceon [5]
		431 Glameow [E]	207 Gligar [4]	472 Gliscor [1, 4]	297 Hariyama [1, 4]	449 Hippopotas [1]	450 Hippowdon [1]	135 Jolteon [5]
		140 Kabuto [21]	141 Kabutops [21]	552 Krokorok [1, 7]	553 Krookodile [1, 7]	470 Leafeon [5]	510 Liepard [1, 10]	506 Lillipup [E]
		264 Linoone [1, 7]	296 Makuhita [4]	179 Mareep [E]	262 Mightyena [1, 7]	290 Nincada [9]	291 Ninjask [1, 9]	504 Patrat [13]
		018 Pidgeot [1, 5]	017 Pidgeotto [1, 5]	016 Pidgey [5]	261 Poochyena [7]	509 Purrloin [10]	524 Roggenrola [7]	551 Sandile [7]
		027 Sandshrew [3]	028 Sandslash [1, 3]	586 Sawsbuck [1, 7]	560 Scrafty [1, 5]	559 Scraggy [5]	292 Shedinja [9]	227 Skarmory [6]
		451 Skorupi [E]	234 Stantler [16]	396 Starly [E]	700 Sylveon [5]	255 Torchic [10]	328 Trapinch [1]	568 Trubbish [E]
		197 Umbreon [5]	134 Vaporeon [5]	329 Vibrava [1]	505 Watchog [13]	263 Zigzagoon [7]		
	Sand Tomb	438 Bonsly [E]	051 Dugtrio [26]	557 Dwebble [E]	330 Flygon [12]	444 Gabite [19]	445 Garchomp [19]	443 Gible [19, E]
		207 Gligar [E]	449 Hippopotas [25, E]	450 Hippowdon [25]	552 Krokorok [13]	553 Krookodile [13]	095 Onix [37]	204 Pineco [E]
		551 Sandile [13]	027 Sandshrew [23]	028 Sandslash [24]	213 Shuckle [E]	185 Sudowoodo [E]	328 Trapinch [12]	387 Turtwig [E]
		329 Vibrava [12]						
Rock	Sandstorm (TM37)	359 Absol [TM]	617 Accelgor [TM]	142 Aerodactyl [TM]	306 Aggron [TM]	698 Amaura [TM]	347 Anorith [TM]	493 Arceus [TM]
		566 Archen [TM]	567 Archeops [TM]	348 Armaldo [TM]	304 Aron [TM]	144 Articuno [TM]	699 Aurorus [TM]	482 Azelf [TM]
		343 Baltoy [40, TM]	689 Barbaracle [TM]	339 Barboach [TM]	411 Bastiodon [TM]	688 Binacle [TM]	625 Bisharp [TM]	242 Blissey [TM]
		525 Boldore [42, TM]	438 Bonsly [TM]	437 Bronzong [TM]	436 Bronzor [TM]	659 Bunnelby [TM]	331 Cacnea [50, TM]	332 Cacturne [54, TM]
		323 Camerupt [TM]	703 Carbink [TM]	565 Carracosta [TM]	351 Castform [TM]	251 Celebi [TM]	113 Chansey [TM]	344 Claydol [46, TM]
		638 Cobalion [TM]	222 Corsola [TM]	346 Cradily [TM]	408 Cranidos [TM]	558 Crustle [TM]	104 Cubone [TM]	483 Dialga [TM]
		719 Diancie [TM]	660 Diggersby [TM]	050 Diglett [TM]	232 Donphan [TM]	149 Dragonite [TM]	529 Drilbur [40, TM]	051 Dugtrio [TM]
		632 Durant [TM]	557 Dwebble [TM]	244 Entei [TM]	530 Excadrill [49, TM]	598 Ferrothorn [TM]	330 Flygon [36, TM]	205 Forretress [TM]
		444 Gabite [13, TM]	445 Garchomp [1, 13, TM]	423 Gastrodon [TM]	074 Geodude [TM]	443 Gible [13, TM]	526 Gigalith [42, TM]	207 Gligar [TM]
		472 Gliscor [TM]	076 Golem [TM]	075 Graveler [TM]	383 Groudon [TM]	130 Gyarados [TM]	695 Heliolisk [TM]	694 Helioptile [TM]
		449 Hippopotas [TM]	450 Hippowdon [TM]	237 Hitmontop [TM]	250 Ho-Oh [TM]	385 Jirachi [TM]	140 Kabuto [TM]	141 Kabutops [TM]
		115 Kangaskhan [TM]	600 Klang [TM]	599 Klink [TM]	601 Klinklang [TM]	552 Krokorok [44, TM]	553 Krookodile [48, TM]	305 Lairon [TM]
		645 Landorus [61, TM]	246 Larvitar [5, TM]	380 Latias [TM]	381 Latios [TM]	463 Lickilicky [TM]	108 Lickitung [TM]	345 Lileep [TM]
		249 Lugia [TM]	337 Lunatone [TM]	219 Magcargo [TM]	473 Mamoswine [TM]	105 Marowak [TM]	303 Mawile [TM]	481 Mesprit [TM]
		376 Metagross [TM]	375 Metang [TM]	151 Mew [TM]	150 Mewtwo [TM]	241 Miltank [TM]	146 Moltres [TM]	446 Munchlax [TM]
		034 Nidoking [TM]	031 Nidoqueen [TM]	290 Nincada [TM]	291 Ninjask [TM]	299 Nosepass [34, TM]	322 Numel [TM]	138 Omanyte [TM]
		139 Omastar [TM]	095 Onix [52, TM]	484 Palkia [TM]	624 Pawniard [TM]	231 Phanpy [TM]	221 Piloswine [TM]	204 Pineco [TM]
		476 Probopass [34, TM]	247 Pupitar [1, 5, TM]	195 Quagsire [TM]	243 Raikou [TM]	409 Rampardos [TM]	384 Rayquaza [TM]	377 Regirock [TM]
		379 Registeel [TM]	369 Relicanth [TM]	112 Rhydon [TM]	111 Rhyhorn [TM]	464 Rhyperior [TM]	524 Roggenrola [33, TM]	551 Sandile [40, TM]
		027 Sandshrew [42, TM]	028 Sandslash [48, TM]	212 Scizor [TM]	292 Shedinja [TM]	410 Shieldon [TM]	213 Shuckle [TM]	227 Skarmory [TM]
		143 Snorlax [TM]	338 Solrock [TM]	208 Steelix [52, TM]	618 Stunfisk [TM]	185 Sudowoodo [TM]	245 Suicune [TM]	220 Swinub [TM]
		128 Tauros [TM]	639 Terrakion [TM]	564 Tirtouga [TM]	389 Torterra [TM]	328 Trapinch [36, TM]	248 Tyranitar [1, 5, TM]	697 Tyrantrum [TM]
		696 Tyrunt [TM]	480 Uxie [TM]	329 Vibrava [36, TM]	340 Whiscash [TM]	194 Wooper [TM]	413 Wormadam (Sand) [TM]	145 Zapdos [TM]
		718 Zygarde [35, TM]						

	Move	Pokémon that can learn it						
Water	Scald (TM55)	594 Alomomola [TM]	184 Azumarill [TM]	298 Azurill [TM]	689 Barbaracle [TM]	339 Barboach [TM]	550 Basculin [TM]	400 Bibarel [TM]
		688 Binacle [TM]	009 Blastoise [TM]	418 Buizel [TM]	565 Carracosta [TM]	318 Carvanha [TM]	351 Castform [TM]	170 Chinchou [TM]
		366 Clamperl [TM]	692 Clauncher [TM]	693 Clawitzer [TM]	341 Corphish [TM]	222 Corsola [TM]	342 Crawdaunt [TM]	159 Croconaw [TM]
		502 Dewott [TM]	691 Dragalge [TM]	580 Ducklett [TM]	500 Emboar [TM]	395 Empoleon [TM]	349 Feebas [TM]	160 Feraligatr [TM]
		456 Finneon [TM]	419 Floatzel [TM]	592 Frillish [TM]	656 Froakie [TM]	657 Frogadier [TM]	423 Gastrodon [TM]	118 Goldeen [TM]
		055 Golduck [TM]	368 Gorebyss [TM]	658 Greninja [TM]	130 Gyarados [TM]	116 Horsea [TM]	367 Huntail [TM]	593 Jellicent [TM]
		140 Kabuto [TM]	141 Kabutops [TM]	647 Keldeo [TM]	230 Kingdra [TM]	099 Kingler [TM]	098 Krabby [TM]	382 Kyogre [TM]
		171 Lanturn [TM]	271 Lombre [TM]	270 Lotad [TM]	272 Ludicolo [TM]	457 Lumineon [TM]	370 Luvdisc [TM]	490 Manaphy [TM]
		226 Mantine [TM]	458 Mantyke [TM]	183 Marill [TM]	259 Marshtomp [TM]	284 Masquerain [TM]	151 Mew [TM]	350 Milotic [TM]
		258 Mudkip [TM]	224 Octillery [TM]	138 Omanyte [TM]	139 Omastar [TM]	501 Oshawott [TM]	536 Palpitoad [TM]	515 Panpour [22, TM]
		279 Pelipper [TM]	489 Phione [TM]	393 Piplup [TM]	186 Politoed [TM]	060 Poliwag [TM]	061 Poliwhirl [TM]	062 Poliwrath [TM]
		394 Prinplup [TM]	054 Psyduck [TM]	195 Quagsire [TM]	211 Qwilfish [TM]	369 Relicanth [TM]	223 Remoraid [TM]	503 Samurott [TM]
		117 Seadra [TM]	119 Seaking [TM]	537 Seismitoad [TM]	319 Sharpedo [TM]	422 Shellos [TM]	516 Simipour [1, TM]	690 Skrelp [TM]
		080 Slowbro [TM]	199 Slowking [TM]	079 Slowpoke [TM]	007 Squirtle [TM]	121 Starmie [TM]	120 Staryu [TM]	618 Stunfisk [TM]
		245 Suicune [TM]	283 Surskit [TM]	260 Swampert [TM]	581 Swanna [TM]	072 Tentacool [TM]	073 Tentacruel [TM]	564 Tirtouga [TM]
		158 Totodile [TM]	535 Tympole [TM]	134 Vaporeon [TM]	320 Wailmer [TM]	321 Wailord [TM]	008 Wartortle [TM]	340 Whiscash [TM]
		278 Wingull [TM]	194 Wooper [TM]					
Normal	Scary Face	142 Aerodactyl [1]	566 Archen [11]	567 Archeops [11]	168 Ariados [1, 5]	610 Axew [16]	371 Bagon [39]	550 Basculin [41]
		625 Bisharp [22]	626 Bouffalant [21]	628 Braviary [19]	318 Carvanha [29]	006 Charizard [21]	004 Charmander [19]	005 Charmeleon [21]
		563 Cofagrigus [34]	534 Conkeldurr [41]	408 Cranidos [19]	159 Croconaw [15]	633 Deino [50]	483 Dialga [1]	232 Donphan [37]
		452 Drapion [43]	621 Druddigon [13]	023 Ekans [E]	160 Feraligatr [15]	136 Flareon [29]	611 Fraxure [16]	092 Gastly [E]
		443 Gible [E]	487 Giratina (Alt) [1]	487 Giratina (Ori) [1]	711 Gourgeist [4]	210 Granbull [1]	088 Grimer [E]	383 Groudon [5]
		533 Gurdurr [41]	612 Haxorus [16]	485 Heatran [41]	367 Huntail [9]	635 Hydreigon [55]	588 Karrablast [40]	552 Krokorok [36]
		553 Krookodile [36]	382 Kyogre [5]	646 Kyurem [43]	246 Larvitar [23]	404 Luxio [43]	405 Luxray [49]	068 Machamp [53]
		067 Machoke [53]	066 Machop [43]	473 Mamoswine [1, 58]	284 Masquerain [22]	376 Metagross [35]	375 Metang [35]	262 Mightyena [28]
		322 Numel [E]	484 Palkia [1]	624 Pawniard [22]	261 Poochyena [25]	710 Pumpkaboo [4]	247 Pupitar [23]	409 Rampardos [19]
		020 Raticate [20]	384 Rayquaza [5]	112 Rhydon [1, 9]	111 Rhyhorn [9]	464 Rhyperior [1, 9]	627 Rufflet [19]	373 Salamence [42]
		551 Sandile [34]	560 Scrafty [34]	559 Scraggy [34]	336 Seviper [E]	319 Sharpedo [29]	372 Shelgon [42]	410 Shieldon [E]
		403 Shinx [37]	451 Skorupi [41]	209 Snubbull [1]	021 Spearow [E]	167 Spinarak [5]	434 Stunky [E]	128 Tauros [11]
		532 Timburr [37]	158 Totodile [15]	248 Tyranitar [23]	217 Ursaring [38]	629 Vullaby [E]	571 Zoroark [21]	570 Zorua [21]
		634 Zweilous [55]						
	Scratch	359 Absol [1]	190 Aipom [1]	424 Ambipom [1]	347 Anorith [1]	348 Armaldo [1]	610 Axew [1]	689 Barbaracle [1]
		688 Binacle [1]	625 Bisharp [1]	257 Blaziken [1]	654 Braixen [1]	006 Charizard [1]	004 Charmander [1]	005 Charmeleon [1]
		390 Chimchar [1]	256 Combusken [1]	159 Croconaw [1]	655 Delphox [1]	050 Diglett [1]	529 Drilbur [1]	621 Druddigon [1]
		051 Dugtrio [1]	677 Espurr [1]	530 Excadrill [1]	653 Fennekin [1]	160 Feraligatr [1]	611 Fraxure [1]	162 Furret [1]
		431 Glameow [5]	055 Golduck [1]	612 Haxorus [1]	392 Infernape [1]	140 Kabuto [1]	141 Kabutops [1]	352 Kecleon [1]
		510 Liepard [1]	056 Mankey [1]	678 Meowstic (F) [1]	678 Meowstic (M) [1]	052 Meowth [1]	391 Monferno [1]	031 Nidoqueen [1]
		029 Nidoran ♀ [1]	030 Nidorina [1]	290 Nincada [1]	291 Ninjask [1]	515 Panpour [1]	511 Pansage [1]	513 Pansear [1]
		046 Paras [1]	047 Parasect [1]	624 Pawniard [1]	053 Persian [1]	057 Primeape [1]	054 Psyduck [1]	509 Purrloin [1]
		432 Purugly [1, 5]	302 Sableye [1]	027 Sandshrew [1]	028 Sandslash [1]	161 Sentret [1]	292 Shedinja [1]	435 Skuntank [1]
		289 Slaking [1]	287 Slakoth [1]	215 Sneasel [1]	434 Stunky [1]	216 Teddiursa [1]	255 Torchic [1]	158 Totodile [1]
		217 Ursaring [1]	288 Vigoroth [1]	461 Weavile [1]	335 Zangoose [1]	571 Zoroark [1]	570 Zorua [1]	
	Screech	190 Aipom [25, E]	424 Ambipom [25]	347 Anorith [E]	024 Arbok [17]	304 Aron [E]	354 Banette [1, 4]	522 Blitzle [E]
		318 Carvanha [18]	170 Chinchou [E]	222 Corsola [E]	408 Cranidos [42]	169 Crobat [1]	159 Croconaw [42]	104 Cubone [E]
		633 Deino [E]	050 Diglett [E]	206 Dunsparce [13]	632 Durant [E]	023 Ekans [17]	125 Electabuzz [42]	466 Electivire [42]
		101 Electrode [13]	239 Elekid [36]	295 Exploud [15]	160 Feraligatr [50]	330 Flygon [22]	596 Galvantula [7]	649 Genesect [1]
		207 Gligar [35]	472 Gliscor [35]	042 Golbat [1]	055 Golduck [29]	088 Grimer [37]	253 Grovyle [63]	367 Huntail [5]
		595 Joltik [7]	140 Kabuto [E]	588 Karrablast [E]	352 Kecleon [38]	600 Klang [40]	599 Klink [39]	601 Klinklang [40]
		109 Koffing [E]	402 Kricketune [34]	246 Larvitar [10]	165 Ledyba [E]	463 Lickilicky [49]	108 Lickitung [49]	294 Loudred [15]
		240 Magby [E]	081 Magnemite [35]	082 Magneton [39]	462 Magnezone [39]	056 Mankey [21]	179 Mareep [E]	052 Meowth [17]
		200 Misdreavus [E]	089 Muk [37]	446 Munchlax [20]	198 Murkrow [E]	291 Ninjask [20]	714 Noibat [1]	715 Noivern [1]
		095 Onix [31]	501 Oshawott [E]	046 Paras [E]	504 Patrat [E]	053 Persian [17]	057 Primeape [21]	054 Psyduck [25]
		247 Pupitar [1, 10]	409 Rampardos [51]	019 Rattata [E]	223 Remoraid [E]	447 Riolu [24]	254 Sceptile [69]	545 Scolipede [1, 8]
		336 Seviper [13]	540 Sewaddle [E]	319 Sharpedo [18]	090 Shellder [E]	410 Shieldon [E]	353 Shuppet [4]	451 Skorupi [E]
		435 Skuntank [7]	215 Sneasel [32]	208 Steelix [31]	434 Stunky [7]	072 Tentacool [37]	073 Tentacruel [40]	158 Totodile [36]
		252 Treecko [49]	248 Tyranitar [1, 10]	197 Umbreon [29]	543 Venipede [8]	048 Venonat [E]	329 Vibrava [22]	100 Voltorb [13]
		461 Weavile [32]	544 Whirlipede [1, 8]	293 Whismur [15]	193 Yanma [46]	469 Yanmega [46]		
Fire	Searing Shot	494 Victini [1]						
Normal	Secret Power (TM94)	460 Abomasnow [TM]	063 Abra [TM]	359 Absol [TM]	617 Accelgor [TM]	681 Aegislash [TM]	142 Aerodactyl [TM]	306 Aggron [TM]
		190 Aipom [TM]	065 Alakazam [TM]	594 Alomomola [TM]	334 Altaria [TM]	698 Amaura [TM]	424 Ambipom [TM]	591 Amoonguss [TM]
		181 Ampharos [TM]	347 Anorith [TM]	024 Arbok [TM]	059 Arcanine [TM]	493 Arceus [TM]	566 Archen [TM]	567 Archeops [TM]
		168 Ariados [TM]	348 Armaldo [TM]	683 Aromatisse [TM]	304 Aron [TM]	144 Articuno [TM]	531 Audino [25, TM]	699 Aurorus [TM]
		713 Avalugg [TM]	610 Axew [TM]	482 Azelf [TM]	184 Azumarill [TM]	298 Azurill [TM]	371 Bagon [TM]	343 Baltoy [TM]
		354 Banette [TM]	689 Barbaracle [TM]	339 Barboach [TM]	550 Basculin [TM]	411 Bastiodon [TM]	153 Bayleef [TM]	614 Beartic [TM]
		267 Beautifly [TM]	015 Beedrill [TM]	606 Beheeyem [TM]	182 Bellossom [TM]	069 Bellsprout [TM]	712 Bergmite [TM]	400 Bibarel [TM]
		399 Bidoof [TM]	688 Binacle [TM]	625 Bisharp [TM]	009 Blastoise [TM]	257 Blaziken [TM]	242 Blissey [TM]	522 Blitzle [TM]

	Move	Pokémon that can learn it						
Normal	Secret Power (TM94)	525 Boldore [TM]	438 Bonsly [TM]	626 Bouffalant [TM]	654 Braixen [TM]	628 Braviary [TM]	286 Breloom [TM]	437 Bronzong [TM]
		436 Bronzor [TM]	406 Budew [TM]	418 Buizel [TM]	001 Bulbasaur [TM]	427 Buneary [TM]	659 Bunnelby [TM]	012 Butterfree [TM]
		331 Cacnea [TM]	332 Cacturne [TM]	323 Camerupt [TM]	703 Carbink [TM]	455 Carnivine [TM]	565 Carracosta [TM]	318 Carvanha [TM]
		351 Castform [TM]	251 Celebi [TM]	609 Chandelure [TM]	113 Chansey [TM]	006 Charizard [TM]	004 Charmander [TM]	005 Charmeleon [TM]
		441 Chatot [TM]	421 Cherrim [TM]	420 Cherubi [TM]	652 Chesnaught [TM]	650 Chespin [TM]	152 Chikorita [TM]	390 Chimchar [TM]
		358 Chimecho [TM]	170 Chinchou [TM]	433 Chingling [TM]	573 Cinccino [TM]	366 Clamperl [TM]	692 Clauncher [TM]	693 Clawitzer [TM]
		344 Claydol [TM]	036 Clefable [TM]	035 Clefairy [TM]	173 Cleffa [TM]	091 Cloyster [TM]	638 Cobalion [TM]	563 Cofagrigus [TM]
		256 Combusken [TM]	534 Conkeldurr [TM]	341 Corphish [TM]	222 Corsola [TM]	546 Cottonee [TM]	346 Cradily [TM]	408 Cranidos [TM]
		342 Crawdaunt [TM]	488 Cresselia [TM]	453 Croagunk [TM]	169 Crobat [TM]	159 Croconaw [TM]	558 Crustle [TM]	615 Cryogonal [TM]
		613 Cubchoo [TM]	104 Cubone [TM]	155 Cyndaquil [TM]	491 Darkrai [TM]	555 Darmanitan [TM]	554 Darumaka [TM]	702 Dedenne [TM]
		585 Deerling [TM]	633 Deino [TM]	301 Delcatty [TM]	225 Delibird [TM]	655 Delphox [TM]	386 Deoxys (Atk) [TM]	386 Deoxys (Def) [TM]
		386 Deoxys (Nor) [TM]	386 Deoxys (Spd) [TM]	087 Dewgong [TM]	502 Dewott [TM]	483 Dialga [TM]	719 Diancie [TM]	660 Diggersby [TM]
		050 Diglett [TM]	085 Dodrio [TM]	084 Doduo [TM]	232 Donphan [TM]	680 Doublade [TM]	691 Dragalge [TM]	148 Dragonair [TM]
		149 Dragonite [TM]	452 Drapion [TM]	147 Dratini [TM]	426 Drifblim [TM]	425 Drifloon [TM]	529 Drilbur [TM]	096 Drowzee [TM, E]
		621 Druddigon [TM]	580 Ducklett [TM]	051 Dugtrio [TM]	206 Dunsparce [TM, E]	578 Duosion [TM]	632 Durant [TM]	356 Dusclops [TM]
		477 Dusknoir [TM]	355 Duskull [TM]	269 Dustox [TM]	557 Dwebble [TM]	603 Eelektrik [TM]	604 Eelektross [TM]	133 Eevee [TM]
		023 Ekans [TM]	125 Electabuzz [TM]	466 Electivire [TM]	309 Electrike [TM]	101 Electrode [TM]	239 Elekid [TM]	605 Elgyem [TM]
		500 Emboar [TM]	587 Emolga [TM]	395 Empoleon [TM]	244 Entei [TM]	589 Escavalier [TM]	196 Espeon [TM]	677 Espurr [TM]
		530 Excadrill [TM]	102 Exeggcute [TM]	103 Exeggutor [TM]	295 Exploud [TM]	083 Farfetch'd [TM]	022 Fearow [TM]	349 Feebas [TM]
		653 Fennekin [TM]	160 Feraligatr [TM]	597 Ferroseed [TM]	598 Ferrothorn [TM]	456 Finneon [TM]	180 Flaaffy [TM]	669 Flabébé [TM]
		136 Flareon [TM]	662 Fletchinder [TM]	661 Fletchling [TM]	419 Floatzel [TM]	670 Floette [TM]	671 Florges [TM]	330 Flygon [TM]
		590 Foongus [TM]	205 Forretress [TM]	611 Fraxure [TM]	592 Frillish [TM]	656 Froakie [TM]	657 Frogadier [TM]	478 Froslass [TM]
		676 Furfrou [TM]	162 Furret [TM]	444 Gabite [TM]	475 Gallade [TM]	596 Galvantula [TM]	569 Garbodor [TM]	445 Garchomp [TM]
		282 Gardevoir [TM]	092 Gastly [TM]	423 Gastrodon [TM]	649 Genesect [TM]	094 Gengar [TM]	074 Geodude [TM]	443 Gible [TM]
		526 Gigalith [TM]	203 Girafarig [TM, E]	487 Giratina (Alt) [TM]	487 Giratina (Ori) [TM]	471 Glaceon [TM]	362 Glalie [TM]	431 Glameow [TM]
		207 Gligar [TM]	472 Gliscor [TM]	044 Gloom [TM]	673 Gogoat [TM]	042 Golbat [TM]	118 Goldeen [TM]	055 Golduck [TM]
		076 Golem [TM]	622 Golett [TM]	623 Golurk [TM]	706 Goodra [TM]	704 Goomy [TM]	368 Gorebyss [TM]	574 Gothita [TM]
		576 Gothitelle [TM]	575 Gothorita [TM]	711 Gourgeist [TM]	210 Granbull [TM]	075 Graveler [TM]	658 Greninja [TM]	088 Grimer [TM]
		388 Grotle [TM]	383 Groudon [TM]	253 Grovyle [TM]	058 Growlithe [TM]	326 Grumpig [TM]	316 Gulpin [TM]	533 Gurdurr [TM]
		130 Gyarados [TM]	440 Happiny [TM]	297 Hariyama [TM]	093 Haunter [TM]	701 Hawlucha [TM]	612 Haxorus [TM]	631 Heatmor [TM]
		485 Heatran [TM]	695 Heliolisk [TM]	694 Helioptile [TM]	214 Heracross [TM]	507 Herdier [TM]	449 Hippopotas [TM]	450 Hippowdon [TM]
		107 Hitmonchan [TM]	106 Hitmonlee [TM]	237 Hitmontop [TM]	430 Honchkrow [TM]	679 Honedge [TM]	250 Ho-Oh [TM]	163 Hoothoot [TM]
		187 Hoppip [TM]	116 Horsea [TM]	229 Houndoom [TM]	228 Houndour [TM]	367 Huntail [TM]	635 Hydreigon [TM]	097 Hypno [TM]
		174 Igglybuff [TM]	314 Illumise [TM]	392 Infernape [TM]	686 Inkay [TM]	002 Ivysaur [TM]	593 Jellicent [TM]	039 Jigglypuff [TM]
		385 Jirachi [TM]	135 Jolteon [TM]	595 Joltik [TM]	189 Jumpluff [TM]	124 Jynx [TM]	140 Kabuto [TM]	141 Kabutops [TM]
		064 Kadabra [TM]	115 Kangaskhan [TM]	588 Karrablast [TM]	352 Kecleon [TM]	647 Keldeo [TM]	230 Kingdra [TM]	099 Kingler [TM]
		281 Kirlia [TM]	600 Klang [TM]	707 Klefki [TM]	599 Klink [TM]	601 Klinklang [TM]	109 Koffing [TM]	098 Krabby [TM]
		402 Kricketune [TM]	552 Krokorok [TM]	553 Krookodile [TM]	382 Kyogre [TM]	646 Kyurem (Blk) [TM]	646 Kyurem (Wht) [TM]	646 Kyurem [TM]
		305 Lairon [TM]	608 Lampent [TM]	645 Landorus [TM]	171 Lanturn [TM]	131 Lapras [TM]	636 Larvesta [TM]	246 Larvitar [TM]
		380 Latias [TM]	381 Latios [TM]	470 Leafeon [TM]	542 Leavanny [TM]	166 Ledian [TM]	165 Ledyba [TM]	463 Lickilicky [TM]
		108 Lickitung [TM]	510 Liepard [TM]	345 Lileep [TM]	549 Lilligant [TM]	506 Lillipup [TM]	264 Linoone [TM]	667 Litleo [TM]
		607 Litwick [TM]	271 Lombre [TM]	428 Lopunny [TM]	270 Lotad [TM]	294 Loudred [TM]	448 Lucario [TM]	272 Ludicolo [TM]
		249 Lugia [TM]	457 Lumineon [TM]	337 Lunatone [TM]	370 Luvdisc [TM]	404 Luxio [TM]	405 Luxray [TM]	068 Machamp [TM]
		067 Machoke [TM]	066 Machop [TM]	240 Magby [TM]	219 Magcargo [TM]	126 Magmar [TM]	467 Magmortar [TM]	081 Magnemite [TM]
		082 Magneton [TM]	462 Magnezone [TM]	296 Makuhita [TM]	687 Malamar [TM]	473 Mamoswine [TM]	490 Manaphy [TM]	630 Mandibuzz [TM]
		310 Manectric [TM]	056 Mankey [TM]	226 Mantine [TM]	458 Mantyke [TM]	556 Maractus [TM]	179 Mareep [TM]	183 Marill [TM]
		105 Marowak [TM]	259 Marshtomp [TM]	284 Masquerain [TM]	303 Mawile [TM]	308 Medicham [TM]	307 Meditite [TM, E]	154 Meganium [TM]
		648 Meloetta [TM]	678 Meowstic (F) [TM]	678 Meowstic (M) [TM]	052 Meowth [TM]	481 Mesprit [TM]	376 Metagross [TM]	375 Metang [TM]
		151 Mew [TM]	150 Mewtwo [TM]	619 Mienfoo [TM]	620 Mienshao [TM]	262 Mightyena [TM]	350 Milotic [TM]	241 Miltank [TM]
		439 Mime Jr. [TM]	572 Minccino [TM]	312 Minun [TM]	200 Misdreavus [TM]	429 Mismagius [TM]	146 Moltres [TM]	391 Monferno [TM]
		414 Mothim [TM]	122 Mr. Mime [TM]	258 Mudkip [TM]	089 Muk [TM]	446 Munchlax [TM]	517 Munna [TM, E]	198 Murkrow [TM]
		518 Musharna [TM]	177 Natu [TM]	034 Nidoking [TM]	031 Nidoqueen [TM]	029 Nidoran ♀ [TM]	032 Nidoran ♂ [TM]	030 Nidorina [TM]
		033 Nidorino [TM]	290 Nincada [TM]	038 Ninetales [TM]	291 Ninjask [TM]	164 Noctowl [TM]	714 Noibat [TM]	715 Noivern [TM]
		299 Nosepass [TM]	322 Numel [TM]	274 Nuzleaf [TM]	224 Octillery [TM]	043 Oddish [TM, E]	138 Omanyte [TM]	139 Omastar [TM]
		095 Onix [TM]	501 Oshawott [TM]	417 Pachirisu [TM]	484 Palkia [TM]	536 Palpitoad [TM]	674 Pancham [TM]	675 Pangoro [TM]
		515 Panpour [TM]	511 Pansage [TM]	513 Pansear [TM]	046 Paras [TM]	047 Parasect [TM]	504 Patrat [TM]	624 Pawniard [TM]
		279 Pelipper [TM]	053 Persian [TM]	548 Petilil [TM]	231 Phanpy [TM]	708 Phantump [TM]	489 Phione [TM]	172 Pichu [TM]
		018 Pidgeot [TM]	017 Pidgeotto [TM]	016 Pidgey [TM]	519 Pidove [TM]	499 Pignite [TM]	025 Pikachu [TM]	221 Piloswine [TM]
		204 Pineco [TM]	127 Pinsir [TM]	393 Piplup [TM]	311 Plusle [TM]	186 Politoed [TM]	060 Poliwag [TM]	061 Poliwhirl [TM]
		062 Poliwrath [TM]	077 Ponyta [TM]	261 Poochyena [TM]	137 Porygon [TM]	233 Porygon2 [TM]	474 Porygon-Z [TM]	057 Primeape [TM]
		394 Prinplup [TM]	476 Probopass [TM]	054 Psyduck [TM, E]	710 Pumpkaboo [TM]	247 Pupitar [TM]	509 Purrloin [TM]	432 Purugly [TM]
		668 Pyroar [TM]	195 Quagsire [TM]	156 Quilava [TM]	651 Quilladin [TM]	211 Qwilfish [TM]	026 Raichu [TM]	243 Raikou [TM]
		280 Ralts [TM]	409 Rampardos [TM]	078 Rapidash [TM]	020 Raticate [TM]	019 Rattata [TM]	384 Rayquaza [TM]	378 Regice [TM]
		486 Regigigas [TM]	377 Regirock [TM]	379 Registeel [TM]	369 Relicanth [TM]	223 Remoraid [TM]	643 Reshiram [TM]	579 Reuniclus [TM]
		112 Rhydon [TM]	111 Rhyhorn [TM]	464 Rhyperior [TM]	447 Riolu [TM]	524 Roggenrola [TM]	315 Roselia [TM]	407 Roserade [TM]
		479 Rotom (Fan) [TM]	479 Rotom (Frost) [TM]	479 Rotom (Heat) [TM]	479 Rotom (Mow) [TM]	479 Rotom (Wash) [TM]	479 Rotom [TM]	627 Rufflet [TM]

Type	Move	Pokémon that can learn it						
Normal	Secret Power (TM94)	302 Sableye [TM]	373 Salamence [TM]	503 Samurott [TM]	551 Sandile [TM]	027 Sandshrew [TM]	028 Sandslash [TM]	539 Sawk [TM]
		586 Sawsbuck [TM]	254 Sceptile [TM]	212 Scizor [TM]	545 Scolipede [TM]	560 Scrafty [TM]	559 Scraggy [TM]	123 Scyther [TM]
		117 Seadra [TM]	119 Seaking [TM]	364 Sealeo [TM]	273 Seedot [TM]	086 Seel [TM]	537 Seismitoad [TM]	161 Sentret [TM]
		497 Serperior [TM]	496 Servine [TM]	336 Seviper [TM]	540 Sewaddle [TM]	319 Sharpedo [TM]	492 Shaymin (Land) [TM]	492 Shaymin (Sky) [TM]
		292 Shedinja [TM]	372 Shelgon [TM]	090 Shellder [TM]	422 Shellos [TM]	616 Shelmet [TM]	410 Shieldon [TM]	275 Shiftry [TM]
		403 Shinx [TM]	285 Shroomish [TM]	213 Shuckle [TM]	353 Shuppet [TM]	561 Sigilyph [TM]	516 Simipour [TM]	512 Simisage [TM]
		514 Simisear [TM]	227 Skarmory [TM]	672 Skiddo [TM]	188 Skiploom [TM]	300 Skitty [TM]	451 Skorupi [TM]	690 Skrelp [TM]
		435 Skuntank [TM]	289 Slaking [TM]	287 Slakoth [TM]	705 Sliggoo [TM]	080 Slowbro [TM]	199 Slowking [TM]	079 Slowpoke [TM]
		218 Slugma [TM]	685 Slurpuff [TM]	238 Smoochum [TM]	215 Sneasel [TM]	495 Snivy [TM]	143 Snorlax [TM]	361 Snorunt [TM]
		459 Snover [TM]	209 Snubbull [TM]	577 Solosis [TM, E]	338 Solrock [TM]	021 Spearow [TM]	363 Spheal [TM]	167 Spinarak [TM]
		327 Spinda [TM]	442 Spiritomb [TM]	325 Spoink [TM]	682 Spritzee [TM]	007 Squirtle [TM]	234 Stantler [TM]	398 Staraptor [TM]
		397 Staravia [TM]	396 Starly [TM]	121 Starmie [TM]	120 Staryu [TM]	208 Steelix [TM]	508 Stoutland [TM]	618 Stunfisk [TM]
		434 Stunky [TM]	185 Sudowoodo [TM]	245 Suicune [TM]	192 Sunflora [TM]	191 Sunkern [TM]	283 Surskit [TM]	333 Swablu [TM]
		541 Swadloon [TM]	317 Swalot [TM]	260 Swampert [TM]	581 Swanna [TM]	277 Swellow [TM]	220 Swinub [TM]	684 Swirlix [TM]
		528 Swoobat [TM]	700 Sylveon [TM]	276 Taillow [TM]	663 Talonflame [TM]	114 Tangela [TM]	465 Tangrowth [TM]	128 Tauros [TM]
		216 Teddiursa [TM]	072 Tentacool [TM]	073 Tentacruel [TM]	498 Tepig [TM]	639 Terrakion [TM]	538 Throh [TM]	642 Thundurus [TM]
		532 Timburr [TM]	564 Tirtouga [TM]	468 Togekiss [TM]	175 Togepi [TM, E]	176 Togetic [TM]	255 Torchic [TM]	324 Torkoal [TM]
		641 Tornadus [TM]	389 Torterra [TM]	158 Totodile [TM]	454 Toxicroak [TM]	520 Tranquill [TM]	328 Trapinch [TM]	252 Treecko [TM]
		709 Trevenant [TM]	357 Tropius [TM]	568 Trubbish [TM]	387 Turtwig [TM]	535 Tympole [TM]	157 Typhlosion [TM]	248 Tyranitar [TM]
		697 Tyrantrum [TM]	236 Tyrogue [TM]	696 Tyrunt [TM]	197 Umbreon [TM]	521 Unfezant [TM]	217 Ursaring [TM]	480 Uxie [TM]
		583 Vanillish [TM]	582 Vanillite [TM]	584 Vanilluxe [TM]	134 Vaporeon [TM]	543 Venipede [TM]	049 Venomoth [TM]	048 Venonat [TM, E]
		003 Venusaur [TM]	416 Vespiquen [TM]	329 Vibrava [TM]	494 Victini [TM]	071 Victreebel [TM]	288 Vigoroth [TM]	045 Vileplume [TM]
		640 Virizion [TM]	666 Vivillon [TM]	313 Volbeat [TM]	637 Volcarona [TM]	100 Voltorb [TM]	629 Vullaby [TM]	037 Vulpix [TM, E]
		320 Wailmer [TM]	321 Wailord [TM]	365 Walrein [TM]	008 Wartortle [TM]	505 Watchog [TM]	461 Weavile [TM]	070 Weepinbell [TM]
		110 Weezing [TM]	547 Whimsicott [TM]	544 Whirlipede [TM]	340 Whiscash [TM]	293 Whismur [TM]	040 Wigglytuff [TM]	278 Wingull [TM]
		527 Woobat [TM]	194 Wooper [TM]	413 Wormadam (Plant) [TM]	413 Wormadam (Sand) [TM]	413 Wormadam (Trash) [TM]	178 Xatu [TM]	716 Xerneas [TM]
		562 Yamask [TM]	193 Yanma [TM, E]	469 Yanmega [TM]	717 Yveltal [TM]	335 Zangoose [TM]	145 Zapdos [TM]	523 Zebstrika [TM]
		644 Zekrom [TM]	263 Zigzagoon [TM]	571 Zoroark [TM]	570 Zorua [TM]	041 Zubat [TM]	634 Zweilous [TM]	718 Zygarde [TM]
Fighting	Secret Sword	647 Keldeo [T]						
Grass	Seed Bomb	460 Abomasnow [BP]	190 Aipom [BP]	424 Ambipom [BP]	591 Amoonguss [BP]	024 Arbok [BP]	153 Bayleef [BP]	182 Bellossom [BP]
		069 Bellsprout [BP]	286 Breloom [44, BP]	406 Budew [BP, E]	001 Bulbasaur [37, BP]	331 Cacnea [BP, E]	332 Cacturne [BP]	455 Carnivine [BP]
		251 Celebi [BP]	421 Cherrim [BP]	420 Cherubi [BP, E]	652 Chesnaught [35, BP]	650 Chespin [32, BP]	152 Chikorita [BP]	573 Cinccino [BP]
		546 Cottonee [BP]	346 Cradily [BP]	585 Deerling [BP]	225 Delibird [BP]	232 Donphan [BP]	023 Ekans [BP]	102 Exeggcute [BP]
		103 Exeggutor [1, BP]	597 Ferroseed [BP, E]	598 Ferrothorn [BP]	669 Flabébé [BP]	670 Floette [BP]	671 Florges [BP]	590 Foongus [BP]
		569 Garbodor [BP]	044 Gloom [BP]	673 Gogoat [30, BP]	711 Gourgeist [48, BP]	388 Grotle [BP]	253 Grovyle [BP]	316 Gulpin [BP]
		187 Hoppip [BP, E]	002 Ivysaur [BP]	189 Jumpluff [BP]	470 Leafeon [BP]	542 Leavanny [BP]	510 Liepard [BP]	345 Lileep [BP]
		549 Lilligant [BP]	264 Linoone [BP]	271 Lombre [BP]	270 Lotad [BP]	272 Ludicolo [BP]	056 Mankey [BP]	226 Mantine [BP]
		556 Maractus [BP, E]	154 Meganium [BP]	052 Meowth [BP]	151 Mew [BP]	572 Minccino [BP]	446 Munchlax [BP]	274 Nuzleaf [BP]
		224 Octillery [BP]	043 Oddish [BP]	417 Pachirisu [BP]	511 Pansage [22, BP]	046 Paras [BP]	047 Parasect [BP]	504 Patrat [BP]
		279 Pelipper [BP]	053 Persian [BP]	548 Petilil [BP]	231 Phanpy [BP]	708 Phantump [BP]	057 Primeape [BP]	710 Pumpkaboo [48, BP]
		509 Purrloin [BP]	651 Quilladin [35, BP]	223 Remoraid [BP]	315 Roselia [BP, E]	407 Roserade [BP]	586 Sawsbuck [BP]	254 Sceptile [BP]
		273 Seedot [BP]	497 Serperior [BP]	496 Servine [BP]	540 Sewaddle [BP]	492 Shaymin (Land) [BP]	492 Shaymin (Sky) [BP]	275 Shiftry [BP]
		285 Shroomish [36, BP, E]	512 Simisage [1, BP]	672 Skiddo [30, BP]	188 Skiploom [BP]	495 Snivy [BP]	143 Snorlax [BP]	459 Snover [BP, E]
		192 Sunflora [BP]	191 Sunkern [43, BP]	541 Swadloon [BP]	317 Swalot [BP]	114 Tangela [BP]	465 Tangrowth [BP]	216 Teddiursa [BP]
		389 Torterra [BP]	252 Treecko [BP]	709 Trevenant [BP]	357 Tropius [BP]	568 Trubbish [BP]	387 Turtwig [BP, E]	217 Ursaring [BP]
		003 Venusaur [BP]	071 Victreebel [BP]	045 Vileplume [BP]	640 Virizion [BP]	505 Watchog [BP]	070 Weepinbell [BP]	547 Whimsicott [BP]
		413 Wormadam (Plant) [BP]	263 Zigzagoon [BP]					
	Seed Flare	492 Shaymin (Land) [100]	492 Shaymin (Sky) [100]					
Fighting	Seismic Toss	493 Arceus [1]	113 Chansey [E]	297 Hariyama [34]	214 Heracross [E]	068 Machamp [15]	067 Machoke [15]	066 Machop [15]
		296 Makuhita [31]	056 Mankey [17]	303 Mawile [E]	241 Miltank [E]	127 Pinsir [8]	057 Primeape [17]	216 Teddiursa [E]
		538 Throh [13]	313 Volbeat [E]					
Normal	Self-Destruct	343 Baltoy [28]	438 Bonsly [E]	344 Claydol [28]	101 Electrode [26]	597 Ferroseed [38]	598 Ferrothorn [38]	205 Forretress [1]
		649 Genesect [77]	074 Geodude [24]	076 Golem [24]	075 Graveler [24]	109 Koffing [23]	446 Munchlax [E]	204 Pineco [6]
		185 Sudowoodo [E]	568 Trubbish [E]	100 Voltorb [26]	110 Weezing [23]			
Ghost	Shadow Ball (TM30)	460 Abomasnow [TM]	063 Abra [TM]	359 Absol [TM]	681 Aegislash [TM]	190 Aipom [TM]	065 Alakazam [TM]	594 Alomomola [TM]
		424 Ambipom [TM]	493 Arceus [TM]	531 Audino [TM]	482 Azelf [TM]	343 Baltoy [TM]	354 Banette [30, TM]	267 Beautifly [TM]
		606 Beheeyem [TM]	400 Bibarel [TM]	399 Bidoof [TM]	242 Blissey [TM]	437 Bronzong [TM]	436 Bronzor [TM]	406 Budew [TM]
		427 Buneary [TM]	012 Butterfree [TM]	351 Castform [TM]	251 Celebi [TM]	609 Chandelure [TM]	113 Chansey [TM]	358 Chimecho [TM]
		433 Chingling [TM]	693 Clawitzer [TM]	344 Claydol [TM]	036 Clefable [TM]	035 Clefairy [TM]	173 Cleffa [TM]	563 Cofagrigus [39, TM]
		222 Corsola [TM]	488 Cresselia [TM]	453 Croagunk [TM]	169 Crobat [TM]	491 Darkrai [TM]	585 Deerling [TM]	301 Delcatty [TM]

Type	Move	Pokémon that can learn it						
Ghost	Shadow Ball (TM30)	655 Delphox [1, TM]	386 Deoxys (Atk) [TM]	386 Deoxys (Def) [TM]	386 Deoxys (Nor) [TM]	386 Deoxys (Spd) [TM]	691 Dragalge [TM]	452 Drapion [TM]
		426 Drifblim [40, TM]	425 Drifloon [36, TM]	096 Drowzee [TM]	206 Dunsparce [TM]	578 Duosion [TM]	356 Dusclops [45, TM]	477 Dusknoir [45, TM]
		355 Duskull [41, TM]	269 Dustox [TM]	133 Eevee [TM]	605 Elgyem [TM]	244 Entei [TM]	196 Espeon [TM]	295 Exploud [TM]
		136 Flareon [TM]	592 Frillish [TM]	478 Froslass [42, TM]	162 Furret [TM]	475 Gallade [TM]	282 Gardevoir [TM]	092 Gastly [29, TM]
		094 Gengar [33, TM]	203 Girafarig [TM]	487 Giratina (Alt) [TM]	487 Giratina (Ori) [TM]	471 Glaceon [TM]	362 Glalie [TM]	431 Glameow [TM]
		042 Golbat [TM]	622 Golett [TM]	623 Golurk [TM]	368 Gorebyss [TM]	574 Gothita [TM]	576 Gothitelle [TM]	575 Gothorita [TM]
		711 Gourgeist [36, 70, TM]	210 Granbull [TM]	088 Grimer [TM]	326 Grumpig [TM]	316 Gulpin [TM]	440 Happiny [TM]	093 Haunter [33, TM]
		507 Herdier [TM]	430 Honchkrow [TM]	250 Ho-Oh [TM]	163 Hoothoot [TM]	229 Houndoom [TM]	228 Houndour [TM]	097 Hypno [TM]
		174 Igglybuff [TM]	314 Illumise [TM]	593 Jellicent [TM]	039 Jigglypuff [TM]	385 Jirachi [TM]	135 Jolteon [TM]	124 Jynx [TM]
		064 Kadabra [TM]	115 Kangaskhan [TM]	352 Kecleon [TM]	281 Kirlia [TM]	109 Koffing [TM]	646 Kyurem (Blk) [TM]	646 Kyurem (Wht) [TM]
		646 Kyurem [TM]	608 Lampent [53, TM]	380 Latias [TM]	381 Latios [TM]	470 Leafeon [TM]	463 Lickilicky [TM]	108 Lickitung [TM]
		510 Liepard [TM]	506 Lillipup [TM]	264 Linoone [TM]	607 Litwick [49, TM]	428 Lopunny [TM]	294 Loudred [TM]	448 Lucario [TM]
		249 Lugia [TM]	337 Lunatone [TM]	490 Manaphy [TM]	630 Mandibuzz [TM]	284 Masquerain [TM]	303 Mawile [TM]	308 Medicham [TM]
		307 Meditite [TM]	648 Meloetta [TM]	678 Meowstic (F) [31, TM]	678 Meowstic (M) [TM]	052 Meowth [TM]	481 Mesprit [TM]	376 Metagross [TM]
		375 Metang [TM]	151 Mew [TM]	150 Mewtwo [TM]	262 Mightyena [TM]	241 Miltank [TM]	439 Mime Jr. [TM]	200 Misdreavus [41, TM]
		429 Mismagius [TM]	414 Mothim [TM]	122 Mr. Mime [TM]	089 Muk [TM]	446 Munchlax [TM]	517 Munna [TM]	198 Murkrow [TM]
		518 Musharna [TM]	177 Natu [TM]	034 Nidoking [TM]	031 Nidoqueen [TM]	290 Nincada [TM]	291 Ninjask [TM]	164 Noctowl [TM]
		714 Noibat [TM]	715 Noivern [TM]	274 Nuzleaf [TM]	504 Patrat [TM]	053 Persian [TM]	708 Phantump [TM]	261 Poochyena [TM]
		137 Porygon [TM]	233 Porygon2 [TM]	474 Porygon-Z [TM]	710 Pumpkaboo [36, TM]	509 Purrloin [TM]	432 Purugly [TM]	211 Qwilfish [TM]
		243 Raikou [TM]	280 Ralts [TM]	020 Raticate [TM]	019 Rattata [TM]	643 Reshiram [TM]	579 Reuniclus [TM]	315 Roselia [TM]
		407 Roserade [TM]	479 Rotom (Fan) [TM]	479 Rotom (Frost) [TM]	479 Rotom (Heat) [TM]	479 Rotom (Mow) [TM]	479 Rotom (Wash) [TM]	479 Rotom [TM]
		302 Sableye [39, TM]	586 Sawsbuck [TM]	273 Seedot [TM]	161 Sentret [TM]	292 Shedinja [33, TM]	275 Shiftry [TM]	353 Shuppet [30, TM]
		561 Sigilyph [TM]	300 Skitty [TM]	451 Skorupi [TM]	690 Skrelp [TM]	435 Skuntank [TM]	289 Slaking [TM]	287 Slakoth [TM]
		080 Slowbro [TM]	199 Slowking [TM]	079 Slowpoke [TM]	238 Smoochum [TM]	215 Sneasel [TM]	143 Snorlax [TM]	361 Snorunt [TM]
		459 Snover [TM]	209 Snubbull [TM]	577 Solosis [TM]	338 Solrock [TM]	327 Spinda [TM]	442 Spiritomb [TM]	325 Spoink [TM]
		234 Stantler [TM]	508 Stoutland [TM]	434 Stunky [TM]	245 Suicune [TM]	283 Surskit [TM]	317 Swalot [TM]	528 Swoobat [TM]
		700 Sylveon [TM]	468 Togekiss [TM]	175 Togepi [TM]	176 Togetic [TM]	454 Toxicroak [TM]	709 Trevenant [TM]	197 Umbreon [TM]
		480 Uxie [TM]	134 Vaporeon [TM]	494 Victini [TM]	288 Vigoroth [TM]	313 Volbeat [TM]	629 Vullaby [TM]	505 Watchog [TM]
		461 Weavile [TM]	110 Weezing [TM]	547 Whimsicott [TM]	293 Whismur [TM]	040 Wigglytuff [TM]	527 Woobat [TM]	413 Wormadam (Plant) [TM]
		413 Wormadam (Sand) [TM]	413 Wormadam (Trash) [TM]	178 Xatu [TM]	562 Yamask [37, TM]	193 Yanma [TM]	469 Yanmega [TM]	717 Yveltal [TM]
		335 Zangoose [TM]	644 Zekrom [TM]	263 Zigzagoon [TM]	571 Zoroark [TM]	570 Zorua [TM]	041 Zubat [TM]	
	Shadow Claw (TM65)	359 Absol [TM]	681 Aegislash [TM]	306 Aggron [TM]	190 Aipom [TM]	424 Ambipom [TM]	493 Arceus [TM]	566 Archen [TM]
		567 Archeops [TM]	304 Aron [TM]	371 Bagon [TM]	354 Banette [TM]	689 Barbaracle [TM]	614 Beartic [TM]	688 Binacle [TM]
		625 Bisharp [TM]	257 Blaziken [TM]	628 Braviary [TM]	006 Charizard [1, TM]	004 Charmander [TM]	005 Charmeleon [TM]	652 Chesnaught [TM]
		650 Chespin [TM]	390 Chimchar [TM]	256 Combusken [TM]	159 Croconaw [TM]	558 Crustle [TM]	613 Cubchoo [TM]	491 Darkrai [TM]
		483 Dialga [TM]	050 Diglett [TM]	680 Doublade [TM]	529 Drilbur [TM]	621 Druddigon [TM]	051 Dugtrio [TM]	632 Durant [TM]
		557 Dwebble [TM]	395 Empoleon [TM]	530 Excadrill [TM]	160 Feraligatr [TM]	598 Ferrothorn [TM]	611 Fraxure [TM]	162 Furret [TM]
		444 Gabite [TM]	445 Garchomp [TM]	649 Genesect [TM]	094 Gengar [TM]	443 Gible [TM]	487 Giratina (Alt) [42, TM]	487 Giratina (Ori) [42, TM]
		431 Glameow [TM]	055 Golduck [TM]	383 Groudon [TM]	093 Haunter [TM]	612 Haxorus [TM]	631 Heatmor [TM]	214 Heracross [TM]
		679 Honedge [TM]	392 Infernape [TM]	115 Kangaskhan [TM]	352 Kecleon [33, TM]	552 Krokorok [TM]	553 Krookodile [TM]	646 Kyurem (Blk) [TM]
		646 Kyurem (Wht) [TM]	646 Kyurem [TM]	305 Lairon [TM]	380 Latias [TM]	381 Latios [TM]	542 Leavanny [TM]	510 Liepard [TM]
		264 Linoone [TM]	448 Lucario [TM]	648 Meloetta [TM]	052 Meowth [TM]	151 Mew [TM]	391 Monferno [TM]	034 Nidoking [TM]
		031 Nidoqueen [TM]	029 Nidoran ♀ [TM]	032 Nidoran ♂ [TM]	030 Nidorina [TM]	033 Nidorino [TM]	714 Noibat [TM]	715 Noivern [TM]
		484 Palkia [TM]	674 Pancham [TM]	675 Pangoro [TM]	515 Panpour [TM]	511 Pansage [TM]	513 Pansear [TM]	624 Pawniard [TM]
		053 Persian [TM]	708 Phantump [TM]	394 Prinplup [TM]	054 Psyduck [TM]	509 Purrloin [TM]	432 Purugly [TM]	651 Quilladin [TM]
		384 Rayquaza [TM]	379 Registeel [TM]	643 Reshiram [TM]	112 Rhydon [TM]	464 Rhyperior [TM]	447 Riolu [TM]	627 Rufflet [TM]
		302 Sableye [29, TM]	373 Salamence [TM]	027 Sandshrew [TM]	028 Sandslash [TM]	161 Sentret [TM]	292 Shedinja [TM]	372 Shelgon [TM]
		516 Simipour [TM]	512 Simisage [TM]	514 Simisear [TM]	435 Skuntank [TM]	289 Slaking [TM]	287 Slakoth [TM]	215 Sneasel [TM]
		434 Stunky [TM]	216 Teddiursa [TM]	255 Torchic [TM]	158 Totodile [TM]	709 Trevenant [55, TM]	157 Typhlosion [TM]	248 Tyranitar [TM]
		217 Ursaring [TM]	288 Vigoroth [TM]	461 Weavile [TM]	717 Yveltal [TM]	335 Zangoose [TM]	644 Zekrom [TM]	571 Zoroark [TM]
	Shadow Force	487 Giratina (Alt) [46]	487 Giratina (Ori) [46]					
	Shadow Punch	356 Dusclops [37]	477 Dusknoir [37]	094 Gengar [25]	622 Golett [13]	623 Golurk [13]	088 Grimer [E]	093 Haunter [25]
	Shadow Sneak	681 Aegislash [1]	168 Ariados [19]	354 Banette [13]	680 Doublade [20]	356 Dusclops [17]	477 Dusknoir [17]	355 Duskull [17]
		487 Giratina (Alt) [19]	487 Giratina (Ori) [19]	711 Gourgeist [30]	658 Greninja [23]	088 Grimer [E]	679 Honedge [20, E]	352 Kecleon [7]
		200 Misdreavus [E]	710 Pumpkaboo [30]	280 Ralts [E]	302 Sableye [16]	292 Shedinja [21]	353 Shuppet [13, E]	167 Spinarak [19]
		442 Spiritomb [1, E]						
Normal	Sharpen	713 Avalugg [20]	712 Bergmite [20]	703 Carbink [8]	615 Cryogonal [9]	719 Diancie [8]	137 Porygon [1]	
Ice	Sheer Cold	460 Abomasnow [58]	144 Articuno [1, 78]	614 Beartic [1, 66]	615 Cryogonal [1, 61]	613 Cubchoo [57]	087 Dewgong [34]	362 Glalie [1, 61]
		382 Kyogre [65]	131 Lapras [50]	364 Sealeo [52]	459 Snover [46]	363 Spheal [46]	583 Vanillish [58]	582 Vanillite [53]
		584 Vanilluxe [1, 67]	365 Walrein [60]					

	Move	Pokémon that can learn it						
Normal	Shell Smash	689 Barbaracle [1]	688 Binacle [1]	565 Carracosta [40]	366 Clamperl [50]	091 Cloyster [1]	558 Crustle [1, 43]	557 Dwebble [37]
		219 Magcargo [38]	138 Omanyte [50]	139 Omastar [67]	090 Shellder [56]	213 Shuckle [34]	564 Tirtouga [38]	324 Torkoal [47]
Steel	Shift Gear	600 Klang [52]	599 Klink [48]	601 Klinklang [54]				
Electric	Shock Wave	063 Abra [BP]	359 Absol [BP]	681 Aegislash [BP]	306 Aggron [BP]	190 Aipom [BP]	065 Alakazam [BP]	424 Ambipom [BP]
		181 Ampharos [BP]	493 Arceus [BP]	304 Aron [BP]	610 Axew [BP]	482 Azelf [BP]	354 Banette [BP]	411 Bastiodon [BP]
		606 Beheeyem [BP]	400 Bibarel [BP]	399 Bidoof [BP]	242 Blissey [BP]	522 Blitzle [11, BP, E]	654 Braixen [BP]	427 Buneary [BP]
		351 Castform [BP]	251 Celebi [BP]	609 Chandelure [BP]	113 Chansey [BP]	358 Chimecho [BP]	170 Chinchou [BP, E]	433 Chingling [BP]
		573 Cinccino [BP]	036 Clefable [BP]	035 Clefairy [BP]	173 Cleffa [BP]	563 Cofagrigus [BP]	408 Cranidos [BP]	491 Darkrai [BP]
		702 Dedenne [BP]	633 Deino [BP]	301 Delcatty [BP]	655 Delphox [BP]	386 Deoxys (Atk) [BP]	386 Deoxys (Def) [BP]	386 Deoxys (Nor) [BP]
		386 Deoxys (Spd) [BP]	483 Dialga [BP]	680 Doublade [BP]	691 Dragalge [BP]	148 Dragonair [BP]	149 Dragonite [BP]	147 Dratini [BP]
		426 Drifblim [BP]	425 Drifloon [BP]	621 Druddigon [BP]	206 Dunsparce [BP]	578 Duosion [BP]	603 Eelektrik [BP]	604 Eelektross [BP]
		125 Electabuzz [15, BP]	466 Electivire [15, BP]	309 Electrike [BP, E]	101 Electrode [BP]	239 Elekid [15, BP]	605 Elgyem [BP]	587 Emolga [22, BP, E]
		677 Espurr [BP]	295 Exploud [BP]	180 Flaaffy [BP]	611 Fraxure [BP]	592 Frillish [BP]	478 Froslass [BP]	162 Furret [BP]
		475 Gallade [BP]	596 Galvantula [BP]	282 Gardevoir [BP]	649 Genesect [BP]	203 Girafarig [BP]	487 Giratina (Alt) [BP]	487 Giratina (Ori) [BP]
		431 Glameow [BP]	622 Golett [BP]	623 Golurk [BP]	706 Goodra [BP]	704 Goomy [BP]	574 Gothita [BP]	576 Gothitelle [BP]
		575 Gothorita [BP]	210 Granbull [BP]	088 Grimer [BP]	383 Groudon [BP]	326 Grumpig [BP]	316 Gulpin [BP]	440 Happiny [BP]
		612 Haxorus [BP]	695 Heliolisk [BP]	694 Helioptile [BP]	507 Herdier [BP]	679 Honedge [BP]	250 Ho-Oh [BP]	635 Hydreigon [BP]
		174 Igglybuff [BP]	314 Illumise [BP]	593 Jellicent [BP]	039 Jigglypuff [BP]	385 Jirachi [BP]	135 Jolteon [BP]	595 Joltik [BP]
		064 Kadabra [BP]	115 Kangaskhan [BP]	352 Kecleon [BP]	281 Kirlia [BP]	600 Klang [BP]	599 Klink [BP]	601 Klinklang [BP]
		109 Koffing [BP]	382 Kyogre [BP]	305 Lairon [BP]	608 Lampent [BP]	171 Lanturn [BP]	131 Lapras [BP]	380 Latias [BP]
		381 Latios [BP]	463 Lickilicky [BP]	108 Lickitung [BP]	506 Lillipup [BP]	264 Linoone [BP]	607 Litwick [BP]	428 Lopunny [BP]
		294 Loudred [BP]	249 Lugia [BP]	404 Luxio [BP]	405 Luxray [BP]	081 Magnemite [BP]	082 Magneton [BP]	462 Magnezone [BP]
		310 Manectric [BP]	179 Mareep [BP]	648 Meloetta [BP]	678 Meowstic (F) [BP]	678 Meowstic (M) [BP]	052 Meowth [BP]	481 Mesprit [BP]
		151 Mew [BP]	150 Mewtwo [BP]	241 Miltank [BP]	439 Mime Jr. [BP]	572 Minccino [BP]	312 Minun [BP]	200 Misdreavus [BP]
		429 Mismagius [BP]	122 Mr. Mime [BP]	089 Muk [BP]	446 Munchlax [BP]	517 Munna [BP]	518 Musharna [BP]	034 Nidoking [BP]
		031 Nidoqueen [BP]	029 Nidoran ♀ [BP]	032 Nidoran ♂ [BP]	030 Nidorina [BP]	033 Nidorino [BP]	299 Nosepass [BP]	417 Pachirisu [BP]
		484 Palkia [BP]	504 Patrat [BP]	279 Pelipper [BP]	053 Persian [BP]	172 Pichu [BP]	025 Pikachu [BP]	311 Plusle [BP]
		137 Porygon [BP]	233 Porygon2 [BP]	474 Porygon-Z [BP]	476 Probopass [BP]	432 Purugly [BP]	211 Qwilfish [BP]	026 Raichu [BP]
		243 Raikou [BP]	280 Ralts [BP]	409 Rampardos [BP]	020 Raticate [BP]	019 Rattata [BP]	384 Rayquaza [BP]	378 Regice [BP]
		486 Regigigas [BP]	377 Regirock [BP]	379 Registeel [BP]	579 Reuniclus [BP]	112 Rhydon [BP]	111 Rhyhorn [BP]	464 Rhyperior [BP]
		479 Rotom (Fan) [22, BP]	479 Rotom (Frost) [22, BP]	479 Rotom (Heat) [22, BP]	479 Rotom (Mow) [22, BP]	479 Rotom (Wash) [22, BP]	479 Rotom [22, BP]	302 Sableye [BP]
		161 Sentret [BP]	410 Shieldon [BP]	403 Shinx [BP, E]	353 Shuppet [BP]	561 Sigilyph [BP]	300 Skitty [BP]	690 Skrelp [BP]
		289 Slaking [BP]	287 Slakoth [BP]	705 Sliggoo [BP]	143 Snorlax [BP]	209 Snubbull [BP]	577 Solosis [BP]	327 Spinda [BP]
		442 Spiritomb [BP]	325 Spoink [BP]	234 Stantler [BP]	508 Stoutland [BP]	618 Stunfisk [BP, E]	317 Swalot [BP]	528 Swoobat [BP]
		114 Tangela [BP]	465 Tangrowth [BP]	128 Tauros [BP]	642 Thundurus [25, BP]	468 Togekiss [BP]	175 Togepi [BP]	176 Togetic [BP]
		248 Tyranitar [BP]	480 Uxie [BP]	494 Victini [BP]	288 Vigoroth [BP]	313 Volbeat [BP]	100 Voltorb [BP]	505 Watchog [BP]
		110 Weezing [BP]	293 Whismur [BP]	040 Wigglytuff [BP]	278 Wingull [BP]	527 Woobat [BP]	562 Yamask [BP]	335 Zangoose [BP]
		145 Zapdos [BP]	523 Zebstrika [11, BP]	644 Zekrom [BP]	263 Zigzagoon [BP]	634 Zweilous [BP]	718 Zygarde [BP]	
Bug	Signal Beam	063 Abra [BP]	617 Accelgor [BP]	065 Alakazam [BP]	181 Ampharos [51, BP]	493 Arceus [BP]	168 Ariados [BP]	144 Articuno [BP]
		531 Audino [BP]	482 Azelf [BP]	343 Baltoy [BP]	267 Beautifly [BP]	606 Beheeyem [BP]	009 Blastoise [BP]	522 Blitzle [BP]
		437 Bronzong [BP]	436 Bronzor [BP]	012 Butterfree [BP]	251 Celebi [BP]	358 Chimecho [BP]	170 Chinchou [28, BP]	433 Chingling [BP]
		344 Claydol [BP]	036 Clefable [BP]	035 Clefairy [BP]	173 Cleffa [BP]	091 Cloyster [BP]	488 Cresselia [BP]	615 Cryogonal [BP]
		702 Dedenne [BP]	225 Delibird [BP]	655 Delphox [BP]	386 Deoxys (Atk) [BP]	386 Deoxys (Def) [BP]	386 Deoxys (Nor) [BP]	386 Deoxys (Spd) [BP]
		087 Dewgong [1, 7, BP]	096 Drowzee [BP]	578 Duosion [BP]	269 Dustox [BP]	603 Eelektrik [BP]	604 Eelektross [BP]	125 Electabuzz [BP]
		466 Electivire [BP]	309 Electrike [BP]	101 Electrode [BP]	239 Elekid [BP]	605 Elgyem [BP]	587 Emolga [BP]	395 Empoleon [BP]
		589 Escavalier [BP]	196 Espeon [BP]	677 Espurr [BP]	456 Finneon [BP, E]	180 Flaaffy [47, BP]	330 Flygon [BP]	205 Forretress [BP]
		478 Froslass [BP]	475 Gallade [BP]	596 Galvantula [34, BP]	282 Gardevoir [BP]	649 Genesect [40, BP]	203 Girafarig [BP]	471 Glaceon [BP]
		362 Glalie [BP]	118 Goldeen [BP, E]	055 Golduck [BP]	622 Golett [BP]	623 Golurk [BP]	368 Gorebyss [BP]	574 Gothita [BP]
		576 Gothitelle [BP]	575 Gothorita [BP]	326 Grumpig [BP]	695 Heliolisk [BP]	694 Helioptile [BP]	250 Ho-Oh [BP]	116 Horsea [BP, E]
		635 Hydreigon [BP]	097 Hypno [BP]	385 Jirachi [BP]	135 Jolteon [BP]	595 Joltik [34, BP]	124 Jynx [BP]	064 Kadabra [BP]
		588 Karrablast [BP]	230 Kingdra [BP]	281 Kirlia [BP]	600 Klang [BP]	599 Klink [BP]	601 Klinklang [BP]	382 Kyogre [BP]
		646 Kyurem (Blk) [BP]	646 Kyurem (Wht) [BP]	646 Kyurem [BP]	171 Lanturn [29, BP]	131 Lapras [BP]	636 Larvesta [BP]	542 Leavanny [BP]
		249 Lugia [BP]	457 Lumineon [BP]	337 Lunatone [BP]	404 Luxio [BP]	405 Luxray [BP]	081 Magnemite [BP]	082 Magneton [BP]
		462 Magnezone [BP]	687 Malamar [BP]	490 Manaphy [BP]	310 Manectric [BP]	226 Mantine [1, BP]	458 Mantyke [BP, E]	179 Mareep [39, BP]
		284 Masquerain [BP]	308 Medicham [BP]	307 Meditite [BP]	648 Meloetta [BP]	678 Meowstic (F) [45, BP]	678 Meowstic (M) [BP]	481 Mesprit [BP]
		376 Metagross [BP]	375 Metang [BP]	151 Mew [BP]	150 Mewtwo [BP]	439 Mime Jr. [BP]	312 Minun [BP]	414 Mothim [BP]
		122 Mr. Mime [BP]	517 Munna [BP]	518 Musharna [BP]	177 Natu [BP]	224 Octillery [34, BP]	489 Phione [BP]	172 Pichu [BP]
		025 Pikachu [BP]	393 Piplup [BP]	311 Plusle [BP]	137 Porygon [29, BP]	233 Porygon2 [29, BP]	474 Porygon-Z [29, BP]	394 Prinplup [BP]
		054 Psyduck [BP]	211 Qwilfish [BP, E]	026 Raichu [BP]	243 Raikou [BP]	280 Ralts [BP]	378 Regice [BP]	223 Remoraid [30, BP]
		579 Reuniclus [BP]	479 Rotom (Fan) [BP]	479 Rotom (Frost) [BP]	479 Rotom (Heat) [BP]	479 Rotom (Mow) [BP]	479 Rotom (Wash) [BP]	479 Rotom [BP]
		302 Sableye [BP]	545 Scolipede [BP]	117 Seadra [BP]	119 Seaking [BP]	364 Sealeo [BP]	086 Seel [BP, E]	540 Sewaddle [BP]
		616 Shelmet [BP]	403 Shinx [BP, E]	561 Sigilyph [BP]	080 Slowbro [BP]	199 Slowking [BP]	079 Slowpoke [BP]	238 Smoochum [BP]
		577 Solosis [BP]	338 Solrock [BP]	363 Spheal [BP, E]	167 Spinarak [BP, E]	325 Spoink [BP]	234 Stantler [BP]	121 Starmie [BP]
		120 Staryu [BP]	245 Suicune [BP]	283 Surskit [BP, E]	541 Swadloon [BP]	528 Swoobat [BP]	468 Togekiss [BP]	175 Togepi [BP]

Type	Move	Pokémon that can learn it						
Bug	Signal Beam	176 Togetic [BP]	328 Trapinch [BP, E]	480 Uxie [BP]	583 Vanillish [BP]	582 Vanillite [BP]	584 Vanilluxe [BP]	134 Vaporeon [BP]
		543 Venipede [BP]	049 Venomoth [37, BP]	048 Venonat [35, BP, E]	416 Vespiquen [BP]	329 Vibrava [BP]	494 Victini [BP]	666 Vivillon [BP]
		313 Volbeat [26, BP]	637 Volcarona [BP]	100 Voltorb [BP]	365 Walrein [BP]	505 Watchog [BP]	544 Whirlipede [BP]	527 Woobat [BP]
		413 Wormadam (Plant) [BP]	413 Wormadam (Sand) [BP]	413 Wormadam (Trash) [BP]	178 Xatu [BP]	193 Yanma [BP, E]	469 Yanmega [BP]	145 Zapdos [BP]
		523 Zebstrika [BP]	644 Zekrom [BP]					
	Silver Wind	267 Beautifly [25]	012 Butterfree [28]	269 Dustox [25]	456 Finneon [49]	314 Illumise [E]	166 Ledian [29]	165 Ledyba [25, E]
		457 Lumineon [59]	284 Masquerain [32]	414 Mothim [38]	290 Nincada [E]	123 Scyther [E]	540 Sewaddle [E]	049 Venomoth [1]
		313 Volbeat [E]	637 Volcarona [50]	193 Yanma [E]				
Normal	Simple Beam	531 Audino [45]	606 Beheeyem [29]	605 Elgyem [29]	083 Farfetch'd [E]	649 Genesect [62]	686 Inkay [E]	177 Natu [E]
		054 Psyduck [E]	300 Skitty [E]	325 Spoink [E]	263 Zigzagoon [E]			
	Sing	334 Altaria [1, 5]	298 Azurill [E]	242 Blissey [31]	113 Chansey [31]	441 Chatot [13]	573 Cinccino [1]	036 Clefable [1]
		035 Clefairy [7]	173 Cleffa [7]	301 Delcatty [1]	174 Igglybuff [1]	039 Jigglypuff [1]	402 Kricketune [18]	131 Lapras [1]
		648 Meloetta [16]	572 Minccino [21]	312 Minun [E]	311 Plusle [E]	300 Skitty [7]	238 Smoochum [18]	333 Swablu [5]
		040 Wigglytuff [1]						
	Sketch	235 Smeargle [1, 11, 21, 31, 41, 51, 61, 71, 81, 91]						
Psychic	Skill Swap	063 Abra [BP, E]	065 Alakazam [BP]	683 Aromatisse [44, BP]	531 Audino [BP]	482 Azelf [BP]	343 Baltoy [BP]	354 Banette [BP]
		606 Beheeyem [BP]	242 Blissey [BP]	654 Braixen [BP]	437 Bronzong [BP]	436 Bronzor [BP]	012 Butterfree [BP]	703 Carbink [40, BP]
		251 Celebi [BP]	113 Chansey [BP]	358 Chimecho [BP, E]	433 Chingling [BP, E]	344 Claydol [BP]	563 Cofagrigus [BP]	488 Cresselia [BP]
		655 Delphox [BP]	386 Deoxys (Atk) [BP]	386 Deoxys (Def) [BP]	386 Deoxys (Nor) [BP]	386 Deoxys (Spd) [BP]	719 Diancie [40, BP]	426 Drifblim [BP]
		425 Drifloon [BP]	096 Drowzee [BP, E]	578 Duosion [43, BP]	356 Dusclops [BP]	477 Dusknoir [BP]	355 Duskull [BP, E]	605 Elgyem [BP, E]
		196 Espeon [BP]	102 Exeggcute [BP, E]	103 Exeggutor [BP]	475 Gallade [BP]	282 Gardevoir [BP]	092 Gastly [BP]	094 Gengar [BP]
		203 Girafarig [BP, E]	574 Gothita [BP]	576 Gothitelle [BP]	575 Gothorita [BP]	711 Gourgeist [BP]	326 Grumpig [BP]	093 Haunter [BP]
		097 Hypno [BP]	385 Jirachi [BP]	124 Jynx [BP]	064 Kadabra [BP]	352 Kecleon [BP, E]	281 Kirlia [BP]	249 Lugia [BP]
		337 Lunatone [BP]	490 Manaphy [BP]	648 Meloetta [BP]	481 Mesprit [BP]	151 Mew [BP]	150 Mewtwo [BP]	439 Mime Jr. [BP]
		200 Misdreavus [BP, E]	429 Mismagius [BP]	414 Mothim [BP]	122 Mr. Mime [BP]	517 Munna [BP]	518 Musharna [BP]	177 Natu [BP, E]
		708 Phantump [BP]	710 Pumpkaboo [BP]	280 Ralts [BP, E]	579 Reuniclus [45, BP]	353 Shuppet [BP]	561 Sigilyph [BP, E]	080 Slowbro [BP]
		199 Slowking [BP]	079 Slowpoke [BP]	238 Smoochum [BP]	577 Solosis [40, BP]	338 Solrock [BP]	327 Spinda [BP]	325 Spoink [BP, E]
		682 Spritzee [44, BP]	234 Stantler [BP]	121 Starmie [BP]	528 Swoobat [BP]	700 Sylveon [25, BP]	709 Trevenant [BP]	480 Uxie [BP]
		049 Venomoth [BP]	048 Venonat [BP, E]	494 Victini [BP]	527 Woobat [BP]	413 Wormadam (Plant) [BP]	413 Wormadam (Sand) [BP]	413 Wormadam (Trash) [BP]
		178 Xatu [BP]	562 Yamask [BP]					
Normal	Skull Bash	713 Avalugg [1, 60]	689 Barbaracle [1, 65]	399 Bidoof [E]	009 Blastoise [39]	626 Bouffalant [E]	001 Bulbasaur [E]	104 Cubone [E]
		529 Drilbur [E]	118 Goldeen [E]	029 Nidoran ♀ [E]	369 Relicanth [E]	111 Rhyhorn [E]	319 Sharpedo [51]	459 Snover [E]
		007 Squirtle [31]	324 Torkoal [E]	008 Wartortle [36]				
Flying	Sky Attack	142 Aerodactyl [BP]	334 Altaria [1, 59, BP]	567 Archeops [BP]	144 Articuno [BP]	628 Braviary [BP]	441 Chatot [BP]	169 Crobat [BP]
		225 Delibird [BP]	085 Dodrio [BP]	083 Farfetch'd [BP]	022 Fearow [BP]	472 Gliscor [BP]	701 Hawlucha [48, BP]	430 Honchkrow [BP]
		250 Ho-Oh [99, BP]	163 Hoothoot [BP, E]	249 Lugia [99, BP]	630 Mandibuzz [BP]	151 Mew [BP]	146 Moltres [1, 78, BP]	198 Murkrow [BP, E]
		177 Natu [BP]	164 Noctowl [1, BP]	714 Noibat [BP]	715 Noivern [BP]	279 Pelipper [BP]	018 Pidgeot [BP]	017 Pidgeotto [BP]
		016 Pidgey [BP]	519 Pidove [50, BP]	561 Sigilyph [50, BP]	227 Skarmory [BP, E]	021 Spearow [BP, E]	398 Staraptor [BP]	333 Swablu [BP]
		581 Swanna [BP]	277 Swellow [BP]	528 Swoobat [BP]	276 Taillow [BP, E]	468 Togekiss [1, BP]	520 Tranquill [59, BP]	521 Unfezant [66, BP]
		278 Wingull [BP]	178 Xatu [BP]	717 Yveltal [93, BP]	145 Zapdos [BP]			
	Sky Drop (TM58)	142 Aerodactyl [49, TM]	144 Articuno [TM]	628 Braviary [50, TM]	006 Charizard [TM]	149 Dragonite [TM]	701 Hawlucha [55, TM]	250 Ho-Oh [TM]
		249 Lugia [TM]	151 Mew [TM]	146 Moltres [TM]	279 Pelipper [TM]	384 Rayquaza [TM]	627 Rufflet [50, TM]	227 Skarmory [TM]
		642 Thundurus [TM]	641 Tornadus [TM]	717 Yveltal [TM]	145 Zapdos [TM]			
Fighting	Sky Uppercut	257 Blaziken [57]	286 Breloom [39]	427 Buneary [E]	256 Combusken [53]	207 Gligar [45]	472 Gliscor [45]	107 Hitmonchan [41]
		674 Pancham [48]	675 Pangoro [52]	447 Riolu [E]				
Normal	Slack Off	390 Chimchar [41]	449 Hippopotas [E]	391 Monferno [49]	289 Slaking [1, 9]	287 Slakoth [9]	080 Slowbro [36]	079 Slowpoke [36]
	Slam	190 Aipom [E]	298 Azurill [20, E]	069 Bellsprout [41]	455 Carnivine [E]	408 Cranidos [E]	633 Deino [28]	232 Donphan [24]
		148 Dragonair [21]	149 Dragonite [21]	147 Dratini [21]	023 Ekans [E]	162 Furret [28]	253 Grovyle [33]	635 Hydreigon [28]
		099 Kingler [44]	098 Krabby [35, E]	463 Lickilicky [29]	108 Lickitung [29]	226 Mantine [E]	458 Mantyke [E]	303 Mawile [E]
		572 Minccino [37]	138 Omanyte [E]	095 Onix [28]	504 Patrat [36]	231 Phanpy [24]	025 Pikachu [37]	195 Quagsire [15]
		254 Sceptile [33]	086 Seel [E]	161 Sentret [25]	497 Serperior [28]	496 Servine [28]	495 Snivy [25]	208 Steelix [28]
		185 Sudowoodo [15]	114 Tangela [41]	465 Tangrowth [43]	564 Tirtouga [E]	252 Treecko [29]	357 Tropius [E]	505 Watchog [43]
		070 Weepinbell [41]	194 Wooper [15]	634 Zweilous [28]				
	Slash	359 Absol [22]	681 Aegislash [1]	347 Anorith [34]	348 Armaldo [25, 34]	610 Axew [20]	689 Barbaracle [13]	614 Beartic [33]
		688 Binacle [13]	625 Bisharp [30]	257 Blaziken [44]	628 Braviary [28]	418 Buizel [E]	006 Charizard [41]	004 Charmander [34]
		005 Charmeleon [39]	256 Combusken [42]	488 Cresselia [47]	159 Croconaw [39]	558 Crustle [31]	615 Cryogonal [41]	613 Cubchoo [33]
		483 Dialga [15]	050 Diglett [37]	680 Doublade [29]	529 Drilbur [26]	621 Druddigon [21]	051 Dugtrio [45]	557 Dwebble [31]
		589 Escavalier [32]	530 Excadrill [26]	083 Farfetch'd [19]	160 Feraligatr [45]	611 Fraxure [20]	444 Gabite [28]	475 Gallade [17]
		596 Galvantula [26]	445 Garchomp [28]	649 Genesect [29]	443 Gible [25]	487 Giratina (Alt) [15]	487 Giratina (Ori) [15]	431 Glameow [37]
		207 Gligar [27]	612 Haxorus [20]	631 Heatmor [41]	679 Honedge [29]	686 Inkay [43]	595 Joltik [26]	141 Kabutops [40]
		588 Karrablast [32]	352 Kecleon [25]	402 Kricketune [26]	646 Kyurem (Blk) [36]	646 Kyurem (Wht) [36]	646 Kyurem [36]	542 Leavanny [29]
		510 Liepard [34]	264 Linoone [32]	687 Malamar [43]	052 Meowth [33]	291 Ninjask [23]	484 Palkia [15]	674 Pancham [20]
		675 Pangoro [20]	046 Paras [27]	047 Parasect [29]	624 Pawniard [30]	053 Persian [37]	509 Purrloin [30]	432 Purugly [37]
		643 Reshiram [36]	627 Rufflet [28]	503 Samurott [36]	027 Sandshrew [26]	028 Sandslash [28]	212 Scizor [29]	123 Scyther [29]
		161 Sentret [E]	319 Sharpedo [30]	227 Skarmory [39]	451 Skorupi [E]	435 Skuntank [22]	287 Slakoth [E]	215 Sneasel [35]

ADVENTURE DATA

	Move	Pokémon that can learn it						
Normal	Slash	434 Stunky [22]	216 Teddiursa [29]	255 Torchic [37]	158 Totodile [34]	217 Ursaring [29]	416 Vespiquen [21]	288 Vigoroth [23]
		469 Yanmega [43]	335 Zangoose [19]	644 Zekrom [36]				
Grass	Sleep Powder	069 Bellsprout [13]	406 Budew [E]	001 Bulbasaur [13]	012 Butterfree [12]	455 Carnivine [E]	102 Exeggcute [23]	044 Gloom [15]
		187 Hoppip [16]	002 Ivysaur [13]	189 Jumpluff [16]	043 Oddish [15]	548 Petilil [10]	315 Roselia [E]	188 Skiploom [16]
		114 Tangela [4]	465 Tangrowth [4]	049 Venomoth [29]	048 Venonat [29]	003 Venusaur [13]	071 Victreebel [1]	666 Vivillon [1]
		070 Weepinbell [13]						
Normal	Sleep Talk (TM88)	460 Abomasnow [TM]	063 Abra [TM]	359 Absol [TM]	617 Accelgor [TM]	681 Aegislash [TM]	142 Aerodactyl [TM]	306 Aggron [TM]
		190 Aipom [TM]	065 Alakazam [TM]	594 Alomomola [TM]	334 Altaria [TM]	698 Amaura [TM]	424 Ambipom [TM]	591 Amoonguss [TM]
		181 Ampharos [TM]	347 Anorith [TM]	024 Arbok [TM]	059 Arcanine [TM]	493 Arceus [TM]	566 Archen [TM]	567 Archeops [TM]
		168 Ariados [TM]	348 Armaldo [TM]	683 Aromatisse [TM]	304 Aron [TM]	144 Articuno [TM]	531 Audino [TM, E]	699 Aurorus [TM]
		713 Avalugg [TM]	610 Axew [TM]	482 Azelf [TM]	184 Azumarill [TM]	298 Azurill [TM]	371 Bagon [TM]	343 Baltoy [TM]
		354 Banette [TM]	689 Barbaracle [TM]	339 Barboach [TM]	550 Basculin [TM]	411 Bastiodon [TM]	153 Bayleef [TM]	614 Beartic [TM]
		267 Beautifly [TM]	015 Beedrill [TM]	606 Beheeyem [TM]	182 Bellossom [TM]	069 Bellsprout [TM]	712 Bergmite [TM]	400 Bibarel [TM]
		399 Bidoof [TM, E]	688 Binacle [TM]	625 Bisharp [TM]	009 Blastoise [TM]	257 Blaziken [TM]	242 Blissey [TM]	522 Blitzle [TM]
		525 Boldore [TM]	438 Bonsly [TM]	626 Bouffalant [TM]	654 Braixen [TM]	628 Braviary [TM]	286 Breloom [TM]	437 Bronzong [TM]
		436 Bronzor [TM]	406 Budew [TM]	418 Buizel [TM]	001 Bulbasaur [TM]	427 Buneary [TM]	659 Bunnelby [TM]	012 Butterfree [TM]
		331 Cacnea [TM]	332 Cacturne [TM]	323 Camerupt [TM]	703 Carbink [TM]	455 Carnivine [TM]	565 Carracosta [TM]	318 Carvanha [TM]
		351 Castform [TM]	251 Celebi [TM]	609 Chandelure [TM]	113 Chansey [TM]	006 Charizard [TM]	004 Charmander [TM]	005 Charmeleon [TM]
		441 Chatot [TM, E]	421 Cherrim [TM]	420 Cherubi [TM]	652 Chesnaught [TM]	650 Chespin [TM]	152 Chikorita [TM]	390 Chimchar [TM]
		358 Chimecho [TM]	170 Chinchou [TM]	433 Chingling [TM]	573 Cinccino [TM]	366 Clamperl [TM]	692 Clauncher [TM]	693 Clawitzer [TM]
		344 Claydol [TM]	036 Clefable [TM]	035 Clefairy [TM]	173 Cleffa [TM]	091 Cloyster [TM]	638 Cobalion [TM]	563 Cofagrigus [TM]
		256 Combusken [TM]	534 Conkeldurr [TM]	341 Corphish [TM]	222 Corsola [TM]	546 Cottonee [TM]	346 Cradily [TM]	408 Cranidos [TM]
		342 Crawdaunt [TM]	488 Cresselia [TM]	453 Croagunk [TM]	169 Crobat [TM]	159 Croconaw [TM]	558 Crustle [TM]	615 Cryogonal [TM]
		613 Cubchoo [TM, E]	104 Cubone [TM]	155 Cyndaquil [TM]	491 Darkrai [TM]	555 Darmanitan [TM]	554 Darumaka [TM, E]	702 Dedenne [TM]
		585 Deerling [TM, E]	633 Deino [TM]	301 Delcatty [TM]	225 Delibird [TM]	655 Delphox [TM]	386 Deoxys (Atk) [TM]	386 Deoxys (Def) [TM]
		386 Deoxys (Nor) [TM]	386 Deoxys (Spd) [TM]	087 Dewgong [TM]	502 Dewott [TM]	483 Dialga [TM]	719 Diancie [TM]	660 Diggersby [TM]
		050 Diglett [TM]	085 Dodrio [TM]	084 Doduo [TM]	232 Donphan [TM]	680 Doublade [TM]	691 Dragalge [TM]	148 Dragonair [TM]
		149 Dragonite [TM]	452 Drapion [TM]	147 Dratini [TM]	426 Drifblim [TM]	425 Drifloon [TM]	529 Drilbur [TM]	096 Drowzee [TM]
		621 Druddigon [TM]	580 Ducklett [TM]	051 Dugtrio [TM]	206 Dunsparce [TM, E]	578 Duosion [TM]	632 Durant [TM]	356 Dusclops [TM]
		477 Dusknoir [TM]	355 Duskull [TM]	269 Dustox [TM]	557 Dwebble [TM]	603 Eelektrik [TM]	604 Eelektross [TM]	133 Eevee [TM]
		023 Ekans [TM]	125 Electabuzz [TM]	466 Electivire [TM]	309 Electrike [TM]	101 Electrode [TM]	239 Elekid [TM]	605 Elgyem [TM]
		500 Emboar [TM]	587 Emolga [TM]	395 Empoleon [TM]	244 Entei [TM]	589 Escavalier [TM]	196 Espeon [TM]	677 Espurr [TM]
		530 Excadrill [TM]	102 Exeggcute [TM]	103 Exeggutor [TM]	295 Exploud [42, TM]	083 Farfetch'd [TM]	022 Fearow [TM]	349 Feebas [TM]
		653 Fennekin [TM]	160 Feraligatr [TM]	597 Ferroseed [TM]	598 Ferrothorn [TM]	456 Finneon [TM]	180 Flaaffy [TM]	669 Flabébé [TM]
		136 Flareon [TM]	662 Fletchinder [TM]	661 Fletchling [TM]	419 Floatzel [TM]	670 Floette [TM]	671 Florges [TM]	330 Flygon [TM]
		590 Foongus [TM]	205 Forretress [TM]	611 Fraxure [TM]	592 Frillish [TM]	656 Froakie [TM]	657 Frogadier [TM]	478 Froslass [TM]
		676 Furfrou [TM]	162 Furret [TM]	444 Gabite [TM]	475 Gallade [TM]	596 Galvantula [TM]	569 Garbodor [TM]	445 Garchomp [TM]
		282 Gardevoir [TM]	092 Gastly [TM]	423 Gastrodon [TM]	649 Genesect [TM]	094 Gengar [TM]	074 Geodude [TM]	443 Gible [TM]
		526 Gigalith [TM]	203 Girafarig [TM]	487 Giratina (Alt) [TM]	487 Giratina (Ori) [TM]	471 Glaceon [TM]	362 Glalie [TM]	431 Glameow [TM]
		207 Gligar [TM]	472 Gliscor [TM]	044 Gloom [TM]	673 Gogoat [TM]	042 Golbat [TM]	118 Goldeen [TM, E]	055 Golduck [TM]
		076 Golem [TM]	622 Golett [TM]	623 Golurk [TM]	706 Goodra [TM]	704 Goomy [TM]	368 Gorebyss [TM]	574 Gothita [TM]
		576 Gothitelle [TM]	575 Gothorita [TM]	711 Gourgeist [TM]	210 Granbull [TM]	075 Graveler [TM]	658 Greninja [TM]	088 Grimer [TM]
		388 Grotle [TM]	383 Groudon [TM]	253 Grovyle [TM]	058 Growlithe [TM]	326 Grumpig [TM]	316 Gulpin [TM]	533 Gurdurr [TM]
		130 Gyarados [TM]	440 Happiny [TM]	297 Hariyama [TM]	093 Haunter [TM]	701 Hawlucha [TM]	612 Haxorus [TM]	631 Heatmor [TM, E]
		485 Heatran [TM]	695 Heliolisk [TM]	694 Helioptile [TM]	214 Heracross [TM]	507 Herdier [TM]	449 Hippopotas [TM, E]	450 Hippowdon [TM]
		107 Hitmonchan [TM]	106 Hitmonlee [TM]	237 Hitmontop [TM]	430 Honchkrow [TM]	679 Honedge [TM]	250 Ho-Oh [TM]	163 Hoothoot [TM]
		187 Hoppip [TM]	116 Horsea [TM]	229 Houndoom [TM]	228 Houndour [TM]	367 Huntail [TM]	635 Hydreigon [TM]	097 Hypno [TM]
		174 Igglybuff [TM, E]	314 Illumise [TM]	392 Infernape [TM]	686 Inkay [TM]	002 Ivysaur [TM]	593 Jellicent [TM]	039 Jigglypuff [TM]
		385 Jirachi [TM]	135 Jolteon [TM]	595 Joltik [TM]	189 Jumpluff [TM]	124 Jynx [TM]	140 Kabuto [TM]	141 Kabutops [TM]
		064 Kadabra [TM]	115 Kangaskhan [TM]	588 Karrablast [TM]	352 Kecleon [TM]	647 Keldeo [TM]	230 Kingdra [TM]	099 Kingler [TM]
		281 Kirlia [TM]	600 Klang [TM]	707 Klefki [TM]	599 Klink [TM]	601 Klinklang [TM]	109 Koffing [TM]	098 Krabby [TM]
		402 Kricketune [TM]	552 Krokorok [TM]	553 Krookodile [TM]	382 Kyogre [TM]	646 Kyurem (Blk) [TM]	646 Kyurem (Wht) [TM]	646 Kyurem [TM]
		305 Lairon [TM]	608 Lampent [TM]	645 Landorus [TM]	171 Lanturn [TM]	131 Lapras [TM, E]	636 Larvesta [TM]	246 Larvitar [TM]
		380 Latias [TM]	381 Latios [TM]	470 Leafeon [TM]	542 Leavanny [TM]	166 Ledian [TM]	165 Ledyba [TM]	463 Lickilicky [TM]
		108 Lickitung [TM, E]	510 Liepard [TM]	345 Lileep [TM]	549 Lilligant [TM]	506 Lillipup [TM]	264 Linoone [TM]	667 Litleo [TM]
		607 Litwick [TM]	271 Lombre [TM]	428 Lopunny [TM]	270 Lotad [TM]	294 Loudred [41, TM]	448 Lucario [TM]	272 Ludicolo [TM]
		249 Lugia [TM]	457 Lumineon [TM]	337 Lunatone [TM]	370 Luvdisc [TM]	404 Luxio [TM]	405 Luxray [TM]	068 Machamp [TM]
		067 Machoke [TM]	066 Machop [TM]	240 Magby [TM]	219 Magcargo [TM]	126 Magmar [TM]	467 Magmortar [TM]	081 Magnemite [TM]
		082 Magneton [TM]	462 Magnezone [TM]	296 Makuhita [TM]	687 Malamar [TM]	473 Mamoswine [TM]	490 Manaphy [TM]	630 Mandibuzz [TM]
		310 Manectric [TM]	056 Mankey [TM, E]	226 Mantine [TM]	458 Mantyke [TM]	556 Maractus [TM]	179 Mareep [TM]	183 Marill [TM]
		105 Marowak [TM]	259 Marshtomp [TM]	284 Masquerain [TM]	303 Mawile [TM]	308 Medicham [TM]	307 Meditite [TM]	154 Meganium [TM]
		648 Meloetta [TM]	678 Meowstic (F) [TM]	678 Meowstic (M) [TM]	052 Meowth [TM]	481 Mesprit [TM]	376 Metagross [TM]	375 Metang [TM]
		151 Mew [TM]	150 Mewtwo [TM]	619 Mienfoo [TM]	620 Mienshao [TM]	262 Mightyena [TM]	350 Milotic [TM]	241 Miltank [TM, E]
		439 Mime Jr. [TM]	572 Minccino [TM, E]	312 Minun [TM]	200 Misdreavus [TM]	429 Mismagius [TM]	146 Moltres [TM]	391 Monferno [TM]
		414 Mothim [TM]	122 Mr. Mime [TM]	258 Mudkip [TM]	089 Muk [TM]	446 Munchlax [TM]	517 Munna [TM, E]	198 Murkrow [TM]
		518 Musharna [TM]	177 Natu [TM]	034 Nidoking [TM]	031 Nidoqueen [TM]	029 Nidoran ♀ [TM]	032 Nidoran ♂ [TM]	030 Nidorina [TM]

	Move	Pokémon that can learn it						
Normal	Sleep Talk (TM88)	033 Nidorino [TM]	290 Nincada [TM]	038 Ninetales [TM]	291 Ninjask [TM]	164 Noctowl [TM]	714 Noibat [TM]	715 Noivern [TM]
		299 Nosepass [TM]	322 Numel [TM]	274 Nuzleaf [TM]	224 Octillery [TM]	043 Oddish [TM]	138 Omanyte [TM]	139 Omastar [TM]
		095 Onix [TM]	501 Oshawott [TM]	417 Pachirisu [TM]	484 Palkia [TM]	536 Palpitoad [TM]	674 Pancham [TM]	675 Pangoro [TM]
		515 Panpour [TM]	511 Pansage [TM]	513 Pansear [TM, E]	046 Paras [TM]	047 Parasect [TM]	504 Patrat [TM]	624 Pawniard [TM]
		279 Pelipper [TM]	053 Persian [TM]	548 Petilil [TM]	231 Phanpy [TM]	708 Phantump [TM]	489 Phione [TM]	172 Pichu [TM]
		018 Pidgeot [TM]	017 Pidgeotto [TM]	016 Pidgey [TM]	519 Pidove [TM]	499 Pignite [TM]	025 Pikachu [TM]	221 Piloswine [TM]
		204 Pineco [TM]	127 Pinsir [TM]	393 Piplup [TM]	311 Plusle [TM]	186 Politoed [TM]	060 Poliwag [TM]	061 Poliwhirl [TM]
		062 Poliwrath [TM]	077 Ponyta [TM]	261 Poochyena [TM, E]	137 Porygon [TM]	233 Porygon2 [TM]	474 Porygon-Z [TM]	057 Primeape [TM]
		394 Prinplup [TM]	476 Probopass [TM]	054 Psyduck [TM, E]	710 Pumpkaboo [TM]	247 Pupitar [TM]	509 Purrloin [TM]	432 Purugly [TM]
		668 Pyroar [TM]	195 Quagsire [TM]	156 Quilava [TM]	651 Quilladin [TM]	211 Qwilfish [TM]	026 Raichu [TM]	243 Raikou [TM]
		280 Ralts [TM]	409 Rampardos [TM]	078 Rapidash [TM]	020 Raticate [TM]	019 Rattata [TM]	384 Rayquaza [TM]	378 Regice [TM]
		486 Regigigas [TM]	377 Regirock [TM]	379 Registeel [TM]	369 Relicanth [TM, E]	223 Remoraid [TM]	643 Reshiram [TM]	579 Reuniclus [TM]
		112 Rhydon [TM]	111 Rhyhorn [TM]	464 Rhyperior [TM]	447 Riolu [TM]	524 Roggenrola [TM]	315 Roselia [TM]	407 Roserade [TM]
		479 Rotom (Fan) [TM]	479 Rotom (Frost) [TM]	479 Rotom (Heat) [TM]	479 Rotom (Mow) [TM]	479 Rotom (Wash) [TM]	479 Rotom [TM]	627 Rufflet [TM]
		302 Sableye [TM]	373 Salamence [TM]	503 Samurott [TM]	551 Sandile [TM]	027 Sandshrew [TM]	028 Sandslash [TM]	539 Sawk [TM]
		586 Sawsbuck [TM]	254 Sceptile [TM]	212 Scizor [TM]	545 Scolipede [TM]	560 Scrafty [TM]	559 Scraggy [TM]	123 Scyther [TM]
		117 Seadra [TM]	119 Seaking [TM]	364 Sealeo [TM]	273 Seedot [TM]	086 Seel [TM, E]	537 Seismitoad [TM]	161 Sentret [TM]
		497 Serperior [TM]	496 Servine [TM]	336 Seviper [TM]	540 Sewaddle [TM]	319 Sharpedo [TM]	492 Shaymin (Land) [TM]	492 Shaymin (Sky) [TM]
		292 Shedinja [TM]	372 Shelgon [TM]	090 Shellder [TM]	422 Shellos [TM]	616 Shelmet [TM]	410 Shieldon [TM]	275 Shiftry [TM]
		403 Shinx [TM]	285 Shroomish [TM]	213 Shuckle [TM]	353 Shuppet [TM]	561 Sigilyph [TM]	516 Simipour [TM]	512 Simisage [TM]
		514 Simisear [TM]	227 Skarmory [TM]	672 Skiddo [TM]	188 Skiploom [TM]	300 Skitty [TM]	451 Skorupi [TM]	690 Skrelp [TM]
		435 Skuntank [TM]	289 Slaking [TM]	287 Slakoth [TM, E]	705 Sliggoo [TM]	080 Slowbro [TM]	199 Slowking [TM]	079 Slowpoke [TM, E]
		218 Slugma [TM]	685 Slurpuff [TM]	238 Smoochum [TM]	215 Sneasel [TM]	495 Snivy [TM]	143 Snorlax [33, TM]	361 Snorunt [TM]
		459 Snover [TM]	209 Snubbull [TM]	577 Solosis [TM]	338 Solrock [TM]	021 Spearow [TM]	363 Spheal [TM, E]	167 Spinarak [TM]
		327 Spinda [TM]	442 Spiritomb [TM]	325 Spoink [TM]	682 Spritzee [TM]	007 Squirtle [TM]	234 Stantler [TM]	398 Staraptor [TM]
		397 Staravia [TM]	396 Starly [TM]	121 Starmie [TM]	120 Staryu [TM]	208 Steelix [TM]	508 Stoutland [TM]	618 Stunfisk [TM, E]
		434 Stunky [TM]	185 Sudowoodo [TM]	245 Suicune [TM]	192 Sunflora [TM]	191 Sunkern [TM]	283 Surskit [TM]	333 Swablu [TM]
		541 Swadloon [TM]	317 Swalot [TM]	260 Swampert [TM]	581 Swanna [TM]	277 Swellow [TM]	220 Swinub [TM]	684 Swirlix [TM]
		528 Swoobat [TM]	700 Sylveon [TM]	276 Taillow [TM]	663 Talonflame [TM]	114 Tangela [TM]	465 Tangrowth [TM]	128 Tauros [TM]
		216 Teddiursa [TM, E]	072 Tentacool [TM]	073 Tentacruel [TM]	498 Tepig [TM, E]	639 Terrakion [TM]	538 Throh [TM]	642 Thundurus [TM]
		532 Timburr [TM]	564 Tirtouga [TM]	468 Togekiss [TM]	175 Togepi [TM]	176 Togetic [TM]	255 Torchic [TM]	324 Torkoal [TM, E]
		641 Tornadus [TM]	389 Torterra [TM]	158 Totodile [TM]	454 Toxicroak [TM]	520 Tranquill [TM]	328 Trapinch [TM]	252 Treecko [TM]
		709 Trevenant [TM]	357 Tropius [TM]	568 Trubbish [TM]	387 Turtwig [TM]	535 Tympole [TM, E]	157 Typhlosion [TM]	248 Tyranitar [TM]
		697 Tyrantrum [TM]	236 Tyrogue [TM]	696 Tyrunt [TM]	197 Umbreon [TM]	521 Unfezant [TM]	217 Ursaring [TM]	480 Uxie [TM]
		583 Vanillish [TM]	582 Vanillite [TM]	584 Vanilluxe [TM]	134 Vaporeon [TM]	543 Venipede [TM]	049 Venomoth [TM]	048 Venonat [TM]
		003 Venusaur [TM]	416 Vespiquen [TM]	329 Vibrava [TM]	494 Victini [TM]	071 Victreebel [TM]	288 Vigoroth [TM]	045 Vileplume [TM]
		640 Virizion [TM]	666 Vivillon [TM]	313 Volbeat [TM]	637 Volcarona [TM]	100 Voltorb [TM]	629 Vullaby [TM]	037 Vulpix [TM]
		320 Wailmer [TM, E]	321 Wailord [TM]	365 Walrein [TM]	008 Wartortle [TM]	505 Watchog [TM]	461 Weavile [TM]	070 Weepinbell [TM]
		110 Weezing [TM]	547 Whimsicott [TM]	544 Whirlipede [TM]	340 Whiscash [TM]	293 Whismur [36, TM]	040 Wigglytuff [TM]	278 Wingull [TM]
		527 Woobat [TM]	194 Wooper [TM, E]	413 Wormadam (Plant) [TM]	413 Wormadam (Sand) [TM]	413 Wormadam (Trash) [TM]	178 Xatu [TM]	716 Xerneas [TM]
		562 Yamask [TM]	193 Yanma [TM]	469 Yanmega [TM]	717 Yveltal [TM]	335 Zangoose [TM]	145 Zapdos [TM]	523 Zebstrika [TM]
		644 Zekrom [TM]	263 Zigzagoon [TM, E]	571 Zoroark [TM]	570 Zorua [TM]	041 Zubat [TM]	634 Zweilous [TM]	718 Zygarde [TM]
Poison	Sludge	001 Bulbasaur [E]	569 Garbodor [18]	088 Grimer [15]	316 Gulpin [10]	109 Koffing [18]	258 Mudkip [E]	089 Muk [15]
		422 Shellos [E]	317 Swalot [1, 10]	568 Trubbish [18]	110 Weezing [18]			
	Sludge Bomb (TM36)	617 Accelgor [TM]	591 Amoonguss [TM]	024 Arbok [TM]	493 Arceus [TM]	168 Ariados [TM]	689 Barbaracle [TM]	015 Beedrill [TM]
		182 Bellossom [TM]	069 Bellsprout [TM]	688 Binacle [TM]	286 Breloom [TM]	406 Budew [TM]	001 Bulbasaur [TM]	659 Bunnelby [TM]
		455 Carnivine [TM]	652 Chesnaught [TM]	650 Chespin [TM]	692 Clauncher [TM]	693 Clawitzer [TM]	341 Corphish [TM]	346 Cradily [TM]
		342 Crawdaunt [TM]	453 Croagunk [45, TM]	169 Crobat [TM]	491 Darkrai [TM]	660 Diggersby [TM]	050 Diglett [TM]	691 Dragalge [38, TM]
		452 Drapion [TM]	529 Drilbur [TM]	621 Druddigon [TM]	051 Dugtrio [TM]	269 Dustox [TM]	023 Ekans [TM]	530 Excadrill [TM]
		102 Exeggcute [TM]	103 Exeggutor [TM]	590 Foongus [TM]	592 Frillish [TM]	569 Garbodor [29, TM]	092 Gastly [TM]	423 Gastrodon [TM]
		094 Gengar [TM]	207 Gligar [TM]	472 Gliscor [TM]	044 Gloom [TM]	042 Golbat [TM]	706 Goodra [TM]	704 Goomy [TM]
		711 Gourgeist [TM]	210 Granbull [TM]	088 Grimer [29, TM]	316 Gulpin [33, TM]	093 Haunter [TM]	229 Houndoom [TM]	228 Houndour [TM]
		002 Ivysaur [TM]	593 Jellicent [TM]	109 Koffing [34, TM]	552 Krokorok [TM]	553 Krookodile [TM]	645 Landorus [TM]	345 Lileep [TM]
		303 Mawile [TM]	376 Metagross [TM]	375 Metang [TM]	151 Mew [TM]	089 Muk [29, TM]	034 Nidoking [TM]	031 Nidoqueen [TM]
		029 Nidoran ♀ [TM]	032 Nidoran ♂ [TM]	030 Nidorina [TM]	033 Nidorino [TM]	224 Octillery [TM]	043 Oddish [TM]	536 Palpitoad [TM]
		674 Pancham [TM]	675 Pangoro [TM]	046 Paras [TM]	047 Parasect [TM]	710 Pumpkaboo [TM]	195 Quagsire [TM]	651 Quilladin [TM]
		211 Qwilfish [TM]	315 Roselia [TM]	407 Roserade [TM]	551 Sandile [TM]	545 Scolipede [TM]	560 Scrafty [TM]	559 Scraggy [TM]
		537 Seismitoad [TM]	336 Seviper [TM]	616 Shelmet [TM]	285 Shroomish [TM]	213 Shuckle [TM]	451 Skorupi [TM]	690 Skrelp [38, TM]
		435 Skuntank [TM]	705 Sliggoo [TM]	209 Snubbull [TM]	167 Spinarak [TM]	618 Stunfisk [TM]	434 Stunky [TM]	192 Sunflora [TM]
		191 Sunkern [TM]	317 Swalot [37, TM]	114 Tangela [TM]	465 Tangrowth [TM]	072 Tentacool [TM]	073 Tentacruel [TM]	642 Thundurus [TM]
		324 Torkoal [TM]	641 Tornadus [TM]	454 Toxicroak [54, TM]	568 Trubbish [29, TM]	535 Tympole [TM]	543 Venipede [TM]	049 Venomoth [TM]
		048 Venonat [TM]	003 Venusaur [TM]	416 Vespiquen [TM]	071 Victreebel [TM]	045 Vileplume [TM]	070 Weepinbell [TM]	110 Weezing [34, TM]
		544 Whirlipede [TM]	194 Wooper [TM]	041 Zubat [TM]				

Type	Move	Pokémon that can learn it						
Poison	Sludge Wave (TM34)	024 Arbok [TM]	689 Barbaracle [TM]	688 Binacle [TM]	692 Clauncher [TM]	693 Clawitzer [TM]	346 Cradily [TM]	342 Crawdaunt [TM]
		453 Croagunk [TM]	691 Dragalge [TM]	051 Dugtrio [TM]	023 Ekans [TM]	592 Frillish [TM]	569 Garbodor [TM]	423 Gastrodon [TM]
		706 Goodra [TM]	704 Goomy [TM]	088 Grimer [32, TM]	316 Gulpin [TM]	593 Jellicent [TM]	645 Landorus [TM]	259 Marshtomp [TM]
		151 Mew [TM]	258 Mudkip [TM]	089 Muk [32, TM]	034 Nidoking [TM]	031 Nidoqueen [TM]	224 Octillery [TM]	536 Palpitoad [TM]
		195 Quagsire [TM]	211 Qwilfish [TM]	537 Seismitoad [TM]	336 Seviper [TM]	213 Shuckle [TM]	690 Skrelp [TM]	705 Sliggoo [TM]
		618 Stunfisk [TM]	317 Swalot [TM]	260 Swampert [TM]	072 Tentacool [43, TM]	073 Tentacruel [48, TM]	642 Thundurus [TM]	641 Tornadus [TM]
		454 Toxicroak [TM]	568 Trubbish [TM]	535 Tympole [TM]	194 Wooper [TM]	718 Zygarde [TM]		
Rock	Smack Down (TM23)	142 Aerodactyl [TM]	306 Aggron [TM]	347 Anorith [13, TM]	566 Archen [TM]	567 Archeops [TM]	348 Armaldo [13, TM]	343 Baltoy [TM]
		689 Barbaracle [TM]	411 Bastiodon [TM]	688 Binacle [TM]	009 Blastoise [TM]	525 Boldore [23, TM]	438 Bonsly [TM]	659 Bunnelby [TM]
		703 Carbink [12, TM]	565 Carracosta [31, TM]	652 Chesnaught [TM]	650 Chespin [TM]	692 Clauncher [39, TM]	693 Clawitzer [42, TM]	344 Claydol [TM]
		534 Conkeldurr [TM]	346 Cradily [TM]	408 Cranidos [TM]	558 Crustle [17, TM]	104 Cubone [TM]	555 Darmanitan [TM]	719 Diancie [12, TM]
		660 Diggersby [TM]	621 Druddigon [TM]	557 Dwebble [17, TM]	500 Emboar [TM]	295 Exploud [TM]	656 Froakie [29, TM]	657 Frogadier [33, TM]
		569 Garbodor [TM]	074 Geodude [18, TM]	526 Gigalith [23, TM]	076 Golem [18, TM]	075 Graveler [18, TM]	658 Greninja [TM]	383 Groudon [TM]
		533 Gurdurr [TM]	297 Hariyama [TM]	214 Heracross [TM]	140 Kabuto [TM]	141 Kabutops [TM]	553 Krookodile [TM]	645 Landorus [TM]
		246 Larvitar [TM]	345 Lileep [TM]	294 Loudred [TM]	337 Lunatone [TM]	068 Machamp [TM]	067 Machoke [TM]	066 Machop [TM]
		219 Magcargo [TM]	296 Makuhita [TM]	056 Mankey [TM]	105 Marowak [TM]	151 Mew [TM]	034 Nidoking [TM]	031 Nidoqueen [TM]
		299 Nosepass [TM]	224 Octillery [TM]	138 Omanyte [TM]	139 Omastar [TM]	095 Onix [22, TM]	127 Pinsir [TM]	057 Primeape [TM]
		476 Probopass [TM]	247 Pupitar [TM]	651 Quilladin [TM]	409 Rampardos [TM]	486 Regigigas [TM]	377 Regirock [TM]	369 Relicanth [TM]
		223 Remoraid [TM]	112 Rhydon [13, TM]	111 Rhyhorn [13, TM]	464 Rhyperior [13, TM]	524 Roggenrola [23, TM]	560 Scrafty [TM]	559 Scraggy [TM]
		410 Shieldon [TM]	213 Shuckle [TM]	561 Sigilyph [TM]	289 Slaking [TM]	143 Snorlax [TM]	338 Solrock [TM]	208 Steelix [22, TM]
		185 Sudowoodo [TM]	639 Terrakion [13, TM]	642 Thundurus [TM]	532 Timburr [TM]	564 Tirtouga [31, TM]	641 Tornadus [TM]	248 Tyranitar [TM]
		217 Ursaring [TM]						
Normal	Smelling Salts	304 Aron [E]	331 Cacnea [E]	453 Croagunk [E]	297 Hariyama [30]	108 Lickitung [E]	066 Machop [E]	296 Makuhita [28]
		056 Mankey [E]	619 Mienfoo [E]	209 Snubbull [E]	327 Spinda [E]	532 Timburr [E]	255 Torchic [E]	293 Whismur [E]
Poison	Smog	609 Chandelure [1]	500 Emboar [20]	136 Flareon [33]	092 Gastly [E]	316 Gulpin [E]	229 Houndoom [1, 8]	228 Houndour [8]
		109 Koffing [4]	608 Lampent [1, 5]	607 Litwick [5]	240 Magby [1]	219 Magcargo [1]	126 Magmar [1]	467 Magmortar [1]
		499 Pignite [20]	218 Slugma [1]	434 Stunky [E]	498 Tepig [19]	324 Torkoal [4]	110 Weezing [1, 4]	
Normal	Smokescreen	006 Charizard [1, 10]	004 Charmander [10]	005 Charmeleon [10]	155 Cyndaquil [6]	691 Dragalge [1]	656 Froakie [18]	657 Frogadier [20]
		658 Greninja [20]	116 Horsea [5]	230 Kingdra [1, 5]	109 Koffing [7]	240 Magby [8]	126 Magmar [8]	467 Magmortar [1, 8]
		156 Quilava [1, 6]	117 Seadra [1, 5]	690 Skrelp [1]	435 Skuntank [14]	218 Slugma [E]	442 Spiritomb [E]	434 Stunky [14]
		324 Torkoal [15]	157 Typhlosion [1, 6]	110 Weezing [1, 7]	293 Whismur [E]			
Dark	Snarl (TM95)	359 Absol [TM]	059 Arcanine [TM]	493 Arceus [TM]	625 Bisharp [TM]	318 Carvanha [TM]	342 Crawdaunt [TM]	491 Darkrai [TM]
		452 Drapion [TM]	621 Druddigon [TM]	309 Electrike [TM]	244 Entei [TM]	676 Furfrou [TM]	210 Granbull [TM]	058 Growlithe [TM]
		507 Herdier [TM]	430 Honchkrow [TM]	229 Houndoom [TM]	228 Houndour [TM]	552 Krokorok [TM]	553 Krookodile [TM]	246 Larvitar [TM]
		510 Liepard [TM]	506 Lillipup [TM]	667 Litleo [TM]	404 Luxio [TM]	405 Luxray [TM]	630 Mandibuzz [TM]	310 Manectric [TM]
		151 Mew [TM]	262 Mightyena [18, TM]	198 Murkrow [TM]	274 Nuzleaf [TM]	675 Pangoro [TM]	624 Pawniard [TM]	261 Poochyena [TM]
		247 Pupitar [TM]	509 Purrloin [TM]	668 Pyroar [TM]	243 Raikou [TM]	302 Sableye [TM]	551 Sandile [TM]	560 Scrafty [TM]
		559 Scraggy [TM]	319 Sharpedo [TM]	275 Shiftry [TM]	403 Shinx [TM]	435 Skuntank [TM]	215 Sneasel [TM]	209 Snubbull [TM]
		442 Spiritomb [TM]	508 Stoutland [TM]	434 Stunky [TM]	245 Suicune [TM]	248 Tyranitar [TM]	197 Umbreon [TM]	629 Vullaby [TM]
		461 Weavile [TM]	717 Yveltal [18, TM]	571 Zoroark [TM]	570 Zorua [TM]			
Dark	Snatch	063 Abra [BP]	359 Absol [BP]	190 Aipom [BP]	065 Alakazam [BP]	424 Ambipom [BP]	024 Arbok [BP]	531 Audino [BP]
		354 Banette [46, BP]	606 Beheeyem [BP]	625 Bisharp [BP]	242 Blissey [BP]	522 Blitzle [BP, E]	654 Braixen [BP]	286 Breloom [BP]
		113 Chansey [BP]	358 Chimecho [BP]	433 Chingling [BP]	036 Clefable [BP]	035 Clefairy [BP]	563 Cofagrigus [BP]	453 Croagunk [BP]
		169 Crobat [BP]	491 Darkrai [BP]	555 Darmanitan [BP]	554 Darumaka [BP, E]	655 Delphox [BP]	386 Deoxys (Atk) [BP]	386 Deoxys (Def) [37, BP]
		386 Deoxys (Nor) [37, BP]	386 Deoxys (Spd) [BP]	660 Diggersby [BP]	096 Drowzee [BP]	621 Druddigon [BP, E]	578 Duosion [1, 10, BP]	356 Dusclops [BP]
		477 Dusknoir [BP]	355 Duskull [BP]	023 Ekans [BP, E]	605 Elgyem [BP]	677 Espurr [BP]	662 Fletchinder [BP]	661 Fletchling [BP, E]
		656 Froakie [BP]	657 Frogadier [BP]	478 Froslass [BP]	475 Gallade [BP]	282 Gardevoir [BP]	092 Gastly [BP]	094 Gengar [BP]
		431 Glameow [BP, E]	042 Golbat [BP]	574 Gothita [BP]	576 Gothitelle [BP]	575 Gothorita [BP]	658 Greninja [BP]	326 Grumpig [BP]
		316 Gulpin [BP]	093 Haunter [BP]	631 Heatmor [26, BP]	430 Honchkrow [BP]	229 Houndoom [BP]	228 Houndour [BP]	367 Huntail [BP]
		097 Hypno [BP]	686 Inkay [BP]	039 Jigglypuff [BP]	064 Kadabra [BP]	352 Kecleon [BP, E]	281 Kirlia [BP]	552 Krokorok [BP]
		553 Krookodile [BP]	510 Liepard [47, BP]	667 Litleo [BP, E]	687 Malamar [BP]	630 Mandibuzz [BP]	303 Mawile [BP]	648 Meloetta [BP]
		678 Meowstic (F) [BP]	678 Meowstic (M) [BP]	052 Meowth [BP, E]	151 Mew [BP]	150 Mewtwo [BP]	262 Mightyena [BP]	439 Mime Jr. [BP]
		200 Misdreavus [BP]	429 Mismagius [BP]	122 Mr. Mime [BP]	446 Munchlax [50, BP]	198 Murkrow [BP]	714 Noibat [BP, E]	715 Noivern [BP]
		674 Pancham [BP]	675 Pangoro [BP]	624 Pawniard [BP]	053 Persian [BP]	261 Poochyena [BP, E]	509 Purrloin [39, BP]	432 Purugly [BP]
		668 Pyroar [BP]	280 Ralts [BP]	579 Reuniclus [1, 10, BP]	479 Rotom (Fan) [BP]	479 Rotom (Frost) [BP]	479 Rotom (Heat) [BP]	479 Rotom (Mow) [BP]
		479 Rotom (Wash) [BP]	479 Rotom [BP]	302 Sableye [BP]	551 Sandile [BP]	545 Scolipede [BP]	560 Scrafty [BP]	559 Scraggy [BP]
		497 Serperior [BP]	496 Servine [BP]	336 Seviper [BP]	285 Shroomish [BP]	353 Shuppet [42, BP]	435 Skuntank [BP]	215 Sneasel [40, BP]
		495 Snivy [BP]	577 Solosis [10, BP]	327 Spinda [BP]	442 Spiritomb [BP]	325 Spoink [BP]	434 Stunky [BP]	317 Swalot [BP]
		663 Talonflame [BP]	454 Toxicroak [BP]	197 Umbreon [BP]	629 Vullaby [BP]	461 Weavile [40, BP]	040 Wigglytuff [BP]	562 Yamask [BP]
		523 Zebstrika [BP]	571 Zoroark [BP]	570 Zorua [BP, E]	041 Zubat [BP]			
Normal	Snore	460 Abomasnow [BP]	063 Abra [BP]	359 Absol [BP]	617 Accelgor [BP]	681 Aegislash [BP]	142 Aerodactyl [BP]	306 Aggron [BP]
		190 Aipom [BP]	065 Alakazam [BP]	594 Alomomola [BP]	334 Altaria [BP]	698 Amaura [BP]	424 Ambipom [BP]	591 Amoonguss [BP]
		181 Ampharos [BP]	347 Anorith [BP]	024 Arbok [BP]	059 Arcanine [BP]	493 Arceus [BP]	566 Archen [BP]	567 Archeops [BP]
		168 Ariados [BP]	348 Armaldo [BP]	683 Aromatisse [BP]	304 Aron [BP]	144 Articuno [BP]	531 Audino [BP]	699 Aurorus [BP]

ADVENTURE DATA

	Move	Pokémon that can learn it						
Normal	Snore	713 Avalugg [BP]	610 Axew [BP]	482 Azelf [BP]	184 Azumarill [BP]	298 Azurill [BP]	371 Bagon [BP]	343 Baltoy [BP]
		354 Banette [BP]	689 Barbaracle [BP]	339 Barboach [25, BP]	550 Basculin [BP]	411 Bastiodon [BP]	153 Bayleef [BP]	614 Beartic [BP]
		267 Beautifly [BP]	015 Beedrill [BP]	606 Beheeyem [BP]	182 Bellossom [BP]	069 Bellsprout [BP]	712 Bergmite [BP]	400 Bibarel [BP]
		399 Bidoof [BP]	688 Binacle [BP]	625 Bisharp [BP]	009 Blastoise [BP]	257 Blaziken [BP]	242 Blissey [BP]	522 Blitzle [BP]
		525 Boldore [BP]	438 Bonsly [BP]	626 Bouffalant [BP]	654 Braixen [BP]	628 Braviary [BP]	286 Breloom [BP]	437 Bronzong [BP]
		436 Bronzor [BP]	406 Budew [BP]	418 Buizel [BP]	001 Bulbasaur [BP]	427 Buneary [BP]	659 Bunnelby [BP]	412 Burmy [BP]
		012 Butterfree [BP]	331 Cacnea [BP]	332 Cacturne [BP]	323 Camerupt [BP]	703 Carbink [BP]	455 Carnivine [BP]	565 Carracosta [BP]
		318 Carvanha [BP]	351 Castform [BP]	010 Caterpie [BP]	251 Celebi [BP]	609 Chandelure [BP]	113 Chansey [BP]	006 Charizard [BP]
		004 Charmander [BP]	005 Charmeleon [BP]	441 Chatot [BP]	421 Cherrim [BP]	420 Cherubi [BP]	652 Chesnaught [BP]	650 Chespin [BP]
		152 Chikorita [BP]	390 Chimchar [BP]	358 Chimecho [BP]	170 Chinchou [BP]	433 Chingling [BP]	573 Cinccino [BP]	366 Clamperl [BP]
		692 Clauncher [BP]	693 Clawitzer [BP]	344 Claydol [BP]	036 Clefable [BP]	035 Clefairy [BP]	173 Cleffa [BP]	091 Cloyster [BP]
		638 Cobalion [BP]	563 Cofagrigus [BP]	415 Combee [BP]	256 Combusken [BP]	534 Conkeldurr [BP]	341 Corphish [BP]	222 Corsola [BP]
		546 Cottonee [BP]	346 Cradily [BP]	408 Cranidos [BP]	342 Crawdaunt [BP]	488 Cresselia [BP]	453 Croagunk [BP]	169 Crobat [BP]
		159 Croconaw [BP]	558 Crustle [BP]	615 Cryogonal [BP]	613 Cubchoo [BP]	104 Cubone [BP]	155 Cyndaquil [BP]	491 Darkrai [BP]
		555 Darmanitan [BP]	554 Darumaka [BP]	702 Dedenne [31, BP]	585 Deerling [BP]	633 Deino [BP]	301 Delcatty [BP]	225 Delibird [BP]
		655 Delphox [BP]	386 Deoxys (Atk) [BP]	386 Deoxys (Def) [BP]	386 Deoxys (Nor) [BP]	386 Deoxys (Spd) [BP]	087 Dewgong [BP]	502 Dewott [BP]
		483 Dialga [BP]	719 Diancie [BP]	660 Diggersby [BP]	050 Diglett [BP]	085 Dodrio [BP]	084 Doduo [BP]	232 Donphan [BP]
		680 Doublade [BP]	691 Dragalge [BP]	148 Dragonair [BP]	149 Dragonite [BP]	452 Drapion [BP]	147 Dratini [BP]	426 Drifblim [BP]
		425 Drifloon [BP]	529 Drilbur [BP]	096 Drowzee [BP]	621 Druddigon [BP]	580 Ducklett [BP]	051 Dugtrio [BP]	206 Dunsparce [BP, E]
		578 Duosion [BP]	632 Durant [BP]	356 Dusclops [BP]	477 Dusknoir [BP]	355 Duskull [BP]	269 Dustox [BP]	557 Dwebble [BP]
		603 Eelektrik [BP]	604 Eelektross [BP]	133 Eevee [BP]	023 Ekans [BP]	125 Electabuzz [BP]	466 Electivire [BP]	309 Electrike [BP]
		101 Electrode [BP]	239 Elekid [BP]	605 Elgyem [BP]	500 Emboar [BP]	587 Emolga [BP]	395 Empoleon [BP]	244 Entei [BP]
		589 Escavalier [BP]	196 Espeon [BP]	677 Espurr [BP]	530 Excadrill [BP]	102 Exeggcute [BP]	103 Exeggutor [BP]	295 Exploud [BP]
		083 Farfetch'd [BP]	022 Fearow [BP]	349 Feebas [BP]	653 Fennekin [BP]	160 Feraligatr [BP]	597 Ferroseed [BP]	598 Ferrothorn [BP]
		456 Finneon [BP]	180 Flaaffy [BP]	669 Flabébé [BP]	136 Flareon [BP]	662 Fletchinder [BP]	661 Fletchling [BP]	419 Floatzel [BP]
		670 Floette [BP]	671 Florges [BP]	330 Flygon [BP]	590 Foongus [BP]	205 Forretress [BP]	611 Fraxure [BP]	592 Frillish [BP]
		656 Froakie [BP]	657 Frogadier [BP]	478 Froslass [BP]	676 Furfrou [BP]	162 Furret [BP]	444 Gabite [BP]	475 Gallade [BP]
		596 Galvantula [BP]	569 Garbodor [BP]	445 Garchomp [BP]	282 Gardevoir [BP]	092 Gastly [BP]	423 Gastrodon [BP]	649 Genesect [BP]
		094 Gengar [BP]	074 Geodude [BP]	443 Gible [BP]	526 Gigalith [BP]	203 Girafarig [BP]	487 Giratina (Alt) [BP]	487 Giratina (Ori) [BP]
		471 Glaceon [BP]	362 Glalie [BP]	431 Glameow [BP]	207 Gligar [BP]	472 Gliscor [BP]	044 Gloom [BP]	673 Gogoat [BP]
		042 Golbat [BP]	118 Goldeen [BP]	055 Golduck [BP]	076 Golem [BP]	622 Golett [BP]	623 Golurk [BP]	706 Goodra [BP]
		704 Goomy [BP]	368 Gorebyss [BP]	574 Gothita [BP]	576 Gothitelle [BP]	575 Gothorita [BP]	210 Granbull [BP]	075 Graveler [BP]
		658 Greninja [BP]	088 Grimer [BP]	388 Grotle [BP]	383 Groudon [BP]	253 Grovyle [BP]	058 Growlithe [BP]	326 Grumpig [35, BP]
		316 Gulpin [BP]	533 Gurdurr [BP]	130 Gyarados [BP]	440 Happiny [BP]	297 Hariyama [BP]	093 Haunter [BP]	701 Hawlucha [BP]
		612 Haxorus [BP]	631 Heatmor [BP]	485 Heatran [BP]	695 Heliolisk [BP]	694 Helioptile [BP]	214 Heracross [BP]	507 Herdier [BP]
		449 Hippopotas [BP]	450 Hippowdon [BP]	107 Hitmonchan [BP]	106 Hitmonlee [BP]	237 Hitmontop [BP]	430 Honchkrow [BP]	679 Honedge [BP]
		250 Ho-Oh [BP]	163 Hoothoot [BP]	187 Hoppip [BP]	116 Horsea [BP]	229 Houndoom [BP]	228 Houndour [BP]	367 Huntail [BP]
		635 Hydreigon [BP]	097 Hypno [BP]	174 Igglybuff [BP]	314 Illumise [BP]	392 Infernape [BP]	686 Inkay [BP]	002 Ivysaur [BP]
		593 Jellicent [BP]	039 Jigglypuff [BP]	385 Jirachi [BP]	135 Jolteon [BP]	595 Joltik [BP]	189 Jumpluff [BP]	124 Jynx [BP]
		140 Kabuto [BP]	141 Kabutops [BP]	064 Kadabra [BP]	115 Kangaskhan [BP]	588 Karrablast [BP]	352 Kecleon [BP]	647 Keldeo [BP]
		230 Kingdra [BP]	099 Kingler [BP]	281 Kirlia [BP]	600 Klang [BP]	707 Klefki [BP]	599 Klink [BP]	601 Klinklang [BP]
		109 Koffing [BP]	098 Krabby [BP]	401 Kricketot [BP]	402 Kricketune [BP]	552 Krokorok [BP]	553 Krookodile [BP]	382 Kyogre [BP]
		646 Kyurem (Blk) [BP]	646 Kyurem (Wht) [BP]	646 Kyurem [BP]	305 Lairon [BP]	608 Lampent [BP]	645 Landorus [BP]	171 Lanturn [BP]
		131 Lapras [BP]	636 Larvesta [BP]	246 Larvitar [BP]	380 Latias [BP]	381 Latios [BP]	470 Leafeon [BP]	542 Leavanny [BP]
		166 Ledian [BP]	165 Ledyba [BP]	463 Lickilicky [BP]	108 Lickitung [BP, E]	510 Liepard [BP]	345 Lileep [BP]	549 Lilligant [BP]
		506 Lillipup [BP]	264 Linoone [BP]	667 Litleo [BP]	607 Litwick [BP]	271 Lombre [BP]	428 Lopunny [BP]	270 Lotad [BP]
		294 Loudred [BP]	448 Lucario [BP]	272 Ludicolo [BP]	249 Lugia [BP]	457 Lumineon [BP]	337 Lunatone [BP]	370 Luvdisc [BP]
		404 Luxio [BP]	405 Luxray [BP]	068 Machamp [BP]	067 Machoke [BP]	066 Machop [BP]	240 Magby [BP]	219 Magcargo [BP]
		126 Magmar [BP]	467 Magmortar [BP]	081 Magnemite [BP]	082 Magneton [BP]	462 Magnezone [BP]	296 Makuhita [BP]	687 Malamar [BP]
		473 Mamoswine [BP]	490 Manaphy [BP]	630 Mandibuzz [BP]	310 Manectric [BP]	056 Mankey [BP]	226 Mantine [BP]	458 Mantyke [BP]
		556 Maractus [BP]	179 Mareep [BP]	183 Marill [BP]	105 Marowak [BP]	259 Marshtomp [BP]	284 Masquerain [BP]	303 Mawile [BP]
		308 Medicham [BP]	307 Meditite [BP]	154 Meganium [BP]	648 Meloetta [BP]	678 Meowstic (F) [BP]	678 Meowstic (M) [BP]	052 Meowth [BP]
		481 Mesprit [BP]	376 Metagross [BP]	375 Metang [BP]	151 Mew [BP]	150 Mewtwo [BP]	619 Mienfoo [BP]	620 Mienshao [BP]
		262 Mightyena [BP]	350 Milotic [BP]	241 Miltank [BP]	439 Mime Jr. [BP]	572 Minccino [BP]	312 Minun [BP]	200 Misdreavus [BP]
		429 Mismagius [BP]	146 Moltres [BP]	391 Monferno [BP]	414 Mothim [BP]	122 Mr. Mime [BP]	258 Mudkip [BP]	089 Muk [BP]
		446 Munchlax [BP]	517 Munna [BP]	198 Murkrow [BP]	518 Musharna [BP]	177 Natu [BP]	034 Nidoking [BP]	031 Nidoqueen [BP]
		029 Nidoran ♀ [BP]	032 Nidoran ♂ [BP]	030 Nidorina [BP]	033 Nidorino [BP]	290 Nincada [BP]	038 Ninetales [BP]	291 Ninjask [BP]
		164 Noctowl [BP]	714 Noibat [BP]	715 Noivern [BP]	299 Nosepass [BP]	322 Numel [BP]	274 Nuzleaf [BP]	224 Octillery [BP]
		043 Oddish [BP]	138 Omanyte [BP]	139 Omastar [BP]	095 Onix [BP]	501 Oshawott [BP]	417 Pachirisu [BP]	484 Palkia [BP]
		536 Palpitoad [BP]	674 Pancham [BP]	675 Pangoro [BP]	515 Panpour [BP]	511 Pansage [BP]	513 Pansear [BP]	046 Paras [BP]
		047 Parasect [BP]	504 Patrat [BP]	624 Pawniard [BP]	279 Pelipper [BP]	053 Persian [BP]	548 Petilil [BP]	231 Phanpy [BP, E]
		708 Phantump [BP]	489 Phione [BP]	172 Pichu [BP]	018 Pidgeot [BP]	017 Pidgeotto [BP]	016 Pidgey [BP]	519 Pidove [BP]
		499 Pignite [BP]	025 Pikachu [BP]	221 Piloswine [BP]	204 Pineco [BP]	127 Pinsir [BP]	393 Piplup [BP, E]	311 Plusle [BP]
		186 Politoed [BP]	060 Poliwag [BP]	061 Poliwhirl [BP]	062 Poliwrath [BP]	077 Ponyta [BP]	261 Poochyena [BP]	137 Porygon [BP]
		233 Porygon2 [BP]	474 Porygon-Z [BP]	057 Primeape [BP]	394 Prinplup [BP]	476 Probopass [BP]	054 Psyduck [BP]	247 Pupitar [BP]
		509 Purrloin [BP]	432 Purugly [BP]	668 Pyroar [BP]	195 Quagsire [BP]	156 Quilava [BP]	651 Quilladin [BP]	211 Qwilfish [BP]

Type	Move	Pokémon that can learn it						
Normal	Snore	026 Raichu [BP]	243 Raikou [BP]	280 Ralts [BP]	409 Rampardos [BP]	078 Rapidash [BP]	020 Raticate [BP]	019 Rattata [BP]
		384 Rayquaza [BP]	378 Regice [BP]	486 Regigigas [BP]	377 Regirock [BP]	379 Registeel [BP]	369 Relicanth [BP, E]	223 Remoraid [BP, E]
		643 Reshiram [BP]	579 Reuniclus [BP]	112 Rhydon [BP]	111 Rhyhorn [BP]	464 Rhyperior [BP]	447 Riolu [BP]	524 Roggenrola [BP]
		315 Roselia [BP]	407 Roserade [BP]	479 Rotom (Fan) [BP]	479 Rotom (Frost) [BP]	479 Rotom (Heat) [BP]	479 Rotom (Mow) [BP]	479 Rotom (Wash) [BP]
		479 Rotom [BP]	627 Rufflet [BP]	302 Sableye [BP]	373 Salamence [BP]	503 Samurott [BP]	551 Sandile [BP]	027 Sandshrew [BP]
		028 Sandslash [BP]	539 Sawk [BP]	586 Sawsbuck [BP]	254 Sceptile [BP]	212 Scizor [BP]	545 Scolipede [BP]	560 Scrafty [BP]
		559 Scraggy [BP]	123 Scyther [BP]	117 Seadra [BP]	119 Seaking [BP]	364 Sealeo [31, BP]	273 Seedot [BP]	086 Seel [BP]
		537 Seismitoad [BP]	161 Sentret [BP]	497 Serperior [BP]	496 Servine [BP]	336 Seviper [BP]	540 Sewaddle [BP]	319 Sharpedo [BP]
		492 Shaymin (Land) [BP]	492 Shaymin (Sky) [BP]	292 Shedinja [BP]	372 Shelgon [BP]	090 Shellder [BP]	422 Shellos [BP]	616 Shelmet [BP]
		410 Shieldon [BP]	275 Shiftry [BP]	403 Shinx [BP]	285 Shroomish [BP]	213 Shuckle [BP]	353 Shuppet [BP]	561 Sigilyph [BP]
		516 Simipour [BP]	512 Simisage [BP]	514 Simisear [BP]	227 Skarmory [BP]	672 Skiddo [BP]	188 Skiploom [BP]	300 Skitty [BP]
		451 Skorupi [BP]	690 Skrelp [BP]	435 Skuntank [BP]	289 Slaking [BP]	287 Slakoth [BP, E]	705 Sliggoo [BP]	080 Slowbro [BP]
		199 Slowking [BP]	079 Slowpoke [BP, E]	218 Slugma [BP]	685 Slurpuff [BP]	238 Smoochum [BP]	215 Sneasel [BP]	495 Snivy [BP]
		143 Snorlax [28, BP]	361 Snorunt [BP]	459 Snover [BP]	209 Snubbull [BP, E]	577 Solosis [BP]	338 Solrock [BP]	021 Spearow [BP]
		363 Spheal [31, BP]	167 Spinarak [BP]	327 Spinda [BP]	442 Spiritomb [BP]	325 Spoink [33, BP]	682 Spritzee [BP]	007 Squirtle [BP]
		234 Stantler [BP]	398 Staraptor [BP]	397 Staravia [BP]	396 Starly [BP]	121 Starmie [BP]	120 Staryu [BP]	208 Steelix [BP]
		508 Stoutland [BP]	618 Stunfisk [BP]	434 Stunky [BP]	185 Sudowoodo [BP]	245 Suicune [BP]	192 Sunflora [BP]	191 Sunkern [BP]
		283 Surskit [BP]	333 Swablu [BP]	541 Swadloon [BP]	317 Swalot [BP]	260 Swampert [BP]	581 Swanna [BP]	277 Swellow [BP]
		220 Swinub [BP]	684 Swirlix [BP]	528 Swoobat [BP]	700 Sylveon [BP]	276 Taillow [BP]	663 Talonflame [BP]	114 Tangela [BP]
		465 Tangrowth [BP]	128 Tauros [BP]	216 Teddiursa [43, BP]	072 Tentacool [BP]	073 Tentacruel [BP]	498 Tepig [BP]	639 Terrakion [BP]
		538 Throh [BP]	642 Thundurus [BP]	532 Timburr [BP]	564 Tirtouga [BP]	468 Togekiss [BP]	175 Togepi [BP]	176 Togetic [BP]
		255 Torchic [BP]	324 Torkoal [BP]	641 Tornadus [BP]	389 Torterra [BP]	158 Totodile [BP]	454 Toxicroak [BP]	520 Tranquill [BP]
		328 Trapinch [BP]	252 Treecko [BP]	709 Trevenant [BP]	357 Tropius [BP]	568 Trubbish [BP]	387 Turtwig [BP]	535 Tympole [BP, E]
		157 Typhlosion [BP]	248 Tyranitar [BP]	697 Tyrantrum [BP]	236 Tyrogue [BP]	696 Tyrunt [BP]	197 Umbreon [BP]	521 Unfezant [BP]
		217 Ursaring [49, BP]	480 Uxie [BP]	583 Vanillish [BP]	582 Vanillite [BP]	584 Vanilluxe [BP]	134 Vaporeon [BP]	543 Venipede [BP]
		049 Venomoth [BP]	048 Venonat [BP]	003 Venusaur [BP]	416 Vespiquen [BP]	329 Vibrava [BP]	494 Victini [BP]	071 Victreebel [BP]
		288 Vigoroth [BP]	045 Vileplume [BP]	640 Virizion [BP]	666 Vivillon [BP]	313 Volbeat [BP]	637 Volcarona [BP]	100 Voltorb [BP]
		629 Vullaby [BP]	037 Vulpix [BP]	320 Wailmer [BP, E]	321 Wailord [BP]	365 Walrein [31, BP]	008 Wartortle [BP]	505 Watchog [BP]
		461 Weavile [BP]	070 Weepinbell [BP]	110 Weezing [BP]	547 Whimsicott [BP]	544 Whirlipede [BP]	340 Whiscash [25, BP]	293 Whismur [BP, E]
		040 Wigglytuff [BP]	278 Wingull [BP]	527 Woobat [BP]	194 Wooper [BP]	413 Wormadam (Plant) [BP]	413 Wormadam (Sand) [BP]	413 Wormadam (Trash) [BP]
		265 Wurmple [BP]	178 Xatu [BP]	716 Xerneas [BP]	562 Yamask [BP]	193 Yanma [BP]	469 Yanmega [BP]	717 Yveltal [BP]
		335 Zangoose [BP]	145 Zapdos [BP]	523 Zebstrika [BP]	644 Zekrom [BP]	263 Zigzagoon [BP]	571 Zoroark [BP]	570 Zorua [BP]
		041 Zubat [BP]	634 Zweilous [BP]	718 Zygarde [BP]				
Water	Soak	594 Alomomola [33]	298 Azurill [E]	550 Basculin [32]	418 Buizel [E]	170 Chinchou [E]	456 Finneon [54]	118 Goldeen [40]
		055 Golduck [38]	457 Lumineon [1, 66]	224 Octillery [64]	279 Pelipper [1]	054 Psyduck [36]	223 Remoraid [50]	119 Seaking [46]
		320 Wailmer [E]	278 Wingull [E]					
Normal	Soft-Boiled	242 Blissey [16]	113 Chansey [16]					
Grass	Solar Beam (TM22)	460 Abomasnow [TM]	306 Aggron [TM]	190 Aipom [TM]	334 Altaria [TM]	424 Ambipom [TM]	591 Amoonguss [49, TM]	059 Arcanine [TM]
		493 Arceus [TM]	168 Ariados [TM]	531 Audino [TM]	343 Baltoy [TM]	153 Bayleef [54, TM]	267 Beautifly [TM]	015 Beedrill [TM]
		182 Bellossom [TM]	069 Bellsprout [TM]	257 Blaziken [TM]	242 Blissey [TM]	654 Braixen [TM]	286 Breloom [TM]	437 Bronzong [TM]
		436 Bronzor [TM]	406 Budew [TM]	001 Bulbasaur [TM]	427 Buneary [TM]	012 Butterfree [TM]	331 Cacnea [TM]	332 Cacturne [TM]
		323 Camerupt [TM]	455 Carnivine [TM]	351 Castform [TM]	251 Celebi [TM]	609 Chandelure [TM]	113 Chansey [TM]	006 Charizard [TM]
		421 Cherrim [43, TM]	420 Cherubi [37, TM]	652 Chesnaught [TM]	650 Chespin [TM]	152 Chikorita [45, TM]	344 Claydol [TM]	036 Clefable [TM]
		035 Clefairy [TM]	173 Cleffa [TM]	546 Cottonee [46, TM]	346 Cradily [TM]	488 Cresselia [TM]	558 Crustle [TM]	615 Cryogonal [53, TM]
		555 Darmanitan [TM]	554 Darumaka [TM]	585 Deerling [51, TM]	301 Delcatty [TM]	655 Delphox [TM]	386 Deoxys (Atk) [TM]	386 Deoxys (Def) [TM]
		386 Deoxys (Nor) [TM]	386 Deoxys (Spd) [TM]	206 Dunsparce [TM]	269 Dustox [TM]	557 Dwebble [TM]	500 Emboar [TM]	244 Entei [TM]
		102 Exeggcute [43, TM]	103 Exeggutor [TM]	295 Exploud [TM]	653 Fennekin [TM]	597 Ferroseed [TM]	598 Ferrothorn [TM]	669 Flabébé [48, TM]
		670 Floette [58, TM]	671 Florges [TM]	330 Flygon [TM]	590 Foongus [43, TM]	205 Forretress [TM]	162 Furret [TM]	569 Garbodor [TM]
		649 Genesect [TM]	526 Gigalith [TM]	044 Gloom [TM]	673 Gogoat [TM]	623 Golurk [TM]	711 Gourgeist [TM]	210 Granbull [TM]
		388 Grotle [TM]	383 Groudon [60, TM]	253 Grovyle [TM]	316 Gulpin [TM]	440 Happiny [TM]	631 Heatmor [TM]	485 Heatran [TM]
		250 Ho-Oh [TM]	187 Hoppip [TM]	229 Houndoom [TM]	228 Houndour [TM]	174 Igglybuff [TM]	314 Illumise [TM]	392 Infernape [TM]
		002 Ivysaur [44, TM]	039 Jigglypuff [TM]	189 Jumpluff [TM]	115 Kangaskhan [TM]	352 Kecleon [TM]	608 Lampent [TM]	636 Larvesta [TM]
		380 Latias [TM]	381 Latios [TM]	470 Leafeon [TM]	542 Leavanny [TM]	166 Ledian [TM]	165 Ledyba [TM]	463 Lickilicky [TM]
		108 Lickitung [TM]	345 Lileep [TM]	549 Lilligant [TM]	667 Litleo [TM]	607 Litwick [TM]	271 Lombre [TM]	428 Lopunny [TM]
		270 Lotad [TM]	294 Loudred [TM]	272 Ludicolo [TM]	219 Magcargo [TM]	467 Magmortar [TM]	556 Maractus [50, TM]	284 Masquerain [TM]
		303 Mawile [TM]	154 Meganium [66, TM]	151 Mew [TM]	150 Mewtwo [TM]	241 Miltank [TM]	439 Mime Jr. [TM]	146 Moltres [71, TM]
		414 Mothim [TM]	122 Mr. Mime [TM]	446 Munchlax [TM]	177 Natu [TM]	290 Nincada [TM]	038 Ninetales [TM]	291 Ninjask [TM]
		714 Noibat [TM]	715 Noivern [TM]	274 Nuzleaf [TM]	043 Oddish [TM]	511 Pansage [TM]	513 Pansear [TM]	046 Paras [TM]
		047 Parasect [TM]	548 Petilil [TM]	708 Phantump [TM]	499 Pignite [TM]	204 Pineco [TM]	077 Ponyta [TM]	137 Porygon [TM]
		233 Porygon2 [TM]	474 Porygon-Z [TM]	710 Pumpkaboo [TM]	668 Pyroar [TM]	651 Quilladin [TM]	078 Rapidash [TM]	384 Rayquaza [TM]
		643 Reshiram [TM]	315 Roselia [TM]	407 Roserade [TM]	586 Sawsbuck [60, TM]	254 Sceptile [TM]	545 Scolipede [TM]	273 Seedot [TM]
		161 Sentret [TM]	497 Serperior [TM]	496 Servine [TM]	540 Sewaddle [TM]	492 Shaymin (Land) [TM]	492 Shaymin (Sky) [TM]	292 Shedinja [TM]
		275 Shiftry [TM]	285 Shroomish [TM]	561 Sigilyph [TM]	512 Simisage [TM]	514 Simisear [TM]	672 Skiddo [TM]	188 Skiploom [TM]
		300 Skitty [TM]	289 Slaking [TM]	287 Slakoth [TM]	495 Snivy [TM]	143 Snorlax [TM]	459 Snover [TM]	209 Snubbull [TM]

Type	Move	Pokémon that can learn it						
Grass	Solar Beam (TM22)	338 Solrock [41, TM]	167 Spinarak [TM]	234 Stantler [TM]	192 Sunflora [34, TM]	191 Sunkern [34, TM]	283 Surskit [TM]	333 Swablu [TM]
		541 Swadloon [TM]	317 Swalot [TM]	663 Talonflame [TM]	114 Tangela [TM]	465 Tangrowth [TM]	128 Tauros [TM]	498 Tepig [TM]
		468 Togekiss [TM]	175 Togepi [TM]	176 Togetic [TM]	324 Torkoal [TM]	389 Torterra [TM]	328 Trapinch [TM]	252 Treecko [TM]
		709 Trevenant [TM]	357 Tropius [56, TM]	387 Turtwig [TM]	157 Typhlosion [TM]	480 Uxie [TM]	543 Venipede [TM]	049 Venomoth [TM]
		048 Venonat [TM]	003 Venusaur [53, TM]	329 Vibrava [TM]	494 Victini [TM]	071 Victreebel [TM]	288 Vigoroth [TM]	045 Vileplume [64, TM]
		640 Virizion [TM]	666 Vivillon [TM]	313 Volbeat [TM]	637 Volcarona [TM]	070 Weepinbell [TM]	547 Whimsicott [TM]	544 Whirlipede [TM]
		293 Whismur [TM]	040 Wigglytuff [TM]	413 Wormadam (Plant) [TM]	178 Xatu [TM]	193 Yanma [TM]	469 Yanmega [TM]	335 Zangoose [TM]
Normal	Sonic Boom	418 Buizel [1]	101 Electrode [1, 4]	419 Floatzel [1]	330 Flygon [1]	081 Magnemite [11]	082 Magneton [1, 11]	462 Magnezone [1, 11]
		517 Munna [E]	167 Spinarak [E]	329 Vibrava [1]	100 Voltorb [4]	193 Yanma [14]	469 Yanmega [14]	
Dragon	Spacial Rend	484 Palkia [46]						
Electric	Spark	339 Barboach [E]	522 Blitzle [25]	170 Chinchou [23]	603 Eelektrik [1]	309 Electrike [13]	101 Electrode [1, 9]	587 Emolga [13]
		171 Lanturn [23]	404 Luxio [13]	405 Luxray [13]	081 Magnemite [19]	082 Magneton [19]	462 Magnezone [19]	310 Manectric [13]
		312 Minun [7]	299 Nosepass [19]	417 Pachirisu [13]	025 Pikachu [26]	311 Plusle [7]	476 Probopass [19]	243 Raikou [29]
		403 Shinx [13]	618 Stunfisk [E]	602 Tynamo [1]	100 Voltorb [9]	523 Zebstrika [25]		
Bug	Spider Web	168 Ariados [32]	596 Galvantula [1]	595 Joltik [1]	167 Spinarak [29]			
Normal	Spike Cannon	091 Cloyster [13]	222 Corsola [20]	139 Omastar [40]				
Ground	Spikes	406 Budew [E]	659 Bunnelby [E]	331 Cacnea [30]	332 Cacturne [30]	650 Chespin [E]	091 Cloyster [28]	225 Delibird [E]
		386 Deoxys (Def) [25]	557 Dwebble [E]	597 Ferroseed [E]	205 Forretress [28]	658 Greninja [28]	707 Klefki [15]	556 Maractus [E]
		138 Omanyte [E]	204 Pineco [28]	211 Qwilfish [1]	315 Roselia [E]	616 Shelmet [E]	227 Skarmory [28]	361 Snorunt [E]
		568 Trubbish [E]	543 Venipede [E]					
Grass	Spiky Shield	332 Cacturne [32]	652 Chesnaught [36, 75]	556 Maractus [1]				
Normal	Spit Up	024 Arbok [27]	455 Carnivine [37]	346 Cradily [52]	426 Drifblim [34]	425 Drifloon [32]	023 Ekans [25]	088 Grimer [E]
		316 Gulpin [28]	631 Heatmor [50]	449 Hippopotas [E]	109 Koffing [E]	171 Lanturn [27]	345 Lileep [46]	303 Mawile [41]
		322 Numel [E]	279 Pelipper [33]	211 Qwilfish [25]	086 Seel [E]	336 Seviper [E]	422 Shellos [E]	218 Slugma [E]
		363 Spheal [E]	317 Swalot [30]	387 Turtwig [E]	071 Victreebel [1]	194 Wooper [E]		
Ghost	Spite	359 Absol [BP]	681 Aegislash [BP]	306 Aggron [BP]	190 Aipom [BP, E]	424 Ambipom [BP]	024 Arbok [BP]	304 Aron [BP]
		354 Banette [1, 10, BP]	625 Bisharp [BP]	331 Cacnea [BP]	332 Cacturne [BP]	318 Carvanha [BP]	609 Chandelure [BP]	563 Cofagrigus [BP]
		341 Corphish [BP]	408 Cranidos [BP]	342 Crawdaunt [BP]	453 Croagunk [BP]	159 Croconaw [BP]	491 Darkrai [BP]	633 Deino [BP]
		680 Doublade [BP]	426 Drifblim [BP]	425 Drifloon [BP]	206 Dunsparce [7, BP]	356 Dusclops [BP]	477 Dusknoir [BP]	355 Duskull [BP]
		023 Ekans [BP, E]	160 Feraligatr [BP]	592 Frillish [BP]	656 Froakie [BP]	657 Frogadier [BP]	478 Froslass [BP]	569 Garbodor [BP]
		092 Gastly [5, BP]	094 Gengar [1, 5, BP]	487 Giratina (Alt) [BP]	487 Giratina (Ori) [BP]	362 Glalie [BP]	711 Gourgeist [BP]	658 Greninja [BP]
		130 Gyarados [BP]	093 Haunter [1, 5, BP]	430 Honchkrow [BP]	679 Honedge [BP]	229 Houndoom [BP]	228 Houndour [BP, E]	635 Hydreigon [BP]
		686 Inkay [BP]	593 Jellicent [BP]	115 Kangaskhan [BP]	109 Koffing [BP, E]	552 Krokorok [BP]	553 Krookodile [BP]	305 Lairon [BP]
		608 Lampent [BP]	246 Larvitar [BP]	510 Liepard [BP]	607 Litwick [BP]	687 Malamar [BP]	056 Mankey [BP]	052 Meowth [BP, E]
		151 Mew [BP]	262 Mightyena [BP]	200 Misdreavus [5, BP, E]	429 Mismagius [1, BP]	198 Murkrow [BP]	290 Nincada [BP]	038 Ninetales [BP]
		291 Ninjask [BP]	274 Nuzleaf [BP]	674 Pancham [BP]	675 Pangoro [BP]	624 Pawniard [BP]	053 Persian [BP]	708 Phantump [BP]
		261 Poochyena [BP]	057 Primeape [BP]	710 Pumpkaboo [BP]	247 Pupitar [BP]	509 Purrloin [BP]	409 Rampardos [BP]	112 Rhydon [BP]
		111 Rhyhorn [BP]	464 Rhyperior [BP]	479 Rotom (Fan) [BP]	479 Rotom (Frost) [BP]	479 Rotom (Heat) [BP]	479 Rotom (Mow) [BP]	479 Rotom (Wash) [BP]
		479 Rotom [BP]	302 Sableye [BP]	551 Sandile [BP]	560 Scrafty [BP]	559 Scraggy [BP]	273 Seedot [BP]	319 Sharpedo [BP]
		292 Shedinja [17, BP]	275 Shiftry [BP]	353 Shuppet [10, BP]	215 Sneasel [BP, E]	361 Snorunt [BP]	442 Spiritomb [1, BP]	234 Stantler [BP, E]
		618 Stunfisk [BP, E]	128 Tauros [BP]	158 Totodile [BP]	454 Toxicroak [BP]	709 Trevenant [BP]	568 Trubbish [BP]	248 Tyranitar [BP]
		197 Umbreon [BP]	037 Vulpix [BP, E]	461 Weavile [BP]	110 Weezing [BP]	562 Yamask [BP]	571 Zoroark [BP]	570 Zorua [BP]
		634 Zweilous [BP]	718 Zygarde [BP]					
Normal	Splash	298 Azurill [1]	427 Buneary [1]	692 Clauncher [1]	693 Clawitzer [1]	173 Cleffa [E]	225 Delibird [E]	349 Feebas [1]
		456 Finneon [E]	326 Grumpig [1]	187 Hoppip [1]	116 Horsea [E]	189 Jumpluff [1]	428 Lopunny [1]	370 Luvdisc [E]
		129 Magikarp [1]	226 Mantine [E]	458 Mantyke [E]	060 Poliwag [E]	188 Skiploom [1]	325 Spoink [1]	320 Wailmer [1]
		321 Wailord [1]	360 Wynaut [1]					
Grass	Spore	591 Amoonguss [62]	590 Foongus [50]	046 Paras [22]	047 Parasect [22]	285 Shroomish [40]		
Rock	Stealth Rock	142 Aerodactyl [BP]	306 Aggron [BP]	698 Amaura [BP]	347 Anorith [BP]	493 Arceus [BP]	566 Archen [BP]	567 Archeops [BP]
		348 Armaldo [BP]	304 Aron [BP, E]	699 Aurorus [BP]	482 Azelf [BP]	343 Baltoy [BP]	689 Barbaracle [BP]	411 Bastiodon [BP]
		400 Bibarel [BP]	399 Bidoof [BP]	688 Binacle [BP]	625 Bisharp [BP]	242 Blissey [BP]	525 Boldore [36, BP]	438 Bonsly [BP, E]
		437 Bronzong [BP]	436 Bronzor [BP]	323 Camerupt [BP]	703 Carbink [21, BP]	565 Carracosta [BP]	251 Celebi [BP]	113 Chansey [BP]
		390 Chimchar [BP]	344 Claydol [BP]	036 Clefable [BP]	035 Clefairy [BP]	638 Cobalion [BP]	222 Corsola [BP]	346 Cradily [BP]
		408 Cranidos [BP]	558 Crustle [24, BP]	104 Cubone [BP]	386 Deoxys (Atk) [BP]	386 Deoxys (Def) [BP]	386 Deoxys (Nor) [BP]	386 Deoxys (Spd) [BP]
		483 Dialga [BP]	719 Diancie [21, BP]	050 Diglett [BP]	232 Donphan [BP]	529 Drilbur [BP]	621 Druddigon [BP]	051 Dugtrio [BP]
		206 Dunsparce [BP]	557 Dwebble [24, BP]	395 Empoleon [BP]	530 Excadrill [BP]	597 Ferroseed [BP, E]	598 Ferrothorn [BP]	205 Forretress [BP]
		444 Gabite [BP]	445 Garchomp [BP]	074 Geodude [28, BP]	443 Gible [BP]	526 Gigalith [36, BP]	207 Gligar [BP]	472 Gliscor [BP]
		076 Golem [30, BP]	622 Golett [BP]	623 Golurk [BP]	075 Graveler [30, BP]	388 Grotle [BP]	383 Groudon [BP]	485 Heatran [BP]
		449 Hippopotas [BP]	450 Hippowdon [BP]	392 Infernape [BP]	039 Jigglypuff [BP]	385 Jirachi [BP]	140 Kabuto [BP]	141 Kabutops [BP]
		352 Kecleon [BP]	552 Krokorok [BP]	553 Krookodile [BP]	305 Lairon [BP]	645 Landorus [BP]	246 Larvitar [BP, E]	345 Lileep [BP, E]
		337 Lunatone [BP]	219 Magcargo [BP]	473 Mamoswine [BP]	105 Marowak [BP]	259 Marshtomp [BP]	303 Mawile [BP]	481 Mesprit [BP]
		376 Metagross [BP]	375 Metang [BP]	151 Mew [BP]	241 Miltank [BP]	391 Monferno [BP]	034 Nidoking [BP]	031 Nidoqueen [BP]

	Move	Pokémon that can learn it						
Rock	Stealth Rock	299 Nosepass [BP, E]	322 Numel [BP]	138 Omanyte [BP]	139 Omastar [BP]	095 Onix [16, BP, E]	536 Palpitoad [BP]	624 Pawniard [BP, E]
		231 Phanpy [BP]	221 Piloswine [BP]	204 Pineco [BP, E]	127 Pinsir [BP]	393 Piplup [BP]	394 Prinplup [BP]	476 Probopass [BP]
		247 Pupitar [BP]	409 Rampardos [BP]	377 Regirock [BP]	379 Registeel [BP]	369 Relicanth [BP]	112 Rhydon [BP]	111 Rhyhorn [BP]
		464 Rhyperior [BP]	524 Roggenrola [30, BP]	551 Sandile [BP]	027 Sandshrew [BP]	028 Sandslash [BP]	537 Seismitoad [BP]	410 Shieldon [BP, E]
		213 Shuckle [BP]	227 Skarmory [BP, E]	338 Solrock [BP]	208 Steelix [16, BP]	618 Stunfisk [BP]	185 Sudowoodo [BP, E]	260 Swampert [BP]
		220 Swinub [BP, E]	639 Terrakion [BP]	564 Tirtouga [BP]	324 Torkoal [BP]	389 Torterra [BP]	387 Turtwig [BP]	248 Tyranitar [BP]
		697 Tyrantrum [15, BP]	696 Tyrunt [15, BP]	480 Uxie [BP]	040 Wigglytuff [BP]	413 Wormadam (Sand) [BP]	413 Wormadam (Trash) [BP]	
Bug	Steamroller	076 Golem [10]	545 Scolipede [39]	543 Venipede [33]	544 Whirlipede [37]			
Steel	Steel Wing (TM51)	142 Aerodactyl [TM, E]	334 Altaria [TM]	566 Archen [TM, E]	567 Archeops [TM]	144 Articuno [TM]	606 Beheeyem [TM]	628 Braviary [TM]
		006 Charizard [TM]	441 Chatot [TM, E]	169 Crobat [TM]	085 Dodrio [TM]	084 Doduo [TM]	149 Dragonite [TM]	580 Ducklett [TM, E]
		605 Elgyem [TM]	395 Empoleon [TM]	083 Farfetch'd [TM, E]	022 Fearow [TM]	662 Fletchinder [55, TM]	661 Fletchling [48, TM]	330 Flygon [TM]
		487 Giratina (Alt) [TM]	487 Giratina (Ori) [TM]	207 Gligar [TM]	472 Gliscor [TM]	042 Golbat [TM]	701 Hawlucha [TM]	430 Honchkrow [TM]
		250 Ho-Oh [TM]	163 Hoothoot [TM]	635 Hydreigon [TM]	646 Kyurem (Blk) [TM]	646 Kyurem (Wht) [TM]	646 Kyurem [TM]	380 Latias [TM]
		381 Latios [TM]	542 Leavanny [TM]	249 Lugia [TM]	630 Mandibuzz [TM]	151 Mew [TM]	146 Moltres [TM]	198 Murkrow [TM]
		177 Natu [TM, E]	164 Noctowl [TM]	714 Noibat [TM]	715 Noivern [TM]	279 Pelipper [TM]	018 Pidgeot [TM]	017 Pidgeotto [TM]
		016 Pidgey [TM, E]	519 Pidove [TM, E]	643 Reshiram [TM]	627 Rufflet [TM]	373 Salamence [TM]	212 Scizor [TM]	123 Scyther [TM, E]
		561 Sigilyph [TM, E]	227 Skarmory [34, TM]	021 Spearow [TM, E]	398 Staraptor [TM]	397 Staravia [TM]	396 Starly [TM, E]	333 Swablu [TM, E]
		581 Swanna [TM]	277 Swellow [TM]	528 Swoobat [TM]	276 Taillow [TM, E]	663 Talonflame [60, TM]	468 Togekiss [TM]	176 Togetic [TM]
		520 Tranquill [TM]	357 Tropius [TM]	521 Unfezant [TM]	329 Vibrava [TM]	629 Vullaby [TM, E]	278 Wingull [TM]	527 Woobat [TM]
		178 Xatu [TM]	193 Yanma [TM]	469 Yanmega [TM]	717 Yveltal [TM]	145 Zapdos [TM]	644 Zekrom [TM]	041 Zubat [TM, E]
Bug	Sticky Web	168 Ariados [58]	596 Galvantula [1, 65]	402 Kricketune [44]	540 Sewaddle [31]	213 Shuckle [1, 53]	167 Spinarak [50]	283 Surskit [38]
Normal	Stockpile	024 Arbok [27]	455 Carnivine [37]	346 Cradily [52]	426 Drifblim [25]	425 Drifloon [25]	023 Ekans [25]	569 Garbodor [23]
		088 Grimer [E]	316 Gulpin [28]	631 Heatmor [50]	449 Hippopotas [E]	109 Koffing [E]	171 Lanturn [27]	345 Lileep [46]
		303 Mawile [41]	446 Munchlax [28]	322 Numel [E]	279 Pelipper [33]	211 Qwilfish [25]	086 Seel [E]	336 Seviper [E]
		422 Shellos [E]	218 Slugma [E]	363 Spheal [E]	317 Swalot [30]	568 Trubbish [23]	387 Turtwig [E]	071 Victreebel [1]
		194 Wooper [E]						
	Stomp	304 Aron [E]	522 Blitzle [29]	626 Bouffalant [E]	408 Cranidos [E]	244 Entei [29]	103 Exeggutor [1]	295 Exploud [23]
		203 Girafarig [14]	115 Kangaskhan [E]	099 Kingler [25]	098 Krabby [25]	246 Larvitar [E]	463 Lickilicky [21]	108 Lickitung [21]
		294 Loudred [23]	241 Miltank [8]	258 Mudkip [E]	322 Numel [E]	077 Ponyta [17]	078 Rapidash [17]	378 Regice [1]
		377 Regirock [1]	379 Registeel [1]	112 Rhydon [17]	111 Rhyhorn [17]	464 Rhyperior [17]	079 Slowpoke [E]	459 Snover [E]
		234 Stantler [13]	357 Tropius [10]	697 Tyrantrum [10]	696 Tyrunt [10]	293 Whismur [22]	523 Zebstrika [31]	
Rock	Stone Edge (TM71)	359 Absol [TM]	142 Aerodactyl [TM]	306 Aggron [TM]	698 Amaura [TM]	493 Arceus [TM]	566 Archen [TM]	567 Archeops [TM]
		348 Armaldo [TM]	699 Aurorus [TM]	713 Avalugg [TM]	689 Barbaracle [1, 60, TM]	411 Bastiodon [TM]	614 Beartic [TM]	712 Bergmite [TM]
		688 Binacle [TM]	625 Bisharp [TM]	257 Blaziken [TM]	525 Boldore [48, TM]	626 Bouffalant [TM]	286 Breloom [TM]	659 Bunnelby [TM]
		323 Camerupt [TM]	703 Carbink [49, TM]	565 Carracosta [TM]	652 Chesnaught [TM]	650 Chespin [TM]	344 Claydol [TM]	638 Cobalion [TM]
		534 Conkeldurr [49, TM]	222 Corsola [TM]	346 Cradily [TM]	408 Cranidos [TM]	558 Crustle [TM]	555 Darmanitan [TM]	483 Dialga [TM]
		719 Diancie [49, TM]	660 Diggersby [TM]	232 Donphan [TM]	149 Dragonite [TM]	051 Dugtrio [TM]	632 Durant [TM]	557 Dwebble [TM]
		500 Emboar [TM]	244 Entei [TM]	330 Flygon [TM]	444 Gabite [TM]	475 Gallade [TM]	445 Garchomp [TM]	423 Gastrodon [TM]
		074 Geodude [42, TM]	443 Gible [TM]	526 Gigalith [48, TM]	487 Giratina (Alt) [TM]	487 Giratina (Ori) [TM]	207 Gligar [TM]	472 Gliscor [TM]
		076 Golem [54, TM]	623 Golurk [TM]	210 Granbull [TM]	075 Graveler [54, TM]	383 Groudon [TM]	533 Gurdurr [49, TM]	130 Gyarados [TM]
		297 Hariyama [TM]	701 Hawlucha [TM]	485 Heatran [88, TM]	214 Heracross [TM]	450 Hippowdon [TM]	107 Hitmonchan [TM]	106 Hitmonlee [TM]
		237 Hitmontop [TM]	635 Hydreigon [TM]	392 Infernape [TM]	141 Kabutops [TM]	647 Keldeo [TM]	552 Krokorok [TM]	553 Krookodile [TM]
		646 Kyurem (Blk) [TM]	646 Kyurem (Wht) [TM]	646 Kyurem [TM]	305 Lairon [TM]	645 Landorus [73, TM]	246 Larvitar [50, TM]	448 Lucario [TM]
		337 Lunatone [37, TM]	068 Machamp [TM]	219 Magcargo [TM]	473 Mamoswine [TM]	105 Marowak [TM]	303 Mawile [TM]	648 Meloetta [TM]
		151 Mew [TM]	150 Mewtwo [TM]	619 Mienfoo [TM]	620 Mienshao [TM]	034 Nidoking [TM]	031 Nidoqueen [TM]	299 Nosepass [40, TM]
		139 Omastar [TM]	095 Onix [46, TM]	484 Palkia [TM]	674 Pancham [TM]	675 Pangoro [TM]	499 Pignite [TM]	221 Piloswine [TM]
		127 Pinsir [TM]	057 Primeape [TM]	476 Probopass [40, TM]	247 Pupitar [60, TM]	195 Quagsire [TM]	651 Quilladin [TM]	409 Rampardos [TM]
		384 Rayquaza [TM]	486 Regigigas [TM]	377 Regirock [43, TM]	369 Relicanth [TM]	643 Reshiram [TM]	112 Rhydon [41, TM]	111 Rhyhorn [41, TM]
		464 Rhyperior [41, TM]	524 Roggenrola [36, TM]	373 Salamence [TM]	551 Sandile [TM]	028 Sandslash [TM]	539 Sawk [TM]	560 Scrafty [TM]
		559 Scraggy [TM]	410 Shieldon [TM]	213 Shuckle [49, TM]	338 Solrock [37, TM]	208 Steelix [46, TM]	618 Stunfisk [TM]	185 Sudowoodo [43, TM]
		260 Swampert [TM]	128 Tauros [TM]	639 Terrakion [67, TM]	538 Throh [TM]	532 Timburr [43, TM]	564 Tirtouga [TM]	324 Torkoal [TM]
		389 Torterra [TM]	454 Toxicroak [TM]	248 Tyranitar [63, TM]	697 Tyrantrum [TM]	696 Tyrunt [TM]	217 Ursaring [TM]	640 Virizion [TM]
		340 Whiscash [TM]	644 Zekrom [TM]	718 Zygarde [TM]				
Psychic	Stored Power	358 Chimecho [E]	433 Chingling [E]	035 Clefairy [28]	173 Cleffa [E]	133 Eevee [E]	475 Gallade [1, 58]	282 Gardevoir [1, 58]
		281 Kirlia [51]	380 Latias [10]	381 Latios [10]	678 Meowstic (F) [1, 53]	517 Munna [47]	177 Natu [17]	280 Ralts [42]
		561 Sigilyph [E]	175 Togepi [E]	494 Victini [89]	527 Woobat [E]	178 Xatu [17]		
Fighting	Storm Throw	674 Pancham [E]	127 Pinsir [36]	538 Throh [25]				

	Move	Pokémon that can learn it						
Normal	Strength (HM04)	460 Abomasnow [HM]	359 Absol [HM]	142 Aerodactyl [HM]	306 Aggron [HM]	190 Aipom [HM]	424 Ambipom [HM]	181 Ampharos [HM]
		024 Arbok [HM]	059 Arcanine [HM]	493 Arceus [HM]	348 Armaldo [HM]	304 Aron [HM]	713 Avalugg [HM]	610 Axew [HM]
		184 Azumarill [HM]	371 Bagon [HM]	689 Barbaracle [HM]	411 Bastiodon [HM]	153 Bayleef [HM]	614 Beartic [HM]	712 Bergmite [HM]
		400 Bibarel [HM]	688 Binacle [HM]	009 Blastoise [HM]	257 Blaziken [HM]	242 Blissey [HM]	525 Boldore [HM]	626 Bouffalant [HM]
		628 Braviary [HM]	286 Breloom [HM]	437 Bronzong [HM]	418 Buizel [HM]	001 Bulbasaur [HM]	659 Bunnelby [HM]	332 Cacturne [HM]
		323 Camerupt [HM]	565 Carracosta [HM]	113 Chansey [HM]	006 Charizard [HM]	004 Charmander [HM]	005 Charmeleon [HM]	652 Chesnaught [HM]
		650 Chespin [HM]	390 Chimchar [HM]	344 Claydol [HM]	036 Clefable [HM]	035 Clefairy [HM]	638 Cobalion [HM]	256 Combusken [HM]
		534 Conkeldurr [HM]	341 Corphish [HM]	222 Corsola [HM]	346 Cradily [HM]	408 Cranidos [HM]	342 Crawdaunt [HM]	453 Croagunk [HM]
		159 Croconaw [HM]	558 Crustle [HM]	613 Cubchoo [HM]	104 Cubone [HM]	491 Darkrai [HM]	555 Darmanitan [HM]	554 Darumaka [HM]
		633 Deino [HM]	301 Delcatty [HM]	386 Deoxys (Atk) [HM]	386 Deoxys (Def) [HM]	386 Deoxys (Nor) [HM]	386 Deoxys (Spd) [HM]	483 Dialga [HM]
		660 Diggersby [HM]	232 Donphan [HM]	149 Dragonite [HM]	452 Drapion [HM]	529 Drilbur [HM]	621 Druddigon [HM]	206 Dunsparce [HM]
		632 Durant [HM]	356 Dusclops [HM]	477 Dusknoir [HM]	557 Dwebble [HM]	604 Eelektross [HM]	023 Ekans [HM]	125 Electabuzz [HM]
		466 Electivire [HM]	309 Electrike [HM]	500 Emboar [HM]	395 Empoleon [HM]	244 Entei [HM]	530 Excadrill [HM]	102 Exeggcute [HM]
		103 Exeggutor [HM]	295 Exploud [HM]	160 Feraligatr [HM]	598 Ferrothorn [HM]	180 Flaaffy [HM]	136 Flareon [HM]	419 Floatzel [HM]
		330 Flygon [HM]	205 Forretress [HM]	611 Fraxure [HM]	656 Froakie [HM]	657 Frogadier [HM]	162 Furret [HM]	444 Gabite [HM]
		475 Gallade [HM]	445 Garchomp [HM]	423 Gastrodon [HM]	094 Gengar [HM]	074 Geodude [HM]	443 Gible [HM]	526 Gigalith [HM]
		203 Girafarig [HM]	487 Giratina (Alt) [HM]	487 Giratina (Ori) [HM]	471 Glaceon [HM]	207 Gligar [HM]	472 Gliscor [HM]	673 Gogoat [HM]
		055 Golduck [HM]	076 Golem [HM]	622 Golett [HM]	623 Golurk [HM]	706 Goodra [HM]	210 Granbull [HM]	075 Graveler [HM]
		658 Greninja [HM]	088 Grimer [HM]	388 Grotle [HM]	383 Groudon [HM]	253 Grovyle [HM]	058 Growlithe [HM]	316 Gulpin [HM]
		533 Gurdurr [HM]	130 Gyarados [HM]	297 Hariyama [HM]	701 Hawlucha [HM]	612 Haxorus [HM]	485 Heatran [HM]	214 Heracross [HM]
		507 Herdier [HM]	449 Hippopotas [HM]	450 Hippowdon [HM]	107 Hitmonchan [HM]	106 Hitmonlee [HM]	237 Hitmontop [HM]	250 Ho-Oh [HM]
		229 Houndoom [HM]	635 Hydreigon [HM]	392 Infernape [HM]	002 Ivysaur [HM]	039 Jigglypuff [HM]	135 Jolteon [HM]	115 Kangaskhan [HM]
		352 Kecleon [HM]	647 Keldeo [HM]	099 Kingler [HM]	098 Krabby [HM]	402 Kricketune [HM]	552 Krokorok [HM]	553 Krookodile [HM]
		382 Kyogre [HM]	646 Kyurem (Blk) [HM]	646 Kyurem (Wht) [HM]	646 Kyurem [HM]	305 Lairon [HM]	645 Landorus [HM]	131 Lapras [HM]
		470 Leafeon [HM]	166 Ledian [HM]	463 Lickilicky [HM]	108 Lickitung [HM]	264 Linoone [HM]	667 Litleo [HM]	271 Lombre [HM]
		428 Lopunny [HM]	294 Loudred [HM]	448 Lucario [HM]	272 Ludicolo [HM]	249 Lugia [HM]	404 Luxio [HM]	405 Luxray [HM]
		068 Machamp [HM]	067 Machoke [HM]	066 Machop [HM]	219 Magcargo [HM]	126 Magmar [HM]	467 Magmortar [HM]	296 Makuhita [HM]
		473 Mamoswine [HM]	310 Manectric [HM]	056 Mankey [HM]	183 Marill [HM]	105 Marowak [HM]	259 Marshtomp [HM]	303 Mawile [HM]
		308 Medicham [HM]	307 Meditite [HM]	154 Meganium [HM]	648 Meloetta [HM]	376 Metagross [HM]	375 Metang [HM]	151 Mew [HM]
		150 Mewtwo [HM]	619 Mienfoo [HM]	620 Mienshao [HM]	262 Mightyena [HM]	241 Miltank [HM]	391 Monferno [HM]	258 Mudkip [HM]
		089 Muk [HM]	446 Munchlax [HM]	034 Nidoking [HM]	031 Nidoqueen [HM]	029 Nidoran ♀ [HM]	032 Nidoran ♂ [HM]	030 Nidorina [HM]
		033 Nidorino [HM]	299 Nosepass [HM]	322 Numel [HM]	274 Nuzleaf [HM]	095 Onix [HM]	484 Palkia [HM]	674 Pancham [HM]
		675 Pangoro [HM]	231 Phanpy [HM]	708 Phantump [HM]	499 Pignite [HM]	025 Pikachu [HM]	221 Piloswine [HM]	204 Pineco [HM]
		127 Pinsir [HM]	186 Politoed [HM]	061 Poliwhirl [HM]	062 Poliwrath [HM]	077 Ponyta [HM]	057 Primeape [HM]	394 Prinplup [HM]
		476 Probopass [HM]	054 Psyduck [HM]	668 Pyroar [HM]	195 Quagsire [HM]	156 Quilava [HM]	651 Quilladin [HM]	026 Raichu [HM]
		243 Raikou [HM]	409 Rampardos [HM]	078 Rapidash [HM]	020 Raticate [HM]	384 Rayquaza [HM]	378 Regice [HM]	486 Regigigas [HM]
		377 Regirock [HM]	379 Registeel [HM]	643 Reshiram [HM]	579 Reuniclus [HM]	112 Rhydon [HM]	111 Rhyhorn [HM]	464 Rhyperior [HM]
		447 Riolu [HM]	524 Roggenrola [HM]	627 Rufflet [HM]	373 Salamence [HM]	503 Samurott [HM]	027 Sandshrew [HM]	028 Sandslash [HM]
		539 Sawk [HM]	254 Sceptile [HM]	212 Scizor [HM]	545 Scolipede [HM]	560 Scrafty [HM]	559 Scraggy [HM]	364 Sealeo [HM]
		537 Seismitoad [HM]	497 Serperior [HM]	336 Seviper [HM]	319 Sharpedo [HM]	372 Shelgon [HM]	410 Shieldon [HM]	275 Shiftry [HM]
		403 Shinx [HM]	213 Shuckle [HM]	672 Skiddo [HM]	451 Skorupi [HM]	435 Skuntank [HM]	289 Slaking [HM]	287 Slakoth [HM]
		080 Slowbro [HM]	199 Slowking [HM]	079 Slowpoke [HM]	215 Sneasel [HM]	143 Snorlax [HM]	209 Snubbull [HM]	363 Spheal [HM]
		327 Spinda [HM]	007 Squirtle [HM]	208 Steelix [HM]	508 Stoutland [HM]	185 Sudowoodo [HM]	317 Swalot [HM]	260 Swampert [HM]
		220 Swinub [HM]	465 Tangrowth [HM]	128 Tauros [HM]	216 Teddiursa [HM]	498 Tepig [HM]	639 Terrakion [HM]	538 Throh [HM]
		642 Thundurus [HM]	532 Timburr [HM]	564 Tirtouga [HM]	255 Torchic [HM]	324 Torkoal [HM]	641 Tornadus [HM]	389 Torterra [HM]
		454 Toxicroak [HM]	328 Trapinch [HM]	252 Treecko [HM]	709 Trevenant [HM]	357 Tropius [HM]	387 Turtwig [HM]	157 Typhlosion [HM]
		248 Tyranitar [HM]	697 Tyrantrum [HM]	236 Tyrogue [HM]	696 Tyrunt [HM]	217 Ursaring [HM]	134 Vaporeon [HM]	003 Venusaur [HM]
		329 Vibrava [HM]	288 Vigoroth [HM]	640 Virizion [HM]	320 Wailmer [HM]	321 Wailord [HM]	365 Walrein [HM]	008 Wartortle [HM]
		505 Watchog [HM]	461 Weavile [HM]	340 Whiscash [HM]	040 Wigglytuff [HM]	335 Zangoose [HM]	644 Zekrom [HM]	634 Zweilous [HM]
		718 Zygarde [HM]						
Bug	String Shot	168 Ariados [1]	010 Caterpie [1]	596 Galvantula [1]	595 Joltik [1]	636 Larvesta [1, E]	542 Leavanny [1]	664 Scatterbug [1]
		540 Sewaddle [1]	167 Spinarak [1]	541 Swadloon [1]	637 Volcarona [1]	013 Weedle [1]	265 Wurmple [1]	
	Struggle Bug (TM76)	617 Accelgor [16, TM]	347 Anorith [TM]	168 Ariados [TM]	348 Armaldo [TM]	267 Beautifly [TM]	015 Beedrill [TM]	012 Butterfree [TM]
		558 Crustle [TM]	452 Drapion [TM]	632 Durant [TM]	269 Dustox [TM]	557 Dwebble [TM]	589 Escavalier [TM]	330 Flygon [TM]
		205 Forretress [TM]	596 Galvantula [TM]	649 Genesect [TM]	207 Gligar [TM]	472 Gliscor [TM]	214 Heracross [TM]	314 Illumise [15, TM]
		595 Joltik [TM]	588 Karrablast [TM]	401 Kricketot [6, TM]	402 Kricketune [TM]	636 Larvesta [TM]	542 Leavanny [22, TM]	166 Ledian [TM]
		165 Ledyba [TM]	284 Masquerain [TM]	151 Mew [TM]	414 Mothim [TM]	290 Nincada [TM]	291 Ninjask [TM]	046 Paras [TM]
		047 Parasect [TM]	204 Pineco [TM]	127 Pinsir [TM]	212 Scizor [TM]	545 Scolipede [TM]	123 Scyther [TM]	540 Sewaddle [22, TM]
		292 Shedinja [TM]	616 Shelmet [16, TM]	213 Shuckle [12, TM]	451 Skorupi [TM]	167 Spinarak [TM]	283 Surskit [TM]	541 Swadloon [TM]
		328 Trapinch [TM]	543 Venipede [TM]	049 Venomoth [TM]	048 Venonat [TM]	416 Vespiquen [TM]	329 Vibrava [TM]	666 Vivillon [12, TM]
		313 Volbeat [15, TM]	637 Volcarona [TM]	544 Whirlipede [TM]	413 Wormadam (Plant) [TM]	413 Wormadam (Sand) [TM]	413 Wormadam (Trash) [TM]	469 Yanmega [TM]

	Move	Pokémon that can learn it						
Grass	Stun Spore	267 Beautifly [15]	182 Bellossom [1]	069 Bellsprout [17]	286 Breloom [1, 5]	406 Budew [10]	012 Butterfree [12]	455 Carnivine [E]
		546 Cottonee [10]	102 Exeggcute [19]	590 Foongus [E]	044 Gloom [14]	187 Hoppip [14]	189 Jumpluff [14]	284 Masquerain [26]
		043 Oddish [14]	046 Paras [6]	047 Parasect [1, 6]	548 Petilil [22]	315 Roselia [10]	664 Scatterbug [6, E]	285 Shroomish [5]
		188 Skiploom [14]	114 Tangela [30]	465 Tangrowth [30]	049 Venomoth [23]	048 Venonat [23]	045 Vileplume [1]	666 Vivillon [1]
		070 Weepinbell [17]						
Fighting	Submission	390 Chimchar [E]	529 Drilbur [E]	068 Machamp [37]	067 Machoke [37]	066 Machop [33]	127 Pinsir [29]	062 Poliwrath [1]
Normal	Substitute (TM90)	460 Abomasnow [TM]	063 Abra [TM]	359 Absol [TM]	617 Accelgor [TM]	681 Aegislash [TM]	142 Aerodactyl [TM]	306 Aggron [TM]
		190 Aipom [TM]	065 Alakazam [TM]	594 Alomomola [TM]	334 Altaria [TM]	698 Amaura [TM]	424 Ambipom [TM]	591 Amoonguss [TM]
		181 Ampharos [TM]	347 Anorith [TM]	024 Arbok [TM]	059 Arcanine [TM]	493 Arceus [TM]	566 Archen [TM]	567 Archeops [TM]
		168 Ariados [TM]	348 Armaldo [TM]	683 Aromatisse [TM]	304 Aron [TM]	144 Articuno [TM]	531 Audino [TM]	699 Aurorus [TM]
		713 Avalugg [TM]	610 Axew [TM]	482 Azelf [TM]	184 Azumarill [TM]	298 Azurill [TM]	371 Bagon [TM]	343 Baltoy [TM]
		354 Banette [TM]	689 Barbaracle [TM]	339 Barboach [TM]	550 Basculin [TM]	411 Bastiodon [TM]	153 Bayleef [TM]	614 Beartic [TM]
		267 Beautifly [TM]	015 Beedrill [TM]	606 Beheeyem [TM]	182 Bellossom [TM]	069 Bellsprout [TM]	712 Bergmite [TM]	400 Bibarel [TM]
		399 Bidoof [TM]	688 Binacle [TM]	625 Bisharp [TM]	009 Blastoise [TM]	257 Blaziken [TM]	242 Blissey [TM]	522 Blitzle [TM]
		525 Boldore [TM]	438 Bonsly [TM]	626 Bouffalant [TM]	654 Braixen [TM]	628 Braviary [TM]	286 Breloom [TM]	437 Bronzong [TM]
		436 Bronzor [TM]	406 Budew [TM]	418 Buizel [TM]	001 Bulbasaur [TM]	427 Buneary [TM]	659 Bunnelby [TM]	012 Butterfree [TM]
		331 Cacnea [TM]	332 Cacturne [TM]	323 Camerupt [TM]	703 Carbink [TM]	455 Carnivine [TM]	565 Carracosta [TM]	318 Carvanha [TM]
		351 Castform [TM]	251 Celebi [TM]	609 Chandelure [TM]	113 Chansey [TM]	006 Charizard [TM]	004 Charmander [TM]	005 Charmeleon [TM]
		441 Chatot [TM]	421 Cherrim [TM]	420 Cherubi [TM]	652 Chesnaught [TM]	650 Chespin [TM]	152 Chikorita [TM]	390 Chimchar [TM]
		358 Chimecho [TM]	170 Chinchou [TM]	433 Chingling [TM]	573 Cinccino [TM]	366 Clamperl [TM]	692 Clauncher [TM]	693 Clawitzer [TM]
		344 Claydol [TM]	036 Clefable [TM]	035 Clefairy [TM]	173 Cleffa [TM]	091 Cloyster [TM]	638 Cobalion [TM]	563 Cofagrigus [TM]
		256 Combusken [TM]	534 Conkeldurr [TM]	341 Corphish [TM]	222 Corsola [TM]	546 Cottonee [TM]	346 Cradily [TM]	408 Cranidos [TM]
		342 Crawdaunt [TM]	488 Cresselia [TM]	453 Croagunk [TM]	169 Crobat [TM]	159 Croconaw [TM]	558 Crustle [TM]	615 Cryogonal [TM]
		613 Cubchoo [TM]	104 Cubone [TM]	155 Cyndaquil [TM]	491 Darkrai [TM]	555 Darmanitan [TM]	554 Darumaka [TM]	702 Dedenne [TM]
		585 Deerling [TM]	633 Deino [TM]	301 Delcatty [TM]	225 Delibird [TM]	655 Delphox [TM]	386 Deoxys (Atk) [TM]	386 Deoxys (Def) [TM]
		386 Deoxys (Nor) [TM]	386 Deoxys (Spd) [TM]	087 Dewgong [TM]	502 Dewott [TM]	483 Dialga [TM]	719 Diancie [TM]	660 Diggersby [TM]
		050 Diglett [TM]	085 Dodrio [TM]	084 Doduo [TM]	232 Donphan [TM]	680 Doublade [TM]	691 Dragalge [TM]	148 Dragonair [TM]
		149 Dragonite [TM]	452 Drapion [TM]	147 Dratini [TM]	426 Drifblim [TM]	425 Drifloon [TM]	529 Drilbur [TM]	096 Drowzee [TM]
		621 Druddigon [TM]	580 Ducklett [TM]	051 Dugtrio [TM]	206 Dunsparce [TM]	578 Duosion [TM]	632 Durant [TM]	356 Dusclops [TM]
		477 Dusknoir [TM]	355 Duskull [TM]	269 Dustox [TM]	557 Dwebble [TM]	603 Eelektrik [TM]	604 Eelektross [TM]	133 Eevee [TM]
		023 Ekans [TM]	125 Electabuzz [TM]	466 Electivire [TM]	309 Electrike [TM]	101 Electrode [TM]	239 Elekid [TM]	605 Elgyem [TM]
		500 Emboar [TM]	587 Emolga [TM]	395 Empoleon [TM]	244 Entei [TM]	589 Escavalier [TM]	196 Espeon [TM]	677 Espurr [TM]
		530 Excadrill [TM]	102 Exeggcute [TM]	103 Exeggutor [TM]	295 Exploud [TM]	083 Farfetch'd [TM]	022 Fearow [TM]	349 Feebas [TM]
		653 Fennekin [TM]	160 Feraligatr [TM]	597 Ferroseed [TM]	598 Ferrothorn [TM]	456 Finneon [TM]	180 Flaaffy [TM]	669 Flabébé [TM]
		136 Flareon [TM]	662 Fletchinder [TM]	661 Fletchling [TM]	419 Floatzel [TM]	670 Floette [TM]	671 Florges [TM]	330 Flygon [TM]
		590 Foongus [TM]	205 Forretress [TM]	611 Fraxure [TM]	592 Frillish [TM]	656 Froakie [35, TM]	657 Frogadier [38, TM]	478 Froslass [TM]
		676 Furfrou [TM]	162 Furret [TM]	444 Gabite [TM]	475 Gallade [TM]	596 Galvantula [TM]	569 Garbodor [TM]	445 Garchomp [TM]
		282 Gardevoir [TM]	092 Gastly [TM]	423 Gastrodon [TM]	649 Genesect [TM]	094 Gengar [TM]	074 Geodude [TM]	443 Gible [TM]
		526 Gigalith [TM]	203 Girafarig [TM]	487 Giratina (Alt) [TM]	487 Giratina (Ori) [TM]	471 Glaceon [TM]	362 Glalie [TM]	431 Glameow [TM]
		207 Gligar [TM]	472 Gliscor [TM]	044 Gloom [TM]	673 Gogoat [TM]	042 Golbat [TM]	118 Goldeen [TM]	055 Golduck [TM]
		076 Golem [TM]	622 Golett [TM]	623 Golurk [TM]	706 Goodra [TM]	704 Goomy [TM]	368 Gorebyss [TM]	574 Gothita [TM]
		576 Gothitelle [TM]	575 Gothorita [TM]	711 Gourgeist [TM]	210 Granbull [TM]	075 Graveler [TM]	658 Greninja [43, TM]	088 Grimer [TM]
		388 Grotle [TM]	383 Groudon [TM]	253 Grovyle [TM]	058 Growlithe [TM]	326 Grumpig [TM]	316 Gulpin [TM]	533 Gurdurr [TM]
		130 Gyarados [TM]	440 Happiny [TM]	297 Hariyama [TM]	093 Haunter [TM]	701 Hawlucha [TM]	612 Haxorus [TM]	631 Heatmor [TM]
		485 Heatran [TM]	695 Heliolisk [TM]	694 Helioptile [TM]	214 Heracross [TM]	507 Herdier [TM]	449 Hippopotas [TM]	450 Hippowdon [TM]
		107 Hitmonchan [TM]	106 Hitmonlee [TM]	237 Hitmontop [TM]	430 Honchkrow [TM]	679 Honedge [TM]	250 Ho-Oh [TM]	163 Hoothoot [TM]
		187 Hoppip [TM]	116 Horsea [TM]	229 Houndoom [TM]	228 Houndour [TM]	367 Huntail [TM]	635 Hydreigon [TM]	097 Hypno [TM]
		174 Igglybuff [TM]	314 Illumise [TM]	392 Infernape [TM]	686 Inkay [TM]	002 Ivysaur [TM]	593 Jellicent [TM]	039 Jigglypuff [TM]
		385 Jirachi [TM]	135 Jolteon [TM]	595 Joltik [TM]	189 Jumpluff [TM]	124 Jynx [TM]	140 Kabuto [TM]	141 Kabutops [TM]
		064 Kadabra [TM]	115 Kangaskhan [TM]	588 Karrablast [TM]	352 Kecleon [42, TM]	647 Keldeo [TM]	230 Kingdra [TM]	099 Kingler [TM]
		281 Kirlia [TM]	600 Klang [TM]	707 Klefki [TM]	599 Klink [TM]	601 Klinklang [TM]	109 Koffing [TM]	098 Krabby [TM]
		402 Kricketune [TM]	552 Krokorok [TM]	553 Krookodile [TM]	382 Kyogre [TM]	646 Kyurem (Blk) [TM]	646 Kyurem (Wht) [TM]	646 Kyurem [TM]
		305 Lairon [TM]	608 Lampent [TM]	645 Landorus [TM]	171 Lanturn [TM]	131 Lapras [TM]	636 Larvesta [TM]	246 Larvitar [TM]
		380 Latias [TM]	381 Latios [TM]	470 Leafeon [TM]	542 Leavanny [TM]	166 Ledian [TM]	165 Ledyba [TM]	463 Lickilicky [TM]
		108 Lickitung [TM]	510 Liepard [TM]	345 Lileep [TM]	549 Lilligant [TM]	506 Lillipup [TM]	264 Linoone [TM]	667 Litleo [TM]
		607 Litwick [TM]	271 Lombre [TM]	428 Lopunny [TM]	270 Lotad [TM]	294 Loudred [TM]	448 Lucario [TM]	272 Ludicolo [TM]
		249 Lugia [TM]	457 Lumineon [TM]	337 Lunatone [TM]	370 Luvdisc [TM]	404 Luxio [TM]	405 Luxray [TM]	068 Machamp [TM]
		067 Machoke [TM]	066 Machop [TM]	240 Magby [TM]	219 Magcargo [TM]	126 Magmar [TM]	467 Magmortar [TM]	081 Magnemite [TM]
		082 Magneton [TM]	462 Magnezone [TM]	296 Makuhita [TM]	687 Malamar [TM]	473 Mamoswine [TM]	490 Manaphy [TM]	630 Mandibuzz [TM]
		310 Manectric [TM]	056 Mankey [TM]	226 Mantine [TM]	458 Mantyke [TM]	556 Maractus [TM]	179 Mareep [TM]	183 Marill [TM]
		105 Marowak [TM]	259 Marshtomp [TM]	284 Masquerain [TM]	303 Mawile [TM]	308 Medicham [TM]	307 Meditite [TM]	154 Meganium [TM]
		648 Meloetta [TM]	678 Meowstic (F) [TM]	678 Meowstic (M) [TM]	052 Meowth [TM]	481 Mesprit [TM]	376 Metagross [TM]	375 Metang [TM]
		151 Mew [TM]	150 Mewtwo [TM]	619 Mienfoo [TM]	620 Mienshao [TM]	262 Mightyena [TM]	350 Milotic [TM]	241 Miltank [TM]
		439 Mime Jr. [29, TM]	572 Minccino [TM]	312 Minun [TM]	200 Misdreavus [TM]	429 Mismagius [TM]	146 Moltres [TM]	391 Monferno [TM]
		414 Mothim [TM]	122 Mr. Mime [29, TM]	258 Mudkip [TM]	089 Muk [TM]	446 Munchlax [TM]	517 Munna [TM]	198 Murkrow [TM]

	Move	Pokémon that can learn it						
Normal	Substitute (TM90)	518 Musharna [TM]	177 Natu [TM]	034 Nidoking [TM]	031 Nidoqueen [TM]	029 Nidoran ♀ [TM]	032 Nidoran ♂ [TM]	030 Nidorina [TM]
		033 Nidorino [TM]	290 Nincada [TM]	038 Ninetales [TM]	291 Ninjask [TM]	164 Noctowl [TM]	714 Noibat [TM]	715 Noivern [TM]
		299 Nosepass [TM]	322 Numel [TM]	274 Nuzleaf [TM]	224 Octillery [TM]	043 Oddish [TM]	138 Omanyte [TM]	139 Omastar [TM]
		095 Onix [TM]	501 Oshawott [TM]	417 Pachirisu [TM]	484 Palkia [TM]	536 Palpitoad [TM]	674 Pancham [TM]	675 Pangoro [TM]
		515 Panpour [TM]	511 Pansage [TM]	513 Pansear [TM]	046 Paras [TM]	047 Parasect [TM]	504 Patrat [TM]	624 Pawniard [TM]
		279 Pelipper [TM]	053 Persian [TM]	548 Petilil [TM]	231 Phanpy [TM]	708 Phantump [TM]	489 Phione [TM]	172 Pichu [TM]
		018 Pidgeot [TM]	017 Pidgeotto [TM]	016 Pidgey [TM]	519 Pidove [TM]	499 Pignite [TM]	025 Pikachu [TM]	221 Piloswine [TM]
		204 Pineco [TM]	127 Pinsir [TM]	393 Piplup [TM]	311 Plusle [TM]	186 Politoed [TM]	060 Poliwag [TM]	061 Poliwhirl [TM]
		062 Poliwrath [TM]	077 Ponyta [TM]	261 Poochyena [TM]	137 Porygon [TM]	233 Porygon2 [TM]	474 Porygon-Z [TM]	057 Primeape [TM]
		394 Prinplup [TM]	476 Probopass [TM]	054 Psyduck [TM]	710 Pumpkaboo [TM]	247 Pupitar [TM]	509 Purrloin [TM]	432 Purugly [TM]
		668 Pyroar [TM]	195 Quagsire [TM]	156 Quilava [TM]	651 Quilladin [TM]	211 Qwilfish [TM]	026 Raichu [TM]	243 Raikou [TM]
		280 Ralts [TM]	409 Rampardos [TM]	078 Rapidash [TM]	020 Raticate [TM]	019 Rattata [TM]	384 Rayquaza [TM]	378 Regice [TM]
		486 Regigigas [TM]	377 Regirock [TM]	379 Registeel [TM]	369 Relicanth [TM]	223 Remoraid [TM]	643 Reshiram [TM]	579 Reuniclus [TM]
		112 Rhydon [TM]	111 Rhyhorn [TM]	464 Rhyperior [TM]	447 Riolu [TM]	524 Roggenrola [TM]	315 Roselia [TM]	407 Roserade [TM]
		479 Rotom (Fan) [36, TM]	479 Rotom (Frost) [36, TM]	479 Rotom (Heat) [36, TM]	479 Rotom (Mow) [36, TM]	479 Rotom (Wash) [36, TM]	479 Rotom [36, TM]	627 Rufflet [TM]
		302 Sableye [TM]	373 Salamence [TM]	503 Samurott [TM]	551 Sandile [TM]	027 Sandshrew [TM]	028 Sandslash [TM]	539 Sawk [TM]
		586 Sawsbuck [TM]	254 Sceptile [TM]	212 Scizor [TM]	545 Scolipede [TM]	560 Scrafty [TM]	559 Scraggy [TM]	123 Scyther [TM]
		117 Seadra [TM]	119 Seaking [TM]	364 Sealeo [TM]	273 Seedot [TM]	086 Seel [TM]	537 Seismitoad [TM]	161 Sentret [TM]
		497 Serperior [TM]	496 Servine [TM]	336 Seviper [TM]	540 Sewaddle [TM]	319 Sharpedo [TM]	492 Shaymin (Land) [TM]	492 Shaymin (Sky) [TM]
		292 Shedinja [TM]	372 Shelgon [TM]	090 Shellder [TM]	422 Shellos [TM]	616 Shelmet [TM]	410 Shieldon [TM]	275 Shiftry [TM]
		403 Shinx [TM]	285 Shroomish [TM]	213 Shuckle [TM]	353 Shuppet [TM]	561 Sigilyph [TM]	516 Simipour [TM]	512 Simisage [TM]
		514 Simisear [TM]	227 Skarmory [TM]	672 Skiddo [TM]	188 Skiploom [TM]	300 Skitty [TM]	451 Skorupi [TM]	690 Skrelp [TM]
		435 Skuntank [TM]	289 Slaking [TM]	287 Slakoth [TM]	705 Sliggoo [TM]	080 Slowbro [TM]	199 Slowking [TM]	079 Slowpoke [TM]
		218 Slugma [TM]	685 Slurpuff [TM]	238 Smoochum [TM]	215 Sneasel [TM]	495 Snivy [TM]	143 Snorlax [TM]	361 Snorunt [TM]
		459 Snover [TM]	209 Snubbull [TM]	577 Solosis [TM]	338 Solrock [TM]	021 Spearow [TM]	363 Spheal [TM]	167 Spinarak [TM]
		327 Spinda [TM]	442 Spiritomb [TM]	325 Spoink [TM]	682 Spritzee [TM]	007 Squirtle [TM]	234 Stantler [TM]	398 Staraptor [TM]
		397 Staravia [TM]	396 Starly [TM]	121 Starmie [TM]	120 Staryu [TM]	208 Steelix [TM]	508 Stoutland [TM]	618 Stunfisk [TM]
		434 Stunky [TM]	185 Sudowoodo [TM]	245 Suicune [TM]	192 Sunflora [TM]	191 Sunkern [TM]	283 Surskit [TM]	333 Swablu [TM]
		541 Swadloon [TM]	317 Swalot [TM]	260 Swampert [TM]	581 Swanna [TM]	277 Swellow [TM]	220 Swinub [TM]	684 Swirlix [TM]
		528 Swoobat [TM]	700 Sylveon [TM]	276 Taillow [TM]	663 Talonflame [TM]	114 Tangela [TM]	465 Tangrowth [TM]	128 Tauros [TM]
		216 Teddiursa [TM]	072 Tentacool [TM]	073 Tentacruel [TM]	498 Tepig [TM]	639 Terrakion [TM]	538 Throh [TM]	642 Thundurus [TM]
		532 Timburr [TM]	564 Tirtouga [TM]	468 Togekiss [TM]	175 Togepi [TM]	176 Togetic [TM]	255 Torchic [TM]	324 Torkoal [TM]
		641 Tornadus [TM]	389 Torterra [TM]	158 Totodile [TM]	454 Toxicroak [TM]	520 Tranquill [TM]	328 Trapinch [TM]	252 Treecko [TM]
		709 Trevenant [TM]	357 Tropius [TM]	568 Trubbish [TM]	387 Turtwig [TM]	535 Tympole [TM]	157 Typhlosion [TM]	248 Tyranitar [TM]
		697 Tyrantrum [TM]	236 Tyrogue [TM]	696 Tyrunt [TM]	197 Umbreon [TM]	521 Unfezant [TM]	217 Ursaring [TM]	480 Uxie [TM]
		583 Vanillish [TM]	582 Vanillite [TM]	584 Vanilluxe [TM]	134 Vaporeon [TM]	543 Venipede [TM]	049 Venomoth [TM]	048 Venonat [TM]
		003 Venusaur [TM]	416 Vespiquen [TM]	329 Vibrava [TM]	494 Victini [TM]	071 Victreebel [TM]	288 Vigoroth [TM]	045 Vileplume [TM]
		640 Virizion [TM]	666 Vivillon [TM]	313 Volbeat [TM]	637 Volcarona [TM]	100 Voltorb [TM]	629 Vullaby [TM]	037 Vulpix [TM]
		320 Wailmer [TM]	321 Wailord [TM]	365 Walrein [TM]	008 Wartortle [TM]	505 Watchog [TM]	461 Weavile [TM]	070 Weepinbell [TM]
		110 Weezing [TM]	547 Whimsicott [TM]	544 Whirlipede [TM]	340 Whiscash [TM]	293 Whismur [TM]	040 Wigglytuff [TM]	278 Wingull [TM]
		527 Woobat [TM]	194 Wooper [TM]	413 Wormadam (Plant) [TM]	413 Wormadam (Sand) [TM]	413 Wormadam (Trash) [TM]	178 Xatu [TM]	716 Xerneas [TM]
		562 Yamask [TM]	193 Yanma [TM]	469 Yanmega [TM]	717 Yveltal [TM]	335 Zangoose [TM]	145 Zapdos [TM]	523 Zebstrika [TM]
		644 Zekrom [TM]	263 Zigzagoon [TM]	571 Zoroark [TM]	570 Zorua [TM]	041 Zubat [TM]	634 Zweilous [TM]	718 Zygarde [TM]
Dark	Sucker Punch	359 Absol [45, E]	168 Ariados [28]	354 Banette [40]	438 Bonsly [36]	331 Cacnea [34]	332 Cacturne [35]	453 Croagunk [31]
		050 Diglett [23]	621 Druddigon [E]	051 Dugtrio [23]	023 Ekans [E]	676 Furfrou [42]	162 Furret [36]	596 Galvantula [46]
		092 Gastly [22]	094 Gengar [22]	431 Glameow [41]	093 Haunter [22]	631 Heatmor [E]	430 Honchkrow [1]	228 Houndour [E]
		367 Huntail [23]	595 Joltik [40]	115 Kangaskhan [49]	352 Kecleon [46]	510 Liepard [55]	556 Maractus [42]	303 Mawile [37, E]
		678 Meowstic (F) [48]	678 Meowstic (M) [48]	262 Mightyena [48]	200 Misdreavus [E]	198 Murkrow [55]	177 Natu [E]	032 Nidoran ♂ [E]
		624 Pawniard [E]	261 Poochyena [40, E]	509 Purrloin [46]	020 Raticate [19]	019 Rattata [19]	302 Sableye [E]	161 Sentret [31]
		353 Shuppet [38]	300 Skitty [E]	167 Spinarak [26]	327 Spinda [28]	442 Spiritomb [31]	185 Sudowoodo [36]	498 Tepig [E]
		454 Toxicroak [31]	717 Yveltal [80]	570 Zorua [E]				
Fire	Sunny Day (TM11)	063 Abra [TM]	359 Absol [TM]	681 Aegislash [TM]	142 Aerodactyl [TM]	306 Aggron [TM]	190 Aipom [TM]	065 Alakazam [TM]
		334 Altaria [TM]	424 Ambipom [TM]	591 Amoonguss [TM]	347 Anorith [TM]	024 Arbok [TM]	059 Arcanine [TM]	493 Arceus [TM]
		168 Ariados [TM]	348 Armaldo [TM]	683 Aromatisse [TM]	304 Aron [TM]	144 Articuno [TM]	531 Audino [TM]	610 Axew [TM]
		482 Azelf [TM]	371 Bagon [TM]	343 Baltoy [TM]	354 Banette [TM]	411 Bastiodon [TM]	153 Bayleef [TM]	267 Beautifly [TM]
		015 Beedrill [TM]	182 Bellossom [1, TM]	069 Bellsprout [TM]	400 Bibarel [TM]	399 Bidoof [TM]	257 Blaziken [TM]	242 Blissey [TM]
		438 Bonsly [TM]	626 Bouffalant [TM]	654 Braixen [51, TM]	628 Braviary [TM]	286 Breloom [TM]	437 Bronzong [1, TM]	436 Bronzor [TM]
		406 Budew [TM]	001 Bulbasaur [TM]	427 Buneary [TM]	012 Butterfree [TM]	331 Cacnea [TM]	332 Cacturne [TM]	323 Camerupt [TM]
		703 Carbink [TM]	455 Carnivine [TM]	351 Castform [20, TM]	251 Celebi [TM]	609 Chandelure [TM]	113 Chansey [TM]	006 Charizard [TM]
		004 Charmander [TM]	005 Charmeleon [TM]	441 Chatot [TM]	421 Cherrim [22, TM]	420 Cherubi [22, TM]	652 Chesnaught [TM]	650 Chespin [TM]
		152 Chikorita [TM]	390 Chimchar [TM]	358 Chimecho [TM]	433 Chingling [TM]	573 Cinccino [TM]	344 Claydol [TM]	036 Clefable [TM]
		035 Clefairy [TM]	173 Cleffa [TM]	256 Combusken [TM]	534 Conkeldurr [TM]	222 Corsola [TM]	546 Cottonee [40, TM]	346 Cradily [TM]
		408 Cranidos [TM]	488 Cresselia [TM]	453 Croagunk [TM]	169 Crobat [TM]	104 Cubone [TM]	155 Cyndaquil [TM]	491 Darkrai [TM]
		555 Darmanitan [TM]	554 Darumaka [TM]	702 Dedenne [TM]	585 Deerling [TM]	633 Deino [TM]	301 Delcatty [TM]	655 Delphox [55, TM]
		386 Deoxys (Atk) [TM]	386 Deoxys (Def) [TM]	386 Deoxys (Nor) [TM]	386 Deoxys (Spd) [TM]	483 Dialga [TM]	719 Diancie [TM]	050 Diglett [TM]

	Move	Pokémon that can learn it						
Fire	Sunny Day (TM11)	085 Dodrio [TM]	084 Doduo [TM]	232 Donphan [TM]	148 Dragonair [TM]	149 Dragonite [TM]	452 Drapion [TM]	147 Dratini [TM]
		426 Drifblim [TM]	425 Drifloon [TM]	096 Drowzee [TM]	621 Druddigon [TM]	051 Dugtrio [TM]	206 Dunsparce [TM]	356 Dusclops [TM]
		477 Dusknoir [TM]	355 Duskull [TM]	269 Dustox [TM]	133 Eevee [TM]	023 Ekans [TM]	500 Emboar [TM]	244 Entei [TM]
		196 Espeon [TM]	677 Espurr [TM]	102 Exeggcute [TM]	103 Exeggutor [TM]	295 Exploud [TM]	083 Farfetch'd [TM]	022 Fearow [TM]
		653 Fennekin [43, TM]	597 Ferroseed [TM]	598 Ferrothorn [TM]	669 Flabébé [TM]	136 Flareon [TM]	662 Fletchinder [TM]	661 Fletchling [TM]
		670 Floette [TM]	671 Florges [TM]	330 Flygon [TM]	590 Foongus [TM]	205 Forretress [TM]	611 Fraxure [TM]	676 Furfrou [TM]
		162 Furret [TM]	444 Gabite [TM]	475 Gallade [TM]	569 Garbodor [TM]	445 Garchomp [TM]	282 Gardevoir [TM]	092 Gastly [TM]
		094 Gengar [TM]	074 Geodude [TM]	443 Gible [TM]	203 Girafarig [TM]	487 Giratina (Alt) [TM]	487 Giratina (Ori) [TM]	471 Glaceon [TM]
		431 Glameow [TM]	207 Gligar [TM]	472 Gliscor [TM]	044 Gloom [TM]	673 Gogoat [TM]	042 Golbat [TM]	076 Golem [TM]
		706 Goodra [TM]	704 Goomy [TM]	711 Gourgeist [TM]	210 Granbull [TM]	075 Graveler [TM]	088 Grimer [TM]	388 Grotle [TM]
		383 Groudon [TM]	253 Grovyle [TM]	058 Growlithe [TM]	326 Grumpig [TM]	316 Gulpin [TM]	533 Gurdurr [TM]	440 Happiny [TM]
		297 Hariyama [TM]	093 Haunter [TM]	701 Hawlucha [TM]	612 Haxorus [TM]	631 Heatmor [TM]	485 Heatran [TM]	214 Heracross [TM]
		507 Herdier [TM]	449 Hippopotas [TM]	450 Hippowdon [TM]	107 Hitmonchan [TM]	106 Hitmonlee [TM]	237 Hitmontop [TM]	430 Honchkrow [TM]
		250 Ho-Oh [29, TM]	163 Hoothoot [TM]	187 Hoppip [TM]	229 Houndoom [TM]	228 Houndour [TM]	635 Hydreigon [TM]	097 Hypno [TM]
		174 Igglybuff [TM]	314 Illumise [TM]	392 Infernape [TM]	686 Inkay [TM]	002 Ivysaur [TM]	039 Jigglypuff [TM]	385 Jirachi [TM]
		135 Jolteon [TM]	189 Jumpluff [TM]	064 Kadabra [TM]	115 Kangaskhan [TM]	352 Kecleon [TM]	281 Kirlia [TM]	707 Klefki [TM]
		109 Koffing [TM]	402 Kricketune [TM]	646 Kyurem (Blk) [TM]	646 Kyurem (Wht) [TM]	646 Kyurem [TM]	305 Lairon [TM]	608 Lampent [TM]
		636 Larvesta [TM]	246 Larvitar [TM]	380 Latias [TM]	381 Latios [TM]	470 Leafeon [37, TM]	542 Leavanny [TM]	166 Ledian [TM]
		165 Ledyba [TM]	463 Lickilicky [TM]	108 Lickitung [TM]	510 Liepard [TM]	345 Lileep [TM]	549 Lilligant [TM]	506 Lillipup [TM]
		264 Linoone [TM]	667 Litleo [TM]	607 Litwick [TM]	271 Lombre [TM]	428 Lopunny [TM]	270 Lotad [TM]	294 Loudred [TM]
		448 Lucario [TM]	272 Ludicolo [TM]	249 Lugia [TM]	068 Machamp [TM]	067 Machoke [TM]	066 Machop [TM]	240 Magby [36, TM]
		219 Magcargo [TM]	126 Magmar [42, TM]	467 Magmortar [42, TM]	081 Magnemite [TM]	082 Magneton [TM]	462 Magnezone [TM]	296 Makuhita [TM]
		687 Malamar [TM]	630 Mandibuzz [TM]	056 Mankey [TM]	556 Maractus [45, TM]	105 Marowak [TM]	284 Masquerain [TM]	303 Mawile [TM]
		308 Medicham [TM]	307 Meditite [TM]	154 Meganium [TM]	648 Meloetta [TM]	678 Meowstic (F) [TM]	678 Meowstic (M) [TM]	052 Meowth [TM]
		481 Mesprit [TM]	376 Metagross [TM]	375 Metang [TM]	151 Mew [TM]	150 Mewtwo [TM]	619 Mienfoo [TM]	620 Mienshao [TM]
		262 Mightyena [TM]	241 Miltank [TM]	439 Mime Jr. [TM]	572 Minccino [TM]	200 Misdreavus [TM]	429 Mismagius [TM]	146 Moltres [57, TM]
		391 Monferno [TM]	414 Mothim [TM]	122 Mr. Mime [TM]	089 Muk [TM]	446 Munchlax [TM]	198 Murkrow [TM]	177 Natu [TM]
		034 Nidoking [TM]	031 Nidoqueen [TM]	029 Nidoran ♀ [TM]	032 Nidoran ♂ [TM]	030 Nidorina [TM]	033 Nidorino [TM]	290 Nincada [TM]
		038 Ninetales [TM]	291 Ninjask [TM]	164 Noctowl [TM]	714 Noibat [TM]	715 Noivern [TM]	299 Nosepass [TM]	322 Numel [TM]
		274 Nuzleaf [TM]	224 Octillery [TM]	043 Oddish [TM]	095 Onix [TM]	484 Palkia [TM]	674 Pancham [TM]	675 Pangoro [TM]
		511 Pansage [TM]	513 Pansear [TM]	046 Paras [TM]	047 Parasect [TM]	504 Patrat [TM]	053 Persian [TM]	548 Petilil [40, TM]
		231 Phanpy [TM]	708 Phantump [TM]	018 Pidgeot [TM]	017 Pidgeotto [TM]	016 Pidgey [TM]	519 Pidove [TM]	499 Pignite [TM]
		204 Pineco [TM]	127 Pinsir [TM]	077 Ponyta [TM]	261 Poochyena [TM]	137 Porygon [TM]	233 Porygon2 [TM]	474 Porygon-Z [TM]
		057 Primeape [TM]	476 Probopass [TM]	710 Pumpkaboo [TM]	247 Pupitar [TM]	509 Purrloin [TM]	432 Purugly [TM]	668 Pyroar [TM]
		156 Quilava [TM]	651 Quilladin [TM]	243 Raikou [TM]	280 Ralts [TM]	409 Rampardos [TM]	078 Rapidash [TM]	020 Raticate [TM]
		019 Rattata [TM]	384 Rayquaza [TM]	486 Regigigas [TM]	377 Regirock [TM]	379 Registeel [TM]	223 Remoraid [TM]	643 Reshiram [TM]
		112 Rhydon [TM]	111 Rhyhorn [TM]	464 Rhyperior [TM]	447 Riolu [TM]	315 Roselia [TM]	407 Roserade [TM]	479 Rotom (Fan) [TM]
		479 Rotom (Frost) [TM]	479 Rotom (Heat) [TM]	479 Rotom (Mow) [TM]	479 Rotom (Wash) [TM]	479 Rotom [TM]	627 Rufflet [TM]	302 Sableye [TM]
		373 Salamence [TM]	027 Sandshrew [TM]	028 Sandslash [TM]	539 Sawk [TM]	586 Sawsbuck [TM]	254 Sceptile [TM]	212 Scizor [TM]
		545 Scolipede [TM]	560 Scrafty [TM]	559 Scraggy [TM]	123 Scyther [TM]	273 Seedot [27, TM]	161 Sentret [TM]	497 Serperior [TM]
		496 Servine [TM]	336 Seviper [TM]	540 Sewaddle [TM]	492 Shaymin (Land) [TM]	492 Shaymin (Sky) [TM]	292 Shedinja [TM]	372 Shelgon [TM]
		410 Shieldon [TM]	275 Shiftry [TM]	285 Shroomish [TM]	213 Shuckle [TM]	353 Shuppet [TM]	512 Simisage [TM]	514 Simisear [TM]
		227 Skarmory [TM]	672 Skiddo [TM]	188 Skiploom [TM]	300 Skitty [TM]	451 Skorupi [TM]	435 Skuntank [TM]	289 Slaking [TM]
		287 Slakoth [TM]	705 Sliggoo [TM]	080 Slowbro [TM]	199 Slowking [TM]	079 Slowpoke [TM]	218 Slugma [TM]	685 Slurpuff [TM]
		215 Sneasel [TM]	495 Snivy [TM]	143 Snorlax [TM]	209 Snubbull [TM]	338 Solrock [TM]	021 Spearow [TM]	167 Spinarak [TM]
		327 Spinda [TM]	442 Spiritomb [TM]	325 Spoink [TM]	682 Spritzee [TM]	234 Stantler [TM]	398 Staraptor [TM]	397 Staravia [TM]
		396 Starly [TM]	208 Steelix [TM]	508 Stoutland [TM]	434 Stunky [TM]	185 Sudowoodo [TM]	245 Suicune [TM]	192 Sunflora [40, TM]
		191 Sunkern [40, TM]	283 Surskit [TM]	333 Swablu [TM]	541 Swadloon [TM]	317 Swalot [TM]	277 Swellow [TM]	684 Swirlix [TM]
		700 Sylveon [TM]	276 Taillow [TM]	663 Talonflame [TM]	114 Tangela [TM]	465 Tangrowth [TM]	128 Tauros [TM]	216 Teddiursa [TM]
		498 Tepig [TM]	538 Throh [TM]	532 Timburr [TM]	468 Togekiss [TM]	175 Togepi [TM]	176 Togetic [TM]	255 Torchic [TM]
		324 Torkoal [TM]	389 Torterra [TM]	454 Toxicroak [TM]	520 Tranquill [TM]	328 Trapinch [TM]	252 Treecko [TM]	709 Trevenant [TM]
		357 Tropius [TM]	568 Trubbish [TM]	387 Turtwig [TM]	157 Typhlosion [TM]	248 Tyranitar [TM]	697 Tyrantrum [TM]	236 Tyrogue [TM]
		696 Tyrunt [TM]	197 Umbreon [TM]	521 Unfezant [TM]	217 Ursaring [TM]	480 Uxie [TM]	134 Vaporeon [TM]	543 Venipede [TM]
		049 Venomoth [TM]	048 Venonat [TM]	003 Venusaur [TM]	416 Vespiquen [TM]	329 Vibrava [TM]	494 Victini [TM]	071 Victreebel [TM]
		288 Vigoroth [TM]	045 Vileplume [TM]	640 Virizion [TM]	666 Vivillon [TM]	313 Volbeat [TM]	637 Volcarona [TM]	629 Vullaby [TM]
		037 Vulpix [TM]	505 Watchog [TM]	461 Weavile [TM]	070 Weepinbell [TM]	110 Weezing [TM]	547 Whimsicott [TM]	544 Whirlipede [TM]
		293 Whismur [TM]	040 Wigglytuff [TM]	413 Wormadam (Plant) [TM]	413 Wormadam (Sand) [TM]	413 Wormadam (Trash) [TM]	178 Xatu [TM]	716 Xerneas [TM]
		193 Yanma [TM]	469 Yanmega [TM]	717 Yveltal [TM]	335 Zangoose [TM]	145 Zapdos [TM]	263 Zigzagoon [TM]	571 Zoroark [TM]
		570 Zorua [TM]	041 Zubat [TM]	634 Zweilous [TM]	718 Zygarde [TM]			

	Move	Pokémon that can learn it						
Normal	Super Fang	400 Bibarel [43, BP]	399 Bidoof [37, BP]	659 Bunnelby [42, BP]	318 Carvanha [BP]	652 Chesnaught [BP]	650 Chespin [BP]	453 Croagunk [BP]
		169 Crobat [BP]	702 Dedenne [BP]	660 Diggersby [48, BP]	603 Eelektrik [BP]	604 Eelektross [BP]	162 Furret [BP]	362 Glalie [BP]
		431 Glameow [BP]	042 Golbat [BP]	210 Granbull [BP]	229 Houndoom [BP]	228 Houndour [BP]	367 Huntail [BP]	264 Linoone [BP]
		303 Mawile [BP]	151 Mew [BP]	262 Mightyena [BP]	034 Nidoking [BP]	031 Nidoqueen [BP]	029 Nidoran ♀ [BP]	032 Nidoran ♂ [BP]
		030 Nidorina [BP]	033 Nidorino [BP]	714 Noibat [43, BP]	715 Noivern [43, BP]	417 Pachirisu [37, BP]	504 Patrat [21, BP]	261 Poochyena [BP]
		432 Purugly [BP]	651 Quilladin [BP]	020 Raticate [34, BP]	019 Rattata [28, BP]	027 Sandshrew [BP]	028 Sandslash [BP]	560 Scrafty [BP]
		559 Scraggy [BP]	364 Sealeo [BP]	161 Sentret [BP]	319 Sharpedo [BP]	209 Snubbull [BP]	363 Spheal [BP]	528 Swoobat [BP]
		454 Toxicroak [BP]	365 Walrein [BP]	505 Watchog [22, BP]	527 Woobat [BP]	263 Zigzagoon [BP]	041 Zubat [BP]	
Fighting	Superpower	359 Absol [BP]	306 Aggron [BP]	348 Armaldo [BP]	304 Aron [BP, E]	713 Avalugg [BP]	610 Axew [BP]	184 Azumarill [46, BP]
		689 Barbaracle [BP]	550 Basculin [BP]	614 Beartic [1, BP]	400 Bibarel [48, BP]	399 Bidoof [41, BP]	257 Blaziken [BP]	626 Bouffalant [BP]
		628 Braviary [1, 51, BP]	286 Breloom [BP]	332 Cacturne [BP]	565 Carracosta [BP]	652 Chesnaught [BP]	650 Chespin [BP]	638 Cobalion [BP]
		534 Conkeldurr [57, BP]	341 Corphish [BP, E]	408 Cranidos [BP]	342 Crawdaunt [BP]	159 Croconaw [57, BP]	613 Cubchoo [BP]	555 Darmanitan [47, BP]
		554 Darumaka [39, BP]	633 Deino [BP]	386 Deoxys (Atk) [37, BP]	660 Diggersby [BP]	232 Donphan [BP]	149 Dragonite [BP]	621 Druddigon [55, BP]
		632 Durant [BP]	604 Eelektross [BP]	500 Emboar [BP]	160 Feraligatr [71, BP]	136 Flareon [BP]	330 Flygon [BP]	611 Fraxure [BP]
		074 Geodude [BP]	526 Gigalith [BP]	673 Gogoat [BP]	076 Golem [BP]	622 Golett [BP]	623 Golurk [BP]	706 Goodra [BP]
		210 Granbull [BP]	075 Graveler [BP]	388 Grotle [BP]	533 Gurdurr [57, BP]	297 Hariyama [BP]	701 Hawlucha [BP]	612 Haxorus [BP]
		631 Heatmor [BP]	449 Hippopotas [BP]	450 Hippowdon [BP]	106 Hitmonlee [BP]	430 Honchkrow [BP]	635 Hydreigon [BP]	686 Inkay [48, BP]
		141 Kabutops [BP]	647 Keldeo [BP]	099 Kingler [BP]	098 Krabby [BP]	553 Krookodile [BP]	305 Lairon [BP]	645 Landorus [BP]
		246 Larvitar [BP]	405 Luxray [BP]	068 Machamp [BP]	067 Machoke [BP]	066 Machop [BP]	296 Makuhita [BP]	687 Malamar [1, 48, BP]
		473 Mamoswine [BP]	183 Marill [40, BP, E]	259 Marshtomp [BP]	151 Mew [BP]	258 Mudkip [BP]	446 Munchlax [BP]	034 Nidoking [BP]
		031 Nidoqueen [1, 58, BP]	674 Pancham [BP]	675 Pangoro [BP]	231 Phanpy [BP]	499 Pignite [BP]	221 Piloswine [BP]	127 Pinsir [47, BP, E]
		247 Pupitar [BP]	651 Quilladin [BP]	409 Rampardos [BP]	378 Regice [61, BP]	486 Regigigas [BP]	377 Regirock [61, BP]	379 Registeel [61, BP]
		579 Reuniclus [BP]	112 Rhydon [BP]	111 Rhyhorn [BP]	464 Rhyperior [BP]	627 Rufflet [BP]	503 Samurott [BP]	539 Sawk [BP]
		212 Scizor [BP]	545 Scolipede [BP]	516 Simipour [BP]	512 Simisage [BP]	514 Simisear [BP]	143 Snorlax [BP]	209 Snubbull [BP]
		508 Stoutland [BP]	260 Swampert [BP]	220 Swinub [BP]	216 Teddiursa [BP]	498 Tepig [BP, E]	639 Terrakion [BP]	538 Throh [48, BP]
		642 Thundurus [BP]	532 Timburr [49, BP]	324 Torkoal [BP, E]	641 Tornadus [BP]	389 Torterra [BP]	158 Totodile [48, BP]	328 Trapinch [40, BP]
		387 Turtwig [BP, E]	248 Tyranitar [BP]	697 Tyrantrum [BP]	696 Tyrunt [BP]	217 Ursaring [BP]	329 Vibrava [BP]	640 Virizion [BP]
		634 Zweilous [BP]	718 Zygarde [BP]					
Normal	Supersonic	142 Aerodactyl [1]	012 Butterfree [18]	441 Chatot [E]	170 Chinchou [1]	366 Clamperl [E]	091 Cloyster [1]	169 Crobat [1, 5]
		084 Doduo [E]	147 Dratini [E]	295 Exploud [18]	330 Flygon [19]	042 Golbat [1, 5]	118 Goldeen [5]	163 Hoothoot [E]
		171 Lanturn [1]	166 Ledian [1, 6]	165 Ledyba [6]	463 Lickilicky [5]	108 Lickitung [5]	294 Loudred [18]	370 Luvdisc [E]
		081 Magnemite [5]	082 Magneton [1, 5]	462 Magnezone [1, 5]	490 Manaphy [16]	226 Mantine [1, 3]	458 Mantyke [3]	183 Marill [E]
		029 Nidoran ♀ [E]	032 Nidoran ♂ [E]	714 Noibat [1]	715 Noivern [1]	138 Omanyte [E]	536 Palpitoad [1, 5]	279 Pelipper [5]
		489 Phione [16]	393 Piplup [E]	211 Qwilfish [E]	223 Remoraid [E]	119 Seaking [1, 5]	537 Seismitoad [1, 5]	090 Shellder [8]
		276 Taillow [E]	072 Tentacool [4]	073 Tentacruel [1, 4]	535 Tympole [5]	049 Venomoth [1, 5]	048 Venonat [5]	329 Vibrava [19]
		666 Vivillon [21]	293 Whismur [18]	278 Wingull [5]	527 Woobat [E]	193 Yanma [22]	469 Yanmega [22]	041 Zubat [5]
Water	Surf (HM03)	306 Aggron [HM]	594 Alomomola [HM]	493 Arceus [HM]	531 Audino [HM]	713 Avalugg [HM]	184 Azumarill [HM]	298 Azurill [HM]
		689 Barbaracle [HM]	339 Barboach [HM]	550 Basculin [HM]	614 Beartic [HM]	712 Bergmite [HM]	400 Bibarel [HM]	688 Binacle [HM]
		009 Blastoise [HM]	626 Bouffalant [HM]	418 Buizel [HM]	659 Bunnelby [HM]	565 Carracosta [HM]	318 Carvanha [HM]	170 Chinchou [HM]
		366 Clamperl [HM]	692 Clauncher [HM]	693 Clawitzer [HM]	091 Cloyster [HM]	341 Corphish [HM]	222 Corsola [HM]	342 Crawdaunt [HM]
		159 Croconaw [HM]	613 Cubchoo [HM]	087 Dewgong [HM]	502 Dewott [HM]	660 Diggersby [HM]	691 Dragalge [HM]	148 Dragonair [HM]
		149 Dragonite [HM]	147 Dratini [HM]	621 Druddigon [HM]	580 Ducklett [HM]	395 Empoleon [HM]	295 Exploud [HM]	349 Feebas [HM]
		160 Feraligatr [HM]	456 Finneon [HM]	419 Floatzel [HM]	592 Frillish [HM]	656 Froakie [HM]	657 Frogadier [HM]	676 Furfrou [HM]
		162 Furret [HM]	445 Garchomp [HM]	423 Gastrodon [HM]	673 Gogoat [HM]	118 Goldeen [HM]	055 Golduck [HM]	368 Gorebyss [HM]
		658 Greninja [HM]	130 Gyarados [HM]	297 Hariyama [HM]	612 Haxorus [HM]	695 Heliolisk [HM]	694 Helioptile [HM]	507 Herdier [HM]
		116 Horsea [HM]	367 Huntail [HM]	635 Hydreigon [HM]	593 Jellicent [HM]	140 Kabuto [HM]	141 Kabutops [HM]	115 Kangaskhan [HM]
		647 Keldeo [HM]	230 Kingdra [HM]	099 Kingler [HM]	098 Krabby [HM]	382 Kyogre [HM]	171 Lanturn [HM]	131 Lapras [HM]
		380 Latias [HM]	381 Latios [HM]	463 Lickilicky [HM]	108 Lickitung [HM]	264 Linoone [HM]	271 Lombre [HM]	270 Lotad [HM]
		272 Ludicolo [HM]	249 Lugia [HM]	457 Lumineon [HM]	370 Luvdisc [HM]	296 Makuhita [HM]	490 Manaphy [HM]	226 Mantine [HM]
		458 Mantyke [HM]	183 Marill [HM]	259 Marshtomp [HM]	151 Mew [HM]	350 Milotic [HM]	241 Miltank [HM]	258 Mudkip [HM]
		446 Munchlax [HM]	034 Nidoking [HM]	031 Nidoqueen [HM]	224 Octillery [HM]	138 Omanyte [HM]	139 Omastar [HM]	501 Oshawott [HM]
		484 Palkia [HM]	536 Palpitoad [HM]	674 Pancham [HM]	675 Pangoro [HM]	515 Panpour [HM]	279 Pelipper [HM]	489 Phione [HM]
		393 Piplup [HM]	186 Politoed [HM]	060 Poliwag [HM]	061 Poliwhirl [HM]	062 Poliwrath [HM]	394 Prinplup [HM]	054 Psyduck [HM]
		195 Quagsire [HM]	211 Qwilfish [HM]	409 Rampardos [HM]	384 Rayquaza [HM]	369 Relicanth [HM]	223 Remoraid [HM]	112 Rhydon [HM]
		464 Rhyperior [HM]	503 Samurott [HM]	117 Seadra [HM]	119 Seaking [HM]	364 Sealeo [HM]	086 Seel [HM]	537 Seismitoad [HM]
		161 Sentret [HM]	319 Sharpedo [HM]	090 Shellder [HM]	422 Shellos [HM]	516 Simipour [HM]	672 Skiddo [HM]	690 Skrelp [HM]
		080 Slowbro [HM]	199 Slowking [HM]	079 Slowpoke [HM]	685 Slurpuff [HM]	215 Sneasel [HM]	143 Snorlax [HM]	363 Spheal [HM]
		007 Squirtle [HM]	121 Starmie [HM]	120 Staryu [HM]	508 Stoutland [HM]	618 Stunfisk [HM]	245 Suicune [HM]	260 Swampert [HM]
		581 Swanna [HM]	684 Swirlix [HM]	128 Tauros [HM]	072 Tentacool [HM]	073 Tentacruel [HM]	564 Tirtouga [HM]	158 Totodile [HM]
		535 Tympole [HM]	248 Tyranitar [HM]	134 Vaporeon [HM]	320 Wailmer [HM]	321 Wailord [HM]	365 Walrein [HM]	008 Wartortle [HM]
		461 Weavile [HM]	340 Whiscash [HM]	194 Wooper [HM]	263 Zigzagoon [HM]			

	Move	Pokémon that can learn it						
Normal	Swagger (TM87)	460 Abomasnow [17, TM]	063 Abra [TM]	359 Absol [TM]	617 Accelgor [TM]	681 Aegislash [TM]	142 Aerodactyl [TM]	306 Aggron [TM]
		190 Aipom [TM]	065 Alakazam [TM]	594 Alomomola [TM]	334 Altaria [TM]	698 Amaura [TM]	424 Ambipom [TM]	591 Amoonguss [TM]
		181 Ampharos [TM]	347 Anorith [TM]	024 Arbok [TM]	059 Arcanine [TM]	493 Arceus [TM]	566 Archen [TM]	567 Archeops [TM]
		168 Ariados [TM]	348 Armaldo [TM]	683 Aromatisse [TM]	304 Aron [TM]	144 Articuno [TM]	531 Audino [TM]	699 Aurorus [TM]
		713 Avalugg [TM]	610 Axew [TM]	482 Azelf [TM]	184 Azumarill [TM]	298 Azurill [TM]	371 Bagon [TM]	343 Baltoy [TM]
		354 Banette [TM]	689 Barbaracle [TM]	339 Barboach [TM]	550 Basculin [TM]	411 Bastiodon [24, TM]	153 Bayleef [TM]	614 Beartic [29, TM]
		267 Beautifly [TM]	015 Beedrill [TM]	606 Beheeyem [TM]	182 Bellossom [TM]	069 Bellsprout [TM]	712 Bergmite [TM]	400 Bibarel [TM]
		399 Bidoof [TM]	688 Binacle [TM]	625 Bisharp [TM]	009 Blastoise [TM]	257 Blaziken [TM]	242 Blissey [TM]	522 Blitzle [TM]
		525 Boldore [TM]	438 Bonsly [TM]	626 Bouffalant [TM]	654 Braixen [TM]	628 Braviary [TM]	286 Breloom [TM]	437 Bronzong [TM]
		436 Bronzor [TM]	406 Budew [TM]	418 Buizel [TM]	001 Bulbasaur [TM]	427 Buneary [TM]	659 Bunnelby [TM]	012 Butterfree [TM]
		331 Cacnea [TM]	332 Cacturne [TM]	323 Camerupt [TM]	703 Carbink [TM]	455 Carnivine [TM]	565 Carracosta [TM]	318 Carvanha [22, TM]
		351 Castform [TM]	251 Celebi [TM]	609 Chandelure [TM]	113 Chansey [TM]	006 Charizard [TM]	004 Charmander [TM]	005 Charmeleon [TM]
		441 Chatot [TM]	421 Cherrim [TM]	420 Cherubi [TM]	652 Chesnaught [TM]	650 Chespin [TM]	152 Chikorita [TM]	390 Chimchar [TM]
		358 Chimecho [TM]	170 Chinchou [TM]	433 Chingling [TM]	573 Cinccino [TM]	366 Clamperl [TM]	692 Clauncher [TM]	693 Clawitzer [TM]
		344 Claydol [TM]	036 Clefable [TM]	035 Clefairy [TM]	173 Cleffa [TM]	091 Cloyster [TM]	638 Cobalion [TM]	563 Cofagrigus [TM]
		256 Combusken [TM]	534 Conkeldurr [TM]	341 Corphish [TM]	222 Corsola [TM]	546 Cottonee [TM]	346 Cradily [TM]	408 Cranidos [TM]
		342 Crawdaunt [TM]	488 Cresselia [TM]	453 Croagunk [24, TM]	169 Crobat [TM]	159 Croconaw [TM]	558 Crustle [TM]	615 Cryogonal [TM]
		613 Cubchoo [TM]	104 Cubone [TM]	155 Cyndaquil [TM]	491 Darkrai [TM]	555 Darmanitan [17, TM]	554 Darumaka [TM]	702 Dedenne [TM]
		585 Deerling [TM]	633 Deino [TM]	301 Delcatty [TM]	225 Delibird [TM]	655 Delphox [TM]	386 Deoxys (Atk) [TM]	386 Deoxys (Def) [TM]
		386 Deoxys (Nor) [TM]	386 Deoxys (Spd) [TM]	087 Dewgong [TM]	502 Dewott [TM]	483 Dialga [TM]	719 Diancie [TM]	660 Diggersby [TM]
		050 Diglett [TM]	085 Dodrio [TM]	084 Doduo [TM]	232 Donphan [TM]	680 Doublade [TM]	691 Dragalge [TM]	148 Dragonair [TM]
		149 Dragonite [TM]	452 Drapion [TM]	147 Dratini [TM]	426 Drifblim [TM]	425 Drifloon [TM]	529 Drilbur [TM]	096 Drowzee [45, TM]
		621 Druddigon [TM]	580 Ducklett [TM]	051 Dugtrio [TM]	206 Dunsparce [TM]	578 Duosion [TM]	632 Durant [TM]	356 Dusclops [TM]
		477 Dusknoir [TM]	355 Duskull [TM]	269 Dustox [TM]	557 Dwebble [TM]	603 Eelektrik [TM]	604 Eelektross [TM]	133 Eevee [TM]
		023 Ekans [TM]	125 Electabuzz [TM]	466 Electivire [TM]	309 Electrike [TM]	101 Electrode [TM]	239 Elekid [TM]	605 Elgyem [TM]
		500 Emboar [TM]	587 Emolga [TM]	395 Empoleon [24, TM]	244 Entei [43, TM]	589 Escavalier [TM]	196 Espeon [TM]	677 Espurr [TM]
		530 Excadrill [TM]	102 Exeggcute [TM]	103 Exeggutor [TM]	295 Exploud [TM]	083 Farfetch'd [TM]	022 Fearow [TM]	349 Feebas [TM]
		653 Fennekin [TM]	160 Feraligatr [TM]	597 Ferroseed [TM]	598 Ferrothorn [TM]	456 Finneon [TM]	180 Flaaffy [TM]	669 Flabébé [TM]
		136 Flareon [TM]	662 Fletchinder [TM]	661 Fletchling [TM]	419 Floatzel [TM]	670 Floette [TM]	671 Florges [TM]	330 Flygon [TM]
		590 Foongus [TM]	205 Forretress [TM]	611 Fraxure [TM]	592 Frillish [TM]	656 Froakie [TM]	657 Frogadier [TM]	478 Froslass [TM]
		676 Furfrou [TM]	162 Furret [TM]	444 Gabite [TM]	475 Gallade [TM]	596 Galvantula [TM]	569 Garbodor [TM]	445 Garchomp [TM]
		282 Gardevoir [TM]	092 Gastly [TM]	423 Gastrodon [TM]	649 Genesect [TM]	094 Gengar [TM]	074 Geodude [TM]	443 Gible [TM]
		526 Gigalith [TM]	203 Girafarig [TM]	487 Giratina (Alt) [TM]	487 Giratina (Ori) [TM]	471 Glaceon [TM]	362 Glalie [TM]	431 Glameow [TM]
		207 Gligar [TM]	472 Gliscor [TM]	044 Gloom [TM]	673 Gogoat [TM]	042 Golbat [TM]	118 Goldeen [TM]	055 Golduck [TM]
		076 Golem [TM]	622 Golett [TM]	623 Golurk [TM]	706 Goodra [TM]	704 Goomy [TM]	368 Gorebyss [TM]	574 Gothita [TM]
		576 Gothitelle [TM]	575 Gothorita [TM]	711 Gourgeist [TM]	210 Granbull [TM]	075 Graveler [TM]	658 Greninja [TM]	088 Grimer [TM]
		388 Grotle [TM]	383 Groudon [TM]	253 Grovyle [TM]	058 Growlithe [TM]	326 Grumpig [TM]	316 Gulpin [TM]	533 Gurdurr [TM]
		130 Gyarados [TM]	440 Happiny [TM]	297 Hariyama [TM]	093 Haunter [TM]	701 Hawlucha [TM]	612 Haxorus [TM]	631 Heatmor [TM]
		485 Heatran [TM]	695 Heliolisk [TM]	694 Helioptile [TM]	214 Heracross [TM]	507 Herdier [TM]	449 Hippopotas [TM]	450 Hippowdon [TM]
		107 Hitmonchan [TM]	106 Hitmonlee [TM]	237 Hitmontop [TM]	430 Honchkrow [25, TM]	679 Honedge [TM]	250 Ho-Oh [TM]	163 Hoothoot [TM]
		187 Hoppip [TM]	116 Horsea [TM]	229 Houndoom [TM]	228 Houndour [TM]	367 Huntail [TM]	635 Hydreigon [TM]	097 Hypno [45, TM]
		174 Igglybuff [TM]	314 Illumise [TM]	392 Infernape [TM]	686 Inkay [12, TM]	002 Ivysaur [TM]	593 Jellicent [TM]	039 Jigglypuff [TM]
		385 Jirachi [TM]	135 Jolteon [TM]	595 Joltik [TM]	189 Jumpluff [TM]	124 Jynx [TM]	140 Kabuto [TM]	141 Kabutops [TM]
		064 Kadabra [TM]	115 Kangaskhan [TM]	588 Karrablast [TM]	352 Kecleon [TM]	647 Keldeo [TM]	230 Kingdra [TM]	099 Kingler [TM]
		281 Kirlia [TM]	600 Klang [TM]	707 Klefki [TM]	599 Klink [TM]	601 Klinklang [TM]	109 Koffing [TM]	098 Krabby [TM]
		402 Kricketune [TM]	552 Krokorok [25, TM]	553 Krookodile [25, TM]	382 Kyogre [TM]	646 Kyurem (Blk) [TM]	646 Kyurem (Wht) [TM]	646 Kyurem [TM]
		305 Lairon [TM]	608 Lampent [TM]	645 Landorus [TM]	171 Lanturn [TM]	131 Lapras [TM]	636 Larvesta [TM]	246 Larvitar [TM]
		380 Latias [TM]	381 Latios [TM]	470 Leafeon [TM]	542 Leavanny [TM]	166 Ledian [TM]	165 Ledyba [TM]	463 Lickilicky [TM]
		108 Lickitung [TM]	510 Liepard [TM]	345 Lileep [TM]	549 Lilligant [TM]	506 Lillipup [TM]	264 Linoone [TM]	667 Litleo [TM]
		607 Litwick [TM]	271 Lombre [TM]	428 Lopunny [TM]	270 Lotad [TM]	294 Loudred [TM]	448 Lucario [TM]	272 Ludicolo [TM]
		249 Lugia [TM]	457 Lumineon [TM]	337 Lunatone [TM]	370 Luvdisc [TM]	404 Luxio [28, TM]	405 Luxray [28, TM]	068 Machamp [TM]
		067 Machoke [TM]	066 Machop [TM]	240 Magby [TM]	219 Magcargo [TM]	126 Magmar [TM]	467 Magmortar [TM]	081 Magnemite [TM]
		082 Magneton [TM]	462 Magnezone [TM]	296 Makuhita [TM]	687 Malamar [12, TM]	473 Mamoswine [TM]	490 Manaphy [TM]	630 Mandibuzz [TM]
		310 Manectric [TM]	056 Mankey [33, TM]	226 Mantine [TM]	458 Mantyke [TM]	556 Maractus [TM]	179 Mareep [TM]	183 Marill [TM]
		105 Marowak [TM]	259 Marshtomp [TM]	284 Masquerain [TM]	303 Mawile [TM]	308 Medicham [TM]	307 Meditite [TM]	154 Meganium [TM]
		648 Meloetta [TM]	678 Meowstic (F) [TM]	678 Meowstic (M) [TM]	052 Meowth [TM]	481 Mesprit [TM]	376 Metagross [TM]	375 Metang [TM]
		151 Mew [TM]	150 Mewtwo [TM]	619 Mienfoo [TM]	620 Mienshao [TM]	262 Mightyena [20, TM]	350 Milotic [TM]	241 Miltank [TM]
		439 Mime Jr. [TM]	572 Minccino [TM]	312 Minun [TM]	200 Misdreavus [TM]	429 Mismagius [TM]	146 Moltres [TM]	391 Monferno [TM]
		414 Mothim [TM]	122 Mr. Mime [TM]	258 Mudkip [TM]	089 Muk [TM]	446 Munchlax [TM]	517 Munna [TM]	198 Murkrow [TM]
		518 Musharna [TM]	177 Natu [TM]	034 Nidoking [TM]	031 Nidoqueen [TM]	029 Nidoran ♀ [TM]	032 Nidoran ♂ [TM]	030 Nidorina [TM]
		033 Nidorino [TM]	290 Nincada [TM]	038 Ninetales [TM]	291 Ninjask [TM]	164 Noctowl [TM]	714 Noibat [TM]	715 Noivern [TM]
		299 Nosepass [TM]	322 Numel [TM]	274 Nuzleaf [32, TM]	224 Octillery [TM]	043 Oddish [TM]	138 Omanyte [TM]	139 Omastar [TM]
		095 Onix [TM]	501 Oshawott [TM]	417 Pachirisu [TM]	484 Palkia [TM]	536 Palpitoad [TM]	674 Pancham [TM]	675 Pangoro [TM]
		515 Panpour [TM]	511 Pansage [TM]	513 Pansear [TM]	046 Paras [TM]	047 Parasect [TM]	504 Patrat [TM]	624 Pawniard [TM]

Type	Move	Pokémon that can learn it						
Normal	Swagger (TM87)	279 Pelipper [TM]	053 Persian [TM]	548 Petilil [TM]	231 Phanpy [TM]	708 Phantump [TM]	489 Phione [TM]	172 Pichu [TM]
		018 Pidgeot [TM]	017 Pidgeotto [TM]	016 Pidgey [TM]	519 Pidove [39, TM]	499 Pignite [TM]	025 Pikachu [TM]	221 Piloswine [TM]
		204 Pineco [TM]	127 Pinsir [TM]	393 Piplup [TM]	311 Plusle [TM]	186 Politoed [27, TM]	060 Poliwag [TM]	061 Poliwhirl [TM]
		062 Poliwrath [TM]	077 Ponyta [TM]	261 Poochyena [19, TM]	137 Porygon [TM]	233 Porygon2 [TM]	474 Porygon-Z [TM]	057 Primeape [35, TM]
		394 Prinplup [TM]	476 Probopass [TM]	054 Psyduck [TM]	710 Pumpkaboo [TM]	247 Pupitar [TM]	509 Purrloin [TM]	432 Purugly [38, TM]
		668 Pyroar [TM]	195 Quagsire [TM]	156 Quilava [TM]	651 Quilladin [TM]	211 Qwilfish [TM]	026 Raichu [TM]	243 Raikou [TM]
		280 Ralts [TM]	409 Rampardos [TM]	078 Rapidash [TM]	020 Raticate [TM]	019 Rattata [TM]	384 Rayquaza [TM]	378 Regice [TM]
		486 Regigigas [TM]	377 Regirock [TM]	379 Registeel [TM]	369 Relicanth [TM]	223 Remoraid [TM]	643 Reshiram [TM]	579 Reuniclus [TM]
		112 Rhydon [TM]	111 Rhyhorn [TM]	464 Rhyperior [TM]	447 Riolu [TM]	524 Roggenrola [TM]	315 Roselia [TM]	407 Roserade [TM]
		479 Rotom (Fan) [TM]	479 Rotom (Frost) [TM]	479 Rotom (Heat) [TM]	479 Rotom (Mow) [TM]	479 Rotom (Wash) [TM]	479 Rotom [TM]	627 Rufflet [TM]
		302 Sableye [TM]	373 Salamence [TM]	503 Samurott [TM]	551 Sandile [25, TM]	027 Sandshrew [TM]	028 Sandslash [TM]	539 Sawk [TM]
		586 Sawsbuck [TM]	254 Sceptile [TM]	212 Scizor [TM]	545 Scolipede [TM]	560 Scrafty [16, TM]	559 Scraggy [16, TM]	123 Scyther [TM]
		117 Seadra [TM]	119 Seaking [TM]	364 Sealeo [32, TM]	273 Seedot [TM]	086 Seel [TM]	537 Seismitoad [TM]	161 Sentret [TM]
		497 Serperior [TM]	496 Servine [TM]	336 Seviper [1, TM]	540 Sewaddle [TM]	319 Sharpedo [22, TM]	492 Shaymin (Land) [TM]	492 Shaymin (Sky) [TM]
		292 Shedinja [TM]	372 Shelgon [TM]	090 Shellder [TM]	422 Shellos [TM]	616 Shelmet [TM]	410 Shieldon [24, TM]	275 Shiftry [TM]
		403 Shinx [25, TM]	285 Shroomish [TM]	213 Shuckle [TM]	353 Shuppet [TM]	561 Sigilyph [TM]	516 Simipour [TM]	512 Simisage [TM]
		514 Simisear [TM]	227 Skarmory [TM]	672 Skiddo [TM]	188 Skiploom [TM]	300 Skitty [TM]	451 Skorupi [TM]	690 Skrelp [TM]
		435 Skuntank [TM]	289 Slaking [36, TM]	287 Slakoth [TM]	705 Sliggoo [TM]	080 Slowbro [TM]	199 Slowking [41, TM]	079 Slowpoke [TM]
		218 Slugma [TM]	685 Slurpuff [TM]	238 Smoochum [TM]	215 Sneasel [TM]	495 Snivy [TM]	143 Snorlax [TM]	361 Snorunt [TM]
		459 Snover [17, TM]	209 Snubbull [TM]	577 Solosis [TM]	338 Solrock [TM]	021 Spearow [TM]	363 Spheal [TM]	167 Spinarak [TM]
		327 Spinda [TM]	442 Spiritomb [TM]	325 Spoink [TM]	682 Spritzee [TM]	007 Squirtle [TM]	234 Stantler [TM]	398 Staraptor [TM]
		397 Staravia [TM]	396 Starly [TM]	121 Starmie [TM]	120 Staryu [TM]	208 Steelix [TM]	508 Stoutland [TM]	618 Stunfisk [TM]
		434 Stunky [TM]	185 Sudowoodo [TM]	245 Suicune [TM]	192 Sunflora [TM]	191 Sunkern [TM]	283 Surskit [TM]	333 Swablu [TM]
		541 Swadloon [TM]	317 Swalot [TM]	260 Swampert [TM]	581 Swanna [TM]	277 Swellow [TM]	220 Swinub [TM]	684 Swirlix [TM]
		528 Swoobat [TM]	700 Sylveon [TM]	276 Taillow [TM]	663 Talonflame [TM]	114 Tangela [TM]	465 Tangrowth [TM]	128 Tauros [48, TM]
		216 Teddiursa [TM]	072 Tentacool [TM]	073 Tentacruel [TM]	498 Tepig [TM]	639 Terrakion [TM]	538 Throh [TM]	642 Thundurus [7, TM]
		532 Timburr [TM]	564 Tirtouga [TM]	468 Togekiss [TM]	175 Togepi [TM]	176 Togetic [TM]	255 Torchic [TM]	324 Torkoal [TM]
		641 Tornadus [7, TM]	389 Torterra [TM]	158 Totodile [TM]	454 Toxicroak [24, TM]	520 Tranquill [45, TM]	328 Trapinch [TM]	252 Treecko [TM]
		709 Trevenant [TM]	357 Tropius [TM]	568 Trubbish [TM]	387 Turtwig [TM]	535 Tympole [TM]	157 Typhlosion [TM]	248 Tyranitar [TM]
		697 Tyrantrum [TM]	236 Tyrogue [TM]	696 Tyrunt [TM]	197 Umbreon [TM]	521 Unfezant [49, TM]	217 Ursaring [TM]	480 Uxie [TM]
		583 Vanillish [TM]	582 Vanillite [TM]	584 Vanilluxe [TM]	134 Vaporeon [TM]	543 Venipede [TM]	049 Venomoth [TM]	048 Venonat [TM]
		003 Venusaur [TM]	416 Vespiquen [49, TM]	329 Vibrava [TM]	494 Victini [TM]	071 Victreebel [TM]	288 Vigoroth [TM]	045 Vileplume [TM]
		640 Virizion [TM]	666 Vivillon [TM]	313 Volbeat [TM]	637 Volcarona [TM]	100 Voltorb [TM]	629 Vullaby [TM]	037 Vulpix [TM]
		320 Wailmer [TM]	321 Wailord [TM]	365 Walrein [32, TM]	008 Wartortle [TM]	505 Watchog [TM]	461 Weavile [TM]	070 Weepinbell [TM]
		110 Weezing [TM]	547 Whimsicott [TM]	544 Whirlipede [TM]	340 Whiscash [TM]	293 Whismur [TM]	040 Wigglytuff [TM]	278 Wingull [TM]
		527 Woobat [TM]	194 Wooper [TM]	413 Wormadam (Plant) [TM]	413 Wormadam (Sand) [TM]	413 Wormadam (Trash) [TM]	178 Xatu [TM]	716 Xerneas [TM]
		562 Yamask [TM]	193 Yanma [TM]	469 Yanmega [TM]	717 Yveltal [TM]	335 Zangoose [TM]	145 Zapdos [TM]	523 Zebstrika [TM]
		644 Zekrom [TM]	263 Zigzagoon [TM]	571 Zoroark [TM]	570 Zorua [TM]	041 Zubat [TM]	634 Zweilous [TM]	718 Zygarde [TM]
	Swallow	024 Arbok [27]	455 Carnivine [37]	346 Cradily [52]	426 Drifblim [34]	425 Drifloon [32]	023 Ekans [25]	569 Garbodor [23]
		088 Grimer [E]	316 Gulpin [28]	631 Heatmor [50]	449 Hippopotas [E]	109 Koffing [E]	171 Lanturn [27]	345 Lileep [46]
		303 Mawile [41]	446 Munchlax [33]	322 Numel [E]	279 Pelipper [33]	086 Seel [E]	336 Seviper [E]	422 Shellos [E]
		218 Slugma [E]	363 Spheal [E]	317 Swalot [30]	568 Trubbish [23]	387 Turtwig [E]	071 Victreebel [1]	194 Wooper [E]
Fairy	Sweet Kiss	683 Aromatisse [6]	531 Audino [E]	427 Buneary [E]	173 Cleffa [10]	456 Finneon [E]	440 Happiny [12]	174 Igglybuff [9]
		370 Luvdisc [31]	312 Minun [E]	417 Pachirisu [29]	172 Pichu [10]	311 Plusle [E]	492 Shaymin (Land) [82]	492 Shaymin (Sky) [82]
		238 Smoochum [8]	682 Spritzee [6]	175 Togepi [9]	176 Togetic [1, 9]			
Normal	Sweet Scent	591 Amoonguss [24]	683 Aromatisse [1]	153 Bayleef [32]	182 Bellossom [1]	069 Bellsprout [29]	001 Bulbasaur [21]	455 Carnivine [17]
		420 Cherubi [E]	152 Chikorita [28]	415 Combee [1]	590 Foongus [24]	044 Gloom [1, 5]	314 Illumise [5]	002 Ivysaur [23]
		270 Lotad [E]	556 Maractus [3]	284 Masquerain [1, 9]	303 Mawile [13]	154 Meganium [34]	043 Oddish [5]	046 Paras [E]
		548 Petilil [E]	315 Roselia [31]	407 Roserade [1]	492 Shaymin (Land) [37]	492 Shaymin (Sky) [37]	213 Shuckle [E]	685 Slurpuff [1]
		495 Snivy [E]	682 Spritzee [1]	191 Sunkern [E]	283 Surskit [9]	684 Swirlix [1]	216 Teddiursa [22]	357 Tropius [6]
		217 Ursaring [22]	003 Venusaur [23]	416 Vespiquen [1]	071 Victreebel [1]	070 Weepinbell [29]		
	Swift	617 Accelgor [25]	190 Aipom [22]	424 Ambipom [22]	482 Azelf [21]	550 Basculin [E]	418 Buizel [21]	318 Carvanha [E]
		342 Crawdaunt [30]	169 Crobat [24]	155 Cyndaquil [31]	386 Deoxys (Spd) [37]	133 Eevee [10]	125 Electabuzz [12]	466 Electivire [12]
		309 Electrike [E]	101 Electrode [20]	239 Elekid [12]	196 Espeon [17]	419 Floatzel [21]	042 Golbat [24]	385 Jirachi [10]
		166 Ledian [41]	165 Ledyba [33]	481 Mesprit [21]	150 Mewtwo [8]	619 Mienfoo [21]	620 Mienshao [21]	572 Minccino [19]
		312 Minun [16]	517 Munna [E]	417 Pachirisu [21]	053 Persian [28]	204 Pineco [E]	311 Plusle [16]	156 Quilava [31]
		223 Remoraid [E]	027 Sandshrew [17]	028 Sandslash [17]	403 Shinx [E]	227 Skarmory [23]	121 Starmie [1]	120 Staryu [16]
		700 Sylveon [17]	157 Typhlosion [31]	480 Uxie [21]	100 Voltorb [20]	041 Zubat [23]		
Dark	Switcheroo	190 Aipom [E]	566 Archen [E]	688 Binacle [E]	418 Buizel [E]	427 Buneary [E]	331 Cacnea [E]	341 Corphish [E]
		546 Cottonee [E]	655 Delphox [1]	023 Ekans [E]	309 Electrike [E]	097 Hypno [1]	686 Inkay [23]	707 Klefki [E]
		264 Linoone [1]	687 Malamar [23]	312 Minun [13]	714 Noibat [E]	053 Persian [1]	336 Seviper [E]	361 Snorunt [E]
Normal	Swords Dance (TM75)	460 Abomasnow [TM]	359 Absol [25, TM]	681 Aegislash [1, TM]	347 Anorith [TM]	493 Arceus [TM]	348 Armaldo [TM]	610 Axew [46, TM]
		689 Barbaracle [TM]	153 Bayleef [TM]	614 Beartic [TM]	015 Beedrill [TM]	182 Bellossom [TM]	069 Bellsprout [TM]	688 Binacle [TM]
		625 Bisharp [63, TM]	257 Blaziken [TM]	626 Bouffalant [56, TM]	286 Breloom [TM]	406 Budew [TM]	001 Bulbasaur [TM]	331 Cacnea [TM]
		332 Cacturne [TM]	455 Carnivine [TM]	251 Celebi [TM]	006 Charizard [TM]	004 Charmander [TM]	005 Charmeleon [TM]	421 Cherrim [TM]

Type	Move	Pokémon that can learn it						
Normal	Swords Dance (TM75)	420 Cherubi [TM]	652 Chesnaught [TM]	650 Chespin [TM]	152 Chikorita [TM]	390 Chimchar [TM]	692 Clauncher [25, TM]	693 Clawitzer [25, TM]
		638 Cobalion [49, TM]	256 Combusken [TM]	341 Corphish [37, TM]	346 Cradily [TM]	408 Cranidos [TM]	342 Crawdaunt [40, TM]	159 Croconaw [TM]
		558 Crustle [TM]	104 Cubone [TM]	491 Darkrai [TM]	502 Dewott [49, TM]	660 Diggersby [1, TM]	680 Doublade [1, TM]	452 Drapion [TM]
		529 Drilbur [36, TM]	557 Dwebble [TM]	395 Empoleon [11, TM]	589 Escavalier [52, TM]	530 Excadrill [42, TM]	102 Exeggcute [TM]	103 Exeggutor [TM]
		083 Farfetch'd [25, TM]	160 Feraligatr [TM]	598 Ferrothorn [TM]	662 Fletchinder [TM]	661 Fletchling [TM]	611 Fraxure [48, TM]	475 Gallade [26, TM]
		445 Garchomp [TM]	207 Gligar [50, TM]	472 Gliscor [50, TM]	044 Gloom [TM]	388 Grotle [TM]	383 Groudon [TM]	253 Grovyle [TM]
		701 Hawlucha [60, TM]	612 Haxorus [50, TM]	214 Heracross [TM]	679 Honedge [1, TM]	187 Hoppip [TM]	392 Infernape [TM]	002 Ivysaur [TM]
		189 Jumpluff [TM]	141 Kabutops [TM]	588 Karrablast [52, TM]	647 Keldeo [49, TM]	099 Kingler [TM]	098 Krabby [TM]	402 Kricketune [TM]
		645 Landorus [37, TM]	470 Leafeon [29, TM]	542 Leavanny [46, TM]	166 Ledian [TM]	165 Ledyba [TM]	463 Lickilicky [TM]	108 Lickitung [TM]
		345 Lileep [TM]	549 Lilligant [TM]	271 Lombre [TM]	270 Lotad [TM]	448 Lucario [19, TM]	272 Ludicolo [TM]	105 Marowak [TM]
		303 Mawile [TM]	154 Meganium [TM]	151 Mew [TM]	619 Mienfoo [TM]	620 Mienshao [TM]	391 Monferno [TM]	291 Ninjask [41, TM]
		274 Nuzleaf [TM]	043 Oddish [TM]	501 Oshawott [41, TM]	674 Pancham [TM]	675 Pangoro [TM]	046 Paras [TM]	047 Parasect [TM]
		504 Patrat [TM]	624 Pawniard [57, TM]	127 Pinsir [40, TM]	651 Quilladin [TM]	409 Rampardos [TM]	020 Raticate [1, TM]	384 Rayquaza [TM]
		112 Rhydon [TM]	111 Rhyhorn [TM]	464 Rhyperior [TM]	447 Riolu [TM]	315 Roselia [TM]	407 Roserade [TM]	503 Samurott [57, TM]
		027 Sandshrew [38, TM]	028 Sandslash [43, TM]	586 Sawsbuck [TM]	254 Sceptile [TM]	212 Scizor [57, TM]	545 Scolipede [TM]	123 Scyther [57, TM]
		273 Seedot [TM]	497 Serperior [TM]	496 Servine [TM]	492 Shaymin (Land) [TM]	492 Shaymin (Sky) [TM]	275 Shiftry [TM]	285 Shroomish [TM]
		227 Skarmory [TM]	188 Skiploom [TM]	451 Skorupi [TM]	215 Sneasel [TM]	495 Snivy [TM]	459 Snover [TM]	192 Sunflora [TM]
		191 Sunkern [TM]	663 Talonflame [TM]	114 Tangela [TM]	465 Tangrowth [TM]	216 Teddiursa [TM]	072 Tentacool [TM]	073 Tentacruel [TM]
		639 Terrakion [49, TM]	255 Torchic [TM]	389 Torterra [TM]	158 Totodile [TM]	454 Toxicroak [TM]	252 Treecko [TM]	357 Tropius [TM]
		387 Turtwig [TM]	217 Ursaring [TM]	003 Venusaur [TM]	071 Victreebel [TM]	045 Vileplume [TM]	640 Virizion [49, TM]	505 Watchog [TM]
		461 Weavile [TM]	070 Weepinbell [TM]	335 Zangoose [47, TM]	571 Zoroark [TM]	570 Zorua [TM]		
Psychic	Synchronoise	606 Beheeyem [1, 63]	441 Chatot [49]	358 Chimecho [1, 52]	096 Drowzee [37]	133 Eevee [E]	605 Elgyem [53]	295 Exploud [53]
		163 Hoothoot [41]	097 Hypno [37]	352 Kecleon [50]	294 Loudred [50]	517 Munna [25]	177 Natu [E]	164 Noctowl [47]
		054 Psyduck [E]	280 Ralts [E]	561 Sigilyph [31]	293 Whismur [43]	527 Woobat [E]		
Grass	Synthesis	460 Abomasnow [BP]	591 Amoonguss [35, BP]	153 Bayleef [12, BP]	182 Bellossom [BP]	069 Bellsprout [BP, E]	286 Breloom [BP]	406 Budew [BP, E]
		001 Bulbasaur [33, BP]	331 Cacnea [BP]	332 Cacturne [BP]	455 Carnivine [BP, E]	251 Celebi [BP]	421 Cherrim [BP]	420 Cherubi [BP]
		652 Chesnaught [BP]	650 Chespin [BP, E]	152 Chikorita [12, BP]	346 Cradily [BP]	585 Deerling [BP, E]	102 Exeggcute [BP, E]	103 Exeggutor [BP]
		669 Flabébé [BP]	670 Floette [BP]	671 Florges [BP]	590 Foongus [35, BP]	044 Gloom [BP]	673 Gogoat [20, BP]	711 Gourgeist [BP]
		388 Grotle [37, BP]	253 Grovyle [BP]	187 Hoppip [4, BP]	002 Ivysaur [39, BP]	189 Jumpluff [1, 4, BP]	470 Leafeon [33, BP]	542 Leavanny [BP]
		345 Lileep [BP]	549 Lilligant [1, BP]	271 Lombre [BP]	270 Lotad [BP, E]	272 Ludicolo [BP]	556 Maractus [15, BP]	154 Meganium [12, BP]
		151 Mew [BP]	274 Nuzleaf [BP]	043 Oddish [BP, E]	511 Pansage [BP]	046 Paras [BP]	047 Parasect [BP]	548 Petilil [17, BP]
		710 Pumpkaboo [BP]	651 Quilladin [BP]	315 Roselia [46, BP, E]	407 Roserade [BP]	586 Sawsbuck [BP]	254 Sceptile [BP]	273 Seedot [21, BP]
		497 Serperior [BP]	496 Servine [BP]	540 Sewaddle [BP]	492 Shaymin (Land) [28, BP]	492 Shaymin (Sky) [BP]	275 Shiftry [BP]	285 Shroomish [BP]
		512 Simisage [BP]	672 Skiddo [20, BP]	188 Skiploom [1, 4, BP]	495 Snivy [BP]	459 Snover [BP]	192 Sunflora [BP]	191 Sunkern [28, BP]
		541 Swadloon [BP]	114 Tangela [BP]	465 Tangrowth [BP]	389 Torterra [39, BP]	252 Treecko [BP, E]	357 Tropius [50, BP, E]	387 Turtwig [33, BP]
		003 Venusaur [45, BP]	071 Victreebel [BP]	045 Vileplume [BP]	640 Virizion [BP]	070 Weepinbell [BP]	413 Wormadam (Plant) [BP]	

T

Type	Move	Pokémon that can learn it						
Normal	Tackle	306 Aggron [1]	181 Ampharos [1]	304 Aron [1]	713 Avalugg [1]	184 Azumarill [1]	550 Basculin [1]	411 Bastiodon [1]
		153 Bayleef [1]	712 Bergmite [1]	400 Bibarel [1]	399 Bidoof [1]	009 Blastoise [1]	525 Boldore [1]	286 Breloom [1]
		437 Bronzong [1]	436 Bronzor [1]	001 Bulbasaur [1]	659 Bunnelby [1]	412 Burmy [10]	323 Camerupt [1]	703 Carbink [1]
		351 Castform [1]	010 Caterpie [1]	421 Cherrim [1]	420 Cherubi [1]	652 Chesnaught [1]	650 Chespin [1]	152 Chikorita [1]
		222 Corsola [1]	155 Cyndaquil [1]	555 Darmanitan [1]	554 Darumaka [1]	702 Dedenne [1]	585 Deerling [1]	633 Deino [1]
		502 Dewott [1]	719 Diancie [1]	660 Diggersby [1]	680 Doublade [1]	691 Dragalge [1]	133 Eevee [1]	309 Electrike [1]
		101 Electrode [1]	500 Emboar [1]	395 Empoleon [1]	196 Espeon [1]	349 Feebas [15]	597 Ferroseed [1]	598 Ferrothorn [1]
		180 Flaaffy [1]	669 Flabébé [1]	136 Flareon [1]	662 Fletchinder [1]	661 Fletchling [1]	670 Floette [1]	205 Forretress [1]
		676 Furfrou [1]	444 Gabite [1]	445 Garchomp [1]	074 Geodude [1]	443 Gible [1]	526 Gigalith [1]	203 Girafarig [1]
		471 Glaceon [1]	673 Gogoat [1]	076 Golem [1]	706 Goodra [1]	704 Goomy [1]	210 Granbull [1]	075 Graveler [1]
		388 Grotle [1]	297 Hariyama [1]	701 Hawlucha [1]	631 Heatmor [1]	214 Heracross [1]	507 Herdier [1]	449 Hippopotas [1]
		450 Hippowdon [1]	679 Honedge [1]	163 Hoothoot [1]	187 Hoppip [8]	314 Illumise [1]	686 Inkay [1]	002 Ivysaur [1]
		135 Jolteon [1]	189 Jumpluff [1, 8]	707 Klefki [1]	109 Koffing [1]	305 Lairon [1]	470 Leafeon [1]	542 Leavanny [1]
		166 Ledian [1]	165 Ledyba [1]	506 Lillipup [1]	264 Linoone [1]	667 Litleo [1]	337 Lunatone [1]	370 Luvdisc [1]
		404 Luxio [1]	405 Luxray [1]	129 Magikarp [15]	081 Magnemite [1]	082 Magneton [1]	462 Magnezone [1]	296 Makuhita [1]
		687 Malamar [1]	310 Manectric [1]	226 Mantine [1]	458 Mantyke [1]	179 Mareep [1]	183 Marill [1]	259 Marshtomp [1]
		154 Meganium [1]	262 Mightyena [1]	241 Miltank [1]	414 Mothim [1]	258 Mudkip [1]	446 Munchlax [1]	164 Noctowl [1]
		714 Noibat [1]	715 Noivern [1]	299 Nosepass [1]	322 Numel [1]	095 Onix [1]	501 Oshawott [1]	674 Pancham [1]
		675 Pangoro [1]	504 Patrat [1]	231 Phanpy [1]	708 Phantump [1]	018 Pidgeot [1]	017 Pidgeotto [1]	016 Pidgey [1]
		499 Pignite [1]	204 Pineco [1]	077 Ponyta [1]	261 Poochyena [1]	137 Porygon [1]	233 Porygon2 [1]	474 Porygon-Z [1]
		394 Prinplup [1]	476 Probopass [1]	668 Pyroar [1]	156 Quilava [1]	651 Quilladin [1]	211 Qwilfish [1]	020 Raticate [1]
		019 Rattata [1]	369 Relicanth [1]	524 Roggenrola [1]	503 Samurott [1]	586 Sawsbuck [1]	664 Scatterbug [1]	497 Serperior [1]
		496 Servine [1]	540 Sewaddle [1]	090 Shellder [1]	410 Shieldon [1]	403 Shinx [1]	285 Shroomish [1]	672 Skiddo [1]
		188 Skiploom [1, 8]	300 Skitty [1]	690 Skrelp [1]	705 Sliggoo [1]	080 Slowbro [1]	199 Slowking [1]	079 Slowpoke [1]
		685 Slurpuff [1]	495 Snivy [1]	143 Snorlax [1]	209 Snubbull [1]	338 Solrock [1]	327 Spinda [1]	007 Squirtle [1]

ADVENTURE DATA

	Move	Pokémon that can learn it						
Normal	Tackle	234 Stantler [1]	398 Staraptor [1]	397 Staravia [1]	396 Starly [1]	120 Staryu [1]	208 Steelix [1]	508 Stoutland [1]
		618 Stunfisk [1]	541 Swadloon [1]	260 Swampert [1]	220 Swinub [1]	684 Swirlix [1]	700 Sylveon [1]	663 Talonflame [1]
		128 Tauros [1]	498 Tepig [1]	389 Torterra [1]	709 Trevenant [1]	387 Turtwig [1]	602 Tynamo [1]	157 Typhlosion [1]
		697 Tyrantrum [1]	236 Tyrogue [1]	696 Tyrunt [1]	197 Umbreon [1]	134 Vaporeon [1]	049 Venomoth [1]	048 Venonat [1]
		003 Venusaur [1]	313 Volbeat [1]	100 Voltorb [1]	008 Wartortle [1]	505 Watchog [1]	110 Weezing [1]	413 Wormadam (Plant) [1]
		413 Wormadam (Sand) [1]	413 Wormadam (Trash) [1]	265 Wurmple [1]	193 Yanma [1]	469 Yanmega [1]	263 Zigzagoon [1]	
Bug	Tail Glow	490 Manaphy [1]	313 Volbeat [22]					
	Tail Slap	418 Buizel [E]	573 Cinccino [1]	572 Minccino [25]	037 Vulpix [E]			
Normal	Tail Whip	190 Aipom [1]	424 Ambipom [1]	184 Azumarill [1, 2]	298 Azurill [2]	550 Basculin [1]	009 Blastoise [1, 4]	242 Blissey [5]
		522 Blitzle [4]	654 Braixen [1]	113 Chansey [5]	104 Cubone [3]	702 Dedenne [1]	655 Delphox [1]	502 Dewott [1, 5]
		691 Dragalge [9]	133 Eevee [1]	500 Emboar [1, 3]	587 Emolga [7]	196 Espeon [1]	653 Fennekin [1]	136 Flareon [1]
		676 Furfrou [15]	471 Glaceon [1]	431 Glameow [E]	673 Gogoat [9]	118 Goldeen [1]	055 Golduck [1, 4]	210 Granbull [1]
		694 Helioptile [1]	187 Hoppip [6]	135 Jolteon [1]	189 Jumpluff [1, 6]	115 Kangaskhan [10]	352 Kecleon [1]	470 Leafeon [1]
		264 Linoone [1, 5]	183 Marill [2]	105 Marowak [1, 3]	052 Meowth [E]	572 Minccino [E]	031 Nidoqueen [1]	029 Nidoran ♀ [7]
		030 Nidorina [7]	501 Oshawott [5]	417 Pachirisu [E]	172 Pichu [5]	499 Pignite [1, 3]	025 Pikachu [1]	077 Ponyta [4]
		054 Psyduck [4]	195 Quagsire [1]	026 Raichu [1]	078 Rapidash [1, 4]	020 Raticate [1]	019 Rattata [1]	112 Rhydon [1]
		111 Rhyhorn [1]	464 Rhyperior [1]	503 Samurott [1, 5]	119 Seaking [1]	672 Skiddo [9]	188 Skiploom [1, 6]	300 Skitty [1]
		690 Skrelp [9]	209 Snubbull [1]	007 Squirtle [4]	700 Sylveon [1]	128 Tauros [3]	498 Tepig [3]	697 Tyrantrum [1]
		696 Tyrunt [1]	197 Umbreon [1]	134 Vaporeon [1]	037 Vulpix [4]	008 Wartortle [1, 4]	194 Wooper [1]	523 Zebstrika [1, 4]
		263 Zigzagoon [5]						
Flying	Tailwind	142 Aerodactyl [BP, E]	334 Altaria [BP]	493 Arceus [BP]	566 Archen [BP]	567 Archeops [BP]	144 Articuno [1, 64, BP]	267 Beautifly [BP]
		015 Beedrill [BP]	628 Braviary [37, BP]	012 Butterfree [30, BP]	351 Castform [BP]	006 Charizard [BP]	441 Chatot [BP]	415 Combee [BP]
		546 Cottonee [BP]	169 Crobat [BP]	149 Dragonite [BP]	426 Drifblim [BP]	425 Drifloon [BP, E]	580 Ducklett [37, BP]	269 Dustox [BP]
		587 Emolga [BP]	083 Farfetch'd [BP]	022 Fearow [BP]	456 Finneon [BP]	662 Fletchinder [51, BP]	661 Fletchling [45, BP, E]	330 Flygon [BP]
		487 Giratina (Ori) [BP]	207 Gligar [BP]	472 Gliscor [BP]	042 Golbat [BP]	701 Hawlucha [BP]	430 Honchkrow [BP]	250 Ho-Oh [BP]
		163 Hoothoot [BP]	635 Hydreigon [BP]	314 Illumise [BP]	380 Latias [BP]	381 Latios [BP]	166 Ledian [BP]	165 Ledyba [BP, E]
		249 Lugia [BP]	457 Lumineon [BP]	630 Mandibuzz [37, BP]	226 Mantine [BP]	458 Mantyke [E]	284 Masquerain [BP]	151 Mew [BP]
		146 Moltres [BP]	414 Mothim [BP]	198 Murkrow [50, BP]	177 Natu [BP]	164 Noctowl [BP]	714 Noibat [35, BP, E]	715 Noivern [35, BP]
		279 Pelipper [1, 44, BP]	018 Pidgeot [50, BP]	017 Pidgeotto [47, BP]	016 Pidgey [41, BP]	519 Pidove [46, BP]	384 Rayquaza [BP]	643 Reshiram [BP]
		627 Rufflet [37, BP]	373 Salamence [BP]	212 Scizor [BP]	123 Scyther [BP]	492 Shaymin (Sky) [BP]	275 Shiftry [BP]	561 Sigilyph [11, BP]
		227 Skarmory [BP]	021 Spearow [BP]	398 Staraptor [BP]	397 Staravia [BP]	396 Starly [BP]	245 Suicune [1, 57, BP]	333 Swablu [BP]
		581 Swanna [40, BP]	277 Swellow [BP]	528 Swoobat [BP]	276 Taillow [BP]	663 Talonflame [55, BP]	468 Togekiss [BP]	176 Togetic [BP]
		641 Tornadus [1, 55, BP]	520 Tranquill [54, BP]	357 Tropius [BP]	521 Unfezant [60, BP]	049 Venomoth [BP]	416 Vespiquen [BP]	329 Vibrava [BP]
		666 Vivillon [BP]	313 Volbeat [BP]	637 Volcarona [BP]	629 Vullaby [37, BP]	547 Whimsicott [28, BP]	278 Wingull [BP]	527 Woobat [BP]
		178 Xatu [1, BP]	193 Yanma [BP]	469 Yanmega [BP]	717 Yveltal [BP]	145 Zapdos [BP]	644 Zekrom [BP]	041 Zubat [BP]
Normal	Take Down	142 Aerodactyl [41]	306 Aggron [28]	334 Altaria [23]	698 Amaura [15]	181 Ampharos [20]	304 Aron [28]	531 Audino [33]
		699 Aurorus [15]	713 Avalugg [15]	339 Barboach [E]	550 Basculin [20]	411 Bastiodon [15]	374 Beldum [1]	712 Bergmite [15]
		400 Bibarel [38]	399 Bidoof [33]	242 Blissey [27]	522 Blitzle [E]	001 Bulbasaur [15]	659 Bunnelby [15]	323 Camerupt [31]
		318 Carvanha [43]	113 Chansey [27]	421 Cherrim [35]	420 Cherubi [31]	652 Chesnaught [30]	650 Chespin [27]	358 Chimecho [19]
		170 Chinchou [39]	638 Cobalion [19]	408 Cranidos [15]	554 Darumaka [E]	585 Deerling [20]	087 Dewgong [39]	660 Diggersby [15]
		206 Dunsparce [22]	133 Eevee [25]	500 Emboar [28]	180 Flaaffy [20]	205 Forretress [12]	676 Furfrou [35]	444 Gabite [15]
		445 Garchomp [15]	443 Gible [15]	203 Girafarig [E]	673 Gogoat [22]	058 Growlithe [23]	214 Heracross [34]	507 Herdier [15]
		449 Hippopotas [19]	450 Hippowdon [19]	163 Hoothoot [29]	002 Ivysaur [15]	140 Kabuto [E]	588 Karrablast [37]	647 Keldeo [19]
		305 Lairon [28]	171 Lanturn [43]	636 Larvesta [20]	506 Lillipup [15]	667 Litleo [20]	370 Luvdisc [37]	473 Mamoswine [28]
		226 Mantine [27]	458 Mantyke [27]	179 Mareep [18, E]	259 Marshtomp [42]	376 Metagross [1]	375 Metang [1]	262 Mightyena [40]
		258 Mudkip [36]	029 Nidoran ♀ [E]	032 Nidoran ♂ [E]	164 Noctowl [32]	322 Numel [31]	231 Phanpy [28]	499 Pignite [28]
		221 Piloswine [28]	204 Pineco [12]	077 Ponyta [29]	261 Poochyena [34]	668 Pyroar [20]	651 Quilladin [30]	211 Qwilfish [41]
		409 Rampardos [15]	078 Rapidash [29]	369 Relicanth [31]	112 Rhydon [37]	111 Rhyhorn [37]	464 Rhyperior [37]	524 Roggenrola [E]
		586 Sawsbuck [20]	273 Seedot [E]	086 Seel [37]	090 Shellder [E]	410 Shieldon [15]	403 Shinx [E]	672 Skiddo [22]
		234 Stantler [21]	398 Staraptor [33]	397 Staravia [33]	396 Starly [29]	508 Stoutland [15]	333 Swablu [23]	260 Swampert [44]
		220 Swinub [28, E]	128 Tauros [41]	216 Teddiursa [E]	498 Tepig [25]	639 Terrakion [19]	568 Trubbish [25]	543 Venipede [E]
		003 Venusaur [15]	640 Virizion [19]	293 Whismur [E]	716 Xerneas [1]	263 Zigzagoon [31]		
Dark	Taunt (TM12)	063 Abra [TM]	359 Absol [13, TM]	142 Aerodactyl [TM]	306 Aggron [TM]	190 Aipom [TM]	065 Alakazam [TM]	424 Ambipom [TM]
		566 Archen [TM]	567 Archeops [TM]	610 Axew [36, TM]	482 Azelf [TM]	354 Banette [TM]	689 Barbaracle [TM]	550 Basculin [TM]
		411 Bastiodon [1, 6, TM]	614 Beartic [TM]	400 Bibarel [TM]	399 Bidoof [TM]	688 Binacle [TM]	625 Bisharp [TM]	626 Bouffalant [TM]
		318 Carvanha [TM]	609 Chandelure [TM]	441 Chatot [1, 25, TM]	652 Chesnaught [TM]	650 Chespin [TM]	390 Chimchar [9, TM]	358 Chimecho [TM]
		433 Chingling [TM]	638 Cobalion [TM]	534 Conkeldurr [TM]	341 Corphish [34, TM]	546 Cottonee [TM]	342 Crawdaunt [36, TM]	453 Croagunk [10, TM]
		169 Crobat [TM]	491 Darkrai [TM]	555 Darmanitan [39, TM]	554 Darumaka [35, TM]	633 Deino [TM]	386 Deoxys (Atk) [19, TM]	386 Deoxys (Def) [TM]
		386 Deoxys (Nor) [TM]	386 Deoxys (Spd) [TM]	502 Dewott [TM]	085 Dodrio [TM]	452 Drapion [TM]	096 Drowzee [TM]	621 Druddigon [TM]
		356 Dusclops [TM]	477 Dusknoir [TM]	355 Duskull [TM]	466 Electivire [TM]	101 Electrode [TM]	500 Emboar [TM]	587 Emolga [TM]
		295 Exploud [TM]	662 Fletchinder [TM]	661 Fletchling [TM]	419 Floatzel [TM]	611 Fraxure [36, TM]	592 Frillish [TM]	656 Froakie [TM]
		657 Frogadier [TM]	478 Froslass [TM]	475 Gallade [TM]	282 Gardevoir [TM]	092 Gastly [TM]	094 Gengar [TM]	362 Glalie [TM]
		431 Glameow [TM]	207 Gligar [TM]	472 Gliscor [TM]	042 Golbat [TM]	574 Gothita [TM]	576 Gothitelle [TM]	575 Gothorita [TM]
		210 Granbull [TM]	658 Greninja [TM]	088 Grimer [TM]	326 Grumpig [TM]	533 Gurdurr [TM]	130 Gyarados [TM]	093 Haunter [TM]

ADVENTURE DATA

Type	Move	Pokémon that can learn it						
Dark	Taunt (TM12)	701 Hawlucha [TM]	612 Haxorus [36, TM]	631 Heatmor [TM]	485 Heatran [TM]	430 Honchkrow [TM]	229 Houndoom [TM]	228 Houndour [TM]
		635 Hydreigon [TM]	097 Hypno [TM]	392 Infernape [1, 9, TM]	686 Inkay [TM]	593 Jellicent [TM]	124 Jynx [TM]	064 Kadabra [TM]
		647 Keldeo [TM]	281 Kirlia [TM]	109 Koffing [TM]	402 Kricketune [38, TM]	552 Krokorok [TM]	553 Krookodile [TM]	608 Lampent [TM]
		246 Larvitar [TM]	510 Liepard [38, TM]	667 Litleo [TM]	607 Litwick [TM]	294 Loudred [TM]	467 Magmortar [TM]	687 Malamar [TM]
		630 Mandibuzz [TM]	056 Mankey [TM]	303 Mawile [1, TM]	052 Meowth [25, TM]	151 Mew [TM]	150 Mewtwo [TM]	619 Mienfoo [TM]
		620 Mienshao [TM]	262 Mightyena [36, TM]	439 Mime Jr. [TM]	200 Misdreavus [TM]	429 Mismagius [TM]	391 Monferno [9, TM]	122 Mr. Mime [TM]
		089 Muk [TM]	198 Murkrow [31, TM]	034 Nidoking [TM]	031 Nidoqueen [TM]	714 Noibat [TM]	715 Noivern [TM]	299 Nosepass [TM]
		095 Onix [TM]	501 Oshawott [TM]	675 Pangoro [65, TM]	515 Panpour [25, TM]	511 Pansage [TM]	513 Pansear [TM]	624 Pawniard [TM]
		053 Persian [25, TM]	519 Pidove [25, TM]	499 Pignite [TM]	261 Poochyena [31, TM]	057 Primeape [TM]	476 Probopass [TM]	247 Pupitar [TM]
		509 Purrloin [TM]	432 Purugly [TM]	668 Pyroar [TM]	651 Quilladin [TM]	211 Qwilfish [TM]	280 Ralts [TM]	020 Raticate [TM]
		019 Rattata [TM]	302 Sableye [TM]	503 Samurott [TM]	551 Sandile [TM]	539 Sawk [TM]	560 Scrafty [TM]	559 Scraggy [TM]
		497 Serperior [TM]	496 Servine [TM]	336 Seviper [TM]	319 Sharpedo [56, TM]	410 Shieldon [6, TM]	353 Shuppet [TM]	516 Simipour [TM]
		512 Simisage [TM]	514 Simisear [TM]	227 Skarmory [TM]	451 Skorupi [TM]	435 Skuntank [TM]	289 Slaking [TM]	215 Sneasel [1, TM]
		495 Snivy [TM]	209 Snubbull [TM]	442 Spiritomb [TM]	325 Spoink [TM]	208 Steelix [TM]	434 Stunky [TM]	185 Sudowoodo [TM]
		528 Swoobat [TM]	663 Talonflame [TM]	216 Teddiursa [TM]	498 Tepig [TM]	639 Terrakion [TM]	538 Throh [TM]	642 Thundurus [TM]
		532 Timburr [TM]	641 Tornadus [TM]	454 Toxicroak [10, TM]	520 Tranquill [27, TM]	248 Tyranitar [TM]	197 Umbreon [TM]	521 Unfezant [27, TM]
		217 Ursaring [TM]	583 Vanillish [22, TM]	582 Vanillite [22, TM]	584 Vanilluxe [22, TM]	494 Victini [TM]	288 Vigoroth [TM]	640 Virizion [TM]
		100 Voltorb [TM]	629 Vullaby [TM]	461 Weavile [1, TM]	110 Weezing [TM]	547 Whimsicott [TM]	527 Woobat [TM]	717 Yveltal [1, TM]
		335 Zangoose [43, TM]	571 Zoroark [25, TM]	570 Zorua [25, TM]	041 Zubat [TM]	634 Zweilous [TM]		
Normal	Techno Blast	649 Genesect [1]						
	Teeter Dance	427 Buneary [E]	331 Cacnea [E]	326 Grumpig [32]	549 Lilligant [10]	270 Lotad [E]	648 Meloetta [21]	439 Mime Jr. [E]
		122 Mr. Mime [E]	043 Oddish [E]	327 Spinda [32]				
Psychic	Telekinesis	065 Alakazam [33]	574 Gothita [40]	576 Gothitelle [45]	575 Gothorita [43]	064 Kadabra [33]	381 Latios [36]	517 Munna [43]
	Teleport	063 Abra [1]	065 Alakazam [1]	344 Claydol [1]	386 Deoxys (Atk) [13]	386 Deoxys (Def) [13]	386 Deoxys (Nor) [13]	605 Elgyem [E]
		475 Gallade [1, 9]	282 Gardevoir [1, 9]	064 Kadabra [1]	281 Kirlia [1, 9]	177 Natu [9]	280 Ralts [9]	178 Xatu [1, 9]
Dark	Thief (TM46)	063 Abra [TM]	359 Absol [TM]	142 Aerodactyl [TM]	190 Aipom [TM]	065 Alakazam [TM]	334 Altaria [TM]	424 Ambipom [TM]
		024 Arbok [TM]	059 Arcanine [TM]	168 Ariados [TM]	354 Banette [TM]	689 Barbaracle [TM]	267 Beautifly [TM]	015 Beedrill [TM]
		606 Beheeyem [TM]	069 Bellsprout [TM]	400 Bibarel [TM]	399 Bidoof [TM]	688 Binacle [TM]	625 Bisharp [TM]	438 Bonsly [TM]
		654 Braixen [TM]	659 Bunnelby [TM]	012 Butterfree [TM]	455 Carnivine [TM]	318 Carvanha [TM]	351 Castform [TM]	609 Chandelure [TM]
		441 Chatot [TM]	573 Cinccino [TM]	563 Cofagrigus [TM]	408 Cranidos [TM]	453 Croagunk [TM]	169 Crobat [TM]	104 Cubone [TM]
		491 Darkrai [TM]	555 Darmanitan [TM]	554 Darumaka [TM]	702 Dedenne [TM]	633 Deino [TM]	225 Delibird [TM]	655 Delphox [TM]
		087 Dewgong [TM]	660 Diggersby [TM]	050 Diglett [TM]	085 Dodrio [TM]	084 Doduo [TM]	452 Drapion [TM]	426 Drifblim [TM]
		425 Drifloon [TM]	096 Drowzee [TM]	051 Dugtrio [TM]	206 Dunsparce [TM]	356 Dusclops [TM]	477 Dusknoir [TM]	355 Duskull [TM]
		269 Dustox [TM]	023 Ekans [TM]	125 Electabuzz [TM]	466 Electivire [TM]	309 Electrike [TM]	101 Electrode [TM]	239 Elekid [TM]
		605 Elgyem [TM]	102 Exeggcute [TM]	103 Exeggutor [TM]	083 Farfetch'd [TM]	022 Fearow [TM]	653 Fennekin [TM]	662 Fletchinder [TM]
		661 Fletchling [TM]	656 Froakie [TM]	657 Frogadier [TM]	162 Furret [TM]	475 Gallade [TM]	596 Galvantula [TM]	569 Garbodor [TM]
		282 Gardevoir [TM]	092 Gastly [TM]	094 Gengar [TM]	203 Girafarig [TM]	431 Glameow [TM]	207 Gligar [TM]	472 Gliscor [TM]
		042 Golbat [TM]	622 Golett [TM]	623 Golurk [TM]	574 Gothita [TM]	576 Gothitelle [TM]	575 Gothorita [TM]	711 Gourgeist [TM]
		210 Granbull [TM]	658 Greninja [TM]	088 Grimer [TM]	058 Growlithe [TM]	326 Grumpig [TM]	093 Haunter [TM]	631 Heatmor [TM]
		214 Heracross [TM]	107 Hitmonchan [TM]	106 Hitmonlee [TM]	237 Hitmontop [TM]	430 Honchkrow [TM]	163 Hoothoot [TM]	229 Houndoom [TM]
		228 Houndour [TM]	635 Hydreigon [TM]	097 Hypno [TM]	314 Illumise [TM]	686 Inkay [TM]	595 Joltik [TM]	124 Jynx [TM]
		140 Kabuto [TM]	141 Kabutops [TM]	064 Kadabra [TM]	115 Kangaskhan [TM]	352 Kecleon [1, TM]	099 Kingler [TM]	281 Kirlia [TM]
		707 Klefki [TM, E]	109 Koffing [TM]	098 Krabby [TM]	552 Krokorok [TM]	553 Krookodile [TM]	608 Lampent [TM]	166 Ledian [TM]
		165 Ledyba [TM]	463 Lickilicky [TM]	108 Lickitung [TM]	510 Liepard [TM]	264 Linoone [TM]	667 Litleo [TM]	607 Litwick [TM]
		271 Lombre [TM]	270 Lotad [TM]	272 Ludicolo [TM]	404 Luxio [TM]	405 Luxray [TM]	068 Machamp [TM]	067 Machoke [TM]
		066 Machop [TM]	240 Magby [TM]	126 Magmar [TM]	467 Magmortar [TM]	687 Malamar [TM]	630 Mandibuzz [TM]	310 Manectric [TM]
		056 Mankey [TM]	105 Marowak [TM]	284 Masquerain [TM]	052 Meowth [TM]	151 Mew [TM]	262 Mightyena [1, TM]	439 Mime Jr. [TM]
		572 Minccino [TM]	200 Misdreavus [TM]	429 Mismagius [TM]	414 Mothim [TM]	122 Mr. Mime [TM]	089 Muk [TM]	198 Murkrow [TM]
		177 Natu [TM]	034 Nidoking [TM]	031 Nidoqueen [TM]	029 Nidoran ♀ [TM]	032 Nidoran ♂ [TM]	030 Nidorina [TM]	033 Nidorino [TM]
		291 Ninjask [TM]	164 Noctowl [TM]	714 Noibat [TM]	715 Noivern [TM]	274 Nuzleaf [TM]	224 Octillery [TM]	138 Omanyte [TM]
		139 Omastar [TM]	675 Pangoro [TM]	515 Panpour [TM]	511 Pansage [TM]	513 Pansear [TM]	046 Paras [TM]	047 Parasect [TM]
		624 Pawniard [TM]	279 Pelipper [TM]	053 Persian [TM]	708 Phantump [TM]	018 Pidgeot [TM]	017 Pidgeotto [TM]	016 Pidgey [TM]
		127 Pinsir [TM]	186 Politoed [TM]	060 Poliwag [TM]	061 Poliwhirl [TM]	062 Poliwrath [TM]	261 Poochyena [TM]	137 Porygon [TM]
		233 Porygon2 [TM]	474 Porygon-Z [TM]	057 Primeape [TM]	710 Pumpkaboo [TM]	509 Purrloin [TM]	432 Purugly [TM]	668 Pyroar [TM]
		195 Quagsire [TM]	026 Raichu [TM]	280 Ralts [TM]	409 Rampardos [TM]	020 Raticate [TM]	019 Rattata [TM]	223 Remoraid [TM]
		112 Rhydon [TM]	111 Rhyhorn [TM]	464 Rhyperior [TM]	479 Rotom (Fan) [TM]	479 Rotom (Frost) [TM]	479 Rotom (Heat) [TM]	479 Rotom (Mow) [TM]
		479 Rotom (Wash) [TM]	479 Rotom [TM]	302 Sableye [TM]	551 Sandile [TM]	027 Sandshrew [TM]	028 Sandslash [TM]	212 Scizor [TM]
		560 Scrafty [TM]	123 Scyther [TM]	086 Seel [TM]	161 Sentret [TM]	336 Seviper [TM]	319 Sharpedo [TM]	292 Shedinja [TM]
		275 Shiftry [TM]	403 Shinx [TM]	353 Shuppet [TM]	561 Sigilyph [TM]	516 Simipour [TM]	512 Simisage [TM]	514 Simisear [TM]
		227 Skarmory [TM]	451 Skorupi [TM]	435 Skuntank [TM]	685 Slurpuff [TM]	238 Smoochum [TM]	215 Sneasel [TM]	209 Snubbull [TM]
		021 Spearow [TM]	167 Spinarak [TM]	327 Spinda [TM]	442 Spiritomb [TM]	325 Spoink [TM]	234 Stantler [TM]	398 Staraptor [TM]
		397 Staravia [TM]	396 Starly [TM]	434 Stunky [TM]	185 Sudowoodo [TM]	283 Surskit [TM]	333 Swablu [TM]	277 Swellow [TM]
		684 Swirlix [TM]	528 Swoobat [TM]	276 Taillow [TM]	663 Talonflame [TM]	114 Tangela [TM]	465 Tangrowth [TM]	216 Teddiursa [TM]
		072 Tentacool [TM]	073 Tentacruel [TM]	642 Thundurus [TM]	641 Tornadus [TM]	454 Toxicroak [TM]	709 Trevenant [TM]	568 Trubbish [TM]
		236 Tyrogue [TM]	217 Ursaring [TM]	049 Venomoth [TM]	048 Venonat [TM]	416 Vespiquen [TM]	071 Victreebel [TM]	666 Vivillon [TM]
		313 Volbeat [TM]	100 Voltorb [TM]	629 Vullaby [TM]	461 Weavile [TM]	070 Weepinbell [TM]	110 Weezing [TM]	547 Whimsicott [TM]

	Move	Pokémon that can learn it						
Dark	Thief (TM46)	278 Wingull [TM]	527 Woobat [TM]	413 Wormadam (Plant) [TM]	413 Wormadam (Sand) [TM]	413 Wormadam (Trash) [TM]	178 Xatu [TM]	562 Yamask [TM]
		193 Yanma [TM]	469 Yanmega [TM]	717 Yveltal [TM]	335 Zangoose [TM]	263 Zigzagoon [TM]	571 Zoroark [TM]	570 Zorua [TM]
		041 Zubat [TM]	634 Zweilous [TM]					
Normal	Thrash	566 Archen [50]	567 Archeops [61]	371 Bagon [E]	339 Barboach [E]	550 Basculin [1, 56]	614 Beartic [1, 59]	522 Blitzle [43]
		626 Bouffalant [50]	628 Braviary [1, 70]	318 Carvanha [E]	408 Cranidos [E]	159 Croconaw [48]	613 Cubchoo [53]	104 Cubone [31]
		155 Cyndaquil [E]	555 Darmanitan [27]	554 Darumaka [27]	085 Dodrio [59]	084 Doduo [49]	603 Eelektrik [74]	604 Eelektross [1]
		160 Feraligatr [58]	443 Gible [E]	058 Growlithe [E]	130 Gyarados [1]	552 Krokorok [52]	636 Larvesta [90]	246 Larvitar [28]
		473 Mamoswine [41]	056 Mankey [41]	105 Marowak [33]	034 Nidoking [35]	221 Piloswine [41]	127 Pinsir [43]	077 Ponyta [E]
		057 Primeape [47]	247 Pupitar [28]	627 Rufflet [64]	551 Sandile [46]	327 Spinda [55]	234 Stantler [E]	128 Tauros [50]
		216 Teddiursa [50]	498 Tepig [E]	642 Thundurus [1, 85]	641 Tornadus [1, 85]	158 Totodile [41, E]	387 Turtwig [E]	248 Tyranitar [28]
		697 Tyrantrum [42]	696 Tyrunt [40]	217 Ursaring [58]	637 Volcarona [1]	320 Wailmer [E]	523 Zebstrika [53]	
Electric	Thunder (TM25)	359 Absol [TM]	306 Aggron [TM]	190 Aipom [TM]	424 Ambipom [TM]	181 Ampharos [62, TM]	493 Arceus [TM]	683 Aromatisse [TM]
		531 Audino [TM]	699 Aurorus [TM]	482 Azelf [TM]	354 Banette [TM]	411 Bastiodon [TM]	400 Bibarel [TM]	399 Bidoof [TM]
		242 Blissey [TM]	522 Blitzle [TM]	351 Castform [TM]	113 Chansey [TM]	170 Chinchou [TM]	573 Cinccino [TM]	036 Clefable [TM]
		035 Clefairy [TM]	408 Cranidos [TM]	491 Darkrai [TM]	702 Dedenne [45, TM]	301 Delcatty [TM]	386 Deoxys (Atk) [TM]	386 Deoxys (Def) [TM]
		386 Deoxys (Nor) [TM]	386 Deoxys (Spd) [TM]	483 Dialga [TM]	691 Dragalge [TM]	148 Dragonair [TM]	149 Dragonite [TM]	147 Dratini [TM]
		426 Drifblim [TM]	425 Drifloon [TM]	206 Dunsparce [TM]	578 Duosion [TM]	603 Eelektrik [TM]	604 Eelektross [TM]	125 Electabuzz [55, TM]
		466 Electivire [55, TM]	309 Electrike [49, TM]	101 Electrode [TM]	239 Elekid [43, TM]	587 Emolga [TM]	598 Ferrothorn [TM]	180 Flaaffy [56, TM]
		478 Froslass [TM]	162 Furret [TM]	596 Galvantula [TM]	649 Genesect [TM]	094 Gengar [TM]	203 Girafarig [TM]	487 Giratina (Alt) [TM]
		487 Giratina (Ori) [TM]	431 Glameow [TM]	706 Goodra [TM]	210 Granbull [TM]	088 Grimer [TM]	383 Groudon [TM]	130 Gyarados [TM]
		695 Heliolisk [1, TM]	694 Helioptile [TM]	250 Ho-Oh [TM]	314 Illumise [TM]	039 Jigglypuff [TM]	385 Jirachi [TM]	135 Jolteon [45, TM]
		115 Kangaskhan [TM]	352 Kecleon [TM]	601 Klinklang [TM]	109 Koffing [TM]	382 Kyogre [TM]	171 Lanturn [TM]	131 Lapras [TM]
		380 Latias [TM]	381 Latios [TM]	463 Lickilicky [TM]	108 Lickitung [TM]	264 Linoone [TM]	428 Lopunny [TM]	249 Lugia [TM]
		404 Luxio [TM]	405 Luxray [TM]	081 Magnemite [TM]	082 Magneton [TM]	462 Magnezone [TM]	310 Manectric [54, TM]	056 Mankey [TM]
		179 Mareep [46, TM]	648 Meloetta [TM]	052 Meowth [TM]	481 Mesprit [TM]	151 Mew [TM]	150 Mewtwo [TM]	241 Miltank [TM]
		439 Mime Jr. [TM]	312 Minun [43, TM]	200 Misdreavus [TM]	429 Mismagius [TM]	122 Mr. Mime [TM]	089 Muk [TM]	446 Munchlax [TM]
		034 Nidoking [TM]	031 Nidoqueen [TM]	029 Nidoran ♀ [TM]	032 Nidoran ♂ [TM]	030 Nidorina [TM]	033 Nidorino [TM]	299 Nosepass [TM]
		417 Pachirisu [TM]	484 Palkia [TM]	053 Persian [TM]	172 Pichu [TM]	025 Pikachu [58, TM]	311 Plusle [43, TM]	137 Porygon [TM]
		233 Porygon2 [TM]	474 Porygon-Z [TM]	057 Primeape [TM]	476 Probopass [TM]	432 Purugly [TM]	026 Raichu [TM]	243 Raikou [85, TM]
		409 Rampardos [TM]	020 Raticate [TM]	019 Rattata [TM]	384 Rayquaza [TM]	378 Regice [TM]	486 Regigigas [TM]	377 Regirock [TM]
		379 Registeel [TM]	579 Reuniclus [TM]	112 Rhydon [TM]	111 Rhyhorn [TM]	464 Rhyperior [TM]	479 Rotom (Fan) [TM]	479 Rotom (Frost) [TM]
		479 Rotom (Heat) [TM]	479 Rotom (Mow) [TM]	479 Rotom (Wash) [TM]	479 Rotom [TM]	410 Shieldon [TM]	403 Shinx [TM]	353 Shuppet [TM]
		300 Skitty [TM]	289 Slaking [TM]	287 Slakoth [TM]	143 Snorlax [TM]	209 Snubbull [TM]	577 Solosis [TM]	234 Stantler [TM]
		121 Starmie [TM]	120 Staryu [TM]	508 Stoutland [TM]	618 Stunfisk [TM]	128 Tauros [TM]	642 Thundurus [67, TM]	248 Tyranitar [TM]
		480 Uxie [TM]	494 Victini [TM]	288 Vigoroth [TM]	313 Volbeat [TM]	100 Voltorb [TM]	505 Watchog [TM]	110 Weezing [TM]
		040 Wigglytuff [TM]	716 Xerneas [TM]	335 Zangoose [TM]	145 Zapdos [78, TM]	523 Zebstrika [TM]	644 Zekrom [78, TM]	263 Zigzagoon [TM]
	Thunder Fang	142 Aerodactyl [1]	024 Arbok [1]	059 Arcanine [1]	633 Deino [E]	232 Donphan [1]	452 Drapion [1]	621 Druddigon [E]
		632 Durant [E]	309 Electrike [19, E]	295 Exploud [1]	472 Gliscor [1]	210 Granbull [1]	450 Hippowdon [1]	229 Houndoom [1]
		228 Houndour [E]	135 Jolteon [20]	506 Lillipup [E]	404 Luxio [33]	405 Luxray [35]	310 Manectric [19]	303 Mawile [E]
		261 Poochyena [E]	243 Raikou [50]	111 Rhyhorn [E]	373 Salamence [1]	551 Sandile [E]	403 Shinx [29, E]	209 Snubbull [1, E]
		208 Steelix [1]	508 Stoutland [1]	248 Tyranitar [1]	696 Tyrunt [E]	644 Zekrom [1]		
	Thunder Punch	063 Abra [BP, E]	306 Aggron [BP]	190 Aipom [BP]	065 Alakazam [BP]	424 Ambipom [BP]	181 Ampharos [30, BP]	531 Audino [BP]
		482 Azelf [BP]	257 Blaziken [BP]	242 Blissey [BP]	654 Braixen [BP]	286 Breloom [BP]	427 Buneary [BP, E]	331 Cacnea [BP]
		332 Cacturne [BP]	113 Chansey [BP]	006 Charizard [BP]	004 Charmander [BP]	005 Charmeleon [BP]	652 Chesnaught [BP]	650 Chespin [BP]
		390 Chimchar [BP, E]	036 Clefable [BP]	035 Clefairy [BP]	256 Combusken [BP]	534 Conkeldurr [BP]	408 Cranidos [BP]	453 Croagunk [BP]
		104 Cubone [BP]	702 Dedenne [BP]	655 Delphox [BP]	386 Deoxys (Nor) [BP]	386 Deoxys (Spd) [BP]	660 Diggersby [BP]	149 Dragonite [1, BP]
		096 Drowzee [BP, E]	621 Druddigon [BP]	356 Dusclops [1, BP]	477 Dusknoir [1, BP]	604 Eelektross [BP]	125 Electabuzz [29, BP]	466 Electivire [29, BP]
		239 Elekid [29, BP]	500 Emboar [BP]	295 Exploud [BP]	180 Flaaffy [BP]	330 Flygon [BP]	162 Furret [BP]	475 Gallade [BP]
		282 Gardevoir [BP]	092 Gastly [BP, E]	094 Gengar [BP]	074 Geodude [BP]	076 Golem [BP]	622 Golett [BP]	623 Golurk [BP]
		706 Goodra [BP]	210 Granbull [BP]	075 Graveler [BP]	088 Grimer [BP]	383 Groudon [BP]	253 Grovyle [BP]	326 Grumpig [BP]
		316 Gulpin [BP]	533 Gurdurr [BP]	297 Hariyama [BP]	093 Haunter [BP]	701 Hawlucha [BP]	631 Heatmor [BP]	695 Heliolisk [BP]
		107 Hitmonchan [36, BP]	097 Hypno [BP]	314 Illumise [BP]	392 Infernape [BP]	039 Jigglypuff [BP]	385 Jirachi [BP]	064 Kadabra [BP]
		115 Kangaskhan [BP]	352 Kecleon [BP]	281 Kirlia [BP]	166 Ledian [BP]	165 Ledyba [BP]	463 Lickilicky [BP]	108 Lickitung [BP]
		271 Lombre [BP]	428 Lopunny [BP]	294 Loudred [BP]	448 Lucario [BP]	272 Ludicolo [BP]	068 Machamp [BP]	067 Machoke [BP]
		066 Machop [BP, E]	240 Magby [BP, E]	126 Magmar [BP]	467 Magmortar [1, BP]	296 Makuhita [BP]	056 Mankey [BP]	105 Marowak [BP]
		303 Mawile [BP]	308 Medicham [1, BP]	307 Meditite [BP, E]	648 Meloetta [BP]	481 Mesprit [BP]	376 Metagross [BP]	375 Metang [BP]
		151 Mew [BP]	150 Mewtwo [BP]	241 Miltank [BP]	312 Minun [BP]	391 Monferno [BP]	122 Mr. Mime [BP]	089 Muk [BP]
		446 Munchlax [BP]	034 Nidoking [BP]	031 Nidoqueen [BP]	299 Nosepass [BP]	417 Pachirisu [BP]	674 Pancham [BP]	675 Pangoro [BP]
		172 Pichu [BP, E]	499 Pignite [BP]	025 Pikachu [BP]	311 Plusle [BP]	057 Primeape [BP]	476 Probopass [BP]	651 Quilladin [BP]
		026 Raichu [BP]	280 Ralts [BP]	409 Rampardos [BP]	378 Regice [BP]	486 Regigigas [1, BP]	377 Regirock [BP]	379 Registeel [BP]
		579 Reuniclus [BP]	112 Rhydon [BP]	464 Rhyperior [BP]	447 Riolu [BP]	302 Sableye [BP]	539 Sawk [BP]	254 Sceptile [BP]
		560 Scrafty [BP]	559 Scraggy [BP, E]	161 Sentret [BP]	289 Slaking [BP]	287 Slakoth [BP]	143 Snorlax [BP]	209 Snubbull [BP]
		327 Spinda [BP]	185 Sudowoodo [BP]	317 Swalot [BP]	216 Teddiursa [BP]	538 Throh [BP]	642 Thundurus [BP]	532 Timburr [BP]
		454 Toxicroak [BP]	252 Treecko [BP]	157 Typhlosion [BP]	248 Tyranitar [BP]	217 Ursaring [BP]	480 Uxie [BP]	494 Victini [BP]
		288 Vigoroth [BP]	313 Volbeat [BP]	505 Watchog [BP]	293 Whismur [BP]	040 Wigglytuff [BP]	335 Zangoose [BP]	644 Zekrom [BP]

Type	Move	Pokémon that can learn it						
Electric	Thunder Shock	181 Ampharos [1, 8]	702 Dedenne [7]	125 Electabuzz [1, 5]	466 Electivire [1, 5]	239 Elekid [5]	587 Emolga [1]	180 Flaaffy [1, 8]
		694 Helioptile [6]	135 Jolteon [9]	600 Klang [1, 11]	599 Klink [11]	601 Klinklang [1, 11]	081 Magnemite [7]	082 Magneton [1, 7]
		462 Magnezone [1, 7]	179 Mareep [8]	172 Pichu [1]	025 Pikachu [1]	026 Raichu [1]	243 Raikou [8]	479 Rotom (Fan) [1]
		479 Rotom (Frost) [1]	479 Rotom (Heat) [1]	479 Rotom (Mow) [1]	479 Rotom (Wash) [1]	479 Rotom [1]	618 Stunfisk [9]	642 Thundurus [1]
		145 Zapdos [1]						
	Thunder Wave (TM73)	063 Abra [TM]	359 Absol [TM]	306 Aggron [TM]	190 Aipom [TM]	065 Alakazam [TM]	698 Amaura [5, TM]	424 Ambipom [TM]
		181 Ampharos [1, 4, TM]	493 Arceus [TM]	531 Audino [TM]	699 Aurorus [5, TM]	482 Azelf [TM]	354 Banette [TM]	606 Beheeyem [TM]
		400 Bibarel [TM]	399 Bidoof [TM]	625 Bisharp [TM]	242 Blissey [TM]	522 Blitzle [15, TM]	427 Buneary [TM]	351 Castform [TM]
		251 Celebi [TM]	113 Chansey [TM]	358 Chimecho [TM]	170 Chinchou [6, TM]	433 Chingling [TM]	573 Cinccino [TM]	036 Clefable [TM]
		035 Clefairy [TM]	173 Cleffa [TM]	638 Cobalion [TM]	488 Cresselia [TM]	491 Darkrai [TM]	702 Dedenne [23, TM]	585 Deerling [TM]
		633 Deino [TM]	301 Delcatty [TM]	386 Deoxys (Atk) [TM]	386 Deoxys (Def) [TM]	386 Deoxys (Nor) [TM]	386 Deoxys (Spd) [TM]	483 Dialga [TM]
		148 Dragonair [1, 5, TM]	149 Dragonite [1, 5, TM]	147 Dratini [5, TM]	426 Drifblim [TM]	425 Drifloon [TM]	096 Drowzee [TM]	206 Dunsparce [TM]
		578 Duosion [TM]	632 Durant [TM]	603 Eelektrik [1, TM]	604 Eelektross [TM]	125 Electabuzz [19, TM]	466 Electivire [19, TM]	309 Electrike [1, TM]
		101 Electrode [TM]	239 Elekid [19, TM]	605 Elgyem [TM]	587 Emolga [TM]	677 Espurr [TM]	597 Ferroseed [TM]	598 Ferrothorn [TM]
		180 Flaaffy [1, 4, TM]	478 Froslass [TM]	676 Furfrou [TM]	475 Gallade [TM]	596 Galvantula [1, 4, TM]	282 Gardevoir [TM]	649 Genesect [TM]
		203 Girafarig [TM]	487 Giratina (Alt) [TM]	487 Giratina (Ori) [TM]	574 Gothita [TM]	576 Gothitelle [TM]	575 Gothorita [TM]	210 Granbull [TM]
		383 Groudon [TM]	326 Grumpig [TM]	130 Gyarados [TM]	440 Happiny [TM]	695 Heliolisk [TM]	694 Helioptile [31, TM]	507 Herdier [TM]
		430 Honchkrow [TM]	250 Ho-Oh [TM]	635 Hydreigon [TM]	097 Hypno [TM]	174 Igglybuff [TM]	314 Illumise [TM]	039 Jigglypuff [TM]
		385 Jirachi [TM]	135 Jolteon [33, TM]	595 Joltik [4, TM]	064 Kadabra [TM]	352 Kecleon [TM]	281 Kirlia [TM]	600 Klang [TM]
		707 Klefki [TM]	599 Klink [TM]	601 Klinklang [TM]	382 Kyogre [TM]	171 Lanturn [1, 6, TM]	380 Latias [TM]	381 Latios [TM]
		510 Liepard [TM]	506 Lillipup [TM]	264 Linoone [TM]	428 Lopunny [TM]	249 Lugia [TM]	404 Luxio [TM]	405 Luxray [TM]
		081 Magnemite [13, TM]	082 Magneton [13, TM]	462 Magnezone [13, TM]	310 Manectric [1, TM]	179 Mareep [4, TM]	648 Meloetta [TM]	678 Meowstic (F) [TM]
		678 Meowstic (M) [TM]	481 Mesprit [TM]	151 Mew [TM]	150 Mewtwo [TM]	241 Miltank [TM]	439 Mime Jr. [TM]	572 Minccino [TM]
		312 Minun [1, TM]	200 Misdreavus [TM]	429 Mismagius [TM]	122 Mr. Mime [TM]	517 Munna [TM]	198 Murkrow [TM]	518 Musharna [TM]
		177 Natu [TM]	299 Nosepass [13, TM]	224 Octillery [TM]	417 Pachirisu [33, TM]	484 Palkia [TM]	624 Pawniard [TM]	172 Pichu [18, TM]
		025 Pikachu [18, TM]	311 Plusle [1, TM]	137 Porygon [TM]	233 Porygon2 [TM]	474 Porygon-Z [TM]	476 Probopass [13, TM]	509 Purrloin [TM]
		211 Qwilfish [TM]	026 Raichu [TM]	243 Raikou [TM]	280 Ralts [TM]	020 Raticate [TM]	019 Rattata [TM]	384 Rayquaza [TM]
		378 Regice [TM]	486 Regigigas [TM]	377 Regirock [TM]	379 Registeel [TM]	223 Remoraid [TM]	579 Reuniclus [TM]	479 Rotom (Fan) [1, TM]
		479 Rotom (Frost) [1, TM]	479 Rotom (Heat) [1, TM]	479 Rotom (Mow) [1, TM]	479 Rotom (Wash) [1, TM]	479 Rotom [1, TM]	586 Sawsbuck [TM]	403 Shinx [TM]
		353 Shuppet [TM]	561 Sigilyph [TM]	300 Skitty [TM]	080 Slowbro [TM]	199 Slowking [TM]	079 Slowpoke [TM]	209 Snubbull [TM]
		577 Solosis [TM]	325 Spoink [TM]	234 Stantler [TM]	121 Starmie [TM]	120 Staryu [TM]	508 Stoutland [TM]	618 Stunfisk [TM]
		528 Swoobat [TM]	642 Thundurus [TM]	468 Togekiss [TM]	175 Togepi [TM]	176 Togetic [TM]	602 Tynamo [1, TM]	248 Tyranitar [TM]
		480 Uxie [TM]	494 Victini [TM]	313 Volbeat [TM]	100 Voltorb [TM]	505 Watchog [TM]	040 Wigglytuff [TM]	527 Woobat [TM]
		178 Xatu [TM]	716 Xerneas [TM]	145 Zapdos [8, TM]	523 Zebstrika [1, 15, TM]	644 Zekrom [TM]	263 Zigzagoon [TM]	634 Zweilous [TM]
	Thunderbolt (TM24)	359 Absol [TM]	306 Aggron [TM]	190 Aipom [TM]	698 Amaura [TM]	424 Ambipom [TM]	181 Ampharos [TM]	493 Arceus [TM]
		683 Aromatisse [TM]	531 Audino [TM]	699 Aurorus [TM]	482 Azelf [TM]	354 Banette [TM]	411 Bastiodon [TM]	606 Beheeyem [TM]
		400 Bibarel [TM]	399 Bidoof [TM]	242 Blissey [TM]	522 Blitzle [TM]	427 Buneary [TM]	351 Castform [TM]	113 Chansey [TM]
		170 Chinchou [TM]	573 Cinccino [TM]	036 Clefable [TM]	035 Clefairy [TM]	408 Cranidos [TM]	491 Darkrai [TM]	702 Dedenne [TM]
		301 Delcatty [TM]	386 Deoxys (Atk) [TM]	386 Deoxys (Def) [TM]	386 Deoxys (Nor) [TM]	386 Deoxys (Spd) [TM]	483 Dialga [TM]	691 Dragalge [TM]
		148 Dragonair [TM]	149 Dragonite [TM]	147 Dratini [TM]	426 Drifblim [TM]	425 Drifloon [TM]	206 Dunsparce [TM]	603 Eelektrik [44, TM]
		604 Eelektross [TM]	125 Electabuzz [49, TM]	466 Electivire [49, TM]	309 Electrike [TM]	101 Electrode [TM]	239 Elekid [40, TM]	605 Elgyem [TM]
		587 Emolga [TM]	677 Espurr [TM]	597 Ferroseed [TM]	598 Ferrothorn [TM]	180 Flaaffy [TM]	478 Froslass [TM]	162 Furret [TM]
		475 Gallade [TM]	596 Galvantula [TM]	569 Garbodor [TM]	282 Gardevoir [TM]	092 Gastly [TM]	649 Genesect [TM]	094 Gengar [TM]
		203 Girafarig [TM]	487 Giratina (Alt) [TM]	487 Giratina (Ori) [TM]	431 Glameow [TM]	623 Golurk [TM]	706 Goodra [TM]	704 Goomy [TM]
		574 Gothita [TM]	576 Gothitelle [TM]	575 Gothorita [TM]	210 Granbull [TM]	088 Grimer [TM]	383 Groudon [TM]	130 Gyarados [TM]
		093 Haunter [TM]	695 Heliolisk [TM]	694 Helioptile [49, TM]	507 Herdier [TM]	250 Ho-Oh [TM]	314 Illumise [TM]	686 Inkay [TM]
		039 Jigglypuff [TM]	385 Jirachi [TM]	135 Jolteon [TM]	595 Joltik [TM]	115 Kangaskhan [TM]	352 Kecleon [TM]	281 Kirlia [TM]
		600 Klang [TM]	599 Klink [TM]	601 Klinklang [TM]	109 Koffing [TM]	382 Kyogre [TM]	171 Lanturn [TM]	131 Lapras [TM]
		380 Latias [TM]	381 Latios [TM]	463 Lickilicky [TM]	108 Lickitung [TM]	506 Lillipup [TM]	264 Linoone [TM]	428 Lopunny [TM]
		249 Lugia [TM]	404 Luxio [TM]	405 Luxray [TM]	467 Magmortar [TM]	081 Magnemite [TM]	082 Magneton [TM]	462 Magnezone [TM]
		687 Malamar [TM]	310 Manectric [TM]	056 Mankey [TM]	179 Mareep [TM]	648 Meloetta [TM]	678 Meowstic (F) [TM]	678 Meowstic (M) [TM]
		052 Meowth [TM]	481 Mesprit [TM]	151 Mew [TM]	150 Mewtwo [TM]	241 Miltank [TM]	439 Mime Jr. [TM]	572 Minccino [TM]
		312 Minun [TM]	200 Misdreavus [TM]	429 Mismagius [TM]	122 Mr. Mime [TM]	089 Muk [TM]	446 Munchlax [TM]	034 Nidoking [TM]
		031 Nidoqueen [TM]	029 Nidoran ♀ [TM]	032 Nidoran ♂ [TM]	030 Nidorina [TM]	033 Nidorino [TM]	299 Nosepass [TM]	417 Pachirisu [TM]
		484 Palkia [TM]	504 Patrat [TM]	053 Persian [TM]	172 Pichu [TM]	025 Pikachu [42, TM]	311 Plusle [TM]	137 Porygon [TM]
		233 Porygon2 [TM]	474 Porygon-Z [TM]	057 Primeape [TM]	476 Probopass [TM]	432 Purugly [TM]	026 Raichu [1, TM]	243 Raikou [TM]
		280 Ralts [TM]	409 Rampardos [TM]	020 Raticate [TM]	019 Rattata [TM]	384 Rayquaza [TM]	378 Regice [TM]	486 Regigigas [TM]
		377 Regirock [TM]	379 Registeel [TM]	112 Rhydon [TM]	111 Rhyhorn [TM]	464 Rhyperior [TM]	479 Rotom (Fan) [TM]	479 Rotom (Frost) [TM]
		479 Rotom (Heat) [TM]	479 Rotom (Mow) [TM]	479 Rotom (Wash) [TM]	479 Rotom [TM]	161 Sentret [TM]	410 Shieldon [TM]	403 Shinx [TM]
		353 Shuppet [TM]	300 Skitty [TM]	690 Skrelp [TM]	289 Slaking [TM]	287 Slakoth [TM]	705 Sliggoo [TM]	685 Slurpuff [TM]
		143 Snorlax [TM]	209 Snubbull [TM]	682 Spritzee [TM]	234 Stantler [TM]	121 Starmie [TM]	120 Staryu [TM]	508 Stoutland [TM]
		618 Stunfisk [45, TM]	684 Swirlix [TM]	128 Tauros [TM]	642 Thundurus [TM]	248 Tyranitar [TM]	480 Uxie [TM]	494 Victini [TM]
		288 Vigoroth [TM]	313 Volbeat [TM]	100 Voltorb [TM]	505 Watchog [TM]	110 Weezing [TM]	040 Wigglytuff [TM]	716 Xerneas [TM]
		335 Zangoose [TM]	145 Zapdos [TM]	523 Zebstrika [TM]	644 Zekrom [22, TM]	263 Zigzagoon [TM]		

	Move	Pokémon that can learn it						
Normal	Tickle	190 Aipom [15]	594 Alomomola [E]	424 Ambipom [15]	298 Azurill [E]	069 Bellsprout [E]	688 Binacle [E]	420 Cherubi [E]
		573 Cinccino [1]	173 Cleffa [E]	546 Cottonee [E]	133 Eevee [E]	587 Emolga [E]	349 Feebas [E]	456 Finneon [E]
		574 Gothita [7]	576 Gothitelle [1, 7]	575 Gothorita [1, 7]	631 Heatmor [E]	098 Krabby [E]	131 Lapras [E]	345 Lileep [E]
		270 Lotad [E]	066 Machop [E]	303 Mawile [E]	439 Mime Jr. [1]	572 Minccino [9]	043 Oddish [E]	138 Omanyte [43]
		139 Omastar [48]	515 Panpour [E]	511 Pansage [E]	513 Pansear [E]	172 Pichu [E]	300 Skitty [E]	287 Slakoth [E]
		114 Tangela [44]	465 Tangrowth [46]	072 Tentacool [E]	387 Turtwig [E]	320 Wailmer [E]	340 Whiscash [1]	263 Zigzagoon [E]
Dark	Topsy-Turvy	686 Inkay [15]	687 Malamar [15]					
	Torment (TM41)	063 Abra [TM]	359 Absol [TM]	142 Aerodactyl [TM]	065 Alakazam [TM]	024 Arbok [TM]	566 Archen [TM]	567 Archeops [TM]
		683 Aromatisse [TM]	482 Azelf [TM]	354 Banette [TM]	689 Barbaracle [TM]	411 Bastiodon [TM]	688 Binacle [TM]	625 Bisharp [1, 14, TM]
		659 Bunnelby [TM]	318 Carvanha [TM]	441 Chatot [TM]	390 Chimchar [25, TM]	358 Chimecho [TM]	433 Chingling [TM]	091 Cloyster [TM]
		453 Croagunk [TM]	169 Crobat [TM]	491 Darkrai [TM]	555 Darmanitan [TM]	633 Deino [TM]	386 Deoxys (Atk) [TM]	386 Deoxys (Def) [TM]
		386 Deoxys (Nor) [TM]	386 Deoxys (Spd) [TM]	660 Diggersby [TM]	085 Dodrio [TM]	452 Drapion [TM]	096 Drowzee [TM]	621 Druddigon [TM]
		356 Dusclops [TM]	477 Dusknoir [TM]	355 Duskull [TM]	023 Ekans [TM]	466 Electivire [TM]	101 Electrode [TM]	677 Espurr [TM]
		295 Exploud [TM]	419 Floatzel [TM]	478 Froslass [TM]	475 Gallade [TM]	282 Gardevoir [TM]	092 Gastly [TM]	094 Gengar [TM]
		362 Glalie [TM]	431 Glameow [TM]	207 Gligar [TM]	472 Gliscor [TM]	042 Golbat [TM]	574 Gothita [TM]	576 Gothitelle [TM]
		575 Gothorita [TM]	210 Granbull [TM]	088 Grimer [TM]	326 Grumpig [TM]	130 Gyarados [TM]	093 Haunter [TM]	701 Hawlucha [TM]
		485 Heatran [TM]	430 Honchkrow [TM]	229 Houndoom [TM]	228 Houndour [TM]	635 Hydreigon [TM]	097 Hypno [TM]	392 Infernape [TM]
		686 Inkay [TM]	124 Jynx [TM]	064 Kadabra [TM]	281 Kirlia [TM]	707 Klefki [32, TM]	109 Koffing [TM]	552 Krokorok [10, TM]
		553 Krookodile [10, TM]	246 Larvitar [TM]	510 Liepard [19, TM]	294 Loudred [TM]	467 Magmortar [TM]	687 Malamar [TM]	630 Mandibuzz [TM]
		303 Mawile [TM]	678 Meowstic (F) [TM]	678 Meowstic (M) [TM]	052 Meowth [TM]	151 Mew [TM]	150 Mewtwo [TM]	262 Mightyena [TM]
		439 Mime Jr. [TM]	200 Misdreavus [TM]	429 Mismagius [TM]	391 Monferno [29, TM]	122 Mr. Mime [TM]	089 Muk [TM]	517 Munna [TM]
		198 Murkrow [61, TM]	518 Musharna [TM]	034 Nidoking [TM]	031 Nidoqueen [TM]	714 Noibat [TM]	715 Noivern [TM]	299 Nosepass [TM]
		274 Nuzleaf [16, TM]	095 Onix [TM]	674 Pancham [TM]	675 Pangoro [TM]	515 Panpour [TM]	511 Pansage [25, TM]	513 Pansear [TM]
		624 Pawniard [14, TM]	053 Persian [TM]	261 Poochyena [TM]	476 Probopass [TM]	247 Pupitar [TM]	509 Purrloin [19, TM]	432 Purugly [TM]
		280 Ralts [TM]	302 Sableye [TM]	551 Sandile [10, TM]	560 Scrafty [TM]	559 Scraggy [TM]	497 Serperior [TM]	496 Servine [TM]
		319 Sharpedo [TM]	410 Shieldon [TM]	275 Shiftry [TM]	353 Shuppet [TM]	516 Simipour [TM]	512 Simisage [TM]	514 Simisear [TM]
		227 Skarmory [TM]	451 Skorupi [TM]	435 Skuntank [TM]	215 Sneasel [TM]	495 Snivy [TM]	209 Snubbull [TM]	442 Spiritomb [TM]
		325 Spoink [TM]	682 Spritzee [TM]	208 Steelix [TM]	434 Stunky [TM]	185 Sudowoodo [TM]	528 Swoobat [TM]	216 Teddiursa [TM]
		642 Thundurus [TM]	641 Tornadus [TM]	454 Toxicroak [TM]	248 Tyranitar [TM]	197 Umbreon [TM]	217 Ursaring [TM]	100 Voltorb [TM]
		629 Vullaby [TM]	461 Weavile [TM]	110 Weezing [TM]	527 Woobat [TM]	717 Yveltal [TM]	571 Zoroark [34, TM]	570 Zorua [33, TM]
		041 Zubat [TM]	634 Zweilous [TM]					
Poison	Toxic (TM06)	460 Abomasnow [TM]	063 Abra [TM]	359 Absol [TM]	617 Accelgor [TM]	681 Aegislash [TM]	142 Aerodactyl [TM]	306 Aggron [TM]
		190 Aipom [TM]	065 Alakazam [TM]	594 Alomomola [TM]	334 Altaria [TM]	698 Amaura [TM]	424 Ambipom [TM]	591 Amoonguss [32, TM]
		181 Ampharos [TM]	347 Anorith [TM]	024 Arbok [TM]	059 Arcanine [TM]	493 Arceus [TM]	566 Archen [TM]	567 Archeops [TM]
		168 Ariados [TM]	348 Armaldo [TM]	683 Aromatisse [TM]	304 Aron [TM]	144 Articuno [TM]	531 Audino [TM]	699 Aurorus [TM]
		713 Avalugg [TM]	610 Axew [TM]	482 Azelf [TM]	184 Azumarill [TM]	298 Azurill [TM]	371 Bagon [TM]	343 Baltoy [TM]
		354 Banette [TM]	689 Barbaracle [TM]	339 Barboach [TM]	550 Basculin [TM]	411 Bastiodon [TM]	153 Bayleef [TM]	614 Beartic [TM]
		267 Beautifly [TM]	015 Beedrill [TM]	606 Beheeyem [TM]	182 Bellossom [TM]	069 Bellsprout [TM]	712 Bergmite [TM]	400 Bibarel [TM]
		399 Bidoof [TM]	688 Binacle [TM]	625 Bisharp [TM]	009 Blastoise [TM]	257 Blaziken [TM]	242 Blissey [TM]	522 Blitzle [TM]
		525 Boldore [TM]	438 Bonsly [TM]	626 Bouffalant [TM]	654 Braixen [TM]	628 Braviary [TM]	286 Breloom [TM]	437 Bronzong [TM]
		436 Bronzor [TM]	406 Budew [TM]	418 Buizel [TM]	001 Bulbasaur [TM]	427 Buneary [TM]	659 Bunnelby [TM]	012 Butterfree [TM]
		331 Cacnea [TM]	332 Cacturne [TM]	323 Camerupt [TM]	703 Carbink [TM]	455 Carnivine [TM]	565 Carracosta [TM]	318 Carvanha [TM]
		351 Castform [TM]	251 Celebi [TM]	609 Chandelure [TM]	113 Chansey [TM]	006 Charizard [TM]	004 Charmander [TM]	005 Charmeleon [TM]
		441 Chatot [TM]	421 Cherrim [TM]	420 Cherubi [TM]	652 Chesnaught [TM]	650 Chespin [TM]	152 Chikorita [TM]	390 Chimchar [TM]
		358 Chimecho [TM]	170 Chinchou [TM]	433 Chingling [TM]	573 Cinccino [TM]	366 Clamperl [TM]	692 Clauncher [TM]	693 Clawitzer [TM]
		344 Claydol [TM]	036 Clefable [TM]	035 Clefairy [TM]	173 Cleffa [TM]	091 Cloyster [TM]	638 Cobalion [TM]	563 Cofagrigus [TM]
		256 Combusken [TM]	534 Conkeldurr [TM]	341 Corphish [TM]	222 Corsola [TM]	546 Cottonee [TM]	346 Cradily [TM]	408 Cranidos [TM]
		342 Crawdaunt [TM]	488 Cresselia [TM]	453 Croagunk [TM]	169 Crobat [TM]	159 Croconaw [TM]	558 Crustle [TM]	615 Cryogonal [TM]
		613 Cubchoo [TM]	104 Cubone [TM]	155 Cyndaquil [TM]	491 Darkrai [TM]	555 Darmanitan [TM]	554 Darumaka [TM]	702 Dedenne [TM]
		585 Deerling [TM]	633 Deino [TM]	301 Delcatty [TM]	225 Delibird [TM]	655 Delphox [TM]	386 Deoxys (Atk) [TM]	386 Deoxys (Def) [TM]
		386 Deoxys (Nor) [TM]	386 Deoxys (Spd) [TM]	087 Dewgong [TM]	502 Dewott [TM]	483 Dialga [TM]	719 Diancie [TM]	660 Diggersby [TM]
		050 Diglett [TM]	085 Dodrio [TM]	084 Doduo [TM]	232 Donphan [TM]	680 Doublade [TM]	691 Dragalge [32, TM]	148 Dragonair [TM]
		149 Dragonite [TM]	452 Drapion [TM]	147 Dratini [TM]	426 Drifblim [TM]	425 Drifloon [TM]	529 Drilbur [TM]	096 Drowzee [TM]
		621 Druddigon [TM]	580 Ducklett [TM]	051 Dugtrio [TM]	206 Dunsparce [TM]	578 Duosion [TM]	632 Durant [TM]	356 Dusclops [TM]
		477 Dusknoir [TM]	355 Duskull [TM]	269 Dustox [32, TM]	557 Dwebble [TM]	603 Eelektrik [TM]	604 Eelektross [TM]	133 Eevee [TM]
		023 Ekans [TM]	125 Electabuzz [TM]	466 Electivire [TM]	309 Electrike [TM]	101 Electrode [TM]	239 Elekid [TM]	605 Elgyem [TM]
		500 Emboar [TM]	587 Emolga [TM]	395 Empoleon [TM]	244 Entei [TM]	589 Escavalier [TM]	196 Espeon [TM]	677 Espurr [TM]
		530 Excadrill [TM]	102 Exeggcute [TM]	103 Exeggutor [TM]	295 Exploud [TM]	083 Farfetch'd [TM]	022 Fearow [TM]	349 Feebas [TM]
		653 Fennekin [TM]	160 Feraligatr [TM]	597 Ferroseed [TM]	598 Ferrothorn [TM]	456 Finneon [TM]	180 Flaaffy [TM]	669 Flabébé [TM]
		136 Flareon [TM]	662 Fletchinder [TM]	661 Fletchling [TM]	419 Floatzel [TM]	670 Floette [TM]	671 Florges [TM]	330 Flygon [TM]
		590 Foongus [32, TM]	205 Forretress [TM]	611 Fraxure [TM]	592 Frillish [TM]	656 Froakie [TM]	657 Frogadier [TM]	478 Froslass [TM]
		676 Furfrou [TM]	162 Furret [TM]	444 Gabite [TM]	475 Gallade [TM]	596 Galvantula [TM]	569 Garbodor [39, TM]	445 Garchomp [TM]
		282 Gardevoir [TM]	092 Gastly [TM]	423 Gastrodon [TM]	649 Genesect [TM]	094 Gengar [TM]	074 Geodude [TM]	443 Gible [TM]
		526 Gigalith [TM]	203 Girafarig [TM]	487 Giratina (Alt) [TM]	487 Giratina (Ori) [TM]	471 Glaceon [TM]	362 Glalie [TM]	431 Glameow [TM]
		207 Gligar [TM]	472 Gliscor [TM]	044 Gloom [39, TM]	673 Gogoat [TM]	042 Golbat [TM]	118 Goldeen [TM]	055 Golduck [TM]
		076 Golem [TM]	622 Golett [TM]	623 Golurk [TM]	706 Goodra [TM]	704 Goomy [TM]	368 Gorebyss [TM]	574 Gothita [TM]

ADVENTURE DATA

Type	Move	Pokémon that can learn it						
Poison	Toxic (TM06)	576 Gothitelle [TM]	575 Gothorita [TM]	711 Gourgeist [TM]	210 Granbull [TM]	075 Graveler [TM]	658 Greninja [TM]	088 Grimer [TM]
		388 Grotle [TM]	383 Groudon [TM]	253 Grovyle [TM]	058 Growlithe [TM]	326 Grumpig [TM]	316 Gulpin [25, TM]	533 Gurdurr [TM]
		130 Gyarados [TM]	440 Happiny [TM]	297 Hariyama [TM]	093 Haunter [TM]	701 Hawlucha [TM]	612 Haxorus [TM]	631 Heatmor [TM]
		485 Heatran [TM]	695 Heliolisk [TM]	694 Helioptile [TM]	214 Heracross [TM]	507 Herdier [TM]	449 Hippopotas [TM]	450 Hippowdon [TM]
		107 Hitmonchan [TM]	106 Hitmonlee [TM]	237 Hitmontop [TM]	430 Honchkrow [TM]	679 Honedge [TM]	250 Ho-Oh [TM]	163 Hoothoot [TM]
		187 Hoppip [TM]	116 Horsea [TM]	229 Houndoom [TM]	228 Houndour [TM]	367 Huntail [TM]	635 Hydreigon [TM]	097 Hypno [TM]
		174 Igglybuff [TM]	314 Illumise [TM]	392 Infernape [TM]	686 Inkay [TM]	002 Ivysaur [TM]	593 Jellicent [TM]	039 Jigglypuff [TM]
		385 Jirachi [TM]	135 Jolteon [TM]	595 Joltik [TM]	189 Jumpluff [TM]	124 Jynx [TM]	140 Kabuto [TM]	141 Kabutops [TM]
		064 Kadabra [TM]	115 Kangaskhan [TM]	588 Karrablast [TM]	352 Kecleon [TM]	647 Keldeo [TM]	230 Kingdra [TM]	099 Kingler [TM]
		281 Kirlia [TM]	600 Klang [TM]	707 Klefki [TM]	599 Klink [TM]	601 Klinklang [TM]	109 Koffing [TM]	098 Krabby [TM]
		402 Kricketune [TM]	552 Krokorok [TM]	553 Krookodile [TM]	382 Kyogre [TM]	646 Kyurem (Blk) [TM]	646 Kyurem (Wht) [TM]	646 Kyurem [TM]
		305 Lairon [TM]	608 Lampent [TM]	645 Landorus [TM]	171 Lanturn [TM]	131 Lapras [TM]	636 Larvesta [TM]	246 Larvitar [TM]
		380 Latias [TM]	381 Latios [TM]	470 Leafeon [TM]	542 Leavanny [TM]	166 Ledian [TM]	165 Ledyba [TM]	463 Lickilicky [TM]
		108 Lickitung [TM]	510 Liepard [TM]	345 Lileep [TM]	549 Lilligant [TM]	506 Lillipup [TM]	264 Linoone [TM]	667 Litleo [TM]
		607 Litwick [TM]	271 Lombre [TM]	428 Lopunny [TM]	270 Lotad [TM]	294 Loudred [TM]	448 Lucario [TM]	272 Ludicolo [TM]
		249 Lugia [TM]	457 Lumineon [TM]	337 Lunatone [TM]	370 Luvdisc [TM]	404 Luxio [TM]	405 Luxray [TM]	068 Machamp [TM]
		067 Machoke [TM]	066 Machop [TM]	240 Magby [TM]	219 Magcargo [TM]	126 Magmar [TM]	467 Magmortar [TM]	081 Magnemite [TM]
		082 Magneton [TM]	462 Magnezone [TM]	296 Makuhita [TM]	687 Malamar [TM]	473 Mamoswine [TM]	490 Manaphy [TM]	630 Mandibuzz [TM]
		310 Manectric [TM]	056 Mankey [TM]	226 Mantine [TM]	458 Mantyke [TM]	556 Maractus [TM]	179 Mareep [TM]	183 Marill [TM]
		105 Marowak [TM]	259 Marshtomp [TM]	284 Masquerain [TM]	303 Mawile [TM]	308 Medicham [TM]	307 Meditite [TM]	154 Meganium [TM]
		648 Meloetta [TM]	678 Meowstic (F) [TM]	678 Meowstic (M) [TM]	052 Meowth [TM]	481 Mesprit [TM]	376 Metagross [TM]	375 Metang [TM]
		151 Mew [TM]	150 Mewtwo [TM]	619 Mienfoo [TM]	620 Mienshao [TM]	262 Mightyena [TM]	350 Milotic [TM]	241 Miltank [TM]
		439 Mime Jr. [TM]	572 Minccino [TM]	312 Minun [TM]	200 Misdreavus [TM]	429 Mismagius [TM]	146 Moltres [TM]	391 Monferno [TM]
		414 Mothim [TM]	122 Mr. Mime [TM]	258 Mudkip [TM]	089 Muk [TM]	446 Munchlax [TM]	517 Munna [TM]	198 Murkrow [TM]
		518 Musharna [TM]	177 Natu [TM]	034 Nidoking [TM]	031 Nidoqueen [TM]	029 Nidoran ♀ [TM]	032 Nidoran ♂ [TM]	030 Nidorina [TM]
		033 Nidorino [TM]	290 Nincada [TM]	038 Ninetales [TM]	291 Ninjask [TM]	164 Noctowl [TM]	714 Noibat [TM]	715 Noivern [TM]
		299 Nosepass [TM]	322 Numel [TM]	274 Nuzleaf [TM]	224 Octillery [TM]	043 Oddish [35, TM]	138 Omanyte [TM]	139 Omastar [TM]
		095 Onix [TM]	501 Oshawott [TM]	417 Pachirisu [TM]	484 Palkia [TM]	536 Palpitoad [TM]	674 Pancham [TM]	675 Pangoro [TM]
		515 Panpour [TM]	511 Pansage [TM]	513 Pansear [TM]	046 Paras [TM]	047 Parasect [TM]	504 Patrat [TM]	624 Pawniard [TM]
		279 Pelipper [TM]	053 Persian [TM]	548 Petilil [TM]	231 Phanpy [TM]	708 Phantump [TM]	489 Phione [TM]	172 Pichu [TM]
		018 Pidgeot [TM]	017 Pidgeotto [TM]	016 Pidgey [TM]	519 Pidove [TM]	499 Pignite [TM]	025 Pikachu [TM]	221 Piloswine [TM]
		204 Pineco [TM]	127 Pinsir [TM]	393 Piplup [TM]	311 Plusle [TM]	186 Politoed [TM]	060 Poliwag [TM]	061 Poliwhirl [TM]
		062 Poliwrath [TM]	077 Ponyta [TM]	261 Poochyena [TM]	137 Porygon [TM]	233 Porygon2 [TM]	474 Porygon-Z [TM]	057 Primeape [TM]
		394 Prinplup [TM]	476 Probopass [TM]	054 Psyduck [TM]	710 Pumpkaboo [TM]	247 Pupitar [TM]	509 Purrloin [TM]	432 Purugly [TM]
		668 Pyroar [TM]	195 Quagsire [TM]	156 Quilava [TM]	651 Quilladin [TM]	211 Qwilfish [TM]	026 Raichu [TM]	243 Raikou [TM]
		280 Ralts [TM]	409 Rampardos [TM]	078 Rapidash [TM]	020 Raticate [TM]	019 Rattata [TM]	384 Rayquaza [TM]	378 Regice [TM]
		486 Regigigas [TM]	377 Regirock [TM]	379 Registeel [TM]	369 Relicanth [TM]	223 Remoraid [TM]	643 Reshiram [TM]	579 Reuniclus [TM]
		112 Rhydon [TM]	111 Rhyhorn [TM]	464 Rhyperior [TM]	447 Riolu [TM]	524 Roggenrola [TM]	315 Roselia [40, TM]	407 Roserade [TM]
		479 Rotom (Fan) [TM]	479 Rotom (Frost) [TM]	479 Rotom (Heat) [TM]	479 Rotom (Mow) [TM]	479 Rotom (Wash) [TM]	479 Rotom [TM]	627 Rufflet [TM]
		302 Sableye [TM]	373 Salamence [TM]	503 Samurott [TM]	551 Sandile [TM]	027 Sandshrew [TM]	028 Sandslash [TM]	539 Sawk [TM]
		586 Sawsbuck [TM]	254 Sceptile [TM]	212 Scizor [TM]	545 Scolipede [44, TM]	560 Scrafty [TM]	559 Scraggy [TM]	123 Scyther [TM]
		117 Seadra [TM]	119 Seaking [TM]	364 Sealeo [TM]	273 Seedot [TM]	086 Seel [TM]	537 Seismitoad [TM]	161 Sentret [TM]
		497 Serperior [TM]	496 Servine [TM]	336 Seviper [TM]	540 Sewaddle [TM]	319 Sharpedo [TM]	492 Shaymin (Land) [TM]	492 Shaymin (Sky) [TM]
		292 Shedinja [TM]	372 Shelgon [TM]	090 Shellder [TM]	422 Shellos [TM]	616 Shelmet [TM]	410 Shieldon [TM]	275 Shiftry [TM]
		403 Shinx [TM]	285 Shroomish [33, TM]	213 Shuckle [TM]	353 Shuppet [TM]	561 Sigilyph [TM]	516 Simipour [TM]	512 Simisage [TM]
		514 Simisear [TM]	227 Skarmory [TM]	672 Skiddo [TM]	188 Skiploom [TM]	300 Skitty [TM]	451 Skorupi [TM]	690 Skrelp [32, TM]
		435 Skuntank [27, TM]	289 Slaking [TM]	287 Slakoth [TM]	705 Sliggoo [TM]	080 Slowbro [TM]	199 Slowking [TM]	079 Slowpoke [TM]
		218 Slugma [TM]	685 Slurpuff [TM]	238 Smoochum [TM]	215 Sneasel [TM]	495 Snivy [TM]	143 Snorlax [TM]	361 Snorunt [TM]
		459 Snover [TM]	209 Snubbull [TM]	577 Solosis [TM]	338 Solrock [TM]	021 Spearow [TM]	363 Spheal [TM]	167 Spinarak [TM]
		327 Spinda [TM]	442 Spiritomb [TM]	325 Spoink [TM]	682 Spritzee [TM]	007 Squirtle [TM]	234 Stantler [TM]	398 Staraptor [TM]
		397 Staravia [TM]	396 Starly [TM]	121 Starmie [TM]	120 Staryu [TM]	208 Steelix [TM]	508 Stoutland [TM]	618 Stunfisk [TM]
		434 Stunky [27, TM]	185 Sudowoodo [TM]	245 Suicune [TM]	192 Sunflora [TM]	191 Sunkern [TM]	283 Surskit [TM]	333 Swablu [TM]
		541 Swadloon [TM]	317 Swalot [25, TM]	260 Swampert [TM]	581 Swanna [TM]	277 Swellow [TM]	220 Swinub [TM]	684 Swirlix [TM]
		528 Swoobat [TM]	700 Sylveon [TM]	276 Taillow [TM]	663 Talonflame [TM]	114 Tangela [TM]	465 Tangrowth [TM]	128 Tauros [TM]
		216 Teddiursa [TM]	072 Tentacool [TM]	073 Tentacruel [TM]	498 Tepig [TM]	639 Terrakion [TM]	538 Throh [TM]	642 Thundurus [TM]
		532 Timburr [TM]	564 Tirtouga [TM]	468 Togekiss [TM]	175 Togepi [TM]	176 Togetic [TM]	255 Torchic [TM]	324 Torkoal [TM]
		641 Tornadus [TM]	389 Torterra [TM]	158 Totodile [TM]	454 Toxicroak [TM]	520 Tranquill [TM]	328 Trapinch [TM]	252 Treecko [TM]
		709 Trevenant [TM]	357 Tropius [TM]	568 Trubbish [36, TM]	387 Turtwig [TM]	535 Tympole [TM]	157 Typhlosion [TM]	248 Tyranitar [TM]
		697 Tyrantrum [TM]	236 Tyrogue [TM]	696 Tyrunt [TM]	197 Umbreon [TM]	521 Unfezant [TM]	217 Ursaring [TM]	480 Uxie [TM]
		583 Vanillish [TM]	582 Vanillite [TM]	584 Vanilluxe [TM]	134 Vaporeon [TM]	543 Venipede [36, TM]	049 Venomoth [TM]	048 Venonat [TM]
		003 Venusaur [TM]	416 Vespiquen [33, TM]	329 Vibrava [TM]	494 Victini [TM]	071 Victreebel [TM]	288 Vigoroth [TM]	045 Vileplume [TM]
		640 Virizion [TM]	666 Vivillon [TM]	313 Volbeat [TM]	637 Volcarona [TM]	100 Voltorb [TM]	629 Vullaby [TM]	037 Vulpix [TM]
		320 Wailmer [TM]	321 Wailord [TM]	365 Walrein [TM]	008 Wartortle [TM]	505 Watchog [TM]	461 Weavile [TM]	070 Weepinbell [TM]
		110 Weezing [TM]	547 Whimsicott [TM]	544 Whirlipede [41, TM]	340 Whiscash [TM]	293 Whismur [TM]	040 Wigglytuff [TM]	278 Wingull [TM]
		527 Woobat [TM]	194 Wooper [TM]	413 Wormadam (Plant) [TM]	413 Wormadam (Sand) [TM]	413 Wormadam (Trash) [TM]	178 Xatu [TM]	716 Xerneas [TM]

	Move	Pokémon that can learn it						
Poison	Toxic (TM06)	562 Yamask [TM]	193 Yanma [TM]	469 Yanmega [TM]	717 Yveltal [TM]	335 Zangoose [TM]	145 Zapdos [TM]	523 Zebstrika [TM]
		644 Zekrom [TM]	263 Zigzagoon [TM]	571 Zoroark [TM]	570 Zorua [TM]	041 Zubat [TM]	634 Zweilous [TM]	718 Zygarde [TM]
	Toxic Spikes	015 Beedrill [25]	091 Cloyster [1]	452 Drapion [34]	205 Forretress [1]	656 Froakie [E]	569 Garbodor [1, 7]	109 Koffing [E]
		029 Nidoran ♀ [31]	032 Nidoran ♂ [31]	030 Nidorina [35]	033 Nidorino [35]	138 Omanyte [E]	204 Pineco [E]	211 Qwilfish [21]
		315 Roselia [28]	451 Skorupi [34]	690 Skrelp [E]	167 Spinarak [E]	072 Tentacool [13]	073 Tentacruel [13]	568 Trubbish [7]
		543 Venipede [E]	048 Venonat [E]	562 Yamask [E]				
Normal	Transform	132 Ditto [1]	151 Mew [1]					
	Tri Attack	085 Dodrio [25]	051 Dugtrio [1]	649 Genesect [44]	635 Hydreigon [1]	082 Magneton [30]	137 Porygon [50]	233 Porygon2 [50]
		474 Porygon-Z [50]	021 Spearow [E]					
Psychic	Trick	063 Abra [BP]	065 Alakazam [46, BP]	493 Arceus [BP]	482 Azelf [BP]	343 Baltoy [BP]	354 Banette [58, BP]	606 Beheeyem [BP]
		654 Braixen [BP]	437 Bronzong [BP]	436 Bronzor [BP]	251 Celebi [BP]	609 Chandelure [BP]	358 Chimecho [BP]	433 Chingling [BP]
		344 Claydol [BP]	036 Clefable [BP]	035 Clefairy [BP]	173 Cleffa [BP]	563 Cofagrigus [BP]	488 Cresselia [BP]	491 Darkrai [BP]
		655 Delphox [BP]	386 Deoxys (Atk) [BP]	386 Deoxys (Def) [BP]	386 Deoxys (Nor) [BP]	386 Deoxys (Spd) [BP]	426 Drifblim [BP]	425 Drifloon [BP]
		096 Drowzee [BP]	578 Duosion [BP]	356 Dusclops [BP]	477 Dusknoir [BP]	355 Duskull [BP]	605 Elgyem [BP]	196 Espeon [BP]
		677 Espurr [BP, E]	592 Frillish [BP]	478 Froslass [BP]	162 Furret [BP]	475 Gallade [BP]	282 Gardevoir [BP]	092 Gastly [BP]
		094 Gengar [BP]	203 Girafarig [BP]	574 Gothita [BP]	576 Gothitelle [BP]	575 Gothorita [BP]	711 Gourgeist [1, BP]	326 Grumpig [BP]
		093 Haunter [BP]	097 Hypno [BP]	593 Jellicent [BP]	385 Jirachi [BP]	124 Jynx [BP]	064 Kadabra [46, BP]	352 Kecleon [BP, E]
		281 Kirlia [BP]	608 Lampent [BP]	380 Latias [BP]	381 Latios [BP]	510 Liepard [BP]	264 Linoone [BP]	607 Litwick [BP]
		249 Lugia [BP]	308 Medicham [BP]	307 Meditite [BP]	648 Meloetta [BP]	678 Meowstic (F) [BP]	678 Meowstic (M) [BP]	481 Mesprit [BP]
		376 Metagross [BP]	375 Metang [BP]	151 Mew [BP]	150 Mewtwo [BP]	439 Mime Jr. [36, BP, E]	200 Misdreavus [BP]	429 Mismagius [BP]
		122 Mr. Mime [36, BP, E]	517 Munna [BP]	518 Musharna [BP]	177 Natu [BP]	708 Phantump [BP]	137 Porygon [BP]	233 Porygon2 [BP]
		474 Porygon-Z [BP]	710 Pumpkaboo [1, BP]	509 Purrloin [BP]	280 Ralts [BP]	579 Reuniclus [BP]	479 Rotom (Fan) [1, BP]	479 Rotom (Frost) [1, BP]
		479 Rotom (Heat) [1, BP]	479 Rotom (Mow) [1, BP]	479 Rotom (Wash) [1, BP]	479 Rotom [1, BP]	302 Sableye [BP, E]	161 Sentret [BP, E]	292 Shedinja [BP]
		353 Shuppet [50, BP]	561 Sigilyph [BP]	080 Slowbro [BP]	199 Slowking [BP]	079 Slowpoke [BP]	238 Smoochum [BP]	577 Solosis [BP, E]
		327 Spinda [BP, E]	442 Spiritomb [BP]	325 Spoink [BP, E]	121 Starmie [BP]	528 Swoobat [BP]	468 Togekiss [BP]	175 Togepi [BP]
		176 Togetic [BP]	709 Trevenant [BP]	480 Uxie [BP]	494 Victini [BP]	313 Volbeat [BP, E]	527 Woobat [BP]	178 Xatu [BP]
		562 Yamask [BP]	263 Zigzagoon [BP, E]	571 Zoroark [BP]	570 Zorua [BP]			
	Trick Room (TM92)	063 Abra [TM]	065 Alakazam [TM]	493 Arceus [TM]	683 Aromatisse [TM]	531 Audino [TM]	482 Azelf [TM]	343 Baltoy [TM]
		354 Banette [TM]	606 Beheeyem [TM]	437 Bronzong [TM]	436 Bronzor [TM]	703 Carbink [TM]	251 Celebi [TM]	609 Chandelure [TM]
		358 Chimecho [TM]	433 Chingling [TM]	344 Claydol [TM]	563 Cofagrigus [TM]	488 Cresselia [TM]	655 Delphox [TM]	386 Deoxys (Atk) [TM]
		386 Deoxys (Def) [TM]	386 Deoxys (Nor) [TM]	386 Deoxys (Spd) [TM]	483 Dialga [TM]	719 Diancie [46, TM]	096 Drowzee [TM]	578 Duosion [TM]
		356 Dusclops [TM]	477 Dusknoir [TM]	355 Duskull [TM]	605 Elgyem [TM]	196 Espeon [TM]	677 Espurr [TM]	102 Exeggcute [TM]
		103 Exeggutor [TM]	592 Frillish [TM]	475 Gallade [TM]	282 Gardevoir [TM]	092 Gastly [TM]	094 Gengar [TM]	203 Girafarig [TM]
		574 Gothita [TM]	576 Gothitelle [TM]	575 Gothorita [TM]	711 Gourgeist [TM]	326 Grumpig [TM]	093 Haunter [TM]	097 Hypno [TM]
		686 Inkay [TM]	593 Jellicent [TM]	385 Jirachi [TM]	124 Jynx [TM]	064 Kadabra [TM]	352 Kecleon [TM]	281 Kirlia [TM]
		601 Klinklang [TM]	608 Lampent [TM]	607 Litwick [TM]	337 Lunatone [TM]	687 Malamar [TM]	648 Meloetta [TM]	678 Meowstic (F) [TM]
		678 Meowstic (M) [TM]	481 Mesprit [TM]	151 Mew [TM]	150 Mewtwo [TM]	439 Mime Jr. [TM]	200 Misdreavus [TM]	429 Mismagius [TM]
		122 Mr. Mime [TM]	517 Munna [TM]	518 Musharna [TM]	177 Natu [TM]	484 Palkia [TM]	708 Phantump [TM]	137 Porygon [TM]
		233 Porygon2 [TM]	474 Porygon-Z [1, TM]	710 Pumpkaboo [TM]	280 Ralts [TM]	579 Reuniclus [TM]	353 Shuppet [TM]	561 Sigilyph [TM]
		080 Slowbro [TM]	199 Slowking [TM]	079 Slowpoke [TM]	238 Smoochum [TM]	577 Solosis [TM]	338 Solrock [TM]	327 Spinda [TM]
		325 Spoink [TM]	682 Spritzee [TM]	234 Stantler [TM]	121 Starmie [TM]	528 Swoobat [TM]	709 Trevenant [TM]	480 Uxie [TM]
		494 Victini [TM]	547 Whimsicott [TM]	527 Woobat [TM]	178 Xatu [TM]	562 Yamask [TM]		
Ghost	Trick-or-Treat	711 Gourgeist [6, 23, 40, 63]	710 Pumpkaboo [6, 23, 40]					
Fighting	Triple Kick	237 Hitmontop [19]						
Normal	Trump Card	341 Corphish [E]	206 Dunsparce [E]	133 Eevee [45]	083 Farfetch'd [E]	115 Kangaskhan [E]	312 Minun [40]	501 Oshawott [E]
		422 Shellos [E]	199 Slowking [49]					
Bug	Twineedle	015 Beedrill [16]	589 Escavalier [1, 13]	090 Shellder [E]	451 Skorupi [E]	167 Spinarak [E]	543 Venipede [E]	
Dragon	Twister	371 Bagon [E]	691 Dragalge [1, 67]	148 Dragonair [1, 11]	149 Dragonite [1, 11]	147 Dratini [11]	443 Gible [E]	130 Gyarados [29]
		116 Horsea [17]	230 Kingdra [17]	226 Mantine [E]	458 Mantyke [E]	350 Milotic [14]	018 Pidgeot [22]	017 Pidgeotto [22]
		016 Pidgey [21]	384 Rayquaza [1]	117 Seadra [17]	495 Snivy [E]	278 Wingull [E]		

U•V

	Move	Pokémon that can learn it						
Normal	Uproar	306 Aggron [BP]	190 Aipom [BP]	334 Altaria [BP]	424 Ambipom [BP]	566 Archen [BP]	567 Archeops [BP]	304 Aron [BP]
		531 Audino [BP]	482 Azelf [31, BP]	298 Azurill [BP]	550 Basculin [4, BP]	606 Beheeyem [BP]	182 Bellossom [BP]	438 Bonsly [BP]
		626 Bouffalant [BP]	406 Budew [BP]	427 Buneary [BP]	318 Carvanha [BP]	251 Celebi [BP]	441 Chatot [45, BP]	390 Chimchar [BP]
		358 Chimecho [32, BP]	433 Chingling [32, BP]	573 Cinccino [BP]	173 Cleffa [BP]	408 Cranidos [BP]	169 Crobat [BP]	159 Croconaw [BP]
		104 Cubone [BP]	555 Darmanitan [BP]	554 Darumaka [17, BP]	633 Deino [BP]	301 Delcatty [BP]	660 Diggersby [BP]	050 Diglett [E]
		085 Dodrio [47, BP]	084 Doduo [41, BP]	580 Ducklett [BP]	309 Electrike [BP, E]	239 Elekid [BP]	605 Elgyem [BP]	102 Exeggcute [1, BP]
		295 Exploud [27, BP]	083 Farfetch'd [BP]	022 Fearow [BP]	160 Feraligatr [BP]	330 Flygon [40, BP]	676 Furfrou [BP]	162 Furret [BP]
		092 Gastly [BP]	094 Gengar [BP]	203 Girafarig [BP]	042 Golbat [BP]	574 Gothita [BP, E]	576 Gothitelle [BP]	575 Gothorita [BP]
		383 Groudon [BP]	130 Gyarados [BP]	440 Happiny [BP]	093 Haunter [BP]	485 Heatran [BP]	507 Herdier [BP]	430 Honchkrow [BP]

	Move	Pokémon that can learn it						
Normal	Uproar	163 Hoothoot [13, BP]	229 Houndoom [BP]	228 Houndour [BP]	635 Hydreigon [BP]	174 Igglybuff [BP]	385 Jirachi [BP]	115 Kangaskhan [BP, E]
		600 Klang [BP]	599 Klink [BP]	601 Klinklang [BP]	109 Koffing [BP]	401 Kricketot [BP]	402 Kricketune [BP]	552 Krokorok [BP]
		553 Krookodile [BP]	382 Kyogre [BP]	305 Lairon [BP]	246 Larvitar [BP]	166 Ledian [BP]	165 Ledyba [BP]	506 Lillipup [BP]
		271 Lombre [32, BP]	428 Lopunny [BP]	270 Lotad [BP]	294 Loudred [27, BP]	272 Ludicolo [BP]	240 Magby [BP]	490 Manaphy [BP]
		310 Manectric [BP]	056 Mankey [BP]	556 Maractus [BP]	105 Marowak [BP]	259 Marshtomp [BP]	648 Meloetta [BP]	052 Meowth [BP]
		151 Mew [BP]	262 Mightyena [BP]	439 Mime Jr. [BP]	572 Minccino [BP]	312 Minun [BP]	200 Misdreavus [BP]	429 Mismagius [BP]
		258 Mudkip [BP, E]	446 Munchlax [BP]	198 Murkrow [BP]	034 Nidoking [BP]	031 Nidoqueen [BP]	291 Ninjask [BP]	164 Noctowl [13, BP]
		714 Noibat [BP]	715 Noivern [BP]	417 Pachirisu [BP]	536 Palpitoad [23, BP]	674 Pancham [BP]	675 Pangoro [BP]	515 Panpour [BP]
		511 Pansage [BP]	513 Pansear [BP]	279 Pelipper [BP]	053 Persian [BP]	489 Phione [BP]	172 Pichu [BP]	018 Pidgeot [BP]
		017 Pidgeotto [BP]	016 Pidgey [BP, E]	519 Pidove [BP, E]	311 Plusle [BP]	261 Poochyena [BP]	474 Porygon-Z [BP]	057 Primeape [BP]
		247 Pupitar [BP]	409 Rampardos [BP]	020 Raticate [BP]	019 Rattata [BP, E]	384 Rayquaza [BP]	112 Rhydon [BP]	111 Rhyhorn [BP]
		464 Rhyperior [BP]	479 Rotom (Fan) [8, BP]	479 Rotom (Frost) [8, BP]	479 Rotom (Heat) [8, BP]	479 Rotom (Mow) [8, BP]	479 Rotom (Wash) [8, BP]	479 Rotom [8, BP]
		551 Sandile [BP, E]	537 Seismitoad [23, BP]	161 Sentret [BP]	319 Sharpedo [BP]	516 Simipour [BP]	512 Simisage [BP]	514 Simisear [BP]
		300 Skitty [BP, E]	238 Smoochum [BP]	021 Spearow [BP, E]	327 Spinda [37, BP]	442 Spiritomb [BP]	234 Stantler [BP]	398 Staraptor [BP]
		397 Staravia [BP]	396 Starly [BP, E]	508 Stoutland [BP]	618 Stunfisk [BP]	192 Sunflora [BP]	191 Sunkern [BP]	333 Swablu [BP]
		260 Swampert [BP]	581 Swanna [BP]	528 Swoobat [BP]	128 Tauros [BP]	642 Thundurus [1, BP]	175 Togepi [BP]	641 Tornadus [1, BP]
		158 Totodile [BP]	520 Tranquill [BP]	535 Tympole [23, BP]	248 Tyranitar [BP]	236 Tyrogue [BP]	521 Unfezant [BP]	217 Ursaring [BP]
		583 Vanillish [1, 10, BP]	582 Vanillite [10, BP]	584 Vanilluxe [1, 10, BP]	329 Vibrava [40, BP]	494 Victini [BP]	288 Vigoroth [1, 9, BP]	110 Weezing [BP]
		293 Whismur [25, BP]	278 Wingull [BP]	527 Woobat [BP]	413 Wormadam (Plant) [BP]	413 Wormadam (Sand) [BP]	413 Wormadam (Trash) [BP]	193 Yanma [27, BP]
		469 Yanmega [27, BP]	571 Zoroark [BP]	570 Zorua [BP]	041 Zubat [BP]	634 Zweilous [BP]		
Bug	U-turn (TM89)	617 Accelgor [40, TM]	190 Aipom [TM]	424 Ambipom [TM]	566 Archen [41, TM]	567 Archeops [45, TM]	144 Articuno [TM]	482 Azelf [TM]
		267 Beautifly [TM]	015 Beedrill [TM]	628 Braviary [TM]	659 Bunnelby [TM]	012 Butterfree [TM]	251 Celebi [TM]	441 Chatot [TM]
		390 Chimchar [TM]	573 Cinccino [TM]	692 Clauncher [TM]	693 Clawitzer [TM]	169 Crobat [TM]	555 Darmanitan [TM]	554 Darumaka [TM]
		702 Dedenne [TM]	660 Diggersby [TM]	269 Dustox [TM]	603 Eelektrik [TM]	604 Eelektross [TM]	587 Emolga [TM]	083 Farfetch'd [TM]
		022 Fearow [TM]	456 Finneon [42, TM]	662 Fletchinder [TM]	661 Fletchling [TM]	330 Flygon [TM]	656 Froakie [TM]	657 Frogadier [TM]
		676 Furfrou [TM]	162 Furret [TM]	649 Genesect [TM]	431 Glameow [TM]	207 Gligar [30, TM]	472 Gliscor [30, TM]	042 Golbat [TM]
		658 Greninja [TM]	701 Hawlucha [TM]	695 Heliolisk [TM]	694 Helioptile [TM]	187 Hoppip [37, TM]	635 Hydreigon [TM]	314 Illumise [TM]
		392 Infernape [TM]	385 Jirachi [TM]	189 Jumpluff [49, TM]	645 Landorus [TM]	636 Larvesta [TM]	166 Ledian [TM]	165 Ledyba [TM]
		510 Liepard [TM]	457 Lumineon [48, TM]	490 Manaphy [TM]	630 Mandibuzz [TM]	056 Mankey [TM]	284 Masquerain [TM]	648 Meloetta [43, TM]
		052 Meowth [TM]	481 Mesprit [TM]	151 Mew [TM]	619 Mienfoo [41, TM]	620 Mienshao [41, TM]	572 Minccino [TM]	146 Moltres [TM]
		391 Monferno [TM]	414 Mothim [TM]	177 Natu [TM]	291 Ninjask [TM]	714 Noibat [TM]	715 Noivern [TM]	417 Pachirisu [TM]
		279 Pelipper [TM]	053 Persian [TM]	489 Phione [TM]	018 Pidgeot [TM]	017 Pidgeotto [TM]	016 Pidgey [TM]	519 Pidove [TM]
		057 Primeape [TM]	509 Purrloin [TM]	432 Purugly [TM]	020 Raticate [TM]	019 Rattata [TM]	627 Rufflet [TM]	212 Scizor [TM]
		123 Scyther [TM]	161 Sentret [TM]	188 Skiploom [44, TM]	021 Spearow [TM]	398 Staraptor [TM]	397 Staravia [TM]	396 Starly [TM]
		277 Swellow [TM]	528 Swoobat [TM]	276 Taillow [TM]	663 Talonflame [TM]	642 Thundurus [TM]	641 Tornadus [TM]	520 Tranquill [TM]
		521 Unfezant [TM]	480 Uxie [TM]	049 Venomoth [TM]	416 Vespiquen [TM]	329 Vibrava [TM]	494 Victini [TM]	666 Vivillon [TM]
		313 Volbeat [TM]	637 Volcarona [TM]	629 Vullaby [TM]	547 Whimsicott [TM]	278 Wingull [TM]	527 Woobat [TM]	178 Xatu [TM]
		193 Yanma [49, TM]	469 Yanmega [49, TM]	717 Yveltal [TM]	145 Zapdos [TM]	571 Zoroark [1, TM]	570 Zorua [TM]	041 Zubat [TM]
Fighting	Vacuum Wave	453 Croagunk [E]	107 Hitmonchan [26]	447 Riolu [E]	123 Scyther [1]	236 Tyrogue [E]		
Poison	Venom Drench	168 Ariados [1]	316 Gulpin [E]	089 Muk [38]	029 Nidoran ♀ [E]	032 Nidoran ♂ [E]	708 Phantump [E]	407 Roserade [1]
		545 Scolipede [47]	336 Seviper [25]	690 Skrelp [E]	544 Whirlipede [43]	527 Woobat [E]	041 Zubat [E]	
Poison	Venoshock (TM09)	617 Accelgor [TM]	591 Amoonguss [TM]	024 Arbok [TM]	168 Ariados [TM]	267 Beautifly [TM]	015 Beedrill [TM]	182 Bellossom [TM]
		069 Bellsprout [TM]	286 Breloom [TM]	406 Budew [TM]	001 Bulbasaur [TM]	012 Butterfree [TM]	331 Cacnea [TM]	332 Cacturne [TM]
		692 Clauncher [TM]	693 Clawitzer [TM]	453 Croagunk [36, TM]	169 Crobat [43, TM]	691 Dragalge [TM]	452 Drapion [27, TM]	269 Dustox [20, TM]
		023 Ekans [TM]	590 Foongus [TM]	205 Forretress [TM]	569 Garbodor [TM]	092 Gastly [TM]	094 Gengar [TM]	207 Gligar [TM]
		472 Gliscor [TM]	044 Gloom [TM]	042 Golbat [43, TM]	088 Grimer [TM]	316 Gulpin [TM]	093 Haunter [TM]	214 Heracross [TM]
		002 Ivysaur [TM]	109 Koffing [TM]	151 Mew [TM]	414 Mothim [TM]	089 Muk [TM]	034 Nidoking [TM]	031 Nidoqueen [TM]
		029 Nidoran ♀ [TM]	032 Nidoran ♂ [TM]	030 Nidorina [TM]	033 Nidorino [TM]	043 Oddish [TM]	046 Paras [TM]	047 Parasect [TM]
		204 Pineco [TM]	211 Qwilfish [TM]	315 Roselia [TM]	407 Roserade [TM]	212 Scizor [TM]	545 Scolipede [28, TM]	537 Seismitoad [TM]
		336 Seviper [16, TM]	616 Shelmet [TM]	285 Shroomish [TM]	213 Shuckle [TM]	451 Skorupi [27, TM]	690 Skrelp [TM]	435 Skuntank [TM]
		167 Spinarak [TM]	434 Stunky [TM]	317 Swalot [TM]	072 Tentacool [TM]	073 Tentacruel [TM]	454 Toxicroak [36, TM]	568 Trubbish [TM]
		543 Venipede [26, 38, TM]	049 Venomoth [TM]	048 Venonat [TM]	003 Venusaur [TM]	416 Vespiquen [TM]	071 Victreebel [TM]	045 Vileplume [TM]
		070 Weepinbell [TM]	110 Weezing [TM]	544 Whirlipede [28, TM]	413 Wormadam (Plant) [TM]	413 Wormadam (Sand) [TM]	413 Wormadam (Trash) [TM]	041 Zubat [37, TM]
Normal	Vice Grip	692 Clauncher [9]	693 Clawitzer [9]	341 Corphish [7]	342 Crawdaunt [1, 7]	632 Durant [1]	099 Kingler [1, 5]	600 Klang [1]
		599 Klink [1]	601 Klinklang [1]	098 Krabby [5]	303 Mawile [17]	127 Pinsir [1]		
Grass	Vine Whip	069 Bellsprout [1]	001 Bulbasaur [9]	455 Carnivine [11]	652 Chesnaught [5]	650 Chespin [5]	152 Chikorita [E]	669 Flabébé [1]
		670 Floette [1]	673 Gogoat [7]	002 Ivysaur [9]	511 Pansage [10]	651 Quilladin [5]	497 Serperior [1, 7]	496 Servine [1, 7]
		672 Skiddo [7]	495 Snivy [7]	114 Tangela [7]	465 Tangrowth [7]	003 Venusaur [1, 9]	071 Victreebel [1]	070 Weepinbell [1]
Fighting	Vital Throw	297 Hariyama [22]	068 Machamp [25]	067 Machoke [25]	066 Machop [25]	296 Makuhita [22]	619 Mienfoo [E]	674 Pancham [27]
		675 Pangoro [27]	127 Pinsir [18]	538 Throh [17]				

	Move	Pokémon that can learn it						
Electric	Volt Switch (TM72)	181 Ampharos [TM]	522 Blitzle [TM]	170 Chinchou [TM]	638 Cobalion [TM]	702 Dedenne [26, TM]	603 Eelektrik [TM]	604 Eelektross [TM]
		125 Electabuzz [TM]	466 Electivire [TM]	309 Electrike [TM]	101 Electrode [TM]	239 Elekid [TM]	587 Emolga [42, TM]	180 Flaaffy [TM]
		205 Forretress [TM]	596 Galvantula [TM]	695 Heliolisk [TM]	694 Helioptile [40, TM]	135 Jolteon [TM]	595 Joltik [TM]	600 Klang [TM]
		599 Klink [TM]	601 Klinklang [TM]	171 Lanturn [TM]	404 Luxio [TM]	405 Luxray [TM]	081 Magnemite [TM]	082 Magneton [TM]
		462 Magnezone [TM]	310 Manectric [TM]	151 Mew [TM]	312 Minun [TM]	299 Nosepass [TM]	417 Pachirisu [TM]	172 Pichu [TM]
		025 Pikachu [TM]	311 Plusle [TM]	476 Probopass [TM]	026 Raichu [TM]	243 Raikou [TM]	479 Rotom (Fan) [TM]	479 Rotom (Frost) [TM]
		479 Rotom (Heat) [TM]	479 Rotom (Mow) [TM]	479 Rotom (Wash) [TM]	479 Rotom [TM]	403 Shinx [TM]	642 Thundurus [TM]	100 Voltorb [TM]
		145 Zapdos [TM]	523 Zebstrika [TM]	644 Zekrom [TM]				
	Volt Tackle	172 Pichu [E] ◆						

W

	Move	Pokémon that can learn it						
Fighting	Wake-Up Slap	594 Alomomola [29]	035 Clefairy [22]	534 Conkeldurr [20]	453 Croagunk [E]	478 Froslass [37]	431 Glameow [E]	533 Gurdurr [20]
		297 Hariyama [38]	039 Jigglypuff [28]	124 Jynx [33]	068 Machamp [27]	067 Machoke [27]	066 Machop [27]	296 Makuhita [34, E]
		648 Meloetta [50]	241 Miltank [50]	439 Mime Jr. [E]	572 Minccino [31]	122 Mr. Mime [E]	060 Poliwag [35]	061 Poliwhirl [43]
		285 Shroomish [E]	300 Skitty [28]	238 Smoochum [E]	532 Timburr [20]			
Water	Water Gun	347 Anorith [7]	348 Armaldo [1, 7]	184 Azumarill [1]	298 Azurill [1]	689 Barbaracle [4]	339 Barboach [9]	550 Basculin [1]
		400 Bibarel [15]	688 Binacle [4]	009 Blastoise [1, 7]	418 Buizel [15]	565 Carracosta [1]	351 Castform [10]	170 Chinchou [12]
		366 Clamperl [1]	692 Clauncher [1]	693 Clawitzer [1]	159 Croconaw [1, 6]	502 Dewott [1, 7]	691 Dragalge [1]	580 Ducklett [1]
		160 Feraligatr [1, 6]	456 Finneon [6]	419 Floatzel [15]	055 Golduck [1, 8]	116 Horsea [13]	230 Kingdra [1, 13]	171 Lanturn [12]
		131 Lapras [1]	270 Lotad [E]	457 Lumineon [1, 6]	370 Luvdisc [4]	183 Marill [1]	259 Marshtomp [1, 4]	350 Milotic [1]
		258 Mudkip [4]	224 Octillery [1]	138 Omanyte [10]	139 Omastar [10]	501 Oshawott [7]	515 Panpour [10]	279 Pelipper [1]
		060 Poliwag [5]	061 Poliwhirl [1, 5]	054 Psyduck [8]	195 Quagsire [1]	211 Qwilfish [1]	369 Relicanth [1, 10]	223 Remoraid [1]
		503 Samurott [1, 7]	117 Seadra [1, 13]	364 Sealeo [1]	690 Skrelp [1]	080 Slowbro [9]	199 Slowking [9]	079 Slowpoke [9]
		363 Spheal [1]	007 Squirtle [7]	121 Starmie [1]	120 Staryu [4]	618 Stunfisk [1]	260 Swampert [1, 4]	581 Swanna [1]
		564 Tirtouga [1]	158 Totodile [6]	134 Vaporeon [9]	320 Wailmer [7]	321 Wailord [1, 7]	365 Walrein [1]	008 Wartortle [1, 7]
		340 Whiscash [1, 9]	278 Wingull [1]	194 Wooper [1]				
	Water Pledge	009 Blastoise [T]	159 Croconaw [T]	502 Dewott [T]	395 Empoleon [T]	160 Feraligatr [T]	656 Froakie [T]	657 Frogadier [T]
		658 Greninja [T]	259 Marshtomp [T]	258 Mudkip [T]	501 Oshawott [T]	393 Piplup [T]	394 Prinplup [T]	503 Samurott [T]
		007 Squirtle [T]	260 Swampert [T]	158 Totodile [T]	008 Wartortle [T]			
	Water Pulse	460 Abomasnow [BP]	359 Absol [BP]	306 Aggron [BP]	190 Aipom [BP]	594 Alomomola [25, BP]	698 Amaura [BP]	424 Ambipom [BP]
		347 Anorith [BP, E]	493 Arceus [BP]	348 Armaldo [BP]	304 Aron [BP]	144 Articuno [BP]	699 Aurorus [BP]	713 Avalugg [BP]
		482 Azelf [BP]	184 Azumarill [BP]	298 Azurill [BP]	689 Barbaracle [BP]	339 Barboach [17, BP]	614 Beartic [BP]	712 Bergmite [BP]
		400 Bibarel [BP]	688 Binacle [BP]	009 Blastoise [28, BP]	242 Blissey [BP]	418 Buizel [BP]	427 Buneary [BP]	565 Carracosta [BP]
		318 Carvanha [BP]	351 Castform [BP]	251 Celebi [BP]	113 Chansey [BP]	170 Chinchou [BP, E]	366 Clamperl [BP, E]	692 Clauncher [34, BP]
		693 Clawitzer [34, BP]	036 Clefable [BP]	035 Clefairy [BP]	173 Cleffa [BP]	091 Cloyster [BP]	341 Corphish [BP]	222 Corsola [BP, E]
		342 Crawdaunt [BP]	159 Croconaw [BP]	615 Cryogonal [BP]	613 Cubchoo [BP]	301 Delcatty [BP]	225 Delibird [BP]	386 Deoxys (Atk) [BP]
		386 Deoxys (Def) [BP]	386 Deoxys (Nor) [BP]	386 Deoxys (Spd) [BP]	087 Dewgong [BP]	502 Dewott [25, BP]	691 Dragalge [25, BP]	148 Dragonair [BP]
		149 Dragonite [BP]	147 Dratini [BP, E]	580 Ducklett [13, BP]	206 Dunsparce [BP]	395 Empoleon [BP]	295 Exploud [BP]	349 Feebas [BP]
		160 Feraligatr [BP]	456 Finneon [22, BP]	419 Floatzel [BP]	592 Frillish [22, BP]	656 Froakie [14, BP]	657 Frogadier [14, BP]	478 Froslass [BP]
		162 Furret [BP]	423 Gastrodon [1, 7, BP]	471 Glaceon [BP]	362 Glalie [BP]	431 Glameow [BP]	118 Goldeen [16, BP]	055 Golduck [18, BP]
		706 Goodra [BP]	704 Goomy [BP]	368 Gorebyss [14, BP]	210 Granbull [BP]	658 Greninja [14, BP]	316 Gulpin [BP]	130 Gyarados [BP]
		440 Happiny [BP]	449 Hippopotas [BP]	450 Hippowdon [BP]	116 Horsea [BP, E]	367 Huntail [14, BP]	174 Igglybuff [BP]	314 Illumise [BP]
		593 Jellicent [22, BP]	039 Jigglypuff [BP]	385 Jirachi [BP]	124 Jynx [BP]	140 Kabuto [BP]	141 Kabutops [BP]	115 Kangaskhan [BP]
		352 Kecleon [BP]	647 Keldeo [BP]	230 Kingdra [BP]	099 Kingler [BP]	098 Krabby [BP]	382 Kyogre [1, BP]	305 Lairon [BP]
		171 Lanturn [BP]	131 Lapras [14, BP]	380 Latias [BP]	381 Latios [BP]	463 Lickilicky [BP]	108 Lickitung [BP]	264 Linoone [BP]
		271 Lombre [BP]	428 Lopunny [BP]	270 Lotad [BP]	294 Loudred [BP]	448 Lucario [BP]	272 Ludicolo [BP]	249 Lugia [BP]
		457 Lumineon [22, BP]	370 Luvdisc [17, BP]	490 Manaphy [46, BP]	226 Mantine [19, BP]	458 Mantyke [19, BP]	183 Marill [BP]	259 Marshtomp [BP]
		284 Masquerain [BP]	052 Meowth [BP]	481 Mesprit [BP]	151 Mew [BP]	150 Mewtwo [BP]	350 Milotic [17, BP]	241 Miltank [BP]
		258 Mudkip [BP]	446 Munchlax [BP]	034 Nidoking [BP]	031 Nidoqueen [BP]	029 Nidoran ♀ [BP]	032 Nidoran ♂ [BP]	030 Nidorina [BP]
		033 Nidorino [BP]	714 Noibat [BP]	715 Noivern [BP]	224 Octillery [BP]	138 Omanyte [BP, E]	139 Omastar [BP]	501 Oshawott [23, BP]
		484 Palkia [6, BP]	536 Palpitoad [BP]	515 Panpour [BP]	279 Pelipper [15, BP]	053 Persian [BP]	489 Phione [46, BP]	393 Piplup [BP]
		186 Politoed [BP]	060 Poliwag [BP, E]	061 Poliwhirl [BP]	062 Poliwrath [BP]	394 Prinplup [BP]	054 Psyduck [18, BP]	432 Purugly [BP]
		195 Quagsire [BP]	211 Qwilfish [BP, E]	384 Rayquaza [BP]	369 Relicanth [BP]	223 Remoraid [26, BP, E]	302 Sableye [BP]	503 Samurott [25, BP]
		117 Seadra [BP]	119 Seaking [16, BP]	364 Sealeo [BP]	086 Seel [BP, E]	537 Seismitoad [BP]	161 Sentret [BP]	319 Sharpedo [BP]
		090 Shellder [BP, E]	422 Shellos [7, BP]	516 Simipour [BP]	300 Skitty [BP]	690 Skrelp [25, BP]	289 Slaking [BP]	287 Slakoth [BP]
		705 Sliggoo [BP]	080 Slowbro [28, BP]	199 Slowking [28, BP]	079 Slowpoke [28, BP]	238 Smoochum [BP]	143 Snorlax [BP]	361 Snorunt [BP]
		459 Snover [BP]	209 Snubbull [BP]	363 Spheal [BP, E]	327 Spinda [BP, E]	442 Spiritomb [BP]	007 Squirtle [25, BP]	121 Starmie [BP]
		120 Staryu [BP]	618 Stunfisk [BP]	245 Suicune [BP]	283 Surskit [BP]	317 Swalot [BP]	260 Swampert [BP]	581 Swanna [13, BP]
		128 Tauros [BP]	072 Tentacool [16, BP]	073 Tentacruel [16, BP]	564 Tirtouga [BP, E]	468 Togekiss [BP]	175 Togepi [BP]	176 Togetic [BP]
		158 Totodile [BP, E]	535 Tympole [BP, E]	248 Tyranitar [BP]	480 Uxie [BP]	583 Vanillish [BP]	582 Vanillite [BP, E]	584 Vanilluxe [BP]
		134 Vaporeon [17, BP]	288 Vigoroth [BP]	313 Volbeat [BP]	320 Wailmer [19, BP]	321 Wailord [19, BP]	365 Walrein [BP]	008 Wartortle [28, BP]
		340 Whiscash [17, BP]	293 Whismur [BP]	040 Wigglytuff [BP]	278 Wingull [15, BP]	194 Wooper [BP]	335 Zangoose [BP]	263 Zigzagoon [BP]
	Water Shuriken	617 Accelgor [1]	658 Greninja [36, 75]					

◆ To obtain an Egg from which a Pokémon that has learned Volt Tackle will hatch, one of the Pokémon at the Pokémon Day Care needs to be a Pikachu or Raichu holding the Light Ball. Sometimes wild Pikachu are holding this item.

Type	Move	Pokémon that can learn it						
Water	Water Sport	594 Alomomola [1]	184 Azumarill [1, 5]	298 Azurill [5, E]	339 Barboach [6]	399 Bidoof [E]	688 Binacle [E]	406 Budew [7]
		418 Buizel [7]	692 Clauncher [7]	693 Clawitzer [7]	502 Dewott [1, 11]	580 Ducklett [3]	419 Floatzel [1, 7]	592 Frillish [1]
		656 Froakie [E]	118 Goldeen [1]	055 Golduck [1]	368 Gorebyss [5]	593 Jellicent [1]	380 Latias [4]	271 Lombre [20]
		370 Luvdisc [E]	490 Manaphy [1]	226 Mantine [E]	458 Mantyke [E]	183 Marill [5, E]	284 Masquerain [1, 14]	350 Milotic [4]
		501 Oshawott [11]	515 Panpour [16]	279 Pelipper [1]	489 Phione [1]	393 Piplup [11]	060 Poliwag [1, E]	061 Poliwhirl [1]
		394 Prinplup [11]	054 Psyduck [1]	369 Relicanth [E]	503 Samurott [1, 11]	119 Seaking [1]	086 Seel [7]	363 Spheal [E]
		283 Surskit [14]	581 Swanna [1, 3]	158 Totodile [E]	340 Whiscash [1, 6]	278 Wingull [E]		
	Water Spout	592 Frillish [61]	593 Jellicent [1, 69]	382 Kyogre [90]	223 Remoraid [E]	007 Squirtle [E]	320 Wailmer [41]	321 Wailord [33]
	Waterfall (HM05)	594 Alomomola [HM]	493 Arceus [HM]	184 Azumarill [HM]	298 Azurill [HM]	339 Barboach [HM]	550 Basculin [HM]	400 Bibarel [HM]
		009 Blastoise [HM]	418 Buizel [HM]	565 Carracosta [HM]	318 Carvanha [HM]	170 Chinchou [HM]	366 Clamperl [HM]	692 Clauncher [HM]
		693 Clawitzer [HM]	341 Corphish [HM]	342 Crawdaunt [HM]	159 Croconaw [HM]	087 Dewgong [HM]	502 Dewott [HM]	691 Dragalge [HM]
		148 Dragonair [HM]	149 Dragonite [HM]	147 Dratini [HM]	395 Empoleon [HM]	349 Feebas [HM]	160 Feraligatr [HM]	456 Finneon [HM]
		419 Floatzel [HM]	592 Frillish [HM]	656 Froakie [HM]	657 Frogadier [HM]	423 Gastrodon [HM]	118 Goldeen [32, HM]	055 Golduck [HM]
		368 Gorebyss [HM]	658 Greninja [HM]	130 Gyarados [HM]	116 Horsea [HM]	367 Huntail [HM]	593 Jellicent [HM]	140 Kabuto [HM]
		141 Kabutops [HM]	230 Kingdra [HM]	382 Kyogre [HM]	171 Lanturn [HM]	131 Lapras [HM]	380 Latias [HM]	381 Latios [HM]
		271 Lombre [HM]	272 Ludicolo [HM]	249 Lugia [HM]	457 Lumineon [HM]	370 Luvdisc [HM]	490 Manaphy [HM]	226 Mantine [HM]
		458 Mantyke [HM]	183 Marill [HM]	259 Marshtomp [HM]	151 Mew [HM]	350 Milotic [HM]	258 Mudkip [HM]	224 Octillery [HM]
		138 Omanyte [HM]	139 Omastar [HM]	501 Oshawott [HM]	515 Panpour [HM]	489 Phione [HM]	393 Piplup [HM]	186 Politoed [HM]
		060 Poliwag [HM]	061 Poliwhirl [HM]	062 Poliwrath [HM]	394 Prinplup [HM]	054 Psyduck [HM]	195 Quagsire [HM]	211 Qwilfish [HM]
		384 Rayquaza [HM]	369 Relicanth [HM]	223 Remoraid [HM]	503 Samurott [HM]	117 Seadra [HM]	119 Seaking [32, HM]	364 Sealeo [HM]
		086 Seel [HM]	319 Sharpedo [HM]	516 Simipour [HM]	690 Skrelp [HM]	363 Spheal [HM]	007 Squirtle [HM]	121 Starmie [HM]
		120 Staryu [HM]	245 Suicune [HM]	260 Swampert [HM]	072 Tentacool [HM]	073 Tentacruel [HM]	564 Tirtouga [HM]	158 Totodile [HM]
		134 Vaporeon [HM]	320 Wailmer [HM]	321 Wailord [HM]	365 Walrein [HM]	008 Wartortle [HM]	340 Whiscash [HM]	194 Wooper [HM]
Normal	Weather Ball	069 Bellsprout [E]	351 Castform [25]	420 Cherubi [E]	425 Drifloon [E]	250 Ho-Oh [1]	249 Lugia [1]	407 Roserade [1]
		361 Snorunt [E]	584 Vanilluxe [1]					
Water	Whirlpool	339 Barboach [E]	550 Basculin [E]	418 Buizel [31]	170 Chinchou [E]	366 Clamperl [1]	395 Empoleon [39]	456 Finneon [38]
		419 Floatzel [35]	368 Gorebyss [1]	367 Huntail [1]	131 Lapras [E]	457 Lumineon [42]	490 Manaphy [39]	258 Mudkip [33, E]
		138 Omanyte [E]	489 Phione [39]	393 Piplup [32]	394 Prinplup [37]	090 Shellder [40]	564 Tirtouga [E]	320 Wailmer [13]
		321 Wailord [13]						
Normal	Whirlwind	142 Aerodactyl [E]	267 Beautifly [30]	628 Braviary [1, 57]	012 Butterfree [22]	408 Cranidos [E]	269 Dustox [30]	297 Hariyama [16]
		449 Hippopotas [E]	250 Ho-Oh [1]	163 Hoothoot [E]	249 Lugia [1]	296 Makuhita [16]	630 Mandibuzz [1, 57]	284 Masquerain [1, 48]
		446 Munchlax [E]	198 Murkrow [E]	714 Noibat [40]	715 Noivern [40]	018 Pidgeot [17]	017 Pidgeotto [17]	016 Pidgey [17]
		627 Rufflet [55]	275 Shiftry [1]	561 Sigilyph [14]	227 Skarmory [E]	451 Skorupi [E]	143 Snorlax [E]	021 Spearow [E]
		325 Spoink [E]	398 Staraptor [23]	397 Staravia [23]	396 Starly [21]	276 Taillow [E]	357 Tropius [21]	637 Volcarona [40]
		629 Vullaby [55]	193 Yanma [E]	041 Zubat [E]				
Rock	Wide Guard	142 Aerodactyl [E]	594 Alomomola [1, 53]	565 Carracosta [25]	557 Dwebble [E]	475 Gallade [23]	074 Geodude [E]	106 Hitmonlee [41]
		237 Hitmontop [46]	679 Honedge [E]	099 Kingler [1]	068 Machamp [1]	296 Makuhita [E]	226 Mantine [23, E]	458 Mantyke [23, E]
		620 Mienshao [45]	122 Mr. Mime [1]	258 Mudkip [E]	299 Nosepass [E]	046 Paras [E]	476 Probopass [1]	486 Regigigas [40]
		524 Roggenrola [E]	410 Shieldon [E]	538 Throh [45]	532 Timburr [E]	564 Tirtouga [25]	387 Turtwig [E]	278 Wingull [E]
Electric	Wild Charge (TM93)	181 Ampharos [TM]	059 Arcanine [TM]	531 Audino [TM]	242 Blissey [TM]	522 Blitzle [39, TM]	626 Bouffalant [TM]	659 Bunnelby [TM]
		113 Chansey [TM]	170 Chinchou [TM]	155 Cyndaquil [TM]	702 Dedenne [TM]	585 Deerling [TM]	301 Delcatty [TM]	660 Diggersby [TM]
		206 Dunsparce [TM]	603 Eelektrik [59, TM]	604 Eelektross [TM]	125 Electabuzz [TM]	466 Electivire [TM]	309 Electrike [39, TM]	101 Electrode [TM]
		239 Elekid [TM]	500 Emboar [TM]	587 Emolga [TM]	180 Flaaffy [TM]	676 Furfrou [TM]	596 Galvantula [TM]	673 Gogoat [TM]
		210 Granbull [TM]	058 Growlithe [TM]	695 Heliolisk [TM]	694 Helioptile [TM]	507 Herdier [TM]	174 Igglybuff [TM]	039 Jigglypuff [TM]
		135 Jolteon [TM]	595 Joltik [TM]	600 Klang [TM]	599 Klink [TM]	601 Klinklang [TM]	171 Lanturn [TM]	636 Larvesta [TM]
		506 Lillipup [TM]	667 Litleo [TM]	404 Luxio [53, TM]	405 Luxray [63, TM]	081 Magnemite [TM]	082 Magneton [TM]	462 Magnezone [TM]
		310 Manectric [42, TM]	179 Mareep [TM]	151 Mew [TM]	312 Minun [TM]	714 Noibat [TM]	715 Noivern [TM]	172 Pichu [TM]
		499 Pignite [TM]	025 Pikachu [50, TM]	311 Plusle [TM]	077 Ponyta [TM]	668 Pyroar [TM]	156 Quilava [TM]	026 Raichu [TM]
		243 Raikou [TM]	078 Rapidash [TM]	020 Raticate [TM]	019 Rattata [TM]	586 Sawsbuck [TM]	403 Shinx [45, TM]	672 Skiddo [TM]
		300 Skitty [TM]	143 Snorlax [TM]	209 Snubbull [TM]	327 Spinda [TM]	234 Stantler [TM]	508 Stoutland [TM]	128 Tauros [TM]
		498 Tepig [TM]	642 Thundurus [TM]	157 Typhlosion [TM]	494 Victini [TM]	637 Volcarona [TM]	100 Voltorb [TM]	040 Wigglytuff [TM]
		145 Zapdos [TM]	523 Zebstrika [47, TM]	644 Zekrom [TM]				
Fire	Will-O-Wisp (TM61)	359 Absol [TM]	059 Arcanine [TM]	493 Arceus [TM]	354 Banette [16, TM]	257 Blaziken [TM]	654 Braixen [45, TM]	323 Camerupt [TM]
		609 Chandelure [TM]	006 Charizard [TM]	004 Charmander [TM]	005 Charmeleon [TM]	390 Chimchar [TM]	563 Cofagrigus [21, TM]	256 Combusken [TM]
		155 Cyndaquil [TM]	491 Darkrai [TM]	555 Darmanitan [TM]	554 Darumaka [TM]	655 Delphox [47, TM]	426 Drifblim [TM]	425 Drifloon [TM]
		356 Dusclops [25, TM]	477 Dusknoir [25, TM]	355 Duskull [25, TM]	500 Emboar [TM]	244 Entei [TM]	653 Fennekin [38, TM]	136 Flareon [TM]
		662 Fletchinder [TM]	592 Frillish [TM]	475 Gallade [TM]	282 Gardevoir [TM]	092 Gastly [TM]	094 Gengar [TM]	487 Giratina (Alt) [TM]
		487 Giratina (Ori) [TM]	711 Gourgeist [TM]	058 Growlithe [TM]	093 Haunter [TM]	631 Heatmor [TM]	485 Heatran [TM]	250 Ho-Oh [TM]
		229 Houndoom [TM]	228 Houndour [TM]	392 Infernape [TM]	593 Jellicent [TM]	281 Kirlia [TM]	109 Koffing [TM]	608 Lampent [16, TM]
		636 Larvesta [TM]	667 Litleo [TM]	607 Litwick [16, TM]	240 Magby [TM]	219 Magcargo [TM]	126 Magmar [TM]	467 Magmortar [TM]
		151 Mew [TM]	150 Mewtwo [TM]	200 Misdreavus [TM]	429 Mismagius [TM]	146 Moltres [TM]	391 Monferno [TM]	038 Ninetales [TM]
		322 Numel [TM]	513 Pansear [TM]	708 Phantump [31, TM]	499 Pignite [TM]	077 Ponyta [TM]	710 Pumpkaboo [TM]	668 Pyroar [TM]
		156 Quilava [TM]	280 Ralts [TM]	078 Rapidash [TM]	643 Reshiram [TM]	479 Rotom (Fan) [TM]	479 Rotom (Frost) [TM]	479 Rotom (Heat) [TM]
		479 Rotom (Mow) [TM]	479 Rotom (Wash) [TM]	479 Rotom [TM]	302 Sableye [TM]	292 Shedinja [TM]	353 Shuppet [16, TM]	514 Simisear [TM]
		218 Slugma [TM]	338 Solrock [TM]	442 Spiritomb [TM]	663 Talonflame [TM]	498 Tepig [TM]	255 Torchic [TM]	324 Torkoal [TM]
		709 Trevenant [31, TM]	157 Typhlosion [TM]	494 Victini [TM]	637 Volcarona [TM]	037 Vulpix [20, TM]	110 Weezing [TM]	562 Yamask [21, TM]

Type	Move	Pokémon that can learn it						
Flying	Wing Attack	142 Aerodactyl [1]	566 Archen [1]	567 Archeops [1]	628 Braviary [1, 10]	006 Charizard [36]	169 Crobat [13]	149 Dragonite [55]
		580 Ducklett [9]	207 Gligar [E]	042 Golbat [13]	701 Hawlucha [8]	430 Honchkrow [1]	163 Hoothoot [E]	226 Mantine [14]
		458 Mantyke [14]	146 Moltres [1]	198 Murkrow [15, E]	714 Noibat [16]	715 Noivern [16]	279 Pelipper [1, 8]	018 Pidgeot [38]
		017 Pidgeotto [37]	016 Pidgey [33]	627 Rufflet [10]	123 Scyther [21]	398 Staraptor [1, 9]	397 Staravia [9]	396 Starly [9]
		581 Swanna [1, 9]	277 Swellow [13]	276 Taillow [13]	278 Wingull [8]	193 Yanma [43]	041 Zubat [13]	
Normal	Wish	594 Alomomola [37]	531 Audino [E]	358 Chimecho [E]	433 Chingling [E]	173 Cleffa [E]	133 Eevee [E]	653 Fennekin [E]
		669 Flabébé [20]	670 Floette [20]	671 Florges [1]	282 Gardevoir [14]	203 Girafarig [E]	174 Igglybuff [E]	314 Illumise [22]
		385 Jirachi [1]	380 Latias [1]	312 Minun [E]	177 Natu [28]	172 Pichu [E]	519 Pidove [E]	311 Plusle [E]
		300 Skitty [E]	685 Slurpuff [45]	238 Smoochum [E]	327 Spinda [E]	682 Spritzee [E]	684 Swirlix [45]	175 Togepi [29]
		176 Togetic [29]	178 Xatu [29]					
Water	Withdraw	689 Barbaracle [7]	688 Binacle [7]	009 Blastoise [1, 10]	565 Carracosta [1]	091 Cloyster [1]	558 Crustle [1, 7]	557 Dwebble [7]
		388 Grotle [1, 5]	138 Omanyte [1]	139 Omastar [1]	090 Shellder [4]	213 Shuckle [1]	080 Slowbro [37]	007 Squirtle [10]
		564 Tirtouga [1]	324 Torkoal [7]	389 Torterra [1, 5]	387 Turtwig [5]	008 Wartortle [10]		
Psychic	Wonder Room	063 Abra [BP]	065 Alakazam [BP]	334 Altaria [BP]	482 Azelf [BP]	343 Baltoy [BP]	606 Beheeyem [1, 68, BP]	654 Braixen [BP]
		437 Bronzong [BP]	436 Bronzor [BP]	703 Carbink [BP]	251 Celebi [BP]	344 Claydol [BP]	036 Clefable [BP]	035 Clefairy [BP]
		173 Cleffa [BP]	563 Cofagrigus [BP]	491 Darkrai [BP]	655 Delphox [BP]	386 Deoxys (Atk) [BP]	386 Deoxys (Def) [BP]	386 Deoxys (Nor) [BP]
		386 Deoxys (Spd) [BP]	719 Diancie [BP]	578 Duosion [53, BP]	356 Dusclops [BP]	477 Dusknoir [BP]	355 Duskull [BP]	605 Elgyem [56, BP]
		677 Espurr [BP]	475 Gallade [BP]	282 Gardevoir [BP]	092 Gastly [BP]	094 Gengar [BP]	055 Golduck [60, BP]	093 Haunter [BP]
		064 Kadabra [BP]	352 Kecleon [BP]	281 Kirlia [BP]	381 Latios [BP]	249 Lugia [BP]	648 Meloetta [BP]	678 Meowstic (F) [BP]
		678 Meowstic (M) [BP]	481 Mesprit [BP]	151 Mew [BP]	150 Mewtwo [BP]	439 Mime Jr. [BP]	200 Misdreavus [BP, E]	429 Mismagius [BP]
		122 Mr. Mime [BP]	517 Munna [BP]	518 Musharna [BP]	137 Porygon [BP]	233 Porygon2 [BP]	054 Psyduck [50, BP]	280 Ralts [BP]
		579 Reuniclus [59, BP]	302 Sableye [BP]	080 Slowbro [BP]	199 Slowking [BP]	079 Slowpoke [BP, E]	577 Solosis [48, BP]	338 Solrock [49, BP]
		442 Spiritomb [BP]	121 Starmie [BP]	197 Umbreon [BP]	480 Uxie [BP]	716 Xerneas [BP]	562 Yamask [BP]	
Grass	Wood Hammer	460 Abomasnow [36]	652 Chesnaught [55]	650 Chespin [48]	103 Exeggutor [37]	556 Maractus [E]	708 Phantump [49]	651 Quilladin [55]
		459 Snover [36]	185 Sudowoodo [1]	389 Torterra [1]	709 Trevenant [49]			
Normal	Work Up	638 Cobalion [1, 61]	555 Darmanitan [25]	554 Darumaka [25]	633 Deino [38]	676 Furfrou [E]	507 Herdier [20]	635 Hydreigon [38]
		647 Keldeo [61]	506 Lillipup [19]	667 Litleo [8]	674 Pancham [10]	675 Pangoro [10]	504 Patrat [26]	668 Pyroar [8]
		508 Stoutland [20]	128 Tauros [29]	639 Terrakion [1, 61]	640 Virizion [1, 61]	634 Zweilous [38]		
Grass	Worry Seed	460 Abomasnow [BP]	591 Amoonguss [BP]	153 Bayleef [BP]	182 Bellossom [BP]	069 Bellsprout [BP, E]	286 Breloom [BP]	406 Budew [16, BP]
		001 Bulbasaur [31, BP]	331 Cacnea [BP, E]	332 Cacturne [BP]	455 Carnivine [BP, E]	251 Celebi [BP]	421 Cherrim [30, BP]	420 Cherubi [28, BP]
		652 Chesnaught [BP]	650 Chespin [BP]	152 Chikorita [BP]	546 Cottonee [BP, E]	346 Cradily [BP]	585 Deerling [BP, E]	102 Exeggcute [33, BP]
		103 Exeggutor [BP]	597 Ferroseed [BP, E]	598 Ferrothorn [BP]	669 Flabébé [BP]	670 Floette [BP]	671 Florges [BP]	590 Foongus [BP]
		044 Gloom [BP]	673 Gogoat [16, BP]	055 Golduck [BP]	711 Gourgeist [11, BP]	388 Grotle [BP]	253 Grovyle [BP]	187 Hoppip [40, BP, E]
		002 Ivysaur [36, BP]	189 Jumpluff [54, BP]	470 Leafeon [BP]	542 Leavanny [BP]	345 Lileep [BP]	549 Lilligant [BP]	556 Maractus [BP, E]
		154 Meganium [BP]	151 Mew [BP]	517 Munna [BP]	518 Musharna [BP]	274 Nuzleaf [BP]	043 Oddish [BP]	511 Pansage [BP]
		046 Paras [BP]	047 Parasect [BP]	548 Petilil [BP, E]	708 Phantump [BP]	054 Psyduck [BP]	710 Pumpkaboo [11, BP]	651 Quilladin [BP]
		315 Roselia [BP]	407 Roserade [BP]	586 Sawsbuck [BP]	254 Sceptile [BP]	273 Seedot [BP, E]	497 Serperior [BP]	496 Servine [BP]
		540 Sewaddle [BP]	492 Shaymin (Land) [55, BP]	492 Shaymin (Sky) [55, BP]	275 Shiftry [BP]	285 Shroomish [22, BP, E]	512 Simisage [BP]	672 Skiddo [16, BP]
		188 Skiploom [48, BP]	495 Snivy [BP]	459 Snover [BP]	192 Sunflora [19, BP]	191 Sunkern [19, BP]	541 Swadloon [BP]	114 Tangela [BP]
		465 Tangrowth [BP]	389 Torterra [BP]	252 Treecko [BP, E]	709 Trevenant [BP]	357 Tropius [BP]	387 Turtwig [BP, E]	003 Venusaur [39, BP]
		071 Victreebel [BP]	045 Vileplume [BP]	640 Virizion [BP]	070 Weepinbell [BP]	547 Whimsicott [BP]	413 Wormadam (Plant) [BP]	
Normal	Wrap	024 Arbok [1]	069 Bellsprout [11]	358 Chimecho [1]	433 Chingling [1]	386 Deoxys (Atk) [1]	386 Deoxys (Def) [1]	386 Deoxys (Nor) [1]
		386 Deoxys (Spd) [1]	148 Dragonair [1]	149 Dragonite [1]	147 Dratini [1]	023 Ekans [1]	631 Heatmor [E]	463 Lickilicky [17]
		108 Lickitung [17]	350 Milotic [1]	497 Serperior [1, 10]	496 Servine [1, 10]	336 Seviper [1]	213 Shuckle [9]	495 Snivy [10]
		072 Tentacool [19]	073 Tentacruel [19]	070 Weepinbell [1, 11]				
	Wring Out	069 Bellsprout [47]	455 Carnivine [47]	152 Chikorita [E]	346 Cradily [1, 61]	592 Frillish [55]	316 Gulpin [44]	593 Jellicent [1, 61]
		124 Jynx [49]	140 Kabuto [50]	141 Kabutops [63]	463 Lickilicky [1, 57]	108 Lickitung [57]	345 Lileep [52, E]	224 Octillery [28]
		138 Omanyte [E]	497 Serperior [50]	496 Servine [44]	336 Seviper [49, E]	495 Snivy [37]	317 Swalot [1, 54]	114 Tangela [46]
		465 Tangrowth [49]	072 Tentacool [49]	073 Tentacruel [1, 56]	070 Weepinbell [47]			

X·Y·Z

Type	Move	Pokémon that can learn it						
Bug	X-Scissor (TM81)	359 Absol [TM]	347 Anorith [44, TM]	493 Arceus [TM]	168 Ariados [TM]	348 Armaldo [46, TM]	610 Axew [TM]	689 Barbaracle [TM]
		015 Beedrill [TM]	688 Binacle [TM]	625 Bisharp [TM]	638 Cobalion [TM]	341 Corphish [TM]	342 Crawdaunt [TM]	453 Croagunk [TM]
		169 Crobat [TM]	558 Crustle [38, TM]	491 Darkrai [TM]	502 Dewott [TM]	452 Drapion [TM]	529 Drilbur [TM]	632 Durant [51, TM]
		557 Dwebble [35, TM]	589 Escavalier [44, TM]	530 Excadrill [TM]	611 Fraxure [TM]	475 Gallade [TM]	596 Galvantula [TM]	649 Genesect [51, TM]
		207 Gligar [40, TM]	472 Gliscor [40, TM]	253 Grovyle [43, TM]	701 Hawlucha [TM]	612 Haxorus [TM]	595 Joltik [TM]	141 Kabutops [TM]
		588 Karrablast [44, TM]	647 Keldeo [TM]	099 Kingler [TM]	098 Krabby [TM]	402 Kricketune [30, TM]	470 Leafeon [TM]	542 Leavanny [39, TM]
		151 Mew [TM]	290 Nincada [TM]	291 Ninjask [47, TM]	714 Noibat [TM]	715 Noivern [TM]	501 Oshawott [TM]	675 Pangoro [TM]
		046 Paras [54, TM]	047 Parasect [66, TM]	624 Pawniard [TM]	127 Pinsir [33, TM]	503 Samurott [TM]	027 Sandshrew [TM]	028 Sandslash [TM]
		254 Sceptile [45, TM]	212 Scizor [41, TM]	545 Scolipede [TM]	123 Scyther [41, TM]	336 Seviper [TM]	292 Shedinja [TM]	275 Shiftry [TM]
		227 Skarmory [TM]	451 Skorupi [TM]	215 Sneasel [TM]	167 Spinarak [TM]	639 Terrakion [TM]	454 Toxicroak [TM]	709 Trevenant [TM]
		416 Vespiquen [TM]	640 Virizion [TM]	461 Weavile [TM]	335 Zangoose [40, TM]			

	Move	Pokémon that can learn it						
Normal	Yawn	531 Audino [E]	400 Bibarel [28]	399 Bidoof [25]	323 Camerupt [39]	358 Chimecho [13]	433 Chingling [13]	613 Cubchoo [E]
		554 Darumaka [E]	206 Dunsparce [16]	133 Eevee [E]	677 Espurr [E]	316 Gulpin [5]	449 Hippopotas [13]	450 Hippowdon [1, 13]
		230 Kingdra [1]	506 Lillipup [E]	667 Litleo [E]	219 Magcargo [1]	258 Mudkip [E]	517 Munna [7]	322 Numel [36, E]
		513 Pansear [16]	393 Piplup [E]	261 Poochyena [E]	054 Psyduck [E]	509 Purrloin [E]	195 Quagsire [31]	369 Relicanth [35]
		422 Shellos [E]	616 Shelmet [25]	289 Slaking [1]	287 Slakoth [1]	080 Slowbro [1]	199 Slowking [1]	079 Slowpoke [1]
		218 Slugma [1]	143 Snorlax [20]	363 Spheal [E]	007 Squirtle [E]	618 Stunfisk [E]	317 Swalot [1, 5]	684 Swirlix [E]
		216 Teddiursa [E]	498 Tepig [E]	175 Togepi [13]	176 Togetic [13]	324 Torkoal [E]	480 Uxie [31]	194 Wooper [29]
Electric	Zap Cannon	181 Ampharos [1]	386 Deoxys (Atk) [61]	603 Eelektrik [69]	604 Eelektross [1]	205 Forretress [1, 64]	649 Genesect [66]	600 Klang [60]
		599 Klink [54]	601 Klinklang [1, 66]	081 Magnemite [49]	082 Magneton [1, 63]	462 Magnezone [1, 63]	299 Nosepass [43]	137 Porygon [62]
		233 Porygon2 [1, 62]	474 Porygon-Z [1, 62]	476 Probopass [43]	378 Regice [55]	377 Regirock [55]	379 Registeel [55]	145 Zapdos [1, 92]
Psychic	Zen Headbutt	063 Abra [BP]	359 Absol [BP, E]	065 Alakazam [BP]	698 Amaura [BP]	493 Arceus [BP]	566 Archen [BP]	567 Archeops [BP]
		531 Audino [BP]	699 Aurorus [BP]	482 Azelf [BP]	371 Bagon [34, BP]	343 Baltoy [BP]	550 Basculin [BP]	606 Beheeyem [32, BP]
		374 Beldum [BP]	009 Blastoise [BP]	242 Blissey [BP]	626 Bouffalant [BP]	654 Braixen [BP]	628 Braviary [BP]	437 Bronzong [BP]
		565 Carracosta [BP]	318 Carvanha [BP]	251 Celebi [BP]	113 Chansey [BP]	652 Chesnaught [BP]	650 Chespin [BP]	358 Chimecho [BP]
		433 Chingling [BP]	344 Claydol [BP]	036 Clefable [BP]	035 Clefairy [BP]	173 Cleffa [BP]	638 Cobalion [BP]	563 Cofagrigus [BP]
		408 Cranidos [37, BP]	488 Cresselia [BP]	169 Crobat [BP]	555 Darmanitan [BP]	554 Darumaka [BP]	633 Deino [BP]	301 Delcatty [BP]
		655 Delphox [BP]	386 Deoxys (Atk) [49, BP]	386 Deoxys (Def) [49, BP]	386 Deoxys (Nor) [49, BP]	386 Deoxys (Spd) [49, BP]	096 Drowzee [41, BP]	206 Dunsparce [BP]
		578 Duosion [BP]	605 Elgyem [32, BP]	500 Emboar [BP]	196 Espeon [BP]	677 Espurr [BP]	103 Exeggutor [BP]	295 Exploud [BP]
		676 Furfrou [BP]	475 Gallade [BP]	282 Gardevoir [BP]	649 Genesect [BP]	203 Girafarig [32, BP]	673 Gogoat [BP]	042 Golbat [BP]
		055 Golduck [25, BP]	623 Golurk [BP]	574 Gothita [BP]	576 Gothitelle [BP]	575 Gothorita [BP]	326 Grumpig [26, BP]	440 Happiny [BP]
		701 Hawlucha [BP]	250 Ho-Oh [BP]	163 Hoothoot [37, BP]	635 Hydreigon [BP]	097 Hypno [41, BP]	314 Illumise [33, BP]	385 Jirachi [35, BP]
		124 Jynx [BP]	064 Kadabra [BP]	281 Kirlia [BP]	646 Kyurem (Blk) [BP]	646 Kyurem (Wht) [BP]	646 Kyurem [BP]	131 Lapras [BP]
		636 Larvesta [BP, E]	380 Latias [41, BP]	381 Latios [41, BP]	463 Lickilicky [BP]	108 Lickitung [BP, E]	271 Lombre [40, BP]	270 Lotad [33, BP]
		294 Loudred [BP]	448 Lucario [BP]	272 Ludicolo [BP]	249 Lugia [BP]	337 Lunatone [BP]	308 Medicham [1, BP]	307 Meditite [BP]
		648 Meloetta [BP]	678 Meowstic (F) [BP]	678 Meowstic (M) [BP]	481 Mesprit [BP]	376 Metagross [32, BP]	375 Metang [32, BP]	151 Mew [BP]
		150 Mewtwo [BP]	241 Miltank [29, BP]	122 Mr. Mime [BP]	446 Munchlax [BP, E]	517 Munna [23, BP]	518 Musharna [BP]	177 Natu [BP, E]
		038 Ninetales [BP]	164 Noctowl [42, BP]	674 Pancham [BP]	675 Pangoro [BP]	504 Patrat [BP]	499 Pignite [BP]	137 Porygon [BP]
		233 Porygon2 [BP]	474 Porygon-Z [BP]	054 Psyduck [32, BP]	651 Quilladin [BP]	280 Ralts [BP]	409 Rampardos [43, BP]	020 Raticate [BP]
		019 Rattata [BP]	486 Regigigas [50, BP]	369 Relicanth [BP, E]	643 Reshiram [BP]	579 Reuniclus [BP]	447 Riolu [BP]	302 Sableye [34, BP]
		373 Salamence [35, BP]	539 Sawk [BP]	560 Scrafty [BP]	559 Scraggy [BP, E]	319 Sharpedo [BP]	492 Shaymin (Land) [BP]	492 Shaymin (Sky) [BP]
		372 Shelgon [35, BP]	561 Sigilyph [BP]	672 Skiddo [BP]	300 Skitty [BP, E]	080 Slowbro [32, BP]	199 Slowking [32, BP]	079 Slowpoke [32, BP, E]
		238 Smoochum [BP]	143 Snorlax [BP]	577 Solosis [BP]	338 Solrock [BP]	327 Spinda [BP]	325 Spoink [26, BP, E]	007 Squirtle [BP]
		234 Stantler [38, BP, E]	528 Swoobat [BP]	128 Tauros [35, BP]	498 Tepig [BP]	639 Terrakion [BP]	538 Throh [BP]	564 Tirtouga [BP]
		468 Togekiss [BP]	175 Togepi [BP]	176 Togetic [BP]	697 Tyrantrum [BP]	696 Tyrunt [BP]	480 Uxie [BP]	049 Venomoth [41, BP]
		048 Venonat [37, BP]	494 Victini [49, BP]	640 Virizion [BP]	313 Volbeat [33, BP]	637 Volcarona [BP]	037 Vulpix [BP]	320 Wailmer [BP, E]
		321 Wailord [BP]	008 Wartortle [BP]	505 Watchog [BP]	340 Whiscash [30, BP]	293 Whismur [BP]	527 Woobat [BP]	178 Xatu [BP]
		716 Xerneas [BP]	562 Yamask [BP]	717 Yveltal [BP]	644 Zekrom [43, BP]	041 Zubat [BP, E]	634 Zweilous [BP]	718 Zygarde [BP]

ÉMON ABILITIES REVERSE LOOKUP

Hidden Abilities are included. Note that Basculin, Giratina, Kyurem, Landorus, Meowstic, Shaymin, Thundurus, and Tornadus have different Abilities depending on their forms, which are indicated in parentheses.

Ability	Pokémon that have this Ability							
Adaptability	550 Basculin (Blue)	550 Basculin (Red)	341 Corphish	342 Crawdaunt	691 Dragalge	133 Eevee	349 Feebas	
	015 Mega Beedrill	448 Mega Lucario	474 Porygon-Z	690 Skrelp				
Aerilate	127 Mega Pinsir	373 Mega Salamence						
Aftermath	426 Drifblim	425 Drifloon	101 Electrode	569 Garbodor	435 Skuntank	434 Stunky	568 Trubbish	100 Voltorb
Air Lock	384 Rayquaza							
Analytic	606 Beheeyem	605 Elgyem	081 Magnemite	082 Magneton	462 Magnezone	504 Patrat	137 Porygon	233 Porygon2
	474 Porygon-Z	121 Starmie	120 Staryu	505 Watchog				
Anger Point	323 Camerupt	552 Krokorok	553 Krookodile	056 Mankey	057 Primeape	551 Sandile	128 Tauros	
Anticipation	339 Barboach	453 Croagunk	133 Eevee	598 Ferrothorn	454 Toxicroak	340 Whiscash	413 Wormadam	
Arena Trap	050 Diglett	051 Dugtrio	328 Trapinch					
Aroma Veil	683 Aromatisse	682 Spritzee						
Aura Break	718 Zygarde							

Ability	Pokémon that have this Ability							
Bad Dreams	491 Darkrai							
Battle Armor	347 Anorith	348 Armaldo	104 Cubone	452 Drapion	140 Kabuto	141 Kabutops	105 Marowak	451 Skorupi
Big Pecks	441 Chatot	580 Ducklett	661 Fletchling	630 Mandibuzz	018 Pidgeot	017 Pidgeotto	016 Pidgey	519 Pidove
	581 Swanna	520 Tranquill	521 Unfezant	629 Vullaby				
Blaze	257 Blaziken	654 Braixen	006 Charizard	004 Charmander	005 Charmeleon	390 Chimchar	256 Combusken	155 Cyndaquil
	655 Delphox	500 Emboar	653 Fennekin	392 Infernape	391 Monferno	513 Pansear	499 Pignite	156 Quilava
	514 Simisear	498 Tepig	255 Torchic	157 Typhlosion				
Bulletproof	652 Chesnaught	650 Chespin	651 Quilladin					

Ability	Pokémon that have this Ability							
Cheek Pouch	659 Bunnelby	702 Dedenne	660 Diggersby					
Chlorophyll	182 Bellossom	069 Bellsprout	001 Bulbasaur	420 Cherubi	546 Cottonee	585 Deerling	102 Exeggcute	103 Exeggutor
	044 Gloom	187 Hoppip	002 Ivysaur	189 Jumpluff	470 Leafeon	542 Leavanny	549 Lilligant	556 Maractus
	274 Nuzleaf	043 Oddish	548 Petilil	586 Sawsbuck	273 Seedot	540 Sewaddle	275 Shiftry	188 Skiploom
	192 Sunflora	191 Sunkern	541 Swadloon	114 Tangela	465 Tangrowth	357 Tropius	003 Venusaur	071 Victreebel
	045 Vileplume	070 Weepinbell	547 Whimsicott					
Clear Body	374 Beldum	703 Carbink	719 Diancie	600 Klang	599 Klink	601 Klinklang	376 Metagross	375 Metang
	378 Regice	377 Regirock	379 Registeel	072 Tentacool	073 Tentacruel			
Cloud Nine	334 Altaria	055 Golduck	463 Lickilicky	108 Lickitung	054 Psyduck	333 Swablu		
Color Change	352 Kecleon							
Competitive	574 Gothita	576 Gothitelle	575 Gothorita	174 Igglybuff	039 Jigglypuff	678 Meowstic (F)	350 Milotic	040 Wigglytuff
Compound Eyes	012 Butterfree	269 Dustox	596 Galvantula	595 Joltik	290 Nincada	664 Scatterbug	048 Venonat	666 Vivillon
	193 Yanma							
Contrary	686 Inkay	687 Malamar	497 Serperior	496 Servine	213 Shuckle	495 Snivy	327 Spinda	
Cursed Body	354 Banette	592 Frillish	478 Froslass	593 Jellicent	353 Shuppet			
Cute Charm	573 Cinccino	036 Clefable	035 Clefairy	173 Cleffa	301 Delcatty	174 Igglybuff	039 Jigglypuff	428 Lopunny
	350 Milotic	572 Minccino	300 Skitty	700 Sylveon	040 Wigglytuff			

Ability	Pokémon that have this Ability							
Damp	592 Frillish	055 Golduck	116 Horsea	593 Jellicent	230 Kingdra	259 Marshtomp	258 Mudkip	046 Paras
	047 Parasect	186 Politoed	060 Poliwag	061 Poliwhirl	062 Poliwrath	054 Psyduck	195 Quagsire	117 Seadra
	260 Swampert	194 Wooper						
Dark Aura	717 Yveltal							
Defeatist	566 Archen	567 Archeops						

Ability	Pokémon that have this Ability							
Defiant	625 Bisharp	628 Braviary	395 Empoleon	083 Farfetch'd	056 Mankey	624 Pawniard	393 Piplup	057 Primeape
	394 Prinplup	432 Purugly	642 Thundurus (Incarnate)	641 Tornadus (Incarnate)				
Delta Stream	384 Mega Rayquaza							
Desolate Land	383 Primal Groudon							
Download	649 Genesect	137 Porygon	233 Porygon2	474 Porygon-Z				
Drizzle	382 Kyogre	186 Politoed						
Drought	383 Groudon	006 Mega Charizard Y	038 Ninetales	037 Vulpix				
Dry Skin	453 Croagunk	695 Heliolisk	694 Helioptile	124 Jynx	046 Paras	047 Parasect	454 Toxicroak	

E

Ability	Pokémon that have this Ability							
Early Bird	085 Dodrio	084 Doduo	203 Girafarig	229 Houndoom	228 Houndour	115 Kangaskhan	166 Ledian	165 Ledyba
	177 Natu	274 Nuzleaf	273 Seedot	275 Shiftry	192 Sunflora	191 Sunkern	178 Xatu	
Effect Spore	591 Amoonguss	286 Breloom	590 Foongus	046 Paras	047 Parasect	285 Shroomish	045 Vileplume	

F

Ability	Pokémon that have this Ability							
Fairy Aura	716 Xerneas							
Filter	306 Mega Aggron	439 Mime Jr.	122 Mr. Mime					
Flame Body	609 Chandelure	662 Fletchinder	608 Lampent	636 Larvesta	607 Litwick	240 Magby	219 Magcargo	
	126 Magmar	467 Magmortar	077 Ponyta	078 Rapidash	218 Slugma	663 Talonflame	637 Volcarona	
Flare Boost	426 Drifblim	425 Drifloon						
Flash Fire	059 Arcanine	609 Chandelure	155 Cyndaquil	136 Flareon	058 Growlithe	631 Heatmor	485 Heatran	
	229 Houndoom	228 Houndour	608 Lampent	607 Litwick	038 Ninetales	077 Ponyta	156 Quilava	078 Rapidash
	157 Typhlosion	037 Vulpix						
Flower Gift	421 Cherrim							
Flower Veil	669 Flabébé	670 Floette	671 Florges					
Forecast	351 Castform							
Forewarn	096 Drowzee	097 Hypno	124 Jynx	517 Munna	518 Musharna	238 Smoochum		
Friend Guard	035 Clefairy	173 Cleffa	440 Happiny	174 Igglybuff	039 Jigglypuff	664 Scatterbug	665 Spewpa	666 Vivillon
Frisk	354 Banette	356 Dusclops	477 Dusknoir	355 Duskull	162 Furret	574 Gothita	576 Gothitelle	575 Gothorita
	711 Gourgeist	714 Noibat	715 Noivern	708 Phantump	710 Pumpkaboo	161 Sentret	353 Shuppet	234 Stantler
	709 Trevenant	040 Wigglytuff	193 Yanma	469 Yanmega				
Fur Coat	676 Furfrou							

G

Ability	Pokémon that have this Ability							
Gale Wings	662 Fletchinder	661 Fletchling	663 Talonflame					
Gluttony	069 Bellsprout	326 Grumpig	316 Gulpin	631 Heatmor	264 Linoone	446 Munchlax	515 Panpour	511 Pansage
	513 Pansear	213 Shuckle	516 Simipour	512 Simisage	514 Simisear	143 Snorlax	325 Spoink	317 Swalot
	071 Victreebel	070 Weepinbell	263 Zigzagoon					
Gooey	706 Goodra	704 Goomy	705 Sliggoo					
Grass Pelt	673 Gogoat	672 Skiddo						
Guts	534 Conkeldurr	136 Flareon	533 Gurdurr	297 Hariyama	214 Heracross	246 Larvitar	404 Luxio	405 Luxray
	068 Machamp	067 Machoke	066 Machop	296 Makuhita	020 Raticate	019 Rattata	403 Shinx	277 Swellow
	276 Taillow	538 Throh	532 Timburr	236 Tyrogue	217 Ursaring			

H

Ability	Pokémon that have this Ability							
Harvest	102 Exeggcute	103 Exeggutor	708 Phantump	709 Trevenant	357 Tropius			
Healer	594 Alomomola	683 Aromatisse	531 Audino	182 Bellossom	242 Blissey	113 Chansey	531 Mega Audino	682 Spritzee
Heatproof	437 Bronzong	436 Bronzor						
Heavy Metal	306 Aggron	304 Aron	437 Bronzong	436 Bronzor	305 Lairon			
Honey Gather	415 Combee	216 Teddiursa						
Huge Power	184 Azumarill	298 Azurill	659 Bunnelby	660 Diggersby	183 Marill	303 Mega Mawile		

ADVENTURE DATA

Ability	Pokémon that have this Ability							
Hustle	415 Combee	222 Corsola	554 Darumaka	633 Deino	225 Delibird	632 Durant	029 Nidoran ♀	032 Nidoran ♂
	030 Nidorina	033 Nidorino	020 Raticate	019 Rattata	223 Remoraid	627 Rufflet	468 Togekiss	175 Togepi
	176 Togetic	634 Zweilous						
Hydration	617 Accelgor	594 Alomomola	339 Barboach	087 Dewgong	580 Ducklett	706 Goodra	704 Goomy	368 Gorebyss
	131 Lapras	370 Luvdisc	490 Manaphy	536 Palpitoad	489 Phione	086 Seel	616 Shelmet	705 Sliggoo
	238 Smoochum	581 Swanna	535 Tympole	134 Vaporeon	340 Whiscash			
Hyper Cutter	341 Corphish	342 Crawdaunt	207 Gligar	472 Gliscor	099 Kingler	098 Krabby	303 Mawile	127 Pinsir
	328 Trapinch							

I

Ability	Pokémon that have this Ability							
Ice Body	713 Avalugg	712 Bergmite	087 Dewgong	471 Glaceon	362 Glalie	364 Sealeo	086 Seel	
	361 Snorunt	363 Spheal	583 Vanillish	582 Vanillite	584 Vanilluxe	365 Walrein		
Illuminate	170 Chinchou	171 Lanturn	121 Starmie	120 Staryu	313 Volbeat	505 Watchog		
Illusion	571 Zoroark	570 Zorua						
Immunity	207 Gligar	143 Snorlax	335 Zangoose					
Imposter	132 Ditto							
Infiltrator	609 Chandelure	546 Cottonee	169 Crobat	677 Espurr	042 Golbat	187 Hoppip	686 Inkay	189 Jumpluff
	608 Lampent	607 Litwick	687 Malamar	678 Meowstic (F)	678 Meowstic (M)	291 Ninjask	714 Noibat	715 Noivern
	336 Seviper	188 Skiploom	442 Spiritomb	547 Whimsicott	041 Zubat			
Inner Focus	063 Abra	065 Alakazam	625 Bisharp	169 Crobat	554 Darumaka	149 Dragonite	096 Drowzee	083 Farfetch'd
	203 Girafarig	362 Glalie	042 Golbat	107 Hitmonchan	097 Hypno	064 Kadabra	115 Kangaskhan	448 Lucario
	475 Mega Gallade	619 Mienfoo	620 Mienshao	624 Pawniard	447 Riolu	539 Sawk	215 Sneasel	361 Snorunt
	538 Throh	197 Umbreon	041 Zubat					
Insomnia	168 Ariados	354 Banette	225 Delibird	096 Drowzee	711 Gourgeist	430 Honchkrow	163 Hoothoot	
	097 Hypno	150 Mega Mewtwo Y	198 Murkrow	164 Noctowl	710 Pumpkaboo	353 Shuppet	167 Spinarak	
Intimidate	024 Arbok	059 Arcanine	023 Ekans	210 Granbull	058 Growlithe	130 Gyarados	507 Herdier	237 Hitmontop
	552 Krokorok	553 Krookodile	645 Landorus (Therian)	404 Luxio	405 Luxray	284 Masquerain	303 Mawile	310 Mega Manectric
	262 Mightyena	211 Qwilfish	373 Salamence	551 Sandile	560 Scrafty	559 Scraggy	403 Shinx	209 Snubbull
	234 Stantler	398 Staraptor	397 Staravia	508 Stoutland	128 Tauros			
Iron Barbs	597 Ferroseed	598 Ferrothorn						
Iron Fist	390 Chimchar	534 Conkeldurr	622 Golett	623 Golurk	533 Gurdurr	107 Hitmonchan	392 Infernape	166 Ledian
	391 Monferno	674 Pancham	675 Pangoro	532 Timburr				

J

Ability	Pokémon that have this Ability							
Justified	359 Absol	059 Arcanine	638 Cobalion	475 Gallade	058 Growlithe	647 Keldeo	448 Lucario	639 Terrakion
	640 Virizion							

K

Ability	Pokémon that have this Ability							
Keen Eye	628 Braviary	441 Chatot	452 Drapion	580 Ducklett	677 Espurr	083 Farfetch'd	022 Fearow	162 Furret
	431 Glameow	107 Hitmonchan	163 Hoothoot	678 Meowstic (F)	678 Meowstic (M)	164 Noctowl	504 Patrat	279 Pelipper
	018 Pidgeot	017 Pidgeotto	016 Pidgey	627 Rufflet	302 Sableye	161 Sentret	227 Skarmory	451 Skorupi
	435 Skuntank	215 Sneasel	021 Spearow	396 Starly	434 Stunky	581 Swanna	505 Watchog	278 Wingull
Klutz	531 Audino	427 Buneary	622 Golett	623 Golurk	428 Lopunny	528 Swoobat	527 Woobat	

L

Ability	Pokémon that have this Ability							
Leaf Guard	153 Bayleef	406 Budew	152 Chikorita	187 Hoppip	189 Jumpluff	470 Leafeon	549 Lilligant	154 Meganium
	548 Petilil	315 Roselia	188 Skiploom	541 Swadloon	114 Tangela	465 Tangrowth		
Levitate	482 Azelf	343 Baltoy	437 Bronzong	436 Bronzor	455 Carnivine	358 Chimecho	433 Chingling	344 Claydol
	488 Cresselia	615 Cryogonal	355 Duskull	603 Eelektrik	604 Eelektross	330 Flygon	092 Gastly	094 Gengar
	487 Giratina (Origin)	093 Haunter	635 Hydreigon	109 Koffing	380 Latias	381 Latios	337 Lunatone	380 Mega Latias
	381 Mega Latios	481 Mesprit	200 Misdreavus	429 Mismagius	479 Rotom	338 Solrock	602 Tynamo	201 Unown
	480 Uxie	329 Vibrava	110 Weezing					

Ability	Pokémon that have this Ability							
Light Metal	374 Beldum	376 Metagross	375 Metang	212 Scizor				
Lightning Rod	522 Blitzle	104 Cubone	309 Electrike	118 Goldeen	310 Manectric	105 Marowak	254 Mega Sceptile	172 Pichu
	025 Pikachu	311 Plusle	026 Raichu	112 Rhydon	111 Rhyhorn	464 Rhyperior	119 Seaking	523 Zebstrika
Limber	427 Buneary	132 Ditto	431 Glameow	701 Hawlucha	106 Hitmonlee	510 Liepard	428 Lopunny	053 Persian
	509 Purrloin	618 Stunfisk						
Liquid Ooze	316 Gulpin	317 Swalot	072 Tentacool	073 Tentacruel				

M

Ability	Pokémon that have this Ability							
Magic Bounce	196 Espeon	359 Mega Absol	719 Mega Diancie	302 Mega Sableye	177 Natu	178 Xatu		
Magic Guard	063 Abra	065 Alakazam	036 Clefable	035 Clefairy	173 Cleffa	578 Duosion	064 Kadabra	579 Reuniclus
	561 Sigilyph	577 Solosis						
Magician	654 Braixen	655 Delphox	653 Fennekin	707 Klefki				
Magma Armor	323 Camerupt	219 Magcargo	218 Slugma					
Magnet Pull	081 Magnemite	082 Magneton	462 Magnezone	299 Nosepass	476 Probopass			
Marvel Scale	148 Dragonair	147 Dratini	350 Milotic					
Mega Launcher	692 Clauncher	693 Clawitzer	009 Mega Blastoise					
Minus	309 Electrike	600 Klang	599 Klink	601 Klinklang	310 Manectric	312 Minun		
Mold Breaker	610 Axew	550 Basculin (Blue)	550 Basculin (Red)	408 Cranidos	529 Drilbur	621 Druddigon	530 Excadrill	611 Fraxure
	701 Hawlucha	612 Haxorus	181 Mega Ampharos	130 Mega Gyarados	674 Pancham	675 Pangoro	127 Pinsir	409 Rampardos
	539 Sawk	538 Throh						
Moody	400 Bibarel	399 Bidoof	362 Glalie	224 Octillery	223 Remoraid	235 Smeargle	361 Snorunt	
Motor Drive	522 Blitzle	466 Electivire	587 Emolga	523 Zebstrika				
Moxie	130 Gyarados	214 Heracross	430 Honchkrow	552 Krokorok	553 Krookodile	667 Litleo	262 Mightyena	127 Pinsir
	668 Pyroar	373 Salamence	551 Sandile	560 Scrafty	559 Scraggy			
Multiscale	149 Dragonite	249 Lugia						
Multitype	493 Arceus							
Mummy	563 Cofagrigus	562 Yamask						

N

Ability	Pokémon that have this Ability							
Natural Cure	334 Altaria	242 Blissey	406 Budew	251 Celebi	113 Chansey	222 Corsola	440 Happiny	708 Phantump
	315 Roselia	407 Roserade	492 Shaymin (Land)	121 Starmie	120 Staryu	333 Swablu	709 Trevenant	
No Guard	680 Doublade	622 Golett	623 Golurk	679 Honedge	588 Karrablast	068 Machamp	067 Machoke	066 Machop
	018 Mega Pidgeot							
Normalize	301 Delcatty	300 Skitty						

O

Ability	Pokémon that have this Ability							
Oblivious	339 Barboach	349 Feebas	314 Illumise	124 Jynx	463 Lickilicky	108 Lickitung	473 Mamoswine	322 Numel
	221 Piloswine	364 Sealeo	080 Slowbro	199 Slowking	079 Slowpoke	238 Smoochum	363 Spheal	220 Swinub
	320 Wailmer	321 Wailord	365 Walrein	340 Whiscash				
Overcoat	412 Burmy	091 Cloyster	578 Duosion	589 Escavalier	205 Forretress	542 Leavanny	630 Mandibuzz	204 Pineco
	579 Reuniclus	540 Sewaddle	372 Shelgon	090 Shellder	616 Shelmet	577 Solosis	541 Swadloon	629 Vullaby
	413 Wormadam							
Overgrow	153 Bayleef	001 Bulbasaur	652 Chesnaught	650 Chespin	152 Chikorita	388 Grotle	253 Grovyle	002 Ivysaur
	154 Meganium	511 Pansage	651 Quilladin	254 Sceptile	497 Serperior	496 Servine	512 Simisage	495 Snivy
	389 Torterra	252 Treecko	387 Turtwig	003 Venusaur				
Own Tempo	713 Avalugg	712 Bergmite	677 Espurr	431 Glameow	326 Grumpig	463 Lickilicky	108 Lickitung	549 Lilligant
	271 Lombre	270 Lotad	272 Ludicolo	322 Numel	548 Petilil	432 Purugly	080 Slowbro	199 Slowking
	079 Slowpoke	235 Smeargle	327 Spinda	325 Spoink				

P

Ability	Pokémon that have this Ability							
Parental Bond	115 Mega Kangaskhan							
Pickpocket	689 Barbaracle	688 Binacle	274 Nuzleaf	273 Seedot	275 Shiftry	215 Sneasel	461 Weavile	

ADVENTURE DATA

Ability	Pokémon that have this Ability						
Pickup	190 Aipom	424 Ambipom	659 Bunnelby	702 Dedenne	660 Diggersby	711 Gourgeist	506 Lillipup	264 Linoone
	052 Meowth	446 Munchlax	417 Pachirisu	231 Phanpy	710 Pumpkaboo	216 Teddiursa	263 Zigzagoon	
Pixilate	334 Mega Altaria	282 Mega Gardevoir	700 Sylveon					
Plus	181 Ampharos	702 Dedenne	180 Flaaffy	600 Klang	599 Klink	601 Klinklang	179 Mareep	311 Plusle
Poison Heal	286 Breloom	472 Gliscor	285 Shroomish					
Poison Point	406 Budew	691 Dragalge	034 Nidoking	031 Nidoqueen	029 Nidoran ♀	032 Nidoran ♂	030 Nidorina	033 Nidorino
	211 Qwilfish	315 Roselia	407 Roserade	545 Scolipede	117 Seadra	690 Skrelp	543 Venipede	544 Whirlipede
Poison Touch	453 Croagunk	691 Dragalge	088 Grimer	089 Muk	537 Seismitoad	690 Skrelp	454 Toxicroak	
Prankster	546 Cottonee	314 Illumise	707 Klefki	510 Liepard	354 Mega Banette	678 Meowstic (M)	198 Murkrow	509 Purrloin
	447 Riolu	302 Sableye	642 Thundurus (Incarnate)	641 Tornadus (Incarnate)	313 Volbeat	547 Whimsicott		
Pressure	359 Absol	142 Aerodactyl	144 Articuno	625 Bisharp	386 Deoxys	483 Dialga	356 Dusclops	477 Dusknoir
	244 Entei	487 Giratina (Altered)	250 Ho-Oh	646 Kyurem	249 Lugia	150 Mewtwo	146 Moltres	484 Palkia
	624 Pawniard	243 Raikou	442 Spiritomb	245 Suicune	416 Vespiquen	320 Wailmer	321 Wailord	461 Weavile
	145 Zapdos							
Primordial Sea	382 Primal Kyogre							
Protean	656 Froakie	657 Frogadier	658 Greninja	352 Kecleon				
Pure Power	308 Medicham	307 Meditite	308 Mega Medicham					

Q

Ability	Pokémon that have this Ability						
Quick Feet	210 Granbull	135 Jolteon	264 Linoone	262 Mightyena	261 Poochyena	285 Shroomish	216 Teddiursa	217 Ursaring
	263 Zigzagoon							

R

Ability	Pokémon that have this Ability						
Rain Dish	009 Blastoise	271 Lombre	270 Lotad	272 Ludicolo	279 Pelipper	007 Squirtle	283 Surskit	072 Tentacool
	073 Tentacruel	008 Wartortle	278 Wingull					
Rattled	438 Bonsly	366 Clamperl	613 Cubchoo	206 Dunsparce	210 Granbull	165 Ledyba	129 Magikarp	261 Poochyena
	209 Snubbull	185 Sudowoodo	293 Whismur					
Reckless	550 Basculin (Red)	626 Bouffalant	500 Emboar	106 Hitmonlee	619 Mienfoo	620 Mienshao	112 Rhydon	111 Rhyhorn
	464 Rhyperior	398 Staraptor	397 Staravia	396 Starly				
Refrigerate	698 Amaura	699 Aurorus	362 Mega Glalie					
Regenerator	594 Alomomola	591 Amoonguss	531 Audino	222 Corsola	578 Duosion	590 Foongus	250 Ho-Oh	619 Mienfoo
	620 Mienshao	579 Reuniclus	080 Slowbro	199 Slowking	079 Slowpoke	577 Solosis	114 Tangela	465 Tangrowth
	641 Tornadus (Therian)							
Rivalry	610 Axew	267 Beautifly	611 Fraxure	612 Haxorus	667 Litleo	404 Luxio	405 Luxray	034 Nidoking
	031 Nidoqueen	029 Nidoran ♀	032 Nidoran ♂	030 Nidorina	033 Nidorino	519 Pidove	668 Pyroar	403 Shinx
	520 Tranquill	521 Unfezant						
Rock Head	142 Aerodactyl	306 Aggron	304 Aron	371 Bagon	550 Basculin (Blue)	438 Bonsly	104 Cubone	074 Geodude
	076 Golem	075 Graveler	305 Lairon	105 Marowak	095 Onix	369 Relicanth	112 Rhydon	111 Rhyhorn
	372 Shelgon	208 Steelix	185 Sudowoodo	697 Tyrantrum				
Rough Skin	318 Carvanha	621 Druddigon	444 Gabite	445 Garchomp	443 Gible	319 Sharpedo		
Run Away	190 Aipom	427 Buneary	010 Caterpie	085 Dodrio	084 Doduo	206 Dunsparce	133 Eevee	162 Furret
	401 Kricketot	506 Lillipup	290 Nincada	043 Oddish	417 Pachirisu	504 Patrat	077 Ponyta	261 Poochyena
	078 Rapidash	020 Raticate	019 Rattata	161 Sentret	209 Snubbull	048 Venonat	013 Weedle	265 Wurmple

S

Ability	Pokémon that have this Ability						
Sand Force	525 Boldore	050 Diglett	529 Drilbur	051 Dugtrio	530 Excadrill	423 Gastrodon	526 Gigalith	449 Hippopotas
	450 Hippowdon	645 Landorus (Incarnate)	445 Mega Garchomp	208 Mega Steelix	299 Nosepass	476 Probopass	524 Roggenrola	422 Shellos
Sand Rush	529 Drilbur	530 Excadrill	507 Herdier	027 Sandshrew	028 Sandslash	508 Stoutland		
Sand Stream	449 Hippopotas	450 Hippowdon	248 Mega Tyranitar	248 Tyranitar				
Sand Veil	331 Cacnea	332 Cacturne	050 Diglett	232 Donphan	051 Dugtrio	444 Gabite	445 Garchomp	074 Geodude
	443 Gible	207 Gligar	472 Gliscor	076 Golem	075 Graveler	695 Heliolisk	694 Helioptile	246 Larvitar
	231 Phanpy	027 Sandshrew	028 Sandslash	618 Stunfisk				
Sap Sipper	184 Azumarill	298 Azurill	522 Blitzle	626 Bouffalant	585 Deerling	203 Girafarig	673 Gogoat	706 Goodra
	704 Goomy	183 Marill	241 Miltank	586 Sawsbuck	672 Skiddo	705 Sliggoo	234 Stantler	523 Zebstrika

Ability	Pokémon that have this Ability							
Scrappy	295 Exploud	507 Herdier	115 Kangaskhan	294 Loudred	428 Mega Lopunny	241 Miltank	674 Pancham	675 Pangoro
	508 Stoutland	277 Swellow	276 Taillow					
Serene Grace	242 Blissey	113 Chansey	585 Deerling	206 Dunsparce	440 Happiny	385 Jirachi	648 Meloetta	586 Sawsbuck
	492 Shaymin (Sky)	468 Togekiss	175 Togepi	176 Togetic				
Shadow Tag	574 Gothita	576 Gothitelle	575 Gothorita	094 Mega Gengar	202 Wobbuffet	360 Wynaut		
Shed Skin	024 Arbok	412 Burmy	268 Cascoon	148 Dragonair	147 Dratini	023 Ekans	014 Kakuna	588 Karrablast
	401 Kricketot	011 Metapod	247 Pupitar	560 Scrafty	559 Scraggy	336 Seviper	266 Silcoon	665 Spewpa
Sheer Force	371 Bagon	628 Braviary	534 Conkeldurr	408 Cranidos	159 Croconaw	555 Darmanitan	621 Druddigon	160 Feraligatr
	533 Gurdurr	297 Hariyama	099 Kingler	098 Krabby	645 Landorus (Incarnate)	296 Makuhita	303 Mawile	323 Mega Camerupt
	034 Nidoking	031 Nidoqueen	409 Rampardos	627 Rufflet	208 Steelix	128 Tauros	532 Timburr	158 Totodile
	328 Trapinch							
Shell Armor	366 Clamperl	091 Cloyster	341 Corphish	342 Crawdaunt	558 Crustle	502 Dewott	557 Dwebble	589 Escavalier
	388 Grotle	099 Kingler	098 Krabby	131 Lapras	080 Mega Slowbro	138 Omanyte	139 Omastar	501 Oshawott
	503 Samurott	090 Shellder	616 Shelmet	324 Torkoal	389 Torterra	387 Turtwig		
Shield Dust	010 Caterpie	269 Dustox	664 Scatterbug	049 Venomoth	666 Vivillon	013 Weedle	265 Wurmple	
Simple	400 Bibarel	399 Bidoof	322 Numel	528 Swoobat	527 Woobat			
Skill Link	190 Aipom	424 Ambipom	573 Cinccino	091 Cloyster	214 Mega Heracross	572 Minccino	090 Shellder	
Slow Start	486 Regigigas							
Sniper	168 Ariados	689 Barbaracle	015 Beedrill	688 Binacle	452 Drapion	022 Fearow	116 Horsea	230 Kingdra
	224 Octillery	223 Remoraid	117 Seadra	451 Skorupi	021 Spearow	167 Spinarak		
Snow Cloak	614 Beartic	613 Cubchoo	478 Froslass	471 Glaceon	473 Mamoswine	221 Piloswine	220 Swinub	
Snow Warning	460 Abomasnow	460 Mega Abomasnow	459 Snover					
Solar Power	006 Charizard	004 Charmander	005 Charmeleon	695 Heliolisk	694 Helioptile	229 Mega Houndoom	192 Sunflora	191 Sunkern
	357 Tropius							
Solid Rock	323 Camerupt	565 Carracosta	464 Rhyperior	564 Tirtouga				
Soundproof	460 Abomasnow	411 Bastiodon	626 Bouffalant	101 Electrode	295 Exploud	294 Loudred	439 Mime Jr.	122 Mr. Mime
	410 Shieldon	459 Snover	100 Voltorb	293 Whismur				
Speed Boost	257 Blaziken	318 Carvanha	256 Combusken	257 Mega Blaziken	291 Ninjask	545 Scolipede	319 Sharpedo	255 Torchic
	543 Venipede	544 Whirlipede	193 Yanma	469 Yanmega				
Stall	302 Sableye							
Stance Change	681 Aegislash							
Static	181 Ampharos	125 Electabuzz	309 Electrike	101 Electrode	239 Elekid	587 Emolga	180 Flaaffy	310 Manectric
	179 Mareep	172 Pichu	025 Pikachu	026 Raichu	618 Stunfisk	100 Voltorb		
Steadfast	475 Gallade	237 Hitmontop	448 Lucario	068 Machamp	067 Machoke	066 Machop	150 Mega Mewtwo X	447 Riolu
	123 Scyther	236 Tyrogue						
Stench	569 Garbodor	044 Gloom	088 Grimer	089 Muk	435 Skuntank	434 Stunky	568 Trubbish	
Sticky Hold	617 Accelgor	423 Gastrodon	088 Grimer	316 Gulpin	089 Muk	422 Shellos	317 Swalot	568 Trubbish
Storm Drain	346 Cradily	456 Finneon	423 Gastrodon	345 Lileep	457 Lumineon	556 Maractus	422 Shellos	
Strong Jaw	319 Mega Sharpedo	697 Tyrantrum	696 Tyrunt					
Sturdy	306 Aggron	304 Aron	713 Avalugg	411 Bastiodon	712 Bergmite	525 Boldore	438 Bonsly	703 Carbink
	565 Carracosta	558 Crustle	232 Donphan	557 Dwebble	205 Forretress	074 Geodude	526 Gigalith	076 Golem
	075 Graveler	305 Lairon	081 Magnemite	082 Magneton	462 Magnezone	299 Nosepass	095 Onix	204 Pineco
	476 Probopass	369 Relicanth	524 Roggenrola	539 Sawk	410 Shieldon	213 Shuckle	227 Skarmory	
	208 Steelix	185 Sudowoodo	564 Tirtouga	696 Tyrunt				
Suction Cups	346 Cradily	686 Inkay	345 Lileep	687 Malamar	224 Octillery			
Super Luck	359 Absol	430 Honchkrow	198 Murkrow	519 Pidove	468 Togekiss	175 Togepi	176 Togetic	520 Tranquill
	521 Unfezant							
Swarm	168 Ariados	267 Beautifly	015 Beedrill	632 Durant	589 Escavalier	596 Galvantula	214 Heracross	595 Joltik
	588 Karrablast	402 Kricketune	636 Larvesta	542 Leavanny	166 Ledian	165 Ledyba	414 Mothim	212 Scizor
	545 Scolipede	123 Scyther	540 Sewaddle	167 Spinarak	543 Venipede	313 Volbeat	637 Volcarona	544 Whirlipede
Sweet Veil	685 Slurpuff	684 Swirlix						
Swift Swim	347 Anorith	348 Armaldo	614 Beartic	418 Buizel	565 Carracosta	349 Feebas	456 Finneon	419 Floatzel
	118 Goldeen	055 Golduck	368 Gorebyss	116 Horsea	367 Huntail	140 Kabuto	141 Kabutops	230 Kingdra
	271 Lombre	270 Lotad	272 Ludicolo	457 Lumineon	370 Luvdisc	129 Magikarp	226 Mantine	458 Mantyke
	260 Mega Swampert	138 Omanyte	139 Omastar	536 Palpitoad	060 Poliwag	061 Poliwhirl	062 Poliwrath	054 Psyduck
	211 Qwilfish	369 Relicanth	119 Seaking	537 Seismitoad	283 Surskit	564 Tirtouga	535 Tympole	
Symbiosis	669 Flabébé	670 Floette	671 Florges					
Synchronize	063 Abra	065 Alakazam	606 Beheeyem	605 Elgyem	196 Espeon	282 Gardevoir	064 Kadabra	281 Kirlia
	151 Mew	517 Munna	518 Musharna	177 Natu	280 Ralts	197 Umbreon	178 Xatu	

T

Ability	Pokémon that have this Ability							
Tangled Feet	441 Chatot	085 Dodrio	084 Doduo	018 Pidgeot	017 Pidgeotto	016 Pidgey	327 Spinda	
Technician	424 Ambipom	286 Breloom	573 Cinccino	237 Hitmontop	402 Kricketune	212 Mega Scizor	052 Meowth	439 Mime Jr.
	572 Minccino	122 Mr. Mime	053 Persian	407 Roserade	212 Scizor	123 Scyther	235 Smeargle	
Telepathy	606 Beheeyem	483 Dialga	605 Elgyem	282 Gardevoir	487 Giratina (Altered)	281 Kirlia	308 Medicham	307 Meditite
	517 Munna	518 Musharna	714 Noibat	715 Noivern	484 Palkia	280 Ralts	202 Wobbuffet	360 Wynaut
Teravolt	646 Kyurem (Black)	644 Zekrom						
Thick Fat	184 Azumarill	298 Azurill	087 Dewgong	326 Grumpig	297 Hariyama	296 Makuhita	473 Mamoswine	183 Marill
	003 Mega Venusaur	241 Miltank	446 Munchlax	499 Pignite	221 Piloswine	432 Purugly	364 Sealeo	086 Seel
	143 Snorlax	363 Spheal	325 Spoink	220 Swinub	498 Tepig	365 Walrein		
Tinted Lens	012 Butterfree	163 Hoothoot	314 Illumise	414 Mothim	164 Noctowl	561 Sigilyph	049 Venomoth	048 Venonat
	469 Yanmega							
Torrent	009 Blastoise	159 Croconaw	502 Dewott	395 Empoleon	160 Feraligatr	656 Froakie	657 Frogadier	658 Greninja
	259 Marshtomp	258 Mudkip	501 Oshawott	515 Panpour	393 Piplup	394 Prinplup	503 Samurott	516 Simipour
	007 Squirtle	260 Swampert	158 Totodile	008 Wartortle				
Tough Claws	689 Barbaracle	688 Binacle	142 Mega Aerodactyl	006 Mega Charizard X	376 Mega Metagross			
Toxic Boost	335 Zangoose							
Trace	282 Gardevoir	281 Kirlia	065 Mega Alakazam	137 Porygon	233 Porygon2	280 Ralts		
Truant	632 Durant	289 Slaking	287 Slakoth					
Turboblaze	646 Kyurem (White)	643 Reshiram						

U·V·W

Ability	Pokémon that have this Ability							
Unaware	400 Bibarel	399 Bidoof	036 Clefable	195 Quagsire	528 Swoobat	527 Woobat	194 Wooper	
Unburden	617 Accelgor	426 Drifblim	425 Drifloon	253 Grovyle	701 Hawlucha	106 Hitmonlee	510 Liepard	509 Purrloin
	254 Sceptile	685 Slurpuff	684 Swirlix	252 Treecko				
Unnerve	142 Aerodactyl	024 Arbok	610 Axew	023 Ekans	611 Fraxure	596 Galvantula	612 Haxorus	229 Houndoom
	228 Houndour	595 Joltik	667 Litleo	284 Masquerain	052 Meowth	150 Mewtwo	053 Persian	668 Pyroar
	248 Tyranitar	217 Ursaring	416 Vespiquen					
Victory Star	494 Victini							
Vital Spirit	225 Delibird	125 Electabuzz	466 Electivire	239 Elekid	506 Lillipup	240 Magby	126 Magmar	467 Magmortar
	056 Mankey	057 Primeape	236 Tyrogue	288 Vigoroth				
Volt Absorb	170 Chinchou	135 Jolteon	171 Lanturn	312 Minun	417 Pachirisu	642 Thundurus (Therian)		
Water Absorb	331 Cacnea	332 Cacturne	170 Chinchou	592 Frillish	593 Jellicent	171 Lanturn	131 Lapras	226 Mantine
	458 Mantyke	556 Maractus	536 Palpitoad	186 Politoed	060 Poliwag	061 Poliwhirl	062 Poliwrath	195 Quagsire
	537 Seismitoad	535 Tympole	134 Vaporeon	194 Wooper				
Water Veil	418 Buizel	456 Finneon	419 Floatzel	118 Goldeen	367 Huntail	457 Lumineon	226 Mantine	458 Mantyke
	119 Seaking	320 Wailmer	321 Wailord					
Weak Armor	558 Crustle	557 Dwebble	569 Garbodor	140 Kabuto	141 Kabutops	219 Magcargo	630 Mandibuzz	138 Omanyte
	139 Omastar	095 Onix	227 Skarmory	218 Slugma	583 Vanillish	582 Vanillite	584 Vanilluxe	629 Vullaby
White Smoke	631 Heatmor	324 Torkoal						
Wonder Guard	292 Shedinja							
Wonder Skin	301 Delcatty	561 Sigilyph	300 Skitty	049 Venomoth				

Z

Ability	Pokémon that have this Ability							
Zen Mode	555 Darmanitan							

Type Matchup Chart

Types are assigned both to moves and to the Pokémon themselves. These types can greatly affect the amount of damage dealt or received in battle, so if you learn how they line up against one another, you'll give yourself an edge in battle. If your Pokémon has two types, the strengths and weaknesses of both types will be used to calculate that Pokémon's weaknesses and strengths. If both types share the same weakness, the Pokémon will take four times the damage. (For example, Grass types and Ice types are both weak to Fire, and each will take 2× damage from a Fire-type move. A Grass- and Ice-type Pokémon will be twice as weak, and take 4× the damage from a Fire-type move.) However, two resistances can combine in the same way. (Fire types and Water types are both resistant to Fire-type attacks, taking only 1/2 the usual damage. A Fire- and Water-type Pokémon would be twice as resistant, and only take 1/4 the usual damage from a Fire-type move.) Finally, a strength and weakness will cancel each other out. (Grass types take 2× damage from Fire-type attacks, and Water types take 1/2 damage from Fire-type attacks. A Grass- and Water-type Pokémon will simply take normal damage from a Fire-type attack, not more or less.)

Attacking Pokémon's Move Type \ Defending Pokémon's Type	Normal	Fire	Water	Grass	Electric	Ice	Fighting	Poison	Ground	Flying	Psychic	Bug	Rock	Ghost	Dragon	Dark	Steel	Fairy
Normal													▲	×			▲	
Fire		▲	▲	◉		◉						◉	▲		▲		◉	
Water		◉	▲	▲					◉				◉		▲			
Grass		▲	◉	▲				▲	◉	▲		▲	◉		▲		▲	
Electric			◉	▲	▲				×	◉					▲			
Ice		▲	▲	◉		▲			◉	◉					◉		▲	
Fighting	◉					◉		▲		▲	▲	▲	◉	×		◉	◉	▲
Poison				◉				▲	▲				▲	▲			×	◉
Ground		◉		▲	◉			◉		×		▲	◉				◉	
Flying				◉	▲		◉					◉	▲				▲	
Psychic							◉	◉			▲					×	▲	
Bug		▲		◉			▲	▲		▲	◉			▲		◉	▲	▲
Rock		◉				◉	▲		▲	◉		◉					▲	
Ghost	×										◉			◉		▲		
Dragon															◉		▲	×
Dark							▲				◉			◉		▲		▲
Steel		▲	▲		▲	◉							◉				▲	◉
Fairy		▲					◉	▲							◉	◉	▲	

Key

◉	Very effective "It's super effective!"	× 2
No icon	Normal damage	× 1
▲	Not too effective "It's not very effective..."	× 1/2
×	No effect "It doesn't affect..."	× 0

Ineffective status conditions and moves depending on type

Type	Effect
Fire	• Cannot be afflicted with the Burned condition
Grass	• Immune to Leech Seed • Immune to powder and spore moves
Electric	•Cannot be afflicted with the Paralyzed condition
Ice	• Immune to the Frozen condition • Take no damage from hail
Poison	• Immune to the Poison and Badly Poisoned conditions • Immune to the Poison and Badly Poisoned conditions, when switching in with Toxic Spikes in play • Nullify Toxic Spikes (unless these Pokémon are also Flying type or have the Levitate Ability)
Ground	• Immune to Thunder Wave* • Take no damage from sandstorms
Flying	• Cannot be damaged by Spikes when switching in • Cannot be afflicted with a Poison or Badly Poisoned condition due to switching in with Toxic Spikes in play
Rock	• Take no damage from sandstorms • Sp. Def goes up in a sandstorm
Ghost	• Cannot be affected by moves that prevent Pokémon from fleeing from battle
Steel	• Take no damage from sandstorms • Immune to the Poison and Badly Poisoned conditions • Immune to the Poison and Badly Poisoned conditions, when switching in with Toxic Spikes in play

* Types usually don't have effects on status moves, but Thunder Wave won't work against Ground-type Pokémon.

ADVENTURE DATA

Inverse Type Matchup Chart

An Inverse Battle is a Pokémon battle in which type matchups will be reversed. For example, a Flying-type Pokémon is immune to Ground-type moves in a normal battle, but in an Inverse Battle, a Ground-type move can inflict twice the damage on a Flying-type Pokémon. You can try Inverse Battles at the Inverse Battle Stop on Mauville City's first floor.

Attacking Pokémon's Move Type \ Defending Pokémon's Type	Normal	Fire	Water	Grass	Electric	Ice	Fighting	Poison	Ground	Flying	Psychic	Bug	Rock	Ghost	Dragon	Dark	Steel	Fairy
Normal													◉	◉			◉	
Fire		◉	◉	▲		▲						▲	◉		◉		▲	
Water		▲	◉	◉					▲				▲		◉			
Grass		◉	▲	◉				◉	▲	◉		◉	▲		◉		◉	
Electric			▲	◉	◉				◉	▲					◉			
Ice		◉	◉	▲		◉			▲	▲					▲		◉	
Fighting	▲					▲		◉		◉	◉	◉	▲	◉		▲	▲	◉
Poison				▲				◉	◉				◉	◉			◉	▲
Ground		▲		◉	▲			▲		◉		◉	▲				▲	
Flying				▲	◉		▲					▲	◉				◉	
Psychic							▲	▲			◉					◉	◉	
Bug		◉		▲			◉	◉		◉	▲			◉		▲	◉	◉
Rock		▲				▲	◉		◉	▲		▲					◉	
Ghost	◉										▲			▲		◉		
Dragon															▲		◉	◉
Dark							◉				▲			▲		◉		◉
Steel		◉	◉		◉	▲							▲				◉	▲
Fairy		◉					▲	◉							▲	▲	◉	

Key

◉	Very effective "It's super effective!"	× 2
No icon	Normal damage	× 1
▲	Not too effective "It's not very effective..."	× 1/2

Credits

Content from Original Japanese Pokédex
Planning, Page Layout, Writing & Map Development: Shusuke Motomiya and ONEUP, Inc.
Art Direction, Design & Layout: RAGTIME CO., LTD.
DTPR: Plane Dot

Editors
Kellyn Ballard
Blaise Selby
Eric Haddock
Rachel Payne
(Volt Workforce Solutions)

Technical Advisor
Jillian Nonaka

Researchers & Translators
Hisato Yamamori
Mikiko Ryu
Sayuri Munday
Ben Regal

Screenshots
Antoin Johnson
Jeff Hines
Tadasu Hasegawa
Marvin Andrews

Cover Designers
Eric Medalle
Bridget O'Neill

Project Manager
Emily Luty

Design & Production
Prima Games
Jesse Anderson
Donato Tica
Elise Winter
Vanessa Perez
Mark Hughes

Acknowledgements
Heather Dalgleish
Yutaka Kamai
Phaedra Long
Yasuhiro Usui

THE OFFICIAL NATIONAL

ISBN: 978-1-10189-828-4

Published in the United States by
The Pokémon Company International
601 108th Ave NE Suite 1600
Bellevue, WA 98004 USA

1st Floor Building 4, Chiswick Park
566 Chiswick High Road
London, W4 5YE United Kingdom

Printed in the United States of America.